D0917391

The
EUROPA WORLD OF LEARNING
2012

FOREWORD

It gives us great pleasure to introduce the 2012 edition of THE EUROPA WORLD OF LEARNING. First published in 1947, it has since become established as an authoritative reference work on academic institutions all over the world.

THE EUROPA WORLD OF LEARNING is unique in offering information over the entire spectrum of academic activity. Our listings cover not just universities and colleges, but also research institutes, libraries and archives, museums and galleries and learned societies. Further to this, regulatory and representative bodies are covered in a section which also has details of relevant ministries, accrediting bodies and funding organizations. Each chapter has an introductory survey outlining the country's higher education system.

Each year we invite entrants to review and update their entries. Entrants may do so online at updates.worldoflearning.com, or by sending an email to wol@informa.com. We are, as ever, grateful to those who help bring our information up to date with their prompt replies. Continuous research on the internet and in the world's press, as well as contact with official sources worldwide, supplements this method of revision.

In addition to the regular updating of our entries, this edition has expanded coverage of institutions in Western Europe. Chapters covering Austria, Belgium, Denmark, Finland, France, Germany, Iceland, Ireland, Italy, Liechtenstein, Luxembourg, Malta, Monaco, Netherlands, Norway, Portugal, San Marino, Spain, Sweden, Switzerland and the United Kingdom all have specially expanded chapters.

THE EUROPA WORLD OF LEARNING also contains a collection of essays on themes pertinent to international higher education. In this edition subjects covered include the higher education sector's use of social media, academic integrity in the digital age, changes to higher education funding and a global move towards the privatization of higher education, whether education is getting lost in university mergers, and the scholarship of teaching and learning in higher education. For details of the authors contributing to this edition see page ix in Volume 1.

In the sections on Universities and Colleges, our classification follows the practice of the country concerned. This in no way implies any official evaluation on our part. Readers who are interested in the matter of the equivalence of institutions, degrees or diplomas should correspond directly with the institutions concerned, or with the national or international bodies set up for this purpose. Further information on these can be found in the Regulatory and Representative Bodies section of each chapter under the subheading Accreditation.

The online version of THE EUROPA WORLD OF LEARNING offers quarterly updates of content and an unprecedented level of access to institutions of higher education and learning worldwide, and to the people who work within them. See page vi or visit www.worldoflearning.com for further details.

August 2011

CONTENTS

ABBREVIATIONS

AB	Alberta
Abog.	Abogado (lawyer)
Acad.	Academician; Academy
ACT	Australian Capital Territory
Admin.	Administration; Administrative
AIDS	acquired immunodeficiency syndrome
AK	Alaska
AL	Alabama
Apdo	Apartado (Post Box)
approx.	approximately
AR	Arkansas
Arq.	Arquitecto (Spanish); Arquiteto (Portuguese)
Asscn	Association
Assoc.	Associate
Asst	Assistant
Atty	Attorney
Avda	Avenida
Ave	Avenue
Avv.	Avvocato (Advocate)
AZ	Arizona
BA	Bachelor of Arts
BC	British Columbia
Bd	Boulevard
Bdul	Bulevardul
BEng	Bachelor of Engineering
Bld	Boulevard
Bldg	Building
Blv	Boulevard
Blvd	Boulevard
Blvr	Bulevar
BP	Boîte postale
Br.	Branch
BRGM	Bureau de Recherches Géologiques et Minières
Brig.	Brigadier
Bro.	Brother
Brs	Branches
BSc	Bachelor of Science
Bul.	Bulvar (boulevard)
bulv.	bulvarȳs (boulevard)
c.	circa (approximately)
c/o	care of
CA	California
CAR	Central African Republic
Ccl	Council
CD-ROM	compact disc read-only memory
CEA	Commissariat à l'Energie Atomique
CEO	Chief Executive Officer
Chair.	Chairman; Chairperson; Chairwoman
CIRAD	Centre de Coopération Internationale en Recherche Agronomique pour le Développement
Cmdr	Commander
CNR	Consiglio Nazionale delle Ricerche
cnr	corner
CNRS	Centre National de la Recherche Scientifique
CO	Colorado
Co	Company; County
Col	Colonel
Col.	Colonia (District)
colln	Collection
Comm.	Commission
Commr	Commissioner
Conf.	Conference
Corpn	Corporation
Corresp.	Correspondent; Corresponding
CP	Caixa postal; Case postale; Casella postale (Post Box)
Cr	Contador
CRC	Cooperative Research Centre
CT	Connecticut
Cttee	Committee
cu	cubic
DC	District of Colombia
DE	Delaware
Del.	Delegate; Delegation
Dept	Department
Deptl	Departmental
devt	development
DF	Distrito Federal
Dipl.	Diploma
Dir	Director
Dist.	District
Div.	Division
Divs	Divisions
Doc.	Docent
Dott.	Dottore
Dott.ssa	Dottoressa
Doz.	Dozent (lecturer)
Dr	Doctor
Dr Hab.	Doktor Habilitowany (Assistant Professor)
Dr.	Drive
Dra	Doctora
Drs	Doctorandus (Dutch or Indonesian higher degree)
DVD	digital versatile disc
E	East; Eastern
e.g.	exempli gratia
Edif.	Edificio (Building)
edn	edition
Eng.	Engineer
EngD	Doctor of Engineering
esp.	especially
Est.	Established
etc.	et cetera
EU	European Union
Exec.	Executive
f.	founded
F.t.e.	Full-time equivalent
FAO	Food and Agriculture Organization
Fed.	Federal; Federation
FL	Florida
fmr	former
fmrly	formerly
Fr	Father
ft	feet
GA	Georgia
Gdns	Gardens
Gen.	General
Gov.	Governor
Govt	Government
GPOB	Government Post Office Box
HE	His (Her) Excellency; His Eminence
HEI	Higher Education Institution
HI	Hawaii
HIV	human immunodeficiency virus
HM	His (Her) Majesty
HND	Higher National Diploma
Hon.	Honorary; Honourable
HQ	Headquarters
HRH	His (Her) Royal Highness
IA	Iowa
ID	Idaho
IL	Illinois
ILO	International Labour Organization
IN	Indiana
Inc.	Incorporated
incl.	include; includes; including
Ind.	Independent
Ing.	Ingénieur (Engineer)
Instn	Institution
Int.	International
Ir	Insinyur (Engineer)
irreg.	irregular
Jl	Jalan (street)
Jr	Junior
JSC	Joint Stock Company
jt	joint
jtly	jointly
küç.	küçasi (street)
km	kilometre(s)
KS	Kansas
kv.	kvartal (apartment block); kvartira (apartment)
KY	Kentucky
LA	Louisiana
Lic.	Licenciado
Licda	Licenciada
Lt	Lieutenant
Ltd	Limited
m	metre(s)
m.	million
MA	Massachusetts; Master of Arts
Mag.	Magister (Masters degree)
Man.	Manager; Managing
MB	Manitoba
MBA	Master of Business Administration
MD	Maryland
ME	Maine
Mem.	Member
Mems	Members
MEng	Master of Engineering
Mgr	Monseigneur; Monsignor
MI	Michigan
Min.	Minister; Ministry
misc.	miscellaneous
mm	millimetre(s)
MN	Minnesota
MO	Missouri
MRC	Medical Research Council
MS	Mississippi
MSc	Master of Science
MSS	Manuscripts
MT	Montana
N	North; Northern
nám	náměstí (square)
NASA	National Aeronautics and Space Administration
Nat.	National
NB	New Brunswick
NC	North Carolina
ND	North Dakota
NE	Nebraska; Northeast; Northeastern

NGO	Non-Governmental Organization
NH	New Hampshire
NJ	New Jersey
NL	Newfoundland and Labrador
NM	New Mexico
NS	Nova Scotia
NSW	New South Wales
NT	Northwest Territories
NU	Nunavut Territory
NV	Nevada
NW	Northwest; Northwestern
NY	New York
NZ	New Zealand
obl.	oblast
Of.	Oficina
OH	Ohio
OK	Oklahoma
ON	Ontario
OR	Oregon
Org.	Organization
PA	Pennsylvania
PE	Prince Edward Island
PEN	Poets, Playwrights, Essayists, Editors and Novelists (Club)
PhD	Doctor of Philosophy
pl.	place; platz; ploshchad (square)
PMB	Private Mail Bag
POB	Post Office Box
pr.	prospekt (avenue)
Pres.	President
Prin.	Principal
Prof.	Professor
Profa	Professora
Publ.	Publication
Publs	Publications

QC	Québec
q.v.	quod vide (to which refer)
rd	road
Rep.	Representative
retd	retired
Rev.	Reverend
RI	Rhode Island
RP	Révérend Père
Rr.	Rruga
Rt Hon.	Right Honourable
Rt Rev.	Right Reverend
S	South; Southern
s/n	sin número (without number)
SA	South Africa(n); South Australia
SAR	Special Administrative Region
SC	South Carolina
SD	South Dakota
SDI	Selective Dissemination of Information
SE	Southeast; Southeastern
Sec.	Secretary
Sis.	Sister
SK	Saskatchewan
Soc.	Society
spec.	special
Sq.	Square
Sr	Senior
St	Saint; Sint; Street
Sta	Santa
Ste	Sainte
str.	stradă; strada; Strasse (street)
SW	Southwest; Southwestern
tel.	telephone
TN	Tennessee

Treas.	Treasurer
TRNC	Turkish Republic of Northern Cyprus
TX	Texas
u.	utca (street)
UK	United Kingdom
ul.	ulica; ulitsa (street)
UN	United Nations
UNESCO	United Nations Educational, Scientific and Cultural Organization
Univ.	Universidad; Universidade; Università; Universität; Université; Universitas; Universitat; Universitatea; Universiteit; Universitet; Universiteti; Universiti; University; Univerza; Univerzita; Univerzitet; Uniwersytet
USA	United States of America
UT	Utah
VA	Virginia
Vols	Volumes
VT	Vermont
vul.	vulitsa; vulytsa (sreet)
W	West; Western
WA	Washington (State); Western Australia
WI	Wisconsin
WV	West Virginia
WY	Wyoming
YT	Yukon Territory

INTERNATIONAL TELEPHONE CODES

To make international calls to telephone and fax numbers listed in *The Europa World of Learning*, dial the international code of the country from which you are calling, followed by the appropriate country code for the institution you wish to call (listed below), followed by the area code (if applicable) and telephone or fax number listed in the entry.

	Country code	+ or – GMT*
Afghanistan	93	+4½
Albania	355	+1
Algeria	213	+1
Andorra	376	+1
Angola	244	+1
Antigua and Barbuda	1 268	–4
Argentina	54	–3
Armenia	374	+4
Australia	61	+8 to +10
Austria	43	+1
Azerbaijan	994	+5
Bahamas	1 242	–5
Bahrain	973	+3
Bangladesh	880	+6
Barbados	1 246	–4
Belarus	375	+2
Belgium	32	+1
Belize	501	–6
Benin	229	+1
Bhutan	975	+6
Bolivia	591	–4
Bosnia and Herzegovina	387	+1
Botswana	267	+2
Brazil	55	–3 to –4
Brunei	673	+8
Bulgaria	359	+2
Burkina Faso	226	0
Burundi	257	+2
Cambodia	855	+7
Cameroon	237	+1
Canada	1	–3 to –8
Cape Verde	238	–1
Central African Republic	236	+1
Chad	235	+1
Chile	56	–4
China, People's Republic	86	+8
Hong Kong	852	+8
Macao	853	+8
China (Taiwan)	886	+8
Colombia	57	–5
Comoros	269	+3
Congo, Democratic Republic	243	+1
Congo, Republic	242	+1
Costa Rica	506	–6
Côte d'Ivoire	225	0
Croatia	385	+1
Cuba	53	–5
Cyprus	357	+2
'Turkish Republic of Northern Cyprus'	90 392	+2
Czech Republic	420	+1
Denmark	45	+1
Faroe Islands	298	0
Greenland	299	–1 to –4

	Country code	+ or – GMT*
Djibouti	253	+3
Dominica	1 767	–4
Dominican Republic	1 809	–4
Ecuador	593	–5
Egypt	20	+2
El Salvador	503	–6
Equatorial Guinea	240	+1
Eritrea	291	+3
Estonia	372	+2
Ethiopia	251	+3
Fiji	679	+12
Finland	358	+2
Åland Islands	358	+2
France	33	+1
French Guiana	594	–3
French Polynesia	689	–9 to –10
Guadeloupe	590	–4
Martinique	596	–4
New Caledonia	687	+11
Réunion	262	+4
Gabon	241	+1
Gambia	220	0
Georgia	995	+4
Germany	49	+1
Ghana	233	0
Greece	30	+2
Grenada	1 473	–4
Guatemala	502	–6
Guinea	224	0
Guinea-Bissau	245	0
Guyana	592	–4
Haiti	509	–5
Honduras	504	–6
Hungary	36	+1
Iceland	354	0
India	91	+5½
Indonesia	62	+7 to +9
Iran	98	+3½
Iraq	964	+3
Ireland	353	0
Israel	972	+2
Italy	39	+1
Jamaica	1 876	–5
Japan	81	+9
Jordan	962	+2
Kazakhstan	7	+6
Kenya	254	+3
Kiribati	686	+12 to +13
Korea, Democratic People's Republic (North Korea)	850	+9
Korea, Republic (South Korea)	82	+9
Kosovo	381†	+3
Kuwait	965	+3

	Country code	+ or – GMT*
Kyrgyzstan	996	+5
Laos	856	+7
Latvia	371	+2
Lebanon	961	+2
Lesotho	266	+2
Liberia	231	0
Libya	218	+1
Liechtenstein	423	+1
Lithuania	370	+2
Luxembourg	352	+1
Macedonia, former Yugoslav republic	389	+1
Madagascar	261	+3
Malawi	265	+2
Malaysia	60	+8
Maldives	960	+5
Mali	223	0
Malta	356	+1
Marshall Islands	692	+12
Mauritania	222	0
Mauritius	230	+4
Mexico	52	–6 to –7
Micronesia, Federated States	691	+10 to +11
Moldova	373	+2
Monaco	377	+1
Mongolia	976	+7 to +9
Montenegro	382	+1
Morocco	212	0
Mozambique	258	+2
Myanmar	95	+6½
Namibia	264	+2
Nauru	674	+12
Nepal	977	+5¾
Netherlands	31	+1
Aruba	297	–4
Netherlands Antilles	599	–4
New Zealand	64	+12
Nicaragua	505	–6
Niger	227	+1
Nigeria	234	+1
Norway	47	+1
Oman	968	+4
Pakistan	92	+5
Palau	680	+9
Palestinian Autonomous Areas	970 or 972	+2
Panama	507	–5
Papua New Guinea	675	+10
Paraguay	595	–4
Peru	51	–5
Philippines	63	+8
Poland	48	+1
Portugal	351	0
Qatar	974	+3
Romania	40	+2
Russian Federation	7	+2 to +12
Rwanda	250	+2
Saint Christopher and Nevis	1 869	–4
Saint Lucia	1 758	–4
Saint Vincent and the Grenadines	1 784	–4
Samoa	685	–11
San Marino	378	+1
São Tomé and Príncipe	239	0
Saudi Arabia	966	+3
Senegal	221	0

	Country code	+ or – GMT*
Serbia	381	+1
Seychelles	248	+4
Sierra Leone	232	0
Singapore	65	+8
Slovakia	421	+1
Slovenia	386	+1
Solomon Islands	677	+11
Somalia	252	+3
South Africa	27	+2
Spain	34	+1
Sri Lanka	94	+5½
Sudan	249	+2
Suriname	597	–3
Swaziland	268	+2
Sweden	46	+1
Switzerland	41	+1
Syria	963	+2
Tajikistan	992	+5
Tanzania	255	+3
Thailand	66	+7
Timor-Leste	670	+9
Togo	228	0
Tonga	676	+13
Trinidad and Tobago	1 868	–4
Tunisia	216	+1
Turkey	90	+2
Turkmenistan	993	+5
Tuvalu	688	+12
Uganda	256	+3
Ukraine	380	+2
United Arab Emirates	971	+4
United Kingdom	44	0
Northern Ireland	44	0
Bermuda	1 441	–4
Gibraltar	350	+1
Guernsey	44	0
Isle of Man	44	0
Jersey	44	0
United States of America	1	–5 to –10
Guam	1 671	+10
Puerto Rico	1 787	–4
United States Virgin Islands	1 340	–4
Uruguay	598	–3
Uzbekistan	998	+5
Vanuatu	678	+11
Vatican City	39	+1
Venezuela	58	–4
Viet Nam	84	+7
Yemen	967	+3
Zambia	260	+2
Zimbabwe	263	+2

* Time difference in hours + or – Greenwich Mean Time (GMT). The times listed compare the standard (winter) times. Some countries adopt Summer (Daylight Saving) Time — i.e. +1 hour — for part of the year.

† Mobile telephone numbers for Kosovo use either the country code for Monaco (377) or the country code for Slovenia (386).

Note: Telephone and fax numbers using the Inmarsat ocean region code 870 are listed in full. No country or area code is required, but it is necessary to precede the number with the international access code of the country from which the call is made.

PART FOUR

Namibia–Zimbabwe

NAMIBIA

The Higher Education System

From 1925 Namibia was under South African control, first as a League of Nations protectorate and then as a de facto province. Independence was finally achieved in 1990. The University of Namibia was founded in 1992, based on the former Windhoek Academy of Education, following a report by a Presidential commission into the state of higher education in Namibia. Higher education is also provided by the Technicon of Namibia, a vocational college, and four teacher-training colleges. The Ministry of Basic Education, Sport and Culture and The Ministry of Higher Education, Training and Employment Creation were combined in 2005 to form the Ministry of Education, which is responsible for higher education and vocational training. In 2005/06 13,185 students were enrolled in tertiary education.

Admission to the University is based upon results in the International General Certificate of Secondary Education examinations; however, Higher International General Certificate of Secondary Education passes are given more weight when applicants are being evaluated. Non-degree university-level qualifications include two- or three-year Certificate courses and three- or four-year Diploma courses. Undergraduate Bachelors degree programmes last four years and are offered in most subject fields. The two foremost postgraduate degrees are the Masters and the Doctorate; the former is a one-year (full-time) or three-year (part-time) course, and the latter requires at least two years of study following the Masters.

Post-secondary technical and vocational education is offered by the Polytechnic of Namibia (founded 1980), and qualifications include Certificate (one year), Diploma (three years) and Bachelor of Technology.

The Ministry of Education has developed a 15-year strategic plan for 2005/06–2020, titled the Education and Training Sector Improvement Programme (ETSIP). Its aim is to comprehensively reform the education and training sectors.

Regulatory Bodies

GOVERNMENT

Ministry of Education: Troskie House, Uhland St, PMB 13186, Windhoek; tel. (61) 2933111; fax (61) 224277; Minister NANGOLO MBUMBA.

Ministry of Youth, National Service, Sport and Culture: Windhoek; Minister JOHN MUTORWA.

Goethe-Zentrum/Namibisch-Deutsche Stiftung für kulturelle Zusammenarbeit (Goethe-Centre/Namibian-German Institute for Cultural Cooperation): 1–5 Fidel Castro St, POB 1208, 9000 Windhoek; tel. (61) 225700; fax (61) 221256; e-mail il@nads.org.na; internet www.goethe.de/af/win/deindex.htm; f. 1988; affiliated to Goethe-Institut (see chapter on Germany); promotes use of the German language in Nambia and cultural exchange between Namibia and Germany; Dir SABINE ERLENWEIN.

Learned Societies

GENERAL

Namibia Scientific Society: POB 67, Windhoek 9000; tel. (61) 225372; fax (61) 226846; e-mail nwg@iafrica.com.na; f. 1925; ornithology, speleology, botany, archaeology, herpetology, astronomy, ethnology; 1,100 mems (900 ordinary, 200 exchange); library of 8,000 vols; Pres. B. GUHRING; publs *Journal* (1 a year), *Mitteilungen / Newsletter / Nuusbrief*, *Mitteilungen der Ornithologischen Arbeitsgruppe*.

UNESCO Office Windhoek: Windhoek 9000, POB 24519, Windhoek; located at: Oppenheimer House, 5 Brahms St, Windhoek West, Windhoek; tel. (61) 2917220; fax (61) 2917000; e-mail windhoek@unesco.org; designated Cluster Office for Angola, Lesotho, Namibia, South Africa and Swaziland; Dir JOHNNY MCCLAIN.

ARCHITECTURE AND TOWN PLANNING

Namibia Institute of Architects: Love St, POB 1478, Windhoek; tel. (61) 231559; fax (61) 232007; e-mail nia@mweb.com.na; f. 1952; 98 mems; Pres. DEON PRETORIUS.

LANGUAGE AND LITERATURE

British Council: 1–5 Fidel Castro St, Windhoek; tel. (61) 226776; fax (61) 227530; e-mail general.enquiries@britishcouncil.org.na; internet www.britishcouncil.org/namibia; the office in Pretoria, South Africa, is responsible for all British Council work in Namibia (see chapter on South Africa); Officer in Charge PATIENCE MAHLALELA.

Research Institutes

NATURAL SCIENCES

Biological Sciences

Gobabeb Training and Research Centre: POB 953, Walvis Bay; tel. (64) 694199; fax (64) 205197; e-mail gobabeb@gobabeb.org; internet www.gobabeb.org; f. 1963; research in Namib Desert and semi-arid Namibia, emphasizing basic and applied research, conservation biology, community applications, training and environmental education; library of 18,700 off-print colln, 13,000 bibliographic entries, 25 journals; Exec. Dir JOHN R. HENSCHEL; Librarian INGE A. HENSCHEL.

National Botanical Research Institute: c/o Ministry of Agriculture, Water and Forestry, Private Bag 13184, Windhoek; tel. (61) 2029111; fax (61) 258153; e-mail info@nbri.org.na; f. 1953; herbarium colln of 74,000 plant specimens; gene bank colln of 2,500 seed accessions; botanical reference library; incorporates National Botanic Garden; library of 3,053 books, 320 periodicals; Head Dr GILLIAN L. MAGGS-KÖLLING.

Libraries and Archives

Swakopmund

Sam Cohen Library: POB 361, Swakopmund; tel. (64) 402695; fax (64) 400763; e-mail office@swakopmund-museum.de; internet www.swakopmund-museum.de; f. 1977; attached to Museum Swakopmund; 10,000 vols on SW Africa and Africana, 20,000 historical pics, old Namibian maps; Chair. Prof. E. FOERTSCH; Man. P. BRÜGGEMANN; publs *Der Wahrheit eine Gasse*, *Precolonial times in South West Africa*, *Swakopmund—eine kleine Chronik*.

Windhoek

Namibian Agriculture and Water Information Centre: c/o Ministry of Agriculture, Water and Forestry, Govt Park Office, Private Bag 13184, Windhoek 9000; tel. (61) 2087111; fax (61) 221733; e-mail info@nbri.org.na; internet www.mawf.gov.na; f. 1966; 30,555 books, 600 periodical titles; 284 theses, 69 video cassettes, 4,200 pamphlets, 1,960 govt reports, 3,065 audiovisual items; depository for FAO publs; Librarian (vacant).

National Archives of Namibia: Private Bag 13250, 1–9 Eugene Marais St, Windhoek 9000; tel. (61) 2935211; fax (61) 2935217; e-mail natarch@mec.gov.na; internet www.natarch.edu.na; f. 1939; houses 7 km of govt records, private collns, 6,000 maps, 20,000 photographs, microforms, films, sound recordings, posters; 1,000 periodical titles and 9,000 other publs; Chief Archivist WERNER HILLEBRECHT; Sr Archivist ERASMUS NYANGA.

National Library of Namibia: Eugene Marais St, Private Bag 13349, Windhoek; tel. (61) 2935111; fax (61) 2935308; e-mail jloubser@mec.gov.na; internet www.nln.gov.na; f. 1994; legal deposit and general reference library; deposit library for UN, WTO and World Bank publications; Head JOHAN LOUBSER; Sr Librarian PAUL ZULU; publ. *National Bibliography of Namibia* (every 3 years).

Windhoek Public Library: Private Bag 13183, Windhoek 9000; tel. (61) 224899; f. 1924; 75,000 vols; Librarian L. HANSMANN.

Museums and Art Galleries

Lüderitz

Lüderitz Museum: POB 512, Lüderitz 9000; tel. (63) 202346; fax (63) 2346; f. 1966; incorporates finds of Friedrich Eberlanz of archaeological, herpetological, botanical and mineralogical interest, incl. Bushman Stone Age tools; Supervisor G. SCHEELE-SCHMIDT.

Swakopmund

Museum Swakopmund: POB 361, Strand St, Swakopmund; tel. and fax (64) 402046; e-mail info@swakopmund-museum.org.na; internet www.swakopmund-museum.org.na; f. 1951; natural history, mineralogy, marine life, history, archaeology, ethnology, technology; Chair. Prof. E. FÖRTSCH.

Windhoek

National Art Gallery of Namibia: POB 994, Windhoek 9000; tel. (61) 231160; fax (61) 240930; e-mail nagn@mweb.com.na; internet www.nagn.org.na; f. 1947; exhibitions, lectures, educational programmes; Dir A. H. EINS.

National Museum of Namibia: POB 1203, Windhoek; tel. (61) 276800; fax (61) 228636; internet www.natmus.cul.na; f. 1907; natural history, history, anthropology, archaeology, education; library of 6,000 vols, 600 journal titles; Dir E. MOOMBOLAH GOAGOSES (acting); publ. *Cimbebasia*.

University

UNIVERSITY OF NAMIBIA

Private Bag 13301, 340 Mandume Ndemufayo Ave, Pioneerspark, Windhoek

Telephone: (61) 2063111

Fax: (61) 2063866

E-mail: registrar@unam.na

Internet: www.unam.na

Founded 1992 upon the dissolution of the Academy, Windhoek

State control

Language of instruction: English

Academic year: January to November

Chancellor: HE Dr SAM S. NUJOMA

Vice-Chancellor: Prof. LAZARUS HANGULA

Pro-Vice-Chancellor for Academic Affairs and Research: ZACH J. N. KAZAPUA

Pro-Vice-Chancellor for Admin. and Finance: GEOFREY KIANGI

Registrar: (vacant)

Librarian: M. M. VILJOEN

Library of 132,334 vols, 40,000 UNIN books and documents, 498 periodicals

Number of teachers: 343

Number of students: 6,444 (4,017 full-time, 2,427 distance-learning)

DEANS

Faculty of Agriculture and Natural Resources: Prof. I. LUPANGA (acting)

Faculty of Economics and Management Science: Prof. ANDRE DU PISANI

Faculty of Education: Prof. P. K. WAINAINA

Faculty of Humanities and Social Science: Prof. A. G. BEHRENS

Faculty of Law: Prof. M. O. HINZ

Faculty of Medical and Health Sciences: Prof. A. VAN DYK

Faculty of Science: Prof. E. M. R. KIREMIRE

NAURU

The Higher Education System

During 1947–68 Nauru was a UN Trusteeship, administered by Australia on behalf of Australia, New Zealand and the United Kingdom. Independence was declared in 1968. There is a branch campus of the University of the South Pacific on the island but most Nauruans receive tertiary level education overseas.

Australia's annual performance report for Nauru 2007–08 stated that a great deal of external support was still required. A local person was being mentored to take over the role of Director of Education, but the managerial and professional capacity of the Department of Education would still need assistance to develop further.

Regulatory Body

GOVERNMENT

Ministry of Education: Yaren; tel. 444-3130; fax 444-3718; e-mail minister .education@naurugov.nr; Minister ROLAND KUN.

Museums and Galleries

Aiwo

Arts and Crafts Centre: Aiwo, Nauru; tel. 444-3292; f. 1993; baskets, stone tools, fishing nets, a pandanus grater, *ingurig* (grass skirts made from hibiscus), paintings, photographs; spec. collns shells, written materials; organizes craft classes; access by arrangement with Ministry of Internal Affairs.

Nauru Phosphate Corporation Museum: Aiwo, Nauru; tel. 444-3382; fax 444-3791; f. 1995 by the Nauru Phosphate foundation; photographs and items from 20th century, particularly the Second World War, incl. Japanese weapons and ammunition, colonial-era cannons, Japanese pottery; access by arrangement with Ministry of Internal Affairs; reported to be closed pending settlement of island-wide land disputes.

University

UNIVERSITY OF THE SOUTH PACIFIC, NAURU CAMPUS

Private Bag, Nauru Post Office, Aiwo, Nauru 00674

Telephone and fax 444-3774

E-mail: lauti_a@usp.ac.fj

Internet: www.usp.ac.fj/index .php?id=usp_nauru_home

Founded 1987

Campus Dir: ALAMANDA LAUTI

Library Officer: DALYS DANNANG

Library: periodicals, video cassettes and reference books; all documents in English.

NEPAL

The Higher Education System

There are five state universities in Nepal, the oldest of which is Tribhuvan University (founded in 1959). The main Beljhundi campus of the state-run Mahendra Sanskrit University (founded in 1986) was badly damaged during an arson attack in 2002, during which buildings, administrative records and library holdings were destroyed. There is one private university in Banepa. In 2006/07 there were 255,400 students enrolled in tertiary education. While the Ministry of Education and Sports administers the education system at the primary and secondary levels, Tribhuvan University is responsible for developing curriculums at college and Bachelors degree level.

Admission to higher education is on the basis of successful completion of the School Leaving Certificate or the Higher Secondary Certificate. Students with the Higher Secondary Certificate may enter directly Bachelors degree courses, whereas students with the School Leaving Certificate must obtain the Proficiency Certificate, a university-level course lasting two years, which is regarded as the first cycle of university education. The second cycle of university-level education is the Bachelors degree, which lasts four years in most disciplines but slightly longer (five-and-a-half years) in disciplines such as medicine, veterinary medicine and animal husbandry. Following the Bachelors degree the first postgraduate degree is the Masters, which is a two- to three-year course. Students seeking the Masters must undertake one year of National Development Service. The highest university-level degree is the Doctor of Philosophy, awarded after a final three-year period of study following the Masters.

The Directorate of Technical and Vocational Education is the government agency with overall responsibility for provision of technical and vocational education, which is offered at various secondary levels.

Regulatory and Representative Bodies

GOVERNMENT

Ministry of Education: Keshar Mahal, Kantipath, Kathmandu; tel. (1) 4411704; fax (1) 4423252; e-mail infomoe@moe.gov.np; internet moe.gov.np/new; Min. GANGA LAL TULADHAR.

Ministry of Tourism and Civil Aviation: Bhrikutimandap, Kathmandu; tel. (1) 4256217; fax (1) 4227281; e-mail info@tourism.gov.np; internet www.tourism.gov.np; Min. KHADGA BAHADUR BISHWAKARMA.

Ministry of Youth and Sports: Kamalpokhari, Kathmandu; tel. (1) 4416788; fax (1) 4416489; e-mail info@mocs.gov.np; internet www.moys.gov.np; Min. HIT BAHADUR TAMANG.

FUNDING

University Grants Commission: Sanothimi, Bhaktapur, POB 10796, Kathmandu; tel. (1) 6638434; fax (1) 6638552; e-mail info@ugcnepal.edu.np; internet www.ugcnepal.edu.np; f. 1994; 11 mems; Chair. Dr KAMAL KRISHNA JOSHI.

Learned Societies

GENERAL

Nepal Academy: GPOB 23058, Kamaladi, Kathmandu; tel. (1) 4221283; fax (1) 4221175; e-mail rnacademy@wlink.com.np; internet www.nrpp.org.np; f. 1957 as Royal Nepal Academy; promotes Nepalese drama, music and literature; awards prizes annually; 178 mems; library of 10,562 vols, 4,697 periodicals; Vice-Chancellor Prof. Dr BASU DEV TRIPATHI; publs *Kabita* (on Nepalese poetry, 4 a year), *Prajna* (4 a year).

Nepal Academy of Science and Technology: GPOB 3323, Khumaltar, Lalitpur; tel. (1) 5547714; fax (1) 5547713; e-mail info@nast.org.np; internet www.nast.org.np; f. 1982 as Royal Nepal Academy of Science and Technology; 157 mems; library of 10,000 vols, 150 periodicals; Chancellor Rt Hon. PRIME MINISTER OF NEPAL; Vice-Chancellor Prof. Dr HOM NATH BHATTARAI; Sec. Prof. Dr DILIP SUBBA; publs *NAST Communicator* (4 a year), *SAT Journal* (1 a year).

UNESCO Office Kathmandu: Sanepa-2, Lalitpur, POB 14391, Lalitpur; Ring Rd, Bansbari, Kathmandu; tel. (1) 5554396; fax (1) 5554450; e-mail kathmandu@unesco.org; internet www.unesco.org/kathmandu; f. 1998; library of 4,500 books, periodicals, reports, audio-visual materials; Head of Office and UNESCO Rep. AXEL PLATHE.

LANGUAGE AND LITERATURE

Alliance Française: Ganeshman Singh Path, Tripureshwar, POB 452 Kathmandu; tel. (1) 4242832; fax (1) 4242621; e-mail dafk@afk.wlink.com.np; internet www.france-in-nepal.org/frenchalliance; offers courses and exams in French language and culture and promotes cultural exchange with France; Dir CHANTAL LAMA.

British Council: POB 640, Lainchaur, Kathmandu; tel. (1) 4410798; fax (1) 4410545; e-mail library@britishcouncil.org.np; internet www.britishcouncil.org/nepal; f. 1959; teaching centre; offers courses and exams in English language and British culture and promotes cultural exchange with the UK; 6,774 mems; library of 15,036 vols, 30 periodicals, 54 video cassettes, 219 audio items, DVDs and CD-ROMs; Dir JOHN FRY; Information Services Man. RAJU SHAKYA.

Research Institute

GENERAL

International Centre for Integrated Mountain Development (ICIMOD): GPOB 3226, Khumaltar, Kathmandu, Lalitpur; tel. (1) 5003222; fax (1) 5003277; e-mail info@icimod.org; internet www.icimod.org; f. 1983; autonomous org. sponsored by govts of the regional mem. countries, Austria, Denmark, Germany, the Netherlands, Norway and Switzerland, to help promote an economically and environmentally sound ecosystem, and to improve the living standards of the mountain people in the Hindu Kush–Himalayan region; aims to serve as a focal point for multi-disciplinary documentation, training and applied research, and as a consultative centre in scientific and practical matters pertaining to mountain devt; mem. countries: Afghanistan, Bangladesh, Bhutan, People's Republic of China, India, Myanmar, Nepal, Pakistan; Dir-Gen. ANDREAS SCHILD.

Libraries and Archives

Kathmandu

National Archives: Ram Shah Path, Kathmandu; tel. (1) 4251315; f. 1967; 35,000 MSS, 60,000 microfilm copies of MSS in private collections, 16,000 historical documents, 10,000 vols; facilities for researchers; Archivist SANI MAIYA; publ. *Abhilekh*.

Nepal-India Cultural Centre and Library: Embassy of India, RNAC Bldg, New Rd, Kathmandu; tel. (1) 4243497; fax (1) 4255414; e-mail nbsk@mos.com.np; f. 1952; 60,000 vols; Librarian SANJAY K. BIHANI.

Tribhuvan University Central Library: Kirtipur, Kathmandu 2; tel. (1) 4212834; fax (1) 4226964; e-mail tucl@healthnet.org.np; internet www.tucl.org.np; f. 1959; 300,000 vols; depository for the UN; Chief Librarian KRISHNA MANI BHANDARY (acting); publs *Bulletin* (4 a year), *Education Quarterly*, *Journal of Tribhuvan University*, *Nepalese National Bibliography*.

Lalitpur

Madan Puraskar Pustakalaya: Lalitpur; tel. (1) 5521393; fax (1) 5536390; e-mail info@mpp.org.np; internet www.mpp.org.np; f. 1941; 23,700 vols, 4,300 periodical titles, monographs, ephemera in Nepali language; Librarian KAMAL MANI DIXIT.

Nepal National Library: Harihar Bhawan, Pulchowk, POB 182, Lalitpur; tel. (1) 5521132; fax (1) 5010061; e-mail nnl@nnl.wlink.com.np; internet www.nnl.gov.np; f. 1957; 90,000 vols, 96 periodicals, 1,000 rare books and manuscripts, 7,000 children's books, 400 other items; Chief Librarian DASHARATH THAPA.

Museums and Art Galleries

Kathmandu

National Museum of Nepal: Museum Rd, Chhauni, Kathmandu; tel. (1) 4211504; f. 1928; art, history, culture, ethnology, philately, natural history; art gallery; illustrates the art history of Nepal; library of 10,000 vols; Chief SANU NANI KANSAKAR; publ. *Nepal Museum*.

Patan Museum: Patan Darbar, Kathmandu; tel. and fax (1) 5521492; e-mail ptmuseum@mos.com.np; internet www.patanmuseum.gov.np; f. 1997; 18th-century fmr royal palace housing Hindu and Buddhist sacred art of Nepal, Nepalese metalwork, photographs of Nepal taken in 1899, and a Hindu Tantric MS; Dir BHIM PRASAD NEPAL.

Universities

KATHMANDU UNIVERSITY

POB 6250, Dhulikhel, Kavre, Kathmandu
Telephone: (11) 661399
Fax: (11) 661443
E-mail: kuweb@ku.edu.np
Internet: www.ku.edu.np
Founded 1991
State-funded, autonomous control
Academic year: August to June
Language of instruction: English
Chancellor: Rt Hon. PRIME MINISTER OF NEPAL
Pro-Chancellor: Hon. MINISTER FOR EDUCATION
Vice-Chancellor: Dr SURESH RAJ SHARMA
Registrar: Dr SITARAM ADHIKARY
Library of 25,000 vols and 150 periodicals
Number of students: 4,890 (incl. 3,107 enrolled in affiliated colleges)

DEANS

School of Arts: Dr BHADRA MAN TULADHAR
School of Education: Dr KEDAR NATH SHRESTHA
School of Engineering: Dr DINESH CHAPAGAIN
School of Management: Dr BIJAY K. C.
School of Medical Sciences: Dr NARENDRA RANA
School of Science: Dr PUSHPA RAJ ADHIKARY
There are 11 affiliated colleges

MAHENDRA SANSKRIT UNIVERSITY

POB 5003, Kathmandu
Telephone: (1) 4221510
Fax: (1) 4221510
Founded 1986
State control
Languages of instruction: English, Nepali, Sanskrit
Academic year: July to May
Chancellor: (vacant)
Vice-Chancellor: MADHAV RAJ GAUTAM
Rector: Dr BABU RAM POKHAREL
Registrar: Dr BHAJ RAJ PANT
Librarian: KHEM RAJ GYNAWALI
Number of teachers: 315
Number of students: 2,400
Publications: *Maryada* (1 a year), *Ritumbara* (4 a year)
Depts of ayurveda, Buddhist philosophy and tantra, darshna, dernashast, economics, english, hindi and maithali, itihasa purana, karmakanda, mathematics, nepali, nyaya, political science, purva mamamsa, veda, vedanta, vyakarana, yoga.

POKHARA UNIVERSITY

Lekhnath Municiplity-12, Dhungepatan, Kaski, Lekhnath
Telephone: (61) 561046
Fax: (61) 560392
E-mail: info@pu.edu.np
Internet: www.pu.edu.np
Founded 1996
State-funded, autonomous control
Languages of instruction: English, Nepali
Academic year: August to June
Faculties of Engineering, Humanities, Management, Science; 26 affiliated colleges
Chancellor: Rt Hon. PRIME MINISTER OF NEPAL
Pro-Chancellor: Hon. MINISTER FOR EDUCATION
Vice-Chancellor: Dr KESHAR JUNG BARAL
Information Officer: LOK PRASAD DHAKAL
Number of teachers: 1,530
Number of students: 16,666
Publication: *Pokhara University Bulletin*, *Brochure*

DEANS

Faculty of Humanities and Social Science: Prof. Dr GEETA PRADHAN
Faculty of Science and Technology: ISHWOR CHANDRA BANIYAN

PURBANCHAL UNIVERSITY

POB 142, Biratnagar, Eastern Region
Telephone: (21) 22165
Fax: (21) 21204
E-mail: info@puniv.edu.np
Internet: www.puniv.edu.np
Founded 1995
State-funded, autonomous control
Academic year: August to June
Languages of instruction: English, Nepali
Chancellor: Rt Hon. PRIME MINISTER OF NEPAL
Pro-Chancellor: Hon. MINISTER FOR EDUCATION
Publications: *Bulletin* (12 a year), *Business Horizon*, *Expressions*
Faculties of arts, education, management, science and technology
There are 65 affiliated colleges.

TRIBHUVAN UNIVERSITY

POB 8212, Kirtipur, Kathmandu
Telephone: (1) 4330433
Fax: (1) 4331964
E-mail: vcoffice@healthnet.org.np
Internet: www.tribhuvan-university.edu.np
Founded 1959
Autonomous control
Languages of instruction: English, Nepali
Academic year: July to June
60 Constituent campuses and 616 affiliated campuses under Tribhuvan Univ.
Chancellor: Rt Hon. PRIME MINISTER OF NEPAL
Vice-Chancellor: Prof. Dr MADHAB PRASAD SHARMA
Rector: Prof. Dr SOORYA LAL AMATYA
Registrar: Prof. Dr BHIMA RAJ ADHIKAREE
Chief Librarian: KRISHNA MANI BHANDARY
Library: see Libraries and Archives
Number of teachers: 7,950
Number of students: 172,375
Publications: *Contributions to Nepalese Studies*, *Economic Journal of Development Issues* (2 a year), *Education and Development* (CERID, 1 a year), *Journal of Development and Administrative Studies* (CEDA, 1 a year), *Nepalese Journal of Development and Rural Studies* (Central Department of Rural Development (Kirtipur), 2 a year), *Tribhuvan University Today* (1 a year), *TU Journal* (Research Division, 2 a year)

DEANS

Faculty of Education: Prof. Dr PRAKASH MAN SHRESTHA
Faculty of Humanities and Social Science: Prof. Dr NAVA RAJ KANEL
Faculty of Law: Prof. Dr AMBAR PRASAD PANT
Faculty of Management: Prof. Dr GOVIND PRASAD ACHARYA
Institute of Agriculture and Animal Science: Prof. Dr SUNDAR MAN SHRESTHA
Institute of Eng.: HARI DEV CHOUDHARI (acting)
Institute of Forestry: Dr KESHAB DUTTA AVASTHI
Institute of Medicine: Prof. Dr ARUN SAYAMI
Institute of Science and Technology: Prof. Dr MUKUNDA GAJUREL

NETHERLANDS

The Higher Education System

Universiteit Leiden (Leiden University—founded in 1575) is the oldest existing university in the Netherlands. It was founded when the Low Countries or Netherlands were under Spanish rule. In 1579 the seven northernmost provinces of the Netherlands formed the Treaty of Utrecht, declared their independence from Spain in 1581 and in 1648 were recognized as the independent United Provinces or Dutch Republic under the terms of the Treaty of Westphalia. Institutions established in the period 1579–1648 include Rijksuniversiteit Groningen (the University of Groningen—founded in 1614), Universiteit van Amsterdam (the University of Amsterdam—founded in 1632) and Universiteit Utrecht (Utrecht University—founded in 1636).

The modern higher education system is subject to a number of different legislative acts, including the Higher Professional Education Act, the University Education Act (both 1986) and the Higher Education and Research Act (1993). The last of these granted greater autonomy to institutions and introduced a 'credit'-based system for the award of degrees. The Netherlands participates in the Bologna Process to establish a European Higher Education Area, the first phase of which is to adopt a credit-based system of comparable degrees with two main cycles (undergraduate and graduate). The new system of Bachelors and Masters degrees is expected to be fully implemented soon. Higher education institutions are either universities (Universiteiten) or universities of professional education (Hogescholen). The Minister of Education, Culture and Science, advised by an Education Council, is responsible for educational legislation and its enforcement. A system of accreditation was introduced in 2002, for which the new Accreditation Organization of The Netherlands and Flanders is responsible. In 2007/08 212,700 students were enrolled at the Netherlands' 13 universities, while some 374,400 students were enrolled at the 51 institutes of higher vocational education. In addition, 21,004 students were registered with the Open University in 2003.

There are also public and private universities in the Dutch Dependencies of Aruba and Netherlands Antilles; the public universities are the Universiteit van Aruba (founded in 1988) and University of the Netherlands Antilles (founded in 1970; current status since 1979). In Aruba there were an estimated 1,704 students in higher education in 2003/04, and in Netherlands Antilles there were 795 students enrolled in university-level institutions in 2000/01.

The two-tier system of undergraduate Bachelors and postgraduate Masters degrees was first introduced in 2002 and is expected to be adopted by all university-level institutions. The undergraduate Bachelors degree is a three-year programme of study, starting with one year of general studies. The first postgraduate degree is the Masters, a one- to three-year course of study involving research, a written thesis or final test. A Masters in medicine lasts three years and students are required to study for a further three to six years to qualify for independent practice. Following completion of the Masters, the Doctorate is awarded after a minimum of four years of research and public defence of a thesis.

Other than the universities, undergraduate Bachelors degrees are also offered by the Hogescholen, which have mostly been founded since 1986. The main focus of the Hogescholen is on professional degrees and titles in several subject areas, including economics and management, engineering and technology, healthcare, behavioural science and social studies, agriculture and the environment, fine arts, performing arts and education. Since 2002 Hogescholen have also offered Masters degrees. A short cycle programme within the first cycle was introduced as a pilot programme from 2006 and was due to become a permanent part of the education system in 2010. This short-cycle degree is called an Associate degree and comprises a minimum of 120 ECTS points. The Association of Hogescholen is responsible for quality assurance and accreditation.

Post-secondary technical and vocational education (middelbaar beroepsonderwijs—MBO) is administered according to the Adult and Vocational Education Act (1996). The MBO is divided into four levels of qualifications (in ascending order): assistant training (six months to one year), basic vocational training (two to three years), vocational training (two to four years) and management training (three to four years). Alternatively, school-leavers with 10 years of primary and secondary education may undertake apprenticeships based in the workplace.

Regulatory and Representative Bodies

GOVERNMENT

Ministry of Education, Culture and Science: POB 16375, 2500 BJ The Hague; Rijnstraat 50, 2515 XP The Hague; tel. (70) 4123456; fax (70) 4123450; internet www.rijksoverheid.nl/ministeries/ocw; Min. MARJA VAN BIJSTERVELDT-VLIEGENTHART; Sec. HALBE ZIJLSTRA.

ACCREDITATION

ENIC/NARIC Netherlands: Int. Recognition Dept, POB 29777, 2502 LT The Hague; Kortenaerkade 11, 2518 AX The Hague; tel. (70) 4260260; fax (70) 4260399; e-mail info@nuffic.nl; internet www.nuffic.nl; f. 1952; provides information on postgraduate int. courses; advises various educational and govt bodies on matters of academic equivalence and the recognition of professional credentials; promotes int. cooperation in several European and nat. exchange programmes; offers educational and scientific help to developing countries; Dir-Gen. Drs SANDER VAN DEN EIJNDEN; publs *Nieuwsbrief* (4 a year), *Study in the Netherlands: Your Gateway to Europe* (1 a year).

Nederlands-Vlaamse Accreditatieorganisatie (Accreditation Organisation of the Netherlands and Flanders): POB 85498, 2508 CD The Hague; Parkstraat 28, 2514 JK The Hague; tel. (70) 3122300; fax (70) 3122301; e-mail info@nvao.net; internet www.nvao.net; independently ensures the quality of higher education in the Netherlands and Flanders by assessing and accrediting programmes; Chair. K. L. L. M. (KARL) DITTRICH; Vice-Chair. GUIDO LANGOUCHE; Man. Dir RUDY DERDELINCKX.

NATIONAL BODIES

HBO-raad (Netherlands Association of Universities of Applied Sciences): POB 123, 2501 CC The Hague; Prinsessegracht 21, 2514 AP The Hague; tel. (70) 3122121; fax (70) 3122100; e-mail post@hbo-raad.nl; internet www.hbo-raad.nl; works to strengthen the social position of the univs of applied sciences; Pres. (vacant); Sec. Drs A. DE GRAAF.

Nederlandse Vereniging van Pedagogen en Onderwijskundigen (NVO) (Dutch Society of Educational Psychologists): St Jacobsstraat 331, 3511 BP Utrecht; tel. (30) 2322407; fax (30) 2369749; e-mail secretariaat@nvo.nl; internet www.nvo.nl; f. 1962; maintenance of standards in univ. education; Chair. Dr XAVIER MOONEN; Vice-Chair. Drs MARJOLIJN WILSCHUT; Treas. Drs ROBBERT VAN KAMPEN; Dir Drs HANS BOSMAN; publs *Nederlands Tijdschrift voor Opvoeding, Vorming en Onderwijs* (6 a year).

Rectoren College (Rectors' Conference of the Netherlands): POB 19270, 3501 DG Utrecht; tel. (71) 5273130; fax (71) 5273052; e-mail hj.graafland@bb.leidenuniv.nl; Chair. D. F. J. BOSSCHER; Sec. F. VAN STEIJN.

Vereniging van Universiteiten (VSNU) (Association of Universities in the Netherlands): POB 13739, 2501 ES The Hague; Lange Houtstraat 2, 2511 CW The Hague; tel. (70) 3021400; fax (70) 3021495; e-mail post@vsnu.nl; internet www.vsnu.nl; f. 1985; promotes common interests of univs vis-à-vis Dutch and European politicians, govt and civil society orgs to create a forum for discussion; Pres. Dr SIJBOLT NOORDA; Dir JOSEPHINE SCHOLTEN.

Learned Societies

GENERAL

Koninklijke Hollandsche Maatschappij der Wetenschappen (Royal Holland Society of Sciences and Humanities): POB 9698, 2003 LR Haarlem; Spaarne 17, 2011 CD Haarlem; tel. (23) 5321773; fax (23) 5362713; e-mail hollmij@wxs.nl; internet www.hollmij.nl; f. 1752, present bldg 1841; furthers contact between scientists and laymen by arranging lectures, confs, symposia on scientific subjects; awards annual prizes and subsidies for research and publ. of scientific work; 350 mems, 350 dirs, 30 foreign mems; Chair. Dr A. H. G. RINNOOY KAN; Vice-Chair. M. E. BIERMAN-BEUKEMA TOE WATER; Treas. R. E. ROGAAR; publ. *Haarlem Presentations* (1 a year).

Koninklijke Nederlandse Akademie van Wetenschappen (Royal Netherlands Academy of Arts and Sciences): POB 19121, 1000 GC Amsterdam; Kloveniersburgwal 29, 1011 JV Amsterdam; tel. (20) 5510700; fax (20) 6204941; e-mail knaw@bureau.knaw.nl; internet www.knaw.nl; f. 1808, present name 1938; advises govt on matters related to scientific research; assesses the quality of scientific research (peer review); provides a forum for the scientific world and promotes int. scientific cooperation; acts as an umbrella org. for the institutes primarily engaged in basic and strategic scientific research and disseminates information; 300 mems (200 ordinary, 40 corresp., 60 foreign); Pres. Prof. Dr ROBBERT H. DIJKGRAAF; Vice-Pres. Prof. J. W. M. VAN DER MEER; Vice-Pres. Prof. D. G. YNTEMA; Sec.-Gen. Prof. Dr J. J. A. THOMASSEN; Dir for Gen. Affairs, Finance and Operations Dr K. HANS CHANG; Dir for Research Prof. Dr THEO W. MULDER; publs *Akademienieuws*, *Mededelingen der Afdeling Letterkunde*, *Verhandelingen der Afdeling Letterkunde*, *Verhandelingen Eerste en Tweede Reeks der Afdeling Natuurkunde*, *Verslag van de Gewone Vergaderingen der Afdeling Natuurkunde*.

Zuid-Afrikahuis (South Africa House): Keizersgracht 141, 1015 CK Amsterdam; tel. (20) 6249318; fax (20) 6382596; e-mail info@zuidafrikahuis.nl; internet www.zuidafrikahuis.nl; f. 1939; study of Afrikaans language and literature, history and culture of South Africa; attached institutes: Netherlands-South African Soc., South African Institute; library of 34,000 vols; Librarian CORINE DE MAIJER; publ. *Maandblad Zuid-Afrika* (12 a year).

AGRICULTURE, FISHERIES AND VETERINARY SCIENCE

Groei & Bloei (Growth and Bloom): POB 485, 2700 AL Zoetermeer; Louis Pasteurlaan 6, 2719 EE Zoetermeer; tel. (79) 3681215; fax (79) 3681245; e-mail info@groei.nl; internet www.groei.nl; f. 1873 as Royal Soc. of Horticulture and Botany; 146 brs; 60,000 mems; Gen. Sec. J. P. VAN LEEUWEN; publ. *Groei & Bloei* (11 a year).

KLV Wageningen Alumni Netwerk (KLV Wageningen Alumni Network): POB 79, 6700 AB Wageningen; Gen. Foulkesweg 1A, 6703 BG Wageningen; tel. (317) 485191; fax (317) 483976; e-mail secretariaat.klv@wur.nl; internet www.klv.nl; f. 1886, present name 2009; network for Wageningen Univ. graduates and for other professionals with links to Wageningen; workshops, lectures; 7,700 8,000 mems; Pres. MARGRIET TIEMSTRA; Vice-Pres. TINY VAN BOEKEL; Sec. ELMAR THEUNE; Treas. CAREL JASPERS; Dir PAUL DEN BESTEN; Vice-Dir ELVIRE SCHLÖSSER.

Koninklijke Nederlandse Bosbouw Vereniging (Royal Dutch Forestry Association): Parkweg 27, 2585 JH The Hague; tel. (70) 3688222; fax (70) 4162959; e-mail secretaris@knbv.nl; internet www.knbv.nl; f. 1910; promotes forestry, landscape management, nature conservation; advocates functions and values of forests, such as carbon sequestration, historical monuments, nature, recreation, timber production, water, etc.; organises thematic meetings, symposia, excursions and study tours abroad; 600 mems; Chair. Dr Ir HANK H. BARTELINK; Vice-Chair. Ir ERWIN J. AL; Sec. Ing. MARLEEN VAN DEN HAM; publ. *Vakblad Natuur Bos Landschap* (10 a year).

Nederlandse Tuinbouwraad (Netherlands Horticultural Council): POB 1000, 1430 BA Aalsmeer; Legmeerdijk 313, 1431 GB Aalsmeer; tel. (29) 7395005; fax (29) 7395012; e-mail informatie@tuinbouwraad.nl; internet www.tuinbouwraad.nl; f. 1908; represents the common technical and economic interests of the mem. orgs; mems: 12 nat. orgs of cooperatives and producers of edible and non-edible horticultural products; Chair. Dr NICO KOOMEN; Sec. Dr GEORGE TH. FRANKE.

ARCHITECTURE AND TOWN PLANNING

Erfgoedvereniging Heemschut: Nieuwezijds Kolk 28, 1012 PV Amsterdam; tel. (20) 6225292; fax (20) 6240571; e-mail info@heemschut.nl; internet www.heemschut.nl; f. 1911; asscn for safeguarding the architectural heritage of the Netherlands; 12 provincial sub-cttees; 6,500 mems; Chair. P. BREUKINK; Dir KAREL LOEFF; Sec. K. LOEFF; publ. *Heemschut* (6 a year).

Genootschap Architectura et Amicitia: Duke Ellingtonstraat 34, 2324 LA Leiden; e-mail mail@aeta.nl; internet www.aeta.nl; f. 1855; asscn of architects and individuals from related disciplines; 380 mems; Chair. RENS SCHULZE; Sec. FRANCISCA BENTHEM; publ. *FORUM* (1 a year).

Koninklijke Maatschappij tot Bevordering der Bouwkunst Bond van Nederlandse Architekten (BNA) (Royal Institute of Dutch Architects): POB 19606, 1000 GP Amsterdam; Jollemanhof 14, 1019 GW Amsterdam; tel. (20) 5553666; fax (20) 5553699; e-mail bna@bna.nl; internet www.bna.nl; f. 1919 by merger of Soc. for the Advancement of Architecture (f. 1842) and Asscn of Dutch Architects (f. 1908), present status 1957; promotes cultural, economic, skills, social profile of architect and architecture; 3,000 mems; Chair. BJARNE MASTENBROEK; Vice-Chair. FREERK HOEKSTRA; Exec. Sec MARIJKE ZANDHUIS; publ. *BNABlad* (12 a year).

Nederlands Architectuur Instituut (Netherlands Architecture Institute): POB 237, 3000 AE Rotterdam; Museum Park 25, 3015 CB Rotterdam; tel. (10) 4401358; fax (10) 4366975; e-mail info@nai.nl; internet www.nai.nl; f. 1988, present location 1993; museum, archives, collns; 100 mems; library of 35,000 vols; Dir OLE BOUMAN; Man. Dir PETER HAASBROEK; publs *Delft Architectural Studies on Housing Design (DASH)* (2 a year), *Hunch* (2 a year), *OASE* (3 a year), *Open* (2 a year), *Positions* (irregular).

Raad voor Cultuur (Council for Culture): POB 61243, 2506 AE The Hague; RJ Schimmelpennincklaan 3, 2517 JN The Hague; tel. (70) 3106686; fax (70) 3614727; e-mail info@cultuur.nl; internet www.cultuur.nl; f. 1995; statutory advisory body to the govt and both Chambers of Parliament for cultural and media policy; 9 mems; Chair. ELS H. SWAAB; Gen. Sec. KEES WEEDA.

Rijksdienst voor het Cultureel Erfgoed (National Heritage Board): POB 1600, 3800 BP Amersfoort; Smallepad 5, 3811 MG Amersfoort; tel. (33) 4217421; fax (33) 4217799; e-mail info@cultureelerfgoed.nl; internet www.cultureelerfgoed.nl; f. 1918, present name and status 2009; attached to Min. of Education, Culture and Science; conservation of nat. heritage; Dir Drs CEES VAN 'T VEEN; publ. *Tijdschrift van de Rijksdienst voor het Cultureel Erfgoed* (4 a year).

BIBLIOGRAPHY, LIBRARY SCIENCE AND MUSEOLOGY

FOBID Netherlands Library Forum: POB 90407, 2509 LK The Hague; tel. (70) 3140511; fax (70) 3140651; e-mail fobid@kb.nl; internet sitegenerator.bibliotheek.nl/fobid; f. 1974; library umbrella org. for advocacy and devt in the field of legal matters, professional education, classification standards, int. affairs; promotion of cooperation and integration among public, research and spec. libraries in the Netherlands; mems: Netherlands Public Library Asscn (VOB), Netherlands Asscn for Library, Information and Knowledge Professionals (NVB), Nat. Library of the Netherlands (KB) and UKB, the cooperative Asscn of 13 univ. libraries, the Nat. Library and the Library of the Royal Dutch Acad. of Science; Dir and Sec. Dr MARIAN KOREN.

Nederlandse Museumvereniging (Netherlands Museums Association): POB 2975, 1000 CZ Amsterdam; Rapenburgerstraat 123, 1011 VL Amsterdam; tel. (20) 5512900; fax (20) 5512901; e-mail info@museumvereniging.nl; internet www.museumvereniging.nl; f. 1926; devt of museums in terms of professionalism and quality; 450 mems; Chair. ERIC FISCHER; Vice-Chair. and Sec. WILLEM BIJLEVELD; Treas. PETER VERHOEVEN; publ. *Museumvisie* (Museum Vision, 4 a year).

Nederlandse Vereniging voor Beroepsbeoefenaren in de bibliotheek-, informatie- en kennissector (NVB) (Netherlands Association for Library, Information and Knowledge Professionals): Mariaplaats 3, 3511 LH Utrecht; tel. (30) 2330050; fax (30) 2380030; e-mail info@nvbonline.nl; internet www.nvbonline.nl; f. 1912; maintenance of lawful regulation of library system; arrangement of meetings and int. cooperation; professional education; 2,500 individual, 700 institutional mems; Pres. Drs BART VAN DER MEIJ; Chair. M. G. WESSELING; Man. Dir Drs JAN VAN DER BURG; Sec. C. KORLVINKE; Treas. HUIB VERHOEFF; publs *NVB—Nieuwsbrief*, *Informatie Professional*.

Vereniging Openbare Bibliotheken (Netherlands Public Library Association): POB 16146, 2500 BC The Hague; Grote Marktstraat 43, 2511 BH The Hague; tel. (70) 3090500; fax (70) 3090599; e-mail vereniging@debibliotheken.nl; internet www.debibliotheken.nl; f. 1972; defends common interests of the public library sector; 300 mem. instns; Chair. Prof. ERIK JURGENS; Vice-Chair. and Treas. CHARLES NOORDAM; Sec. MARION MERTENS; publ. *Bibliotheekblad* (26 a year).

ECONOMICS, LAW AND POLITICS

Internationaal Juridisch Instituut (International Legal Institute): Spui 186, 2511 BW The Hague; tel. (70) 3460974; fax (70) 3625235; e-mail info@iji.nl; internet www.iji.nl; f. 1918; supplies legal opinions regarding private int. law and foreign (also mostly private) law to the Netherlands judiciary, the Netherlands bar and to other mems of the legal profession, such as civil law notaries; also gives information to judges and lawyers outside the Netherlands; Chair. Prof. A. V. M. STRUYCKEN; Vice-Chair. L. STRIKWERDA; Dir Prof. W. G. HUIJGEN; Deputy Dir E. N. FROHN; Sec. A .C. OLLAND; Treas. G. J. C. VAN ENGELEN.

Koninklijke Vereniging voor de Staathuishoudkunde (Royal Netherlands Economic Association): c/o De Nederlandsche Bank NV, POB 98, 1000 AB Amsterdam; tel. (20) 5242280; fax (20) 5242500; e-mail info@kvsweb.nl; internet www.kvsweb.nl; f. 1849; promotes economic knowledge; 1,550 mems; Chair. Prof. Dr A. W. A. BOOT; Sec. and Treas. Prof. Dr L. H. HOOGDUIN; publs *De Economist* (4 a year), *Preadviezen* (1 a year).

Nederlandse Vereniging voor Internationaal Recht (Netherlands Branch of International Law Association): POB 9520, 2300 RA Leiden; Steenschuur 25, 2311 ES Leiden; tel. (71) 5277748; fax (71) 5277383; e-mail info@nvir.org; internet www.nvir.org; f. 1910; practices and promotes int. public and private law; 475 mems; Pres. Prof. Dr N. J. SCHRIJVER; Hon. Sec. Prof. Dr M. M. T. A. BRUS; publ. *Mededelingen* (1 a year).

Vereniging voor Agrarisch Recht (Agrarian Law Society): Maliesingel 20, 3581 BE Utrecht; tel. (30) 2320826; fax (30) 2341644; e-mail hvanbasten@verenigingagrarischrecht.nl; internet www.verenigingagrarischrecht.nl; f. 1959; promotes scientific and practical practice of agricultural law; 300 mems; Chair. Prof. G. M. F. SNIJDERS; Sec. and Treas. H. A. VAN BASTEN; publ. *Agrarisch Recht* (Agrarian Law).

Vereniging voor Arbeidsrecht (Labour Law Society): De Eem 15, 3448 DS Woerden; fax (348) 422635; e-mail info@verenigingvoorarbeidsrecht.nl; internet www.verenigingvoorarbeidsrecht.nl; f. 1946; acts as a forum for those who practice labour law; 940 mems; Chair. Prof. WILLEM H. A. C. M. BOUWENS; Sec. P. DE CASPARIS; Treas. R. J. KOOIJ.

FINE AND PERFORMING ARTS

Arti et Amicitiae: Rokin 112, 1012 LB Amsterdam; tel. (20) 6245134; fax (20) 6225206; e-mail arti@arti.nl; internet www.arti.nl; f. 1839; a nat. soc. of painters, sculptors and graphic artists; exhibition gallery; 1,550 mems (incl. 550 artist mems); Chair. ARIE VAN DEN BERG; Vice-Chair. ROBERT SAMKALDEN; Sec DIRK JAN JAGER; publ. *De Nieuwe* (6 a year).

Koninklijke Nederlandse Toonkunstenaars Vereniging (Royal Dutch Musician's Union): Grote Bickersstraat 50A, 1013 KS Amsterdam; tel. (20) 5221020; fax (20) 6200229; e-mail office@kntv.nl; internet www.kntv.nl; f. 1875; promotes the interests of professional musicians working in the field of performing arts and education; 3,400 mems; Dir GUSTA KORTEWEG; publ. *KNTV-Magazine* (6 a year).

Rijksbureau voor Kunsthistorische Documentatie (Netherlands Institute for Art History): POB 90418, 2509 LK The Hague; Prins Willem-Alexanderhof 5, 2595 BE The Hague; tel. (70) 3339777; fax (70) 3339789; e-mail info@rkd.nl; internet www.rkd.nl; f. 1932, present status 1995; art-historical information centre; administers colln of documentary, library and archive material on Western art from late Middle Ages to present; library of 450,000 vols, periodicals and catalogues, and press-cuttings, archives, 7m. photos and reproductions; Chair. Prof. P. SCHNABEL; Dir Prof. Dr RUDI E.O. EKKART; publs *Oud-Holland* (4 a year), *RKD Bulletin* (2 a year).

Theater Instituut Nederland (Netherlands Theatre Institute): POB 10783, 1001 ET Amsterdam; Sarphatistraat 53, 1018 EW Amsterdam; tel. (20) 5513300; fax (20) 5513303; e-mail info@tin.nl; internet www.theaterinstituut.nl; f. 1924 as Theatre Museum, present name and status 1992; service org. and research institute for the professional theatre; theatre library; supports and promotes Dutch theatre and theatre persons nationally and internationally; organizes debates and exhibitions; library of 100,000 vols and sound archives and 6,000 video cassettes of the Dutch theatre; Chair. HANS ANDERSSON; Dir HENK SCHOLTEN; publs *Bulletin* (2 a year), *Carnet* (in French and English), *Nederlands Theaterjaarboek* (1 a year).

Vereniging Toonkunst Nederland (Society for the Advancement of Music): Atlantisplein 1, Room 2.04, 1093 NE Amsterdam; tel. (20) 6713091; e-mail info@toonkunstnederland.nl; internet www.toonkunstnederland.nl; f. 1829, present status 2007; assen of amateur choirs and orchestras; 5,000 mems; Chair. GERARD BROEKMANS; Sec. RIA ROELANDS.

Wagnergenootschap Nederland (Wagner Society Netherlands): De Helling 79, 1502 GE, Zaandam; tel. (75) 6157793; e-mail bestuur@wagnergenootschap.nl; internet www.wagnergenootschap.nl; f. 1961; promotes and studies works and life of composer Richard Wagner; 300 mems; Chair. TON HOGENES; Sec. JACK VAN DONGEN; Treas. JAN BURGER; publ. *Wagner After All* (5 a year).

HISTORY, GEOGRAPHY AND ARCHAEOLOGY

Centraal Bureau voor Genealogie (Central Bureau for Genealogy): POB 11755, 2502 AT The Hague; Prins Willem-Alexanderhof 22, 2595 BE The Hague; tel. (70) 3150570; fax (70) 3478394; internet www.cbg.nl; f. 1945; large genealogical and heraldic collns; 14,350 mems; library of 100,000 vols; Chair. Dr PIETER WINSEMIUS; Deputy Chair. Dr ELS M. KLOEK; Dir Dr A. J. LEVER; publs *Genealogie* (4 a year), *Jaarboek* (yearbook).

Internationaal Instituut voor Sociale Geschiedenis (International Institute of Social History): POB 2169, 1000 CD Amsterdam; Cruquiusweg 31, 1019 AT Amsterdam; tel. (20) 6685866; fax (20) 6654181; e-mail info@iisg.nl; internet www.iisg.nl; f. 1935; attached to Royal Netherlands Acad. of Arts and Sciences; documentation and research centre in the field of social history; colln, preservation and availability of heritage of social movements worldwide; library of 1,000,000 vols, archives, especially on the labour movement, 60,000 periodicals; Gen. Dir Prof. Dr ERIK-JAN ZÜRCHER; Dir for Collns and Digital Infrastructure TITIA VAN DER WERF-DAVELAAR; Dir for Research MARCEL VAN DER LINDEN; Exec. Sec. MONIQUE KRUITHOF; publ. *International Review of Social History* (3 a year, plus supplement).

Koninklijk Fries Genootschap voor Geschiedenis en Cultuur/Keninklik Frysk Genoatskip foar Skiednis en Kultuer (Royal Frisian Society for History and Culture): Turfmarkt 11, 8911 KS Leeuwarden; tel. (58) 2555500; e-mail fries.genootschap@friesmuseum.nl; internet www.friesgenootschap.nl; f. 1827, present name 2003; promotes history and culture of Friesland; supports research in that field; 1,800 mems; Chair. Dr PIET HEMMINGA; Sec. LOURENS OLDERSMA; Treas. Drs DIRK VAN DER BIJ; publs *De Vrije Fries* (yearbook), *Fryslân* (4 a year).

Koninklijk Nederlands Aardrijkskundig Genootschap (Royal Dutch Geographical Society): POB 805, 3500 AV Utrecht; Ganzenmarkt 6, 3512 GD Utrecht; tel. (30) 2361202; fax (30) 2621290; e-mail info@knag.nl; internet www.knag.nl; f. 1873; promotes geography as subject and profession; organizes confs, workshops, lectures, seminars; publishes scientific journals and books; 3,500 mems; Dir Drs EELKO POSTMA; Chair. HENK OTTENS; Treas. LEON BUSSCHOPS; publs *Geografie* (9 a year), *Tijdschrift voor Economische en Sociale Geografie (TESG)* (Journal of Economic and Social Geography, 5 a year).

Koninklijk Nederlands Historisch Genootschap (Royal Netherlands Historical Society): POB 90406, 2509 LK The Hague; Prins Willem-Alexanderhof 5, 2595 BE The Hague; tel. (70) 3140363; fax (70) 3140637; e-mail info@knhg.nl; internet www.knhg.nl; f. 1845; promotes historical studies and dissemination of historical research with spec. regard to history of low countries; 1,600 mems; Chair. Prof. Dr A. F. (LEX) HEERMA VAN VOSS; Dir Dr L. M. L. M. DE GOEI; Treas. Prof. Dr JORIS VAN EIJNATTEN; publs *Bijdragen en Mededelingen betreffende de Geschiedenis der Nederlanden* (The Low Countries' Historical Review, 4 a year), *HG-Nieuws* (4 a year, digital).

Koninklijk Oudheidkundig Genootschap (Royal Dutch Antiquarian Society): POB 74888, 1070 DN Amsterdam; Frans van Mierisstraat 92, 1071 RZ Amsterdam; tel. (20) 6747380; e-mail kog@rijksmuseum.nl; internet www.kog.nu; f. 1858; colln of applied art (furniture, silver, sculpture, etc.), paintings, objects of historical value, prints and drawings concerning the topography of Amsterdam, manners and customs of the Netherlands; coins, medals, books; 540 mems; library of 6,100 vols; Pres. Drs NORBERT P. VAN DEN BERG; Sec. H. H. MANGER CATS-VAN DEN BERG; Treas. Dr J. KAMP.

Nederlandsch Economisch-Historisch Archief (NEHA) (Netherlands Economic-Historical Archives Society): Cruquiusweg 31, 1019 AT Amsterdam; tel. (20) 6685866; fax (20) 6654111; e-mail info@neha.nl; internet www.neha.nl; f. 1914; attached to Royal Netherlands Acad. of Arts and Sciences; specializes in economic history and business studies; 400 mems; library: see Libraries and Archives; Pres. Prof. Dr J. L. VAN ZANDEN; Sec. Dr E. A. G. VAN DEN BENT; Archivist JACK HOFMAN; Treas. Drs J. A. DE JONGH; publ. *Tijdschrift voor Sociale en Economische Geschiedenis* (4 a year).

Vereniging Gelre: Markt 1, 6811 CG Arnhem; e-mail info@verenigingelre.nl; internet www.vereniginggelre.nl; f. 1897; promotes practice of archeology, history and law of Gelderland; organizes seminars and symposia; Pres. Dr J. A. H. BOTS; Sec. Dr F. J. W. VAN KAN; Treas. DE HEER M. GRAS; publs *Bijdragen en Mededelingen* (1 a year), *Werken*.

LANGUAGE AND LITERATURE

Alliance Française: POB 75736, 1070 AS Amsterdam; tel. (35) 6237667; e-mail info@alliance-francaise.nl; internet www.alliance-francaise.nl; f. 1888; offers courses and exams in French language and culture and promotes cultural exchange with France; attached offices in Alkmaar, Amersfoort, Apeldoorn, Arnhem, Baarland, Bergen-op-Zoom, Betuwe, Boskoop, Brakel, Breda, Den Haag, Den Helder, Deventer, Dordrecht, Eindhoven, Enschede, Friesland, Hart van Zeeland, Hoorn, Kennemerland, Maastricht, Meppel, Nijmegen, Ommen, Roermond, Roosendaal, Rotterdam, Twente, Utrecht, Vorden, Walcheren, Zutphen and Zwolle; Pres.

E. J. A. VAN TINTEREN-AMERICA; publs *En France* (4 a year), *En Route* (1 a year).

British Council: Weteringschans 85A, 1017 RZ Amsterdam; tel. (20) 5506060; fax (20) 6207389; e-mail exams@britishcouncil.nl; internet www.britishcouncil.org/netherlands; offers exams in English language and British culture and promotes cultural exchange with the UK; not open to gen. public; Dir MARTIN HOPE.

Goethe-Institut: Herengracht 470, 1017 CA Amsterdam; tel. (20) 5312900; fax (20) 6384631; e-mail info@amsterdam.goethe.org; internet www.goethe.de/ins/nl/ams/deindex.htm; offers courses and exams in German language and culture; promotes cultural exchange with Germany; attached centre in Rotterdam; Dir Dr BARBARA HONRATH.

Instituto Cervantes: Domplein 3, 3512 JC Utrecht; tel. (30) 2428477; fax (30) 2332970; e-mail cenutr@cervantes.es; internet utrecht.cervantes.es; f. 1992; offers courses and exams in Spanish language and culture and promotes cultural exchange with Spain and Spanish-speaking Latin and Central America; library of 14,000 vols; Dir PATRICIA IZQUIERDO IRANZO.

Maatschappij der Nederlandse Letterkunde (Society of Netherlands Literature): POB 9501, 2300 RA Leiden; Witte Singel 27, 2300 RA Leiden; tel. (71) 5272109; fax (71) 5272836; e-mail mnl@library.leidenuniv.nl; internet www.maatschappijdernederlandseletterkunde.nl; f. 1766; library administered by the library of Leiden Univ.; 1,500 mems; Chair. PETER SIGMOND; Vice-Chair. LUC DEVOLDERE; Sec. BERRY DONGELMANS; Treas. AAD GROOS; publs *Jaarboek der Maatschappij* (1 a year), *Nieuw Letterkundig Magazijn* (2 a year), *Tijdschrift voor Nederlandse Taal- en Letterkunde* (4 a year).

Netherlands Centre of the International PEN: Emmalaan 29, 3051 JC Rotterdam; tel. (10) 4229805; e-mail secretaariat@pencentrum.nl; f. 1923; 350 mems; Pres. HESTER KNIBBE; Sec. RENÉ APPEL; publ. *PEN Nieuwsbrief* (2 a year).

MEDICINE

Genootschap ter bevordering van Natuur-, Genees- en Heelkunde (Association for Advancement of Natural, Medical and Surgical Sciences): POB 94248, 1090 GE Amsterdam; tel. (20) 5255055; e-mail b.e.fabius@uva.nl; internet www.science.uva.nl/ngh; f. 1790; encourages physics, medicine, surgery; awards individuals who contribute original research of great interest; Pres. Prof. Dr C. J. F. VAN NOORDEN; Sec. Prof. Dr J. J. O. O. WIEGERINCK; Treas. Prof. Dr D. ROOS.

Koninklijke Nederlandsche Maatschappij tot bevordering der Geneeskunst (Royal Dutch Medical Association): POB 20051, 3502 LB Utrecht; Domus Medica, Mercatorlaan 1200, 3528 BL Utrecht; tel. (30) 2823800; fax (30) 2823326; e-mail info@fed.knmg.nl; internet knmg.artsennet.nl; f. 1849; professional org. for physicians of The Netherlands; improves quality of medical care and healthcare; library on history of medicine in the Netherlands; 49,000 mems; Chair. Prof. Dr ARIE C. NIEUWENHUIJZEN KRUSEMAN; publs *Arts in Spe* (4 a year), *Medisch Contact* (52 a year).

Koninklijke Nederlandse Maatschappij ter Bevordering der Pharmacie (Royal Dutch Association for the Advancement of Pharmacy): POB 30460, 2500 GL The Hague; Alexanderstraat 11, 2514 JL The Hague; tel. (70) 3737373; fax (70) 3106530; e-mail communicatie@knmp.nl; internet www.knmp.nl; f. 1842; promotes the interests of professional and industrial pharmacists; c. 3,500 mems; Pres. JAN SMITS; Vice-Pres. MAAYKE FLUITMAN; Dir-Gen. LÉON TINKE; Sec. JARD BALJET; Treas. BART SMALS; publ. *Pharmaceutisch Weekblad*.

Nederlandse Vereniging voor Heelkunde (Association of Surgeons of the Netherlands): POB 20061, 3502 LB Utrecht; Domus Medica, Mercatorlaan 1200, 3528 BL Utrecht; tel. (30) 2823327; fax (30) 2823329; e-mail nvvh@nvvh.knmg.nl; internet www.heelkunde.nl; f. 1902; promotes surgery and interests of gen. surgeons; 1,330 mems (incl. 15 hon. mems, 200 assoc. mems, 490 asst mems); Chair. Dr P. J. VAN DEN AKKER; Dir Drs B. X. OUDE ELBERINK; Vice-Chair. Prof. Dr R. A. E. M. TOLLENAAR; Sec.-Gen. Dr G. A. P. NIEUWENHUIJZEN; Treas. Dr M. H. A. BEMELMANS; publ. *Nederlands Tijdschrift voor Heelkunde* (12 a year); publ. *The European Journal of Surgery* (English, 12 a year).

Nederlandse Vereniging voor Microbiologie (Netherlands Society for Microbiology): POB 214, 2600 AE Delft; tel. (10) 7509766; fax (62) 2607479; e-mail secretariaat@nvvm-online.nl; internet www.nvvm-online.nl; f. 1911; attached to Fed. of European Microbiological Socs; promotes microbiology in the Netherlands and Flanders; organizes symposia; 1,176 mems; Chair. Prof. Dr. H. A. B. WOSTEN; Vice-Chair. Prof. Dr J. A. G. VAN STRIJP; Sec. Dr B. DUIM; Treas. Dr J. W. SANDERS.

Nederlandse Vereniging voor Neurologie (Netherlands Society for Neurology): POB 20050, 3502 LB Utrecht; Mercatorlaan 1200, 3528 BL Utrecht; tel. (30) 2823343; e-mail bureau@neurologie.nl; internet www.neurologie.nl; f. 1871, reorganized 1974; monitors, promotes and optimizes professional quality of care for people with diseases of the nervous system or muscles; 800 mems; Pres. Prof. Dr M. DE VISSER; Sec. Prof. Dr C. H. POLMAN; publ. *Clinical Neurology and Neurosurgery*.

Nederlandse Vereniging voor Orthodontische Studie (Netherlands Orthodontics Society): Mahatma Gandhistraat 10, 3066 VA Rotterdam; tel. (10) 2020006; e-mail info@nvos.info; internet www.nvos.info; f. 1946; offers guidance, training and information on changing insights and new methods; 700 mems; Chair. HERMAN VAN BEEK; Vice-Chair. CARINE CARELS; Sec. MANFRED LEUNISSE; publ. *Chain Nieuwsbrief* (2 a year).

Nederlandse Vereniging voor Psychiatrie (Netherlands Psychiatric Association): POB 20062, 3502 LB, Utrecht; Mercatorlaan 1200, 3528 BL, Utrecht; tel. (30) 2823303; fax (30) 2888400; e-mail info@nvvp.net; internet www.nvvp.net; f. 1871, reorganized 1973; 3,409 mems; Pres. Prof. Dr R. J. VAN DER GAAG; Vice-Pres. P. M. F. J. J. KNAPEN; Dir PETER NIESINK; Treas. J. A. VAN WAARDE; publ. *Tijdschrift voor Psychiatrie*.

Nederlandse Vereniging voor Tropische Geneeskunde en Internationale Gezondheidszorg (Netherlands Society for Tropical Medicine and International Health): POB 5032, 1200 MA Hilversum; tel. (63) 4306672; e-mail nvtg@xs4all.nl; internet www.nvtg.org; f. 1907; supports research; provides education; promotes exchange of expertise and knowledge in the field of tropical medicine and int. health for improvement of health care in low- and middle-income countries; 1,000 mems; Chair. Dr PIETER VAN DEN HOMBERGH; Sec. Dr J. F. WENDTE; Treas. Drs JAN VISSCHEDIJK; publ. *MT Bulletin of the Netherlands Society of Tropical Medicine and International Health* (4 a year).

Vereniging van Orthodontisten (Association of Orthodontists): Simon Vestdijkstraat 67, 3842 LK Harderwijk; tel. (65) 3264175; e-mail info@orthodontist.nl; internet www.orthodontist.nl; f. 1962; Chair. Drs N. E. P. BENNITT; Vice-Chair. Dr C. M. KORSTJENS; Sec. Drs G. P. STEENVOORDEN; Treas. Drs P. C. M. ZUURBIER.

Vereniging voor Volksgezondheid en Wetenschap (Netherlands Society of Public Health and Science): Lindelaan 4, 2282 EX Rijswijk; tel. (70) 3030045; fax (70) 7168270; e-mail secretariaat@verenigingvenw.nl; internet www.verenigingvenw.nl; f. 1985, fmrly Algemene Nederlandse Vereniging voor Sociale Gezondheidszorg; scientific approach to health and health care questions; 800 mems; Pres. Prof. Dr J. SCHUIT; Sec. Ir I. THIEN; Treas. Ir J. JANSEN; publs *European Journal of Public Health* (4 a year), *Tijdschrift voor Gezondheidswetenschappen* (8 a year).

NATURAL SCIENCES

General

Koninklijke Nederlandse Natuurhistorische Vereniging (Royal Dutch Society for Natural History): POB 310, 3700 AH Zeist; Blvd 12, 3707 BM Zeist; tel. (30) 2314797; fax (30) 2368907; e-mail bureau@knnv.nl; internet www.knnv.nl; f. 1901; field biology; supports active participation in and with nature through natural history studies, by enjoying nature and through nature conservation; 8,300 mems; Chair. K. D. WATERREUS; Sec. F. J. M. VAN BUSSEL; Treas. C. J. ANKERSMIT; publ. *Natura* (6 a year).

Natuurmonumenten: POB 9955, 1243 ZS 's-Graveland; Schaep en Burgh, Noordereinde 60, 1243 JJ 's-Graveland; tel. (35) 6559933; fax (35) 6563174; internet www.natuurmonumenten.nl; f. 1905; preserves nature, landscape and cultural history; controls 355 nature reserves; 830,000 mems; Pres. Prof. Dr CEES VEERMAN; Vice-Pres. and Sec. Prof. Dr MARTIN WASSEN; Dir-Gen. Ir JAN JAAP DE GRAEFF; Dir for Finance and Operations Drs FEDDE KOSTER; Treas. JAN VAN DEN BELT; publ. *Natuurbehoud* (4 a year).

Stichting Natuur en Milieu (Society for Nature and Environment): POB 1578, 3500 BN Utrecht; Hamburgerstraat 28A, 3512 NS Utrecht; tel. (30) 2331328; fax (30) 2331311; internet www2.natuurenmilieu.nl; f. 1972, present location 2007; nature conservation and environmental protection; Chair. M. VAN LIER LELS; Dir TJERK WAGENAAR; publ. *Natuur en milieu* (12 a year).

Thijmgenootschap (Society of Christian Scholars in the Netherlands): Groesbeekseweg 125, 6524 CT Nijmegen; e-mail contact@thijmgenootschap.nl; internet www.thijmgenootschap.nl; f. 1904 as Vereeniging tot het Bevorderen van de Beoefening der Wetenschap onder de Katholieken in Nederland, present name 1947; promotes scientific reflection from a Christian perspective on devts in culture and soc.; 1,500 mems; Pres. Prof. Dr WIM B. H. J. VAN DE DONK; Sec. Prof. Drs J. S. L. A. W. B. ROES; Treas. ROLAND E. C. VAN DER PLUYM; publ. *Annalen van het Thijmgenootschap* (4 a year).

Biological Sciences

Koninklijke Nederlandse Botanische Vereniging (Royal Botanical Society of the Netherlands): c/o Dr. Ir. N. Smits, Alterra WUR, POB 47, 6700 AA Wageningen; e-mail nina.smits@wur.nl; internet www.knbv.eu; f. 1845; promotes knowledge of plants through education and research in areas such as plant ecology, plant molecular biology, plant physiology, plant taxonomy, vegetation science; 350 mems; Chair. Prof. Dr JOOP H. J.

SCHAMINÉE; Vice-Chair. Prof. Dr THEO ELZENGA; First Sec. Dr TON PEETERS; Second Sec. Dr NINA SMITS; Treas. Dr TIJS KETELAAR; publ. *Plant Biology*.

Koninklijke Nederlandse Dierkundige Vereniging (Royal Dutch Zoological Society): c/o Dr. P. H. M. Klaren, Radboud Univ. Nijmegen, Faculty of Science, Dept of Organismal Animal Physiology, Heyendaalseweg 135, 6525 AJ Nijmegen; tel. (24) 3653245; fax (24) 3653229; e-mail p.klaren@science.ru.nl; internet www.kndv.nl; f. 1872; promotes zoological research; organizes symposia; 250 mems; Pres. Prof. Dr NICO M. VAN STRAALEN; Sec. Dr PETER H. M. KLAREN; Treas. Dr KATJA J. TEERDS; publs *Animal Biology* (online, www.brill.nl/ab), *Bionieuws* (24 a year).

Natura Artis Magistra (Royal Zoological Society): POB 20164, 1000 HD Amsterdam; Plantage Kerklaan 38–40, Amsterdam; tel. (900) 2784796; fax (20) 5233637; e-mail info@artis.nl; internet www.artis.nl; f. 1838; promotes humans connection with nature, relationship between nature and culture and degree of human interaction in this position; 8,000 mems; Dir Dr HAIG BALIAN; publs *Artis* (5 a year), *Contributions to Zoology, Artis Library* (4 a year), *Tijdschrift van Natura Artis Magistra* (4 a year).

Nederlandse Entomologische Vereniging (Netherlands Entomological Society): Sj. Tiemersma, Vlasakker 2, 8091 MP Wezep; tel. (38) 3758275; e-mail secretaris@nev.nl; internet www.nev.nl; f. 1845; promotes entomology; 5 regional brs; library of 21,000 vols, 4,400 journals, 100,000 reprints; 700 mems; Pres. Dr MATTY P. BERG; Vice-Pres. Prof. Dr MARCEL DICKE; Sec. SJ. TIEMERSMA; Treas. Dr P. OOSTERBROEK; publs *Entomologia Experimentalis et Applicata* (12 a year), *Entomologische Berichten* (6 a year), *Tijdschrift voor Entomologie* (4 a year).

Nederlandse Mycologische Vereniging (Dutch Mycological Society): Centraalbureau voor Schimmelcultures, POB 85167, 3508 AD Utrecht; Uppsalalaan 8, 3584 CT Utrecht; tel. (30) 2122600; e-mail nmv@mycologen.nl; internet www.mycologen.nl; f. 1908; studies fungi; 800 mems; Chair. ROB CHRISPIJN; Sec. JAC N. J. GELDERBLOM; Treas. AAD J. TERMORSHUIZEN; publ. *Coolia* (4 a year).

Nederlandse Ornithologische Unie (Dutch Ornithological Union): Sloet Marke 41, 8016 CJ Zwolle; e-mail nou.ledenadmin@gmail.com; internet nou.natuurinfo.nl; f. 1901; study of ornithology; 1,067 mems; library: c. 120 periodicals; Pres. Prof. Dr J. M. TINBERGEN; Sec. PETER MILDERS; publs *Ardea* (2 a year), *Limosa* (4 a year).

Nederlandse Vereniging voor Parasitologie (Netherlands Society for Parasitology): c/o Dr J.J. Verweij, Laboratorium voor Parasitologie, L4-Q, LUMC, POB 9600, 2300 RC Leiden; e-mail j.j.verweij@lumc.nl; internet www.parasitologie.nl; f. 1961; promotes and exchanges scientific knowledge of infectious diseases caused by parasites; 250 mems; Pres. Prof. Dr ROBERT SAUERWEIN; Sec. Dr JACO. VERWEIJ; Treas. Dr CLEMENS KOCKEN.

Nederlandse Zoötechnische Vereniging (Netherlands Association for Animal Husbandry): POB 79, 6700 AB Wageningen; tel. (317) 483487; fax (317) 483976; e-mail info@nzvnet.nl; internet www.nzvnet.nl; f. 1930; platform for issues in the field of animals, people and environment; 530 mems; Pres. Ir GERT HEMKE; Sec. Ir G. H. JANSEN.

Mathematical Sciences

Koninklijk Wiskundig Genootschap (Royal Dutch Mathematical Society): CWI, POB 94079, 1090 GB Amsterdam; tel. (20) 5924226; fax (20) 5924199; e-mail wiskgenoot@wiskgenoot.nl; internet www.wiskgenoot.nl; f. 1778; organizes confs and symposia; 1,400 mems; library of 16,400 vols and journals of mathematics and its applications; Pres. Prof. Dr GERT VEGTER; Sec. Prof. Dr ROB D. VAN DER MEI; Treas. Dr SANDJAI BHULAI; publs *Nieuw Archief voor Wiskunde* (4 a year), *Pythagoras* (6 a year).

Vereniging voor Statistiek en Operationele Research (Netherlands Society for Statistics and Operations Research): POB 2095, 2990 DB Barendrecht; tel. (180) 623796; fax (180) 623670; e-mail admin@vvs-or.nl; internet www.vvs-or.nl; f. 1945; promotes study and application of statistics, operations research, relevant devts in mathematics in service of science and soc.; 800 mems; Chair. Prof. Dr R. D. GILL; Sec. Dr C. G. H. DIKS; Treas. Prof. Dr C. A. G. M. VAN MONTFORT; publs *Statistica Neerlandica* (4 a year), *Stator* (4 a year).

Physical Sciences

Koninklijk Nederlands Geologisch Mijnbouwkundig Genootschap (Royal Geological and Mining Society of the Netherlands): POB 30424, 2500 GK The Hague; Prinsessegracht 23, 2514 AP The Hague; tel. (70) 3919892; fax (70) 3919840; e-mail kngmg@mac.com; internet web.mac.com/kngmg; f. 1912; promotes the interests of earth sciences in the Netherlands; awards Van Waterschoot van der Gracht medal (an award for outstanding scientific achievement) and organizes the annual Staring lecture; sections for petroleum geology, paleobiolology, palynology, mineralogy, sedimentology, engineering geology and geochemistry; section for female professional earth scientists (GAIA) and various regional earth science asscns; 800 mems; Pres. MENNO DE RUIG; Sec. BARTHOLD SCHROOT; Treas. ARIAN STEENBRUGGEN; publs *Geo.brief* (8 a year), *Geologie en Mijnbouw* (Netherlands Journal of Geosciences, 4 a year).

Koninklijk Nederlands Meteorologisch Instituut (Royal Netherlands Meteorological Institute): POB 201, 3730 AE De Bilt; Wilhelminalaan 10, 3732 GK De Bilt; tel. (30) 2206911; fax (30) 2210407; e-mail prv@knmi.nl; internet www.knmi.nl; f. 1854, present location 1897; attached to Min. of Infrastructure and the Environment; meteorology, climatology, oceanography, seismology; conducts research on climate change; library of 140,000 vols, spec. collns incl. Polar expeditions; Dir-Gen. Dr Ir FRITS J. J. BROUWER; Exec. Dir. Drs D. R. VAN HATTEM; publs *Maandover zicht van het weer, Seismological Bulletin*, scientific reports and technical reports, daily weather maps, rain observations.

Koninklijke Nederlandse Chemische Vereniging (Royal Netherlands Chemical Society): POB 249, 2260 AE Leidschendam; Synthesium, Castellum C, Loire 150, 2491 AK The Hague; tel. (70) 3378790; fax (70) 3378799; e-mail kncv@kncv.nl; internet www.kncv.nl; f. 1903, present location 2006; promotes molecular sciences; 8,500 mems; Pres. Dr MARTIN POST; Vice-Pres. Drs JAN APOTHEKER; Sec. and Dir for Bureau Dr GABRIËLLE DONNÉ; Treas. Dr LENE HVIID; publs *Chemisch 2 Weekblad* (26 a year), *European Journal of Inorganic Chemistry* (12 a year), *European Journal of Organic Chemistry* (12 a year).

Koninklijke Nederlandse Vereniging voor Weer- en Sterrenkunde (Royal Dutch Society for Meteorology and Astronomy): Stichting De Koepel, Sterrenwacht 'Sonnenborgh', Zonnenburg 2, 3512 GB Utrecht; tel. (30) 2311360; fax (30) 2342852; e-mail info@dekoepel.nl; internet www.dekoepel.nl; f. 1901; public lectures, meetings, confs, observing sessions; 5,000 mems; Dir EDWIN MATHLENER; publs *Sterren & Planeten* (11 a year), *Sterrengids* (1 a year), *Zenit* (12 a year).

Nederlandse Natuurkundige Vereniging (Netherlands Physical Society): POB 41882, 1009 DB Amsterdam; Science Park 105, Kamer N227, 1098 XG Amsterdam; tel. (20) 5922211; fax (20) 5925155; e-mail bureau@nnv.nl; internet www.nnv.nl; f. 1921; improves study of physics and safeguards interests of physicists; 3,800 mems; Chair. Prof. Dr G. VAN DER STEENHOVEN; Sec. Prof. Dr P. J. G. MULDERS; Treas. Dr J. A. M. M. VAN HAAREN; publ. *Nederlands Tijdschrift voor Natuurkunde* (12 a year).

PHILOSOPHY AND PSYCHOLOGY

Algemene Nederlandse Vereniging voor Wijsbegeerte (General Netherlands Philosophical Society): c/o Erasmus Universiteit, Faculty of Philosophy, POB 1738, 3000 DR Rotterdam; Faculty of Philosophy, Campus Woudestein, H-Bldg, 5th fl., Burgemeester Oudlaan 50, 3062 PA Rotterdam; e-mail anvw@fwb.eur.nl; internet www.eur.nl/fw; f. 1933; 150 mems; Pres. Dr J. A. VAN RULER; Sec. Dr H. A. KROP; publ. *Algemeen Tijdschrift voor Wijsbegeerte*.

Affiliated Societies:

Internationale School voor Wijsbegeerte (International School of Philosophy): Dodeweg 8, 3832 RD Leusden; tel. (33) 4650700; fax (33) 4650541; e-mail info@isvw.nl; internet www.isvw.nl; f. 1916; courses and confs in philosophy; 3,000 mems; library of 3,000 vols; Man. Dir RENÉ GUDE; Dir for Operations CHANTAL ORTH.

KIVI Aftdeling Filosofie en Techniek: 23 Prinsessegracht, POB 30424, 2500 GK The Hague; f. 1847; Chair. R. E. C. H. TIEPEL; Sec. J. GROENHOEF.

Nederlands Genootschap voor Esthetica (Dutch Association for Aesthetics): Grevingaheerd 181, 9737 SL Groningen; internet www.nge.nl; f. 1997; asscn for theoretical, philosophical, critical reflection on the arts and aesthetic dimensions of contemporary culture; Chair. SANDER VAN MAAS; Vice-Chair. HANS MAES; Sec. RII DALITZ; publ. *Esthetica: Tijdschrift voor Kunst en Filosofie* (online).

Nederlandse Vereniging voor Godsdienstwijsbegeerte: Ring 34, 3227 AS Oudenhoorn; f. 1995.

Nederlandse Vereniging voor Logica en Wijsbegeerte der Exacte Wetenschappen: POB 407, 9700 AK Groningen; tel. (50) 3636334; e-mail rineke@ai.rug.nl; internet www.verenigingvoorlogica.nl; f. 1947; organizes scientific symposia; 150 mems; Chair. Prof. Dr RINEKE VERBRUGGE; Sec. Dr FEMKE VAN RAAMSDONK.

Nederlandse Vereniging voor Wetenschapsfilosofie (Dutch Society for Philosophy of Science): Faculty of Philosophy, Univ. of Groningen, Oude Boteringestr. 52 Groningen; tel. (50) 3636148; fax (50) 3636160; e-mail info@nvwf.nl; internet www.nvwf.nl; f. 1979; org. of confs, workshops and lectures; 80 mems; Pres. F. A. MULLER; Sec. Dr JAN-WILLEM ROMEIJN.

Stichting voor Reformatorische Wijsbegeerte (Association for Reformational Philosophy): POB 3206, 3760 DE Soest; tel. (35) 5880205; fax (35) 5880981; e-mail directie@christelijkefilosofie.nl; internet www.christelijkefilosofie.nl; f. 1935; asscn for Christian philosophy, based on thinking of philosophers such as Dutch Dooyeweerd, Schuurman, Van Riessen, Vollenhoven, foreign philosophers such as

Chaplin (UK), Clouser (USA), Strauss (South Africa); 535 mems; Pres. Drs A. Berger; Vice-Pres. Drs D. A. Meinema; Sec. Drs W. Vollbehr; publs *Philosophia Reformata* (in English, 2 a year), *Sophie* (in Dutch, 6 a year).

Vereniging voor Filosofie en Geneeskunde: p/a VUmc (MF) Afdeling Metamedica, Kamer D-322, t.a.v. E.J. Ettema Van der Boechorststraat 7 1081 BT Amsterdam; tel. (6) 27490195; e-mail m.vanzwol@vumc.nl; internet www.filosofieengeneeskunde.nl; f. 1981; Pres. Prof. Dr Tsjalling Swierstra; Sec. Drs Marjanne van Zwol.

Vereniging 'Het Spinozahuis': Paganinidreef 66, 2253 SK Voorschoten; tel. and fax (71) 5612759; e-mail info@spinozahuis.nl; internet www.spinozahuis.nl; f. 1897; promotes life and works of philosopher Benedictus de Spinoza; cultural monument, library, museum; library of 4,000 vols; 1,100 mems; Pres. L. van Bunge; Sec. Theo van der Werf; publ. *Mededelingen vanwege het Spinozahuis* (1 a year).

Vereniging voor Wijsbegeerte van het Recht: Faculty of Law, Kamerlingh Onnes Bldg, Steenschuur 25, Lorentzzaal, 2311 ES Leiden; e-mail penningmeester@verenigingrechtsfilosofie.nl; internet www.verenigingrechtsfilosofie.nl; f. 1919; promotes practice of legal philosophy and legal theory; Pres. Sanne Taekema; Sec. Gerard Drosterij; publ. *Nederlands Tijdschrift voor Rechtsfilosofie & Rechtstheorie* (3 a year).

Vereniging voor Wijsbegeerte te 's-Gravenhage: Nassau Dillenburgstraat 33, 2596 AC 's-Gravenhage; tel. (20) 6322644; e-mail frankwitzen@restricted.nl; internet www.verenigingvoorwijsbegeerte.nl; f. 1907; 100 mems; Pres. Ir J. M. Albers; Sec. F. Witzen R. A.

Wijsgerige Vereniging Thomas van Aquino: POB 37, 5260 AA Vught; Aloysiuslaan 2, 5262 AH Vught; tel. (73) 6579017; f. 1933; philosophical confs; 160 mems; Pres. Prof. Dr A. Leijen; Sec. Prof. Dr R. A. te Velde.

Bataafsch Genootschap der Proefondervindelijke Wijsbegeerte (Experimental Natural Philosophy Society): POB 597, 3000 AN Rotterdam; tel. (10) 4117947; e-mail secretariaat@bataafschgenootschap.nl; internet www.bataafschgenootschap.nl; f. 1769; organizes 6 lectures for mems each year; awards biannual prizes and an int. Steven Hoogendijk Award every 2 years; 400 mems; Pres. Prof. Ir L. van der Sluis; Dir Prof. Dr Ir J. K. Vrijling; Dir Prof. Dr F. B. de Waard-van der Spek; Dir Prof. Dr Huug W. Tilanus; Sec. Ir G. H. G. Lagers; Sec. Drs A. S. Sijsma.

Nederlands Psychoanalytisch Genootschap (Netherlands Psychoanalytical Association): Maliestraat 1a, 3581 SH Utrecht; tel. (30) 2307080; fax (30) 2343883; e-mail npg@npsai-utrecht.nl; internet www.npg-utrecht.nl; f. 1947; organizes scientific meetings, lectures and symposia; 136 mems; library of 60,000 vols; Sec. Ria Haentjens Dekker.

RELIGION, SOCIOLOGY AND ANTHROPOLOGY

Fryske Akademy: POB 54, 8900 AB Ljouwert; Doelestraat 8, 8911 DX Ljouwert; tel. (58) 2131414; fax (58) 2131409; e-mail fa@fryske-akademy.nl; internet www.fryske-akademy.nl; f. 1938; attached to Royal Netherlands Acad. of Arts and Science; devoted to the scientific study of Friesland, the Frisians and their language, history and culture; 450 mems; library of 20,000 vols; Dir Prof. Dr R. Salverda; publs *De Vrije Fries* (history, 1 a year), *It Beaken* (scientific, 4 a year), *Ut de Smidte fan de Fryske Akademy* (information, 4 a year).

TECHNOLOGY

Economisch Instituut voor de Bouw (Economic Institute for the Building): POB 58248, 1040 HE Amsterdam; Basisweg, 10 1043 AP Amsterdam; tel. (20) 5831900; fax (20) 5831999; e-mail eib@eib.nl; internet www.eib.nl; f. 1956 as Economic Institute for the Bldg Industry; promotes applied research org. bldg and economic analysis; Chair. Carel A. Adriaansens; Dir Drs T. H. van Hoek; Deputy Dir Drs O. M. Vries; Sec. Debbie van Amerongen; Sec. G. Kramer; publs *Algemene kosten in het bouwbedrijf* (1 a year), *Bedrijfseconomische kencijfers* (1 a year), *Bedrijfseconomische kencijfers in de gww-sector* (1 a year), *Verwachtingen bouwproductie en werkgelegenheid* (1 a year).

Koninklijk Instituut van Ingenieurs (KIVI NIRIA) (Royal Institute of Engineers (KIVI NIRIA)): POB 30424, 2500 GK The Hague; Prinsessegracht 23, 2514 AP The Hague; tel. (70) 3919900; fax (70) 3919840; e-mail info@kiviniria.nl; internet www.kiviniria.net; f. 2004, by merger of Dutch NIRIA Engineers Asscn and Royal Institute of Engineers; asscn for engineers and engineering students; promotes technology; 25,000 mems; Pres. Martin C. J. van Pernis; Vice-Pres. Joost J. Wentink; Dir Ir P. L. M. Gilissen; Sec. Jacky C. Gersie; publ. *De Ingenieur Technologiemagazine* (26 a year); publs *Kivi-nieuws* (26 a year), *Technisch Weekblad* (52 a year), *Techno!.*

Technologiestichting STW (Technology Foundation): POB 3021, 3502 GA Utrecht; Van Vollenhovenlaan 661, 3527 JP Utrecht; tel. (30) 6001211; fax (30) 6014408; e-mail info@stw.nl; internet www.stw.nl; f. 1981; improves and stimulates applied sciences and engineering by sponsoring research at (technical) univs in the Netherlands and promotes cooperation between those institutes and industry; also assists in implementing spec. governmental research programmes; Dir Dr Eppo E. W. Bruins; Deputy Dir Dr Chris A. M. Mombers; publ. *!nterval.*

Research Institutes

GENERAL

Adhesion Institute: Kluyverweg 1, 2629 HS Delft; tel. (15) 2785353; fax (15) 2787151; e-mail info@hechtingsinstituut.nl; internet www.adhesioninstitute.com; attached to Faculty of Aerospace Engineering, Delft Univ. of Technology; research focuses on latest devts on surface pre-treatment of metals and plastics, durability of adhesive bonds, the application of adhesive(s) and adhesive bond design, as well as (FEM)-calculations on structural adhesive bonding technology; Dir Dr J. A. Poulis.

Amsterdam Business School (ABS): Plantage Muidergracht, Room M2.42, 1018 WB Amsterdam; tel. (20) 5257384; fax (20) 5255092; e-mail abs-ri@uva.nl; internet www.abs.uva.nl; f. 2002; attached to Univ. of Amsterdam; research concerning accounting, business, finance, management; Dir Prof. Dr Allan Hodgson.

Amsterdam Center for Career Research (ACCR): De Boelelaan 1105, 1081 HV Amsterdam; tel. (20) 5986000; e-mail loopbanen@feweb.vu.nl; internet www.feweb.vu.nl/en/departments-and-institutes/accr; f. 2006; attached to VU Univ. Amsterdam; researches into factors contributing to growth of careers, in terms of devt and job level, within orgs.

Amsterdam Center for Entrepreneurship at VU: De Boelelaan 1085, 1081 Amsterdam; tel. (20) 5989906; fax (20) 5989904; e-mail infoacevu@feweb.vu.nl; internet www.feweb.vu.nl/acevu; research focuses on entrepreneurship as new venture creation, wealth creation as dominant motive to create new ventures, and entrepreneur as instigator of entrepreneurship; Dir Prof. Enno Masurel.

Amsterdam Institute for International Development (AIID): Trinity Bldg C, 3rd Fl., Room XT-3.17, Pietersbergweg 17, 1105 BM Amsterdam; tel. (20) 5661596; fax (20) 5665997; e-mail info@aiid.org; internet www.aiid.org; f. 2000; attached to Univ. of Amsterdam, Vrije Univ. Amsterdam; links the two univ. experts in int. devt and engages in policy debates; research on causes and consequences of poverty, human devt, governance and poverty, environment and devt, globalisation and devt assistance.

Brabant Centre of Entrepreneurship: POB 513, 5600 MB Eindhoven; Multimedia-Paviljoen, Room 0.21, Horsten 1, 5612 AX Eindhoven; tel. (40) 4663320; e-mail info@bc-e.nl; internet www.bc-e.nl; attached to Tilburg Univ.; Academic Dir Dr Geert Duysters; Business Dir Kees Kokke.

Centre for Innovation Research: Faculty of Social and Behavioural Sciences, POB 90153, 5000 LE Eindhoven; Prisma Bldg, Warandelaan 2, 5037 AB Eindhoven; tel. (13) 4663057; fax (13) 4663002; e-mail cir@uvt.nl; internet www.tilburguniversity.nl/cir; attached to Tilburg Univ.; fundamental research on innovation; research themes incl. innovation strategy, org. of innovation, organizational learning; Dir Prof. Dr X. Y. F. Martin; Dir Prof. Dr M. T. H. Meeus.

Centre for Development Studies (CDS): POB 800, Landleven 1, 9747 AD Groningen; tel. (50) 3637224; fax (50) 3633720; e-mail cds@rug.nl; internet www.rug.nl/cds/index; attached to Univ. of Groningen; fosters public debate on a wide range of topics varying from globalization, North–South relations and sustainable devt; Dir Pieter van Hensbroek.

Centrum voor Justitiepastoraat (Inter-university Centre for Pastoral Justice): POB 90153, 5000 LE Tilburg; Prof. Cobbenhagelaan 225, 5037 DB Tilburg; tel. (13) 4662609; e-mail info@centrumvoorjustitiepastoraat.nl; internet www.centrumvoorjustitiepastoraat.nl; f. 2009; attached to Tilburg Univ.; researches on issues relevant for the work of prison chaplains; Chair. and Dir Prof. Dr Theo W. A. de Wit; Chair. Prof. Dr Evert R. Jonker; Sec. Drs A. A. T. van Eijk.

Competence Centre for Pension Research: POB 90153, 5000 LE Tilburg; Montesquieu Bldg, Warandelaan 2, Room M612, 5037 AB Tilburg; tel. (13) 4662412; fax (13) 4663073; e-mail frw.ccp@uvt.nl; internet www.tilburguniversity.nl/ccp; attached to Faculty of Law, Tilburg Univ.; research in the fields of tax and civil law aspects of pensions and other retirement provisions; Chair. Prof. Dr Gerry Dietvorst; Sec. Tonia Nelen.

European Banking Centre: Tilburg Univ., POB 90153, 5000 LE Tilburg; Koopmans Bldg, Room 3 16, Warandelaan 2, 5037 AB Tilburg; tel. (13) 4662468; e-mail ebc@uvt.nl; internet www.tilburguniversity.nl/ebc; attached to Tilburg Univ.; stimulates and disseminates banking research, with three essential areas of expertise: central banking and financial supervision, European banking and regulation, and int. banking and finance; Chair. Prof. Dr THORSTEN BECK.

European Institute of Retailing and Services Studies (EIRASS): POB 513, Vertigo 8.18, 5600 MB Eindhoven; tel. (40) 2472594; fax (40) 2438488; e-mail eirass@bwk.tue.nl; internet w3.bwk.tue.nl/nl/onderzoek/urban_planning/eirass; attached to Eindhoven Univ. of Technology; organizes confs; progress in retailing and consumer services (tourism, recreation, banking, aspects of transportation, etc.); Dir Prof. HARRY TIMMERMANS; Sec. LINDA VAN DE VEN.

European Research Institute in Service Science (ERISS): Room K 731, POB 90153, 5000 LE Tilburg; Warandelaan 2, 5037 AB Tilburg; tel. (13) 4663020; fax (13) 4663069; e-mail eriss@uvt.nl; internet www.tilburguniversity.nl/eriss; attached to Tilburg Univ.; research in innovation, service science with a focus on critical business process areas that span several knowledge-intensive business services within vertical industries; Chair. of Advisory Board Prof. Dr PIET RIBBERS; Scientific Dir Prof. Dr Ir M. P. PAPAZOGLOU; Man. Dir Prof. Dr W. J. A. M. VAN DEN HEUVEL; Sec. ALICE KLOOSTERHUIS.

European Values Study (EVS): Dept of Sociology, Tilburg Univ., POB 90153, 5000 LE Tilburg; Faculty of Social and Behavioural Sciences, Tilburg Univ., Prisma Bldg, Warandelaan 2, 5037 AB Tilburg; tel. (13) 4662554; fax (13) 4663002; e-mail evs@uvt.nl; internet www.europeanvaluesstudy.eu; f. 1981; attached to Tilburg Univ.; research on basic human values; provides insights into the ideas, beliefs, preferences, attitudes, values and opinions of citizens all over Europe; how Europeans think about life, family, work, religion, politics and society; Chair. Prof. Dr JAAK BILLIET; Sec. LOEK HALMAN.

EXPres: Van der Boechorststraat 9, 1081 Amsterdam; e-mail expres@fbw.vu.nl; internet www.expertisecentrum-expres.nl; f. 1989; attached to Vrije Univ. Amsterdam; research on rehabilitation, ergonomics and sports.

Het Zijlstra Center: De Boelelaan 1105, 1081 HV Amsterdam; tel. (20) 5989865; e-mail info@hetzijlstracenter.nl; internet www.feweb.vu.nl/nl/afdelingen-en-instituten/het-zijlstra-center; f. 2009; attached to Univ. of Amsterdam; research focuses on management and operations of non-profits and govts that focus on solving social problems; contributes results to improvement of management of govts and civil society orgs; Dir Prof. Dr G. D. MINDERMAN; Sec. ANJA VAN EIJK.

iCRiSP—Centre for Conflict, Risk and Safety Perception: Citadel H 444, POB 217, 7500 AE Enschede; Citadel Bldg, H 444, Drienerlolaan 5, 7522 NB Enschede; tel. (53) 4896052; fax (53) 4892388; e-mail icrisp@utwente.nl; internet www.utwente.nl/ibr/icrisp; f. 2009; attached to Univ. of Twente; focuses on the implementation of knowledge from social and behavioural sciences regarding issues of conflict, risk, safety in public and private sectors of society; Dir Prof. Dr ELLEN GIEBELS; Dir Dr JAN GUTTELING.

Institute for Sport & Leisure: Univ. of Twente, bld. CTW - Z-115, Drienerlolaan 5, 7522 NB Enschede; tel. (53) 4893606; e-mail info@sportandleisure.nl; internet www.sportandleisure.nl; attached to Univ. of Twente; innovation, devt, prototyping, engineering for products within the field of sport and leisure.

Instituut voor Bedrijfs- en Industriële Statistiek (IBIS) (Institute for Business and Industrial Statistics): Plantage Muidergracht 12, 1018 TV Amsterdam; tel. (20) 5255203; e-mail info@ibisuva.nl; internet www.ibisuva.nl; f. 1994; attached to Univ. of Amsterdam; statistical methodology, business economic context of quality and efficiency improvement; Man. Dir Prof. Dr RONALD J. M. M. DOES.

International Victimology Institute Tilburg (INTERVICT): Room M734, POB 90153, 5000 LE Tilburg; Montesquieu Bldg, 7th Fl., Warandelaan 2, 5037 AB Tilburg; tel. (13) 4663526; fax (13) 4663546; e-mail intervict@uvt.nl; internet www.tilburguniversity.nl/intervict; attached to Tilburg Univ.; research areas incl. victims of abuse of power, crime and disaster; rights of victims; psychological effects of victimization; help provided to victims; social reactions to victims; Dir Prof. MARC S. GROENHUIJSEN; Deputy Dir Assoc. Prof. RIANNE M. LETSCHERT; Gen. Man. BARBARA M. VAN GORP.

IPIT Instituut voor Maatschappelijke Veiligheidsvraagstukken: Universiteit Twente, POB 217, 7500 AE Enschede; Capitool 15, Room C-201, Enschede; tel. (53) 4893280; fax (53) 4892159; e-mail ipit@bbt.utwente.nl; internet www.ipit.nl; attached to Univ. of Twente; law, public safety studies, law, risk analysis, risk management; research incl. functioning of insecurity and society, public safety maintenance system; Dir Prof. Dr M. JUNGER; Sec. J.L.M. (ANNETTE) VAN DER TUUK.

IVA Beleidsonderzoek en Advies: POB 90153, 5000 LE Tilburg; Campus Tilburg Univ., Bldg T, Warandelaan 2, 5037 AB Tilburg; tel. (13) 4668466; fax (13) 4668477; e-mail iva@uvt.nl; internet www.iva.nl; f. 1957; attached to Tilbug Univ.; applied scientific research, consultancy, implementation concerning current social devts, particularly in the domains of education, care and welfare, security, art, media and culture, labour and organizational issues; Pres. Prof. Dr MARC VERMEULEN; Man. Dir and Vice-Pres. MYLÈNE ZWAANS; Exec. Sec. ANNELIES VAN LEEUWEN.

IVO—Instituut voor Ontwikkelingsvraagstukken/Instituto de Estudios Para El Desarrollo (Development Research Institute): POB 90153, 5000 LE Tilburg; Tias Bldg, Office T-231, Warandelaan 2, 5037 AB Tilburg; tel. (13) 4662264; fax (13) 4663015; e-mail secr.ivo@uvt.nl; internet www.uvt.nl/ivo; f. 1963; attached to Tilburg Univ.; applied socio-economic research, training and capacity building in support of poverty alleviation in developing countries; Dir GERARD DE GROOT; Man. MARIA JOSÉ RODIL.

Kohnstamm Instituut (Kohnstamm Institute): POB 94208, 1090 GE Amsterdam; Plantage Muidergracht 24, 1018 TV Amsterdam; tel. (20) 5251226; fax (20) 5254029; e-mail secr@kohnstamm.uva.nl; internet www.kohnstamminstituut.uva.nl; f. fmrly as SCO-Kohnstamm Institute, present status 2009; attached to Univ. of Amsterdam; research areas incl. child rearing, child welfare, education; Man. Dir Drs J. E. KRAMER; Scientific Dir Drs G. LEDOUX; Deputy Dir Drs M. VAN ERP.

Kosmopolis Institute: POB 797, 3500 AT Utrecht; Univ. for Humanistics, Kromme Nieuwegracht 29, 3512 HD Utrecht; tel. (30) 2390100; e-mail kosmopolis@uvh.nl; internet www.uvh.nl; f. 2004; attached to Univ. for Humanistics; focuses on interdisciplinary teaching; training, research, networking on cosmopolitan dimensions of humanism in the world; Gen. Dir Prof. Dr HENK MANSCHOT; Deputy Dir Dr CAROLINE SURANSKY; Exec. Sec. DOROTHÉ VAN DRIEL.

Netspar, Network for Studies on Pensions, Aging and Retirement: POB 90153, 5000 MB Tilburg; Tilburg Univ. Campus, Tias Bldg, Warandelaan 2, 5037 AB Tilburg; tel. (13) 4662109; fax (13) 4663066; e-mail secretariaat@netspar.nl; internet www.netspar.nl; f. 2005; attached to Tilburg Univ.; research areas incl. ageing, pensions, retirement; Chair. Prof. Dr FRANK VAN DER DUYN SCHOUTEN; Scientific Dir THEO NIJMAN; Man. Dir DOMINIQUE DE VET; publ. *Netspar Magazine* (2 a year).

Nexus Instituut (Nexus Institute): POB 90153, 5000 LE Tilburg; Tilburg Univ., Room T203-209, Warandelaan 2, 5037 AB Tilburg; tel. (13) 4663450; fax (13) 4663434; e-mail nexus@nexus-instituut.nl; internet www.nexus-instituut.nl; f. 1994; attached to Tilburg Univ.; centre for intellectual reflection; organizes confs and lectures; Chair. of Supervisory Board Dr WIM VAN DEN GOORBERGH; Pres. and CEO ROB RIEMAN; Vice-Pres. KIRSTEN WALGREEN; publ. *Nexus* (3 a year).

Nikos—Dutch Institute for Knowledge Intensive Entrepreneurship: Univ. of Twente, POB 217, 7500 AE Enschede; Drienerlolaan 5, 7522 NB Enschede; tel. (53) 4894512; fax (53) 4893919; e-mail nikos@mb.utwente.nl; internet www.utwente.nl/mb/nikos; attached to Univ. of Twente; innovative entrepreneurship, int. management, marketing, strategic management; Scientific Dir Prof. Dr AARD J. GROEN; Sec. GLORIA ROSSINI.

Onderzoekscentrum Preventie Overgewicht Zwolle (Research Centre for the Prevention of Overweight Zwolle): VU-Windesheim, Campus 2–6, POB 10090, 8000 GB Zwolle; tel. (88) 4699096; e-mail preventieovergewicht@windesheim.nl; research on designing, implementing, evaluating and disseminating knowledge related to prevention of obesity in 0–19 year old children; Man. Dir Dr SASKIA VAN HELDEN.

Rathenau Instituut (Rathenau Institute): POB 95366, 2509 CJ The Hague; Anna van Saksenlaan 51, 2593 HW The Hague; tel. (70) 3421542; fax (70) 3633488; e-mail info@rathenau.nl; internet www.rathenau.nl; f. 1986 as Netherlands Org. for Technology Assessment, present name 1994; attached to Royal Netherlands Acad. of Arts and Sciences; supports social and political opinion-forming on issues arising from scientific and technological devt; Chair. WIM VAN VELZEN; Sec. Drs JAN STAMAN.

Research Center voor Examinering en Certificering (RCEC) (Research Center for Examinations and Certification (RCEC)): POB 217, 7500 AE Enschede; tel. (53) 4893555; fax (53) 4894239; e-mail rcec@gw.utwente.nl; internet www.rcec.nl; f. 2007; attached to Univ. of Twente; stimulates and facilitates ind. research into examinations and certification; conducts research projects for public and private orgs; gives training in educational measurement; disseminates information by organizing confs on issues in examinations; Dir BERNARD P. VELDKAMP; Dir Dr PIET F. SANDERS.

Research Institute for Flexicurity, Labour Market Dynamics and Social Cohesion (ReflecT): Tilburg Univ., S 424, POB 90153, 5000 LE Tilburg; Simon Bldg (entrance at Prof. Verbernelaan), 4th Fl., Room S 424, 5000 LE Tilburg; tel. (13) 4662181; e-mail reflect@uvt.nl; internet www.tilburguniversity.nl/reflect; attached to Tilburg Univ.; combines legal, economic, sociological and psychological approaches and adopts a multi-level perspective in studying the interplay between various regulatory and institutional levels in society: the European/int., nat., sector and company/

individual level; Dir Prof. A. C. J. M. (TON) WILTHAGEN; Sec. A. I. (ANNET) VAN HUIJKELOM.

Tilburg Centre of Finance: Loes de Groot, K 916, POB 90153, 5000 LE Tilburg; tel. (13) 4663041; fax (13) 4662875; e-mail tcf@uvt.nl; internet www.tilburguniversity.edu/research/institutes-and-research-groups/tcf; attached to Tilburg Univ.; research areas incl. actuarial profession, finance, governance and supervision; Mem. of Board Prof. Dr BAS WERKER; Mem. of Board Prof. Dr FRANK DE JONG; Mem. of Board Prof. Dr FRANS DE ROON.

Tilburg Sustainability Center (TSC): Tilburg Univ., POB 90153, 5000 LE Tilburg; Tilburg Univ., Koopmans Bldg, K405, Warandelaan 2, 5037 AB Tilburg; tel. (13) 4664148; e-mail tsc@uvt.nl; internet www.tilburguniversity.nl/tsc; f. 2009; attached to Tilburg Univ.; collaborative research between economists, legal scientists, sociologists and related disciplines on fundamental and applied problems in relation to sustainability; Scientific Dir Prof. Dr AART DE ZEEUW; Man. Dir Drs Ir HILDE BAERT.

Transport Infrastructure and Logistics (TRAIL) Research School: POB 5017, 2600 GA Delft; Delft Transport Centre, Kluyverweg 4, 2629 HT Delft; tel. (15) 2786046; fax (15) 2784333; e-mail info@rstrail.nl; internet www.rstrail.nl; f. 1997; collaboration of five Dutch univ.; research in mobility, transport, logistics, traffic, infrastructure and transport systems; Scientific Dir H. L. BEN IMMERS; Managing Dir and Deputy Scientific Dir VINCENT A. W. J. MARCHAU.

Tranzo—Scientific Centre for Care and Welfare: Faculty of Social Sciences, Tilburg Univ., POB 90153, 5000 LE Tilburg; Room T 515, Tias Bldg, Warandelaan 2, 5037 AB Tilburg; tel. (13) 4662969; fax (13) 4663637; e-mail tranzo@uvt.nl; internet www.tilburguniversity.nl/tranzo; attached to Tilburg Univ.; fundamental and applied research in care and services; Chair. Prof. Dr HENK GARRETSEN.

AGRICULTURE, FISHERIES AND VETERINARY SCIENCE

Alterra: POB 47, 6700 AA Wageningen; Droevendaalsesteeg 3, Bldg 101, 6708 PB Wageningen; tel. (317) 480700; fax (317) 419000; e-mail info.alterra@wur.nl; internet www.alterra.wur.nl; f. 2000 by merger of DLO Winand Staring Centre for Integrated Land, Soil and Water Research, Instuut voor Bos- en Natuuronderzoek and part of DLO-Instituut voor Agrobiologisch Onderzoek; attached to Wageningen Univ. and Research Centre; practical and scientific research in disciplines related to the green world and the sustainable use of our living environment: knowledge of water, nature, biodiversity, climate, landscape, forest, ecology, environment, soil, landscape and spatial planning, geo-information, remote sensing, flora and fauna, urban green, man and soc. etc.; Man. Dir Ir C. T. (KEES) SLINGERLAND; Dir for Operations Ir AUKE H. DE BRUIN; publ. *Alterra Scientific Contributions*.

Centre for Development Innovation: POB 88, 6700 AB Wageningen; Lawickse Allee 11, Bldg 425, 6711 AN Wageningen; tel. (317) 486800; fax (317) 486801; e-mail info.cdi@wur.nl; internet www.cdi.wur.nl; attached to Wageningen Univ. and Research Centre; works on processes of innovation and change in areas of secure and healthy food, adaptive agriculture, sustainable markets and ecosystem governance; Dir Dr JIM WOODHILL; Deputy Dir WOUTER LEEN HIJWEEGE; Sec. ANNETTE VAN 'T HULL.

Food & Biobased Research: POB 17, 6700 AA Wageningen; Wageningen Campus, Bornse Weilanden 9, Bldg 118, 6708 WG Wageningen; tel. (317) 480084; fax (317) 483011; e-mail info.fbr@wur.nl; internet www.fbr.wur.nl; attached to Wageningen Univ. and Research Centre; research and devt org. for sustainable innovation in areas of healthy food, sustainable fresh food chains and biobased products; Man. Dir Prof. Dr RAOUL J. BINO; Dir for Operations Drs INGE T. J. GRIMM.

IMARES: POB 68, 1970 AB IJmuiden; Haringkade 1, 1976 CP IJmuiden; tel. (317) 480900; fax (317) 487326; e-mail imares@wur.nl; internet www.imares.wur.nl; f. 1912; attached to Wageningen Univ. and Research Centre; concentrates on research into strategic and applied marine ecology in areas covering aquaculture, coastal zone management, ecology, ecosystem based economy, environmental conservation and protection, fisheries, marine governance; Dir DICK POUWELS; Dir MARTIN SCHOLTEN.

International Institute for Land Reclamation and Improvement (Alterra–ILRI): POB 47, 6700 AA Wageningen; Droevendaalsesteeg 3, Wageningen; tel. (317) 495584; fax (317) 419000; e-mail ilri@ilri.nl; f. 1955; collects and disseminates information on land reclamation and improvement and undertakes supplementary research work; postgraduate courses; 30 staff; Dir Ir C. B. DE ZEEUW.

LEI: POB 29703, 2502 LS The Hague; Alexanderveld 5, 2585 DB The Hague; tel. (70) 3358330; fax (70) 3615624; e-mail informatie.lei@wur.nl; internet www.lei.wur.nl; f. 1940; attached to Wageningen Univ. and Research Centre; develops economic expertise for govt and industry in the field of food, agriculture and natural environment; offers a solid basis for socially and strategically justifiable policy choices; library of 20,000 vols; Dir-Gen. Prof. Dr Ir RUUD B. M. HUIRNE; Dir for Operations Ir LAAN C. VAN STAALDUINEN; Sec. R. VAN DEN BERG; Sec. S. FONTIJN; publ. *Leidraad* (6 a year).

Livestock Research: POB 65, 8200 AB Lelystad; Edelhertweg 15, 8219 PK Lelystad; tel. (320) 238238; fax (320) 238050; e-mail info.livestockresearch@wur.nl; internet www.livestockresearch.wur.nl; f. 1970, present status 2008, present name 2009; attached to Wageningen Univ. and Research Centre; 9 experimental farms in the Netherlands; develops knowledge, solutions for contemporary issues in the livestock sector; areas incl. animal nutrition, animal behaviour and welfare, genetics and genomics, innovation processes, livestock and environment; 140 mems; library of 20,000 vols; Gen. Dir Ir PAUL W. J. VRIESEKOOP; Man. for Operations JAN DIJK; publs *Rapporten* (6 a year), *Publikaties* (10 a year), *Jaarverslag* (1 a year), *Periodiek* (6 a year).

Nederlands Agronomisch-Historisch Instituut (Dutch Institute of Agricultural History): Oude Kijk in 't Jatstraat 26, 9712 EK Groningen; POB 716, 9700 AS Groningen; tel. (50) 3637672; e-mail nahi@rug.nl; internet www.rug.nl/let/nahi; f. 1949, present status 1998; advances study of and facilitates scientific research in agricultural history by maintaining institute at Groningen Univ. and Wageningen Univ. and Research Centre; library of 12,000 vols; Dir Prof. Dr PIM KOOIJ; Man. Dir Dr ERWIN H. KAREL; publ. *Historia Agriculturae* (1 or 2 a year).

Plant Research International: POB 16, 6700 AA Wageningen; Droevendaalsesteeg 1, Radix (Bldg 107), 6708 PB Wageningen; tel. (317) 486001; fax (317) 418094; e-mail info.plant@wur.nl; internet www.pri.wur.nl; f. 1991; attached to Wageningen Univ. and Research Centre; strategic and applied research in agrosystems, bioinformatics, crop ecology, crop protection, genetics and reproduction, genomics, metabolomics, proteomics; offers unique new perspectives for govts and private cos, for agriculture and horticulture, and for rural and environmental devt; library of 50,000 vols; Dir-Gen. Dr ERNST VAN DEN ENDE; Dir for Management Ir TON VAN SCHEPPINGEN; publs *Descriptive List of Fruit Varieties* (every 5 years), *Descriptive List of Ornamental Crops* (every 2 years), *Descriptive List of Trees* (every 5 years), *Descriptive List of Varieties of Field Crops*, *Descriptive List of Varieties of Vegetable Crops* (1 a year).

Plantenziektenkundige Dienst (Plant Protection Service): Geertjesweg 15, POB 9102, 6700 HC Wageningen; tel. (317) 496911; fax (317) 421701; f. 1899; activities incl. phytosanitary inspection of plants, issue of plant health certificates and design of laws for disease and pest prevention and control, integrated plant protection, diagnostics of diseases and pests; location offices, 3 per district; Dir Prof. Dr. L. VAN VLOTEN-DOTING; publs *Newsletter* (in Dutch, 8 a year), *Verslagen en Mededelingen Plantenziektenkundige Dienst* (Reports and Communications of the Plant Protection Service).

ARCHITECTURE AND TOWN PLANNING

Netherlands Graduate School of Urban and Regional Research: POB 80115, 3508 TC Utrecht; Willem C. van Unnikgebouw, Room 725A, Heidelberglaan 2, 3584 CS Utrecht; tel. (30) 2532250; fax (30) 2532037; e-mail nethur@geo.uu.nl; internet www.nethur.nl; urban, regional, housing research; joint initiative of 6 univ.; Scientific Dir Prof. Dr PIETER HOOIMEIJER; Dir for Education Dr D. F. ETTEMA.

Onderzoeksinstituut OTB (OTB Research Institute for the Built Environment): POB 5030, 2600 GA Delft; Jaffalaan 9, Bldg 30, 2628 BX Delft; tel. (15) 2783005; fax (15) 2784422; e-mail mailbox@otb.tudelft.nl; internet www.otb2.tudelft.nl; attached to Delft Univ. of Technology; research in the field of housing, construction, built environment; Academic Dir Prof. Dr PETER J. BOELHOUWER; Dir Prof. WILLEM KORTHALS ALTES; publ. *European Journal of Spatial Development*.

ECONOMICS, LAW AND POLITICS

Amsterdam Center for Entrepreneurship: Univ. of Amsterdam, Roetersstraat 11, Room E 2.28, 1018 WB Amsterdam; tel. (20) 5254110; fax (20) 5255652; e-mail ace-feb@uva.nl; internet www.ace-uva.nl; attached to Univ. of Amsterdam; research focuses on understanding the determinants of successful entrepreneurship; Scientific Dir CELINE MIRJAM VAN PRAAG; Exec. Dir ERIK BOER.

Amsterdam Center for Finance and Insurance: Finance Group, UvA Business School, Faculty of Economics and Business, Univ. of Amsterdam, Roetersstraat 11, 1018 WB Amsterdam; tel. (20) 5254256; fax (20) 5255285; e-mail acfi@uva.nl; internet www.feb.uva.nl/acfi; attached to Univ. of Amsterdam; researches in areas of quantitative finance and insurance and stimulates interaction between practitioners and academic researchers; Dir ANTOON PELSSER.

Amsterdam Center for Law & Economics (ACLE): Universiteit van Amsterdam, Roetersstraat 11, 1018 WB Amsterdam; tel. (20) 5254162; fax (20) 5255318; e-mail acle@uva.nl; internet www.acle.nl; attached to

Univ. of Amsterdam; research areas incl. foundations of law and economics, competition and regulation, corporate governance and law; Dir Prof. Dr ARNOUD BOOT.

Amsterdam Centre for Corporate Finance (ACCF): Chandra Doest, Roetersstraat 11, 1018 WB Amsterdam; tel. (20) 5254162; fax (20) 5255318; e-mail office@accf.nl; internet www.accf.nl; promotes research on the interface between financial theory and corporate policy; provides a forum for dialogue between academics and practitioners; Dir Prof. Dr ARNOUD BOOT; Dir Prof. Dr JOSEPH MCCAHERY.

Amsterdam Centre for Environmental Law and Sustainability (ACELS): POB 1030, 1000 BA Amsterdam; Oudemanhuispoort 4–6, 1000 BA Amsterdam; tel. (20) 5253075; fax (20) 5254742; e-mail milieurecht-fdr@uva.nl; internet www.jur.uva.nl/cvm; f. 1988, fmrly Centre for Environmental Law, present name 2010; attached to Faculty of Law, Univ. of Amsterdam; research focuses on environmental law as a means of orienting market processes towards sustainable devt, especially problem of climate change; Dir Prof. ROSA UYLENBURG.

Amsterdam Centre for International Law (ACIL): Faculty of Law, Univ. of Amsterdam, POB 1030, 1000 BA Amsterdam; Faculty of Law, Univ. of Amsterdam, Oudemanhuispoort 4, 1012 CN Amsterdam; tel. (20) 5253361; fax (20) 5253495; e-mail acil-fdr@uva.nl; internet www.jur.uva.nl/aciluk/home.cfm; attached to Faculty of Law, Univ. of Amsterdam; research on int. constitutional law (incl. human rights law), int. responsibility, int. criminal justice, reception of int. law in domestic legal order; Exec. Dir Dr YVONNE DONDERS; publ. *Legal Issues of Economic Integration*.

Amsterdam Centre for Research in International Finance (CIFRA): Univ. of Amsterdam, Business Studies, Finance Group, Room E4.26, Roetersstraat 11, 1018 WB Amsterdam; tel. (20) 5254256; fax (20) 5255285; e-mail j.a.p.gompel@uva.nl; internet www1.fee.uva.nl/fm/cifra/cifra.htm; f. 1998; research areas incl. int. capital market integration and corporate finance and banking; Dir Prof. Dr ENRICO PEROTTI; Dir Prof. Dr STIJN CLAESSENS; Sec. JOLINDA GOMPEL.

Amsterdam Centre for Service Innovation (AMSI): Amsterdam Business School, Faculty of Economics and Business, Univ. of Amsterdam, Roetersstraat 11, 1018 WB Amsterdam; tel. (20) 5258620; fax (20) 5254177; e-mail w.vanderaa@uva.nl; internet www.abs.uva.nl/amsi/home.cfm; f. 2008; attached to Univ. of Amsterdam; research focuses on management of innovation in service firms and service orgs; Dir Dr WIETZE VAN DER AA; Chair. Prof. Dr M. W. DE JONG.

Amsterdam Institute for Business and Economic Research Foundation (AMBER): Main Bldg, VU Univ., 5th Fl., Room 5A-38, De Boelelaan 1105, 1081 HV Amsterdam; tel. (20) 5986080; fax (20) 5986127; e-mail amber@feweb.vu.nl; internet www.feweb.vu.nl/amber; attached to Faculty of Economics and Business Admin., VU Univ. Amsterdam; facilitates research for faculty of economics and business admin.; supports application for nat. and int. grants for research; Man. Dir Dr A. M. GROENENDIJK; Chair. Prof. Dr E. J. BARTELSMAN.

Amsterdams Instituut voor ArbeidsStudies (AIAS) (Amsterdam Institute for Advanced Labour Studies): Univ. of Amsterdam, Plantage Muidergracht 12, 1018 TV Amsterdam; tel. (20) 5254199; fax (20) 5254301; e-mail aias@uva.nl; internet www.uva-aias.net; f. 1998; attached to Univ. of Amsterdam; combines law, economics, sociology, psychology, occupational health studies for labour studies; Dir Dr WIEMER SALVERDA.

CentER Applied Research: Tilburg Univ., POB 90153, 5000 LE Tilburg; tel. (13) 4662347; fax (13) 4668780; internet www.tilburguniversity.nl/center-ar; f. 1931; attached to Tilburg Univ.; applied economic research; Dir Prof. Dr H. FLEUREN; Dir Drs J. DE RANITZ.

Centre for Company Law: Tilburg Univ., Tilburg Law School, Dept of Business Law, POB 90153, 5000 LE Tilburg; Montesquieu Bldg, Warandelaan 2, 5037 AB Tilburg; tel. (13) 4662672; fax (13) 4662182; e-mail a.huijben@uvt.nl; internet www.tilburguniversity.nl/ccl; attached to Tilburg Univ.; research in the fields of corporate, property, securities, tax, insolvency law; also focuses on doing research in nat., int. and European aspects of the 'firm', its various legal forms, financing, governance, reorganization and accounting; Dir Prof. E. C. C. M. KEMMEREN; Dir Assoc. Prof. GER J. H. VAN DER SANGEN; Dir Prof. Dr P. H. J. ESSERS; Dir M. J. G. C. RAAIMAKERS; Management Asst ANJA M. H. J. HUIJBEN-VAN DER ZANDEN.

Center for e-Government Studies (CFES): Univ. of Twente, Cubicus Bldg, POB 217, 7500 AE Enschede; Univ. of Twente, Cubicus Bldg, Drienerlolaan 5, 7522 NB Enschede; tel. (53) 4893299; fax (53) 4894259; e-mail an.vandijk@utwente.nl; internet www.utwente.nl/ibr/cfes; f. 2009; attached to Univ. of Twente; research on the electronic govt; advises governmental agencies, policy makers, politicians, stakeholders; Dir Prof. Dr JAN VAN DIJK.

CentER for Economic Research: POB 90153, 5000 LE Tilburg; tel. (13) 4663050; fax (13) 4663066; e-mail center@uvt.nl; internet center.uvt.nl; f. 1988, present status 1992; attached to Tilburg Univ.; academic research into economics, econometrics, finance and accounting, information management, marketing, operations research, organization; Dir Prof. Dr F. A. DE ROON.

Center for Nonlinear Dynamics in Economics and Finance (CeNDEF): Faculty of Economics and Econometrics, Univ. of Amsterdam, Roetersstraat 11, 1018 WB Amsterdam; tel. (20) 5254217; fax (20) 5254349; e-mail kesec-feb@uva.nl; internet www1.fee.uva.nl/cendef; f. 1998; research areas incl. non-linear dynamics in economics and finance; Dir Prof. Dr CARS HOMMES.

Center for Research in Experimental Economics and Political Decision-Making (CREED): Faculty of Economics and Econometrics, Univ. of Amsterdam, Bldg E2, 6th Fl., Roetersstraat 11, Amsterdam; tel. (20) 5254126; fax (20) 5255283; e-mail creed-fee@uva.nl; internet www1.fee.uva.nl/creed; attached to Univ. of Amsterdam; research programmes incl. economics of political decision making, bounded rationality and institutions, experimental economics; Dir ARTHUR SCHRAM.

Centre for Transboundary Legal Development: Tilburg Univ., POB 90153, 5000 LE Tilburg; Tilburg Univ., Montesquieu Bldg, 5th Fl., Warandelaan 2, 5037 AB Tilburg; tel. (13) 4668033; fax (13) 4668047; e-mail frw.eip.secretariaat@uvt.nl; internet www.tilburguniversity.nl/ctld; f. 2000; attached to Tilburg Univ.; ethics and jurisprudence, history of law, int. and European law, philosophy of law, social law; Dir Prof WILLEM VAN GENUGTEN; Coordinator Asst Prof. ANNA MEIJKNECHT.

Centraal Bureau voor de Statistiek (Central Bureau of Statistics): POB 24500, 2490 HA The Hague; Henri Faasdreef 312, 2492 JP The Hague; tel. (70) 3373800; fax (70) 3877429; e-mail infoserv@cbs.nl; internet www.cbs.nl; f. 1899, present status 2004; economic and social statistical research; br office in Heerlen; library not accessible to public; library of 410,000 vols, 100,000 microfiche; Dir-Gen. G. VAN DER VEEN; Deputy Dir G. BRUINOOGE; publs *Historical Statistics of the Netherlands*, *Statistical Yearbook of the Netherlands*, *Statistisch Bulletin* (52 a year).

Centre for International Cooperation (CIS): De Boelelaan 1105, 1081 HV Amsterdam; Metropolitan Bldg, 4th Fl., Buitenveldertselaan 3–7, 1082 VA Amsterdam; tel. (20) 5989090; fax (20) 5989095; e-mail cis@vu.nl; internet www.cis.vu.nl; attached to VU Univ. Amsterdam; int. devt cooperation with partners in Asia, Africa and Latin America; contributes to capacity bldg efforts in developing countries; Dir KEES KOUWENAAR.

Centre for the Study of Democracy (CSD): Univ. of Twente, POB 217, 7500 AE Enschede; tel. (53) 4893270; fax (53) 4892590; e-mail j.k.vanderwoude@utwente.nl; internet www.utwente.nl/mb/csd; attached to Univ. of Twente; research on functioning of contemporary democracies; provides insight on innovation of democratic institutions; Dir Prof. Dr J. J. A. THOMASSEN; Exec. Dir Dr A. K. WARNTJEN; Exec. Dir Dr M. ROSEMA; Sec. JANINE VAN DER WOUDE.

Centrum van Procesrecht (Centre for Legal Procedure and Litigation): Tilburg Univ., POB 90153, 5000 LE Tilburg; Tilburg Univ., Montesquieu Bldg, Warandelaan 2, 5037 AB Tilburg; tel. (13) 4662254; fax (13) 4668102; e-mail m.j.w.dejong@uvt.nl; internet www.uvt.nl/cvp; attached to Tilburg Univ.; research in criminal law; Dir Prof. Dr C. J. C. F. FIJNAUT; Dir Prof. M. S. GROENHUIJSEN.

Centrum voor Recht, Bestuur en Samenleving (CRBS) (Centre for Law, Administration and Society): POB 716, 9700 AS Groningen; Harmonie, bldg 11, Oude Kijk in't Jatstraat 26, 9712 EK Groningen; tel. (50) 3636145; fax (50) 3636735; e-mail b.m.e.hallebeek@rug.nl; internet www.rug.nl/crbs/index; f. 1990; attached to Faculty of Law, Univ. of Groningen; 3 legal areas transcending, interdisciplinary and internationally orientated research lines are brought together in 3 research centres; Admin. Dir Dr JOOP HOUTMAN; Academic Dir Prof. Dr O. COUWENBERG.

Economics Network for Competition and Regulation (ENCORE): Faculty of Economics, Univ. of Amsterdam, Roetersstraat 11, 1018 WB Amsterdam; tel. (20) 5257162; fax (20) 5255318; e-mail info@encore.nl; internet www.encore.nl; f. 2003; attached to Faculty of Economics, Univ. of Amsterdam; int. research network; researches on available scientific knowledge on competition and regulation to benefit and improve policy making; Dir Prof. Dr MAARTEN PIETER SCHINKEL.

ECORYS: POB 4175, 3006 AD Rotterdam; Watermanweg 44, 3067 GG Rotterdam; tel. (10) 4538800; fax (10) 4530768; e-mail netherlands@ecorys.com; internet www.ecorys.nl; f. 1929 as Netherlands Economic Institute (NEI), present name and status 2000; economic research and policy advice; consulting and training; programme management and implementation; monitoring and evaluation; areas covered incl. economics and competitiveness, regions, cities and real estate, transport, mobility and infrastructure, social policy and govt; Chair. MARTEN VAN DEN BOSSCHE.

Fiscaal Instituut Tilburg (FIT) (Tilburg Institute of Fiscal Law): POB 90153, 5000 LE Tilburg; Warandelaan 2, Montesquieu Bldg, Room M612, 5037 AB Tilburg; tel. (13) 4662412; fax (13) 4663073; e-mail fit@uvt.nl; internet www.uvt.nl/fit; f. 1968; attached to Tilburg Univ.; research in the field of Dutch and int. taxation, tax law system.

Groningen Centre for Law and Governance: Attn. Eelke van der Ree, POB 716, 9700 AS Groningen; Harmonie bldg, Oude Kijk in 't Jatstraat 26, 9712 EK Groningen; tel. (50) 3639341; e-mail gcl@rug.nl; internet www.rug.nl/gcl; f. 2008; attached to Faculty of Law, Univ. of Groningen; contributes to legal research into the relationship between public and private interests; focuses on the interaction between public and private law and the function of law in the regulatory state; Gen. Academic Dir Prof. Dr AURELIA CIACCHI; Academic Dir Prof. Dr LEON VERSTAPPEN.

Groningen Centre of Energy Law: POB 716, 9700 AS Groningen; tel. (50) 3635736; e-mail m.m.roggenkamp@rug.nl; internet www.rug.nl/rechten/onderzoek/gcel/index; f. 2007; attached to Faculty of Law, Univ. of Groningen; research covers the entire energy chain ('from well to burner tip') and incl. all legislation and regulation applying to the production, transmission and supply of energy, promotion of renewable energy sources, need to secure energy supply as well as issues concerning climate change and environmental protection; Dir Prof. MARTHA ROGGENKAMP.

Hugo Sinzheimer Instituut (HSUIK) (Hugo Sinzheimer Institute): Law Faculty, Univ. of Amsterdam, Oudemanhuispoort 4–6, 1012 CN Amsterdam; tel. (20) 5253560; fax (20) 5253648; e-mail hsi@jur.uva.nl; internet www.jur.uva.nl/hsiuk; attached to Law Faculty, Univ. of Amsterdam; coordinates, implements and stimulates interdisciplinary research into the practice of labour law and social security law; Scientific Dir Dr ROBERT KNEGT.

Institute for Innovation and Governance Studies (IGS): Univ. of Twente, POB 217, 7500 AE Enschede; Univ. of Twente, Bldg Ravelijn, 7522 NH Enschede; tel. (53) 4893423; fax (53) 4892159; e-mail info@igs.utwente.nl; internet www.utwente.nl/onderzoek/igs; attached to Univ. of Twente; multi-disciplinary research, postgraduate research training in the field of governance and management of technological and social innovation; Scientific Dir Prof. KEES AARTS; Exec. Dir SJOERD VAN TONGEREN; Sec. MARCIA CLIFFORD.

Institute for Management Research: POB 9108, 6500 HK Nijmegen; Thomas van Aquinostraat 5.0.39, 6525 GD Nijmegen; tel. (24) 3615995; fax (24) 3611568; e-mail imr@fm.ru.nl; internet www.ru.nl/imr; attached to Radbound Univ. Nijmegen; conducts fundamental and applied research on devt, design and effectiveness of the public and private structures that regulate, govern, manage human interaction.

Institute of Social Studies: see under Colleges.

Instituut voor Informatierecht (Institute for Information Law): Kloveniersburgwal 48, 1012 CX Amsterdam; Korte Spinhuissteeg 3, 1012 CG Amsterdam; tel. (20) 5253406; fax (20) 5253033; e-mail ivir@ivir.nl; internet www.ivir.nl; f. 1989; attached to Faculty of Law, Univ. of Amsterdam; information society related legal areas such as advertising law, commercial speech, digital consumer issues, domain names, freedom of expression, intellectual property law, internet regulation, media law, privacy, patents, telecommunications and broadcasting regulation, etc.

International Institute for Asian Studies: POB 9500, 2300 RA Leiden; Rapenburg 59, 2311 GJ Leiden; tel. (71) 5272227; fax (71) 5274162; e-mail iias@iias.nl; internet www.iias.nl; f. 1993 by Royal Netherlands Acad. of Arts and Sciences and 3 Dutch univs; postdoctoral research in humanities and social sciences; promotes interdisciplinary and comparative study of Asia and nat. and int. cooperation; Chair. Prof. H. SCHULTE NORDHOLT; Dir PHILIPPE PEYCAM; Deputy Dir MANON OSSEWEIJER; Sec. AMPARO DE VOGEL.

Nederlands Instituut voor Internationale Betrekkingen 'Clingendael' (Netherlands Institute of International Relations 'Clingendael'): POB 93080, 2509 AB The Hague; Clingendael 7, 2597 VH The Hague; tel. (70) 3245384; fax (70) 3282002; e-mail info@clingendael.nl; internet www.clingendael.nl; f. 1983; research on int. issues; lectures; postgraduate courses, training in int. negotiation; information and documentation; library of 26,000 vols, 300 periodicals, 150 current journals; Pres. Dr BERNARD R. BOT; Vice-Pres. Lt. Gen. M. L. M. URLINGS; Treas. H. D. A. HAKS; Sec. Prof. Dr JAAP W. DE ZWAAN; publ. *Internationale Spectator* (12 a year).

Nederlands Interdisciplinair Demografisch Instituut (NIDI-KNAW) (Netherlands Interdisciplinary Demographic Institute): POB 11650, 2502 AR The Hague; Lange Houtstraat 19, 2511 CV The Hague; tel. (70) 3565200; fax (70) 3647187; e-mail info@nidi.nl; internet www.nidi.nl; f. 1970, present status 2003; attached to Royal Netherlands Acad. of Arts; research, training, information and documentation in the field of population studies; 60 mems; library of 6,000 vols, 2,500 reprints, 15,000 articles, etc.; Dir Prof. Dr LEO J. G. VAN WISSEN; Deputy Dir Drs NICO VAN NIMWEGEN; publs *Bevolking en Gezin* (Population and Family, 3 a year), *Demos* (10 a year, also online).

Nederlands Studiecentrum Criminaliteit en Rechtshandhaving (NCSR) (Netherlands Institute for the Study of Crime and Law Enforcement): POB 71304, 1008 BH Amsterdam; Room 0D-07, De Boelelaan 1105, 1081 HV Amsterdam; tel. (20) 5985239; fax (20) 5983975; e-mail nscr@nscr.nl; internet www.nscr.nl; f. 1992, reorganized 1999; attached to Netherlands Org. for Scientific Research; fundamental research, dissemination of knowledge in the field of crime and law enforcement; Chair. Prof. Y. BURUMA; Scientific Dir Prof. Dr G. J. N. BRUINSMA; Sec. ARIENA H. VAN POPPEL-VAN DIJK.

Research Amsterdam School of Economics: Universiteit van Amsterdam, Roetersstraat 11, Room E5.31, 1018 WB Amsterdam; tel. (20) 5254276; fax (20) 5254254; e-mail resam-ase@uva.nl; internet www.ase.uva.nl/aseresearch; f. fmrly as Research in Economics & Econometrics Amsterdam (RESAM); attached to Univ. of Amsterdam; research focuses to improve understanding of the operation of economic systems, behaviour of agents in the economy and the effects of economic policies; Dir Prof. Dr PETER BOSWIJK.

Research Group for Methodology of Law and Legal Research: Faculty of Law, Tilburg Univ., Room M225, Montesquieu Bldg, POB 90153, 5000 LE Tilburg; Montesquieu Bldg, Warandelaan 2, Room M225, 5037 AB Tilburg; tel. (13) 4662745; fax (13) 4662537; e-mail frw.methodology@uvt.nl; internet www.tilburguniversity.nl/legalmethodology; f. 2007; attached to Faculty of Law, Tilburg Univ.; research in methodology of judicial lawmaking and legal research; Dir Dr H. E. B. TIJSSEN; Sec. AUDREY WEISMANN.

SEO Economisch Onderzoek (SEO Economic Research): Univ. of Amsterdam, Gijsbert van Tienhoven Bldg, Roetersstraat 29, 1018 WB Amsterdam; tel. (20) 5251630; e-mail secretariaat@seo.nl; internet www.seo.nl; f. 1949; attached to Univ. of Amsterdam; ind. applied economic research for govt and industry; Chair. JACQUES SCHRAVEN; Dir Prof. Dr B. E. BAARSMA; Treas. WALTER ETTY.

SOM Research Institute: POB 800, 9700 AV Groningen; Nettelbosje 2, Duisenberg Bldg, 9747 AE Groningen; tel. (50) 3633749; fax (50) 3633720; e-mail a.c.koning@rug.nl; internet www.rug.nl/som/index; attached to Faculty of Economics and Business, Univ. of Groningen; coordinating institute of 6 research programmes: human resource management and organisational behaviour; int. economics, business and management; economics, econometrics and finance; innovation and org.; marketing; operations management and operations research; Chair. Prof. ELMER STERKEN; Scientific Dir Prof. Dr TAMMO BIJMOLT.

Tilburg Graduate Law School: Tilburg Univ., POB 90153, 5000 LE Tilburg; Montesquieu Bldg, Warandelaan 2, 5037 AB, Tilburg; tel. (13) 4662694; fax (13) 4662537; e-mail law.tgls@uvt.nl; internet www.tilburguniversity.nl/law/graduateschool; f. fmrly as Schoordijk Institute; attached to Tilburg Univ.; interdisciplinary study of law, legal methodology; Dir Prof. J. HAN SOMSEN.

Tilburg Institute for Behavioural Economics Research (TIBER): Tilburg Univ., POB 90153, 5000 LE Tilburg; tel. (13) 4668394; fax (13) 4662067; e-mail d.a.stapel@uvt.nl; internet www.tilburguniversity.nl/tiber; attached to Tilburg Univ.; interdisciplinary research in psychological processes underlying individual choice and economic decision; Dir Prof. DIEDERIK A. STAPEL; Man. Dir Dr TON HEINEN.

Tilburg Institute for Interdisciplinary Studies of Civil Law and Conflict Resolution Systems (TISCO): Faculty of Law, Tilburg Univ., Montesquieu Bldg, Room M 928, POB 90153, 5000 LE Tilburg; Montesquieu Bldg, Warandelaan 2, Room M 928, 5037 AB Tilburg; tel. (13) 4662281; fax (13) 4662323; e-mail law.tisco@uvt.nl; internet www.tilburguniversity.nl/tisco; attached to Faculty of Law, Tilburg Univ.; interdisciplinary, empirical-based research in civil law; develops, integrates, and applies insight from negotiation theory, conflict research, dispute system design, (comparative) legal research, network theory, behavioural law, and law and economics; Academic Dir Prof. J. M. (MAURITS) BARENDRECHT; Man. Dir C. M. C. (CORRY) VAN ZEELAND.

Tilburg School of Politics and Public Administration: Tilburg School of Politics and Public Admin., Tilburg Univ., POB 90153, 5000 LE Tilburg; Montesquieu Bldg, Warandelaan 2, 5037 AB Tilburg; tel. (13) 4662128; fax (13) 4668149; e-mail frw.tspb.secretariaat@tilburguniversity.edu; internet www.tilburguniversity.nl/tspb; attached to Tilburg School of Politics and Public Admin., Tilburg Univ.; researches into legitimacy, multiplicity, vitality of public sector; Dept Chair. Prof. Dr G. J. M. (GABRIËL) VAN DEN BRINK; Dir Prof. Dr P. H. A. FRISSEN.

TILEC—Tilburg Law and Economics Centre: Tilburg Univ., POB 90153, 5000 LE Tilburg; Prof. Cobbenhagenlaan 221, Montesquieu Bldg, Room M512A 5037 DE, Tilburg; tel. (13) 4668789; e-mail tilec@uvt.nl; internet www.tilburguniversity.nl/tilec;

attached to Tilburg Univ.; research on economic regulation of markets; Dir Prof Dr ERIC VAN DAMME; Dir Prof. Dr PIERRE LAROUCHE; Man. NICOLA HEEREN.

Tinbergen Institute: Gustav Mahlerplein 117, 1082 MS Amsterdam; tel. (20) 5251600; e-mail tinbergen@tinbergen.nl; internet www.tinbergen.nl; f. 1987; also located in Rotterdam; research areas incl. institutions and decision analysis, financial and international markets, labour, region and the environment, econometrics; Gen. Dir Prof. BAUKE VISSER.

EDUCATION

Centre for European Studies (CES): POB 217, 7500 AE Enschede; tel. (53) 4894106; fax (53) 4892159; e-mail n.s.groenendijk@utwente.nl; internet www.utwente.nl/mb/ces; f. 1998; attached to School of Management and Governance, Univ. of Twente; Dir for Educational Programmes Dr BERT DE VROOM; Dir for Research Prof. Dr NICO GROENENDIJK.

Centre for Higher Education Policy Studies (CHEPS): POB 217, 7500 AE Enschede; tel. (53) 4893263; fax (53) 4340392; e-mail cheps@mb.utwente.nl; internet www.utwente.nl/mb/cheps; f. 1986; attached to Univ. of Twente; research focuses on dynamics of the transformation of higher education and research in the knowledge society; Dir Prof. Dr JÜRGEN ENDERS; Sec. INGRID VAN DER SCHOOR.

Centre for International Cooperation: De Boelelaan 1105, 1081 HV Amsterdam; Metropolitan Bldg, 4th Fl., Buitenveldertselaan 3–7, 1082 VA Amsterdam; tel. (20) 5989090; fax (20) 5989095; e-mail cis@vu.nl; internet www.cis.vu.nl; attached to Vrije Univ.; education and devt in higher education; ICT in teaching and research; management and org. in higher education; natural resource management; Chair. Prof. Dr H. A. VERHOEF; Dir KEES KOUWENAAR; Sec. HENNY KEPPEL.

Groningen Institute for Educational Research: Grote Rozenstraat 3, 9712 TG Groningen; tel. (50) 3636631; fax (50) 3636670; internet www.rug.nl/gion/index; attached to Faculty of Behavioural and Social Studies, Univ. of Groningen; fundamental and contract research in teaching and education; Scientific Dir Prof. Dr ROEL BOSKER.

ICT in het Onderwijs (ICTO) (ICT in Education): Kanaalweg 2B, 2628 EB Delft; tel. (15) 2784686; e-mail icto@tudelft.nl; internet www.icto.tudelft.nl; attached to Delft Univ. of Technology.

Instituut voor Internationale Studien (Institute for International Studies): POB 9555, 2333 AK Leiden; tel. 5273411; fax 5273619; f. 1970; attached to Leiden Univ.; promotes cooperation in teaching between univ. depts; research on contemporary int. affairs; Dir Dr PH. P. EVERTS.

Top Institute for Evidence Based Education Research (TIER): Roetersstraat 11, 1018 WB Amsterdam; tel. (20) 5254311; fax (20) 5254310; e-mail s.m.postma@uva.nl; internet www.tierweb.nl; conducts and promotes research in the field of evidence based education; Scientific Coordinator Prof. Dr HENRIËTTE MAASSEN VAN DEN BRINK.

Twente Centre for Career Research (TCCR): Univ. of Twente, Bldg Cubicus, POB 217, 7500 AE Enschede; Univ. of Twente, Bldg Cubicus, Drienerlolaan 5, 7522 NB Enschede; tel. (53) 4893580; fax (53) 4892255; e-mail k.sanders@utwente.nl; internet www.utwente.nl/ibr/tccr; attached to Univ. of Twente; research programmes in the field of professional devt of teachers within education and health care; Dir Prof. Dr KARIN SANDERS.

FINE AND PERFORMING ARTS

Piet Zwart Institute: POB 1272, 3000 BG Rotterdam; Mauritsstraat 36, 3012 CJ Rotterdam; tel. (10) 7947405; internet pzwart.wdka.nl; attached to Willem de Kooning Acad. Rotterdam Univ.; offers int. Masters study and research programmes into professional practice of art, design, media and education.

HISTORY, GEOGRAPHY AND ARCHAEOLOGY

Centrum voor Technische Geowetenschappen (Centre for Technical Geoscience): Stevinweg 1, 2628 CN Delft; tel. (15) 2789511; fax (15) 2781189; e-mail ctg@tudelft.nl; internet www.citg.tudelft.nl; attached to Delft Univ. of Technology; integration of applied geosciences.

Groningen Institute of Archaeology: Poststraat 6, 9712 ER Groningen; tel. (50) 3636712; fax (50) 3636992; e-mail gia@rug.nl; internet www.rug.nl/let/onderzoek/onderzoekinstituten/gia/index; f. 1995; attached to Faculty of Arts, Univ. of Groningen; fundamental archaeological research with strong ecological component in Eurasia, Mediterranean and Arctic; stimulates and integrates fundamental research on past human societies and their environments, from the level of Palaeolithic hunter-gatherers to that of historical complex urban societies; library of 20,000 e-journals; Dir Prof. D. C. M. RAEMAEKERS; publs *Paleo-aktueel* (Dutch, 1 a year), *Palaeohistoria* (English, 1 a year), *Tijdschrift voor Mediterrane Archeologie* (Dutch, 1 a year).

Instituut voor Milieuvraagstukken (IVM) (Institute for Environmental Studies): De Boelelaan 1087, 1081 HV Amsterdam; De Boelelaan 1085, 1081 HV Amsterdam; tel. (20) 4449555; fax (20) 4449553; e-mail info@ivm.falw.vu.nl; internet www.ivm.vu.nl; f. 1971; attached to Vrije Univ.; multidisciplinary research in chemistry and biology, environmental economics, environmental policy and governance, spatial analysis and decision support; Dir Prof. Dr FRANS G. H. BERKHOUT.

Koninklijk Instituut voor Taal-, Land- en Volkenkunde (Royal Netherlands Institute of Southeast Asian and Caribbean Studies): POB 9515, 2300 RA Leiden; Reuvensplaats 2, 2311 BE Leiden; tel. (71) 5272295; fax (71) 5272638; e-mail kitlv@kitlv.nl; internet www.kitlv.nl; f. 1851; attached to Royal Netherlands Acad. of Arts and Sciences; advances the study of the social sciences and humanities of SE Asia and the Caribbean, particularly the fmr Dutch colonies of Indonesia and Suriname, and the fmr Netherlands Antilles and Aruba; library of 500,000 vols; spec. collns incl. Indonesia; Chair. Prof. Dr P. J. M. NAS; Vice-Chair. Dr H. DE JONGE; Dir Prof. Dr G. J. OOSTINDIE; publs *Bijdragen tot Taal-, Land- en Volkenkunde* (3 a year, in English), *Nieuwe West-Indische Gids* (2 a year, in Dutch), *OSO* (2 a year, in Dutch), *Tijdschrift voor Surinamistiek* (in Dutch).

NIOD Instituut voor Oorlogs-, Holocaust- en Genocide Studies (NIOD Institute for War, Holocaust and Genocide Studies): Herengracht 380, 1016 CJ Amsterdam; tel. (20) 5233800; fax (20) 5233888; e-mail info@niod.knaw.nl; internet www.niod.knaw.nl; f. 1945, merger of Center for Holocaust and Genocide Studies and Netherlands Institute for War Documentation in 2010; attached to Royal Netherlands Acad. of Arts and Sciences; Dutch, German and Allied collns on the history of Second World War; conducts research on war, large-scale violence in the twentieth century; library of 60,000 vols; Dir Prof. Dr MARJAN SCHWEGMAN.

Roosevelt Study Center: POB 6001, 4330 LA Middelburg; Abdij 8, 4331 BK Middelburg; tel. (118) 631590; fax (118) 631593; e-mail rsc@zeeland.nl; internet www.roosevelt.nl; f. 1986; attached to Royal Netherlands Acad. of Arts and Sciences; research institute, conf. centre and library on modern US history and Dutch–US relations; Pres. GEORGE R. J. VAN HEUKELOM; Sec. REIN JAN HOEKSTRA; Treas. JAN G. F. VELDHUIS; Dir Prof. Dr CORNELIS A. VAN MINNEN; Asst Dir Dr HANS KRABBENDAM; publ. *The Roosevelt Review* (1 a year).

Spatial Information Laboratory (SPINlab): De Boelelaan 1087, 1081 HV Amsterdam; tel. (20) 5989569; fax (20) 5989553; e-mail spinlab@ivm.vu.nl; internet www.feweb.vu.nl/gis/spinlab_website; attached to Vrije Univ.; research on spatial, geo-information with enphasis on their added value to environmental protection, health care, emergency and risk management, field work, transport, distribution, logistics, and marketing; Scientific Dir HENK SCHOLTEN; Sec. JESSICA ENDENDIJK.

Vening Meinesz Research School of Geodynamics: c/o Institute of Earth Sciences, Budapestlaan 4, 3584 CD Utrecht; tel. (30) 2535031; fax (30) 2535030; e-mail vmsg@geo.uu.nl; internet vmsg.geo.uu.nl; promotes and carries out geodynamic research, with spec. attention for the integration of geophysical, geological and Earth-oriented space research; Scientific Dir Prof. Dr RINUS WORTEL; Exec. Sec. Drs. JAN-WILLEM DE BLOK.

LANGUAGE AND LITERATURE

Amsterdam Centre for Language and Communication (ACLC): Spuistraat 210–212, Room 1.11, 1012 VT Amsterdam; tel. (20) 5252543; fax (20) 5253052; e-mail aclc-fgw@uva.nl; internet www.hum.uva.nl/aclc; attached to Faculty of Humanities, Univ. of Amsterdam; focuses on study of both functionally and formally oriented linguistic research; Academic Dir Prof. Dr KEES HENGEVELD; Man. Dir Dr ELS VERHEUGD-DAATZELAAR; Vice-Dir Dr ROB SCHOONEN; publ. *Linguistics in Amsterdam series*.

Center for Language and Cognition Groningen (CLCG): POB 716, 9700 AS Groningen; e-mail clcg@let.rug.nl; internet www.rug.nl/let/onderzoek/onderzoekinstituten/clcg/index; f. 1994; attached to Faculty of Arts, Univ. of Groningen; linguistic research; interaction between other linguistic research groups; Dir Prof. Dr Ir JOHN NERBONNE.

Centre for Language Studies: POB 9103, 6500 HD Nijmegen; Erasmusplein 1, 6525 HT Nijmegen; tel. (24) 3611807; fax (24) 3615481; e-mail cls@let.ru.nl; internet www.ru.nl/cls; attached to Faculty of Arts, Radbound Univ. Nijmegen; research in linguistics, language and speech technology and communication studies; Dir ANS VAN KEMENADE.

Max Planck Institute for Psycholinguistics: POB 310, 6500 AH Nijmegen; Wundtlaan 1, 6525 XD Nijmegen; tel. (24) 3521911; fax (24) 3521213; e-mail info@mpi.nl; internet www.mpi.nl; attached to German Max Planck Society; basic research on psychological, social and biological foundations of language; library of 30,000 vols, 20,000 bound journals, 30,000 online journals; Dir PETER HAGOORT.

MEDICINE

Academic Centre for Dentistry Amsterdam: Gustav Mahler Laan 3004, 1081 LA Amsterdam; tel. (20) 5980380; e-mail info@acta.nl; internet www.acta.nl; br. at Almere; conducts scientific research, provides educational programmes, and delivers patient care in field of dentistry; research focuses on physiology and pathology of tissues in and around oral cavity; Dean Prof. Dr A. J. FEILZER; Dir for Research Prof. Dr V. EVERTS.

Academisch Medisch Centrum (AMC): POB 22660, 1100 DD Amsterdam; Meibergdreef 9, 1105 AZ Amsterdam; tel. (20) 5669111; fax (20) 5664440; internet www.amc.uva.nl; f. 1983; attached to Universiteit van Amsterdam; clinical and translational research; works as medical centre; Pres. and Dean Prof. Dr M. M LEVI; Vice-Pres. Dr R. J. M. HOPSTAKEN; publ. *AMC Magazine* (10 a year).

Centre for Healthcare Operations Improvement & Research (CHOIR): POB 217, 7500 AE Enschede; tel. (53) 4893447; fax (53) 4894858; e-mail e.w.hans@utwente.nl; internet www.utwente.nl/choir; attached to Univ. of Twente; research on healthcare; research areas incl. decision theory, logistics and operations management, information technology and management, operations research, purchase management, quality and safety management.

Centre of Research on Psychology in Somatic Diseases (CoRPS): POB 90153, 5000 LE Tilburg; Warandelaan 2, 5037 AB Tilburg; tel. (13) 4668720; fax (13) 4662067; e-mail corps@uvt.nl; internet www.tilburguniversity.nl/corps; attached to Tilburg Univ.; research on issues in the interface between medical and behavioural sciences; Academic Dir Prof. Dr JOHAN DENOLLET; Man. Dir J. H. (HANS) DIETEREN.

Centrum voor Ouderenonderzoek (CVO) (Center for Research on Aging): De Boelelaan 1081, 1081 HV Amsterdam; Metropolitan, Room Z-427, Buitenveldertselaan 3, 1081 HV Amsterdam; tel. (20) 5986891; fax (20) 5986810; internet www.cvo.vu.nl; f. 1996; attached to Vrije Univ. Amsterdam; research and education in gerontology and geriatrics; Head Dr F. J. M. MEILAND.

EMGO+ Institute for Health and Care Research: van der Boechorststraat 7, 1081 BT Amsterdam; tel. (20) 4448180; fax (20) 4448181; e-mail secretariaat.emgo@vumc.nl; internet www.emgo.nl; attached to Vrije Univ.; research in public and occupational health, primary care, rehabilitation, long-term care; Dir Prof. JOHANNES BRUG; Vice-Dir Prof. Dr PIM CUIJPERS; Vice-Dir Prof. Dr WILLEM VAN MECHELEN.

Graduate School of Neurosciences Amsterdam, Rotterdam:; tel. (20) 4449641; e-mail els.borghols@cncr.vu.nl; internet www.onwar.nl; research in the field of neurosciences; Chair. of Advisory Board Prof. Dr F. H. LOPES DA SILVA; Dir Prof. Dr A. B. SMIT; Chair. of Teaching Cttee Dr C. N. LEVELT.

GUIDE—Research Institute for Chronic Diseases and Drug Innovation: POB 196, 9700 AD Groningen; Ant. Deusinglaan 1, Bldg 3217 'De Brug', Room 7.31, 9713 AV Groningen; tel. (50) 3633163; fax (50) 3632612; e-mail guideoffice@med.umcg.nl; internet www.graduateschoolguide.nl; attached to Univ. of Groningen; integrates clinical, biomedical and pharmaceutical research, which promotes education of researchers with a keen eye on the complete spectrum of biomedical research in a unique research and teaching environment: from bed to bench to drugs; Scientific Dir Prof. Dr HAN MOSHAGE.

Het Nederlands Kanker Instituut—Antoni van Leeuwenhoek Ziekenhuis (Netherlands Cancer Institute—Antoni van Leeuwenhoek Hospital): POB 90203, 1006 BE Amsterdam; Plesmanlaan 121, 1066 CX Amsterdam; tel. (20) 5129111; fax (20) 6172625; e-mail nkilib@nki.nl; internet www.nki.nl; f. 1916, present bldg 1959; library of 15,000 vols; basic and translational cancer research, clinical cancer research, diagnostic, surgical and medical oncology, radiotherapy; Patron HKH QUEEN BEATRIX; Chair. and Scientific Dir Prof. Dr A. J. M. BERNS; Sec. P. BELTMAN; Library Dir SUZANNE BAKKER; publ. *Scientific Report* (1 a year).

Institute for Cardiovascular Research: POB 7057, 1007 MB Amsterdam; Van der Boechorststraat 7, 1081 BT Amsterdam; tel. (20) 4448111; fax (20) 4448255; e-mail icar@vumc.nl; internet www.vumc.nl/afdelingen/icar-vu; f. 1992; attached to Vrije Univ.; research into aspects of cardiovascular diseases, cardiovascular function; Dir Prof. Dr V. W. M. VAN HINSBERGH.

Institute for Genetic and Metabolic Disease: Radboud Univ. Nijmegen Medical Centre, Geert Grooteplein Zuid 10, POB 9101, 6500 HB Nijmegen; Radboud Univ. Nijmegen Medical Centre, Geert Grooteplein 10, 6525 GA Nijmegen; tel. (24) 3619118; fax (24) 3668532; internet www.igmd.nl; attached to Radboud Univ. Nijmegen Medical Centre; clinical, applied and fundamental research on genetic and metabolic diseases; Dir Prof. Dr JAN SMEITINK.

Institute of Technical Medicine: Noordhorst, POB 217, 7500 AE Enschede; tel. (53) 4893300; fax (53) 4893288; e-mail j.a.dutrieux-schuit@utwente.nl; internet www.utwente.nl/tnw/itm; attached to Univ. of Twente; basic science and technology with clinical practice in medicine.

Instituut Beleid & Management Gezondheidszorg (iBMG) (Institute of Health Policy & Management): POB 1738, 3000 DR Rotterdam; J-Bldg, Campus Woudestein, Burgemeester Oudlaan 50, 3062 PA Rotterdam; tel. (10) 4081169; e-mail research@remove-this.bmg.eur.nl; internet www.bmg.eur.nl; f. 1982; attached to Erasmus Univ.; research school and educational programmes of Netherlands Institute for Health Sciences (Nihes) and Netherlands School of Public Health (NSPH); researches on competition and regulation in health care, quality and efficiency in health care, adaptation of orgs to competitive environment; Assoc. Dean Prof. Dr W. R. F. NOTTEN; Man. Dir Dr M. S. VEENSTRA; Dir for Research Prof. Dr W. B. F. (WERNER) BROUWER.

Instituut voor Fundamentele en Klinische Bewegingswetenschappen (Institute for Fundamental and Clinical Human Movement Sciences): van der Boechorststraat 9, 1081 BT Amsterdam; tel. (20) 5982000; e-mail ifkb@fbw.vu.nl; internet www.ifkb.nl; f. 1995; attached to Vrije Univ.; research into nature and significance of human movement; research themes incl. control, mechanics, metabolism; Chair. of Board Prof. Dr P. J. BEEK; Dir Dr Ir L. BLANKEVOORT; Dir Prof. Dr ARNOLD DE HAAN; Dir Prof. Dr Ir D. F. STEGEMAN.

Interuniversitair Cardiologisch Instituut Nederland (Interuniversity Cardiology Institute of the Netherlands): POB 19258, 3501 DG Utrecht; Catharijnesingel 52, 3511 GC Utrecht; tel. (30) 2333600; fax (30) 2315940; e-mail info@icin.knaw.nl; internet www.icin.nl; attached to Royal Netherlands Acad. of Arts and Sciences; scientific research in the field of cardiovascular diseases; alliance of 8 univ. cardiology depts; Dir Prof. Dr WIEK H. VAN GILST; Dir Prof. Dr ERNST E. VAN DER WALL; Gen. Man. JAN WEIJERS.

Koninklijk Instituut voor de Tropen (KIT) (Royal Tropical Institute): POB 95001, 1090 HA Amsterdam; Mauritskade 63, 1092 AD Amsterdam; tel. (20) 5688711; fax (20) 6684579; e-mail ils@kit.nl; internet www.kit.nl; f. 1910 as Colonial Institute, present bldg 1926, present name 1950; health policy and tropical medicine; int. research and training org. that focuses on improving communication between the W and non-Western world; collects and disseminates information on the developing world; library: see Libraries and Archives; Tropical Museum: see Museums and Art Galleries; Chair. Prof. Dr RUDY RABBINGE; Vice-Chair. PETER J. GROENENBOOM; Pres. Dr JAN DONNER.

Nederlands Instituut voor Neurowetenschappen (Netherlands Institute for Neuroscience): AMC, Meibergdreef 47, 1105 BA Amsterdam; tel. (20) 5665500; fax (20) 5666121; e-mail secretariaat@nin.knaw.nl; internet www.nin.knaw.nl; f. 2005; attached to Royal Netherlands Acad. of Arts and Sciences; carries out fundamental neuroscience research with spec. emphasis on the brain and the visual system; 18 research groups; Scientific Dir Dr PIETER R. ROELFSEMA; Man. Dir Dr RONALD VAN DER NEUT; Vice-Dir Dr CHRIS I. ZEEUW.

Nijmegen Centre for Evidence Based Practice (NCEBP): Radboud Univ. Nijmegen Medical Centre, Post 148, NCEBP, POB 9101, 6500 HB Nijmegen; Radboud Univ. Nijmegen Medical Centre, NCEBP, Geert Grooteplein 21, 6525 EZ Nijmegen; tel. (24) 3614639; e-mail info@ncebp.umcn.nl; internet www.ncebp.eu; attached to Radboud Univ.; conducts research that is aimed at individual patients and patient population, and in a preventative sense also at healthy population; Scientific Dir Prof. Dr PAUL SMITS; Asst Scientific Dir Dr. GERDI EGBERINK.

Nijmegen Intitute for Infection, Inflammation and Immunity: POB 9101, Route 463, 6500 HB Nijmegen; tel. (24) 3668015; e-mail a.peters@aig.umcn.nl; internet www.n4i.nl; attached to Radboud Univ. Nijmegen Medical Centre; performs clinical translational and basic research on the interaction between microorganisms and the host, the inflammatory response and immune mechanisms as occur in autoimmune disorders and transplantation; Scientific Dir Prof. Dr JOS VAN DER MEER; Sec. GONNY PETERS.

Onderzoekschool Oncologie Amsterdam (Oncology Graduate School): c/o Dr. Esther M. Ruhé-Hoogervorst , De Boelelaan 1117, 1081 HV Amsterdam; tel. (20) 4443113; fax (20) 4442964; e-mail e.ruhe@vumc.nl; internet www.ooa-graduateschool.org; attached to Vrije Univ.; research in basic and clinical oncology; Chair. of Board Prof. Dr ANTON BERNS; Chair. Prof. Dr GERRIT A. MEIJER.

TNO Preventie en Zorg (TNO Prevention and Care): POB 2215, 2301 CE Leiden; Wassenaarseweg 56, 2333 AL Leiden; tel. (88) 8669000; e-mail info-zorg@tno.nl; internet www.tno.nl; f. 1932; scientific research in the fields of public health and prevention of illness; postgraduate courses in occupational health; library of 20,000 vols; Chair. Ir JAN H. J. MENGELERS; Chair for Defence Research Board JAN WILLEM KELDER; Chair for Supervisory Board Ir J. M. LEEMHUIS-STOUT; publ. *TNO Magazine* (4 a year).

VU Medisch Centrum (VU University Medical Center): POB 7057, 1007 MB Amsterdam; De Boelelaan 1117, 1081 HV Amsterdam; tel. (20) 4444444; fax (20) 4444645; e-mail uhp@vumc.nl; internet www.vumc.nl/meg; f. 2001 by merger of medical school and VU hospital; attached to Vrije Universiteit Medical Centre; research into magnetoencephalography; Chair. Drs E. B. MULDER; Vice-Chair. Prof. Dr T. J. F. SAVELKOUL; Dean Prof. Dr W. A. B. STALMAN.

W. Kahn Institute of Theoretical Psychiatry and Neuroscience: Het Nateland 1, 3911 XZ Rhenen Utrecht; tel. and fax (317) 618708; e-mail wimkahn1@hotmail.com; internet kahn-institute.tripod.com; f. 1997; 25 mems; develops theoretical models in the fields of psychiatry, psychology, neuroscience and philosophy, for the diagnosis and treatment of mental health disorders; 10 depts; Chair. Dr WILLEM H. J. MARTENS; Pres. Prof. Dr W. KAHN; Sec. W. A. TUIJTEN; publ. *WKITPN–Publication* (4 a year).

W. J. Kolff Institute for Biomedical Engineering and Materials Science: Antonius Deusinglaan 1, FB41, 9713 AV Groningen; tel. (50) 3633140; fax (50) 3633159; e-mail h.j.busscher@med.umcg.nl; internet www.rug.nl/umcg/onderzoek/interfacultaireinstituten/bmsa/index; f. 1997; establishes a centre of expertise for the entire stage of biomedical materials science and its application involving basic materials science, medical product devt and clinical evaluation that contributes to the long-lasting well-being of patients in need of biomaterials implants and extra-corporal support systems; Scientific Dir Prof. Dr H. J. BUSSCHER.

NATURAL SCIENCES

General

CEDLA—Centrum voor Studie en Documentatie van Latijns-Amerika (CEDLA—Centre for Latin American Research and Documentation): Keizersgracht 395–397, 1016 EK Amsterdam; tel. (20) 5253498; fax (20) 6255127; e-mail secretariat@cedla.nl; internet www.cedla.uva.nl; f. 1964, present status 1971; social science research on Latin America; library: see Libraries and Archives; Dir Prof. Dr MICHIEL BAUD; publ. *ERLACS: European Review of Latin American and Caribbean Studies* (Revista Europea de Estudios Latinoamericanos y del Caribe, 2 a year, in English and Spanish).

CentERdata—Instituut voor Dataverzameling en Onderzoek (CentERdata—Institute for Data Collection and Research): POB 90153, 5000 LE Tilburg; Koopmans Bldg, Warandelaan 2, 5037 AB Tilburg; tel. (13) 4668325; fax (13) 4662764; e-mail centerdata@uvt.nl; internet www.centerdata.nl; attached to Tilburg Univ.; data colln, methodological and applied research; Dir Prof. Dr MARCEL DAS.

Groningen Research Institute of Pharmacy (GRIP): Dept of Pharmacy, Antonius Deusinglaan 1 9713 AV Groningen; tel. (50) 3633275; fax (50) 3637943; e-mail ; internet www.rug.nl/farmacie/index; attached to Faculty of Mathematics and Natural Sciences, Univ. of Groningen; organises research in 11 pharmacy research groups; Scientific Dir Prof. Dr W.J. QUAX.

Kapteyn Astronomical Institute: POB 800, 9700 AV Groningen; Landleven 12, Zernike bldg, 9747 AD Groningen; tel. (50) 3634073; fax (50) 3636100; internet www.rug.nl/sterrenkunde/onderzoek/index; f. 1896 as an astronomical laboratory; astronomical research; Scientific Dir Prof. Dr J. M. VAN DER HULST.

Nederlandse Organisatie voor Toegepast—Natuurwetenschappelijk Onderzoek (TNO) (Netherlands Organization for Applied Scientific Research): POB 6050, 2600 JA Delft; Schoemakerstraat 97, 2628 VK Delft; tel. (88) 8660000; fax (15) 2612403; e-mail wegwijzer@tno.nl; internet www.tno.nl; f. 1932; strategic policy and innovation consultancy; bldg, materials and information technology, mechanical and production engineering, product design and development, telecommunications, quality control, health and safety, nutrition, environment and energy; library of 16,000 vols; Chair. JAN MENGELERS; Sec. Drs S. J. VLAAR; publs *TNO Magazine* (in English), *Toegepaste Wetenschap* (in Dutch).

Nederlandse Organisatie voor Wetenschappelijk Onderzoek (NWO) (Netherlands Organization for Scientific Research): POB 93138, 2509 AC The Hague; Laan van Nieuw Oost Indië 300, 2593 CE The Hague; tel. (70) 3440640; fax (70) 3850971; e-mail nwo@nwo.nl; internet www.nwo.nl; f. 1988; stimulates and coordinates pure and applied research in all fields of learning; Chair. Dr JOS ENGELEN; Dir-Gen. and Sec. Dr CEES DE VISSER; publ. *Jaarboek*.

Netherlands Graduate Research School of Science, Technology and Modern Culture (WTMC): Univ. Maastricht, Faculteit der Cultuur-en Maatschappijwetenschappen, WTMC, POB 616, 6200 MD Maastricht; e-mail wtmc@maastrichtuniversity.nl; internet www.wtmc.net; science and technology studies; study of devt of science, technology and modern culture; Scientific Dir Prof. Dr SALLY WYATT.

Netherlands Research School in Process Technology: OSPT Secretariat, Faculty of Engineering Technology, Bldg 'De Meander', POB 217, 7500 AE Enschede; OSPT office, Univ. of Twente, Bldg 'De Meander', Room ME-116, 7500 AE Enschede; tel. (53) 4894626; fax (53) 4894233; e-mail ospt@tudelft.nl; internet ospt.tnw.utwente.nl; research in chemical engineering and process technology; five participant univ.; Scientific Dir Prof. Dr H. E. A. VAN DEN AKKER.

Oldendorff Research Institute: POB 90153, 5000 LE Tilburg; Prisma Bldg, Warandelaan 2, 5037 AB, Tilburg; tel. (13) 4663140; fax (13) 4668183; e-mail e.j.simons@uvt.nl; f. 2001; attached to Tilburg Univ.; int., multi-disciplinary, multi-level research in social sciences; Dir Prof. Dr KLAAS SIJTSMA; Man. A. G. J. J. (TON) HEINEN.

Radionuclide Centre (RNC): De Boelelaan 1085C, 1081 HV Amsterdam; tel. (20) 4449101; fax (20) 4449121; internet www.rnc.vu.nl; attached to Vrije Univ. Amsterdam; research on chemical, biological and medical research with Radionuclides at Type-2-level; facilitation and cooperation in processing and transport of radioactive waste and first aid with radioactive accidents; laundering of radioactive working clothes.

Stichting voor Wetenschappelijk Onderzoek van de Tropen (WOTRO) (WOTRO Science for Global Development): POB 93120, 2509 AC The Hague; Laan van Nieuw Oost Indië 131, 2593 CE The Hague; tel. (70) 3440763; fax (70) 3819874; e-mail wotro@nwo.nl; internet www.nwo.nl; f. 1964; attached to Nederlandse Organisatie voor Wetenschappelijk Onderzoek (NWO); supports scientific research on development issues, in particular poverty alleviation and sustainable development; advancement of tropical research both pure and applied by awarding grants; Chair. Prof. WILLEM J. M. VAN GENUGTEN.

Stratingh Institute for Chemistry: Nijenborgh 4, 9747 AG Groningen; tel. (50) 3634233; fax (50) 3634296; e-mail stratingh@rug.nl; internet www.rug.nl/scheikunde/onderzoek/scholen/stratingh/index; f. 1997; attached to Faculty of Mathematics and Natural Sciences, Univ. of Groningen; research in molecular chemistry; Scientific Dir Prof. Dr B. L. FERINGA.

Tilburg Centre for Logic and Philosophy of Science (TILPS): POB 90153, 5000 LE Tilburg; Dante Bldg, Warandelaan 2, 5037 AB Tilburg; e-mail tilps@tilburguniversity.nl; internet www.tilburguniversity.nl/tilps; f. 2007; attached to Tilburg Univ.; Dir Prof. STEPHAN HARTMANN.

Van der Waals-Zeeman Institute: POB 94485, 1090 GL Amsterdam; Science Park 904, 1098 XH Amsterdam; tel. (20) 5255663; fax (20) 5255788; e-mail secr-wzi-science@uva.nl; internet www.science.uva.nl/research/wzi; attached to Univ. of Amsterdam; research areas incl. atomic physics, hard condensed matter, materials science, quantum optics, soft condensed matter; Dir Prof. Dr M. S. GOLDEN; Man. L. LUSINK.

Biological Sciences

Behavioural and Cognitive Sciences: POB 196, 9700 AD Groningen; A. Deusinglaan 2, Bldg 3111, 1st Fl., Room 108, 9713 AW Groningen; tel. (50) 3634734; fax (50) 3638875; e-mail e.t.kuiper-drenth@med.umcg.nl; internet www.rug.nl/bcn; attached to Univ. of Groningen; participation of five faculties and a number of research institutes; Scientific Dir Prof. Dr H. W. G. M. BODDEKE.

Center for Behaviour and Neurosciences: Kerklaan 30, 9751 NN Haren; tel. (50) 3632053; e-mail d.g.m.beersma@rug.nl; internet www.rug.nl/fwn/onderzoek/programmas/cbn; attached to Faculty of Mathematics and Natural Sciences, Univ. of Groningen; integral part of the Research School for Behavioural and Cognitive Neurosciences (BCN) of Univ. of Groningen; Dir Prof. Dr DOMIEN BEERSMA.

Centraalbureau voor Schimmelcultures (CBS—KNAW Fungal Biodiversity Centre): POB 85167, 3508 AD Utrecht; Uppsalalaan 8, 3584 CT Utrecht; tel. (30) 2122600; fax (30) 2512097; e-mail info@cbs.knaw.nl; internet www.cbs.knaw.nl; f. 1904, present location 2000; attached to Royal Netherlands Acad. of Arts and Sciences; researches on biosystematics of the fungal kingdom; maintains a world-renowned colln of filamentous fungi, yeasts and bacteria; research focus on the taxonomy and evolution of fungi, functional aspects of fungal biology and ecology, using molecular and genomics approaches; Dir Prof. Dr PEDRO W. CROUS; publs *CBS Biodiversity Series* (2–3 a year), *IMA Fungus* (2 a year), *Persoonia* (2 a year), *Studies in Mycology* (3 a year).

Centre for Synthetic Biology: Nijenborgh 4, 9747 AG Groningen; tel. (50) 3633941; fax (50) 3634165; e-mail syntheticbiology@rug.nl; internet www.rug.nl/fwn/onderzoek/instituten/csb/index; f. 2008; attached to Faculty of Mathematics and Natural Sciences, Univ. of Groningen; design, construction of cellular and biohybrid systems; founded by three leading research institutes of the faculty; Scientific Dir Prof. Dr BERT POOLMAN.

Donders Institute for Brain, Cognition and Behaviour: POB 9101, 6500 HB Nijmegen; Kapittelweg 29, 6525 EN Nijmegen; tel. (24) 3610750; fax (24) 3610989; e-mail info@donders.ru.nl; internet www.ru.nl/donders/; attached to Radbound Univ. Nijmegen; consists of the Centre of Cognition, the Centre for Cognitive Neuroimaging and the Centre for Neuroscience; Administrative Dir ARTHUR WILLEMSEN.

Groningen Biomolecular Science and Biotechnology Institute: Nijenborgh 7, 9747 AG Groningen; tel. (50) 3634203; fax (50) 3632154; e-mail t.hummel@rug.nl; internet www.rug.nl/gbb/organisation/index; f. 1993; attached to Faculty of Mathematics and Natural Sciences, Univ. of Groningen; originates from collaboration between dept of biology and chemistry; composed of 13 research groups; Dir Prof. Dr A. J. M. DRIESSEN.

Hortus botanicus: POB 9516, 2300 RA Leiden; Rapenburg 73, 2311 GJ Leiden; tel. (71) 5277249; fax (71) 5275199; e-mail hortus@hortus.leidenuniv.nl; internet www.hortusleiden.nl; f. 1590; attached to Universiteit Leiden; research in the field of botany; Scientific Dir Prof. Dr E. F. SMETS.

Hortus Haren Holland: POB 179, 9750 AD Haren; Kerklaan 34, 9751 NN Haren; tel. (50) 5370053; fax (50) 5371223; e-mail info@hortusharen.nl; internet www.hortusharen.nl; f. 1642, renewed 1929; 8,000 species; CEO Drs J. C. KAPPENBURG.

Hubrecht Institute: POB 85164, 3508 AD Utrecht; Uppsalalaan 8, 3584 CT Utrecht; tel. (30) 2121800; fax (30) 2516464; e-mail nimwegen@niob.knaw.nl; internet www.hubrecht.eu; f. 1916 as Hubrecht Laboratory, present location 2000, present name 2007; attached to Royal Netherlands Acad. of Arts and Sciences; research on developmental and stem cell biology of animals; 17 research groups; Dir Prof. HANS CLEVERS; Business Dir Dr JOS KOELMAN; Deputy Dir Prof. JEROEN DEN HERTOG.

Nederlands Instituut voor Onderzoek in de Katalyse (Netherlands Institute for Catalysis Research): 51 Anna v. Saksenlaan, POB 93223 2509 AE Hague; tel. (70) 3440740; e-mail office@niok.nl; internet www.niok.nl; f. 1991; virtual institute consists of major catalysis groups of seven Dutch univ.; Scientific Dir Prof. BERT WECKHUYSEN.

Instituut voor Plantenziektenkundig Onderzoek (IPO–DLO) (DLO–Research Institute for Plant Protection): POB 9060, 6700 WG Wageningen; tel. (317) 476000; fax (317) 410113; e-mail info@ipo.dlo.nl; f. 1949; prevention, management and control of plant diseases and pests; library of 24,000 vols; Dir Dr Ir N. G. HOGENBOOM.

Nationaal Herbarium Nederland (National Herbarium of the Netherlands): POB 9514, 2300 RA Leiden; Van Steenis Bldg, Einsteinweg 2, 2333 CC Leiden; tel. (71) 5273515; fax (71) 5273511; e-mail dewolf@nhn.leidenuniv.nl; internet www.nhn.leidenuniv.nl; f. 1999 by merger of Herbarium Vadense, Rijksherbarium Leiden and Utrecht Univ. Herbarium; attached to Universiteit Leiden; investigation of flora (taxonomy, geography), particularly of the Netherlands and the Tropics; br and research centre in Wageningen; library of 45,000 vols, 100,000 journal vols, 100,000 reprints, 90,000 microfiches, 40,000 plant illustrations; Chair. Prof. Dr S. B. MENKEN; Dir Prof. Dr E. F. SMETS; Sec. Dr J. B. MOLS; publs *Blumea* (in English), *Flora Malesiana* (Phanerog., ferns), *Flora Malesiana Bulletin*, *Gorteria* (Netherlands flora), *IAWA Journal* (4 a year), *Persoonia* (Mycology).

Nijmegen Centre for Molecular Life Sciences (NCMLS): 259 NCMLS, POB 9101, 6500 HB Nijmegen; Geert Grooteplein 28, 6525 GA Nijmegen; tel. (24) 3610707; fax (24) 3610909; e-mail info@ncmls.ru.nl; internet www.ncmls.edu; attached to Radbound Univ. Nijmegen Medical Centre; multidisciplinary research within molecular mechanisms of disease and molecular medicine, cell biology, translational research; Dir Prof. Dr RENÉ BINDELS.

Swammerdam Institute for Life Sciences: POB 94216, 1090 GE Amsterdam; Science Park 904, 1098 XH Amsterdam; tel. (20) 5257678; fax (20) 5257675; e-mail info-science@uva.nl; internet www.science.uva.nl/sils; attached to Univ. of Amsterdam; research related to cellular processes and interactions; multidisciplinary research in biology, (bio)chemistry, (bio)physics, data analysis technology, information technology, medicine; Dir Prof. Dr WILLEM. J. STIEKEMA.

Mathematical Sciences

Casimir Onderzoekschool (Casimir Research School): Management Office, Casimir Research School, Maddy Lansbergen, Lorentzweg 1, 2628 CJ Delft; tel. (15) 2787213; fax (15) 2781413; e-mail info@casimir.researchschool.nl; internet casimir.researchschool.nl; f. 2004 by Leiden Institute of Physics and Kavli Institute of Nanoscience; graduate school for interdisciplinary physics and strong focus on nanoscience; Dir Prof. Dr Ir TEUN KLAPWIJK.

Centre for Theoretical Physics: Chemistry-Physics Bldg, Nijenborgh 4, 5111.0153, 9747 AG Groningen; tel. (50) 3634950; fax (50) 3634947; e-mail secrctn@rug.nl; internet www.rug.nl/natuurkunde/onderzoek/instituten/ctn/index; consists of four research groups: computational physics, theory of condensed matter, high energy physics, statistical physics.

CentrumWiskunde & Informatica (CWI) (Centre for Mathematics and Computer Science): POB 94079, 1090 GB Amsterdam; Science Park 123, 1098 XG Amsterdam; tel. (20) 5929333; fax (20) 5924199; e-mail info@cwi.nl; internet www.cwi.nl; f. 1946; fundamental scientific research in mathematics and computer science; library: see Libraries and Archives; Gen. Dir Prof. Dr JAN KAREL LENSTRA; Chair. PETER VAN LAARHOVEN; publs *CWI Quarterly*, *CWI Syllabi*.

Euler Institute for Discrete Mathematics and its Applications: c/o Dept of Mathematics and Computing Science, Eindhoven Univ. of Technology, POB 513, 5600 MB Eindhoven; tel. (40) 2472254; fax (40) 2475366; e-mail eidma@tue.nl; internet www.win.tue.nl/wsk/eidma; f. 1994; attached to Eindhoven Univ. of Technology; coding theory, combinatorial optimization and algorithms, discrete algebra and geometry, graph theory, information theory and cryptology; Chair. Prof. Dr A. M. COHEN; Scientific Dir Prof. Dr Ir HENK C. A. VAN TILBORG.

Eurandom: POB 513, 5600 MB Eindhoven; Den Dolech 2, 5612 AZ Eindhoven; tel. (40) 2478100; fax (40) 2478190; e-mail office@eurandom.tue.nl; internet www.eurandom.tue.nl; attached to Eindhoven Univ. of Technology; probability theory, statistics, stochastic operations research; Chair. Prof. Dr FRANK VAN DER DUYN SCHOUTEN; Scientific Dir Prof. Dr Ir ONNO J. BOXMA; Man. Dir Drs CONNIE M. M. CANTRIJN.

Institute for Mathematics, Astrophysics and Particle Physics: POB 9010, 6500 GL Nijmegen; Huygens Bldg, Room HG03.830, Heyendaalseweg 135, 6525 AJ Nijmegen; tel. (24) 3652099; fax (24) 3652191; e-mail secr@hef.ru.nl; internet www.ru.nl/imapp; f. 2005; attached to Faculty of Science, Radbound Univ. Nijmegen; research in mathematics, astrophysics and elementary particle physics; Dir Prof. Dr SIJBRAND DE JONG.

Instituut voor Hoge Energie Fysica (IHEF) (Institute for High Energy Physics): POB 41882, 1009 DB Amsterdram; Science Park 105, 1098 XG Amsterdam; tel. (20) 5925169; fax (20) 5925054; e-mail j.berger@nikhef.nl; internet www.nikhef.nl/onderwijs/universitaire-partners/uva-ihef; attached to Univ. of Amsterdam; high energy particle physics, subatomic physics, instrumentation; Dir Prof. Dr S. C. M. BENTVELSEN.

Instituut voor Programmatuurkunde en Algoritmiek (Institute for Programming Research and Algorithmics): Dept of Mathematics and Computing Science, IPA Secretariat, POB 513, 5600 MB Eindhoven; Den Dolech 2, Room HG 7.22, 5600 MB Eindhoven; tel. (40) 2474124; fax (40) 2436685; e-mail ipa@tue.nl; internet www.win.tue.nl/ipa; attached to Eindhoven Univ. of Technology; research areas incl. algorithms and complexity, formal methods, software technology and engineering; Scientific Dir Prof. Dr J. C. M. BAETEN.

Instituut voor Theoretische Fysica (Institute for Theoretical Physics): POB 94485, 1090 GL Amsterdam; Science Park 904, Amsterdam; tel. (20) 5255773; fax (20) 5255778; e-mail itf@science.uva.nl; internet www.science.uva.nl/research/itf; f. 1949; attached to Univ. of Amsterdam; Dir Prof. Dr KARELJAN SCHOUTENS.

Johann Bernoulli Institute of Mathematics and Computing Science (JBI): POB 407, 9700 AK Groningen; Nijenborgh 9, 9747 AG Groningen; tel. (50) 3633973; fax (50) 3633800; e-mail research@math.rug.nl; internet www.rug.nl/informatica/onderzoek/bernoulli; attached to Faculty of Mathematics and Natural Science, Univ. of Groningen; 6 mathematics, 6 computer research programmes.

Kernfysisch Versneller Instituut (KVI) (Nuclear Physics Accelerator Institute): Zernikelaan 25 9747 AA Groningen; tel. (50) 3633600; fax (50) 3634003; e-mail info@kvi.nl; internet www.rug.nl/kvi/index; f. 1971; attached to Univ. of Groningen; international institute in fundamental and applied atomic and subatomic physics; Dir Prof. Dr KLAUS JUNGMANN.

Korteweg-de Vries Instituut voor Wiskunde (Korteweg-de Vries Institute for Mathematics): POB 94248, 1090 GE Amsterdam; Fl. 4C, Science Park 904, 1098 XH Amsterdam; tel. (20) 5255217; fax (20) 5257820; internet www.science.uva.nl/research/math; f. 1997, present location 2009; attached to Univ. of Amsterdam; research in mathematics; Dir Prof. Dr JAN J. O. O. WIEGERINCK; Man. J. L. (HANNEKE) PENTINGA; Sec. EVELIEN WALLET.

Sterrenkundig Instituut Anton Pannekoek (Anton Pannekoek Astronomical Institute): POB 94249, 1090 GE Amsterdam; Science Park 904, 1098 XH Amsterdam; tel. (20) 5257491; fax (20) 5257484; e-mail secr-astro-science@uva.nl; internet www.astro.uva.nl; attached to Univ. of Amsterdam; research in high-energy astrophysics; Dir Prof. Dr MICHIEL VAN DER KLIS.

Physical Sciences

Centre for Ecological and Evolutionary Studies (CEES): POB 14, 9750 AA Haren; Biological Centre, Kerklaan 30, 9750 AA Haren; tel. (50) 3638357; fax (50) 3632295; e-mail cees-office@rug.nl; internet www.rug.nl/biologie/onderzoek/onderzoekinstituten/cees/index; attached to Faculty of Mathematics and Natural Sciences, Univ. of Groningen; seven research groups; coordinates the local research school ecology and evolution; Dir Prof. Dr LEONARDUS BEUKEBOOM.

IMPACT—Institute for Energy and Resources: Meander Bldg, POB 217, 7500 AE Enschede; Meander Bldg, Drienerlolaan 5, 7522 NB Enschede; tel. (53) 4892489; fax (53) 4894233; e-mail impact@utwente.nl; internet www.utwente.nl/impact; attached to Univ. of Twente; research focuses on new materials based on renewable resources, reduction of energy demand and consumption by optimization of products, processes and methods, reduction of environmental footprints of processes and products, sustainable energy generation; Scientific Dir Prof. Dr Ir L. LEFFERTS; Man. Dir Ir J. P. EMMERZAAL.

Institute for Molecules and Materials (IMM): POB 9010, 6500 GL Nijmegen; Huygens bldg , Heyendaalseweg 135, 6525 AJ Nijmegen; tel. (24) 3652121; fax (24) 3652190; e-mail imm@science.ru.nl; internet www.ru.nl/imm; f. 2005; attached to Faculty of Science, Radbound Univ. Nijmegen; research in functional molecular structures and materials; Managing Dir Prof. Dr IWAN HOLLEMAN.

Institute for Wetland and Water Research (IWWR): POB 9010, 6500 GL Nijmegen; Heijendaalseweg 135, 6525 AJ Nijmegen; tel. (24) 3652294; fax (24) 3652830; e-mail m.frieling@science.ru.nl; internet www.ru.nl/iwwr; attached to Faculty of Science, Radbound Univ. of Nijmegen; joint research in microbiology, ecology, plant and environmental sciences; Dir Prof. Dr HANS DE KROON.

Instituut voor Biodiversiteit en Ecosysteem Dynamica (Institute for Biodiversity and Ecosystem Dynamics): POB 94248, 1090 GE Amsterdam; Science Park 904, 1098 XH Amsterdam; tel. (20) 5256635; fax (20) 5257832; e-mail ibed-dir-science@uva.nl; internet www.science.uva.nl/ibed; attached to Univ. of Amsterdam; research on biodiversity and evolution, geo-ecology and community dynamics; Dir Prof. Dr PETER TIENDEREN.

Nationaal Instituut voor Subatomaire Fysica (NIKHEF) (National Institute for Subatomic Physics): POB 41882, 1009 DB Amsterdam; Science Park 105, 1098 XG Amsterdam; tel. (20) 5922000; fax (20) 5925155; e-mail info@nikhef.nl; internet www.nikhef.nl; f. fmrly Nat. Institute for Nuclear Physics and High-Energy Physics, present name 1998; has a 900 MeV pulse stretcher and storage ring (AmPs) and auxiliary instrumentation for basic research in (astro) particle physics; Dir F. LINDE.

Nederlands Instituut voor Ecologie (Nederlands Institute of Ecology): POB 1299, 3600 BG Maarssen; Rijksstraatweg 6, 3631 AC Nieuwersluis; tel. (294) 239300; fax (294) 232224; e-mail m.albers@nioo.knaw.nl; internet www.nioo.knaw.nl; f. 1992 as Netherlands Institute for Ecological Research, present name 2002; attached to Royal Netherlands Acad. of Arts and Sciences; studies animal ecology, plant ecology, microbial ecology in terrestrial, freshwater and marine environments; incorporates Centre for Estuarine and Coastal Ecology (in Yerseke), Centre for Limnology (in Nieuwersluis) and Centre for Terrestrial Ecology (in Heteren); Dir Prof. Dr L. E. M. VET.

Netherlands Institute of Applied Geoscience TNO—National Geological Survey: POB 80015, 3508 TA Utrecht; Princetonlaan 6, 3584 CB Utrecht; tel. (30) 2564256; fax (30) 2564475; e-mail info@nitg.tno.nl; f. 1903; Dir Dr M. J. VAN BRACHT; publs *Geological Maps*, *Netherlands Journal of Geosciences* (4 a year).

NIOZ Koninklijk Nederlands Instituut voor Zeeonderzoek (NIOZ Royal Netherlands Institute for Sea Research): POB 59, 1790 AB Den Burg, Texel; Landsdiep 4, 1797 SZ 't Horntje, Texel; tel. (22) 2369300; fax (22) 2319674; e-mail cpr@nioz.nl; internet www.nioz.nl; f. 1876, present bldg 1976; attached to Netherlands Org. for Scientific Research; scientific marine research; ships; Chair. Prof. Dr PIER VELLINGA; Gen. Dir Prof. Dr CARLO H. R. HEIP; Deputy Dir Prof. Dr Ir HERMAN RIDDERINKHOF; Sec. Prof. Dr E.A. (WARD) KOSTER; Treas. GUUS F.C. VAN DER KAMP; publ. *Journal of Sea Research* (4 a year).

Sterrekundig Instituut Utrecht (Astronomical Institute Utrecht): Utrecht Univ., POB 80000, 3508 TA Utrecht; Buys Ballotlaboratorium, Princetonplein 5, 3584 CC Utrecht; tel. (30) 2535200; fax (30) 2535201; e-mail m.n.wijburg@astro-uu.nl; internet www.astro.uu.nl/siu; f. 1642, fmrly Sonnenborgh Observatory, present location 1987; studies in solar physics, stellar atmospheres, plasma and high energy astrophysics, space research, astrophysical instrumentation, astroparticle physics, massive stars, nucleosynthesis, stellar evolution, galaxies; library of 30,000 vols; Scientific Dir Prof. Dr CHRISTOPH U. KELLER; Sec. MARION N. WIJBURG.

SRON Netherlands Institute for Space Research: Sorbonnelaan 2, 3584 CA Utrecht; tel. (88) 7775600; fax (88) 7775601; e-mail info@sron.nl; internet www.sron.nl; f. 1983 as Space Research Org. Netherlands, present name 2005; attached to Netherlands Org. for Scientific Research; develops and exploits equipment for space research and for terrestrial research from space; br. in Groningen; Chair. Ir P. A. O. G. KORTING; Vice-Chair. Prof. Dr W. J. VAN DER ZANDE; Scientific Dir and Gen. Dir Prof. Dr RENS WATERS; Man. Dir and Deputy Gen. Dir Dr ROEL GATHIER.

Stichting voor Fundamenteel Onderzoek der Materie (FOM) (Foundation for Fundamental Research on Matter): POB 3021, 3502 GA Utrecht; Van Vollenhovenlaan 659, 3527 JP Utrecht; tel. (30) 6001211; fax (30) 6014406; e-mail info@fom.nl; internet www.fom.nl; f. 1946; promotes, coordinates and finances fundamental physics research in the Netherlands through 200 univ. teams in 2 institutes of its own, and 1 used jtly with univs; Chair. Prof. Dr N. J. LOPES CARDOZO; Vice-Chair. Prof. Dr C. W. J. BEENAKKER; Dir Dr Ir WIM VAN SAARLOOS; Sec. PETRA VAN LULING.

Attached Institutes:

FOM-Instituut voor Atoom- en Moleculfysica (FOM Institute of Atomic and Molecular Physics (AMOLF)): POB 41883, 1009 DB Amsterdam; Science Park 104, 1098 XG Amsterdam; tel. (20) 7547100; fax (20) 7547290; e-mail info@amolf.nl; internet www.amolf.nl; f. 1949 as FOM Laboratory for Mass Spectrography, present name 1966; facilities incl. mass-spectrometers, spectrographs, molecular beam apparatus, microwave interferometers, laser equipment, beam plasma experiments, a PDP 11 computer and a nanocentre; library of 2,200 vols; Gen. Dir Dr ALBERT POLMAN; Man. BART VAN LEIJEN.

FOM-Instituut voor Plasmafysica Rijnhuizen (FOM Institute of Plasma Physics Rijnhuizen): POB 1207, 3430 BE Nieuwegein; Edisonbaan 14, 3439 MN Nieuwegein; tel. (30) 6096999; fax (30) 6031204; e-mail info@rijnhuizen.nl; internet www.rijnhuizen.nl; f. 1959; research in plasma physics, plasma containment, heating, free electron laser, molecular cooling, plasma surface interaction, EUV mirrors; library of 7,000 vols, 13,000 reports; Dir Dr A. J. H. DONNÉ.

KVI (Nuclear-Physics Accelerator Institute): Zernikelaan 25, 9747 AA Groningen; tel. (50) 3633600; fax (50) 3634003; e-mail info@kvi.nl; internet www.kvi.nl; f. 1968; fundamental and applied atomic and subatomic physics; AVF cyclotron, ion sources, traps for short-living isotopes; Chair. Prof. K. DUPPEN; Dir Prof. KLAUS JUNGMANN; Exec. Sec. Dr MARJAN KOOPMANS.

Twente Water Centre: Horst Bldg, W 114, POB 217, 7500 AE Enschede; Horst Bldg, Drienerlolaan 5, 7522 NB Enschede; tel. (53) 4894320; fax (53) 4895377; e-mail water@utwente.nl; internet www.utwente.nl/water; attached to Univ. of Twente; water systems and governance; Chair. for Scientific Programme Council Prof. Dr Ir ARJEN Y. HOEKSTRA; Sec. JOKE MEIJER-LENTELINK.

Van't Hoff Institute for Molecular Sciences: POB 94157, 1090 GD Amsterdam; Science Park 904, 1098 XH Amsterdam; tel. (20) 5255265; fax (20) 5255604; e-mail r.b.hippert@uva.nl; internet www.science.uva.nl/hims; research themes incl. bio-molecular synthesis, catalysis, computational chemistry, macromolecular and biosystems analysis, molecular photonics; Scientific Dir Prof. Dr AART W. KLEIJN.

Zernike Institute for Advanced Materials: POB 221, 9700 AE Groningen; Nijenborgh 4, 9747 AG Groningen; tel. (50) 3634843; fax (50) 3637732; e-mail t.t.m.palstra@rug.nl; internet www.rug.nl/zernike/index; f. 2007 by merger of Materials Science Centre and Materials Science Centre plus; attached to Faculty of Mathematics and Natural Sciences, Univ. of Groningen; symbiotic studies of functional materials involving researchers from different disciplines; Scientific Dir Prof. Dr T. T. M. PALSTRA.

PHILOSOPHY AND PSYCHOLOGY

Amsterdam Centre for Child Studies: c/o Dr Dorien Graas, Van der Boechorststraat 1, 1081 BT Amsterdam; tel. (20) 5988785; e-mail info@ack.vu.nl; internet www.ack.vu.nl; f. 2002; attached to Vrije Univ. Amsterdam; research on insights in disturbed processes of child rearing and devt, and application and implementation of findings for policies and programs concerning parents and children.

Behavioural Science Institute: POB 9104, 6500 HE Nijmegen; Montessorilaan 3, A.08.29, 6525 HR Nijmegen; tel. (24) 3610082; fax (24) 3615937; e-mail secr@bsi.ru.nl; internet www.ru.nl/bsi; attached to Faculty of Social Sciences, Radbourne Univ. Nijmegen; research on principles and processes of human behaviour; Dir Prof. Dr MICHIEL KOMPIER.

Centre for Philosophy of Technology and Engineering Science: POB 217, 7500 AE Enschede; tel. (53) 4893297; e-mail p.bruulsema@utwente.nl; internet www.utwente.nl/gw/ceptes; attached to Univ. of Twente; research in philosophy of engineering science, technology; Dir PHILIP BREY; Sec. PETRA BRUULSEMA.

Heymans Institute for Psychological Research: Grote Kruisstraat 2/1, 9712 TS Groningen; tel. (50) 3638210; fax (50) 3636304; e-mail secr-onderzoekpsych@rug.nl; internet www.rug.nl/psy/onderzoek; attached to Dept. of Psychology, Univ. of Groningen; psychological research conducted within seven research programmes, participates in six research schools; Scientific Dir RITSKE DE JONG.

Psychology Research Institute: Roetersseiland-Bldg A , Roetersstraat 15, 1018 WB Amsterdam; tel. (20) 5256739; fax (20) 5256710; e-mail ozipsychologie-fmg@uva.nl; internet www.fmg.uva.nl/psy_research; attached to Univ. of Amsterdam; research, bachelors and masters courses in psychology; Scientific Dir Prof. Dr G. A. KERKHOF; Sec. RENÉE VELDHUIS.

Research Institute for Philosophy: POB 9103, 6500 HD Nijmegen; Erasmusplein 1,

6525 HT Nijmegen; tel. (24) 36124 74; fax (24) 3615564; e-mail secretariaat@unie.ru.nl; internet www.ru.nl/english/research/research_institutes/vm/research_institute_0; research programmes-rationality and cognition, hermeneutic philosophy, natural philosophy to science; includes centre for ethics.

RELIGION, SOCIOLOGY AND ANTHROPOLOGY

Amsterdam Institute for Social Science Research: Kloveniersburgwal 48, 1012 CX Amsterdam; Nieuwe Prinsengracht 130, 1018 VZ Amsterdam; tel. (20) 5252262; fax (20) 5252446; e-mail aissr@uva.nl; internet www.aissr.uva.nl; f. 2010 by merger of Amsterdam Institute for Metropolitan and International Development, Amsterdam School for Social science Research, Institute for Migration and Ethnic Studies; attached to Univ. of Amsterdam; research in social sciences incl. anthropology, devt studies, geography and planning, political science, sociology; Academic Dir Prof. ANITA HARDON; Exec. Dir JOSE KOMEN.

Amsterdam School for Cultural Analysis: Spuistraat 210, Room 113, 1012 VT Amsterdam; tel. (20) 5253874; fax (20) 5254773; e-mail asca-fgw@uva.nl; internet www.hum.uva.nl/asca; attached to Univ. of Amsterdam; interdisciplinary, comparative studies across cultural and linguistic areas; Academic Dir CHRISTOPH LINDNER; Man. Dir Dr ELOE KINGMA; Vice-Dir Dr WANDA STRAUVEN.

Babylon, Centre for Studies of Multicultural Society: POB 90153, 5000 LE Tilburg; Tilburg Univ., Warandelaan 2, Dante Bldg, 2nd Fl., 5037 AB Tilburg; tel. (13) 4662668; fax (13) 4662892; e-mail babylon@uvt.nl; internet www.tilburguniversity.nl/babylon; f. 2002; attached to Tilburg Univ.; research on characteristics and management of cultural, linguistic, religious diversity in multicultural society, taken from an int. comparative perspective; Dir Prof. Dr JAN BLOMMAERT; Assoc. Dir Prof. Dr FONS VAN DE VIJVER; Sec. KARIN BERKHOUT.

Centrum voor Patristisch Onderzoek (Centre for Patristic Research): POB 80101, 3508 TC Utrecht; tel. (30) 2532928, e-mail info@patristiek.eu; internet www.patristiek.eu; attached to Tilburg Univ.; research themes incl. early devt of Christian thinking about man, society, creation, the triune God; Dir Prof. Dr PAUL VAN GEEST.

Centre for Intercultural Ethics: POB 90153, 5000 LE Tilburg; Warandelaan 2, Dante Bldg, Room D103, 5037 AB Tilburg; tel. (13) 4662782; fax (13) 4662892; attached to Tilburg Univ.; Dir Prof. Dr HERMAN BECK; Sec. MARCIA SMITS.

Franciscaans Studiecentrum (Franciscan Study Centre): W.C. van Unnik Bldg, Heidelberglaan 2, 3584 CS Utrecht; tel. (13) 4663818; e-mail info@franciscaans-studiecentrum.nl; internet www.franciscaans-studiecentrum.nl; attached to Tilburg Univ.; research in Franciscan Spirituality, history, theology; examines spirituality of St Francis and St Clare of Assisi; Dir Prof. Dr G. P. FREEMAN.

Globus Competence Centre for Globalization and Sustainable Development: POB 90153, 5000 LE Tilburg; Warandelaan 2, 5037 AB, Tilburg; tel. (13) 4669111; fax (13) 4668699; e-mail viv.mestdagh@uvt.nl; internet www.tilburguniversity.nl/globus; attached to Tilbug Univ.; globalization, sustainable devt; Chair. Prof. Dr K. ZOETEMAN; Exec. Dir PAUL VAN SETERS.

Groningen Research Institute for the Study of Culture (ICOG): POB 716, NL-9700 AS Groningen; Oude Kijk in 't Jatstraat 26, 9712 EK Groningen; tel. (50) 3635918; fax (50) 3635821; e-mail icog@rug.nl; internet www.rug.nl/let/onderzoek/onderzoekinstituten/icog; attached to Faculty of Arts, Univ. of Groningen; research on study of cultural processes, their manifestations and discussion of these subjects in Europe, Americas, E Mediterranean, Asian regions; Dir Prof. Dr GOFFE JENSMA.

Institute for Historical, Literary and Cultural Studies: POB 9103, 6500 HD Nijmegen; Erasmusplein 1, 6525 HT Nijmegen; tel. (24) 3612336; fax (24) 3615481; e-mail hlcs@let.ru.nl; internet www.ru.nl/english/research/research_institutes/vm/institute_for_4; attached to Faculty of Arts, Radbound Univ. Nijmegen; research programmes on ancient world, Islamic culture, Christian cultural heritage, middle ages and literature, culture, media.

Institute for Migration and Ethnic Studies: Oudezijds Achterburgwal 185, 1012 DK Amsterdam; tel. (20) 5253627; fax (20) 5253628; e-mail imes@uva.nl; internet www.imes.uva.nl; attached to Univ. of Amsterdam; focuses on int. migration and the integration of immigrants and their descendants in host societies in a comparative perspective; Dir Prof. JAN RATH.

Instituut voor Liturgische en Rituele Studies (ILRS) (Institute for Liturgical and Ritual Studies): POB 90153, 5000 LE Tilburg; Dante Bldg, Room 132, Warandelaan 2, 5037 AB, Tilburg; tel. (13) 4662056; fax (13) 4662892; e-mail ilrs@uvt.nl; internet www.tilburguniversity.nl/ilrs; attached to Tilburg Univ.; research areas incl. rituals, Christian liturgy, sacred places, sacraments, folk religious rites; Chair. Prof. Dr G. ROUWHORST; Sec. Dr PETRA VERSNEL; publs *Jaarboek voor liturgieonderzoek*, *Liturgia condenda*, *Meander*, *Netherlands Studies in Ritual and Liturgy*.

Interuniversity Centre for Social Science Theory and Methodology (ICS): ICS, Department of Sociology, Grote Rozenstraat 31, 9712 TG Groningen; tel. (50) 3636469; fax (50) 3636226; e-mail s.simon@rug.nl; internet www.ics-graduateschool.nl; f. 1986; jt project of Univ. of Groningen, Utrecht Univ. and Radboud Univ. Nijmegen; located in sociology dept. of all three univs; Scientific Dir Prof. RAFAEL WITTEK.

LUCE—Centrum voor Religieuze Communicatie (LUCE—Centre for Religious Communication): POB 80101, 3508 TC Utrecht; Heidelberglaan 2, Utrecht; tel. (30) 2531882; fax (30) 2533665; e-mail luce-crc@uvt.nl; f. 2007; attached to Tilburg Univ.; Dir HENK VAN HOUT.

Meertens Instituut: POB 94264, 1090 GG Amsterdam; Joan Muyskenweg 25, 1096 CJ Amsterdam; tel. (20) 4628500; fax (20) 4628555; e-mail info@meertens.knaw.nl; internet www.meertens.knaw.nl; f. 1926, present status 1952; attached to Royal Netherlands Acad. of Arts and Sciences; research into diversity and documentation of Dutch language and culture; incl. ethnological studies, structural, dialectological and sociolinguistic study of language variation; organizes workshops, symposiums and confs; library of 70,000 vols, 4,000 journals; Dir Prof. Dr H. J. BENNIS.

Nederlandse Onderzoekschool voor Theologie en Religiewetenschap (NOSTER) (Netherlands School for Advanced Studies in Theology and Religion): POB 80.105, 3508 TC Utrecht; W.C. van Unnik Bldg, Heidelberglaan 2, 3584 CS Utrecht; tel. (30) 2533105; fax (30) 2533241; e-mail noster@uu.nl; internet www.noster.org; attached to Tilburg Univ.; research in theology, religious studies; Pres. Prof. Dr PETER J. A. NISSEN; Dir Prof. Dr A. J. A. C. M. (ANNE-MARIE) KORTE; Sec. ANJA H. HAVINGA; 200 teachers; 50 students; publ. *STAR*.

Netherlands Institute for Advanced Study in the Humanities and Social Sciences (NIAS): Meijboomlaan 1, 2242 PR Wassenaar; tel. (70) 5122700; fax (70) 5117162; e-mail nias@nias.knaw.nl; internet www.nias.knaw.nl; f. 1970, present status 1998; attached to Royal Netherlands Acad. of Arts and Sciences; encourages research in the humanities and social sciences; fellowships awarded annually (25 to foreign scholars, 25 to Dutch scholars); Rector Prof. AAFKE C. J. HULK; publs *Jelle Zijlstra Lecture* (1 a year), *KB Lecture* (1 a year), *Ortelius Lecture* (every 2 years), *Uhlenbeck Lecture* (1 a year), *Willem F. Duisenberg Lecture* (1 a year).

Nijmeegs Instituut voor Sociaal en Cultureel Onderzoek (NISCO) (Nijmegen Institute for Social and Cultural Research): POB 9104, 6500 HE Nijmegen; Thomas van Aquinostraat 4, 6525 GD Nijmegen; tel. (24) 3615568; fax (24) 3612351; e-mail e.vanwijk@maw.ru.nl; internet www.ru.nl/english/research/research_institutes/vm/nijmegen_-institute; f. 2003; attached to Faculty of Social Sciences, Radbound Univ. Nijmegen; comparative questions on cohesion, inequality, rationalization within and between societies; Dir PAUL HOEBINK.

Research Institute for Theology and Religious Studies: POB 9103, 6500 HD Nijmegen; Erasmusplein 1, 6525 HT Nijmegen; tel. (24) 3612474; e-mail secretariaat@unie.ru.nl; internet www.ru.nl/english/research/research_institutes/vm/research_-institute; attached to Radbound Univ. Nijmegen; study of religious identities in multi-religious societies.

SISWO—Instituut voor Maatschappijwetenschappen (SISWO—Institute for the Social Sciences): Plantage Muidergracht 4, 1018 TV Amsterdam; tel. (20) 5270600; fax (20) 6229430; e-mail siswo@siswo.uva.nl; internet www.siswo.uva.nl/angloam; f. 1960; initiates and coordinates policy-relevant social science research; Dir Prof. Dr H. G. DE GIER; publs *FACTA*, *KWALON*, *Tijdschrift voor Criminologie*.

Telos Brabants Centrum voor Duurzame Ontwikkeling (TELOS—Brabant Centre for Sustainable Development): POB 90153, 5000 LE Tilburg; Warandelaan 2, 5037 AB, Tilburg; tel. (13) 4668712; fax (13) 4663499; e-mail telos@uvt.nl; internet www.telos.nl; f. 1999; attached to Tilburg Univ.; research into sustainable system innovations, transitions in Brabant; Chair Prof. Dr Ir J. T. MOMMAAS.

Thomas Instituut te Utrecht: Heidelberglaan 2, 3584 CS Utrecht; tel. (73) 6135665; fax (73) 5482049; e-mail info@instituut-thomas.nl; internet www.thomasinstituut.org; f. 1990, present status 2006; attached to Tilburg Univ.; study of work of St Thomas Aquinas; Dir Prof. Dr H. J. M. SCHOOT; Sec. for Studies Dr C. M. PUMPLUN.

TECHNOLOGY

3TU Centre for Ethics and Technology: POB 5015, 2600 GA Delft; tel. (15) 2787210; fax (15) 2786439; e-mail info@ethicsandtechnology.eu; internet www.ethicsandtechnology.eu; studies ethical issues in devt, use and regulation of technology; Man. Dir Dr SABINE ROESER.

Advanced School for Computing and Imaging: TU Delft, EWI, Mekelweg 4, 2628 CD Delft; tel. (15) 2788032; fax (15) 2786632;

e-mail asci@ewi.tudelft.nl; internet www.asci.tudelft.nl; research in computer systems; Scientific Dir Prof. Dr Ir A. W. M. SMEULDERS.

BatchKennisCentrum (Batch Knowledge Centre): POB 5015, 2600 GA Delft; Jaffalaan 5, 2628 GX Delft; tel. (15) 2781147; fax (15) 2783422; e-mail bkc@batchcentre.tudelft.nl; internet www.batchcentre.tudelft.nl; attached to Delft Univ. of Technology; provides information on batch literature, batch research, batch software, batch tutorials; Project Leader Dr Z. VERWATER-LUKSO.

Beta Research School for Operations Management and Logistics: Paviljoen C 07, POB 513, 5600 MB Eindhoven; tel. (40) 2474733; fax (40) 2472607; e-mail beta@tue.nl; internet beta.ieis.tue.nl; f. 1995, present status 1998; attached to Eindhoven Univ. of Technology; operational processes, computer science, labour psychology, mathematics, organizational behaviour; Scientific Dir Prof. Dr Ir G. J. VAN HOUTUM.

CIM Centrum Delft (CIM Centre Delft): Mekelweg 2, 2628 CD Delft; tel. (15) 2786876; fax (15) 2783910; e-mail b.r.meijer@tudelft.nl; f. 1985; attached to Delft Univ. of Technology; training and knowledge centre in the fields of computer integrated manufacturing (CID), automated production systems, robotics in corporate economic and organizational context.

Centre for Plasma Physics and Radiation Technology: Dept of Applied Physics, POB 513, 5600 MB Eindhoven; tel. (40) 2472779; fax (40) 2438060; e-mail office.cps@tue.nl; internet www.phys.tue.nl/cps; attached to Eindhoven Univ. of Technology; research in the field of astrophysical plasmas, cold etching and deposition plasmas, hot thermonuclear plasmas, micro-discharges, physics; devt, applications of radiation sources; Scientific Dir Prof. Dr M. C. M. VAN DE SANDEN; Sec. A. M. M. LOONEN.

Centre for Telematics and Information Technology: POB 217, 7500 AE Enschede; Zilverling Bldg, Drienerlolaan 5, 7522 NB Enschede; tel. (53) 4898031; fax (53) 4891070; e-mail office@ctit.utwente.nl; internet www.ctit.utwente.nl; attached to Univ. of Twente; research on design of advanced ICT systems and their application in a variety of application domains; Chair. of Supervisory Board Prof. Dr E. H. L. AARTS; Scientific Dir PETER M. G. APERS; Man. Dir IDDO BANTE.

Centrum voor Schone Technologie en Milieubeleid (Twente Centre for Studies in Technology and Sustainable Development): POB 217, 7500 AE Enschede; Ravelijn Bldg, Drienerlolaan 5, 7522 NB Enschede; tel. (53) 4893203; fax (53) 4894850; e-mail secr@cstm.utwente.nl; internet www.utwente.nl/mb/cstm; f. 1988; attached to Univ. of Twente; environmental quality, governance, sustainable devt, technological innovation; Scientific Dir Prof. Dr HANS TH. A. BRESSERS; Man. Dir Dr MAARTEN J. ARENTSEN.

Communication Technology Basic Research and its Applications (COBRA): Bldg Potentiaal, Room PT 12.35, POB 513, 5600 MB Eindhoven; Bldg Potentiaal, Room PT 12.35, Den Dolech 2, 5612 AZ Eindhoven; tel. (40) 2475801; fax (40) 2455197; e-mail cobra@tue.nl; internet w3.ele.tue.nl/en/cobra; f. 1994; attached to Eindhoven Univ. of Technology; communication technologies basic research and applications; Chair. of Board Drs P. MAIJ; Scientific Dir Prof. Dr H. J. S. DORREN; Scientific Sec. Ir J. J. B. KWAAITAAL.

Delft Centre for Engineering Design: Mekelweg 2, 2628 CD Delft; tel. (15) 278 6794; fax (15) 278 4717; e-mail j.w.m.tournoij@tudelft.nl; internet www.tudelft.nl; attached to Delft Univ. of Technology; Advanced Masters in Engineering Design; industry research; Dir Prof. Dr T. TOMIYAMA.

Delft Centre for Aviation: Jaffalaan 5, 2628 BX Delft; tel. (12) 2787553; e-mail a.r.c.dehaan@tudelft.nl; internet www.tudelft.nl; aviation research centre of Delft Univ. of Technology; researches air traffic systems, aviation processes, airport systems, landslide accessibility, sustainability analysis; Managing Dir Dr ALEXANDER DE HAAN.

Delft Institute for Earth-Oriented Space Research: POB 5058, Delft; Kluyverweg 1, 2600 GB Delft; tel. (15) 2782558; fax (15) 2782348; e-mail teunissen@deos.tudelft.nl; attached to Delft Univ. of Technology; incorporates field of spacecraft system integration and design that is essential for the devt of earth observation systems; Scientific Dir Prof. Dr Ir P. J. G. TEUNISSEN.

Delft Institute of Microsystems and Nanoelectronics (Dimes): Feldmannweg 17, 2628 CT Delft; tel. (15) 2786234; fax (15) 2787369; e-mail info@dimes.tudelft.nl; internet www.dimes.tudelft.nl; attached to Delft Univ. of Technology; research and education in microsystems and nanoelectronics through PhD programme; Scientific Dir Prof. Dr KEES BEENAKKER.

Delft University Wind Energy Research Institute: Kluyverweg 1, 2629 HS Delft; tel. (15) 2785170; fax (15) 2785347; e-mail duwind@tudelft.nl; internet www.duwind.tudelft.nl; f. 1999; attached to Delft Univ. of Technology; research on modern wind turbine technology.

Delft University Research Centre of Intelligent Sensor Microsystems: POB 5031, 2600 GA Delft; Mekelweg 4, EWI Bldg, 2628 CD Delft; tel. (15) 2785745; fax (15) 2785755; e-mail disens@tudelft.nl; internet www.disens.tudelft.nl; attached to Delft Univ. of Technology; research on sensors and actuators in microsystem technology; Dir Prof. Dr P. M. SARRO; Man. Dir Prof. Dr Ir J. H. HUIJSING; Sec. G. HOUWELING.

Delft Institute for Information Technology in Service Engineering: Stevinweg 1, 2628 CN Delft; tel. (15) 2785170; fax (15) 2785347; e-mail info@duwind.tudelft.nl; attached to Delft Univ. of Technology; Dir Prof. Dr H. G. SOL.

Drebbel Institute for Mechatronics: POB 217, 7500 AE Enschede; internet www.drebbel.utwente.nl; f. 1989 as Mechatronics Research Institute Twente; attached to Univ. of Twente; research in mechatronics activities; research topics incl. advanced robotics, control theory and control engineering, embedded control systems, mechatronic design, mechatronic measuring systems, modelling and simulation; Scientific Dir Prof. JOB VAN AMERONGEN.

Dutch Institute of Systems and Control: Delft Centre for Systems and Control, Delft Univ. of Technology, DISC, Mekelweg 2, 2628 CD Delft; tel. (15) 2785572; fax (15) 2786679; e-mail s.m.vandermeer@tudelft.nl; internet www.disc.tudelft.nl; f. 1995 by Delft and Eindhoven Univ. of Technology and Univ. of Twente; interuniv. research institute, graduate school unites all academic research active in systems and control theory and engineering; Dir Prof. Dr Ir PAUL VAN DEN HOF.

Dutch National Research School Combination Catalysis Controlled by Chemical Design (NRSC-Catalysis): POB 513, 5600 MB Eindhoven; Den Dolech 2, Helix W 3.23, Eindhoven; tel. (40) 2473071; fax (40) 2475054; e-mail m.j.m.j.jong@tue.nl; internet www.nrsc-catalysis.nl; f. 1999; attached to Eindhoven Univ. of Technology; Dir Prof. Dr RUTGER A. VAN SANTEN; Man. Dr GABRIELA E. DIMA.

Energieonderzoek Centrum Nederland (ECN) (Energy Research Centre of the Netherlands (ECN)): POB 1, 1755 ZG Petten; Westerduinweg 3, 1755 LE Petten; tel. (22) 4564949; fax (22) 4568486; e-mail info@ecn.nl; internet www.ecn.nl; f. 1955 as Reactor Centrum Nederland—RCN; carries out energy research; under contract from the govt, nat. and int. orgs and industry; Man. Dir Ir PAUL A. O. G. KORTING; Dir Dr C. A. M. (KEES) VAN DER KLEIN; Dir PEDRO J. SAYERS.

Graduate School on Engineering Mechanics: c/o Dr. ir. J. A. W. van Dommelen, Dept of Mechanical Engineering, Eindhoven Univ. of Technology, POB 513, W-hoog 4.133, 5600 MB Eindhoven; tel. (40) 2474060; fax (40) 2447355; e-mail engineering.mechanics@tue.nl; internet www.em.tue.nl; f. 1996; attached to Eindhoven Univ. of Technology; description, analysis, optimization of static and dynamic behaviour of materials, products, processes in variety of engineering applications; Scientific Dir Prof. MARC G. D. GEERS.

Hechtingsinstituut (The Adhesion Institute): Kluyverweg 1, 2629 HS Delft; tel. (15) 2785353; e-mail info@hechtingsinstituut.nl; internet www.adhesioninstitute.com; f. 1990; attached to Delft Univ. of Technology; research in the field of structural adhesive bonds; part of the Faculty of Aerospace Engineering; Dir Dr J. A. POULIS.

IBR Centre for eHealth Research and Disease Management: Citadel H 411, POB 217, 7500 AE Enschede; Citadel Bldg H 411, Drienerlolaan 5, 7522 NB Enschede; tel. (53) 4892398; fax (53) 4892388; e-mail j.vangemert-pijnen@utwente.nl; internet www.utwente.nl/ibr/ehealth; attached to Univ. of Twente; examines technology's contribution to healthy lifestyle.

IBR Research Institute for Social Sciences and Technology: Citadel Bldg H 411, POB 217, 7500 AE Enschede; tel. (53) 4892398; fax (53) 4894259; e-mail ibr@utwente.nl; internet www.utwente.nl/ibr; attached to Univ. of Twente; research on human behaviour; research themes incl. health assessment and promotion, learning, organization and communication, product design, safety and security, technical cognition; Scientific Dir Prof. Dr E. R. SEYDEL; Man. Dir Dr O. PETERS; Sec. M. G. STEGEHUIS-DE VEGTE.

Institute for Biomedical Technology and Technical Medicine: Zuidhorst Bldg, POB 217, 7500 AE Enschede; Zuidhorst Bldg, Drienerlolaan 5, 7522 NB Enschede; tel. (53) 4893367; fax (53) 4892319; e-mail mira@utwente.nl; internet www.utwente.nl/mira; attached to Univ. of Twente; Scientific Dir Prof. Dr CLEMENS A. VAN BLITTERSWIJK; Man. Dir Dr Ir MARTIJN KUIT; Medical Dir Prof. Dr G. P. (PETER) VOOIJS; Dir for Education Drs HELEEN A. T. MIEDEMA.

Institute for Computing and Information Sciences: POB 9010, 6500 GL Nijmegen; Heyendaalseweg 135, 6525 AJ Nijmegen; tel. (24) 3652643; fax (24) 3652728; e-mail info@cs.ru.nl; internet www.ru.nl/icis; attached to Faculty of Science, Radbound Univ. Nijmegen; research on computer systems through model based system development, digital security and intelligent systems; Research Dir Prof. Dr T. M. HESKES.

Institute for Logic, Language and Computation: POB 94242, 1090 GE Amsterdam; Science Park 904, 1098 XH Amsterdam; tel. (20) 5256051; fax (20) 5255206; e-mail illc@uva.nl; internet www.illc.uva.nl; f. 1986 as Institute for Language, Logic and Information, present status 1991; attached to Univ. of Amsterdam; research in fundamental principles of encoding, transmission and comprehension of information; Dir LEEN TORENVLIET; Man. INGRID VAN LOON; publ. *ILLC magazine* (1 a year).

Institute for Medical Technology Assessment (iMTA): POB 1738, 3000 DR Rotterdam; Burgemeester Oudlaan 50, 3062 PA Rotterdam; tel. (10) 4088571; fax (10) 4089081; e-mail deklerk@bmg.eur.nl; internet www.bmg.eur.nl/imta; f. 1988; attached to Erasmus Univ.; medical technology assessment, incl. health economics and health outcomes research; provides teaching and training in economic evaluation and MTA research; Vice-Dir Prof. Dr MAUREEN RUTTEN-VAN MÖLKEN; Sec. I. DE KLERK.

Institute for Science, Innovation and Society (ISIS): POB 9010, 6500 GL Nijmegen; Huygens Bldg, Room 02.832, Heijendaalseweg 135, 6525 AJ Nijmegen; tel. (24) 3653155; fax (24) 3553450; e-mail h.zwart@science.ru.nl; internet www.ru.nl/science/isis; f. 2005; attached to Faculty of Science, Radboud Univ. Nijmegen; analyses, assesses and improves societal embedding of science and technology; Dir Prof. Dr HUB ZWART.

Instituut voor Milieu en Agritechniek (IMAG-DLO) (Institute of Agricultural and Environmental Engineering): POB 43, 6700 AA Wageningen; Mansholtlaan 10–12, 6708 PA Wageningen; tel. (317) 476300; fax (317) 425670; e-mail postkamer@imag.dlo.nl; f. 1974; Dir Dr Ir AAD A. JONGEBREUR.

International Research Centre for Telecommunications and Radar: c/o Delft Univ. of Technology, POB 5031, 2600 GA Delft; Mekelweg 4, EWI Bldg, 2628 CD Delft; tel. (15) 2781034; fax (15) 2784046; e-mail d.a.u.meijer@tudelft.nl; f. 1994; attached to Delft Univ. of Technology; Dir Prof. Dr Ir LEO P. LIGTHART; Sec. DOMINIQUE A. U. MEIJER.

International Research Institute for Simulation, Motion and Navigation: POB 5058, 2600 GB Delft; Anthony Fokkerweg 1, 2629 HC Delft; tel. (15) 2782094; fax (15) 2786480; e-mail info@simona.tudelft.nl; attached to Delft Univ. of Technology; research institute in the field of simulation and transport; Man. Dir Ir MEINE P. OOSTEN; Management Asst VERA M. VAN BRAGT.

J. F. Schouten School for User-System Interaction Research: POB 513, 5600 MB Eindhoven; Paviljoen, R. 1.40, ingang Het Eeuwsel, Eindhoven; tel. (40) 2475938; fax (40) 2472607; e-mail jfs@tue.nl; internet www.industrialdesign.tue.nl/jfschouten; f. 1993; attached to Eindhoven Univ. of Technology; Scientific Dir Prof. Dr DON G. BOUWHUIS.

J. M. Burgerscentrum—Onderzoekschool voor Stromingsleer (JMBC) (J. M. Burgerscentrum—Research School for Fluid Mechanics): c/o TU Delft, Mekelweg 2, 2628 CD Delft; tel. (15) 2783216; e-mail jmburgerscentrum@tudelft.nl; internet www.jmburgerscentrum.nl; 60 research groups, 250 PhD students; Dir Prof. Dr Ir G. OOMS.

Kavli Institute of Nanoscience: Postbus 5046, 2600 GA Delft; Lorentzweg 1, 2628 CJ Delft; tel. (15) 2783163; fax (15) 2786600; e-mail nanoscience@tnw.tudelft.nl; internet www.tnw.tudelft.nl; f. 2004; attached to Delft Univ. of Technology; 6 research units, one nanofacility cleanroom; founded on grant by Kavli foundation; Dir Prof. Dr HANS MOOIJ.

Koiter Institute Delft: Kluyverweg 1, 2629 HS Delft; tel. (15) 2785460; fax (15) 2611465; e-mail r.deborst@lr.tudelft.nl; internet www.kid.tudelft.nl; attached to Delft Univ. of Technology; promotes mono-disciplinary activity in engineering mechanics.

Materials Analysis, Testing, Technology and Research: POB 513, 5600 MB Eindhoven; tel. (40) 2474950; fax (40) 2445619; e-mail i.m.j.j.v.d.ven-lucassen@tue.nl; attached to Eindhoven Univ. of Technology; Sec. Dr Ir I. M. M. J. VAN DE VEN-LUCASSEN.

Materials Innovation Institute (M2i): POB 5008, 2600 GA Delft; Mekelweg 2, 2628 CD Delft; tel. (15)-2782535; fax (15)-2782591; e-mail info@m2i.nl; internet www.m2i.nl; devt of new materials for sustainable economic growth; partnership between industy, govt, academia.

MESA+ Institute for Nanotechnology: POB 217, 7500 AE Enschede; NanoLab Bldg, Hallenweg 15, 7522 NB Enschede; tel. (53) 4892715; fax (53) 4892575; e-mail info@mesaplus.utwente.nl; internet www.utwente.nl/mesaplus; attached to Univ. of Twente; research in nanotechnology; Scientific Dir Prof. Dr Ing DAVE BLANK.

Nationaal Lucht- en Ruimtevaartlaboratorium (NLR) (National Aerospace Laboratory): POB 90502, 1006 BM Amsterdam; Anthony Fokkerweg 2, 1059 CM Amsterdam; tel. (20) 5113113; fax (20) 5113210; e-mail info@nlr.nl; internet www.nlr.nl/public; f. 1919; fluid dynamics, flight mechanics, flight testing and operations, structures and materials, space technology, remote sensing, information technology, electronics and instrumentation; br. in Flevoland; library of 7,000 vols, 4,800 conf. proceedings, 2,500 theses, 112,000 reports, etc.; Chair. Drs ARIE KRAAIJEVELD; Gen. Dir Ir MICHEL PETERS; Gen. Sec. ERNST FOLKERS.

National Dutch Graduate Research School of Polymer Science and Technology (PTN): POB 6284, 5600 HG Eindhoven; tel. (40) 2475262; fax (40) 2475430; e-mail info@ptn.nu; internet www.ptn.nu; cooperation foundation stage for polymer research in univ. and industry.

National Dutch Graduate School of Polymer Science and Technology (PTN): POB 6284, 5600 HG Eindhoven; tel. (40) 2475262; fax (40) 2475430; e-mail nfo@ptn.nu; internet www.ptn.nu; Chair. Ir DICK MEDEMA.

Onderzoekschool Engineering Mechanics (Graduate School on Engineering Mechanics): c/o Dr.Ir J. A. W. van Dommelen, POB 513, WH 4.125, 5600 MB Eindhoven; tel. (40) 2474521; e-mail engineering.mechanics@tue.nl; internet www.em.tue.nl; f. 1996; research and education in engineering mechanics; works with Eindhoven Univ. of Technology, Delft Univ. of technology and Univ. of Twente; Scientific Dir Prof. Dr Ir M. G. D. (MARC) GEERS.

OnderzoekSchool ProcesTechnologie (Research School in Process Technology): De Meander Bldg, POB 217, 7500 AE Enschede; De Meander Bldg, Room ME 116, Drienerlolaan 5, 7522 NB Enschede; tel. (53) 4893034; fax (53) 4891199; e-mail ospt@tnw.utwente.nl; internet ospt.tnw.utwente.nl/ospt4; chemical engineering, process technology; Chair. of the Board Prof. Dr G. VAN DER STEENHOVEN; Scientific Dir Prof. Dr Ir H. E. A. VAN DEN AKKER; Exec. Sec. Ing. GERT H. BANIS.

Onderzoekschool voor Integrale Product Vernieuwing (Graduate School of Integrated Product Innovation): Universiteit Twente, Faculteit der Werktuigbouwkunde, Centrum voor Integrale, Productie Vernieuwing, POB 217 7500 AE Enschede; tel. (53) 4892520; research programme for research groups in product innovation; Dir Prof. Dr Ir F. J. A. M. VAN HOUTEN.

Reactor Institute Delft: Mekelweg 15, 2629 JB Delft; tel. (15) 2785052; fax (15) 2786422; e-mail secretary-rid@tudelft.nl; attached to Delft Univ. of Technology; fundamental and applied scientific research in various fields, both nationally and internationally; houses Hoger Onderwijs Reactor (HOR); Dir Prof. Dr Ir TIM H. J. J. VAN DER HAGEN; Gen. Man Drs Ir RIK J. LINSSEN; Sec. LINDA HOOGENDONK-DEN OTTER.

Research School Integral Design of Structures: POB 5048, 2600 GA Delft; Faculty of Civil Engineering and Geosciences, Delft Univ. of Technology, Stevinweg 1, 2628 CN Delft; tel. (15) 2784578; fax (15) 2787438; e-mail info@osbouw.nl; internet www.osbouw.nl; f. 1994; inter-univ. research institute for structural design, structural engineering and building processes; Dir Prof. Dr Ir J. C. WALRAVEN.

School for Information and Knowledge Systems: Utrecht Univ., Dept of Information and Computing Sciences, Corine Jolles, Buys Ballot Laboratory, Princetonplein 5, Office 574, 3584 CC Utrecht; tel. (30) 2534083; fax (30) 2513791; e-mail office@siks.nl; internet www.siks.nl; f. 1996; research school for information and communication technology; network institute with 11 collaborating univs; Man. Dir Dr R. J. C. M. STARMANS.

ThermoPlastic Composite Research Centre: Horst Bldg, POB 217, 7500 AE Enschede; tel. (53) 4891051; fax (53) 4894784; internet www.tprc.nl; f. 2008; attached to Univ. of Twente.

TICER—Tilburg Innovation Centre for Electronic Resources: POB 90153, 5000 LE Tilburg; tel. (13) 4662620; fax (13) 4668383; e-mail m.a.schuurman@uvt.nl; internet www.tilburguniversity.nl/ticer; f. 1995; attached to Tilburg Univ.; digital libraries and IT infrastructure; Man. JOLA PRINSEN; Logistics Man. MERRILEE SCHUURMAN.

Tilburg Centre for Cognition and Communication (TICC): POB 90153, 5000 LE Tilburg; Dante Bldg, Warandelaan 2, 5037 AB Tilburg; tel. (13) 4668118; e-mail ticc@uvt.nl; internet www.tilburguniversity.nl/ticc; attached to Tilburg Univ.; artificial intelligence, cognitive modelling, gaming, human–computer interaction; Dir Prof. Dr H. J. VAN DEN HERIK.

Tilburg Institute for Law, Technology and Society (TILT): POB 90153, 5000 LE Tilburg; Montesquieu Bldg, Warandelaan 2, 5037 AB Tilburg; tel. (13) 4668199; fax (13) 4663750; e-mail v.carter@uvt.nl; internet www.tilburguniversity.nl/tilt; attached to Tilburg Univ.; transnational study of law, society, technology; research areas incl. devts in ICT, biotechnology, other technologies; Gen. Dir Prof. Dr HAN SOMSEN; Dir for Research and Deputy Dir Prof. Dr RONALD E. LEENES; Dir for Studies Dr ANTON H. VEDDER; Dir for Human Resources Dr SIMONE VAN DER HOF; Sec. VIVIAN CARTER.

Twente Embedded Systems Initiative: POB 217, 7500 AE Enschede; tel. (53) 4894173; fax (53) 4893770; e-mail t.krol@cs.utwente.nl; internet www.tesi.utwente.nl;

attached to Univ. of Twente; research activities in the field of embedded systems, embedded systems design; Head Prof. Dr Ir THIJS KROL.

Vakgroep Verkeer, Vervoer & Ruimte (Centre for Transport Studies): POB 217, 7500 AE Enschede; Bldg Horst, Drienerlolaan 5, 7522 NB Enschede; tel. (53) 4894322; fax (53) 4894040; e-mail d.alink-olthof@utwente.nl; internet www.vvr.ctw.utwente.nl; attached to Univ. of Twente; provides traffic engineering courses in Bachelors programme; civil engineering and track traffic engineering and management within the Masters programme; Head Prof. Dr ERIC VAN BERKUM; Sec. DORETTE ALINK-OLTHOF.

Vermogenselektronica en Elektromagnetisch Conversie Centrum (Power Electronics and Electromagnetic Power Conversion Centre): Mekelweg 4, 2628 CD Delft; tel. (15) 2786259; fax (15) 2782968; attached to Delft Univ. of Technology.

Virtual Reality Initiative Twente: c/o Dr Ir H. van der Kooij, POB 217, 7500 AE Enschede; tel. (53) 4894779; internet vrint.ctit.utwente.nl; attached to Univ. of Twente; platform for all research groups involved with the devt and application of virtual reality tools.

Libraries and Archives

Alkmaar

Regionaal Archief (Regional Record Office): Bergerweg 1, POB 9232, 1815 AC Alkmaar; Hertog Aalbrechtweg 5, 1823 DL Alkmaar; tel. (72) 8508200; fax (72) 8508252; e-mail regionaal@archiefalkmaar.nl; internet www.archiefalkmaar.nl; f. 1990; municipal archives, books about Alkmaar and N Holland, etc.; also regional archives for the area; pictures, prints, maps, relating to Alkmaar and surroundings; 50,000 vols; Librarian M. JOUSTRA; publ. *Inventories of Archives*.

Amersfoort

Bibliotheek van het Oud-Katholiek Seminarie (Library of the Old Catholic Seminary): Heidelberglaan 3, 3584 CS Amersfoort; tel. (33) 4617569; fax (33) 4619340; e-mail l.nieuwenhuiz@hetnet.nl; internet seminarie.okkn.nl; f. 1725; attached to Dept of Theology, Utrecht Univ.; 11,000 vols; Old Catholicism, Jansenism, Port-Royal, Church history of the Netherlands and Old-Catholic churches, ecumenism, titles edited before 1900 have been moved to the Library of Utrecht Univ.; Librarian L. NIEUWENHUIZEN.

Openbare Leeszaal en Bibliotheek (Public Library): Zonnehof 12, 3811 ND Amersfoort; tel. (33) 631914; f. 1913; 190,000 vols; Librarian E. A. MURRIS.

Amsterdam

Bibliotheca Philosophica Hermetica (Library of Hermetic Philosophy in Amsterdam): Bloemgracht 13–19, 1016 KC Amsterdam; tel. (20) 6258079; fax (20) 6200973; e-mail bph@ritmanlibrary.nl; internet www.ritmanlibrary.nl; f. 1984; private library, open to researchers by appt; 22,000 vols, incl 5,000 vols printed before 1800, 600 MSS, 17,000 modern titles; specialises in early printed books and MSS in the field of the Christian-hermetic tradition (alchemy, hermetism, mysticism and rosicrucianism); also modern biographical and bibliographical reference works, text-editions, scholarly works, books on the modern esoteric tradition; Man. Dir and Librarian ESTHER OOSTERWIJK-RITMAN; Curator Dr CIS VAN HEERTUM; Curator Drs JOSÉ BOUMAN.

Bibliotheek Centrum Wiskunde & Informatica (Library of the Centre for Mathematics and Computer Science): POB 94079, 1090 GB Amsterdam; Science Park 123, 1098 XG Amsterdam; tel. (20) 5924027; e-mail bibl@cwi.nl; internet www.cwi.nl/library; f. 1946; spec. scientific library on non-elementary mathematics and its applications and computer science; 45,700 vols, 1,000 current periodicals, 10,000 e-books, 158,000 reports; Library Man. AY-LING ONG.

Bibliotheek van het Koninklijk Instituut voor de Tropen (Library of the Royal Tropical Institute): POB 95001, 1090 HA Amsterdam; Mauritskade 63, 1092 AD Amsterdam; tel. (20) 5688462; fax (20) 6654423; e-mail library@kit.nl; internet www.kit.nl; f. 1910; 450,000 vols, 12,000 periodicals, 27,000 maps; Head of Information, Library and Documentation Drs J. H. W. VAN HARTEVELT.

Boekmanstichting Bibliotheek (Library of the Boekman Foundation): Herengracht 415, 1017 BP Amsterdam; tel. (20) 6243739; fax (20) 6385239; e-mail library@boekman.nl; internet www.boekman.nl; f. 1963; all fields of art and culture, and related policy; 65,000 vols, 150 current periodicals; Librarian SASKIA LEEFSMA.

Centre for Latin American Research and Documentation: Keizersgracht 395–397, 1016 EK Amsterdam; tel. (20) 5253248; fax (20) 6255127; e-mail library@cedla.nl; internet www.cedla.uva.nl/60_library/library_index.html; attached to Univ. of Amsterdam; social sciences, economy and history of Latin America; 1,222 journals, spec. collns incl. 20,000 microfiches, 3,500 microfilms.

Economisch-Historische Bibliotheek Amsterdam (Economic-Historical Library Amsterdam): Cruquiusweg 31, 1019 AT Amsterdam; tel. (20) 6685866; fax (20) 6654181; e-mail cse@iisg.nl; internet www.neha.nl; f. 1914; attached to Netherlands Economic-Historical Archives Foundation; 120,000 vols, spec. colln of 16th–18th-century books on commerce and book-keeping, and on Dutch business history and companies, 3,000 periodicals; Librarian J. J. SEEGERS; publ. *Tijdschrift voor Sociale en Economische Geschiedenis*.

Historical Documentation Centre for Dutch Protestantism: De Boelelaan 1105, 1081 HV Amsterdam; tel. (20) 5985270; e-mail hdc@ubvu.vu.nl; internet www-old.vu.nl/hdc; f. 1971; attached to Vrije Univ. Amsterdam; collects and manages archives of persons and instns in protestant circles; promotes historical research, organizes symposia and workshops and publs; provides information and advice, and collaborates in educational and academic projects; Dir Prof. Dr G. HARINCK.

KIT Library—Royal Tropical Institute: POB 95001, 1090 HA Amsterdam; Mauritskade 63, 1092 AD Amsterdam; tel. (20) 5688298; fax (20) 6654423; e-mail ils@kit.nl; internet www.kit.nl/smartsite.shtml?id=27569; information on international cooperation, sustainable social and economic development, poverty alleviation, health, cultural exchange and heritage, capacity building, and on the history of the former Dutch colonies; 260,000 vols, 4,500 journals, 30,000 articles, 25,000 maps, 800 atlases; Dir HANS VAN HARTEVELT.

Openbare Bibliotheek Amsterdam (Amsterdam Public Library): Oosterdokstraat 110, 1011 DK Amsterdam; Oosterdokskade 143, 1011 DL Amsterdam; tel. (20) 5230701; fax (20) 5230955; e-mail dir@oba.nl; internet www.oba.nl; f. 1919; central library, 27 br libraries; 1.7m. vols and pieces of sheet music, spec. collns incl. AdamNet libraries, Hella Haasse, children's books in Spanish and home language, Europe Direct centres, international gay and lesbian information centre and archives, music collns; Dir HANS VAN VELZEN.

Rijksakademie van Beeldende Kunsten Bibliotheek (Library of the State Academy of Fine Arts): Sarphatistraat 470, 1018 GW Amsterdam; tel. (20) 5270303; fax (20) 5270301; e-mail infodesk@rijksakademie.nl; internet www.rijksakademie.nl; f. 1870, present status 1999; 33,000 vols, 85 magazines, 1,400 video cassettes and DVDs; art historic library; large colln of monographs, catalogues of exhibitions and books on visual arts, photography, video, applied art and architecture; Head MARIETTA DIRKER.

The Academy Library: POB 2169, 1000 CD Amsterdam; Cruquiusweg 31, 1019 AT Amsterdam; tel. (20) 6685866; fax (20) 6654181; e-mail ask@iisg.nl; internet www.iisg.nl/collections/akademiebibliotheek; f. 1808; attached to International Institute of Social History; formerly part of Library KNAW; contains library collns of Royal Netherlands Academy of Arts and Sciences collected in 19th century; 200,000 vols; spec. collns incl. collns of Willem Bilderdijk, Jacob van Lennep, Johannes Wertheim Salomonson; 15th, 16th century printings; western, eastern MSS; travel accounts and expedition reports; numismatics; Head CO SEEGERS.

Universiteitsbibliotheek Amsterdam (University of Amsterdam Library): POB 19185, 1000 GD Amsterdam; Singel 425, 1012 WP Amsterdam; tel. (20) 5252301; fax (20) 5252311; e-mail secr-uba@uva.nl; internet cf.uba.uva.nl/nl; f. 1578; incl. Bibliotheca Rosenthaliana (f. 1880, 100,000 vols, 850 MSS), Réveil-Archives, Vondel, Frederik van Eeden and Albert Verwey collns; Tetterode colln; several historical Church collns; libraries of Royal Dutch Book Trade Asscn, Royal Geographical Soc., Royal Netherlands Soc. of Medicine; 4m. vols, 145,000 maps, 160 medieval and 70,000 modern MSS, 500,000 letters; Head of Information Services A. DOEK; Dir Drs A. J. H. A. VERHAGEN; Chief Curator S. C. G. T SCHOLTEN.

Universiteitsbibliotheek Vrije Universiteit (Free University Amsterdam University Library): De Boelelaan 1103, 1081 HV Amsterdam; De Boelelaan 1105, 1081 HV Amsterdam; tel. (20) 5985200; fax (20) 5985259; e-mail info@ubvu.vu.nl; internet www.ubvu.vu.nl; f. 1880; 1m. book titles in print; 2,560,991 eBooks, 15,681 electronic journals, 70,000 documents produced prior to 1901, 36,000 maps; Chief Librarian JOSÉ H. M. FRIJNS; Deputy Librarian Prof. Dr AUGUST DEN HOLLANDER.

Arnhem

Gelders Archief (Gelders Archives): Markt 1, 6811 CG Arnhem; tel. (26) 3521600; fax (26) 3521699; e-mail info@geldersarchief.nl; internet www.geldersarchief.nl; f. 1877; contains archives of the Dukes of Gelders and succeeding provincial admins, and of other regional and local authorities; of private persons, families, enterprises, religious bodies, etc. (since 12th century); archive material for northern Limburg before 1580; Dir-Gen. Dr FRED J. W. VAN KAN.

Stichting Arnhemse Openbare en Gelderse Wetenschappelijke Bibliotheek (Arnhem Public and Learned Library): POB 1168, 6801 ML Arnhem; Koningstraat 26, 6811 DG, Arnhem; tel. (26) 3543111; fax (26) 4458616; e-mail secretariaat@bibliotheekarnhem.nl; internet www.biblioarnhem.nl; f. 1856; dist. libraries in Kronenburg, Presikhaaf; 14 regional libraries; 750,000 vols, 130 MSS; Library Dir RIA OUDEGA.

Assen

Drents Archief (Drenthe Archive): POB 595, 9400 AN Assen; Brink 4, 9401 HS Assen; tel. (59) 2313523; e-mail info@drentsarchief.nl; internet www.drentsarchief.nl; f. 1879, present status 2005; public records of the Province of Drenthe; archives of private persons, institutions and enterprises; 7,500 vols; Dir DOUWE HUIZING.

Breda

De Bibliotheek Breda (Breda Public Library): POB 90192, 4800 RN Breda; Molenstraat 6, 4811 GS Breda; tel. (76) 5299500; fax (76) 5299502; e-mail aam.weterings@breda.nl; internet www.bibliotheekbreda.nl.

Sifria—van de Joodse Gemeente Breda (Sifria—library of the Jewish Congregation of Breda): NIG Breda, POB 1934, 4801 BX Breda; tel. (13) 5086008; e-mail info@joodsbreda.nl; internet www.joodsbreda.nl/bibliotheek.html; f. 1997; books on Jewish religion, tradition, history, philosophy; collns on holocaust, anti-Semitism, contemporary history of Israel; nonfiction science books, reference dept; works by Jewish writers.

Breukelen

Nyenrode Business Universiteit Library: Straatweg 25, POB 130, 3620 AC Breukelen; tel. (46) 291310; fax (46) 291230; e-mail library@nyenrode.nl; internet www.nyenrode.nl/education/services/library/pages/default.aspx; attached to Nyenrode Business Univ.; library colln covers relevant areas of management studies; 25,000 vols; 350 printed journals; Library Head OMNO MASTENBROEK.

Bussum

Bibliotheek Narden-Bussum (Nard-Bussum Library): Wilhelminaplantsoen 18, 1404 JB Bussum; tel. (35)-6973000; fax (35)-6916772; e-mail info@bibliotheeknaardenbussum.nl; internet www.bibliotheeknaardenbussum.nl.

Brunssum

Parkstad Limburg Bibliotheken: Rumpenerstraat 147, 6443 CC Brunssum; tel. (45) 4007560; e-mail info@parkstadlimburgbibliotheken.nl; internet www.obparkstad.nl; consortium of 23 brs in Bocholtz, Brunssum, Heerlen, Hoensbroek, Hulsberg, Kerkrade, Klimmen, Landgraaf, Merkelbeek, Nuth, Ransdaal, Schimmert, Schinveld, Simpelveld and Voerendaal.

De Bilt

Bibliotheek van het Koninklijk Nederlands Meteorologisch Instituut (Library of the Royal Netherlands Meteorological Institute): POB 201, 3730 AE De Bilt; Wilhelminalaan 10, 3732 GK De Bilt; tel. (30) 2206855; fax (30) 2210407; e-mail bibliotheek@knmi.nl; internet www.knmi.nl/bibliotheek; f. 1854; holds the nat. meteorological colln; 180,000 vols on meteorology, physical oceanography and geophysics (esp. seismology, ionosphere and geomagnetism); Librarian W. J. JANSEN.

Delft

Erfgoed Delft en omstreken (Heritage of Delft and Surroundings): POB 78, 2600 ME Delft; Schoolstraat 7, 2611 HS Delft; tel. (15) 2602358; fax (15) 2138744; e-mail erfgoeddelft@delft.nl; internet www.erfgoed-delft.nl; f. 1859; 40,000 vols mainly on history of Delft, genealogy and heraldry; spec. collns: Delft early printed books, House of Orange-Nassau, Naundorff, 17th-century Dutch art, vols about Indonesia, contemporary art, archeology; protects cultural heritage of Delft and its surroundings; consists of Archaeology of Delft, Archives of Delft, Museum Lambert van Meerten, Museum Nusantara, Museum Het Prinsenhof, Kouwenhoven's little shop; Dir J. A. METER; Head Librarian M. P. SCHOEMAKER- VAN WEEZENBERG.

TU Delft Library (Library of the Delft University of Technology): POB 98, 2600 MG Delft; Prometheusplein 1, 2628 ZC Delft; tel. (15) 2785678; fax (15) 2785706; e-mail library@tudelft.nl; internet www.library.tudelft.nl; f. 1842; largest technical and scientific library in the Netherlands; approx. 1m. vols, 4,242 periodicals (3,567 electronic), 3,880 eBooks; Librarian Drs MARIA A. M. HEIJNE.

Deventer

Stadsarchief en Athenaeumbibliotheek Deventer (City Archives and Deventer Municipal Library): POB 351, 7400 AJ Deventer; Klooster 12, 7411 NH Deventer; tel. (570) 693713; e-mail info.sab@saxion.nl; internet www.sabinfo.nl; f. 1560; 250,000 vols, 550 MSS, 380 incunabula, 400 post-incunabula; municipal archives 1241–1950, judicial archives 1423–1811, archives of chapter 1123–1591, church registers 1542–1811, notarial archives 1811–1905; library for town of Deventer and province of Overijssel and Saxion Univ. of applied sciences; Dir G. E. TULP.

Dordrecht

Erfgoedcentrum DiEP (Municipal Archives of Dordrecht): Stek 13, POB 8, 3300 AA Dordrecht; tel. (78) 6492311; fax (78) 6492388; e-mail erfgoedcentrumdiep@dordrecht.nl; internet www.erfgoedcentrumdiep.nl; f. 1885, present name 2007; archives of the City of Dordrecht and of nearby towns; books and prints of Dordrecht and its environs; 40,000 vols, 800 periodicals; Archivist Drs TEUN DE BRUIJN; Librarian JAN ALLEBLAS.

Eindhoven

Informatie Expertise Centrum/Bibliotheek Technische Universiteit Eindhoven (Information Expertise Centre/Library of the Eindhoven University of Technology): POB 90159, 5600 RM Eindhoven; 'De Hal' Bldg, Het Kranenveld, 5612 AZ Eindhoven; tel. (40) 2472381; fax (40) 2447015; e-mail helpdesk.bib@tue.nl; internet w3.tue.nl/nl/diensten/bib; f. 1956; 415,000 vols, 550 current print journals, 10,800 electronic journals, 3,200 full-text TU/e dissertations, 1,500 microfiches and 66,000 other items; Head Librarian Drs JEANNE C. M. FIGDOR; Sec. CAROLA M. J. L. TAK.

Openbare Bibliotheek Eindhoven (Eindhoven Public Library): POB 488, 5600 AL Eindhoven; Gebouw de Witte Dame, Emmasingel 22, 5611 AZ Eindhoven; tel. (40) 2604260; fax (40) 2461225; e-mail info@bibliotheekeindhoven.nl; internet www.bibliotheekeindhoven.nl; f. 1916; 9 brs; 800,000 vols; Man. and Dir Drs THIJS TORREMAN.

Enschede

ITC Library (Faculty of Geo-Information Science and Earth Organization Library): POB 217, 7500 AE Enschede; Hengelosestraat 99, 3rd Fl., Room 3-036, 7514 AE Enschede; tel. (53) 4874202; fax (53) 4874396; e-mail library@itc.nl; internet www.itc.nl/pub/home/library; attached to Univ .of Twente; specialized scientific library on remote sensing and geographical information sciences; Archivist HOMME MARTINUS.

University of Twente Library and Archive: POB 217, 7500 AE Enschede; Drienerlolaan 5, 7522 NB AE Enschede; tel. (53) 4892777; fax (53) 4893599; e-mail infoub@utwente.nl; internet www.utwente.nl/ub; f. 1964; 375,000 vols, 2,700 periodicals, 250 printed journals, 14,000 e-journals; Librarian Drs P. G. G. M. DAALMANS; Sec. J. VROOM-VAN GORCUM.

Gouda

De Bibliotheek Gouda (Gouda Library): Spieringstraat 1, 2801 ZH Gouda; tel. (82) 590101; internet www.bibliotheekgouda.nl; central library and 3 br. libraries; 119,892 materials incl. 300,000 CDs, 10,000 music DVDs; Dir NAN VAN SCHENDEL.

Groningen

Bibliotheek der Rijksuniversiteit te Groningen (Library of the State University): POB 559, 9700 AN Groningen; Broerstraat 4, 9712 CP Groningen; tel. (50) 3635020; fax (50) 3634996; e-mail bibliotheek@rug.nl; internet www.rug.nl/bibliotheek; f. 1615; 3m. vols, 1,100 MSS, 210 incunabula; Librarian MARJOLEIN NIEBOER.

Regionaal Historisch Centrum Groninger Archieven (RHC Groninger Archives): POB 30040, 9700 RM Groningen; Cascadeplein 4, 9726 AD Groningen; tel. (50) 5992000; fax (50) 5992050; e-mail info@groningerarchieven.nl; internet www.groningerarchieven.nl; f. 2002 by merger of Nat. Archives Groningen and Municipal Archive Groningen; information centre for history of city and province of Groningen; about 12.5 miles of documents, maps, prints, books, newspapers, photos, film- and video cassettes from governmental bodies and private individuals; 35,000 vols; Chair. Drs J. A. J. STAM; Dir EDDY DE JONGE; Deputy Dir HARRY ROMIJN.

Haarlem

Bibliotheek van Teylers Museum (Teyler Museum Library): Spaarne 16, 2011 CH Haarlem; tel. (23) 5160960; fax (23) 5342004; e-mail info@teylersmuseum.nl; internet www.teylersmuseum.nl; f. 1784; 125,000 vols (natural sciences); Head Librarian Drs M. A. M. VAN HOORN.

Hbo-opleidingen Hogeschool Inholland Bibliotheek (Inholland University of Applied Sciences Library): Inholland University Haarlem, attn Library, POB 558, 2003 RN Harleem; Bijdorplaan 15, 2015 CE Harleem; tel. (23) 5412700; e-mail bibliotheek@inholland.nl; internet www.inholland.nl/bibliotheek; Head of Library RIA PAULIDES.

Noord-Hollands Archief (North Holland Archives): POB 3006, 2001 DA Haarlem; Jansstraat 40, 2011 RX Haarlem; tel. (23) 5172700; fax (23) 5172720; e-mail info@noord-hollandsarchief.nl; internet www.noord-hollandsarchief.nl; f. 2005 by merger of Archives of Kennemerland and State Archives in North Holland; documentary heritage of province of North Holland, Kennemerland region (in particular the municipalities of Aalsmeer, Beverwijk, Bloemendaal, Haarlemmerliede and Spaarnwoude, Haarlemmermeer, Heemskerk, Heemstede, Uitgeest, Uithoorn, Velsen and Zandvoort) and of provincial capital Haarlem; Chair. B. B. SCHNEIDERS; Dir Drs L. ZOODSMA.

De Bibliotheek Haarlem en Omstreken: POB 204, 2000 AE Haarlem; Gasthuisstraat 32, 2011 XP Haarlem; tel. (23) 5115300; fax (23) 5115390; e-mail stadsbibliotheek@

haarlem.nl; internet www.sbhaarlem.nl; f. 1596, present status 2008; 452,000 vols, 280 MSS, 192 incunabula; Dir L. SLUYSER.

Kampen

Gemeentearchief Kampen (Record Office Kampen): Molenstraat 28, 8261 JW Kampen; tel. (38) 3370770; fax (38) 3370779; e-mail gemeentearchief@kampen.nl; internet www.gemeentearchiefkampen.nl; archives of the town 1251–1955; Dir Drs H. DIJK; Archivist M. VINK; publ. *De Archieven der gemeente Kampen, I, II* and *III*.

Leeuwarden

Historisch Centrum Leeuwarden (Leeuwarden History Centre): Groeneweg 1, 8911 EH Leeuwarden; tel. (58) 2338399; fax (58) 2332315; e-mail historischcentrum@leeuwarden.nl; internet www.historischcentrumleeuwarden.nl; f. 1838, fmrly Leeuwarden Municipal Archives; archives, publs, MSS about Leeuwarden; topographical colln, mainly historical; 18,000 vols; Man. Drs G. DE VRIES.

TRESOAR Fries Historisch en Letterkundig Centrum (TRESOAR Frisian Historical and Literary Centre): POB 2637, 8901 AC Leeuwarden; Boterhoek 1, 8911 DH Leeuwarden; tel. (58) 7890789; fax (58) 7890777; e-mail info@tresoar.nl; internet www.tresoar.nl; f. 2002 by merger of the Frysk Letterkundich Museum en Dokumintaasjesintrum (FLMD), the Provincial and Buma library (PBF) and the Public Records Office in Friesland (RAF); collns mainly relating to Frisian literature and history; Chair. Drs J. A. DE VRIES; Dir Drs B. LOOPER; publ. *Letterhoeke*.

Leiden

Bibliotheek van de Maatschappij der Nederlandse Letterkunde (Library of the Society of Dutch Literature): POB 9501, 2300 RA Leiden; tel. (71) 5272854; fax (71) 5272836; e-mail mnl@library.leidenuniv.nl; internet www.maatschappijdernederlandseletterkunde.nl/bibliotheek.php; f. 1766, managed by Leiden Univ. Library since 1876; 110,000 vols, 3,300 MSS; Librarian Dr KURT DE BELDER.

NCB Naturalis Library: POB 9517, 2300 RA Leiden; Darwinweg 2, 2333 CR Leiden; tel. (71) 5687668; fax (71) 5687666; e-mail library@ncbnaturalis.nl; internet science.naturalis.nl/library; formed by merger of Zoological Museum Amsterdam, National Museum of Natural History Naturalis and brs of National Herbarium of the Netherlands; 65,000 vols, 8,000 journals, 200,000 zoology and geology papers.

Universiteitsbibliotheek Leiden (Leiden University Library): POB 9501, 2300 RA Leiden; Witte Singel 27, 2311 BG Leiden; tel. (71) 5272814; fax (71) 5272836; e-mail helpdesk@library.leidenuniv.nl; internet library.leiden.edu; f. 1575; 3.5m. vols, 1m. e-books, 16,000 e-journals, 50,000 MSS, 70,000 maps; Librarian KURT DE BELDER; Deputy Dir JOSJE CALFF.

Maastricht

Regionaal Historisch Centrum Limburg (Regional Historic Centre Limburg): St Pieterstraat 7, 6211 JM Maastricht; tel. (43) 3285500; fax (43) 3255640; e-mail info@rhcl.nl; internet www.rhcl.nl; f. 2004 by merger of State Archives in Limburg and Municipal Archives; 60,000 vols; Dir Drs LITA WIGGERS.

Stadsbibliotheek Maastricht, Centre Céramique (Municipal Library): POB 1992, 6201 BZ Maastricht; Ave Céramique 50, 6221 KV Maastricht; tel. (43) 3505600; fax (43) 3505599; e-mail mail@sbm.nl; internet www.centreceramique.nl; f. 1662; 774,000 vols, incl. 107 incunabula, 297 post-incunabula, 1,600 periodicals, spec. collns and documentation relating to the Province of Limburg, devotional material and chess literature; Dir Dr ERIC P. G. WETZELS; publ. *Limburgensia*.

Universiteitsbibliotheek Maastricht (Maastricht University Library): POB 616 6200 MD Maastricht; Inner City Library, Grote Looiersstraat 17 6211 JH Maastricht; Randwyck Library, Universiteitssingel 50 6229 ER Maastricht; tel. (43) 3885000; fax (43) 3884888; e-mail i.wijk@maastrichtuniversity.nl; internet www.maastrichtuniversity.nl/web/library/home.htm; attached to Maastricht Univ.; includes digital library; 11,703 e-journals, 11,279 digital univ. publs; spec. collns incl. Jesuit colln of 265,000 vols; Univ. Librarian I. WIJK.

Middelburg

Zeeuws Archief (Zeeland Archives): POB 70, 4330 AB Middelburg; Hofplein 16, 4331 CK Middelburg; tel. (118) 678800; fax (118) 628094; e-mail info@zeeuwsarchief.nl; internet www.zeeuwsarchief.nl; f. 2000 by merger of State Archives in the province of Zeeland, Middelburg Municipal Archives and Veere Municipal Archives; contains documents on the history of Zeeland in gen.; Man. Dir Dr J. L. (HANNIE) KOOL-BLOKLAND.

Zeeuwse Bibliotheek (Zeeland Library): POB 8004, 4330 EA Middelburg; Kousteensedijk 7, 4331 JE Middelburg; tel. (118) 654000; fax (118) 654001; e-mail info@zeeuwsebibliotheek.nl; internet www.zeeuwsebibliotheek.nl; f. 1985; 880,000 vols, 7,500 MSS, 2,900 periodicals; Pres. Ir P. G. BOERMA; Vice-Pres. Drs G. A. EGAS REPÁRAZ; Dir Dr J. A. BRANDENBARG.

Nijkerk

Bibliotheek Nijkerk (Nijkerk Library): POB 198, 3860 AD Nijkerk; Frieswijkstraat 99 3861 BK Nijkerk; tel. (33) 2451756; fax (33) 2460985; e-mail info@bibliotheeknijkerk.nl; internet www.bibliotheeknijkerk.nl.

Nijmegen

Universiteitsbibliotheek, Radboud Universiteit Nijmegen (Library of Radboud University Nijmegen): POB 9100, 6500 HA Nijmegen; Erasmuslaan 36, Nijmegen; tel. (24) 3612428; fax (24) 3615944; e-mail secretariaat@ubn.ru.nl; internet www.ru.nl/ubn; f. 1923; 6 library brs; 2m. vols; Librarian Drs H. P. A. SMIT.

Oss

Bibliothek Oss (Oss Library): POB 815, 5340 AV Oss; Raadhuislaan 10, 5341 GM Oss; tel. (12) 622618; fax (12) 646950; e-mail contact@oboss.nl; internet www.oboss.nl; brs in Berghem, Heesch, Heeswijk-Dinther, Nistelrode, Lith, Ravenstein, Schaijk and Zeeland.

Rotterdam

Bibliotheek Gemeente Rotterdam (Rotterdam Library): Hoogstraat 110, 3011 PV Rotterdam; tel. (10) 2816100; fax (10) 2816181; e-mail communicatie@bibliotheek.rotterdam.nl; internet www.bibliotheek.rotterdam.nl; f. 1604; 23 dist. brs; 1,550,000 vols, 200 MSS, Erasmus colln 5,000 vols, 1,500 journals, 300,000 CDs; Dir Ir F. H. MEIJER.

Gemeentearchief Rotterdam (Municipal Archives of Rotterdam): POB 71, 3000 AB Rotterdam; Hofdijk 651, 3032 CG Rotterdam; tel. (10) 2675555; fax (10) 2675556; e-mail info@gar.rotterdam.nl; internet www.gemeentearchief.rotterdam.nl; f. 1857; 17 linear kms of archives; city archives, church records, notarial archives, Chamber of Commerce records 1797–1922, family archives, business archives, topographical colln, sound archives, historical library; Archivist and Man. Dir Drs JANTJE STEENHUIS.

Rotterdamsch Leeskabinet (Rotterdam Reading Cabinet): POB 1738, 3000 DR Rotterdam; Burgemeester Oudlaan 50, 3062 PA Rotterdam; tel. (10) 4081195; e-mail kabinet@ubib.eur.nl; internet www.eur.nl/rlk; f. 1859; attached to Erasmus Univ.; history, art, art history, language and literature, biography, theology, philosophy, social sciences, geography; 250,000 vols; Chair. A. DUPAIN; Deputy Chair. Prof. Dr W. M. LAMMERTS VAN BUEREN; Sec. and Treas. J. DE MUINCK KEIZER; Librarian Drs PIERRE N. G. PESCH; publ. *Kwartaalbericht*.

Universiteitsbibliotheek Erasmus Universiteit Rotterdam (Library of the Erasmus University of Rotterdam): POB 1738, 3000 DR Rotterdam; Burgemeester Oudlaan 50, 3062 PA Rotterdam; tel. (10) 4081223; fax (10) 4089052; e-mail documentverwerking@ubib.eur.nl; internet www.eur.nl/ub; f. 1913; economics and management, medicine and health, law, culture and soc.; 1m. vols, 5,400 current journals; Univ. Librarian Dr PAUL E. L. J. SOETAERT; Deputy Librarian Drs G. GORIS; Deputy Librarian Drs J. L. DE VRIES.

's-Hertogenbosch

Brabants Historisch Informatie Centrum (Brabant Historical Information Centre): POB 81, 5201 AB 's-Hertogenbosch; Zuid-Willemsvaart 2, 5211 NW 's-Hertogenbosch; tel. (73) 6818500; fax (73) 6146439; e-mail info@bhic.nl; internet www.bhic.nl; f. 1860 as Rijksarchief in de Provincie Noord Brabant; records since 13th century; record office contains approx. 200,000 vols; 40,000 vols, 8,000 charters; Dir Drs R. BASTIAANSE; Librarian F. VAN DE POL; publ. *Inventarisreeks*.

Openbare Bibliotheek 's-Hertogenbosch: POB 1253, 5200 BH 's-Hertogenbosch; Hinthamerstraat 72, 5211 MR 's-Hertogenbosch; tel. (73) 6802900; fax (73) 6144925; e-mail stadsbibliotheek@bibliotheekdenbosch.nl; internet www.sbdenbosch.nl; f. 1915; 270,000 vols, 18,000 CDs; Dir J. J. T. E. (HANS) DERKS; Deputy Dir P. C. J. M. (ELLY) HUFF-MEULENBROEKS.

The Hague

Bibliotheek Den Haag (The Hague Public Library): POB 12653, 2500 DP The Hague; Spui 68, 2511 BT The Hague; tel. (70) 3534455; fax (70) 3534504; e-mail secr@dobdenhaag.nl; internet www.dobdenhaag.nl; f. 1906; 980,000 vols, 190,000 children's books, music library of 55,000 vols and 60,000 CDs, 21,000 audio-visual items; 16 br., 2 mobile libraries; Dir CHARLES NOORDAM.

Bibliotheek van het Centraal Bureau voor de Statistiek (Library of Statistics Netherlands): POB 24500, 2490 HA The Hague; Henri Faasdreef 312, 2492 JP The Hague; tel. (70) 3375151; fax (70) 3375984; e-mail acquisitiev@cbs.nl; internet www.cbs.nl; f. 1899; not accessible to public from 2005; available for scientific research with prior appointment; 380,000 vols; Librarian D. L. M. WEIJERS.

Bibliotheek van het Vredespaleis (Peace Palace Library): Carnegieplein 2, 2517 KJ The Hague; tel. (70) 3024242; fax (70) 3024166; e-mail peacelib @ ppl.nl; internet www.ppl.nl; f. 1913; int. public and municipal law, diplomatic history, int. relations; Grotius Colln; 700,000 vols; Dir JEROEN VERVLIET.

Koninklijke Bibliotheek (National Library of the Netherlands): POB 90407,

2509 LK The Hague; Prins Willem-Alexanderhof 5, 2595 BE The Hague; tel. (70) 3140310; fax (70) 3140450; e-mail info@kb.nl; internet www.kb.nl; f. 1798, present status 1993; responsible for the devt, documentation and management of the nat. cultural heritage; depository for all Dutch publs and the nat. bibliography; research library for the humanities and social sciences; centre of expertise in preservation and restoration; focal point of inter-library cooperation; 2.2m. books, 15,000 current periodicals, newspapers, MSS; spec. collns incl. chess, cookery, children's books; Chair. Drs L. C. BRINKMAN; Dir-Gen. Drs J. S. M. (BAS) SAVENIJE; publ. *Nederlandse Bibliografie*.

Nationaal Archief (National Archives): POB 90520, 2509 LM The Hague; Prins Willem Alexanderhof 20, 2595 BE The Hague; tel. (70) 3315400; fax (70) 3315540; e-mail info@nationaalarchief.nl; internet www.nationaalarchief.nl; f. 1802; 93 km of archives; 80,000 vols, 700 journals; Gen State Archivist MARTIN BERENDSE; publ. *Inventories of Archives*.

Tweede Kamer der Staten-Generaal; Dienst Bibliotheek en Dienst Documentatie (Dutch House of Representatives; Library Department and Documentation Department): Plein 2, POB 20018, 2500 EA The Hague; tel. (70) 3183040; fax (70) 3182307; internet www.houseofrepresentatives.nl; f. 1815; 100,000 vols; Librarian J. C. KEUKENS; Head of Documentation P. VAN RIJN.

Tilburg

Universiteit van Tilburg Bibliotheek (Tilburg University Library): POB 90153, 5000 LE Tilburg; Warandelaan 2, 5037 AB Tilburg; tel. (13) 662124; fax (13) 662996; e-mail library@uvt.nl; internet www.uvt.nl/bibliotheek; f. 1927; economics, applied computer sciences, social sciences, law, history, philosophy, linguistics; 900,000 vols; Dir Ir M. J. VAN DEN BERG.

Utrecht

Bibliotheek Utrecht (Public Library): POB 80, 3500 AB Utrecht; Oude Gracht 167, Utrecht; tel. (30) 2861800; fax (30) 2861801; e-mail klantenservice@bibliotheek-utrecht.nl; internet www.bibliotheek-utrecht.nl; f. 1892; 14 br libraries and art library; 795,000 vols, music library; Dir A. G. J. VAN VLIMMEREN.

Het Utrechts Archief (Utrecht Archives): POB 131 3500 AC Utrecht; Hamburgerstraat 28, 3512 NS Utrecht; tel. (30) 2866611; fax (30) 2866600; e-mail inlichtingen@hetutrechtsarchief.nl; internet www.hetutrechtsarchief.nl; f. 1805; records of the City and Province of Utrecht, church history, political pamphlets, regional newspapers, nat. railway history; 70,000 vols, 500,000 maps, drawings, prints and photographs, 18 km archival documents; Chair. ALEID WOLFSEN; Deputy Chair. VINCENT VAN DER BURG; Dir Drs SASKIA VAN DOCKUM; Head Archivist Dr K. VAN VLIET; Librarian L. JURRITSMA-VAN DER SPELT.

Universiteitsbibliotheek Utrecht (Library of Utrecht University): POB 80124, 3508 TC Utrecht; Heidelberglaan 3, 3584 CS Utrecht; tel. (30) 2536601; fax (30) 2538398; e-mail info@library.uu.nl; internet www.uu.nl/university/library; f. 1584; 4.5m. vols, 2,500 MSS, 900 incunabula, 110,000 vols printed before 1800, MSS and printed books of the medieval libraries of the Utrecht churches and religious houses, 2 16th-century private libraries; special collns in the fields of literature, theology, history, botany, medicine, 18th and 19th-century science libraries, and on the province and city of Utrecht; Univ. Librarian Drs H. P. A. SMIT.

Vlaardingen

Vlaardingen City Archives: Plein Emaus 5, 3135 JN Vlaardingen; tel. (10) 2484999; fax (10) 2484980; e-mail stadsarchief@vlaardingen.nl; internet www.vlaardingen.nl/stadsarchief; f. 1948; 500 archives and collns related to city; oldest document from 1276.

Wageningen

Bibliotheek Wageningen UR (Wageningen UR Library): POB 9100, 6700 HA Wageningen; Droevendaalsesteeg 2, Wageningen; tel. (31) 7484440; fax (31) 7484761; e-mail servicedesk.library@wur.nl; internet library.wur.nl; f. 1873; colln of scientific literature esp. in fields of agrotechnology, food sciences, plant and animal sciences, soil science, geo-information, landscape and spatial planning, water and climate, ecosystem studies; 1.5m. vols, 15,000 current periodicals; Chief Librarian D. VAN ZAANE; publ. *Wageningen Agricultural University Papers*.

Zwolle

Historisch Centrum Overijssel (Historic Centre of Overijssel): POB 1510, 8001 BM Zwolle; Eikenstraat 20, 8021 WX Zwolle; tel. (38) 4266300; fax (38) 4266333; e-mail infohco@historischcentrumoverijssel.nl, internet www.historischcentrumoverijssel.nl; f. 2000; 60,000 vols; 18 km archive, 15,000 charters; 15,000 maps, prints, posters and drawings; 150,000 photographs; collns incl. provincial archives 1528–1948, judicial archives 1333–1979, notarial archives 1811–1915, old church registers and civil registers 1592–1942, archives of monasteries 1225–1811, industrial archives 1850–1980, Zwolle municipal archives 1265–1970, notarial archives 1811–1925, cadastral archives 1811–1980, family archives since 13th century; Chair. C. G. A. A. BREKELMANS; Dir Drs A. G. DE VRIES.

Museums and Art Galleries

Alkmaar

Stedelijk Museum Alkmaar: Canadaplein 1, 1811 KE Alkmaar; tel. (72) 5489789; e-mail museum@alkmaar.nl; internet stedelijkmuseumalkmaar.nl; f. c. 1550; municipal museum; antiquarian and art colln from Alkmaar and its environs, paintings by van Heemskerck, van de Velde the Elder, Allart and Caesar B. van Everdingen, Honthorst; objects incl. old silver, glass, pottery, porcelain, tiles and modern art; colln of antique toys and dolls; Dir LIDEWIJ DE KOEKKOEK; Curator CHRISTI KLINKERT.

Amstelveen

Cobra Museum voor Moderne Kunst (Cobra Museum of Modern Art): POB 2028, 1180 EA Amstelveen; Sandbergplein 1, 1181 ZX Amstelveen; tel. (20) 5475050; fax (20) 5475025; e-mail info@cobra-museum.nl; internet www.cobra-museum.nl; works by artists of CoBrA group (1948–51) and Dutch artists, incl. artists of Vrij Beelden (1945) and Creatie (1950–55) movements; Artistic Dir Dr K. WEITERING; Exec. Dir E. OTTENHOF.

Museum Jan van der Togt: Dorpstraat 50, 1182 JE Amstelveen; tel. and fax (20) 6415754; e-mail info@jvdtogt.nl; internet www.jvdtogt.nl; f. 1991; colln of paintings, sculpture and glass; incl. architectural museum designs; temporary exhibitions; Curator TOMAS HILLEBRAND.

Amsterdam

Allard Pierson Museum: POB 94057, 1090 GB Amsterdam; Oude Turfmarkt 127, 1012 GC Amsterdam; tel. (20) 5252556; fax (20) 5252561; e-mail allard.pierson.museum@uva.nl; internet www.allardpiersonmuseum.nl; f. 1934, present location 1994; attached to Univ. of Amsterdam; archaeological museum; scientific research centre for students of archaeology and history of art, and public museum; archaeology of ancient Egypt, Near East, Greece, Etruria, Roman Empire; Dir-Gen. Prof. Dr W. HUPPERETZ; Scientific Dir Prof. Dr H. A. G. BRIJDER; publ. *Mededelingenblad van de Vereniging van Vrienden*.

Amsterdams Historisch Museum (Amsterdam Historical Museum): POB 3302, 1001 AC Amsterdam; Nieuwezijds Voorburgwal 357, Kalverstraat 92, Amsterdam; tel. (20) 5231822; fax (20) 6207789; e-mail info@ahm.nl; internet www.ahm.nl; f. 1926; exhibits of the city's history over 700 years incl. archaeological finds, artefacts, paintings, prints and models; spec. colln: Jan and Casper Luyken colln; library of 18,000 vols on history of Amsterdam, Dutch art history and applied industrial arts; Chair. Drs HENK J. BROUWER; Vice-Chair. BEN VAN DER VEER; Dir RUTGER J. GRAAF SCHIMMELPENNINCK; Curator LAURA VAN HASSELT.

Anne Frank Museum: POB 730, 1000 AS Amsterdam; Prinsengracht 267, 1000 AS Amsterdam; tel. (20) 5567100; fax (20) 6207999; internet www.annefrank.org; f. 1960; Anne's hiding place, secret annexe; original MSS of diaries and samples of other writings Anne produced during her time in hiding; film exhibition; Exec. Dir HANS WESTRA; Man. Dir KLEIS BROEKHUIZEN.

Hermitage Amsterdam: POB 11675, 1001 GR Amsterdam; Amstel 51, 1001 GR Amsterdam; tel. (20) 5307488; e-mail mail@hermitage.nl; internet www.hermitage.nl; exhibition devoted to Alexander the Great; has archive; Dir Prof. Dr MIKHAIL PIOTROVSKI.

Hortus Botanicus Amsterdam: Plantage Middenlaan 2A, 1081 DD Amsterdam; tel. (20) 6259021; fax (20) 6257006; e-mail info@dehortus.nl; internet en.dehortus.nl; f. 1638, present status 1987; colln of species of plants from different countries; greenhouse; historic herb garden; Dir LENA EUWENS; publs *Het Hortusbericht*, *Hortuskrant* (4 a year).

Joods Historisch Museum (Jewish Historical Museum): POB 16737, 1001 RE Amsterdam; Nieuwe Amstelstraat 1, 1001 RE Amsterdam; tel. (20) 5310310; fax (20) 5310311; e-mail info@jhm.nl; internet www.jhm.nl; f. 1930; colln of 13,000 works of art, ceremonial items and historical objects related to Jewish history and culture; library of 43,000 vols; Dir JOËL CAHEN.

Museum Van Loon: Keizersgracht 672, 1017 ET Amsterdam; tel. (20) 6245255; e-mail info@museumvanloon.nl; internet www.museumvanloon.nl; f. 1672; colln of paintings, furniture, precious silver and porcelain from different centuries; canal house, coach house and garden; Chair. PHILIPPA VAN LOON.

Nederlands Scheepvaartmuseum Amsterdam (Netherlands Maritime Museum Amsterdam): POB 15443, 1001 MK Amsterdam; Kattenburgerstraat 7, Amsterdam; tel. (20) 5232222; fax (20) 5232213; e-mail info@scheepvaartmuseum.nl; internet www.scheepvaartmuseum.nl; f. 1916; closed until mid-2011 for reconstruction; models, paintings, charts, globes, technical drawings, nautical instruments, arms and relics, full-size replica East-Indiaman; library of 60,000 vols, spec. collns: early navigation textbooks, voyages and travel, navigation, Dutch sea atlases; Dir Dr WILLEM BIJLEVELD; Business Dir KARIN BRANDT; Dir for Collns Drs HENK DESSENS; publ. *Zee Magazijn* (4 a year).

NEMO: POB 421, 1000 AK Amsterdam; Oosterdok 2, 1011 VX Amsterdam; tel. (20) 5313233; fax (20) 5313535; e-mail info@e-nemo.nl; internet www.e-nemo.nl; f. 1997; science centre; organizes exhibitions, theatre performances, films, workshops and demonstrations related to science and technology; Gen. Dir MICHIEL BUCHEL; Dir R. V. M VAN HATTUM.

Ons' Lieve Heer op Solder Museum (Our Lord in the Attic Museum): Oudezijds Voorburgwal 40, 1012 GE Amsterdam; tel. (20) 6246604; fax (20) 6381822; e-mail info@opsolder.nl; internet www.opsolder.nl; f. 1888; merchant's house of 1661 with a clandestine Catholic church in the attic; exhibits of ecclesiastical art since 16th century; library of 1,500 vols; Chair. Drs M. A. M. ELSENBURG; Dir Drs J. KIERS; Exec. Sec. M. AARDEWIJN; Curator Drs T. BOERS.

Persmuseum: Zeeburgerkade 10, 1019 HA Amsterdam; tel. (20) 6928810; fax (20) 4680505; e-mail info@persmuseum.nl; internet www.persmuseum.nl; colln of newspapers and magazines from 1600, posters and other advertisements in press, political cartoons and press graphics, archives, photos of journalists, editors and publishers, and library; Dir ANGELIE SENS; publ. *Jaarverslag*.

Rembrandthuis Museum (Rembrand House Museum): Jodenbreestr. 4, 1011 NK Amsterdam; tel. (20) 5200400; fax (20) 5200401; e-mail museum@rembrandthuis.nl; internet www.rembrandthuis.nl; f. 1907; Rembrandt's etchings and drawings, and paintings by his teacher and pupils; the artist lived here 1639–58; Dir JANRENSE BOONSTRA; Deputy Dir MICHIEL KERSTEN; Curator BOB VAN DEN BOOGERT; publ. *Kroniek van het Rembrandthuis* (Rembrandt House Chronicle, 2 a year).

Rijksmuseum (State Museum): POB 74888, 1070 DN Amsterdam; Stadhouderskade 42, 1071 ZD Amsterdam; tel. (20) 6747000; fax (20) 6747001; e-mail info@rijksmuseum.nl; internet www.rijksmuseum.nl; f. 1800; colln incl. major works by Rembrandt, Vermeer, Jan Steen, Frans Hals and other artists; paintings, sculpture, drawings, history, porcelain, glass, costumes, silver, furniture, Asiatic art (main museum closed till 2013 while major renovation work is undertaken; masterpieces colln of 400 of the most important works on display in the Philips Wing during this period); library of 80,000 vols; Chair. A. RUYS; Gen. Dir Prof. Drs W. M. J. PIJBES; Man. Dir J. W. SIEBURGH; Dir for Collns Drs T. D. W. DIBBITS; Curator for Paintings Dr J. P. FILEDT KOK; Curator for Sculpture and Applied Art Dr R. J. BAARSEN; Curator for Nat. Historical Colln Dr C. J. ZANDVLIET; Curator for Prints Drs G. LUIJTEN; Curator for Asiatic Art Drs P. C. M. LUNSINGH SCHEURLEER; Librarian Drs G. J. M. KOOT; publ. *Bulletin* (4 a year).

Stedelijk Museum: POB 75082, 1070 AB Amsterdam; Paulus Potterstraat 13, 1071 CX Amsterdam; tel. (20) 5732911; fax (20) 6752716; e-mail info@stedelijk.nl; internet www.stedelijkmuseum.nl; f. 1895; modern paintings and sculpture, esp. American and European trends since 1950; graphics and drawings; applied arts and industrial design; temporary exhibitions on contemporary art; library of 170,000 vols, 210 periodicals; Dir ANN GOLDSTEIN (acting); publ. *Bulletin* (in Dutch and English).

Tropenmuseum (Museum of the Royal Tropical Institute): POB 95001, 1090 HA Amsterdam; Linnaeusstraat 2, 1092 CK Amsterdam; tel. (20) 5688200; fax (20) 5688548; e-mail info@tropenmuseum.nl; internet www.tropenmuseum.nl; f. 1916, present location 1926; attached to Royal Tropical Institute; 175,000 objects, 155,000 photographs and 10,000 drawings, paintings, documents etc; presents a picture of life and work in the tropics and sub-tropics; children's museum; library of 18,000 vols; Dir LEJO SCHENK.

Van Gogh Museum: POB 75366, 1070 AJ Amsterdam; Stadhouderskade 55, 1072 AB Amsterdam; tel. (20) 5705200; fax (20) 5705222; e-mail info@vangoghmuseum.nl; internet www.vangoghmuseum.nl; f. 1973; collns of the Vincent van Gogh Foundation; paintings and drawings by van Gogh and his contemporaries; van Gogh's personal colln incl. English and French prints and graphics, Japanese woodcuts, documents and personal correspondence with his brother, Theo van Gogh; Theo's personal colln; Western paintings, sculptures, drawings and prints from the period 1840 to 1920; archives of the art historian M. E. TRALBAUT; spec. colln: 19th century literature (mainly French) read by van Gogh; library of 24,000 vols; Chair. TRUDE MAAS-DE BROUWER; Dir AXEL RÜGER; Treas. PETER TIELEMAN; publs *Cahier Vincent* (scientific research, 1 a year), *Van Gogh Bulletin* (4 a year).

Verzetsmuseum Amsterdam: Plantage Kerklaan 61, 1018 CX Amsterdam; tel. (20) 6202535; fax (20) 6202960; e-mail info@verzetsmuseum.org; internet www.verzetsmuseum.org/museum; f. 1985; colln of objects, photos and documents, film and sound fragments related to Second World War; temporary exhibitions on historical or contemporary themes; Pres. HANS BLOM; Sec. CARLA BASTIAANSEN; Treas. HANS HOEK; Dir LIESBETH VAN DER HORST.

Apeldoorn

CODA museum: Vosselmanstraat 299, 7311 CL Apeldoorn; tel. (55) 5268400; fax (55) 5268499; e-mail mail@coda-apeldoorn.nl; internet www.coda-apeldoorn.nl; f. 1978; colln exhibits contemporary art and regional history, esp. jewellery and paper art; image bank; Dir Dr CARIN E. M. REINDERS.

Paleis Het Loo (Loo Palace): Koninklijk Park 1, 7315 JA Apeldoorn; tel. (55) 5772400; fax (55) 5772408; e-mail info@paleishetloo.nl; internet www.paleishetloo.nl; f. 1984; colln of portraits, furniture, documents, etc., relating to the Dutch royal family, the House of Orange-Nassau; library of 20,000 vols; Dir Prof. Dr J. R. TER MOLEN.

Arnhem

Historisch Museum Arnhem (Arnhem Historical Museum): Bovenbeekstraat 21, 6811 CV Arnhem; tel. (26) 3775300; fax (26) 3775398; e-mail hma@arnhem.nl; internet www.hmarnhem.nl; f. 1995; pre-1900 applied art, history, archaeology, glass and silver, Delftware, topographic colln of Gelderland; Head of Public Affairs PETER DE KOK; publ. *Museumkrant* (2 a year).

Museum voor Moderne Kunst (Museum for Modern Art): Utrechtseweg 87, 6812 AA Arnhem; tel. (26) 3775300; fax (26) 3775353; e-mail mmka@arnhem.nl; internet www.mmkarnhem.nl; f. 1920; post-1900 sculpture, Dutch realist paintings, design, jewellery, contemporary art; Dir M. MEYER; Head of Public Affairs PETER DE KOK.

Nederlands Openluchtmuseum (Netherlands Open Air Museum): POB 649, 6800 AP Arnhem; Schelmseweg 89, 6816 SJ Arnhem; tel. (26) 3576111; fax (26) 3576147; e-mail info@openluchtmuseum.nl; internet www.openluchtmuseum.nl; f. 1912, present status 1991; history of daily life; information retrieval; library of 26,000 vols, 146 periodicals; Chair. Ir Drs JEROEN VAN DER VEER; Dir-Gen. Drs PIETER-MATTHIJS GIJSBERS; Man. Dir ADELHEID M. C. J. PONSIOEN.

Assen

Drents Museum: POB 134, 9400 AC Assen; Brink 8, 9401 HS Assen; tel. (592) 377773; internet www.drentsmuseum.nl; f. 1854, present status 1999; temporarily closed until autumn 2011; exhibits bog bodies, Pesse dugout canoe, Terracotta army of Xi'an; colln art nouveau, art deco and figurative art; photo archive; Dir MICHEL VAN MAARSEVEEN.

Brill

Historisch Museum Den Briel: Markt 1, 3231 AH Brill; tel. (181) 475475; fax (181) 475476; e-mail info@historischmuseumdenbriel.nl; internet www.historischmuseumdenbriel.nl; f. 1912, present status 1998; colln of art historical prints by patron Alexander Verhuell; Curator Dr MARIJKE HOLTROP.

Delft

Leger Museum (Army Museum): POB 90004, 3509 AA Delft; Korte Geer 1, 2611 CA Delft; tel. (15) 2150500; fax (15) 2150544; e-mail info@legermuseum.nl; internet www.legermuseum.nl; f. 1913, present location 1984; contains more than 500,000 objects, incl. personal books, handwritten documents, prints and photographs, vehicles; exhibition covering 2,000 years of Netherlands' military history; weapons from prehistory to the present; uniforms, equipment, medals, paintings; library of 225,000 vols and colln of prints; Dir-Gen. CHRIS RONTELTAP; Dir for Collns DIRK STAAT; publ. *Armamentaria* (1 a year).

Museum Het Prinsenhof: POB 78, 2600 ME Delft; St Agathaplein 1, 2611 HR Delft; tel. (15) 2602358; fax (15) 2138744; e-mail gemeentemusea@delft.nl; internet www.prinsenhof-delft.nl; f. 1948; historical colln of City of Delft, paintings of the Delft School, Eighty Years' War, William the Silent; Dir ERIK DE GROOT.

Museum Lambert van Meerten: POB 78, 2600 ME Delft; Oude Delft 199, 2611 HD Delft; tel. (15) 2602358; fax (15) 2138744; e-mail gemeentemusea@delft.nl; internet www.lambertvanmeerten-delft.nl; f. 1909; 19th-century art collector's house; 16th–19th-century Dutch tiles, Delft faience, paintings, furniture; Dir ERIK DE GROOT; Curator Drs RONALD E. BROUWER.

Museum Nusantara: POB 78, 2600 ME Delft; Sint Agathaplein 4, 2611 HR, Delft; tel. (15) 2602358; fax (15) 2138744; e-mail gemeentemusea@delft.nl; internet www.nusantara-delft.nl; f. as Ethnographic Museum of Delft; history and culture of the Indonesian archipelago; colln incl. exhibitions of Dutch involvement in Indonesia since the 17th century, incl. the Dutch East India Co. (1602–1799) and the Colonial Period (1800–1949); Indonesian art, culture, religion, musical instruments, puppets, jewellery, wooden carvings, masks, textiles; maquettes of 19th century, Indonesian houses and ships; Dir ERIK DE GROOT.

Den Helder

Marinemuseum (Dutch Naval Museum): Hoofdgracht 3, 1781 AA Den Helder; tel. (223) 657534; fax (223) 657282; e-mail info@

marinemuseum.nl; internet www .marinemuseum.nl; f. 1962; attached to Min. of Defence; history of the Royal Netherlands Navy since 1813, collns of models, navigational instruments, paintings, photographs, etc.; three-cylinder submarine 'Tonijn' (1966), minesweeper 'Abraham Crynssen' (1937), ironclad ram ship 'Schorpioen' (1868), and other craft; Dir Cmdr HARRY DE BLES.

Deventer

Gemeentemusea Deventer (Municipal Museums of Deventer): POB 5000, 7400 GC Deventer; tel. (570) 693783; fax (570) 693788; e-mail info@deventermusea.nl; internet www .deventermusea.nl; f. 1963; Dir C. F. C. G. BOISSEVAIN.

Associated Museums:

Historisch Museum Deventer (Historical Museum Deventer): POB 5000, 7400 GC Deventer; Brink 58, 7411 BV Deventer; tel. (570) 693783; fax (570) 693788; e-mail info@deventermusea.nl; internet www .historischmuseumdeventer.nl; f. 1915; local history, paintings, drawings, applied arts, bicycles; Dir C. F. C. G. BOISSEVAIN; publ. *Deventer jaarboek* (yearbook).

Speelgoedmuseum Deventer (Deventer Toy Museum): POB 5000, 7400 GC Deventer; Brink 47, 7411 BV Deventer; tel. (570) 693783; fax (570) 693788; e-mail info@ deventermusea.nl; internet www .speelgoedmuseumdeventer.nl; f. 1982; dolls, mechanical toys, toys, trains; Dir C. F. C. G. BOISSEVAIN.

Dordrecht

Dordrechts Museum: POB 1170, 3300 BD Dordrecht; Museumstraat 40, 3311 XP Dordrecht; tel. (78) 7708708; internet www .dordrechtsmuseum.nl; f. 1842; colln of paintings, drawings, prints, photos, sculptures and ceramics; conducts research and restoration work; Man. Dir P. J. SCHOON.

Drechterland

Museum Mohlmann for Representational Art: Westersingel 102–104, 9901 GK Drechterland (Appingedam); tel. (596) 682856; e-mail info@museummohlmann.nl; internet www.robmohlmann.nl; 3 permanent collns: canto-colln, Møhlmann-colln I (present-day realistic and figurative works) and Møhlmann-colln II (work of painter); Owner ROB MØHLMANN.

Eindhoven

Museum Kempenland: St. Antoniusstraat 7, 5616 RT Eindhoven; tel. (40) 2529093; fax (40) 2522344; e-mail secretariaat@ museumkempenland.nl; internet www .museumkempenland.nl; f. 1932; closed until mid-2011; colln of material culture of Eindhoven and region, Brabant painting, drawing and graphic arts and photography, Dutch small sculpture from 19th and 20th centuries; organizes lectures, choir performances, publ., courses, tours; has library; Man. JAN VAN LAARHOVEN.

Van Abbemuseum: POB 235, 5600 AE Eindhoven; Bilderdijklaan 10, 5611 NH Eindhoven; tel. (40) 2381000; fax (40) 2460680; e-mail info@vanabbemuseum.nl; internet www.vanabbemuseum.nl; f. 1936; large colln of modern and contemporary art incl. works and archives by Lissitzky, Picasso, Kokoschka, Chagall, Beuys, McCarthy, Daniëls and Körmeling; library of 130,000 vols; Dir CHARLES ESCHE; Deputy Dir ULRIKE ERBSLÖH.

Enschede

Rijksmuseum Twenthe, Enschede (Twenthe Estate Museum, Enschede): Lasondersingel 129–131, 7514 BP Enschede; tel. (53) 4358675; fax (53) 4359002; e-mail info@ rijksmuseumtwenthe.nl; internet www .rijksmuseumtwenthe.nl; f. 1930, present status 1994; 8,000 art objects from the 13th century up to the present day; library of 15,000 vols; Dir LISETTE PELSERS; Curator for Fine Arts PAUL KNOLLE; Curator for Modern Art TON GEERTS; publs *Bulletin* (4 a year), *MUSE Rijksmuseum Twenthe* (2 a year).

Gouda

museumgoudA 'Het Catharina Gasthuis' (St Catherine Hospital, Municipal Museum): Achter de Kerk 14, 2801 JX Gouda; tel. (182) 331000; fax (182) 331019; e-mail info@ museumgouda.nl; internet www .museumgouda.nl; f. 1874; 18th-century town dispensary; antique toys, surgeons' Guild Room, decorative art since late 16th century, Gasthuis kitchen and chapel, important colln of art since 15th century; Dir GERARD DE KLEIJN.

Nationaal Farmaceutisch Museum (National Pharmaceutical Museum): Westhaven 29, 2801 PJ Gouda; tel. (182) 687142; fax (182) 331019; e-mail info@ farmaceutischmuseum.nl; internet www .farmaceutischmuseum.nl; f. 1938 reopened in 2008; exhibiting the history of Dutch apothecaries and the devt of the pharmaceutical profession; fmrly the 'The Blackmoor' Stedeljik Museum containing and managing authentic 18th-century tobacco shop, colln of Dutch clay pipes and Gouda pottery now transferred to Het Catharina Gasthuis en De Moriaan; Chair. Prof. Dr A. H. L. M. PIETERS; Deputy Chair. Dr R. H. A. SOREL; Dir Drs P. H. VREE; Treas. Drs C. B. M. HEERKENS.

Groningen

Groninger Museum: POB 90, 9700 ME Groningen; Museumeiland 1, 9711 ME Groningen; tel. (50) 3666555; fax (50) 3120815; e-mail info@groningermuseum.nl; internet www.groningermuseum.nl; f. 1894; prehistory and history; paintings of local school; Dutch and Flemish of 16th and 17th centuries: Fabritius, Jordaens, Rubens, Sweerts, Teniers; drawings: Rembrandt, Averkamp, Van Goyen, Cuyp, Lievens; painting since 19th century; extensive colln of Far-Eastern ceramics; colln of applied art; photography, design and fashion collns; library of 38,000 vols incl. book colln on modern art and artists and colln of modern art since 1979; Man. Dir KEES VAN TWIST; Dir PATTY WAGEMAN.

Noordelijk Scheepvaartmuseum (Northern Maritime Museum): Brugstraat 24, 9711 HZ Groningen; tel. (50) 3122202; fax (50) 3183751; e-mail info@ noordelijkscheepvaartmuseum.nl; internet www.noordelijkscheepvaartmuseum.nl; f. 1932; colln related to N Dutch shipping and shipbuilding history from Middle Ages to present, archives, library, photographs; Dir J. W. VAN VEEN; Curator and Deputy Dir W. KERKMEIJER.

Haarlem

Frans Hals museum (Frans Hals Museum): POB 3365, 2001 DJ Haarlem; Groot Heiligland 62, 2011 ES Haarlem; tel. (23) 5115775; fax (23) 5115776; e-mail office@ franshalsmuseum.nl; internet franshalsmuseum.nl; f. 1913; pictures since 15th century, focusing on the Haarlem school and Frans Hals; applied arts; Dir KAREL SCHAMPERS; Sec. JUDITH HARREN.

Teylers Museum: Spaarne 16, 2011 CH Haarlem; tel. (23) 5160960; fax (23) 5342004; e-mail info@teylersmuseum.nl; internet www .teylersmuseum.nl; f. 1784; paintings, drawings, palaeontology, geology, mineralogy, natural history, physics, numismatics; library of 125,000 vols (natural science); Dir Drs M. SCHARLOO; publs *Archives du Musée Teyler*, *Verhandelingen van Teylers Godgeleerd Genootschap*, *Verhandelingen van Teylers Tweede Genootschap*.

Heerlen

Thermenmuseum Heerlen: POB 1, 6400 AA Heerlen; Coriovallumstraat 9, 6411 CA Heerlen; tel. (45) 5605100; fax (45) 5603915; e-mail info@thermenmuseum.nl; internet www.thermenmuseum.nl; f. 1977; colln incl. Roman bath house excavated in 1940–41 and other objects from Roman period; Curator Dr KAREN JENESON.

Helmond

Gemeentemuseum Helmond: Kasteelplein 1, 5701 PP Helmond; tel. (492) 587716; fax (492) 587717; e-mail info@ gemeentemuseumhelmond.nl; internet www .gemeentemuseumhelmond.nl; colln of int. modern and contemporary art incl. works from 1970 to present; exhibits popular visual culture, incl. film and advertising; works of Alma, Burtynsky, Heijenbrock, Isaac Israels, Kollwitz, Meunier, Jan en Chartley Toorope and Van der Leck; Curator ANNEMIEKE HOGERVORST.

Hoorn

Westfries Museum: Achterom 2–4, 1621 KV Hoorn; Roode Steen 1, 1621 CV Hoorn; tel. (229) 280028; fax (229) 280029; e-mail info@wfm.nl; internet www.wfm.nl; f. 1879, baroque bldg dates from 1632; 17th- and 18th-century painting, prints, oak panelling, glass, pottery, silver, furniture, costumes, interiors, objects of trade, navigation and business, folk art, historical objects from Hoorn and West Friesland, prehistoric finds; Dir AD GEERDINK.

Leerdam

Nationaal Glasmuseum—De Glasblazerij (National Glass Museum—The Glass Factory): POB 78, 4140 AB Leerdam; Lingedijk 28–30, 4142 LD Leerdam; tel. (345) 614960; e-mail info@stichtingglas.nl; internet www.nationaalglasmuseum.nl; f. 1953, present status 2007; art glass, industrial glass and bottles, contemporary Dutch colln and works from other European countries and America; small library; Chair. AUBERT VAN ENGELEN; Dir ARNOUD ODDING; Curator HÉLÈNE BESANÇON.

Leeuwarden

Fries Museum: POB 1239, 8900 CE Leeuwarden; Turfmarkt 11, 8911 KS Leeuwarden; tel. (58) 2555500; fax (58) 2132271; e-mail info@friesmuseum.nl; internet www .friesmuseum.nl; f. 1827; painting, local history, archaeology, decorative arts, prints and drawings, Second World War, Mata Hari gallery, modern art; Chair. Prof. Dr L. KOOPMANS; Dir-Gen. Drs SASKIA BAK; Man. Dir Ir ROEL WOERING; publ. *Visitor's Guide* (in English, French and German).

Keramiekmuseum Princessehof (Princessehof National Museum of Ceramics): Grote Kerkstraat 11, POB 1239, 8900 CE Leeuwarden; tel. (58) 2948958; fax (58) 2948968; e-mail info@princessehof.nl; internet www .princessehof.nl; f. 1917; Asian and European ceramics and tiles, contemporary ceramics; library of 20,000 vols; Dir-Gen. Drs SASKIA BAK; Man. Dir Ir ROEL WOERING; publ. *Keramika* (3 a year).

Leiden

Museum Boerhaave/Rijksmuseum voor de Geschiedenis van de Natuurwetenschappen en van de Geneeskunde

(Museum Boerhaave/National Museum of the History of Science and Medicine): POB 11280, 2301 EG Leiden; Lange St Agnietenstraat 10, 2312 WC Leiden; tel. (71) 5214224; fax (71) 5120344; e-mail informatie@museumboerhaave.nl; internet www.museumboerhaave.nl; f. 1907; historical scientific and medical instruments and documents, anatomical preparations, portraits; library of 25,000 vols, 12,100 periodicals, MSS; Dir Prof. Dr DIRK VAN DELFT; Exec. Sec. FRANCISCA PARMENTIER.

Museum Volkenkunde (National Museum of Ethnology): POB 212, 2300 AE Leiden; Steenstraat 1, 2312 BS Leiden; tel. (71) 5168800; fax (71) 5128437; e-mail pr@volkenkunde.nl; internet www.volkenkunde.nl; f. 1837 as Ethnographic Museum in Leiden; collns from Africa, the Middle E, the Islamic and Indian cultural areas, the Far E, Pacific, SE Asia, the Americas and the circumpolar regions; library of 60,000 vols; Dir Dr STEVEN B. ENGELSMAN; Business Dir MIEP HUIVENAAR; Dir for Public Programmes and Devt JOHN SIJMONSBERGEN; publ. *Mededelingen*.

NCB Naturalis (Netherlands Centre for Biodiversity Naturalis): POB 9517, 2300 RA Leiden; Darwinweg 2, 2333 CR Leiden; tel. (71) 5687600; fax (71) 5687666; e-mail contact@ncbnaturalis.nl; internet www.ncbnaturalis.nl; f. 1820, merger of Zoological Museum Amsterdam, Nat. Museum of Natural History Naturalis and brs of Nat. Herbarium of the Netherlands; colln incl. more than 11m. objects related to fossils, insects, invertebrates, vertebrates; library of 108,000 vols, 8,000 periodical (zoology library 78,000 vols, 5,000 periodicals; geology library 30,000 vols, 3,000 periodicals), palaeontology; Gen. Dir Dr Ir BERT M. GEERKEN; Scientific Dir Prof. Dr ERIK F. SMETS; publs *Entomologische tabellen, Nederlandse Faunistische Mededelingen, Scripta Geologica, Technical Bulletin NNM, Zoölogische Bijdragen, Zoölogische Mededelingen, Zoölogische Verhandelingen*.

Rijksmuseum van Oudheden (National Museum of Antiquities): POB 11114, 2301 EC Leiden; Rapenburg 28, 2311 EW Leiden; tel. (71) 5163163; fax (71) 5149941; e-mail info@rmo.nl; internet www.rmo.nl; f. 1818; prehistoric, Roman and Medieval periods in the Netherlands; Egyptian, Mesopotamian, Greco-Roman and ancient European collns; library of 30,000 vols, 25 periodicals; Dir Drs WIM WEIJLAND.

Stedelijk Museum de Lakenhal Leiden (Cotton Hall Museum, Leiden): POB 2044, 2301 CA Leiden; Oude Singel 28–32, 2312 RA Leiden; tel. (71) 5165360; fax (71) 5134489; e-mail postbus@lakenhal.nl; internet www.lakenhal.nl; f. 1874; pictures of Leiden school; memorial table (triptych) and altar pieces by Lucas van Leyden and C. Engebrechtsz; Rembrandt, Jan Steen, Jan van Goyen, van Mieris, Dou, modern Leiden school: Verster, Kamerlingh Onnes and contemporary Dutch art; furniture, silver, glass, tapestry, etc.; period rooms; history of the town; library of 4,604 vols, 10,500 catalogues; Dir META KNOL.

Limburg

Museum Het Domein Sittard: POB 230, 6130 AE Sittard; Kapittelstraat 6, 6131 ER Sittard; tel. (46) 4513460; fax (46) 4529111; e-mail info@hetdomein.nl; internet www.hetdomein.nl; colln of archaeological and historical artefacts, int. avant-garde, with emphasis on photography, video and crossover art; Dir PETER FRANSMAN.

Maastricht

Bonnefantenmuseum (Provincial Museum): POB 1735, 6201 BS Maastricht; Ave Céramique 250, 6221 KX Maastricht; tel. (43) 3290190; fax (43) 3290199; e-mail info@bonnefanten.nl; internet www.bonnefanten.nl; f. 1863, refounded 1968; early Italian paintings (1300–1550); Neutelings colln (medieval sculpture and applied arts; Maasland sculpture (incl. works by Jan van Steffeswert); contemporary art (incl. works by René Daniëls, Peter Duig, Gary Hume, Sol LeWitt and Roman Signer); Chair. Drs J. H. H. MANS; Vice-Chair. Prof. Dr K. OTTENHEYM; Artistic Dir ALEXANDER M. U. VAN GREVENSTEIN; Man. Dir HARRIE DRAGSTRA; Treas. L. J. J. RULKENS; Sec. Drs J. VAN DEN BELT.

Natuurhistorisch Museum Maastricht (Maastricht Natural History Museum): De Bosquetplein 6–7, 6211 KJ Maastricht; De Bosquetplein 7, 6211 KJ Maastricht; tel. (43) 3505490; fax (43) 3505475; e-mail museum@maastricht.nl; internet www.nhmmaastricht.nl; f. 1912; colln of 550,000 objects; flora, fauna and soils of the Limburg area, late Cretaceous fossils; library of 30,000 vols; Dir-Gen. Drs ERIC P. G. WETZELS; Man. CORRIEN DERKSEN; publ. *Natuurhistorisch Maandblad* (12 a year).

Muiden

Muiderslot: Stichting Rijksmuseum Muiderslot, Herengracht 1, 1398 AA Muiden; tel. (294) 256262; fax (294) 261056; e-mail info@muiderslot.nl; internet www.muiderslot.nl; 13th-century castle furnished in early 17th-century style: paintings, tapestries, furniture and armoury; Dir TIES HILGERS-MICHIELS VAN KESSENICH; Chair. H. J. E. BRUINS SLOT.

Naarden

Comenius Museum: Kloosterstraat 33, 1411 RS Naarden; tel. (35) 6943045; fax (35) 6941949; e-mail info@comeniusmuseum.nl; internet www.comeniusmuseum.nl; f. 1924; J. A. Comenius mausoleum and museum; library of 2,500 vols; Chair. H. VAN OOSTVEEN; Dir HANS VAN DER LINDE; Sec. H. VERHOEF; Treas. H. RÖRIK.

Nijmegen

Museum Het Valkhof: POB 1474, 6501 BL Nijmegen; Kelfkensbos 59, 6511 TB Nijmegen; tel. (24) 3608805; fax (24) 3608656; e-mail mhv@museumhetvalkhof.nl; internet www.museumhetvalkhof.nl; f. 1999; archaeology, cultural history and fine art, mainly related to Nijmegen and the province of Gelderland; modern art, mainly related to the Netherlands; library of 22,400 vols in art library and 11,000 titles in archaeological library; Dir Drs MARIJKE BROUWER; Chair. R. MIGO.

Opmeer

Scheringa Museum voor Realisme (Scheringa Museum of Realist Art): Spanbroekerweg 162, 1715 GV Spanbroek; tel. (226) 351111; fax (226) 351859; e-mail info@scheringamuseum.nl; internet www.scheringamuseum.nl; f. 1997; coll of paintings and drawings by Carel Willink, paper, sculptures, fashion creations, photographs, objects, and contemporary works of Realism; Dir BELIA VAN DER GIESSEN.

Oss

Museum Jan Cunen: Molenstraat 65, 5341 GC Oss; tel. (412) 629328; fax (412) 629335; e-mail museumjancunen@oss.nl; internet www.museumjancunen.nl; f. 1935; exhibits contemporary art focused on local history, archeology and industrial history; Dir NICOLETTE BARTELINK.

Otterlo

Kröller-Müller Museum: POB 1, 6730 AA Otterlo; Houtkampweg 6, 6731 AW Otterlo; tel. (318) 591241; fax (318) 591515; e-mail info@kmm.nl; internet www.kmm.nl; f. 1938; large colln of paintings by van Gogh, paintings and sculpture since 19th century, old masters, open-air modern sculpture colln (Moore, Serra, Volten), ceramics, drawings, graphic art; library of 40,000 vols; Dir Dr EVERT J. VAN STRAATEN; Exec. Sec. Drs WANDA VERMEULEN.

Nederlands Tegelmuseum (Dutch Tile Museum): Eikenzoom 12, 6731 BH Otterlo; tel. (318) 591519; fax (318) 592000; e-mail info@nederlandstegelmuseum.nl; internet www.nederlandstegelmuseum.nl; f. 1963; extensive colln of Netherlands tiles since 1500; library of 930 vols; Dir M. H. VAN MEURS.

Roermond

Het Cuypershuis (The House of Cuypers): POB 900, 6040 AX Roermond; Pieter Cuypersstraat 1, 6041 XG Roermond; tel. (475) 359584; fax (475) 336299; e-mail museum@roermond.nl; internet museum.roermond.nl; f. 1932; archaeology, historical and contemporary art and design, architecture and art of Dr P. J. H. Cuypers (1827–1921); museum closed for renovation until spring 2011; Head Dr HANS VAN DE MORTEL.

Rotterdam

Chabotmuseum Rotterdam: Museumpark 11, 3015 CB Rotterdam; tel. (10) 4363713; fax (10) 4360355; e-mail mail@chabotmuseum.nl; internet www.chabotmuseum.nl; f. 1993, present status 2000; private Grootveld colln incl. paintings, sculptures, drawings and graphics by Chabot; Schortemeijer colln; enthnographic objects; artists' works, notes, letter, photographs and original sketches.

Historisch Museum Rotterdam (Rotterdam Historical Museum): Korte Hoogstraat 31, 3011 GK Rotterdam Centrum; tel. (10) 2176767; fax (10) 4782376; e-mail info@hmr.rotterdam.nl; internet www.hmr.rotterdam.nl; more than 100,000 objects; archaeology, art, domestic life, history, technology; Dir HANS WALGENBACH; publ. *Historisch Nu*.

Kunsthal Rotterdam: POB 23077, 3015 AA Rotterdam; Westzeedijk 341, 3015 AA Rotterdam; tel. (10) 4400301; e-mail communicatie@kunsthal.nl; internet www.kunsthal.nl; works of impressionism, Leonardo da Vinci, Blackfoot Indians, jewels of the orient, pop-art; 2 annual exhibitions: for children and on historico-cultural theme; Dir EMILY ANSENK; Curator JANNET DE GOEDE; Curator CHARLOTTE VAN LINGEN.

Maritiem Museum Rotterdam (Rotterdam Maritime Museum): POB 988, 3000 AZ Rotterdam; Leuvehaven 1, 3011 EA Rotterdam; tel. (10) 4132680; fax (10) 4137342; e-mail info@maritiemmuseum.nl; internet www.maritiemmuseum.nl; f. 1874, new bldg 1986; models of ships since 15th century, globes, atlases, 20,000 books; ironclad warship 'Buffel'; spec. children's exhibition; library of 35,000 vols, 25,000 journals; Chair. Ir P. O. VERMEULEN; Dir-Gen. FRITS LOOMEIJER; Man. Dir FRANS VAN HAMBURG; publ. *MM Journaal* (2 a year).

Museum Boijmans Van Beuningen: POB 2277, 3000 CG Rotterdam; Museumpark 18–20, 3015 CX Rotterdam; tel. (10) 4419400; fax (10) 4360500; e-mail info@boijmans.nl; internet www.boijmans.nl; f. 1849; approx. 140,000 objects; Dutch School incl. paintings by van Eyck, Bosch, Pieter Brueghel, Hals, Rembrandt, van Ruysdael, Hobbema, Jan Steen; Baroque School, French School, Impressionists; old, modern and contemporary paintings and sculpture; drawings since 15th century from Dutch, Flemish, French, German, Italian and Spanish schools, old and modern prints; glass, Dutch silver, old pewter, laces and ceramics, among which an important colln of Persian, Spanish, Italian and Dutch pottery and tiles; furniture, industrial design; library of 125,000 vols and catalogues, 200 periodical titles; Chair. H. R. OKKENS; Gen. Man. SJAREL EX.

Nederlands Architectuurinstituut: POB 237, 3000 AE Rotterdam; Museumpark 25, 3015 CB Rotterdam; tel. (10) 4401358; fax (10) 4366975; e-mail collection@nai.nl; internet www.nai.nl; f. 1988, by merger of Stichting Architectuurmuseum, Nederlands Documentatiecentrum voor de Bouwkunst, and Stichting Wonen; Sonneveld house museum; maintains archive; library of 42,000 vols, 1,000 periodicals; Chair. WILLEM HEIN SCHENK; Vice-Chair. SANDER MIRCK.

Nederlands Fotomuseum: POB 23383, 3001 KJ Rotterdam; Wilhelminakade 332, 3072 AR Rotterdam; tel. (10) 2030405; fax (10) 2030406; e-mail info@nederlandsfotomuseum.nl; internet www.nederlandsfotomuseum.nl; 3m. negatives and colln of slides, prints and documents about life and work of Dutch photographers, amateur photography exhibition; archives of Katharina Eleonore Behrend and Hein Wertheimer; conserves and restores photographic material and provides advice about archival storage material; library of 11,000 vols; Dir RUUD VISSCHEDIJK.

Stedelijk Museum Schiedam: POB 208, 3100 AE Schiedam; Hoogstraat 112–114, 3111 HL Schiedam; tel. (10) 2463666; fax (10) 2463664; e-mail info@stedelijkmuseumschiedam.nl; internet www.stedelijkmuseumschiedam.nl; f. 1899; Major Gerrit Visser Bastiaansz's private colln of modern and contemporary art and historical artefacts; Dir DIANA A. WIND.

Wereldmuseum Rotterdam (World Museum Rotterdam): POB 361, 3000 AJ Rotterdam; Willemskade 25, 3016 DM Rotterdam; tel. (10) 2707172; fax (10) 2707182; e-mail info@wereldmuseum.nl; internet www.wereldmuseum.nl; f. 1885; exhibitions on regional collns, festivities, music, arts and crafts, modern non western art; ethnological and archaeological collns from Indonesia, realm of Islam, Asia, Africa, America and Oceania; 100,000 objects and 100,000 photographs dating from 1860; Dir STANLEY BREMER.

Witte de With, Centre for Contemporary Art: Witte de Withstraat 50, 3012 BR Rotterdam; tel. (10) 4110144; fax (10) 4117924; e-mail info@wdw.nl; internet www.wdw.nl; f. 1990; contemporary art and theory in context of Rotterdam and Netherlands; Dir NICOLAUS SCHAFHAUSEN; Curator JUAN GAITAN; Curator ZOË GRAY.

's-Hertogenbosch

Noordbrabants Museum (North Brabant Museum): POB 1004, 5200 BA 's-Hertogenbosch; Verwersstraat 41, 5211 HT 's-Hertogenbosch; tel. (73) 6877877; fax (73) 6877899; e-mail info@noordbrabantsmuseum.nl; internet www.noordbrabantsmuseum.nl; f. 1981; North Brabant prehistorical, historical and folklore collns, paintings, sculpture, metalwork, prints, coins, etc.; Chair. W. M. VAN DEN GOORBERGH; Dir CHARLES DE MOOIJ; Gen. Man. LEO VAN ROZENDAAL; publ. *Noordbrabants Museum Nieuws* (4 a year).

The Hague

Escher in Het Paleis (Escher in The Palace): Lange Voorhout 74, 2514 EH The Hague; tel. (70) 4277730; fax (70) 4277731; e-mail info@escherinhetpaleis.nl; internet www.escherinhetpaleis.nl; f. 2002; works of Escher; exhibits works of art with biographical material incl. slide show, photographs, letters, studies of divisions of plane and preliminary sketches.

Fotomuseum Den Haag (The Hague Museum of Photography): POB 72, 2501 CB The Hague; Stadhouderslaan 43, 2517 HV The Hague; tel. (70) 3381144; fax (70) 3381155; e-mail info@fmdh.nl; internet www.fotomuseumdenhaag.nl; f. 2002; attached to Stichting Gemeentemuseum Den Haag; contemporary photography as well as photographs from the colln of the Gemeentemuseum; Dir BENNO TEMPEL; Deputy Dir HANS BUURMAN; Curator WIM VAN SINDEREN.

Gemeentemuseum Den Haag: POB 72, 2501 CB The Hague; Stadhouderslaan 41, 2517 HV The Hague; tel. (70) 3381111; fax (70) 3381112; e-mail info@gemeentemuseum.nl; internet www.gemeentemuseum.nl; f. 1862, present status 1999; Modern Art (since 19th century); Decorative Arts (ceramics, glass, silver, furniture) and design since early 20th century; costumes and fashion from 1750 to the present; musical instruments from 15th century to the present; art and music library; Chair. JOOP N. A. VAN CALDENBORGH; Dir BENNO TEMPEL; Deputy Dir HANS BUURMAN.

Mauritshuis, Het Koninklijk Kabinet van Schilderijen Mauritshuis (Mauritshuis, Royal Picture Gallery): POB 536, 2501 CM The Hague; Korte Vijverberg 8, 2513 AB The Hague; tel. (70) 3023456; fax (70) 3653819; e-mail communicatie@mauritshuis.nl; internet www.mauritshuis.nl; f. 1822, present status 1995; 15th-, 16th- and 17th-century Dutch and Flemish masters (Rembrandt, Vermeer, Hals, Rubens, Ruisdael, Ter Borch, van Dyck, Holbein, R. v.d. Weyden); Chair. A. BURGMANS; Sec. J. W. WINTER; Dir E. E. S. GORDENKER; Deputy Dir V. J. E. MOUSSAULT.

Museon: POB 30313, 2500 GH The Hague; Stadhouderslaan 37, 2517 HV The Hague; tel. (70) 3381338; fax (70) 3381339; e-mail info@museon.nl; internet www.museon.nl; f. 1904 as Museum for Education, present status and name 1985; astronomy and geology, biology and ecology, history and archaeology, geography and ethnology, science and technology; library; Dir Dr BERT MOLSBERGEN.

Museum Bredius: Lange Vijverberg 14, 2513 AC The Hague; tel. (70) 3620729; fax (70) 3639978; e-mail info@museumbredius.nl; internet www.museumbredius.nl; f. 1895; colln of paintings, drawings, German and Chinese ceramics, Dutch and English silver; Chair. Prof. Dr P. SCHNABEL; Man. R. R. D. SWART; Sec. A. H. VERMEULEN; Treas. F. CH. M. TILMAN; Curator Dr J. HOOGSTEDER.

Museum Meermanno: Prinsessegracht 30, 2514 AP The Hague; tel. (70) 3462700; fax (70) 3630350; e-mail info@meermanno.nl; internet www.meermanno.nl; f. 1848; medieval MSS, incunabula; modern typography, book plates, private press books; Dir MAARTJE DE HAAN; publ. *Leeslint* (2 a year).

Museum Mesdag: Laan van Meerdervoort 7F, 2517 AB The Hague; tel. (70) 3621434; fax (70) 3614026; e-mail uildriks@vangoghmuseum.nl; internet www.museummesdag.nl; f. 1903; attached to Van Gogh Museum, Amsterdam; Dutch pictures 1860–1920; French pictures of the Barbizon school; Oriental objects; Dir AXEL RÜGER; publs *Catalogue de l'école française XIX siècle, Museum Mesdag Nederlandse 19e eeuwse Schilderijen*.

Museum Rijswijk: Herenstraat 67, 2282 BR Rijswijk; tel. (70) 3903617; fax (70) 3368880; e-mail musryszh@xs4all.nl; internet www.museumryswyk.nl; temporary exhibitions; colln of excavated artefacts, mementos of the poet Hendrik Tollens, engravings, medals and treaty documents commemorating event that took place in 1697; Curator ARJAN KWAKERNAAK.

Museum voor Communicatie (Museum of Communication): Zeestraat 82, 2518 AD The Hague; tel. (70) 3307500; fax (70) 3608926; e-mail info@muscom.nl; internet www.muscom.nl; f. 1929, present name 1999; objects and documents, etc., concerning the history and working of the services of posts, telegraphs and telephones in the Netherlands; int. stamp gallery; library of 20,000 vols; Dir TITUS YOCARINI.

Utrecht

Cavaleriemuseum: Barchman Wuytierslaan 198, Amersfoort; tel. (33) 4661996; fax (33) 4661493; internet www.cavaleriemuseum.nl; colln of uniforms, small arms, silver, paintings, miniatures, scale, cavalry vehicles, tanks and armoured cars.

Centraal Museum Utrecht: POB 2106, 3500 GC Utrecht; Nicolaaskerkhof 10, 3512 XC Utrecht; tel. (30) 2362362; fax (30) 2332006; e-mail info@centraalmuseum.nl; internet www.centraalmuseum.nl; f. 1838; oldest municipal museum in the Netherlands; colln divided into 5 depts: old masters, modern art, design, fashion and local history; paintings and sculpture incl. old masters works by Saenredam, van Scorel and the Utrecht Caravaggists, incl. Ter Brugghen and van Honthorst; modern art colln from 20th century incl. works by van Doesburg, van der Leck and the Magic Realists Koch, Willink and Moesman; doll's house, 11th-century Utrecht ship, applied art and design; Rietveld colln, Dick Bruna colln; Dir EDWIN JACOBS; Deputy Dir MARCO GROB.

Geld Museum (Money Museum): POB 2407, 3500 GK Utrecht; Leidseweg 90, 3531 BG Utrecht; tel. (30) 2910492; fax (30) 2910467; e-mail info@geldmuseum.nl; internet www.geldmuseum.nl; f. 1816 as Rijksmuseum Het Koninklijk Penningkabinet, merged with Nederlands Muntmuseum 2004; coins from Greek and Roman times to the present, medals, paper money, engraved gems: serves as nat. and int. monetary institute for the main Dutch numismatics; library of 12,000 vols on numismatics and glyptics; Chair. Drs CEES MAAS; Dir HELEEN BUIJS; Curator Drs A. POL; Man. Div. Collns and Research CHRITSEL SCHOLLAARDT; Librarian ANS TER WOERDS; publs *De Beeldenaar* (6 a year), *Jaarboek voor Munt- en Penningkunde*.

Mondriaanhuis: POB 699, 3800 SR Amersfoort; Kortegracht 11, 3811 KG Amersfoort; tel. (33) 4600170; fax (33) 4614087; e-mail info@mondriaanhuis.nl; internet www.mondriaanhuis.nl; f. 1992; works of art from early figurative period of Piet Mondrian; exhibition of works by contemporary artists; colln of geometric abstract art and structural concrete art.

Veere

Museum 'De Schotse Huizen' (Museum of Scottish Homes): Kaai 25–27, 4351 AA Veere; tel. (118) 501744; e-mail info@deltacultureel.nl; internet www.schotsehuizen.nl; f. 1950; Chinese and Japanese ceramics; prints, nat. costumes, furniture, statues, exhibitions of paintings; sited in 16th-century merchants' houses; Dir JAN VAN DEN BROEKE.

Polderhuis Westkapelle Dijk- en Oorlogsmuseum: Zuidstraat 154–156, 4631 AK

Westkapelle; tel. (118) 570700; e-mail info@polderhuiswestkapelle.nl; internet www.polderhuiswestkapelle.nl/wie-zijn-we; f. 1999; presentation of history of dam village and its inhabitants; history of dike village: Second World War with bombing of dikes in Walcheren in 1944, flooding, closing dike and reconstruction of dike village; liberty bridge; temporary exhibitions in art and cultural and historical heritage; publ. *Polderhuisblad*.

Stadhuismuseum De Vierschaar (Town Hall Museum Vierschaar): Markt 5, 4351 AA Veere; tel. (118) 506064; e-mail info@deltacultureel.nl; internet www.schotsehuizen.nl/devierschaar; f. 1881; tribunal, council-chamber and exhibition rooms; old standards and flags; pictures; golden cup of Maximilian from Burgundy (1546); memorabilia from the house of Oranje-Nassau; Dir PETER BLOM.

Venlo

Limburgs Museum: POB 1203, 5900 BE Venlo; Keulsepoort 5, 5911 BX Venlo; tel. (77) 3522112; fax (77) 3548396; e-mail info@limburgsmuseum.nl; internet www.limburgsmuseum.nl; f. 2000; prehistory, Roman and medieval colln, history of Limburg, art and applied art; coins and medals; Chair. W. AERTS; Vice-Chair. M. DE LOO; Sec. and Treas. S. S. HUIJS; Dir Drs JOS SCHATORJÉ.

Vlissingen

Zeeuws Maritiem Muzeeum Vlissingen (Maritime Museum of Zeeland in Vlissingen): Nieuwendijk 15, 4381 BV Vlissingen; Nieuwendijk 11, 4381 BV Vlissingen; tel. (118) 412498; fax (118) 430307; e-mail info@muzeeum.nl; internet www.muzeeum.nl; f. 2002, originally Stedelijk Museum Vlissingen (f. 1890); maritime colln (pilotage, lighthouses, marine archaeology, fishery); local history (souvenirs of Admiral de Ruyter, paintings, ceramics, wood carvings, engravings, tiles, coins and medals); library of 700 vols; Dir Drs WILBERT WEBER; Gen. Man. LEO DINGEMANSE.

Universities

DE HAAGSE HOGESCHOOL
(The Hague University of Applied Sciences)

Johanna Westerdijkplein 75, 2521 EN The Hague
Telephone: (70) 4458888
Fax: (70) 4458825
Internet: www.dehaagsehogeschool.nl
Chair.: ROB K. BRONS
Number of teachers: 1,700
Number of students: 20,000

ERASMUS UNIVERSITEIT ROTTERDAM
(Erasmus University)

POB 1738, 3000 DR Rotterdam
Burgemeester Oudlaan 50, 3062 PA Rotterdam
Telephone: (10) 4081111
E-mail: info@smc.eur.nl
Internet: www.eur.nl
Founded 1973 by merger of Nederlandse Economische Hogeschool (f. 1913) and Medische Faculteit Rotterdam (f. 1966)
Academic year: September to July
Chair. of Supervisory Board: Drs A. VAN ROSSUM
Chair. of Exec. Board: P. F. M. VAN DER MEER MOHR
Rector Magnificus: Prof. HENK SCHMIDT
Sec. of Supervisory Board: J. T. A. VAN MAURIK
Librarian: Dr P. E. L. J. SOETAERT
Library: see Libraries and Archives
Number of students: 23,867

DEANS

Erasmus MC (Medical Center): Prof. Dr HUIB POLS
Erasmus School of Economics: Prof. PHILIP HANS FRANSES
Erasmus School of Law: Prof. MAARTEN KROEZE
Faculty of History and Arts: Prof. Dr DICK DOUWES
Faculty of Philosophy: Prof. L. (WIEP) VAN BUNGE
Faculty of Social Sciences: Prof. Dr H. T. VAN DER MOLEN
Rotterdam School of Management: Prof. Dr GEORGE S. YIP

FONTYS HOGESCHOLEN
(Fontys University of Applied Sciences)

POB 347, 5600 AH Eindhoven
Telephone: (877) 877877
Fax: (877) 876233
E-mail: info@fontys.nl
Internet: www.fontys.nl
Pres.: MARCEL J. G. WINTELS
Sec.: H. J. M. (LENY) SCHEEPERS
Sec.: PIETER G. JANSSEN
Number of teachers: 3,111 (f.t.e.)
Number of students: 38,313

HOGESCHOOL LEIDEN

POB 382, 2300 AJ Leiden
Zernikedreef 11, 2333 CK Leiden
Telephone: (71) 5188800
Fax: (71) 5188801
E-mail: infohl@hsleiden.nl
Internet: www.hsleiden.nl
Br. in Rotterdam
Chair.: PAUL VAN MAANEN
Sec.: LISETTE VAN DE WEIJER
Number of teachers: 700
Number of students: 7,300

HOGESCHOOL ZEELAND
(HZ University of Applied Sciences)

Edisonweg 4, 4382 NW Vlissingen
Telephone: (118) 489155
E-mail: study@hz.nl
Internet: hz.nl
State control
Chair.: Drs H. J. SIMONS
Pres.: Drs PETER C. A. VAN DONGEN
Sec.: M. (RIEN) DE KLERK
Number of students: 4,000

HOGESCHOOL ZUYD
(Zuyd University)

POB 550, 6400 AN Heerlen
Nieuw Eyckholt, Heerlen
Telephone: (45) 4006060
E-mail: info@hszuyd.nl
Internet: www.hszuyd.nl
Campuses in Maastricht, Sittard-Geleen
Chair.: J. J. FRANSEN VAN DE PUTTE
Sec.: BERT NELISSEN
Number of teachers: 1,099
Number of students: 13,955

HOTELSCHOOL THE HAGUE—INTERNATIONAL UNIVERSITY OF HOSPITALITY MANAGEMENT

Brusselselaan 2, 2587 AH The Hague
Telephone: (70) 3512481
Fax: (70) 3512155
E-mail: info@hdh.nl
Internet: www.hotelschool.nl
Founded 1929
Campus in Amsterdam
Private control
Pres.: WIM DOOGE
Number of teachers: 180
Number of students: 1,900

NYENRODE BUSINESS UNIVERSITEIT
(Nyenrode Business University)

POB 130, 3620 AC Breukelen
Straatweg 25, 3621 BG Breukelen
Telephone: (346) 291211
Fax: (346) 264204
E-mail: info@nyenrode.nl
Internet: www.nyenrode.nl
Founded 1946
Private control
Languages of instruction: Dutch, English
Academic year: September to July
Rector: Prof. Dr MAURITS VAN ROOIJEN
Dean: Prof. Dr LEEN PAAPE
Registrar: R. GUIJT
Librarian: Dr ONNO MASTENBROEK
Library of 25,000 vols, 350 printed journals
Number of teachers: 68
Number of students: 350

OPEN UNIVERSITEIT
(Open University)

POB 2960, 6401 DL Heerlen
Valkenburgerweg 177, 6419 AT Heerlen
Telephone: (45) 5762888
Fax: (45) 5711486
E-mail: info@ou.nl
Internet: www.ou.nl
Founded 1984
State control
Language of instruction: Dutch
Chair.: Drs T. J. F. M. BOVENS
Chair. of Supervisory Board: A. H. BROUWER-KORF
Rector: Prof. Dr Ir F. MULDER
Pro-Rector: Prof. Dr W. M. G. JOCHEMS
Registrar: Y. SMEETS-BERKERS
Librarian: Y. SMEETS-BERKERS
Library of 30,000 vols
Number of teachers: 751
Number of students: 26,182
Publications: *Modulair*, *OnderwijsInnovatie* (4 a year)

DEANS

Educational Technology Expertise Centre: Prof. Dr W. M. G. JOCHEMS
School of Cultural Studies: Prof. Dr JAAP VAN MARLE
School of Education: Prof. Dr ELS BOSHUIZEN
School of Informatics: Prof. Dr A. (LEX) BIJLSMA
School of Law: Prof. EVERT STAMHUIS
School of Management: Prof. Dr HERMAN VAN DEN BOSCH
School of Natural Science: Prof. Dr PAQUITA PÉREZ SALGADO
School of Psychology: Prof. Dr R. VAN HEZEWIJK

PROFESSORS

Educational Technology Expertise Centre:
JOCHEMS, W. M. G.
KIRSCHNER, P. A.

Koper, E. J. R.
van Merrienboer, J. J. G.

Rude de Moor Centre:
Coonen, H. W. A. M.
Stijnen, P. J. J.
Vermeulen, M. J. M.
Zwaneveld, G.

School of Cultural Studies:
Marle, J. van
Wessel, L. H. M.
van der Dussen, W. J.

School of Education:
Boshuizen, H. P. A.

School of Informatics:
Bakker, R. R.
Jeuring, J. T.
Joosten, S. M. M.
Udink ten Cate, A.
van de Craats, J.

School of Law:
Boon, P. J.
Rinkes, J. G. J.
Sloot, B. P.
Spoormans, H. C. G.

School of Management:
Heemstra, F. J.
Herst, A. C. C.
Homan, T.
Jepma, C. J.
Korsten, A. F. A.
Kusters, R. J.
Peer, H. W. G. M.
Semeijn, J. J. S.
Storm, P. M.
van den Aardema, H. M. J.
van den Bosch, H. M. J.
van den Heijden, B. I. J. M.
Verstegen, B. H. J.

School of Psychology:
Claessen, J. F. M.
van der Molen, H. T.
von Grumbkow, J.
van Hezewijk, R. W. J.
van Kemenade, J. A.

School of Science:
Glasbergen, P.
Martens, P.
Perez Salgado, F.
Reijnders, L.
van Dam-Mieras, M. C. E.

RADBOUD UNIVERSITEIT NIJMEGEN
(Radboud University, Nijmegen)

POB 9102, 6500 HC Nijmegen
Comeniuslaan 4, 6525 HP Nijmegen
Telephone: (24) 3616161
Fax: (24) 3564606
E-mail: info@communicatie.ru.nl
Internet: www.ru.nl

Founded 1923 as Katholieke Universiteit Nijmegen, present name 2004
Private control
Languages of instruction: Dutch, English
Academic year: September to July

Trustees: Stichting Katholieke Univ.
Pres. of the Univ. Board: Ir R. J. de Wijkerslooth de Weerdesteyn
Vice-Pres. of the Univ. Board: A. A. J. M. Franken
Rector Magnificus: Prof. Dr S. C. J. J. Kortmann
Sec.-Gen.: Drs J. J. A. van de Riet
Librarian: Dr G. P. Jefcoate

Number of teachers: 2,352
Number of students: 19,137

Publications: *Radbond Magazine* (4 a year), *Vox* (96 a year)

DEANS

Faculty of Arts: Prof. Dr P. L. Sars
Faculty of Law: Prof. Dr P. P. T. Bovend'Eert
Faculty of Medical Sciences: Prof. Dr F. H. M. Corstens
Faculty of Philosophy, Theology and Religious Studies: Prof. Dr J. Thijssen
Faculty of Religious Studies: Prof. Dr J. M. M. H. Thijssen
Faculty of Science: Prof. C. C. A. M. Gielen
Faculty of Social Sciences: Prof. H. P. J. M. Dekkers
Faculty of Theology: Prof. Dr J. M. M. H. Thijssen
Nijmegen School of Management: Prof. Dr Ir R. E. C. M. van der Heijden

RIJKSUNIVERSITEIT GRONINGEN
(University Of Groningen)

POB 72, 9700 AB Groningen
Broerstraat 5, 9700 AB Groningen
Telephone: (50) 3639111
Fax: (50) 3635380
E-mail: communicatie@rug.nl
Internet: www.rug.nl

Founded 1614
State control
Languages of instruction: Dutch, English
Academic year: September to September

Chair.: Prof. Dr Sibrand Poppema
Chair. of Supervisory Board: R. J. Hoekstra
Rector Magnificus: Prof. Dr Frans Zwarts
Registrar: C. G. M. van Spanje
Librarian: Marjolein Nieboer

Number of teachers: 413
Number of students: 27,699

Publication: *Broerstraat 5* (4 a year)

DEANS

Faculty of Arts: Prof. Dr Gerry C. Wakker
Faculty of Behavioural and Social Sciences: Prof. Dr Henk A. L. Kiers
Faculty of Economics and Business: Prof. Dr J. H. Garretsen
Faculty of Law: Prof. Dr Jan Berend Wezeman
Faculty of Mathematics and Natural Sciences: Prof. Dr Jasper. S. Knoester
Faculty of Medical Science: Prof. Dr Folkert Kuipers
Faculty of Philosophy: Prof. Dr Michel R. M. ter Hark
Faculty of Spatial Sciences: Prof. Dr Piet H. Pellenbarg
Faculty of Theology: Prof. Dr Geurt Henk van Kooten

TECHNISCHE UNIVERSITEIT DELFT
(Delft University of Technology)

POB 5, 2600 AA Delft
Julianalaan 134, 2628 BL Delft
Telephone: (15) 2789111
Fax: (15) 2786522
E-mail: info@tudelft.nl
Internet: www.tudelft.nl

Founded 1842, present name 1986
State control
Language of instruction: Dutch
Academic year: September to July

Pres.: Drs D. J. van den Berg
Vice-Pres. and Rector Magnificus: Prof. Ir K. Ch. A. M. Luyben
Vice-Pres. for Education: Drs P. M. M. Rullmann
Sec. Gen.: J. Krul
Librarian: M. A. M. Heijne

Library: see Libraries and Archives
Number of teachers: 2,683
Number of students: 16,427

Publications: *Delft Integraal, Delft Outlook, Delta, Jaarverslag, Quarterly Progress Report, Statistisch Jaarboek, Studiegids, Wetenschappelijk Verslag*

DEANS

Faculty of Aerospace Engineering: Prof. Dr Ir Jacco M. Hoekstra
Faculty of Applied Sciences: Prof. Dr Ir Tim van der Hagen (acting)
Faculty of Architecture: Prof. Ir Wytze Patijn
Faculty of Civil Engineering and Geosciences: Prof. Ir Louis de Quelerij
Faculty of Electrical Engineering, Mathematics and Computer Science: Prof. Dr Daan Lenstra
Faculty of Industrial Design Engineering: Prof. Dr Cees J. P. M. de Bont
Faculty of Mechanical, Maritime and Materials Engineering: Prof. Drs M. Waas
Faculty of Technology, Policy and Management: Prof. Dr Th. A. J. Toonen

TECHNISCHE UNIVERSITEIT EINDHOVEN
(Eindhoven University of Technology)

POB 513, 5600 MB Eindhoven
Den Dolech 2, 5612 AZ Eindhoven
Telephone: (40) 2479111
Fax: (40) 2475187
E-mail: csc@tue.nl
Internet: w3.tue.nl

Founded 1956
State control
Languages of instruction: Dutch, English
Academic year: September to August

Chair. of Supervisory Board: Ir R. L. van Iperen
Pres. of Exec. Board: Dr Ir A. J. H. M. Peels
Sec. of Univ.: Ir H. P. J. M. Roumen
Rector Magnificus: Prof. Dr Ir C. J. van Duijn
Chair. of the Univ. Council: Ir M. E. Segers
Librarian: Drs J. C. M. Figdor

Library: see Libraries and Archives
Number of teachers: 169
Number of students: 7,215

Publication: *Matrix* (4 a year)

DEANS

Dept of Applied Physics: Prof. Dr Ir K. Kopinga
Dept of Architecture, Building and Planning: Prof. Ir J. Westra
Dept of Biomedical Engineering: Prof. Dr P. A. J. Hilbers
Dept of Chemical Engineering and Chemistry: Prof. Dr P. J. Lemstra
Dept of Electrical Engineering: Prof. Dr Ir A. C. P. M. Backx
Dept of Industrial Design: Prof. Dr Ir Aarnout Brombacher
Dept of Industrial Engineering and Innovation Sciences: Prof. Dr A. G. L. Romme
Dept of Mathematics and Computer Science: Prof. Dr A. M. Cohen
Dept of Mechanical Engineering: Prof. Dr Ir R. de Borst

UNIVERSITEIT LEIDEN
(Leiden University)

POB 9500, 2300 RA Leiden
Rapenburg 70, 2311 EZ Leiden
Telephone: (71) 5272727
Fax: (71) 5273118
E-mail: info@leidenuniv.nl
Internet: www.leidenuniv.nl

Founded 1575
State control
Language of instruction: Dutch
Academic year: September to July

Rector Magnificus and Pres.: Prof. Dr P. F. VAN DER HEIJDEN
Vice-Rector: Prof. Dr M. C. E. VAN DAM-MIERAS
Vice-Pres.: Drs H. W. TE BEEST
Librarian: KURT DE BELDER

Library: see Libraries and Archives
Number of teachers: 1,125 (f.t.e.)
Number of students: 18,778

DEANS

Faculty of Archaeology: Prof. Dr WILLEM J. H. WILLEMS
Faculty of Humanities: Prof. Dr H. W. VAN DEN DOEL
Faculty of Science: Prof. SJOERD M. VERDUYN LUNEL
Faculty of Social Science: Prof. Dr P. SPINHOVEN
Leiden Law School: Prof. C. J. J. M. STOLKER
Leiden University Medical Center: Prof. Dr E. C. KLASEN (Chair. of Exec. Bd)

UNIVERSITEIT MAASTRICHT
(University of Maastricht)

POB 616, 6200 MD Maastricht
Minderbroedersberg 4–6, 6211 LK Maastricht

Telephone: (43) 3882222
Fax: (43) 3884898
E-mail: communicatie@maastrichtuniversity.nl
Internet: www.maastrichtuniversity.nl

Founded 1976 as State Univ. of Limburg, present name 2008, Univ. of Limburg (www.tul.edu) was est. in 2001, in partnership with Hasselt Universiteit (see chapter on Belgium)
State control
Languages of instruction: Dutch, English
Academic year: September to June

Chair. of Supervisory Board: Drs A. H. A. VEENHOF
Pres. of Exec. Board: Dr Ir J. M. M. RITZEN
Rector: Prof. Dr G. P. M. F. MOLS
Vice-Pres. of Exec. Board: Drs A. POSTEMA
Librarian: Dr I. M. WIJK

Publication: *Doc UM ent* (research and devts in problem-based learning, 2 a year)

Library of 410,000 vols, 2,400 current periodicals
Number of teachers: 2,060
Number of students: 14,500

DEANS

Faculty of Arts and Social Sciences: Prof. Dr. REIN DE WILDE
Faculty of Cultural Studies: Prof. Dr Ir W. E. BIJKER, Prof. Dr P. TUMMEC
Faculty of Health, Medicine and Life Sciences: Prof. Dr MARTIN PAUL
Faculty of Humanities and Sciences: Prof. Dr LOUIS BOON
Faculty of Law: Prof. Dr A. W. HERINGA
Faculty of Psychology and Neurosciences: Prof. Dr BERNADETTE JANSMA
School of Business and Economics: Prof. Dr JOS LEMMINK

UNIVERSITEIT TWENTE
(University of Twente)

POB 217, 7500 AE Enschede
Drienerlolaan 5, 7522 NB Enschede

Telephone: (53) 4899111
Fax: (53) 4892000
E-mail: info@utwente.nl
Internet: www.utwente.nl

Founded 1961

Chair. of Supervisory Board: Drs H. J. VAN ESSEN
Pres.: Dr A. H. FLIERMAN
Rector Magnificus: Prof. Dr H. BRINKSMA
Vice-Pres.: K. J. VAN AST
Sec. of the Univ.: ERIK VAN KEULEN
Librarian: Drs P. G. G. M. DAALMANS

Library: see Libraries and Archives
Number of students: 9,000

DEANS

Faculty of Behavioural Sciences: Prof. Dr HUBERT COONEN
Faculty of Electrical Engineering, Mathematics and Computer Science: Prof. Dr Ir A. J. MOUTHAAN
Faculty of Engineering Technology: Prof. Dr F. EISING
Faculty of Geo-Information Science and Earth Observation: ERNA LEURINK (Man. Dir)
Faculty of Science and Technology: (vacant)
School of Management and Governance: PAUL VAN LOON

UNIVERSITEIT UTRECHT
(Utrecht University)

POB 80125, 3508 TC Utrecht
Heidelberglaan 8, 3584 CS Utrecht

Telephone: (30) 2539111
Fax: (30) 2533388
E-mail: studievoorlichting@uu.nl
Internet: www.uu.nl

Founded 1636
Languages of instruction: Dutch, English
Academic year: September to July

Pres.: YVONNE C. M. T. VAN ROOY
Chair. of Supervisory Board: M. H. (RIEN) MEIJERINK
Rector Magnificus and Vice-Pres.: Prof. HANS STOOF
Sec.-Gen.: Dr JOOP J. M. KESSELS

Library: see Libraries and Archives
Number of teachers: 3,000
Number of students: 29,927

Publication: *Ublad* (univ. magazine, 52 a year)

DEANS

Faculty of Geosciences: Prof. Dr BERT VAN DER ZWAAN
Faculty of Humanities: Prof. Dr WILJAN VAN DEN AKKER
Faculty of Law, Economics and Governance: Prof. H. R. B. M. (HENK) KUMMELING
Faculty of Science: Prof. Dr JAN VAN REE
Faculty of Social and Behavioural Sciences: Prof. Dr WILLEM KOOPS
Faculty of Veterinary Medicine: Prof. Dr A. PIJPERS
University Medical Centre: Prof. Dr F. MIEDEMA

PROFESSORS

Faculty of Arts (Kromme Nieuwegracht 46, 3512 HJ Utrecht):

BRAIDOTTI, R., Comparative Women's Studies
DE GROOT, R., Music of the Low Countries after 1600
DE JONG, F., Islamic Languages and Cultures
EDEL, D. R., Celtic Languages
GERRITSEN, W. P., Dutch Medieval Literature
HART, P., Utrecht Studies
HECHT, P. A., History of Visual Arts in Renaissance and Modern Times
HERRLITZ, W., German Language
JANSSEN, H. L., Studies of Medieval Castles
JONG, M. B., Medieval History
KLAMT, J. C. J. A., History of Medieval Art
KLOEK, J. J., Social History of Literature
LANDSBERGEN, S. P. J., Language and Speech Automation
LASARTE, F. J., Latin-American Studies
MEYER, B. W., Visual Arts during the Renaissance in Italy and the Netherlands and their Underlying Relationship
MIJNHARDT, W. W., Post-Middle Ages History
MOORTGAT, J., Linguistics, Language Informatics
NOOTEBOOM, S. G., Linguistics, in particular Phonetics
OP DE COUL, P. M., History of Music after 1600
ORBÁN, A. P., Vulgar and Medieval Latin
OTTENHEYM, K. A., History of Architecture
POLLMANN, M. M. W., Social Functions of Language Disciplines
PRAK, M. R., Post-Medieval History (Social Relationships)
REULAND, E. J., Linguistics, specifically Syntax
RIGHART, J. A., Post-Medieval History, in particular Internal Political Relations
SANCISI-WEERDENBURG, H. W. A. M., Ancient History and Culture
SCHENKEVELD VAN DER DUSSEN, M. A., Dutch Renaissance Literature
SCHOENMAKERS, H., Theatre Science
SCHWEGMAN, M. J., Women's History
SICCAMA, J. G., History of Security Issues
STUMPEL, J. F. H. J., Iconology and Art Theory
URICCHIO, W., History of Film and Television
VAN BUUREN, M. B., Modern Literature (French)
VAN DEN HOVEN, P. J., Linguistics
VAN DER VOORT, C. M. M.
VAN EIJCK, D. J. N., Logical Aspects of Computational Linguistics
VAN ZANDEN, J. L., Post-Medieval History (Social Relationships)
VELLEKOOP, C., History of Music before 1600
VERKUIJL, H. J., Dutch Language
VOOGD, P. J. DE, Modern Literature
WESTHOFF, G. J., Didactics of Modern Languages
ZONNEVELD, W., Linguistics, in particular Phonology, English Linguistics

Faculty of Biology (Sorbonnelaan 16, 3584 CA Utrecht; tel. (30) 2532276):

BOERSMA, K. TH., Didactics of Biology
DURSTON, A. J., Organismal Embryology
GOOS, H. J. TH., Comparative Endocrinology
HOEKSTRA, W. P. M., Microbiology
HOGEWEG, P., Theoretical Biology
KOLLÖFFEL, CHR., Botany
LAAT, S. W. DE, Developmental Biology
LAMBERS, J. T., Ecophysiology
SAYER, J. A., International Aspects of Nature Protection
SEINEN, W., Biological Toxicology
VAN DAMME, J. M. M., Ecological Population Genetics
VAN DE GRIND, W. A. P. F. L., Comparative Physiology
VAN DEN BIGGELAAR, J. A. M., Experimental Embryology
VAN DER HORST, D. J., Metabolic Physiology
VAN DER MAAS, P. J. M., Plant Taxonomy
VAN HOOFF, J. A. R. A. M., Comparative Physiology
VAN LEEUWEN, C. J., Biological Toxicology (Ecological Risk Assessment)
VAN LOON, L. C., Phytopathology
VAN NOORDWIJK, A. J., Population Ecology of Animals
VERKLEIJ, A. J., Electromicroscopy
VERRIPS, C. T., Applied Molecular Biology
VISSCHER, H., Palaeobotany
VOORMA, H. O., Molecular Biology
WEISBEEK, P. J., Molecular Genetics
WERGER, M. J. A., Botanical Ecology

Faculty of Chemistry (Sorbonnelaan 16, 3584 CA Utrecht; tel. (30) 2533791; fax (30) 2533072):

BRANDSMA, L., Organic Chemistry
DE HAAS, G. H., Biophysics
DE KRUIJF, H. A. M., Toxicology and Society
DE KRUIJFF, B., Molecular Biology of Biomembranes
EGMOND, M. R., Applied Enzymology
FRENKEL, D., Physical Computer Simulation
GEUS, J. W., Inorganic Chemistry
HAVERKAMP, J., Analytical Chemistry
HOLLANDER, J. A., In vivo NMR Spectroscopy
JENNESKENS, L. W., Physical Organic Chemistry
KAMERLING, J. P., Organic Chemistry of Natural Substances
KAPTEIN, R., NMR Spectroscopy
KELLY, J. J., Electrochemistry
KONINGSBERGER, D. C., Inorganic Chemistry
KROON, J., Chemistry
LEKKERKERKER, H. N. W., Physical Chemistry
MEIJERINK, A., Chemistry of Solids
PHILIPSE, A. P., Physical Chemistry
TURKENBURG, W. C., Science and Society
VAN DE VEN, J., Materials Science
VAN DEN BOSCH, H., Biochemistry
VAN DER MAAS, J. H., Spectrochemical Analysis
VAN DUIJNEVELDT, F. B., Theoretical Chemistry
VAN EERDEN, J. P. J. M., Macroscopic Physical Chemistry
VAN EIJNDHOVEN, J. C. M., Technological Research of Aspect
VAN KOTEN, G., Organic Chemistry
VELDINK, G. A., Organic Aspects of Bio-Catalysis
VERHEIJ, H. M., Biochemistry
VLIEGENTHART, J. F. G., Bio-Organic Chemistry
WIRTZ, K. W. A., Biochemistry

Faculty of Earth Sciences (Budapestlaan 4, 3584 CD Utrecht; tel. (30) 2535050; fax (30) 2535030):

DAS, H. A., Radioanalysis in Geochemistry
EISMA, D., Marine Sedimentology
JONG, B. M. W. S. DE, Petrology and Experimental Petrology
LEEUW, J. W. DE, Organic Geochemistry
MEULENKAMP, J. E., Stratigraphy and Palaeontology
MONDT, J. C., Exploratory Geophysics
OONK, H. A. J., Thermodynamics
PRIEM, H. N. A., Isotope Geology
SNIEDER, R. K., Seismology
SPIERS, CH. J., Experimental Rock-Deformation
VAN DER WEIJDEN, C. H., Marine Geochemistry and Hydrochemistry
WHITE, S. H., Structural Geology and Tectonics
WONG, TH. E., Sedimentary Geology of Subsoils in the Netherlands
WORTEL, M. J. R., Tectonophysics

Faculty of Geosciences (Heidelberglaan 2, 3584 CS Utrecht; tel. (30) 2532044; fax (30) 2540604):

BURROUGH, P. A., Physical Geography of Landscapes
DIELEMAN, F. M. J., Human Geography of Urban Industrialized Countries
GLASBERGEN, P., Environmental Policies
GROENEWEGEN, P. P., Environmental and Social Aspects of Health and Health Care
HAUER, J., Methods and Techniques in Geographical Research
HOEKVELD, G. A., Education and Regional Geography
HOOIMEIJER, P., Regional Aspects of Population Issues
KOSTER, E. A., Landscape Architecture
KREUKELS, A. M. J., Urban and Regional Planning
LAMBOOY, J. G., Geographical Economics
LUNING, H. A., Town and Country Planning in Developing Countries
NIEUWENHUIS, J. D., Soil Mechanics of Natural Systems
ORMELING, F. J., Cartography
OTTENS, H. F. L., Human Geography
SCHILDER, G. G., History of Cartography
TERWINDT, J. H. J., Physiogeographical Processes
VAN DEN AKKER, C., Ground and Surface Water Quality
VAN DEN BERG, M., Urban and Regional Planning
VAN GINKEL, J. A., Human Geography
VAN RIJN, L. C., Mechanics of Fluids (Geographical Modelling)
VAN WEESEP, J., Human Geography
VELLINGA, M. L., Human Geography (Developing Countries)
VONKEMAN, G. H., Environmental Studies
WEVER, E., Human Geography (Economic Geography and International Economics)

Faculty of Law (Janskerhof 3, 3512 BK Utrecht; tel. (30) 2537017; fax (30) 2537300):

ANDRIESSEN, F. H. J. J., European Integration
BACKES, CH. W., Environmental Law
BAEHR, P. R., Human Rights
BAHLMAN, J. P., Business Economics
BOELE-WOELKI, K. S. R. D., International and Comparative Private Law
BOON, D., Animals and Law
BOVENKERK, F., Criminology
BOVENS, M. A. P., Philosophy of Law
BRANTS, C. H., Penal Law and Law of Criminal Procedure
BRINKHOFF, J. J., Industrial Property
BRUINSMA, J. F., Sociology of Law
CURTIN, D. M., Law of International Organizations
DALHUISEN, J. H., International Commercial Law
GROSHEIDE, F. W., Private Law
HARTKAMP, A. S., Private Law, particularly Civil Law
HEYMAN, H. W., Notarial Law
HOL, A. M., Theory of Law
HONDIUS, E. H., Civil Law
IDENBURG, PH. A., Management Sciences
IN 'T VELD, R. I., Management of Public Government
JASPERS, A. PH. C. M., Social Law
KABEL, J. J. C., Mass Media Law
KELK, C., Penitentiary Law
KOERS, A. W., International Law
KUMMELING, H. R. B. M., Constitutional and Administrative Law
KWIATKOWSKA, B., International Maritime Law
MEIJKNECHT, P. A. M., Civil Law
MOOIJ, A. W. M., Forensic Psychiatry
MORTELMANS, K. J. M., Social Economic Law
NIEUWENBURG, C. K. F., Political Economy
ROSCAM ABBING, H. D. C., Health Law
SCHILFGAARDE, P., Business Law
SIEGERS, J. J., Economics
SOONS, A. H. A., International Law
SPRUIT, J. E., History of Roman Law
STILLE, A. L. G. A., Notarial Law
SWART, A. H. J., Penitentiary Law
TEN BERGE, J. B. J. M., Administrative Law
VAN BUUREN, P. J. J., Governmental Law
VAN DEN BERGH, R., Economics of Law
VAN HALL, A., Law of Public Water and Water Boards
VAN HOOF, G. J. H., Social Economic Law
VAN HUIZEN, P. H. J. G., Commercial Traffic Law
VAN MENS, K. L. H., Fiscal Law
VAN REENEN, P., Causes of Violations of Human Rights
VERVAELE, J. A. E., Maintenance of Law and Order
VREE, J. K. DE, International and Political Relations

Faculty of Mathematics and Informatics (Budapestlaan 6, 3584 CD Utrecht; tel. (30) 2531515; fax (30) 2518394):

DE LANGE, J., Didactics of Teaching Mathematics and Computer Science
DIEKMANN, O., Applied Mathematics
DUISTERMAAT, J. J., Pure and Applied Mathematics
GILL, R. D., Stochastics
HAZEWINKEL, M., Algebraic Chemistry
LOOIJENGA, E. J. N., Pure Mathematics
MARS, J. G. M., Mathematics
MEERTENS, L. T. G., Programming Technology
MEIJER, J. J. CH., Informatics
OORT, F., Mathematics
OVERMARS, M. H., Computer Science
SIERSMA, D., Mathematics
SWIERSTRA, S. D., Informatics
TREFFERS, A., Field-Specific Education
VAN DALEN, D., Logic and Philosophy of Mathematics
VAN DER VORST, H. A., Mathematics
VAN LEEUWEN, J., Informatics
VERHULST, F., Quantitative Analysis of Dynamic Systems
ZAGIER, D. B., Pure Mathematics

Faculty of Medicine (Universiteitsweg 100, 3584 CG Utrecht; tel. (30) 2538888; fax (30) 2539025):

AKKERMANS, L. M. A., Gastrointestinal Physiology
BÄR, P. R., Experimental Neurology
BATTERMAN, J. J., Radiotherapy
BAX, N. M. A., Paediatric Surgery
BEEMER, F. A., Clinical Genetics
BERGER, R., Chemistry of Hereditary Metabolic Diseases
BERNARDS, R. A., Molecular Carcinogenesis
BIJLSMA, J. W. J., Rheumatology
BLIJHAM, G. H., Clinical Medicine
BORST, C., Experimental Cardiology
BOS, J. L., Physiological Chemistry
BOSMAN, F., Dental Physics
BOUMA, B. N., Biochemistry of Haemostasis
BREDEE, J. J., Cardio-pulmonic Surgery
BRUYNZEEL-KOOMEN, C. A. F. M., Dermatology-Allergology
BUITELAAR, I. K., Biopsychosocial Determinants in Human Behaviour
BURBACH, J. P. H., Molecular Biology of Neuropeptides
CAPEL, P. J. A., Experimental Immunology
CLEVERS, J. C., Clinical Immunology
COHEN-KETTENIS, P. T., Gender Development and Child and Youth Psychopathology
DEJONCKERE, P. H., Speech Therapy and Phoniatrics
DE PUTTER, C., Special Dental Surgery
DE WILDT, D. J., Medical Pharmacology
DUIJNSTEE, M. S. H., Innovations in Home Care
DUURSMA, S. A., Clinical Medicine
EIKELBOOM, B. C., Vascular and Transplant Surgery
ERKELENS, D. W., Clinical Medicine
FELDBERG, M. A. M., Radiodiagnostics
GAST, G. C. DE, Haematology
GEUZE, J. J., Cytology
GISPEN, W. H., Molecular Pharmacology and Neuro-Pharmacology
GOOSZEN, H. G., Surgery
GROBBEE, D. E., Clinical Epidemiology
GRYPDONCLE, M. H. F., Nursing Science

HAUER, R. N. W., Clinical Electrophysiology
HEEREN, TH. J., Psychogeriatrics
HEINTZ, A. P. M., Oncological Gynaecology
HELDERS, P. J. M., Physiotherapy
HENGEVELD, M. W., Sexology
HILLEN, B., Functional Anatomy
HORDIJK, G. J., Oto-rhino-laryngology
TEN HORN, G. H. M. M., Psychiatric Care-Management
HUIZING, E. H., Oto-rhino-laryngology
JONGSMA, H. J., Medical Physiology
KAHN, R. S., Clinical and Biological Psychiatry
KATER, L., Clinical Immunopathology
KNAPE, J. TH. A., Anaesthesiology
KOERSELMAN, G. F., Psychotherapy
KON, M., Plastic and Reconstructive Surgery
KOOMANS, H. A., Nephrology
LAMMERS, J. W. J., Pulmonary Diseases
MALI, W. P. TH. M., Radiodiagnostics
MARX, J. J. M., General Internal Medicine
MOSTERD, W. L., Clinical Sports Medicine
OKKEN, A., Paediatrics
PEARSON, P. L., Medical Molecular Genetics
PETERS, A. C. B., Paediatric Neurology
PETERS, P. W. J., Teratology
POLL-THE, B. E., Clinical Congenital Metabolic Diseases
ROBLES DE MEDINA, E. O., Clinical Cardiology
SANGSTER, B., Health Protection
SAVELKOUL, T. J. F., Toxicology
SCHRIJVERS, A. J. P., General Health Care
SCHULPEN, T. W. J., Social Paediatrics
SITSEN, J. M. A., Clinical Pharmacology
SIXMA, J. J., Haematology
SLOOTWEG, P. J., Oral Pathology
SMOORENBURG, G. F., Experimental Audiology
SMOUT, A. J. P. M., Pathophysiology
STAAL, G. E. J., Enzymology
STILMA, J. S., Ophthalmology
STROUS, G. J. A. M., Cellular Biology
SUSSENBACH, J. S., Molecular Biology
TE VELDE, E. R., Desirable Fertility
THIJSSEN, J. J. H., Clinical Chemistry
TREFFERS, W. F., Ophthalmology
TULLEKEN, C. A. F., Neurosurgery
VAN BEL, F., Neonatology
VAN BERGE HENEGOUWEN, G. P., Gastroenterology
VAN BRONSWIJK, J. E. M. H., Biological Agents in Domestic Hygiene
VAN DE WAL, H. J. C. M., Cardiopulmonic Surgery of Infants and Children
VAN DEN TWEEL, J. G., Pathology
VAN DER DONK, J. A. W. M., Cell Biology
VAN DER VLIET, P. C., Physical Chemistry
VAN DER WERKEN, CHR., Acute Surgery
VAN DER WINKEL, J. G. J., Immunotherapy
VAN ENGELAND, H., Psychiatry of Children
VAN GIJN, J., Neurology
VAN HUFFELEN, A. C., Clinical Neurophysiology
VAN LONDEN, J., General Health Care
VAN NIEUWENHUIZEN, O., Paediatric Neurology in relation to Functional Morphology
VAN NORREN, D., Ophthalmological Physics
VAN REE, J. M., Psychopharmacology
VAN VEELEN, C. W. M., Functional Neurosurgery
VAN VLOTEN, W. A., Dermatology
VAN VROONHOVEN, TH. J. M. V., General Surgery
VAN WAES, P. F. G. M., Röntgen Diagnostics
VAN WIMERSMA GREIDANUS, TJ. B., Neuroendocrinology
VELDMAN, J. E., Experimental Otology and Otoimmunology
VERBOUT, A. J., Orthopaedic Aspects of Spinal and Neuromuscular Disorders
VERHEIJ, T. J. M., Family Medicine
VERHOEF, J., Clinical Microbiology
VERSTEEG, D. H. G., Medical Pharmacology
VIERGEVER, M. A., Image-processing in Medicine
VISSER, G. H. A., Obstetrics
VOORN, TH. B., General Practice
WESTENBERG, H. G. M., Neurochemical Aspects of Psychiatry
WINNUBST, J. A. M., Psychology of Health and Illness
WOKKE, J. H. J., Neurology focusing on Neuromuscular Diseases
WOLTERS, W. H. G., Paediatric Psychology
ZEGERS, B. J. M., Paediatric Immunology
ZONNEVELD, F. W., Medical Representation Techniques

Faculty of Pharmacy (Sorbonnelaan 16, 3584 CA Utrecht; tel. (30) 2532525; fax (30) 2533953):

BAKKER, A., Pharmaceutical Practice
BEIJNEN, J. H., Bio-Analysis (Research in Clinical Medicine)
BULT, A., Pharmaceutical Analysis
CLERCK, F. F. P., Applied Pulmonary and Cardiovascular Pharmacology
CROMMELIN, D. J. A., Biopharmacy
DE JONG, J. G. A. M., Management Aspects of Pharmaceutical Practice
GLERUM, J. H., Clinical Pharmacy
HENNINK, W. E., Pharmaceutical Technology
JANSSEN, L. H. M., Pharmaceutical Chemistry
LABADIE, R. P., Pharmacognosy
LISKAMP, R. M. J., Molecular Medicinal Chemistry
MAES, R. A. A., Toxicology
NIJKAMP, F. P., Molecular Pharmacology
OLIVIER, B., Applied Pharmacology of the Central Nervous System
PORSIUS, A. J., Pharmacotherapy
RUITER, A., Food Chemistry and Bromatology
THIJSSEN, J. H. H., Clinical Chemistry
TOLLENAERE, J. P. A. E., Computational Medicinal Chemistry
VAN DIJK, H., Immunology of Phytochemicals
VERBATEN, M. N., Human Psychophysiology and Psychopharmacology

Faculty of Philosophy (Heidelberglaan 8, 3584 CS Utrecht; tel. (30) 2531831; fax (30) 2532816):

BERGSTRA, J. A., Applied Logic
GEERTSEMA, H. P., Calvinist Philosophy
MANSFELD, J., History of Philosophy in the Ancient World and the Middle Ages
MIDDELBURG, C. A., Applied Logic
RUNIA, D. T., The Tradition of Platonism in Relation to Early Christianity
SCHUHMANN, K. J., History of Modern and Renaissance Philosophy
VAN DALEN, D., Logic and Philosophy
VAN REIJEN, W. L., Political and Social Philosophy
VERBEEK, TH. H. M., 17th-Century Ideology from the Dutch Perspective

Faculty of Physics and Astronomy (Princetonplein 5, 3584 CC Utrecht; tel. (30) 2533284; fax (30) 2539282):

ANDRIESSE, C. D., Electricity Supplies
BEIJERINCK, H. C. W., Atomic and Interface Physics
BLEEKER, J. A. M., Space Research
BUIJS, A., Experimental Physics
BUILTJES, P. J. H., Chemistry of the Atmosphere
CROWE, A., Medical and Physiological Physics
DE RUIJTER, W. P. M., Physical Oceanography
DE WIJN, H. W., Solid State Physics
DE WIT, B. Q. P. J., Theoretical Physics
DE WITT HUBERTS, P. K. A., Reactor Physics
DIEKS, D. G. B. J., Foundations and Philosophy of the Natural Sciences
DIJKHUIS, J. I., Semiconductor Laser Optics
DRONKERS, J., Physics of Coastal Systems
ERKELENS, C. J., Human Physics
ERNÉ, F. C., Current Issues in Physics
ERNST, M. H. J. J., Theoretical Physics
FEINER, L. F., Theory of Condensed Materials
HABRAKEN, F. H. P. M., Physics Education
HEARN, A. G., Astrophysics
HEIDEMAN, H. G. M., Experimental Physics
HOLTSLAG, A. A. M., Meteorology (Forecasting) Techniques
HOOFT, T. W. J. M., Theory of Solids
KAMERMANS, R., Experimental Physics and Experimental Nuclear Physics
KOENDERINK, J. J., Human Physics
KUPERUS, M., Astrophysics
LAMERS, H. J. G. L. M., Astronomy
LELIEVELD, J., Atmospheric Chemistry
LEVINE, Y. K., Biophysics
LIJNSE, P. L., Development of Physics Concepts and Methods in Education
LOURENS, W., Physics Informatics
NIEHAUS, A., Experimental Physics
OERLEMANS, J., Dynamics of the Climate
POLMAN, A., Advancement of Atomic and Interface Physics
RUIJGROK, TH. W., Theoretical Physics and Mechanics
SARIS, F. W., Atomic and Molecular Physics
SCHÜLLER, F. C., Plasma Physics
SCHUURMANS, C. J. E., Meteorology
SINKE, W. C., Physical and Chemical Properties of Thin Layers
SMIT, J., Theoretical High-Energy Physics
'T. JANSSEN, G., Theoretical Physics
TJON, J. A., Theoretical Physics
VAN BEIJEREN, H., Theoretical Physics
VAN DER WEG, W. F., Technical Physics
VAN HIMBERGEN, J. E. J. M., Theoretical Physics
VERBUNT, F. W. M., High-Energy Astrophysics
VERLINDE, E. P., Theoretical Physics
ZIMMERMAN, J. TH. F., Physical Oceanography

Faculty of Social Sciences (Heidelberglaan 1, 3584 CS Utrecht):

ADRIAANSENS, H. P. M., Social Sciences and Social Processes and Structures
BANCK, G. A., Anthropology of Brazil
BECKER, H. A., Sociology
BENSING, J. M., Clinical Psychology and Health Psychology
BIERMAN, D. J., Parapsychology
BRINKGEVE, C. D. A., Primary forms of Cohabitation, Life-course and Identity
Dr COENEN, H. M. H., Labour Issues
DEEN, N., Theory and Practice of Pupil Accompaniment
DERCKSEN, W. J., Social Sciences (Socio-Economic Policy)
DUBBELDAM, L. F. B., Education in Developing Countries
ELBERS, E. P. J. M., Communication, Thought and Culture Issues
ENGBERSEN, G. B. M., Welfare State System
ENTZINGER, H. B., Studies of Multi-Ethnic Societies
GRIENSVEN, G. J. P., Social Epidemiology with respect to HIV/AIDS
GROEBEL, F. J., Social Sciences (Psychology of Mass Communication)
HAAN, E. H. F. DE, Applied Experimental Psychology
HAGENDOORN, A. J. M. W., Social Sciences
HART, H. 'T, Statistics and Methodology of Pedagogical Research
HEIJMANS, P. G., Life Psychology
HOKSBERGEN, R. A. C., Adoption
HOX, J. J., Survey Research
IDENBURG, PH. A., Management Sciences

IMELMAN, J. D., Principles of Pedagogics
INGLEBY, J. D., Life Psychology
KANSELAAR, G., Educational Sciences, in particular Educational Psychology
KNULST, W. P., Education in Arts and Cultural Participation
KRUIJT, D. A. N. M., Development Issues
LAGERWEIJ, N. A. J., Pedagogics and Innovation in Teaching
LEEUW, F. L., Empirical Theoretical Analysis of the Social Effects of Government Policy
MANTE MEIJEE, E. A., Management and Renewal Processes in Large Organizations
OOSTINDIE, G. J., Anthropology of Comparative Sociology (Caribbean)
PILOT, A., Didactics
RAUB, W., Theoretical Sociology
RISPENS, J., Education of Problem Children
ROBBEN, A. C. G. M., Anthropology of Comparative Sociology (Latin America)
RUIJTER, A. DE, Social Anthropology
SCHAUFELI, W. B., Organizational Psychology
SCHETTKAT, R., Social and Institutional Economics
SCHNABEL, P., Mental Health Care
SCHOFFELEERS, J. H., Socio-Economic Changes and Forms of Meaning-Making
SEVENHUYSEN, S. L., Comparative Women's Studies
STEVENS, L. M., Orthopedagogics
STROEBE, W., Social and Organizational Psychology
TAZELAAR, F., Sociology
THIJSSEN, J. G. L., Business and Professional Education
TIELMAN, R. A. P., Social and Cultural Aspects of Humanism
TREFFERS, A., Field-Specific Education
VAN DEN BOUT, J., Bereavement Acceptance Process
VAN DER HEIJDEN, P. G. M., Statistics for Social Sciences
VAN DER LAAN, G., Foundations of Social Work
VAN DER ZWAN, A., Development of Views on the Adjustment of the Welfare State
VAN SON, M. J. M., Clinical and Health Care Psychology
VAN WAARDEN, B. F., Intervention, Organization and Policy Issues in Social Sciences
VAN WIJNGAARDEN, P. J., Sociological Aspects of Social Security Issues
VAN WYNGAARDEN, P. J., Social Security Issues
VAN ZANTWIJK, R. A. M., Anthropology and Ethno-History of the Indian Peoples of Latin America
VEENHOVEN, R., Humanism
VERMEER, A., Remedial Education
VRIENS, L. J. A., Peace Studies
VROON, P., Theoretical Psychology
WERTHEIM, A. H., Cognitive Ergonomics
WILTERDINK, N. A., Study of Long-term Processes in Social Sciences
WINTER, M. DE, Innovations in Primary Parent and Child Care
WUBBELS, TH., Teacher Behaviour as a factor in the Learning Environment

Faculty of Theology (Heidelberglaan 2, 3584 CS Utrecht; tel. (30) 2531853; fax (30) 2533241):

ANDREE, T. G. I. M., Ideological Upbringing and Formation in a Multi-religious Context
BECKING, B. E. H. J., Old Testament
BRÜMMER, V., Philosophy of Religion
DE REUVER, A., Education in Calvinist Theology
DEN BOEFT, J., Religious History of Hellenism
HEEGER, F. R., Ethics
HOUTEPEN, A. W. P., Ecumenics
IMMINK, F. G., Practical Theology
JONGENEEL, J. A. B., Missiology
KLOPPENBORG, M. A. G. T., History of Religions and Comparative Religious Studies
MAAS, T. A., Relationships between Christianity and Modern Culture
MUIS, J., Dogmatics
OTTEN, W., Church History
SCHROTEN, E., Christian Ethics
TIELEMAN, H. J., Sociology of Religions
VAN BELZEN, J. A., Psychology of Religion
VAN DER HORST, P. W., New Testament
VAN LEEUWEN, TH. M., Science of the Old Testament and History of Israelite Religion
VRIES, O. H. DE, History and Dogmas of the Baptism

Faculty of Veterinary Medicine (Yalelaan 1, 3584 CL Utrecht; tel. (30) 2534851; fax (30) 2537727):

BARNEVELD, A., General Surgery and Surgery of Large Domestic Animals
BEYNEN, A. C., Experimental Animals
BREUKINK, H. J., Clinical Veterinary Medicine
COLENBRANDER, B., Fertility
CORNELISSEN, A. W. C. A., Parasitology
DE VRIES, H. W., Medicine of Small Domestic Animals
DEN OTTER, W., Cell Biology and Histology
DIK, K. J., Radiology
EVERTS, M. F., Veterinary Physiology
FERON, V. J., Biological Toxicology
FINK-GREMMELS-GEHRMANN, J., Pharmacology of Domestic Animals
GIELKENS, A. J. L., Veterinary Medicine for Poultry Farms
GROMMERS, F. J., Relationship between Man and Animal
GRUYS, E., Pathology of Domestic Animals
HELLEBREKERS, L. J., Anaesthesiology of Laboratory Animals
HORZINEK, M. C., Virology
HUIS IN 'T VELD, J. H. J., Microbiology of Food Products of Animal Origin
JANSSEN, J., Knowledge of Veterinary Law
KROES, R., Biological Toxicology
MELOEN, R. H., Biomedical Identification
MOUWEN, J. M. V. M., Pathology
OSTERHAUS, A. D. M. E., Environmental Virology
PIJPERS, A., Veterinary Medicine for Poultry Farms
ROTTIER, P. J. M., Molecular Virology
RUITENBERG, E. J., Veterinary Immunology
RIJNBERK, A., Medicine of Small Domestic Animals
SCHALKEN, J. A., Veterinary Oncology
SLUYS, F. J., Medicine of Domestic Animals, Reproduction and Surgery
SPRUIJT, B. M., Good Health of Animals
TIELEN, M. J. M., Lodging and Provision of Animals
VAN DER WEYDEN, G. C., Obstetrics
VAN DER ZEIJST, B. A. M., Veterinary Bacteriology
VAN DER ZUTPHEN, L. F. M., Animals and Experimental Application
VAN DIJK, J. E., Pathology of Rare Animals/Spontaneous Laboratory Animal Pathology
VAN EDEN, W., Veterinary Immunology
VAN GOLDE, L. M. G., Veterinary Biochemistry
VAN KNAPEN, F., Hygiene of Food of Animal Origin
VAN MIERT, A. S. J. P. A. M., Veterinary Pharmacology
VAN OIRSCHOT, J. T., Veterinarian Vaccinology
VAN OOST, B. A., Clinical and Molecular Genetics of Domestic Animals
VERHEIJDEN, J. H. M., Medicine of Pigs
VOS, J. G., Toxicological Pathology
WEIJS, W. A., Veterinary Anatomy and Embryology

UNIVERSITEIT VAN AMSTERDAM
(University of Amsterdam)

POB 19268, 1000 GG Amsterdam
Spui 21, 1012 WX Amsterdam
Telephone: (20) 5259111
Fax: (20) 5252136
E-mail: info@uva.nl
Internet: www.uva.nl

Founded 1632 as Athenaeum Illustre, present name and status 1877
State control
Languages of instruction: Dutch, English
Academic year: September to July

Pres.: Dr KAREL VAN DER TOORN
Rector Magnificus: Prof. DYMPH VAN DEN BOOM
Vice-Pres.: P. W. DOOP
Sec.-Gen.: M. ZAANEN
Librarian: Drs A. J. H. A. VERHAGEN

Library: see Libraries and Archives
Number of teachers: 4,062 (f.t.e)
Number of students: 30,825

Publications: *Athenaeum Illustre* (4 a year), *Gids van de Universiteit van Amsterdam* (1 a year)

DEANS

Faculty of Dentistry: Prof. Dr A. J. FEILZER
Faculty of Economics and Business: Prof. E. J. FISCHER
Faculty of Humanities: Prof. Dr J. F. T. M. VAN DIJCK
Faculty of Law: Prof. C. E. DU PERRON
Faculty of Medicine: Prof. Dr M. M. LEVI
Faculty of Science: Prof. Dr L. D. NOORDAM
Faculty of Social and Behavioural Sciences: Prof. Dr E. H. F. DE HAAN

UNIVERSITEIT VAN TILBURG
(Tilburg University)

POB 90153, 5000 LE Tilburg
Warandelaan 2, 5037 AB Tilburg
Telephone: (13) 4669111
Fax: (13) 4663019
E-mail: tilburguniversity@uvt.nl
Internet: www.tilburguniversity.nl

Founded 1927 as Roomsch Katholieke Handelshoogeschool, present status 2006
State control
Languages of instruction: Dutch, English
Academic year: September to August

Chair.: R. F. M. LUBBERS
Pres. of Exec. Board: H. M. C. M. VAN OORSCHOT
Rector: Prof. Dr PHILIP EIJLANDER
Chief Admin. Officer: Drs M. J. A. M. WIJNHOVEN
Chief Information Officer: Ir M. VAN DEN BERG
Sec.-Gen.: Drs HUUB DEKKERS

Library of 800,000 , 11,000 periodical vols
Number of teachers: 992 (f.t.e.)
Number of students: 12,500 students

Publications: *Tilburg Research* (irregular), *UNIVERS* (52 a year), *Until* (irregular)

DEANS

Law School: Prof. Dr RANDALL LESAFFER
School of Economics and Management: Prof. Dr KEES KOEDIJK
School of Humanities: Prof. Dr ARIE DE RUIJTER
School of Social and Behavioural Sciences: Prof. Dr DIEDERIK STAPEL
School of Theology: Prof. Dr ADELBERT DENAUX

TiasNimbas Business School: Prof. Dr Ir RAMON O'CALLAGHAN

UNIVERSITEIT VOOR HUMANISTIEK
(University for Humanistics)

POB 797, 3500 AT Utrecht
Kromme Nieuwegracht 29, 3512 HD Utrecht
Telephone: (30) 2390100
Fax: (30) 2340738
E-mail: info@uvh.nl
Internet: www.uvh.nl

Founded 1989
State control
Academic year: September to June

Chair.: Prof. Dr ARIE DE RUIJTER
Rector: Prof. Dr HANS A. ALMA
Librarian: M. A. M. BOERBOOM

Library of 22,000 vols
Number of teachers: 100
Number of students: 350

PROFESSORS

COENEN, H. L. M., Sciences of Man, Society and Culture
ELDERS, A. D. M., Theories of World Views
HOUTEN, D. J. VAN, Social Policy, Planning and Organization
KUNNEMAN, H. P., Practical Humanist Studies
MANSCHOT, H. A. M., Philosophy and Ethics
MASO, I., Philosophy of Science, Methodology and the Theory of Research
VRIES, T. DE, Regional Health Care

VRIJE UNIVERSITEIT, AMSTERDAM
(Free University, Amsterdam)

De Boelelaan 1105, 1081 HV Amsterdam
Telephone: (20) 5989898
Fax: (20) 5989899
E-mail: international@dienst.vu.nl
Internet: www.vu.nl

Founded 1880
Languages of instruction: Dutch, English
Academic year: September to September

Chair. of Supervisory Board: P. BOUW
Chair. of Exec. Board: R. M. SMIT
Rector: LEX BOUTER
Mem. of Exec. Board: H. J. RUTTEN

Library: see under Libraries and Archives
Number of teachers: 2,000
Number of students: 25,000
Publication: *VU Magazine*

DEANS

Faculty of Arts: Prof. Dr DOUWE G. YNTERNA
Faculty of Dentistry: Prof. A. FEILZER
Faculty of Earth and Life Sciences: Prof. BAUKE OUDEGA
Faculty of Economics and Business Administration: Prof. H. VERBRUGGEN
Faculty of Human Movement Sciences: Prof. P. J. BEEK
Faculty of Law: Prof. Dr E. SLIEDREGT
Faculty of Medicine: Prof. W. STALMAN
Faculty of Philosophy: Prof. R. VAN WOUDENBERG
Faculty of Psychology and Education: Prof. J. PASSCHIER
Faculty of Sciences: Prof. Dr H. IRTH
Faculty of Social Sciences: Prof. ANTON C. HEMERIJCK
Faculty of Theology: Prof. Dr WIM JANSE

WAGENINGEN UNIVERSITEIT
(Wageningen University)

POB 9101, 6700 HB Wageningen
Bldg no. 400, Costerweg 50, 6701 BH Wageningen
Telephone: (317) 480100
Fax: (317) 484884
E-mail: info@wur.nl
Internet: www.wageningenuniversity.nl

Founded 1876, present status 1918; attached to Wageningen Univ. and Research Centre
State control
Languages of instruction: Dutch, English
Academic year: September to August

Chair.: Dr A. A. DIJKHUIZEN
Rector Magnificus and Vice-Pres.: Prof. Dr M. J. KROPFF
Mem. of Exec. Board: Dr IJ. J. H. (TIJS) BREUKINK
Chair. of Supervisory Board: M. DE BOER
Chief Librarian: D. VAN ZAANE
Information Officer: S. VINK

Library: see Libraries and Archives
Number of teachers: 500
Number of students: 6,427
Publication: *Wb*

MANAGING DIRECTORS OF DEPARTMENTS

Agrotechnology and Food Sciences Group: Dr R. J. (RAOUL) BINO
Animal Sciences Group: Dr M. C. TH. (MARTIN) SCHOLTEN
Environmental Sciences Group: Ir C. T. (KEES) SLINGERLAND
Plant Sciences Group: Dr Ir J. E. (ERNST) VAN DEN ENDE
Social Sciences Group: Prof. Dr Ir R. B. M. (RUUD) HUIRNE

PROFESSORS

ANTONIDES, G., Economics of Consumers and Households
BAKKER, J., Nematology, Physiology and Molecular Ecology of Nematodes
BEERS, G., Supply Chain Management
BERENDSE, F., Nature Conservation and Plant Ecology
BERG, J. A. VAN DEN, Genomics
BEULENS, A. J. M., Information Technology
BIGMAN, D., Global Food Security and Int. Trade
BINDELS, J., Nutrition during Growth and Devt
BINO, R. J., Metabolomica of Plants
BISSELING, A. H. J., Molecular Biology, Devt Biology of Plants
BLADEREN, P. J. VAN, Toxico-kinetics and Biotransformation
BLANS, G. H. T., Philosophy
BONGERS, F., Forest Ecology and Forest Management Group
BOOM, R. M., Food Process Engineering
BOT, G. P. A., Technical Physics
BOEKEL, M. A. J. S. VAN, Product Design and Quality Management
BREEMEN, N. VAN, Soil Formation and Ecopedology
BRINK, A. VAN DEN, Policy and Management in Land Use Planning
BREGT, A. K., Geo-information Science, Geographical Information Systems
BRUGGEN, A. H. C. VAN, Biological Farming Systems
BRUSSAARD, L., Soil Biology and Biological Soil Quality
CAPELLE, A., Agrification
CLEEF, A. M., Tropical Nature Conservation and Vertebrate Ecology
COHEN STUART, M. A., Physical Chemistry and Colloid Chemistry
CROUS, P. W., Evolutionary Phytopathology
DENNY, P., Aquatic Ecology
DICKE, M., Entomology
DIJK, G. VAN, Theory and Practice of Agricultural Cooperative Organizations
DONS, H. J. M., Entrepreneurship in Life Sciences
ELFRING, T., Innovative Entrepreneurship
EMONS, A. M. C., Plant Cell Biology
FEDDES, R. A., Soil Physics, Ecohydrology and Groundwater Management
FLEER, G. J., Physical and Colloid Chemistry
FOLMER, H., General Economics
FOLSTAR, P., Knowledge Management of Innovation Processes in Food Production
FRERKS, G. E., Disaster Management
FREWER, L. J., Food Safety and Consumer Behaviour
GIJZEN, H. J., Environmental Biotechnology
GILLER, K. E., Plant Production Systems
GOEWIE, E. A., Social Aspects of Biological Farming
GOLDBACH, R. W., Virology
GORRIS, L. G. M., Food Safety Microbiology
GOVERDE, H. J. M., Political Science in Agriculture and Environment
GRASMAN, J., Mathematical and Statistical Methods
GROENEN, M. A. M., Animal Breeding and Genetics
HAMER, R. J., Technology of Cereal Proteins
HARTOG, L. A. DEN, Developments in Animal Production
HEIDE, D. VAN DER, Human and Animal Physiology
HEIJMAN, W. J. M., Rural Economics, Spatial Aspects of Rural Devt and Transformation
HEYTING, C., Molecular Cell Genetics
HIDDINK, G. J., Nutritional Extension by Intermediary
HOEKSTRA, R. F., Genetics, Populations and Quantitative Genetics
HOLTSLAG, B., Meteorology and Air Quality
HOOG, C. DE, Sociology of the Family
HOWARD-BORJAS, P. L., Gender Studies in Agriculture
HUIRNE, R. B. M., Economics of Animal Health and Food Safety
IERLAND, E. C. VAN, Environmental Economics and Natural Resources
JACOBSEN, E., Plant Breeding
JONGEN, W. M. F., Product Design and Quality Management
KATAN, M. B., Nutrition and Epidemiology
KEMP, B., Adaptation Physiology
KOK, F. J., Nutrition and Health
KOOIJ, D. VAN DER, Environmental Microbiology, Drinking Water Supply
KOOIJ, P., Agricultural History
KOORNNEEF, M., Genetics
KOOTEN, O. VAN, Horticultural Production Chains
KORTHALS, M. J. J. A. A., Applied Philosophy
KROEZE, J. H. A., Psychological and Sensorial Aspects of Food and Nutrition
KROMHOUT, D., Public Health Research
KROPFF, M. J., Crop and Weed Ecology
LANKVELD, J. M. G., Dairy Science
LEEMANS, R., Analysis of Environmental Systems
LEENTVAAR, J., Integrated Water Management
LEEUWEN, J. L. VAN, Experimental Zoology
LEEUWIS, C., Communication and Innovation Studies
LEIJNSE, A., Groundwater Quality
LENGKEEK, J., Socio-spatial Analysis of Land Use (Recreation and Tourism)
LEUNISSEN, J. A. M., Bio-informatics
LENTEREN, J. C. VAN, Entomology
LINDEN, E. VAN DER, Food Physics
MAESEN, L. J. G. VAN DER, Plant Taxonomy and Geography
METZ, J. H. M., Technical Design of Farm Systems in Animal Husbandry
MEULEN, B. M. J. VAN DER, Law and Governance
MILITZ, H., Wood Science
MOHREN, G. M. J., Forest Ecology and Forest Management Group
MOL, A. P. J., Environmental Policy
MUISWINKEL, W. B. VAN, Cell Biology and Immunology
MULDER, B. M., Theoretical Cell Physics
MULDER, M., Agricultural Education
MÜLLER, J., Farm Technology
MÜLLER, M., Nutrition, Metabolism and Genomics

NIEHOF, A., Sociology of Consumers and Households
OENEMA, O., Management of Nutrient Fluxes and Soil Fertility
OMTA, S. W. F., Management Studies
OOYEN, A. J. J. VAN, Genetics in Food Technology
OPDAM, P. F. M., Landscape Ecology, Spatial Population Ecology
OSKAM, A. J., Agricultural Economics and Rural Policy
OUDE LANSINK, A. G. J. M., Business Economics
PENNINGS, J. M. E., Future Markets
PERDOK, U. D., Soil Technology
PLAS, L. H. W. VAN DER, Plant Physiology
PLOEG, J. D. VAN DER, Rural Sociology
PRINS, H. H. T., Resource Ecology
PUTTEN, W. H. VAN DER, Functional Biodiversity
RAATS, P. A. C., Continuum Mechanics
RABBINGE, R., Sustainable Devt and System Innovation
RICHARDS, P., Technology and Agrarian Devt
RIEMSDIJK, W. H. VAN, Soil Chemistry and Chemical Soil Quality
RIETJENS, I. M. C. M., Toxicology
RULKENS, W. H., Environmental Technology
SANDERS, J. P. M., Valorisation of Plant Production Chains
SAVELKOUL, H. F. J., Cell Biology and Immunology
SCHAAFSMA, G. J., Nutrition and Food
SCHAEPMAN, M. E., Geo-information Science, Remote Sensing
SCHANZ, H., Forest Policy and Forest Management
SCHEFFER, J. J. C., Medicinal and Aromatic Plant Science
SCHEFFER, M., Aquatic Ecology and Water Quality
SCHIPPERS, J. C., Water Supply Technology (IHE)
SCHOUTEN, M. G. C., Ecology of Nature Conservation
SCHULTZ, E., Land and Water Devt (IHE)
SCHUURMAN, E., Reformational Philosophy
SKIDMORE, A. K., Vegetation and Agricultural Land Use Survey
SLANINA, J., Measuring Methods in Atmospheric Research
SMIT, G., Molecular Flavour Science
SMITS, M. A., Animal Breeding and Genetics
SNOO, G. R. DE, Agri-environment Schemes
SOSEF, M., Biosystematics
SPIERTZ, J. H. J., Crop Ecology, Nutrient and Metabolic Flows
SPRUIJT, B. M., Ethology and Animal Welfare
STAM, P., Plant Breeding, Selection Methods and Sustainable Resistance
STAMS, A. J. M., Microbiology
STAVEREN, W. A. VAN, Nutrition and Gerontology
STEIN, A., Spatial Statistics
STIEKEMA, W. J., Genome Informatics
STRATEN, G. VAN, Systems and Control
STROOSNIJDER, L., Erosion and Soil and Water Conservation
STRUIK, P. C., Crop Physiology
SUDHÖLTER, E. J. R., Organic Chemistry
SYKORA, K. V., Ecological Organisation and Management of Infrastructure
TAMMINGA, S., Animal Nutrition, Ruminants
TERPSTRA, M. J., Consumer Technology and Product Use
TRAMPER, J., Bioprocess Engineering
TRIJP, J. C. M. VAN, Marketing and Consumer Behaviour
TROCH, P. A., Hydrology and Quantitative Water Management
VALK, A. J. J. VAN DER, Land Use Planning
VAN ARENDONK, J. A. M, Animal Genetics and Breeding
VEER, P. VAN 'T, Human Nutrition and Epidemiology
VELDKAMP, A., Soil and Land Evaluation
VERRETH, J. A. J., Fish Culture and Fisheries
VERSTEGEN, M. W. A., Animal Nutrition, Monogastrics
VERVLOET, J. A. J., Historical Geography of Landscaping in the Netherlands
VET, L. E. M., Evolutionary Ecology
VIERSSEN, W. VAN, Aquatic Ecology
VINCENT, L. F., Irrigation and Water Engineering
VISSER, L. E., Rural Devlopment Sociology
VISSER, R. G. F., Plant Breeding
VLAK, J. M., Virology
VORAGEN, A. G. J., Food Chemistry
VOS, W. M. DE, Microbiology
VRIES, S. C. DE, Biochemistry
WAGENBERG, A. F. VAN, Facility Management
WIT, P. J. G. M. DE, Phytopathology, Plant-Pathogen Interactions
WOERKUM, C. M. J. VAN, Communication Management
ZACHARIASSE, L. C., Strategic Economics in Agribusiness
ZEE, S. E. A. T. M. VAN DER, Soil Chemistry and Chemical Soil Quality
ZIJPP, A. J. VAN DER, Animal Production Systems
ZWIETERING, M. H., Food Microbiology

Institutes of University Standing

ABC HOGESCHOOL

POB 8118, 3301 CC Dordrecht
Telephone: (78) 6186662
Fax: (78) 6181904
E-mail: info@abc-opleidingen.nl
Internet: www.abc-opleidingen.nl; attached to ABC Opleidingen.

ACADEMIE VERLOSKUNDE MAASTRICHT (University of Midwifery Education and Studies Maastricht)

POB 1256, 6201 BG Maastricht
Universiteitssingel 60, 6229 ER Maastricht
Telephone: (43) 3885410
Fax: (43) 3885451
E-mail: info@av-m.nl
Internet: www.av-m.nl
Founded 1913
Man. Dir: R. W. A. A. VAN CRIMPEN
Sec.: S. NORDHAUSEN.

ACADEMIE VOOR OVERHEIDSJURISTEN (Academy for Government Lawyers)

Lange Voorhout 62, 2514 EH The Hague
Telephone: (70) 3129850
Fax: (70) 3129849
E-mail: academie@acjur.nl
Internet: www.academievooroverheidsjuristen.nl
Founded 2009
Chair.: R. J. HOEKSTRA
Dean: Drs PETER VAN LOCHEM.

ACADEMIE VOOR WETGEVING (Academy for Legislation)

Lange Voorhout 62, 2514 EH The Hague
Telephone: (70) 3129830
Fax: (70) 3129849
E-mail: academie@acwet.nl
Internet: www.academievoorwetgeving.nl
Founded 2001
Chair.: R. J. HOEKSTRA
Dean: Drs PETER VAN LOCHEM.

AMSTERDAM SCHOOL OF REAL ESTATE

POB 140, 1000 AC Amsterdam
Huys Azië , Jollemanhof 5, 1019 GW Amsterdam
Telephone: (20) 6681129
Fax: (20) 6680361
E-mail: info@asre.uva.nl
Internet: www.asre.nl
Founded 1987
Chair.: Ir J. D. DOETS
Dir and Sec of the Board: Drs L. B. UITTENBOGAARD.

BUSINESS SCHOOL NETHERLANDS

POB 709, 4116 ZJ Buren
De Raadskamer, Herenstraat 25, 4116 BK Buren
Telephone: (344) 579030
Fax: (344) 579050
E-mail: international@bsn.eu
Internet: www.bsn.eu
Founded 1988
Dean: FRANCIS BLUM.

BUSINESS SCHOOL NOTENBOOM—INSTITUTE FOR BUSINESS, HOTEL AND LEISURE MANAGEMENT

POB 307, 5600 AH Eindhoven
Telephone: (40) 2520620
E-mail: hogeschool@notenboom.nl
Internet: www.notenboom.nl
Brs in Hilversum, Maastricht
Man: JAN THEO MELLEMA
Number of teachers: 120

CHRISTELIJKE AGRARISCHE HOGESCHOOL DRONTEN

De Drieslag 1, 8251 JZ Dronten
Telephone: (321) 386100
Fax: (321) 313040
E-mail: info@cah.nl
Internet: www.cah.nl
Br. in Almere
Dir: Ir W. VAN DE WEG
Exec. Sec.: DAALMEIJER VAN VUUREN.

CHRISTELIJKE HOGESCHOOL EDE

POB 80, 6710 BB Ede
Oude Kerkweg 100, 6717 JS Ede
Telephone: (318) 696300
Fax: (318) 696396
E-mail: info@che.nl
Internet: www.che.nl
Founded 1950, present status 1994, present name 1997
State control
Chair. of Supervisory Board: R. C. ROBBERTSEN
Head: Dr C. P. (KEES) BOELE
Number of teachers: 400
Number of students: 4,000

CHRISTELIJKE HOGESCHOOL WINDESHEIM

POB 10090, 8000 GB Zwolle
Campus 2–6, 8017 CA Zwolle
Telephone: (88) 4699777
Fax: (88) 4688822
E-mail: info@windesheim.nl
Internet: www.windesheim.nl
State control
Chair.: Prof. Dr A. W. C. A. CORNELISSEN
Sec.: Drs W. A. HOBBELEN
Number of teachers: 1,700
Number of students: 20,000

DRIESTAR HOGESCHOOL
(University for Teacher Education)

POB 368, 2800 AJ Gouda
Burg. Jamessingel 2, 2803 PD Gouda
Telephone: (182) 540333
Fax: (182) 538449
E-mail: internationaloffice@driestar-educatief.nl
Internet: www.driestar-hogeschool.nl
Founded 1944, present status 2005; attached to Driestar Educatief
Chair.: Drs L. N. (Rens) Rottier
Number of teachers: 275
Number of students: 1,400

EUROPORT BUSINESS SCHOOL

POB 21510, 3001 AM Rotterdam
Complex Weenahof, Schaatsbaan 61–91, Rotterdam
Telephone: (10) 2012320
Fax: (10) 2012321
E-mail: info@epbs.nl
Internet: www.epbs.nl
Chair.: Jelle Marchand.

FEDERATIE BELASTINGACADEMIE BV

Brenkmanweg 6, 4105 DH Culemborg
Telephone: (345) 547024
Fax: (345) 547024
E-mail: fba@rb.nl
Internet: www.fbacademie.nl.

FONTYS BESTUURSACADEMIE—INSTITUUT VOOR BESTUURLIJKE INNOVATIE

POB 90903, 5000 GD Tilburg
Professor Gimbrerelaan 16, 5037 EK Tilburg
Telephone: (13) 4651351
Fax: (13) 4651379
E-mail: bestuursacademie@fontys.nl
Internet: www.bazn.nl
Founded 2002 as BAZN de bestuursacademie, present name and status 2011
Br in Amsterdam
Dir: Pieter Bon.

GEREFORMEERDE HOGESCHOOL

POB 10030, 8000 GA Zwolle
Grasdorpstraat 2, 8012 EN Zwolle
Telephone: (38) 4255542
Fax: (38) 4230785
E-mail: info@gh-gpc.nl
Internet: www.gh.nl
Chair.: A. van der Veer
Vice-Chair.: B. Wesseling
Sec.: D. de Jonge
Number of teachers: 125
Number of students: 1,450

GERRIT RIETVELD ACADEMIE

Frederik Roeskestraat 96, 1076 ED Amsterdam
Telephone: (20) 5711600
Fax: (20) 5711654
E-mail: secretariaatcvb@grac.nl
Internet: www.gerritrietveldacademie.nl
Founded 1924, present status 1968, present name 1965
Private control
Chair.: Tijmen van Grootheest
Dir of Sandberg Institute: Jurgen Bey
Dir of Education: Ben Zegers
Dir of Operations: Annelies van Eennennaam
Sec.: Steven Jongejan
Dean of Fine Arts and Design: Ben Zegers
Library of 8,000 vols
Number of students: 1,000

HANZEHOGESCHOOL GRONINGEN, UNIVERSITY OF APPLIED SCIENCES
(Hanze University Groningen, University of Applied Sciences)

POB 30030, 9700 RM Groningen
Zernikeplein 7, 9747 AS Groningen
Telephone: (50) 5955555
Fax: (50) 5710634
E-mail: info@org.hanze.nl
Internet: www.hanze.nl
Founded 1798, present status 1993
Brs in offices in Amsterdam, Assen, Leeuwarden; 21 attached institutes
Chair.: Drs H. J. Pijlman
Number of teachers: 24,000
Number of students: 2,700

HBO NEDERLAND

Kortestraat 1, 6811 EN Arnhem
Telephone: (26) 3516379
Fax: (26) 4451023
E-mail: info@hbonederland.com
Internet: www.hbonederland.com
Founded 1987
Private control
Language of instruction: Dutch
Number of students: 3,000

HOGESCHOOL DIRKSEN ARNHEM

POB 3090, 6802 DB Amsterdam
Parkstraat 27, 6828 JC Arnhem
Telephone: (26) 3544644
Fax: (26) 3544698
E-mail: info@dirksen.nl
Internet: www.dirksen.nl.

HOGESCHOOL E3 ICT

Oranjeplein 97, 6224 KV Maastricht
Telephone: (43) 3638333
E-mail: info@e3.nl
Internet: www.e3.nl
Private control
Dir: Marcel Snel.

HOGESCHOOL EDITH STEIN—ONDERWIJSCENTRUM TWENTE

POB 568, 7550 AN Hengelo
M.A. de Ruyterstraat 3, 7556 CW Hengelo
Telephone: (74) 8516100
Fax: (74) 8516161
E-mail: info@edith.nl
Internet: www.edith.nl
Founded 1984, by merger of Pedagogische Academie Hoogveld and KLOS (Kleuter-Leidster OpleidingsSchool), present name 1986
Private control
Language of instruction: Dutch
Dir: Manon Ketz
Chair.: Henk Mulders
Number of teachers: 110
Number of students: 1,100

HOGESCHOOL HAS DEN BOSCH

POB 90108, 5223 DE 's-Hertogenbosch
Onderwijsboulevard 221, 5223 DE 's-Hertogenbosch
Telephone: (73) 6923600
Fax: (73) 6923699
E-mail: hasdb@hasdb.nl
Internet: www.hasdenbosch.nl
Languages of instruction: Dutch, English
Chair.: Stef Valk (acting)
Number of teachers: 300
Number of students: 1,700
Publication: *HAS Beats Hogeschoolgeluiden* (10 a year).

HOGESCHOOL HELICON

Socrateslaan 22A, 3707 GL Zeist
Telephone: (30) 6937900
Fax: (30) 6911440
E-mail: info@hhelicon.nl
Internet: www.hhelicon.nl
Founded 1995, by merger of Vrije Pedagogische Akademie te Zeist and Akademie voor Eurythmie te Den Haag, 1998 Vrije Muziek-Akademie te Zeist merged
Chair.: B. Holvast.

HOGESCHOOL INHOLLAND

POB 93043, 2509 AA The Hague
Theresiastraat 8, 2593 AN The Hague
Telephone: (70) 3120100
E-mail: info@inholland.nl
Internet: www.inholland.nl
Private control
Chair.: D. Terpstra
Pres.: Geert Dales
Number of teachers: 2,900
Number of students: 37,500

HOGESCHOOL IPABO

POB 90506, 1006 BM Amsterdam
Jan Tooropstraat 136, 1061 AD Amsterdam
Telephone: (20) 6137079
Fax: (20) 6134645
E-mail: receptie@hs-ipabo.edu
Internet: www.hs-ipabo.edu
Private control
Language of instruction: Dutch
Chair.: Dr Ing. Jan W. M. A. Houben
Number of teachers: 120
Number of students: 1,000

HOGESCHOOL ISBW

POB 266, 5300 AG Zaltbommel
Internet: www.isbw.nl
Founded 1931
Private control
Language of instruction: Dutch.

HOGESCHOOL IVA DRIEBERGEN

POB 33, 3970 AA Driebergen
Hogesteeg 2A, 3972 JT Driebergen
Telephone: (343) 512780
Fax: (343) 532187
E-mail: info@iva-driebergen.nl
Internet: www.iva-driebergen.nl
Founded 1930
Private control
Publication: *LIVA Post*.

HOGESCHOOL NOVI

POB 2068, 3500 GB Utrecht
Kobaltweg 44, 3542 CE Utrecht
Telephone: (30) 7115615
Fax: (30) 7115614
E-mail: info@novi.nl
Internet: www.novi.nl
Founded 1958, present status 1997
Dir: Kees Louwman.

HOGESCHOOL NTI

POB 2222, 2301 CE Leiden
Schipholweg 101, 2301 XC Leiden
Telephone: (71) 7501040
Fax: (71) 5612550

E-mail: vragen@nti.nl
Internet: www.nti.nl
Founded 1997, present status 2000
Head: MARIANNE VAN WESTRIENEN
Number of teachers: 125
Number of students: 70,000

HOGESCHOOL PBNA

POB 68, 3330 AB Zwijndrecht
H.A. Lorentzstraat 1A, 3331 EE Zwijndrecht
Telephone: (78) 6253889
Fax: (78) 6253827
E-mail: examens@pbna.com
Internet: www.pbna.com
Founded 1912, present status 1999
Private control
Languages of instruction: Dutch, English, French, German, Polish, Portuguese
Number of students: 50,000

HOGESCHOOL THIM VAN DER LAAN

Newtonbaan 6, 3439 NK Nieuwegein
Telephone: (30) 2886670
Fax: (30) 2898811
E-mail: info@thimvanderlaan.nl
Internet: www.thim.nl
Founded 1974, as Thim van der Laan Hogeschool voor Fysiotherapie
Private control
Languages of instruction: Dutch, German
Dir of Education Affairs: R. M. VAN ECK
Number of students: 650

HOGESCHOOL TIO

Oudenoord 2, 3513 ER Utrecht
Telephone: (30) 6668836
Fax: (30) 6668397
Internet: www.tio.nl
Private control
Languages of instruction: Dutch, English
Dir: Ir M. W. DÜTHLER
Number of teachers: 250

HOGESCHOOL UTRECHT (HU)

Oudenoord 330, 3513 EX Utrecht
Telephone: (88) 4818181
E-mail: info@hu.nl
Internet: www.hu.nl
Founded 1995, present name 2005
Private control
Chair.: GERI BONHOF
Number of teachers: 3,500
Number of students: 30,000
Publication: *magazine van Hogeschool Utrecht*.

HOGESCHOOL VAN AMSTERDAM

POB 1025, 1000 BA Amsterdam
Spui, 21 1021 WX Amsterdam
Telephone: (20) 5953200
E-mail: voorzittercvb@uva.nl
Internet: www.hva.nl
Chair.: Dr KAREL VAN DER TOORN
Sec.: ARJAN P. TROMMEL
Number of teachers: 3,101
Number of students: 41,770

HOGESCHOOL VAN ARNHEM EN NIJMEGEN

POB 5375, 6802 EJ Arnhem
Ruitenberglaan 31, 6826 CC Arnhem
Telephone: (26) 3691555
Fax: (26) 3691514
E-mail: info@han.nl
Internet: www.han.nl
Founded 1996, by merger of 3 instns
Chair.: Drs RON BORMANS
Number of teachers: 2,900
Number of students: 28,000

HOGESCHOOL VAN HALL LARENSTEIN
(Van Hall Larenstein University of Applied Sciences)

POB 1528, 8901 BV Leeuwarden
Agora 1, 8934 CJ Leeuwarden
Telephone: (58) 2846100
Fax: (58) 2846423
E-mail: info@vanhall-larenstein.nl
Internet: www.vanhall-larenstein.nl
Founded 2003
Campuses in Velp, Wageningen
Languages of instruction: English, Dutch; attached to Wageningen UR
Man. Dir: ELLEN MARKS
Dirs of Education: GEARTSJE OOSTERHOF, GERRIT JEURING, HANS HARDUS, HANS VAN HAEREN, HANS VAN ROOIJEN, JAN VAN DER VALK, JOS WINTERMANS
Number of teachers: 450
Number of students: 4,500

HOGESCHOOL WEST-NEDERLAND VOOR VERTALER EN TOLK

Chr. Scholengemeenschap Zandvliet, Bezuidenhoutseweg, 40, 2594 AW The Hague
Internet: www.west-nederland.nl
Founded 1994
Gen. Man.: A. MINKMAN.

HOGESCHOOL WITTENBORG

Laan van de Mensenrechten 500, 7331 VZ Apeldoorn
Telephone: (88) 6672688
Fax: (88) 6672699
Internet: www.wittenborg.nl
Founded 1987
State control
Language of instruction: English
Chair.: PETER BIRDSALL
Gen. Man.: KAREN PENNINGA
Number of teachers: 22
Number of students: 220

INHOLLAND SELECT STUDIES

POB 23145, 3001 KC Rotterdam
Posthumalaan 90, 3072 AG Rotterdam
Telephone: (10) 4399491
E-mail: selectstudies@inholland.nl
Internet: www.inholland.nl/select+studies.

INSTITUUT VOOR PSYCHOSYNTHESE

Biltstraat 200, 3572 BS Utrecht
Telephone: (30) 2714634
Fax: (30) 2762979
E-mail: info@psychosynthese.nl
Internet: www.psychosynthese.nl
Founded 1985, present status 1999
Dir-Gen.: DIEDERIK VAN ROSSUM
Dean of Student Affairs: INGRID VAN BEEK-VELDKAMP.

INTERCOLLEGE BUSINESS SCHOOL

Zeestraat 62, 2518 AC The Hague
Telephone: (70) 3451110
E-mail: denhaag@intercollege.nl
Internet: www.intercollege.nl
Founded 1979
Campuses in Amsterdam, Rotterdam, Utrecht
Private control.

ITV HOGESCHOOL VOOR TOLKEN & VERTALEN
(ITV School of Interpretation and Translation)

POB 14007 3508 SB Utrecht
Padualaan 97 3508 SB Utrecht
Telephone: (30) 2730818
Fax: (30) 2721497
E-mail: admin@itv-hogeschool.nl
Internet: www.itv-h.nl
Founded 1983
College of translation; uses premises, facilities of Utrecht univ.
Private control
Dir: SJOKEAN OOSTERBAAN
Number of teachers: 70
Number of students: 750

KATHOLIEKE THEOLOGISCHE UNIVERSITEIT TE UTRECHT
(Catholic Theologic University of Utrecht)

POB 80101, 3508 TC Utrecht
Heidelberglaan 2, 3584 TC Utrecht
Telephone: (30) 4663800
Fax: (30) 2533665
E-mail: bureau@ktu.nl
Internet: www.ktu.nl
Founded 2007 by merger of Catholic Theological Univ. in Utrecht and Tilburg Faculty of Theology; attached to Tilburg Univ.
Academic year: September to September
Chair. of the Board: Prof. Dr E. M. H. HIRSCH BALLIN
Dean: Prof. Dr. A. J. DENAUX
Vice-Dean for Research: Prof. Dr P. H. A. I. JONKERS
Vice-Dean for Education: Dr. H. P. J. WITTE
Registrar: Ir J. J. VAN DE PAS
Number of teachers: 58
Number of students: 300

PROFESSORS

BEENTJES, P. C., Old Testament
FRISHMAN, J., Rabbinic Literature and Judaism
HELLEMANS, G. A. F., Social Sciences
JONKERS, P. H. A. I., Philosophy and History of Philosophy
MENKEN, M. J. J., New Testament
MÜLLER, D., Church History
RIKHOF, H. W. M., Systematic Theology and History of Theology
ROUWHORST, G. A. M., History of Liturgy
VOSMAN, F. J. H., Moral Theology
WISSINK, J. B. M., Practical Theology

LANDELIJK EXPERTISECENTRUM SOCIALE INTERVENTIE

c/o Utrecht Univ., FSW/ASW, POB 80140, 3508 TC Utrecht
Van Unnikgebouw, Heidelberglaan 2, 3584 CS Utrecht
Telephone: (30) 2534920
E-mail: nfo@lesi.nl
Internet: www.lesi.nl
Founded 2004; attached to Utrecht Univ.
Dir: Prof. Dr ROELOF HORTULANUS
Publication: *Tijdschrift voor Sociale Interventies*.

MARKUS VERBEEK BUSINESS ACADEMY

POB 6546 4802 HM Breda
Telephone: (76) 5499998
Fax: (76) 5425074
E-mail: info@mvba.nl

Internet: www.mvba.nl
Private control

Masters courses in business, management and finance

Dir: W. HAIR.

MARKUS VERBEEK PRAEHEP

Paasheuvelweg 35 1105 BG Amsterdam Zuidoost

Telephone: (20) 5677800
Fax: (20) 5677810
E-mail: amsterdam@mvp.nl
Internet: www.markusverbeek.nl/

Founded 1896
Private control

Brs in Amsterdam, Rotterdam, Rijswijk, Zwolle, Eindhoven, Utrecht; provides Bachelors Masters and training in finance-related courses.

NHTV INTERNATIONAAL HOGER ONDERWIJS BREDA
(NHTV Breda University of Applied Sciences)

POB 3917 4800 DX Breda

Telephone: (76) 5332203
Fax: (76) 5332205
E-mail: communicatie@nhtv.nl
Internet: www.nhtv.nl

Founded 1966 as the Dutch Scientific Institute for Tourism
Private control

Specialist disciplines of games and media, hotel and facility, leisure, tourism, urban devt, logistics and mobility

Rector Magnificus: Prof. Dr JAAP LENGKEEK
Number of students: 7,000

NOORDELIJKE HOGESCHOOL LEEUWARDEN
(NHL University)

POB 1080 8900 CB Leeuwarden
Rengerslaan 10 8917 DD Leeuwarden

Telephone: (58) 2512345
Fax: (58) 2511950
E-mail: infocentrum@nhl.nl
Internet: www.nhl.nl
Private control
Number of students: 10,000

PRO EDUCATION

POB 22799, 1100 DG Amsterdam
Atlas Complex, Gebouw Azië, Hoogoorddreef 5, 1101 BA Amsterdam

Telephone: (20) 5677999
Fax: (20) 5677901
E-mail: info@proeducation.nl
Internet: www.proeducation.nl

Founded 2002 by Univ. of Amsterdam; independent in 2004
Private control.

PROTESTANTSE THEOLOGISCHE UNIVERSITEIT
(Protestant Theological University)

POB 5021, 8260 GA Kampen
Koornmarkt 1, Kampen

Telephone: (38) 3371600
Fax: (38) 3371613
E-mail: bureau@mail.thuk.nl
Internet: www.thuk.nl

Founded 2007 by merger of Theological University Kampen (ThUK), Theological Research Institute (ThWI), Utrecht and Leiden, Evangelical Lutheran Seminary (ELS), Utrecht, Theological Seminary, Doorn; attached to Protestant Church in The Netherlands

Languages of instruction: Dutch, English
Academic year: September to August

Pres.: Dr HENK C. VAN DER SAR
Rector: Prof. Dr F. G. IMMINK
Dean of Students: Drs T. A. STRUIK
Head Librarian: J. W. PUTTENSTEIN

Library of 187,500 vols
Number of teachers: 30
Number of students: 172

Publications: *Documentatieblad voor de Geschiedenis van de Nederlandse zending en overzeese kerken* (2 a year, in Dutch), *Zeitschrift für Dialektische Theologie* (2 a year, in German)

PROFESSORS

DE LANGE, F., Ethics
HOLTROP, P. N., Missiology
HOUTMAN, C., Old Testament
JONKER, E. R., Pastoral Theology
KIRN, H.-M., Church History
KOFFEMAN, L. J., Church Polity
NEVEN, G. W., Dogmatics
ROUKEMA, R., New Testament

SAXION HOGESCHOLEN
(Saxion University of Applied Sciences)

POB 501 7400 AM Deventer
Handelskade 75 7417 DH Deventer

Telephone: (70) 603663
Fax: (70) 603123
E-mail: info@saxion.nl
Internet: www.saxion.nl

Founded 1998 by merger of Hogeschool Enschede and Hogeschool IJselland
State control

Campuses in Deventer, Enschede and Apeldoorn

Chair.: WIM BOOMKAMP
Number of teachers: 1,200
Number of students: 22,000

Publication: *Sax* (11 a year; online at sax.nu).

SCHOEVERS

Papiermolen 10, 3994 DK Houten

Telephone: (30) 2808770
Fax: (30) 2808775
E-mail: info@schoevers.nl
Internet: www.schoevers.nl

Founded 1913

Dir: RIA VAN 'T KLOOSTER.

SOD-OPLEIDINGEN

POB 544, 3440 AM Woerden
De Bleek 6, 3447 GV Woerden

Telephone: (348) 485151
Fax: (348) 485148
E-mail: info@sod-opleidingen.nl
Internet: www.sod-opleidingen.nl
Private control
Languages of instruction: Dutch, English

Pres.: Drs J. C. M. COX
Sec.: R. DE NIEUWE
Dir: CASPER MOLMANS.

STENDEN HOGESCHOOL

POB 1298 8900 CG Leeuwarden
Rengerslaan 8 8917 DD Leeuwarden

Telephone: (58) 2441441
Fax: (58) 2441401
E-mail: info@stenden.com
Internet: www.stenden.com

Founded 2008 from merger of Christelijke Hogeschool Nederland and Hogeschool Drenthe
Private control

Pres.: PIM BREEBAART
Number of students: 11,000

STICHTING OPLEIDINGEN MUSCULOSKELETALE THERAPIE
(Musculoskeletal Therapy Foundation Training)

POB 585 3800 AN Amersfoort
Softwareweg 5 3821 BN Amersfoort

Telephone: (33) 4560737
Fax: (33) 4511769
E-mail: info@somt.nl
Internet: www.somt.nl

Education, research and clinic; offers Masters in manual therapy, basin physiotherapy, sports physiotherapy, physiotherapy in geriatrics and ultrasound

Dir: WILY SMEETS.

STOAS HOGESCHOOL

POB 245, 6710 BE Ede
Bovenbuurtweg 27, 6710 BE Ede

Telephone: (318) 675611
Fax: (318) 640420
E-mail: info@aeres.nl
Internet: www.stoashogeschool.nl

Founded 1981

Number of teachers: 71
Number of students: 774

THEOLOGISCHE UNIVERSITEIT APELDOORN
(The Theological University of Apeldoorn)

Wilhelminapark 4, 7316 BT Apeldoorn

Telephone: (55) 5775700
Fax: (55) 5226339
E-mail: info@tua.nl
Internet: www.tua.nl

Founded 1894, present name 1992

Pres.: Ir J. J. EBERWIJN
Rector: Prof. Dr G. C. DEN HERTOG
Vice-Rector: Prof. H. G. L. PEELS
Librarian: Prof. Dr N. VAN DER MIJDEN-GROENENDIJK

Library of 45,000 vols
Number of teachers: 11 (6 full-time, 10 part-time)
Number of students: 98 full-time

Publications: *Apeldoornse Studies* (2 a year), *Oikodomē* (4 a year), *TUA Conned* (3 a year).

THEOLOGISCHE UNIVERSITEIT VAN DE GEREFORMEERDE KERKEN
(Theological University of the Reformed Churches)

POB 5026, 8260 GA Kampen
Broederweg 15, 8261 GS Kampen

Telephone: (38) 4471710
Fax: (38) 4471711
E-mail: secretariaat@tukampen.nl
Internet: www.tukampen.nl

Founded 1854

Pres.: Prof. Dr M. TE VELDE
Man. Dir: N. VERSTEEG
Rector: Prof. Dr C. J. DE RUIJTER
Librarian: Drs G. D. HARMANNY

Library of 150,000 vols
Number of teachers: 16
Number of students: 80

PROFESSORS

DE BRUIJNE, A. L. TH., Ethics and Spirituality
DE RUIJTER, C. J., Pastoral Theology
KAMPHUIS, B., Dogmatics
KWAKKEL, G., Old Testament Exegesis
TE VELDE, M., Church History and Polity
VAN DER POL, F., Church History and History of Dogma
VAN HOUWELINGEN, P. H. R., New Testament Exegesis

TIASNIMBAS BUSINESS SCHOOL

POB 90153, 5000 LE Tilburg
Tias Bldg, Warandelaan 2, 5037 AB Tilburg
Telephone: (13) 4668600
Fax: (13) 4668699
E-mail: information@tiasnimbas.edu
Internet: www.tiasnimbas.edu

Founded 1982 as Tilburg Institute for Advanced Studies; attached to Tilburg Univ.

Br in Bonn, Eindhoven, Taipei, Utrecht
Private control

Chair.: Prof. Dr Ir R. O'CALLAGHAN
Chair. of Supervisory Board: RICK HARWIG
Deputy Chair. of Supervisory Board: PHILIP EIJLANDER
Dean: Prof. Dr Ir RAMON O'CALLAGHAN
Man. Dir: JAN HENK VAN DER WERFF
Academic Dean: PHILIP JOOS.

TRANSFERGROEP ROTTERDAM (Transfer Group Rotterdam)

POB 420 3000 AK Rotterdam
Hogeschool Rotterdam, locatie Museumpark, Burgemeester s'Jacobplein 1 3015 CA Rotterdam
Telephone: 10) 794 68 00
Fax: 10) 794 68 01
E-mail: transfergroep@hro.nl
Internet: www.transfergroep.nl

Founded 1996; attached to Hogeschool Rotterdam
Private control

Undergraduate and postgraduate courses in business and management, coaching skills, health, education and training, welfare; specialist in organizational consulting and individual counselling programmes.

UNIVERSITY COLLEGE UTRECHT

POB 80145, 3508 TC Utrecht
Campusplein 1, 3584 ED Utrecht
Telephone: (30) 2539900
Fax: (30) 2539905
E-mail: ucu.info@uu.nl
Internet: www.uu.nl/university/college

Founded 1997; attached to Utrecht Univ.
State control

Dean: ROB VAN DER VAART

Number of teachers: 165
Number of students: 723

WEBSTER UNIVERSITY LEIDEN

Boommarkt 1 2311 EA Leiden
Telephone: (71) 5168000
E-mail: info@webster.nl
Internet: www.webster.nl

Founded 1983
Private control

Dir: Prof. Dr JEAN MARISSING

Library of 19,000 e-books, 23,000 academic journals
Number of students: 400

Institutes of International Education

EUROPEAN INSTITUTE OF PUBLIC ADMINISTRATION

POB 1229, 6201 BE Maastricht
Telephone: (43) 3296222
Fax: (43) 3296296
E-mail: info@eipa.eu
Internet: www.eipa.eu

Founded 1981

Languages of instruction: English, French, German

Centres in Luxembourg, Barcelona; supported by mem. states of the European Union and the Commission of the EU; personal and organizational devts and policy support in European policy-making and implementation, EU institutions and political integration, European public management, community policies and internal markets, legal systems of the EU

Chair.: HENNING CHRISTOPHERSEN
Dir-Gen.: Prof. Dr MARGA PRÖHL
Dir for Finance and Org.: WIM VAN HELDEN

Library of 30,000 vols, 350 periodicals; European documentation centre; depositing library of the Council of Europe
Number of teachers: 60
Number of students: 15,000

Publications: *Conference Proceedings*, *Current European Issues*.

HOGESCHOOL ROTTERDAM (Rotterdam University, University of Applied Sciences)

POB 25035, 3001 HA Rotterdam
Kralingse Zoom 91, 3063 ND Rotterdam
Telephone: (10) 7949494
Fax: (10) 7944211
E-mail: tudievoorlichting@hr.nl
Internet: www.hro.nl

Founded 1988, present status 2002
State control
Languages of instruction: English, Dutch
Academic year: September to July

Pres.: Drs J. A. C. F. TUYTEL
Asst Dir: MARJOLEIN BAKKER
Dir for Gen. and Admin. Affairs: HERMAN A. VEENEMA
Dir for Communications and External Relations: Drs J. E. (ANS) HUURMAN-VAN BUREN

Number of teachers: 3,000
Number of students: 28,500

Publication: *Profielen* (College Profiles magazine).

HOGESCHOOL VAN HALL LARENSTEIN (Van Hall Larenstein, University of Professional Education)

POB 411, 6700 AK Wageningen
Droevendaalsesteeg 2, Wageningen
Telephone: (317) 486262
Fax: (317) 486280
E-mail: info@vanhall-larenstein.com
Internet: www.larenstein.com

Founded 2003; attached to Wageningen Univ. and Research Centre

Brs in Velp, Leeuwarden; offers courses in areas related to nature and environment, human and animal health, responsible entrepreneurship
Academic year: August to July

Man. Dir: ELLEN MARKS

Library of 12,000 vols
Number of teachers: 450
Number of students: 4,500

INTERNATIONAL INSTITUTE OF SOCIAL STUDIES

POB 29776, 2502 LT The Hague
Kortenaerkade 12, 2518 AX The Hague
Telephone: (70) 4260460
Fax: (70) 4260799
E-mail: info@iss.nl
Internet: www.iss.nl

Founded 1952, present status 2009; attached to Erasmus Univ. Rotterdam
Language of instruction: English

Rector: Prof. LEO DE HAAN
Chair. of Advisory Board: Prof. Dr J. A. VAN GINKEL
Deputy Rector for Academic Affairs: WILL HOUT
Deputy Rector for Resources: RENÉE DE LOUW
Exec. Sec.: LINDA JOHNSON

Library of 100,000 vols, 400 print journals, 20,000 e-journals
Number of teachers: 80
Number of students: 350

Publication: *Development and Change* (5 a year)

PROFESSORS

BJÖRKMAN, J. W., Public Policy and Administration
DE LA RIVE BOX, L., International Cooperation
DIJK, M. P. VAN, Urban Management
ELSON, D., Feminist Development Economics
FITZGERALD, V., Development Economics
GRIMM, M., Development Economics
HAAR, G. TER, Religion and Development
HELMSING, B., Local and Regional Development
MURSHED, M., Economics of Conflict and Peace
OPSCHOOR, H., Economics of Environment and Development
PRONK, J., Theory and Practice of International Development
SAITH, A., Rural Economics
SALIH, M., Politics of Development
SCHRIJVER, N., International Law
WHITE, B., Rural Sociology
WUYTS, M., Applied Quantitative Economics

MAASTRICHT SCHOOL OF MANAGEMENT (MSM)

POB 1203, 6201 BE Maastricht
Endepolsdomein 150, 6229 EP Maastricht
Telephone: (43) 3870808
Fax: (43) 3870800
E-mail: info@msm.nl
Internet: www.msm.nl
Private control

Founded 1952
Language of instruction: English
Academic year: September to September

Chair. of the Board: Prof. P. R. H. M. VAN DER LINDEN
Vice-Chair. of the Board: F. J. M. TUMMERS
Man. Dir: KLAAS N. H. J. E. C. VAN MIERLO
Dean Dir: Prof. Dr PETER P. DE GIJSEL

Library of 15,000 books
Number of teachers: 140 (40 resident, 100 visiting)
Number of students: 2,500

Publication: *MSM Research Papers: Management & Development* (2 a year)

PROFESSORS

DE WIT, B., Strategic Management
FOSTER, S. F., Organizational Behaviour
GANS, M., International Projects and Programmes
HELING, G. W. J., Organizational Behaviour
NIKOLIK, D., Management Information System
RWEGASIRA, K. S. P., Financial Management and Accounting
SAMSON, R., General and Strategic Management
TUNINGA, R. S. J., International Business and Marketing
VAN DER HEIJDEN, B. I. J. M., Organizational Behaviour
VAN GEFFEN, L. M. J. H., Organizational Behaviour

TRANSNATIONALE UNIVERSITEIT LIMBURG

c/o Maastricht Univ., POB 616, 6200 MD Maastricht

Telephone: (43) 3882222
E-mail: info@unimaas.nl
Internet: www.tul.edu

Founded 2001.

UNESCO–IHE, INSTITUTE FOR WATER EDUCATION

POB 3015, 2601 DA Delft
Westvest 7, 2611 AX Delft

Telephone: (15) 2151715
Fax: (15) 2122921
E-mail: info@unesco-ihe.org
Internet: www.unesco-ihe.org

Founded 1957 as IHE, present name and status 2003
State control
Language of instruction: English
Academic year: October to September

Postgraduate and PhD programmes; short courses; online courses in environmental science and technology, environmental planning and management, limnology and wetland ecosystems, water quality management, sanitary engineering, urban water engineering and management, water supply engineering, water quality management, water services management, water resources management, water conflict management, hydrology and water resources, hydraulic engineering and river basin devt, hydraulic engineering—coastal engineering and port devt, hydraulic engineering—land and water devt, hydroinformatics—modelling and information systems for water management

Chair.: MARGREETH DE BOER
Rector: Prof. ANDRÁS SZÖLLÖSI-NAGY
Dir: Prof. Dr A. MEGANCK
Deputy Dir: JOOP DE SCHUTTER

Library of 25,000 vols
Number of teachers: 100
Number of students: 500

Schools of Art, Architecture and Music

Academie van Bouwkunst (Academy of Architecture): Waterlooplein 211, 1011 PG Amsterdam; tel. (20) 5318218; fax (20) 5318240; e-mail info@bwk.ahk.nl; internet www.ahk.nl/bouwkunst; f. 1908, present status 1987; attached to Amsterdam School of the Arts; offers courses in architecture, urban design and landscape architecture; library: 10,000 vols; 150 teachers; 200 students; Dir Drs AART OXENAAR.

Academie van Bouwkunst Maastricht (Maastricht Academy of Architecture): Brusselsestraat 75, 6211 PC Maastricht; tel. (43) 3219645; e-mail abm@hszuyd.nl; internet www.academievanbouwkunst.com; f. 1947, present status 2002; attached to Zuyd Univ.; offers Masters degree in architecture and related fields; 43 teachers; 55 students; Dir NIEK BISSCHEROUX.

Academie voor Architectuur en Stedebouw (School of Architecture and Urban Design): POB 90907, 5000 GJ Tilburg; Bisschop Zwijsenstraat 5, 5038 VA Tilburg; tel. (877) 874922; fax (877) 873522; e-mail aas@fontys.nl; internet www.fontyshogeschoolvoordekunsten.nl/architectuur_stedenbouw.aspx; f. 1936; attached to Fontys Univ. of Arts; architecture and town planning/design; library: 8,000 vols; 50 teachers; 80 students; Dir MARC K. T. M. GLAUDEMANS.

AKV – St Joost Breda: POB 90116, 4800 RA Breda; Beukenlaan 1, 4834 CR Breda; tel. (76) 5250302; fax (76) 5250305; e-mail info.akvstjoost@avans.nl; internet www.akvstjoost.nl; f. 1945; attached to Avans Univ.; br. in 's-hertogenbosch; offers Bachelors and Masters courses in fine art, design; publ. *Leporello*.

Amsterdamse Hogeschool voor de Kunsten (Amsterdam School of the Arts): POB 15079, 1001 MB Amsterdam; Jodenbreestraat 3, Amsterdam; tel. (20) 5277710; fax (20) 5277712; e-mail info@ahk.nl; internet www.ahk.nl; f. 1987 by merger of Academy of Fine Art in Education, Amsterdam Academy of Architecture, Conservatorium van Amsterdam, Netherlands Film and Television Academy, Reinwardt Academy, Theatre School; offers Bachelors and Masters degrees in architecture, dance, film and television, fine art and design, music, theatre, museum studies; Chair. OLCHERT BROUWER; 750 teachers; 3,000 students.

ArtEZ Academie voor Art & Design (ArtEZ Academy of Art & Design): POB 1440, 7500 BK Enschede; Campus Univ. of Twente, Hallenweg 5, 7522 NH Enschede; tel. (53) 4824400; fax (53) 4824463; e-mail artdesign.enschede@artez.nl; internet www.artez.nl; f. 1949; attached to ArtEZ Institute of the Arts; fine arts, design, fashion, architecture; library: 8,000 vols; Chair. DINGEMAN KUILMAN; Dir S. HUISMANS.

ArtEZ Hogeschool voor de Kunsten (ArtEZ Institute of the Arts): POB 49, 6812 CE Arnhem; Onderlangs 9, 6812 CE Arnhem; tel. (26) 3535600; fax (26) 3535677; e-mail communicatie@artez.nl; internet www.artez.nl; f. 2002; architecture, design, dance, drama, fine arts, fashion, music; institutes in Arnhem, Enschede, Zwolle; Chair. DINGEMAN KUILMAN; Sec. LAURIEN TIMMERMANS; 600 teachers (420 f.t.e.); 3,059 students.

Avans Hogeschool (Avans University of Applied Sciences): POB 732, 5201 AS 's-Hertogenbosch; Onderwijsboulevard 215, 5223 DE 's-Hertogenbosch; tel. (73) 6295295; fax (73) 6214725; e-mail internationaloffice@avans.nl; internet www.studyatavans.com; f. 2004 by merger of Hogeschool Brabant and Hogeschool 's-Hertogenbosch; offers courses in painting, sculpture, graphic art, ceramics, environmental art, illustration, graphic design; brs in Breda, Tilburg; 19 attached schools, 4 support units, 1 learning and innovation centre; library: 10,000 vols; 2,000 teachers; 23,000 students; Chair. Drs PAUL L. A. RÜPP; Vice-Chair. Drs FRENCH J. M. VAN KALMTHOUT.

Codarts, Hogeschool voor de Kunsten (Codarts University for the Arts): Kruisplein 26, 3012 CC Rotterdam; tel. (10) 2171100; fax (10) 2171101; e-mail codarts@codarts.nl; internet www.codarts.nl; consists of the Rotterdams' Conservatorium and the Rotterdamse Dansacademie; library: 15,000 copies of sheet music; 300 teachers; 1,100 students; Pres. CAREL VAN EYKELENBURG; Dir JIKKIE VAN DER GIESSEN; publ. *Codarts Magazine* (4 a year).

Conservatorium Maastricht (Hogeschool Zuyd): Bonnefantenstraat 15, 6211 KL Maastricht; tel. (43) 3466680; fax (43) 3466689; e-mail info.conservatorium@hszuyd.nl; internet www.hszuyd.nl; f. 1956; Bachelors and Masters degrees; library: 30,000 vols; 110 teachers; 450 students; Dir HARRY CUSTERS (acting).

Attached Institutes:

Conservatorium Gent: Hoogpoort 64, 9000 Ghent, Belgium; Dir JAN RISPENS.

Fontys Conservatorium: Postbus 90907, 5000 GJ Tilburg; Dir JAN WIRKEN.

Conservatorium van Amsterdam: POB 78022, 1070 LP Amsterdam; Oosterdokskade 151, 1011 DL Amsterdam; tel. (20) 5277550; fax (20) 6761506; e-mail cva-info@ahk.nl; internet www.ahk.nl/conservatorium; f. 1884, present bldg 2008; attached to Amsterdam School of the Arts; offers courses in classical music, early music, jazz, opera, latin and popular music; library: 30,000 vols; 200 teachers; 800 students; Dir HANS VAN BEERS; Vice-Dir MICHEL DISPA; Vice-Dir RUUD VAN DIJK; publ. *Gebouwd voor Muziek*.

Design Academy Eindhoven: POB 2125, 5600 CC Eindhoven; Emmasingel 14, 3rd Fl., 5611 AZ Eindhoven; tel. (40) 2393939; fax (40) 2393940; e-mail info@designacademy.nl; internet www.designacademy.nl; f. 1950; offers Bachelors and Masters courses in contextual design, information design, social design; 200 teachers; 700 students; Chair. ANNE MIEKE EGGENKAMP.

Hogeschool Dansacademie Lucia Marthas (Dance Academy Lucia Marthas): Rustenburgerstraat 436, 1072 HK Amsterdam; tel. (20) 6761370; fax (20) 6707698; e-mail info@luciamarthas.nl; internet www.luciamarthas.nl; f. 1983; offers accredited HBO (higher vocational education) degrees and MBO degrees (intermediate vocational education); Man. C. VAN DER LOOP-MEESTERMAN; Man. LUCIA MARTHAS; Man. RUUD VAN DER KOOIJ.

Hogeschool der Kunsten (University of the Arts): Juliana van Stolberglaan 1, 2595 CA The Hague; tel. (70) 3151515; fax (70) 3151518; e-mail info@koncon.nl; internet www.koncon.nl; f. 1826 by merger of Royal Conservatory and the Royal Acad. of Fine Arts 1990, present name 2010; faculties of fine arts and design, music and dance; interfaculty of art and science; school for young talent; library: 50,000 vols; 265 teachers; 1,023 students; Chair. JACK VERDUYN LUNEL; Dir HENK VAN DER MEULEN.

Hogeschool voor de Kunsten Utrecht (Utrecht School of the Arts): POB 1520, 3500 BM Utrecht; Lange Viestraat 2B, Utrecht; tel. (30) 2349440; fax (30) 2349484; e-mail info@ssc.hku.nl; internet www.hku.nl; f. 1987 by merger of Utrechts Conservatorium, Academie voor Beeldende Kunsten Utrecht and Academie voor Expressie en door Woord en Gebaar; faculties of art and economics; art, media and technology; music; theatre; visual arts and design; interfaculty of art and economics; library: 36,000 vols; 350 teachers; 3,800 students; Chair. of Supervisory Board Drs P. C. KLAVER; Deputy Chair. of Supervisory Board Drs W. KARDUX; Pres. AD WISMAN; Dir CÉCILE DE VOS; publ. *Mahkuzine* (2 a year).

IHS—Institute for Housing and Urban Development Studies: Burgemeester Oudlaan 50, Bldg T, 14th Fl., 3062 PA Rotterdam; POB 1935, 3000 BX Rotterdam; tel. (10) 4089825; fax (10) 4089826; e-mail admission@ihs.nl; internet www.ihs.nl; f. 1948, present name 1991, present status 2003; attached to Erasmus Univ.; library: 15,000 vols; 53 teachers; 120 students; Dir KEES VAN ROOIJEN; Deputy Dir JAN FRANSEN.

Rijksakademie van Beeldende Kunsten (State Academy of Fine Arts): Sarphatistraat 470, 1018 GW Amsterdam; tel. (20) 5270300; fax (20) 5270301; e-mail info@rijksakademie.nl; internet www.rijksakademie.nl; f. 1870, present location 1992, present status 1999; 1 and 2 year courses; organizes the Prix de Rome, the Netherlands; library: 33,000 vols, 85 magazines, 1,400 video cassettes and DVDs, large colln of monographs, catalogues of exhibitions and art theory books on visual arts, photography, video, applied art and architecture; Chair. of Board of Supervisors

Prof. Dr L. J. GUNNING-SCHEPERS; Dir ELS VAN ODIJK; Librarian MARIETTA DIRKER.

Rotterdamse Academie van Bouwkunst (Rotterdam Academy of Architecture): POB 25035, 3001 HA Rotterdam; Heijplaatstraat 23, 3089 JB Rotterdam; tel. (10) 7944855; e-mail info@ravb.nl; internet www.ravb.nl; f. 1965; attached to Rotterdam Univ.; architecture and urban design; library: 10,000 vols; 225 students; Dir CHRIS VAN LANGEN; Business Dir BERT HOOIJER.

Sandberg Instituut: Fred. Roeskestraat 98, 1076 ED Amsterdam; tel. (20) 5882400; fax (20) 5882401; e-mail contact@sandberg.nl; internet www.sandberg.nl; f. 1990; attached to Gerrit Rietveld Acad.; Masters programmes in fine arts, applied arts and design; courses validated by accreditation cttee NVAO; 41 students; Dir JURGEN BEY.

University of the Arts, The Hague: Juliana van Stolberglaan 1, 2595 CA The Hague; tel. (70) 3151515; fax (70) 3151518; e-mail secrcvb@kabk.nl; internet www.koncon.nl; f. 1990 as Academy of Fine Arts, Music and Dance by merger of The Royal Conservatory and Royal Academy of Arts; present name 2010; Bachelors and Masters courses in classical music, early music, jazz, composition, sonology, art of sound, art science, music education, theory of music and dance, master in opera and PhD (Arts); bachelors, masters and preparatory courses in fine arts, design etc.; Dir HENK MEULEN.

Willem de Kooning Academie (Willem de Kooning Academy): POB 1272, 3000 BG Rotterdam; Blaak 10 and Wijnhaven 61, Rotterdam; tel. (10) 7904750; fax (10) 7944766; e-mail wdka.communicatie@hro.nl; internet abk.hro.nl; f. 1773, present name 1998; attached to Rotterdam Univ.; 120 staff; library: 6,000 vols; Pres. RICHARD E. OUWERKERK.

ARUBA

Regulatory Bodies

GOVERNMENT

Ministry of Economic Affairs, Social Affairs and Culture: L. G. Smith Blvd 76, Oranjestad; tel. 5885455; fax 5827526; e-mail minszi@setarnet.aw; Minister Drs MICHELLE JANICE HOOYBOER-WINKLAAR.

Ministry of Justice and Education: L. G. Smith Blvd 76, Oranjestad; tel. 5830004; fax 5827518; e-mail macs@setarnet.aw; Minister ARTHUR LAWRENCE DOWERS.

Libraries and Archives

Oranjestad

Archivo Nacional Aruba (National Archives of Aruba): Sabana Banco 60, Oranjestad; tel. 5834880; fax 5839275; e-mail ana@aruba.gov.aw; f. 1994; preservation and conservation of nat. and cultural heritage of Aruba; manages transferred govt and private records; supervises and inspects governmental archives; makes archival information accessible for public use; supplies information about records to public; conducts historical research and publishes result; promotes historical interest of the public by organizing exhibitions, presentations regarding history and culture; Dir Drs RAYMOND R. HERNANDEZ.

Biblioteca Nacional Aruba (National Library of Aruba): George Madurostr. 13, Oranjestad; tel. 5821580; fax 5825493; e-mail info@bibliotecanacional.aw; internet www.bibliotecanacional.aw; f. 1908 as first Public Library of Aruba 1949, mobile library 1968, present bldg 1982, present name and status 1986; 100,000 books; nat. library, with functions of public library and nat. information centre; br. in San Nicolas; 2 bookmobiles; Dir ASTRID J. T. BRITTEN.

Museums and Art Galleries

Oranjestad

Museo Arquelogico Aruba (Archaeological Museum of Aruba): J. E. Irausquinplein 2A, Oranjestad; tel. 5828979; fax 5838267; e-mail archeo@setarnet.aw; internet www.institutodicultura-aruba.com; attached to Instituto di Cultura Aruba; permanent colln of ceramic artefacts, shell and stone tools, ornaments from the first cultures of Aruba; research, documentation, preservation of heritage and indigenous culture of Aruba.

Museo Historico Arubano (Aruban Historical Museum): Fort Zoutman z/n, Oranjestad; tel. and fax 5885199; e-mail museohistoricoarubano@hotmail.com; internet www.institutodicultura-aruba.com; f. fort built in 1798, est. as museum by Cultureel Centrum van Aruba 1983, admin. by Fundacion Museo Arubano since 1992; attached to Instituto di Cultura Aruba; archaeology, architecture, history.

Museo Numismatico Aruba (Aruba Numismatic Museum): Timbalstr. 11, Tarabana, Oranjestad; tel. 5828831; fax 5838246; e-mail numisaruba@hotmail.com; internet www.museumaruba.org; f. 1981; attached to Instituto di Cultura Aruba; holds private colln of Juan Mario Odor; colln of 35,000 items from 400 countries; Pres., J. M. Odor colln RAQUEL MADURO-ODOR; Dir, J. M. Odor colln DESIREE CROES.

San Nicolas

Aruban Model Trains Museum: Koolbaaibergstr. 12, San Nicolas; tel. and fax 5847321; internet www.institutodicultura-aruba.com; f. 2001; attached to Instituto di Cultura Aruba; colln of miniature trains; Dir J. DE VRIES.

Universities and Colleges

AUREUS UNIVERSITY SCHOOL OF MEDICINE

Hato 3E& F, Oranjestad
Telephone: 5832126
Fax: 5832127
E-mail: info@aureusuniversity.com
Internet: www.aureusuniversity.com

Founded 2004, fmrly All Saints Univ. of Medicine
Private control
Language of instruction: English
Academic year: January to December

Exec. Dean: Dr GURMIT CHILANA
Dean of Academic Affairs: Dr LAKHINDER KANWAR
Dean of Clinical Affairs: Dr RICHARD SCOTT

Number of teachers: 17
Number of students: 190 medical, 77 pre-medical

Arubaanse Muziekschool (Aruban School of Music): Vondellaan 2, Oranjestad; tel. 5822888; fax 5836529; e-mail arumuziekschool@setarnet.aw; f. 1953; Government support; educational and recreational activities; centre for information and archive of musical pieces; Dir FELIX RAIMOND HOEK.

UNIVERSIDAD DI ARUBA (University of Aruba)

Dr Schaepmanstr. z/n, San Nicholas
Telephone: 5845287
Fax: 5847274

Founded 1970
Private control
Language of instruction: English
Academic year: September to June

Pres.: Dr CARLIN I. BROWNE
Registrar: HILTONIA PETER
Librarian: LISA WEBB

Library of 6,000 vols
Number of teachers: 20
Number of students: 300

DEANS

College of Business Administration: Dr CARLIN I. BROWNE
College of Education: Dr RACHEL JONES
College of Languages: Dr JOSSY MANSUR
College of Liberal Arts: Rev. Fr WILLIAM LAKE

UNIVERSITEIT VAN ARUBA (University of Aruba)

J. Irausquinplein 4, POB 5, Oranjestad
Telephone: 5823901
Fax: 5831770
E-mail: info@ua.aw
Internet: www.ua.aw

Founded 1988
State control
Languages of instruction: Dutch, English
Academic year: September to June

Pres.: FREDERIC GIBBS
Rector: ERIC MIJTS
Sec.: (vacant)
Librarian: LEONIE PETERSON

Library of 20,000 vols
Number of teachers: 40
Number of students: 500

Publication: *Aruba Iuridica* (2 a year)

DEANS

Faculty of Arts and Sciences: PAULA KIBBELAAR
Faculty of Financial and Economic Studies: JOOST JACOBS
Faculty of Hospitality and Tourism Management: JOHN WARDLAW
Faculty of Law: CARLOS BOLLEN

NETHERLANDS ANTILLES

Regulatory Body

GOVERNMENT

Ministry of Education and Culture: Schouwburgweg 24–26 (APNA gebouw), Willemstad, Curaçao; tel. (9) 4343711; fax (9) 4624471; e-mail minoc@gov.an; internet www.minoc.an; Min. OMAYRA VICTORIA ELISABETH LEEFLANG; Head of Education Dr AIGNALD PANNEFLEK (acting).

Learned Societies

NATURAL SCIENCES

Biological Sciences

CARMABI Foundation: Piscaderabaai z/n, POB 2090, Willemstad, Curaçao; tel. (9) 4624242; fax (9) 4627680; e-mail info@carmabi.org; internet www.carmabi.org; f. 1955 as a marine biological research station, merged with STINAPA 1996; terrestrial and marine ecology; Christoffel Park, Curaçao Marine Park, Savonet Museum, Research Station Carmabi, Carmabi Education (environmental education programmes); library of 3,000 vols; Chair. DITO ABBAD; Sec. JEFFREY SYBESMA; Treas. PETER BONGERS; Dir Ir. PAUL STOKKERMANS.

Physical Sciences

Meteorological Service of the Netherlands Antilles and Aruba: Seru Mahuma, Willemstad, Curaçao; tel. (9) 8393366; fax (9) 8683999; e-mail admin-cur@meteo.an; internet www.weather.an; f. 1950, present location 1976; provides weather forecasts and warnings for the Netherlands Antilles, Aruba and adjacent waters and air space; offers services to sustain social-economic devt; Dir Dr A. A. E. MARTIS; publ. *Statistics of Meteorological Observations in Netherlands Antilles* (1 a year).

Libraries and Archives

Curaçao

Biblioteka Públiko Kòrsou/Openbare Bibliotheek Curaçao (Public Library Curaçao): Abr. M. Chumaceiro Blvd 17, Willemstad, Curaçao; tel. (9) 4345200; fax (9) 4656247; e-mail publiclibrary@onenet.an; internet www.curacaopubliclibrary.an; f. 1922 as part of Government Service of Culture and Education, present ind. status 1973, present location 1988, present status 1997; Antillean and Caribbean colln; adult, children's, mobile and schools' library services, 1 br. library, 2 mobile libraries; 180,000 vols and small colln of audio-visual material; Librarian R. M. DE PAULA; publs *Monthly Acquisition List*, *Quarterly Antillean Caribbean Acquisition List*.

Archivo Nashnal Kòrsou: Scharlooweg 75–79, Willemstad, Curaçao; tel. (9) 4614866; fax (9) 4616794; e-mail na@nationalarchives.an; internet www.nationalarchives.an; f. 1969; repository for all non-current govt records; 15,000 vols; Dir Drs N. C. ROMER-KENEPA; publ. *Lantèrnu*.

Museums and Art Galleries

Curaçao

Curaçao Museum: Van Leeuwenhoekstr., Willemstad, Curaçao; tel. (9) 4623873; fax (9) 4626051; e-mail curmuseum@yahoo.com; internet www.curacaomuseum.an; f. 1946 as The Curaçao Museum Foundation, present name and status 1948; housed in an old Dutch quarantine station, built 1853; paintings by early 20th-century Dutch masters and contemporary Curaçao artists; 19th-century mahogany furniture; folklore colln; Indian artefacts; library of Antillean books; regular exhibitions of local and int. artists; botanical garden and music pavilion; Dir K. DURGUTI; publ. *De Museumbode* (4 a year).

National Archeologisch-Antropologisch Museum van de Netherlandse Antillen (National Archaeological–Anthropological Museum): Johan van Walbeeckplein 13, Pietermaai, Curaçao; tel. (9) 4621933; fax (9) 4621936; e-mail info@naam.an; internet www.naam.an; f. 1998; collns from the five islands of the Netherlands Antilles; 10,000 artefacts; library of 2,000 vols; Chair. GIONEL JANGA; Dir J. WITTEVEEN; Treas. FLORENTINO OVERMAN; publ. *Report* (irregular).

Universities

UNIVERSITY OF SINT EUSTATIUS SCHOOL OF MEDICINE

POB 73, Goldenrock, Sint Eustatius

Telephone: (9) 3182600

Fax: (9) 3182088

E-mail: info@eustatiusmed.edu

Internet: www.eustatiusmed.edu

Founded 1999

Public control

Language of instruction: English

Chair.: Dr CLYDE B. JENSEN

Pres.: LEONARD A. WISNESKI

Provost: EZZELDIN NASSER

CEO: MICHAEL KNOPF

Vice-Pres. for Academic Devt: MARC POULIN

Vice-Pres. for Finance: JOHN BLUETHGEN

Dean of Int. Affairs: THAM NIMAL-RAJ.

UNIVERSITY OF THE NETHERLANDS ANTILLES

Jan Noorduynweg 111, Curaçao

Telephone: (9) 8442222

Fax: (9) 8442100

E-mail: una@una.an

Internet: www.una.an

Founded 1970 as The Law College of the Netherlands Antilles, univ. status 1979

Languages of instruction: Dutch, English

Academic year: September to June

Pres.: Ir H. J. BEHR

Rector: Dr RUPERT E. SILBERIE

Gen. Dir: H. DE FRANÇA

Chief Admin. Officer: R. RAVENSTEIN

Librarian: Drs M. GROENEWOUD

Library of 100,000 vols

Number of teachers: 100

Number of students: 2,104

DEANS

Faculty of Arts: E. ECHTELD

Faculty of Engineering: R. R. BULBAAI

Faculty of Law: Dr V. HEUTGER

Faculty of Social and Behavioural Sciences: (vacant)

Faculty of Social and Economic Sciences: R. J. MADURO

Colleges

Akademia di Músika 'Edgar Palm' (Edgar Palm Music Academy): Koninginnelaan z/n, Emmastad, Curaçao; tel. (9) 7373682; fax (9) 7378882; e-mail info@sentrokultural-korsou.org; internet www.sentrokultural-korsou.org; f. 1960; attached to Sentro Kultural Kòrsou (Cultureel Centrum Curaçao); instrumental, voice and gen. music education; 550 students; Dir ETZEL PROVENCE.

Saba University School of Medicine: POB 1000, Church St, Saba; tel. (9) 4163456; fax (9) 4163458; e-mail info@saba.edu; internet www.saba.edu; private control; f. 1989; library: 8,600 books, 155 periodicals; 79 teachers; 585 students (postgraduate); Chair. of the Board of Trustees Dr PAUL L. DALBEC; Pres. JOSEPH CHU; Assoc. Dean for Basic Sciences HUGH K. DUCKWORTH; Assoc. Dean for Clinical Sciences MICHAEL ELIASTAM; Library Dir SAMUEL JOHNSON.

NEW ZEALAND

The Higher Education System

New Zealand became a dominion, under the British Crown, in 1907 and achieved full independence in 1947, when it accepted the 1931 Statute of Westminster. Most of the major institutions of higher education were founded during the second half of the 19th century, notably the University of Otago (founded in 1869), the University of Canterbury (founded in 1873), Lincoln University (founded in 1878; current name and status since 1990) and the University of Auckland (founded in 1882; current status since 1962). Higher education consists of universities, polytechnic institutions, colleges of education and schools of art and music. In 2003 there were eight state universities and 20 polytechnics. In 2007 there were 146,931 students enrolled at the universities and 206,965 students in the polytechnic system. There is a parallel education system for the indigenous Maori population, who account for 20% of school enrolment. Three Maori institutions (wänanga) in the tertiary sector provide higher learning in ahuatanga Maori (Maori tradition) according to tikanga Maori (Maori custom). In 2007 42,352 students were enrolled in the wänanga. Students from the Dependent Territory of Tokelau and the Associated States of the Cook Islands and Niue may receive higher education either through branches and campuses of the University of the South Pacific or through scholarships to study in New Zealand, Australia, Fiji and other Pacific countries.

Under the Education Act (1989) the Ministry of Education is the supreme body for the provision of education at all levels. The Tertiary Education Commission determines public higher education policy and administers funding, and the New Zealand Qualifications Authority (NZQA) oversees private education providers and government training establishments. The NZQA has established a New Zealand Register of Quality Assured Qualifications ('The Register') which lists all quality-assured programmes of study and their international equivalency. It accredits and audits tertiary education providers, excluding universities, and other registered learning establishments that offer approved courses and award credits for registered qualifications. The universities are autonomous institutions, each governed by a Council, consisting of elected, appointed or co-opted members, and headed by a Vice-Chancellor. The Senate is an academic board with responsibility for academic affairs. In addition to Government funding dispersed by the Tertiary Education Commission, the universities are also financed by tuition fees, which are subsidized by the State. Universities in New Zealand are not self-accrediting and must apply to offer new qualifications or new subjects to the Committee on University Academic Programmes of the New Zealand Vice-Chancellors' Committee, which acts under statutory authority in lieu of NZQA in the university sector. Following the Education Amendment Act (1990) the polytechnics, colleges of education and wänanga became autonomous institutions and award their own degrees.

Admission to higher education is on the basis of the National Certificate of Educational Achievement. The standard university-level degree system consists of Bachelors, Masters and Doctorate degrees but aspects such as period of study and criteria for award vary among the institutions due to their autonomy. The Bachelors is often a three-year degree, although some disciplines such as medicine require upwards of five years, and is awarded on the basis of 'credits' accrued. An 'Honours' Bachelors degree is a four-year programme of study. The Masters is the first postgraduate degree, and varies in length from one to three years of full-time study. The PhD or DPhil is the highest university-level degree, awarded after a minimum two years of research-based study leading to submission of a thesis. There are also 'higher' doctorates such as the DSc or DLitt awarded after publication of a corpus of work. Institutions of higher education operate a credit-transfer system which allows students to complete their degree in an institution other than the one in which they started.

Post-secondary technical and vocational education is offered by the universities, institutes of technology, polytechnics, colleges of education, professional institutes and the wänanga. The main qualifications are the National Certificate (four levels) and National Diploma.

During 2009 the Government strengthened the performance of institutes of technology and polytechnics by reshaping the nature of their governing councils and introducing a new investment-based approach to quality assurance.

Regulatory and Representative Bodies

GOVERNMENT

Ministry for Culture and Heritage: Level 5, Radio NZ House, 155 The Terrace, POB 5364, Wellington; tel. (4) 499-4229; fax (4) 499-4490; e-mail info@mch.govt.nz; internet www.mch.govt.nz; Min. CHRISTOPHER FINLAYSON; Librarian FRAN MCGOWAN.

Ministry of Education: 45–47 Pipitea St, POB 1666, Thorndon, Wellington 6140; tel. (4) 463-8000; fax (4) 463-8001; e-mail enquiries.national@minedu.govt.nz; internet www.minedu.govt.nz; Min. ANNE TOLLEY.

Ministry of Research, Science and Technology: Level 10, 2 The Terrace, POB 5336, Wellington 6145; tel. (4) 917-2900; fax (4) 471-1284; e-mail info@morst.govt.nz; internet www.morst.govt.nz; f. 1992; Min. Hon. Dr WAYNE MAPP.

ACCREDITATION

ENIC/NARIC New Zealand: New Zealand Qualifications Authority, POB 160, Wellington 6140; tel. (4) 463-3000; fax (4) 802-3401; e-mail pamela.hulston@nzqa.govt.nz; internet www.nzqa.govt.nz; Man. PAMELA HULSTON.

New Zealand Qualifications Authority: POB 160, Wellington 6140; Level 13, 125 The Terrace, Wellington 6011; tel. (4) 463-3000; fax (4) 463-3112; e-mail helpdesk@nzqa.govt.nz; internet www.nzqa.govt.nz; co-ordinates the admin. and quality assurance of nat. qualifications in NZ; Chair. SUE SUCKLING; Chief Exec. Dr KAREN POUTASI.

NATIONAL BODIES

Distance Education Association of New Zealand: 78C White Rd, RD2, Otane, Central Hawkes Bay 4277; tel. and fax (6) 856-8022; e-mail admin@deanz.org.nz; internet www.deanz.org.nz; promotes growth, devt, research and good practice in distance education; Pres. Dr BILL ANDERSON; Sec. ANNA WEATHERSTONE; publ. *Journal of Distance Learning* (1 a year).

Institutes of Technology and Polytechnics of New Zealand: POB 10-344, Wellington; Level 12, St John House, 114 The Terrace, Wellington; tel. (4) 471-1162; fax (4) 473-2350; e-mail enquiries@itpnz.ac.nz; internet www.itpnz.ac.nz; 19 mem. institutes of technology and polytechnics; develops and promotes policies, acts as an advocacy body, and promotes academic quality on behalf of its mems; Exec. Dir DAVID GUERIN.

Tertiary Education Commission: Level 10, 44 The Terrace, POB 27048, Wellington 6011; tel. (4) 462-5200; fax (4) 462-5400; e-mail info@tec.govt.nz; internet www.tec.govt.nz; f. 2003; Chair. KAYE TURNER; Chief Exec. ROY SHARP.

Universities New Zealand—Te Pōkai Tara: POB 11915, Manners St, Wellington 6142; Level 9, 142 Lambton Quay, Wellington; tel. (4) 381-8500; fax (4) 381-8501; e-mail jackie.bailey@universitiesnz.ac.nz; internet www.universitiesnz.ac.nz; f. 1961; Chair. Prof. DEREK MCCORMACK; Exec. Dir PENNY FENWICK.

Learned Societies

GENERAL

Royal Society of New Zealand: POB 598, Wellington 6140; tel. (4) 472-7421; fax (4) 473-1841; internet www.royalsociety.org.nz; f. 1867; science, technology, humanities; 1,300 mems, 368 fellows, 70 constituent socs; Pres. Dr GARTH CARNABY; CEO Dr DIANNE MCCARTHY; publs *Journal of the Royal Society of New Zealand* (4 a year), *Kotuitui: New Zealand Journal of Social Sciences Online* (2 a year), *New Zealand Journal of Agricultural Research* (4 a year), *New Zealand Journal of Botany* (4 a year), *New Zealand Journal of Crop and Horticultural Science* (4 a year), *New Zealand Journal of Geology and Geophysics* (4 a year), *New Zealand Journal of Marine and Freshwater Research* (4 a year), *New Zealand Journal of Zoology* (4 a year).

AGRICULTURE, FISHERIES AND VETERINARY SCIENCE

Agronomy Society of New Zealand: Institute of Natural Resources, Seed Technology Building, Private Bag 11-222, Massey University, Palmerston North; e-mail c.r.mcgill@massey.ac.nz; internet nzsap.rsnz.org; f. 1970; promotes the advancement of scientific research and the practice of agronomy in New Zealand, and encourages the flow of agronomic information; 150 mems; Pres. Dr BRUCE MCKENZIE; Sec. CRAIG MCGILL; publ. *Agronomy New Zealand* (1 a year).

New Zealand Institute of Agricultural and Horticultural Science: POB 121063, Henderson, Waitakere City; tel. (9) 812-8506; fax (9) 812-8503; e-mail secretariat@agscience.org.nz; internet www.agscience.org.nz; f. 1954; 750 mems; Sec. JENNY TAYLOR; publ. *AgScience* (6 a year).

New Zealand Institute of Forestry: POB 10-513, Wellington; tel. (4) 974-8421; fax (4) 473-9330; e-mail admin@nzif.org.nz; internet www.nzif.org.nz; f. 1926; promotes the best use of NZ's resources and encourages wise use of forest lands; 824 mems; Pres. ANDREW MCEWEN; Sec. JAMES BARTON; publs *New Zealand Forestry* (4 a year), *NZIF Handbook* (1 a year).

New Zealand Society of Animal Production Inc.: c/o Dr Jane Kay, Dexcel, Private Bag 3221, Hamilton; tel. (7) 824-0916; fax (7) 824-0916; e-mail nzsap.animal@xtra.co.nz; internet nzsap.org.nz; f. 1940; 530 mems; Exec. Sec. Dr JANE KELLY; publ. *Proceedings* (1 a year).

New Zealand Society of Soil Science Inc.: c/o Dr Trish Fraser, Plant and Food Research, Private Bag 4704, Christchurch; tel. (3) 325-9604; fax (3) 325-2074; e-mail trish.fraser@plantandfood.co.nz; internet nzsss.rsnz.org; f. 1952; encourages the advancement of soil science; organizes annual conf; promotes knowledge of soil science; lobbies govt on science funding and scientific issues; 400 mems; Pres. Dr ALLAN HEWITT; Sec. Dr TRISH FRASER; publ. *Soil News* (6 a year).

New Zealand Veterinary Association (Inc.): Level 2, 44 Victoria St, POB 11-212, Wellington; tel. (4) 471-0484; fax (4) 471-0494; e-mail nzva@vets.org.nz; internet www.vets.org.nz; f. 1923; represents, provides services and promotes standards for and on behalf of veterinarians; 1,750 mems; Pres. RICHARD WILD; Chief Exec. JULIE HOOD; publs *New Zealand Veterinary Journal* (6 a year, also online), *Vetscript* (11 a year).

Royal Agricultural Society of New Zealand (Inc.): POB 54, Woodend, North Canterbury; tel. (3) 313-1004; fax (3) 313-1003; e-mail enquiries@ras.org.nz; internet www.ras.org.nz; f. 1924; promotes the development of agricultural, pastoral, horticultural, stock-raising and forestry resources in New Zealand; 1,000 individual mems, 170 institutional mems; library of 1,000 vols; Pres. MICK LESTER; Exec. Officer CHRIS MASON; publ. *On Show* (2 a year).

ARCHITECTURE AND TOWN PLANNING

New Zealand Institute of Architects: D72 Bldg (Suite 1.5), Dominion Rd, POB 2516, Auckland; tel. (9) 623-6080; fax (9) 623-6081; e-mail info@nzia.co.nz; internet www.nzia.co.nz; f. 1905; supports the needs of its member architects, and promotes architecture and the living environment of all New Zealanders; 2,889 mems; Chief Exec. BEVERLEY MCRAE.

New Zealand Institute of Surveyors: 5th Fl., St John House, 114 The Terrace, Wellington; tel. (4) 471-1774; fax (4) 471-1907; e-mail nzis@surveyors.org.nz; internet www.surveyors.org.nz; f. 1888; concerned with the professional and ethical conduct of surveyors; 1,300 mems; Pres. MARK DYER; publs *NZ Surveyor* (1 a year), *Survey Quarterly* (4 a year).

BIBLIOGRAPHY, LIBRARY SCIENCE AND MUSEOLOGY

Museums Aotearoa Te Tari o Nga whare Taonga o Te Motu-The Museums of New Zealand (Inc.): POB 10-928, Wellington; tel. (4) 499-1313; fax (4) 499-6313; e-mail mail@museums-aotearoa.org.nz; internet www.museums-aotearoa.org.nz; f. 1947; ind. professional body; represents museums and museum employees in NZ; 327 mems; Exec. Dir PHILLIPA TOCKER; publs *e-museum NEWS* (12 a year), *Museums Aotearoa Quarterly*, *New Zealand Directory of Museums* (1 a year), *Te Ara—Journal of Museums Aotearoa* (online).

New Zealand Book Council: Level 7, Alan Burns Insurance House, 69 Boulcott St, Wellington; tel. (4) 499-1569; fax (4) 499-1424; e-mail admin@bookcouncil.org.nz; internet www.bookcouncil.org.nz; f. 1972; promotes love for books and reading through a wide range of programmes; 2,500 mems (individuals, schools, libraries, booksellers, publishers); Chair. PETER BIGGS; Chief Exec. NOEL MURPHY; publ. *Booknotes* (4 a year).

New Zealand Library Association (Inc.): Level 7, Navigate House, 69 Boulcott St, POB 12-212, Wellington; tel. (4) 473-5834; fax (4) 499-1480; e-mail office@lianza.org.nz; internet www.lianza.org.nz; f. 1910; 2,281 (1,884 individual mems, 397 institutional mems); Pres. BARBARA GARRIOCK; Sec. ALLI SMITH; publs *Library Life* (26 a year), *The NZ Library & Information Management Journal* (2 a year).

ECONOMICS, LAW AND POLITICS

New Zealand Institute of International Affairs: c/o Victoria Univ. of Wellington, Rm 507, Level 5, W Wing Railways, Pipitea Campus, POB 600, Wellington 6140; tel. (4) 463-5356; e-mail nziia@vuw.ac.nz; internet www.vuw.ac.nz/nziia; f. 1934; promotes understanding of int. questions and problems, particularly those relating to New Zealand, the Pacific, Asia, and the Commonwealth; Pres. Hon. RUSSELL MARSHALL; Dir BRIAN LYNCH; Exec. Officer NGAIRE FLYNN; publ. *New Zealand International Review* (6 a year).

New Zealand Law Society: POB 5041, Lambton Quay, Wellington 6145; tel. (4) 472-7837; fax (4) 473-7909; e-mail inquiries@lawsociety.org.nz; internet www.lawsociety.org.nz; f. 1869; has statutory responsibility for regulating the legal profession (barristers and solicitors) in New Zealand; offers membership services to those lawyers who also choose to be mems; 11,100 mems; Exec. Dir CHRISTINE GRICE (acting); publ. *LawTalk* (24 a year).

Population Association of New Zealand: POB 225, Wellington; tel. (4) 471-6146; fax (4) 471-4412; internet panz.rsnz.org; f. 1974; promotes population research, understanding and policy devt; 122 mems; Pres. WARD FRIESEN; Sec. LESLEY BADDON; Treas. PETER HIMONA; publs *Monographs* (irregular), *New Zealand Population Review* (1 a year), *Technical Papers*.

FINE AND PERFORMING ARTS

Creative New Zealand (Arts Council of New Zealand Toi Aotearoa): Old Public Trust Bldg, 131–135 Lambton Quay, POB 3806, Wellington; tel. (4) 473-0880; fax (4) 471-2865; e-mail info@creativenz.govt.nz; internet www.creativenz.govt.nz; f. 1994; statutory body formed to encourage and promote the practice and appreciation of the arts; invests in a wide variety of artists and artistic orgs involved with all areas of the arts; 7 mems; Chair. ALASTAIR CARRUTHERS; Chief Exec. STEPHEN WAINWRIGHT.

New Zealand Maori Arts and Crafts Institute: Hemo Rd, POB 334, Rotorua; tel. (7) 348-9047; fax (7) 348-9045; e-mail education@maci.co.nz; internet www.nzmaori.co.nz; f. 1963; aims: the appreciation, promotion, preservation and perpetuation of Maori arts, crafts and culture; 70 mems; Chief Exec. ANDREW TE WHAITI.

HISTORY, GEOGRAPHY AND ARCHAEOLOGY

New Zealand Archaeological Association (Inc.): POB 6337, Dunedin 9059; tel. (3) 474-7474 ext. 819; fax (3) 477-5993; internet www.nzarchaeology.org; f. 1954; 500 mems; Pres. R. CLOUGH; Sec. M. WHITE; publs *Archaeology in New Zealand* (4 a year), *Journal of Pacific Archaeology* (2 a year), *Monograph series* (irregular), *New Zealand Journal of Archaeology* (1 a year).

New Zealand Cartographic Society (Inc.): ENV, Univ. of Auckland, Private Bag 92019, Auckland; tel. (9) 373-7599; fax (9) 373-7434; e-mail info@cartography.org.nz; internet www.cartography.org.nz; f. 1971; promotes devt of cartography; Pres. GEOFF AITKEN; Sec. Dr TONY MOORE; publ. *Cartogram Newsletter* (irregular).

New Zealand Geographical Society Inc.: School of Environment, Univ. of Auckland, PMB 92019, Auckland; tel. (9) 373-7599, ext. 88464; fax (9) 373-7434; e-mail nzgs@auckland.ac.nz; internet www.nzgs.co.nz; f. 1944; promotes and encourages the study of geography; brs in Auckland, Christchurch, Dunedin, Hamilton, Palmerston N and Wellington; biennial conf.; 450 mems. (425 in NZ, 25 overseas); Pres. Prof. TONY BINNS; Vice-Pres. JOHN OVERTON; Sec. MARIA BOROVNIK; publ. *New Zealand Geographer* (3 a year).

New Zealand Historic Places Trust: Antrim House, 63 Boulcott St, POB 2629, Wellington 1; tel. (4) 472-4341; fax (4) 499-0669; e-mail information@historic.org.nz; internet www.historic.org.nz; f. 1955; independent trust with statutory responsibilities; identifies, investigates, registers and preserves historic places, incl. archaeological sites, traditional sites and old European and Maori heritage; 25,000 national mems; Chair. Dame ANNE SALMOND; Chief Exec. BRUCE CHAPMAN; publ. *Heritage New Zealand* (4 a year).

New Zealand Historical Association: c/o Department of History, University of Auckland, Private Bag 92019, Auckland; internet historians.rsnz.govt.nz; f. 1979; promotes historical study, teaching and research; holds regular national and regional conferences, gives financial or other assistance to the publication of historical research in NZ, expresses opinion on issues of public policy which concern historical study, teaching or research; 300 mems; Pres. Assoc. Prof. LINDA BRYDER; Sec. Dr MALCOLM CAMPBELL.

LANGUAGE AND LITERATURE

Alliance Française Wellington: The Dominion Bldg Level 3, 78 Victoria St, POB 3002, Wellington 6140; tel. (4) 472-1272; fax (4) 472-2936; e-mail alliance@paradise.net.nz; internet www.french.co.nz; offers courses and exams in French language and culture and promotes cultural exchange with France; centres in Auckland, Christchurch, Dunedin, Hamilton, Nelson, North Shore, Palmerston North, Rotorua, Timaru and Whangerei; library of 7,000 vols, 1500 books for children, 150 audio-books, 880 CDs, 750 DVDs, 15 magazines; Dir JEAN- VICTOR MARTIN.

British Council: POB 91488 AMSC, Auckland 1142; 5E Endeans Bldg, 2 Queen St, Auckland; tel. (9) 302-3560; fax (9) 307-3670; e-mail enquiries@britishcouncil.org.nz; internet www.britishcouncil.org.nz; offers courses and exams in English language and British culture and promotes cultural exchange with the UK; attached office in Auckland; Dir PAULA MIDDLETON.

New Zealand Society of Authors (PEN NZ Inc.): POB 67013, Mt Eden, Auckland 3; tel. and fax (9) 356-8332; e-mail nzsa@clear.net.nz; internet www.authors.org.nz; f. 1934; promotes cooperation and support amongst writers; encourages writing in New Zealand and works to protect the interests of writers; awards annual and biannual prizes; has representatives on major literary bodies; 1,000 mems; Pres. CHRIS ELSE; Exec. Dir LIZ ALLEN; publ. *The New Zealand Author* (6 a year).

MEDICINE

Dietitians NZ: POB 5065, Wellington; tel. (4) 473-3061; e-mail office@dietitians.org.nz; internet www.dietitians.org.nz; f. 1943; professional asscn of registered dietitians and assoc. nutrition professionals; aims to ensure that mems are recognized as the most credible source of food and nutrition knowledge within New Zealand, and to promote good health through appropriate food and nutrition, using evidence-based scientific research; 550 mems; Pres. ANNETTE NISTOR; Exec. Dir JAN MILNE; publ. *Nutrition & Dietetics* (published jtly with Dietitians Asscn of Australia).

New Zealand Medical Association: POB 156, Wellington 6140; tel. (4) 472-4741; fax (4) 471-0838; e-mail nzma@nzma.org.nz; internet www.nzma.org.nz; f. 1887; provides advocacy on behalf of doctors and their patients and provides support and services to mems and their practices; 5,000 mems; Chair. Dr PETER FOLEY; Chief Exec. CAMERON MCIVER; publ. *New Zealand Medical Journal* (20 a year).

Physiological Society of New Zealand (Inc.): c/o Assoc. Prof. Simon Malpas, Dept of Physiology, Faculty of Medical and Health Sciences, Univ. of Auckland, Private Bag 92019, Auckland; e-mail s.malpas@auckland.ac.nz; internet www.bioeng.auckland.ac.nz/psnz; f. 1972; aims to enhance the quality of physiological and related research, and to establish links with similar research societies throughout the world; 180 mems; Pres. Assoc. Prof. BRUCE SMAILL; Sec. Assoc. Prof. SIMON MALPAS; publ. *Proceedings* (1 a year).

NATURAL SCIENCES

General

New Zealand Association of Scientists: POB 1874, Wellington 6140; e-mail pgandar@paradise.net.nz; internet www.scientists.org.nz; f. 1940; promotes and increases public awareness of science; debates scientific issues and influences govt science policy; improves working conditions for scientists and promotes the free exchange of knowledge and int. cooperation; Pres. Dr JAMES RENWICK; Sec. Dr FIONA MCDONALD; publ. *New Zealand Science Review* (4 a year).

Biological Sciences

Entomological Society of New Zealand (Inc.): Bioprotection and Ecology Div., POB 84, Lincoln Univ., Canterbury 7647; tel. (3) 384-0163; e-mail secretary@ento.org.nz; internet www.ento.org.nz; f. 1951; 250 mems; Sec. PAULINE SYRETT; publ. *New Zealand Entomologist* (1 a year).

New Zealand Ecological Society (Inc.): POB 25178, Christchurch; tel. (3) 318-1056; fax (3) 318-1061; e-mail nzecosoc@paradise.net.nz; internet nzes.org.nz; f. 1951; membership open to any person interested in ecology; holds annual conf.; 594 mems; Sec. RUTH GUTHRIE; publ. *New Zealand Journal of Ecology* (2 a year).

New Zealand Freshwater Sciences Society (Inc.): c/o Janine Wech, NIWA, Private Bag 8602, Christchurch; tel. (3) 348-8987; fax (3) 348-5548; internet freshwater.science.org.nz; f. 1968 as New Zealand Limnological Soc., present name 2005; promotes interest in all aspects of fresh and brackish water research in New Zealand; 420 mems; Pres. Prof. DAVID HAMILTON; Sec. and Treas. Dr BRIAN SORRELL.

New Zealand Marine Sciences Society: c/o Vicki Seager, 42 Carlyon Rd, RD 1, Upper Moutere, Nelson 7152; fax (3) 543-2109; e-mail secretary@nzmss.rsnz.org; internet nzmss.rsnz.org; f. 1960; concerned with all aspects of marine science in New Zealand; 400 mems, 47 inst. mems; Sec. VICKI SEAGER; publ. *Marine Sciences Review* (1 a year).

New Zealand Microbiological Society (Inc.): Dept of Oral Sciences, University of Otago, POB 647, Dunedin 9001; tel. (3) 479-5471; fax (3) 479-7078; e-mail geoffrey.tompkins@stonebow.otago.ac.nz; internet www.nzms.org.nz; f. 1956; 422 mems; Pres. Dr ANDREW HUDSON; Sec. Dr GEOFFREY TOMPKINS; publ. *New Zealand Microbiology* (3 a year).

New Zealand Society for Parasitology: c/o Tania Waghorn, Private Bag 11008, Palmerston North; tel. (6) 351-8086; fax (6) 351-8134; e-mail tania.waghorn@agresearch.co.nz; internet nzsp.rsnz.org.nz; f. 1972; study of parasites of plants and animals; 100 mems; Pres. Dr COLIN MCKAY; Sec. Dr TANIA WAGHORN; Treas. Dr DEAN REYNECKE; publ. *Proceedings in NZ journal of Zoology* (1 a year).

New Zealand Society of Plant Physiologists: HortResearch, Te Puke Research Centre, 412 No. 1 Rd, RD2 Te Puke; tel. (7) 573-3873; fax (7) 573-3871; e-mail mclearwater@hortresearch.co.nz; internet nzspp.hort.cri.nz; f. 1978; 160 mems; Pres. Dr MATTHEW TURNBULL; Sec. and Treasurer Dr MIKE CLEARWATER.

Ornithological Society of New Zealand (Inc.): c/o POB 834, Nelson 7040; e-mail secretary@osnz.org.nz; internet www.osnz.org.nz; f. 1939; encourages, organizes and promotes the study of birds and their habitat; 1,000 mems; Pres. DAVID LAWRIE; Exec. Officer INGRID HUTZLER; Sec. PETER GAZE; publs *Notornis* (4 a year), *Southern Bird* (4 a year).

Mathematical Sciences

New Zealand Mathematical Society: c/o Dept of Maths and Stats, Univ. of Canterbury, Private Bag 4800, Christchurch; e-mail a.james@math.canterbury.ac.nz; internet nzmathsoc.org.nz; f. 1974; 226 mems; Pres. Assoc. Prof. CHARLES SEMPLE; Sec. Dr ALEX JAMES; publ. *NZ Journal of Mathematics* (2 a year).

New Zealand Statistical Association (Inc.): POB 1731, Wellington; internet nzsa.rsnz.org; f. 1950; to promote good statistical practice; 400 mems; small library; Pres. Dr JENNIFER BROWN; Sec. RICHARD PENNY; publ. *Australian and New Zealand Journal of Statistics* (published jtly with Statistical Society of Australia (Inc.), 4 a year).

Physical Sciences

Geoscience Society of New Zealand: POB 38951, Wellington Mail Centre; e-mail admin@gsnz.org.nz; internet www.gsnz.org.nz; f. 1955 by merger of New Zealand Geophysical Soc.; encourages the advancement of geological sciences in NZ; confs, lecture series, field trips, br. meetings; 8 brs; 740 mems; Pres. JAN LINDSAY; Vice-Pres. ANDREW GORMAN; Vice-Pres. SCOTT NODDER; Sec. KAT HOLT; Treas. DAVID SKINNER.

Meteorological Society of New Zealand: POB 6523, Marion Sq., Wellington; internet metsoc.rsnz.org; f. 1979; 300 mems; Pres. MIKE REVELL; Sec. SIMON KJELLBERG; publ. *Weather and Climate* (1 a year).

New Zealand Geophysical Society (Inc.): POB 30368, Lower Hutt; tel. (4) 570-1444; fax (4) 570-4603; internet www.gns.cri.nz; f. 1980; now merged with the Geological Soc. of New Zealand to form the Geoscience Soc. of New Zealand; 140 mems; Pres. G. LAMARCHE; Sec. CAROLINE HOLDEN.

New Zealand Institute of Chemistry (Inc.): c/o Richard Rendle, POB 39-112, Harewood, Christchurch; tel. (3) 359-7275; fax (3) 359-7248; e-mail nzic.office@nzic.org.nz; internet www.nzic.org.nz; f. 1931; 1,000 mems; promotes the study, practice, teaching and management of chemistry; 6 brs; Pres. KEITH GORDON; Hon. Gen. Sec. RICHARD RENDLE; publ. *Chemistry in New Zealand* (4 a year).

New Zealand Institute of Physics: c/o Geoff Willmott, Industrial Research Ltd, POB 31-310, Lower Hutt; e-mail secretary@nzip.org.nz; internet www.nzip.org.nz; promotes the study, practice and teaching of physics; 6 brs; 310 mems; Pres. Dr BEN RUCK; Sec. Dr GEOFF WILLMOTT; Treas. Prof. MICHELE GOVERNALE.

New Zealand Society for Biochemistry and Molecular Biology (Inc.): Animal and Food Sciences Div., Lincoln Univ., POB 84, Canterbury; 400 mems (230 full mems, 170 student mems); Pres. Prof. DAVID PALMER; Sec. JIM MORTON; publ. *NZ BioScience* (4 a year).

Royal Astronomical Society of New Zealand (Inc.): POB 3181, Wellington; e-mail secretary@rasnz.org.nz; internet www.rasnz.org.nz; f. 1920, Royal Charter 1946; promotion and extension of knowledge of astronomy and related branches of science; 200 mems; Pres. G. ROWE; Exec. Sec. RORY O'KEEFFE; publ. *Southern Stars* (4 a year).

PHILOSOPHY AND PSYCHOLOGY

New Zealand Psychological Society (Inc.): POB 4092, Wellington 6140; tel. (4)

473-4884; fax (4) 473-4889; e-mail office@psychology.org.nz; internet www.psychology.org.nz; f. 1967; promotes the discipline of psychology as a science, high standards of ethical and professional practice, and provides professional support and devt to mems.; 1,000 full mems, 200 student and subscriber mems.; Exec. Dir Dr PAMELA HYDE; publs *NZ Journal of Psychology* (3 a year, online), *Professional Practice of Psychology in Aotearoa New Zealand*, *Psychology Aotearoa* (2 a year).

RELIGION, SOCIOLOGY AND ANTHROPOLOGY

Polynesian Society:; tel. (9) 373-7599 ext. 87463; fax (9) 373-5409; e-mail jps@auckland.ac.nz; internet www.arts.auckland.ac.nz/ant/jps/polysoc.html; f. 1892; promotes studies and publs about the Polynesians and other Pacific peoples past and present; library deposited in the Alexander Turnbull Library; 1,000 mems; Pres. Dr RICHARD BENTON; Hon. Sec. RANGIMARIE RAWIRI; publs *Journal* (4 a year), *Memoirs* (irregular).

TECHNOLOGY

Institution of Professional Engineers New Zealand: POB 12241, 101 Molesworth St, Wellington; tel. (4) 473-9444; fax (4) 474-8933; e-mail ipenz@ipenz.org.nz; internet www.ipenz.org.nz; f. 1914; 9,300 mems; 15 brs; Pres. Dr IAN PARTON; Chief Exec. Dr ANDREW CLELAND; publ. *e.nz* (6 a year).

New Zealand Computer Society (Inc.): Ground Fl., 158 The Terrace, Wellington; tel. (4) 473-1043; fax (4) 473-1025; e-mail nzcs@nzcs.org.nz; internet www.nzcs.org.nz; f. 1960; develops the professional skills of its members and promotes excellence in information and communication technology; 1,650 mems; Pres. RICHARD DONALDSON; Chief Exec. DOUGLAS WHITE.

New Zealand Hydrological Society: POB 12300, Thorndon, Wellington 6144; tel. and fax (3) 319-7211; e-mail admin@hydrologynz.org.nz; internet www.hydrologynz.org.nz; f. 1961; publishes books; organizes annual conf.; 570 mems.; Pres. JOSEPH THOMAS; Sec. GIL ZEMANSKY; Admin. LINDSAY ROWE; publ. *Journal of Hydrology (New Zealand)* (2 a year).

New Zealand Society for Earthquake Engineering: POB 2193, Wellington, 6140; tel. (4) 565-3650; e-mail exec@nzsee.org.nz; internet www.nzsee.org.nz; f. 1968; promotes the advancement of the science and practice of earthquake engineering, and cooperation among scientists, engineers and other professionals in the field; 700 mems; Pres. PETER WOOD; Sec. DEREK WILSHIRE; publ. *Bulletin* (4 a year).

Operational Research Society of New Zealand (Inc.): POB 6544, Wellesley St, Auckland; internet www.orsnz.org.nz; f. 1964; promotes operational research and management science in New Zealand in both academic and industrial aspects; 150 mems; Pres. DAVID RYAN; Sec. GEOFFREY PRITCHARD.

Research Institutes

AGRICULTURE, FISHERIES AND VETERINARY SCIENCE

AgResearch: 5th Fl., Tower Block, Ruakura Research Centre, East St, Private Bag 3123, Hamilton; tel. (7) 834-6600; fax (7) 834-6640; internet www.agresearch.co.nz; f. 1992 as New Zealand Pastoral Agriculture Research Institute Ltd; groups for Agriculture and Environment, Applied Biotechnologies and for Food and Health; Chief Exec. ANDREW WEST; publ. *AgResearch Now* (4 a year).

Plant & Food Research – New Zealand Institute for Plant & Food Research, Ltd: Private Bag 92169, 120 Mt Albert Rd, Mt Albert, Auckland 1142; tel. (9) 926-3543; fax (9) 925-7001; internet www.plantandfood.co.nz; f. 2008 by merger of HortResearch—Horticulture and Food Research Institute of New Zealand, Ltd (f. 1992) and New Zealand Institute for Crop and Food Research Ltd (f. 1992); integrated fruit research using resources in fruit, plants and sustainable production systems to develop technologies and innovative fruit and food products; library of 16,000 monograph titles, 5,500 periodical titles.

Scion Research: Private Bag 3020, Rotorua 3201; tel. (7) 343-5899; fax (7) 358-0952; e-mail info@scionresearch.com; internet www.scionresearch.com; f. 1947; a govt-owned Crown Research Institute providing research and technology development for the forestry and wood products industries as well as focusing on the development of biomaterials from plants; library of 300,000 vols (incl. monographs and periodicals); Chief Exec. Dr WARREN PARKER; Librarian CLAIRE MILLER; publ. *NZ Journal of Forestry Science* (3 a year).

New Zealand Institute of Food Science and Technology (Inc.): POB 5574, Terrace End, Palmerston North; tel. (6) 356-1686; fax (6) 356-1687; e-mail rosemary@nzifst.org.nz; internet www.nzifst.org.nz; f. 1965; professional body for the food science and technology industry in NZ; divs of dairy, food marketing, food safety, nutrition and sensory evaluation; regular branch meetings, technical sessions and an annual conference; education and vocational guidance for young people; 1,000 student, standard and professional mems; Pres. DAVID POOCH; Exec. Man. ROSEMARY HANCOCK; publs *Food NZ* (6 a year), *NZIFST Nibbles* (e-mail bulletin, 26 a year).

ECONOMICS, LAW AND POLITICS

New Zealand Institute of Economic Research: 8 Halswell St, Thorndon, POB 3479, Wellington; tel. (4) 472-1880; fax (4) 472-1211; e-mail econ@nzier.org.nz; internet www.nzier.org.nz; f. 1958; economic consultation, forecasting and research in New Zealand and overseas; Dir BRENT LAYTON; Chief Exec. JEAN-PIERRE DE RAAD; Chair. MICHAEL WALLS; publs *New Zealand Industry and Regions* (1 a year), *Quarterly Predictions* (4 a year), *Quarterly Survey of Business Opinion* (4 a year), *Update* (12 a year).

EDUCATION

New Zealand Council for Educational Research: 10th Fl., West Block, Education House, 178–182 Willis St, POB 3237, Wellington; tel. (4) 384-7939; fax (4) 384-7933; internet www.nzcer.org.nz; f. 1934; fosters the study of, and research into, educational matters; prepares and publishes reports for teachers and others in the profession; library of 7,900 vols; Chair. Dr MARY HILL; Dir ROBYN BAKER; publs *Curriculum Matters* (1 a year), *New Zealand Annual Review of Education* (2 a year), *New Zealand Journal of Educational Studies* (2 a year), *set—Research Information for Teachers* (2 a year).

MEDICINE

Auckland Medical Research Foundation: Level 8, Bldg 13, Greenlane Clinical Centre, Private Bag 92189, Auckland 1010; tel. (9) 923-1701; fax (9) 362-0458; internet www.medicalresearch.co.nz; f. 1956; financed by public subscription to sponsor and encourage medical research; Chair. BRUCE COLE; Exec. Dir KIM MCWILLIAMS.

Canterbury Medical Research Foundation: Van der Veer Institute, POB 2682, 16 St Asaph St, Christchurch; tel. (3) 378-6052; fax (3) 378-6057; e-mail health@cmrf.org.nz; internet www.cmrf.org.nz; f. 1960; promotion and support of all aspects of medical research; privately financed; Pres. ROBERT JOHNSON; Dir GUY STEWART.

Hawke's Bay Medical Research Foundation (Inc.): POB 596, Napier; tel. and fax (6) 879-9199; e-mail jmbax@xtra.co.nz; internet www.hawkesbaymedicalresearch.org.nz; f. 1961 to foster and support medical research and health education in and outside Hawke's Bay; Pres. ANDREW WARES; Sec. J. M. BAXTER.

Health Research Council of New Zealand: POB 5541, Wellesley St, Auckland; tel. (9) 379-8227; fax (9) 377-9988; e-mail info@hrc.govt.nz; internet www.hrc.govt.nz; f. 1990; initiates, funds and supports health research; advises the govt on issues of health research ethics; Chair. Prof. GRAEME FRASER; Chief. Exec. Dr BRUCE SCOGGINS; publs *Ethics Notes* (irregular), *HRC News* (3 a year), *Panui* (Maori health research issues, irregular), *Update* (e-mail bulletin, 26 a year).

Palmerston North Medical Research Foundation: c/o POB 648, Palmerston North; tel. (6) 357-0640; fax (6) 358-9105; e-mail ml@naylorlawrence.co.nz; internet www.pnmrf.org.nz; f. 1959; privately financed; gen. medical research; Sec. MICHAEL LAWRENCE.

Wellington Medical Research Foundation: c/o The Secretary, POB 51-211, Wellington; tel. (4) 232-5475; fax (4) 232-5494; e-mail info@wmrf.co.nz; internet www.wmrf.co.nz; f. 1960; privately financed; supports all forms of medical research; Sec. ROSS MACDONALD.

NATURAL SCIENCES

Biological Sciences

Cawthron Institute: 98 Halifax St East, Private Bag 2, Nelson; tel. (3) 548-2319; fax (3) 546-9464; e-mail info@cawthron.org.nz; internet www.cawthron.org.nz; f. 1919; scientific and technological research into the management and development of New Zealand's coastal and freshwater systems; library of 4,500 vols; Chief Exec. GILLIAN WRATT; publ. *Cawthron Lectures* (1 a year).

Institute of Environmental Science and Research Ltd (ESR): Kenepuru Science Centre, 34 Kenepuru Dr., POB 50-348, Porirua, Wellington; tel. (4) 914-0700; fax (4) 914-0770; e-mail enquiries@esr.cri.nz; internet www.esr.cri.nz; f. 1992; provides scientific research and consulting services related to public health, environmental health and forensic science to public and private sectors in New Zealand and the Asia-Pacific region; research centres in Auckland, Wellington and Christchurch; Chief Exec. Dr JOHN HAY; publ. *Briefing Newsletter* (2 a year).

Landcare Research New Zealand Ltd: Canterbury Agriculture and Science Centre, Gerald St, POB 40, Lincoln; tel. (3) 325-6700; fax (3) 325-2127; internet www.landcareresearch.co.nz; f. 1992 as a Crown Research Institute (CRI); research, consultancy services and technology devt focused on enhancing natural, productive and urban environments to ensure the future economic prosperity of New Zealand; other activities incl. environmental sciences, remote-sensing and GIS; attached specialist library; Chief Exec. Dr WARREN PARKER; publ. *Discovery* (4 a year).

Physical Sciences

Carter Observatory: POB 2909, Wellington; tel. (4) 472-8167; fax (4) 472-8230; e-mail info@carterobs.ac.nz; internet www.carterobs.ac.nz; f. 1938; the nat. observatory; astronomical research and planetarium; nat. centre for receipt and distribution of astronomical information; co-operation with schools, colleges and universities for education in astronomy; library of 20,000 vols, 434 journals; Chair. RICHARD J. BENTLEY; Senior Astronomer BRIAN CARTER.

GNS Science: POB 30-368, Lower Hutt; 1 Fairway Dr., Avalon, Lower Hutt; tel. (4) 570-1444; fax (4) 570-4600; e-mail webmaster@gns.cri.nz; internet www.gns.cri.nz; f. 1865 as New Zealand Geological Survey; DSIR Geology & Geophysics 1990; Institute of Geological and Nuclear Sciences Ltd 1992; GNS Science 1995; a crown research institute; earth and isotope research and consultancy; maintains collns of rocks, minerals and fossils of NZ and other countries, including Suter colln of NZ Mollusca; responsible for nat. geological mapping, geophysics and hazard studies, and all applied geology incl. petroleum exploration, geothermal energy, and groundwater; 340 staff; library of 40,000 vols, 15,000 photos; Chair. CON ANASTASIOU; Chief Exec. Dr ALEX MALAHOFF; publs *Globe Magazine* (1 a year), *NZ Volcanological Record* (1 a year).

Mount John University Observatory: POB 56, Lake Tekapo 8770; tel. (3) 680-6000; fax (3) 680-6005; e-mail mjuo@phys.canterbury.ac.nz; internet www.phys.canterbury.ac.nz/research/astronomy; f. 1963; operated by Univ. of Canterbury; research especially into variable stars, stellar spectroscopy and gravitational microlensing; 4 telescopes in total with apertures of 1.8 m, 1.0 m and 2 of 0.6 m; Dir Prof. J. B. HEARNSHAW.

National Institute of Water and Atmospheric Research Ltd–NIWA: Private Bag 99940, 41 Market Pl., Viaduct Harbour, 1149 Auckland; tel. (9) 375-2090; fax (9) 375-2091; e-mail scicomm@niwa.co.nz; internet www.niwa.co.nz; f. 1992; manages and makes use of the natural environment in a sustainable manner; Nat. Climate Centre; Nat. Centre for Fisheries and Aquaculture; Nat. Centre for Climate–Energy Solutions; Nat. Centre for Water Resources; Nat. Centre for Aquatic Biodiversity and Biosecurity; Nat. Centre for Coasts and Oceans; Natural Hazards Centre; Chief Exec. Dr RICK PRIDMORE.

New Plymouth Astronomical Society Observatory: POB 818, New Plymouth; e-mail kruseco@xtra.co.nz; f. 1920; 60 mems; Sec. ROBYN CADE; Treas. MICHAEL KRUSE.

TECHNOLOGY

New Zealand Institute for Industrial Research and Development (Industrial Research Ltd): Gracefield Research Centre, 69 Gracefield Rd, POB 31-310, Lower Hutt 5040; tel. (4) 931-3000; fax (4) 566-6004; e-mail info@irl.cri.nz; internet www.irl.cri.nz; f. 1992; Crown Research Institute; conducts research and devt into science and technology, and advises on implementing its results commercially; Chair. BRIAN RHOADES; Chief Exec. SHAUN COFFEY.

Libraries and Archives

Auckland

Auckland Libraries: POB 92300, Auckland 1142; tel. (9) 377-0209; fax (9) 307-7741; e-mail allison.dobbie@aucklandcouncil.govt.nz; internet www.aucklandlibraries.govt.nz; f. 1880, merger of local authorities in Auckland region 2010; 54 community libraries,4 mobile libraries, central library; libraries of Auckland, Franklin, Manukau, North Shore, Papakura, Rodney, and Waitakere; 3,400,000 vols, incls approx. 3.4m. books, music scores, music sound recordings, and DVD and video cassettes; 133 online databases; spec. collns incl. founding donation from Sir George Grey; medieval MSS, incunabula, early printed books, maps, sheet music, photographs, early Maori MSS and printed works; Man. ALLISON DOBBIE.

University of Auckland Library: Private Bag 92019, Auckland; tel. (9) 373-7999; fax (9) 373-7565; internet www.library.auckland.ac.nz; f. 1884; 2,215,000 vols; consists of General Library, 9 divisional libraries and 12 subject specialist libraries, 3 Information Commons facilities; Librarian JANET COPSEY.

Christchurch

Christchurch City Libraries: POB 3845 Christchurch 8140; tel. (3) 941-7459; fax (3) 941-7075; e-mail library@ccc.govt.nz; internet christchurchcitylibraries.com; f. 1859; 19 libraries and 1 mobile library; 1,105,903 vols, incl. 360,000 vols; Library Man. CAROLYN ROBERTSON; Librarian for Serials and Preservation COLLEEN FINNERTY.

Library, Teaching and Learning George Forbes Memorial Library Lincoln University: POB 64, Lincoln Univ., Lincoln, Canterbury 7647; tel. (3) 325-2811; fax (3) 325-2944; internet library.lincoln.ac.nz; f. 1960; specializes in agriculture, commerce and management, primary production, science and engineering, social sciences incl. landscape architecture, and tourism, environment and natural resource management; 229,657 vols, 114,504 books, 1,357 current print periodicals, 53,336 electronic periodicals; Univ. Librarian Prof. PENNY CARNABY; publ. *Lincoln University Research Archive*.

University of Canterbury Library: Private Bag 4800, Christchurch; tel. (3) 366-7001; fax (3) 364-2055; e-mail helpdesk@libr.canterbury.ac.nz; internet library.canterbury.ac.nz; f. 1873; 1,800,000 items; spec. collns incl. Macmillan Brown Colln of New Zealand and Pacific Materials; Univ. Librarian S. MCKNIGHT.

Dunedin

Dunedin Public Libraries: POB 5542, Moray Pl., Dunedin; tel. (3) 474-3690; fax (3) 474-3660; e-mail library@dcc.govt.nz; internet www.dunedinlibraries.com; f. 1908; 709,992 vols; heritage collns incl. McNab New Zealand colln (90,509 vols) and numerous spec. collns, incl. illuminated MSS and Bibles, Samuel Johnson, Sir Walter Scott, Charles Dickens, Walt Whitman, Farjeon, hymn books, autographed letters; Library Services Man. BERNIE HAWKE.

New Zealand Law Society Library, Otago Branch: Private Bag 1901, Dunedin; tel. (3) 477-0596; fax (3) 474-1886; e-mail otago@nzlslibrary.org.nz; internet www.lawsociety.org.nz/home/for_lawyers/law_library; f. 1859; 13,500 vols, consisting of statutes, regulations, law reports, unreported judgments, treaties; and a representative selection of New Zealand secondary sources (textbooks, law journals, dictionaries and encyclopedias); Librarian KIRSTEN FRANCIS.

University of Otago Library: POB 56, Dunedin 9054; tel. (3) 479-8932; fax (3) 479-8947; e-mail library@otago.ac.nz; internet www.library.otago.ac.nz; f. 1869; Consists of several libraries: Central (arts, humanities, social sciences, commerce), Law, Dental, Medical, Science, Education, Hocken (major NZ and Pacific research collns incl. archives, pictorial collns, exhibition gallery); special collns incl. early European imprints, de Beer Exhibition Gallery and Otakou Press; 1,094,165 vols, 525,512 serials, 6,813 (print) titles, 111,919 (electronic); Librarian HOWARD AMOS.

Hamilton

University of Waikato Library: Private Bag 3105, Hamilton 3240; tel. (7) 838-4111; fax (7) 838-4017; e-mail library@waikato.ac.nz; internet www.waikato.ac.nz/library; f. 1964; incorporates Central, Education, Law and Map libraries, and New Zealand Colln; 857,540 print vols, 1,807 print serial titles and 76,000 electronic resources; Librarian ROSS HALLETT.

Palmerston North

Palmerston North City Library: POB 1948, Palmerston North; tel. (6) 351-4100; fax (6) 351-4102; e-mail pncl@pncc.govt.nz; internet citylibrary.pncc.govt.nz; f. 1876; 250,000 vols; lending, reference, children's, audio-visual, archives sections; 4 brs; 1 mobile library; Librarian ANTHONY LEWIS.

Tauranga

Tauranga City Libraries: Private Bag 12022, Tauranga 3143; Library Arcade, Willow St, Tauranga; tel. (7) 577-7177; fax (7) 578-6787; e-mail library@tauranga.govt.nz; internet library.tauranga.govt.nz; f. 1906 from Mechanics Institute (f. 1871); reference, New Zealand and local history collns; 4 brs, 1 mobile; 300,000 items; General Man., Libraries JILL BEST.

Wellington

Archives New Zealand: POB 12-050, Wellington; located at: 10 Mulgrave St, Wellington; tel. (4) 499-5595; fax (4) 495-6210; e-mail info@archives.govt.nz; internet www.archives.govt.nz; f. 1926; attached to Dept of Internal Affairs; 76,652 linear metres of archives, 1,578,074 photographs, 21,987 films and video cassettes, 534,368 maps and plans; legislative, exec. and judicial records of New Zealand govt (incl. provincial govts); ministerial papers; Nat. War Art Colln; Treaty of Waitangi; public reference services in Wellington and at regional offices in Auckland, Christchurch and Dunedin; gateway at Wellington office; Chief Archivist and Gen. Man. JOHN ROBERTS (acting).

Museum of New Zealand, Te Papa Tongarewa, Te Aka Matua Research Library: Cable St, Wellington; tel. (4) 381-7000; fax (4) 381-7370; e-mail library@tepapa.govt.nz; internet tinyurl.com/te-aka-matua-library; f. 1867; 150,000 vols; Knowledge Man. SHARMAN BUCKLE.

National Library of New Zealand, Te Puna Matauranga o Aotearoa, The Department of Internal Affairs Te Tari Taiwhenua: POB 1467, Wellington 6140; tel. (4) 474-3000; fax (4) 474-3035; e-mail information@dia.govt.nz; internet www.natlib.govt.nz; f. 1966; 940,863 vols, 10,466 current print periodical titles, 12 main microform collns, 16,812 audio titles in the Gen. Collns, 778 e-books, 35 databases, 33,418 e-journals, 593,249 items in the schools collns; Nat. Librarian BILL MACNAUGHT.

Constituent Library:

Alexander Turnbull Library: POB 12-349, Wellington 6144; tel. (4) 474-3120; fax (4) 474-3063; e-mail alexander.turnbull-library@dia.govt.nz; internet www.natlib.govt.nz; f. 1920; spec. collns incl. New Zealand and the Pacific, Milton, Katherine Mansfield; 30,000 oral history audio cassettes; 10,000 linear metre of

MSS; 105,000 drawings, paintings, prints and cartoons; 4,964,446 photographic prints, negatives and albums; 60,000 maps; 50,000 sound recordings; 7,000 video cassettes; 1,100 computer files; 195,000 items of ephemera (incl. 19,500 posters); 458,000 newspaper issues; 1,216,000 vols of periodicals; 3,740 music scores; 30,000 online publs; 3,500 websites; 387,500 vols, incl. 32,000 rare books, chiefly in English literature; Chief Librarian CHRIS SZEKELY; publs *Off the Record* (1 a year), *Turnbull Library Record* (1 a year).

Parliamentary Library: PMB 18041, Parliament Bldgs, Wellington 6160; tel. (4) 817-9647; fax (4) 471-2551; e-mail parlinfo@parliament.govt.nz; internet www.parliament.nz; f. 1858; research, reference and information services for mems of parliament and parliamentary staff; services to the public incl. Parliamentary Information Service and Int. Documents Service; 500,000 vols, spec. collns: New Zealand, incl. official publs, overseas official and parliamentary publs; Parliamentary Librarian and Group Man., Information and Knowledge MOIRA FRASER; publs *Bills Digests* (online), *Electorate Profiles* (online), *Research Papers* (online), *Monthly Economic Review* (online).

Victoria University of Wellington Library: POB 3438, Wellington; tel. (4) 463-5249; fax (4) 471-2070; e-mail library@vuw.ac.nz; internet www.vuw.ac.nz/library; f. 1899; 1,000,000 printed vols; 25,000 current print and electronic periodicals; Univ. Librarian SUE ROBERTS.

Wellington City Libraries: POB 1992, Wellington; tel. (4) 801-4040; fax (4) 801 4047; e-mail librariesadmin@wcc.govt.nz; internet www.wcl.govt.nz; f. 1893; 600,000 vols, 450,000 bound periodicals, 85,000 audiovisual items; 12 br. libraries; Man., Libraries JANE HILL.

Museums and Art Galleries

Auckland

Auckland Art Gallery Toi o Tāmaki: POB 5449, Auckland 1; tel. (9) 307-7700; fax (9) 302-1096; e-mail gallery@aucklandartgallery.govt.nz; internet www.aucklandartgallery.govt.nz; f. 1888; European paintings since 12th century, sculpture, prints and drawings, Frances Hodgkins colln, Colin McCahon colln, Fuseli drawings, New Zealand painting since 19th century, sculpture and prints; photographs and artists' books, audio- and video-tapes; John Weeks archive; library: research library of 33,000 vols; Dir CHRIS SAINES.

Auckland War Memorial Museum: Private Bag 92018, Auckland 1142; tel. (9) 306-7076; fax (9) 379-9956; e-mail info@aucklandmuseum.com; internet www.aucklandmuseum.com; f. 1852; natural history, ethnology (especially NZ Maori and Oceanic), applied arts (especially Asian, European and NZ ceramics, English furniture, textiles), social and war history; conservation laboratory; war memorial for the province; library of 100,000 vols; Dir (vacant); Library Services Man. BRUCE RALSTON; publs *Bulletin* (irregular), *Records* (1 a year).

Museum of Transport and Technology (MOTAT): Great North Rd, Western Springs, Auckland; tel. (9) 815-5800; fax (9) 846-4242; e-mail enquiries@motat.org.nz; internet www.motat.org.nz; f. 1964; operates on 2 sites, exhibiting vehicles, aircraft, machinery and equipment of historical and technical interest, incl. an extensive aircraft colln, vintage agricultural and military vehicles, steam and diesel engines, a working tram line and travelling exhibitions; library: Walsh Memorial Library 12,000 vols, 1,500 serial titles, technical manuals, photographs, maps, plans, archives, Whites Aviation Photographic prints, archives relating to pioneer aviators Jean Batten and Richard Pearse, Les Downey rail photograph colln, Air New Zealand, TEAL, National Airways Corpn, New Zealand Flying School Archives; Dir JEREMY HUBBARD.

Christchurch

Canterbury Museum: Rolleston Ave, Christchurch 8013; tel. (3) 366-5000; fax (3) 366-5622; e-mail info@canterburymuseum.com; internet www.canterburymuseum.com; f. 1867; cultural and natural history of the Canterbury region, in NZ and global contexts; Antarctic age of discovery and exploration; archaeology, ethnology, geology, zoology, extinct bird studies; Asian and European arts; Canterbury archives; pictorial history; library: research library, and spec. research library on the Antarctic; Dir ANTHONY E. WRIGHT; publ. *Records of the Canterbury Museum* (1 a year).

Christchurch Art Gallery Te Puna o Waiwhetu: Worcester Blvd, Christchurch 8001; tel. (3) 941-7300; fax (3) 941-7301; internet www.christchurchartgallery.org.nz; f. 1932, as Robert McDougall Art Gallery and McDougall Contemporary Art Annex, present name and location 2003; one of the largest art collns in New Zealand; nat. and int. touring exhibitions; works by local artists; Dir JENNY HARPER; publ. *Bulletin* (4 a year).

Dunedin

Dunedin Public Art Gallery: 30 The Octagon, POB 566, Dunedin; tel. (3) 474-3240; fax (3) 474-3250; e-mail dpagmail@dcc.govt.nz; internet www.dunedin.art.museum; f. 1884; maintains a conservation laboratory; holdings incl.: 14th–19th century European paintings, NZ paintings from 1870, Australian paintings 1900–70, British watercolours, portraits and landscapes; Japanese prints since the 18th century, NZ prints since the 19th century; old and modern masters, incl. oils by Claude Lorrain and Monet; decorative arts collns of furniture, ceramics, glass, oriental rugs, gallery dedicated to works of painter Frances Hodgkins; Dir PRISCILLA PITTS.

Otago Museum: 419 Great King St, POB 6202, Dunedin; tel. (3) 474-7474; fax (3) 477-5993; internet www.otagomuseum.govt.nz; f. 1868; natural sciences, NZ and Pacific anthropology, classical archaeology, European and Asian ceramics, 'Discovery World' Science Centre, NZ crafts, southern geology and fossils; Dir S. C. PAUL.

Theomin Gallery, Dunedin: 'Olveston', 42 Royal Terrace, Dunedin; tel. (3) 477-3320; fax (3) 479-2094; e-mail olveston@xtra.co.nz; internet www.olveston.co.nz; built 1904–06; Jacobean-style house designed by British architect Sir Ernest George for David Edward Theomin; bequeathed to the city by his daughter, Dorothy, 1966; opened to the public 1967; antique furniture, ceramics, crystal, bronzes, Persian rugs, silver, early English, European and NZ oils and watercolours; Man. GRANT BARRON.

Gisborne

Tairawhiti Museum: POB 716, Gisborne; Kelvin Rise, Stout St, Gisborne; tel. (6) 867-3832; fax (6) 867-2728; e-mail info@tairawhitimuseum.org.nz; internet www.tairawhitimuseum.org.nz; f. 1954; social history, Maori treasures (taonga Maori), fine arts, photography, surfboards, 'Star of Canada' wreck colln, natural history, oral history archive, textiles; local archives, cards and postcards, maps, plans, theatrical programmes; temporary exhibitions of fine arts and crafts, C-Co 12th Maori Battalion; Dir Dr DAVID BUTTS.

Gore

Eastern Southland Gallery (Inc.): Cnr Main and Norfolk Sts, POB 305, Gore, Southland; tel. (3) 208-9907; fax (3) 208-9968; e-mail jgeddes@goredc.govt.nz; f. 1983; exhibitions: art works, craft work, historical displays; cultural centre for presentation of films, lectures, music, poetry, etc.; Dir JIM GEDDES; publ. *Activities Bulletin* (2 a year).

Hokitika

West Coast Historical Museum: Hamilton St, POB 171, Hokitika 7842, Westland; tel. (3) 755-6898; fax (3) 755-5011; e-mail enquiries@hokitikamuseum.co.nz; internet www.westland.govt.nz; f. 1960; social exhibits, working models; audiovisual programme on 19th-century West Coast gold-mining industry and colonial settlement; Poutini Maori and 19th-century immigrant histories; pounamu (NZ greenstone), gold; maintains research centre with local history archives and large photograph colln; Curator JULIA BRADSHAW.

Invercargill

Anderson Park Art Gallery (Inc.): POB 5095, Invercargill 9843; tel. (3) 215-7432; fax (3) 215-7472; e-mail andersonparkgallery@xtra.co.nz; f. 1951; mainly New Zealand works; Dir JOHN HUSBAND; Deputy Dir HELEN NICOLL.

Southland Museum and Art Gallery: 108 Gala St, Invercargill; tel. (3) 219-9069; fax (3) 218-3872; e-mail office@southlandmuseum.co.nz; internet www.southlandmuseum.com; f. 1915; natural history; Maori and colonial history; 'Victoriana'; 4 art galleries; astronomical observatory; Tuatara breeding colony; sub-Antarctic centre; education programmes; Man. GAEL RAMSAY.

Napier

Hawke's Bay Cultural Trust: POB 248, Napier; tel. (6) 835-7781; fax (6) 835-9249; e-mail info@hbmag.co.nz; internet www.hawkesbaymuseum.co.nz; f. 1989; Man. DOUGLAS LLOYD JENKINS.

Institutions Under the Trust's Control:

Faraday Centre: 1 Faraday St, Napier; tel. (6) 835-7781; fax (6) 835-9249; e-mail faraday@hbct.co.nz; internet www.faraday.hbmag.co.nz; f. 1979; science and technology education (stationary, hot-air and steam engines; steam traction engines, horse-drawn phaeton and hearse, bath-chairs; audio recording and broadcasting equipment; printing presses; early hospital and surgical equipment; high voltage displays, Wimshurst machine, Tesla coil); workshops for young people; Man. DAVID PREBENSEN.

Hawke's Bay Museum and Art Gallery: 9 Herschell St, Napier; tel. (6) 835-7781; fax (6) 835-9249; e-mail info@hbmag.co.nz; internet www.hbmag.co.nz; f. 1936; Maori and NZ art and material culture, painting, pottery and sculpture, decorative arts, 1931 earthquake and dinosaur exhibitions; regional archives; library; Museum Man. DOUGLAS LLOYD JENKINS.

Nelson

Nelson Provincial Museum: Town Acre 445, POB 853, Nelson; tel. (3) 548-9588; fax

(3) 548-9589; e-mail enquiries@museumnp.org.nz; internet www.nelsonmuseum.org.nz; f. 1841; Maori and European history; reference library, 1,200,000 photographs (since 1860s), archives (since 1840s).

The Suter Art Gallery te Aratoi o Whakatu: 208 Bridge St, POB 751, Nelson 7040; tel. (3) 548-4699; fax (3) 548-1236; e-mail info@thesuter.org.nz; internet www.thesuter.org.nz; f. 1895; New Zealand and international art works; early New Zealand watercolours; programme of exhibitions, events, performances and films; Dir JULIE CATCHPOLE; publ. *The Suter Programme* (4 a year).

Oamaru

Forrester Gallery: Waitaki District Council, Private Bag 50058, Oamaru; tel. (3) 434-1653; fax (3) 434-1654; internet www.forrestergallery.com; f. 1983; housed in a neo-classical building constructed in 1884; works of art and architectural drawings related to North Otago and New Zealand; programme of exhibitions and cultural events; Dir WARWICK SMITH.

Paihia

Waitangi Treaty Grounds: Waitangi National Trust, Paihia, Bay of Islands; tel. (9) 402-7437; fax (9) 402-8303; e-mail waitangiestate@waitangi.net.nz; internet www.waitangi.net.nz; f. 1932; historic Treaty House; carved Maori meeting house and war canoe; exhibits of NZ historical interest up to 1840; visitor centre complex and audiovisual programme on signing of Treaty of Waitangi between Maori Chiefs and British Crown on 6 February 1840; live Maori theatre and spec. education programmes; Retail and Business Man. ANDY LARSEN.

Timaru

Aigantighe Art Gallery: 49 Wai-iti Rd, Timaru; tel. (3) 688-4424; internet www.timaru.govt.nz/art-gallery; f. 1956; New Zealand and European paintings, prints, sculpture and ceramics; Dir FIONA CIARAN; publ. *Members' Newsletters* (4 a year).

Wanganui

Sarjeant Gallery: Queen's Park, POB 998, Wanganui; tel. (6) 349-0506; fax (6) 349-0507; e-mail info@sarjeant.queenspark.org.nz; internet www.sarjeant.org.nz; f. 1919; European and English watercolours since 18th century; representative New Zealand colln; Gilfillan colln, Barraud colln, drawings after Bernardino Poccetti, colln of First World War cartoons; contemporary Maori art; sculpture, particularly wooden photography; Colln Man. DENIS RAINFORTH.

Whanganui Regional Museum: POB 352, Watt St, Wanganui; tel. (6) 349-1110; fax (6) 347-6512; e-mail info@museum.queenspark.org.nz; internet www.wanganui-museum.org.nz; f. 1895; Taonga Maori, natural history, local social history; archives; Dir S. E. DELL.

Wellington

New Zealand Academy of Fine Arts: 1 Queens Wharf, Wellington; tel. (4) 499-8807; fax (4) 499-2612; e-mail info@nzafa.com; internet www.nzafa.com; f. 1882; art gallery promoting New Zealand artists and the visual arts in New Zealand through 8 annual exhibitions; Dir JUSTIN MORGAN; publ. *Academy Arts News* (4 a year).

Te Papa: Cable St, POB 467, Wellington; tel. (4) 381-7000; fax (4) 381-7070; e-mail mail@tepapa.govt.nz; internet www.tepapa.govt.nz; f. 1992 by merger of the Nat. Art Gallery and the Nat. Museum; art, history, Maori culture, natural environment; colln of Maori taonga, incl. Te Hau-ki-Turanga (oldest extant Maori building in NZ); Polynesian, Micronesian and Melanesian art and culture; paintings, drawings, graphic art, photography and sculpture by NZ and foreign artists; colls of works by Natalia Gontcharova, Frances Hodgkins, Raymond McIntyre and Colin McCahon; maintains Hector Library (systematic biology, ethnology, early European South Pacific exploration and art reference material); Chief Exec. (vacant).

Universities

AUCKLAND UNIVERSITY OF TECHNOLOGY

Private Bag, 92006, Auckland 1142

Telephone: (9) 917-9999
Fax: (9) 917-9981
Internet: www.aut.ac.nz

Founded 1895 as Auckland Technical School; became Seddon Memorial Technical College 1913, Auckland Technical Institute 1960, Auckland Institute of Technology 1989; present name 2000

State control

Academic year: January to December

Vice-Chancellor: Dr. DEREK MCCORMACK
Pro Vice-Chancellor for Learning and Teaching: Dr. ROBERT ALLEN
Pro Vice-Chancellor for Applied Humanities: NIGEL HEMMINGTON
Pro Vice-Chancellor for Research: Prof. IAN SHIRLEY
Pro Vice-Chancellor for Te Ahurei—Maori Devt: PARE KEIHA
Dir of Univ. Relations: VIVIEN SUTHERLAND BRIDGWATER
Univ. Librarian: Dr. LARRAINE SHEPHERD

Library of 244,746 vols
Number of teachers: 929
Number of students: 23,288 (22,796 undergraduate, 492 postgraduate)

DEANS

Faculty of Applied Humanities: Prof. NIGEL HEMMINGTON
Faculty of Business and Law: DES GRAYDON
Faculty of Design and Creative Technologies: Dr KATHRYN GARDEN
Faculty of Health and Environmental Sciences: Prof. MAX ABBOTT
Faculty of Science and Engineering: Prof. ROY GEDDES
Te Ara Poutama (Faculty of Maori Development): Assoc. Prof. PARE KEIHA

LINCOLN UNIVERSITY

POB 84, Lincoln Univ., Christchurch

Telephone: (3) 325-2811
Fax: (3) 325-2965
Internet: www.lincoln.ac.nz

Founded 1878, fmrly the Canterbury Agricultural College and from 1961 to 1989 Lincoln College, a constituent college of the Univ. of Canterbury, from 1990 an autonomous univ.

State control

Academic year: February to October

Chancellor: THOMAS LAMBIC
Vice-Chancellor: Prof. ROGER FIELD
Deputy Vice-Chancellor: Dr CHRIS KIRK
Librarian: ADRIANT DE GROOT

Library: see Libraries
Number of teachers: 219
Number of students: 3,323

Publications: *Alumni News* (1 a year), *Infolinc* (12 a year), *Landforms* (1 a year)

DEANS

Faculty of Agriculture and Life Sciences: Prof. BRUCE MCKENZIE
Faculty of Commerce: Dr PATRICK ALDWELL
Faculty of Environment, Society and Design: Dr STEFANIE RIXECKER

PROFESSORS

BOND, S., Property Studies
CONDRON, L., Biochemistry
CULLEN, R., Resource Economics
DI, H., Soil And Environmental Science
EASON, C., Wildlife Management
EDWARDS, G., Dairy Production
FALLOON, R., Plant And Food
HUGHLEY, K., Environmental Management
LIYANARACHICHI, G., Accounting
MATEAR, S., Marketing
MATUNGA, H., Maori Studies
MCKENZIE, B., Agronomy
MOOT, J., Crop And Pasture Physiology
PALMER, D., Biochemical Pathology
PERKINS, H., Human Geography
SAUNDERS, C., Economics
SMALLMAN, C., Business Management

MASSEY UNIVERSITY

Private Bag 11-222, Tennent Drive, Palmerston North 5301

Telephone: (6) 356-9099
Fax: (6) 350-2263
E-mail: contact@massey.ac.nz
Internet: www.massey.ac.nz

Founded 1926 as Massey Agricultural College and merged with the Palmerston North Branch of the Victoria Univ. of Wellington 1963; full autonomy granted 1964; absorbed Wellington Polytechnic 1998

State control

Academic year: February to November

Chancellor: N. J. GOULD
Vice-Chancellor: Prof. JUDITH KINNEAR
Deputy Vice-Chancellor for Academic Affairs: Prof. N. LONG
Deputy Vice-Chancellor for Research and External Relations: Prof. N. LONG
Univ. Registrar: S. D. MORRISS
Librarian: J. W. REDMAYNE

Number of teachers: 1,255
Number of students: 39,657

PRO VICE-CHANCELLORS

College of Business: Prof. JACK DOWDS
College of Design, Fine Arts and Music: Dr. D. A. JOINER
College of Education: Prof. L. MEYER
College of Humanities and Social Sciences: Prof. B. K. MACDONALD
College of Sciences: Prof. R. D. ANDERSON

PROFESSORS

ANDERSON, R. D., Sciences
BAILEY, W. C., Food Nutrition and Human Health
BARRY, T., Veterinary, Animal and Biomedical Sciences
BIRKBECK, J., Food Nutrition and Human Health
BLAIR, H. T., Veterinary, Animal and Biomedical Sciences
BODDY, J., Health Sciences
BRIGHT, G., Mechatronics
BRODIE, A. M., Fundamental Sciences
BROWN, I., History
CAHAN, S. F., Accountancy
CARRYER, J. B., Health Sciences
CHAMBERLAIN, K. P., Psychology
CHAPMAN, J. W., Learning and Teaching
CHATTERJEE, S., Applied and International Economics
CHETTY, S., Commerce
CHISTI, Y., Biotechnology

CLELAND, D. J., Technology and Engineering
CODD, J. A., Social and Policy Studies in Education
CORBALLIS, R. P., English and Media Studies
CRESSWELL, M. J., History, Philosophy and Politics
CROPP, G. M., Language Studies
CULLEN, J. L., Learning and Teaching
DAVIES, C., Particle Technology
DE BRUIN, A., Commerce
DEVLIN, M., Management
DURIE, M. H., Maori Studies
ENGELBRECHT, H.-J., Applied and International Economics
EVANS, I., Psychology
FIRTH, E. C., Veterinary, Animal and Biomedical Sciences
FLENLEY, J. R., People, Environment and Planning
FREYBURG, C., Information Systems
GARRICK, D. J., Veterinary, Animal and Biomedical Sciences
GENDALL, P. J., Marketing
GILL, H. S., Food, Nutrition and Animal Health
GUILFORD, W. G., Veterinary, Animal and Biomedical Sciences
HARGREAVES, R. V., Finance, Banking and Property Studies
HARKER, R. K., Education
HAWICK, K., Computer Science
HENDY, M. D., Mathematics
HERMANSSON, G. L., Health and Human Development
HEWETT, E. W., Food, Nutrition and Human Health
HODGSON, J., Natural Resources
HODGSON, R. M., Information Sciences and Technology
HOLMES, C. W., Veterinary, Animal and Biomedical Sciences
HOWE, K. R., History, Philosophy and Politics
HUNT, G. J., Aviation
HUNTER, J. J., Information and Mathematical Sciences
INKSON, J. H., Management and International Business
INKSON, K., Management and International Business
JAMESON, P., Plant Biology
LAGROW, S. J., Health Sciences
LAMBERT, D. M., Molecular Biosciences
LASWAD, F., Accountancy
LEATHERN, J., Neuropsychology
LOCK, A. J., Psychology
LONG, N., Psychology
MACDONALD, B. K., Humanities and Social Sciences
MCKIBBIN, R., Information and Mathematical Sciences
MCLACHLAN, R., Mathematics
MADDOX, I., Industrial Bioscience
MALLON, M., Human Resource Management
MEISTER, A. D., Applied and International Economics
MELLOR, D. J., Food, Nutrition and Human Health
MERRICK, P. L., Psychology
MILNE, K. S., Sciences
MOORE, C. I., Finance, Banking and Property Studies
MORGAN, S., Fine Arts
MORRIS, R. S., Veterinary, Animal and Biomedical Sciences
MOUGHAN, P. J., Food, Nutrition and Human Health
MUNFORD, R. E., Sociology, Social Policy and Social Work
MURPHY, B., Commerce
NASH, R., Social and Policy Studies in Education
OFFICER, D., Chemistry
ONO, K., Language Studies
OPENSHAW, R., Social and Policy Studies in Education
OVERTON, J. D., People, Environment and Planning
PARRY, D. A., Fundamental Sciences
PEARCE, N. E., Public Health Research
PENNY, E. D., Molecular Biosciences
PERERA, H. M. B., Accountancy
RAE, A. N., Applied and International Economics
REEVES, R., Chemistry
ROCHE, M., Health Sciences
ROSE, L. C., Commerce
SCHEWE, K.-D., Information Systems
SCOTT, D. B., Molecular Biosciences
SHOUKSMITH, G., Psychology
SIGNAL, A., Physics
SINGH, H., Food, Nutrition and Human Health
SISSONS, J. D., People, Environment and Planning
SPOONLEY, P., Social and Cultural Studies
SPRINGETT, B. P., Natural Resources
STABLEIN, R., Management
SULLIVAN, P. A., Molecular Biosciences
TENNANT, M., Health Sciences
THOMSON, D. W., History, Philosophy and Politics
TILLMAN, R. W., Natural Resources
TRAWICK, M. J., People, Environment and Planning
TUNMER, W. E., Learning and Teaching
VAN DER WALT, N. T., Management and International Business
VITALIS, T., Management
WATERS, J., Chemistry
WILLIAMSON, N. B., Veterinary, Animal and Biomedical Sciences
WINGER, R. J., Food, Nutrition and Human Health

UNIVERSITY OF AUCKLAND

PMB 92019, Auckland 1142
Telephone: (9) 373-7999
Fax: (9) 373-7400
E-mail: contactus@auckland.ac.nz
Internet: www.auckland.ac.nz

Founded 1882 as Auckland University College; university status 1962
Academic year: January to November
Chancellor: ROGER FRANCE
Pro-Chancellor: LINDSAY CORBAN
Vice-Chancellor: Prof. STUART MCCUTCHEON
Deputy Vice-Chancellor for Academic Affairs: Prof. JOHN MORROW
Deputy Vice-Chancellor for Research: Prof. JANE HARDING
Registrar: TIM GREVILLE
Dir of Admin.: ADRIENNE CLELAND
Library: see under Libraries and Archives
Number of teachers: 1,981 (full-time)
Number of students: 38,551
Publication: *University of Auckland Research Report* (1 a year)

DEANS

Faculty of Arts: Assoc. Prof. JAN CROSTHWAITE
Business School: Prof. GREG WHITTRED
Nat. Institute of Creative Arts and Industries: Prof. JENNY DIXON
Faculty of Education: Assoc. Prof. GRAEME AITKEN
Faculty of Engineering: Prof. MICHAEL DAVIES
Faculty of Law: Prof. PAUL RISHWORTH
Faculty of Medical and Health Sciences: Prof. IAIN MARTIN
Faculty of Science: Prof. GRANT GUILFORD
School of Theology: Prof. ELAINE WAINWRIGHT (Head)

PROFESSORS

ADAMS, P., Applied Behavioural Science
ANAE, M., Pacific Studies
ANDERSON, C. A., Medicine
ASHER, I., Paediatrics
AUSTIN, G. L., Physics
BAKER, E. N., Biological Sciences, Chemistry
BAKER, M., Sociology
BELICH, J. C., History
BELLAMY, A. R., Biological Sciences
BHATTACHARYYA, D., Mechanical Engineering
BISHOP, J. C., Philosophy
BLACK, P. M., Geology
BOOTH, G., Creative and Performing Arts
BOOTH, R., Molecular Medicine and Pathology
BOWMAKER, G., Chemistry
BOWMAN, R. G., Accounting and Finance
BOXALL, P., Management and Employment Relations
BOYS, J. T., Electrical and Electronic Engineering
BRIMBLE, M. A., Chemistry
BRODIE, R. J., Marketing
BROWETT, P., Pathology
BROWNE, P., Geology
BYBLEW, W., Sport and Exercise Science
CALUDE, C. S., Computer Science
CANNELL, M., Physiology
CARMICHAEL, H., Physics
CARTER, I. R., Sociology
CARTWRIGHT, R. W., International Business
CHEN, J. J. J., Chemical and Materials Engineering
CHEN, X. D., Chemical and Materials Engineering
CLARK, G., Chemistry
CLARK, P. J. A., Chinese
CLARK, R. G., Molecular Medicine
COLLINS, I. F., Engineering Science
COOPER, G. J. S., Biological Sciences and Medicine
CORBALLIS, M. C., Psychology
CORRADO, C., Accounting and Finance
COSTER, G. D., General Practice
COVIELLO, N., Marketing
CRAIG, J. L., Geography and Environmental Science
CROSIER, K. E., Molecular Medicine and Pathology
CROSTHWAITE, J., European Languages and Literatures
DANAHER, P. J., Marketing
DAVISON, M. C., Psychology
DENNY, W., Cancer Society Research Centre
DIXON, J., Planning
DRAGUNOW, M., Pharmacology and Clinical Pharmacology
DUFFY, G. G., Chemical and Materials Engineering
DUNN, M. R., Fine Arts
DUNN, W., Business
DURING, M. J., Molecular Medicine
EAGLES, I. G., Commercial Law
ELLIS, R., Applied Language Studies and Linguistics
EMANUEL, D. M., Accounting and Finance
EVANS, P. J., Law
FAULL, R. L. M., Anatomy
FERGUSON, L., Auckland Cancer Society Research Centre
FERGUSON, W. G., Chemical and Materials Engineering
FLAY, R., Mechanical Engineering
FORER, P. C., Geography and Environmental Science
FRASER, J., Molecular Medicine
GAO, W., Chemicals and Materials Engineering
GARDNER, R. C., Biological Sciences
GAULD, D. B., Mathematics
GEERTSHUIS, S., Continuing Education
GILMOUR, R. S., Liggins Institute
GLUCKMAN, P. D., Liggins Institute
GONZALEZ-CASANOVAS, R., Spanish
GORMAN, D., Medicine
GRANTHAM, R., Commercial Law
GRAY, V. J., Classics and Ancient History
GRUNDY, J., Computer Science

GUSTAFSON, B. S., Political Studies
HAARHOF, E. J., Architecture
HARDING, J. E., Obstetrics and Gynaecology
HARRIS, B. V., Law
HARVEY, J. D., Physics
HATCHER, S., Psychiatry
HATTIE, J. A., Education
HAWORTH, N. A. F., International Business
HAZLEDINE, T. J., Economics
HOLLIS, S., English
HOOL, R. B., Economics
HORROCKS, R., Film, Television and Media Studies
HOSKING, J., Computer Science
HOUSLEY, G., Physiology
HUNT, J. G., Architecture
HUNTER, P. J., Bioengineering Institute
HURSTHOUSE, R., Philosophy
IRWIN, G. J., Anthropology
JACKSON, M. P., English
JACKSON, P. S., Mechanical Engineering
JACKSON, R., Community Health
JACOBS, R., Optometry and Vision Science
JENSEN, C., Anatomy with Radiology
KALLONIATIS, M., Optometry
KELSEY, J., Law
KILPATRICK, J., Nursing
KIRKNESS, A. C., Applied Language Studies and Linguistics
KISTLER, J., Biological Sciences
KLETTE, R., Computer Science
KYDD, R. R., Psychiatry
LARSEN, K., English
LEES, H., Music
LE HERON, R. B., Geography and Environmental Science
LENNON, D. R., Paediatrics
LIPSKI, J., Physiology
LORRIGAN, G., Business
LUCIANO, B., Italian
MCCARTHY, D. C., Psychology
MCCORMICK, R., Goodfellow Unit
MCGHEE, C., Ophthalmology
MCKECHNIE, P., Classics and Ancient History
MCNAUGHTON, S., Education
MACPHERSON, C., Sociology
MANTELL, C. D., Maori and Pacific Health
MARTIN, G. J., Mathematics
MARTIN, I., Surgery
MAXTON, J. K., Law
MELLSOP, G., South Auckland Clinical School
MELVILLE, B., Civil and Resource Engineering
MERRY, A., Anaesthesiology
MITCHELL, E. A., Paediatrics
MITCHELL, M. D., Pharmacology and Clinical Pharmacology
MOLLOY, M. A., Women's Studies
MONTGOMERY, J. C., Biological Sciences
MORIARTY, S., Accounting and Finance
MORROW, J., Political Studies
MUTU, M., Maori Studies
MYERS, M., Management Science and Information Systems
NEICH, R., Anthropology
NEILL, M. A. F., English
NEVILLE, R., Property
NICHOLSON, T., Education
O'CONNOR, C. J., Chemistry
O'SULLIVAN, M., Engineering Science
OWENS, R. G., Psychology
PARRY, B. R., Surgery
PAVLOV, B., Mathematics
PAXTON, J., Pharmacology and Clinical Pharmacology
PENDER, M. J., Civil and Resource Engineering
PERRY, N., Film, Television and Media Studies
PETERS, M., Education
PETRIE, K., Health Psychology
PHILPOTT, A., Engineering Science
POWELL, M. J., Management and Employment Relations
RAMSAY, R. L., French
RANKIN, E. A., Art History
REA, H. H., Medicine
REAY, B. G., History
REID, I. R., Medicine
REILLY, I. L., Mathematics
ROBINSON, V., Education
RUSSELL, D. K., Chemistry
RYAN, D. M., Engineering Science
SALCIC, Z., Electrical and Electronic Engineering
Dame SALMOND, M. A., Anthropology, Maori Studies
SCHWERDTFEGER, P., Chemistry
SCOTT, A. J., Statistics
SCOTT, D., Statistics
SCRIVEN, M., Education
SHARP, R. A., Political Studies
SHAW, J., Pharmacy
SHEPHEARD, C., Fine Arts
SIMPSON, I. J., Medicine
SLEIGH, J., Anaesthesia
SMALL, J., Economics
SMITH, G., Education
SMITH, L., Education
SMITH, W., Geography and Environmental Science
SPALINGER, A., Classics and Ancient History
SPICER, B. H., Accounting and Finance
SRINIVASAN, A., Management Science and Information Systems
STONE, P., Obstetrics and Gynaecology
STURM, T. L., English
SUTTON, D. G., Anthropology
TAGGART, M. B., Law
THOMAS, D. R., Community Health
THOMBORSON, C. D., Computer Science
THORNE, P., Audiology
TIBBLES, J., Music
TINDLE, C., Physics
VALE, B. A., Architecture
VOIT, F., German Languages and Literature
VOWLES, J., Political Studies
WAINWRIGHT, E., Theology
WATTS, P., Law
WELLS, R. M. G., Biological Sciences
WENDT, A., English
WILD, C., Statistics
WILLIAMS, P. W., Geography and Environmental Science
WILLIAMSON, A. G., Electrical and Electronic Engineering
WILSON, M. G., Management and Employment Relations
WILSON, M. J., Classics and Ancient History
WILSON, W., Auckland Cancer Society Research Centre
WILTON, R., Accounting and Finance
WONG, J., Accounting and Finance
ZHANG, Y., Asian Studies

UNIVERSITY OF CANTERBURY

Private Bag 4800, Christchurch 8140
Telephone: (3) 366-7001
Fax: (3) 364-2999
E-mail: info@canterbury.ac.nz
Internet: www.canterbury.ac.nz

Founded 1873
State control
Academic year: February to November

Chancellor: REX WILLIAMS
Vice-Chancellor: Dr ROD CARR
Deputy Vice-Chancellor: Prof. IAN TOWN
Asst Vice-Chancellor for Māori Affairs: Sir TIPENE O'REGAN
Registrar: JEFF FIELD
Chief Financial Officer: Dr YVONNE SHANAHAN
Dir of Human Resources: PAUL O'FLAHERTY
Pro Vice-Chancellor for Arts: Prof. ED ADELSON
Pro Vice-Chancellor for Business and Economics: Prof. NIGEL HEALEY
Pro Vice-Chancellor for Education: Prof. GAIL GILLON
Pro Vice-Chancellor for Engineering: Prof. PETER JACKSON
Pro Vice-Chancellor for Law: Prof. JAN EVANS-FREEMAN
Pro Vice-Chancellor for Science: Prof. PAUL FLEMING
Pro Vice-Chancellor for Int./Student Services: Dr NELLO ANGERILLI
Pro Vice-Chancellor for Learning Resources: Prof. SUE MCKNIGHT
Librarian: GAIL PATTIE

Library: see Libraries and Archives
Number of teachers: 605 (f.t.e.)
Number of students: 22,001

DEANS

Commerce: Dr SONIA MAZEY
Creative Arts: CATHRYN SHINE
Education: Assoc. Prof. LINDSEY CONNOR (Assoc. Dean)
Engineering and Forestry: Dr HAMISH COCHRANE
Humanities and Social Sciences: COLIN G. GOODRICH
Law: Assoc. Prof. RICHARD SCRAGG (acting)
Science: Assoc. Prof. PETER COTTRELL
Postgraduate Studies: Prof. STEVE WEAVER

PROFESSORS

College of Arts:

BERCOVITCH, J., Political Science
CARSTAIRS-MCCARTHY, A. D., Linguistics
COPELAND, B. J., Philosophy and Religious Studies
FRANCIS, M., Political Science
HEMPENSTALL, P. J. A., History
KUIPER, K., Linguistics
MACDONALD, G. F., Philosophy
MCNAUGHTON, H. D., English
MAJOR, M., Music
MONDRY, H., Russian
ROCHFORT, A. D., Fine Arts
THORNS, D. C., Sociology and Anthropology
WILLIAMS, M., Culture, Literature and Society
ZANKER, G., Classics

College of Business and Economics:

BALL, A., Accountancy
CLARKE, B. J., Accountancy, Finance and Information Systems
CRAGG, P., Accountancy
HALL, C. M., Management
HAMILTON, R. T., Management
MILNE, M., Accountancy
OXLEY, L., Economics

College of Engineering and Forestry:

BLAKIE, R. J., Electrical and Computer Engineering
BODGER, P., Electrical and Computer Engineering
BRIDGES, D. S., Mathematics and Statistics
BUCHANAN, A. H., Civil Engineering
CARR, A. J., Civil and Natural Resources
DAVID, T., Mechanical Engineering
FEE, C. J., Chemical and Process Engineering
GOUGH, P. T., Electrical and Computer Engineering
MILLANE, R. P., Electrical and Computer Engineering
PAWLIKOWSKI, K., Computer Science and Software Engineering
SIRISENA, H. R., Electrical and Computer Engineering
STEEL, M., Mathematics and Statistics
TAKOAKA, T., Computer Science and Software Engineering
TAYLOR, D. P., Electrical and Electronic Engineering
WALKER, J. C., Forestry
WALL, D., Mathematics and Statistics

College of Science:

BAGGALEY, W. J., Physics and Astronomy
BLUNT, J. W., Chemistry

BUTLER, P. H., Physics and Astronomy
COLE, J. W., Geological Sciences
COXON, J. M., Chemistry
DAVIDSON, W., Biological Sciences
FLETCHER, G., Psychology
GERRARD, J., Biological Sciences
HARLAND, P. W., Chemistry
HEARNSHAW, J., Physics and Astronomy
HUGHES, R., Psychology
JACKSON, R. R., Biological Sciences
JAMESON, P. E., Biological Sciences
KELLY, D., Biological Sciences
KEMP, S., Psychology
MCEWAN, M., Chemistry
MUNROE, M. H., Chemistry
PAWSON, E. J., Geography
PHILLIPS, L. F., Chemistry
ROBB, M. P., Communication Disorders
SCHIEL, D. R, Biological Sciences
STEEL, P., Chemistry
STURMAN, A. P., Geography
TAYLOR, R. P., Physics and Astronomy
WEAVER, S. D., Geology
WILLIAMSON, B., Chemistry

School of Law:
FINN, J., Law
JOSEPH, P. A., Law
TODD, S. M. D., Law
WEBB, D., Law

UNIVERSITY OF OTAGO

POB 56, Dunedin 9054
Telephone: (3) 479-1100
Fax: (3) 474-8692
E-mail: university@otago.ac.nz
Internet: www.otago.ac.nz
Founded 1869
Public control
Language of instruction: English
Academic year: February to November
Chancellor: J. F. WARD
Pro-Chancellor: S. J. MCLAUCHLAN
Vice-Chancellor: V. H. HAYNE
Deputy Vice-Chancellor for Research and Enterprise: R. J. BLAIKIE
Deputy Vice-Chancellor for Academic and Int. Affairs: V. A. SQUIRE
Pro-Vice-Chancellor for Commerce: G. L. BENWELL
Pro-Vice-Chancellor for Health Sciences: P. R. CRAMPTON
Pro-Vice-Chancellor for Humanities: B. D. MOLOUGHNEY
Pro-Vice-Chancellor for Sciences: K. A. HUNTER
Pro-Vice-Chancellor Int. Affairs: S. J. TODD
Sec. to the Ccl and Registrar: J. A. FLOOD
Librarian: H. B. AMOS
Library: see Libraries and Archives
Number of teachers: 1,451
Number of students: 22,139

DEANS

College of Education: H. MAY
Dunedin School of Medicine: J. B. ADAMS
Faculty of Law: R. M. HENAGHAN
Faculty of Medicine: P. R. CRAMPTON
Otago School of Medical Sciences: H. D. NICHOLSON
School of Dentistry: G. J. SEYMOUR
School of Maori, Pacific and Indigenous Studies: P. J. TAPSELL
School of Pharmacy: S. B. DUFFULL
School of Physical Education: D. G. BOOTH
School of Physiotherapy: G. D. BAXTER
School of Surveying: G. B. HALL
Univ. of Otago, Christchurch: P. R. JOYCE
Univ. of Otago, Wellington: C. D. COLLINGS

PROFESSORS

ABRAHAM, W. C., Psychology
ACKERLEY, C., English
ADLER, R. W., Accountancy and Business Law
AHDAR, R., Law
AN HUEF, A., Mathematics
ANDERSON, J. S., Law
ANDERSON, T. J., Medicine
ANSTEY, P., Philosophy
ARDAGH, M. W., Surgery
ATKINSON, M. D., Computer Science
BALLAGH, R. J., Physics
BARKER, R., Mathematics and Statistics
BARTLETT, R., Physical Education
BARUSCH, A., Social Work
BAXTER, G. D., Physiotherapy
BEAUTRAIS, A., Psychological Medicine
BEGG, E., Medicine
BENNETT, J., History
BENWELL, G., Information Science
BHATIA, M., Pathology
BILKEY, D., Psychology
BINNS, J. A., Geography
BLAKELY, A., Public Health
BOOTH, D., Physical Education
BRADSTOCK, A., Theology and Public Issues
BRAITHWAITE, A. W., Pathology
BREMER, P., Science
BROOKER, S., Chemistry
BROOKES, B., History
BROOKING, T. W. H., History
BURGESS, C. D., Medicine
BURNS, C. W., Zoology
CAMPBELL, A. J., Medicine
CAMPBELL-HUNT, C., Management
CANNON, R., Oral Sciences
CHAMBERS, S. T., Pathology
CLEMENTS, K., Peace and Conflict Studies
COLOMBO, M., Psychology
COOK, G., Microbiology and Immunology
COOPER, A. F., Geology
CRACK, T. F., Finance and Quantitative Analysis
CRAMPTON, P., Public Health
CRANE, J., Medicine
CRAW, D., Geology
CROOKS, T. J., Education
DARLOW, B. A., Paediatrics
DAVIS, D. K., Communication Studies
DAWKINS, K., Law
DAWSON, J. B., Law
DELAHUNT, B., Pathology
DENNIS, J., Music
DICKINSON, K., Botany
DOMINIK, W. J., Classics
DOWELL, A. C., General Practice
DOYLE, T. C. A., Medicine
DRUMMOND, J. D., Music
DUFFULL, S., Pharmacy
ECCLES, R., Pathology
ECONOMIDES, K., Law
EDWARDS, P., Public Health
ELLIS, P. M., Psychological Medicine
ENDRE, Z. H., Medicine
EVANS, D. M., Biomedical Ethics
FARELLA, M., Oral Sciences
FERGUSON, M. M., Stomatology
FERGUSSON, D. M., Psychological Medicine
FIELDING, D. J., Economics
FLEMING, J., Zoology
FOX, A. G., English
FRASER, R., Pathology
FRAUENDIENER, J., Mathematics and Statistics
FRIZELLE, F. A., Surgery
GARDINER, C., Physics
GEARE, A. J., Economics
GEMMELL, N., Anatomy and Structural Biology
GIBSON, R. S., Human Nutrition
GILLETT, G. R., Neurosurgery and Biomedical Ethics
GLUE, P., Psychological Medicine
GORDON, K., Chemistry
GRATTAN, D., Anatomy and Structural Biology
GRAY, B., Marketing
GREEN, D. P. L., Anatomy and Structural Biology
GRIFFIN, J. F. T., Microbiology
GROVER, S., Management
HALL, C. M., Tourism
HALL, G., Law
HANNAH, J., Surveying
HANNAH, R., Classics
HANTON, L., Chemistry
HAROLD, G., Childhood Studies
HARRIS, W., Politics
HAUG, A., Economics
HAYNE, H., Psychology
HENAGHAN, R. M., Law
HERBISON, A. E., Physiology
HERBISON, G., Preventive and Social Medicine
HIGHAM, J., Tourism
HIGHTON, J., Medical and Surgical Sciences
HILL, P., Preventive and Social Medicine
HOEK, J., Marketing
HOWDEN-CHAPMAN, P., Public Health
HUNTER, K. A., Chemistry
HUTTON, J. D., Obstetrics and Gynaecology
JACKSON, S., Physical Education
JOHANNESSON, A., Paediatrics and Child Health
JOHNSON, H., Music
JONES, D., Bioethics
JOYCE, P. R., Psychological Medicine
KARDOS, T. B., Oral Studies and Orthodontics
KEARSLEY, G. W., Social Science
KENNEDY, M., Pathology
KETTLE, A., Pathology
KIESER, J. A., Oral Sciences and Orthodontics
KNIGHT, R. G., Psychology
KRAUSE, K., Biochemistry
KÜCH, P., Irish Studies
LAI, K., Education
LAING, R. M., Clothing and Textile Science
LAMONT, I., Biochemistry
LANGLEY, J. D., Preventive and Social Medicine
LAWSON, R. W., Marketing
LOVER, M., Oral Diagnostic and Surgical Sciences
MCCALL, J., Medical and Surgical Sciences
MCCARTHY, A., History
MCGEE, R., Preventive and Social Medicine
MCILVANNEY, L., Scottish Studies
MCNAUGHTON, N., Psychology
MCQUILLAN, A., Chemistry
MAHONEY, R., Law
MANN, J., Human Nutrition
MATISOO-SMITH, E., Anatomy and Structural Biology
MAY, H., Education
MEHIGAN, T., Languages and Cultures
MERCER, A., Microbiology and Immunology
MERCER, A., Zoology
MILLER, J., Psychology
MOLLER, H., Agriculture, Food and Environment
MOLOUGHNEY, B., Humanities
MOLTENO, A., Medical and Surgical Sciences
MORGAN, R., Geography
MORISON, I., Pathology
MULDER, R., Psychological Medicine
MURDOCH, D., Pathology
MUSGRAVE, A., Philosophy
NACEY, J., Surgery and Anaesthesia
NEL, P., Politics
NICHOLLS, M., Medicine
NICHOLSON, H., Anatomy and Structural Biology
NORRIS, P., Pharmacy
NORRIS, R., Geology
OEY, I., Food Science
OWEN, P., Economics
PATMAN, R., Politics
PAUL, C., Preventive and Social Medicine
PEART, N., Law
PORTER, R., Psychological Medicine
POULIN, R., Zoology
POULTON, R., Preventive and Social Medicine
PRINGLE, K., Obstetrics and Gynaecology

PURVIS, M., Information Science
RADES, T., Pharmacy
RADNER, H., Media, Film and Communication
RAEBURN, I., Mathematics and Statistics
REEVE, A., Biochemistry
REILLY, M., Maori, Pacific and Indigenous Studies
RICHARDS, A., Medicine
ROAKE, J., Surgery
ROBERTON, D., Medicine
ROBERTSON, S., Paediatrics and Child Health
ROBINSON, B., Chemistry
RONSON, C., Microbiology and Immunology
ROTH, P., Law
SELLMAN, J., Psychological Medicine
SEYMOUR, G., Higher Education Development CentreDentistry
SHEPHARD, K., Higher Education Development Centre
SHIPTON, E., Anaesthesia
SIMPSON, J., Chemistry
SKEAFF, C., Human Nutrition
SKEGG, P., Law
SMILLIE, J., Law
SMITH, J., Education
SMITH, L., Education
SMITH, P., Pharmacology and Toxicology
SMITH, R., Chemistry
SPENCER, H., Zoology
SQUIRE, V., Mathematics and Statistics
STRINGER, M., Anatomy and Structural Biology
SULLIVAN, S., Physiotherapy
SUMMERHAYES, G., Anthropology
SWAIN, M., Oral Rehabilitation
TAGG, J., Microbiology and Immunology
TANNOCK, G., Microbiology and Immunology
TAPSELL, P., Maori, Pacific and Indigenous Studies
TATE, W., Biochemistry
TAYLOR, B., Women's and Children's Health
TAYLOR, D., Medical and Surgical Sciences
THOMSON, C., Human Nutrition
THOMSON, W., Oral Sciences
TILYARD, M., General Practice
TODD, S., Marketing
TOOP, L., Public Health and General Practice
TOWNSEND, C., Zoology
TREBILCO, P., Theology and Religion
TRIBBLE, E., English
TUCKER, I., Pharmacy
VAN RIJ, A., Medical and Surgical Sciences
WALKER, R., Medical and Surgical Sciences
WALLIS, G., Zoology
WEISS, H., Preventive and Social Medicine
WHITE, K., Psychology
WICKENS, J., Anatomy and Structural Biology
WILKINSON, T., Medicine
WILSON, G., Marine Science
WILSON, J., Botany
WILSON, P., Women's and Children's Health
WINTERBOURN, C., Pathology
WYVILL, G., Computer Science
YOON, H., Pathology

UNIVERSITY OF WAIKATO

Private Bag 3105, Hamilton
Telephone: (7) 856-2889
Fax: (7) 838-4370
E-mail: info@waikato.ac.nz
Internet: www.waikato.ac.nz

Founded 1964
Academic year: February to November

Chancellor: JOHN GALLAGHER
Vice-Chancellor: ROY CRAWFORD
Asst to the Vice-Chancellor: HELEN PRIDMORE
Librarian: S. PHARO

Library: see Libraries and Archives
Number of teachers: 780
Number of students: 14,405

DEANS

Faculty of Arts and Social Sciences: Prof. D. ZIRKER
School of Computing and Mathematical Sciences: Prof. M. APPERLEY
School of Education: Prof. N. ALCORN
School of Law: Prof. J. FARRAR
School of Maori and Pacific Development: Prof. A. YATES-SMITH
School of Science and Engineering: Prof. R. PRICE
Waikato Management School: Prof. M. J. PRATT

PROFESSORS

APPERLEY, M. D., Computing and Mathematical Sciences
BARRATT, A. A. T., English
BARTON, B., Law
BEARDON, C., Computer Sciences
BEDFORD, R. D., Geography
BING, D., Political Science and Public Policy
BISHOP, R., Maori Education
BOOTH, D., Sport and Leisure Studies
CARY, C., Biological Sciences
CLARK, D., Management
CLEARY, J. G., Computer Sciences
CORNER, J., Management Systems
CRAIG, I., Mathematics
CUBITT, S., Screen and Media Studies
DANIEL, R. M., Biological Sciences
EGGLETON, I., Accounting
ERICKSEN, N., International Global Change Institute
FARRAR, J. H., Law
FARRELL, R. L., Biological Sciences
FOULDS, L. R., Management Systems
GILLESPIE, A. M., Law
GILSON, C. H. J., Strategic Management and Leadership
GLYNN, E. L., Human Development and Counselling
GRANT, B., Sport and Leisure Studies
GREEN, T. G. A., Biological Sciences
HAMILTON, D., Biological Sciences
HARCOURT, M., Strategic Management and Leadership
HEALY, T. R., Earth Sciences
HOLMES, M. J., Economics
JOHN, N., Statistics
JONES, A. T., Wilf Malcolm Institute of Educational Research
KALNINS, E. G., Mathematics
KAMP, P. J. J., Earth Sciences
KOOPMAN-BOYDEN, P. G., Arts and Social Sciences
LAWRENCE, S., Accounting
LEITCH, S., Public Relations and Marketing
LOWE, A., Accounting
MCGEE, C., Wilf Malcolm Institute of Educational Research
MCKIE, D., Management Communication
MCQUEEN, B., Management Systems
MAY, S., Arts and Language Education
MIDDLETON, S. C., Policy, Cultural and Social Studies in Education
MOLAN, P. C., Biological Sciences
MORGAN, H. W., Biological Sciences
MOTION, J., Management Communication
NELSON, C. S., Earth Sciences
NICHOLSON, B. K., Chemistry
O'DRISCOLL, M., Psychology
POOL, D. I., Population Studies
POOT, J., Population Studies
PRATT, M. J., Management Studies
PRICE, R., Science and Engineering
QUICK, S. P., Biological Sciences
REEDY, T., Maori Sustainable Enterprise
REEVES, S., Computer Science
RICHARDSON, N. A., Management
RITCHIE, J., Psychology
ROA, T. C., Maori and Pacific Development
RYAN, C. A., Tourism Management
SCARPA, R., Economics
SCRIMGEOUR, F. G., Economics
SILVESTER, W. B., Biological Sciences
SMYTH, J., Wilf Malcolm Institute of Educational Research
SNEYD, A. D., Mathematics
SPILLER, P. R., Law
STOKES, E. M., Geography, Tourism and Environmental Planning
TE AWEKOTUKWU, N. A., Maori and Pacific Development
VAREY, R. J., Marketing and International Management
VOS, E. A. J., Finance
WALKER, G. M., English
WILKINS, A. L., Chemistry
WILKINS, R. J., Biological Sciences
WITTEN, I. H., Computer Science
YATES-SMITH, G. R. A., Maori and Pacific Development
ZIRKER, D., Arts and Social Sciences
ZORN, T. E., Management Communication

VICTORIA UNIVERSITY OF WELLINGTON

POB 600, Wellington 6140
Telephone: (4) 472-1000
Fax: (4) 499-4601
Internet: www.victoria.ac.nz.

Founded 1897
Languages of instruction: English, Maori
Academic year: March to February (3 trimesters)

Chancellor: Emeritus Prof. IAN MCKINNON
Pro-Chancellor: HELEN SUTCH
Vice-Chancellor: Prof. PAT WALSH
Deputy Vice-Chancellor: Prof. PENNY BOUMELHA
Pro-Vice-Chancellor: Prof. PIRI SCIASCIA
Pro-Vice-Chancellor: Prof. BOB BUCKLE
Pro-Vice-Chancellor: Prof. DEBORAH WILLIS
Pro-Vice-Chancellor: Prof. NEIL QUIGLEY
Pro-Vice-Chancellor: Prof. DIANE BRAND
Pro-Vice-Chancellor: Prof. TONY SMITH
Pro-Vice-Chancellor: Prof. DUGALD SCOTT
Asst Vice-Chancellor for Academic Affairs: Assoc. Prof. DAVID CRABBE
Chief Financial Officer: WAYNE MORGAN
Chief Operating Officer: ANDREW SIMPSON
Dir for Campus Services: JENNY BENTLEY
Dir for Human Resources: ANNEMARIE DE CASTRO

Library: see Libraries and Archives
Number of teachers: 856
Number of students: 22,310

Publications: *Staff and Student Research* (1 a year), *Victorious* (3 a year)

DEANS

Faculty of Architecture and Design: Prof. DAVID MACKAY (acting)
Faculty of Commerce and Admin.: Prof. BOB BUCKLE
Faculty of Education: Prof. DUGALD SCOTT
Faculty of Humanities and Social Sciences: Prof. D. WILLIS
Faculty of Law: Prof. TONY SMITH
Faculty of Maori: Prof. PIRI SCIASCIA
Faculty of Science: Prof. D. BIBBY

PROFESSORS

Faculty of Architecture and Design (tel. (4) 463-6200; fax (4) 463-6204; e-mail architecture@vuw.ac.nz; internet www.victoria.ac.nz/architecture):

BRAND, D., Architecture
FRASER, S., Design

Faculty of Commerce and Administration (tel. (4) 463-5376; fax (4) 463-5360; e-mail fca-sao@vuw.ac.nz; internet www.victoria.ac.nz/fca):

BOSTON, J., Govt
BROCKLESBY, J., Management
CORBETT, L., Management
CUMMINGS, S., Management
DAVIES, J., Management
EVANS, L. T., Economics and Finance
GORMAN, G., Information Management
HALL, V. B., Economics and Finance

HUFF, S., Information Management
LOVE, N., Management
PEARCE, D., Tourism Management
SCOTT, C. D., Govt
STOKES, T., Govt
VAN ZIJL, T., FCA

Faculty of Education (tel. (4) 463-9500; fax (4) 463-9649; e-mail teaching@vuw.ac.nz; internet www.victoria.ac.nz/education):

HALL, C. G. W.
MEYER, L.
SIGAFOOS, J.

Faculty of Humanities and Social Sciences (tel. (4) 463-5208; fax (4) 463-5209; e-mail hum-socsci-office@vuw.ac.nz; internet www.victoria.ac.nz/fhss):

BAUER, L., Linguistics and Applied Language Studies
CLARK, M., History, Philosophy, Political Science and Int. Relations
DAVIDSON, J. F., Art History, Classics and Religious Studies
HOLMES, J., Linguistics and Applied Language Studies
LEVINE, S., History, Philosophy, Political Science and Int. Relations
MORRIS, P., Art History, Classics and Religious Studies
NATION, P., Linguistics and Applied Languages
PRATT, J., Social and Cultural Studies
STERELNY, K., History, Philosophy, Political Science and Int. Relations

Faculty of Law (tel. (4) 463-6366; fax (4) 463-6365; e-mail law-enquiries@vuw.ac.nz; internet www.victoria.ac.nz/law):

ANDERSON, G.
ANGELO, A. H.
ATKIN, B.
MCLACHLAN, C.
MCLAUCHLAN, D. W.
PREBBLE, J.
SMITH, T.

Faculty of Science (tel. (4) 463-5101; fax (4) 463-5122; e-mail science-faculty@vuw.ac.nz; internet www.victoria.ac.nz/science):

BARRETT, P. J., Earth Sciences
CALLAGHAN, P., Chemical and Physical Sciences
DOWNEY, R., Mathematics, Statistics and Operations Research
GARNOCK-JONES, P., Biological Sciences
GOLDBLATT, R. I., Engineering and Computer Science
HINE, J., Mathematics, Statistics and Computer Science
JOHNSTON, J., Chemical and Physical Sciences
KAISER, A., Chemical and Physical Sciences
KHMALADZE, E., Mathematics, Statistics and Operations Research
LEKNER, J., Chemical and Physical Sciences
SCHENK, S., Psychology
SMITH, E., Earth Sciences
TALLON, J., Chemical and Physical Sciences
WARD, C., Psychology
WARD, T., Psychology
WHITTLE, G., Mathematics, Statistics and Operations Research

Polytechnic Institutions

Central Institute of Technology: Private Box 40740, Upper Hutt; tel. (4) 527-6398; fax (4) 527-6359; f. 1960; full-time technician and professional education; 330 staff; 5,000 enrolments; library: 29,000 vols, 800 periodicals (570 current); CEO T. BOYLE.

Christchurch Polytechnic Institute of Technology: Madras St, POB 22-095, Christchurch 8032; tel. (3) 379-8150; fax (3) 366-6544; e-mail info@cpit.ac.nz; internet www.cpit.ac.nz; f. 1965; courses at trade technician, professional and degree levels, recreational and community courses; specializes in information technology, with pathways to Monash Univ. (Australia) Masters programmes; library: 48,000 items; 1,180 teachers (350 full-time, 830 part-time); 17,600 students; Dir JOHN W. SCOTT; publ. *Prospectus* (1 a year).

Hutt Valley Polytechnic: Private Bag 39803, Te Puni Mail Centre, Petone, nr Wellington; tel. (4) 568-3419; fax (4) 568-6849; f. 1976; courses in trades, commercial and technical subjects; 180 staff, 10,000 enrolments; library of 20,000 items; Chief Exec. W. J. MATTHEW.

Manukau Institute of Technology: Private Bag 94006, Manukau City; tel. (9) 968-8000; fax (9) 968-8701; e-mail info@manukau.ac.nz; internet www.manukau.ac.nz; f. 1970; courses in trade, technical and professional subjects; library: 55,000 vols; 409 teachers; 32,674 students; Chief Exec. Dr GEOFFREY PAGE.

Open Polytechnic of New Zealand: Wyndrum Ave, Private Bag 31914, Lower Hutt; tel. (4) 913-5300; fax (4) 913-5308; e-mail brochurecentre@openpolytechnic.ac.nz; internet www.openpolytechnic.ac.nz; f. 1946; certificate- to degree-level courses by distance and open learning methods in business, social science, professional, technical, agriculture/horticulture, trades and self-improvement subjects; 37,000 students; Chief Exec. PAUL GRIMWOOD.

Otago Polytechnic: Private Bag, Dunedin; tel. (3) 477-3014; fax (3) 471-6870; e-mail info@tekotago.ac.nz; internet www.tekotago.ac.nz; f. 1966; degrees, diplomas and certificates in fine arts, business, engineering, architectural technology, health sciences, tourism and sports; 236 teachers; 9,000 students; library: 30,000 vols; CEO PHIL KER.

UNITEC Institute of Technology: Private Bag 92025, Auckland; tel. (9) 849-4180; fax (9) 815-2901; e-mail ceo@unitec.ac.nz; internet www.unitec.ac.nz; f. 1976; faculties of Architecture and Design, Arts and Social Sciences, Business, Health and Environmental Sciences; Applied Technology Institute; library: 88,834 vols; 496 teachers (full-time); 18,179 students; Dir Dr JOHN A. WEBSTER; Registrar REBECCA EWERT.

Waikato Institute of Technology: Private Bag HN 3036, Hamilton 2020; tel. (7) 834-8888; fax (7) 838-0707; e-mail info@wintec.ac.nz; internet www.wintec.ac.nz; f. 1968; courses at Masters degree, diploma, certificate, professional technician and trades levels, also community education; library: 62,800 vols; 365 teachers; 13,100 students (4,500 full-time, 8,600 part-time); CEO MARK FLOWERS.

Schools of Art and Music

Elam School of Fine Arts: Faculty of Fine Arts, University of Auckland, Private Bag 92019, Auckland; tel. (9) 373-7599; fax (9) 308-2302; e-mail enquiries@elam.auckland.ac.nz; internet www.elam.auckland.ac.nz; f. 1950; library: 35,000 vols; 35 teachers; 450 students; Head of School Prof. MICHAEL DUNN; publ. *Fine Arts Library Bulletin*.

School of Fine Arts: Faculty of Visual and Performing Arts, University of Canterbury, Christchurch; tel. (3) 364-2161; fax (3) 364-2858; e-mail postmaster@fina-canterbury.ac.nz; internet www.canterbury.ac.nz; f. 1882; BA, BA (Hons), BFA, BFA (Hons), MA, MFA and PhD degrees; courses in art theory, art history, film, graphic design, painting, photography, printmaking and sculpture; library: 10,000 vols, including index of NZ historic buildings, 100,000 slides; 20 teachers; 785 students; Head Prof. DESMOND ROCHFORT.

NICARAGUA

The Higher Education System

The oldest institution of higher education in Nicaragua is the Universidad Nacional Autónoma de Nicaragua (founded in 1812), which dates from the Spanish colonial period. Nicaragua became part of the Central American Federation in 1821 and declared its independence in 1838. There are many commercial schools and eight universities. In 2003/04 a total of 103,577 students attended universities and other higher education institutes. The National Council of Universities is the body responsible for all strategic planning.

Admission to higher education is on the basis of the Bachillerato, the leading secondary school qualification, and an entrance examination. The Licenciado, the main undergraduate degree, is a four- or five-year course of study; a professional title may also be awarded depending on the subject. Following the Licenciado, the first postgraduate degree is the Maestría, which lasts two years and culminates with the submission of a thesis.

Institutions of higher education also offer two- or three-year courses in technical and vocational education. The main qualification studied for is the Técnico Superior.

Regulatory and Representative Bodies

GOVERNMENT

Ministry of Education: Complejo Cívico Camilo Ortega Saavedra, Managua; tel. 265-1451; e-mail rivash@mecd.gob.ni; internet www.mined.gob.ni; Min. Dr Miriam Ráudez.

NATIONAL BODY

Consejo Nacional de Universidades (National Council of Universities): De donde fue el Sandy, Carretera a Masaya, 2 cuadras arriba y 1 cuadra al lago, Managua; tel. 278-1053; fax 278-3385; e-mail cnuni@ibw.com.ni; internet www.cnu.edu.ni; f. 1990; 14 mems; Pres. Ing. Telémaco Talavera Siles; Sec. Ing. Arturo Collado Maldonado; publ. *Universidad y Sociedad*.

Learned Societies

BIBLIOGRAPHY, LIBRARY SCIENCE AND MUSEOLOGY

Asociación Nicaragüense de Bibliotecarios y Profesionales afines: Apdo postal 3257, Calle F. Guzman Bolanos, Altamira del Est, Casa 120, Managua; e-mail anibipa@yahoo.com; f. 1983.

LANGUAGE AND LITERATURE

Academia Nicaragüense de la Lengua (Nicaraguan Academy of Letters): Apdo 2711, Managua; located at: Avda del Campo 42, Las Colinas, Managua; fax 249-5389; e-mail pavsa@munditel.com.ni; internet www.anl.edu.ni; f. 1928; corresp. of the Real Academia Española (Madrid); 13 mems; Dir Jorge Eduardo Arellano Sandino; Sec. Francisco Arellano Oviedo.

Alliance Française: Apdo 2370, Managua; Planes de Altamira, De la Embajada de México ½ Cuadra al Norte, Managua; tel. 2267-2811; fax 2267-8287; e-mail culturalafmga@gmail.com; internet www.alianzafrancesa.org.ni; f. 1951; offers courses and examinations in French language and culture and promotes cultural exchange with France; attached teaching centre in León and Granada; Dir Nicolas Blasquez; Sub Dir Marie-Pierre Baylocq; Culture Coordinator Sara Bolt Kalfon.

MEDICINE

Sociedad de Oftalmología Nicaragüense: Clínica Especializada, Managua; f. 1949; Pres R. Lacayo G.

Sociedad Nicaragüense de Psiquiatría y Psicología: Centro Médico, Managua; f. 1962; Pres. Dr R. Gutiérrez.

Research Institutes

ECONOMICS, LAW AND POLITICS

Instituto Nicaragüense de Investigaciones Económicas y Sociales (INIES): Apdo postal C-16, Managua; Avda Bolívar, Antojitos 2 cuadra al sur Managua; tel. 266-2485; fax 266-8503; e-mail inies@sdnnic.apc.org; f. 1981 to inform and conduct research on developing alternatives for the more vulnerable sectors of the national population; documentation centre of 8,000 items, 250 periodicals; Dir Bladimir Varela Hidalgo; publs *Boletín Socioeconómico* (4 a year), *Cuadernos de Investigación* (irregular).

NATURAL SCIENCES

Physical Sciences

Observatorio Geofísico: Apdo postal 1761, Managua; tel. 225-1023; f. 1980; geophysics, geology, seismology, vulcanology; publ. *Boletín Sismológico* (1 a year).

Libraries and Archives

Bluefields

Biblioteca Raití: Alcaldía Municipal, Bluefields, Zelaya; tel. 822-2502; Librarian Janice Taylor.

Chinandega

Biblioteca 'Eduardo Montealegre': Parque Las Rosas 2 cuadras al sur, Chinandega; tel. 341-2950; Librarian Ana Luisa Paniagua González.

León

Biblioteca Rubén Dario de la Universidad Nacional Autónoma de Nicaragua: Frente a la panadería León Dorado, León; tel. 311-3508; f. 1816; 36,000 vols; Dir Norma Flores.

Managua

Archivo Nacional de Nicaragua: Del Cine Cabrera 2½ Cuadras al Lago, Managua; tel. 222-6290; fax 222-2722; e-mail binanic@tmx.com.ni; internet http://manfut.org/museos/archivonacional.html; f. 1882; 40,356 vols; Dir Alfredo González Vilchez; publs *Boletín Técnico Informativo*, *Gaceta Oficial*.

Biblioteca del INCAE Business School: Apdo 2485, Managua; tel. 2265-8141 ext. 228; fax 2265-8617; e-mail antonio.acevedo@incae.edu; internet conocimiento.incae.edu/es/biblioteca; f. 1968 as Depositary Library Food and Agricultural Organization of the United Nations and the World Bank; academic business library of 34,417 vols and 111 periodical titles on business admin., economic devt and Central American social and economic conditions; colln of 16,000 case materials for teaching of management; Dir Lic. Antonio Acevedo; publs *Bibliografía de Casos* (1 a year), *Gerencia—Artículos Nuevos* (irregular), *INCAE Business Review* (4 a year), *Mini-Bibliografía* (12 a year), *Nuevas Adquisiciones* (12 a year), *Revistas—Números Temáticos* (irregular).

Biblioteca Nacional 'Rubén Dario': Apdo Postal 3514, Managua; Palacio Nacional de la Cultura, Antigua Catedral, Managua; tel. and fax 222-2722; e-mail dibinacr@racsa.co.cr; internet www.abinia.org/nicaragua; f. 1880; 80,000 vols; Dir Jimmy Alvarado Moreno.

Masaya

Biblioteca 'El Ateneo': Masaya; f. 1941; new collection of literature on philately and numismatics; Dir Dr Santiago Fajardo F.

Nagarote

Biblioteca Municipal: Costado sur Parque Central, Nagarote, León; tel. 313-2244; Dir Prof. José Ángel Palacios.

Museums and Art Galleries

Managua

Museo Nacional de Nicaragua: Apdo 416, Colonia Dambach, Managua; tel. 222-5291; internet manfut.org/museos/nacional.html; f. 1896; archaeology, ceramics, zoology, botany and geology; library of 500 vols; Dir Leonor Martínez de Rocha.

Masaya

Museo 'Tenderí': Villa Nindirí, Masaya; archaeological remains from the Chorotega Indian culture; coins and medals from the Spanish colonial era.

Universities

ESCUELA INTERNACIONAL DE AGRICULTURA Y GANADERÍA

Apdo postal 5, Rivas
Telephone: 453-3551
Fax: 453-3957
E-mail: eiag@tmx.com.ni
Dir: Fr GREGORIO BARREALES

Academic programmes in agriculture, management, veterinary science and zootechnology.

UNIVERSIDAD CENTROAMERICANA

Pista de la Resistencia, Apdo 69, Managua
Telephone: 277-3026
Fax: 267-0106
E-mail: asrector@ns.uca.edu.ni
Internet: www.uca.edu.ni

Founded 1961
Private control
Academic year: February to December

Rector: Dra MAYRA LUZ PÉREZ DÍAZ
Vice-Rector for Gen. Affairs: P. JESÚS MANUEL SARIEGO
Vice-Rector for Academic Affairs: RENATA RODRIGUEZ
Vice-Rector for Research and Postgraduates: SANDRA RUIZ
Sec.-Gen.: P. MIGUEL ÁNGEL RUIZ
Dir of Admin.: Lic. RÓGER URIARTE GÓMEZ
Librarian: Lic. GLORIA MARÍA MORALES

Number of teachers: 324 (72 full-time, 252 part-time)
Number of students: 6,401

Publications: *Cuadernos de Sociología*, *Diakonía*, *Encuentro* (24 a year), *Envío* (12 a year), *WANI* (4 a year)

DEANS

Faculty of Administration: GUILLERMO BORNEMANN
Faculty of Agriculture and Stockbreeding: VERA AMANDA SOLÍS REYES
Faculty of Communications: Dr GUILLERMO ROTHSCHUH
Faculty of Foreign Languages: RAMÓN BERMÚDEZ
Faculty of Humanities: DONALD MÉNDEZ QUINTANA
Faculty of Law: MANUEL ARKUZ ULLOA

UNIVERSIDAD NACIONAL AGRARIA

Km 12½ Carretera Norte, Managua
Telephone: 233-1619
Fax: 233-1950
Internet: www.una.edu.ni

Founded 1929, present name and status 1990

Rector: Ing. FRANCISCO TELÉMACO TALAVERA SILES
Vice-Rector Gen.: Ing. ALBERTO SEDILES JAEN
Dir for Camoapa Campus: Ing. LUIS HERNÁNDEZ MALUEÑO
Dir for Juigalpa Campus: Ing. ARISTIDES TABLADA CALERO
Registrar: Lic. RONALD QUIROZ OCAMPO

Library of 12,000 vols, 500 periodicals
Number of students: 2,217

Publications: *Boletín Informativo* (12 a year), *La Calera* (2 a year)

DEANS

Faculty of Agronomy: Dr DENNIS SALAZAR CENTENO
Faculty of Animal Sciences: Ing. ELMER GUILLEN CORRALES
Faculty of Natural Resources and the Environment: Lic. ESTHER CARBALLO MADRIGAL
Faculty of Rural Development: Dr ELGIN VIVAS VILLACHICA

UNIVERSIDAD NACIONAL AUTÓNOMA DE NICARAGUA

Apdo Postal 663, Managua
De Enel Central 2½ km al sur, Villa Fontana, Managua
Telephone: 278-6769
Fax: 278-2990
E-mail: unan@unan.edu.ni
Internet: www.unan.edu.ni

Founded 1812
Academic year: June to March
State control

Rector: FRANCISCO GUZMÁN PASOS
Vice-Rector: ELMER CISNEROS MOREIRA
Vice-Rector for Academic Affairs: Dr GUSTAVO SILES GONZÁLEZ
Vice-Rector for Admin. Affairs: Lic. JAIME LÓPEZ LOWERY
Registrar: Dra NÍVEA GONZÁLEZ ROJAS
Library Dir: SIDAR RIVERA MARÍN

Library: see Libraries and Archives
Number of teachers: 709
Number of students: 24,629

Publications: *Cuadernos Universitarios* (4 a year), *Gaceta Universitaria* (6 a year), *Revista Médica* (2 a year)

DEANS

Faculty of Economics: ABEL MEMBREÑO GALEANO
Faculty of Education and Humanities: Lic. ALEJANDRO GENET CRUZ
Faculty of Medicine: Dr FRANCISCO CORTÉZ HERNÁNDEZ
Faculty of Sciences: Lic. HUGO GUTIÉRREZ OCÓN

UNIVERSIDAD NACIONAL DE INGENIERÍA

Avda Universitaria Frente Escuela de Danza, Apdo postal 5595, Managua
Telephone: 277-1650
Fax: 267-3709
Internet: www.uni.edu.ni

Founded 1983
State control
Academic year: March to December

Rector: Ing. ALDO URBINA VILLALTA
Vice-Rector: Ing. SERGIO ENRIQUE ALVAREZ GARCÍA
Vice-Rector for Academic Affairs: Arq. ANA ULMOS VADO
Vice-Rector for Administrative Affairs: Ing. NÉSTOR GALLO ZELEDÓN
Vice-Rector for Research and Development: Lic. SERGIO MARTÍNEZ TRAÑA
Registrar: Ing. DIEGO ALFONSO MUÑOZ LATINO
Librarian: Lic. VIOLETA BONICHE SOMARRIBA

Number of teachers: 409
Number of students: 7,518

Publications: *Campus* (6 a year), *Nexo* (quarterly scientific review), *Teckno* (6 a year)

DEANS

Faculty of Architecture: Arq. VÍCTOR ARCIA GÓMEZ
Faculty of Chemical Engineering: SILVIO ROJAS ZAMBRANA
Faculty of Construction Technology: Ing. JULIO MALTEZ MONTIEL
Faculty of Electrotechnology and Computer Science: Ing. ARIEL ROLDÁN PAREDES
Faculty of Industrial Technology: Ing. DANIEL CUADRA HORNEY
Faculty of Sciences and Systems: RONALD TORRES MERCADO

UNIVERSIDAD POLITÉCNICA DE NICARAGUA

Apdo 3595, Managua
Costado Sur Colonia Rubén Darío, Managua
Telephone: 289-7740
Fax: 249-9232
E-mail: rectoria@upoli.edu.ni
Internet: www.upoli.edu.ni/default.html

Founded 1967 as institute, university status 1977
Private control
Academic year: March to December

Rector: Ing. EMERSON PÉREZ SANDOVAL
Vice-Rector: Dra LIDIA RUTH ZAMORA
Vice-Rector for Academic Affairs: Dra MIRNA CUEVAS RUIZ
Vice-Rector for Students: Lic. BLANCA ROSA GALARZA
Registrar: TOMÁS HANDELL TÉLLEZ RUIZ
Librarian: Licda AURA CELA CORTEZ SILVA

Number of teachers: 101
Number of students: 1,475

DEANS

School of Administration, Commerce and Finance: MIGUEL MURILLO
School of Design: D. I. EDUARDO VANEGAS
School of Economics: EYRA REYES
School of Engineering: Licda GLADYS AGUILAR
School of Law: Dr OSCAR CASTILLO GUIDO
School of Nursing: MARGARITA GUEVARA
School of Tourism: AMPARO MENDOZA

College

Instituto Centroamericano de Administración de Empresas (INCAE): Apdo 2485, Managua; Campus Francisco de Sola Montefresco, Km 15½ Carretera Sur, Managua; tel. 265-8141; fax 265-8617; e-mail incaenic@mail.incae.edu.ni; internet www.incae.ac.cr; f. 1964 with technical assistance from Harvard Business School; 16-month degree programme in business administration; executive training programmes; management research and consulting; 53 teachers; library: see Libraries and Archives; Rector Dr ROBERTO ARTAVIA.

NIGER

The Higher Education System

The Republic of Niger was formerly part of French West Africa and obtained independence from France in 1960. The Ecole Nationale d'Administration du Niger (founded in 1963) is the oldest current institution of higher education and the Université Abdou Moumouni (founded in 1971; formerly Université de Niamey) was the first university-level institution. The other leading institution is the Université Islamique du Niger (founded in 1986). In 2005/06 there were 8,710 students enrolled in these institutions.

The principal officer of a university is the President or Rector, elected by the faculty to serve three-year, renewable terms of office. A Vice-President is also elected to assist the President. Deans of Faculty and Heads of Department are also elected to their posts and serve for three years and two years respectively. The Ministry for Secondary and Higher Education, Research and Technology is responsible for all tertiary education.

The university degree system is based on the French cyclical model. The entry requirement for higher education courses is the Baccalauréat; however, students who do not hold the Baccalauréat can gain admission by taking an entrance examination The first cycle lasts two years and leads to the award of the Diplôme Universitaire d'études Littéraires (arts and humanities), the Diplôme Universitaire d'études Scientifiques (mathematics or sciences) or the Diplôme d'études Economiques Générales (economics). The second cycle lasts either one year for the award of the Licence or two years for the award of the Maîtrise. Professional titles are awarded in fields such as agricultural engineering (Diplôme d'Ingénieur des Techniques Agricole), agronomy (Diplôme d'Ingénieur Agronome or Diplôme d'Agronomie Approfondie) and medicine (Doctorat en Médecine).

Specialist non-university education is offered by institutes attached to the relevant Ministries, including schools and centres for administration, public health, civil aviation and information technology.

Regulatory Bodies

GOVERNMENT

Ministry of Culture, the Arts and Communication: BP 452, Niamey; tel. 20-72-28-74; fax 20-73-36-85; Minister OUMAROU HADARY.

Ministry of Secondary and Higher Education, Research and Technology: BP 628, Niamey; tel. 20-72-26-20; fax 20-72-40-40; e-mail mesnt@intnet.ne; Minister Prof. SIDIKOU OUMAROU.

Learned Society

LANGUAGE AND LITERATURE

Alliance Française: BP 126, Agadez; tel. 20-44-05-82; offers courses and examinations in French language and culture and promotes cultural exchange with France; attached teaching centre in Maradi.

Research Institutes

GENERAL

Institut de Recherche pour le Développement (IRD): Ave de Maradi BP 11416, Niamey; tel. 20-75-38-27; fax 20-75-20-54; e-mail irdniger@ird.ne; internet www.ird.ne; medical entomology, hydrology, genetics, ecology, soil sciences, botany, agronomy, economics, linguistics, sociology; in co-operation with Org. for Co-ordination and Co-operation in the Fight against Endemic Diseases; library: documentation centre of 2,500 vols; Dir FRANCIS KAHN; (see main entry under France).

Institut de Recherches en Sciences Humaines (IRSH) de l'Université Abdou Moumouni: BP 318, Niamey; tel. 20-73-51-41; f. 1975 as successor to Institut Français d'Afrique Noire and Centre Nigérien de Recherches en Sciences Humaines; 6 sections: art and archaeology, history and popular traditions, linguistics and nat. languages, Arabic MSS, geography and environmental devt, sociology of devt, devt economics; library of 30,000 vols; Dir ABDOULAYE MAGA; publs *Etudes Nigériennes* (irregular), *Mu Kara Sani* (2 a year).

AGRICULTURE, FISHERIES AND VETERINARY SCIENCE

Institut de Recherches sur les Fruits et Agrumes (IRFA): BP 886, Niamey; Dir C. LENORMAND; (see main entry under France).

Institut National de Recherches Agronomiques au Niger (INRAN): BP 149, Niamey; e-mail inran@intnet.ne; soil science; stations at Tarna and Kolo; Dir J. NABOS.

Laboratoire Vétérinaire de Niamey: Niamey.

Station Avicole et Centre d'Elevage Caprin: Maradi; f. 1961; Dir HASSANE BAZA.

Station Sahélienne Expérimentale de Toukounous: Service d'Elevage du Niger, Toukounous/Filingué; f. 1931; selection and breeding of Zebu Azaouak cattle and distribution of selected bulls to improve the local heterogeneous breed; Dir Dr MANFRED LINDAU; publ. *Berlin Münchner Tierärztliche Wochenschrift*.

HISTORY, GEOGRAPHY AND ARCHAEOLOGY

Centre d'Etudes Linguistiques et Historiques par Tradition Orale: BP 878, Niamey; tel. 20-73-54-14; fax 20-73-36-54; f. 1974; 25 mems; library of 1,250 vols; oral tradition, African languages and cultures; publishes works in African languages, French and English; publ. *Les Cahiers du CELHTO*.

TECHNOLOGY

Bureau de Recherches Géologiques et Minières (BRGM): BP 11458, Niamey; tel. 20-72-23-25; Dir G. BERNERT; (see main entry under France).

Office National de l'Energie Solaire: BP 621, Niamey; tel. 20-73-45-05; f. 1965; 40 staff; research, post-univ. and technical courses; Dir Eng. ALBERT WRIGHT.

Libraries and Archives

Niamey

Archives de la République du Niger: BP 550, Niamey; tel. 20-72-26-82; fax 20-72-36-54; f. 1913; documents to the end of the 19th century; Dir IDRISSA YANSAMBOU.

Centre d'Information et de Documentation Economique et Sociale (CIDES): Ministère des Finances et du Plan, BP 862, Niamey; tel. 20-72-33-11; fax 20-73-59-83; f. 1988; attached to Min. of Economy, Finance and Planning; 10,500 vols; Dir MALIKI ABDOULAYE; publ. *CIDES-Flash* (6 a year).

Museum

Niamey

Musée National du Niger: BP 248, Niamey; tel. 20-73-43-21; fax 20-73-43-21; f. 1959; representative colln of tribal costumes, crafts, tribal houses; incl. park and zoo, geological and mineral exhibition, ethnographic museum, palaeontology and pre-history museums; also Handicrafts Centre and Cultural Activities Centre; Curator NÉINO CHAÏBOU.

Universities

UNIVERSITÉ ABDOU MOUMOUNI

BP 237, 10896 Niamey

Telephone: 20-73-27-13
Fax: 20-73-38-62

Founded 1971; univ. status as Univ. de Niamey 1973; present name 1999
State control
Language of instruction: French
Academic year: October to June

Rector: Prof. BOULI ALI DIALLO
Sec.-Gen.: MAÏGA DJIBO
Librarian: SAIDOU HAROUNA

Library of 62,000
Number of teachers: 260
Number of students: 3,700

Publications: *Annales de l'Université Abdou Moumouni* (1 a year), *Etudes Nigériennes*, *Mu Kara Sani* (2 a year)

DEANS

Faculty of Agronomy, Arts and Humanities: AMOUKOU IBRAHIM
Faculty of Arts and Humanities: ABOUBACAR ADAMOU
Faculty of Economics and Law: ALHADA ALKACHE
Faculty of Health Sciences: NOUHOU HASSANE
Faculty of Science: FODÉ MADÉ

UNIVERSITÉ ISLAMIQUE DU NIGER
(Islamic University in Niger)

BP 11507, Niamey, Say

Telephone: 20-72-39-03
Fax: 20-73-37-96
E-mail: unislam@intnet.ne
Internet: www.universite.say.ne

Founded 1986 by the Islamic Conf. Org.
Language of instruction: Arabic

Number of teachers: 20
Number of students: 350

Rector: Prof. ABDEL JAOUAD SEKKAT

Faculties of Arabic Language and Islamic Studies.

College

Ecole Nationale d'Administration du Niger: Rue Martin Luther King Jr, BP 542, Niamey; tel. 20-72-31-83; fax 20-72-43-83; e-mail enaniger@intnet.ne; f. 1963 to train civil servants and other officials; library: 27,000 vols; 116 teachers (56 full-time, 60 part-time); 431 students; Dir DJIBO ISSAKA; publ. *Revue* (2 a year).

NIGERIA

The Higher Education System

The oldest institution of higher education in Nigeria is the Federal College of Agriculture, Ibadan (founded in 1921) and the oldest university is the University of Ibadan (founded in 1948; formerly University College, Ibadan), originally founded in conjunction with the University of London (United Kingdom). Expansion of the university system began following Nigeria's independence in 1963, and the universities established during 1960–70 are referred to as the 'first generation' universities, among them the University of Nigeria (founded in 1960), Obafemi Awolowo University (founded in 1961; present name since 1987), Ahmadu Bello University (founded in 1962), the University of Lagos (founded in 1962) and the University of Benin (founded in 1970). Education is partly the responsibility of the state Governments, although the Federal Government has played an increasingly important role since 1970, and universities may be federally, state or privately administered. In 2005 there were 724,856 students enrolled in 80 universities and 237,708 in 178 poly/monotechnics.

The Governing Board or Council is the governing body of the Federal universities, and its members are Government appointees. The chief executive role is taken by the Vice-Chancellor in universities, the Rector in polytechnics and the Provost in colleges of education. Funding for public universities is channelled through different agencies for different types of institution, namely the National Universities Commission (universities), the National Board for Technical Education (polytechnics) and the National Commission for Colleges of Education (colleges). The National Universities Commission is also responsible for accreditation and quality assurance, which takes place on a six-yearly cycle.

Admission to higher education is made on the basis of sufficient passes in the Senior School Certificate and the University Matriculation Examination, administered by the Joint Admissions and Matriculation Board. Most undergraduate Bachelors degrees last four years, but programmes leading to the award of professional titles last five years and degrees in medicine and dentistry take six years to complete. A student awarded a first- or second-class Bachelors degree with Honours may be admitted to the first postgraduate degree, the Masters, study for which lasts for one to two years. Following the Masters, the Doctorate is the highest university-level degree, and consists of a two- or three-year period of research, submission of a thesis and an oral examination (viva).

Polytechnics and colleges offer post-secondary technical and vocational education. The most popular qualifications offered by these institutions are the Ordinary National Diploma, Higher National Diploma and Full Professional Diploma. Programmes are accredited by the National Board for Technical Education (NBTE), which sets standards for non-university further and higher education.

Regulatory and Representative Bodies

GOVERNMENT

Ministry of Culture and Tourism: Phase II Federal Secretariat, Block A, 1st Floor, Shehu Shagari Way, Abuja; tel. (9) 2348311; fax (9) 23408297; e-mail akayode@nigeria.gov.ng; internet www.visit-nigeria.gov.ng; Minister ADETOKUNBO KAYODE.

Ministry of Education: New Federal Secretariat Complex, Shehu Shagari Way, Central Area District, PMB 146, Abuja; tel. (9) 5237838; e-mail enquires@fme.gov.ng; internet www.fme.gov.ng; Minister IGWE AJA-NWACHUKWU.

ACCREDITATION

National Universities Commission: Aja Nwachukwu House, Plot 430, Aguiyi Ironsi St, Maitama District, PMB 237, Garki GPO, Abuja; tel. (9) 4133176; fax (9) 4133520; e-mail webmaster@nuc.edu.ng; internet www.nuc.edu.ng; f. 1962; Exec. Sec. Prof. JULIUS OKOJIE.

Learned Societies

GENERAL

UNESCO Office Abuja: PMB 424, Garki, Abuja; located at: Plot 777, Bouake St (off Herbert Macauley Way), Wuse Zone 6, Abuja; tel. (9) 4618502; fax (9) 5238094; e-mail abuja@unesco.org; Dir HUBERT CHARLES.

AGRICULTURE, FISHERIES AND VETERINARY SCIENCE

Fisheries Society of Nigeria: PMB 12529, Lagos; f. 1976; 500 mems; Pres. OLATUNDE OLANIYI; Gen. Sec. B. B. ADEKOYA; publs *Fishery Bulletin*, *Fish Network* (4 a year), *Proceedings*.

Forestry Association of Nigeria: POB 4185, Ibadan, Oyo State; tel. (64) 626535; internet www.forestrynigeria.org; f. 1970 to further interest in forests and forest resources management and utilization; 61 life mems; 1,000 ordinary mems; 17 corporate mems; Pres. BELLOI ABBA YAKASA; Sec. P. C. OBIAGA; publs *FAN Newsletter*, *Nigerian Journal of Forestry*, *Proceedings of Annual Conference*.

Nigerian Veterinary Medical Association: c/o Nigerian Veterinary Medical Institute, POB 38, Vom, Plateau State; f. 1963 to advance the science and art of veterinary medicine, including its relationship to public health and agriculture; 891 mems; Pres. Dr L. H. LOMBIN; Sec. Dr L. Y. NYAM; publs *Nigerian Veterinary Journal* (2 a year), *Tropical Veterinarian* (2 a year), *Zariya Veterinarian* (2 a year).

West African Association of Agricultural Economics: c/o Dept of Agricultural Economics, University of Ibadan, Ibadan, Oyo State; fax (8) 87222872; f. 1972; 250 mems from Benin Republic, Burkina Faso, Cameroon, Côte d'Ivoire, Ghana, Liberia, Mali, Nigeria, Senegal, Sierra Leone and Togo; Pres. Prof. Dr ANTHONY E. IKPI; Sec. Dr THOMAS EPONOU; publ. *West African Journal of Agricultural Economics*.

ARCHITECTURE AND TOWN PLANNING

Nigerian Institute of Architects: 2 Kukawa Close, Garki II, Abuja; tel. (9) 4802518; e-mail info@niarchitects.org; internet www.niarchitects.org; f. 1960; 87 Fellows, 1,370 full mems; 874 graduate mems; Pres. Arc. ERIC CHUKWUKA; publs *NIA Journals*, *NIA Newsletter*, *NIA Yearbook and Diary*, *Shelter for Nigerians*.

BIBLIOGRAPHY, LIBRARY SCIENCE AND MUSEOLOGY

Nigerian Library Association: c/o National Library of Nigeria, Sanusi Dantata House, Business Central District, PMB 1, Garki GPO 900001, Abuja; tel. (9) 2346773; e-mail info@nla-ng.org; internet www.nla-ng.org; f. 1962; 5,000 mems; established to safeguard and promote the professional interests of librarians; to promote the establishment and development of libraries; to assist in the promotion of legislation considered necessary for the establishment, regulation and management of libraries in Nigeria; to encourage bibliographical study, research and library co-operation; Pres. VICTORIA OKOJIE; publs *Nigerian Libraries* (2 a year), *NLA Newsletter* (2 a year), occasional papers.

ECONOMICS, LAW AND POLITICS

Nigerian Bar Association: Plot 1261, Adeola Hopewell St, Victoria Island, Lagos; tel. and fax (1) 4618287; internet www.nigerianbar.com; f. 1962; Pres. Chief BAYO OJO; Gen. Sec. NIMI WALSON-JACK.

Nigerian Economic Society: Dept of Econ., Univ. of Ibadan, Ibadan; tel. (2) 7800395; e-mail adminofficer@nigerianeconomicsociety.org; internet www.nigerianeconomicsociety.org; f. 1957; advances the study and promotes investigation of economic and social problems, with spec. reference to Nigeria; 3,420 mems comprising 1,944 full mems, 400 assoc. mems,

1,000 life mems, 23 corporate mems, 40 institutional mems and 13 life corporate mems; Pres. Prof. K. S. ADEYEMI; Sec. Dr OMO AREGBEYEN; publs *Nigerian Journal of Economic and Social Studies (NJESS)* (3 a year), *Proceedings of Annual Conferences*.

Nigerian Institute of International Affairs: 13 Kofo Abayomi Rd, Victoria Island, POB 1727, Lagos; tel. (1) 9500983; fax (1) 2611360; e-mail dgeneral@niianet.org; internet www.niianet.org; f. 1961; a non-political and non-profit-making org. for the study of int. affairs, to disseminate and maintain information on int. issues through confs, lectures and discussions; 2,344 mems; library of 69,324 vols, 1,707 periodicals, 20,509 pamphlets, 333,085 press clippings; Dir-Gen. Prof. BOLA A. AKINTERINWA (acting); publs *Nigeria: Bulletin on Foreign Affairs* (4 a year), *Nigerian Forum* (12 a year), *Nigerian Journal of International Affairs* (4 a year).

Nigerian Institute of Management: Plot 22, Idowu Taylor St, POB 2557, Victoria Island, Lagos; tel. (1) 2615105; fax (1) 614116; e-mail registrar@managementnigeria.org; internet www.managementnigeria.org; f. 1961; a professional body for the management profession; aims to determine standards of knowledge and skills to be attained by persons seeking to become management professionals; and to regulate and control the profession of management; academic programmes offered include the Professional Diploma in Management and Postgraduate Diploma in Management (with Obafemi Owalowo University, Ile-Ife—see Federal Universities); 20,000 mems; library of 2,300 vols; Dir-Gen. Chief L. E. A. AIMIUWU; publ. *Management in Nigeria* (4 a year).

Nigerian Political Science Association (NPSA): c/o The Secretariat, School of Social Sciences, University of Port Harcourt, PMB 5323, Port Harcourt; f. 1973 to research in politics and government in Nigeria; 200 mems; Pres. Prof. L. ADELE JINADU; Vice-Pres. Dr Y. R. BARONGO; National Sec. Dr CLIFF EDOGUN; publ. *Newsletter*.

EDUCATION

Committee of Vice-Chancellors of Nigerian Federal Universities: 4, Parakou St, Wuse II, Abuja; tel. (9) 5237655; f. 1962; acts as a coordinating body for Federal Univs; offers advice to govt and univ. governing councils on educational matters; 24 fed. univ. mems; Sec.-Gen. Prof. MUSA ABDULLAHI.

HISTORY, GEOGRAPHY AND ARCHAEOLOGY

Historical Society of Nigeria: c/o Dept. of History, University of Lagos, Lagos; internet www.hsnonline.org; f. 1955 to encourage interest and work in connection with the study of history, especially Nigerian history; Pres. Prof. MONDAY B. ABASIATTAI; Sec. Dr I. R. AMADI; publs *Bulletin of News* (4 a year), *Journal, Tarikh* (2 a year).

Nigerian Geographical Association: c/o Dept of Geography, University of Ibadan, Ibadan; tel. (22) 400550; f. 1955; to further interest in geography and its methods of teaching with special reference to Nigeria; 500 mems; Pres. Prof. ADETOYE FANIRAN; publ. *Nigerian Geographical Journal*.

LANGUAGE AND LITERATURE

Alliance Française: c/o French Consulate, Maison de France 2, Aromire Rd (on Kingsway Rd, opp. Ikoyi Hotel), Ikoyi, Lagos; tel. (1) 2692365; fax (1) 2694181; internet www.maisondefrance-ng.com; offers courses and exams in French language and culture and promotes cultural exchange with France; attached teaching centres in Enugu, Ibadan, Ikoyi, Ikoyi-Yaba, Ilorin, Jos, Kaduna, Kano, Lagos, Lagos-Yaba, Maiduguri, Owerri and Port Harcourt.

British Council: Plot 2935, IBB Way, Maitama, PMB 550, Garki, Abuja; tel. (9) 41378707; fax (9) 4130902; e-mail infonigeria@ng.britishcouncil.org; internet www.britishcouncil.org/nigeria; offers courses and exams in English language and British culture and promotes cultural exchange with the UK; attached offices in Lagos and Kano; Dir, Nigeria and Regional Dir, West Africa Dr JOHN RICHARDS.

Goethe-Institut: 10, Ozumba Mbadiwe Ave, opp. 1004 Flats, Victoria Island, Lagos State; tel. (1) 2610717; fax (1) 2617916; e-mail verw@lagos.goethe.org; internet www.goethe.de/af/lag/deindex.htm; offers courses and exams in German language and culture and promotes cultural exchange with Germany; library of 6,000 vols; Dir MICHAEL MÜLLER-VERWEYEN.

MEDICINE

Nigerian Dental Association: c/o Dept of Oral Pathology and Biology, School of Dental Sciences, University of Lagos, PMB 12003, Lagos; fax (1) 5849582; e-mail ndass1966@yahoo.co.uk; Pres. Dr KOFO WINFUNKE SAVAGE; Sec.-Gen. Dr O. A. OREBANJO.

Nigerian Medical Association: POB 1108, Adeniyi Jones Ave, Ikeja, Marina, Lagos; tel. (1) 4801569; fax (1) 4936854; e-mail info@nigeriannma.org; internet www.nigeriannma.org; f. 1951; 35,000 mems; Chair. (vacant); Pres. Dr WOLE ATOYEBI; Sec.-Gen. Dr WAPADA INUWA BALAMI.

Nigerian Society for Microbiology: c/o Prof. Nduka Okafor, Anambra State University of Technology, PMB 1660 Enugu State; f. 1973 to promote the advancement of medical, veterinary, agricultural and industrial microbiology; holds annual conferences in the Nigerian universities; 130 mems; Pres. Dr A. O. EJIOFOR; publ. *Nigerian Journal for Microbiology* (2 a year).

Nutrition Society of Nigeria: c/o Dept of Human Nutrition, Faculty of Public Health, College of Medicine, University of Ibadan, Ibadan, Oyo State; e-mail nutrisocng@yahoo.com; f. 1963; 350 mems; Pres. Prof. ISAAC O. AKINYELE; publ. *Nigerian Nutrition Newsletter*.

NATURAL SCIENCES

General

Nigerian Academy of Science: NSPRI House, 32–36 Barikisu Iyede St, PMB 1004, University of Lagos Post Office, Akoko, Yaba, Lagos; tel. (1) 7916130; e-mail info@nas.org.ng; internet www.nas.org.ng; f. 1977; 120 fellows; Pres. Prof. D. U. U. OKALI; Academic Sec. (Physical Sciences) Prof. A. O. ESOGBUE; Academic Sec. (Biological Sciences) Prof. N. M. GADAZAMA; publs *Discourses* (2 a year), *Newsletter* (2 a year), *Nigerian Journal of Agricultural Sciences* (1 a year), *Nigerian Journal of Medical Sciences* (1 a year), *Nigerian Journal of Natural Sciences* (1 a year), *Proceedings of the Nigerian Academy of Science* (4 a year).

Biological Sciences

Ecological Society of Nigeria: c/o Department of Biological Sciences, University of Lagos, Lagos; f. 1973; 373 mems; Pres. Prof. J. K. EGUNJOBI; Sec. C. CHIKE OKAFO; publs *Newsletter, Proceedings*.

Entomological Society of Nigeria: c/o Department of Crop Protection, Ahmadu Bello University, PMB 1044, Samaru, Zaria, Kaduna State; f. 1965 to further the study of insects in Nigeria; 250 mems; Pres. Prof. S. N. OKIWELU; Sec. O. O. ADU; publs *Nigerian Entomologists' Magazine* (1 a year), *Nigerian Journal of Entomology* (1 a year).

Genetics Society of Nigeria: c/o International Institute of Tropical Agriculture, Oyo Rd, PMB 5320, Ibadan, Oyo State; f. 1972 to further interest in genetics for the benefit of mankind and in the various areas of crops, livestock and medicine; 75 mems; Pres. Dr O. A. OJOMO; Sec. Dr A. O. ABIFARIN; publ. *Proceedings*.

Physical Sciences

Geological Survey of Nigeria: PMB 2007, Kaduna South; tel. (62) 212003; f. 1919; geological mapping; mineral exploration; geophysical and geochemical surveys and consultation on geological problems; library of 34,000 vols; Chief Officer J. I. NEHIKHARE.

TECHNOLOGY

Nigerian Society of Engineers: 1 Engineering Close, PMB 72667, Victoria Island, Lagos; tel. (1) 2617349; fax (1) 2617315; e-mail se@nse.org.ng; internet www.nse.org.ng; f. 1958; 15,000 mems; library of 1,500 vols; Pres. Eng. FOLUSEKE ABIDEMI SOMOLU; publ. *The Nigerian Engineer* (4 a year).

Research Institutes

GENERAL

Lake Chad Research Institute (LCRI): Maidugur, PMB 1293, Maiduguri, Borno State; tel. (76) 960300; fax (76) 923441; e-mail executivedirector@lcresmaid.org; internet www.lcresmaid.org; f. 1975; researches into the hydrological behaviour and characteristics of Lake Chad and the limnology of the associated surface and ground waters; the abundance, distribution and other biological characteristics of species of fish and other aquatic life in the lake and practical methods of their exploitation; the behaviour and characteristics of the wildlife associated with the lake and its conservation; ecology and methods of control of crop pests and diseases of economic importance; improvement of the methods of control of dry farming and livestock husbandry in the severe environmental condition around the lake; improvement of cultivation of wheat, barley, and other crops by irrigation; the socioeconomic and public health effects of the introduction of large-scale irrigation schemes and improved methods of animal husbandry and fishing on the rural populations around the lake; genetic improvement, investigation of problems of all agricultural food crops grown, agricultural extension and research services with relevant fed. and state ministries, primary agricultural producers, industries and other users, technical services to farmers, agro-based industries; library of 16,000 vols; Exec. Dir Prof. BUKAR BABABE; publ. *LCRI Newsletter* (4 a year).

AGRICULTURE, FISHERIES AND VETERINARY SCIENCE

Cocoa Research Institute of Nigeria: Onigambari, PMB 5244, Ibadan, Oyo State; tel. (22) 410040; f. 1964; research into cocoa, cola, coffee, cashew and tea; research aspects include entomology, plant-breeding, plant pathology, soil chemistry and biochemistry; library of 15,000 vols; Dir S. T. OLATOYE; publs *CRIN News* (12 a year), *Progress Report* (4 a year).

Forestry Research Institute of Nigeria (FRIN): PMB 5054, Ibadan, Oyo State; tel. (2) 413327; fax (2) 2410515; e-mail dfrin@skannet.com; internet www.frin-ng.org; f. 1954; conducts intensive research into all aspects of forestry and forest products utilization; Federal Colleges of Forestry at Ibadan and Jos, Federal College of Wildlife Management at New Bussa and Federal College of Forestry Mechanization at Afaka in Kaduna State; library of 17,798 vols, 590 periodicals; Exec. Dir Prof. S. O. O. BADEJO; publs *Journal of Forestry Research and Management* (2 a year), *Newsletter* (4 a year).

Institute for Agricultural Research (IAR): Ahmadu Bello University, PMB 1044, Samaru, Zaria, 810261; tel. (69) 551335; fax (69) 550563; e-mail iar20002001@yahoo.com; internet www.iarsamaru.org; f. 1924; improvement of production of sorghum, millet, wheat, groundnuts, cotton and fibres, cowpea, sesame, soyabean and vegetables; maintenance of soil fertility; land resources assessment; crop environment; cropping systems and intercropping; crop-livestock integration; mechanization; soil and water management; socio-economic studies of small farm management, marketing, credit, supply systems and extension; sub-stations at: Kano in Kano State, Kadawa in Kano State and Talata Mafara in Zamfara State; library of 18,000 vols; Dir Prof. SHEHU GARKI ADO; publs *Samaru Journal of Agricultural Research* (1 a year), *Samaru Miscellaneous Papers* (2 a year), *Samaru Research Bulletins* (4 a year), *Soil Survey Reports*.

Institute of Agricultural Research and Training (IART): Obafemi Awolowo University, Moor Plantation, PMB 5029, Ibadan, Oyo State; tel. (2) 2312523; fax (2) 2316857; e-mail drart@infoweb.abs.net; f. 1921, univ. institute 1970; comprises research div. and 2 federal colleges of agriculture and animal health production; serves as nat. centre for research into crops, cereals, grains, soyabean, jute, kenaf, livestock, soils and water management; library of 45,000 vols; Dir Prof. E. A. ADEBOWALE; publ. *Moor Journal of Agricultural Research* (2 a year).

National Agricultural Extension and Research Liaison Services: Ahmadu Bello University, PMB 1067, Zaria; tel. (69) 879449; fax (69) 552198; e-mail director@naerls.gov.ng; internet www.naerls.gov.ng; f. 1963; agricultural performance and evaluation, agricultural economics and resources management, agricultural extension research, extension training and outreach and agricultural communication research; library of 2,000 vols, 1,400 periodicals; Exec. Dir Prof. SADIQ ZUBAIAR ABUBAKAR; Exec. Dir Dr O. A. OYEDOKUN; publ. *The Nigerian Journal of Agricultural Extension* (2 a year).

National Animal Production Research Institute (NAPRI): Ahmadu Bello University, Shika, POB 1096, Zaria; tel. (69) 550435; fax (69) 551272; f. 1928; research into dairy, beef, sheep, goat, swine, rabbit and poultry production, management and breeding, range and pasture research and improvement, livestock economics and rural sociology of pastoral nomadic peoples; library of 23,624 vols; Dir Prof. A. M. ADAMU; publs *Bulletin* (4 a year), *Journal of Animal Production Research* (1 a year).

National Centre for Agricultural Mechanization: Federal Ministry of Agriculture, PMB 1525, Ilorin, Kwara State; tel. (33) 649168; e-mail info@ncam.gov.ng; internet www.ncam.gov.ng; f. 1977; testing and developing of agricultural machinery; standardization, extension and training services in the field of agricultural mechanization; Exec. Dir Ing. IKE AZOGU.

National Centre for Genetic Resources and Biotechnology (NACGRAB): Moor Plantation, PMB 5382, Ibadan, Oyo State; tel. (2) 2312622; e-mail nacgrab@skannet.com; f. 1986; research, data gathering and dissemination of information on matters relating to plant genetic resources, genetic engineering and biotechnology; library of 1,500 vols; Project Man. LANRE GBADAMOSI.

National Cereals Research Institute (NCRI): PMB 8, Badeggi, Bida, Niger State; tel. (66) 461233; tel. (66) 461234; e-mail ncri@skannet.com; f. 1975, fmrly Federal Department of Agricultural Research; conducts research into the production, processing and industrial capacity utilization of rice, digitaria, oilseeds (soybean and beniseed) and sugarcane; mechanization and improvement of methods of cultivating, harvesting, processing and storage of crops; improving the utilization of by-products; ecology of crop pests and diseases and improved methods of their control; integration of crop cultivation into farming systems in different ecological zones and its socio-economic effects on the rural population; distributes farming implements, machinery and cultivated varieties of rice and soybean; library of 6,078 vols; incl. a Plant Quarantine Training Centre; Head of Station A. S. GANA; publs *Information Papers* (12 a year), *Memoranda* (irregular), *Research Bulletins* (4 a year).

National Horticultural Research Institute (NIHORT): Idi-Ishin, PMB 5432, Ibadan, Oyo State; tel. and fax (2) 2412230; e-mail nihortinfo@yahoo.com; internet www.nihort.org; f. 1975; two sub-stations at Mbato, near Okigwe, Imo State and at Bagauda, near Tiga, Kano State; conducts research into fruit and vegetable production and consumption, in particular improvement of the genetic potentials of the cultivated, semi-cultivated and wild crops; improvement of agronomic and husbandry practices; mechanization and improvement of methods of cultivating, harvesting, processing and storage; improvement of the utilization of by-products; ecology of crop pests and diseases and improved methods of their control; integration of crop cultivation into farming systems in different ecological zones of the country; library of 23,000 vols; Dir ADEMOLA ADESEYE IDOWU; publs *Information Papers* (12 a year), technical bulletins, production guides, training manuals (irregular).

National Institute for Freshwater Fisheries Research (NIFFR): PMB 6006, New Bussa, Niger State; tel. (31) 670 444; f. 1968; research into the limnological behaviour and characteristics of the man-made lakes and their effects on the fish and other aquatic life; the abundance, distribution and other biological characteristics of species of fish and practical methods of their exploitation; the socio-economic effects of the construction of man-made lakes on rural populations; technical and vocational training in freshwater fishing and related fields; library of 20,000 vols, 40 periodicals; Dir Prof. B. M. B. LADU; publs *Newsletter* (4 a year), *Nigerian Fisheries and Aquatic Sciences Abstract* (1 a year).

National Root Crops Research Institute (NRCRI): Umudike, PMB 7006, Umuahia, Abia State; tel. and fax (82) 440471; e-mail keninwrosu_nrcri@yahoo.com; internet www.nrcri.org.ng; f. 1923; research for the genetic improvement of yams, cocoyams, cassava, sweet potato, Irish potato, ginger and other root-crops; farming systems research and middle manpower training; library of 3,113 books, 25,665 periodicals; Dir Dr KEN I. NWOSU; publs *Advisory Bulletins* (12 a year), *Gazette*, *News Bulletin* (4 a year), *Newsletter*, *Programmes of Work* (1 a year).

National Veterinary Research Institute (NVRI): PMB 01, Vom, near Jos, Plateau State; tel. (55) 578876; fax (81) 817080; e-mail edvr@nvri.gov.ng; f. 1924; intensive research into all aspects of animal diseases and their treatment and control; all aspects of animal nutrition; production of vaccine and sera; introduction of exotic stock to improve meat, milk and egg production; standardization and quality control of manufactured animal feeds; training livestock superintendents, laboratory technicians and technologists; library of 14,000 vols, 4,000 reports, etc.; Exec. Dir Dr MOHAMMED SANI AHMED; publs *Index of Veterinary Research* (1 a year), *Newsletter* (4 a year), *Research Papers* (irregular).

Nigerian Institute for Oil Palm Research (NIFOR): PMB 1030, Benin City, Edo State; tel. (52) 602485; fax (52) 602486; f. 1939; research into the production and products of oil palm and other palms of economic importance and recommendation of improved methods; library of 13,000 vols; Dir Dr U. OMOTI; publ. *Nigerian Journal of Palms and Oil Seeds* (irregular).

Nigerian Stored Products Research Institute (NSPRI): Km. 3, Asa Dam Rd, PMB 1489, Ilorin, Kwara State; tel. (31) 222143; fax (31) 221639; e-mail nspriheadquarters@yahoo.com; internet www.nspriilorin.com; f. 1960; research into stored-product pests and primary processing; training, analytical services and advisory work, design and construction of storage structures; 450 mems; library of 3,610 vols; Exec. Dir Dr M. A. ADESIDA; publs *Journal* (4 a year), *Newsletter* (4 a year), *Nigerian Post-Harvest Technology Abstract* (1 a year), *Research News* (4 a year).

Rubber Research Institute of Nigeria (RRIN): Iyanomo, PMB 1049, Benin City, Edo State; tel. (68) 226591; e-mail rubberresearchnig@yahoo.com; f. 1961; researches on natural rubber (*Hevea brasiliensis*), gum arabic (*Acacia Spp.*) and other latex bearing plants of economic importance; dissemination of vital research information to farmers; production; sub-station at Akwete near Aba in Anambra; library of 1,000 vols; Exec. Dir Prof. OSAYANMO IGBINOSA EGUAVOEN; publs *Information Booklets* (4 a year), *RRIN's Advisory Leaflets* (12 a year).

BIBLIOGRAPHY, LIBRARY SCIENCE AND MUSEOLOGY

Institute of Archaeology and Museum Studies: PMB 2031, Jos, Plateau State; tel. (73) 453516; e-mail iamsjos2000@yahoo.co.uk; f. 1963; library of 1,500 vols, 500 journals; Dir MONICA ABADOM; publ. *The Museologist* (1 a year).

ECONOMICS, LAW AND POLITICS

Centre for Management Development: PMB 21578, Ikeja Lagos; tel. (1) 7748165; fax (1) 4978390; e-mail infor@cmdonline.org; internet www.cmdonline.org; f. 1973 to promote and coordinate the activities of institutions engaged in the education and training of managerial manpower; advises government on policy, formulates policies and guidelines, monitors standards of management education, accredits and registers management trainers, assesses training programmes, provides advisory and consultancy service to Nigerian businesses; library of 46,000 vols, 700 periodicals, also general publs and serials, teaching materials library, and audiovisual unit; Dir-Gen. Dr KABIR KABO USMAN; Asst Dir of Library S. S. OGUNNOWO; publs *Journal of Economic Man-*

agement, *Nigerian Management Review* (2 a year).

Nigerian Institute of Social and Economic Research: PMB 5, University Post Office, Ibadan; tel. (2) 8102904; fax (2) 8101194; e-mail dg@niser.org.ng; internet www.nisernigeria.org; f. 1950 as WA Institute of Social and Economic Research, present name 1960; government-financed; applied research on problems of immediate and long-term relevance to Nigerian development: economic planning and development, agricultural and industrial development, business and technology, foreign and international trade, public finance and social, physical and manpower planning and development; political development, population studies; training for staff of planning organizations; consultancy service for federal and state governments, private organizations and international bodies; library of 75,000 vols; Dir-Gen. Prof. BANKOLE ONI; publ. *Research for Development* (1 a year).

EDUCATION

Nigerian Educational Research Council: POB 8058, Lagos; f. 1965; curriculum development and general educational research; 30 mems; library of 12,000 vols; Chair. Prof. S. N. NWOSU; Sec. J. M. AKINTOLA; publs conference and workshop reports.

MEDICINE

National Institute of Pharmaceutical Research and Development (NIPRD): PMB 21, Idu, Abuja; tel. (9) 5239089; f. 1989; research into medical plants, herbs and drug development and formulary; drug information centre; nat. centre for drugs; regulates the standardization of pharmaceutical substances; library of 2,350 vols, 2,389 journals, 6,000 CD-ROMs; Dir Dr UFORD S. INYANG; publ. *Journal of Phytomedicine and Therapeutics (JOPAT)* (1 a year).

Nigerian Institute of Medical Research (NIMR): Edmund Crescent, PMB 2013, Yaba, Lagos; tel. (1) 800090; fax (1) 862865; e-mail director@nimr-ng.org; internet www.nimr-ng.org; f. 1973; identifies major health problems of the country and their determinants; research into environmental hazards and their effect on the population's health; library of 13,000 vols; Dir-Gen. Dr ONI IDIGBE.

Nigerian Institute for Trypanosomiasis Research (NITR): PMB 2077, Kaduna, Kaduna State; tel. (62) 238074; fax (62) 238705; e-mail nitrng@yahoo.com; internet www.nitr-ng.org; f. 1951; research into trypanosomiasis and onchocerciasis generally; the pathology, immunology and methods of treatment of the diseases; the ecology and life-cycle of the vectors and the mode of transmission of the disease; chemical, biological and other methods of vector control, the socio-economic effects of the disease on the rural populations; maintains 6 zonal offices, 2 field stations; library of 10,000 vols; Dir Prof. M. MAMMAN.

NATURAL SCIENCES

General

Nigerian Institute for Oceanography and Marine Research (NIOMR): Victoria Island, PMB 12729, Lagos; tel. (1) 2617385; fax (1) 2619517; e-mail niomr@linkserve.com.ng; f. 1975; research into the resources and physical characteristics of the Nigerian territorial waters and the high seas beyond; library of 10,000 vols; Dir J. G. TOBOR; publ. *Newsletter* (4 a year).

TECHNOLOGY

Federal Institute of Industrial Research (FIIRO): PMB 21023, Ikeja, Lagos; Blind Centre St, Cappa Bus Stop, off Agege Motor Rd, Oshodi, Ikeja, Lagos; tel. (1) 8947094; fax (1) 4525880; e-mail info@fiiro-ng.org; internet www.fiiro-ng.org; f. 1956; food technology, industrial fermentation through biotechnology, pulp and paper research, domestic and industrial water treatment, environmental studies, ceramic and engineering materials research, machinery and equipment design and fabrication; consultancy, analytical services, technical services to industry, scientific and industrial information service; library of 14,500 vols; Dir-Gen./CEO Dr OLUWOLE OLATUNJI; publs *Journal of Industrial Research and Technology* ((irregular)), *Profile on FIIRO Commercializable Technologies* (irregular), *Research Report* (irregular).

National Centre for Energy Research and Development: University of Nigeria, Nsukka, Enugu State; tel. (42) 771853; fax (42) 771855; e-mail misunn@aol.com; f. 1982; federal government-funded centre for research and development of solar and other renewable and non-renewable energy such as photovoltaic, photothermal, wind energy, radiation measurement, biomass, coal, energy management, etc.; Dir Dr O. V. EKECHUKWU.

National Research Institute for Chemical Technology (NARICT): PMB 1052, Zaria, Kaduna State; tel. (69) 334503; fax (69) 334835; f. 1988; research and development work in chemicals, leather and allied fields; short-term training courses in chemical technology, laboratory management, chemistry laboratory practicals, safety; four extension centres, at Kano, Jos, Maiduguri and Sokoto for extension services; serves as national information centre on leather and chemical technology; Dir-Gen. Dr E. M. OKONKWO; publs *Journal of Leather and Chemical Technology* (1 a year), *NARICT Bulletin* (1 a year), *NARICT Newsletter* (12 a year).

Nigerian Building and Road Research Institute (NBRRI): PMB 5065, Wuse General Post Office, Abuja FCT; 3 Gabes str., Wuse Zone 2, Abuja FCT; tel. and fax (9) 5237466-7; e-mail servicomunit@nbrri.gov.ng; internet www.nbrri.gov.ng; f. 1978; conducts applied research and devt into the use of local materials and methods in road and bldg construction; library of 12,000 vols; Dir-Gen. Dr J. A. ALI; publs *Journal of Construction and Materials Technology* (2 a year), *Technical Digest* (2 a year).

Projects Development Institute (PRODA): Emene Industrial Layout, PMB 01609, Enugu State; tel. (42) 301306; fax (42) 457691; e-mail info@proda-ng.org; internet www.proda-ng.org; f. 1970 as Project Devt Agency, present status 1977; accredited by Federal Min. of Science and Technology; conducts research into various areas of science, ceramics, energy and engineering with the aim of advancing industialization; promotes the establishment of new industrial projects through laboratory and pilot investigations to the construction of large-scale commercial plants, uses local raw materials and labour; library of 4,500 vols; Dir-Gen. Prof. G. N. ONUOHA; publs *PRODA Annual Report*, *PRODA Investment Profile*, *PRODA Quarterly Report*.

Raw Materials Research and Development Council (RMRDC): Plot 17, Aguiyi Ironsi St, Maitama District, PMB 232, Garki, Abuja; tel. (9) 8213090; fax (9) 4136034; e-mail ceo@rmrdc.gov.ng; internet www.rmrdc.gov.ng; f. 1987; supports and expedites industrial devt and self-sufficiency through maximum utilization of local materials; draws up policy guidelines and action programmes on raw materials acquisition, exploitation and devt; advises on adaptation of machinery and process for raw materials utilization; library of 3,000 vols; Chief Exec. and Dir-Gen. Prof. PETER AZIKIWE ONWUALU; publs *Journal of Raw Materials* (1 a year), *Research Reports* (8 a year), *RMRDC Newsletter* (4 a year).

Libraries and Archives

Abeokuta

Ogun State Library: PMB 2060, Abeokuta, Ogun State; f. 1976; 21,736 vols; special collection on Ogun State; Chief Librarian Alhaji BAYO YISA ODULAJA.

Akure

Ondo State Library Board: PMB 719, Akure; tel. (34) 230561; f. 1976, renamed 1985; reading and reference services, mobile- and school-library services, training of library assistants; 62,546 vols; Dir T. A. AJUMOBI.

Bauchi

Bauchi State Library Board: Ministry of Education, Bauchi; f. 1976; lending and reference services, special services to rehabilitation centres, training of library staff; 35,000 vols, 3,475 periodicals; Dir MUSA M. DEDE.

Benin

Edo State Library Board: Sapele Rd, PMB 1127, Benin City; tel. (52) 234-255176; f. 1971; 311,680 vols; Central Reference Library with emphasis on the needs of the State Govt; Readers Services Div. (22 brs). Technical Service Div.; School Library Div.; hospital trolley services; Dir JOSEPH O. UDUEBOR; publs *Edo Library Accessions List* (2 a year), *Legal Deposit Bulletin* (2 a year), *Newsletter* (4 a year), *Index to The Observer* (2 a year).

Enugu

Enugu State Library Board: PMB 01026, Enugu; tel. (42) 254103; f. 1955; Dir of Library Services ISAAC OGBONNA..

Attached Library:

State Central Library: Market Rd, Enugu; f. 1956; lending and reference library activities; legal deposit and regional centre for bibliographical information and research; Nigeriana colln; 1 mobile library unit; divisional library at Onueke; zonal libraries at Awgu, Agbani and Nsukka; 83,000 vols.

Ibadan

Federal Ministry of Science and Technology, Library and Documentation Centre: Moor Plantation, PMB 5382, Ibadan, Oyo State; f. 1973; 2,000 vols, 700 current periodicals, 22 microfiches, 350 reprints; newspaper clippings; the Liaison Office in Nigeria for both AGRIS (International Information System for Agricultural Sciences and Technology) and CARIS (Current Agricultural Research Information Service); Librarian O. A. ADIGUM; publs *List of Reprints*, *List of Serials* (1 a year).

Forestry Research Institute of Nigeria Library: PMB 5054, Ibadan; tel. (2) 2414441; fax (2) 2410515; e-mail dfrin@skannet.com; internet www.frin-ng.org; f. 1954; spec. collns: Nigerian silvicultural records and working plans, postgraduate theses colln, and Harold Young Library of rare materials on forest mensuration, biometrics, photogrammetry and technometrics; 17,798 vols, 590 periodicals; Head of Library Dr B. A. AKINTOLA; publs *Current Awareness Service on Agricultural Research and Development Bulletin* (12 a year), *Current Contents* (12 a year), *Library Accession Lists* (4 a year).

Kenneth Dike Library, University of Ibadan: University of Ibadan, Ibadan; tel. (2) 8101100; fax (2) 8103118; internet www.ui.edu.ng/unitslibrary.htm; f. 1948; 700,000 vols, 1,500 current periodicals; depository for OAU and UN specialized agencies publs; special collection of Africana, private papers of eminent Nigerians; Librarian OLUFUNMILAYO G. TAMUNO; publ. *Library Record*.

National Archives of Nigeria: PMB 4, University of Ibadan Post Office, Ibadan; f. 1951, legally recognized 1957; charged with collection, rehabilitation, reproduction and preservation of all public records including private papers under the Ministry of Information and National Orientation; 3 major (zonal) offices at Enugu, Ibadan and Kaduna; other brs are located at Abeokuta, Akure, Benin, Calabar, Ilorin, Jos, Lagos Maiduguri, Oweri, Port-Harcourt and Sokoto; 8,500 vols; Dir COMFORT AINA UKWU; publ. *Special Lists*.

Ife

Hezekiah Oluwasanmi Library, Obafemi Awolowo University: Ile-Ife; tel. (36) 230290; f. 1961; 640,567 vols, 6,905 periodicals; spec. collns of Africana, audiovisual materials and govt documents; Librarian B. O. ASUBIOJO; publs *Abstracts of Theses* (1 a year), *Research in Progress at the Obafemi Awolowo University* (1 a year).

Ikeja

Industrial Information Centre and Extension Services (FIIRO Indices): PMB 21023, Ikeja, Cappa Bus Stop, Agege Motor Rd, Lagos State; tel. (1) 4522905; fax (1) 4525880; f. 1956; scientific, technical and industrial information, documentation and dissemination, current awareness, publication services; 14,500 vols; spec. collns: UNIDO, NTIS, FOS publs, nat. and int. standards; Librarian P. O. DEKWE; publs *Journal of Industrial Research and Technology*, industrial and corporate profiles, reports on selected FIIRO technologies for rural industrialization.

Ilorin

Kwara State Library Board: Sulu Gambari Rd, PMB 1561, Ilorin, Kwara State; f. 1968; 45,000 vols; Dir Deacon BENSON BABATUNDE ODEWALE.

Jos

Plateau State Library Services: c/o Bureau for Information, POB 2053, Jos, Plateau State; f. 1976; 45,293 vols; brs at Akwanga, Keffi, Lafia, Pankshin and Shendam; Librarian TIMOTHY P. A. ANGBA (acting).

Kaduna

Kaduna State Library Board: PMB 2061, Kaduna; f. 1953, renamed 1976; 200,000 vols; Dir JOSEPH AHMADU MAIGARI; publs *Bibliographies*, *Current Awareness Bulletin*, *Legal Deposit Collection*, *Public Enlightenment*, *Readers' Guides*.

Kano

Kano State Library Board: PMB 3094, Ahmadu Bello Way, Kano; tel. (64) 645614; e-mail nassarawa2001@yahoo.com; f. 1968; includes mobile and school library services, cultural programmes, outreach services to government departments, reference and documentation services, audiovisual services, internet services; 1m. vols; Exec. Dir Alhaji SANUSI ABDULLAH NASSARAWA.

Lagos

Central Medical Library: Federal Ministry of Health, PMB 2003, Yaba, Lagos; f. 1946; serves the entire country; 30,000 vols, 600 journals; Librarian M. O. ORIMOLADE.

Lagos City Libraries: PMB 2025, Lagos; f. 1950; 229,150 vols; Librarian Mrs B. B. OGUNLANA.

National Library of Nigeria: 4 Wesley St, PMB 12626, Lagos; tel. (1) 2600220; fax (1) 2631563; f. 1964; 12 brs; 140,000 vols in main library, 18,000 at branches; special collections of Nigerian and UK government publications, UN documents, Rhodes House Library Collection (private papers of past colonial civil servants), Ranfurly Library Collection; depository for UN, OAU and Canadian publs; Chair. FRANCIS Z. GANA; National Librarian Alhaji MU'AZU H. WALI.

University of Lagos Library: Lagos; tel. and fax (1) 4932552; internet www.unilag.edu; f. 1962; 375,000 vols, 4,500 periodicals; legal depository for Lagos State; depository for all publications of ECA, GATT, ICJ and ILO; collections on UNESCO, WHO and FAO; Librarian Dr S. O. OLANLOKUN (acting); publs *Library Notes*, *Reader's Guide*, *Unilag: Quarterly News Bulletin*.

Maiduguri

Borno State Library Board: PMB 1443, Maiduguri, Borno State; tel. (76) 231389; f. 1968; became library board 1984; 86,535 vols; 11 brs; provides information for the public, trains library staff, organizes school libraries, annual book exhibition, etc.; Dir JOHN YADU MALGWI.

Nsukka

University of Nigeria, Nsukka Libraries: Nnamdi Azikiwe Library, Nsukka, Enugu State; tel. (42) 771444; fax (42) 270644; e-mail misunn@aol.com; f. 1960; 717,000 vols at Nsukka and Enugu campuses, medical library at Enugu with 42,000 vols, Africana collection of 30,000 vols; Librarian EMENIKE IKEGBUNE (acting); publs *Nsukka Library Notes* (irregular), *UNLAN*.

Owerri

Imo State Library Board: PMB 1118, Owerri, Imo State; tel. (83) 230280; f. 1976; lending, reference, children's library and library for the disabled, bibliographic and information consultancy services, rural library services and school library resource centre; 123,000 vols; Dir of Library Services AGATHA C. NWACHUKWU; publ. *The Light* (1 a year).

Port Harcourt

British Council Information Centre: Plot 127, Olu Obasanjo Way, GRA II, Port Harcourt; tel. (84) 237173; fax (84) 237172; e-mail info.portharcourt@ng.britishcouncil.org; Centre Man. PATIENCE EZINWOKE.

Museums and Art Galleries

Benin

National Museum, Benin: Benin; tel. and fax (52) 252675; e-mail natmusben@yahoo.com; f. 1973; Benin antiquities, bronzes, ivory, terracotta, wood, beads, masks, masquerades, ancestral figures, materials for warfare, etc.; Curator MARTINS OGUNTAYO AKANBIEMU.

Esie

Esie Museum: PMB 301, Kwara State; f. 1945; stone antiquities (800 half life-size human figures); Dir (vacant).

Ife

Natural History Museum, Obafemi Awolowo University: Ile-Ife, Osun State; tel. (36) 230291 ext. 2451; e-mail oige@oauife.edu.ng; f. 1971 as sub-unit of Dept. of Biological Sciences of University of Ife, present status 1982; research, outreach activities, teaching, exhibition and identification of animal and plant specimens; botanical, entomological, geological, palaeontological and zoological collections; archaeological artifacts; offers MSc in conservation and MSc and PhD in biosystematics; Dir Prof. AKIN IGE.

Jos

National Museum, Jos: PMB 2031, Jos, Plateau State; f. 1982; ethnography, architecture and archaeology of Nigeria; terracotta Nok figurines, modern and traditional Nigerian pottery; zoological and botanical gardens; museum of traditional architecture; transport museum; craft village; open-air theatre; library of 10,000 vols and 2,000 Arabic MSS; Dir M. DANDAURA.

Kaduna

National Museum, Kaduna: PMB 2127, Kaduna; tel. (62) 211180; fax (1) 2633890; f. 1975; archaeology and ethnography; houses the 'Craft Village', where traditional hair-plaiting, weaving, pottery, calabash decoration, wood carving, leather work, brass casting and smithery are done; library of 1,500 vols; Dir Dr K. S. CHAFE; publ. *Tambari*.

Kano

Gidan Makama Museum: POB 2023, Kano; tel. (64) 645170; e-mail yusufadamu2000@yahoo.com; internet www.kanoonline.com/gidan_makama; f. 1959; local art work; history of Kano and the Kanawas from 15th–19th centuries; Curator MUSA O. HAMBOLU.

Lagos

National Museum, Lagos: Onikan Rd, Lagos; tel. (1) 2634045; e-mail museumlagos@yahoo.com; f. 1957; ethnography, archaeology and traditional art; library of 9,247 vols; Dir-Gen. MALLAM YUSUF ABDALLAH USMAN; publ. *Nigerian Heritage* (1 a year).

Oron

National Museum, Oron: PMB 1004, Oron, Akwa Ibom State; f. 1958; rebuilt after civil war in 1975; wooden sculptures and ethnographic artefacts and materials; Chief Curator ANIEFIOK UDO AKPAN.

Owo

Owo Museum: Federal Dept of Antiquities, POB 84, Owo, Ondo State; f. 1959; arts and crafts; some ethnographic relics mainly from the Eastern part of the Yoruba region; Curator E. OLA ABEJIDE.

Universities

FEDERAL UNIVERSITIES

ABUBAKAR TAFAWA BALEWA UNIVERSITY

PMB 0248, Bauchi

Telephone: (77) 543500

Fax: (77) 542095

E-mail: info@atbunet.org

Internet: www.atbu.edu.ng
Founded 1988
Federal government control
Language of instruction: English
Academic year: October to September
Vice-Chancellor: Prof. MUHAMMAD HAMISU MUHAMMAD
Deputy Vice-Chancellor for Academic Affairs: Prof. MOHAMMAD IBRAHIM ONOGU
Deputy Vice-Chancellor for Admin.: Prof. USMAN ALIYU EL-NATATY
Bursar and Registrar: Alhaji ALI A. DEBA
Librarian: Prof. MANSUR USMAN MALUMFASHI
Number of teachers: 260
Number of students: 12,000 (8,000 full-time, 4,000 part-time)
Publication: *University Bulletin* (4 a year)

DEANS

School of Agriculture and Agricultural Technology: Prof. ISYAKU MUHAMMAD
School of Engineering Technology: Prof. GERRY EGBO
School of Environment and Environmental Technology: Prof. UMAR ABDULLAHI
School of Management Technology: ABUBAKAR YUSUF DUTSE
School of Science and Science Education: Prof. EDIGA B. AGBO
School of Technology Education: Prof. JOSEPH D. ENEMALI

PROFESSORS

ABAYEH, O. J., Chemistry
ABUBAKAR, M. M., Animal Science
ADEBITAN, S. A., Crop Production
ADEGBOLA, T. A., Animal Science
ALIYU, U. O., Electrical Engineering
BABAJI, G. A., Crop Production
BOGOVO, S., Crop Production
DIKE, E. F. C., Geology
ELINWA, A. U., Civil Engineering
GANI, A. M., Biological Sciences
HAQUE, M. F., Physics
IBRAHIM, S. A., Crop Production
JATAU, J. S., Mechanical and Production Engineering
KELA, S. L., Biological Sciences
MATAWAL, D. S., Civil Engineering
MBAP, S. T., Animal Production
OCHI, J. E., Agricultural Economics and Extension
OGIDI, J. A., Biological Sciences
ONOGU, M. I., Electrical Engineering and Electronics
ORAZULIKE, D. M., Geology
OYAWOYE, E. O., Animal Production
OYAWOYE, E. O., Biological Sciences
SANI, R. M., Agricultural Economics and Extension
SAWA, F. J., Biological Sciences
SESAY, M. S., Mathematical Sciences
SHEHU, L. M., Animal Production
SHEHU, Y., Animal Production
SULEIMAN, M. M., Biological Sciences
UBA, A., Biological Sciences
YUSUF, I. Z., Biological Sciences

UNIVERSITY OF ABUJA

PMB 117, Abuja, Federal Capital City
Telephone: (9) 8821380
Fax: (9) 8821605
E-mail: vc@uniabuja.edu.ng
Founded 1988
Language of instruction: English
Academic year: October to September
Chancellor: (vacant)
Vice-Chancellor: Prof. A. L. GAMBO
Registrar: Mallam YAKUBU HASSAN HABI
Librarian: Dr FAB. A. J. AKHIDIME
Number of teachers: 150
Number of students: 5,400

DEANS

College of Arts and Education: Dr JOSEPH N. UKWEDEH
College of Law, Management and Social Sciences: Dr NANA M. TANKO
College of Science and Agriculture: Prof. SIMON I. OKWUTE
Postgraduate School: Dr MICHAEL A. ADEWALE

PROFESSORS

ADELABU, J. A., Physics
AMDII, I. E. S., Political Science
BIRAI, U. M., Political Science
IKEOTUONYE, A. I., Education
OKWUTE, S. I., Chemistry
UJO, A. A., Political Science

UNIVERSITY OF AGRICULTURE, ABEOKUTA

PMB 2240, Abeokuta, Ogun State
Telephone: (39) 08033490946
E-mail: registrar@unaab.edu.ng
Internet: www.unaab.edu.ng
Founded 1988 (previously a college of University of Lagos)
Federal control
Language of instruction: English
Academic year: October to July
Chancellor: Prof. JOSEPH CHIKE EDOZIEN
Vice-Chancellor: Prof. OLUWAFEMI OLAIYA BALOGUN ADU
Deputy Vice-Chancellor (Academic): Prof. C. F. I. ONWUKA
Deputy Vice-Chancellor (Development): Prof. S. T. O. LAGOKE
Registrar: A. O. ADEBOYE (acting)
Librarian: A. T. AGBOOLA
Number of teachers: 519
Number of students: 9,723
Publications: *Agricultural Sciences, Science, Environment and Technology (ASSET)* (2 a year), *UNAAB News*

DEANS

College of Agricultural Management, Rural Development: Prof. S. O. APANTAKU
College of Animal Science and Livestock Production: Prof. D. ERUVBETINE
College of Engineering: Prof. E. S. A. AJISEGIRI
College of Environmental Resources Management: Prof. T. A. AROWOLO
College of Food Science and Human Ecology: Prof. F. O. HENSHAW
College of Natural Sciences: Prof. T. O. S. POPOOLA
College of Plant Science and Crop Production: Prof. O. B. KEHINDE
College of Veterinary Medicine: Prof. M. DIPEOLU
Postgraduate School: Prof. S. O. AFOLAMI
Student Affairs: Prof. S. A. OLUWALANA

PROFESSORS

ADAMSON, I., Chemistry
ADDO, A. A., Home Science and Management
ADEBAMBO, O. A., Animal Breeding and Genetics
ADETUNJI, M. T., Soil Science and Agricultural Mechanisation
ADU, I. F., Animal Nutrition
AKINGBALA, J. O., Food Science and Technology
AKINLADE, O., Physics
ARIYO, O. J., Plant Breeding and Seed Technology
AWONORIN, S. O., Food Science and Technology
BAMIRO, F. O., Chemistry
BELLO, N. J., Water Management and Agricultural Meteorology
EROMOSELE, I. C., Chemistry
ERUVBETINE, D., Animal Nutrition
KADIRI, M., Biological Sciences
LADEINDE, T. A. O., Plant Breeding and Seed Technology
MARTINS, O., Water Management and Agricultural Meteorology
OGUNTONA, C. R. B., Home Science and Management
OJANUGA, A. G., Soil Science and Agricultural Mechanisation
OKUNEYE, P. A., Agricultural Economics and Farm Management
OLADOKUN, M. A. O., Horticulture
OLAGOKE, S. T. O., Crop Protection
OLASANTAN, F. O., Horticulture
ONWUKA, C. F., Animal Nutrition
PHILLIP, D., Agricultural Economics and Farm Management
TAYO, T. O., Plant Physiology and Crop Production

UNIVERSITY OF AGRICULTURE, MAKURDI

PMB 2373, Makurdi, Benue State
Telephone: (44) 533204
Founded 1988, previously campus of the University of Jos, now a fully independent university
Federal control
Language of instruction: English
Academic year: October to September
Chancellor: HRH, Igwe (Barr) I. U. NNAJI (Eze Odezurigbo III of Nike, Enugu)
Vice-Chancellor: Prof. D.V. UZA
Registrar: Dr S. A. EDE
Librarian: SUGH LOHO
Number of teachers: 446
Number of students: 7,654
Publication: *Journal of Agriculture, Science and Technology* (2 a year)

DEANS

College of Agricultural Economics and Mgt: Prof. O.J. OKWO
College of Agricultural Engineering and Engineering Technology: Dr I. O. AGBEDE
College of Agricultural Science Education: Prof. A. A. EKOJA
College of Agronomy: Dr M. O. ADEYEMO
College of Animal Science: Prof. O.I.A. OLUREMI
College of Food Science and Technology: Prof. C.C. ARIAHU
College of Forestry and Fisheries: Dr L.O. TIAMIYU
College of Veterinary Medicine: Prof. P.A. ONYEYILI
School of Postgraduate Studies: Prof. E.I. KUCHA

AHMADU BELLO UNIVERSITY

Zaria
Telephone: (69) 550581
Fax: (69) 550022
E-mail: registrar@abu.edu.ng
Founded 1962
Federal control
Language of instruction: English
Academic year: November to August
Vice-Chancellor: Prof. ABDULLAHI MUSTAPHA
Deputy Vice-Chancellor for Academic Affairs: Prof. ALI MOSES ADAMU
Deputy Vice-Chancellor for Admin.: Prof. IDRIS ISA FUNTUA
Registrar: Dr ISAH MOHAMMED ABBASS
Librarian: Prof. ZAKARI MOHAMMAD
Number of teachers: 2,064
Number of students: 35,783
Publications: *Inaugural Lectures* (4 a year), *University Bulletin* (26 a year), *University*

Gazette, *University Public Lectures* (12 a year), *University Research Report*

DEANS

Faculty of Administration: Dr B. SABO
Faculty of Agriculture: Prof. M. C. DIKE
Faculty of Arts: Dr M. L. AMIN
Faculty of Education: Prof J. GWANI
Faculty of Engineering: Prof. O. J. MUDIARE
Faculty of Environmental Design: Prof. M. B. YUNUSA
Faculty of Law: Prof. N. M. JAMO
Faculty of Medicine: Dr S. SHEHU
Faculty of Pharmaceutical Sciences: Dr M. I. SLE
Faculty of Science: Prof. A. J. NOK
Faculty of Social Sciences: Prof. R. A. DUNMOYE
Faculty of Veterinary Medicine: Prof. N. D. G. IBRAHIM
School of Postgraduate Studies: Prof. J. ADEBAYO

PROFESSORS

Faculty of Administration (Kongo Campus, Zaria):
ABDULLAHI, S., Business Administration
ABDULSALAMI, I., Public Administration

Faculty of Agriculture (Agricultural Complex, A. B. U. Main Campus, Zaria):
ATALA, T. K., Rural Sociology
DIKE, M. C., Crop Protection
OGUNLELA, V. B., Agronomy
OLAREWAJU, J. D., Plant Science
OLUFAJO, O. O., Agronomy
OLUKOSI, J. O., Agricultural Economics
VOH, J. P., Rural Sociology

Faculty of Arts (tel. (69) 551540):
ABAH, O. S., English
MAHADI, A., History
MOHAMMED, A., English
NASIDI, Y. A., English

Faculty of Education (e-mail deaneduc@yahoo.com):
ADEYANJU, F. B., Physical and Health Education
CHADO, M. A., Physical and Health Education
KOLO, F. D., Education
LADAN, B. A., Physical and Health Education
OLAOFE, I. A., Education
VENKATESWARLU, K., Physical and Health Education
ZAKARI, M., Library Science

Faculty of Engineering (e-mail deaneng@abu.edu.ng):
ADEFILA, S. S., Chemical Engineering
AKU, S. Y., Mechanical Engineering
FOLAYAN, C. O., Mechanical Engineering
OKUOFU, C. A., Water Resources and Environmental Engineering
OYINOLA, A. K., Metallurgical Engineering

Faculty of Environmental Design (e-mail deanen@abu.edu.ng):
OGUNTONA, T., Industrial Design
SA'AD, H. T., Architecture

Faculty of Law:
CHUKKOL, K., Public Law

Faculty of Medicine:
ADEKEYE, E. A., Dental Surgery
AHMED, M. H., Psychiatry
AIKHIONBARE, H. A., Paediatrics
ALI, M. A., Human Physiology
OGALA, W. N., Paediatrics
ONYEMELUKWE, G. C., Medicine
YAKUBU, A. M., Paediatrics

Faculty of Pharmaceutical Sciences (tel. (69) 951209; e-mail emabdu@abu.edu.ng):
AGUYE, I. A., Pharmacy and Clinical Pharmacy
HUSSEIN, I., Pharmacology and Clinical Pharmacy
ILYAS, M., Pharmacy and Medicinal Chemistry
MUSTAPHA, A., Pharmaceutical and Medicinal Chemistry
ONAOLAPO, J. A., Pharmaceutical Science and Microbiology

Faculty of Science (tel. (69) 551886; e-mail science@abu.edu.ng):
AHMAD, A., Microbiology
AMUPITAN, J. O., Chemistry
ARIYO, J. A., Geography
AWODI, S., Biological Sciences
BELLO, K. O., Textile Science and Technology
IKE, E. C., Geology
IYUN, J. F., Chemistry
KOLAWOLE, E. G., Textile Science and Technology
NKEONYE, P. O., Textile Science and Technology
OSAZUWA, I. B., Physics

Faculty of Social Sciences (tel. (69) 551540; fax (69) 550022):
DUNMOYE, A., Political Science
KWANASHIE, M., Economics
NKOM, S., Sociology

Faculty of Veterinary Medicine (tel. (69) 551358; e-mail deanvet@abu.edu.ng):
ABDULLAHI, U., Veterinary Surgery and Medicine
AGBEDE, R. I. S., Parasitology and Entomology
ESIEVO, K. A. N., Veterinary Pathology and Medicine
GHAJI, A., Veterinary Anatomy
HAMBOLU, J. O., Anatomy
KWAGA, J. P. K., Veterinary Public Health and Preventive Medicine
OGWU, D., Veterinary Surgery and Medicine
OJO, S. A., Veterinary Anatomy
UMOH, J. U., Veterinary Public Health and Preventive Medicine
ZARIA, L. T., Veterinary Pathology and Microbiology

Centres:
ABUBAKAR, S., National Agricultural Research and Liaison ServicesADAMU, A. M., National Animal Production Research Institute
ADEGBEHIN, J. D., National Agricultural Research and Liaison Services
ALIYU, J. S., Institute of Education
BAIKIE, A., Institute of Education
EDUVIE, L. V., National Animal Production Research Institute
GEFU, J. O., National Animal Production Research Institute
OTCHERE, E. O., National Animal Production Research Institute
VOH, A., National Animal Production Research Institute

BAYERO UNIVERSITY

PMB 3011, Kano
Telephone: (64) 666023
Fax: (64) 665904
E-mail: registrar@buk.edu.ng
Founded 1977
Federal control
Language of instruction: English
Academic year: October to July (two semesters)
Chancellor: HRH OBA SIJUWADE OKUNADE OLUBUSE II (Ooni of Ife)
Chair. of Council: MUHD ADAMU JUMBA
Vice-Chancellor: Prof. ABUBAKAR ADAMU RASHID
Deputy Vice-Chancellor for Academic Affairs: Prof. MUHD YAHUZA BELLO
Deputy Vice-Chancellor for Admin.: Prof. ABDULRASHID GARBA
Registrar: SANI IBRAHIM AMIN
Librarian: MISBAHU NA'YA KATSINA

Library of 170,000 vols, 2,200 periodicals
Number of teachers: 793
Number of students: 27,939

Publications: *Bayero University Quarterly News*, *University Public Lectures* (1 a year)

DEANS

Faculty of Agriculture: Prof. AUWALU MANSUR BINDAWA
Faculty of Arts and Islamic Studies: Prof. SAIDU A. BABURA
Faculty of Education: Dr IBRAHIM M. YAKASAI
Faculty of Law: Dr A. B. AHMAD
Faculty of Medicine: Dr ABDU LAWAN
Faculty of Science: M. S. SULE
Faculty of Social and Management Sciences: Prof. SULEIMAN ALIYU KANTUDU
Faculty of Technology: Dr A. U. ALHAJI
Postgraduate School: Prof. SADIQ ISA RADDA
General Studies Unit: Dr LAWAN S. TAURA (Dir)

PROFESSORS

ABBA, I. A., History
ABDULKADIR, D., Centre for the Study of Nigerian Languages
ABDULKADIR, M. S., History
ABDULLAHI, M., Sociology
ABUBAKAR, M. A., Arabic
ABUBAKAR, M. M.
ADAMU, U. A., Education
AHMED, K., Geography
AJIBERO, M., Library Science
AYODELE, J. T., Chemistry
AZARE, G. D., Education
BICHI, A. Y., Centre for the Study of Nigerian Languages
BICHI, M. Y., Education
DAMBATTA, B. B., Chemistry
DANGAMBO, A., Nigerian Languages
DISO, S. I., Mechanical Engineering
DUZE, M. C., Sociology
EGBON, M., Mass Communication
ESSIET, E. U., Geography
FAGBEMI, A. O., Education
FALOLA, J. A., Geography
FATOPE, M. O., Physics
GUSAU, S. M., Nigerian Languages
HASHIM, I., Political Science
IBRAHIM, M., Paediatrics
JEGA, A. M., Political Science
JIBRIL, M. M., English Language
JOWITT, D. R., English and European Languages
KATANDE, J., Electrical Engineering
MAIWAQDA, D. A., Education
MUHAMMAD, A. R., History
OCHOGWU, M., Library Science
OLOFIN, E. A., Geography
PEDRO, I. A., Economics
RUJBANI, S. M., Mathematics
SALIHI, A., Mechanical Engineering
SALIM, B. A., Nigerian Languages
SANI, M. A. Z., Nigerian Languages
SHEA, P. J., History
SULEIMAN, M. D., History
TABI'U, M., Islamic Law
UMAR, I. H., Physics
YADUDU, A. H., Law
YAHAYA, D., History
ZAHRADEEN, M. S., Islamic Studies
ZAHRADEEN, U., Management Science

UNIVERSITY OF BENIN

Ugbowo-Lagos Rd, Ugbowo, PMB 1154, Benin City
Telephone: (52) 600443
Fax: (52) 241156
E-mail: registrar@uniben.edu
Internet: www.uniben.edu

Founded 1970
Federal control
Language of instruction: English
Academic year: October to June
Chancellor: HRH Alhaji Dr MUHAMMADU BARKINDO ALIYU MUSDAFA
Pro-Chancellor: Sir GABRIEL TOBY
Vice-Chancellor: Prof. O. G. OSHODIN
Deputy Vice-Chancellor for Academic Affairs: Prof. E. A. ONIBERE
Deputy Vice-Chancellor for Admin.: Prof. J. A. OKHUOYA
Registrar: G. O. OGBOGHODO
Librarian: S. A. OGUNROMBI (acting)
Library of 265,144 vols
Number of teachers: 1,182
Number of students: 31,247
Publications: *Benin Journal of Educational Studies*, *Faculty of Arts Journal* (4 a year), *Faculty of Education Journal* (2 a year), *Journal of the Humanities*, *Physical Health Education and Recreational Journal*, *University of Benin Law Journal* (1 a year)

DEANS

Faculty of Agriculture: Prof. U. J. IKHATUA
Faculty of Arts: Prof. A. O. ASAGBA
Faculty of Education: Prof. MON NWADIANI
Faculty of Engineering: Prof. F. O. EDEKO
Faculty of Law: Prof. A. ATSEGBUA
Faculty of Life Sciences: Prof. C. C. OSUDOR
Faculty of Management Sciences: Prof. B. A. AGBONIFOH
Faculty of Pharmacy: Prof. E. O. OSAZUWA
Faculty of Physical Sciences: Prof. S. M. OGBONNWAN
Faculty of Social Sciences: Prof. C. O. OKOLOCHA
School of Dentistry: Prof. B. D. O. SAHEED
School of Medicine: Prof. D. E. OVIASU
School of Postgraduate Studies: Prof. R. O. ELAIHO

PROFESSORS

ABIODUN, P. O., Child Health
ADEMOROTI, C. M. A., Chemistry
AFE, J. O., Educational Psychology and Curriculum Studies
AGBADUDU, A. B., Business Administration
AGBAKWURU, E. O. P., Pharmaceutical Chemistry
AGHENTA, J. A., Educational Administration and Foundations
AHONKHAI, S. I., Chemistry
AJISAFE, M. O., Physical and Health Education
AKERELE, A., Business Administration
ALAKIJA, W., Community Health
ANAO, A. R., Accounting
ASALOR, J. O., Mechanical Engineering
AUDU, T. O. K., Chemical Engineering
AWANBOR, D., Educational Psychology and Curriculum Studies
AWARITEFE, A. A., Mental Health
AYANRU, D. K. G., Microbiology
AYANRU, J. O., Ophthalmology
BADMUS, G. A., Educational Psychology and Curriculum Studies
BAFOR, B. E., Geology
EBEIGBE, A. B., Physiology
EBEWELE, R. O., Chemical Engineering
ECHENIM, K., Modern Languages
EGHAFONA, N. O., Microbiology
EGUDU, R. N., English and Literature
EHIAMETALOR, E. T., Educational Administration and Foundations
EKUNDAYO, J. A., Microbiology
GRILLO, B. O., Anatomy
HUGBO, P. G., Pharmaceutical Microbiology
IGBAFE, A. I., History
IGENE, J. O., Animal Science
IKEDIUGWU, F. E. O., Microbiology
IKENEBOMEH, M. J., Microbiology
IKHATUA, J. U., Animal Science
ILOHA, M. A., Economics and Statistics
IMEOKPARIA, G. E., Geology
IMOGIE, A. I., Educational Psychology and Curriculum Studies
IREMIREN, G. O., Crop Science
IWU, G. O., Chemistry
KUALE, P. A., Civil Engineering
NDIOKWERE, C. L., Chemistry
NWAGWU, N. A., Educational Administration and Foundations
NWANZE, E. C., Biochemistry
NWOKOYE, D. N., Civil Engineering
OBADAN, M. I., Economics and Statistics
OBASEIKI-EBOR, E. E., Pharmaceutical Microbiology
OBASOHAN, A. O., Medicine
OBIANWU, H. O., Pharmacology and Toxicology
OBIKA, L. F., Physiology
OBUEKWE, C. O., Microbiology
ODEBUNMI, A., Educational Psychology and Curriculum Studies
ODIME, O., Surgery
OFOEGBU, R. O., Surgery
OFUANI, O. A., English and Literature
OGBEIDE, N. O., Chemistry
OGBEIDE, O., Community Health
OGBIMI, A. O., General Studies
OGONOR, J. I., Pharmaceutical Chemistry
OGUDE, S. E., English and Literature
OHWOVORIOLE, E. N., Mechanical Engineering
OJUGWU, L. I., Medicine
OKAFOR, F. C., Geography and Regional Planning
OKEH, P. I., Modern Languages
OKEKE, E. O., Mathematics
OKHAMAFE, A. O., Pharmaceutics and Pharmaceutical Technology
OKHUOYA, J. A., Botany
OKIEIMEN, F. E., Chemistry
OKOH, S. E. N., Economics and Statistics
OKOJIE, C. E., Economics and Statistics
OKOLO, A. A., Child Health
OKOLOKO, G., Botany
OKONOFUA, F.E., Obstetrics and Gynaecology
OKOR, R. S., Pharmaceutics and Pharmaceutical Technology
OLA, R. F., Physics
OLOMU, J. M., Animal Science
OMIUNU, F. G. I., Geography and Regional Planning
OMU, F. I. A., History
OMUTA, G. E. D., Geography and Regional Planning
ONOKERHORAYE, A. G., Geography and Regional Planning
OPUTE, F. I., Botany
OROBATOR, S. E., Physics
ORONSAYE, A. U., Obstetrics and Gynaecology
OSAGIE, A. U., Biochemistry
OSAZE, R. E., Business Administration
OSHODIN, O. G., Physical and Health Education
OWIE, I., Physical and Health Education
OYAIDE, W. J., Agricultural Economics and Extension Services
SADA, P. O., Geography and Regional Planning
SALAMI, L. A., Mechanical Engineering
SANNI, B. S., Chemistry
UCHE, C., Sociology and Anthropology
UFOMATA, D., Restorative Dentistry
URAIH, N., Microbiology
WEMAMBU, S. N. C., Medical Microbiology

UNIVERSITY OF CALABAR

PMB 1115, Calabar, Cross River State
Telephone: (87) 232790
Fax: (87) 231766
E-mail: webadmin@unicaledu.org
Internet: www.unicaledu.org

Founded 1975; previously a campus of the University of Nigeria
Federal control
Language of instruction: English
Academic year: October to July
Chancellor: HRH IGWE KINGSLEY CHIME (Eze of Abia)
Vice-Chancellor: Prof. IVARA EJEMOT ESU
Deputy Vice-Chancellor for Academic Affiars: Prof. A. I. ESSIEN
Deputy Vice-Chancellor for Admin.: Prof. JOHN O. OFEM
Registrar: E. E. EFFIOM
Librarian: Dr OLU OLAT LAWAL
Number of teachers: 707
Number of students: 22,678 full-time

DEANS

Faculty of Agriculture: Prof. A. I. ESSIEN
Faculty of Arts: Prof. CHRIS NWAMUO
Faculty of Basic Medical Sciences: Prof. I. B. UMOH
Faculty of Clinical Sciences: Dr C. E. ANTIA-OBONG (acting)
Faculty of Education: Prof. S. C. UCHE (acting)
Faculty of Laboratory and Allied Health Sciences: Prof. A. E. UDOH (acting)
Faculty of Law: N. O. ITA (acting)
Faculty of Science: Prof. JOHN O. OFFEM
Faculty of Social Sciences: Prof. JOHN E. NDEBBIO
College of Medical Sciences: Prof. SPENCER EFEM
Graduate School: Prof. EBONG W. MBIPOM

PROFESSORS

Faculty of Agriculture:

AMALU, U. C., Soil Science
ASUQUO, B. O., Animal Science
ESSIEN, A. I., Animal Science
ESU, I., Soil Science

Faculty of Arts:

ABASIATTAI, M. B., History
EKO, E. O., English and Literary Studies
ERIM, E. O, History
ESSIEN, O. E. A., Languages and Linguistics
IKONNE, C. U. E., English and Literary Studies
IWE, N. S. S., Religious Studies and Philosophy
JOHN, E. E., Languages and Linguistics
NOAH, M. E., History
NWAMUO, C. I., Theatre Arts
ORISAWAYI, D., English and Literary Studies
UKA, K., Theatre Arts
UYA, O. E., History

Faculty of Education:

ABODERIN, A. O., Curriculum and Teaching
AMADI, L. E., Curriculum and Teaching
DENGA, D. I., Educational Foundations and Administration
ENUKOHA, O. I.
ESU, A. E.
IKPAYA, B. O.
NWACHUKWU, D. N., Guidance and Counselling
OMOJUWA, J. O.
UCHE, S. C.

College of Medical Sciences:

AKPAN, J. O., Pharmacology
ANDY, J. J., Medicine
ATTAH, E. B., Pathology
BASSEY, O. O., Surgery
BOLARIN, D. M., Chemical Pathology
BRAIDE, V. B., Pharmacology
EFEM, S., Surgery
EJEZIE, G. C., Medical Microbiology and Parasitology
EKA, O. U., Biochemistry
ESSIEN, E. U., Biochemistry
ONUBA, O. O., Surgery
OSIM, E. E., Physiology

Otu, A. A., Surgery
Umoh, I. B., Biochemistry
Utsalo, S. J., Medical Microbiology, Parasitology

Faculty of Science:
Akpan, E. B., Geology
Braide, E. I., Parasitology
Ekpa, O. D., Chemistry
Ekpe, U. J., Chemistry
Ekwere, S. J., Geology
Ekwueme, B. N., Geology
Ibok, U. J., Chemistry
Lipcsy, Z.
Mbipom, E. W., Physics
Menkiti, A. I., Physics
Offem, J. O., Chemistry
Okwueze, E. E., Physics
Peters, S. W., Geology
Usua, E. J., Biological Sciences
Uwah, E. J., Physics

Faculty of Social Sciences:
Bassey, C. O., Political Science
Ebong, M. O., Geography, Regional Planning
Etuk, E. J., Management Studies
Ndebbio, J. E. U., Economics
Obot, J. U., Geography, Regional Planning
Ottong, J. G., Sociology
Sule, R. A. O., Geography, Regional Planning

Institute of Oceanography:
Antai, E. E.
Holzloner, S.
Obiekezie, A. I.

Institute of Public Policy and Administration:
Uya, O. E.

FEDERAL UNIVERSITY OF TECHNOLOGY, AKURE

PMB 704, Akure, Ondo State
Telephone: (34) 243744
Fax: (34) 230450
Internet: futa-edu.ng
Founded 1981
State control
Language of instruction: English
Academic year: October to September
Chancellor: Emir of Lafia Isa Mustapha Agwai II
Vice-Chancellor: Prof. Peter O. Adeniyi
Deputy Vice-Chancellor for Academic: Prof. O. C. Ademosun
Deputy Vice-Chancellor for Devt: Prof. A. M. Balogun
Registrar: Dr E. F. Oyebade
Librarian: O. A. Oke (acting)
Number of teachers: 442
Number of students: 13,432
Publications: *Journal of Applied Tropical Agriculture* (4 a year), *Journal of Urban and Environmental Research* (every 2 years), *Nigerian Journal of Pure and Applied Physics* (4 a year)

DEANS

School of Agriculture and Agricultural Technology: Prof. J. A. Fuwape
School of Engineering and Engineering Technology: Prof. C. O. Adegoke
School of Environmental Technology: Prof. D. O. Olanrewaju
School of Mines and Earth Sciences: Prof. J. S. Ojo
School of Sciences: Prof. K. O. Ipinmoroti
School of Postgraduate Studies: Prof. V. A. Aletor

FEDERAL UNIVERSITY OF TECHNOLOGY, MINNA

PMB 65, Minna, Niger State
Telephone and fax (66) 222422
E-mail: futmx@skannet.com
Internet: www.futminna.net
Founded 1983
Fed. control
Language of instruction: English
Academic year: October to September (2 semesters)
Chancellor: The Olu of Warri, HRH Ogiame Atuwase II
Pro-Chancellor: Prof. Rufa'i Ahmed Alkali
Vice-Chancellor: Prof. Muhammed Salihu Audu
Deputy Vice-Chancellor: Dr Akim O. Osunde
Registrar: Mallam M. D. Usman
Bursar: M. A. Bello
Librarian: Muhammad Ibn Muhammad
Number of teachers: 698
Number of students: 13,589
Publications: *Journal of Agricultural Technology* (2 a year), *Journal of Science, Technology and Mathematics Education* (2 a year), *Nigeria Journal of Technological Research* (2 a year), *Proceedings of the National Engineering Conference* (1 a year)

DEANS

School of Agriculture and Agricultural Technology: Prof. K. M. Baba
School of Engineering and Engineering Technology: Prof. J. O. Odiguore
School of Environmental Technology: Prof. O. O. Morenkeji
School of Science and Science Education: Prof. Musa Galadima
Postgraduate School: Prof. Samuel L. Lamai

FEDERAL UNIVERSITY OF TECHNOLOGY, OWERRI

PMB 1526, Owerri, Imo State
Telephone: (83) 233228
E-mail: vc@futo.edu.ng
Founded 1980
Federal control
Language of instruction: English
Academic year: October to July
Chancellor: HRH Dr Shekarau Angyu Massa-Ibi
Pro-Chancellor: Vita O. Abba
Vice-Chancellor: Prof. Celestine O. E. Onwuliri (acting)
Deputy Vice-Chancellor for Academic Affairs: Prof. E. T. Eshett
Deputy Vice-Chancellor for Admin.: Prof. M. I. Nwufo
Registrar: C. O. Omeire
Bursar: R.-U. Akujobi
Librarian: J. E. Nwogu
Library of 68,345 vols
Number of teachers: 699
Number of students: 21,307
Publications: *Annual Review*, *Centre for Industrial Studies*, *Erosion News* (4 a year)

DEANS

School of Agriculture and Agricultural Technology: Prof. C. C. Asiabaka
School of Engineering and Engineering Technology: Prof. O. N. Oguoma
School of Management Technology: Prof. G. E. Nworuh
School of Science: Dr F. C. Eze (acting)
Postgraduate School: Prof. C. D. Okereke

PROFESSORS

Achi, P., Mechanical Engineering
Agbogu, A., Political Science
Agwu, E., Transport Management Technology
Akpan, E., Engineering
Akujor, C., Astrophysics and Space Physics
Alaezi, O., Curriculum and Vocational Education
Ananaba, S., Geophysics
Aneke, L., Chemical Engineering
Anunuso, C., Analytical Chemistry
Anyanwu, B., Microbiology
Anyanwu, E., Mechanical Engineering
Aririatu, L., Industrial Microbiology
Asiabaka, C., Agricultural Extension
Asiegbu, L., Ethical Philosophy
Duru, J., Water Resources Engineering
Eheduru, G., Information Management Technology
Ejike, E., Chemistry
Emeharole, P., Public Health Technology
Enyiegbulam, M., Polymer Science and Technology
Eshett, E., Pedology
Esonu, B., Animal Nutrition
Eze, F., Physics
Ibe, K., Geology
Iheonye, A., Polymer and Textile Engineering
Iloeje, M., Animal Genetics
Iwuagwu, C., Geology
Iwuala, M., Biology
Iwuoha, C., Food Science and Technology
Mbakwe, R., Forestry and Wildlife Management
Nduka, A., Theoretical Physics and Applied Mathematics
Njoku, J., Agricultural Economics
Njoku, O., Biology
Njiribeako, I., Chemical Engineering
Ntamere, C., Economics
Nwabueze, R., Microbiology
Nwachukwu, B., Civil Engineering
Nwachukwu, E., Computer Science
Nwadiaro, C., Fisheries and Aquaculture
Nwafor, O., Mechanical Engineering
Nwankiti, A., Crop Science and Technology
Nwankwor, G., Geology
Nwigwe, H., Biotechnology
Nworuh, G., Statistics
Nwufo, M., Plant Pathology
Obah, B., Petroleum Engineering
Obiefuna, J., Horticulture
Ofoh, M., Crop Science Technology
Ogbobe, O., Polymer and Textile Engineering
Ogbogu, S., Electrical/Electronic Engineering
Ogbulie, J., Microbiology
Oguoma, O., Mechanical Engineering
Ogweuegbu, M., Industrial Chemistry
Ogwude, I., Transport Management
Ogwude, S., English Literature
Okereke, C., Environmental Engineering
Okpala, K., Chemical Engineering
Okorafor, O., Metallurgical Engineering
Ononiwu, J., Solid State Physics
Onu, N., Geophysics
Onuoha, G., Chemistry
Onwuagba, B., Physics
Onwuliri, C., Zoology/Parasitology/Biotechnology
Onwuliri, V., Biochemistry
Onyeagoro, E., Mechanical Engineering
Onyejekwe, D., Mechanical Engineering
Onyejiekwe, E., Public Health Technology
Onyemaobi, O., Material and Metallurgical Engineering
Onyeze, G., Industrial Biochemistry
Onyiriuka, S., Organic Chemistry
Orebiyi, J., Agricultural Economics
Osondu, K., Pure Mathematics
Osuala, F., Biotechnology
Osuagwu, O., Information Management Technology
Osuji, G., Soil Science
Owuama, O., Environmental Technology

OZOH, P., Environmental Management and Toxicology
UBBAONU, C., Food Processing and Product Development
UDEDIBIE, A., Animal Nutrition
UFODIKE, E., Fisheries and Aquaculture
UKOHA, A., Biochemistry

FEDERAL UNIVERSITY OF TECHNOLOGY, YOLA

PMB 2076, Yola, Adamawa State
Telephone: (75) 624416
Fax: (75) 624416
E-mail: vcfuty@yahoo.com
Internet: www.futy.edu.ng

Founded 1981, present status 1988
Federal control
Language of instruction: English
Academic year: October to September

Chancellor: HH Oba GABRIEL ADEKUNLE AROMOLARAN II
Vice-Chancellor: Prof. ABDULLAHI YUSUFU RIBADU
Registrar: Alh. AHMED USMAN W/CHEKKE
Librarian: Prof. B. S. H. WOMBOH

Library of 29,000 vols
Number of teachers: 345
Number of students: 9,701

Publication: *Technology and Development* (1 a year)

DEANS

School of Agriculture and Agricultural Technology: Prof. A. KADAMS
School of Engineering and Engineering Technology: Prof. P. B. OMAJI
School of Environmental Sciences: Dr F. ILLESANMI
School of Management and Information Technology: Prof. S. O. ANYANWU
School of Pure and Applied Sciences: Dr A. OKOLO
School of Technology and Science Education: Dr L. C. EZUGU
School of Post-Graduate Studies: Prof. G. FAKUADE

UNIVERSITY OF IBADAN

Ibadan
Telephone: (2) 7511988
E-mail: vc@mail.ui.edu.ng
Internet: www.ui.edu.ng

Founded 1948 as University College, Ibadan, a constituent College of the University of London, UK; present name and status 1962
Federal control
Language of instruction: English
Academic year: September to July

Chancellor: HH ALHAJI ADO BAYERO
Vice-Chancellor: Prof. OLUFEMI A. BAMIRO
Deputy Vice-Chancellor for Academics: Prof. A. A. B. AGBAJE
Deputy Vice-Chancellor for Admin.: Prof. ELIJAH A. BAMGBOYE
Registrar: OMOTAYO O. IKOTUN
Librarian: Dr B. A. OLADELE

Library: see Libraries and Archives
Number of teachers: 1,214
Number of students: 19,521

Publications: *Digest of Statistics*, *Ivory Tower*, *Official Bulletin*, *Official Gazette*, *Order of Proceedings*, *Pocket Statistics*, *Research Bulletin of the Centre for Arabic Documentation* (2 a year), *Student Information Handbook*, *University Calendar*

DEANS

Faculty of Agriculture and Forestry: Prof. F. K. EWETE
Faculty of Arts: Prof. P. A. OGUNDEJI
Faculty of Basic Medical Sciences: Prof. O. D. OLALEYE
Faculty of Clinical Sciences: Prof. O. M. OLUWATOSIN
Faculty of Dentistry: Prof. GHEMISOLA A. OKE
Faculty of Education: Prof. J. B. BABALOLA
Faculty of Law: Prof. OLUYEMISI A. BAMGBOSE
Faculty of Pharmacy: Prof. J. O. MOODY
Faculty of Science: Prof. K. O. ADEBOWALE
Faculty of Social Sciences: Prof. KASSEY GARBA
Faculty of Technology: Prof. A. E. OLULEYE
Faculty of Veterinary Medicine: Prof. V. O. TAIWO
Postgraduate School: Prof. L. POPOOLA
Student Affairs: Prof. A. E. FALAYE

PROFESSORS

Faculty of Agriculture and Forestry:
ADEJUMO, O., Animal Science
ADEOYE, G., Agronomy
AIYELARI, E., Agronomy
AKEN'OVA, M., Agronomy
AKINSOYINU, A., Animal Science
AKORODA, M., Agronomy
ATIRI, G., Crop Protection and Environmental Biology
AYODELE, A., Wildlife and Fisheries
BADA, S., Forest Resources Management
EKPO, E., Crop Protection and Enviromental Biology
EWETE, F., Crop Protection and Enviromental Biology
FALAYE, A., Wildlife and Fisheries
FALUSI, A., Agricultural Economics
FATUROTI, E., Wildlife and Fisheries
FAWOLE, B., Crop Protection and Enviromental Biology
IKOTUN, B., Crop Protection and Enviromental Biology
IKPI, A., Agricultural Economics
IYAYI, E., Animal Science
LADELE, A., Agricultural Extension and Rural Development
LONGE, O., Animal Science
LUCAS, E., Agronomy
OGUNKUNLE, A., Agronomy
OGUNYEMI, S., Crop Protection and Enviromental Biology
OLAWOYE, J., Agricultural Extension and Rural Development
OLOGHOBO, A., Animal Science
OMUETI, J., Agronomy
OSHO, J., Forest Resources Management
POPOOLA, L., Forest Resources Management
TEWE, O., Animal Science
TIJANI-ENIOLA, H., Agronomy
TOGUN, A., Crop Protection and Enviromental Biology

Faculty of Arts:
ABDULRAHMON, M., Arabic and Islamic Studies
ADEBAYO, A., European Studies
ADEKOYA, O., English
ADESANOYE, F., Communication and Language Arts
AKINYEYE, O., History
DASYLVA, A., English
DRURGBA, A., Religious Studies
EGBOKHARE, F., Linguistics and African Languages
ELUGBE, B., Linguistics and African Languages
IRELE, J., Philosophy
LAWAL, O., History
ODEJIDE, I., Communication and Language Arts
OGUNDEJI, P., Linguistics and African Languages
OLADIPO, O., Philosophy
OMAMOR, P., Linguistics and African Languages
OMOSINI, O., History
OSOFISAN, B., Theatre Arts
OWOLABI, D., Linguistics and African Languages
OYELEYE, A., English
OYETADE, S., Linguistics and African Languages

Faculty of Basic Medical Sciences:
ADENIYI, F., Chemical Pathology
AGBEDANA, E., Chemical Pathology
AKANG, E., Pathology
AKEN'OVA, Y., Haematology
BAKARE, R., Medical Microbiology and Parasitology
BOLARINWA, A., Physiology
FAROMBI, E., Biochemistry
MADUAGWU, E., Biochemistry
OGUNBIYI, J., Pathology
OLALEYE, D., Virology
OLORUNSOGO, O., Biochemistry
OSOTIMEHIN, B., Chemical Pathology
OYEBOLA, D., Physiology
SHOKUNBI, W., Haematology
SHOKUNBI, M., Anatomy
SOWUNMI, A., Pharmacy and Therapeutics

Faculty of Clinical Sciences:
ADEBAMOWO, C., Surgery
ADEGBOYE, V., Surgery
ADEKUNLE, A., Obstetrics and Gynaecology
ADEWOLE, I., Obstetrics and Gynaecology
AJAIYEOBA, A., Ophthalmology
AKINYINKA, O., Paediatrics
AMANOR-BOADU, S., Anaesthesia
ARIJE, A., Medicine
AROWOJOLU, A., Obstetrics and Gynaecology
ASUZU, M., Community Medicine
BAIYEROJU, A., Ophthalmology
BAIYEWU, O., Psychiatry
CAMPBELL, O., Radiotherapy
FALADE, A., Paediatrics
GEORGE, A., Medicine
GUREJE, O., Psychiatry
IJADUOLA, G., Otorhinolaryngology
ILESANMI, A., Obstetrics and Gynaecology
KADIRI, S., Medicine
NWAORGU, O., Otorhinolaryngology
OGUNNIYI, A., Medicine
OGUNSEYINDE, A., Radiology
OJENGBEDE, O., Obstetrics and Gynaecology
OLUWATOSIN, O., Surgery
OMIGBODUN, A., Obstetrics and Gynaecology
OMOKHODION, S., Paediatrics
OMOKHODION, F., Community Medicine
OSINUSI, K., Paediatrics
SALAKO, B., Medicine
SANYA, A., Physiotherapy
SHITTU, O., Surgery
SOYANNWO, O., Anaesthesia

Faculty of Dentistry:
AROWOJOLU, M. O., Preventive Dentistry
LAWOYIN, J. O., Oral Pathology
OBIECHINA, A. E., Oral & Maxillo. Surgery
OKE, G. A., Preventive Dentistry

Faculty of Education:
AJAYI, E., Educational Management
AKINTAYO, M., Adult Education
ALEGBELEYE, G., Library, Archival and Information Studies
ATINMO, M., Library, Archival and Information Studies
AYODELE-BAMISAIYE, O., Teacher Education
BABALOLA, J., Educational Management
MABAWONKU, I., Library, Archival and Information Studies
NWAZUOKE, A., Special Education
OGUNDELE, B., Human Kinetics and Health Education
OGUNSANYA, M., Educational Management
UWAKWE, C., Guidance and Counselling

Faculty of Law:
AGBEDE, I., Private and Business Law
ANIFALAJE, J., Private and Business Law

Bamgbose, O., Private and Business Law
Omorogbe, O., Public and International Law
Owoade, M., Public and International Law

Faculty of Pharmacy:
Ajaiyeoba, E. O., Pharmacognosy
Babalola, C. P., Pharmaceutical Chemistry
Erhun, W. O., Clinical Pharmacy and Pharmacy Administration
Itiola, O. A., Pharmaceutical and Industrial Pharmacy
Jaiyeoba, K. T., Pharmaceutical and Industrial Pharmacy
Moody, J. O., Pharmacognosy

Faculty of Public Health:
Akinyele, I. O., Human Nutrition and Dietetics
Atinmo, T., Human Nutrition and Dietetics
Ayeni, O., Epidemiology, Medical Statistics and Environmental Health
Bamgboye, E. A., Epidemiology, Medical Statistics and Environmental Health
Oladepo, O., Health Promotion and Education

Faculty of Science:
Adebowale, K., Chemistry
Adeleke, B., Chemistry
Adesomoju, A., Chemistry
Bamiro, F., Chemistry
Ekhaguere, G., Mathematics
Ekundayo, O., Chemistry
Elueze, A., Geology
Farai, I., Physics
Folorunso, C., Archaeology and Anthropology
Hassan, A., Zoology
Hussain, L., Physics
Ilori, S., Mathematics
Lawuyi, O., Archaeology and Anthropology
Odaibo, A., Zoology
Oderinde, R., Chemistry
Odiaka, T., Chemistry
Odunfa, S., Botany and Microbiology
Okunade, A., Physics
Oladiran, E., Physics
Olayinka, A., Geology
Onianwa, P., Chemistry
Osibanjo, O., Chemistry
Osofisan, A., Computer Science
Osonubi, O., Botany and Microbiology
Oyelaran, P., Archaeology and Anthropology
Sanni, A., Botany and Microbiology
Ugwumba, O., Zoology
Woods, J., Chemistry

Faculty of Social Sciences:
Adenikinju, A., Economics
Afolayan, A., Geography
Agbaje, A., Political Science
Agbola, S., Urban and Regional Planning
Ariyo, A., Economics
Aweto, A., Geography
Ayeni, M., Geography
Balogun, S., Psychology
Egwaikhide, F., Economics
Ehigie, B., Psychology
Garba, A., Economics
Garba, P., Economics
Gbadegesin, A., Geography
Gboyega, E., Political Science
Ikporukpo, C., Geography
Isiugo-Abanihe, U., Sociology
Iwayemi, A., Economics
Ogunkola, E., Economics
Okafor, S., Geography
Oke, E., Sociology
Okunade, A., Political Science
Olofin, S., Economics
Osinowo, H., Psychology
Oyejide, T., Economics
Soyibo, A., Economics
Suberu, R., Political Science
Sunmola, A., Psychology

Faculty of Technology:
Adegoke, G., Food Technology
Adekoya, L., Mechanical Engineering
Agbede, O., Civil Engineering
Alabi, B., Mechanical Engineering
Aworh, O., Food Technology
Bamiro, O., Mechanical Engineering
Charles-Owaba, O., Industrial and Production Engineering
Olorunsola, A., Agricultural Engineering
Oluleye, A., Industrial & Production Enging
Onilude, M., Agricultural Engineering
Sangodoyin, A., Agricultural Engineering

Faculty of Veterinary Medicine:
Abatan, M., Veterinary Physiology and Pharmacy
Adeyefa, C., Veterinary Medicine
Agbede, S., Veterinary Public Health
Akinboade, O., Veterinary Microbiology and Parasitology
Akpavie, S., Veterinary Pathology
Anosa, V., Veterinary Pathology
Arowolo, R., Veterinary Physiology and Pharmacy
Fagbemi, B., Veterinary Microbiology and Parasitology
Fayemi, O., Veterinary Surgery and Reproduction
Nottidge, H., Veterinary Medicine
Obi, T., Veterinary Medicine
Ogundipe, G., Veterinary Public Health
Oke, B., Veterinary Anatomy
Oladosu, L., Veterinary Medicine
Olufemi, B., Veterinary Medicine
Onwuka, S., Veterinary Anatomy
Oyewale, J., Veterinary Physiology and Pharmacy
Taiwo, V., Veterinary Pathology

UNIVERSITY OF ILORIN

PMB 1515, Ilorin, Kwara State
Telephone: (31) 221691
Fax: (31) 221937
E-mail: registra@unilorin.edu.ng
Internet: www.unilorin.edu.ng

Founded 1975
Federal control
Language of instruction: English
Academic year: September to June

Chancellor: HRH Ambrose Allagoa
Vice-Chancellor: Prof. Shamsudeen Onyilokwu Onche Amali
Deputy Vice-Chancellor for Academic Affairs: Prof. Ishaq Olanrewaju Oloyede
Deputy Vice-Chancellor for Admin.: Prof. Luke Dayo Edungbola
Registrar: O. O. Oyeyemi
Librarian: Prof. M. I. Ajibero

Library of 155,000 vols, 2,800 periodicals
Number of teachers: 644
Number of students: 18,488

Publications: *News Bulletin* (52 a year), *University Calendar*

DEANS

Faculty of Agriculture: Prof. J. O. Atteh
Faculty of Arts: Prof. R. D. Abubakre
Faculty of Business and Social Sciences: Prof. I. O. Taiwo
Faculty of Education: Prof. E. A. Ogunsakin
Faculty of Engineering and Technology: Prof. O. A. Adetifa
Faculty of Health Sciences: Prof. M. A. Araoye
Faculty of Law: Prof. Z. O. Aje
Faculty of Science: Prof. T. O. Opoola
Post-Graduate School: Prof. J. A. Morakinyo

UNIVERSITY OF JOS

PMB 2084, Jos, Plateau State
Telephone: (73) 610514
Fax: (73) 610514
Internet: www.uiowa.edu/intlinet/unijos

Founded 1975
Federal control
Language of instruction: English
Academic year: September to June (2 semesters)

Chancellor: HRH Oba Dr Festus Ibidapo Adedinsewo Adesanoye Osemawe of Ondoland
Pro-Chancellor: Prof. Musa Abdullahi
Vice-Chancellor: Prof. Monday Mangywat
Deputy Vice-Chancellor for Academic Affairs: Prof. A. O. Malu
Deputy Vice-Chancellor for Admin.: Prof. J. O. A. Onyeka
Registrar: Z. D. Galam
Librarian: Dr A. Ochai

Number of teachers: 745
Number of students: 14,378

DEANS AND DIRECTORS

Faculty of Arts: Prof. E. B. Ajulo
Faculty of Education: Prof. I. J. Ihenacho
Faculty of Environmental Sciences: Prof. A. A. Adepetu
Faculty of Law: Dr J. M. Nasir
Faculty of Medical Sciences: Prof. J. O. Ogunranti
Faculty of Natural Sciences: Prof. M. S. Audu
Faculty of Pharmaceutical Sciences: Prof. F. Okwuasaba
Faculty of Social Sciences: Prof. S. G. Tyoden
School of Postgraduate Studies: Prof. G. A. Ubom
Institute of Education: Dr A. Y. Mallum
Centre for Continuing Education: Dr E. A. Abama
Centre for Development Studies: Dr J. S. Illah

PROFESSORS

Faculty of Arts:
Aire, Y. O., Languages and Lingusitics
Aje, A. O., Languages and Linguistics
Ajulo, E. B., English
Amali, S. O. O., Theatre Studies
Bashir, I. L., History
Cyril, I. O., Religious Studies
James, I., History
Jemkur, J. F., History
Mangvwat, M. Y., History
Yahya, M. T., Religious Studies

Faculty of Education:
Abang, T., Special Education
Adewole, M. A., Philosophy of Education
Akinnade, C. T. O., Science and Technical Education
Akpan, E. U. U., Science and Technology Education
Awotunde, P. O., Science Education
Ihenacho, I. J., Special Education
Lassa, P. N., Mathematics Education
Mallum, M. P., Guidance and Counselling
Ozoji, E., Special Education
Udoh, S. U., Social Science Education

Faculty of Environmental Sciences:
Adepetu, A. A., Geography and Planning
Kolawole, J. O., Building

Faculty of Law:
Aduba, J. N., Public and Law

Faculty of Medical Sciences:
Adoga, G. I., Biochemistry
Anakwe, G. E., Biochemistry
Idoko, J. A., Medicine
Ihezue, C. H., Surgery
Isichei, H. U., Psychiatry
Malu, A. O., Medicinal Radiology
Okoye, Z. S. C., Biochemistry

UBOM, G. A., Enzymology and Molecular Biology

Faculty of Natural Sciences:

AGINA, S. E., Botany
AJAYI, J., Zoology
AKUESHI, C. O., Plant Pathology
AUDU, M. S., Mathematics
DUHLINSKA, D. D., Protozoology, Insect Pathology
EGILA, J. N., Chemistry
EKPENYONG, K. I., Chemistry
EKWENCHI, M. M., Chemistry
HUSAINI, S. W. H., Plant Taxonomy and Cytogenetics
IFENKWE, O. P., Botany
LIVERPOOL, L. S. O., Mathematics
NWUFO, B. T., Chemistry
OGBONNA, C. I., Botany
OGEZI, I. E., Geology and Mining
OJOJEKWU, P. C., Zoology
ONUMANYI, P., Mathematics
ONWULIRI, C. O. E., Zoology
ONYEKA, J. O. A., Zoology
POPOV, T. V., Zoology
SHAMBE, T. S., Chemistry
UFODIKE, E. B. C., Zoology
UTAH, E. U., Physics

Faculty of Pharmaceutical Sciences:

IRANLOYE, T. A., Pharmacology and Pharmaceutical Technology
OKWUASABA, F., Pharmacology and Clinical Pharmacy
SOKOMBA, E. N., Pharmacology

Faculty of Social Sciences:

ALLI, W. O., International Relations
ALUBO, S. O., Sociology
ETANNIBI, E. O., Sociology
IBANGA, U. A., Sociology
NWEZE, A., Psychology
TYODEN, G. S., Political Economy

Centre for Development Studies:

OJOWU, O., Economics

UNIVERSITY OF LAGOS

Lagos
Telephone: (1) 4932660
Fax: (1) 4932667
E-mail: vc@unilag.edu
Internet: www.unilag.edu
Founded 1962
Fed. control
Language of instruction: English
Academic year: October to June
Chancellor: HRH Alhaji Dr ALIYU O. OBAJE (the Attah Igala)
Pro-Chancellor: Chief AFE BABALOLA
Vice-Chancellor: Prof. OYE IBIDAPO-OBE
Deputy Vice-Chancellor for Academic Affairs and Research: Prof. OLUSOGA A. SOFOLA
Deputy Vice-Chancellor for Management: (vacant)
Registrar: C. F. A. OLUMIDE
Librarian: S. O. OLANLOKUN
Library: see Libraries and Archives
Number of teachers: 969
Number of students: 39,783
Publications: *Imodoye, A Journal of Africa Philosophy* (1 a year), *Journal of Economics and Policy Analysis* (1 a year), *Journal of Engineering Research* (1 a year), *Journal of Private and Property Law* (1 a year), *Journal of Society, Development and Public Health* (1 a year), *LAANGBASA (Jona Ise Akadani Ede Yoruba)* (African Studies, 1 a year), *Lagos Historical Review* (1 a year), *Lagos Journal of Environmental Studies* (1 a year), *Lagos Review of English Studies* (1 a year), *Nigerian Journal of Business and Social Science* (1 a year), *Nigerian Journal of Health and Biomedical Sciences* (2 a year), *Nigerian Journal of Industrial Relations* (1 a year), *Nigerian Journal of Management Studies* (1 a year), *Nigerian Journal of Philosophy* (1 a year), *UNILAG Communication Review* (1 a year), *UNILAG Journal of Business* (1 a year), *UNILAG Journal of Politics* (1 a year), *UNILAG Sociological Review* (1 a year)

DEANS

College of Medicine: Prof. S. O. ELEHSA (Provost)
Faculty of Arts: Prof. C. S. MOMOH
Faculty of Business Administration: Prof. W. ADEWUNMI
Faculty of Education: Prof. DURO ADENAYO AJEYALEMI
Faculty of Engineering: Prof. O. O. AKINDELE
Faculty of Environmental Sciences: Prof. R. O. IYAGBA
Faculty of Law: Prof. CHIOMA AGOMO
Faculty of Pharmacy: Prof. H. A. B. COKER
Faculty of Science: Prof. O. O. AMUND
Faculty of Social Sciences: Prof. L. OLURODE
School of Basic Medical Sciences: Prof. S. A. ADIGUN
School of Clinical Sciences: Prof. A. O. GRANGE
School of Dental Sciences: Prof. J. A. AKINWANDE
School of Postgraduate Studies: Prof. F. O. OLATUNJI

PROFESSORS

ABAELU, A. M., Biochemistry
ABASS, O., Computer Science
ABIDOYE, R. O., Community Health
ABUDU, O. O., Obstetrics and Gynaecology
ADEBAYO, N., Sociology
ADEDIMILA, A. S., Civil Engineering
ADEGBENRO, O., Electrical and Electronics Engineering
ADEGBOLA, O., Geography
ADEGOKE, K. A., Curriculum Studies (Education)
ADEJUGBE, M. O. A., Economics
ADEKOLA, S. A., Electrical and Electronics Engineering
ADELEMO, I. A., Geography
ADENIYI, P. O., Geography
ADEOGUN, A. A., Commercial and Industrial Law
ADE-OJO, S., European Languages
ADEPOJU, J. A., Mathematics
ADEROGBA, K., Mathematics
ADEWALE, A. O., Adult Education
ADEWUNMI, W., Banking and Finance
ADEYEMI, A. A., Public Law
ADEYEMI, J. D., Psychiatry
ADEYEMI, S. D., Surgery
ADEYEMI-DORO, H. O., Surgery
ADIGUN, S. A., Physiology
ADU, D. I., Mathematics
AGOMO, C. K., Commercial and Industrial Law
AJAYI, O., Mathematics
AJEYALEMI, S. D., Curriculum Studies (Education)
AKEJU, T. A., Civil Engineering
AKERE, J. F., English
AKINDELE, O. O., Mechanical Engineering
AKINFELEYE, R. A., Mass Communication
AKINGBADE, J. F., Business Administration
AKINOLA, M. O., European Languages (French)
AKINSETE, I., Haematology and Blood Transfusion
AKINTOLA-ARIKAWE, J. O., Geography
AKINTONWA, A., Pharmacology
AKINWADE, J. A., Oral and Maxillofacial Surgery
AKINWANDE, A. I., Biochemistry
AKO, C. T., Chemical Engineering
AKPATA, T. V. I., Botany and Microbiology
ALABA, I. O., African Languages and Literature (Yoruba)
ALABA OGUNSANWO, Political Science
ALO, B. I., Chemistry
AMUND, O. O., Botany and Microbiology
ARIGBABU, S. O., Surgery
ASIKA, M. N., Business Administration
AWONUSI, V. O., English
AWOSOPE, C. O., Electrical and Electronics Engineering
AYENI, J. O., Computer Science
AYENI, O. O., Surveying
BALOGUN, O. Y., Geography
BALOGUN, S. A., Metallurgical Engineering
BANDELE, E. O., Medicine
BELLO, R. A., Chemical Engineering
COKER, A. O., Medical Microbiology and Parasitology
COKER, H. A. B., Pharmaceutical Chemistry
DANESI, M. A., Medicine
DENLOYE, A. O., Chemical Engineering
DON-PEDRO, K., Zoology, Marine Biology and Fisheries
DUROSIMI-ETTI, F. A., Radiation biology, Radiotherapy and Radiodiagnosis
EDEBIRI, U., European Languages (French)
EGBERONGBE, F. O. A., Surveying and Geoinformatics
EJIOGU, A. M., Educational Administration
ELESHA, S. O., Morbid Anatomy
ERUVBETINE, A. E., English
EZE, L. N., Psychology
EZEIGBO, C. U., Surveying and Geoinformatics
EZEIGBO, T. A., English
FAGBAMIYE, E. O., Educational Administration
FAGBENRO-BEYIOKU, A. F., Microbiology and Parasitology
FAJEMIROKUN, F. A., Surveying and Geoinformatics
FAMUYIWA, O. O., Psychiatry
FOGAM, P. K., Commercial and Industrial Law
FOLARIN, B. A., Psychology
FOLAWIYO, A. F. A., Physical and Health Education
GBADAMOSI, T. G. O., History
GIWA-OSAGIE, O. O. F., Obstetrics and Gynaecology
GRANGE, A. O., Clinical Pathology
IBIDAPO-OBE, O., Systems Engineering
IFUDU, N. D., Pharmacy and Pharmaceutical Technology
IGWILO, C. I., Pharmacy and Pharmaceutical Technology
IJAOLA, O. O., Electrical and Electronics Engineering
IKULAYO, P. B., Physical and Health Education
ISIEKWE, M. C., Dental Sciences
IYAGBA, R. O., Building
IYIEGBUNIWE, W. C., Finance
JEBODA, S. O., Preventive Dentistry
JOHNSON, M. A., European Languages (French)
JOHNSON, T. O., Medicine
KAMMA, C. M., Mechanical Engineering
KAZEEM, A. A., Clinical Pathology
KENKU, M. A., Mathematics
KUKOYI, A. A., European Languages (French)
KUSEMIJU, K., Marine Science
KWOFIE, E. N., European Languages (French)
LAWAL, A. A., History
LAWAL, O. O., Education
MAJEKODUNMI, A. A., Surgery
MAKANJU, O. O. A., Psychology
MAKANJUOLA, W. A., Zoology
MALAKA, S. L. O., European Languages (French)
MOMOH, C. S., Philosophy
MOREGBE, J. I., Philosophy
NINALOWO, A., Sociology
NWANKO, D. I., Zoology, Marine Biology and Fisheries
OBEBE, B. J., Curriculum Studies
ODEIGAH, P. G. C., Zoology, Marine Biology and Fisheries

ODIETE, W. O., Zoology, Marine Biology and Fisheries
ODUGBEMI, T., Medical Microbiology and Parasitology
ODUKOYA, O. O., Oral Pathology
ODUTOLA, T. A., Medicine
OGBOJA, O., Chemical Engineering
OGEDENGBE, O. K., Obstetrics and Gynaecology
OGUNDOWOLE, E. K., Philosophy
OGUNLESI, M. M., Chemistry
OGUNSANWO, A. C. A., Political Science
OGUNTOYE, A. O., Educational Administration
OHWOVORIOLE, A. E., Medicine
OJO, S. A., European Languages (French)
OJO, S. O., Geography
OKENIMKPE, M. N., Adult Education
OKEOWO, P. A., Surgery
OKORO, C. C., Electrical and Electronics Engineering
OKOTORE, R. O., Biochemistry
OLATUNJI, F. O., Chemical Engineering
OLOWOKUDEJO, J. O., Botany and Microbiology
OLUKOJU, A. O., History
OLUMIDE, Y. M., Medicine
OLUNLOYO, V. O. S., Mechanical Engineering
OLURODE, O., Sociology
OLUSANYA, O., Architecture
OLUWAFEMI, C. O., Physics
OMOLUABI, P. F., Psychology
OMO-MALAKA, S. L., Zoology, Marine Biology and Fisheries
OMOREGBE, J., Philosophy
OMOTOLA, J. A., Private and Property Law
OSEGBE, D. N., Surgery
OSIBOGUN, A. O., Community Health
OSINBAJO, Y., Public Law
OSIPITAN, T. A. I., Public Law
OSUNTOKUN, J. O., History
OTOBO, D., Industrial Relations and Personnel Management
OWHOTU, V. B., Curriculum Studies
OWOEYE, I. O., Physiotherapy
OYEBANDE, L., Geography
OYEBODE, A., Jurisprudence and International Law
OYEDIRAN, M. A., Child Health and Primary Care
OYEKANMI, F. A. D., Sociology
OYELELE, D. A., Geography
DA ROCHA-AFODU, J. T., Surgery
SOFOLA, O. A., Physiology
SOFOLUWE, A. B., Computer Science
SOTE, E. O., Child Dental Health
SOTE, G. A., Psychology
SOWEMIMO, G. O. A., Surgery
SUSU, A. A., Chemical Engineering
TALABI, S. O., Mechanical Engineering
TAYO, F., Clinical Pharmacy
TOMORI, S., Economics
UCHE, L. U., Mass Communication
UCHEGBU, A., Jurisprudence and International Law
UNAH, J. I., Philosophy
UTUAMA, A. A., Private and Property Law
UZOCHUKWU, S., African Languages and Literature (Igbo)
UZODIKE, E. N. U., Private and Property Law
VINCENT, T., English
WILLIAMS, G. O., Zoology, Marine Biology and Fisheries

UNIVERSITY OF MAIDUGURI

PMB 1069, Maiduguri, Borno State
Telephone: (76) 232949
E-mail: root@unimaid.edu.ng
Internet: www.unimaid.edu.ng

Founded 1975
Fed. control
Language of instruction: English
Academic year: October to June

Chancellor: His Royal Majesty Dr EKPENYONG OKONKO UDOUTUN
Pro-Chancellor and Chairman of Council: Dr BOLANLE OLAWALE BABALAKIN
Vice-Chancellor: Prof. MOHAMMED MALA DAURA
Deputy Vice-Chancellor for Academic Services: (vacant)
Deputy Vice-Chancellor for Central Admin.: (vacant)
Registrar: Dr LAWAN BUKAR ALHAJI
Librarian: JAMES ABAYOMI AGAJA (acting)

Number of teachers: 700
Number of students: 30,000

Publications: *Annals of Borno, Inaugural Lecture and Convocation Speeches*

DEANS

College of Medical Sciences: Prof. A. A. TAHIR
Faculty of Agriculture: Prof. J. D. KWARI
Faculty of Arts: Prof. YAKUBU MUKHTAR
Faculty of Education: Prof. IBRAHIM NJODI
Faculty of Engineering: Prof. M. I. BUGAJE
Faculty of Law: Dr YUSUF M. YUSUF (acting)
Faculty of Management Sciences: Prof. AMINU AYUBA (acting)
Faculty of Science: Prof. M. Y. BALLA (acting)
Faculty of Social Sciences: Prof. S. S. IFAH (acting)
Faculty of Veterinary Medicine: Prof. A. G. AMBALI

PROFESSORS

ABAH, J. O., English
ABUBAKAR, A., Languages and Linguistics
ABUBAKAR, S., History
ADENIJI, F. A., Agricultural Engineering
AGUOLU, C. C., Library Science
AL-AMIN, J.D.
ALKALI, M. NUR, History
AMALI, I. O. O., English
AMBALI, A. G., Veterinary Medicine
ANASO, A. B., Crop Science
AYUBA, A., Management Science
AZEKE, T. O., Education
BABU, S. S., Veterinary Medicine, Microbiology and Parasitology
BADEJO, B. R., Languages and Linguistics
BRANN, C. M. B., Language and Linguistics
BWALA, S. A., Medicine
CAREW, P. F. C., Education
CHHANGANI, R. C., Common Law
CHIBUZO, G. A., Veterinary Anatomy
DAWHA, E. M. K., Library Science
DLAKWA, H., Social Science
EGWU, G. O., Veterinary Anatomy
ENYIKWOLA, O., Human Physiology
GADZAMA, M. N., Science
GOPAL, B. V., Biological Sciences
GUKAS, G. H., Industrial Design
HARRY, T. O., Microbiology
HASSAN, A. W., Surgery
HUSSAINI, I. M., Pharmacy
IDOKO, E. F., Theatre Arts
IGBOKWE, I. O., Veterinary Pathology
IGUN, U. A., Sociology and Anthropology
JACKS, J. W., Medicine
JIBOYEWA, D. A., Education
KAGU, B., Education
KALU, A. U., Veterinary, Public Health and Preventive Medicine
KOROMA, D. S. M., History
MALGWI, D., Physics
MBAHI, A. A., Creative Arts
MOHAMMED, I., Medicine
MSHELIA, B., P. H. E.
MSHELIA, E. D., Physics
ODO, P. E., Crop Science
OGUNBAMERU, B. O.
OHU, J. O., Agricultural Engineering
OMOTARA, B., Community Medicine
ONI, A., Continuing Education
PATE, U., Mass Communication
PINDIGA, H. U., Medicine
RICHARDS, W. S., Biological Sciences
SHEHU, U., Community Medicine
SODIPO, W., Biochemistry
TIJANI, K., Political Science and Administration
UBOSI, C. O., Animal Science
WAZIRI, I., History
ZARIA, L. T., Veterinary Microbiology and Parasitology

MICHAEL OKPARA UNIVERSITY OF AGRICULTURE, UMUDIKE

PMB 7267, Umuahia, Umuahia, Abia State
Telephone: (82) 440555
Fax: (82) 440555

Founded 1992 as Federal University of Agriculture, Umudike; present name and status 2000

Vice-Chancellor: Prof. OGBINNAYA C. ONWUDIKE
Deputy Vice-Chancellor: Prof. HILARY O. EDEOGA
Registrar: JULIA N. UCHE
Librarian: ALOYSIUS ONONOGBO

Library of 8,500 vols
Number of teachers: 158
Number of students: 1,248

DEANS

College of Agricultural Economics, Rural Sociology and Extension: Prof. ALOYSIUS NWOSU
College of Animal Science and Animal Health: Prof. JOHN IBEAWUCHI
College of Biological and Physical Sciences: Dr OBIOHA EZEREONYE
College of Crop and Soil Sciences: Dr CHIDA AMADIOHA
College of Food Processing and Storage Technology: Prof. ENOCH AKOBUNDU
College of Natural Resources and Environmental Management: Prof. EME AKACHUKU
School of Postgraduate Studies: Prof. SYLVESTER IBE

PROFESSORS

AKACHUKU, E. A., Natural Resources and Environmental Management
AKOBUNDU, E. N. T., Food Processing and Storage Technology
ALUKO, P., Natural Resources and Environmental Management
ANASO, H. U., Crop and Soil Sciences
ASIEGBU, J. C., Crop and Soil Sciences
CHIBOKA, V. O., Biological and Physical Sciences
EDEOGA, H. O., Biological and Physical Sciences
EKWUEME, B. N., Biological and Physical Sciences
ELUWA, M. C., Biological and Physical Sciences
IBE, S. N., Animal Science and Animal Health
IBEAWUCHI, J. A., Animal Science and Animal Health
MENKITI, A. I., Biological and Physical Sciences
NJOKU, P. C., Animal Science and Animal Health
NWAGBO, E. C., Agricultural Economics, Rural Sociology and Extension
NWOKE, B. E. B., Biological and Physical Sciences
NWOSU, A. C., Agricultural Economics, Rural Sociology and Extension
OBIZOBA, I. C., Food Processing and Storage Technology
OKERE, L. C., Agricultural Economics, Rural Sociology and Extension
OKOH, P. N., Biological and Physical Sciences
ONWUDIKE, O. C., Animal Science and Animal Health
ONYENWEAKU, C. E., Agricultural Economics, Rural Sociology and Extension

UWAEGBUTE, A. C., Food Processing and Storage Technology
UWAKAH, C. T., Agricultural Economics, Rural Sociology and Extension

NATIONAL OPEN UNIVERSITY OF NIGERIA

14–16 Ahmadu Bello Way, PMB 80067, Victoria Island, Lagos
Telephone: (1) 8188849
Fax: (1) 2712665
Kaduna Campus Fmr NETC Campus, Kaduna-Zaria Rd, Rigachikun Kaduna
E-mail: centralinfo@nou.ed.ng
Internet: www.nou.edu.ng

Founded 1983; suspended by government 1984; re-opened 2001
Vice-Chancellor: Prof. OLUGBEMIRO JEGEDE
Registrar: JOSEPHINE O. AKINYEMI
Number of students: 78,935

Courses for adults by correspondence and distance teaching at 40 study centres serving each state and local government area of Nigeria; Schools of Arts and Social Sciences, Business and Human Resource Management, Education and Science and Technology; Centre for Continuing Education; Regional Training and Research Institute for Open and Distance Learning (RETRIDAL).

UNIVERSITY OF NIGERIA

Nsukka, Enugu State
Telephone: (42) 771911
Internet: www.unn.edu.org

Founded 1960
Fed. control
Language of instruction: English
Academic year: September to June
Chancellor: Emir of Zazzau Alhaji Dr SHEHU IDRIS
Pro-Chancellor: Prof. BOLANLE AWE
Vice-Chancellor: Prof. BARTO N. OKOLO
Deputy Vice-Chancellor for Academic Affairs: Prof. I. U. ASUZU
Deputy Vice-Chancellor for Admin.: Prof. EGBEKE AJA
Deputy Vice-Chancellor (Enugu Campus): Prof. R. E. UMEH
Registrar: A. I. OKONTA (acting)
Librarian: Dr CHARLES O. OMEKWU

Library: see Libraries and Archives
Number of teachers: 1,122
Number of students: 29,482

DEANS

College of Medicine: Prof. B. J. C. ONWUBERE
Faculty of Agriculture: Prof. K. P. BAIYERI
Faculty of Arts: Prof. I. U. NWADIKE
Faculty of Biological Sciences: Prof. C. E. A. OKEZIE
Faculty of Business Administration: Prof. IKE E. NWOSU
Faculty of Dentistry: Prof. E. NDIOKWELU
Faculty of Education: Prof. S. A. EZEUDU
Faculty of Engineering: Prof. J. C. AGUWAMBA
Faculty of Environmental Studies: Prof. J. U. OGBUEFI
Faculty of Health Sciences and Technology: Prof. G. C. OKOYE
Faculty of Law: Prof. F. N. MONYE
Faculty of Medical Sciences: Prof. F. U. EZEPUE
Faculty of Pharmaceutical Sciences: Prof. P. O. OSADEBE
Faculty of Physical Sciences: Prof. M. O. OYESANYA
Faculty of Social Sciences: Prof. E. O. EZEANI
Faculty of Veterinary Medicine: Prof. C. N. UCHENDU
School of General Studies: Prof. E. OGBONNA
School of Postgraduate Studies: Prof. A. N. AKWANYA

PROFESSORS

ADEILUYI, J. O., Civil Engineering
AGAJELU, S. I., Geoinformatics and Surveying
AGHAJI, M. A. C., Medical Sciences and Dentistry
AGU, C. C., Economics
AGUWA, C. N., Clinical Pharmacy and Pharmacy Management
AKAH, P. A., Pharmacology and Toxicology
AKAMIGBO, F. O. R., Soil Science
AKUBUE, A. U., Educational Foundations
ALI, A., Institute of Education
AMAZIGO, J. C., Mathematics
AMUCHEAZI, E. C., Political Science
AMUCHIE, F. A., Health and Physical Education
ANATSUI, E. K., Fine and Applied Arts
ANIAKOR, C. C., Fine and Applied Arts
ANIKA, S. M., Veterinary Physiology and Pharmacology
ANYADIKE, R. N. C., Geography
ANYANWU, S. U., Health and Physical Education
ARUA, E. O., Agricultural Economics
ASIEGBU, J. E., Crop Science
ASUZU, I. U., Veterinary Physiology and Pharmacology
ATTAH, C. A., Surgery
AZUBUIKE, J. C., Paediatrics
CHIDEBELU, S. A. N. D., Agricultural Economics
CHIDUME, C. E., Mathematics
CHIEJINA, S. N., Veterinary Parasitology and Entomology
CHIKWENDU, V. E., Archaeology
CHUKWU, C. C., Veterinary Medicine
EBIGBO, P. O., Psychological Medicine
EDOKA, B. E., Library and Information Science
EGBUNIWE, N., Civil Engineering
EGONU, I. T. K., Foreign Languages and Literature
EGWIM, P. O., Medical Biochemistry
EJIOFOR, L. J. C., Political Science
EKE, E. I., Educational Foundations
EKECHUKWU, O. V., Mechanical Engineering
ENEKWE, O., English
ESEDEBE, P. O., History
EYO, I. E., Psychology
EZEASOR, D. N., Veterinary Anatomy
EZEILO, B. N., Psychology
EZEJI, S. C. O. A., Vocational Teacher Education
EZEKWE, C. I., Mechanical Engineering
EZEOKE, A. C. J., Chemical Pathology
EZEPUE, M. C., Geology
EZE-UZOMAKA, O. J., Civil Engineering
HARBOR-PETERS, V. F., Science Education
IBEMESSI, J. A., Pure and Industrial Chemistry
IGBOELI, G., Animal Science
IGWILO, B. N., Fine and Applied Arts
IHEKORONYE, A. I., Food Science and Technology
IHEZUE, U. H., Psychological Medicine
IJOMA, J. O., History
IKEJIANI-CLARK, M. I. O., Public Administration and Local Government
IKENE, A. I., Home Science and Technology
IKPEZE, A. I., Economics
ILOABACHIE, G. C., Obstetrics and Gynaecology
ILOBA, C., Crop Science
ILOEJE, O. C., Mechanical Engineering
IMAGA, E. U. L., Management
KENE, R. O. C., Veterinary Surgery and Obstetrics
MADUBUNYI, L. C., Veterinary Parasitology and Entomology
MADUEWESI, E. J., Educational Foundations
MBAGWU, J. S. C., Soil Science
MODUM, E. P., Languages
MODUM, U., Accountancy
NGODDY, P. O., Food Science and Technology
NJOKO, O. N., History
NWABUEZE, E. P., Dramatic Arts
NWACHUKWU, P A., Linguistics and Nigerian Languages
NWACHUKWU, T. A., Educational Foundations
NWAFOR, J. C., Geography
NWAGBO, E. C., Agricultural Economics
NWAKOBY, B. A. N., Community Medicine
NWALA, T. U., Philosophy
NWANKITI, O. C., Botany
NWOSU, I. E., Marketing
NZE, C. B., Philosophy
NZEAKO, A. N., Electronic Engineering
OBANU, Z. A., Food Science and Technology
OBI, I. U., Crop Science
OBI, M .E., Soil Science
OBI, S. K. C., Microbiology
OBIANYO, N. E. N., Surgery
OBIDOA, O., Biochemistry
OBIKEZE, D. S., Sociology and Anthropology
OBIZOBA, I. C., Home Science and Nutrition
OBOEGBULAM, S. I., Veterinary Pathology and Microbiology
ODIGBOH, E. U., Agricultural Engineering
ODUKWE, A. O., Mechanical Engineering
OGBAZI, J. N., Vocational Teacher Education
OGBUJI, R. O., Crop Science
OHAEGBU, A. U., Languages
OKAFOR, B. C., Otolaryngology
OKAFOR, C. O., Pure and Industrial Chemistry
OKAFOR, E. C., Pure and Industrial Chemistry
OKAFOR, F. C., Zoology
OKAFOR, F. O., Banking and Finance
OKAFOR, F. U., Philosophy
OKEKE, C. E., Physics and Astronomy
OKEKE, E. A. C., Education
OKEKE, F. N., Physics and Astronomy
OKEKE, P. N., Physics and Astronomy
OKOGBUE, C. O., Geology
OKOLI, F. C., Public Administration and Local Government
OKONKWO, P. O., Pharmacology and Therapeutics
OKORAFOR, A. E., Economics
OKORE, A. O., Economics
OKORIE, J. U., Vocational Teacher Education
OKORJI, E. C., Agricultural Economics
OKORO, B. A., Paediatrics
OKORO, O. M., Vocational Teacher Education
OKOYE, J. O. A., Veterinary Pathology and Microbiology
OKPALA, J. I. N., Education
OKPARA, E., Psychology
OKPOKO, A. I., Archaeology
OLAITAN, S. O., Vocational Teacher Education
OLI, J. M., Medicine
OLOIDI, O., Fine and Applied Arts
ONAH, J. O., Marketing
ONONOGBU, I. C., Biochemistry
ONUKOGU, I. B., Statistics
ONUOHA, K. M., Geology
ONWU, N., Religion
ONYEGEGBU, S. O., Mechanical Engineering
ONYEJEKWE, D. C., Mechanical Engineering
ORANU, R. N., Vocational Teacher Education
OSUAGWU, C. C., Electronic Engineering
OSUALA, E. C., Vocational Teacher Education
OSUALA, J. D. C., Adult Education and Extramural Studies
OYEOKU, O. K., Fine and Applied Arts
OZIOKO, J. O. C., Psychology
OZUMBA, B. C., Obstetrics and Gynaecology
PAL, S., Physics and Astronomy
SOLUDO, C. C., Economics
UCHE, P. I., Statistics
UKAEJIOFO, E. O., Medical Laboratory Science
UME, J. A., Estate Management
UMEH, L. C., Urban and Regional Planning
UMEH, T. A., Adult Education and Extramural Studies

ATTACHED INSTITUTES

Centre for Energy Research and Development: Nsukka; Dir Prof. E. C. OKORJI (acting).

Centre for Equipment Maintenance and Development: Nsukka; Dir Prof. I. C. OBIZOBA.

Institute of African Studies: Nsukka; Dir Prof. O. O. ENEKWE.

Institute for Development Studies: University of Nigeria, Enugu Campus, Enugu; Dir Prof. E. U. L. IMAGA.

Institute of Education: Nsukka; Dir Prof. E. A. C. OKEKE.

Veterinary Teaching Hospital: Nsukka; Dir Dr L. J. E. ORAJAKA (acting).

NNAMDI AZIKIWE UNIVERSITY

PMB 5025, Awka, Anambra State
Telephone: (80) 60492273
E-mail: info@unizik.edu.ng

Founded 1992
Federal govt control
Languages of instruction: English, French, Hausa, Igbo, Yoruba
Academic year: October to June

Chancellor: Emir of Ilorin Alhaji SULU GAMBARI
Pro-Chancellor: SENAS UKPANAH
Vice-Chancellor: Prof. B. C. E. EGBOKA
Deputy Vice-Chancellor for Academic Affairs: Prof. J. E. AHANEKU
Deputy Vice-Chancellor for Admin.: Prof. BEN C. OKEKE
Registrar: C. C. OKEKE (acting)
Librarian: EMMA ONWUKA (acting)
Provost, College of Health Sciences: Prof. OKEY IKPEZE
Bursar: U. J. AGU (acting)

Library of 65,000 vols
Number of teachers: 842
Number of students: 36,000

Publications: *Journal of Arts and Humanities, Journal of Economic Studies, Journal of Education Management, Journal of Management Studies, Journal of Vocational and Adult Education, Tropical Journal of Medical Research, UNIZIK Law Journal*

DEANS

Faculty of Agriculture: Prof. NONSO NNABUIFE
Faculty of Arts: Prof. DAN AGU
Faculty of Basic Medical Sciences: Prof. ED NWOBODO
Faculty of Education: Prof. SAM OKEKE
Faculty of Engineering and Technology: Prof. D. O. ONUKWULI
Faculty of Environmental Sciences: Prof. C. C. EGOLUM
Faculty of Health Sciences and Technology: Dr C. C. ONYENEKWE (acting)
Faculty of Law: Prof. KEN NWOGU
Faculty of Management Sciences: Prof. C. I. ONWUCHEKWA
Faculty of Medicine: Prof. A. M. E. NWOFOR
Faculty of Natural Sciences: Prof. P. A. C. OKOYE
Faculty of Pharmaceutical Sciences: Prof. C. O. ESIMONE
Faculty of Physical Sciences: Prof. F. C. ODIBO
Faculty of Social Sciences: Prof. E. A. EGBOH
Postgraduate School: Prof. LUKE ANIKE

PROFESSORS

Confucius Institute:
NENGWEN, J.

Faculty of Arts:
AGBODIKE, C.
AGU, D.
ANAGBOGU, P.
ANIZOBA, O.
DUKOR, E.
EKPUNOBI, D.
EYISI, J.
MADU, J.
MBANUGO, C.
NDUKA, D.
NZOMIWU, J.
OKEKE, D.
ONYEKAONWU, G.
UMEASIEGBU, R.
UMEH, O.

Faculty of Education:
ABONE, O.
AKUDOLU, L.
AKUEZUILO, E.
ANAGBOGU, M.
EBENEBE, R.
EZE, T.
IKE, A.
NDINECHI, G.
NDU, A.
NNADOZIE, J.
OGBALU, A.
OKAFOR, J.
OKONKWO, O.
ORAEMESI, J.
UMEDUM, S.
UMEASIEGBU, G.
UNACHUKWU, G.

Faculty of Engineering and Technology:
IGBOKWE, P.
IJOMAH, M.
INYIAMA, H.
KATCHY, E.
NNUKA, E.
NWOBU, R.
OFODILE, E.
OGBUAGU, J.
OKEKE, S.
ONUKWULI, O.
UBA NWUBA, E.

Faculty of Law:
OKAFOR, I.

Faculty of Management Sciences:
IKEZUE, C.
MBACHU, A.
NZE, F.
OKAFOR, F.
ONWUCHEKWA, C.
OSISIOMA, B.
UMEBALI

Faculty of Medicine:
ADINMA, J.
AGBATA, A.
AHANEKU, J.
ANYANWU, S.
EGBUONU, I.
EKEJINDU, G.
EMELE, F.
EZECHUKWU, C.
IKPEZE, O.
MBONU, O.
MELUDU, S.
NWOFOR, A.
NWOFOR, A.
NWOSU, S.
OFIAELI, R.
OKAFOR, P.
OKONKWO, J.
ORAKWE, J.
OSUIGWE, A.
UMEH, B.
UWAKWE, R.

Faculty of Natural Sciences:
AJIWE, V.
AKPUAKA, M.
ANASO, H.
ANENE, G.
ANIZOBA, M.
ANYAKOHA, M.
CHUKWURAH, E.
EBOATU, A.
EKEJIUBA, I.
EKPUNOBI, A.
ENEANYA, C.
EZEKWE, N.
EZEONU, E.
MBANUGO, J.
MOORE, C.
NWAORGU, O.
ODIBO, F.
OGUM, G.
OKAKA, A.
OKEREKE, G.
OKOYE, P.
ONOCHIE, C.
ONYALI, O.
ONYEAGU, S.
ORAJAKA, I.
OYEKA, C.
OYEKA, I.
UMEGO, M.
UMEH, C.

Faculty of Pharmaceutical Sciences:
ESIMONE, C. O.

Faculty of Social Sciences:
DIKE, M.
EYIUCHE, A.
NWANUNOBI, C.
NWUNELI, O.
OBI, A.
OKUNNA, C.

OBAFEMI AWOLOWO UNIVERSITY

Ile-Ife
Telephone: (36) 230290
Fax: (36) 232401
E-mail: registra@oauife.edu.ng
Internet: www.oauife.edu.ng

Founded 1961 as University of Ife, present name 1987
Federal control
Language of instruction: English
Academic year: September to July

Chancellor: Alhaji KABIR USMAN
Pro-Chancellor: Alhaji SHETIMA A. M. LIBERTY
Vice-Chancellor: Prof. ROGER MAKANJUOLA
Deputy Vice-Chancellor for Academic Affairs: Prof. A. A. ADEDIRAN
Deputy Vice-Chancellor for Admin.: Prof. L. O. KEHINDE
Registrar: B. O. ILUYOMADE
University Bursar: O. ODEYEMI
University Librarian: M. O. AFOLABI

Library: see Libraries and Archives
Number of teachers: 1,343
Number of students: 22,742

Publications: *Calendar*, *Gazette*, *Handbook*, *Ife Studies in English Language*, *Odu: A Journal of West African Studies* (2 a year), *Quarterly Journal of Administration*, *Second Order* (2 a year), *University Bulletin*

PROVOSTS

College of Health Sciences: M. O. BALOGUN
Postgraduate College: S. K. ADESINA

DEANS

Faculty of Administration: O. OJO
Faculty of Agriculture: R. ADEYEMO
Faculty of Arts: O. T. AKINRINADE
Faculty of Basic Medical Sciences: M. A. DUROSINMI
Faculty of Clinical Sciences: J. A. OWA
Faculty of Dentistry: O. D. OTUYEMI (acting)
Faculty of Education: D. K. AKANBI
Faculty of Environmental Design and Management: C. A. AJAYI
Faculty of Law: M. O. ADEDIRAN
Faculty of Pharmacy: A. O. OGUNDAINI
Faculty of Science: M. A. BADEJO

Faculty of Social Sciences: J. A. FABAYO
Faculty of Technology: M. O. FABORODE

PROFESSORS

Faculty of Administration:
ERERO, E. J., Public Administration
OJO, O., International Relations
OMOPARIOLA, O., Management and Accounting
ORIBABOR, P. E., Management and Accounting
SESAY, A., International Relations
SOREMEKUN, O., International Relations

Faculty of Agriculture:
ADEBAYO, A. A., Soil Science
ADEPETU, J. A., Soil Science
ADERIBIGBE, A. O., Animal Science
ADEYEMO, R., Agricultural Economics
ADUAYI, E. A., Soil Science
AINA, P. O., Soil Science
AJOBO, O., Agricultural Economics
AKINGBOHUNGBE, A. E., Plant Science
AKINYEMIJU, O. A., Plant Science
ALOFE, C. O., Plant Science
FAKOREDE, M. A., Plant Science
ILORI, J. O., Animal Science
JIBOWO, A. A., Agricultural Extension and Rural Sociology
LADIPO, J. L., Plant Science
LAOGUN, E. A., Agricultural Extension and Rural Sociology
MATANMI, B. A., Plant Science
OBISESAN, I. O., Plant Science
OKUSAMI, T. A., Soil Science
OLAYINKA, A., Soil Science
SONAIYA, E. B., Animal Science

Faculty of Arts:
ADEDIRAN, A. A., History
ADEWOLE, L. O., African Languages and Literature
AJUWON, B., African Languages and Literature
AKINRINADE, O. T., History
IBITOKUN, B. M., English
ILESANMI, T. M., Religious Studies
KOLAWOLE, M. E. M., English
MAKINDE, M. A., Philosophy
MANUS, C. U., Modern European Languages
NWEZEH, E. C., Foreign Languages
OLANIYAN, R. A., History
OLAYIWOLA, D. O., Religious Studies
OLOMOLA, G. O. I., History
OLORUNFEMI, A., History
OMOSINI, O., History
ONIBERE, S. G. A., Religious Studies
VIDAL, A. O., Music

Faculties of Basic Medical Sciences, Clinical Sciences and Dentistry:
ADEJUYIGBE, O., Surgery
ADELEKAN, D. A., Community Health
ADEYEMO, A. O., Surgery
AKINOLA, D. O., Surgery
AKINSOLA, A., Medicine
ARIGBABU, O., Surgery
BALOGUN, M. O., Medicine
CAXTON-MARTINS, A. E., Anatomy and Cell Biology
DARE, F. O., Obstetrics and Gynaecology
DUROSINMI, M. A., Haematology and Immunology
ELEGBE, R. A., Physiological Sciences
FAJEWONYOMI, B. A., Community Health
FAKUNLE, J. B., Chemical Pathology
JINADU, M. I., Nursing
MAKANJUOLA, R. O. A., Mental Health
ODESANMI, W. O., Morbid Anatomy and Forensic Medicine
OGUNBODEDE, E. O., Preventive Dentistry
OGUNNIYI, S. O., Obstetrics and Gynaecology
OJO, O. S., Morbid Anatomy and Forensic Medicine
OJOFEITIMI, E. O., Community Health and Nutrition
ONWUDIEGWU, U., Obstetrics and Gynaecology
OTUYEMI, O. D., Child Dental Health
OWA, J. A., Paediatrics and Child Health
OYEDEJI, G. A., Paediatrics and Child Health

Faculty of Education:
ADEYANJU, S. A., Physical and Health Education
AKANBI, D. K., Educational Technology
EHINDERO, O. J., Institute of Education
FASOKUN, T. O., Continuing Education
FAWOLE, J. O., Physical Education
OBIDI, S. S., Education, Foundation and Counselling
OGUNDARI, J. T., Physical and Health Education
OKUNROTIFA, E. B., Physical and Health Education

Faculty of Environmental Design and Management:
AJAYI, C. A., Estate Management
AMOLE, S. A., Architecture
AREMU, P. S. O., Fine Arts
FADARE, S. O., Urban and Regional Planning
IGHALO, J. I., Estate Management
OGUNJUMO, A., Urban and Regional Planning
OLAJUYIN, L. O., Urban and Regional Planning

Faculty of Law:
ADEDIRAN, M. O., Public Law
FABUNMI, J. O., Business Law
OKORODUDU-FUBARA, M. T., International Law

Faculty of Pharmacy:
ADESANYA, S. A., Pharmacognosy
ADESINA, S. K., Drug Research
ADEWUNMI, C. O., Drug Research
ALADESANMI, J. A., Pharmacognosy
ELUJOBA, A. A., Pharmacognosy
LAMIKANRA, A., Pharmaceutics
OGUNBONA, F. A., Pharmaceutical Chemistry
OGUNDAINI, A. O., Pharmaceutical Chemistry
OGUNDARI, O., Pharmaceutical Chemistry
OLUGBADE, T. O., Pharmaceutical Chemistry
ONAWUNMI, G. O., Pharmaceutics
ONYEJI, O. C., Pharmaceutical Chemistry
ORAFIDIYA, O. O., Pharmaceutics
SOFOWORA, E. A., Pharmacognosy

Faculty of Science:
ADEDOKUN, J. A., Physics
ADEGOKE, J. A., Zoology
ADESULU, E. A., Zoology
ADEWUSI, S. R. A., Chemistry
AFOLAYAN, A., Biochemistry
AFUWAPE, M. A., Mathematics
AJAYI, E. O. B., Physics
AJAYI, T. R., Geology
AKANNI, M. S., Chemstry
AKINRELERE, E. A., Mathematics
AKO, B. D., Geology
AKO-NAI, K. A., Microbiology
ALADEKOMO, J. B., Physics
AMIRE, O. A., Chemistry
AMUSA, A., Physics
ARAWOMO, G. A. O., Zoology
ASAOLU, S. O., Zoology
AUBICJO, F. O. I., Chemistry
BALOGUN, E. E., Physics
BALOGUN, R. A., Zoology
FAKUNLE, C. O., Chemistry
IGE, W. J., Chemistry
IMORU, C. O., Mathematics
ISAWUMI, M. A. (Natural History Museum)
ISICHEI, A. O., Botany
KOLAWOLE, D. O., Microbiology
NWACHUKWU, J. I., Geology
OBAFEMI, C. A., Chemistry
ODEYEMI, O., Microbiology
ODU, E. A., Botany
OGUNKOYA, L. O., Chemistry
OJO, J. F., Chemistry
OKON, E. E., Zoology
OLANIYI, H. B., Physics
OLAREWAJU, V. O., Geology
OLOMO, J. B., Physics
OLORODE, O., Botany
OLORUNFEMI, M. O., Geology
OLUTIOLA, P. O., Microbiology
ONAJOBI, F. D., Biochemistry
OSADEBE, F. A. N., Physics
OSHOBI, E. O., Mathematics
RAHAMAN, M. A., Geology
SALAMI, M. B., Geology
SALAU, A. A. M., Physics
SHONUKAN, O. O., Microbiology

Faculty of Social Sciences:
ADESINA, F. A., GeographyADEWUYI, A. A., Demography and Social Statistics
AFONJA, S., Sociology and Anthropology
EBIGBOLA, J. A., Demography and Social Statistics
EKANADE, O., Geography
FABAYO, J. A., Economics
JEJE, L. K., Geography
ODEBIYI, A. I., Sociology and Anthropology
OGUNBADEJO, F. O., Political Science
OGUNKOYA, O. O., Geography
OLORUNTIMEHIN, O., Sociology and Anthropology
OLOWU, A. A., Psychology
TOGONU-BICKESTETH, T., Psychology

Faculty of Technology:
ADEGBOYEGA, G. A., Electronic and Electrical Engineering
ADEKOYA, L. O., Mechanical Engineering
AFONJA, A. A., Metallurgical and Materials Engineering
AJAYI, G. O., Electronic and Electrical Engineering
AJIBOLA, O. A., Agricultural Engineering
BURAIMAH-IGBO, L. A., Electronic and Electrical Engineering
FABORODE, M. O., Agricultural Engineering
FAPOHUNDA, M. O., Agricultural Engineering
FASHAKIN, J. B., Food Science and Technology
IGE, M. T., Agricultural Engineering
ILLORI, M. O., Technology, Planning and Development Unit
KEHINDE, L. O., Electronic and Electrical Engineering
KUKU, T. A., Electronic and Electrical Engineering
LASISI, F., Agricultural Engineering
LAYOKUN, S. K., Chemical Engineering
MAKANJUOLA, G. A., Agricultural Engineering
MOJOLA, O. O., Mechanical Engineering
OGEDENGBE, M. O., Civil Engineering
OGUNSUA, A. O., Food Science and Technology
SANNI, S. A., Chemical Engineering
SOLOMON, B. O., Chemical Engineering
TAIWO, O., Chemical Engineering

AFFILIATED INSTITUTES

Institute of Agricultural Research and Training (IART), Ibadan: see under Research Institutes.

Institute of Education: Ile-Ife; f. 1962; sponsored by the University, the Oyo State Ministry of Education and the Association of Principals of Teacher Training Colleges and Secondary Schools in the State; a mobile library equipped with books, audio-visual aids and film aids demonstration among colleges and secondary schools; Dir O. J. EHINDERO; publ. *News Bulletin* (4 a year).

UNIVERSITY OF PORT HARCOURT

PMB 5323, Port Harcourt, Rivers State
Telephone: (84) 335218
Fax: (84) 230903
E-mail: registrar@uniport.edu.ng
Internet: www.uniport.edu.ng

Founded 1975
Federal control
Language of instruction: English
Academic year: October to July

Chancellor: HRH Alhaji MUSTAPHA UMAR EL-KANEMI (Shehu of Borno)
Pro-Chancellor: Prof. (Emer.) ALHAJI L. A. K. JIMOH
Vice-Chancellor: Prof. NIMI DIMPKA BRIGGS
Deputy Vice-Chancellor for Academic Affairs: Prof. J. D. OKOH
Deputy Vice-Chancellor for Admin.: Prof. M. O. C. ANIKPO
Registrar: Dr CHRIS ALAFONYEKA TAMUNO
Librarian: Prof. E. O. AYALOGU

Library of 90,000 vols, 220 foreign current journals, depository rights for UN publications
Number of teachers: 560
Number of students: 26,672

Publications: *Biologia Africana* (2 a year), *Journal of Education in Developing Areas—JEDA* (1 a year), *Kiabara* (2 a year), *Library Waves* (2 a year)

DEANS

Faculty of Basic Medical Sciences: Prof. O. O. EBONG
Faculty of Clinical Sciences: Prof. K. E. O. NKANGINIEME
Faculty of Dentistry: Prof. F. OKOISOR
Faculty of Engineering: Prof. C. UMEZURIKE
Faculty of Humanities: Prof. S. I. UDOIDEM
Faculty of Management Sciences: Prof. D. P. S. ASECHEMIE
Faculty of Pharmacy: Prof. O. K. UDEALA
Faculty of Science: Prof. C. M. OJINNAKA
Faculty of Social Sciences: Prof. W. J. OKOWA
College of Health Sciences: Prof. O. J. ODIA (Provost)
School of Graduate Studies: Prof. W. I. BELL-GAM

PROFESSORS

Faculty of Education:
AWOTUA-EFEBO, E. B., Educational Technology
BARIKOR, C. N., Adult Education
DIENYE, N. E., Science Education
DIKE, H. I., Curriculum and Educational Technology
EHEAZU, B. A., Adult and Non-Formal Education
ENAOWHO, J. O., Educational Management and Planning
GBAMANJA, S. P. T., Curriculum and Educational Technology
JOE, A. I., Psychology, Guidance and Counselling
OKEKE, B. S., Education Administration
OKOH, J. D., History and Philosophy of Education
UKWUIJE, R. P. I., Educational Psychology, Guidance and Counselling

Faculty of Engineering:
AJIENKA, J. A., Petroleum Engineering
EBONG, M. B., Civil Engineering
KUYE, A. O., Chemical Engineering
NWAOGAZIE, I. L., Civil Engineering
ONYEKONWU, M. A., Petroleum Engineering
UMEZURIKE, C., Mechanical Engineering

Faculty of Humanities:
BESTMAN, M. T., French
CHUKWUMA, H. O., Oral Literature
EJITUWU, N. C., History
EJIZU, C. I., Religious Studies
EKWELIE, S. A., Linguistics
EMENANJO, E. N., Linguistics
IKONNE, C., English
ILEGA, D., Religious Studies
MADUKA, C. T., Comparative Literature
NNOLIM, C. E., Literature
NWODO, C. S., Philosophy
UDOIDEM, S. I., Philosophy

Faculty of Management Sciences:
ASECHEMIE, D. P. S., Accounting
BARIDAM DON, O. M., Management
NWACHUKWU, C. C., Management

Faculty of Science:
ABBEY, B. W., Biochemistry
AKPOKODJE, E. A., Geology
AMAJOR, L. C., Geology
ANOSIKE, E. O., Enzymology and Protein Chemistry
ANUSIEM, A. C. I., Thermochemistry and Biophysical Chemistry
ARENE, F. O. I., Animal and Environmental Biology
ARINZE, A. E., Plant Science and Biotechnology
AYALOGU, E. O., Biochemistry
EBENIRO, J. O., Physics
EFIU-VWEVWERE, B. J. O., Biodegradation and Environmental Toxicology
EKEKE, G. I., Biochemistry
ETU-EFEOTOR, J. O., Sedimentology, Sedimentary Geochemistry
KINAKO, P. D. S., Botany
LALE, N. E. S., Crop Science
NYANANYO, B. L., Plant Science and Biotechnology
OJINNAKA, C. M., Organic and Natural Products Chemistry
OKIWELU, S. N., Entomology
OKOLI, B. S., Genetics
OKPOKWASILI, G. S. C., Microbiology
OTI, M. N., Geology

Faculty of Social Sciences:
AGIOBENEBO, T. J., Economics
ANIKPO, M. O. C., Sociology
BELL-GAM, W. I., Geography
EKPENYONG, S., Sociology
ETENG, I. A., Sociology
GBOSI, A. A., Economics
IBODJE, S. W. E., Political and Administrative Studies
OKOKO, K. A. B., Political and Administrative Studies
OJO, O. J. B., Political and Administrative Studies
OKOWA, W. J., Economics

College of Health Sciences:
ANAH, C. O., Cardiology
ASOGWA, S. E., Preventative and Social Medicine
BRAMBAIFA, N., Pharmacology
BRIGGS, N. D., Obstetrics and Gynaecology
DATUBO-BROWN, D. D., Surgery
EBONG, O. O., Pharmacology
EKE, N., Surgery
ELECHI, E. N., Surgery
EKE, F., Paediatrics
ESSIEN, E. N., Haematology
JOHN, T., Obstetrics and Gynaecology
NKANGINIEME, K. E. O., Paediatrics
NWANKWOALA, R. N. P., Pharmacology
ODIA, O. J., Medicine
OKOISOR, F., Dentistry
ORUAMABO, R. S., Paediatrics
UDEALA, O. K., Pharmacy
WAKWE, V. C., Chemical Pathology

USMANU DANFODIYO UNIVERSITY

Dundaye Village, PMB 234, Sokoto
Telephone: (60) 234042
Fax: (60) 235519
E-mail: registrar@udusok.edu.ng
Internet: www.udusok.edu.ng

Founded 1975
Federal control
Language of instruction: English
Academic year: November to July

Chancellor: (vacant)
Vice-Chancellor: Prof. A.S. MIKAILA
Deputy Vice-Chancellor for Academic Affairs: Dr A. A. ZURU
Registrar: A. S. USMAN
Librarian: AHMED ABDU BALARABE (acting)

Number of teachers: 371
Number of students: 11,617

Publications: *Calendar*, *Convocation Speeches*, *News Bulletin* (12 a year), *Student Handbook* (1 a year), *University Lecture Series*

DEANS

Faculty of Agriculture: Dr H. M. TUKUR (acting)
Faculty of Arts and Islamic Studies: Dr M. M. DANGANA (acting)
Faculty of Education and Extension Services: Dr F. A. KALGO (acting)
Faculty of Law: Mal. M. I. SAID
Faculty of Management and Administration: Prof. S. A. DIYO
Faculty of Science: Dr U. ABUBAKAR
Faculty of Social Sciences: (vacant)
Faculty of Veterinary Medicine: Dr A. I. DANEJI
College of Health Sciences: Dr W. E. K. OPARA
Postgraduate School: Dr R. A. SHEHU

PROFESSORS

ABDULKAREEM, A., Health Sciences
ABDULRAHMAN, D. A., Sociology
ABDULRAHMAN, F. W., Chemistry
ABUBAKAR, M. K., Biochemistry
ADAMU, M., History
ADEYANJU, J. B., Veterinary Medicine
AGALEA, A. S., Arabic
AUDU, M. S., Mathematics
BADEJO, O. A., Health Sciences
BANDE, T. M., Political Science
BASHAR, M. L. A., Economics
BASHIR, A. M., Accounting
BILBIS, L. S., Biochemistry
BIRNIWA, H. A., Nigerian Languages
DANIEL, S. O., Community Health
DORA, J. S., Geography
ILIYA, M. A., Geography
IPINJOLU, J. K., Forestry and Fisheries
JUNAID, M. I., Education
KALGO, F. A., Education
KAURA, J. M., Islamic Studies
KYIOGWON, U. B., Agricultural Economics and Extension
MAGAJI, M. D., Crop Science
MAJEED, Q., Biological Sciences
MAMMAN, A. B., Geography
MIKAILU, A. S., Business Administration
MUKOSHY, I. A., Nigerian Languages
OBEMBE, A. Y. O., Medicine
OPARA, W. E., Surgery
SALAWU, A. A., Education
SHEHU, B., Surgery
SHEIDU, A. D., Accounting
YAQUB, N. O., Political Science
ZURU, A. A., Chemistry

UNIVERSITY OF UYO

1 Ikpa Rd, PMB 1017, Uyo, Akwa Ibom State
Telephone: (85) 200303
Fax: (85) 202694
E-mail: vc@uniuyo.edu.ng
Internet: www.uniuyo.edu.ng

Founded 1983 as University of Cross River State, then renamed University of Akwa Ibom State; present name 1991
Fed. govt control
Language of instruction: English

Academic year: October to July
Chancellor: The Emir of Fika, Haj. Dr ABALI IBN MUHAMMADU
Vice-Chancellor: Prof. AKPAN H. EKPO
Deputy Vice-Chancellor for Academic Affairs: Prof. UDO I. ANWANA
Deputy Vice-Chancellor for Admin.: Prof. UDO ETUK
Dean of Student Affairs: ETOK O. EKANEM
Registrar: PETER J. EFIONG
Librarian: Dr OFFIONG O. UDOH
Library of 46,745 vols, 271 periodicals
Number of teachers: 769
Number of students: 16,707
Publications: *Journal of Humanities*, *Journal of Research in Education and the Humanities*, *Uyo Social Science Journal*

DEANS

Faculty of Agriculture: Prof. BASSEY A. NDON
Faculty of Arts: Prof. UDO A. ETUK
Faculty of Basic Medical Sciences: Prof. A. ABODERIN
Faculty of Business Administration: Prof. EDET B. AKPAKPAN
Faculty of Education: Prof. GEORGE S. IBE-BASSEY
Faculty of Engineering: Prof. E. U. NWA
Faculty of Environmental Studies: AKANINYENE MENDIE
Faculty of Law: Prof. ENEFIOK E. ESSIEN
Faculty of Pharmacy: Prof. ETIENE E. ESSIEN
Faculty of Social Sciences: Prof. IMO E. UKPONG
Postgraduate School: Prof. IME S. IKIDDEH

PROFESSORS

ABASIATTAI, M. B., History
ABASIEKONG, E. M., Sociology
ABODERIN, A., Chemistry
ACHALU, O. E., Health Education
AFOLABI, M., Library Science
ANWANA, U. I., Guidance and Counselling
EKA, D., English
EKONG, E. E., Sociology
EKPENYONG, S., Sociology and Anthropology
EKPO, A. H., Economics
EKPO, N. M., Physics
EKPO, O. E., Curriculum Studies
ENOH, C. O. E., Geography
ESHIET, I. T., Chemistry and Education
ESSIEN, E. E., Pharmaceutical Chemistry
ETTE, S. I., Biochemistry
ETUK, U. A., Philosophy
EZE, O. C., Law
IBE-BASSEY, G. S., Educational Technology
IKKIDEH, I. S., English
IWOK, E. R., Accounting
NWA, E. U., Engineering
OKON, E. D., Zoology
UDO, E. J., Soil Science
UDOFOT, M. A., Curriculum Studies
UKPONG, I. I., Economics
UMOH, J. E., Animal Science
UMOH, P. U., Law
USORO, E., Geography

STATE UNIVERSITIES

ABIA STATE UNIVERSITY

PMB 2000, Uturu, Abia State
Telephone: (88) 220785
Internet: www.abia-state-uni.net
Founded 1981 as Imo State University; present name c. 1993
State control
Language of instruction: English
Academic year: October to August
Chancellor: Ambassador Dr Chief M. T. MBU
Vice-Chancellor: Prof. OGWO E. OGWO
Deputy Vice-Chancellor: Prof. STELLA OGBUAGU
Pro-Chancellor: EMEKA NWANKPA
Registrar: O. E. ONUOHA
Librarian: HERBERT I. IWUJI
Library of 27,000 vols
Number of teachers: 640
Number of students: 7,050

DEANS

College of Agriculture and Veterinary Medicine: Dr V. O. IMOH
College of Biological and Physical Sciences: Dr C. I. OGBONNAYA
College of Business Administration: Dr I. AJA-NWACHUKU
College of Education: Prof. V. C. NWACHUKU
College of Engineering and Environmental Studies: Dr M. A. IJIOMA (acting)
College of Humanities and Social Sciences: Prof. J. O. J. NWACHUKWU-ABADA
College of Legal Studies: M. O. UNEGBU (acting)
College of Medicine and Health Sciences: A. U. MBANASO (Provost)

PROFESSORS

AKPUAKA, F. C., Medicine and Health Sciences
ALEZI, O., Education
EBEOGU, A. N., Humanities and Social Sciences
EKE, F., Medicine and Health Sciences
MADUABUM, M. A., Education
MBATA, G. N., Biological and Physical Sciences
MKPA, M. A., Education
NWACHUKU, V. C., Education
NWACHUKWU-AGBADA, J. O. J., Humanities and Social Sciences
OGBONNAYA, C. I., Biological and Physical Sciences
OGBUAGU, S. C., Humanities and Social Sciences
OGWO, E. O., Marketing
ONOFEGHARA, N., Education
ONOH, J. K., Finance
ONUIGBO, W. I., Medicine and Health Sciences
OPARA-NADI, O. I., Agriculture and Veterinary Medicine
UWAKAH, C. T., Agriculture and Veterinary Medicine

ADAMAWA STATE UNIVERSITY

PMB 25, Mubi, Adamawa State
Telephone: (805) 8421126
Fax: (803)6131590
E-mail: info@adsu.edu.ng
Internet: www.adsu.edu.ng
Founded 2002
State control
Language of instruction: English
Academic year: October to August, (2 semesters)
Vice-Chancellor: Dr ALKASUM ABBA
Deputy Vice-Chancellor: Dr SAIDU IBRAHIM
Registrar: J. M. GARNVWA
Bursar: M. B. ABUBAKAR
Univ. Librarian: BELLO Y. DAHIRU
Dir for Academic Planning: S. M. MORUPPA
Library of 35,089 vols, 60 journals, 5,000 vols of electronic books, 2,000 electronic journals
Number of teachers: 311
Number of students: 5,719
Publications: *Adamawa Business Journal* (2 a year), *Adamawa Journal of Management and Decision Analysis* (2 a year), *ADSU Journal of Social and Development Studies* (2 a year)

DEANS

Faculty of Agriculture: Dr NEILS SHELLENG
Faculty of Science: Dr O. N. MAITERA
Faculty of Social and Management Sciences: Dr ABDULSALAM JIBRIL
Postgraduate School: Prof. MERCY OGUNSOLA-BANDELE
School of Remedial and Basic Studies: ELI TARTIYUS (Dir)

UNIVERSITY OF ADO-EKITI

PMB 5363, Ado-Ekiti, Ekiti State
Telephone: (30) 250026
E-mail: registrar@unad.edu.ng
Internet: www.unadportal.com
Founded 1982
Vice-Chancellor: Prof. DIPO KOLAWOLE
Deputy Vice-Chancellor for Academics: Prof. O. OLAOFE
Deputy Vice-Chancellor for Devt: Prof. J. A. ADEGUN
Dir for Directorate of Distance Learning: Prof. R. O SEWEJE
Dir for General Studies Unit: Prof. K. AJAYI
Dir for Pre-Degree Programmes: Prof. E. O. OLANIPEKUN
Registrar: OMOJOLA AWOSUSI
Bursar: F. M. FAPOHUNDA
Librarian: G. O. OGUNLEYE
Library of 110,000 vols
Number of teachers: 445
Number of students: 14,652 (full-time; 5,700 part-time)
Publication: *Nigerian Journal of Banking and Financial Issues* (2 a year)

DEANS

College of Medicine: Prof. D. D. OYEBOLA
Faculty of Agricultural Sciences: Prof. A.S. FASINA
Faculty of Arts: Dr T. F. JEMIRIYE (acting)
Faculty of Education: Prof. G. A. AKINLEYE
Faculty of Engineering: Dr S. B. ADEYEMO (acting)
Faculty of Law: T. I. AKOMOLEDE
Faculty of Management Sciences: Prof. J. A. OLOYEDE
Faculty of Science: Prof. S. S. ASAOLU
Faculty of Social Sciences: Prof. A. L. ADESINA (acting)
School of Postgraduate Studies: Prof. J. O. ARIBISALA

PROFESSORS

ADEBAYO, W., Social Sciences
ADELOWO, E., Arts
ADERIBIGBE, E., Science
ADERIBIGBE, F., Science
ADERIYE, J., Science
ADETIFA, O., Engineering
ADEYOJU, K., Agricultural Sciences
AFOLABI, F., Social Sciences
AGAGU, A., Political Science
AJAJA, O., Engineering
AKINDUTIRE, I., Education
AKINLEYE, G., Education
AKINTAYO, E., Science
ALONGE, M., Education
BANDELE, S., Education
ESAN, G., Medicine
FAKUNLE, J., Science
FALUYI, M., Science
FAMUREWA, O., Science
IBIJOLA, E., Mathematical Sciences
KAYODE, J., Science
KOLAWOLE, D., Social Sciences
LUCAS, E., Agricultural Sciences
MUKOLU, I., Physics
OGUNLADE, A., Education
OGUNSINA, J., Arts
OJO, S., Faculty of Engineering
OKE, G., Faculty of Law
OLOMOLA, G., History and International Studies
OLORUNSOLA, S., Science
OMOSINI, O., Arts
OWOLABI, I., Elect/Elect. Engineering
OWUAMANAM, D., Education

OWUAMANAM, T., Education
OYINLOYE, A., Science
UKOYEN, J., Arts

AMBROSE ALLI UNIVERSITY

PMB 14, Ekpoma, Edo State
Telephone: (55) 98448

Founded 1981
State control
Language of instruction: English
Academic year: September to August

Chancellor: HRH Alhaji Dr UMARU FARUQ BAHAGO (Emir of Minna)
Vice-Chancellor and Chief Executive: Prof. D. O. AIGBOMIAN
Deputy Vice-Chancellor for Academic Affairs: Dr G. B. EFOGHE
Deputy Vice-Chancellor for Admin.: (vacant)
Provost, College of Medicine: Prof. G. O. AKPEDE
Registrar: G. T. OLAWOLE
Librarian: M. E. OJO-IGBINOBA

Library of 94,000 vols
Number of teachers: 500
Number of students: 18,000

Publications: *AAU* (journal of the Faculty of Education, 1 a year), *Iroro* (journal of the Faculty of Arts and Social Sciences, 1 a year)

DEANS

Faculty of Agriculture: Dr P. O. ONOLEMHEMHEN (acting)
Faculty of Arts: Prof. F. I. EMORDI
Faculty of Clinical Sciences: F. ALUFOHAI
Faculty of Education: Prof. M. O. OMO-OJUGO
Faculty of Engineering and Technology: Prof. C. A. AJUWA
Faculty of Environmental Studies: Dr Ing. S. O. IZOMOH (acting)
Faculty of Law: Prof. A. D. BADAIKI
Faculty of Medicine: Dr C. P. ALOAMAKA
Faculty of Natural Sciences: Prof. F. EGHAREVBA (acting)
Faculty of Social Sciences: Prof. B. E. AIGBOKHAN

PROFESSORS

AGBONLAHOR, D. E., Microbiology
AIGBOKHAN, B. E., Economics
AIGBOMIAN, D. O., Educational Foundations
AKINBODE, A., Geography and Regional Planning
ALOAMAKA, C. P., Physiology
DIME, C. A., Religious and Cultural Management
ECHEKWUBE, A. O., Philosophy
EFOGHE, G. B., Psychology
EGUAVOEN, O. I., Chemistry
EMIOLA, A., Law
EMORDI, F. I., Modern Languages
IJOMAH, B. I. C., Sociology
IMOBIGHE, T. A., Political Science
KURNOW, K., History
LONGE, J. B., Economics
OAIKHINAN, E. P., Engineering, Technology and Development
OKECHA, S. A., Chemistry
OMO-OYUGO, M. O., Curriculum and Instruction
OSEMEIKHIAN, J. E. A., Physics
REMISON, S. U., Crop Science
SEGYNOLA, A. A., Geography and Regional Planning
UNOMAH, A. C., History
YESUFU, A. K., Electrical and Electronic Engineering

BENUE STATE UNIVERSITY

PMB 102119, Makurdi, Benue State
Telephone: (44) 533811
Fax: (44) 534040
E-mail: root@bensu.edu.ng

Founded 1992
Language of instruction: English
Accredited by National Universities Commission, Abuja

Vice-Chancellor: Prof. AKASE P. SORKA
Deputy Vice-Chancellors: Prof. TONY EDOH (Admin), Prof. TYOHDZUAH P. AKOSU (Academic)
Registrar: TIMOTHY I. UTILE
Librarian: JOHNATHAN A. OCHEIBI

Library of 67,000 vols
Number of teachers: 558
Number of students: 12,070 full-time, 1,579 part-time

Publications: *Faculty of Arts Journal*, *Faculty of Education Journal*

DEANS

Faculty of Allied Sciences: EMMANUEL O. NWOKEDI
Faculty of Arts: Dr JOSEPH T. KERKER
Faculty of Clinical Sciences: MARGARET M. ARAOYE
Faculty of Education: Dr NANCY AGBE
Faculty of Law: AKAA T. IMBWASEH
Faculty of Management Science: SYLVESTER ORSAAH
Faculty of Science: Prof. EMMANUEL AGBA
Faculty of Social Science: Prof. ADAGBA OKPAGA
Postgraduate School: Prof. JOSEPH FIASE

PROFESSORS

ACHUA, J., Accounting
ADEJIR, T., Languages And Linguistics
AGBA, E. H., Physics
ANGYA, C. A., Theatre Arts
ANYANDE, G., Economics
APAM, J., Political Science
CHIAWA, M., Maths And Computer Science
GAFFA, T., Biological Science
GYUSE, T., Geography
KEGHKU, T., Mass Communication
KPELAI, T., Business Management
MOTI, J. S., Religion And Philosophy
NEVKAA, J. N., Educational Foundations
NYITSE, L. M., English
ODEY, M. O., History
SAMBA, J. N., Commercial And Property Law
SHINDI, J. A., Psychology
UTULU, R. E., Curriculum And Teaching
WEGH, F. S., Sociology
YIASE, S. G., Chemistry

EBONYI STATE UNIVERSITY

PMB 053, Abakaliki, Ebonyi State
Telephone: (43) 221093
E-mail: vc@ebsu-edu.net
Internet: www.ebsu-edu.net

Founded 1999
Language of instruction: English

Vice-Chancellor: Eng. Prof. FRANK I IDIKE
Deputy Vice-Chancellor: Prof. EGWU U. EGWU
Registrar: SAM NTE EGWU
Librarian: FRIDAY U. IBIAM

Library of 27,000 vols
Number of teachers: 792
Number of students: 22,029 (11,441 full-time; 10,588 part-time)

DEANS

Faculty of Agriculture and Natural Resources Management: Prof. EKUMA O. EKUMANKAMA
Faculty of Applied and Natural Sciences: Prof. JAMES C. OGBONNA
Faculty of Arts: Dr CLEMENT MGBADA
Faculty of Basic Medical Sciences: Prof. SUNDAY O. ELOM
Faculty of Biological Sciences: Dr IBIAM UDU
Faculty of Clinical Medicine: Prof. ESTHER U. AJULUCHUKWU
Faculty of Education: Prof. BERNARD ALUMODE
Faculty of Health Science and Technology: Asst Prof. C. O. EDEOGU
Faculty of Law: M. AJA NWACHUKWU
Faculty of Management Sciences: Dr FIDELIS OKPATA
Faculty of Physical Sciences: Prof. OBINI EKPE
Faculty of Social Sciences: Dr EUGENE NWEKE
School of Postgraduate Studies: Prof. SUNDAY N. AGWU

PROFESSORS

AKUBILO, C. J. C., Agricultural Economics, Management and Extension
ALAKU, S. O., Animal Production and Fisheries Management
ALI, A., Computer Science Education
AMUCHIE, F. A., Human Kinetics and Health Education
ANEZI-ONWU, O. N., Medicine
ATTAH, C. A., Surgery
AZUBUIKE, M. M., Computer Science Education
DIRIBE, C. O., Medical Biochemistry
EGWU, E. U., Management and Marketing
EGWUATU, V. E., Obstetrics and Gynaecology
EKUMANKAMA, E. O., Food Science
EZEIFEKA, G. O., Applied Microbiology
EZEILO, J. O., Industrial Mathematics and Applied Statistics
IBE, S., Animal Production and Fisheries Management
IBEMISI, J. A., Industrial Chemistry
IHEME, B. A., Law
INYIAMA, H. C., Computer Science
MARIRE, B. N., Animal Production and Fisheries Management
MGBODILE, M. U. K., Chemical Pathology
NDU, U., Applied Biology
NNOKE, F. N., Soil and Environmental Management
OBI, I. U., Crop Production and Landscape Management
OBIAKO, M. N., Surgery
OBIDOA, O., Medical Biochemistry
OBINNA, O. E., Economics
OBIONU, C. N., Community Medicine
OGAH, F., Crop Production and Landscape Management
OGBONNA, J. C., Biochemistry and Biotechnology
OJI, C., Surgery
OKAGBUE, R. N., Applied Microbiology
OKAKA, A. N. C., Biochemistry and Biotechnology
OKAKA, J. C., Food Science
OKANY, M. C., Law
OKOGBUE, C. O., Geology and Exploration Geophysics
OKOLI, E. C., Food Science
OKOLI, F. C., Political Science and Public Administration
OKORJI, E. C., Agricultural Economics, Management and Extension
OLUIKPE, B. O., English
ONUAGULUCHI, G., Pharmacology and Therapeutics
ONYENEKE, C. E., Biochemistry and Biotechnology
OSISIOMA, B. C., Accountancy
UBAH, C. N., History and International Relations
UCHE, C. U., Banking and Finance
UKPABI, S. C., History and International Relations
UKWU, U. I., Economics
UMEH, E. D., Crop Production and Landscape Management
UMEJI, A. C., Geology and Exploration Geophysics
UMEZUIKE, I. A., Law
UMOH, S. M., Management and Marketing

ENUGU STATE UNIVERSITY OF SCIENCE AND TECHNOLOGY

PMB 01660, Enugu

Telephone: (42) 451244
Fax: (42) 335705
E-mail: esut@compuserve.com
Internet: www.esut.edu.ng

Founded 1980

Campuses at Enugu and Nsukka
State control
Academic year: January to October (two semesters)
Language of instruction: English
Chancellor: Dr Chief ERNEST ADEGUNLE OLADEINDE SHONEKAN
Pro-Chancellor: Igwe Dr C. A. ABANGWU
Vice-Chancellor: Prof. SAMUEL CHUKWU
Deputy Vice-Chancellor: Prof. Rev. Canon CHINEDU NEBO
Registrar: B. N. UZOIGWE
Librarian: Dr N. ENE
Number of teachers: 472
Number of students: 29,827
Publication: *Journal of Science and Technology* (2 a year)

DEANS

Faculty of Agriculture: Prof. B. N. MARIRE
Faculty of Applied Natural Sciences: Prof. A. C. OKONKWO
Faculty of Basic Medical Sciences: Prof. S. E. ASOGWA
Faculty of Education: Prof. O. O. ONOWOR
Faculty of Law: Dr OBI S. OGENE
Faculty of Management Sciences: P. E. EMEKEKWUE
Faculty of Social Sciences: Dr D. N. NWATU
School of Engineering: Prof. G. N. ONOH
School of Environmental Sciences: Prof. A. N. AGU
School of Postgraduate Studies: Prof. R. C. OKAFOR

PROFESSORS

ADIBE, E. C., Geography and Meteorology
AGAJELU, S. I., Surveying and Photography
AGU, N., Geography and Meteorology
AKUBUILO, C. J. C., Agriculture
ALAKU, S. O., Animal Science
ANEKE, L. E., Chemical Engineering
ANOWOR, O. O., Foundations of Education
ASOGWA, S. E., Community Medicine
CHIDOBEM, I. J., Animal Science
CHUKWU, S. C., Cooperatives
ENE, J. C., Applied Natural Sciences
MADUEWESI, J. N. C., Applied Natural Sciences
MARIRE, B. N., Animal Science
MOGBO, J. O., Foundations of Education
NEBO, C. O., Mechanical and Materials Engineering
NWORGY, O. C., Applied Biology
OCHO, L. O., Foundations of Education
OHUCHE, R. O., Industrial Mathematics and Statistics
OKAFOR, N., Applied Microbiology and Brewing
OKAFOR, R. C., Foundations of Education
OKAKA, J. C., Agriculture
OKONKWO, C. A. C., Applied Biology
OKORIE, B. A., Mechanical and Materials Engineering
ONOH, G. N., Electrical and Electronic Engineering
ONYEHALU, A. S., Foundations of Education
UGWU, I. C., Urban and Regional Planning
UMEH, E. D., Applied Biology

IMO STATE UNIVERSITY

PMB 2000, Owerri, Imo State

Telephone: (83) 221687
Fax: (83) 232716

Founded 1981

Vice-Chancellor: Prof. TONY G. ANWUKAH
Registrar: FRANCIS E. NWANKWO
Number of teachers: 230
Number of students: 15,991

DEANS

Faculty of Agriculture and Veterinary Medicine: A. ONWEAGBA
Faculty of Business Administration: INNOCENT OKONKWO
Faculty of Education: D. A. ONYEJEMEZI
Faculty of Engineering and Environmental Sciences: U. O. NKWOGU
Faculty of Humanities: ROSE ACHOLONU
Faculty of Law: U. S. F. NNABUE
Faculty of Science: E. N. MGBENU
Faculty of Social Sciences: C. B. NWACHUKWU
College of Medical and Health Sciences: B. C. JIBURUM
Postgraduate School: F. N. MADUBUIKE

KANO STATE UNIVERSITY OF TECHNOLOGY, WUDIL

PMB 3244, Kano, Kano State

Telephone: (64) 241149
Fax: (64) 241175

Founded 2001

Chancellor: ALHAJI ALIKO DANGOTE
Vice-Chancellor: SHAWKI A. A. SEOUD
Registrar: A. U. ABDURAHIM.

LADOKE AKINTOLA UNIVERSITY OF TECHNOLOGY

PMB 4000, Ogbomoso, Oyo State

Telephone: (38) 720285
Fax: (38) 720750

Founded 1990 as Oyo State University of Technology; present name 1991

Vice-Chancellor: Prof. AKINOLA M. SALAU
Registrar: Y. O GBADAMOSI

Library of 19,604 vols
Number of teachers: 439
Number of students: 12,245

DEANS

Faculty of Agriculture: J. I. OLAIFA
Faculty of Engineering and Technology: J. O. OJEDIRAN (acting)
Faculty of Environmental Sciences: R. O. R. KALILU
Faculty of Medical Sciences: P. O. AKINWISU (acting)
Faculty of Pure and Applied Sciences: R. O. AYENI

LAGOS STATE UNIVERSITY

PMB 1087, Apapa, Lagos State

Telephone: (1) 5884048
Fax: (1) 5884048
E-mail: veecee@lasu.org

Founded 1983
State control
Language of instruction: English
Academic year: October to July

Vice-Chancellor: Prof. ABISOGUN OLUBODE LEIGH
Registrar: OLUWATOYIN GLADSTONE OSHUN
Librarian: T. A. B. SERIKI

Library of 63,000 vols
Number of teachers: 513
Number of students: 35,544 (16,422 full-time, 19,122 part-time)
Publications: *ECOFLASH*, *Educational Perspectives*, *Enhancing Quality Education in Nigeria*, *Journal of Humanities* (2 a year), *Journal of Prospects in Science*, *LASU Jurist*, *LASU Law Journal*, *LASU Social Science Journal*, *Nigerian Journal of Research & Review in Science*

DEANS

Faculty of Arts: Dr KUMLE LAWAL
Faculty of Education: Prof. ADEMOLA ONIFADE
Faculty of Engineering: Prof. P. A. O. ADEGBUYI
Faculty of Law: Prof. B. A. SUSU
Faculty of Management Science: Prof. O. J. FAPOHUNDA
Faculty of Sciences: Prof. MARTIN A. ANATEKHAI
Faculty of Social Sciences: Prof. TAYO ODUMOSU
College of Medicine: Prof. WOLE ALAKIJA
Postgraduate School: Prof. C. O. OSHUN

PROFESSORS

ABDUL-KUREEM, H., Medical Biochemistry
ADARAMOLA, F., International Law and Jurisprudence
AJAJA, O., Mechanical Engineering
AJOSE, S. O., Electronics and Computer Engineering
AKINRIMISI, E. O., Haematology and Blood Transfusion
ALAKIJA, W., Community and Primary Healthcare
ANETEKHAI, M. A., Fisheries Science
ASHIRU, O. A., Anatomy
BAMGBOYE, O. A., Chemistry
DADA, O. A., Chemical Pathology
FAPOHUNDA, O. J., Business Administration
HUNPONU-WUSU, O. O., Community and Primary Healthcare
IKHARIALE, M. A., Public Law
MATANMI, S. O., Industrial Relations and Personnel Management
OBAFUNWA, J. O., Pathology
ODERINDE, B. B., Curriculum Studies
ODUBUNMI, E. O., Curriculum Studies
ODUMOSU, A. O., Geography and Planning
ODUMOSU, T., Communications
OKANLAWON, A., Anatomy
OKEBUKOLA, P. A. O., Curriculum Studies
OLUKOYE, A. O., Chemical Pathology
ONABANJO, A. O., Medical Microbiology
ONIFADE, A., Public Law
OSINBAJO, O. O., Public Law
OYERINDE, J. P. O., Medical Biochemistry
SAGOE, A. O., Haematology and Blood Transfusion
TUNDE, S., Communications and Educational Management
YEROKUN, O. A., Business Law

NIGER DELTA STATE UNIVERSITY

PMB 1, Abraka, Delta State

Telephone: (54) 66027

Founded 1992

Vice-Chancellor: Prof. F. M. A. UKOLI
Registrar: E. E. AVBIOROKOMA
Librarian: LAWRENCE OGBENI

OLABISI ONABANJO UNIVERISTY

PMB 2002, Ago-Iwoye, Ogun State

Telephone: (37) 432384
Fax: (37) 432384
Internet: www.oou-ng.com

Founded 1982
State Government control
Academic year: October to July

Chancellor: Dr AYOOLA OBA OTUDEKO
Pro-Chancellor: Prof. BIYI AFONJA
Vice-Chancellor: Prof. AFOLABI SOYODE
Deputy Vice-Chancellors: Prof. E. O. A. AJAYI, Prof. ODUTOLA OSILESI
Registrar: APOSTLE SAMUEL O. AJAYI
Librarian: O. K. ODUSANYA

Library of 106,709 vols
Number of teachers: 699

Number of students: 43,382 (28,221 full-time, 15,161 part-time)

Publications: *Ago-Iwoye Journal of Social and Behavioural Sciences* (2 a year), *GEGE Journal of the English Department* (1 a year), *International Journal of Accountancy, Finance and Management Sciences* (2 a year), *Journals of History and Diplomatic Studies* (1 a year), *Journal of Philosophy and Development.* (1 a year), *Journal of Public Law and Practice* (1 a year), *Journal of Social and Management Sciences* (1 a year), *Nigerian Journal of Private and Commercial Law* (1 a year), *OSU Journal of Educational Studies* (1 a year), *OYE Journal of Arts* (1 a year), *Private and Commercial Law Additional Information* (1 a year), *Studies in Curriculum* (4 a year)

DEANS

Faculty of Agricultural Management and Rural Development: Dr AIHONSU JOHN (Provost)
Faculty of Agricultural Production and Renewable Resources: Prof. S. O. OSUNLAJA
Faculty of Arts: Prof. KAMALDEEN BALOGUN
Faculty of Basic Medical Sciences: Prof. JIDE OLOWOOKERE
Faculty of Clinical Sciences: Prof. FEMI ADELOWO
Faculty of Education: Prof. OLATUNJI ODEDEYI
Faculty of Engineering: Prof. J. AKINYEMI
Faculty of Environmental Technology: Prof. TOYIN OGUNTONA
Faculty of Law: Prof. JUSTUS SOKEFUN
Faculty of Management Sciences: Dr S. A. TELLA (acting)
Faculty of Pharmacy: Prof. M. N. FEMI-OYEWO
Faculty of Science: Prof. AFOLABI ADEBANJO
Faculty of Social Sciences: Dr WALE OLAITAN
College of Agricultural Sciences: Prof. S. F. ADEDOYIN (Provost)
College of Engineering and Technology: Prof. R. O. FAGBENLE (Provost)
Obafemi Awolowo College of Health Sciences: Prof. M. A. OLANREWAJU (Provost)
Postgraduate School: Prof. O. O. KEHINDE PHILLIPS (Provost)

PROFESSORS

ADEBANJO, A., Chemical Sciences
ADEDIPE, V. O., Educational Foundations and Management
ADEDOYIN, S. F., Agricultural Extension and Rural Sociology
ADEJONWO, K. O., Crop Production
ADESEMOWO, P. O., Educational Foundations and Management
ADESIMI, A. A., Agribusiness and Farm Management
ADETORO, O. O., Obstetrics and Gynaecology
AFEJUKU, D. H., Private and Commercial Law
AJAYI, E. O. A., Educational Foundations and Management
AJIBADE, E. S., Educational Foundations and Management
ALAUSA, O. K., Community Medicine and Primary Care
AWODERU, V. A., Biological Sciences
AYANLAJA, S. A., Soil Science and Farm Mechanisation
BALOGUN, K A., Religious Studies
BENEDICT, J. N., Curriculum Studies and Instructional Technology
DADA, O. A., Haematology and Blood Transfusion
DADA, S. S., Earth Sciences
EJIWUNMI, A. B., Anatomy
ERINOSHO, O. A., Sociology
FEMI, O. M. N., Pharmaceutics and Pharmaceutical Technology
HASSAN, T., Educational Foundations and Management
IYANIWURA, J. O., Mathematical Sciences
JAYESIMI, A. E. A., Medicine
KEHINDE-PHILLIPS, O. O., Earth Sciences
ODEDEYI, TUNJI, Sports Science and Health Education
ODUGBEMI, O. O., Geography and Regional Planning
ODUMUYIWA, E. A., Religious Studies
OGUNBA, OYIN, English
OGUNDERO, V. W., Biological Sciences
OGUNYEMI, E. O., Chemical Pathology and Haematology
OLAGUNJU, O. P., Educational Foundations and Management
OLANREWAJU, D. M., Paediatrics
OLOWOOKERE, J. O., Biochemistry
OLOWU, A. O., Paediatrics
OLUDIMU, O. L., Agricultural Economics
OSILESI, O., Biochemistry
OSONUBI, O., Biological Sciences
OSUNLAJA, S. O., Crop Production
OWORU, O. O., Crop Production
OYEDEJI, O. A., Curriculum Studies and Instructional Technology
OYEGUNLE, O. A., Anaesthesia
OYESIKU, O. O., Geography and Regional Planning
SANWO, J. O., Crop Production
SOSANWO, O. A., Mathematical Sciences
SULE-ODU, A. O., Obstetrics and Gynaecology
TAIWO, A., Educational Foundations and Management

RIVERS STATE UNIVERSITY OF SCIENCE AND TECHNOLOGY

PMB 5080, Port Harcourt, Rivers State
Telephone: (84) 233288
Fax: (84) 230720
E-mail: info@ust.edu.ng

Founded 1971, univ. status 1980
State control
Language of instruction: English
Academic year: October to July

Chancellor: (vacant)
Pro-Chancellor: Hon. Justice (rtd) ADOLPHUS KARIBI-WHYTE
Vice-Chancellor: Prof. B. B. FAKAE
Deputy Vice-Chancellor: Prof. H. I. HART
Registrar: DABA C. ODIMABO
Librarian: Dr B. E. AHIAUZU

Library of 2,000 vols
Number of teachers: 496
Number of students: 20,060

Publication: *News Bulletin* (4 a year)

DEANS

Faculty of Agriculture: Prof. J. P. ALAWA
Faculty of Engineering: Prof. ALEX J. AKOR
Faculty of Environmental Sciences: VICTOR A. AKUJURU (acting)
Faculty of Law: F. O. AKAAKAR (acting)
Faculty of Management Sciences: Prof. SETH ACCRA-JAJA (acting)
Faculty of Science: Prof. FRIDAY B. SIGALO
Faculty of Technical and Science Education: Prof. W. AMAEWHULE (acting)
Postgraduate School: Prof. EMMANUEL N. AMADI

PROFESSORS

Faculty of Agriculture:

ACHINEWHU, S. C., Food Science
AMAKIRI, M. A., Soil Science
AMAKIRI, S. F., Animal Science
GIAMI, S., Food Science
IGBEN, M. S., Agricultural Economics/Extension
ISIRIMAH, N. O., Crop/Soil Science
MONSI, A., Animal Science
OGBURIA, M. N., Food Science
ONUEGBU, B. A., Crop/Soil Science
OPUWARIBO, E. E., Crop/Soil Science
ORUWARI, B. M., Animal Science
WAHUA, T. A. T., Crop/Soil Science
WEKHE, S. N, Animal Science

Faculty of Engineering:

ABOWEI, M. F. N.
CHINWAH, J. G.
HART, H. I., Mechanical Engineering
IDERIAH, F. J. K., Mechanical Engineering
IDONIBOYE-OBU, K. I., Chemical/Petrochemical Engineering
JOHNARRY, T., Civil Engineering
ODI-OWEI, S., Mechanical Engineering
WAMI, E. N.

Faculty of Environmental Sciences:

FUBARA, D. M. J., Geodesy
TEME, S. C., Geology

Faculty of Management Sciences:

ACCRA-JAJA, S., Business Administration
AHIAUZU, A. I., Business Administration
FUBARA, B. A., Business Administration
GBOSI, A. N., Management Science
JOHNNIE, P. B., Business Administration
ONOH, J. K., Banking & Finance

Faculty of Science:

ABBEY, S. D., Medical Laboratory
AMADI, E. N., Biology
EKWEOZOR, I. K. E., Biology
NWANKWO, S. I., Chemistry
OKWAKPAM, B. A., Biology
OMUARU, V. O. T., Chemistry

Faculty of Technical and Science Education:

AHIAKWO, M. J., Science and Technical Education
AMAEHULE, W. A., Business Education
KOKO, M. N., Business Education
WOKOCHA, A. M., Educational Foundations

PRIVATE UNIVERSITIES

ABTI AMERICAN UNIVERSITY OF NIGERIA

2 Ahmed Onibudo St, POB 73688, Victoria Island, Lagos
Telephone: (1) 3200695
E-mail: abtiuniversity@yahoo.com
Internet: www.abti-american.edu.ng

Founded 2005 in partnership with the American University, Washington, DC, USA
Number of students: 200

President: Dr DAVID HUWILER
Dean of Students and Registrar: Dr BARRY MORRIS.

BABCOCK UNIVERSITY

Ilishan-Remo, Ogun
Telephone: (1) 7613797
E-mail: registrar@babcockuni.edu.ng
Internet: www.babcockuni.edu.ng

Founded 1999, fmrly Adventist Seminary of West Africa
Seventh-Day Adventist Church control
Language of instruction: English

Pres. and Vice-Chancellor: Prof. JAMES KAYODE MAKINDE

Number of teachers: 233
Number of students: 5,600

Library of 58,000 vols, 664 periodicals

DEANS

School of Education and Humanities: Prof. JOSHUA M. A. OYINLOYE
School of Law and Security Studies: ZAC O. OLOMOJOBI
School of Management and Social Sciences: (vacant)
School of Science and Technology: Prof. GRACE OLUWATOYIN TAYO

PROFESSORS

School of Education and Humanities

Department of History and International Studies:

ADEWOYE, O., Legal History
NENGEL, J. G., Intergroup Relations

Department of Languages and Literary Studies:

AKPOROBARO, I. A., Literary Studies, African and European Literature
OSISANWO, I. A., English Language, Phonetics and Grammar

Department of Mass Communication:

AKANBI, D. K., Instructional Media and Communication
ALAO, D., Journalism and International Communication
KIO, J., Speech Communication and Human Relations

School of Law and Security Studies:

AGEDE, I. S., Alternative Dispute Resolution, Arbitration, Conflict of Law and Jurisprudence
OLIYIDE, S., Banking, Commercial Law and Law of International Trade
OLOMOJOBO, Z. O., Military and Constitutional Law

School of Management and Social Sciences:

AINA, A., Political Science, Political Strategies
AJAYI, F., Political Science
AKINOLA, J., Educational Management
ASIKA, N., Business Management, Research Methods
MAKINDE, J., Political Science, Political History
OGUNDAIRO, M., Economics
OLALOKU, F., Economics

School of Science and Technology

Department of Agriculture:

DARAMOLA, D. S., Soil Science
TAYO, G. O., Animal Nutrition

Department of Biosciences and Biotechnology:

FAPOHUNDA, S. O., Industrial Microbiology
KOLAWOLE, D. O., Medical Microbiology

Department of Chemical and Environmental Sciences:

ESAN, E. B., Botany and Biotechnology
OGUNWENMO, K. O., Biosystematics and Cytogenetics
ONAJOBI, F. D., Lipids and Membrane Biochemistry

Department of Computer and Mathematics:

ADELODUN, J. F., Mathematics
OMOTOSHO, O. J., Computer Engineering and Instrumentation

Department of Nursing Sciences:

FASHINA, E. M., Clinical Psychology and Nursing

Department of Public and Allied Health:

AKINBOYE, D. O., Medical Parasitology
FAJEWONYOMI, B. A., Community Health and Epidemiology

BENSON IDAHOSA UNIVERSITY

PMB 1100, University Way, Off Upper Adesuwa Grammar School Rd, Benin City
Telephone: (52) 253764
E-mail: biuportal@biuportal.com
Internet: www.idahosauniversity.com

Founded 2002

President: Rev. F. E. B. IDAHOSA II.

COVENANT UNIVERSITY

10 km Idiroko Rd,, Canaan Land, Ota, Ogun State
Telephone: (1) 7900724
E-mail: contact@covenantuniversity.com
Internet: www.covenantuniversity.com

Founded 2002

Chancellor: Dr DAVID OYEDEPO
Vice-Chancellor: Prof. AIZE OLOHIGBE IMOUOKHOME OBAYAN

Colleges of Business and Social Sciences, Human Development and Science and Technology.

IGBINEDION UNIVERSITY

PMB 0006, Okada, Benin-City

Telephone and fax (52) 260005
E-mail: pefs@skannet.com
Internet: www.igbinedionuniversity.edu.ng

Founded 1999

Vice-Chancellor: Prof. EGHOSA EMMANUEL OSAGHAE
Deputy Vice-Chancellor: Prof. L. C. CHIEDOZI
Dean of Student Affairs: Prof. GILBERT O. NWOBU
Registrar: Dr SALLY AKWUGO ASAGWARA
Librarian: Dr R. OLORUNSOLA (acting)

DEANS AND PROVOSTS

College of Agriculture: Prof. ADETOKUNBO ADEOLA (Dean)
College of Arts and Social Sciences: Dr ANGELU M. ONWUEJEOGU (Dean)
College of Business and Management Studies: Prof. A. E. OKOYE (Dean)
College of Engineering: Dr T. S. WARA (acting) (Dean)
College of Health Sciences: Prof. TUNDE DARAMOLA (Provost)
College of Law: Prof. M. O. OGUNGBE (Dean)
College of Natural and Applied Sciences: Prof. ALEXANDER E. ODAIBO (Dean)
College of Pharmacy: Prof. SAMSON ESEZOBOR (Dean)
School of Basic Medical Sciences: Prof. A. A. ODUTOGA (Dean)
School of Clinical Medicine: Prof. L. C. CHIEDOZIE (Dean)
School of Postgraduate Studies: Prof. ABAYOMI ONI (Dean)

PROFESSORS

ADELUSI, Pharmacy
ADEOLA, A., Wildlife and Forestry
AGBA, M., Microbiology
AGBONLAHOR, D., Microbiology and Medical Laboratory Sciences
AIBONI, S., Law
AWOGUN, I., Medical Microbiology
BAXTER-GRILLO, D., Anatomy
CHIEDOZIE, L., Surgery
DARAMOLA, T., Community Health
EKEH, J., Electrical and Electronic Engineering
EKUNDARE, R., Economics
ESEZOBOR, S., Pharmacy
NAREBO, D., Law
NWOBU, G., Medical Laboratory Sciences
ODAIBO, A., Biological Sciences: Zoology
ODUTUGA, A., Biochemistry
OFUOROFO, I., Chemical Pathology
OGUNBIYI, J., Morbid Anatomy
OGUNGBE, M., Law
OKOYE, A., Accountancy
OLUOHA, U., Chemical Pathology
ONI, A., Mechanical Engineering
ONWUJEOGWU, A., Sociology and Anthropology
OSAGHAE, Political Science
OSENI, T., Agronomy
OSIFO, N., Pharmacology
PADONU, M., Community Health
YESUFU, English

PAN-AFRICAN UNIVERSITY

2 Ahmed Onibudo St, POB 73688, Victoria Island, Lagos
Telephone: (1) 3200695

Founded 2002

Vice-Chancellor: Prof. ALBERT J. ALOS

Postgraduate degree programmes in business administration and economics.

Polytechnics and Colleges

FEDERAL POLYTECHNIC, ADO-EKITI

PMB 5351, Ado-Ekiti, Ekiti State
Telephone: (30) 250523
E-mail: fedpolyado@fedpolyado.org
Internet: www.fedpolyado.org

Founded 1977

Academic year: February to November

Rector: Prof. O. AJAJA
Registrar: A. I. AJAYI
Librarian: M. O. OLASEHINDE

Library of 15,706 vols, 845 periodicals
Number of teachers: 290
Number of students: 6,161

Publications: *Expertus* (sustainable development, 2 a year), *Research Journal* (1 a year)

HEADS OF SCHOOLS

Business Studies: A. O. AKINYEMI
Engineering: D. A. T. ADEGBOYEGA
Environmental Studies: G. S. OLORUNOJE
Science and Computer Studies: D. O. ORIMAYE

AKANU IBIAM FEDERAL POLYTECHNIC, UNWANA

PMB 1007, Afikpo, Ebonyi State
Telephone: (90) 500180

Founded 1981

Rector: G. I. AMASIATU
Registrar: IHEANACHOR V. OBI OBI
Librarian: J. A. EKEH (acting)

Library of 12,217 vols
Number of teachers: 132
Number of students: 2,500

Publications: *Information Bulletin* (4 a year), *Student Handbook*

DIRECTORS

School of Business: A. I. IBIAM
School of Engineering: S. EGBUCHULAMI
School of Industrial Technology: M. I. ANUNA
School of Science and General Studies: O. U. L. IBE-URO

FEDERAL POLYTECHNIC, AUCHI

PMB 13, Auchi, Edo State
Telephone: (57) 200148
Fax: (57) 200148

Founded 1973

Rector: Sir O. F. EBOREIME
Registrar: F. O. OGUNBOR
Librarian: J. O. AGHOJA

Library of 38,250 vols
Number of teachers: 305
Number of students: 9,500

DIRECTORS OF SCHOOLS

Applied Sciences and Technology: P. AWERIALE
Art and Design: Prince OSAGIE-ERESE
Business Studies: J. EDEMODE
Engineering: S. OHIMAI
Environmental Studies: C. V. AJOKU

FEDERAL POLYTECHNIC, BAUCHI

PMB 0231, Bauchi
Telephone: (77) 543630
Fax: (77) 540465
E-mail: registrar@bauchipoly.edu.ng
Internet: www.bauchipoly.edu.ng

Founded 1979
Academic year: October to July

Rector: Surv. I. S. JAHUN
Registrar: Alhaji LABARAN IBRAHIM
Librarian: Mallam N. O. TOYYO

Library of 35,900 vols
Number of teachers: 257
Number of students: 8,667

DEANS

School of Business Studies: C. P. EJIKEME
School of Engineering Technology: Eng. J. D. KONNI
School of Environmental Technology: J. A. ALEREGE
School of General Studies: Mal. M. L. GARBA
School of Technology: S. M. KUMO

BENUE STATE POLYTECHNIC, UGBOKOLO

PMB 2215, Otukpo, Benue State

Founded 1976
State control
Language of instruction: English
Academic year: October to September

Rector: Dr Y. W. AWODI
Deputy Rector: A. T. IKEREVE
Registrar: D. O. ONA
Librarian: M. A. SHINYI

Number of teachers: 115
Number of students: 1,505

Publication: *New Bulletin* (12 a year)

DEANS

School of Art and Design: B. Y. EBUTE (acting)
School of Business and Administrative Studies: E. A. ADEGBE
School of Engineering: P. E. AGBESE
School of Technology: P. U. ANYOGO

FEDERAL POLYTECHNIC, BIDA

PMB 55, Bida, Niger State
Telephone: (66) 461707

Founded 1977
Academic year: October to July

Rector: Eng. UMARU SANI-ANGO
Registrar: S. F. IKO
Librarian: S. A. KASIMU

Library of 26,105 vols
Number of teachers: 377
Number of students: 9,097

Publication: *Polymath Journal*

DIRECTORS

School of Applied Arts and Science: Dr S. O. ADEYEMO
School of Business and Management: P. KARICKSON
School of Engineering: Engr A. SULE
School of Environmental Studies: S. M. OB'LAMA
School of Preliminary Studies: ABDULLAHI MANN

POLYTECHNIC, BIRNIN KEBBI

PMB 1034, Birnin Kebbi, Kebbi State
Telephone: (68) 320597
Fax: (68) 320597
E-mail: kbpoly@skannet.com.ng

Founded 1976
Academic year: October to July

Rector: Arc. MUHAMMAD KABIR NABADE
Registrar: BELLO BAGUDU ABUBAKAR
Librarian: YUSUF ABUBAKAR ARGUNGU

Library of 13,761 vols
Number of teachers: 350
Number of students: 3,678

ND and HND courses; postgraduate diplomas in management and public administration

DEANS

School of Accounting and Finance: UMARU SULE
School of Business and Public Administration: UMAR M. S. RAHA
School of Environmental Design: TIMOTHY O. IBIRONKE
School of Industrial Engineering: ISHAYA H. JOSHUA
School of Natural Resources Engineering: ABUBAKAR MIKAIL
School of Sciences: ABUBAKAR UMAR BASHAR
School of Surveying and Land Administration: (vacant)
School of Vocational and Technical Education: UMAR A. RUFAI

POLYTECHNIC, CALABAR

PMB 1110, Calabar, Cross River State
Telephone: (87) 222303

Founded 1973
State control
Language of instruction: English
Academic year: October to June

Rector: Engr R. E. EKANEM
Deputy Rector: Dr R. A. ITAM
Registrar: G. F. A. ONUGBA
Librarian: J. S. UMOH

Library of 25,000 vols
Number of teachers: 213
Number of students: 5,000

DIRECTORS OF SCHOOLS AND CENTRES

School of Agriculture: Dr E. J. OROK
School of Applied Science: U. U. ASUQUO
School of Business and Management: P. O. N. ABANG
School of Communication Arts: Dr M. E. EKERE
School of Education: Dr JOE IBANGA
School of Engineering: Dr E. U. UYE
School of Environmental Studies: A. DIAWUO
Computer Centre: T. O. EYO (acting)
Continuing Education Centre: N. U. UMOH
Centre for General and Preliminary Studies: L. O. I. OGUEZE
Industrial Coordination and Public Relations Unit: M. J. MBONG (acting)
Polytechnic Industrial Consultancy Services Unit: Dr I. U. UGOT

FEDERAL POLYTECHNIC, EDE

PMB 231, Ede, Osun State
Telephone: (35) 360096
Fax: (35) 360640
E-mail: edepoly@pinet.net

Vice-Chancellor: Deacon JOSEPH S. OKE.

POLYTECHNIC, IBADAN

PMB 022, U.I. Post Office, Ibadan
Telephone: (22) 8133356769
Fax: (22) 8101122
E-mail: rector@polyibadan.edu.ng

Founded 1961, polytechnic status 1971
State control
Language of instruction: English

Rector: Prof. O. A. ODUNOLA
Deputy Rector: N. A. ADEBAYO
Registrar: TOSHO AYANWALE
Bursar: G. O. D. OLOJEDE
Chief Librarian: O. A. OBIKOYA

Library of 68,000 vols
Number of teachers: 576
Number of students: 9,250

Publications: *Calendar/Prospectus* (1 a year), *PolyNews*

DEANS

Faculty of Business and Communication Studies: FEMI ARAMIDE
Faculty of Engineering: Eng. T. I. OYEDEMI
Faculty of Environmental Studies: T. A. OLURIN
Faculty of Financial and Management Studies: S. B. BABARINDE
Faculty of Science: O. A. OLUBAMIWA

FEDERAL POLYTECHNIC, IDAH

PMB 1037, Idah, Kogi State
Telephone: (58) 800128

Founded 1977

Rector: Dr JOSEPH EGILA
Deputy Rector: Dr D. O. BELLO
Registrar: S. A. OGUNLEYE
Librarian: J. I. ITANYI

Library of 19,489 vols
Number of teachers: 136
Number of students: 3,200

Publication: *News Bulletin* (12 a year)

DIRECTORS OF SCHOOLS

School of Business Studies: M. A. OKPANACHI
School of Engineering: Surv. P. IYAJI
School of Technology: E. O. NDA-SULEIMAN

FEDERAL POLYTECHNIC, ILARO

PMB 50, Ilaro, Ogun State
Telephone: (39) 440005

Founded 1979

Rector: Dr Prince S. A. OLATERU-OLAGBEGI
Vice-Rector: Dr K. O. JIBODU
Registrar: R. O. EGBEYEMI
Librarian: R. OLA BELLO

Library of 16,000 vols
Number of students: 3,000

DIRECTORS

School of Applied Science: Dr J. O. A. OMOLE
School of Business Studies: J. O. ABIBU
School of Engineering: F. O. AREGBE

INSTITUTE OF MANAGEMENT AND TECHNOLOGY

PMB 01079, Enugu, Enugu State
Telephone: (42) 250416

Founded 1973
Academic year: October to August

Rector: Prof. E. C. ONYENEJE
Deputy Rector: Dr JOHN ORJIH
Registrar: BARTH O. EZEA
Librarian: DONALD M. OZOALOR

Library of 50,000 vols
Number of teachers: 360
Number of students: 20,000

Publications: *IMT News* (4 a year), *Journal of Financial Studies* (1 a year), *Journal of Technology Education* (1 a year)

DIRECTORS OF SCHOOLS

Business Studies: Rev. Canon SAM EZUGWU
Communication Arts: HENRY U. ANIUGBO
Distance Learning and Continuing Education: NICK A. OBODO
Engineering: Dr CHARLES N. UDE
Financial Studies: Dr WILSON ANI
General Studies: UMEAYO S. MADUKWE
Technology: EMEKA G. ANI

KADUNA POLYTECHNIC

PMB 2021, Kaduna
Telephone: (62) 211551
Internet: kadpoly.edu.ng
Founded 1968
Rector: Eng. Dr D. I. Isah
Deputy Rector for Academics: Mal Muhammadu Lawal Jibbin
Deputy Rector for Admin.: Jenny Yohanna Mivanyi
Registrar: Abdullahi Ahman
Librarian: Aliyu Idris Guragi
Library on three campuses of 56,000 vols
Number of teachers: 1,123
Number of students: 17,320

DIRECTORS

College of Administration Studies and Social Sciences: Dr Hajiya Asmau Sani Maikudi
College of Business and Management Studies: Dr Aliyu Mamman
College of Engineering: Eng. Abu Bakar Salihu Ovajimoh
College of Environmental Studies: Kefas Jericho
College of Science and Technology: Moses Obafunmi (acting)

KANO STATE POLYTECHNIC

PMB 3401, B. U. K. Rd, Kano
Telephone: (64) 666058
Founded 1976
Rector: Arch. Hamza Said
Registrar: Sulaiman Abdullahi
Chief Librarian: Alhaji Wada Tafida Kurawa
Library of 30,276 vols
Number of teachers: 510
Number of students: 12,826
Publication: *News Bulletin* (12 a year)

DIRECTORS

School of Management Studies: Hajiya Asabe B. Borodo
School of Social and Rural Development: Sulaiman Hashim
School of Technology: Yusufu Sule Gaya

HASSAN USMAN KATSINA POLYTECHNIC

PMB 2052, Katsina
Telephone: (65) 32816
Founded 1983
Rector: Kabir Ibrahim Matazu
Registrar: Abdu Halliru Abdullahi
Director, Library Services: Mannir Isa Batagarawa
Library of 18,000 vols
Number of teachers: 501
Number of students: 3,506

DIRECTORS OF COLLEGES

College of Administration and Management Studies: Alhaji Abdullahi Bawa
College of Legal and General Studies: Alhaji Musa Sule
College of Science and Technology: Aliyu Abubakar Bakori

FEDERAL POLYTECHNIC, KAURA NAMODA

PMB 1012, Kaura-Namoda, Zamfara State
Telephone: (63) 60452
E-mail: namodapoly@plet.net
Founded 1983
Academic year: October to July
Rector: Eng. Na'inna Mohammad Audi
Vice-Rector: C. Apraku
Registrar: A. Danboyi
Librarian: Alhaji Sanusi Umar Ksauri
Library of 11,450 vols
Number of teachers: 152
Number of students: 3,268
Publications: *Kanajoge* (2 a year), *Namoda Telescope* (2 a year), *Polytechnic News Bulletin* (12 a year)

DIRECTORS

School of Business Management: Amos Oyeyiola
School of Engineering: Eng. Abubakar Lugard
School of Environmental Studies: Tajudeen Yusuf
School of General Studies: Alhaji Ibrahim Kamba
School of Science and Technology: Isa Mohammad Kutigi

KWARA STATE POLYTECHNIC

PMB 1375, Ilorin
Telephone: (31) 221441
Founded 1972
Academic year: October to July
Rector: Alhaji Mas'ud Elelu
Deputy Rector for Academics: M. O. Olasehinde
Deputy Rector for Admin.: Ibrahim Olayinka
Registrar: M. O. Salami
Librarian: Opaleke
Library of 50,155 vols
Number of teachers: 650
Number of students: 17,000
Publication: *Techforum* (2 a year)

DIRECTORS

Centre For Continuous Education: Olubunmi Ajibade
Directorate Of Student Services: F. O. Oyewole
Industrial Liaison Placement Of Guidance And Counselling Unit: A. A. Aminu
Entrepreneurial Centre: B. A. Ibrahim
Institute of Administration: K. G. Shittu
Institute of Basic and Applied Sciences: Dr A. J. Bello
Institute of Business and Vocational Studies: J. A. Awolola
Institute of Environmental Studies (IES): S. B. Fadipe
Institute Of Finance & Management Studies (IFMS): Yousouf Razak
Institute of General Studies (IGS): Idowu O. O.
Institute of Technology: Eng. Y. O. Oyebode

LAGOS STATE POLYTECHNIC

PMB 21606, Ikeja, Lagos State
Telephone: (1) 523528
Founded 1977
Rector: B. Oloro
Deputy Rector: J. B. Agunbiade
Registrar: Oluwole O. Ojikutu
Chief Librarian: E. O. Soyinka
Library of 29,558 vols, 1,880 in spec. colln
Number of teachers: 222
Number of students: 4,287
Publications: *Laspotech News* (4 a year), *Poly Handbook* (1 a year).

MOSHOOD ABIOLA POLYTECHNIC, ABEOKUTA

PMB 2210, Abeokuta, Ogun State
Telephone: (80) 33230941
E-mail: mapolylib2002@yahoo.com
Internet: www.mapoly.educ.ng
Founded 1979
Rector: Alhaji Waheed A. Kadiri
Deputy Rector: Arch. Olatokunbo Fowode
Registrar: Maj. (retd) A. B. Badmos
Librarian: Bola Adeosun
Library of 22,097 vols
Number of teachers: 165
Number of students: 15,000
Publications: *Liberal Forum* (1 a year), *Polymath* (1 a year), *Social Philosophy* (1 a year)

DIRECTORS

School of Business and Management Studies: O. A. Sobande
School of Communication and General Studies: S. O. Famuyiwa
School of Engineering: Dr M. O. Abdul
School of Environmental Studies: A. A. Jegede
School of Pure and Applied Science: A. S. Arowolo
Centre for Part-time Studies: O. A. Soile

FEDERAL POLYTECHNIC, MUBI

PMB 35, Mubi, Adamawa State
Telephone: (75) 882771
Founded 1979
Academic year: October to July
Rector: Alhaji M. A. Abba
Deputy Rector: E. E. Etuk
Registrar: B. Bello
Librarian: T. S. Tarfa
Library of 23,601 vols
Number of teachers: 184
Number of students: 3,338
Publications: *Applied Science and Management* (1 a year), *Sabon Dale* (1 a year)

DIRECTORS

School of Business Studies and General Studies: A. S. Yahaya
School of Engineering: I. Dagwa
School of Science and Technology: A. Bawa

FEDERAL POLYTECHNIC, NASARAWA

PMB 001, Nasarawa, Nasarawa State
Telephone: (47) 66707
E-mail: fpnas@yahoo.com
Founded 1983
Rector: Dr Idris Bugaje.

FEDERAL POLYTECHNIC, NEKEDE

PMB 1036, Owerri, Imo State
Telephone: (83) 231516
Founded 1978
Rector: Eng. O. I. Nwankwo
Registrar: C. D. Onukogu
Librarian: J. U. Obasi
Library of 24,837 vols
Number of teachers: 257
Number of students: 30,000

DEANS

School of Business and Public Administration: S. C. Nsofor
School of Engineering Technology: J. N. Amadi
School of Environmental Design: G. O. C. Nwachukwu
School of General Studies: Dr N. C. Anumihe
School of Industrial Sciences: C. A. Omenka

FEDERAL POLYTECHNIC, OFFA

PMB 420, Offa, Kwara State
Telephone: (31) 800160
Founded 1979
Rector: Dr Abdul-Razaq Bello.

FEDERAL POLYTECHNIC, OKO

PMB 21, Aguata, Anambra State

Telephone: (48) 911144

Founded 1979

Rector: Dr U. C. NZEWI
Registrar: Sir O. C. A. OFOCHEBE
Librarian: Dr OBIORA NWOSU

Library of 150,000 vols
Number of students: 9,298

Publications: *Federal Polytechnic Library* (4 a year), *Journal of Accountancy* (Nigerian edition, 2 a year), *The Polytechnic Accountant* (1 a year)

Courses in accountancy, architecture, banking and finance, business administration and management, business studies, environmental design, estate management and building technology, information technology, library science, marketing, mass communication, secretarial studies, technology.

ONDO STATE POLYTECHNIC

POB 1019, Owo, Ondo State

Telephone: (51) 241045

Founded 1980

Rector: Prof. A. S. ADEDIMILA
Deputy Rector: KEHINDE ALAO
Registrar: R. F. AKERELE
Librarian: M. O. POPOOLA

Library of 25,000 vols
Number of teachers: 173
Number of students: 9,710

DEANS

Business Studies: Chief A. O. OLALEYE
Engineering: Rev. S. A. ADEGBEMIRO
Environmental Studies: E. A. ARIGBEDE
Food Technology: J. K. AJAYI

PETROLEUM TRAINING INSTITUTE

PMB 20, Effurun, Delta State

Telephone: (53) 250774
Fax: (53) 250774
Internet: pti.nigeria.org

Founded 1972
Federal control
Language of instruction: English
Academic year: October to July

Principal and Chief Exec.: N. C. DENNAR
Director of Finance and Supplies: A. O. IKIMI
Director of Studies: G. I. ORAKA
Registrar: A. S. EWERE
Chief Librarian: E. M. A. DUDU

Library of 54,013 vols
Number of teachers: 189
Number of students: 2,520

Publication: *PTI News* (4 a year).

PLATEAU STATE POLYTECHNIC, BARKIN LADI

PMB 02023, Bukuru, Plateau State

Founded 1978, present status 1980

Rector: Eng. ALEXANDER A. T. KEBANG
Registrar: TIMOTHY A. ANJIDE
Director of Administration: LAMI A. ENATTO
Librarian: J. E. KOTSO

Library of 11,393 vols
Number of teachers: 121
Number of students: 2,260

Publication: news bulletins and student's handbook

DEANS

School of Administration and General Studies: L. A. ENATTO
School of Engineering and Environmental Studies: Dr R. JATAU
School of Management Studies: ELIZABETH PAM
School of Science and Technology: K. D. DABER

DIRECTORS

Centre for Continuing Education: ELIZABETH K. PAM
Consultancy and Applied Research Division: Eng. O. O. OLUSANYA

YABA COLLEGE OF TECHNOLOGY

PMB 2011, Yaba, Lagos State 234

Telephone: (1) 7742155
Fax: (1) 7917565
Internet: www.yabatech.edu.ng

Founded 1948
Federal control
Academic year: October to July

Rector: O. OWOSO
Registrar: F. F. TAIWO (acting)
Deputy Rector for Academic Affairs: A. O. AGBAJE-WILLIAMS
Deputy Rector for Admin.: Eng. A. I. ABIODUN
Polytechnic Librarian: R. I. OLOGBONSAIYE

Library of 70,000 vols
Number of teachers: 800
Number of students: 14,000

Publications: *Newsletter*, *Prospectus* (1 a year), *Yabatech News* (4 a year), *YCT Academic Journal* (published by various departments, each semester)

DIRECTORS

School of Art, Design and Printing: MAO OMOIGHE
School of Engineering: Eng. P. K. ADEGBOYEGA
School of Environmental Studies: Arch. A. A. ADENIJI
School of Management: IFY MAFINZE
School of Science: I. A. ABIODUN
School of Technology: O. AKINJAIYEJU

Federal College of Agriculture, Akure: Ado-Ekiti Rd, Akure, Ondo State; tel. and fax (34) 240891; f. 1957; library: 10,000 vols; 30 teachers; 1,000 students; Principal Dr A. O. AYODELE.

Federal College of Agriculture, Ibadan: Institute of Agricultural Research and Training, PMB 5029, Moor Plantation, Ibadan; tel. (2) 2312070; f. 1921; 33 teachers; 319 students; Provost Dr D. S. DARAMOLA.

Federal College of Forestry: Forestry Research Institute of Nigeria, PMB 5054, Ibadan; tel. (22) 411035; f. 1941; technical forestry training, National and Higher National Diploma courses; vocational courses; library: 4,800 vols; 20 teachers; 520 students; Dir Dr ISAAC I. ERO.

Federal School of Dental Hygiene: 1 Broad St, PMB 12562, Lagos; f. 1957; Principal Dr S. JOHNSON.

National Eye Centre: Off Nnamdi Azikiwe Way, PMB 2267, Kaduna; tel. and fax (62) 313956; e-mail neckad@yahoo.com; f. 1979; provides postgraduate ophthalmic training (medical and surgical), TOT IOL microsurgical course, ophthalmic nursing training, clinical services; 9 teachers; 16 students; Chief Medical Dir Dr C. P. OZEMELA; publs *Newsletter* (4 a year), *Pharmacy News* (12 a year).

NORWAY

The Higher Education System

The oldest current institutions of higher education were founded before Norway declared its independence from Swedish rule in 1905. The state Universitetet i Oslo (founded in 1811) is the oldest university; the next oldest university is the state Universitetet for Miljø- og Biovitenskap (Norwegian University of Life Sciences—founded in 1859). The first institution founded in the independent period was the private Teologiske Menighetsfakultet (Norwegian Lutheran School of Theology—founded in 1907). Higher education is administered according to the Universities and Colleges Act (1995). Norway participates in the Bologna Process to establish a European Higher Education Area, the first phase of which is to adopt a credit-based system of comparable degrees with two main cycles (undergraduate and graduate). The Norwegian Agency for Quality Assurance in Education (NOKUT) is an independent government body established in 2003 to monitor and develop the quality of higher education in Norway through evaluation, accreditation and recognition of quality assurance systems, institutions and study programmes. The primary responsibility for quality assurance rests with the individual higher education institution, but internal quality assurance systems must adhere to nationally set standards and are externally evaluated by NOKUT. Institutions and programmes are not accredited for a defined period; accreditation is valid until revoked. NOKUT makes its decisions independently of the Ministry of Education and Research. In October 2003 130,148 students were enrolled at colleges of higher education; in 2006 86,366 were enrolled at universities and their equivalent.

Admission to higher education is on the basis of successful completion of secondary education, however since 2000 applicants have also been admitted with non-formal qualifications. In 2003 a two-tier Bachelors and Masters degree system was implemented in accordance with the principles of the Bologna Process. Norwegian institutions award degrees on the basis of the European Credit Transfers System, and each year is equivalent to 60 'credits'. The standard undergraduate degree is the Bachelors, which lasts three years, and the first postgraduate degree is the Masters, a course lasting one-and-a-half to two years. The final postgraduate and highest university degree is the Doctorate, awarded after three to four years of study. The title of the Doctorate may vary depending on the subject area.

Post-secondary vocational and technical education is available at technical colleges (Teckniske Fagskoler), university colleges and state colleges. Programmes at these institutions last for two to three years.

Regulatory and Representative Bodies

GOVERNMENT

Ministry of Culture: POB 8030 Dep., 0030 Oslo; Akersgt. 59, Oslo; tel. 22-24-90-90; fax 22-24-95-50; e-mail postmottak@kud.dep.no; internet www.regjeringen.no/kud; Minister ANNIKEN HUITFELDT.

Ministry of Education and Research: POB 8119 Dep., 0032 Oslo; Akersgt. 44, Oslo; tel. 22-24-90-90; fax 22-24-27-64; e-mail postmottak@kd.dep.no; internet www.regjeringen.no/kd; Minister of Education KRISTIN HALVORSEN; Minister of Research and Higher Education TORA AASLAND; Sec.-Gen. TROND FEVOLDEN.

ACCREDITATION

ENIC/NARIC Norway: NOKUT—Norwegian Agency for Quality Assurance in Education, POB 1708 Vika, 0121 Oslo; tel. 21-02-18-60; fax 21-02-18-01; e-mail postmottak@nokut.no; internet www.nokut.no; Dir-Gen. TERJE MØRLAND.

Nasjonalt Organ for Kvalitet i Utdanningen (Norwegian Agency for Quality Assurance in Education): POB 1708 Vika, 0121 Oslo; Kronprinsensgt. 9, Oslo; tel. 21-02-18-00; fax 21-02-18-01; e-mail postmottak@nokut.no; internet www.nokut.no; f. 2002; ind. governmental agency; controls and develops the quality of Norwegian higher education instns through the evaluation, accreditation and recognition of quality assurance systems, instns and education programmes; Chair. Prof. PETTER AASLESTAD; CEO PER ARNE SYRRIST.

NATIONAL BODIES

Norges Forskningsråd (The Research Council of Norway): POB 2700, St Hanshaugen, 0131 Oslo; Stensberggt 26, Oslo; tel. 22-03-70-00; fax 22-03-70-01; e-mail post@forskningsradet.no; internet www.forskningsradet.no; attached to Ministry of Education and Research; promotes and supports basic and applied research in all areas of science, technology, medicine and the humanities; awards research grants and fellowships and runs its own research establishments (see elsewhere under Research Institutes); Chair. GEIR STENE-LARSEN; publ. *Forskning* (4 a year).

Norsk Forbund for Fjernundervisning og Fleksibel Utdanning (NFF) (Norwegian Association for Distance Education and Flexible Education): Lilleakerveien 23, 0283 Oslo; tel. 22-51-04-80; fax 22-51-04-81; e-mail nade@nade-nff.no; internet www.nade-nff.no; f. 1968; Chair. SVEIN QVIST-ERIKSEN; Gen. Man. TORHILD SLÅTTO; publ. *Synkron* (magazine).

Senter for Internasjonalisering av Høgre Utdanning (SIU) (Norwegian Centre for International Cooperation in Higher Education): POB 1093, 5809 Bergen; Vaskerelven 39, 5014 Bergen; tel. 55-30-38-00; fax 55-30-38-01; e-mail siu@siu.no; internet siu.no; f. 2004; promotes int. cooperation in education and research; Chair. Prof. SONNI OLSEN; Dir ALF RASMUSSEN (acting); publ. *Global Knowledge* (magazine on politics and global implication in research and higher education).

Universitets- og Høgskolerådet (Norwegian Association of Higher Education Institutes): Pilestredet 46B, 0167 Oslo; tel. 22-45-39-50; e-mail uhr@uhr.no; internet www.uhr.no; f. 2000 by merger of the Norwegian Ccl of State Colleges and the Norwegian Ccl of Univs; 46 mem. institutions; Chair. JAN I. HAALAND; Gen. Sec. JOHN SPELL.

Learned Societies

GENERAL

Det Kongelige Norske Videnskabers Selskab (Royal Norwegian Society of Sciences and Letters): Erling Skakkesgt. 47C, Postuttak, 7491 Trondheim; tel. 73-59-21-57; fax 73-59-58-95, e-mail post@dknvs.no; internet www.dknvs.no; f. 1760; 683 mems (521 Norwegian, 144 foreign, 1 hon., 18 assoc.); Pres. Prof. KRISTIAN FOSSHEIM; Gen. Sec. KRISTIAN OVERSKAUG; publ. *Skrifter*.

Norske Videnskaps-Akademi (Norwegian Academy of Science): Drammensveien 78, 0271 Oslo; tel. 22-12-10-90; fax 22-12-10-99; e-mail dnva@online.no; internet www.dnva.no; f. 1857; sections: Mathematics and Natural Sciences, Historical and Philosophical Sciences; 885 mems (476 Norwegian, 409 foreign); Pres. Prof. NILS CHRISTIAN STENSETH; Sec.-Gen. Prof. ØIVIND ANDERSEN; publs *Årbok*, *Avhandlinger*, *Physica Scripta* (12 a year), *Zoologica Scripta* (6 a year).

ARCHITECTURE AND TOWN PLANNING

Norske Arkitekters Landsforbund (NAL) (Norwegian Architects' Association): Josefines gt. 34, 0351 Oslo; tel. 23-33-25-00; fax 23-33-25-01; e-mail nal@arkitektur.no; internet www.arkitektur.no; f. 1911; 4,300 mems; Pres. KJERSTI NERSETH; publs *Arkitektnytt* (20 a year), *Byggekunst* (8 a year), *Norske Arkitektkonkurranser*.

BIBLIOGRAPHY, LIBRARY SCIENCE AND MUSEOLOGY

Norsk Bibliotekforening (Norwegian Library Association): POB 6540, Etterstad, 0606 Oslo; tel. 23-24-34-30; fax 22-67-23-68; e-mail nbf@norskbibliotekforening.no; internet www.norskbibliotekforening.no; f. 1913; 3,200 mems; Pres. SVEIN ARNE TINNESAND; Sec.-Gen. HEGE NEWTH NOURI; publ. *Bibliotekforum* (10 a year).

ECONOMICS, LAW AND POLITICS

Norsk Forening for Internasjonal Rett (International Law Association, Norwegian Branch): c/o Wiersholm Mellbye and Bech, POB 1400 Vika, 0115 Oslo; Ruseløkkveien 26, 0115 Oslo; tel. 21-02-10-00; fax 21-02-10-01; e-mail veem@wiersholm.no; internet www.nfir.no; f. 1925; 77 mems; Pres. ROLF EINAR FIFE; Sec. VEGARD EMAUS.

Statsøkonomisk Forening (Economic Association of Norway): Ullern Alle 59, 0381 Oslo; tel. and fax 63-90-05-76; f. 1883; approx. 300 mems; Pres. Prof. KJELL STORVIK; Sec. BJÖRN STENSETH.

FINE AND PERFORMING ARTS

Arts Council Norway: POB 101 Sentrum, 0102 Oslo; tel. 22-47-83-30; fax 22-33-40-42; e-mail post@kulturrad.no; internet www.kulturrad.no; f. 1965, merged with ABM-utvikling—Statens Senter for Arkiv, Bibliotek og Museum 2011; aims, in connection with the Cultural Fund, to encourage artistic life and cultural activities in Norway and to distribute the resources of the Fund in grants and subsidies; 9 mems appointed by the Statsraid (Council of State) and 4 by the Storting (parliament) all for a period of 4 years; Chair. BENTEIN BAARDSON; Dir GURI SKJELDAL; publs *Notatserien* (irregular), *Rapportserien* (irregular).

MIC Norsk Musikkinformasjon (Music Information Centre Norway): POB 2674 Solli, 0203 Oslo; Henrik Ibsensgt. 110, Solli Pl., Oslo; tel. 23-27-63-00; fax 23-27-63-01; e-mail info@mic.no; internet www.mic.no; f. 1979; promotes and offers information on Norwegian music of all genres, composers, music instns, performing groups and artists; aims to build up a representative colln of contemporary Norwegian music; mem. of the Int. Asscn of Music Information Centres; comprises a MSS library, orchestral materials, reference library, copying service; library: MSS colln of more than 7,000 Norwegian musical works; Dir MARTIN REVHEIM; publ. *Ballade* (in Norwegian, online).

Norske Billedkunstnere (Association of Norwegian Visual Arts): Grubbegt. 14, 0179 Oslo; tel. 23-25-60-30; fax 23-25-60-49; e-mail nbk@billedkunst.no; internet www.billedkunst.no; f. 1889, reorganized 1979 and 1988; a nat. asscn of professional artists' orgs; the Norwegian Govt's Advisory Bd on questions relating to graphic arts; mem. of UNESCO's Int. Artists Ascn (IAA); 2,700 mems; Chair. HILDE ROGNSKOG; Sec. GJERT GJERTSEN; publ. *Billedkunstneren* (7 a year).

HISTORY, GEOGRAPHY AND ARCHAEOLOGY

Fortidsminneforeningen (Foreningen til norske Fortidsminnesmerkers Bevaring) (Society for the Preservation of Ancient Monuments in Norway): Dronningensgt. 11, 0152 Oslo; tel. 23-31-70-70; fax 23-31-70-50; e-mail post@fortidsminneforeningen.no; internet www.fortidsminneforeningen.no; f. 1844; works towards protecting Norwegian cultural heritage sites and creating a common understanding of their value; owns and cares for 40 properties, among those 8 stave churches incl. the World Heritage site at Urnes; 7,500 mems; Sec.-Gen. ELISABETH SEIP; Head of Org. FREDRIC MONCLAIR; publs *Årbok* (1 a year), *Fortidsvern* (4 a year), *Gode Råd serien* (irregular).

Kirkehistorisk Samfunn (Church History Society): Markalléen 7, 1368 Stabekk; e-mail peder.eidberg@baptist.no; f. 1956; 43 mems; Pres. Prof. JAN SCHUMACHER; Sec. Prof. Dr PEDER A. EIDBERG.

Landslaget for Lokalhistorie (National Association of Local History): Institutt for Historie og Klassiske Fag, NTNU, 7491 Trondheim; tel. 73-59-63-95; fax 73-59-64-41; e-mail post@historielag.org; internet www.historielag.org; f. 1920; 415 mem. historical socs; Pres. KURT TVERLI; Man. JOSTEIN MOLDE; publs *Heimen* (4 a year), *Lokalhistorisk* (4 a year).

Norsk Arkeologisk Selskap (Norwegian Archaeological Society): Huk Aveny 35, 0287 Oslo; tel. 22-43-87-92; fax 22-13-52-86; e-mail nas@arkeologi.no; internet www.arkeologi.no; f. 1936; 800 mems; Pres. CHRISTEN AASS; Sec.-Gen. EGIL MIKKELSEN; publ. *Viking* (1 a year).

Norsk Lokalhistorisk Institutt: POB 8045 Dep, 0031 Oslo; Observatoriegt. 1B, 0254 Oslo; tel. 22-92-51-30; fax 22-92-51-31; e-mail nli@lokalhistorie.no; internet www.lokalhistorie.no; f. 1955; guidance for local historians, research in local history incl. publication of sources, etc., valuable for research; library of 20,000 vols; Dir KNUT SPRAUTEN.

Norsk Slektshistorisk Forening (Norwegian Genealogical Society): Øvre Slottsgt. 2B, 0157 Oslo; tel. 22-33-30-30; e-mail kontor@genealogi.no; internet www.genealogi.no; f. 1926; 2,100 mems; Chair. RUNE NEDRUD; Sec. JAN I. KRISTIANSEN; publs *Genealogen* (2 a year), *Norsk Slektshistorisk Tidsskrift* (2 a year).

Norske Historiske Forening (Norwegian Historical Society): Avdeling for historie, POB 7805, 5020 Bergen; tel. 22-85-67-59; fax 22-85-52-78; e-mail hifo@sv.uit.no; internet hifo.b.uib.no; f. 1869; 1,000 mems; Pres. DAY HUNDSTAD; Sec. ELISE NICOLAISEN; publ. *Historisk Tidsskrift* (4 a year).

LANGUAGE AND LITERATURE

Alliance Française: POB 34, Sentrum, 5803 Bergen; Vågsallmenningen 12, Gamle Norges Bank, 3. etasje, Bergen; e-mail alliance.francaise@uib.no; internet www.france-bergen.no; offers courses and examinations in French language and culture and promotes cultural exchange with France; 100 mems.

British Council: Storgaten 10B, 0155 Oslo; tel. 22-39-61-90; fax 22-42-40-39; e-mail british.council@britishcouncil.no; internet www.britishcouncil.org/norway; offers courses and examinations in English language and British culture and promotes cultural exchange with the UK; Country Man. KAROLINE TELLUM-DJARRAYA.

Goethe-Institut: Grønland 16, 0188 Oslo; tel. 22-05-78-80; fax 22-17-20-04; e-mail info@oslo.goethe.org; internet www.goethe.de/oslo; offers courses and examinations in German language and culture and promotes cultural exchange with Germany; library of 6,000 vols, 30 periodicals; Dir Dr KRISTIAN ZAPPEL.

Norsk PEN (Norwegian Centre of International PEN): Wergelandsveien 29, 0167 Oslo; tel. 22-60-74-50; fax 22-60-74-51; e-mail pen@norskpen.no; internet www.norskpen.no; f. 1922; contact for Norwegian writers with the rest of the writing world; defends freedom of expression worldwide, with a spec. focus on Afghanistan, Belarus, People's Republic of China, Tunisia, Turkey and the Middle East; 370 mems; Pres. ANDERS HEGER; Sec.-Gen. CARL MORTEN IVERSEN.

Norske Forfatterforening (Norwegian Authors' Union): POB 327 Sentrum, 0103 Oslo; tel. 23-35-76-20; fax 22-42-11-07; e-mail post@forfatterforeningen.no; internet www.forfatterforeningen.no; f. 1893; 563 mems; Chair. ANNE OTERHOLM.

Riksmålsforbundet—Det Norske Akademi for Sprog og Litteratur (Norwegian Academy for Language and Literature): Rosenborggaten 3, 0356 Oslo; tel. 22-60-88-59; fax 22-60-03-74; e-mail ordet@riksmalsforbundet.no; internet www.riksmalsforbundet.no; f. 1907; protects and authorizes dictionaries of the traditional 'Riksmaal'; Chair. TROND VERNEGG; Sec. Prof. SISSEL LANGE-NIELSEN.

MEDICINE

Norsk Farmasøytisk Selskap (Norwegian Pharmaceutical Society): POB 5070, Majorstuen, 0301 Oslo; tel. 21-62-02-23; fax 22-60-81-73; e-mail farm-sel@online.no; internet www.nfs.no; f. 1924; furthers scientific and practical devt of pharmacy; 550 mems; Chair. BRITT WOLDEN; Sec. RØNNAUG LARSEN.

Norsk Kirurgisk Forening (Norwegian College of Surgeons): POB 1152 Sentrum, 0107 Oslo; Legenes hus, Akersgt. 2, Oslo; tel. 23-10-90-00; fax 22-10-91-80; e-mail trazumo@legeforeningen.no; internet www.legeforeningen.no/nkf; f. 1911; 1,135 mems; Chair. OLAUG VILLANGER; Sec. TATJANA RAZUMOVA; publ. *Vitenskapelige forhandlinger* (1 a year).

Norske Laegeforening (Norwegian Medical Association): POB 1152 Sentrum, 0107 Oslo; tel. 23-10-90-00; fax 23-10-90-10; e-mail informasjon@legeforeningen.no; internet www.legeforeningen.no; f. 1886; 27,164 mems; Pres. Dr TORUNN JANBU; Sec.-Gen. Dr GEIR RIISE; publ. *Tidsskrift for den norske lægeforening* (24 a year).

Det norske medicinske Selskab (Norwegian Medical Society): POB 1130 Blindern, 0318 Oslo; tel. 22-85-06-73; e-mail oivind.larsen@medisin.uio.no; internet www.dnms.no; f. 1833, as continuation of a medical reading soc.; 400 mems; Chair. Prof. Dr ØIVIND LARSEN; Sec. ASTRID LAVOLL-NYLENNA; publ. *Michael Quarterly*.

Norske Tannlegeforening (NTF) (Norwegian Dental Association): POB 3063 Elisenberg, 0207 Oslo; Frederik Stangsgt. 20, 0264 Oslo; tel. 22-54-74-00; fax 22-55-11-09; e-mail tannlegeforeningen@tannlegeforeningen.no; internet www.tannlegeforeningen.no; f. 1884; 4,500 mems, 21 local asscns; Pres. LYNGSTAD GUNNAR; Sec.-Gen. DAG E. REITE (acting); publ. *Den norske tannlegeforenings Tidende* (12 a year).

NATURAL SCIENCES

General

Polytekniske Forening (Polytechnical Society): Rosenkrantzgt. 7, 0159 Oslo; tel. 22-42-68-70; fax 22-42-58-87; e-mail polyteknisk@polyteknisk.no; internet www.polyteknisk.no; f. 1852; 7,000 mems; Chair. J. R. WAALER; Sec.-Gen. FREDRIK EVJEN; publ. *Teknisk Ukeblad* (52 a year).

Selskapet til Vitenskapenes Fremme (Society for the Advancement of Science): Noreidstraumen 31, c/o Guldborg, 5251 Søreidgrend; e-mail guldborg.sovik@biomed.uib.no; internet www.vitenskap-bergen.no; f. 1927; promotes and encourages intellectual activities generally by regular series of lectures, excursions; 200 mems; Pres. Prof. DAG E. HELLAND; Gen. Sec. Prof. GULDBORG SØVIK.

Biological Sciences

Norsk Botanisk Forening (Norwegian Botanical Association): Naturhistorisk Museum, POB 1172 Blindern, 0318 Oslo; tel. 22-85-17-01; fax 22-85-18-35; e-mail post@botaniskforening.no; internet www

.botaniskforening.no; f. 1935; 1,500 mems; Pres. MARIT ERIKSEN; Sec. MARIANNE KARLSEN; publ. *Blyttia* (4 a year).

Physical Sciences

Norsk Geologisk Forening (Geological Society of Norway): NGU, POB 6315 Sluppen, 7491 Trondheim; tel. 73-90-40-00; fax 73-92-16 20; e-mail ngf@geologi.no; internet www.geologi.no; f. 1905; 1,400 mems; Pres. ARVID NØTTVEDT; Sec.-Gen. GUNN KRISTIN HAUKDAL; publ. *Norsk Geologisk Tidsskrift* (4 a year).

Norsk Kjemisk Selskap (Norwegian Chemical Society): POB 1107 Blindern, 0317 Oslo; tel. 22-85-55-56; fax 22-85-54-41; internet www.kjemi.no; f. 1893; 2,000 mems; Pres. KENNETH RUUD; Gen. Sec. HARALD WALDERHAUG; publ. *Kjemi*.

TECHNOLOGY

Norges Tekniske Vitenskapsakademi (Norwegian Academy of Technological Sciences): Lerchendal Gård, 7491 Trondheim; tel. 73-59-54-63; fax 73-59-08-30; e-mail ntvamail@ntva.ntnu.no; internet www.ntva.no; f. 1955; 500 mems; Pres. Dr KJELL ARNE INGEBRIGTSEN; Sec.-Gen. HEIN JOHNSON.

Teknisk-Naturvitenskapelig Forening (Tekna) (Norwegian Society of Chartered Technical and Scientific Professionals (Tekna)): POB 2312 Solli, 0201 Oslo; Dronning Mauds gate 15, Oslo; tel. 22-94-75-00; fax 22-94-75-01; e-mail post@tekna.no; internet www.tekna.no; f. 1874; professional society; promotes research and development; represents engineering profession in its relations with other organizations and countries; 53,104 mems; Pres. MARIANNE HARG; Sec.-Gen. KENNETH STIEN; publs *Magasinet Tekna* (10 a year), *Sivilingeniøren* (10 a year), *Teknisk Ukeblad* (52 a year), *Våre veger* (10 a year).

Research Institutes

GENERAL

Chr. Michelsens Institutt: POB 6033 Bedriftssenteret, 5892 Bergen; Jekteviksbakken 31, Bergen; tel. 47-93-80-00; fax 47-93-80-01; e-mail cmi@cmi.no; internet www.cmi.no; f. 1930; independent, non-profit research institution with a focus on Sub-Saharan Africa, South and Central Asia, the Middle East, Balkans and South America; library of 70,000 vols; Dir OTTAR MÆSTAD.

Nordlandsforskning (Nordland Research Institute): POB 1490, 8049 Bodø; tel. 75-51-76-00; fax 75-51-72-34; e-mail nf@nforsk.no; internet www.nordlandsforskning.no; f. 1979; inter-disciplinary research across a wide range of fields, with a particular focus on social sciences and business management; Admin. Dir AGNETE ALSOS.

Norsk Samfunnsvitenskapelig Datatjeneste (NSD) (Norwegian Social Science Data Services): Harald Hårfagres gt. 29, 5007 Bergen; tel. 55-58-21-17; fax 55-58-96-50; e-mail nsd@nsd.uib.no; internet www.nsd.uib.no; f. 1971; attached to Universitetet i Bergen; Dir BJØRN HENRICHSEN.

Stein Rokkan Senter for Flerfaglige Samfunnsstudier (Stein Rokkan Centre for Professional Social Studies): Nygårdsgt. 5, 5015 Bergen; tel. 55-58-97-10; fax 55-58-97-11; e-mail rokkansenteret@uni.no; internet rokkan.uni.no; f. 2002 by merger of Senter for Samfunnsforskning (Centre for Social Research) and Norsk Senter for Forskning i Ledelse, Organisasjon og Styring (Norwegian Centre for Research in Organization and Management); attached to Universitetet i Bergen; multi-disciplinary research centre for social and cultural studies; Dir JAN ERIK ASKILDSEN; publ. *Tidsskrift for Velferdsforskning* (Journal of Social Research, 4 a year).

ECONOMICS, LAW AND POLITICS

Centre for Peace Studies: Faculty of Humanities, Social Sciences and Education, Universitetet i Tromsø, 9037 Tromsø; tel. 77-64-43-00; fax 77-64-59-19; e-mail mail@peace.uit.no; internet www.peace.uit.no; f. 2002; attached to Universitetet i Tromsø; examines, promotes and facilitates dialogue pertaining to non-violent conflict resolution and the creation of peace; Dir TONE BLEIE.

Norsk Utenrikspolitisk Institutt (Norwegian Institute of International Affairs): POB 8159 Dep., 0033 Oslo; C. J. Hambros pl. 2D, Oslo,; tel. 22-99-40-00; fax 22-36-21-82; e-mail internett@nupi.no; internet www.nupi.no; f. 1959; int. economics, devt studies, European integration, collective security, Russian studies, UN, peacekeeping; library of 20,000 vols; Dir JAN EGELAND; publs *Forum for Development Studies* (3 a year), *Hvor Hender Det?* (24 a year), *Internasjonal Politikk* (4 a year), *Nordisk Østforum* (4 a year).

Norske Nobelinstitutt (Norwegian Nobel Institute): Henrik Ibsens gt. 51, 0255 Oslo; tel. 22-12-93-00; fax 22-12-93-17; e-mail postmaster@nobel.no; internet www.nobel.no; f. 1903; follows devt of int. relations (especially work for the pacific settlement of them) in order to advise the Nobel Peace Prize Cttee; research dept; library of 200,000 vols, 200 periodicals; Dir GEIR LUNDESTAD.

Peace Research Institute Oslo (PRIO): POB 9229 Grønland, 0134 Oslo; Hausmanns gt. 7, 0186, Oslo; tel. 22-54-77-00; fax 22-54-77-01; e-mail info@prio.no; internet www.prio.no; f. 1959; multi-disciplinary research on peace- and conflict-related topics; library of 22,000 vols, 340 journals; Chair. BERNT AARDAL; Dir KRISTIAN BERG HARPVIKEN; publs *Journal of Peace Research* (6 a year), *Security Dialogue* (6 a year).

Statistisk Sentralbyrå (Statistics Norway): POB 8131 Dep., 0033 Oslo; Kongens gt. 6, Oslo; tel. 21-09-00-00; fax 21-09-49-73; e-mail ssb@ssb.no; internet www.ssb.no; f. 1876; library of 160,000 vols; Dir-Gen. HANS HENRIK SCHEEL; publs *Norges offisielle statistikk* (series, Official Statistics of Norway, irregular), *Økonomiske analyser* (Economic Survey), *Sosiale og Økonomiske studier* (Social and Economic Studies), *Statistiske analyser* (Statistical Survey), *Statistisk årbok* (Statistical Yearbook).

EDUCATION

Centre for Flexible Education (U-vett): Teorifagsbygget hus 1, Universitetet i Tromsø, 9037 Tromsø; tel. 77-64-65-58; fax 77-64-55-50; e-mail postmottak@uvett.uit.no; internet uit.no/uvett; attached to Universitetet i Tromsø; Asst Dir INGER ANN HANSSEN.

HISTORY, GEOGRAPHY AND ARCHAEOLOGY

Roald Amundsen Centre for Arctic Research: 9037 Tromsø; tel. 77-64-52-41; e-mail arctic.info@arctic.uit.no; internet uit.no/amundsen/438; f. 1989; attached to Universitetet i Tromsø; aims to encourage inter-disciplinary cooperation in Arctic research and teaching; Head of Admin. GEIR GOTAAS.

LANGUAGE AND LITERATURE

Center for Advanced Study in Theoretical Linguistics (CASTL): Faculty of Humanities, Social Sciences and Education, Universitetet i Tromsø, 9037 Tromsø; tel. 77-64-47-51; fax 77-64-42-39; e-mail tore.bentz@uit.no; internet castl.uit.no; f. 2002; attached to Universitetet i Tromsø; aims to foster a greater understanding of the nature of syntactic, morphological and phonological variation, in order to be able to determine along which grammatical parameters any two languages vary; Dir MARIT WESTERGAARD.

MEDICINE

Helseøkonomi Bergen (HEB) (Health Economics Bergen): Herman Fossgt. 6, 5007 Bergen; tel. 55-58-92-00; fax 55-58-92-10; e-mail oddvar.kaarboe@econ.uib.no; internet heb.rokkan.uib.no; attached to Universitetet i Bergen; economic analysis of health; assessment of profitability and distributional effects of health care and treatment; Dir ODDVAR KAARBØ.

Nasjonalt Forskningssenter innen Komplementær og Alternativ Medisin (NaFKAM) (National Research Centre in Complementary and Alternative Medicine): Forskningsparken I, Sykehusveien 23, 9037 Tromsø; tel. 77-64-66-50; fax 77-64-68-66; e-mail nafkam@helsefak.uit.no; internet uit.no/nafkam; f. 2000; conducts inter-disciplinary research into a wide range of fields, incl. clinical studies and patients' use of alternative treatments; Dir VINJAR MAGNE FØNNEBØ; publ. *NAFKAM skriftserie* (irregular).

Nasjonalt Senter for Distriktsmedisin (NSDM) (National Centre of Rural Medicine): Institutt for Samfunnsmedisin, Universitetet i Tromsø 9037 Tromsø; tel. 77-64-48-16; fax 77-64-48-31; e-mail ivar.aaraas@uit.no; internet www.nsdm.no; f. 2007; attached to Universitetet i Tromsø; aims to promote research, professional devt projects, education and networking among physicians and health personnel in rural and remote areas to bridge the gap between academia and practice and contribute to quality, recruitment and stability in rural health services; Gen. Man. Prof. IVAR J. AARAAS.

Research Centre for Health Promotion: Faculty of Psychology, Christies gt. 13, 5020 Bergen; tel. 55-58-28-08; e-mail adm-hemil@psych.uib.no; internet www.uib.no/rg/hemil; f. 1988; attached to Universitetet i Bergen; Head of Institute MAURICE B. MITTELMARK.

Senter for Samisk Helseforskning (Centre for Sami Health Research): POB 71, Storgt. 39, 9735 Karasjo; tel. 78-46-89-00; fax 78-46-89-10; e-mail ragnhild.kalstad@ism.uit.no; internet uit.no/medsamisk; f. 1999; attached to Universitetet i Tromsø; aims to promote inter-disciplinary and multi-disciplinary research and development on the health and living conditions among the Sami population in Norway; Dir RAGNHILD V. KALSTAD.

NATURAL SCIENCES

Biological Sciences

Havforskningsinstituttet (Institute of Marine Research): POB 1870 Nordnes, 5817 Bergen; Nordnesgt. 50, 5005 Bergen; tel. 55-23-85-00; fax 55-23-85-31; e-mail post@imr.no; internet www.imr.no; f. 1900; attached to Min. of Fisheries and Coastal Affairs; applied research related to fisheries; divisions: marine environment, marine living research, aquaculture (with two experimental stations), coastal zone; library of 80,000 vols; Man. Dir TORE NEPSTAD; publs *Facts and Figures* (every 2 years), *Fisken og Havet*.

Marine Biological Station: Espelamdsveien 232, 5258 Blomsterdalen; attached to Universitetet i Bergen; open to research workers from all countries; equipped for large-scale experimental work on primary and secondary production; Man. AGNES AADNESEN.

Norwegian Structural Biology Centre (NorStruct): Faculty of Sciences, University of Tromsø, 9037 Tromsø; tel. 77-64-40-70; e-mail norstruct@chem.uit.no; internet uit.no/norstruct; attached to Universitetet i Tromsø; Dir ARNE O. SMALÅS.

Physical Sciences

Centre for Theoretical and Computational Chemistry: Universitetet i Oslo, Department of Chemistry, POB 1033 Blindern, 0315 Oslo; Universitetet i Tromsø, Department of Chemistry, 9037 Tromsø; tel. 77-62-31-00; e-mail post@ctcc.no; internet www.ctcc.no; f. 2007; collaborative project between Universitetet i Oslo and the Universitetet i Tromsø; aims to be an internationally renowned contributor to the devt and application of quantum-mechanical modelling in chemistry and materials science; Head of Admin. STIG EIDE.

Meteorologiske Institutt (Norwegian Meteorological Institute): POB 43 Blindern, 0313 Oslo; Niels Henrik Abels vei 40, Oslo; tel. 22-96-30-00; fax 22-96-30-50; e-mail post@met.no; internet www.met.no; f. 1866; library of 30,000 vols; Dir ANTON ELIASSEN; publs *Klimatologisk månedsoversikt* (12 a year), *Technical Report* (irregular).

Nansen Environmental and Remote Sensing Center: Thormøhlensgt. 47, 5006 Bergen; tel. 55-20-58-00; fax 55-20-58-01; e-mail admin@nersc.no; internet www.nersc.no; attached to Universitetet i Bergen; aims to make significant contribution to the understanding, monitoring and forecasting of the environment and climate on regional and global scales through coordination and participation in nat. and int. research programmes; Dir STEIN SANDVEN.

Norges Geologiske Undersøkelse (Geological Survey of Norway): POB 6315 Sluppen, 7491 Trondheim; Leiv Eirikssons vei 39, 7040 Trondheim; tel. 73-90-40-00; fax 73-92-16-20; e-mail ngu@ngu.no; internet www.ngu.no; f. 1858; library of 120,000 vols and 950 periodicals; Man. Dir MORTEN SMELROR; publs *Bulletin* (irregular, in English, online only), *Gråsteinen* (irregular, in Norwegian).

Norsk Polarinstitutt (Norwegian Polar Institute): Framsenteret, 9296 Tromsø; Hjalmar Johansens gt. 14, Tromsø; tel. 77-75-05-00; fax 77-75-05-01; e-mail post@npolar.no; internet www.npolar.no; f. 1928; preparation and publication of maps of Norwegian territories in the polar regions; scientific investigations in the fields of geology, geophysics and biology; responsible for Norwegian Antarctic Research expeditions; scientific logistical support; administration and maintenance of an all-year scientific station Ny-Ålesund, Svalbard; library of 13,000 vols and 12,000 pamphlets and authors' MSS; Dir JAN-GUNNAR WINTHER; publ. *Polar Research* (irregular).

RELIGION, SOCIOLOGY AND ANTHROPOLOGY

Instituttet for Sammenlignende Kulturforskning (Institute for Comparative Research in Human Culture): POB 2832 Solli, 0204 Oslo; Drammensveien 78, Oslo; tel. and fax 22-55-42-07; e-mail kulturfo@online.no; internet kulturfo.webhotell.no; f. 1922; comparative study of languages, religions, folklore, law, ethnology, archaeology, and sociology, sponsoring research programmes and publishing; Chair. Prof. ARNE BUGGE AMUNDSEN; Vice-Chair. AUD TALLE; Sec. IDA SLETTA; publ. *Institute for Comparative Research in Human Culture. Series B* (irregular).

Senter for Aldersforskning (Centre for Research on the Elderly): Institutt for Klinisk Medisin, Medisinske Fakultet, Universitetet i Tromsø, 9037 Tromsø; tel. 77-62-08-94; e-mail sat@fagmed.uit.no; internet uit.no/172; f. 2000; attached to Universitetet i Tromsø; multi-disciplinary research into the medical, health and social concerns of the elderly; Dir MAGNHILD NICOLAISEN (acting).

Senter for Kvinne og Kjønnsforskning (Kvinnforsk): Universitetet i Tromsø, 9037 Tromsø; tel. 77-64-52-40; fax 77-64-64-20; e-mail kvinnforsk@skk.uit.no; internet uit.no/kvinnforsk; f. 1995; attached to Universitetet i Tromsø; Dir LISE NORDBRØND; publ. *Kvinnforsk Skritserie* (irregular).

Senter for Kvinne og Kjønnsforskning (SKOK) (Centre for Women's and Gender Research): POB 7805, 5020 Bergen; Ida Bloms hus, Allégt. 34, 5007 Bergen; tel. 55-58-24-71; fax 55-58-96-64; e-mail post@skok.uib.no; internet www.uib.no/skok; attached to Universitetet i Bergen; research fields incl. feminist theory, gender theory, women's studies, philosophy, sociology, anthropology, cultural studies, psychoanalysis, sexuality, development studies, migration studies and family history; Dir Prof. ELLEN MORTENSEN.

TECHNOLOGY

Institutt for Energiteknikk (Institute for Energy Technology): POB 40, 2027 Kjeller; Instituttveien 18, 2007 Kjeller; tel. 63-80-60-00; fax 63-81-63-56; e-mail firmapost@ife.no; internet www.ife.no; f. 1948; int. research institute for energy and nuclear technology; undertakes research and devt within the energy and petroleum sectors, carries out assignments in nuclear technology, safety and environmental research; Man. Dir EVA S. DUGSTAD.

NIVA—Norsk Institutt for Vannforskning (NIVA—Norwegian Institute for Water Research): Gaustadalléen 21, 0349 Oslo; tel. 22-18-51-00; fax 22-18-52-00; e-mail niva@niva.no; internet www.niva.no; f. 1958; research and contract projects on technical, economical and sanitary problems in connection with water supply, waste water and pollution in rivers and lakes/fjords; library of 5,000 vols, 25 periodicals in print, 3,900 online periodicals; Admin. Dir GRETA BENTZEN; publ. *Årbok*.

Norges Geotekniske Institutt (NGI) (Norwegian Geotechnical Institute): POB 3930 Ullevaal Stadion, 0806 Oslo; Sognsveien 72, Oslo; tel. 22-02-30-00; fax 22-23-04-48; e-mail ngi@ngi.no; internet www.ngi.no; f. 1953; soil, rock and snow mechanics, foundation engineering, dams, offshore structures, instrumentation, rock engineering, geoenvironmental engineering; library of 20,000 vols, 300 periodicals, Terzaghi Library, Peck Library; Admin. Dir SUZANNE LACASSE.

NORSAR: POB 53, 2027 Kjeller; Gunnar Randers vei 15, 2007 Kjeller; tel. 63-80-59-00; fax 63-81-87-19; internet www.norsar.no; f. 1968; research on a wide range of topics within the field of seismology and seismic exploration; Dir ANDERS DAHLE; publ. *Technical Summary* (2 a year).

Norsk Institutt for By- Og Regionforskning (Norwegian Institute for Urban and Regional Research): Gaustadalléen 21, 0349 Oslo; tel. 22-95-88-00; fax 22-60-77-74; e-mail nibr@nibr.no; internet www.nibr.no; f. 1967; 90 mems; library of 23,000 vols, 200 periodicals; Dir HILDE LORENTZEN; publ. *Regionale Trender* (irregular).

Norsk Institutt for Luftforskning (Norwegian Institute for Air Research): POB 100, 2027 Kjeller; Instituttveien 18, 2007 Kjeller; tel. 63-89-80-00; fax 63-89-80-50; e-mail nilu@nilu.no; internet www.nilu.no; f. 1969; nat. and int. research and consultation in air pollution, atmospheric dispersion and measurements, meteorological measurements and analysis, instrumentation and chemical analysis; library of 9,000 vols, 130 periodicals; Dir KARI NYGAARD.

Norsk Regnesentral (Norwegian Computing Centre): POB 114 Blindern, 0314 Oslo; Gaustadalléen 23 A–B, 0373 Oslo; tel. 22-85-25-00; fax 22-69-76-60; e-mail nr@nr.no; internet www.nr.no; f. 1952; contract research and devt projects in information and communication technology and applied statistical modelling; library of 4,000 vols, 250 periodicals; Man. Dir LARS HOLDEN.

Norwegian Marine Technology Research Institute (MARINTEK): POB 4125 Valentinlyst, 7450 Trondheim; Otto Nielsens veg 10, 7052 Trondheim; tel. 73-59-55-00; fax 73-59-57-76; e-mail marintek@marintek.sintef.no; internet www.sintef.no/home/marintek; f. 1984; mem. of the SINTEF Group; research, devt and technical consultancy in the maritime sector for industry and the public sector; develops and verifies technological solutions for the shipping and maritime equipment industries and offshore petroleum production; library of 11,000 vols, 365 periodicals; Pres. ODDVAR EIDE; publ. *Marintek Review* (irregular).

NUTEC—Norsk Undervannsteknologisk Senter A/S (FALCK NUTEC—Norwegian Underwater Technology Centre): Gravdalsveien 255, POB 6, Ytre Laksevåg, 5848 Bergen; tel. 55-94-20-00; fax 55-94-20-01; e-mail companymail@falcknutec.no; internet www.nutec.no; f. 1976, present name adopted 1981; test and research centre for underwater technology, full-scale testing, diving, hyperbaric medicine and physiology, safety analysis, education and training; consulting services; library of 5,000 vols, 170 periodicals; Man. Dir ELI MOEN SÆTER.

Papirindustriens Forskningsinstitutt (PFI) (Paper and Fibre Research Institute): Høgskoleringen 6B, 7491 Trondheim; tel. 73-60-50-65; fax 73-55-09-99; e-mail firmapost@pfi.no; internet www.pfi.no; f. 1923; Pres. Dr PHILIP ANDRÉ REME.

Senter for Internasjonal Økonomi og Skipsfart (SIØS) (Centre for International Economics and Shipping): Norwegian School of Economics and Business Administration, Helleveien 30, 5035 Bergen; tel. 55-95-92-62; fax 55-95-93-50; e-mail sasamndm@debetmhs.no; f. 1958; aims to provide a centre for research fellows in sea transport, shipping economics and int. economics from Norway and abroad, and to promote cooperation with similar institutions; library of 3,500 vols, 1,600 periodicals, reports, etc.; Dir Prof. GUTTORM SCHJELDERUP; Sec. ANNE LIV SCRASE.

SINTEF: POB 4760 Sloop, 7465 Trondheim; Strindveien 4, Trondheim; tel. 73-59-30-00; fax 73-59-33-50; e-mail info@sintef.no; internet www.sintef.no; f. 1950 as Stiftelsen for Industriell og Teknisk Forskning ved Norges Tekniske Høgskole (Foundation for Scientific and Industrial Research at the Norwegian Institute of Technology); present name adopted 2007; undertakes contracts in science and technology research for industry and others; 7 affiliated research institutes; Pres. UNNI M. STEINSMO.

SINTEF Byggforsk (SINTEF Building and Infrastructure): POB 124 Blindern, 0314 Oslo; Forskningsveien 3B, Oslo; tel. 22-96-55-55; fax 22-69-94-38; e-mail byggforsk@sintef.no; internet www.sintef.no; f. 1953, reorganized 1985 as an ind. institute; merged with Norges byggforskningsinstitutt (NBI)

2007; library of 25,000 vols, 250 periodicals; Exec. Dir HANNE RØNNEBERG.

SINTEF Energi (SINTEF Energy): 7034 Trondheim; tel. 73-59-72-00; fax 73-59-72-50; e-mail energy.research@sintef.no; internet www.sintef.no; f. 1958 as Elektrisitetsforsyningens Forskningsinstitutt; renamed SINTEF Energiforskning 1998; present name adopted 2010; research and devt in the field of energy, esp. electricity generation, transmission, distribution and consumption; Man. Dir SVERRE AAM.

Transportøkonomisk Institutt (Institute of Transport Economics): Gaustadalléen 21, 0349 Oslo; tel. 22-57-38-00; fax 22-60-92-00; e-mail toi@toi.no; internet www.toi.no; f. 1958 as a govt dept; reorganized as ind. institute 1964; library of 30,000 vols, 200 periodicals; Chair. SIGURD LARSEN; publ. *Samferdsel* (Communication, 10 a year).

VilVite, Bergen Vitensenter (VilVite, Bergen Science Centre): HIB, Thormøhlensgt. 51, 5006 Bergen; tel. 55-59-45-00; e-mail post@vilvite.no; f. 2005; attached to Universitetet i Bergen; research and learning centre of technology, natural sciences and mathematics; Dir SVEIN ANDERS DAHL.

Libraries and Archives

Arendal

Arendal Bibliotek (Arendal Library): Torvet 6, POB 786 Stoa, 4809 Arendal; tel. 37-01-39-13; fax 37-01-30-80; e-mail arendal@arendal.folkebibl.no; internet www.arendal.folkebibl.no; f. 1832, inc. *Aust-Agder Fylkesbibliotek* (East Agder County Library) 1972; 200,000 vols; Head Librarian OLA EIKSUND.

Ås

Universitetet for Miljø- og Biovitenskap, Biblioteket (Norwegian University of Life Sciences, Library): POB 5003, 1432 Ås; Chr. M. Falsens vei 18, Tårnbygningen, Ås; tel. 64-96-50-00; fax 64-96-55-01; e-mail biblioteket@umb.no; internet www.umb.no/biblioteket; f. 1859; literature concerning all branches of agricultural science and forestry, conservation of natural resources, biology, etc.; 500,000 vols; Head Librarian DAG GUTTORMSEN (acting).

Bergen

Bergen offentlige Bibliotek (Municipal and County Library): Strømgt. 6, 5015 Bergen; tel. 55-56-85-00; fax 55-56-85-55; e-mail post@bergenbibliotek.no; internet bergenbibliotek.no; f. 1872; 600,000 vols; Grieg colln of 135 MSS and 5,700 letters; 6 brs and 1 mobile library; City Librarian TRINE KOLDERUP FLATEN.

Universitetsbiblioteket i Bergen (University of Bergen Library): POB 7808, 5020 Bergen; Stein Rokkans hus, Nygårdsgt. 5, 5015 Bergen; tel. 55-58-25-32; fax 55-58-46-20; e-mail post@ub.uib.no; internet www.uib.no/ub; f. 1825 as Bergens Museums Bibliotek; 1,780,000 books and journals, 240,000 photographs, 110,600 microforms, 42,800 maps and atlases, 6,400 audio recordings, 3,600 MSS; Library Dir RANDI E. TAXT.

Drammen

Drammensbiblioteket (Drammen Library): POB 3554, 3007 Drammen; Grønland 58B, 3045 Drammen; tel. 32-04-54-00; fax 32-80-64-53; e-mail bibliotek@drmk.no; internet www.dbib.no; f. 1916 as Drammen Bibliotek; present name adopted 2007 following merger with Buskerud fylkesbibliotek (Buskerud County Library) and the library at Høgskolen i Buskerud (Buskerud University College); 300,000 vols; Faculty Librarian HUGO HØYMO.

Hamar

Statsarkivet i Hamar (Regional State Archives): POB 533, 2317 Hamar; Lille Strandgt. 3, 3. etasje, 2317 Hamar; tel. 62-55-54-40; fax 62-52-94-48; e-mail sahamar@arkivverket.no; internet www.arkivverket.no/arkivverket/hamar; f. 1917; public record office, archives; public reading room open on weekdays; 23,000 vols; Chief Archivist VIGDIS STENSBY.

Kristiansand

Kristiansands Folkebibliotek (Municipal Library): POB 476, 4665 Kristiansand; Rådhusgt. 11, 4611 Kristiansand; tel. 38-12-49-10; fax 38-12-49-49; e-mail post.folkebibliotek@kristiansand.kommune.no; internet www.kristiansand.folkebibl.no; f. 1909; 3 brs; 300,000 vols; Chief Librarian ANNE KRISTIN UNDLIEN.

Oslo

Deichmanske Bibliotek (Oslo Public Library): Arne Garborgs pl. 4, 0179 Oslo; tel. 23-43-29-00; fax 22-11-33-89; e-mail postmottak.deichman@kul.oslo.kommune.no; internet www.deichmanske-bibliotek.oslo.kommune.no; f. 1785; 1,378,109 vols, incl. 1,118,274 books, 22,231 audio books, 31,438 music recordings, 19,239 video cassettes and DVDs; Chief Librarian LIV SÆTEREN.

Patentstyret (Norwegian Industrial Property Office): POB 8160 Dep., 0033 Oslo; Sandakerveien 64, 0484 Oslo; tel. 22-38-73-00; fax 22-38-73-01; e-mail mail@patentstyret.no; internet www.patentstyret.no; f. 1911; 25,000 vols of scientific and technical books and periodicals of reference for patent research; Head of Dept OTTO SCHARFF; publs *Designtidende* (Design Gazette), *Norsk Varemerketidende*, *Patenttidende* (Patent Gazette, 52 a year), *Varemerketidende* (Trademark Gazette, 52 a year).

Riksarkivet (National Archives of Norway): Folke Bernadottes vei 21, 4013 Ullevål Stadion, 0806 Oslo; tel. 22-02-26-00; fax 22-23-74-89; e-mail riksarkivet@arkivverket.no; internet www.arkivverket.no; f. 1817; takes charge of the archives of the mins and other brs of the central admin.; collns incl. medieval documents, maps and drawings, MSS and transcripts; more than 60,000 vols; Nat. Archivist IVAR FONNES; publ. *Arkivmagasinet* (3 a year).

Statistisk Sentralbyrås Bibliotek og Informasjonssenter (Statistics Norway, Library and Information Centre): POB 8131 Dep., 0153 Oslo; Kongensgt. 6, Oslo; tel. 21-09-46-42; fax 21-09-45-04; e-mail biblioteket@ssb.no; internet www.ssb.no/biblioteket; f. 1917; open to the public; OECD deposit library; European Statistical Data Support; 150,000 vols: mainly economic, demographic and statistical literature (incl. official and int. statistics); Librarian BJØRG GLESNE; publ. *Biblioteksnytt* (12 a year, online only).

Universitetsbiblioteket i Oslo (University of Oslo Library): POB 1085, Blindern, 0317 Oslo; tel. 22-85-40-50; fax 22-84-41-50; e-mail postmottak@ub.uio.no; internet www.ub.uio.no; f. 1811; depositary library; spec. collns of papyri and orientalia; 3,613,049 vols; Library Dir BENTE R. ANDREASSEN.

Utenriksdepartementets Dokumentasjonssenter (Documentation Centre of the Ministry of Foreign Affairs): POB 8114 Dep., 0032 Oslo; 7 Juni-Plassen 1, Oslo; tel. 22-24-36-00; fax 22-24-95-80; e-mail post@mfa.no; internet www.ud.dep.no; f. 1900; literature on foreign affairs, int. law and int. relations; not open to the public; Head Librarian RITA AARS-NICOLAYSEN.

Rjukan

Rjukan Bibliotek (Public Library of Rjukan): POB 93, 3661 Rjukan; Torget 1, 3660 Rjukan; tel. 35-08-25-60; fax 35-08-25-65; e-mail utlaan@rjukan.folkebibl.no; internet www.tinn.kommune.no; f. 1914; 3 brs; 120,000 vols; colln on history, philosophy and sociology of the working class; colln on local and regional history; Chief Librarian PER ESPELAND.

Stavanger

Stavanger Bibliotek (Stavanger Library): POB 310, 4002 Stavanger; Sølvberggt. 2, Stavanger; tel. 51-50-74-65; fax 51-50-70-25; e-mail biblioteket@stavanger-kulturhus.no; internet www.stavanger-kulturhus.no/stavanger_bibliotek; f. 1885; municipal library for the town of Stavanger, central library for the county of Rogaland; 500,000 vols; music and picture colln; Librarian KURT KRISTENSEN.

Tønsberg

Tønsberg og Nøtterøy Bibliotek (Tønsberg and Nøtterøy Public Library): Storgt. 16, 3126 Tønsberg; tel. 33-35-49-00; fax 33-35-49-69; e-mail tbg@tnb.no; internet www.tnb.no; f. 1909; 220,000 vols; Chief Librarian VIGDIS G. JAKOBSEN.

Trondheim

Universitetsbiblioteket i Trondheim (NTNU library): Høgskoleringen 1, 7491 Trondheim; tel. 73-59-51-10; fax 73-59-51-03; e-mail ubit@ub.ntnu.no; internet www.ntnu.no/ub; f. 1768; attached to Norges Teknisk-Naturvitenskapelige Universitet (NTNU); receives deposit copies of all Norwegian books; comprises 10 faculty libraries, incl. arts, social sciences, science, technology, architecture, medicine; nat. resource library for architecture and technology; 2,878,000 books and periodicals, 421,500 photographs, 84,500 electronic books, 32,500 maps, 19,500 MSS, 12,000 electronic journals; Dir LISBETH TANGEN.

Ulefoss

Telemark Fylkesbibliotek/Nome Folkebibliotek (Telemark/Nome County Library): Ringsevja 2, 3830 Ulefoss; tel. 35-94-89-20; fax 35-94-89-40; e-mail telfy@t-fk.no; internet www.tm.fylkesbibl.no; f. 1942; 150,000 vols, 200 periodicals; Librarian LILLIAN NILSSEN.

Museums and Art Galleries

Bergen

Bergen Museum, Universitetet i Bergen: POB 7800, 5020 Bergen; H. Hårfagresgt. 1, 5007 Bergen; tel. 55-58-93-60; fax 55-58-93-64; e-mail publikum@bm.uib.no; internet www.uib.no/bergenmuseum; f. 1825, part of University 1948; comprises two units, Cultural History Collns (Norwegian culture and folk art) and Natural History Collns (anthropology, archaeology, botany, geology and zoology); Dir SIRI JANSEN; publ. *Årbok for Bergen Museum* (Bergen Museum Yearbook).

Vestlandske Kunstindustrimuseum (West Norway Museum of Decorative Art): Nordahl Brungt. 9, 5014 Bergen; tel. 55-33-66-33; fax 55-33-66-30; e-mail permanenten@kunstmuseene.no; internet www.vk.museum

.no; f. 1887; 20,000 objects incl. Norwegian and European furniture, glass, porcelain, silver and textiles from the Renaissance to modern times; Gen. Munthe's colln of Chinese art; library of 20,000 vols; Dir JORUNN HAAKESTAD; Curators ANNE BRITT YLVISÅKER, TROND INDAHL.

Bodø

Norsk Luftfartsmuseum (National Norwegian Aviation Museum): POB 1124, 8001 Bodø; Olav V gt., Bodø; tel. 75-50-78-50; fax 75-50-78-51; e-mail flymuseum@luftfart.museum.no; internet www.luftfart.museum.no; f. 1998; depicts cultural and technical background of Norway's civil and military aviation history; Dir SVEN SCHEIDERBAUER.

Salten Museum: Prinsensgt. 116, 8005 Bodø; tel. 75-50-35-00; fax 75-52-58-05; e-mail post@saltenmuseum.no; internet www.saltenmuseum.no; f. 1888; covers most aspects of life in the county of Nordland; 80,000 items, specialities: fisheries, boats, etc.; 9 br. museums; library of 6,000 vols; Dir HARRY ELLINGSEN.

Drammen

Drammens Museum–Fylkesmuseum for Buskerud: Konnerudgt. 7, 3045 Drammen; tel. 32-20-09-30; e-mail post@drammens.museum.no; internet www.drammens.museum.no; f. 1908; merged with Drammen Art Society 1996; 50,000 artefacts of art and cultural history, incl. paintings, furniture, glass, ceramics; library of 16,000 vols; Dir ASMUND THORKILDSEN; publ. *Årbok* (Yearbook).

Fredrikstad

Fredrikstad Museum: Tøihusgt. 41, 1632 Fredrikstad; tel. 69-30-40-30; fax 69-95-85-01; e-mail fredrikstadmuseum@ostfoldmuseene.no; internet www.fredrikstad.kommune.no/museet; f. 1903; cultural and military history of the town and district; Curator TOVE M. THØGERSEN.

Hamar

Hedmarksmuseet: Strandvegen 100, 2315 Hamar; tel. 62-54-27-00; fax 62-54-27-13; e-mail post@domkirkeodden.no; internet www.hedmarksmuseet.no; f. 1906 as Opplandenes Folkemuseum; renamed Hedmarksmuseet og Domkirkeodden 1945, and subsequently as above; comprises 50,000 artefacts; colln of 2m. photographs; open-air museum and medieval colln; ruins of the medieval cathedral, bishop's palace (now housing a modern exhibition), and other medieval ruins; excavations in progress; farm buildings depicting local history and domestic life; library of 14,000 vols; Dir STEINAR BJERKESTRAND; Chief Curator BJØRN SVERRE HOL HAUGEN; publ. *Årbok Fra Kaupang og bygd*.

Attached Museums:

Kirsten Flagstad Museum: POB 1053, 2305 Hamar; Kirkegt. 11, 2305 Hamar; tel. 62-54-27-00; fax 62-54-27-13; e-mail post@kirsten-flagstad.no; internet www.kirsten-flagstad.no; f. 1985; dedicated to the life and work of opera singer Kirsten Flagstad (1895–1962), born in Hamar; Chair. RAGNHILD NYHUS.

Norsk Utvandrermuseum (Norwegian Emigrant Museum): Åkershagan, 2312 Ottestad; tel. 62-57-48-50; fax 62-57-48-51; e-mail admin@emigrantmuseum.no; internet www.emigrantmuseum.no; f. 1955; Chair. GEORG A. BROCH.

Lillehammer

Lillehammer Kunstmuseum (Lillehammer Art Museum): Stortorget 2, POB 264, 2602 Lillehammer; tel. 61-05-44-60; fax 61-25-19-44; e-mail post@lillehammerartmuseum.com; internet www.lillehammerartmuseum.com; f. 1927 as Lillehammer City Colln of Paintings; present name adopted 1994; contains collns of Norwegian paintings, sculpture and graphic art, historical and contemporary art exhibitions; Chair. GUNNAR K. HAGEN.

Sandvigske Samlinger på Maihaugen (Sandvig Collections, Maihaugen): Maihauvegen 1, 2609 Lillehammer; tel. 61-28-89-00; fax 61-26-95-93; e-mail post@maihaugen.no; internet www.maihaugen.no/maihaugen; f. 1887; open-air museum with 185 old houses of historical interest, and 30 old workshops in a new exhibition hall; exhibitions of Norwegian history and folk culture; library of 20,000 vols; Dir OLAV AARAAS; publ. *Årbok* (Yearbook).

Oslo

Astrup Fearnley Museet for Moderne Kunst (Astrup Fearnley Museum of Modern Art): POB 1158 Sentrum, 0107 Oslo; Dronningsgt. 4, Oslo; tel. 22-93-60-60; fax 22-93-60-65; e-mail info@fearnleys.no; internet afmuseet.no; f. 1993; Norwegian and int. contemporary art; Dir GUNNAR B. KVARAN.

Forsvarsmuseet (Armed Forces Museum): Oslo mil Akershus, 0015 Oslo; tel. 23-09-35-82; fax 23-09-31-90; e-mail fmu.kontakt@mil.no; internet www.fmu.mil.no; f. 1978; depicts technical and historical progress of the Norwegian military from Viking era to cold war years; library of 175,000 vols; Dir RUNAR GJERALD; Curator NINI FRITZNER; publs *Fosvarsmuseets Årbok*, *Forsvarsmuseets skrifter* (irregular).

Kon-Tiki Museet (Kon-Tiki Museum): Bygdøynesveien 36, 0286 Oslo; tel. 23-08-67-67; fax 23-08-67-60; e-mail kon-tiki@kon-tiki.no; internet www.kon-tiki.no; archaeology of Easter Island, eastern Polynesia, the Galapagos Islands and Peru; boats and artefacts from Thor Heyerdahl's expeditions; library of 12,000 vols; Dir MAJA BAUGE.

Munch Museum: POB 2823 Tøyen, 0608 Olso; Tøyengt. 53, 0578 Oslo; tel. 23-49-35-00; fax 23-49-35-01; e-mail info.munch@munch.museum.no; internet www.munch.museum.no; f. 1963; colln of 1,100 paintings, 4,700 drawings and 15,500 prints, bequeathed to the city of Oslo by Edvard Munch; library of 22,000 vols, incl. colln of Munch's private letters, notes and diaries, and Munch's private book colln; Dir STEIN OLAV HENRICHSEN.

Nasjonalmuseet for Kunst, Arkitektur og Design (National Museum of Art, Architecture and Design): POB 7014, St. Olavs plass, 0130 Oslo; Kristian Augusts gt. 23, Oslo; tel. 21-98-20-00; fax 21-98-20-93; e-mail info@nasjonalmuseet.no; internet www.nasjonalmuseet.no; f. 2003 by merger of the Norwegian Museum of Architecture, the Museum of Decorative Arts and Design, the Museum of Contemporary Art and the Nat. Gallery; library of 30,000 vols; Dir AUDUN ECKHOFF.

Naturhistorisk museum, Universitetet i Oslo (Natural History Museum, University of Oslo): POB 1172 Blindern, 0318 Oslo; tel. 22-85-16-30; fax 22-85-17-09; e-mail informasjon@nhm.uio.no; internet www.nhm.uio.no; houses 7.4m. artefacts (c. 65% of the total natural history collns nationwide); Dir Prof. ARNE BJØRLYKKE.

Constituent Museums:

Botanisk hage og Botanisk museum (Botanical Garden and Botanical Museum): POB 1172 Blindern, 0318 Oslo; Sarsgt. 1, 0562 Oslo; tel. 22-85-17-00; fax 22-85-18-35; e-mail informasjon@nhm.uio.no; internet www.nhm.uio.no/om-museet/museets-bygninger/botanisk-museum; f. 1814 (garden), 1863 (museum); attached to Universitetet i Oslo; taxonomy and plant ecology; museum not open to the general public; library of 45,000 vols; publ. *Sommerfeltia* (irregular).

Geologisk museum (Geological Museum): POB 1172 Blindern, 0318 Oslo; Sarsgt. 1, 0562 Oslo; tel. 22-85-17-00; fax 22-85-17-09; e-mail informasjon@nhm.uio.no; internet www.nhm.uio.no/om-museet/museets-bygninger/geologisk-museum; f. 1920; attached to Universitetet i Oslo; rocks, minerals and fossils; research laboratories in mineralogy, petrology, geochemistry and palaeontology; library of 75,000 vols.

Zoologisk museum (Zoological Museum): POB 1172 Blindern, 0318 Oslo; Sarsgt. 1, 0562 Oslo; tel. 22-85-17-00; fax 22-85-18-37; e-mail informasjon@nhm.uio.no; internet www.nhm.uio.no/om-museet/museets-bygninger/zoologisk-museum; f. 1910; attached to Universitetet i Oslo; public exhibitions of Norwegian and world fauna; Norwegian vertebrates and invertebrates, Arctic, Antarctic and exotic, particularly Australian, research collns; library of 28,000 vols, 53,000 pamphlets.

Norsk Folkemuseum (Norwegian Museum of Cultural History): POB 720 Skøyen, 0214 Oslo; Museumsveien 10, Bygdøy, Oslo; tel. 22-12-37-00; fax 22-12-37-77; e-mail post@norskfolkemuseum.no; internet www.norskfolkemuseum.no; f. 1894; consists of indoor and open-air sections comprising 230,000 objects; spec. exhibits in the indoor section incl. rural culture (incl. display of folk dresses and folk art), church history, toys, Sámi (Lapp) colln; open-air museum consists of: 155 old bldgs (incl. 13th-century Gol stave church and four other medieval bldgs), examples of different farms from most of Norway, urban structures arranged as an old town quarter, museum shop, artisans; library of 45,000 vols; Dir OLAV AARAAS; Librarian ALEXANDER LINDBÄCK.

Norsk Maritimt Museum (Norwegian Maritime Museum): Bygdøynesvn. 37, 0286 Oslo; tel. 24-11-41-50; fax 24-11-41-51; e-mail fellespost@marmuseum.no; internet www.marmuseum.no; f. 1914; museum opened 1974; Norwegian maritime history and coastal culture; colln of ship portraits, maritime paintings, models, instruments, historic ships (Amundsen's 'Gjøa' and traditional small craft), full-size original ship interiors; library of 30,000 vols, archives of photographs and plans, MSS, maps, occasional papers, research reports; Dir PER G. NORSENG; Asst Dir EYVIND BAGLE; publs *Årbok* (Yearbook), *Norsk Maritimt Museum. Skrifter* (series, irregular).

Norsk Teknisk Museum (Norwegian Museum of Science and Technology): Kjelsåsveien 143, 0491 Oslo; tel. 22-79-60-00; internet www.tekniskmuseum.no; f. 1914; library of 40,000 vols; Man. Dir HANS WEINBERGER; publ. *Yearbook*.

Riksantikvaren (Directorate for Cultural Heritage): Dronningensgt. 13, POB 8196 Dep., 0034 Oslo; tel. 22-94-04-00; fax 22-94-04-04; e-mail postmottak@ra.no; internet www.riksantikvaren.no; f. 1912; directorate responsible for nat. monuments and sites, medieval bldgs; archives; library of 60,000 vols, 700,000 photographs; special collns incl. Norwegian churches, restoration and conservation of paintings and sculptures; Dir-Gen. JØRN HOLME; publs *La stå!* (Let Stand!, 2 a year), *Arringer* (Tree Rings, 1 a year).

Kulturhistorisk Museum (Museum of Cultural Heritage): POB 6762 St Olavs plass,

0130 Oslo; Frederiksgt. 2, 0164 Oslo (Historical Museum); Huk Aveny 35, 0287 Oslo (Viking Ship Museum); tel. 22-85-19-00; fax 22-85-19-38; e-mail postmottak@khm.uio.no; internet www.khm.uio.no; f. 1999; attached to Universitetet i Oslo; exhibits from prehistoric and Viking times, incl. Viking ships (at Bygdøy), and the Middle Ages, Norwegian coins, collns from Africa, South America, North America, East Asia and the Arctic; collns incl. 1,647,592 artefacts pertaining to cultural history, 4,504 art history works, 558,000 photographs; library of 70,000 vols; Dir Prof. Dr EGIL MIKKELSEN; publs *KHM skrifter* (1 a year), *Norske Oldfunn* (Norwegian Archaeological Finds, irregular), *Nytt om runer* (Rune News, 1 a year), *Varia* (irregular).

Vigeland-museet: Nobelsgt. 32, 0268 Oslo; tel. 23-49-37-00; fax 23-49-37-01; e-mail postmottak.vigeland@vigeland.museum.no; internet www.vigeland.museum.no; f. 1947; life and work of sculptor Gustav Vigeland; colln comprises 1,600 sculptures, 12,000 drawings and 400 woodcarvings; museum closed to public between Aug. 2010 and May 2011 owing to major renovation work; Dir JARLE STRØMODDEN; Curator GURI SKUGGEN; Curator TRINE OTTE BAK NIELSEN.

Sandefjord

Kommandør Chr. Christensens Hvalfangstmuseum (Commdr Chr. Christensen's Whaling Museum): POB 396, 3201 Sandefjord; Museumsgt. 39, 3210 Sandefjord; tel. 33-48-46-50; fax 33-46-37-84; e-mail museene@sandefjord.kommune.no; internet www.hvalfangstmuseet.no; f. 1917; shows the devt of whaling from primitive to modern times; geography, ethnology, zoology, maritime history, etc.; incl. photograph colln comprising some 150,000 images; Dir DAG INGEMAR BØRRESEN.

Skien

Telemark Museum: Øvregt. 41, 3715 Skien; tel. 35-54-45-00; fax 35-52-01-59; e-mail post@telemark.museum.no; internet telemarkmuseum.no; f. 1909 as Fylkesmuseet for Telemark og Grenland (County Museum of Telemark and Grenland); present name adopted 1998; conservation and research on items of historical interest from the Telemark region; situated in Brekkeparken, with open-air museum (log houses dating from the Middle Ages) and a manor house furnished in 17th-, 18th- and 19th-century styles; collns on folk art, handicrafts, navigation, church art, Ibsen Colln and Ibsen's childhood home, Venstøp Farm; library of 6,000 vols; Dir LENE E. WALLE.

Stavanger

Arkeologisk Museum i Stavanger (Museum of Archaeology, Stavanger): POB 478, 4002 Stavanger; Peder Klowsgt 30A, Stavanger; tel. 51-84-60-00; fax 51-84-61-99; e-mail ams@ark.museum.no; internet www.ark.museum.no; f. 1975; own library, scientific archive; Dir ARNE JOHAN NERØY (acting); publ. *Frá haug ok heiðni* (scientific magazine, 4 a year).

Museum Stavanger (MUST): Muségt. 16, 4010 Stavanger; tel. 51-84-27-00; fax 51-84-27-01; e-mail post@stavanger.museum.no; internet www.stavanger.museum.no; f. 1877 as Stavanger Museum; present name adopted 2010, following merger with Rogaland Art Museum; urban and rural culture, zoology, ornithology; a maritime museum, a canning museum, a medical museum, a children's museum, a printing museum and the mansions of Ledaal and Breidablikk are in the museum's care; library of 65,000 vols; Man. Dir GRO PERSSON.

Tromsø

Tromsø Museum (Universitetetsmuseet): Lars Thøringsvei 10, 9037 Tromsø; tel. 77-64-50-00; fax 77-64-55-20; e-mail museumspost@uit.no; internet uit.no/tmu; f. 1872; attached to Universitetet i Tromsø; 6 sections: Archaeology, Botany, Cultural History, Geology, Sami Ethnography, Zoology; library of 180,000 vols; Dir MARIT ANNE HAUAN; publs *Ottar* (5 a year, in Norwegian), *Skrifter* (irregular, in Norwegian), *Tromura* (scientific reports, irregular, in Norwegian), *Way North* (irregular, in English).

Trondheim

Nordenfjeldske Kunstindustrimuseum (National Museum of Decorative Arts): Munkegt. 5, 7013 Trondheim; tel. 73-80-89-50; fax 73-80-89-51; e-mail post@nkim.museum.no; internet www.nkim.no; f. 1893; depts of furniture, textiles, glass, ceramics, metalwork from the 14th century onwards; special colln of Japanese art and textiles; Dir JAN-LAURITZ OPSTAD.

NTNU Vitenskapsmuseet (Museum of Natural History and Archaeology, of the Norwegian University of Science and Technology): 7491 Trondheim; Erling Skakkes gt. 47A, Trondheim; tel. 73-59-21-45; fax 73-59-22-23; e-mail post@vm.ntnu.no; internet www.ntnu.no/vitenskapsmuseet; f. 1760; graduate and research instn of the univ.; archaeological, botanical and zoological depts; mineralogical and numismatic collns; marine station; schools service; Dir Prof. AXEL CHRISTOPHERSEN; publs *Fauna norvegica* (peer-reviewed journal, 1 a year, in English), *Gunneria* (original works in archaeology, cultural history, botany and zoology, irregular, in English and Norwegian), *Vitark—Acta Archaelogica Nidrosiensi* (Norwegian and Nordic research and insight into archaeological problems, irregular, in English and Norwegian).

Universities

NORGES TEKNISK-NATURVITENSKAPELIGE UNIVERSITET (NTNU) (Norwegian University of Science and Technology)

7491 Trondheim
Telephone: 73-59-50-00
Fax: 73-59-53-10
E-mail: postmottak@adm.ntnu.no
Internet: www.ntnu.no

Founded 1996 to replace the Univ. of Trondheim (which included the Norwegian Institute of Technology, the College of Arts and Science and the Museum of Natural History and Archaeology)

Academic year: August to June

Chair.: MARIT ARNSTAD
Rector: TORBJØRN DIGERNES
Pro-Rector for Education and Quality of Learning: BERIT KJELDSTAD
Pro-Rector for Research: KARI MELBY
Pro-Rector for External Relations and Innovation: JOHAN E. HUSTAD
Dir for Finance and Property: FRANK ARNTSEN
Dir for Organization and Information: TROND SINGSAAS

Number of teachers: 2,800
Number of students: 20,000

Publications: *Gemini* (irregular), *Spor* (2 a year)

DEANS

Faculty of Architecture and Fine Art: TORE I. HAUGEN
Faculty of Engineering Science and Technology: INGVALD STRØMMEN
Faculty of Humanities: KATHRINE SKRETTING
Faculty of Information Technology, Mathematics and Electrical Engineering: GEIR ØIEN
Faculty of Medicine: STIG A. SLØRDAHL
Faculty of Natural Sciences and Technology: BJØRN HAFSKJOLD
Faculty of Social Sciences and Technology Management: JAN MORTEN DYRSTAD

PROFESSORS

Faculty of Architecture and Fine Art (tel. 73-55-02-75; e-mail fak-adm@ab.ntnu.no; internet www.ntnu.no/ab):

BERGAUST, K., Fine Art
BJØNNESS, H. C., Urban Design and Planning
BLEIKLIE, S., Architectural Design and Management
BOOKER, C. A., Architectural Design, Form and Colour Studies
BRAND, P., Architectural Design, Form and Colour Studies
FISKAA, H., Urban Design and Planning
FURUNES, A.-K., Fine Art
GAMDRUP, M., Fine Art
GRYTLI, E. R., Architectural Design, History and Technology
GUSTAVSEN, A., Architectural Design, History and Technology
HESTNES, A. G., Architectural Design, History and Technology
HØYEM, H., Architectural Design, History and Technology
JAUKKURI, M. H., Fine Art
LARSEN, K., Architectural Design and Management
LARSEN, K. E., Architectural Design, History and Technology
LUND, F., Architectural Design, Form and Colour Studies
MATUSIAK, B., Architectural Design, Form and Colour Studies
MEDALEN, T., Urban Design and Planning
RØE, B., Urban Design and Planning
SAMBOLEC, D., Fine Art
SHETELIG, C. F. L., Architectural Design and Management
SIEM, J. H., Architectural Design, History and Technology
STEEN, O., Architectural Design and Management
STØA, E., Architectural Design and Management
SVENDSEN, S. E., Architectural Design and Management

Faculty of Engineering Science and Technology (tel. 73-59-45-01; fax 73-59-47-90; e-mail postmottak@ivt.ntnu.no; internet www.ivt.ntnu.no):

AMDAHL, J., Marine Structures
ANDERSEN, B., Production and Quality Engineering
ANDERSSON, H. I., Fluids Engineering
ASHEIM, H. A., Petroleum Engineering, Production
BAKKEN, L. E., Thermal Engineering
BARDAL, E., Machine Design and Materials Technology
BELL, K., Structural Engineering, Structural Mechanics
BERGE, S., Marine Structures
BOLLAND, O., Thermal Engineering
BRATTEBØ, H., Environmental Engineering
BRATTELAND, E., Marine Technology
BRATTLI, B., Engineering Geology
BREDESEN, A. M., Refrigeration Engineering
BREVIK, I. H., Fluids Engineering
BROCH, E., Engineering Geology

BRULAND, A., Project Management and Construction Engineering
DIGERNES, T., Marine Systems Design
EIKEVIK, T. M., Food Engineering in the Marine Sector
ENDAL, A., Marine Systems Design
ERTESVÅG, I. S., Thermal Energy
FALTINSEN, O. M., Marine Hydrodynamics
FIKSDAL, L., Urban Water Systems
FJELDAAS, S., Machine Design
GJØRV, O. E., Structural Engineering, Concrete
GOLAN, M., Petroleum Engineering, Production
GRANDE, L. O., Marine Geotechnical Engineering
GUDMUNDSSON, J. S., Petroleum Engineering Production
GUNDERSEN, T., Process, Energy and Systems Engineering
GUSTAFSON, C.-G., Materials and Processes, Materials Technology
HAAGENSEN, P. J., Structural Engineering, Steel and Light Metal
HAAVALDSEN, T., Bldg Technologies
HALMØY, E., Materials and Processes, Materials Technology
HANSSEN, S. O., Heating, Ventilation and Sanitary Engineering
HÅRKEGÅRD, G., Machine Design and Materials Technology
HERTWICH, E., Thermal Energy
HOLM, K. R., Geomatics
HOLT, R. M., Petroleum Engineering, Drilling Technology
HOLTHE, K. H., Structural Engineering, Structural Mechanics
HØISETH, K. V., Structural Engineering, Concrete
HOPPERSTAD, O. S., Structural Engineering, Steel and Light Metal
HORVLI, I., Highway Engineering
HOVD, A., Highway Engineering
HOVDE, P. J., Bldg Technologies
HUSTAD, J. E., Thermal Energy
IRGENS, F., Structural Engineering, Structural Mechanics
JELMERT, T. A., Petroleum Engineering, Reservoir Technology
JOHANNESSEN, S., Transport Engineering
JOHNSEN, R., Corrosion and Surface Technology
KANSTAD, T., Structural Engineering, Concrete
KILLINGTVEIT, Å., Engineering Hydrology
KLEPPE, J., Petroleum Engineering, Reservoir Technology
KOCH, W. H., Production and Quality Engineering
KRAMMER, G., Environmental Engineering
KRILL, A., Geology
KRISTIANSEN, S., Marine Systems Design
KROGSTAD, P.-Å., Fluids Engineering
LANDRØ, M., Applied Geophysics
LANGSETH, M., Structural Engineering, Sheet and Light Metal
LARSEN, C. M., Marine Structures
LARSEN, P. K., Structural Engineering, Sheet and Light Metal
LEIRA, B. J., Marine Structures
LI, C., Mining Engineering
LIEN, T. K., Production and Quality Engineering
LILE, O. B., Petroleum Engineering, Applied Geophysics
LIPPARD, S. J., Petroleum Geology
LØSET, S., Arctic Technology
MAGNUSSEN, O. M., Industrial Fish Processing
MALO, K. A., Structural Engineering, Sheet and Light Metal
MALVIK, T., Resources Geology
MATHISEN, K. M., Structural Engineering, Structural Mechanics
MIDTBØ, T., Geomatics
MINSAAS, K. J., Marine Hydrodynamics
MOAN, T., Marine Structures
MOE, G., Port and Ocean Engineering
MYRAN, T., Engineering Geology
MYRHAUG, D., Marine Hydrodynamics
NIELSEN, K. O., Mining Engineering
NIELSEN, T. K., Fluids Engineering
NILSEN, B., Engineering Geology
NORDAL, S., Geotechnical Engineering
NOREM, H. A., Transport Engineering
NOVAKOVIC, V., Heating, Ventilation and Sanitary Engineering
NYDAL, O. J., Indoor Environmental Engineering
NÆSS, A., Marine Technology
NØRSTRUD, H., Fluids Engineering
OKSMAN, K., Materials and Processes
PETTERSEN, B., Marine Hydrodynamics
PRESTVIK, T., Geology, Petrology
RASCH, F. O., Production and Quality Engineering
RASMUSSEN, M., Marine Engineering
RAUSAND, M., Production and Quality Engineering
REMSETH, S. N., Structural Engineering, Structural Mechanics
ROALD, S., Project Management and Construction Engineering
ROKOENGEN, K., Engineering Geology
ROLSTADÅS, A., Production and Quality Engineering
RØDLAND, A., Petroleum Engineering (Drilling Technology)
RØLVÅG, T., Computer-aided Engineering
SAGER, T. Ø., Transport Engineering
SAMSET, K. F., Project Management and Construction Engineering
SANDVIK, K. L., Mineral Dressing
SANGESLAND, S., Petroleum Engineering (Drilling Technology)
SCHILLING, W., Urban Water Systems
SELLEVOLD, E. J., Structural Engineering, Concrete
SINDING-LARSEN, R., Resources Geology
SIVERTSEN, O. I., Machine Design
SKALLERUD, B. H., Structural Engineering, Structural Mechanics
STEEN, S., Marine Technology and Experience Hydrodynamics
STRØMMEN, E. N., Structural Engineering, Structural Mechanics
STRØMMEN, I., Refrigeration Engineering
STØLE, H., Hydro Power Devt
STØREN, S., Materials and Processes, Materials Technology
SYVERTSEN, T. G., Structural Engineering, Structural Mechanics
SÆTRAN, L. R., Fluids Engineering
SØNJU, O. K., Thermal Energy
SØRENSEN, A. J., Marine Hydrodynamics
SØRENSEN, S. I., Structural Engineering, Concrete
THAULOW, C., Materials Processes, Materials Technology
THUE, J. V., Building Technology
TJELFLAAT, P. O., Indoor Environmental Engineering
TORSÆTER, O., Petroleum Engineering, Reservoir Technology
TØNDER, K., Machine Design, Materials Technology
URSIN, B., Petroleum Engineering, Seismatics
VALBERG, H. S., Materials and Processes, Materials Technology
VALLAND, H., Marine Engineering
VATN, J., Production and Quality Engineering
VENNESLAND, Ø., Structural Engineering, Concrete
WANG, K., Production and Quality Engineering
WESTBY, O., Marine System Design
WHITE, M. F., Marine Engineering
WHITSON, C. H., Petroleum Engineering, Reservoir Technology
YTREHUS, T., Fluids Engineering
ZHANG, Z., Solid State Mechanics
ØDEGAARD, H., Environmental Engineering, Urban Water Systems

Faculty of Humanities (tel. 73-59-65-95; fax 73-59-10-30; e-mail postmottak@hf.ntnu.no; internet www.ntnu.no/hf):

AARSET, H. E., Literature
AASLESTAD, P., Scandinavian Studies and Comparative Literature
ÅFARLI, T. A., Scandinavian Studies and Comparative Literature
ALTERHAUG, B., Musicology
ANDERSEN, H. W., History
BAKKA, E., Musicology
BENDER JØRGENSEN, L., Archaeology
BERGMANN, S., Religious Studies
BORGERSEN, T., Media Studies
BULL, I, History
DAHL, S. L., History
DOMMELEN, W. A. VAN, Linguistics
DYBVIG, M., Philosophy
ELIASSEN, K. O., Literature
EVENSEN, L. S., Applied Linguistics
FAUSKEVÅG, S. E., Romance Literature
FEIGS, W. G., Germanic Languages
FINDAL, W., History of Art
FINKE, S., Philosophy
FISKUM, B., Musicology
FOSS, G., General Literature
FRETHEIM, T., Literature
GIMNES, S., Scandinavian Literature
HAGLAND, J. R., Scandinavian Literature and Comparative Literature
HALVORSEN, A., Romance Studies
HANKELN, R., Medieval Music
HAUG, A., Medieval Studies
HAWTHORN, J., English Literature
HELLAN, L., Applied Linguistics
HERNÆS, P. O., History
HETLAND, J., Germanic Languages
IMSEN, S., History
IVERSEN, G., Film Studies
JASINSKI, M. E., Maritime Architecture
JONSSON, L. S., Musicology
KALDAL, I., History
KNOWLES, J., Philosophy
LEDANG, O. K., Musicology
LIE, M., Social Anthropology
LIE, S., Literature
MÆHLUM, B. K., Norwegian Language
MELBY, K., History, Women's Research
MITCHELL, D., English Literature
MOLANDER, B., Philosophy
NEUMANN, B. O., German Literature
NILSEN, H. N., Literature
NORDGÅRD, T., Linguistics
NYLANDER, L., Literature
ØFSTI, A., Philosophy
ØSTBY, P., History of Technology
ØSTERUD, E., Literature
PETERI, G. G., History
RASMUSSEN, B., Drama and Theatre
RISE, H., Church Music
SAWYER, B., History
SHERRY, R. G., English
SIMENSEN, J., History
SKRETTING, K., Media Studies
SØRENSEN, K. H., History of Technology
SØRENSSEN, B., Film Studies
STUGU, O. S., History
SUPPHELLEN, S., History
TVINNEREIM, H. S., History of Art
ULRICHSEN, J. H., Religious Studies
VIDEN, G., History
VULCHANOVA, M. D., English Language
WYLLER, T., Philosophy

Faculty of Information Technology, Mathematics and Electrical Engineering (tel. 73-59-42-02; fax 73-59-36-28; e-mail postmottak@ime.ntnu.no; internet www.ime.ntnu.no):

AAGESEN, F. A., Telematics
AAMODT, A., Artificial Intelligence
AARNES, J. F., Mathematics
AAS, E. J., Physical Electronics

ANDRESEN, S. H., Telematics
BAAS, N. A., Mathematics
BLAKE, R., Image Processing
BRATSBERG, S. E., Database Systems
BRATBERGSENGEN, K., Database Systems
BRÆK, R., Telematics
CONRADI, R., Software Engineering
DIGERNES, T., Mathematics
DIVITINI, M., Software Engineering
DO, V. T., Telematics
DONG, H., Telecommunications
DOWNING, K., Artificial Intelligence
EGELAND, O., Engineering Cybernetics
EMSTAD, P. J., Telematics
ENGAN, H. E., Physical Electronics
ENGEN, S., Mathematical Statistics
FAANES, H. H., Electrical Power Engineering
FIMLAND, B.-O., Physical Electronics
FJELDLY, T. A., Physical Electronics
FORSSELL, B., Telecommunications
FOSS, B. A., Engineering Cybernetics
FOSSEN, T. I., Engineering Cybernetics
FOSSO, O. B., Electrical Power Engineering
GREPSTAD, J., Physical Electronics
GULLA, F. A., Database Systems
GUTTEBERG, O., Satellite Communications
HAG, K., Mathematics
HALAAS, A., Algorithm Theory and Construction
HELVIK, B. E., Telematics
HENRIKSEN, R., Engineering Cybernetics
HOLDEN, H., Mathematics
HOLEN, A. T., Electrical Power Engineering
HOLTE, N., Telecommunications
HOVD, M., Engineering Cybernetics
HOVEM, J. M., Telecommunications
HUGHES, P., Database Systems
HVASSHOVD, S.-O., Database Systems
ILSTAD, E., Electric Power Engineering
JACCHERI, M. L., Software Engineering
JOHANSEN, T. A., Engineering Cybernetics
KNAPSKOG, S. J., Telematics
KRISTIANSEN, L., Telematics
KRISTIANSEN, U. R., Telecommunications
KROGSTAD, H. E., Mathematics
KURE, Ø., Telematics
LANDSTAD, M. B., Mathematics
LINDQUIST, B. H., Mathematical Statistics
LINDQVIST, L. P., Mathematics
LORENTZEN, L., Mathematics
LYUBARSKII, Y., Mathematics
MALVIG, K. E., Engineering Cybernetics
MJØLSNES, S. F., Telematics
MONTEIRO, E., Human–Computer Interaction
MÜLLER, R. R., Wireless Networks
NATVIG, L., Computer Architecture and Design
NILSEN, R., Electrical Power Engineering
NILSSEN, R., Electrical Power Engineering
NORUM, L. E., Electrical Power Engineering
NYGÅRD, M., Database Systems
NYSVEEN, A., Electrical Power Engineering
NÆSS, A., Mathematical Statistics
NØRSETT, S. P., Mathematics
OMRE, K. H., Mathematical Statistics
ONSHUS, T. E., Engineering Cybernetics
OWREN, B., Mathematics
PERKIS, A., Digital Image Processing
PETTERSEN, K. Y., Engineering Cybernetics
PETTERSEN, O., Engineering Cybernetics
RAMSTAD, T. A., Telecommunications
REITEN, I., Mathematics
ROUDAKOV, A., Mathematics
RUE, H., Mathematical Statistics
RØNNEKLEIV, A., Physical Electronics
RØNNINGEN, L. A., Telematics
RØNQVIST, E., Mathematics
SEIP, K., Mathematics
SINDRE, G., Information Systems
SKAAR, J., Photonics
SKAU, C. F., Mathematics
SKRAMSTAD, T., Human–Computer Interaction
SMALØ, S. O., Mathematics
SOLBERG, Ø., Mathematics
STRAUME, E., Mathematics
STÅLHANE, T., Software Engineering
SVENDSEN, T., Telecommunications
SVENSSON, P., Telecommunications
SVAASAND, L. O., Physical Electronics
SÆTHER, T., Physical Electronics
SØLVBERG, A., Information Systems
SØLVBERG, I., Information Management
UNDELAND, T. M., Electrical Power Engineering
WANGENSTEEN, I., Electrical Power Engineering
YTTERDAL, T., Physical Communications
ØIEN, G. E., Telecommunications

Faculty of Medicine (tel. 73-59-88-59; fax 73-59-88-65; e-mail dmf-post@medisin.ntnu.no; internet www.medisin.ntnu.no):

AADAHL, P., Anaesthesiology
ANGELSEN, B. A. J., Biomedical Engineering
AUSTGULEN, R., Cancer Research and Molecular Medicine
BACKE, B., Laboratory Medicine, Children's and Women's Health
BASSØE, C. F., Neuroscience
BENTZEN, N., Public Health and General Practice
BERGH, K., Laboratory Medicine, Children's and Women's Health
BOVIM, G., Neurology
BRATLID, D., Laboratory Medicine, Children's and Women's Health
BRUBAKK, A.-M., Laboratory Medicine, Children's and Women's Health
BRUBAKK, A. O., Physiology
CHEN, D., Cancer Research and Molecular Medicine
CLIFFORD, G., Child Psychiatry
DALE, O., Anaesthesiological Pharmacology
DRABLØS, F., Cancer Research and Molecular Medicine
ELLINGSEN, Ø., Physiology
ESPEVIK, T., Cancer Research and Molecular Medicine
FARUP, P. G., Applied Clinical Research
FINSEN, V., Neuroscience
GRILL, V., Cancer Research and Molecular Medicine
GRIMSMO, A., Public Health and General Practice
GRØNBECK, J. E., Surgery Gastroenterology
GØTESTAM, K. G., Neuroscience
HARALDSETH, O., MR/Radiology
HAUGEN, O. A., Morphology
HELGERUD, J., Sports Physiology
HOLMEN, J., Nord-Trøndelag Health Study
IVERSEN, O.-J., Laboratory Medicine, Children's and Women's Health
JACOBSEN, G., Public Health and General Practice
JOHNSEN, R., Public Health and General Practice
JYNGE, P., Physiology
KAASA, S., Cancer Research and Molecular MedicineKLEPP, O., Oncology
KLUNGLAND, H., Laboratory Medicine, Children's and Women's Health
KROKAN, H. E., Cancer Research and Molecular Medicine
LAMVIK, J., Cancer Research and Molecular Biology
LARSSON, B. S., Child Psychiatry
LEIVSETH, G., Neuroscience
LYDERSEN, S., Cancer Research and Molecular Medicine
LÆGREID, A., Microarray
LØVIK, M., Public Health
MIDELFART, A., Neuroscience
MOSER, M.-B., Neuroscience
NILSEN, O. G., Cancer Research and Molecular Medicine
OTTERLEI, M., Cancer Research and Molecular Medicine
PETERSEN, H., Public Health and General Practice
RYGNESTAD, T., Laboratory Medicine
RØNNINGEN, H., Neuroscience
SAND, T., Neurology
SANDVIK, A. K., Cancer Research and Molecular Medicine
SCHEI, B., Public Health and General Practice
SKORPEN, F., Nord-Trøndelag Health Study
SLUPPHAUG, G., Cancer Research and Molecular Medicine
SLØRDAHL, S. A., Physiology
SLØRDAL, L., Laboratory Medicine, Children's and Women's Health
SONNEWALD, U., Neuroscience
STOVNER, L. J., Neuroscience
SUNDAN, A., Cancer Research and Molecular Medicine
SVEBAK, S., Neuroscience
SYVERSEN, T., Neuroscience
SYVERSEN, U., Cancer Research and Molecular Medicine
TORP, H., Biomedical Engineering
VATTEN, L. J., Public Health and General Practice
VIDEM, V., Laboratory Medicine, Children's and Women's Health
VIK, T., Public Health and General Practice
WAAGE, A., Haematology
WALDUM, H., Cancer Research and Molecular Medicine
WESTIN, S., Public Health and General Practice
WIBE, A., Cancer Research and Molecular Medicine
WIDERØE, T.-E., Nephrology
WITTER, M., Neuroscience

Faculty of Natural Sciences and Technology (tel. 73-59-41-97; fax 73-59-14-10; e-mail postmottak@nt.ntnu.no; internet www.ntnu.no/nt):

ALSBERG, B. K., Physical Chemistry
AMUNDSEN, T., Etology
ANDERSEN, R., Terrestrial Ecology
ANDERSEN, R., Zoo Physiology
ANTHONSEN, T., Organic Chemistry
ARMBRUSTER, W. S., Evolution, Ecology
ÅRNBERG, L., Process Metallurgy
ÅSTRAND, P. O., Physical Chemistry
BAKKE, J. M., Organic Chemistry
BAKKEN, J. A., Process Metallurgy
BECH, C., Zoology
BERG, O. K., Freshwater Ecology
BLEKKAN, E. A., Chemical Engineering, Catalysis and Petrochemistry
BONES, A., Cell and Molecular Biology
BORG, A., Surface Physics
BRATAAS, A., Theoretical Physics
CARLSEN, P. H., Organic Chemistry
CHEN, D., Chemical Engineering, Catalysis and Petrochemistry
CHRISTENSEN, B. E., Biopolymer Chemistry
DAVIES, C., Biophysics and Medical Technology
EINARSRUD, M.-A., Inorganic Chemistry
ELGSÆTER, A., Biological Physics
ENGH, T. A., Metallurgy
FIKSDAHL, A., Organic Chemistry
FOOSNÆS, T., Inorganic Chemistry
FOSSHEIM, K., Material Physics
FOSSUM, J. O., Condensed-Matter Physics
GRANDE, T., Inorganic Chemistry
GREGERSEN, Ø. W., Chemical Engineering, Pulp and Paper Technology
GRONG, Ø., Process Metallurgy
HAARBERG, G. M., Electrochemistry
HAFSKJOLD, B., Physical Chemistry
HAGEN, K., Physical Chemistry
HANSEN, A., Theoretical Physics
HERTZBERG, T., Chemical Engineering, Process Systems Engineering
HOGSTAD, O., Zoology

HOLMEN, A., Chemical Engineering, Catalysis and Petrochemistry
HOLMESTAD, R., Material Physics
HUNDERI, O., Surface Physics
HYTTERBORN, H., Plant Ecology
HÆGG, M.-B., Chemical Engineering, Separation Technology
HØYE, J. S., Theoretical Physics
IVERSEN, T.-H., Cell Biology
JAKOBSEN, H. A., Chemical Engineering, Reactor Technology
JENSSEN, B. M., Ecotoxicology
JOHANSEN, B., Cell and Molecular Biology
JOHNSSON, A., Biophysics and Medical Technology
KJELSTAD, B. J., Ultraviolet Radiation
KJELSTRUP, S., Physical Chemistry, Thermodynamics
KOCH, H., Physical Chemistry
KOLBEINSEN, L., Process Metallurgy
KOLBENSTVEDT, H., Theoretical Physics
LANGELAND, A. L., Freshwater Ecology
LEVINE, D. W., Biochemical Engineering
LINDGREN, M., Experimental Optics
LINDMO, T., Biophysics and Medical Technology
LJONES, T., Biophysical Chemistry
LOHNE, O., Physical Metallurgy
LØKBERG, O. J., Applied Optics
MARTHINSEN, K., Physical Metallurgy
MELØ, T. B., Biophysics and Medical Technology
MIKKELSEN, A., Biophysics and Medical Technology
MO, F., Crystallography
MOKSNES, A., Terrestrial Ecology
MORK, K. J., Theoretical Physics
MUSTAPARTA, H., Neurophysiology
MYRHEIM, J., Anyons
MØRK, P., Chemical Engineering, Polymer and Colloid Chemistry
NAQVI, K. R., Biophysics and Medical Technology
NES, E.-A., Physical Metallurgy
NESSE, N., Chemical Engineering, Separation Technology
NICHOLSON, D. G., Materials Science
NILSSEN, K. J., Zoophysiology, Aquaculture
NISANCIOGLU, K., Electrochemistry
OLAUSSEN, K., Anyons
OLSEN, Y., Marine Biology
ØSTGAARD, K., Environmental Biotechnology
ØSTVOLD, T., Inorganic Chemistry
ØYE, H. A., Inorganic Chemistry
PREISIG, H., Chemical Engineering, Process Systems Engineering
REINERTSEN, H., Aquaculture, Marine Biology
ROSENQVIST, G., Etology
ROVEN, H. J., Physical Metallurgy
RYUM, N., Physical Metallurgy
RØSKRAFT, E., Evolutionary Biology
RAAEN, S., Experimental Condensed Matter Physics
SAKSHAUG, E., Marine Biology
SAMUELSEN, E. J., Material Physics
SCHRØDER, K. H., Analytical Chemistry
SJØBLOM, J., Chemical Engineering, Polymer and Colloid Chemistry
SKAGERSTAM, B.-S., Theoretical Physics
SKJÅK-BRÆK, G., Biotechnology, Biopolymer Chemistry
SKOGESTAD, S., Chemical Engineering, Process Systems Engineering
SKULLERUD, H., Electron and Ion Physics
SMIDSRØD, O., Biotechnology, Biopolymer Chemistry
SOLBERG, J. K., Physical Metallurgy
STEINNES, E., Environmental Technology
STOKKE, B. T., Biophysics and Medical Technology
STRØM, A. R., Biotechnology, Molecular Genetics
STØLEVIK, R. E., Physical Chemistry
SUDBØ, A., Theoretical Physics
SUNDE, S., Hydrogen Technology
SVENDSEN, H. F., Chemical Engineering, Reactor Technology
SÆTHER, B.-E., Terrestrial Ecology
TANGSTAD, M., Process Metallurgy
TUNOLD, R., Electrochemistry
VADSTEIN, O., Biotechnology
VALBERG, A., Biophysics and Medical Technology
VALLA, S., Biotechnology, Molecular Genetics
VÅRUM, K., Marine Biochemistry
WRIGHT, J., Marine Biochemistry
YSTENES, M., Inorganic Chemistry
ZACHARIASSEN, K. E., Zoophysiology

Faculty of Social Sciences and Technology Management (tel. 73-59-19-00; fax 73-59-19-01; e-mail postmottak@svt.ntnu.no; internet www.ntnu.no/svt):

ALMÅS, R., Sociology
BERG, N. G., Human Geography
BERGE, E., Sociology
BJØRGEN, I. A., Psychology
BORGE, L.-E., Economics
BRANDTH, B., Sociology
BRØGGER, J. C., Social Anthropology
CHRISTIANSEN, M., Industrial Economics
DAHL-JØRGENSEN, C., Social Anthropology
DALE, B. E., Geography
DYRSTAD, J. M., Economics
ERRING, B. B., Social Anthropology
ESPNES, G. A., Programme for Social Work
ETTERMA, G., Sports Sciences
FET, A. M., Organizational Studies
GAIVORONSKI, A. A., Industrial Economics
HESTAD, K., Psychology
HOEL, T. L., Education
HOPMANN, S., Education
HOVDEN, J., Organizational Studies
HVINDEN, B., Sociology
HAAVELSRUD, M., Education
IMSEN, G. M., Education
INGVALDSEN, R. P., Sports Sciences
JACOBSEN, K. H., Psychology
JENSEN, A.-M., Sociology
JENSSEN, A. T., Political Science
JONES, M. R. H., Geography
KARLSEN, A., Economic Geography
KAUL, H., Psychology
KNUTSEN, T., Political Science
KOLSTAD, A., Psychology
KREKLING, S., Psychology
KVANDE, E., Sociology
LEIULFSRUD, H., Sociology
LEVIN, M., Organizational Studies
LISTHAUG, O., Political Science
LORENTZEN, S., Education
LUND, R., Geography
LUNHEIM, R., Organizational Studies
MARTINUSSEN, W. M., Sociology
MEER, A. L. VAN DER, Psychology
MOSER, E., Neuroscience
MOSER, M.-B., Neuroscience
MOSES, J., Political Science
MOXNES, K., Sociology
NORDAHL, H. M., Psychology
NORDVIK, H., Psychology
NYGREEN, B., Industrial Economics
QVORTRUP, J., Sociology
RAMET, S., Political Science
RASMUSSEN, B., Sociology
RASMUSSEN, K., Psychology
RATTSØ, J. G., Economics
RINGDAHL, G. I., Health Psychology
RINGDAL, K., Sociology
RUNDMO, T., Psychology
SAKSVIK, P. Ø., Psychology
SCHIEFLOE, P.-M., Sociology
SIGMUNDSSON, H., Sociology
SIMKUS, A., Sociology
SJØBERG, B.-M. D., Psychology
SKAALVIK, E. M., Education
SKONHOFT, A., Economics
SOLEM, K. E., Political Science
SOLEM, O., Organizational Studies
STEINSHOLT, K., Education
STILES, T. C., Psychology
SÆTNAN, A. R., Sociology
TORVIK, R., Economics
TØSSEBRO, J., Programme for Social Work
VEREIJKEN, E., Sports Sciences
VIKAN, A., Psychology
WAAGØ, S., Organizational Studies
WEEL, F. VAN DER, Psychology
WESTGAARD, R. H., Organizational Studies
WICHSTRØM, L., Psychology
WIJST, D. VAN DER, Industrial Economics

Museum of Natural History and Archaeology (tel. 73-59-21-45; fax 73-59-22-23; e-mail post@vm.ntnu.no; internet www.ntnu.no/vitenskapsmuseet):

CHRISTOPHERSEN, A., Archaeology
FLATBERG, K. I., Botany
HOGSTAD, O., Zoology
JASINKSI, M. E., Maritime Archaeology
JOHANSEN, A. B., Archaeology
MOEN, A., Botany
MORK, J., Population Genetics
OLSEN, Y., Marine Physiology
SAKSHAUG, E., Marine Botany
SOGNES, K., Archaeology
SOLEM, J. O., Zoology

UNIVERSITETET FOR MILJØ- OG BIOVITENSKAP (UMB)
(Norwegian University of Life Sciences)

POB 5003, 1432 Ås

Telephone: 64-96-50-00
Fax: 64-96-50-01
E-mail: postmottak@umb.no
Internet: www.umb.no

Founded 1859 as State College, present name and status 2005, plans mooted for merger with Norges Veterinærhøgskole (Norwegian School of Veterinary Science)
Language of instruction: English, Norwegian
Academic year: August to August

Rector: Prof. HANS FREDRIK HOEN
Vice-Rectors: Prof. RUTH HAUG, Asst Prof. MARI SUNDLI TVEIT
Univ. Dir: SIRI MARGRETHE LÖKSA
Dir of Human Resources: ANDERS AUTHEN
Dir of Research: RAGNHILD SOLHEIM
Dir of Studies: OLE-JØRGEN TORP
Library Dir: DAG GUTTORMSE

Number of teachers: 640 , incl. 80 full professors
Number of students: 3,800 , plus 460 postgraduates

UNIVERSITETET I AGDER
(University of Agder)

POB 422 Kristiansand, 4604 Grimstad

Telephone: 38-14-10-00
Fax: 38-14-10-01
E-mail: post@uia.no
Internet: www.uia.no

Founded 1994 as Høgskolen i Agder (Agder University College) by merger of 6 regional colleges; univ. status acquired and present name adopted 2007

Rector: TORUNN LAUVDAL
Vice-Rector for Education: MARIT AAMODT NIELSEN
Vice-Rector for Research, Devt and Innovation: DAG G. AASLAND
Man. Dir: TOR A. AAGEDAL
Chief Librarian: ELSE-MAGRETHE BREDLAND

Library of 200,000 vols, 1,500 periodicals
Number of teachers: 600
Number of students: 8,000

UNIVERSITETET I BERGEN
(University of Bergen)

POB 7800, 5020 Bergen
Telephone: 55-58-00-00
Fax: 55-58-96-43
E-mail: post@uib.no
Internet: www.uib.no

Founded 1946
State control
Academic year: August to June

Rector: Prof. SIGMUND GRØNMO
Deputy Rector: Prof. BERIT ROKNE
Vice-Rector for Education: Prof. KUVVET ATAKAN
Vice-Rector for Int. Relations: Prof. ASTRI ANDRESEN
University Dir: KARI TOVE ELVBAKKEN
Library Dir: JAN S. VAAGEN

Library: see Libraries and Archives
Number of teachers: 1,900
Number of students: 14,500

Publications: *Ilicifolia* (irregular), *Naturen* (popular scientific review, 6 a year), *Sarsia* (6 a year)

DEANS

Faculty of Humanities: Prof. GJERT KRISTOFFERSEN
Faculty of Law: Prof. ASBJØRN STRANDBAKKEN
Faculty of Mathematics and Natural Sciences: Prof. DAG RUNE OLSEN
Faculty of Medicine and Dentistry: Prof. NINA LANGELAND
Faculty of Psychology: Prof. GERD KVALE
Faculty of Social Sciences: Prof. KNUT HELLAND

PROFESSORS

Faculty of Humanities (tel. 55-58-93-80; fax 55-58-93-83; e-mail post@hf.uib.no; internet www.uib.no/hf):

ÅDLAND, E., General Literature
AKSELBERG, G., Nordic Language
ALVER, B. G., Folklore
ANGVIK, B., Spanish
ARMSTRONG, C. I., British Literature
ÅRSETH, A., Nordic Language
BAGGE, S. H., History
BELL, J. N., Arabic
BERGGREEN, B., Ethnology
BJØRGO, N., Archaeology
BJØRKELO, A., History
BONDEVIK, J., Nordic Language
BØRTNES, J., Russian Literature
BREIVIK, L. E., English Philology
BROWN, E., Philosophy
BUVIK, P., General Literature
CHRISTENSEN, K. K., General Linguistics
DANBOLT, G., History of Art
DE CUZZANI, P. M., Philosophy
DYRVIK, S., History
DYVIK, H. J., General Linguistics
ENDSJØ, D., Religious Studies
FJELL, T. I., Cultural Studies and History of Art
FLØTTUM, K., French Language
FORSBERG, L. L., Archaeology
GILHUS, A. I. S., Religion
GRØNLIE, T., History
GULLVEIG, B. A., Folklore
HAAVERT, I. E., History
HÄGG, T., Classical Philology
HÅLAND, R., African Archaeology
HALMØY, O., French Language
HALVERSEN, S., Philology
HAUG, E., History
HAUGEN, O. E., Nordic Language
HELLE, L. J., Russian Language
HENSHILWOOD, C., Archaeology
HESTVIK, A., General Linguistics
HOLGERNES, B., Philosophy
HOLM, H. V., Philology
HOVLAND, E., History
HUBBARD, W. H., History
JANICKI, K., English Philology
JOHANNESSEN, H., Philosophy
JOHANNESSEN, K. S., Philosophy
JOHNSEN, K. O., Philosophy
KILERICH, B. K., History of Art
KITTANG, A., General Literature
KOLLER, W., German Language
KRISTOFFERSEN, G., Nordic Language
KROEPELIEN, B., History of Art
LIE, R. K., Philosophy
LINNEBERG, A., General Literature
LUNDE, I., Russian Language and Literature
MCCAFFERTY, K., British Literature
MELVE, L., History
MEYER, J. C., History of Art
MEYER, S., European Culture
MIKAELSSON, L., Religion
MORTENSEN, E., General Literature
MUNDAL, E., Nordic Languages
NAGEL, A.-H., History
NORDENSTAM, T., Philosophy
O'FAHEY, R. S., History
ØSTBY, E., Archaeology
ØVERLAND, O., American Literature
ØYE, I., Archaeology
PIERCE, R., Egyptology
QUESEDA-PACHECO, M. A., Spanish
ROKSTAD, K., Philosophy
RYDVING, L. O. H., Religion
SÄÄTELÄ, S. T. S., Philosophy
SÆTRE, L., General Literature
SANAKER, J. K., French Language
SANDBERG, B., German Literature
SANDØY, H., Nordic Language
SCHRØTER, H. G., History
SELBERG, T., Folklore
SILLARS, S. J., English Philology
SKÅNLAND, M. H., Linguistics
SKARSTEN, R., Humanistic Informatics
SKILLEÅS, O. M., Philosophy
SKIRBEKK, G., Philosophy
SKULSTAD, A. S., English Philology
STEGANE, I., Nordic Language
STRAUSBERG, M., Religion
SVENDSEN, L. F., Philosophy
THOMASSEN, E., Religion
UTAKER, A., Philosophy
VELAND, R. M., French Language
VENNESLAN, K., Philosophy
VIKØR, K. S., History
WINTHER, T., French Language
WÆRNESS, K. E., Sociology

Faculty of Law (tel. 55-58-95-00; fax 55-58-95-71; e-mail post@jurfa.uib.no; internet www.uib.no/jur):

ÅLL, J.
ÅSEN, H. S.
ASKELAND, B.
BERNT, J. F.
FRANTZEN, T.
GIERTSEN, J.
HOLGERSEN, G.
HUSABØ, E. J.
KONOW, B.-E.
KRÜGER, K.
LUNDE, T.
MÆLAND, H. J.
MONSEN, E.
NORDTVEIT, E.
NYGAARD, N.
RASMUSSEN, Ø.
SÆBO, R.
SØVIG, K. H.
SUNDE, J.
TRUYEN, F.

Faculty of Mathematics and Natural Sciences (tel. 55-58-20-62; fax 55-58-96-66; e-mail post@mnfa.uib.no; internet www.uib.no/matnat):

AKSNES, D., Chemistry
AKSNES, D. L., Fisheries Biology
ANDERSEN, Ø. M., Chemistry
BÅMSTEDT, U., Fisheries Biology
BERG, C. C., Botany
BERGE, G., Mathematics
BERNTSEN, J., Mathematics
BEZEM, M. A., Computer Science
BIRKELAND, N.-K., Microbiology
BIRKS, H. J. B., Botany
BJØRSTAD, P. E., Computer Science
BRATBAK, G., Microbiology
BRIX, O., Zoology
CSERNAI, L., Physics
DAHLE, H. K., Mathematics
DYSTHE, K., Mathematics
ECKHOFF, K. S., Mathematics
ECKHOFF, R. K., Physics
EIGEN, G., Physics
ENDRESEN, C., Fisheries Biology
ENGEVIK, L. E., Mathematics
ESPEDAL, M., Mathematics
ESPELID, T. O., Computer Science
FERNØ, A., Fisheries Biology
FJOSE, A., Molecular Biology
FOSSEN, F., Geology
FRANCIS, G. W., Organic Chemistry
FRODESEN, A. G., Physics
FURNES, H., Petroleum Geology
FYHN, H. J., Milieu Physiology
GABRIELSEN, R., Petroleum Geology
GADE, H. G., Physical Oceanography
GAMMELSRØD, T., Physical Oceanography
GISKE, J., Fisheries Biology
GRAHL-NIELSEN, O., Chemistry
GRAUE, A., Physics
GRØNÅS, S., Meteorology
GUDMUNDSSON, A., Geology
HAMMER, E. A., Physics
HANSEN, J. P., Physics
HANYGA, A., Applied Geophysics
HAUGAN, P. M., Geophysics
HAVSKOV, J., Applied Geophysics
HELLAND, D. E., Molecular Biology
HELLAND-HANSEN, W., Geology
HELLESETH, T., Computer Science
HEUCH, I., Mathematics
HOBÆK, H., Physics
HØGSTEDT, G., Zoology
HOFFMAN, A. C., Physics
HØILAND, H., Physical Chemistry
HOLME, A., Mathematics
HUSEBYE, E., Applied Geophysics
HUSEBYE, S., Chemistry
JAKOBSEN, P. J., Zoology
JANSEN, E., Geology
JENSEN, H. B., Molecular Biology
JOHANNESEN, O. M., Physical Oceanography
JOHNSEN, T., Mathematics
JØRGENSEN, P. M., Botany
KALAND, P. E., Botany
KLØVE, T., Computer Science
KNUDSEN, L. R., Computer Science
KNUTSEN, G., Microbiology
KOCBACH, L., Physics
KOLLTVEIT, K., Physics
KRISTOFFERSEN, Y., Seismology
KRYVI, H., Zoology
KVALHEIM, O. M., Chemistry
KVAMME, B., Physics
LARSSON, P., Zoology
LAURITZEN, S.-E., Geology
LIEN, T., Microbiology
LILLEHAUG, J., Molecular Biology
LILLESTØL, E., Physics
LØVLIE, R., Geomagnetism
MAALØE, S. B., Geology
MÆLAND, E., Applied Geophysics
MALYSHEV, A., Computer Science
MANGERUD, J., Quaternary Geology
MANNE, R. E., Chemistry
MJELDE, R., Applied Geophysics
MOE, D., Botany
MUNTHE-KAAS, H., Computer Science
MYKLEBOST, K., Physics
NÆVDAL, G., Fisheries Biology
NEMEC, W., Geology
NESJE, A., Geology
NYLUND, A., Fisheries Biology
ØIEN, A. H., Mathematics

OSLAND, P., Physics
PAULSEN, J., Mathematics
PEDERSEN, R.-B., Geology
RAAE, A. J., Molecular Biology
ROBINS, B., Geology
RØDSETH, Ø. J., Mathematics
RØHRICH, D., Physics
RYE, N. M., Geology
SÆTHER, O. A., Zoology
SÆTHRE, L. J., Chemistry
SALVANES, A. G. V.
SCHRADER, H., Geology
SEJRUP, H. P., Geology
SKARTVEIT, A., Physical Oceanography
SKOGEN, A., Botany
SKORPING, A., Zoology
SLETTEN, E., Physical Chemistry
SLETTEN, J., Inorganic Chemistry
SONGSTAD, J., Inorganic Chemistry
SØRÅS, F., Physics
SØREVIK, T., Computer Science
STAMNES, J. J., Physics
STEFANSSON, S., Fisheries Biology
STEIHAUG, T., Informatics
STORETVEDT, K. M., Geomagnetism
STORØY, S., Computer Science
STRAY, A., Mathematics
STRØMME, S. A., Mathematics
STUGU, B., Physics
SUNDVOR, E., Seismology
SVENDSEN, H., Physical Oceanography
SVENDSEN, J.-I., Geology
SYDNES, L. K., Chemistry
TAI, X.-C., Mathematics
TALBOT, M. R., Petroleum Geology
TELLE, J. A., Computer Science
THINGSTAD, T. F., Microbiology
TJØSTHEIM, D. B., Statistics
TØNSBERG, T., Botany
TORSVIK, V. L., Microbiology
TOTLAND, G. K., Zoology
TVERBERG, H., Mathematics
ULLTANG, Ø., Fisheries Biology
VÅGEN, J. S., Physics
WALTHER, B. T., Molecular Biology
WILLASSEN, E., Zoology
YTREHUS, Ø., Computer Science

Faculty of Medicine and Dentistry (tel. 55-58-20-86; fax 55-58-96-82; e-mail post@mofa.uib.no; internet www.uib.no/mofa):

ÅKSNES, L., Clinical Medicine
ÅRLI, J. A., Clinical Medicine
ÅRSTAD, H. J., Surgical Sciences
ÅRVIDSON, K. F., Dentistry
ÅSTROM, A. N., Dentistry
BÆRHEIM, A., General Practice
BAKKE, M., Biomedicine
BAKKEN, V., Oral Microbiology
BERG, E., Prosthesis
BERGE, M. E., Prosthodontics
BERGE, T. I., Dentistry
BERGGREEN, E., Biomedicine
BINDOFF, L., Clinical Medicine
BJERKNES, R., Clinical Medicine
BJERKVIG, R., Biomedicine
BJØRGE, T., Epidemiology
BJØRVATN, B., General Practice
BLYSTAD, A., Nursing Science
BØ, L., Clinical Medicine
BOLSTAD, A. I., Dental Research
BOMAN, H., Clinical Medicine
BRAMHAM, C. R. E., Biomedicine
BRÅTVEIT, M., Physiology
BRUDVIK, P., Dentistry
DALTVEIT, A. K., Epidemiology
DØSKELAND, S. E., Biomedicine
EIDE, R., Dental Materials
ENGESÆTER, L. B., Surgical Sciences
ESPELID, I., Paedodontics
FASMER, O. B., Clinical Medicine
GERDES, H.-H., Biomedicine
GJENGEDAL, E., Praxeology
GJERDET, N. R., Dental Materials
GJESDAL, S., Public Health
GREVE, G., Clinical Medicine
GRONG, K., Surgical Sciences
GULLBERG, D., Biomedicine
HAAVIK, R., Biomedicine
HALSE, A., Oral Radiology
HARTVEIT, E., Biomedicine
HAUG, K., General Practice
HAUKAAS, S. A., Surgical Sciences
HAVER, B., Clinical Medicine
HELLE, K. B., Biomedicine
HELLEM, S., Oral Surgery
HOLSTEN, F., Clinical Medicine
HØVDING, G., Clinical Medicine
HUSBY, P., Surgical Sciences
IVERSEN, O.-E., Clinical Medicine
JOHANNESSEN, A. C., Oral Pathology
JONUNG, J. A. T., Surgical Sciences
JØRGENSEN, H., Clinical Medicine
KETTUNEN, P., Biomedicine
KISERUD, T., Clinical Medicine
KLOCK, K., Dentistry
KROHN, J., Clinical Medicine
KRÜGER, P. G., Biomedicine
KUSCHE-GULLBERG, M., Biomedicine
LARSEN, T., Biomedicine
LEKNES, K., Dentistry
LEKVEN, J., Surgical Sciences
LORENS, J., Biomedicine
LUND, A., Clinical Medicine
LUNDERVOLD, A., Biomedicine
LUND-JOHANSEN, M., Surgical Sciences
LUUKKO, K. A., Biomedicine
MÆLAND, J., Social Medicine
MARTINEZ, A., Biomedicine
MELAND, E., General Practice
MOE-NILSSEN, R., Physiotherapy
MOEN, B. E., Occupational and Environmental Medicine
MØLLER, P., Surgical Sciences
MUSTAFA, K., Dentistry
MYKLEBUST, R., Biomedicine
NATVIG, G., Nursing Science
NJØLSTAD, P. R., Clinical Medicine
NORGÅRD, G., Clinical Medicine
NORHEIM, O. F., Medical Ethics
NYLAND, H. I., Clinical Medicine
OLOFSSON, J., Surgical Sciences
ØYMAR, K., Clinical Medicine
PETERSEN, K. A., Praxeology
PRYME, I. F., Biomedicine
RÅDAL, M. J., Odontophobia and Paedodontics
RASMUSSEN, S., Clinical Medicine
RØDAHL, E, Clinical Medicine
RØRVIK, J., Surgical Sciences
ROSLAND, J. H., Surgical Sciences
SALVESEN, H. B., Clinical Medicine
SARASTE, J., Biomedicine
SØNDENAA, K., Surgical Sciences
STEEN, V. M., Clinical Medicine
STRAND, G., Dentistry
TANG, T., Clinical Medicine
TAXT, T., Biomedicine
TENSTAD, O., Biomedicine
TJØLSEN, A., Biomedicine
VASSTRAND, E., Dentistry
VEDELER, A., Biomedicine
VISTE, A., Surgical Sciences
WESTER, K., Surgical Sciences
WIIG, H., Biomedicine
WIK, G., Clinical Medicine
WISTH, P. J., Orthodontics

Faculty of Psychology (tel. 55-58-27-10; fax 55-58-98-71; e-mail post@psyfa.uib.no; internet www.uib.no/psyfa):

AARØ, L. E., Social Psychology
ANDERSSEN, N., Social Psychology
ASBJØRNSEN, A E., Biological and Medical Psychology
BØHM, G., Social Psychology
DALLAND, T., Social Psychology
EID, J., Social Psychology
EINARSEN, S., Social Psychology
HAVIK, O. E., Clinical Psychology
HELLAND, T., Biological and Medical Psychology
HUGDAHL, K., Somatic Psychology
JOHNSEN, B. H., Social Psychology
KVALE, G., Clinical Psychology
LABERG, J. C., Clinical Psychology
LÆNG, B., Biological and Medical Psychology
LINSTRØM, T. C., Social Psychology
LUNDERVOLD, A., Biological and Medical Psychology
MANGER, T., Social Psychology
MATTHIESEN, S., Social Psychology
MURISON, R., Physiological Psychology
NIELSEN, G. H., Clinical Psychology
NORDHUS, I. H., Clinical Psychology
PALLESEN, S., Social Psychology
REBER, R., Biological and Medical Psychology
SAM, D. L., Personal Psychology
SANDAL, G. M., Social Psychology
SKOGSTAD, A., Social Psychology
STORMARK, K. M., Childl Psychology
SUNDBERG, H., Physiological Psychology
VOLLMER, F., Personal Psychology
WICKLUND, R. A., Social Psychology

Faculty of Social Sciences (tel. 55-58-90-50; fax 55-58-90-52; e-mail post@svfa.uib.no; internet www.uib.no/svf):

ÅMUNDSEN, E. S., Economics
ÅRRESTAD, J., Economics
ÅSE, T. H., Geography
BAKKE, M., Media Studies
BJELLAND, A. K., Social Anthropology
BLEIKLIE, I., Administration and Organization Theory
DAVIDSEN, P., Geography
EIDE, M., Media Studies
FIMREITE, A., Administration and Organization Theory
FLÅM, S. D., Economics
FLØYSAND, A., Geography
GOODNOW, K. J., Media Studies
GRAN, T., Administration and Organization Theory
GRIPSRUD, J., Media Studies
GRØNHAUG, R., Social Anthropology
GRØNMO, S., Sociology
GULBRANDSEN, Ø., Social Anthropology
HENRIKSEN, G., Social Anthropology
HOLT-JENSEN, A., Geography
HVIDING, E., Social Anthropology
HÅLAND, G., Social Anthropology
JOHANSEN, A., Media Studies
KAPFERER, B., Social Anthropology
KAPFERER, J., Sociology
KJELDSEN, J. E., Media Studies
KNUDSEN, J. C., Social Anthropology
KORSNES, O., Sociology
KUHNLE, S., Comparative Politics
LÆGREID, P., Administration and Organization Theory
LARSEN, P. L., Media Studies
LILLEHAUG, B. W., Media Studies
LINDSTRØM, U. A., Comparative Politics
LINDKVIST, K. B., Geography
LITHMAN, Y., Sociology
LOMMERUD, K. E., Economics
LUNDBERG, A., Geography
MANGER, L. O., Social Anthropology
MIDTBØ, T., Comparative Politics
MOXNES, E., Geography
NILSEN, A., Sociology
OPDAHL, A. L., Information Science
ØSTBYE, H., Media Studies
RISA, A. E., Economics
RONESS, P. G., Administration and Organization Theory
RUSTEN, G., Geography
STRAND, T., Administration and Organization Theory
SVÅSAND, L. G., Comparative Politics
SÆTREN, H., Administration and Organization Theory
STRAND, T., Administration and Organization Theory
TESSEM, B., Information Science

TJØTTA, S., Economics
TORSVIK, G., Economics
TVEDT, T., Geography
UHDE, A., Economics
ØYEN, E., Sociology

Bergen Museum (tel. 55-58-93-60; fax 55-58-93-64; e-mail publikum@bm.uib.no; internet www.uib.no/bergenmuseum):

ACHEN, H. VON, Art History
BERG, C. C., Botany
FOSSEN, H., Geology
INDRELID, S., Archaeology
JØRGENSEN, P. O., Botany
MOE, D., Botany
ØVSTEDAL, D. O., Botany
SÆTHER, O. A., Zoology
TØNSBERG, T., Botany
WILLASSEN, E., Zoology

UNIVERSITETET I OSLO (University of Oslo)

POB 1072, Blindern, 0316 Oslo
Telephone: 22-85-50-50
Fax: 22-85-44-42
E-mail: informasjon@uio.no
Internet: www.uio.no

Founded 1811
State control
Academic year: August to June (two semesters)

Rector: Prof. OLE-PETTER OTTERSEN
Pro-Rector: Dr INGA BOSTAD
Dir: Dr GUNN-ELIN AA. BJØRNEBOE
Vice-Rectors: Prof. RAGNHILD HENNUM, Prof. DORIS JORDE
Library Dir: BENTE R. ANDREASSEN

Library: see Libraries
Number of teachers: 2,400
Number of students: 27,700

Publications: *Apollon* (4 a year, in Norwegian, 1 a year, in English), *Uniforum* (16 a year)

DEANS

Faculty of Dentistry: Prof. PÅL BRODIN
Faculty of Education: Prof. VIBEKE GRØVER AUKRUST
Faculty of Humanities: Prof. TRINE SYVERTSEN
Faculty of Law: Prof. HANS PETTER GRAVER
Faculty of Mathematics and Natural Sciences: Prof. KNUT FÆGRI
Faculty of Medicine: Prof. FINN G. B. WISLØFF
Faculty of Social Sciences: Prof. KNUT HEIDAR
Faculty of Theology: Prof. TRYGVE E. WYLLER

PROFESSORS

Faculty of Dentistry (POB 1142 Blindern, 0317 Oslo
Geitmyrsvn. 69-71, 0455 Oslo; tel. 22-85-20-00; fax 22-85-23-32; e-mail infoskranke@odont.uio.no):

BARKVOLL, P., Dental Surgery
BJØRNLAND, T., Oral Surgery and Medicine
BRODIN, P., Physiology
BRYNE, M., Oral Biology
DEMBIK, Z., Dentistry
ELLINGSEN, J. E., Prosthetic Dentistry
ERIKSEN, H. M., Cariology
ESPELAND, L. V., Dentistry
ESPELID, L., Dentistry
GRYTTEN, J. I., Community Dentistry, Health Economics
HALTENSEN, T. S., Oral Biology
HANSEN, B., Periodontology
HOLST, D. J., Social Dentistry
HAANÆS, H. R., Dental Surgery
HAAPASALO, M., Endodontics
JACOBSEN, I., Pedodontics
JOKSTAD, A., Dentistry
KLINGE, R. F., General and Oral Anatomy
KOPPANG, H. S., General and Oral Pathology
KOPPANG, R., Material Sciences
LARHEIM, T. A., Dentistry
LYNGSTADAAS, S. P., Dentistry
ØGAARD, B., Orthodontics
OLSEN, I., Microbiology
OSMUNDSEN, H., Biochemistry
PREUS, H. R., Periodontology
RISNES, S., General and Oral Anatomy
RYKKE, M., Dentistry
RØED, A., Physiology
SCHEIE, A. AA, Microbiology
SCHENCK, K., Immunology
SKOGLUND, L. A., Dental Pharmacology
SOLHEIM, T., Oral Pathology
STENVIK, A., Orthodontics
THRANE, P. S., Oral Pathology
TRONSTAD, L., Endodontics
TVEIT, A. B., Dentistry
VASSEND, O., Behavioural Science
WÅLER, S. M., Dentistry

Faculty of Education (Helga Engs hus, Sem Sælands vei 7, POB 1161 Blindern, 0318 Oslo; tel. 22-85-82-76; fax 22-85-82-41; e-mail postmottak@uv.uio.no):

BEFRING, E., Special Education
BIRKEMO, A., Pedagogy
BRÅTEN, I., Pedagogy
BROCK-UTNE, B., Pedagogy
DALE, E. L., Pedagogy
DALEN, M., Special Education
ENGELSEN, B. U., General Didactics
GJESME, T., Pedagogy
GJONE, G., Teacher Education and School Development
HAGTVET, B. E., Education, Dyslexia
HANDAL, G., Pedagogy
HAUGE, T. E., Pedagogy
HERTZBERG, F., Teacher Education
JENSEN, K., Pedagogy
JORDE, D., Teacher Education
JORDELL, K. Ø., Pedagogy
LAHN, L. C., Pedagogy
LIE, S., Pedagogy
LIEBERG, S., Pedagogy
LUND, T., Special Education
LYCKE, K. H., Pedagogy
LØVLIE, L., Pedagogy
MARTINSEN, H., Psychology
NIELSEN, H. B., Pedagogy
OSTAD, S., Pedagogy
ØSTERUD, S., Pedagogy
ØZERK, K., Pedagogy
RUDBERG, M., Pedagogy
RYE, H., Special Education
SIMENSEN, A. M., Teacher Education
SJØBERG, S., Pedagogy (Natural Science)
SKOGEN, K., Special Education
STAFSENG, O., Pedagogy
TELLEVIK, J. M., Special Education
TJELDVOLL, A., Pedagogy
TVEIT, K., Pedagogy
ULVUND, S. E., Pedagogy
VONEN, A. M., Pedagogy, Linguistics
WIGGEN, G., Pedagogy

Faculty of Humanities (Administrasjonsbygn., 8 et., POB 1079 Blindern, 0316 Oslo; tel. 22-85-62-93; fax 22-85-45-50):

AKSNES, H., Musical Theory
ALLERN, S., Media and Communication Research
AMUNDSEN, A. B., Folklore
ANDERSEN, Ø., Classical Philology (Greek)
ANDERSEN, P. T., Nordic Literature
ASHEIM, O., Philosophy
ASKEDAL, J. O., German Language
ASZTALOS, M. M., Classical Philology (Latin)
AUESTAD, R. A., Japanese Language
AÚKRÚST, K. H., History of Religions
BACHE-WIIG, H., Nordic Literature
BAUNE, Ø., Philosophy
BENSKIN, M., English Language
BERGE, K. L., Nordic Language
BJERKE, Ø. L. S., Fine Art History
BJØRDAL, F., Philosophy
BJØRGUM, J., History
BJORVAND, H., German Linguistics
BJØRKVOLD, J. R., Musicology
BJØRNFLATEN, J. J., Slavonic Languages
BLIKSRUD, L., Nordic Literature
BRAAVIG, J., History of Religion
BRANDT, J. R., Classical Archaeology
BRENDEMOEN, B., Turkish Language
BRULAND, K., History
BRYNHILDSVOLL, K., Research on Ibsen
BØ, G., Norwegian Literature
BØ-RYGG, A., General Aesthetics
COLLETT, F. P., History
DAHL, H. F., Media and Communication Research
DIMAS, P., Philosophy
EDZARD, L. E., Hebrew and Semitic Languages
EGGE, Å., History
EIFRING, H., Modern Chinese Languages
ELSNESS, J., English Language
EMILSSON, E. K., Ancient Philosophy
ENGER, H.-O., Scandinavian Languages and Linguistics
ERIKSEN, A., Folklore
ERIKSEN, T. B., History of Ideas
FAARLUND, J. T., Nordic Language and Literature
FARNER, G., Dutch
FEHR, D., Literature
FJELD, R. E. V., Lexicography
FØRLAND, T. E., History
FREIIN VON VILLIEZ, C., Philosophy
FRELLESVIG, B., Japanese Language and Culture
FRICKE, C., Philosophy
FRIEDMAN, R. M., History
FUGLESTAD, F., History
GAMMELGAARD, K., Central and Eastern European Languages
GJELSVIK, O., Philosophy
GLAMBEK, I., Art History
GODØY, R. I., Musical Theory
GULDBRANDSEN, E. E., Music History
GUNDERSEN, K., French Literature
GUSTAVSSON, A., Ethnology
GUTH, S., Arabic and Middle Eastern Studies
HAARBERG, F., Nordic Literature
HAGEMANN, G., History
HANSEN, C. F., German Language
HANSEN, J. E. E., History of Ideas
HARBSMEIER, C. H., East Asian Languages
HAREIDE, J., Nordic Literature
HAREIDE, S., Philosophy
HASSELGÅRD, H., English Language
HAWKINS, S., Music
HEDEAGER, L., Nordic Archaeology
HELLAND, H. P., French
HEYERDAHL, G. B., History of Ideas
HJELDE, S., History of Religions
HOBÆK HAFF, M., French Language
HODNE, B., Folklore
HOEL, K., Fine Art History
IMENES, O., Philosophy
IVERSEN, I., General Literary Science
JERVELL, H. R., Computer Science
JOHANNESSEN, F. E., History
JOHANNESSEN, J. B., Linguistics
JOHANSEN, K. E., Philosophy
JOHANSSON, A., Modern Economic History
JØRGENSEN, J. G., Nordic Literature
KAARE, B. H., Folklore
KELLER, J. C., Nordic Archaeology
KJELDSTADLI, K., Modern History
KJETSAA, G., Russian Literature
KOLSTØ, P., Russian and East European Studies
KRISTOFFERSEN, K. E., Linguistics, Philology
KROGH, T., History of Ideas
KROGSETH, O., History of Christianity
KVÆRNE, P., History of Religions
KVIFTE, T., Folk Music
LANGE, E., History
LANGHOLM, T., Computer Science

LANZA, E., Linguistics
LAÚK, E., Media and Communication
LIE, S., Norwegian Language
LIEPE, L., Art History
LOTHE, J., British Literature
LYCHE, C., French, Phonetics
LØDRUP, H., Linguistics
LØNNING, J. T., Computer Science
MELBERG, B. A. E., Literature
MOEN, I., Linguistics
MORGAN, N., Fine Art History
MYHRE, J., History
MØNNESLAND, S., Slavonic Languages
NAGUIB, S. N., Cultural History, Cultural Analysis
NEDKVITNE, A., History
NYGAARD, J., Theatre Science
OTTOSSON, K., Icelandic
PEDERSEN, A., Philosophy
PETTERSON, E. R., Fine Art History
PHARO, H., History
PRELL, H.-P., German Language
PRICE, P. G., History
QUILLER, B., History of Ideas
RAMBERG, B., Philosophy
RAND, K. A., English Language
RASMUSSEN, T., Media and Communication
REINTON, R., Literary Theory
REM, T., English Literature
RIAN, Ø., History
RINDAL, M., Nordic Onomastics
ROGAN, B., Ethnology
RUUD, E., Musicology
RØNNING, H., Media and Communication Research
SAGMO, I., German Literature
SALBERG, T. K., French
SANDE, S., Classical Archaeology
SAÚGSTAD, F., Philosophy
SCHAANNING, E., History of Ideas
SCHMIDT, T., Nordic Literature
SERCK-HANSSEN, C., Philosophy
SIMONSEN, H. G., Linguistics
SIRGES, T., German Language
SKAUG, E., Art Conservation
SKATTURN, I., Francophone Studies
SKEI, H. H., Literary Theory
SKOGERBØ, E., Media and Communication Research
SKRE, D., Archaeology
SLETSJØE, A., Portuguese Language
STEINFELD, T., Nordic Language and Literature
STEINSLAND, G. S., History of Religions
STENE-JOHANSEN, K., Literary Theory
STENGAARD, B., Ibero-Romance Philology
STENSVOLD, A., History of Religions
SYVERTSEN, T., Media and Communication
SØRENSEN, Ø., Modern History
SÆBØ, K. J., German Language
TEEUWEN, M. J., Japanese
THEIL, R., English Literature
THORSEN, L. E., Ethnology
TORP, A., Nordic Languages
URSTAD, T. S., British Literature
VETLESEN, A. J., Philosophy
VIKØR, L. S., Nordic Linguistics
VOLLSNES, A., Music
WALDAHL, R., Media and Communication Research
WERENSKIOLD, M., Fine Art History
WICHSTRØM, A., Fine Art History
WIKSHÅLAND, S., Musicology
WORREN, D., Nordic Linguistics
YSTAD, V., Nordic Literature
YTREBERG, E., Media and Communication
ZOLLER, C. P., South Asian Studies
ZWARTJES, O., Spanish Language

Faculty of Law (POB 6706 St Olavs plass 5, 0130 Oslo
Karl Johans gt. 47, 0162 Oslo; tel. 22-85-93-00; fax 22-85-01-80; e-mail postmottak@jus.uio.no; internet www.jus.uio.no):

ANDENÆS, K., Sociology of Law
ANDENÆS, M., European Law
ANDREASSEN, B., Human Rights and Governance
ARNESEN, F., European Law
BAILLIET, C. M., International Law
BING, J., Law
BOE, E., Law
BUGGE, H. CHR., Law
BULL, H. J., Law
BULL, K. S., Law
CORDERO-MOSS, G., International Law
EIDE, E., Economics and Statistics
ENG, S., Law
ERICSSON, K., Criminology
ESKELAND, S., Criminal Law
EVJU, S., Civil Law
FAUCHALD, O. K., International Law
FINSTAD, L., Criminology
FØLLESDAL, A., Human Rights Law
GIERTSEN, H., Criminology
GJEMS-ONSTAD, O., Tax Law
GRAVER, H. P., Sociology of Law
HAGSTRØM, V., Civil Law
HELLUM, A., Women's Law
HJELMENG, E. J., Tort Law
HOV, J., Civil Law
HØIGÅRD, I. C., Criminology
JOHANSEN, P. O., Criminology
JOHNSEN, J. T., Law
KAASEN, K., Law
KJØNSTAD, A., Law
LARSEN, A., Criminology
LILLEHOLT, K., Civil Law
MESTAD, O., European Law
MICHALSEN, D., Law History
PRIEUR, A. I., Criminology
ROBBERSTAD, A., European Law
ROGNSTAD, O.-A., Private Law
RØSÆG, E., Transportation Law
SAND, I. J., Public Law
SANDBERG, K., Children's and Women's Law
SCHARTUM, D. W., Administrative Informatics
SEJERSTED, F., European Law
SIMONSEN, L., Private Law
SMITH, E., Constitutional Law
STENVIK, A., Private Law
STRIDBECK, U., Criminology
SVERDRUP, T., Family Law
TORVUND, O., Private Law
TRONVOLL, K., Law
ULFBECK, V., Law
ULFSTEIN, G., International Law
WILHELMSEN, T. L., Insurance Law
WOXHOLTH, G., Civil Law
ZIMMER, F., Tax Law

Faculty of Mathematics and Natural Sciences (Fysikkbygn., POB 1032 Blindern, 0315 Oslo; tel. 22-85-52-00; fax 22-85-43-67; e-mail postmottak@matnat.uio.no; internet www.matnat.uio.no):

AAGAARD, P., Geology
AALEN, R., Biology
AARNES, H., Biology
AASEN, A. J., Pharmacy
AASHAMAR, K., Physics
AKSNES, K., Astrophysics
ALBREGTSEN, F., Computer Science
ALVE, E., Geology
ANDERSEN, T. B., Geology
ANDERSSON, K. K., Biochemistry
ANDRESEN, A., Geology
AUSTRHEIM, H., Geology
BAKKE, O., Biology
BEDOS, E. CHR., Mathematics
BENNECHE, T., Chemistry
BERG, T., Cell Biology
BERG, Y., Informatics
BERTELSEN, A., Mechanics
BEUTH, F. E., Mathematics
BJØRLYKKE, K. O., Geology
BORGAN, Ø., Statistics
BRATTELI, O., Mathematics
BRAVINA, L., Physics
BRODERSEN, H., Mathematics
BUGGE, L., Physics
BURAN, T., Physics
BYE, R., Chemistry
BØLVIKEN, E., Statistics
CARLSSON, M., Astrophysics
CHRISTOPHERSEN, N., Informatics
CORFU, F., Geology
DAHL, G., Informatics
DAHLBACK, A., Physics
DALE, B., Geology
DÆHLEN, M., Mathematical Modelling
DØVING, K., Zoophysiology
EEG, J. O., Physics
ELIASSEN, F., Computer Science
ELLINGSRUD, G., Mathematics
ELVERHØI, A., Quaternary Geology
ENGVOLD, O., Astrophysics
ESKILD, W., Biochemistry
FALEIDE, J. I., Geology
FEDER, J. G., Physics
FINSTAD, T., Physics
FJELLVÅG, H., Chemistry
FLEKKØY, E. G., Physics
FLOATER, M. S., Informatics
FURUSETH, S., Chemistry
FÆGRI, K., Chemistry
GABRIELSEN, O. S., Biochemistry
GALPERINE, I., Physics
GELIUS, L.-J., Geophysics
GJESSING, S., Computer Science
GJEVIK, B., Hydrodynamics
GOEBEL, V. H., Informatics
GOTTSCHALK, L., Geophysics
GRAY, J. S., Marine Zoology
GREIBROKK, T., Analytical Chemistry
GRUE, J., Mechanics
GUNDERSEN, G., Chemistry
GUNDERSEN, K., Biology (Physiology)
GUNDERSEN, L.-L., Chemistry
GUTTORMSEN, M., Physics
GØRBITZ, C. H., Chemistry
HAALAND, A., Chemistry
HAGELBERG, E., Zoology
HAGEN, J. O. M., Geography
HANSEN, E. W., Chemistry
HANSEN, F. K., Chemistry
HANSETH, O., Informatics
HANSTEEN, V., Astrophysics
HELGAKER, T., Chemistry
HELLAND, I., Statistics
HELLESLAND, J., Mechanics
HESSEN, D., Zoology
HESTMARK, G., Biology
HJORT, N. L., Statistics
HJORTH-JENSEN, M., Nuclear Physics
HOFF, P., Chemistry
HOLE, E. O., Physics
HOLM, P., Mathematics
HOLM, S., Signal Processing
HOLTET, J. A., Physics
HUMLUM, O., Geography
HØEG, K., Geology
HØGÅSEN, H., Theoretical Physics
HØILAND, K., Biology
INGEBRETSEN, F., Physics
ISAKSEN, I., Meteorology
IVERSEN, T., Geophysics
JAHREN, B., Mathematics
JAKOBSEN, K. S., Biology
JAMTVEIT, B., Geology
JOHANSEN, H. T., Pharmacy
JOHANSEN, T. H., Physics
JØRGENSEN, M., Informatics
KAARTVEDT, S., Marine Biology
KAASBØLL, F. F., Informatics
KAREN, P., Chemistry
KARLSEN, J., Pharmacy
KJELDSETH-MOE, O., Astrophysics
KLAVENESS, D., Biology
KLAVENESS, J., Pharmacy
KOLSTØ, A. B., Microbiology
KOOMEY, J. M., Pharmacology
KRISTENSEN, T. A., Biochemistry
KRISTJANSSON, F. E., Geophysics
KROGDAHL, S., Computer Science
LAANE, C. M., Botany

LAMBERTSSON, A., Genetics
LAMPE, H. M., Biology
LANDE, T. S., Computer Science
LANGTANGEN, H. P., Informatics
LEER, E., Astrophysics
LEINAAS, H. P., Zoology
LEINAAS, J. M., Physics
LIESTØL, K., Mathematical Modelling
LILJE, P. V., Astrophysics
LILLERUD, K. P., Chemistry
LINDQVIST, B. H., Zoology
LINDSTRØM, T., Mathematics
LUND, W., Chemistry
LUNDANES, E., Chemistry
LUTKEN, C. A., Physics
LYCHE, T. J. W., Mathematical Modelling
LYSNE, O., Communication Systems
LØVHØIDEN, G., Physics
LØW, E., Mathematics
MALTERUD, K. E., Pharmacognosy
MARTINSEN, Ø. G., Physics
MAUPIN, V., Geophysics
MOEN, J. I., Physics
MYHRE, A. M., Geology
MØLLENDAL, H., Chemistry
MØLLER-PEDERSEN, B., Informatics
MØRKEN, K., Numerical Analysis
MÅLØY, K. J., Physics
NAGY, J., Geology
NATVIG, B., Mathematical Statistics
NEUMANN, E. R., Geology
NIELSEN, C. J., Chemistry
NILSSON, G. E., Biology (Physiology)
NISSEN-MEYER, J., Biochemistry
NORBY, P. Æ., Chemistry
NORBY, T. E., Chemistry
NORDAL, I., Botany
NORMANN, D., Mathematical Logic
NYSTRØM, B., Organic Chemistry
ØKSENDAL, B., Mathematics
OLSBYE, U., Chemistry
OLSEN, A., Physics
OMTVEDT, F. P., Chemistry
OSNES, E., Physics
OWE, O., Computer Science
PAULSEN, B. S., Pharmacognosy
PAULSEN, R. E., Pharmacy (Microbiology)
PECSELI, H., Physics
PEDERSEN, G. K., Mathematics
PEDERSEN-BJERGAARD, S., Pharmacy
PETTERSEN, E. O., Physics
PIENE, R., Mathematics
PLAGEMANN, T. P., Informatics
PODLADTCHIKOV, Y., Geology
PRYDZ, K., Biochemistry
RANESTAD, K., Mathematics
RASMUSSEN, K. E., Pharmaceutical Analysis
RAVNDAL, F., Theoretical Physics
READ, A. L., Physics
REKSTAD, J. B., Physics
RISE, F., Chemistry
RISEBRO, N. H., Mathematics
ROGNES, J., Mathematics
ROOS, N., Cell Biology
ROOTS, J., Chemistry
RUENESS, J., Marine Biology
RUSTAN, A., Pharmacy
SAATCIOGLU, F., Biology
SAGSTUEN, E., Physics
SAHAY, S., Informatics
SAMDAL, S., Chemistry
SAND, O., Zoophysiology
SANDE, S. A., Pharmacy
SANDHOLT, P. E., Physics
SANDLIE, I., Biology
SCHUMACHER, T., Botany
SEIP, H. M., Chemistry
SIREVÅG, R., Microbiology
SJØBERG, D., Informatics
SKAALI, T. B., Physics
SKRAMSTAD, J., Chemistry
SLAGSVOLD, T., Zoology
SMISTAD, G., Pharmacy
SPILLING, P., Telematics and Telecommunications
STABELL, B., Geology
STABELL, R., Astrophysics
STAPNES, S., Physics
STEEN, H., Biology
STENERSEN, J. H. V., Biology
STENSETH, N. C., Zoology
STORDAL, F., Meteorology
STØLEN, S., Chemistry
STØRMER, E., Mathematics
SUDBØ, AA., Optoelectronics
SVENSSON, B. G., Physics
SWENSEN, A. R., Mathematics (Statistics)
SÆTRE, G.-P., Biology
SØRÅSEN, O., Microelectronics
TAFTØ, J., Physics
THRONDSEN, J., Marine Biology
TILSET, M., Chemistry
TOMTER, P., Mathematics
TOVERUD, E., Pharmacy
TRULSEN, J., Astrophysics
TVEITO, A., Informatics
TVETER, T. S., Physics
TØNNESEN, H. H., Clinical Pharmacy
UGGERUD, E., Chemistry
VESETH, L., Physics
VØLLESTAD, A. L., Biology (Zoology)
WEBER, J. E., Geophysics
WINTHER, R., Mathematical Modelling

Faculty of Medicine (POB 1018 Blindern, 0315 Oslo
Domus Medica, Sognsvannsvn.9, Oslo; tel. 22-85-05-00; fax 22-85-05-01; e-mail delarkiv-sekretariatet@medisin.uio.no; internet www.med.uio.no):

AALEN, O. O., Statistics
AASEN, A., Surgery
AGARTZ, I., Psychiatry
AURSNES, I. A., Pharmacology
BENESTAD, H. B., Physiology
BERG, O. T., Health Administration
BERG, T., Physiology
BJERTNESS, E., Epidemiology
BJUNE, G. A., International Health
BJÅLIE, E. G., Anatomy
BLOMHOFF, H. K., Medical Biochemistry
BLOMHOFF, R., Nutrition Research
BOE, J., Respiratory Medicine
BOGEN, B., Immunology
BOTTEN, G. S., Health Administration
BRANTZAEG, P., Immunology
BREIVIK, H., Anaesthesiology
BRODAL, P., Anatomy
BROSSTAD, F. R., Internal Medicine Research
BRUUSGAARD, D., Social Security Medicine
BUKHOLM, G., Bacteriology
CARLSEN, K.-H., Paediatrics
CHRISTOFFERSEN, T., Pharmacology
CLAUSEN, O. P. F., Pathology
COLLAS, P., Biochemistry
COLLINS, A. R., Nutrition Research
DANBOLT, N. C., Physiology
DREVON, C., Nutrition Research
DUTTAVOY, A. K., Nutrition Research
EVENSEN, S. A., Haematology
FINSET, A., Medical Behavioural Research
FOSSUM, S., Anatomy
FRIGESSI, A., Medical Statistics
FRØLAND, S. S., Clinical Medicine
FUGELLI, P., Social Medicine
FYRAND, O. L., Dermatology
GEIRAN, O., Cardiovascular Surgery
GIESDAL, K., Cardiology
GLOVER, J., Physiology
GORDELADZE, J. O., Medical Biochemistry
GRØHOLT, B., Psychiatry
GRØTTUM, P., Medical Computer Science
HAGEN, T. P., Health Administration
HANSSON, V., Medical Biochemistry
HAUG, F. M., Anatomy
HEGGELUND, P., Neurophysiology
HEIBERG, A. N., Psychiatry
HJORTDAHL, P., Medicine
HOLCK, P., Anatomy
HORN, R., Medical Biochemistry
HUITFELDT, H., Pathology
HUSBY, G., Rheumatology
HØGLEND, P. A., Psychiatry
HØSTMARK, T. A., Preventive Medicine
ILEBEKK, A. B., Experimental Medicine
INGSTAD, B., Social Medicine
IVERSEN, I. G. H., Physiology
IVERSEN, P. O., Nutrition Research
IVERSEN, T., Health Economics
JAHNSEN, T., Biochemistry
JELLUM, E., Clinical Biochemistry
KASE, B. F., Paediatrics
KIERULF, P., Clinical Chemistry
KIRKEVOLD, M., Medicine
KJEKSHUS, J., Cardiology
KLEPP, K. I., Nutrition Research
KOLBENSTVEDT, A. N., Radiology
KOLSET, S. O., Nutrition Research
KVITTINGEN, E. A., Clinical Biochemistry
LAAKE, P., Medical Statistics
LARSEN, Ø., Medical History
LEVY, F. O., Pharmacology
LIE, S. O., Paediatrics
LINDEGAARD, K., Neurosurgery
LOGE, F. H., Medical Behavioural Research
LORENSEN, M., Nursing Science
LÆRUM, F., Clinical Medicine
LØVSTAD, R., Medical Biochemistry
MADSHUS, I. H., Molecular Biology
MENGSHOEL, A. M., Health Science
MEYER, H. E., Social Medicine
MOUM, T., Medical Behavioural Research
MULLER, F., Pharmacology
NAFSTAD, P., Social Medicine
NATVIG, J. B., Immunology
NICOLAYSEN, G., Physiology
NJÅ, A., Neurophysiology
NYBERG-HANSEN, R., Neurology
NÆSS, O., Pathology
ORMSTAD, K., Forensic Medicine
OS, I., Pharmacology
OSNES, J. B., Pharmacology
ØSTVOLD, A. C., Neurochemistry
OTTERSEN, O. P., Anatomy
PEDERSEN, J. I., Nutrition Research
REIBERÅS, O., Orthopaedics
REIKVAM, Å., Pharmacotherapy
REINHOLT, F. P., Pathology
RINVIK, E., Anatomy
ROGDE, S., Forensic Medicine
ROGNUM, T. O., Forensic Medicine
ROLLAG, H., Bacteriology
ROLSTAD, B., Anatomy
SAGVOLDEN, T., Neurophysiology
SANDANGER, B., Medical Behavioural Research
SANDNES, D. L., Pharmacology
SAUGSTAD, O. D., Paediatrics
SEJERSTED, O. M., Experimental Research
SKOMEDAL, T., Pharmacology
SOLBAKK, J. H., Medical Ethics
SOLLID, L. M., Transplantation Immunology
STEEN, P. A., Anaesthesiology
STOKKE, O., Clinical Biochemistry
STORM, J., Physiology
STORM-MATHISEN, J., Anatomy
STRAAND, F., Social Medicine
STRAY-PEDERSEN, B., Obstetrics and Gynaecology
SØRENSEN, T., Psychiatry
TASKÉN, K., Medical Biochemistry
TELLNES, G., Social Security Medicine
TØNJUM, T., Microbiology
UNDLIEN, D. E., Medical Genetics
URSIN, G., Nutrition Research
VAAGE, I. F., Traumatology
VAGLUM, P., Psychiatry
VATN, M. H., Clinical Epidemiology
VØLLESTAD, N. K., Health Science
WAAL, H., Psychiatry
WALAAS, S. I., Biochemistry
WALLØE, L., Physiology
WANDEL, M., Nutrition Research

Faculty of Social Sciences (Eilert Sundts hus, 3. et., POB 1084 Blindern, 0317 Oslo; tel. 22-85-62-64; fax 22-85-48-25; e-mail sv-info@sv.uio.no; internet www.sv.uio.no):

ALBUM, D., Sociology
ANDRESEN, S. E., Political Science
ARCHETTI, E. P., Social Anthropology
ASHEIM, G. B., Economics
BALDERSHEIM, H., Political Science
BERKAAK, O. A., Social Anthropology
BIRKELUND, G. E., Sociology
BIØRN, E., Economics
BJERKHOLT, O., Economics
BJØRKLÚND, R., Psychology
BJØRKLÚND, T., Political Science
BLAKAR, R. M., Social Psychology
BORGE, A. I. H., Psychology
BREKKE, K. A., Economics
BRENNEN, T., Psychology
BROCH, H. B., Social Anthropology
BROCHMANN, G., Sociology
CHECKEL, F. T., Political Science
CHRISTENSEN, T., Political Science
CHRISTIANSEN, V., Economics
DUCKERT, F., Psychology
EGEBERG, M., Political Science
ENGELSTAD, F., Sociology
ERIKSEN, G. T. H., Social Anthropology
FEHR, N. H., Economics
FJELL, A., Psychology
FØRSUND, F., Economics
FRØNES, I., Sociology
FURST, E. L., Social Anthropology
GULLESTAD, S. E., Psychology
HAAVIND, H., Psychology
HAGTVET, B., Political Science
HAGTVET, K. A., Psychology
HANSEN, M. N., Sociology
HANSEN, T., Political Science
HARTMANN, E. F., Psychology
HEIDAR, K., Political Science
HELLEVIK, O., Political Science
HESSELBERG, J., Social Geography
HOEL, M. O., Economics
HOLDEN, S., Economics
HOVI, J., Political Science
HOWELL, S. L., Social Anthropology
HVEEM, H., Political Science
HYLLAND, AA., Economics
KALLAND, A., Social Anthropology
KALLENBERG, R., Sociology
KEILMAN, N. W., Demography
KIRKEBØEN, G., Psychology
KNUTSEN, O., Political Science
KRAVDAL, Ø., Demographics
KROGSTAD, A., Sociology
LANDRØ, N. I., Psychology
LEIRA, A., Sociology
LUND, D., Economics
LUND, S. E., Social Anthropology
MAGNUSSEN, S. J., Psychology
MALNES, R. S., Political Science
MASTEKAASA, A., Sociology
MATLARY, F. H., Political Science
MEHLUM, H., Economics
MELHUS, M., Social Anthropology
MJØSET, L., Sociology
MOENE, K. O., Economics and Statistics
MONSEN, J., Psychology
MYDSKE, P. K., Political Science
NARUD, H. M., Political Science
NIELSEN, T. H., Social Sciences and Humanities
NILSSEN, T., Economics
NORDBY, T., Political History
NYBORG, K., Economics
NYMOEN, R., Economics
OMMUNDSEN, R., Psychology
ØSTERUD, Ø., Conflict and Peace Research
OTNES, P., Sociology
PEDERSEN, W., Social Geography
PONS, F., Psychology
RASCH, B. E., Political Science
REINVANG, I., Psychology
RØDSETH, A., Economics
RØNNESTAD, H., Psychology
ROSE, L. E., Political Science
RØYSAMB, E., Psychology
SCHWEDER, T., Statistics
SKJEIE, H., Political Science
SKOE, E. E. A., Psychology
SKOG, O., Sociology
STEEN, A., Political Science
STOKKE, K., Social Geography
STORESLETTEN, K., Economics
STRAND, J., Economics
SUNDET, J. M., Psychology
SUNDET, K. S., Psychology
SYDSÆTER, K., Mathematics
SØRENSON, T., Sociology
SØRUM, A., Social Anthropology
TALLE, A., Social Anthropology
TEIGEN, K. H., Psychology
TETZCHNER, S. V., Psychology
TJERSLAND, O. A., Psychology
TORGERSEN, S. O., Psychology
TØRNQUIST, O., Political Science
ULLTVEIT-MOE, K. H., Economics
UNDERDAL, A., Political Science
VASSEND, O., Psychology
VISLIE, J., Economics
VOLLRATH, M., Psychology
WALHOVD, K., Psychology
WESSEL, T., Social Geography
WIDERBERG, K., Sociology
WIKAN, U., Social Anthropology
WILLASSEN, Y., Economics
WOLD, A. H., Psychology

Faculty of Theology (POB 1023 Blindern, 0315 Oslo
Domus Theologica, Blindernvn. 9, 0371 Oslo; tel. 22-85-03-00; fax 22-85-03-01; e-mail postmottak@teologi.uio.no; internet www.tf.uio.no):

CHRISTOFFERSEN, S. A., Systematic Theology
DOKKA, T. S., New Testament and Systematic Theology
ELSTAD, H., Church History and Religious Sociology
FRØYSHOV, S. R., Liturgy and Ancient Christianity
HAFSTAD, K., Systematic Theology
KVANVIG, H. S., Old Testament
LEIRVIK, O. B., Inter-religious Studies
MOXNES, H., New Testament
NODERVAL, Ø., Ancient Christianity
RASMUSSEN, T., History of the Church
RUYTER, K., Religious Ethics
SALOMONSEN, J., Religious Anthropology
STORDALEN, T., Old Testament
THORKILDSEN, D., Church History
TØNNESEN, A. V., Church History
WYLLER, T. E., Systematic Theology

Biotechnology Centre of Oslo (EMBIO) (POB 1125 Blindern, 0317 Oslo
Forskringsparken, Gaustadalleen 21, 0349 Oslo; tel. 22-84-05-00; fax 22-84-05-01; e-mail postmottak@biotek.uio.no; internet www.biotek.uio.no):

TASKÉN, K. (Dir)

Natural History Museum and Botanical Gardens (POB 1172 Blindern, 0318 Oslo
Sars' gt. 1, Monradgt., 0562 Oslo; tel. 22-85-16-30; fax 22-85-17-09; e-mail informasjon@nhm.uio.no; internet www.nhm.uio.no):

ANDERSEN, K. I., Zoology
BACHMANN, L., Zoology
BAKKE, T. A., Zoology
BJORKLUND, K. R., Palaeontology
BORGEN, L., Botany
BROCHMANN, C., Botany
BRUTON, D. L., Palaeontology
ELVEN, R., Botany
GULDEN, G., Botany
HALVORSEN, O., Zoology
LIFJELD, J. T., Zoology
ØKLAND, R. H., Botany
SUNDING, P., Botany
VAN BERGEN, I. J., Mineralogy
WIIG, Ø., Zoology and Mammalogy

Kulturhistorisk Museum (POB 6762 St Olavs plass, 0130 Oslo; tel. 22-85-19-00; fax 22-85-19-38; e-mail postmottak@khm.uio.no; internet www.khm.uio.no):

CHRISTENSEN, A. E., Scandinavian Archaeology
KNIRK, J. E., Medieval History
MIKKELSEN, E., Nordic Archaeology
ØSTMO, E., Stone Age and Bronze Age
PLATHER, U., Art Conservation Chemistry
RESI, H. G., Iron Age
SVENSSON, T. G., Social Anthropology

UNIVERSITET I STAVANGER
(University of Stavanger)

4036 Stavanger
Arne Rettedal hus, Kjell Arholmsgt. 41, Stavanger
Telephone: 51-83-10-00
Fax: 51-83-30-50
E-mail: post@uis.no
Internet: www.uis.no

Founded 1994 as Høgskolen i Stavanger; univ. status acquired and present name adopted 2005
State control
Languages of instruction: Norwegian, English

Rector: ASLAUG MIKKELSEN
Vice-Rector: EGIL GABRIELSEN
University Dir: PER RAMVI
Strategy and Communication Dir: ANNE SELNES
Librarian: ESPEN SKJOLDAL

Number of teachers: 1,200
Number of students: 8,300

Library of 250,000 vols, 3,000 periodicals

DEANS

Faculty of Humanities: TOR HAUKEN
Faculty of Natural Science and Technology: ARNE BJØRKUM
Faculty of Social Sciences: MARIT BOYESEN

UNIVERSITETET I TROMSØ
(University of Tromsø)

9037 Tromsø
Telephone: 77-64-40-00
Fax: 77-64-49-00
E-mail: postmottak@uit.no
Internet: uit.no

Founded 1968, merged with Høgskolen i Tromsø (Tromsø University College) 2009
State control
Academic year: August to June (two semesters)

Rector: Prof. JARLE AARBAKKE
Pro-Rector for Education: Prof. BRITT VIGDIS EKELI
Pro-Rector for Research and Devt: CURT RICE
Univ. Dir: LASSE LØNNUM
Library Dir: HELGE SALVESEN

Number of teachers: 1,900
Number of students: 6,700

Publications: *Journal of Department of Community Medicine*, *Journal of Faculty of Law*, *Nordlit* (literature), *Ottar* (popular science), *Poljarnyj Vestnik* (Russian language and literature), *Ravnetrykk* (univ. library journal), *Speculum Boreale* (history), *Troll* (literature), *Uvett* (education)

DEANS

Faculty of the Arts: KJELL MAGNE MÆLEN
Faculty of Health Sciences: ARNFINN SUNDSFJORD
Faculty of Humanities, Social Sciences and Education: PETTER NAFSTAD
Faculty of Law: HEGE BRÆKHUS

Faculty of Life Sciences, Fisheries and Economics: EDEL ELVEVOLL
Faculty of Science and Technology: MORTEN HALD

PROFESSORS

Faculty of the Arts (tel. 77-66-03-04; fax 77-61-88-99; e-mail postmottak@kunstfak.uit.no):

LUNDBERG, L., Creative Writing
SIEPEN, N., Contemporary Art
SONJASDOTTER, A., Contemporary Art

Faculty of Health Sciences (tel. 77-64-46-01; fax 77-64-53-00; e-mail postmottak@helsefak.uit.no):

ANDERSEN, T., Community Medicine
ARNESEN, E., Community Medicine
BJØRKLID, E., Medical Biology
BLIX, A. S., Medical Biology
BRANDL, M., Pharmacy
DAHL, S. G., Medical Biology
EL-GEWELY, M. R., Medical Biology
FOLKOW, L., Medical Biology
FØNNEBØ, V., Community Medicine
FØRDE, O. H., Community Medicine
GRAM, I. T., Community Medicine
GREINER-TOLLERSRUD, O. K., Medical Biology
HASVOLD, T., Community Medicine
HOLTEDAHL, K., Community Medicine
HUSEBEKK, A., Medical Biology
HUSEBY, N.-E., Medical Biology
HØYER, G., Community Medicine
JACOBSEN, B. K., Community Medicine
JENSEN, E., Pharmacy
JOHANSEN, S., Medical Biology
JOHANSEN, T., Medical Biology
LARSEN, T., Medical Biology
LOENNECHEN, T., Pharmacy
NIELSEN, K. M., Pharmacy
LUND, E., Community Medicine
MERCER, J., Medical Biology
MELBYE, H., Community Medicine
MJØS, O. D., Medical Biology
MOENS, U., Medical Biology
NIELSEN, K. M., Pharmacy
NJØLSTAD, I., Community Medicine
NORDØY, E., Medical Biology
OLSEN, J. A., Community Medicine
OLSVIK, Ø., Medical Biology
ØRBO, A., Medical Biology
REKVIG, O.-P., Medical Biology
RINNE, A., Medical Biology
SAGER, G., Medical Biology
SMEDSRØD, B., Medical Biology
STOKKAN, K.-A., Medical Biology
SUNDSFJORD, A., Medical Biology
SYLTE, I., Medical Biology
WILLASSEN, N. P., Medical Biology
WINBERG, J.-O., Medical Biology
YTREHUS, K., Medical Biology

Faculty of Humanities, Social Sciences and Education (tel. 77-64-43-00; e-mail postmottak@hsl.uit.no):

AARSÆTHER, N.
ANDERSSON, D. T.
ALHAUG, G.
BARSTAD, G.
BERTELSEN, R.
BLANKHOLM, P.
BOUVRIE, S. DES
BULL, T.
DAMM, C.
DRIVENES, E.-A.
EGEBERG, E. H.
ENGELSTAD, E.
GAASLAND, R.
HOFSTEN, H. W. VON
KARLSEN, O.
KONSTANTINOV, Y.
LIEPE, L.
LINDGREN, A.-R.
LUND, N. W.
LÖNNGREN, L.
MØRCK, E.
MYRSTAD, A.
NESSET, T.
OLSEN, B.
RAMCHAND, G.
RICE, C.
SCHMIDT, M.
STARKE, M.
SVENONIUS, P.
SVONNI, M.
SWAN, T.
TARALDSEN, K. T.
VALESTRAND, H.
WESTVIK, O. M. J.
WÆRP, H. H.

Faculty of Law (tel. 77-64-41-97; fax 77-64-47-75; e-mail postmottak@jus.uit.no):

CHRISTIANSEN, P.
HAUGLI, T.

Faculty of Life Sciences, Fisheries and Economics (tel. 77-64-60-00; e-mail eksped@nfh.uit.no):

AMUNDSEN, P.-A., Aquatic Biology
BØGWALD, J., Marine Biotechnology
CLARK, D., Economics and Management
EILERTSEN, H. C., Aquatic Biology
ELVEVOLL, E. O., Marine Biotechnology
FALK-PETERSEN, I. B., Aquatic Biology
FEVOLDEN, S.-E., Aquatic Biology
FLÅTEN, O., Economics and Management
GULLIKSEN, B., Aquatic Biology
HERSOUG, B., Economics and Management
HOLM, P., Economics and Management
JENTOFT, S., Economics and Management
JOBLING, M., Aquatic Biology
JOHNSEN, H. K., Aquatic Biology
JØRGENSEN, E., Aquatic Biology
JØRGENSEN, J. B., Marine Biotechnology
JØRGENSEN, T. Ø., Marine Biotechnology
KLEMETSEN, J., Aquatic Biology
KRISTIANSEN, S., Aquatic Biology
OLAFSEN, J. A., Marine Biotechnology
OLSEN, K. K., Aquatic Biology
OLSEN, R. L., Marine Biotechnology
OLSEN, S. O., Economics and Management
ROBERTSEN, B., Marine Biotechnology
SCHULZ, C.-E., Economics and Management
TANDE, K., Aquatic Biology
TRONDSEN, T., Social and Marketing Studies
VASSDAL, T., Economics and Management
WASSMANN, P., Aquatic Biology

Faculty of Science and Technology (tel. 77-64-40-01; fax 77-64-47-65; e-mail postmottak@nt.uit.no):

ANDERSEN, J., Biology
ANSHUS, O. J., Computer Science
ASLAKSEN, T., Physics
BERGH, S., Geology
BHUVANESWARI, T. V., Biology
CARLSON, R., Chemistry
DAHL, D., Chemistry
ELTOFT, T., Physics
ESSER, R., Physics
FLÅ, T., Mathematics and Statistics
FOLSTAD, I., Biology
GHOSH, A., Chemistry
GODTLIBSEN, F., Mathematics and Statistics
HALD, M., Geology
HANSEN, L. K., Chemistry
HANSSEN, A., Physics
HARTVIGSEN, G., Computer Science
HAVNES, O., Physics
HOUGH, E., Chemistry
IMS, R. A., Biology
JACOBSEN, S., Physics
JOHANSEN, D., Computer Science
JOHNSEN, B., Mathematics and Statistics
JUNTILLA, O., Biology
KRUGLIKOV, B., Mathematics and Statistics
LA HOZ, C., Physics
LYCHAGIN, V., Mathematics and Statistics
MELANDSØ, F., Physics
MIENERT, J., Geology
MJØLHUS, E., Mathematics and Statistics
OLSON, L., Mathematics and Statistics
PRASOLOV, A., Mathematics and Statistics
RAVNA, E. K., Geology
RUUD, K., Chemistry
RYPDAL, K., Physics
RØEGGEN, I., Physics
SMALÅS, A., Chemistry
SVENDSEN, J. S., Chemistry
SVENNING, M., Biology
VORREN, K.-D., Biology
VORREN, T., Geology
YOCCOZ, N., Biology

Colleges of University Standing

ARKITEKTHØGSKOLEN I OSLO
(Oslo School of Architecture)

POB 6768 St Olavs plass, 0130 Oslo
Maridalsveien 29, 0175 Oslo

Telephone: 22-99-70-00
Fax: 22-99-71-90
E-mail: postmottak@aho.no
Internet: www.aho.no

Founded 1945
State control
Academic year: September to June

Rector: KARL OTTO ELLEFSEN
Vice-Rector: BIRGER SEVALDSON
Dir: EINAR FAGERÅ
Library Dir: SISSEL MOUM

Library of 40,000 vols
Number of teachers: 120
Number of students: 700

Publication: *Research Magazine* (1 a year)

HEADS OF FACULTY

Faculty of Architecture: BØRRE SKODVIN
Faculty of Design: JONATHAN ROMM
Faculty of Form, Theory and History: MARI LENDING
Faculty of Urbanism and Landscape: NETTEN ØSTBERG

PROFESSORS

DAHL, K. E., Urbanism and Landscape
DAHLE, E., Architectural Design
DOBLOUG, M., Architectural Design
DUNIN-WOYSETH, H., Form, Theory and History
EDEHOLT, H., Design
FJELD, P. O., Architectural Design
GERSTLAUER, R., Architectural Design
HERMANSEN, C., Architectural Design
HJELTNES, K., Architectural Design
HØLMEBAKK, B., Form, Theory and History
HVATTUM, M., Form, Theory and History
JENSEN, J., Architectural Design
KLEVEN, B., Architectural Design
LØKSE, O., Form and Design
MICHL, J., Industrial Design
MORRISON, A., Design
ROBBINS, E., Urbanism and Landscape
SANDAKER, B., Building Technology
SEVALDSON, B., Design
SKJØNSBERG, T., Form and Design
THIIS-EVENSEN, T., Architectural Theory and History
TOSTRUP, E., Form, Theory and History
TVILDE, D., Urbanism and Landscape

BERGEN ARKITEKT SKOLE
(Bergen School of Architecture)

POB 39, 5841 Bergen
Sandviksboder 59–61A, 5035 Bergen
Telephone: 55-36-38-80
Fax: 55-36-38-81

E-mail: adm@bergenarkitektskole.no
Internet: www.bergenarkitektskole.no

Founded 1986, fully recognized 1990
Private control

Accredited by Norwegian Agency for Quality Assurance in Education

Rector: MARIANNE SKJULHAUG
Head of Student Affairs: SIV GJERDE AARDAL
Head of Library: LINE FRØYLAND

Library of 3,000 books, 20 int. magazines, spec. focus on architecture, soc., art, landscape, architecture, history and bldgs in northern climate, bldg history of Norway's W coast, foreign culture and disaster risk migration

Number of teachers: 50 (incl. part-time)
Number of students: 150

HANDELSHØYSKOLEN BI
(BI Norwegian School of Management)

0442 Oslo
Nydalsveien 37, 0484 Oslo

Telephone: 46-41-00-00
Fax: 21-04-80-00
E-mail: info@bi.no
Internet: www.bi.no

Founded 1943
Private control
Languages of instruction: Norwegian, English
Academic year: September to June

Rector: TOM COLBJØRNSEN
Deputy-Rector: DAG MORTEN DALEN
Vice-Rector: ULF HENNING OLSSON
Exec. Dir: JENS PETTER TØNDEL
Library Dir: DAGMAR LANGEGGEN

Number of teachers: 370
Number of students: 19,931 (incl. part-time)

HØGSKOLEN I BODØ
(Bodø University College)

POB 1490, 8049 Bodø
Mørkvedtråkket 30, 8049 Bodø

Telephone: 75-51-72-00
Fax: 75-51-74-57
E-mail: postmottak@hibo.no
Internet: www.hibo.no

Founded 1994 by merger of 3 univ. colleges in Bodø
State control
Languages of instruction: Norwegian, English
Academic year: August to June

Rector: PÅL A. PEDERSEN
Dir: STIG FOSSUM
Registrar and Dir for Marketing and Communications: HEGE NERDAL RASCH
Exec. Librarian: GUNNLAUG HANSTEEN, HEIDI PEDERSON

Number of teachers: 305
Number of students: 5,000

DEANS

Bodø Graduate School of Business: FRANK LINDBERG
Faculty of Biosciences and Aquaculture: TERJE SOLBERG
Faculty of Social Sciences: TERJE HALVORSEN
School of Professional Studies: ARNE FJALSTAD

HØGSKOLEN I NARVIK
(Narvik University College)

POB 385, 8505 Narvik
Lodve Langesgt. 2, Narvik
Alta campus: Follumsvei 33, 9510 Alta

Telephone: 76-96-60-00 (Narvik)
Fax: 76-96-68-10 (Narvik)
E-mail: postmottak@hin.no
Internet: www.hin.no

Founded 1955

Vice-Chanchellor: ARNE ERIK HOLDØ
Admin. Dir: KNUT RAVLO (acting)
Library Dir: ELLEN JULIN

Library of 20,000 items
Number of teachers: 170
Number of students: 1,300

DEANS

Faculty of Health and Society: ÅSE BERIT VRENNE
Faculty of Technology: ARNE LAKSÅ

NORGES HANDELSHØYSKOLE
(Norwegian School of Economics and Business Administration)

Helleveien 30, 5045 Bergen

Telephone: 55-95-90-00
Fax: 55-95-91-00
E-mail: nhh.postmottak@nhh.no
Internet: www.nhh.no

Founded 1936
State control
Academic year: September to June

Rector: JAN I. HAALAND
Vice-Rector: GUNNAR E. CHRISTENSEN
Dir: OLE HOPE
Library Dir: SISSEL HAFSTAD

Library of 280,000 vols, 1,600 periodicals
Number of teachers: 210
Number of students: 3,000

DEANS

Faculty of Accounting, Auditing and Law: KATARINA ÖSTERGREN
Faculty of Economics: ØYSTEIN THØGERSEN
Faculty of Finance and Management Science: FRODE SÆTTEM
Faculty of Professional and Intercultural Communication: SUNNIVA WHITTAKER
Faculty of Strategy and Management: TOR FREDRIKSEN

PROFESSORS

Faculty of Accounting, Auditing and Law:
- BJØRNENAK, T., Management Accounting
- EILIFSEN, A., Financial Accounting and Auditing
- GJESDAL, F., Management and Financial Accounting
- JOHNSEN, A., N., Financial Accounting
- MONSEN, N., Governmental Accounting
- ÖSTERGREN, K., Cost Accounting and Project Management
- STUART, I., Auditing

Faculty of Economics:
- BASBERG, B., Economic History
- BIVAND, R., Economic and Quantitative Geography
- BJORVATN, K., Economic Development and Geography
- BREKKE, K., Health Economics
- BRUNSTAD, R., Macroeconomics
- BRUNT, L., Economic History
- CAPPELEN, A., Experimental Economics
- GRYTTEN, O., Macroeconomic History
- HAGEN, K. P., Public Economics
- HANNESSON, R., Fisheries Economics
- HÅLAND, J. I., International Economics
- KIND, H. J., Industrial Organization and International Economics
- KLOVLAND, J. T., Macroeconomics and Economic History
- KRISTIANSEN, E. G., Microeconomics
- MATHIESEN, L., General Equilibrium Modelling
- NILSEN, O. A., Labour Economics and Investment
- NORMAN, V. D., International Economics
- SALVANES, K. G., Labour Economics and Industrial Organization
- SCHROTYEN, F., Public Economics
- SØRGARD, L., Industrial Organization
- STEEN, F., Econometrics and Industrial Organization
- STRANDENES, S. P., International and Shipping Economics
- THØGERSEN, O., Macroeconomics and Social Security
- TUNGODDEN, B., Social Choice Theory and Development Economics
- VATNE, E., Economic Geography

Faculty of Finance and Management Science:
- ÅSE, K. K., P., Finance and Insurance Mathematics
- BJERKSUND, P., Investment and Risk Management
- BJØRNDAL, M. H., C., Operations Research and Management
- EKERN, S., Finance
- ESKELAND, G. S., Environmental Economics and Public Finance
- FOROS, O., Industrial Organization and Management Science
- GJERDE, O., Finance and Operations Management
- HANSEN, T., Personal Finance and Management Control Systems
- JÖRNSTEN, KURTJOHNSEN, T., Finance
- JÖRNSTEN, K., Production Planning and Control
- LEITE, T., Financial Markets and Intermediation
- LENSBERG, T., Decision Theory
- LILLESTØL, J., Statistics and Probability
- MØEN, J., Microeconometrics and Productivity Analysis
- OLSEN, T. E., Financial Contracting
- PERSSON, S.-A., Finance and Economics of Insurance
- RÖNNQVIST, M., Operations Research and Logistics
- SANDAL, L. K., Applied Mathematics and Management Science
- SCHJELDERUP, G., Microeconomics
- STENSLAND, G., Investment and Risk Management
- SÆTTEM, F., Finance
- UBØE, J., Mathematics and Statistics

Faculty of Professional and Intercultural Communication:
- DAHL, T., English
- MARTÍNEZ, J. A., Spanish
- SIMONNÆS, I., German
- WHITTAKER, S., French

Faculty of Strategy and Management:
- BREIVIK, E., Brand Management and Consumer Trends
- BROCHS-HAUKEDAL, W., Management and Organizational Behaviour
- ESPEDAL, B., Organizational Learning and Adaptation
- FOSS, K., Competitive Strategy
- FUGLSETH, A.-M., System Development
- GOODERHAM, P., International and Knowledge Management
- GREVE, A., Organization Theory
- HAUGLAND, S., Strategic Management and Organization Theory
- HEM, L., Brand Management and Consumer Trends
- IMS, K., Business Ethics and Management
- LINES, R., Market Research and Strategy
- MEYER, C., Strategy, Merger and Acquisitions
- NORDHAUG, O., Organization Theory and Management
- NYSVEEN, H., Interactive Marketing and Product Development
- PEDERSON, P. E., Innovation and Information Management
- ROGNES, J. K., Negotiation
- SELART, M., Organizational Behaviour and Human Resources Management
- SUPPHELLEN, M., Brand Management and Consumer Trends

THORBJØRNSEN, H., Consumer Psychology and Trends
TROYE, S., Market Research and Consumption Patterns

NORGES IDRETTSHØGSKOLE (Norwegian School of Sport Sciences)

POB 4014 Ullevål Stadion, 0806 Oslo
Sognsveien 220, Oslo

Telephone: 23-26-20-00
Fax: 22-23-42-20
E-mail: postmottak@nih.no
Internet: www.nih.no

Founded 1968
State control
Academic year: August to June

Rector: SIGMUND LOLAND
Vice-Rector: INGER-ÅSHILD BY
Dir: BAARD WIST
Library Dir: HEGE UNDERTHUN

Library of 70,000 vols
Number of teachers: 100
Number of students: 1,500

Publication: *Moving Bodies* (2 a year)

HEADS OF DIVISION

Division of Coaching and Psychology: NICOLAS LEMYRE
Division of Culture and Society: DAG VIDAR HANSTAD
Division of Physical Education and Paedagogy: GUNN ENGELSRUD
Division of Physical Performance: JAN CABRI
Division of Sports Medicine: ROALD BAHR

NORGES VETERINÆRHØGSKOLE (Norwegian School of Veterinary Science)

POB 8146 Dep, 0033 Oslo

Telephone: 22-96-45-00
Fax: 22-59-73-09
E-mail: post@nvh.no
Internet: www.nvh.no

Founded 1935; plans mooted for merger with Universitetet for Miljø- og Biovitenskap (Norwegian University of Life Sciences)
Academic year: August to June

Rector: YNGVILD WASTESON
Vice-Rector: HALVOR HEKTOEN
Admin. Dir: BIRGER KRUSE
Head of Secretariat: HANS GRAN
Head Librarian: ANNE CATHRINE MUNTHE

Library of 77,000 vols
Number of teachers: 114
Number of students: 470 , incl. 80 postgraduate

HEADS OF FACULTY

Faculty of Basic Sciences and Aquatic Medicine: MONA ALEKSANDERSEN
Faculty of Companion Animal Clinical Sciences: KRISTIN THORUD
Faculty of Food Safety and Infection Biology: GUDMUND HOLSTAD
Faculty of Livestock Medicine: OLAV REKSEN

PROFESSORS

ALESTRØM, P., Biochemistry
ANDRESEN, Ø., Reproduction
ANSOK, S. B., Anatomy and Pathology
AULIE, A., Physiology
BERG, K. A., Reproduction
BJERKÅS, I., Anatomy
DOLVIK, N. I., Large Animal Clinical Sciences
EVENSEN, Ø., I., Aquatic Medicine and Nutrition
ELIASSEN, K., Biochemistry and Physiology
FARSTAD, W., Reproduction
FRØSLIE, A., Forensic Medicine
GJERDE, B., Parasitology
GODFROID, J., Arctic Veterinary Medicine
GRANUM, P. E., Food Hygiene
GRAVE, K., Pharmacology and Toxicology
GRØNDALEN, J., Small Animal Clinical Sciences
GRØNSTØL, H., Large Animal Clinical Sciences
HARBITZ, I., Biochemistry
HORSBERG, T. E., Pharmacology
KARLBERG, K., Reproduction
KROGDAHL, A., Nutrition
LANDSVERK, T., Pathology
LARSEN, J. J., Microbiology
LINGAAS, F., Animal Genetics
LØKEN, T., Large Animal Clinical Sciences
MOE, L., Small Animal Clinical Sciences
NESBAKKEN, T., Food Hygiene
ØDEGAARD, S., Reproduction
PAULSON, J. E., Food Hygiene
POPPE, T., Anatomy and Pathology
REIMERS, E., Anatomy and Pathology
REITE, O. B., Aquaculture and Fish Diseases
RIMSTAD, E., Virology
ROPSTAD, E., Reproduction
RØED, K. H., Animal Genetics
RØNNINGEN, K., Animal Genetics
SIMENSEN, E., Research Farm
SJAASTAD, Ø., Physiology
SKJERVE, E., Food Hygiene
SMITH, A., Laboratory Animals
SØLI, N., Pharmacology and Toxicology
SØRUM, H., Microbiology
TEIGE, J., Pathology
TRANULIS, M., Biochemistry and Physiology
TRYLAND, M., Arctic Veterinary Medicine
TVERDAL, A., Animal Genetics
ULVUND, M., Sheep and Goat Research
WALDELAND, H., Sheep and Goat Research
WASTESON, Y., Food Hygiene
YNDESTAD, M., Food Hygiene

TEOLOGISKE MENIGHETSFAKULTET (MF Norwegian School of Theology)

POB 5144 Majorstuen, 0302 Oslo
Gydasvei 4, 0302 Oslo

Telephone: 22-59-05-00
Fax: 22-59-05-05
E-mail: post@mf.no
Internet: www.mf.no

Founded 1907
Private control

Accredited by the Norwegian Agency for Quality Assurance in Education (NOKUT) and ENQA—the European Assn for Quality Assurance in Higher Education
Languages of instruction: Norwegian, English
Academic year: August to June

Rector: Prof. Dr VIDAR L. HAANES
Dir: Cand. jur. BEATE PETTERSEN
Dean of Research: Prof. KARL OLAV SANDNES
Dean of Studies: Dr ØYSTEIN LUND
Librarian: ELNA OLINE STRANDHEIM

Library of 73,000 vols and 500 periodicals
Number of teachers: 90
Number of students: 1,100

Publications: *Studia Theologica* (2 a year), *Nordic Journal for Religion and Society* (2 a year)

HEADS OF FACULTY

Faculty of Theology: SVEIN OLAF THORBJØRNSEN
Faculty of Religion and Education: ANN MIDTTUN
Faculty of Religion and Science: GUNNAR HEIENE

PROFESSORS

AFDAL, G., Philosophy of Religious Education
ENGEDAL, L. G., Psychology of Religion
ENGELSVIKEN, T., Missiology
GRAVEM, P., Systematic Theology
HEGSTAD, H., Systematic Theology
HEIENE, G., Systematic Theology
HENRIKSEN, J.-O., Systematic Theology
HVALVIK, R., The New Testament
KÖRTING, C., The Old Testament
KVALBEIN, H., The New Testament
MOGSTAD, S. D., Philosophy of Religious Education
OFTESTAD, B. T., Church History
SANNES, K. O., Systematic Theology
SKARSAUNE, O., Church History
THORBJØRNSEN, S. O., Systematic Theology
WEYDE, K. W., The Old Testament

Schools of Art and Music

Griegakademiet (Grieg Academy): Humanistiske fakultet, POB 7805, 5020 Bergen; Lars Hillesgt. 3, 5015 Bergen; tel. 55-58-69-50; fax 55-58-69-60; e-mail post@grieg.uib.no; internet www.uib.no/grieg; f. 1905; education of musicians, music teachers and organists; offers teacher-training and Bachelors and Masters degree courses; 120 students; Head of Institute FRODE THORSEN.

Kunstakademiet i Trondheim, Norges Teknisk-Naturvitenskaplige Universitet (Trondheim Academy of Fine Art, Norwegian University of Science and Technology): NTNU, 7491 Trondheim; Innherredsveien 7, Trondheim; tel. 73-59-79-00; fax 73-59-79-20; e-mail adm@kit.ntnu.no; internet www.kit.ntnu.no; f. 1946; offers Bachelors and Masters degree courses in fine art; 11 staff; 58 students; library: 5,000 vols; Pres. IVAR SMEDSTAD; publ. *Kitsch* (4 a year).

Kunsthøgskolen i Bergen (KHIB) (Bergen National Academy of the Arts): Strømgt. 1, 5015 Bergen; tel. 55-58-73-00; fax 55-58-73 10; e-mail khib@khib.no, internet www.khib.no; offers Bachelors and Masters degree courses in ceramics, fine arts, interior and furniture design, photography, textiles and printmaking, visual communication; library: 15,000 vols, 200 periodicals; 45 teachers; 300 students; Pres. KETIL SCHREINER EVJEN.

Kunsthøgskolen i Oslo (KHiO) (National Academy of Oslo): POB 6853 St Olavs plass, 0130 Oslo; Fossveien 24, 0551 Oslo; tel. 22-99-55-80; fax 22-99-55-85; e-mail khio@khio.no; f. 1996 by merger of Statens Håndverks og Kunstindustriskole (Nat. College of Art and Design), Statens Kunstakademi (Nat. Academy of Fine Arts), Statens Balletthøgskole (Nat. College of Ballet), Statens Teaterhøgskole (State University of Theatre) and Statens Operahøgskole (State Opera Academy); offers Bachelors and Masters degree courses; comprises faculties of design, visual arts and performing arts; library: 80,000 vols; 138 teachers; 496 students; Pres. GYRID GARSHOL.

Norges Musikkhøgskole (Norwegian Academy of Music): POB 5190 Majorstua, 0302 Oslo; Slemdalsveien 11, 0369 Oslo; tel. 23-36-70-00; fax 23-36-70-01; e-mail mh@nmh.no; internet www.nmh.no; f. 1973, merged with Eastern Norway Conservatory of Music 1996; offers Bachelors, Masters and PhD degree courses; library: 75,000 books and items of sheet music, 31,000 audio recordings, 750 video cassettes and DVDs; 130 teachers; 541 students; Dir INGEBORG HARSTEN.

OMAN

The Higher Education System

Until independence was confirmed in 1951, Oman had a special relationship with the United Kingdom. The first institutions of higher education were founded in the 1980s, notably Sultan Qaboos University (founded 1986). In 2007/08 there were 14,722 students enrolled at the University. In 2004/05 there were 23,286 students enrolled in 34 other institutions of higher education (six teacher-training colleges, the College of Shari'a and Law, five technical colleges, Oman Tourism and Hospitality Academy, the College of Banking and Financial Studies, 16 institutes of health and four vocational training centres). The Ministry of Education has supreme authority over general education, but the Ministry of Higher Education is responsible for tertiary education, the Ministry of Manpower oversees most vocational and technical training and the Ministry of Health coordinates health sciences, nursing and pharmaceutical education. The Ministries sponsor an estimated 6,000 students per year to attend higher education.

Success in the secondary school leaving certificate (thanawiya amma) examinations is the main basis for admission to higher education. Prior to commencing the undergraduate Bachelors degree students are required to take a one-year Foundation course; this consists of English language, information technology (IT) and study skills training. The Bachelors degree is usually a four-year course and students must accrue at least 120 'credits' in order to graduate. Medical students must first complete a four-year Bachelor of Health Sciences degree before proceeding to a three-year postgraduate programme in Clinical Medicine. The first postgraduate degree is the Diploma, which is approximately equivalent to half a Masters degree. Following completion of the Masters, the PhD is the highest university degree. In 2009 there were 15 doctoral programmes on offer at Sultan Qaboos University.

Technical and vocational education at the post-secondary level is offered by technical industrial colleges, vocational training centres, professional institutes and a higher college of technology. The technical industrial colleges award National Diplomas after upwards of two years of study and workplace training; admission is on the basis of the thanawiya amma. The vocational training centres offer one- or two-year programmes of training for skilled and semi-skilled workers, and qualifications are equivalent to the United Kingdom National Vocational Qualification (NVQ). The Ministry of Health administers Institutes of Health Sciences, Pharmacy, Public Health and Medical Records.

In 2009 there were 25 private tertiary education providers under licence from the Ministry of Higher Education. These institutions are classified into private universities, private university colleges and private colleges. Most of these were established by foreign providers to meet the demand of school leavers entering higher education as the existing provision for higher education in the public sector is insufficient. The three private university colleges—Caledonian College of Engineering, Majan College and Sur University College—are affiliated to recognized overseas degree providers. Caledonian College of Engineering offers an undergraduate Diploma, a Bachelors (Ordinary) and a Bachelors (Honours) degree in Engineering validated by Glasgow Caledonian University. The awards align to levels within the Scottish Credit and Qualifications Framework. Majan University College offers Bachelors (Honours) degrees in IT, Business and Marketing and Finance, which are validated by the University of Bedfordshire. Sur University College offers Australian Bachelors (Honours) degrees in IT and Commerce, which are validated by Bond University in Queensland. There are 20 private colleges in Oman, some of which have ties with overseas institutions. They do not offer Bachelors degrees but two-year Diploma and three-year Advanced Diploma programmes, the majority of which are in Business, IT and Engineering.

Established in 2001, the Oman Accreditation Council (OAM) is responsible for the external quality assurance and quality enhancement of higher education institutions and programmes. The OAM created a National Qualifications Framework in 2005 to standardize qualifications offered by tertiary education providers in terms of level, learning outcomes and volume of study.

Regulatory and Representative Bodies

GOVERNMENT

Ministry of Education: POB 3, Muscat 113; tel. 24775334; fax 24704465; e-mail moe@moe.gov.om; internet www.moe.gov.om; Min. MADINA BINT AHMED BIN NASIR AL-SHIBANIYAH.

Ministry of Heritage and Culture: POB 668, Muscat 113; tel. 24641300; fax 24641331; e-mail info@mhc.gov.om; internet www.mhc.gov.om; Min. Sayyid HAITHM BIN TARIQ AL-SAID.

Ministry of Higher Education: POB 82, Ruwi 112; tel. 24755999; internet www.mohe.gov.om; Minister Dr RAWYA BINT SAUD BIN AHMAD AL BURAIDIYAH.

ACCREDITATION

Oman Accreditation Council: POB 1255, Al Khuwair 133; tel. 24475170; fax 24475168; e-mail enquiries@oac.gov.om; internet www.oac.gov.om; accredits public institutes, and public and private colleges and univs; 11 mems; Chair. Dr HAMED AL-DHAHAB.

Learned Societies

HISTORY, GEOGRAPHY AND ARCHAEOLOGY

Historical Association of Oman: POB 3941, Ruwi 112; tel. 24141674; fax 24143212; e-mail artsdean@hotmail.com; internet www.hao.org.om; f. 1971; study of history, monuments and natural history of Oman; organizes lectures and field trips to places of interest; library of 400 vols; 200 mems; Pres. Dr ISAM BIN ALI BIN AHMED AL-RAWAS; publs *Geology of Oman*, *The Journal of Oman Studies*, *The Sambuq*, *Traditional Spinning and Weaving in the Sultanate of Oman*, *Turtles in the Sultanate of Oman*.

LANGUAGE AND LITERATURE

British Council: Road One, Madinat al Sultan, Qaboos West, POB 73, Muscat 115; tel. 24681000; fax 24681090; e-mail bc.muscat@om.britishcouncil.org; internet www.britishcouncil.org/me-oman.htm; teaching centre; offers courses and exams in English language and British culture and promotes cultural exchange with the UK; attached office in Seeb; Dir JIM SCARTH; Dir, Teaching and Examination Services MARY STANSFIELD.

Research Institutes

AGRICULTURE, FISHERIES AND VETERINARY SCIENCE

Directorate of Water Resources Research: c/o Min. of Regional Municipalities and Water Resources, POB 323, Muscat; activities include hydrological surveys, water conservation, etc.

Marine Sciences and Fisheries Centre: c/o Ministry of Agriculture and Fisheries, POB 467, Muscat; tel. 24740062; fax 24740159; f. 1987; biological research, conservation, ecology, food technology, oceanography; includes a library and aquarium.

Libraries and Archives

Bowshar

Central Medical Library: Min. of Health-Royal Hospital, POB 1331, Seeb, Bowshar 111; tel. 24595971 ext. 454; fax 24594247; f. 1970; 7,000 vols, 122 periodicals; spec. collns: Min. of Health reports, health reports, WHO collns; Head of Medical Library AFFRA SAID AL SHAMSI; Librarian IMAN MAHFOODH AL HARTHY.

Muscat

Archives of the Directorate General of Heritage: Min. of Heritage and Culture, POB 668, Muscat 113; f. 1976; 5,000 MSS, 50,000 archives; Dir-Gen. MOHAMMED SAID AL-WOHAIBI.

Museums and Art Galleries

Muscat

Oman Natural History Museum (ONHM): Ministry of Heritage and Culture, Al Khuwair, Muscat; tel. 24641510; f. 1983; incl. the Nat. Herbarium of Oman and the Nat. Shell and Coral Colln, and the Insect and Osteological Collns.

Qurm

Oman Museum, Qurm: c/o Min. of Heritage and Culture, POB 668, Muscat 113; Al Alam St, behind Ministry of Information, Madinat Sultan Qaboos, Muscat; tel. 24600946; attached to Min. of Heritage and Culture; Oman's 5,000-year history with displays on shipbuilding, Islam and fort architecture.

Ruwi

National Museum at Ruwi: Way 3123, off Al'Noor St, near Al Fallaj Hotel, Ruwi, Muscat; tel. 24701289; f. 1978; formerly the Museum of Bait Assayed, Nadir bin Faisal bin Turki; exhibits incl. silver ornaments, copper crafts and samples from Omani ships; holy relics incl. a letter sent by The Prophet to the rulers of Oman A'bd and Jaiifer, sons of Al Julanda, dated 8th century Hijri; belongings of the Al Busaidi dynasty, rulers of Zanzibar; attached to Ministry of Heritage and Culture.

Universities

DHOFAR UNIVERSITY

POB 2509, Salalah 211
Telephone: 23225061
Fax: 23225064
E-mail: du@du.edu.om
Internet: www.du.edu.om

Founded 2004

Vice-Chancellor: MUHAMMAD FAOUR

DEANS

College of Arts and Applied Sciences: HUSSEIN YAGHI
College of Commerce and Business Administration: NIMR EID
College of Engineering: FARID CHAABAN

GERMAN UNIVERSITY OF TECHNOLOGY IN OMAN

POB 1816, Athaibah 130
Telephone: 24493051
Fax: 24495568
E-mail: info@gutech.edu.om
Internet: www.gutech.edu.om; attached to RWTH Aachen University, Germany

Founded 2006
Private control

Faculties of economics and planning, information technology and mathematics, sciences.

NIZWA UNIVERSITY

POB 33, Birkat al Mouz 616
Telephone: 25446318
E-mail: alsabahi@unizwa.edu.om
Internet: www.unizwa.edu.om

Founded 2004

Pres.: Dr AHMED BIN KHALFAN AL RAWAHI
Library Dir: Dr MOID A. SIDDIQUI

DEANS

College of Arts and Sciences: Dr MOHAMED ISMAIL
College of Economics, Business Management and Information Systems: Dr ABDALLAH OMEZZINE
College of Nursing and Pharmacy: Prof. Dr SOBHI ALI SAID

SOHAR UNIVERSITY

POB 44, Sohar 311
Telephone: 26720101
Fax: 26720102
E-mail: soharuni@omantel.net.om
Internet: www.soharuni.edu.om

Founded 1998 as Sohar College of Applied Sciences; univ. status 2001

Private control

Affiliated to Queensland University, Australia

Vice-Chancellor: Dr ABOOD HAMAD AL SAWAFI

DEANS

Faculty of Business: Dr MOHIT KUMAR KOLAY
Faculty of Computing and Information Technology: Dr WAIL M. OMAR
Faculty of Engineering: (vacant)
Faculty of Humanities and Social Sciences: (vacant)

SULTAN QABOOS UNIVERSITY

POB 50, 123, Al-Khod, Muscat
Telephone: 24141111
Fax: 24413391
E-mail: webmaster@squ.edu.om
Internet: www.squ.edu.om

Founded 1986
State control
Academic year: September to May

Vice-Chancellor: Dr ALI AL-BEMANI
Dean of Admissions and Registration: Dr. HAIDER ALI RAMADAN
Library Dir: Dr MOOSA NASSER AL-MUFARAJI

Library of 120,698 vols
Number of teachers: 964
Number of students: 12,591

Publications: *Journal of Scientific Research: Agricultural Marine Sciences* (2 a year), *Journal of Scientific Research: Medical Sciences* (2 a year), *Journal of Scientific Research: Science and Technology* (2 a year)

DEANS

College of Agriculture and Marine Sciences: Dr SANMUGAM A. PRATHAPAR
College of Arts and Social Sciences: Dr ISSAM ALI AL-RAWAS
College of Commerce and Economics: Dr DARWISH AL-MOHARBY
College of Education: Dr THUWAYBA AHMED AL-BARWANI
College of Engineering: Dr ALI AL-HARETHI
College of Law: Dr MOHAMED SAMI GAMALELDIN
College of Medicine and Health Sciences: Dr BAZDAWI AL-RIYAMI
College of Nursing: Prof. BAZDAWI M. S. AL-RIYAMI (acting)
College of Science: Dr ADEL YOUSSEF

DIRECTORS

Centre for Environmental Studies and Research: Prof. REGINALD VICTOR
Centre for Human Resources and Staff Development: ABDUL BASIT TALIB RAJAB AL-HAMMADI
Centre of Educational Technology: KHALID KHAMIS AL-SAADI
Centre of Information Systems: ALI OBAID AL-MAJEENI
Language Centre: Dr WILLIAM HARSBARGER
Remote Sensing Centre: Dr ANDY KWARTENG
Student Counselling Centre: SAUD MOHAMMAD ALI SULAIMAN
Water Research Centre: Dr SANMUGAM A. PRATHAPAR

Colleges

Al Buraimi University College: tel. 25641866; fax 25641855; e-mail info@buc.edu.om; internet www.buc.edu.om; private control; diploma, advanced diploma and Bachelor degree levels; depts of business administration and accounting, English language and literature, information technology; Dir YAQOOB M. FAKEER.

College of Banking and Financial Studies: POB 3122, Ruwi 112; tel. 24505796; fax 24502525; e-mail info@cbfs.edu.om; internet www.cbfs.edu.om; f. 1998 as Institute of Banking and Financial Studies; present name and status 2004; state control; courses in accounting, banking, business, computing, English, insurance; Chair. IQBAL ALI KHAMIS AL LAWATI; Dean Dr ASHRAF NABHAN AL NABHANI.

Higher College of Technology: POB 74, Al Khuwair 133; tel. 24473600; fax 24473611; internet www.hct.edu.om; f. 1984 as Oman Technical Industrial College; present name and status 2001; under control of the Ministry of Manpower; Bachelors degree; depts of applied sciences, business studies, engineering, fashion design, information technology, pharmacy, photography; 600 teachers; 7,300 students; Dean Dr OBAID AL SAEEDI.

Institute of Health Sciences: POB 3720, 112 Ruwi, Muscat; tel. 24560085; fax 24560384; f. 1982; under the Ministry of Health; library: 5,000 vols; 36 teachers; 244 students; Dean ALYA MOHAMMED MUSALLEM AL-RAWAHY; publ. *Quarterly Medical News Journal*.

Institute of Public Administration: POB 1994, Ruwi 112; tel. 24600205; fax 24602066; e-mail ipa@ipa.gov.om; internet www.ipa.gov.om; f. 1977; training, research and consultancy; library of 12,000 Arabic vols, 3,800 foreign; 70 Arabic periodicals, 5 foreign; 1,000 students per year attend courses; 57 staff; Dir-Gen. SULEIMAN BIN HILAL AL-ALAWI; publ. *Al-Edari* (4 a year).

Mazoon University College: POB 101, Muscat 133; tel. 24513301; e-mail mazoonco@omantel.net.om; internet www.mazooncollege.edu.om; private control; f. 1999; affiliated to Missouri University of Science and technology, USA in partnership with Banasthali Vidyapith, Jaipur, India; Masters Degree, Bachelors Degree and Associate Diploma in Accounting, Business Administration, Computer Science, Economics, English, Information Science and Technology, Management Information Systems and Psychology; Man. Dir Dr JUMA S. AL GHAILANI; Dir of Student Affairs and Registration JIHAD IBRAHIM JABARIN.

Middle East College of Information Technology: POB 79, al Rusayl 124; tel. 24446698; fax 24446028; e-mail info@mecit.edu.om; internet www.mecit.edu.om; Private control; f. 2000; affiliated to Coventry Univ., UK; depts of business studies, computing, cultural studies, design technology, electronics and communication, mathematics and applied sciences.

Modern College of Business and Science: POB 100, al Khuwair 133; tel. 24482802; fax 24482729; e-mail info@mcbs.edu.om; internet www.mcbs.edu.om; f. 1996; private control; Assoc. of Science in business admin., computer science, information communication technology; BA in arts; BSc in business admin., computer science; Dean BADR EL DIN A. IBRAHIM.

Muscat College: POB 2910, Ruwi 112; tel. 24503821; fax 24504954; e-mail info@mctcollege.com; internet www.mctcollege.com; f. 1996; private control; affiliated to University of Stirling, UK and Scottish Qualifications Authority; Bachelor degrees in accountancy and finance, business studies, computing science; Chair. Dr AHMED BIN ABDULLA AL-GHAZALI.

Oman Dental College: POB 835, Muscat 116; tel. 24696171; fax 24696174; e-mail info@omandentalcollege.org; internet www.omandentalcollege.org; private control; affiliated to AB Shetty Memorial Institute of Dental Sciences, India.

Oman Medical College: POB 620, Azaiba 130; tel. 24504608; fax 24504820; e-mail admissions@omc.edu.om; internet www.omc.edu.om; f. 2000; private control; affiliated to West Virginia Univ., USA; degrees in Doctor of Medicine and Bachelor of Pharmacy; Dean of Boshwar Campus Dr DIANA BEATTIE; Dean of Sohar Campus Dr SALEH MOHAMMED AL KHUSAIBY.

Oman Tourism and Hospitality Academy: POB 822, al Khoud 132; tel. 521105; fax 522283; e-mail office@otha.edu.om; internet www.otha.edu.om; f. 2001; affiliated to the International Institute of Tourism and Management, Krems and the International Management Centre, University of Applied Sciences, Krems, Austria.

Salalah College of Technology: Thumrait Rd, Salalah, Dhofar 211; e-mail webmasterl@sct.edu.om; internet www.sct.edu.om; state control; f. 1979 as a Vocational Training Centre; 1993 became Technical Industrial College; present name 2001; attached to Ministry of Manpower; depts of business, engineering, information technology; 197 teachers; 2,132 students; Dean Dr HASSAN KASHOOB.

Sur University College: POB 400, Sur 411; tel. 25542888; fax 25540737; internet www.suc.edu.om; private control; affiliated to Bond Univ., Australia; depts of business administration and commerce, information systems and technology; Chair. MUBARAK JUMA BAHWAN; Dean Dr AHMAD ABDEL-AZIZ SHARIEH.

Waljat Colleges of Applied Sciences: POB 197, Muscat 124; tel. 24446660; fax 24449196; e-mail info@waljatcolleges.edu.om; internet www.waljatcolleges.edu.om; in partnership with Birla Institute of Technology; Dean Dr A. M. AGRAWAL.

PAKISTAN

The Higher Education System

In 1947 Pakistan declared its independence from the former British Indian Empire. The oldest current institutions of higher education were established during the period of British rule, among them the Government College University (founded in 1864), Liaquat University of Medical and Health Sciences (founded in 1881; present name and status since 2001) and the University of the Punjab (founded in 1882). Consequently, the university system is closely based on the late 19th-century British model (particularly the University of London) of federal institutions, consisting of a centralized administration and affiliated colleges. Universities and degree-awarding institutions are broadly divided into 'general' and 'professional' categories. In 2007/08 there were 120 universities and degree-awarding institutions with an estimated 666,639 students. There were also 3,592 arts and science colleges and 1,329 professional colleges (including educational colleges); enrolment totalled 983,000 and 377,767 respectively. The Open University has been established with the technical support of the British Open University.

In late 2002 the Higher Education Committee (HEC) replaced the University Grants Commission (UGC) as the national controlling body of higher education. The HEC is responsible for, inter alia, dispersal of government funding, formation of higher education policy, evaluation, accreditation and quality assurance. It has authority over both public and private institutions, although universities are still autonomous institutions. The chairman of the university is the Chancellor and the chief executive and academic officer is the Vice-Chancellor, aided by Pro-Vice-Chancellors. Bodies of institutional and academic control include the Senate, Syndicate, Academic Council, Boards of Faculty and Study, Selection Board, Advanced Studies and Research Board, Finance and Planning Committee, Affiliation Committee and Disciplinary Committee.

Admission to higher education is based on the secondary school leaving certificate. Colleges affiliated to universities conduct most undergraduate teaching, particularly the two-year Bachelors (Pass) degree. The Bachelors (Honours) degree is a three-year course of study conducted by both affiliated colleges and universities. Specialist degrees leading to professional titles in architecture and medicine are five-year programmes of study. Bachelors degrees in law, education and library science are postgraduate degrees taken after the Bachelors (Pass). Postgraduate diplomas are one-year courses taken following a relevant first degree. The Masters is a postgraduate degree requiring two years of study following the Bachelors (Pass) and one year following the Bachelors (Honours); it consists of coursework and final examinations. The Master of Philosophy (MPhil) lasts two years, and is a research-based degree taken after a Masters in arts, commerce or science. The highest university degree is the PhD, requiring three years of study after award of the Masters.

Technical and vocational education at the post-secondary level is available at polytechnics and colleges of technology, which are the responsibility of the National Institute of Science and Technical Education. At a provincial level Boards of Technical Education are the responsible bodies. Polytechnics specialize in three-year Diploma courses and colleges of technology offer degree courses to holders of the Polytechnic Diplomas (in addition to the Diploma). Several professional bodies are authorized to issue Diplomas and certificates, among them the Pakistan College of Physicians and Surgeons, the Institute of Chartered Accountants of Pakistan, the Institute of Cost and Management Accountants of Pakistan and the Pakistan Nursing Council.

Regulatory and Representative Bodies

GOVERNMENT

Ministry of Culture: Green Trust Tower, Blue Area, Jinnah Ave, Islamabad; tel. (51) 9206127; fax (51) 9224697; e-mail contact@culture.gov.pk; internet www.culture.gov.pk; Minister SARDAR SIKANDAR HAYAT KHAN JOGEZAI; Federal Sec. SHAHID RAFI.

Ministry of Education: Block D, Pakistan Secretariat, Islamabad; tel. (51) 9208880; fax (51) 9202851; e-mail info@moe.gov.pk; internet www.moe.gov.pk; Minister Prof. MIR HAZAR KHAN BIJARANI; Federal Sec. ABDUR RAUF CHAUDHRY.

Attached Departments:

Department of Libraries.

Federal Directorate of Education: Rohtas Rd, Mauve Ave, Sector G-9/4, Islamabad; tel. (51) 9260230; e-mail info@fde.gov.pk; internet www.fde.gov.pk; Dir-Gen. ATIQUE-UR-REHMAN.

National Book Foundation: 6 Mauve Area, G-8/4, Taleemi Chowk, POB 1169, Islamabad; tel. (51) 2255572; fax (51) 9261534; e-mail books@nbf.org.pk; internet www.nbf.org.pk; f. 1972.

ACCREDITATION

Higher Education Committee: Sector H-9, Islamabad; tel. (51) 9040000; e-mail info@hec.gov.pk; internet www.hec.gov.pk; f. 2002 as a govt body to evaluate, improve and promote Pakistan's higher education and research sector; has established accreditation councils in the areas of computing, agricultural education, teachers' education and business education; has established a Quality Assurance Agency to develop policies and guidelines to ensure improvement in the quality of higher education throughout the country; 17 mems; Chair. Prof. Dr ATTAR-UR-RAHMAN; Exec. Dir Prof. Dr S. SOHAIL H. NAQVI; publ. *News and Views* (online newsletter, 12 a year).

Learned Societies

GENERAL

Quaid-i-Azam Academy: 297 M. A. Jinnah Rd, Karachi 74800; tel. (21) 99215238; fax (21) 99215236; e-mail info@quaidiazamacademy.com; internet www.quaidiazamacademy.com; f. 1976; research on Quaid-i-Azam Mohammad Ali Jinnah, on the historical background (incl. cultural, religious, literary, linguistic, social, economic and political aspects) of the Pakistan Movement, and various aspects of Pakistan; gives scholarships and professorships; awards Quaid-i-Azam Academic and Literary Prizes for scholarly works; holds seminars and lectures; photostat vols of Archives of Freedom Movement; photostat files of Quaid-i-Azam Papers; 52 photostat vols of Shamsul Hasan collns, Sadar Abdur Rab Nishtar collns, 2,000 microfilms of various pre-partition newspapers and other collns; publishes bibliographies, research studies, biographies, monographs and documents (in English, Urdu and dialects); library of 30,000 vols; Dir Dr SHEHLA KAZMI.

UNESCO Office Islamabad: St 8 House 17 Sector F 7/3, Islamabad 2034; tel. (51) 2611170; fax (51) 2611175; e-mail islamabad@unesco.org; internet www.un.org.pk/unesco; f. 1945; education, basic sciences, culture, communication, information, social sciences; Dir JORGE SEQUEIRA.

ARCHITECTURE AND TOWN PLANNING

Pakistan Council of Architects and Town Planners: Suite 111, 1st Floor, RSM Square, E-1 Shaheed-e-Millat Rd, Karachi 75350; tel. (21) 4523129; fax (21) 4541099; internet www.pcatp.org.pk; f. 1983 as a statutory body by the Government of Pakistan; regulation of the professions of architecture and town planning; Chair. SHAHAB GHANI KHAN.

BIBLIOGRAPHY, LIBRARY SCIENCE AND MUSEOLOGY

Library Promotion Bureau: Head Office, 1239/9 Dastgir Society, Federal B Area, Karachi 75270; tel. and fax (21) 6321959; internet lpbpk.com; f. 1965; aims to promote librarianship in Pakistan; coordinates with all the other organizations engaged in promotional activities; publs reference books, books on library and information science, text books on library science, bibliographies, directories, etc.; Pres. M. ADIL USMANI; Sec.-Gen. Dr NASIM FATIMA; publ. *Pakistan Library and Information Science Journal* (4 a year).

National Book Foundation: 6 Mauve Area, G-8/4, Taleemi Chowk, Islamabad; tel. (51) 9261533; fax (51) 9261534; e-mail books@nbf.org.pk; internet www.nbf.org.pk; f. 1972; aims to make books available at moderate prices, promotes writing, research and publication, promotes literacy, organizes book festivals and exhibitions, operates book promotion schemes, publishes Braille books; 128 mems; Man. Dir GHIASUDDIN AHMED; Sec. MUHAMMAD ASLAM RAO; publ. *Kitab* (in English and Urdu).

Pakistan Library Association: c/o Office of Executive Committee, PLA Headquarters, Quetta Balochistan; tel. (51) 9214041; fax (51) 9210006; e-mail info@pla.org.pk; internet www.pla.org.pk; f. 1957; to advance the cause of the library movement throughout Pakistan; office of Exec. council rotates every two years between PLA branches in Balochistan, Sindh, Punjab and the North-West Frontier Province; 1,329 mems; Pres. ABDUL JALIL KHAN BAZAI; Sec.-Gen. ABDUR RAHMAN QAISARANI; publs *Conference Proceedings* (1 a year), *PLA Journal* (2 a year), *Newsletter* (6 a year).

Regional Branches:

Balochistan Branch: Quetta; e-mail bb@pla.org.pk; Pres. ABDUR RAHMAN QAISARANI.

Federal Branch: Islamabad; e-mail fb@pla.org.pk; Pres. MUSHAHID HUSSAIN.

NWFP Branch: Peshawar; e-mail nwfp@pla.org.pk; Pres. MUHAMMAD KHAN MARAWAT.

Punjab Branch: Lahore; e-mail pb@pla.org.pk; Pres. MUHAMMAD AHSAN.

Sindh Branch: Karachi; e-mail sb@pla.org.pk; Pres. RAEES AHMAD SAMDANI.

ECONOMICS, LAW AND POLITICS

Institute of Cost and Management Accountants of Pakistan: St 18/C, Block-6, Gulshan-e-Iqbal, POB 17642, Karachi 75300; tel. (21) 99243900; fax (21) 99243342; e-mail ed@icmap.com.pk; internet www.icmap.com.pk; f. 1951; regulates management accountancy profession in Pakistan and arranges professional devt programmes; collects data, analyses it, plans for future, puts in place an effective control mechanism and operates emergency alarm system; 4,620 mems; 15,000 registered students; library of 32,000 vols; Pres. HASAN A BILGRAMI; Exec. Dir MUSHTAQ AHMED MADRASWALA; publs *Cost Audit Handbook*, *Glossary of Management Accounting*, *History of Management Accounting Profession in Pakistan*, *Students' Handbook* (1 a year).

Pakistan Institute of International Affairs: Aiwan-e-Sadar Rd, POB 1447, Karachi 74200; tel. (21) 5682891; fax (21) 5686069; e-mail info@piia.org.pk; internet www.piia.org.pk; f. 1947 to study int. affairs and to promote the scientific study of int. politics, Pakistan foreign policy, economics and jurisprudence; library: see Libraries and Archives; 650 mems; conducts research and surveys; maintains clipping files of chronology of events; organizes lectures, roundtable discussions, and seminars on relevant subjects; Chair. FATEHYAB KHAN; Sec. MINAL JAFRI; publ. *Pakistan Horizon* (4 a year).

EDUCATION

Higher Education Commission: Sector H/9, Islamabad; tel. (51) 9259201; fax (51) 9259203; internet www.hec.gov.pk; f. 1974 as Univ. Grants Commission, for the promotion and coordination of univ. education, the maintenance of standards of teaching, examinations and research in univs, and the orientation of univ. courses to nat. needs; library of 41,000 vols, 232 periodicals; Chair. SHAHNAZ WAZIR ALI; publs *Guide to the Equivalence of Qualifications in Pakistan* (irregular), *Handbook of Centres of Excellence and Advanced Studies*, *Handbook of Colleges*, *Handbook of Universities of Pakistan* (every 2 years), *Higher Education News* (4 a year), *Statistics on Higher Education in Pakistan*.

Punjab Bureau of Education: Punjab Public Service Commission, Lahore; tel. (42) 9202762; fax (42) 9202766; e-mail info@ppsc.gop.pk; internet www.ppsc.gop.pk; f. 1958; clearing house for information on education of all aspects and levels, within Pakistan and abroad; Documentation Section, Statistical Section, Publication Section and Research Section; library of 10,000 vols and periodicals; Dir SAJJAD HUSSAIN NAQVI; publ. *Educational Statistics* (1 a year).

FINE AND PERFORMING ARTS

Arts Council of Pakistan: M. R. Kayani Rd, Karachi 74200; tel. (21) 9213090; fax (21) 9213074; e-mail arts_council_khi@yahoo.com; f. 1956 to foster the development of fine arts and crafts, drama, music, and to promote the study and appreciation thereof by sponsoring exhibitions, lectures, etc.; 2,700 mems; Pres. SHAFIQ-UR-REHMAN PARACHA; Exec. Dir SHAMIM ALAM; Sec. ANEEQ AHMED; publ. *Khabar Nama*; publ. *Newsletter* (12 a year).

Lok Virsa (National Institute of Folk and Traditional Heritage): POB 1184, Shakarparian, Islamabad; tel. (51) 9252097; fax (51) 9252096; e-mail info@lokvirsa.net; internet www.lokvirsa.net; f. 1974; museum, publishing house, media centre, sound archive; library: over 20,000 vols on Pakistani culture, ethnology, folklore; films, video-cassettes and publications on folk heritage and culture; Dir MAZHAR-UL-ISLAM; publs *Lok Punjab*, *Mai Ni Main Kinno Akhan*, *Rag Swaroop*.

Music Foundation of Pakistan: Buch Terrace, Preedy St, Karachi 74400; tel. (21) 7722743; f. 1964 to serve the cause of classical music through academic instruction, promote it by means of concerts, and foster an international exchange of ideas; Dir FEROSE BUCHOME.

HISTORY, GEOGRAPHY AND ARCHAEOLOGY

Department of Archaeology and Museums: 27-A, Central Union Commercial, Shaheed-e-Millat Rd, Karachi; tel. and fax (21) 4526458; f. 1947; explores, excavates and scientifically conserves the archaeological, historical and cultural wealth of the country; develops a documentary and published record; and exhibits material in the museums for the purpose of educational research and amusement; Dir-Gen. Dr SAEED-UR-REHMAN; publ. *Pakistan Archaeology* (1 a year).

Pakistan Historical Society: Bait al-Hikmah, Hamdard University campus, Madinat al-Hikmah, Karachi 74600; tel. (21) 36616001; fax (21) 36611755; e-mail phs@hamdard.edu.pk; f. 1950; historical studies and research, particularly history of Islam and the sub-continent; library of 10,000 vols, 80 MSS; Pres. SADIA RASHID; Gen. Sec. Dr ANSAR ZAHID KHAN; publ. *Journal of the Pakistan Historical Society (Historicus)* (4 a year).

LANGUAGE AND LITERATURE

Alliance Française: House 9, St 49, F 6/4, Islamabad; tel. (51) 2825218; fax (51) 9213730; e-mail contact@afislamabad.org; internet www.afislamabad.org; offers courses and exams in French language and culture and promotes cultural exchange with France; attached teaching centres in Karachi, Lahore and Peshawar; library of 1,500 vols; Dir MATTHIEU DECLERCQ; Asst Dir NAUMAN AHMED.

Anjuman Taraqqi-e-Urdu Pakistan: D-159, Block 7, Gulshan-e-Iqbal, Karachi 75300; tel. (21) 7724023; f. 1903 in pre-partition India, 1948 in Pakistan; promotion of the Urdu language and literature; preparing a 6-volume bibliography of Urdu books, in collaboration with UNESCO; library: lending library of 20,000 vols, research library of 26,000 vols and 4,000 MSS; Pres. AFTAB AHMED KHAN; Hon. Sec. JAMILUDDIN A'ALI; publs *Qaumi Zaban* (12 a year), *Urdu* (4 a year).

Balochi Academy: Adalat Rd, Quetta, Balochistan; tel. (81) 829566; f. 1958 to promote Balochi language and literature; publishes books on Balochi history, poetry, culture, folk stories, and a Balochi–Urdu dictionary and encyclopaedia; 48 mems; library of 40,000 vols; Chair. JAN MOHAMMAD DASHTI; Gen. Sec. ABDUL QADIR SHAHWANI ASEER.

British Council: POB 1135, Islamabad; fax (51) 111425425; e-mail info@britishcouncil.org.pk; internet www.britishcouncil.org/pakistan; offers courses and exams in English language and British culture and promotes cultural exchange with the UK; attached offices in Faisalabad, Karachi, Lahore, Multan, Peshawar and Quetta; Dir Dr TOM CRAIG-CAMERON.

Goethe-Institut: 2 Brunton Rd, Civil Lines, Karachi; tel. (21) 5661633; fax (21) 5661632; e-mail info@karachi.goethe.org; internet www.goethe.de/karachi; f. 1956; offers courses and exams in German language; cultural activities incl. lectures, seminars, workshops and concerts from Germany; library of 3,715 vols, 20 periodicals; Dir Dr MARKUS LITZ; Admin. Man. S. A. FAROOQ.

Institute of Islamic Culture: 2 Club Rd, Lahore; tel. (42) 6363127; f. 1950; publications on Islamic subjects in English and Urdu; Dir Dr RASHID AHMAD JULLUNDHRI; publ. *Al-Ma'arif* (in Urdu, 4 a year).

Iqbal Academy: POB 1308, 6th Fl., Academy Blk, Aiwan-e-Iqbal Complex, off Egerton Rd, Lahore; tel. (42) 6314510; fax (42) 6314496; e-mail info@iap.gov.pk; internet www.allamaiqbal.com; f. 1951; publishes books and pamphlets on Dr Allama Iqbal; library: research library of 30,000 vols; Pres. FEDERAL MINISTER FOR CULTURE, SPORTS, TOURISM AND YOUTH AFFAIRS; Dir MUHAMMED SUHEYL UMAR; publs *Iqbaliat* (2 a year, in Urdu, 1 a year, in Arabic, Farsi and Turkish), *Iqbal Review* (2 a year, in English).

National Language Authority: Pitras Bukhari Rd, H-8/4, Islamabad; tel. (51) 9250311; fax (51) 9250310; e-mail nlapak@apollo.net.pk; internet www.nla.gov.pk; f. 1979; promotes Urdu as the nat., official, judicial and instructional language of Pakistan; organizes seminars and conferences; offers courses; develops Urdu terminology in various disciplines; compiles dictionaries; library of 25,000 vols; Chair. Prof. IFTIKHAR ARIF; publ. *Akhbar-e-Urdu* (12 a year).

Attached Centre:

Centre of Excellence for Urdu Informatics:tel. (51) 9250317; e-mail nlauit@apollo.net.pk; internet www.nlauit.gov.pk; Urdu IT Wing of the NLA; develops Urdu keyboard lay-outs for computers and computer codes (Standardized Urdu Code Plate), and localization of Microsoft Urdu Office and Windows XP; member of UNICODE, Inc.; Project Dir Dr ATTASH DURRANI; Project Man. AGHA ABID HUSSAIN MEMON.

Pakistan Academy of Letters: H 8/1, Islamabad; tel. (51) 9250570; fax (51) 9250590; e-mail info@academy.gov.pk; internet academy.gov.pk; f. 1976; promotion of literary works; determination of research priorities in literature; evaluation of the performance of literary bodies; setting up of Bureau of Translation; introduction of Pakistani literature to foreign readers; organizes seminars on literary and academic issues; advises the Government on international literary gatherings; nominates recipients for various literary awards and distinctions; provides financial assistance to scholars; Chair. FAKHAR ZAMAN; publs *Academy* (12 a year), *Adbiyat* (4 a year, in Urdu), *Akhbar-e-Adab* (newsletter, 12 a year), *Pakistani Literature* (2 a year).

Regional Offices:

Karachi Office: 80A, Blk 2, PECHS, Khalid Bin Waleed Rd, Karachi; tel. (21) 4531588; Resident Dir AGHA NOOR MUHAMMAD PATHAN.

Lahore Office: A-7 Hunza Blk, Allama Iqbal Town, Lahore; tel. (42) 7831237; Resident Dir QAZI JAVED.

Quetta Office: Flat 301, 3rd Fl., Universal Complex, opp. Saleem Medical Complex, M. A. Jinnah Rd, Quetta; tel. (81) 9202405; Resident Dir AFZAL MURAD.

Pakistan Writers Guild: Guild House, 1 Montgomery Rd, Lahore; tel. (42) 6367124; e-mail info@pakwritersguild.org; internet www.pakwritersguild.org; f. 1959; 4 regional offices; promotes authorship, dispenses literary prizes, concerned with welfare of writers; Sec. AHMED OMAR SHARIF; publ. *Ham Qalam* (12 a year).

Pashto Academy: University of Peshawar, Peshawar; tel. (91) 9216486; fax (91) 5704272; e-mail pashtoacademy@yahoo.com; internet pashto.upesh.edu.pk; f. 1955; research into Pashto language and literature, history, art and culture; a research cell for the study of the life and works of Khushal Khan Khattak and his contemporaries; research library; Dir Dr SALMA SHAHEEN; Librarian SARFARAZ KHAN MARWAT; publ. *Pukhto* (12 a year).

Sindhi Adabi Board: POB 12, Jamshorro, Sindh, 76070; tel. (222) 2771276; fax (222) 2771602; e-mail bookinfo@sindhiadabiboard.org; internet www.sindhiadabiboard.org; f. 1951; autonomous literary and cultural institution set up by the government to foster the language, literature and culture of the Sindh region; publishes books in English, Sindhi, Urdu, Persian and Arabic; library of 10,000 vols, 450 MSS; Chair. HAMIDA KHUHRO; Sec. AIJAZ AHMED MANGI; publs *Mehran* (4 a year), *Gul Phul* (children's, 12 a year), *Sartyoon* (women's, 12 a year).

Urdu Academy: 33C Model Town 'A', Bahawalpur; f. 1959 to develop Urdu literature and language; publishes books in English and Urdu; Sec. MASUD HASSAN SHIHAB; publ. *Az-Zubair* (4 a year, in Urdu).

Urdu Dictionary Board: ST-18/A, Block 5, Gulshan-e-Iqbal, Off Karachi University Rd, Karachi 75300; tel. (21) 4988887; f. 1958 by Government of Pakistan; projects include a comprehensive, 23-vol. Urdu Dictionary; Chair. FEDERAL MINISTER FOR EDUCATION; Pres. Dr JAMILUDDIN AALI.

Urdu Science Board: 299 Upper Mall, Lahore 54000; tel. (42) 5758475; fax (42) 5789215; e-mail ubfi@urdusciencebord.com; internet www.urduscienceboard.com; f. 1962; aims to remove deficiencies in the Urdu language, particularly in the fields of technology, natural and social sciences, so that Urdu can be used as the medium of instruction in higher education, and to coordinate the work of other organizations engaged in related fields; to prepare standard dictionaries of scientific and technical terms; library of 10,000 vols; Dir-Gen. Dr ABDUL GHAFOOR RASHID; publ. *Urdu Science Magazine* (4 a year).

MEDICINE

College of Physicians and Surgeons, Pakistan: 7th Central St, Defence Housing Authority Phase II, Karachi 75500; tel. (21) 5892801; fax (21) 5887513; e-mail library@cpsp.edu.pk; internet www.cpsp.edu.pk; f. 1962; promotes specialist practice of medicine, surgery and gynaecology and allied disciplines by means of improvement in hospital teaching and methods; arranges postgraduate medical, surgical and other specialist training; provides for medical research and organizes scientific confs for Pakistani and foreign medical experts; awards diplomas of MCPS and FCPS; 9,366 mems (MCPS), 6,900 fellows (FCPS); short course on research methodology, biostatistics, medical writing and computer learning, CME for medical and allied health teachers, CME in RH primary care providers (medical), computer training workshop for medical librarians in Pakistan, diploma in health system management; 12 regional centres; library of 10,000 books, 10,000 journals, 7,000 periodicals, 7,500 dissertations, 375 CD-ROMs, 1,300 audio journals, 1,322 video tapes, 600 WHO books and monagrams, 171 slides, 1,835 x-rays, medical databases and journals; 18,390 mems; Pres. Prof. ZAFAR ULLAH CHAUDHRY; Vice-Pres. Prof. TARIQ MAHMOOD KHAN; Vice-Pres. Prof. KHALID MASOOD; Sec. Capt. Dr QAZI JALALUDDIN AHMED; Registrar Prof. GHULAM ASGHAR CHANNA; Chief Librarian BAIBA AWAN; publs *CPSP Bulletin* (12 a year), *Journal of the College of Physicians and Surgeons Pakistan* (12 a year).

Regional Centres:

Regional Centre, Hyderabad: Adj. Sir Cowasji Jehangir Institute of Psychiatry, Hyderabad Sindh; tel. (22) 3860056; fax (22) 3860057; e-mail rc_hyderabad@cpsp.edu.pk.

Regional Centre, Islamabad: P.I.M.S., Sector G 8/3, Ravi Rd, Islamabad; tel. (51) 9262590; fax (51) 9262592; e-mail rc_islamabad@cpsp.edu.pk.

Regional Centre, Lahore: Inmol Hospital, Blk D, New Muslim Town, Lahore; tel. (42) 9231320; fax (42) 9231327; e-mail rc_lahore@cpsp.edu.pk.

Regional Centre, Peshawar: Hayatabad Medical Complex, Hayatabad Phase IV, Peshawar; tel. (91) 9217011; fax (91) 9217062; e-mail rc_peshawar@cpsp.edu.pk.

Regional Centre, Quetta: Near Cenar Hospital, off Brewery Rd, Quetta; tel. (81) 9213434; e-mail rc_quetta@cpsp.edu.pk; Asst Man. MIR ZAMAN KASI.

Pakistan Academy of Medical Sciences: 238 Jinnah Colony, Faisalabad; tel. (411) 31795; f. 1975 for the advancement of medical sciences and arts, for the recognition of merit and scholarly achievement, for cooperation among professionals and with other similar orgs; awards annual Gold Medal and holds annual PAMS Lecture; 56 Fellows; Pres. Prof. KHALID J. AWAN; Sec.-Gen. IFTIKHAR A. MALIK; publs *Bulletin* (2 a year), *Pakistan Journal of Ophthalmology* (4 a year).

Pakistan Medical Association: PMA House, Garden Rd, POB 7267, Karachi 74400; tel. and fax (21) 2226443; e-mail editor@jpma.org.pk; internet www.jpma.org.pk; f. 1948; Chair. Dr MASOOD A. SHAIKH; Editor-in-Chief FATEMA JAWAD; publ. *Journal of Pakistan Medical Association*.

NATURAL SCIENCES

General

Pakistan Academy of Sciences: 3 Constitution Ave, G-5/2, Islamabad; tel. (51) 9204657; fax (51) 9206770; e-mail pasisb@yahoo.com; internet www.paspk.org; f. 1953; to promote research in pure and applied sciences, establish and maintain libraries; awards grants and fellowships and gold medals; 103 mems (80 fellows, 23 foreign fellows); Pres. Dr ISHFAQ AHMAD; Sec.-Gen. Prof. Dr IFTIKHAR A. MALIK; publs *Proceedings of the Pakistan Academy of Sciences* (4 a year), *Newsletter* (4 a year), *Proceedings of Symposia, Monographs* (irregular), *Yearbook*.

Pakistan Association for the Advancement of Science: 1st Floor, 67 Shadman Plaza, Shadman Market, Lahore; tel. (42) 7532014; fax (42) 7532014; e-mail cmsaleem@wol.net.pk; f. 1947 for the promotion of science in all its branches, including its application to practical problems and research; organizes national conferences; 1,500 mems; Pres. Prof. Dr MUHAMMAD SALEEM CHAUDHRY; Gen. Sec. Dr MUHAMMAD ARSHAD; publs *Pakistan Journal of Science* (4 a year), *Pakistan Journal of Scientific Research* (4 a year), *Proceedings of the All Pakistan Science Conference* (every 3 years), *Proceedings of the National Seminars* (every 3 years).

Scientific Society of Pakistan: Karachi University Campus, Karachi 32; tel. (21) 4463144; f. 1954 to promote science through the national language (Urdu); 3,500 mems; Pres. Dr SYED IRTIFAQ ALI; Sec. Maj. (retd) AFTAB HASAN; publs *Jadeed Science* (6 a year, in Urdu), *Proceedings of Annual Science Conferences* (in Urdu), *Science Bachchon Key Liye* (12 a year, in Urdu), *Science Nama* (26 a year, in Urdu).

PHILOSOPHY AND PSYCHOLOGY

Pakistan Philosophical Congress: Dept of Philosophy, University of the Punjab, New Campus, Lahore 20; tel. (42) 5863984; f. 1954 for the promotion of philosophical studies; Pres. Dr ABDUL KHALIQ; Sec. Dr NAEEM AHMAD; publ. *Pakistan Philosophical Journal* (1 a year).

RELIGION, SOCIOLOGY AND ANTHROPOLOGY

Hamdard Foundation Pakistan: Al Majeed, Hamdard Centre, Nazimabad 3, Karachi 74600; tel. (21) 36616001; fax (21) 36611755; e-mail hfp@hamdardfoundation.org; internet www.hamdardfoundation.org; f. 1964; administers and controls the charitable and philanthropic work of Hamdard Laboratories (WAQF) Pakistan; oversees the establishment of academic and educational institutes; 7 mems; library: see Libraries and Archives; Pres. SADIA RASHID; Dir-Gen FURQAN AHMAD SHAMSI; publs *Hamdard-i-Sehat* (12 a year), *Hamdard Islamicus* (4 a year),

Hamdard Medicus (4 a year), *Hamdard Naunehal* (12 a year), *Historicus* (4 a year).

Jamiyat-ul-Falah: Akbar Rd, Saddar, POB 7141, Karachi 74400; internet www.jamiatulfalah.com; f. 1950 to work for the exposition, propagation and implementation of Islam; Tamizuddin Khan Memorial Library (8,000 vols), Quran, Tafseer, Hadees, and Seerat collection; Falah Islamic Centre, Falah Social Service Centre, Falah Majlis-e-Adab (literary society), Falah Pakistan Studies Centre, Falah Muslim World Studies Centre, Falah Science Studies Centre; Sec.-Gen. SHAMSUDDIN KHALID AHMED; publ. *Voice of Islam* (12 a year, in English).

Karachi Theosophical Society: Jamshed Memorial Hall, M. A. Jinnah Rd, Karachi 74200; tel. (21) 2721275; e-mail secretary@tospakistan.com; internet www.tospakistan.com/khi_tos_society.html; f. 1896; 150 mems; activities incl. study of comparative religion, philosophy and science; investigation of unexplained laws of nature; library of 20,000 vols; Pres. AMANULLAH AMIR; Hon. Sec. K. J. DINSHAW; publs *Theosophy in Karachi* (6 a year), *The Karachi Theosophist*.

Society for the Preservation of Muslim Heritage: E6 Fourth Gizri St, DHA 4, Karachi 75500; tel. (21) 5834215; fax (21) 5863474; e-mail info@heritagefoundationpak.org; internet www.heritagefoundationpak.org; f. 1980; engages in research, publication and conservation of Pakistan's cultural heritage; outreach programme KaravanPakistan, est. 2000, involves youth and communities in safeguarding heritage; attached research institute; Chair. and CEO YASMEEN LARI.

TECHNOLOGY

Institution of Electrical and Electronics Engineers Pakistan: 4 Lawrence Rd, Lahore 54000; tel. (42) 6305289; fax (42) 6360287; f. 1969; lectures, seminars and publications on electrical and electronic telecommunication engineering; 2,300 corporate mems, 2,150, individual mems; library of 2,050 vols, 6,000 periodicals; Pres. BASHIR AHMAD ABBASI; publs *The Electrical Engineer* (12 a year), *Newsletter*, *Quarterly Electrical Journal*.

Institution of Engineers (Pakistan): 5th Fl., IEP HQ Bldg, Engineering Centre, Gulberg III, Lahore 54660; tel. (42) 5756974; fax (42) 5759449; e-mail ieplahore@yahoo.com; internet www.iepkc.org; f. 1948; Chair. ZAFFARUDDIN A. ZUBERI; 50,000 mems (corporate and individual); publ. *The Pakistan Engineers* (12 a year).

Regional Centre:

Karachi Centre: 4th Fl., IEP Building; 177/2, Liaquat Barracks, Karachi 75530; tel. (21) 2780233; fax (21) 2783442; e-mail info@iepkc.org.

Research Institutes

AGRICULTURE, FISHERIES AND VETERINARY SCIENCE

Central Cotton Research Institute: Pakistan Central Cotton Committee, 47-A Hussain Centre, Darul Aman Housing Society, Main Shahrah-e-Faisal, Karachi,; tel. (61) 9201128; e-mail pccc@super.net.pk; internet www.ccri.org.pk; f. 1970; divs: agronomy, breeding and genetics, cytogenetics, entomology, pathology, physiology, fibre technology, statistics, transfer of technology; processing of cotton varieties and their release for cultivation in the local environment; library of 1,530 vols; Dir Dr M. ARSHAD; publ. *The Pakistan Cottons*.

Pakistan Agricultural Research Council: Headquarters, Plot 20 Sector G-5/1, Islamabad; tel. (51) 9203966; fax (51) 9202968; e-mail chair@comsats.net.pk; internet www.parc.gov.pk; f. 1978; aims to undertake, aid, promote and coordinate agricultural research; set up research establishments; arrange the training of high-level scientists in agricultural sciences; and to generate, acquire and disseminate information relating to agriculture; library of 21,000 vols, 1,166 periodicals; Chair. Dr ZAFAR ALTAF; publs *Pakistan Journal of Agricultural Research* (4 a year), *Pakistan Journal of Agricultural Social Sciences* (2 a year), *PARC News* (12 a year), *Progressive Farming* (6 a year).

Pakistan Forest Institute: Peshawar University Campus, Peshawar, NWFP 25000; tel. (91) 49580; tel. (91) 71260; f. 1947; library: see Libraries and Archives; Forestry Museum; training courses leading to BSc and MSc in Forestry; Dir-Gen. Dr K. M. SIDDIQUI; publ. *Pakistan Journal of Forestry* (2 a year).

Punjab Veterinary Research Institute: Ghazi Rd, Lahore Cantt.; tel. (42) 9220140; fax (42) 9220142; f. 1963; aims to promote and improve the development of the livestock industry and control diseases; production of vaccines, research on animal health problems; disease diagnosis and investigation; development of improved laboratory techniques; part of the Punjab Livestock and Dairy Development Department.

Rice Research Institute Dokri: Dokri 77080, Larkana, Sindh; tel. (74) 4080328; fax (74) 4080283; f. 1938; research on various aspects of rice incl. varietal improvement, control of insect pests, diseases and weeds, grain quality; library of 4,426 vols, 1,523 periodicals.

Veterinary Research Institute: NWFP, Bacha Khan Chowk, Charsadda Rd, POB 367, Peshawar 25000; tel. (91) 9210218; fax (91) 9210220; f. 1949 to undertake research on livestock and poultry diseases, production of veterinary biologics and diagnostic agents; 45 mems; library of 1,000 vols on aspects of livestock and poultry; Dir Dr SAADULLAH JAN; publ. *Journal of Animal Health and Production* (4 a year).

ECONOMICS, LAW AND POLITICS

Applied Economics Research Centre: University of Karachi, POB 8403, Karachi 75270; tel. (21) 99261541; fax (21) 99261545; e-mail pjae@aerc.edu.pk; internet www.aerc.edu.pk; f. 1973; policy-orientated quantitative research on problems in applied economics; courses leading to MPhil and PhD in Economics; library of 40,000 vols; 250 periodicals; Dir Prof. Dr NUZHAT AHMAD; publ. *Pakistan Journal of Applied Economics* (2 a year).

Centre for South Asian Studies: Univ. of the Punjab, Quaid-i-Azam Campus, Lahore 54590; tel. (42) 99231143; fax (42) 99232039; e-mail director@csas.pu.edu.pk; f. 1973; interdisciplinary research on South Asia, incl. economics, politics, sociology, foreign affairs, and other social devts of the area; programme incl. data colln and analysis; sponsors seminars; library of 12,000 vols; Dir Dr UMBREEN JAVAID; publ. *South Asian Studies* (2 a year, in English).

Federal Bureau of Statistics: Statistics Division, Government of Pakistan, 5-SLIC Bldg, F-6/4, Blue Area, Islamabad; tel. (51) 9208489; fax (51) 9203233; e-mail statpak@statpak.gov.pk; internet www.statpak.gov.pk; f. 1950; library of 4,600 vols, 41,200 periodicals; Dir-Gen. Dr NOOR MUHAMMAD LARIK; publs *Census of Manufacturing Industries* (1 a year), *Foreign Trade Statistics of Pakistan* (separate series for imports and exports, each 1 a year), *Macro Economic Indicators of Pakistan* (4 a year), *Monthly Statistical Bulletin*, *National Accounts* (1 a year), *Newsletter* (12 a year), *Pakistan Statistical Yearbook* (1 a year), *Reviews of Foreign Trade* (12 a year), *Statistical Pocket Book of Pakistan* (1 a year).

Institute of Strategic Studies: Sector F-5/2, Islamabad; tel. (51) 9204423; fax (51) 9204658; e-mail strategy@issi.org.pk; internet www.issi.org.pk; f. 1973; provides a broad-based and informed public understanding of vital strategic and allied issues affecting Pakistan and the int. community at large; library of 11,000 vols and 70 foreign periodicals; Dir-Gen. Ambassador TANVIR AHMAD KHAN; Dir for Americas NAJAM RAFIQUE; Dir for East Asia FAZAL-UR-RAHMAN; Dir for Russia and Central Asia SIMBAL KHAN (acting); Dir for South Asia FAHMIDA ASHRAF; publ. *Strategic Studies* (4 a year).

National Institute of Public Administration: 78 Shahrah-e-Quaid-e-Azam, Lahore; tel. (42) 9200921; fax (42) 9200926; internet www.niplahore.gov.pk; f. 1961; training in public administration for officers of federal and provincial govt; research in public administration; consultancy services to the govt; library of 30,000 vols; Dir-Gen. Maj.-Gen. (Retd) SIKANDAR SHAMI; publ. *Public Administration Review* (4 a year).

Punjab Economic Research Institute (PERI): 24 Mianmir Rd, Upper Mall Scheme, Lahore 15; internet www.pndpunjab.gov.pk/page.asp?id=31; f. 1955 to undertake socioeconomic investigations and coordinate research in economic problems of Pakistan; attached to Planning and Development Dept, Govt of Punjab; collects, compiles and interprets statistical data; publishes the results and findings of investigations; Dir AZIZ A. ANWAR; Sec. A. R. ARSHAD; publ. Research Papers.

Pakistan Institute of Development Economics: Quaid-i-Azam University campus, POB 1091, Islamabad 44000; tel. (51) 9201140; fax (51) 9210886; e-mail pide@pide.org.pk; internet www.pide.org.pk; f. 1957; provides in-service training in economic analysis, research methods, and project planning, preparation, appraisal, implementation and evaluation techniques; PhD programme in economics; library of 33,750 vols, 220 current periodicals, 6,200 microfiches, 22,700 research papers and reports; Vice-Chancellor Dr RASHID AMJAD; Chief Librarian ZAFAR JAVED NAQVI; publ. *Pakistan Development Review* (4 a year).

Pakistan Institute of Human Rights: Waqar Plaza, St 67, F-10/3, Islamabad; tel. (51) 2212845; fax (51) 2212846; e-mail pihr@pihr.org; internet www.pihr.org; f. 1998, on the 50th anniversary of the Universal Declaration of Human Rights; non-profit, non-aligned research-based academic institution promoting human rights; Chair. and Founder Dr SYED MOHAMMED ANWER; Dirs ABDUR REHMAN, FAZAL I RABBI, HINA BASHARAT, MUHAMMAD RAUF CHAUDHRY, NIAZ. A. ABASSI, SYED TANVER HAIDER.

HISTORY, GEOGRAPHY AND ARCHAEOLOGY

National Institute of Historical and Cultural Research (Quaid-e-Azam University): POB 1230, H. 605, St 29, G-10/2, Islamabad; tel. (51) 9266055; fax 9266055; e-mail info@nihcr.edu.pk; internet www.nihcr.edu.pk; f. 1973, name changed 1983; promotes studies on the history and culture of South Asian Muslims, and the genesis and growth of the Muslim freedom movement; publishes research studies in history and culture, bibliographies, indices etc.; library of 50,000 vols, a collection of historical records, old newspapers, journals, photocopies of rare material, microfilms, microfiches; Dir Dr RIAZ AHMAD; Librarian HAZOOR BAKHSH CHANNA; publs *Majallah-i-Tarikh wa Thaqafat* (2 a year, in Urdu), *Pakistan Journal of History and Culture* (2 a year).

Research Society of Pakistan: c/o the Vice Chancellor, Univ. of the Punjab, Lahore; tel. (42) 9211631; f. 1963 to organize research in national affairs, particularly in the nat. struggle that led to the establishment of Pakistan; research on cultural, political, literary, linguistic, economic, historical, topographical and archaeological features of Pakistan; library: reference library of 12,000 vols; Pres. Prof. Dr MUJAHID KAMRAN (Vice-Chancellor, Univ. of the Punjab); Dir AFZAL HAQ; publs *Journal* (2 a year), research results.

MEDICINE

Cancer Research Institute: Dept and Institute of Radiotherapy, Jinnah Postgraduate Medical Centre, Rafiqui (H.J.) Shaheed Rd, Karachi 75510; tel. (21) 9201300; e-mail edojpmc@jpmc.com.pk; internet www.jpmc.com.pk; f. 1954.

Pakistan Medical Research Council: Shahrah-e-Jamhuriat G-5/2, Islamabad; tel. (51) 9216793; fax (51) 9216774; e-mail pmrc@comsats.net.pk; internet www.pmrc.org.pk; f. 1953; reconstituted 1962; aims to promote research in fields of medicine and public health, to disseminate and arrange for utilization of this research, and to establish liaison with national and international organizations; has established research centres in medical colleges in Lahore, Karachi, Peshawar, Islamabad, Multan and Quetta; 19 mems; library of 4,800 vols; Pres. MIR AIJAZ HUSSAIN JAKHRANI; Exec. Dir Dr HUMA QURESHI; Librarian FAYYAZ AHMAD PIRZADO; publ. *Pakistan Journal of Medical Research* (4 a year).

NATURAL SCIENCES

General

Fazl-i-Omar Research Institute: Rabwah, Chenabnagar, P.C. 35460, District Jhang; tel. (4524) 211082; fax (4524) 212296; f. 1946; objectives: to promote the study of science and the development of industries in the country; library of 10,000 vols; Dir MUBARAK MUSLEH-UD-DIN AHMAD.

Pakistan Council for Science and Technology: Shahrah-e-Jamhuriat, off Constitution Ave, Bank Rd, Sector G-5/2, Islamabad; tel. (51) 9205157; fax (51) 9205171; e-mail info@pcst.org.pk; internet www.pcst.org.pk; f. 1961; advises the Govt on science and technology policy; devises measures for the promotion, devt and application of science and technology in Pakistan; library of 1,200 vols; Chair. Dr TARIQ-UR-RAHMAN; Librarian SHAGUFTA SHAHEEN; publs *Science*, *Science and Technology in the Islamic World* (4 a year), *Technology and Development* (6 a year).

Pakistan Council of Scientific and Industrial Research (PCSIR): Head Office, Constitution Ave, Sector G-5/2, Islamabad 74200; tel. (51) 9225395; fax (51) 9225372; e-mail pcsirheadoffice@yahoo.com; internet www.pcsir.gov.pk; f. 1953; promotes scientific and industrial research and its applications to the devt of the nat. industries and the utilization of the natural resources of the country; Scientific and Technical Information Centre: see Libraries and Archives; Chair. Dr ANWARUL HAQ; Sec. AHMAD SAGHIR; publs *Pakistan Journal of Scientific and Industrial Research* (6 a year), *PCSIR News Bulletin* (12 a year).

Attached Research Institutes:

Institute of Industrial Electronic Engineering: St-22/C, Block 6, Gulshan-e-Iqbal, Karachi; tel. (21) 9924421820; e-mail principal@iiee.edu.pk; general research and devt work, quality control, design and devt of electronic components; Prin. Dr RIAZUDDIN ABRO.

PCSIR Fuel Research Centre: PCSIR Laboratories Campus, off University Rd, Karachi; tel. (21) 8141738; fax (21) 8141754; e-mail frc@khi.sdnpk.org; coal analysis, upranking of coal, making of briquettes, hydrogen and alternative fuels division, coal conversion and combustion; Dir Dr M. A. DAMANI.

PCSIR Laboratories Complex Karachi: off University Rd, Karachi; tel. (21) 4642894; fax (21) 4641847; e-mail klcpcsir@khi.paknet.com.pk; fish technology, pharmaceuticals, applied physics, paints, plastics, bldg materials, chemical engineering; rural technology and water decontamination; library of 45,000 vols, 900 journals and periodicals; Dir-Gen. TANZIL HAIDER USMANI.

PCSIR Laboratories Complex Lahore: Ferozepur Rd, Lahore 54600; tel. (42) 9230704; fax (42) 9230705; e-mail pcsir@brain.net.pk; metallurgical, industrial fermentation, oils and fats, glass and ceramics, food technology research divs and solar energy and environmental research; Dir-Gen. Dr SYED ASAD MUSTAFA.

PCSIR Laboratories Complex Peshawar: Jamrud Rd, POB Peshawar Univ., Peshawar; tel. (91) 9216240; fax (91) 9216232; e-mail dgplc@yahoo.com; indigenous drugs, fruit technology, minerals evaluation, wool and rural technology, process design and fabrication divisions, dimension stones evaluation, calibration of equipment; Dir-Gen. Eng. LIAQAT ALI.

PCSIR Laboratories Hyderabad: POB 356, GPO Hyderabad, Hyderabad; tel. (221) 871434; product development and dissemination of solar energy technology, solar refrigeration and photovoltaic applications, solar water desalination, solar air-conditioning and solar architecture, solar energy storage and power generation, wind energy converters, devt of tidal wave and geothermal energy; Officer in Charge Dr RIAZUDDIN ABRO.

PCSIR Laboratories Quetta: POB 387, Mian Ghundi, Mastung Rd, Quetta; tel. (81) 447840; fax (81) 440880; e-mail pcsirqta@qta.paknet.com.pk; mineral processing and fruit technology; Dir Dr K. KHAN.

PCSIR Leather Research Centre: D/102, SITE, South Ave, Karachi 75700; tel. (21) 2570765; fax (21) 2578748; e-mail lrcpcsirkar@hotmail.com; leather technology, with special reference to tanning and upgrading of leathers, training in leather technology; Dir GHULAM ABBAS.

PCSIR National Physical and Standards Laboratory: 16 Sector H/9, Islamabad; tel. (51) 9257462; fax (51) 9258162; e-mail npsllab@isb.comsts.net.pk; maintains primary standards of physical measurements; develops sets of secondary standards; supplies standard materials for industrial calibration and standardization; Dir KHALID ISLAM.

Biological Sciences

Centre of Excellence in Marine Biology: University of Karachi, Karachi 75270; tel. (21) 9261300; e-mail jmst@cyber.net.pk; internet www.uok.edu.pk/research_institutes/cemb/index.php; f. 1975; 20 mems; library of 3,000 vols, 50 periodicals; Dir Prof. Dr JAVED MUSTAQUIM; Chair. Prof. Dr PIRZADA QASIM RAZA SIDDIQUI; publs *CEMB News* (2 a year), *Pakistan Journal of Marine Biology* (2 a year).

Department of Plant Protection: Jinnah Ave, Malir Halt, Karachi 27; tel. (21) 9248612; fax (21) 9248673; e-mail info@plantprotection.gov.pk; internet www.plantprotection.gov.pk; f. 1947; survey and control of desert locust population, control of crop pests by air; executes Plant Quarantine Act 1976 and Pakistan Agriculture Pesticide Ordinance 1971 and its rules 1973; advises Federal and Provincial Govts on plant protection matters; library of 22,085 vols, 13 current periodicals; Dir-Gen. ALLAH RAKHA ASI; publ. *Locust Situation Bulletin* (26 a year).

Zoological Survey Department: Government of Pakistan, Kalma Chowk, Bhara Kahu, Islamabad 44000; tel. (51) 2233121; fax (51) 2233511; e-mail zoology@isb.comsats.net.pk; internet www.zsd.gov.pk; f. 1948; research in ecology, biodiversity, marine biology, and wildlife of Pakistan; library of 10,810 vols, 125 periodicals, 1,600 reprints; Dir ABDUL WAHAB; publ. *Records / Zoological Survey of Pakistan* (1 a year).

Research Laboratory:

Marine Biological Research Laboratory: Block 67, Pakistan Secretariat, Shahrah-e-Iraq, Saddar, Karachi 74200; tel. (21) 9203334; e-mail zsd6167@imulti.net.pk; f. 1962.

Physical Sciences

Astronomical Observatory of the University of the Punjab: c/o Dept of Space Science, Quaid-i-Azam Campus, Univ. of the Punjab, 54590, Lahore; tel. (42) 9230370; e-mail chairman@spsc.pu.edu.pk; f. 1920, reorganized in 1986 within the Univ. Dept of Space Science; teaching and research in astronomy, remote sensing, GIS, telecommunication and atmospheric science; courses at undergraduate and graduate level; works in cooperation with nat. and int. institutes; Chair. Dr MUHAMMAD ALI.

Pakistan Atomic Energy Commission (PAEC): POB 1114, Islamabad; tel. (51) 9204276; fax (51) 9204908; e-mail sipr@paec.gov.pk; internet www.paec.gov.pk; f. 1956; responsible for the devt of nuclear technology as part of Pakistan's nuclear power programme; operates nuclear power plants in Karachi and Chashma; promotes peaceful use of atomic energy in agriculture, medicine, industry and hydrology; searches for indigenous mineral deposits suitable for the production of atomic energy; trains project personnel; Chair. Dr ANSAR PARVEZ; Sec. JAVED IQBAL KHWAJA; publ. *The Nucleus* (4 a year).

Attached Research Institutes:

Atomic Energy Medical Centre (AEMC): Jinnah Post Graduate Medical Centre, Karachi; tel. (21) 9205965; fax (21) 9201354; Dir Dr SHAHID KAMAL.

Atomic Energy Minerals Centre (AEMC): POB 658, Lahore; tel. (42) 9230746; fax (42) 9230745; Dir-Gen. Dr KHURSHID ALAM BUTT.

Bahawalpur Institute of Nuclear Medicine and Oncology (BINO): POB 35, Noor Mahal Rd, Bahawalpur; tel. (62) 9255327; fax (62) 9255331; e-mail bino@ntc.net.pk; Dir Dr SHAHAB FATMI.

Centre for Nuclear Medicine (CENUM): Mayo Hospital, POB 53, Lahore; tel. (42) 7324141; fax (42)

7313267; e-mail cenol@lhr.comsats.net.pk; internet www.paec.gov.pk/cenum/cenum-index.htm; Dir Dr MUHAMMAD NAEEM.

Centre for Nuclear Medicine and Radiotherapy (CENAR): POB 17, Brewery Rd, Quetta; tel. (81) 9202367; fax (81) 9202416; e-mail cenar123@qta.paknet.com.pk; Dir Dr G. M. BURDY.

Chashma Nuclear Power Plant (C-1): PO Chashma Barrage Colony, Mianwali; tel. (459) 924270; fax (459) 924301; e-mail chasnupp@fsd.paknet.com.pk; Dir-Gen. SAFDAR HABIB.

Chashma Nuclear Power Plant (C-2): POB 3094, Islamabad; tel. (51) 9212738; fax (51) 924396; Dir-Gen. MUHAMMAD ATIQUE.

Chasnupp Centre of Nuclear Training (CHASCENT): Chashma Barrage Colony, Kundian Dist., Mianwali; tel. (459) 241727; fax (459) 241505; Sr Man. SYED JAVED MUNAWAR.

Computer Training Centre (CTC): POB 1659, Islamabad; tel. (51) 9258517; fax (51) 9258593; Dir NASEEM AKHTAR BHATTI.

Institute of Nuclear Medicine and Oncology (INMOL): Wahdat Rd, POB 10068, Lahore; tel. (42) 9230274; fax (42) 9230778; Dir Dr SYED WAQAR HYDER.

Institute of Nuclear Medicine, Oncology and Radiotherapy (INOR): POB 110, Abbottabad; tel. (992) 383349; fax (992) 384377; Dir Dr AMJAD AZIZ KHAN.

Institute of Radiotherapy and Nuclear Medicine (IRNUM): University Campus, Peshawar; tel. (91) 9216118; fax (91) 9216119; Dir Dr AYUB KHAN.

Karachi Institute of Nuclear Power and Engineering (KINPOE): POB 3183, Karachi; tel. (21) 9202288; fax (21) 9202250; Dir Dr KHALID MEHMOOD BUKHARI.

Karachi Institute of Radiotherapy and Nuclear Medicine (KIRAN): POB 3913, Karachi 75530; tel. (21) 9261609; fax (21) 9261610; Dir Dr ABID HAMEED.

Karachi Nuclear Power Complex (K-1): POB 3183, Karachi 75400; tel. (21) 9202244; fax (21) 9202240; Dir-Gen. WAQAR MURTAZA BUTT.

Larkana Institute of Nuclear Medicine and Radiotherapy (LINAR): POB 05, Larkana; tel. (741) 9410322; fax (741) 9410729; Dir Dr KHAN MUHAMMAD.

Multan Institute of Nuclear Medicine and Radiotherapy (MINAR): Nishtar Medical College and Hospital, POB 377, Multan; tel. (61) 9200252; fax (61) 9200942; Dir Dr DURR-E-SABIH.

National Institute for Biotechnology and Genetic Engineering (NIBGE): Jhang Rd, POB 577, Faisalabad; tel. (41) 2651471; fax (41) 2651472; internet www.nibge.org; Dir Dr ZAFAR M. KHALID.

Nuclear Institute for Agriculture and Biology (NIAB): Jhang Rd, POB 128, Faisalabad; tel. (41) 2654210; fax (41) 2654213; e-mail niabmail@niab.org.pk; internet www.niab.org.pk; library of 6,990 vols; Dir Dr SYED ANWAR SHAH (acting).

Nuclear Institute for Food and Agriculture (NIFA): POB 446, Peshawar; tel. (91) 2964060; fax (91) 2964059; e-mail mails@nifa.org.pk; internet www.nifa.org.pk; f. 1982; basic and applied research in food science, entomology, soil science, crop breeding; library of 1,400 books, 1300 technical reports, 300 IAEA publs, 200 journals; Dir Dr FAROOQ-E-AZAM.

Nuclear Institute of Agriculture (NIA): Tandojam; tel. (222) 765514; fax (222) 765284; e-mail niatjam@gmail.com; f. 1963; Dir MUHAMMAD AFZAL ARAIN.

Nuclear Institute of Medical Radiotherapy (NIMRA): NIMRA, Liaquat Medical College and Hospital, Jamshoro; tel. (22) 2771148; fax (22) 2771411; internet www.paec.gov.pk/nimra/nimra-index.htm; Dir Dr AKHTAR AHMED.

Nuclear Medicine, Oncology and Radiotherapy Institute (NORI): POB 1590, Hanna Rd, Sector G 8/3, Islamabad; tel. (51) 9261313; fax (51) 9260616; e-mail nori@ntc.net.pk; internet www.paec.gov.pk/nori/nori-index.htm; Dir Dr JAVAID IRFAN ULLAH.

Pakistan Institute of Engineering and Applied Sciences (PIEAS): PO Nilore, Islamabad; tel. (51) 2207380; fax (51) 2208070; e-mail registrar@pieas.edu.pk; internet www.pieas.edu.pk; f. 1968; Rector Dr M. ASLAM.

Pakistan Institute of Nuclear Science and Technology (PINSTECH): PO Nilore, Islamabad; tel. (51) 2207201; fax (51) 9290275; operates a 10-MW research reactor of swimming-pool type; Dir-Gen. Dr MUSTANSAR JAHANGIR (acting).

Pakistan Welding Institute (PWI): PWI, Plot 234, St 7, I-9/2, Industrial Area, Islamabad; tel. (51) 9257347; fax (51) 9258524; e-mail pwi@comsats.net.pk.

Punjab Institute of Nuclear Medicine (PINUM): POB 2019, Jail Rd, Faisalabad; tel. (41) 9210171; fax (41) 9210180; e-mail pinum@fsd.comsats.net.pk; Dir Dr MUHAMMAD SAEED AKHTAR.

Pakistan Meteorological Department: Headquarters Office, POB 1214, Sector H-8/2, Islamabad; tel. (51) 9250367; fax (51) 9250368; e-mail pmd@pakmet.com.pk; internet www.pakmet.com.pk; f. 1947; provides hydrometeorological and geophysical services for protection of life, property and the environment, increased safety on land, at sea and in the air, sustainable economic growth; issues of different types of weather and flood forecasts, warnings and advisories; investigates the behaviour of the atmosphere and exploits this knowledge for short- and long-term weather predictions; undertakes research and devt activities in various disciplines such as weather modifications and the wind potential of coastal and northern areas of Pakistan; Dir-Gen. Dr QAMAR-UZ-ZAMAN CHAUDHRY; publs *Agromet Bulletin of Pakistan* (12 a year), *Pakistan Journal of Meteorology* (2 a year), *Quarterly News Bulletin* (incl. climate news).

RELIGION, SOCIOLOGY AND ANTHROPOLOGY

Institute of Sindhology: Allama I. I. Kazi Campus, University of Sindh, Jamshoro 76070, Sindh; tel. (22) 2771386; fax (22) 2772494; e-mail director@sindhology.usindh.edu.pk; internet www.sindhology.com.pk; f. 1962 as Sindhi Academy, name changed 1964; aims to interpret Sindh and its contribution to history and civilization, encourage translation and original work in the fields of social and natural sciences; to project Sindh on an international level by publishing relevant research material in foreign languages, to develop working tools (dictionaries, historical surveys, etc.) for scholars, to advance research in history, culture, literature and fine arts; includes a bureau of production, publication and translation, a documentation, information and research cell, a research library, a dept of preservation of documents and rare material, anthropological research centre with Sindh Art Gallery and Museum, a dept of performing arts, sound and film with ethnomusical gallery; photographic and microform sections; 84 staff; library: see Libraries; Dir SHOUKAT HUSSAIN SHORO; publs *Sindhi Adab* (1 a year, in Sindhi), *Sindhological Studies* (2 a year, in English).

Islamic Research Institute: POB 1035, Islamabad 44000; tel. (51) 2281289; fax (51) 2250821; internet www.iiu.edu.pk/iri/iri.htm; f. 1960, research arm of Islamic International University since 1980; aims to develop and disseminate methodology for research in various fields of Islamic learning, to interpret the teachings of Islam so as to bring out its dynamic character in the context of the intellectual and scientific progress of the modern world; to study contemporary problems of the world of Islam; contribute to the revival of Islamic heritage; organizes study groups, serves as a clearing-house on various aspects of Islam, organizes seminars, conferences, etc.; 24 research staff; library of 55,000 vols and periodicals, 550 microfilms, 140 MSS, 760 photostats, 150 cassettes; Chair. Dr ANWAR HUSSAIN SIDDIQI; Dir Dr Z. I. ANSARI; publs *Al-Dirasat al-Islamiyyah* (4 a year), *Fikr-o-Nazar* (4 a year), *Islamic Studies* (4 a year, in English).

TECHNOLOGY

Hydrocarbon Development Institute of Pakistan: 18, Street 6, Sector H-9/1, POB 1308, Islamabad; tel. (51) 9258301; fax (51) 9258310; e-mail hdip@apollo.net.pk; internet www.hdip.com.pk; f. 1975; research and services in petroleum geology and geochemistry, resource estimation, enhanced oil recovery, petroleum products testing and evaluation, petroleum processing technology, coal utilization technology, interfuel substitution, energy conservation, environmental control, compressed natural gas, energy database, oil and gas advisory and training services; 225 mems; library of 1,500 vols, 44 periodicals; Dir-Gen. HILAL A. RAZA; publs *Pakistan Journal of Hydrocarbon Research* (every 2 years), *Pakistan Energy Yearbook* (1 a year).

Attached Laboratories:

Islamabad Laboratories Complex: 18, Sector H-9, Islamabad; tel. (51) 9257472; fax (51) 9257307; e-mail hdipopsi@apollo.net.pk; General Man. S. MANSHOOR ALI.

Karachi Laboratories Complex: St 3, Sector 47, Near Pakistan Refinery Ltd, Korangi Creek, Karachi 75400; tel. (21) 5090834; fax (21) 5120496; e-mail hdip@multi.net.pk; General Man. HABIB-UR-REHMAN.

Irrigation Research Institute: Shahrah-e-Quaid-e-Azam, Lahore; f. 1925; attached to Pakistan Institute of Science and Technology; deals with irrigation and allied engineering problems in Pakistan; 2 field model stations, 2 substations and subsidiary laboratories for soils, foundation engineering, tube well experiments, etc.; library of 20,000 vols; Administrator SAAD HARROON; publs reports, records, memoirs.

Pakistan Council of Research in Water Resources: Khyaben e Johar Rd, Sector H 8/1, Islamabad; tel. (51) 9258247; fax (51) 9258963; e-mail pcrwr@isb.comsats.net.pk; internet www.pcrwr.gov.pk; f. 1964; attached to Ministry of Science and Technology; aims to promote research in the fields of water and environment, hydraulics, irrigation, drainage, reclamation, tube wells and flood control; library of 9,820 vols; Chair. Dr SABIH UR-REHMAN; Chief of Research Dr MUHAMMAD ABDULLAH; publs *Fresh Arrivals and Periodicals Content Service* (4 a year), *Journal of*

Drainage and Water Management (2 a year), *Reservoir* (newsletter, 4 a year).

Regional Centres and Laboratory:

Drainage Research Centre: Tandojam; f. 1975; library of 2,112 vols; research in drainage and reclamation of waterlogged and salt affected soils, ground-water resources development and management, soil and water management; Dir MUHAMMAD KHAN MARRI.

Regional Office, Bahawalpur:water resources management and desertification control.

Regional Office, Lahore:conducts site-specific research on problems of irrigated agriculture in Northern Indus Plains; water requirements of major crops in the irrigated areas; efficient use of land and water resources; Regional Dir ABDUR RAUF.

Water Resources Research Centre (WRRC): Peshawar; f. 2003.

Water Resources Research Centre (WRRC): Quetta; Dir Eng. ABDUL JABBAR KHAN.

Pakistan Institute of Cotton Research and Technology: Moulvi Tamizuddin Khan Rd, Karachi 74200; tel. (21) 9202558; fax (21) 9205941; e-mail pccc@super.net.pk; f. 1956; to carry out fundamental and applied research work on cotton fibres, yarns and fabrics; provides testing facilities and training to agriculture, trade and industry; library of 30,000 vols, 350 periodicals; Dir I. H. RESHAMWALA; publ. *The Pakistan Cottons* (4 a year).

Pakistan Institute of Management: Management House, Shahrah-e-Iran, Clifton, Karachi 75600; tel. (21) 9251711; fax (21) 9251715; e-mail registration@pim.com.pk; internet www.pim.com.pk; f. 1954; 900 institutional and 250 individual mems; dedicated to the management development programme in Pakistan; offers 140 short courses in functional and integrated aspects of management each year; br. in Lahore; library of 6,000 vols, 60 films, 60 periodicals; Dir ZARRAR R. ZUBAIR; publ. *Pakistan Management Review* (4 a year).

Pakistan Standards and Quality Control Authority: Blk 77, Pak Secretariat, Saddar Karachi; tel. (21) 9206290, fax (21) 9206263; e-mail psqcadg@super.net.pk; internet www.psqca.com.pk; f. 1951; member of ISO, International Electrotechnical Commission (IEC), Organisation Internationale de Métrologie Légale (OIML); objectives: to recommend national standards for the measurement of length, weight, volume and energy, to prepare and promote general adoption of standards on national and international basis relating to materials and commodities, and simplification in industry and commerce, enforcement of standards, etc.; library of 1,852 technical books, 148,955 national and international standards; Dir-Gen. Dr ABDUL GHAFFAR SOOMRO; publs *Pakistan Standards Specification*, *PSI Yearbook*, *Test Methods and Code of Practice*.

Libraries and Archives

Bahawalpur

Central Library: Bahawalpur; tel. (621) 80658; f. 1948; 105,960 vols (36,070 Urdu, 61,730 English, 8,160 other languages); 175 MSS (120 Arabic, 55 Persian and Urdu); 34 microfilms, 70 films; mobile library; audiovisual and microfiche sections; language laboratory; collections: books, newspapers and periodicals since 1948; some 19th-century newspapers and periodicals; map gallery; children's library of 22,400 vols; Braille library of 1,100 vols; computer training centre; Chief Librarian MUHAMMAD ASHRAF JALAL.

Islamia University Central Library: Bahawalpur; tel. (62) 9255482; e-mail info@iub.edu.pk; f. 1975; 186,000 vols, 40,000 e-books; Librarian TARIQ MAHMOOD CHOHAN.

Dera Ismail Khan

Gomal University Central Library: D. I. Khan, NWFP; tel. (966) 750424 extn 3057; f. 1974; 60,000 vols; Librarian MUHAMMAD ZUBAIR ASGHAR.

Faisalabad

University of Agriculture Library: Faisalabad 38040; tel. (41) 9200161; e-mail luaf98@yahoo.com; internet www.uaf.edu.pk/lib.htm; f. 1961; internet access, audiovisual section, Global Information Centre (GIC), Information Resource Centre (IRC), access to HEC Digital Library; 253,496 vols, 22,320 MSS; Head Library Dept Prof. ASGHAR ALI; publ. *News Bulletin* (4 a year).

Hyderabad

Pakistan National Central Library and Culture Centre: Hyderabad, Sindh; f. 1958; 19,000 vols; Dir M. R. SIDDIQI.

Shamsul Ulema Daudpota Sindh Government Library: Hyderabad; f. 1951; attached to Culture and Tourism Dept, Sindh; reference and general; 59,000 vols; Librarian (vacant).

Islamabad

Allama Iqbal Open University Central Library: Sector H-8, Islamabad; tel. (51) 9250040; e-mail reacmsf@gmail.com; internet www.aiou.edu.pk; f. 1974; 1m. vols; colln of theses, monographs and term papers; archives and govt papers colln; Librarian Dr SHAH FARRUKH (acting); publs *Ilm Ki Roshni* (2 a year, in Urdu), *Journal of Social Sciences and Humanities* (2 a year), *Maarif-e-Islami* (2 a year, in Urdu), *Pakistan Journal of Education* (2 a year).

International Islamic University Central Library:; e-mail principal.librarian@iiu.edu.pk POB 1243, H-10 Campus, Islamabad; tel. (51) 9257955; fax (51) 9258054; e-mail principal.librarian@iiu.edu.pk; internet www.iiu.edu.pk; f. 1980; 0.3m. vols, 108 periodicals and journals; teaching and research facilities; Prin. Librarian MUHAMMAD RAFIQ; Sr Librarian for Reader Services MUHAMMAD SAJID MIRZA; Sr Librarian for Periodicals SYED FAYYAZ ALI.

Islamabad Public Library: Block 12-A, G-8 Markaz, Islamabad; tel. (51) 9221382; e-mail nlpiba@isb.paknet.com.pk; internet www.nlp.gov.pk/html/ipl.htm; f. 1950; 34,000 vols; spec. collns incl. central and provincial govt publs; Asst Dir IQRAR HUSSAIN SHAIKH; Sr Librarian MUHAMMAD TARIQ.

Ministry of Agriculture and Works Library: Ministry of Agriculture, Food and Underdeveloped Areas Library, Government of Pakistan, Islamabad; f. 1947; 26,000 vols; 159 periodicals; Librarian S. S. FATIMI; publs *Economic Survey of the Muslim Countries*, *Food and Forestry*.

National Archives of Pakistan: Administrative Block Area, Block N, Pak Secretariat, Islamabad; tel. (51) 9202044; fax (51) 9203545; e-mail info@nap.gov.pk; internet www.nap.gov.pk; f. 1951; acquisition, classification and preservation of public and private records of permanent and historical value; provides reference service and assistance to accredited scholars; promotes ideology of Pakistan by projecting the Muslim efforts in acquiring independence; 35,000 vols, 325 MSS, 400 oral archives (300 cassettes, 150 video cassettes), 1,614 titles of newspapers and periodicals, gazetteers of 109 districts, 31,000 govt publs, Quaid-i-Azam Papers, Muslim League Records; Dir-Gen. Prince HABIB AHMED KHAN; Dir SYED RIAZUL HASAN; Deputy Dir IRSHAD AHMED; Deputy Dir TAHIRA TANVEER; Deputy Dir ZAHIR GUL; publs *Archival Sources in South Asia*, *Archives News* (4 a year), *The Pakistan Archives* (2 a year).

National Assembly Library: Islamabad; tel. (51) 9205626; fax (51) 9206220; internet www.na.gov.pk; f. 1947; 80,000 vols, 160 current periodicals, UN publications; Librarian Haji HATTAR.

National Library of Pakistan: Constitution Ave, POB 1982, Islamabad 44000; tel. (51) 9214523; fax (51) 9221375; e-mail nlpiba@isb.paknet.com.pk; internet www.nlp.gov.pk; f. 1993; depository library for all Pakistani publs, ISBN agency for Pakistani publs; 180,000 vols, 600 MSS, 80,000 microfiches, 500,000 pages on microfilm; Dir-Gen. MUHAMMAD NAZIR; publs *Pakistan National Biography* (1 a year), *Directory of Periodicals and Newspapers* (irregular).

Pakistan Scientific and Technological Information Centre (PASTIC): PASTIC National Centre, Quaid-i-Azam University Campus, POB 1217 Islamabad 44000; tel. (51) 9201340; fax (51) 9207211; e-mail dg@pastic.gov.pk; internet www.pastic.gov.pk; f. 1956 as PANSDOC under Pakistan Council of Scientific and Industrial Research, reorganized 1974 under Pakistan Science Foundation; sub-centres at Karachi, Lahore, Peshawar, Quetta, Faisalabad and Muzaffarabad; facilities include documentation services, scientific and technical information services, scientific and technical publications and compilation of scientific bibliographies, patent services, environmental information service, reprographic services; 8,000 vols, 600 bound periodicals, 300 current periodicals, 300,000 patents, 1,340 NTIS reports; Dir-Gen. Dr MOHAMMAD AFZAL; Dir NAGEEN AINUDDIN; Sr Librarian SYED HABIB AKHTAR JAFRI; publ. *Pakistan Science Abstracts* (agriculture (1 a year), animal sciences (1 a year), biology and biotechnology (1 a year), chemistry (1 a year), earth sciences (1 a year), information (1 a year), communication and space sciences (1 a year), mathematics and statistics (1 a year), medicine (1 a year), pharmaceutics (1 a year), plant sciences (1 a year)).

Quaid-i-Azam University 'Dr Raziuddin Siddiqi' Memorial Library: Islamabad 45320; tel. (51) 2872563; fax (51) 2821397; e-mail librarian@qau.edu.pk; internet www.qau.edu.pk/lib; f. 1966; 195,000 vols, 223 current periodicals, 11,200 online journals; special collection of 29,000 vols on Indo–Pakistani history and Oriental literature; 269 MSS; 20,000 abstracts provided by Higher Education Commission of Pakistan; Librarian MEHBOOB HUSSAIN KHAN.

Jamshoro

Allama I. I. Kazi Central Library (University of Sindh): Allama I. I. Kazi Campus, Jamshoro, Sindh; tel. (22) 9213239; fax (22) 9213181; e-mail chief@library.usindh.edu.pk; internet www.library.usindh.edu.pk; f. 1947; 356,843 vols, 23 current periodicals, 700 MSS; Librarian QURBAN ALI MUGHAL; Asst Librarian ASGHAR ALI.

Institute of Sindhology Library: Allama I. I. Kazi Campus, University of Sindh, Jamshoro 76070; tel. (22) 2771386; fax (22) 2772494; e-mail director@sindhology.usindh.edu.pk; internet www.sindhology.com.pk; f.

1962; 109,000 vols (Arabic, Balochi, English, Pashito, Persian, Sindhi, Urdu and other languages); 14,500 periodical bound vols, 32,000 rare books, 500 microfilms; 2,200 audio tapes, 3,500 slides, 1,700 MSS, 700 bound vols; 3,800 bound vols of newspapers; Librarian GUL MUHAMMED N. MUGHAL; publs *Sindhi Adab* (2 a year, in Sindhi), *Sindhological Studies* (2 a year, in English).

Mehran University of Engineering and Technology Library: Jamshoro, Sindh; tel. and fax (221) 2772250; e-mail mumtaz@uunet.uu.net; internet www.muet.edu.pk/resources/library.html; f. 1977; 125,000 vols, including journals; Librarian MUMTAZ S. MUNSHI.

Karachi

All Pakistan Educational Conference Library: 1-5-45/100 Altaf Brelvi Rd, Karachi 18-74600; tel. (21) 621195; f. 1886 by Sir Sayed Ahmed Khan; 35,000 vols on Aligarh and Pakistan Movement; Sec. SAYED MUSTAFA ALI BRELVI.

Bait al-Hikmah—The Hamdard Library: Madinat al-Hikmah, Muhammad bin Qasim Avenue, off Sharae Madinat al-Hikmah, Karachi 74700; tel. (21) 6440055; internet www.ihikmah.com; f. 1989; 434,693 vols, 28,010 periodicals, 2,300 current periodicals, 1,626 MSS, 1,827 rare books, 690 microfilms, 2,163 audio tapes, photographs, 16,357 stamps, maps and charts; 3,610,000 newspaper clippings covering 1,210 subjects; specializes in medicine, science, history, Indo–Pakistani history, Islamic studies, literature, management and social sciences; Dir AFZAL AHMED; Chief Librarian SAYED AKHTAR ALI.

Dr Mahmud Hussain Library, University of Karachi: Karachi 75270; tel. (21) 9261300 ext. 2243; e-mail librarian@uok.edu.pk; internet www.uok.edu.pk/library; f. 1952; 358,417 vols, 22,000 vols in seminar libraries, 8,000 theses and reports; Deputy Librarian RASHIDA AMAN.

Islamic Documentation and Information Centre (IDIC): SS College of Liberal Arts and Social Sciences, opp. Safari Park, University Rd, Karachi 75000; tel. (21) 4978274; fax (21) 4976181; f. 1983; 5,250 vols in English and Urdu, 60 current periodicals; Dir-Gen. Dr MANZOOR AHMAD.

Khalikdina Hall Library Association: M. A. Jinnah Rd, Karachi; tel. (21) 7732228; fax (21) 2638000; f. 1856; language classes, social and cultural events; 50,218 vols; Pres. TARIQ RAHMANI; Chief Librarian QARI HILAL AHMED RABBANI.

Liaquat Hall Library: Bagh-e-Jinnah, Abdullah Haroon Rd, Karachi 4; f. 1852 as Frere Hall Library; 52,000 vols; Asst Dir SYEDA SHAHANA ALVI.

Liaquat Memorial Library: c/o Tourism and Cultural Department, Govt. of Sindh, Stadium Rd, Karachi 5; tel. (21) 9230116; f. 1950; 150,000 vols; Principal Librarian I. A. S. BOKHARI.

National Bank of Pakistan, Head Office Library: Central Directorate of State Bank of Pakistan, I. I. Chundrigar Rd, Karachi 2; tel. (21) 2414783; f. 1949; 60,000 vols (45,000 English, 15,000 Oriental); colln of books, technical reports, govt documents, periodicals and magazines relating mainly to the subjects of economics, banking, finance, management and commerce; Librarian SALIHA MOIN; publs *Index of Economic Literature* (12 a year), *List of Acquisitions* (4 a year).

NED University of Engineering and Technology Central Library: University Rd, Karachi 75270; tel. (21) 9243261; fax (21) 9243255; e-mail libadmin@neduet.edu.pk; internet www.neduet.edu.pk/library; f. 1977; 123,361 vols, 121 current periodicals; Chief Librarian MEHER YASMEEN KHAN.

Pakistan Institute of International Affairs Library: Aiwan-e-Sadar Rd, POB 1447, Karachi 74200; tel. (21) 5682891; fax (21) 5686069; e-mail info@piia.org.pk; internet www.piia.org.pk; f. 1947; 35,000 vols, 44 microfilms, 210 audio tapes; newspaper clippings on int. politics, econ. and jurisprudence; Information Resource Librarian MUNAWAR SULTANA RAZIUDDIN; publ. *Pakistan Horizon* (scholarly articles, chronology of events and other documents relating to Pakistan, 4 a year).

Scientific Information Centre: PCSIR Laboratories Campus, Shahrah-e-Dr Salimuzzaman Siddiqui, Karachi 75280; tel. (21) 4651739; fax (21) 4651738; e-mail info@pjsir.org; internet www.pjsir.org; f. 1958; attached to Pakistan Council of Scientific and Industrial Research; Dir Dr KANIZ FIZZA AZHAR; publs *Pakistan Journal of Scientific and Industrial Research* (6 a year), *PCSIR Bulletin* (12 a year), *PCSIR Research and Development Programme* (1 a year).

State Bank of Pakistan Library: I. I. Chundrigar Rd, Karachi 74000; tel. (21) 9212460; fax (21) 9211009; e-mail bashir.zia@sbp.org.pk; internet lib.sbp.org.pk; f. 1949; 80,000 books, 40,000 bound periodicals; Chief Librarian BASHIR AHMAD ZIA; publs *Current Contents Bulletin* (12 a year), *Fresh Arrivals* (12 a year), *Fresh Arrivals Bulletin* (12 a year).

Lahore

Atomic Energy Minerals Centre Library: POB 658, Lahore; tel. (42) 5758661; fax (42) 5757903; f. 1961; Dir MUHAMMAD MANSOOR.

Dyal Singh Trust Library: 25 Nisbet Rd, Lahore; tel. (42) 7229483; fax (42) 7233631; e-mail info@dyalsingh.org.pk; internet www.dyalsingh.org.pk; f. 1908; 146,000 vols; Senior Librarian NUSRAT ALI ATHEER; publs *Bulletin*, *Minhaj* (4 a year).

Ewing Memorial Library: Forman Christian College, Ferozepur Rd, Lahore 54600; tel. (42) 9231581; fax (42) 9230703; e-mail fcclibrary@gmail.com; internet fccollege.edu.pk/officesandservices_ewinglibrary.php; f. 1864; 100,000 vols; Chief Librarian MANZOOR AHMAD KHAN ANJUM.

GC University Libraries: GC Univ. Library, Katchery Rd, Lahore 54000; tel. (42) 99213348; fax (42) 99213349; e-mail chieflibrarian@gcu.edu.pk; internet www.gcu.edu.pk/library; f. 1872 as Fazal-i-Hussain Library; 308,438 vols, 236 journals; Chief Librarian ABDUL WAHEED; publ. *GCU Lahore Newspapers Index*.

Islamia College Library: Civil Lines, Lahore 54000; f. 1958 after split of Old Islamia College; 50,061 vols, 53 current periodicals; Librarian MUNIR AHMAD NAEEM; publs *College Bulletin* (6 a year), *Faran* (1 a year).

National Library of Engineering Sciences: University of Engineering and Technology, Grand Trunk Rd, Lahore 54890; tel. (42) 9029243; fax (42) 9230222; e-mail lib@uet.edu.pk; internet www.uet.edu.pk; f. 1961; 125,000 vols, 60,000 bound copies of scientific and technical periodicals; Librarian MUHAMMAD SAEED.

Pakistan Administrative Staff College Library: Shahrah-e-Quaid-e-Azam, Lahore; tel. (42) 9202916; e-mail pasclibrary@yahoo.com; internet www.pasc.gov.pk/library.htm; f. 1960; 37,000 vols, 150 periodicals, 1,500 audio tapes; Librarian TALAT ALI SHER.

Punjab Public Library: Adj. Lahore Museum, Shahrah-e-Quaid-e-Azam, Lahore; tel. (42) 9211649; e-mail zilpk@yahoo.com; f. 1884; 300,000 vols, 5,000 bound vols of periodicals, 1,100 MSS, 121 English and 115 Oriental language periodicals; Bait-ul-Quran Section with Quranic MSS, rare material on the Quran, audio visual units; ladies' and children's section; arranges seminars and lectures for the promotion of library activities; Chief Librarian and Sec. ZIL-E-HASNAIN; publ. *Bulletin* (4 a year).

Quaid-e-Azam Library, Lahore: Bagh-e-Jinnah, The Mall, Lahore; tel. (42) 9201007; fax (42) 9201004; e-mail qal@brain.net.pk; internet www.brain.net.pk/~qal; f. 1984; research and reference facilities; 110,000 vols, 350 current periodicals; special colln: dissertations on Pakistan and Islam; Chief Librarian MUHAMMAD TAJ; publs *Bulletin* (4 a year), *Informit* (4 a year), *Makhzan* (2 a year).

University of the Punjab Library: Quaid-e-Azam Campus, Lahore 54590; tel. (42) 9230834; fax (42) 9230892; e-mail info@library.pu.edu.pk; internet www.pulibrary.edu.pk; f. 1882; 402,634 vols, incl. 22,000 MSS; Chief Librarian MUHAMMAD HANIF.

Multan

Bahauddin Zakariya University Library: Bosan Rd, Multan; e-mail libraryscbzu.edu.pk; f. 1975; 109,000 vols, 20 current periodicals, 20 slides; Chair. Dr MUMTAZ HUSSAIN BOKHARI; publs *Journal of Research* (humanities), *Journal of Research* (sciences), *Law Research Journal*, *News Bulletin* (12 a year).

Muzaffarabad

University of Azad Jammu and Kashmir Central Library: Muzaffarabad; tel. (300) 5228090; fax (51) 9259152; e-mail chief.librarian@ajku.edu.pk; f. 1980; 120,000 vols; Chief Librarian MUHAMMAD YAQUB CHAUDHARY.

Peshawar

Archival Museum: Directorate of Archives, Govt of NWFP, Peshawar; tel. (521) 274831; f. 1950; library of 71,000 items; Dir TARIQ MANSOOR JALALI.

Central Forest Library: Pakistan Forest Institute, Peshawar; tel. (91) 9216196; fax (91) 9216203; e-mail dg_pfi@yahoo.com; f. 1947; 25,000 vols, 20,000 periodicals; Librarian YOUSAF KHAN; publ. *Pakistan Journal of Forestry* (2 a year).

Peshawar University Library: Peshawar; tel. (91) 9216701; fax (91) 9216470; f. 1951; 153,652 vols, 10,400 periodicals, 693 Persian, Arabic and Pashto MSS; Librarian MOHAMMAD IBRAR.

Quetta

University of Balochistan Library: Sariab Rd, Quetta; tel. (81) 9211247; fax (81) 9211277; f. 1971; 120,000 vols, 1,000 rare books, 4,000 microfiche cards, periodicals, depository library of World Bank, UNESCO and UNICEF; Librarian ABDUL JALIL KHAN.

Taxila

Archaeological Library: Taxila Museum, Taxila; f. 1960; 1,450 vols on history and arts, especially the ancient history and archaeology of Pakistan; Custodian GULZAR MOHAMMAD KHAN.

Museums and Art Galleries

Harappa

Archaeological Museum: Harappa, Dist. Sahiwal, Punjab; f. 1967; antiquities from site of the prehistoric city; Curator MOHAMMAD BAHADAR KHAN.

Karachi

National Museum of Pakistan:; e-mail zubairam@hamdard.net.pk Burns Garden, Dr Ziauddin Ahmed Rd, Karachi 74200; tel. (21) 9212839; fax (21) 9212798; f. 1950; Pakistan's cultural heritage from Stone Age to the birth of Pakistan; Supt QASIM ALI QASIM; publs *Museum Journal*, *Pakistan Archaeology*.

Quaid-i-Azam Birthplace, Reading Room, Museum and Library: Wazir Mansion, Chagla St, Kharadar, Karachi; tel. (21) 2434904; f. 1953; library of 5,000 vols (incl. spec. colln on Indo-Pakistani history); Custodian TAHIR SAEE.

Lahore

Directorate of Archives and Archival Museum: Punjab Civil Secretariat, Lahore; tel. (42) 7322381; fax (42) 212693; f. 1924; consists of Historical Record Office, Central Record Office and Museum; library of 150,000 vols; Dir SYED ISHRAT ALI SHAH; publ. *Urdu Nama* (12 a year).

Industrial and Commercial Museum: Poonch House, Multan Rd, Lahore; f. 1950; permanent up-to-date collection of the raw material resources, handicrafts, art-ware and manufactured products of Pakistan; industrial library, reading-room and auditorium attached; provides free economic intelligence to trade and industry; Curator MUSHTAQ AHMAD.

Lahore Fort Museum: Lahore 54000; Mughal Gallery: Mughal paintings, coins, calligraphy, MSS, carving; Sikh Gallery: arms and armour, paintings of Sikh period; Sikh Painting Gallery: oil paintings from the Princess Bamba Collection; Dir SAEED-UR RAHMAN; Curator IRSHAD HUSSAIN.

Lahore Museum: Opp. old University Hall, Shahrah-i-Quaid-i-Azam, Lahore; tel. (42) 7322835; f. 1864; collections of Graeco-Buddhist sculpture, Indo-Pakistani coins and miniature paintings of the Mughal, Rajput, Kangra and Pahari schools; Hindu, Buddhist and Jaina sculpture, local arts, Chinese porcelain, armoury, fabrics, Pakistani postage stamps, modern paintings, oriental MSS, Islamic calligraphy, archives and photographs on Pakistan Movement; library of 35,000 vols; Dir Dr SAIFUR RAHMAN DAR; publs *Catalogue of Coins*, *Catalogue of Miniatures*, *Guide Book*, *Guide to Gandhara Gallery*, *Guide to Manuscripts*, *Lahore Museum Bulletin* (2 a year).

Lahore Zoological Gardens: 92 Shahrah-e-Quaid-i-Azam, Mall Rd, Lahore; tel. (42) 6314684; fax (42) 6304683; e-mail info@lahorezoo.com.pk; internet www.lahorezoo.com.pk; f. 1872; houses animals of 136 species incl. 82 species of birds, 8 species of reptiles and 45 species of mammals; Dir RAJA MUHAMMAD JAVED.

Larkana

Archaeological Museum: Moenjodaro, Larkana, Sindh; tel. (741) 459051; f. 1924; a variety of antiquities unearthed from the prehistoric site of Moenjodaro, dating from 3,000 BC; Curator SAEED JATOI.

Peshawar

Peshawar Museum: Near Old Deans Hotel, Peshawar; f. 1906; the collections of this museum are devoted mainly to the sculptures of the Gandhara School; they comprise an unrivalled collection of images of the Buddha, the Bodhisattvas, Buddhist deities, reliefs illustrating the life of the Buddha and Jataka stories, architectural pieces and minor antiquities excavated at Charsadda, Sahri-Bahlol, Shahji-ki-Dheri, Takht-i-Bahi and Jamal Garhi; a Muslim gallery of Quranic MSS and MSS in Arabic and Persian languages; ethnological section; Dir AURANGZEB KHAN.

Taxila

Archaeological Museum: Taxila, Rawalpindi; tel. and fax (596) 9314270; e-mail nasiraladand2003@yahoo.com; f. 1928; Gandhara sculptures in stone and stucco; gold and silver ornaments; household utensils, pottery; antiquities of every description from the sites of Taxila and monastic area from 6th century BC to 5th century AD; library: see Libraries and Archives; Curator ABDUL NASIR KHAN.

Universities

AGA KHAN UNIVERSITY

Stadium Rd, POB 3500, Karachi 74800
Telephone: (21) 4930051
Fax: (21) 4934294
E-mail: aku@aku.edu
Internet: www.aku.net

Founded 1983
Private control (Aga Khan Foundation, Geneva)
Language of instruction: English
Academic year: January to August

Chancellor: HH The Aga Khan
Pres.: FIROZ RASUL
Provost and Chief Academic Officer: Dr WILLIAM DOE (acting)
Vice President, Health and Operational Services: ALLAUDIN MERALI
Dir-Gen. for Resource Devt: ZAHIR JANMOHAMED (acting)
Dir-Gen. and Chief Financial Officer: AL-KARIM HAJI
Vice-Pres. for Human Resources: CAROL JOAN ARIANO
Registrar: LOUIS R. ARIANO
Library of 137,000 vols 265 print journal titles, 70,500 online books, 27,000 online periodicals
Number of teachers: 650
Number of students: 1,580

DEANS

Faculty of Arts and Sciences, East Africa: Dr RAFIQUE KESHAVJEE
Institute for Educational Development, East Africa: Prof. PAULINE REA-DICKINS
Institute for Educational Development, Karachi: Dr MUHAMMAD MEMON
Institute for the Study of Muslim Civilisations: Dr FAROUK TOPAN (Dir)
Medical College: Dr FARHAT ABBAS
Medical College, East Africa: ROBERT ARMSTRONG
Nursing and Midwifery, East Africa: Dr YASMIN AMARSI
Research and Graduate Studies: Dr EL-NASIR MA LALANI
School of Nursing, Karachi: Dr ROZINA KARMALIANI (Dir)

PROFESSORS

AMARSI, Y., Nursing
BADRUDDIN, S. H., Community Health Sciences
BAIG, S. M., Medicine
BHUTTA, A. B., Paediatrics
BILLOO, A. G., Paediatrics
CHOHAN, U., Anaesthesia
CONNOR, J. D., Pharmacology
FARAH, I., Education
FILALI-ANSARY, A., Education (London)
FROSSARD, P., Biochemistry
GILANI, A. H., Pharmacology
HAMID, S., Medicine
HARLEEH-JONES, B. A., Education
HASAN, R., Microbiology
HASAN, S. H., Pathology
HUSSAIN, R., Microbiology
IQBAL, M. P., Biochemistry
JABBAR, A., Medicine
JAFRI, S. M. W., Medicine
KAMAL, R., Anaesthesia
KARIM, M. S., Community Health Sciences
KAYANI, N., Pathology
KHAN, F. A., Anaesthesia
KHAN, F. H., Anaesthesia
KHAN, I. A., Paediatrics
KHAN, J. A., Medicine
KHAN, K. M., Anatomy
KHAN, M. A., Medicine
KHAN, M. M., Psychiatry
KHAN, S. M., Surgery
KHURSHID, M., Pathology
KING, L., Nursing (Kenya)
MACLEOD, G., Education
MEMON, M., Education
NIZAMI, S. Q., Paediatrics
PARDHAN, S., Education
PERVEZ, S., Pathology
QURESHI, R. H., Family Medicine
RAJA, A. J., Surgery (Kenya)
REES, J., Radiology (Kenya)
RIZVI, J. H., Obstetrics and Gynaecology
SIDDIQUI, A. A., Biochemistry
TALATI, J., Surgery
VELLANI, C. W., Medicine
ZUBERI, R. W., Family Medicine

ATTACHED RESEARCH INSTITUTES

Institute for Educational Development: IED-PDC, 1-5/B-VII, F.B. Area, POB 13688, Karimabad, Karachi 75950; tel. (21) 6347611; fax (21) 6347616; e-mail ied@aku.edu; f. 1993; Dir Prof. MUHAMMAD MEMON; publ. *Research and Policy Studies*.

Institute for the Study of Muslim Civilisations: 4–5 Bedford Sq., London WC1B 3RA, United Kingdom; tel. (20) 7907-1020; fax (20) 7907-1030; e-mail ismc@aku.edu; Dir Prof. ABDOU FILALI-ANSARY; Librarian WASEEM FAROOQ.

UNIVERSITY OF AGRICULTURE, FAISALABAD

Faisalabad
Telephone and fax (41) 9200161
E-mail: vc@uaf.edu.pk
Internet: www.uaf.edu.pk

Founded 1909 as Punjab Agricultural College, present name 1973
Public control
Language of instruction: English
Academic year: October to September

Chancellor: THE GOV. OF THE PUNJAB
Vice-Chancellor: Prof. Dr IQRAR AHMAD KHAN
Registrar: CH. MUHAMMAD HUSSAIN
Treas.: ABDUL GHAFOOR KHAN
Controller of Examinations: Prof. Dr TANWIR AHMAD MALIK
Librarian: Prof. Dr ASGHAR ALI

Library: see under Libraries and Archives
Number of teachers: 598
Number of students: 11,745

Publications: *Journal of Agricultural Sciences* (4 a year), *Journal of Veterinary*

Science, Pakistan Entomologist, Research Studies

DEANS

Faculty of Agriculture: Prof. Dr MUHAMMAD ASHFAQ
Faculty of Agricultural Economics and Rural Sociology: Prof. Dr MUHAMMAD IQBAL ZAFA
Faculty of Agricultural Engineering and Technology: Prof. Dr RAI NIAZ AHMAD
Faculty of Animal Husbandry: Prof. Dr MUHAMMAD SARWAR
Faculty of Sciences: Prof. Dr MUHAMMAD ASHRAF
Faculty of Veterinary Science: Prof. Dr LAEEQ AKBAR LODHI

DIRECTORS

Advanced Studies: Dr MUMTAZ AKHTAR CHEEMA
Centre of Agricultural Biochemistry and Biotechnology: Prof. Dr IQRAR AHMAD KHAN
Division of Education and Extension: SHER MUHAMMAD
Institute of Animal Nutrition and Feed Technology: Prof. Dr MUHAMMAD SARWAR
Institute of Horticultural Sciences: MUHAMMAD ASLAM PERVEZ
Institute of Soil and Environmental Sciences: Prof. Dr MUHAMMAD ARSHAD
National Institute of Food Science and Technology: Prof. Dr FAQIR MUHAMMAD ANJUM (Dir-Gen.)
Research: ABDUL GHAFOOR

PROFESSORS

Faculty of Agriculture (tel. (41) 9200193; fax (41) 614335; e-mail deanagri@fsd.paknet.com.pk):

Department of Agricultural Entomology:

RANA, M. A.

Department of Agronomy:

AKHTAR, M.
ALI, A.
ATTA, Z
HUSSAIN, A.
MALIK, M. A.

Department of Horticulture:

IBRAHIM, M.
KHAN, I. A.
KHAN, M. A.

Department of Plant Breeding and Genetics:

AZHAR, F. M.
ASLAM, M.
KHAN, I. A.
MEHDI, S.
SALEEM, A.
SALEEM, M.

Department of Plant Pathology:

CHOHAN, R. A.
KHAN, S. M.

Department of Soil Science:

ARSHAD, M.
GHAFOOR, A.
GILL, M. A.
HASSAN, A. U.
RANJHA, A. M.

Faculty of Agricultural Economics and Rural Sociology (tel. (41) 9200196):

Department of Agricultural Economics:

HUSSAIN, Z.

Faculty of Agricultural Engineering and Technology (tel. (41) 9200194; e-mail mssabir_uaf@yahoo.com):

Department of Farm Machinery and Power:

SABIR, M. S.

Department of Food Technology:

ANJUM, F. M.

Department of Irrigation and Drainage:

CHAUDHRY, M. R.

Department of Structural and Environmental Engineering:

ALI, M. A.
SIAL, J. K.

Faculty of Animal Husbandry (tel. (41) 9200195):

Department of Animal Nutrition:

SARWAR, M.

Department of Livestock Management:

GONDAL, K. Z.
YOUNAS, M.

Department of Poultry Husbandry:

HAQ, A.

Faculty of Sciences (tel. (41) 9200197):

Department of Botany:

ASHRAF, M.

Department of Chemistry:

NAWAZ, R.
SHEIKH, M. A.

Department of Mathematics and Statistics:

KHAN, M. I.

Department of Physics:

CHAUDHRY, M. A.

Department of Zoology and Fisheries:

QURESHI, J. I.

Faculty of Veterinary Science (tel. (41) 9200725; e-mail drmsakhter@hotmail.com):

Department of Animal Reproduction:

LODHI, L. A.
SAMAD, H. A.

Department of Physiology and Pharmacology:

AKHTAR, M. S.
NAWAZ, M.

Department of Veterinary Microbiology:

SIDDIQU, M.

Department of Veterinary Pathology:

ANJUM, A. D.

Division of Education and Extension (tel. (41) 9200186):

Department of Rural Home Economics:

ALMAS, K.

College of Agriculture, Dera Ghazi Khan (POB 79, Dera Ghazi Khan; constituent college of the Univ.):

IQBAL, M.

There are 31 affiliated colleges and institutes

AIR UNIVERSITY

Sector E-9, PAF Complex, Islamabad 44000
Telephone: (51) 9262557
Fax: (51) 9260158
E-mail: admissions@mail.au.edu.pk
Internet: www.au.edu.pk

Founded 2002
State control
Academic year: September to August
Vice-Chancellor: Air Cdre (retd) Dr IJAZ AHMAD MALIK
Registrar: Air Cdre (retd) ZAFAR AHMED
Director for Academic Affairs: Dr Q. ISA DAUDPOTA
Librarian: MAMOONA KOUSAR

Library of 12,000 vols
Number of teachers: 78
Number of students: 816

DEANS

Faculty of Administrative Sciences: I. U. SHAD
Faculty of Basic and Applied Sciences: Dr ABDULLAH SADIQ
Faculty of Engineering: Dr ZAFAR-ULLAH KORESHI
Faculty of Social Sciences: ABIDA HASSAN (acting)

ATTACHED INSTITUTE

Institute of Avionics and Aeronautics: e-mail dgiaa@mail.au.edu.pk; Dir-Gen. Air Cdre Dr KHALID M TAHIR.

AFFILIATED INSTITUTES

Air War College: PAF Faisal, Karachi; science degrees in War Studies.

Bilquis College of Education for Women: PAF Chaklala, Rawalpindi; tel. (51) 9525593; f. 1984.

College of Education for Women: PAF 56-B, The Mall, Peshawar Cantt, Peshawar; tel. (91) 9212719; f. 2003.

Fazaia Degree College: Risalpur.

ALLAMA IQBAL OPEN UNIVERSITY

Sector H-8, Islamabad
Telephone: (51) 9250111
Fax: (51) 9250102
E-mail: reg@aiou.edu.pk
Internet: www.aiou.edu.pk

Founded 1974 as People's Open University, renamed 1977
Autonomous control
Languages of instruction: English, Urdu
Academic year: April to March
Chancellor: THE PRESIDENT OF PAKISTAN
Pro-Chancellor: THE MINISTER OF EDUCATION
Vice-Chancellor: Prof. Dr MAHMOOD H.BUTT
Registrar: ILYAS AHMAD
Librarian: Prof. Dr SHAH FARRUKH (acting)
Library: see Libraries and Archives
Number of teachers: 166
Number of students: 512,635
Publications: *Ilm Ki Roshni* (2 a year), *Jamia Nama* (12 a year, in English and Urdu), *Journal of Social Sciences and Humanities* (2 a year), *Marif-I-Islami* (2 a year), *Pakistan Journal of Education* (2 a year), *Sehen Ujala* (2 a year)

DEANS

Faculty of Arabic and Islamic Studies: Prof. Dr M. BAQIR KHAN KHAKWANI
Faculty of Education: Prof. Dr REHANA MASRUR
Faculty of Sciences: Prof. Dr MUHAMMAD KALIM TAHIR
Faculty of Social Sciences and Humanities: Prof. INAM UL HAQ JAVAID

UNIVERSITY OF ARID AGRICULTURE RAWALPINDI

Shamsabad, Muree Rd, Rawalpindi
Telephone: (51) 9290151
Fax: (51) 9290160
E-mail: registrar@uaar.edu.pk
Internet: www.uaar.edu.pk

Founded 1979; present name and status 1994
Vice-Chancellor: Prof. Dr KHALID MEHMOOD KHAN
Registrar: MALIK MAQBOOL HUSSAIN AWAN
Librarian: MUHAMMAD ZAMMURAD IQBAL AHMAD

DEANS

Faculty of Crop and Food Sciences: Dr ABDUL KHALIQ
Faculty of Forestry Range Management and Wildlife: Prof. Dr SARWAT N. MIRZA
Faculty of Sciences: Dr AZRA KHANUM
Faculty of Veterinary and Animal Sciences: Prof. Dr NEMAT ULLAH
Division of Continuing Education, Home Economics and Women's Development: Dr AFSAR MIAN (Dir)

University Institute of Education and Research
University Institute of Information Technology: Dr MUHAMMAD AFZAL (Dir)
University Institute of Management Sciences: Dr RAUF-I-AZAM

AFFILIATED INSTITUTE

Barani Institute of Information Technology: Umair Plaza, 3rd Fl., 6th Rd Chowk, Murree Rd, Rawalpindi; tel. (51) 9290407; fax (51) 9290409; e-mail admin@biit.edu.pk; internet www.biit.edu.pk; Dir Dr MOHAMMAD JAMIL SAWAR.

UNIVERSITY OF AZAD JAMMU AND KASHMIR

City Campus, CMH Rd, Muzaffarabad 13100
Telephone: (58810) 49273
Fax: (58810) 49274
E-mail: vice.chancellor@ajku.edu.pk
Founded 1980
State control
Languages of instruction: English, Urdu
Academic year: September to October
Chancellor: SARDAR MUHAMMAD IBRAHIM KHAN
Vice-Chancellor: Prof. Dr HABIB-UR-REHMAN
Registrar: Prof. Dr RAJA MUHAMMAD QAYYUM KHAN
Chief Librarian: MUHAMMAD YAQUB CHAUDHARY
Library: see Libraries
Number of teachers: 256
Number of students: 1,800
Publications: *Al-Muhaqqiq* (1 a year), *Kashmir Economics Review* (1 a year), *Kashmir Journal of Geology* (1 a year), *Kashmir Journal of Language Research* (1 a year), *Kashmir Research Journal of Natural Sciences* (1 a year)

DEANS

Muzaffarabad Campus (Main Campus):
Faculty of Arts: Prof. Dr MUHAMMAD SALEEM KHAN
Faculty of Sciences: Dr GHAZANFAR ALI ABBASI
Kotli Campus:
Faculty of Administrative Sciences: Prof. Dr MUSHTAQ AHMED MALIK
Mirpur Campus:
Faculty of Engineering and Technology: Prof. CH. NAIB HUSSAIN
Faculty of Home Economics: RAFIA KHANAM
Rawalakot Campus:
Faculty of Agriculture: Prof. Dr MUHAMMAD KALEEM ABBASI

CONSTITUENT INSTITUTES

Institute of Economics: Muzaffarabad Campus; tel. (58810) 44983; e-mail kie@ajku.edu.pk; Dir Dr JAVED IQBAL KHAN.

Institute of Geology: Muzaffarabad Campus; tel. (58810) 43119; e-mail geology@ajku.edu.pk; Dir Prof. Dr MUHAMMAD SABIR KHAN.

Institute of Islamic Studies: Mirpur Campus; tel. (58610) 44849; e-mail iis@ajku.edu.pk; Dir Dr ABDUL KHALIQ KHAN.

RESEARCH DEPARTMENTS

Dept of Agronomy and Soil Sciences: Rawalakot Campus; tel. (58710) 42688; fax (58710) 42688; e-mail ass@ajku.edu.pk; Chair. Prof. Dr M. KALEEM ABBASI.

Dept of Art and Design: Muzaffarabad Campus; fax (58810) 47912; e-mail arts@ajku.edu.pk; Chair. SAFIA DAR.

Dept of Entomology and Plant Pathology: Rawalakot Campus; tel. (58710) 42688; fax (58710) 42688; e-mail pp@ajku.edu.pk; Chair. Dr KHALID MAHMOOD KHAN.

Dept of Food Science and Technology: Rawalakot Campus; tel. (33450) 98846; e-mail habibrathore2006@yahoo.com; Chair. Prof. Dr HABIB AHMED RATHORE.

Dept of Plant Breeding and Molecular Genetics: Rawalakot Campus; tel. (58710) 42688; fax (58710) 42688; e-mail pbmg@ajku.edu.pk; Chair. Dr DILNAWAZ AHMED GARDEZI.

Dept of Veterinary and Animal Sciences: Rawalakot Campus; Chair. Dr MUHAMMAD AKHTER QURESHI.

RESOURCE CENTRE

International Resource Centre: IRC, University of Azad Jammu and Kashmir City Campus, CMH Rd, Muzaffarabad 13100; tel. (58810) 4283; e-mail coordinator.irc@ajku.edu.pk; internet www.ajku.edu.pk/irc.php; Coordinator WAHEED AHMAD QURESHI.

There are 67 affiliated colleges

BAHAUDDIN ZAKARIYA UNIVERSITY

University Campus, Bosan Rd, Multan 60800
Telephone: (61) 9210097
Fax: (61) 9210098
E-mail: regbzu@brain.net.pk
Internet: www.bzu.edu.pk
Founded 1975 as University of Multan; present name 1979
State control
Languages of instruction: Urdu, English
Academic year: October to September
Chancellor: SALMAN TASEER
Vice-Chancellor: Prof. Dr MUHAMMAD ZAFARULLAH
Registrar: MALIK MUNIR HUSSAIN
Librarian: MAQBOOL AHMAD CHAUDHRY
Library: see Libraries and Archives
Number of teachers: 360
Number of students: 6,997
Publications: *Journal of Research (Humanities)*, *Journal of Research (Science)*, *Journal of Research of the Faculty of Islamic Studies and Languages*, *Journal of Research of Business Management*, *News Bulletin*

DEANS

Faculty of Arts and Social Science: Prof. Dr S. KHAWAJA ALQAMA
Faculty of Commerce, Law and Business Administration: Prof. Dr HAYAT M. AWAN
Faculty of Engineering and Technology: Prof. Dr ABDUL AZIZ MAZHAR
Faculty of Islamic Studies and Languages: Prof. Dr ZAFAR IQBAL
Faculty of Medicine and Dentistry: Prof. Dr SHABBIR AHMAD NASIR
Faculty of Pharmacy: Prof. Dr KHALID HUSSAIN JANBAZ
Faculty of Science and Agriculture: Prof. Dr SHAHIDA B. NIAZI
Faculty of Veterinary Sciences: Prof. Dr CH. SIKANDAR HAYAT

ATTACHED RESEARCH INSTITUTES

Centre for Advanced Studies in Pure and Applied Mathematics: e-mail caspam@bzu.edu.pk; Dir Prof. Dr MUHAMMAD ANWAR CH..

Centre for Undergraduate Studies: e-mail undergraduate@bzu.edu.pk; Dir Dr EJAZ AHMED.

Institute of Advanced Materials: tel. (61) 9210454; fax (61) 9210071; e-mail iam@bzu.edu.pk; Dir Prof. Dr SHABBAR ATIQ.

Institute of Management Sciences: tel. (61) 9210058; fax (61) 4745540; e-mail info@ims-bzu.edu.pk; internet www.ims-bzu.edu.pk; f. 1977; Dir Prof. Dr MUHAMMAD ZAFARULLAH.

Institute of Pure and Applied Biology: e-mail biology@bzu.edu.pk; Dir Prof. Dr ABDUL SALAM.

Information Technology Centre: Dir Prof. Dr SAJID IQBAL.

Siraiki Research Centre: Dir Prof. Dr ANWAR AHMAD.

CONSTITUENT COLLEGES

University College of Agriculture: Multan; f. 1990; Principal Prof. Dr MUSHTAQ AHMAD SALEEM.

University College of Engineering and Technology: f. 1994; Principal Prof. Dr AKHTAR ALI MALIK.

University College of Fine Arts: f. 2004; Principal ZAFAR H. GILANI.

University College of Textile Engineering: f. 2004; Vice-Principal Dr MUHAMMAD TAHIR SAJID BAPPI.

University Gilani Law College: Multan; e-mail uglaw@bzu.edu.pk; f. 1971; In-charge Prof. Dr MUHAMMAD SALEEM SHEIKH.

There are 126 affiliated colleges

BAHRIA UNIVERSITY

Main Campus: Shangrila Rd, Sector E-8, Islamabad 44000
Telephone: (51) 9260002
Fax: (51) 9260885
Karachi Campus: 13, Stadium Rd, Karachi
Telephone: (21) 9240002
Fax: (21) 9240351
E-mail: info@bahria.edu.pk
Internet: www.bahria.edu.pk
Founded 2000
State control
Rector: Vice Admiral (retd) MOHAMMAD HAROON
Pro-Rector: Rear Admiral (retd) SHAHID LATIF
Registrar: Cmdr (retd) MUMTAZ RAZA
Librarian: AAMIR RASUL
Library of 13,500 vols
Number of students: 6,000

DEANS

Islamabad Campus:
Internet: www.bci.edu.pk
Faculty of Engineering: Prof. Dr MOHAMMAD MUNIR HASSAN
Faculty of Sciences: Dr MUHAMMAD RIAZ
Karachi Campus:
E-mail: src@bimcs.edu.pk
Internet: www.bimcs.edu.pk
Computer Science and Engineering: Prof. NAEEM JANJUA
Management Sciences: NAVEED MOHAMMAD KHAN

CONSTITUENT UNITS

Bahria Institute of Management and Computer Sciences, Islamabad: Shangrila Rd, Naval Complex, Sector E-8, Islamabad; tel. (51) 9260002; fax (51) 9260889; e-mail director@bci.edu.pk; Dir Cmdr (retd) SAJID WASEEM QURESHI.

Bahria Institute of Management and Computer Sciences, Karachi: 13 National Stadium Rd, Karachi; tel. (21) 9240002; fax (21) 9240351; e-mail director@bimcs.edu.pk; Dir Capt. ASHFAQ AGA.

Bahria Institute of Professional Psychology: PNS SHIFA, Karachi Cantt, Karachi; tel. (21) 9204889; fax (21) 9205065; e-mail ippbu@hotmail.com; internet ipp.bahria.edu.pk; Dir Dr ZAINAB F. ZADEH.

National Centre of Maritime Policy Research: 13 National Stadium Rd, Karachi; tel. (21) 9240816; fax (21) 9240351; e-mail info@ncmpr.org.pk; internet www.ncmpr.org.pk; Dir Capt. RAJA JAVED AFZAL.

Pakistan Naval Academy: PNS Rahbar, Karachi; tel. (21) 4850501; fax (21) 9210053; internet www.paknavy.gov.pk; Dir Cmd Capt. ZAFAR MAHMOOD ABBASI.

AFFILIATED UNITS

Frontier Medical College: PO Public School, Mansehra Rd, Abbottabad; tel. (992) 383568; fax (992) 381053; e-mail info@fmc.edu.pk; internet www.fmc.edu.pk; Principal Prof. Dr A. J. KHAN; Dean Prof. Dr MUJAHID AKBAR; library of 9,000 vols.

Institute of Teachers Education (ITE): 150 Westridge 1, Peshawar Rd, Rawalpindi 46000; tel. (51) 5380386; e-mail info@kef.org.pk; internet www.kef.org.pk; Dir Dr AYESHA KAMRAN.

Islamabad Medical and Dental College: Main Muree Rd, Bhara Khuo, Islamabad; tel. (51) 2807200; tel. (51) 2807201; e-mail yasir.niazi@imdcollege.com; internet www.imdc.edu.pk; Principal Prof. Dr QAZI MUHAMMAD RIZWAN; Dir YASIR NIAZI; Librarian ZAFAR. H. NAQVI.

Shifa College of Medicine: Pitras Bukhari Rd, Sector H-8/4, Islamabad; tel. (51) 4446801; fax (51) 4435046; e-mail sf_scm@hotmail.com; Dean Dr MUHAMMAD AMIN.

Shifa College of Nursing: Pitras Bukhari Rd, Sector H-8/4, Islamabad; tel. (51) 4446801; fax (51) 4435046; e-mail sf_scm@hotmail.com; Dir ZAHIRA LADHANI.

UNIVERSITY OF BALOCHISTAN

Sariab Rd, Quetta
Telephone: (81) 9211268
Fax: (81) 9211277
E-mail: netadmin@uob.edu.pk
Internet: www.uob.edu.pk

Founded 1970
State control
Languages of instruction: English, Urdu
Academic year: March to December

Chancellor: NAWAB ZULFIQAR ALI MAGSSI
Vice-Chancellor: Prof. MUHAMMAD MASOOM YASINZAI
Registrar: HAJI ABDUL WASAY ABID (acting)
Librarian: ABDUL JALIL KHAN BAZAI

Number of teachers: 255
Number of students: 3,650

Publications: *Acta Mineralogica Pakistanica* (2 a year), *Middle East Journal of Area Studies Centre*

DEANS

Faculty of Arts: Prof. GHULAM NABI ACHAKZAI
Faculty of Science: Dr NAEEM M. HASSAN

ATTACHED INSTITUTES

Area Studies Centre: to promote co-operation with the Middle Eastern and Arab countries; Dir Dr MUNIR AHMED BALOCH.

Centre of Excellence in Mineralogy: Dir Dr ABDUL SALAM.

Pakistan Study Centre: Dir Prof. BAHADUR KHAN RODINI.

University Law College: Principal MIR AURANGZEB.

Institute of Biochemistry Research and Postgraduate studies: Dir Dr ABBAS HAIDER.

BALOCHISTAN UNIVERSITY OF ENGINEERING AND TECHNOLOGY

Khuzdar, Balochistan
Telephone: (848) 412524
Fax: (848) 413197
E-mail: info@buetk.edu.pk
Internet: www.buetk.edu.pk

Founded 1987 as Balochistan Engineering College; present name and status 1994
State control

Vice-Chancellor: Col MUKHTAR AHMAD KHAN
Registrar: SHER AHMED QAMBRANI
Librarian: MOHAMMAD ANWAR
Dean of Engineering: Eng. SAEED AHMED SHEIKH.

BALOCHISTAN UNIVERSITY OF INFORMATION TECHNOLOGY AND MANAGEMENT SCIENCES

Sumungli Rd, Jinnah Town, Quetta, Balochistan
Telephone: (81) 9202463
Fax: (81) 9201064
E-mail: info@buitms.edu.pk
Internet: www.buitms.edu.pk

Vice-Chancellor: Eng. AHMED FAROOQ BAZAI
Registrar: MOHAMMAD AFZAL KASI
Librarian: GULAM MURTAZA SHAHWANI

DEANS

Faculty of Basic Sciences: Prof. Dr SYED ARIF KAZMI
Faculty of Biotechnology and Informatics: Prof. Dr M. K. MALGHANI
Faculty of Computer and Emerging Sciences: Prof. Dr SABIR USMANI
Faculty of Management Sciences: Prof. Dr ZAFFARYAB

UNIVERSITY OF EDUCATION

Township Campus, College Rd, Township, Lahore 5400, Punjab
Telephone: (42) 5216530
Fax: (42) 5216524
Internet: www.ue.edu.pk

Founded 2002

Three campuses in Lahore; further campuses in Attock, Faisalabad, Jauharabad, Multan, Okara and Vehari

Vice-Chancellor: Dr MUNAWAR S MIRZA
Registrar: MUHAMMAD SAEED AKHTAR (acting)
Librarian: NAEEM SARWAR

Publication: *Journal of Research and Reflections in Education* (2 a year)

DIRECTORS

Arts and Social Sciences: Prof. Dr MUZAFFAR ABBAS
Education: Prof. Dr BASHARAT ALI
Islamic and Oriental Learning: (vacant)
Management and Administrative Sciences: (vacant)
Science and Technology: Prof. Dr F.M. NAZAR

There are 33 affiliated colleges

UNIVERSITY OF ENGINEERING AND TECHNOLOGY, LAHORE

Grand Trunk Rd, Lahore 54890
Telephone: (42) 9250201
Fax: (42) 9029205
E-mail: registrar@uet.edu.pk
Internet: www.uet.edu.pk

Founded 1961
Language of instruction: English
Academic year: January to December

Chancellor: THE GOVERNOR OF THE PUNJAB
Vice-Chancellor: Lt-Gen. (retd) MUHAMMAD AKRAM KHAN
Registrar: MUHAMMAD ASHRAF BAJWA

Library: see Libraries and Archives
Number of teachers: 310
Number of students: 8,248

Publications: *ECHO* (1 a year), *Research Bulletin* (4 a year), *Varsity News* (26 a year)

DEANS

Faculty of Architecture and Planning: Prof. Dr SHABIH-UL-HASSAN ZAIDI
Faculty of Chemical and Metallurgical Engineering: Prof. Dr FAIZ UL HASAN
Faculty of Civil Engineering: Prof. Dr WARIS ALI
Faculty of Electrical Engineering: Prof. Dr NOOR MUHAMMAD SHEIKH
Faculty of Mechanical Engineering: Prof. Dr ARSHAD HUSSAIN QURESHI
Faculty of Natural Sciences, Humanities and Islamic Studies: Prof. Dr NAWAZISH ALI SHAH

PROFESSORS

Department of Architecture (tel. (42) 9029223; e-mail chairdoa@uet.edu.pk):
AKBAR, S.
AWAN, M. Y.
GELANI, I. A. S.
HUSSAIN, M.
MALIK, R. A.
REHMAN, A.

Department of Chemical Engineering (tel. (42) 9029488; e-mail chairmanchemical@uet.edu.pk):
AHMAD, M. M.
KHAN, J. R.
MAMOOR, G. M.
NAVEED, S.
SALARYA, A. K.
SALEEMI, A. R.

Department of Chemistry (tel. (42) 9029239; e-mail chairchemistry@uet.edu.pk):
AMJAD, M.
HAQ, I. U.
TAHIRA, F.

Department of City and Regional Planning (tel. (42) 9029203):
ANJUM, G. A.
BAJWA, E. U.
ISLAM, Q. U.
MALIK, T. H.
ZAIDI, S.-UL-H.

Department of Civil Engineering (tel. (42) 9029202; e-mail chairmancivil@uet.edu.pk):
ASHRAF, M.
CHAUDHRY, M. Y.
CHISHTY, F. A.
ILYAS, M.
MIAN, Z.
RIZWAN, S. A.
SHAKIR, A. S.
SHEIKH, A. S.
TAHIR, M. A.

Department of Computer Science and Information Technology (tel. (42) 9029260; e-mail chairmancse@uet.edu.pk):
ASIM, M. R.
MALIK, A. A.

Department of Electrical Engineering (tel. (42) 9029229; e-mail chairmanee@uet.edu.pk):
BUKHARI, S. H.
CHUGHTAI, M. A.
KHAN, Z. A.
QURESHI, S. A.
SALEEM, M. M.
SHAH, A. H.
SHAMI, T. A.
SHEIKH, N. M.

Department of Humanities and Social Sciences (tel. (42) 9029291; e-mail chairmanhmss@uet.edu.pk):
ZAIDI, M. H.

Department of Islamic Studies (tel. (42) 9029246; e-mail chairmanislamic@uet.edu.pk):

YAHYA, M. A.

Department of Mathematics (tel. (42) 9029210; e-mail chairmanmath@uet.edu.pk):

AHMAD, M. O.
CH., N. M.
SHAH, N. A.

Department of Mechanical Engineering (tel. (42) 9029208; e-mail chairmanmech@uet.edu.pk):

ALI, S.
CHAUDHRY, I. A.
HUSSAIN, I.
KHAN, M. I.
MIRZA, M. R.
PIRACHA, J. L.
QURESHI, A. H.
SHAH, F. H.
TABASSUM, S. A.

Department of Metallurgical and Materials Engineering (tel. (42) 9029207; e-mail chairmanmet@uet.edu.pk):

AJMAL, M.
HASSAN, F.
IQBAL, J.
ZAIDI, S. Q. H.

Department of Mining and Geological Engineering (tel. (42) 9029212; e-mail chairmanmining@uet.edu.pk):

AKRAM, M.
CHATTAH, N. H.
HUSSAIN, S. A.
KIRMANI, F. A.
RANA, M. T.

Department of Petroleum and Gas Engineering (tel. (42) 9029271; e-mail chairmanpetroleum@uet.edu.pk):

KHAN, A. S.

Department of Physics (tel. (42) 9029204; e-mail chairmanphy@uet.edu.pk):

REHMAN, M. K. (Chair)

Institute of Environmental Engineering and Research (tel. (42) 9029248; e-mail ajbari57@hotmail.com):

AHMAD, K.
ALI, W.
AZIZ, J. A.
BARI, A. J.
HYAT, S.
ZIAI, K. H.

UNIVERSITY OF ENGINEERING AND TECHNOLOGY, TAXILA

Taxila 47050, Punjab
Telephone: (596) 9314216
Fax: (596) 9047420
E-mail: registrar@uettaxila.edu.pk
Internet: www.uettaxila.edu.pk

Vice-Chancellor: Prof. Dr M. ABBAS CHOUDHARY
Registrar: AZIZ UR REHMAN
Library of 25,000 vols

DEANS

Faculty of Civil and Environmental Engineering: Prof. SHAUKAT ALI KHAN
Faculty of Electronics and Electrical Engineering: Prof. Dr MUHAMMAD AMIN
Faculty of Mechanical and Aeronautical Engineering: Prof. MUKHTAR HUSSAIN SAHIR
Faculty of Telecommunications and Information Engineering: Prof. Dr ZAFRULLAH

PROFESSORS

AHMAD, S., Mechanical Engineering
AHMED, S., Civil Engineering
AMIN, M., Electrical Engineering
CHOWDHRY, M. A., Electrical Engineering
FAROOQ, U., Electrical Engineering
GHUMMAN, A. R., Civil Engineering
IQBAL ALVI, M. S., Mechanical Engineering
JAMAL, H., Electrical Engineering
JAVAID, M. A., Basic Sciences
KAMAL, M. A., Civil Engineering
KHAN, A. K., Electrical Engineering
KHAN, M. A., Mechanical Engineering
KHAN, S. A., Civil Engineering
KHUSHNOOD, S., Mechanical Engineering
NISAR, H., Civil Engineering
SAHIR, M. H., Mechanical Engineering
ZAFRULLAH, Electrical Engineering

ATTACHED CENTRES

Centre of Excellence for ASIC Design: e-mail haroon@uettaxila.edu.pk; internet web.uettaxila.edu.pk/uet/asic.

Network Administration and Research Centre: e-mail farhan@uettaxila.edu.pk; internet web.uettaxila.edu.pk/uet/narc; Dir Eng. FARHAN A. NADEEM.

AFFILIATED INSTITUTES

Centre for Advanced Studies in Engineering: Sir Syed Memorial Bldg, 19-Atta-turk Ave., G-5/1, Islamabad.; tel. (51) 8432273; fax (51) 8314660; e-mail info@case.edu.pk; internet www.case.edu.pk; Pres. Dr SAEED UR REHMAN; Registrar KHALID JAVED (acting).

Dr A. Q. Khan Institute of Computer Sciences & Information Technology (KICSIT): POB 502, Sumbal Gah Kahuta, Rawalpindi 47320; tel. and fax (51) 9285059; e-mail admin@kicsit.edu.pk; internet www.kicsit.edu.pk; library of 4,000 vols; Dir Dr MUHAMMAD AFZAL.

FAISALABAD GOVERNMENT COLLEGE UNIVERSITY

Allama Iqbal Rd, Faisalabad
Telephone: (41) 9200670
Fax: (41) 9200671
E-mail: info@gcuf.edu.pk
Internet: www.gcuf.edu.pk

Founded 1897

Vice-Chancellor: Dr ASIF IQBAL
Registrar: MUSHTAQ CHUNDRAY
Librarian: GHULAM GHOUS

Library of 80,400 vols.

ATTACHED INSTITUTE

Faisalabad Institute of Textile and Fashion Design: New Civil Lines, Mall Rd, Faisalabad; tel. (41) 2408005; fax (41) 2610783; e-mail info@fitfd.edu.pk; internet www.gcuf.edu.pk/fitfd/fitfd.html; Dir TEHMINA AFZAL; Librarian SOHAIL HASHMAT.

FATIMA JINNAH WOMEN UNIVERSITY

Old Presidency, The Mall, Rawalpindi, Punjab 4600
Telephone: (51) 9271162
Fax: (51) 9271168
E-mail: fjwuadmin@comsats.net.pk
Internet: www.fjwu.edu.pk

Founded 1998
State control

Vice-Chancellor: Prof. Dr SAEEDA ASADULLAH KHAN
Registrar: MARYAM RAB
Librarian: JULIE RASHID

Library of 23,000 vols

DEANS

Faculty of Arts and Social Sciences: Prof. Dr SAMINA AMIN QADIR
Faculties of Law, Commerce, Management and Administration Sciences, Science and Technology: Prof. Dr NAHEED ZIA KHAN

FEDERAL URDU UNIVERSITY FOR ARTS, SCIENCE AND TECHNOLOGY

Plot St 1 St 2, Block 9, Gulshan-e-Iqbal, Karachi 75300
Telephone: (21) 9243986
E-mail: info@fuuast.edu.pk
Internet: www.fuuast.edu.pk

Other campuses in Abdul Haq and Islamabad

Founded 2002

Vice-Chancellor: Prof. Dr MUHAMMAD QAISER
Registrar: Prof. Dr QAMAR UL HAQ
Dir of Islamabad Campus: Prof. Dr ZAHID SALEEM
Librarian: MUHAMMAD AYYAZ

DEANS

Faculty of Arts, Commerce and Law (Abdul Haq): Prof. Dr ZAFAR IQBAL
Faculty of Pharmacy (Gulshan): (vacant)
Faculty of Science and Business Management (Islamabad): Dr KHAIRAT CHUDHARY
Faculty of Science and Technology (Gulshan): Prof. MUHAMMAD SAEED

GOMAL UNIVERSITY

Dera Ismail Khan, North West Frontier Province
Telephone: (966) 750424
Fax: (966) 750255
E-mail: vc@gu.edu.pk
Internet: www.gu.edu.pk

Founded 1974
State control
Language of instruction: English
Academic year: September to June

Chancellor: THE GOVERNOR OF NWFP
Vice-Chancellor: MUHAMMAD FARID KHAN
Registrar: MUHAMMAD JAN KHAN
Librarian: MUHAMMAD SADIQ

Library: see Libraries and Archives
Number of teachers: 359
Number of students: 5,570

Publication: *Gomal University Journal of Research* (2 a year)

DEANS

Faculty of Agriculture: Prof. Dr QASIM KHAN
Faculty of Arts: Prof. Dr AISHA BIBI
Faculty of Pharmacy: Dr GUL MAJID KHAN
Faculty of Sciences: Prof. Dr MUHAMMAD AYUB

PROFESSORS

AHMAD, H. K., Agriculture
BALOCH, J. J., Physics
KHAN, A. G., Agriculture
KHAN, A. S., Pharmacy
KHAN, I. U., Pharmacy
KHAN, K. Z., Economics
KHAN, L. U., Agriculture
KHAN, M. A., Physics
KHAN, M. F., Pharmacy
KHAN, M. K., Chemistry
KHAN, M. Q., Agriculture
KHAN, Z. A., Chemistry
QAZI, N. S., Pharmacy
SAEED, A., Biological Sciences

CONSTITUENT COLLEGES

Gomal College of Veterinary Sciences: tel. (966) 9280469; fax (966) 750255.

Law College: tel. (966) 9280348; fax (966) 750255.

ATTACHED CENTRE

Gomal Centre of Biochemistry and Biotechnology: tel. (966) 750424; fax (966) 750255.

There are 10 private institutes affiliated to the University

GOVERNMENT COLLEGE UNIVERSITY

Katchery Rd, Lahore 54000, Punjab
Telephone: (42) 9213340
Fax: (42) 9213341
E-mail: registrar@gcu.edu.pk
Internet: www.gcu.edu.pk

Founded 1864

Vice-Chancellor: Prof. Dr KHALID AFTAB
Registrar: SAHIBZADA FAISAL KHURSHID
Treas.: MUHAMMAD SHAFIG MUGHAL
Controller of Examinations: ASHRAF SHABBIR BOKHARI
Chief Librarian: ABDUL WAHEED

Library: see Libraries and Archives
Number of teachers: 275
Number of students: 6,504

DEANS

Arts and Social Sciences: Prof. Dr M. KHALID PERVAIZ
Languages, Islamic and Oriental Learning: Prof. Dr SOHAIL AHMAD KHAN
Science and Technology: Prof. Dr AMIN-UL-HAQ KHAN

INSTITUTES, SCHOOLS AND CENTRES

Abdus Salam School of Mathematical Sciences (ASSMS): GC Univ., Lahore, 35 C II, Gulberg III, Lahore; tel. (42) 9263018; fax (42) 9263020; e-mail info@sms.edu.pk; internet www.sms.edu.pk; f. 2003 as centre for fundamental research in mathematical and allied sciences; library of 2,000 vols; Dir-Gen. A. D. R. CHOUDHARY; Librarian SHOUKAT ALI REHMAT; publ. *Journal of Prime Research in Mathematics (JPRM)* (Mathematics Magazine), *Math Track* (Mathematics Magazine).

Centre for Advanced Studies in Physics (CASP): GC Univ., Lahore; e-mail dr .imghauri@gcu.edu.pk; f. 1954 for research in Atomic and Nuclear Physics; Dir Prof. Dr IJAZ MUJTABA GHAURI; Rafi M. Chaudhry Chair. Dr (Sitara-e-Imtiaz) NISAR AHMAD.

Institute of Industrial Biotechnology: GC Univ., Lahore; e-mail dr.ikramulhaq@ gcu.edu.pk; f. 1990 as Biotechnology Research Centre, Dept of Botany; acquired present status in 2005; aims to develop indigenous manpower experts in the field of Biotechnology; Dir Prof. Dr IKRAM UL HAQ.

Sustainable Development Centre: Science Blk Bldg, GC Univ., Lahore; e-mail dr .aminulhaq@gcu.edu.pk; tel. (42) 9213357; f. 2003; Dir Prof. Dr AMIN-UL-HAQ KHAN.

HAMDARD UNIVERSITY

Madinat al-Hikmah, Shahrah-e-Madinat al-Hikmah, Muhammad bin Qasim Avenue, Karachi 75600
Telephone: (21) 6996001
E-mail: huvc@hamdard.edu.pk
Internet: www.hamdard.edu.pk

Other campuses in Faisalabad and Islamabad

Founded 1991 by the Hamdard Foundation (see Learned Societies)
Private control

Chancellor: Sen. S. M. ZAFAR
Vice-Chancellor: Prof. Dr NASIM A. KHAN
Registrar: Col (retd) RAFIQ AHMED

Library of 400,000 vols, 1,629 manuscripts
Number of students: 5,000

DEANS

Faculty of Eastern Medicine: Prof. Dr HK. ABDUL HANNAN
Faculty of Engineering Sciences and Technology: Prof. Dr ABDUL REHMAN MEMON
Faculty of Health and Medical Sciences: Prof. Dr MUHAMMAD SARWAR
Faculty of Humanities and Social Sciences: (vacant)
Faculty of Legal Studies: Justice (retd) NASIR ASLAM ZAHID
Faculty of Management Sciences: Prof. Dr MATIN A. KHAN
Faculty of Pharmacy: Prof. Dr WAQAR HUSSEIN

DIRECTORS AND PRINCIPALS

Al-Majeed College of Eastern Medicine: HAKIM ABDUL HANNAN
Cisco Regional Academy: SHAZIA HASNIE
College of Medicine and Dentistry: Dr ALAY HASSAN ZAIDI
Institute of Education and Social Sciences: Dr SYED ABDUL AZIZ (acting)
Institute of Information Technology, Islamabad: Col. MUSTAQ AHMED QURASHI
Institute of Information Technology, Karachi: Prof. Dr NAZEER AHMED
Institute of Management Sciences, Karachi: AMEER HAIDER ALI
School of Law: Dr RASHID MUNIR AHMED
Usman Institute of Technology: JAMSHED UR-REHMAN

AFFILIATED INSTITUTES

Plastic Technology Centre: St 2/1, Sector 30, Korangi Industrial Area, Karachi 74900; tel. (21) 5063589; fax (21) 5060373; e-mail info@ptc.org.pk; internet www.ptc.org.pk; f. 1987; Dir Prof. AHSAN SIDDIQI.

Synthetic Fibre Development and Application Centre: St 2, Sector 30, Korangi Industrial Area, Karachi 74900; tel. (21) 5066390; fax (21) 5060400; e-mail info@ sfdac.org.pk; internet www.sfdac.org.pk; f. 1994; Dir Prof. AHSAN SIDDIQI.

HAZARA UNIVERSITY

Mansehra, North West Frontier Province
Telephone: (997) 530732
Fax: (997) 530046
E-mail: registrar@hu.edu.pk
Internet: www.hu.edu.pk

Founded 2002
State control
Academic year: January to December (two semesters)

Vice-Chancellor: Prof. Dr IHSAN ALI
Registrar: Dr SHER ALI KHAN

Publications: *Newsletter* (4 a year), *University Magazine and Student Activities Report*

26 Affiliated colleges

DEANS

Faculty of Arts: Prof. Dr SAEED ANWAR
Faculty of Health Sciences: Prof. Dr MUHAMMAD SULEMAN
Faculty of Law and Administrative Sciences: Prof. Dr BAHADAR SHAH
Faculty of Science: Prof. Dr HABIB AHMAD

UNIVERSITY OF HEALTH SCIENCES

Shaikh Zayed Hospital Medical Complex, Khayaban-e-Jamia, Lahore 54600, Punjab
Telephone: (42) 9231304
Fax: (42) 9230870
E-mail: info@uhs.edu.pk
Internet: www.uhs.edu.pk

Vice-Chancellor: Prof. MALIK HUSSAIN MUBBASHAR
Registrar: Prof. MUHAMMAD ZAFAR IQBAL
Librarian: ABID ALI GILL.

AFFILIATED INSTITUTES

Allama Iqbal Medical College, Lahore: Allama Shabbir Ahmed Usmani Rd, Lahore 54550; tel. (42) 9231400; fax (42) 9231442; Principal Prof. JAVAID AKRAM.

De Montmorency College of Dentistry, Lahore: Campus 1, Punjab Dental Hospital Fort Rd, Lahore;Campus 2, Govt Nawaz Sharif Hospital, Yakki Gate, Lahore; tel. (42) 7662715; fax (42) 7630476; Principal Prof. Dr M. RAFIQUE CHATHA.

Nishtar Medical College, Multan: Nishtar Rd, Multan; tel. (61) 9200238; fax (61) 9200227; Principal Dr LAIQ HUSSAIN.

Punjab Medical College, Faisalabad: Sargodha Rd, Faisalabad; tel. (41) 9210080; fax (41) 9210081; Principal Dr ASGHAR ALI RANDHAWA.

Quaid-i-Azam Medical College, Bahawalpur: Circular Rd, Bahawalpur; tel. (621) 9250411; fax (621) 9250432; Principal Prof. ALI AJWAD SHAH.

Rawalpindi Medical College: Tipu Rd, Rawalpindi; tel. (51) 9280403; fax (51) 9280462; Principal Prof. Dr MUHAMMAD MUSSADIQ KHAN.

There are 17 public and 20 private sector institutes affiliated to the University.

INTERNATIONAL ISLAMIC UNIVERSITY

POB 1243, Islamabad
Telephone: (51) 850751
Fax: (51) 250821
E-mail: rector@iiu.edu.pk
Internet: www.iiu.edu.pk

Founded 1980, present name 1985
Academic year: September to August

Chancellor: THE PRESIDENT OF PAKISTAN
Pro-Chancellor: (vacant)
Rector: Dr MANZOOR AHMED
President: Dr ANWAR HUSSAIN SIDDIQUI
Vice-Presidents: Dr MUHAMMAD KHALIFA HASSAN AHMAD (Academic), Dr ANWAR HUSSAIN SIDDIQUI (Administration, Finance and Planning), Dr ZAFAR ISHAQ ANSARI (Higher Studies and Research)
Librarian: YAQUB ALI

Library: see Libraries and Archives
Number of teachers: 97
Number of students: 3,458

Publications: *Al-Dirasat Al-Islamiya* (4 a year, in English), *Fikr-O-Nazar* (4 a year, in Urdu), *Islamic Studies* (4 a year, in English)

DEANS

Faculty of Arabic Language: Prof. Dr MAHMOOD A. A. SHARFUDDIN
Faculty of Basic and Applied Sciences: Prof. Dr MUHAMMAD SHER
Faculty of Engineering and Technology: Prof. Dr I. M. QURESHI
Faculty of Languages and Literature: Prof. MUNAWAR IQBAL AHMED
Faculty of Management Sciences: Prof. DANISHMAND
Faculty of Shariah and Law: Dr MUHAMMAD YUSUF FARUQI
Faculty of Social Sciences: Dr SYED TAHIR HIJAZI
Faculty of Usuluddin: Dr ABDUL KHALIQ KAZI PROFESSOR

ATTACHED INSTITUTES

Darwah Academy: Dir-Gen. Prof. Dr KHALID ALVI.

International Institute of Islamic Economics: tel. (51) 9257936; fax (50) 9019423;

e-mail iiie@paknet.com.pk; f. 1983; Dir Dr NASIM SHAH SHERAZI.

IQRA Centre for Technical Education: tel. (51) 9258042; fax (51) 9258041; offers the Diploma of Associate Engineers (DAE) and other short technical courses; Principal Eng. MUHAMMAD SALEEM SADDOZAI.

Islamic Research Institute: tel. (51) 2281289; fax (51) 2250821; e-mail ziansari@gmail.com; f. 1960; Dir Dr ZAFAR ISHAQ ANSARI.

Shariah Academy: Dir-Gen. Prof. Dr MUHAMMAD YUSUF FARUQI.

ISLAMIA UNIVERSITY BAHAWALPUR

Bahawalpur
Telephone: (62) 9250231
Fax: (62) 9250232
E-mail: vc@iub.edu.pk
Internet: www.iub.edu.pk

Founded 1975
State control
Languages of instruction: English, Urdu
Academic year: September to August

Chancellor: THE GOVERNOR OF PUNJAB
Vice-Chancellor: Prof. Dr BELAL A. KHAN
Registrar: MUHAMMAD ISHTIAQ
Librarian: MUHAMMAD RAFIQ AWAN (acting)

Library: see Libraries and Archives
Number of teachers: 505
Number of students: 13,000

Publications: *Journal of Pure and Applied Sciences* (2 a year, in English), *Mujullah Uloom-e-Islamia* (2 a year, in English, Persian and Urdu)

DEANS

Faculty of Arts: Prof. Dr NAJEEB-UD-DIN JAMAL
Faculty of Education: Prof. Dr M. ASLAM ADEEB
Faculty of Islamic Learning: Prof. Dr SALEEM TARIQ KHAN
Faculty of Management Sciences: Prof. Dr BELAL A. KHAN
Faculty of Pharmacy and Alternative Medicine: Prof. Dr MAHMOOD AHMED
Faculty of Science: MUHAMMAD MOAZZAM

DIRECTORS

Cholistan Institute of Desert Studies: Dr RANA MUHAMMAD IQBAL
Khawaja Farid Chair: Dr NASRULLAH KHAN NASIR (Head)
Modern Progressive Centre Of Excellence In Islamic Studies: Prof. Dr SHAMSUL BASAR
Seerat Chair: Prof. Dr ABDUR RAUF ZAFAR
University College of Agriculture and Environmental Sciences: Dr MOAZZAM JAMIL (Principal (Acting))
University College of Conventional Medicine: Dr NAVEED AKHTAR (Principal (Acting))
University College of Engineering and Technology: Prof. Dr SHAHID RAHIM (Principal)
University College of Veterinary and Animal Sciences: Prof. Dr ABDUS SAMAD (Principal (Acting))

UNIVERSITY OF KARACHI

University Campus, Karachi 75270
Telephone: (21) 9261300
Fax: (21) 9261340
E-mail: info@uok.edu.pk
Internet: www.uok.edu.pk

Founded 1951
State control
Languages of instruction: Urdu, English
Academic year: September to August

Chancellor: THE GOVERNOR OF SINDH
Vice-Chancellor: Prof. Dr PIRZADA QASIM RAZA SIDDIQUI
Registrar: Prof. Dr MUHAMMAD RAIS ALVI

Library: see Libraries
Number of teachers: 479
Number of students: 20,000

Publications: *Jareeda* (Journal of the Bureau of Composition, Compilation and Translation, annual), *Journal of Science* (2 a year), *Pakistan Journal of Botany* (2 a year), *Pakistan Journal of Nematology* (2 a year), *Pakistan Journal of Psychology* (4 a year)

DEANS

Faculty of Arts: Prof. Dr M. SHAMSUDDIN
Faculty of Education: Prof. Dr M. ISMAIL BROHI
Faculty of Islamic Studies: Prof. Dr JALALUD-DIN A. NOORI
Faculty of Law: Prof. MAMOON HUSAN
Faculty of Management and Administrative Sciences: Prof. Dr M. ABUZAR WAJIDI
Faculty of Medicine: Prof. Dr SADIYA AZIZ KARIM
Faculty of Pharmacy: Prof. Dr S. WASEEMUD-DIN AHMED
Faculty of Science: Prof. Dr SHAHANA UROOJ KAZMI

PROFESSORS

Faculty of Arts:

AHMED, N., Islamic History
ANSARI, A. M. S., Urdu
ARAB, A. K., Arabic
FATIMA, N., Library and Information Science
HAQ, I., Arabic
HUMAYUN, S., Public Administration
HUSAIN, F., Sindhi
HUSAIN, S. M. A., Economics
HUSSAIN, J., General History
MEHDI, S. S., International Relations
MEMON, S., Sindhi
MIRZA, S. Q., Mass Communication
MURTAZA, M. R., Mass Communication
REHMAN, K., Sociology
SAJDIN, M., Commerce
SHAHEED, M. A., Arabic
SHAMSUDDIN, M., Mass Communication
SHERWANI, M. K., Library and Information Science
TAFHIMI, S., Persian
WAJIDI, M. A., Public Administration
WAZARAT, T. A., International Relations

Faculty of Islamic Studies:

RASHID, A., Islamic Studies
SIDDIQUI, M. A. S., Islamic Learning

Faculty of Pharmacy:

AHMED, M., Pharmacognosy
AHMED, M. A., Pharmaceutics
AHMED, S. P., Pharmacology
AHMED, T., Pharmaceutics
ALI, S. A., Pharmaceutics
BAIG, A. E., Pharmaceutics
HUSSAIN, W., Pharmaceutical Chemistry
MANZAR, K. N., Pharmaceutical Chemistry
REHMAN, S. B., Pharmacology
SAIFY, S. Z., Pharmaceutical Chemistry
SHAIKH, D., Pharmaceutics
SULTANA, N., Pharmaceutical Chemistry

Faculty of Science:

AFTAB, N., Biochemistry
AHMED, A., Applied Chemistry
AHMED, E., Statistics
AHMED, F., Physics
AHMED, I., Zoology
AHMED, I. K., Physics
AHMED, N., Genetics
AHMED, S., Botany
AKHTAR, S. K., Physics
AKHTAR, W., Physics
ALI, S. I., Applied Chemistry
ANIS, K., Physics
ANSARI, A. A., Applied Physics
ARAYN, M. S., Chemistry
ARSHAD, R., Physiology
ATHAR, H. S. A., Biochemistry
AZEEM, A., Physiology
AZHAR, A., Biochemistry
AZIZ, K., Botany
AZMATULLAH, M., Geology
BARKATI, S., Zoology
BURNI, S. M. A., Computer Science
FAHIMUDDIN, Chemistry
FARID, A., Philosophy
HALEEM, M. A., Biochemistry
HAMEED, S., Applied Chemistry
HASAN, H., Zoology
HASNAIN, S. N., Biochemistry
HASNI, S., Biochemistry
HUSAIN, V., Geology
HUSSAIN, M. R., Physics
IQBAL, M., Zoology
IQBAL, Z., Botany
JABEEN, D., Biochemistry
JAHANGIR, S., Biochemistry
JAVED, W., Zoology
KAZMI, M. A., Zoology
KAZMI, Q. B., Zoology
KAZMI, S. A., Chemistry
KAZMI, S. U., Microbiology
KHAN, A. F., Microbiology
KHAN, F., Applied Chemistry
KHAN, K. R., Physiology
KHAN, M. A., Botany
KHAN, M. ALTAF, Microbiology
KHAN, M. I., Botany
KHAN, N., Mathematics
KHANUM, A., Biochemistry
KHATOON, H., Microbiology
KHATOON, K., Botany
MAHMOOD, Z., Statistics
MALIK, A., Research Institute of Chemistry
MALIK, S. A., Chemistry
MAQSOOD, Z. T., Chemistry
MEHDI, F., Botany
MOHSIN, S. I., Geology
MUHAMMAD, I., Biochemistry
NAEEM, R. K., Mathematics
NAQVI, I. I., Chemistry
NAQVI, S. M. M. R., Physics
NAQVI, S. R. R., Chemistry
NAZAMI, S. S., Chemistry
NOOR, F., Chemistry
NUSRAT, J., Microbiology
QADEER, A., Applied Physics
QADRI, M. U., Geology
QAISER, M., Botany
QAMAR, J., Mathematics
QASIM, R., Biochemistry
QIDWAI, A. A., Physics
QIDWAI, I. M., Biochemistry
QURESHI, M. A., Physiology
QURESHI, N. M., Physiology
RAFI, F., Physiology
RAOOF, M. A., Physics
RASOOL, S. A., Microbiology
RAZZAQI, T. F., Biotechnology
REHMAN, A. U., Research Institute of Chemistry
RIZVI, N., Zoology
SAIFULLAH, S. M., Botany
SHAIKH, S. A., Geology
SHAHEEN, B., Research Institute of Chemistry
SHAMEEL, M. M., Botany
SHAMS, N., Applied Chemistry
SHAUKAT, S. S., Botany
SIDDIQUI, A. J., Statistics
SIDDIQI, J. S., Statistics
SIDDIQUI, K. A., Physics
SIDDIQI, N. S., Biochemistry
SIDDIQI, P. A., Zoology
SIDDIQI, P. Q. R., Physiology
SIDDIQI, R., Microbiology
SIDDIQI, S. A., Chemistry
SIDDIQI, Z., Chemistry
ULLAH, N., Geology
USMAN, M., Botany
USMANI, A. A., Chemistry
VAHIDY, A. A., Genetics

VAHIDY, R., Microbiology
YASMEN, N., Zoology
ZAIDGHAM, N. A., Geology
ZAIDI, S. A. H., Applied Chemistry
ZAIDI, S. S. H., Applied Physics
ZEENAT, I., Psychology

ATTACHED INSTITUTES

Applied Economics Research Centre: see under Research Institutes.

Centre for European Studies: Dir Dr NAVID TAHIR.

Centre for Molecular Genetics: tel. and fax (21) 4966045; e-mail cmg@uok.edu.pk; Dir Dr N. AHMED.

Centre of Excellence in Marine Biology: see under Research Institutes.

Centre of Excellence in Women's Studies: e-mail cews@uok.edu.pk; Dir Dr NASREEN ASLAM SHAH.

Hussein Ibrahim Jamal Research Institute of Chemistry: tel. (21) 4824925; fax (21) 4819018; e-mail info@iccs.edu; internet www.iccs.edu; attached to International Center for Chemical and Biological Sciences; Dir Prof. Dr ATTA-UR-REHMAN.

Institute of Clinical Psychology: tel. (21) 4613584; e-mail icp@uok.edu.pk; Dir Prof. M. SHAMSUDDIN; publ. *Pakistan Journal of Psychology (PJP)* (official journal), *Pakistan Journal of Clinical Psychology (PJCP)* (2 a year).

Institute of Environmental Sciences: tel. (21) 9261386; fax (21) 9261386; e-mail ies@uok.edu.pk; Dir Dr MOAZZAM ALI KHAN.

Institute of Marine Science: e-mail ims@uok.edu.pk; f. 1981; Dir Dr S. N. SAIF ULLAH.

Institute of Sustainable Halophyte Utilization: tel. (21) 7700930; fax (21) 4820922; e-mail halophyte@uok.edu.pk; internet halophyte.org; Dir Dr M. AJMAL KHAN.

M. A. H. Qadri Biological Research Centre: Dir Dr A. A. VAHIDY.

Marine Reference Collection and Research Centre: tel. (21) 9243680,; e-mail mrrcc@uok.edu.pk; Dir Dr QUDDUSI B. KAZMI; library of 500 vols.

National Nematological Research Centre: tel. and fax (21) 9261387; e-mail nnrc@uok.edu.pk; Dir Dr SHAHINA FAYYAZ; publ. *Pakistan Journal of Nematology (PJN)* (journal and newsletter).

Pakistan Study Centre: tel. (21) 9261300; e-mail psc@uok.edu.pk; f. 1977; Dir Dr S. AHMED JAFFAR (acting).

Pure and Applied Physics Research Centre: Dir Dr NAQVI RAZA MUNIR MEHDI.

Shahik Zajed Islamic Research Centre: e-mail szic@uok.edu.pk; Dir Dr M. A. SHAHEED.

There are 110 affiliated colleges

KARAKORAM INTERNATIONAL UNIVERSITY

Gilgit, North West Frontier Province
Telephone: (5811) 50440
Fax: (5811) 58245
E-mail: vcoffice@kiu.edu.pk
Internet: www.kiu.edu.pk

Founded 2002

Vice-Chancellor: AZIZ ALI NAJAM

Faculties of humanities and social sciences, mountain area development studies and science.

KOHAT UNIVERSITY OF SCIENCE AND TECHNOLOGY

Bannu Rd, off Jerma, Kohat 26000, North West Frontier Province
Telephone: (922) 554565
Fax: (922) 554556
Internet: www.kust.edu.pk

Founded 2001

Vice-Chancellor: Dr LUTFULLAH KAKAKHEIL
Registrar: Prof. Dr IHSAN ELLAHI
Director for Academic Affairs: MUNAWAR ALI SHAH
Director for Administration: Lt Col (Rtd) ABDUL KARIM
Director for Finance and Planning: MUHAMMAD ZAKIR
Librarian: MURAD ALI

Institutes of education and research, information technology, management sciences and microbiology; faculties in arts, sciences and medicine.

LAHORE COLLEGE FOR WOMEN UNIVERSITY

Jail Rd, Lahore 54600, Punjab
Telephone: (42) 9203801
Fax: (42) 9203077
E-mail: vc@lcwu.edu.pk
Internet: www.lcwu.edu.pk

Founded 1922; present name and status 2002

Vice-Chancellor: Prof. Dr BUSHRA MATEEN
Registrar: SHAISTA VINE
Librarian: HINA AZIZ

Number of teachers: 260
Number of students: 5,000

DEANS

Faculty of Engineering and Technology: Prof. Dr FARHAT SALEEMI
Faculty of Humanities, Islamic and Oriental Learning: Dr HUMALA S. KHALID
Faculty of Natural Sciences: Prof. Dr KAUSER JAMAL CHEEMA
Faculty of Social Sciences: Prof. RIFFAT SAQLAIN

PROFESSORS

ALI, Y., Physics
CHEEMA, K. J., Environmental Sciences
CHEEMA, K. J., Zoology
GOHAR, K., Economics
MAHMOOD, A. S., Mathematics
MATEEN, B., Environmental Sciences
NAVQI, R. F., Fine Arts
NAWAZ, R., Islamic Studies

LAHORE UNIVERSITY OF MANAGEMENT SCIENCES

Opposite Sector U, DHA, Lahore Cantt, Lahore 54792
Telephone: (42) 5722670
Fax: (42) 5722591
E-mail: admissions@lums.edu.pk
Internet: www.lums.edu.pk

Founded 1985
Private control
Language of instruction: English
Academic year: September to June

Chancellor: PRESIDENT OF PAKISTAN (ex-officio)
Pro-Chancellor: SYED BABAR ALI
Pro-Vice-Chancellor: Dr AHMAD J. DURRANI
Rector: ABDUL RAZAK DAWOOD
Librarian: MUHAMMAD RAMZAN

Library of 47,000 vols
Number of teachers: 123
Number of students: 1,750

Publications: *Asian Journal of Management Cases* (2 a year), *LUMS Business Recorder* (1 a year), *PLUMS* (1 a year)

DEANS

School of Humanities, Social Sciences and Law: Dr ANJUM NASIM
School of Science and Engineering: ASAD A. ABIDI
Suleman Dawood School of Business: Dr SHAUKAT ALI BRAH

PROFESSORS

ALI, I., Business History and Business Policy
BABRI, H. A., Computer Science
BEG, I., Mathematics
GHANI, J. A., Strategy and Marketing
HASSAN, S. Z., Management Information Systems and Management of Technology
IQBAL, M. A., Computer Science and Mathematics
KHURSHID, A., Technology and Organizational Management
MAUD, M. A., Computer Science
NASIM, A., Business–Government Relations
SARWAR, S. M., Computer Science
SIPRA, N., Finance
ZAMAN, A., Econometrics
ZAMAN, A., Mathematics

ATTACHED RESEARCH INSTITUTES

Case Research Centre: tel. (42) 5722670; fax (42) 5722591; e-mail sipra@lums.edu.pk; Dir Prof. Dr NAEEM SIPRA.

Centre for Advanced Studies in Mathematics: tel. (42) 5722670; fax (42) 5722591; e-mail ibeg@lums.edu.pk; Dir Prof. Dr ISMAT BEG.

Centre for Management and Economic Research: tel. (42) 5722670; e-mail burki@lums.edu.pk; internet ravi.lums.edu.pk/cmer; f. 1992; Dir Dr ABID A. BURKI.

Entrepreneurship, Small and Medium Enterprise Centre: tel. (42) 5722679; e-mail esmec@lums.edu.pk; Dir Dr FAISAL BARI.

Social Enterprise Development Centre: tel. (42) 5722670; fax (42) 5722591; e-mail sedc@lums.edu.pk; internet sedc.org.pk/portal; Dir SYED MUBASHIR ALI.

LIAQUAT UNIVERSITY OF MEDICAL AND HEALTH SCIENCES

Jamshoro, Sindh
Telephone: (22) 2772230
Fax: (22) 2772827
E-mail: registrar@lumhs.edu.pk
Internet: www.lumhs.edu.pk

Founded 1881; present name and status 2001

Vice-Chancellor: Prof. Dr NOSHAD A. SHAIKH
Registrar: Prof. SYED GHULAM KADIR SHAH

Publications: *Bulletin*, *Journal of Liaquat University of Medical and Health Sciences (JLUMHS)*

DEANS

Faculty of Basic Medical Sciences: Prof. SHAHEEN SHAH
Faculty of Community Medicine and Public Health Sciences: Prof. RAFIQUE AHMED SOOMRO
Faculty of Dentistry: Prof. RAFQUE AHMED MEMON
Faculty of Medicine and Allied Sciences: Prof. ALLAH BACHAYO MEMON
Faculty of Surgery and Allied Sciences: Prof. GHULAM ALI MEMON

UNIVERSITY OF MALAKAND

Chakdara, Dir, Malakand, North West Frontier Province
Telephone: (936) 763441
Fax: (936) 763491

Founded 2001

Vice-Chancellor: Prof. Dr RASUL JAN

Registrar: AMIR ZADA ASAD.

MEHRAN UNIVERSITY OF ENGINEERING AND TECHNOLOGY

Jamshoro, 76062 Sindh
Telephone: (22) 2772250
Fax: (221) 2771382
E-mail: vc@muet.edu.pk
Internet: www.muet.edu.pk
Founded 1963 as constituent college of University of Sindh; present status 1977
State control
Language of instruction: English
Academic year: October to August
Chancellor: THE GOVERNOR OF SINDH
Vice-Chancellor: Dr ABDUL QADEER KHAN RAJPUT
Registrar: MOHAMMAD ASLAM UQAILI
Library: see Libraries and Archives
Number of teachers: 270
Number of students: 3,702
Publication: *Research Journal of Engineering and Technology* (4 a year)

DEANS

Faculty of Architecture, Planning, Arts and Design: Prof. Dr DOST ALI KHOWAJA
Faculty of Electrical, Electronics and Computer Engineering: Prof. Dr MUHAMMAD RAFIQUE ABRO
Faculty of Engineering: Prof. Dr RIAZ AHMED SOHAG
Faculty of Science, Technology and Humanities: Prof. Dr MOHAMMAD IBRAHIM PANHWAR

DIRECTORS

Computer Centre: SHUJAUDDIN SIDDIQUI
Continuing Education: Dr MUJEEBUDDIN MEMON
Industrial Liaison: Dr ABDUL KARIM BALOCH
Institute of Environmental Engineering and Management: ABDUL RASHID MEMON
Institute of Irrigation and Drainage Engineering: Prof. BAKHSHAL KHAN LASHARI
Institute of Petroleum and Natural Gas Engineering: Prof. Dr H. R. MEMON
Institute of Science and Technology Development: Dr S. M. QURESHI
Planning and Development: ABDUL RAZZAQUE KAZI
Postgraduate Studies: Dr GHOUS BUX KHASKELI

There are 2 affiliated colleges

NATIONAL TEXTILE UNIVERSITY

Sheikhupura Rd, Faisalabad 37610, Punjab
Telephone: (41) 9230081
Fax: (41) 9230098
E-mail: info@ntu.edu.pk
Internet: www.ntu.edu.pk
Founded 1959 as Institute of Textile Technology; renamed National College of Textile Engineering 1965; present name and status 2002
Federal
Rector: Dr MUKHTAR AHMED
Registrar: Prof. JAVAID IQBAL (acting)
Librarian: MUSHTAQ AHMAD SIDDIQUI
Library of 13,373 vols
Number of teachers: 35
Number of students: 600

NATIONAL UNIVERSITY OF MODERN LANGUAGES

Main Campus, Sector H-9, Islamabad 44000
Telephone: (51) 9257636
Fax: (51) 9257679
E-mail: info@numl.edu.pk
Internet: www.numl.edu.pk
Founded 1970; present name and status 2000
Academic year: January to December (two semesters)
Rector: Brig. Dr AZIZ AHMAD KHAN
Dir for Academic Affairs: RIASAT HUSSAIN
Dir for Admin.: MUHAMMAD YASIN
Dir (Library): MUHAMMAD ABBAS
Dir-Gen. for Int. Relations: KAMRAN JAHANGIR
Project Director: Col MUHAMMAD NAVEED
Registrar: Dr OBAIDULLAH RANJHA
Number of teachers: 315
Number of students: 12,422
Publications: *Research Magazine* (2 a year), *Daryaft* (1 a year), *Takhleeqi Adab* (1 a year).

NATIONAL UNIVERSITY OF SCIENCES AND TECHNOLOGY

Tamiz-ud-din Rd, POB 297, Rawalpindi, Punjab
Telephone: (51) 9271581
Fax: (51) 9271577
E-mail: info@nust.edu.pk
Internet: www.nust.edu.pk
Other campuses in Islamabad, Karachi and Risalpur
Rector: MUHAMMAD ASGHAR
Publication: *Newsletter* (12 a year)
Colleges of aeronautical engineering (Risalpur), civil engineering (Risalpur), electrical and mechanical engineering (Rawalpindi), marine engineering (Karachi), medical sciences (Rawalpindi), telecommunication engineering (Rawalpindi).

UNIVERSITY INSTITUTES

Centre for Cyber Technology and Spectrum Management: H. No. 295, St, No. 35, Sector F-11/3, Islamabad; tel. (51) 9266480; fax (51) 2103427; e-mail cctsm@nust.edu.pk.

Institute of Environmental Science and Engineering: Tamiz-ud-din Rd, Rawalpindi; tel. (51) 9271597; fax (51) 9271597; Principal ISHTIAQ AHAMAD QAZI.

Institute of Geographical Information System: 112-A St 37, Sector F-10/1, Islamabad; tel. (51) 9267241; fax (51) 9267245; e-mail info@igis.edu.pk; internet www.igis.edu.pk; Principal Dr M. UMAR KHATTAK.

Institute of Information Technology: 166-A St 9, Chaklala Scheme-III, Rawalpindi; tel. (51) 9280443; fax (51) 9280782; e-mail info@niit.edu.pk; internet www.niit.edu.pk; Dir-Gen. ARSHAD ALI.

Institute of Management Sciences: Tamiz-ud-din Rd, Rawalpindi; tel. (51) 9271610; fax (51) 9271610.

International Institute for Peace and Conflict Resolution: 112-A St 37, Sector F-10/1, Islamabad; tel. (21) 5892055; fax (51) 9267224; Hon. Chair. JAVED JABBAR.

National Institute of Transportation: Risalpur Cantt, Risalpur 24080; tel. (923) 631211; fax (923) 631594; e-mail sa-nit@nust.edu.pk; Dir Dr TAYYEB AKRAM.

Technology Incubation Centre: 112-B St 37, Sector F-10/1, Islamabad 4400; tel. (51) 9267241; fax (51) 9267245; e-mail info@tic.org.pk; internet www.tic.org.pk; Dir-Gen. Dr ABID PERVEZ GHUMAN.

NED UNIVERSITY OF ENGINEERING AND TECHNOLOGY

University Rd, Karachi 75270
Telephone: (21) 9243261
Fax: (21) 9243255
E-mail: vc@neduet.edu.pk
Internet: www.neduet.edu.pk
Founded 1922 as NED Government Engineering College, university status 1977
Language of instruction: English
Academic year: February to December
Chancellor: THE GOVERNOR OF SINDH
Vice-Chancellor: Eng. ABUL KALAM
Pro-Vice Chancellor: Prof. Dr SHAMSUL HAQUE
Registrar: Prof. Dr SAROSH HASHMAT LODI
Library: see Libraries and Archives
Number of teachers: 150
Number of students: 4,000
Publications: *NED University of Engineering and Research* (2 a year), *Research Journal* (4 a year), *Versity News* (12 a year)

DEANS

Chemical and Material Engineering: Prof. Dr MUHAMMAD TUFAIL
Civil Engineering and Architecture: Prof. Dr. SAHIBZADA FAROOQ AHMED RAFEEQI
Electrical and Computer Engineering: Prof. Dr TALAT ALTAF
Information Sciences and Humanities: Dr MAHMOOD KHAN PATHAN
Mechanical and Manufacturing Engineering: Prof. Dr NAZIMUDDIN QURESHI

PROFESSORS

AHMAD, A., Mechanical Engineering
AHMED, S. F., Civil Engineering
AHSAN, P. F., Civil Engineering
ALTAF, T., Electrical Engineering
HUSSAIN, S. G., Electrical Engineering
KHAN, A. A., Mathematics and Sciences
KHAN, A. S., Civil Engineering
MAHMOOD, K., Mechanical Engineering
MAHMOOD, M., Mechanical Engineering
MIRZA, S. H., Computer Systems Engineering
QURESHI, N., Mechanical Engineering
SHAIKH, N., Electrical Engineering
SIDDIQUI, A. A., Computer Systems Engineering
SOOMRO, A. G., Mechanical Engineering

AFFILIATED COLLEGES

Dawood College of Engineering and Technology: see under Colleges.

Government College of Technology: Plot No. F-13, Sindh Industrial Trading Estate, SITE, Karachi 75700; tel. (21) 2562888; fax (21) 2564503; e-mail info@gctkarachi.com; internet www.gctkarachi.com; Principal Prof. RAJA GHULAM HUSSAIN.

ATTACHED INSTITUTES

Institute of Environmental Engineering and Research: Chair. SAEED AHMED KHAN.

Institute of Industrial Electronics Engineering: St-22/C, Block-6, Gulshan-e-Iqbal, Karachi; tel. (21) 4966274; Principal Eng. SYED NAIMAT ALI RIZVI.

Institute of Material Sciences and Research: Principal MOINUDDIN ALI KHAN.

KANUPP Institute of Nuclear Power Engineering: POB No. 3183, Paradise Pt, Karachi; tel. (21) 9202222; fax (21) 9202240; e-mail kinpoe@kinpoe.edu.pk; internet www.kinpoe.edu.pk; Dir Dr KHALID M. BUKHARI; library of 3,400 vols.

PAF Institute of Aviation Technology: PAF Base, Korangi Creek, Karachi; tel. (21) 5090250; fax (21) 9231453; library of 3,400 vols; Principal Group Capt. HAROON RAFI.

NORTH WEST FRONTIER PROVINCE AGRICULTURAL UNIVERSITY

Peshawar
Telephone: (91) 9216572
Fax: (91) 9216520
E-mail: ayazjan@hotmail.com
Internet: www.aup.edu.pk

Founded 1981
Language of instruction: English
Academic year: January to December

Chancellor: OWAIS AHMED GHANI
Vice-Chancellor: Prof. Dr SAID KHAN KHALIL
Registrar: MOHAMMAD DILAWAR
Librarian: ATTAULLAH

Library of 79,000 vols
Number of teachers: 200
Number of students: 8,000

Publications: *Journal of Development Studies* (irregular), *Sarhad Journal of Agriculture* (6 a year)

DEANS

Faculty of Animal Husbandry and Veterinary Sciences: Prof. Dr GHULAM HABIB
Faculty of Crop Production Sciences: Prof. Dr MUHAMMAD SARIRULLAH SARIR
Faculty of Crop Protection Sciences: Prof. Dr MUHAMMAD NAEEM
Faculty of Nutrition Sciences: Prof. Dr HAMID ULLAH SHAH
Faculty of Rural Social Sciences: MUNIR KHAN

NORTH WEST FRONTIER PROVINCE UNIVERSITY OF ENGINEERING AND TECHNOLOGY

POB 814, University Campus, Peshawar 25120
Telephone: (91) 9216796
Fax: (91) 9216663
E-mail: registrar@nwfpuet.edu.pk
Internet: www.nwfpuet.edu.pk

Founded 1980
Language of instruction: English
Academic year: November to September

Campuses at Abbottabad, Bannu and Mardan

Chancellor: OWAIS AHMED GHANI
Vice-Chancellor: SYED IMTIAZ HUSSAIN GILLANI
Registrar: Lt-Col IMTIAZ AHMAD KHAN
Dean: Prof. AZZAM UL ASSAR
Librarian: ABDUR RASHID

Library of 110,000 vols
Number of teachers: 347
Number of students: 3,365

Publication: *Journal of Engineering and Applied Sciences* (2 a year)

PROFESSORS

AKBAR SHAH, S. R., Mechatronics Engineering
GUL JADOON, K., Mining Engineering
HUSSAIN, I., Industrial Engineering
INAYATULLAH KHAN BABAR, M., Computer Science and Information Technology (Non Engineering)
JADOON, K. G., Chemical Engineering
MAHMOOD, Z., Agricultural Engineering
NAEEM KHAN, A., Civil Engineering
TAJIK, S. J., Mechanical Engineering
UR REHMAN, S., Basic Science and Islamiat
YAHYA, K. M., Computer System Engineering
ZAHIR KHAN, M., Electrical and Electronics Engineering

UNIVERSITY OF PESHAWAR

Peshawar, NWFP
Telephone: (91) 9216701
Fax: (91) 9216470
E-mail: vice_chancellor@upesh.edu.pk
Internet: www.upesh.edu

Founded 1950
State control
Languages of instruction: Arabic, English, Pashto, Persian, Urdu
Academic year: September to June

Chancellor: THE GOV. OF THE NORTH WEST FRONTIER PROVINCE
Vice-Chancellor: Prof. Dr AZMAT HAYAT KHAN
Registrar and Dir of Admissions: SHIREEN ZADA KHATTAK (acting)
Provost: Dr MOHAMMAD FAROOQ SWATI
Controller of Examination: MUHAMMAD ISLAM
Dir of Admin.: IFTHIKHAR HUSSAIN KHAN
Dir of QEC: MUHAMMAD TAIMUR KHAN
Dir of Sports: BAHRE KARAM
Dir of Works: Majr. (Retd) Eng. MOH. AYAZ
Librarian: IBRAR MOHAMMAD

Library: see Libraries and Archives
Number of teachers: 583
Number of students: 18,500

Publications: *Geological Bulletin* (1 a year), *Journal of Humanities and Social Sciences* (1 a year), *Journal of Law and Society* (1 a year), *Peshawar University Review* (1 a year)

DEANS

Faculty of Arts and Humanities: Prof. Dr TAJ ALI
Faculty of Islamic and Oriental Studies: Prof. Dr GHULAM NASIR MARWAT
Faculty of Life and Environmental Sciences: Prof. Dr MUHAMMAD JAVED
Faculty of Management and Information Sciences: Prof. Dr SHAH JEHAN SYED
Faculty of Numerical and Physical Sciences: Prof. Dr MUHAMMAD IQBAL
Faculty of Social Sciences: Prof. Dr NAEEM-UR-REHMAN

PROFESSORS

ABBASI, J. A., Geology
ADEEL, M. A., Institute of Education and Research
ALI, A., Law
ALI, T., Archaeology
AYAZ, Q., Islamic Studies
BANGASH, G. T., History
GILANI, S. Z., Education (Psychology)
HANIF, M., Islamic Studies
HUSSAIN, F., Biotechnology
IQBAL, M., Statistics
JAN, A.-H., Zoology
JAN, M. Q., Geology
KHAN, A., Geography
KHAN, M., Chemistry
KHAN, M. A., Chemistry
KHAN, M. J., Geology
KHAN, Z. A., Mathematics
KHATTAK, N. S., Electronics
MAJID, M., Geology
MIAN, I., Geology
NAWAZ, A., Geography
NASIR, G., Persian
NOOR, I., Mathematics
QAZI, S., Islamic Studies
RAFIQ, M., Geology
RAHMAN, C., English
RAHMAN, F., Physics
RAHMAN, M., English
RASHID, H., Chemistry
REHANA, N., Chemistry
REHMAN, S. S., Environmental Sciences
RIAZ, M., Physics
RIAZ, M. N., Psychology
SHAH, R., Pashto
SULAIMAN, M., Zoology

CONSTITUENT COLLEGES

College of Home Economics: University of Peshawar; tel. (91) 9216882; e-mail hec@upesh.edu.pk; f. 1954; Principal Dr FANILA FAR.

Islamia College: Peshawar; e-mail icp@upesh.edu.pk; f. 1913; Principal AJMAL KHAN.

Jinnah College for Women: Peshawar; e-mail jcw@upesh.edu.pk; f. 1964; Principal Prof. Dr NELOFAR ZEB.

Law College: Peshawar; Principal Prof. Dr MISAL ZADA; publ. *Law & Society* (48 a year).

Quaid-e-Azam College of Commerce: Peshawar; e-mail qcc@upesh.edu.pk; f. 1962; Principal IKHTIAR MUHAMMAD.

ATTACHED INSTITUTES AND CENTRES

Area Study Centre: Peshawar; tel. (91) 9216764; e-mail asc@upesh.edu.pk; internet asc.upesh.edu.pk; f. 1976; Dir Dr AZMAT HAYAT KHAN; library of 18,880 .

Centre of Biotechnology: Peshawar; tel. (91) 9216485; e-mail biotech@upesh.edu.pk; internet biotech.upesh.edu.pk; f. 2001; Dir Assoc. Prof. Dr BASHIR AHMAD.

Centre of Excellence in Geology: Peshawar; e-mail ncegeo@upesh.edu.pk; Dir Prof. Dr MUHAMMAD ASIF KHAN.

Centre of Excellence in Physical Chemistry: Peshawar; e-mail ncepc@upesh.edu.pk; Dir Dr MUHAMMAD MUSTAFA.

Institute of Chemical Sciences: Peshawar; tel. (91) 9216652; e-mail chemistry@upesh.edu.pk; f. 1955; Dir Dr MUHAMMAD NISAR AHMAD.

Institute of Education and Research: Peshawar; tel. (91) 9216756; e-mail ier@upesh.edu.pk; f. 1980; Dir Prof. Dr SHAH JEHAN.

Pakistan Study Centre: tel. (91) 9216765; e-mail psc@upesh.edu.pk; Dir PERVAZ AHMAD KHAN TORU.

Pashto Academy: see under Learned Societies.

Shaikh Zayed Islamic Centre: Peshawar; tel. (91) 9216746; e-mail islamic_centre@upesh.edu.pk; Dir Prof. Dr DOSAT MUHAMMAD.

There are 92 govt and 108 private colleges affiliated to the University

UNIVERSITY OF THE PUNJAB

Quaid-e-Azam Campus, POB 54590, Lahore
Telephone: (42) 9231099
Fax: (42) 9231101
E-mail: registrar@pu.edu.pk
Internet: www.pu.edu.pk

Founded 1882
State control
Languages of instruction: English, Urdu
Academic year: begins September

Chancellor: THE GOVERNOR OF THE PUNJAB
Vice-Chancellor: Prof. Dr MUJAHID KAMRAN
Pro-Vice-Chancellor: (vacant)
Registrar: Prof. Dr MUHAMMAD NAEEM KHAN

Library: see Libraries and Archives
Number of teachers: 381
Number of students: 10,047

Publications: various faculty and institute bulletins

DEANS

Faculty of Arts and Humanities: Prof. SHAISTA SONNU SIRAJ UD DIN
Faculty of Behavioural and Social Sciences: Prof. Dr MUGHEES-UDDIN SHEIKH
Faculty of Commerce: Prof. Dr LIAQAT ALI
Faculty of Economics and Management Sciences: Prof. Dr MUHAMMAD EHSAN MALIK
Faculty of Education: Prof. Dr HAFIZ MUHAMMAD IQBAL
Faculty of Engineering and Technology: Prof. Dr JAVAID AHMAD
Faculty of Islamic Studies: Prof. Dr HAFIZ MAHMOOD AKHTAR
Faculty of Law: Prof. Dr MUJAHID KAMRAN
Faculty of Life Sciences: Prof. Dr SHAHIDA HASNAIN
Faculty of Medicine and Dentistry: Prof. Dr ANWAAR A. KHAN

Faculty of Oriental Learning: Prof. Dr MUHAMMAD SALEEM MAZHAR
Faculty of Pharmacy: Prof. Dr M. JAMSHAID
Faculty of Science: Prof. Dr CH. JAMIL ANWAR

PROFESSORS

Faculty of Arts and Humanities (Quaid-e-Azam Campus, Lahore; tel. (42) 9231167; e-mail dean.ahs@pu.edu.pk):

ABID, M., Pakistan Studies Centre
ABID, Q., History
AHMAD, A., Philosophy
AHMAD, N., Philosophy
AHSAN, A. S., Research Society of Pakistan
BUTT, A. R., Economics
CHAUDHRY, M. A., Economics
GILL, S. A., History
HAFEEZ, M., Philosophy
HASNAT, S. F., Political Science
JABEEN, N., Administrative Sciences
JADOON, M. Z. I., Administrative Sciences
JAVED, M. A., Sports Sciences and Physical Education
JULLANDHRY, M. S., Mass Communication
MALIK, M. E., Business Administration
MALIK, M. H., Social Sciences
MIRZA, M. S., Women Studies
SHEIKH, M. D., Mass Communication
SIRAJUDDIN, S. S., English Language and Literature
ZAKAR, M. Z., Sociology

Faculty of Commerce (Quaid-e-Azam Campus, Lahore; tel. (42) 9231154; fax (42) 9231259; e-mail dean.commerce@pu.edu.pk; internet www.pu.edu.pk/commerce):

ALI, L.
BUTT, Z. A.
CHAUDHARY, N. A.
SAEED, K. A.

Faculty of Education (Quaid-e-Azam Campus, Lahore; tel. (42) 9231264; fax (42) 9231156; e-mail dean.education@pu.edu.pk; internet www.pu.edu.pk/education):

HAMEED, A.
IQBAL, M. Z.
KHALID, M. I.
KHAN, Z. A.
MIRZA, M. S.
ZAIDI, S. N. R.

Faculty of Engineering and Technology (Quaid-e-Azam Campus, Lahore; tel. (42) 9230343; fax (42) 9231159; e-mail dean .engg@pu.edu.pk):

AHMAD, J.
AKHTAR, N. A.
BUTT, M. A.
BUTT, M. T. Q.
DILAWARI, A. H.
NAWAZ, S.
RIZVI, S. Z. H.

Faculty of Islamic Studies (Allama Iqbal Campus, Lahore; tel. (42) 9210837; fax (42) 9210837; e-mail dean.is@pu.edu.pk; internet www.pu.edu.pk/islamic):

AKHTAR, H. M., Islamic Studies
CHAUDHARY, M. A., Arabic
FATIMA, S., Islamic Studies
HASAN, M., Urdu
HASHMI, R., Urdu
KHAN, S. A., Urdu
MOEEN, M., Arabic
SHAH, M. A., Iqbal Studies
SHAUKAT, J., Islamic Studies

Faculty of Law (Quaid-e-Azam Campus, Lahore; tel. (42) 9231276; fax (42) 9231278; e-mail dean.law@pu.edu.pk; internet www .pu.edu.pk/law):

MALIK, D. M.
NAEEM, M.

Faculty of Pharmacy (Allama Iqbal Campus, Lahore; tel. (42) 9211617; e-mail dean .pharmacy@pu.edu.pk; internet www.pu.edu .pk/pharmacy):

RIAZ, M.

Faculty of Science (Quaid-e-Azam Campus, Lahore; tel. (42) 9231162; fax (42) 9230242; e-mail dean.science@pu.edu.pk; internet www.pu.edu.pk/science):

ABBASI, G. Q., Mathematics
ABDULLAH, T., Solid-State Physics
AHMAD, Z., Geology
AKHTAR, M. W., Biochemistry and Biotechnology
AKHTER, A. S., Statistics
ALEEM, F., High-Energy Physics
ANWAR, C. J., Chemistry
ASGHAR, R., Business and Information Technology
AZHAR, S., Business and Information Technology
BHATTI, S. A., Mathematics
BUTT, A. R., Business and Information Technology
DIN, S., Business and Information Technology
DIN, S., Mathematics
FAROOQ, U., Geology
GHAZANFAR, M., Geology
GULZAR, F., Geography
HAFEEZ, M., Business and Information Technology
HASNAIN, S., Botany
IDREES, M., Business and Information Technology
IKRAM, N., Solid-State Physics
IQBAL, J., Chemistry
JAMAL, K., Business and Information Technology
KAMRAN, M., Physics
KHAN, Z. A., Business and Information Technology
LATIF, S., Business and Information Technology
MANSOOR, G. D., Business and Information Technology
NAZAR, F. M., Solid-State Physics
RAO, A. A., Business and Information Technology
RASHID, K. H., High-Energy Physics
RAZA, A., Business and Information Technology
RIAZUDDIN, S., Advanced Molecular Biology
SHAKOORI, A. R., Microbiology and Molecular Genetics
SIDDIQI, S. A., Solid-State Physics
SOHAIL, M., Business and Information Technology
SOHAIL, S., Business and Information Technology
ZAIDI, N. R., Business and Information Technology

Research Departments:

AHSAN, A. R. S., Research Society of Pakistan
AKRAM, S. M., Iqbaliyat
ALEEM, F., Centre for High-Energy Physics
ALI, M., Space Sciences
ANWAR, J., Institute of Chemistry
ANWAR, M., Social Sciences Research Centre
ARIF, M., Urdu Encyclopaedia of Islam
FAROOQ, U., Institute of Geology
GILL, S. A., South Asian Study Centre
JADOON, M. Z. I., Institute of Administrative Sciences
JAMSHAID, M., College of Pharmacy
MALIK, D. M., University Law College
MALIK, M. E., Institute of Business Administration
MIRZA, M., Institute of Education and Research
NAZAR, F. M., Centre for Solid-State Physics
RAHMAN, N. K., Centre for Clinical Psychology
SHAUKAT, J., Sheikh Zayed Islamic Centre
ZAIDI, H. S., College of Arts and Design

ATTACHED INSTITUTES AND CONSTITUENT COLLEGES

College of Arts and Design: Allama Iqbal Campus, Lahore 54000; tel. (42) 9211608; fax (42) 9211604; e-mail principal@cad.pu.edu .pk; internet www.pu.edu.pk/cad/site/history .html; f. 1940; Principal HASAN SHAHNAWAZ ZAIDI.

College of Pharmacy: Allama Iqbal Campus, Lahore; f. 1944; Principal Dr MUHAMMAD JAMSHAID.

Hailey College of Banking and Finance: Lahore; f. 2003; Principal Prof. Dr KHAWAJA AMJAD SAEED.

Hailey College of Commerce: Quaid-i-Azam Campus, Lahore; f. 1927; Principal Prof. Dr LIAQAT ALI.

Institute of Administrative Sciences: Quaid-e-Azam Campus, Lahore 54590; tel. (42) 9231164; fax (42) 9230622; e-mail info@ ias.pu.edu.pk; internet ias.pu.edu.pk; f. 1962; Dir Prof. Dr MUHAMMAD ZAFAR IQBAL JADOON.

Institute of Biochemistry and Biotechnology: Quaid-i-Azam Campus, Lahore; f. 1997; Dir Dr AMIN ATHAR.

Institute of Business Administration: Quaid-e-Azam Campus, Lahore 54590; tel. (42) 9231257; f. 1972; Dir Prof. Dr MUHAMMAD EHSAN MALIK.

Institute of Business and Information Technology: Quaid-e-Azam Campus, Lahore 54590; tel. (42) 9230825; fax (42) 9230557; e-mail info@ibitpu.edu.pk; internet ibitpu.edu.pk; f. 2001; Dir Prof. Dr NAYYAR RAZA ZAIDI.

Institute of Chemical Engineering and Technology: Quaid-e-Azam Campus, Lahore 54590; f. 1917; Dir Prof. Dr SYED ZAHOOR-UL-HASSAN RIZVI.

Institute of Chemistry: Lahore; tel. (42) 9230463; fax (42) 9231269; e-mail snagra@ gmail.com; internet www.chemistrypu.edu .pk; f. 1923; Dir Dr SAEED AHMAD NAGRA.

Institute of Education and Research: Quaid-i-Azam Campus, Lahore; f. 1960; Dir Dr HAFIZ MUHAMMAD IQBAL.

Institute of Environmental Science: Lahore; f. 2000; Dir Dr IFTIKHAR HUSSAIN BALOCH.

Institute of Geology: Quaid-i-Azam Campus, Lahore; f. 1951; Dir Prof. Dr NASIR AHMED.

Institute of Statistics: Lahore; f. 1950; Dir Dr SHAHID KAMAL.

Punjab University College of Information Technology: Allama Iqbal Campus, Lahore; f. 1987; Principal Dr SYED MANSOOR SARWAR.

University Law College: Quaid-i-Azam Campus, Lahore; f. 1968; Dir Dr SHAZIA QURESHI.

University Oriental College: Allama Iqbal Campus, Lahore; f. 1882; Principal Prof. Dr MAZHAR MOEEN.

There are 434 affiliated colleges

QUAID-E-AWAM UNIVERSITY OF ENGINEERING, SCIENCES AND TECHNOLOGY

Nawabshah 67480, Sindh
Telephone: (241) 9370382
Fax: (241) 9370367
E-mail: info@quest.edu.pk
Internet: www.quest.edu.pk
State control
Founded 1963

Vice-Chancellor: Prof. WAHID BUX SOOMRO
Registrar: GHULAM RASOOL KHASKHELI
Librarian: M. RAUF MUGHAL

Library of 50,000 vols; 25,000 online research journals

DEANS

Faculty of Engineering: Prof. Dr ALI BUX SOOMRO

Faculty of Technology: Prof. Dr SADARUDDIN SHAIKH

QUAID-I-AZAM UNIVERSITY

Islamabad 45320
Telephone: (51) 90642002
E-mail: vco@qau.edu.pk
Internet: www.qau.edu.pk

Founded 1965; incorporated 1967; name changed 1976

Postgraduate students only
State control
Language of instruction: English

Chancellor: THE PRESIDENT OF THE ISLAMIC REPUBLIC OF PAKISTAN
Vice-Chancellor: Dr M. QASIM JAN
Registrar: AURANGZEB HASAN
Librarian: MEHBOOB HUSSAIN KHAN

Library: see Libraries and Archives
Number of teachers: 195
Number of students: 3,995

Publications: *Prospectus*, *Scrutiny* (2 a year), *Journal of Social Science*, *Journal of Science* (2 a year)

DEANS

Faculty of Medicine: Dr SYED FAZLE HADI
Faculty of Natural Sciences: Dr KHAWAJA AZAM ALI
Faculty of Social Sciences: Dr IJAZ HUSSAIN

ATTACHED INSTITUTES

Area Study Centre (US Studies).

Centre for Central Asian Studies.

Centre for Nuclear Studies (PINSTECH).

National Institute of Historical and Cultural Research.

National Institute of Modern Languages.

National Institute of Pakistan Studies: tel. (51) 90644010; e-mail trahman@nips.qau.edu.pk; internet www.qau.edu.pk/nips/main.html; Dir Prof. Dr TARIQ RAHMANf. 1983.

National Institute of Psychology: tel. (51) 90644033; e-mail nip@nip.edu.pk; internet www.nip.edu.pk; Dir NAEEM TARIQ; publ. *Pakistan Journal of Psychological Research* (2 a year).

Pakistan Institute of Medical Sciences.

Taxila Institute of Asian Civilization: e-mail support@tiac.edu.pk; internet www.tiac.edu.pk; Dir HUGH VAN SKYHAWK (acting); publ. *Journal of Asian Civilizations*.

UNIVERSITY OF SARGODHA

Sargodha, Punjab
Telephone: (451) 9230811
Fax: (451) 222121
E-mail: info@uos.edu.pk
Internet: www.uos.edu.pk

Founded 2002

Vice-Chancellor: Dr MOHAMMAD AKRAM CHAUDHARY
Registrar: M. B AWAN
Treasurer: MIAN MUHAMMAD SARWAR

Number of teachers: 205
Number of students: 7,000

DEANS

Faculty of Agriculture: ZAKIR HUSSAIN RANA
Faculty of Arts and Social Sciences: Prof. Dr ISHTIAQ AHMED CHAUDHARY
Faculty of Islamic and Oriental Learning: Prof. Dr MAQBOOL HUSSAIN SIAL
Faculty of Management and Administrative Sciences: Prof. Dr MAQBOOL HUSSAIN SIAL
Faculty of Science and Technology: Prof. Dr GHULAM HUSSAIN

PROFESSORS

AHMED, I., Arts and Social Sciences
ALI, M., Chemistry
ARIF, S., English
BUKHARI, A., Islamic and Oriental Learning
HAQ, F., Chemistry
IQBAL, M., Science and Technology
SULTANA, N., Mathematics
TAHIR, M., Chemistry

CONSTITUENT COLLEGE

Sargodha Medical College: University of Sargodha; tel. (48) 9230811; fax (48) 3768595; e-mail smc@uos.edu.pk; internet smc.uos.edu.pk; Principal Prof. Dr M. ZAHOOR UL HASSAN DOGAR.

University College of Agriculture: University of Sargodha; tel. (48) 3703661; e-mail agriculture@uos.edu.pk; internet agriculture.uos.edu.pk; depts of agricultural economics and marketing, agro-forestry and agricultural extension education, agronomy, animal sciences, entomology, genetics and molecular biology, horticulture, plant breeding, plant pathology, soil and environmental sciences; Principal Prof. Dr MUHAMMAD AFZAL.

There are 92 affiliated colleges

SHAH ABDUL LATIF UNIVERSITY

Khairpur, Sindh
Telephone: (243) 9280051
Fax: (243) 9280060
E-mail: info@salu.edu.pk
Internet: www.salu.edu.pk

Founded 1975 as campus and 1987 as university
State control
Languages of instruction: English, Sindhi, Urdu
Academic year: September to June

Chancellor: THE GOVERNOR OF SINDH
Vice-Chancellor: Dr NILOFER SHAIKH
Registrar: Prof. SYED AHMED HUSSAIN SHAH
Librarian: MUHAMMAD SALEH BHATTI

Library of 40,311 vols
Number of teachers: 186
Number of students: 4,608

Publications: *Aashikar* (research, in Sindhi, 1 a year), *Ancient Sindh* (research, 1 a year), *Bhittai* (research, in Sindh, 1 a year), *The Commerce and Economic Review* (research, 1 a year), *The Diplomat* (2 a year), *Scientific Sindh* (research, 1 a year)

DEANS

Faculty of Arts and Social Sciences: Prof. SAYED AHMED HUSSAIN SHAH
Faculty of Commerce and Business Administration: Prof. SHAH MUHAMMAD LOHRANI
Faculty of Law: (vacant)
Faculty of Natural Science: Prof. MIAN DAD ZARDARI

ATTACHED RESEARCH INSTITUTES

Date Palm Research Institute: fax (243) 9280344; e-mail gsmarkhand@yahoo.com; Dir Prof. Dr GHULAM SARWAR MARKHAND.

Indus Developing Research Centre: f. 1992.

UNIVERSITY OF SINDH

Allama I.I. Kazi Campus, Jamshoro 76080, District Dadu
Telephone: (22) 2772681
Fax: (22) 2772002
E-mail: info@usindh.edu.pk
Internet: www.usindh.edu.pk

Founded 1947 in Karachi
Languages of instruction: English, Sindhi, Urdu

Chancellor: THE GOVERNOR OF SINDH
Vice-Chancellor: MAZHARUL HAQ SIDDIQUI
Registrar: Prof. Dr SAEED AHMED SOOMRO
Controller of Examinations: Dr PERVAIZ AHMED PAHTAN
Director of Finance: FAIZ MUHAMMAD HINGORO
Director of Planning: MUHAMMAD HUSSAIN SHAIKH

Library: see Libraries and Archives
Number of teachers: 423
Number of students: 12,800

Publications: *Ariel* (1 a year, in English), *Grassroot* (2 a year, English), *Kinjhar* (1 a year, in Sindhi), *Sindhi Arab* (1 a year, in Sindhi), *Sindhological Studies* (1 a year, in English), *Sindh University Journal of Education* (1 a year, in English), *Sindh University Research Journal (Science)*, *Sindh University Research Journal (Social Sciences)* (1 a year, in English), *SU Bulletin* (4 a year), *Tahqiq* (1 a year, in Urdu), *University of Sindh Arts Research Journal* (1 a year, in English)

DEANS

Faculty of Arts: Prof. Dr M. QASIM BUGHIO
Faculty of Commerce and Business Administration: Prof. Dr ANWAR ALI SHAH G. SAYED
Faculty of Education: Assoc. Prof. MUNSHI PARVEEN (acting)
Faculty of Islamic Studies: Prof. Dr SANAULLAH BHUTTO
Faculty of Law: Prof. AHMED ALI SHAIKH
Faculty of Natural Sciences: Prof. SEEHAR GHULAM MUSTAFA
Faculty of Pharmacy: Prof. Dr DAYO ABDULLAH
Faculty of Social Sciences: Prof. Dr IQBAL AHMED PANHWAR

DIRECTORS

Centre for Environmental Sciences: Prof. Dr BALOCH MUSHTAQUE AHMED
Centre for Excellence in Analytical Chemistry: Prof. Dr M. IQBAL AHMED BHANGAR
Centre for Health and Physical Education: YASMEEN IQBAL QURESHI
Centre for Rural Development Communication: SYED IBADULLAH RASHDI
Far East and South East Asia Study Centre: HIDAYATULLAH SOOMRO
Institute of Art and Design: Dr MUHAMMAD ALI BHATTI
Institute of Biochemistry: Prof. Dr ALLAH NAWAZ MEMON
Institute of Biotechnology and Genetic Engineering: Prof. Dr MUHAMMAD UMAR DAHOT
Institute of Business Administration: Prof. FEROZUDDIN KAZI
Dr. M. A. Kazi Institute of Chemistry: Prof. Dr ABBASI UBEDULLAH
Institute of Information Technology: Prof. Dr HAJI KHAN SOOMRO
Institute of Languages: Prof. Dr ABDUL GHANI SHAIKH
Institute of Mathematics and Computer Science: Prof. NOOR AHMED SHAIKH
Institute of Pharmacy: Prof. Dr MUHAMMAD USMAN MEMON
Institute of Sindhology: SHAUKAT HUSSAIN SHORO
Pakistan Study Centre: Prof. CHAND BIBI SULTANA BAKHTIARZAI
Sindh Development Studies Centre: Prof. Dr ABIDA TAHIRANI

Women Development Studies Centre: Prof. PARVEEN SHAH

PROFESSORS

Department of Botany:

ABRO, H.
AHMED, B.
HASSANI, S. S.
MEMON, A. H.
RAJPUT, M. T.
SAHITO, M. A.
SHAIKH, W.
TIRMIZI, S. A.
YASMIN, S.

Department of Comparative Religion and Islamic Culture:

BHUTTO, S.

Department of Fine Arts:

BHATTI, M. A.

Department of Muslim History:

ANSARI, A. S.
BHUTTO, M.
BUGHIO, M. M.

Department of Sindhi:

BUGHIO, M. Q.
HUSSAIN, K. K.
IMDAD, S.
KHUWAJA, N. A.

ATTACHED SCHOOLS

Dr N. A. Baloch Model School, Hyderabad: Principal AKHTAR AHMED MEMON.

Syed Pannah Ali Shah Model School, Jamshoro: Principal Prof. SAHAR IMDAD.

There are 13 private and 67 govt colleges and institutes affiliated to the University

SINDH AGRICULTURE UNIVERSITY, TANDOJAM

Tandojam District, Hyderabad, Sindh
Telephone: (22) 2765870
Fax: (22) 2765300
E-mail: info@sau.edu.pk
Internet: www.sau.edu.pk

Founded 1977
State control
Language of instruction: English
Academic year: October to March

Chancellor: ISHRAT-UL-IBAD KHAN (Governor of Sindh Province)
Vice-Chancellor: Dr A. Q. MUGHAL
Registrar: HAFEEZ ULLAH MEMON
Librarian: ABDUL LATIF ANSARI

Library of 75,000 vols
Number of teachers: 222
Number of students: 3,930

Publications: *Pakistan Journal of Agriculture, Agricultural Engineering and Veterinary Sciences* (2 a year, in English), *SARANG Magazine* (1 a year, in English, Sindhi and Urdu), *SAUNI News* (4 a year, in English, Sindhi and Urdu), *Seerat Supplement* (1 a year, in English, Sindhi and Urdu), *Zarat Sindh* (4 a year)

DEANS

Faculty of Agricultural Engineering: Dr HUSSAIN BAKHSK G. BHUTTO
Faculty of Agricultural Social Sciences: Assoc. Prof KHALID AHMED MAHAR
Faculty of Animal Husbandry and Veterinary Sciences: Dr GUL MOHAMMAD BALOCH
Faculty of Crop Production: Dr SHAMSUDDIN TUNIO
Faculty of Crop Protection: Dr SHAFI MUHAMMAD NIZAMANI

PROFESSORS

ABRO, G. H., Entomology
ABRO, H. K., Plant Breeding and Genetics
ANSARI, N. N., Poultry Husbandry
ARAIN, M. H., Plant Pathology
BALOCH, A. F., Horticulture
BALOCH, G. M., Animal Nutrition
BHUTTO, H. B., Irrigation and Drainage
BURIRO, U. A., Agronomy
CHANDIO, B. A., Land and Water Management
CHANG, M. A., Plant Breeding and Genetics
CHANNA, A. N., Plant Physiology and Biochemistry
DEHO, N. A., Horticulture
DEVERAJANI, B. T., Land and Water Management
JAKHARO, A. A., Soil Science
KADRI, A. A., English
KALHORO, A. B., Surgery and Obstetrics
KHAN, M. M., Entomology
KUMBAHAR, M. I., Animal Breeding and Genetics
KUMBHAR, M. B., Plant Breeding and Genetics
LARIK, A. S., Plant Breeding and Genetics
LEGHARI, N. H., Farm Power and Machinery
LOHAR, M. K., Entomology
MAHAR, S., Farm Power and Machinery
MEMON, K. S., Soil Science
MEMON, M. A., Animal Physiology and Biochemistry
MEMON, N. A., Land and Water Management
MEMON, R. A., Agricultural Education Extension and Short Courses
MIRBAHAR, K. B., Animal Reproduction
MIRBAHAR, R. B., Plant Physiology and Biochemistry
MIRJAT, M. S., Irrigation and Drainage
MUGHAL, A. Q., Farm Power and Machinery
NENWANI, K. L., Soil Science
NIZAMANI, S. M., Plant Protection
PARDEHI, M., Anatomy and Histology
PATHAN, M. A., Plant Pathology
PHULLAN, M. S., Parasitology
PHULPOTO, P. B., Agricultural Economics
PUNO, H. K., Soil Science
QAYYUN KHAN, S. M., Agronomy
RAHU, G. M., Entomology
RAJPER, M. M., Biotechnology
RIZVI, N.-UL-H., Entomology
SAIF, M. S., Soil Science
SHAH, A. J., Plant Breeding and Genetics
SHAIKH, B. A., Animal Physiology and Biochemistry
SIDDIQUI, L. A., Veterinary Microbiology
SIYAL, N. B., Soil Science
SOOMRO, A. L., Soil Science
SOOMRO, M. S., Energy and Environment
TNIO, K., Agronomy
WAGGAN, M. R., Soil Science

ATTACHED INSTITUTE

Institute of Science and Food Technology: tel. (22) 2765554; e-mail sasheikhsau@hotmail.com; Dir Prof. Dr SAGHIR AHMED SHEIKH.

UNIVERSITY OF VETERINARY AND ANIMAL SCIENCES

Syed Abdul Qadir Jillani Rd, Lahore 54600, Punjab
Telephone: (42) 9211374
Fax: (42) 9211461
E-mail: helpline@uvas.edu.pk
Internet: www.uvas.edu.pk

Founded 1882; present name and status 2002

Vice-Chancellor: Prof. Dr MUHAMMAD NAWAZ
Registrar: ATTIQUE AHMAD
Librarian: MIAN MUHAMMAD ILYAS

DEANS

Faculty of Animal Production and Technology: Prof. Dr MUHAMMAD ABDULLAH
Faculty of Biosciences: Prof. Dr MUHAMMAD ASHRAF
Faculty of Fisheries and Wildlife: Prof. Dr NAUREEN AZIZ QURESHI
Faculty of Life Sciences Business Management: Prof. Dr TALAT NASEER PASHA
Faculty of Veterinary Sciences: Prof. Dr ZAFAR IQBAL CHAUDHRY

ATTACHED INSTITUTES

Bioequivalence Study (BeSt) Centre: Lahore 54000; tel. (42) 9211449; f. 2008.

Institute of Continuing Education and Extension: f. 2002; offers courses on Social Sciences and Livestock Extension Education; Dir Prof. Dr ZAFAR IQBAL CHAUDHRY.

Colleges

Dawood College of Engineering and Technology: M. A. Jinnah Rd, Karachi 74800; tel. (21) 9231195; fax (21) 9230710; e-mail registrar@dcet.edu.pk; internet www.dcet.edu.pk; faculties of architecture, basic sciences, chemical engineering, electronic engineering, humanities, industrial engineering, management, materials engineering, mathematics, metallurgy; f. 1962; library: 30,269 vols; 70 teachers; 1,451 students; Principal Dr MUHAMMAD NASIM; Registrar RANA SINGH RAJPUT.

Government College of Technology: Rasul, Mandi Baha-ud-Din, Punjab; tel. (546) 553216; fax (546) 553110; e-mail gctrasul@yahoo.com; internet www.gctrasul.edu.pk; f. 1912; diploma and degree courses in technology and civil engineering; library: 25,076 vols; 90 teachers; 4,062 students; Principal MAZHAR ABBAS NAQVI.

Government Polytechnic Institute: Paris Rd, Sialkot; tel. (52) 9250199; 3-year diploma courses in electrical, mechanical, civil engineering, auto and diesel technologies; library: 12,999 vols.

Jinnah Postgraduate Medical Centre: Rafiqui (H. J.) Shaheed Rd, Karachi 75510; tel. (21) 9201300; e-mail edojpmc@jpmc.com.pk; internet www.jpmc.com.pk; f. 1958; provides postgraduate training and education (including to doctorate) in the basic medical subjects, leading potentially to Membership of the College of Physicians and Surgeons (FCPS, MCPS) of Pakistan; also degrees in medical technology, occupational therapy and physiotherapy, diplomas in general and postgraduate nursing, and other full-time certificate courses; library: 19,000 books, 21,000 bound periodicals, 500,000 loose periodicals; Dir Dr ABDUL SHAKOOR QAZI; publ. *Annals* (4 a year).

National School of Public Policy (National Management College): Shahrah-i-Quaid-i-Azam, Lahore 54000; tel. (42) 9202941; fax (42) 9202932; e-mail pasc@lhr.comsats.net.pk; internet www.pasc.gov.pk; f. 1960 as Pakistan Administrative Staff College; present name and status 2002; training in administrative management for senior executives from govt and public enterprises, private sector, Commonwealth and third world countries; also research and publications on the subject; consultancy and advisory service in public administration; library: see Libraries and Archives; Rector and Principal Lt Gen. (retd) JAVED HASSAN; publ. *Pakistan Administration* (2 a year).

Pakistani–Swedish Institute of Technology: Landhi, GPO Box 186, Karachi 22; f. 1955; training in electrical, mechanical, woodworking, welding and clothing technology; library: 20,000 vols; 35 teachers; Dir IMAM ALI SOOMRO.

Rawalpindi Government College of Technology: Shahrah-e-Shershah, Rawalpindi; f. 1958; 3-year diploma courses in various subjects, degree courses in electrical power technology, electronics and communication technology; library: 22,000 vols; 1,700 students; Principal Col MUHAMMAD AFSAR; publ. *Technician* (1 a year).

Swedish–Pakistani Institute of Technology: Rehman Shaheed Rd, Near Service More, Gujrat 50700; tel. (53) 3524819; fax (53) 3524819; e-mail contact@spitgujrat.com; internet www.spitgujrat.com; f. 1966; 3-year diploma courses in electrical engineering, mechanical engineering, electronics, instrumentation, foundry, pattern making, metallurgy and welding technology, auto and diesel technology, automation and control technology; 1-year post-diploma course in biomedical technology; library: 15,000 vols; 46 teachers; 593 students; Principal MUHAMMAD IQBAL DUGAL.

Textile Institute of Pakistan: *City campus*: 10/E Blk 6, P.E.C.H.S., Karachi 75400; *Bin Qasim campus*: EZ/1/P-8, Eastern Zone, Bin Qasim Karachi; tel. (21) 4549734 (City); tel. (302) 8285456 (Bin Qasim); fax (21) 4533525 (City); e-mail info@tip.edu.pk; internet www.tip.edu.pk; f. 1994; degree programmes: textile science, textile design technology, textile management and marketing, textile technology; Facilities: 2 science laboratories, 3 textile laboratories (spinning, weaving, wet processing), computer laboratories; library: 4,000 books, journals; Chancellor ARIF HASAN; Pres. Dr ZUBAIR BANDUKDA.

PALAU

The Higher Education System

The Republic of Palau's independence in 1994, under a Compact of Free Association with the USA, marked the end of the US-administered Trust Territory of the Pacific Islands that had been established in 1947. The Ministry of Education is the responsible body of higher education. The Palau Scholarship Programme assists those students who wish to pursue their post-secondary education abroad but intend to return to Palau. The Palau Community College (founded in 1993) is accredited by the Western Association of Schools and Colleges (USA). In 2005 there were an estimated 545 students in tertiary education. The Ministry of Education Bureau of Curriculum and Programme Development is responsible for providing adult and community education.

Regulatory Bodies

GOVERNMENT

Ministry of Community and Cultural Affairs: POB 100, Koror 96940; tel. 488-1126; fax 488-3354; e-mail mcca@palaunet.com; internet www.palaugov.net/mincommunity; Minister ALEXANDER R. MEREP.

Ministry of Education: POB 189, Koror 96940; tel. 488-1464; fax 488-1465; e-mail moe@palaumoe.net; internet www.palaumoe.net; Minister MARIO KATOSANG.

Learned Society

NATURAL SCIENCES

Biological Sciences

Palau Conservation Society: POB 1811, Koror 96940; tel. 488-3993; fax 488-3990; e-mail pcs@palaunet.com; internet palau-pcs.org; f. 1994; works with the community to preserve the nation's unique natural environment and perpetuate its conservation ethic for the economic and social benefit of present and future generations of Palauans and for the enjoyment and education of all; Exec. Dir TIARE TURANG HOLM.

Research Institutes

NATURAL SCIENCES

Biological Sciences

Coral Reef Research Foundation (CRRF): POB 1765, Koror 96940; tel. 488-5123; fax 488-5513; e-mail crrf@palaunet.com; internet www.coralreefresearchfoundation.org; f. 1991 to increase knowledge of coral reefs and other tropical marine environments in order to allow intelligent conservation and management decisions; special emphasis on species diversity work, collection for biomedical screening, environmental monitoring, reef fish spawning biology, and innovative development of new techniques for marine research work; Dir and Pres. Dr PATRICK L. COLIN.

Palau International Coral Reef Center: POB 7086, Koror 96940; tel. 488-6950; fax 488-6951; e-mail picrc@palaunet.com; internet www.picrc.org; f. 1999 to address critical global challenges to protect marine environments and raise awareness about the importance of preserving coral reef ecosystems; centre for marine research, training and educational activities; indoor gallery displays several closed-system aquariums exhibiting marine organisms; outdoor marine park features open-system aquariums that exhibit the different plant and animal dwellers of these habitats; CEO FRANCIS M. MATSUTARO.

Libraries and Archives

Koror

Palau Congress Library: POB 8, Koror 96940; tel. 488-2507; fax 488-5653; f. 1981; 5,000 vols of committee reports, journals and legislative history on all public laws enacted by the Palau Nat. Congress; Librarian HARRY BESEBES.

Palau National Archives: POB 1886, Koror 96940; tel. 488-4720; fax 488-4502; e-mail archives@palaunet.com; internet www.palaugov.net/mincommunity/natlarch.html; f. 1988; 2,200 16-mm and 110 35-mm cartridges/rolls of microfilms processed during the Trust Territory era; Chief Archivist NAOMI NGIRAKAMERANG; publ. *Newsletter* (online, 12 a year).

Palau Public Library: POB 189, Koror 96940; tel. 488-2973; fax 488-2830; e-mail publiclibrary@palaumoe.net; 17,000 vols; spec. collns: Pacific area, legislative records of Palau House of Delegates, nuclear topics; Librarian BEDEBII SADANG.

Museum

Koror

Belau National Museum: POB 666, Koror 96940; Ngerbeched Hamlet, Koror; tel. 488-2265; fax 488-3183; e-mail bnm@palaunet.com; internet www.belaunationalmuseum.org; f. 1955; preserves, promotes nat. heritage; exhibits natural, cultural, social and historical values; develops arts at all levels; 4,000 cultural objects relating to anthropology, traditional and contemporary art, history and natural history, media colln of 20,000 photographic slides, 6,000 prints, negatives, films, videos and sound recordings, traditional men's meeting hall, botanical garden; library of 2,000 vols, and periodicals, maps, posters, research papers and articles; Dir and Curator OLYMPIA ESEL MOREI.

College

Palau Community College: POB 9, Koror 96940; tel. 488-2470; fax 488-2447; e-mail alvina@palau.edu; internet www.palau.edu; f. 1969; independent, two-year post-secondary vocational/technical institution; school of arts and sciences; school of business; school of technical education; library: 26,000 items, incl. books, periodicals, govt documents, video cassettes, maps and CD-ROMs; 34 teachers; 650 students; Pres. Dr PATRICK U. TELLEI.

PALESTINIAN AUTONOMOUS AREAS

The Higher Education System

Palestinian education has been severely disrupted since 1987, when the university sector in the Gaza Strip and the West Bank was closed by military order. The universities were not re-opened until 1992. Since late 2000 the al-Aqsa intifada has led to further strain on relations between the Palestinian Authority (PA) and Israel. All aspects of political, social and economic life in the occupied territories have been affected by the deteriorating security situation, including the higher education sector. The oldest university is Hebron University, which was founded in 1971. In 2006/07 there were 11 universities and 23 other institutions of higher education in the Palestinian Autonomous Areas. In 2007/08 there were a total of 167,984 students enrolled in tertiary education.

In May 1994 the PA assumed responsibility for education in Gaza and parts of the West Bank. Higher education is regulated by the Ministry of Higher Education under Law 11 of 1998. The specific requirements for the completion of undergraduate and postgraduate degrees are set out in Article 20 of Law 11 (1998). The Accreditation and Quality Assurance Commission (AQAC) was established in 2002 as an autonomous body functioning under the Ministry of Education and Higher Education. Its main duties include the licensing and accreditation of new higher education institutions, the accreditation of undergraduate and postgraduate programmes and the promoting of quality assurance within the higher education sector. In its first year of operation, the AQAC conducted evaluations of 69 separate degree programmes in the allied health subjects. Programme accreditation is not yet compulsory at all institutions.

In order to proceed to higher education students are required to pass the Tawjihi (Secondary School Certificate) examinations. Arts and science undergraduate degree programmes require a score of at least 65% in the Tawjihi for entry, while engineering, medical technology, pharmacy and veterinary degrees require at least 80%. Medicine and dental programmes require at least 90% in the Tawjihi. Some programmes, e.g. medicine and dentistry, also require the applicant to pass an English proficiency test as well as an interview for entry.

Undergraduates may study for a Diploma. Some Diplomas represent roughly half the content of a Bachelors degree in the same subject. Others are more vocational in their nature and are regarded as post-secondary non-tertiary qualifications. Study for a Diploma may last anything from a few months to three years. The main undergraduate qualification is the Bachelors degree, which is generally awarded after four years of study, and requires the completion of at least 120 credit hours following the Tawjihi. Students are required to select three categories of subjects: those specific to a degree programme (offered by the appropriate departments), those relevant to a degree programme (offered by faculties) and those of a more general nature (offered centrally by the university). Examples of the latter include Islamic studies and the History of Jerusalem. With the exception of dentistry, only two degree titles are awarded on completion of a Bachelor degree—Bachelor of Arts and Bachelor of Science. Degrees in dentistry, engineering, pharmacy and veterinary medicine require five years' study, and degrees in medicine six years'. Degree programmes in these subjects are only available at selected universities.

The first postgraduate qualification is the Higher Diploma, which is awarded after the completion of at least 30 credit hours (one year) of study following the Bachelors degree. Higher Diplomas are offered only by the Birzeit University and available only in selected subjects (development, gender studies, law, medical laboratory technology, primary healthcare supervision and training).

Study for a Masters degree is generally one to two years in length following the award of the Bachelors degree, and may include the submission of a thesis. For most Masters programmes taught courses make up the majority of the required credit hours. At some universities where a thesis is required, candidates may be awarded a Higher Diploma should their thesis not meet the required standard, or if the comprehensive examination is failed.

Doctoral studies are typically three years in duration, and require the completion of a minimum of 45 credit hours following the completion of a Masters degree (with a minimum grade of 'very good'). Doctoral degrees are only offered by the Faculty of Graduate Studies at An-Najah National University, and currently the only doctorate available is in the field of chemistry. This doctorate is divided evenly between taught courses and a research project. Candidates must obtain a grade of at least 75% in the taught courses in order to proceed to the research component. A submitted dissertation must be defended by the candidate in front of a panel of specialists from the department.

Regulatory Bodies

GOVERNMENT

Ministry of Culture: POB 147, Ramallah; tel. (2) 2986205; fax (2) 2986204; Minister SIHAM AL-BARGHOUTHI.

Ministry of Education and Higher Education: POB 576, Al-Masioun, Ramallah; tel. (2) 2983200; fax (2) 2983222; e-mail irp@mohe.gov.ps; internet www.moe.gov.ps; Minister LAMIS AL-ALAMI.

ACCREDITATION

Accreditation and Quality Assurance Commission: Ministry of Education and Higher Education, POB 1932, Ramallah; tel. (2) 2980140; fax (2) 2954518; e-mail aqac@p-ol.com; internet www.aqac.mohe.gov.ps; f. 2002; autonomous body attached to the Min.; board of 12 mems; Dir Prof. MOHAMMED M. A ALSUBU; Sec. GHADEER A'LI ZA'AL AHMAD.

Learned Societies

GENERAL

UNESCO Office Ramallah: POB 2154, Ramallah, West Bank; 17 Ahliyya College St, Ramallah, West Bank; tel. (2) 2959740; fax (2) 2959741; e-mail ramallah@unesco.org; Dir BECHIR LAMINE.

LANGUAGE AND LITERATURE

Alliance Française: Peace Centre, POB 1166, Bethlehem; e-mail afbeth@p-ol.com; tel. (2) 2750777; offers courses and exams in French language and culture and promotes cultural exchange with France; Pres. PAULINE ANASTAS.

British Council: 31 Nablus Rd, POB 19136, 97200 Jerusalem; tel. (2) 6267111; fax (2) 6283021; e-mail information@ps.britishcouncil.org; internet www.britishcouncil.org/ps.htm; offers courses and exams in English language and British culture and promotes cultural exchange with the UK; attached offices in Gaza (building destroyed during civil unrest in March 2006), Hebron, Khan Yunis, Nablus and Ramallah; Dir-Gen. KEN CHURCHILL.

Research Institutes

GENERAL

Applied Research Institute, Jerusalem: Caritas St., Bethlehem; tel. (2) 2741889; fax (2) 2776966; e-mail pmaster@arij.org; internet www.arij.org; f. 1990; dedicated to promoting applied research, technology transfers, sustainable devt and the self-reliance of the Palestinian people through greater control over their natural resources; Pres. Eng. DAOUD ISTANBULI; Vice-Pres. SALIM ZUGBI; Treas. Dr NASRI QUMSIYEH; Sec. Dr NABEEL 'EDEILY; publ. *Report* (12 a year).

Health, Development, Information and Policy Institute: POB 1351, Ramallah; tel. (2) 2985372; fax (2) 2985917; e-mail hdip@hdip.org; internet www.hdip.org; f. 1989; policy research and planning regarding the Palestinian health care and development system in the West Bank and Gaza Strip.

Muwatin/The Palestinian Institute for the Study of Democracy: POB 1845, Ramallah; tel. (2) 2951108; fax (2) 2960285; e-mail muwatin@muwatin.org; internet www.muwatin.org; f. 1992 to promote the study and development of democracy in Palestine; Dir Dr GEORGE GIACAMAN.

Palestinian Academic Society for the Study of International Affairs: POB 19545, Jerusalem; 18 Hatem Al-Ta'i St., Wadi Al-Joz; tel. 2-6264426; fax 2-6282819; e-mail passia@passia.org; internet www.passia.org; f. 1987; deals with nat., Arab and int. aspects of the Palestinian Question through academic research, dialogue and publs; library of 2,000 vols; Chair. Dr MAHDI ABDUL HADI.

Libraries

Nablus

Nablus Municipality Public Library: Shwetreh St, Nablus, West Bank; tel. (9) 2383356; fax (9) 2374690; e-mail nab_lib@nablus.org; internet www.nablus.org; f. 1969; 70,000 vols, mainly in Arabic and English; Librarian ALI TOUQAN.

Ramallah

Public Library: Ramallah, West Bank; f. 1962; 3,500 vols; Librarian ADEL UWAIS.

Museums

Bethlehem

Baituna al-Talhami Museum/Bethlehem Folklore Museum: c/o Arab Women's Society, POB 19, Star St, Bethlehem; tel. (2) 2742431; fax (2) 2742589; f. 1948 as centre for Palestinian refugees, museum established 1979; two houses of typical Palestinian architecture, furnished with colln of traditional Palestinian household items and colln of photographs, furniture, and works of art illustrating life of Bethlehem residents in 1900–1932; open daily except Thursdays and Sundays.

Gaza

Al-Math'af/Recreational Cultural House: Sodaniya, Rasheed St, Gaza; tel. (8) 2858444; fax (8) 2858440; e-mail info@almathaf.ps; internet www.almathaf.ps; f. 2008; archaeology and antiquities; Dir JAWDAT AL-KHOUDARY.

Universities

AL-AQSA UNIVERSITY

POB 4051 Gaza
Telephone: (8) 282826809
Fax: (8) 2082826819
E-mail: it_affairs@alaqsa.edu.ps
Internet: www.alaqsa.edu.ps
Founded 1991
State control
Academic year: July to January

Faculties of admin. sciences, arts, education, fine arts, media, physical education, sciences; (Educational Studies Campus destroyed by Israeli military in March 2004)

Pres.: SALAM ALAGHA
Number of teachers: 350
Number of students: 21,000
Library of 113,200 vols.

AL-AZHAR UNIVERSITY

POB 1277, Jamal Abdl Naser St, Gaza
Telephone: (8) 2824020
Fax: (8) 2823180
E-mail: alazhar@alazhar-gaza.edu
Internet: www.alazhar-gaza.edu
Founded 1991
State control
Languages of instruction: Arabic, English

Pres.: Prof. Dr JAWAD WADI
Vice-Pres. for Academic Affairs: Prof. Dr ABDELKAREEM NIJIM
Vice-Pres. for Admin. and Financial Affairs: Dr JABR EL DAOUR
Vice-Pres. for Planning and Quality Assurance: Dr MAHMOUD OKASHA

Number of teachers: 396
Number of students: 18,156

DEANS

Faculty of Agriculture: Prof. Dr KHALIL TUBAIL
Faculty of Applied Sciences: Dr ABDEL NASSER ABU SHAHLA
Faculty of Arts and Human Sciences: Dr MOHAMMED SALAH ABU HAMAIDA
Faculty of Economics and Administrative Sciences: MARWAN S. EL-AGHA
Faculty of Dentistry: Dr SALAH JODA
Faculty of Education: Dr SOHAIB EL-AGHA
Faculty of Engineering and Information Technology: Dr SAMY ABU NASSER
Faculty of Information Technology: Dr NABIL ABU SHABAN
Faculty of Intermediate Studies: Dr HAZIM SAKEEK
Faculty of Law: Dr SALEM EL KORD
Faculty of Medicine: Dr SUHAIL EL MADBAK
Faculty of Pharmacy: Dr AMEEM HAMED
Faculty of Science: Dr HASSAN TAMOUS
Faculty of Sharia: Dr NAEIM EL MASRY

ATTACHED CENTRES

Centre for Continuing Education: Dir Dr WAEL THADET.

Centre for Drug Analysis and Research: Dir Dr SULAIMAN AL JOBOUR.

Centre for Food Analysis: Dir Dr ABED EL-RAZEQ SALAMA.

Centre for Information Technology: Dir Dr MONTASER EL HALABI.

Institute of Water and Environment: Dir Dr YOUSIF ABU MAYLA.

AL-QUDS OPEN UNIVERSITY

POB 51800, Sheikh Jarrah, Musa Feidi St, East Jerusalem
Telephone: (2) 5816239
Fax: (2) 5816734
E-mail: administrative@qou.edu
Internet: www.qou.edu
Founded 1991
State control

Pres.: Prof. YOUNIS AMIR
Vice-Pres. for Academic Affairs: Prof. SUFIAN KAMAL
Vice-Pres. for Admin.: Dr SAMIR NAJDI

Library of 20,800 vols (16,000 in Arabic, 4,800 in English), 80 periodicals
Number of teachers: 356 academic supervisors apart from part-time instructors
Number of students: 60,699

Programmes in agriculture, education, management and entrepreneurship, social and family devt and technology and applied science; campus in Riyadh, Saudi Arabia, open to Palestinian nationals or people of Palestinian origin; 22 educational regions and study centres in the West Bank and Gaza Strip, in addition to a br. in Saudi Arabia; also has 5 centres that deal with IT, media production and education.

AL-QUDS UNIVERSITY

POB 51000, Jerusalem
Telephone: (2) 5838652
Fax: (2) 5838653
E-mail: president@alquds.edu
Internet: www.alquds.edu
Founded 1979
Private control
Language of instruction: English
Academic year: October to August

Pres.: Prof. SARI NUSSEIBEH
Vice-Pres.: Prof. HASAN DWEIK
Asst to the Pres. for Academic Affairs: Dr SAED ZEEDANI
Asst to the Pres. for Planning and Devt: Dr BADIE SARTAWI
Dean of Scientific Research: Dr SAMIRA BARGHOUTHI
Librarian: HAKIM BESHAWI

Library of 100,000 vols
Number of teachers: 431
Number of students: 11,631

DEANS

Faculty of Admin. and Economics Sciences: Dr MAHMOOD ALJAFARE
Faculty of Arts: Dr MUNTHER DAJANI
Faculty of Dentistry: Dr MUSA BAJALI
Faculty of Engineering: Dr HUSSEIN JADDU
Faculty of Health Professions: Dr VARSEEN SHAHEEN
Faculty of Islamic Studies: Dr SAID AL-QEEQ
Faculty of Law: Prof. ALI KHASHAN
Faculty of Medicine: Prof. HANI ABDEEN
Faculty of Pharmacy: Dr RAFIK KARAMAN
Faculty of Public Health: Dr SHAHEEN MOHAMMAD
Faculty of Science and Technology: Dr AMIN AHMAD LEGHROUZ

ATTACHED RESEARCH INSTITUTES

Abu-Jihad Centre for Political Prisoners' Affairs: tel. and fax (2) 2792515; e-mail info@aj-museum.alquds.edu; internet www.aj-museum.alquds.edu.

Al-Quds Human Rights Clinic: tel. (2) 2790417; fax (2) 2799717; e-mail info@aqhrclinic.alquds.edu; f. 2006; Dir MUNIR NUSEIBAH.

Al-Quds Nutrition and Health Research Institute: tel. (2) 6289798; fax (2) 6289849; e-mail enquire@anahri.alquds.edu; internet anahri.alquds.edu; Dir ZIAD ABDEEN.

American Studies Institute: tel. (2) 2989184; fax (2) 2957072; e-mail info@americanstudiespalestine.org; internet asi.arts.alquds.edu; Dir Prof. MOHAMMED S. DAJANI DAOUDI.

Centre for Chemical and Biological Analysis: tel. (2) 2796961; f. 1999; Dir Dr MUSTAFA KHAMIS.

Centre for Development in Primary Health Care: tel. (2) 2952767; fax (2) 2981526; e-mail cdphc@palnet.com; internet cdphc.alquds.edu.

Centre for Human Rights and Humanitarian Law: f. 2006; Dir Dr MOHAMMAD SHALALDEH.

Centre for Jerusalem Studies: tel. (2) 6287517; fax (2) 6284920; e-mail huda@planet.edu; internet www.jerusalem-studies.alquds.edu; Dir HUDA IMAM.

Centre for Radiation Science and Technology: e-mail lahham@crst.alquds.edu;

internet www.crst.alquds.edu; Dir Dr A. LAHHAM.

Child Institute: tel. (2) 5859955; fax (2) 6569182; e-mail pci@admin.alquds.edu; Dir Dr KHULOUD KHAYYAT DAJANI.

Community Action Centre: internet www.cac-alquds.org.

Ethnomusicology Research and Studies Centre: e-mail adileh@art.alquds.edu; Dir Prof. MUTASEM ADILEH.

INSAN Centre for Gender and Women's Studies: tel. (2) 2791344; e-mail fadwal@arts.alquds.edu; Dir Dr FADWA ALLABADI.

Institute of Archaeology: tel. (2) 2959276; Dir Dr MARWAN ABU KHALAF.

Institute of Area Studies: Dir Dr AZIZ HEIDER.

Institute of Business and Economic Studies: tel. and fax (2) 2799497; e-mail mjafari@admin.alquds.edu; Dir MAHMOUD K. EL-JAFARI.

Institute of Modern Media: tel. (2) 2964213; fax (2) 2959275; e-mail info@imm.ps; internet www.imm.ps.

Islamic Research Centre: tel. (2) 6275228; f. 1987; Dir Dr MOSTAFA ABU SWAI.

Issam Sartawi Centre: tel. (2) 5859955; fax (2) 5853918; e-mail msdajani@art.alquds.edu; f. 1998; Dir Prof. MUNTHER S. DAJANI.

Jericho Local Urban Observatory Centre: tel. (2) 2799753; fax (2) 2796960; e-mail juoc@admin.alquds.edu; internet www.jluo.alquds.edu; Dir Dr FAYEZ FREIJAT.

Language Resource Centre: tel. (2) 6275228; f. 1995; Dir Dr OMAR ABU HOMOS.

Medical Research Centre: Dir Dr MYSA EL-AZZEH.

Said Khoury IT Centre of Excellence: tel. (2) 2790852; fax (2) 2791508; internet www.itce.alquds.edu.

Science and Technology Centre: tel. (2) 2799234; f. 1998; Dir Dr HASAN DWEIK.

Science Discovery Centre: e-mail info@sep.alquds.edu; internet www.sep.alquds.edu.

AN-NAJAH NATIONAL UNIVERSITY

Omar Ibn Khattab St, POB 7, Nablus, West Bank
Telephone: (9) 2345113
Fax: (9) 2345982
E-mail: info@najah.edu
Internet: www.najah.edu

Founded 1977
Public control
Academic year: September to June
Languages of instruction: Arabic, English(for science faculties)
Academic year: September to June

Chair., Bd of Trustees: SABIH AL-MASRI
Pres.: Prof. RAMI HAMDALLAH
Vice-Pres. for Academic Affairs: Prof. MAHER NATSHEH
Vice-Pres. for Administrative Affairs: Dr SHAKER BITAR
Vice-Pres. for Community Affairs: Dr MOHAMAD HANOON
Dir for Public Relations: ALAA ABU DHEER (acting)
Dean of Admission and Registration: Dr JABR ABU JUOKHA
Dean of Scientific Research: Prof. SAMI JAB
Dean of Student Affairs: MUSA ABU DIYEH
Librarian: HANI JABER

Library of 201,000 vols, 2,200 periodicals
Number of teachers: 541 (408 full-time, 133 part-time)
Number of students: 19,000

Publications: *An-Najah 'A base of Science and Technology'* (in Arabic and English), *An-Najah Journal of Research* (separate series for natural sciences and humanities)

DEANS

Faculty of Agriculture: Dr MUNQIZ ISHTAEH (acting)
Faculty of Arts: Prof. KHALIL ODEH
Faculty of Economics and Administrative Sciences: Dr SA'ED AL KOUNI
Faculty of Educational Sciences: Dr FAIZ AQEL
Faculty of Engineering: Dr NABLIL DOMAIDI
Faculty of Fine Arts: Dr HASAN M. NAIRAT
Faculty of Graduate Studies: Dr MOHAMMAD ABU JAFAR
Faculty of Information Technology: Dr RA'ED AL-QADI
Faculty of Islamic Law (Shari'a): Dr HASSAN KHADIR
Faculty of Law: Dr AKRAM DAOUD
Faculty of Medicine: Dr ANWAR DOODEEN
Faculty of Nursing: Dr ADNAN SARHAN
Faculty of Optometry: Dr KHERIEH RASSAS
Faculty of Pharmacy: Dr MOHAMMED J. MUSMAR
Faculty of Science: Prof. SULEIMAN AL-KHALIL
Faculty of Veterinary Medicine: Dr RATEB AREF

ATTACHED RESEARCH INSTITUTES

Academic Programme for the Study of Involuntary Migration: e-mail frc@najah.edu; Dir SAMER AQROUQ.

Centre for Continuing Education: e-mail cec@najah.edu; Dir Dr MUSADDAQ ALMASRI.

Centre for Urban and Regional Planning: e-mail abhamid@najah.edu; Dir Dr ALI ABDUL HAMEED.

Central Medical Laboratory: e-mail cml@najah.edu; Dir Dr SULAIMAN KHALIL.

Chemical, Biological and Drugs Analysis Centre: e-mail nidalzatar@najah.edu; Dir Dr NIDAL ZATAR.

Community Service Centre: Dir BILAL SALAMEH.

Computer Research Centre: e-mail cc@najah.edu; Dir NAJEH ABU SAFYYEH.

Construction and Transport Research Centre: e-mail alsahili@yahoo.com; Dir Dr KHALED AL-SAHILI.

Earth Sciences and Seismic Engineering Centre: e-mail seiscen@najah.edu; Dir Dr JALAL ALDABEEK.

Energy Research Centre: Dir Dr EMAD BRAIK.

Korean Palestinian IT Institute of Excellence (KPITIE): e-mail kaitie@najah.edu; Dir KHALID BARHAM.

Measurement and Evaluation Centre: e-mail mec2006@najah.edu; Dir Dr ABDELNASSER ALQADDOUMI.

Opinion Polls and Survey Studies Centre: e-mail polls@najah.edu; Dir Dr HUSSEIN AHMAD.

Poison Control and Drug Information Centre (PCDIC): e-mail poison@najah.edu; Dir Dr ANSAM SAWALHA.

UNESCO Chair on Human Rights and Democracy: e-mail uchrdn@najah.edu; Dir SAMER AQROUQ.

Water and Environmental Studies Institute: e-mail wesi@najah.edu; Dir Dr MARWAN HADDAD.

ARAB AMERICAN UNIVERSITY—JENIN

Jenin
E-mail: asaleh@aauj.edu
Internet: www.aauj.edu

Founded 2000
Private control

Faculties of admin. and financial sciences, allied medical sciences, arts and sciences, dentistry, engineering and information technology, law

Pres.: Dr ADLI SALEH
Vice-Pres. for Academic Affairs: Dr NASER HAMAD
Vice-Pres. for Planning and Devt: Dr ZAKI M. SALEH

Library of 60,000 vols.

BETHLEHEM UNIVERSITY

POB 9, Bethlehem, West Bank
Rue des Frères, Bethlehem, West Bank
Telephone: (2) 2741241
Fax: (2) 2744440
E-mail: info@bethlehem.edu
Internet: www.bethlehem.edu

Founded 1973
Private control (Roman Catholic)
Languages of instruction: Arabic, English
Academic year: September to June

Chancellor: Archbishop ANTONIO FRANCO
Vice-Chancellor: Br DANIEL CASEY
Pres.: Archbishop FOUD TWAL
CEO: Br PETER BRAY
Vice-Pres. for Academic Affairs: Br ROBERT SMITH
Vice-Pres. for Devt: Br JACK CURRAN
Vice-Pres. for Finance and Planning: SAMI EL-YOUSEF
Dean of Students: MAHMOUD HAMMAD
Registrar: MARY JUHA
Librarian: Dr MELLIE BRODRETH

Library of 90,000 vols
Number of teachers: 184 (132 full-time, 52 part-time)
Number of students: 3,000

DEANS

College of Arts: JAMAL DAIBES
College of Business Administration: Dr FADI KATTAN
College of Education: RIZEK SLEIBI
College of Nursing and Health Sciences: AMAL ABU NIJMEH
College of Sciences: Dr HAIFA KONKAR

ATTACHED RESEARCH INSTITUTES

Hereditary Research Laboratory: tel. (2) 2744233; fax (2) 2744440; e-mail mkanaan@bethlehem.edu; internet hrl.bethlehem.edu; f. 1993; Dir Dr MOIEN KANAAN.

Institute for Community Partnership: tel. (2) 2770936; fax (2) 2745559; e-mail icp@bethlehem.edu; internet icp.bethlehem.edu; f. 1989; Dir MOUSSA RABADI.

UNESCO Biotechnology Educational and Training Centre: tel. (2) 2765404; fax (2) 2765404; e-mail niraki@bethlehem.edu; f. 1995; Dir Dr NAIM IRAKI.

Water and Soil Environmental Research Unit: e-mail wseru@bethlehem.edu; internet wseru.bethlehem.edu; f. 1988; Dir Dr ALFRED ABED RABBO.

BIRZEIT UNIVERSITY

POB 14, Birzeit, West Bank
Telephone: (2) 2982000
Fax: (2) 2810656Also Birzeit Univ. Liaison Office, POB 950666, Amman, Jordan
Telephone: (6) 5527181
Fax: (6) 5527202
E-mail: pr@birzeit.edu
Internet: www.birzeit.edu

Founded 1924 as school, 1951 college, present status 1975
Private autonomous control
Languages of instruction: Arabic, English

Academic year: September to June (two semesters), summer session July–August

Pres.: Dr NABEEL KASSIS
Vice-Pres. for Academic Affairs: Dr ADNAN AL-YEHYA
Vice-Pres. for Admin. and Financial Affairs: Dr SAMI AL-SAYRAFI
Vice-Pres. for Community Outreach: Dr MUNEER QAZZAZ (acting)
Head Librarian: DIANA SAYEJ

Library of 17,000 vols, 1,653 periodicals
Number of teachers: 294
Number of students: 8,700

Publication: *Birzeit Human Rights Record* (in English)

DEANS

Faculty of Arts: Dr MAHER AL-HASHWEH
Faculty of Commerce and Economics: Dr NIDAL SABRI
Faculty of Engineering: Dr FAISAL AWADALLAH
Faculty of Graduate Studies: Dr LIZA TARAKI
Faculty of Information Technology: Dr ADNAN AL-YEHYA
Faculty of Law and Public Administration: Dr SALEH ABDEL-JAWWAD
Faculty of Nursing and Allied Health Professions: Dr TAMER ESSAWI
Faculty of Science: Dr SIMON KUTTAB

ATTACHED RESEARCH INSTITUTES

Continuing Education Centre: tel. (2) 2984810; fax (2) 2954383; e-mail cce@birzeit.edu; internet cceweb.birzeit.edu; Dir MARWAN TARAZI.

I. Abu Lughod Institute of International Studies: POB 14, Birzeit, West Bank; tel. (2) 2982009; fax (2) 2982137; e-mail akhalil@birzeit.edu; internet home.birzeit.edu/giis/giis/index.php; offers courses focused on forced migration and refugee studies; research in peace studies and conflict resolution strategies and diplomacy; organizes lectures and confs in issues related to Palestine; Dir Dr ASEM KHALIL (acting).

Institute of Community and Public Health: tel. (2) 2982019; fax (2) 2982079; e-mail icph@birzeit.edu; internet icph.birzeit.edu; f. 1982; Dir Dr RANA KHATIB.

Institute of Environmental and Water Studies: tel. and fax (2) 2982120; e-mail wsi@birzeit.edu; internet home.birzeit.edu/iws; Dir Dr ZIAD AL-MIMI.

Institute of Law: tel. (2) 2982009; fax (2) 2982137; e-mail iol@birzeit.edu; internet lawcenter.birzeit.edu; Dir GHASSAN FARAMAND.

Institute of Women's Studies: Birzeit, West Bank; tel. (2) 2982013; fax (2) 2982958; e-mail women-inst@birzeit.edu; internet www.home.birzeit.edu/wsi; library of 7,200 vols; Dir ISLAH JAD; publ. *Institute of Women Studies*.

Media Development Centre: tel. (2) 2982979; fax (2) 2982180; e-mail mdc@birzeit.edu; internet home.birzeit.edu/media; Dir NEBAL THAWABTEH.

HEBRON UNIVERSITY

POB 40, Hebron, West Bank
Telephone: (2) 2220995
Fax: (2) 2229303
E-mail: info@hebron.edu
Internet: www.hebron.edu

Founded 1971
Ind. nat. univ.
Languages of instruction: Arabic, English
Academic year: October to June

Chair., Board of Trustees: Dr NABEEL AL-JABARI
Pres.: Dr AWNI A. KHATIB
Vice-Pres. for Academic Affairs: Dr AHMAD ATAWNEH
Vice-Pres. for Foreign Affairs: Dr NIMER ABUZAHRA
Vice-Pres. for Planning and Quality Assurance: Dr SALMAN TALAHMEH
Registrar: M. ZIAD JA'ABARI
Librarian: SALAH ABU SNANEH

Library of 60,000 vols
Number of teachers: 129
Number of students: 6,273

DEANS

Faculty of Agriculture: Dr RIZQ BASHEER
Faculty of Arts: Dr SALAH ALSHROUF
Faculty of Education: Dr NABEEL JUNDI
Faculty of Finance and Management: Dr SHAREEF ABU KHARSH
Faculty of Islamic Studies: Dr HUSSEIN AL-TARTORI
Faculty of Nursing: ZAINAB SULAIMAN
Faculty of Postgraduate Studies: Dr RADWAN BARAKAT
Faculty of Science and Technology: Dr MAHMOUD EDHEIDEL

ISLAMIC UNIVERSITY OF GAZA

POB 108, Gaza
Telephone: (8) 2860700
Fax: (8) 2860800
E-mail: pres@iugaza.edu.ps
Internet: www.iugaza.edu.ps

Founded 1978
Academic year: September to June

Pres.: Dr KAMALAIN SHAATH
Vice-Pres. for Academic Affairs: Prof. MOHAMMED SHABAT
Vice-Pres. for Admin. Affairs: Prof. SALEM HELLES
Vice-Pres. for External Relations: Prof. RIFAT RUSTOM
Dean of Library: Dr WALEED AL-AMOUDY
Dean of Planning and Devt: Dr ABDELMAJEED NASSAR
Dean of Student Affairs: Dr KAMAL GHNAIM

Library of 100,300 vols in central library
Number of students: 20,888

Publication: *Journal* (2 a year)

DEANS

College of Arts: Prof. MAHMOUD EL-AMOUDI
College of Business: Prof. MAJED EL-FARRA
College of Education: Prof. ELYAN AL-HOLY
College of Engineering: Prof. SHAFIQ JENDYA
College of Foundations of Religion: Dr SALEM SALAMEH
College of Information Technology: Prof. NABEEL HEWAIHY
College of Islamic Law: Dr MAHER AL-HOLY
College of Medicine: Dr MOFEED MOKHALLATI
College of Nursing: Dr ASHRAF EL-JEDI
College of Religion Foundation: Dr MOHAMMED BKHAIT
College of Science: Dr NIZAM AL-ASHQAR

PROFESSORS

College of Arts:
ABO ALI, N. KH.
AMOUDI, M. A.
OLWAN, M. SH.
OLWAN, N. S.

College of Business:
EDWAN, A. I.

College of Education:
ASQOUL, M.
EL-HELOU, M. W.

College of Engineering:
AWAD, M.
ENSHASSI, A.
KUHAIL, Z. S.

College of Religion Foundation:
HALABIYA, A. A.
HAMMAD, N. H.

College of Science:
ABDEL-LATIF, M.
ASHOUR, M. M.
EL-ATRASH, M. S.
EL-AZIZ, E. E. A.
EL-NAKHAL, H. A.
HABIL, E.
SARSOUR, M. E.
SHABAT, M. M.
SHUBAIR, M. E.

PALESTINE POLYTECHNIC UNIVERSITY

Hebron, West Bank
Telephone: (2) 2229812
Fax: (2) 2217248
E-mail: info@ppi.edu
Internet: www.ppu.edu

Founded 1978
State control

Pres.: DAWOD AL-ZATARY

Colleges of admin. sciences and informatics, applied professions, applied sciences, engineering and technology
Number of students: 5,000

Colleges

Bethlehem Bible College: POB 17166, 91190 Jerusalem; tel. (2) 2741190; fax (2) 2743278; e-mail info@bethlehembiblecollege.edu; internet www.bethlehembiblecollege.edu; f. 1979; Private control; Christian Bible College; accredited by Ministry for Higher Education and Middle East Association of Theological Education; Pres. Prof. BISHARA AWAD.

Community College of Applied Sciences: POB 1415, Gaza; tel. (8) 2868999; fax (8) 2847404; e-mail info@ccast.edu.ps; internet www.ccast.edu.ps; f. 1998; State control; accredited by Ministry for Higher Education; Dean YEHIA ROSHDI SIRAJ.

Ibrahimieh Community College: POB 19014, 91190 Jerusalem; tel. (8) 6286361; fax (8) 6262984; e-mail icc@ibrahimieh.edu; internet www.ibrahimieh.edu; f. 1998; State control; accredited by Ministry for Higher Education.

National Institute for Administration: Al-Bireh; f. 2004; Palestinian Economic Council for Development and Construction; public admin. training for Palestinian Ministries, public orgs, private sector; Dir Dr MOHAMMED DAJANI.

National Institute for Technology: Ramallah; f. 2001; Palestinian Economic Council for Development and Construction; higher education courses in software engineering, web and e-commerce solutions devt, system engineering, database devt and network engineering; English language courses; Dir ADEL LAFI.

Palestine Technical College, Deir al-Balah: POB 6037, Deir al-Balah; tel. (8) 2531171; fax (8) 2538101; e-mail eng_ptc@ptcdb.edu.ps; internet www.ptcdb.edu.ps; State control; accredited by Ministry for Higher Education.

Tulkarm Community College: West Bank; f. 1931; library: 30,000 vols; 27 teachers; 400 students; teacher training college preparing teachers of agriculture, science, mathematics, computer science, Arabic, Islamic and social studies, English and physical education; Dean Dr M. Z. GHAZALEH.

PANAMA

The Higher Education System

In 1821 Panama became independent from Spain as part of Gran Colombia, declaring its separate independence in 1903. The Universidad de Panamá (founded in 1935) is the oldest university. There are four public universities, with regional centres in the provinces, and 11 private universities, including one specializing in distance learning. In 2006/07 there were 32,660 students enrolled in tertiary education at 24 institutions. Higher education is centralized under the authority of the Ministry of Education.

Admission to higher education is made on the basis of a specialized secondary school certificate (Bachillerato) relevant to the intended field of study. Applicants must also pass an entrance examination. Undergraduates study for four or five years for the Licenciado degree or a professional title. Following the Licenciado a further two years of study is required for the postgraduate Masters (Maestría) degree.

Technical and vocational education is offered by institutions of higher education; the leading programme of study is the Técnico, which requires two to three years of study. Adult education is administered by the Institute for Training and Utilization of Human Resources.

Regulatory and Representative Bodies

GOVERNMENT

Ministry of Education: Edif. Poli y Los Rios, Avda Justo Arosemena, Calles 26 y 27, Apdo 0816-04049, Panamá 3; tel. 511-4400; fax 262-9087; e-mail meduca@meduca.gob.pa; internet www.meduca.gob.pa; Minister LUCINDA MOLINAR.

NATIONAL BODY

Consejo de Rectores de Panamá (Panama Rectors' Council): Albrook, Ancón, Edificio Nº 868, Panamá; tel. 315-0959; fax 315-1601; e-mail rectores@cwpanama.net; internet www.pa/consejo; f. 1995; Pres. Dra NOEMÍ LUCILA CASTILLO JAÉN; Exec. Sec. NURIA ARAGUAS SAMBRANO.

Learned Societies

HISTORY, GEOGRAPHY AND ARCHAEOLOGY

Academia Panameña de la Historia (Panama Academy of History): Apdo 973, Zona 1, Panamá; f. 1921; Pres. MIGUEL A. MARTÍN; Sec. ROGELIO ALFARO; publ. *Boletín*.

LANGUAGE AND LITERATURE

Academia Panameña de la Lengua (Panama Academy of Language): Apdo 0816-06740, Panamá; Calle Manuel María Icaza, esquina con Calle 50, Panamá; tel. 223-0717; fax 263-3910; e-mail aplengua@cwpanama.net; corresp. of the Real Academia Española (Madrid); 4 mems, 14 elected mems; Dir BERNA PÉREZ AYALA DE BURRELL; Sec. MARGARITA J. VÁSQUEZ Q.; publ. *Boletín*.

Alliance Française: Apdo Postal 4305, Zona 5, Panamá; Calle 49, por la Avda Federico Boyd, entrando por la bolsa de valores, Bella Vista, Panamá; tel. 223-7376; fax 264-1931; e-mail alliance@cableonda.net; internet www.afpanama.org; offers courses and exams in French language and culture and promotes cultural exchange with France; attached teaching centres in David.

Research Institutes

AGRICULTURE, FISHERIES AND VETERINARY SCIENCE

Instituto de Investigación Agropecuaria de Panamá (Institute of Agricultural Research): Ciudad del Saber, Clayton, Panamá 6-4391; tel. 317-0519; fax 317-0510; f. 1975; to increase the yields and productivity of agricultural producers; establishes rules for agricultural research carried out in the public sector; advises the govt on the formulation and application of scientific policies and on agricultural technology; promotes technical training at all levels in the agricultural sector; Dir Dr REYNALDO PÉREZ-GUARDIA.

EDUCATION

Instituto para la Formación y Aprovechamiento de los Recursos Humanos (Institute for the Training and Development of Human Resources): Apdo 6337, Zona 5, Panamá; Vía España, al lado de la agencia Thrifti Car Rental, Panamá; tel. 269-6666; fax 263-6101; internet www.ifarhu.gob.pa; f. 1965 for the devt of technical training and the rational use of the country's human resources in order to improve its economic and social devt; 9 regional agencies, 8 student centres and an Information and Documentation Centre (see below); Dir-Gen. Licda GLORIA ROVIRA; publs *Cidinforma* (12 a year), *Mujer al Cambio* (1 a year), *Orientifarhu* (4 a year).

MEDICINE

Instituto Conmemorativo Gorgas de Estudios de la Salud (Gorgas Commemorative Institute of Health Research): Apdo 6991, Zona 5, Panamá; Avda Justo Arosemena entre Calle 35 y 36, Panamá; tel. 227-4111; fax 225-4366; e-mail igorgas@gorgas.gob.pa; internet www.gorgas.gob.pa; f. 1921; library of 50,000 vols; Dir Dr JORGE MOTTA; publ. *Boletín Informativo* (4 a year, online).

NATURAL SCIENCES

Biological Sciences

Smithsonian Tropical Research Institute: Apdo Postal 0843-03092, Balboa, Ancón; Roosevelt Ave, Building 401, Tupper, Balboa, Ancón; tel. 212-8000; fax 212-8148; internet www.stri.org; f. 1923; administered by the Smithsonian Institution; researches and promotes tropical biology, education and conservation; the institute has extensive marine and terrestrial research facilities; library of 66,000 vols, 850 periodicals; Dir Dr IRA RUBINOFF.

Libraries and Archives

Panamá

Archivo Nacional: Apdo 6618, Zona 5, Panamá; Avda Perú entre Calle 31 y 32, Zona 5, 6618 Panamá; tel. 225-0944; fax 225-1937; e-mail arnapa@cwpanama.net; internet www.registro-publico.gob.pa; f. 1912; 3,400 vols; Dir FLORENCIO R. MUNOZ B.; publ. *Boletín Informativo* (2 a year).

Biblioteca del Instituto Nacional de Estadística y Censo: Apdo 0816-01521, Panamá; tel. 510-4829; fax 510-4801; e-mail elsid@contraloria.gob.pa; internet www.contraloria.gob.pa/inec; f. 1949; compiles and publishes statistical information about Panama and its provinces incl. details of the Nat. Census; 60,000 vols; Dir DANIS P. CEDEÑO H.; Librarian ELSI P. DE MEJÍA; publs *Censo Nacional Agropecuario* (every 10 years, also on CD-ROM), *Censos Nacionales de Población y Vivienda* (every 10 years, also on CD-ROM), *Censos Nacionales Económicos* (every 10 years), *Compendios Estadísticas Provinciales* (every 2 years), *Estadística Panameña* (32 series, each 1 a year), *Informe del Contralor* (1 a year, also on CD-ROM), *Panamá en Cifras* (1 a year, also on CD-ROM).

Biblioteca Interamericana Simón Bolívar: Estafeta Universitaria, Panamá; tel. 223-8786; fax 223-3734; e-mail biblis1@ancon.up.ac.pa; f. 1935 as Biblioteca de la Universidad de Panamá, name changed 1978; 285,855 vols incl. 9,000 vols in medical library; maintains interchange with 200 institutions; Dir Prof. DAYSI DE JEAN FRANÇOISE; publ. *Boletín Bibliográfico* (2 a year).

Biblioteca Nacional (National Library): Apdo 7906, Zona 9, Panamá; Parque Recreativo y Cultural Omar, Vía Porras, San Francisco, Panamá; tel. 224-9466; fax 224-9988; internet www.binal.ac.pa; f. 1892 as Biblioteca Colón, reorganized as Biblioteca Nacional 1942; a branch of the Ministry of Education's Public Libraries system, its special function is to provide a Government information service; 200,000 vols (incl. bound reviews and periodicals); Admin. Dir MARÍA MAJELA BRENES; publ. *LOTERIA*.

Centro de Información y Documentación Institucional: Apdo 6337, Zona 5, Panamá; tel. 262-2109; fax 262-1179; e-mail cidi@ifarhu.gob.pa; internet www.ifarhu.gob

.pa; f. 1980; 5,000 vols; Dir Lic. INES PERALTA DE VARGAS; publs *Orientifarhu*, *Cidinforma* (bibliographical information), *Alertas* (specialized bibliographical information), *Mujer al Cambio* (women's psychological and social issues, 1 a year).

Museums and Art Galleries

Panamá

Dirección Nacional del Patrimonio Histórico: Apdo 0816-07812, Zona 5, Panamá; tel. 232-7485; fax 232-7644; internet www.inac.gob.pa; f. 1974; conservation and admin. of Panama's historical heritage; library of 8,000 vols; Dir Lic. LINETTE MONTENEGRO.

Instituto Panameño de Arte/Museo de Arte Contemporáneo: Apdo 4211, Zona 5, Panamá; tel. 262-8012; fax 262-3376; e-mail info@macpanama.org; internet www.macpanama.org; f. 1962; museum; library of 3,000 vols; Dir REINIER RODRÍGUEZ FERGUSON.

Museo de Arte Religioso Colonial: Apdo 662, Zona 1, Panamá; Avda A y Calle 3ra., San Felipe, Panamá; tel. and fax 228-2897; f. 1974; sited in restored 17th-century Dominican chapel; varied collection of objects of religious art of the Colonial period; cultural programmes and lectures; Dir Prof. NORIS NÚÑEZ DE ALVAREZ.

Museo de Ciencias Naturales: Apdo 662, Zona 1, Panamá; Avda Cuba, Calle 29 y 30, Calidonia, Panamá; tel. 225-0645; fax 225-0646; e-mail museocienciasnaturales@yahoo.com; internet www.pa/cultura/museos/ciencias; f. 1975; natural history, geology and palaeontology; fauna of Panama and other countries; library of 300 vols; Dir Profa NURIA ESQUIVEL DE BARILLAS.

Museo de Historia de Panamá: Apdo 662, Zona 1, Panamá; Palacio Municipal, Avda Central, entre Calles 6 y 7 Oeste, Panamá; tel. and fax 228-6231; f. 1977; Dir Licda NILKA FUENTES; publ. guide books.

Public Universities

UNIVERSIDAD AUTÓNOMA DE CHIRIQUÍ

El Cabrero, David, Chiriquí
Telephone: 775-1114
Fax: 774-4050
E-mail: rectoria@unachi.ac.pa
Internet: www.unachi.ac.pa

Founded 1994; present name and status 1995
State control

Rector: VIRGILIO A. OLMOS APARICIO
Vice-Rector for Academic Affairs: DANIEL CARRILLO
Vice-Rector for Admin.: ETELVINA DE BONAGAS
Vice-Rector for Research and Postgraduate Affairs: Dra JUANA RAMOS CHUE
Sec.-Gen.: BLANCA RÍOS

Number of teachers: 560
Number of students: 8,500

Publications: *Bitacora* (society, culture and science, 4 a year), *Econometrín* (economics), *El Observator* (social communication), *Revista*, *Senda Universitaria* (12 a year), *Supra* (Spanish language)

Faculties of business administration and accountancy, economics, education sciences, humanities, law, medicine, natural sciences, nursing, public administration, social communication; School of Chemistry; campuses in Boquete, Oriente and Barú.

UNIVERSIDAD ESPECIALIZADA DE LAS AMERICAS (Specialized University of the Americas)

Albrook Edificio 808, Apdo 0843-01041, Panamá
Telephone: 501-1000
Fax: 501-1041
E-mail: rectoria@udelas.ac.pa
Internet: www.udelas.ac.pa

Founded 1997
State control
Language of instruction: Spanish

Rector: Dra BERTA TORRIJOS DE AROSEMENA
Vice-Rector: Dr JUAN BOSCO BERNAL
Gen. Sec.: ERIC GARCÍA
Librarian: YISELA ARROCHA

Library of 10,000 vols
Number of teachers: 873
Number of students: 6,222

DEANS

Faculty of Integrated Health and Rehabilitation: GRACIELA AMBULO
Faculty of Social and Special Education: ELIZABETH DE TAM

UNIVERSIDAD DE PANAMÁ

Ciudad Universitaria 'Dr Octavio Méndez Pereira', El Cangrejo, Apdo Estafeta Universitaria, Panamá
Telephone: 263-6133
Fax: 264-3733
Internet: www.up.ac.pa

Founded 1935
State control
Language of instruction: Spanish
Academic year: March to December

Rector: Dr GUSTAVO GARCÍA DE PAREDES
Vice-Rector for Academic Affairs: Dr JUSTO MEDRANO
Vice-Rector for Admin.: Dr CARLOS BRANDARIZ ZÚÑIGA
Vice-Rector for Extension: Dr ARIOSTO E. ARDILLA MARTÍNEZ
Vice-Rector for Research and Graduate Studies: Dra BETTY ANN ROWE DE CATSAMBANIS
Vice-Rector for Student Affairs: Dr NELSON NOVARRO
Registrar: ONFALA LÓPEZ DE BELLO
Librarian: Prof. DAYSI DE JEAN FRANÇOISE

Number of teachers: 3,662
Number of students: 65,225

Publications: *Boletines Estadísticos*, *Campus*, *ECO*, *EDU*, *Hacia La Luz*, *Memoria*, *Revistas Jurídicas Panameñas*, *Revista Universidad*, *Scientia*

DEANS

Faculty of Agriculture: Dr JUAN MIGUEL MIGUEL OSORIO
Faculty of Architecture: Arq. MARÍA T. DE BENAVIDES
Faculty of Business Administration and Accountancy: RUTH E. MATA
Faculty of Computer Science, Electronics and Communication: Dra DIANA CHEN
Faculty of Economics: Prof. GABRIEL VELÁSQUEZ
Faculty of Education: Prof. TOMÁS GARIBALDI
Faculty of Fine Arts: Prof. EFRAIN CASTRO
Faculty of Humanities: Dr MIGUEL ÁNGEL CANDANEDO ORTEGA
Faculty of Law and Political Sciences: Dr ROLANDO MURGAS TORRAZZA
Faculty of Medicine: Dr SERGIO FUENTES
Faculty of Natural and Exact Sciences and Technology: Prof. RAMIRO GÓMEZ
Faculty of Nursing: ELBA E. DE ISAZA
Faculty of Odontology: Dra OMAR LÓPEZ
Faculty of Pharmacy: Dra ANGELA DE AGUILAR
Faculty of Public Administration: NICOLÁS JEROME
Faculty of Social Communication: Prof. HARRY IGLESIAS
Faculty of Veterinary Medicine: Dr CARLOS G. MORÁN R.

UNIVERSIDAD TECNOLOGICA DE PANAMÁ

Campus 'Víctor Levi Sasso', Apdo Postal 0819-07289, El Dorado, Panamá
Telephone: 560-3178
Fax: 560-3181
E-mail: utp@utp.ac.pa
Internet: www.utp.ac.pa

Founded 1981
State control
Academic year: March to December

Pres.: Ing. MARCELA PAREDES DE VÁSQUEZ
Vice-Pres. for Academic Affairs: Ing. LUIS BARAHONA
Vice-Pres. for Admin. Affairs: Ing. MYRIAM GONZÁLEZ BOUTET
Vice-Pres. for Research and Graduate Studies: Dr MARTÍN CANDANEDO
Dir of External Affairs: Ing. JAIME JAEN
Librarian: Lic. EDILDA F. DE MORALES

Number of teachers: 1,428
Number of students: 17,000

Publications: *Boletín Informativo* (12 a year), *El Tecnológico* (bulletin, 12 a year), *I+D Tecnológico* (1 a year), *International Affairs Bulletin* (12 a year), *Memorias* (1 a year)

DEANS

Faculty of Civil Engineering: Ing. MARINA SAVAL DE GUERRA
Faculty of Computer Science Engineering: Ing. RAUL BARAHONA
Faculty of Electrical Engineering: Ing. CELSO SPENCER
Faculty of Mechanical Engineering: Dr VÍCTOR SÁNCHEZ
Faculty of Science and Technology: Dr ELEICER CHING

Private Universities

UNIVERSIDAD ABIERTA Y A DISTANCIA DE PANAMÁ (Open and Distance Learning University of Panama)

Apdo 87-2526, Panamá 7
Calle 39 Este, Bella Vista Edif. 5–57 entre Ave Cuba y Ave Perú, Panamá
Telephone: 227-7242
Fax: 227-7243
E-mail: generalunadp@cwpanama.net
Internet: www.unadp.ac.pa

Founded 1994
Private control
Language of instruction: Spanish.

UNIVERSIDAD CATÓLICA SANTA MARÍA LA ANTIGUA

Apdo 0819-08550, Panamá
Telephone: 230-8200
Fax: 230-3433
E-mail: rectoria@usma.ac.pa
Internet: www.usmapanama.com

Founded 1965, reorganized 1973
Private control
Language of instruction: Spanish (except the Hotel and Restaurant Management programme)

Academic year: January to December (three semesters)
Chancellor: Mgr JOSÉ DOMINGO ULLOA MENDIETA
Rector: Mgr CARLOS ALBERTO VOLOJ PEREIRA
Vice-Rector for Academic Affairs: Mgr. DIMAS QUIEL REYES
Vice-Rector for Admin. Affairs: Prof. LUIS PABÓN ORDOÑES
Vice-Rector for Research and Postgraduate Affairs: Mgr. MARÍA EUGENIA PÉREZ DE ALEMÁN
Registrar: Mgr. INGRID MIROSLAVA CHANG VALDÉS
Librarian: Lic. IRENE DE CARVAJAL
USMA Colon Br. Dir: Prof. NEDELKA NUÑEZ
USMA Chiriquí Br. Dir: Prof. FATIMA PITTI
USMA Los Santos Br. Dir: Prof. FULVIA OCAÑA
Library of 65,000 vols
Number of teachers: 400
Number of students: 4,500
Publications: *Boletín Informativo* (1 a year), *Iustitia et Pulchritudo* (1 a year), *Revista La Antigua* (2 a year)

DEANS
Administrative Sciences: Prof. LÍA CORDOBA
Humanities and Religious Studies: Prof. FRANCISCO BLANCO
Law and Political Science: Prof. VICTOR DELGADO
Natural Sciences and Technology: Prof. HUMBERTO MENA
Social Sciences: Prof. MELVA PALACIOS DE MON

UNIVERSIDAD DEL ISTMO

Av. Justo Arosemena, Calle 40 y 41, Panamá
Telephone: 227-8822
Fax: 227-8831
E-mail: informacion@udi.edu
Internet: www.udi.edu
Founded 1963
Private control
Rector: PABLO MICHELSEN
Campuses in Chiriquí, David and La Chorrera.

UNIVERSIDAD INTERAMERICANA DE PANAMÁ

Avda Manuel Espinosa Batista, Panamá
Telephone: 208-4444
Internet: www.uip.edu.pa
Founded 1992
Private control
Language of instruction: Spanish
Academic year: January to December
Pres.: WILLIAM J. SALOM
Rector: NOEMÍ CASTILLO JAÉN
Number of teachers: 500
Number of students: 5,800

UNIVERSIDAD LATINA DE PANAMÁ

Apdo 87-0887, Via Ricardo J. Alfaro, Calle Aragón, Catilla, Panamá 7
Telephone: 230-8600
Fax: 230-8686
E-mail: web@ulat.ac.pa
Internet: www.ulat.ac.pa
Founded 1989, present status 1991
Private control
Rector: Dr MODALDO TUÑON
Registrar: CLAUDIA MARÍN
Library Dir: AURA AROSEMENA
Number of teachers: 600
Number of students: 7,000
Campuses in Chitré, David and Santiago

DEANS
Faculty of Administrative and Economic Sciences: AUGUSTO A. CORRO
Faculty of Communication Sciences: NEDELKA GALVEZ
Faculty of Computer Sciences and Telecommunications: LUJAN GONZALES
Faculty of Education Sciences: GLADYS DE JAÉN
Faculty of Health Sciences: Dr JORGE MEDRANO
Faculty of Law and Political Sciences: OCTAVIO DEL MORAL
Faculty of Social Sciences: (vacant)

Schools of Arts and Music

Escuela Nacional de Danzas: Apdo 662, Zona 1, Panamá; f. 1948.

Escuela Nacional de Teatro: Apdo 662, Zona 1, Panamá; f. 1974; 10 teachers; 40 students; Dir Prof. IVÁN R. GARCÍA.

PAPUA NEW GUINEA

The Higher Education System

In 1906 the Territory of Papua came under Australian control, and in 1914 the former German possession of New Guinea became a Trust Territory, also under Australian control. A joint administration for the two territories was established by Australia in July 1949, and the name Papua New Guinea was adopted in 1971. Independence was achieved in 1975. Major institutions of higher education were first established in the 1960s, including the Papua New Guinea Institute of Public Administration (founded in 1963), the University of Papua New Guinea, the Papua New Guinea University of Technology and the Papua New Guinea University of Natural Resources and Environment (all founded in 1965). In addition to the universities there are also teacher-training colleges and higher education institutions that cater for specific professional training, such as a medical school, which had a total enrolment of 656 students in early 2005. In 1999 there were 13,761 students enrolled in tertiary education.

Admission to higher education is on the basis of the Grade 12 Higher School Certificate. In addition to the standard undergraduate Bachelors degree, which is a four-year programme of study, universities offer two- to four-year diploma and certificate-level courses. Degree courses in medicine and law are five years in duration. Following the Bachelors, the Masters is the first postgraduate degree and lasts between one and three years. Finally, the PhD is the highest university-level degree and requires a minimum of three years' study and research for the preparation and submission of a thesis.

Most technical and vocational education starts at the secondary Grade 10-level, and consists of two- to three-year diploma and certificate programmes at technical colleges and specialized professional institutes.

Regulatory Body

GOVERNMENT

Department of Education: POB 446, Waigani, NCD 131, Fin Corp Haus; tel. 3013555; fax 3254648; internet www.education.gov.pg; Min. for Education JAMES MARABE (acting); Min. for Higher Education, Research, Science and Technology PARU AIHI.

Learned Societies

BIBLIOGRAPHY, LIBRARY SCIENCE AND MUSEOLOGY

Papua New Guinea Library Association: c/o National Library Service, POB 734, Waigani, NCD; f. 1973; 200 mems; Pres. MARGARET J. OBI; Sec. JENNY WAL; publs *Directory of Libraries in Papua New Guinea*, *PNGLA Nius* (2 a year), *PNG Librarians' Calendar* (12 a year), *Toktok bilong haus buk* (Journal, 4 a year).

ECONOMICS, LAW AND POLITICS

Papua New Guinea Institute of Banking and Business Management: ToRobert Centre, Vanama Crescent, POB 1721, Port Moresby NCD; tel. 3221000; fax 3212960; e-mail info@ibbm.com.pg; internet www.ibbm.com.pg; f. 1965; training in all aspects of management and development; Exec. Dir. RAY CLARK.

LANGUAGE AND LITERATURE

Alliance Française: ADF Haus, Musgrave St, POB 5877, Port Moresby; tel. and fax 3210994; e-mail alliance@daltron.com.pg; internet ambfrance-pg.org; offers courses and exams in French language and culture and promotes cultural exchange with France.

NATURAL SCIENCES

General

Papua New Guinea Scientific Society: c/o National Museum and Art Gallery, POB 5560, Boroko; tel. 3252422; fax 3251779; e-mail pngmuseum@global.net.pg; f. 1949; promotes sciences, exchange scientific information, preserve scientific collns and establish museums; 203 mems; Pres. H. SAKULAS; publ. *Proceedings*.

Research Institutes

GENERAL

National Research Institute: POB 5854, Boroko, NCD 111; tel. 3260300; fax 3260213; e-mail nri@global.net.pg; internet www.nri.org.pg; f. 1989; promotion of research into social, political, economic, educational and cultural issues in Papua New Guinea; practical research opportunities for trainee research workers; library of 10,000 vols; Dir Dr TOM WEBSTER; publs *Current Issues* (4 a year), *Post Courier Index* (1 a year), *Taim-Lain: A Journal of Contemporary Melanesian Studies*.

AGRICULTURE, FISHERIES AND VETERINARY SCIENCE

Lowlands Agricultural Experiment Station: Kerevat, POB 204, Kokopo, East New Britain Province; tel. 9839145; fax 9839129; f. 1928; food crops, spices, soil and land management, entomology and plant pathology.

ECONOMICS, LAW AND POLITICS

Institute of National Affairs: POB 1530, Port Moresby; tel. 3211045; fax 3217223; e-mail inapng@daltron.com.pg; internet www.inapng.com; f. 1979; aims to foster the devt of the nat. economy by encouraging discussion and research on issues which are important in the public and private sectors; undertakes research in matters of interest to management in both sectors, the findings of which are published; organizes seminars, public meetings, etc., on matters of importance to economic devt; 80 mems; Pres. PHIL FRANKLIN; Exec. Dir and Treas. and Sec. PAUL BARKER; Deputy Dir MARJORIE ANDREW.

MEDICINE

Papua New Guinea Institute of Medical Research: POB 60, Goroka EHP 441; tel. 7322800; fax 7321998; e-mail general@pngimr.org.pg; internet www.pmgimr.org.pg; f. 1968; medical, human biological, nutritional and sociological research, all matters relating to research into human health and disease within Papua New Guinea; library of 5,000 vols; Dir Prof. JOHN C. REEDER.

Libraries and Archives

Boroko

National Archives and Public Records Service: POB 1089, Boroko; tel. 3256200; fax 3254251; f. 1957; br. of Nat. Library Service, Division of the Dept of Education; repository for the public archives and records of Papua New Guinea; Reference Service and Microfilm Unit, Records Management Service and Records Centre Service for govt offices and statutory bodies; br. repository in Lae: 10,000 linear m and 1,000 maps and plans, and photographic archives; Chief Archivist JACOB HELEVAWA; publs *Guides to Groups of Records in the National Archives* (irregular), *Patrol Reports* (microfiche, irregular).

Lae

Matheson Library, Papua New Guinea University of Technology: Private Mail Bag, Lae; fax 4734355; f. 1965; 120,000 monograph vols, 600 serial titles, 4,000 audiovisual items; spec. colln: Papua New Guinea; microfilm unit produces microfiche edns of all major PNG serial publs; Univ. Librarian D. TEMU.

Waigani

National Library Service: POB 734, Waigani; tel. 3256200; fax 3251331; f. 1975; nat. reference library; legal deposit library; ISBN agency for Papua New Guinea; advisory services, lending and educational services; important holdings of New Guineana, particularly govt publs; Papua New Guinea colln; films and videos of Papua New Guinea; mobile school library service; 50,000 vols, 4,000 films and video recordings; Dir-Gen. DANIEL PARAIDE; publs *Directory of Libraries in Papua New Guinea* (irregular), *OLA Nius* (6 a year), *Papua New Guinea Directory of Information Sources in Science and Technology* (irregular), *Papua New Guinea National Bibliography* (1 a year), *Selective Times Index to PNG* (1 a year).

University of Papua New Guinea 'Michael Somare Library': POB 319, University Post Office, Waigani; tel. 3267280; fax 3267187; f. 1965; 458,000 vols, 2,000 current periodicals; spec. collns: law, New Guinea; Librarian IVARATURE KIVIA; publs *New Guinea Archives: A Listing* (microfiche), *New Guinea Photographic Index* (microfiche).

Subordinate library:

Medical Library: POB 5623, Boroko; f. 1976; 65,000 vols; Librarian L. WANGATAU; publ. *Papua New Guinea Medical Journal*.

Museum and Art Gallery

Boroko

Papua New Guinea National Museum and Art Gallery: POB 5560, Boroko; tel. 3252422; fax 3251779; e-mail pngmuseum@global.net.pg; f. 1954; field research in archaeology, cultural anthropology, natural history; educational tours, public programmes, broadcasts, etc.; aims to implement the National Cultural Property (Preservation) Act to protect Papua New Guinea's cultural heritage, and establish museums; library of 4,500 vols; Dir SIMON PAUL PORAITUK.

Universities

DIVINE WORD UNIVERSITY

POB 483, Madang

Telephone: 4222907

Fax: 4222812

E-mail: info@dwu.ac.pg

Internet: www.dwu.ac.pg

Founded 1979 by the Society of the Divine Word, university status granted by Act of Parliament 1980

Private control (funded by Catholic Church)

Language of instruction: English

Academic year: February to October (2 semesters)

Pres.: Fr JAN CZUBA

Vice-Pres.: Dr CECILIA NEMBOU

Vice-Pres. for Academics: ANDREW SIMPSON

Vice-Pres. for Admin.: BENJAMIN NAING

Dean of Studies: Assoc. Prof. PAMELA NORMAN

Registrar: CECILIA N'DROWER

Head Librarian: MONICA ROTHLISBERGER

Library of 43,320 vols, 1,350 e-books and 1659 e-journals

Publication: *DWU Research Journal* (2 a year)

DEANS

Faculty of Arts: Dr LINDA SUE CROWL

Faculty of Business and Management: Dr ROMULO LINDIO

Faculty of Education: Dr CATHERINE NONGKAS

Faculty of Flexible Learning: PHIL SMITH

Faculty of Health Sciences: Dr PASCAL MICHON

UNIVERSITY OF GOROKA

POB 1078, Goroka, EHP

Telephone: 7311700

Fax: 7322620

E-mail: amaras@uog.ac.pg

Internet: www.uog.ac.pg

Founded 1995

State control

Language of instruction: English

Academic year: January to December

Chancellor: Sir EBIA OLEWALE

Vice-Chancellor: Dr MICHAEL MEL (acting)

Pro-Vice-Chancellor for Academic Affairs and Devt: Dr GAIRO ONAGI (acting)

Pro-Vice-Chancellor for Admin.: Dr JERRY SEMOS (acting)

Librarian: N. AMARASINGHE

Library of 107,000 books, 110 periodicals

Number of teachers: 80

Number of students: 1,100

Publication: *Papua New Guinea Journal of Teacher Education* (1 a year)

DEANS

Faculty of Education: Dr ARNOLD KUKARI

Faculty of Humanities: Dr GAIRO ONAGI

Faculty of Science: Dr POORANALINGHAM JEYARATHAN

PACIFIC ADVENTIST UNIVERSITY

Private Mail Bag, Boroko, National Capital District 111

Telephone: 3280200

Fax: 3281257

E-mail: administration@pau.ac.gp

Internet: www.pau.ac.gp

Founded 1984 as Pacific Adventist College, present status 1997

Private (funded by Church of Christ)

Language of instruction: English

Academic year: February to August

Vice-Chancellor: Dr BRANIMIR SCHUBERT

Number of teachers: 41

Number of students: 379

UNIVERSITY OF PAPUA NEW GUINEA

Box 320, University Post Office, Waigani

Telephone: 3267200

Fax: 3267187

E-mail: pr&m@upng.ac.pg

Internet: www.upng.ac.pg

Founded 1965

Language of instruction: English

State control

Academic year: February to November (2 semesters)

Chancellor: Sir ALKAN TOLOLO

Pro-Chancellor: Dr ROSEMARY KEKEDO

Vice-Chancellor: Dr L. R. EASTCOTT

Deputy Vice-Chancellor: N. R. KUMAN

Registrar: VINCENT MALAIBE

Library: see Libraries and Archives

Number of teachers: 700

Number of students: 4,416

Publications: *Melanesian Law Journal* (2 a year), *PNG Law*, *Research in Melanesia* (2 a year), *Science in New Guinea* (4 a year), *South Pacific Journal of Psychology* (1 a year), *Yagl-Ambu*

DEANS

School of Business Administration: Dr ALBERT MELLAM

School of Humanities and Social Science: Dr KENNETH SUMBUK

School of Law: Prof. LAWRENCE KALINOE

School of Medicine and Health Sciences: Prof. MATHIAS SAPURI

School of Natural and Physical Sciences: Prof. KIRPAL SINGH

School of Research and Postgraduate Studies: Dr SIMON SAULEI

PAPUA NEW GUINEA UNIVERSITY OF NATURAL RESOURCES AND ENVIRONMENT

PMB, Rabaul, E New Britain Province

Telephone: 9839144

Fax: 9839166

E-mail: lythia@global.net.pg*Popondetta Campus*, POB 131, Popondetta, Oro Province

Telephone: 3297457

Fax: 3297239

E-mail: oroacademic@global.net.pg

Founded 1965 as Vudal Agricultural College, became Univ. of Vudal 1997

Language of instruction: English

Academic year: February to November

State control

Language of instruction: English

Depts of agriculture, fisheries, forestry

Vice-Chancellor: Prof. PHILIP SIAGURU

Registrar: HENRY GIOVEN

Bursar: JACKSON RODGERS

Popondetta Campus Dir: JACK LAPAUVE

Dean of School of Natural Resources and Environment: Dr ALAN QUARTERMAN

Librarian: BRUCE NINGAKUN

Library of 25,000

Number of teachers: 20

Number of students: 380

PAPUA NEW GUINEA UNIVERSITY OF TECHNOLOGY

Private Mail Bag, Lae

Telephone: 4734999

Fax: 4757667

E-mail: nkalimda@pro.unitech.ac.pg

Internet: www.unitech.ac.pg

Founded 1965

Language of instruction: English

State control

Academic year: February to November (2 semesters)

Chancellor: A. TOLOLO

Pro-Chancellor: R. KEKEDO

Vice-Chancellor: M. BALOILOI

Registrar: T. CHAN

Librarian: RAPHAEL TOPAGUR (acting)

Library: see Libraries and Archives

Number of teachers: 92

Number of students: 2,600

Publications: *Reporter*, *Research Report*, *Vice-Chancellor's Report*.

College

Papua New Guinea Institute of Public Administration: POB 1216, Boroko; tel. 3260433; fax 3261654; f. 1963; diploma, certificate and short courses in public and land admin., public finance and accountancy, local govt, management, law, social devt, library studies, business devt, communication skills, mathematics and statistics, rural devt; library: 75,000 vols; 60 teachers; 700 students; Dir GEI ILAGI; publs *Administration for Development* (2 a year), *Handbook* (1 a year).

PARAGUAY

The Higher Education System

Paraguay, ruled by Spain from the 16th century, achieved independence in 1811. The oldest institution of higher education is the Universidad Nacional de Asunción (founded in 1889). The next oldest university was not opened until the 1960s. Following the end of military rule in 1989, university-level education expanded in the 1990s with the opening of several universities. The governing law of higher education is Law 136/93 (1993), which led to the creation of the Council of Universities. In 2004/05 there were an estimated 156,167 students enrolled in university-level education at 111 institutions.

Applicants must have the Bachillerato in order to gain admission to higher education, and universities may set individual entry requirements. The Título de Licenciatura is the main undergraduate degree, and is awarded after four years of study. Under Law 136/93 the Título de Licenciatura is both an academic and a professional title. Undergraduate degrees in professional fields of study, such as economics, engineering, law and medicine, may last upwards of four years. There is no uniform system of postgraduate degrees, which were not available in Paraguay before 1991. However, the Universidad Nacional de Asunción has established a system that is being considered by the Council of Universities, consisting of: Diploma (Diplomado), a postgraduate short course in a professional field of study; Specialization (Especialización), undertaken as part of the undergraduate degree; Masters (Maestría), which lasts two years; and Doctorate (Título de Doctorado) or Doctor of Sciences (Doctor en Ciencias), which is available at nine universities.

Post-secondary technical and vocational education is available mainly at higher technical institutions (instituciones técnicas superiores) under the authority of the Directorate of Higher Technical Institutes (Dirección de Institutos Técnicos Superiores). The qualification Título de Técnico Superior is awarded after completion of two years or 1,500 classroom hours of study.

The National Agency for Evaluation and Accreditation of Higher Education (Agencia Nacional de Evaluación y Acreditación de la Educación Superior—ANEAES) was founded in 2003 following the enactment of Law 2072/03. ANEAES is the national body for quality assurance and accreditation of higher education at undergraduate and postgraduate levels. Paraguay also participates in the Mecanismo Experimental de Acreditación de Carreras del MERCOSUR.

Regulatory and Representative Bodies

GOVERNMENT

Consejo Nacional de Educación y Cultura (CONEC) (National Council for Education and Culture): Tte. Aponte 609 y Juan de Salazar, Asunción; tel. (21) 226-341; e-mail secret_conec@webmail.com.py; internet www.mec.gov.py/conec; autonomous org. working with the Min. of Education and Culture on the formulation and implementation of nat. policy on education and culture; proposes ways to develop and improve the educational system; mems are appointed by the Pres. of the Republic and serve a term of 3 years; 12 mems; Pres. THE MINISTER OF EDUCATION AND CULTURE; Admin. Dir Lic. MIRTA ELIZABETH ARMOA.

Dirección General de Educación Superior (Directorate of Higher Education): O'Leary 615 esq. Gral. Díaz, Edif. Lider II, Piso 4, Asunción; tel. (21) 498-716; e-mail info@educacionsuperior.mec.gov.py; internet educacionsuperior.mec.gov.py; Dir-Gen. Dr DOMINGO PEDROZO.

Ministry of Education and Culture: Chile, Humaitá y Piribebuy, Asunción; tel. (21) 44-3078; fax (21) 44-3919; internet www.paraguaygobierno.gov.py/mec; Minister MARÍA ESTER JIMÉNEZ.

ACCREDITATION

Agencia Nacional de Evaluación y Acreditación de la Educación Superior (ANEAES) (National Agency for Evaluation and Accreditation of Higher Education): 25 de Mayo 640 esq. Antequera Edificio 'Garantía', Piso 2 ofic. 203, Asunción; tel. (21) 444-644; e-mail info@aneaes.gov.py; internet www.aneaes.gov.py; f. 2003; Pres. Dra CARMEN QUINTANA-HORÁK.

Learned Societies

GENERAL

Academia de la Lengua y Cultura Guaraní (Academy of the Guaraní Language and Culture): Calle España y Mompox, Asunción; f. 1975; Pres. Dr RUFINO AREVALO PARIS; Sec. ANTONIO E. GONZÁLEZ; publ. *Revista*.

LANGUAGE AND LITERATURE

Academia Paraguaya de la Lengua Española (Paraguayan Academy of the Spanish Language): Avda España 1098, Asunción; tel. (21) 206-048; fax (21) 224-106; e-mail acapales@sce.cnc.una.py; internet www.aparle.org; f. 1927; corresp. of the Real Academia Española (Madrid); 26 mems; Pres. JOSÉ ANTONIO MORENO RUFFINELLI; Gen. Sec. Dra RENÉE FERRER DE ARRÉLLAGA; publ. *Anales*.

Alliance Française: Estigarribia 1039, Calle Estados Unidos, Casilla de Correo 2076, Asunción; tel. (21) 210-503; fax (21) 212-697; e-mail info@alianzafrancesa.edu.py; internet www.alianzafrancesa.edu.py; offers courses and exams in French language and culture and promotes cultural exchange with France; Dir FERNAND DEFOURNIER.

MEDICINE

Sociedad Paraguaya de Pediatría (Paediatrics Society): Mcal Estigarribia 1764 c/ Rca Francesa, Asunción; tel. (21) 447-493; fax (21) 226-795; e-mail sppsecre@spp.org.py; internet www.spp.org.py; f. 1938; Pres. Dr RAÚL ALBERTO OLMEDO SISUL; Gen. Sec. Dra MARÍA DEL ROCÍO BOGADO.

RELIGION, SOCIOLOGY AND ANTHROPOLOGY

Asociación Indigenista del Paraguay: Mompox y Manuel Gondra, CC 1838, 1209 Asunción; tel. (21) 448-592; fax (21) 448-592; e-mail aindigenistadelpy@tigo.com.py; internet www.aip.org.py; f. 1942; anthropology, devt of indigenous communities; 170 mems; library of 1,640 vols; Pres. Dr RICARDO AZORERO MORENO; Sec. MARIA JOSÉ MORENO.

Research Institutes

ECONOMICS, LAW AND POLITICS

Centro Interdisciplinario de Derecho Social y Economía Política (CIDSEP): Alberdi 855 casi Piribebuy, Asunción; tel. (21) 445-429; e-mail cidsep@conexion.com.py; internet www.cidsep.org; f. 1986; attached to Universidad Católica 'Nuestra Señora de la Asunción'; Dir Dr CARLOS ALBERTO GONZÁLEZ.

Centro Paraguayo de Estudios de Desarrollo Económico y Social: Mariscal Estigarribia, 1050 Asunción.

HISTORY, GEOGRAPHY AND ARCHAEOLOGY

Instituto Geográfico Militar: Av. Artigas 920 casi Saltos del Guaira, Asunción; tel. (21) 222-443; fax (21) 204-959; e-mail disergemil@highway.com.py; Dir Coronel ÓSCAR ANTONIO NÚÑEZ; Sec. E. LÓPEZ MOREIRA.

MEDICINE

Instituto Nacional de Parasitología (National Institute of Parasitology): Instituto de Microbiología, Facultad de Medicina, Casilla Correo 1102, Asunción; f. 1963; 5 mems; library; Dir Dr ARQUIMEDES CANESE; publ. *Revista Paraguaya de Microbiología* (1 a year).

RELIGION, SOCIOLOGY AND ANTHROPOLOGY

Centro de Estudios Antropológicos de la Universidad Católica: Casilla de Correo 1718, Asunción; fax (21) 441-044; e-mail ceaduc@uca.edu.py; f. 1950, affiliated to Universidad Católica 1971; 25 mems; Dir JOSÉ ZANARDINI; Sec. MYRIAN AURORA GAONA MARTÍNEZ; publs *Estudios Paraguayos, Suple-*

mento Antropológico, Universidad Católica (2 a year).

Centro Paraguayo de Estudios Sociológicos: Eligio Ayala 973 e/ Brasil y EE.UU., Asunción; tel. (21) 443-734; fax (21) 446-617; e-mail cpes@cpes.org.py; f. 1964; research and development in social sciences: migration, bi-lingualism, population structure, rural development, role of women in the work force, education, etc.; library: specialized library of 5,000 vols, 4,000 documents; Dir MARÍA MAGDALENA RIVAROLA; publ. *Revista Paraguaya de Sociología* (3 a year).

TECHNOLOGY

Centro Paraguayo de Ingenieros: Avda España 959, Casilla 336, Asunción; tel. 202-424; fax 205-019; e-mail cpi@supernet.com.py; internet www.cpi.org.py; f. 1939; Pres. Ing. NICANOR FLEITAS BAREIRO; Sec. Ing. CÉSAR MANUEL LÓPEZ BOSIO; publ. *Ingeniería 2000* (1 a year).

Instituto Nacional de Tecnología, Normalización y Metrología (INTN): Avda Artigas 3973 y Gral Roa, Asunción; tel. (21) 290-160; fax (21) 290-873; e-mail intn@intn.gov.py; internet www.intn.gov.py; f. 1965; carries out research and technological studies, and lays down technical norms; Dir Ing. OSCAR SALAZAR YARYES; publ. *Normas Técnicas Paraguayas*.

Libraries and Archives

Asunción

Archivo del Ministerio de Relaciones Exteriores (Archive of the Ministry of Foreign Affairs): Calle Juan E. Oleary 222 esq. Pdte Franco, Asunción; tel. (21) 493-928; fax (21) 493-210; e-mail smareski@mre.gov.py; internet www.mre.gov.py; contains 200 linear m of documents incl. Colecciones de los Documentos Diplomáticos from 1870 and the Archivo General de las Indias from 1545.

Archivo Nacional de Asunción: Mcal. Estigarribia esq. Iturbe, Asunción; tel. and fax (21) 447-311; e-mail info@archivonacionaldeasuncion.org; internet archivonacionaldeasuncion.org; f. 1544; attached to Dirección General de Archivos, Bibliotecas y Museos of the Secretaría de Cultura; c. 7,000 vols of documents and 2.5m. records dating from 1534; Dir NORMA IBÁÑEZ DE YEGROS.

Biblioteca Americana (American Library): Mariscal Estigarribia e Iturbe, Asunción; attached to the Museo Nacional de Bellas Artes (*q.v.*).

Biblioteca de la Sociedad Científica del Paraguay (Library of the Paraguayan Scientific Society): Andrés Barbero 230 esq. Artigas, Asunción; tel. (21) 205-438; f. 1921; 29,300 vols on science.

Biblioteca Nacional: De la Residenta 820 casi Perú, Asunción; tel. (21) 204-670; e-mail info@bibliotecanacional.org; internet www.bibliotecanacional.org; f. 1887; 44,000 vols; Dir Lic. RAMÓN ROLANDI TORRES.

Biblioteca Pública del Ministerio de Defensa Nacional (Public Library of the Ministry of Defence): Avda Mariscal López y Vicepresidente Sánchez, Planta baja, Asunción; tel. (21) 223-965; fax (21) 210-052; e-mail mendozah@cu.com.py; internet www.mdn.gov.py; 2,000 vols, 7,000 photographs; Dir Col HUGO RAMÓN MENDOZA MARTÍNEZ.

Museums and Art Galleries

Asunción

Casa de la Independencia: 14 de Mayo esq. Pdte Franco, Asunción; tel. (21) 493-918; e-mail info@casadelaindependencia.org.py; internet www.casadelaindependencia.org.py; f. 1965; historical museum of the colonial period; Pres. Dr GERARDO FOGEL; Dir Prof. CARLOS ALBERTO PUSINERI SCALA.

Colección Carlos Alberto Pusineri Scala: Hernandarias 1313, Asunción; tel. (21) 81855; f. 1950; collections of Guaraní archaeology, trophies of Paraguayan wars, colonial objects; small library of Paraguayan history, numismatics and anthropology; Dir CARLOS ALBERTO PUSINERI SCALA.

Jardín Botánico y Museo de Historia Natural (Botanical Gardens and Natural History Museum): Artigas y Av. Primer Presidente, Asunción; tel. (21) 290-269; fax (21) 291-255; f. 1914; herbarium, zoological garden and museum, bacteriological laboratory, agricultural experimental station; Dir Ing. GILDO INSFRÁN GUERROS; publ. *Revista*.

Museo Etnográfico 'Andrés Barbero': España 217, Asunción; tel. and fax (21) 441696; e-mail museobarbero@museobarbero.org.py; internet www.museobarbero.org.py; f. 1929; archaeology, ethnography, ethnology, history, archives, MSS, photographs, world music; library of 30,000 vols; Dir Lic. ADELINA PUSINERI; Sec. RAQUEL ZALAZAR.

Museo Histórico Militar (Museum of Military History): Avda Mariscal López 140 y Vicepresidente Sánchez, Planta baja del edificio del Ministerio de Defensa Nacional, Asunción; tel. (21) 223-965; fax (21) 210-052; e-mail mendozah@cu.com.py; internet www.mdn.gov.py; f. 1942; recent war colins; Dir Col HUGO RAMÓN MENDOZA MARTÍNEZ.

Museo Nacional de Bellas Artes: Mariscal Estigarribia esq. Iturbe, Asunción; tel. (21) 447-716; f. 1887; the paintings and sculpture of Juan Silvano Godoy form the basis of the collection; Dir JOSÉ LATERZA PARODI.

Yaguarón

Museo Doctor Francia: Yaguarón; f. 1968; relics of Paraguay's first dictator, 'El Supremo'; Pres. Dr FABIO RIVAS; Dir Dr JULIO CÉSAR CHAVES.

Universities

UNIVERSIDAD AMERICANA

Avda Brasilia 1100, Asunción
Telephone and fax (21) 295-710
E-mail: universidad@uamericana.edu.py
Internet: www.uamericana.edu.py

Founded 1994

School of administration and economics

Pres.: Dr ANDRÉS BENKÖ KAPUVÁRY
Rector: Dr BENJAMÍN FERNÁNDEZ BOGADO
Vice-Rector for Academic Affairs: Ing. EDMUNDO DURÁN
Vice-Rector for Administration and Finance: Ing. RODOLFO CORTHORN
Vice-Rector for International Relations: Lic. SERGIO SOMERVILLE

Library of 5,000 vols, 100 periodicals
Number of teachers: 200
Number of students: 4,000

UNIVERSIDAD AUTÓNOMA DE ASUNCIÓN

Jejuí 667, entre O'Leary y 15 de Agosto, Asunción
Telephone: (21) 440-980
Fax: (21) 497-299
E-mail: info@uaa.edu.py
Internet: www.uaa.edu.py

Founded 1978 as Escuela Superior de Administración de Empresas; present name and status 1991
Private control
Language of instruction: Spanish
Academic year: March to December

Rector: KITTY GAONA FRANCO
Vice-Rector: Lic. JUAN DE DIOS GARBETT SCHAERER
Secretary-General: Lic. MARÍA LUISA PUERTAS LÓPEZ

Library of 15,000 vols
Number of teachers: 400
Number of students: 6,000

DEANS

Faculty of Communication and Art: (vacant)
Faculty of Economics and Business Administration: Dr SALVIO GÓMEZ ZORRILLA
Faculty of Health Sciences: Dr GRACIELA MOREIRA
Faculty of Humanities and Educational Sciences: MARIEN PEGGY MARTÍNEZ
Faculty of Law, Politics and Social Science: Dr EUGENIO JIMÉNEZ R.
Faculty of Science and Technology: Lic. HUGO CORREA

UNIVERSIDAD AUTÓNOMA DEL PARAGUAY

Gen. Díaz 1053, Colón 568, Asunción
Telephone: (21) 441-924
Fax: (21) 447-579
E-mail: rectorado@uap.edu.py
Internet: www.uap.edu.py

Founded 1991

Rector: Dr CARLOS LAHAYE AGUIAR
Vice-Rector: Dr ARNALDO LATAZA MIGONE

DEANS

Faculty of Behavioural Sciences: Prof. Dr JOSÉ ANTONIO ARIAS
Faculty of Obstetrics: Prof. Dr REINALDO BARRETO M.
Faculty of Optics: Lic. LEONARDO GARCÍA
Pierre Fauchard Faculty of Dentistry: Prof. Dr ARMANDO MERCADO B.

UNIVERSIDAD CATÓLICA 'NUESTRA SEÑORA DE LA ASUNCIÓN'

Cantaluppi y G. Molinas, Asunción
Telephone: (21) 441-044
Fax: (21) 445-245
E-mail: relinter@uc.edu.py
Internet: www.uc.edu.py

Founded 1960
Private control
Language of instruction: Spanish
Academic year: March to December

Chancellor: Mgr IGNACIO GORGOZA (Bishop of Encarnación)
Rector: Mgr Dr MICHEL MARCEL GIBAUD WESTERMANS
Vice-Rector for Academic Affairs: Prof. Dra CARMEN QUINTANA DE HORAK
Vice-Rector for Administrative Affairs: Prof. Lic. CARLOS L. AYALA VERA
Secretary-General: (vacant)
Director of the Office of Institutional Relations: Abog. MINERVA IZQUIERDO
Librarian: Licda MARGARITA KALLSEN

Number of teachers: 1,922
Number of students: 18,000

Publications: *Anuario* (university), *Anuario* (Faculty of Law and Diplomatic Science), *Anuario* (Faculty of Philosophy and Human Sciences), *Cuadernos de Discusión* (Faculty of Philosophy and Human Sciences), *Estudios Antropológicos* (Anthropological Studies), *La Quincena* (Faculty of Philosophy and Human Sciences), *Lila* (Faculty of Business, Administration and Accounting), *Revista Jurídica* (Juridical Review), *Universitas* (Tomás Moro Institute of the Faculty of Law and Diplomatic Science), *Ventana Abierta* (Faculty of Philosophy and Human Sciences)

DEANS

Admissions Courses (Asunción): Prof. Lic. XENIA JERMOLIEF DE CATTONI (Dir)
Conservatoire (Asunción): Prof. Abog. GLORIA MAZÓ (Dir)
Department of Theology and Pastoral Action (Asunción): Pbro SILVIO SUÁREZ (Dir)
Faculty of Accounting (Alto Paraná): Lic. ARMÍN NICOLÁS VILLAGRA
Faculty of Accounting, Administration and Economics (Asunción): Prof. Lic. HÉCTOR ENRIQUE ALMIRÓN FIGUEREDO
Faculty of Accounting, Administration and Economics (Concepción): Lic. MARÍA VICTORIA COELHO DE SOUZA DE PÉREZ
Faculty of Accounting and Administration (Guairá): Lic. DAXI SILVANA DUARTE DE GARCÍA
Faculty of Agriculture (Caaguazú): Ing. Agr. PAULINO INVERNIZZI
Faculty of Chemistry (Guairá): Quim. NILSA BATTAGLIA DE MARECOS
Faculty of Economics (Itapúa): Lic. FRANCISCO SOLANO MACIEL
Faculty of Education (Guairá): Lic. RICARDA AIDEÉ JIMÉNEZ DE CABRERA
Faculty of Education (Itapúa): Lic. MARÍA ISABEL MADRAZZO DE GARAY
Faculty of Education, Law and Early Education (Concepción): Lic. JOSEFINA OVELAR DE BENÍTEZ
Faculty of Health Sciences (Alto Paraná): Dra PETRONA VÁZQUEZ DE CARDOZO
Faculty of Health Sciences (Asunción): Prof. Dr JOSÉ CORVALÁN
Faculty of Law (Alto Paraná): Dr PORFIRIO ZACARÍAS LEÓN
Faculty of Law (Caaguazú): Abog. SILVIO MARTÍNEZ JIMÉNEZ
Faculty of Law (Guairá): Abog. ESTHER LISBOA VDA. DE BOGADO
Faculty of Law (Itapúa): Abog. SERGIO MARTYNIUK
Faculty of Law and Diplomatic Science (Asunción): Prof. Abog. JOSÉ MARÍA CABRAL ALCARAZ
Faculty of Medicine (Guairá): Dr FRANCISCO DUARTE LEGAL
Faculty of Philosophy and Human Sciences (Asunción): Prof. Lic. ILDE SILVERO ÁLVAREZ
Faculty of Science and Technology (Asunción): Prof. Ing. JUAN ALBERTO GONZÁLEZ MEYER
Faculty of Science and Technology (Itapúa): Arq. MARIO ZAPUTOVICH RUOSH
Faculty of Technology (Alto Paraná): Ing. MANUEL CHAMORRO ALDERETE
Higher Institute of Theology (Asunción): Pbro JOAQUÍN MEDINA (Dir)

CAMPUSES

Alto Paraná: Pro-Rector Lic. HUGO EUGENIO RIVAROLA GODOY.

Asunción: Pro-Rector Ing. GERÓNIMO BELLASSAI BAUDO.

Caaguazú: Pro-Rector Abog. ALBERTO GODOY VERA.

Carapegúa: Pro-Rector (vacant).

Concepción: Pro-Rector Lic. MARGARITA MARÍA PÁEZ DE COMELLI.

Guairá: Pro-Rector Lic. RUFINO FERNÁNDEZ RAMOS.

Itapúa: Pro-Rector Dr JESÚS RENÉ HAURÓN.

UNIVERSIDAD COLUMBIA DEL PARAGUAY

25 de Mayo 658 y Antequera, Asunción
Telephone: (21) 206-526
Fax: (21) 490-811
Internet: www.columbia.edu.py
Founded 1991
Rector: ROBERTO ELÍAS CANESE
Courses offered in accountancy and business studies, computer engineering, hotel management and tourism, law, marketing, organizational psychology, social engineering.

UNIVERSIDAD COMUNERA

San José 630 y Artigas, Asunción
Telephone: (21) 223-892
Founded 1992
Rector: ADRIANO IRALA BURGOS
Faculties of agricultural administration, tourism.

UNIVERSIDAD DEL CONO SUR DE LAS AMÉRICAS

Avda España 372 Calle Brasil, Asunción
Telephone: (21) 213-872
Fax: (21) 212-658
E-mail: ucsa@ucsa.py
Internet: www.ucsa.edu.py
Founded 1996
Rector: Ing. LUIS ALBERTO LIMA
Academic Director: Lic. ANDRÉS ANTONIO VILLALBA COLMÁN
Vice-Rector for Administration: Lic. HELGA MARÍA DE SARUBBI
Vice-Rector for Postgraduate Studies: Lic. JUDITH FARIAS DA FONSECA
Vice-Rector for Research and Development: Lic. JOSÉ BLÁS VILLALBA

SUBJECT COORDINATORS

Business: Lic. CLARISSA MELINA RODRIGUEZ CAÑETE
Engineering: Ing. JOSÉ JUAN RICART BOSSI
Social Studies: Lic. NANCY MIRIAN CAÑETE DE GINZO

UNIVERSIDAD DEL NORTE

Avda España 676, entre Rosa Peña y Boquerón, Asunción
Telephone: (21) 229-450
Fax: (21) 228-217
E-mail: info@uninorte.edu.py
Internet: www.uninorte.edu.py
Founded 1991
Academic year: March to December
Rector: JUAN MANUEL MARCOS
Library of 20,000 vols

DEANS

Faculty of Business Administration: CÉSAR CRUZ ROA
Faculty of Chemistry: ANA KALENIUSKA
Faculty of Education and Humanities: SERGIO MARCOS GUSTAFSON
Faculty of Engineering: LUIS FERNANDO MEYER CANILLAS
Faculty of Health Sciences: CARLOS MICHELETTO
Faculty of Law and Politics: CARMEN GUBETICH DE CATTONI
Faculty of Medicine: JUAN CARLOS CHAPARRO
Faculty of Technology: CARLOS CABALLERO
Postgraduate Faculty: JUAN MANUEL MARCOS

UNIVERSIDAD DEL PACÍFICO

México 775, Asunción
Telephone: (21) 450-287.

UNIVERSIDAD EVANGÉLICA DEL PARAGUAY

José Berges 459, Asunción
Telephone: (21) 223-496
Fax: (21) 223-496
E-mail: unievangelica@rieder.net.py
Internet: www.uep.edu.py
Founded 1994
Academic year: February to December
Faculties of accounting, administration and economics, health sciences, humanities and educational sciences, modern languages, music, nursing, psychology and human development, theology
Rector: DIONISIO ÓRTIZ MUTTI
Vice-Rector: MELITA WALL
Sec.-Gen.: ESTEBAN MISSENA DEL CASTILLO
Number of teachers: 193
Number of students: 1,374

UNIVERSIDAD NACIONAL DE ASUNCIÓN

Avda España, Asunción
Telephone: (21) 507-080
Fax: (21) 213-734
E-mail: sgeneral@rec.una.py
Internet: www.una.py
Founded 1889
State control
Language of instruction: Spanish
Academic year: March to December
Rector: Prof. Ing. Agr. PEDRO GERARDO GONZÁLEZ GONZÁLEZ
Vice-Rector: Prof. Arq. AMADO FRANCO NAVONI
Gen. Sec.: Prof. Ing. Agr. JULIO RENÁN PANIAGUA
Librarian: Lic. JULIA ROMÁN RODRÍGUEZ
Library of 15,288 vols, 93 audiovisual material, 313 periodicals
Number of teachers: 6,200
Number of students: 42,000
Publications: *Researches and UNA studies* (2 a year), *UNA Revista* (2 a year, electronic)

DEANS

Faculty of Agricultural Engineering: Prof. Ing. Agr. LORENZO MEZA LÓPEZ
Faculty of Architecture, Design and Art: Prof. Arq. RICARDO MANUEL MEYER CANILLAS
Faculty of Chemistry: Prof. Dr ANDRÉS AMARILLA
Faculty of Dentistry: Prof. Dr RUBÉN DI TORE AQUINO
Faculty of Economics: Prof. Dr ANTONIO RAMÓN RODRÍGUEZ ROJAS
Faculty of Engineering: Prof. Ing. ISACIO EUSEBIO VALLEJOS AQUINO
Faculty of Exact and Natural Sciences: Prof. CONSTANTINO NICOLAS GUEFOS KAPSALIS
Faculty of Law and Social Sciences: Prof. Dr ANTONIO FRETES
Faculty of Medicine: Prof. Dr ANÍBAL PASTOR FILÁRTIGA LACROIX
Faculty of Philosophy: Prof. Lic. MARÍA ANGÉLICA GONZÁLEZ DE LEZCANO
Faculty of Veterinary Sciences: Prof. Dr FROILÁN ENRIQUE PERALTA TORRES
Polytechnic Faculty: Prof. ABEL BERNAL CASTILLO

DIRECTORS

Andrés Barbero Institute: Prof. Lic. ROSALÍA RODRÍGUEZ DE LÓPEZ
Health Sciences Research Institute: Dra GRACIELA VELÁZQUEZ

Higher Institute of Art: Prof. Arq. WILLIANS PAATS
Higher Institute of Languages: Prof. Lic. BEATRIZ DE SCHVARTZMAN
National Atomic Energy Commission: Prof. Lic. ZULMA VILLANUEVA DE DÍAZ (President)
National Computing Centre: Prof. Ing. CARLOS LUIS FILIPPI SANABRIA
Paraguay-Brazil Experimental College: Prof. Lic. EMILIANO RAMÍREZ MENCIA
Service Training Centre: Prof. Lic. EUFEMIO DANIEL GONZÁLEZ

UNIVERSIDAD NACIONAL DEL ESTE

POB 389, Calle 3 y Los Palmitos, Ciudad del Este, Alto Paraná
Telephone: (61) 63804
Fax: (61) 68664
Internet: www.une.edu.py
Founded 1993
Rector: Dr GLIBERTO RUIZ CARVALLO
Vice-Rector: Lic. VÍCTOR ALFREDO BRÍTEZ CHAMORRO
Faculties of agricultural engineering, economics, health sciences, law and social sciences, philosophy.

PERU

The Higher Education System

From the 16th century Peru was under Spanish control until independence was declared in 1821 and achieved in 1824. The oldest universities date from the period of Spanish rule, notably the Universidad Nacional Mayor de San Marcos de Lima (founded in 1551) and the Universidad Nacional de San Cristóbal de Huamanga (founded in 1677). The Universidad Nacional de la Libertad (founded in 1824) was the first university established in the independent period; its founder was Simón Bolívar. The Universidad Nacional de San Agustín de Arequipa (founded in 1828) followed shortly after. Higher education consists of pre-university and university levels. The Constitution of 1993 abolished the right to free university education. In 2000 there were 435,637 students in university-level education, and in 2008 there were 343,321 students enrolled at other institutions of higher education. In the same year 286,677 students were enrolled in vocational institutions and 20,472 attended specialist institutions.

Students must hold the certificate of completion of secondary education (Certificado de Educación Secundaria Común Completa) in order to sit the university entrance examination. The first undergraduate degree is the Bachelors (Bachiller), awarded after a three- to five-year period of specialization. Upon completion of a thesis the Licenciado or professional title is then awarded. Not every university awards postgraduate degrees, which are primarily the Masters (Maestría) and the Doctorate (Doctorado); both degrees require completion of two years of study.

Post-secondary technical and vocational education is provided by Teacher Training Institutes (Institutos Superiores Pedagógicos) and Higher Technological Institutes (Institutos Superiores Tecnológicos). The Especialista Profesional and Título de Bachiller Profesional are the main qualifications offered by Higher Technological Institutes.

Regulatory and Representative Bodies

GOVERNMENT

Ministry of Education: Avda Van De Velde 160, cuadra 33, Avda Javier Prado Este, San Borja, Lima 41; tel. (1) 435-3900; fax (1) 437-0471; e-mail postmaster@minedu.gob.pe; internet www.minedu.gob.pe; Minister José Antonio Chang Escobedo; Permanent Sec. José Enrique Cabrera García.

NATIONAL BODY

Asamblea Nacional de Rectores (Rectors' National Assembly): Calle Aldabas 337, Urb. Las Gardenias, Surco, Lima 33; tel. (1) 275-4608; e-mail webmaster@anr.edu.pe; internet www.anr.edu.pe; f. 1983; 34 mems; library of 30,000 vols; Pres. Dr Iván Rodríguez Chávez; Exec. Dir Ing. José Torres Vásquez; publs *Universidad, Escuelas y/o Carreras Profesionales, Grados y Títulos* (statistical bulletin), *Desarrollo Universitario* (bulletin).

Learned Societies

GENERAL

Academia Peruana de la Lengua (Peruvian Academy of Language): Palacio de Osambela, Conde de Superunda 298, Lima 1; fax (1) 427-7987; internet academiaperuanadelalengua.org; f. 1887; corresp. of the Real Academia Española (Madrid); 30 mems; Dir Dr Luis Jaime Cisneros; Sec. Dr Martha Hildebrandt; publ. *Boletín* (1 a year).

UNESCO Office Lima: Avda Javier Prado Este 2465, San Borja, Lima 41; tel. (1) 224-2526; fax (1) 476-9872; e-mail unescope@amauta.rcp.net.pe; internet www.unesco.org/lima; Rep. Patricia Uribe Arango.

ARCHITECTURE AND TOWN PLANNING

Colegio de Arquitectos del Perú: Avda San Felipe 999, Jesús María, Lima 11; tel. (1) 265-4098; fax (1) 471-5058; internet www.cap.org.pe; f. 1962; 3,717 mems; library of 3,500 vols; Dean Javier Sota Nadal.

BIBLIOGRAPHY, LIBRARY SCIENCE AND MUSEOLOGY

Asociación Peruana de Archiveros (Peruvian Association of Archivists): Archivo General de la Nación, Calle Manuel Cuadros s/n, Palacio de Justicia, Apdo 3124, Lima.

Colegio de Bibliotecólogos del Perú: Avda 2 de Mayo 1545, Oficina 218, Lima 27; fax (1) 442-7513; e-mail cbperu@gmail.com; internet cbp.tripod.com.pe; f. 1990; 320 mems; Dean Norma Altamirano de Hurtado.

EDUCATION

Asociación Nacional de Educadoras Sampedranas: Máximo Abril 695, Jesús María, Lima 11; tel. (1) 310562; f. 1910; aims to contribute to the development and improvement of national education; educational research, 'Education for Peace', educational innovation, institutional development; 6,200 mems; library of 1,000 vols with special collection: 'Education for Peace'; Pres. Peregrina Morgan de Goñi; Sec. Nanete Pérez de Pilco.

FINE AND PERFORMING ARTS

Asociación de Artistas Aficionados: Jr. Ica 323, Centro Histórico, Lima Cercado; tel. (1) 428-0432; e-mail aaaasociacion@yahoo.com; internet aaasociacion.iespana.es; f. 1938; 254 mems; presentation of plays, classical ballet and varied music programmes.

Instituto de Arte Peruano 'José Sabogal' (José Sabogal Institute of Peruvian Art): Avda Alfonso Ugarte 650, Apdo. 3048, Lima 1; tel. (1) 423-5892; fax (1) 423-5892; e-mail mncp@inictel.gob.pe; internet museodelacultura.perucultural.org.pe; f. 1946; under the auspices of the Museo Nacional de la Cultura Peruana; publ. *Revista del Museo Nacional* (1 a year).

Instituto Nacional de Cultura: Avda Javier Prado este 2465, Lima 41; tel. (1) 476-9933; fax (1) 476-9888; e-mail comunicaciones@inc.gob.pe; internet www.inc.gob.pe; f. 1971; official cultural institute; 24 brs; Dir Dr Luis Guillermo Lumbreras; publs *Revista Arqueológicas, Revista Gaceta Cultural, Revista de Historia y Cultura, Revista del Museo Nacional*.

Instituto Peruano de Cultura Hispánica (Peruvian Institute of Hispanic Culture): Calle de la Riva 426, Lima; f. 1947; 280 mems; publ. *Boletín*.

HISTORY, GEOGRAPHY AND ARCHAEOLOGY

Centro de Estudios Histórico-Militares del Perú (Centre of Historico-Military Studies of Peru): Paseo Colón 150, Lima 1; tel. (1) 230415; f. 1944; 1,098 mems; library of 13,800 vols; publ. *Revista*.

Centro de Investigación y Restauración de Bienes Monumentales del Instituto Nacional de Cultura: Casilla 5247, Jr. Ancash 769, Lima.

Instituto Geográfico Nacional (National Geographic Institute): Avc A. Aramburú 1190–1198, Surquillo, Lima 34; tel. (1) 475-3030; fax (1) 475-9960; e-mail jefatura@ign.gob.pe; internet www.ign.gob.pe; f. 1921; 300 mems; library of 3,200 vols; Man. Gral Div Carlos Alfonso Tafur Ganoza; publ. topographical, physical and political maps of Peru, *Boletín Informativo*.

Instituto Vizcardo de Estudios Históricos (Vizcardan Institute of Historical Studies): Porta 540, Miraflores, Lima; f. 1954; study of revolutionary movements for Spanish-American independence (1781–1820); publ. *Revista*.

Sociedad Geográfica de Lima (Lima Geographical Society): Jirón Puno 450, Apdo 1176, Lima 100; tel. (1) 427-3723; fax (1) 426-9930; e-mail antunez@socgeolima.org; f. 1888; library of 13,400 vols, also archives, maps and museum; 750 mems, including corresp. and hon.; Pres. Dr Santiago Antúnez de Mayolo Rynning; Vice-Pres. Ing. Zaniel Novoa Goicochea; publs *Anuario Geográfico del Perú, Boletín* (1 a year), *Diccionario Geográfico del Perú, Forjando los Genios del Mañana* (1 a year).

LANGUAGE AND LITERATURE

Alliance Française de Lima: Avda Arequipa 4595, Casilla 18, 1667 Lima; tel. (1) 610-8000; fax (1) 610-8020; e-mail informes@alianzafrancesa.org.pe; internet www.alianzafrancesa.org.pe; offers courses and exams in French language and culture and promotes cultural exchange with France; attached teaching centres in Arequipa, Chiclayo, Cusco, Huancayo, Iquitos, Piura and Trujillo; Dir of Operations, Peru PAUL-ÉLIE LÉVY.

British Council: 22nd fl., Torre Parque Mar, Avda Jose Larco 1301, Miraflores, Lima 18; tel. (1) 617-3060; fax (1) 617-3065; internet www.britishcouncil.org/peru; offers courses and examinations in English language and British culture and promotes cultural exchange with the UK; Dir FRANK FITZPATRICK.

Goethe-Institut: Jr. Nazca 722, Jesús María, Lima 100; tel. (1) 433-3180; fax (1) 431-0494; e-mail info@lima.goethe.org; internet www.goethe.de/ins/pe/lim/esindex.htm; offers courses and exams in German language and culture and promotes cultural exchange with Germany; library of 7,500 vols, 24 periodicals; Dir PETRA BEHLKE-CAMPOS; Dir for Admin. FRANK MEYER.

MEDICINE

Academia de Estomatología del Perú (Peruvian Academy of Stomatology): Calle Los Próceres 261, 2do Piso, Urb. Sta Constanza, Lima 33; tel. (1) 435-1623; fax (1) 435-1623; e-mail academiadeestomatologia@terra.com.pe; internet www.academiadeestomatologiadelperu.com; f. 1929; 165 mems; library of 600 vols; Pres. Dra ESTHER FLORES MUBARAK; Sec. PATRICIA FRY OROPEZA; publ. *Estomatología Integrada* (2 a year).

Academia Nacional de Medicina (National Academy of Medicine): Avda Belén 331, San Isidro, Lima; tel. (1) 441-3938; e-mail academia.nac@speedy.com.pe; internet www.acadnacmedicina.org.pe; f. 1884; 40 mems; 40 associate mems; 40 corresp. and hon. mems; Pres. Dr GINO COSTA ELICE; Perm. Sec. Dr JAVIER MARIATEGUI; publ. *Boletín de la Academia Nacional de Medicina*.

Academia Peruana de Cirugía: Malecón Armendáriz 791, Miraflores; f. 1940; activities relate to the development of surgery in Peru; national and foreign membership; 100 titular mems and unlimited number of associates; Pres. Dr LUIS GURMENDI; publ. *Revista*.

Asociación Médica Peruana (Peruvian Medical Association): Jirón Camaná 381, of. 207, Lima 1; tel. (1) 427-4590; fax (1) 321-0037; e-mail amp@amp.pe; internet www.amp.pe; f. 1920; 1,499 mems; Pres. Dr HERBERTH CUBA GARCÍA; Gen. Sec. Dr JULIO CÉSAR SÁNCHEZ TONOHUYE; publ. *Revista Médica Peruana*.

Federación Médica Peruana (Peruvian Medical Federation): Jr. Almirante Guisse 2165, Lince, Lima; tel. (1) 470-5036; fax (1) 265-2890; e-mail federacion_medica_peruana@yahoo.es; internet www.federacionmedicaperuana.org; f. 1942; 1,230 mems; Pres. Dr LEONCIO DIAZ DIAZ; Gen. Sec. Dr MANUEL ALVAREZ LARRAONDO; publ. *Boletín de la Federación Médica Peruana*.

Sociedad Peruana de Neumología (Peruvian Society of Respiratory Medicine): Avda Guardia Civil 236, San Isidro, Lima 27; tel. (1) 226-2867; internet www.spneumologia.org.pe; f. 1935; 280 mems; Pres. Dr ALBERTO MATSUNO FUCHIGAMI; Gen. Sec. Dr ANTONIO TOKUMOTO KISHABA; publs *Boletín Informativo*, *Revista SPN*.

NATURAL SCIENCES

Biological Sciences

Sociedad Entomológica del Perú: Apartado Postal 14-0413, Lima; Universidad Nacional Agraria La Molina, Avda La Universidad s/n, Museo de Entomología, Lima 14; tel. (1) 349-5647 ext. 330; e-mail sepperu@sepperu.net; internet www.sepperu.net; f. 1956; 700 mems; library of 9,500 vols; Pres. ELIZABETH YOLANDA NÚÑEZ SACARÍAS DE DIOSES; Sec. MÓNICA NARREA CANGO; publ. *Revista Peruana de Entomología* (1 a year).

Mathematical Sciences

Instituto Nacional de Estadística (National Institute of Statistics): Avda Gral Garzón 662, Jesús María, Lima 11; tel. (1) 433-3104; fax (1) 433-3159; e-mail infoinei@inei.gob.pe; internet www.inei.gob.pe; f. 1975; involved in population, housing, socio-economic and agricultural censuses and surveys; plans statistical policy of country; library of 9,000 vols; Dir FARID MATUK CASTRO; publs *Compendio Económico* (1 a year), *Cuentas Nacionales—PBI Nacional* (1 a year), *Indice de precios al consumidor* (12 a year), *Informe Económico Mensual* (12 a year).

Physical Sciences

Asociación Peruana de Astronomía: Morro Solar s/n, Chorrillos, Lima 9; fax (1) 431-3084; e-mail wcentauri@apa.com.pe; internet www.apa.com.pe; f. 1946; 550 mems; library of 1,000 vols, 1,000 periodicals; Pres. Ing. VÍCTOR ESTREMADOYRO; Sec. Dr JOSÉ DOMINGO GÓMEZ SÁNCHEZ; publ. *Boletín* (3 a year).

Sociedad Geológica del Perú (Peruvian Geological Society): Arnaldo Marquez 2277, Distrito de Jesús María, Lima 11; tel. (1) 461-2362; fax (1) 461-5272; e-mail sgp@sgp.org.pe; internet www.sgp.org.pe; f. 1924; 800 mems; library of 40,000 vols; Pres. Ing. CARLOS MORALES BERMÚDEZ LÁMPARO; publs *Boletín* (1 a year), *Resumenes Extendidos* (conference proceedings, every 3 years).

Sociedad Peruana de Espeleología y Carstología (Peruvian Speleological and Karstological Society): Casilla 18-1209, Lima 18; La Mariscala 115, Lima 27; fax (1) 261-5305; e-mail peru.spec@gmail.com; f. 1965; Pres. Ing. CARLOS MORALES-BERMÚDEZ LÁMPARO; publ. *Cavernas Peruanas*.

Sociedad Química del Perú (Peruvian Chemistry Society): Avda Nicolas de Aranibar 696, Sta. Beatriz, Lima; tel. (1) 472-3925; internet www.sqperu.com; f. 1933; 1,200 mems; library of 5,600 vols; Pres. Dr JUAN JOSÉ LEÓN CAM; Gen. Sec. Dr JORGE REINALDO ANGULO CORNEJO; publ. *Revista* (4 a year).

RELIGION, SOCIOLOGY AND ANTHROPOLOGY

Centro Amazónico de Antropología y Aplicación Práctica (CAAAP): Apdo 14-0166, Lima 14; Avda González Prada 626, Magdalena del Mar, Lima; tel. (1) 460-0763; fax (1) 463-8846; e-mail caaapdirec@caaap.org.pe; internet www.caaap.org.pe; f. 1974; defends the cultural identity and the way of life of marginalized Amazonian people and seeks to protect natural resources in the Amazonian region; library of 5,000 vols; Dir FABIOLA LUNA; publs *Amazonía Peruana* (2 a year), *El Trueno* (4 a year), *Nuestra Tierra—Nuestra Vida* (4 a year).

Instituto de Estudios Etnológicos (Institute of Ethnological Studies): Avda Alfonso Ugarte 650, Apdo. 3048, Lima 1; tel. (1) 423-5892; fax (1) 423-5892; e-mail mncp@inictel.gob.pe; internet museodelacultura.perucultural.org.pe; f. 1946; under auspices of Museo Nacional de la Cultura Peruana; publ. *Revista del Museo Nacional* (1 a year).

Instituto de Estudios Islámicos: Calle Rey de Bahamonde 121, Vista Alegre, Surco, Lima 33; tel. (1) 489720; f. 1959; sound archives, numismatic collection, etc.; interests include economics, sociology and politics of contemporary Muslim world, the Palestinian problem, the Iranian Islamic revolution, the al-Fateh (Jamahiriya) revolution, and the diffusion of Islamic religious values in South America; special interest in Islamic-America relations in 16th and 17th centuries and nowadays; Pres. Dr RAFAEL GUEVARA BAZÁN; Chief Officer Prof. ELVA ZEGARRA TORREBLANCA.

Instituto Indigenista Peruano (Peruvian Institute of Indian Affairs): c/o Ministerio de Agricultura, Avda Salaverry s/n, Jesús María, Lima 11; f. 1946; studies the specific problems of indigenous groups; library of 1,500 vols, 1,046 periodicals; Dir Ing. CARLOS EDUARDO MENDOZA SALDIVAR; publ. *Perú-Indígena* (1 a year).

TECHNOLOGY

Asociación de Ingenieros Civiles del Perú: Nicolás de Piérola 788, 4° piso, Casilla 1314, Lima.

Asociación Electrotécnica Peruana: Av. República de Chile 284, Oficina 201, Jesús María, Lima; tel. (1) 330-4635; fax (1) 433-6543; e-mail informes@aep-peru.org; internet www.aep-peru.org; f. 1943; Pres. Ing. ALEX SALAZAR MARZAL; Sec. Ing. JORGE FLORES MARCHENA.

Instituto Peruano de Ingenieros Mecánicos: Avda República de Chile 284, Of. 201, Lima; Dir ROBERTO HEREDIA ZAVADA.

Sociedad de Ingenieros del Perú (Society of Peruvian Engineers): Avda Nicolás Piérola 788, Casilla 20085, Lima Cercado; tel. (1) 423-3804; fax (1) 424-6514; e-mail soc_ing_peru@terra.com.pe; library of 15,000 vols; Pres. Ing. RAUL GUERRA PÉREZ; Exec. Sec. Arq. CÉSAR SILVA HURTADO; publ. *Ingeniería* (3 a year).

Research Institutes

GENERAL

Institut de Recherche pour le Développement (IRD): Casilla 18-1209, Lima 18; Calle Teruel 357, Mirafolores, Lima 18; tel. (1) 441-3223; fax (1) 441-3223; e-mail perou@ird.fr; internet www.peru.ird.fr; f. 1967; research in geology, agronomy, botany, ecology, economy, archaeology, geography; 15 staff; library of 950 vols; natural history museum; Rep. GÉRARD HÉRAIL; publ. *Boletín Sistemas Agrarios*; (see main entry under France).

AGRICULTURE, FISHERIES AND VETERINARY SCIENCE

Estación Experimental Vista Florida: km 8 Carretera a Ferreñafe, Chiclayo; tel. (74) 238753; fax (74) 272950; e-mail vflorida@inia.gob.pe; f. 1970; crops research (plant protection, rice, corn, beans, sorghum); 26 staff; library of 5,000 vols; Dir Ing. SEGUNDO FERNÁNDEZ ROMERO.

Instituto Nacional de Investigación y Promoción Agropecuaria (National Agricultural Research Institute): Avda Guzmán Blanco 390, Lima 5; tel. (1) 317159; f. 1929; library of 50,000 vols; technical staff 350; Exec. Dir Dr JAVIER GAZZO FERNÁNDEZ DÁVILA; publs *Revista de Investigación Avances en Investigación*, *Serie de Boletín Investigación*, *Avances en Investigación*, *Serie de Boletín Técnico*, *Informes Especiales*, *Divulgaciones*, *Boletín Bibliográfico*.

ECONOMICS, LAW AND POLITICS

Instituto Peruano para la Investigación de la Estadística: Avda Benavides 190, Lima 18; tel. (1) 464064; f. 1974; study of statistics in general, and especially in relation to economics; library of 5,000 vols; organizes symposia, seminars, courses, etc.

EDUCATION

Instituto Experimental de Educación Primaria No. 1: Barranco, Avda Miraflores 200, Lima; f. 1940; studies systems and methods for the development of learning and the means to evaluate and control the results; library of scholastic texts; Dir Prof. NARCISO GONZÁLEZ CH.; publ. *Boletín*.

MEDICINE

Instituto de Cultura Alimentaria Birchner-Benner: Diez Canseco 487, Miraflores, Lima; fax (1) 444-4250; f. 1979; research into diet, especially of meat-substitutes and high-nutrition and low-cost food mixtures; warns about inadequate diet; promotes agriculture by biological methods; film and sound archives; Pres. CÉSAR MORALES GARCÍA; Sec. MARCELA CÁRDENAS.

Instituto de Investigaciones Alérgicas 'Dr Luis E. Betetta' ('Dr Luis E. Betetta' Allergy Research Institute): Avda La Marina 2501, San Miguel, Lima; tel. and fax (1) 578-1083; e-mail www.alergia.betetta@speedy.com.pe; f. 1965.

Instituto Nacional de Salud (National Institute of Health): Cápac Yupanqui No. 1400, Jesús Maria, Lima 11; tel. (1) 471-3254; fax (1) 471-7443; internet www.ins.gob.pe; f. 1936; communicable diseases, occupational diseases, nutritional disorders, food and drug quality control, research, production of vaccines and reagents, traditional medicine; library of 5,000 books, 30,000 journals, 1,000 theses; Head Dr CÉSAR NÁQUIRA VELARDE; publs *Boletín* (52 a year), *Revista Peruana de Medicina Experimental y Salud Pública* (4 a year).

NATURAL SCIENCES

General

Instituto del Mar del Perú (IMARPE) (Peruvian Marine Institute): Esq. Gral. Valle y Gamarra, Apdo 22, Callao; tel. (51) 420-2000; internet www.imarpe.gob.pe; f. 1964; oceanography, marine biology, fisheries, aquaculture, aquatic ecotoxicology, hydroacoustics, biodiversity; library of 75,000 vols; Pres. Contra-Almirante HUGO ARÉVALO ESCARÓ; Exec. Dir Econ. GODOFREDO CAÑOTE SANTAMARINA; Scientific Dir Biol. RENATO GUEVARA-CARRASCO; publs *Boletín* (scientific papers, 1 or 2 a year), *Informe* (research results, 6 a year), *Informe Progresivo* (current research activities, 12 a year).

Biological Sciences

Instituto de Biología Andina (Institute of Andean Biology): Facultad de Medicina de San Fernando, Universidad Nacional Mayor de San Marcos, Avda Grau 755, Lima 1; tel. (1) 619-7000; e-mail ofinfmed@unmsm.edu.pe; f. 1930; affiliated to the Faculty of Medicine, San Marcos Univ.; laboratories in Lima, Morococha and Puno; mobile laboratory research on physiology of inhabitants of the Andes and their resistance to high altitudes, acclimatization and fertility of animals taken to high altitudes with a view to industrial use, methods of hygiene, adaptive faculties of humans at great heights, chronic mountain sickness and remedies, ecology and sociological problems; library of 1,091 vols, 400 periodicals; Dir Dr TULIO VELÁSQUEZ; publ. *Archivos del Instituto de Biología Andina* (4 a year).

Physical Sciences

Dirección General de Meteorología del Perú (National Meteorological Service): Jr. Cahuide 785, Jesús María, Lima 11; tel. (1) 614-1414; e-mail webmaster@senamhi.gob.pe; internet www.senamhi.gob.pe; f. 1928; 79 primary stations; publ. *Boletín* (1 a year).

Instituto Geofísico del Perú (Geophysical Institute): Calle Badajoz 169, Mayorazgo IV Etapa, Lima; tel. (1) 317-2300; e-mail web@geo.igp.gob.pe; internet www.igp.gob.pe; f. 1919 as Huancayo Magnetic Observatory of the Carnegie Institution of Washington, transferred to the Peruvian Government 1947; education sector; observatories in Huancayo, Jicamarca, Ancón, Arequipa and Lima; basic and mission-oriented research; international programmes in geomagnetism, seismology, atmospheric sciences, solar activity and natural hazards; Pres. Dr MANUEL CHANG.

TECHNOLOGY

Instituto Geológico, Minero y Metalúrgico (Institute of Geology, Mining and Metallurgy): Apdo 889, Avda Canadá 1470, San Borja, Lima; tel. (1) 224-2965; fax (1) 225-4540; e-mail info@ingemmet.gob.pe; internet www.ingemmet.gob.pe; f. 1978; carries out and coordinates geological mapping at regional scale and evaluates mineral resources; environmental assessment and ecological zonification; provides mining and metallurgical information; library of 33,098 vols; Pres. ROMULO MUCHO MAMANI; Dir HUGO RIVERA MANTILLA; publs *Boletín Serie A: Carta Geológica Nacional* (irregular), *Boletín Serie B: Geología Económica* (irregular), *Boletín Serie C: Geodinámica e Ingeniería Geológica* (irregular), *Boletín Serie D: Estudios Regionales* (irregular), *Informes Técnicos* (irregular), *Newsletter* (electronic, 12 a year).

Instituto Peruano de Energía Nuclear (Peruvian Nuclear Energy Institute): Av. Canadá 1470, San Borja, Lima 41; tel. (1) 226-0030; fax (1) 226-0026; e-mail sege@ipen.gob.pe; internet www.ipen.gob.pe; f. 1975; researches into peaceful uses of nuclear energy in medicine, biology, agriculture and industry, prospecting, mining and processing of uranium ores; management of nuclear reactor and operation of a radioisotope production plant; nucleo-electricity planning; training and research; library: information and documentation centre of 75,000 vols, periodicals, monographs; Pres. JORGE DU BOIS GERVASI; Exec. Dir Dr CONRADO SEMINARIO ARCE; publs *Boletín de Informaciones* (4 a year), *Informes*.

Affiliated Institute:

Centro Superior de Estudios Nucleares: Avda Canadá 1470, San Borja, Lima 41; tel. (1) 226-0030; fax (1) 224-8991; e-mail csen@ipen.gob.pe; f. 1972; information and training centre on nuclear energy and its applications; Dir Prof. EDGARD MEDINA FLORES.

Libraries and Archives

Arequipa

Biblioteca de la Universidad Nacional de San Agustín: Calle Santa Catalina 117, Arequipa; f. 1900; 430,000 vols, 1,204 pamphlets and 535 periodicals; in addition the University has 12 specialized libraries; Dir Dr JORGE DÍAZ ENCINAS; publ. *Revista de Investigación de la Universidad*.

Biblioteca Pública Municipal de Arequipa: Portal de la Municipalidad 110, Arequipa; f. 1879; 51,500 vols; Librarian WALTER ALVAREZ THOMAS; also houses *Casa de la Cultura*.

Callao

Biblioteca de la Escuela Naval del Perú (Naval School Library): La Punta, Callao; f. 1914; Librarian ABEL ULLOA FERNÁNDEZ-PRADA; specialized library of 6,500 vols.

Biblioteca Pública Municipal Piloto: Esq. Ruiz y Colón, Apdo 270, Callao; tel. (14) 290558; f. 1936, reorganized 1957; 48,312 vols; 42 mems; Dir ROSA SÁNCHEZ DE WU.

Lima

Archivo General de la Nación (National Archives): Jr. Camaná 125 con Pasaje Piura, Lima; tel. (1) 427-5930; fax (1) 426-7221; e-mail agn.peru@mail.pol.com.pe; internet archivogeneral.gob.pe; f. 1861; 2 sections, Administrative and Historical; Dir Dr LIZARDO PASQUEL COBOS; publs *Legislación Archivística Peruana*, *Revista del AGN*.

Archivo Histórico Municipal: Jr. Conde de Superunda 141, 2do piso, Palacio Municipal, Lima; tel. (1) 315-1540; e-mail biblioteca@munlima.gob.pe; internet www.munlima.gob.pe/biblioteca/archivo_municipal; f. 1963; documents, certificates from the 19th century; Librarian LUIS E. WUFFARDEN.

Biblioteca Central de la Universidad Nacional de Ingeniería: Avda Tupac Amaru 210, El Rimac, Lima 25; tel. (1) 481-1070; e-mail webmaster@uni.edu.pe; internet www.lisnet.uni.edu.pe; 29,000 vols; Librarian JUANA PAREJA MARMANILLO.

Biblioteca Central de la Universidad Nacional Mayor de San Marcos (San Marcos National University General Library): Avda Germán Amézaga s/n, Lima 1; tel. (1) 619-7000 ext. 7618; e-mail achoquem@unmsm.edu.pe; internet sisbib.unmsm.edu.pe; f. 1551; the colln corresponding to the colonial period was incorporated in the *Biblioteca Pública*—now the *Biblioteca Nacional*—when the latter was founded in 1821; the Peruvian Section has valuable material on history, law, and literature; Head of Library System Lic. ALEJANDRO SALOMÓN CHOQUE MARTÍNEZ; 450,000 vols; publ. *Boletín Bibliográfico* (1 a year).

Biblioteca de la Municipalidad de Lima: Jr. Conde de Superunda 141, 2do piso, Palacio Municipal, Lima; tel. (1) 315-1540; e-mail biblioteca@munlima.gob.pe; f. 1935; gen. reference about Lima and its municipal govt; 22,000 vols; Librarian LUZMILA TELLO.

Biblioteca del Ministerio de Relaciones Exteriores (Library of the Ministry of Foreign Affairs): Palacio Torre-Tagle, Jirón Ucayali 363, Lima; tel. (1) 311-2952; f. 1921; 30,000 vols; Dir MANUEL G. GALDO; publ. *Maris Aestus*.

Biblioteca Nacional del Perú (National Library): Avda Abancay 4ta Cdra s/n, Lima 01; tel. (1) 428-7690; fax (1) 427-7331; internet www.binape.gob.pe; f. 1821 by José de San Martín; possesses copies of the first printed works in Peru and the Americas; 736,465 vols, 32,500 MSS, 12,499 maps, 11,000 photographs, 2,164,413 periodicals; Dir Dr SINESIO LÓPEZ JIMÉNEZ; publs *Bibliografía Peruana* (1 a year), *Bibliografías de intelectuales Peruanos* (irregular), *Boletín de la Biblioteca Nacional* (irregular), *Gaceta Bibliotecaria del Perú* (irregular), *Fénix* (1 a year), *Revista Libros y Artes* (4 a year).

Sistema de Bibliotecas de la Pontificia Universidad Católica del Perú: Apdo 1761, Lima; tel. (1) 626-2000 ext. 3400; fax (1) 626-2861; e-mail biblio@pucp.edu.pe;

internet biblioteca.pucp.edu.pe; f. 1917; 800,000 vols, 26,049 audiovisual items, 2,260 electronic items; Dir CARMELA VILLANUEVA; System Librarian RAUL SIFUENTES.

Museums and Art Galleries

Arequipa

Museo Arqueológico (Archaeological Museum): Avda Independencia s/n, Ciudad Universitaria, Arequipa; tel. (54) 229719; f. 1933; ceramics, mummies; Dir Dr E. LINARES MÁLAGA.

Ayacucho

Museo Histórico Regional de Ayacucho (Regional Historical Museum of Ayacucho): Jirón, Calle 28 de Julio Noi 106, Ayacucho; tel. (66) 912056; f. 1946; archaeology, anthropology, history and popular crafts; library of 4,724 vols (incl. bound periodicals); Dir FREDY LAGOS ARRIARÁN; publ. *Anuario*.

Callao

Museo del Ejército del Perú (Army Museum of Peru): Fortaleza del Real Felipe, Plaza de la Independencia s/n, Callao; tel. (14) 429-0532; f. 1984; Dir LUIS LOAYZA MORALES.

Museo Naval del Perú (Naval History Museum): Avda Jorge Chávez 123, Plaza Grau, Callao; tel. (14) 613-6868 ext. 6794; fax (14) 429-4793; e-mail informes@museonaval.com.pe; internet www.museonaval.com.pe; f. 1958; library: specialist library of 7,948 vols; Dir Contralmirante FERNANDO CASARETTO ALVARADO; publ. *Fuentes para la Historia Naval*.

Cuzco

Museo Arqueológico: Cuesta del Almirante 103 esq. Calle Ataúd, Cusco; tel. (84) 237380; remains from the Inca period incl. stone objects, funerary metalwork, ceramics, textiles, vessels, evidence of trepanning, embalming, gold, silver, copper and turquoise idols, ceremonial objects, jugs; 17th-century portraits of Incas and Indian chiefs; Dir Dr LUIS A. PARDO.

Museo Histórico Regional del Cusco: Calle Heladeros s/n, Cusco; tel. (84) 223-245; fax (84) 223-831; f. 1946; Peruvian colonial art, Cusco schools of painting affiliated to Inst. Nacional de Cultura; Dir ANTONIA VEGA CENTENO B.; publ. *Revista del Museo Histórico Regional*.

Huancayo

Museo Arqueológico 'Federico Gálvez Durand' de la Gran Unidad Escolar 'Santa Isabel': Jr. Santa Isabel 567, San Carlos, Huancayo; tel. (64) 231061; f. 1952; 1,654 archaeological specimens from Nazca and other Peruvian cultures; examples of weaving, gold and bronze ornaments, fossils.

Huánuco

Museo Regional 'Leoncio Prado': Calle 2 de Mayo 680, Huánuco; f. 1945; natural history; Curator RICARDO E. FLORES.

Huaráz

Museo Arqueologico de Ancash: Avda Luzuriaga 762, Plaza de Armes, Huaráz, Ancash; tel. (43) 42-1551; fax (43) 42-4849; e-mail museoarqueologicodeancash@hotmail.com; internet www.mcultura.gop.pe; f. 1935; pre-Hispanic history of the Ancash region; exhibits incl. ceramics, metalwork, textiles, human remains; collns from the Chavín, Recuay, Moche, Wari, Chimu and Inca cultures; largest Lithic Park in South America, incl. stone carvings and megalithic statues from the Recuay culture; Dir Arq. RAFAEL PALOMINO PRADO; publ. *Cuadernillo de Difusión*.

Ica

Museo Cabrera: Plaza de Armas, Calle Bolívar 174, Ica; tel. (56) 231933; f. 1966; collection of ancient engraved stones and pottery; library of 100,000 vols; Dir (vacant).

Lambayeque

Museo Regional Arqueológico 'Bruning' de Lambayeque (Bruning Archaeological Museum): Avda Huamachuco s/n, Lambayeque; tel. (74) 232-110; fax (74) 233-440; f. 1924; nearly 8,000 exhibits, of which 1,366 gold, 110 silver; textile, ceramic, wooden and stone pieces; 2 unique blue and black granite mortars incised with mythological figures in 'Chavin' style; Dir WALTER ALVA.

Lima

Museo de Arte de Lima (Museum of Art): Paseo Colón 125, Lima; tel. (1) 423-6332; fax (1) 331-0126; e-mail prensa@museodearte.org.pe; internet www.museodearte.org.pe; inaugurated in its present form in 1961; exhibits of Peruvian art from its origins to the present day; Pre-Columbian Dept: ceramics, carvings, Paracas woven material dating from 400BC; Colonial Dept: furniture, sculpture, paintings, religious art, silver; Modern Dept: furniture and paintings since 19th century; an important film archive; studio art courses; library of 4,000 items; restoration and conservation laboratory; Dir NATALIA MAJLUF BRAHIM; publ. *Bulletin* (6 a year).

Museo de Arte Italiano: Paseo de la República 250, Lima 1; tel. (1) 423-9932; fax (1) 423-9932; f. 1923; 1920s Italian art donated by the Italian colony in Peru; organizes courses and conferences; library of 500 vols; Dir IRENE VELAOCHAGA REY.

Museo de Historia Natural de la Universidad Nacional Mayor de San Marcos (Natural History Museum of the National University of San Marcos): Apartado 14-0434, Lima 14; Avda Arenales 1256, Jesús María, Lima; tel. (1) 471-0117; fax (1) 265-6819; e-mail museohn@unmsm.edu.pe; internet museohn.unmsm.edu.pe; f. 1918; incl. Herbario San Marcos (USM), with 300,000 specimens largely of Peruvian flora and units of zoology, botany, ecology, and geosciences; zoological collns; library of 8,000 vols; Dir Prof. Dr GERARDO LAMAS MÜLLER; publs *Boletín del Museo de Historia Natural UNMSM, Nueva Serie* (irregular), *Memorias, Serie 'A' Zoología, Serie 'B' Botánica, Serie 'C' Geología, Serie de Divulgación* (irregular).

Museo del Virreinato (Museum of the Viceroys): Quinta de Presa, Jirón Chira 344, Rímac, Lima; tel. (1) 481-3867; f. 1935; sited in an 18th-century mansion; exhibits relating to the period of the Spanish Viceroys; Dir JOSÉ FLORES ARAOS; publ. *Revista*.

Museo Geológico de la Universidad Nacional de Ingeniería del Perú (Geological Museum of the National University of Engineering): Campus Universitario, Av. Túpac Amaru km 4.5, Rimac, Lima; tel. (1) 481-1070 ext. 364; fax (1) 382-2174; e-mail cpinto@uni.edu.pe; f. 1891 as Museo de Yacimentos Minerales y Metalíferos de la Escuela Nacional de Ingenieros, name changed 1955; incorporates the Raymondi collections; Chief of Dept. of Geology JULIO DAVILA V.

Museo Larco (Larco Museum): Avda Bolívar 1515, Pueblo Libre, Lima 21; tel. (1) 461-1312; fax (1) 461-5640; e-mail webmaster@museolarco.org; internet museolarco.org; f. 1926; Peruvian pre-Columbian history; colln of gold, silver, erotica; 45,000 classified archaeological objects; library of 10,000 vols; Exec. Dir ANDRÉS ALVAREZ CALDERÓN; Curator ULLA HOLMQUIST.

Branch Museum:

Museo de Arte Precolombino: Plaza de Las Nazarenas 231, Cusco; tel. (84) 233-210; fax (84) 233-210; e-mail amap@infonegocio.net.pe; internet map.perucultural.org.pe; f. 2003; arts of ancient Peruvian cultures; 450 objects from 1250BC to AD 1532; Dir ANDRÉS ALVAREZ CALDERÓN; Exec. Dir EDGAR CASAVERDE.

Museo Nacional de Arqueología, Antropología e Historia del Perú (National Museum of Archaeology, Anthropology and History): Plaza Bolívar s/n, Pueblo Libre, Lima 21; tel. (1) 463-5070; fax (1) 463-2009; f. 1945; library of 30,000 vols; colln contains pre-Inca and Inca remains, and artefacts from the colonial and republican periods; Dir FERNANDO ROSAS MOSCOSO; publs *Boletines, Arqueológicas, Historia y Cultura, Cuadernos de Investigaciones*.

Museo Nacional de la Cultura Peruana: Avda Alfonso Ugarte 650, Apdo 3048, Lima 1; tel. (1) 423-5892; fax (1) 423-5892; e-mail mncp@inc.gob.pe; internet museodelacultura.perucultural.org.pe; f. 1946; responsible for Instituto de Estudios Etnológicos and the Instituto de Arte Peruano 'José Sabogal'; popular art and ethnography; ethno-historical library and a photographic archive; Dir GLADYS ROQUEZ DIAZ; publs *Revista del Museo Nacional* (1 a year), *Boletín* (4 a year).

Museo Postal y Filatélico del Perú (Postal and Philatelic Museum): Pasaje Piura, Lima 1; tel. (1) 428-0400; f. 1931; library of 100 vols; Dir DORA IBERICO CASTRO.

Trujillo

Museo de Arqueología e Historia de la Universidad Nacional de Trujillo: Jr. Junín 682, Trujillo; tel. (44) 249322; f. 1946; Dir Dr JORGE ZEVALLOS QUIÑONES; publ. *Chimor*.

National Universities

UNIVERSIDAD NACIONAL AGRARIA LA MOLINA

Avda La Molina s/n, La Molina, Lima 12
Telephone: (1) 349-5647
E-mail: orgi@lamolina.edu.pe
Internet: www.lamolina.edu.pe

Founded 1902, fmrly Escuela Nacional de Agricultura
Language of instruction: Spanish
Academic year: April to December (2 semesters)

Rector: Ing. FRANCISCO DELGADO DE LA FLOR BADARACCO
Dir for Postgraduate School: Dr SALOMÓN HELFGOTT
Dir for Int. Office: Ing. ROBERTO UGAS
Number of teachers: 495
Number of students: 4,100
Publication: *Anales Científicos* (3 a year)

DEANS

Agricultural Engineering: Dr ABEL MEJIA MARCACUZCO
Agronomy: Dr LEONOR MATTOS CALDERÓN
Economics and Planning: Ing. LUÍS JÍMENEZ DÍAZ
Fisheries: Ing. RAÚL PORTURAS OLAECHEA

Food Science and Technology: Dr AUGUSTO MONTEZ GUTIÉRREZ
Forestry: Ing. JOSÉ DANCE CABALLERO
Postgraduate School: Dr SALOMÓN HELFGOTT
Sciences: Dr EDUARDO GÓMEZ-CORNEJO BELGRANO
Zootechnics: Dr MAÑUEL ROSEMBERG BARRON

UNIVERSIDAD NACIONAL AGRARIA DE LA SELVA

Avda Universitaria s/n km 1.5, Tingo María Huánuco
Telephone: (62) 562342
Fax: (62) 561156
E-mail: unas@unas.edu.pe
Internet: www.unas.edu.pe
Founded 1964
State control
Language of instruction: Spanish
Academic year: April to December
Rector: Dr MILTHON MUÑOZ BERROCAL
Vice-Rector for Academic Affairs: Dr JOSÉ WILFREDO ZAVALA SOLORZANO
Vice-Rector for Admin. Affairs: Ing. JYTAVCLERH VARGAS CLEMENTE
Sec.-Gen.: TITO F. GONZÁLEZ MANRIQUE DE LARA
Central Library Dir: KARINA DEL AGUILA VELA
Number of teachers: 190
Number of students: 1,533
Publication: *Tropicultura*

DEANS
Agronomy: Ing. SEGUNDO RODRIGUEZ DELGADO
Animal Breeding: Ing. MIGUELPEREZ OLANO
Economics and Administration: Lic. VICTOR CHACON LOPEZ
Food Industries: Ing. RAUL NATIVIDAD FERRER
Information Systems: Dr MAXIMO DIONISIO GARMA
Renewable Natural Resources: Ing. LUCIO MANRIQUE DE LARA SUÁREZ

UNIVERSIDAD NACIONAL DEL ALTIPLANO

Av. Floral 1153, Puno
Telephone: (51) 352-206
E-mail: webmaster@unap.edu.pe
Internet: www.unap.edu.pe
Founded 1856
Academic year: March to December
Rector: Dr VICTOR TORRES ESTEVES
Admin. Vice-Rector for Econ.: FRANCISCO GUTIERREZ GUTIERREZ
Vice-Rector: Prof. VICTOR GALLEGOS MONROY
Head of Personnel and Gen. Services: HERMOGENES MENDOZA ANCCO
Librarian: Prof. SERAFÍN CALSIN MAMANI
Number of teachers: 623
Number of students: 10,202
Publications: *Revistas problemáticas*, *Revista Universitaria*, *Revista Visión Agraria*

DEANS
Accounting and Administration: E. PINEDA QUISPE
Agriculture: R. SERRUTO COLQUE
Agricultural Engineering: W. SALAS PALMA
Biological Sciences: S. ATENCIO LIMACHI
Chemical Engineering: N. VILLAFUERTE PRUDENCIO
Civil Engineering, Architecture and Systems: P. ARROYO GONZALES
Economic Engineering: L. AVILA ROJAS
Education: J. L. CACERES MONROY
Health Sciences: R. LÓPEZ VELÁSQUEZ
Law and Political Science: J. VALDEZ PEÑARANDA
Metallurgy and Geological Engineering: H. MANRIQUE MEZA
Mining Engineering: V. NAVARRO TORRES
Nursing: N. CALSIN CHIRINOS
Postgraduate School: F. CÁCEDA DÍAZ
Social Sciences: M. CANO OJEDA
Social Work: G. PINTO SOTELO
Statistics for Engineering: E. CALMET URIA
Veterinary Medicine and Stockbreeding: Prof. C. SÁNCHEZ VIVEROS

UNIVERSIDAD NACIONAL DE LA AMAZONÍA PERUANA

Apdo 496, Iquitos
Sargento Lores 385, Iquitos, Loreto
Telephone: (65) 234140
E-mail: infounap@unapiquitos.edu.pe
Internet: www.unapiquitos.edu.pe
Founded 1962
State control
Language of instruction: Spanish
Academic year: April to February (2 terms)
Rector: Dr ANTONIO PASQUEL RUIZ
Vice-Rector for Academic Affairs: Econ. CARLOS HERNÁN ZUMAETA VÁSQUEZ
Gen. Sec.: Ing. MARÍA ISABEL MAURY LAURA
Librarian: MARGARITA FASANANDO VÁSQUEZ
Number of teachers: 400
Number of students: 3,200
Publication: *Conocimiento*

DEANS
Faculty of Administration and Accountancy: Prof. HEDMER PASQUEL CHONG
Faculty of Agronomy Science: Ing. JULIO VÁSQUEZ RAMÍREZ
Faculty of Biology: ANDRÉS URTEAGA CAVERO
Faculty of Chemistry: Ing. JESÚS LÓPEZ SANGAMA
Faculty of Education and Humanities: Prof. JOSÉ ZUMAETA TORRES
Faculty of Food Sciences: Ing. JORGE TORRES LUPERDI
Faculty of Forestry: Ing. JOSÉ TORRES VÁSQUEZ
Faculty of Human Medicine: Dr MARIO THEMME RUNCIMAN
Faculty of Nursing: Enf. PABLO CASTRO TRELLES
Faculty of Zootechnics: Ing. FERNANDO ARAUJO PAREDES

UNIVERSIDAD NACIONAL DE ANCASH 'SANTIAGO ANTÚNEZ DE MAYOLO'

Apdo 70, Huáraz, Ancash
Telephone: (43) 422-085
Fax: (43) 421-393
E-mail: jnunez00@yahoo.com
Internet: www.unasam.edu.pe
Founded 1977
State control
Language of instruction: Spanish
Academic year: April to December
Rector: Dr FERNANDO CASTILLO PICON
Vice-Rector for Academic Affairs: Mag. ROOSWELT VILLALOBOS
Vice-Rector for Admin.: Mag. CARLOS REYES PAREJA
Sec.: Econ. WILMER SICCHA CUSTODIO
Librarian: Ing. OSCAR RUIZ CASIMIRO
Number of teachers: 400
Number of students: 6,500
Publications: *Avance Santiaguino* (12 a year), *Informativo UNASAM*, *Revista de Investigacion de la UNASAM* (3 a year)

DEANS
Faculty of Agricultural Sciences: Ing. PEDRO COLONIA CERNA
Faculty of Civil Engineering: Ing. FELISMERO SALINAS FERNÁNDEZ
Faculty of Economic and Administrative Sciences: Econ. DARIO VAREAS ARCE
Faculty of Education: Lic. VICTOR PAREDES ESTEÍA
Faculty of Environmental Sciences: Ing. CESAR DAVILA PAREDES
Faculty of Food Industry Engineering: Ing. DANIEL REEVES ITA
Faculty of Law and Political Science: Abog. FABIAN ANICETO LUCERO
Faculty of Medicine: Lic. RIBIANA LEÓN HUERTA
Faculty of Mining, Geological and Metallurgical Engineering: Ing. JACINTO ISIDRO GIRALDO
Faculty of Science: Lic. ESMELIN NIGUIN ALAYO

UNIVERSIDAD NACIONAL DE CAJAMARCA

Avda Atahualpa 1050, Cajamarca
Telephone: (76) 363263
Fax: (76) 362796
E-mail: webmaster@unc.edu.pe
Internet: www.unc.edu.pe
Founded 1962
State control
Language of instruction: Spanish
Academic year: March to December (2 semesters)
Rector: Prof. CÉSAR A. PAREDES CANTO
Vice-Rectors: Dr HOMERO BAZÁN ZURITA, Ing. AURELIO MARTOS DÍAZ
Librarian: LUIS RONCAL
Number of teachers: 387
Number of students: 5,700

DEANS
Agriculture: Dr ISIDORO SÁNCHEZ VEGA
Animal Husbandry: Ing. TULIO MONDRAGÓN RONCAL
Economics, Administration and Accountancy: Prof. SEGUNDO CIEZA YAÑEZ
Education: Dr JOSUÉ TEJADA ATALAYA
Engineering: Ing. JULIO GUZMÁN PERALTA
Health: Dr JORGE CÉSPEDES ABANTO
Social Sciences: Prof. ALIDOR LUNA TELLO
Veterinary Medicine: Dr ROBERTO ACOSTA GÁLVEZ

UNIVERSIDAD NACIONAL DEL CALLAO

Saenz Peña 1060, Apdo 138, Callao
Telephone: (14) 296-608
Fax: (14) 296-607
E-mail: rector@redunac.unac.edu.pe
Internet: www.unac.edu.pe
Founded 1966
State control
Language of instruction: Spanish
Academic year: April to December (2 terms)
Rector: ALBERTO ARROYO VIALE
Vice-Rector: VICTOR MEREA LLANOS
Vice-Rector: GLORIA SAENZ ORREGO
Registrar: PABLO ARELLANO UBILLUZ
Librarian: LUIS CARRASCO VEREGAS
Number of teachers: 550
Number of students: 12,000
Publications: *Catálogo de Informes de Investigación* (1 a year), *Ciencia y Tecnología* (1 a year)

DEANS
Accounting: CARLOS HÚRTADO CRIADO
Administration: CÉSAR ANGULO RODRÍGUEZ
Chemical Engineering: PABLO DIAZ BRAVO
Economics: JUAN NUNURA CHULLY
Electrical and Electronic Engineering: FRANCO VELIZ LIZÁRRAGA
Environmental Engineering: MARIA TERESA VALDERRAMA ROJAS

Fish and Food Engineering: JUVENCIO VRIOS AVENDOÑO
Health Sciences: ARCELIA ROJAS SALAZAR
Industrial and Systems Engineering: MANUEL MORI PAREDES
Mathematics and Physics: ROEL MARIA VIDAL GUZMÁN
Mechanical Engineering: FELIX GUERRERO ROLDAN
Postgraduate School: LIDA SANÉZ FALCÓN

UNIVERSIDAD NACIONAL DEL CENTRO DEL PERÚ

Ciudad Universitaria, Avda Mariscal Castilla s/n km. 5, El Tambo Huancayo
Telephone: (64) 481062
E-mail: rrpp@uncp.edu.pe
Internet: www.uncp.edu.pe
Founded 1959
State control
Language of instruction: Spanish
Academic year: April to December (2 terms)
Rector: Ing. ESAÚ TIBERIO CARO MEZA
Vice-Rector for Academic Affairs: Ing. HUGO AYALA SÍNCHEZ
Chief Admin. Officer: Prof. KRÜGER SARAPURA YUPANQUI
Librarian: Dr FERNANDO ARAUCO VILLAR
Number of teachers: 705
Number of students: 8,395
Publications: *Boletín Informativo* (12 a year), *Ciencias Agrarias*, *Proceso* (irregular)

DEANS

Accountancy: CPC HERNANDO PAYANO ROJAS
Administration: Lic. ANDRÉS ILDEFONSO SUÁREZ
Agronomy: Ing. GLICERIO LÓPEZ ORIHUELA
Anthropology: Ing. JULIO BARRERA YUPANQUI
Architecture: Arq. FELIPE ARIAS MATOS
Chemical Engineering: Ing. ANTONIO COCHACHI GUADALUPE
Economics: Econ. MANUEL LARRAURI ROJAS
Education and Humanities: Lic. CARLOS GAMBOA DEL CARPIO
Electrical, Electronic and Systems Engineering: Ing. HÉCTOR TORRES MARAVÍ
Food Engineering: Ing. LIBIA GUTIÉRREZ GONZALES
Forestry: Ing. PEDRO ARIZAPANA ANCCASI
Mechanical Engineering: Ing. RAÚL MAYCO CHÁVEZ
Medicine: Dr RIGOBERTO ZÚÑIGA MERA
Metallurgical Engineering: Ing. EUGENIO MUCHA BENITO
Mining Engineering: Ing. ÓRISON DELZO SALOMÉ
Nursing: Lic. HÉCTOR ZAPATA RIVERA
Social Work: Lic. LIDIA LAGONES MIRANDA
Stockbreeding: Ing. HUMBERTO RODRÍGUEZ LANDEO
Postgraduate School: Dr PABLO MOSOMBITE PINEDO

UNIVERSIDAD NACIONAL DANIEL ALCIDES CARRIÓN

Edificio Estatal No. 4, San Juan Pampa, Cerro de Pasco, Pasco
Telephone and fax (63) 422197
E-mail: webmaster@undac.edu.pe
Internet: www.undac.edu.pe
Founded 1965
Rector: Prof. NORBERTO GONZALES PERALTA
Number of teachers: 90
Number of students: 1,000
Faculties of economics, education, mining, metallurgy.

UNIVERSIDAD NACIONAL DE EDUCACIÓN 'ENRIQUE GUZMÁN Y VALLE'

Avda Enrique Guzmán y Valle s/n, La Cantuta, Chosica, Lima 15
Telephone: (1) 313-3700
Internet: www.une.edu.pe
Founded 1967
State control
Language of instruction: Spanish
Pres.: Dra DORALIZA TOVAR TORRES
First Vice-Pres. for Academic Affairs: Dra LUZ DORIS SÁNCHEZ PINEDO
Second Vice-Pres. for Admin.: VIDAL BAUTISTA CARRASCO
Gen. Sec.: Dra GLADYS RAMÍREZ ADRIANZÉN
Registrar: Prof. MIREIA SOLÉ ALABART
Librarian: MARGARITA LÓPEZ M.
Library of 16,500 vols
Number of teachers: 190
Number of students: 9,744
Publication: *Cantuta*

DEANS

Faculty of Humanities: HUMBERTO VARGAS SALGADO
Faculty of Sciences: LILIANA SUMARRIVA BUSTINZA
Faculty of Technology: JOSÉ ASTOLAZA DE LA CRUZ
Postgraduate School: Dr JORGE JHONCON KOOYIP (Dir)

UNIVERSIDAD NACIONAL FEDERICO VILLARREAL

Jr. Carlos Gonzáles 285, Maranga, San Miguel, Lima
Telephone: (14) 720-9720
E-mail: rector@unfv.edu.pe
Internet: www.unfv.edu.pe
Founded 1963
Public control
Language of instruction: Spanish
Academic year: April to December
Rector: DAGOBERTO SÁNCHEZ MANTILLA
Vice-Rector for Academic Affairs: Dr GABRIEL HUERTA DÍAZ
Vice-Rector for Admin.: Dr EULOGIO PISFIL CHAVESTA
Gen. Sec.: Lic. CARLOS HERÁCLIDES PAJUELO CAMONES
Librarian: Lic. ANA DORIS TERRONES SILVA
Number of teachers: 2,354
Number of students: 22,449
Publications: *Hipótesis*, *Villarreal en el tercer milenio*, *Síntesis Academica*, *Villarreal al Futuro*, *Wiñay Yachay*, *Yachaywasi*

DEANS

Architecture, Town Planning and Arts: Mag. RAQUEL CARO ZALDIVAR
Civil Engineering: Dr ROQUE ALBERTO SÁNCHEZ CRISTOBÁL
Economics: Dr OSCAR PONGO AGUILA
Education: Dra NANCY OLIVERO PACHECO
Electronic Engineering and Information Science: Dr JUSTO PASTOR SOLIS FONSECA
Finance and Accountancy: Dra ELENA MARÑOS LINARES
Geographical and Environmental Engineering: Dr LUIS ALBERTO VILCHEZ LARA
Humanities: Mag. GIOVANNI MITROVIC DE RISI
Industrial and Systems Engineering: Ing. JOSÉ RAMÍREZ ROSILLO
Law and Political Sciences: Dr VÍCTOR TAQUIA VILA
Medicine: Dr JESÚS FERNÁNDEZ URDAY
Medical Technology: Mg. CÉSAR ENRIQUE GUERRERO BARRANTES
Natural Sciences and Mathematics: Mag. MILVIO CASAVERDE RÍOS
Oceanography, Fisheries and Food Sciences: Dr JUAN ACOSTA POLO
Odontology: Mag. JUVENAL ÁNGEL QUIÑONES MORENO
Psychology: Lic. BELIZARDO SILVA DÍAZ
Public and Private Administration: Dr FELICIANO ONCEVAY ESPINOZA
Social Sciences: Dr ISAAC ROBERTO ÁNGELES LAZO

UNIVERSIDAD NACIONAL DE HUANCAVELICA

Ciudad Universitaria Paturpampa, Huancavelica
Telephone: (67) 751-380
Fax: (67) 751-551
E-mail: secretaria@unh.edu.pe
Internet: www.unh.edu.pe
Founded 1990
Rector: MANUEL J. BASTO SÁEZ
Vice-Rector for Academic Affairs: Dr ALFONSO CORDERO FERNÁNDEZ
Vice-Rector for Admin.: ADOLFO R. CORTAVARRIA
Sec.-Gen.: Lic. ALEJANDRO RODRIGO QUILCA

DEANS

Faculty of Business Administration: RAÚL RUA SULCA
Faculty of Education: ZEIDA P. HOCES LA ROSA
Faculty of Engineering: Dr OMAR BURGA MOSTACERO
Faculty of Nursing: Lic. BENJAMINA ORTIZ ESPINAR

UNIVERSIDAD NACIONAL HERMILIO VALDIZÁN

Av. Universitaria 601, Cayhuayna, Huánuco
Telephone: (62) 512-341
Fax: (62) 513-360
Internet: www.unheval.edu.pe
Founded 1964
State control
Language of instruction: Spanish
Academic year: April to July;August to December (2 semesters)
Rector: Dr VICTOR PEDRO CUADROS OJEDA
Vice-Rector for Academic Affairs: Dr PEDRO GETULIO VILLAVICENCIO GUARDIA
Vice-Rector for Admin.: ERASMO FERNÁNDEZ SIXTO
Head of Admin.: Lic. ESTEBAN MEDINA AVILA
Dir of Post Degree: Dr LORENZO PASQUEL LOARTE
Librarian: Lic. AURORA AMPUDIA DÁVILA
Library of 25,967 vols
Number of teachers: 568
Number of students: 9,606

DEANS

Accountancy and Financial Sciences: GUILLERMO AREVALO RÍOS
Administrative Sciences and Tourism: Dr ROGER WILFREDO CÉSPEDES REVELO
Agrarian Sciences: DAVID ALCIDES MAQUERA LUPACA
Business Management: CPC ARTURO RIVERA Y CALDAS
Civil Engineering and Architecture: Ing. CLIFTON PAUCARY MONTENEGRO
Economic sciences: EMIGIDIO RAMOS CORNELIO
Health Sciences: EDILBERTO ENRIQUE SUERO ROJAS
Industrial Engineering: Dr GUILLERMO AUGUSTO BOCANGEL WEYDERT
Law and Political Science: Dr ARMANDO PIZARRO ALEJANDRO
Nursing: NANCY GUILLERMINA VERAMENDI VILLAVICENCIO
Obstetrics: VÍCTOR QUISPE SULCA

Sciences of Education and Humanities: ARTURO LUCAS CABELLO
Social Sciences: ORTZY FORTUNATO LOVÓN RONDÓN
Veterinary Medicine and Zootechnics: AUGUSTO BAZAN GARCÌA

UNIVERSIDAD NACIONAL DE INGENIERÍA

Avda Túpac Amaru 210, Rimac, Lima 25
Telephone: (1) 481-1070
E-mail: webmaster@uni.edu.pe
Internet: www.uni.edu.pe

Founded 1896 as Escuela Nacional de Ingenieros del Perú, present name 1955
State control
Language of instruction: Spanish
Academic year: April to December

Rector: Dr JOSÉ IGNACIO LÓPEZ SORIA
Vice-Rectors: Ing. MIGUEL ANGEL SAENZ LIZARZABURU, Dr CASIO ORE ORE
Sec.-Gen.: Dr ABELARDO LUDEÑA LUQUE

Library: see Libraries and Archives
Number of teachers: 996
Number of students: 12,241

Publications: *Boletín 'Quilca'*, *Revista Técnica 'Tecnia'*, *Revista Artes y Ciencias 'Amaru'*

DEANS

Faculty of Architecture, Town Planning and Fine Arts: Arq. JAVIER SOTA NADAL
Faculty of Chemical and Manufacturing Engineering: Ing. LUCIO RAMOS BENAVENTE
Faculty of Civil Engineering: Ing. GENARO HUMALA AYBAR
Faculty of Economics and Social Sciences: Lic. JORGE ABADIE LINARES
Faculty of Electrical and Electronic Engineering: Ing. JUBERT CHÁVEZ SERRANO
Faculty of Environmental Engineering: Ing. JORGE PFLUCKER
Faculty of Geology, Mining and Metallurgical Engineering: Ing. PEDRO MÁXIMO ANGELES BETETA
Faculty of Industrial and Systems Engineering: Ing. LUIS FLORES FONSECA
Faculty of Mechanical Engineering: Ing. JUAN HORI ASANO
Faculty of Petroleum Engineering: Ing. ARTURO BURGA ACOSTA
Faculty of Science: Dr JAIME AVALOS SÁNCHEZ

UNIVERSIDAD NACIONAL JORGE BASADRE GROHMANN

Calle Alto Lima 1594, Tacna
Telephone: (52) 583000
E-mail: sredo@unjbg.edu.pe
Internet: www.unjbg.edu.pe

Founded 1971 as Universidad Nacional de Tacna
State control
Language of instruction: Spanish
Academic year: April to December

Chancellor: Dr CARLOS VALENTE ROSSI
Rector: Dr hab VICENTE M. CASTAÑEDA CHÁVEZ
Vice-Rectors: Mgr DANTE MANZANARES CÁCERES, Dr ELÍ ESPINOZA ATENCIA
Sec.-Gen.: Lic. CARLOS POLO BRAVO
Librarian: Ing. ALBERTO PACHECO PACHECO

Library of 29,000 vols
Number of teachers: 457
Number of students: 4,903

Publications: *Ciencia y Tecnología* (1 a year), *Memoria de Gestión* (1 a year), *Revista Materno Infantil* (1 a year)

DEANS

Accounting: CPC BETTY COHAILA CALDERÓN
Administration: Ing. Eco. JESÚS OLIVERA CÁCERES
Agriculture: Ing. ELOY CASILLA GARCÍA
Education: Prof. OLIVER BALLÓN MONTESINOS
Fishing Engineering: Dr ELÍ ESPINOZA ATENCIA
Food Industry Engineering: Dr MIGUEL LARREA CÉSPEDES
Law and Arts: Psic. CARLOS PAUCA LAZO
Medicine: Dr JORGE LÓPEZ CLAROS
Metallurgical Engineering: Ing. RAÚL DEL POZO TELLO
Mining Engineering: Ing. DANTE MORALES CABRERA
Nursing: Mgr. DALILA SALAS ROMERO
Obstetrics: Obst. MIRIAM RÍOS MORENO
Science: Lic. RAMÓN VERA ROALCABA
Postgraduate School: Mgr PELAYO DELGADO TELLO

UNIVERSIDAD NACIONAL JOSÉ FAUSTINO SÁNCHEZ CARRIÓN

Ciudad Universitaria, Avda Mercedes Indacochea s/n, Huacho, Lima
Telephone: (1) 232-6097
Internet: www.unjfsc.edu.pe

Founded 1968

Rector: Lic. SEVERO LLANOS BAYONA

Library of 5,000 vols
Number of teachers: 100
Number of students: 3,000

Depts of administration, engineering, fisheries, nutrition, sociology.

UNIVERSIDAD NACIONAL MAYOR DE SAN MARCOS

Edificio Jorge Basadre, Ciudad Universitaria, Lima 1
Telephone: (1) 619-7000
E-mail: cooperacion.unmsm@gmail.com
Internet: www.unmsm.edu.pe

Founded 1551
Public control
Language of instruction: Spanish
Academic year: March to December

Rector: Dr LUIS FERNANDO IZQUIERDO VÁSQUEZ
Vice-Rector for Academic Affairs: Dr VÍCTOR PEÑA RODRÍGUEZ
Vice-Rector for Research: Dr AURORA MARROU ROLDÁN

Library of 470,448 vols
Number of teachers: 3,059
Number of students: 28,041

Publications: *Boletín*, *Compendios*, *Revista de San Marcos*

DIRECTORS OF THE GRADUATE SCHOOL

Accountancy: Dr J. C. TRUJILLO MEZA
Accounting Studies: Dr JULIO TRUJILLO MEZA
Administration: Dr A. PAÚCAR CARBAJAL
Administrative Sciences: Dr PABLO WILLINS MAURICIO PACHAS
Biological Sciences: Dr PABLO SERGIO RAMÍREZ ROCA
Biology: Dra B. LIZÁRRAGA DE OLARTE
Chemistry and Chemical Engineering: Ing D. SÁNCHEZ MANTILLA
Completion Studies: Dr M. VELASCO VERÁSTEGUI
Dentistry: Dr JUAN ADOLFO MERINO MARTIJENA
Economics: Dr A. MENDOZA DIEZ
Economic Sciences: Dr RAYMUNDO PACHECO MEXZON
Education: CARLOS BARRIGA HERNÁNDEZ
Electronic Engineering: Dr RUBÉN ALARCÓN MATUTTI
Engineering: Dr P. MATÍAS ATÚNCAR
Geology and Geography: Dr A. ALBERCA CEVALLOS
Geology, Mining, Metallurgy and Geographical Sciences: Dr CARLOS CABRERA CARRANZA
Human Medicine: JUAN ERNESTO DENEGRI ARCE
Human Science: Dr RAYMUNDO PRADO REDÓNDEZ
Industrial Engineering: Mg JORGE INCHE MITMA
Law and Political Science: Dr PERCY PEÑARANDA PORTUGAL
Linguistics, Literature and Philology: Dr M. MARTOS CARRERA
Mathematical Sciences: Dr RENATO BENAZIC TOME
Mathematics and Physics: Dr R. MOSQUERA RAMÍREZ
Medicine: Dr J. CAMPOS REY DE CASTRO
Metallurgy: Ing. M. CHÁVEZ AGUILAR
National School of Librarianship and Information Science: M. BONILLA DE GAVIRIA
Nutrition: Dr T. AGUILAR FAJARDO
Pharmacy and Biochemistry: Dr PABLO ENRIQUE BONILLA RIVERA
Philosophy, Psychology and Art: Dr A. CASTRILLÓN VIZCARRA
Physical Sciences: Dr PABLO LAGOS ENRIQUEZ
Psychology: Dr NICOLÁS MEDINA CURI
Social Science: Dra ALIDA ISIDORA DÍAZ ENCINAS
Systems Engineering: CAYO LEÓN FERNÁNDEZ
Veterinary Science: Dr FELIPE SAN MARTÍN HOWARD

UNIVERSIDAD NACIONAL MICAELA BASTIDAS DE APURIMAC

Avda Arenas 121, Abancay
Telephone: (83) 322-577
Internet: www.unamba.edu.pe

Founded 2000
State control

Pres.: Dr CARROLL DALE SALINAS
Vice-Pres. for Academic Affairs: DALIN OMAR ENCOMENDEROS
Vice-Pres. for Admin.: ALFONSO VÍCTOR BUSTINZA CHOQUE
Sec.-Gen.: Abog. CORINA VELÁSQUEZ SÁNCHEZ

Number of teachers: 104
Number of students: 1,500

COORDINATORS OF ACADEMIC PROGRAMMES

Agricultural Engineering: Ing. FULGENCIO VILCANQUI PÉREZ
Business Administration: Lic. YUDBERTO VILCA COLQUE
Education: Ing. JESÚS MANUEL IBARRA CABRERA
Mining: Ing. NELSON PALEMON MEZA PEÑA

UNIVERSIDAD NACIONAL PEDRO RUIZ GALLO

Avda Juan XXIII 339, Lambayeque
Telephone: (74) 590-393
E-mail: webmaster@unprg.edu.pe
Internet: www.unprg.edu.pe

Founded 1970
State control
Language of instruction: Spanish

Rector: Ing. ANGEL DIAZ CELIS
Vice-Rector: Ing. PEDRO CASANOVA CHIRINOS
Librarian: Dr GUILLERMO BACA AGUINAGA

Number of teachers: 261
Number of students: 5,460

Publications: *Boletín Informativo* (12 a year), *Universidad* (1 a year)

DIRECTORS OF ACADEMIC PROGRAMMES

Accounting: Ing. A. GIRALDO ESPINOSA
Administration: Ing. M. MORENO MESTA
Agriculture: Ing. D. OJEDA PEÑA
Agricultural Engineering: Ing. O. VIVAR PÁRRAGA

Animal Husbandry: Ing. F. VILLENA RODRÍGUEZ
Biology: Ing. A. DÍAZ CELIS
Civil Engineering: Ing. J. SALAZAR CASTILLO
Economics: Econ. G. NINAHUAMAN MUCHA
Human Medicine: Dr A. BURGA HERMÁNDEZ
Law: Ab. C. VELA MARQUILLO
Mathematics and Statistics: Mat. N. LÓPEZ SEGURA
Mechanical and Electrical Engineering: Ing. J. SAENZ QUIROGA
Nursing: Enf. C. ROMERO DE CARCELEN
Sociology: M. RAMOS BAZÁN
Veterinary Medicine: Vet J. GUTIÉRREZ REYES

UNIVERSIDAD NACIONAL DE PIURA

Esquina Apurimac-Tacna 719–743, Apdo 295, Piura
Telephone: (74) 324603
Fax: (74) 321931
E-mail: postmast@tallan.unp.edu.pe
Internet: www.unp.edu.pe

Founded 1961
State control
Language of instruction: Spanish
Academic year: March to December

Rector: Ing. FREDDY APONTE GUERRERO
Vice-Rector for Academic Affairs: Ing. LUÍS GUZMÁN FARFÁN
Vice-Rector for Admin.: Ing. ORLANDO ZAPATA COLOMA
Admin. Dir: Lic. JORGE RODRÍGUEZ RIVERA
Librarian: Dr LUÍS VEGA FARFÁN

Number of teachers: 481
Number of students: 8,503

Publications: *Boletines*, *Universalia* (scientific journal, 2 a year)

DEANS

Faculty of Accounting and Finance: MÁXIMO MÁRQUEZ TACURA
Faculty of Administrative Sciences: Lic. VICENTE SÁNCHEZ JUÁREZ
Faculty of Agronomy: Dr CÉSAR DELGADILLO FUKUSAKI
Faculty of Animal Husbandry: ADRIÁN GUZMÁN ZAGARRO
Faculty of Architecture: MIGUEL ADRIANZÁN HUANCAS
Faculty of Civil Engineering: Ing. RICARDO CARRASCO SOTOMAYOR
Faculty of Economics: Econ. JOSÉ ORDINOLA BOYER
Faculty of Fisheries Engineering: MANUEL MOGOLLÓN LÓPEZ
Faculty of Human Medicine: Dr RAÚL CASTILLO ZÚÑIGA
Faculty of Industrial Engineering: Lic. MARK SADOWSKY SMITH
Faculty of Law and Political Sciences: Dr CARLOS CORNEJO GUERRERO
Faculty of Mining Engineering: Ing. RICARDO DILLON LONG
Faculty of Sciences: SAUL CÉSPEDES LOMPARTE
Faculty of Social Sciences and Education: Econ. LORENZO ALVILES VALEZMORO

UNIVERSIDAD NACIONAL DE SAN AGUSTÍN DE AREQUIPA

Calle Santa Catalina 117, Arequipa
Telephone: (54) 237808
Fax: (54) 237808
Internet: www.unsa.edu.pe

Founded 1828
State control
Language of instruction: Spanish
Academic year: April to December

Rector: Dr ROLANDO CORNEJO CUERVO
Vice-Rector for Academic Affairs: Dr VALDEMAR MEDINA HOYOS
Vice-Rector for Admin.: Dr MILTON TALAVERA SOTO
Gen. Sec.: LUIS ALBERTO VALDIVIA RODRÍGUEZ
Library: see Libraries

Number of teachers: 1,453
Number of students: 22,899

Publications: *Boletín Bibliográfico*, *Boletín Estadístico* (1 a year)

DEANS

Accounting and Administration: EDGAR RÍOS VILLENA
Architecture and Town Planning: CÉSAR MÁRQUEZ MARES
Biological and Agricultural Sciences: VALDEMAR MEDINA HOYOS
Civil Engineering: ENRIQUE CAMPOS MATTOS
Economics: EDGAR ACOSTA Y GUTIÉRREZ
Education: VÍCTOR HUGO LINARES HUACO
Geology and Geophysics: MELECIO LAZO ANGULO
History and Social Sciences: VÍCTOR RAÚL SACCA ABUSABAL
Law: RAYMUNDO NÚÑEZ LOZADA
Medicine: BENJAMÍN PAZ ALIAGA
Natural and Formal Sciences: ANDRÉS REYNOSO ORTIZ
Nursing: ESPERANZA VALDIVIA AMPUERO
Philosophy and Humanities: TERESA ARRIETA TRONCOSO DE GUZMÁN
Process Engineering: MARIO LOZADA REYNOSO
Production and Services Engineering: JOSÉ HERNÁNDEZ VALLEJOS
Psychology and Industrial and Public Relations: CÉSAR SALAS MORALES

UNIVERSIDAD NACIONAL DE SAN ANTONIO ABAD DEL CUSCO

Apdo 921, Cusco
Avda de la Cultura 733, Cusco
Telephone: (84) 604-100
Fax: (84) 238-156
E-mail: webmaster@unsaac.edu.pe
Internet: www.unsaac.edu.pe

Founded 1962, reorganized 1969

Depts of accountancy, animal husbandry, economics, education, geology and mining, technology

Rector: Ing. CARLOS CHACON GALINDO

Number of teachers: 450
Number of students: *c.* 16,000

Publication: *Revista Universitaria* (1 a year).

UNIVERSIDAD NACIONAL DE SAN CRISTÓBAL DE HUAMANGA

Portal Independencia No. 57, Ayacucho
Telephone: (66) 312-230
Fax: (66) 312-510
E-mail: postmaster@unsch.edu.pe
Internet: www.unsch.edu.pe

Founded 1677, reopened 1959
State control
Language of instruction: Spanish
Academic year: March to July,August to December

Rector: MV JORGE DEL CAMPO CAVERO
Vice-Rector for Academic Affairs: Dr RAMIRO PALOMINO MALPARTIDA
Vice-Rector for Admin.: MSc JORGE SOTERO GARCÍA BLÁSQUEZ MOROTE
Gen. Sec.: Ing. MAURO VARGAS CAMARENA
Librarian: MARIA ISABEL MATTA DURAN

Number of teachers: 450
Number of students: 6,000

Publications: *Boletín UNSCH*, *Guamangengis, Signos y Obras*

DEANS

Agronomy: Ing. CÉSAR ROLANDO RUIZ CANALES
Biological Sciences: VICTOR ALEGRIA VALERIANO
Chemical and Metallurgical Engineering: Ing. CLEMENTE LIMAYLLA AGUIRRE
Economics and Administration: AURELIO ELORRIETA ESPINOZA
Education: Prof. HECTOR ELIAS VEGA LEON
Law and Political Sciences: Dr DANIEL QUISPE PÉREZ
Mining and Civil Engineering: Ing. CARLOS AUBERTO PRADO PRADO
Nursing: Prof. VICENTE VALVERDE BALTAZAR
Obstetrics: Dr SADOT TORRES RAMOS
Social Sciences: TULA RUTH ALARCON ALARCON

UNIVERSIDAD NACIONAL SAN LUIS GONZAGA DE ICA

Prolongación Ayabaca C-9, Urb. San José, Ica
Telephone: (56) 228-406
E-mail: webmaster@unica.edu.pe
Internet: www.unica.edu.pe

Founded 1961

Academic programmes in agronomy, arts and education, civil engineering, dentistry, economic and social sciences, fisheries and biological sciences, law, mechanical engineering and electricity, medicine, pharmacy and biochemistry, veterinary medicine

Rector: Dr CESAR ANGELES CABALLERO
Sec.-Gen.: Dr MIGUEL CALDERÓN REINA

Number of teachers: 459
Number of students: 6,295

Publications: *Educación Dental*, *Letras y Educación*.

UNIVERSIDAD NACIONAL DE SAN MARTÍN

Jr. Maynas 177, Tarapoto
Telephone: (42) 524253
E-mail: informes@unsm.edu.pe
Internet: www.unsm.edu.pe

Founded 1979

Rector: Ing. M.Sc. ALFREDO QUINTEROS GARCÍA
Sec.-Gen.: Ing. JAIME RAMÍREZ NAVARRO
Librarian: JORGE YUNGBLUTH ZEGARRA

Number of teachers: 41
Number of students: 410

UNIVERSIDAD NACIONAL DEL SANTA

Avda Pacífico 508, Urb. Buenos Aires Apdo 10, Nuevo Chimbote
Telephone: (44) 311249
Fax: (44) 311556
Internet: www.uns.edu.pe

Founded 1984; present status 1998

Rector: ESTEBAN HORNA BANCES
Vice-Rector for Academic Affairs: PEDRO MONCADA BECERRA
Vice-Rector for Admin.: Ing. PEDRO GAMARRA LEIVA

Number of teachers: 160
Number of students: 3,100

DEANS

Faculty of Education and Humanities: Lic. BETTY RISCO RODRÍGUEZ
Faculty of Engineering: Ing. VICTOR CASTRO ZAVALETA
Faculty of Science: Lic. AMÉRICA ODAR ROSARIO

UNIVERSIDAD NACIONAL DE TRUJILLO

Jr. Independencia 389, Trujillo
Telephone: (44) 205-513

Fax: (44) 256-629
E-mail: rectorado@unitru.edu.pe
Internet: www.unitru.edu.pe

Founded 1824 by Simón Bolívar and José Faustino Sánchez Carrión
State control
Language of instruction: Spanish
Academic year: April to December

Rector: Dr VÍCTOR CARLOS SABANA GAMARRA
Vice-Rector for Academic Affairs: Dr JUAN CÉSAR MURO MOREY
Vice-Rector for Admin.: Dr ORLANDO VELÁSQUEZ BENITES
Librarian: Dr CESAR GAMARRA SÁNCHEZ

Library of 28,000 vols
Number of teachers: 980
Number of students: 15,000

Publications: *Amauta—Archivos de Oftalmología del Norte del Perú*, *Lenguaje y Ciencia*, *Memoria Rectoral*, *Revista de Derecho*, *Revista del Museo de Arqueología y Antropología*

DEANS

Agricultural Sciences: NELSON RÍOS CAMPOS
Chemical Engineering: Dr JUAN GUERRERO LLUNCOR
Biological Sciences: Dr JOSÉ MOSTACERO LEÓN
Economic Sciences: Dr ENRIQUE RODRÍGUEZ RODRÍGUEZ
Education and Communication Sciences: Dr JULIO ALDAMA FLORES
Engineering: Ing. JUAN SÁNCHEZ BUSTAMANTE
Law and Political Sciences: Dr TEÓDULO SANTOS CRUZ
Medical Sciences: Dra LOURDES ARMAS FAVA
Nursing: Dra FLOR LUNA VICTORIA MORI
Pharmacy and Biochemistry: Dr SEGUNDO RONCAL SALDAÑA
Physical and Mathematical Sciences: Dr MARCIAL VÁSQUEZ ARTEAGA
Social Sciences: Dr GUILLERMO GUTIÉRREZ CHACÓN

UNIVERSIDAD NACIONAL DE TUMBES

Centro Cívico, 3er Piso, Tumbes

Telephone: (72) 522810
E-mail: oginf@untumbes.edu.pe
Internet: www.untumbes.edu.pe

Founded 1984

Rector: Dr ADÁN ALVARADO BERNUY
Vice-Rector for Academic Affairs: Dr CÉSAR MANTILLA AVALOS
Vice-Rector for Admin.: AUBERTO HIDALGO MOGOLLÓN

DEANS

Faculty of Agrarian Sciences: FRANCISCO ALBURQUEQUE VIERA
Faculty of Economics: MANUEL PAZ LÓPEZ
Faculty of Fishery: CÉSAR ESTUARDO POMA SÁNCHEZ
Faculty of Health Sciences: GINO ANTONIO MORETTI OTOYA
Faculty of Law and Social Sciences: RICARDO NOBLECILLA MORÁN

UNIVERSIDAD NACIONAL DE UCAYALI

Avda Centenario km. 6, Pucallpa

Telephone: (61) 579962
Fax: (61) 592236
E-mail: imagen@unu.edu.pe
Internet: www.unu.edu.pe

Founded 1979
State control
Language of instruction: Spanish

Rector: Dr VICTOR CHÁVEZ VÁSQUEZ
Vice-Rector for Academic Affairs: Ing. DANIEL BALAREZO INFANTE
Vice-Rector for Admin.: Dr MIGUEL NOLTE MANZANARES
Registrar: Ing. Admin. ROMEL PINEDO RÍOS
Librarian: RAUL JAVIER GUTIÉRREZ PINEDA

Number of teachers: 178
Number of students: 1,400

DEANS

Administration and Accountancy: Lic. Admin. PEDRO ORMEÑO CARMONA
Agronomy: OSCAR LLAPAPASCA PAUCAR
Forest Sciences: Ing. CARLOS FACHIN MATOS
Health: ISABEL ESTEBAN ROBLADILLO

Private Universities

PONTIFICIA UNIVERSIDAD CATÓLICA DEL PERÚ

Apdo 1761, Lima 100
Avda Universitaria, Cdra 18 s/n, San Miguel, Lima 32

Telephone: (1) 626-2000
Fax: (1) 626-2847
E-mail: secgen@pucp.edu.pe
Internet: www.pucp.edu.pe

Founded 1917
Private control
Language of instruction: Spanish
Academic year: March to December (2 terms)

Rector: Ing. LUIS GUZMÁN BARRÓN SOBREVILLA
Vice-Rector for Academic Affairs: Dr MARCIAL RUBIO CORREA
Vice-Rector for Admin.: EFRAÍN GONZALES DE OLARTE
Sec.-Gen.: Dr RENÉ ORTIZ CABALLERO
Registrar: ANGELITA BASSO
Dir for Int. Relations and Cooperation: LUIS JAIME CASTILLO BUTTERS
Librarian: Dra CARMEN VILLANUEVA

Library: see Libraries and Archives
Number of teachers: 2,572
Number of students: 17,000

Publications: *Agenda Internacional* (2 a year), *Análisis Económico de Coyuntura* (12 a year), *Anthropológica* (1 a year), *Areté* (philosophy, 2 a year), *Boletín de Arqueología* (archaeology, 1 a year), *Boletín del Instituto Riva-Agüero* (1 a year), *Debates en Sociología* (sociology, 2 a year), *Derecho* (law, 1 a year), *Economía* (economics, 1 a year), *Educación* (education, 2 a year), *Electro Electrónica* (2 a year), *Espacio y Desarrollo* (1 a year), *Histórica* (2 a year), *Lexis* (linguistic and literary review, 2 a year), *Pensamiento Constitucional* (1 a year), *Pro Matemática* (2 a year), *Revista de Psicología* (psychology, 2 a year), *Revista de Química* (chemistry, 2 a year), *Synergies Pérou* (didactology of languages and cultures, 1 a year), *Tren de Sombras* (cinema, 4 a year)

DEANS

Arts (General Studies Programme): Dr ROBERTO CRIADO ALZAMORA
Faculty of Administration and Accounting: NELSON SANTOS
Faculty of Architecture and Planning: FREDERICK COOPER (Government Commission's President)
Faculty of Communication Arts and Sciences: Dr LUIS PEIRANO FALCONÍ
Faculty of Education: JORGE CAPELLA
Faculty of Fine Arts: ALEJANDRO ALAYZA
Faculty of Humanities: Dra LILIANA REGALADO DE HURTADO
Faculty of Law: Dr ARMANDO ZOLEZZI MÖLLER
Faculty of Science and Engineering: EDUARDO ISMODES
Faculty of Social Sciences: ADOLFO FIGUEROA
Graduate School: Dr MÁXIMO VEGA CENTENO (Dir)
Science (General Studies Programme): Dr LUIS MONTESTRUQUE ZEGARRA

UNIVERSIDAD FEMENINA DEL SAGRADO CORAZÓN

Avda Los Frutales 954, Urb. Santa Magdalena Sofía, La Molina, Apdo 0005, Lima 41

Telephone: (1) 436-4641
Fax: (1) 436-3247
E-mail: postmast@unife.edu.pe
Internet: www.unife.edu.pe

Founded 1962
Private control
Language of instruction: Spanish
Academic year: April to December (2 semesters)

Rector: Dra R. M. ELGA GARCÍA ASTE
Vice-Rector for Admin.: Dra GRACIELA RUIZ DURÁN
Vice-Rector for Academic Affairs: Dra ROSA MARÍA REUSCHE LARI
Librarian: Lic. MARÍA LA SERNA DE MÁS

Library of 67,340 vols
Number of teachers: 321
Number of students: 2,292

Publications: *Revista de Educación*, *Cuaderno de Psicología*, *Revista de Psicología*, *Puente*, *Consensus*, *Avances en Psicología*, *Comunifé*

DEANS

Architecture: Arq. CARMEN ÁNGELA SALVADOR WADSWORTH
Education: Dr AGUSTÍN CAMPOS ARENAS
Engineering: Mg. JUAN MANUEL FERNÁNDEZ CHAVESTA
Law and Political Sciences: Dr LUIS FELIPE ALMENARA BRYSON
Psychology and Humanities: Dra. VICTORIA GARCÍA GARCÍA
Translation, Interpreting and Communications: Lic. ROSSANA SORLANO VERGARA
Postgraduate School: Dra GLORIA BENAVIDES VÍA

UNIVERSIDAD DE HUÁNUCO

Jr. Hermilio Valdizán 871, 2° Piso, Huánuco

Telephone and fax (62) 513-154
E-mail: info@udh.edu.pe
Internet: www.udh.edu.pe

Founded 1984

Rector: RAUL ISRAEL OLIVERA
Vice-Rector: RAFAEL ISRAEL OLIVERA
Admin. Officer: MANUEL MANRIQUE MARCOS
Librarian: MARY DIAZ PAIVA

Number of teachers: 55
Number of students: 1,700

DEANS

Faculty of Forestry Engineering: NILO LÓPEZ TELLO
Faculty of Law and Politics: EMERICO ISRAEL OLIVERA
Faculty of Obstetrics: MANUEL ISRAEL OLIVERA

UNIVERSIDAD INCA GARCILASO DE LA VEGA

Avda San Felipe 890, Jesús María, Lima

Telephone: (1) 471-1784
E-mail: vrac@uigv.edu.pe
Internet: www.uigv.edu.pe

Founded 1964
Private control

Rector: Dr LUIS CERVANTES LINAN
Sec.-Gen.: Dr ALFONSO CARRIZALES ULLOA
Librarian: NANCY HARMAN DE ALVARADO

Number of teachers: 240

Number of students: 7,000
Publication: *Garcilaso*

DIRECTORS

Accountancy: T. MOYA DE ROJAS
Administration: G. SUXE MONTERO
Economics: M. DELGADO ULLOQUE
Education: A. CASTRO URBINA
Industrial Engineering: L. TITO ATAURIMA
Law: R. CASTRO NESTAREZ
Social Sciences: A. CASTRO URBINA
Social Work: B. CORDOVA SUÁREZ

UNIVERSIDAD DE LIMA

Apdo 852, Lima 100
Telephone: (1) 437-6767
Fax: (1) 437-8066
E-mail: postmaster@ulima.edu.pe
Internet: www.ulima.edu.pe

Founded 1962
Private control
Language of instruction: Spanish
Academic year: April to December

Rector: Dra ILSE WISOTZKI LOLI
Vice-Rector: Mag. CÉSAR VIALARDI SACÍN
Admin. and Gen. Services: Ing. JOSÉ ANTONIO LIZÁRRAGA
Librarian: NELLY CASAS PASTOR

Number of teachers: 900
Number of students: 14,000

Publications: *Ciencia Económica* (2 a year), *Contratexto* (1 a year), *Ingeniería Industrial*, *Ius et Praxis* (2 a year), *Lienzo* (1 a year), *Noticias* (12 a year), *Persona* (1 a year)

DEANS

Administration: CARLOS BRESANI
Communication Sciences: ÓSCAR QUÉZADA
Economics: ALBERTO TOKESHI
General Studies: CÉSAR VIALARDI
Industrial Engineering: JAIME LEÓN
Law: OSWALDO HUNDSKOPF
Psychology: EDWIN SALAS
Systems Engineering: JORGE CHUE

UNIVERSIDAD DEL PACÍFICO

Avda Salaverry 2020, Jesús María, Apdo 4683, Lima 11
Telephone: (1) 471-2485
Fax: (1) 219-0140
E-mail: dri@up.edu.pe
Internet: www.up.edu.pe

Founded 1962
Private control
Language of instruction: Spanish
Academic year: January to February,March to July,August to December

Rector: Prof. FELIPE PORTOCARRERO
Vice-Rector: Prof. MATILDE SCHWALB
Sec.-Gen.: Prof. CARLOS LUIS AGUSTI
Dir Institutional Relations: CECILIA MONTES
Registrar: Prof. MIGUEL CHANG
Librarian: ROSA DORIVAL

Number of teachers: 190
Number of students: 1,681 full-time
Number of students: 1,700 part-time

Publications: *Apuntes*, *Punto de Equilibrio*

DEANS

Administration and Accountancy: Prof. EDUARDO MINDREAU
Business Engineering: Prof. OSCAR DE AZAMBUJA
Economics: Prof. ARLETTE BELTRAN
Graduate School: Prof. ELSA DEL CASTILLO
Law: Prof. FERNANDO CANTUARIAS

UNIVERSIDAD PERUANA CAYETANO HEREDIA

Av. Honorio Delgado 430, Urb. Ingeniería, Lima
Telephone: (1) 319-0000
E-mail: postmaster@upch.edu.pe
Internet: www.upch.edu.pe

Founded 1961
Private control
Language of instruction: Spanish
Academic year: April to March

Rector: Dr OSWALDO ZEGARRA ROJAS
Vice-Rector for Academic Affairs: Dr DAVID LOZA FERNÁNDEZ
Vice-Rector for Research: Dr ALBERTO RAMÍREZ RAMOS
Vice-Rector for Admin. Affairs: Dr RODOLFO ZAVALA ULFFE
Sec.-Gen.: JUAN JIMÉNEZ BENDEZU

Number of teachers: 450
Number of students: 4,264

Publications: *Acta Herediana*, *Boletín UPCH*, *Revista Acta Andina*, *Revista Estomatológica*, *Revista Médica Herediana*

DEANS

Faculty of Education: Dr MAÑUEL BELLO DOMINGUEZ
Faculty of Medicine: Dr LUIS CARAVEDO REYES
Faculty of Nursing: Dr MARGOT ZARATE LEÓN
Faculty of Public Health and Administration: Dr ALEJANDRO LLANOS CUENTAS
Faculty of Sciences and Philosophy: Dr ABRAHAM VAISBERG WOLACH
Faculty of Stomatology: Dr FERNANDO DONAYRE GONZALES
School of Postgraduate Studies: Dr ENRIQUE MACHICADO ZAVALA

UNIVERSIDAD DE PIURA

Avda Ramón Mugica 131, Urbanización San Eduardo, POB 353, Piura
Telephone: (73) 284-500
Fax: (73) 284-510
E-mail: info@udep.edu.pe
Internet: www.udep.edu.pe

Founded 1969
Private control
Language of instruction: Spanish
Academic year: March to December

Pres.: Dr ANTONIO ABRUÑA PUYOL
Vice-Pres.: ANTONIO MABRES TORELLÓ
Vice-Pres.: DANTE GUERRERO CHANDUVÍ
Vice-Pres.: JESÚS CHIYÓN DE MARES
Vice-Pres.: SERGIO BALAREZO SALDAÑA
Gen. Sec.: WILLIAM ZAPATA JIMÉNEZ
Librarian: Dr MARÍA JOSÉ ANDRADE DE HAKANSSON

Number of teachers: 233
Number of students: 5,400

Publications: *Boletín electrónico DesdelCampus*, *Libro de Humanidades*, *Mercurio Peruano*, *Periódico Campus*, *Revista Amigos*, *Revista de Investigacion de Derecho*, *Revista de Investigacion de Comunicacion*

DEANS

Faculty of Communications: MELA SALAZAR VELARDE
Faculty of Economics and Business Administration: MARIELA GARCÍA ROJAS
Faculty of Education: FLOR HAU YON PALOMINO
Faculty of Engineering: Dra. SUSANA VEGAS CHIYÓN
Faculty Of Humanities: Arq. ERNESTO MAVILA UGARTE
Faculty of Law: Dr CARLOS HAKANSSON NIETO
Faculty of Sciences and Humanities: Arq. ERNESTO MAVILA UGARTE

UNIVERSIDAD RICARDO PALMA

Avda Benavides 5440, Urb. Las Gardenias, Santiago de Surco, Apdo 18-0131, Lima
Telephone: (1) 275-0450
Fax: (1) 275-0468
E-mail: webmaster@urp.edu.pe
Internet: www.urp.edu.pe

Founded 1969
Private control
Language of instruction: Spanish
Academic year: April to December

Rector: Dr IVÁN RODRÍGUEZ CHÁVEZ
Vice-Rectors: Dr HUGO SÁNCHEZ CARLESSI, Arq. ROBERTO CHANG CHAO
Sec.-Gen.: Lic. GERARDO CHOQUE MARTINEZ
Librarian: Mg. ROSARIO VALDIVIA PAZ SOLDÁN

Number of teachers: 650
Number of students: 9,000

Publications: *Revista*, *Revista Arquitextos*, *Revista Biotempus*, *Revista de la Facultad de Ciencias Económicas*, *Revista de la Faculdad de Lenguas Modernas*, *Revista de la Facultad de Psicología*, *Revista Perfiles de Ingeniería*, *Tradición*

DEANS

Faculty of Architecture and Town Planning: Arq. OSWALDO VELÁSQUEZ HIDALGO
Faculty of Biological Sciences: Dra REINA ZUÑIGA DE ACLETO
Faculty of Economics: Dr RONALD FIGUEROA AVILA
Faculty of Engineering: Mg. LEONARDO ALCAYHUAMAN ACCOSTUPA
Faculty of Medicine: Dr MANUEL HUAMÁN GUERRERO
Faculty of Modern Languages: Dra DORA BAZÁN DE DEVOTO
Faculty of Psychology: Dr RAÚL YAÑEZ CANNON

UNIVERSIDAD DE SAN MARTÍN DE PORRES

Ciuadad Universitaria, Avda Las Calandrias s/n, Santa Anita, Lima
Telephone: (1) 362-0064
E-mail: rectorado@usmp.edu.pe
Internet: www.usmp.edu.pe

Founded 1969

Rector: Ing. JOSE ANTONIO CHANG

Depts of arts, education; institutes of philosophy and social sciences, history, geography.

College

UNIVERSIDAD ESAN

Apdo 1846, Lima 100
Telephone: (1) 317-7200
Fax: (1) 345-1328
E-mail: cendoc@esan.edu.pe
Internet: www.esan.edu.pe

Founded 1963, as a jt venture between the Peruvian Govt and the US Dept of State Agency for Int. Devt to promote the socio-economic devt of the region; training in management at graduate level and for executives

Dir: JORGE TALAVERA TRAVERSO

Library of 50,000 vols
Number of teachers: 37
Number of students: 3,000

Publications: *Cuadernos de Difusión* (2 a year), *Documentos de Trabajo*, *INFORMESAN* (institutional bulletin, 26 a year).

Schools of Art and Music

Conservatorio Nacional de Música (National Conservatory of Music): Jr. Carabaya 429, Lima; tel. (1) 426-9677; fax (1) 426-5658; e-mail cnmdg@terra.com.pe; f. 1908 as Academia Nacional de Música 'Alcedo', autonomous since 1966; performance, musicology, education, composition; choir and orchestra; library: 14,000 books and musical scores, and record library; 87 teachers; 400 students; Dir Gen. ENRIQUE ITURRIAGA ROMERO; Acad. Dir CARMEN ESCOBEDE REVOREDO; publ. *Conservatorio* (1 a year).

Affiliated Institutes:

Conservatorio Regional de Música del Norte 'Carlos Valderrama': Independencia 572 (2° piso), Trujillo; tel. (44) 235392; fax (44) 235392; e-mail crmncv@qnet.com.pe; f. 1946; 42 teachers; 450 students; Dir CARLOS E. PAREDES ABAD.

Escuela Regional de Música de Huánuco: Dir JAIME DÍAZ.

Escuela Superior de Formación Artística 'Mario Urteaga': km. 3.5 Carretera Baños del Inca, Cajamarca; tel. (44) 826010; fax (44) 821209; e-mail esfamusica@yahoo.com; f. 1984; 9 teachers; 89 students; Dir RAMÓN BAZÁN FIGUEROA.

Escuela Superior de Música 'Condorcunca': Jirón 28 de Julio No 122, Ayacuche; tel. (64) 812598; e-mail esma@goalsnet.com.pe; f. 1957; 33 teachers; 152 students; Dir PEDRO RAMÓN CASTILLA HUAYHUA.

Escuela Superior de Música 'José María Valle Riestra': Avda Bolognesi No 890, Piura; tel. (74) 322632; e-mail esmjmvr@lanet.com.pe; f. 1951; 23 teachers; 203 students; Dir REYNALDO E. BURGO PÉREZ.

Escuela Superior de Música 'Luis Duncker Lavalle': Calle 4 s/n, Coop. Labramara J. L. Bustamante y Rivero, Arequipa; tel. (54) 424510; fax (54) 425723; e-mail esma@terra.com.pe; f. 1945; 33 teachers; 251 students; Dir ELÍAS ADOLFO CHÁVEZ.

Escuela Superior Pública de Formación Artística 'Francisco Lase': Avda 2 de Mayo No 412, Tacna; tel. (54) 711601; fax (54) 711601; e-mail esfafl@correoweb.com; internet www.geocities.com/esfafl; f. 1989; 45 teachers; 315 students; Dir DAVID ORTIZ OVIEDO.

Instituto Superior de Música 'Leandre Alviña Miranda': Tocuyeres 526, San Blas, Cusco; tel. (84) 231621; fax (84) 231621; e-mail ismlam.cusco@latinmail.com.pe; f. 1950; 36 teachers; 192 students; Dir ESTEBAN ITUPA LLAVINA.

Escuela Nacional Superior Autónoma de Bellas Artes del Perú (Autonomous National School of Fine Arts): Jirón Ancash 681, Lima; tel. (1) 427-2200; internet www.ensabap.edu.pe; f. 1918; to train artists and teachers; library: 5,000 vols; Dir PEDRO BENITO ROTTA BISSO; publ. *Anuario Académico*.

Escuela Regional de Bellas Artes 'Diego Quispe Tito': Calle Márquez 271, Cusco; tel. (84) 231-491.

Escuela Superior Pública de Arte Carlos Baca Flor: Calle Sucre 111, Cercado, Arequipa; tel. (54) 281-291; f. 1951.

PHILIPPINES

The Higher Education System

From the 16th century until 1898 the Philippines were under Spanish control. They were ceded to the USA under the terms of the Treaty of Paris (1898) and remained under US control until independence was achieved in 1946. The Philippines' colonial inheritance is reflected in its higher education system. The two oldest institutions, the University of San Carlos (founded in 1595; current status since 1948) and the University of Santo Tomás (founded in 1611), are both private Catholic universities, while universities founded during or after the period of US control are modelled on US institutions. The Commission on Higher Education is the supreme national body for public and private universities. In 2004/05 there were 2,402,315 students enrolled in 1,619 university-level institutions.

Admission to higher education is on the basis of satisfactory performance in the High School Diploma and the university entrance examination. Most Filipino degrees are awarded on a 'credit–semester' basis; students are expected to accrue a specified number of credits each semester throughout the duration of the degree in order to graduate. Associate degrees are offered by community colleges and universities and are two-year programmes of study in the arts and sciences. The first full undergraduate degree is the Bachelors, usually a four-year course, but degrees in certain subjects may require longer periods of study, such as law and medicine (eight years). The postgraduate degrees are the Masters and PhD. The Masters lasts for two years and consists of full-time study and the submission of a thesis. For a PhD, students are required to undertake at least three years of study and research, and to complete a dissertation.

The Technical Education and Skills Development Authority is the controlling body of post-secondary technical and vocational education, which is offered by public and private technical/vocational institutes and specialist institutions. The duration of programmes varies from one to three years; in some instances programmes are geared towards a Certificate system of four levels. There is no mandatory system of accreditation for higher education, but the Commission on Higher Education encourages institutions to seek accreditation from one of four agencies, namely Philippine Accrediting Association of Schools, Colleges and Universities, Philippine Association of Colleges and Universities—Commission on Accreditation, Association of Christian Schools and Colleges—Accrediting Agency, Inc. and Accrediting Agency of Chartered Colleges and Universities in the Philippines. All of the above-listed bodies are members of the Federation of Accreditation Agencies of the Philippines.

Regulatory and Representative Bodies

GOVERNMENT

Department of Education: DepED Complex, Meralco Ave, Pasig City, 1600 Metro Manila; tel. (2) 632-13-61; fax (2) 638-86-34; internet www.deped.gov.ph; Sec. of Education ARMIN A. LUISTRO.

ACCREDITATION

Accrediting Agency of Chartered Colleges and Universities in the Philippines, Inc. (AACCUP): 812 Future Point Plaza 1, 112 Panay Ave, South Triangle, Quezon City; tel. (2) 415-9016; fax (2) 415-8995; e-mail aaccup@axti.com; internet www.aaccupqa.org.ph; f. 1987; accredits curricular programmes in the Philippines, particularly for state univs and colleges; 107 mems (104 state univs and colleges, 3 local colleges); Pres. and Chair. of Board of Trustees Dr RUPERTO S. SANGALANG; Exec. Dir Dr MANUEL T. CORPUS.

Federation of Accrediting Agencies of the Philippines (FAAP): Unit 302 Puno Building, 47 Kalayaan Ave, Diliman, Quezon City; tel. (2) 927-9645; f. 1976; NGO founded to improve the quality of education by means of voluntary accreditation for private higher education instns; Pres. Dr FELICIANA A. REYES.

Philippine Accrediting Association of Schools, Colleges and Universities (PAASCU): Unit 107, The Tower at Emerald Sq., J. P. Rizal corner P. Tuazon Sts, 1109 Quezon City; tel. (2) 911-2845; fax (2) 911-0807; e-mail info@paascu.org.ph; internet www.paascu.org.ph; f. 1957; private org. accrediting academic programmes that meet commonly accepted standards of quality education; has accredited programmes in 229 instns; Chair. of Board of Dirs Dr RAMON C. REYES; Exec. Dir CONCEPCION V. PIJANO.

Philippine Association of Colleges and Universities, Commission on Accreditation (PACUCOA): Suite 7M Eagle Star Condominium, Dela Rosa St, Loyola Heights, Katipunan Ave, Quezon City; tel. (2) 426-0089; e-mail pacucoa@yahoo.com; f. 1967; accredits private colleges and univs; 125 mem. schools with 799 programmes; Chair. Dr ROSITA L. NAVARRO; Exec. Dir Dr ADLAI C. CASTIGADOR.

FUNDING

Fund Assistance to Private Education (FAPE): 7th Floor, Concorde Condominium, Salcedo cnr Benavides Sts, Legaspi Village, Makati City; tel. (2) 816-4136; fax (2) 818-0013; f. 1968; perpetual trust fund set up by the Philippines govt with help from the US govt; funds are provided by interest earned on the initial capital augmented by donations and grants; Exec. Dir CAROLINA PORIO.

NATIONAL BODIES

Association of Catholic Universities of the Philippines, Inc.: University of Santo Tomás (Room 111, Main Bldg), España, Manila; tel. (2) 731-35-44; fax (2) 740-97-27; f. 1973 to serve the interests of the 21 Catholic univs in the Philippines; Pres. Fr TAMERLANE R. LANA; Sec. Gen. Prof. GIOVANNA V. FONTANILLA; publ. *ACUP Newsletter* (1 a year).

Catholic Educational Association of the Philippines (CEAP): 7 Road 16, Bagong Pag-asa, 1105 Quezon City; tel. (2) 426-2679; fax (2) 426-2670; e-mail ceap@edsamail.com.ph; internet www.eccceonline.org/ceap; f. 1941; Pres. Fr RODERICK SALAZAR, Jr.

Commission on Higher Education: 5th Floor, DAP Bldg, San Miguel Ave, Ortigas Centre, Pasig City; tel. (2) 634-6836; fax (2) 633-1980; e-mail info@ched.gov.ph; internet www.ched.gov.ph; f. 1994; governing body covering public and private higher education instns as well as degree-granting programmes in all tertiary educational insts in the Philippines; Chair. ROMULO L. NERI; Exec. Dir Dr WILLIAM C. MEDRANO.

Coordinating Council for Private Educational Association (COCOPEA): 89-C 9th Ave, Cubao, Quezon City; tel. (2) 913-2932; fax (2) 911-5888; promotes excellence in private higher education instns; Pres. JUANITO M. ACANTO.

Philippine Association of Colleges and Universities (PACU): Unit 601 Richmonde Plaza, Ortigas Centre, San Miguel Ave, Pasig City; tel. (2) 638-5635; fax (2) 637-6795; e-mail pacuinc@yahoo.com; internet www.pacu.org.ph; f. 1932; Pres. Dr VICENTE K. FABELLA; Sec. Dr PATRICIA B. LAGUNDA.

Philippine Association of Private Schools, Colleges and Universities (PAPSCU): 10th Fl., Bldg 7, Emilio Aguinaldo College, 113 Gonzales cnr San Marcelino Sts, UN Ave, Ermita, Manila; tel. (2) 522-0097; fax (2) 523-3117; e-mail papscu2005@yahoo.com.ph; internet www.papscu.org.ph; f. 1956; Pres. Dr JOSE PAULO E. CAMPOS.

Philippine Association of State Universities and Colleges: 2nd Fl., ITC Bldg, EARIST Compound, Valencia St, Sta Mesa, Manila; tel. (2) 716-0944; fax (2) 716-0430; f. 1967; ind. but attached to Dept of Education; aims to foster excellence in higher education, to promote communication among its mem. institutions, to encourage studies on higher education, to secure adequate government support for education, to encourage inter-institutional assistance through fellowships, grants, teacher exchange, accreditation; 75 mem. institutions; library with special collections on education; Pres. ELDIGARIO D. GONZALES; Exec. Dir Dr FREDERICK S. PADA; publ. *Baliham* (4 a year).

Learned Societies

GENERAL

Academia Filipina (Philippine Academy): 47 Juan Luna St, San Lorenzo Village, 1200 Makati, Metro Manila; tel. (2) 817-1128; fax (2) 817-1135; f. 1924; corresp. of the Real Academia Española (Madrid); 15 mems; Dir ALEJANDRO ROCES; Sec. SALVADOR B. MALIG.

AGRICULTURE, FISHERIES AND VETERINARY SCIENCE

Crop Science Society of the Philippines: c/o Phil Rice, Los Baños, Pili Drive, College, Laguna; tel. (49) 536-3635; e-mail asian@laguna.net; internet www.cssp.org.ph; f. 1970; 3,000 mems; Pres. NORVIE L. MANIGBAS; Vice-Pres. RENATO A. REANO; publ. *Philippine Journal of Crop Science* (3 a year).

Philippine Society of Agricultural Engineers: ATI Bldg Elliptical Rd, Diliman, Quezon City; tel. and fax (2) 920-4071; e-mail contact@psae.net; internet psae.net; f. 1950; 5,800 mems; Pres. Dr TERESITO G. AGUINALDO.

Philippine Veterinary Medical Association: Unit 233, Union Square Condominium, 15th Ave, Cubao, Quezon City; tel. (2) 911-3159; internet www.pvma.com.ph; f. 1907; 5,274 mems; Pres. Dr TOMAS C. LAZARO II.

ARCHITECTURE AND TOWN PLANNING

United Architects of the Philippines (UAP): 53 Scout Rallos St, Diliman, Quezon City 1103; tel. (2) 412-6374; fax (2) 372-1796; e-mail uap@united-architects.org; internet www.united-architects.org; f. 1974 following merger of Philippine Institute of Architects, League of Philippine Architects and Association of Philippine Government Architects; Pres. EDRIC MARCO C. FLORENTINO; Sec.-Gen. GIL C. EVASCO.

BIBLIOGRAPHY, LIBRARY SCIENCE AND MUSEOLOGY

Association of Special Libraries of the Philippines (ASLP): Room 301, National Library Bldg, Kalaw St, Ermita, Manila; tel. (2) 524-4611; e-mail ladladj@dlsu.edu.ph; internet www.aczafra.com; f. 1954; 556 mems; Pres. JOCELYN L. LADAD; Sec. ARLENE Y. GONZALES; publs *ASLP Bulletin* (4 a year), *ASLP Newsletter* (4 a year), *Directory of Special Libraries*.

HISTORY, GEOGRAPHY AND ARCHAEOLOGY

Philippine Historical Association: c/o Office of External Affairs, St Mary's College, 37 M. Ignacia Ave, 1103 Quezon City; tel. 413-4076 ext. 222; fax 374-3073; e-mail glo.santos@yahoo.com; f. 1955; 500 mems; Pres. Prof. AMBETH OCAMPO; Exec. Dir Dr GLORIA M. SANTOS; publs *Philippine Historical Bulletin* (1 a year), *PHA Balita* (2 a year).

LANGUAGE AND LITERATURE

Alliance Française: POB 2899, 128 Manila; located at: 209 Nicanor Garcia St, Bel Air II, 1209 Makati City; tel. (2) 895-75-85; fax (2) 899-36-54; e-mail info@alliance.ph; internet www.alliance.ph; offers courses and examinations in French language and culture and promotes cultural exchange with France; Dir PHILIPPE NORMAND.

British Council: 10th Fl., Taipan Pl., F. Ortigas Jr Ave, Ortigas Centre, Pasig City 1605, Manila; tel. (2) 914-1011; fax (2) 914-1020; e-mail britishcouncil@britishcouncil.org.ph; internet www.britishcouncil.org/philippines; teaching centre; offers courses and examinations in English language and British culture and promotes cultural exchange with the UK; library; Dir GILL WESTAWAY.

Goethe-Institut: POB 1744, Makati Central Post Office, 1257 Makati City; 4-5/F Adamson Centre, 121 Leviste St, Salcedo Village, 1227 Makati City; tel. (2) 817-0978; fax (2) 817-0979; e-mail goetheinfo@manila.goethe.org; internet www.goethe.de/manila; f. 1961; offers courses and examinations in German language and culture and promotes cultural exchange with Germany; library of 3,000 vols; Dir RICHARD KÜNZEL.

Instituto Cervantes: 855 T. M. Kalaw St, Ermita, 1000 Manila; tel. (2) 526-14-82; fax (2) 526-14-49; e-mail cenmni@cervantes.es; internet manila.cervantes.es; f. 1991; offers courses and examinations in Spanish language and culture and promotes cultural exchange with Spain and Spanish-speaking countries; library of 23,000 vols, 1,500 CDs and audio cassettes, 2,000 video cassettes and 500 DVDs; Dir JOSÉ RODRÍGUEZ; Sec. KATERINA VENERACIÓN.

Komisyon sa Wikang Filipino: Watson Bldg, 1610 J. P. Laurel St, San Miguel, Manila; tel. (2) 734-55-46; fax (2) 736-03-15; internet www.komfil.gov.ph; f. 1991 (fmrly Institute of Philippine Languages); aims to develop, promote and standardize Filipino and other Philippine languages; library of 5,000 vols; Chair. Dr PONCIANO B. P. PINEDA; publ. *Sangwika* (newsletter, 4 a year).

MEDICINE

Manila Medical Society: 800 Taft Ave, Manila; tel. (2) 524-9944; fax (2) 525-6771; e-mail mmsi@yahoo.com; internet www.geocities.com/mmsi1902; f. 1902; 1,249 mems; Pres. Dr ASCENSION F. BAUTISTA; Sec. Dr FELICISIMA B. BACON.

Philippine Medical Association: PMA Bldg, North Ave, Quezon City; tel. (2) 929-6366; fax (2) 929-6951; e-mail medical@pma.com.ph; internet www.pma.com.ph; f. 1903; 107 component societies, 60 affiliated speciality societies; Pres. Dr MODESTO O. LLAMAS; Sec.-Gen. Dr REY MELCHOR SANTOS; publ. *Journal*.

Philippine Paediatric Society, Inc.: POB 3527, Manila; f. 1947; 620 mems; Pres. Dr JOEL S. ELISES; Sec. Dr VICTOR S. DOCTOR; publ. *Philippine Journal of Paediatrics* (6 a year).

Philippine Pharmaceutical Association: 815 R. Papa St. Sampaloc, 1008 Manila; tel. (2) 50-9006; fax (2) 522-3230; f. and incorporated 1920; 8,000 mems; Pres. Dr LOURDES TALAG ECHAUZ; Exec. Sec. Dr NORMA V. LERMA.

NATURAL SCIENCES

General

National Academy of Science and Technology: 2nd Fl., Philippine Science Heritage Centre, DOST Complex, Gen. Santos Ave, Bicutan, Taguig City, 1631 Metro Manila; tel. (2) 837-2071; fax (2) 837-3170; e-mail secretariat@nast.ph; internet www.nast.dost.gov.ph; f. 1976; advises the Pres. and Cabinet on policies concerning science and technology nationally; Pres. Dr EMIL Q. JAVIER; Sec. Dr EVELYN MAE TECSON-MENDOZA.

Physical Sciences

Philippine Council of Chemists: 2227 Severino Reyes St, Sta Cruz, POB 1202, Manila 2805; f. 1958; 200 mems; Nat. Pres. MIGUEL G. AMPIL; Gen. Sec. P. B. CARBONELL; publ. *Bulletin*.

TECHNOLOGY

Philippine Institute of Mining, Metallurgical and Geological Engineers: POB 1595, Manila; f. 1940; 117 mems; Pres. JONES R. CASTRO; Sec.-Treas. LEOPOLDO F. ABAD.

Philippine Society of Civil Engineers: c/o Bureau of Public Works, Bonifacio Drive, Manila; f. 1918; assumed present title 1933; Pres. FLORENCIO MORENO; Sec.-Treas. TOMAS DE GUZMÁN; publ. *The Philippine Engineering Record* (4 a year).

Philippine Society of Mechanical Engineers: 19 Scout Bayoran St, South Triangle, Quezon City; tel. (2) 371-1819; fax (2) 372-4341; e-mail info@psme.org; internet www.psme.org; f. 1952; Pres. Eng EDIMAR V. SALCEDO.

Research Institutes

GENERAL

Advanced Science and Technology Institute: ASTI Bldg., C. P. Garcia Ave., Technology Park Complex, U.P. Campus, Diliman, Quezon City, 1101; tel. (2) 426-9755; fax (2) 925-8598; e-mail info@asti.dost.gov.ph; internet www.asti.dost.gov.ph; conducts research and devt in information and communications technology and microelectronics; Dir DENIS F. VILLORENTE.

Institute of Philippine Culture, Ateneo de Manila University: Frank Lynch Hall, Social Devt Complex, Loyola Heights, Quezon City 1108; tel. and fax 426-6067; e-mail ipc@admu.edu.ph; internet www.ipc-ateneo.org; f. 1960 as a univ. research org.; undertakes studies directed towards solving devt problems, particularly in the areas of upland devt, local governance, agrarian reform, community health, resources management, irrigation, forestry, women and sustainable agriculture; assists devt agencies; trains agency personnel and local communities in the use of research methodologies; library of 7,000 vols, 3,000 reprints and 104 multimedia vols; Dir Dr WILFREDO F. ARCE; publs *Culture and Development Series*, *IPC Discussion Papers*, *IPC Final Reports*, *IPC Monograph Series*, *IPC Papers*, *IPC Social Explorations Series*.

National Research Council of the Philippines: General Santos Ave, Bicutan, Taguig City; tel. (2) 837-6141; fax (2) 837-6143; e-mail nrcpinfo@dost.gov.ph; internet mis.dost.gov.ph/nrcp; f. 1933; supports basic research in a wide variety of fields; 12 scientific divisions; 2,250 mems; library of 1,300 vols; Pres. Prof. FORTUNATO T. DELA PEÑA; Exec. Dir Dr PACIENTE A. CORDERO Jr; publs *Newsletter* (4 a year), *NRCP Research Journal* (4 a year), *Technical Bulletin* (irregular).

AGRICULTURE, FISHERIES AND VETERINARY SCIENCE

Bureau of Plant Industry: 692 San Andres St, Malate, Manila; tel. (2) 525-7857; fax (2) 521-7650; e-mail cu.bpi@da.gov.ph; internet bpi.da.gov.ph; f. 1930; conserves and develops Philippine plant genetic resources and ensures the protection and development of the plant industry; library of 10,000 vols; Dir LEALYN A. RAMOS.

Forest Products Research and Development Institute (FPRDI): Narra St, Forestry Campus, UP College, Los Baños, Laguna 4031; tel. (49) 536-2360; fax (49) 536-3630; e-mail fprdi@dost.gov.ph; internet www.fprdi.dost.gov.ph; f. 1957; conducts basic and applied research on forestry, forest products and other related areas; undertakes the transfer of completed research; provides technical services and industrial manpower training; library of 17,000 vols, 8,042 books, 3,431 reports, 4,500 vols of periodicals; Dir IV Dr ROMULO T. AGGANGAN; Sec. Dr MARIO G. MONTEJO; publs *Forest Products Technoflow*, *FPRDI Journal* (1 a year), *Lexicon of Philippine Trees*.

Philippine Rice Research Institute: Central Experiment Station Maligaya, Science City of Muñoz, Nueva Ecija; tel. (44) 456-0277; e-mail prri@philrice.gov.ph; internet www.philrice.gov.ph; f. 1960; aims to sustain the country's self-sufficiency in rice; undertakes and funds a national research and development programme for rice and rice-based farming systems; trains scientists, farmer leaders and agribusiness managers; Exec. Dir Dr LEOCADIO S. SEBASTIAN.

EDUCATION

Science Education Institute: c/o Department of Science and Technology, 3rd PTRI Bldg, Bicutan, Taguig, 1604, Metro Manila; tel. (2) 837-1359; fax (2) 837-1924; e-mail webmaster@sei.dost.gov.ph; internet www.sei.dost.gov.ph; Dir Dr ESTER B. OGENA.

Southeast Asian Ministers of Education Organization Regional Center for Educational Innovation and Technology (SEAMEO INNOTECH): Commonwealth Ave, Diliman, Quezon City 1101; tel. (2) 924-7681; fax (2) 921-0224; e-mail info@seameo-innotech.org; internet www.seameo-innotech.org; f. 1970; identifies basic educational problems common to the SE Asian region and assists the SE Asian Mins of Education Org. mem. countries in the solution of these problems; conducts training, devt, research, evaluation, information and communications technology and other spec. programmes; library of 18,000 vols; Dir Dr ERLINDA C. PEFIANCO; publs *INNOTECH Journal* (2 a year), *INNOTECH Newsletter* (2 a year).

MEDICINE

Food and Nutrition Research Institute: c/o Department of Science and Technology, Gen. Santos Ave, Bicutan, Taguig 1604, Metro Manila; tel. (2) 837-2934; fax (2) 837-3164; e-mail mvc@fnri.dost.gov.ph; internet www.fnri.dost.gov.ph; f. 1987; Dir Dr MARIO V. CAPANZANA.

NATURAL SCIENCES

Physical Sciences

Philippine Institute of Volcanology and Seismology: PHIVOLCS Bldg, C. P. Garcia Ave, U.P. Campus, Diliman, Quezon City; tel. (2) 426-14-68; fax (2) 929-83-66; e-mail phivolcs@x5.phivolcs.dost.gov.ph; internet www.phivolcs.dost.gov.ph; f. 1952; library of 3,000 vols; Dir RENATO U. SOLIDUM, Jr.

TECHNOLOGY

Industrial Technology Development Institute: DOST Compound, Gen. Santos Ave, Bicutan, Taguig 1631, Metro Manila; tel. (2) 837-2071; fax (2) 837-6156; e-mail nea@dost.gov.ph; internet www.mis.dost.gov.ph/itdi; f. 1951; carries out research and development in the areas of food processing, materials science, chemicals and minerals, electronics and process control, fuels and energy, microbiology and genetics, and the environment; Dir Dr NUNA E. ALMANZOR.

Metals Industry Research and Development Centre: MIRDC Compound, Gen. Santos Ave, Bicutan, Taguig 1604, Metro Manila; tel. (2) 837-0431; fax (2) 837-0430; e-mail adcruz@dost.gov.ph; internet www.mirdc.dost.gov.ph; f. 1972; research and devt, quality control, and testing of metal products; Exec. Dir ARTHUR LUCAS D. CRUZ; publ. *Metals Industry Trends and Events* (newsletter, 3 a year).

Mines and Geosciences Bureau: North Ave, Diliman, Quezon City, 1100, Metro Manila; tel. (2) 920-91-20; fax (2) 920-16-35; e-mail central@mgb.gov.ph; internet www.mgb.gov.ph; f. 1898; administers the utilization and management of the country's mineral wealth; conducts geological, mining, metallurgical, chemical and other research; undertakes geological and mineral exploration surveys; library of 4,200 vols; Dir JEREMIAS DOLINO; publs *Mineral Gazette* (2 a year), *Mineral Industry Indicators* (2 a year), *National Directory of Producing Mines and Quarries in the Philippines* (1 a year), *Philippine Mineral Industry Review* (4 a year), *Philippine Mineral Statistics* (1 a year).

Philippine Nuclear Research Institute: Commonwealth Ave, Diliman, Quezon City 1101; tel. (2) 920-8787; fax (2) 920-1646; e-mail nrlsd@pnri.dost.gov.ph; internet www.pnri.dost.gov.ph; f. 1958; peaceful applications of nuclear energy; library of 19,069 vols; Dir Dr ALUMANDA M. DELA ROSA (acting); publ. *Philippines Nuclear Journal* (1 a year).

Philippine Textile Research Institute: Gen. Santos Ave, Bicutan, Taguig City, Metro Manila; tel. and fax (2) 837-1325; e-mail ptri@dost.gov.ph; internet www.ptri.dost.gov.ph; f. 1967; conducts applied research and development for the textile industry; provides technical services and training programmes; Dir Dr CARLOS C. TOMBOC.

Libraries and Archives

Bacalod City

Bacalod City Library: Bacalod City, Negros Occidental; e-mail mcorpuz@bacolodcity.gov.ph; 50,000 vols.

Cagayan de Oro City

Cagayan de Oro City Public Library: Apolinar Velez St, Cagayan de Oro City; tel. (8822) 72-55-60; Librarian MYRNA F. ACEDERA.

Xavier University Library: Ateneo de Cagayan, Corrales Ave, Cagayan de Oro City 9000; tel. (8822) 72-31-16 ext. 2302; fax (8822) 72-71-63; e-mail librarytech@xu.edu.ph; internet library.xu.edu.ph; f. 1933; 121,500 vols, 376 periodicals; Dir, Univ. Libraries ANNABELLE P. ACEDERA; publ. *Kinaadman*.

Cebu City

Cebu City Public Library: Osmeña Blvd., Cebu City; tel. (32) 253-1526; Librarian CIRILA A. DELOS REYES.

University of San Carlos Library: P. del Rosario St, 6000 Cebu City; tel. (32) 253-1000 ext. 133; fax (32) 254-04-32; e-mail direklib@usc.edu.ph; internet www.usc.edu.ph; f. 1947; 269,705 vols incl. 21,320 vols of Filipiniana, 3,360 titles of periodicals (44,992 vols total); 3,502 audiovisual items; spec. colln for local studies held in Cebuano Studies Centre at above address; Dir of Libraries Dr MARILOU P. TADLIP.

Davao City

Davao City Library: 3rd Fl., SP Building, San Pedro St, Davao City; tel. (82) 227-3137; fax (82) 226-8913; Librarian NORA FE ALAJAR.

Dumaguete

Silliman University Library: 6200 Dumaguete City, Negros Oriental; tel. and fax (35) 422-7208; internet su.edu.ph; f. 1906; 200,000 items; Librarian LORNA YSO; publs *Convergence* (arts and sciences, irregular), *Silliman Journal* (humanities, social sciences and sciences, 2 a year).

Makati City

Asian Institute of Management, Knowledge Resource Centre: 123 Paseo de Roxas, POB 2095, Makati City 1260; tel. (2) 892-4011; fax (2) 817-2663; e-mail vong@aim.edu; internet www.aim.edu; f. 1968; 20,000 vols; Knowledge Resource Officer VIRGINIA ONG; Chief Librarian VIRGINIA G. ONG.

Filipinas Heritage Library: Nielson Tower, Ayala Triangle Makati Ave, Makati City, 1224; tel. (2) 892-1801; fax (2) 892-1810; e-mail asklibrarian@filipinaslibrary.org.ph; internet www.filipinaslibrary.org.ph; f. 1996; research library specializing in Philippine art, culture, history, language, religion and social sciences; also covers management, marketing, information technology, human resources and literature; 13,000 vols; Dir MA. ANTONIA C.

Manila

Adamson University Library: 900 San Marcelino St, Ermita, 1000 Manila; tel. (2) 524-2011 ext. 131; fax (2) 524-8038; e-mail hdecastro@adamson.edu.ph; internet www.adamson.edu.ph; f. 1933; Dir of Libraries HELEN C. DE CASTRO.

Ateneo de Manila University Rizal Library: Katipunan Ave, Loyola Heights, Quezon City 1108; tel. (2) 426-6001; fax (2) 426-5961; e-mail ltdavid@ateneo.edu; internet rizal.lib.admu.edu.ph; f. 1967; 240,000 vols, 36,000 bound periodicals, 325,000 microforms; preservation of spec. collns, incl. Filipiniana colln, Rizaliana, American Historical colln, Pardo de Tavera colln and the Ateneo Library of Women's Writings; Dir Prof. LOURDES T. DAVID; publs *Asian Perspectives in the Humanities and the Arts*, *Journal of Philippine Studies*.

Far Eastern University Library: POB 609, Quezon Blvd, Manila 1008; 3rd Fl., NRH Bldg, Nicanor Reyes Sr St, Sampaloc, Manila 1008; tel. (2) 735-5649; e-mail evelyn_sf@hotmail.com; f. 1928; 82,243 vols; Librarian Dr EVELYN S. FABITO.

Manila City Library: 2nd Fl., Sining Kayumanggi Bldg, Mehan Garden, Malate, Manila; tel. (2) 523-8688; Chief Librarian FILEMON L. GECOLEA.

National Library of the Philippines: POB 2926, T. M. Kalaw St, 1000 Ermita, Manila; tel. (2) 525-3196; fax (2) 524-2329; e-mail amb@nlp.gov.ph; internet www.nlp.gov.ph; f. 1900; 207,703 books, 6,250 periodicals, 813,095 MSS, 51,680 vols of theses and disserations, 10,332 cassette tapes, 6,004 microfilms, 2,190 sheet maps, 388 CD-ROMs; also 762,459 vols in public libraries and 8,579 vols in bookmobiles; Dir PRUDENCIANA C. CRUZ; publs *Philippine National Bibliography* (1 a year), *TNL Newsletter* (irregular).

Philippine Women's University Library: Taft Ave, Manila 1004; internet www.pwu.edu.ph; nine br. libraries; 87,620 vols; medicine, pure sciences, Filipiniana, music, the arts, literature, archive collection; Librarian DIONISIA M. ANGELES.

Science and Technology Information Institute, Department of Science and Technology: DOST Complex, Gen. Santos Ave, Upper Bicutan, Taguig City, Metro Manila; tel. (2) 837-2191; fax (2) 837-7518; e-mail litanobleza@yahoo.com; internet www

.stii.dost.gov.ph; f. 1988; acquisition of science and technology information materials, technical information processing, library and reference services, science information services, training in science and technology information and computer applications; training on ScINET Integrated LibraryManagement System (SILMS); provides communication and publication services, prepares audiovisual materials on science and technology, press releases, documentary films/video, coordinates and facilitates radio and television interviews of scientists and science managers; 10,534 vols, 2,549 periodicals, 1,903 theses and dissertations, 1,661 nonprints, 32,708 analytics and 251 investigative projects, 411 technical reports; Dir RAYMUND E. LIBORO; publs *Philippine Journal of Science* (2 a year), *Philippine Men and Women of Science* (1 a year), *Philippine Science and Technology Abstracts* (2 a year), *S&T Post* (4 a year), *Specialized Bibliographies* (on request).

Technological University of the Philippines Library: Ayala Blvd, Ermita, Manila 1000; tel. (2) 302-7750 ext. 601; internet www.tup.edu.ph; 34,170 items; Dir Dr WILHELMINA G. BORJAL.

University of the East Library: 2219 Claro M. Recto Ave, Manila 2806; internet online.ue.edu.ph/manila/library; 183,000 vols; Dir of Libraries NORMA I. JIOCSON.

University of Manila Central Library: 546 Dr M. V. de los Santos St, Sampaloc, Manila; internet www.dlsu.edu.ph/library; f. 1913; 28,600 vols; other libraries; 23,000 vols; Assistant Chief Librarian JUAN MARTIN GUASCH.

University of the Philippines Manila, University Library: 650 Pedro Gil St, Ermita, Manila 1000; tel. (2) 526-4253; fax (2) 526-5847; e-mail tdugenia@mail.upm.edu.ph; internet lib.upm.edu.ph; main library and nine br. libraries; Librarian THERESA P. DUGENIA.

University of Santo Tomás Library: España St, Manila 1015; tel. (2) 731-30-34; fax (2) 740-97-09; e-mail library@mnl.ust.edu.ph; internet library.ust.edu.ph; 391,120 vols; collections of Filipiniana and rare and ancient books; special libraries of Ecclesiastical Faculties, Medicine, Music, Engineering, Fine Arts and Commerce; High School and Elementary School libraries; Prefect of Libraries Fr ANGEL APARICIO; Chief Librarian Prof. ERLINDA F. FLORES.

Quezon City

Loyola School of Theology Library: POB 240, U.P. Quezon City; tel. (2) 426-5966; e-mail lwakefield@admu.edu.ph; internet www.lst.edu/library.asp; f. 1965; 69,000 vols, 18,000 vols of periodicals; Librarian CRISANTA C. ROSALES; publ. *Landas (The Way)* (2 a year).

University of the Philippines Diliman University Library: Gonzalez Hall, Diliman, Quezon City 1101; tel. (2) 926-1877; fax (2) 926-1876; e-mail salvacion.arlante@up.edu.ph; internet www.mainlib.upd.edu.ph; f. 1922; 1,055,048 vols, 32,671 periodical titles; 26 brs; Dir SALVACION M. ARLANTE; publ. *Index to Philippine Periodicals* (4 a year).

Museums and Art Galleries

Cebu City

CAP Art Centre and President Osmeña Memorabilia: 60 Osmeña Blvd, Cebu City; tel. (32) 217-519; fax (32) 218-102; f. 1986; work by artists from all parts of the Philippines; memorabilia concerning the late President Osmeña; Curator MARY F. ABAD.

Casa Gorordo Museum: 35 Lopez Jaena St., Cebu City; tel. (32) 255-5645; fax (32) 253-2380; fmr home of the first Filipino Bishop of Cebu, now restored as a typical 19th century residence; furniture, paintings, religious relics, pottery and ceramics; Exec. Dir CHARLES MUERTEGUI.

Southwestern University Museum: Urgello Rd, Cebu City 6000; tel. and fax (32) 253-6500; internet www.cebu-online.com/swum; prehistoric, archaeological, ethnographic, ecclesiastical and art objects; Dir TONETTE S. PAÑARES.

University of San Carlos Museum: P. del Rosario St, Cebu City 6000; tel. (32) 253-1000 loc 191; fax (32) 253-1000; e-mail museum@usc.edu.ph; internet www.usc.edu.ph; f. 1967; Spanish colonial, ethnographic, archaeological and natural science objects; Curator MARLENE SOCORRO SAMSON.

Davao City

Davao Museum: Zonta Bldg, Insular Village Phase I, Lanang, Davao City; f. 1977; tribal art, local costumes, jewellery, textiles, handicrafts, musical instruments; Curator Dr HEIDI K. GLORIA.

Makati City

Ayala Museum: Makati Avenue, Greenbelt Park, Ayala Center, Makati City 1224; tel. (2) 757-7117; fax (2) 757-3588; e-mail museum_inquiry@ayalamuseum.org; internet www.ayalamuseum.org; f. 1967; archaeological, ethnographic and fine arts collections; paintings by Philippine artists Juan Luna, Fernando Amorsolo and Fernando Zobel; 60 dioramas illustrating Philippine history; models of ships and watercraft; Dir Dr FLORINA H. CAPISTRANO-BAKER.

Makati Museum: J. P. Rizal St, Población, Makati City; tel. (2) 896-0277; native arts and crafts, paintings by contemporary Filipino artists; Curator LINGLING CERVANTES.

Manila

Lopez Memorial Museum: Benpres Bldg, Ground Floor, Exchange Rd, cnr Meralco Ave, Ortigas Centre, Pasig City, Manila; tel. (2) 631-24-17; e-mail pezseum@skyinet.net; internet www.lopezmuseum.org.ph; f. 1960; paintings by the Filipino painters Juan Luna, Felix Resureccion Hidalgo and others; letters and MSS of Jose Rizal; library of 16,000 vols, including rare Filipiniana; Dir MERCEDES LOPEZ VARGAS.

Malacañang Palace Presidential Museum: J. P. Laurel St, San Miguel, Manila; tel. 521-2301; internet www.op.gov.ph/museum; f. 1993; memorabilia of all former Philippine presidents; Dir MA. EDNA S. GAFFUD.

Metropolitan Museum of Manila: Bangko Sentral ng Pilipinas Complex, Roxas Blvd, Manila 1004; tel. (2) 536-1566; fax (2) 523-0613; e-mail info@metmuseum.ph; internet metmuseum.ph; f. 1976; fine arts museum: painting, sculpture, graphic arts, decorative arts, prehistoric gold, pottery; Museum Dir ERIC ZERRUDO; Exhibition and Education Programme Man. CRUZ MAY LYN.

Museo ng Arkidiyosesis ng Maynila (MANA): 121 Arzobispo St, Intramuros, Manila; tel. (2) 527-7631; fax (2) 530-4815; f. 1987, fmrly Archdiocesan Museum of Manila; history of the Catholic Church in the Philippines; Dir Fr ALBERT C. A. FLORES.

Museum of the University of Santo Tomas (UST Museum): 3rd Fl., Main Bldg, Univ. of Santo Tomás, España Blvd, Sampaloc Manila 1015; tel. (2) 781-1815; fax (2) 740-9718; e-mail museum@mnl.ust.edu.ph; internet www.ustmuseum.ust.edu.ph; f. 1871; sections on natural history, Philippine ethnography, Philippine religious images, coins, medals and memorabilia, visual arts, and archeology; Dir Fr ISIDRO C. ABAÑO; publ. *UST Museum Newsletter* (2 a year).

National Museum of the Philippines: P. Burgos Ave, Padre Burgos St, Manila 1000; tel. (2) 527-1215; fax (2) 527-0306; e-mail directornatmuse@yahoo.com; internet www.nationalmuseum.gov.ph; f. 1901; divs of anthropology, archaeology, botany, geology, zoology, museum education, restoration and engineering, arts, cultural properties, planetarium; 19 br. museums and sites; museology training, workshops, outreach activities, lectures; library of 5,442 vols; Dir JEREMY R. BARNS; Dir CECILIO G. SALCEDO; Dir MAHARLIKA A. CUEVAS; Chief Admin. Officer DIONISIO O. PANGILINAN; publ. *National Museum Papers* (scientific journal, 1 a year).

Attached Sites:

Angono Petroglyphs Site: Binangonan, Rizal, Luzon; the most ancient Filipino work of art, dating from c. 1000BC; 127 drawings of human and animal figures; declared a nat. cultural treasure.

Balanghai Site: Libertad, Butuan City, Mindanao; remains of the earliest known watercraft in the country, dating from AD 320.

Bolinao Branch: Bolinao, Pangasinan, Luzon; archaeological and general museum; Head GINA DE VERA.

Butuan City Branch: Butuan City, Mindanao; archaeological artefacts from Agusan del Norte and ethnographic materials from several local ethnic communities; Head MARGARITA CEMBRANO.

Cagsawa Branch: Albay, Luzon; geological materials from the Mayon volcano, archaeological and ethnographic collns; Head ALICE ALAURIN.

Cotabato City Branch: Cotabato City, Mindanao; ethnographic colln of local tribal materials; Head DANIEL LACERNA.

Fort Pilar Branch: Zamboanga City, Mindanao; f. 1985; material culture of 3 ethnic groups, traditional boats; dioramas depicting 400 species of marine life; Head EUFEMIA CATOLIN.

Fort San Pedro Branch: Cebu City, Cebu; ceramics, archaeological artefacts depicting the history of a sunken 16th-century Spanish galleon; Head VICENTE SECUYA.

Jolo Branch: Jolo, Sulu, Mindanao; material culture of Sulu; Head BELEN UDDIN.

Kabayan Branch: Kabayan, Benguet, Luzon; material culture of the Ibalois and the Kankana-ey; Head JULIET IGLOSO.

Kiangan Branch: Kiangan, Ifugao, Luzon; anthropological materials, Ifugao house.

Lubuagan Branch: Lubuagan, Kalinga, Luzon; ethnographic colln on culture of the Kalinga.

Magsingal Branch: Vigan City, Ilocos Sur, Luzon; ethnographic colln on the Ilocano people and liturgical arts; Head REMEDIOS PALACPAC.

Peñablanca Branch: Peñablanca, Cagayan, Luzon; finds from the cave sites of Peñablanca.

Puerto Galera Branch: Puerto Galera, Oriental Mindoro, Luzon; archaeological history of Puerto Galera; Head MAMERTO CONTRERAS.

Tabon Caves Branch: Tabon, Quezon, Palawan; natural heritage of the region; ethnographic materials from 3 local ethnic groups; archaeological artefacts from the Tabon Caves; Head VIVIAN BROWN.

Tuguegarao Branch: Tuguegarao City, Cagayan, Luzon; prehistory of the Cagayan Valley; ethnographic exhibits; Head AIREEN MELAD.

Vigan Branch: Vigan City, Ilocos Sur, Luzon; culture of the Ilocano people through archaeological and ethnographic materials; Head REMEDIOS PALACPAC.

San Agustín Museum: POB 3366, General Luna St, Intramuros, Manila 1002; tel. and fax (2) 527-4060; f. 1972; located in 400-year-old San Agustín monastery; Hispano-Philippino religious art (paintings, sculptures, etc.); library of 3,000 vols; Dir Dr PEDRO G. GALENDE.

Marikina City

Philippine Science Centrum: E-Com Bldg, Riverbanks Centre, 84 Andres Bonifacio Ave, Barangka, Marikina City, 1803 Metro Manila; tel. (2) 942-5136; fax (2) 942-5091; e-mail pfst@science-centrum.ph; internet www.science-centrum.ph; f. 1990; attached to Philippine Foundation for Science and Technology; interactive museum with sections on earth science, human body, light, vision and perception, mechanics, electricity and magnetism, liquids and mathematics; Exec. Dir MAY PAGSINOHIN; Head of Operations EDICEL HERRERA; publs *DISCOVER!* (28 a year), *PFST Update* (4 a year), *PSC Manual of Exhibits*.

Pasay City

Cultural Centre of the Philippines Museum/Museo ng Kalinangang Pilipino: CCP Complex, Roxas Blvd, Pasay City, Metro Manila; tel. (2) 832-5094; fax (2) 832-3683; e-mail museo@culturalcenter.gov.ph; internet www.culturalcenter.gov.ph; f. 1988; traditional Filipino art and traditional Asian musical instruments; Officer-in-Charge SONITA MAGANTE-REINOSO.

Quezon City

Ateneo Art Gallery: Ateneo de Manila University, Katipunan Ave, Loyola Heights, Quezon City 1108; tel. (2) 426-6001 ext. 4160; fax (2) 426-6488; e-mail yarambulo@ateneo.edu; internet www.admu.edu.ph/?p=221; f. 1960; works by Filipino artists since 1945; Curator RAMON E. S. LERMA.

Jorge B. Vargas Museum and Filipiniana Research Centre: Roxas Ave, Univ. of the Philippines, Diliman, Quezon City 1101; tel. (2) 928-1927; fax (2) 928-1925; e-mail vargasmuseum@gmail.com; internet www.vargasmuseum.org; f. 1987; Philippine oil paintings, watercolours, pastels, drawings and sculpture from the 1880s to the 1960s, incl. work by the artists Lorenzo Guerrero, Simon Flores, Juan Luna, Felix Resurrecion Hidalgo, Fabian de la Rosa, Fernando Amorsolo, Jorge Pineda, Vicente Rivera y Mir, Victorio Edades, Juan Aralleno and Diosdado Lorenzo, and by the sculptors Guillermo Tolentino and Graciano Nepomuceno; archives, newspaper cuttings, photographs; colln also incl. Vargas archives and philatelic and numismatic memorabilia; library of 3,193 vols, 1,542 vols of periodicals; Curator Dr PATRICK FLORES.

Universities

ADAMSON UNIVERSITY

900 San Marcelino St, Ermita, 1000 Manila
Telephone: (2) 524-20-11
Fax: (2) 524-73-23
E-mail: glbanaga@adamson.edu.ph
Internet: www.adamson.edu.ph

Founded 1932
Private (Roman Catholic)
Languages of instruction: English, Filipino
Academic year: June to March

Pres.: Fr GREGORIO L. BAÑAGA
Vice-Pres. for Finance: Fr MAXIMINO RENDON
Vice-Pres. for Academic Affairs: Fr FRANCISCO NICOLAS MAGNAYE, JR
Vice-Pres. for Student Affairs: Fr ANDREW BAYAL
Registrar: Sr NILDA IBAÑEZ
Librarian: HELEN DE CASTRO

Library: See Libraries and Archives
Number of teachers: 460
Number of students: 28,390

Publications: *Adamson Chronicle* (12 a year), *Adamson News* (12 a year), *Touchstone* (4 a year)

DEANS

College of Architecture: Arch PETER VILLANUEVA
College of Business Administration: Dr VIRGINIA CALABRIA
College of Education: Dr SERVILLANO MARQUEZ
College of Engineering: JESUS MANALASTAS
College of Law: ANTONIO ABAD
College of Liberal Arts: Dr SERVILLANO MARQUEZ
College of Nursing: Prof. NARESSIA BALLENA
College of Pharmacy: RYAN PEKSON
College of Sciences: Dr GLADIOLA SANTOS
Graduate School: JOSE GENARO YAP-AYSON

AKLAN STATE UNIVERSITY

Banga, Aklan 5601, Western Visayas
Telephone: (36) 267-6567
Fax: (36) 267-5801
E-mail: webmaster@asu.edu.ph
Internet: www.asu.edu.ph

Founded 1918 as Capiz Farm School, present name and status 2001
State control
Academic year: June to March

Pres.: Dr BENNY A. PALMA
Vice-Pres. for Academic Affairs: Dr ERSYL T. BIRAY
Vice-Pres. for Admin.: Eng. MERLINE I. MARCELINO
Vice Pres. for Research, Extension, Training and ICT: ROBERTO L. SALADAR
Univ. Sec.: MICHELLE M. TAN
Dir for Library and Information Technology: EDELINA L. MATEO
Dir. for Student Affairs: EDILBERTO L. SOLIDUM

DEANS

College of Agriculture, Forestry and Environmental Sciences: Dr MARILYN E. ROMAQUIN (acting)
College of Fisheries and Marine Sciences: Prof. EDUARDO B. PASTRANA (acting)
College of Hospitality and Rural Resource Management: Prof. MARIVEL S. VILLORENTE (acting)
College of Industrial Technology: Eng. LESLIE S. CABANEZ (acting)
College of Teacher Education: Dr EDNA I. GONZALES
School of Arts and Sciences: Dr MARY EDEN M. TERUEL (acting)
School of Management Sciences: Dr CECILE O. LEGASPI
School of Veterinary Medicine: Dr CECILIA T. REYES (acting)

ANGELES UNIVERSITY FOUNDATION

Angeles City
Telephone: (2) 845-1491
Fax: (2) 845-1491
Internet: www.auf.edu.ph

Founded 1962
Private control
Languages of instruction: English, Filipino
Academic year: June to March

Chancellor: Dr EMMANUEL Y. ANGELES
Pres.: Dr RICARDO P. PAMA
Vice-Pres. for Academic Affairs: Dr RUBEN C. UMALY
Vice-Pres. for Admin.: Prof. SYLVIA M. SORIANO
Vice-Pres. for Finance: LORETO A. CANLAS
Registrar: Dr ARCHIMEDES T. DAVID
Librarian: TERESITA M. MANARANG

Library of 38,569 vols
Number of teachers: 317
Number of students: 7,500

Publications: *Alumnews*, *AUF Journal*, *AUF News*, *Datalink*, *MPA Perspective*, *Nurscene*, *The Pioneer*

DEANS

College of Allied Medical Professions: CONSUELO P. MACALALAD
College of Arts and Sciences: Dr NUNILON G. AYUYAO
College of Business Administration: LEONIDA F. CAYANAN
College of Computer Science: CAESAR R. MANALAC
College of Criminology: LUCIA M. HIPOLITO
College of Education: LUCENA P. SAMSON
College of Engineering and Technology: Eng. JOSÉ L. MACAPAGAL, Jr
College of Medicine: Dr REYNALDO V. LOPEZ
College of Nursing: ZENAIDA S. FERNANDEZ
Graduate School: Dr CONCESA MILAN BADUEL

AQUINAS UNIVERSITY OF LEGAZPI

Rawis, Legazpi City 4500
Telephone and fax (52) 482-0540
E-mail: secgen@aq.edu.ph
Internet: www.aq.edu.ph

Founded 1948, present status 1968
Private (Roman Catholic) control
Languages of instruction: Bikol, English, Filipino
Academic year: June to May

Pres.: Very Rev. Dr RAMONCLARO G. MENDEZ
Vice-Pres.: Fr ROBERTO G. REYES
Sec.-Gen.: VIRGILIO S. PERDIGON, Jr
Registrar: LETICIA R. ROQUE
Librarian: JANE L. BEBENG

Library of 54,992 vols
Number of teachers: 237
Number of students: 4,137

Publications: *Aquinas University Research Journal*, *Balintataw* (Mind; student ccl newsletter), *Gimata* (New Moon; Awakening; admin. newsletter), *Tagba* (Harvest; research journal), *Phoenix* (college student organ), *The Prism* (high school student organ)

DEANS

College of Arts, Sciences and Education: Dr SUSAN G. BOBADILLA
College of Business Administration: Dr JEAN C. DELA TORRE
College of Law: Atty EMERSON B. AQUENDE
College of Nursing and Health Sciences: VICENTE B. PERALTA

Graduate School: Dr ROSALINDA B. BARQUEZ
Polytechnic Institute (Engineering, Architecture, Computer Science): MARIA TERESA P. BONDAD

ARELLANO UNIVERSITY

2600 Legarda St, Sampaloc, Manila
Telephone: 60-74-41
Internet: www.arellano.edu.ph

Founded 1938
Language of instruction: English
Private control

Chair., Board of Trustees: Atty FLORENTINE CAYCE, Jr
Pres.: JOSE T. ENRIQUEZ
Exec. Vice-Pres.: PAULINO F. CAYCO
Registrar: JOSEFA V. LEBRON
Librarian: ALFREDO C. VALDEZ

Number of teachers: 335
Number of students: 10,326

Publications: *Arellano Standard*, *Philippine Education Quarterly*

DEANS

Arellano Law College: Atty MARIANO M. MAGSALIN
College of Arts and Sciences: Dr SERGIA G. ESGUERRA
College of Commerce: FRANCISCO P. CAYCO
College of Education and Normal College: Dr AMPARO S. LARDIZABAL
College of Nursing: Dr PRAXEDES S. M. DELA ROSA
Graduate School: Dr AMPARO S. LARDIZABAL

ATENEO DE DAVAO UNIVERSITY

E. Jacinto St, 8000 Davao City
Telephone: (82) 221-2411
Fax: (82) 226-4116
E-mail: admissions@addu.edu.ph
Internet: www.addu.edu.ph

Founded 1948
Language of instruction: English
Private control
Academic year: June to March

Pres.: Rev. EDMUNDO M. MARTINEZ
Registrar: Atty RENE ALEXIS VILLARENTE
Librarian: LEONISA P. SALES

Library of 104,857 vols
Number of teachers: 512 (372 full-time, 140 part-time)
Number of students: 7,925

Publications: *Tambara* (1 a year), *Journal of Business and Governance* (4 a year)

DEANS

Law School: Atty HILDEGARDO F. IÑIGO
School of Arts and Sciences: Dr PERLA E. FUNA
School of Business and Governance: JOSE ISAGANI M. LACSON

ATENEO DE MANILA UNIVERSITY

POB 154, Manila
Telephone: 924-4601
Internet: www.ateneo.edu

Founded 1859; Univ. status 1959
Languages of instruction: English, Filipino
Private control
Academic year: June to March (two semesters and a summer term)

Pres.: Rev. BIENVENIDO F. NEBRES
Vice-Pres. for Admin. and Planning: Dr EDNA P. FRANCO
Vice-Pres. for Finance and Treas.: JOSE F. SANTOS
Vice-Pres. for Loyola Schools: Dr JOHN PAUL C. VERGARA
Vice-Pres. for Professional Schools: Dr ALFREDO R. A. BENGZON
Dir. of Library: LOURDES T. DAVID

Library of 228,846 vols, 32 databases, 45,000 e-books, 14,000 e-journals, 800 print journals, 32, 493 other materials
Number of teachers: 1,026 , 609 F.t.e.
Number of students: 7,731 undergraduate, 3978 graduate/post graduate

Publications: *Alumni Guidon*, *Guidon*, *IPC Reports*, *Kritika Kultura*, *Landas—Journal of Loyola School of Theology*, *Loyola Schools Review*, *Pantas* (2 a year), *Philippine Studies* (4 a year)

DEANS

Ateneo Graduate School of Business: ALBERT BUENVIAJE
Ateneo Law School: Atty CESAR VILLANUEVA
Ateneo School of Medicine and Public Health: Dr ALFREDO R. A. BENGZON
John Gokongwei School of Management: RODOLFO P. ANG
School of Government: Dr ANTONIO G. LA VINA
School of Humanities: Dr MARIA LUZ C. VILCHES
School of Science and Engineering: Dr FABIAN C. DAYRIT
School of Social Sciences: Fr JOSE M. CRUZ

UNIVERSITY OF BAGUIO

General Luna Rd, Baguio City 2600
Telephone: (74) 4423071
Fax: (74) 4423071
E-mail: ub@ubaguio.edu
Internet: www.ubaguio.edu

Founded 1948 as a Technical School
Private control; granted deregulated status by the Philippine Comm. on Higher Education
Languages of instruction: English, Filipino
Academic year: June to March

Pres.: HERMINIO C. BAUTISTA
Vice-Pres. for Academic Affairs: Dr PERFECTO M. LOPEZ
Vice-Pres. for Admin.: Dr REBECCA C. CAJILOG
Registrar: Eng. MELBA E. BALIWAN
Librarian: BIRGIT S. SANTIAGO

Library of 75,223 vols
Number of teachers: 415
Number of students: 18,085

Publications: *University of Baguio Journal* (2 a year), *The Leaven* (4 a year)

DEANS

College of Commerce: MARY HAYDEE AGNES E. DABUCOL
College of Dentistry: Dr VERONICA S. GARCIA
College of Education: Dr AGNES T. BAUTISTA
College of Engineering: Eng. RENATO D. TANDOC
College of Hotel and Restaurant Management: JANE P. LIU
College of Information and Communications Technology: Eng. LAKAN-ASA R. BAUTISTA
College of Law: DANIEL T. FARIÑAS
College of Liberal Arts: Dr TERESITA DE GUZMAN
College of Medical Technology: CONSTANTINO WI
College of Nursing: CATALINA B. ALINDUZA
College of Physical Therapy and Optometry: ESMERELDA M. GATCHALLAN
Graduate School: Dr AGNES T. BAUTISTA
Law Enforcement Academy: Dr MILLER F. PECKLEY

BATANGAS STATE UNIVERSITY

Rizal Ave, Batangas City 4200
Telephone: (43) 778-2170
Fax: (43) 778-2170
E-mail: webmaster@batstate-u.edu.ph
Internet: www.batstate-u.edu.ph

Founded 1903 as Manual Training School; present name and status 2001
State control
Academic year: June to March

Pres.: Dr ERNESTO M. DE CHAVEZ
Sr Exec. Vice-Pres.: Dr ROLANDO L. LONTOC, Sr
Exec. Vice-Pres.: Dr PORFIRIO C. LIGAYA
Vice-Pres.: Dr MARITESS D. MANLOÑGAT (Academic Affairs), LUZVIMINDA ROSALES (Admin. and Finance), Dr FELIX M. PANOPIO (Extension Campus Operation), Dr JESSIE A. MONTALBO (ICT, Infrastructure Devt and External Affairs), Dr ROLANDO M. LONTOK, Jr (Research, Public Relations, Planning and Devt, and Univ. Sec.)
Dir (Library Services): Prof. ARACELI H. LUNA

Central campuses in Batangas City (Don Pablo Borbon Campuses 1 and 2) and extension campuses in Balayan, Calaca, Lipa City (Don Claro M. Recto Campus), Lobo, Malvar (Jose P. Laurel Polytechnic College Campus), Nasugbu (ARASOF Campus), Padre Garcia, Rosario, San Juan and Taysan

DEANS

College of Accountancy (Don Pablo Borbon Campus 1 and Lipa City): Prof. MARIA CARMEN L. VIDAL
College of Arts and Science: Prof. RACHEL EVANGELIO
College of Engineering (Lipa City): Eng. ERMA QUINAY
College of Engineering, Architecture and Fine Arts (Don Pablo Borbon Campus 2): Prof. ROGELIO A. ANTENOR
College of Industrial Technology (Don Pablo Borbon Campuses 1 and 2): Dr ROLANDO M. LONTOK, Jr
College of Industrial Technology (Calaca, Balayan and Lipa City Campuses): Prof. MAXIMO PANGANIBAN
College of Liberal Arts: Dr GLORIA G. MENDOZA
College of Physical Education and Human Kinetics: Prof. EDUARDO EVANGELIO
Graduate School: Dr ROLANDO L. LONTOC
School of Business and Economics: Prof. MARITESS D. MANLOÑGAT
School of Developmental Communication: Prof. CYNTHIA Q. MANALO
School of Energy, Earth and Transportation Engineering: Dr JESSIE A. MONTALBO
School of Food and International Hospitality Management: Prof. TERESA KALALO
School of Governance, Peace and Development Studies: Prof. RACHEL EVANGELIO
School of Informatics and Computing Sciences: Dr JESSIE A. MONTALBO

ATTACHED RESEARCH CENTRE

Batangas Centre for Research and Special Studies: Dir Prof. JOCELYN R. CASTILLO.

BENGUET STATE UNIVERSITY

La Trinidad, Benguet 2601
Telephone: (74) 422-24-01
Fax: (74) 442-22-81
E-mail: cip@bsu.edu.ph
Internet: www.bsu.edu.ph

Founded 1916, univ. status 1985
Language of instruction: English
Academic year: June to May

Pres.: Dr CIPRIANO C. CONSOLACION
Vice-Pres.: Dr FRANCO T. BAWANG
Designated Vice-Pres.: Dr MARCOS A. BULIYAT (Academic Affairs), Dr ROGELIO D. COLTING (Research and Extension), Dr TESSIE M. MERESTELA (Planning and Devt)
Dir of Admissions: VIRGINIA R. DUGAT
Dir of Student Affairs: Prof. WILFREDO B. MINA

Registrar: (vacant)
Librarian: Dr NORA J. CLARAVALL

Library of 34,000 vols
Number of teachers: 290
Number of students: 6,598 on degree courses

Publications: *BSU Research Journal, BSU Extension, BSU Newsletter, Highland Express, college publications*

DEANS

College of Agriculture: Dr DANILO P. PADUA
College of Arts and Sciences: Dr EDNA A. CHUA
College of Engineering and Applied Technology: GENARO W. MACASIEB, Jr
College of Forestry: MELECIO A. BALANGEN
College of Home Economics and Technology: Dr JANE K. AVILA
College of Nursing: Dr FLORENCE C. CAWAON
College of Teacher Education: Dr PERCYVERANDA A. LUBRICA
College of Veterinary Medicine: Dr RUTH C. DIEGO
Graduate School: Dr DOMINADOR S. GARIN

BICOL UNIVERSITY

Rizal St, Legazpi City 4500
Telephone: (5221) 449-13
Internet: www.bicol-u.edu.ph

Founded 1970
State control
Languages of instruction: English, Filipino
Academic year: June to May (two semesters and a summer term)

Pres.: LYLIA CORPORAL-SENA
Vice-Pres.: EMILIANO A. ABERIN
Vice-Pres. for Academic Affairs: NELIA S. CIOCSON
Registrar: CARMELINA O. BALLARES
Librarian: EXALTACION R. RESONTOC

Library of 35,380 vols
Number of teachers: 568
Number of students: 12,572

Publications: *The Bicol Universitarian* (4 a year), *Graduate Forum* (2 a year), *The Gearcast, The Net, R & D Journal, The Cassette, The Mentor, Research Monitor* (2 a year), *Outreach* (4 a year), *BU Bulletin* (6 a year)

DEANS

Agriculture: JUSTINO R. ARBOLEDA
Arts and Sciences: SUSANA C. CABREDO
Education: OSCAR L. LANDAGAN
Engineering: EDUARDO M. LORIA
Fisheries: OFELIA S. VEGA
Nursing: PAZ G. MUÑOZ
Graduate School: NELIA S. CIOCSON
Institute of Communication and Cultural Studies: RAMONA B. RAÑESES
School of Arts and Trades: EDGAR R. CAMBA

BULACAN STATE UNIVERSITY

Malolos, Bulacan 3000
Telephone: (44) 791-0153
Fax: (44) 791-0153
E-mail: bsu-ice@bulsu.edu.ph
Internet: www.bulsu.edu.ph

Founded 1904 as Bulacan Trade School; present name and status 1993
State control
Academic year: June to March

Pres.: Dr ROSARIO PIMENTEL
Vice-Pres.t (Academic Affairs): Dr MARIANO C. DE JESUS
Vice-Pres. (Planning and Devt): Dr FRANCISCO L. CRUZ
Dean (Student Affairs): TRINIDAD P. PANGAN
Registrar: LEILANI M. LIZARDO
Librarian: VIRGINIA C. MIRANDA

Regional campuses in Bambang, Bustos, Hagonoy and Sarmiento

DEANS

College of Arts and Sciences: Dr NORMA C. MORALA
College of Education: Dr DANILO D. FAUSTINO
College of Engineering: Dr CECILIA A. GERONIMO
College of Industrial Technology: Dr SALVADOR P. PEREDO
College of Law: (vacant)
Graduate School: Dr DANILO S. HILARIO

DIRECTORS

Distance Education: EDGARDO MATEO
Institute of Architecture and Fine Arts: SATURNINA C. PARUNGAO
Institute of Computer Education: FAUSTO S. HILARIO
Institute of Home Economics: FIDELITA P. ESTRADA
Institute of Physical Education and Sports: RACQUEL M. MENDOZA

CAGAYAN STATE UNIVERSITY

Carig, Tuguegarao City 3500
Telephone: (78) 844-01-07
Fax: (78) 844-41-19
E-mail: abcortes@scan.com.ph

Founded 1978 by merger of Northern Luzon State College of Agriculture and Cagayan Valley College of Arts and Trades
Academic year: June to March

Pres.: Dr ARMANDO B. CORTES
Vice-Pres. for Academic Affairs: Dr ELEUTERIO C. DE LEON
Dir for Research: ROMILLO N. TRINIDAD

Number of teachers: 500
Number of students: 10,300

Publications: *Research Journal of the Graduate School, Faculty Journal* (1 a year), *CSU Research Journal* (2 a year)

Colleges of agriculture, arts and sciences, engineering, fisheries, industrial technology, medicine, teacher training, and graduate school.

CAVITE STATE UNIVERSITY

Bancod, Indang, Cavite 4122
Telephone: (46) 4150-010
Fax: (46) 4150-013
E-mail: cvsu_rc@cavite.net

Founded 1906; fmrly Don Severino Agricultural College; present name and status 1998

Pres.: Dr RUPERTO S. SANGALANG

Colleges of arts, trades, fisheries; courses in agriculture, business administration, development studies, economics, education, engineering, environmental studies, food technology, hotel and restaurant management, mass communication, mathematics and computer science, natural sciences and technology.

CEBU NORMAL UNIVERSITY

Osmeña Blvd, Cebu City, Cebu 6000
Telephone and fax (32) 253-9611
E-mail: info@cnu.vis.ph
Internet: www.cnu.edu.ph

Founded 1902, as Cebu Normal Secondary School; present name and status 1998
State control
Academic year: June to March

Pres.: Dr MARCELO T. LOPEZ
Vice-Pres. for Academic Affairs: Dr MERLEA A. CABALQUINTO
Vice-Pres. for Admin.: Dr BIBIANA T. ISOK
Registrar: ALFREDO V. ALBARICO
Dean for Student Affairs: GWENDELINA A. VILLARANTE
Univ. Librarian: MARILYN LASPIÑAS

Number of students: 6,910

DEANS

College of Arts and Sciences: Dr FLORIZA N. LAPLAP
College of Nursing: Dr DAISY R. PALOMPON (acting)
College of Teacher Education: Dr FILOMENA T. DAYAGBIL
Graduate School: Dr BERNADITA M. SOLEDAD

CENTRAL LUZON STATE UNIVERSITY

Muñoz, Nueva Ecija 3120
Telephone: (6344) 456-0107
Fax: (6344) 456-5187
Internet: www.clsu.edu.ph

Founded 1907, attained univ. status 1964
State control
Languages of instruction: English, Filipino
Academic year: June to March

Pres.: Dr RODOLFO C. UNDAN
Vice-Pres.: Dr RUBEN C. SEVILLEJA (Academic Affairs), Prof. REYNALDO S. GUTIERREZ (Admin.), Prof. ONOFRE F. RINGOR (Business Affairs), Dr HONORATO L. ANGELES (Research, Extension and Training)
Dean of Students: Dr ZENAIDA M. SERNA
Dir of Admissions: Dr MELISSA E. AGULTO
Librarian: Prof. CELIA D. DE LA CRUZ

Number of teachers: 373
Number of students: 6,489

Publications: *CLSU Collegian* (2 a year), *CLSU Newsletter* (12 a year), *CLSU Scientific Journal* (2 a year), *CLSU Research Digest* (2 a year)

DEANS

College of Agriculture: Dr FEDERICO O. PEREZ
College of Arts and Sciences: Dr MARILOU G. ABON
College of Business Administration and Accountancy: Dr DANILO S. CASTRO
College of Education: Dr DANILO G. TAN
College of Engineering: Dr IRENEO C. AGULTO
College of Fisheries: Dr ARSENIA G. CAGAUAN
College of Home Science and Industry: Dr HILARIA T. CUARESMA
College of Veterinary Science and Medicine: Dr JESUS S. DE LA ROSA
Institute of Graduate Studies: Dr CYNTHIA C. DIVINA

CENTRAL MINDANAO UNIVERSITY

University Town, Musuan, Bukidnon 8710
Telephone: (88) 3561910
Fax: (88) 8442520
E-mail: cmu.musuan@eudora.com
Internet: www.cmu.edu.ph

Founded 1952 as the Mindanao Agricultural College; Univ. 1965
State control
Languages of instruction: English, Filipino
Academic year: June to March (two semesters and a summer school)

Pres.: Dr MARDONIO M. LAO
Vice-Pres.: Dr EMMANUEL A. LARIOSA (Academic Affairs), Dr PORFERIO M. BALANAY (Admin.), Dr HERMINIO M. PAUA (Research and Extension)
Registrar: Prof. NELLIE C. LASTIMOSA
Librarian: Prof. ESTHER E. DINAMPO

Library of 23,000 vols
Number of teachers: 311
Number of students: 5,371

Publications: *CMU Journal of Food, Agriculture and Nutrition* (4 a year), *Barangay Balita* (4 a year), *Newsletter* (4 a year)

DEANS

College of Arts and Sciences: Dr CECILIA B. AMOROSO
College of Agriculture: Dr CELSO C. TAUTHO
College of Education: Dr MARINA I. LIZARDO
College of Engineering: Prof. REYNALDO G. JUAN
College of Home Economics: Dr NERISSA A. MACARAYAN
College of Forestry: Dr JAMES O. LACANDULA
College of Veterinary Medicine: Dr JOSE ALEXANDER C. ABELLA
Graduate School: Dr EVELYN L. BARRIDO

DEPARTMENT CHAIRMEN

College of Agriculture (tel. (88) 3561881; fax (88) 3561910):
Agribusiness: Dr JOSEFINO M. MAGALLANES
Agricultural Economics: Dr ISABELO O. MUGOT
Agricultural Education: Dr JUDITH O. INTONG
Agronomy: Dr DELFIN UALLADOR
Animal Science: Dr MARIA LUZ L. SORIANO
Development Communication: Prof. NELIA T. ESCARLOS
Entomology: Prof. ESTELITO CATLI
Horticulture: Dr LOUELLA CABAHUG
Plant Pathology: Dr LOLITO CAPILI
Soil Science: Dr NONILONA DAQUIADO

College of Arts and Sciences (tel. (88) 3561911):
Behavioural Sciences: Prof. ZENAIDA CAINTIC
Biological Sciences: Prof. VICTORIA T. QUIMPANG
Chemistry: Dr LORDINO CABIGON
Languages and Literature: Prof. MARICHU CATERIAL
Mathematics: Prof. LETICIA J. TAN
Physics: JUSEMIE V. ORTELANO
Social Science: ELEUTERIO D. TANO

College of Education (tel. (88) 3561890):
Business Education: Prof. MAGDALENA R. REDOBLE
Educational Services: Prof. LOURDES BAGO
Physical Education: Prof. MARYLOU C. VILORIA

College of Engineering (tel. (22) 3561812):
Agricultural Engineering: Prof. ARNOLD VILLAMOR
Civil Engineering: Prof. PAULINO REOMERO
Electrical Engineering: Prof. LESLIE S. CABAÑEZ
Mechanical Engineering: Prof. COSTANCIO VERULA

College of Forestry (tel. (88) 3561872):
Forest Biological Science: Prof. DEOLITO T. CLAVEJO
Forest Resources Management: Prof. ANTONIO O. ECUACION
Wood Science Technology: Prof. GEORGE R. PUNO

College of Home Economics (tel. (88) 3561885):
Education and Family Life: Prof. INES B. GEWAN
Food Science and Nutrition: Prof. ANGELITA R. BOKINGO

College of Veterinary Medicine (tel. (88) 3561883):
Anatomy, Physiology and Pharmacology: JOSE ESCARLOS, Jr
Medicine and Surgery: Prof. PETER R. ORBASE
Microbiology, Parasitology, Pathology and Public Health: Dr ROY V. VILLOREJO

CENTRAL PHILIPPINE UNIVERSITY

POB 231, Iloilo City 5000
Telephone: (33) 7-34-71
Fax: (33) 20-36-85
Internet: www.cpu.edu.ph

Founded 1905
Language of instruction: English
Private control
Academic year: June to March (two terms)

Pres.: AGUSTIN A. PULIDO
Treas.: ROSALENE J. MADERO
Vice-Pres. for Academic Affairs: ELMA S. HERRADURA
Registrar: ESTHER S. BASIAO
Librarian: VICTORY D. GABAWA

Number of teachers: 280
Number of students: 9,280

Publications: *The Central Echo* (student paper), *Centralite* (student annual), *Link* (Alumni organ), *Southeast Asia Journal*

DEANS

College of Agriculture: ENRIQUE S. ALTIS
College of Arts and Sciences: LYNN J. PAREJA
College of Commerce: MILAGROS V. DIGNADICE
College of Education: LORNA D. GELLADA
College of Engineering: WALDEN S. RIO
College of Law: JUANITO M. ACANTO
College of Nursing: BETTY T. POLIDO
College of Theology: JOHNNY V. GUMBAN
School of Graduate Studies: MIRIAM M. TRAVIÑA

CENTRO ESCOLAR UNIVERSITY

9 Mendiola St, San Miguel, Manila
Telephone: (2) 735-59-91
Fax: (2) 735-59-91
E-mail: ceu1@galileo.fapenet.org
Internet: www.ceu.edu.ph

Founded 1907
Languages of instruction: English, Filipino
Private control
Academic year: June to March

Pres.: Dr ROSITA L. NAVARRO
Vice-Pres.: Dr ROSITA L. NAVARRO (Academic Affairs, concurrent with Univ. Presidency), LUCILA C. TIONGCO (Alumni Affairs), CARMELITA E. LA O' (Business Affairs), Dr MARIA L. AYUYAO (Exec.), JOSEPHINE E. MAPE (Finance)
Registrar: LUCIA D. GONZALES
Librarian: Dr TERESITA G. HERNANDEZ

Number of teachers: 800
Number of students: 22,691

Publications: *Academe*, *Ciencia y Virtud* (4 a year), *The Clarion* (4 a year), *Graduate and Faculty Studies* (1 a year), *Rose and the Leaf* (1 a year)

DEANS

School of Accountancy, Business, Secretarial and Public Administration: Dr CONRADO E. IÑIGO, Jr
School of Arts and Humanities: Dr CECILIA G. VALMONTE
School of Education, Music and Social Work: Dr PAZ I. LUCIDO
School of Pharmacy: Dr OLIVIA M. LIMUACO
School of Tourism, Family Economics and Nutrition: Dr CARMINA P. CATAPANG
College of Dentistry: Dr RENATO M. SISON
College of Medical Technology: Dr PRISCILLA A. PANLASIGUI
College of Nursing: MERLINA V. LOCQUIAO
College of Optometry: Dr JESSICA L. FLOR
College of Science: Dr ZENAIDA M. AUSTRIA
Graduate School: Dr ROSITA L. NAVARRO

DE LA SALLE UNIVERSITY

2401 Taft Ave, Malate, Manila 1004
Telephone: (2) 523-4148
Fax: (2) 521-9094
E-mail: quebengcoc@dlsu.edu.ph
Internet: www.dlsu.edu.ph

Founded 1911
Private control
Languages of instruction: English, Filipino
Academic year: May to April

Pres.: Bro. ARMIN A. LUISTRO
Chancellor: Dr CARMELITA I. QUEBENGCO
Vice-Chancellor for Academics: Dr JULIUS B. MARIDABLE
Vice-Chancellor for Research: Dr WYONA C. PATALINGHUG
Vice-Chancellor for Admin.: Dr CARMELITA I. QUEBENGCO
Asst Vice-Chancellor for Academic Services: AGNES G. YUHICO
Asst Vice-Chancellor for Campus Services: ENRICO J. CORDERO
Asst Vice-Chancellor for Campus Devt: AURELLANO O. DE LA CRUZ, Jr
Registrar: EDWIN P. SANTIAGO
Dir of Library: ANA MARIA B. FRESNIDO

Library of 258,591
Number of teachers: 950
Number of students: 14,400 (12,000 undergraduate, 2,400 postgraduate)

Publications: *Asia-Pacific Social Science Review* (2 a year), *Ideya* (2 a year), *DLSU Business and Economics Review* (2 a year), *Journal of Research in Science, Computing and Engineering* (3 a year), *Asia–Pacific Education Researcher* (2 a year), *URCO Digest* (3 a year), *Maluy* (2 a year)

DEANS

College of Business and Economics: Dr MYRNA S. AUSTRIA
College of Computer Studies: Dr CASLON L. CHUA
College of Education: Dr ROSE MARIE SALAZAR-CLEMEÑA
College of Engineering: Dr PAG-ASA D. GASPILLO
College of Liberal Arts: Dr ANTONIO P. CONTRERAS
College of Science: Dr GERARDO C. JANAIRO

PROFESSORS

ABELLA, L. C., Chemical Engineering
AUSTRIA, M. S., Economics
AZCARRAGA, A. P., Software Technology
BERNARDO, A. B. I., Counselling and Educational Psychology
CABRERA, E. C., Biology
CARANDANG, J. S. R. V., Biology
CLAVERIA, F. G., Biology
CONTRERAS, A. P., Political Science
CORPUZ, C. C., History
CRUZ, I. R., Literature
CULABA, A. B., Mechanical Engineering
DADIOS, E. P., Manufacturing Engineering Management
DEL MUNDO, C. A., Jr, Communication
DIESTO, S. D., Mathematics
EDRALIN, D. M., Business Management
ESTAÑERO, R. A., Civil Engineering
EVASCO-PERNIA, M., Literature
GALLARDO, S. M., Chemical Engineering
GARCIA, L. R., Jr, Marketing Management
GASPILLO, P. D., Chemical Engineering
GERVACIO, S. V., Mathematics
GRIPALDO, R. M., Philosophy
HILA, A. C., History
INTAL, P. S., Jr, Economics
JANAIRO, G. C., Chemistry
LAMBERTE, E. E., Behavioural Sciences
LICUANAN, W. R. Y., Biology
MAGLAYA, A. B., Mechanical Engineering
ORETA, A. W. C., Civil Engineering
PALISOC, S. T., Physics
PASCASIO, A. A., Mathematics
PATALINGHUG, W. C., Chemistry
PRUDENTE, M. S., Science Education
RAGASA, C. Y., Chemistry
ROBLES, A. C., JR, International Studies
ROCES, S. A., Chemical Engineering

SALAZAR-CLEMEÑA, R. M., Counselling and Educational Psychology
SANTOS, P. V. M., Literature
SISON, R. C., Software Technology
TULLAO, T. S., Jr, Economics
UNITE, A. A., Economics

DON MARIANO MARCOS MEMORIAL STATE UNIVERSITY

Bacnotan, La Union 2515
Telephone: (72) 888-5677
Fax: (72) 888-3191
Internet: www.dmmmsu.edu.ph
Founded 1960 as La Union Agricultural School; present name and status 1980
State control
Academic year: June to March
Pres.: Dr ERNESTO R. GAPASIN
Vice-Pres. (Academic Affairs): Dr AMELIA O. BACUNGAN
Vice-Pres. (Admin.): (vacant)
Vice-Pres. (Planning and Devt): Dr ELVI C. BUGAOAN
Vice-Pres. (Research and Public Relations): Dr FLORENTINA S. DUMLAO

HEADS OF OPERATING UNITS

Apiculture Training and Development Center: Dr APOLONIO S. SITO (Dir)
Graduate College: Dr NORMA B. NATINO (Dean)
Mid La Union Campus: Dr RODOLFO R. APIGO (Chancellor)
North La Union Campus: Dr ORLANDO O. ALMOITE (Chancellor)
Open University System: Dr CONCEPCION L. BEDERIO (Dir)
Sericulture Research Development Institute: Dr RICARDO C. BRIONES (Dir)
South La Union Campus: Dr INOCENCIO I. MANGAOANG, Jr

UNIVERSITY OF THE EAST

Main Campus, 2219 Claro M. Recto Ave, Manila 1008
Telephone: (2) 735-5471
Fax: (2) 735-6972
E-mail: admission@ue.edu.ph
Internet: www.ue.edu.ph
Caloocan Campus, 105 Samson Rd, Caloocan City, Metro Manila 1400
Telephone: (2) 367-4572
Fax: (2) 364-2659
E-mail: admissions_cal@ue.edu.ph
Internet: www.ue.edu.ph/caloocan
Academic year: June to April
Founded 1946 as the Philippine College of Commerce and Business Admin.; Univ. of the East 1951
Private control
Chair. of the Board and Chief Exec. Officer: LUCIO C. TAN
Pres. and Chief Academic Officer: Dr ESTER A. GARCIA
Exec. Vice-Pres. and Chief Admin. Officer: CARMELITA G. MATEO
Chancellor of UE Caloocan: Dr ZOSIMO M. BATTAD
Chancellor of UE Manila: Dr LINDA P. SANTIAGO
Dirs of Student Affairs: CLEMENTE A. DIWAS (UE Caloocan): MERCY L. CANDELARIA (UE Manila)
Registrar: ERWIN B. BERMILLO
Dir of Libraries: LORETO GARCIA
Library: see Libraries and Archives
Number of teachers: 725
Number of students: 19,000
Publications: *Graduate School Research Journal*, *Law Update*, *Research Bulletin*, *UE Panorama Yearbook*, *UE Today*

DEANS

Caloocan Campus:
College of Arts and Sciences: JULIAN E. ABUSO
College of Business Administration: Dr ROGELIO V. PAGLOMUTAN
College of Engineering: Dr VICTOR R. MACAM Jr
College of Fine Arts: CELINO B. SANTIAGO
Elementary and Secondary Laboratory Schools: BENILDA L. SANTOS (Principal)
Physical Education Department: FERNANDO Z. OLONA (acting)

Manila Campus:
College of Arts and Sciences: JUSTINA M. EVANGELISTA
College of Business Administration: Dr VERONICA N. ELIZALDE (acting)
College of Computer Studies and Systems: RODANY A. MERIDA
College of Dentistry: Dr RHODORA H. LUCIANO
College of Education: Dr EVELINA M. VICENCIO
College of Engineering: Dr DOMINADOR S. PAGBILAO
College of Fine Arts: GERARDO M. TAN
College of Law: Justice AMADO D. VALDEZ
Elementary and Secondary Laboratory Schools: NIEVA J. DISCIPULO (Principal)
Graduate School: Dr AVELINA A. DE LA REA
Physical Education Department: RODRIGO M. ROQUE (acting) (Asst Dir)

AFFILIATED MEDICAL CENTRE

University of the East Ramon Magsaysay Memorial Medical Centre
64–68 Aurora Blvd, Barangay Doña Imelda, Quezon City 1113
Telephone: (2) 715-0861
E-mail: registrar@uerm.edu.ph
Internet: www.uerm.edu.ph
Founded 1957
Affiliated to Univ. of the East
Chief Librarian: JULIANA M. NOCES-GASMEN
Library of 31,150 vols, 342 periodicals

DEANS

Graduate School: Dr TERESA S. LUDOVICE-YAP
College of Medicine: Dr ALFARETTA LUISA T. REYES
College of Nursing: Dr CARMELITA C. DIVINAGRACIA
College of Physical Therapy: Dr RAQUEL S. CABAZOR

UNIVERSITY OF EASTERN PHILIPPINES

University Town, Northern Samar 6400
Founded 1918
State control
Languages of instruction: English, Filipino
Pres.: Dr PEDRO D. DESTURA
Vice-Pres.: Dr NILO E. COLINARES (Academic Affairs), Dr PEDRO A. BASILOY (Admin.), Dr NESTOR L. RUBENECIA (External Affairs)
Registrar: ROGELIO L. NOBLE
Librarian: FE G. BAOY
Number of teachers: 339
Number of students: 7,511
Publications: *UEP Graduate Journal*, *The Pacific Journal of Science and Technology*, *The Pillar*

DEANS

College of Agriculture: Prof. LEON A. GUEVARA
College of Arts and Communication: Dr LYDIA E. DE LA ROSA
College of Business Administration: Dr LOURDES O. MOSCARE
College of Education: Dr ZENAIDA S. LUCERO
College of Engineering: ROMEO D. ATENCIO
College of Law: Mar P. DE ASIS
College of Nursing: Dr ELBIE Y. BALDO
College of Science: Dr NESTOR L. RUBENECIA
College of Veterinary Medicine: Dr EDUARDO L. ALVAREZ
Graduate School: Dr MINDANILLA B. BROTO

FAR EASTERN UNIVERSITY

POB 609, Manila
Telephone: (2) 735-56-21
Fax: (2) 735-02-32
Internet: www.feu.edu.ph
Founded 1928 as Institute of Accountancy, incorporated in 1934 as Far Eastern Univ.
Private control
Language of instruction: English
Academic year: June to March
Pres.: EDILBERTO C. DE JESUS
Vice-Pres. on Academic Affairs: LYDIA A. PALAYPAY
Registrar: JOHN J. MACASIO (acting)
Chief Librarian: ZENAIDA M. GALANG
Library: see Libraries and Archives
Number of teachers: 1,320
Number of students: 25,106
Publications: *Far Eastern University Journal* (2 a year), *Transition* (1 a year), *Ambon* (1 a year), *Arts and Science Review* (2 a year), *Cultural Forum* (irregular), *FEU Newsletter* (4 a year), *Papers Etcetera* (2 a year)

DEANS

Institute of Accounts, Business and Finance: DANNY A. CABULAY
Institute of Architecture and Fine Arts: VICTORIANO O. AVIGUETERO, Jr
Institute of Arts and Sciences: ANGEL O. ABAYA
Institute of Education: JOVITO B. CASTILLO
Institute of Graduate Studies: JOVITO B. CASTILLO (Co-ordinator)
Institute of Law: ANDRES D. BAUTISTA
Institute of Nursing: NORMA M. DUMADAG

FOUNDATION UNIVERSITY

Dumaguete City 6200
Telephone: (35) 422-9167
Fax: (35) 225-0167
E-mail: op@foundationu.com
Internet: www.foundationu.com
Founded 1949
Language of instruction: English
Private control
Academic year: June to March (two semesters)
Pres.: Dr MIRA D. SINCO (acting)
Vice-Pres. for Academic Affairs: Dr EVA C. MELON
Vice Pres. for Finance and Admin.: VICTOR VICENTE G. SINCO
Vice-Pres. for Student Life and External Affairs: DINNO WILLIE D. DEPOSITARIO
Registrar: GLENE MAY D. LUSARES
Librarian: LILIBETH D. BUSLON
Library of 55,023 vols
Number of teachers: 169
Number of students: 4,000
Publications: *Foundation Time* (12 a year), *FU Recorder* (12 a year), *Graduate Journal* (2 a year), *Greyhound* (Magazine), *University Recorder* (2 a year), *Law Forum* (2 a year), *Pillar* (1 a year)

DEANS

College of Agriculture: LILIAN P. SUMAGAYSAY
College of Arts and Sciences: Dr MIRA D. SINCO

College of Business and Economics: Dr Eva C. Melon
College of Education: Dr Thelma E. Florendo
College of Law and Jurisprudence: Eleuterio E. Chiu (Retd)
College of Nursing: Nenita P. Tayko
Graduate School: Dr Aparicio H. Mequi
Habalo School of Hospitality Management: Charlotte V.
School of Computer Studies: Dae P.
School of Industrial Engineering: Eng. Marlon A. Tanilon

GREGORIO ARANETA UNIVERSITY FOUNDATION

Araneta University Post Office, Malabon, Metro Manila 1404
Telephone: 366-90-53
Fax: 361-90-54
E-mail: gauf@gauf.curricula.net
Internet: www.gauf.curricula.net
Founded 1946; reorganized as a foundation 1965
Private control
Languages of instruction: English, Filpino
Academic year: June to March
Pres.: Dr Manuel D. Punzal
Exec. Vice-Pres.: Dr Rosenda A. de Gracia
Dir for Academic Affairs: Dr Ma. Corazon V. Tadena
Registrar: Prof. Teresita R. Gutierrez
Librarian: Prof. Felisa W. Dador
Number of teachers: 156 (69 full-time, 87 part-time)
Number of students: 3,012
Publications: *Araneta Research Journal* (4 a year), *Tinig* (12 a year), *Harvest* (1 a year), *Compendium of Veterinary Research* (1 a year), *The Philippine Veterinarian* (4 a year)

DEANS

College of Agriculture and Forestry: Dr Anastacio T. Mercado
College of Arts and Sciences: Dr Lillian L. Pena
College of Business and Accountancy: Dr Nellie A. Asuncion
College of Education: Dr Lydia S. Jusay
College of Engineering and Technology: Dr Leovigildo A. Manalo
College of Veterinary Medicine: Dr Daniel C. Ventura, Jr
Graduate School: Dr Ma. Corazon V. Tadena

ISABELA STATE UNIVERSITY

San Fabian, Echague, Isabela 1318
Telephone: 22013
Founded 1978
State control
Language of instruction: English
Academic year: June to May
Pres.: Dr Rodolfo C. Nayga
Vice-Pres.: Dr Mariano P. Baluag
Registrar: Thelma T. Lanuza
Librarian: Romula P. Romero
Library of 11,818 vols
Number of teachers: 477
Number of students: 4,340
Publications: *Research Journal*, *CVIARS Monitor*, *Forum*, *Mediator*, *Hexachord*, *Geyser*

DEANS

College of Agriculture: Dr Francisco M. Basuel
College of Arts and Sciences: Dr Jesus B. Gollayan
College of Forestry: Dr Roberto R. Araño
School of Business Administration: Prof. Relli C. Pableo
School of Development Communication: Prof. Lolita G. Sarangay
School of Engineering: Jose J. Lorenzana
Polytechnic College: Dr Esperanza Bueno
Teachers' College: Dr Sacrificia T. Catabui
Graduate Studies: Dr Nelson T. Binag

LEYTE NORMAL UNIVERSITY

Paterno St, Tacloban City, Leyte 6500
Telephone: (53) 321-2176
Fax: (53) 325-6122
Internet: lnu.evis.net.ph
Founded 1921 as Leyte Normal School; present name and status 1995
State control
Academic year: June to March
Pres.: Dr Crescencia V. Chan-Gonzaga
Publication: *LNU Research Journal* (1 a year)
Colleges of arts and sciences, commerce, education, engineering and management, development and entrepreneurship.

LEYTE STATE UNIVERSITY

Visca, Baybay, Leyte 6521
Telephone: (53) 335-2601
Fax: (53) 335-2601
Internet: www.lsu.visayas.org
Founded 1924 as Baybay Agricultural School; present name and status 2001
State control
Academic year: June to March
Pres.: Dr Paciencia P. Milan
Number of teachers: 261
Colleges of agriculture, arts and science, education, engineering and agri-industries, forestry and veterinary medicine; Graduate School; Open Univ. system.

UNIVERSITY OF MANILA

546 Dr M. V. de los Santos St, Sampaloc, Manila 1008
Telephone: 7413637
Fax: 7413640
Founded 1913
Private, non-sectarian instn
Language of instruction: English
Academic year: June to May (three terms)
Pres.: Dr Virgilio de los Santos
Exec. Vice-Pres.: Atty Ernesto Ll. de los Santos
Vice-Pres. for Academic Affairs: Dr Emily D. de Leon
Registrar: Dr Virgilio de los Santos
Chief Librarian: Corazon G. Payte
Number of teachers: 250
Number of students: 7,500
Publications: *The University of Manila Graduate School Journal*, *The UM Law Gazette*, *The Gold Leaf*

DEANS

College of Business Administration and Accountancy: Nelson S. Abeleda
College of Criminology: Fortunato S. Rivera
College of Education: Emily D. de Leon
College of Engineering: Arsenio A. Ronquillo
College of Foreign Service: Benjamin D. Quineri
College of Law: Michael P. Moralde
College of Liberal Arts: Rosalia V. Molina
Graduate Studies: Emily D. de Leon

MANILA CENTRAL UNIVERSITY

Edsa, 1400 Caloocan
Telephone: 364-10-71
Internet: www.mcu.edu.ph
Founded 1904
Private control
Language of instruction: English
Academic year: June to March
Pres.: Dr Aristotle T. Malabanan
Vice-Pres. for Academic Affairs: Dr Lydia L. Taganguin
Vice-Pres. for Admin. Affairs: Dr Renato C. Tanchoco, Jr
Dir for Finance: Mila Perez
Registrar: Aini Salvadora
Librarian: Ophelia Enriquez
Number of teachers: 240
Number of students: 5,500
Publications: *Gold and Purple*, *Research Journal*, *The Pharos*, *The Pulse*

DEANS

College of Arts and Sciences: Dr Eva Javier
College of Business Administration: Dr Dennis Sandoval
College of Dentistry: Dr Jerome Alcazaren
College of Medical Technology: Petrona Benitez
College of Medicine: Dr Divina Beato
College of Nursing: Dr Lina Salarda
College of Optometry: Dr Francisco Baetiong, Jr
College of Pharmacy: Maricon Boie
College of Physical Therapy: Eduardo Peregrino
Graduate School: Dr Jose Mallari
School of Midwifery: Dr Lina Salarda

MARIANO MARCOS STATE UNIVERSITY

Batac, Ilocos Norte
Telephone: 792-31-91
Fax: (77) 792-31-31
Internet: www.mmsu.edu.ph
Founded 1978
State control
Language of instruction: English
Academic year: June to March
Pres.: Dr Elias L. Calacal
Vice-Pres. for Academic Affairs: Dr Nancy B. Balantac
Vice-Pres. for Admin.: Dr Heraldo L. Layaoem
Vice-Pres. for Research and Extension: Dr Rodolfo A. Natividad
Registrar: Dr Nenita P. Blanco
Admin. Officer: Manuel B. Corpuz
Librarian: Prof. Bucalen C. Saboy
Library of 55,511 vols
Number of teachers: 485
Number of students: 11,761

DEANS

College of Agriculture and Forestry: Dr Salud F. Barroga
College of Aquatic Sciences and Technology: Prof. Rodolfe V. Laddaran
College of Arts and Sciences: Dr Anabelle C. Felipe
College of Business, Economics and Accountancy: Dr Marietta M. Bonoan
College of Education: Dr Vicente A. Bondan
College of Engineering and Technology: Engr Carlos F. Ungson
College of Technology: Prof. Nestor M. Agngarayngay
Graduate School: Dr Lorenza S. Matias
Institute of Health Sciences: Prof. Violeta M. Glova

ATTACHED CENTRES

Business Resource Development Centre: Head Prof. Lorna Fernandez.

Centre for Applied Research and Technology Transfer: Dir Prof. Felipe R. Esta.

Fulbright American Studies Resource Centre: Dir Prof. Bucalen C. Saboy.

Iloko Research and Information Centre: Dir Dr Ernesto Ma. Cadiz.

Regional Science Teaching Centre: Dir Prof. Leo Ver Domingo.

MINDANAO STATE UNIVERSITY

MSU Campus, Marawi City 9700
Telephone: (63) 3521002
E-mail: op@msumain.edu.ph
Internet: www.msumain.edu.ph

Founded 1961
Language of instruction: English
Academic year: June to May

Pres.: Dr Camar A. Umpa
Exec. Vice-Pres. and Chancellor: Dr Datumanong A. Sarangani
Vice-Pres. for Academic Affairs: Prof. Yusoph Latip
Vice-Pres. for Admin. and Finance: Dr Datumanong Sarangani (acting)
Vice-Pres. for Planning and Devt: Prof. Saidale Mohamad
Registrar: Jessie Silang
Librarian: Lawansan Mangorac

Number of teachers: 1,220
Number of students: 12,000

Publications: *Alumni Monitor*, *CSSH Graduate Research Journal*, *Darangen*, *Mindanao Arts and Culture Professional Papers Publication*, *Mindanao Journal*, *Mindanao Varsitarian* (12 a year), *Ongangen*, *OVCRE Bulletin*, *Pagsibol*, *Piglas*, *Unirescent*

DEANS

College of Agriculture: Dr Camar Mikunug
College of Business Administration: Dr Merlyn Tan
College of Education: Dr Pendililang Gunting
College of Engineering: Prof. Rodrigo Baid (acting)
College of Fisheries: Dr Julieta Lagmay
College of Forestry and Environmental Sciences: Dr Gerardo Gavine
College of Health Sciences: Dr Mindamora Mutin
College of Hotel and Restaurant Management: Dr Cecille Mambuay
College of Law: Basari D. Mapupuno
College of Medicine: Dr Angelo Manalo
College of Natural Sciences and Mathematics: Prof. Rambe Ramel
College of Public Affairs: Dr Nasroden Guro
College of Social Sciences and Humanities: Prof. Bonifacio R. Tacata
College of Sports and Physical Recreation: Prof. Hasan Maranda
Graduate School: Dr Cosain Derico
Institute of Science Education: Dr Emerita Moti
King Faisal Centre for Islamic and Arabic Studies: Prof. Talib Benito
Regional Science Training Centre: Dr Dolores Pattuinan
School of Information Technology: Dr Pepe L. Madrid

ATTACHED INSTITUTE OF TECHNOLOGY

Iligan Institute of Technology of the Mindanao State University

Andres Bonifacio Ave, Tibanga, Iligan City 9200
Telephone: (63) 2214056
Fax: (63) 2214056
E-mail: mpsalazar50@gmail.com
Internet: www.msuiit.edu.ph

Founded 1968
State control
Languages of instruction: English, Filipino
Academic year: June to April

Chancellor: Prof. Marcelo P. Salazar
Vice-Chancellor for Academic Affairs: Dr Arnulfo P. Supe
Vice-Chancellor for Admin. and Finance: Dr Polaus M. Bari
Vice-Chancellor for Research and Extension: Dr Olga M. Nuñeza
Registrar: Dr Lydie D. Paderanga
Librarian: Meles F. Castillano

Library of 58,975 vols
Number of teachers: 490
Number of students: 7,778

Publications: *Gazette* (4 a year), *Mindanao Forum* (1 a year)

DEANS

College of Arts and Social Sciences: Prof. Nora A. Clar
College of Business Admin.: Dr Julita W. Bokingo
College of Education: Prof. Esmar N. Sedurifa
College of Engineering: Dr Feliciano B. Alagao
College of Science and Mathematics: Dr Jinky B. Bornales
Integrated Development School: Dr Manuel B. Barquilla
School of Engineering Technology: Prof. Santiago R. Evasco
School of Graduate Studies: Dr Jerson N. Orejudos

UNIVERSITY OF MINDANAO

Bolton St, Davao City, Mindanao
Telephone: (82) 227-54-56
Fax: (82) 221-73-35
E-mail: um@mozcom.com
Internet: www.umindanao.edu.ph

Founded 1946
Private control
Language of instruction: English
Academic year: June to March

Pres.: Guillermo P. Torres, Jr.
Exec. Vice-Pres. for Academic Affairs: Dr Pedro B. San Jose
Exec. Vice-Pres. for Operations: Gloria E. Detoya
Sr Vice-Pres. for Academic Planning and Services: Dr Eugenio S. Guhao, Jr.
Sr Vice-Pres. for Treasury: Sandra G. Angeles
Vice-Pres. for ICT: Edgardo O. Castillo
Vice-Pres. for Institutional Affairs: Maria Julieta R. Torres
Vice-Pres. for Student Personnel Services/ Registrar: Dr Carmencita E. Vidamo
Vice Pres. for Physical Plant: Felicisimo Ramos

Number of teachers: 620
Number of students: 19,720

Publications: *Communique*, *Journal of Arts and Sciences*, *The Frontier*, *Journal of the Graduate School*, *UM Research and Publication Journal*

DEANS

Arts and Sciences: Gerlieta S. Ruiz
College of Architecture: Iluminado C. Quinto
College of Business Administration: Vicente Salvador E. Montaño
College of Criminology: Dr Carmelita B. Chavez
College of Education: Dr Marilou T. Lozarita (Asst Dean)
College of Engineering: Leo Largo
College of Law: Melchor Quitain
College of Nursing: Ofelia B. Lariego
Graduate School: Eugenio S. Guhao
Technical School: Gerardo Salas

NATIONAL UNIVERSITY

551 Mariano F. Jhocson St, Sampaloc, Manila
Telephone: 61-34-31
Internet: www.nu.edu.ph

Founded 1900
Language of instruction: English
Private control
Academic year: June to March

Pres.: Jesus M. Jhocson
Registrar: Leticia J. Paguia
Head of Graduate Studies: Zenaida N. Magiba
Librarian: Consuelo J. Miguel

DEANS

College of Architecture: Fernando Abad
College of Civil, Chemical and Sanitary Engineering: Romulo D. Coloma
College of Commerce: Leticia J. Paguia (acting)
College of Dentistry: Dr Gregorio D. Gabriel
College of Education: Domingo L. Diaz
College of Electrical, Industrial and Mechanical Engineering: Romulo D. Coloma
College of Liberal Arts: Zenaida N. Magiba
College of Pharmacy: Celia V. Lansang

UNIVERSITY OF NEGROS OCCIDENTAL-RECOLETOS

Lizares Ave, POB 214, 6100 Bacolod City
Telephone: 433-2449
Fax: 433-1709
E-mail: unorpro@yahoo.com
Internet: www.uno-r.edu.ph

Founded 1941
Private control
Language of instruction: English
Academic year: June to March

Pres.: Fr Dionisio Cachero
Comptroller: Fr Eduardo Celiz
Registrar: Dr Carmenda Leonoras
Librarian: Arabella M. Ananoria

Number of teachers: 330
Number of students: 7,879

Publications: *The Tolentine Star* (2 a semester), *UNO-R Journal of the Graduate School (Raison d'Etre)* (4 a year)

DEANS

Graduate School: Joel A. Alve
College of Arts and Sciences: Nieves Hibaler-Pepito
College of Business and Accountancy: Dr John Clifford Salugsugan
College of Criminal Justice Education: Jasmin Parreno
College of Education: Dr Ofelia Posecion
College of Engineering: Eng. Christopher G. Taclobos
Elementary Dept: Sunya Phi Sumalde
High School Dept: Sol Abellar
School of Agriculture: Dr Evangeline O. Aboyo
School of Law: Atty John Paolo Villasor

UNIVERSITY OF NORTHERN PHILIPPINES

Vigan, Ilocos Sur
Telephone: 28-10
Internet: www.unp.edu.ph
Founded 1965
State control
Languages of instruction: English, Filipino
Academic year of two semesters
Pres.: Dr DOROTEA C. FILART
Exec. Vice-Pres.: Prof. LEO OANDASAN
Vice-Pres. for Academic Affairs: Dr PACITA B. ANTIPORDA
Univ. Sec.: Prof. RAMONA VEGA
Dir of Admissions: ELEUTERIA REMUCAL
Dir of Research: Prof. NORMA I. CACHOLA
Librarian: PEROMA L. PACIS
Library of 28,369 vols
Number of teachers: 392
Number of students: 7,017
Publications: *New Vision* (4 a year), *Tandem* (6 a year)

DEANS

Faculty of Arts and Sciences: Dr FRANCISCO C. MACANAS
Faculty of Business Administration: Dr LUMEN ALMACHAR
Institute of Criminology: Prof. PLACIDO UNCIANO
Institute of Engineering: Eng. ROGELIO ANINAG
Institute of Fine Arts: Prof. FLORO PERLAS
Institute of Nursing and Paramedical Services: Prof. LILIA SALVADOR
Faculty of Teacher Education: Dr CIRILO PARRA
Institute of Social Work and Community Development: DANIEL COLCOL
Institute of Technical Education and Cottage Industries Development: Prof. WILHELMINA VERGARA
Faculty of the Graduate School: SALVADOR S. EDER

UNIVERSITY OF NUEVA CACERES

Jaime Henandez Ave, Naga City 4400
Telephone: 21-21-84
Internet: www.unc.edu.ph
Founded 1948
Private control
Languages of instruction: English, Filipino
Academic year: June to March (two semesters)
Pres.: Dr DOLORES H. SISON
Exec. Vice-Pres.: PERFECTO O. PALMA
Vice-Pres. for Admin.: JAIME HERNÁNDEZ, Jr
Registrar: NELIA E. SAN JOSE
Librarian: Dr PERPETUA S. PORCALLA
Number of teachers: 327
Number of students: 8,061
Publications: *Nueva Caceres Review*, *Nueva Caceres Bulletin* (6 a year), *Red and Gray* (1 a year), *The Trailblazer* (12 a year)

DEANS

College of Arts and Sciences and Education: LOURDES S. ANONAS
College of Engineering: MAXIMINO O. PANELO, Jr
College of Law and Commerce: PERFECTO O. PALMA
School of Graduate Studies and Research: MILAGROS Z. REYES

PROFESSORS

ALMOITE, G. E. O., Public Administration
ANONAS, L. S., Methods of Research
BARIAS, A. M.
CADAG, D., Engineering Management, Highway Engineering, Water Resources Engineering, Hydrology
CONDA, A., Development of the Novel
ENOJADO, V. F., Human Relations, Principles of Guidance
EVORA, M., Electrical Engineering, Refrigeration Engineering
FORTUNO, R. Z., Production, Planning Control
GROYON, S., Psychology
PALMA, M. B., Civil Procedure, Special Proceedings
PORCALLA, P., Library Science
REYES, M., Educational Planning, Personnel Administration, Inferential Statistics
SEPTIMO, C., Power Plant Design, Steam Power Engineering, Industrial Plant Design

NUEVA ECIJA UNIVERSITY OF SCIENCE AND TECHNOLOGY

Gen. Tinio St, Cabanatuan City 3100, Central Luzon
Telephone: (44) 463-1201
Fax: (44) 463-0226
E-mail: president@nuest.edu.ph
Internet: www.nuest.edu.ph
Founded 1929 as Nueva Ecija Trade School; present name and status 1998
State control
Academic year: June to March
Pres.: Dr GEMILIANO C. CALLING
Campuses at Fort Magsaysay, Gabaldon, San Isidro and Sumacab; Colleges of arts and science, business and management technology, computer studies, education, engineering and industrial technology; Graduate School.

PALAWAN STATE UNIVERSITY

Tiniguiban Heights, Puerto Princesa City 5300
Telephone: (48) 433-2379
Fax: (48) 433-5303
E-mail: psu@pal-onl.com
Internet: www.psu.itgo.com
Founded 1972 as Palawan Teacher's College; present name and status 1994
State control
Academic year: June to March
Pres.: Dr TERESITA L. SALVA
Exec. Vice-Pres.: Dr CARLOS A. ALCANTARA
Vice-Pres. for Academic Affairs: Dr ELIZABETH J. MAGAY
Vice-Pres. for Admin.: MARILYN GONZALES PABLICO
Vice-Pres. for Finance: DESTIDCHADO S. VILLASARIO
Registrar: VENERANDA L. LAGROSA
Univ. Librarian: LOURDES C. SALVADOR.

PAMANTASAN NG LUNGSOD NG MAYNILA (University of the City of Manila)

Intramuros, Manila 1002
Telephone: (2) 527-79-41
E-mail: info@plm.edu.ph
Internet: www.plm.edu.ph
Founded 1965
City government control
Languages of instruction: English, Filipino
Academic year: June to March (two semesters); summer term for graduate schools; trimestral for graduate programmes in management and engineering
Pres. (CEO): Atty RAFAELITO M. GARAYBLAS (acting)
Exec. Vice Pres. (COO): Atty GLADYS FRANCE J. PALARCA
Vice-Pres. for Academic Affairs: Dr VIRGINIA N. SANTOS
Vice-Pres. for Admin.: DANILO A. BALUYOT
Univ. and Board Sec.: Dr ANCHELA BIAG
Vice-Pres. for Finance and Planning: ANGELITA G. SOLIS
Registrar: Dr ESTER D. JIMENEZ
Librarian: REBECCA JOCSON
Univ. Treasurer: ANGELES RAMOS
Library of 52,000 vols, 3,400 periodicals
Number of teachers: 822 incl. 301 full-time, 521 part-time
Number of students: 9,283
Publications: *Ang Pamantasan*, *PLM Review*, *PLM Star Post*

DEANS

College of Accountancy and Economics: Prof. NONALYN V. GESALAN
College of Architecture and Urban Planning: GIL C. EVASCO
College of Arts and Sciences: Dr DOLORES B. LIWAG
College of Business and Public Administration: NILO D. BULADACO
College of Education: MYRNA G. GIL
College of Engineering and Technology: Prof. RICHARD C. REGALA Jr
College of Human Devt: Dr DAISY P. HICARTE
College of Law: Atty ERNESTO P. MACEDA Jr.
College of Liberal Arts: Prof. EVELYN L. SEBASTIAN
College of Management and Entrepreneurship: Prof. NEIL B. GAMUS
College of Mass Communication: Prof. LUDMILA R. LABAGNOY
College of Medicine: Dr EUGENIO A. PICAZO
College of Nursing: Prof. MARILYN R. NILO A. CAPANGPANGAN
College of Physical Education, Recreation and Sports: Prof. SUSAN C. MERCADO
College of Physical Therapy: Prof. PRIME ROSE TEODULICE M. LANETE
College of Science: Prof. PROCULA B. AMARILLO
College of Tourism, Hotel and Travel Industry Management: Prof. MA. CRISTINA A. MAPUYAN
Emeritus College: Prof. ESPERANZA B. BAUTISTA
Graduate School of Arts, Sciences, Education and Nursing: Dr TERESITA P. SALVADOR
Graduate School of Business and Government: Dr ROBERT G. ONG
Graduate School of Engineering: Engr. FELIX F. ASPIRAS
Graduate School of Law: ANGELINA SANDOVAL-GUTIERREZ
Graduate School of Management: Dr NERI S. PESCADERA

PANGASINAN STATE UNIVERSITY

Lingayen, Pangasinan
Telephone: (75) 542-6103
Fax: (75) 542-8694
Internet: www.psu.edu.ph
Founded 1979
State control
Languages of instruction: English, Filipino
Academic year: June to May
Pres.: Dr RUFINO O. ESLAO
Vice-Pres. for Academic Affairs: Dr REYNALDO P. SEGUI
Vice-Pres. for Research and Extension: Dr PORFERIO L. BASILIO
Vice-Pres. for Admin.: Dr ALFREDO F. AQUINO
Admin. Officer: EMERITO J. URBANO
Librarian (Lingayen): ARACELI P. UNTALAN
Library of 50,000 vols
Number of teachers: 308
Number of students: 5,830
Publications: *Banyuhay* (2 a year), *PSU Chronicle*, *PSU Graduate School Journal*, *Research and Extension Bulletin* (4 a year), *The Aqua Sounds*, *The Farm Breeze*, *The Golden Harvest*, *The Green Hills*, *The*

Ocean View, *The Reflections*, *The Technologist*, *The Technotrends*

DEANS

College of Agriculture, PSU-Infanta: Prof. ARTEMIO M. REBUGIO
College of Agriculture: PSU-San Carlos City: Dr LEONARDO E. MONGE
College of Agriculture, PSU-Santa Maria: Dr LYDIO E. CALONGE
College of Arts, Sciences and Technology, PSU-Lingayen: Dr VICTORIANO C. ESTIRA
College of Arts, Trades and Technology, PSU-Asingan: Prof. ESTER E. LOMBOY
College of Education, PSU-Bayambang: Dr APOLINARIO G. BAUTISTA
College of Engineering and Technology, PSU-Urdaneta: Dr EUSEBIO E. MICLAT
College of Fisheries, PSU-Binmaley: Dr PORFERIO L. BASILIO
Graduate School (Urdaneta Centre, Bayambang Center, Lingayen Centre): Dr RODOLFO C. ASANION

UNIVERSITY OF PANGASINAN

Arellano St, Dagupan City
Telephone: (75) 522-5635
Fax: (75) 522-2496
E-mail: registrar@upang.edu.ph
Internet: www.upang.edu.ph

Founded 1925; Univ. status 1968
Private control
Languages of instruction: English, Filipino
Academic year: June to March

Pres.: CESAR T. DUQUE
Registrar: TERESITA R. VISTRO
Librarian: IDA F. ROSARIO

Library of 20,500 vols
Number of teachers: 218
Number of students: 10,340

Publication: *The Researcher* (2 a year)

DEANS

College of Accountancy, Commerce, Secretarial Administration and Management Accounting: MARIETTA B. SORIO
College of Architecture: FREDDIE O. ARCALAS
College of Computer Science and Technology: MARIETTA B. SORIO
College of Education: Dr TITO G. ROCABERTE
College of Engineering: Dr LUIS M. ORTEGA
College of Law: HERMOGENES S. DECANO
College of Liberal Arts: Dr OFELIA C. RAYOS
College of Medical Technology: MARIA D. AVELINO
College of Nursing: Dr VIRTUD P. OLOAN
College of Physical Therapy: Dr MELECIO M. PENA III
School of Graduate Studies: Dr ALELI N. CORNISTA
University Elementary Laboratory School: NENITA Y. VICTORIO
University High School: NENITA T. RAYOS (Principal)

PARTIDO STATE UNIVERSITY

San Juan Bautista, Goa, Camarines Sur 4422
Telephone: (54) 453-0235
Fax: (54) 453-1301
E-mail: psu-goa@asia.com
Internet: ecommunity.ncc.gov/psu

Founded 1941 as Partido High School; present name and status 2001
State control
Academic year: June to March

Pres.: Dr MODESTO D. DETERA
Vice-Pres. for Academic Affairs: Dr MINDA P. FORMALEJO
Vice-Pres. for Admin.: LEONCIO P. OBIAS

Campuses in Caramoan, Lagonoy, Sagñay, Salogon, San Jose and Tinambac; Depts of business education, engineering, graduate studies, teacher education and technology.

PHILIPPINE NORMAL UNIVERSITY

Taft Ave, Cnr Ayala Blvd, Manila 1000
Telephone: (2) 527-0374
Fax: (2) 536-6471
Internet: www.pnumanila.com.ph

Founded 1901; present name and status 1991
State control
Academic year: June to March

Pres.: Dr NILO L. ROSAS.

PHILIPPINE WOMEN'S UNIVERSITY

Taft Ave, 1004 Manila
Telephone: (2) 526-69-34
Fax: (2) 536-81-69
Internet: www.pwu.edu.ph

Founded 1919
Private control
Language of instruction: English
Academic year: June to March

Chair. of the Board of Trustees: Hon. HELENA Z. BENITEZ
Pres.: Dr JOSE CONRADO BENITEZ
Chancellor, Cavite Campus: Dr AMELIA REYES
Chancellor, Manila Campus, and Vice-Pres. for Academic Affairs: Dr DOLORES LASAN
Chancellor, Quezon City Campus: Dr SYLVIA MONTES
Vice-Pres.: JULITA DADO (Admin. and Finance), ENCARNACION RARALIO (Planning, Devt and External Affairs)
Registrar: LILIA ROBOSA
Librarian: DIONISIA ANGELES

Library: see Libraries and Archives
Number of teachers: 479
Number of students: 10,675

Publications: *Journal on the Environment and Habitat*, *Journal on Women's Health*, *Philippine Educational Forum* (2 a year), *PWU Bulletin* (4 a year), *PWU Research Journal* (2 a year), *The Maroon and White* (1 a year), *The Philwomenian* (12 a year)

DEANS

College of Arts and Sciences: Dr ELIZABETH DELA CRUZ
College of Distance Education: LUMEN LARGOZA
College of Education: Dr CECILIO DUKA
College of Music: MERCEDES DUGAN (Head)
College of Nursing: CONSTANCIA P. PITPITAN
College of Pharmacy: ZENAIDA SADIWA
Conrado Benitez Institute of Business Education: Dr CONSUELO ANG
Institute of Fine Arts and Design: LORNA SALUTAL (Head)
Institute of Medical Sciences and Technology: Dr NINI FESTIN LIM
Philippine Institute of Nutrition, Food Science and Technology: ROMUALDA GUIRRIEC
Philippine School of Social Work: Dr NENITA M. CURA (Dir)

UNIVERSITY OF THE PHILIPPINES SYSTEM

UP Diliman, Quezon City
Telephone and fax (2) 926-15-72
E-mail: op@up.edu.ph
Internet: www.up.edu.ph

Founded 1908
Public control
Languages of instruction: English, Filipino
Academic year: June to March (two terms, one summer session)

Pres.: Dr ALFREDO PASCUAL
Vice-Pres. for Academic Affairs: Prof. GISELA CONCEPCION
Vice-Pres. for Admin.: Prof. ARLENE A. SAMANIEGO
Vice-Pres. for Devt: Prof. ARMIN B. SARTHOU Jr
Vice-Pres. for Planning and Finance: Prof. EDGARDO G. ATANACIO
Vice-Pres. for Public Affairs: Prof. ISABELITA O. REYES
Vice-Pres. for Legal Affairs: Prof. MARAGTAS AMANTE
Sec.: Prof. LILIAN DE LAS LLAGAS

Library: see Libraries and Archives
Number of teachers: 3,952
Number of students: 50,668

Publications: *The Carillon* (online), *UP Forum* (28 a year), *UP Newsletter* (12 a year), *UP Statistics* (1 a year).

CONSTITUENT CAMPUSES

UP at Baguio

Internet: www.upb.edu.ph

Chancellor: Prof. PRISCILLA SUPNET-MACANSANTOS
Vice Chancellor for Academic Affairs: Prof. ALIPIO T. GARCIA
Vice Chancellor for Admin.: Prof. BIENVENIDO C. MARZAN
Registrar: Prof. JOCELYN R. RAFANAN
Librarian: BRENDA A. DOGUP

DEANS

College of Arts and Communication: Prof. PURIFICACION DELIMA
College of Science: Prof. WILFREDO V. ALANGUI
College of Social Sciences: Prof. RAYMUNDO D. ROVILLOS
Institute of Management: Prof. SANTOS JOSE O. DACANAY III

UP at Diliman

Internet: www.upd.edu.ph

Chancellor: SERGIO S. CAO
Vice Chancellor for Academic Affairs: Prof. LORNA I. PAREDES
Vice Chancellor for Admin.: Prof. MARY DELIA G. TOMACRUZ
Vice Chancellor for Community Affairs: Prof. CYNTHIA GRACE C. GREGORIO
Vice Chancellor for Research and Devt: Prof. LUIS G. SISON
Vice Chancellor for Student Affairs: Prof. ELIZABETH L. ENRIQUEZ
Registrar: Prof. PAMELA C. CONSTANTINO
Librarian: SALVACION M. ARLANTE

DEANS

Archeological Studies Program: Prof. VICTOR J. PAZ
Asian Centre: Prof. MARIO I. MICLAT
Asian Institute of Tourism: Prof. CORAZON P. RODRIGUEZ
College of Architecture: Prof. DANILO A. SILVESTRE
College of Arts and Letters: Prof. FLORA ELENA R. MIRANO
College of Business Administration: Prof. ERLINDA S. ECHANIS
College of Education: Prof. VIVIEN M. TALISAYON
College of Engineering: Prof, ROWENA CRISTINA L. GUEVARA
College of Fine Arts: Prof. ROWENA CRISTINA L. GUEVARA
College of Home Economics: Prof. ADELAIDA V. MAYO
College of Human Kinetics: Prof. LEILANI L. GONZALO
College of Law: Prof. MARVIC MARIO VICTOR F. LEONEN

College of Mass Communication: Prof. Roland B. Tolentino
College of Music: Prof. Ramón Ma. G. Acoymo
College of Science: Prof. Caesar A. Saloma
College of Social Science and Philosophy: Zosimo E. Lee
College of Social Work and Community Development: Prof. Amery llis Torres
Institute of Islamic Studies: Prof. Mashur Bin-Ghalib Jundam
National College of Public Administration and Governance: Prof. Alex B. Brillantes Jr
School of Economics: Emmanuel S. De Dios
School of Labour and Industrial Relations: Prof. Jorge V. Sibal
School of Library and Information Science: Prof. Vyva Aguirre
School of Statistics: Prof. Erniel Barrios
School of Urban and Regional Planning: Prof. Candido A. Cabrido Jr
UP Extension Programme in Pampanga: Prof. Julieta C. Mallari

UP at Los Baños

Internet: www.uplb.edu.ph
Chancellor: Prof. Luis Rey I. Velasco
Vice Chancellor for Admin.: Prof. Roberto F. Rañola Jr
Vice Chancellor for Community Affairs: Prof. Virginia R. Cardenas
Vice Chancellor for Instruction: Prof. Rita P. Laude
Vice Chancellor for Planning and Devt: Prof. Ruben D. Tanqueco
Vice Chancellor for Research and Extension: Prof. Enrico P. Supangco
Registrar: Prof. Myrna G. Carandang
Librarian: Concepcion DL. Saul

DEANS
College of Agriculture: Prof. Domingo E. Angeles
College of Arts and Sciences: Prof. Asuncion K. Raymundo
College of Development Communication: Prof. Cleofe S. Torres
College of Economics and Management: Prof. Liborio S. Cabanilla
College of Engineering and Agro-Industrial Technology: Prof. Victor B. Cruz
College of Forestry and Natural Resources: Prof. Rex Victor O. Cruz
College of Human Ecology: Prof. Sue Liza C. Saguiguit
College of Public Affairs: Prof. Agnes C. Rola
College of Veterinary Medicine: Prof. Conrado A. Valdez
Graduate School: Prof. Oscar B. Zamora
School of Environmental Science and Management: Prof. Maria Victoria O. Espaldon

UP at Manila

Internet: www.upm.edu.ph
Chancellor: Prof. Dr Ramon L. Arcadio
Vice Chancellor for Academic Affairs: Prof. Josefina G. Tayag
Vice Chancellor for Admin.: Prof. Orlino O. Talens
Vice Chancellor for Planning and Devt: Prof. Zorayda E. Leopando
Vice Chancellor for Research: Prof. Lulu C. Bravo
Registrar: Susan B. Villegas
Librarian: Theresa P. Dugenia
Library: see Libraries and Archives

DEANS
College of Allied Medical Professions: Prof. Concepcion C. Cabatan
College of Arts and Sciences: Prof. Reynaldo H. Imperial
College of Dentistry: Prof, Vicente O. Medina
College of Medicine: Prof. Alberto B. Roxas
College of Nursing: Prof. Josefina A. Tuazon
College of Pharmacy: Prof. Jocelyn S. Bautista-Palacpac
College of Public Health: Prof. Nina G. Gloriani
Graduate School: Lilia A. Reyes
National Institutes of Health: Prof. Lulu C. Bravo
National Teacher-Training Centre for the Health Professions: Prof. Erlyn A. Sana
School of Health Sciences: Prof. Jusie Lydia J. Siega-Sur

UP on Mindanao

Internet: www.upmin.edu.ph
Chancellor: Prof. Gilda C. Rivero
Vice Chancellor for Academic Affairs: Prof. Emma Ruth V. Bayogan
Vice Chancellor for Admin.: Prof. Miguel D. Soledad
Registrar: Prof. Karen Joyce G. Cayamanda
Librarian: Briccio M. Merced

DEANS
College of Humanities and Social Sciences: Prof. Ma. Araceli Dans-Lee
College of Science and Mathematics: Prof. Reynaldo G. Abad
School of Management: Prof. Sylvia B. Concepcion

UP in the Visayas

Internet: www.upv.edu.ph
Chancellor: Prof. Minda J. Formacion
Vice Chancellor for Academic Affairs: Prof. Leonor M. Santos
Vice Chancellor for Admin.: Prof. Louise Annette B. Escoto
Vice Chancellor for Planning and Devt: Prof. Alice Joan G. Ferrer
Vice Chancellor for Research and Extension: Prof. Jane S. Geduspan
Registrar: Prof. Marilyn Z. Alcarde
Librarian: Ana T. Mones

DEANS
College of Arts and Sciences: Prof. Rommel A. Espinosa
College of Fisheries and Ocean Sciences: Prof. Carlos C. Baylon
College of Management: Prof. Joy C. Lizada
School of Technology: Prof. Luzette T. Teruel
UPV Cebu College: Prof. Enrique M. Avila
UPV Tacloban College: Prof. Margarita Dela Cruz

UP Open University

Internet: www.upou.org
Chancellor: Prof. Grace Javier Alfonso
Vice Chancellor for Academic Affairs: Prof. Maria Fe V. Mendoza
Vice Chancellor for Finance and Admin.: Prof. Melinda F. Lumanta
Registrar: Prof. Ricardo T. Bagarinao
Librarian: Audrey Anday

DEANS
Faculty of Education: Prof. Ma. Theresa de Villa
Faculty of Information and Communication Studies: Prof. Melinda dP. Bandalaria
Faculty of Management and Development Studies: Prof. Inocencio E. Buot, Jr

POLYTECHNIC UNIVERSITY OF THE PHILIPPINES

Anonas St, Santa Mesa, Manila
Telephone: (2) 716-26-44
Fax: (2) 716-11-43
E-mail: omcaragu e@edsamail.com.ph
Internet: www.pup.edu.ph

Founded 1904
State control
Languages of instruction: English, Filipino
Academic year: June to March

Pres.: Dr Ofelia M. Caragu e
Vice-Pres. for Academic Affairs: Dr Samuel M. Salvador
Vice-Pres. for Admin.: Dr Dante G. Guevarra
Vice-Pres. for Student Services: Dr Moises S. Garcia
Vice-Pres. for Finance: Dr Carmela S. Perez
Vice-Pres. for Research and Devt: Dr Normita A. Villa
Registrar: Prof. Melba D. Abaleta
Library Officer: Dr Irene D. Amores

Library of 205,365 vols
Number of teachers: 1,381
Number of students: 42,988

Publications: *BISIG* (Journal of Labour and Industrial Relations), *Campus Circular*, *CLMC Update*, *Graduate Forum*, *Journal of Economics and Politics* (4 a year), *Journal of Open and Distance Education*, *PUP Monograph* (1 a year), *PUP Open University Newsletter* (12 a year), *PUP Studies*, *Statistical Bulletin*, *The Catalyst* (12 a year), *Trends* (4 a year)

DEANS
College of Accountancy and Law: Dr Gloria T. Baysa
College of Architecture and Fine Arts: Arch. Gloria T. Baysa
College of Arts: Dr Amalia C. Rosales
College of Business: Dr Erlinda C. Garcia
College of Computer Management and Information Technology: Prof. Gisela May A. Albano
College of Economics, Finance and Politics: Dr Roman R. Dannug
College of Engineering and Architecture: Vicky S. Cruz
College of Languages and Mass Communication: Prof. Wilhelmina N. Cayanan
College of Office Administration and Business Teacher Education: Prof. Avelina C. Bucao
College of Physical Education and Sports: Prof. Maripres P. Pascua
College of Science: Adela Jamorabo-Ruiz
College of Tourism, Hotel and Restaurant Management: Ma. Teresa C. Villar
Commonwealth: Doris B. Gatan
Graduate School: Dr Victoria C. Naval
Institute of Cooperatives: Elenita S. Mantalaba
Open University: Dr Carmencita L. Castolo
Technical School: Josefina R. Tan
Taguig Campus: Amelita A. Laurente

MANUEL L. QUEZON UNIVERSITY

916 R. Hidalgo, Quiapo, Manila
Telephone: (2) 734-0121
Fax: (2) 733-7976
E-mail: mlq@mlqu.edu.ph
Internet: www.mlqu.edu.ph

Founded 1947

Pres.: Amado C. Dizon
Vice-Pres. for Academic Affairs: Martha A. Mogol
Exec. Officer, Regent: Ma. Victoria O. Chan
Registrar: Prof. Gregorio A. del Valle , Jr
Treas., Regent: Amador P. Alvendia
Chief Librarian: Prof. Flordeliza M. Torres

Number of teachers: 291
Number of students: 8,355

Publications: *MLQU Newsletter*, *Junior Quezonian*, *MLQU Graduate Journal*, *MLQU Law Quarterly*

DEANS

Faculty of Accountancy and Business: ENRIQUE A. B. GABRIEL
Faculty of Architecture: CARLOS B. BANAAG
Faculty of Arts and Science: LETICIA L. LAVA
Faculty of Criminology: CLETO B. SENOREN
Faculty of Education: VIRGINIA P. GANIR
Faculty of Engineering: ANTERO P. MANGUNDAYAO
Faculty of Graduate Studies: MARTHA A. MOGOL
Faculty of Law: NORBERTO S. GONZALES
Faculty of Secretarial Education and Technology: PILAR E. SOTO
Faculty of the Institute of Computer Education: JUANITA M. UMAGAT

RAMON MAGSAYSAY TECHNOLOGICAL UNIVERSITY

Iba, Zambales 2201, Central Luzon
Telephone: (47) 811-1683
Fax: (47) 811-1683

Founded 1910; present name and status 2001
State control

Courses in biology, education, engineering, hotel and restaurant management, mathematics and computer science, psychology, public administration, technology
Academic year: June to March

Pres.: Dr FELICIANO S. ROSETE.

RIZAL TECHNOLOGICAL UNIVERSITY

Boni Ave, Mandaluyong City 1550
Telephone: (2) 533-6041
Fax: (2) 532-0665
E-mail: riztech@mnl.cyberspace.com.ph

Founded 1969
State control
Academic year: June to March

Pres.: Dr JOSÉ Q. MACABALLUG

Courses in architecture, business administration, education, engineering, english, industrial and organizational psychology, mathematics, natural sciences, political science, statistics, technology.

UNIVERSITY OF RIZAL SYSTEM

URS Tanay Main Campus, J. P. Rizal St, Sampaloc, Tanay, Rizal 1980
Telephone: (2) 401-4900
Fax: (2) 674-2543URS Morong Campus, Sumulong St, Morong, Rizal 1960
Telephone: (2) 653-1735
E-mail: urstanay_main@yahoo.com
Internet: www.urs.edu.ph

Founded 1959 as Rizal Agricultural School; present name and status 2001
State control
Academic year: June to May (two semesters)
Number of teachers: 15,407
Number of students: 582

Pres.: Dr OLIVIA F. DE LEON
Vice-Pres. for Academic Affairs: Dr ARACELI M. BOBADILLA
Vice-Pres. for Admin. and Finance: Dr DEMETRIA A. SAN JUAN
Vice-Pres. for Research, Devt, Extension and Production: Dr HERMY D. ESTRABO
Chancellor for Cluster 1 (Tanay, Cardona, Rodriguez): Dr ALLEN U. BAUTISTA
Chancellor for Cluster 2 (Morong, Cainta, Taytay): Dr RENEECILIA B. PAZ DE LEON
Chancellor for Cluster 3 (Angono, Antipolo, Binangonan, Pililla): Dr GLORIA P. SARABIA

CAMPUS DIRECTORS

URS Main Campus (Tanay): Dr FLORIE B. GAPIDO
URS Angono: Dr ROWENA A. LAROZA
URS Antipolo: Prof. ALLEN U. BAUTISTA
URS Binangonan: Dr DEMETRIA A. SAN JUAN
URS Cainta: Dr MANUEL S. ORDONEZ
URS Morong: Dr HERMY D. ESTRABO
URS Pililla: Dr GLORIA P. SARABIA
URS Rodriguez: Dr TERESITA BUENVIAJE

SAINT LOUIS UNIVERSITY

POB 71, 2600 Baguio City
Telephone: (74) 442-2793
Fax: (74) 442-2842
E-mail: picrodir@slu.edu.ph
Internet: www.slu.edu.ph

Founded 1911
Private control (Roman Catholic)
Languages of instruction: English, Filipino
Academic year: June to March (two semesters)

Pres.: Fr PAUL VAN PARIJS
Vice-Pres. for Academic Affairs: Engr JOSE MARIA PANGILINAN
Vice-Pres. for Finance: EVANGELINE O. TRINIDAD
Vice-Pres. for Admin.: ARNULFO SORIANO
Registrar: VIOLETA GARCIA
Dean, Student Affairs: GIL ESPIRITU
Dir of Libraries (College-Level): VIRGILIO C. FUERTE

Library of 107,214 vols
Number of teachers: 669
Number of students: 23,584

Publications: *Buhay SLU* (12 a year), *Cordillera Researches and Studies* (1 a year), *SLU Chronicle* (4 a year), *SLU Research Journal* (2 a year)

DEANS

College of Accountancy and Commerce: NOEL B. DE LEON
College of Education: ROQUE Q. BERNARDEZ
College of Engineering and Architecture: JOSELITO BUHANGIN
College of Human Sciences: TERESITA AZARCON
College of Information and Computing Sciences: RANDY FLORES
College of Law: CEAZAR ORACION
College of Medicine: ROBERTO LEGASPI
College of Natural Science: GAUDELIA A. REYES
College of Nursing: MARY GRACE LACANARIA

UNIVERSITY OF SAN AGUSTÍN

General Luna St, 5000 Iloilo City
Telephone: (33) 337-4841
Fax: (33) 337-4403
E-mail: info@usa.edu.ph
Internet: www.usa.edu.ph

Founded 1904, Univ. status 1953
Private control
Languages of instruction: English, Filipino
Academic year: June to March

Pres.: Fr RAUL M. MARCHAN
Vice-Pres. for Academic Affairs: Fr GENEROUS P. GONESTO
Vice-Pres. for Admin.: Fr EDGARDO L. LAZO
Vice-Pres. for Student Affairs: Fr PEDERITO A. APARECE
Registrar: GEMMA B. HALILI
Librarian: EPIFANIA A. PACLIBAR

Number of teachers: 524
Number of students: 10,250

Publications: *Augustinian Interdisciplinary Journal* (2 a year), *Augustinian Legacy* (1 a year), *Augustinian Research Journal* (1 a year), *Communitas* (2 a year), *The Augustinian* (6 a year), *The Augustinian Mirror* (2 a year)

DEANS

College of Arts and Sciences: Dr ISIDORO CRUZ
College of Business Admin. and Accountancy: Dr LUCIO ENCIO
College of Commerce: NEOMISIA GONZALES
College of Education: Dr ALEX FACINABAO
College of Engineering and Architecture: Ing. REYNALDO ASUNCION
College of Nursing: SOFIA COSETTE MONTEBLANCO
College of Pharmacy and Medical Technology: VICTORIA SUSTENTO
College of Law: JUANA JUDITA P. NAFARRETE
Conservatory of Music: Fr JONAS MEJARES
Graduate School: Dr RUBY CATALAN

UNIVERSITY OF SAN CARLOS

Cebu City 6000
Telephone: (32) 253-1000
Fax: (32) 255-4341
E-mail: president@usc.edu.ph
Internet: www.usc.edu.ph

Founded 1595; Univ. status 1948
Private (Roman Catholic) control
Language of instruction: English
Academic year: June to March (two terms)

Pres.: Fr DIONISIO M. MIRANDA
Vice-Pres. for Academic Affairs: Fr ANTHONY SALAS,
Vice-Pres. for Admin.: Fr ELENO BUCIA
Vice-Pres. for Finance: Fr GENEROSO RICARDO Jr REBAYLA
Registrar: Sencio ROMEO E. YAP
Dir of Library System: Dr MARIOLOU P. TADLIP

Library of 303,049 vols, 41698 periodicals
Number of teachers: 1,086 (591 full-time, 495 part-time)
Number of students: 17,619

Publications: *Journal of Business Studies* (2 a year), *Philippine Quarterly of Culture and Society* (4 a year), *Philippine Scientist* (1 a year), *The University Bulletin* (26 a year), *USC Graduate Journal* (2 a year)

DEANS

College of Architecture and Fine Arts: JOSEPH MICHAEL P. ESPINA
College of Arts and Sciences: Fr RAMON S. DEL FIERRO
College of Commerce: Fr RENE R. PAQUIBUT
College of Education: Dr ANTONIO E. BATOMALAQUE
College of Engineering: ANDRESA S. ALLERA
College of Law: Atty ALEX L. MONTECLAR
College of Nursing: ANTONIA F. PASCUAL
College of Pharmacy: YOLANDA C. DELIMAN

UNIVERSITY OF SAN JOSE-RECOLETOS

Corner Magallanes and P. Lopez Sts, 6000 Cebu City
Telephone: (32) 253-7900
Fax: (32) 254-1720
E-mail: usjr@usjr.edu.ph
Internet: www.usjr.edu.ph

Founded 1947, univ. status 1984
Private (Roman Catholic) control
Language of instruction: English
Academic year: June to March

Pres.: Rev. Fr CONSTANTINO B. REAL
Vice-Pres. for Admin.: Rev. Fr CORNELIO E. MORAL
Vice-Pres. for Academics: Rev. Fr SIXTO M. BITANGJOL

Vice-Pres. for Business and Finance: Rev. Fr LEONARDO P. PAULIGUE
Vice-Pres. for Student Welfare: Rev. Fr ANTHONY A. MORILLO
Dir of Basak Campus: Rev. Fr RAUL M. BUHAY
Registrar: DEMETRIO QUIRANTE
Librarian: EVELYN A. LIM

Library of 190,000 vols
Number of teachers: 500
Number of students: 13,000

Publications: *Forward* (1 a year), *Josenian* (1 a year), *Faculty Research Journal* (1 a year), *Precedent* (2 a year), *USJ-R Journal of Research* (Graduate School publication, 2 a year), *USJ-R Updates* (newsletter, 4 a year)

DEANS

College of Arts and Sciences: Dr CORAZON A. TAN
College of Commerce: Dr SUSAN CHUNG
College of Education: Dr ALMA ANG
College of Engineering: Dr EVANGELINE EVANGELISTA
College of Law: ALICIA E. BATHAN
College of Nursing: RAOUL
Graduate School: (vacant)
Grade School Department: PURA S. WAGAS
High School Department: SONIA F. PAGLINAWAN
Religious Education Centre: Fr CORNELIO E. MORAL

UNIVERSITY OF SANTO TOMÁS

España St, Manila
Telephone: 731-31-01
Fax: 732-74-86
Internet: www.ust.edu.ph

Founded 1611
Private (Roman Catholic) control
Academic year: June to March

Grand Chancellor: Very Rev. TIMOTHY RADCLIFFE
Vice-Chancellor: Very Rev. QUIRICO PEDREGOSA
Rector: Fr TAMERLANE R. LANA
Vice-Rector: Fr ERNESTO M. ARCEO
Sec.-Gen.: Fr RODEL ALIGAN
Registrar: Prof. RODOLFO N. CLAVIO
Prefect of Libraries: Fr ANGEL APARICO
Chief Librarian: Prof. ERLINDA FLORES

Number of teachers: 1,438
Number of students: 32,061

Publications: *Academia*, *Thomasian*, *Varsitarian*, *Journal of Medicine*, *Law Review*, *Unitas*, *Boletín Eclesiástico*, *Commerce Journal*, *Nursing Journal*, *Education Journal*, *Science Journal*, *Philippiniana Sacra*, *Acta Manilana*, *Journal of Graduate Research*

DEANS

Faculty of Arts and Letters: Dr ARMANDO DE JESUS
Faculty of Canon Law: Fr JAVIER GONZALES
Faculty of Civil Law: Dr AMADO DIMAYUGA
Faculty of Engineering: Dr MARILYN MABINI
Faculty of Medicine and Surgery: Dr ANGELES TAN-ALORA
Faculty of Pharmacy: Dr ROSALINDA SOLEVILLA
Faculty of Philosophy: Fr ERNESTO ARCEO
Faculty of Sacred Theology: Fr FAUSTO GOMEZ
College of Architecture and Fine Arts: LUIS FERRER
College of Commerce and Business Administration: Prof. AMELIA HALILI
College of Education: Dr CLOTILDE ARCANGEL
College of Nursing: Prof. GLENDA VARGAS
College of Science: Dr GLORIA BERNAS
Graduate School: Fr JOSE ANTONIO AUREADA
Institute of Religion: Fr RODEL ALIGAN
Conservatory of Music: Prof. ERLINDA FULE

SILLIMAN UNIVERSITY

6200 Dumaguete City, Negros Oriental
Telephone: (35) 4227195
Fax: (35) 2254768
E-mail: pres@su.edu.ph
Internet: www.su.edu.ph

Founded 1901
Private control
Language of instruction: English
Academic year: June to May

Pres.: Dr AGUSTIN A. PULIDO
Vice-Pres. for Academic Affairs: Dr BETTY C. ABREGANA
Vice-Pres. for Finance: JEAN G. ESPINO
Registrar: ANNABELLE E. PAA
Librarian: LORNA TUMULAK-YSO

Library: see Libraries and Archives
Number of teachers: 253
Number of students: 6,500

Publications: *Silliman Journal* (humanities, social sciences and sciences, 2 a year), *Sillimanian Magazine* (1 a year), *Sands and Corals* (literary magazine, 1 a year), *Convergence* (1 a year), *Educator* (every 5 years), *Infoline* (12 a year), *Ingenium* (2 a year), *Insights* (2 a year), *Nurse* (2 a year), *Scoop* (1 a year), *Stones and Pebbles* (1 a year), *SUCN Abstracts* (irregular)

DEANS

College of Agriculture: Prof. EDNA DUMANCAS
College of Arts and Sciences: Prof. CARLOS MAGTOLIS
College of Business Administration: TABITHA TINAGAN
College of Education: Dr JESUSA CORAZON GONZALES
College of Engineering: Dr BENJAMIN TOBIAS
College of Law: MYLES BEJAR
College of Nursing and Allied Medical Sciences: Dr MARIA TERESITA S. SINDA
College of Performing Arts: Prof. JOSEPH BASA
Divinity School: Dr NORIEL CAPULONG
School of Basic Education: Prof. LETICIA ALCALA
School of Communication: CELIA ACEDO

UNIVERSITY OF SOUTHEASTERN PHILIPPINES

Bo. Obrero, Davao City 8000
Telephone: (82) 225-4696
Fax: (82) 221-7737
E-mail: pio@usep.edu.ph
Internet: www.usep.edu.ph

Founded 1978
State control
Language of instruction: English
Academic year: June to March

Pres.: Dr PERFECTO A. ALIBIN
Vice-Pres. for Academic Affairs: Dr MARCELO M. ANGELIA
Vice-Pres. for Admin.: Dr RODULFO C. SUMUGAT
Univ./Board Sec.: MARNIE GRACE I. SONICO
Chancellor (Tagum-Mabini Campus): Prof. CEFERINO T. BASTIAN
Vice-Pres. for Research, Devt and Extension: Dr SOPHREMIANO B ANTIPOLO
Registrar: VIC JEAN A. SOLLER
Librarian: MARIVIC I. DUMARAN

Number of teachers: 400
Number of students: 12,000

Publications: *Headlight* (2 a year), *Newsletter*

DEANS

College of Arts and Sciences: Dr PATRICIA O. ELBANBUENA
College of Education: Prof. DENNIS A. ALONZO
College of Engineering: Ing. RICARDO FORBES ABEAR
College of Governance Business and Economics: Dr SHERLITO SABLE
College of Technology: Dr ANNWEDA C. MINA
Institute of Computing: VAL A. QUIMNO (acting)

UNIVERSITY OF SOUTHERN MINDANAO

Kabacan 9407, North Cotabato
Telephone: (64) 248-21-38
Fax: (64) 248-21-38
Internet: www.usm.edu.ph

Founded 1954 as Institute of Technology, present name 1980
State control
Languages of instruction: English, Filipino
Academic year: June to December (2 semesters)

Colleges of agriculture, engineering, home and ecological sciences, education, arts and sciences, trade and industry; institutes of veterinary science, Middle Eastern and Asian studies, development economics management, animal science and aquaculture, nursing

Pres.: Dr JESUS ANTONIO GAMIDO DERIJE
Vice-Pres.: Dr NAOMI G TANGONAN
Vice Pres.: ABRAHAM G CASTILLO
Vice Pres.: Dr PALASIG U AMPANG
Vice Pres.: ANTONIO N TACARDON
Registrar: Dr PRISCILLA P COSTES
Librarian: ANITA SORNITO

Number of teachers: 434
Number of students: 9,152

Publications: *CA Research Journal*, *USMARC Monitor*, *USM Research and Development Journal* (2 a year).

UNIVERSITY OF SOUTHERN PHILIPPINES

Mabini St, Cebu City
Telephone: (32) 232-5939
Fax: (32) 231-0178
Internet: www.usp.ph

Founded 1927; Univ. status 1949
Private control

Pres.: OSCAR JEREZA
Registrar: ERLINDA M. CAMPOS

Number of teachers: 197
Number of students: 7,439

DEANS

College of Arts and Sciences: INOCENTA GO
College of Commerce: GERONIMO S. ANA
College of Education: ISABELITA CONALES (acting)
College of Engineering: ROMULO JEREZA
Graduate School: Dr ROSETTA MANTE
Graduate School of Law: RONALD DUTERTE
School of Social Work: INOCENTA GO

SOUTHWESTERN UNIVERSITY

Villa Aznar, Urgello St, Cebu City 6000
Telephone: (32) 256-27-43
Fax: (32) 253-75-01
E-mail: president@swu.edu.ph
Internet: www.swu.edu.ph

Founded 1946
Private control
Languages of instruction: English, Filipino
Academic year: June to March

Pres.: Dr ALICIA P. CABATINGAN
Vice-Pres. for Academic Affairs: Dr FRANCES F. LUMAIN
Vice-Pres. for Admin.: THELMA G. GARCIA
Vice-Pres. for Finance: LASSI MATTI A. HOLOPAINEN

Registrar: FRANCISCO B. BACALLA
Librarian: VIRGINIA P. MOLLANEDA

Number of teachers: 540
Number of students: 10,768

Publications: *SWU Research Digest* (2 a year), *SWU Graduate School Journal* (1 a year)

DEANS

College of Arts and Sciences: CATALINO C. ABOS
College of Commerce: FLORDELIS R. RIVERA
College of Dentistry: Dr CORNELIA R. NOVAL
College of Engineering: CARLOS S. SATIEMBRE
College of Law: Atty JONAH S. VILLAGONZALO
College of Medical Technology: ALMA A. HOLOPAINEN
College of Medicine: Dr MARILYN T. ZARRAGA
College of Nursing: Dr CARMEN V. N. SAN LORENZO
College of Optometry: Dr ARLEN O. DORIO
College of Pharmacy: Dr ALTHEA R. ARENAJO
College of Physical Therapy: DAVID M. MATHEU
College of Veterinary Medicine: Dr JOCELYN A. TINGSON
Graduate School: Dr ALICIA P. CABATINGAN
Institute of Computer Science: Eng. AL BENJIE C. LOZADA
Institute of Physical Education and Sports: MELQUIADES B. GONZALEZ
Maritime College: Comm. CARMELO T. SIMOLDE
Teachers' College: Dr FRANCES F. LUMAIN

TARLAC STATE UNIVERSITY

Romulo Blvd, Tarlac City, Tarlac 2300

Telephone: (45) 982-0110
Fax: (45) 982-3317
E-mail: tsu@mozcom.com.ph

Founded 1906 as Tarlac Trade School; present name and status 1989
State control
Academic year: June to March

Pres.: Dr DOLORES G. MATIAS

Courses in architecture, business administration, education, engineering, fine arts, journalism, mathematics and computer science, natural sciences, nutrition, social sciences, technology, theatre.

TECHNOLOGICAL UNIVERSITY OF THE PHILIPPINES

POB 3171, Ayala Blvd, Ermita, Metro Manila

Telephone: (2) 523-22-93
Fax: (2) 523-22-93
Internet: www.tup.edu.ph

Founded 1901
State control
Languages of instruction: English, Filipino
Academic year: June to March

Pres.: Dr FEDESERIO C. CAMARAO
Vice-Pres. for Academic Affairs: Prof. JOSEFINO P. GASCON
Vice-Pres. for Admin. and Finance: Prof. RADAMES M. DOCTOR
Vice-Pres. for Planning and Devt: Prof. PERLA S. ROXAS
Vice-Pres. for Research and Extension: Dr EMILIANA V. R. TADEO
Dir, TUP Cavite: Prof. ENRICO R. HILARIO
Dir, TUP Taguig: Dr FEDERICO RAMOS
Dir, TUP Visayas: Dr LEONCIO JAMERA
Registrar: Dr MILAGROS I. CACHOLA
Library Dir: Dr WILHELMINA G. BORJAL

Library: see Libraries and Archives
Number of teachers: 573
Number of students: 18,915

Publications: *Philippine Journal of Industrial Education and Technology* (2 a year), *TUP.com* (4 a year), *TUP Graduate Journal* (1 a year)

DEANS

College of Architecture and Fine Arts: Dr DIONISIO A. ESPRESSION, Jr
College of Engineering: Prof. FLORENCIO G. BALANAY, Jr
College of Industrial Education: Dr OLYMPIO V. CAPARAS
College of Industrial Technology: Prof. BUENAVENTURA V. SABATER
College of Liberal Arts: Dr MARCELO B. APAR
College of Sciences: Dr ADORA S. PILI

PROFESSORS

AGBAYANI, J., Economics
ALTO, R., Education
APAR, M., Filipino
ARRIETA II, C., Tool and Die Technology
BALUYUT, F., Education
BELEN, V., English
BELGICA, A., Career Education
BUAQUIÑA, V., Mathematics
CACHOLA, M., Foods
CALO, R., Physical Education
CAMARO, G., Research, Life Sciences, Ecology
CAPARAS, O., Industrial Arts
DE LEON, L., Education
DELOS REYES, V., Education
DIMAYUGA, Z., Education
DOMANTAY, D., Education
GABRIEL, P., English
GALANG, E., Family and Community Education
GARINO, N., Electrical Technology, Technology Management
GATMAYTAN, R., Chemistry
GOLLAYAN, R., Chemistry
GRAZA, N., Mechanical Engineering
HILARIO, E., Education
HUANG, A., Mathematics
IGNACIO, M., Mathematics
IMLAN, J., Public Administration
JANIER, J., Mathematics
JOAQUIN, A., Drafting Technology
LABUGUEN, F., Foods
LEJANO, B., Civil Engineering
MACAM, Jr, V., Civil Engineering
MANALASTAS, J., Civil Engineering
MANALASTAS, S., Chemistry Education
MANGAO, F., Mathematics
MATIC, V., Chemistry
MENDOZA, M., Social Studies
OBNAMIA, C., English, Journalism, Education
PACIO, A., Mathematics Education
PANGAN, M., Mathematics
PANGILINAN, M., Social Studies
PEREDA, P., Education
PEREZ, J., Sociology
PILI, A., Chemistry
RIVERA, A., Education
ROLLUQUI, G., Electronic Engineering Technology, Computer Technology
SALTIVAN, L., Physics
TABANERA, M. D., Physics
TRACENA, M., English
VALDERRAMA, L., Public Administration
VELAS, F., Cultural Affairs
VERAYO, E., Education
VILLAMEJOR, S., English
ZARATAN, L., Education Research

UNIVERSITY OF THE VISAYAS

6000 Cebu City

Telephone: (32) 253-28-85
Internet: www.uv.edu

Founded 1919
Private control
Languages of instruction: English, Filipino
Academic year: June to May

Pres.: EDUARDO R. GULLAS
Exec. Vice-Pres.: JOSE R. GULLAS
Registrar: JOSEFINA T. ARREZA
Librarian: EDNA CAGA

Number of teachers: 600
Number of students: 18,214

Publications: *Spectrum* (Graduate Research Journal), *Statistical Bulletin*, *Strategies* (Education Journal), *The Visayanian*, etc

DEANS

College of Arts and Sciences: ERLINDA L. PEPITO
College of Commerce: SOLEDAD CUMBRA
College of Criminology: EMMANUEL PEPITO
College of Engineering and Architecture: MARCIALITO VALENZONA
College of Law: AMADEO SENO
College of Medicine: RENATO ESPINOSA
College of Nursing: LOURDES FERNAN
College of Pharmacy: CARMEN YAP
Graduate School: FE NECESARIO
Nautical School: GODOFREDO COSIDO
Teachers' College: AURORA A. ECONG

WEST VISAYAS STATE UNIVERSITY

Luna St, La Paz, Iloilo City, Iloilo 5000

Telephone: (33) 320-0870
Fax: (33) 320-0879
Internet: www.wvsu.edu.ph

Founded 1924 as Iloilo Normal School; present name and status 1986
State control
Academic year: June to March

Pres.: Dr LOURDES C. ARAÑADOR

Colleges of arts and sciences, education, mass communications, medicine and nursing; Institute of information and communications technology.

WESTERN MINDANAO STATE UNIVERSITY

Normal Rd, Baliwasan, 7000 Zamboanga City

Telephone: 991-1040
Fax: 991-3065
Internet: www.wmsu.edu.ph

Founded 1918
State control
Languages of instruction: English, Filipino
Academic year: June to March (two semesters)

Pres.: Dr ELDIGARIO D. GONZALES
Vice-Pres. for Academic Affairs: Dr MARLENE C. TILLAH
Vice-Pres. for Admin. and Finance: Dr CLEMENCIO M. BASCAR
Vice-Pres. for Research Extension and Training: (vacant)
Registrar: JULIETA A. DEL ROSARIO
Librarian: SALUD C. LAQUIO

Library of 50,000 vols
Number of teachers: 436
Number of students: 12,397

Publication: *Bulletin*

DEANS

Admissions: Prof. RUTH N. JUNIO
College of Agriculture: ERIBERTO D. SALANG
College of Arts and Sciences: Dr RAIMUNDA J. BANICO
College of Criminology: Prof. EFFRENDY ESTIPONA
College of Education: Prof. FELICITAS F. FALCATAN
College of Engineering and Technology: Eng. MOHAMMAD NUR MOHAMMAD
College of Forestry: Prof. DINO A. SABELLINA
College of Home Economics: Prof. NOEMI S. ENRIQUEZ
College of Law: Atty EDUARDO F. SANSON
College of Nursing: Prof. TERESITA C. MARBELLA

College of Science and Mathematics: Dr ELBIA P. AQUINO
College of Social Work: Prof. BAGIAN ABDULKARIM
Extension Services: Dr ABDULAJID A. IBBA
Graduate School: Prof. OFELIO R. MENDOZA
Institute of Asian and Islamic Studies: Prof. NURUDDIN I. UNGGANG
Institute of Physical Education, Sports and Cultural Affairs: Prof. ALICIA LOURDES SORIANO
Research Center: Dr ALFREDO DUCANES
Student Affairs: Eng. ARMANDO ARQUIZA

XAVIER UNIVERSITY

Ateneo de Cagayan, Corrales Ave, 9000 Cagayan de Oro City
Telephone: (8822) 72-27-25
Fax: (8822) 72-63-55
E-mail: pres@xu.edu.ph
Internet: www.xu.edu.ph

Founded 1933
Private control
Language of instruction: English
Academic year: June to March (two terms)

Pres.: Fr JOSE RAMON T. VILLARIN
Registrar: AURORA M. GAPUZ
Librarian: ANNABELLE P. ACEDERA

Number of teachers: 407
Number of students: 9,897

Publications: *Kinaadman (Wisdom)* (1 a year), *XU Graduate School Journal* (2 a year)

DEANS

Faculty of Agriculture: GUADALUPE M. CALALANG
Faculty of Arts and Sciences: Fr ANTONIO F. MORENO
Faculty of Commerce: Dr ALFONSO B. HORTELANO
Faculty of Education: Dr AMOR Q. DE TORRES
Faculty of Engineering: ANTONIO C. SEVILLANO, Jr
Faculty of Law: RAUL R. VILLANUEVA
Faculty of Medicine: Dr CANDIDA D. CANCEKO
Faculty of Nursing: Dr RAMONA HEIDI C. PALAD
Graduate School: Dr ESTER L. RAAGAS

DIRECTORS

Appropriate Technology for Small Farmers: RACHEL POLESTICO
Centre for Industrial Technology: ANTONIO C. SEVILLANO, Jr
Institute for the Development of Educational Administrators: Dr ALFONSO B. HORTELANO
Legal Aid and Research Centre for Human Rights: NEIL Y. PACAMALAN
Mindanao Lumad and Muslim Development Centre: Rev. EMETERIO J. BARCELON
Philippine Folklife and Folklore Research and Archives: LUIS OSTIQUE
Research Institute for Mindanao Culture: Dr ISIAS S. SEALZA
Southeast Asia Rural Social Leadership Institute: Dr ANSELMO B. MERCADO
Sustainable Agriculture Centre: VICTORIANO I. TAGUPA

Colleges

GENERAL

San Beda College: Mendiola St, Manila; tel. 735-60-11; fax 735-59-94; e-mail sbc@dns.sbc.edu.ph; f. 1901; private control; constituent grade and high schools and colleges of law, arts and sciences; library: 120,464 vols; 276 teachers; 6,006 students; Rector Rev. BERNARDO M. PEREZ; Librarian MARLO CHAVEZ.

St Paul College of Manila: 680 Pedro Gil St, Malate, Manila, POB 3062; tel. (2) 524-56-87; fax (2) 525-66-20; e-mail spcm@spcm.edu.ph; internet www.spcm.edu.ph; f. 1912; private control; first degree courses in computer science, hotel and restaurant management, psychology, education, commerce, secretarial administration, nursing, communication arts, music; library: 47,898 vols; 148 teachers; 2,800 students; Pres. Sis. NATIVIDAD DE JESUS FERAREN.

St Scholastica's College: 2560 Leon Guinto St, Malate, Metro Manila 1004, POB 3153; tel. (2) 524-7686; fax (2) 521-2593; e-mail maryjohn@ssc.edu.ph; internet www.ssc.edu.ph; f. 1906; private control (sectarian); schools of accountancy, arts and sciences, commerce, music, music education; 516 teachers; 6,601 students; Pres. Sis. MARY JOHN MANANZAN.

State Polytechnic College of Palawan: Aborlan, 5302 Palawan; tel. 433-4480; f. 1910; courses in agriculture, forestry, fisheries, environmental management, engineering and technology, education, arts, science, rural development; library: 22,500 vols; Pres. Dr CONCEPTO B. MAGAY; publs *SPCP-IMS Research Journal* (2 a year), *SPCP Research Journal* (irregular), *SPCP Newsletter* (12 a year).

ECONOMICS

Asian Institute of Management: Eugenio Lopez Foundation Bldg, Joseph R. McMicking Campus, 123 Paseo de Roxas, Makati City, 1260; tel. (632) 8924011; fax (632) 8179240; e-mail admissions@aim.edu.ph; internet www.aim.edu.ph; f. 1968 by Ateneo de Manila Univ., De La Salle University, the Harvard Business School and the Ford Foundation; academic units and degree programmes: Washington SyCip Graduate School of Business (MBA, Master in Management), Centre for Development Management (Master in Development Management), Asian Centre for Entrepreneurship (Master in Entrepreneurship), Executive Education and Life Long Learning Centre (Executive MBA, Certificate Programmes); library: more than 25,000 books and periodicals, more than 30,000 learning material items; 61 teachers; Pres. ROBERTO F. DE OCAMPO; Dean VICTORIA S. LICUANAN.

MEDICINE

Bicol Christian College of Medicine: AMEC-BCCM Postal Station, Rizal St, Legazpi City 4901; tel. (5221) 44433; fax (5221) 455058; f. 1980; 4-year undergraduate courses; library: 30,052 vols; Pres. EMMANUEL F. AGO; Dean, College of Medicine Dr ANGELITA F. AGO.

Cebu Doctors' University College of Medicine: CDU Administrative Offices Bldg, Gov. M. Roa St, Cebu City 6000; tel. and fax (32) 253-4919; e-mail cdu-cm@cebudoctorsuniversity.edu; internet www.cebudoctorsuniversity.edu/medicine; f. 1977; library: 11,800 vols; 160 staff; 360 students; Pres. POTENCIANO V. LARRAZABAL; Sec. POTENCIANO S. D. LARRAZABAL, III; Treas. PHILIP ANTHONY S. D. LARRAZABAL; Dean ENRICO B. GRUET; publ. *Proceedings* (2 a year).

TECHNOLOGY

Leyte Institute of Technology: Salazar St, Tacloban City; f. 1965; courses in engineering, science, industrial technology, education and vocational training; postgraduate courses; 309 staff; library: 17,000 vols; Pres. GREGORIO T. DE LA ROSA; Registrar FRANKLIN A. COLASITO; publs *College Journal*, *Graduate School Bulletin*, *Industrial Wheel*.

Lyceum of the Philippines: Real and Muralla Sts, Intramuros, POB 1264, Manila; tel. (2) 527-55-48; fax (2) 527-17-61; internet www.lyceumphil.edu.ph; f. 1952; private control; Faculties of law, graduate studies, mechanical engineering, mass communication, journalism, arts and sciences, foreign service, economics, business administration, office management, technical vocational, hotel and restaurant management, secretarial science, computer engineering, electronics and communication engineering, political science, legal studies, Filipino, literature, history, humanities, mathematics, psychology, biology, tourism, accountancy, legal secretarial administration, computer science, secondary education, banking and finance, management, marketing, computer data management and processing, tax and customs administration, cruise line management, nursing and medical transcription; library: 45,000 vols; 300 teachers; 10,000 students; Pres. ROBERTO P. LAUREL.

Mapùa Institute of Technology: Muralla St, Intramuros, Manila; tel. (832) 527-7916; fax (832) 527-5161; f. 1925; private control; Faculties of architecture and planning, industrial design, industrial engineering, mining and metallurgical engineering, civil engineering, electrical engineering, electronics and communications engineering, mechanical engineering, geology, environmental and sanitary engineering, chemical engineering and chemistry, computer engineering; 13,000 students; Pres. OSCAR B. MAPÙA, Sr.

Namei Polytechnic Institute: 123 A Mabini St, Mandaluyong, Metro Manila; tel. 531-73-28; fax 815-63-37; f. 1947; private control; courses in naval architecture and marine engineering, B. S. marine transportation, marine engineering, mechanical engineering, electrical engineering; Pres. MARIA VICTORIA P. ESTRELLA; Registrar PERLA G. CRUZ.

Naval Institute of Technology: Naval, Biliran 6543; f. 1972; library: 10,000 vols; 83 teachers; 2,500 students; Pres. Dr JUANITO S. SISON.

Palompon Institute of Technology: Palompon, Leyte; tel. (53) 5559841; fax (53) 3382501; e-mail pit@glinesnx.com.ph; internet foo.ncc.gov.ph/ecommunity/pit; f. 1972; courses in marine transportation and engineering; engineering technology; technical and vocational education; customs administration; radio communication; domestic science; industrial technology, shipping management, teacher education, information technology, industrial engineering, Doctor and Master programmes; library: 10,434 vols; 114 teachers; 2,776 students; Pres. Dr JUANITO S. SISON.

POLAND

The Higher Education System

Higher education in Poland dates from the 14th century, with the establishment of Uniwersytet Jagielloński (Jagiellonian University—founded in 1364), the country's oldest university. Several institutions of higher education were founded in the 18th and 19th centuries, including Uniwersytet Wrocławski (the University of Wrocław—founded in 1702), Akademia Muzycna im. Fryderyka Chopina w Warszawie (the Frederick Chopin Academy of Music in Warsaw—founded in 1810) and Uniwersytet Warszawki (the University of Warsaw—founded in 1816). Many institutions of higher education were founded during the period of Communist rule (1948–89) and by 2003/04 there were 400 higher education establishments in Poland, including 17 universities and 22 technical universities, which by 2006/07 had a total of 2,146,900 students.

The Ministry of National Education is the state authority responsible for higher education; most institutions of higher education are funded from the state budget. Higher education is administered according to the Higher Education Act (1990) and Act of Academic Title and Degrees (1990). Higher education is provided by universities (uniwersytet), technical universities (politechnika) and non-university level institutions (wyzsze szkoly zawodowe). Poland participates in the Bologna Process to establish a European Higher Education Area, the first phase of which is to adopt a credit-based system of comparable degrees with two main cycles (undergraduate and graduate).

The main criterion for admission to higher education is the secondary school 'maturity' certificate (swiadectwo dojrzalosci) and some institutions may set entrance examinations. Poland has implemented a two-tier Bachelors and Masters degree system, in accordance with the principles of the Bologna Process, but some old-style degree programmes are still offered, mostly by institutions of professional education. The primary examples of these types of degree are the Licencjat and Inzynier, which are awarded after three- to four-year courses of higher professional education. The undergraduate Bachelors degree is a three- or four-year course of study equivalent to the initial stages of the old-style Masters (Magistr). The new Masters is now a separate postgraduate degree lasting one to two years; however, students in mainly professional fields of study continue to work towards integrated Masters programmes. Admission to the highest level of university degree, the Doctorate (Doktor), requires the Masters. The Doctorate is awarded following the submission and defence of a thesis and success in doctoral examinations.

Technical and vocational education at the post-secondary level is offered by Post-Secondary Schools (Szkoly policealne or Szkoly pomaturalne) and Schools of Higher Professional Education (Wyzsze Szkoly Zawodowe); the latter were established following the Act on Schools of Higher Vocational Education (1997).

The Act of 1997 established the Accreditation Commission for Higher Vocational Education, and the State Accreditation Committee (created on the basis of the amended Higher Education Act of 1990) has been in operation since 2002.

Regulatory and Representative Bodies

GOVERNMENT

Ministry of Culture and National Heritage: ul. Krakowskie Przedmieście 15/17, 00-071 Warsaw; tel. (22) 4210100; fax (22) 8260726; e-mail rzecznik@mkidn.gov.pl; internet www.mkidn.gov.pl; Minister BOGDAN ZDROJEWSKI; Gen. Dir GRAŻYNA OŻAREK.

Ministry of National Education: Al. Szucha 25, 00-918 Warsaw; tel. (22) 3474100; fax (22) 5224100; e-mail informacja@men.gov.pl; internet www.men.gov.pl; Minister KATARZYNA HALL; Gen. Dir ROBERT BARTOLD.

Ministry of Science and Higher Education: ul. Wspólna 1/3, 00-529 Warsaw; tel. (22) 5292718; fax (22) 6280922; e-mail sekretariat.bm@nauka.gov.pl; internet www.nauka.gov.pl; Min. Prof. BARBARA KUDRYCKA; Gen. Dir MAREK KUCIŃSKI.

ACCREDITATION

Centralna Komisja do Spraw Stopni i Tytułów (Central Commission for Degrees and Titles): pl. Defilad 1 (PKiN), 00-091 Warsaw; tel. (22) 826-82-38; fax (22) 620-33-24; e-mail kancelaria@ck.gov.pl; internet www.ck.gov.pl; defines fields and disciplines within sciences and the arts in which academic and professional titles and degrees are awarded; grants relevant instns the right to award such titles and degrees; ratifies awards of Dr hab. degrees; Pres. Prof. Dr hab. TADEUSZ KACZOREK; Sec. Prof. OSMAN ACHMATOWICZ.

ENIC/NARIC Poland: Dept of Int. Programmes and Recognition of Dipls, Min. of Science and Higher Education, ul. Wspólna 1/3 00-529 Warsaw; tel. (22) 628-67-76; fax (22) 628-35-34; e-mail hanna.reczulska@mnisw.gov.pl; internet www.enic-naric.net/index.aspx?c=poland; Head HANNA RECZULSKA.

Państwowa Komisja Akredytacyjna (State Accreditation Committee): ul. Żurawia 32/34, 00-515 Warsaw; tel. (22) 622-07-18; fax (22) 621-15-84; internet www.pka.edu.pl; f. 2001; supports Polish public and non-public higher education instns in the devt of educational standards matching the best models adopted in Europe and the world; conducts obligatory assessments of the quality of education and gives opinions on applications submitted by higher education instns to provide degree programmes; Pres. Dr Hab. ZBIGNIEW MARCINIAK; Sec. Dr Hab. MIECZYSŁAW WACŁAW SOCHA.

Uniwersytecka Komisja Akredytacyjna (University Accreditation Commission): Uniwersytet im. A. Mickiewicza, ul. Wieniawskiego 1, 61-712 Poznań; tel. (61) 829-25-02; fax (61) 829-24-92; e-mail pkaz@amu.edu.pl; internet www.uka.amu.edu.pl; f. 1998; matches the quality of univ. education in Poland with that in the EU; promotes high quality courses of study and the univs offering them; harmonizes the standards of educational quality at univs; 21 mems; Chair. Prof. Dr hab. MAREK WĄSOWICZ; Sec. Prof. Dr hab. ZBIGNIEW PALKA.

FUNDING

Komitet Badań Naukowych (State Committee for Scientific Research): ul. Wspólna 1/3, 00-529 Warsaw; tel. (22) 529-27-18; fax (22) 628-09-22; e-mail dip@kbn.gov.pl; internet kbn.icm.edu.pl; f. 1991; draws up guidelines on scientific policy, submits plans for budgetary expenditure in the area of science and technology, distributes funds among instns and research teams and controls spending, and signs int. agreements on co-operation in science and technology; Chair. MICHAŁ KLEIBER; Gen. Dir KRYSTYN WEREMOWICZ.

NATIONAL BODIES

Konferencja Rektorów Akademickich Szkół Polskich (Conference of Rectors of Academic Schools in Poland): ul. Wybrzeze Wyspianskiego 27, 50-370 Wrocław; tel. (71) 320-29-60; fax (71) 320-32-22; e-mail krasp@pwr.wroc.pl; internet www.krasp.org.pl; f. 1997; voluntary asscn of rectors representing those instns of higher education awarding doctorates (or equivalent) in at least one scientific discipline; 105 mems, 3 assoc. instns; Pres. Prof. TADEUSZ LUTY; Sec. Gen. Prof. ANDRZEJ KRASNIEWSKI.

Rada Główna Szkolnictwa Wyższego (Central Council for Higher Education): ul. Wspólna 1/3, 00-529 Warsaw; tel. (22) 529-25-64; fax (22) 529-27-68; e-mail radaglowna@mnisw.gov.pl; internet www.rgsw.edu.pl; formulates opinions on how higher education should be developed and on all proposed legislation concerning higher education; Pres. Prof. Dr hab. JERZY BŁAŻEJOWSKI.

Learned Societies

GENERAL

Bydgoskie Towarzystwo Naukowe (Bydgoszcz Scientific Society): ul. Jezuicka 4, 85-102 Bydgoszcz; tel. and fax (52) 322-22-68; e-mail btn@um.bydgoszcz.pl; f. 1959; 553 mems; library of 17,500 vols; Pres. Prof. Dr hab. HENRYK Z. WREMBEL; Sec.-Gen. Dr GRZEGORZ DOMINIAK; publs *Ekologia i Technika* (6 a year), *Prace Wydziału Nauk Humanistycznych* (1 a year), *Prace Wydziału Nauk Przyrodniczych* (1 a year), *Prace Wydziału Nauk Technicznych* (1 a year), *Przegląd Bydgoski* (1 a year), *Bydgostiana Kolokwium Wiedzy o Ziemi* (irregular).

Gdańskie Towarzystwo Naukowe (Gdańsk Scientific Society): ul. Grodzka 12, 80-841 Gdańsk; tel. (58) 301-21-24; fax (58) 305-81-31; e-mail gtn@3net.pl; f. 1922 as Gdańsk Society of Friends of Science and Art; sections of social sciences and humanities, biological and medical sciences, mathematical, physical and chemical sciences, technical sciences, earth sciences; 572 mems; Pres. Prof. JAN DRWAL; Sec. Prof. JERZY BŁAŻEJOWSKI; publ. *Acta Biologica et Medica*.

Kieleckie Towarzystwo Naukowe (Kielce Scientific Society): ul. Zamkowa 5, 25-009 Kielce; tel. (41) 344-54-53; fax (41) 344-54-53; e-mail ktn@pu.kielce.pl; internet www.pu.kielce.pl/ktn; f. 1958; regional scientific research in history, philology, medicine, geology, geography and nature conservation, psychology, sociology and education, physics, mathematics, engineering; 464 mems; library of 4,620 vols; Pres. Prof. Dr hab. ADAM MASSALSKI; Sec. Prof. Dr hab. MAREK JÓŹWIAK; publs *Rocznik Świętokrzyski* (Yearbook), *Studia Kieleckie* (irregular).

Łomżyńskie Towarzystwo Naukowe im. Wagów (The Brothers Waga Łomża Scientific Society): ul. Długa 13, 18-400 Łomża; tel. and fax (86) 216-32-56; e-mail zegalska@poczta.onet.pl; internet www.ltn.lomza.pl; f. 1975; agriculture, economics, environmental protection, ethnology, geography, history, linguistics, natural history, veterinary science, settlement of NE Poland, sociology; 250 mems; library of 20,000 vols; Pres. Prof. Dr hab. HALINA KARAŚ; Dir Mgr inż ELŻBIETA ŻEGALSKA; publs *Pogranicze w Jezyku i Kulturze* (1 a year), *Polszczyzna Mazowsza i Podlasia* (1 a year), *Studia Łomżyńskie* (1 a year).

Lubelskie Towarzystwo Naukowe (Lublin Scientific Society): Pl. Litewski 2, 20-080 Lublin; tel. and fax (81) 532-13-00; e-mail biuro@ltn.lublin.pl; f. 1957; 722 mems; five sections: humanities, biology, mathematics-physics-chemistry, technical science, mining and geography; Pres. Prof. Dr hab. EDMUND K. PROST; Sec.-Gen. Prof. Dr JAN MALARCZYK.

Polska Akademia Nauk (PAN) (Polish Academy of Sciences): Pałac Kultury i Nauki, Plac Defilad 1, POB 24, 00-901 Warsaw; tel. (22) 620-49-70; fax (22) 620-49-10; e-mail barbara.szoltyk@pan.pl; internet www.pan.pl; f. 1952; divisions of agricultural, forestry and veterinary sciences (Chair. Prof. ANDRZEJ GRZYWACZ), biological sciences (Chair. Prof. ANDRZEJ B. LEGOCKI), earth and mining sciences (Chair. Prof. BOGDAN NEY), mathematical, physical and chemical sciences (Chair. Prof. JANUSZ JURCZAK), medical sciences (Chair. Prof. WOJCIECH KOSTOWSKI), social sciences (Chair. Prof. STANISŁAW MOSSAKOWSKI) and technical science (Chair. Prof. WŁADYSŁAW WŁOSIŃSKI); attached research institutes: see Research Institutes; collection: science and technology, future studies, praxiology, library and information science, bibliography; 523 mems (178 ordinary, 147 corresp., 198 foreign); library of 413,697 vols; Pres. Prof. MICHA I. KLEIBER; Vice-Pres Prof. ANDRZEJ GÓRSKI, Prof. KAROL MODZELEWSKI, Prof. WOJCIECH J. STEC; publs *Academia. The Magazine of the Polish Academy of Sciences* (English and Polish versions, each 4 a year), *Acta Arithmetica* (4 a year), *Acta Biochimica Polonica* (4 a year), *Acta Geologica Polonica* (4 a year), *Acta Neurobiologicale Experimentalis* (4 a year), *Acta Physica Polonica* (4 a year), *Acta Poloniae Historica* (2 a year), *Acta Protozoologica* (4 a year), *Acta Physiologiae Plantarum* (4 a year), *Archeologia* (1 a year), *Archives of Metallurgy and Materials* (4 a year), *Archivum Immunologiae et Therapiae Experimentalis* (6 a year), *Bulletin of the Polish Academy of Sciences*: Series: *Technical Sciences* (4 a year), *Chemia Analityczna* (4 a year), *Chemical and Process Engineering* (4 a year), *Ethnologia Polonia* (1 a year), *Etudes et Travaux* (1 a year), *Folia Neuropathologica* (4 a year), *Fundamenta Mathematicae* (4 a year), *Journal of Animal and Feed Sciences* (4 a year), *Nauka* (4 a year), *Oceanologia* (4 a year), *Onomastica* (1 a year), *Pamiętnik Literacki* (4 a year), *Polish Journal of Food and Nutrition Sciences* (4 a year), *Polish Journal of Pharmacology* (6 a year), *Polish Journal of Veterinary Sciences* (4 a year), *Studia Logica* (4 a year), *Studia Mathematica* (4 a year).

Poznańskie Towarzystwo Przyjaciół Nauk (Poznań Society of Friends of Arts and Sciences): ul. Sew. Mielżyńskiego 27/29, 61-725 Poznań; tel. (61) 852-74-41; fax (61) 852-22-05; e-mail sekretariat@ptpn.poznan.pl; internet www.ptpn.poznan.pl; f. 1857; 1,070 mems; library of 197,176 books, 5,024 periodical titles, 1,432 MSS, 15,157 old books incl. incunabula, 1,839 maps and atlases, 711 microfilms; Pres. Prof. Dr hab. JACEK WIESIOŁOWSKI; Sec.-Gen. Dr LECH TORLIŃSKI; publs *Badania Fizjograficzne nad Polską Zachodnią* (Series A (Geography) Series B (Botany) Series C (Zoology)), *Bulletin de la Société des Amis des Sciences et des Lettres de Poznań—Série D: Sciences Biologiques*, *Lingua Posnaniensis*, *Roczniki Dziejów Społecznych i Gospodarczych*, *Slavia Antiqua*, *Slavia Occidentalis*, *Sprawozdania Poznańskiego Towarzystwa Przyjaciół Nauk*.

Towarzystwo Naukowe Płockie (Płock Scientific Society): plac Narutowicza 8, 09-402 Płock; tel. (24) 366-99-50; fax (24) 262-26-04; e-mail aktnp@interia.pl; internet www.tnp.org.pl; f. 1820; 416 mems; library of 328,149 vols; Pres. Dr hab. inż. ZBIGNIEW KRUSZEWSKI; Sec.-Gen. Dr WIESŁAW KOŃSKI; publs *Notatki Płockie* (4 a year), *Sprawozdanie z działalności* (Yearbook).

Towarzystwo Naukowe w Toruniu (Scientific Society of Toruń): ul. Wysoka 16, 87-100 Toruń; tel. (56) 622-39-41; fax (56) 622-39-41; e-mail tnt.biuro@wp.pl; internet www.tnt.torun.pl; f. 1875; concerned with historical, legal and social studies, philology, philosophy and natural sciences; 490 mems; library of 112,340 vols; Pres. Prof. MARIAN BISKUP; Gen. Sec. Prof. MARIAN KALLAS; publs include *Roczniki*, *Fontes* (irregular), *Prace Archaeologiczne* (irregular), *Prace Popularnonaukowe* (irregular), *Prace Wydziału Filologiczno-Filozoficznego* (irregular), *Sprawozdania* (1 a year), *Studia Iuridica* (irregular), *Studia Societatis Scientiarum Toruniensis* (various series: geography and geology, botany, zoology, astronomy, physiology, medicine, all irregular), *Zapiski Historyczne* (4 a year, concerned chiefly with Pomeranian problems).

Towarzystwo Naukowe Warszawskie (Warsaw Scientific Society): ul. Nowy Świat 72, 00-330 Warsaw; tel. (22) 657-27-18; fax (22) 657-28-26; e-mail sekretariat@tnw.waw.pl; internet www.tnw.waw.pl; f. 1907; 430 mems; Pres. Prof. JANUSZ LIPKOWSKI; Sec.-Gen. Prof. EWA WOLNICZ-PAWŁOWSKA; publ. *Rocznik TNW* (1 a year).

Towarzystwo Przyjaciół Nauk w Przemyślu (Society of Science and Letters of Przemyśl): ul. Kościuszki 7, 37-700 Przemyśl; tel. (16) 678-56-01; e-mail tpntpn@wp.pl; internet www.tpn.vt.pl; f. 1909; 266 mems; library of 60,000 vols; Pres. Prof. Dr hab. ZDZISŁAW BUDZYŃSKI; Sec.-Gen. Dr MACIEJ DALECKI; publs *Acta Medica Premisliensia*, *Biblioteka Przemyska*, *Polska południowo-wschodnia w epoce nowożytnej Źródła dziejowe*, *Rocznik Przemyski*.

Towarzystwo Wiedzy Powszechnej (Universal Education Society): Pałac Kultury i Nauki, Plac Defilad 1, VI flor, Room 602, 00-901 Warsaw; tel. (22) 826-56-30; fax 620-33-06; e-mail twp@twp.pl; internet www.twp.pl; f. 1950; general adult education; runs private schools providing vocational, secondary and post-secondary education; founded five schools of higher education of which two award Masters qualifications; organizes discussions, lectures, seminars, confs, popular science and training sessions; 6,000 mems; library of 2,000 vols; Pres. EDWARD BALAWEJDER; Gen. Dir ZENON GAWORCZUK; publ. *Edukacja Dorosłych* (12 a year).

Towarzystwo Wolnej Wszechnicy Polskiej (Society of the Polish Free University): ul. Górnośląska 20, 00-484 Warsaw; tel. (22) 621-73-55; fax (22) 625-38-34; e-mail mlipowski@mercury.ci.uw.cdu.pl; f. 1882; permanent education, research and application services, specialized interests clubs; 1,000 mems; library of 10,000 vols; Pres. Dr inż. MIKOŁAJ Ł. LIPOWSKI; Sec.-Gen. (vacant); publs *Człowiek w Społeczeństwie* (irregular), *Kalendarz Samorządowy* (1 a year), *Zeszyty Naukowe* (irregular).

Wrocławskie Towarzystwo Naukowe (Wrocław Scientific Society): ul. Parkowa 13, 51-616 Wrocław; tel. (71) 348-40-61; e-mail wtn@wtn.wroc.pl; internet zts.ita.pwr.wroc.pl/wtn; f. 1946 to study social and exact sciences; 482 mems; Pres. Prof. MARIAN PIEKARSKI; Sec. Prof. JAN ZARZYCKI; publs include *Prace Wrocławskiego Towarzystwa Naukowego* (Series A: Humanistic Sciences, Series B: Exact Sciences), *Annales Silesiae*, *Litteraria*, *Rozprawy Komisji Historii Sztuki*, *Rozprawy Komisji Językowej*, *Śląskie Prace Bibliologiczne i Bibliotekoznawcze*, *Sprawozdania* (series A and B).

AGRICULTURE, FISHERIES AND VETERINARY SCIENCE

Polskie Towarzystwo Gleboznawcze (Polish Society of Soil Science): ul. Wiśniowa 61, 02-520 Warsaw; tel. (22) 849-48-16; f. 1937; 750 mems; Pres. Prof. Dr hab. PIOTR SKŁODOWSKI; Sec. Prof. Dr hab. JÓZEF CHOJNICKI; publ. *Roczniki Gleboznawcze* (4 a year).

Polskie Towarzystwo Leśne (Polish Forest Society): ul. Bitwy Warszawskiej 1920r. 3, 02-362 Warsaw; tel. (22) 822-14-70; e-mail sylwan@ibles.waw.pl; f. 1882; 4,451 mems; library of 2,005 vols; Pres. Prof. Dr ANDRZEJ GRZYWACZ; Sec. Dr JAN ŁUKASZEWICZ; publ. *Sylwan* (12 a year).

Polskie Towarzystwo Nauk Weterynaryjnych (Polish Society of Veterinary Sciences): Zarząd Główny PTNW, ul. Nowoursynowska 159c, 03-776 Warsaw; tel. (22) 59-31-606; fax (22) 59-31-606; e-mail ptnw@sggw.pl; internet www.ptnw.pl; f. 1952; lectures and seminars in 12 divs throughout Poland; congress every 4 years; 1,360 mems; library of 2,500 vols; Pres. Prof. Dr ZYQMUNT PEJSAK; Sec. Dr JWONA MAR-

KOWSKA-DANIEL; publ. *Medycyna Weterynaryjna* (12 a year).

Polskie Towarzystwo Zootechniczne (Polish Society of Animal Production): Kaliska 9, 02-316 Warsaw; tel. (22) 822-17-23; e-mail ptz_redakcja@alpha.sggw.waw.pl; f. 1922; 1,200 mems; library of 2,630 vols; Pres. Prof. ZYGMUNT REKLEWSKI; Dir Inż. ANNA ZABŁOCKA-IDCZAK; publs *Animal Production Review* (12 a year), *Animal Production Review Applied Science Reports* (1 a year).

ARCHITECTURE AND TOWN PLANNING

Stowarzyszenie Architektów Polskich (Association of Polish Architects): ul. Foksal 2, 00-950 Warsaw; tel. (22) 827-87-12; fax (22) 827-87-13; e-mail sarp@sarp.org.pl; internet sarp.org.pl; f. 1934; 5,100 mems; Sec.-Gen. DARIUSZ MIECHOWSKI; publ. *Komunikat SARP* (12 a year).

Towarzystwo Urbanistów Polskich (Society of Polish Town Planners): ul. Lwowska 5, lokal 100, 00-660 Warsaw; tel. (22) 875-97-56; fax (22) 875-97-56; e-mail zg@tup.org.pl; internet www.tup.org.pl; f. 1923; conducts and supports activity serving spatial management of Poland; realizes principles of sustainable devt and ensures spatial order; advertises new research and design methods; 1,300 mems; Pres. Prof. Dr hab. TADEUSZ MARKOWSKI; Sec.-Gen. Dr Ing. TOMASZ MAJDA; publ. *Przeglad Urbanistyczny* (4 a year).

BIBLIOGRAPHY, LIBRARY SCIENCE AND MUSEOLOGY

Stowarzyszenie Archiwistów Polskich (Polish Archivists Association): ul. Bonifraterska 6 lok. 21, 00-213 Warsaw; tel. (22) 831-83-63; fax (22) 831-31-71; e-mail sap@sap.waw.pl; internet www.sap.waw.pl; Pres. Dr WŁADYSŁAW STĘPNIAK; Sec.-Gen. (vacant); publ. *Archiwista* (4 a year).

Stowarzyszenie Bibliotekarzy Polskich (Polish Librarians Association): National Library, al. Niepodleglosci 213, 02-086 Warsaw; tel. (22) 608-24-51; fax (22) 825-91-57; e-mail biurozgsbp@wp.pl; internet ebib.oss.wroc.pl/sbp/english/index_en.html; f. 1917; 8,300 mems in 16 regional divs; Pres. JAN WOŁOSZ; Sec.-Gen. ELŻBIETA STEFAŃCZYK; publs *Bibliotekarz* (12 a year), *Poradnik Bibliotekarza* (12 a year), *Przegląd Biblioteczny* (4 a year), *Zagadnienia Informacji Naukowej* (4 a year).

ECONOMICS, LAW AND POLITICS

Polskie Towarzystwo Demograficzne (Polish Demographic Society): al. Niepodległości 164, room 3, 02-554 Warsaw; tel. 48-22-3379273; e-mail ewaf@sgh.waw.pl; f. 1982; 250 mems; Pres. ZBIGNIEW STRZELECKI; Sec. LUCYNA NOWAK; publ. *Polish Population Review* (2 a year).

Polskie Towarzystwo Ekonomiczne (Polish Economic Society): Nowy Świat 49, 00-042 Warsaw; tel. (22) 827-99-04; fax (22) 827-99-04; e-mail zk@pte.pl; internet www.pte.pl; f. 1945; 6,220 mems; Pres. Prof. Dr hab. ZDZISŁAW SADOWSKI; Gen.-Sec. Prof. Dr hab. URSZULA PŁOWIEC; publ. *Ekonomista* (6 a year).

Polskie Towarzystwo Towaroznawcze (Polish Society for Commodity Science): ul. Sienkiewicza 4, 30-033 Cracow; tel. (12) 633-08-21; e-mail adamczyw@ae.krakow.pl; internet www.ae.krakow.pl; f. 1963; 500 mems; Pres. Prof. WACŁAW ADAMCZYK; Sec. Dr STANISŁAW POPEK; publ. *Towaroznawstwo—Problemy Jakości* (1 a year).

EDUCATION

Polskie Towarzystwo Pedagogiczne (Polish Pedagogics Society): ul. Smulikowskiego 6/8, 00-389 Warsaw; tel. (22) 826-10-11, ext. 249; internet pedagog.umcs.lublin.pl/~ptp-ol; f. 1981; 800 mems; Chair. Prof. Dr hab. ZBIGNIEW KWIECIŃSKI; Sec.-Gen. Prof. Dr hab. MARIAN WALCZAK; publs *Forum Oświatowe* (Educational Forum, 2 a year), *Przegląd Historyczno-Oświatowy* (Historical-Educational Review, 4 a year).

FINE AND PERFORMING ARTS

Polskie Stowarzyszenie Filmu Naukowego (Polish Association of Scientific Film): ul. Mokotowska 58 pok. 1, 00-534 Warsaw; tel. (22) 629-08-32; internet galaxy.uci.agh.edu.pl/~kpfn; Pres. GRZEGORZ KOWALEWSKI; Sec.-Gen. STANISŁAW ŚLEDŹ; publ. *Film Naukowy* (2 a year).

Stowarzyszenie Historyków Sztuki (Art Historians Association): Rynek Starego Miasta 27, 00-272 Warsaw; tel. (22) 635-96-99; fax (22) 635-90-74; e-mail shs@shs.pl.pl; internet www.shs.pl; f. 1934; search and publication, popularization of art history; 1,406 mems; library of 28,492 vols; Pres. Prof. Dr hab. MARIA POPRZĘCKA; Sec.-Gen. Dr KATARZYNA NOWAKOWSKA-SITO; publs *Materiały Sesii SHS*, *Materiały do Dziejów Rezydencji w Polsce*, *Materiały Seminariów Metodologicznych*, *Materiały Sesji Oddziałowych*.

Towarzystwo im. Fryderyka Chopina (Fryderyk Chopin Society): Pl. Pilsudskiego 9, 00-078 Warsaw; tel. (22) 826-65-49; tel. (22) 826-65-49; e-mail info@chopin.pl; internet www.tifc.chopin.pl; f. 1934; 600 mems; permanent Secretariat of the Int. Chopin Record Competitions 'Grand Prix du Disque-Frédéric Chopin'; central Chopin museum, library, phototheque and phonotheque for study of Chopin's life and preparation of complete edition of his works; organization of concerts; Gen. Dir ANTONI GRUDZIŃSKI; publs *Annales Chopin*, *Chopin Studies*.

Warszawskie Towarzystwo Muzyczne (Music Society in Warsaw): ul. Morskie Oko 2, 02-511 Warsaw; tel. (22) 849-68-56; e-mail wtm@wtm.org.pl; internet www.wtm.org.pl; f. 1871; 300 mems; Pres. ANNA MALEWICZ-MADEY; Sec. ZOFIA KOSTROWSKA-STAŃCZYKOWSKA.

HISTORY, GEOGRAPHY AND ARCHAEOLOGY

Polskie Towarzystwo Geograficzne (Polish Geographical Society): Krakowskie Przedmieście 30, 00-927 Warsaw; tel. (22) 826-17-94; fax (22) 826-17-94; e-mail ptg@uw.edu.pl; internet www.ptg.pan.pl/mainen.htm; f. 1918; 1,500 mems; library of 17,000 vols; Pres. Prof. Dr JERZY BAŃSKI; Sec. Dr ANNA BILIK; publs *Czasopismo Geograficzne* (Geographical Journal, 4 a year), *Polski Przegląd Kartograficzny* (Polish Cartographical Review, 4 a year), *Prace Komisji Geografii Komunikacji* (1 a year), *Studia Obszarów Wiejskich* (Rural Studies, 1 a year), *Teledetekcja Srodowiska* (1 a year).

Polskie Towarzystwo Historyczne (Polish Historical Society): Rynek Starego Miasta 29/31, 00-272 Warsaw; tel. (22) 831-63-41; e-mail pth@ihpan.edu.pl; internet http://historicus.umk.pl/pth; f. 1886; 4,137 mems; 53 local brs, 4 research centres; Pres. Prof. Dr KRZYSTOF MIKULSKI; Sec.-Gen. Mgr ZOFIA T. KOZŁOWSKA; publs *Komunikaty Mazursko-Warmińskie* (4 a year), *Przegląd Historyczny* (4 a year), *Sobótka-Śląski Kwartalnik Historyczny* (4 a year), *Studia i Materialy do dziejów Wielkopolski i Pomorza* (series), and several annuals.

Polskie Towarzystwo Numizmatyczne (Polish Numismatic Society):; tel. and fax (22) 831-39-28; e-mail ptn@ptn.pl; internet www.ptn.pl; f. 1991; 2,500 mems; library of 3,645 vols; Pres. Prof. Dr hab. MARIUSZ MIELCZAREK; Sec. ADAM ZAJĄC; publ. *Biuletyn Numizmatyczny* (4 a year).

Stowarzyszenie Miłośników Dawnej Broni i Barwy (Historic Arms and Uniforms Association): al. 3 Maja 1, 30-062 Cracow; tel. (12) 295-55-77; fax (12) 633-97-67; f. 1957; 320 mems; Pres. Prof. Dr hab. ALEKSANDER GUTERCH; publ. *Studia do dziejów dawnego uzbrojenia i ubioru wojskowego*.

Towarzystwo Miłośników Historii i Zabytków Krakowa (Society of Friends of the History and Monuments of Cracow): ul. Sw. Jana 12, 31-018 Cracow; tel. (12) 421-27-83; fax (12) 423-10-74; e-mail tmhzk@tmhzk.krakow.pl; internet www.tmhzk.krakow.pl; f. 1896; 650 mems; Pres. Prof. Dr hab. JERZY WYROZUMSKI; Sec. OLGA DYBA; publs *Rocznik Krakowski*, *Biblioteka Krakowska*, *Kraków Dawniej i Dziś*, *Rola Krakowa w dziejach narodu*.

LANGUAGE AND LITERATURE

Alliance Française: AF, BUW, ul. Dobra 56/66, 00-312 Warsaw; tel. (22) 552-71-65; fax (22) 552-71-67; e-mail alliance.francaise@neostrada.pl; internet www.af-enpologne.pl; offers courses and exams in French language and culture and promotes cultural exchange with France; attached offices in Białystok, Cieszyn, Gdańsk, Gorzow, Katowice, Łódź, Lublin, Opole, Poznań, Rybnik, Rzeszów, Szczecin, Toruń, Wałbrzych and Wrocław; Dir PATRICK RENARD.

British Council: 00-697 Warsaw, Al Jerozolimskie 59; tel. (22) 695-59-00; fax (22) 621-99-55; e-mail bc.warsaw@britishcouncil.pl; internet www.britishcouncil.pl; teaching centre and library; offers courses and exams in English language and British culture and promotes cultural exchange with the UK; attached teaching centre in Kraków; Dir SUSAN MAINGAY.

Goethe-Institut: ul. Chmielna 13A, 00-021 Warsaw; tel. (22) 505-90-00; fax (22) 505-90-10; e-mail sekretariat@warschau.goethe.org; internet www.goethe.de/warschau; f. 1990; offers courses and exams in German language and culture and promotes cultural exchange with Germany; attached centre in Krakow; library of 15,000 vols, 30 periodicals; Dir Dr MARTIN WÄLDE.

Instituto Cervantes: ul. Myśliwiecka 4, 00-459 Warsaw; tel. (22) 622-54-22; fax (12) 622-54-13; e-mail cenvar@cervantes.es; internet varsovia.cervantes.es; offers courses and exams in Spanish language and culture and promotes cultural exchange with Spain and Spanish-speaking Latin and Central America; library of 16,000 vols; Dir JOSEP MARIA DE SAGARRA ANGEL.

Polskie Towarzystwo Filologiczne (Polish Philological Society): Al Mickiewicza 9/11, VI p., 31-120 Kraków; tel. (12) 633-63-77 ext. 2324; f. 1893; promotes classical studies; 500 mems; library of 2,500 vols; Pres. Prof. Dr hab. KAZIMIERZ KORUS; Sec. Dr HUBERT WOLANIN; publ. *EOS* (1 a year).

Polskie Towarzystwo Fonetyczne (Polish Phonetic Association): Instytut Lingwistyki UAM, ul. Międzychodzka 5, 60-371 Poznań; tel. (61) 829-27-06; fax (61) 829-27-00; e-mail fonetyka@amu.edu.pl; internet www.staff.amu.edu.pl/~fonetyka; f. 1980; linguistic phonetics, phonetics in medicine and technology; 112 mems; Pres. GRAŻYNA DEMENKO; Sec. MARIUSZ OWSIANNY.

Polskie Towarzystwo Językoznawcze (Polish Linguistic Society): al. A. Mickiewicza

31, 31-120 Cracow; e-mail ptj@civ.pl; internet www.ptj.civ.pl; f. 1925; 585 mems; organizes meetings for mems and annual scientific confs; Pres. Prof. RENATA PRZYBYLSKA; Sec. Dr RENATA BURA; publ. *Biuletyn* (1 a year).

Polskie Towarzystwo Neofilologiczne (Modern Language Association of Poland): UAM, Collegium Novum, al. Niepodległości 4, pok. 014, 61-874 Poznań; tel. (61) 853-37-64; e-mail poltowneo@gmail.com; internet www.poltowneo.org; f. 1929; 184 mems; Pres. WERONIKA WILCZYŃSKA; Sec. ANNA BARBARA CIEŚLICKA; publ. *Neofilolog* (2 a year).

Towarzystwo Literackie im. Adama Mickiewicza (Mickiewicz Literary Society): Nowy Świat 72, 00-330 Warsaw; tel. 22 65-72-879; e-mail towarzystwo_literackie@wp.pl; internet www.towarzystwo_literackie.webpark.pl; f. 1886; 1,600 mems; arranges lectures on literature mainly in the provinces; Pres. Prof. Dr hab. GRAŻYNA BORKOWSKA; Vice-Pres. Dr JACEK WØJCICKI; Sec. Dr IRENA SZYPOWSKA.

Związek Literatów Polskich (Union of Polish Writers): Krakowskie Przedmieście 87/89, 00-079 Warsaw; tel. (22) 826-57-85; e-mail owzlp@o2.pl; internet literatura.waw.pl; f. 1920; 700 mems; library of 40,000 vols and cuttings; Pres. MAREK WAWRZKIEWICZ; Gen. Sec. GRZEGORZ WIŚNIEWSKI.

MEDICINE

Polskie Lekarskie Towarzystwo Radiologiczne (Polish Medical Society of Radiology): c/o Assoc. Prof. Jan Baron, Nuklearnej Śląskiej Akademii Medycznej – SP CSK AM, ul. Medyków 14, 40-752 Katowice; tel. and fax (32) 252-55-66; e-mail gwawrzonek@csk.katowice.pl; internet www.polradiologia.org; f. 1925; 1,700 mems; Pres. Asst Prof. JAN BARON; Vice-Pres. Prof. MAREK SĄSIADEK; Vice-Pres. ANDRZEJ URBANIK; Treas. Dr JOANNA GIBIŃSKA; Sec. Dr MAGDALENA MACHNIKOWSKA-SOKOŁOWSKA; publ. *Polski Przegląd Radiologiczny* (4 a year).

Polskie Towarzystwo Anatomiczne (Polish Anatomical Society): ul. Chałubińskiego 5, 02-004 Warsaw; tel. (22) 629-52-82; fax (22) 629-52-82; e-mail mbruska@ump.edu.pl; internet www.pta.info.pl; f. 1923; 400 mems; Pres. MAŁGORZATA BRUSKA; Sec. Dr AGNIESZKA PRZYSTAŃSKA; publs *Folia Morphologica*, *Postępy Biologii Komórki* (Advances in Cell Biology).

Polskie Towarzystwo Anestezjologii i Intensywnej Terapii (Polish Society of Anaesthesiology and Intensive Therapy): Katedra i Klinika Anestezjologii i Intensywnej Terapii AM SPSK Nr 4, ul. Jaczewskiego 8, 20-954 Lublin; tel. (81) 724-43-32; fax (81) 742-52-56; internet www.anestezjologia.org.pl; f. 1959; Pres. Prof. Dr hab. n. med. ANDRZEJ NESTOROWICZ; Sec.-Gen. Dr n. med. ANNA FIJAŁKOWSKA; publ. *Anestezjologia Intensywna Terapia* (6 a year).

Polskie Towarzystwo Badań Radiacyjnych im. Marii Skłodowskiej-Curie (M. Skłodowska-Curie Polish Society for Radiation Research): ul. Chocimska 24, 00-791 Warsaw; tel. (22) 849-77-74; fax (22) 849-29-64; e-mail ptbr@pzh.gov.pl; internet www.ptbr.pzh.gov.pl; f. 1967; 229 mems; Pres. Prof. Dr hab. ANTONI GAJEWSKI; Sec. Dr MAŁGORZATA ROCHALSKA.

Polskie Towarzystwo Chirurgów Dziecięcych (Polish Association of Paediatric Surgeons): Dept of Pediatric Surgery, Medical Univ. of Bialystok, L. Zamenhof Children's Univ. Hospital, ul. Waszyngtona 17, 15-274 Bialystok; tel. (48)857-45-09-21; fax (48)857-45-09-20; e-mail ptchdsek@gmail.com; internet www.ptchd.pl; f. 1965; 600 mems; Pres. Assoc. Prof. Dr WOJCIECH DEBEK; Sec.-Gen. Dr DZIENIS-KORONKIEWICZ EWA; publs *Roczniki Dziecięcej Chirurgii Urazowej* (1 a year), *Surgery in Childhood International* (4 a year).

Polskie Towarzystwo Chorób Płuc (Polish Phthisiopneumonological Society): ul. Płocka 26, 01-138 Warsaw; tel. (32) 271-56-08; fax (32) 274-56-64; internet www.ptchp.org; f. 1934; research into tuberculosis and chest diseases; Pres. Prof. Dr hab. med. WŁADYSŁAW PIERZCHAŁA; publ. *Pneumonologia i Alergologia Polska* (12 a year).

Polskie Towarzystwo Diagnostyki Laboratoryjnej (Polish Laboratory Diagnostics Society): c/o Dr n. med. Andrzej Marszałek, Zakład Diagnostyki Laboratoryjnej 10 WSK z Polikliniką SPZOZ, ul. Powstańców Warszawy 5, 85-680 Bydgoszcz; tel. (52) 378-48-87; fax (52) 377-33-10; internet www.diagnostykalab.pl/diagnost/ptdl/teren.htm; f. 1963; 3,500 mems; Pres. Prof. Dr n. med. MAREK PARADOWSKI; Sec. Dr n. med. ANDRZEJ MARSZAŁEK; publ. *Diagnostyka Laboratoryjna* (4 a year).

Polskie Towarzystwo Epidemiologów i Lekarzy Chorób Zakaźnych (Polish Society of Epidemiology and Infectious Diseases): ul. Św. Floriana 12, 85-030 Bydgoszcz; tel. (52) 322-48-70; fax (52) 345-71-95; e-mail kikchzak@amb.bydgoszcz.pl; f. 1958; 1,200 mems; Pres. Prof. WALDEMAR HALOTA; Sec. Dr EWA TOPCZEWSKA-STAUBACH; publ. *Przegląd Epidemiologiczny* (4 a year).

Polskie Towarzystwo Farmaceutyczne (Polish Pharmaceutical Society): ul. Długa 16, 00-238 Warsaw; tel. and fax (22) 831-15-42; e-mail zarzad@ptfarm.pl; internet www.ptfarm.pl; f. 1947; 7,000 mems; Pres. Prof. Dr hab. JANUSZ PLUTA; publs *Acta Poloniae Pharmaceutica* (6 a year), *Bromatologia i Chemia Toksykologiczna* (4 a year), *Farmacja Polska* (26 a year).

Polskie Towarzystwo Farmakologiczne (Polish Pharmacological Society): Katedra i Zakład Patofizjologii, Uniwersytet Medyczny, Jaczewskiego 8, 00-927 Warszawa; tel. (12) 662 32 58; fax (22) 826-21-16, e-mail lason@if-pan.krakow.pl; internet pharmacology.slam.katowice.pl; f. 1965; 341 mems; Pres. Prof. Dr WLADYSLAW LASON; Sec. Prof. Dr BOGUSLAWA BUDZISZEWSKA; publ. *Pharmacological Reports* (abstracts of the Int. Congresses of the Polish Pharmacological Soc.).

Polskie Towarzystwo Fizjologiczne (Polish Physiological Society): 16 Grzegórzecka St, 31-531 Cracow; tel. (12) 421-10-06; fax (12) 421-15-78; e-mail mpbrzozo@cyf-kr.edu.pl; internet www.ptf.ifzz.pl; f. 1936; promotes scientific activity in all fields of physiology incl. most gastrointestinal, endocrine, cardiovascular, neural, respiratory and kidney physiology; 300 mems; Pres. Prof. Dr WIESLAW W. PAWLIK; Sec. Prof. Dr TOMASZ BRZOZOWSKI; publ. *Journal of Physiology and Pharmacology*.

Polskie Towarzystwo Fizyki Medycznej (Polish Society of Medical Physics): c/o Dr Ewa Zalewska, Instytut Biocybernetyki i Inżynierii Biomedycznej PAN, ul. Ks. Trojdena 4, 02-109 Warsaw; e-mail k.zaremba@ire.pw.edu.pl; internet ptfm.ire.pw.edu.pl; f. 1965; 150 mems; Pres. Prof. GRZEGORZ PAWLICKI; Sec. Dr EWA ZALEWSKA; publ. *Polish Journal of Medical Physics and Engineering*.

Polskie Towarzystwo Gerontologiczne (Polish Society of Gerontology): Wisniowa St 41/66D, 02-520 Warsaw; tel. and fax (50) 101-63-65; fax (22) 812-11-89; e-mail gerontologia@gerontologia.org.pl; internet www.borgis.pl/ptg; f. 1973; 320 mems; Pres. Pres. PIOTR BTEDOWSKI; Vice-Pres. for Medical Cttee Prof. BARBARABIEN; Vice-Pres. for Social Cttee Prof. MAEGORZATA HALICKA; publ. *Gerontologia Polska* (4 a year).

Polskie Towarzystwo Ginekologiczne (Polish Gynaecological Society): Klinika Onkologii Ginekologicznej Małgorzata Skowrońska, ul. Polna 33, 60-535 Poznań; tel. (61) 841-92-65; fax (61) 841-94-65; e-mail ptgzg@gpsk.am.poznan.pl; internet www.gpsk.am.poznan.pl/ptg; br. in Wrocław; Pres. Prof. Dr hab. MAREK SPACZYŃSKI; Sec. Prof. Dr hab. LESZEK PAWELCZYK; publ. *Ginekologia Polska* (12 a year).

Polskie Towarzystwo Higieniczne (Polish Hygiene Society): ul. Karowa 31, 00-324 Warsaw; tel. (22) 826-63-20; fax (22) 826-82-36; internet www.pth.pl; f. 1898; Pres. Assoc. Prof. CEZARY W. KORCZAK; Sec. Dr PAWEŁ GORYŃSKI; publs *Druk Bibliofilski 'Hygeia'* (all irregular), *Problemy Higieny*, *Problemy Higieny Pracy*.

Polskie Towarzystwo Higieny Psychicznej (Polish Mental Health Society): Targowa 59/16, 03-729 Warsaw; tel. (22) 818-65-99; e-mail pthp@poczta.onet.pl; safeguarding the mental and moral health of the individual; f. 1935; 1,250 mems; library of 2,500 vols; Pres. ANDRZEJ BAŁANDYNOWICZ; publ. *Zdrowie Psychiczne* (4 a year).

Polskie Towarzystwo Immunologii Doswiadczalnej i Klinicznej (Polish Society for Experimental and Clinical Immunology): ul. Garbary 15, 61-866 Poznań; tel. (61) 854-06-65; fax (61) 852-85-02; internet www.immuno.pl; f. 1969; 500 mems; Pres. Prof. Dr hab. ANDRZEJ MACKIEWICZ; Scientific Sec. Dr hab. DARIUSZ KOWALCZYK; Technical Sec. Dr hab. PIOTR WYSOCKI; publs *Central European Journal of Immunology* (4 a year, in English), *Integryna—Biuletyn PTI* (4 a year, in Polish).

Polskie Towarzystwo Kardiologiczne (Polish Cardiological Society): ul. Stawki 3A/1, 00-193 Warsaw; tel. (22) 887-18-56; fax (22) 887-18-58; e-mail zarzad.glowny@ptkardio.pl; internet www.ptkardio.pl; Pres. Prof. Dr hab. ADAM TORBICKI; Sec. Prof. Dr hab. TOMASZ PASIERSKI, publs *Folia Cardiologica* (12 a year), *Kardiologia Polska* (12 a year).

Polskie Towarzystwo Lekarskie (Polish Medical Association): Al. Ujazdowskie 24, 00-478 Warsaw; tel. and fax (22) 628-86-99; e-mail ptl@interia.pl; internet www.ptl.org.pl; f. 1951; 25,000 mems; Pres. Prof. Dr hab. med. JERZY WOY-WOJCIECHOWSKI; Secs Dr FELICJA ŁAPKIEWICZ, Dr ZBIGNIEW MILLER; publs *Polski Tygodnik Lekarski* (52 a year), *Przegląd Lekarski* (12 a year), *Wiadomości Lekarskie* (26 a year).

Polskie Towarzystwo Medycyny Pracy (Polish Society of Occupational Medicine): ul. Teresy 8, 90-950 Łódź; tel. (42) 631-47-75; fax (42) 631-47-19; e-mail jolantaw@imp.lodz.pl; internet www.imp.lodz.pl/ptmp/ptmp.htm; f. 1969; Pres. Prof. Dr hab. RYSZARD ANDRJEZAK; Sec. Dr JOLANTA WALUSIAK; publs *International Journal of Occupational Medicine and Environmental Health* (4 a year, in English), *Medycyna Pracy* (6 a year).

Polskie Towarzystwo Medycyny Sądowej i Kryminologii (Polish Society of Forensic Medicine and Criminology): ul. Sędziowska 18A, 91-304 Łóź; tel. (42) 654-45-36; fax (42) 654-42-93; e-mail ptmsik@ptmsik.pl; internet www.ptmsik.pl; f. 1938; forensic medicine, toxicology, genetics, other forensic science; 200 mems; Chair. Prof. JAROSŁAW BERENT; Vice-Chair. Doc. MARIA KAŁA; Vice-Chair. Prof. PAWEŁ KRAJEWSKI; publ. *Archiwum Medycyny Sądowej i Kryminologii* (4 a year).

Polskie Towarzystwo Medycyny Społecznej i Zdrowia Publicznego (Polish

Society of Social Medicine and Public Health): ul. Chodźki 1, 20-093 Lublin; tel. (81) 740-57-53; fax (81) 740-57-52; e-mail mchbt@eskulap.am.lublin.pl; f. 1916; 1,800 mems; Pres. Prof. Dr hab. n. med. LESZEK WDOWIAK; publ. *Problemy Medycyny Społecznej* (Problems in Social Medicine, 2 or 3 a year).

Polskie Towarzystwo Medycyny Sportowej Zarząd Główny (Polish Society of Sports Medicine): Plac Hallere 1 90-647 Łódź; tel. (42) 639-32-15; fax (42) 639-32-18; e-mail sekretariat@ptms.org.pl; internet www.ptms.org.pl; f. 1937; Pres. Prof. ARTUR DZIAK; Sec. WOJCIECH DRYGAS; publ. *Medycyna Sportowa* (4 a year).

Polskie Towarzystwo Nauk Żywieniowych (Polish Society of Nutritional Sciences): ul. Nowoursynowska 159C, 02-776 Warsaw; tel. (22) 59-37-110; fax (22) 59-37-117; e-mail ptnz@sggw.pl; internet ptnz.sggw.pl; f. 1980; 300 mems; Pres. Prof. Dr hab. ANNA BRZOZOWSKA; Sec. Dr hab JERZY BERTRANDT; publ. *Polish Journal of Food and Nutrition Sciences* (4 a year).

Polskie Towarzystwo Neurochirurgów (Polish Society of Neurosurgeons): ul. Żeromskiego 113, 90-549 Łódź; tel. (42) 639-35-51; f. 1964; 279 mems; Pres. Prof. Dr hab. ANDRZEJ RADEK; publ. *Neurologia i Neurochirurgia Polska* (6 a year).

Polskie Towarzystwo Neurologiczne (Polish Neurological Society): ul. Jaczewskiego 8, 20-950 Warsaw; tel. (81) 742-54-20; fax (81) 742-54-20; e-mail neurolog@asklepios.am.lublin.pl; internet www.neurologiapolska.pl; f. 1934; Pres. Prof. ZBIGNIEW STELMASIAK; Sec. ANNA SZCZPAŃSKA-SZEREJ; publ. *Neurologia i Neurochirurgia Polska* (6 a year).

Polskie Towarzystwo Onkologiczne (Polish Oncological Society): ul. Garncarska 11, 31-115 Cracow; tel. and fax (12) 422-87-60; internet www.pto.io.gliwice.pl; f. 1921; 720 mems; Pres. Prof. Dr hab. MARIAN REINFUSS; Sec. Prof. Dr hab. JAN KULPA; publ. *Nowotwory* (4 a year).

Polskie Towarzystwo Ortopedyczne i Traumatologiczne (Polish Orthopaedic and Traumatological Society): ul. Konarskiego 13, 05-400 Otwock; tel. and fax (22) 779 54 18; internet www.ptoitr.pl; f. 1928; Pres. Prof. Dr hab. TADEUSZ SZYMON GAŹDZIK; Sec. Dr MAREK BOŻEK; publs *Chirurgia Narządów Ruchu i Ortopedia Polska* (6 a year), *Kwartalnik Ortopedyczny* (4 a year).

Polskie Towarzystwo Patologów (Polish Society of Pathologists): ul. Unii Lubelskiej 1, 71-252 Szczecin; tel. and fax (91) 487-00-32; e-mail polpat@ams.edu.pl; internet www.pol-pat.pl; f. 1958; 581 mems; Pres. Prof. Dr hab. WENANCJUSZ DOMAGAŁA; Sec. Dr ELŻBIETA URASIŃSKA; publ. *Patologia Polska* (4 a year, in English).

Polskie Towarzystwo Pediatryczne (Polish Paediatric Society): ul. Sporna 36/50, 91-738 Łódź; tel. (42) 617-29-29; fax (42) 617-28-82; e-mail ptpzg@csk.am.lodz.pl; internet csk.am.lodz.pl/ptpzg; f. 1908; 4,500 mems; Pres. Prof. Dr hab. KRYSTYNA WĄSOWSKA-KRÓLIKOWSKA; Sec. Prof. Dr hab. JERZY STAŃCZYK; publs *Pediatria Polska* (12 a year), *Przegląd Pediatryczny* (4 a year).

Polskie Towarzystwo Pielęgniarskie (Polish Nurses Association): Reymonta 8/12, 01-842 Warsaw; tel. (22) 663-63-45; fax (22) 388-18-51; internet www.ptp.na1.pl; f. 1924, revived 1954; 3,500 mems; library of 3,000 vols; Pres. DOROTA KILANSKA; Sec. GRAZYNA WYSIADECKA; publs *Biuletyn Polskiego Towarzystwa Pielęgniarskiego* (4 a year), *Problemy Pielęgniarstwa* (Nursing Topics).

Polskie Towarzystwo Psychiatryczne (Polish Psychiatric Association): Al. Sobieskiego 1/9, 02-957 Warsaw; tel. and fax (22) 842-40-87; e-mail wciorka@ipin.edu.pl; internet www.psychiatria.org.pl; f. 1920; 1,400 mems; Pres. Prof. Dr JACEK WCIORKA; publs *Archives of Psychiatry and Psychotherapy* (4 a year), *Psychiatria Polska* (6 a year), *Psychoterapia* (4 a year).

Polskie Towarzystwo Stomatologiczne (Polish Dental Association): ul. Montelupich 4, 30-155 Kraków; tel. (12) 424-54-42; fax (12) 424-54-94; e-mail biurozgpts@gmail.com; internet www.pts.net.pl; f. 1951; 6,000 mems; Pres. Assoc. Prof. Dr hab. BARTLOMIEJ W. LOSTER; Vice-Pres. Prof. Dr hab. HONORATA SHAW; Vice-Pres. Prof. Dr hab. ELZBIETA MIERZWINSKA-NASTALSKA; Vice-Pres. Prof. Dr hab. MAREK ZIETEK; Sec. Dr MAŁGORZATA RADWAN-OCZKO; publs *Czasopismo Stomatologiczne* (12 a year), *Dental and Medical Problems* (4 a year), *Dental Forum* (2 a year), *Implantoprotetyka* (4 a year), *Protetyka Stomatologiczna* (6 a year).

Polskie Towarzystwo Toksykologiczne (Polish Toxicological Society): POB 199, 90-950 Łódź; ul. Św. Teresy od Dzieciątka Jezus 8, 90-950 Łódź; tel. (42) 631-45-02; fax (42) 656-83-31; e-mail impx@imp.lodz.pl; internet www.imp.lodz.pl/nowy_pttox; f. 1978; 305 mems; Pres. Prof. Dr hab. KONRAD RYDZYŃSKI; Sec. Dr JOLANTA GROMADZIŃSKA; publ. *Acta Poloniae Toxicologica* (2 a year).

Polskie Towarzystwo Urologiczne (Polish Urological Society): ul. Burszynowa 2, 04-749 Warsaw; tel. and fax (22) 815-68-61; e-mail info@pturol.org.pl; internet www.pturol.org.pl; f. 1949; 800 mems; Pres. Prof. Dr hab. ANDRZEJ BORÓWKA; Sec. Prof. ROMUALD ZDROJOWY; publs *Urologia Polska* (4 a year), *Przegląd Urologiczny* (6 a year).

Polskie Towarzystwo Walki z Kalectwem (Polish Society for Rehabilitation of the Disabled): ul. Oleandrów 4 m. 10, 00-629 Warsaw; tel. and fax (22) 825-70-50; e-mail twk@idn.org.pl; internet twk.idn.org.pl; f. 1960; popularizing progressive ideas in prophylaxis and changing social attitudes towards the disabled; Pres. Dr PIOTR JANASZEK; Sec. Dr ZBIGNIEW KAŹMIERAK; publ. *Life of the Polish Society for Rehabilitation of the Disabled Information Bulletin*.

Stowarzyszenie Neuropatologów Polskich (Association of Polish Neuropathologists): ul. Pawińskiego 5, 02-106 Warsaw; tel. (61) 661-92-34; fax (61) 661-98-12; e-mail jszymas@ampat.amu.edu.pl; internet snp.amu.edu.pl; f. 1964; 51 mems; Pres. Prof. Dr JANUSZ SZYMAŚ; Sec. Dr HALINA WEINRAUDER; publ. *Folia Neuropathologica* (4 a year).

Towarzystwo Chirurgów Polskich (Society of Polish Surgeons): ul. Banacha 1A, 02-097 Warsaw; tel. and fax (22) 658-36-62; e-mail tchp@mp.pl; internet tchp.org.pl; f. 1889; 3,150 mems; Pres. Prof. ZBIGNIEW PUCHALSKI; Sec.-Gen. Prof. MAREK KRAWCZYK; publ. *Polski Przegląd Chirurgiczny* (12 a year).

Towarzystwo Internistów Polskich (Polish Society of Internal Medicine): Skawińska 8, 31-066 Krakow; tel. (12) 430-54-15; fax (12) 293-42-28; e-mail tip@mp.pl; internet tip.org.pl; f. 1906; advances knowledge of internal medicine, represents Polish internal medical physicians; organizes Congress (every 4 years), annual Nat. Educational Conf. on Internal Medicine and Polish–Slovak Conf. on Internal Medicine; 3,000 mems; Pres. JACEK MUSIAŁ; Sec. PIOTR GAJEWSKI; publ. *Polskie Archiwum Medycyny Wewnętrznej* (Polish Archives of Internal Medicine, 12 a year, in English).

NATURAL SCIENCES

Biological Sciences

Polskie Towarzystwo Biochemiczne (Polish Biochemical Society): ul. Pasteura 3, 02-093 Warsaw; tel. (22) 589-23-52; fax (22) 589-24-99; e-mail ptbioch@nencki.gov.pl; internet www.ptbioch.edu.pl; f. 1958; 1,200 mems; Pres. Prof. ANDRZEJ DZUGAJ; Sec. Prof. MARIA JOLANTA REDOWICZ; publs *Acta Biochimica Polonica* (online, 4 a year), *Postępy Biochemii* (Advances in Biochemistry, 4 a year).

Polskie Towarzystwo Biofizyczne (Polish Biophysical Society): ul. Chałubińskiego 10, 50-368 Wrocław; tel. (71) 784-14-15; fax (71) 784-00-88; e-mail hendrich@biofiz.am.wroc.pl; internet www.ptbf.am.wroc.pl; f. 1972; 250 mems; Pres. Prof. Dr hab. MARIA KOTER-MICHALAK; Sec. Dr ANETA KOCEVA-CHYLA; publ. *Current Topics in Biophysics* (2 a year, in English, supplement in Polish).

Polskie Towarzystwo Biometryczne (Polish Biometric Society): Poznan Univ. of Life Sciences, Wojska Polskiego 28, 60-637 Poznan; tel. and fax (61) 848-71-40; e-mail smejza@up.poznan.pl; f. 1961; biometry, applied mathematical statistics in medicine, agriculture, biology; 230 mems; Pres. Prof. Dr hab. STANISLAW MEJZA; Sec Dr JOLANTA KRZYSZKOWSKA; Sec Dr KATARZYNA AMBROZY; publs *Biometrical Letters* (2 a year), *Colloquium Biometricum* (1 a year).

Polskie Towarzystwo Botaniczne (Polish Botanical Society): Al. Ujazdowskie 4, 00-478 Warsaw; f. 1922; 1,320 mems; library of 24,651 vols; Pres. Prof. Dr JAN J. RYBAZYŃSKI; publs *Acta Agrobotanica*, *Acta Mycologica*, *Acta Societatis Botanicorum Poloniae*, *Biuletyn Ogrodów Botanicznych Muzeów i Zbiorów*, *Monographiae Botanicae*, *Rocznik Sekcji Dendrologicznej Pol. Tow. Bot.*, *Wiadomości Botaniczne*.

Polskie Towarzystwo Entomologiczne (Polish Entomological Society): Dabrowskiego 159, 60-594 Poznan; tel. (61) 848-79-19; e-mail bunalski@up.poznan.pl; internet pte.au.poznan.pl; f. 1923; theoretical and applied entomology; 500 mems; library of 11,000 vols; Pres. Dr hab. MAREK BUNALSKI; Vice-Pres. Prof. Dr Hab. JAROSŁAW BUSZKO; Vice-Pres. Prof. Dr Hab. RYSZARD SZADZIEWSKI; Sec. Dr PAWEŁ SIENKIEWICZ; publs *Klucze do Oznaczania Owadów Polski* (Keys for Identification of Polish Insects, irregular), *Polish Entomological Monographs* (irregular), *Polskie Pismo Entomologiczne* (Polish Journal of Entomology, 4 a year), *Wiadomości Entomologiczne* (Entomological News, 4 a year).

Polskie Towarzystwo Fitopatologiczne (Polish Phytopathological Society): ul. Wojska Polskiego 71c, 60-625 Poznań; tel. (61) 848-77-08; fax (61) 848-77-11; e-mail mmanka@up.poznan.pl; internet www.up.poznan.pl/ptfit; f. 1971; scientific meetings, field days, confs and symposia of sections incl. nomenclature and teaching, biological control of plant diseases, plant virology, seed pathology, mycology and mycotoxins, biochemistry and genetics of plant pathogens, woody plant diseases, bacteriology, new pathogens and diseases; 300 mems; Pres. Prof. Dr hab. MAŁGORZATA MAŃKA; Sec. Dr Ing. DOROTA SZOPIŃSKA; publ. *Phytopathologia* (4 a year, in English).

Polskie Towarzystwo Genetyczne (Polish Genetics Society): ul. Ciszewskiego 8 , 02-786 Warsaw; tel. and fax (22) 853-09-31; fax (22) 853-09-31; e-mail k_charon@hotmail.com; internet jay.au.poznan.pl/ptg; f. 1963; 762 mems; Pres. Prof. Dr hab. MAREK SWITONSKI; Sec. Prof. Dr hab. KRYSTYNA MAŁGORZATA CHARON; publ. *Genetica Polonica* (4 a year).

Polskie Towarzystwo Hydrobiologiczne (Polish Hydrobiological Society): ul. Banacha 2, 02-097 Warsaw; tel. (22) 554-64-43; fax (22) 554-64-26; internet www.pth.home.pl; f. 1959; 12 brs nationally; 500 mems; Pres. Prof. Dr hab. MARCIN PLIŃSKI; Sec. Dr JAN IGOR RYBAK; publs *Fauna Słodkowodna Polski*, *Wiadomości Hydrobiologiczne* (4 a year, *Wiadomości Ekologiczne*).

Polskie Towarzystwo Mikrobiologów (Polish Society of Microbiologists): ul. Chocimska 24, 00-791 Warsaw; tel. (22) 542-12-38; fax (22) 542-13-07; internet www.microbiology.pl; f. 1927; 800 mems; Pres. Prof. DANUTA DZIERŻANOWSKA; Sec. Dr JOLANTA SZYCH; publs *Journal of Polish Microbiology* (English, 4 a year), *Medycyna Doświadczalna i Mikrobiologia* (Experimental Medicine and Microbiology, Polish, 4 a year), *Postępy Mikrobiologii* (Advances in Microbiology, Polish, 4 a year).

Polskie Towarzystwo Parazytologiczne (Polish Parasitological Society): Twarda 51–55, 00-818 Warsaw; tel. (22) 697-89-95; fax (22) 620-62-27; internet www.ptparasit.org.pl; f. 1948; 390 mems; Pres. Prof. PIOTR KURNATOWSKI; publs *Katalog Fauny Pasozytniczej Polski* (irregular), *Monografie Parazytologiczne* (irregular), *Wiadomości Parazytologiczne* (4 a year).

Polskie Towarzystwo Zoologiczne (Polish Zoological Society): Sienkiewicza 21, 50-335 Wrocław; tel. (71) 375-40-49; fax (71) 322-50-44; e-mail ptzol@biol.uni.wroc.pl; f. 1935; 750 mems; library of 55,000 vols; Pres. Dr hab. Prof. MARTA BOROWIEC; Sec. ANDRZEJ JABŁOŃSKI; publs *Notatki Ornitologiczne*, *Przegląd Zoologiczny*, *The Ring* (4 a year), *Zoologica Poloniae*.

Mathematical Sciences

Polskie Towarzystwo Matematyczne (Polish Mathematical Society): ul. Śniadeckich 8, 00-956 Warsaw; tel. (22) 522-81-46; e-mail zgptm@ptm.org.pl; internet www.ptm.org.pl; f. 1919; 1,300 mems; Pres. Prof. STEFAN JACKOWSKI; publs *Annales Societatis Mathematicae Polonae: Series I Commentationes Mathematicae*, *Popularny Miesięcznik Matematyczno-Fizyczno-Astronomiczny DELTA* (Mathematical and Physical Popular, 12 a year), *Series II Wiadomości Matematyczne* (Mathematical News), *Series III Matematyka Stosowana* (Applied Mathematics), *Series IV Fundamenta Informaticae*, *Series V Didactica Mathematicae* (Didactics of Mathematics), *Series VI Antiquitates Mathematicae* (History of Mathematics).

Polskie Towarzystwo Statystyczne (Polish Statistical Association): Al. Niepodległości 208, 00-925 Warsaw; tel. (22) 625-42-89; f. 1912; statistics, informatics, economics and econometrics; c. 1,000 mems; Pres. Prof. CZESŁAW DOMAŃSKI; Sec. JÓZEF GWOZDOWSKI; publs *Biuletyn Informacyjny* (Bulletin of Information, 4 a year), *Wiadomości Statystyczne* (Statistics in Transition, 4 a year).

Physical Sciences

Polskie Towarzystwo Astronomiczne (Polish Astronomical Society): ul. Bartycka 18, 00-716 Warsaw; tel. (22) 841-00-41 ext. 146; fax (22) 841-00-46; e-mail pta@pta.edu.pl; internet www.pta.edu.pl/pta; f. 1923; 219 mems; Pres. Prof. Dr hab. ANDRZEJ WOSZCZYK; Sec. Dr ADAM MICHALEC; publs *Urania – Postępy Astronomii* (Progress in Astronomy), *Delta*.

Polskie Towarzystwo Chemiczne (Polish Chemical Society): ul. Freta 16, 00-227 Warsaw; tel. (22) 831-13-04; fax (22) 831-13-04; e-mail zgptchem@chemix.ch.pw.edu.pl; internet www.ptchem.lodz.pl; f. 1919; 2,350 mems; library of 2,400 vols; Pres. Prof. JERZY KONARSKI; Sec. Prof. ROMAN MIERZECKI; publs *Wiadomości Chemiczne* (Chemical News), *Polish Journal of Chemistry*, *Orbital* (Society News, 6 a year), *Chemical Analysis* (6 a year).

Polskie Towarzystwo Fizyczne (Polish Physical Society): ul. Hoża 69, 00-681 Warsaw; tel. and fax (22) 621-26-68; e-mail ptf@fuw.edu.pl; internet ptf.fuw.edu.pl; f. 1920; 1,800 mems; library of 1,300 vols; Pres. Prof. Dr hab. MACIEJ KOLWAS; Gen. Sec. Doc. HELENA BIAŁKOWSKA; publs *Acta Physica Polonica A and B* (12 a year, in English, French, German and Russian), *Delta* (12 a year, in Polish), *Postępy Fizyki* (Advances in Physics, 6 a year), *Reports on Mathematical Physics* (6 a year, in English).

Polskie Towarzystwo Geofizyczne (Polish Geophysical Society): ul. Podleśna 61, 01-673 Warsaw; tel. (22) 569-45-62; f. 1947; devt of geophysical sciences and their popularization; 450 mems; library of 5,000 vols; Pres. Dr ALFRED DUBICKI; Sec.-Gen. Dr JERZY SZKUTNICKI; publ. *Przegląd Geofizyczny* (Geophysical Review, 4 a year).

Polskie Towarzystwo Geologiczne (Polish Geological Society): Oleandry 2A, 30-063 Cracow; tel. (12) 633-20-41; fax (12) 633-22-70; e-mail ptg@uj.edu.pl; internet www.ptgeol.pl; f. 1921; 875 mems; library of 9,397 vols, 25,883 journals; Pres. Dr hab. MARIAN ADAM GASINSK; Sec. Dr inż. JOZEF CHOWANIEC; publ. *Annales Societatis Geologorum Poloniae/Rocznik Polskiego Towarzystwa Geologicznego/Annals of the Polish Geological Society* (3 a year).

Polskie Towarzystwo Miłośników Astronomii (Polish Amateur Astronomical Society): ul. św. Tomasza 30/8, 31-027 Cracow; tel. (12) 422-38-92; internet ptma-zg.astronomia.pl; f. 1919; 3,000 mems; amateur observations, instrument-making, popularization of astronomy; Pres. Prof. ZBIGNIEW KOWALSKI; Sec. Dr HENRYK BRANCEWICZ; publ. *Urania* (12 a year) and reports.

Polskie Towarzystwo Mineralogiczne (Mineralogical Society of Poland): Al. Mickiewicza 30, 30-059 Cracow; tel. (12) 617-24-36; fax (12) 633-43-30; e-mail szydlak@uci.agh.edu.pl; internet uranos.cto.us.edu.pl/~ptmin; f. 1969; 195 mems; Pres. Prof. PIOTR WYSZOMIRSKI; Sec. Dr TADEUSZ SZYDŁAK; publ. *Mineralogia Polonica* (2 a year).

Polskie Towarzystwo Nautologiczne (Polish Nautological Society): ul. 3 Maja 12a m 7, 81-357 Gdynia; tel. and fax (58) 620-49-75; internet www.ptn-nautologia.pl; f. 1958; history of human involvement with the sea; 150 mems; library of 2,800 vols; Pres. Prof. Dr DANIEL DUDA; Sec. Dr ELŻBIETA SKUPIŃSKA-DYBEK; publ. *Nautologia* (4 a year).

PHILOSOPHY AND PSYCHOLOGY

Polskie Towarzystwo Filozoficzne (Polish Philosophical Society): Pałac Staszica, ul. Nowy Świat 72, p.160, 00-330 Warsaw; tel. (22) 826-52-31, ext. 759; fax (22) 657-27-59; internet www.ptfilozofia.pl; f. 1904; study of all traditional philosophical disciplines; 826 mems; library of 7,200 vols; Pres. Prof. Dr hab. WŁADISŁAW STRÓŻEWSKI; Sec. Dr WANDA KAMIŃSKA; publ. *Ruch Filozoficzny* (Philosophical Movement, 4 a year).

Polskie Towarzystwo Psychologiczne (Polish Psychological Association): Stawki 5/7, 00-183 Warsaw; tel. and fax (22) 831-13-68; e-mail ptp@engram.psych.uw.edu.pl; internet www.ptp.org.pl; f. 1948; 2,000 mems; Pres. Prof. ADAM NIEMCZYNSKI; Gen. Sec. Dr TERESA PANAS; publs *Nowiny Psychologiczne* (Psychological Newsletter, 4 a year), *Przegląd Psychologiczny* (Psychological Review, 4 a year).

Polskie Towarzystwo Semiotyczne (Polish Semiotic Society): c/o Institute of Philosophy, Warsaw Univ., ul. Krakowskie Przedmieście 3, 00-927 Warsaw; tel. (22) 826-57-34; fax (22) 826-57-34; e-mail pts1@pts.edu.pl; internet www.pts.edu.pl; f. 1968; all aspects of semiotics: signs, sign systems, information, communication, indirect cognition; applied semiotics; philosophy of language, linguistics, logic; 150 mems; library of 1,700 vols; Pres. Prof. JERZY PELC; Sec.-Gen. Dr TADEUSZ CIECIERSKI; publ. *Studia Semiotyczne* (irregular).

RELIGION, SOCIOLOGY AND ANTHROPOLOGY

Polskie Towarzystwo Antropologiczne (Polish Anthropological Society): Umultowska 89, 61-614 Poznań; tel. (61) 829-57-13; e-mail pta@antropo.uni.wroc.pl; internet www.pta.uni.maszt.pl; f. 1925; 317 mems; library of 10,000 vols; Chair. MARIA KACZMAREK; Sec. Dr ANITA SZWED; publ. *Przegląd Antropologiczny* (Anthropological Review, 1 a year).

Polskie Towarzystwo Kryminalistyczne (Polish Society of Criminologists): ul. Zgoda 11 lok. 300, 00-018 Warsaw; tel. (22) 692-43-85; fax (22) 692-83-81; e-mail biuro@kryminalistyka.pl; internet www.kryminalistyka.pl; f. 1973; forensic science; 350 mems; Pres. Prof. Dr hab. MARIUSZ KULICKI; Sec. Mgr inż. TOMASZ BEDNAREK; publ. *Z Zagadnień Współczesnej Kryminalistyki* (irregular).

Polskie Towarzystwo Ludoznawcze (Polish Ethnological Society): Szczytnicka 11, 50-382 Wrocław; tel. (71) 321-16-10; fax (71) 321-16-14; e-mail ptl@ptl.info.pl; internet www.ptl.info.pl; f. 1895; cultural anthropology, folklore; 680 mems; library of 44,068 vols; Pres. MICHAŁ BUCHOWSKI; Sec. JERZY ADAMCZEWSKI; Librarian ALEKSANDRA MICHAŁOWSKA; publs *Archiwum Etnograficzne*, *Atlas Polskich Strojów Ludowych*, *Biblioteka Literatury Ludowej*, *Biblioteka Popularna*, *Biblioteka Zesłańca*, *Dziedzictwo Kulturowe*, *Dzieła Wszystkie O. Kolberga*, *Komentarze do Polskiego Atlasu Etnograficznego*, *Literatura Ludowa* (6 a year), *Łódzkie Studia Etnograficzne* (1 a year), *Lud* (1 a year), *Prace Etnologiczne*, *Prace i Materiały Etnograficzne*.

Polskie Towarzystwo Orientalistyczne (Polish Oriental Society): c/o Wydział Orientalistyczny UW, ul. Krakowskie Przedmieście 26/28, 00-927 Warsaw; tel. (22) 552-03-53; e-mail pto.orient@uw.edu.pl; internet www.orient.uw.edu.pl/pto; f. 1922; 139 mems; Pres. MAREK MEJOR; Sec.-Gen. MARIA KOZLOWSKA; publ. *Przegląd Orientalistyczny* (4 a year).

Polskie Towarzystwo Religioznawcze (Polish Society for the Science of Religions): 30 skr. poczt. 151, Jaracza 1 Lok. 6, 00-959 Warsaw; tel. (22) 625-26-42; e-mail prof2aw@yahoo.com; f. 1958; history, theory, methodology, sociology, psychology of religions; 165 mems; Pres. Prof. Dr hab. ZBIGNIEW STACHOWSKI; Scientific Sec. Prof. Dr hab. ANDRZEJ WÓJTOWICZ; publ. *Przegląd Religioznawczy* (4 a year).

Polskie Towarzystwo Socjologiczne (Polish Sociological Association): ul. Nowy Świat 72, 00-330 Warsaw; tel. and fax (22) 826-77-37; e-mail pts@ifispan.waw.pl; internet www.pts.org.pl; f. 1957; the main professional org. of sociologists in Poland; 1,040 mems; Pres. Prof. PIOTR GLIŃSKI; Exec.-Sec. Prof. ZBIGNIEW RYKOWSKI; publs *Informacja Bieżąca* (Current Bibliographical Information, 2 a year), *Polish Sociological Review* (4 a year).

Polskie Towarzystwo Teologiczne (Polish Theological Society): ul. Kanonicza 3, 31-

002 Cracow; tel. (12) 394-56-76; fax (12) 422-56-90; e-mail zarzad@ptt.net.pl; internet www.ptt.net.pl; f. 1924; Pres. Rev. Prof. KAZIMIERZ PANUŚ; Sec. Rev. KAZIMIERZ MOSKALA; publ. *Ruch Biblijny i Liturgiczny* (4 a year).

Towarzystwo Naukowe Organizacji i Kierownictwa (Scientific Society for Organization and Management): ul. Górska 6/10 lok. 71 00-740 Warsaw; tel. (22) 625-44-85; fax (22) 629-21-27; e-mail bzg@tnoik.org; internet www.tnoik.org; f. 1925; 32,000 individual mems, 5,000 collective mems; library of 15,000 vols; Pres. Prof. Dr hab. RYSZARD BOROWIECKI; Gen. Sec. Mgr WŁODZIMIERZ HAUSNER; publ. *Przegląd Organizacji* (12 a year).

TECHNOLOGY

Akademia Inżynierska w Polsce (Academy of Engineering in Poland): ul. Czackiego 3/5, 00-950 Warsaw; tel. (22) 828-64-45; fax (22) 827-29-49; e-mail aip@aip.medianet.pl; internet www.aip.medianet.pl; f. 1992; Pres. Prof. Dr hab. BOGDAN JERZY NEY; Gen. Sec. Prof. Dr JANUSZ DYDUCH.

Federacja Stowarzyszeń Naukowo-Technicznych–Naczelna Organizacja Techniczna (FSNT-NOT) (Polish Federation of Engineering Associations): ul. Czackiego 3/5, 00-950 Warsaw; tel. (22) 826-74-61; fax (22) 827-29-49; e-mail notdgz@not.org.pl; internet not.org.pl; 230,000 mems; Pres. Dr WOJCIECH RATYNSKI; Sec.-Gen. KAZIMIERZ WAWRZYNIAK; publ. *Przegląd Techniczny* (52 a year).

Polskie Towarzystwo Akustyczne (Polish Acoustical Society): Umultowska 85, 61-614 Poznań; tel. (58) 626-28-72; fax (58) 625-48-46; e-mail kozaczka@pg.gda.pl; internet www.ippt.gov.pl/akustyka; Pres. Prof. Dr hab. inż. EUGENIUSZ KOZACZKA; Sec.-Gen. Dr inż. GRAŻYNA GRELOWSKA; publ. *Archives of Acoustics* (continuous).

Polskie Towarzystwo Astronautyczne (Polish Astronautical Society): Bartycka 18a, 00-716 Warsaw; tel. (22) 840-37-66; fax (22) 840-31-31; e-mail poczta@ptastronaut.org.pl; internet www.ptastronaut.org.pl; f. 1954; scientific, educational, and popular astronautics, planetology, bio-astronautics, space physics, CETI, and space law; 40 mems; Pres. MACIEJ MROCZKOWSKI; Vice-Pres. ANDRZEJ KOTARSKI; Vice-Pres. Prof. RUDOLF KLEMENS; publ. *Postępy Astronautyki* (Progress in Astronautics, irregular).

Polskie Towarzystwo Elektrotechniki Teoretycznej i Stosowanej (Polish Society for Theoretical and Applied Electrical Engineering): ul. Koszykowa 75, Politechnika Warszawska, Wydz. Elektryczny, Gmach Electrotechniki p. 310, 00-662 Warsaw; tel. and fax (22) 625-67-25; e-mail ptetis@ien.pw.edu.pl; internet www.ee.pw.edu.pl/ptetis; f. 1961; brs in 13 major towns; 750 mems; Pres. Prof. Dr hab. inż. KRZYSZTOF KLUSZCZYŃSKI; Gen. Sec. Dr inż. WŁODZIMIERZ KAŁAT.

Polskie Towarzystwo Ergonomiczne (Polish Ergonomics Society): ul. Narbutta 85 p. 103, 02-524 Warsaw; tel. and fax (22) 234-82-09; e-mail sekretariat@ergonomia-polska.com; internet www.ergonomia-polska.com; f. 1977; Pres. Prof. EWA GÓRSLUZ; Gen. Sec. MACIEJ MAJEWSKI; publ. *Ergonomia* (2 a year).

Polskie Towarzystwo Mechaniki Teoretycznej i Stosowanej (Polish Society of Theoretical and Applied Mechanics): Dept of Civil Engineering, Warsaw University of Technology, Al. Armii Ludowej 16, p. 650, 00-637 Warsaw; tel. (22) 825-71-80; fax (22) 825-71-80; e-mail biuro@ptmts.org.pl; internet www.ptmts.org.pl; f. 1958; 976 mems; brs in 17 other towns; Pres. Prof. JÓZEF KUBIK; Gen. Sec. Dr WIESŁAW NAGÓRKO; publ. *Journal of Theoretical and Applied Mechanics* (4 a year).

Research Institutes

GENERAL

Instytut Kultury (Institute of Culture):e-mail info@instytutkultury.pl; internet instytutkultury.pl; f. 1974; library of 35,000 vols; Dir JAN STANISLAW WOJCLECHOWSKI; publ. *Prace Instytutu Kultury*.

Instytut Podstaw Inżynierii Środowiska PAN (Institute of Environmental Engineering): ul. M. Skłodowskiej-Curie 34, 41-819 Zabrze; tel. (32) 271-64-81; fax (32) 271-74-70; e-mail ipis@ipis.zabrze.pl; internet www.ipis.zabrze.pl; f. 1961; attached to Polish Acad. of Sciences; air and water pollution control, land reclamation, energy conservation, influence of pollutants on plants; library of 14,000 vols; Dir Prof. Dr hab. inż. CZESŁAWA-ROSIK DULEWSKA (acting); Dir Doc. Dr hab. inż. JOANNA KYZIOŁ (acting); publs *Archiwum Ochrony Środowiska* (Archives of Environmental Protection, 4 a year, with summaries in English and Russian), *Prace i Studia* (irregular).

Instytut Slawistyki PAN (Institute of Slavic Studies): ul. Bartoszewicza 1 B m. 17, 00-337 Warsaw; tel. and fax (22) 826-76-88; e-mail ispan@ispan.waw.pl; internet www.ispan.waw.pl; f. 1954; attached to Polish Acad. of Sciences; library of 124,000 vols; Dir Prof. Dr hab. GRAZYNA SZWAT-GYŁYBOW; Vice-Dir ANNA ENGELKING; publs *Acta Baltico-Slavica*, *Cognitive Studies/Etudes Cognitives*, *Colloquia Humanistica*, *Studia z Filologii Polskiej i Słowiańskiej*, *Slavia Meridionalis*, *Sprawy Narodowościowe*.

Instytut Sportu (Institute of Sport): ul. Trylogii 2/16, 01-982 Warsaw; tel. (22) 834-08-12; fax (22) 835-09-77; e-mail insp@insp.waw.pl; internet www.insp.pl/default.htm; f. 1978; library of 6,130 vols; Dir Prof. Dr hab. RYSZARD GRUCZA; publ. *Biology of Sport* (4 a year).

Zakład Badań Narodowościowych PAN (Centre for the Study of Nationalities): Stary Rynek 78/79, 61-772 Poznań; tel. and fax (61) 852-09-50; e-mail zbnpan@man.poznan.pl; f. 1973; attached to Polish Acad. of Sciences; library of 1,800 vols; Dir Prof. Dr hab. WOJCIECH J. BURSZTA; publ. *Sprawy Narodowościowe* (Issues of Nationality, 2 a year).

Zakład Krajów Pozaeuropejskich PAN (Centre for Studies on Non-European Countries): Nowy Świat 72, 00-330 Warsaw; tel. (22) 826-63-56; fax (22) 826-63-56; e-mail csnec@zkppan.waw.pl; f. 1978; attached to Polish Acad. of Sciences; library of 16,000 vols; Dir Dr JERZY ZDANOWSKI; publs *Acta Asiatica Varsoviensia* (in English and French, 1 a year), *Hemispheres* (in English and French, 1 a year).

AGRICULTURE, FISHERIES AND VETERINARY SCIENCE

Instytut Agrofizyki im. Bohdana Dobrzańskiego PAN (Institute of Agrophysics): ul. Doświaczalna 4, 20-290 Lublin; tel. (81) 744-50-61; fax (81) 744-50-67; internet www.ipan.lublin.pl; f. 1968; attached to Polish Acad. of Sciences; library of 3,000 vols; Dir Prof. Dr hab. JÓZEF HORABIK; publs *Acta Agrophysica* (2 a year), *International Agrophysics* (4 a year), *Polish Journal of Soil Science* (2 a year).

Instytut Badawczy Leśnictwa (Forestry Research Institute): ul. Bitwy Warszawskiej 1920 r. 3, 00-973 Warsaw; tel. (22) 823-45-65; fax (22) 822-49-35; e-mail ibl@ibles.waw.pl; internet www.ibles.waw.pl; f. 1930; comprises 14 scientific sections covering all aspects of forestry, especially factors of environment, silviculture and selection, tree-planting, forest economics, management, forest work organization, protection, forest plant pathology, game management, water economy, logging mechanization and transport; main documentation and information centre of forestry; brs at Cracow, Białowieża and Katowice; library of 69,000 vols; Dir Prof. Dr hab. eng. A. KLOCEK; publs *Folia Forestalia Polonica* (Series A—Forestry, in English, irregular), *Leśne Prace Badawcze* (Forest Research Papers, 4 a year), *Notatnik Naukowy*, *Nowości Piśmiennictwa Leśnego* (12 a year).

Instytut Biotechnologii Przemysłu Rolno-Spożywczego (Institute of Agricultural and Food Biotechnology): ul. Rakowiecka 36, 02-532 Warsaw; tel. (22) 849-02-24; fax (22) 849-04-26; e-mail ibprs@ibprs.pl; internet www.ibprs.pl; f. 1949; biotechnology: improvement of microbial strains, fermentation processes (beer, wine, spirits, organic acids), malt, yeasts, enzymatic preparations, microbial preparations; technology of fruit and vegetable products, food analysis, food concentration, storage and processing of grain, bread and pastry baking; culture collection of industrial micro-organisms; library of 22,000 vols; Dir Prof. ROMAN GRZYBOWSKI; publ. *Prace Instytutów i Laboratoriów Badawczych Przemysłu Spożywczego* (in Polish with summaries in English, 1 a year).

Instytut Budownictwa, Mechanizacji i Elektryfikacji Rolnictwa (Institute for Building, Mechanization and Electrification in Agriculture): ul. Rakowiecka 32, 02-532 Warsaw; tel. (22) 49-32-31; fax (22) 49-17-37; e-mail selian@ibmer.waw.pl; f. 1950; research into the mechanization of farming, economics and management, land reclamation, farm building and energy sources; library of 47,783 vols; Dir ALEKSANDER SZEPTYCKI; publs *Inżynieria Rolnicza* (irregular), *Prace NaukowoBadawcze IBMER* (1 a year), *Problemy Inżynierü Rolniczej* (4 a year), *Przegląd Dokumentacyjny—Technika Rolnicza* (6 a year).

Instytut Ekonomiki Rolnictwa i Gospodarki Żywnościowej (Institute of Agricultural and Food Economics): ul. Świętokrzyska 20, 00-002 Warsaw; tel. (22) 505-44-44; fax (22) 827-19-60; e-mail ierigz@ierigz.waw.pl; internet www.ierigz.waw.pl; f. 1983, fmrly Inst. of Agricultural Economics; library of 41,000 vols; scientific and research work, focused on issues of economic production and social situation of rural areas in Poland, agriculture and broadly conceived food economy; Dir Prof. Dr ANDRZEJ KOWALSKI; publs *Analizy Rynkowe* (Market Analyses, 2 a year for main commodities), *Rynek Rolny* (Agricultural Market, 12 a year), *Zagadnienia Ekonomiki Rolnej* (Problems of Agricultural Economics, 6 a year).

Instytut Fizjologii i Żywienia Zwierząt im. Jana Kielanowskiego PAN (Kielanowski Institute of Animal Physiology and Nutrition): ul. Instytucka 3, 05-110 Jabłonna; tel. (22) 782-41-75; fax (22) 774-20-38; f. 1955; attached to Polish Acad. of Sciences; study of nutrition of ruminants, pigs and poultry, digestive processes, neuroendocrinology, endocrinology of reproduction; library of 5,000 vols; Dir Dr JACEK SKOMIAT.

Instytut Fizjologii Roślin im. Franciszka Górskiego PAN (Institute of Plant Physiology): ul. Niezapominajek 21, 30-239 Cracow; tel. (12) 425-18-33; fax (12) 425-18-

44; e-mail ifr@ifr-pan.krakow.pl; internet www.ifr-pan.krakow.pl; f. 1956; attached to Polish Acad. of Sciences; laboratories; plant growth and development, photosynthesis, biology of stress, metabolism of fungi; myxomycetes; Dir Prof. Dr hab. FRANCISZEK DUBERT; publ. *Acta Physiologiae Plantarum* (4 a year).

Instytut Genetyki i Hodowli Zwierząt PAN (Institute of Genetics and Animal Breeding): Jastrzębiec ul. Postępu 1, 05-552 Wólka Kosowska; tel. (22) 756-17-11; fax (22) 756-16-99; e-mail e.dymnicki@ighz.pl; internet www.ighz.edu.pl/index.htm; f. 1955; attached to Polish Acad. of Sciences; research work in animal genetics with special reference to farm animals; 130 mems; library of 6,000 vols, 5,640 journals; Dir Prof. EDWARD DYMNICKI; publs *Prace i Materiały Zootechniczne* (irregular), *Animal Science Papers and Reports* (4 a year).

Instytut Genetyki Roślin PAN (Institute of Plant Genetics): ul. Strzeszyńska 34, 60-479 Poznań; tel. (61) 823-35-11; fax (61) 823-36-71; e-mail office@igr.poznan.pl; internet www.igr.poznan.pl; f. 1961; attached to Polish Acad. of Sciences; basic genetic research on cultivated plants, genomics, biometrics, molecular biology, plant stresses; Dir Prof. WOJCIECH K. ŚWIĘCICKI; publ. *Journal of Applied Genetics* (4 a year).

Instytut Meteorologii i Gospodarki Wodnej (Institute of Meteorology and Water Management): ul. Podleśna 61, 01-673 Warsaw; tel. (22) 569-42-99; fax (22) 569-43-01; e-mail sekretariat@imgw.pl; internet www.imgw.pl; f. 1973 from fmr State Institute of Hydrology and Meteorology and the Institute of Water Management; collections of data from 61 meteorological stations, 149 meteorological posts, 893 hydrological posts, 1,027 pluviometric posts and 100 groundwater posts; library of 98,500 vols; Dir Prof. Dr eng. JAN ZIELIŃSKI; publ. *Wiadomości Instytutu Meteorologii i Gospodarki Wodnej* (Reports, 4 a year).

Instytut Nawozów Sztucznych (Fertilizers Research Institute): 24-110 Puławy; tel. (81) 473-14-00; fax (81) 473-14-10; e-mail ins@ins.pulawy.pl; internet www.ins.pulawy.pl; f. 1948; research in synthesis gases and hydrogen, nitric acid and its salts, mineral fertilizers, catalysts and sorbents, derivatives of methanol and urea, super-critical carbon dioxide extraction, environmental protection, unit operations, new processes and products; library of 36,960 vols; Gen. Dir CEZARY MOZEŃSKI; publ. *Przemysł Nawozowy* (4 a year).

Instytut Przemysłu Cukrowniczego (Institute of the Sugar Industry): ul. Inzynierskiej 4, 05-084 Leszno k Blonia, Warsaw; tel. (22) 725-90-88; tel. and fax (22) 725-66-61; e-mail dyrektor@inspcukr.pl; internet www.inspcukr.bip.waw.pl; f. 1898; research into all brs of the sugar industry; raw product, sugar beet, technological, analytical, mechanical, environmental protection depts; library of 1,500 vols; Dir ANTONI LAUDAŃSKI; publs *Burak cukrowy—gazeta dla plantatorów* (irregular), *Informacja dekadowa z przebiegu Kampanii* (9 a year), *Informacja o wynikach produkcyjnych i danych techniczo-technologicznych przemysłu cukrowniczego* (1 a year).

Instytut Roślin i Przetworów Zielarskich (Research Institute of Medicinal Plants): ul. Libelta 27, 61-707 Poznań; tel. (61) 665-95-40; fax (61) 665-95-51; e-mail iripz@iripz.pl; internet www.iripz.pl; f. 1947; botany, plant breeding, agrotechnology, pest control, phytochemistry, pharmaceutical analysis, technology of plant drugs, pharmacology; library of 13,000 vols; Dir PRZEMYSŁAW MROZIKIEWICZ; publ. *Herba Polonica* (4 a year).

Instytut Rozwoju Wsi i Rolnictwa PAN (Institute of Rural and Agricultural Development PAS): Nowy Świat 72, 00-330 Warsaw; tel. (22) 826-63-71; fax (22) 657-27-50; e-mail irwir@irwirpan.waw.pl; internet www.irwirpan.waw.pl; f. 1971; attached to Polish Acad. of Sciences; researches into the process of developing agriculture and rural soc.; 42 mems; library of 7,000 vols; Dir Prof. ANDRZEJ ROSNER; publs *Problems of Rural and Agricultural Development* (4 or 5 a year in Polish, summaries in English), *Village and Agriculture* (4 a year in Polish, 1 a year supplement of selected papers in English), studies and monographs (research series).

Instytut Rybactwa Śródlądowego im. Stanisława Sakowicza (Inland Fisheries Institute): ul. Oczapowskiego 10, 10-719 Olsztyn; tel. (89) 524-01-71; fax (89) 524-05-05; e-mail irs@infish.com.pl; internet www.infish.com.pl; f. 1951; Dir Prof. Dr hab. BOGUSŁAW ZDANOWSKI; publs *Archives of Polish Fisheries* (2 a year), *Komunikaty Rybackie* (6 a year).

Instytut Sadownictwa i Kwiaciarstwa (Institute of Pomology and Floriculture): ul. Pomologiczna 18, 96-100 Skierniewice; tel. (46) 833-20-21; fax (46) 833-32-28; e-mail isad@insad.pl; internet www.insad.pl; f. 1951; three divisions; pomology, floriculture, bee-keeping, covering field of applied research; five interdivisional laboratories: chemical, botanical, physiological, biochemical and isotopes; experimental greenhouses, phytotrone, cold storage and freezing facilities; 6 field stations; library of 37,578 vols; Dir Prof. Dr hab. DANUTA GOSZCZYŃSKA; publs *Journal of Fruit and Ornamental Plant Research* (1 a year), *Pszczelnicze Zeszyty Naukowe* (Bee Research Bulletin), *Sprawozdanie Roczne* (1 a year), *Zeszyty Naukowe Instytutu Sadownictwa i Kwiaciarstwa* (1 a year).

Instytut Środowiska Rolniczego i Leśnego PAN (Institute for Agricultural and Forest Environment): ul. Bukowska 19, 60-809 Poznań; tel. (61) 847-5603; fax (61) 847-3668; e-mail kedan@man.poznan.pl; internet www.isrl.poznan.pl; f. 1979; attached to Polish Acad. of Sciences; study of energy flow and cycling of matter, evaluation of ecological guidelines for landscape management, and strategy for nature conservancy; library of 35,000 vols; Vice-Dir Prof. Dr hab. ANDRZEJ KĘDZIORA.

Instytut Technologiczno-Przyrodniczy (Institute of Technology and Life Sciences): Falenty, Al. Hrabska 3, 05-090 Raszyn; tel. (22) 720-05-31; fax (22) 628-37-63; e-mail itep@itep.edu.pl; internet www.itep.edu.pl; f. 2010; advocacy, devt, education, research, training and innovation in agriculture; flood and drought management, grassland farming, land devt, sustainable devt of rural areas, rural sanitation, water management in agriculture; library of 47,200 vols and 8,900 vols in spec. collns; Dir Prof Dr hab. inż. EDMUND KACA; publs *Journal of Water and Land Development* (1 a year), *Problemy Inżynierii Rolniczej* (4 a year), *Water – Environment – Rural Areas* (2 a year).

Instytut Technologii Drewna (Wood Technology Institute): ul. Winiarska 1, 60-654 Poznań; tel. (61) 849-24-00; fax (61) 822-43-72; e-mail office@itd.poznan.pl; internet www.itd.poznan.pl; f. 1952; responsible for solving problems of the wood processing industry and for developing new technical processes; library of 27,351 vols; Dir Dr WŁADYSŁAW STRYKOWSKI; publ. *Drewno (Wood)* (2 a year).

Instytut Uprawy, Nawożenia i Gleboznawstwa—Państwowy Instytut Badawczy (Institute of Soil Science and Plant Cultivation—State Research Institute): Czartoryskich 8, 24-100 Puławy; tel. (81) 886-34-21; fax (81) 886-45-47; e-mail iung@iung.pulawy.pl; internet www.iung.pulawy.pl; f. 1917; pedology; utilization and protection of agricultural land; soil chemistry, plant physiology, biochemistry, microbiology, soil and crop management, production technology of cereals, forage crops, tobacco and hops, etc.; Dir Prof. Dr hab. SEWERYN KUKUŁA; publs *Monografie i Rozprawy Naukowe* (in Polish and summaries in English), *Pamiętnik Puławski* (2 or 3 a year), *Polish Journal of Agronomy* (2–4 a year), *Studia i Raporty IUNG-PIB* (in Polish), *Zalecenia Agrotechniczne* (every 5 years).

Instytut Warzywnictwa (Research Institute of Vegetable Crops): ul. Konstytucji 3 Maja 1/3, 96-100 Skierniewice; tel. (46) 833-22-11; fax (46) 833-31-86; e-mail iwarz@iwarz.pl; internet www.iwarz.pl; f. 1964; research into the devt of practical guidelines for the rational and economic devt of vegetable production; Dir Prof. Dr hab. FRANCISZEK ADAMICKI; publs *Biuletyn Warzywniczy* (Vegetable Research Bulletin, 2 a year), *Nowości Warzywnicze* (Vegetable Crops News, 2 a year).

Instytut Zootechniki (Institute of Animal Husbandry): k. Krakowa, 32-083 Balice; tel. (12) 258-81-11; fax (12) 285-67-33; e-mail izooinfo@izoo.krakow.pl; internet www.izoo.krakow.pl; f. 1950; 5 scientific depts, 11 experimental stations; library of 125,000 vols; Dir Prof. J. KRUPIŃSKI; publs *Annals of Animal Science* (4 a year), *Reports on Animal Performance Testing* (1 a year), *Wiadomosci Zootechniczne* (4 a year).

Morski Instytut Rybacki w Gdyni (Sea Fisheries Institute in Gdyni): ul. Kołłątaja 1, 81-332 Gdynia; tel. (58) 735-61-00; fax (58) 735-61-10; e-mail sekrdn@mir.gdynia.pl; internet www.mir.gdynia.pl; f. 1923; departments of ichthyology, oceanography, fishing technique, technology of fish processing, seafishery economics, scientific information; two branches at Szczecin and Swinoujście; library of 24,000 vols; Dir Doc. Dr hab. TOMASZ LINKOWSKI; publ. *Bulletin of the Sea Fisheries Institute*.

Państwowy Instytut Badawczy (National Veterinary Research Institute): ul. Partyzantów 57, 24-100 Puławy; tel. (81) 886-30-51; fax (81) 886-25-95; e-mail t.wijaszka@piwet.pulawy.pl; internet www.piwet.pulawy.pl; f. 1945; veterinary microbiology, immunology, parasitology, toxicology, etc.; 16 scientific departments including those at Bydgoszcz and Zduńska Wola, and 4 specialized laboratories; library of 18,345 vols; Dir Dr TADEUSZ WIJASZKA; publ. *Bulletin of the Veterinary Institute in Puławy* (4 a year).

ARCHITECTURE AND TOWN PLANNING

Instytut Gospodarki Mieszkaniowej (Housing Research Institute): ul. Filtrowa 1, 00-925 Warsaw; tel. (22) 825-09-53; fax (22) 825-06-83; e-mail igmuchm@polbox.com; internet www.orgmasz.waw.pl/w/jbr/k7.htm; f. 1952; research and development in housing problems: dwelling construction and stock, investment process, construction market; library of 8,770 vols, 76 periodicals; Dir Dr RYSZARD UCHMAN; publs *Problemy Rozwoju Budownictwa* (4 a year), *Sprawy Mieszkaniowe* (4 a year).

Instytut Gospodarki Przestrzennej i Mieszkalictwa (Institute of Spatial Management and Housing): ul. Targowa 45, 03-728 Warsaw; tel. (22) 619-13-50; fax (22) 619-

24-84; e-mail igpik@igpik.waw.pl; internet www.igpik.waw.pl; f. 1986; physical planning, architecture, municipal economy; library of 70,000 vols, including several special collns; Dir WŁODZIMIERZ BUCHALSKI; publ. *Geospatial information–key asset of spatial planning* (2 a year).

Instytut Techniki Budowlanej (Building Research Institute): ul. Filtrowa 1, 00-611 Warsaw; tel. (22) 825-04-71; fax (22) 825-52-86; e-mail itb@itb.pl; internet www.itb.pl; f. 1945; research in the use of building materials and methods of construction; library of 104,000 vols; Dir MAREK KAPROŃ; publ. *Prace Instytutu Techniki Budowlanej* (4 a year).

ECONOMICS, LAW AND POLITICS

Instytut Badań Rynku, Konsumpcji i Koniunktur (Institute for Market, Consumption and Business Cycles Research): Al. Jerozolimskie 87, 02-001 Warsaw; tel. (22) 628-55-85; fax (22) 628-24-79; e-mail sekretariat@ibrkk.pl; internet ibrkk.pl; f. 1950; 135 mems; library of 40,000 vols; Dir Dr hab. RYSZARD MICHALSKI; publs *Bieżąca informacja o publikacjach z zakresu rynku w kraju i na świecie* (12 a year), *Biuletyn Informacyjny COINTE* (6 a year), *Materiały Informacyjno-Szkolebiowe* (series), *Przedsiębiorstwo i Rynek* (4 a year), *Przegląd Dokumentacyjny* (4 a year), *Rocznik IRWIK* (series).

Instytut Ekspertyz Sądowych (Institute of Forensic Research): ul. Westerplatte 9, 31-033 Cracow; tel. (12) 422-87-55; fax (12) 422-38-50; e-mail ies@ies.krakow.pl; internet www.ies.krakow.pl; f. 1929; depts of criminalistics, traffic accident investigation, forensic toxicology, forensic psychology, forensic haemogenetics; library of 9,862 vols; Dir Assoc. Prof. MARIA KAŁA; publs *Paragraf na Drodze* (12 a year), *Z Zagadnień Nauk Sądowych* (Problems of Forensic Sciences, 4 a year).

Instytut Przedsiębiorstwa (Institute of Entrerprise): ul. Madalińskiego 6/8, pok.106, 02-554 Warsaw; tel. 848-59-28; fax 564-86-71; e-mail rstach@sgh.waw.pl; internet www.sgh.waw.pl; f. 2006; research on enterprise devt and competitiveness of enterprises and regions; organizes lectures for general audience, doctoral seminars, and confs; Dir Prof. Dr hab. IRENA LICHNIAK; Sec. RENATA STACHOWICZ; publs *Studia i Analizy* (3 or 4 a year), *Mongrafie i Opracowania* (2 a year), *Szara Seria* (3 or 4 a year).

Instytut Nauk Ekonomicznych PAN (Institute of Economics of the Polish Academy of Sciences): Pałac Staszica, ul. Nowy Świat 72, 00-330 Warsaw; tel. (22) 657-27-07; fax (22) 826-72-54; e-mail inepan@inepan.waw.pl; internet www.inepan.waw.pl; f. 1981; attached to Polish Acad. of Sciences; researches contemporary economic theory, economic policy, analysis, forecasts and strategic studies concerning the Polish economy; analyzes world economy and European integration and their influence on the devt of the Polish economy; library of 15,000 vols; Scientific Ccl Chair. Prof. JERZY OSIATYŃSKI; Dir Prof. LESZEK JASIŃSKI; publs *Gospodarka Polski – Prognozy i Opinie* (Polish Economy – Forecasts and Opinions, 2 a year), *Monografie* (irregular), *Opera Minora* (irregular), *Raport o innowacyjności gospodarki* (Report on Innovation in the Polish Economy, 1 a year), *Studia Ekonomiczne* (4 a year), *Working Papers* (irregular).

Instytut Nauk Prawnych PAN (Institute of Legal Studies): Pałac Staszica, ul. Nowy Świat 72, 00-330 Warsaw; tel. (22) 826-75-71; fax (22) 826-78-53; e-mail inp@inp.pan.pl; internet www.inp.pan.pl; f. 1956; attached to Polish Acad. of Sciences; legal research; 66 mems; library of 44,000 vols; Dir Prof. Dr hab. WŁADYSŁAW CZAPLIŃSKI; publs *Archiwum Kryminologii* (irregular), *Droit Polonais Contemporain* (4 a year, in French and English), *Orzecznictwo sądów polskich* (12 a year), *Polish Yearbook of International Law* (in English), *Polska Bibliografia Prawnicza* (yearbook), *Studia Prawnicze* (4 a year).

Instytut Organizacji i Zarządzania w Przemyśle 'ORGMASZ' (Institute of Organization and Management in Industry): ul. Żelazna 87, 00-879 Warsaw; tel. (22) 654-60-61; fax (22) 620-43-60; e-mail instytut@orgmasz.waw.pl; internet www.orgmasz.waw.pl; f. 1953; library of 11,200 vols, spec. colln; Dir Inż RYSZARD WIECZORKOWSKI; publ. *Ekonomika i Organizacja Przedsiębiorstwa* (Business Economics and Organization, 12 a year).

Instytut Pracy i Spraw Socjalnych (Institute of Labour and Social Studies): Bellottiego 3B, 01-022 Warsaw; tel. (22) 636-72-00; fax (22) 636-72-00; e-mail instprac@ipiss.com.pl; internet www.ipiss.com.pl; f. 1963; research into labour, wages, income distribution, living standards, social security and social insurance, labour law, human resources management, collective labour relations, family problems and family policy; Dir BOŻENNA BALCERZAK-PARADOWSKA; publs *Materiały z Zagranicy* (irregular), *Opracowania PCZ* (irregular), *Polityka Społeczna* (Social Policy,12 a year), *Raport IPiSS* (irregular), *Zarządzanie Zasobami Ludzkimi* (Human Resources Management, 6 a year).

Instytut Studiow Politycznych PAN (Institute of Political Studies): ul. Polna 18/20, 00-625 Warsaw; tel. (22) 825-52-21; fax (22) 825-21-46; e-mail politic@isppan.waw.pl; internet www.isppan.waw.pl; f. 1990; attached to Polish Acad. of Sciences; develops theoretical work and empirical studies of post-communist societies; library of 17,330 vols; Dir Prof. WOJCIECH MATERSKI; publs *Civitas* (1 a year), *Europa Środkowo-Wschodnia* (Central-Eastern Europe Yearbook), *Kultura i Społeczeństwo* (Culture and Society, 4 a year), *Rocznik Polsko-Niemiecki* (Polish-German Yearbook), *Studia Polityczne* (Political Studies, 2 a year).

Instytut Turystyki (Institute of Tourism): ul. Merliniego 9a, 02-511 Warsaw; tel. (22) 844-63-47; fax (22) 844-12-63; e-mail it@intur.com.pl; internet www.intur.com.pl; f. 1972; social, economic and spatial aspects of tourism, professional training and provision of information; library of 12,609 vols, 3,304 periodicals, special collns of 3,280 vols; Dir Dr KRZYSZTOF ŁOPACIŃSKI; publ. *Problemy Turystyki* (4 a year).

Instytut Wymiaru Sprawiedliwości (Institute of Justice): ul. Krakowskie Przedmieście 25, 00-950 Warsaw; tel. (22) 826-03-63; fax (22) 826-24-01; e-mail iws@iws.org.pl; internet www.iws.org.pl; f. 1992; financed and supervised by the Min. of Justice but operates independently; sections of civil law, criminal law and criminology, and statistical analysis and methodology; library of 5,500 vols; Dir Prof. Dr hab. ANDRZEJ SIEMASZKO.

Instytut Zachodni im. Zygmunta Wojciechowskiego (Institute for Western Affairs): Mostowa 27, 61-854 Poznań; tel. (61) 852-76-91; fax (61) 852-49-05; e-mail izpozpl@rose.man.poznan.pl; internet www.iz.poznan.pl; f. 1945; for the study of Polish–German relations up to the acquisition of Polish western territories, and since 1945, and of Western European economic, political, historical, juridical, social and cultural matters; library of 100,000 vols; Dir Prof. Dr Hab. ANDRZEJ SAKSON; publ. *Przegląd Zachodni* (4 a year).

Państwowy Instytut Naukowy–Instytut Śląski w Opolu (Government Research Institute–Silesian Institute in Opole): ul. Piastowska 17, 45-081 Opole; tel. and fax (77) 453-60-32; e-mail instytutslaski@wp.pl; internet www.instytutslaski.opole.pl; f. 1957; departments: historical and German–Polish relationships research, regional research; library of 72,000 vols (history since 19th century, contemporary history, social economics, Silesiana); Dir Prof. Dr hab. STANISŁAW SENFT; publs *Region and Regionalism* (in English, irregular), *Śląsk Opolski* (4 a year), *Studia Śląskie* (1 a year), *Zeszyty Odrzańskie* (1 a year).

Polski Instytut Spraw Międzynarodowych (Polish Institute of International Affairs): 1, POB 1010, ul. Warecka 1, 00-950 Warsaw; tel. (22) 556-80-00; fax (22) 556-80-99; e-mail pism@pism.pl; internet www.pism.pl; f. 1996; research in int. affairs; courses for civil servants, conferences; library of 156,000 vols; Dir Dr SŁAWOMIR DĘBSKI (acting); publs *Biuletyn* (in Polish, irregular), *Europa* (journal, in Russian, 4 a year), *Polish Quarterly of International Affairs* (4 a year), *Polski Przegląd Dyplomatyczny* (in Polish, 6 a year), *Sprawy Międzynarodowe* (in Polish, 4 a year).

EDUCATION

Centrum Badań Polityki Naukowej i Szkolnictwa Wyższego (Centre for Science Policy and Higher Education): ul. Nowy Świat 69, 00-046 Warsaw; tel. and fax (22) 826-07-46; e-mail crphe@plearn.pl; f. 1973; planning and forecasting development of higher education; modernization of instruction and organization of higher education; Dir Prof. IRENEUSZ BIAŁECKI; publ. *Nauka i Szkolnictwo Wyższe* (Science and Higher Education, 2 a year).

Instytut Badań Edukacyjnych (Institute for Educational Research): ul. Górczewska 8, 01-180 Warsaw; tel. (22) 241-71-00; fax (22) 241-71-11; e-mail ibe@ibe.edu.pl; internet ibe.edu.pl; f. 1952; conducts research and devt work for education; prepares analyses, expert opinions, reports and forecasts for the Min. of Nat. Education; library of 100,000 vols; Dir Prof. MICHAL FEDEROWICZ; publ. *Edukacja* (4 a year).

Instytut Kształcenia Zawodowego (Institute of Vocational Education): ul. Jana Pawła II 14, 47-220 Kędzierzyn-Koźle; tel. (77) 483-40-53; fax (77) 483-40-53; f. 1972; 113 staff; library of 18,000 vols; Dir STANISŁAW KACZOR; publs *Biblioteka Kształcenia Zawodowego*, *Pedagogika Pracy* (1 a year), *Szkoła-Zawód-Praca* (1 a year).

FINE AND PERFORMING ARTS

Instytut Sztuki PAN (Institute of Art): ul. Długa 26/28, 00-950 Warsaw; tel. (22) 504-82-18; fax (22) 831-31-49; e-mail ispan@ispan.pl; internet www.ispan.pl; f. 1949; attached to Polish Acad. of Sciences; fine arts, architecture, music, theatre, film, cultural anthropology; 125 mems; library of 140,000 vols; photographic archive of 450,000 negatives; phonographic library of 80,000 items; 16,000 tapes; Dir Dr hab. LECH SOKÓŁ; publs *Almanach Sceny Polskiej* (Almanack of the Polish Stage, 1 a year), *Biuletyn Historii Sztuki* (4 a year), *Dagerotyp* (Daguerrotype, 1 a year), *Konteksty. Polska Sztuka Ludowa* (4 a year), *Kwartalnik Filmowy* (4 a year), *Muzyka* (4 a year), *Pamiętnik Teatralny* (4 a year), *Rzeczy Teatralne* (Theatre Miscellaneous, 1 a year).

HISTORY, GEOGRAPHY AND ARCHAEOLOGY

Instytut Archeologii i Etnologii PAN (Institute of Archaeology and Ethnology of the Polish Academy of Sciences): Al. Solidarności 105, 00-140 Warsaw; tel. (22) 620-28-81; fax (22) 624-01-00; e-mail director@iaepan.edu.pl; internet www.iaepan.edu.pl; f. 1953; attached to Polish Acad. of Sciences; prehistoric, classical, early medieval and industrial archaeology, medieval and modern history of material culture, ethnography, ethnology; library of 185,000 vols; Dir Prof. ANDRZEJ BUKO; publs *Archaeologia Polona, Archaeology, Archaeology of Poland, Archaeologia Urbium, Archaeological Reports, Archaeological Review, Bibliotheca Antiqua, Culture of Early Medieval Europe, Ethnologia Polona, Inventaria Archaeologica, Library of Polish Ethnography, Polish Archaeological Abstracts, Polish Archaeological Researches, Polish Ethnographic Atlas, Polish Ethnography, Quarterly Journal of the History of Material Culture, Studia Ethnica, Studies and Materials of the History of Material Culture*.

Instytut Geodezji i Kartografii (Institute of Geodesy and Cartography): ul. Modzelewskiego 27, 02-679 Warsaw; tel. (22) 329-19-00; fax (22) 329-19-50; e-mail igik@igik.edu.pl; internet www.igik.edu.pl; f. 1945; cartography, geodesy, photogrammetry, remote sensing, GIS; library of 16,200 vols; Dir Dr MAREK BARANOWSKI; Chief of Library BARBARA SMYL; publs *Biuletyn Informacyjny Branżowego Ośrodka Informacji Naukowej, Informacja Bibliograficzna Geodezji i Kartografii* (12 a year), *Monographic Series* (1–3 a year), *Prace IGIK* (2–3 a year), *Proceedings of Institute of Geodesy and Cartography* (1–3 a year), *Rocznik Astronomiczny* (1 a year), *Technicznej i Ekonomicznej Geodezji i Kartografii* (4 a year).

Instytut Geografii i Przestrzennego Zagospodarowania im. S. Leszczyckiego PAN (Stanisław Leszczycki Institute of Geography and Spatial Organization): ul. Twarda 51/55, 00-818 Warsaw; tel. (22) 697-88-41; fax (22) 620-62-21; e-mail igipzpan@twarda.pan.pl; internet www.igipz.pan.pl; f. 1953; attached to Polish Acad. of Sciences; geomorphology, hydrology, climatology, geoecology, economic geography, urban and population studies, geography of agriculture and rural areas, global development, political geography, regional planning, environmental management, ecodevelopment, European studies, cartography, geographic information systems; library of 132,113 vols, 50,804 vols of periodicals, 4,483 atlases, 80,180 maps, 1,149 antique; Dir Prof. Dr PIOTR KORCELLI; publs *Atlas Warszawy* (irregular), *Bibliografia Geografii Polskiej* (1 a year), *Dokumentacja Geograficzna* (irregular), *Europa XXI* (irregular), *Geographia Polonica* (2 a year), *Geopolitical Studies* (irregular), *Monografie* (irregular), *Prace Geograficzne* (irregular), *Przegląd Geograficzny* (4 a year).

Instytut Historii im. Tadeusza Manteuffla PAN (Institute of History): Rynek Starego Miasta 29/31, 00-272 Warsaw; tel. and fax (22) 831-36-42; e-mail ihpan@ihpan.edu.pl; internet www.ihpan.edu.pl; f. 1953; attached to Polish Acad. of Sciences; studies political and social history from the Middle Ages to the modern era; specific fields of research: Poland and Central-Eastern Europe, origins and history of modern Poland, history of Polish culture, social changes in post-Second World War Poland, history of mass migrations in 19th and 20th centuries, history of totalitarian systems and the Second World War; library of 60,000 vols; Dir Assoc. Prof. ADAM MANIKOWSKI; Chief of Research Org. Dept HANNA KORDOWICZ; publs *Acta Poloniae Historica* (2 a year, in English), *Czasopismo Prawno-Historyczne* (2 a year), *Dzieje Najnowsze* (4 a year), *Kwartalnik Historyczny* (4 a year), *Odrodzenie i Reformacja w Polsce* (1 a year), *Roczniki Dziejów Społecznych i Gospodarczych* (1 a year), *Roczniki Historyczne* (1 a year), *Studia Zródłoznawcze. Commentationes* (1 a year), *Studia z Dziejów Rosji i Europy Środkowo-Wschodniej* (1 a year).

Zakład Archeologii Śródziemnomorskiej PAN (Research Centre for Mediterranean Archaeology): Nowy Świat 72, Pałac Staszica (pok. 33), 00-330 Warsaw; tel. and fax (22) 826-65-60; e-mail zaspan@zaspan.waw.pl; internet zaspan.waw.pl; f. 1956; attached to Polish Acad. of Sciences; study, documentation and publ. of results of Polish and foreign excavations in the Middle East, Nubian studies, incl. surveys and excavations; publs of ancient objects in Polish museums; library of 13,600 books, 6,900 vols of periodicals; Dir Prof. KAROL MYŚLIWIEC; Vice-Dir Prof. ZSOLT KISS; publs *Alexandrie* (irregular), *Deir el-Bahari* (irregular), *Etudes et Travaux, Nea Paphos* (irregular), *Nubia* (irregular), *Saqqara* (irregular), *Tell Atrib* (irregular), *Travaux du Centre d'Archéologie Méditerranéenne*.

LANGUAGE AND LITERATURE

Instytut Badań Literackich PAN (Institute of Literary Research): Nowy Świat 72, Pałac Staszica, 00-330 Warsaw; tel. and fax (22) 826-99-45; e-mail ibadlit@ibl.waw.pl; internet www.ibl.waw.pl; f. 1948; attached to Polish Acad. of Sciences; 20 scientific departments, and sections in Poznań, Toruń and Wrocław; research in the theory of literature, history of Polish literature, and sociology of literature; library of 450,000 vols, spec. colln: 85,000 vols; Dir Prof. ELŻBIETA SARNOWSKA-TEMERIUSZ; publs *Pamiętnik Literacki* (Literary Journal, 4 a year), *Teksty Drugie* (Texts, 6 a year).

Instytut Języka Polskiego PAN (Polish Language Institute): al. Mickiewicza 31, 31-120 Cracow; tel. and fax (12) 632-87-13; internet www.ijp-pan.krakow.pl; f. 1973; attached to Polish Acad. of Sciences; library of 20,000 vols; Dir Prof. Dr hab. PIOTR ŻMIGRODZKI; publs *Antroponimia Polski od XVI do końca XVIII w., Nazwy miejscowe Polski, Nazwy wodne Polski* (electronic version), *Onomastica* (1 a year), *Polonica* (1 a year), *Prace* (series), *Prace Instytutu Języka Polskiego PAN* (series), *Słownik gwar polskich* (1 a year), *Socjolingwistyka* (1 a year), *Słownik gwar Ostródzkiego, Słownik języka polskiego XVII i I polowy XVIII wieku, Słownik laciny średniowiecznej w Polsce, Studies in Polish Linguistics* (1 a year), *Słownik polskich leksemów potocznych, Słownik polszczyzny Jana Kochanowskiego, Wielki słownik języka polskiego* (electronic version).

MEDICINE

Centrum Onkologii, Instytut im. Marii Skłodowskiej-Curie (Marie Sklodowska-Curie Memorial Cancer Centre and Institute of Oncology): ul. Roentgena 5, 02-781 Warsaw; tel. (22) 546-20-00; internet www.coi.waw.pl; f. 1932; brs at Cracow and Gliwice; fundamental cancer research, clinical research, diagnosis and treatment, epidemiology; co-ordinates Nat. Cancer Programme; 247 scientific staff; library of 23,458 vols; Dir Prof. Dr hab. MAREK P. NOWACKI; publs *Nowotwory* (4 a year), *Journal of Oncology* (6 a year).

Instytut Biocybernetyki i Inżynierii Biomedycznej PAN (Institute of Biocybernetics and Biomedical Engineering): ul. Trojdena 4, 02-109 Warsaw; tel. (22) 659-91-43; fax (22) 659-70-30; e-mail ibib@ibib.waw.pl; internet www.ibib.waw.pl; f. 1975; attached to Polish Acad. of Sciences; collaborates with WHO; mem. of UNESCO Global Network for Molecular and Cell Biology; field of activities: biomeasurements, artificial internal organs, mathematical and physical modelling of physiological systems and processes, computerized image analysis, computer-aided medical diagnosis; library of 23,800 vols; Dir Prof. ANDRZEJ WERYŃSKI; publs *Biocybernetics and Biomedical Engineering* (4 a year), *Prace IBIB PAN* (IBIB PAN Reports, irregular).

Attached Centre:

Miedzynarodowe Centrum Biocybernetyki (International Centre for Biocybernetics): 02-109 Warsaw, ul. Trojdena 4; tel. (22) 659-91-43; fax (22) 658-28-72; e-mail maciej.nalecz@ibib.waw.pl; internet www.ibib.waw.pl/icb.html; f. 1988; attached to Polish Acad. of Sciences; int. centre for research and training in biocybernetics and biomedical engineering; organizes five seminars a year; Dir Prof. MACIEJ NAŁECZ; publ. *Lecture Notes of the ICB Seminars*.

Instytut Farmaceutyczny (Pharmaceutical Research Institute): ul. Rydygiera 8, 01-793 Warsaw; tel. (22) 456-39-00; fax (22) 456-38-38; e-mail kontakt@ifarm.waw.pl; internet www.ifarm.waw.pl; f. 1952; organic synthesis of pharmaceutically active substances, process development, pharmaceutical finished forms, bioequivalence and bioavailability of drug products; library of 12,200 vols, 350 periodical titles; Dir Dr WIESŁAW SZELEJEWSKI.

Instytut Farmakologii PAN (Institute of Pharmacology): ul. Smętna 12, 31-343 Cracow; tel. (12) 637-40-22; fax (12) 637-45-00; e-mail ifpan@if-pan.krakow.pl; internet www.if-pan.krakow.pl; f. 1954; attached to Polish Acad. of Sciences; behavioural, biochemical, molecular, electrophysiological, pharmacokinetic and histochemical aspects of psychopharmacology and neuropsychopharmacology; modelling and synthesis of potential, centrally acting agents; acclimatization of medicinal plants and their phytochemical investigation; library of 11,322 vols, 15,055 periodicals; Dir Prof. Dr hab. KRZYSZTOF WEDZONY; publ. *Pharmacological Reviews* (6 a year).

Instytut Genetyki Człowieka PAN (Institute of Human Genetics): ul. Strzeszyńska 32, 60-479 Poznań; tel. (61) 823-30-11; fax (61) 823-32-35; e-mail igcz@man.poznan.pl; internet www.igcz.poznan.pl; f. 1974; attached to Polish Acad. of Sciences; Dir Prof. Dr JERZY NOWAK.

Instytut Hematologii i Transfuzjologii (Institute of Haematology and Blood Transfusion): ul. Chocimska 5, 00-957 Warsaw; tel. (22) 849-85-07; fax (22) 848-89-70; e-mail hematol@ihit.waw.pl; internet www.ihit.waw.pl; f. 1951; Dir Prof. KRZYSZTOF WARZOCHA; publs *Acta Haematologica Polonica* (4 a year), *Sprawozdania Roczne z Działalności Instytutu* (1 a year).

Instytut Immunologii i Terapii Doświadczalnej im. Ludwika Hirszfelda PAN (L. Hirszfeld Institute of Immunology and Experimental Therapy): ul. Rudolfa Weigla 12, 53-114 Wrocław; tel. (71) 337-11-72; fax (71) 337-13-82; e-mail bednorz@iitd.pan.wroc.pl; internet www.iitd.pan.wroc.pl; f. 1952; attached to Polish Acad. of Sciences; research work in basic and clinical immunology, microbiology, immunochemistry, immunogenetics, experimental and bacteriophage therapy; library of 24,000 vols; Dir Prof. Dr ANDRZEJ GÓRSKI; publs *Archivum Immunologiae et Therapiae Experimentalis* (English, 6 a year), *Postępy Higieny i Medycyny Doświadczalnej* (Polish, 6 a year).

Instytut Kardiologii im. Prymasa Tysiąclecia Stefana Kardynała Wyszyńskiego (Cardinal Stefan Wyszyński Institute of Cardiology): ul. Alpejska 42, 04-628 Warsaw; tel. (22) 343-46-00; fax (22) 343-45-00; e-mail bn@ikard.pl; internet www.ikard.pl; f. 1980; library of 4,344 vols; Dir-Gen. Prof. WITOLD RUŻYŁŁO; publ. *Biblioteka Kardiologiczna* (Cardiological Library, irregular).

Instytut Matki i Dziecka (Mother and Child Research Institute): ul. Kasprzaka 17A, 01-211 Warsaw; tel. (22) 327-70-00; fax (22) 327-70-01; internet www.imid.med.pl; f. 1948; research into the physiology and medicine of reproduction; Dir Prof. Dr hab. WOJCIECH WOŹNIAK; publ. *Development Period Medicine* (4 a year).

Instytut Medycyny Doświadczalnej i Klinicznej im. M. J. Mossakowskiego PAN (Medical Research Centre): ul. Pawińskiego 5, 02-106 Warsaw; tel. (22) 608-64-93; fax (22) 668-55-32; e-mail sekretariat@cmdik.pan.pl; internet www.cmdik.pan.pl; f. 1967; attached to Polish Acad. of Sciences; depts of physiology and neurophysiology, neuroimmunology, neurochemistry, neuropathology, neurology, neurosurgery, experimental transplantology, endocrinology and cellular biology at the ultrastructural (immunocytochemical and histochemical) level located at the Ochota campus, attached to the Bielanski Hospital; one unit (Dept of Endocrinology) located at the Warsaw Medical Univ.; library of 10,000 vols, 164 periodicals; Dir Prof. Dr hab. ZBIGNIEW CZERNICKI; publ. *Folia Neuropathologica* (4 a year).

Instytut Medycyny Morskiej i Tropikalnej (Institute of Maritime and Tropical Medicine): ul. Powstania Styczniowego 9B, 81-519 Gdynia; tel. and fax (58) 622-33-54; e-mail poczta@immt.gdynia.pl; f. 1939; attached to Medical University of Gdańsk; research in maritime occupational health, tropical medicine and epidemiology, toxicology, microbiology, travel medicine; clinic; postgraduate courses; 340 staff; WHO Inter-Regional Collaborating Centre on Maritime Occupational Health; Dir Dr W. NAHORSKI; publ. *International Maritime Health* (4 a year).

Instytut Medycyny Pracy i Zdrowia Środowiskowego (Institute of Occupational Medicine and Environmental Health): ul. Kościelna 13, 41-200 Sosnowiec; tel. (32) 266-08-85; fax (32) 266-11-24; internet www.imp.sosnowiec.pl; f. 1950; occupational toxicology; Dir Prof. Dr hab. JERZY A. SOKAL.

Instytut Medycyny Pracy im. prof. dra med. Jerzego Nofera (Nofer Institute of Occupational Medicine): ul. Św. Teresy 8, 91-348 Łódź; tel. (42) 631-45-02; fax (42) 656-83-31; e-mail impx@imp.lodz.pl; internet www.imp.lodz.pl; f. 1954; research in occupational medicine and hygiene, physiology, psychology, toxicology, neurotoxicology, carcinogenesis, pathology and epidemiology, management of occupational health service, radiation protection and the diagnosis and treatment of occupational diseases and acute poisonings, scientific information; Dir Prof. KONRAD RYDZYŃSKI; publs *Medycyna Pracy* (Occupational Medicine, 6 a year), *International Journal of Occupational Medicine and Environmental Health* (in English, 4 a year), *Informacja Expresowa–Ostre Zatrucia* (Express Information–Acute Poisoning, 4 a year).

Instytut Medycyny Wsi im. Witolda Chodźki (W. Chodźko Institute of Agricultural Medicine): POB 185, ul. Jaczewskiego 2, 20-950 Lublin; tel. (81) 747-80-27; fax (81) 747-86-46; e-mail imw@galen.imw.lublin.pl; internet www.imw.lublin.pl; f. 1951; environmental and agricultural medicine, family doctor training, health service organization in rural areas; library of 14,000 vols; Dir Prof. Dr hab. JERZY ZAGÓRSKI; publs *Medycyna Ogólna* (electronic and 4 a year), *Sprawozdania z działalności Instytutu* (1 a year), *Annals of Agricultural and Environmental Medicine* (electronic and 2 a year), *Zdrowie Publiczne* (electronic and 4 a year).

Instytut Psychiatrii i Neurologii (Institute of Psychiatry and Neurology): ul. Sobieskiego /9, 02-957 Warsaw; tel. (22) 458-28-00; e-mail ipin@ipin.edu.pl; internet www.ipin.edu.pl; f. 1951; library of 26,300 vols; Dir Prof. STANISŁAW PUŻYŃSKI; publs *Postępy Psychiatrii i Neurologii* (4 a year), *Farmakoterapia w Psychiatrii i Neurologii* (4 a year), *Alkoholizm i Narkomania* (4 a year).

Instytut Zdrowia Publicznego (Institute for Public Health): ul. Chełmska 30/34, 00-725 Warsaw; tel. (22) 851-43-69; fax (22) 841-06-52; e-mail sekretariat@il.waw.pl; internet www.il.waw.pl; pharmaceutical microbiology and laboratory accreditation; library of 7,000 vols; Dir Prof. Dr hab. ZBIGNIEW E. FIJAŁEK; publs *Biuletyn Informacyjny Instytutu Leków* (irregular), *Biuletyn Leków* (4 a year).

Instytut Żywności i Żywienia (National Food and Nutrition Institute): ul. Powsińska 61/63, 02-903 Warsaw; tel. (22) 842-21-71; fax (22) 842-11-03; e-mail jarosz@izz.waw.pl; internet www.izz.waw.pl; f. 1963; multidisciplinary scientific research in the field of human nutrition; library of 15,000 vols; Dir MIROSŁAW JAROSZ; publs *Żywienie Człowieka i Metabolizm* (4 a year), *Żywność, Żywienie a Zdrowie* (4 a year).

Państwowy Zakład Higieny (National Institute of Hygiene): ul. Chocimska 24, 00-791 Warsaw; tel. (22) 849-76-12; fax (22) 849-74-84; internet www.pzh.gov.pl; f. 1918; 15 departments covering all aspects of epidemiology, bacteriology, virology, parasitology, vaccines and sera control, medical statistics, radiologic control and radiobiology, immunopathology, communal hygiene, foodstuffs, environmental toxicology, school hygiene, health education, biological contamination control; courses in public health; library of 45,000 vols; Dir-Gen. Prof. JAN K. LUDWICKI; publs *Roczniki Państwowego Zakładu Higieny* (4 a year), *Medycyna Doświadczalna i Mikrobiologia* (4 a year), *Przegląd Epidemiologiczny* (4 a year).

NATURAL SCIENCES

General

Instytut Historii Nauki PAN (Institute for the History of Science): Pałac Staszica, Nowy Świat 72, pok. 9, 00-330 Warsaw; tel. (22) 657-27-46; fax (22) 826-61-37; e-mail ihn@ihnpan.waw.pl; internet www.ihnpan.waw.pl; f. 1954; attached to Polish Acad. of Sciences; library of 20,000 vols; Dir Prof. Dr hab. KALINA BARTNICKA; publs *Analecta* (2 a year), *Archiwum Dziejów Oświaty* (1 a year), *Kwartalnik Historii Nauki i Techniki* (4 a year), *Medycyna Nowożytna* (2 a year), *Organon* (in French, English and Russian, 1 a year), *Rozprawy z Dziejów Nauki i Techniki* (1 a year).

Instytut Oceanologii PAN (Institute of Oceanology): ul. Powstańców Warszawy 55, POB 68, 81-712 Sopot; tel. (58) 551-72-81; fax (58) 551-21-30; e-mail office@iopan.gda.pl; internet www.iopan.gda.pl; f. 1953; attached to Polish Acad. of Sciences; marine physics, hydrodynamics, marine chemistry, marine ecology, genetics of marine organisms; library of 7,000 vols, 240 periodicals; Dir Prof. STANISLAW MASSEL; publ. *Oceanologia* (4 a year, in English).

Biological Sciences

Centrum Badań Ekologicznych PAN (Centre for Ecological Research): Dziekanów Leśny, Ul. M. Konopnickiej 1, 05-092 Łomianki; tel. (22) 751-30-46; fax (22) 751-31-00; e-mail cbe@cbe-pan.pl; internet www.cbe-pan.pl; f. 2002; attached to Polish Acad. of Sciences; population and community studies, landscape ecology, ecological bioenergetics, biogeochemistry, agroecology, polar research, hydrobiology, plant ecology, soil ecology, vertebrate ecology, modelling of ecological processes; library of 75,000 vols; Dir Prof. JANUSZ UCHMAŃSKI; publs *Polish Journal of Ecology* (original papers in English, 4 a year), *Wladomości Ekologiczne* (with English summary).

Instytut Biochemii i Biofizyki PAN (Institute of Biochemistry and Biophysics): ul. Pawińskiego 5A, 02-106 Warsaw; tel. (22) 659-70-72; fax (22) 592-21-90; e-mail secretariate@ibb.waw.pl; internet www.ibb.waw.pl; f. 1957; attached to Polish Acad. of Sciences; research work in the fields of molecular genetics, biotechnology, biochemistry, biophysics, bioinformatics; library of 16,000 vols, 140 periodicals, 1,000 online periodicals; Dir Prof. WŁODZIMIERZ ZAGÓRSKI-OSTOJA.

Instytut Biologii Doświadczalnej im M. Nenckiego (M. Nencki Institute of Experimental Biology): ul. Pasteura 3, 02-093 Warsaw; tel. (22) 822-28-31; fax (22) 822-53-42; internet www.nencki.gov.pl; f. 1918; attached to Polish Acad. of Sciences; scientific research work in the fields of biochemistry, cell biology, molecular biology, neurophysiology and experimental psychology; library of 68,000 vols; Dir Prof. JERZY DUSZYŃSKI; publs *Acta Neurobiologiae Experimentalis* (4 a year), *Acta Protozoologica* (4 a year).

Instytut Botaniki im. Władysława Szafera PAN (W. Szafer Institute of Botany): Lubicz 46, 31-512 Cracow; tel. (12) 421-51-44; fax (12) 421-97-90; internet bobas.ib-pan.krakow.pl; f. 1954; attached to Polish Acad. of Sciences; library of 164,533 vols; Dir Prof. Dr ZBIGNIEW MIREK; publs *Acta Palaeobotanica* (International Journal of Palaeobotany), *Fragmenta Floristica et Geobotanica Polonica* (Material on the Flora and Vegetation of Poland, in Polish), *Polish Botanical Journal*.

Instytut Chemii Bioorganicznej PAN (Institute of Bio-organic Chemistry): ul. Noskowskiego 12/14, 61-704 Poznań; tel. and fax (61) 852-85-03; e-mail ibch@ibch.poznan.pl; internet ww.ibch.poznan.pl; f. 1980; attached to Polish Acad. of Sciences; bio-organic chemistry, crystallochemistry of nucleic acids, proteins and their components; molecular biology, genetics and genetic engineering of plants, applied phytochemistry, biochemistry, bioinformatics; library of 3,300 vols; Dir Prof. Dr WOJCIECH T. MARKIEWICZ.

Instytut Dendrologii PAN (Institute of Dendrology): ul. Parkowa 5, 62-035 Kórnik; tel. (61) 817-00-33; fax (61) 817-01-66; e-mail idkornik@man.poznan.pl; internet www.idpan.poznan.pl; f. 1952; attached to Polish Acad. of Sciences; dendrology, acclimatization, systematics and geography of woody plants, tree genetics, tree physiology, seed physiology, tree resistance to pathogens, frost and pollution; 40 scientists; library of 40,000 vols; Dir Prof. JACEK OLEKSYN; publ. *Dendrobiology* (2 a year).

Instytut Ochrony Przyrody PAN (Institute of Nature Conservation): ul. A. Mickiewicza 33, 31-120 Cracow; tel. (12) 632-22-21; fax (12) 632-24-32; e-mail sekretariat@iop.krakow.pl; internet www.iop.krakow.pl; f. 1920; attached to Polish Acad. of Sciences; research work on all problems relating to nature conservation, biological conservation, landscape ecology, interaction between human activity and the biosphere; field stations in Wrocław and Zakopane; library of 21,000 vols, 19,000 periodicals, 19,000 maps and photographs; Dir Prof. HENRYK OKARMA; publs *Chrońmy Przyrodę Ojczystą* (Let Us Protect the Nature of our Homeland, 6 a year), *Nature Conservation* (in English, 1 a year), *Studia Naturae* (irregular).

Instytut Paleobiologii im. Romana Kozłowskiego PAN (Institute of Palaeobiology): ul. Twarda 51/55, 00-818 Warsaw; tel. (22) 697-88-50; fax (22) 620-62-25; e-mail paleo@twarda.pan.pl; internet www.paleo.pan.pl; f. 1952; attached to Polish Acad. of Sciences; library of 11,000 vols, 27,000 vols of periodicals; Dir Prof. HUBERT SZANIAWSKI; publs *Palaeontologia Polonica* (irregular), *Acta Palaeontologica Polonica* (4 a year).

Instytut Parazytologii im Witolda Stefańskiego PAN (W. Stefański Institute of Parasitology): ul. Twarda 51/55, 00-818 Warsaw; tel. (22) 620-62-26; fax (22) 620-62-27; e-mail iparpas@twarda.pan.pl; f. 1952; attached to Polish Acad. of Sciences; scientific research work in parasitology, including animal parasitism, its origin, prevalence, manifestations and effects in natural and experimental parasite-host systems; departments of biodiversity, molecular biology, epizootiology and pathology, and deer farming; library: documentation centre and library of 25,666 vols (e-mail: libripar@twarda.pan.pl); Dir Prof. ANDRZEJ MALCZEWSKI; Librarian Dr hab. WŁADYSŁAW CABAJ; publ. *Acta Parasitologica* (4 a year).

Instytut Systematyki i Ewolucji Zwierząt PAN (Institute of Systematics and Evolution of Animals): ul. Sławkowska 17, 31-016 Cracow; tel. (12) 422-19-01; fax (12) 422-42-94; e-mail office@isez.pan.krakow.pl; internet www.isez.pan.krakow.pl; f. 1865; attached to Polish Acad. of Sciences; library of 85,000 vols; Dir Prof. ADAM NADACHOWSKI; publs *Folia Biologica* (4 a year), *Acta Zoologica Cracoviensia* (4 a year).

Zakład Badania Ssaków PAN (Mammal Research Institute): ul. Gen. Waszkiewicza 1C, 17-230 Białowieża; tel. (85) 682-77-50; fax (85) 682-77-52; e-mail mripas@zbs.bialowieza.pl; internet www.zbs.bialowieza.pl; f. 1954; attached to Polish Acad. of Sciences; scientific research in biomorphology, ecology, ecophysiology, genetics, taxonomy and fauna of mammals; colln of 180,000 specimens; library of 34,000 vols; Dir Prof. Dr hab. JAN M. WÓJCIK; publ. *Acta Theriologica* (4 a year).

Zakład Biologii Wód im. Karola Starmacha PAN (Institute of Freshwater Biology): ul. Sławkowska 17, 31-016 Cracow; tel. (12) 421-50-82; fax (12) 422-21-15; f. 1952; attached to Polish Acad. of Sciences; study of the plant and animal communities in ponds, rivers and dam reservoirs and productivity of these ecosystems, hydrochemistry and fisheries; hydrobiological station at Goczałkowice; biological fisheries station at Brzączowice; library of 29,000 vols and 1,520 periodicals; Dir Dr GRAŻYNA MAZURKIEWICZ-BOROŃ; publs *Supplementa ad Acta Hydrobiologica*, *Ecohydrology and Hydrobiology*.

Mathematical Sciences

Instytut Matematyczny PAN (Institute of Mathematics): ul. Śniadeckich 8, POB 21, 00-956 Warsaw; tel. (22) 522-81-00; fax (22) 629-39-97; e-mail im@impan.gov.pl; internet www.impan.gov.pl; f. 1948; attached to Polish Acad. of Sciences; scientific research work in mathematics and applications; local brs in Cracow, Gdańsk, Katowice, Łódź, Poznań, Toruń and Wrocław; 100 mems; library of 134,000 vols; Dir Prof. Dr hab. STANISŁAW JANECZKO; publs *Acta Arithmetica* (online), *Annales Polonici Mathematici* (online), *Applicationes Mathematicae* (online), *Bulletin* (online), *Colloquium Mathematicum* (online), *Dissertationes Mathematicae* (online), *Fundamenta Mathematicae* (online), *Studia Mathematica* (online).

Attached Centre:

Międzynarodowe Centrum Matematyczne im. Stefana Banacha (Stefan Banach International Mathematical Centre): ul. Śniadeckich 8, POB 21, 00-956 Warsaw; tel. (22) 522-82-32; fax (22) 622-57-50; e-mail office@impan.pl; internet www.impan.pl/bc; f. 1972 by an agreement of Academies of East European countries; br. of the Institute of Mathematics; promotion of int. cooperation in mathematics through organizing research and training semesters, workshops, confs and symposia in different fields of mathematics; no permanent staff; Dir Prof. Dr hab. STANISŁAW JANECZKO.

Physical Sciences

Centrum Astronomiczne im. Mikołaja Kopernika PAN (Copernicus Astronomical Centre): ul. Bartycka 18, 00-716 Warsaw,; tel. (22) 841-10-86; fax (22) 841-00-46; e-mail camk@camk.edu.pl; internet www.camk.edu.pl; f. 1957; attached to Polish Acad. of Sciences; astronomy and astrophysics; library of 20,000 vols; Dir Prof. Dr hab. MAREK SARNA.

Centrum Badań Kosmicznych PAN (Space Research Centre): ul. Bartycka 18A, 00-716 Warsaw; tel. (22) 840-37-66; fax (22) 840-31-31; e-mail cbk@cbk.waw.pl; internet www.cbk.waw.pl; f. 1977; attached to Polish Acad. of Sciences; space physics, planetary geodesy, remote sensing; library of 9,000 vols; Dir Dr Hab. MAREK BANASZKIEWICZ; publ. *Artificial Satellites—Journal of Planetary Geodesy* (4 a year).

Centrum Fizyki Teoretycznej PAN (Centre for Theoretical Physics): Al. Lotników 32/46, 02-668 Warsaw; tel. (22) 847-09-20; fax (22) 843-13-69; e-mail cft@cft.edu.pl; internet www.cft.edu.pl; f. 1980; attached to Polish Acad. of Sciences; classical and quantum field theory, gen. relativity, statistical physics, quantum and atom optics, particle astrophysics; Dir Prof. LECH MANKIEWICZ.

Centrum Materiałów Polimerowych i Węglowych PAN (Centre of Polymer and Carbon Materials PAS): Marii Curie-Skłodowskiej 34, POB 20, 41-819 Zabrze; tel. (32) 271-60-77; fax (32) 271-29-69; e-mail sekretariat@cmpw-pan.edu.pl; internet www.cmpw-pan.edu.pl; f. 1968; attached to Polish Acad. of Sciences; divs of polymeric materials (3 laboratories), chemistry and physics of conducting and optical materials (3 laboratories), carbonaceous and polymer-carbon materials (1 laboratory) and clean energy (1 laboratory); library of 15,000 vols; Dir Prof. ANDRZEJ DWORAK; Dir for Scientific Affairs ANDRZEJ F. BOROWSKI; publ. *Journal of Applied Chemistry* (4 a year).

Institute of High Pressure Physics: POB 65, 01-142 Warsaw; located at: ul. Sokołowska 29/37, 01-142 Warsaw; tel. (22) 632-50-10; fax (22) 632-42-18; e-mail sylvek@unipress.waw.pl; internet www.unipress.waw.pl; f. 1972; attached to Polish Acad. of Sciences; effects of high pressure on metals and semiconductors, high pressure metal formation and crystal growth, cold isostatic pressing, hot isostatic pressing and sintering; manufacture of high pressure laboratory equipment; Dir Prof. Dr hab. SYLWESTER POROWSKI.

Instytut-Centrum Badań Molekularnych i Makromolekularnych PAN (Centre of Molecular and Macromolecular Studies): ul. Sienkiewicza 112, 90-363 Łódź; tel. (42) 684-71-13; fax (42) 684-71-26; e-mail cbmm@bilbo.cbmm.lodz.pl; internet www.cbmm.lodz.pl; f. 1972; attached to Polish Acad. of Sciences; hetero-organic chemistry, organic chemistry of sulphur, bio-organic chemistry, polymer physics, polymer chemistry, hetero-organic polymers, instrumental and elemental analysis; library: over 15,000 vols; Dir Prof. MARIAN MIKOŁAJCZYK.

Instytut Chemii Fizycznej PAN (Institute of Physical Chemistry): Kasprzaka 44/52, 01-224 Warsaw; tel. (22) 343-31-08; fax (22) 343-33-33; e-mail ichf@ichf.edu.pl; internet ichf.edu.pl; f. 1955; attached to Polish Acad. of Sciences; research work in physico-chemical fundamentals incl. chemical engineering and chemical technology as follows: physical chemistry of metal-hydrogen systems including surface science and heterogeneous catalysis, analytical physical chemistry and instrumentation, experimental thermodynamics of organic mixtures, spectroscopy, including special-purpose apparatus, calorimetry including special-purpose apparatus and instrumentation, theory of chemical kinetics, electrochemistry and corrosion, fuel cells, molten salts, process kinetics, statistical mechanics and thermodynamics of irreversible phenomena; library of 99,147 vols; Dir Prof. ALEKSANDER JABLONSKI.

Instytut Chemii Organicznej PAN (Institute of Organic Chemistry PAS): Kasprzaka 44/52, 01-224 Warsaw; tel. (22) 631-87-88; fax (22) 632-66-81; e-mail icho-s@icho.edu.pl; internet www.icho.edu.pl; f. 1954; attached to Polish Acad. of Sciences; research in synthetic organic chemistry and natural products chemistry; library of 28,648 vols; Dir Prof. SŁAWOMIR JAROSZ; Research Dir Prof. WITOLD DANIKIEWICZ; Deputy Dir Dr PIOTR LIPKOWSKI.

Instytut Fizyki PAN (Institute of Physics): Al. Lotników 32/46, 02-668 Warsaw; tel. (22) 843-70-01; fax (22) 843-09-26; e-mail director@ifpan.edu.pl; internet www.ifpan.edu.pl; f. 1953; attached to Polish Acad. of Sciences; research in condensed matter physics: semiconductors, magnetics, superconductors, atomic and molecular physics, quantum optics, spectroscopy, x-ray crystallography, crystal growth; 350 mems; library of 28,000 vols; Dir Prof. Dr hab. JACEK KOSSUT; publs *Acta Physica Polonica* (12 a year), *Monographs in Physics* (irregular), *Proceedings of Conferences in Physics* (irregular).

Instytut Fizyki Plazmy i Laserowej Mikrosyntezy im. Sylwestra Kaliskiego (S. Kaliski Institute of Plasma Physics and Laser Microfusion): ul. Hery 23, 01-497 Warsaw; tel. (22) 638-14-60; fax (22) 666-83-72; e-mail office@ifpilm.pl; internet www.ifpilm.waw.pl; f. 1976; library of 1,000 vols; Dir Prof. ANDRZEJ GAŁKOWSKI.

Instytut Fizyki Jądrowej im. Henryka Niewodniczańskiego Polskiej Akademii Nauk (Henryk Niewodniczański Institute of Nuclear Physics of Polish Academy of Sciences (IFJ PAN)): ul. Radzikowskiego 152, 31-342 Cracow; tel. (12) 662-80-00; fax (12) 662-84-58; e-mail dyrektor@ifj.edu.pl;

internet www.ifj.edu.pl; f. 1955; attached to Polish Acad. of Sciences; particle physics and astrophysics, nuclear physics and strong interactions physics, condensed matter physics, interdisciplinary research, physics methods in radiation and environmental biology, environmental physics, medical physics, dosimetry, nuclear geophysics, econophysics, radiochemistry and engineering of nano-materials; library of 19,000 vols; 8,000 journals; Dir-Gen. Prof. MAREK JEŻABEK.

Instytut Fizyki Molekularnej PAN (Institute of Molecular Physics): ul. Mariana Smoluchowskiego 17, 60-179 Poznań; tel. (61) 869-51-00; fax (61) 868-45-24; e-mail office@ifmpan.poznan.pl; internet www.ifmpan.poznan.pl; f. 1975; attached to Polish Acad. of Sciences; physics of magnetics, ferroelectrics and liquid crystals; molecular interactions in liquids; molecular electronics; nanostructures; radiospectroscopy (EPR, NMR, NQR); superconductivity and low-temperature physics; library of 23,500 vols; Dir Prof. Dr hab. ANDRZEJ JEZIERSKI; publ. *Molecular Physics Reports* (4 a year).

Instytut Geofizyki PAN (Institute of Geophysics): ul. Księcia Janusza 64, 01-452 Warsaw; tel. (22) 691-59-54; fax (22) 691-59-15; e-mail sn@igf.edu.pl; internet www.igf.edu.pl; f. 1952; attached to Polish Acad. of Sciences; seismology and physics of the Earth's interior, geomagnetism, palaeomagnetism, physics of the atmosphere, hydrology and polar research; library of 44,000 vols; Dir Prof. Dr hab. PAWEŁ ROWIŃSKI; publs *Acta Geophysica Polonica* (4 a year), *Publications* (irregular).

Instytut Katalizy i Fizykochemii Powierzchni PAN (Institute of Catalysis and Surface Chemistry): ul. Niezapominajek 8, 30-239 Cracow; tel. (12) 639-51-01; fax (12) 425-19-23; e-mail ncikifp@cyf-kr.edu.pl; internet www.ik-pan.krakow.pl; f. 1968; attached to Polish Acad. of Sciences; kinetics and mechanism of heterogeneous, homogeneous and enzymatic catalytic reactions, solid state chemistry, properties and dynamics of colloids, inter-facial phenomena, electrochemistry of interfaces; library of 9,000 vols; Dir Prof. MAŁGORZATA WITKO.

Instytut Mechaniki Górotworu PAN (Strata Mechanics Research Institute): ul. Reymonta 27, 30-059 Cracow; tel. (12) 637-62-00; fax (12) 637-28-84; e-mail dziurzyn@img-pan.krakow.pl; internet www.img-pan.krakow.pl; f. 1954; attached to Polish Acad. of Sciences; mechanics of granular media, rock deformation, gas and rock-mass outbursts, low-speed flow of fluids, dynamics of air flow, flow through porous media, micromeritics; library of 23,000 vols; Dir Prof. WACŁAW DZIURZYŃSKI; publ. *Archives of Mining Sciences* (4 a year).

Instytut Nauk Geologicznych PAN (Institute of Geological Sciences): Twarda 51/55, 00-818 Warsaw; tel. (22) 697-87-01; fax (22) 620-62-23; e-mail ingpan@twarda.pan.pl; internet www.ing.pan.pl; f. 1956; attached to Polish Acad. of Sciences; stratigraphy, sedimentology, tectonics, petrography, mineralogy and isotope geochemistry, quaternary geology, hydrogeology, micropalaeontology; runs undergraduate and PhD courses; library: (in Warsaw and Cracow) 42,700 books, 100,700 periodicals, 11,030 maps; Dir Prof. TERESA MADEYSKA; publs *Archiwum Mineralogiczne* (irregular), *Geologia Sudetica* (1 a year), *Studia Geologica Polonica* (irregular), *Studia Quaternaria* (1 a year).

Instytut Niskich Temperatur i Badań Strukturalnych PAN (Institute of Low Temperature and Structure Research PAS): POB 1410, 50-950 Wrocław 2; ul. Okólna 2, 50-422 Wrocław; tel. (71) 343-50-21; fax (71) 344-10-29; e-mail intibs@int.pan.wroc.pl; internet www.int.pan.wroc.pl; f. 1966; attached to Polish Acad. of Sciences; physics and chemistry of solids: electronic and crystallographic structure, low temperature phenomena, magnetism, superconductivity; library of 22,000 vols; Dir Prof. Dr hab. ANDRZEJ JEŻOWSKI; Scientific Sec. ANDRZEJ KOCZARSKI.

Instytut Problemów Jądrowych im. Andrzeja Sołtana (A. Sołtan Institute for Nuclear Studies): 05-400 Świerk/Otwock; tel. (22) 718-05-83; fax (22) 779-34-81; e-mail sins@ipj.gov.pl; internet www.ipj.gov.pl; f. 1983, fmrly part of Institute of Nuclear Research; library of 27,000 vols; nuclear physics, elementary particle physics, plasma physics, accelerator physics and technology, material research using nuclear technology, spectrometric technology and nuclear electronics; Dir Prof. ZIEMOWID SUJKOWSKI.

Państwowy Instytut Geologiczny (Polish Geological Institute): ul. Rakowiecka 4, 00-975 Warsaw; tel. (22) 849-53-51; fax (22) 849-53-42; e-mail sekretariat@pgi.gov.pl; internet www.pgi.gov.pl; f. 1919, name changed 1987; geological, hydrogeological and geo-environmental mapping; geological and hydrogeological national survey; central chemical laboratory; eight brs; geological museum; library of 160,000 vols, 32,000 bound periodicals, 520,000 maps and atlases, 326,000 geological documents; Dir Prof. TADEUSZ PERYT; publs *Bibliografia Geologiczna Polski* (Geological Bibliography of Poland, 1 a year), *Biuletyn* (irregular), *Geological Quarterly*, *Prace* (Memoirs, irregular).

Zakład Karbochemii PAN (Institute of Coal Chemistry): ul. Sowińskiego 5, 44-121 Gliwice; tel. (32) 238-07-80; fax (32) 231-28-31; e-mail inbox@karboch.gliwice.pl; internet www.karboch.gliwice.pl; f. 1954; attached to Polish Acad. of Sciences; research on structure, properties and reactivity of coals and studies on coal conversion methods; thermodynamics data banks, membrane separation processes, conducting polymers; library of 5,000 vols; Dir Prof. Dr hab. Inż. ZBIGNIEW FLORJAŃCZYK.

PHILOSOPHY AND PSYCHOLOGY

Instytut Filozofii i Socjologii PAN (Institute of Philosophy and Sociology): Nowy Świat 72, 00-330 Warsaw; tel. (22) 826-71-81; fax (22) 826-78-23; internet www.ifispan.waw.pl; f. 1956; attached to Polish Acad. of Sciences; library of 173,258 vols; Dir Prof. HENRYK DOMAŃSKI; publs *Archiwum Historii Filozofii i Myśli Spolecznej* (irregular), *ASK—Społeczeństwo—Badania—Metody* (irregular), *Etyka* (irregular), *Mediaevalia Philosophica Polonorum* (irregular), *Prakseologia* (irregular), *Studia Logica* (in English, 4 a year), *Studia Mediewistyczne* (irregular), *Studia Socjologiczne* (4 a year).

Instytut Psychologii PAN (Institute of Psychology): ul. Chodakowska 19/31, 03-815 Warsaw; tel. (22) 517-99-16; fax (22) 517-99-17; e-mail sekretariat@psychpan.waw.pl; f. 1980; attached to Polish Acad. of Sciences; social psychology, personality, general psychology, psycholinguistics, cognitive and decision processes, political psychology, ecological psychology, cross-cultural psychology; library of 8,000 vols; Dir Prof. BOGDAN WOJCISZKE; publ. *Studia Psychologiczne* (4 a year).

RELIGION, SOCIOLOGY AND ANTHROPOLOGY

Zakład Antropologii PAN (Institute of Anthropology): ul. Kuźnicza 35, 50-951 Wrocław 56; tel. (71) 343-86-75; fax (71) 343-81-50; e-mail sekretaria@antro.pan.wroc.pl; internet www.antro.pan.wroc.pl; f. 1952; attached to Polish Acad. of Sciences; biological aspects of social stratification, human growth and developmental, indicators of individual biological conditions, biological basis of human behaviour and reproduction; library of 18,500 vols; Dir Assoc. Prof. BOGUSŁAW PAWEŁOWSKI.

Żydowski Instytut Historyczny im. Emanuela Ringelbluma (Emanuel Ringelblum Jewish Historical Institute): ul. Tłomackie 3/5, 00-090 Warsaw; tel. (22) 827-92-21; fax (22) 827-83-72; e-mail secretary@jhi.pl; internet www.jhi.pl; f. 1947; incl. a museum of Jewish art and martyrology, archives; library of 60,000 vols, 600 MSS; Dir Dr ELEONORA BERGMAN; publs *Biuletyn* (4 a year, summary in English), *Kwartalnik Historii Zydow*.

TECHNOLOGY

Centralny Instytut Ochrony Pracy–Państwowy Instytut Badawczy (CIOP-PIB) (Central Institute for Labour Protection—National Research Institute): ul. Czerniakowska 16, 00-701 Warsaw; tel. (22) 623-36-78; fax (22) 623-36-95; e-mail oinip@ciop.pl; internet www.ciop.pl; f. 1950; research and devt on occupational health and safety; determination of exposure limits; standardization; testing and certification of machinery and manufacturing devices as well as personal and collective protective equipment; implementation and certification of occupational health and safety management systems; certification of the competence of personnel and educational bodies active in occupational health and safety; education and training; consultations; promotion; information and publishing; 281 mems; library of 30,000 vols; Dir Prof. DANUTA KORADECKA; publs *Bezpieczeństwo Pracy–Nauka i Praktyka* (Occupational Safety–Science and Practice, 12 a year), *International Journal of Occupational Safety and Health* (in English, 4 a year), *Podstawy i Metody Oceny Srodowiska Pracy* (Principles and Methods of Assessing the Working Environment, 4 a year).

Główny Instytut Górnictwa (Central Mining Institute): Plac Gwarków 1, 40-166 Katowice; tel. (32) 258-16-31; fax (32) 259-65-33; e-mail gig@gig.katowice.pl; internet www.gig.katowice.pl; f. 1945; research work in rock mechanics, mining systems, blasting technique, gas, dust, water and rock burst hazards, clean coal technologies utilization and recovery of waste water, material engineering, noise and vibration control, environmental protection; 608 mems; library of 390,000 vols; Gen.-Dir Prof. JÓZEF DUBIŃSKI; publs *Prace Naukowe* (Transactions, irregular, about 20 papers a year), *Prace Naukowe—Górnictwo i Srodowisko* (4 a year).

Instytut Automatyki Systemów Energetycznych (Institute of Power Systems Automation): ul. Wystawowa 1, 51-618 Wrocław; tel. (71) 348-42-21; fax (71) 348-21-83; e-mail bujko@iase.wroc.pl; internet www.iase.wroc.pl; f. 1949; automatic control systems, computer systems and networks, database systems, data communication for electric power system operation, expert systems, exploitation and management; library of 21,000 vols, 5,400 vols of reports; Dir Prof. Dr Ing. JAN BUJKO; publs *Biuletyn IASE* (2 a year in 12 a year *Energetyka* journal), *Informator Patentowy Energetyki* (4 a year), *Prace IASE* (1 a year).

Instytut Badań Systemowych PAN (Systems Research Institute): ul. Newelska 6, 01-447 Warsaw; tel. (22) 381-02-75; fax (22) 381-01-05; e-mail ibapan@ibspan.waw.pl;

internet www.ibspan.waw.pl; f. 1977; attached to Polish Acad. of Sciences; control and optimization theory and applications, methods of systems analysis, information technology; library of 45,000 vols; Dir Prof. Dr hab. ZBIGNIEW NAHORSKI; Deputy Dir for Scientific Research Prof. Dr hab. SLAWOMIR ZADROZNY; publs *Control and Cybernetics* (4 a year), *Working Papers IBS PAN* (continuous), *Badania Systemowe* (series of monographs).

Instytut Badawczy Dróg i Mostów (Road and Bridge Research Institute): ul. Jagiellońska 80, 03-301 Warsaw; tel. (22) 811-32-31; fax (22) 811-17-92; e-mail ibdim@ibdim.edu.pl; internet ibdim.edu.pl; Dir Prof. Dr hab. Inż. LESZEK RAFALSKI; publs *Drogi i Mosty* (Roads and Bridges, 4 a year), *Nowości Zagranicznej Techniki Drogowej* (3–4 a year), *Prace Instytutu Badawczego Dróg i Mostów* (4 a year), *Studia i Materiały* (irregular).

Instytut Biopolimerów i Włókien Chemicznych (Institute of Biopolymers and Chemical Fibres): ul. M. Skłodowskiej-Curie 19/27, 90-570 Łódź; tel. (42) 637-67-44; fax (42) 637-62-14; e-mail ibwch@ibwch.lodz.pl; internet www.ibwch.lodz.pl; f. 1952; chemistry, technology, application of chemical fibres, environmental protection, natural polymers, their modification, applied biotechnology, medical and agricultural applications of polymers and fibres; library of 9,548 vols; Man. Dir Dr DANUTA CIECHAŃSKA; publ. *Fibres and Textiles in Eastern Europe*.

Instytut Budownictwa Wodnego PAN (Institute of Hydroengineering): ul. Kościerska 7, 80-328 Gdańsk; tel. (58) 522-29-00; fax (58) 552-42-11; e-mail sekr@ibwpan.gda.pl; internet www.ibwpan.gda.pl; f. 1953; attached to Polish Acad. of Sciences; river, estuary and reservoir hydraulics, maritime hydraulics, soil mechanics and foundation engineering, environmental engineering; library of 24,000 vols; Dir Prof. ANDRZEJ SAWICKI; publs *Archives of Hydroengineering and Environmental Mechanics* (4 a year), *Proceedings* (irregular).

Instytut Chemii Nieorganicznej (Institute of Inorganic Chemistry): ul. Sowińskiego 11, 44-100 Gliwice; tel. (32) 231-30-51; fax (32) 231-75-23; e-mail sekret@ichn.gliwice.pl; internet www.ichn.gliwice.pl; f. 1948; library of 18,000 vols; Dir Dr Inż. BOŻENNA PISARSKA; publ. *Bieżąca Informacja Chemiczna seria—NIEORGANIKA* (Bibliography selected from current papers, 12 a year).

Instytut Chemii Przemysłowej (Industrial Chemistry Research Institute): Rydygiera 8, 01-793 Warsaw; tel. (22) 633-97-98; fax (22) 633-82-95; e-mail ichp@ichp.pl; internet www.ichp.pl; f. 1922; research into carbo- and petrochemistry, organic synthesis, polymer and plastics technology, industrial catalysis, household chemistry products and disinfectants, environmental impact technology, process safety, chemical process engineering, instrumental analysis, medical diagnostic tests, biotechnology; Bureau for Ozone Layer Protection; Nat. Centre for Ecological Management in the Chemical Industry; library of 49,600 vols, 55,540 periodicals; Dir Prof. JOZEF MENES; publ. *Polimery* (12 a year).

Instytut Chemii i Techniki Jądrowej (Institute of Nuclear Chemistry and Technology): ul. Dorodna 16, 03-195 Warsaw; tel. (22) 504-12-05; fax (22) 811-15-32; e-mail sekdyrn@ichtj.waw.pl; internet www.ichtj.waw.pl; f. 1955; library of 41,000 vols; Dir Prof. ANDRZEJ G. CHMIELEWSKI; publs *INCT Reports* (Series A and B, irregular), *Nukleonika* (4 a year, with 2 or 3 supplements).

Instytut Elektrotechniki (Electrotechnical Institute): ul. Pożaryskiego 28, 04-703 Warsaw; tel. (22) 812-20-00; fax (22) 615-75-35; e-mail iel@iel.waw.pl; internet www.iel.waw.pl; f. 1946; research and manufacture of electric machines, apparatus and appliances; library of 45,000 vols, 500 periodicals; Gen. Dir Dr WIESŁAW WILCZYŃSKI; publs *Nowa Elektrotechnika* (12 a year), *Prace Instytutu Elektrotechniki* (Proceedings of the Electrotechnical Institute).

Instytut Energetyki (Institute of Power Engineering): ul. Mory 8, 01-330 Warsaw; tel. (27) 211-02-00; fax (22) 836-63-63; e-mail instytut.energetyki@ien.com.pl; internet www.ien.com.pl; f. 1953; library of 53,000 vols; Man. Dr JACEK WAŃKOWICZ; publs *Biuletyn Instytutu Energetyki* (6 a year), *Prace Instytutu Energetyki* (irregular).

Instytut Energii Atomowej (Institute of Atomic Energy): 05-400 Otwock-Świerk; tel. (22) 718-00-01; fax (22) 779-38-88; e-mail iea@cyf.gov.pl; internet www.iea.cyf.gov.pl; f. 1983; fmrly Inst. of Nuclear Research; reactor technology, radiation protection and dosimetry, quality standards for nuclear reactors, condensed matter physics, nuclear power plants, radioactive waste management; library of 16,000 vols, 685 periodicals; Dir Prof. Dr hab. KRZYSZTOF WIETESKA.

Instytut Informatyki Teoretycznej i Stosowanej PAN (Institute of Theoretical and Applied Informatics): ul. Bałtycka 5, 44-100 Gliwice; tel. (32) 231-73-19; fax (32) 231-70-26; e-mail office@iitis.gliwice.pl; internet www/iitis.gliwice.pl; f. 1969; attached to Polish Acad. of Sciences; 35 staff; research areas: performance evaluation of computer networks, computer vision, quantum informatics; library of 6,000 vols; Dir Prof. Dr TADEUSZ CZACHORSKI; publ. *Archiwum Informatyki Teoretycznej i Stosowanej* (4 a year).

Instytut Inżynierii Chemicznej PAN (Institute of Chemical Engineering): ul. Bałtycka 5, 44-100 Gliwice; tel. (32) 234-69-15; fax (32) 231-03-18; e-mail secret@iich.gliwice.pl; internet www.iich.gliwice.pl; f. 1958; attached to Polish Acad. of Sciences; chemical and process engineering: chemical reaction engineering, adsorption, membrane separation, mass and heat transfer, environmental and bioprocess engineering, renewable energy sources; library of 6,580 vols; Dir Prof. Dr hab. inż. KRZYSZTOF WARMUZINSKI; publs *Inżynieria Chemiczna i Procesowa* (4 a year), *Prace Naukowe* (research papers, 1 a year).

Instytut Łączności (National Institute of Telecommunications): ul. Szachowa 1, 04-894 Warsaw; tel. (22) 512-81-00; fax (22) 512-86-25; e-mail info@itl.waw.pl; internet www.itl.waw.pl; f. 1951; telecommunications, data transmission, satellite telecommunications, optical transmission, information technology, radiocommunications, EMC; library of 56,405 vols; Dir WOJCIECH HALKA; publs *Journal of Telecommunications and Information Technology* (4 a year), *Telekomunikacja i Techniki Informacyjne* (4 a year).

Instytut Lotnictwa (Institute of Aviation): Al. Krakowska 110/114, 02-256 Warsaw; tel. (22) 846-00-11; fax (22) 846-44-32; e-mail ilot@ilot.edu.pl; internet www.ilot.edu.pl; f. 1926; library of 72,000 vols; Dir Dr WITOLD WIŚNIOWSKI; publs *Informacja Ekspresowa Lotnicza i Silnikowa* (12 a year), *Opracowania Problemowe* (15–20 a year), *Prace Instytutu Lotnictwa* (4 a year), *Prace Przemysłu Lotniczego* (1 a year), *Przegląd Dokumentacyjny* (12 a year), *Tematy Prac Wykonawczych w Instytucie Lotnictwa* (1 a year).

Instytut Maszyn Matematycznych (Institute of Mathematical Machines): ul. Ludwika Krzywickiego 34, 02-078 Warsaw; tel. (22) 621-84-41; fax (22) 629-92-70; e-mail imasmat@imm.org.pl; internet bi.imm.org.pl; f. 1957; computer science and technology, training and education; library of 28,000 vols; Dir ROMAN CZAJKOWSKI; publ. *Techniki Komputerowe—Biuletyn Informacyjny* (irregular).

Instytut Maszyn Przepływowych im. R. Szewalskiego PAN (R. Szewalskiego Institute of Fluid Flow Machinery): ul. Gen. J. Fiszera 14, 80-952 Gdańsk; tel. (58) 341-12-71; fax (58) 341-61-44; e-mail imp@imp.gda.pl; internet www.imp.gda.pl; f. 1956; attached to Polish Acad. of Sciences; fundamental research, design methods, construction and development of machines and equipment for energy conversion in flow, measuring techniques and instrumentation in connection with fluid-flow machines, solid-state mechanics, machinery diagnostics, plasma physics; library of 23,000 vols; Dir Prof. Dr hab. JAROSŁAW MIKIELEWICZ; publs *Transactions* (2 a year), *Zeszyty Naukowe* (bulletin, irreg.), *Archives of Thermodynamics* (4 a year), *Archives of Energetics* (2 a year).

Instytut Maszyn Spożywczych (Institute of Food Processing Machinery): ul. Otwocka 1B, 03-759 Warsaw; tel. (22) 619-12-61; fax (22) 619-87-94; e-mail ims@orgmasz.waw.pl; internet www.orgmasz.waw.pl/w/ims/ims_a.htm; f. 1954; research and application in all fields of food processing, marketing and catering machinery and equipment; automation; energy-saving techniques; library of 4,984 vols, 141 periodicals, 20,066 leaflets; Dir Assoc. Prof. WALDEMAR P. RACZKO; publs *Postępy Techniki* (Developments in Food Processing Technology, 3 a year), *Biuletyn Informacyjny* (Bulletin of Food Processing Machinery, irregular).

Instytut Mechanizacji Budownictwa i Górnictwa Skalnego (Institute for Mechanized Construction and Rock Mining): ul. Racjonalizacji 6/8, 02-673 Warsaw; tel. (22) 843-02-01; fax (22) 843-21-80; e-mail imb@imbigs.org.pl; internet www.imbigs.org.pl; f. 1951; mechanized construction, industry of construction material machinery, construction and road-building machinery; rock mining machinery; waste management and recycling; normalization, using systems and techniques of machines and equipment; quality systems and product certification; protection of man and environment in construction; construction materials, rock mining and road-building industry; training of building machinery operators; library of 6,997 vols, 49 periodicals; Dir STEFAN GORALCZYK; publs *Działalność Instytutu Mechanizacji Budownictwa* (1 a year), *Przegląd Mechaniczny*, *Wiadomości IMB* (4 a year).

Instytut Metali Niezelaznych (Institute of Non-ferrous Metals): ul. Sowińskiego 5, 44-100 Gliwice; tel. (32) 238-02-00; fax (32) 231-69-33; e-mail imn@imn.gliwice.pl; internet www.imn.gliwice.pl; f. 1952; processing of non-ferrous ores and other mineral materials; pyro- and hydrometallurgical processes of metals recovery from ores and concentrates, and recovery of accompanying metals; waste treatment and utilisation; new alloys and composites; processing of metals and alloys; environmental protection; analytical chemistry of metals; 422 mems; library of 35,000 vols, 270 current periodicals, 15,000 reports; Dir Prof. Dr ZBIGNIEW ŚMIESZEK; publ. *Biuletyn Instytutu Metali Nieżelaznych* (12 a year).

Instytut Metalurgii i Inżynierii Materiałowej im. Aleksandra Krupkowskiego PAN (A. Krupkowski Institute of Metallurgy and Materials Science): ul. W. Reymonta 25, 30-059 Cracow; tel. (12) 295-28-00; fax (12) 295-28-04; e-mail office@imim-pan.krakow.pl; internet www.imim.pl; f. 1953; attached to Polish Acad. of Sciences; metallurgical thermodynamics, physical metallurgy, metal working; library of 25,000 vols; Dir Prof. Dr hab. Inż. BOGUSŁAW MAJOR; publ. *Archives of Metallurgy and Materials* (4 a year).

Instytut Metalurgii Żelaza im. Stanisława Staszica (Stanislaw Staszic Institute of Ferrous Metallurgy): ul. K. Miarki 12–14, 44-100 Gliwice; tel. (32) 234-52-05; fax (32) 234-53-00; e-mail imz@imz.pl; internet www.imz.pl; f. 1945; library: 34,800 books, 21,850 vols of periodicals; Dir Dr ADAM SCHWEDLER; publ. *Prace Instytutu Metalurgii Żelaza* (transactions, 4 a year).

Instytut Mineralnych Materiałow Budowlanych (Institute of Mineral Building Materials): ul. Oświęcimska 21, 45-641 Opole; tel. (77) 456-3201; fax (77) 456-2661; e-mail immb@immb.opole.pl; internet www.immb.opole.pl; f. 1954; basic and applied research in mineral building materials technology, thermal engineering and environmental protection; br. in Cracow; library of 11,800 vols, 4,000 vols of reports; Dir Assoc. Prof. JERZY DUDA; publ. *Prace IMMB* (2 a year).

Instytut Morski (Maritime Institute): ul. Długi Targ 41/42, 80-830 Gdańsk; tel. (58) 301-16-41; fax (58) 301-35-13; internet www.im.gda.pl; f. 1950; economic and technical research in shipping, harbour and coastal engineering, corrosion, maritime law; 120 staff; library of 80,000 vols; Dir Asst Prof. Dr Eng. JAN CURZYTEK; Scientific Dir Prof. zw. Dr hab. Inż. BOLESŁAW MAZURKIEWICZ; publs *Informacja ekspresowa, Materiały Instytutu Morskiego, Prace Instytutu Morskiego, Przegląd Informacji, Zeszyty Problemowe Gospodarki Morskiej*.

Instytut Nafty i Gazu (Oil and Gas Institute): ul. Lubicz 25A, 31-503 Cracow; tel. (12) 421-00-33; fax (12) 421-00-50; e-mail office@inig.pl; internet www.igng.krakow.pl; f. 1945; oil and gas recovery industry, gas transport and storage, gas use, and related topics; library of 110,000 vols; Dir Prof. Dr hab Inż. MARIA CIECHANOWSKA; publs *Nafta-Gaz* (12 a year), *Prace, Przegląd Bibliograficzno-Faktograficzny 'Nafta-Gaz'* (4 a year).

Instytut Obróbki Plastycznej (Metal Forming Institute): ul. Jana Pawła 14, 61-139 Poznań; tel. (61) 657-05-55; fax (61) 657-07-21; e-mail inop@inop.poznan.pl; internet www.inop.poznan.pl; f. 1948; research and devt works on non-metallurgical metal forming; library of 24,500 vols; Dir HANNA WISNIEWSKA-WEINERT; publ. *Obróbka Plastyczna Metali* (4 a year).

Instytut Odlewnictwa (Foundry Research Institute): ul. Zakopiańska 73, 30-418 Cracow; tel. (12) 266-26-19; fax (12) 266-08-70; e-mail iod@iod.krakow.pl; internet czapla.iod.krakow.pl/infocast/inst_odl.html; f. 1946; research into foundry materials, technological processes, alloys and additives; library of 10,000 vols, 45 periodicals; Pres. Dr JERZY TYBULCZUK; publ. *Odlewnictwo – Nauka i Praktyka* (6 a year).

Instytut Podstaw Informatyki Polskiej Akademii Nauk (Institute of Computer Science Polish Academy of Sciences): ul. J. K. Ordona 21, 01-237 Warsaw; tel. (22) 836-28-41; fax (22) 837-65-64; e-mail ipi@ipipan.waw.pl; internet www.ipipan.waw.pl; f. 1976; attached to Polish Acad. of Sciences; library of 16,400 vols, 250 periodicals; research depts of Theoretical Foundations of Computer Science and Artificial Intelligence; Dir-Gen. Prof. JACEK KORONACKI; Dir (Scientific Affairs) BEATA KONIKOWSKA; Dir (Economic Affairs) BOGUSLAW MARTYNIAK; Sec. MICHAL CIESIOLKA; publs *Machine Graphics and Vision* (4 a year), *Prace IPI PAN* (ICS PAS Reports, irreg.).

Instytut Podstawowych Problemów Techniki PAN (Institute of Fundamental Technological Research): ul. Pawińskiego 5B, 02-106 Warsaw; tel. (22) 826-12-81; fax (22) 826-98-15; e-mail director@ippt.gov.pl; internet www.ippt.gov.pl; f. 1953; attached to Polish Acad. of Sciences; applied mechanics, vibrations, ultrasonics, ultrasound in medicine, acoustics, electromagnetic fields, mechanical systems, energy problems, automatics and robotics, building structures, computational science and engineering; library of 80,000 vols; Dir Prof. ANDRZEJ NOWICKI; Scientific Ccl Chair. Prof. KAZIMIERZ SOBCZYK; publs *Archives of Acoustics* (4 a year), *Archives of Civil Engineering* (4 a year), *Archives of Mechanics* (6 a year), *Biblioteka Akustyki i Ultradźwięków* (Acoustics and Ultrasound Series), *Biblioteka Mechaniki Stosowanej* (Applied Mechanics Series), *CAMES–Computer Assisted Mechanics and Engineering Sciences* (4 a year), *Engineering Transactions* (4 a year), *Prace IPPT* (IFTR Reports).

Instytut Przemysłu Gumowego 'Stomil' ('Stomil' Rubber Research Institute): ul. Harcerska 30, 05-820 Piastów; tel. (22) 723-60-25; fax (22) 723-71-96; internet www.ipgum.pl; f. 1953; research in all brs of rubber technology and its development; library of 6,000 vols; Dir Dr JACEK MAGRYTA; Scientific Board Chair. Prof. Dr hab. ZBIGNIEW FLORJAŃCZYK; publs *Elastomery* (6 a year), *Guma–Elastomery–Przetwórstwo Informacje bieżace* (12 a year), *Rubber–Elastomers–Processing Technology* (in English, 12 a year).

Instytut Przemysłu Organicznego (Institute of Industrial Organic Chemistry): ul. Annopol 6, 03-236 Warsaw; tel. (22) 811-12-31; fax (22) 811-07-99; e-mail ipo@ipo.waw.pl; internet www.ipo.waw.pl; f. 1947; research on plant pesticides and biocides, auxiliary chemical products, organic intermediate products, blasting materials, chemical safety, toxicology and ecotoxicology; 235 mems; library of 36,700 vols, 171 periodicals; Dir Dr KAROL BUCHALIK; publs *Central European Journal of Energetic Materials* (4 a year), *Organika—Prace Naukowe Instytutu Przemysłu Organicznego* (1 a year), *Pestycydy* (4 a year).

Instytut Spawalnictwa (Institute of Welding): ul. Bł. Czesława 16–18, 44-100 Gliwice; tel. (32) 231-00-11; fax (32) 231-46-52; e-mail is@is.gliwice.pl; internet www.is.gliwice.pl; f. 1945; fundamental and developmental research, acceptance tests, certification, consulting, training, safety of welders, standardization, manufacture; library of 12,000 vols, 36 periodicals; Dir Prof. JAN PILARCZYK; publ. *Biuletyn Instytutu Spawalnictwa* (6 a year).

Instytut Systemów Sterowania (Institute of Control Systems): ul. Długa 1-3, 41-506 Chorzów; tel. (32) 247-28-20; fax (32) 246-25-91; e-mail office@iss.pl; internet www.iss.pl; f. 1977; Dir LESZEK E. ŻYCHOŃ; publs *Prace Naukowe Instytutu Systemów Sterowania* (irregular), *Komunikaty Naukowe ISS*.

Instytut Szkła, Ceramiki, Materiałów Ogniotrwałych i Budowlanych w Warszawie (Institute of Glass, Ceramics, Refractory and Construction Materials in Warsaw): ul. Postępu 9, 02-676 Warsaw; tel. (22) 843-74-21; fax (22) 843-17-89; e-mail info@isic.waw.pl; internet www.isic.waw.pl; f. 1952; basic research on all aspects of glass and ceramics technology; library of 15,000 vols and spec. colln of 5,000 vols; Dir ZDZISŁAW STACHURA; publ. *Szkło i Ceramika* (6 a year).

Instytut Technologii Elektronowej (Institute of Electron Technology): Al. Lotników 32/46, 02-668 Warsaw; tel. (22) 548-77-00; fax (22) 847-06-31; e-mail cambroz@ite.waw.pl; internet www.ite.waw.pl; f. 1966; research and devt in physics and technology of low dimensional semiconductor structures for photonics, silicon semiconductor nanostructures and microsystems, sensors; designing of integrated schemes and systems; hybrid microelectronics; characterization of nanostructures; library of 11,000 vols; Dir Prof. Dr hab. inż. CEZARY A. AMBROZIAK; publs *Electron Technology Internet Journal* (online), *Biblioteka Elektroniki* (irregular).

Instytut Technologii Materiałów Elektronicznych (Institute of Electronic Materials Technology): ul. Wólczyńska 133, 01-919 Warsaw; tel. (22) 835-30-41; fax (22) 864-54-96; e-mail itme@itme.edu.pl; internet www.itme.edu.pl; f. 1979; library of 20,000 vols; Gen. Man. Dr ZYGMUNT ŁUCZYŃSKI; Scientific Dir Prof. ANDRZEJ JELEŃSKI; publs *Materiały Elektroniczne* (4 a year), *MST News – Poland* (4 a year).

Instytut Technologii Nafty im. Prof. Stanisława Pilata (Institute of Petroleum Processing): ul. Łukasiewicza 1, 31-429 Cracow; tel. (12) 617-75-28; fax (12) 617-75-22; e-mail itn@itn.com.pl; internet www.itn.com.pl; f. 1958; petroleum refining and petrochemistry, standardization of products and testing methods, new methods of analysis and production, fuel and oil additives; library of 20,000 vols; Man. Dir Dr LESZEK ZIEMIAŃSKI; publs *Nafta Gaz* (12 a year), *Biuletyn* (4 a year).

Instytut Transportu Samochodowego (Motor Transport Institute): ul. Jagiellońska 80, 03-301 Warsaw; tel. (22) 811-09-44; fax (22) 811-09-06; e-mail awojciech@its.waw.pl; internet www.its.home.pl; f. 1952; focuses on operation of motor transport in the market economy, road traffic organization, and environmental protection; library of 22,000 vols, 50 periodicals; Dir Dr ANDRZEJ WOJCIECHOWSKI; Scientific Cttee Chair. Prof. Dr hab. Inż. JERZY MERKISZ; publs *Transport Samochodowy* (4 a year), *Bezpieczeństwo Ruchu Drogowego* (4 a year), *Biuletyn Informacyjny* (6 a year).

Instytut Włókien Naturalnych (Institute of Natural Fibres): ul. Wojska Polskiego 71b, 60-630 Poznań; tel. (61) 845-58-00; fax (61) 841-78-30; e-mail sekretar@inf.poznan.pl; internet www.inf.poznan.pl; f. 1930; complex research on production and processing of natural fibres (flax, hemp, kenaf, jute, silk), environmental protection, processing of waste products, plant biotechnology, properties of fibre, yarn, fabrics and textiles, composites, flame retardants, plant protection; cultivation and harvesting of fibrous plants and natural dyestuffs; library of 20,278 vols, 7,800 in special collns; Gen.–Dir Prof. Dr RYSZARD KOZŁOWSKI; Scientific Board Chair. Prof. Dr BOGUMIL LASZKIEWICZ; publs *Euroflax* (2 a year), *Journal of Natural Fibers* (4 a year), *Natural Fibres, Włókna Naturalne* (1 a year).

Instytut Włókiennictwa (Textile Research Institute): ul. Brzezińska 5/15, 92-103 Łódź; tel. (42) 616-31-95; fax (42) 679-26-38; e-mail info@mail.iw.lodz.pl; internet www.iw.lodz.pl; f. 1945; textile raw materials, technology of yarn manufacturing, non-woven fabrics, textile chemical processing; library of 17,559 vols and 12,879 in spec. colln; Dir JOLANTA MAMENAS; Scientific Council Chair. Prof. Dr hab. KAZIMIERZ KOPIAS; publ. *Prace Instytutu Włókiennictwa* (1 a year).

Instytut Wzornictwa Przemysłowego (Institute of Industrial Design): ul. Świętojerska 5/7, 00-236 Warsaw; tel. (22) 860-00-66; fax (22) 831-64-78; e-mail iwp@iwp.com.pl; internet www.iwp.com.pl; f. 1950; research into design and ergonomics of industrial products; ergonomic research and data selection; design for the disabled; standardization; technical information service; organization of national and foreign exhibitions, seminars, conferences etc.; library of 42,000 vols, 270 titles of periodicals, collection of special editions, etc.; Dir Prof. HALINA WALTER; Scientific Council Pres. Prof. JERZY WUTTKE; publs *Studies and Materials*, *Express News*, *Design Library Series*.

Polski Komitet Normalizacyjny (Polish Committee for Standardization): Świętokrzyska 14, 00-050 Warsaw; tel. (22) 556-76-00; fax (22) 556-77-80; e-mail prezeskr@pkn.pl; internet www.pkn.pl; f. 1924; library has collections of Polish National Standards, ISO, IEC, EN and foreign standards; Pres. JANUSZ SZYMAŃSKI; publ. *Normalizacja* (12 a year).

Przemysłowy Instytut Automatyki i Pomiarów (Industrial Research Institute of Automation and Measurements): Al. Jerozolimskie 202, 02-486 Warsaw; tel. (22) 874-00-00; fax (22) 874-02-20; e-mail piap@piap.pl; internet www.piap.pl; f. 1965; development of automation equipment, measuring instruments and industrial robots; library of 24,000 vols; Dir Prof. STANISŁAW KACZANOWSKI; publ. *Pomiary Automatyka Robotyka* (12 a year).

Przemysłowy Instytut Elektroniki (Industrial Institute of Electronics): ul. Długa 44/50, 00-241 Warsaw; tel. (22) 831-52-21; fax (22) 831-30-14; e-mail pie@pie.edu.pl; academic year pie.edu.pl; automatic production lines and technical equipment, equipment for thermal and chemical processes, test and measuring systems; Dir Dr Inż. JÓZEF WIECHOWSKI; Scientific Board Chair. Prof. Dr hab. Inż. MIECZYSŁAW HERING; publ. *Prace PIE* (4 a year).

Przemysłowy Instytut Maszyn Budowlanych (Construction Equipment Research Institute): ul. Napoleona 2, 05-230 Kobyłka; tel. (22) 786-23-26; fax (22) 786-18-30; e-mail pimb@pimb.com.pl; internet www.pimb.com.pl; f. 1952; library of 14,000 vols; Dir Dr ANDRZEJ MACHNIEWSKI; publ. *Prace PIMB* (irregular).

Przemysłowy Instytut Maszyn Rolniczych (Industrial Institute of Agricultural Machinery): ul. Starołęcka 31, 60-963 Poznań; tel. (61) 871-22-00; fax (61) 879-32-62; e-mail office@pimr.poznan.pl; internet www.pimr.poznan.pl; f. 1946; design and testing of agricultural machines and equipment; library of 11,000 vols; Man. Dir Dr Inż. TADEUSZ PAWŁOWSKI; Scientific Council Chair. Prof. zZw. Dr Inż. ZDZISŁAW KOŚMICKI; publs *Ciągniki i maszyny rolnicze. Budowa, przeznaczenie* (every 2 years), *Journal of Research and Applications in Agricultural Engineering* (4 a year), *Katalog—cennik ciągników i maszyn rolniczych* (2 a year).

Przemysłowy Instytut Motoryzacji (Automotive Industry Institute): ul. Jagiellońska 55, 03-301 Warsaw; tel. (22) 811-14-21; fax (22) 811-60-28; e-mail info@pimot.org.pl; internet www.pimot.org.pl; f. 1972; Dir Dr Inż LECH SOKALSKI; Scientific Council Chair. Prof. Dr hab. Inz. JERZY BARZYKOWSKI.

Przemysłowy Instytut Telekomunikacji (Telecommunications Research Institute): ul. Poligonowa 30, 04-051 Warsaw; tel. and fax (22) 810-23-81; e-mail office@pit.edu.pl; internet www.pit.edu.pl; f. 1934; radar technology, microwave technology and antennas, command control communication, intelligent systems (C3I); library of 22,000 vols; Dir Dr ROMAN DUFRENE; Scientific Ccl Chair. Prof. Dr STANISŁAW SŁAWIŃSKI; publs *Postępy Radiotechniki* (2 a year), *Prace Przemysłowego Instytutu Telekomunikacji* (2 a year).

Libraries and Archives

Białystok

Biblioteka Politechniki Białostockiej (Library of Białystok University of Technology): ul. Wiejska 45C, 15-351 Białystok; tel. (85) 746-93-30; fax (85) 746-93-32; e-mail biblioteka@pb.edu.pl; internet biblioteka.pb.edu.pl; f. 1951; 236,525 books, 687 periodicals (print), 99,792 spec. collns; Chief Custodian JOANNA PUTKO; Deputy Dir GRAŻYNA BOŻEK.

Bydgoszcz

Wojewódzka i Miejska Biblioteka Publiczna im. dr. Witolda Bełzy w Bydgoszczy (Bydgoszcz Dr W. Bełza Voivodship and Public Municipal Library): ul. Długa 39, 85-034 Bydgoszcz; tel. (52) 323-80-08; fax (52) 328-73-90; e-mail sekretariat@wimbp.bydgoszcz.pl; internet www.wimbp.man.bydgoszcz.pl; f. 1903; 1,057,752 vols, incl. 8,220 old books, 6,520 maps and atlases, 1,826 MSS; Dir EWA STELMACHOWSKA; publ. *Bibliotekarz Kujawsko-Pomorski* (2 a year).

Cracow

Biblioteka Główna Akademii Pedagogicznej im. KEN (Main Library of the Pedagogical University of Cracow): ul. Podchorążych 2, 30-084 Cracow; tel. (12) 662-63-61; fax (12) 637-22-43; e-mail info@tessa.wsp.krakow.pl; internet www.ap.krakow.pl/biblio/; f. 1946; 654,504 vols, 48,526 periodicals, 1,857 sound recordings; also audiovisual materials, CD-ROMs and microforms; Dir TERESA WILDHARDT.

Biblioteka Jagiellońska (Jagiellonian Library): al. Mickiewicza 22, 30-059 Cracow; tel. (12) 663-35-55; fax (12) 633-09-03; e-mail ujbj@uj.edu.pl; internet www.bj.uj.edu.pl; f. 1364; colln: nat. library for books before 1800, central library of general scientific, Polish affairs, humanities, Polish writing of the 15th–18th centuries; 4,851,214 vols, 2,288,469 books, 862,664 periodicals, 35,266 online journals, 106,036 old prints (3,666 incunabula), 32,216 MSS, 38,588 music prints, 58,295 drawings and items of graphic art, 50,097 maps and atlases, and also flysheets and microforms; 44 univ. institute libraries; 1,961,321 units; Dir Prof. Dr ZDZISŁAW PIETRZYK; publs *Bibliotheca Iagellonica, Fontes et Studia* (irregular), *Bulletin of the Jagiellonian Library* (1 a year).

Biblioteka Naukowa PAU i PAN w Krakowie (Scientific Library of the Polish Academy of Arts and Sciences and the Polish Academy of Sciences in Cracow): ul. Sławkowska 17, 31-016 Cracow; tel. (12) 431-00-21; fax (12) 422-29-15; e-mail biblioteka@pau.krakow.pl; f. 1856; 339,570 annual vols of periodicals relating to the social and biological sciences, 147,066 MSS, old prints, cartography, graphic arts; 715,024 vols, 153,549 MSS, 345,069 periodicals; Dir KAROLINA GRODZISKA; publ. *Rocznik Biblioteki Naukowej PAU i PAN w Krakowie* (Yearbook).

Wojewódzka Biblioteka Publiczna w Krakowie (Cracow Voivode Public Library): ul. Rajska 1, 31-124 Cracow; tel. (12) 632-59-07; fax (12) 633-22-10; e-mail biblioteka@wbp.krakow.pl; internet www.wbp.krakow.pl; f. 1945; 550,000 vols; 771 regional brs; Dir Dr ARTUR PASZKO; publ. *Notes Biblioteczny* (2 a year).

Częstochowa

Biblioteka Główna Politechniki Częstochowskiej (Central Library of Częstochowa University of Technology): Al. Armii Krajowej 36, 42-200 Częstochowa; tel. (34) 361-44-73; fax (34) 365-15-07; e-mail biblioteka@adm.pcz.czest.pl; internet www.bg.pcz.czest.pl; f. 1950; 483,146 vols, incl. 151,182 books, 76,872 periodicals, 255,092 standards, patents, etc.; Dir Mgr MAŁGORZATA HANKIEWICZ.

Gdańsk

Biblioteka Gdańska PAN (Gdańsk Library of the Polish Academy of Sciences): Wałowa 15, 80–858 Gdańsk; tel. (58) 301-22-51; fax (58) 301-55-23; e-mail bgpan@task.gda.pl; internet www.bgpan.gda.pl; former City Library; f. 1596; collection: humanities, social sciences, maritime, Pomeranian and Gdańsk affairs; 539,542 vols, incl. 55,114 old books, 634 incunabula, 80,284 periodicals, 5,275 MSS, 9,542 maps, 8,000 graphics; Dir Dr MARIA PELCZAR; publ. *Libri Gedanenses* (1 a year).

Biblioteka Główna Politechniki Gdańskiej (Central Library of Gdańsk Technical University): ul. G. Narutowicza 11/12, 80-952 Gdańsk; tel. 47-25-75; fax 47-27-58; e-mail library@sunrise.pg.gda.pl; 1,096,000 vols incl. 494,000 books, 113,000 periodicals, 491,000 standards, patents; Librarian Mgr JANINA LIGMAN; publs *Bibliografia Publikacji Pracowników Naukowych Politechniki Gdańskiej* (Bibliography of Publications of Scientific Workers of the Technical University of Gdańsk, irregular), *Raport Politechniki Gdańskiej* (Report of the Technical University of Gdansk, 1 a year), *Wykaz Nabytków* (List of Acquisitions, 12 a year).

Gliwice

Biblioteka Główna Politechniki Śląskiej (Central Library of Silesian University of Technology): ul. Kaszubska 23, 44-100 Gliwice; tel. (32) 237-12-69; fax (32) 237-15-51; e-mail bg.sekr@polsl.pl; internet www.bg.polsl.pl; f. 1945; 589,063 vols in main library and 201,198 vols in departmental libraries, 92,223 journals and periodicals, 19,8704 spec. collns; collns incl. technical and technology sciences, mathematics, physics, chemistry, materials technology, metallurgy, chemistry, building, architecture, mineral and mining, geology, traffic, sanitary, environmental, civil, power, electrical and electronics, informatics, telecommunications and mechanical engineering, bioengineering; Dir Dr inz. KRZYSZTOF ZIOLO; Vice-Dir mgr MARIA RYCHLEWSKA; publ. *Biuletyn Biblioteki Głównej Politechniki Śląskiej*.

Katowice

Biblioteka Główna Śląskiego Uniwersytetu Medycznego w Katowicach (Main Library of the Medical University of Silesia): ul. Poniatowskiego 15, 40-055 Katowice; tel. (32) 208-35-37; fax (32) 208-35-87; e-mail biblio@sum.edu.pl; internet www.sum.edu.pl; f. 1948; 163,000 vols; Head of Library (vacant) EWA NOWAK; Librarian KATARZYNA BOJKO; publ. *Biuletyn Informacyjny SUM* (irregular).

Biblioteka Śląska (Silesian Library): Plac Rady Europy 1, 40-021 Katowice; tel. (32) 208-37-40; fax (32) 208-37-20; e-mail bsl@bs.katowice.pl; internet www.bs.katowice.pl; f. 1922; colln: social science, economics, literature relating to Silesia; 1,425,459 books (incl. 28,701 old vols), 200,416 vols of periodicals, 13,400 MSS, 17,758 maps and atlases, 8,047 drawings and prints, 26,842 postcards, 15,442 photographs, 242,645 documents of social life; Dir Prof. Dr hab. JAN MALICKI; publs *Bibliografia Bieżąca Województwa Śląskiego* (4 a year), *Bibliografia Śląska* (1 a year), *Bibliografia Województwa Śląskiego* (1 a year), *Książnica Śląska* (irregular).

Kielce

Biblioteka Główna Politechniki Świętokrzyskiej (Central Library of

Świętokrzyska Technical University): Al. Tysiąclecia Państwa Polskiego 7, 25-314 Kielce; tel. (41) 342-44-83; fax (41) 344-76-35; e-mail library@eden.tu.kielce.pl; internet lib.tu.kielce.pl; f. 1966; 115,425 books, 34,468 vols of periodicals, 50,881 standards; Dir DANUTA KAPINOS.

Łódź

Biblioteka Uniwersytetu Łódzkiego (Library of Łódź University): ul. Matejki 34/38, 90-237 Łódź; tel. (42) 635-60-02; fax (42) 665-57-42; e-mail bulinf@lib.uni.lodz.pl; internet www.lib.uni.lodz.pl/library; f. 1945; 1,073,217 books, 423,499 vols of periodicals, 3,676 MSS, 18,847 maps and atlases, 59,017 vols of music, 47,321 iconographic items, 3,026 microfilms, 31,934 microfiches; Dir MARIA WROCŁAWSKA.

Wojewódzka i Miejska Biblioteka Publiczna im. Marszałka Józefa Piłsudskiego w Łodzi (The Jozef Pilsudski Regional and Municipal Public Library in Lodz): ul. Gdańska 100/102, 90-508 Łódź; tel. (42) 636-68-35; fax (42) 637-21-02; e-mail sekretariat@hiacynt2.wimbp.lodz.pl; internet www.wimbp.lodz.pl; f. 1917; general; special subjects socio-economic science and the arts; 755,000 vols, 545,000 periodicals, 129,000 vols in special collns; Dir BARBARA CZAJKA; publ. *Sprawozdanie z działalności WiMBP* (1 a year).

Lublin

Biblioteka Główna Uniwersytetu Marii Curie-Skłodowskiej w Lublinie (Central Library of the M. Curie-Skłodowska University): ul. I. Radziszewskiego 11, 20-950 Lublin; tel. and fax (81) 537-58-35; e-mail kasbo@eos.umcs.lublin.pl; internet www.bg.umcs.lublin.pl; f. 1944; general scientific colln of 2,527,251 vols, including 494,867 vols of periodicals, 16,000 online journals, 803 MSS, 369,207 patents, 40,272 maps and atlases, 33,707 drawings and illustrations, 14,954 music scores, 19,215 ancient books, 4 incunabula, 2,814 dissertations, 4,900 audio cassettes and records; Dir Dr BOGUSŁAW KASPEREK.

Wojewódzka i Miejska Biblioteka Publiczna im H. Łopacińskiego (H. Łopacińskiego Voivodship and City Public Library): ul. Narutowicza 4, 20-950 Lublin; tel. (81) 532-39-47; fax (81) 532-39-47; f. 1907; scientific and educational collection; 710,000 vols, 16,000 old vols, 35,000 periodicals, 2,800 MSS, 3,500 maps and atlases, 18,000 drawings and illustrations, 2,600 microfilms; Dir ZOFIA CIURUŚ; publs *Bibliotekarz Lubelski* (1 a year), *Dostrzegacz Biblioteczny* (irregular).

Poznań

Biblioteka Kórnicka PAN (Library of the Polish Academy of Sciences, Kórnik): 62-035 Kórnik, near Poznań; tel. (61) 817-00-81; fax (61) 817-19-30; e-mail bkpan@amu.edu.pl; internet www.bkpan.poznan.pl; f. 1828; 191,784 books, 79,680 periodicals, 15,222 MSS, 30,055 old prints, 14,000 graphics; collections on history, history of Polish literature, history of art, history of culture; attached literary museum; Dir Prof. Dr hab. STANISŁAW SIERPOWSKI; publ. *Pamiętnik Biblioteki Kórnickiej*.

Biblioteka Raczyńskich (Raczyńsky Library): Plac Wolności 19, 61-739 Poznań; tel. (61) 852-94-42; fax (61) 852-98-68; e-mail sekret@bracz.edu.pl; internet www.bracz.edu.pl; f. 1829; scientific and educational collection; 1,592,654 vols, 17,854 old books, 44,851 periodicals, 10,038 MSS, 11,596 maps and atlases, 37,083 ex-libris, 21,374 photos, 1,514 drawings and illustrations, 164 microfilms, 84,517 audio and video items; Dir WOJCIECH SPALENIAK.

Biblioteka Uniwersytecka (Library of Adam Mickiewicz University): Skr. Poczt. 526, ul. Ratajczaka 38/40, 61-816 Poznań; tel. (61) 829-38-20; fax (61) 829-38-24; e-mail library@amu.edu.pl; internet lib.amu.edu.pl; f. 1919; supports the academic programmes of the University and the University's curriculum in natural sciences, the humanities, mathematics, chemistry, physics, social science, law and languages; supports research activity of the academic community; acquisition, organization and dissemination of information; provides training in computer literacy and web-based searches; 2,731,000 vols in central library, incl. 100,240 ancient vols, 5,600 MSS, 30,000 maps and atlases, 2,059,000 vols in departmental libraries; Dir Dr ARTUR JAZDON; publ. *Biblioteka* (1 a year).

Rzeszów

Biblioteka Główna Politechniki Rzeszowskiej (Central Library of Rzeszów University of Technology): ul. Pola 2, 35-959 Rzeszów; tel. (17) 854-25-33; fax (17) 854-25-33; e-mail bgprz@prz.rzeszow.pl; internet www.prz.rzeszow.pl/biblio/biblio.htm; f. 1951; 143,500 books, 33,600 vols of periodicals, 139,000 items in spec. colln; Dir Mgr ELŻBIETA KAŁUŻA.

Sopot

Biblioteka Uniwersytetu Gdańskiego (Library of the University of Gdansk): ul. Wita Stwosza 53, 80-308 Gdańsk; tel. (58) 523-32-10; fax (58) 523-32-09; e-mail bib@bg.ug.gda.pl; internet www.bg.univ.gda.pl; f. 1970; 882,200 books, 156,568 items in spec. collns, 295,443 vols of periodicals, 31,100 electronic journals; Dir GRAŻYNA JAŚKOWIAK.

Szczecin

Biblioteka Główna Uniwersytetu Szczecińskiego (Library of University of Szczecin): ul. A. Mickiewicza 16, 70-384 Szczecin; tel. (91) 444-23-60; fax (91) 444-23-62; internet bg.univ.szczecin.pl; f. 1985; 1,300,000 vols; Dir JOLANTA GOC; publs *Wykaz ważniejszych nabytków* (irregular), *Bibliografia publikacji pracowników Uniwersytetu Szczecińskiego*.

Książnica Pomorska im. Stanisława Staszica (Stanisław Staszic Pomeranian Library): ul. Podgórna 15, 70-205 Szczecin; tel. (91) 481-91-10; fax (91) 481-91-15; e-mail ksiaznica@ksiaznica.szczecin.pl; internet www.ksiaznica.szczecin.pl; f. 1905; 848,087 vols, 157,930 vols of periodicals, 3,243 MSS, 30,410 early books, 250,010 govt documents, 38,287 standards, 9,036 maps and atlases, 19,032 records, 4,755 tapes, 2,407 CDs, 3,986 microforms; Dir LUCJAN BĄBOLEWSKI; publs *Bibliografia Pomorza Zachodniego. Piśmiennictwo polskie i Piśmiennictwo zagraniczne* (Bibliography of Western Pomerania. Polish Literature and Foreign Literature), *Bibliotekarz Zachodniopomorski* (The West Pomeranian Librarian, 4 a year).

Toruń

Wojewódzka Biblioteka Publiczna – Książnica Kopernikańska w Toruniu (Copernicus Library of Toruń): ul. Słowackiego 8, 87-100 Toruń; tel. (56) 622-66-42; fax (56) 622-55-13; e-mail ksiaznica@ksiaznica.torun.pl; internet www.ksiaznica.torun.pl; f. 1923; international exchange of information, bibliographic enquiries, archival research, research on cultural and political history of Pomerania; 769,419 books, incl. 26,300 old books, 92,926 vols of periodicals, 700 MSS, 3,807 cartographic units; Dir Mgr TERESA E. SZYMOROWSKA; publs *Folia Toruniensia* (irregular), *Regional Bibliography of Kujawy-Pomerania* (on CD-ROM, 1 a year).

Warsaw

Archiwum Akt Nowych (Central Archive of Modern Records): ul. Hankiewicza 1, 02-103 Warsaw; tel. (22) 589-31-18; fax (22) 589-30-01; e-mail sekretariat@aan.gov.pl; internet www.aan.gov.pl; f. 1919; Dir TADEUSZ KRAWCZAK.

Archiwum Główne Akt Dawnych (Central Archives of Historical Records): ul. Długa 7, 00-263 Warsaw; tel. (22) 831-54-19; fax (22) 831-16-08; e-mail archagad@poczta.onet.pl; internet www.archiwa.gov.pl/agad; f. 1808; archives from 13th century to 1918; 22,946 vols, 412,704 records; Dir Dr HUBERT WAJS.

Archiwum Polskiej Akademii Nauk (Archives of the Polish Academy of Sciences): ul. Nowy Świat 72, 00-330 Warsaw; tel. (22) 657-28-48; fax (22) 826-81-30; e-mail archiwum@apan.waw.pl; internet www.apan.waw.pl; f. 1953; 26,000 vols; brs in Cracow, Poznań, Katowice; Dir Dr HANNA KRAJEWSKA; publ. *Biuletyn Archiwum PAN* (1 a year).

Biblioteka Narodowa (National Library): al. Niepodległości 213, 02-086 Warsaw; tel. (22) 608-29-99; fax (22) 825-52-51; e-mail biblnar@bn.org.pl; internet www.bn.org.pl; f. 1928; State central library; colln of writings in Polish and relating to Poland; basic foreign publications in the social sciences and humanities; library science literature; houses the Bibliographic Institute, the Institute of the Book and Reading; 2,609,188 books, 930,642 vols of periodicals, 27,366 MSS, 161,994 old books, 122,480 maps and atlases, 489,412 drawings, photographs, illustrations, leaflets and posters, 121,049 music scores, 2,311,044 items of social ephemera, 268,676 reels of microfilm; Dir Dr TOMASZ MAKOWSKI; publs *Biuletyn Informacyjny Biblioteki Narodowej* (Information Bulletin, 4 a year), *Polish Libraries Today* (in English, irregular), *Rocznik Biblioteki Narodowej* (National Library Yearbook, scientific library science periodical, electronic, with English summaries).

Biblioteka Publiczna m. st. Warszawy–Biblioteka Główna Województwa Mazowieckiego (Warsaw Public Library—Central Library of Masovia Province): ul. Koszykowa 26–28, POB 365, 00-950 Warsaw; tel. (22) 621-78-52; fax (22) 621-19-68; e-mail biblioteka@biblpubl.waw.pl; internet www.biblpubl.waw.pl; f. 1907; gen. colln; 1,249,083 vols, 13,000 old prints, 4,000 MSS, 18,400 maps and atlases, 39,600 standards, 3,933 drawings, 5,900 records; Dir MICHAŁ STRĄK; publ. *Bibliotekarz* (The Librarian, 12 a year).

Biblioteka Sejmowa (Sejm Library): ul. Wiejska 4, 00-902 Warsaw; tel. (22) 694-24-29; fax (22) 694-17-78; e-mail parlib@sejm.gov.pl; internet parlib.sejm.gov.pl; f. 1919; law, political and social sciences, modern history, economics; 507,000 vols, 291,000 books, 113,000 vols of periodicals, 97,000 parliamentary, official and int. publs, 1,067m. archival documents, 61,000 sound and video recordings of Sejm meetings; Dir Dr WOJCIECH KULISIEWICZ.

Biblioteka Szkoły Głównej Handlowej (Library of Warsaw School of Economics): ul. Rakowiecka 22B, 02-521 Warsaw; tel. (22) 564-95-05; fax (22) 564-86-90; e-mail infnauk@sgh.waw.pl; internet www.sgh.waw.pl/biblioteka; f. 1906; colln: economics, sociology, social policy, geography, economic history, politics, statistics and demography, accounting, finance, cooperative movement, law, labour problems, foreign trade, marketing, industry, agriculture, transport, business and management; 1,003,112 vols; Dir MARIA REKOWSKA; publs *Bibliografia Opublikowanego Dorobku Pracowników Naukowo-*

Dydaktycznych SGH, *Przegląd Bibliograficzny Czasopiśmiennictwa Ekonomicznego* (4 a year).

Biblioteka Uniwersytecka w Warszawie (Warsaw University Library): Dobra 56–66, 00-312 Warsaw; tel. (22) 552-56-60; fax (22) 552-56-59; e-mail buw@uw.edu.pl; internet www.buw.uw.edu.pl; f. 1816; 2,937,104 vols, incl. 130,342 early imprints, 676,477 periodicals, 6,990 MSS, 12,052 maps, 35,475 maps and prints, 17,839 microforms, 72,797 vols of printed music, 112,137 vols ephemera; Dir EWA KOBIERSKA-MACIUSZKO; publ. *Prace Biblioteki Uniwersyteckiej w Warszawie* (irregular).

Centralna Biblioteka Rolnicza 'Michała Oczapowskiego' (Central Agricultural Library named Michael Oczapowski): POB 360, 00-950 Warsaw; ul. Krakowskie Przedmieście 66, 00-950 Warsaw; tel. (22) 826-60-41; fax (22) 826-01-57; e-mail listy@cbr.net.pl; internet www.cbr.edu.pl; f. 1955; br. at Puławy; mem. of Agris-FAO, IAALD; centre for information and documentation in agriculture and for exchange with scientific instns abroad; 311,100 vols and 605 current periodical titles on agriculture and related sciences; Dir Dr RYSZARD MIAZEK; publs *Bibliography of Polish Agricultural and Food Economy Literature* (12 a year), *Current Information on Agriculture in the World* (52 a year).

Centralna Biblioteka Statystyczna (Central Statistical Library): al. Niepodległości 208, 00-925 Warsaw; tel. (22) 608-31-43; fax (22) 608-31-88; e-mail b.lazowska@stat.gov.pl; internet statlibr.stat.gov.pl; f. 1918; colln: scientific and specialized (economic and social subjects, with emphasis on statistics); 475,000 books, 1,500 periodical titles, 5,000 maps and atlases; Dir Mgr BOŻENA ŁAZOWSKA; publs *Bibliografie Piśmiennictwa Demograficznego*, *Bibliografia Polskiego Piśmiennictwa Statystycznego* (irregular), *Bibliografia Wydawnictw Głównego Urzędu Statystycznego* (irregular), *Biuletyn Nabytków*, *Roczniki zagraniczne w zbiorach Centralnej Biblioteki Statystycznej*.

Centralna Biblioteka Wojskowa im. Marszałka Józefa Piłsudskiego (Marshal Joseph Pilsudski Central Military Library): ul. Ostrobramska 109, 04-041 Warsaw; tel. (22) 681-79-52; fax (22) 681-69-40; e-mail informacja@cbw.pl; internet www.cbw.pl; f. 1919; 610,482 vols, 143,313 periodicals; special collection: 162,942 vols; Dir Col. Dr ALEKSANDRA SKRABACZ; publs *Informator Naukowy Centralnej Biblioteki Wojskowej* (irregular), *Polska Bibliografia Wojskowa* (Polish Military Bibliography, 4 a year).

Główna Biblioteka Lekarska (Central Medical Library): ul. Chocimska 22, 00-791 Warsaw; tel. (22) 849-78-51; fax (22) 849-78-02; e-mail gbl@gbl.waw.pl; internet www.gbl.waw.pl; f. 1945; collection of medical items, drawings and illustrations; 422,279 vols, 4,000 old vols, 1,156 MSS and 154,442 periodicals, 44,246 microforms; Dir Dr ALEKSANDER TULCZYŃSKI; publs *Biuletyn Głównej Biblioteki Lekarskiej* (2 a year), *Polska Bibliografia Lekarska* (yearbook).

Główna Biblioteka Pracy i Zabezpieczenia Społecznego (Central Library of Labour and Social Security): ul. Limanowskiego 23, 02-943 Warsaw; tel. (22) 642-04-73; fax (22) 642-19-27; e-mail gbpizs@gbpizs.gov.pl; internet www.gbpizs.gov.pl; f. 1974; attached to Min. of Labour and Social Policy; colln: labour, wages, social affairs and related matters; 55,988 vols, 16,661 periodicals; Dir ANNA PASZEK; publs *Bibliography of economic and social problems of labour* (1 a year), *Documentation Review* (12 a year), *Special Bibliographies* (irregular).

Naczelna Dyrekcja Archiwów Państwowych (Head Office of State Archives): ul. Rakowiecka 2D, 02-517 Warsaw; tel. (22) 565-46-00; fax (22) 565-46-14; e-mail ndap@archiwa.gov.pl; internet www.archiwa.gov.pl; f. 1951; 21,433 vols; Gen. Dir Dr ANDRZEJ BIERNAT (acting); publs *Archeion* (2 a year), *Miscellanea Historico-Archivistica* (1 a year), *Nowe Miscellanea Historyczne* (1 a year).

Ośrodek Informacji Naukowej Polskiej Akademii Nauk (Centre for Information Science of the Polish Academy of Sciences): Pałac Staszica, ul. Nowy Świat 72, 00-330 Warsaw; f. 1953; 23,000 vols, 900 scientific periodicals from all over the world on social science and other scientific disciplines; Dir Dr ANDRZEJ GROMEK; publs *Przegląd Informacji o Naukoznawstwie* (Review of Information on Science of Science, 4 a year), *Zagadnienia Informacji Naukowej* (Problems of Information Science, 2 a year), *Przegląd Literatury Metodologicznej* (Review of Methodological Literature, 2 a year).

Ośrodek Przetwarzania Informacji (Information Processing Centre): ul. Niepodległości 188B, 00-950 Warsaw; tel. (22) 825-12-40; fax (22) 825-33-19; e-mail opi@opi.org.pl; internet www.opi.org.pl; f. 1990; international co-operation, technology transfer, information services on research and development; database management; Dir Dr OLAF GAJL; publ. *Informator Nauki Polskiej* (Polish Research Directory, every 2 years).

Wrocław

Biblioteka Uniwersytecka we Wrocławiu (Wrocław University Library): Karola Szajnochy, 10 St, 50-076 Wrocław; tel. (71) 346-31-20; fax (71) 346-31-66; e-mail sekretariat1@bu.uni.wroc.pl; internet www.bu.uni.wroc.pl; f. 1945; Silesiaca and Lusatica; bibliography, int. relations between Poland and other Slavonic countries and Germany; 3,895,727 vols, 1,230,628 books, 369,488 journals, 42,363 microfilms, 475,777 spec. collns; Dir GRAŻYNA PIOTROWICZ; publs *Bibliografia Piśmiennictwa o Uniwersytecie Wrocławskim* (irregular), *Bibliografia Publikacji Pracowników Uniwersytetu Wrocławskiego* (1 a year), *Bibliothecalia Wratislaviensia* (irregular).

Dolnośląska Biblioteka Publiczna im. Tadeusza Mikulskiego we Wrocławiu (T. Mikulski Dolnoslaska Public Library): Rynek 58, 50-116 Wrocław; tel. (71) 344-39-03; fax (71) 344-18-08; e-mail wbp@wbp.wroc.pl; internet wbp.wroc.pl; 253,000 vols, 128,000 spec. colln; Dir Mgr ANDRZEJ TYWS; publ. *Książka i Czytelnik* (2 a year).

Zakład Narodowy im. Ossolińskich (Ossoliński National Institute): ul. Szewska 37, 50-139 Wrocław; tel. (71) 344-44-71; fax (71) 344-85-61; e-mail znio@znio.pl; internet www.oss.wroc.pl; f. 1817; 1,800,000 vols; colln incl. MSS, old prints, graphics, drawings, bookplates, postcards, numismatic material, decorative items, badges, social documents, microforms, digitalized objects; Dir Dr ADOLF JUZWENKO; Sr Librarian JOANNA GRZESKOWIAK-STEPOWICZ; publs *Czasopismo Zakładu Narodowego im. Ossolińskich* (1 a year), *Rocznik Wrocławski* (1 a year).

Museums and Art Galleries

Bydgoszcz

Muzeum Okręgowe im. Leona Wyczółkowskiego (L. Wyczółkowski Museum): Gdańska 4, 85-006 Bydgoszcz; tel. and fax (52) 585-98-16; e-mail muzeum@muzeum.bydgoszcz.pl; internet www.muzeum.bydgoszcz.pl; f. 1880; Polish art since 19th century; paintings and graphic art of Leon Wyczółkowski and gallery of contemporary Polish paintings; Archaeological and Local History brs and Coin Room; library of 46,000 vols; Dir Dr MICHAL WOŹNIAK.

Bytom

Muzeum Górnośląskie w Bytomiu (Upper Silesian Museum): Pl. Jana III Sobieskiego 2, 41-902 Bytom; tel. (32) 281-82-94; fax (32) 281-34-01; e-mail mgbytom@us.edu.pl; internet www.muzeum.bytom.pl; f. 1927 in Katowice, transferred in 1945; history, archaeology, ethnography, natural history, Polish and foreign art; branch museum (ul. W. Korfantego 34, Bytom); library of 51,300 vols; Dir MIECZYSŁAW DOBKOWSKI; publ. *Rocznik Muzeum Górnośląskiego w Bytomiu* (annals).

Cracow

Muzeum Archeologiczne w Krakowie (Archaeological Museum in Cracow): ul. Senacka 3, 31-002 Cracow; tel. (12) 422-75-60; fax (12) 422-77-61; e-mail mak@ma.krakow.pl; internet www.ma.krakow.pl; f. 1850; library of 11,753 vols, 16,726 periodicals; Dir Dr JACEK RYDZEWSKI; publs *Materiały Archeologiczne* (1 a year), *Materiały Archeologiczne Nowej Huty* (1 a year).

Muzeum Etnograficzne im. S. Udzieli w Krakowie (Ethnographic Museum in Cracow): ul. Krakowska 46, 31-066 Cracow; tel. (12) 430-60-23; fax (12) 430-63-30; internet www.mek.krakow.pl; f. 1910; folk art and folk culture of Poland; also foreign collections from Europe, Asia, Africa, S. America; archives; library of 30,000 vols; Dir MARIA ZACHOROWSKA; publ. *Rocznik Muzeum Etnograficznego w Krakowie* (1 a year).

Muzeum Historyczne m. Krakowa (Historical Museum of the City of Crakow): Krzysztofory, Rynek Główny 35, 31-011 Crakow; tel. and fax (12) 422-32-64; e-mail promocja@mhk.pl; internet www.mhk.pl; f. 1899; traditions, history and culture of the city of Crakow, model houses, arms and clocks, history of the theatre in Crakow, history and culture of the Jews in Crakow, history of the Crakow Fowler Brotherhood, upheaval and martyrdom of the Polish people in the period 1936–1956; special collection of 1,171 items; library of 23,810 vols; Dir MICHAŁ NIEZABITOWSKI; publ. *Krzysztofory-Zeszyty Naukowe* (1 a year).

Muzeum Narodowe w Krakowie (National Museum in Cracow): 3 Maja ave 1, 30-062 Cracow; tel. (12) 295-56-20; fax (12) 295-55-55; e-mail dyrekcja@muz-nar.krakow.pl; internet www.muzeum.krakow.pl; f. 1879; history, fine art, costume and textiles, arms and armour, numismatics, house-museums of Matejko, Wyspiański, Mehoffer and Szymanowski, Japanese art and technology; library of 300,000 vols and Czartoryski Library; Dir ZOFIA GOŁUBIEW; publs *Notae Numismaticae Zapiski Numizmatyczne* (Numismatic Notes, 1 a year), *Rozprawy i Sprawozdania Muzeum Narodowego w Krakowie* (yearbook).

Zamek Królewski na Wawelu (Wawel Royal Castle): Wawel 5, 31-001 Cracow; tel. (12) 422-51-55; fax (12) 422-19-50; e-mail zamek@wawel.krakow.pl; internet www.wawel.krakow.pl; f. 1930; collns of art in the Royal Castle: Italian Renaissance furniture, King Sigismund August's 16th-century colln of Flemish tapestries, Italian and Dutch painting, Polish carpets; Royal treasury: crown jewels, historical relics, banners, gold objects; armoury: Polish and West European weapons; objects of Oriental art: Persian and Turkish weaponry and tents; oriental rugs,

Chinese and Japanese pottery; colln relating to the history of Wawel Hill, other archaeological materials, Polish stove tiles from 15th to 18th centuries; 18th-century Meissen porcelain; library of 15,000 vols, 390 periodicals; Dir Prof. Dr hab. JAN OSTROWSKI; publs *Acta Archaeologica Waweliana*, *Biblioteka Wawelska*, *Studia Waweliana* (1 a year).

Frombork

Muzeum Mikołaja Kopernika (Nicholas Kopernik Museum): ul. Katedralna 8, 14-530 Frombork; tel. (55) 244-00-71; fax (55) 244-00-72; e-mail frombork@frombork.art.pl; internet www.frombork.art.pl; f. 1948; biographical exhibits; history of astronomy; astronomical observatory; example of Foucault's pendulum; planetarium; modern art gallery; history of medicine; herb garden; library of 20,500 vols; Dir Mgr HENRYK SZKOP; publ. *Komentarze Fromborskie* (1 a year).

Gdańsk

Centralne Muzeum Morskie (Polish Maritime Museum): ul. Olowianka 9–13, 80-751 Gdańsk; tel. (58) 301-86-11; fax (58) 301-84-53; e-mail info@cmm.pl; internet www.cmm.pl; f. 1960; depts of ports development, history of shipbuilding, history of maritime shipping and trade, marine fine arts, history of yachting, underwater archaeology, educational services; special vessel for underwater archaeological investigations; laboratory for conservation of artefacts recovered from sea; Lighthouse Museum in Rozewie; also br. in Hel (history of Polish fishery; open-air exhibition of types of fishing boats); br. in Tczew (history of Polish inland navigation); four historic ships (incl. sailing ship 'Dar Pomorza', fmr Polish school-ship); library of 42,000 vols, archives: plans, drawings, photos, documents; Dir Dr inż. JERZY LITWIN.

Muzeum Archeologiczne w Gdańsku (Archaeological Museum in Gdańsk): ul. Mariacka 25/26, 80-958 Gdańsk; tel. (58) 301-50-31; fax (58) 301-52-28; e-mail mag@archeologia.pl; internet www.archeologia.pl; f. 1953; library of 23,000 vols; Dir HENRYK PANER; publs *Pomorania Antiqua*, *Gdańsk Archaeological Museum African Reports*.

Muzeum Historyczne Miasta Gdańska (History Museum of the City of Gdańsk): ul. Długa 46/47, 80-831 Gdańsk; tel. (58) 767-91-00; e-mail kancelaria@mhmg.pl; internet www.mhmg.gda.pl; f. 1970; Dir ADAM KOPERKIEWICZ.

Muzeum Narodowe w Gdańsku (National Museum in Gdańsk): ul. Toruńska 1, 80-822 Gdańsk; tel. (58) 301-70-61; fax (58) 301-11-25; e-mail info@muzeum.narodowe.gda.pl; internet www.muzeum.narodowe.gda.pl; f. 1872; art since 12th century, craftwork since 15th century, photography, ethnography (collns held at various locations); library of 19,224 vols, 3,506 periodicals; Dir TADEUSZ PIASKOWSKI.

Kielce

Muzeum Narodowe w Kielcach (National Museum in Kielce): Pl. Zamkowy 1, 25-010 Kielce; tel. (41) 344-40-14; fax (41) 344-82-61; e-mail poczta@mnki.pl; internet www.mnki.pl; f. 1908; brs: Museum of Stefan Żeromski's early years, Henryk Sienkiewicz Museum in Oblęgorek; library of 40,000 vols; Dir Dr ROBERT KOTOWSKI; publ. *Rocznik Muzeum Świętokrzyskiego* (1 a year) from vol 10 *Rocznik Muzeum Narodowego w Kielcach*.

Łódź

Centralne Muzeum Włókiennictwa (Central Museum of Textiles): ul. Piotrkowska 282, 93-034 Łódź; tel. (42) 683-26-84; fax (42) 684-33-55; e-mail sekretariat@muzeumwlokiennictwa.pl; internet www.muzeumwlokiennictwa.pl; f. 1960; collections of textile tools and machines, documents of history of textile industry, Polish and foreign artistic textiles, industrial textiles, ancient and modern clothes, folk textiles; Łódź Wooden Architecture Open-Air Museum; library of 12,500 vols; Dir NORBERT ZAWISZA.

Muzeum Archeologiczne i Etnograficzne: Pl. Wolności 14, 91-415 Łódź; tel. (42) 632-84-40; fax (42) 632-97-14; f. 1956; archaeology, ethnography, numismatics; radio-chemical laboratory; library of 47,000 vols; Dir Dr hab. RYSZARD GRYGIEL; publ. *Prace i Materiały Muzeum Archeologicznego i Etnograficznego* (archaeology, ethnography, numismatics and conservation series).

Muzeum Sztuki w Łodzi (Art Museum): ul. Więckowskiego 36, 90-743 Łódź; tel. (42) 633-97-90; fax (42) 632-99-41; e-mail muzeum@muzeumsztuki.lodz.pl; internet www.muzeumsztuki.lodz.pl; f. 1929; departments: Gothic art; foreign painting of the 15th to 19th centuries; Polish painting since 17th century; international modern and contemporary art; Księży Młyn house with late 19th-century interior décor; library of 36,000 vols; Dir MIROSŁAW BORUSIEWICZ.

Lublin

Muzeum Lubelskie w Lublinie (Lublin Provincial Museum): The Castle (Zamek), ul. Zamekowa 9, 20-117 Lublin; tel. and fax (81) 532-17-43; e-mail kancelaria@zamek-lublin.pl; internet www.zamek-lublin.pl; f. 1906; regional archaeological, historical and ethnographic collection, Polish and foreign paintings and decorative art; armoury; numismatics; conservation dept; 14th-century Holy Trinity Chapel, with 15th-century paintings; 13th-century dungeon; library of 20,000 vols; Dir ZYGMUNT NASALSKI; publ. *Studia i Materiały Lubelskie*.

Państwowe Muzeum na Majdanku (State Museum at Majdanek): ul. Droga Męczenników Majdanka 67, 20-325 Lublin; tel. (81) 710-28-21; fax (81) 710-28-65; e-mail sekretariat@majdanek.pl; internet www.majdanek.pl; f. 1944; fmr Nazi concentration camp; Dir TOMASZ KRANZ; publ. *Zeszyty Majdanka* (irregular).

Olsztynek

Muzeum Budownictwa Ludowego — Park Etnograficzny w Olsztynku (The Folk Architecture Museum and Ethnographic Park in Olsztynek): ul. Leśna 23, 11-015 Olsztynek; tel. and fax (89) 519-21-64; e-mail mbl@muzeumolsztynek.com.pl; internet www.muzeumolsztynek.com.pl; f. 1962; protection of folk culture; 9,885 exhibits; library of 10,768 vols; Dir MARIAN JUSZCZYŃSKI.

Oświęcim

Państwowe Muzeum Auschwitz-Birkenau w Oświęcimiu/Auschwitz-Birkenau Memorial and Museum in Oświęcim: ul. Więźniów Oświęcimia 20, 32-603 Oświęcim; tel. (33) 844-81-02; fax (33) 843-19-34; e-mail muzeum@auschwitz.org.pl; internet www.auschwitz.org.pl; f. 1947; former Nazi concentration camp at Auschwitz-Birkenau, illustrating system of mass extermination; colln incl. concentration camp documents and objects; library of 30,000 vols, 2,500 periodicals and archives; Dir Mgr JERZY WRÓBLEWSKI; publs *Zeszyty Oświęcimskie* (in Polish and German), *Pro Memoria* (in Polish and English).

Poznań

Muzeum Archeologiczne w Poznaniu (Poznań Archaeological Museum): ul. Wodna 27, 61-781 Poznań; tel. (61) 852-82-51; fax (61) 852-82-51; e-mail muzarp@man.poznan.pl; internet www.muzarp.poznan.pl; f. 1857; archaeology of Greater Poland and the Nile basin; library of 54,087 vols; Dir Prof. Dr MARZENA SZMYT; publs *Biblioteka Fontes Archaeologici Posnanienses* (irregular), *Fontes Archaeologici Posnanienses* (1 a year), *Studies in African Archaeology* (irregular).

Muzeum Narodowe (National Museum): Al. Marcinkowskiego 9, 61-745 Poznań; tel. (61) 856-80-00; fax (61) 851-58-98; e-mail mnp@mnp.art.pl; internet www.mnp.art.pl; f. 1857; medieval art, European paintings 14th–19th centuries, Polish paintings since 15th century, prints and drawings, sculpture, numismatics, modern art; br. museums specializing in ethnography, Poznań history, military history, musical instruments, applied arts; library of 89,000 vols; Dir Prof. Dr hab. WOJCIECH SUCHOCKI; publs *Monographs*, *Studia Muzealne* (1 a year).

Sanok

Muzeum Budownictwa Ludowego w Sanoku (Museum of Folk Architecture in Sanok): ul. Traugutta 3, 38-500 Sanok; tel. (13) 463-09-04; fax (13) 463-53-81; e-mail skansen.sanok@pro.onet.pl; f. 1958; traditional architecture, interiors, folk arts and crafts, icons; library of 18,900 vols on the Orthodox church and ethnography; Dir Mgr JERZY GINALSKI; publs *Materiały Muzeum Budownictwa Ludowego w Sanoku* (every 2 years), *Acta Scansenologica* (every 2 years).

Szczecin

Muzeum Narodowe w Szczecinie (National Museum in Szczecin): ul. Staromłyńska 27, 70-561 Szczecin; tel. (91) 431-52-00; fax (91) 431-52-04; e-mail biuro@muzeum.szczecin.pl; internet www.muzeum.szczecin.pl; f. 1945; Pomeranian art and archaeology, Polish art since 19th century, African and Asian art, maritime and ethnological collections; library of 77,831 vols; Dir LECH KARWOWSKI; publs *Mare Articum—The Baltic Art Magazine* (2 a year), *Materiały Zachodniopomorskie* (1 a year).

Sztutowo

Państwowe Muzeum Stutthof w Sztutowie (State Museum in Sztutowo): ul. Muzealna 6, 82-110 Sztutowo; tel. (55) 247-83-53; fax (55) 247-83-58; e-mail stutthof@stutthof.pl; internet www.stutthof.pl/en/main.htm; former Nazi concentration camp of Stutthof; f. 1962; Dir ROMUALD DRYNKO; publ. *Zeszyty Muzeum Stutthof* (1 a year).

Toruń

Muzeum Etnograficzne w Toruniu (Ethnographical Museum in Toruń): Wały gen. Sikorskiego 19, 87-100 Toruń; tel. (56) 622-80-91; fax (56) 622-89-44; internet www.zabytki.pl/sources/muzea/t/torun-etnograf.html; f. 1959; folk culture of northern Poland; library of 18,142 vols; Dir Dr HUBERT CZACHOWSKI; publ. *Rocznik Muzeum Etnograficznego w Toruniu* (1 a year).

Muzeum Okręgowe w Toruniu (District Museum in Toruń): Rynek Staromiejski 1, Ratusz, 87-100 Toruń; tel. (56) 622-36-84; fax (56) 622-40-29; e-mail muzeum@muzeum.torun.pl; internet www.muzeum.torun.pl; f. 1861; 14th- to 20th-century art (painting, graphics, sculpture, handicrafts), Far-Eastern art, history, archaeology, militaria, numismatics, Copernicus museum; library of 25,000 vols; Dir Dr ANNA KOSICKA; publs *Rocznik Muzeum w Toruniu* (Toruń Museum Yearbook), *Biuletyn* (Bulletin, 4 a year).

Warsaw

Muzeum Historyczne m. st. Warszawy (History Museum of the City of Warsaw): Rynek Starego Miasta 28, 00-272 Warsaw; tel. (22) 635-16-25; fax (22) 831-94-91; f. 1948; exhibits relating to the history of Warsaw from the 10th century; library of 42,000 vols; Dir Prof. JANUSZ DURKO; publ. *Almanach Muzealny* (every 2 years).

Muzeum i Instytut Zoologii PAN (Institute of Zoology): ul. Wilcza 64, 00-679 Warsaw; tel. (22) 629-32-21; fax (22) 629-63-02; e-mail sekretariat@miiz.waw.pl; internet www.miiz.waw.pl; f. 1819; attached to Polish Acad. of Sciences; research in various fields of zoology; molecular and three-dimensional morphometrics laboratory; research station at Łomna near Warsaw; zoological collections of 8,178,000 specimens; archives and documents; library of 117,696 vols, 696 current periodicals, 4,953 maps; Dir Prof. WIESŁAW BOGDANOWICZ; publs *Annales Zoologici* (4 a year), *Fragmenta Faunistica* (2 a year), *Acta Ornithologica* (2 a year), *Acta Chiropterologica* (2 a year).

Muzeum Literatury im. Adama Mickiewicza (Adam Mickiewicz Museum of Literature): Rynek Starego Miasta 20, 00-272 Warsaw; tel. (22) 831-40-61; fax (22) 831-76-92; e-mail sekretariat@muzeumliteratury.pl; internet www.muzeumliteratury.pl; f. 1951; museum of literary history of Poland especially 19th and 20th centuries; library of 110,000 vols; Dir JANUSZ ODROWĄŻ-PIENIĄŻEK; publ. *Blok-Notes Muzeum Literatury*.

Muzeum Narodowe w Warsawie (National Museum in Warsaw): ul. Jerozolimskie 3, 00-495 Warsaw; tel. (22) 621-10-31; fax (22) 622-85-59; e-mail muzeum@mnw.art.pl; internet www.mnw.art.pl; f. 1862; paintings and sculpture; prints and drawings; numismatics; decorative arts and crafts; photography; Egyptian, Greek, Roman and Byzantine (Nubian) art; medieval and modern Polish art since 12th century; 14th- to 19th-century foreign painting; also administers the Poster Museum at Wilanów, Królikarnia Palace in Warsaw and, outside Warsaw, Nieborów Palace; Otwock Palace; library of 130,000 vols; Dir FERDYNAND RUSZCZYC; Dir for Colln, Research and Education Dr DOROTA FOLGA JANUSZEWSKA; publ. *Bulletin du Musée National de Varsovie* (4 a year).

Muzeum Niepodległości (Museum of Independence): ul. Solidarności 62, 00-240 Warsaw; tel. (22) 827-37-70; fax (22) 827-03-23; e-mail promocja@muzeumniepodleglosci.art.pl; internet www.muzeumniepodleglosci.art.pl; f. 1990; history of Polish independence movements; library of 29,230 vols, 3,960 periodicals; Dir Dr ANDRZEJ STAWARZ.

Muzeum Techniki w Warszawie (Warsaw Museum of Technology): Pałac Kultury i Nauki, 00-901 Warsaw; tel. (22) 656-67-59; fax (22) 620-47-10; f. 1875; popularization of science and technology and their history, preservation of monuments of technology; planetarium; cinema; local branches: Museum of Ancient Metallurgy in Nowa Słupia, Museum of the old Polish Basin in Sielpia, water-powered forges in Stara Kuźnica and Gdańsk, 19th-century blast furnace in Chlewiska, Museum of Industry in Old Rolling Mill, Warsaw; library of 17,160 vols; Dir JERZY JASIUK.

Muzeum Wojska Polskiego (Polish Military Museum): ul. Jerozolimskie 3, 00-495 Warsaw; tel. (22) 629-52-71; fax (22) 629-58-43; e-mail muzeumwp@muzeumwp.pl; internet www.muzeumwp.pl; f. 1920; colln of 79,000 weapons, uniforms, banners, decorations, etc; permanent exhibition showing Polish military history since 10th century; militaria from Asia, Africa, Australia; colln of modern paintings, sculptures and graphics; iconographic colln; conservation workshops for metal, textile, wooden, leather and paper exhibits; library of 40,000 vols; Dir Prof. JANUSZ CISEK; publ. *Muzealnictwo Wojskowe* (Military Museology, irreg.).

Polska Akademia Nauk Muzeum Ziemi w Warszawie (Museum of the Earth): ul. Na Skarpie 20–26, 00-488 Warsaw; tel. (22) 629-80-63; fax (22) 629-74-97; e-mail sekretariat@mz-pan.pl; internet www.mz-pan.pl; f. 1932; attached to Polish Acad. of Sciences; most important collections: Polish minerals, rocks, meteorites, fossil flora and fauna, Baltic amber; Dir Dr RYSZARD SZCZĘSNY; publ. *Prace Muzeum Ziemi PAN*.

Ogród Botaniczny – Centrum Zachowania Różnorodności Biologicznej PAN (Botanical Garden—Centre for the Conservation of Biological Diversity): 76, ul. Prawdziwka 2, POB 45, 02-973 Warsaw; tel. (22) 648-38-56; fax (22) 757-66-45; e-mail obpan@ikp.atm.com.pl; internet www.obpanwar.pl; f. 1974; attached to Polish Acad. of Sciences; conservation and evaluation of genetic resources of plants; library of 8,000 vols; Dir JERZY PUCHALSKI; publs *Biuletyn* (1 a year), *Prace* (reports, irregular).

Państwowe Muzeum Archeologiczne (State Archaeological Museum): ul. Długa 40, 00-950 Warsaw; tel. (22) 831-32-21; fax (22) 831-51-95; e-mail pma@pma.pl; internet www.pma.pl/main.html; f. 1923; prehistoric and proto-historic exhibits; organizes regional and field exhibitions, and carries out archaeological excavations throughout Poland; archaeological stores at Rybno; library of 55,000 vols; Dir Dr WOJCIECH BRZEZINSKI; publ. *Wiadomości Archeologiczne* (irregular).

Państwowe Muzeum Etnograficzne w Warszawie (State Ethnographic Museum in Warsaw): ul. Kredytowa 1, 00-056 Warsaw; tel. (22) 827-76-41; fax (22) 827-66-69; e-mail pme@pme.art.pl; internet www.pme.art.pl; f. 1888; Polish and non-European ethnographical collection; library of 23,000 vols; Dir Dr JAN WITOLD SULIGA; publ. *Zeszyty Państwowego Muzeum Etnograficznego w Warszawie* (Reports, 1 a year).

Zamek Królewski w Warszawie—Pomnik Historii i Kultury Narodowej (Royal Castle in Warsaw, National History and Culture Memorial): Pl. Zamkowy 4, 00-277 Warsaw; tel. (22) 657-21-70; fax (22) 657-21-27; e-mail zamek@zamek-krolewski.art.pl; internet www.zamek-krolewski.art.pl; f. 1980; furniture, carpets and rugs, paintings, sculpture, applied arts, drawings, numismatics; library of 25,000 vols; Dir ANDRZEJ ROTTERMUND; publ. *Kronika Zamkowa* (2 a year).

Wieliczka

Muzeum Żup Krakowskich Wieliczka (Cracow Saltworks Museum in Wieliczka): Zamkowa 8, 32-020 Wieliczka; tel. (12) 422-19-47; fax (12) 278-30-28; e-mail promocja@muzeum.wieliczka.pl; internet www.muzeum.wieliczka.pl; f. 1951; history, archaeology, geology, history of art and ethnography, archives, metal conservation laboratory; library of 18,000 vols, spec. collns: photographs, mining maps; Dir Prof. ANTONI JODŁOWSKI; publ. *Studia i Materiały do Dziejów Żup Solnych w Polsce* (1 a year).

Wrocław

Muzeum Architektury (Museum of Architecture): ul. Bernardyńska 5, 50-156 Wrocław; tel. (71) 343-36-75; fax (71) 344-65-77; e-mail muzeum@ma.wroc.pl; internet www.ma.wroc.pl; f. 1965; Polish and other architecture; modern art; library of 7,000 vols; Dir Dr JERZY ILKOSZ.

Muzeum Historyczne we Wrocławiu (Historical Museum in Wrocław): ul. Sukiennice 14/15, 50-107 Wrocław; tel. (71) 44-57-30; fax (71) 44-47-85; f. 1970; Dir MACIEJ ŁAGIEWSKI.

Muzeum Narodowe we Wrocławiu (National Museum in Wrocław): Pl. Powstańców Warszawy 5, 50-153 Wrocław; tel. (71) 372-51-50; fax (71) 343-56-43; e-mail muzeumnarodowe@wr.onet.pl; internet www.mnwr.art.pl; f. 1948; collection of medieval art, Polish painting since 17th century, European painting since 16th century, decorative arts, prints, photographs, ethnography and history relating to Silesia, panoramic painting 'Battle of Racławice'; numismatics; library of 92,889 vols; Dir MARIUSZ HERMANSDORFER; publ. *Roczniki Sztuki Śląskiej* (1 a year).

Zakopane

Muzeum Tatrzańskie im. Tytusa Chałubińskiego (T. Chałubiński Tatra Museum): ul. Krupówki 10, 34-500 Zakopane; tel. (18) 201-52-05; fax (18) 206-38-72; e-mail biuro@muzeumtatrzanskie.pl; internet www.muzeumtatrzanskie.pl; f. 1888; main museum: geology, regional flora, fauna, history and ethnography; glass paintings, pottery, sculpture, wooden, metal and leather ware, costumes, musical instruments, etc.; museum of the Zakopane style—inspirations (local culture sources of the style); museum of the Zakopane style (architecture, furniture, textiles, ceramics and jewellery plus pastels by St Ignacy Witkiewicz); Wł. Hasior Art Gallery; Kornel Makuszyński Museum; art gallery in Koziniec (temporary exhibitions) and 4 brs across Podhale and Spisz regions; library of 50,000 vols; Dir Mgr TERESA JABŁOŃSKA; publ. *Rocznik Podhalański*.

Universities

UNIWERSYTET W BIAŁYMSTOKU (University of Białystok)

ul. Marii Skłodowskiej-Curie 14 15-097 Białystok

Telephone: (85) 745-70-01
Fax: (85) 744-77-49
E-mail: rektorat@uwb.edu
Internet: www.uwb.edu.pl

Founded 1997
State control
Academic year: October to June 2 semesters

Rector: Prof. JERZY NIKITOROWICZ
Vice-Rector for Economic Affairs and Regional Contacts: Prof. Dr MAREK PRONIEWSKI
Vice-Rector for Research and International Relations: Prof. Dr BEATA GODLEWSKA-ŻYŁKIEWICZ
Vice-Rector for Students and Teaching Affairs: Prof. Dr ELŻBIETA AWRAMIUK
Vice-Rector for Univ. Organization and Development: Prof. Dr DARIUSZ KIJOWSKI
Libriarian: HALINA BRZEZIŃSKA-STEC

Library of 559,575 vols, 74,784 periodicals
Number of teachers: 908
Number of students: 18,308

DEANS

Faculty of Administration in Siedlce: Prof. STANISŁAW BOŻYK
Faculty of Biology and Chemistry: Prof. ANATOL KOJŁO
Faculty of Economics and Informatics in Vilnius: Prof. JAROSLAV VOLKONOVSKI
Faculty of Economics and Management: Prof. Dr ROBERT CIBOROWSKI

Faculty of History and Sociology: Prof. ANDRZEJ SADOWSKI
Faculty of Law: Prof. LEONARD ETEL
Faculty of Mathematics and Informatics: Prof. ANATOL ODZIJEWICZ
Faculty of Pedagogy and Psychology: Prof. Dr ELWIRA JOLANTA KRYŃSKA
Faculty of Philology: Prof. BOGUSŁAW NOWOWIEJSKI
Faculty of Physics: Prof. EUGENIUSZ ŻUKOWSKI

UNIWERSYTET MEDYCZNY W BIAŁYMSTOKU
(Medical University of Białystok)

ul. Kilińskiego 1, 15-089 Białystok

Telephone: (85) 748-54-00
Internet: www.amb.edu.pl

Founded 1950

Faculties: medicine with divisions of dentistry and medical education, pharmacy with division of laboratory medicine, health sciences

Rector: Prof. Dr hab. JACEK NIKLIŃSKI

Library of 235,000 vols
Number of teachers: 660
Number of students: 1,762

Publication: *Annals*.

UNIWERSYTET TECHNOLOGICZNO-PRZYRODNICZY IM. J. J. ŚNIADECKICH W BYDGOSZCZY
(University of Technology and Agriculture in Bydgoszcz)

ul. Kordeckiego 20, 85-225 Bydgoszcz

Telephone: (52) 373-14-50
Fax: (52) 374-93-27
E-mail: rektor@utp.edu.pl
Internet: www.utp.edu.pl

Founded 1951

Faculties: agriculture, animal husbandry, chemical technology and engineering, civil engineering, electronics and telecommunication, environmental engineering, management and marketing, mechanics and machine construction, technical physics

Rector: Prof. Dr hab. inż. ANTONI BUKALUK

Library of 239,706 vols, 51,243 periodicals
Number of teachers: 656
Number of students: 9,900

Publications: *Image Processing and Communications* (in English, 4 a year), *Zeszyty Naukowe* (in Polish, with Russian and English summaries, irregular).

UNIWERSYTET JAGIELLOŃSKI
(Jagiellonian University)

ul. Gołębia 24, 31-007 Cracow

Telephone: (12) 422-10-33
Fax: (12) 422-63-06
E-mail: rektor@adm.uj.edu.pl
Internet: www.uj.edu.pl

Founded 1364
Academic year: October to June

Rector: Prof. Dr hab. KAROL MUSIOŁ
Vice-Rector (Collegium Medicum): Prof. Dr hab. WIESŁAW PAWLIK
Vice-Rector (Devt): Prof. Dr hab. PIOTR TWORZEWSKI
Vice-Rector (Educational Affairs): Prof. Dr hab. MARIA SZEWCZYK
Vice-Rector (Personal and Financial Affairs): Prof. Dr hab. WŁADYSŁAW MIODUNKA
Vice-Rector (Research and Int. Relations): Prof. Dr hab. SZCZEPAN BILINSKI
Administrator: Dr TADEUSZ SKARBEK
Librarian: Prof. Dr hab. ZDZISŁAW PIETRZYK

Library: see Libraries and Archives
Number of teachers: 3,407
Number of students: 41,086

Publications: *Acta Physica Polonica B* (12 a year), *Ad Americam* (1 a year), *Alma Mater* (12 a year), *Biuletyn Biblioteki Jagiellońskiej* (1 a year), *Cracow Indological Studies* (irregular), *Estetyka i Krytyka* (4 a year), *Eurasian Prehistory* (2 a year), *Forum Europejskie* (4 a year), *Foton* (4 a year), *Kronika* (1 a year), *Kwartalnik Religioznawczy NOMOS* (4 a year), *Management in Culture* (2 a year), *Materiały Edukacyjne Bibliotekoznawstwa i Informacji Naukowej* (1 a year), *MODUS Prace z Historii Sztuki* (1 a year), *Nowy Filomata* (4 a year), *Politea* (1 a year), *Prace Archeologiczne* (irregular), *Prace Archeologiczne—Studies in Ancient Art and Civilization* (irregular), *Prace Geograficzne* (irregular), *Prace Historyczne* (1 a year), *Principia* (2 a year), *Przekładaniec* (literary translation, 2 a year), *Peregrinus Cracoviensis* (irregular), *Recherches Archéologiques* (irregular), *Reports on Mathematical Logic* (1 a year), *Reports on Philosophy* (1 a year), *Romanica Cracoviensia* (1 a year), *Schedae Informaticae*, *Studia z zakresu Prawa Pracy i Polityki Społecznej* (1 a year), *Universitatis Jegellonicae Acta Mathematica* (1 a year), *Zeszyty Naukowe Uniwersytetu Jagiellońskiego* (1 a year in 26 series), *Zeszyty Prasoznawcze* (4 a year), *Zmieniające się przedsiębiorstwo w zmieniającej się politycznie Europie* (1 a year)

DEANS

Faculty of Biology and Earth Sciences: Prof. Dr hab. KAZIMIERZ KRZEMIEŃ
Faculty of Biotechnology: Prof. Dr hab. KAZIMIERZ STRZAŁKA
Faculty of Chemistry: Prof. Dr hab. LEONARD M. PRONIEWICZ
Faculty of Health Care: Prof. Dr hab. JOLANTA JAWOREK
Faculty of History: Prof. Dr hab. ANDRZEJ BANACH
Faculty of International and Political Studies: Prof. Dr hab. WIESŁAW KOZUB-CIEMBRONIEWICZ
Faculty of Law and Administration: Prof. Dr hab. TADEUSZ WŁUDYKA
Faculty of Management and Social Communication: Prof. Dr hab. MICHAŁ DU VALL
Faculty of Mathematics and Computer Science: Prof. Dr hab. MAREK JARNICKI
Faculty of Medicine: Prof. Dr hab. WOJCIECH NOWAK
Faculty of Pharmacy: Prof. Dr hab. JOANNA SZYMURA-OLEKSIAK
Faculty of Philology: Prof. Dr hab. MARCELA SEWIĄTKOWSKA
Faculty of Philosophy: Prof. Dr hab. MARIA FLIS
Faculty of Physics, Astronomy and Applied Computer Science: Prof. Dr hab. JERZY SZWED
Faculty of Polish Studies: Prof. Dr hab. JACEK POPIEL

PROFESSORS

Faculty of Biology and Earth Sciences (tel. (12) 422-63-48; fax (12) 430-14-73; e-mail binoz@adm.uj.edu.pl; internet www.uj.edu.pl/uj-guide/biol.en.html):

BILIŃSKA, B., Animal Physiology
BILIŃSKI, SZ., Cell Biology
BOBEK, B., Wildlife Research
CHEŁMICKI, W., Geography
DĄBROWSKI, Z., Animal Physiology
DOMANSKI, B., Geography
DZWONKO, Z., Plant Ecology
FALNIOWSKI, A., Malacology
GÓRECKI, A., Ecology
GREGORASZCZUK, E., Animal Physiology
GUZIK, CZ., Population and Agricultural Geography
JACKOWSKI, A., Geography of Religion
KACZANOWSKI, K., Anthropology
KOZŁOWSKI, J., Hydrobiology
KRZEMIEŃ, K., Geomorphology
KUTA, E., Cytology and Embryology of Plants
LASKOWSKI, R., Ecology
LITYŃSKA, A., Glycobiology
ŁOMNICKI, A., Population Ecology
MARCHLEWSKA-KOJ, A., Mammalian Reproduction
MORYCOWA, E., Palaeozoology
MYDEL, R., Geographical Studies on Japan
OBRĘBSKA-STARKEL, B., Climatology
OLECH, M., Plant Taxonomy
OSZCZYPKO, N., Geology
PETRYSZAK, B., Systematic Zoology and Zoological Geography
PŁYTYCZ, B., Evolutionary Immunology
PRZYWARA, L., Plant Cytology and Embryology
RADOMSKI, A., Geology
RAFIŃSKI, J., Evolutionary Biology
SAWICKA-KAPUSTA, K., Ecology, Environmental Protection
ŚKIBA, S., Soil Geography and Pedology
SŁĄCZKA, A., Tectonics and Stratigraphy
SZOŁTYS, M., Zoology
SZYMURA, J. M., Zoology
TRZCIŃSKA-TACIK, H., Botany
TURNAU, K., Plant Taxonomy and Phytogeography
UCHMAN, A., Geology, Sedimentology, Ichnology
WEINER, J., Ecological Bioenergetics and Evolutionary Ecosystems
WIDACKI, W., Geography
WOJTUSIAK, J., Zoology
WOYCIECHOWSKI, M., Ecology and Evolution
ŻABIŃSKI, W., Geology
ZAJĄC, A., Plant Taxonomy and Phytogeography
ZAJĄC, M., Phytogeography
ZEMANEK, A., Botany
ZEMANEK, B., Phytogeography
ZUCHIEWICZ, W., Geology

Faculty of Biotechnology (ul. Gronostajowa 7, 30-387 Cracow; tel. (12) 252-60-02; fax (12) 252-69-02; e-mail sekretariat@mol.uj.edu.pl; internet www.mol.uj.edu.pl):

DUBIN, A., Biochemistry
FRONCISZ, W., Biophysics
GABRYŚ, H., Plant Physiology
KLEIN, A., Biochemistry
KOJ, A., Biochemistry
KOROHODA, WŁ., Cell Biology
ŁUKIEWICZ, S., Biophysics
PASENKIEWICZ-GIERULA, M., Molecular Biophysics
POTEMPA, J., Biochemistry, Biotechnology
PRYJMA, J., Microbiology and Immunology
SARNA, T., Biophysics
STRZAŁKA, K., Biochemistry
WASYLEWSKI, Z., Physical Biochemistry
WIĘCKOWSKI, S., Plant Physiology
ŻAK, Z., Animal Biochemistry

Faculty of Chemistry (ul. Ingardena 3, 30-060 Cracow; tel. (12) 633-63-77 ext. 2215; fax (12) 634-05-15; e-mail sekretar@chemia.uj.edu.pl; internet www.ch.uj.edu.pl):

BARAŃSKI, A., Chemical Kinetics
BOGDANOWICZ-SZWED, K., Chemistry of Heterocyclic Compounds
DATKA, J., Inorganic Chemistry and Infrared Spectroscopy
DZIEMBAJ, R., Catalysis, Solid State Chemistry and Technology
HODOROWICZ, S. A., Crystallography and Solid State Chemistry
JUSZKIEWICZ, A., Physical and Environmental Chemistry

KOŚCIELNIAK, P., Analytical and Forensic Chemistry
NAJBAR, J., Physical Chemistry, Photophysics and Photochemistry
NAJBAR, M., Inorganic and Environmental Catalysis
NALEWAJSKI, R. F., Theoretical Chemistry, Quantum Chemistry
NOWAKOWSKA, M., Physical Chemistry, Photochemistry of Polymers
OLEKSYN, B., Crystallography and Crystal Chemistry
PALUCH, M., Physical Chemistry, Surface Chemistry
PARCZEWSKI, A., Chemometrics and Analytical Chemistry
PAWLIKOWSKI, M., Theoretical Chemistry, Molecular Spectroscopy
PETELENZ, P., Theoretical Chemistry
PRONIEWICZ, L.M., Chemical Physics, Molecular Spectroscopy
SILBERRING, J., Biochemistry and Neurochemistry
STASICKA, Z., Inorganic and Coordination Chemistry
STOCHEL, G., Inorganic and Bioinorganic Chemistry
WÓJCIK, M., Physical Chemistry, Molecular Spectroscopy

Faculty of Health Care (ul. Michałowskiego 12, 31-126 Cracow; tel. (12) 421-41-41; fax (12) 421-41-41; e-mail kbrzezns@cm-uj.krakow.pl; internet www.cm-uj.krakow.pl):

CZABAŁA, J., Psychology
GOLINOWSKA, S., Health Economics
HAŁUSZKA, J., Environmental Health
PILC, A., Pharmacology
SPODARYK, K., Physiotherapy
SZAFRAN, Z., Biochemistry
WŁODARCZYK, W., Health Policy

Faculty of History (tel. (12) 422-77-62; fax (12) 430-14-67; e-mail historia@adm.uj.edu.pl; internet www.uj.edu.pl/uj-guide/history.en.html):

BACZKOWSKI, K., General Medieval History
BAŁUS, K., History of Late Modern Art
BRZOZA, Cz., Modern Polish History
CENTAROWICZ, A., General Modern History
CHOCHOROWSKI, J., Archaeology
CHWALBA, A., Documentation of Polish Independence Movements
CIAŁOWICZ, K, Archaeology
DĄBROWA, E., Ancient History
DYBIEC, J., History of Science and Culture
DZIELSKA, M., Byzantine History
FABIAŃSKI, M., History of Modern Art
GĄSOWSKI, T., Polish Modern History
GEDL, M., Archaeology
GINTER, B., Archaeology
GRYGLEWICZ, T., History of Contemporary Art
JARZĘBSKA, A., 20th-century Polish History
KACZANOWSKI, P., Archaeology
KOZŁOWSKI, J., Archaeology
MAŁKIEWICZA, A., History of Modern Art
MICHALEWICZ, A., Economic and Social History
OSTROWSKI, JAN, History of Art
OSTROWSKI, JANUSZ, Classical Archaeology
PAJA-STACH, J., Contemporary Polish Music
PAPUCI-WŁADYKA, E., Archaeology
PARCZEWSKI, M., Polish and Modern Archaeology
PIROŻYŃSKI, J., General Modern History
QUIRINI-POPŁAWSKA, D., Medieval History
ROBOTYCKI, Cz., Polish Ethnography, Anthropology of Culture
ROJEK, W., General Modern History
ŚLIWA, J., Mediterranean Archaeology
SNIEŻYŃSKA-STOLOT, E., History of Ideas
SZCZUR, S., Medieval History

Faculty of International and Political Studies (tel. (12) 422-02-25; fax (12) 422-02-25; e-mail wsmip@adm.uj.edu.pl; internet www.uj.edu.pl/wydzmiedzpol):

BABIŃSKI, G., Sociology of Interethnic Relationships
CZIOMER, E., International Relations
FLORKOWSKA-FRANCIĆ, H., History of International Migration Movements
KAPISZEWSKI, A., Middle East Studies
KOZUB-CIEMBRONIEWICZ, M., Modern Political Movements and Political Thought
MACH, Z., Anthropology
MAJCHROWSKI, J. M., Recent Political History of Poland, History of Political and Legal Doctrines, Religious Policy
MANIA, A., World History of the 20th Century
MIODUNKA, W., Applied Linguistics in Polish Language Teaching
PURCHLA, J., Economic History and History of Art
RAŹNY, A., East Slavonic Philology
STAWOWY-KAWKA, I., History of Balkan Countries
SUCHANEK, L., Russian and Soviet Literature
WALASZEK, A., History of International Migration Movements
ZIĘBA, A., Constitutional Law
ZYBLIKIEWICZ, L., International Relations

Faculty of Law and Administration (tel. (12) 422-37-42; fax (12) 423-11-21; e-mail prawo@adm.uj.edu.pl; internet www.uj.edu.pl/uj-guide/law&adm.en.html):

BARAN, KA., General Legal History
BARAN, KRZ., Labour Law
BIERNAT, S., European Law
BŁACHUT, J., Criminology
BRZEZIŃSKI, B., Financial Law
CHOJNICKA, K., History of Political and Legal Thought
ĆWIĄKALSKI, K., Criminal Law
CZAJOWKI, J., Modern Political Systems
DROZD, E., Civil Law, Private International Law
GABERLE, A., Criminology
GAWLIK, B., Civil Law
GIZBERT-STUDNICKI, T., Theory and Philosophy of Law
GRZYBOWSKI, M., Modern Political Systems
HOFMAŃSKI, P., Criminal Procedure
HOŁDA, Z., Sentencing and Penal Procedure
JASKÓLSKI, M., History of Political and Legal Thought
KISIEL, W., Territorial Self-Government
KRAJEWSKLI, K., Criminology
KUBAS, A., Civil Law
LANKOSZ, K., International Public Law
LICHOROWICZ, A., Agricultural Law
MĄCZYŃSKI, A., Civil and International Private Law
MALEC, J., History of Administration
PAŁECKI, K., Theory and Sociology of Law
PŁESZKA, K., Theory and Philosophy of Law
PREUSSNER-ZAMORSKA, J., Civil Law
PYZIOŁ, W., Private Business Law
SARKOWICZ, R., Theory and Philosophy of Law
SARNECKI, P., Constitutional Law
SONDEL, J., Roman Law
STEC, M., Private Business Law
STELMACH, J., Theory and Philosophy of Law
ŞZEWCZYK, M., Criminal Law
ŚWIĄTKOWSKI, A., Labour Law
SZUMAŃSKI, A., International Business Law
TRAPLE, E., Civil Law
URUSZCZAK, W., History of Ecclesiastical Law
WAGNER, B., Labour Law
WALASZEK-PYZIOŁ, A., Public Business Law
WASILEWSKI, A., Environmental Protection Law
WŁUDYKA, T., Economics Policy
WOJCIKIEWICZ, J., Forensic and Police Science
WOŚ, T., Administration Law, Administration Procedures Law
ZAWADA, K., Civil Law and International Private Law
ZIMMERMAN, J., Administrative Procedures
ZOLL, A., Criminal Law

Faculty of Management and Social Communication (tel. (12) 422-10-33 ext. 1132; fax (12) 421-49-75; e-mail orzech@adm.uj.edu.pl; internet gemini.miks.uj.edu.pl):

BAŃKA, A., Organizational Psychology
BARTA, J., Copyright Law, Press Law and Information Law
BEDNARCZYK, M., Tourism Management
BOBROWSKI, J., Linguistics, Communication
GOBAN-KLAS, T., Theory of Mass Communication, Public Relations
GODZIC, W., Media and Film Studies
HELMAN, A., Film Studies
LASKOWSKI, R., Linguistics, Slavic Language and Social Communication
LIBERSKA, B., International Economics
LUBASZEWSKI, W., Electrical Transformation of Information
LUBELSKI, T., Film Studies
MAREK, T., Psychology of Work, Organization and Management
MARKIEWICZ, R., Copyright Law, Information Law and Industrial Property Law
MATCZEWSKI, A., Industrial Management
NĘCKI, Z., Social Psychology
OKOŃ-HORODYŃSKA, E., Economics, Management
ORZECHOWSKI, E., Arts Management, History of Theatre
PISAREK, W., Media Research, Social Linguistics
PLEŚNIAROWICZ, K., Arts Management, Performance Theory
PRZEWŁOCKI, R., Medical Science, Neuroscience, Pharmacology
SOWA, K., Management of Higher Education, Sociology
STACHÓWNA, G., Film Studies
STĘPNIEWSKI, J., Accounting, Auditing, Operational Management
SURDYKOWSKA, S., International Accounting and Corporate Finance, Management, Accounting, Comparative Economics Systems
SZUMPICH, S., Management, Accounting, Comparative Economics Systems
SZWAJA, J., Civil and Commercial Law, Industrial Property Law
WIDACKI, J., Criminal Law, Management of Public Security
WILK, E., Media and Film Studies
WITKOWSKI, L., Philosophy, Theory of Arts and Education
WOJCIECHOWSKI, J., Communication and Librarianship

Faculty of Mathematics and Computer Science (tel. (12) 422-10-33 ext. 1145; fax (12) 430-14-67; e-mail matinf@adm.uj.edu.pl; internet www.mat-inf.uj.edu.pl):

DENKOWSKI, Z., Optimization and Control Theory
DRUŻKOWSKI, L. M., Analytic and Algebraic Geology
FLASIŃSKI, M., Artificial Intelligence Systems
GANCARZEWICZ, J., Differential Geometry
IDZIAK, P. M, Foundations of Computer Science
JARNICKI, M., Complex Analysis
MROZEK, M., Numerical Methods
OMBACH, J., Dynamical Systems
OPOZDA, B., Differential Geometry
PAWŁUCKI, W., Singularity Theory
PELCZAR, A., Analysis, Differential Equations

PLEŚNIAK, W., Complex Analysis, Theory of Approximations
RUSEK, K., Algebraic Geometry
SĘDZIWY, S., Numerical Methods
SICIAK, J., Complex Analysis
SRZEDNICKI, R., Differential Equations
STOCHEL, J., Functional Analysis, Theory of Operators
SZAFIRSKI, B., Differential Equations, Theory of Turbulence
SZAFRANIEC, F. H., Functional Analysis, Theory of Operators
TWOREWSKI, P., Analytical and Algebraic Geometry
WINIARSKI, T., Analytic and Algebraic Geometry

Faculty of Medicine (ul. Św. Anny 6, 31-008 Cracow; tel. (12) 422-54-44; fax (12) 422-40-06; e-mail dziekwl@cm-uj.krakow.pl; internet www.cm-uj.krakow.pl/pliki/en_lekarski.html):

ADAMEK-GUZIK, T., Internal Medicine
ALEKSANDROWICZ, J., Psychotherapy, Psychiatry
ANDRES, J., Anaesthesiology
BASTA, A., Gynaecology and Oncology
BOGDAŁ, J., Gastroenterology, Internal Medicine
BOGDASZEWSKA-CZABANOWSKA, J., Dermatology
BOMBA, J., Psychiatry
BRZOZOWSKI, T., Physiology
CICHOCKI, T., Histology
DEMBIŃSKA-KIEĆ, A., Clinical Biochemistry
DEMBIŃSKI, A., Physiology
DOBROWOLSKI, Z., Urology
DUBIEL, J. S., Cardiology
GIEROWSKI, J., Pyschiatry
GRODZIŃSKA, L., Pharmacology
HECZKO, P., Microbiology
KACIŃSKI, M., Neurology
KARCZ, D., Surgery
KAWECKA-JASZCZ, K., Cardiology
KLIMEK, R., Gynaecology, Obstetrics
KONIECZNY, L., Biochemistry
KORBUT, R., Pharmacology
KULIG, J., Surgery
LAUTERBACH, R., Paediatrics
LITWIN, J., Histology
MAJEWSKI, S., Dental Prosthetics
MALEC, E., Paediatric Cardiac Surgery
MARCINKIEWICZ, J., Immunology
MIODOŃSKI, A., Laryngology
MIRECKA, J., Histology
MUSIAŁ, J., Internal Medicine
NASKALSKI, J., Clinical Biochemistry
NIŻANKOWSKA-MOGILNICKA, E., Pulmonology
OBTUŁOWICZ, K., Internal Medicine
PACH, J., Toxicology
PAWLĘGA, J., Oncology
PAWLICKI, R., Histology
PAWLIK, W., Physiology
PIETRZYK, J., Paediatrics
PIWOWARSKA, W., Cardiology
POPIELA, T., Gastroenterological Surgery
RATAJCZAK, M., Transplantology
REROŃ, E., Laryngology
ROKITA, E., Medical Physics
RYN, Z., Psychiatry
SIERADZKI, J., Metabolic Diseases
SKŁADZIEŃ, J., Otolaryngology
SKOTNICKI, A., Haematology
SŁADEK, K., Internal Medicine
STACHURA, J., Pathomorphology
STARZYCKA, M., Ophthalmology
SUŁOWICZ, W., Nephrology
SZCZEKLIK, A., Internal Medicine
THOR, P., Physiopathology
TOBIASZ-ADAMCZYK, B., Epidemiology and Preventive Medicine
TRACZ, W., Cardiology
WYSOCKI, A., Surgery
ZARZYCKI, D., Orthopaedics
ZEMBALA, M., Microbiology, Immunology
ZIĘBA, A., Psychiatry

Faculty of Pharmacy (ul. Medyczna 9, 30-688 Cracow; tel. (12) 657-54-56; fax (12) 657-02-62; e-mail mfdmicha@cyf-kr.edu.pl; internet www.cm-uj.krakow.pl):

BOJARSKI, J., Organic Chemistry
BRANDYS, J., Toxicology
BUDAK, A., Pharmaceutical Microbiology
CZARNECKI, R., Pharmacodynamics
JAŚKIEWICZ, J., Biochemical Analysis
KIEĆ-KONOWICZ, K., Chemical Technology of Drugs
PAWŁOWSKI, M., Pharmaceutical Chemistry
RZESZUTKO, W., Inorganic Chemistry
STAREK, A., Biochemical Toxicology
SZYMURA-OLEKSIAK, J., Pharmacokinetics
ZACHWIEJA, Z., Food Chemistry, Nutrition
ZIEJA, A., Pharmaceutical Chemistry

Faculty of Philology (tel. (12) 422-11-03; fax (12) 422-11-03 ext. 1102; e-mail filolog@adm.uj.edu.pl; internet www.filg.uj.edu.pl):

BALBUS, S., Theory of Literature
BOCHENEK-FRANCZAKOWA, R., French Literature
BOROWSKI, A., Polish Philology
BORYŚ, W., Comparative and Historical Slavic Etymology, Serbo-Croatian Linguistics
BRZEZINA, M., Linguistics
BUJNICKI, T., History of Polish Literature
DUNAJ, B., Linguistics
FIUT, A., Polish Philology
GIBIŃSKA-MARZEC, M., English Literature
HOMBEK, D., Polish Philology
JARZĘBSKI, J., History of Polish Literature
JAWORSKI, S., History of Polish Literature
KAPUŚCIK, J., Russian Literature and History
KŁAŃSKA, M., German Philology
KORNHAUSER, J., Slavonic Philology
KORPANTY, J., Classical Philology
KORUS, K., Classical Philology
KORYTOWSKA, M., Comparative Literature
KOWALIKOWA, J., Methodology of Teaching Polish Literature
KULAWIK, A., Theory of Literature
KUREK, H., Polish Philology
LABOCHA, J., Polish Philology
LIPIŃSKI, K., German Philology, History of German Literature, Translation
MAŃCZAK-WOHLFELD, E., English Linguistics
MARKOWSKI, M., History of Polish Literature
MELANOWICZ, M., Japanese Literature
MICHALAK-PIKULSKA, B., Arabic Literature
MICHALIK, J., Theatre Studies
MIODOŃSKA-BROOKES, E., Polish Philology
MUSKAT-TABAKOWSKA, E., Cognitive Linguistics and Theory of Translation
NAUMOW, A., Slavonic Philology
NYCZ, R., Polish Philology
PISOWICZ, A., Iranian and Armenian Linguistics
PRZEBINDA, G., Russian Literature and History, Ukrainian Culture and History
ŚKARŻYŃSKI, M., Polish Philosophy
ŚLIWIŃSKI, W., Polish Philology
SMOCZYŃSKI, W., General and Indo-European Linguistics
STABRYŁA, S., Classical Philology
STACHOWSKI, M., Turkic and Altaic Linguistics
STALA, M., History of Polish Literature
STYKA, J., Classical Philology
ŚUGIERA, M., Theatre Studies
ŚWIĄTKOWSKA, M., Romance Philology
SZCZUKIN, W., Russian Literature, Culture and History, Theory of Literature
SZTURC, W., Comparative Literature
WALECKI, W., History of Polish Literature
WIDŁAK, S., Romance Philology
WŁODARSKI, M., History of Polish Literature
WRÓBEL, H., Polish and Czech Philology
WYKA, M., History of Polish Literature
ZABORSKI, A., Chamito-Semitic Linguistics
ZAJADA, A., Polish Philology
ZARĘBIANKA, Z., History of Polish Language
ZIEJKA, F., History of Polish Philology

Faculty of Philosophy (tel. (12) 422-11-36; fax (12) 430-14-75; e-mail filozof@adm.uj.edu.pl; internet www.phils.uj.edu.pl):

ALEKSANDER, T., Adult Education
DRABINA, J., History of Christianity
FLIS, A., Sociology of Culture
FLIS, M., Sociology of Culture, Anthropology
FRYSZTACKI, K., Sociology
GALEWICZ, W., Philosophy
GORLACH, K., Sociology
GROTT, B., Religious Studies
GRYZMAŁA-MOSZCZYŃSKA, H., Psychology of Religion
KOCIK, L., Sociology
KUBIAK, H., Sociology of Politics
LEGUTKO, R., Political Philosophy
LIPIEC, J., Philosophy
MIKLASZEWSKA, J., Philosophy
NÊCKA, E., Psychology
OCHMANN, J., Religious Studies
PACZKOWSKA-ŁAGOWSKA, E., Philosophy
PALKA, S., Methodological Elements of Education
PALUCH, A., Sociology
PERZANOWSKI, J., Philosophy and Logic
PIĄTEK, Z., Philosophy of Natural Sciences
PILECKA, W., Psychology
RODZIŃSKI, S., Pedagogy
SKOCZYŃSKI, J., Philosophy
SLANY, K., Sociology
STRÓŻEWSKI, W., Philosophy, Ontology
SUCHOŃ, W., Philosophy
SZTOMPKA, P., Sociological Theory
SZYMAŃSKA-ALEKSANDROWICZ, B., Philosophy
SZYMAŃSKI, M., Pedagogy, Sociology
URBAN, B., Pedagogy
WILKOSZEWSKA, K., Philosophy of Aesthetics
WOLEŃSKI, J., Philosophy, Epistemology
WROŃSKI, A., Logic and Philosophy

Faculty of Physics, Astronomy and Applied Computer Science (ul. Reymonta 4, 30-059 Cracow; tel. (12) 632-48-88 ext. 5703; fax (12) 433-70-86; e-mail fais@adm.uj.edu.pl; internet www.fais.uj.edu.pl):

ARODŹ, H., Field Theory
BAŁANDA, A., Nuclear Physics
BARA, J., Nuclear Physics
BIAŁAS, A., Theory of Elementary Particles, Astrophysics
BLICHARSKI, J. S., Radiospectroscopy, Biophysics
BODEK, K., Nuclear Physics
DOHNALIK, T., Atomic and Optical Physics
FIAŁKOWSKI, K., Theoretical Physics
FULIŃSKI, A., Statistical Physics
GAWLIK, W., Atomic and Optical Physics, Photonics
JURKIEWICZ, J., Theoretical Physics
KAMYS, B., Nuclear Physics
KOTAŃSKI, A., Computer Science, High Energy Physics
KRÓLAS, K., Nuclear Physics
KULESSA, R., Nuclear Physics
KUTSCHERA, M., Astrophysics
ŁĄTKA, K., Experimental Physics
LONGA, L., Statistical Physics
MACHALSKI, J., Radioastronomy and Extragalactic Astronomy
MAJKA, Z., Hot Matter
MALEC, E., Relativity, Astrophysics
MASŁOWSKI, J., Radioastronomy and Cosmic Physics
MICEK, S., Experimental Computer Physics
MOŚCICKI, J., Soft Matter Physics
MUSIOŁ, K., Atomic Physics
NOWAK, M., Theoretical Physics
OLEŚ, A. M., Theoretical Physics

OSTROWSKI, M., Astronomy
PĘDZIWIATR, A., Experimental Physics
RICHTER-WĄS, E., Applied Numerical Methods, High Energy Physics
ROKITA, E., Medical Physics, Environmental Physics
ROŚCISZEWSKI, K., Condensed Matter Theory
SPAŁEK, J., Condensed Matter Theory
STANEK, J., Solid State Physics
STARUSZKIEWICZ, A., General Relativity, Electrodynamics, Astrophysics
SZWED, J., Applied Numerical Methods, High Energy Physics
SZYMOŃSKI, M., Experimental Physics
SZYTUŁA, A., Solid State Physics, Magnetism
TOMALA, K., Radiospectroscopy
URBAN, S., Solid State Physics
WALUŚ, W., Nuclear Physics
WARCZAK, A., Experimental Physics
WITAŁA, H., Nuclear Physics
WOSIEK, J., Theoretical Computer Physics
WRÓBEL, S., Solid State Physics
ZAKRZEWSKI, J., Atomic and Optical Physics, Photonics
ZALEWSKI, K., Particle Theory

UNIWERSYTET GDAŃSKI (University of Gdańsk)

Ul. Bażyńskiego 1A, 80-952 Gdańsk
Telephone: (58) 523-24-00
Fax: (58) 552-03-11
E-mail: rekug@ug.gda.pl
Internet: www.ug.edu.pl

Founded 1970
State control
Academic year: October to June

Rector: Prof. Dr hab. BERNARD LAMMEK
Pro-Rectors: Prof. Dr hab. MARIA MENDEL, Prof. Dr hab. GRZEGORZ WĘGRZYN, Prof. Dr hab. MIROSŁAW KRAJEWSKI, Prof. Dr hab. JÓZEF WŁODARSKI
Admin. Dir: Dr JERZY GWIZDAŁA
Librarian: Mgr URSZULA SAWICKA

Library: see Libraries and Archives
Number of teachers: 1,700
Number of students: 32,000

Publications: *Prace Habilitacyjne*, *Skrypty*, *Zeszyty Naukowe*

DEANS

Faculty of Biology: Prof. Dr hab. DARIUSZ SZLACHETKO
Faculty of Chemistry: Prof. Dr hab. inż. ANDRZEJ WIŚNIEWSKI
Faculty of Economics: Prof. Dr hab. KRZYSZTOF DOBROWOLSKI
Faculty of History: Prof. Dr hab. ZBIGNIEW OPACKI
Faculty of Languages: Prof. Dr hab. ANDRZEJ CEYNOWA
Faculty of Law and Administration: Prof. Dr hab. JAROSŁAW WARYLEWSKI
Faculty of Management: Prof. Dr hab. JERZY BIELIŃSKI
Faculty of Mathematics, Physics and Informatics: Prof. Dr hab. WŁADYSŁAW ADAM MAJEWSKI
Faculty of Oceanography and Geography: Prof. Dr hab. ADAM KRĘŻEL
Faculty of Social Sciences: Prof. Dr hab. BEATA PASTWA-WOJCIECHOWSKA
Intercollegiate Faculty of Biotechnology of University of Gdańsk and Medical University of Gdańsk: Prof. Dr hab. EWA ŁOJKOWSKA

UNIWERSYTET ŚLĄSKI W KATOWICACH (University of Silesia in Katowice)

Bankowa 12, 40-007 Katowice
Telephone: (32) 359-20-52
Fax: (32) 359-11-78
E-mail: admission@us.edu.pl
Internet: www.us.edu.pl

Founded 1968
State control
Language of instruction: Polish
Academic year: October to June

Rector: Prof. WIESŁAW BANYŚ
Pro-Rectors: Prof. Dr hab. BARBARA KOŻUSZNIK, Prof. Dr hab. STANISŁAW KUCHARSKI, Prof. Dr hab. CZESŁAW MARZYSZ, Dr hab. ANDRZEJ KOWALCZYK
Registrar and Chief Admin. Officer: Dr JAN JELONEK
Librarian: Dr DARIUSZ PAWELEC

Library of 1,441,224 vols, 15,300 periodicals
Number of teachers: 1,935
Number of students: 38,357

Publication: *Zeszyty Naukowe Wydziałów*

DEANS

Faculty of Biology and Environmental Protection: Prof. Dr hab. IWONA SZAREJKO
Faculty of Computer and Materials Sciences: Prof. JAN ILCZUK
Faculty of Earth Sciences: Prof. ADAM IDZIAK
Faculty of Education and Psychology: Assoc. Prof. ZBIGNIEW SPENDEL
Faculty of Ethnology and Sciences of Education: Prof. Dr hab. ZIGMUNT KŁODNICKI
Faculty of Fine Arts and Music: Prof. WIESŁAW CIENCIAŁA
Faculty of Law and Administration: Prof. ZBIGNIEW TOBOR
Faculty of Mathematics, Physics and Chemistry: Prof. Dr hab. MACIEJ SABLIK
Faculty of Philology: Prof. UŚ Dr hab. PIOTR WILCZEK
Faculty of Radio and Television: Prof. KRYSTYNA DOKTOROWICZ
Faculty of Social Sciences: Prof. Dr hab. WIESŁAW KACZANOWICZ
Faculty of Theology: Prof. Dr hab. ANDRZEJ ŻĄDŁO

PROFESSORS

Faculty of Biology and Environmental Protection (ul Jagielońska 28, 40-032 Katowice; tel. (32) 200-94-61; fax (32) 200-93-61; e-mail biologia@us.edu.pl):

CABAŁA, S., Ecology
CIEPAŁ, R., Ecology
GAJ, N., Genetics
GORCZYCA, J., Zoology
HERCZEK, A., Zoology
KARCZ, W., Genetics
KLAG, J., Histology and Animal Embryology
KURCZYŃSKA, E., Cell Biology
ŁABUŻEK, S., Biochemistry
MAŁUSZYŃSKA, J., Plant Anatomy and Cytology
MAŁUSZYŃSKI, M., Genetics
MIGULA, P., Animal Physiology and Ecotoxicology
PALOWSKI, B., Ecology
PIOTROWSKA-SEGET, Z., Microbiology
RADZIEJEWSKA-LEBRECHT, J., Microbiology
STRZELEC, M., Hydrobiology
SZAREJKO, I., Genetics
WĘGIEREK, P., Zoology
WIKA, S., Geobotany and Nature Protection
WOJCIECHOWSKI, W., Zoology

Faculty of Computer and Materials Sciences (ul. Żeromskiego 3, 41-200 Sosnowiec; tel. (32) 291-84-59; fax (32) 291-85-49; e-mail dwt@us.edu.pl):

BUDNIOK, A., Material Science
CYBO, J., Material Science
CZECH, Z., Computer Science
CZEKLAJ, D., Material Science
HANECZOK, G., Material Science
ILCZUK, J., Material Science
KOTARSKI, W., Computer Science
ŁAGIEWKA, E., Material Science
LELĄTKO, J., Material Science
MORAWIEC, H., Material Science
PAJĄK, L., Material Science
RASEK, J., Material Science
SKONECZNY, W., Material Science
STOLARZEWICZ, A., Material Science
SZEWC, A., Computer Science
TOMAWSKI, L., Computer Science
WAKULICZ-DEJA, A., Computer Science
WOKULSKA, K., Material Science
WOKULSKI, Z., Material Science
WRÓBEL, Z., Computer Science

Faculty of Earth Sciences (ul. Będzińska 60, 41-200 Sosnowiec; tel. (32) 291-83-81 ext. 324; fax (32) 291-58-65; e-mail dz-wnoz@ultra.cto.us.edu.pl):

CZAJA, S., Physical Geography
CZYLOK, A., Physical Geography
GŁUCHOWSKI, E., Stratygraphy and Paleontology
IDZIAK, A., Applied Geology
JANECZEK, J., Geochemistry
JANIA, J., Geomorphology
JANKOWSKI, A., Physical Geography
KARWOWSK, Ł., Geochemistry
KLIMEK, K., Quaternary Paleogeography and Paleoecology
KOWALCZYK, A., Hydrogeology and Engineering Geology
KRUSZEWSKA, K., Geochemistry
ŁAJCZAK, A., Quaternary Paleogeography and Paleoecology
NIEDŹWIEDŹ, T., Klimatology
PULINOWA, M., Physical Geography
RACKI, G., Stratygraphy and Paleontology
ŚNIESZKO, Z., Geomorphology
SZCZYPEK, T., Physical Geography
TEPER, L., Applied Geology
WÓJCIK, A., General Geology
ŻABA, J., General Geology
ZUBEREK, W., Applied Geology

Faculty of Education and Psychology (ul. Grażyńskiego 53, 40-126 Katowice; tel. (32) 258-94-82; fax (32) 258-94-82; e-mail pips@us.edu.pl):

BAŃKA, A., Psychology
BOROWSKA, T., Education
JUSZCZYK, S., Education
KOJS, W., Education
PETLAK, E., Education
PILCH, T., Education
RADZIEWICZ-WINNICKI, A., Education
RATAJCZAK, Z., Psychology
TOKARZ, M., Logic
VASEK, A., Education
ZIELIŃSKI, J., Education

Faculty of Ethnology and Science of Education (ul. Bielska 62, 43-400 Cieszyn; tel. (33) 854-61-14; fax (33) 858-11-28; e-mail artped@mail.filus.edu.pl):

BUKOWSKA-FLOREŃSKA, I., Ethnology and Cultural Anthropology
KASACOVA, B., Pedagogy
KIEDOS, J., Pedagogy
KORZENIOWSKA, W., Pedagogy
MURZYN, A., Pedagogy
REMIN, M., Pedagogy
STOLICNA, R., Ethnology and Cultural Anthropology
ŽILINEK, M., Pedagogy

Faculty of Fine Arts and Music (62 Bielska St, 43-400 Cieszyn; tel. (33) 854-61-16; fax (33) 854-61-02):

DELEKTA, E., Graphic Arts
DROZD, H., Instrumentation
FOBER, J., Sculpture

GONIEWICZ - URBAŚ, H., Conducting and Music Education
HOŁARD, J., Graphic Design
JACYKÓW, W., Interdisciplinary Artistic Creation
KOWALCZYK-KLUS, A., Theory of Arts and Artistic Education
ŁUSZCZAK, M., Interdisciplinary Artistic Creation
MICHALAK, R., Instrumentation
PICHURA, J., Instrumentation
SZAREK, A., Sculpture
TUREK, K., Composition and Theory of Music

Faculty of Law and Administration (ul. Bankowa 11b, 40-007 Katowice; tel. (32) 359-20-60; fax (32) 359-20-61; e-mail akrawcz@us.edu.pl):

CHEŁMICKI-TYSZKIEWICZ, L.
CIĄGWA, J.
DOLNICKI, B.
FELUŚ, A.
GÓRNIOK, O.
GRABOWSKA, G.
GRABOWSKI, J.
KAŁUS, S.
KNOSALA, E.
KRAJEWSKI, K.
KUDEJ, M.
LIPIŃSKI, A.
LITYŃSKI, A.
MAŁAJNY, R.
MARSZAŁ, K.
NOWACKI, J.
PAZDAN, M.
SOBAŃSKI, R.
STRZĘPKA, J.
WIDŁA, T.
ZWIERZCHOWSKI, E.

Faculty of Mathematics, Physics and Chemistry (ul. Bankowa 14, 40-007 Katowice; tel. (32) 359-16-52; e-mail basia@dz.wmfch.us.edu.pl):

BARON, K., Mathematics
BŁASZCZYK, A., Mathematics
BORGIEŁ, W., Theoretical Physics
BURIAN, A., Biophysics and Molecular Physics
CHEŁKOWSKA, G., Solid State Physics
CHOLEWA, J., Mathematics
CZYŻ, H., Field Theory and Elementary Particle Physics
DEC, J., Experimental Physics
DŁOTKO, T., Mathematics
DRZAZGA, Z., Medical Physics
FLAKUS, H., Chemistry
FUGIEL, B., Biophysics and Molecular Physics
GBURSKI, Z., Computational Physics and Electronics
GROŃ, T., Physics of Crystals
HACURA, A., Biophysics and Molecular Physics
JOHN, E., Chemistry
KISIEL, J., Nuclear Physics
KOCOT, A., Biophysics and Molecular Physics
KOŁODZIEJ, K., Field Theory and Elementary Particle Physics
KOMINEK, Z., Mathematics
KOWALSKA, T., Chemistry
KROK-KOWALSKI, J., Physics of Crystals
KROMPIEC, S., Chemistry
KUCHARSKI, S., Chemistry
KULPA, W., Mathematics
LIGĘZA, J., Mathematics
ŁUCZKA, J., Theoretical Physics
MARCZAK, W., Chemistry
MAŚKA, M., Theoretical Physics
MATKOWSKI, J., Mathematics
MATLAK, M., Theoretical Physics
MIERZEJEWSKI, M., Theoretical Physics
MROWIEC, H., Chemistry
NOWAK, A., Mathematics
PALUCH, M., Biophysics and Molecular Physics
PLEWIK, S., Mathematics
POLAŃSKI, J., Chemistry
RATUSZNA, A., Solid State Physics
ROLEDER, K., Experimental Physics
ROMAN GER, R., Mathematics
RUDNICKI, R., Mathematics
RZOSKA, S., Biophysics and Molecular Physics
SABLIK, M., Mathematics
SIEMASZKO, M., Nuclear Physics
SKRZYPEK, D., Solid State Physics
ŚŁADEK, A., Mathematics
ŚLEBARSKI, A., Solid State Physics
SUŁKOWSKI, W., Chemistry
SZADE, J., Solid State Physics
SZAREK, T., Mathematics
SZOPA, M., Theoretical Physics
SZOT, K., Experimental Physics
SZYMICZEK, K., Mathematics
TALIK, E., Solid State Physics
UJMA, Z., Experimental Physics
WALCZAK, B., Chemistry
WARCZEWSKI, J., Physics of Crystals
WESTWAŃSKI, B., Theoretical Physics
WIKTOR ZIPPER, W., Nuclear Physics
ZAREK, W., Solid State Physics
ZIOŁO, J., Biophysics and Molecular Physics
ZIPPER, E., Theoretical Physics
ZRAŁEK, M., Field Theory and Elementary Particle Physics

Faculty of Philology (plac Sejmu Śląskiego 1, 40-032 Katowice; tel. (32) 255-12-60 ext. 267; fax (32) 255-32-29; e-mail filologia@homer.fil.us.edu.pl):

ABŁAMOWICZ, A., French Philology
ARABSKI, J., English Philology
BANYŚ, W., French Philology
BEDNARSKI, M., Philology
CZAPIK-LITYŃSKA, B., Slavonic Philology
CZERWIŃSKI, P., Russian Philology
FAST, P., Russian Philology
FONTAŃSKI, H., Russian Philology
GONDEK, E., Philology
GWÓŹDŹ, A., Philology
HESKA-KWAŚNIEWICZ, K., Polish Philology
HUCZEK, M., Economics
ILUK, J., German Philology
JĘDRZEJKO, E., Polish Philology
KALAGA, W., English Philology
KAKIETEK, P., English Philology
KLESZCZ, K., Polish Philology
KŁOSIŃSKI, K., Polish Philology
KORPANTY, J., Classical Philology
KOSOWSKA, E., Philology
MALICKI, J., Polish Philology
MICZKA, T., Polish Philology
OCIECZEK, R., Polish Philology
OPACKA, A., Polish Philology
OPACKI, I., Polish Philology
PASZEK, J., Polish Philology
PIECHOTA, M., Philology
PIKALA-TOKARZ, B., Slavonic Philology
POLAŃSKI, E., Polish Philology
POLAŃSKI, K., English Philology
ROSTROPOWICZ, J., Classical Philology
SIERADZKA, D., Philology
SŁAWEK, T., English Philology
SOCHA, I., Philology
STEFANIAK, B., Philology
STYKA, J., Classical Philology
SZEWCZYK, G., German Philology
UDALSKA, E., Philology
WANDZIOCH, M., French Philology
WILKOŃ, A., Philology
WILKOSZEWSKA, K., Polish Philology
WÓJCIK, W., Polish Philology
WOJTYNEK-MUSIK, K., French Philology
WRÓBEL, H., Polish Philology

Faculty of Radio and Television (1B Bytkowska Street, 40-955 Katowice; tel. (32) 258-24-20; fax (32) 258-70-70; e-mail writv@us.edu.pl; internet www.writv.us.edu.pl):

BAJON, F., Film and Television Directing
BIENIOK, H., Media Management and Production
CZYŻEWSKI, S., Cinematography
DOKTOROWICZ, K., Media Management and Production
DZIWORSKI, B., Cinematography
HUDON, W., Cinematography
ŁUKASZEWICZ, J., Cinematography
MORSKI, K., Film and Television Directing
STUHR, J., Film and Television Directing
ŻAKOWICZ, A., Cinematography
ZANUSSI, K., Film and Television Directing

Faculty of Social Sciences (ul. Bankowa 11, 40-007 Katowice; tel. (32) 258-04-11; fax (32) 258-04-11; e-mail dziekan@wns.us.edu.pl):

BAŃKA, J., Philosophy
DOBROWOLSKI, P., Political Science
DŁUGAJCZYK, E., History
FRĄCKIEWICZ, L., Political Science
GŁOMBIK, C., Philosophy
GLUCHAŁĄ, J., History
JACHER, W., Sociology
KACZANOWICZ, W., History
KANTYKA, J., History
KIEPAS, A., Philosophy
KRAKOWSKI, J., Economics and Finance
MIKUŁOWSKI-POMORSKI, J., Political Science
PANIC, I., History
PROMIEŃSKA, H., Philosophy
PRZEWŁOCKI, J., History
SZCZEPAŃSKI, M., Sociology
SZTUMSKI, J., Sociology
ŚLĘCZKA, K., Philosophy
ŚWIĄTKIEWICZ, W., Sociology
WANATOWICZ, M., History
WÓDZ, J., Sociology
WÓDZ, K., Sociology
ŻECHOWSKI, Z., Sociology

Faculty of Theology (ul. Wita Stwosza 17A, 40-042 Katowice; tel. (32) 257-20-67; e-mail wtl@quest.kuria.katowice.pl):

DROŻDŻ, A., Moral Theology and Spirituality
GÓRSKI, J., Missiology and Theology of Religion
KRĘTOSZ, J., Pastoral Theology and History of Pastoral Ministry
KRZYSTECZKO, H., Catechetic Education
MYSZOR, J., Patristic Theology and History of the Church
MYSZOR, W., Patristic Theology and History of the Church
SŁOMKA, J., Dogmatic Theology
SZYMIK, J., Dogmatic Theology
ZĄDŁO, A.

UNIWERSYTET ŁÓDZKI
(University of Łódź)

Narutowicza 65, 90-131 Łódź
Telephone: (42) 365-40-00
Fax: (42) 678-39-58
E-mail: rektorat@uni.lodz.pl
Internet: www.uni.lodz.pl

Founded 1945
State control
Language of instruction: Polish
Academic year: October to September

Rector: Prof. Dr hab. WLODZIMIERZ NYKIEL
Pro-Rector (Economic Relations): Prof. Dr hab. BOGDAN GREGOR
Pro-Rector (Int. Relations): Prof. Dr hab. ZOFIA WYSOKINSKA
Pro-Rector (Research): Prof. Dr hab. JOANNA JABLKOWSKA
Pro-Rector (Students): Prof. Dr hab. PAWEL MASLANKA
Pro-Rector (Teaching): Prof. Dr hab. ANTONII ROZALSKI
Admin. Dir: Dr JAROSLAW GRABARCZYK
Librarian: Dr JAN JANIAK

Library: see Libraries and Archives
Number of teachers: 2,355

Number of students: 43,000

Publications: *Acta Universitatis Lodziensis* (Research Bulletin), *Kronika Uniwersitetu Łódzkiego*

DEANS

Faculty of Biology and Environmental Protection: Prof. Dr hab. ELZBIETA ZADZINSKA
Faculty of Chemistry: Prof. Dr hab. BOGUSLAW KRYCZKA
Faculty of Economics and Sociology: Prof. Dr hab. JAN GAJDA
Faculty of Educational Sciences: Prof. Dr hab. GRZEGORZ MICHALSKI
Faculty of Geographical Sciences: Prof. Dr hab. TADEUSZ MARSZAL
Faculty of International and Political Studies: Prof. Dr hab. TOMASZ DOMANSKI
Faculty of Law and Administration: Prof. Dr hab. AGNIESZKA LISZEWSKA
Faculty of Management: Prof. Dr hab. EWA WALINSKA
Faculty of Mathematics: Prof. Dr hab. RYSZARD PAWLAK
Faculty of Philology: Prof. Dr hab. PIOTR STALMASZCZYK
Faculty of Philosophy and History: Prof. Dr hab. ZBIGNIEW ANUSIK
Faculty of Physics and Applied Informatics: Prof. Dr ANNA URBANIAK-KUCHARCZYK

PROFESSORS

Faculty of Philology (ul. Kósciuszki 65, 90-514 Łódź; tel. (42) 639-02-53; fax (42) 639-02-54; e-mail filolog@uni.lodz.pl):

BIEŃKOWSKA, D., Polish Language
BOLECKI, W., Romance Literature and Contemporary Literature
CYBULSKI, M., Polish and Slavonic Languages
CZYŻEWSKI, S., Theory of Literature
DEJNA, K., Polish and Slavonic Languages
DUNIN-HORKAWICZ, J., Research on Books
GALA, A., Polish Language
GAZDA, G., Theory of Literature
HELMAN, A., Film
JABŁKOWSKA, J., German Philology
JANICKA-ŚWIDERSKA, I., English Philology
JANISZEWSKA-ZEIDLER, A., Theory of Literature, Theatre and Film
KAMIŃSKA, M., Polish and Slavonic Languages
KORYTKOWSKA, M., Slavonic Studies
KULIGOWSKA-KORZENIEWSKA, A., History of Theatre
LEWANDOWSKA-TOMASZCZYK, B., English Language
MAŁEK, E., Russian Literature
MUCHA, B., Russian Literature
NOWIKOW, W., Spanish Philology
NURCZYŃSKA-FIDELSKA, E., Theory of Literature
OKOŃ, J., Old Polish Literature
POKLEWSKA, K., Polish Literature
PUSZ, W., History of Polish Literature
RATAJCZAK, D., Theory of Literature
SADZIŃSKI, R., German Philology
STARNAWSKI, J., Old Polish Literature
SYPNICKI, J., French Language
TADEUSIEWICZ, H., Research on Books
TARANTOWICZ, A., German Philology
UMIŃSKA-TYTOŃ, E., Polish Language
WIŚNIEWSKI, B., Classical Philology
WOLSKA, B., History of 18th- and 19th-century Polish Literature
WRÓBLEWSKI, W., Classical Philology and Philosophy

Faculty of Philosophy and History (ul. Lindleya 3/5, 90-131 Łódź; tel. (42) 635-43-50; fax (42) 678-39-58):

BRZEZIŃSKI, A., Archaeology
CERAN, W., Prehistory and Medieval History
GAJDA-KRYNICKA, J., Philosophy
GŁOSEK, M., Prehistory
GROMCZYŃSKI, W., History of 19th- and 20th-century Philosophy
HASSAN ALI JAMSHEER, Near East Studies
HUNGER, R., History of Art
KAJZER, L., Medieval History, Archaeology
KRAWCZYK-WASILEWSKA, V., Cultural Anthropology, Ethnography
LIPIŃSKA, J., History of Art
MĄCZYŃSKA, M., Archaeology
MALINOWSKI, G., Logic
MATERSKI, W., Recent World History
NOWACZYK, A., Logic
PANASIUK, R., History of 19th-century Philosophy
PIÓRCZYŃSKI, J., Philosophy
PUŚ, P., 19th- and 20th-century Economic History of Poland
SAMUŚ, W., Recent Polish History
STYCZYŃSKI, M., History of Russian Philosophy
SZCZYGIELSKI, W., Modern Polish History
SZTABIŃSKI, G., Aesthetics
SZYNKIEWICZ, S., Ethnology
TUCHAŃSKA, B., Philosophy of Science
WIERUSZEWSKA-ADAMCZYK, M., Ethnography
WIŚNIEWSKI, E., Russian History
ZAJĄCZKOWSKI, S. M., Medieval Polish History

Faculty of Educational Sciences (ul. Kopernika 55, 90-553 Łódź; tel. (42) 639-07-76; fax (42) 639-07-77):

BŁASZCZYK, J., Physical Education
BŁASZCZYK, T., Science of Art
BUCZYŃSKI, A., Physical Education
DOWLASZ, B., Music Education
FLORKOWSKI, A., Psychology
JAŁMUŻNA, T., Pedagogy
KACZOROWSKI, S., Science of Art
KĘDZIORA, J., Biochemistry
KOCUR, J., Psychiatry
MARYNOWICZ-HETKA, E., Social Pedagogy
ORKISZ, S., Physical Education and Health
PAŃCZYK, J., Pedagogy
ŚLIWERSKI, B., Pedagogy
WIERZBIŃSKI, A., Music Education
WÓDKA, B., Science of Art

Faculty of Physics and Chemistry (ul. Pomorska 149/153, 90-236 Łódź; tel. (42) 635-57-00; fax (42) 678-70-87; e-mail dziekanat@fic.uni.lodz.pl):

BALD, E., Chemistry, Analysis
BARTCZAK, W., Theoretical Physics
BARTNIK, R., Organic Chemistry
CIBOROWSKI, J., Theoretical Physics
EPSZTAJN, J., Organic Chemistry
GILLER, M., Experimental Physics
JANKOWSKI, J., Experimental Nuclear Physics
KAPUŚCIK, E., Physics
KOSIŃSKI, P., Theoretical Physics
ŁAWRYNOWICZ, J., Complex Analysis
MAŚLANKA, P., Theoretical Physics
MLOSTOŃ, G., Organic Chemistry
PIEKARSKI, H., Physical Chemistry
PŁAZA, S., Inorganic Chemistry
REMBIELIŃSKI, J., Theoretical Physics
ROMANOWSKI, S., Physical and Theoretical Chemistry
SCHOLL, H., Physical Chemistry
SKOWROŃSKI, R., Organic Chemistry
SUKIENNICKI, A., Solid State Physics
TYBOR, W., Theoretical Physics
WOJTCZAK, L., Solid State Physics
ZAKRZEWSKI, J., Organic Chemistry

Faculty of Mathematics (ul. Banacha 22, 90-238 Łódź; tel. (42) 635-59-49; fax (42) 635-42-66; e-mail facmath@imul.uni.lodz.pl):

BALCERZAK, M., Real Analysis
CHĄDZYŃSKI, J., Complex Variables
GOLDSTEIN, S., Functional Analysis
JAJTE, R., Probability Theory
JAKUBOWSKI, Z., Analytical Functions
MIKOŁAJCZYK, L., Analytical Functions
NOWAKOWSKI, A., Optimization Theory
PASZKIEWICZ, A., Functional Analysis
PAWLAK, R., Functional Analysis
WALCZAK, P., Geometry
WALCZAK, S., Analytical Functions
WALISZEWSKI, W., Geometry
WILCZYŃSKI, W., Real Analysis
WŁODARCZYK, K., Functional Analysis, Complex Analysis

Faculty of Biology and Environmental Protection (ul. Pilarskiego 14, 90-231 Łódź; tel. (42) 635-40-16; fax (42) 635-45-06; e-mail dziekan@biol.uni.lodz.pl):

BAŃBURA, J., Biology, Ecology
BARTOSZ, G., Biophysics
BŁASIAK, J., Molecular Genetics
BRYSZEWSKA, M., Biophysics
DŁUGOŃSKI, J., Microbiology
DUDA, W., Biochemistry
GABARA, B., Cytology and Cytochemistry
GALICKA, W., Ecology and Zoology of Vertebrates
GAŹDZICKI, A., Geology
GRZYBKOWSKA, M., Zoology, Ecology
GWOŹDZIŃSKI, K., Molecular Biology
HEREŹNIAK, J., Biology
JAKUBOWSKA-GABARA, J., Geobotany
JANAS, K., Plant Physiology
JAWORSKI, A., Microbiology
JAŻDŻEWSKI, K., Zoology
JÓŹWIAK, Z., Biochemistry
KACA, W., Microbiology
KILIAŃSKA, Z., Biochemistry
KONOPACKI, J., Neurophysiology
KRAJEWSKA, W., Biochemistry
KUKULSKA-GOŚCICKA, T., Immunology
KWIATKOWSKA, M., Plant Cytology and Cytochemistry
LIGOWSKI, R., Biology, Oceanography
LIPIŃSKA, A., Biochemistry
LISZEWSKI, S., Economic Geography
ŁAWRYNOWICZ, M., Botany, Mycology
MARKOWSKI, J., Biology, Theriology
MASZEWSKI, J., Cell Biology
OLACZEK, R., Plant Systems and Geography
PENCZAK, T., Zoology, Fish Ecology
PIECHOCKI, A., Zoology
ROMANIUK, A., Animal Physiology and Neurophysiology
RÓŻALSKA, B., Infectious Biology
RÓŻALSKI, A., Microbiology
RUDNICKA, W., Immunology
SIDORCZYK, Z., Microbiology
SZWEDA-LEWANDOWSKA, Z., Molecular Biophysics
URBANEK, H., Biochemistry
WACHOWICZ, B., Biochemistry
ZALEWSKI, M., Biology

Faculty of Law and Administration (ul. Składowa 43, 90-127 Łódź; tel. (42) 635-40-21; fax (42) 678-45-33; e-mail dziekanat@wpia.uni.lodz.pl):

BIŃCZYCKA-MAJEWSKA, T., Labour Law
BORKOWSKI, J., Administrative Law
BRONIEWICZ, W., Civil Procedure
CHRÓŚCIELEWSKI, W., Administrative Procedure
DĘBOWSKA-ROMANOWSKA, T., Financial Law
GRZEGORCZYK, T., Penal Procedure
HOŁYST, B., Criminology
JANKOWSKI, J., Civil Law
KATNER, W., Civil Law
KMIECIAK, Z., Administrative Procedure
LELENTAL, S., Penal Law
LEWANDOWSKI, H., Labour Law
LEWASZKIEWICZ-PETRYKOWSKA, B., Civil Law
MARCINIAK, A., Civil Procedure
MATUSZEWSKI, J., Medieval History, History of Law
MATUSZEWSKI, J., History of State and Law
NYKIEL, W., Financial Law
PYZIAK-SZAFNICKA, M., Civil Law

RYMASZEWSKI, Z., History of State and the Law
SEWERYŃSKI, M., Labour Law
SZYMCZAK, T., Constitutional Law
TYLMAN, J., Penal Procedure
WŁODARCZYK, W., Social Insurance and Social Policy Law
ZIRK-SADOWSKI, M., Theory of State and Law

Faculty of Economics and Sociology (ul. Polskiej Organizacji Wojskowej 3/5, 90-255 Łódź; tel. (42) 635-51-12; fax (42) 635-50-32; e-mail dziekes@uni.lodz.pl):

BOKSZAŃSKI, Z., Cultural Sociology
BORKOWSKA, S., Business Administration
BUCHNER-JEZIORSKA, A., Sociology
DĘBSKI, W., Commerce and International Finance
DOKTÓR, K., Industrial Sociology
DOMAŃSKI, C., Statistics
DURAJ, J., Economics and Organization of Industry
GAJDA, J., Economics
JÓZEFIAK, C., Economics
KOCIK, L., Sociology
KRYŃSKA, E., Economics, Economic Policy
KUCHARSKA-STASIAK, E., Economics of Urban Development
KULPIŃSKA, J., Industrial Sociology
KWIATKOWSKI, E., Theory of Economy
LEWANDOWSKA, L., Economics, Industrial Economics
MARSZAŁEK, A., Economics
MILO, W., Econometrics, Statistics
MORTIMER-SZYMCZAK, H., Planning and Economic Policy
PIĄTKOWSKI, W., History of Economic Theory
PIOTROWSKA-MARCZAK, K., Finance
RUDOLF, S., Political Economy of Capitalism
SKODLARSKI, J., International Economic Relations
SUCHECKA, J., Economics
SUŁKOWSKI, B., Cultural Sociology
TOMASZEWICZ, Ł., Econometrics
TRZASKALIK, T., Economics
WARZYWODA-KRUSZYŃSKA, W., Sociology
WELFE, A., Econometrics
WELFE, W., Econometrics and Statistics
WOJCIECHOWSKI, E., Economics of Urban Development

Faculty of Management (ul. Matejki 22/26, 90-237 Łódź; tel. (42) 635-50-50; fax (42) 635-53-06; e-mail wzdziek@uni.lodz.pl):

DIETL, J., Commercial Economics
GREGOR, W., Organization and Management, Marketing
GREGORCZYK, B., Organization and Management, Banking
JANOWSKA, Z., Human Resources, Management Accountancy
JARUGA, A., Cost Accounting, Management Accountancy
KOBYLIŃSKI, W., Quality Management
ŁAŃCUCKI, J., Management
MARKOWSKI, T., Economics of Urban Development
MIKOŁAJCZYK, Z., Theory of Organization and Management
PIASECKI, B., Economics and Organization of Industry
SIKORSKI, C., Organization and Management
SZYMCZAK, J., Management
ZIELIŃSKI, J. S., Computer Science

Faculty of International and Political Studies (ul. Składowa 41/43, 90-127 Łódź; tel. (42) 675-42-74; fax (42) 678-49-16; e-mail interul@uni.lodz.pl):

DE LAZARI, A., Eastern Studies
DOMAŃSKI, T., Euromarketing
DUBICKI, T., History
DZIEKAN, M., History of Arabic Literature
KMIECIŃSKI, J., Archaeology
KUCZYŃSKI, K. A., German Literature
MICHOWICZ, W., History of International Relations (Dir)
OLEKSY, E., American Literature
PRZEBINDA, G., Russian Philology

Faculty of Geographical Sciences (ul. Pilarskiego 14/16, 90-231 Łódź; tel. (42) 635-45-09; e-mail dziekan@geo.uni.lodz.pl):

BACHVAROV, M., Urban Geography and Tourism
HEFFNER, K., Political Geography and Regional Studies
JELONEK, A., Social and Economic Geography
KŁYSIK, C., Climatology and Meteorology
KOTER, M., Environmental Biophysics
KOWALCZYK, A., Urban Geography and Tourism
KOŻUCHOWSKI, K., Physical Geography
LASKOWSKI, S., Pedology
LISZEWSKI, S., Economic Geography
MARSZAŁ, T., Social and Economic Geography
MATCZAK, A., Urban Geography
WERWICKI, A., Economic Geography

UNIWERSYTET MEDYCZNY W ŁODZI (Medical University of Łódź)

ul. Kościuszki 4, 90-419 Łódź
Telephone: (42) 632-51-00
Fax: (42) 630-07-07
E-mail: rektor@rkt.am.lodz.pl
Internet: www.umed.lodz.pl

Founded 2002 by the merger of Łódź Medical Acad. and Łódź Military Medical Acad.
State control
Rector: Prof. ANDRZEJ LEWIŃSKI
Number of teachers: 1,177
Number of students: 23,127

DEANS

Faculty of Medicine: Prof. KAZIMIERZ JĘDRZEJEWSKI
Faculty of Medicine and Dentistry: Prof. WIELISŁAW PAPIERZ
Faculty of Military Medicine: Prof. JAN BŁASZCZYK
Faculty of Pharmacy: Prof. JADWIGA SZYMAŃSKA
Faculty of Physiotherapy: Prof. JUREK OLSZEWSKI
Faculty of Public Health: Prof. ANNA JEGIER

KATOLICKI UNIWERSYTET LUBELSKI JANA PAWŁA II (John Paul II Catholic University of Lublin)

ul. Racławickie 14, 20-950 Lublin
Telephone: (81) 445-41-05
Fax: (81) 445-41-91
E-mail: dwz@kul.lublin.pl
Internet: www.kul.lublin.pl

Founded 1918
Private control
Academic year: October to June
Chancellor: Archbp Prof. Dr hab. JÓZEF ŻYCIŃSKI
Rector: Rev. Prof. Dr hab. STANISŁAW WILK
Vice-Rector (Admin. and Finances): Prof. Dr hab. STANISŁAW ZIĘBA
Vice-Rector (Research, and Int. and Public Relations): Rev. Prof. Dr hab. SŁAWOMIR NOWOSAD
Vice-Rector (Didactics and Education): Prof. Dr hab. JÓZEF FERT
Librarian: Rev. Dr TADEUSZ STOLZ
Library of 1,800,000 vols (incl. dept libraries) of which 1,000,000 books, 50,000 old books, 35,000 vols of periodicals, 5,000 MSS, 3,000 maps and atlases, 10,000 music scores, 10,000 audio cassettes and records, 15,000 graphic items
Number of teachers: 1,185
Number of students: 18,672
Publications: *Acta Mediaevalia*, *Człowiek i Przyroda* (2 a year), *Ethos* (4 a year), *KERYGS* (2 a year), *Law–Administration–Church* (4 a year), *Przegląd Uniwersytecki* (6 a year), *Roczniki Filozoficzne* (1 a year), *Roczniki Humanistyczne* (1 a year), *Roczniki Nauk Prawnych* (1 a year), *Roczniki Nauk Społecznych* (1 a year), *Roczniki Psychologiczne* (1 a year), *Roczniki Teologiczne* (1 a year), *Studia Norwidiana* (1 a year), *Studia Polonijne* (1 a year), *Summarium*, *Zeszyty Naukowe KUL* (4 a year), *Vox Patrum* (2 a year)

DEANS

Faculty of Humanities: Prof. Dr hab. KRZYSZTOF NARECKI
Faculty of Law, Canon Law and Administration: Rev. Prof. Dr hab. ANTONI DĘBIŃSKI
Faculty of Mathematics and Natural Sciences: Rev. Prof. Dr hab. RYSZARD SMARZEWSKI
Faculty of Philosophy: Prof. Dr hab. STANISŁAW JANECZEK
Faculty of Social Sciences: Prof. Dr hab. ANDRZEJ SĘKOWSKI
Faculty of Theology: Rev. Prof. Dr hab. MIROSŁAW KALINOWSKI
Off-Campus Faculty of Legal and Economic Sciences: Rev. Prof. Dr hab. JAN ZIMNY (Stalowa Wola): Rev. Prof. Dr hab. TADEUSZ GUZ (Tomaszów Lubelski)
Satellite Faculty of Social Sciences: Rev. Prof. Dr hab. MARIAN WOLICKI

PROFESSORS

Faculty of Humanities (tel. (81) 445-41-45; fax (81) 445-41-90):

ANDRUSIW, S., Ukrainian Literature
CHODKOWSKI, R., Classical Linguistics, Greek Literature
DEPTUA, C., History of Medieval Culture
ECKMANN, A., Classical Linguistics, Ancient Christian Literature
KACZMAREK, W., Drama and Theatre
KNAPIŃSKI, R., Art History
KONEFAŁ, J., 19th – 20th Centuries History of Social and Political Movements
KUCZYŃSKA, J., Medieval Polish Art
LAMEŃSKI, L., Modern Art History
MAZURCZAK, M., General Medieval Art History
MAKARSKI, W., Linguistics
OŁDAKOWSK, M., Contemporary Literature
PODBIELSKI, H., Classical Greek Philology
WOŹNIAK, A., Russian Literature

Faculty of Law, Canon Law and Administration (tel. (81) 445-37-31; fax (81) 445-37-26; e-mail prawa@kul.lublin.pl):

CIOCH, H., Civil Law
DĘBIŃSKI, A., Roman Law
HRYSZCZUK, W., Medical Law and Forensic Medicine
KOŚĆ, A., Philosophy of Law
KRUKOWSKI, J., Canon Law
ŁĄCZKOWSKI, W., Financial Law, Administrative Law
MISZTAL, H., Canon Law, Law and Religion
SZAJKOWSKI, A., Commercial Law
TYSZCZYK, B., History of State and Law
WITCZAK, W., Forensic Medicine
ZUBERT, B., Canon Law

Faculty of Mathematics and Natural Sciences (tel. (81) 445-45-52; fax (81) 445-35-36):

CICHOCKA, E., Agriculture
FISCHER-MALANOWSKA, Z., Ecology
GOSZCZYŃSKI, W., Horticulture
HOŁUBIEC, J., Numerical Analysis and Programming
JANICKI, A., Information Technology

MATUS, P., Mathematics
RZYMOWSKI, W., Mathematics Application
SKOWRONSKI, T., Toxicology
STĘPNIEWSKA, Z., Agricultural Engineering
SZESZKO, M., Mathematics and Computer Science
SZYSZKA, R., Molecular Biology
URBANOWICZ, P., Computer Science
WOJCIECHOWSKA, W., Ecology, Hydrobiology
ZIĘBA, S., Humanistic Ecology

Faculty of Philosophy (tel. (81) 445-42-51; fax (81) 445-41-90; e-mail filozofia@kul.lublin.pl):

BRONK, A., Philosophy of Science
GAŁKOWSKI, J., Ethics, Political Philosophy
KICZUK, S., Logic
MARYNIARCZYK, A., Metaphysics
SZOSTEK, A., Ethics
WIELGUS, S., History of Philosophy, Medieval Philosophy
ZIELIŃSKI, E., History of Ancient and Medieval Philosophy
ŻYCIŃSKI, J., Philosophy of Nature, Philosophy of Science

Faculty of Social Sciences (tel. (81) 445-35-48; fax (81) 445-42-93; e-mail wns@kul.lublin.pl):

BIELA, A., Experimental Psychology, Industrial Psychology, Environmental Psychology
BRAUN-GAŁKOWSKA, M., Educational Psychology, Family Psychology
DYCZEWSKI, L., Sociology of Culture, Sociology of Family
GILOWSKA, Z., Economics, Local Finance
MARIAŃSKI, J., Sociology of Religion, Sociology of Morals
SĘKOWSKI, A., Rehabilitative Psychology
WÓJCIK, S., Sociology, Local Policy
ZALESKI, Z., Experimental Psychology

Faculty of Theology (tel. (81) 445-38-41; fax (81) 445-38-45; e-mail teolog@kul.lublin.pl):

DRĄCZKOWSKI, F., Patristics
GŁOWA, W., Pastoral Theology, Liturgy
KAMIŃSKI, R., Pastoral Theology, Organization of Pastoral Care
PACIOREK, A., Biblical Studies
RUBINKIEWICZ, R., Biblical Studies
RUSECKI, M., Fundamental Theology
TRONINA, A., Biblical Studies
WITCZYK, H., Biblical Studies
WILK, S., History of Monasteries
ZASĘPA, T., Contemporary Forms of Communication of the Faith
ZIMOŃ, H., Religious Studies

Off-Campus Faculty of Legal and Economic Sciences (ul. Lwowska 68, 22-600 Tomaszow Lubelski; tel. and fax (84) 664-45-74):

ANTONOWICZ, L., International Public Law
CZEREWKO, G., Theory of Economics
KOSSAK, W., Civil Law
KRUKOWSKI, J., Theory of Law
MISZTAL, H., Canon Law
ŚRUTWA, J., Church History of Law
WOJCIECHOWSKI, W., Econometrics and Statistics

Satellite Faculty of Social Sciences (ul. Ofiar Katynia 6, 37-450 Stalowa Wola; tel. (15) 642-25-35):

NYCZKAŁO, N., Education
WOLICKI, M., Education

UNIWERSYTET PRZYRODNICZY W LUBLINIE
(Lublin University of Life Sciences)

ul. Akademicka 13, 20-950 Lublin
Telephone: (81) 445-66-22
Fax: (81) 533-35-49
E-mail: poczta@up.lublin.pl
Internet: www.ar.lublin.pl

Founded 1955

Faculties: agricultural engineering, agriculture, animal husbandry, horticulture, veterinary science

Rector: Prof. Dr hab. MARIAN WESOŁOWSKI

Library of 336,000 vols
Number of teachers: 640
Number of students: 6,000

Publications: *Annales UMCS*, *Excerpta Veterinaria Lublin* (in English), *Sectio DD Medicina Veterinaria*, *Sectio E Agricultura*, *Sectio EE Zootechnica*, *Sectio EEE Horticulture*.

UNIWERSYTET MEDYCZNY W LUBLINIE
(Medical University in Lublin)

ul. Aleje Racławickie 1, 20-059 Lublin
Telephone: (81) 528-84-00
Internet: www.umlub.pl

Founded 1950

Rector: Prof. Dr hab. ANDRZEJ KSIĄŻEK

Library of 250,000 vols
Number of teachers: 1,180
Number of students: 3,535

Faculties: Medicine, Pharmacy and Nursing.

UNIWERSYTET MARII CURIE-SKŁODOWSKIEJ
(Marie Curie-Skłodowska University)

Plac Marii Curie-Skłodowskiej 5, 20-031 Lublin
Telephone: (81) 537-51-07
Fax: (81) 537-51-02
E-mail: rector@ramzes.umcs.lublin.pl
Internet: www.umcs.lublin.pl

Founded 1944

Academic year: October to June

Rector: Prof. Dr hab. WIESŁAW ANDRZEJ KAMIŃSKI
Pro-Rector (Devt): Prof. Dr hab. JERZY WĘCŁAWSKI
Pro-Rector (Gen.): Prof. Dr hab. TADEUSZ BOROWIECKI
Pro-Rector (Scientific Research, Int. Relations and Off-Campus Centres): Prof. Dr hab. ANNA TUKIENDORF
Pro-Rector (Students and Teaching): Prof. Dr hab. ANNA PAJDZIŃSKA
Chief Admin. Officer: Inż. MACIEJ GRUDZIŃSKI
Librarian: Dr BOGUSŁAW KASPEREK

Library: gen. scientific colln of 2,528,340 vols, including 338,853 vols of periodicals, 10,168 online journals, 803 MSS, 369,207 patents, 40,272 maps and atlases, 14,954 music scores, 19,215 ancient books, 2,814 dissertations, 4,822 audio cassettes and records

Number of teachers: 1,805
Number of students: 34,758

Publication: *Annales Universitatis Mariae Curie-Skłodowska*

DEANS

Faculty of Biology and Earth Sciences: Prof. Dr hab. RYSZARD DĘBICKI
Faculty of Chemistry: Prof. Dr hab. ANDRZEJ DĄBROWSKI
Faculty of Economics: Prof. Dr hab. ELŻBIETA SKRZYPEK
Faculty of Fine Arts: Prof. Dr hab. URSZULA BOBRYK
Faculty of Humanities: Prof. Dr hab. HENRYK GMITEREK
Faculty of Law and Administration: Prof. Dr hab. ANTONI PIENIĄŻEK
Faculty of Mathematics, Physics and Computer Science: Prof. Dr hab. KRZYSZTOF POMORSKI
Faculty of Philosophy and Sociology: Prof. Dr hab. JACEK PAŚNICZEK
Faculty of Political Science: Prof. Dr hab. STANISŁAW MICHAŁOWSKI
Faculty of Psychology and Pedagogy: Prof. Dr hab. ZDZISŁAW BARTKOWICZ

PROFESSORS

Faculty of Biology and Earth Sciences (ul. Akademicka 19, 20-030 Lublin; tel. (81) 537-52-16; fax (81) 537-52-14; internet binoz.umcs.lublin.pl):

BEDNARA, J., Anatomy and Plant Cytology
BYSTREK, J., Plant Systematics
DĘBICKI, A., Soil Science
DERNAŁOWICZ-MALARCZYK, E., Biochemistry
DROŻAŃSKI, W., Microbiology
FIEDERUK, J., Microbiology
GRANKOWSKI, N., Molecular Biology
HARASIMIUK, M., Geomorphology
JAKUBOWICZ, T., Biochemistry and Immunology
KAŁKOWSKA, K., Animal Physiology
KANDEFER-SZERSZEŃ, M., Microbiology
KRUPA, Z., Plant Physiology
KUREK, E., Environmental Microbiology
LEONOWICZ, A., Biochemistry
MICHALCZYK, Z., Hydrography
PĘKALA, K., Physical Geography and Geomorphology
ROGALSKI, J., Molecular Biology
RUSSA, R., Microbiology
SIRKO, M., Cartography
SKORUPSKA, A., Microbiology
ŚNIEZKO, R., Botany
ŚWIĘS, F., Botany
SZCZODRAK, J., Microbiology
TRĘBACZ, K., Biology and Biophysics
WOJCIECHOWSKI, K., Geography
WOJTANOWICZ, J., Physical Geography and Geomorphology
ZAWADZKI, T., Plant Physiology

Faculty of Chemistry (Plac Marii Curie-Skłodowskiej 3, 20-030 Lublin; tel. (81) 537-57-16; fax (81) 533-33-48; e-mail chemia@hermes.umcs.lublin.pl; internet chemia.umcs.lublin.pl):

BOROWIECKI, T., Chemical Technology
BORÓWKO, M., Physical Chemistry
CHIBOWSKI, E., Physical Chemistry
CHIBOWSKI, S., Physical Chemistry
DAWIDOWICZ, A., Physical Chemistry
DĄBROWSKI, A., Theoretical Chemistry
FERENC, W., Inorganic Chemistry
GAWDZIK, B., Physical Chemistry
GOWOREK, J., Physical Chemistry
HUBICKA, H., Inorganic Chemistry
HUBICKI, Z., Inorganic Chemistry
JAŃCZUK, B., Physical Chemistry
KOZIOŁ, A., Chemistry, X-ray Crystallography
LEBODA, R., Physical Chemistry of Surfaces and Chromatography
MACHOKI, A., Heterogeneous Catalysis, C1 Chemistry
MATYNIA, T., Organic Chemistry
NARKIEWIEZ-MICHAŁCK, J., Theoretical Chemistry
NAZIMEK, D., Physical Chemistry
PATRYKIEJEW, A., Physical Chemistry
PIETRUSIEWICZ, K., Organic Chemistry
PIKUS, S., X-ray Crystallography-powder Diffraction
PODKOŚCIELNY, W., Organic Chemistry
RAYSS, J., Physical Chemistry
RÓŻYŁŁO, J., Physical Chemistry
RUDZINSKI, W., Theoretical Chemistry
SOKOŁOWSKI, S., Theoretical Chemistry
STASZCZUK, P., Physical Chemistry
WOLIŃSKI, K., Quantum Chemistry, Methods and Applications
WÓJCIK, W., Physical Chemistry

Faculty of Economics (tel. (81) 537-54-62; fax (81) 537-54-62; e-mail ekonomia@ramzes.umcs.lublin.pl; internet ekonomia.umcs.lublin.pl):

GRABOWIECKI, J., Political Economy
KARPUŚ, P., Economics
KOZŁOWSKI, S., Economics
MAMEARZ, M., Economics, Financial Markets
MUCHA-LESZKO, B., Political Economy, Economic Planning
POMORSKA, A., Finances
RONCK, H., Economics
RUDNICKI, M., Economics of Agriculture
SIKORSKI, C., Economics
SKOWRONEK, Cz., Industrial Economics
SKRZYPEK, E., Economics
SOBCZYK, G., Economics
SZYMAŃSKI, Z., Economics, History of Economic Thought
SZYNAL, J., Economics, Banking
WĘCŁAWSKI, J., Economics, Banking
WICH, U., Urban Planning
ZALEWA, J., Agricultural Economics
ZUKOWSKI, M., Economics

Faculty of Fine Arts (ul. Kraśnicka 2b, 20-718 Lublin; tel. (81) 523-53-91; fax (81) 523-53-91; e-mail warto@klio.umcs.lublin.pl):

BERNATOWICZ, M., Conducting
BOBRYK, U., Conducting
DĄBROWSKA, B., Conducting
GÓRSKI, K., Conducting
GRYKA, J., Graphics
HERMAN, M., Painting
JAWORSKA, A., Conducting
JAWORSKI, L., Conducting
KIERSKI, J., Sculpture
KOŁODZIEJ, R., Graphics
LECH, P., Graphics
MAZUREK, G., Graphics
MIELESZKO, S., Teaching of Sculpture
NALEPKA, J., Music Education
NAWROT-TRZCIŃSKA, I., Photographics
NIEDŹWIEDŹ, Z., Graphics
ORDYK-CZYZŻEWSKA, E., Conducting
POPEK, A., Graphics
PRZYCHODZIŃSKA-KACICZAK, M., Music Education
RZECHOWSKA-KLAUZA, G., Conducting
SMOCZYŃSKI, M., Painting
SNOCH, M., Graphics
ŞTYKA, A., Painting
SWIECA, C., Music Education
WOJCIECHOWSKI, J., Painting
WRÓBLEWSKI, W., Painting
ZAWADZKI, T., Painting
ŻUKOWSKI, S., Painting

Faculty of Humanities (Plac Marii Curie-Skłodowskiej 4, 20-031 Lublin; tel. (81) 537-54-66; fax (81) 537-54-66; internet www.umcs.lublin.pl):

BARTMIŃSKI, J., History of Polish Literature
BLAIM, A., English Literature
BONIECKA, B., History of Polish Literature
GMITEREK, M., Modern History
GRABIAS, S., Applied and Sociolinguistics
KARDELA, H., English Philology
KĘSIK, M., French Linguistics
KOKOWSKI, A., Archaeology
KOLEK, L., English Literature
KOLODZIEJ, E., Archiving
KORDELA, H., English Philology
KOSYL, Cz., Polish Philology
KRAJKA, W., Theory of Literature, History of English Literature
KRUK, S., History of Polish Theatre
LEWANDOWSKI, J., Modern History
LEWICKI, R., Linguistics
MAZUR, J., Polish Linguistics
MIKULEC, B., Modern History
MISIEWICZ, J., Theory of Literature
MYRDZIK, B., History of Polish Literature
NIEZNANOWSKI, S., Old Polish Literature
ORŁOWSKI, J., History of Russian Literature
PLISIECKI, J., Film
POMORSKI, J., Methodology and History of Historiography
RADZIK, T., Contemporary History
SAWECKA, H., Theory of Romance Literature
ŚLADKOWSKI, W., Modern History
SWIĘCH, W., Modern Polish Literature
STĘPNIK, K., Polish Literature
SZCZYGIEŁ, R., Medieval History
SZYMAŃSKI, J., Auxiliary Sciences of History
TOKARSKI, R., Polish Language
TRELIŃSKA, B.
WIŚNIEWSKA, H., Polish Linguistics
WOŹNIAKIEWICZ-DZIADOSZ, M., Theory of Literature

Faculty of Law and Administration (tel. (81) 537-51-26; fax (81) 537-54-05; internet pia.umcs.lublin.pl):

BOJARSKI, T., Penal Law
CHORĄŻY, K., Administrative Law
GDULEWICZ, E., Constitutional Law
KIDYBA, A., Economic Law
KMIECIK, R., Penal Law
KOROBOWICZ, A., History of State and Law
KURYŁOWICZ, M., Roman Law
LESZCZYŃSKI, L., Theory of State and Law
OLESZKO, A., Civil Law
POŹNIAK-NIEDZIELSKA, M., Economic Law
SAWCZUK, M., Civil Procedure
SKRĘTOWICZ, E., Penal Law
SKUBISZ, R., European Community Law
SZRENIAWSKI, J., Administrative Law and Administrative Science
TOKARCZYK, R., History of Political Thought
WĄSEK, A., Penal Law and Criminology
WITKOWSKI, W., History of State and Law
WÓJTOWICZ, W., Financial Law
WRÓBEL, A., European Community Law
ZDYB, M., Administrative Law

Faculty of Mathematics, Physics and Computer Science (Plac Marii Curie-Skłodowskiej 2, 20-031 Lublin; tel. (81) 537-52-12; fax (81) 537-52-71; internet mfi.umcs.lublin.pl):

ADAMCZYK, B., Physics
BARAN, A., Computer Science
BUDZYŃSKI, M., Experimental Physics
GLADYSZEWSKI, L., Theoretical Physics
GOEBEL, K., Differential Equations
GOWOREK, T., Nuclear Physics
GÓŹDŹ, A., Theoretical Physics
GRUSZECKI, W., Biophysics
HAŁAS, ST., Experimental Physics
JAŁOCHOWSKI, M., Experimental Physics
KAMIŃSKI, W., Nuclear Physics
KOMOROWSKI, T., Differential Equations
KORCZAK, Z., Solid Body Physics
KOZICKI, J., Computer Science
KRAWCZYK, W., Biophysics
KRZYŻ, J., Analytic Functions
KUCZUMOW, T., Differential Equations
KUREK, J., Differential Geometry
MĄCZKA, D., Experimental Physics
MICHALAK, L., Experimental Physics
MIKOŁAJCZAK, P., Solid Body Physics
MURAWSKI, K., Computer Science
NOWAK, M., Analytic Functions
POMORSKA, B., Theoretical Physics
POMORSKI, K., Theoretical Physics
PRUS, S., Functional Analysis
RYCHLIK, Z., Probability Theory
RZYMOWSKI, W., Differential Equations
SIELANKO, J., Nuclear Physics
SIELEWIESIUK, J., Physics and Biophysics
SYZNAL, D., Probability Theory
SZEZERBA, J., Computer Science
TARANKO, E., Theoretical Physics
TARANKO, R., Theoretical Physics
WANIURSKI, J., Analytical Functions
WÓJCIK, L., Experimental Physics
WYSOKIŃSKI, K., Theoretical Physics
ZĄBEK, S., Numerical Methods
ZAŁUŹNY, M., Theoretical Physics
ZIĘBA, W., Probability Theory
ZŁOTKIEWICZ, E., Analytic Functions
ŻUK, J., Experimental Physics

Faculty of Philosophy and Sociology (Plac Marii Curie-Skłodowskiej 4, 20-030 Lublin; tel. (81) 537-54-79; fax (81) 537-54-81; e-mail dziekfis@ramzes.umcs.lublin.pl; internet bacon.umcs.lublin.pl):

CZARNECKI, Z., History of Philosophy
FILIPIAK, M., Sociology
JEDYNAK, S., Ethics
KOSIŃSKI, S., Sociology
LIBISZEWSKA-ZÓŁTKOWSKA, M., Sociology
MIZIŃSKA, J., Epistemology
OGRYZKO-WIEWIÓROWSKA, M., Sociology
PAŚNICZEK, J., Logic
STYK, J., Sociology
SYMOTIUK, S., Philosophy of Culture
TOKARSKI, S., Sociology of Medicine

Faculty of Political Science (Plac Litewski 3, 20-080 Lublin; tel. (81) 532-42-78; fax (81) 533-66-10; e-mail poldziek@sokrates.umcs.lublin.pl; internet www.politologia.pl):

CHAŁUPCZAK, H., International Relations
CZARNOCKI, A., International Relations
HOŁDA, Z., Human Rights
HUDZIK, J., Political Philosophy
JACHYMEK, J., Political Thought
JANUSZ, G., International Relations
JELENKOWSKI, M., Political Doctrines
KUCHARSKI, W., National Minorities
MAJ, Cz., International Relations
MAJ, F., Contemporary History
MICH, W., Contemporary History
MICHAŁOWSKI, S., Local Government
MIECZKOWSKI, A., Contemporary History
OLSZEWSKI, E., Political Movements
PIETRAŚ, M., International Relations
PIETRAŚ, Z. J., International Relations
STĘPICŃ, S., Contemporary History
SZELIGA, Z., Constitutional Law
WÓJCIK, A., Contemporary History
ŻMIGRODZKI, M., Political Systems

Faculty of Psychology and Pedagogy (ul. Narutowicza 12, 20-950 Lublin; tel. (81) 537-63-04; fax (81) 537-04-27; internet pip.umcs.lublin.pl):

BARTKOWICZ, Z., Pedagogy
CACKOWSKA, M., Didactics
CHODKOWSKA, M., Sociology
GAJDA, M., Pedagogy
GAŚ, Z., Psychopathology
GUZ, S., Pedagogy
HERZYK, A., Neuropsychology
KACZMAREK, B., Psychology
KĘPSKI, Cz., Pedagogy
KIRENKO, J., Pedagogy
KRASOWICZ-KUPIS., G., Psychology
KUCHA, R., History of Learning and Education
KWIATKOWSKA, G., Philosophy
OCHMAŃSKI, M., High School Pedagogy
PALAK, Z., Pedagogy
POPEK, S., Psychology
SARAN, J., Pedagogy
STACHYRA, J., Pedagogy
WĘGLIŃSKI, A., Pedagogy

UNIWERSYTET WARMIŃSKO-MAZURSKI W OLSZTYNIE (University of Warmia and Mazury in Olsztyn)

ul. M. Oczapowskiego 2, 10-719 Olsztyn
Telephone: (89) 523-33-30
Fax: (89) 523-44-56
E-mail: rektor@uwm.edu.pl
Internet: www.uwm.edu.pl

Founded 1999 through merger of Olsztyn University of Agriculture and Technology, Higher School of Pedagogy, and Warmian Theological Institute

State control

Rector: Prof. Dr hab. JÓZEF GÓRNIEWICZ
Pro-Rector: Dr WOJCIECH JANCZUKOWICZ
Pro-Rector for Devt: Dr SZCZEPAN FIGIEL
Pro-Rector for Staff Affairs: Dr TADEUSZ RAWA
Pro-Rector for Research and Cooperation with Nat. Economy: Dr WŁADYSŁAW KORDAN
Pro-Rector for Student Affairs: Dr TADEUSZ RAWA
Dir of Admin.: Dr WOJCIECH CYMERMAN

Library of 823,374 vols, 1,811 periodicals
Number of teachers: 1,680
Number of students: 30,000

Publications: *Forum Oświatowe* (1 or 2 a year), *Humanistyka i Przyrodoznawstwo* (1 or 2 a year), *Prace Językoznawcze* (1 or 2 a year), *Echa Przeszłości* (1 or 2 a year), *Forum Teologiczne* (1 or 2 a year), *Acta Polono-Ruthenica* (1 or 2 a year), *Acta Neophoilologica* (1 or 2 a year), *Economic Sciences* (1 or 2 a year), *Technical Sciences* (1 or 2 a year), *Natural Sciences* (1 or 2 a year)

DEANS

Faculty of Agriculture and Environmental Management: Prof. JAN KUCHARSKI
Faculty of Animal Bioengineering: Prof. MANFRED LOREK
Faculty of Arts and Educational Sciences: Dr EUGENIUSZ ŁAPIŃSKI
Faculty of Biology: Prof. JADWIGA PRZAŁA
Faculty of Engineering and Technical Sciences: Prof. KAZIMIERZ WIERZBICKI
Faculty of Environmental Sciences and Fisheries: Dr IRENA WOJNOWSKA-BARYŁA
Faculty of Food Sciences: Prof. ZBIGNIEW SMIETANA
Faculty of Geodesy and Land Management: Dr RYSZARD ŻRÓBEK
Faculty of Humanities: Prof. ANDRZEJ STANISZEWSKI
Faculty of Management and Business Administration: Dr HENRYK LELUSZ
Faculty of Theology: Rev. Prof. ALOJZY SZORC
Faculty of Veterinary Medicine: Prof. TOMASZ JANOWSKI

UNIWERSYTET OPOLSKI (Opole University)

pl. Kopernika 11a, 45-058 Opole
Telephone: (77) 454-58-71
Fax: (77) 454-51-22
E-mail: sekretariat@uni.opole.pl
Internet: www.uni.opole.pl

Founded 1994 by the merger of Opole Teacher Training College and the Theological-Pastoral Institute of Opole
State control
Chancellor: ANDRZEJ KIMLA
Deputy Chancellor: GRZEGORZ KŁOSIŃSKI

DEANS

Faculty of Economics: Prof. JANUSZ SŁODCZYK
Faculty of History and Education: Prof. STEFAN MAREK GROCHALSKI
Faculty of Mathematics, Physics and Chemistry: Prof. HUBERT WOJTASEK
Faculty of Natural Sciences and Technology: Prof. ANDRZEJ GAWDZIK
Faculty of Philology: Prof. IRENA JOKIEL
Faculty of Theology: Prof. TADEUSZ DOLA

UNIWERSYTET IM. ADAMA MICKIEWICZA W POZNANIU (Adam Mickiewicz University in Poznań)

ul. H. Wieniawskiego 1, 61-712 Poznań
Telephone: (61) 852-64-25
Fax: (61) 829-41-11
E-mail: rectorof@amu.edu.pl
Internet: www.amu.edu.pl

Founded 1919
Rector: Prof. Dr hab. STANISŁAW LORENC
Pro-Rectors: Prof. Dr hab. BRONISŁAW MARCINIAK, Prof. Dr hab. BOGUSŁAW MRÓZ, Prof. Dr hab. KAZIMIERZ PRZYSZCZYPKOWSKI, Prof. Dr hab. BOGDAN WALCZAK, Prof. Dr hab. JANUSZ WIŚNIEWSKI
Registrar: Mgr STANISŁAW WACHOWIAK
Librarian: Dr ARTUR JAZDON

Library: see Libraries and Archives
Number of teachers: 2,634
Number of students: 51,677

DEANS

Faculty of Biology: Prof. Dr hab. ANDRZEJ LESICKI
Faculty of Chemistry: Prof. Dr hab. GRZEGORZ SCHROEDER
Faculty of Education and Fine Arts in Kalisz: Prof. JERZY RUBIŃSKI
Faculty of Educational Studies: Prof. Dr hab. WIESŁAW AMBROZIK
Faculty of Geography and Geology: Prof. Dr hab. JANUSZ CHOIŃSKI
Faculty of History: DANUTA MINTA-TWORZOWSKA
Faculty of Law and Administration: ANDRZEJ SZWARC
Faculty of Mathematics and Computer Science: Prof. Dr hab. ZBIGNIEW PALKA
Faculty of Modern Languages and Literature: Prof. Dr hab. JÓSEF DARSKI
Faculty of Physics: Prof. Dr hab. ANDRZEJ DOBEK
Faculty of Polish and Classical Philologies: Prof. Dr hab. ANTONI SMUSZKIEWICZ
Faculty of Social Sciences: Prof. Dr hab. JAN GRAD
Faculty of Theology: Prof. Dr hab. PAWEŁ BORTKIEWICZ

PROFESSORS

Faculty of Biology (ul. Umultowska 89, 61-614 Poznań; tel. (61) 829-55-52; fax (61) 829-55-50; e-mail dziekan@amu.edu.pl):

AUGUSTYNIAK, H., Biochemistry
BALCERKIEWICZ, S., Plant Ecology
BEDNORZ, J., Animal Ecology
BIELAWSKI, J., Animal Cytology
BŁASZAK, Cz., Animal Ecology
BOBOWICZ, M., Plant Genetics
BUJAKIEWICZ, A., Mycology
BURCHARDT, L., Hydrobiology
CIEŚLIK, J., Anthropology
GOŹDZICKA-JÓZEFIAK, A., Biochemistry
GWÓŹDŹ, E., Plant Ecophysiology
HRYNIEWIECKA, L., Biochemistry
JACKOWIAK, B., Botany
KRASKA, M., Hydrobiology
KRZAK, M., Plant Genetics
LATOWSKI, K., Plant Taxonomy
LISIEWSKA, M., Mycology
NIEDBAŁA, W., Animal Ecology
PIONTEK, J., Anthropology
PRUS-GŁOWACKI, W., Plant Genetics
RATAJCZAK, L., Plant Physiology
RATAJCZAK, W., Plant Physiology
STĘPCZAK, K., Zoology
STRZAŁKO, J., Anthropology
SZWEYKOWSKA-KULIŃSKA, Z., Biochemistry
WOJTASZEK, P., Biochemistry
WOŹNY, A., Plant Cytology
ŻUKOWSKI, W., Plant Taxonomy

Faculty of Chemistry (ul. Grunwaldzka 6, 60-780 Poznań; tel. (61) 829-13-35; fax (61) 865-80-08; e-mail depchem@amu.edu.pl):

BRZEZIŃSKI, B., Bio-organic Physical Chemistry
BUREWICZ, A., Teaching of Chemistry
DEGA-SZAFRAN, Z., Physical Organic Chemistry
FIEDOROW, R., Catalysis
GAWROŃSKI, J., Organic Chemistry, Stereochemistry
JARCZEWSKI, A., Physical Organic Chemistry
JASKÓLSKI, M., Crystallography and Biological Chemistry
KATRUSIAK, A., Crystallography
KONARSKI, J., Theoretical Chemistry
KOPUT, J., Physical Chemistry
KORONIAK, H., Synthesis and Structure of Organic Compounds
KOWALAK, S., Catalysis
LIS, S., Rare Earths
ŁOMOZIK, L., Coordination Chemistry, Bioinorganic Chemistry
MARCINIAK, B., Photochemistry
MARCINIEC, B., Organometallic Chemistry, Molecular Catalysis
NAWROCKI, J., Water Treatment Technology
PARYZEK, Z., Organic and Natural Products Chemistry
RADECKA-PARYZEK, W., Coordination and Macrocyclic Chemistry, Bioinorganic Chemistry
ROZWADOWSKA, M., Asymmetric Synthesis, Alkaloid Chemistry
RYCHLEWSKA, U., Crystallography
SARBAK, Z., Adsorption and Catalysis, Environmental Protection
SCHROEDER, G., Organic Chemistry
SIEPAK, J., Water and Soil Analysis
SZAFRAN, M., Physical Organic Chemistry
WACHOWSKA, H., Chemistry of Coal
WASIAK, W., Instrumental Analysis
WOJCIECHOWSKA, M., Heterogeneous Catalysis
WOLSKA, E., Solid-state Chemistry and Magnetochemistry
WYRZYKIEWICZ, E., Mass Spectrometry of Organic Compounds
WYSOCKA, W., Natural Products Chemistry
ZIOŁEK, M., Heterogeneous Catalysis

Faculty of Education and Fine Arts in Kalisz (62-800 Kalisz; tel. (62) 767-07-30; fax (62) 764-57-21; e-mail wpa@amu.edu.pl):

JANKOWSKI, D., Education
NAWROT, A., Fine Arts
NIEKRASZ, A., Methodology of Art
WERNER, B., Music Arts

Faculty of Educational Studies (ul. Szamarzewskiego 89, 60-569 Poznań; tel. (61) 847-49-00; fax (61) 847-49-00):

DUDZIKOWA, M., School Education
FRĄCKOWIAK, T., Social Education
GNITECKI, J., Methodology of Education
MELOSIK, Z., Comparative Education
POTULICKA, E., Comparative Education
PRZYSZCZYPKOWSKI, K., Adult Education
SKRZYPCZAK, J., Adult Education
STRYKOWSKI, W., Educational Technology
ZANDECKI, A., Youth Educational Problems
ŻOŁĄDŹ-STRZELCZYK, D., Pedagogy, History of Education

Faculty of Geography and Geology (ul. Fredry 10, 61-701 Poznań; tel. (61) 852-02-98; fax (61) 853-02-10; e-mail dziego@amu.edu.pl):

CHOIŃSKI, J. A., Hydrology
CIERNIEWSKI, J., Remote Sensing
FEDOROWSKI, J., Palaeozoology
GŁAZEK, J., Dynamic and Regional Geology
GŁĘBOCKI, B., Economic Geography
GÓRSKI, J., Hydrogeology
KANIECKI, A., Hydrology
KOSTRZEWSKI, A., Dynamic Geomorphology, Geoecology
KOZACKI, L., Integrated Physical Geography
LORENC, S., Geology, Petrography
MUSZYŃSKI, A., Mineralogy, Petrography
NOWACZYK, B., Geomorphology
PARYSEK, J., Socioeconomic Geography
ROGACKI, H., Spatial Management

SKOCZYLAS, J., Petroarchaeology, Archometry
TOBOLSKI, K., Palaeobotany
WOŚ, A., Climatology, Meteorology

Faculty of History (ul. Sw. Marcin 78, 61-809 Poznań; tel. (61) 852-87-79; fax (61) 852-47-82; e-mail dhist@amu.edu.pl):

BŁASZCZYK, G., East European History
BUCHOWSKI, M., European Ethnology, Theory of Anthropology
FOGEL, J., Bronze and Early Iron Age Prehistory
HAUSER, P., Contemporary History
JASIEWICZ, Z., Ethnology of Poland and Central Asia
JASIŃSKI, T., Medieval History
KOŚKO, A., Prehistory of Poland
KOTŁOWSKI, T., Contemporary History
KOWAL, S., Economic History
LABUDA, A., History of Art
ŁAZUGA, W., Modern History
MOLIK, W., Modern Polish History
MROZEWICZ, L., Ancient History
OLEJNIK, K., Military History
OLSZEWSKI, W., Modern and Contemporary History
PIOTROWSKI, P., History of Contemporary Art
POSERN-ZIELIŃSKI, A., Ethnology of the Americas, Anthropology of Ethnicity
SCHRAMM, T., Modern History
SERWAŃSKI, M., Modern History
SIERPOWSKI, S., Contemporary History
SKIBIŃSKI, S., History of Medieval Art
STRZELCZYK, J., Medieval History
WYRWA, A., History
ZAWADZKI, S., Ancient History

Faculty of Law and Administration (ul. Św. Marcin 90, 61-809 Poznań; tel. (61) 853-68-43):

CHOBOT, A., Labour Law
GOMUŁOWICZ, A., Financial Law
GULCZ, M., Economics
KĘPIŃSKI, M., European Law
KIJOWSKI, A., Labour Law
KOŁECKI, H., Criminal Law
ŁĄCZKOWSKI, W., Financial Law
MAŁECKI, J., Financial Law
NIEDBAŁA, Z., Labour Law
OWOC, M., Criminal Law
PATRYAS, W., Theory of State and Law
SMYCZYŃSKI, T., Civil Law
SOŁTYSIŃSKI, S., Civil Law
STACHOWIAK, S., Criminal Procedure
SZWARC, A. J., Criminal Law
TYRANOWSKI, J., International Law
WRONKOWSKA-JAŚKIEWICZ, S., Theory of State and Law
ZEDLER, F., Civil Procedure

Faculty of Mathematics and Information Sciences (ul. Umultowska 87, 61-614 Poznań; tel. (61) 829-53-11; fax (61) 829-53-15; e-mail wmiuam@math.amu.edu.pl):

BATÓG, T., Mathematical Logic, Mathematical Linguistics
BUSZKOWSKI, W., Logic, Linguistics, Computation Theory
DOMAŃSKI, P., Functional Analysis
DREWNOWSKI, L., Functional Analysis
HUDZIK, H., Functional Analysis
KACZOROWSKI, J., Number Theory
KĄKOL, J., Functional Analysis, Topology
KAROŃSKI, M., Discrete Mathematics and Probability
KRZYŚKO, M., Mathematical Statistics
KUBIACZYK, I., Mathematics
ŁUCZAK, T., Discrete Mathematics and Probability
MARZANTOWICZ, W., Mathematics
MASTYŁO, M., Functional Analysis
MURAWSKI, R., Mathematical Logic, Philosophy of Mathematics
PYCH-TABERSKA, P., Approximation Theory
RUCIŃSKI, A., Discrete Mathematics and Probability
SZUFLA, ST., Differential Equations
WASZAK, A., Functional Analysis

Faculty of Modern Languages and Literature (ul. Niepodległości 4, 61-874 Poznań; tel. (61) 852-22-03; fax (61) 853-69-33; e-mail spuppel@amu.edu.pl):

ANDRUSZKO, CZ., Russian Literature
BAŃCZEROWSKI, J., General Linguistics
DARSKI, J., German Linguistics
DZIUBALSKA-KOŁACZYK, K., English Linguistics
FISIAK, J., English Linguistics
GUSSMANN, E., English Linguistics
KALISZAN, J., Russian Linguistics
KAROLAK, CZ., German Literature
KASZYŃSKI, S., Austrian Literature and Culture
KOPCEWICZ, A., American Literature
KOPYTKO, R., English Linguistics
KRYSZTOFIAK-KASZYŃSKA, M., Danish Literature
ŁABĘDZKA, I., Romance Literature
LIPOŃSKI, W., Anglo-Saxon Studies
ŁOBACZ, P., General Linguistics
MAJEWICZ, A., Oriental Linguistics
MALINOWSKI, W., Romance Literature
MARKUNAS, A., Methodology of Russian Language Teaching
ORŁOWSKI, H., German Literature
PAPIÓR, J., German Literature and Culture
PFEIFFER, W., Applied Linguistics
PIOTROWSKI, B., History of Scandinavia
POGONOWSKI, J., Mathematical Linguistics
PUPPEL, S., English Linguistics
SCHATTE, CH., German Linguistics
SIEK-PISKOZUB, T., English Linguistics
SIKORSKA, L., English Literature
SOBKOWIAK, W., English Linguistics
STEFFEN-BATOGOWA, M., General Linguistics
SYPNICKI, J., Romance Linguistics
TOMASZKIEWICZ, T., Romance Linguistics
WĄSIK, Z., General Linguistics
WILCZYŃSKA, W., Applied Linguistics
WÓJTOWICZ, M., Russian Linguistics
ZGÓŁKA, T., General Linguistics

Faculty of Physics (ul. Umultowska 85, 61-614 Poznań; tel. (61) 829-51-56; fax (61) 829-51-55; e-mail dobek@amu.edu.pl):

BARNAS, J., Solid-state Physics
BŁASZAK, M., Mathematical Physics
BŁASZCZAK, Z., Molecular Optics
DOBEK, A., Biophysics
HOJAN, E., Electroacoustics
JACYNA-ONYSZKIEWICZ, Z., Quantum Physics
JURGA, K., Radiospectroscopy
JURGA, S., Radiospectroscopy and Molecular Physics
KAMIENIARZ, G., Computer Physics
KOZIEROWSKI, M., Nonlinear Optics
KURZYŃSKI, M., Statistical Physics
ŁABOWSKI, M., Molecular Acoustics
MAKAREWICZ, R., Environmental Acoustics
MICNAS, R., Solid-state Physics
MRÓZ, B., Ferroelectrics
NAWROCIK, W., Physics
OZIMEK, E., Psychoacoustics
PARZYŃSKI, R., Quantum Electronics
PATKOWSKI, A., Molecular Biophysics
PUSZKARSKI, H., Solid-state Physics
ROBASZKIEWICZ, S., Solid-state Physics
SCHWARZENBERG-CZERNY, A., Astronomy
STANKOWSKA, J., Molecular Physics
ŚLIWIŃSKA-BARTKOWIAK, M., Physics
TANAŚ, R., Nonlinear Optics
WĄSICKI, J., Physics
WNUK, E., Astronomy

Faculty of Polish and Classical Philologies (ul. Niepodległości 4, 67-874 Poznań; tel. (61) 852-71-27; fax (61) 852-71-27):

ABRAMOWSKA, J., Polish Literature, Historical Poetics
ADAMCZYK, M., Old Polish Literature
BĄBA, S., Idioms and Culture of Polish Language
BAKUŁA, B., 20th-century Literature
BALCERZAN, E., Polish Literature, Theory of Literature and 20th-century Literature
BARTOL, K., Classical Philology
BOREJSZO, M., Polish Linguistics
CHRZĄSTOWSKA, B., New Teaching Methods, History of Polish Literature
CZAPLIŃSKI, P., Theory of Literature, Literary Criticism
DANIELEWICZ, J., Hellenistic Philology
DWORACKI, S., Hellenistic Philology
HENDRYKOWSKA, M., Film History and Theory
KRĄŻYŃSKA, Z., Polish Linguistics
LEGEŻYŃSKA, A., Theory of Literature
LEWANDOWSKI, I., Latin Philology
LEWANDOWSKI, T., Polish Literature
NOWAK, H., Polish Dialectology
POKRZYWNIAK, J. T., Old Polish Literature
PRZYBYLSKI, R. K., Theory of Literature, History of Literature
RATAJCZAK, D., Polish Drama
RZEPKA, W., Polish Linguistics
SMUSZKIEWICZ, A., Teaching of Polish Language and Literature
TROJANOWICZ, Z., 19th-century Polish Literature
WALCZAK, B., Polish Linguistics
WIEGANDT, E., History of Contemporary Literature
WYDRA, W., Editorial and Bibliography
WYSŁOUCH, S., Polish Literature, Theory of Literature and 20th-century Literature
ZGÓŁKA, T., General Linguistics
ZGÓŁKOWA, H., Polish Linguistics

Faculty of Social Sciences (ul. Szamarzewskiego 89, 60-568 Poznań; tel. (61) 847-25-71; fax (61) 847-15-55; e-mail socuam@amu.edu.pl):

ANDRZEJEWSKI, B., History of German Philosophy
BRZEZIŃSKA, A., Development
BRZEZIŃSKI, J., Methodology of Psychology
BUKSIŃSKI, T., Social Philosophy, Philosophy of History
CHYŁA, W., Culture
DROZDOWICZ, Z., Philosophy of Religion
GOLKA, M., Sociology of Culture, Social Anthropology
JAMROZIAKOWA, A., Aesthetics
KOSMAN, M., History
KOSMANOWA, B., History of Science
KOSZEL, B., History and Political Science
MALENDOWSKI, W., Political Science
NOWAK, L., Philosophy of Science, Political Philosophy
NOWAKOWA, I., Philosophy of Science
ORCZYK, J., Economics and History
PAŁUBICKA, A., Theory of Culture
PUŚLECKI, Z., International Economic Relations
SAKSON, A., Sociology of Ethnic Minorities, Sociology of Youth
SĘK, H., Health and Clinical Psychology
SOBCZAK, J., Law
STACHOWSKI, R., History of Psychological Thought
TITTENBRUN, J., Theory and Practice of Privatization
WOŹNIAK, Z., Sociology of Medicine
ZAMIARA, T., Philosophy of Science
ZIÓŁKOWSKI, M., Sociological Theory

Faculty of Theology (ul. Wieżowa 2–4, 61-111 Poznań; tel. (61) 829-39-90; fax (61) 851-97-35; e-mail thfac@man.poznan.pl):

BRANIAK, J., Sociology
CZĘSZ, B., Theology, Patristic Theology
LEWEK, A., Theology, Religious Communication
NIPARKO, R., Christian Pedagogy

PONIŻY, B., Theology, Old Testament Exegisis
PYTEL, J., Theology, New Testament Exegisis
STEFAŃSKI, J., Theology
SZPET, J., Theology, Religious Education
TARNOWSKI, K., Philosophy
WĘCŁAWSKI, T., Theology, Fundamental Theology
WEJMAN, H., Theology of Spirituality

UNIWERSYTET PRZYRODNICZY W POZNANIU (Poznan University of Life Sciences)

ul. Wojska Polskiego 28, 60-637 Poznań
Telephone: (61) 848-72-00
Fax: (61) 848-71-46
E-mail: rektorat@up.poznan.pl
Internet: www.au.poznan.pl

Founded 1951

Faculties: agronomy, animal breeding and biology, food science and nutrition, forestry, horticulture, land reclamation and environmental engineering, wood technology

Rector: Prof. GRZEGORZ SKRZYPCZAK

Library of 641,000 vols
Number of teachers: 782
Number of students: 9,016

UNIWERSYTET RZESZOWSKI (Rzeszów University)

ul. Rejtana 16C, 35-959 Rzeszów
Telephone: (17) 872-10-00
Fax: (17) 852-20-44
E-mail: rektor@univ.rzeszow.pl
Internet: www.univ.rzeszow.pl

Founded 2001 through the merger of the Pedagogical Univ. of Rzeszów, the Marie Curie Skłodowska Univ., Lublin (Rzeszów branch) and the Economics Faculty of the Agricultural Acad. of Krakow
State control

Rector: Prof. WŁODZIMIERZ BONUSIAK
Pro-Rector for Education: Prof. STANISŁAW KRAWCZYK
Pro-Rector for Foreign Relations: Prof. STANISŁAW SAGAN
Pro-Rector for Scientific Research and Finances: Prof. JERZY KITOWSKI
Pro-Rector for Student Affairs and Accreditation: Prof. EWA ORLOF

DEANS

Faculty of Agriculture and Biology: Prof. CZESŁAW PUCHALSKI
Faculty of Arts and Education: Prof. MIECZYSŁAW RADOCHOŃSKI
Faculty of Economics: Prof. SYLWESTER MAKARSKI
Faculty of Health Sciences: Prof. RYSZARD CIEŚLIK
Faculty of History and Sociology: Prof. ALEKSANDER BOBKO
Faculty of Law: Prof. JAN ŁUKASIEWICZ
Faculty of Mathematics and Natural Sciences: Prof. JERZY TOCKI
Faculty of Philology: Prof. STANISŁAW ULIASZ
Faculty of Physical Education: Prof. KAZIMIERZ OBODYŃSKI
External Faculty of Biotechnology (Kolbuszowa): Prof. IGOR Z. ZUBRZYCKI

UNIWERSYTET SZCZECIŃSKI (Szczecin University)

ul. Papieża Jana Pawła II 22A, 70-453 Szczecin
Telephone: (91) 444-11-72
Fax: (91) 444-11-74
E-mail: rektorat@univ.szczecin.pl
Internet: www.us.szc.pl

Founded 1985
State control
Language of instruction: Polish
Academic year: October to September

Rector: Prof. Dr hab. ZDZISŁAW CHMIELEWSKI
Vice-Rectors: Prof. Dr hab. WALDEMAR TARCZYŃSKI (Academic Affairs), Prof. Dr hab. HENRYK BABIS (Education Affairs), Prof. Dr hab. STANISŁAW CZEPITA (Devt and Org.)
Admin. Officer: EUGENIUSZ KISIEL

Library: see Libraries and Archives
Number of teachers: 1,008
Number of students: 26,793

Publication: *Przegląd Uniwersytecki* (The Univ. Review, 6 a year)

DEANS

Faculty of Arts: Prof. Dr hab. EDWARD WŁODARCZYK
Faculty of Economics and Management: Prof. Dr hab. TERESA LUBIŃSKA
Faculty of Law and Administration: Prof. Dr hab. ZBIGNIEW OFIARSKI
Faculty of Management and Economics of Services: Prof. Dr hab. JÓZEF PERENC
Faculty of Mathematics and Physics: Prof. Dr hab. RYSZARD LEŚNIEWICZ
Faculty of Natural Sciences: Prof. Dr hab. LUCJAN AGAPOW

PROFESSORS

ALEKSIEJENKO, M., Arts
BĄKOWSKI, W., Economics
BIAŁECKI, T., Arts
BRONK, H., Economics
CHMIELEWSKI, Z., Arts
CHWESIUK, K., Economics
CZAPLEWSKI, R., Economics
CZERNIATIN, W., Mathematics
DEPTUŁA, W., Natural Sciences
DOROZIK, L., Economics
DUDZIŃSKI, J., Economics
DZIEDZICZAK, I., Economics
FARYŚ, J., Arts
GIZA, A., Arts
GŁODEK, Z., Economics
GŁOWACKI, A., Arts
GÓRBIEL, A., Law
GRANOWSKI, J., Physics
GRZYWACZ, W., Economics
HADACZEK, B., Arts
HŁYŃCZAK, A. J., Natural Sciences
HOZER, J., Economics
JANASZ, W., Economics
JASKOT, K., Arts
JASZCZANIN, J., Natural Sciences
KARWOWSKI, J., Economics
KĘPCZYŃSKI, J., Natural Sciences
KIZIUKIEWICZ, T., Economics
KOPYCIŃSKA, D., Economics
KOROBOW, W., Mathematics
KOŹMIAN, D., Arts
KUCHARSKA, E., Arts
LUKS, K., Economics
MEJBAUM, W., Arts
MOŁCZANOWA, O., Arts
NOWAKOWSKI, A., Economics
PERENC, J., Economics
PRUSAK, F., Law
RADOMSKA-TOMCZUK, M., Fine Arts
ROGALSKA, S., Natural Sciences
ROGALSKI, M., Natural Sciences
RZEPA, T., Social Sciences
SIERGIEJEW, N., Physics
ŚŁAWIK, K., Law
ŚLIAŻAS, J., Natural Sciences
STANIELEWICZ, J., Arts
SULIKOWSKI, A., Arts
SUŁKOWSKI, CZ., Economics
SYGIT, M., Medical Sciences
SZAŁEK, B., Economics, Arts
SZLAUER, L., Natural Sciences
URBAŃCZYK, E., Economics
WAŚNIEWSKI, T., Economics
WIERZBICKI, T., Economics
WOŹNIAK, R., Arts
ZALEWSKI, P., Economics
ZAWADZKI, J., Economics

UNIWERSYTET MIKOŁAJA KOPERNIKA W TORUNIU (Nicholas Copernicus University of Toruń)

ul. Gagarina 11, 87-100 Toruń
Telephone: (56) 654-29-51
Fax: (56) 654-29-44
E-mail: rektor@uni.torun.pl
Internet: www.uni.torun.pl

Founded 1945
State control
Language of instruction: Polish
Academic year: October to September (two terms)

Rector: Prof. Dr hab. ANDRZEJ RADZIMIŃSKI
Vice-Rectors: Prof. Dr hab. ANDRZEJ TRETYN, Prof. Dr hab. DANUTA JANICKA, Prof. Dr hab. WŁODZIMIERZ KARASZEWSKI, Prof. Dr hab. WITOLD WOJDYŁO, Prof. Dr hab. MAŁGORZATA TAFIL-KLAWE
Registrar: Dr PAWEŁ MODRZYŃSKI
Librarian: Dr KRZYSZTOF NIERZWICKI

Library of 1,155,888 vols, 563,862 vols of periodicals, 54,912 old books, 82,117 manuscripts, 14,227 cartographic publications, 62,711 graphics and posters, 87,376 musical scores, 11,366 records; 754,086 vols in departmental libraries; special collns: Pomeranica, Copernicana, Baltica, Polish Emigration Archives
Number of teachers: 2,222
Number of students: 31,000

Publications: *Bulletin of Geography, Socio-economic Series, Chaotic and Regular Dynamics, Comparative Law Review, Eastern European Countryside, Logic and Logical Philosophy, Medical and Biological Sciences, Open Systems and Information Dynamics, Prussia Sacra* (published jointly with Max-Planck-Institut, Göttingen), *Reports on Mathematical Physics, Topological Methods in Nonlinear Analysis, Theoria et Historia Scientiarum, Toruński Rocznik Praw Człowieka i Pokoju*

DEANS

Faculty of Biology and Earth Sciences: Prof. Dr hab. WIESAW KOZAK
Faculty of Chemistry: Prof. Dr hab. JERZY ŁUKASZEWICZ
Faculty of Education Sciences: Prof. Dr hab ALEKSANDER NALASKOWSKI
Faculty of Economics and Management: Prof. Dr hab. JÓZEF STAWICKI
Faculty of Fine Arts: Prof. Dr hab. PIOTR KLUGOWSKI
Faculty of Health Sciences: Prof. Dr hab ZBIGNIEW BARTUZI
Faculty of History: Prof. Dr hab. JACEK GZELLA
Faculty of Humanities: Prof. Dr hab. ANDRZEJ SZAHAJ
Faculty of Languages: Prof. Dr hab. ADAM BEDNAREK
Faculty of Law and Administration: Prof. Dr hab. ANDRZEJ SOKALA
Faculty of Mathematics and Computer Science: Prof. Dr hab. ANDRZEJ ROZKOSZ
Faculty of Medicine: Prof. Dr hab. HENRYK KAŹMIERCZAK
Faculty of Pharmacy: Prof. Dr hab BRONISŁAW GRZEGORZEWSKI
Faculty of Political Sciences and Int. Studies: Prof. Dr hab. ROMAN BÄCKER
Faculty of Physics, Astronomy and Informatics: Prof. Dr hab. STANISŁAW CHWIROT
Faculty of Theology: Rev. Prof. Dr hab. JAN PERSZON

PROFESSORS

Faculty of Biology and Earth Sciences (ul. Gagarina 9, 87-100 Toruń; tel. (56) 611-44-41; fax (56) 611-47-72; e-mail baranow@biol.uni.torun.pl; internet www.biol.uni.torun.pl):

BEDNAREK, R., Soil Science
BEDNARSKA, E., Plant Cytology
BUSZKO, J., Entomology, Zoogeography
CAPUTA, M., Animal Physiology
CEYNOWA-GIEŁDON, M., Plant Taxonomy, Geobotany
CHWIROT, B., Plant and Animal Cytology
DAHM, H., Microbiology
DONDERSKI, W., Microbiology, Biotechnology
FALKOWSKI, J., Economic Geography, Spatial Management
GIZIŃSKI, A., Hydrobiology
GNIOT-SZULŻYCKA, J., Biochemistry
GÓRSKA-BRYLASS, A., Plant Cytology
KOPCEWICZ, J., Plant Physiology
KRIESEL, G., Anthropology
MAIK, W., Social Geography
NIEWAROWSKI, W., Physical Geography, Palaeogeography
REJEWSKI, M., Plant Ecology
SADURSKI, A., Hydrobiology and Environmental Protection
SZUPRYCZYŃSKI, J., Geomorphology
TRETYN, A., Plant Physiology

Faculty of Chemistry (ul. Gagarina 7, 87-100 Toruń; tel. (56) 654-29-38; fax (56) 654-24-77; e-mail wydzial@chem.uni.torun.pl; internet www.chem.uni.torun.pl):

BUSZEWSKI, B., Analytical Chemistry
CHOSTENKO, A., Nuclear Chemistry
GRODZICKI, A., Inorganic Chemistry
KITA, P., Inorganic Chemistry
ROZWADOWSKI, M., Physical Chemistry
RYCHLICKI, G., Physical Chemistry
SADLEJ, A., Theoretical Chemistry
TRYPUĆ, M., Chemical Technology
ZAIDLEWICZ, M., Organic Chemistry

Faculty of Economics and Management (ul. Gagarina 13A, 87-100 Toruń; tel. (56) 611-46-08; fax (56) 654-24-50; e-mail krystyna@econ.uni.torun.pl; internet www.econ.uni.torun.pl):

BOGDANIENKO, J., Investment Economics
DREWIŃSKI, M., Management
GŁUCHOWSKI, J., Finance Management
JAWOROWSKI, P., Agricultural Economics
KACZMARCZYK, S., Marketing
MELLER, J., Human Resources Management
SMOLEŃSKI, S., Marketing
SOJAK, S., Accounting
STANKIEWICZ, M., Strategic Management and Planning
SUDOŁ, S., Industrial Management
SZULCE, H., Marketing
WIŚNIEWSKI, Z., Employment Policy
ZIELIŃSKI, Z., Econometrics

Faculty of Fine Arts (ul. Sienkiewicza 30/32, 87-100 Toruń; tel. (56) 622-70-51; fax (56) 622-59-71; internet www.uni.torun.pl/wydzialy/wszp):

BEBARSKA, J., Sculpture
CANDER, K., Painting
CHMIELEWSKI, B., Drawing
CHMIELEWSKI, W., Drawing
FLIK, J., Painting
GUTTFELD, A., Painting
KILJAŃSKI, L., Graphics
KRUSZELNICKI, Z., History of Art
LIMONT, W., Art Education
MALINOWSKI, J., History of Art
PAWŁOWSKI, M., Graphics
PRĘGOWSKI, J., Painting
PRZYBYLIŃSKI, B., Graphics
ROUBA, B., Restoration of Painting
SKIBIŃSKI, S., Medieval Art and Architecture
SŁOBOSZ, J., Graphics
STRZELCZYK, A., Conservation on Painting and Leather
SZAŃKOWSKI, M., Sculpture
TAJCHMAN, J., Restoration of Architectural Monuments
WOLSKI, L., Painting
ZIOMEK, M., Painting

Faculty of History (Pl. Teatralny 2A, 87-100 Toruń; tel. (56) 622-62-03; fax (56) 622-28-44; e-mail atom@his.uni.torun.pl; internet www.his.uni.torun.pl):

CHUDZIAK, J., Archaeology of Buildings
DYGDAŁA, J., 16th- to 18th-century Polish History
KALEMBKA, S., Polish and General History
KOZŁOWSKI, R., Modern Polish History
KUTZNER, M., Polish and General Medieval History of Art
MALISZEWSKI, K., 16th- to 18th-century Polish and General History
MAŁŁEK, K., 16th- to 18th-century Polish and General History
MIELCZAREK, M., Classical Archaeology and Numismatics
NOWAKOWSKI, A., Medieval Archaeology and Military History
OLCZAK, J., Medieval Archaeology and History of Glass
POMIAN, K., Polish and General Modern History of Art and Culture
RADZIMIŃSKI, A., Medieval Church History
REZMER, W., Polish Army between the Two World Wars
STASZEWSKI, J., 16th- to 18th-century Polish and General History
SUDZIŃSKI, R., Modern Polish History
SYMONIDES, J., EU and International Law
TANDECKI, J., Polish-German Relationship
TONDEL, J., History of the Book
WAŻBIŃSKI, Z., History of Art
WENTA, J., Medieval History
WOJCIECHOWSKI, M., 19th- and 20th-century Polish and General History
WOŹNICZKA-PARUZEL, B., Bibliotherapy
ZAREMSKA, H., Cultural History

Faculty of Humanities (ul. Fosa Staromiejska 1A, 87-100 Toruń; tel. (56) 611-36-10; fax (56) 652-27-69; e-mail whminus@ped.uni.torun.pl; internet www.uni.torun.pl/wydzialy/wh):

ADAMSKI, W., Social Structures and Transformations
BAŃKA, A., Psychology
BOROWICZ, R., Sociology of Education
BYBLUK, M., Teaching of Languages
HUBNER, P., History of Science, Sociology of Institutions
KALETA, A., Rural Sociology
KOWALIK, S., Special Education
KWIECIŃSKI, Z., Sociology of Education
ŁUKASZEWICZ, R., School Education
MELOSIK, Z., General Education
MUCHA, J., Social Anthropology and History of Sociology
NALASKOWSKI, A., General Education
PAWLAK, J., History of Philosophy and Social Thought
PERZANOWSKI, J., Logic and Philosophy
PÓŁTURZYCKI, J., General Education
SCHULZ, R., General Education
SIEMIENIECKI, B., Technology in Education
SZAHAJ, A., Political Philosophy, Philosophy of Culture
SZULAKIEWICZ, M., Political Culture
TEMPCZYK, M., Philosophy of Natural Science
TYBURSKI, W., Ethics
WINCŁAWSKI, W., History of Sociology
ZANDECKI, A., General Education
ZELAZNY, M., Aesthetics, History of Philosophy

Faculty of Languages (Coll. Maius, ul. Fosa Staromiejska 3, 87-100 Toruń; tel. (56) 611-35-10; fax (56) 622-66-59; internet www.uni.torun.pl/wydzialy/wf):

BEZWIŃSKI, A., Russian Literature
BRZOZA, H., Russian Literature
FRIEDEL, T., Slavonic and Polish Linguistics
GROCHOWSKI, M., General Linguistics, Semiotics
HARTMANN, H., German Literature
KALLAS, K., Contemporary Polish Syntax
KRYSZAK, J., Contemporary Polish Poetry
SAUERLAND, K., German Literature
SAWICKA, I., Slavonic Linguistics
SKUCZYŃSKI, J., History of Polish Literature and Theatre
SPEINA, J., 20th-century Polish Prose
SZARMACH, M., Greek Literature, Second Sophistry
SZUPRYCZYŃSKA, M., Contemporary Polish Syntax
WĄSIK, Z., English Linguistics
WISZNIOWSKA-MAJCHRZYK, M., English Drama
WRÓBLEWSKI, W., Classical Philology

Faculty of Law and Administration (ul. Gagarina 15, 87-100 Toruń; tel. (56) 611-41-10; fax (56) 611-40-05; e-mail kandydat_wpia@cc.uni.torun.pl; internet www.law.uni.torun.pl):

BORODO, A., Financial Law
BRZEZIŃSKI, B., Public Finance Law
BULSIEWICZ, A., Criminal Law
FILAR, M., Penal Law
JASUDOWICZ, T., Human Rights
JUSTYŃSKI, J., Political and Legal Doctrines
KALLAS, M., History of the Polish State
KOLASIŃSKI, K., Labour Law
KULICKI, M., Crime Detection
LANG, A., Theory of Law and State
ŁASZEWSKI, R., History of Law
LUBIŃSKI, K., Civil Law
MAREK, A., Criminal Law
MIK, C., European Law, Human Rights
MORAWSKI, L., Theory of Law and State
NESTEROWICZ, M., Civil Law
OCHENDOWSKI, E., Administrative Law

Faculty of Mathematics and Computer Science (ul. Chopina 12/18, 87-100 Toruń; tel. (56) 611-34-10; fax (56) 622-89-79; e-mail wmii@mat.uni.torun.pl; internet www.mat.uni.torun.pl):

GÓRNIEWICZ, L., Nonlinear Analysis
JAKUBOWSKI, A., Theory of Probability
KAMIŃSKI, B., Ergodic Theory
KWIATKOWSKI, J., Ergodic Theory
LEMAŃCZYK, M., Ergodic Theory
NAGAJEW, A., Theory of Probability, Statistics
SIMSON, D., Algebra
SKOWROŃSKI, A., Algebra
TYC, A., Algebra

Faculty of Physics, Astronomy and Informatics (ul. Grudziądzka 5/7, 87-100 Toruń; tel. (56) 611-33-10; fax (56) 611-53-97; e-mail lidia@phys.uni.torun.pl; internet www.phys.uni.torun.pl):

BĄCZYNSKI, A., Molecular Spectroscopy, Optoelectronics
BALTER, A., Molecular Spectroscopy, Photophysics, Molecular Biophysics
BIELSKI, A., Atomic and Molecular Physics, History of Physics
CHWIROT, S., Atomic and Optical Physics
DEMBIŃSKI, S., Quantum Optics, Chaos Theory
DUCH, W., Computational Intelligence, Cognitive Science and Theoretical Physics
JANKOWSKI, K., Atomic and Molecular Physics, Computational Methods in Physics
JASKÓLSKI, W., Atomic and Molecular Physics, Physics of Low-dimensional Structures

KARWOWSKI, J., Atomic and Molecular Physics
KOSSAKOWSKI, A., Theoretical Physics, Statistical Physics
KREŁOWSKI, J., Astrophysics
KUS, A., Radio Astronomy
MĘCZYŃSKA, H., Solid State Physics
RACZYŃSKI, A., Atomic and Molecular Physics
ROZPŁOCH, F., Condensed Matter Physics, Physics of Carbon
SZUDY, J., Atomic and Molecular Physics, Optical Collisions
WOJTOWICZ, A., Solid State Physics, Optoelectronics
WOLSZCZAN, A., Radio Astronomy, Pulsars
WOSZCZYK, A., Astrophysics, Physics of Comets
WYBOURNE, B., Atomic and Molecular Physics
ZAREMBA, J., Atomic and Molecular Physics

Faculty of Theology (ul. Mickiewicza 121, 87-100 Toruń; tel. (56) 611-49-90; fax (56) 611-49-91; internet www.uni.torun.pl/wydzialy/wt):

BAGROWICZ, J., Catechetic and Religious Education
GRABOWSKI, M., Christian Philosophy
RYCHLICKI, C., Dogmatic and Ecumenical Theology

UNIWERSYTET WARSZAWSKI
(University of Warsaw)

Krakowskie Przedmieście 26–28, 00-927 Warsaw
Telephone: (22) 552-00-00
Fax: (22) 826-32-62
Internet: www.uw.edu.pl

Founded 1816
Academic year: October to June

Rector: Prof. Dr hab. PIOTR WĘGLEŃSKI
Vice-Rectors: Prof. Dr hab. MAREK WĄSOWICZ, Prof. Dr hab. WŁODZIMIERZ BORODZIEJ, Prof. Dr hab. JAN MADEY, Prof. Dr hab. WOJCIECH MACIEJEWSKI
Administrative Director: JERZY PIESZCZURYKOW
Librarian: Dr HENRYK HOLLENDER

Library: see Libraries and Archives
Number of teachers: 2,602
Number of students: 55,790

Publications: *Acta Philologica* (irregular), *Africana Bulletin* (irregular), *American Studies* (irregular), *Barok* (2 a year), *Biuletyn Centrum Europejskiego Uniwersytetu Warszawskiego* (irregular), *Filozofia Nauki* (irregular), *Ikonotheka* (irregular), *Japonica* (irregular), *Journal of Juristic Papyrology* (irregular), *Kwartalnik Pedagogiczny* (4 a year), *Novensia* (irregular), *Orientalia Varsoviensia* (irregular), *Phytocoenosis* (irregular), *Polityka Wschodnia* (irregular), *Przegląd Humanistyczny* (4 a year), *Przegląd Historyczny* (4 a year), *Przegląd Glottodydaktyczny* (irregular), *Stosunki Międzynarodowe* (irregular), *Studia Palmyreńskie* (irregular), *Studia Europejskie* (4 a year), *Studia Politologiczne* (irregular)

DEANS

Faculty of Biology: Prof. Dr hab. MICHAŁ KOZAKIEWICZ
Faculty of Chemistry: Prof. Dr hab. STANISŁAW GŁĄB
Faculty of Journalism and Political Science: Prof. Dr hab. GRAŻYNA ULICKA
Faculty of Physics: Prof. Dr hab. KATARZYNA CHAŁASIŃSKA-MACUKOW
Faculty of Geography and Regional Studies: Prof. Dr hab. MARIA SKOCZEK
Faculty of Geology: Prof. Dr hab. BRONISŁAW MATYJA
Faculty of History: Prof. Dr hab. PIOTR BIELIŃSKI
Faculty of Mathematics, Informatics and Mechanics: Prof. Dr hab. STEFAN JACKOWSKI
Faculty of Economic Science: Prof. Dr hab. MARIAN WIŚNIEWSKI
Faculty of Philosophy and Sociology: (vacant)
Faculty of Modern Languages and Oriental Studies: Prof. Dr EMMA HARRIS
Faculty of Polish Philology: Prof. Dr hab. STANISŁAW DUBISZ
Faculty of Law and Administration: Prof. Dr hab. MIROSŁAW WYRZYKOWSKI
Faculty of Education: Prof. Dr hab. ALICJA SIEMAK-TYLIKOWSKA
Faculty of Applied Linguistics and East Slavonic Languages: Prof. Dr hab. ANTONI SEMCZUK
Faculty of Psychology: Prof. Dr hab. DANUTA KĄDZIELAWA
Faculty of Management: Prof. Dr hab. KAZIMIERZ RYĆ
Faculty of Applied Social Sciences and Social Rehabilitation: Prof. Dr hab. MARCIN KRÓL

PROFESSORS

Faculty of Biology (Miecznikowa 1, 02-096 Warsaw; tel. (22) 554-11-03; fax (22) 554-11-06; internet www.biol.edu.pl):

BARTNIK, E., Molecular Biology, Genetics
BRYŁA, J., Biochemistry—Metabolism
CHARZYŃSKA, M., Embryology
CHRÓST, R., Microbiology
CYMBOROWSKI, B., Animal Physiology
DOBROWOLSKI, K., Zoology Ecology
DOBRZAŃSKA-KACZANOWSKA, J., Zoology
FALIŃSKI, J., Botany, Ecology
GLIWICZ, M., Zoology, Hydrobiology
HREBENDA, J., Microbiology
JERZMANOWSKI, A., Biochemistry
KACPERSKA-LEWAK, A., Plant Physiology, Biochemistry
KACZANOWSKI, A., Zoology
KŁOSOWSKI, S., Ecology of Water Plants
KOZAKIEWICZ, M., Ecology
KURAŚ, M., Experimental Biology
MARKIEWICZ, Z., Microbiology
MORACZEWSKI, J., Zoology
MYCIELSKI, R., Microbiology
PIECZYŃSKA, E., Zoology, Hydrobiology
PIEKAROWICZ, A., Microbiology
POSKUTA, J., Plant Physiology
PREJS, A., Zoology, Hydrobiology
RYCHTER, A., Plant Physiology
SIŃSKI, E., Zoology
STAROŃ, K., Molecular Biology
STĘPIEŃ, P., Molecular Biology, Genetics
SYMONIDES, E., Botany, Ecology
TARKOWSKI, A., Embryology
TOMASZEWICZ, H., Botany
WĘGLEŃSKI, P., Molecular Biology, Genetics
WIŁKOMIRSKY, B., Botany
WŁODARCZYK, M., Microbiology
WOJCIECHOWSKI, Z., Biochemistry
ZIELENKIEWICZ, P., Experimental Biology

Faculty of Chemistry (Pasteura 1, 02-096 Warsaw; tel. (22) 822-02-11; fax (22) 822-59-96; e-mail dziekan@chem.uw.edu.pl; internet www.chem.uw.edu.pl):

BILEWICZ, R., Analytical Chemistry
BORUCKA-BUKOWSKA, J., Physical Chemistry and Molecular Spectroscopy
CHAŁASIŃSKI, G., Theoretical Chemistry
CZERWIŃSKI, A., Physical Chemistry
FIGASZEWSKI, Z., Physical Chemistry
GADOMSKI, W., Physical Chemistry, Optics
GALUS, Z., Mineral Chemistry
GŁĄB, B., Analytical Chemistry
GOLIMOWSKI, J., Analytical Chemistry
IZDEBSKI, J., Organic Chemistry
JAWORSKI, J., Chemistry and Food Technology
JEZIORSKI, B., Analytical Chemistry
JURCZAK, J., Organic Chemistry
KALINOWSKI, M., Physical Chemistry
KASPRZYCKA-GUTTMAN, T., Chemical Technology
KOCZOROWSKI, Z., Electrochemistry
KOLIŃSKI, A., Theoretical Chemistry
KRYGOWSKI, T., Physical Chemistry
KULESZA, P., Electrochemistry
LEŚ, A., Theoretical Chemistry
NIEDZIELSKI, J., Organic Chemistry
OSZCZAPOWICZ, J., Organic Chemistry
PIELA, L., Theoretical Chemistry
SADLEJ, J., Physical Chemistry
SAMOCHOCKA, K., Radiochemistry
STOJEK, Z., Electrochemistry
SZYDŁOWSKI, J., Radiochemistry
TEMERIUSZ, A., Organic Chemistry
TROJANOWICZ, M., Analytical Chemistry
WRONA, P., Analytical Chemistry
ŻYLICZ, M., Biochemistry

Faculty of Geography and Regional Studies (Krakowskie Przedmieście 30, 00-927 Warsaw; tel. (22) 552-06-31; fax (22) 552-15-21; e-mail globus@wgsr.uw.edu.pl; internet www.wgsr.uw.edu.pl):

CIOŁKOSZ, A., Cartography, GIS
DEMBICZ, A., Economic Geography, Socio-economic Geography of Latin America
GRYGORENKO, W., Cartography
GUDOWSKI, J., Economic Geography
GUTRY-KORYCKA, M., Hydrogeology, Hydrology
KOSTROWICKA, A., Economic Geography, Geography of Tourism
KOWALCZYK, A., Economic Geography
MAKOWSKI, J., Regional Geography
MIKULSKI, Z., Hydrogeography, Hydrology
MYCIELSKA-DOWGIAŁŁO, E., Geomorphology
PLIT, F., Regional Geography of Africa
RICHLING, A., Physical Geography, Landscape Ecology
SOCZYŃSKA, U., Hydrology
STOPA-BORYCZKA, M., Climatology

Faculty of Philosophy and Sociology (00-046 Warsaw, Nowy Świat 69; tel. (22) 826-09-62; fax (22) 826-09-62; internet www.is.uw.edu.pl/wfis):

AUGUSTYNEK, Z., Philosophy
CIUPAK, E., Sociology
DEMBIŃSKA-SIURY, D., Philosophy
JADACKI, J., Philosophy
JANKOWSKI, H., Sociology
JASIŃSKA-KANIA, A., Sociology
KOŹMIŃSKI, A., Sociology
KUCZYŃSKA, A., Philosophy
KUCZYŃSKI, J., Philosophy
MARKIEWICZ, B., Philosophy
MARODY, M., Sociology
MORAWSKI, W., Sociology
NOWICKA-RUSEK, E., Sociology
OMYŁA, M., Logic Philosophy
PELC, J., Logic
ROSIŃSKA-ZIELIŃSKA, Z., Philosophy
SIEMEK, M. J., Philosophy
SIEMIEŃSKA-ŻOCHOWSKA, R., Sociology
SMOLICZ, J. J., Sociology
STANISZKIS, J., Sociology
WIATR, J., Sociology

Faculty of Journalism and Political Science (Krakowskie Przedmieście 3, 00-047 Warsaw; tel. (22) 552-02-18; fax (22) 828-94-99; e-mail wdinp@mail.uw.edu.pl; internet www.wdnip.uw.edu.pl):

AULEYTNER, J., Economy
BASZKIEWICZ, J., Political Science
BRALCZYK, J., Journalism
DANECKI, J., Political Economy
DOBRZYCKI, W., Law and International Relations
FILIPIAK, T., Political Science
FILIPOWICZ, S., History of Social-Political Thought
GOLKA, B., Journalism
GOŁĘBIOWSKI, B., Political Science

GOŁEMBSKI, F., Political Science
HALIŻAK, M., Political Science
KASPRZYK, L., International Relations
KUKUŁKA, J., Political Science
KUŹNIAR, R., International Relations
ŁUKASZUK, L., International Law
MICHALSKI, B., Journalism
MROZEK, A. B., Political Science
PARZYMIES, S., International Relations
PIEKARA, A., Social Politics
PRZYBYSZ, K., Political Science
RAJKIEWICZ, A., Political Science
SATKIEWICZ, A. H., Theory of Style, Polish Language
SKRZYPEK, A., History
SOBCZAK, J., Law
SYMONIDES, J., International Relations
WŁADYKA, W., Political History
WOJTASZCZYK, K., Political Science
ZIELIŃSKI, E., Modern Political Systems

Faculty of Polish Philology (Oboźna 8, 00-927 Warsaw; tel. (22) 552-04-28; fax (22) 826-07-83; internet www.polon.uw.edu.pl):

BARTNICKA, B., Polish Philology, Linguistics
CZAPLEJEWICZ, E., Polish Literature
DOMAŃSKI, J., Classical Philology
DREWNOWSKI, T., History of Polish Literature
DUBISZ, S., Polish Philology
FRYBES, S., Polish Literature
GRZEGORCZYKOWA, R., Polish Philology
HANDKE, R., Theory of Literature
KARWACKA, H., Polish Literature
KOWALCZYK, A., History of Literature
KUPISZEWSKI, W. M., Polish Philology, Linguistics
LAM, A., Polish Philology, Literature
MACIEJEWSKI, J., History of Polish Literature
MAKOWSKI, S., History of Literature
MARKOWSKI, A., Polish Philology, Linguistics
MENCWEL, A., Science of Culture
MITOSEK, Z., Theory of Literature
NOWICKA-JEŻOWA, A., Literature, History of Polish Literature
OSIŃSKI, Z., Science of Culture
OWCZAREK, B., Theory of Literature
PELC, J., History of Literature
PUZYNINA, J., Polish Philology, Linguistics
SIATKOWSKA, E., Slavonic Philology, Linguistics
SIATKOWSKI, J., Slavonic Philology, Linguistics
SMOCZYŃSKI, W., Linguistics
SMUŁKOWA, E., Slavonic Philology, Linguistics
STAROWIEYSKI, M., Classical Philology
SUDOLSKI, Z., Polish Philology, Literature
ŞULIMA, R., Science of Culture
SWIDZIŃSKI, M., Polish Literature, Linguistics
TABORSKI, R., Polish Literature
WOJTCZAK-SZYSZKOWSKI, J., Classical Philology

Faculty of Applied Linguistics and East Slavonic Languages (Szturmowa 4, 02-678 Warsaw; tel. (22) 553-42-23; fax (22) 553-42-24; internet www.uw.edu.pl/wlsifw):

GRUCZA, F., Linguistics
KIELAR, B., Linguistics
KOZAK, S., Ukrainian Philology
KRZESZOWSKI, T., Linguistics
LUKSZYN, J., Russian Philology
NAMOWICZ, T., German Philology
ŞEMCZUK, A., Russian Philology
ŚLIWOWSKI, R., Russian Philology
SZYSZKO, T., Russian Philology
WAWRZYŃCZYK, J., Linguistics
ZMARZER, W., Linguistics

Faculty of Modern Languages and Oriental Studies (Browarna 8/10, 00-311 Warsaw; tel. (22) 552-09-50; fax (22) 826-75-28; e-mail dznfilol@mail.uw.edu.pl; internet www.neofilologia.uw.edu.pl):

ASZYK-BANGS, U., Linguistics
BOGACKI, B. K., Italian Philology
BOGUSŁAWSKI, A., Russian Philology
BOJAR, B., Formal Linguistics
BYRSKI, M. K., Oriental Philology
BYSTYDZIEŃSKA, G., English Studies
CZOCHRALSKI, J., German Philology
DANECKI, J., Oriental Philology
KAŁUŻYŃSKI, S., Oriental Philology
KOMOROWSKA-JANOWSKA, H., Linguistics
KOTAŃSKI, W., Oriental Philology
KÜNSTLER, M., Sinology
ŁYCZKOWSKA, K., Oriental Philology
MAJDA, T., Oriental Philology
MAŁCUŻYŃSKI, P., Literature
MANTEL-NIEĆKO, J., Ethiopian Philology
MELANOWICZ, M., Oriental Philology
PIŁASZEWICZ, S., African Philology
POPKO, M., Oriental Philology
RUBACH, J., English Philology
RUSIECKI, J., English Linguistics
SALWA, P., Italian Literature
SAUERLAND, K. K., German Philology
SEMENIUK-POLAKOWSKA, M., Linguistics
SKARŻYŃSKA-BOCHEŃSKA, K., Oriental Philology
SKŁADANEK, B., Iranian Philology
SKŁADANEK, M., Oriental Philology
SŁUPSKI, Z., Oriental Philology
TUBIELEWICZ, J., Oriental Philology
UGNIEWSKA-DOBRZAŃSKA, J., Italian Philology
WEŁNA, J. A., English Philology
WESELIŃSKI, A., English Literature
WIKTOROWICZ, J., German Philology
WIŚNIEWSKI, J., English Literature
ŻABOKLICKI, K., French Philology

Faculty of Geology (Żwirki i Wigury 93, 02-089 Warsaw; tel. (22) 822-58-84; fax (22) 554-00-01; e-mail dziekstu@geo.uw.edu.pl; internet www.geo.uw.edu.pl):

BAŁUK, W. A., Palaeontology
DRĄGOWSKI, A., Environmental Protection
GRABOWSKA-OLSZEWSKA, B., Engineering Geology
KACZYŃSKI, R., Engineering Geology
KOWALSKI, W., Geochemistry, Mineralogy
KRAJEWSKI, S., Hydrogeology
KUTEK, J., Tectonics, Stratigraphy
LINDNER, L., Quaternary Geology
MACIOSZCZYK, A., Hydrogeology
MACIOSZCZYK, T., Hydrogeology
MAŁECKA, D., Hydrogeology
MARCINOWSKI, R., Stratigraphy
MARKS, L., Quaternary Geology
MATYSIAK, S., Mechanics of Solids
MYŚLIŃSKA, E., Engineering Geology
ORŁOWSKI, S., Stratigraphy
PINIŃSKA, J., Engineering Geology, Geomechanics
RADWAŃSKI, A., Geology
RONIEWICZ, P., Sedimentology
SPECZIK, S., Geology of Ore Deposits
SZULCZEWSKI, M., Stratigraphy, Sedimentology
WIERZBOWSKI, A., Stratigraphy
WYRWICKI, R., Geology of Ore Deposits

Faculty of History (tel. (22) 552-05-45; fax (22) 826-21-30; internet www.his.uw.edu.pl/wh):

AUGUSTYNIAK, U., History of Culture
BANASZKIEWICZ, J., Modern History
BIEŃKOWSKA, B., History of Culture, Library Science
BRAVO, B., Ancient History
BUCHWALD-PELC, P., Library Science
BUKO, A., Archaeology
BUKOWSKI, Z., Archaeology
CHMIELEWSKI, W., Archaeology
CHRÓŚCICKI, J., History of Art
CZEKANOWSKA-KUKLIŃSKA, A., Musicology
DASZEWSKI, W., Archaeology
FIAŁKOWSKI, K., Library Science
GARLICKI, A., History
GAWLIKOWSKI, M., Archaeology
GODLEWSKI, W., Archaeology
GOŁĄB, M., Musicology
HELMAN-BEDNARCZYK, Z., Musicology
JAŚKIEWICZ, D., History of the USSR
JUSZCZAK, W., History of Art
KARPOWICZ, M., History of Art
KIZWALTER, T., 19th-Century History
KOLENDO, J., Archaeology
KOŁODZIEJSKA, J., Library Science
KOZŁOWSKI, S., Archaeology
KULA, M., General History
LASOTA-MOSKALEWSKA, A., Biology, Archaeozoology
LENGAUER, W., History
ŁUKASIEWICZ, J., History
MACISZEWSKI, J., History
MĄCZAK, A., Modern History
MICHAŁEK, K., Modern History, History of the USA
MIKOCKI, T., History of Art
MIŁOBĘDZKI, J. A., History of Art
MODZELEWSKI, K., Medieval History
MURASZKIEWICZ, M., Library Science
MYŚLIWIEC, K., Archaeology
NIWIŃSKI, A. S., History, Egyptology
NOWAKOWSKI, W., Archaeology
OKULICZ-KOZARYN, J., Archaeology
PAPUZIŃSKA-BEKSIAK, J., Literature
PERZ, M., Musicology
POKROPEK, M., Ethnography
PONIATOWSKA, I., History of Music
POPPE, A., Medieval History
POPRZĘCKA, M., History of Art
POTKOWSKI, E., History
RAKOWSKI, A., Musical Acoustics
RUDNICKI, S., 19th- and 20th-century Polish History
RUSINOWA, J., Modern History
SAMSONOWICZ, H., Medieval History
SKUBISZEWSKI, P., Medieval History of Art
SOCHACKI, Z., Archaeology
SOKOLEWICZ, Z., Ethnography
SUCHODOLSKI, S., Archaeology
ŞZAFLIK, J., History
ŚWIDERKÓWNA, A., Papyrology
TANTY, M., History of Slavonic Countries
TOMASZEWSKI, J., Political Science
TYMOWSKI, M., Modern History
TYSZKIEWICZ, J., Medieval History
WASILEWSKI, T., Medieval History
WAWRYKOWA, M., Modern History
WIERCIŃSKI, A., Archaeology
WIPSZYCKA-BRAVO, E., Ancient History
WOJCIECHOWSKI, M., Modern History
WYROBISZ, A., Medieval History
ZADROŻYŃSKA-BARĄCZ, A., Ethnography
ŻARNOWSKA, A., Modern Polish History
ŻERAŃSKA-KOMINEK, S., Musicology

Faculty of Mathematics, Informatics and Mechanics (Banacka 2, 02-097 Warsaw; tel. (22) 554-42-14; fax (22) 554-42-00; e-mail mim@mimuw.edu.pl; internet www.mimuw.edu.pl):

BESSAGA, C., Mathematical Analysis
BIAŁYNICKI-BIRULA, A., Mathematics
BOJDECKI, T., Theory of Elasticity
BROWKIN, J., Mathematics
DRYJA, M., Informatics
ENGELKING, R., Mathematics
GRABOWSKI, J., Mathematics
JACKOWSKI, S., Mechanics
KREMPA, J., Mathematics
KWAPIEŃ, S., Mathematics
LIGOCKA, E., Mathematics
MOSZYŃSKA, M., Mathematics
PALCZEWSKI, A., Mathematics
PERADZYŃSKI, Z., Mathematics
POL, R., Mathematics
PUCZYŁOWSKI, E., Mathematics
RYTTER, W., Informatics
SEMADENI, Z., Mathematics
SIEKLUCKI, K., Mathematics

SKOWRON, A., Mathematics
SZAŁAS, A., Informatics
TARLECKI, A., Informatics
TIURYN, J., Mathematics
TORUŃCZYK, H., Mathematics
TURSKI, W., Informatics
WOJTASZCZYK, P., Mathematics
WOŹNIAKOWSKI, H., Informatics
ZBIERSKI, P., Mathematics
ŻOŁĄDEK, H., Mathematics

Faculty of Physics (Hoża 69, 00-681 Warsaw; tel. (22) 553-21-23; fax (22) 625-23-36; e-mail dziekfiz@fuw.edu.pl; internet www.fuw.edu.pl):

BADEŁEK, B., Experimental Physics
BAJ, M., Solid Body Physics
BARANOWSKI, J., Experimental Physics
BAŻAŃSKI, S., Theoretical Physics
BIAŁYNICKI-BIRULA, I., Optics and Mechanics
BLINOWSKI, J., Solid Body Physics
CHAŁASIŃSKA-MACUKOW, K., Optics
CIBOROWSKI, J. A., Experimental Physics
CIEŚLAK-BLINOWSKA, K., Medical Physics
DEMIAŃSKI, M., Theoretical Physics
DOBACZEWSKI, J., Theoretical Physics
DZIEMBOWSKI, W., Astronomy
ERNST, K., Atomic Physics
GAJ, J., Solid Body Physics
GRAD, M., Geophysics
GRYNBERG, M., Solid Body Physics
HAMAN, K., Geophysics
KALINOWSKI, J., Molecule Elementary Physics
KAMIŃSKA, M., Solid Body Physics
KIJOWSKI, J., Theoretical Physics
KOPCZYŃSKI, W., High Energy Physics
KOWALCZYK, P., Experimental Physics
KROLIKOWSKI, J., High Energy Physics
KRÓLIKOWSKI, W., Atomic Physics
KRUSZEWSKI, A., Astronomy
KUBIAK, M., Astrophysics
KURCEWICZ, W., Nuclear Physics
LELIWA-KOPYSTYŃSKI, J., Geophysics
LESYNG, B., Biophysics
MAURIN, K., Mathematical Methods in Physics
MIELNIK, B., Theoretical Physics
NAMYSŁOWSKI, J., Theoretical Physics
NAPIÓRKOWSKI, M., Statistics Physics
NAZAREWICZ, W., Solid Body Physics
PIASECKI, J., Theoretical Physics
POKORSKI, S., Theoretical Physics
RADZEWICZ, C., Experimental Physics
ROHOZIŃSKI, ST., Atomic Physics
RYKACZEWSKI, K., Experimental Physics
SHUGAR, D., Biophysics
SKRZYPCZAK, E., High Energy Physics
SOSNOWSKA, I., Experimental Physics
STĘPIEŃ, K., Astronomy
STĘPNIEWSKI, R., Solid Body Physics
SYM, A., Physics
SZOPLIK, T., Optics
SZYMACHA, A., Atomic Physics
TRAUTMAN, A., Electrodynamics and Theory of Relativity
TWARDOWSKI, A., Solid Body Physics
UDALSKI, A., Astrophysics
WILHELMI, Z., Atomic Physics
WORONOWICZ, S., Mathematical Methods in Physics
WÓDKIEWICZ, K., Optics
WRÓBLEWSKI, A., Experimental Physics
ZAKRZEWSKI, J., High Energy Physics
ŻYLICZ, J., Experimental Physics

Faculty of Education (Mokotowska 16/20, 00-561 Warsaw; tel. (22) 553-08-18; fax (22) 629-89-79; e-mail pedagog@mail.uw.edu.pl; internet www.pedagog.uw.edu.pl):

BARTNICKA, K., Education History
FRĄCZEK, A., Psychology
KRUSZEWSKI, K., Education
KUPISIEWICZ, C., Didactics, Comparative Education
KWIATKOWSKA, H., Education
LEWOWICKI, T., Adult Education
MIESZALSKI, S., Didactics
POŁTURZYCKI, J., Education
PRZECŁAWSKA, A., Social Education
THEISS, W., Education
WILGOCKA-OKOŃ, B., Education
WOJNAR, I., Education
WOYNAROWSKA, B., Social Medicine
ZACZYŃSKI, W., Didactics

Faculty of Psychology (Stawki 5/7, 00-183 Warsaw; tel. (22) 554-97-00; fax (22) 635-79-91; e-mail dean@sci.psych.uw.edu.pl; internet www.psych.uw.edu.pl):

GAŁKOWSKI, T., Educational Psychology
GRZELAK, J., Social Psychology
GRZESIUK, L., Psychopathology and Psychotherapy
JARYMOWICZ, M., Personality Psychology
KOFTA, M., Personality Psychology
KOŚCIELSKA, M., Clinical Psychology
KOZIELECKI, J., Cognitive Psychology
MATCZAK, A., Individual Differences
MATYSIAK, J., Biological Psychology
MIKA, S., Social Psychology
STRELAU, J., Individual Differences
WIECZORKOWSKA-NEJTARDT, G., Social Psychology
ZALEWSKA, M., Clinical Psychology

Faculty of Law and Administration (tel. (22) 552-03-95; fax (22) 826-99-25; internet www.uw.edu.pl/wpia):

BARDACH, J., History of Law
BŁESZYŃSKI, J., Civil Law
DYBOWSKI, T., Civil Law
ERECIŃSKI, T., Civil Law
FLOREK, L., Labour Law
GARDOCKI, L., Penal Law
GARLICKI, L., Constitutional Law
IZDEBSKI, H., History of Law
JĘDRASIK-JANKOWSKA, I., Labour Law
JĘDRZEJEWSKA, M., Civil Law
KRUSZYŃSKI, P., Penal Law
OKOLSKI, J., Civil Law
PIETRZAK, M., History of Law
PIETRZYKOWSKI, K., Civil Law
PIONTEK, E., International Law
RAJSKI, J., Civil Law
REJMAN, G., Penal Law
SAFJAN, M., Civil Law
SALWA, Z., Labour Law
SKOWROŃSKA-BOCIAN, E., Civil Law
SÓJKA-ZIELIŃSKA, K., History of Law
SZYSZKOWSKA, M., Philosophy of Law
TOMASZEWSKI, T., Penal Law
TRZCIŃSKI, J., Constitutional Law
TURSKA, A., Sociology of Law
WĄSOWICZ, M., History of Law
WIERZBOWSKI, M., Administrative Law
WINCZOREK, P., Theory of State and Law
ZABŁOCKA, M., Roman Law
ZIELIŃSKI, A., Civil Law

Faculty of Economic Sciences (Długa 44/50, 00-241 Warsaw; tel. (22) 554-91-44; fax (22) 831-28-46; internet www.wne.uw.edu.pl):

BAKA, W., Banking and Finance
DANILUK, M., Public Finance
DOBROCZYŃSKI, M., International Economics
GMYTRASIEWICZ, M., Economics, Business
GÓRECKI, B., Econometrics
JEZIERSKI, A., Economic History
KASPRZAK, T., Business, Informatics
KLEER, J., Economics
KOTOWICZ-JAWOR, J., Economics
KOZIŃSKI, W., Banking and Finance
LUBBE, A., International Economics
ŁUKASZEWICZ, A., Economic Policy
MACIEJEWSKI, W., Econometrics
MORECKA, Z., Political Economy
OKÓLSKI, M., Statistics, Demography
OPOLSKI, K., Banking and Finance
RUTKOWSKI, J., Political Economy
SADOWSKI, Z., Theory of Economic Development
SIWIŃSKI, W., International Economics
SZEWORSKI, A., Political Economy
SZTYBER, W., Political Economy, Public Finance
TIMOFIEJUK, I., Statistics
WIECZORKIEWICZ, A., Banking and Finance
WILKIN, J., Political Economy, Agricultural Economics

Faculty of Management (Szturmowa 3, 02-678 Warsaw; tel. (22) 553-40-00; fax (22) 553-40-01; internet www.wz.uw.edu.pl):

BOLESTA-KUKUŁKA, K., Sociology of Management
BUCZKOWSKI, L., Techniques of Management
GŁOWACKI, R., Marketing
JAROSZYŃSKI, A., Administrative Law
KISIELNICKI, J., Industrial Economy and Informatics
KRZYŻEWSKI, R., Social Economics
KWIATKOWSKI, S., Theory of Management
MAJCHRZYCKA-GUZOWSKA, A., Financial Law
MUSZALSKI, W., Employment
OBŁÓJ, K., Organization and Management
RYĆ, K., Economic Theory
ŚLIWA, J., Planning
SOBCZAK, K., Administrative Law
SOPOĆKO, A., Theory of Organization
SZPRINGER, W., Administrative Law
ZAWIŚLAK, A., Theory of Management

Faculty of Applied Social Sciences and Social Rehabilitation (Żurawia 4, 00-503 Warsaw; tel. (22) 621-91-22; fax (22) 625-40-86):

BAŁANDYNOWICZ, A., Resocialization, Prevention
BOKSZAŃSKI, Z., Sociology
JAWŁOWSKA, A., Sociology
KACZYŃSKA, E., History of Social Economics
KICIŃSKI, K., Sociology of Morals
KRÓL, M., History of Ideas
KULPIŃSKA, J., Sociology
KURCZEWSKI, J., Sociology, Sociology of Law
KWAŚNIEWSKI, J., Labour Law, Deviation Sociology
MISIAK, W., Sociology
PILCH, T., Education
PRZECŁAWSKI, K., Sociology
RZEPLIŃSKI, A., Law, Criminology
ŚWIDA-ZIEMBA, H., Sociology
SZYMANOWSKI, T., Penal Law
TYMOWSKI, A., Social Politics
WOJCIK, P., Political Science, Social Politics
ZABOROWSKI, Z., Psychology
ZIEMBA, Z., Philosophy

WARSZAWSKI UNIWERSYTET MEDYCZNY
(Medical University of Warsaw)

ul. Żwirki i Wigury 61, 02-091 Warsaw
Telephone: (22) 572-09-13
Fax: (22) 572-01-54
Internet: www.wum.edu.pl

Founded 1789

Rector: Prof. Dr hab. MAREK KRAWCZYK

Library of 400,000 vols
Number of teachers: 1,185
Number of students: 3,200

Faculties: dentistry, health sciences, medicine, pharmacy, postgraduate education

Publication: *Medycyna-dydaktyka-wychowanie* (Medicine-Didactics-Education, 4 a year).

UNIWERSYTET KARDYNAŁA STEFANA WYSZYŃSKIEGO W WARSZAWIE
(Cardinal Stefan Wyszyński University in Warsaw)

ul. Dewajtis 5, 01-815 Warsaw
Telephone: (22) 839-52-21

Fax: (22) 839-52-45
E-mail: rektorat@uksw.edu.pl
Internet: www.uksw.edu.pl

Founded 1954 as Akademia Teologii Katolickiej; present name and status 1999

Academic year: October to June

Rector: Prof. Dr hab. HENRYK SKOROWSKI
Vice-Rector for Gen. Affairs and Scientific Research: Rev. Prof. Dr hab. RYSZARD RUMIANEK
Vice-Rector for Education and Int. Cooperation: Rev. Prof. Dr hab. JAN BIELECKI
Vice-Rector for Devt and Student Affairs: Prof. Dr hab. ZBIGNIEW CIEŚLAK
Admin. Dir: Mgr inż MAREK LEPA
Librarian: Mgr PIOTR LATAWIEC

Library of 200,000 vols
Number of teachers: 520
Number of students: 15,392

Publications: *Collectanea Theologica* (4 a year), *Jus Matrimoniale* (1 a year), *Kroniki UKSW* (4 a year), *Maqom* (2 a year), *Prawo Kanoniczne* (4 a year), *Saeculum Christianum* (2 a year), *Studia Philosophiae Christianae* (2 a year), *Studia Psychologica* (1 a year), *Studia Theologica Varsaviensia* (2 a year), *Studia nad Rodziną* (2 a year), *Wiadomości UKSW* (12 a year), *Zeszyty Prawnicze* (1 a year)

DEANS

Faculty of Canon Law: Rev. Prof. Dr hab. JULIAN KAŁOWSKI
Faculty of Christian Philosophy: Rev. Prof. Dr hab. JÓZEF DOŁĘGA
Faculty of History and Social Sciences: Rev. Prof. Dr hab. HENRYK SKOROWSKI
Faculty of Humanities: Dr TOMASZ CHACHULSKI
Faculty of Law: Prof. Dr hab. CEZARY MIK
Faculty of Mathematics and Science: Prof. Dr hab. MAREK KOWALSKI
Faculty of Theology: Rev. Prof. Dr hab. STANISŁAW URBAŃSKI

PROFESSORS

Faculty of Theology (tel. (22) 839-92-82; e-mail wtdz@uksw.edu.pl):

BALTER, L., Dogmatic Theology
BARTNICKI, R., Biblical Studies
BEŁCH, K., Pastoral Theology
BOKWA, I., Dogmatic Theology
CHROSTOWSKI, W., Biblical Studies
CZAJKOWSKI, M., Biblical Studies
DECYK, J., Liturgy
DURAK, A., Liturgy
DZIUBA, A., Moral Theology
GACKA, B., Dogmatic Theology
GÓRALCZYK, P., Moral Theology
GRACZYK, M., Moral Theology
JABŁOŃSKI, S., Mariology
KARWACKI, R., Fundamental Theology
KULISZ, J., Fundamental Theology
LEWANDOWSKI, J., Dogmatic Theology
LEWEK, A., Theology of Mass Media
MATWIEJUK, K., Liturgics
MĘDALA, S., Biblical Studies
MIERZWIŃSKI, B., Pastoral Theology
MISIASZEK, K., Catechesis
MROCZKOWSKI, I., Moral Theology
MURAWSKI, R., Catechesis
NOWAK, J., Liturgy
OGÓREK, P., Theology of Spirituality
OZOROWSKI, E., Dogmatic Theology
PAZERA, W., Homiletics
PIETRZYK, Z., History of the Church
PIKUS, T., Fundamental Theology
PRZYBYŁOWSKI, J., Pastoral Theology
RUMIANEK, R., Biblical Studies
SAKOWICZ, E., Religion
SALIJ, J., Dogmatic Theology
SEWERYNIAK, H., Fundamental Theology
TYLKI-SZYMAŃSKA, A., Family Studies
URBAŃSKI, S., Theology of Spirituality
WARCHOŁ, E., History of the Church
WARZESZAK, J., Dogmatic Theology
ZABIELSKI, J., Moral Theology
ZAŁĘSKI, J., Biblical Studies

Faculty of Canon Law (tel. (22) 839-52-64; fax (22) 561-88-12; e-mail prawokan@uksw.edu.pl):

BŁESZYŃSKI, J., Civil Law
BRZOZOWSKI, A., Civil Law
DĘBIŃSKI, A., Roman Law
DYBOWSKI, T., Civil Law
GÓRALSKI, W., Ecclesiastical Matrimonial and Family Law
GRĘŹLIKOWSKI, J., History of Law
JEMIELITY, W., History of Ecclesiastical Polish Law
KAŁOWSKI, J., Law of Consecration Life Institutes and Apostolic Life Associations
KIWIOR, W., Procedural Law
KRUKOWSKI, J., Religion and Concordat Law
PASTUSZKO, M., Law of Sacraments
SOBAŃSKI, R., Theory of Ecclesiastical Law
STAWNIAK, H., Law of Teaching Services
SYRYJCZYK, J., Ecclesiastical Criminal Law
SZTYCHMILER, R., Ecclesiastical Procedural Law
WROCEŃSKI, J., Ecclesiastical Law of Persons

Faculty of Christian Philosophy (tel. (22) 561-88-53; fax (22) 561-88-53; e-mail wfch@uksw.edu.pl):

ANDRZEJUK, A., Philosophy
ARANOWSKA, E., Methodology of Psychological Sciences
BIELECKI, J., Psychology of Religion
BOŁOZ, J., Bioethics
BOMBIK, M., Logic
DOŁĘGA, J., Philosophy of Nature
GAŁUSZKO, K., Preservation of Nature
GASIUL, H., Psychology of Personality
GERAS, G., Judicial and Penitentiary Psychology
HAŁACZEK, B., Anthropology, History and Philosophy of Science
JAKUBIK, A., Clinical Psychology
KLIMSKI, T., History of Philosophy
LATAWIEC, A., Philosophy of Nature
LEMAŃSKA, A., Philosophy of Nature
MACEWICZ, J., Genetics
MATCZAK, A., Developmental Psychology
MORAWIEC, E., Philosophy, Metaphysics
NIEZNAŃSKI, E., Logic, Methodology of Sciences
NOWICKA, G., Biochemistry
PODREZ, E., Ethics
PORĘBSKI, S., History of Polish Philosophy
RYŚ, M., Psychology of Marriage and Family
SAREŁO, Z., Ethics
SINIARSKA-WOLAŃSKA, A., Ecology
SOCHOŃ, J., History of Philosophy, Philosophy of Religion
STOJANOWSKA, E., Social Psychology
STRZAŁECKI, A., General Psychology, Psychodiagnosis
TERELAK, J., Psychology of Labour and Stress
TYLKA, J., Clinical Psychology
ZABŁOCKI, K., Pedagogy, Psychology of Revalidation and Rehabilitation

Faculty of History and Social Sciences (tel. (22) 561-88-10; fax (22) 561-88-10; e-mail wnhis@uksw.edu.pl):

BALICKI, J., Political Science
BANIA, Z., History of Medieval and Modern Architecture
CYWIŃSKI, B., Contemporary History
DĄBEK, S., Musicology
DĄBROWSKA, T., Archaeology
DADAK-KOZICKA, K., Musicology
DELUGA, W., History of Art
DROZD, J., International Relations
DYLUS, A., Philosophy and Ethics
GRONKIEWICZ-WALTZ, H., Administrative and Banking Law
GROSFELD, J., Political Economy
JANOCHA, M., History of Art
JUROS, H., Moral Theology, Ethics
KOBIELUS, S., History of Art
KOBYLIŃSKI, Z., Archaeology
KOŁOSOWSKI, T., History of Early Christian Literature
KORAL, J., Political Science
KOZŁOWSKI, S., Archaeology
KRASNODĘBSKI, Z., Philosophy and Sociology
MAJKOWSKI, W., Sociology of the Family
MANDZIUK, J., History of the Church
MAZURKIWEICZ, P., Political Science
MIŚKIEWICZ, M., Archaeology
MOISAN-JABLONSKI, CH., History of Art
NAUMOWICZ, J., History of Early Christian Literature
NAWROT, E., History
OCHOCKI, A., Demography
ODZIEMKOWSKI, J., History
POKORA, H., History of Art
POTOCKI, A., Sociology
REKŁAJTIS, E., Arabic Philology
SKOROWSKI, H., Political Science
SZYMONIK, K., Arts of Music
TRZECIAK, M., Sociology
UERTZ, R., Political Science
WILSKA, M., Archaeology
WÓJTOWICZ, A., Sociology
WYSOCKI, W., History
ZBUDNIEWEK, J., History of the Church
ZIEMER, K., Political Science
ŻYRO, T., Political Science

Faculty of Law (ul. Wóycickiego 1/3, 01-938 Warsaw; tel. (22) 569-96-50; fax (22) 569-97-45; e-mail prawo@uksw.edu.pl):

BORUTA, M., Labour Law
CIEŚLAK, Z., Administrative Law
GRANAT, M., Constitutional Law
JĘDRZEJEWSKA, M., Civil Proceedings
JURCEWICZ, A., Agrarian Law
KACZYŃSKI, L., Labour Law
KALLAS, M., History of the Political System and Law in Poland
LIPOWICZ, I., European Administrative Law
MAJEWSKI, J., Criminal Law
MIK, C., International and European Law
MORAWSKI, L., Theory and Philosophy of Law
NOWAK-FAR, A., Financial Law
OMYŁA, M., Logic and Methodology of Legal Sciences
PRUSAK, F., Criminal Procedure
STOJANOWSKA, W., Family Law
STRZYCZKOWSKI, K., Private Economic Law
SZAJKOWSKI, A., Private Economic Law
SZPOR, G., Informatics Law
ZABŁOCKI, J., Roman Law
ZIELIŃSKI, A., Civil Proceedings

Faculty of Humanities (tel. (22) 839-77-63; e-mail polonistyka@uksw.edu.pl):

BIEŃKOWSKA, E., History of 19th- and 20th-century Literature, Comparative Literature, Literary Criticism
BOBROWSKA, B., History of Literature of the Second Half of the 19th Century
DOPART, B., Romantic Literature
DUMA, J., History of Language
DYBCIAK, K., History of 20th-century Literature, Literary Criticism
JANUS, E., History of Language
KOSTKIEWICZOWA, T., History of 18th-century Literature, Theory of Literature
KUCZYŃSKA-KWAPISZ, J., Education for Handicapped People
ŁUKASZUK-PIEKARA, M, 20th-century Literature
PAWŁOWSKI, K., Classical Philology, Theory of Literature
PISKUREWICZ, J., History of Child-rearing

PRUSSAK, M., Science of Theatre, History of Literature of the Second Half of the 19th Century, Science Publications
SMOLIŃSKA-THEISS, B., Education
SURZYSZKIEWICZ, J., Education
THEISS, W., Social Education
WARZECHA, J., Biblical Studies
WOLNICZ-PAWŁOWSKA, E., History of Language
ZIELIŃSKA, A., Linguistics

Faculty of Mathematics and Natural Science (tel. (22) 561-89-29; e-mail matematyka@uksw.edu.pl):

ALSTER, K., Mathematics
CHEŁMIŃSKI, K., Mathematics
CHOJNACKI, W., Mathematics
CYTOWSKI, J. W., Computer Science
GAJDA, M., Physics
GODLEWSKI, M., Physics
GÓRECKI, J., Chemistry
HERBICH, J., Chemistry
HOŁYST, R., Chemistry
JABŁOŃSKI, A., Chemistry
KARPIŃSKI, Z., Chemistry
KIJOWSKI, J., Physics
KORYBUT-DASZKIEWICZ, B., Chemistry
KOTLARSKI, H., Mathematics
KOWALSKI, M. A., Mathematics
KRYNICKI, M., Mathematics
KULPA, W., Mathematics
KUŚ, M., Physics
KUTNER, W., Chemistry
ŁUNARSKA-BOROWIECKA, E., Chemistry
MACEK, W., Physics
MAINARDI, S., Economy
MAZUR, T., Mathematics
MOSTOWSKI, J., Physics
NANIEWICZ, Z., Mathematics
NOWICKA-TARASZEWSKA, J., Chemistry
RUSINEK, J., Mathematics
RZĄŻEWSKI, K., Physics
SKOŚKIEWICZ, T., Physics
SKWARCZYŃSKI, M., Mathematics
SOCHA, L., Computer Science
TURSKI, L. A., Physics
TURZAŃSKI, M., Mathematics
WALUK, J., Chemistry
ZAGRODNY, D., Mathematics
ZAREMBA, L., Mathematics

UNIWERSYTET WROCŁAWSKI (University of Wrocław)

pl. Uniwersytecki 1, Wrocław
Telephone: (71) 343-68-47
Fax: (71) 3744-34-21
E-mail: rektorat@adm.uni.wroc.pl
Internet: www.uni.wroc.pl

Founded 1702, rebuilt 1945
State control
Language of instruction: Polish
Academic year: October to June (two terms)

Rector: Prof. Dr hab. ZDZISŁAW LATAJKA
Vice-Rector (Scientific Research and Foreign Relations): Prof. Dr hab. KRZYSZTOF WÓJTOWICZ
Vice-Rector (Gen. Affairs): (vacant)
Vice-Rector (Student Affairs): Prof. Dr hab. JERZY MARÓN (acting)
Vice-Rector (Teaching Affairs): Prof. Dr hab. KRYSTYNA GABRYJELSKA
Admin. Officer: Dr BEATA LENKIEWICZ
Librarian: Mgr Inż. GRAŻYNA PIOTROWICZ

Library: see Libraries and Archives
Number of teachers: 1,720
Number of students: 41,663

Publication: *Acta Universitatis Wratislaviensis*

DEANS

Faculty of Chemistry: Prof. Dr hab. JERZY PIOTR HAWRANEK
Faculty of Historical and Pedagogical Sciences: Prof. Dr hab. BOGDAN ROK
Faculty of Law and Administration: Prof. Dr hab. MAREK BOJARSKI
Faculty of Mathematics and Computer Science: Prof. Dr hab. RYSZARD SZEKLI
Faculty of Natural Sciences: Prof. Dr hab. ANDRZEJ WITKOWSKI
Faculty of Philology: Prof. Dr hab. WŁADYSŁAW DYNAK
Faculty of Physics and Astronomy: Prof. Dr hab. HENRYK CUGIER
Faculty of Social Sciences: Prof. Dr hab. BERNARD ALBIN

PROFESSORS

Faculty of Chemistry (ul. F. Joliot-Curie 14, 50-383 Wrocław; tel. (71) 375-72-90; fax (71) 375-74-20; e-mail dziekanat@wchuwr.chem.uni.wroc.pl; internet www.chem.uni.wroc.pl/indexpol.htm):

HAWRANEK, J., Electronic Data Processing
JAKUBAS, R., Physical Chemistry
JEZIERSKI, A., Inorganic Chemistry
KISZA, A., Physical Chemistry
KOLL, A., Physical Chemistry
KONOPIŃSKA, D., Organic Chemistry
KOZŁOWSKI, H., Bioinorganic and Biomedicinal Chemistry
LATAJKA, Z., Theoretical Chemistry and Chemical Physics
LATOS-GRAŻYŃSKI, L., General Chemistry
LIS, T., Crystallography
MROZIŃSKI, J., Methodology of Chemistry
PRUCHNIK, F., Environmental Chemistry and Protection
RATAJCZAK, H., Theoretical Chemistry and Chemical Physics
SIEMION, I., Organic Chemistry
SKRZYPIEC-LEGENDZIEWICZ, J., Analytical Chemistry
SOBCZYK, L., Physical Chemistry
SOBOTA, P., Inorganic Chemistry for Natural Scientists
ZIÓŁKOWSKI, J., Inorganic Chemistry

Faculty of Historical and Pedagogical Sciences (ul. Szewska 48, 50-139 Wrocław; tel. (71) 375-22-23; fax (71) 343-28-55; e-mail dziekan@hist.uni.wroc.pl; internet www.wnhip.hist.uni.wroc.pl):

ADAMCZYK, M., Comparative Pedagogy
BANAŚ, P., Science of Art
CIESIELSKI, M., History of Eastern Europe
CZAPLIŃSKI, M., History of Silesia
DERWICH, M., Centre for Studies of Religious Orders and Church Congregations
KULAK, T., General and Polish History since 19th century
KUSIAK, F., Economic History, Demography and Statistics
MATWIJOWSKI, K., 16th–18th-century General and Polish History
OCHMAN-STANISZEWSKA, S., 16th–18th-century General and Polish History
PIETRZAK, J., 16th–18th-century General and Polish History
POTYRAŁA, B., General Pedagogy
ROK, B., 16th–18th-century General and Polish History
WACHOWSKI, K., Medieval Archaeology
WRZESIŃSKI, W., Contemporary History
ŻABSKI, E., Philosophical and Methodological Foundations of Psychology
ŻERELIK, R., Centre for Studies of Religious Orders and Church Congregations

Faculty of Law and Administration (ul. Uniwersytecka 22–26, 50-145 Wrocław; tel. (71) 343-71-64; fax (71) 375-27-84; internet www.prawo.uni.wroc.pl):

ADAMIAK, B., Administrative Proceedings and Judicial Control of Administrative Activity
BANASZEK, B., Constitutional Law
BŁAS, A., Administrative Law
BEDNARSKI, T., Statistics and Operation Researches
BOĆ, J., Administrative Law
BOGUNIA, L., Criminal Law Practice
BOJARSKI, M., Law of Petty Offences and Penal Fiscal Law
DZIAŁOCHA, K., Constitutional Law
FOJCIK-MASTALSKA, E., Financial Law
FRĄCKOWIAK, J., Economic and Commercial Law
GNIEWEK, E., Civil Law and International Private Law
JENDROŚKA, J., Administrative Proceedings and Judical Control of Administrative Activity
JONCA, K., Political and Legal Doctrines
KACZMAREK, T., Substantive Penal Law
KAŹMIERCZYK, S., Theory and Philosophy of Law
KEGEL, Z., Crime Detection
KIERES, L., Administrative Economic Law
KOLASA, J., International Economic Relations
KONIECZNY, A., History of Administration
MACIEJEWSKI, M., Political and Legal Doctrine
MĄDRZAK, H., Civil Procedure
MASTALSKI, R., Financial Law
OLSZEWSKI, L., International Economic Relations
ORZECHOWSKI, K., History of Polish State and Law
POŁOMSKI, F., History of Polish State and Law
ŚWIDA, Z., Penal Proceedings
SZURGACZ, H., Labour Law
TRZCIŃSKI, J., Crime Detection

Faculty of Mathematics and Computer Science (pl. Grunwaldzki 2–4, 50-384 Wrocław; tel. and fax (71) 375-74-91; e-mail dziekan@math.uni.wroc.pl; internet www.math.uni.wroc.pl/wydzial/index.php):

BILER, P., Differential Equations
BOŻEJKO, M., Mathematical Analysis
DAMEK, E., Geometry
DUDA, R., History and Methodology of Mathematics
HULANICKI, A., Functional Analysis
KISIELEWICZ, A., Algebra and Theory of Numbers
KOPOCIŃSKI, B., Applied Mathematics
NARKIEWICZ, W., Algebra and Theory of Numbers
NEWELSKI, Algebra and Theory of Numbers
PACHOLSKI, L., Programming Languages
PYTLIK, T., Functional Analysis
ROLSKI, T., Stochastic Processes
SYSŁO, M., Programming Methods
SZCZOTKA, W., Applications of Mathematics
SZWARC, R., Mathematical Analysis
URBANIK, K., Theory of Probability

Faculty of Natural Sciences (ul. Kuźnicza 35, 50-138 Wrocław; tel. and fax (71) 343-57-28):

BOROWIEC, L., Animal Systematics
CEBRAT, S., Genome Studies
DŻUGAJ, A., Animal Physiology
KOZUBEK, A., Lipids and Liposomes
KUPRIŃSKI, T., Anthropology
ŁOBODA, J., Social and Economic Geography
OGORZAŁEK, A., Zoology
OTLEWSKI, J., Protein Engineering
POLANOWSKI, A., Biotechnology of Proteins
SACHANBIŃSKI, M., Museum of Mineralogy and Section of Gemmology
SADOWSKA, A., Geology (Palaeobotany)
SIKORSKI, A., Cell Biology
SZOPA-SKÓRKOWSKI, J., Genetic Biochemistry
TOMIAŁOJĆ, L., Natural Museum
WESOŁOWSKI, T., Bird Ecology
WILUSZ, T., Enzymology
WITKOWSKI, A., Avian Ecology
WYRZYKOWSKI, J., Regional Geography and Tourism

Faculty of Philology (pl. Biskupa Nankiera 15, 50-140 Wrocław; tel. and fax (71) 343-30-29; e-mail dziekanat.fil@uni.wroc.pl):

DĄBROWSKA, A., Applied Linguistics
DEGLER, J., Theory of Culture and Performing Arts
DYNAK, W., Methodology of Teaching Polish Language and Literature
JANIKOWSKI, K., Scandinavian Studies, German Language
JASTRZĘBSKI, J., Theory of Culture
KAMIŃSKA-SZMAJ, I., Contemporary Polish
KLIMOWICZ, T., Russian Literature and Culture
KOLBUSZEWSKI, J., History of Polish Literature before 1918
KUNICKI, W., German Literature before 1848
ŁAWIŃSKA-TYSZKOWSKA, J., New Latin Philology
ŁUGOWSKA, J., Theory of Culture and Performing Arts
MIGOŃ, A., Theory and History of Books
MIGOŃ, K., Theory and History of Books
MIODEK, J., History of Polish
PISAREK, L., Russian Studies
PRĘDOTA, S., Dutch Lexicology and Lexicography
PYSZNY, J., Polish Literature since 1918
SAWICKI, P., Italian Studies
SOKOLSKI, J., History of Early Polish Literature
SZASTYŃSKA-SIEMION, A., Greek Philology
TOMICZEK, E., Applied Linguistics
WIECZOREK, D., Ukrainian Studies
ŻABSKI, T., History of Polish Literature before 1918
ZAWADA, A., Polish Literature since 1918

Faculty of Physics and Astronomy (pl. M. Borna 9, 50-204 Wrocław; tel. (71) 375-94-04; fax (71) 321-76-82; e-mail dziekan@ift.uni.wroc.pl; internet www.wfa.uni.wroc.pl):

CISZEWSKI, A., Microstructure Surface Experimental Physics
CUGIER, H., Astrophysics and Classical Astronomy
CZAPLA, Z., Experimental Physics (Dielectrics Physics)
HABA, Z., Theoretical Physics (Field Theory)
KIEJNA, A., Absorption Experimental Physics
KOŁACZKIEWICZ, J., Experimental Physics (Spectroscopy of Field Emission)
LUKIERSKI, J., Theoretical Physics (High-Energy Physics and Theory of Fundamental Particles)
ŁOPUSZAŃSKI, J., Theoretical Physics (Mathematical Methods in Physics)
MRÓZ, S., Experimental Physics (Electron Spectroscopy)
PĘKALSKI, A., Theoretical Physics (Nonlinear Dynamics and Complex Systems)
POPOWICZ, Z., Theoretical Physics (Field Theory)
REDLICH, K., Theoretical Physics (High-Energy Physics and Theory of Fundamental Particles)

Faculty of Social Sciences (ul. Koszarowa 3, 51-149 Wrocław; tel. (71) 375-51-92; fax (71) 326-10-11; e-mail sekretariat@wns.uni.wroc.pl; internet www.wns.uni.wroc.pl):

ALBIN, B., International Studies (Eastern Europe Research)
ANTOSZEWSKI, A., Political Sciences (Political Systems)
BAL, K., Philosophy (German Philosophy)
BOKAJŁO, W., Contemporary Political Ideas
DĄBROWSKI, S., Political Sciences (Contemporary History and Social Movements)
GAJDA-KRYNICKA, J., Philosophy (History of Philosophy)
GELLES, R., International Studies
HULANICKA, B., Sociology of Political Relations
JABŁONSKI, A., Theory of Politics
KOSIAN, J., History of Philosophy in Silesia
ŁOS-NOWAK, T., International Relations
ŁUKASZEWICZ, R., Studies in Alternatives of Human Education
PISAREK, H., Epistemology and Ontology
SIEMIANOWSKI, A., Philosophy of Science and Culture
STANDTMUELLER, E., Studies on European Union
SURMACZYŃSKI, M., Sociology (Sociology of Political Relations)
WOLAŃSKI, M., Research in East European Studies

UNIWERSYTET ZIELONOGÓRSKI
(University of Zielona Góra)

ul. Licealna 9, 65-417 Zielona Góra
Telephone: (68) 328-20-00
Fax: (68) 324-55-97
E-mail: rektorat@uz.zgora.pl
Internet: www.uz.zgora.pl

Founded 2001 through merger of Politechnika Zielonogórska and Wyższa Szkoła Pedagogiczna im. Tadeusza Kotarbińskiego
State control

Rector: Prof. Dr hab. CZESŁAW OSĘKOWSKI
Pro-Rector for Scientific Research and Int. Cooperation: Prof. Dr hab. inż TADEUSZ KUCZYŃSKI
Pro-Rector for Devt: Prof. Dr hab. KRZYSZTOF URBANOWSKI
Pro-Rector for Student Affairs: Prof. Dr hab. LONGIN RYBIŃSKI
Pro-Rector for Educational Quality: Prof. Dr hab. WIELISŁAWA OSMAŃSKA-FURMANEK

Library of 425,255 vols
Number of teachers: 1,177
Number of students: 23,127

Publications: *Applied Mathematics and Computer Science* (4 a year), *Applied Mechanics and Engineering* (4 a year), *Discussiones Mathematicae* (4 series, each 2 a year), *Management* (2 a year), *Studia Zachodnie* (1 a year), *Zeszyty Naukowe* (irregular)

DEANS

Faculty of Arts: Prof. Dr hab. ANDRZEJ TUCHOWSKI
Faculty of Education and Social Sciences: Prof. Dr inż. WIELISŁAWA OSMAŃSKA-FURMANEK
Faculty of Electrotechnology, Informatics and Telecommunications: Prof. Dr hab. inż. JERZY BOLIKOWSKI
Faculty of Exact Sciences: Prof. Dr hab. MIECZYSŁAW BOROWIECKI
Faculty of Humanities: Prof. Dr hab. ANDRZEJ KSENICZ
Faculty of Land and Environmental Engineering: Prof. Dr hab. inż. HENRYK GREINERT
Faculty of Mechanical Engineering: Prof. Dr hab. inż. RYSZARD ROHATYŃSKI
Faculty of Management: Prof. Dr hab. DANIEL FIC

Technical Universities

AKADEMIA GÓRNICZO-HUTNICZA IM. STANISŁAWA STASZICA W KRAKOWIE
(AGH University of Science and Technology)

ul. Mickiewicza 30, 30-059 Cracow
Telephone: (12) 617-20-02
Fax: (12) 633-46-72
E-mail: rektorat@uci.agh.edu.pl
Internet: www.agh.edu.pl

Founded 1919
State control
Languages of instruction: Polish, English
Academic year: October to June

Rector: Prof. RYSZARD TADEUSIEWICZ
Vice-Rector for Gen. Affairs: Prof. ANTONI TAJDUŚ
Vice-Rector for Education: Prof. ANDRZEJ ŁĘDZKI
Vice-Rector for Int. Affairs: Prof. ANDRZEJ KORBEL
Vice-Rector for Science: Prof. JANUSZ KOWAL
Chief Admin. Officer: HENRYK ZIOŁO
Librarian: Mgr EWA DOBRZYŃSKA-LANKOSZ

Library of 407,247 vols, 138,287 vols periodicals, 769,333 items spec. collns
Number of teachers: 2,014
Number of students: 29,237

Publications: *Automatyka* (Automatics, 2 a year), *Computer Science* (1 a year), *Elektrotechnika i Elektronika* (Electrical Engineering, 2 a year), *Geodezja* (Mining Surveying, 2 a year), *Geologia* (Geology, 4 a year), *Górnictwo* (Mining, 4 a year), *Inżynieria Środowiska* (Environmental Engineering, 2 a year), *Kliertnictwo Nafta Gaz* (Drilling Oil and Gas, 1 a year), *Mechanika* (Mechanics, 4 a year), *Metallurgy and Foundry Engineering* (2 a year), *Opuscula Mathematica* (1 a year), *Telekomunikacja Cyfrowa* (1 a year)

DEANS

Faculty of Applied Mathematics: Prof. ADAM PAWEŁ WOJDA
Faculty of Applied Social Sciences: Dr ANNA SIWIK
Faculty of Drilling, Oil and Gas: Prof. STANISŁAW STRYCZEK
Faculty of Electrical Engineering, Automatics, Computer Science and Electronics: Prof. TADEUSZ ORZECHOWSKI
Faculty of Foundry Engineering: Prof. STANISŁAW RZADKOSZ
Faculty of Fuels and Energy: Prof. JANINA MILEWSKA-DUDA
Faculty of Geology, Geophysics and Environmental Protection: Prof. Dr TADEUSZ SŁOMKA
Faculty of Management: Prof. Dr WIESŁAW WASZKIELEWICZ
Faculty of Materials Science and Ceramics: Prof. JERZY LIS
Faculty of Mechanical Engineering and Robotics: Prof. WŁODZIMIERZ KOWALSKI
Faculty of Metallurgy and Materials Science: Prof. Dr ZBIGNIEW MALINOWSKI
Faculty of Mining and Geoengineering: Prof. JERZY KLICH
Faculty of Mining Surveying and Environmental Engineering: Prof. JAN GOCAŁ
Faculty of Non-Ferrous Metals: Prof. WOJCIECH LIBURA
Faculty of Physics and Applied Computer Science: Prof. KAZIMIERZ JELEŃ

POLITECHNIKA CZĘSTOCHOWSKA
(Częstochowa University of Technology)

ul. Dąbrowskiego 69, 42-200 Częstochowa
Telephone: (34) 325-04-98
Fax: (34) 361-23-85
E-mail: rektor@adm.pcz.czest.pl
Internet: www.pcz.pl

Founded 1949
State control
Academic year: October to June

Rector: Prof. Dr hab. Inż. HENRYK DYJA
Pro-Rectors: Prof. Dr hab. Inż. ANDRZEJ RUSEK, Prof. Dr hab. Inż. MARIA NOWICKA-SKOWRON, Prof. Dr hab. Inż. JÓZEF KOSZKUL
Executive Director: Mgr MAREK REMBISZ
Librarian: Mgr MAŁGORZATA HANKIEWICZ

Library: see Libraries and Archives
Number of teachers: 878
Number of students: 20,975
Publication: *Turbulence* (1 a year)

DEANS

Faculty of Civil Engineering: Prof. Dr hab. Inż. SŁAWOMIR KOSIŃSKI
Faculty of Electrical Engineering: Prof. Dr hab. Inż. ANDRZEJ ROMAN
Faculty of Environmental Protection and Engineering: Prof. Dr hab. Inż. MARTA JANOSZ-RAJCZYK
Faculty of Management: Prof. Dr hab. JANUSZ SZOPA
Faculty of Materials Processing Technology and Applied Physics: Prof. Dr hab. Inż. JERZY SIWKA
Faculty of Mechanical Engineering and Computer Science: Prof. Dr hab. Inż. JERZY WŁODARSKI

PROFESSORS

Faculty of Mechanical Engineering and Computer Science (ul. Armii Krajowej 21, 42-200 Częstochowa; tel. (34) 325-05-61; fax (34) 325-05-04; e-mail dziekanat@itm.pcz.czest.pl):

CUPIAŁ, K., Machines and Internal Combustion Engines
DOMAŃSKI, Z., Physics, Biophysics
DROBNIAK, S., Fluid Mechanics, Fluid Flow Machines
GAJEWSKI, W., Thermodynamics
GIERZYŃSKA-DOLNA, M., Mechanical Engineering, Plastics Processing Machines and Technology
JARŻA, A., Fluid Mechanics
KENSIK, R., Welding
KLAJNY, R., Fluid Mechanics
KOMPANEC, L., Informatics
KOSZKUL, J., Plastics Materials
KRIVOI, S., Mathematics
KUBARSKI, J., Mathematics
KUKLA, S., Mathematics, Mechanics
KUKURYK, B., Plastic Working of Metals
MAJCHRZAK, E., Mathematics
MAZANEK, E., Machine Design
MELECHOW, R., Machine-Building Technology
MENDERA, K., Machines and Internal Combustion Engines
MIRKOWSKI, J., Mechanics and Internal Combustion Engines
MOCHNACKI, B., Mathematics
NIESZPOREK, T., Machine-building Technology
PARKITNY, R., Applied Mechanics and Foundry Technology
PIECH, H., Computer Engineering
POSIADAŁA, B., Applied Mechanics
RUTKOWSKA, D., Informatics
RUTKOWSKI, L., Informatics, Cybernetics
SCZYGIOL, N., Applied Mechanics
SEWASTJANOW, P., Mathematics
SUBERLAK, O., Plastics Materials
SZOPA, R., Mathematics
TOMSKI, L., Machine Design, Applied Mechanics
TUBIELEWICZ, K., Machine-Building Technology
WIERZBICKI, E., Applied Mathematics, Mechanics
WŁODARSKI, J., Plastics Processing Machines and Technology
WOLAŃSKI, R., Thermodynamics, Thermal Processes in Welding
WOŹNIAK, C., Mathematics, Mechanics
WYRZYKOWSKI, R., Informatics

Faculty of Materials Processing Technology and Applied Physics (ul. Armii Krajowej 19, 42-200 Częstochowa; tel. (34) 325-07-13; fax (34) 361-38-88; e-mail dziekanat@mim.pcz.czest.pl; internet www.mim.pcz.czest.pl):

BALA, H., Corrosion of Metals
BOCHENEK, A., Metallurgy, Materials Science
BRASZCZYŃSKI, J., Metallurgy, Foundry Technology
BUDZIK, R., Metallurgy of Ferrous Metals
DYJA, H., Plastic Working of Metals
DZILIŃSKI, K., Physics
GOLIS, B., Plastic Working of Metals
HRABAŃSKI, R., Physics
JEZIORSKI, L., Metallurgy, Metals Science
JOWSA, J., Metallurgy
KNAP, F., Plastic Working of Metals
KONOPKA, Z., Metallurgy, Foundry Technology
ŁĘDZKI, A., Metallurgy, Steelmaking
LESIK, L., Metallurgy
LIS, A., Materials Engineering, Metallurgy
MIELCZAREK, E., Thermodynamics in Power Engineering, Heat Engineering
MOREL, S., Heat Engineering
NITKIEWICZ, Z., Metallurgy, Materials Engineering
PIETRZYK, M., Metallurgy
PILARCZYK, J., Metallurgy, Materials Science
PIŁKOWSKI, Z., Foundry, Steelmaking
SIWKA, J., Metallurgy, Steelmaking
SŁUPEK, S., Metallurgy, Heat Engineering
STACHURA, S., Metals Science
WASZKIELEWICZ, W., Organization and Management, Metallurgy
WIERZBICKA, B., Metallurgy, Casting of Non-ferrous Metals
WOLKENBERG, A., Metals Science
WYSŁOCKI, B., Physics of Magnetic Materials
WYSŁOCKI, J., Physics, Physics of Magnetic Materials
ZAPART, M., Physics
ZAPART, W., Physics of Magnetic Materials
ZBROSZCZYK, J., Physics

Faculty of Electrical Engineering (ul. Armii Krajowej 17, 42-200 Częstochowa; tel. (34) 325-08-22; fax (34) 325-08-23; e-mail dziekanat@el.pcz.czest.pl; internet www.el.pcz.czest.pl):

BIERNACKI, Z., Electrotechnics, Measurements, Design of Measuring Equipment
BRZOZOWSKI, W., Electrical Engineering, Power Stations
DOBRZAŃSKA, I., Electrical Engineering, Electrical Power Management
ISKIERKA, S., Electrotechnics
JANICZEK, R., Electrotechnology
KRAWCZYK, A., Electrotechnics
KRUCZININ, A. M., Electrotechnology
MINKINA, W., Electronics
POPOV, B., Informatics
ROJEK, R., Electronics, Automatics
ROLICZ, P., Electrotechnics
ROMAN, A., Electronics, Magnetic Materials
RUSEK, A., Electric Motors
SAWICKI, A., Electrotechnology
SOIŃSKI, M., Magnetic Materials, Material Engineering
SOKALSKI, K., Physics
SOWA, P., Electroenergetics
WYSOCKI, J., Electronics, Computer Engineering
ZĄBKOWSKA-WACŁAWEK, M., Electrotechnology

Faculty of Civil Engineering (ul. Akademicka 3, 42-200 Częstochowa; tel. (34) 325-09-30):

BOBKO, T., Technology, Organization of Building
CZECH, L., Geometrical Construction, Civil Engineering
DREWNOWSKI, S., Materials Engineering, Structural Engineering
KLEIBER, M., Structural Engineering
KONIECZNY, S., Structural Mechanics
KOSIŃSKI, S., Structural Mechanics
KOZŁOWSKI, R., Civil Engineering
KWIATEK, J., Civil Engineering, Geotechnology
PRZYBYŁO, W., Structural Mechanics, Civil Engineering
PUSZKARIOWA, E., Building Materials
RAJCZYK, J., Civil Engineering
SŁUŻALEC, A., Mathematics, Mechanics
SYGUŁA, S., Bridge Construction, Civil Engineering

Faculty of Management (ul. Armii Krajowej 19B, 42-200 Częstochowa; tel. (34) 325-03-25; e-mail wz@zim.pcz.czest.pl; internet zim.pcz.czest.pl):

ANTOSZKIEWICZ, J., Organization and Management
BARTZ, B., Economics, Logistics
BORKOWSKI, S., Organization and Management, Metallurgy
BOROWIECKI, R., Organization and Management
BUKOWSKI, L., Machine Building Technology, Management
BUKUVKA, O., Production Engineering
CHRZAN, P., Econometrics, Statistics
DURAJ, J., Organization and Management
DURLIK, I., Marketing
FIEDOROWICZ, K., Economics
GOŁUCHOWSKI, J., Informatics
GORCZYCKA, E., Economics, Organization and Management
GRZESZCZYK, T., Economics, Law
GUBARIENI, N., Informatics
GURGUL, E., Agrotechnology
JASTRZĘBOWSKI-HOFFMAN, Z., History, Politics
KATKOW, A., Informatics
KIEŁTYKA, L., Automatics in Management
KLIBER, J., Materials Engineering, Metallurgy
KLISIŃSKI, J., Economics, Marketing
KONODYBA-SZYMAŃSKI, B., Metallurgy
LEWANDOWSKI, J., Organization and Management, Machine Building Technology
MALISZEWSKI, J., Economics, Organization and Management
MILIAN, L., Sociology, Organization and Management
MOSZKIEWICZ, M., Economics
NOWAK, C., Agricultural Technology
NOWICKA-SKOWRON, M., Economics, Organization and Management
NOWICKI, A., Organization and Management, Informatics
PABIAN, A., Organization of Building
PARTYKA, M., Mathematics, Informatics
RUBACHOW, A., Organization and Management Economics
SITEK, E., Economics
SOBOLAK, L., Organization and Management
SUCHECKA, J., Economics
SZOPA, J., Theoretical and Applied Mechanics, Applied Mathematics, Computers
SZTUKA, J., Marketing
SZUWALSKI, K., Organization and Management
VARKOLY, L., Materials Engineering, Computer Engineering
WOŹNIAK-SOBCZAK, B., Economics, Organization and Management
ZACHOROWSKA, A., Economics
ZAWISŁAWSKA, D., Economics
ŻÓŁTOWSKI, B., Process Engineering and Organization

Faculty of Environmental Protection and Engineering (tel. (34) 325-04-62; fax (34) 325-04-63; e-mail wiis@adm.pcz.czest.pl):

BIEŃ, J., Geology, Hydrogeology
BIS, Z., Mechanics, Thermodynamics
BOHDZIEWICZ, J., Environmental Engineering
DEWIATOW, W., Mechanics, Structural Engineering
GIRCZYS, J., Sanitary Engineering
GODZIK, S., Environmental Engineering

GUMNITSKY, J., Biochemistry, Biotechnology
HŁAWICZKA, S., Environmental Engineering
JAGIEŁA, K., Electrotechnology
JANIKOWSKI, R., Environmental Engineering
JANOSZ-RAJCZYK, M., Environmental Engineering
KISIEL, A., Sanitary Engineering
KOSIŃSKI, W., Environmental Engineering
KUCHARSKI, R., Environmental Engineering
MALINA, G., Sanitary Engineering
NOWAK, W., Sanitary Engineering
PISAREK, J., Mechanics, Machine Building Technology
SANITSKY, M., Environmental Engineering

POLITECHNIKA GDAŃSKA (Gdańsk University of Technology)

ul. G. Narutowicza 11/12, 80-952 Gdańsk
Telephone: (58) 341-57-91
Fax: (58) 341-58-21
E-mail: rektor@pg.gda.pl
Internet: www.pg.gda.pl
Founded 1945
Academic year: October to July
Rector: Prof. JANUSZ RACHOŃ
Vice-Rectors: Prof. RYSZARD KATULSKI, Prof. ROMUALD SZYMKIEWICZ, Prof. WOJCIECH SADOWSKI, Prof. WŁADYSŁAW KOC
Chief Admin. Officer: EWA MAZUR
Librarian: BOŻENA HAKUĆ
Library: see Libraries and Archives
Number of teachers: 1,200
Number of students: 20,000
Publications: *Advances in Materials Sciences* (Journal, 4 a year), *Inżynieria Morska i Geotechnika* (Journal, 4 a year), *Pismo PG* (Journal, 12 a year), *Polish Maritime Research* (Journal, 4 a year), *Wykazy Nowych Nabytków Biblioteki* (Library Acquisitions Lists, 4 year), *Zeszyty Naukowe Politechniki Gdańskiej* (Scientific Papers of the Technical Univ. of Gdańsk, irregular)

DEANS

Faculty of Applied Physics and Mathematics: JAN GODLEWSKI
Faculty of Architecture: ANDRZEJ BARANOWSKI
Faculty of Chemistry: JACEK NAMIEŚNIK
Faculty of Electrical and Control Engineering: KAZIMIERZ JAKUBIUK
Faculty of Electronics, Telecommunications and Informatics: HENRYK KRAWCZYK
Faculty of Environmental Engineering: KRZYSZTOF WILDE
Faculty of Management and Economics: PIOTR DOMINIAK
Faculty of Mechanical Engineering: ADAM BARYLSKI
Faculty of Ocean Engineering and Ship Technology: (vacant): MAREK DZIDA

PROFESSORS

Faculty of Applied Physics and Mathematics (Narutowicz 11/12, 80-952 Gdańsk; tel. (58) 347-13-10; fax (58) 347-28-21; internet www.mif.pg.gda.pl):

GŁAZUNOW, J., Mathematical Analysis, Applied Mathematics
GODLEWSKI, J., Physics
KALINOWSKI, J., Physics
KAMONT, Z., Differential Equations
LEBLE, S., Theoretical and Mathematical Physics
MURAWSKI, L., Physics, Solid State Physics
ROMANOWSKI, A., Algebra
SADOWSKI, W., Solid State Physics
SIENKIEWICZ, J., Physics, Applied Informatics
SZMYTKOWSKI, CZ., Atomic and Molecular Physics

Faculty of Architecture (Narutowicz 11/12, 80-952 Gdańsk; tel. and fax (58) 347-13-15; e-mail dziekanarch@pg.gda.pl; internet www.pg.gda.pl/architektura):

GÓRA, J., Painting
KITA, A., Painting
STAWICKA-WAŁKOVSKA, M., Healthy Housing (Urban and Building) and Environmental Assessment of Buildings (Sustainable Buildings)

Faculty of Civil and Environmental Engineering (Narutowicz 11/12, 80-952 Gdańsk; tel. (58) 347-22-05; fax (58) 347-20-44; e-mail biuruyd@pg.gda.pl; internet cenwil.bl.pg.gda.pl/wilis/):

BOGDANIUK, B., Traffic Engineering
GODYCKI ĆWINKO, T., Theory of Reinforced and Prestressed Concrete Structures
JUDYCKI, J., Road Construction
KOWALCZYK, Z., Technology and Management in Civil Engineering
KOWALIK, P., Geodesy
KRYSTEK, R., Traffic Engineering
OBARSKA-PEMPKOWIAK, H., Environmental Engineering
OLAŃCZUK-NEYMAN, K., Environmental Engineering
SIKORA, Z., Civil Engineering, Soil Mechanics and Geomechanical Computation
SZYMCZAK, CZ., Structural Mechanics
SZYMKIEWICZ, R., Hydrology
ZADROGA, B., Soil Mechanics and Foundation Engineering
ZIÓŁKO, J., Steel Structures

Faculty of Chemistry (Narutowicz 11/12, 80-952 Gdańsk; tel. (58) 347-13-45; fax (58) 347-26-94; e-mail dzknt@chem.pg.gda.pl; internet www.pg.gda.pl/chem):

BALAS, A., General Chemistry
BIERNAT, J., General Chemistry
BIZIUK, M., Environmental Analytical Chemistry, Elemental Analysis, Spectrophotometric Analysis
BOROWSKI, E., Biochemistry
DAROWICKI, K., Electrochemistry, Corrosion and Corrosion Protection
HĘDRZYCKA, K., Biochemistry
HUPKA, J., Chemical Engineering
KAMIŃSKI, M., Chemical Technology
KAWALEC-PIETRENKO, B., Chemical Engineering
KOŁODZIEJCZYK, A., Organic Chemistry
KONOPA, J., Organic Chemistry
KUR, J., Molecular Biology
LEWANDOWSKI, W., Heat Technology, Chemical Engineering
MAZERSKI, J., Molecular Modelling, Chemometrics, Biophysics
MILEWSKI, S., Biochemistry
NAMIEŚNIK, J., Analytical Chemistry
PACYNA, J., Environmental Chemistry, Environmental Engineering, Environmental Analysis and Monitoring
POŁOŃSKI, T., Organic Chemistry, Stereochemistry, Molecular Modelling, Chiroptical Spectroscopy
RACHOŃ, J., Organic Chemistry
SYNOVIEĆKI, J., Technical Science
WOJNOWSKI, W., Inorganic Chemistry

Faculty of Electrical and Control Engineering (Narutowicz 11/12, 80-952 Gdańsk; tel. (58) 347-12-58; fax (58) 347-18-02; e-mail dean@ely.pg.gda.pl; internet www.ely.pg.gda.pl):

BRDYŚ, M., Control Systems
JAKUBIUK, K., Principles of Electrotechnics, Electrical Apparatus
KOWALSKI, Z., Industrial Automation
KRAWĆZUK, M., Mechanics
KRZEMIŃSKI, Z., Electrical Drives and Power Electronics
MARECKI, J., Electrical Power Engineering
PAZDRO, P., Electrical Apparatus and Traction
SZCZERBA, Z., Electrical Power Engineering
WOLNY, A., High-Voltage Current Switching
ZAJCZYK, R., Power Engineering
ZIMNY, P., Theoretical Electromagnetic Field

Faculty of Electronics, Telecommunications and Informatics (Narutowicz 11/12, 80-952 Gdańsk; tel. (58) 347-12-45; fax (58) 341-61-32; e-mail deans@eti.pg.gda.pl; internet www.eti.pg.gda.pl):

CZYŻEWSKI, A., Sound Engineering
GÓRSKI, J. K., Software Engineering, Informatics
KOWALCZUK, Z., Automatic Control and Robotics
KRAWCZYK, H., Computer Science, Parallel, Architectures and Fault-Tolerance
KUBALE, M., Discrete Optimization
MALINA, W., Computer Science and Pattern Recognition
MAZUR, J., Microwave Techniques
MROZOWSKI, M., Electromagnetic Field Theory, Microwaves
NIEDŹWIECKI, MACIEJ, Automatic Control
NOWAKOWSKI, A., Electronics Technology
POLOWCZYK, M., Telecommunications Technology
RUTKOWSKI, D., Principles of Telecommunications
SOBCZAK, W., Cybernetics
SPIRALSKI, L., Electronic Equipment
STEPNOWSKI, A., Marine Acoustics, Telecommunications
WOŹNIAK, J., Telecommunications, Computer Communication Systems
ZIELONKO, R., Electronic Equipment Technology
ZIENTALSKI, M., Electronic Equipment Technology

Faculty of Management and Economics (Narutowicz 11/12, 80-952 Gdańsk; tel. (58) 347-18-99; fax (58) 347-18-61; e-mail dziekani@mech.pg.gda.pl; internet www.zie.pg.gda.pl):

ADAMKIEWICZ, A., Research and Development of Social, Economic and Technological Systems
DASZKOWSKA, M., Principles of Marketing, Services Marketing, the Service Economy

Faculty of Mechanical Engineering (Narutowicz 11/12, 80-952 Gdańsk; tel. (58) 347-20-32; fax (58) 347-10-25; e-mail dziekani@mech.pg.gda.pl; internet www.mech.pg.gda.pl):

BALCERSKI, A., Marine Diesel Engines and Ship Power Plants
EJSMONT, J., Machine Building and Maintenance
NEYMAN, A., Tribology
PRZYBYLSKI, W., Manufacturing Engineering
PUZYREWSKI, R., Fluid Mechanics
STĄSIEK, J., Thermodynamics and Heat Transfer
WALCZAK, W., Welding
WITTBRODT, E., Mechanics and Machine Dynamics, Applied Mechanics
ZIELIŃSKI, A., Materials Engineering

Faculty of Ocean Engineering and Ship Technology (Narutowicz 11/12, 80-952 Gdańsk; tel. (58) 347-16-62; fax (58) 341-47-12; e-mail sekoce@pg.gda.pl; internet www.oce.pg.gda.pl/wydziai):

BRANDOWSKI, A., Engineering Safety and Reliability, Ship Technology
DOMACHOWSKI, Z., Automatic Control of Power Engineering Plants

GIRTLER, J., Ship Power Plants and Diesel Engines
KOLENDA, J., Mechanics of Ship Structures
ROSOCHOWICZ, K., Ship Technology
SZANTYR, J., Mechanics, Ship Hydrodynamics

POLITECHNIKA KRĄKOWSKA IM. TADEUSZA KOŚCIUSZKI (Cracow University of Technology)

Warszawska 24, 31-155 Cracow
Telephone: (12) 628-20-00
Fax: (12) 628-20-71
E-mail: r-0@admin.pk.edu.pl
Internet: www.pk.edu.pl

Founded 1945
State control
Language of instruction: Polish
Academic year: October to June (two semesters)

Rector: Prof. Dr hab. Inż. JÓZEF GAWLIK
Pro-Rectors: Dr hab. Inż. RAFEŁ PALEJ, Dr hab. Inż. Arch. WOJCIECH KOSINSKI, Prof. Dr hab. Inż. KAZIMIERZ FURTAK, Prof. Dr hab. Inż. JOZEF GAWLIK, Dr hab. Inż. Arch. WACŁAW CELADYN
Chief Admin. Officer: Mgr Inż. ZBIGNIEW SKAWICKI
Librarian: Mgr MAREK GÓRSKI

Library of 234,600 vols, 81,221 periodicals, 422,127 standards, patents, etc.
Number of teachers: 1,167
Number of students: 17,357

Publications: *Czasopismo Techniczne* (Technical Bulletin, irregular; series on Architecture, Civil Engineering, Chemistry, Mechanics, Electrotechnics, Environmental Science), *Zeszyty Naukowe i Monografie Politechniki Krakowskiej* (Scientific Papers, irregular; series on Architecture, Civil Engineering, Environmental Engineering, Mechanics, Electrical and Computer Engineering, Chemical Engineering and Technology, Basic Technical Sciences, Human, Economic and Social Sciences)

DEANS

Faculty of Applied Physics and Computer Modelling: Dr hab. RYSZARD ZACH
Faculty of Architecture: Prof. Zw. Dr hab. Inż. arch. DARIUSZ KOZŁOWSKI
Faculty of Chemical Engineering and Technology: Prof. Zw. Dr hab. Inż. ZBIGNIEW ŻUREK
Faculty of Ciyil Engineering: Prof. Dr hab. Inż. JACEK ŚLIWIŃSKI
Faculty of Electrical and Computer Engineering: Dr hab. Inż. PIOTR DROZDOWSKI
Faculty of Environmental Engineering: Dr hab. Inż. KRZYSZTOF KNAPIK
Faculty of Mechanical Engineering: Dr hab. Inż. KRZYSZTOF SZUWALSKI

PROFESSORS

Faculty of Applied Physics and Computer Modelling (Podchorążych 1, 30-084 Cracow; tel. (12) 638-07-28; fax (12) 638-07-28; e-mail f-0@admin.pk.edu.pl; internet www.pk.edu.pl/wftimk):

ARTEMOWICZ, O., Algebra
CISOWSKI, J., Solid State Physics
GRAFIJCZUK, W., Mechanics
KOZARZEWSKI, B., Theoretical Physics, Quantum Computation
ŁAWRENIUK, S., Differential Equations
ŁOPUSZAŃSKI, O., Spectral Theory of Operators
OSTOJA-GAJEWSKI, A., Applied Mechanics
PLICZKO, A., Mathematics

Faculty of Architecture (tel. (12) 628-20-20; fax (12) 628-20-20; e-mail a-0@admin.pk.edu.pl; internet www.pk.edu.pl/arch):

BARTKOWICZ, B., Urban Design and Spatial Planning
BIEDA, K., Urban Design Theory and Practice
BÖHM, A., Architecture, Landscape Architecture
BULIŃSKI, W., Architectural Design
DOUSA, S., Sculpture
GOŁOGÓRSKA-KUCIA, E., Painting and Drawing
KADŁUCZKA, A., History of Architecture and Monument Preservation
KOZŁOWSKI, D., Architectural Design and Theory
KUŚNIERZ, K., History of Urban Design
LENARTOWICZ, J. K., Design of Industrial Architecture
MITKOWSKA, A., History of Architecture and Urban Design
SERUGA, W., Urban and Architectural Design
SIEWNIAK, M., Landscape Architecture
WYŻYKOWSKI, A., Urban and Architectural Design

Faculty of Chemical Engineering and Technology (tel. (12) 628-20-35; fax (12) 628-20-35; e-mail wiitch@indy.chemia.pk.edu.pl; internet www.chemia.pk.edu.pl):

BARAŃSKI, A., Organic Chemistry and Physical Organic Chemistry
KOWALSKI, Z., Inorganic Chemical Technology
PIELICHOWSKI, J., Chemistry and Technology of Polymers, Organic Synthesis
STOKŁOSA, A., Physical Chemistry, Solid State Physical Chemistry
TABIS, B., Chemical Engineering
ŻUREK, Z., Solid State Chemistry, Materials Science

Faculty of Civil Engineering (tel. (12) 628-20-23; fax (12) 628-20-23; e-mail l-0@admin.pk.edu.pl; internet www.pk.edu.pl/wil):

ADAMSKI, A., Transport Control Computer Systems, Management and Control Decision-making, Optimization Problems
CHRZANOWSKI, M., Fracture Mechanics and Rheology
CICHOŃ, C., Theory of Structure, Numerical Analysis
CZYCZUŁA, W., Rail and Air Transport Infrastructure, Transportation Systems
DYDUCH, K., Reinforced and Prestressed Concrete Structures, Industrial Buildings, Modernization
FLAGA, A., Structural Mechanics, Building Aerodynamics, Wind Engineering
FLAGA, K., Bridges, Tunnels, Concrete Structures, Technology of Concrete, Nondestructive Testing
FURTAK, K., Bridges, Tunnels, Concrete Structures
KAWECKI, J., Structural Mechanics
ORKISZ, J., Theory of Structure, Structural Mechanics
RUDNICKI, A., Traffic and Highway Engineering, Transportation Systems
ŚLIWIŃSKI, J., Concrete Technology, Building Materials
STACHOWICZ, A., Structural Mechanics, General and Industrial Building, Concrete Structures
SZEFER, G., Solid and Structural Mechanics
TRACZ, M., Traffic and Highway Engineering
WASZCZYSZYN, Z., Structural Mechanics, Strength of Materials, Artificial Intelligence, Neurocomputing and Microcomputing

Faculty of Electrical and Computer Engineering (tel. (12) 628-20-43; fax (12) 628-20-43; e-mail e-0@admin.pk.edu.pl; internet www.elektron.pk.edu.pl):

JAGIEŁŁO, A., Electrical Machines
LAYER, E., Electrical Metrology
MALECKI, P., Experimental Particle Physics, Online Computing, Detector Control Systems
MOŚCIŃSKI, J., Computer Systems, Large-scale Computing, Network Security, Wireless Networking
SAPIECHA, K., Computer Architecture and Programming
SIWCZYŃSKI, M., Electrotechnics, Circuit Theory and Signals
SOBCZYK, T., Electrical Machines
SZARANIEC, E., Mathematical Geophysics

Faculty of Environmental Engineering (tel. (12) 628-28-01; fax (12) 628-20-40; e-mail s-0@admin.pk.edu.pl; internet www.wis.pk.edu.pl):

BRYŚ, H., Surveying in Engineering
DĄBROWSKI, W., Water Supply, Waste Water Disposal, Sanitary Engineering
KANDEFER, S., Thermal Engineering, Combustion Processes, Use of Thermal Waste, Air Protection Systems
KOCWA-KALUCH, R., Environmental Biology, Microbiology of Water, Waste Water and Air
MĄCZEK, K., Refrigeration, Air Conditioning, Environmental Engineering
NACHLIK, E., Hydraulics and Water Management
PIASEK, Z., Geodesy and Cartography for Environmental Engineering, Numerical Geodesy
SŁOTA, H., Water Management
WYSOKIŃSKI, L., Geotechnics, Environmental and Geological Engineering, Civil Engineering

Faculty of Mechanical Engineering (Jana Pawła II 37, 31-864 Cracow; tel. (12) 648-14-32; fax (12) 648-14-32; e-mail m-0@admin.pk.edu.pl; internet www.mech.pk.edu.pl):

CYKLIS, J., Production Engineering
DYLĄG, M., Chemical Engineering, Chemical Industry Equipment, Environmental Engineering
GAWLIK, J., Machining, Design of Cutting Tools
GOLEC, K., Internal Combustion Engines, Engine Cold-starting, Feeding Systems, Turbocharging
KAMIEŃSKI, J., Industrial Equipment
KAZIOR, J., Machine Technology, Powder Metallurgy, Stainless Steels
KNAPCZYK, J., Motor Vehicles and Tractors, Robotics, Theory of Machines and Mechanisms
KOZŁOWSKI, R., Physical Metallurgy and Heat Treatment, Power Engineering Materials Science
MATRAS, Z., Fluid Mechanics, Rheology, Chemical Engineering, Power Engineering
MAZURKIEWICZ, S., Experimental Mechanics, Biomechanics
MICHAŁOWSKI, S., Machine Dynamics, Robotics
MUC, A., Plate and Shell Structures, Mechanics of Composite Materials
NIZIOŁ, J., Theoretical and Applied Mechanics, Machine Dynamics
OPRZĘDKIEWICZ, J., Reliability of Mechanical Devices
RUP, K., Fluid Mechanics, Heat and Mass Transfer
RYŚ, J., Machine Design, Gears, Pressure Vessels
SENDYKA, B., Internal Combustion Engines
SKRZYPEK, J., Theory of Plasticity, Rheology, Damage

TALER, J., Power Machines and Engineering, Heat Transfer, Thermodynamics
WANTUCH, E., Production Engineering
WOJNAR, L., Tribology
WOŁKOW, J., Hydraulic and Pneumatic Control and Drives
ZALEWSKI, W., Power Equipment and Systems, Refrigerating and Air-conditioning Systems
ZIELINSKI, A., Computer Methods of Structural Mechanics, Computer-aided Machine Design

POLITECHNIKA ŁÓDZKA (Technical University of Lodz)

116 Żeromskiego St 90-924 Lodz
Telephone: (42) 631-20-80
Fax: (42) 631-85-22
E-mail: office.rector@adm.p.lodz.pl
Internet: www.p.lodz.pl

Founded 1945
Languages of instruction: English, French, Polish
Public control
Academic year: October to June (2 semesters)

Rector: Prof. STANISŁAW BIELECKI
Vice-Rectors: Prof. IRENEUSZ ZBICIŃSKI, Prof. PIOTR SZCZEPANIAK, Dr KRZYSZTOF JÓŹWIK, Prof. WOJCIECH WOLF
Chancellor: Dr STANISŁAW STARZAK
Librarian: Mgr Inż. BŁAŻEJ FERET

Library of 348,456 vols, 755 current periodicals, 231,873 patents and standards
Number of teachers: 1,464
Number of students: 19,880

Publications: *Budownictwo* (in Polish), *Bulletin* (in Polish), *Chemia* (in Polish and English), *Chemia Spożywcza i Biotechnologia* (in Polish and English), *Cieplne Maszyny Przepływowe* (in Polish and English), *Elektryka* (in Polish and English), *Inżynieria Chemiczna i Procesowa* (in Polish and English), *Journal of Applied Computer Science* (in English), *Mechanics and Mechanical Engineering* (in English), *Organizacja i Zarządzanie* (in Polish), *Physics* (in English), *Rozprawy Naukowe* (in Polish and English), *Włókiennictwo* (in Polish), *Zeszyty Naukowe Politechniki Łódzkiej* (in Polish and English)

DEANS

Faculty of Biotechnology and Food Science: Prof. MARIA KOZIOŁKIEWICZ
Faculty of Chemistry: Prof. PIOTR PANETH
Faculty of Civil Engineering, Architecture and Environmental Engineering: Prof. DARIUSZ GAWIN
Faculty of Electrical, Electronic, Computer and Control Engineering: Prof. SŁAWOMIR WIAK
Faculty of Material Technologies and Textile Design: Prof. RYSZARD KORYCKI
Faculty of Mechanical Engineering: Prof. BOGDAN KRUSZYŃSKI
Faculty of Organization and Management: Prof. RYSZARD GRĄDZKI
Faculty of Process and Environmental Engineering: Prof. STANISŁAW LEDAKOWICZ
Faculty of Technical Physics, Computer Science and Applied Mathematics: Prof. GRZEGORZ BĄK
Institute of Papermaking and Printing: Prof. BARBARA SURMA-ŚLUSARSKA, Prof. NADZW

PROFESSORS

Faculty of Biotechnology and Food Science (Wólczańska 171/173, 90-924 Łódź; tel. (42) 631-34-01; fax (42) 631-34-02; e-mail deanbiof@adm.p.lodz.pl; internet www.snack.p.lodz.pl):

AMBROZIAK, W., Fermentation Technology
ANTCZAK, T., Technical Biochemistry
BIELECKI, S., Technical Biochemistry
BUJACZ, G., Protein Crystallography, Structural Biochemistry
CEDZYŃSKA, K., Organic Chemistry, Environmental Protection
GRABKA, J., Food Engineering, Sugar Technology
ICIEK, J., Chemical Food Technology, Food Engineering
KOZIOŁKIEWICZ, M., Biotechnology, Chemistry, Technical Biotechnology
KRÓL, B., Food Technology
KULA, J., Chemical Technology
LIBUDZISZ, Z., Technical Microbiology
NEBESNY, E., Food Technology
OKRUSZEK, A., Biotechnology, Organic Chemistry
SZOPA, J., Technical Microbiology
TURKIEWICZ, M., Biochemistry, Enzymology
TWARDOWSKI, T., Technical Biochemistry
WYSOCKI, S., Physical And Theoretical Chemistry
ŻAKOWSKA, Z., Technical Microbiology

Faculty of Chemistry (Zeromskiego 116, 90-924 Łódź; tel. (42) 631-31-00; fax (42) 631-31-03; e-mail deanchem@adm.p.lodz.pl; internet www.chemia.p.lodz.pl):

ABRAMCZYK, H., Molecular Spectroscopy, Laser Spectroscopy, Physical and Theoretical Chemistry
BEM, H., Physical and Nuclear Chemistry
CZAJKOWSKI, W., Dyes Chemistry and Technology, Organic Chemistry and Technology
GĘBICKI, J. M., Organic Physical Chemistry, Photochemistry, Spectroscopy, Radiation Chemistry, Biocrystallography
GŁÓWKA, M., Biocrystallography
HAWLICKA, E., Physical and Theoretical Chemistry, Computation Chemistry
JANECKI, T., Organic Chemistry
JÓŹWIAK, W., Chemical Catalysis, Environmental Protection
KAMIŃSKI, Z., Organic Chemistry
KAROLAK-WOJCIECHOWSKA, J., Physical and Theoretical Chemistry, Crystallography
MARCINEK, A., Physical Chemistry, Radiation Chemistry
PANETH, P., Physical and Theoretical Chemistry, Biochemistry
ROSIAK, J. M., Biomaterials Engineering, Polymer Chemistry, Radiation Technology
RYNKOWSKI, J., General Chemistry, Chemical Catalysis, Environmental Protection
RZYMSKI, W., Polymer Chemistry and Technology
SOKOŁOWSKA, J., Dyes Chemistry and Technology
ULAŃSKI, J., Physics and Physical Chemistry of Polymers
ZABORSKI, M., Rubber Chemistry and Technology

Faculty of Civil Engineering, Architecture and Environmental Engineering (Politechniki 6, 90-924 Łódź; tel. (42) 631-35-00; fax (42) 631-35-02; e-mail deanarch@p.lodz.pl; internet www.p.lodz.pl/bais):

CZKWIANIANC, A., Concrete Structures
JOCZ, J., Sculpture
JUZWA, J., Industrial Architecture, Planning of Industrial Areas
KAMIŃSKA, M., Concrete Structures
KLEMM, P., Building Physics, Building Materials, Acoustics of the Architectural and Urban Environment
PAWŁOWSKI, P., History of Town Planning, Planning for Urban Revitalization
PRZEWŁOCKI, S., Engineering Geodesy, Building Metrology, Cartography, Descriptive Geometry
ROGOWSKI, B., Fracture Mechanics, Contact and Inclusion Mechanics, Mechanics of Piezo-electro-magneto-elastic Materials, 'Smart' Materials and 'Intelligent' Structures, Coupled Fields
SABINIAK, H., Heating, Air Conditioning and Ventilation Engineering, Powerdriving and Exploitation of Machinery

Faculty of Electrical, Electronic and Control Engineering (B. Stefanowskiego 18/22, 93-924 Łódź; tel. (42) 631-25-02; fax (42) 636-47-02; e-mail deanelec@sir.p.lodz.pl; internet wee.p.lodz.pl):

ANDERS, G., Reliability Analysis, Power Cable Thermal Rating, Asset Management, Project Management
BARTOSZEWICZ, A., Control Engineering and Robotics, Control Theory
JEZIERSKI, E., Control of Robots
KACPRZAK, T., Telecommunications, Electronic Devices and Systems, Neural Networks
KOŁACIŃSKI, Z., Electrical Apparatus, Plasma Technologies
KOSZMIDER, A., Instrument Transformers, Applied Electrical Engineering
KUŚMIEREK, Z., Electrical Metrology
KUŹMIŃSKI, K., Control Theory, Automation
LISIK, Z., Semiconductor Devices, Microelectronic Technology, High Temperature Electronics, Optical and Electrical Integrated Systems
MATERKA, A., Telecommunications, Signals Processing, Medical Electronics
MIELCZARSKI, W., Power Engineering
MOSIŃSKI, F., Stochastic Processes, High Voltage Engineering
NAPIERALSKI, A., Microelectronics, Electronic Circuits, Power Electronics, Computer Engineering, Thermography
NOWACKI, Z., Electrical Drive Control, Power Electronics
NOWICZ, R., Electrical Engineering, Transformers
OSTALCZYK, P., Control Engineering and Robotics, Electric Drive Automation
PAWELSKI, W., Electronic Devices and Circuits, Power Electronics
PAWLIK, M., Thermal Power Plant Energy Economics
SANKOWSKI, D., Computerized Data Measurement, Identification and Control of Electrothermal Systems
STRZELCZYK, A., Electrical Engineering, Power Engineering
TADEUSIEWICZ, M., Circuit Theory, Theoretical Electrotechnology
WIAK, S., Computer-aided Design, Electrodynamics
ZAKRZEWSKI, K., Electric Machines and Transformers, Applied Electrodynamics

Faculty of Material Technologies and Textile Design (Zeromskiego 116, 90-924 Łódź; tel. (42) 631-33-00; fax (42) 636-48-23; e-mail dzw4@adm.p.lodz.pl):

CYGAN, W., Tapestry
DEMS, K., Structural Mechanics
FRYDRYCH, I., Mechanical Technology of Textiles, Clothing
GNIOTEK, K., Automation of Textile Processes, Measurement Science and Systems
JANTAS, R., Chemical Technology
KOWALSKI, K., Knitting Technology
KOPIAS, K., Knitting Technology
KRUCIŃSKA, I., Mechanical Technology of Textiles, Metrology
LIPP-SYMONOWICZ, B., Chemical Technology of Textiles
MASAJTIS, J., Mechanical Technology of Textiles
NAWROT, A., Tapestry
RYBICKI, F. E., Chemical Technology of Textiles
SNYCERSKI, M., Mechanical Technology of Textiles
WYSOKIŃSKA, Z., Economics

ZAJACZKOWSKI, J., Mechanics, Textiles

Faculty of Mechanical Engineering (B. Stefanowskiego 1/15, 90-924 Łódź; tel. (42) 631-22-00; fax (42) 631-22-03; e-mail deanmech@sir.p.lodz.pl; internet www.p.lodz.pl/mechaniczny):

AWREJCEWICZ, J., Dynamics, Control, Biomechanics
BURCAN, J., Precision Engineering, Medical Engineering
CZOLCZYNSKI, K., Mechanics, Machine Engineering
FODEMSKI, T., Thermodynamics, Heat Transfer
GAWROŃSKI, Z., Materials Engineering
GAZICKI-LIPMAN, M., Materials Engineering
GOLĄBCZAK, A., Production Engineering
KAPITANIAK, T., Mechanics, Machine Dynamics
KOLAKOWSKI, Z., Applied Mechanics
KRÓLAK, M., Applied Mechanics
KRUSZYŃSKI, B., Machining, Manufacturing and Machine Tools Surface Technology
KRYSIŃSKI, J., Fluid-flow Machinery
KULA, P., Machine Design, Materials Engineering
MITURA, S., Materials Engineering
NIEZGODZINSKI, T., Mechanics, Applied Mechanics
ORYŃSKI, F., Machine Tools, Machine Dynamics
PAWELSKI, Z., Machine Design
PIETROWSKI, S., Materials Engineering, Foundry
TOMCZYK, I., Machine Design, Control
WALKOWIAK, B., Medical Engineering
WIŚNIEWSKI, M., Machine Design, Tribology

Faculty of Organization and Management (Piotrkowska 266, 90-924 Łódź; tel. (42) 631-37-68; fax (42) 684-79-93; e-mail dz-w9-4@adm.p.lodz.pl; internet www.oizet.p.lodz.pl):

BALENDRA, R., Management
BARANOWSKI, K., Humanities
LACHIEWICZ, S., Management
LECEWICZ-BARTOSZEWSKA, J., Ergonomics
LEWANDOWSKI, J., Management
MARTIN, C., Management
PENC, J., Strategy Management
POMYKALSKI, A., Economics

Faculty of Process and Environmental Engineering (Wólczańska 213, 90-924 Łódź; tel. (42) 631-37-00; fax (42) 636-56-63; e-mail deanev@wipos.p.lodz.pl; internet wipos.p.lodz.pl):

HEIM, A., Mechanical Engineering, Chemical Engineering
KAMIŃSKI, W., Environmental Engineering, Chemical Engineering
LEDAKOWICZ, S., Chemical Engineering and Bioprocess Engineering, Environmental Engineering, Chemical Technology
MUCHA, M., Chemical Engineering, Chemical Technology
PIDDUBNIAK, D., Mechanics
TYCZKOWSKI, J., Materials Science, Chemical Engineering, Chemistry
WODZIŃSKI, P., Chemical Engineering, Mechanical Engineering
ZARZYCKI, R., Environmental Engineering
ZBICIŃSKI, I., Chemical Engineering, Environmental Engineering

Faculty of Technical Physics, Information Technology and Applied Mathematics (Wólczańska 215, 90-924 Łódź; tel. (42) 631-36-01; fax (42) 631-36-02; e-mail dz-w7-7@adm.p.lodz.pl; internet www.ftims.p.lodz.pl; publ. *Intelligent Internet Exploration*):

BĄK, G., Solid State Physics, Dielectrics
BALCERZAK, M., Real Analysis
GAJEK, L., Statistics, Financial and Actuarial Mathematics
JACYMIRSKI, M., Signal Processing Methods and Fast Algorithms, Technical and Medical Diagnosis
JEMEC, W., Cytography, Asymptotic Methods, Integral Equations
KUCHARCZYK, W., Solid State Physics
MIŚKIEWICZ, L., Artistic Composition of Images and Virtual Spaces, Computer Graphics, Visualization
NAKWASKI, W., Semiconductor Laser Physics, Computer Physics
PRZANOWSKI, M., Theory of Relativity, Mathematical Physics
PRZERADZKI, B., Differential Equations, Dynamical Systems
STACHIW, P., Numerical Methods, Methods of Optimization, System Theory
SZCZEPANIAK, P. S., Computational Intelligence, Pattern Recognition, Knowledge Extraction, Technical and Medical Applications

Institute of Papermaking and Printing (Wólczańska 223, 90-924 Łódź; tel. (42) 636-88-22; fax (42) 631-38-01; e-mail inpapsek@p.lodz.pl; internet www.inpap.p.lodz.pl):

KAWKA, W., Processes and Equipment in the Paper Industry
PRZYBYSZ, K., Paper Technology
SURMA-SLUSARSKA, B., Chemistry of Wood, Pulp and Paper Technology
TOPOLNYTSKYY, P., Processes and Equipment in the Paper Industry
WANDELT, P., Pulp and Paper Technology

POLITECHNIKA LUBELSKA
(Technical University of Lublin)

ul. Nadbystrzycka 38D, 20-618 Lublin
Telephone: (81) 538-11-00
Fax: (81) 532-26-12
E-mail: politechnika@pollub.pl
Internet: www.pollub.pl

Founded 1953
State control
Language of instruction: Polish
Academic year: October to June (two semesters)

Rector: Prof. JOZEF KUCMASZEWSKI
Vice-Rectors: Prof. WITOLD STEPNIEWSKI, Prof. MAREK OPIELAK, Prof. ANDRZEJ WACWLORDARCZYK
Chief Admin. Officer: MIECZYSLAW HASIAK
Library Dir: Mgr Inż. STEFAN WÓJTOWICZ

Library of 172,000 vols, 97,000 standards and technical catalogues
Number of teachers: 566
Number of students: 12,000

DEANS

Faculty of Civil and Sanitary Engineering: Prof. BOGUSLAV SZMYGIN
Faculty of Electrical Engineering and Computer Science: Prof. WOLDEMAR WOJCIK
Faculty of Environmental Engineering: Prof. LUCJAN PAWLOWSKI
Faculty of Management Sciences and Principles of Technology: Prof. JERZY LIPSKI
Faculty of Mechanical Engineering: Prof. HENRYK KOMSTA

PROFESSORS

Faculty of Civil and Sanitary Engineering:

BUREK, R., Heating, Ventilation and Automation
CIEŚLAK, W., Mathematics and Engineering Geometry
CIĘŻAK, T., Institute of Civil Engineering and Architecture
FLAGA, A., Structural Mechanics
HALICKA, A., Civil Engineering Structures
KRZOWSKI, Z., Geotechnics
KUKIEŁKA, J., Highway Engineering
OLSZTA, W., Water Supply and Waste Water Removal
POMORSKA, K., Chemical Engineering
SADOWSKI, T., Solid Mechanics

Faculty of Electrical Engineering:

BOBROWSKI, A., Mathematics
GRZEGÓRSKI, S., Informatics
JANOWSKI, T., Institute of Electrical Engineering and Electrotechnologies
KOLANO, J., Electrical Drive Systems
KOSMULSKI, M., Electrochemistry
LOZBIN, V., Automatics and Metrology
MAJKA, K., Power Plants and Energy Management
PIETRZYK, W., Computer and Electrical Engineering
RUTKA, Z., Power Networks and Protection
WOJCIK, W., Electronics
ZIELENSKI, W., Mechanics, Polymer Processing
ŻUKOWSKI, P., Electrical Devices and High-Technology Engineering

Faculty of Environmental Engineering:

KWIETNIEWSKI, M., Water Supply and Sewage Disposal
OLSZTA, W., Water Management
OZONEK, J., Indoor Environment Engineering
PAWLOWSKI, L., Institute of Environmental Production Engineering
PAWLOWSKI, L., Water, Waste Water and Waste Technology
SOBCZUK, H., Thermal Techniques
SOLDATOV, V., Sustainable Development
STEPNIEWSKI, W., Land Protection

Faculty of Management Sciences and Principles of Technology:

BANEK, T., Quantitative Methods
BAUM, T., Ergonomics
BOJAR, E., Economics
LENIK, K., Principles of Technology
LIPSKI, J., Enterprise Organization
OLCHOWIK, J., Institute of Physics
PAWLAK, M., Organization and Management
SITKO, W., Management
SKOWRON, S., Marketing
WANIURSKI, J., Applied Mathematics

Faculty of Mechanical Engineering:

JONAK, J., Machine Design
KOCZAN, L., Mathematics, Analytical Functions
KUCZMASZEWSKI, J., Production Engineering
NIEWCZAS, A., Internal Combustion Engines and Transportation
OPIELAK, M., Food Processing Engineering
SIKORA, R., Mechanics, Polymer Processing
SWIC, A., Institute of Technical Systems of Information
SZABELSKI, K., Applied Mechanics
TARKOWSKI, P., Tribology, Motor Vehicles and Internal Combustion Engines
WEROŃSKI, A., Physical Metallurgy, Heat Treatment
WEROŃSKI, W., Metal Forming

POLITECHNIKA POZNAŃSKA
(Poznań University of Technology)

Pl. Marii Skłodowskiej-Curie 5, 60-965 Poznań
Telephone: (61) 665-35-37
Fax: (61) 665-37-70
E-mail: rector@put.poznan.pl
Internet: www.put.poznan.pl

Founded 1919
State control
Academic year: October to September

Rector: Prof. JERZY DEMBCZYŃSKI
Vice-Rector (Educational Affairs): Prof. TOMASZ ŁODYGOWSKI
Vice-Rector (Gen. Affairs): Prof. BOGDAN MARUSZEWSKI

Vice-Rector (Scientific and Int. Affairs): Prof. ANNA CYSEWSKA-SOBUSIAK
Chief Admin. Officer: Dr MIROSŁAW STROIŃSKI
Registrar: Mgr KRYSTYNA DŁUGOSZ
Librarian: Mgr HALINA GANIŃSKA
Library of 237,680 vols, 74,668 vols of periodicals, 46,811 standards, 154,358 patents
Number of teachers: 1,200
Number of students: 20,000
Publications: *Fasciculi Mathematici* (in English), *Foundations of Computing and Decision Sciences* (in English, 4 a year), *Zeszyty Naukowe Politechniki Poznańskiej* (Faculty Bulletins, in Polish and English)

DEANS

Faculty of Architecture: Prof. WOJCIECH BONENBERG
Faculty of Chemical Technology: Prof. ADAM VOELKEL
Faculty of Civil and Environmental Engineering and Architecture: Prof. JÓZEF JASICZAK
Faculty of Computer Science and Management: Prof. LESZEK PACHOLSKI
Faculty of Electrical Engineering: Prof. RYSZARD NAWROWSKI
Faculty of Mechanical Engineering and Management: Prof. ADAM HAMROL
Faculty of Technical Physics: Prof. DANUTA BAUMAN
Faculty of Working Machines and Transportation: Prof. KAROL NADOLNY

CHAIRS

Atomic Physics: Prof. EWA STACHOWSKA
Basics of Machine Design: Prof. MARIAN DUDZIAK
Drawing, Painting, Sculpture and Visual Arts: Prof. WŁODZIMIERZ WŁOSZKIEWICZ
Optical Spectroscopy: Prof. MIROSŁAW DROZDOWSKI
Public Architecture and Housing: Prof. MARIAN FIKUS
Thermal Engineering: Prof. LEON BOGUSŁAWSKI

POLITECHNIKA RZESZOWSKA
(Rzeszów University of Technology)

POB 85, ul. W. Pola 2, 35-959 Rzeszów
Telephone: (17) 854-12-60
Fax: (17) 854-12-60
E-mail: rektor@prz.rzeszow.pl
Internet: www.prz.rzeszow.pl
Founded 1963 as High School of Engineering; Univ. status 1974
Academic year: October to September
Rector: Assoc. Prof. ANDRZEJ SOBKOWIAK
Vice-Rector (Education): Prof. LESZEK WOŹNIAK
Vice-Rector (Gen. Affairs): Prof. TADEUSZ MARKOWSKI
Vice-Rector (Int. Cooperation): Assoc. Prof. ALEKSANDER KOZŁOWSKI
Vice-Rector (Research): Asst. Prof. JACEK KLUSKA
Admin. Dir: Mgr WACŁAW GAWEŁ
Library Dir: Mgr ELŻBIETA KAŁUŻA
Library: see Libraries and Archives
Number of teachers: 680
Number of students: 11,680
Publications: *Zeszyty Naukowe*, *Folia Scientiarum Universitatis Technicae Resoviensis*

DEANS

Faculty of Chemistry: Prof. HENRYK GALINA
Faculty of Civil and Environmental Engineering: Prof. LEONARD ZIEMIAŃSKI
Faculty of Electrical and Computer Engineering: Assoc. Prof. KAZIMIER BUCZEK
Faculty of Management and Marketing: Assoc. Prof. KAZIMIERZ RAJCHEL
Faculty of Mechanical Engineering and Aeronautics: Prof. FELIKS STACHOWICZ

POLITECHNIKA ŚLĄSKA
(Silesian University of Technology)

ul. Akademicka 2A, 44-100 Gliwice
Telephone: (32) 231-23-49
Fax: (32) 237-16-55
E-mail: rek.sekr@polsl.gliwice.pl
Internet: www.polsl.gliwice.pl
Founded 1945
State control
Academic year: October to June
Rector: Prof. Dr WOJCIECH ZIELIŃSKI
Vice-Rector (Education): Prof. Dr RYSZARD K. WILK
Vice-Rector (Org. and Devt): Prof. Dr WOJCIECH CHOLEWA
Vice-Rector (Research and Industrial Cooperation): Prof. Dr MARIAN DOLIPSKI
Chief Admin. Officer: WOJCIECH WYDRYCHIEWICZ
Library: see Libraries and Archives
Number of teachers: 1,707
Number of students: 30,042
Publication: *Zeszyty Naukowe Politechniki Śląskiej* (Research Review—various titles)

DEANS

Faculty of Architecture: Prof. NINA JUZWA
Faculty of Automatic Control, Electronics and Computer Science: Prof. JERZY RUTKOWSKI
Faculty of Chemistry: Prof. JERZY SUWIŃSKI
Faculty of Civil Engineering: Prof. STANISŁAW MAJEWSKI
Faculty of Electrical Engineering: Assoc. Prof. BOGUSŁAW GRZESIK
Faculty of Materials Science and Metallurgy: Dr LESZEK BLACHA
Faculty of Mathematics and Physics: Dr STANISŁAW KOCHOWSKI
Faculty of Mechanical Engineering: Prof. Dr LESZEK DOBRZAŃSKI
Faculty of Mining and Geology: Assoc. Prof. KRYSTIAN PROBIERZ
Faculty of Organization and Management: Prof. ANDRZEJ KARBOWNIK
Faculty of Power and Environmental Engineering: Prof. Dr MICHAŁ BODZEK
Faculty of Transport: Prof. ANDRZEJ WILK

POLITECHNIKA ŚWIĘTOKRZYSKA
(Kielce University of Technology)

ul. Tysiąclecia Państwa Polskiego 7, 25-314 Kielce
Telephone: (41) 342-41-00
Fax: (41) 344-29-97
E-mail: rek@tu.kielce.pl
Internet: www.tu.kielce.pl/en
Founded 1965
State control
Academic year: October to June
Rector: Prof. Dr hab. STANISŁAW ADAMCZAK
Vice-Rector for Int. Cooperation: Prof. Dr hab. ZBIGNIEW RUSIN
Vice-Rector for Research: Prof. Dr hab. LESZEK PŁONECKI
Vice-Rector for Research Personnel Devt: Prof. Dr hab. CZESŁAW KUNDERA
Vice-Rector for Student Affairs: Prof. Dr hab. MAŁGORZATA SUCHAŃSKA
Admin. Officer: Dr Eng. ANDRZEJ SĘK
Library: see Libraries and Archives
Number of teachers: 382
Number of students: 8,170

DEANS

Faculty of Civil and Environmental Engineering: Prof. Dr hab. JERZY ZBIGNIEW PIOTROWSKI
Faculty of Electrical and Computer Engineering: Prof. Dr hab. ANDRZEJ KAPŁON
Faculty of Management and Computer Modelling: Prof. Dr hab. DARIUSZ BOJCZUK
Faculty of Mechatronics and Machinery Building: Prof. Dr hab. LESZEK RADZISZEWSKI,

PROFESSORS

Faculty of Civil and Environmental Engineering (tel. (41) 342-45-41; fax (41) 344-37-84; e-mail wbldzie@tu.kielce.pl; internet www.tu.kielce.pl/en/wbiis):

BEZAK-MAZUR, E., Environmental Protection
BOROWICZ, T., Structural Mechanics, Computer Methods in Structural Mechanics
DĄBEK, L., Environmental Chemistry
DĄBKOWSKI, SZ., Water Engineering, Hydraulics
DACHOWSKI, R, Technology and Organization in Civil Engineering
FARYNIAK, L., Civil Engineering
GILEWSKI, W., Structural Mechanics
GOŁASKI, L., Strength of Materials
IWAŃSKI, M., Road Construction Technologies
KOWAL, Z., Metal Constructions and Theory of Structures
KOZŁOWSKI, T., Soil Mechanics, Foundation Engineering
KULICZKOWSKI, A., Environmental Engineering, Trenchless Technologies
ŁOMOTOWSKI, J., Water and Sewage Treatment
MIRSKI, J., Theory of Designing Coatings of Structures
NITA, P., Airfield Construction
ORZECHOWSKI, T., Heat Transfer, Heating and Ventilation
OWSIAK, Z., Concrete Technology
PIASTA, J., Concrete Technology and Prefabrication
PIASTA, W. G., Concrete Technology and Prefabrication
PIOTROWSKI, J. Z., Physics of Buildings, Heating and Ventilation
PURGAL, P., Heating and Ventilation
PROSKURIAKOW, V., Architecture
RUDZIŃSKI, L., Building Repair and Maintenance
RUSIN, Z., Building Materials
RYMASZEWSKI, B., History and Theory of Historical Monuments' Conservation
SERUGA, W., Architecture and Urban Planning
SIKORSKI, M., Land Amelioration
STROJ, A., Heating, Ventilation and Air Conditioning
SZCZEPAŃSKI, W., Art Science
TRĄMPCZYŃSKI, W., Strength of Materials, Mechanics
WAWRZEŃCZYK, J., Building Materials, Concrete Technology
WEHLE-STRZELECKA, S., Architecture and Urban Planning
ŻYGADŁO, M., Waste Management, Waste Disposal and Treatment

Faculty of Electrical and Computer Engineering (tel. (41) 342-41-29; fax (41) 344-77-58; e-mail weaii@tu.kielce.pl; internet www.tu.kielce.pl/en/faculties/weaii):

AUGUSTYN, J., Metrology
DENIZIAK, S., Computer Science
GAD, S., Power Electronics, Electrical Engineering
GORZAŁCZANY, M., Electronics and Intelligent Systems, Computer Engineering, Digital Systems
JASTRIEBOW, A., Computer Science
KACZMAREK, Z., Theoretical Electrical Engineering and Metrology
KAPŁON, A., Power Electronics and Electrical Drives, Electrical Engineering
KUŚMIERZ, J., Metrology

ŁASTOWIECKI, J., Power Electronics and Electric Drives
MARCINIAK, M., Telecommunications
NADOLSKI, R., Electrical Machines, Electrical Engineering
NOWICKI, T., Technical Science
RÓŻOWICZ, A., Lighting Technology
SAPIECHA, K., Computer Science
STACHULEC, K., Modern Solid Physics
STEFAŃSKI, T., Management and Control Systems, , Identifications and Control Systems
STĘPIEŃ, J., Power Engineering
SUCHAŃSKA, M., Telecommunications and Photonics
SZCZEŚNIAK, Z., Automatization of Technical Process; Components and Devices of Electronics and Control Systems
TUNIA, H., Power Electronics
WCIŚLIK, M., Automatic Control Devices and Systems, , Automatic Control, Electrical Engineering
WŁODARCZYK, M., Theoretical Electrical Engineering
WORWA, K., Informatics, Technical Science

Faculty of Management and Computer Modelling (tel. (41) 342-44-40; fax (41) 342-43-06; e-mail wzimk@tu.kielce.pl; internet www.tu.kielce.pl/en/wzimk):

BEDNARCZYK, J., Economics and Management
BOJCZUK, D., Production Engineering Optimisation Methods
CICHOŃ, C., Applied Computer Science
GIERULSKI, W., Production Engineering, Process Modelling
GRYSA, K., Mathematics
JASTRZĘBSKA-SMOLAGA, H., Economic Strategies
KOTOWSKA-JELONEK, M., Economics and Management
MATCZYŃSKI, M., Production Engineering, Process Modelling
MEDUCKI, S., Economic Strategies
OKNIŃSKI, A., Physics
OKSANYCH, A., Economics and Management
PIELORZ, A., Mathematics
PŁOSKI, A., Mathematics
STADNYTSKYY, Y., Economics and Management

Faculty of Mechatronics and Machinery Building (tel. (41) 342-44-20; fax (41) 344-86-98; e-mail wmibm@tu.kielce.pl; internet www.tu.kielce.pl/en/wmibm):

ADAMCZAK, S., Machine Design and Maintenance; Engineering Metrology; Quality Systems; Automated Measurement Systems
AMBROZIK, A., Machine design and Maintenance; Motor and Tractor Vehicles; Combustion Piston Engines
ANTOSZEWSKI, B., Machine Design And Maintenance; Tribology; Sealing Technologies
CHAŁUPCZAK, J., Metallurgy; Metal Forming; Mechanical Engineering
DINDORF, R., Machine Design And Maintenance; Automation Of Fluid Systems; Hydraulic And Pneumatic Automation Systems; Mechatronics; Hydraulic Drive And Control Systems
DZIADOŃ, A., Materials Engineering; Metal Science; Heat Treatment
FARANA, R., Industrial Process and Equipment Control
GAJEWSKI, M., Metallurgy; Foundry Engineering
JANECKI, D., Automation And Robotics, Computer Science; Surface Metrology; Control Theory; Modelling And Simulation
KORUBA, Z., Mechanical Engineering; Mechanical System Dynamics; Numerical Methods; Aerial Vehicle Control
KUNDERA, CZ., Machine Design And Maintenance; Machine Dynamics And Control; Mechanical Engineering; Tribology
LISCAK, S., Transport Technology
MIKO, E., Machine Design and Maintenance; Industrial Process Control
MUCHA, Z., Machine Design and Maintenance; Laser Process Control
MYCZUDA, Z., Automation and Robotics, Computational Methods and Control Systems
NEIMITZ, A., Mechanical Engineering; Mechanics of Solids
OZIMINA, D., Machine Design and Maintenance; Tribology
PŁONECKI, L., Machine Design And Maintenance; Hydraulic and Pneumatic Automation Systems; Machine Control; Laser System Control
RADOWICZ, A., Mechanical Engineering; Mechanics of Solids; Engineering Mechanics
RADZISZEWSKI, B., Theoretical Mechanics; Theory of Stability
RADZISZEWSKI, L., Mechanical Engineering; Vibroacoustics
ROKACH, I., ; Machine Design and Maintenance; Fracture Mechanics
SPADŁO, S., Machine Design and Maintenance; Industrial Process Control
STAMIROWSKI, J., Automation and Robotics; Computer Science; Information Technology for Business; Computer-aided Engineering
STAŃCZYK, T. L., Machine Design And Maintenance; Machine Dynamics
WESOŁOWSKI, Z., Mechanical Engineering; Dynamics of Continuous Media; Laser Processing Of Metals
ZOWCZAK, W., Machine Design and Maintenance; Optimization of Mechanical Systems

POLITECHNIKA WARSZAWSKA (Warsaw University of Technology)

Pl. Politechniki 1, 00-661 Warsaw
Telephone: (22) 234-72-11
Fax: (22) 621-68-92
E-mail: soltyski@rekt.pw.edu.pl
Internet: www.pw.edu.pl

Founded 1826
State control
Languages of instruction: English, Polish
Academic year: October to September

Rector: Prof. WŁODZIMIERZ KURNIK
Vice-Rector (Academic Affairs): Prof. LECH CZARNECKI
Vice-Rector (Gen. Affairs): Prof. ROMAN GAWROŃSKI
Vice-Rector (Płock Campus): Prof. JACEK KIJEŃSKI
Vice-Rector (Scientific Affairs): Prof. TADEUSZ KULIK
Vice-Rector (Student Affairs): Prof. WŁADYSŁAW WIECZOREK
Chief Admin. Officer: Dr KRZYSZTOF DZIEDZIC
Librarian: Mgr JOLANTA STĘPNIAK

Library of 1,551,537 vols, 1,200 periodical titles, 7,500 electronic periodical titles, 220,000 special collns, incl. 34,000 Polish, European and int. standards
Number of teachers: 2,538
Number of students: 35,156

Publication: *Prace naukowe—Politechnika Warszawska* (Scientific Works—Warsaw University of Technology)

DEANS

College of Economics and Social Sciences (Płock Campus): Dr JACEK KUBISSA (Dir)
College of Social Science and Administration: Prof. HELENA KISILOWSKA (Dir)
Business School: Dr WITOLD ORŁOWSKI (Dir)
Faculty of Architecture: Prof. STEFAN WRONA
Faculty of Automobile and Construction Machinery Engineering: Prof. JERZY BAJKOWSKI
Faculty of Chemical and Process Engineering: Prof. JERZY BAŁDYGA
Faculty of Chemistry: Prof. ZBIGNIEW BRZÓZKA
Faculty of Civil Engineering: Prof. HENRYK ZOBEL
Faculty of Civil Engineering, Mechanics and Petrochemistry (Płock Campus): Prof. JACEK KIJEŃSKI
Faculty of Electrical Engineering: Prof. STANISŁAW WINCENCIAK
Faculty of Electronics and Information Technology: Prof. JAN SZMIDT
Faculty of Environmental Engineering: Prof. BERNARD ZAWADA
Faculty of Geodesy and Cartography: Prof. WITOLD PRÓSZYŃSKI
Faculty of Management: Prof. TADEUSZ KRUPA
Faculty of Materials Science and Engineering: Prof. JERZY SZAWŁOWSKI
Faculty of Mathematics and Information Science: Prof. IRMINA HERBURT
Faculty of Mechatronics: Prof. KRZYSZTOF LEWENSTEIN
Faculty of Physics: Prof. RAJMUND BACEWICZ
Faculty of Power and Aeronautical Engineering: Prof. JERZY BANASZEK
Faculty of Production Engineering: Prof. ANDRZEJ KOCAŃDA
Faculty of Transport: Prof. WOJCIECH WAWRZYŃSKI

PROFESSORS

Faculty of Architecture (Koszykowa 55, 00-659 Warsaw; tel. (22) 628-28-87; fax (22) 628-32-36; e-mail dziekan@arch.pw.edu.pl; internet www.arch.pw.edu.pl):

BENEDEK, W., Housing Design and Public Utilities
BRYKOWSKA, M., History of Towns and Architecture
CHMIELEWSKI, J. M., Urban Design and Town Planning
GAWLIKOWSKI, A. Z., Urban Design and Town Planning
GZELL, S., Urban Design and Town Planning
HRYNIAK, Z., Urban Design and Town Planning
KŁOSIEWICZ, L., Contemporary Architecture
KUBICA, B., Fine Arts—Sculpture
KUCZA-KUCZYŃSKI, K., Housing Design and Public Utilities
PAWŁOWSKI, Z., Building Structures
ROGUSKA, J., History of Towns and Architecture
SZPARKOWSKI, Z., Industrial Buildings
SZULBORSKI, K., Building Structures
TOMASZEWSKI, A., Conservation of Monuments, History of Architecture
WIŚNIEWSKA, M., Housing Design and Public Utilities
WERNER, W., Economics of Investment Processes and Management
WRONA, S., Computer-Aided Architectural Design

Faculty of Automobile and Construction Machinery Engineering (Narbutta 84, 02-524 Warsaw; tel. (22) 849-03-01; fax (22) 849-03-06; e-mail dzk@simr.pw.edu.pl; internet www.simr.pw.edu.pl):

BIAŁAS, S., Geometrical Accuracy in Machinery Design, Tolerance Technology
BOGACZ, R., Dynamics of Means of Transport
DĄBROWSKI, Z., Machine Design, Vibroacoustics
GOŁOŚ, K., Fatigue in Materials

KURNIK, WŁ., Dynamics of Mechanical Systems, Mechatronics
MADEJ, J., Mechanics of Rail Vehicles
OSIŃSKI, J., Dynamics of Mechanical Systems
RADKOWSKI, ST., Safety in Technical Systems, Technical Diagnostics
STARCZEWSKI, Z., Dynamics of Mechanical Systems, Dynamics of Rotors and Journal Bearing System
SZLAGOWSKI, J., Plastics Design of Structures, Automation of Construction Machinery
SZUMANOWSKI, A., Electromechanical Propulsion Systems, Energy Storage, Hybrid and Electric Vehicles
TYLIKOWSKI, A., Dynamics of Mechanical Systems, Mechatronics
WICHER, J., Mechanics, Dynamics of Mechanical Systems
WRÓBEL, J., Theory of Machine Design

Faculty of Chemical and Process Engineering (Waryńskiego 1, 00-645 Warsaw; tel. and fax (22) 825-14-40; e-mail dziekan@ichip.pw.edu.pl; internet www.ichip.pw.edu.pl):

BAŁDYGA, J., Chemical Reactor Engineering
BIŃ, A. K., Process Kinetics, Environmental Protection Processes
CHMIELEWSKI, A. G., Environmental Engineering, Separation Processes
GAWROŃSKI, R., Membrane Processes
GRADOŃ, L., Chemical Engineering, Aerosol Mechanics
POHORECKI, R., Chemical Reactor Engineering, Bioprocess Engineering
SIENIUTYCZ, S., Process Thermodynamics, Non-equilibrium Thermodynamics
SZEWCZYK, K. W., Biochemical Technology, Bioprocess Engineering
SZWAST, Z., Process Optimization
WOLNY, A., Chemical Engineering

Faculty of Chemistry (Noakowskiego 3, 00-664 Warsaw; tel. and fax (22) 628-27-41; e-mail dziekan@ch.pw.edu.pl; internet www.ch.pw.edu.pl):

BRZÓZKA, Z., Analytical Chemistry
DOMAŃSKA-ŻELAZNA, U., Physical Chemistry
FLORJAŃCZYK, Z., Organic Chemistry, Polymer Science
GRYFF-KELLER, A., Organic Chemistry
GRZYWA, E., General Chemistry
JAROSZ, M., Analytical Chemistry
JOŃCZYK, A., Organic Chemistry and Technology
KASIURA, K., Inorganic and Analytical Chemistry
KIJEŃSKI, J., Organic Chemistry, Catalysis
KSIĄŻCZAK, A., Theory and Technology of Explosives
ŁOBIŃSKI, R., Analytical Chemistry
MĄKOSZA, M., Organic Chemistry and Technology
PLENKIEWICZ, J., Biotransformation in Organic Chemistry
PROŃ, A., Polymer Science, Solid State Technology
ROKICKI, G., Organic Chemistry, Polymer Science
SERWATOWSKI, J., Physical Organic Chemistry
WIECZOREK, W., Solid State Technology

Faculty of Civil Engineering (Armii Ludowej 16, 00-637 Warsaw; tel. (22) 825-59-37; fax (22) 825-88-99; e-mail dziekanat@il.pw.edu.pl; internet www.il.pw.edu.pl):

ABRAMOWICZ, M., Reinforced Concrete Structures
CHRABACZYŃSKI, G., Building Production and Prefabrication
CZARNECKI, L., Technology of Building Materials
GOMULIŃSKI, A., Structural Mechanics
JAWORSKI, K., Technology of Building Materials
KARCZEWSKI, J., Metal Constructions, Spatial Structures
KNAUFF, M., Building Construction
NAGÓRSKI, R., Structural Mechanics
OBRĘBSKI, J., Structural Mechanics
RADOMSKI, W., Bridge Engineering
RUNKIEWICZ, L., Building Construction
SUCHORZEWSKI, W., Construction of Roads, Streets and Bridges
SZCZEŚNIAK, W., Structural Mechanics
WITKOWSKI, M., Structural Mechanics, Computers in Civil Engineering
WOJEWÓDZKI, W., Theory of Elasticity and Plasticity
ŻÓŁTOWSKI, W., Metal Constructions

Faculty of Civil Engineering, Mechanics and Petrochemistry (Płock Campus) (Łukasiewicza 17, 09-400 Płock; tel. (24) 262-62-54; fax (24) 367-22-25; e-mail zielinski@pw.plock.pl; internet www.pw.plock.pl):

BOCHEŃSKI, C., Agricultural Engineering
BUKOWSKI, A., Technology of Plastics
CHOCHOWSKI, A., Solar Power Engineering
DWILIŃSKI, L., Construction and Reliability of Agricultural Machinery
FRĄCZEK, K., Carbon Derivatives Technology, Polymer Chemistry
KAJDAS, CZ., Technology and Processing of Petroleum and its Products, Tribopolymerization
KAMIŃSKI, E., Mechanical Appliances and Machinery
KOSIŃSKI, W., Cartography and Surveying
PONIEWSKI, M., Heat Engines and Thermal Equipment
POWIERŻA, L., Systems Engineering
PYSIAK, J., Physical Solid-State Chemistry
RÓŻYCKI, C., Trace Analysis, Chemometrics
ŚCIŚLEWSKI, Z., Durability
URBANIEC, K., Food Industry Machinery
WŁODARCZYK, W., Building Constructions
WOLSKI, L., Physics of Buildings, Sanitary Systems
ZIELIŃSKI, J., Technology of Petroleum and Plastics
ŻUK, D., Agricultural Engineering

Faculty of Electrical Engineering (pl. Politechniki 1, 00-661 Warsaw; tel. (22) 629-25-31; fax (22) 625-75-24; e-mail ura@dean.ee.pw.edu.pl; internet www.ee.pw.edu.pl):

BĄK, J., Lighting Technology
BARLIK, R., Industrial Electronics and Electrical Drives, Power Electronics
BOLKOWSKI, S., Circuit Theory and Electromagnetic Fields
CELIŃSKI, Z., Nuclear Technology
CICHOCKI, A., Circuit Theory
CIOK, Z., High-voltage Technology
DMOWSKI, A., Industrial Electronics
FLISOWSKI, Z., High-voltage Technology
HERING, M., Electro-heating Technology
KACZOREK, T., Linear Control Systems
KAŹMIERKOWSKI, M., Industrial Electronics and Intelligent Control
KOCZARA, N., Electrical Drives and Generation of Power
KRZEMIŃSKI, S., Circuit Theory
KUJSZCZYK, S., Power Systems and Electrical Networks
MACHOWSKI, J., Power Systems and Electrical Networks
MAKSYMIUK, J., Electrical Apparatus
MIKOŁAJUK, K., Circuit Theory and Electromagnetic Fields
OSOWSKI, S., Artificial Intelligence—Neural Networks
RAWA, H., Circuit Theory and Electromagnetic Fields
SIKORA, J., Circuit Theory and Electromagnetic Fields
SUPRONOWICZ, H., Industrial Electronics
TRZASKA, Z., Circuit Theory and Electromagnetic Fields
TUMAŃSKI, S., Electrical Measurements
WINCENCIAK, S., Circuit Theory and Electromagnetic Fields

Faculty of Electronics and Information Technology (Nowowiejska 15–19, 00-665 Warsaw; tel. (22) 825-37-58; fax (22) 825-19-84; e-mail dziekan@elka.pw.edu.pl; internet www.elka.pw.edu.pl):

DĄBROWSKI, M., Computer Networks and Switching
DOBROWOLSKI, J., Computer-aided Design of Microwave Circuits, Monolithic Microwave Integrated Circuits
EBERT, J., High-power Radiotechnology
GALWAS, B., Microwave Electronics and Photonics
GWAREK, P., Microwave Technology
HOLEJKO, K., Telecommunications and Opto-electronics
JACHOWICZ, R., Measurement Systems and Sensors
JAKUBOWSKI, A., Microelectronics, Metal-oxide-semiconductor Devices
KUDREWICZ, J., Theory of Electronic Systems
KUŹMICZ, W., Microelectronics
ŁUBA, T., Computer Engineering, Digital Systems Design
LUBACZ, J., Information and Communication Technologies
MAJKUSIAK, B., Microelectronics
MALINOWSKI, K., Information Engineering and Control Systems
MODELSKI, J., Microwaves, Satellite and Cable Television
MORAWSKI, R. Z., Measurement and Instrumentation
MORAWSKI, T., Microwave Technology
MULAWKA, J., Computer Science, Artificial Intelligence
MURASZKIEWICZ, M., Information and Knowledge Systems, Databases, Networking
PAWŁOWSKI, Z., Medical and Nuclear Electronics
PIÓRO, M., Information and Communication Technologies
ROSŁONIEC, S., Microwave Technology
RYBIŃSKI, H., Information Systems, Databases
SZCZEPAŃSKI, P., Optoelectronics, Laser Physics
TRACZYK, W., Knowledge-based Systems
WIERZBICKI, A., Optimization and Decision Theory
WOJCIECHOWSKI, J., Electronics, Telecommunication Networks, Signals and Systems
WOŹNICKI, J., Electronics, Optoelectronics
ZABRODZKI, J., Computer Science, Computer Graphics

Faculty of Environmental Engineering (Nowowiejska 20, 00-653 Warsaw; tel. (22) 621-45-60; fax (22) 625-73-77; e-mail dziekan@is.pw.edu.pl; internet www.is.pw.edu.pl):

BIEDUGNIS, S., Water Supply and Sewerage Systems, Sanitary and Environmental Engineering
JĘDRZEJEWSKA-ŚCIBAK, T., Indoor Air Quality, Ventilation and Air Conditioning
KINDLER, J., Water Resources Management and Environmental Systems
MAŃKOWSKI, S., Heat Engineering
MITOSEK, M., Hydraulics, Fluid Mechanics
MIZIELIŃSKI, B., Ventilation and Air Conditioning
NAWALANY, M., Environmental Engineering, Groundwater Protection
OSIADACZ, A., Gas Engineering
PISARCZYK, S., Building Engineering, Geotechnology
ROMAN, M., Water Supply and Sewerage Systems, Sanitary and Environmental Engineering

Faculty of Geodesy and Cartography (pl. Politechniki 1, 00-661 Warsaw; tel. (22) 660-72-23; fax (22) 621-36-80; e-mail dziekanat@gik.pw.edu.pl; internet www.gik.pw.edu.pl):

ADAMCZEWSKI, Z., Theory of Adjustment, Geodetic Computation
BARLIK, M., Geodesy, Gravimetry
BIAŁOUSZ, S., Soil Mapping and Remote Sensing, Geographical Information Systems
CZARNECKI, K., Geodesy
CZICHON, H., Technology of Printing
MACIEJEWSKA, A., Soil Conservation and Land Protection
MAKOWSKI, A., Cartography
MARTUSEWICZ, J., Surveying for Tunnelling
MERWIŃSKI, R., Printing Technology
PRÓSZYŃSKI, W., Engineering Surveying, Theory of Adjustment
ROGOWSKI, J., Geodetic Astronomy, Satellite Geodesy
SKŁODOWSKI, P., Soil Science, Soil Conservation
SKÓRCZYŃSKI, A., Surveying, Theory of Adjustment
ŚLEDZIŃSKI, J., Satellite Geodesy
WILKOWSKI, W., Rural Land Management

Faculty of Materials Science and Engineering (Wołoska 141, 02-507 Warsaw; tel. (22) 849-99-29; fax (22) 660-85-14; e-mail wim@inmat.pw.edu.pl; internet www.inmat.pw.edu.pl):

GRABSKI, M. W., Physics of Plastic Deformation
KURZYDŁOWSKI, K. J., Materials Characterization and Modelling
LEONOWICZ, M., Magnetic Materials
OLSZYNA, A., Ceramic Materials
MICHALSKI, A., Surface Engineering
SZUMMER, A., Functional Construction of Materials
WIERZCHOŃ, T., Surface Engineering

Faculty of Mathematics and Information Science (pl. Politechniki 1, 00-661 Warsaw; tel. (22) 621-93-12; fax (22) 625-74-60; e-mail sekretariat@mini.pw.edu.pl; internet www.mini.pw.edu.pl):

JANECZKO, S., Singularity Theory and Symplectic Geometry
KLEIBER, M., Computer Methods in Mechanics
LONC, Z., Discrete Mathematics
MACUKOW, B., Artificial Intelligence
MĄCZYŃSKI, M., Algebra, Mathematical Foundations of Quantum Theory
MARCINIAK, K., Computer Graphics and Geometry
MUSZYŃSKI, J., Differential Equations
PLUCIŃSKA, A., Probability and Stochastic Processes
ROMANOWSKA, A., Algebra
SPIEŻ, S., Topology

Faculty of Mechatronics (Św. A. Boboli 8, 02-525 Warsaw; tel. (22) 849-07-11; fax (22) 849-99-36; e-mail dean@mchtr.pw.edu.pl; internet www.mchtr.pw.edu.pl):

CIEŚLICKI, K., Fluid Mechanics
DUNAJSKI, Z., Biomedical Engineering
GAMBIN, W., Mechanics
JANISZOWSKI, K., Automatic Control and Robotics, System Identification
JÓŹWICKI, R., Design of Optical Instruments
KOŚCIELNY, J. M., Automatic Control, Fault Detection
KUJAWIŃSKA, M., Applied Optics, Machine Vision
KUREK, J., Automatic Control and Robotics, Control Theory
MRUGALSKI, Z., Design of Precision Devices
OLEKSIUK, T., Design of Precision Devices
PAŁKO, T., Biomedical Engineering
PATORSKI, K., Applied Optics, Design of Optical Instruments
PAWLICKI, W. G., Biomedical Engineering
RATAJCZYK, E., Measuring Apparatus

Faculty of Physics (Koszykowa 75, 00-662 Warsaw; tel. (22) 660-72-67; fax (22) 628-21-71; e-mail dziekan@if.pw.edu.pl; internet www.if.pw.edu.pl):

ADAMCZYK, A., Liquid Crystals
BACEWICZ, R., Solid State Physics
BOGUSZ, W., Solid State Physics
ĆWIOK, S., Nuclear Physics
HOŁYST, J., Physics of Complex Systems
KOSIŃSKI, R., Physics of Magnetism
KROK, F., Solid State Physics
SŁOWIŃSKI, B., Nuclear Physics
STRZAŁKOWSKI, I., Solid State Physics
SUKIENNICKI, A., Physics of Magnetism
WOLIŃSKI, T., Optoelectronics
ŻEBROWSKI, J., Physics of Complex Systems

Faculty of Power and Aeronautical Engineering (Nowowiejska 24, 00-665 Warsaw; tel. (22) 621-53-10; fax (22) 625-73-51; e-mail dziekan@meil.pw.edu.pl; internet www.meil.pw.edu.pl):

ARCZEWSKI, K., Analytical Mechanics, Multibody Systems
BANASZEK, J., Thermodynamics, Mathematical Methods of Heat Transfer
DIETRICH, M. (acting), Mechanical Engineering, Biomedical Engineering
DOMANSKI, R., Heat Transfer, Thermodynamics, Environmental Engineering
FURMAŃSKI, P., Heat Transfer, Thermodynamics, Thermal Properties of Materials
GORAJ, Z., Aerodynamics, Flight Dynamics, Aircraft Design
JEDRAL, W., Power Engineering, Pumping Machinery and Installations
KĘDZIOR, K., Modelling of Human Movement, Systems Dynamics, Robotics and Biomechanics
LEWANDOWSKI, J., Environmental Engineering, Power Engineering, Control of Power Plants
LEWITOWICZ, J., Aircraft Maintenance, Aerospace Engineering
MARYNIAK, J., Flight Mechanics
MILLER, A., Power Engineering, Gas and Steam Turbines
PORTACHA, J., Power Engineering, Power Plants
RYCHTER, T., Internal Combustion Engines, Combustion
SADO, J., Thermodynamics, Refrigeration, Plasma Physics
STUPNICKI, J., Fundamentals of Machine Construction
STYCZEK, A., Mathematical Methods of Fluid Mechanics
SZOPA, T., Safety Engineering
SZUMOWSKI, A., Fluid Mechanics, Gas Dynamics, Aerodynamic Noise Control
WOLAŃSKI, P., Combustion, Aero Engines
ŻOCHOWSKI, M., Strength of Materials

Faculty of Production Engineering (Narbutta 85, 02-524 Warsaw; tel. (22) 849-97-95; fax (22) 849-94-34; e-mail dean@wip.pw.edu.pl; internet www.wip.pw.edu.pl):

BOSSAK, M., Computational Mechanics, Computer-aided Design
GRUDZEWSKI, W., Organization and Management
HEJDUK, J., Organization and Management
JEMIELNIAK, K., Production Engineering
KACZOROWSKI, M., Materials Science and Engineering
KISIELNICKI, J., Organization and Management
KLASZTORNY, M., Applied Mechanics
KOCAŃDA, A., Metal-forming
KOZAK, J., Production Engineering
LEWANDOWSKI, J., Economics
MASŁOWSKI, A., Automation and Robotics
MASŁYK-MUSIAŁ, E., Organization and Management
MONKIEWICZ, J., Organization and Management
NOWICKI, B., Production Engineering
PERZYK, M., Casting Technology
SANTAREK, K., Organization and Management
SZAFARCZYK, M., Machine Tools Control and Drive
SZENAJCH, W., Mechanical Engineering, Automatic Control of Industrial Processes
TKACZYK, S., Organization and Management
WILCZYŃSKI, A., Mechanical Engineering
WŁOSIŃSKI, W., Materials Technology

Faculty of Transport (Koszykowa 75, 00-662 Warsaw; tel. (22) 660-73-11; fax (22) 621-56-87; e-mail dziekan@it.pw.edu.pl; internet www.it.pw.edu.pl):

BORGOŃ, J., Air Traffic Control
CHUDZIKIEWICZ, A., Dynamics and Diagnostics of Means of Transport
DĄBROWA-BAJON, M., Rail Traffic Control
DYDUCH, J., Control Systems
KISILOWSKI, J., Dynamics and Diagnostics of Mechanical Systems
LESZCZYŃSKI, J., Organization and Technology of Transport
MANEROWSKI, J., Flight Mechanics
NIEDZIELA, T., Image Processing
SMALKO, Z., Maintenance and Operation of Vehicles

College of Economics and Social Sciences (Płock Campus) (Łukasiewicza 17, 09-400 Płock; tel. (24) 367-21-26; fax (24) 262-90-08; e-mail knes@pw.plock.pl):

BIAŁOŃ-SOCZYŃSKA, L., Economics of Industry, Economics of Science, Marketing
GÓRALSKI, W., Domestic Relations Law, Canon Law
KRAJEWSKA, A., Economics, Fiscal Policy and Taxation Theory
KRAJEWSKI, S., Innovative and Structural Policies, Enterprise Operation and Privatization
MARCINIAK, S., Economics of Innovation, Macroeconomics
OBRĘBSKI, T., Labour Economics, Industrial Relations
PACHO, W., Financing Strategies of Public Limited Companies
SPYCHALSKI, G., History of Economics, Modern Economics
STAWICKI, J., Econometrics and Statistics
WĄSOWICZ, M., Economic Theory, Environmental Economics
WITKOWSKA, J., International Economics, European Integration
ZIELIŃSKI, R., Economic Theory, Defence Economics

College of Social Science and Administration (Noakowskiego 18/20, 00-668 Warsaw; tel. (22) 621-36-92; fax (22) 825-37-46; e-mail kolegium@kns.pw.edu.pl; internet www.kns.pw.edu.pl):

BIAŁOŃ-SOCZYŃSKA, L., Economics of Industry, Economics of Science, Marketing
MARCINIAK, S., Economics of Innovation, Macroeconomics
NIEWIADOMSKI, Z., Public Administration, Self-government, Physical Planning
OBRĘBSKI, T., Economics, Labour Economics, Industrial Relations
ZAWADZKA, Z., Economics, Finance, Banking

POLITECHNIKA WROCŁAWSKA
(Wrocław University of Technology)

Wybrzeże Wyspiańskiego 27, 50-370 Wrocław
Telephone: (71) 320-26-00

Fax: (71) 322-36-64
E-mail: kancelaria.rektora@pwr.wroc.pl
Internet: www.pwr.wroc.pl

Founded 1945
State control
Languages of instruction: English, Polish
Academic year: October to June

Rector: Prof. TADEUSZ WIĘCKOWSKI
Vice-Rector for General Affairs: Prof. JERZY WALENDZIEWSKI
Vice-Rector: Prof. LUDWIK RUSIŃSKI
Vice-Rector: Dr LUDOMIR JANKOWSKI
Vice-Rector for Teaching: Prof. JERZY ŚWIĄTEK
Vice-Rector for Gen. Affairs: Prof. JERZY WALENDZIEWSKI
Vice-Rector for Research: Prof. EUGENIUSZ RUSIŃSKI
Vice-Rector for Education: Prof. ANDRZEJ KASPRZAK
Vice-Rector for Devt: Prof. CEZARY MADRYAS
Vice-Rector for Student Affairs: Dr ZBIGNIEW SROKA
Chief Admin. Officer: Mgr Inż. JAROSŁAW M. JANISZEWSKI
Librarian: Dr HENRYK SZARSKI

Library of 900,000 vols, incl. 4,500 periodical titles
Number of teachers: 2,000
Number of students: 33,000
Publications: *Acta – Bioengineering and Biomechanics* (2 a year), *Architectus Systems* (2 a year), *Badania Operacyjne i Decyzje* (4 a year), *Environmental Protection Engineering* (4 a year), *Fizykochem. Problemy Mineralurgii* (1 a year), *Geometria Wykreślna i Grafika Inżynierska* (1 a year), *Materials Science* (4 a year), *Optica Applicata* (4 a year), *Pryzmat* (12 a year), *Semestr* (12 a year), *Studia Geotechnica et Mechanica* (4 a year), *Systems – Journal of Transdisciplinary Systems Science* (2 a year), *Systems Science* (4 a year)

DEANS

Department of Fundamental Studies: Assist Prof. JANUSZ GÓRNIAK
Faculty of Architecture: Prof. STANISŁAW MEDEKSZA
Faculty of Chemistry: Prof. ANDRZEJ MATYNIA
Faculty of Civil Engineering: Prof. JERZY HOŁA
Faculty of Computer Science and Management: Prof. JERZY ŚWIĄTEK
Faculty of Electrical Engineering: Prof. MARIAN SOBIERAJSKI
Faculty of Electronics: Prof. JAN ZARZYCKI
Faculty of Environmental Engineering: Prof. JAN DANIELEWICZ
Faculty of Geoengineering, Mining and Geology: Prof. LECH GŁADYSIEWICZ
Faculty of Fundamental Problems of Technology: Prof. ZBIGNIEW OLSZAK
Faculty of Mechanical and Power Engineering: Prof. MACIEJ CHOROWSKI
Faculty of Mechanical Engineering: Prof. EDWARD CHLEBUS
Faculty of Microsystem Electronics and Photonics: Prof. ANDRZEJ DZIEDZIC

ZACHODNIOPOMORSKI UNIWERSYTET TECHNOLOGICZNY W SZCZECINIE
(West Pomeranian University of Technology, Szczecin)

ul. Piastów 17, 70-310 Szczecin
Telephone: (91) 434-67-51
Fax: (91) 449-40-15
E-mail: rektor@zut.edu.pl
Internet: www.zut.edu.pl

Founded 2009, by merger of Akademia Rolnicza w Szczecinie and Politechnika Szczecińska
Language of instruction: Polish
Academic year: October to September

Rector: Prof. Dr hab. Inż. WŁODZIMIERZ KIERNOŻYCKI
Pro-Rector for Organization and Academic Development: Prof. Dr hab. Inż. JAN B. DAWIDOWSKI
Pro-Rector for Science: Prof. Dr hab. Inż. RYSZARD KALENCZUK
Pro-Rector for Education: Prof. Dr hab. Inż. WITOLD BIEDUNKIEWICZ
Pro-Rector for Student Affairs: Prof. Dr hab. Inż. JACEK WRÓBEL
Chancellor: Inż. JAROSŁAW POTACZEK
Bursar: JAROSŁAW POTACZEK
Dir of Library: Mgr ANNA GRZELAK-ROZENBERG

Library of 556,525 vols of special colln, 446,341 books, 156,229 vols of periodicals
Number of teachers: 1,114
Number of students: 13,233
Publications: *Acta Ichthyologica et Piscatoria* (2 a year), *Acta Scientiarum Polonorum. Ser. Piscaria* (4 a year), *Acta Scientiarum Polonorum. Ser. Zootechnica* (4 a year), *Advances in Agricultural Sciences* (irregular), *Electronic Journal of Polish Agricultural Universities. Ser. Fisheries* (4 a year), *Folia Pomeranae Universitatis Technologiae Stetinensis* (4 a year), *Forum Uczelniane* (4 a year), *Polish Journal of Chemical Technology* (4 a year)

DEANS

Dept of Civil Engineering and Architecture: Prof. Dr hab. Inż. HALINA GARBALIŃSKA
Dept of Computer Science: Prof. Dr hab. Inż. ANTONI WILIŃSKI
Faculty of Biotechnology and Animal Husbandry: Dr hab. JAN UDAŁA
Faculty of Chemical Technology and Engineering: Prof. Dr hab. Inż. JACEK SOROKA
Faculty of Economics: Prof. Dr hab. GRAŻYNA KARMOWSKA
Faculty of Electrical Engineering: Prof. Dr hab. Inż. STEFAN DOMEK
Faculty of Environment Management and Agriculture: Prof. Dr hab. ALEKSANDER BRZÓSTOWICZ
Faculty of Food Sciences and Fisheries: Prof. Dr hab. Inż. WALDEMAR DĄBROWSKI
Faculty of Marine Technology: Dr hab. Inż. BOGUSŁAW ZAKRZEWSKI
Faculty of Mechanical Engineering and Mechatronics: Prof. Dr hab. Inż. STEFAN BERCZYŃSKI

Higher Institutes

AGRICULTURE

SZKOŁA GŁÓWNA GOSPODARSTWA WIEJSKIEGO W WARSZAWIE
(Warsaw University of Life Sciences–SGGW(WULS-SGGW))

ul. Nowoursynowska 166, 02-787 Warsaw
Telephone: (22) 593-10-00
Fax: (22) 593-10-87
E-mail: rektor@sggw.pl
Internet: www.sggw.pl

Founded 1816
Languages of instruction: Polish, English
Academic year: October to June

Chancellor: Dr WŁADYSŁAW SKARŻYŃSKI
Rector: Prof. Dr. hab. ALOJZY SZYMAŃSKI
Pro-Rector (Devt): Prof. Dr hab. WIESŁAW SKARŻYŃSKI
Pro-Rector (Science): Prof. Dr hab. JAN NIEMIEC
Pro-Rector (Didactics): Prof. Dr hab. KRYSTYNA GUTKOWSKA
Librarian: Mgr JERZY LEWANDOWSKI

Library of 249,151 books, 149,597 vols of periodicals
Number of teachers: 1,266
Number of students: 27,108
Publication: *Annals* (in 8 series)

DEANS

Faculty of Agriculture and Biology: Prof. Dr hab. GRAŻYNA GARBACZEWSKA
Faculty of Animal Science: Prof. Dr hab. PIOTR BRZOZOWSKI
Faculty of Applied Informatics and Mathematics: Prof. Dr hab. BOLESŁAW BORKOWSKI
Faculty of Economic Sciences: Prof. Dr hab. BOGDAN KLEPACKI
Faculty of Engineering and Environmental Science: Prof. Dr hab. JERZY JEZNACH
Faculty of Food Sciences: Prof. Dr hab. DOROTA WITROWA-RAJCHERT
Faculty of Forestry: Prof. Dr hab. MICHAŁ ZASADA
Faculty of Horticulture and Landscape Architecture: Dr hab. MAREK SZYNDEL
Faculty of Humanities: Dr hab. FRANCISZEK KAMPKA
Faculty of Human Nutrition and Consumer Sciences: Prof. Dr hab. JOANNA GROMADZKA
Faculty of Production Engineering: Prof. Dr hab. ANDRZEJ CHOCHOWSKI
Faculty of Veterinary Medicine: Prof. Dr hab. MARIAN BINEK
Faculty of Wood Technology: Dr hab. ADAM KRAJEWSKI

PROFESSORS

Faculty of Agriculture and Biology (02-776 Warsaw, ul. Nowoursynowska 159; tel. (22) 593-25-19; fax (22) 593-25-06; e-mail dwrb@sggw.pl):

BIELAWSKI, W., Biochemistry
BLASZCZYK, M., Biochemistry
BOGATEK – LESZCZYNSKA, R., Plant Physiology
CHOJNICKI, J., Soil Science
CZEPINSKA – KAMINSKA, D., Soil Science
GARBACZEWSKA, G., Botany
GOLINOWSKI, W., Botany
GWOREK, B., Soil Science
KOZANECKA, T., Soil Science
KUSINSKA, A., Soil Science
LABETOWICZ, J., Agrochemistry
LENART, S., Soil And Land Management
LOBOCKA, M., Biochemistry
MADRY, W., Mathematical Statistics And Experimentation
PIETKIEWICZ, S., Plant Physiology
PODLASKI, S., Plant Physiology
PRACZ, J., Soil Science
RADECKI, A., Soil And Land Management
ROZBICKI, J., Crop Production
RUSSEL, S., Biochemistry
RUTKOWSKA, B., Agrochemistry
STYPINSKI, P., Agronomy
WYSZYNSKI, Z., Crop Production
ZAGDANSKA, B., Biochemistry
ZAGORSKI, Z., Soil Science

Faculty of Veterinary Medicine (02-776 Warsaw, ul. Nowoursynowska 159; tel. and fax (22) 593-60-15; e-mail dwmw@sggw.pl):

BINEK, M., Bacteriology, Molecular Biology
BORYCZKO, Z., Animal Gynaecology, Animal Reproduction
DEBSKI, B., Biochemistry
FRYMUS, T., Veterinary Epidemiology
GRALAK, M., Animal Physiology
KANIA, B., Animal Physiology
KATKIEWICZ, M., Animal Gynaecology, Animal Reproduction
KLECZKOWSKI, M., Clinical Diagnosis, Internal Medicine
KLUCINSKI, W., Clinical Diagnosis, Internal Medicine
KOBRYN, H., Anatomy
LECHOWSKI, R., Internal Medicine

LEONTOWICZ, H., Animal Dietetics
MALINOWSKI, E., Livestock Disease, Internal Medicine
MOTYL, T., Animal Physiology
NIEMIALTOWSKI, M., Preclinical Science, Animal Immunology
ORZECHOWSKI, A., Animal Physiology
OSTASZEWSKI, P., Animal Dietetics
SYSA, P., Histology and Embryology
SZCZAWINSKI, J., Hygiene of Food of Animal Origin
WEDRYCHOWICZ, H., Parasitology
WIECHETEK, M., Pharmacology, Toxicology
ZABIELSKI, R., Animal Physiology

Faculty of Forestry (02-776 Warsaw, ul. Nowoursynowska 159; tel. (22) 593-80-10; fax (22) 593-80-08; e-mail dwl@sggw.pl):

ALEKSANDROWICZ-TRZCINSKA, M., Mycology and Forest Pathology
ANDRZEJCZYK, T., Silviculture
BEDKOWSKI, K., GIS in Forestry
BORECKI, T., Forest Management
BOROWSKI, J., Forest Entomology
BRZEZIECKI, B., Silviculture, Forest Management
DUDEK, A., Dendrometry
GOSZCZYNSKI, J., Forest Zoology
GRZYWACZ, A., Mycology and Forest Pathology
KLAPEC, B., Forestry Economics
MAZUR, S., Entomology and Forest Protection
MISCICKI, S., Forest Management
MOSKALIK., T., Forest Resources Utilisation
MOZGAWA, J., GIS in Forestry
OLENDEREK, H., GIS in Forestry
PASCHALIS-JAKUBOWICZ, P., Forest Resources Utilisation
PLOTKOWSKI, L., Forestry Economics
PORTER, B., Forest Resources Utilisation
SKLODOWSKI, J., Entomology and Forest Protection
STEPIEN, E., Forest Management
TARASIUK, S., Silviculture, Forest Management
TRACZ, H., Forest Entomology and Ecology
WASILEWSKI, M., Forest Zoology
WERKA, J., Forest Zoology
ZAJACZKOWSKI, S., Botany, Tree Physiology
ZAKRZEWSKI, J., Botany
ZYBURA, H., Silviculture, Forest Management

Faculty of Horticulture and Landscape Architecture (02-776 Warsaw, ul. Nowoursynowska 159; tel. (22) 593-20-10; fax (22) 593-20-11; e-mail dwoa@sggw.pl):

BURZA, W., Plant Genetics, Breeding and Biotechnology
DABROWSKI, Z., Applied Entomology
GAJC-WOLSKA, J., Vegetable and Medicinal Plants
GAJEWSKI, M., Vegetable and Medicinal Plants
GAWRONSKA, H., Natural Sciences in Horticulture
GAWRONSKI, W., Natural Sciences in Horticulture
IGNATOWICZ, S., Applied Entomology
JABLONSKA, L., Horticultural Economics
JADCZUK-TOBJASZ, E., Pomology
KARPINSKI, S., Plant Genetics, Breeding and Biotechnology
KIELKIEWICZ, M., Applied Entomology
KOBRYN, J., Vegetable and Medicinal Plants
KOSMALA, M., Landscape Art
KOZLOWSKI, M., Applied Entomology
KROLIKOWSKI, J., Landscape Art
LUKASZEWSKA, A., Ornamental Plants
MALESZY, S., Plant Genetics, Breeding and Biotechnology
NIEMIROWICZ-SZCZYTT, K., Plant Genetics, Breeding and Biotechnology
OSINSKA, E., Vegetable and Medicinal Plants
PADUCH-CICHAL, E., Plant Pathology
PLANDER, W., Plant Genetics, Breeding and Biotechnology
PRZYBECKI, Z., Plant Genetics, Breeding and Biotechnology
PRZYBYLA, A., Pomology
RAKOCZY-TROJANOWSKA, M., Plant Genetics, Breeding and Biotechnology
RYLKE, J., Landscape Art
SZULCZEWSKA, B., Landscape Architecture
SZYNDEL, M., Plant Pathology
SZYSZKO, J., Evaluation and Assessment of Natural Resources
TOMALA, K., Pomology
TOMCZYK, A., Applied Entomology
WAKULINSKI, W., Plant Pathology
WEGLARZ, Z., Vegetable and Medicinal Plants
WYSOCKI, C., Environmental Protection
ZARSKA, B., Environmental Protection

Faculty of Engineering and Environmental Science (02-776 Warsaw, ul. Nowoursynowska 159; tel. (22) 593-50-10; fax (22) 593-50-15; e-mail dwiks@sggw.pl):

BANASIK, K., Hydrology, Erosion and Sedimentation
BUCZKOWSKI, W., Civil Engineering
GARBULEWSKI, K., Environmental Geotechnics
HEWELKE, P., Environmental Improvement
IGNAR, S., Hydrology, Water Management
JEZNACH, J., Environmental Improvement, Drainage and Irrigation
KERNYTSKYY, I., Descriptive Geometry
KUBRAK, J., Hydraulics
LECHOWICZ, Z., Environmental Geotechnics
MOSIEJ, J., Environmental Improvement
NAGORKO, W., Civil Engineering
OKRUSZKO, T., Hydrology
PIEKUT, K., Natural Bases of Environmental Engineering
PIERZGALSKI, E., Environmental Improvement, Drainage and Irrigation
POLONSKI, M., Engineering Management
POPEK, Z., Water Engineering
SZYMANSKI, A., Geotechnical Engineering
WAGROWSKA, M., Civil Engineering
WYSOCKI, J., Geodesy
ZELAZO, J., Water Engineering
ZOLTOWSKI, W., Civil Engineering

Faculty of Wood Technology (02-776 Warsaw, ul. Nowoursynowska 159; tel. (22) 593-85-10; fax (22) 593-85-15; e-mail dwtd@sggw.pl):

BAJKOWSKI, B., Mechanical Processing of Wood
BEER, P., Furniture Quality and Technology
DOLOWY, K., Physics
DZBENSKI, W., Wood Science
GORSKI, J., Mechanical Processing of Wood
KRAJEWSKI, A., Wood Protection
KRAJEWSKI, J., Wood Protection
KRUTUL, D., Wood Science
NICEWICZ, D., Composite Wood Products
OSIPIUK, J., Mechanization and Automatisation
SWACZYNA, I., Construction and Technology of Final Wood Products
ZIELONKA, P., Economics

Faculty of Animal Science (02-786 Warsaw, ul. Ciszewskiego 8; tel. (22) 593-65-06; fax (22) 593-65-10; e-mail dwnz@sggw.pl):

BRZOZOWSKI, M., Fur Animal Breeding
BRZOZOWSKI, P., Cattle Breeding
CHARON, K., Animal Genetics
CHRZANOWSKI, S., Horse Breeding
DYMNICKA, M., Animal Nutrition
GRODZKI, H., Cattle Breeding
KALETA, T., Animal Genetics
KAMIONEK, M., Zoology
KOSLA, T., Animal Hygiene
KULISIEWICZ, J., Swine Breeding
MICHALSKA, E., Animal Genetics
NALECZ-TARWACKA, T., Cattle Breeding
NIEMIEC, J., Poultry Breeding
NIZNIKOWSKI, R., Sheep and Goats Breeding
OLECH-PIASECKA, W., Animal Genetics
OSTASZEWSKA, T., Ichthyobiology and Fisheries
PEZOWICZ, E., Zoology
RADZIK-RANT, A., Sheep and Goats Breeding
REKIEL, A., Animal Breeding
SAWOSZ-CHWALIBOG, E., Animal Nutrition, Biotechnology
SCIESINSKI, K., Animal Breeding
SKOMIAL, J., Animal Nutrition
SOKOL, J., Economics, Animal Nutrition
ZARSKI, T., Animal Hygiene

Faculty of Applied Informatics and Mathematics (02-776 Warsaw, ul. Nowoursynowska 159; tel. (22) 593-72-10; fax (22) 593-72-11; e-mail wzim@sggw.pl):

BINDERMAN, Z., Mathematics
BORKOWSKI, B., Econometrics
CHMIELEWSKI, L., Informatics
CIARKOWSKI, A., Computer Applications
JANOWICZ, M., Physics
JEZIERSKI, J., Mathematics
LAUDANSKI, Z., Biometrics
ORŁOWSKI, A., Physics
RUSEK, M., Physics
SMOLIK, S., Econometrics
STRASBURGER, A., Mathematics
SZCZESNY, W., Informatics
TWARDOWSKA, K., Mathematics
WIERZBICKI, E., Technical Applications
WITKOWSKA, D., Econometrics, Financial Engineering
ZAWISTOWSKI, Z., Computer Applications
ZIELINSKI, W., Statistics and Biometrics
ZUBEREK, W., Informatics

Faculty of Economic Sciences (02-787 Warsaw, ul. Nowoursynowska 166; tel. and fax (22) 593-40-10; e-mail dwne@sggw.pl):

BAGIENSKI, S., Organisation and Management
JEDRZEJCZYK, I., Law and Finances
JUSZCZYK, S., Banking
KLEPACKI, B., Economics of Production and Logistics
KRZYZANOWSKA, K., Communication
KRZYZANOWSKI, J., International Economic Relations
MAJEWSKI, E., Organisation and Management
MANTEUFFEL, H., International Economic Relations
PODSTAWKA, M., Law and Finances
PUDELKIEWICZ, E., Marketing
RUNOWSKI, H., Organisation and Management
SAWICKA, J., Agrarian Policy and Law
SIKORSKA-WOLAK, I., Rural Development
STANKO, S., Agricultural Economics
SZWACKA-MOKRZYCKA, J., Marketing
WASILEWSKI, M., Accountancy, Banking
WOJCICKI, W., Economic Policies
WOLOSZYN, J., Organisation
ZIETARA, W., Organisation and Management

Faculty of Food Sciences (02-776 Warsaw, ul. Nowoursynowska 159C; tel. (22) 593-75-07; fax (22) 593-75-05; e-mail dwnoz@sggw.pl):

BIALECKA-FLORJANCZYK, E., Organic Chemistry
BLAZEJAK, S., Biotechnology, Microbiology
CEGLINSKA, A., Crop Technology
GNIEWOSZ, M., Biotechnology, Microbiology
KAZIMIERCZUK, Z., Food Chemistry
KOWALCZYK, R., Food Engineering
KOWALSKI, B., Food Chemistry
KRYGIER, K., Fats and Oils Technology
LENART, A., Food Engineering
MITEK, M., Fruit and Vegetables Technology
MROCZEK, J., Meat Technology

OBIEDZINSKI, M., Food Quality
ORZESZKO, A., Organic Chemistry
PALACHA, Z., Food Engineering
PISULA, A., Meat Technology
RACZYNSKA, E., Organic Chemistry
SLOWINSKI, M., Meat Technology
WITROWA-RAJCHERT, D., Food Engineering

Faculty of Humanities (02-787 Warsaw, ul. Nowoursynowska 166; tel. (22) 593-47-10; fax (22) 593-47-01; e-mail dwnh@sggw.pl):

BLESZYNSKA, K., Pedagogy
BOBRYK, J., Psychology
CZAPLIGO-SIKORSKA, J., Sociology
GRYKO, C., Sociology
JEDRZEJKO, M., Pedagogy
KAMPKA, F., Sociology, Political Science
KORAB, K., Rural Sociology, Social Communication
LASTAWSKI, K., Political Science
PODEDWORNA, H., Sociology
PRZYCHODZEN, Z., Pedagogy, Sociology
SNIHUR, S., Philosophy
STEPKA, S., Political Science, History
WALKIEWICZ, W., Political Science
WOJTOWICZ, A., Sociology
ZANIEWSKA, T., Pedagogy, Sociology of Culture

Faculty of Human Nutrition and Consumer Sciences (02-776 Warsaw, ul. Nowoursynowska 159C; tel. (22) 593-70-10; fax (22) 593-70-15; e-mail dwnzk@sggw.pl):

BRZOZOWSKA, A., Human Nutrition
FILIP, R., Gastroenterology, Dietetics
GROMADZKA-OSTROWSKA, J., Nutritional Physiology, Dietetics, Reproductive Regulation
GRONOWSKA-SENGER, A., Human Nutrition
GUTKOWSKA, K., Consumer Behaviour, Marketing Research
KAWECKA, W., Human Immunology, Medical Mycology
KOLOZYN-KRAJEWSKA, D., Food Technology, Food Hygiene and Microbiology
KOWRYGO, B., Food Policy and Management
LASKOWSKI, W., Consumption Research
OZIMEK, I., Consumer Protection, Consumer Behaviour
PRZYBYLSKI, W., Catering Technology, Meat Science
REMBIALKOWSKA, M., Organic Agriculture, Food Quality
ROSOLOWSKA-HUSZCZ, D., Dietetics, Nutritional Physiology
SWIDERSKI, F., Functional Food and Commodities
WASZKIEWICZ-ROBAK, B., Functional Food and Commodities
WIERZBICKA, A., Food Engineering; Food Quality

Faculty of Production Engineering (02-787 Warsaw, ul. Nowoursynowska 164; tel. and fax (22) 593-45-01; e-mail dwip@sggw.pl):

BULINSKI, J., Agricultural and Forest Machinery
CHOCHOWSKI, A., Energy Management
FABIRKIEWICZ, A., Production Engineering
GACH, S., Farm Machinery
JAROS, M., Agricultural Engineering
KALETA, A., Technical Sciences
KLIMKIEWICZ, M., Technical Infrastructure
KRAWIEC, F., Production Organization and Management
KUPCZYK, F., Production Organization and Management
LISOWSKI, A., Agricultural and Forest Machinery
MAJEWSKI, Z., Production Engineering
SKROBACKI, A., Production Engineering
SZTYBER, J., Forestry Mechanisation
TRAJER, J., Technical Sciences
WASCINSKI, T., Production Organization and Management
WASZKIEWICZ, C., Farm Machinery
WOJDALSKI, J., Technical Infrastructure

Akademia Rolnicza im. Hugona Kołłątaja w Krakowie (Agricultural University of Cracow): ul. Mickiewicza 21, 31-120 Cracow; tel. (12) 662-42-60; fax (12) 633-62-45; e-mail recint@ar.krakow.pl; internet www.ar.krakow.pl; f. 1890; State control; faculties of agriculture and economics, food technology, animal science, environmental engineering and land surveying, forestry, horticulture, agricultural engineering; language of instruction: Polish; library: 618,576 vols; 747 teachers; 12,646 students; Rector Prof. JANUSZ ŻMIJA; publs *Acta Scientiarum Polonorum* (irregular), *Zeszyty Naukowe* (in Polish or English).

Akademia Rolnicza we Wrocławiu (Agricultural University of Wrocław): Norwida 25, 50-375 Wrocław; tel. (71) 320-51-01; fax (71) 320-54-04; e-mail rektor@ozi.ar.wroc.pl; internet www.ar.wroc.pl; f. 1951; faculties of biology and animal science, environmental engineering and geodesy, veterinary medicine, food science, agriculture; library: 180,000 vols; 750 teachers; 11,500 students; Rector Prof. Dr hab. MICHAL MAZURKIEWICZ; publs *Acta Scientiarum Polonorum* (online), *Electronic Journal of Polish Agricultural Universities* (online), *Zeszyty Naukowe*.

ECONOMICS, SOCIAL SCIENCES

Akademia Ekonomiczna im. Karola Adamieckiego w Katowicach (Karol Adamiecki University of Economics in Katowice): ul. 1 Maja 50, 40-287 Katowice; tel. (32) 257-70-00; e-mail akademia@ae.katowice.pl; internet www.ae.katowice.pl; f. 1937; faculties of management and economics; library: 330,000 vols; 446 teachers; 9,784 students; Rector Prof. Dr hab. JAN PYKA; publ. *Studia Ekonomiczne* (Economic Studies, irregular).

Akademia Ekonomiczna w Krakowie (Cracow University of Economics): Rakowicka 27, 31-510 Cracow; tel. (12) 293-57-00; fax (12) 293-50-17; e-mail akademia@ae.krakow.pl; f. 1925; faculties of economics, management and commodity science; library: 530,000 vols, 1,630 periodicals; 630 teachers; 20,000 students; Rector Prof. Dr hab. TADEUSZ GRABIŃSKI; publs *Argumenta Oeconomica Cracoviensia*, *Zeszyty Naukowe* (Scientific Papers).

Akademia Ekonomiczna w Poznaniu (University of Economics in Poznań): ul. Niepodległości 10, 60-967 Poznań; tel. (61) 856-90-00; fax (61) 866-89-24; internet www.ae.poznan.pl; f. 1926; faculties of management, economics and commodity science; library: 439,356 vols; 608 teachers; 16,860 students; Rector Prof. Dr WITOLD JUREK; publs *Podręczniki*, *Prace Doktorskie Obronione v Akademii Ekonomicznej w Poznaniu* (1 a year), *Debiuty Ekonomiczne*, *The Poznan University Review*, *Zeszyty Naukowe Seria I*, *Zeszyty Naukowe Seria II–Prace habilitacyjne*.

Akademia Ekonomiczna im. Oskara Langego we Wrocławiu (Wrocław University of Economics): Komandorska 118/120, 53-345 Wrocław; tel. (71) 368-01-00; fax (71) 367-27-78; e-mail www@ae.wroc.pl; internet www.ae.wroc.pl; f. 1947; faculties: engineering and economics, national economy, computer science and management, regional economy and tourism; library: 350,000 vols; 683 teachers; 18,644 students (16,144 undergraduate, 2,500 postgraduate); Rector Prof. zw. Dr hab. MARIAN NOGA; publs *Argumenta Oeconomica* (4 a year), *Prace Naukowe Akademii Ekonomicznej im O. Langego we Wrocławiu*.

Akademia Leona Koźmińskiego (Kozminski University): ul. Jagiellońska 57–59, 03-301 Warsaw; tel. (22) 519-21-00; fax (22) 814-11-56; e-mail wspiz@wspiz.edu.pl; internet www.wspiz.edu.pl; f. 1993; MBA degree courses; library: 35,000 vols; 240 teachers; 5,170 students (3,400 undergraduate, 1,770 postgraduate); Rector Prof. ANDRZEJ K. KOŹMIŃSKI.

Szkoła Główna Handlowa (Warsaw School of Economics): ul. Niepodległości 162, 02-554 Warsaw; tel. (22) 337-90-00; fax (22) 849-53-12; e-mail information@sgh.waw.pl; internet www.sgh.waw.pl; f. 1906; economics, European studies, spatial economy, public administration, quantitative methods and information systems, finance and banking, international relations, management and marketing; library: see Libraries and Archives; 900 teachers; 16,451 students (6,544 full-time, 6,131 extra-mural, 2,626 postgraduate, 1,150 PhD); Rector Prof. MAREK ROCKI; Exec. Dir Dr PIOTR WACHOWIAK; publs *National Economy* (12 a year), *Poland: International Economic Report* (1 a year).

MEDICINE

Akademia Medyczna im. Ludwika Rydygiera w Bydgoszczy (Ludwik Rydygier Medical University in Bydgoszcz): ul. Jagiellońska 13, 85-067 Bydgoszcz; tel. (52) 585-33-00; fax (52) 585-33-08; e-mail rektor@amb.bydgoszcz.pl; internet www.amb.bydgoszcz.pl; f. 1984; library: 64,000 vols, 16,000 periodicals; 545 teachers; 3,714 students; Rector Prof. Dr hab. DANUTA MIŚCICKA ŚLIWKA.

Akademia Medyczna w Gdańsku (Medical University of Gdańsk): ul. Marii Skłodowskiej-Curie 3a, 80-210 Gdańsk; tel. (58) 349-10-00; fax (58) 349-12-00; e-mail rektor@amg.gda.pl; internet www.amg.gda.pl; f. 1945; faculties of medicine (with sub-faculties of dentistry and nursing), health sciences, pharmacy and (jointly with Univ. of Gdańsk) biotechnology; library: 544,316 vols; 915 teachers; 2,700 students; Rector Prof. Dr WIESŁAW MAKAREWICZ; publ. *Annales Academiae Medicae Gedanensis* (1 a year).

Akademia Medyczna w Łodzi (Medical University of Łódź): ul. Kościuszki 4, 90-419 Łódź; tel. (42) 632-21-13; fax (42) 632-23-47; e-mail akmed@rkt2.rkt.am.lodz.pl; f. 1945; faculty of medicine (Dean Prof. ANDRZEJ JOSS) with sub-faculties of stomatology, public health, and nursing; faculty of pharmacy (Dean Prof DARIA ORSZULAK-MICHALAK) with sub-faculty of laboratory medicine and college of cosmetology; library: 291,309 vols; 935 teachers; 3,058 students; Rector Prof. HENRYK STĘPIEŃ; publ. *Annales Academiae Medicae Lodziensis* (irregular).

Akademia Medyczna im. Karola Marcinkowskiego w Poznaniu (Karol Marcinkowski University of Medical Sciences in Poznań): ul. Fredry 10, 61-701 Poznań; tel. (61) 852-03-42; fax (61) 852-04-55; e-mail info@usoms.poznan.pl; internet www.usoms.poznan.pl; f. as Univ. faculty 1920; Univ. status 1950; faculties of medicine, pharmacy, health sciences (with nursing, physiotherapy, public health); sections of stomatology, clinical analysis; library: 328,773 vols; 1,013 teachers; 3,714 students; Rector Prof. Dr LEON DROBNIK; publs *Annual* (with supplements), *Annual Medical News*.

Akademia Medyczna we Wrocławiu (Wrocław Medical University): 50-367 Wrocław, ul. Pasteura 1; tel. (71) 784-10-01; fax (71) 784-01-09; e-mail rektor@am.wroc.pl; internet www.am.wroc.pl; f. 1950; faculties of medicine, dentistry, nursing and pharmacy, postgraduate training; library:

190,367 books, 76,322 papers; 884 teachers; 3,900 students; Rector Prof. Dr hab. LESZEK PARADOWSKI; publ. *Advances in Clinical and Experimental Medicine* (4 a year).

Centrum Medyczne Kształcenia Podyplomowego (Medical Centre for Postgraduate Education): ul. Marymoncka 99–103, 01-813 Warsaw; tel. (22) 569-37-00; e-mail dyrektor@cmkp.edu.pl; internet www.cmkp.edu.pl; f. 1970; faculties of basic sciences, clinical medicine, stomatology, pharmacy, family medicine; school of public health and social medicine; library: 46,000 vols; Dir Prof. Dr hab. med. JOANNA JĘDRZEJCZAK.

Collegium Medicum Uniwersytetu Jagiellońskiego (Jagiellonian University, Medical College): ul. Sw. Anny 12, 31-008 Cracow; tel. (12) 422-04-11; fax (12) 422-25-78; e-mail mabertma@cyf-kr.edu.pl; internet www.cm-uj.krakow.pl; f. 1364; faculties of medicine (with division of dentistry), pharmacy (with division of medical analysis), health care (with Institute of Nursing and Institute of Public Health); Vice-Rector Prof. MAREK ZEMBALA; Representatives of the Rector Prof. JACEK S. DUBIEL (Gen. Affairs), Prof. JANUSZ PACH (Clinical Affairs), Prof. WIESŁAW PAWLIK (Education and Foreign Cooperation), Prof. RYSZARD LAUTERBACH (Scientific Research and Postgraduate Training); library 210,000 vols; 1,200 staff, 100 full professors; 4,600 students; publs *Annales Collegii Medici Universitatis Jagiellonicae Cracoviensis* (1 a year), *The Methodical Review* (1 a year).

Pomorska Akademia Medyczna w Szczecinie (Pomeranian Academy of Medicine in Szczecin): ul. Rybacka 1, 70-204 Szczecin; tel. (91) 480-07-00; fax (91) 480-07-05; internet www.pam.szczecin.pl; f. 1948; faculties of dentistry, medicine, nursing; 1,094 teachers; 1,743 students; Rector Prof. Dr hab. n. med. PRZEMYSŁAW NOWACKI; publs *Annales Academiae Medicae Stetinensis*, *Biuletyn* (12 a year).

Śląska Akademia Medyczna w Katowicach (Medical University of Silesia in Katowice): ul. Warszawska 14, 40-006 Katowice; tel. (32) 251-49-64; fax (32) 208-35-61; e-mail rektor@slam.katowice.pl; internet www.slam.katowice.pl; f. 1948; medical, dental, pharmaceutical and nursing faculties, research in medicine and medical analysis, with special interest in cardiology, cardiac surgery, nephrology, gastroenterology, pulmonary diseases, environmental and occupational medicine; library: see Libraries; 1,517 teachers; 4,682 students; Rector Prof. Dr hab. TADEUSZ WILCZOK; publs *Annales Academiae Medicae Silesiensis* (1 a year), *Annales Societatis Doctrinae Studentium* (irregular), *Wiadomości Lekarskie* (12 a year).

Szkoła Wyzsza Psychologii Społecznej (School of Social Psychology): Chodakowska 19/31, 03-815 Warsaw; tel. (22) 517-96-00; fax (22) 517-99-21; e-mail centrum.informacji@swps.edu.pl; internet www.swps.edu.pl; f. 1996; library: 12,000 vols; 243 teachers; 8,314 students; Pres. Prof. ANDRZEJ ELIASZ; publs *Charaktery* (jt publ., 12 a year), *Czasopismo Psychologiczne* (jt publ., 2 a year), *Kultura Popularna* (2 a year), *Psychologia Jakości Życia* (2 a year), *Studia Psychologiczne* (jt publ., 2 a year).

TECHNOLOGY AND ENGINEERING

Akademia Morska w Gdyni (Gdynia Maritime University): ul. Morska 83, 81-225 Gdynia; tel. (58) 620-75-12; fax (58) 620-67-01; e-mail rector@am.gdynia.pl; internet www.am.gdynia.pl; f. 1920; mechanics, navigation, management and marketing, electrical engineering; library: 84,000 vols, 7,000 in spec. colln; 370 teachers; 8,500 students; Rector Prof. JÓZEF LISOWSKI; publs *Joint Proceedings*, *Scientific Journal*, *Zeszyty Naukowe*.

Akademia Morska w Szczecinie (Maritime University of Szczecin): ul. Wały Chrobrego 1–2, 70-500 Szczecin; tel. (91) 480-94-00; e-mail rektor@am.szczecin.pl; internet www.wsm.szczecin.pl; f. 1969; faculties of marine engineering, navigation, transport engineering and economics; library: 93,000 vols; 1,871 students; Rector Prof. and Master Mariner STANISŁAW GUCMA; publ. *Zeszyty Naukowe* (4 a year).

Politechnika Koszalińska (Technical University of Koszalin): Śniadeckich 2, 75-453 Koszalin; tel. (94) 342-60-20; fax (94) 342-03-74; e-mail kupk@tu.koszalin.pl; internet www.tu.koszalin.pl; f. 1968; depts of mechanical engineering, civil and environmental engineering, electronics, and economics and management; Institute of Design; library: 99,800 vols; 512 teachers; 15,767 students; Rector Prof. Dr hab. KRZYSZTOF WAWRYN; publs *Zeszyty Naukowe* (Research Review, annual), *Koszalińskie Studia i Materiały* (2 a year), *Na Temat* (6 a year).

Politechnika Opolska (Technical University of Opole): ul. Stanisława Mikołajczyka 5, 45-271 Opole; tel. (77) 400-60-00; fax (77) 400-60-50; e-mail rektor@po.opole.pl; internet www.po.opole.pl; f. 1966; academic year October to September (first semester); Rector Prof. Dr PIOTR WACH; Pro-Rector for Science Prof. JERZY SKUBIS; Pro-Rector for Students Dr hab. STANISŁAW WITCZAK; Pro-Rector for Organizational Affairs Dr ZYGMUNT KASPERSKI; Dir of Admin. LEON PRUCNAL; library: 370,000 vols; 429 teachers; 12,224 students; publs *Skrypty* (1 a year), *Studies and Monographs* (1 a year), *Zeszyty Naukowe* (Scientific Papers, 1 a year).

Politechnika Radomska im. Kazimierza Pułaskiego (K. Pułaski Technical University in Radom): ul. Malczewskiego 29, 26-600 Radom; tel. (48) 361-70-10; fax (48) 361-70-12; e-mail rektor@kiux.man.radom.pl; internet www.man.radom.pl; f. 1950; faculties of mechanical engineering, transport, materials science and footwear production technology, economics, teacher training, labour, business and finance, banking, mathematics, physics, chemistry, plastics, cosmetic chemistry, art, food industry, fine art education, history, information technology, sociology, statistics, politics, geography, ecology, foodstuffs economy, law; library: 144,000 vols, 66,000 in spec. collns; 506 teachers; 12,500 students; Rector Prof. Dr hab. Inż. WINCENTY LOTKO; publs *Economics* (2 series), *Mechanics* (1 series), *Pedagogics* (2 series), *Prace Naukowe* (4 series, 1, 2, 3 or 4 of each a year), *Transport* (4 series).

THEOLOGY

Chrześcijańska Akademia Teologiczna (Christian Theological Academy): ul. Miodowa 21, 00-246 Warsaw; tel. (22) 831-95-97; fax (22) 635-95-44; e-mail chat@chat.edu.pl; internet www.chat.edu.pl; f. 1954; library: 55,000 vols; 76 teachers; 955 students; Rector Archbishop Prof. Dr hab. JEREMIASZ JAN ANCHIMIUK; publ. *Rocznik Teologiczny* (2 a year).

Schools of Art and Music

Akademia Muzyczna im. Feliksa Nowowiejskiego w Bydgoszczy (F. Nowowiejski Academy of Music in Bydgoszcz): ul. Słowackiego 7, 85-008 Bydgoszcz; tel. (52) 321-11-42; fax (52) 321-23-50; e-mail sekr@amuz.bydgoszcz.pl; internet www.amuz.bydgoszcz.pl; f. 1979; 100 teachers; 402 students; Rector Prof. JERZY KASZUBA.

Akademia Muzyczna im. Stanisława Moniuszki w Gdańsku (Stanisław Moniuszko Academy of Music in Gdańsk): ul. Łakowa 1–2, 80-743 Gdańsk; tel. (58) 300-92-01; fax (58) 300-92-10; e-mail muzyczna@amuz.gda.pl; internet www.amuz.gda.pl; f. 1947; faculties of composition and theory, music performance, music education; 165 teachers; 433 students; library: 92,000 vols; Rector Prof. BOGDAN KUŁAKOWSKI; publs *Bibliografia* (irregular), *Kultura Muzyczna Północynch Ziem Polski* (irregular), *Muzyka Pomorza* (irregular), *Prace Specjalne* (irregular), *Rocznik Informacyjny* (1 a year), *Skrypty i Podręczniki* (irregular), *Zeszyty Naukowe* (irregular).

Akademia Muzyczna im. Karola Szymanowskiego w Katowicach (Academy of Music in Katowice): ul. Zacisze 3, 40-025 Katowice; tel. (32) 255-40-17; fax (32) 256-44-85; internet www.am.katowice.pl; f. 1929; faculties of composition, music theory and education, instrumental music, vocal music and theatrical art, jazz and popular music; library: 100,000 vols; spec. colln: music in Silesia; 170 teachers; 745 students; Rector Prof. JULIAN GEMBALSKI.

Akademia Muzyczna w Krakowie (Academy of Music in Cracow): ul. Sw. Tomasza 43, 31-027 Cracow; tel. (12) 422-32-50; fax (12) 422-23-43; e-mail zbrektor@cyf-kr.edu.pl; internet www.amuz.krakow.pl; f. 1888; faculties of composition, theory and conducting; instrumental performance; vocal technique; teacher training and choir conducting; also postgraduate studies; library: 47,000 vols; 365 teachers; 644 students; Rector Prof. STANISLAW KRAWCZYNISKI.

Akademia Muzyczna im. Grażyny i Kiejstuta Bacewiczów w Łodzi (Academy of Music in Łódź): Gdańska 32, 90-716 Łódź; tel. (42) 662-16-01; fax (42) 662-16-60; e-mail rektorat@amuz.lodz.pl; internet www.amuz.lodz.pl; f. 1945; composition, theory, eurhythmics, music education; instrumental and vocal technique, performance; library: 32,000 scores, 8,000 vols, 6,000 records and CDs, 300 periodicals; 208 teachers; 574 students; Rector Prof. ANTONI WIERZBIŃSKI.

Akademia Muzyczna im. Ignacego Jana Paderewskiego w Poznaniu (Academy of Music in Poznań): ul. Sw. Marcin 87, 61-808 Poznań; tel. (61) 856-89-10; fax (61) 853-66-76; e-mail amuz@amuz.edu.pl; internet www.amuz.edu.pl; f. 1920; faculties of composition, theory, conducting, instrumental technique, vocal technique, music teaching; Rector Prof. BOGUMIŁ NOWICKI.

Akademia Muzyczna im. Fryderyka Chopina w Warszawie (Frederick Chopin Academy of Music in Warsaw): ul. Okólnik 2, 00-368 Warsaw; tel. (22) 827-72-41; fax (22) 827-83-10; e-mail info@chopin.edu.pl; internet www.chopin.edu.pl; f. 1810; 7 faculties: composition, conducting and theory of music, keyboard instruments, orchestral instruments, vocal performance, general music education, sound engineering; teacher training; library: 20,000 books and 71,000 scores; 330 teachers; 814 students; Rector Prof. RYSZARD ZIMAK; publs *Prace Biblioteki Głównej*, *Zeszyty Naukowe*.

Akademia Muzyczna im. Karola Lipińskiego we Wrocławiu (Academy of Music in Wrocław): pl. 1-go Maja 2, 50-043 Wrocław; tel. (71) 355-55-53; fax (71) 355-91-05; e-mail info@amuz.wroc.pl; internet www.amuz.wroc.pl; f. 1948; depts of composition, conducting, music theory and music therapy, instrumental music, vocal music, music education; library: 113,015 vols; 185 teachers; 685 students; Rector Prof. GRZEGORZ KURZYŃSKI.

Akademia Sztuk Pięknych im. Jana Matejki w Krakowie (Academy of Fine Arts in Cracow): pl. Matejki 13, 31-157 Cracow; tel. (12) 422-24-50; fax (12) 422-65-66; e-mail zerektor@cyf-kr.edu.pl; internet www.asp.krakow.pl; f. 1818; faculties of painting, sculpture, conservation and restoration of works of art, graphic arts, industrial design, interior design; postgraduate studies in theatre, film and television stage design; European poster colln up to 1939; library: 86,500 vols, 21,000 graphic items, 7,500 posters; 244 teachers; 845 students; Rector Prof. STANISŁAW RODZIŃSKI; Library Dir JADWIGA WIELGUT-WALCZAK; publ. *Studia i materiały konserwatorskie* (1 a year).

Akademia Sztuk Pięknych w Gdańsku (Academy of Fine Arts in Gdańsk): Targ Węglowy 6, 80-836 Gdańsk; tel. (58) 301-44-40; fax (58) 301-22-00; e-mail office@asp.gda.pl; internet www.asp.gda.pl; f. 1945; faculties of painting, graphics, sculpture, architecture and industrial design; library: 10,450 vols; 130 teachers; 875 students; Rector Prof. TOMASZ BOGUSŁAWSKI.

Akademia Sztuk Pięknych w Poznaniu (Academy of Fine Arts in Poznań): ul. Marcinkowskiego 29, 60-967 Poznań; tel. (61) 855-25-21; fax (61) 852-80-91; e-mail office@asp.poznan.pl; internet www.asp.poznan.pl; f. 1919, state-controlled from 1921; faculties of painting, printmaking, sculpture, interior architecture and design, art education, multimedia communication; library: 60,000 vols; 189 full-time teachers; 1,264 full-time students; Rector Prof. WOJCIECH MÜLLER; Vice-Rectors Prof. ANDRZEJ WIELGOSZ, Prof. ASP MARCIN BERDYSZAK, Prof. PIOTR KURKA; Admin. Dir WIESŁAWA SZOKALEWICZ.

Akademia Sztuk Pięknych w Warszawie (Academy of Fine Arts in Warsaw): Krakowskie Przedmieście 5, 00-068 Warsaw; tel. (22) 826-19-72; fax (22) 826-21-14; f. 1904 as Szkoła Sztuk Pięknych (School of Fine Arts), renamed 1927; depts of painting, sculpture, interior design, graphics, industrial design, conservation of works of art; spec. studies: tapestry, scenography; library: 24,500 books, 5,578 vols of periodicals; 296 teachers; 1,020 students; Rector Prof. ADAM MYJAK; Library Dir Mgr IRENA KURNICKA-KĘPA; publs *Rocznik* (1 a year, in English and Russian), *Zeszyty Naukowe ASP* (Scientific Copy Books ASP).

Akademia Sztuk Pięknych we Wrocławiu (Academy of Fine Arts in Wrocław): ul. Plac Polski 3/4, 50-156 Wrocław; tel. (71) 343-80-31; fax (71) 343-15-58; e-mail info@asp.wroc.pl; internet www.asp.wroc.pl; f. 1946; faculties of painting, sculpture, graphic arts, glass and ceramics design, interior architecture, industrial design; library: 14,000 vols; Rector Prof. JACEK SZEWCZYK.

Akademia Teatralna im. Al. Zelwerowicza w Warszawie (A. Zelwerowicz Academy of Theatre in Warsaw): ul. Miodowa 22/24, 00-246 Warsaw; tel. (22) 831-69-25; fax (22) 831-91-01; e-mail rektorat@at.edu.pl; internet www.at.edu.pl; f. 1932; faculties of acting, directing, theatre studies, puppetry; library: 39,000 vols; 110 teachers; 360 students; Rector Prof. LECH ŚLIWONIK.

Państwowa Wyższa Szkoła Filmowa Telewizyjna i Teatralna im. Leona Schillera w Łodzi (National School of Film, Television and Theatre in Łódź): Targowa 61/63, 90-323 Łódź; tel. (42) 674-39-43; fax (42) 674-81-39; e-mail swzfilm@filmschool.lodz.pl; internet www.filmschool.lodz.pl; f. 1948; faculties of film and television direction, film and television camerawork, acting, production; courses in screen-writing, television production, photography; library: 40,000 vols; 118 teachers (96 full-time, 22 part-time); 825 students (incl. 600 extra-mural); Rector Prof. HENRYK KLUBA.

Akademia Sztuk Pięknych im. Władysława Strzemińskiego w Łodzi (Władysław Strzemiński Academy of Fine Arts in Łódź): Ul. Wojska Polskiego 121, 91-726 Łódź; tel. (42) 656-10-56; fax (42) 656-21-92; e-mail rektorat@asp.lodz.pl; internet www.asp.lodz.pl; f. 1945; textile faculty (depts of textile, fashion, painting, sculpture, drawing and composition); faculty of graphic art and painting (depts of graphic design, printmaking, painting, visual problems); faculty of visual education; faculty of industrial design; library: 30,000 vols; 240 teachers; 1,500 students; Rector Prof. GREG CHOJNACKI; Librarian KRYSTYNA LOREK.

Państwowa Wyższa Szkoła Teatralna im. Ludwika Solskiego w Krakowie (State Theatre Academy in Cracow): ul. Strasewskiego 21–22, 31-109 Cracow; tel. (12) 422-18-55; fax (12) 422-02-09; e-mail rektor@pwst.krakow.pl; internet www.pwst.krakow.pl; f. 1945; faculties of acting and stage craft; puppet theatre section (Wrocław); Rector Prof. EWA KUTRYŚ.

PORTUGAL

The Higher Education System

Portugal was ruled by a monarchy from the 11th century until it was overthrown in 1910 and a republic was declared. The two oldest current universities, Universidade de Lisboa (founded 1288) and Universidade de Coimbra (founded 1290), date from the late 13th century and were the only such institutions until 1911, when Universidade do Porto was founded. Portugal was governed by a dictatorship during 1932–74, the later years of which saw the establishment of several prominent universities, but most institutions of higher education were founded after the restoration of civilian government in 1975. Higher education is divided into two strands, universities and other institutions (polytechnic institutes, higher schools, professional institutes, schools of art and music). Universities offer undergraduate and postgraduate degrees while other institutions offer three-year degrees and one- or two-year diploma programmes.

Universities became autonomous institutions under the University Autonomy Law (1988), which granted them the power to devise curricula, award degrees and define the equivalency of foreign awards. The Ministry of Science, Technology and Higher Education oversees state universities and other institutions of higher education. The Statute of the Private Higher Education Institution is the legislation governing private institutions, which are not allowed to offer degree-level programmes but instead offer five-year diploma courses. The Ministry of Education is the accrediting body for private institutions, overseeing the programmes and curricula available. Portugal participates in the Bologna Process to establish a European Higher Education Area, the first phase of which is to adopt a credit-based system of comparable degrees with two main cycles (undergraduate and graduate). In 2007/08 there were 376,917 students at 305 institutions of higher education (including the Azores and Madeira).

Portuguese students are admitted to higher education on the basis of two examinations, the prova de aferição (counter test) for secondary education and the provas específicas (specific examination) for the intended course of study. In 2006 a two-tier Bachelors (Licenciatura) and Masters (Mestrado) degree system was introduced in both universities and polytechnic institutes in accordance with the principles of the Bologna Process. The Bachelors degree is usually a three-year programme of study, although courses in some subjects may last longer, such as medicine and dentistry (six years). Under the new system, some degrees are integrated courses of study culminating with award of the Masters degree, which is otherwise a separate postgraduate degree lasting up to two years. The Doctorate (Doutor) is the highest university-level degree, and students may spend up to five or six years in study and research. Beyond doctoral studies, students who have shown great ability as researchers and who have special teaching expertise in a certain area can take the examinations for the award of the Agregação. The Ministry of Labour and Social Solidarity is responsible for vocational and technical education. The Decree Law 26/89 (1989) legislated the creation of professional schools (Escolas Profissionais) primarily aimed at upper secondary-level students.

Regulatory and Representative Bodies

GOVERNMENT

Ministry of Culture: Palácio Nacional da Ajuda, 1349-021 Lisbon; tel. (21) 361-45-00; fax (21) 364-98-72; e-mail gmc@mc.gov.pt; internet www.portaldacultura.gov.pt; Min. MARIA GABRIELA CANAVILHAS.

Ministry of Education: Avda. 5 de Outubro 107, 1069-018 Lisbon; tel. (21) 781-18-00; fax (21) 781-18-35; e-mail gme@me.gov.pt; internet www.min-edu.pt; Min. ISABEL ALÇADA; Sec. of State ALEXANDRE VENTURA.

Ministry of Labour and Social Solidarity: Praça de Londres 2, 1049-056 Lisbon; tel. (21) 844-11-00; fax (21) 842-41-08; e-mail gmtss@mtss.gov.pt; internet www.mtss.gov.pt; f. 1916 as Min. of Labour and Social Welfare; Min. MARIA HELENA ANDRÉ; Head of the Office Dr ANA LUCIA REIS.

Ministry of Science, Technology and Higher Education: Palácio de Laranjeiras, Estrada de Laranjeiras 197–205, 1649-018 Lisbon; tel. (21) 723-10-00; fax (21) 727-14-57; e-mail mctes@mctes.gov.pt; internet www.mctes.pt; Min. Prof. JOSÉ MARIANO REBELO PIRES GAGO; Sec. of State MANUEL HEITOR.

ACCREDITATION

ENIC/NARIC Portugal: NARIC Centre, Direcção-Geral do Ensino Superior, Av. Duque de Ávila 137, 1069-016 Lisbon; tel. (21) 312-60-00; fax (21) 312-60-20; e-mail info.naric@dges.mctes.pt; internet www.dges.mctes.pt/dges/pt/reconhecimento/naricenic; f. 1986; establishes and carries out nat. policy on higher education; Dir-Gen. Prof. ANTONIO MORÃO DIAS; Sub-Dir-Gen. Dr CRISTINA JACINTO.

NATIONAL BODIES

Associação Portuguesa do Ensino Superior Privado (Portuguese Association of Private Higher Education Institutions): Av. da República 47, 1° dto, 1050-188 Lisbon; tel. (21) 799-48-60; fax (21) 799-48-69; e-mail contactos@apesp.pt; internet www.apesp.pt; works towards the full integration of non-state higher education in the Portuguese educational system; Pres. Prof. JOÃO DUARTE REDONDO; Vice-Pres. Prof. Dr MIGUEL FARIA.

Conselho Coordenador do Ensino Particular e Cooperativo (Coordinating Council for Private and Cooperative Education): Av. 5 de Outubro 89, 2°, 1050-050 Lisbon; tel. (21) 797-29-10; fax (21) 795-67-93; e-mail ccepc@mail.telepac.pt; f. 1980; works for the integration of private and co-operative education into the nat. educational and training system; Pres. Dr ANTÓNIO DE ALMEIDA COSTA; Dir MARIA DE CONCEIÇÃO REIS.

Conselho Coordenador dos Institutos Superiores Politécnicos (Coordinating Council for Polytechnic Institutes): Av. 5 de Outubro 89, 3°, 1050-050 Lisbon; tel. (21) 792-83-60; fax (21) 792-83-69; e-mail ccisp@ccisp.pt; internet www.ccisp.pt; f. 1979; representative body for public polytechnic instns with influence in all aspects of their operation; Pres. Dr. JOÃO SOBRINHO TEIXEIRA; Vice-Pres. Prof. RUI TEIXEIRA; Sec. CRISTINA ROCHA.

Conselho Nacional de Educação (National Council for Education): Rua Florbela Espanca, 1700-195 Lisbon; tel. (21) 793-52-45; fax (21) 797-90-93; e-mail cnedu@cne.min-edu.pt; internet www.cnedu.pt; f. 1982, present status 1987; ind. advisory body on all aspects of the Portuguese educational system; Pres. Prof. ANA MARIA DIAS BETTENCOURT; Sec.-Gen. MANUEL MIGUÉNS; publs *Estudos e Relatórios* (Studies and Reports), *Pareceres e Recomendações* (Statements and Recommendations, 1 a year).

Conselho de Reitores das Universidades Portuguesas (Council of Rectors of the Portuguese Universities): Edifício O, Campus do Lumiar, Estrada do Paço do Lumiar, 1649-038 Lisbon; tel. (21) 360-29-50; fax (21) 364-00-11; e-mail crup@crup.pt; internet www.crup.pt; creation, integration, modification or termination of educational public univs; Pres. Prof. Dr FERNANDO JORGE RAMA SEABRA SANTOS; Sec.-Gen. Dr JOÃO CARLOS LOPES DE MELO BORGES.

Direcção-Geral de Inovação e de Desenvolvimento Curricular (DGIDC) (Department for Innovation and Curricular Development): Av. 24 de Julho 140, 1399-025 Lisbon; tel. (21) 393-45-00; fax (21) 393-46-95; e-mail dgidc@dgidc.min-edu.pt; internet www.dgidc.min-edu.pt; educational research, innovation in teaching practice, curriculum devt and evaluation, spec. education, and distance learning; library of 23,000 vols, 1,500 periodicals; Pres. Dra CRISTINA PAULO; Dir-Gen. Dr LUÍS CAPUCHA; publs *Inovação* (3 a year), *Noesis* (4 a year).

Learned Societies

GENERAL

Academia das Ciências de Lisboa (Lisbon Academy of Sciences): Rua da Academia das Ciências 19, 1249-122 Lisbon; tel. (21) 321-97-30; fax (21) 342-03-95; e-mail geral@acad-ciencias.pt; internet www.acad-ciencias.pt; f. 1779; attached to Min. of Science, Technology and Higher Education; establishes ongoing, valuable contacts with other academies to promote cultural exchanges, research fellowships and joint programmes to renew their ancestral tradition; weekly lectures on science and humanities topics; 189 nat. mems; library: see Libraries and Archives; Pres. Prof. ADRIANO MOREIRA; Sec.-Gen. Prof. Dr MARIA SALOMÉ PAIS; Librarian LEONOR PINTO; publs *Memórias da Classe de Ciências*, *Memórias da Classe de Letras*.

Sociedade Científica da Universidade Católica Portuguesa (Scientific Society of the Portuguese Catholic University): Gabinete da Reitoria, Universidade Católica Portuguesa, Palma de Cima, 1649-023 Lisbon; tel. (21) 721-41-36; fax (21) 721-41-59; e-mail scientif@lisboa.ucp.pt; internet www.scucp.ucp.pt; f. 1980; attached to Universidade Católica Portuguesa; advances intellectual, artistic, moral and spiritual forms of a Christian-inspired culture as a means to the fulfilment of man, promotes research in a perspective of inter-disciplinarity aiming at a synthesis of knowledge; 15 sections: arts, biology, philosophy, law, history, economics, environmental sciences, literature and linguistics, education, theology, exact and natural sciences, applied sciences and engineering, health sciences and technology, social sciences and politics, communication and information sciences; library of 500 vols; 400 mems; Chair. Prof. MÁRIO JÚLIO BRITO DE ALMEIDA COSTA; Vice-Pres. Prof. Dr ANTÓNIO PEDRO BARBAS HOMEM; Sec. Prof. Dr MARÍLIA PEREIRA LÚCIO DOS SANTOS LOPES HANENBERG; publs *Colecção Cadernos*, *Lumen Veritatis*.

BIBLIOGRAPHY, LIBRARY SCIENCE AND MUSEOLOGY

Associação Portuguesa de Bibliotecários, Arquivistas e Documentalistas (Portuguese Association of Librarians, Archivists and Documentalists): Rua Morais Soares, 43C, 1° dto e frte, 1900-341 Lisbon; tel. (21) 816-19-80; fax (21) 815-45-08; e-mail apbad@apbad.pt; internet www.apbad.pt; f. 1973; promote better policy and practice of information management, improved scientific, technical and cultural devt of its mems; organizes training and refresher courses; 1,500 mems; Pres. ANTÓNIO JOSÉ DE PINA FALCÃO; Vice-Pres. CRISTINA MARIA REALINHO RIBEIRO; Sec. MARIA JOSÉ VITORINO GONÇALVES; Treas. LEONARDA DE JESUS RODRIGUES GALHANAS; publ. *Cadernos BAD* (2 a year).

ECONOMICS, LAW AND POLITICS

Ordem dos Economistas (Economists' Association): Rua da Estrela 8, 1200-669 Lisbon; tel. (21) 392-94-70; fax (21) 396-14-28; e-mail geral@ordemeconomistas.pt; internet www.ordemeconomistas.pt; f. 1976; brs in Azores, Madeira and Norte; 12,500 mems; Dir FRANCISCO MURTEIRA NABO; publs *Anuário do Economista* (1 a year), *Cadernos de Economia* (4 a year), *Carta Informativa* (4 a year).

EDUCATION

Associação das Universidades de Língua Portuguesa (Association of Universities of Portuguese Language): Av. Santos Dumont, 67, 2°, 1050-203 Lisbon; tel. (21) 781-63-60; fax (21) 781-63-69; e-mail aulp@aulp.org; internet www.aulp.org; promotes cooperation between univs and educational and research institutions by facilitating exchange of researchers and students, encouraging reflection on the role of higher education and devt of joint scientific and technological research and the widespread exchange of information; Pres. Prof. Dr CLÉLIO CAMPOLINA DINIZ; Vice-Pres. JOÃO TETA; Vice-Pres. ANTÓNIO LEÃO CORREIA E SILVA; Vice-Pres. JOÃO PINTO GUERREIRO; Vice-Pres. RUI MARTINS.

Instituto Açoriano de Cultura (Azorean Institute of Culture): Apdo 67, 9700-220 Angra do Heroísmo; Alto das Covas, 9700-220 Angra do Heroísmo; tel. and fax (295) 21-44-42; e-mail iac@iac-azores.org; internet www.iac-azores.org; f. 1955; Pres. PAULO ALEXANDRE MARTINS RAIMUNDO; Sec. Dr FILIPA ALEXANDRA DE MOURA MAGALHÃES TAVARES; publs *Atlântida* (1 a year), *Insula* (1 a year).

Instituto Camões (Camões Institute): Rua Rodrigues Sampaio 113, 1150-279 Lisbon; Av. da Liberdade 270, 1250-149 Lisbon; tel. (21) 310-91-00; fax (21) 314-39-87; e-mail icgeral@instituto-camoes.pt; internet www.instituto-camoes.pt; f. 1929 as Junta de Educação Nacional, present name 1992; attached to the Min. of Foreign Affairs; promotes teaching of Portuguese language and culture abroad; awards grants to foreign students in Portugal; publishes works on Portuguese language and culture; 250 mems; library of 4,500 vols; Pres. ANA PAULA LABORINHO; Vice-Pres. MÁRIO JOSÉ FILIPE DA SILVA; Vice-Pres. MARIA DINAH BANDEIRA SANTOS SILVA AZEVEDO NEVES; publ. *Camões* (irregular).

FINE AND PERFORMING ARTS

Academia Nacional de Belas Artes (National Academy of Fine Arts): Largo da Academia Nacional de Belas Artes, 1200-005 Lisbon; tel. (21) 346-70-91; fax (21) 342-75-00; e-mail geral@academiabelasartes.pt; internet www.academiabelasartes.pt; f. 1932; library of 25,000 vols, incl. some 16th-century work; 20 mems; Pres. Prof. Arq. AUGUSTO PEREIRA BRANDÃO; Sec. Arq. ANTÓNIO MARQUES MIGUEL; publs *Inventário Artístico de Portugal*, *Revista-Boletim de Belas Artes*.

Instituto Gregoriano de Lisboa (Gregorian Institute of Lisbon): Av. 5 de Outubro 258, 1600-038 Lisbon; tel. (21) 793-37-37; fax (21) 795-04-15; e-mail secretaria@inst-gregoriano.rcts.pt; internet www.inst-gregoriano.rcts.pt; f. 1953 as the Gregorian Studies Centre, present name and status 1976; public school of music; courses on Gregorian chant, organ, piano, harpsichord, violin, cello and recorder; Dir Dr MARIA LUÍSA OLIVEIRA; Deputy Dir RICARDO MONTEIRO; publ. *Modus* (musicology).

Sociedade Nacional de Belas Artes (National Society of Fine Arts): Palacio das Belas Artes, Rua Barata Salgueiro 36, 1250-044 Lisbon; tel. (21) 313-85-10; fax (21) 313-85-19; e-mail geral@snba.pt; internet www.snba.pt; f. 1901; exhibitions of painting, sculpture, drawing, etc.; organizes courses in design, painting, drawing, visual education, sociology, aesthetics and history of art; 1,350 assocs; 832 mems; library of 5,200 vols; Pres. EMÍLIA NADAL; Vice-Pres. JOSÉ JOÃO BRITO; Sec. Dr CRISTINA AZEVEDO TAVARES; Treas. AMÉRICO SILVA; publ. *Boletim Informativo* (2 a year).

HISTORY, GEOGRAPHY AND ARCHAEOLOGY

Academia Portuguesa da História (Portuguese Academy of History): Palácio dos Lilases, Alameda das Linhas de Torres 198–200, 1769-024 Lisbon; tel. (21) 754-90-60; fax (21) 759-13-82; e-mail acad.port.historia@sapo.pt; internet www.academiaportuguesadahistoria.gov.pt; f. 1720; research on historical topics; providing historical information; 40 mems, 190 corresp. mems; library of 180,000 vols; Pres. Prof. Dra MANUELA MENDONÇA; Sec.-Gen. Prof. Dr MIGUEL CORRÊA MONTEIRO; publs *Anais*, *Boletim*, *Documentos Medievais Portugueses*, *Fontes Narrativas da História Portuguesa*, *Itinerários Régios*, *Subsídios para a História Portuguesa*.

Associação dos Arqueólogos Portugueses (Association of Portuguese Archaeologists): Largo do Carmo 4, 1° dto, 1200-092 Lisbon; tel. and fax (21) 346-04-73; e-mail aap@mail.pt; internet www.museusportugal.org/aap; f. 1863 as Asscn of Portuguese Civil Architects; 640 mems; library of 10,500 vols; Pres. Dr JOSÉ MORAIS ARNAUD; Vice-Pres. Dr JOÃO JOSÉ FERNANDES GOMES; Sec. Dr PAULO DE ALMEIDA FERNANDES; Treas. Dr JOSÉ BAPTISTA DOMINGOS; publ. *Arqueologia e História* (irregular).

Instituto De Gestão Do Património Arquitectónico e Arqueológico (Institute for Management of Architectural and Archaeological Heritage): Palácio Nacional da Ajuda, 1349-021 Lisbon; tel. (21) 361-42-00; fax (21) 363-70-47; e-mail igespar@igespar.pt; internet www.igespar.pt; f. 2007 by merger of Portuguese Architectural Heritage Institute and Portuguese Archaeological Institute; attached to Min. of Culture; manages, safeguards, conserves and enhances those assets that, due to their historical, artistic, landscape, scientific, social and technical value, integrate Portugal's listed architectural and archaeological heritage; Dir GONÇALO COUCEIRO; Deputy Dir JOÃO PEDRO CUNHA RIBEIRO; Deputy Dir LUÍS FILIPE CAPAZ COELHO; publs *Estudos Património* (2 a year), *Portuguesa de Arqueologia*.

Instituto Geográfico Português (Portuguese Geographical Institute): Rua Artilharia Um 107, 1099-052 Lisbon; tel. (21) 381-96-00; fax (21) 381-96-99; e-mail igeo@igeo.pt; internet www.igeo.pt; f. 2002, by merger of Instituto Português de Cartografia e Cadastro and Centro Nacional de Informação Geográfica; attached to Min. of the Environment, Territorial Planning and Regional Devt; nat. cartographic authority, provides official geographical information, fosters training and research; main brs in Ponta Delgada, Beja, Faro, Castelo Branco, Santarém, Funchal and Mirandela; Gen. Dir. Lt-Gen. CARLOS MOURATO NUNES; Librarian MARIA DIAS.

Instituto Histórico da Ilha Terceira (IHIT) (Terceira Island Historical Institute): Convento de São Francisco, Ladeira de São Francisco, Angra do Heroísmo, Terceira, 9700 The Azores; tel. (29) 521-31-47; e-mail ihit@ihit.pt; internet www.ihit.pt; f. 1942, present location 1991; historical, cultural, anthropological, scientific and patrimonial studies and research; consultancy and educational activities; academic partnerships; residential instn for the UNESCO Azores Centre; 70 mems; library of 1,000 vols; Pres. Dr FRANCISCO DOS REIS MADURO-DIAS; Sec. Dr MIGUEL CORTE-REAL DA SILVEIRA MONJARDINO; Treas. Dr ANTÓNIO BENTO FRAGA BARCELOS; publ. *Boletim do Instituto Histórico da Ilha Terceira* (1 a year).

Real Instituto Arqueológico de Portugal (Royal Archaeological Institute of Portugal):

Praça Rainha D. Filipa 4, 6° dto, 1600 Lisbon; tel. (21) 759-11-09; e-mail dphadb@sapo.pt; f. 1868; Pres. and Sec.-Gen. Dr JOSÉ ANTÓNIO FALCÃO; publs *Actas*, *Trabalhos*.

Real Sociedade Arqueológica Lusitana (Royal Lusitanian Archaeological Society): Hospital do Espírito Santo, Praça Conde do Bracial 3, 7540 Santiago do Cacém; tel. (269) 82-63-80; f. 1849; archaeological, historical and ethnological studies; has own museum, archives and library; 150 mems, 97 corresp. mems, 50 fellows; Pres. Dr JOSÉ ANTÓNIO FALCÃO; Gen.-Sec. Dr LÍLIA RIBEIRO DA SILVA TAVARES; publs *Anais*, *Boletim*, *Memórias*, *Repertorium Fontium Studium Artis Historiae Portugaliae Instaurandum*, *Trabalhos*.

Sociedade de Geografia de Lisboa (Lisbon Geographical Society): Rua das Portas de Santo Antão 100, 1150-269 Lisbon; tel. (21) 342-54-01; fax (21) 346-45-53; e-mail geral@socgeografialisboa.mail.pt; internet www.socgeografialisboa.pt; f. 1875; studies geography, history and ethnology of the Portuguese; organizes confs; library of 205,240 vols, 2,020 periodicals, 6,000 MSS, 155 theses/dissertations, 3 sheets printed music, 10,050 maps; 1,500 mems; Pres. Prof. LUÍS AIRES-BARROS; Sec.-Gen. Prof. Dr. JOÃO PEREIRA NETO; Sec.-Gen Prof. ANTÓNIO DIOGO PINTO; Treas. Prof. Dr. CARLOS LOPES BENTO; publs *Boletim* (scientific and literary journal, 1 a year), *Memórias* (irregular), *Relatório* (1 a year).

Sociedade Martins Sarmento (Martins Sarmento Society): Universidade do Minho, Rua Paio Galvão, 4814-509 Guimarães; tel. (253) 41-59-69; fax (253) 51-94-13; e-mail sms@msarmento.org; internet www.csarmento.uminho.pt; f. 1881; archaeology and culture; 600 mems; library of 100,000 vols; Pres. ANTÓNIO AMARO DAS NEVES; publs *Boletim* (4 a year), *Revista de Guimarães* (1 a year).

LANGUAGE AND LITERATURE

Alliance Française: Rua Pinheiro Chagas 60, Apdo 2049, 3000-333 Coimbra; tel. (239) 70-12-52; fax (239) 40-48-50; e-mail afcoimbra@gmail.com; internet www.alliancefr.pt; offers courses and exams in French language and culture and promotes cultural exchange with France; attached offices in the Algarve, Beja, Caldas da Rainha, Entroncamento, Évora, Guimarães, Leiria, Lisbon, Monção, Portalegre, Setúbal, Vila Real and Viseu; Dir of Operations ALAIN DIDIER.

Associação Portuguesa de Escritores (Portuguese Writers' Association): Rua de S. Domingos à Lapa 17, 1200-832 Lisbon; tel. (21) 397-18-99-7; fax (21) 397-23-41; e-mail a.p.escritores@mail.telepac.pt; f. 1973; protects the interests of Portuguese writers, promotes Portuguese literature abroad, supports cultural activities, conferences, debates, confers several literary prizes, etc.; over 600 mems; library of 7,500 vols; Pres. Dr JOSÉ MANUEL MENDES.

British Council: Rua Luís Fernandes 1–3, 1249-062 Lisbon; tel. (21) 321-45-00; fax (21) 347-61-51; e-mail lisbon.enquiries@pt.britishcouncil.org; internet www.britishcouncil.org/portugal; f. 1938; teaching centre; offers courses and exams in English language and British culture and promotes cultural exchange with the UK; attached teaching centres in Almada, Alverca, Cascais, Coimbra, Foz do Douro, Miraflores, Parede and Porto; Dir ROSEMARY HILHORST; publ. *In English*.

Goethe-Institut: Campo dos Mártires da Pátria 37, 1169-016 Lisbon; tel. (21) 882-45-10; fax (21) 885-00-03; e-mail info@lissabon.goethe.org; internet www.goethe.de/portugal; offers courses and exams in German language and culture and promotes cultural exchange with Germany; attached centre in Porto; library of 14,000 vols, 50 periodicals; Dir Dr JOACHIM BERNAUER.

Instituto Cervantes de Lisboa: Rua Santa Marta 43F, 1169-119 Lisbon; tel. (21) 310-50-20; fax (21) 315-22-99; e-mail cenlis@cervantes.es; internet lisboa.cervantes.es; f. 1991 as Spanish Cultural Centre, present name and status 1993; offers courses and exams in Spanish language and culture and promotes cultural exchange with Spain and Spanish-speaking Latin and Central America; library of 30,000 vols; Dir JOSÉ MARÍA MARTÍN VALENZUELA; Sec. PAULA DE SOUSA PRUDÊNCIO; Head Librarian CECILIA GÁNDARAS PÉREZ.

Sociedade Portuguesa de Autores (Portuguese Society of Authors): Av. Duque de Loulé 31, 1069-153 Lisbon; tel. (21) 359-44-00; fax (21) 353-02-57; e-mail geral@spautores.pt; internet www.spautores.pt; f. 1925 as Sociedade de Escritores e Compositores Teatrais Portugueses; copyright protection and authors' rights; cultural activities; 23,000 mems; library of 33,000 vols, 6,000 periodicals; Pres. MANUEL FREIRE; CEO JOSÉ JORGE LETRIA; publ. *Autores* (4 a year).

MEDICINE

Ordem dos Farmacêuticos (Pharmaceutical Society): Rua da Sociedade Farmacêutica 18, 1169-075 Lisbon; tel. (21) 319-13-80; fax (21) 319-13-99; e-mail direccao.nacional@ordemfarmaceuticos.pt; internet www.ordemfarmaceuticos.pt; f. 1835; famous colln of Portuguese pharmacopoeias; unique MS *Historia Pharmaceutica das Plantas Exóticas* by Frei João de Jesus Maria, with permit to print from the Holy Office; 9,950 mems; library of 5,040 vols; Chair. Prof. Dr CARLOS MAURÍCIO GONÇALVES BARBOSA; Pres. JOÃO GONÇALVES DA SILVEIRA; Sec. CARLOS ALBERTO LARANJEIRA HENRIQUES; Sec. MARGARIDA MENDES MARQUES GOMES CARNEIRO; publ. *Revista do Ordem dos Farmacêuticos* (6 a year).

Ordem dos Médicos (Portuguese Medical Association): Av. Almirante Gago Coutinho 151, 1749-084 Lisbon; tel. (21) 842-71-00; fax (21) 842-71-99; e-mail omcne@omcne.pt; internet www.ordemdosmedicos.pt; f. 1938; regulation of medical practice; independence of practitioners; 39,419 mems; Pres. Prof. JOSÉ MANUEL SILVA; publs *Acta Médica Portuguesa* (6 a year), *Revista* (12 a year).

Sociedade Anatómica Portuguesa (Portuguese Anatomical Society): Lab. de Anatomia Normal, Faculdade de Medicina de Coimbra, 3049 Coimbra; f. 1930; 184 mems; Pres. Prof. Dr ANTÓNIO CARLOS MIGUÉIS.

NATURAL SCIENCES

General

Serviço de Informação e Documentação (Information and Documentation Service): Av. D. Carlos I 126, 1249-074 Lisbon; tel. (21) 392-43-00; fax (21) 390-74-81; internet alfa.fct.mctes.pt; f. 1936; attached to Fundação para a Ciência e a Tecnologia; nat. centre of scientific and technical information; library of 3,000 Portuguese, 5,000 foreign books, 350 periodicals; Dir GABRIELA LOPES DA SILVA.

Biological Sciences

Sociedade Broteriana (Botanical Society): Instituto Botânico, Universidade de Coimbra, 3049 Coimbra; tel. (239) 82-28-97; fax (239) 82-07-80; e-mail socbrot@ci.uc.pt; f. 1880; 300 mems; library of 122,000 vols; Chair. Prof. JOSÉ F. M. MESQUITA; publs *Anuário*, *Boletim* (1 a year), *Memórias* (irregular).

Sociedade Portuguesa de Ciências Naturais (Portuguese Natural Science Society): Faculdade de Ciências, Campo Grande, 1749-016 Lisbon; tel. (21) 750-00-00; fax (21) 750-00-09; e-mail spcn@fc.ul.pt; f. 1907; 938 mems; library of 30,000 vols; Pres. HUMBERTO ROSA; publs *Boletim*, *Natura*, *Naturalia*.

Sociedade Portuguesa de Ecologia (Portuguese Society of Ecology): Faculdade de Ciências da Univ. de Lisboa, Edif. C4, 1º Piso, Sala 4.1.10, Campo Grande 1749-016 Lisbon; tel. and fax (21) 7500439; e-mail speco@fc.ul.pt; internet speco.fc.ul.pt; f. 1995; scientific society for environmentalists; Pres. HELENA FREITAS; Sec. PAULA SOBRAL; publs *Revista de biologia* (1 a year), *Cadernos de ecologia* (1 a year).

Mathematical Sciences

Instituto Nacional de Estatística (National Statistical Institute): Av. António José de Almeida, 1000-043 Lisbon; tel. (21) 842-61-00; fax (21) 842-63-80; e-mail ine@ine.pt; internet www.ine.pt; f. 1935; production and dissemination of official statistical information; 750 mems; library of 12,000 vols, 2,500 periodicals; Pres. ALDA MARIA DAS NEVES CARNEIRO DE CAETANO CARVALHO; Vice-Pres. MARIA HELENA DE SOUSA CORDEIRO; Vice-Pres. PEDRO JORGE NUNES DA SILVA DIAS; publs *Statistical Review*, *Statistical Yearbook* (in English and Portuguese).

Physical Sciences

Sociedade Geológica de Portugal (Geological Society): Rua da Escola Politécnica, 56, 58, 1269-102 Lisbon; tel. and fax (21) 294-85-73; e-mail webmaster@socgeol.org; internet socgeol.org; f. 1940; asscn of of individuals and legal entities that promotes devt of knowledge concerning the geological sciences and cooperate with other stakeholders; 600 mems; library of 1,200 vols; Pres. ROGÉRIO BORDALO DA ROCHA; Vice-Pres. FILOMENA DINIZ; Sec. JOSÉ CARLOS KULLBERG; Sec. RUI TABORDA; Treas. JOSÉ MANUEL ROMÃO, publ. *Boletim*.

Sociedade Portuguesa de Química (Portuguese Chemical Society): Av. da República 45–3, 1050-187 Lisbon; tel. (21) 793-46-37; fax (21) 795-23-49; e-mail sede@spq.pt; internet www.spq.pt; f. 1911; holds Chemistry Olympics; brs in Aveiro, Braga, Coimbra and Oporto; 2,800 mems; Pres. MÁRIO NUNO DE MATOS SEQUEIRA BERBERAN E SANTOS; Vice-Pres. MARIA JOSÉ DIOGO DA SILVA CALHORDA; Gen. Sec. JOAQUIM LUÍS BERNARDES MARTINS DE FARIA; Treas. MARIA MANUEL MARTINHO SEQUEIRA BARATA MARQUES; publ. *Química* (4 a year).

RELIGION, SOCIOLOGY AND ANTHROPOLOGY

Academia Internacional da Cultura Portuguesa (International Academy of Portuguese Culture): Rua das Portas de Santo Antão 100, 1150-269 Lisbon; tel. (21) 342-10-81; fax (21) 342-10-33; e-mail aicportuguesa@clix.pt; f. 1965; attached to Min. of Culture; seeks to promote research into the culture of Portuguese communities living outside the nat. territory; 50 mems; Pres. Dr CARLOS MONJARDINO; Vice Pres. Prof. Dr JUSTINO MENDES DE ALMEIDA; Vice Pres. Prof. ÓSCAR BARATA; publ. *Boletim*.

Sociedade Portuguesa de Antropologia e Etnologia (Portuguese Anthropological and Ethnological Society): Faculdade de Ciências do Porto, Praça Gomes Teixeira, 4099-002 Porto; tel. (22) 208-71-49; fax (22) 202-69-03; e-mail vojsoj@sapo.pt; internet spae.no.sapo.pt; stimulates and develops the main anthropological research in its different areas and creates an interdisciplinary perspective; f. 1918; 100 mems; library of 10,000 vols; Pres. Prof. VÍTOR OLIVEIRA JORGE; Sec. PAULO CASTRO SEIXAS; publ. *Trabalhos de Antropologia e Etnologia* (2 a year).

TECHNOLOGY

Ordem dos Engenheiros (Portuguese Association of Engineers): Av. António Augusto de Aguiar 3D, 1069-030 Lisbon; tel. (21) 313-26-00; fax (21) 352-46-32; e-mail secretariageral@ordemdosengenheiros.pt; internet www.ordemengenheiros.pt; f. 1936; holds seminars, conf. etc. on topics useful to engineers; 28,000 mems; library of 23,000 vols, 500 periodical titles; Pres. Eng. CARLOS ALBERTO MATIAS RAMOS; Vice-Pres. JOSÉ MANUEL PEREIRA VIEIRA; Vice-Pres. VICTOR MANUEL GONÇALVES DE BRITO; publ. *Ingenium* (review, 12 a year).

Research Institutes

GENERAL

Centro de Estudos do Território, Cultura e Desenvolvimento (Territory, Culture and Development Research Centre): Universidade Lusófona de Humanidades e Tecnologias, Av. do Campo Grande 376, 1749-024 Lisbon; tel. (21) 751-55-00; fax (21) 751-55-09; e-mail zoran.roca@ulusofona.pt; internet tercud.ulusofona.pt; f. 2008, fmrly Applied Social Sciences Research Unit; attached to Faculty of Architecture, Urban Planning, Geography and Arts, Univ. Lusófona de Humanidades e Tecnologias; planning, management and evaluation of territorial devt in urban and rural settings; valorization of natural and cultural heritage and other components of territorial identities as devt recourses; Dir Dr ZORAN ROCA; publs *Arquitectura e Educação* (online), *Cadernos de Sociomuseologia* (online), *Malha Urbana* (online).

Centro de Estudos Transdisciplinares para o Desenvolvimento (CETRAD) (Transdisciplinary Studies Centre for Development): Av. Almeida Lucena 1, 5000-660 Vila Real; tel. (25) 930-22-00; fax (25) 930-22-49; e-mail cetrad@utad.pt; internet www.cetrad.info; f. 2002; attached to Univ. of Tras-os-Montes and Alto Douro; research incl. globalization and state policies; innovation, markets and orgs; society, territory and resources; Dir CHRISTOPHER GERRY; Deputy Dir FRANCISCO DINIZ; Deputy Dir ALBERTO BAPTISTA.

CERAP—Centre d'Étude et de Recherche Appliquée en Psychopédagogie Perceptive (Centre for Applied Research and Study in Perceptual Psychoeducation): Praça 9 de Abril 349, 4249-004 Porto; e-mail info@cerap.org; internet www.cerap.org; f. 2004; attached to Univ. Fernando Pessoa; studies the particular relationship individuals have to the 'sensible' experience of the body and the place of the 'sensible' body in educational, formative and existential learning processes; Dir Prof. Dr DANIS BOIS; publ. *Réciprocités* (2 a year).

Fundação para a Ciência e a Tecnologia (Science and Technology Foundation): Av. D. Carlos I 126, 1249-074 Lisbon; tel. (21) 392-43-00; fax (21) 390-74-81; e-mail presidencia@fct.mctes.pt; internet www.fct.mctes.pt; f. 1997, fmrly Nat. Board of Scientific and Technological Research; attached to Min. of Science, Technology and Higher Education; evaluates, finances and promotes institutions, programmes and projects in the fields of science and technology; also concerned with the education and qualifications in human resources; library of 15,500 vols; Pres. Prof. JOÃO JOSÉ DOS SANTOS SENTIEIRO.

Instituto de Altos Estudos (Institute for Advanced Studies): c/o Academia das Ciências de Lisboa, Rua Academia das Ciências 19, 1249-122 Lisbon; tel. (21) 321-97-30; fax (21) 342-03-95; e-mail geral@acad-ciencias.pt; internet www.acad-ciencias.pt; f. 1931; attached to Lisbon Acad. of Sciences; Pres. Prof. ADRIANO MOREIRA.

Instituto de Investigação Científica Tropical (Tropical Science Research Institute): Rua da Junqueira 86–1, 1300-344 Lisbon; tel. (21) 361-63-40; fax (21) 363-14-60; e-mail iict@iict.pt; internet www2.iict.pt; f. 1883; develops scientific research in tropical areas of humanities and natural sciences; enhances scientific and technical capacity of countries with which it cooperates; promotes preservation of heritage; Pres. Prof. Dr JORGE BRAGA DE MACEDO; Vice-Pres. Dr ANTÓNIO JOSÉ LOPES DE MELO; Sec. JOÃO NOGUEIRA; publs *Boletim da Filmoteca Ultramarina Portuguesa*, *Comunicações do IICT* (series: Agrarian Sciences; Biological Sciences; Ethnological and Ethnomuseological Sciences; Geographical Sciences; Earth Sciences), *Estudos de Antropologia Cultural e Social*, *Estudos de Ciências Políticas e Sociais*, *Estudos de História e Cartografia Antiga—Memórias*, *Estudos e Ensaios e Documentos*, *Index Seminum*, *Leba* (quaternary, prehistory, archaeology), *Memórias*, *Revista Internacional de Estudos Africanos*, *Separatas do Centro de Estudos de História e Cartografia Antiga*, *Studia*.

Research Centres:

Centro de Ambiente e Ciências da Terra do Instituto de Investigação Científica Tropical (Environment and Earth Sciences Centre): Aleja D. Afonso Henriques 41, 4° dto, 1000-123 Lisbon; tel. (21) 847-64-05; fax (21) 840-79-65; e-mail cgeol@iict.pt; internet www.iict.pt.

Centro de Antropobiologia do Instituto de Investigação Científica Tropical (Anthropobiology Centre): Av. Óscar Monteiro Torres 34, 1° esq, 1000-219 Lisbon; tel. (21) 796-66-70; e-mail cantp@iict.pt; internet www.iict.pt; f. 1954; Dir (vacant).

Centro de Antropologia Cultural e Social do Instituto de Investigação Científica Tropical (Cultural and Social Anthropology Centre): Av. Ilha da Madeira, Edifício Museu, 1400-203 Lisbon; tel. (21) 301-52-64; fax (21) 301-19-45; e-mail cacst@iict.pt; internet www.iict.pt; f. 1962; Dir Dra CLARA SARAIVA.

Centro de Botânica do Instituto de Investigação Científica Tropical (Botany Centre): Travessa Conde da Ribeira 9, 1300-142 Lisbon; tel. (21) 361-63-40; e-mail cbotn@iict.pt; internet www.iict.pt; f. 1948; Dir Dra MARIA ADÉLIA DINIZ.

Centro de Cartografia do Instituto de Investigação Científica Tropical (Cartography Centre): Travessa Conde da Ribeira 7–9, 1300-007 Lisbon; tel. (21) 361-63-40; fax (21) 363-14-60; e-mail ccart@iict.pt; internet www.iict.pt; f. 1946; Dir Prof. Eng. ARMANDO SEPÚLVEDA.

Centro de Cristalografia e Mineralogia do Instituto de Investigação Científica Tropical (Crystallography and Mineralogy Centre): Alameda D. Afonso Henriques 41, 4° esq, 1000-123 Lisbon; tel. (21) 847-65-96; fax (21) 840-79-65; e-mail ccris@iict.pt; internet www.iict.pt; f. 1957; Dir Prof. Dra MARIA ONDINA FIGUEIREDO.

Centro de Desenvolvimento Global do Instituto de Investigação Científica Tropical (Global Development Centre): Rua João de Barros 27, 1300-319 Lisbon; tel. (21) 364-27-32; e-mail des@iict.pt; internet www.iict.pt.

Centro de Detecção Remota para o Desenvolvimento do Instituto de Investigação Científica Tropical (Remote Sensing for Development Centre): Travessa Conde da Ribeira 9, 1300-142 Lisbon; tel. (21) 361-63-40; fax (21) 364-00-46; e-mail ccart@iict.pt; internet www.iict.pt.

Centro de Ecofisiologia, Bioquímica e Biotecnologia Vegetal do Instituto de Investigação Científica Tropical (Ecophysiology, Biochemistry and Vegetal Biotechnology Centre): Av. da República, Quinta do Marquês, 2784-505 Oeiras; tel. (21) 454-46-82; fax (21) 454-46-89; e-mail eco-bio@iict.pt; internet www.iict.pt; Dir. ANTÓNIO EDUARDO BAPTISTA LEITÃO.

Centro de Estudos Africanos e Asiáticos do Instituto de Investigação Científica Tropical (African and Asian Studies Centre): Rua da Junqueira 30, 1°, 1349-007 Lisbon; tel. (21) 362-26-21; fax (21) 362-26-26; e-mail cestaa@iict.pt; internet www.iict.pt; f. 1983; Dir Prof. Dra JILL REANEY DIAS.

Centro de Estudos de Fitossanidade do Armazenamento do Instituto de Investigação Científica Tropical (Research Centre on Plant Health during Storage): Travessa Conde da Ribeira 9, 1300-142 Lisbon; tel. (21) 361-63-40; e-mail cefa@iict.pt; internet www.iict.pt; f. 1955; Dir Prof. Dr ANTÓNIO MARQUES MEXIA.

Centro de Estudos de História e Cartografia Antiga do Instituto de Investigação Científica Tropical (History and Early Cartography Research Centre): Rua da Junqueira 30, r/c, 1349-007 Lisbon; tel. (21) 360-05-82; e-mail cesth@iict.pt; internet www.iict.pt; f. 1961; history of Portuguese expansion overseas, African history; library of 9,200 vols, 430 periodicals; Dir Dra MARIA EMÍLIA MADEIRA SANTOS; publs *Boletim da Filmoteca Ultramarina Portuguesa* (irregular), *Studia* (2 a year).

Centro de Estudos de Pedologia do Instituto de Investigação Científica Tropical (Pedology Studies Centre): Tapada da Ajuda, 1349-018 Lisbon; tel. (21) 365-31-00; e-mail cestp@iict.pt; internet www.iict.pt; f. 1960; Dir Prof. Eng. RUI PINTO RICARDO.

Centro de Estudos de Produção e Tecnologia Agrícolas do Instituto de Investigação Científica Tropical (Agricultural Technology and Production Studies Centre): Tapada da Ajuda, Edifício das Agro-Indústria e Agronomia Tropical, 1349-018 Lisbon; tel. (21) 361-72-40; e-mail cestt@iict.pt; internet www.iict.pt; f. 1960; Dir (vacant).

Centro de Etnologia Ultramarina do Instituto de Investigação Científica Tropical (Overseas Ethnology Centre): Av. Ilha da Madeira, 1400-203 Lisbon; tel. (21) 301-21-18; fax (21) 301-19-45; e-mail cetno@iict.pt; internet www.iict.pt; f. 1962; Dir Dra MARGARIDA LIMA DE FARIA.

Centro de Florestas e Produtos Florestais do Instituto de Investigação Científica Tropical (Forests and Forest Products Centre): Tapada da Ajuda, 1349-017 Lisbon; tel. (21) 363-46-62; fax (21) 364-50-00; e-mail flor@iict.pt; internet www.iict.pt; f. 1948; Dir Prof. Dra HELENA PEREIRA.

Centro de Fotogrametria do Instituto de Investigação Científica Tropical (Photogrammetry Centre): Rua João de Barros 27, 1300-319 Lisbon; tel. (21) 364-27-32; e-mail cfotg@iict.pt; internet www.iict.pt; f. 1983; Dir Prof. Dr ARMANDO SEPÚLVEDA.

Centro de Geodesia do Instituto de Investigação Científica Tropical (Geodesy Centre): Rua da Junqueira 534, 1300-341 Lisbon; tel. (21) 363-18-62; fax (21) 364-19-47; e-mail cgeod@iict.pt; internet www.iict.pt; f. 1983; Dir Eng. JOSÉ FRIAS DE BARROS.

Centro de Geografia do Instituto de Investigação Científica Tropical (Geography Centre): Rua Ricardo Espírito Santo 7, c/v esq, 1200-790 Lisbon; tel. and fax (21) 395-67-72; e-mail cgeog@iict.pt; internet www.iict.pt; f. 1983; Dir Prof. Dr ILÍDIO DO AMARAL.

Centro de Geologia do Instituto de Investigação Científica Tropical (Geology Centre): Alameda D. Afonso Henriques 41, 4° dto, 1000-123 Lisbon; tel. (21) 847-64-05; fax (21) 840-79-65; e-mail cgeol@iict.pt; internet www.iict.pt; f. 1958; Dir Prof. Dr RICARDO AUGUSTO QUADRADO.

Centro de Investigação das Ferrugens do Cafeeiro do Instituto de Investigação Científica Tropical (Coffee Rusts Research Centre): Quinta do Marquês, 2784-505 Oeiras; tel. (21) 454-46-80; fax (21) 454-46-89; e-mail cferc@iict.pt; internet www.iict.pt; f. 1955; Dir MARIA DO CÉU M. L. SILVA.

Centro de Pré-História e Arqueologia do Instituto de Investigação Científica Tropical (Prehistory and Archaeology Centre): Travessa Conde da Ribeira 7, 1300-142 Lisbon; tel. (21) 361-63-40; e-mail cphst@iict.pt; internet www.iict.pt; f. 1954; Dir Prof. Dr A. TEODORO DE MATOS.

Centro de Sociedades e Culturas Tropicais do Instituto de Investigação Científica Tropical (Societies and Tropical Cultures Centre): Rua da Junqueira 30, 1°, 1349-007 Lisbon; tel. (21) 360-05-81; fax (21) 360-05-87; e-mail cestaa@iict.pt; internet www.iict.pt.

Centro de Sócio-Economia do Instituto de Investigação Científica Tropical (Socio-Economics Centre): Travessa Conde da Ponte 9, 1°, 1300-141 Lisbon; tel. (21) 363-57-48; fax (21) 363-96-03; e-mail csoec@iict.pt; internet www.iict.pt; f. 1956; Dir Prof. Dr JORGE BRAGA DE MACEDO.

Centro de Veterinária e Zootecnia do Instituto de Investigação Científica Tropical (Veterinary and Zootechnics Centre): R. João de Barros, 27 1300-319 Lisbon; tel. (21) 364-27-29; fax (21) 363-42-38; e-mail dcn@iict.pt; internet www.iict.pt; f. 1983; Dir Dr LUÍS ALFARO CARDOSO.

Centro de Zoologia do Instituto de Investigação Científica Tropical (Zoology Centre): Rua da Junqueira 14, 1300-343 Lisbon; tel. (21) 363-70-55; e-mail czool@iict.pt; internet www.iict.pt; f. 1948; Dir Dr LUÍS F. MENDES.

Instituto de Orientação Profissional (Institute of Professional Guidance): Rua José Carlos dos Santos 7, 1700-256 Lisbon; tel. (21) 346-33-57; fax (21) 346-33-58; e-mail geral@iop.ul.pt; internet www.iop.ul.pt; f. 1925, present status 1989; attached to Univ. of Lisbon; fundamental and applied research; develops educational tools and techniques; Dir Prof. Dr MARIA EDUARDA DUARTE.

AGRICULTURE, FISHERIES AND VETERINARY SCIENCE

Centro de Ciência Animal e Veterinária (CECAV) (Centre for Animal and Veterinary Sciences (CECAV)): Univ. of Tras-os-Montes and Alto Douro, Apdo 1013, 5001-801 Vila Real; tel. (25) 935-04-08; fax (25) 935-04-82; e-mail arnaldos@utad.pt; internet www.cecav.utad.pt; f. 2002; attached to Univ. of Tras-os-Montes and Alto Douro; fundamental and applied research in veterinary and animal science; disseminates knowledge in animal health and production with emphasis on increasing efficiency and sustainability of livestock production and safety of products of animal origin without compromising on the surrounding environment and economic conditions; main research areas incl. animal production, animal physiology and pathology and quality and food safety of animal products; Dir ARNALDO DIAS DA SILVA; Vice-Dir CRISTINA GUEDES; Vice-Dir JOSÉ MANUEL ALMEIDA.

Centro de Investigação e de Tecnologias Agro-Ambientais e Biológicas (Centre for the Research and Technology of Agro-Environmental and Biological Sciences): Univ. of Trás-os-Montes and Alto Douro, Quinta de Prados, Apdo 1013, 5001-801 Vila Real; tel. (23) 935-04-75; fax (25) 935-06-29; e-mail citab@utad.pt; internet www.citab.utad.pt; f. 2007 by merger of 3 instns; attached to Univ. of Trás-os-Montes and Alto Douro; ecointegrity, integrative biology and quality and biosystems engineering; research focuses on devt and upgrading of agriculture and forestry production chains; Dir EDUARDO AUGUSTO DOS SANTOS ROSA; Vice-Dir PEDRO JOSÉ DE MELO TEIXEIRA PINTO; Vice-Dir RUI MANUEL VÍTOR CORTES.

Estação Agronómica Nacional (National Agronomical Research Station): Av. República, Quinta do Marquês, Nova Oeiras, 2784-505 Oeiras; tel. (21) 440-35-00; fax (21) 441-60-11; e-mail dir.ean@iniap.min-agricultura.pt; f. 1937; comprises depts of agronomy, entomology, experimental statistics, genetics and plant breeding, pedology, phytopathology, plant physiology, microbiology, systematic botany and plant sociology; library of 172,000 vols; Dir Dr MARIA CRISTINA LOPES; Librarian ROSÁRIO SÁ; publs *Agronomia Lusitana*, *Index Seminum*.

Estação Florestal Nacional (National Forestry Research Station): Quinta do Marquês, 2780-159 Oeiras; tel. (21) 446-37-00; fax (21) 446-37-01; e-mail direccao@efn.com.pt; f. 1979; forestry research unit of the Instituto Nacional de Investigação Agrária e das Pescas; 4 research depts; 105 staff; library of 3,500 vols; Dir Dr RUI OLIVEIRA E SILVA; publ. *Silva Lusitana*.

Instituto Nacional de Recursos Biológicos IP (National Institute of Biological Resources IP): R. Barata Salgueiro 37–4°, 1250-042 Lisbon; tel. (21) 313-17-41; fax (21) 313-17-83; e-mail presidencia@inrb.pt; internet www.inrb.pt; f. 2006; attached to Min. of Agriculture, Rural Devt and Fisheries; supports research of public policies for the valuation of biological resources in the defence of nat. interests and in the continuation and deepening of EU common policies; Pres. Dr MARIA ROSA TOBIAS SÁ.

ECONOMICS, LAW AND POLITICS

Centro de Estudos Sociais da Faculdade de Economia da Universidade de Coimbra (Centre for Social Studies): Colégio de São Jerónimo, Apdo 3087, 3001-401 Coimbra; tel. (23) 985-55-70; fax (23) 985-55-89; e-mail ces@ces.uc.pt; internet www.ces.uc.pt; f. 1978, present status 2002; attached to School of Economics, Univ. of Coimbra; research and advanced training in social sciences and humanities; library of 13,000 vols, 800 periodicals; Dir Prof. Dr BOAVENTURA SOUSA SANTOS; Pres. PEDRO HESPANHA; Vice-Pres. SILVIA PORTUGAL; Sec.-Gen. LASSALETE PAIVA; publ. *Revista Crítica de Ciências Sociais* (4 a year).

Centro de Investigação do Instituto de Estudos Políticos (Research Centre of the Institute for Political Studies): Univ. Católica Portuguesa, Palma de Cima, 1649-023 Lisbon; tel. (21) 721-41-29; fax (21) 727-18-36; internet www.iep.lisboa.ucp.pt; f. 2001; attached to Institute for Political Studies, Univ. Católica Portuguesa; supports scientific research in various brs of science policy, incl. int. relations, comparative politics, public policy, history of political thought and political theory; Scientific Dir Prof. Dr JOÃO CARLOS ESPADA; Scientific Coordinator Dr LÍVIA FRANCO.

EDUCATION

ILG—Instituto Leopoldo Guimarães (Leopoldo Guimarães Institute): Rua Fernando Miguel Cabanas, 2950-616 Palmela; e-mail geral@institutolg.com; internet www.institutolg.com; f. 2008; attached to Univ. Fernando Pessoa; promotes lifelong learning in Portugal, cooperating with such instns for higher education, with public and enterprise dedicated to scientific research; provides teacher training and Masters programmes; Pres. Prof. LEOPOLDO GUIMARÃES.

Kie—Associação Conhecimento, Inovação e Educaçã (Kie—Association of Knowledge, Innovation and Education): Edif. Panoramic (Parque das Nações), Av. do Atlântico 1.19.02 A, Escritório 6.05, 1990-096 Lisbon; tel. (21) 894-33-05; fax (21) 214-13-32; e-mail terezaventura@ufp.edu.pt; internet www.kie.pt; f. 2009; attached to Univ. Fernando Pessoa; promotes research and training in continuing education and lifelong learning; provides Masters programmes; Pres. MARIA TEREZA ROMANO VENTURA; Chair. MARIA DE FÁTIMA PAIVA S. COELHO; Treas. HÉLIO JOÃO DA SILVA COELHO.

HISTORY, GEOGRAPHY AND ARCHAEOLOGY

Centro de Estudos do Baixo Alentejo (Centre for Lower Alentejo Studies): c/o Real Sociedade Arqueológica Lusitana, Hospital do Espírito Santo, Praça Conde do Bracial 3, 7540 Santiago do Cacém; tel. (269) 82-63-80; f. 1944; Dir The Pres. of the Royal Lusitanian Archaeological Soc. (*q.v.*); Sec.-Gen. The Gen.-Sec. of the Royal Lusitanian Archaeological Soc. (*q.v.*).

Centro de Estudos Geográficos da Universidade de Lisboa (Centre of Geographical Studies of the University of Lisbon): IGOT - Edif., Faculdade de Letras, Alameda da Universidade, 1600-214 Lisbon; tel. (21) 794-02-18; fax (21) 793-86-90; e-mail ceg@campus.ul.pt; internet www.ceg.ul.pt; f. 1943; funded by the Fundação para a Ciência e Tecnologia (*q.v.*), the European Commission and other nat. and int. orgs; research into human and regional geography, geoecology, physical and environmental geography and fluvial, coastal dynamics; supports teaching activities; library of 35,000 vols; Pres. CARLOS ALBERTO MEDEIROS; Scientific Dir Prof. Dr DIOGO JOSÉ BROCHADO DE ABREU; Sec. LUÍS MANUEL COSTA MORENO; publ. *Finisterra* (2 a year).

Centro de Estudos Históricos e Etnológicos (Centre for Historical and Ethnological Studies): Serra do Balas, Areias, 2240 Ferreira do Zêzere; tel. (249) 39-14-08; f. 1983; Pres. Dr JORGE M. RODRIGUES FERREIRA; Sec. ANABELA BENTO; publ. *Série Arqueológica*.

Centro de Geologia da Universidade do Porto (Geology Centre of the University of Porto): Dept de Geologia da FCUP, Rua do Campo Alegre 687, 4169-007 Porto; tel. (22) 040-24-72; fax (22) 040-24-90; e-mail fmnoronh@fc.up.pt; internet www.cguporto.org; f. 1978; attached to Univ. of Porto; devt of research in earth sciences; Coordinator Prof. FERNANDO NORONHA.

Centro de Investigação em Ciência e Engenharia Geológica (Centre for Research in Science and Engineering Geology): Dept de Ciências da Terra, Faculdade de Ciências e Tecnologia, Quinta da Torre 2829-516 Caparica; tel. (21) 294-85-73; fax (21) 294-85-56; e-mail sec-dct@fct.unl.pt; internet www.cicege.fct.unl.pt; f. by merger of Centre for Geological Studies (CEG) and the Research Centre for Applied Geoscience (CIGA); attached to Univ. Nova de Lisboa; research in areas of sedimentary geology, stratigraphy, paleontology, geological mapping, ornamental rocks, applied geology and engineering geology; publ. *Ciências da Terra*.

Centro de Investigação Marinha e Ambiental (Centre for Marine and Environmental Research): Univ. do Algarve, Faculdade de Ciências e Tecnologia, Edif. 7, Campus de Gambelas, 8005-139 Faro; tel. (28) 980-09-00; fax (28) 980-00-69; e-mail cima@ualg.pt; internet cima.ualg.pt; research areas incl. large-scale geological processes and their local record, marine morphosedimentary processes and impact of environmental changes; Gen. Coordinator TOMASZ BOSKI.

Centro de Petrologia e Geoquímica (Centre for Petrology and Geochemistry): Av. Rovisco Pais 1049-001 Lisbon; tel. and fax (21) 840-08-06; e-mail jose.marques@ist.utl.pt; internet cepgist.ist.utl.pt; research, teaching and consulting in hydrogeology, groundwater quality, isotope hydrology, monument stone decay and conservation, environmental geochemistry, applied mineralogy and petrology; Scientific Coordinator JOSÉ MANUEL MARQUES.

Centro de Vulcanologia e Avaliação de Riscos Geológicos (Centre for Volcanology and Geological Risk Assessment): c/o Univ. dos Açores, Edif. do Complexo Científico, 3º Piso, Ala Sul, 9501-801 Ponta Delgada; tel. (29) 665-01-47; fax (29) 665-01-42; e-mail patricia.ij.raposo@azores.gov.pt; internet www.cvarg.azores.gov.pt; f. 1997; attached to Univ. of Azores; supports research of devt of earth sciences and prediction of disasters, natural calamities; focuses on technical and scientific cooperation nationally and internationally in the field of volcanology and associated phenomena, incl. volcanic eruptions, earthquakes, explosions of steam, toxic gas release, mass movements and tsunamis; mem. of the World Org. of Volcano Observatories (WONO); Dir MARIA GABRIELA PEREIRA DA SILVA.

Evolução Litosférica e Meio Ambiente Superficial: Departamento de Geociências, Universidade de Aveiro, Campus de Santiago, 3810-193 Aveiro; tel. (23) 437-03-57; fax (23) 437-06-05; e-mail sec@geo.ua.pt; internet www.ua.pt/geo; f. 1998; attached to Geosciences Dept, Univ. of Aveiro; interdisciplinary studies in fundamental and applied aspects of geology and biology; Dir JORGE MEDINA.

'Infante D. Luis' Geophysical Institute: Rua da Escola Politécnica 58, 1250-102 Lisbon; tel. (21) 392-18-63; fax (21) 390-81-87; e-mail presidente.igidl@fc.ul.pt; internet www.igidl.ul.pt; f. 1853; attached to Univ. of Lisbon; geophysics, seismology, meteorology, climatology, solar radiation; maintains Portugal's oldest meteorological series; library of 4,000 vols, 1075 journals; Pres. JORGE MIGUEL DE MIRANDA; Sec. ANABELA MARTINS.

Instituto Geofísico (Geophysical Institute): Av. Dr Dias da Silva, 3000-134 Coimbra; tel. (23) 979-34-20; fax (23) 979-34-28; e-mail iguc@ci.uc.pt; internet www1.ci.uc.pt/iguc; f. 1864; attached to Univ. of Coimbra; meteorological, magnetic and seismological observatory; library of 16,000 vols; Dir Prof. Dr ANTÓNIO FERREIRA SOARES; publs *Observações Meteorológicas, Magnéticas e Sismológicas* (1 a year).

LANGUAGE AND LITERATURE

Centro de Estudos em Letras (Centre for Studies in Literature):tel. (25) 935-07-01; fax (25) 935-07-87; e-mail cassunca@utad.pt; internet www.utad.pt/pt/investigacao/cel/index.html; Dir Prof. Dr CARLOS DA COSTA ASSUNÇÃO.

Instituto de Estudos Clássicos (Classical Studies Institute): Faculdade de Letras, Universidade de Coimbra, 3004-530 Coimbra; tel. (23) 985-99-81; fax (23) 983-67-33; e-mail classic@ci.uc.pt; internet www.uc.pt/fluc/eclassicos/iec; f. 1944; attached to Faculty of Arts, Univ. of Coimbra; teaching, research, promotion of classics in Portugal; library of 15,000 vols, 500 periodicals; Dir Dr JOSÉ LUIS LOPES BRANDÃO; Sec. Dr LUÍSA DE NAZARÉ FERREIRA; Sec. Dr SUSANA MARQUES PEREIRA.

Instituto de Lexicologia e Lexicografia da Língua Portuguesa (Institute of Lexicology and Lexicography of the Portuguese Language): c/o Academia das Ciências de Lisboa, Rua da Academia das Ciências 19, 1249-122 Lisbon; tel. (21) 321-97-30; fax (21) 342-03-95; e-mail geral@acad-ciencias.pt; internet www.acad-ciencias.pt; f. 1987; attached to Lisbon Acad. of Sciences; Pres. Prof. Dr ARTUR ANSELMO; Sec. Dr LUÍSA MACEDO.

Instituto Português da Sociedade Científica de Goerres (Portuguese Institute of the Goerres Research Society): Universidade Católica Portuguesa, Reitoria, Palma de Cima, 1649-023 Lisbon; tel. (21) 721-40-00; fax (21) 726-05-46; e-mail mrato@reitoria.ucp.pt; internet www.ucp.pt; f. 1962; research on history, legal history, language and Portuguese literature; also known as Institute Vieira; Office Sec. Dr MARIA EUGÉNIA RATO; library of 9,000 vols; publ. *Portugiesische Forschungen*.

MEDICINE

Association for Innovation and Biomedical Research on Light and Image: Azinhaga Sta. Comba, Celas, 3000-548 Coimbra; tel. (23) 948-01-00; fax (23) 948-01-17; e-mail aibili@aibili.pt; internet www.aibili.pt; f. 1989, present location 1994; develops new products for health imaging, pharmaceutical and biotechnology cos; CEO CECÍLIA MARTINHO; Pres. JOSÉ CUNHA-VAZ.

'Câmara Pestana' Bacteriological Institute: Rua do Instituto Bacteriológico, 1169-110 Lisbon; tel. (21) 882-32-90; fax (21) 885-14-37; e-mail reitoria@reitoria.ul.pt; internet www.ul.pt; f. 1892, present status 1911; attached to Univ. of Lisbon; areas of research incl. several domains of public health, namely diphtheria, streptococci, clinical microbiology and analysis of biology products; nat. lab for anti-tuberculosis vaccine; responsible for Portugal's anti-rabies programme; Dir Prof. JOSÉ MELO CRISTINO.

Centro de Estudos de Vectores e Doenças Infecciosas Doutor Francisco Cambournac (Dr Francisco Cambournac Centre for the Study of Vectors and Infectious Diseases): c/o Instituto Nacional de Sáude Dr Ricardo Jorge, Av. da Liberdade 5, 2965-575 Águas de Moura; tel. (26) 593-82-90; fax (26) 591-22-22; e-mail cevdi@insa.min-saude.pt; internet www.insa.pt; f. 1938 as the Malaria Institute, present name since 1987; attached to Nat. Institute of Health Dr Ricardo Jorge; research and diagnostic activities on vectors and vector-borne diseases incl. hantavirus, arbovirus, phlebovirus, arenavirus, borrelia, francisella, rickettsia, ehrlichia, anaplasma, coxiella and bartonella; vector studies incl. the determination of species present in Portugal and surveillance to prevent or minimize risk of introduction of new species; library of 3,400 vols; Dir Dr MARIA SOFIA NUNCIO.

Centro de Investigação em Desporto, Saúde e Desenvolvimento Humano (Research Centre in Sports, Health and Human Development Science): CIFOP—Sports Dept, Rua Doutor Manuel Cardona, 5000-558 Vila Real; tel. (25) 933-01-05; fax (25) 933-01-68; e-mail cidesd.geral@utad.pt; internet cidesd.org; f. 2007 by merger of 6 research units from the Polytechnic Institute of Bragança; attached to Univ. of Tras-os-Montes and Alto Douro; cross-institutional technical and scientifically multi-disciplinary unity of applied and fundamental research; 3 main domains of sports performance, health, professional and pedagogical intervention; Dir Dr ANTÓNIO JOSÉ SILVA.

Centro de Neurociências e Biologia Celular (Centre for Neuroscience and Cell Biology): Dept of Zoology, Univ. of Coimbra, 3004-51 Coimbra; tel. (23) 985-57-60; fax (23) 985-34-09; e-mail info@cnc.uc.pt; internet www.cnbc.pt; attached to Univ. of Coimbra; translates basic knowledge into clinical applications to improve diagnostics and develop novel therapeutical approaches; Pres CATARINA RESENDE DE OLIVEIRA; Vice-Pres. EUCLIDES PIRES; Vice-Pres. CARLOS FARO; Vice-Pres. LEONOR ALMEIDA.

Instituto de Biologia Molecular e Celular (Institute of Molecular and Cell Biology): Rua do Campo Alegre 823, 4150-180 Porto; tel. (22) 607-49-00; fax (22) 609-91-57; e-mail info@ibmc.up.pt; internet www.ibmc.up.pt; f. 2000; attached to Univ. of Porto; research focuses on genetic diseases, infectious diseases and immunology, neuroscience, stress and structural biology; Dir CLAUDIO SUNKEL; Vice-Dir MARIA JOÃO SARAIVA; Vice-Dir MÓNICA SOUSA; Chair. CHRISTOPHER LEAVER.

Instituto de Ciências Biomédicas de Abel Salazar (Abel Salazar Biomedical Sciences Institute): Largo Prof. Abel Salazar, 2, 4099-003 Porto; tel. (22) 206-22-00; fax (22) 206-22-32; e-mail conped@icbas.up.pt; internet www.icbas.up.pt; f. 1975; attached to Univ. of Porto; fundamental and applied research in health and life sciences; Dir ANTÓNIO SOUSA PEREIRA.

Instituto de Medicina Molecular (Institute of Molecular Medicine): Faculdade de Medicina da Universidade de Lisboa, Av. Professor Egas Moniz, 1649-028 Lisbon; tel. (21) 799-94-11; fax (21) 799-94-12; e-mail imm@fm.ul.pt; internet www.imm.ul.pt; f. 2001; attached to Min. of Science, Technology and Higher Education; research into cell and devt biology, immunology and infectious diseases, neurosciences and oncology; Pres. J. LOBO ANTUNES; Vice-Pres. JOAQUIM ALEXANDRE RIBEIRO; Exec. Dir M. CARMO-FONSECA; Sec. PATRÍCIA DA CUNHA.

Instituto de Patalogia e Imunologia da Universidade do Porto (Institute of Molecular Pathology and Immunology of the University of Porto): Rua Dr Roberto Frias s/n, 4200-465 Porto; tel. (22) 557-07-00; fax (22) 557-07-99; e-mail ipatimup@ipatimup.pt; internet www.ipatimup.pt; f. 1989; attached to Univ. of Porto; associated laboratory of Min. of Science and Higher Education; research focuses on causes and evolution of human oncologic diseases; Dir MANUEL SOBRINHO SIMÕES.

Instituto Gulbenkian de Ciência (Gulbenkian Science Institute): Apdo 14, 2781-901 Oeiras; Rua da Quinta Grande, 6, 2780-156 Oeiras; tel. (21) 440-79-00; fax (21) 440-79-70; internet www.igc.gulbenkian.pt; attached to Fundação Calouste Gulbenkian; biomedical research and education in areas of genetic basis of devt and evolution of complex systems; privileged organism-centred approaches in experimental models that incl. plants, yeast, flies and mice, and on the genetics of complex human diseases; library of 16,868 vols; Chair. for Scientific Advisory Board SYDNEY BRENNER; Dir ANTONIO COUTINHO; Deputy Dir JOSÉ MÁRIO LEITE.

Instituto Nacional de Medicina Legal (National Institute of Legal Medicine): Largo da Sé Nova, 3000-213 Coimbra; tel. (23) 985-42-20; fax (23) 983-64-70; e-mail correio@inml.mj.pt; internet www.inml.mj.pt; f. 1919; attached to Faculty of Medicine, Univ. of Coimbra; nat. instn of reference in forensic science; library of 5,000 vols, 45 periodicals; Dir Prof. Dr DUARTE NUNO PESSOA VIEIRA.

Instituto Nacional de Saúde Dr. Ricardo Jorge (National Institute of Health Dr. Ricardo Jorge): Av. Padre Cruz, 1649-016 Lisbon; tel. (21) 751-92-00; fax (21) 752-64-00; e-mail info@insa.min-saude.pt; internet www.insa.pt; f. 1899 as Central Institute of Hygiene, present status 1971; attached to Min. of Health; research and technological devt; epidemiological and health services research; external quality assurance for laboratories; diffusion of scientific culture; fostering capacities, knowledge and skills and by providing specialized services, incl. prevention of genetic diseases; nat. reference laboratory and nat. health observatory; Pres. JOSÉ PEREIRA MIGUEL.

Observatório de Medicina Integrativa—Centro de Estudos Avançados em Ciências da Saúde (Centre for Integrative Medicine—Centre for Advanced Studies in Health Sciences): Rua Joaquim Bonifácio, 21–2 Andar, 1150-195 Lisbon; tel. (21) 315-11-43; fax (21) 317-44-48; e-mail cidalia.paradelo@omi.pt; internet www.omi.pt; attached to Univ. Fernando Pessoa; promotes creation and devt of an integrative medicine combining conventional and unconventional medicines through practical work and research of multidisciplinary teams; provides advanced modules, Masters courses in alternative forms of medicine; Pres. Prof. ANGELO LUCAS.

NATURAL SCIENCES

General

Centro de Matemática (CM) (Centre for Mathematics):e-mail egs@utad.pt; internet www.utad.pt/pt/investigacao/c_matematica/index.html; attached to Univ. of Tras-os-Montes and Alto Douro; Dir Prof. Dr EMILIA JOAQUINA GIRALDES SOARES.

Centro de Química—Vila Real (CQVR) (Chemistry Centre—Vila Real): Univ. of Trás-os-Montes and Alto Douro, Chemistry Dept, Edif. de Geociências, 2 stage, 5001-801 Vila Real; tel. (25) 935-02-27; e-mail ptavares@utad.pt; internet home.utad.pt/~cqvr; f. 2001; attached to Univ. of Trás-os-Montes and Alto Douro; develops fundamental and applied chemistry research in areas of organic chemistry, natural products and food chemistry, materials chemistry, environmental chemistry; Dir PEDRO MANUEL DE MELO BANDEIRA TAVARES; Vice-Dir JOSÉ ALCIDES SILVESTRE PERES; Vice-Dir MARIA CRISTINA FIALHO OLIVEIRA.

Centro de Recursos Naturais e Ambiente (Centre for Natural Resources and the Environment): Instituto Superior Técnico, Av. Rovisco Pais 1049-001 Lisbon; tel. (21) 841-74-25; fax (21) 841-73-89; e-mail juliar@ist.utl.pt; internet cerena.ist.utl.pt; f. 2006; attached to Instituto Superior Técnico; multi-disciplinary research and advanced activities in natural resources and environment for modelling and management of natural resources, the benefit of raw materials and solid residues, geoengineering, geotechnics, biomonitoring, environmental modelling and environmental remediation; Pres. AMÍLCAR SOARES.

Instituto Botânico 'Dr Júlio Henriques' (Botanical Institute): Arcos do Jardim, 3049 Coimbra; tel. (239) 82-28-97; f. 1775; attached to Univ. of Coimbra; botanical garden, study in botany; library of 114,000 vols; Dir Prof. Dr J. FIRMINO MOREIRA MESQUITA; publs *Boletim*, *Index Seminum*, *Memórias* and *Anuário* of Sociedade Broteriana.

Institution of Marine Research: 'Centro Interdisciplinar de Coimbra', c/o Dept of Zoology, Univ. of Coimbra, 3000 Coimbra; tel. (23) 983-63-86; fax (23) 982-36-03; e-mail imar@ci.uc.pt; internet www.imar.pt; f. 1991; contributes to the scientific basis of policy support; establishes and promotes key areas of scientific research on a multiyear scale; empowers the Portuguese marine sciences community, making it competitive on a European and int. level; Pres. R. SERRÃO SANTOS; Vice-Pres. Prof. J. C. MARQUES; Vice-Pres. Prof. MANUEL GRAÇA; Vice-Pres. Prof. O. FERREIRA.

Instituto da Conservação da Natureza e da Biodiversidade (Institute for Nature Conservation and Biodiversity): Rua de Santa Marta 55, 1169-230 Lisbon; tel. (21) 350-79-00; fax (21) 350-79-84; e-mail icnb@icnb.pt; internet www.icnb.pt; f. 1993 as Instituto da Conservação da Natureza (ICN); attached to Min. of Environment and Territorial Planning; sustainable management of wild animal and plant species; designation of land and marine protected areas; integrates the objectives of nature conservation and sustainable use of natural resources into planning policies and sectorial policies; implements nat. strategy for nature conservation and biodiversity and develops nat. programme for nature conservation; warrants compliance with both EU and int. law in matters related to nature conservation and biodiversity; Pres. TITO ROSA; Vice-Pres. FÁTIMA FERNANDES; Vice-Pres. CARLOS FIGUEIREDO.

Instituto de Investigação Científica 'Bento da Rocha Cabral' (Institute of Scientific Research): Calçada Bento Rocha Cabral 14, 1257-047 Lisbon; tel. and fax (21) 388-29-93; e-mail geral@ircabral.org; internet www.ircabral.org; f. 1922; biochemical research, histology and embryology, bacteriology, physiology, history and philosophy of science; Dir MANUEL DIAMANTINO PIRES BICHO; publs *Relatórios*, *Travaux de Laboratoire*.

Sociedade Afonso Chaves (Afonso Chaves Society): Edifício do Museu Carlos Machado, Rua de Santo André, Apdo 258, Ponta Delgada Codex, 9500-903 The Azores; tel. (296) 28-38-14; f. 1932; ethnography, natural history, geophysics and geology of the Azores; Pres. Prof. ANTÓNIO MANUEL DE FRIAS MARTINS; Sec. Dr CARLOS MEDEIROS; publ. *Açoreana* (1 a year).

Biological Sciences

Centro de Genómica e Biotecnologia (CGB) (Centre for Genomics and Biotechnology):e-mail hgp@utad.pt; internet www.utad.pt/pt/investigacao/cgb/index.html; attached to Univ. of Tras-os-Montes and Alto Douro; Dir Prof. Dr HENRIQUE GUEDES PINTO.

Instituto de Investigação das Pescas e do Mar (INRB) (Institute of Fisheries and Maritime Research): Av. de Brasília, 1449-006 Lisbon; tel. (21) 302-70-00; fax (21) 301-59-48; e-mail ipimar@ipimar.pt; internet inrb.pt/ipimar; f. 1978; attached to Min. of Agriculture, Rural Devt and Fisheries; marine biology, fisheries, aquaculture, marine environment, aquatic products technology; library of 11,000 monographs, 2,000 periodicals; Dir LEONOR NUNES; publs *IPIMAR Divulgação*, *Notícias IPIMAR*, *Publicações Avulsas*, *Relatórios Científicos e Técnicos*.

Jardim Botânico (Botanical Gardens): Jardim Botânico da Universidade de Lisboa, Rua da Escola Politécnica 58, 1250-102 Lisbon; tel. (21) 392-18-00; fax (21) 397-08-82; e-mail jbactividades@museus.ul.pt; internet www.jb.ul.pt; f. 1878; attached to Univ. of Lisbon; taxonomy and systematics, biomonitoring, biodiversity and conservation; library of 18,000 vols; Dir Prof. Dr MARIA AMÉLIA LOUÇÃO; publs *Delectus Sporarum et Seminum* (1 a year), *Portugaliae Acta Biologica* (irregular), *Revista de Biologia* (irregular).

Physical Sciences

Instituto de Plasmas e Fusão Nuclear (Institute for Plasma and Nuclear Fusion): Av. Rovisco Pais, 1049-001 Lisbon; tel. (21) 841-76-96; fax (21) 841-78-19; e-mail ipfn@ipfn.ist.utl.pt; internet www.ipfn.ist.utl.pt; f. 2008, by merger of Centro de Fusão Nuclear (CFN) and Centro de Física de Plasmas (CFP); attached to Instituto Superior Técnico; carries out research projects and supports formation actions and scientific divulgation in its thematic areas; Pres. CARLOS VARANDAS.

Instituto de Meteorologia (Institute of Meteorology): Rua C do Aeroporto, 1749-077 Lisbon; tel. (21) 844-70-00; fax (21) 844-70-40; e-mail informacoes@meteo.pt; internet www.meteo.pt; f. 1946; provides information to the population, socio-economic activities and public entities adjusted to their needs pursuing nat. politics in meteorology, climate and geophysics; library of 34,000 vols; Pres. ADÉRITO VICENTE SERRÃO; publs *Açores* (1 a year), *Anuário Climatológico de Portugal*, *Anuário Sismológico de Portugal* (1 a year), *Boletim Sismológico Preliminar do Continente e Madeira* (12 a year), *Boletim Sismológico Preliminar do Continente e Madeira* (12 a year), *Boletim Meteorológico para a Agricultura* (36 a year), *Boletim Climatológico Mensal dos Açores* (12 a year), *Projecto 12 do PIDDAC* (12 a year), *Resumos Meteorológicos para a Aeronáutica* (12 a year), *Revista do Instituto Nacional de Meteorologia e Geofísica* (4 a year).

Observatório Astronómico da Universidade de Coimbra (Coimbra Univ. Astronomical Observatory): Santa Clara, 3040-004 Coimbra; tel. (239) 80-23-70; fax (239) 80-23-79; e-mail obsastuc@mat.uc.pt; internet www.astro.mat.uc.pt; f. 1772, present location 1951; library of 3,500 vols; education and research; Dir ARTUR SOARES ALVES; publs *Comunicações*, *Efemérides Astronómicas* (1 a year), *Longitudinal Position of Sunspots and Chromospheric Filaments* (12 a year).

Observatório Astronómico de Lisboa (Lisbon Astronomical Observatory): Tapada da Ajuda, 1349-018 Lisbon; tel. (21) 361-67-30; fax (21) 361-67-50; e-mail info@oal.ul.pt;

internet www.oal.ul.pt; f. 1861; part of the Faculty of Sciences, Univ. of Lisbon, since 1995; the country's official timekeeper; carries out scientific research through its attached site; provides astronomical information to the public and civil soc.; promotes teaching of astronomy in schools; library of 13,500 vols; Dir Prof. RUI JORGE AGOSTINHO; Deputy Dir Prof. PAUL CRAWFORD; publs *Dados Astronómicos* (1 a year), *O Observatório* (12 a year).

Attached Site:

Centro de Astronomia e Astrofísica da Universidade de Lisboa (Astronomy and Astrophysics Centre of the University of Lisbon): Tapada da Ajuda, Edifício Leste, 2°, 1349-018 Lisbon; tel. (21) 361-67-39; fax (21) 361-67-52; e-mail caaul@oal.ul.pt; internet www.oal.ul.pt/caaul; f. 2000; research into extragalactic and galactic astrophysics, the Sun, planetary and space sciences, cosmology and gravitational physics; Scientific Coordinator Prof. PAULO CRAWFORD.

RELIGION, SOCIOLOGY AND ANTHROPOLOGY

Centro de Investigação em Antropologia e Saude (Research Centre for Anthropology and Health):; tel. (239) 85-41-00; fax (239) 82-34-91; e-mail cia@ci.uc.pt; internet www.uc.pt/cia; f. 1994; study of human health, disease and well-being in past and living populations from a biocultural perspective; operates through 4 sections: anthropology of past populations; genetics, population and disease; human biology, health and society; studies in material culture; library of 44,790 vols, 330 periodicals; Coordinator Prof. Dra CRISTINA PADEZ; publ. *Antropologia Portuguesa*.

Comissão Nacional de Arte Sacra e do Património Cultural da Igreja (National Committee for Sacred Art and the Cultural Heritage of the Church): Santuário de Fátima, Apdo 31, 2496 Fátima; tel. (249) 53-33-47; fax (249) 53-33-43; f. 1989; Pres. ANTÓNIO FRANCISCO MARQUES; Gen. Sec. Dr JOSÉ ANTÓNIO FALCÃO.

Instituto de Ciências Sociais (Institute of Social Sciences): Av. Prof. Aníbal de Bettencourt 9, 1600-189 Lisbon; tel. (21) 780-47-00; fax (21) 794-02-74; e-mail instituto.ciencias.sociais@ics.ul.pt; internet www.ics.ul.pt; f. 1962, present status 2002, present building 2003; attached to Univ. of Lisbon; studies contemporary socs with spec. emphasis on Portugal and socs and cultures with which Portugal has an historical relationship, either in Europe or in other regions of the world; library of 40,000 books, 313 periodicals; Dir Prof. JORGE VALA.

Instituto Português de Artes e Tradições Populares (Portuguese Institute of Folk Arts and Traditions): Travessa do Passadiço 1, 7540 Santiago do Cacém; tel. (269) 82-63-80; f. 1979; Dir Prof. Dr PERE FERRÉ; Gen. Sec. Dr JOSÉ ANTÓNIO FALCÃO; publs *Biblioteca de Artes e Tradições Populares*, *Novos Inquéritos*.

TECHNOLOGY

Centro Aquicola do Rio Ave (Inland Fisheries Station): 4481 Vila do Conde; tel. (252) 63-12-41; fax (252) 63-25-94; f. 1886; fresh water fisheries and aquaculture; 15 staff; library of 1,000 vols; Dir EUARDO LENCASTRE.

Instituto Hidrográfico (Hydrographic Institute): Rua das Trinas 49, 1249-093 Lisbon; tel. (21) 094-30-00; fax (21) 094-32-99; e-mail mail@hidrografico.pt; internet www.hidrografico.pt; f. 1960; hydrographic surveys, physical oceanography, magnetic compass adjustments, laboratory; library of 12,000 vols; Dir-Gen. Vice-Admiral AGOSTINHO RAMOS DA SILVA; publs *Anais*, *Hidrográfico* (1 a year), *Hidromar*.

Laboratório Nacional de Energia e Geologia (LNEG) (National Laboratory for Energy and Geology): Estrada do Paço do Lumiar 22, 1649-038 Lisbon; tel. (21) 092-46-00; fax (21) 716-09-01; e-mail info@lneg.pt; internet www.lneg.pt; f. 1977; attached to Min. of the Economy, Innovation and Devt; research and devt in technological innovation for application in the fields of energy, new systems, processes and products, environmental management and sustainability, geological resources and hazards, public health and safety, defence and space, laboratory support and testing; library of 38,000 vols; Pres. MARIA TERESA COSTA PEREIRA DA SILVA PONCE DE LEÃO.

Attached Centres:

Campus de Coimbra (Coimbra Branch): Rua Coronel Júlio Veiga Simão-Loreto, 3020 Coimbra; tel. (239) 82-37-97; fax (239) 82-90-00; e-mail info@lneg.pt; internet www.lneg.pt.

Centro de Dados Geológico-Mineiro Alfragide (Geological and Mining Data Centre, Alfragide): Estrada da Portela, Zambujal-Alfragide, Apdo 7586, 2611-901 Amadora; tel. (21) 092-46-00; fax (21) 471-90-18; e-mail atendimento@ineti.pt; internet www.ineti.pt/campus/campus_frameset.aspx.

Centro de Estudos Geológicos e Mineiros de Beja (Geological and Mining Studies Centre, Beja): Rua Frei Amador Arrais 39, r/c, Apdo 104, 7801-902 Beja; tel. (28) 431-13-10; fax (28) 432-59-74; e-mail inetibeja@ineti.pt; internet e-geo.ineti.pt/centros/centro_beja.htm; f. 1944.

Laboratório de S. Mamede de Infesta: Rua da Amieira, Apdo 1089, 4466-901 S. Mamede de Infesta; tel. (22) 040-00-00; fax (22) 951-40-40; e-mail atendimento@ineti.pt; internet www.ineti.pt; f. 1953; Dir MÁRIO RUI MACHADO LEITE.

Museu Geológico de Portugal (Geological Museum of Portugal): see under Museums and Art Galleries.

Laboratório Nacional de Engenharia Civil (National Civil Engineering Laboratory): Av. Brasil 101, 1700-066 Lisbon; tel. (21) 844-30-00; fax (21) 844-30-11; e-mail lnec@lnec.pt; internet www.lnec.pt; f. 1946; attached to Min. of Public Works, Transport and Communications; pursues public policies, which are under the responsibility of the various mins; provides expert support to public authorities in various public admin. sectors, particularly with regard to quality and safety of works, protection and re-qualification of natural and built patrimony, as well as technological upgrading and innovation in bldg construction sector; library of 142,000 vols; Pres. CARLOS ALBERTO DE BRITO PINA; publs *Especificações* (standards, regulations), *Memórias* (technical papers).

Libraries and Archives

Agualva-Cacém

Biblioteca Municipal de Agualva-Cacém (Agualva-Cacém Municipal Library): Praceta das Descobertas 20A, 2735-095 Caçem; tel. (21) 432-80-39; fax (21) 432-80-41; f. 1997; 11,452 vols, 21 periodicals.

Amadora

Bibliotecas Municipais da Amadora (Amadora Municipal Libraries): Rua Capitão Plácido de Abreu, Venteira, 2700 Amadora; tel. (21) 494-80-40; fax (21) 491-49-50; e-mail biblioteca.amadora@clix.pt; internet www.cm-amadora.pt/bibliotecas; f. 1960.

Angra do Heroísmo

Biblioteca Pública e Arquivo Regional de Angra do Heroísmo (Public Library and Archives of Angra do Heroísmo): Palácio Bettencourt, Rua da Rosa 49, 9700-171 Angra do Heroísmo, The Azores; tel. (295) 40-10-00; fax (295) 40-10-09; e-mail bpar.angra.info@azores.gov.pt; internet www.bparah.azores.gov.pt/html/bparah-biblioteca+documental+e+publica.html; f. 1956; 250,000 vols, 3.5m. MSS; Dir Dr MARCOLINO CANDEIAS COELHO LOPES; publs *Arquivo Distrital de Angra do Heroísmo*, *Boletim da Biblioteca Pública*.

Braga

Arquivo Distrital de Braga (Braga District Archives): Universidade do Minho, Largo do Paço, 4704-553 Braga; tel. (253) 60-11-77; fax (253) 60-11-80; e-mail sec@adb.uminho.pt; internet www.adb.uminho.pt; f. 1917, present status 1976; attached to Universidade do Minho; 1,498 linear m of documents since 6th century; Dir Dr ELÍSIO SILVA MAIA ARAÚJO.

Biblioteca Pública de Braga (Braga Public Library): Largo do Paço, 4704-553 Braga; tel. and fax (253) 60-11-35; e-mail bpb@bpb.uminho.pt; internet www.bpb.uminho.pt; f. 1841; attached to Universidade do Minho; 500,000 vols, 27,000 periodicals, 53 incunabula; Dir Dr ELÍSIO MAIA ARAÚJO.

Bragança

Arquivo Distrital de Bragança (Bragança District Archives): Rua Miguel Torga, 5300-037 Bragança; tel. (273) 30-02-70; fax (273) 30-02-79; e-mail mail@adbgc.dgarq.gov.pt; internet adbgc.dgarq.gov.pt; f. 1916; 2,072 linear m of documents; Dir Dr ALDA BERENGUEL.

Cascais

Biblioteca 'Condes de Castro Guimarães': Av. Rei Humberto II de Itália, Parque Marechal Carmona, 2750-327 Cascais; tel. (21) 481-53-26; fax (21) 482-53-81; f. 1930; 25,000 vols; history, art, philosophy, literature, archaeology, local history; Librarian ANTÓNIO MANUEL GONÇALVES DE CARVALHO; publ. *Arquivo de Cascais—Boletim Cultural do Município* (1 a year).

Coimbra

Arquivo da Universidade de Coimbra (Archives of Coimbra University): Universidade de Coimbra, Rua de S. Pedro 2, 3000-370 Coimbra; tel. (239) 85-98-55; fax (239) 82-09-87; e-mail auc-geral@auc.uc.pt; internet www.uc.pt/auc; f. 1901; Dir Prof. Dra MARIA JOSÉ AZEVEDO SANTOS; Deputy Dir JÚLIO RAMOS; publ. *Boletim* (1 a year).

Biblioteca Geral Universidade de Coimbra (General Library University of Coimbra): Largo da Porta Férrea, 3000-447 Coimbra; tel. (23) 985-98-15; fax (23) 982-71-35; e-mail secretaria@bg.uc.pt; internet www.uc.pt/bguc; f. 1291; 800,000 vols, 27,300 periodicals; 7 faculty br. libraries; Dir Prof. Dr CARLOS MANUEL BAPTISTA FIOLHAIS; Deputy Dir ANTÓNIO EUGÉNIO MAIA DO AMARAL; publs *Acta Univ. Conimbrigensis*, *Boletim da Biblioteca Geral da Universidade de Coimbra* (1 a year), *Divulgação Bibliográfica*, *Revista da Universidade de Coimbra* (1 a year), *Sumários das Publicações Periódicas Portuguesas* (10 a year).

Attached Library:

Biblioteca Joanina: Largo da Porta Férrea, 3000-447 Coimbra; tel. (23) 985-

98-41; fax (23) 982-71-35; e-mail joanina@bg.uc.pt; internet bibliotecajoanina.uc.pt; f. 1728; 55,935 vols; Dir Prof. Dr CARLOS FIOLHAIS.

Biblioteca Municipal de Coimbra (Coimbra Public Library): Rua Pedro Monteiro, Apdo 1189, 3000-329 Coimbra; tel. (23) 970-26-30; fax (23) 970-24-96; e-mail biblioteca@cm-coimbra.pt; internet www.cm-coimbra.pt/biblioteca; f. 1922; 600,000 vols, 2,992 video cassettes and DVDs, 7,989 audio cassettes and CDs, 30,000 journals, 955 books in braille, 1,321 audiobooks; public library comprising a network of 7 small annexe libraries and a mobile library; Chief Librarian MARIA-JOSÉ MIRANDA; publ. *Arquivo Coimbrão: boletim da Biblioteca Municipal de Coimbra* (irregular).

Évora

Biblioteca Pública de Évora (Évora Public Library): Largo Conde de Vila Flor, 7000-804 Évora; tel. (26) 676-93-30; fax (26) 676-93-31; e-mail bpevora@bpe.pt; f. 1805; 644,000 vols; Dir JOSÉ ANTÓNIO CALIXTO.

Funchal

Arquivo Regional da Madeira (Madeira Regional Archives): Caminho dos Álamos 35, Santo António, 9020-064 Funchal; tel. (29) 170-84-00; fax (29) 170-84-02; e-mail arm@arquivo-madeira.org; internet www.arquivo-madeira.org; f. 1931, present name 1980, present bldg 2005; 8,500 vols on specialized history, 300,000 MSS; memories of admin. of the islands of Madeira and Porto Santo from dawn of their settlement to rise of process of autonomy in 20th century; Dir MARIA FÁTIMA ARAÚJO DE BARROS FERREIRA; publ. *Arquivo Histórico da Madeira*.

Biblioteca Municipal do Funchal (Municipal Library): Palácio de São Pedro, Rua da Mouraria 31, 9000-047 Funchal; tel. (291) 22-28-49; fax (291) 22-77-30; e-mail bmfunchal@gmail.com; f. 1838; 150,000 vols; Librarian RICARDO ARAUJO.

Biblioteca Pública Regional da Madeira (Madeira Regional Public Library): Caminho dos Álamos 35, Santo António, 9020-064 Funchal, Madeira; tel. (291) 70-84-10; fax (291) 70-84-12; e-mail geral@bprmadeira.org; internet www.bprmadeira.org; f. 1979 as Library of Contemporary Documentation, present name 2003, present status 2007; legal deposit library; 200,000 vols; Dir MARIA DA PAZ DE AZEREDO PAIS.

Guimarães

Biblioteca Municipal Raul Brandão (Municipal Library): Largo Cónego José Maria Gomes, 4800-419 Guimarães; tel. (253) 51-57-10; e-mail biblioteca@cm-guimaraes.pt; internet www.bmrb.pt; f. 1992; 70,000 monographs, 6,600 audiovisual documents, about 1,000 electronic documents, 510 periodicals and a local fund with approx. 21,500 vols and postcards, posters, maps, etc.; incl. local studies library.

Horta

Biblioteca Pública e Arquivo Regional João José da Graça—Horta (João José da Graça—Horta Public Library and Regional Archive): Rua Walter Bensaúde 14, 9900-142 Horta, Faial, The Azores; tel. (292) 20-25-50; fax (292) 39-13-44; e-mail bpar.horta.info@azores.gov.pt; internet edt-gra.azores.gov.pt/portal/pt/entidades/pgra-drcultura-bpah; f. 1886, present location 2008; 60,000 vols; Librarian MANUEL PITA SÃO BENTO.

Leiria

Arquivo Distrital de Leiria (District Archives Leiria): Apdo 1145, 2401-801, Leiria; Rua Marcos Portugal 4, 2400-179 Leiria; tel. (244) 82-00-50; fax (244) 82-00-59; e-mail mail@adlra.dgarq.gov.pt; internet adleiria.pt; f. 1916, present bldg 1997; 30,000 books, 496 microfilms; Dir ACÁCIO FERNANDO DOS SANTOS LOPES DE SOUSA.

Lisbon

Arquivo Histórico Militar (Military Historical Archives): Largo dos Caminhos de Ferro 2, 1100-105 Lisbon; tel. (21) 884-25-63; fax (21) 884-25-14; f. 1921; Dir Tenente-Coronel ANICETO AFONSO; publs *Boletim*, *Noticias* (2 a year).

Arquivo Histórico Parlamentar (Parliamentary Historical Archives): Palácio de S. Bento, 1249-068 Lisbon; tel. (21) 391-90-00; fax (21) 391-74-70; e-mail manuela.magalhaes@ar.parlamento.pt; internet www.parlamento.pt; 180,000 vols; history, law, economics, statistics and texts from int. orgs; Dir MANUELA MAGALHÃES.

Arquivo Municipal de Lisboa (Municipal Archives of Lisbon):internet arquivomunicipal.cm-lisboa.pt; f. 12th century; publ. *Cadernos*.

Constituent Centres:

Arquivo do Arco do Cego: Rua Nunes Claro 8A, 1000-209 Lisbon; tel. (21) 841-11-70; fax (21) 848-46-38; e-mail arqmun.acego@cm-lisboa.pt; f. 1919; documents since 1834.

Arquivo Fotográfico: Rua da Palma 246, 1100-394 Lisbon; tel. (21) 884-40-60; fax (21) 886-16-14; e-mail arqmun.fotografico@cm-lisboa.pt; f. 1942; images since end of 19th century.

Arquivo Histórico: Rua B, Bairro da Liberdade, lote 3 a 6, piso 1, 1070-017 Lisbon; tel. (21) 380-71-00; fax (21) 380-71-12; e-mail dba.dga@cm-lisboa.pt; f. 1931; documents since 12th century.

Arquivo Intermédio: Rua B, Bairro da Liberdade, lote 3 a 6, piso 0, 1070-017 Lisbon; tel. (21) 380-71-00; fax (21) 380-71-99; e-mail arqmun.intermedio@cm-lisboa.pt; f. 1985; city admin. documents.

Biblioteca Central de Marinha (Naval Library): Praça do Império, 1400-206 Lisbon; tel. (21) 365-85-20; fax (21) 365-85-23; e-mail biblioteca.marinha@marinha.pt; internet www.marinha.pt/pt/amarinha/actividade/areacultural/biblioteca; f. 1835; valuable edns; 126,616 vols; Dir Alm. RUI VILAS BOAS TAVARES.

Biblioteca da Academia das Ciências de Lisboa (Library of the Academy of Sciences): Rua da Academia das Ciências 19, 1249-122 Lisbon; tel. (21) 321-97-30; fax (21) 342-03-95; e-mail biblioteca@acad-ciencias.pt; internet www.acad-ciencias.pt; f. 1779; 1,000,000 vols, 3,000 MSS, 100 incunabula; Portuguese language and culture; Dir Prof. Dr JUSTINO MENDES DE ALMEIDA; Librarian LEONOR PINTO.

Biblioteca da Assembleia da República (Library of the Assembly of the Republic): Palácio de S. Bento, 1249-068 Lisbon; tel. (21) 391-41-41; fax (21) 391-41-45; e-mail bib@ar.parlamento.pt; internet sisgerar.parlamento.pt/sitebib/site/homepage.htm; f. 1836, present name 1974; 200,000 vols; spec. collns: nat. legislation and old books from the libraries of religious orders; offers its services to mems of parliament, admin., parliamentary bodies and officials, and staff of parliamentary groups; also open to gen. public; Dir JOSÉ LUÍS M. TOMÉ.

Biblioteca de Ajuda (Ajuda Library): Palácio Nacional da Ajuda, 1349-021 Lisbon; tel. and fax (21) 363-85-92; e-mail bib_ajuda@bnportugal.pt; f. 1756, present location 1880; 100,000 vols, 30,000 MSS, 5,000 music MSS, 213 incunabula; Dir Dr CRISTINA PINTO BASTO.

Biblioteca de Arte da Fundação Calouste Gulbenkian (Art Library of Calouste Gulbenkian Foundation): Av. de Berna 45A, 1067-001 Lisbon; tel. (21) 782-35-98; fax (21) 782-30-44; e-mail artlib@gulbenkian.pt; internet www.biblarte.gulbenkian.pt; f. 1968; 200,000 vols specializing in art, monographs, periodicals, architectural drawings, photographs; reference library for research in the fields of fine arts and architecture; Dir Dr JOSÉ AFONSO FURTADO.

Biblioteca do Exército (Army Library): Largo do Outeirinho da Amendoeira, 1100-386 Lisbon; tel. (21) 884-24-56; fax (21) 884-25-26; e-mail bibex.director@mail.exercito.pt; internet www.exercito.pt; f. 1884; 100,000 vols; Dir Col FRANCISCO DIAS COSTA.

Biblioteca e Arquivo Histórico do Ministério das Obras Públicas, Transportes e Comunicações (Library and Historical Archive of the Ministry of Public Works, Transport and Communications): Rua Vale de Pereiro 4, 1250-271 Lisbon; tel. (21) 319-42-00; fax (21) 319-42-18; e-mail biblioteca@sg.moptc.pt; internet www.moptc.pt; f. 1852; 13,000 vols, documents since 16th century, 200,000 textual documents on industry, agriculture, forestry, trade, public works, etc., 1,100 periodicals; collects, treats and conserves cases completed and printed books and MSS belonging to the min.; Dir Dra MARIA TERESA AZEVEDO MENEZES.

Biblioteca Francisco Pereira de Moura (Higher Institute of Economics and Management Library): Instituto Superior de Economia e Gestão, Rua do Quelhas 6, 1200-781 Lisbon; tel. (21) 392-28-88; fax (21) 397-26-84; e-mail biblio@iseg.utl.pt; internet www.iseg.utl.pt/biblioteca; f. 1911 as Higher Institute of Commerce; attached to Universidade Técnica de Lisboa; European documentation centre of Universidade Técnica de Lisboa and depository library of World Bank; Scientific Dir Prof. Dr JOSÉ PEREIRINHA.

Biblioteca Municipal Central (Central Municipal Library): Palácio Galveias, Largo do Campo Pequeno, 1049-046 Lisbon; tel. (21) 780-30-20; fax (21) 780-30-57; e-mail bib.galveias@cm-lisboa.pt; internet blx.cm-lisboa.pt; f. 1931; 332,673 vols; Dir Dra MANUELA RÊGO.

Biblioteca Nacional de Portugal (National Library of Portugal): Campo Grande 83, 1749-081 Lisbon; tel. (21) 798-20-00; fax (21) 798-21-38; e-mail bn@bnportugal.pt; internet www.bnportugal.pt; f. 1796; 3,000,000 vols, 50,000 newspapers and periodicals, 36,000 MSS; collects, processes and preserves nation's bibliographic heritage and makes it available to intellectual and scientific community; uses latest technologies to conduct online bibliographic research from anywhere in the world; Dir Dr JORGE COUTO; publ. *Leituras* (2 a year).

DGARQ—Direcção-Geral de Arquivos (Directorate General for the Portuguese Archives): Alameda da Universidade, Campo Grande, 1649-010 Lisbon; tel. (21) 781-15-00; fax (21) 793-72-30; e-mail secretariado@dgarq.gov.pt; internet www.dgarq.gov.pt; f. 2007; attached to Min. of Culture; colln dates from 9th century; Nat. Archives network, processing and preservation of conventional and digital records; Dir SILVESTRE LACERDA; publ. *DGARQ Boletim* (news and information, 4 a year).

Serviço de Biblioteca e Documentação Diplomática (Library and Diplomatic Documentation Service): Ministério dos Negócios Estrangeiros, Palácio das Necessidades Largo do Rilvas, 1399-030 Lisbon; tel. (21)

394-63-05; fax (21) 394-60-29; internet www.mne.gov.pt/mne/pt/ministerio/id/biblioteca; f. 1994, present status 2007; attached to Min. of Foreign Affairs; 80,000 vols; Dir MARIA HELENA LOPES DE NEVES PINTO.

Mafra

Biblioteca do Palácio Nacional de Mafra (Mafra National Palace Library): Terreiro de D. João V, 2640-492 Mafra; tel. (261) 81-75-50; fax (261) 81-19-47; e-mail pnmafra@ippar.pt; f. 18th century; 40,000 vols; notable colln of rare books, esp. incunabula and books from the 17th–18th centuries; Dir MARIA MARGARIDA MONTENEGRO.

Ponta Delgada

Biblioteca Pública e Arquivo Regional de Ponta Delgada (Ponta Delgada Public Library and Regional Archive): Largo do Colégio, 9500-054 Ponta Delgada, São Miguel, The Azores; tel. (29) 628-20-85; fax (29) 628-12-16; e-mail bpar.pdelgada.info@azores.gov.pt; internet www.bparpd.azores.gov.pt/index.html; f. 1841; 120,000 vols in spec. collns, 40,000 monographs, 5,000 serials, 3,000 m of archive material; Dir CARLOS GUILHERME RILEY.

Porto

Arquivo Distrital do Porto (District Archives): Rua das Taipas 90, 4050-598 Porto; tel. (22) 339-51-70; fax (22) 339-51-79; e-mail info@adporto.org; internet www.adporto.pt; f. 1931, present location 1995; attached to Min. of Culture; 200,000 vols; Dir MARIA JOÃO PIRES DE LIMA; publ. *Boletim do Arquivo Distrital do Porto*.

Arquivo Histórico Municipal do Porto (Municipal Historical Archives): Rua da Alfândega 10, 4050-029 Porto; tel. (22) 206-04-00; fax (22) 206-04-01; e-mail dmarquivos@cm-porto.pt; internet www.cm-porto.pt; f. 1980; 5,000 vols; colln incl. numerous series handwritten scrolls, illuminated MSS, drawings, photographs, etc.; Head of Section MARIA HELENA DE PAIVA GIL BRAGA.

Biblioteca Pública Municipal do Porto (Municipal Library): Rua D. João IV (ao Jardim de São Lázaro), 4049-017 Porto; tel. (22) 519-34-80; fax (22) 519-34-88; e-mail bpmp@cm-porto.pt; internet www.cm-porto.pt; f. 1833, present location 1842; 1,390,000 vols, 9,411 MSS, 246 incunabula; MSS from the Middle Ages to the present day; Dir SOFIA ALVES; publ. *Biblioteca Portucalensis* (1 a year).

Santarém

Biblioteca Municipal de Santarém (Municipal Library of Santarém): Rua Braamcamp Freire, 2000-094 Santarém; tel. (24) 333-02-40; fax (24) 330-44-79; e-mail biblioteca@cm-santarem.pt; internet www.cm-santarem.pt/cultura/biblioteca/paginas/default.aspx; f. 1880; 100,000 vols; Librarian Dr LUIS NAZARÉ FERREIRA.

Setúbal

Arquivo Distrital de Setúbal (District Archives of Setúbal): Rua Prof. Borges de Macedo, Manteigadas Sul, 2910-001 Setúbal; tel. (26) 570-99-00; fax (26) 570-99-35; e-mail mail@adstb.dgarq.gov.pt; internet adstb.dgarq.gov.pt; f. 1965, present bldg 2001; 4,800 m of documents; documents since 16th century; Dir GLÓRIA SANTOS.

Sintra

Arquivo Municipal de Sintra/Arquivo Histórico (Sintra Municipal Archives/Historical Archives): Palácio Valenças, Rua Visconde de Monserrate 1, 2710-591 Sintra; tel. (21) 923-69-09; fax (21) 923-87-78; e-mail geral@cm-sintra.pt; internet www.cm-sintra.pt; f. 1939; 60,000 documents since 14th century.

Biblioteca Municipal de Sintra: Rua Gomes de Amorim 12/14, 2710-569 Sintra; tel. (21) 923-61-70; fax (21) 923-61-79; e-mail geral@cm-sintra.pt; internet www.cm-sintra.pt; f. 1939; 60,000 vols.

Torres Novas

Biblioteca Municipal Gustavo Pinto Lopes: Jardim das Rosas, 2350-444 Torres Novas; tel. (249) 81-03-10; fax (249) 81-03-19; e-mail biblioteca@cm-torresnovas.pt; internet biblioteca.cm-torresnovas.pt; f. 1937; 70,000 vols; Librarian and Dir Dr LUÍS FILIPE CORREIA DIAS.

Vila Nova de Gaia

Biblioteca Municipal de Vila Nova de Gaia (Municipal Library): Rua de Angola, 4430-014 Vila Nova de Gaia; tel. (22) 374-56-70; fax (22) 374-56-79; e-mail bmgaia@gaianima.pt; internet www.bmgaia.gaianima.pt; f. 1933; 101,000 vols, 2,246 periodicals; Coordinator CRISTINA MARGARIDE.

Vila Real

Arquivo Distrital de Vila Real (Vila Real District Archives): Av. Almeida Lucena 5, 5000-660 Vila Real; tel. (25) 933-08-20; fax (25) 932-57-12; e-mail correio@advrl.org.pt; internet www.advrl.org.pt; f. 1965, present status 2007; 31,590 vols, 3,000 m of documents, 180 m of Portuguese legislation since 1715; Dir PAULO MESQUITA GUIMARÃES; publs *Arquivos de Trás-os-Montes e Alto Douro—Instrumentos de Descrição, Estudos Transmontanos e Durienses, Memórias de Vila Real, Memórias do Tempo*.

Viseu

Arquivo Distrital de Viseu (Viseu District Archives): Largo de Santa Cristina, 3504-515 Viseu; tel. (23) 243-03-80; fax (23) 242-18-00; e-mail mail@advis.dgarq.gov.pt; internet www.ad-viseu.com; f. 1932, present bldg 2003; 450,000 documents; collns of scrolls, books, music and books of liturgy; Dir MARIA DAS DORES ALMEIDA HENRIQUES.

Museums and Art Galleries

Alenquer

Museu Municipal 'Hipólito Cabaço' (Municipal Museum 'Hipólito Cabaço'): Rua Maria Milne e Carmo 2, 2580-319 Alenquer; tel. and fax (26) 373-33-04; e-mail museu@cm-alenquer.pt; f. 1975; archaeological, historical and ethnographical collections; 4,000 exhibits; Dir JOÃO JOSÉ FERNANDES GOMES.

Alpiarça

Casa dos Patudos—Museu de Alpiarça (Alpiarça Museum): Rua José Relvas, 2090-100 Alpiarça; tel. (24) 355-83-21; fax (24) 355-64-44; e-mail cm.alpiarca@mail.telepac.pt; internet www.cm-alpiarca.pt; f. 1904; fine and applied arts, archaeology; library of 41,000 vols incl. historical archive; Dir Dr JOSÉ ANTÓNIO FALCÃO.

Amadora

Centro Ciência Viva de Amadora (Interactive Science Centre of Amadora): Rua Gonçalves Ramos 54B, 2700-036 Amadora; tel. (21) 491-13-13; fax (21) 493-09-00; e-mail info@amadora.cienciaviva.pt; internet amadora.cienciaviva.pt; f. 2003; interactive displays on scientific and technological topics, incl. town planning and electricity; Exec. Dir MARTA VELOSO.

Angra do Heroísmo

Museu de Angra do Heroísmo (Angra do Heroísmo Museum): Ladeira de São Francisco, 9701-875 Angra do Heroísmo, Ilha Terceira, The Azores; tel. (29) 524-08-00; fax (29) 524-08-17; e-mail museu.angra.info@azores.gov.pt; internet museu-angra.azores.gov.pt; f. 1949; historical museum; permanent exhibition on the history of the Azores Islands; paintings, ceramics, furniture, sculpture, ethnography, arms, guns, carriages; Dir MARIA HELENA DE MENESES ORMONDE.

Braga

'D. Diogo de Sousa' Museu Regional de Arqueologia ('D. Diogo de Sousa' Regional Archaeological Museum): Rua dos Bombeiros Voluntários, 4700-025 Braga; tel. (25) 327-37-06; fax (25) 361-23-66; e-mail mdds@imc-ip.pt; internet mdds.imc-ip.pt; f. 1918 as D. Diogo de Sousa Museum of Archaeology and Arts; colln ranges from the Palaeolithic to the Middle Ages; visits to local archaeological sites; library of 8,000 vols; Dir Dra MARIA ISABEL CUNHA E SILVA.

Bragança

Museu do Abade de Baçal (Abbot of Baçal Museum): Rua Conselheiro Abílio Beça 27, 5300-011 Bragança; tel. (27) 333-15-95; fax (27) 332-32-42; e-mail mabadebacal@imc-ip.pt; internet www.ipmuseus.pt; f. 1915 as Regional Museum of Art Works, Parts and Archaeological Numismatics of Bragança, present name 1935; archaeology, epigraphy, sacred art, paintings, gold items, numismatics, furniture, ethnography; Dir ANA MARIA AFONSO.

Cascais

Museu 'Condes de Castro Guimarães': Av. Rei Humberto II de Itália, Parque Marechal Carmona, 2750 Cascais; tel. (21) 481-53-04; fax (21) 482-54-04; e-mail mccg@cm-cascais.pt; internet www.cm-cascais.pt; f. 1931; *Crónica* about the kings of the first dynasty of Duarte Galvão, 16th-century illuminated *Codex* on parchment, 17th-century Indo-Portuguese counting frames, paintings, oriental porcelain; furniture, silverware; library of 2,826 vols; Curator MARIA JOSÉ REGO DE SOUSA.

Castelo Branco

Museu de Francisco Tavares Proença Júnior: Largo Dr José Dias Lopes, 6000-462 Castelo Branco; tel. (27) 234-42-77; fax (27) 234-78-80; e-mail mftpj@ipmuseus.pt; internet www.ipmuseus.pt; f. 1910, present bldg 1971; archaeological colln of objects found in megalithic tombs at Beira Baixa; Bronze-Age weapons and objects from a complete workshop found at Castelo Novo; illustrations of rupestral art in the Tagus sanctuary; Roman epigraphy; art gallery (16th-century Portuguese School and Brussels tapestries); Bishop's Gallery (18th- and 19th-century paintings); ethnographic collns; ceramic collns; regional embroidery workshop; textiles, incl. oriental and Indo-Portuguese embroidered bedcovers; Dir AIDA RECHENA.

Coimbra

Museu da Ciência da Universidade de Coimbra (Museum of Science, University of Coimbra): Laboratorio Chimico, Largo Marquês de Pombal, 3000-272 Coimbra; tel. (23) 985-43-50; fax (23) 985-43-59; e-mail geral@museudaciencia.org; internet www.museudaciencia.pt; f. 2006; attached to Univ. of Coimbra; 240,000 objects in categories of natural history, ethnography, scientific instruments and models.

Museu Nacional de Ciência e Técnica 'Dr Mário Silva' (National Museum of Science and Technology 'Dr Mário Silva'): Palacete Sacadura Botte, Rua dos Coutinhos 23, 3000 Coimbra; tel. (23) 985-19-40; fax (23) 985-19-49; e-mail mnct@mnct.mces.pt; internet www.museudaciencia.pt; f. 1971; attached to Min. of Science, Technology and Higher Education; information science, medicine, physics, graphic arts, photography, cinema, radio, industrial technology; Dir Prof. Dr PAULO GAMA MOTA.

Museu Nacional de 'Machado de Castro' ('Machado de Castro' National Museum): Rua António José de Almeida 208, 3000-042 Coimbra; tel. (23) 948-20-01; fax (23) 948-24-69; e-mail mnmachadodecastro@imc-ip.pt; internet mnmachadodecastro.imc-ip.pt; f. 1919; est. in the old Bishop's Palace built over Roman galleries, renewed in the 16th century and recently adapted; antiquities, sculpture, paintings, silver-work, priests' vestments, tapestries, ceramics, glass, furniture; Dir ANA ALCOFORADO.

Coruche

Coruche Museu Municipal (Municipal Museum Coruche): Rua Júlio Maria de Sousa, 2100-192 Coruche; tel. (24) 361-08-20; fax (24) 361-08-21; e-mail museu .municipal@cm-coruche.pt; internet www .museu-coruche.org; f. 2001; 211,390 pieces, mostly archaeological and ethnographic.

Évora

Museu de Évora: Largo do Conde de Vila Flor, 7000-804 Évora; tel. (26) 670-26-04; fax (26) 670-80-94; e-mail mevora@ipmuseus.pt; internet museudevora.imc-ip.pt; f. 1915; paintings: large collns of 16th-century Flemish and Portuguese works; 17th-century works; local prehistoric tools and Roman art and archaeology; sculpture from middle ages to the 19th century; 18th-century Portuguese furniture and silver; library of 4,000 vols; Dir ANTÓNIO CAMÕES GOUVEIA.

Faro

Museu Arqueológico e Lapidar Infante D. Henrique (Infante D. Henrique Archaeological and Geological Museum): Convento de N.S. da Assunção, Largo Afonso III, 8000-167 Faro; tel. (28) 989-74-00; fax (28) 989-74-19; e-mail dmar.dc@cm-faro.pt; internet www .cm-faro.pt; f. 1894; history, archaeology, ethnography, art from 16th to 19th centuries, photography, toys; also known as Municipal Museum of Faro; Dir Dra DÁLIA PAULO; publ. *Anais do Municipio do Faro* (1 a year).

Museu Marítimo 'Almirante Ramalho Ortigão' (Maritime Museum): Rua da Comunidade Lusíada Capitania do Porto do Faro, 8000-253 Faro; tel. (28) 989-49-90; fax (28) 989-49-96; e-mail biblioteca.dms@clix.pt; f. 1931; regional methods of fishing, instruments, models of ships and equipment, paintings of marine fauna, sailors' handicrafts; Curator Capt. LUÍS FERNANDO TAVARES DOS BEIS ÁGOAS.

Figueira da Foz

Museu Municipal 'Santos Rocha' (Municipal Museum 'Santos Rocha'): Rua Calouste Gulbenkian, 3080-084 Figueira da Foz; tel. (23) 340-28-40; fax (23) 340-28-48; e-mail museu@cm-figfoz.pt; f. 1894; art, archaeology, ethnology, coins and medals, Indo-Portuguese furniture, weapons; library of 14,300 vols; Manager ANA PAULA CARDOSO; Manager MANUELA SILVA; Manager SÓNIA PINTO.

Funchal

Museu de Arte Contemporânea (Museum of Contemporary Art): Fortaleza de São Tiago, Rua do Portão de São Tiago, 9060-250 Funchal, Madeira; tel. (29) 121-33-40; fax (29) 121-33-48; e-mail mac.funchal.drac@ madeira-edu.pt; f. 1966, present location 1992; Portuguese art since the 1960s; Dir JOSÉ MANUEL DE FREITAS SAINZ-TRUEVA.

Museu de Arte Sacra (Museum of Sacred Art): Rua do Bispo 21, 9000-073 Funchal, Madeira; tel. (29) 122-89-00; fax (29) 123-13-41; e-mail masf@netmadeira.com; internet www.museuartesacrafunchal.org; f. 1955; diocesan museum; art of the 15th–18th centuries, Flemish art of the 15th and 16th centuries, sculpture, jewellery; Scientific Dir LUIZA CLODE.

Musee de História Natural do Funchal (Mudeum of Natural History of Funchal): Rua da Mouraria 31, 9004-546 Funchal, Madeira; tel. (29) 122-97-61; fax (29) 122-51-80; e-mail mmf@cm-funchal.pt; f. 1929; natural history museum and marine aquarium; large colln of marine animals, esp. deep-sea fish and crustaceans; library on marine biology; garden of medicinal and aromatic plants; Dir RICARDO ARAÚJO; publs *Bocagiana* (irregular), *Boletim* (1 a year).

Museu da Quinta das Cruzes: Calçada do Pico 1, 9000-206 Funchal, Madeira; tel. (29) 174-06-70; fax (29) 174-13-84; e-mail mqc .drac@madeira-edu.pt; internet www .museuquintadascruzes.com; f. 1946, present status 2004; decorative arts and small clusters of archaeological and ethnographic objects; Dir TERESA PAIS; publs *Porcelana da China—Colecção do Museu Quinta das Cruzes*, *Um Olhar do Porto*.

Guimarães

Museu de Alberto Sampaio (Alberto Sampaio Museum): Rua Alfredo Guimarães, 4800-407 Guimarães; tel. (25) 342-39-10; fax (25) 342-39-19; e-mail masampaio@imc-ip.pt; internet masampaio.imc-ip.pt; f. 1928; religious painting and sculpture, goldsmiths' and silversmiths' art, priestly garments, ceramics; research on industrial archaeology and anthropology; Dir Dr MANUEL SAMPAYO GRAÇA.

Museu da Sociedade Martins Sarmento (Museum of the Martins Sarmento Society): Rua Paio Galvão, 4814-509 Guimarães; tel. (25) 341-59-69; fax (25) 351-94-13; e-mail sms@msarmento.org; internet www .csarmento.uminho.pt; f. 1885; archaeology; numerous exhibits relating to Portuguese Celtic, Roman and Visigothic periods; ethnography, numismatics, contemporary art; Dir Dr J. SANTOS SIMÕES.

Paço dos Duques de Bragança (Palace of the Dukes of Braganza): Rua Conde D. Henrique, 4810-245 Guimarães; tel. (25) 341-22-73; fax (25) 351-72-01; e-mail pduques@imc-ip.pt; internet pduques.imc-ip .pt; f. 1910; attached to Portuguese Institute of Architectural Heritage; 15th-century palace and nat. monument; 17th- and 18th-century art, tapestries, ceramics, faïence, furniture; Dir Dra ANTÓNIO PONTE.

Lamego

Museu de Lamego: Largo de Camões, 5100-147 Lamego; tel. (25) 460-02-30; fax (25) 465-52-64; e-mail mlamego@imc-ip.pt; internet www.ipmuseus.pt; f. 1917 as Museum of Works of Art, Archaeology and Numismatics; colln of 16th-century Brussels tapestries, Portuguese painting of 16th–18th centuries, sculpture, religious ornaments; Dir Dr AGOSTINHO PAIVA RIBEIRO.

Leiria

Museu da Imagem em Movimento (Museum of the Moving Image): Largo de São Pedro, Cerca do Castelo, 2400-235 Leiria; tel. (24) 483-96-75; e-mail mimo@cm-leiria .pt; internet mimo.cm-leiria.pt; f. 1996; commemorates the centenary of the creation of cinema; photographic archive, documentation centre.

Lisbon

Casa-Museu Dr. Anastácio Gonçalves: Avda 5 de Outubro 6–8, 1050-055 Lisbon; tel. (21) 354-08-23; fax (21) 354-87-54; e-mail cmag@ipmuseus.pt; internet www .cmag-ipmuseus.pt; f. 1980; 2,000 works of Portuguese paintings and foreign furniture; Dir JOSÉ RIBEIRO.

Centro de Arte Moderna— Fundação Calouste Gulbenkian (Centre for Modern Art—Calouste Gulbenkian Foundation): Rua Dr Nicolau de Bettencourt, 1050-078 Lisbon; tel. (21) 782-34-74; fax (21) 782-30-34; e-mail camjap@gulbenkian.pt; internet cam .gulbenkian.pt; f. 1983; Portuguese and foreign modern art; documentation and research depts, workshops, outdoor amphitheatre; Dir ISABEL CARLOS.

Jardim e Museu Agrícola Tropical do Instituto de Investigação Científica Tropical (Garden and Museum of Tropical Agriculture): Calçada do Galvão, Belém, 1400-171 Lisbon; tel. (21) 363-70-23; fax (21) 362-02-10; internet www.iict.pt/revista/ rev06/vrev0603.htm; e-mail jmat@iict.pt; f. 1906; Dir MARIA CÂNDIDA LIBERATO.

Museu Arqueológico do Carmo (Archaeological Museum): Largo do Carmo, 1200-092 Lisbon; tel. (21) 347-86-29; fax (21) 342-42-55; e-mail carlavf@mac.pt; internet www .museusportugal.org/aap; f. 1863; administered by Associação dos Arqueólogos Portugueses; prehistoric, Roman, Visigothic and medieval collns; sarcophagi, religious sculpture, coins, etc.

Museu Calouste Gulbenkian: Av. de Berna 45A, 1067-001 Lisbon; tel. (21) 782-30-00; fax (21) 782-30-32; e-mail info@ gulbenkian.pt; internet www.museu .gulbenkian.pt; f. 1969; Gulbenkian art colln containing works since 2800BC; antique classical and oriental art, Egyptian, Assyrian, Greek, Roman, Islamic and Far Eastern art; European painting, sculpture, illuminated MSS, tapestries and fabrics, furniture, silverware, jewellery, glass, medals, coins; Dir Dr JOÃO CASTEL-BRANCO PEREIRA.

Museu da Cidade (City Museum): Palácio Pimenta, Campo Grande 245, 1700-091 Lisbon; tel. (21) 751-32-00; fax (21) 757-18-58; e-mail museudacidade@cm-lisboa.pt; internet www.museudacidade.pt; f. 1942, present location 1979; history of devt of Lisbon shown by archaeological, historical, artistic and ethnological documents and exhibits; an 'ensemble' of the 18th-century period and a large model of Lisbon before the earthquake of 1755; Dir ANA CRISTINA LEITE.

Museu da Música (Music Museum): Estação do Metropolitano Alto dos Moinhos, Rua João de Freitas Branco, 1500-359 Lisbon; tel. (21) 771-09-90; fax (21) 771-09-99; e-mail mmusica@imc-ip.pt; internet www .museudamusica.imc-ip.pt; f. 1994; attached to Instituto dos Museus e da Conservação; more than 1,000 instruments of both classical and popular traditions, European wind, key and percussion instruments of the 16th–19th centuries, Portuguese clavichords, harpsichords and 19th-century string instruments, also African, Asian and Portuguese folk instruments; iconography; sound archive of 6,000 items; printed documents and MSS; Dir MARIA HELENA TRINDADE.

Museu de Arte Popular (Museum of Folk Art): Av. de Brasília, 1400-038 Lisbon; tel. (21) 301-12-82; fax (21) 301-11-28; e-mail museuartepopular@gmail.com; f. 1948; folk art, ethnology; 13,000 objects; Dir ANDREIA GALVAO.

Museu de Artes Decorativas (Museum of Decorative Arts): Fundação Ricardo do Espírito Santo Silva, Largo das Portas do Sol 2, 1100-411 Lisbon; tel. (21) 888-19-91; fax (21) 881-46-83; e-mail museu@fress.pt; internet www.fress.pt; f. 1953; incl. Ricardo do Espírito Santo Silva's private colln of Portuguese furniture, silver, china, paintings, rugs, tapestries etc., and workshops in which craftsmen are trained in all aspects of traditional interior arts; Dir MARIA DA CONCEIÇÃO AMARAL.

Museu de Ciência da Universidade de Lisboa (Museum of Science, University of Lisbon): Rua da Escola Politécnica 56, 1250-102 Lisbon; tel. (21) 392-18-08; e-mail geral@museus.ul.pt; internet www.mc.ul.pt; f. 1985; 10,000 scientific instruments; conducts research and supports postgraduate studies in close collaboration with the Inter-Univ. Centre for the History of Science and Technology (CIUHCT) in the areas of history of science, history of the history of collns and scientific instruments; library of 30,000 vols; Dir ANA MARIA EIRÓ; Asst Dir LUÍS SARAIVA.

Museu de São Roque (Museum of São Roque): Igreja de São Roque, Largo Trindade Coelho (ao Bairro Alto), 1200-470 Lisbon; tel. (21) 323-50-65; fax (21) 323-54-01; e-mail info@museu-saoroque.com; internet www.museu-saoroque.com; f. 1905; collns of religious paintings, Church vessels in precious metals, embroidered vestments by Italian artists of the 18th century; works from the chapel of St John the Baptist in the adjacent museum of the 16th-century Church of St Roque; educational services and temporary exhibitions; Dir TERESA FREITAS MORNA.

Museu do Chiado (Chiado Museum): Rua Serpa Pinto 4, 1200-444 Lisbon; tel. (21) 343-21-48; fax (21) 343-21-51; e-mail mnac-museudochiado@imc-ip.pt; internet www.museudochiado-ipmuseus.pt; f. 1911; painting and sculpture since 1850; library of 6,000 vols; Dir PEDRO LAPA.

Museu Etnológico da Sociedade de Geografia de Lisboa (Ethnological Museum of Geographical Society of Lisbon): Rua das Portas de St Antão 100, 1150-269 Lisbon; tel. (21) 342-54-01; fax (21) 346-45-53; e-mail geral@socgeografialisboa.mail.pt; internet socgeografia-lisboa.planetaclix.pt; f. 1875; native arts, arms, clothing, musical instruments from Africa, India, China, Indonesia and Timor, statues of navigators and historians, relics of voyages of discovery, scientific instruments; Curator Dra MANUELA CANTINHO.

Museu Geológico de Portugal (Geological Museum of Portugal): Rua Academia das Ciências 19, 2, 1200-003 Lisbon; tel. (21) 346-39-15; fax (21) 342-46-09; e-mail museugeol@lneg.pt; internet www.lneg.pt; f. 1848; palaeontology, stratigraphy, archaeology and mineralogy; fossils from the Cambrian to the Tertiary period.

Museu Militar (Military Museum): Largo do Museu de Artilharia, 1100-468 Lisbon; tel. and fax (21) 884-25-69; e-mail museumilitar@portugalmail.pt; internet www.exercito.pt/sites/musmillisboa/paginas/default.aspx; f. 1851, present name 1926; exhibits of Portuguese military history, light arms, ancient artillery and other equipment, paintings since 18th century; Dir Col LUIS SODRE DE ALBUQUERQUE.

Museu Mineralógico e Geológico (Museum of Mineralogy and Geology): Rua da Escola Politécnica 58, 1250-102 Lisbon; tel. (21) 392-18-24; fax (21) 390-58-50; e-mail smineralogia@fc.ul.pt; internet www.mnhn.ul.pt/geologia/geologia.htm; f. 1837; attached to Museu Nacional de História Natural; geology, petrology, mineralogy, palaeontology and museology; Dir Prof. FERNANDO JOSÉ ARRAIANO DE SOUSA BARRIGA; Curator Dr CÉSAR LOPES; Curator Dra LILIANA PÓVOAS; publs *Gaia* (journal of geosciences), *Memórias de Geociencias* (irregular).

Museu Nacional de Arqueologia do Dr Leite de Vasconcelos (National Museum of Archaeology): Praça do Império, 1400-206 Lisbon; tel. (21) 362-00-00; fax (21) 362-00-16; e-mail mnarq.info@imc-ip.pt; internet www.mnarqueologia-ipmuseus.pt; f. 1893; attached to Inst. Português de Museus; library of 25,000 vols; Dir Dr LUÍS RAPOSO; publ. *O Arqueólogo Português*.

Museu Nacional de Arte Antiga (National Museum of Ancient Art): Rua das Janelas Verdes, 1249-017 Lisbon; tel. (21) 391-28-00; fax (21) 397-37-03; e-mail mnarteantiga@imc-ip.pt; internet www.mnarteantiga-ipmuseus.pt; f. 1884; Portuguese and foreign plastic and ornamental art from the 12th century to 19th century; library of 36,000 vols; Dir Prof. Dr ANTÓNIO FILIPE PIMENTEL.

Museu Nacional de Etnologia (National Ethnological Museum): Av. Ilha da Madeira, 1400-203 Lisbon; tel. (21) 304-11-60; fax (21) 301-39-94; e-mail mnetnologia@ipmuseus.pt; internet www.mnetnologia-ipmuseus.pt; f. 1965, present bldg 1976; Portuguese rural artefacts; collns representing the people and cultures of Lusophone Africa, Mali, Côte d'Ivoire, Ghana, Nigeria, Cameroon, Indonesia, Timor, Macau, and the Amazonian Indians; library: 20,000 books and periodicals; Dir Prof. Dr JOAQUIM PAIS DE BRITO.

Museu Nacional de História Natural (National Museum of Natural History): Universidade de Lisboa, Rua da Escola Politécnica 58, 1250-102 Lisbon; tel. (21) 392-18-90; fax (21) 392-18-41; internet www.mnhn.ul.pt; f. 1859; library of 27,000 vols; Dir for Botany Prof MARIA AMELIA MARTINS-LOUCÃO; Dir for Mineralogy and Geology Prof. FERNANDO BARRIGA; Dir for Zoology and Anthropology Dra MARIA GRAÇA RAMALHINHO; publs *Arquivos do Museu Bocage*, *Gaia* (journal of geosciences), *Portugaliae Acta Biologica*, *Revista de Biologia (Lisboa)* (1 a year).

Museu Nacional do Azulejo (National Tile Museum): Rua da Madre de Deus 4, 1900-312 Lisbon; tel. (21) 810-03-40; fax (21) 810-03-69; e-mail mnazulejo@imc-ip.pt; internet mnazulejo.imc-ip.pt; f. 1965; colln of 7,271 tiles, 368 ceramics, 698 prints and engravings, 47 tools; library of 6,000 monographs.

Museu Nacional do Teatro (National Theatre Museum): Estrada do Lumiar 10, 1600-495 Lisbon; tel. (21) 756-74-10; fax (21) 757-57-14; e-mail mnteatro@ipmuseus.pt; internet museudoteatro.imc-ip.pt; f. 1982; 250,000 pieces of costumes, props, sets, posters, programmes, records, sheet music, 120,000 photographs; library of 35,000 vols; Dir JOSÉ ALVAREZ; Librarian SOFIA PATRÃO.

Museu Nacional do Traje (National Museum of Costume): Largo Júlio de Castilho-Lumiar, 1600-483 Lisbon; tel. (21) 756-76-20; fax (21) 759-12-24; e-mail mntraje@imc-ip.pt; internet museudotraje.imc-ip.pt; f. 1977; colln of garments and accessories of Portuguese people since 1882; Dir Dr CLARA PINTO.

Museu Nacional dos Coches (National Coach Museum): Praça Afonso de Albuquerque, Belém, 1300-044 Lisbon; tel. (21) 361-08-50; fax (21) 363-25-03; e-mail mncoches@imc-ip.pt; internet www.museudoscoches.pt; f. 1905 by Queen Amélia in the Riding School of the Royal Palace; comprehensive colln of carriages and coaches since 1619, many by famous craftsmen, incl. those of the Portuguese ex-Royal Family; sedan chairs, harness and equipment, royal liveries, etc., silver trumpets; section of portraits, paintings and engravings; Dir Dra SILVANA BESSONE.

Museu Numismático Português (Portuguese Numismatic Museum): Imprensa Nacional-Casa da Moeda, Av. António José de Almeida, 1000-042 Lisbon; tel. (21) 781-07-00; fax (21) 789-07-08; e-mail mramos@incm.pt; f. 1933; important collns of Portuguese and Colonial, Iberian, Roman and Visigothic coins; also Portuguese and foreign medals; temporarily closed to the public; library of 20,000 vols; consists of Documentation and Information Centre, and Historical Archives of the Nat. Press and the Lisbon Mint; Dir Dr MARGARIDA RAMOS; publ. *Diário da República*.

Museu Rafael Bordalo Pinheiro: Campo Grande 382, 1700-097 Lisbon; tel. (21) 817-06-67; fax (21) 757-18-58; e-mail museu.bordalopinheiro@cm-lisboa.pt; internet www.museubordalopinheiro.pt; f. 1916 as a biographical museum; originals and reproductions of famous caricatures, ceramics, satirical documents; Chief Man. ANA CRISTINA LEITE.

Odivelas

Núcleo Museológico do Posto de Comando do Movimento das Forças Armadas (Command Post of the Armed Forces Movement): Quartel do Regimento de Engenharia 1 Av. do Regimento de Engenharia 1, 1675-103 Pontinha; tel. (21) 932-08-00; e-mail cultura@cm-odivelas.pt; internet www.cm-odivelas.pt; f. 2001; commemorates the revolution of 25 April 1974, covering the main events during 24–26 April 1974.

Pêro Pinheiro

Museu do Ar (Air Museum): Granja do Marquês, 2715-021 Pêro Pinheiro; tel. (21) 967-89-84; fax (21) 967-89-38; e-mail museudoar@emfa.pt; internet www.emfa.pt/www/po/musar/index.php; f. 1969; Air Force museum, 10,000 pieces.

Porto

Museu de Arte Contemporânea de Serralves (Serralves Museum of Contemporary Art): Rua D. João de Castro 210, 4150-417 Porto; tel. (22) 615-65-00; fax (22) 615-65-33; e-mail serralves@serralves.pt; internet www.serralves.com; f. 1999; Portuguese and int. art since the late 1960s; library: reference art library; Dir JOÃO FERNANDES; Asst Dir ULRICH LOOCK.

Museu de Etnologia do Porto (Ethnological Museum of Porto): Largo de São João Novo 11, 4000 Porto; f. 1945 as Museum of Ethnography and History of Douro Litora; ethnology, archaeology and history; temporarily closed to the public; Dir (vacant).

Museu do Carro Eléctrico (Tram Museum): Alameda Basílio Teles 51, 4150-127 Porto; tel. (22) 615-81-85; fax (22) 507-11-50; e-mail dsgalmeida@stcp.pt; internet www.museudocarroelectrico.pt; f. 1992; colln of trams used in Portugal for public transport; Dir CRISTINA PIMENTEL.

Museu Nacional da Imprensa (National Printing Press Museum): Estrada Nacional 108, 206, 4300-316 Porto; tel. (22) 530-49-66; fax (22) 530-10-71; e-mail mni@museudaimprensa.pt; internet www.museudaimprensa.pt; f. 1997; colln incl. materials of foundry, printing, binding and engraving; Dir LUIS HUMBERTO MARCOS; Asst Dir ISABEL GONÇALVES; Sec. JOANA MOTA.

Museu Nacional de Soares dos Reis (National Museum): Palacio dos Carrancas, Rua D. Manuel II, 4050-342 Porto; tel. (22) 339-37-70; fax (22) 208-28-51; e-mail mnsr .div @ imc-ip.pt; internet mnsr.imc-ip.pt; f. 1833; paintings, sculpture, jewellery, furniture, pottery, glass, metalwork; Dir Dra TERESA VIANA.

Attached Museums:

Casa Museu Fernando de Castro: Rua de Costa Cabral 716, 4200-211 Porto; tel. (22) 339-37-70; f. 1952; colln of Fernando de Castro; ceramics, sculpture, painting.

Sacavém

Museu de Cerâmica de Sacavém (Museum of Ceramics Sacavém): Urbanização Real Forte, 2685 Sacavém; tel. (21) 940-98-00; fax (21) 949-98-98; e-mail museu_ceramica@cm-loures.pt; internet www.cm-loures.pt/aa_patrimonioredemuseussacavema.asp; f. 2000; colln of ceramics, fine arts and others.

Setúbal

Museu de Setúbal (Setúbal Museum): Rua do Balneário Dr Paulo Borba, 2900-261 Setúbal; tel. (26) 553-78-90; fax (26) 553-78-93; e-mail museu.setubal@mun-setubal.pt; internet www.ipmuseus.pt; f. 1961; 16th-century art, sacred sculpture, decorative arts, archaeology, numismatics; Dir FERNANDO ANTÓNIO BAPTISTA PEREIRA.

Museu do Trabalho Michel Giacometti (Museum of the Work—Michel Giacometti): Largo Defensores da República, 2910-470 Setúbal; tel. (26) 553-78-80; fax (26) 553-78-89; e-mail museu.trabalho@mun-setubal.pt; internet www.mun-setubal.pt/museutrabalho; f. 1995; ethnographic colln of Michel Giacometti; Dir ISABEL VICTOR.

Sintra

Museu Arqueológico de São Miguel de Odrinhas (São Miguel de Odrinhas Archaeological Museum): Av. Prof. Dr D. Fernando d'Almeida, Odrinhas, 2710 Sintra; tel. (21) 961-35-74; fax (21) 961-35-78; e-mail museudeodrinhas@sapo.pt; internet www .museudeodrinhas.com; f. 1955; epigraphs from Etruscan times to the modern age, important colln of Roman inscriptions and carved stones; archaeological artefacts from the Middle Palaeolithic to the 18th century; publ. *Actividades Ludico-didacticas*.

Sintra Museu de Arte Moderna (Sintra Museum of Modern Art): Av. Heliodoro Salgado, 1270 Sintra; tel. (21) 924-81-70; fax (21) 924-81-77; e-mail info@ sintramodernart.com; internet www .berardomodern.com; f. 1987; art representing 14 movements; Curator PEDRO AGUILAR; Sec. JOANA DE ÁVILA.

Torres Novas

Museu Municipal Carlos Reis (Carlos Reis Municipal Museum): Rua do Salvador 10, 2350-415 Torres Novas; tel. (24) 981-25-35; fax (24) 983-90-99; e-mail museu .municipal@cm-torresnovas.pt; internet www.cm-torresnovas.pt/pt/conteudos/espacoequipamentos/museu; f. 1937; archaeological, historical, fine arts, ethnographical, religious art, numismatics; library of 200 vols; Dir MARIA ELVIRA MARQUES TEIXEIRA.

Vila Nova de Gaia

Casa Museu Teixeira Lopes (Teixeira Lopes House and Museum): Rua Teixeira Lopes 32, 4400-320 Vila Nova de Gaia; tel. (22) 375-12-24; fax (22) 375-20-95; e-mail cmteixeiralopes@gaianima.pt; internet www .cm-gaia.pt; f. 1933; comprises the home of the sculptor António Teixeira Lopes (1866–1942) and the adjacent Galerias Diogo de Macedo; sculpture and paintings since 19th century, furniture, ceramics, tapestries, decorative arts; Dir DOLPHIN SOUSA.

Vila Viçosa

Museu-Biblioteca da Casa de Bragança (Museum and Library of the House of Bragança): Paço Ducal, Terreiro do Paço, 7160-251 Vila Viçosa; tel. (26) 898-06-59; fax (26) 898-98-08; e-mail palacio.vilavicosa@ mail.telepac.pt; internet www.fcbraganca.pt; f. 1933; tapestry, furniture, tiles, European and Chinese ceramics, portraits of the Royal Family, arms, photographs, coaches and carriages; rare 16th-century printed books, Italian 16th-century majolica, and 17th- and 18th-century musical archives; library of 40,000 vols; Curator Dra MARIA DE JESUS MONGE; Curator TIAGO SALGUEIRO; Librarian Dr JOÃO LUÍS DA COSTA RUAS.

Viseu

Museu Grão Vasco: Adro da Sé, 3500-195 Viseu; tel. (23) 242-20-49; fax (23) 242-12-41; e-mail mgv@imc-ip.pt; internet www .ipmuseus.pt; f. 1916; furniture, tapestry, plate, ceramics and glassware, prints and Portuguese paintings; Dir Dra ANA PAULA ABRANTES.

Universities

UNIVERSIDADE ABERTA

Palácio Ceia Rua da Escola Politécnica, 141–147, 1269-001 Lisbon
Telephone: (21) 391-63-00
Fax: (21) 391-65-17
E-mail: contas@univ-ab.pt
Internet: www.uab.pt

Founded 1988
State control
Language of instruction: Portuguese
Academic year: October to July

Number of teachers: 200
Number of students: 9,000

Rector: Dr CARLOS REIS
Vice-Rector: Dr CARLA MARIA BISPO PADREL DE OLIVEIRA
Vice-Rector: ALDA MARIA SIMÕES PEREIRA
Vice-Rector: Dr DOMINGOS JOSÉ ALVES CAEIRO
Pro-Rector: JOÃO CARLOS RELVÃO CAETANO

DIRECTORS

Department of Education And Distance Learning: Dr LÚCIA DA GRAÇA CRUZ DOMINGUES AMANTE
Department of Humanities: Dr CARLOS CARRETO
Department of Science and Technology: Dr ADÉRITO FERNANDES MARCOS
Department of Social Sciences and Management: Dr JOSÉ ANTÓNIO FERREIRA PORFÍRIO

PROFESSORS

Department of Education and Distance Learning:

AMANTE, L.
BASTOS, G.
FRUTUOSO HENRIQUES, S.
GOULÃO, M. DE F.
GRAVE, L.
IVONE GASPAR, M.
LEBRES AIRES, M. L.
MALHEIRO DA SILVA, S.
MANUEL MARTINS MENDES, A.
MANUELA MALHEIRO FERREIRA, M.
MARGARIDA LOUREIRO CARDOSO, T.
MARIA SIMÕES PEREIRA, A.
MIRANDA, B.
MOREIRA, D.
MOREIRA MARTINS, A.
MORGADO, L.
OLIVEIRA, I.
PAULA MARTINS PEREIRA AFONSO, A.
PINTO MARTINS, A.
TINOCA, L.

Department of Humanities:

ALEXANDRE MAGALHÃES NUNES DA SILVA, P.
ANTÓNIO ALVES DOS REIS, C.
AURÉLIA RODRIGUES DE ALMEIDA, C.
BÄR, G.
BÁRBARA DE SOUSA MONTES RODRIGUES MARQUES DIAS, H.
BATORÉO, H.
CARLOS FERNANDES AVELAR, M.
CARLOS PIMENTA GONÇALVES, L.
CASTILHO PAIS, C.
CHENOLL MORA, A.
DE JESUS CRESPO CANDEIAS VELEZ RELVAS, M.
DO CÉU MARTINS MONTEIRO MARQUES, M.
DO ROSÁRIO DA CUNHA DUARTE, M.
DO ROSÁRIO SAMPAIO SOARES DE SOUSA LEITÃO LUPI BELLO, M.
FILIPA PALMA DOS REIS, M.
FONSECA CLAMOTE CARRETO, C.
GÖTTSCHE, K.
ISABEL PEREIRA TEIXEIRA VASCONCELOS, A.
JOAQUIM DE AZEVEDO TEIXEIRA, R.
JOSÉ FILIPE DA SILVA, M.
MALHEIRO, H.
MANUEL LOPES FIRMINO, J.
MARIA DA CONCEIÇÃO FERREIRA DA SILVA, E.
MARIA DE BARROS DIAS, I.
MARIA DE JESUS FERREIRA NOBRE, A.
MARIA DOS SANTOS FALÉ, I.
MARIA FERIN CUNHA DE ALBUQUERQUE VELOSO, M.
MARIA LOUREIRO DE ROBOREDO SEARA, I.
MARIA PONTES CAPITÃO PEDROSA, I.
MARIA SANTOS GRAÇA DE VASCONCELOS RODRIGUES, C.
MARIA SEQUEIRA, R.
MIGUEL GUERREIRO NOBRE, R.
NASCIMENTO PIEDADE, A.
PAULA DA SILVA MACHADO, A.
PAULA S. MENDES COELHO, M.
RITA DE SÁ SOVERAL PADEIRA, A.
SALOMÃO, R.
SCOTT CHILDS, J.
TERESA DE NORONHA CARDOSO ROCHA, M.
VILA MAIOR, D.

Department of Science and Technology:

AMADOR, F.
ARAÚJO, A.
ARAÚJO, J.
AZEITEIRO, U.
BACELAR NICOLAU, P.
BIDARRA DE ALMEIDA, J.
BORGES SEIXAS, S.
CAETANO, F.
CARAPETO, C.
CARDOSO, V.
CARVALHO, G.
CAVIQUE, L.
COELHO, J.
DO ROSÁRIO O. D. RAMOS, M.
FERNANDES MARCOS, A.
GONZAGA ALBUQUERQUE, L.
JOÃO OLIVEIRA, M.
JORGE EDMUNDO, M.
LUCINDA MATOS FERNANDES, M.
LUÍSA CORREIA, A.
MARTINHO MARTINS, C.
MIGUEL MARQUES DE SOUSA, N.
MORAIS, J.
OLIVEIRA, A.
OLIVEIRA, T.
PADREL DE OLIVEIRA, C.
PAULA FERNANDES, A.
PAULA MARTINHO, A.
PESTANA DA COSTA, F.
PINTO DE MOURA, A.
QUARESMA, P.

REMÉDIOS, J.
ROCIO, V.
SÃO MAMEDE, J.
SASPORTES, R.
SHIRLEY, P.
SILVA PEREIRA, P.
SOFIA FERREIRA DA SILVA CAEIRO, S.

Department of Social Sciences and Management:

ALBUQUERQUE, R.
ALEXANDRA GAGO DA CÂMARA, M.
ALEXANDRA GONÇALVES, C.
ALEXANDRE RODRIGUES DIAS DE SOUSA, I.
ALVES, F.
ALVES CAEIRO, D.
ANTÓNIO FERREIRA PORFÍRIO, J.
BÄCKSTRÖM, B.
CAETANO, J.
CARMO, H.
CARRILHO NEGAS, M.
CARRILHO RIBEIRO MENDES, T.
CRISTINA HENRIQUES LOPES DOS REIS, F.
DAS CANDEIAS SALES, J.
DO CARMO TEIXEIRA PINTO, M.
DO ROSÁRIO ALVES DE ALMEIDA, M.
DO ROSÁRIO BASTOS, M.
DO ROSÁRIO DE ABREU DE MATOS BERNARDO, M.
EDUARDO MARTINS, A.
FERREIRA DA SILVA, L.
FILIPE MOUTA LOPES, M.
FILOMENA ANDRADE, M.
FLOR, P.
FONTES, J.
GRONITA, J.
ISABEL DA CONCEIÇÃO JOÃO, M.
JOÃO BRANCO, M.
JOAQUIM, T.
JOAQUIM MARQUES DE ALMEIDA, J.
LUIS CUNHA CARDOSO, J.
MAGANO, O.
MANUEL COSTA, P.
MANUEL TRINDADE, J.
MARIA MILLÁN COSTA, A.
MARIE LUC PHILIPPE JACQUINET, M.
MIGUEL CUSTÓDIO FERRÃO NETO SIMÃO, J.
MIRANDA, J.
NUNES, C.
NUNES, P.
OLIVEIRA RAMOS, P.
PAIVA, A.
PAULA AVELAR, A.
PAULA BEJA HORTA, A.
PAULA CORDEIRO, A.
PAULO GOMES DA SILVA, V.
PEDRO RAMOS DOS SANTOS PINHO, C.
RAFAEL SANTOS BRANCO, C.
RAMOS, N.
RIBEIRO, J.
SOUSA, L.
SOUSA NUNES, T.
TEIXEIRA ISAÍAS, P.
VIDAL, N.
VIEIRA, C.

UNIVERSIDADE ATLÂNTICA
(Atlantic University)

Fábrica da Pólvora de Barcarena, 2730-036 Barcarena
Telephone: (21) 439-82-00
Fax: (21) 430-25-73
E-mail: geral@uatlantica.pt
Internet: www.uatlantica.pt

Founded 1996
State control
Language of instruction: Portuguese
Academic year: October to December

Pres.: Prof. Dr NELSON LOURENÇO
Sec.-Gen.: Dr NATÁLIA DO ESPÍRITO SANTO

DIRECTORS

Department of Management Science: Prof. Dr PIRIQUITO COSTA
Department of Nutritional Sciences: Prof. Dr ANA RITO
Department of Planning, Environment and Society: Prof. Dr JOÃO VILHENA
Department of Post Graduate Studies: Prof. Dr GERMANO DE SOUSA
Department of Science and Information Technology and Communication: Prof. Dr ANTÓNIO AGUIAR
School of Health: Prof. Dr JULIETA ESPERANÇA PINA

PROFESSORS

Department of Planning, Environment and Society:

ALEXANDRE COELHO, J.
ALMEIDA PINTO, G.
AUGUSTO, R.
BARROSO, P.
CANHOTO DA SILVA, J.
CARNEIRO MARTINS, P.
CATARINA AFONSO, A.
CÉLIA GOMES, A.
DE FÁTIMA GEADA, M.
DO ROSÁRIO JORGE, M.
FÉLIX, S.
FONSECA FERREIRA, A.
LOURENÇO, N.
MEIRELLES, I.
MONTEIRO DA CRUZ, P.
PACHECO, D.
PAULO ZBYSZEWSKI, J.
PINTO DA SILVA, P.
PIRIQUITO COSTA, J.
RODRIGUES, L.
RUSSELL, D.
RUSSO MACHADO, C.
SIMÃO, J.
TABORDA, F.
TEIXEIRA D'AZEVEDO, R.
TIRONE, L.
VALENTIM, A.
VILHENA, J.

Department of Science and Information Technology and Communication:

AGUIAR, A.
ALEXANDRE COELHO, J.
AUGUSTO, R.
BARROSO, P.
CABECINHA, F.
CAÇADOR, D.
CALDAS, A.
CANHOTO, J.
CARNEIRO MARTINS, P.
CÉLIA GOMES, A.
CHAVES, M.
CRUZ, P.
DUTSCHKE, G.
FALCATO, A.
GEADA, F.
MEIRELLES, I.
MIGUEL OLIVEIRA, L.
PINTO, G.
PIRIQUITO COSTA, J.
TABORDA, F.
VALENTIM, A.
VALENTIM, J.

School of Health:

AFONSO, A.
ALMEIDA, C.
ALMEIDA, L.
ALMEIDA, L.
ANTÓNIO PESSOA, J.
ANTUNES, V.
BALTAR, C.
BÁRCIA, S.
BARREIROS, P.
BARROS, R.
BORREGO, M.
BRANDÃO, R.
BREDA, J.
CAIADO GOMES, J.
CALISTO, C.
CARDOSO, J.
CARMO, S.
CARVALHAL, A.
CARVALHO, M.
CARVALHO RODRIGUES, L.
CASASNOVAS, A.
CATARINA AFONSO, A.
CLÁUDIA DE SOUSA, A.
COSTA, M.
COUCEIRO, J.
DA LAPA, M.
DUARTE, D.
DURÃO, C.
FAUSTINO, R.
FELICIANO, E.
FÉLIX, S.
FERNANDES, R.
FERNANDES, S.
FIGUEIREDO, P.
FRAGATA, I.
GERMANO, A.
GODINHO, J.
ISABEL FERREIRA, A.
ISABEL RITO, A.
JACOBSOHN, L.
JOÃO FERNANDES, M.
JOÃO SANTOS, M.
JORGE, R.
KOPKE, R.
LEÃO, J.
LOPES, J.
LOPES, N.
LUCAS, L.
LÚCIA SILVA, A.
LÚCIO, I.
MADEIRA, P.
MAGALHÃES, Z.
MAMEDE, R.
MANUEL VIDAL, M.
MARECO, R.
MARQUES, R.
MARTINS, E.
MAURÍCIO, J.
MENDONÇA LIMA, F.
MENEZES, A.
MERCÊS, A.
MESQUITA, A.
MORAIS, T.
MOURA, J.
NASCIMENTO, G.
NETO, T.
OLIVEIRA, C.
OLIVEIRA, I.
PAIXÃO, P.
PASSÃO, V.
PAULA VITAL, A.
PAZ, S.
PERDIGÃO, E.
PEREIRA COUTINHO, A.
PINHO, M.
PINTO, E.
PIRES, A.
POSTOLACHE, G.
RAINHO, A.
RAMALHO, M.
RAMOS, C.
RAMOS, J.
RATO, J.
RATO, J.
RIBEIRO, H.
SANDE LEMOS, P.
SERRA, S.
SERRANO, M.
SILVA NUNES, J.
TECELÃO, S.
TOMÁS, A.
VALENTE, H.
VALENTIM, A.
VANESSA ANTUNES, A.
VASSALO, P.
VITOR, L.
VITOR, L.

UNIVERSIDADE DO ALGARVE
(University of Algarve)

Campus da Penha, 8005-139 Faro

Telephone: (289) 80-01-00
Fax: (289) 80-00-72
E-mail: info@ualg.pt
Internet: www.ualg.pt

Founded 1979
State control
Language of instruction: Portuguese
Academic year: September to July

Rector: Prof. Dr JOÃO PINTO GUERREIRO
Administrator: Dr JOÃO MANUEL PAULO RODRIGUES
Librarian: MARIA JOÃO BARRADAS

Number of teachers: 732
Number of students: 10,000

Publications: *Jornal Algarve Académico* (1 a year), *Revista Encontros Científicos*, *UALGzine*

DEANS

Engineering Institute: Prof. ILIDIO DA ENCARNAÇÃO JESUS NETO MESTRE
Faculty of Economics: Prof. Dr EFIGÉNIO DA LUZ REBELO
Faculty of Human and Social Sciences: Prof. Dr ANTÓNIO MANUEL DA COSTA GUEDES BRANCO
Faculty of Science and Technology: Prof. Dr RUI CABRAL E SILVA
Faro School of Health: Prof. ANA MARIA DE MELO SAMPAIO DE FREITAS
School of Education and Communication: Prof. CAROLINA MOREIRA DA SILVA DE FERNANDES DE SOUSA
School of Management, Hospitality and Tourism: Prof. Dr PAULO MANUEL ROQUE ÁGUAS

UNIVERSIDADE AUTÓNOMA DE LISBOA
(Autonomous University of Lisbon)

Rua de Santa Marta 56, 1169-023 Lisbon

Telephone: (21) 317-76-46
Fax: (21) 317-76-03
E-mail: secgeral@universidade-autonoma.pt
Internet: www.universidade-autonoma.pt

Founded 1985
State controlPortuguese

Rector: Prof. Dr JUSTINO MENDES DE ALMEIDA
Registrar: Prof. Dr JORGE TRACANA DE CARVALHO
Librarian: Prof. Dr MIGUEL FARIA

Library of 20,000 vols
Number of teachers: 500
Number of students: 8,700

DIRECTORS

Department of Architecture: Prof. FLAVIO BARBINI
Department of Communication Science: Prof. Dr ANTÓNIO BERNARDO
Department of Documentation Sciences: Prof. Dr JOSÉ MANUEL SUBTIL
Department of Modern Languages and Literature: Prof. Dr ISABEL MARIA FERNANDES DA SILVA
Department of Psychology and Sociology: Prof. Dr JOÃO HIPÓLITO
Department of Science and Technology: Prof. Dr ALBERTO CARNEIRO
Department of Tourism: GABRIELA MOURA

UNIVERSIDADE DE AVEIRO
(University of Aveiro)

Campus Universitário de Santiago, 3810-193 Aveiro

Telephone: (23) 437-02-00
Fax: (23) 437-09-85
E-mail: sre@ua.pt
Internet: www.ua.pt

Founded 1973
State control
Academic year: September to July

Rector: Prof. MANUEL ANTÓNIO ASSUNÇÃO
Vice-Rector: Prof. Dr JOAQUIM DA COSTA LEITE
Vice-Rector: Prof. Dr EDUARDO ANSELMO FERREIRA DA SILVA
Vice-Rector: Prof. Dr CARLOS DE PASCOAL NETO
Vice-Rector: Prof. JOSÉ FERNANDO FERREIRA MENDES
Vice-Rector: Prof. Dr. JOSÉ ALBERTO DOS SANTOS RAFAEL
Pro-Rector: Prof. Dr ARTUR DA ROSA PIRES
Pro-Rector: Prof. Dr JOSÉ CLAUDINO CARDOSO
Pro-Rector: Prof. Dr LILIANA XAVIER DE SOUSA
Pro-Rector: Prof. Dr OSVALDO ROCHA PACHECO
Pro-Rector: Prof. Dr GILLIAN OWEN MOREIRA
Chief Admin. Officer: Dr JOSÉ DA CRUZ COSTA
Librarian: Dra MARIA EMÍLIA M. FERREIRA ARAÚJO

Number of teachers: 952
Number of students: 13,000

Publication: *Lineas* (4 a year).

UNIVERSIDADE DA BEIRA INTERIOR
(University of Beira Interior)

Convento de Sto. António, 6201-001 Covilhã

Telephone: (27) 531-97-00
Fax: (27) 531-90-57
E-mail: geral@ubi.pt
Internet: www.ubi.pt

Founded 1986
State control
Language of instruction: Portuguese

Rector: JOÃO ANTÓNIO DE SAMPAIO RODRIGUES QUEIROZ
Admin. Officer: Dr JOÃO CARLOS CORREIA LEITÃO
Librarian: Dra JOANA LOPES DIAS

Library of 74,000 vols
Number of teachers: 460
Number of students: 6,000

Publication: *Boletim Informativo 'Urbi@Orbi'*.

UNIVERSIDADE CATÓLICA PORTUGUESA
(Catholic University of Portugal)

Palma de Cima, 1649-023 Lisbon

Telephone: (21) 721-40-00
Fax: (21) 727-02-56
E-mail: info@reitoria.ucp.pt
Internet: www.ucp.pt

Founded 1967
Private control
Language of instruction: Portuguese
Academic year: September to July

Chancellor: Patriarch JOSÉ POLICARPO
Rector: Prof. Dr MANUEL BRAGA DA CRUZ
Vice-Rector: Prof. MARIA LUÍSA HOMEM LEAL DE FARIA GERALDES BARBA
Vice-Rector: Prof. PETER DAMIEN STILWEL
Librarian: Prof. JOSÉ CÂNDIDO DE OLIVEIRA MARTINS

Number of teachers: 1,000
Number of students: 11,300

Publications: *Didaskalia* (2 a year), *Direito e Justiça* (3 a year), *Economia* (3 a year), *Gestão e Desenvolvimento*, *Humanística e Teológica*, *Lusitania Sacra*, *Máthesis*, *Povos e Culturas*, *Revista Portuguesa de Filosofia* (4 a year), *Revista Portuguesa de Humanidades*, *Theologica* (4 a year)

DIRECTORS

Faculty of Arts: Prof. AIRES DO COUTO
Faculty of Economics and Management (Lisbon): Prof. FÁTIMA BARROS
Faculty of Economics and Management (Porto): Prof. ÁLVARO DO NASCIMENTO
Faculty of Engineering: Prof. MANUEL BARATA MARQUES
Faculty of Human Sciences: Prof. ISABEL CAPELOA GIL
Faculty of Law: Prof. RUI MEDEIROS
Faculty of Philosophy: Prof. NUNO DA SILVA GONÇALVES
Faculty of Social Sciences: Prof. MARIA DA GRAÇA DIAS FERREIRA ALVES
Faculty of Theology: Prof. PETER STILWELL
Castro College of Biotechnology: FRANCISCO XAVIER MALCATA
Castro College of Science and Technology: C. PASSOS MORGADO
Education Institute: JOAQUIM AZEVEDO
European Studies Institute: ERNÂNI LOPES
Institute of Bioethics: ANA SOFIA CARVALHO
Institute for Canon Law: Prof. M. SATURNINO GOMES
Institute for Distance Learning: ROBERTO CARNEIRO
Institute of Health Sciences: Prof. A. CASTRO CALDAS
Oriental Studies Institute: LUIS FILIPE THOMAZ
Political Studies Institute: JOÃO CARLOS ESPADA
School of Fine Arts: Prof. JOAQUIM AZEVEDO
University Institute for Development and Social Progress: Prof. J. RIBEIRO GOMES

UNIVERSIDADE DE COIMBRA
(University of Coimbra)

Palácio dos Grilos Rua da Ilha, 3004-531 Coimbra

Telephone: (23) 985-99-00
Fax: (23) 982-79-94
E-mail: ucadmin@adm.uc.pt
Internet: www.uc.pt

Founded 1290 (in Lisbon)
State control
Language of instruction: Portuguese
Academic year: September to July

Rector: Prof. Dr FERNANDO JORGE RAMA SEABRA SANTOS
Vice-Rector: Prof. Dr HENRIQUE DO CARMO SANTOS MADEIRA
Vice-Rector: Prof. Dr ANTONIO MANUEL DE OLIVEIRA GOMES MARTINS
Vice-Rector: Prof. Dra CRISTINA MARIA SILVA ROBALO CORDEIRO
Pro-Rector: Prof. Dr JOSÉ ANTÓNIO OLIVEIRA BANDEIRINHA
Pro-Rector: Prof. Dr MARGARIDA ISABEL MANO TAVARES SIMÕES LOPES MARQUES DE ALMEIDA
Pro-Rector: Prof. Dr JOSÉ ANTÓNIO RAIMUNDO MENDES DA SILVA
Pro-Rector: Prof. Dr FERNANDO ALBERTO DEOMÉTRIO RODRIGUES ALVES GUERRA
Administrator: CÉLIA CRAVO
Registrar: Dr CARLOS JOSÉ LUZIO VAZ
Gen. Library Dir: Prof. Dr CARLOS MANUEL BAPTISTA FIOLHAIS
Dir of Univ. Archives: Prof. Dr MARIA JOSÉ AZEVEDO SANTOS

Library: see Libraries and Archives
Number of teachers: 1,472 , incl. 494 profs
Number of students: 21,165

Publications: *Acta Universitatis Conimbrigensis*, *Anuário da Universidade*, *Biblos*, *Boletim do Arquivo da Universidade*, *Boletim da Biblioteca da Universidade de Coimbra*, *Boletim do Centro de Estudos Geográficos*, *Boletim das Ciências Económicas*, *Boletim da Faculdade de Direito*, *Boletim do Laboratório de Fonética Experimental*, *Brasilia*, *Conimbriga*, *Humanitas*, *Revista Ciência Biológica*, *Revista de His-*

tória Literária de Portugal, Revista Portuguesa de Filologia, Revista Portuguesa de História, Revista Portuguesa de Pedagogia, Revista da Universidade

DEANS

Faculty of Arts: Prof. Dr CARLOS MANUEL BERNARDO ASCENSO ANDRÉ
Faculty of Economics: Prof. Dr JOSÉ JOAQUIM DINIS REIS
Faculty of Law: Prof. Dr ANTÓNIO DOS SANTOS JUSTO
Faculty of Medicine: Prof. Dr MANUEL AMARO DE MATOS SANTOS ROSA
Faculty of Pharmacy: Prof. Dr AMÍLCAR CELTA FALCÃO RAMOS FERREIRA
Faculty of Psychology and Education: Prof. Dr LUÍSA MARIA ALMEIDA MORGADO
Faculty of Science and Technology: Prof. Dr JOÃO GABRIEL MONTEIRO DE CARVALHO E SILVA
Faculty of Sports Science and Physical Education: Profa Dra JOSÉ PEDRO LEITÃO FERREIRA

UNIVERSIDADE DE ÉVORA
(University of Évora)

Largo dos Colegiais 2, 7004-516 Évora
Telephone: (26) 674-08-00
Fax: (26) 674-08-31
E-mail: uevora@uevora.pt
Internet: www.uevora.pt

Founded 1559, present status 1973
State control
Language of instruction: Portuguese
Academic year: September to September

Rector: Prof. CARLOS ALBERTO DOS SANTOS BRAUMANN
Vice-Rector: Prof. HERMÍNIA MARIA VASCONCELOS ALVES VILAR
Vice-Rector: Prof. JOSÉ MANUEL MARTINS CAETANO
Vice-Rector: Prof. MANUEL D'OREY CANCELA D'ABREU
Pro-Rector: JACINTO ANTÓNIO SETÚBAL VIDIGAL DA SILVA
Pro-Rector: MARTA DA CONCEIÇÃO SOARES SILVA DA CRUZ SILVÉRIO
Pro-Rector: PAULO ALEXANDRE NEVES MARTINHO NETO
Administrator: RUI PINGO
Library Dir: ANA CLARA BIRRENTO

Number of teachers: 577
Number of students: 7,625

DIRECTORS

Institute for Research and Advanced Training: SOUMODIP SARKAR
School of Arts: CHRISTOPHER CONSITT BOCHMANN
School of Nursing: MANUEL JOSÉ LOPES
School of Science and Technology: PAULO QUARESMA
School of Social Sciences: JOSÉ MACHADO

PROFESSORS

BRAUMANN, C. A. S., Stochastic Processes
CARVALHO, M. J. G. P. R., Agricultural Sciences
CLARA, M. I. E. DA, Plant Pathology
CORTE-REAL, J. A. M., Physics
FERREIRA, A. A. C. G., Soil Conservation
LOPES, R. M. E. J., Natural Resource Economics
LOURENÇO, M. E. V., Plant Physiology
MACHADO, J. A. S. G., History of Art
MARQUES, C. A. F., Agricultural Economics
MORAIS, J. M. C., Toxicology
OLIVEIRA, M. R. G., Phytotechnics
PINHEIRO, A. C. A., Agricultural Economics
RAMOS, F. M., Social and Cultural Anthropology
ROSA, R. M. V. N., Energetics, Climatology and Materials
SANTOS, M. A. O. P., Physics
SERRALHEIRO, R. P., Soil and Water Engineering
ZORRINHO, J. C. D., Information Systems Analysis

UNIVERSIDADE DE LISBOA
(University of Lisbon)

Alameda da Universidade, Cidade Universitária, 1649-004 Lisbon
Telephone: (21) 796-76-24
Fax: (21) 793-36-24
E-mail: reitoria@reitoria.ul.pt
Internet: www.ul.pt

Founded 1288, restored 1911
State control
Academic year: September to July

Rector: Prof. ANTÓNIO SAMPAIO DA NÓVOA
Vice-Rector: Prof. MARIA AMÉLIA BOTELHO DE PAULO MARTINS CAMPOS
Vice-Rector: Prof. ANTÓNIO EMÍLIO PEIXOTO VASCONCELOS TAVARES
Vice-Rector: Prof. CARLOS BAPTISTA LOBO
Administrator: Dra LUÍS PEDRO GOMES COSTA PAULITOS
Librarian: Dra MARIA LEAL VIEIRA

Number of teachers: 1,797
Number of students: 22,245

Publications: *Agenda* (12 a year), *Boletim*

DIRECTORS

Faculty of Dental Medicine: Prof. Dr JOÃO MANUEL DE AQUINO MARQUES
Faculty of Fine Arts: Prof. LUÍS JORGE GONÇALVES
Faculty of Law: Prof. Dr EDUARDO VERA CRUZ PINTO
Faculty of Letters: Dr ANTÓNIO MARIA MACIEL DE CASTRO FEIJÓ
Faculty of Medicine: Prof. Dr JOSÉ FERNANDES E FERNANDES
Faculty of Pharmacy: Prof. Dr JOSÉ A. GUIMARÃES MORAIS
Faculty of Psychology: Prof. MARIA BARROS
Faculty of Science: Prof. Dr JOSÉ MANUEL PINTO PAIXÃO
Institute of Education: Prof. JOÃO PEDRO DA PONTE
Institute of Social Sciences: Prof. Dr JORGE VALA

UNIVERSIDADE DOS AÇORES
(University of the Azores)

Rua da Mãe de Deus s/n, Apdo 1422, 9501-801 Ponta Delgada The Azores
Telephone: (29) 665-00-00
Fax: (29) 665-00-05
E-mail: uacgeral@uac.pt
Internet: www.uac.pt

Founded 1976, present status 1980
State control
Language of instruction: Portuguese
Academic year: September to June

3 Campuses: Campus de Ponta Delgada, Campus da Horta, Campus de Angra do Heroísmo

Rector: Prof. Dr AVELINO DE FREITAS DE MENESES
Vice-Rector: Prof. Dr JORGE MANUEL ROSA DE MEDEIROS
Vice-Rector: Prof. Dr. JOSÉ LUÍS VASCONCELOS BRANDÃO DA LUZ
Pro-Rector for Mobility and Cooperation: Prof. Dr LUÍS MANUEL VIEIRA DE ANDRADE
Pro-Rector for Activities Coordination of Horta Campus: Dr RICARDO DA PIEDADE ABREU SERRÃO SANTOS
Pro-Rector for Activities Coordination of Angra do Heroísmo Campus: Prof. Dr ALFREDO EMILIO SILVEIRA DE BORBA
Pro-Rector for Area of Evaluation and Quality: Prof. Dr JORGE MANUEL ÁVILA DE LIMA
Pro-Rector for Coordination of Lifelong Learning: Prof. Dr MARIA TERESA PIRES DE MEDEIROS
Administrator: Dra ANA PAULA CARVALHO HOMEM DE GOUVEIA
Librarian: Dra MARIA JOÃO MOTA MELO

Library of 200,000 vols
Number of teachers: 470
Number of students: 6,068

Publication: *Archipélago* (series on human sciences, natural sciences)

DIRECTORS

Department of Agriculture: Prof. ALFREDO E. S. BORBA
Department of Biology: Dr JOÃO ANTÓNIO CÂNDIDO TAVARES
Department of Economics and Administration: Prof. Dr MÁRIO JOSÉ AMARAL FORTUNA
Department of Education: Prof. Dra CARLOS JOÃO PEIXOTO CARDOSO DE OLIVEIRA GOMES
Department of Geosciences: Prof. NICOLAU MARIA BERQUÓ DE AGUIAR WALLENSTEIN
Department of History, Philosophy and Social Sciences: Prof. Dr MARIA GABRIELA COUTO TEVES DE AZEVEDO E CASTRO
Department of Literature and Modern Languages: Prof. Dr PAULO JORGE SOUSA MENESES
Department of Mathematics: Prof. ELISABETE MARIA DA SILVA RAPOSO FREIRE
Department of Oceanography and Fisheries: Prof. Dr RICARDO SERRÃO SANTOS
Department of Technological Sciences: Prof. HELENA CRISTINA DE SOUSA PEREIRA MENESES E VASCONCELOS
Nursing College of Angra Heroism: Prof. NORBERTO FRANCISCO AVILA MESSIAS
Nursing College in Ponta Delgada: MARIA LEONOR MACHADO MELO RAPOSO

UNIVERSIDADE FERNANDO PESSOA
(Fernando Pessoa University)

Praça 9 de Abril 349, 4249-004 Porto
Telephone: (22) 507-13-00
Fax: (22) 550-82-69
E-mail: incoming@ufp.pt
Internet: www.ufp.pt

Founded present status 1996
State control
Languages of instruction: Portuguese, English

Rector: Prof. Dr SALVATO TRIGO.

UNIVERSIDADE LUSÍADA
(Lusíada University)

Rua da Junqueira 188–198, 1349-001 Lisbon
Telephone: (21) 361-15-00
Fax: (21) 363-83-07
E-mail: info@lis.ulusiada.pt
Internet: www.ulusiada.pt

Founded 1986 by Cooperativa de Ensino Univ. Lusíada
Private control
Academic year: October to June

Campuses in Lisbon, Oporto and Vila Nova de Famalição

Rector: Prof. Dr DIAMANTINO DURÃO
Vice-Rector: Prof. Dr JOSÉ J. GONÇALVES DE PROENÇA
Librarian: Dr MADALENA FERNANDES

Library of 15,000 vols
Number of teachers: 986
Number of students: 17,041

Publications: *Boletim Informativo, CDE Bulletin, Pólis* (legal-political studies), *Revista Lusíada de Ciência e Cultura.*

UNIVERSIDADE LUSÓFONA DE HUMANIDADES E TECNOLOGIAS (Lusophone University of Humanities and Technology)

Campo Grande 376, 1749-021 Lisbon
Telephone: (21) 751-55-00
Fax: (21) 757-70-06
Internet: www.ulusofona.pt
State control
Language of instruction: Portuguese
Rector: Prof. Dr MÁRIO C. MOUTINHO
Vice-Rector: Prof. Dr ÁUREA DO CARMO ADÃO
Pro-Rector: Prof. Dr. AUGUSTO PEREIRA BRANDÃO
Library of 1,300 vols, 60,000 monographs

DIRECTORS

Administration School of Lisbon: Prof. Dr RUI TEIXEIRA SANTOS
College of Architecture, Urban Planning, Geography and Arts: Prof. Dr JOSÉ BRAGANÇA DE MIRANDA
Faculty of Economics and Management: Prof. Dr ANA CRISTINA BRASÃO AMADOR
Faculty of Engineering and Natural Sciences: Prof. Dr JOSÉ TEIXEIRA TRIGO
Faculty of Law: Prof. Dr MÁRIO JÚLIO DE ALMEIDA COSTA
Faculty of Philosophy, Mathematics and Cognitive Sciences: Prof. Dr MANUEL COSTA LEITE
Faculty of Physical Education and Sport: Prof. Dr JORGE PROENÇA
Faculty of Political Science, Lusophone and International Relations: Prof. Dr ÂNGELA MONTALVÃO MACHADO
Faculty of Science and Health Technologies: Prof. Dr LUIS MONTEIRO RODRIGUES
Faculty of Social Sciences and Humanities: Prof. Dr JOSÉ FIALHO FELICIANO
Faculty of Veterinary Medicine: Prof. Dr LAURENTINA PEDROSO
Institute of Education: Prof. Dr ANTÓNIO TEODORO
Institute for Security Studies: Prof. Dr JOAQUIM DE CARVALHO
School of Aeronautical Sciences: Prof. Dr ANTÓNIO DA SILVA MENDES
School of Biomedical Sciences: Prof. Dr JOÃO VASCONCELOS COSTA
School of Communication, Arts and Information Technology: Prof. Dr JOSÉ BRAGANÇA DE MIRANDA
School of Fine Arts: Prof. Dr AUGUSTO PEREIRA BRANDÃO
School of Psychology: Prof. Dr CARLOS ALBERTO POIARES

UNIVERSIDADE DA MADEIRA (University of Madeira)

Colégio dos Jesuitas, Rua dos Ferreiros, 9000-082 Funchal, Madeira
Telephone: (29) 120-94-00
Fax: (29) 120-94-10
E-mail: gabinetedareitoria@uma.pt
Internet: www.uma.pt
Founded 1988
State control
Academic year: September to August
Rector: Prof. Dr JOSÉ MANUEL NUNES CASTANHEIRA DA COSTA
Vice-Rector: Prof. Dr GONÇALO NUNO RAMOS FERREIRA DE GOUVEIA
Vice-Rector: Profa Dra SANDRA MARIA FREITAS MENDONÇA
Vice-Rector: Prof. Dr MIGUEL XAVIER JESUS JOSEFAT FERNANDES
Pro-Rector: Prof. Dr BERNARDO GUIDO DE VASCONCELOS
Pro-Rector: Prof. Dr JOAQUIM JOSÉ SANCHES PINHEIRO
Pro-Rector: Prof. Dr MORGADO DIAS
Administrator: Dra CARLA CRÓ ABREU
Librarian: Dra MARIA YOLANDA PEREIRA DA SILVA
Library of 95,400 vols
Number of teachers: 200
Number of students: 2,528

UNIVERSIDADE DO MINHO

Largo do Paço, 4704-553 Braga
Telephone: (25) 360-11-09
Fax: (25) 360-11-05
E-mail: gcii@reitoria.uminho.pt
Internet: www.uminho.pt
Founded 1973
State control
Language of instruction: Portuguese
Academic year: October to July
Rector: Prof. Dr ANTÓNIO M. DA CUNHA
Vice-Rector: Prof. RUI VIEIRA CASTRO
Vice-Rector: Prof. MARGARIDA PROENÇA
Vice-Rector: Prof. JOSÉ F. MENDES
Vice-Rector: Prof. GRACIETE DIAS
Pro-Rector: Prof. VASCO TEIXEIRA
Pro-Rector: Prof. PAULA CRISTINA MARTINS
Pro-Rector: Prof. FELISBELA LOPES
Pro-Rector: Prof. CLAÚDIA VIANA
Chief Admin. Officer: Eng. JOSÉ F. AGUILAR MONTEIRO
Librarian: Dr ELOY RODRIGUES
Number of teachers: 1,200
Number of students: 16,000
Publications: *Cadernos do Noroeste*, *Ciência Jurídica*, *Fórum*, *Revista Portuguesa de Educação*, *UM Boletim*, *UM Jornal*

DIRECTORS

Health Sciences School: Prof. MARIA CECÍLIA LEMOS PINTO ESTRELA LEÃO
Institute of Arts and Human Sciences: Prof. MARIA EDUARDA BICUDO AZEREDO KEATING
Institute of Education: Prof. LEANDRO SILVA ALMEIDA
Institute of Social Sciences: MIGUEL SOPAS MELO BANDEIRA
School of Architecture: Prof. PAULO JORGE SOUSA CRUZ
School of Economics and Management: Prof. JOSÉ ANTÓNIO OLIVEIRA ROCHA
School of Engineering: Prof. PAULO ANTÓNIO ALVES PEREIRA
School of Law: Prof. HEINRICH EWALD HORSTER
School of Nursing: Prof. MARIA ISABEL GOMES SOUSA LAGE
School of Psychology: ÓSCAR FILIPE COELHO NEVES GONÇALVES
School of Sciences: Prof. ESTELITA GRAÇA LOPES RODRIGUES VAZ

PROFESSORS

ALVES BERNARDO, C. A., Polymer Engineering
ALVES FERREIRA, J. F., Physics
ALVES PEREIRA, P. A., Civil Engineering
ARAÚJO, M. D., Textile Engineering
ASSUNÇÃO MONTENEGRO, M. I., Chemistry
BARBOSA FREITAS, V. L., Computer Science
BORGES ALMEIDA, J. M., Physics
CABEÇO SILVA, A. A., Textile Engineering
CADIMA RIBEIRO, J. A., Economics
CALADO FERREIRA, M. I., Physics
CARVALHO PROENÇA, A. J., Computer Science
COUTO TEIXEIRA, J. A., Biological Engineering
DUARTE POUSADA, A. S., Polymer Engineering
EIRAS CAPELA, J. V., History
ESGALHADO VALENÇA, J. M., Computer Science
ESTANQUEIRO ROCHA, A., Philosophy
ESTRELA LEÃO, M. C., Biology
FARHANGMEHR, M., Management and Public Administration
GOMES CORREIA, A., Civil Engineering
GOMES COVAS, J. A., Polymer Engineering
GOMES MENDES, J. F., Civil Engineering
GOMES MOTA, M. J., Biological Engineering
GUIMARÃES ALMEIDA, L. M., Textile Engineering
GUIMARÃES RODRIGUES, A. J., Industrial Engineering
LEMOS MARTINS, M., Communication Science
MACHADO SANTOS, S., Computer Science
MAGALHÃES CUNHA, A. A., Polymer Engineering
MONTEIRO COUTO, C. A., Electronics Engineering
OLIVEIRA CAMPOS, A. M., Chemistry
OLIVEIRA ROCHA, J. A., Management and Public Administration
PEREIRA CARMELO, J. M., Physics
PEREIRA VIEIRA, J. M., Civil Engineering
RAMOS MORGADO, R. J., Electronics Engineering
REGO PAIVA PROENÇA, M. F., Chemistry
ROCHA ARMADA, M. J., Management and Public Administration
ROCHA GOMES, J. I., Textile Engineering
RODRIGUES VAZ, E. G., Mathematics
SALVADOR PINHEIRO, J. D., Biological Engineering
SANCHES SIMÕES, J. M., Childhood Studies
SANTOS SOARES, L. J., Biological Engineering
SILVA FERRAZ, A. M., Economics
SILVA LIMA, N. M., Childhood Studies
SILVA MAIA, H. L., Chemistry
SIMÕES CARVALHO, M. G., Childhood Studies
TAVARES OLIVEIRA, D. R., Biological Engineering
VARELA FREITAS, C. M., Childhood Studies

UNIVERSIDADE NOVA DE LISBOA (New University of Lisbon)

Campus de Campolide, 1099-085 Lisbon
Telephone: (21) 371-56-00
Fax: (21) 371-56-14
E-mail: unl@unl.pt
Internet: www.unl.pt
Founded 1973
State control
Academic year: October to July
Rector: Prof. Dr ANTÓNIO MANUEL BENSABAT RENDAS
Vice-Rector: JOSÉ PEREIRA
Vice-Rector: MARIA ARMÉNIA CARRONDO
Vice-Rector: MIGUEL DE OLIVEIRA CORREIAL
Vice-Rector: JOÃO PAULO CRESPO
Pro-Rector: LUÍS ESPINHA DA SILVEIRA
Pro-Rector: HENRIQUE TEIXEIRA
Pro-Rector: VÁLTER LÚCIO
Pro-Rector: PAULO JOSÉ JUBILADO SOARES DE PINHO
Administrator: Dra FERNANDA ANTÃO
Number of teachers: 1,449
Number of students: 18,233
Publications: *Faculdade de Ciências Médicas: Annual Report*, *Faculdade de Ciências Médicas: Nova Medicina* (4 a year), *Faculdade de Ciências Sociais e Humanas: Bulletin, Portuguese and Japanese Studies* (1 a year), *Faculdade de Ciências Sociais e Humanas: Cadernos de Cultura* (irregular), *Faculdade de Ciências Sociais e Humanas: Cadernos de Filosofia* (2 a year), *Faculdade de Ciências Sociais e Humanas: Ethnologia* (irregular), *Faculdade de Ciências Sociais e Humanas: Faces de Eva: estudos sobre a mulher* (2 a year), *Faculdade de Ciências Sociais e Humanas: Fórum Sociológico* (2 a year), *Faculdade de Ciências Sociais e Humanas: Geolnova* (2 a year), *Faculdade de Ciências Sociais e Humanas: Revista de Estudos Anglo-Portugueses* (1 a year), *Faculdade de Ciências Sociais e Humanas: Revista da FCSH* (1 a year), *Faculdade de Direito Cultura: Revista de História e Teoria das Ideias* (1 a year), *Faculdade de Ciências Sociais e Humanas: Working Paper* (irregular), *Frontal* (irregular), *Instituto de Tecnologia*

Química e Biológica: Revista Portuguesa de Saúde Pública (2 a year, 1 annual themed journal), *Thémis* (2 a year)

DIRECTORS

Faculty of Economics: Prof. Dr JOSÉ ANTÓNIO FERREIRA MACHADO
Faculty of Law: Prof. Dr TERESA PIZARRO BELEZA
Faculty of Medical Sciences: Prof. Dr JOSÉ MIGUEL BARROS CALDAS DE ALMEIDA
Faculty of Sciences and Technology: Prof. Dr FERNANDO JOSÉ PIRES SANTANA
Faculty of Social and Human Sciences: Prof. Dr JOÃO DE DEUS SANTOS SÀÁGUA
Institute of Chemical and Biological Technology: Prof. Dr JOSÉ ARTUR DE SOUSA MARTINHO SIMÕES
Institute of Hygiene and Tropical Medicine: Prof. Dr PAULO DE LYZ GIROU MARTINS FERRINHO
Institute of Statistics and Information Management: Prof. Dr PEDRO MIGUEL PEREIRA SIMÕES COELHO
National School of Public Health: Prof. Dr CONSTANTINO THEODOR SAKELLARIDES

UNIVERSIDADE DO PORTO
(University of Porto)

Praça Gomes Teixeira, 4099-002 Porto
Telephone: (22) 040-80-00
Fax: (22) 040-81-86
E-mail: up@up.pt
Internet: www.up.pt

Founded 1911
Public control
Academic year: September to July
Language of instruction: Portugese

Rector: Prof. Dr JOSÉ CARLOS MARQUES DOS SANTOS
Vice-Rector: ANTÓNIO CARDOSO
Vice-Rector: ANTÓNIO MARQUES
Vice-Rector: JORGE GONÇALVES
Vice-Rector: MARIA DE LURDES CORREIA FERNANDES
Pro-Rector: EMÍDIO GOMES
Pro-Rector: JOSÉ SARSFIELD CABRAL
Pro-Rector: LÍGIA MARIA RIBEIRO
Pro-Rector: MANUEL JANEIRA
Pro-Rector: PATRÍCIA TEIXEIRA LOPES
Administrator: JOSÉ ANGELINO BRANCO

Number of teachers: 1,895
Number of students: 29,896 (12,205 undergraduate, 17,691 postgraduate)

Publications: *Arquivos de Medicina* (medicine), *Arquivos Portugueses de Cirurgia* (surgery), *Cadernos de Consulta Psicologica* (consultant psychology), *Cadernos de Literatura Comparada* (comparative literature), *Douro, Estudos CEJD* (sport), *Mediaevalia* (medieval studies), *Revista Africana Studia* (African studies), *Revista de Filosofia* (philosophy), *Revista de Geografia* (geography), *Revista de História* (history), *Revista de Línguas e Literaturas* (languages and literature), *Revista Educação Sociedade e Cultura* (education, society and culture), *Revista Estudos, Revista Património* (nat. heritage), *Revista População e Sociedade* (population and society), *Revista Portugália, Revista Portuguesa de Ciências do Desporto* (sports sciences), *Sociologia* (sociology), *Terceira Margem* (Brazilian studies)

DIRECTORS

Abel Salazar Institute of Biomedical Sciences: ANTÓNIO SOUSA PEREIRA
Faculty of Architecture: CARLOS ALBERTO ESTEVES GUIMARÃES
Faculty of Arts: Prof. Dr MARIA DE FÁTIMA MARINHO
Faculty of Dental Medicine: Prof. Dr AFONSO MANUEL PINHÃO FERREIRA
Faculty of Economics: JOÃO PROENÇA
Faculty of Engineering: SEBASTIÃO JOSÉ CABRAL FEYO DE AZEVEDO
Faculty of Fine Arts: FRANCISCO LARANJO
Faculty of Law: CÂNDIDO AGRA
Faculty of Medicine: Dr JOSÉ AGOSTINHO MARQUES LOPES
Faculty of Nutrition and Food Sciences: MARIA DANIEL VAZ DE ALMEIDA
Faculty of Pharmacy: JOSÉ COSTA LIMA
Faculty of Psychology and Education: JOSÉ ALBERTO DE AZEVEDO E VASCONCELOS CORREIA
Faculty of Science: ANTÓNIO FERNANDO SILVA
Faculty of Sport Science and Physical Education: JORGE OLÍMPIO BENTO
Porto Business School: BELMIRO MENDES DE AZEVEDO

UNIVERSIDADE PORTUCALENSE INFANTE D. HENRIQUE

Rua Dr António Bernardino de Almeida 541, 4200-072 Porto
Telephone: (22) 557-20-00
Fax: (22) 557-20-10
E-mail: up@upt.pt
Internet: www.upt.pt

Founded 1986
Private control
Language of instruction: Portuguese
Academic year: September to July

Rector: Prof. Dr FRANCISCO DA COSTA DURÃO
Vice-Rector: Prof. Dr AMÍLCAR DA COSTA PEREIRA MESQUITA
Gen.-Sec.: Prof. Dr JOSÉ MANUEL TEDIM
Chief Admin. Officer: ANTÓNIO ALVES MONTEIRO
Librarian: Profa Dra MANUELA BARRETO NUNES

Library of 46,150 vols
Number of teachers: 230
Number of students: 3,100

Publications: *Africana, Revista de Ciências da Educação, Revista de Ciências Históricas, Revista Jurídica*

DIRECTORS

Department of Economics and Business: Prof. Dr LUÍS MIGUEL PACHECO
Department of Education and Heritage: ISABEL VAZ DE FREITAS
Department of Innovation, Science and Technology: Prof. MARIA FILOMENA CASTRO LOPES
Department of Law: Prof. Dr MARIA MANUELA MAGALHÃES SILVA

UNIVERSIDADE TÉCNICA DE LISBOA
(Technical University of Lisbon)

Alameda de Santo António dos Capuchos 1, 1169-047 Lisbon
Telephone: (21) 881-19-01
Fax: (21) 881-19-90
E-mail: gre@reitoria.utl.pt
Internet: www.utl.pt

Founded 1930
State control
Language of instruction: Portuguese
Academic year: September to July

Rector: Prof. FERNANDO MANUEL RAMÔA CARDOSO RIBEIRO
Vice-Rector: Prof. LUÍS MANUEL DOS ANJOS FERREIRA
Vice-Rector: Prof. Dr VÍTOR FERNANDO DA CONCEIÇÃO GONÇALVES
Vice-Rector: Prof. HELENA MARGARIDA NUNES PEREIRA
Pro-Rector: Prof. Dr NUNO PAULO DE SOUSA ARROBAS CRATO
Pro-Rector: Prof. Dr MANUEL ALMEIDA RIBEIRO
Pro-Rector: Prof. Dr PAULO JORGE PIRES FERREIRA
Pro-Rector: Prof. Dr JOSÉ MANUEL FRAGOSO ALVES DINIZ
Administrator: Prof. EDUARDO LOPES RODRIGUES
Librarian: D. UMBELINA NASCIMENTO

Library of 500,000 vols, 28000 periodicals
Number of teachers: 1,822
Number of students: 22,503

Publications: *DAXIYANGGUO, Portuguese Review of Asiatic Studies, Episteme Review, European Review of Economics and Finance, ISEG—Estudes de Economia, ISCSP—Estudes Politicos e Sociais, Portuguese Economic Journal, Portuguese Review of International and Community Relations, Portuguese Review of Veterinary Sciences*

PRESIDENTS OF THE DIRECTIVE COUNCILS

Faculty of Architecture: Prof FRANCISCO JOSÉ GENTIL BERGER
Faculty of Human Kinetics: Prof. Dr CARLOS ALBERTO FERREIRA NETO
Faculty of Veterinary Medicine: Prof. Dr LUÍS MANUEL MORGADO TAVARES
School of Agriculture: Prof. CARLOS JOSÉ DE ALMEIDA NOÉME
School of Economics and Management: Prof. Dr JOÃO LUIS CORREIA DUQUE
School of Engineering: Prof. Dr ANTÓNIO MANUEL DA CRUZ SERRA
School of Social and Political Sciences: Prof. Dr JOÃO ABREU DE FARIA BILHIM

UNIVERSIDADE DE TRÁS-OS-MONTES E ALTO DOURO
(University of Trás-os-Montes and Alto Douro)

Apdo 1013, 5000-801 Vila Real
Telephone: (25) 935-00-00
Fax: (25) 935-04-80
E-mail: reitoria@utad.pt
Internet: www.utad.pt

Founded 1973, present status 1986
State control
Language of instruction: Portuguese
Academic year: September to July

Rector: Prof. Dr CARLOS ALBERTO SEQUEIRA
Vice-Rector: Prof. Dr MARIA SOLINA DE JESUS CURADO QUINTAS DINIS POETA
Vice-Rector: Prof. Dr JORGE MANUEL TEIXEIRA DE AZEVEDO
Vice-Rector: Prof. Dr CARLOS DA COSTA ASSUNÇÃO
Pro-Rector: Prof. Dr ANTÓNIO AUGUSTO FONTAÍNHAS FERNANDES
Pro-Rector: Prof. Dr FERNANDO MANUEL COELHO FRANCO MARTINS
Pro-Rector: Prof. Dr ANTÓNIO JOSÉ ROCHA MARTINS DA SILVA
Pro-Rector: Prof. Dr JOÃO MANUEL PEREIRA BARROSO
Pro-Rector: Prof. Dr ISABEL ALEXANDRA FERREIRA DA SILVA VAZ NICOLAU
Pro-Rector: Prof. Dr ALEXANDRA SOFIA MIGUÉNS FIDALGO ESTEVES
Registrar: Dra ELSA JUSTINO
Administrator: RUI JORGE CORDEIRO DOS SANTOS
Librarian: Dra MARGARIDA CARVALHO

Number of teachers: 502
Number of students: 8,393

Publications: *Annals of UTAD, A UTAD em Números, Boletim Informativo da UTAD, Yearbook of UTAD*

DIRECTORS

School of Agriculture and Veterinary Sciences: Prof. Dr VICENTE DE SEIXAS E SOUSA

School of Humanities and Social Sciences: Prof. Dr CHRISTOPHER GERRY
School of Life Sciences and Environment: Prof. Dr ANTÓNIO FONTAÍNHAS FERNANDES
School of Science and Technology: Prof. Dr JOSÉ AFONSO MORENO BULAS CRUZ

Colleges

Escola Náutica Infante D. Henrique (Infante D. Henrique Nautical School): Av. Eng. Bonneville Franco, 2770-058 Paço d'Arcos; tel. (21) 446-00-10; fax (21) 442-95-46; e-mail info@enautica.pt; internet www.enautica.pt; f. 1972; provides training in merchant navy; Pres. ABEL AMORIM.

Escola Superior de Actividades Imobiliárias (School of Real Estate): Praça Eduardo Mondlane, 7C Edifício Coopemi, 1950-104 Lisbon; tel. (21) 836-70-10; fax (21) 836-70-19; e-mail esai@esai.pt; internet www.esai.pt; f. 1990; Dir Prof. Dr LEANDRO PEREIRA.

Escola Superior de Enfermagem da Cruz Vermelha Portuguesa de Oliveira de Azeméis (School of Nursing of the Portuguese Red Cross Oliveira de Azemeis): Rua da Cruz Vermelha, Cidacos, Apdo 1002, 3720-126 Oliveira de Azeméis; tel. (25) 666-14-30; fax (25) 666-14-32; e-mail secretaria@esenfcvpoa.eu; internet www.esenfcvpoa.eu; f. 2002; polytechnic instn of nursing and health sciences education; Pres. HENRIQUE PEREIRA; Vice-Pres. FERNANDA PRÍNCIPE.

Escola Superior de Enfermagem de Coimbra (Nursing School of Coimbra): *Campus A:* Avda Bissaya Barreto, Apdo 55, 3001-901 Coimbra; *Campus B:* Rua 5 de Outubro, Apdo 55, 3001-901 Coimbra; tel. (23) 980-28-50; fax (23) 944-26-48; internet www.esenfc.pt; f. 2004 by merger of Nursing School of Higher Education Dr. Ângelo da Fonseca (f. 1881) with Nursing School of Higher Education Bissaya Barreto (f. 1971); Pres. MARIA DA CONCEIÇÃO SARAIVA DA SILVA COSTA BENTO; Vice-Pres. FERNANDO MANUEL DIAS HENRIQUES; Vice-Pres. JOSÉ REIS DOS SANTOS ROXO; publ. *Revista Referência*.

Escola Superior de Enfermagem de Lisboa (Lisbon Nursing School): Pólo Maria Fernanda Resende, Parque da Saúde, na Av. do Brasil 53-B, 1700-063 Lisbon; tel. (21) 792-41-00; fax (21) 792-41-97; internet www.esel.pt; f. 2004 by merger of School of Nursing Artur Ravara, School of Nursing Calouste Gulbenkian, Lisbon, School of Nursing and Francisco Garcia College of Nursing Maria Fernanda Resende; library: 22,300 vols, 170 periodicals, 2,500 digital journals; Pres. Prof. Dr MARIA FILOMENA MENDES GASPAR; Vice-Pres. Prof. OLGA MARIA ORDAZ FERREIRA; Vice-Pres. Prof. JOÃO CARLOS BARREIROS DOS SANTOS; publ. *Pensar Enfermagem*.

Escola Superior de Hotelaria e Turismo do Estoril (School of Hospitality and Tourism, Estoril): Av. Condes de Barcelona, 2769-510 Estoril; tel. (21) 004-07-00; fax (21) 004-07-19; e-mail info@eshte.pt; internet www.eshte.pt; offers graduate and postgraduate courses in tourism, travel and hospitality; 110 teachers; Pres. Prof. Dr FERNANDO MOREIRA.

Escola Superior de Saúde Egas Moniz (Egas Moniz School of Health Sciences): Egas Moniz, Cooperativa de Ensino Superior, Crl Campus Universitário, Quinta da Granja, Monte de Caparica, 2829-511 Caparica; tel. (21) 294-68-07; fax (21) 294-68-32; e-mail essem@egasmoniz.edu.pt; internet www.egasmoniz.com.pt; f. 1999; offers Masters courses in health sciences; Dir Prof. Dr JOSÉ A. DE SALIS AMARAL.

Escola Superior de Tecnologia da Saúde de Coimbra (School of Health Technology of Coimbra): Rua 5 de Outubro, S Martinho do Bispo, Apdo 7006, 3046-854 Coimbra; tel. (23) 980-24-30; fax (23) 981-33-95; e-mail geral@estescoimbra.pt; internet www.estescoimbra.pt; f. 1993; clinical analyses, audiology, cardiology, dietetics and nutrition, pharmacy, physiotherapy, radiology and environmental health; library: 4,357 monographs, 6,150 periodicals; 1,000 students; Pres. JORGE CONDE.

Escola Superior de Tecnologia da Saúde do Porto (School of Health Technology Porto): R. Valente Perfeito 322, 4400-330 Vila Nova de Gaia; tel. (22) 206-10-00; fax (22) 206-10-01; e-mail geral@estsp.ipp.pt; internet www.estsp.ipp.pt; f. 1980, present status 2004; offers Masters courses in health technology; Pres. AGOSTINHO CRUZ.

Escola Superior Enfermagem S. José de Cluny (St Joseph of Cluny School of Nursing): Rampa de Quinta de Sant' Ana 22, 9050-282 Funchal, Madeira; tel. (29) 174-34-44; fax (29) 174-36-26; e-mail geral@esesjcluny.pt; internet www.esesjcluny.pt; f. 1940; offers graduate and postgraduate courses in nursing; Pres. IRMÃ SOARES; publ. *O Cluny* (4 a year).

Escola Superior Gallaecia: Largo das Oliveiras, 4920-275 Vila Nova de Cerveira; tel. (25) 179-40-54; fax (25) 179-40-55; e-mail esg@esg.pt; internet www.esg.pt; f. 1992; attached to Fundação Convento da Orada; studies and research in design, ecology and landscape, arts and multimedia; offers Masters degree in architecture and urbanism; Pres. Prof. Dr MARIANA CORREIA.

Escola Universitária Vasco da Gama (Vasco da Gama University School): Mosteiro S. Jorge de Milréu, Estrada da Conraria, Castelo Viegas, 3040-714 Coimbra; tel. (23) 944-44-44; fax (23) 943-76-27; e-mail geral@euvg.net; internet www.euvg.net; f. 2000; attached to Associação Cognitária S. Jorge de Milréu; architecture and veterinary medicine; Pres. Prof. Dr MACHADO FARIA.

Instituto Nacional de Administração (National Institute for Public Administration): Palácio dos Marqueses de Pombal, 2784-540 Oeiras; tel. (21) 446-53-00; fax (21) 446-54-44; e-mail ina@ina.pt; internet www.ina.pt; f. 1979; training and research in public admin., law, European affairs, management, computer science, human resources management; European Documentation Centre; 373 teachers; 11,473 students; library: 19,000 vols, 250 periodicals; Pres. Prof. ANTÓNIO CORREIA DE CAMPOS; publ. *Legislação: Cadernos de Ciência de Legislação* (3 a year).

Instituto Piaget: Quinta de Arreinela de Cima, 2800-305 Almada; tel. (21) 294-62-50; fax (21) 294-62-51; e-mail info@almada.ipiaget.org; internet www.ipiaget.org; f. 1979; offers courses in clinical analysis and public health, social sciences, communications science and intercultural development, chemical sciences and the environment, complementary studies, education, artistic and industrial design, design and management of teaching materials, economics and business, economics and management of health sciences, infant education, nursing, food engineering, civil engineering, contract engineering and maintenance management, electrical engineering, physiotherapy, music, human, social and school nutrition, basic education, psychology, environmental health, sociology.

National Campuses:

Campus Académico de Almada: Quinta de Arreinela de Cima, 2800-305 Almada; tel. (21) 294-62-50; fax (21) 294-62-51; e-mail info@almada.ipiaget.org; internet www.ipiaget.org.

Campus Universitário de Viseu: Estrada do Alto do Gaio, Galifonge, Lordosa, 3515-776 Viseu; tel. (23) 2 91-01-00; fax (23) 2 91-01-80; e-mail info@viseu.ipiaget.org; internet www.ipiaget.org.

Complexo de Ensino Superior de Macedo de Cavaleiros: Rua Dr António Oliveira Cruz, 5340-257 Macedo de Cavaleiros; tel. (27) 842-00-40; fax (27) 842-54-30; e-mail info@macedo.ipiaget.org; internet www.ipiaget.org.

Escola Superior de Saúde—Jean Piaget Silves: Enxerim, 8300-025 Silves; tel. (28) 244-01-70; fax (28) 244-01-71; e-mail info@silves.ipiaget.org; internet www.ipiaget.org.

ESS Jean Piaget: Escola Superior de Sáude, Alameda Jean Piaget, Gulpilhares, 4405-678 Vila Nova de Gaia; tel. (22) 753-66-20; fax (22) 753-66-39; e-mail info@gaia.ipiaget.org; internet www.ipiaget.org.

ISEIT Mirandela: Av. 25 de Abril, 5370-202 Mirandela; tel. (27) 820-01-50; fax (27) 826-52-03; e-mail info@mirandela.ipiaget.org; internet www.ipiaget.org.

Santo André: Bairro das Flores, Apdo 38, 7500-999 Vila Nova de Santo André; tel. (26) 970-87-10; fax (26) 970-87-27; e-mail info@standre.ipiaget.org; internet www.ipiaget.org.

Vila Nova de Gaia: Escola Superior de Educação, Rua António Sérgio, Apdo 551, 4410-269 Canelas, Vila Nova de Gaia; tel. (22) 753-76-00; fax (22) 753-76-81; e-mail info@gaia.ipiaget.org; internet www.ipiaget.org.

International Campuses:

Universidade Jean Piaget de Angola: see separate entry in Angola chapter.

Universidade Jean Piaget de Cabo Verde: see separate entry in Cape Verde chapter.

Instituto Politécnico de Beja: Rua Pedro Soares, Campus do Instituto Politécnico de Beja, Apdo 6155, 7800-295 Beja; tel. (28) 431-44-00; fax (28) 431-44-01; e-mail geral@ipbeja.pt; internet www.ipbeja.pt; f. 1987; 231 teachers; 3,500 students; library: 35,000 vols; Dir Dr JOSÉ LUÍS RAMALHO.

Instituto Politécnico de Bragança: Campus de Santa Apolónia, Apdo 1101, 5301-856 Bragança; tel. (27) 333-06-90; fax (27) 331-36-84; e-mail ipb@ipb.pt; internet www.ipb.pt; f. 1983; agriculture, education, technology, management, communication and health; campus in Mirandela; 310 teachers; 7,000 students; Dir Prof. DIONÍSIO A. GONÇALVES.

Instituto Politécnico de Castelo Branco, Escola Superior Agrária: Quinta da Senhora de Mércules, Apdo 119, 6001-909 Castelo Branco; tel. (27) 233-99-00; fax (27) 233-99-01; e-mail esa@ipcb.pt; internet www.esa.ipcb.pt; f. 1983; higher courses in agriculture (vegetable production, animal production, forestry production, natural resources management, edible oil production); 70 teachers; 1,400 students; library: 22,000 vols; Dir CELESTINO ANTÓNIO MORAIS DE ALMEIDA; publs *AGROforum*, *Bibliografia Temática*, *Boletim Bibliográfico*, *Folha Bibliográfica Mensal*.

Instituto Politécnico da Guarda: Av. Dr Francisco Sá Carneiro 50, 6300-559 Guarda; tel. (27) 122-01-10; fax (27) 122-26-90; e-mail ipg@ipg.pt; internet twintwo.ipg.pt; f. 1980; courses in education, public relations, computer science, civil engineering, mechanical engineering and business management; 258 teachers; 3,700 students; Pres. Prof. Dr

Constantino Mendes Rei; Vice-Pres. Prof. Dr Fernando Augusto Sá Neves Santos; Vice-Pres. Prof. Dr Gonçalo Poeta Fernandes; publs *Educação e Tecnologia* (2 a year), *Revista Egitania Sciencia* (2 a year).

Instituto Politécnico de Lisboa: Estrada de Benfica 529, 1549-020 Lisbon; tel. (21) 710-12-00; fax (21) 710-12-35; e-mail academica@sc.ipl.pt; internet www.ipl.pt; f. 1985; 13,000 students; Pres. Dr Alberto A. Antas de Barros Júnior; Administrator Dr António José Carvalho Marques.

Constituent Institutes:

Escola Superior de Communicação Social: Campus de Benfica do IPL, 1549-014 Lisbon; tel. (21) 711-90-00; fax (21) 716-25-40; e-mail servicos_academicos@escs.ipl.pt; internet www.escs.ipl.pt; f. 1987; academic year September to July; library of 3,919 vols, 8,799 periodicals; 62 teachers; 866 students; Pres. Dr João Pedro Abreu.

Escola Superior de Dança: Rua da Academia das Ciências 5, 1200-003 Lisbon; tel. (21) 324-47-70; fax (21) 324-02-71; e-mail geral@esd.ipl.pt; internet www.esd.ipl.pt; f. 1983; academic year September to July; 17 teachers; 83 students; library of 1,270 vols; Pres. Prof. Fernando Crespo; publ. *Dança*.

Escola Superior de Educação: Campus de Benfica do IPL, 1549-003 Lisbon; tel. (21) 711-55-00; fax (21) 716-61-47; e-mail eselx@eselx.ipl.pt; internet www.eselx.ipt.pt; f. 1985; academic year September to July; library of 28,000 vols, 8,500 periodicals; 96 teachers; 1,065 students; Pres. Dra Amália Garrido Bárrios.

Escola Superior de Música: Campus de Benfica do IPL, 1500-651 Lisbon; tel. (21) 322-49-40; fax (21) 347-14-89; e-mail esml@esm.ipl.pt; internet www.esml.ipl.pt; f. 1983; academic year October to June; library of 1,500 vols and 5,000 music scores; 43 teachers; 140 students; Dir Prof. José João Gomes dos Santos.

Escola Superior de Teatro e Cinema: Av. Marquês de Pombal 22B, 2700-571 Amadora; tel. (21) 498-94-00; fax (21) 498-94-01; e-mail estc@estc.ipl.pt; internet www.estc.ipl.pt; f. 1983; academic year September to July; library of 10,000 vols, 2,000 periodicals; 43 teachers; 208 students; Pres. Prof. Filipe Oliveira.

Escola Superior de Tecnologia da Saúde de Lisboa (ESTeSL): Av. D João II, Lote 4.69.01, 1990-096 Lisbon; tel. (21) 898-04-00; fax (21) 898-04-60; e-mail estesl@estesl.ipl.pt; internet www.estesl.ipl.pt; f. 1981; Pres. Prof. Manuel Correia; publ. *Saúde & Tecnologia*.

Instituto Superior de Contabilidade e Administração de Lisboa (ISCAL): Av. Miguel Bombarda 20, 1069-035 Lisbon; tel. (21) 798-45-00; fax (21) 798-45-98; internet www.iscal.ipl.pt; f. 1754 as Aula de Comércio, present name 1976; academic year September to July; library of 6,566 vols, 211 periodicals; 202 teachers; 3,334 students; Dir of Services Dr Graciette Pinto Correia.

Instituto Superior de Engenharia de Lisboa (ISEL): Rua Conselheiro Emídio Navarro 1, 1959-007 Lisbon; tel. (21) 831-70-00; fax (21) 831-70-01; e-mail isel@isel.ipl.pt; internet www.isel.ipl.pt; f. 1852 as Instituto Industrial de Lisboa, present name 1974; academic year September to July; library of 9,388 vols, 312 periodicals; 551 teachers; 5,495 students; Pres. Dr José Carlos Lourenço Quadrado.

Instituto Politécnico de Portalegre: Praça do Município Apdo 84, 7301-901 Portalegre; tel. (245) 30-15-00; fax (245) 33-03-53; e-mail geral@ipportalegre.pt; internet www.ipportalegre.pt; f. 1985; 250 teachers; 3,000 students; Pres. Joaquim Mourato.

Constituent Schools:

Escola Superior Agrária de Elvas (ESAE): Edifício do Trem Alto, Av. 14 de Janeiro, Apdo 254, 7350-903 Elvas; tel. (26) 862-85-28; fax (26) 862-85-29; e-mail esae@esaelvas.pt; internet www.esaelvas.pt; 5 teachers; 25 students; Dir Eng. Gonçalo J. P. Antunes Barradas.

Escola Superior de Educação (ESE): Praça da República. Apdo 125, 7300-957 Portalegre; tel. (245) 33-94-00; fax (245) 20-46-19; e-mail esep@mail.esep.ipportalegre.pt; internet www.esep.pt; f. 1985; 72 teachers; 671 students; Pres. Dr Carlos Brandão; Librarian Dr Domingos Bucho; publ. *Aprender*.

Escola Superior de Saúde de Portalegre: Av. de Santo António, Apdo 89, 7301-901 Portalegre; tel. (24) 530-04-30; fax (24) 530-04-39; e-mail geral@essp.pt; internet www.essp.pt; Pres. Prof. Francisco Alberto Mourato Vidinha.

Escola Superior de Tecnologia e Gestão (ESTG): Lugar do Abadessa, Apdo 148, 7301-901 Portalegre; tel. (24) 530-02-00; fax (24) 530-02-30; e-mail estg@estgp.pt; internet baco.estgp.pt; 45 teachers; 695 students; Pres. Artur Jorge Romão; Librarian Bac. Catarina Elias Barradas.

Instituto Politécnico de Santarém: Complexo Andaluz, Apdo 279, 2001-904 Santarém; tel. (24) 330-95-20; fax (24) 330-95-38; e-mail relacoes.publicas@ipsantarem.pt; internet www.ipsantarem.pt; f. 1979; colleges of agriculture, education, management, sport, health; Social Services; library: 38,900 vols; 270 teachers; 3,936 students; Pres. Prof. J. A. Guerra Justino; Vice-Pres. Maria Teresa Pereira Serrano; Vice-Pres. Hélder Orlando Cardoso Pereira.

Instituto Politécnico de Setúbal: Largo Defensores da República 1, 2910-470 Setúbal; tel. (26) 554-88-20; fax (26) 523-11-10; e-mail ips@spr.ips.pt; internet www.ips.pt; f. 1981; 5 colleges: Escola Superior de Tecnologia de Setúbal, Escola Superior de Educação, Escola Superior de Ciências Empresariais, Escola Superior de Tecnologia do Barreiro, Escola Superior de Saúde; courses in education, management and technology; Pres. Prof. Dr Armando Pires.

Instituto Politécnico de Viana do Castelo (Viana do Castelo Polytechnic Institute): Praça General Barbosa, 4900-347 Viana do Castelo; tel. (25) 880-96-10; fax (25) 882-90-65; e-mail dmoreira@ipvc.pt; internet www.ipvc.pt; f. 1980; 5 schools offering undergraduate and postgraduate degree courses; teacher-training college, agricultural college, schools of technology and management, nursing, business studies; Pres. Prof. Rui Teixeira.

Instituto Politécnico de Viseu (Polytechnic Institute of Viseu): Av. José Maria Vale de Andrade, 3504-510 Viseu; tel. (23) 248-07-00; fax (23) 248-07-50; e-mail ipv@pres.ipv.pt; internet www.ipv.pt; f. 1979; Schools of education, technology, agrarian, technology and management, health, welfare services; higher training in teacher training, media studies, cultural studies, social service, sports, multimedia, engineering, management, marketing, tourism, agrarian sciences, nursing; 400 teachers; 7,000 students; Dir Eng. Fernando Lopes Rodrigues Sebastião; publs *Forum Media* (2 a year), *Millenium* (4 a year).

Instituto Superior Bissaya Barreto: Campus do Conhecimento e da Cidadania, Apdo 7049, 3046-901 Coimbra; tel. (23) 980-04-50; fax (23) 980-04-95; e-mail isbb@isbb.pt; internet www.isbb.pt; f. 1927; law and public admin.; Dir Prof. Dr Maria Luísa Ferreira Cabral dos Santos Veiga; Pres. Prof. Dr Rui Nogueira Lobo Alarcão e Silva.

Instituto Superior de Ciências da Saúde-Norte (Institute of Health Sciences-North): Coop. de Ensino Superior, Politécnico e Universitário, CRL R. Central de Gandra 1317, 4585-116 Gandra Prd; tel. (22) 415-71-00; fax (22) 415-71-02; e-mail info@cespu.pt; internet www.cespu.pt; f. 1984, present name 1993, present location 1995; attached to Cooperative Education, Polytechnic and University (CESPU); higher education in health related courses; 380 profs; Dir Prof. Dr Jorge Proença.

Instituto Superior de Ciências do Trabalho e da Empresa (Higher Institute of Labour and Enterprise): Avda das Forças Armadas, 1649-026 Lisbon; tel. (21) 790-30-00; fax (21) 796-47-10; e-mail geral@iscte.pt; internet iscte.pt; f. 1972; offers Bachelors, Masters and Doctoral courses in management, social, and technological sciences; library: 56,000 vols, 17,000 periodicals; 400 teachers; 6,000 students; Dir Luís Antero Reto; publ. *Portuguese Journal of Social Science*.

Instituto Superior de Línguas e Administração (ISLA): Quinta do Bom Nome, Estrada da Correia 53, 1500-210 Lisbon; tel. (21) 030-99-08; fax (21) 030-99-17; e-mail jose.inacio@lx.isla.pt; internet www.isla.pt; f. 1962; business management, marketing, human resources, computer science for management, applied mathematics, translation, tourism, secretarial studies; library: 20,000 vols; 260 teachers; 3,000 students; Dir Prof. Dr Tawfiq Rkibi; publ. *Revista Portuguesa de Management*.

Instituto Superior Politécnico Portucalense: Rua do Paço 3, 4560 Penafiel; tel. (25) 571-10-54; fax (25) 571-10-53; f. 1990; courses in local govt admin., accounting, management, computer studies; library: 5,000 vols; 73 teachers; 620 students; Dir Dr Joaquim M. Silva Cunha.

School of Art

Escola Superior Artística do Porto (Art School of Porto): Largo de S. Domingos 80, 4050-545 Porto; tel. (22) 339-21-30; fax (22) 339-21-39; e-mail geral@esap.pt; internet www.esap.pt; f. 1982; 130 teachers; 780 students; Pres. Alexandra Trevisan da Siveira Pacheco.

Escola Superior de Belas-Artes (Higher School of Fine Arts): Av. Rodrigues de Freitas 265, 4049-021 Porto; tel. (22) 519-24-00; fax (22) 536-70-36; e-mail directivo@fba.up.pt; internet www.fba.up.pt; f. 1836, present name and status 1994; attached to Univ. of Porto; design, painting, sculpture, art sciences, drawing, geometry; library: 13,300 vols, 11,000 slides, 160 audiovisual titles, 50 electronic documents, antique book colln; Pres. Prof. José Vaz; Vice-Pres. Heitor Alvelos.

Escola Universitária das Artes de Coimbra (Coimbra University School of Arts): Campus Universitário da ARCA, Lordemão, 3020-244 Coimbra; tel. (23) 949-74-00; fax (23) 983-85-33; e-mail info@arca.pt; internet www.arca.pt; f. 1989, present location 1996; offers Bachelors and Masters degrees in architecture, art and design; Sec. Paula Fonseca.

QATAR

The Higher Education System

Qatar was part of the Ottoman Turkish Empire until 1916 when it came under British protection. British control was extended in 1934 and in 1971 independence was achieved. The traditional education system was based on Koranic and Shari'a (Islamic law) studies, but in 1973 the largely secular College of Education was founded and it became the University of Qatar in 1977. The University consists of six Colleges and degrees are approved by the United Kingdom Quality Assurance Agency. In 2006/07 8,088 students enrolled as undergraduates and 96 as postgraduates. Education City Qatar, the Qatar Foundation for Education, Science and Community Development's flagship project which opened in 2003, hosts branch campuses of five US universities and numerous other educational and research institutions. A Science and Technology Park, designed to establish Qatar as a regional hub for research and development, was officially opened at Education City in 2009.

Admission to undergraduate courses at the University of Qatar is based upon results achieved in the General Secondary Certificate (Al-Thanawaya Al-Amah) examinations. Students are admitted to the University before their applications are considered by the Colleges. Degrees are awarded on a 'credit' basis, and students are required to accumulate a specified number of credits before graduating, depending on the degree applied for. There are mandatory Foundation courses for students in engineering, science, economics and administration, consisting of English, mathematics and IT training. The foremost undergraduate degree is the Bachelors, and the main postgraduate courses are the Postgraduate Diplomas and Certificates, Masters and PhDs. Postgraduate Certificate and Diploma courses are between two and five semesters in duration and are available in education, library science and architectural planning. Masters degree courses last one year and students are required to maintain a specified grade point average. Doctoral degrees (mainly PhD) are not yet widespread.

The main post-secondary qualification for technical and vocational education is the Diploma in Technology, available from Colleges of Technology.

Regulatory Bodies

GOVERNMENT

Ministry of Education: POB 80, Al-Waqf Tower, Dafna, Doha; tel. 1111494; fax 1445494; e-mail e.alhorr@moe.edu.qa; internet www.moe.edu.qa; Minister Sheikha BINT AHMAD AL-MAHMOUD.

NATIONAL BODY

Qatar Museums Authority: POB 2777, Doha; tel. 4525555; fax 4525556; e-mail info@qma.com.qa; internet www.qma.com.qa; coordinating body for nat. museums, incl. Qatar National Museum, Museum of Islamic Art; spec. collns of Orientalist art, Islamic coins, natural history, antique weapons; Chief Exec. Officer ABDULLAH AL-NAJJAR; Exec. Dir Dr ROGER MANDLE.

Learned Societies

GENERAL

UNESCO Office Doha: 66 Lusail St, West Bay, POB 3945, Doha; tel. 4113293; fax 4113015; e-mail doha@unesco.org; internet www.unesco.org/doha; designated Cluster Office for Bahrain, Kuwait, Oman, Qatar, Saudi Arabia and United Arab Emirates; Dir HAMED AL-HAMMAMI.

EDUCATION

Qatar Foundation: POB 5825, Doha; tel. 4540000; fax 4806117; e-mail info@qf.org.qa; internet www.qf.org.qa; education, scientific research and community development; responsible for Education City project; f. 1995; Pres. Dr MOHAMMAD FATHY SAOUD.

LANGUAGE AND LITERATURE

British Council: 93 Al-Sadd St, POB 2992 Doha; tel. 4251888; fax 4423315; e-mail general.enquiries@qa.britishcouncil.org; internet www.britishcouncil.org/me-qatar.htm; offers courses and examinations in English language and British culture and promotes cultural exchange with the UK.

Research Institutes

ECONOMICS, LAW AND POLITICS

Center for International and Regional Studies: POB 23689, Doha; tel. 4578400; fax 4578401; internet cirs.georgetown.edu; attached to School of Foreign Service in Qatar; research into regional and int. issues; Dir MEHRAN KAMRAVA.

RAND-Qatar Policy Institute: POB 23644, Doha; tel. 4927400; fax 4927410; e-mail rand-qatarpolicyinstitute@rand.org; internet www.rand.org/qatar; Private control, attached to RAND Corporation and Qatar Foundation; analysis into public policy; Dir RICHARD E. DARILEK.

HISTORY, GEOGRAPHY AND ARCHAEOLOGY

Gulf Cooperation Council Folklore Centre: POB 7996, Doha; tel. 4861999; fax 4867170; f. 1982 to collect, study, disseminate and protect indigenous local folklore mainly in the fields of literature, customs and traditions, music and dance, arts and crafts; mem. states: Bahrain, Kuwait, Oman, Qatar, Saudi Arabia, UAE; library of 4,853 vols, 110 journals, also video cassettes, cassette recordings and photographic material; Dir-Gen. ABDULRAHMAN AL-MANNAI; publ. *Al Ma'thurat Al Sha'biyyah* (4 a year).

MEDICINE

Doha International Institute for Family Studies and Development: POB 34080, Doha; tel. 4548200; fax 4548249; e-mail diifsd@qf.org.qa; internet www.fsd.org.qa; attached to Qatar Foundation; research and scholarship on the legal, sociological, and scientific basis of the family as the natural and fundamental group unit of society; f. 2004.

Libraries and Archives

Doha

College of the North Atlantic-Qatar Campus Library System: POB 24449, Doha; tel. 4952051; e-mail reference@cna-qatar.edu.qa; internet www.cna-qatar.com/library; incl. Al-Rayyan Library spec. colln of Pre-nursing, Health Sciences, English Language Learning; Dir PATRICIA SUTHERLAND.

Qatar National Library: POB 205, Doha; tel. 4429955; fax 4429976; e-mail qanaly@qatar.net.qa; f. 1962; 218,600 vols in Arabic, 33,800 vols in English, 1,300 Arabic MSS, 454 on microfilm, 1,288 periodicals on microfilm and 10,248 on microfiche, bibliographic services on subjects of local interest; 5 brs; Dir ABDULLA NASSER AL-ANSARI.

Qatar University Library: POB 2713, Doha; tel. 4852406; fax 4835092; e-mail library@qu.edu.qa; internet www.qu.edu.qa/library; f. 1973.

Research and Documents Division: POB 923, Amir's Office, Doha; tel. 4425497; fax 4310518; f. 2003; Dir Dr SULTAN JASIM AL-JABER.

Museums and Art Galleries

Doha

Museum of Islamic Art: POB 2777, Doha; tel. 4224444; e-mail infomia@qma.com.qa; internet www.mia.org.qa; attached to Qatar Museums Authority; Early Islamic Art, Iran and Central Asia (12th–19th century), Egypt and Syria (12th–15th century), Turkey (16th–18th century), India (16th–18th century).

Qatar National Museum: Doha; tel. 4442911; e-mail qnm2000@hotmail.com; internet www.qnm.8m.com; attached to Qatar Museums Authority; opened 1975; consists of 5 major sections: the old Amiri Palace (nine 19th-century buildings), the new palace, aquarium, lagoon, botanical garden; collns: ethnography, archaeo-history, geology, botany, zoology, jewellery, numismatics, perfumery; Dir IBRAHIM JABER AL-JABER.

Universities

CARNEGIE MELLON QATAR

POB 24866 Doha
Telephone: 4548400
Fax: 4548410
E-mail: ug-admission@qatar.cmu.edu
Internet: www.qatar.cmu.edu
Founded 2004; attached to Carnegie Mellon Univ., Pittsburgh, USA and the Qatar Foundation
Private control
Dean: Dr CHUCK THORPE
Librarian: NIKKI KRYSAK
Business and Computer Science.

NORTHWESTERN UNIVERSITY IN QATAR

POB 34102 Doha
Telephone: 4545100
E-mail: nu-qadmissions@northwestern.edu
Internet: www.qatar.northwestern.edu
Founded 2004; attached to Northwestern Univ., Illinois, USA and the Qatar Foundation
Private control
Dean: JOHN D. MARGOLIS
Schools of Communication and Journalism.

STENDEN UNIVERSITY QATAR

POB 36037 Doha
Telephone: 4888116
E-mail: info@chn.edu.qa
Internet: www.stenden.com/en/stenden/locations/qatar; attached to Stenden Univ., Netherlands
International Hospitality Management, Tourism Management, International Business and Management Studies.

TEXAS A&M UNIVERSITY AT QATAR

POB 23874, Doha
Telephone: 4230010
Fax: 4230011
E-mail: info@qatar.tamu.edu
Internet: www.qatar.tamu.edu
Founded 2003; attached to Texas A&M Univ., Texas, USA
Private control
Dean and Chief Exec. Officer: Dr MARK H. WEICHOLD
Librarian: CAROLE THOMPSON
Library of 3,900,000 vols, 90 periodicals
Number of students: 300
Chemical Engineering, Electrical and Computer Engineering, Mechanical Engineering, Petroleum Engineering.

UNIVERSITY OF QATAR

POB 2713, Doha
Telephone: 4852222
Fax: 4835043
E-mail: info@qu.edu.qa
Internet: www.qu.edu.qa
Founded 1973 as College of Education, Univ. status 1977
State control
Language of instruction: Arabic
Academic year: September to June
Chair.: HH Sheikh TAMIN BIN HAMAD AL THANI (Heir Apparent)
Pres.: Prof. Dr SHEIKHA ABDULLAH AL-MISNAD
Vice-Pres. and Chief Financial Officer: Dr HUMAID ABDULLAH AL-MIDFAA
Vice-Pres. and Chief Academic Officer: Dr SHEIKHA JABOR AL-THANI
Vice-Pres. for Student Affairs: Dr OMAR MOHAMED AL-ANSARI
Vice-Pres. for Research: Dr HASSAN AL-DERHAM
Vice-Pres. for Institutional Planning and Devt: Prof. SAIF SAID AL-SOWAIDI
Library Dir: TAG ELSIR IBRAHIM S. KARDAMAN
Library of 360,000 vols (Arabic and English), 1,040 periodicals
Number of teachers: 705
Number of students: 7,245
Publication: *Fruits of Knowledge* (1 a year)

DEANS

College of Arts and Science: Dr SIHAM AL-QARADAWI
College of Business and Economics: Prof. Dr MUHAMMAD K. NAJDAWI (acting)
College of Education: Prof. Dr HESSA AL-SADIQ
College of Engineering: Dr MAZEN HASNAH
College of Law: Dr HASSEN ABDULRAHIM AL-SAYED
College of Pharmacy: Prof. Dr PETER JEWESSON
College of Shari'a Law and Islamic Studies: Dr AISHA YOUSIF AL-MANNAI

ATTACHED INSTITUTES

Computer Centre: Dir Dr JIHAD MUHAMMAD AL-JAAM.

Documentation and Humanities Research Centre: colln, classification and preparation of documents pertaining to the field of humanities as a basic source of research, and the issuing of documented research papers; specialized research on the heritage of the Gulf area in all its aspects: social, cultural, linguistic and literary; Dir Dr SAIF AL-MEREIKHI.

Educational Research Centre: educational research and studies that contribute to the devt of education in the State of Qatar, oriented among other things toward improvement of the educational process, curricula and textbooks; Dir Dr NASRA REDA BAGHER.

Educational Technology Centre: Dir Dr JIHAD MOHAMMED AL-JAAM.

Gulf Studies Centre: Dir Dr HASSAN AL-ANSARI.

Scientific and Applied Research Centre: to develop experience in scientific, industrial and agricultural fields with spec. reference to industries, natural resources, agriculture and animal resources of Qatar; and to contribute to the transfer of technology and adapt it for application in Qatar; Dir Dr MOHSIN ABDULLAH AL-ANSI.

Sirra and Sunna Research Centre: research related to the *Sirra* of the Prophet Mohamed, i.e. his preaching, moral and spiritual values, and his life, and the *Sunna* of the Prophet Muhammad, i.e. his sayings and acts, which are the second source of guidance for the practice of Islam after the holy Koran; Dir Prof. YOUSUF AL-QARADAWI.

VIRGINIA COMMONWEALTH UNIVERSITY IN QATAR

Doha
Telephone: 4927200
E-mail: vcuqadmissions@qatar.vcu.edu
Internet: www.qatar.vcu.edu
Founded 2003; attached to Virginia Commonwealth Univ., USA and the Qatar Foundation
Private control
Dean: ALLYSON VANSTONE
Library of 16,000 vols
Bachelor of Fine Arts degree in Fashion Design, Graphic Design or Interior Design.

Colleges

Centre for GIS: POB 22088 Doha; tel. 4955112; fax 4955011; e-mail masoun@gisqatar.org.qa; internet www.gisqatar.org.qa; attached to Urban Planning and Devt Authority; Regional Training Centre for Geospatial Information Systems.

College of the North Atlantic-Qatar: 68 Al-Tarafa, Duhail North, POB 24449, Doha; tel. 4952222; fax 4952200; e-mail info@cna-qatar.edu.qa; internet www.cna-qatar.com; attached to College of the North Atlantic, Canada; f. 2002; 400 teachers; 2,300 students; Technical College offering 4 programmes in Business Studies, Engineering Technology, Health Sciences, Information Technology; Security Academy, Centre for Banking and Financial Studies; Pres. Dr HAROLD JORCH.

Language Teaching Institute: POB 3224, Doha; tel. 4657690; fax 4665465; f. 1972; part-time courses in Arabic, Persian, English, French, for mature students already in employment; library: 6,000 vols; 29 teachers; 504 students; Dir MUHAMMAD HASSAN AL-SIDDIQI.

Qatar Aeronautical College: POB 4050 Doha; tel. 4408888; fax 4357034; e-mail qacadmn@qatar.net.qa; internet www.qac.edu.qa; Dir-Gen. ALI IBRAHIM AL-MALKI; Dir for Academic Affairs Dr SAID ABDULLAH AL-SULEIMAN.

School of Foreign Service in Qatar: POB 23689 Doha; tel. 4578100; fax 4578241; e-mail sfsqadmissions@georgetown.edu; internet qatar.sfs.georgetown.edu; Private control; attached to Georgetown Univ., USA; Dean of Academic Affairs VICTORIA PEDRICK; Dir of Library FRIEDE WIEBE; Dir of Public Affairs CHARLES NAILEN.

Weill Cornell Medical College in Qatar: Doha; tel. 4928402; fax 4928422; e-mail jadmissions@qatar-med.cornell.edu; internet qatar-weill.cornell.edu; Private control; attached to Cornell Univ., Ithaca, NY, USA; Dir JAVAID I. DHEIKH.

ROMANIA

The Higher Education System

Formerly part of the Ottoman Turkish Empire, Romania became an independent kingdom in 1881. In 1947 King Michael was forced to abdicate and the Romanian People's Republic was proclaimed. Romania became a one-party state under the communist Romanian Workers' Party. Communist rule ended in 1989, when the regime of President Ceauşescu was overthrown in a revolution; multi-party democracy was established in 1991. The oldest current institutions of higher education are mostly specialist establishments dating from the first half of the 19th century, among them the Universitatea 'Politehnica' din Bucureşti (founded in 1818), the Academia de Muzică 'Georghe Dima' (founded in 1819), the Universitatea de Ştiinţe Agronomice şi Medicine Veterinara Bucureşti (founded in 1852) and the Universitatea de Medicină şi Farmacia 'Carol Davila' (founded in 1857; current name since 1990). There was an expansion of higher education during the period of reform (1859–66) initiated by Alexander Ioan Cuza, the first elected Domnitor of the United Principalities of Wallachia and Moldova (which later became independent Romania). Current institutions established during that period include the Unversitatea 'Alexandru Ioan Cuza' Iaşi (founded in 1860), the Universitatea de Arte 'George Enescu' (founded in 1860; current name since 1960), the Universitatea Naţională de Muzica din Bucureşti (founded in 1863) and the Universitaea din Bucureşti (founded in 1864). The Ministry of Education and Research is responsible for higher education, which is governed by the Constitution (1991) and the Education Act (1995). Education at public institutions is free. Romania participates in the Bologna Process to establish a European Higher Education Area, the first phase of which is to adopt a credit-based system of comparable degrees with three main cycles (undergraduate, postgraduate and doctoral). In 2006/07 there were 30,583 students enrolled in 104 institutions of higher education.

Admission to higher education is on the basis of the secondary school diploma (Bacalaureat) and success in the university entrance examination. Higher education is divided into short- and long-term courses. Short-term courses consist solely of the three-year Diploma de Absolvire and are offered by university colleges (Colegii Universitare). Long-term higher education consists of undergraduate and postgraduate degrees, principally the undergraduate Bachelors and postgraduate Masters degrees, in accordance with the principles of the Bologna Process. The Bachelors degree (Diploma de Licenta) is a programme of study lasting four to six years, depending on the field of study. Following the Bachelors degree, graduates may study for one or two years for the award of, principally, the Masters degree or Professional Postgraduate Diploma (Diploma de Studii postuniversitare). Finally, the highest university-level degree is the Doctorate (Doktorat), a programme of study lasting three to seven years.

Post-secondary technical and vocational education (scoala postliceala) consists of two- to three-year training courses at three levels of specialization.

The academic year in Romania usually runs from October until June (the exact date varies from one university—or even one faculty—to another). It is divided into two semesters of approximately 14 weeks each. An examination period of about four weeks follows each semester. The first semester lasts from October until mid-February, with the examination period starting after the Christmas holiday (beginning of January). The second semester (or the Spring semester) starts at the beginning of March. It includes the Easter holiday and a four-week examination session in May–June. Some faculties organize practical activities with compulsory attendance at the end of the second semester. There is also a re-examination period, in September, for students who did not pass their examinations during the previous academic year.

Since 2006 the Agenţia Română de Asigurare a Calităţii în Învăţământul Superior (ARACIS—Romanian Agency for Quality Assurance in Higher Education) has been in charge of university accreditation. ARACIS is a full member of the European Association for Quality Assurance in Higher Education. Accreditation is a two-stage process. The first step is trust licensing, which gives institutions the right to organize admission examinations. The second step is accreditation, which gives institutions the right to administer degree examinations and issue diplomas (degrees) recognized by the Ministry of Education, Research, Youth and Sport.

Regulatory and Representative Bodies

GOVERNMENT

Ministry of Culture and National Heritage: Şos. Kiseleff 30, 011374 Bucharest 1; tel. (21) 224-46-65; fax (21) 222-83-20; e-mail ministru@cultura.ro; internet www.cultura.ro; Minister HUNOR KELEMEN; Sec.-Gen. MIRCEA CRISTIAN STAICU.

Ministry of Education, Research, Youth and Sport: Str. Gen. Berthelot 28–30, Sector 1, 010168 Bucharest; tel. (21) 405-62-00; fax (21) 312-47-19; internet www.edu.ro; Minister DANIEL FUNERIU; Sec.-Gen. GHEORGHE ASĂNICĂ.

ACCREDITATION

Agenţia Română de Asigurare a Calităţii în Învăţământul Superior (ARACIS) (Romanian Agency for Quality Assurance in Higher Education): Str. Spiru Haret 12, 010176 Bucharest; tel. (21) 206-76-00; fax (21) 312-71-35; e-mail mail@aracis.ro; internet www.aracis.ro; f. 2006; draws up procedures and sets accreditation standards for the assessment of different types of programmes and higher education providers, and submits them to the Ministry of Education, Research, Youth and Sport for approval; carries out assessments and submits accreditation reports to the Ministry; draws up and reviews the nat. reference standards and the performance indicators to assess and assure the quality of higher education; devises and promotes policies and strategies to improve the quality of education in Romania; 17 mems; Pres. Prof. Dr IOAN CURTU; Gen. Sec. Prof. Dr MIHAI ARISTOTEL UNGUREANU.

ENIC/NARIC Romania: Nat. Centre for Recognition and Equivalence of Diplomas Granted Abroad, Str. Gen. Berthelot 28–30, Sector 1, 010168 Bucharest; tel. (21) 405-63-22; fax (21) 313-10-13; e-mail cornelmun@yahoo.com; internet www.cnred.edu.ro; Dir CORNELIU MUNTEANU.

NATIONAL BODY

Romanian Council of Rectors: Splaiul Independenţei 313, 060042 Bucharest; tel. (21) 402-91-00; fax (21) 318-10-01; e-mail e_andronescu@rectorat.pub.ro; internet www.upb.ro; Rector Prof. ECATERINA ANDRONESCU.

Learned Societies

GENERAL

Academia Română (Romanian Academy): Calea Victoriei 125, 010071 Bucharest; tel. (21) 212-86-40; fax (21) 211-66-08; e-mail solunca@acad.ro; internet www.acad.ro; f. 1866; sections of Philology and Literature (Chair. EUGEN SIMION), Historical and Archaeology Sciences (Chair. ALEXANDRU ZUB), Mathematical Sciences (Chair. ROMULUS CRISTESCU), Physical Sciences (Chair. HORIA SCUTARU), Chemical Sciences (Chair. MARIUS ANDRUH), Biological Sciences (Chair. MAYA SIMIONESCU), Geonomical Sciences (Chair. MIRCEA SĂNDULESCU), Technical Sciences (Chair. GLEB DRĂGAN), Agricultural Sciences and Forestry (Chair. CRISTIAN HERA), Medical Sciences (Chair. LAURENŢIU POPESCU), Economics, Legal Sciences and Sociology (Chair. MUGUR ISĂRESCU), Philosophical, Theological, Psychological and Pedagogical Science (Chair. ALEXANDRU SURDU), Arts, Architecture and Audiovisual (Chair. MIHNEA GHEORGHIU), Information Science and Technology (Chair. MIHAI DRĂGĂNESCU); 181 mems; attached research institutes: see Research Institutes; library: see Libraries and Archives; Pres. IONEL HAIDUC; Vice Pres. DAN BERINDEI; Sec.-Gen. PĂUN ION OTIMAN; publs *Annuaire Roumain d'Anthropologie*, *Anuar de lingvistică şi istorie literară* (Yearbook of Linguistics and Literary History), *Buletinul Societăţii Numismatice Române* (1 a year), *Cahiers de linguistique théorique et appliquée*, *Calitatea vieţii* (Quality of Life), *Cellulose Chemistry and Technology*, *Cercetări de lingvistică* (Linguistic Researches), *Fonetică şi dialectologie* (Phonetics and Dialectology), *Functional and Architectural Electronics*, *Historia Urbana*, *Limba română* (The Romanian Language), *Mathematica*, *Nyelv- és Irodalomtudományi Közlemények*, *Ocrotirea naturii şi a mediului înconjurător* (The Protection of Nature and of the Environment), *Revista de etnografie şi folclor* (Journal of Ethnography and Folklore), *Revista de psihologie* (Journal of Psychology), *Revista română de demografie* (Romanian Journal of Demography), *Revue d'analyse numérique et de théorie de l'approximation*, *Revue des études sud-est européennes*, *Revue Roumaine de biochimie*, *Revue Roumaine de biologie: Série de biologie animale*, *Revue Roumaine de biologie: Série de biologie végétale*, *Revue Roumaine de chimie*, *Revue Roumaine de géologie, géophysique et géographie* (3 series), *Revue Roumaine de Linguistique*, *Revue Roumaine de mathématiques pures et appliquées*, *Revue Roumaine de philosophie*, *Revue Roumaine de psychologie*, *Revue Roumaine des sciences économiques*, *Revue Roumaine des sciences juridiques*, *Revue Roumaine des sciences techniques: Série de mécanique appliquée*, *Revue Roumaine des sciences techniques: Série électrotechnique et énergétique*, *Romanian Astronomical Journal*, *Romanian Chemical Quarterly Review*, *Romanian Journal of Biophysics*, *Romanian Journal of Sociology*, *Romanian Neurosurgery*, *Romanian Reports of Physics*, *Studii şi cercetări de antropologie* (Studies and Research in Anthropology), *Studii şi cercetări de biochimie* (Studies and Research in Biochemistry), *Studii şi cercetări de biologie: Seria biologie animală* (Studies and Research in Biology: Series of Animal Biology), *Studii şi cercetări de biologie: Seria biologie vegetală* (Studies and Research in Biology: Series of Plant Biology), *Studii şi cercetări de geologie, geofizică şi geografie* (Studies and Research in Geology, Geophysics and Geography, 3 series), *Studii şi cercetări lingvistice* (Studies and Research in Linguistics), *Studii şi cercetări de mecanică aplicată* (Studies and Research in Applied Mechanics), *Studii şi cercetări matematice* (Studies and Research in Mathematics), *Synthesis–Bulletin du Comité National de Littérature comparée*, *Travaux de l'Institut de Spéléologie 'Emile Racovitza'*.

Asociaţia Culturală 'Pro Basarabia şi Bucovina' (Bessarabia and Bucovina Cultural Association): Str. Blănari 23, Sector 3, Bucharest; tel. and fax (21) 314-03-59; e-mail probasarabiasibucovina@yahoo.com; internet www.probasarabia.ro; f. 1990; 60,000 mems; Pres. ION RADU; publ. *Dor E Basarabia*.

Centrul European de Cultură, Bucureşti (European Cultural Centre, Bucharest): Sfinţii Voievozi St 49–51, 4th Fl., Apt. 16, Sector 3, 010965 Bucharest; tel. (21) 650-81-45; fax (21) 650-32-80; e-mail cti@clicknet.ro; internet www.studyabroad.ro; f. 1990; organizes int. postgraduate seminars on European issues; promotes Romania as an attractive cultural tourist destination, through research, publs and study tours; promotes colleges and univs in Western Europe, the USA, Canada and Australia, which offer int. programmes related to undergraduate and postgraduate studies in Romania; 1,300 mems; library of 3,000 vols, 40 periodicals; Pres. Acad. DAN BERINDEI; Exec. Dir MARIA BURS-POPESCU.

Institutul Cultural Român (Romanian Cultural Institute): Aleea Alexandru 38, 011824 Bucharest; tel. (31) 710-06-27; fax (31) 710-06-07; e-mail icr@icr.ro; internet www.icr.ro; f. 2003; promotes Romanian culture abroad; publishes works by Romanian and foreign authors, dictionaries, history texts and other literature; 130 mems; Pres. HORIA-ROMAN PATAPIEVICI; publs *Contrafort* (12 a year), *Curierul Românesc* (12 a year), *Destin Românesc* (4 a year), *Dilema* (48 a year), *Euresis* (4 a year), *Glasul Bucovinei* (4 a year), *Lettres internationales* (4 a year), *Plural* (2 a year), *România Culturală* (online), *Transylvanian Review* (4 a year).

Societatea Cultural-Ştiinţifică 'Getica' (Getica Cultural Scientific Society): POB 37-149, 70060 Bucharest 37; Str. Plantelor 8–10, 023974 Bucharest; tel. (21) 318-47-57; e-mail contact.gandirea@yahoo.com; internet www.gandirea.ro; f. 1990; 87 mems; library of 7,000 vols; Pres. GABRIEL GHEORGHE; publ. *Getica* (irregular).

AGRICULTURE, FISHERIES AND VETERINARY SCIENCE

Academia de Ştiinţe Agricole şi Silvice 'Gheorghe Ionescu-Şişeşti' (Academy of Agricultural and Forestry Sciences 'Gheorghe Ionescu-Şişeşti'): Bdul Mărăşti 61, 011464 Bucharest 1; tel. (21) 318-44-54; fax (21) 318-44-55; e-mail secretariat@asas.ro; internet www.asas.ro; f. 1969; sections of Soil Science, Land Reclamation and Environmental Protection in Agriculture, Field Crops, Horticulture, Animal Husbandry, Veterinary Medicine, Forestry Science, Agrarian Economics and Rural Development, Food Industry, Agricultural Mechanization; 311 mems (81 full and corresp., 40 hon., 90 assoc.); attached research institutes: see Research Institutes; library: see Libraries and Archives; Pres. Prof. Dr GHEORGHE SIN; Sec. Gen. Prof. Dr MARIAN IANCULESCU; publs *Buletinul informativ al Academiei de Ştiinţe Agricole şi Silvice* (1 a year), *Bulletin de l'Académie des Sciences Agricoles et Forestières* (1 a year), *Bulletin of the Academy of Agricultural and Forestry Sciences* (1 a year), *Yearbook* (1 a year).

Asociaţia Economiştilor Agrarieni din România (Agrarian Economists Association of Romania): Bdul Mărăşti 61, 011464 Bucharest; tel. (21) 617-21-80; f. 1990; 42 mems; library of 4,000 vols; Pres. Prof. N. N. CONSTANTINESCU; Gen. Sec. RADU COTIANU.

Societatea Inginerilor Agronomi (Agronomists Society): Bdul Mărăşti 59, 011464 Bucharest; tel. (21) 618-22-30; f. 1990; 3,500 mems; Pres. Prof. Dr MIHAI VÂJIALĂ; Gen. Sec. Dr RUXANDRA CIOFU.

Societatea Naţională Română pentru Ştiinţa Solului (Romanian National Soil Science Society): Bdul Mărăşti 61, 011646 Bucharest; tel. (21) 318-43-49; fax (21) 318-43-48; e-mail mdumitru@icpa.ro; f. 1962; 494 mems; library of 3,592 vols; Pres. Dr MIHAIL DUMITRU; Gen. Sec. CONSTANTIN CRĂCIUN; publs *Bulletin Informativ* (1 a year), *Ştiinţa Solului* (2 a year).

Societatea Română de Zootehnie (Romanian Society of Animal Production): Bdul Mărăşti 59, 011464 Bucharest; tel. (21) 618-22-30; fax (21) 312-56-93; f. 1990; 4,500 mems; Pres. Prof. STEFAN POPESCU-VIFOR; Sr Sec. Dr AGATHA POPESCU.

ARCHITECTURE AND TOWN PLANNING

Uniunea Arhitecţilor din România (Union of Architects of Romania): Str. Dem Dobrescu 5, 010014 Bucharest; tel. and fax (21) 315-60-73; e-mail ma@com.pcnet.ro; internet www.uniuneaarhitectilor.ro; f. 1891; 2,010 mems; library of 13,000 vols; Pres. Arch. PETER DERER; publs *Architectura* (4 a year), *Buletin Informativ* (12 a year).

ECONOMICS, LAW AND POLITICS

Asociaţia de Drept Internaţional şi Relaţii Internaţionale (Association of International Law and International Relations): Şoseaua Kiseleff 47, 011314 Bucharest; tel. (21) 222-44-22; fax (21) 222-74-62; f. 1965; 500 mems; library of 8,000 vols; Pres. CORNELIU MĂNESCU; Sec.-Gen. MIRCEA MALIŢA.

Asociaţia Română de Drept Umanitar (Romanian Association of Humanitarian Law): Piaţa Haralambie Botescu 11–13, 050892 Bucharest; tel. and fax (21) 311-99-19; e-mail ardu.association@gmail.com; internet www.ardu.ro; f. 1990; 200 mems; library of 5,000 vols; Pres. Dr IONEL CLOŞCĂ; Gen. Sec. GHEORGHE BĂDESCU; publ. *Revista română de drept umanitar*.

FINE AND PERFORMING ARTS

Asociaţia Artiştilor Fotografi din Romania (Art Photographers Association): Piaţa Unirii, 2–4, Oradea; e-mail office@aafr.ro; internet www.aafr.ro; f. 1956; 1,615 mems; library of 12,000 photographic magazines; Pres. ŞTEFAN TÓTH; publs *Foto Magazin* (online), *Fotografia şi Video* (6 a year).

Asociaţia Artiştilor Plastici—Bucureşti (Artists Association of Bucharest): Str. Nicolae Balcescu 18, 021051 Bucharest; tel. (21) 613-38-60; f. 1973; 1,800 mems; Pres. Dr Eng. IOAN CEZAR CORÂCI; Gen. Sec. DAN SEGĂRCEANU.

Uniunea Artiştilor Plastici din România (Romanian Union of Fine Arts): Bdul Nicolae Balcescu, 1, 010433 Bucharest; tel. (21) 212-79-54; fax (21) 212-79-58; e-mail office@uappr.ro; internet www.uappr.ro; f. 1972; 4,170 mems; library of 12,000 vols; Pres. Prof. Dr DUMITRU SERBAN; publs *Arta* (art review, 4 a year), *Info* (12 a year).

Uniunea Cineaştilor din România (Romanian Film Makers Union): Str. Mendeleev 28–30, 010365 Bucharest; tel. (21) 316-80-84; fax (21) 311-12-46; e-mail czucin@ucin.ro; internet www.ucin.ro; f. 1963; 900 mems; Pres. MIHNEA GHEORGHIU; Vice Pres. CONSTANTIN PIVNICIERU; Sec. CARMEN ZAMFIRESCU.

Uniunea Compozitorilor şi Muzicologilor din România—Asociatia Pentru Drepturi De Autor (Composers and Musicologists Union of Romania): Calea Victoriei 141, 010071 Bucharest; tel. (21) 316-79-76; fax (21) 316-58-80; e-mail ada@ucmr-ada.ro; internet www.ucmr-ada.ro; f. 1920; 432 mems; library of 50,000 vols incl. spec. colln of Romanian music (printed scores and MSS); Dir Gen. ANA ACHIM; Sec. CARMEN RADULESCU; publs *Muzica* (4 a year), *Actualitatea Muzicală* (24 a year).

Uniunea Teatrală din România (Romanian Association of Theatre Artists): Str. George Enescu 2–4, 010306 Bucharest; tel. (21) 311-32-14; fax (21) 312-09-13; internet www.uniter.ro; f. 1990; 900 mems; Pres. ION CARAMITRU; publs *Semnal teatral* (Theatre Signal, 4 a year), *Anuarul teatrului românesc* (Romanian Theatre Yearbook).

HISTORY, GEOGRAPHY AND ARCHAEOLOGY

Comitetul Naţional al Istoricilor (National Committee for Historical Sciences): Calea Victoriei 125, 010071 Bucharest; tel. (21) 212-86-29; fax (21) 312-02-09; f. 1955; Pres DAN BERINDEI; Sec.-Gen. CONSTANTIN BUŞE; publ. *Nouvelles d'études d'histoire* (irregular).

Federaţia Filatelică Română (Romanian Philatelic Federation): Str. Boteanu 6, POB 1-29, 010027 Bucharest; tel. (21) 313-89-21; fax (21) 310-40-04; e-mail federatia_filatelica@yahoo.com; internet www.federatia-filatelica.ro; f. 1891; 25,000 mems; library of 3,000 vols; Pres. LEONARD PASCANU; Sec.-Gen. SERGIU GABUREAC; publ. *Filatelia* (12 a year).

Societatea de Ştiinţe Geografice din România (Society of Geographical Sciences of Romania): Bdul Bălcescu 1, 010041 Bucharest; tel. (21) 614-93-50; f. 1875; 5,000 mems; library of 4,000 vols; Exec. Pres. POSEA GRIGORE; publs *Terra*, *Bulletin*.

Societatea de Ştiinţe Istorice din România (Society of Historical Sciences of Romania): Bd Regina Elisabeta 4–12, 030018 Bucharest; tel. (21) 313-13-29; fax (21) 321-05-35; e-mail ssi_r@yahoo.com; internet www.societateistorie.ro; f. 1949; 5,000 mems; Chair. Prof. Dr NICHITA ADĂNILOAIE; Pres. Prof. Dr IOAN SCURTU; Sec.-Gen Prof. Dr BOGDAN TEODORESCU; publ. *Studii şi articole de istorie* (1 a year).

Societatea Numismatică Română (Romanian Numismatic Society): Str. Popa Tatu 20, 010805 Bucharest; tel. (21) 642-26-02; f. 1903; 3,000 mems; library of 4,010 vols; Pres. Dr CONSTANTIN PREDA; Sec.-Gen. AURICĂ SMARANDA; publ. *Buletinul* (1 a year).

LANGUAGE AND LITERATURE

Alliance Française: Str. Emile Zola 6, 011847 Bucharest; tel. (21) 231-05-15; fax (21) 231-05-19; e-mail thierry.dumas@diplomatie.fr; offers courses and examinations in French language and culture and promotes cultural exchange with France; attached offices in Braşov, Constanţa, Craiova, Medgidia, Piteşti and Ploieşti.

British Council: Calea Dorobantilor 14, 010572 Bucharest; tel. (21) 307-96-00; fax (21) 307-90-01; e-mail contact@britishcouncil.ro; internet www.britishcouncil.org/romania.htm; teaching centre; offers courses and examinations in English language and British culture and promotes cultural exchange with the UK; attached offices in Brasov, Cluj, Iaşi, and Timişoara; library of 16,000 vols; Dir LILIANA BIGLOU; Teaching Centre Man. DIANA BERLINSCHI.

Goethe-Institut: Str. Tudor Arghezi 8–10, 020945 Bucharest; tel. (21) 311-97-62; fax (21) 312-05-85; e-mail info@bukarest.goethe.org; internet www.goethe.de/ins/ro/buk/deindex.htm; offers courses and examinations in German language and culture and promotes cultural exchange with Germany; also responsible for Goethe-Institut work in Moldova; library in Chisinau; library of 12,000 vols; Dir BEATE KÖHLER.

Instituto Cervantes: Str. Marin Serghiescu 12, 021016 Bucharest; tel. (21) 210-27-37; fax (21) 210-77-67; e-mail cenbuc@cervantes.es; internet bucarest.cervantes.es; offers courses and examinations in Spanish language and culture and promotes cultural exchange with Spain and Spanish-speaking Latin and Central America; library of 20,000 vols; Dir JUAN CARLOS VIDAL GARCÍA.

Institut Français: Bdul Dacia 77, 020051 Bucharest; tel. (21) 316-38-36; fax (21) 316-02-25; e-mail denis.soriot@culture-france.ro; internet www.institut-francais.ro; f. 1936; library of 35,000 vols; Dir DENIS SORIOT; Sec.-Gen. STÉPHANE BERGEOT.

PEN Club: Str. Transilvaniei 56, 010799 Bucharest; tel. (21) 312-58-54; fax (21) 311-11-12; f. 1924, re-f. 1990; 50 mems; Pres. ANA BLANDIANA; Sec. DENISA COMANESCU.

Societatea Română de Lingvistică (Romanian Society of Linguistics): Calea 13 Septembrie 13, 050711 Bucharest; tel. (21) 641-27-57; f. 1941; Pres. Prof. EMANUEL VASILIU; Sec. LAURENŢIU THEBAN.

Societatea Română de Lingvistică Romanică (Romanian Society of Romance Linguistics): Str. Edgar Quinet 7, 010017 Bucharest; f. 1962; 250 mems; library of 2,000 vols; Pres. Dr MARIUS SALA; Gen. Sec. SANDA REINHEIMER RÎPEANU; publ. *Bulletin* (irregular).

Uniunea Scriitorilor din România (Romanian Writers' Union): Calea Victoriei 115, 010071 Bucharest; tel. (21) 316-58-29; fax (21) 312-96-34; e-mail w_u_ro@yahoo.com; internet www.uniuneascriitorilor.ro; f. 1949; 2,400 mems; Pres. NICOLAE MANOLESCU; Dir. Gen. ALEXANDRU ISTRATE; publs *Apostrof*, *Caiete Critice*, *Contrapunct*, *Convorbiri literare* (1 a year), *Helikon*, *Lato*, *Luceafărul*, *Memoria*, *Orizont*, *Ramûri*, *România Literară*, *Secolul 20*, *Vatra*, *Viaţa Românească*.

MEDICINE

Academia de Ştiinţe Medicale (Academy of Medical Sciences): Splaiul Independenţei 99–101, 061621 Bucharest; tel. (21) 311-53-80; fax (21) 311-53-81; e-mail adsm@adsm.ro; internet www.adsm.ro; f. 1935; sections of Fundamental Biomedical Sciences (Pres. Dr NICOLAE MANOLESCU), Internal Medicine (Pres. CONSTANTIN I. POPA), Surgey Clinic (Pres. Prof. Dr IRINEL POPESCU); attached research institutes: see Research Institutes; 82 mems, 14 corresp. mems; Pres. Prof. Dr LAURENTIU POPESCU; Sec.-Gen. Prof. Dr MIHAIL ZAMFIRESCU.

Asociaţia Medicală Română (Romanian Medical Association): Str. Ionel Perlea 10, 010209 Bucharest; tel. and fax (21) 314-10-71; e-mail amr@medica.ro; f. 1873; 38 affiliated socs; Pres. Prof. Dr VALERIU POPESCU; Sec.-Gen. Prof. Dr EMANOIL POPESCU; publs *Buletin A.M.R.* (4 a year), *Despre MÆDICA—a Journal of Clinical Medicine* (4 a year), *Practica Medicala* (4 a year), *Revista Medicala Romana* (4 a year), *Revista Romana de Boli Infectioase* (4 a year), *Revista Romana de Neurologie* (4 a year), *Revista Romana de Pediatrie* (4 a year), *Revista Romana de Reumatologie* (4 a year), *Revista Romana de Stomatologie* (4 a year).

Societatea de Medici şi Naturalişti Iaşi (Society of Physicians and Naturalists in Iaşi): Bdul Independenţei 16, POB 25, 700098 Iaşi; tel. (232) 14-29-80; f. 1830; medicine, pharmacy, dentistry; 1,640 mems; Chair. Prof. ION HĂULICĂ; publ. *Revista Medico-Chirurgicală* (multilingual, English abstracts, 4 a year).

Societatea Română de Stomatologie (Romanian Society of Stomatology): Str. Ionel Perlea 10, 70754 Bucharest; tel. (21) 314-20-80; fax (21) 312-13-57; f. 1923; Pres. Prof. Dr EMILIAN HUTU; Sec. Dr MARION VLADIMIR CONSTANTINESCU; publ. *Stomatologia* (4 a year).

NATURAL SCIENCES

General

Asociaţia Oamenilor de Ştiinţă din România (Academy of Romanian Scientists): Splaiul Independenţei 54, 050094 Bucharest; tel. (21) 314-74-91; fax (21) 314-75-39; e-mail aosromania@yahoo.com; internet www.aos.ro; f. 1956; Pres. Prof. Dr VASILE CÂNDEA; Scientific Sec.-Gen. Prof. Dr DORU-SABIN DELION.

Biological Sciences

Societatea de Ştiinţe Biologice din România (Society of Biological Sciences of Romania): Intrarea Portocalelor 1–3, 060101 Bucharest; f. 1949; 9,000 mems; library of 6,100 vols; Chair. Prof. Dr ION ANGHEL; Sec.-Gen. Dr CONSTANTIN VOICA; publ. *Natura* (4 a year).

Mathematical Sciences

Societatea de Ştiinţe Matematice din România (Romanian Mathematical Society): Str. Academiei 14, 010014 Bucharest; tel. (21) 314-46-53; fax (21) 312-40-72; e-mail office@rms.unibuc.ro; internet www.rms.unibuc.ro; f. 1895; 5,000 mems; Pres. RADU GOLOGAN; Vice-Pres. DORU STEFANESCU; publs *Bulletin Mathématique de la Societe des Sciences Mathematiques de Roumanie* (4 a year), *Gazeta Matematică Seria A, Revista de cultura matematica* (4 a year), *Gazeta Matematică Seria B, Revista de cultura matematica pentru tineret* (12 a year).

Physical Sciences

Societatea Geologică a României (Geological Society of Romania): Str. Caransebeş, 012271 Bucharest; internet www.geosociety.ro; f. 1930; 500 mems; Pres. Dr ANTONETA SEGHEDI; Gen. Sec. TITUS BRUSTUR; publ. *Buletinul* (1 a year).

RELIGION, SOCIOLOGY AND ANTHROPOLOGY

Asociaţia Slaviştilor din România (Slav Studies Association of Romania): Str. Pitar Moş 7–13, 010451 Bucharest; tel. (21) 318-1579; fax (21) 211-9940; e-mail kgeambasu@yahoo.com; internet www.unibuc.ro; f. 1956; promotes comparative Romanian-Slav studies at univ. level, in the fields of culture and civilization, of linguistics, literature, history, anthropology, ethnology, theory and practice of translation; promotes research in the Bulgarian, Croatian, Czech, Polish, Russian, Serbian, Slovakian, Slovenian, Ukrainian languages and literatures; library of 46 vols; 150 mems; Pres. Prof. Dr CONSTANTIN GEAMBAŞU; Vice-Pres. Dr MARIANA MANGIULEA; Vice-Pres. Prof. Dr ANTOANETA OLTEANU; Sec. Dr ANDREEA DUNAEVA; publ. *Romanoslavica* (1 a year).

Institutul Biblic şi de Misiune al Bisericii Ortodoxe Române (Biblical and Missionary Institute of the Romanian Orthodox Church): Intrarea Miron Cristea 6, 040162 Bucharest; tel. (21) 406-71-94; fax (21) 300-05-53; e-mail tipogr.inst.biblic@rdslink.ro; internet www.editurapatriarhiei.ro; f. 1925; publishes the synodal Romanian versions of the Holy Scripture, liturgical books, patristic texts, handbooks and treatises for Romanian theological schools, contemporary Orthodox literature; 14 mems; Dir. AURELIAN MARINESCU; Sec. Fr EUGEN MORARU; publs *Biserica Ortodoxa Româna* (4 a year), *Ortodoxia* (2 a year).

Societatea de Etnologie din România (Ethnology Society of Romania): Str. Zalomit 12, 010151 Bucharest; tel. and fax (21) 311-03-23; e-mail rica_org@yahoo.com; f. 1990; 200 mems; library; Pres. Dr. GEORGE ANCA; Sec. ION MOANŢA; publs *Etnologie românească* (4 a year), *Liber* (4 a year), *Trivium* (4 a year), *School of Indology* (4 a year).

TECHNOLOGY

Asociaţia Generală a Inginerilor din România (General Association of Engineers of Romania): Calea Victoriei 118, 70179 Bucharest; tel. (21) 316-89-94; fax (21) 312-55-31; e-mail office@agir.ro; internet www.agir.ro; f. 1881; 16,300 mems; library of 32,000 vols; Pres. Prof. Dr Ing. MIHAI MIHĂIŢĂ; publs *Univers Ingineresc* (24 a year), *Buletinul Tehnic AGIR* (4 a year), *Anuarul AGIR* (1 a year).

Research Institutes

AGRICULTURE, FISHERIES AND VETERINARY SCIENCE

Aquaproiect, SA: Spl. Independenţei 294, 060031 Bucharest; tel. (21) 316-00-35; fax (21) 316-00-42; e-mail office@aquaproiect.ro; internet www.aquaproiect.ro; f. 1953; design and consulting in environmental engineering and water management; library of 10,000 vols; Technical Dir Dipl. Eng. GHEORGHE BRĂTIANU.

Centrul de Cercetăre-Dezvoltare pentru Cultura Plantelor pe Nisipuri (Central Research Station for Plant Cultivation on Sand): Jud. Dăbuleni, 207220 Dolj; tel. (251) 33-44-02; fax (251) 33-43-47; e-mail ccdcpndabuleni@yahoo.com; f. 1959; attached to Acad. of Agricultural and Forestry Sciences; 111 mems; library of 14,315 vols; Dir-Gen. Dr Eng. AURELIA DIACONU; publ. *Anales* (1 a year).

Centrul Naţional de Geodezie, Cartografie, Fotogrammetrie şi Teledecţie (National Centre of Geodesy, Cartography, Photogrammetry and Remote-Sensing): Bdul Expoziţiei 1A, 012101 Bucharest; tel. (21) 224-42-84; fax (21) 224-19-96; e-mail cngcft@ancpi.ro; internet www.cngcft.ro; f. 1958; library of 6,000 vols; Dir ILEANA SPIROU; publs *Analele CNGCFT* (1 a year), *Buletinul de Fotogrammetrie şi Teledetecţie*, *Revistei de Geodezie*.

Institutul de Cercetări şi Amenajări Silvice (Forest Research and Management Institute): Eroilor Blvd. 128, 077190 Voluntari/Ilfou; tel. (21) 350-32-38; fax (21) 350-32-45; e-mail icas@icas.ro; internet www.icas.ro; f. 1933; attached to Acad. of Agricultural and Forestry Sciences; library of 32,000 vols; Man. GHEORGHE DUMITRIU; Man. HEINRICH FLORENTINA; Sec. VIOLETA TIRON; publs *Analele Ilas*, *Bucovina Forestiera*.

Institutul de Cercetări Dezvoltare pentru Legumicultură şi Floricultură (Research and Development Institute for Vegetable and Flower Growing): Judeţul Ilfov, 077185 Vidra; tel. and fax (21) 361-20-94; e-mail inclf@mediasat.ro; internet www.icdlfvidra.ro; f. 1967; attached to Acad. of Agricultural and Forestry Sciences; research into plant breeding and seed production, soil science, plant protection and flower-growing; library of 500 vols; Dir Dr MARCEL COSTACHE; publ. *Annals*.

Institutul de Cercetări pentru Cereale şi Plante Tehnice (Research Institute for Cereals and Industrial Crops): Judeţul Fundulea, 915200 Călăraşi; tel. (242) 311-07-22; fax (242) 311-07-22; f. 1957; attached to Acad. of Agricultural and Forestry Sciences; library of 12,000 vols; Dir GHEORGHE SIN; publs *Analele* (1 a year), *Probleme de genetică teoretică şi aplicată*, *Probleme de agrofitotehnie teoretică şi aplicată*, *Probleme de protecţia plantelor* (4 a year), *Romanian Agricultural Research* (every 2 years).

Institutul Naţional de Cercetare-Dezvoltare pentru Pedologie, Agrochimie şi Protecţia Mediului—ICPA Bucureşti (National Research and Development Institute for Soil Science, Agrochemistry and Environment Protection—ICPA Bucharest): Bdul Mărăşti 61, 71331 Bucharest; tel. (21) 318-44-63; fax (21) 318-43-48; e-mail office@icpa.ro; internet www.icpa.ro; f. 1970; attached to Acad. of Agricultural and Forestry Sciences; characterization and quantification of natural resources and environment; inventorying and monitoring natural resources and environment; plant nutrition and soil/plant fertilization; sustainable management of natural resources and environment, soil pollution, global change, rural devt; waste management; standards and methodologies on natural resources and environment; soil/land/environment data computing, agricultural/environment information services; library of 9,000 vols; Dir Dr Ing. MIHAIL DUMITRU; Scientific Dir Dr CATALIN SIMOTA; publ. *Anale* (1 a year).

Institutul de Cercetări pentru Viticultură şi Vinificaţie (Research Institute for Viticulture and Wine-Making): Str. Valea Mantei 1, Judeţul Valea Călugărească, 107620 Prahova; tel. (244) 23-66-90; fax (244) 23-63-89; e-mail icvv@xnet.ro; f. 1967; Man Dr Eng. NICOLAE VARGA; attached to Acad. of Agricultural and Forestry Sciences; library of 14,000 vols; publ. *Anale* (research papers).

Institutul de Cercetare-Dezvoltare pentru Apicultură (Research and Development Institute for Beekeeping): Bdul Ficusului 42, 013975 Bucharest; tel. (21) 232-50-60; fax (21) 232-02-87; e-mail secretariat@icdapicultura.ro; f. 1974; attached to Acad. of Agricultural and Forestry Sciences; researches on biology honeybees, beekeeping technologies, melliferous flora and pollination, honeybee pathologies, apitherapy; genetic fund conservation program; production of veterinary medicines for honeybees; production of food supplements and medicines based on bee products; library of 11,300 vols, 4,400 periodicals; Gen. Dir Dr CRISTINA MATEESCU; publ. *România apicolă* (12 a year).

Institutul de Cercetare-Dezvoltare pentru Cultura şi Industrializarea Sfeclei de Zahăr şi Substanţelor Dulci (Research and Development Institute for the Cultivation and Processing of Sugar Beet and Sweet Substances): Judeţul Călarasi, 915200 Fundulea; tel. and fax (242) 64-24-23; f. 1981; attached to Acad. of Agricultural and Forestry Sciences; Dir Dr Ing. AURELIAN POPA; publs *Scientific Works—Beet and Sugar* (1 a year), *Health of Plants* (1–3 a year), *Cereal and Technical Plants* (1–3 a year), *Agricultural Papers* (1–4 a year).

Institutul de Cercetare—Dezvoltare pentru Protecţia Plantelor (Research and Development Institute for Plant Protection): Bdul Ion Ionescu de la Brad 8, Sector 1, 013813 Bucharest; tel. (21) 269-32-34; fax (21) 269-32-39; e-mail secretariat_stiintific@icdpp.ro; internet icdpp.ro; f. 1967; attached to Acad. of Agricultural and Forestry Science; draws up new technologies to increase food chain safety incl. means and methods of biological protection against pathogen attack to accomplish sustainable devt objectives in agriculture and to complete and carry out ecological agriculture systems; application of nat. and int. strategies for research activity in plant protection; devt and improvement of rapid diagnosis techniques for pathogens; eco-toxicology studies and research works necessary to register plant protection products in accordance with EU acquis; library of 9,000 vols; Dir and Gen. Man. Prof. Dr HORIA ILIESCU; publs *Anale ICDPP* (1 a year), *Romanian Journal for Plant Protection* (4 a year).

Institutul de Cercetare şi Dezvoltare pentru Bovine (Institute for Bovine Research and Development): Sect. Agricol Ilfov, 077015 Baloteşti; tel. (21) 266-12-02; fax (21) 266-12-06; e-mail icpcb@k.ro; f. 1970; attached to Acad. of Agricultural and Forestry Sciences; library of 11,000 vols; Dir Dr Ing. IOAN CUREU; publs *Taurine—Scientific Works* (1 a year), *Presentation* (every 5 years).

Institutul de Cercetare şi Dezvoltare pentru Valorificarea Produselor Horticole (Institute of Research and Development for Marketing Horticultural Products): Intrarea Binelui 1A, POB 1-93, 042146 Bucharest; tel. (21) 312-90-37; fax (21) 330-36-85; f. 1967; attached to Acad. of Agricultural and Forestry Sciences; library of 3,575 vols; Dir Dr Eng. ANDREI GHERGHI; publs *Lucrări ştiinţifice* (1 a year), *Horticultura* (12 a year).

Institutul de Cercetare şi Inginerie Tehnologică pentru Irigaţii şi Drenaje (Research and Technological Engineering Institute for Irrigation and Drainage): Judeţul Giurgiu, 087010 Băneasa; tel. (246) 28-50-23; fax (246) 28-50-24; e-mail scdid@easynet.ro; f. 1977; attached to Acad. of Agricultural and Forestry Sciences; library of 5,700 vols, 763 periodicals; Dir Dr Ing. GHEORGHE CRUTU; publ. *Scientific Papers on Irrigation and Drainage* (1 a year).

Institutul de Cercetare şi Producţie pentru Creşterea Ovinelor şi Caprinelor (Research and Production Institute for Sheep and Goat Breeding): Str. I. C. Brătianu 248, Judeţul Constanţa Palas, 900316 Constanţa; tel. and fax (241) 63-95-06; e-mail icdcoc@relsys.ro; f. 1897; attached to Acad. of Agricultural and Forestry Sciences; Dir Ing. RADU RĂDUCU.

Institutul de Cercetare şi Producţie pentru Creşterea Păsărilor şi Animalelor Mici (Research and Production Institute for Poultry and Small Animal Breeding): Sect. Agricol Ilfov, 077015 Baloteşti; fax (21) 795-10-23; f. 1970; attached to Acad. of Agricultural and Forestry Sciences; Dir Ing. GRIGORE MUSCALU.

Institutul de Cercetare şi Producţie pentru Cultura Pajiştilor (Grassland Research and Production Institute): Str. Cucului 5, 500128 Braşov; tel. (268) 47-27-81; fax (268) 47-52-95; f. 1969; attached to Acad. of Agricultural and Forestry Sciences; library of 7,000 vols; Dir-Gen. Dr MARUSCA TEODOR; publ. *Lucrări ştiinţifice* (1 a year).

Institutul de Cercetare Dezvoltare pentru Ecologie Acvatica, Pescuit si Acvacultura (Research and Development Institute for Aquatic Ecology, Fishing and Aquaculture): Str. Portului 54, 800211 Galaţi; tel. (236) 41-69-14; fax (236) 41-42-70; e-mail icdeapa@icdeapa.ro; internet www.icdeapa.ro; f. 1981; attached to Acad. of Agricultural and Forestry Sciences; fundamental and applied research, studies for environmental licences, evaluation in aquaculture and fishing, consulting, technical assistance; Dir Prof. Univ. NECULAI PATRICHE; Scientific Sec. MARILENA TALPES.

Institutul de Cercetare Dezvoltare pentru Pomicultura (Fruit-Growing Research Institute): Mărăcineni, Str. Mărului 402, 117450 Argeş; tel. (248) 27-80-66; fax (248) 27-84-77; e-mail office@icdp-pitesti.ro; internet www.icdp.ro; f. 1967; attached to Acad. of Agricultural and Forestry Sciences; 10 experimental fruit stations; research areas incl. breeding studies, biotechnology, pest control and virology; 33 mems; library of 25,000 vols; Dir Gen. COMAN MIHAIL; publ. *Lucrările Ştiinţifice ale Institutul de Cercetare Dezvoltare pentru Pomicultura* (1 a year).

Institutul de Chimie Alimentară (Research Institute for Food Chemistry): Str. Gârlei 1, 013721 Bucharest; tel. (21) 230-50-90; fax (21) 230-03-11; e-mail ica@sunu.rnc.ro; f. 1950; attached to Acad. of Agricultural and Forestry Sciences; library of 25,000 vols; Dir Prof. Dr GHEORGHE MENCINICOPSCHI; publ. *Ştiinţe şi Tehnologii Alimentare* (Food Sciences and Technology, 4 a year).

Institutul Naţional de Cercetare—Dezvoltare Marină 'Grigore Antipa' (National Institute for Marine Research and Development 'Grigore Antipa'): Bdul Mamaia 300, POB 3, 900001 Constanţa; tel. (41) 54-32-88; fax (41) 83-12-74; e-mail office@alpha.rmri.ro; internet www.rmri.ro; f. 1970; attached to Min. of Water, Forests and Environmental Protection; library of 38,000 vols and periodicals; Dir Dr Ing. SIMION NICOLAEV; Scientific Dir Dr ALEXANDRU S. BOLOGA; publ. *Cercetări Marine* (1 a year).

Institutul Naţional de Cercetare Dezvoltare pentru Cartof si Sfeclă de Zahar (Research and Development Institute for Potato and Sugar Beet): Str. Fundăturii 2, 500470 Braşov; tel. (268) 47-67-95; fax (268) 47-66-08; e-mail icpc@potato.ro; internet www.potato.ro; f. 1967; attached to Acad. of Agricultural and Forestry Sciences, Bucharest; 55 mems; library of 10,000 vols; Gen. Dir Dr SORIN CHIRU; Scientific Dir Dr VICTOR DONESCU; publs *Anale* (scientific papers, 1 a year), *Cartoful în România* (The Potato in Romania, 4 a year), *Tehnologie* (1 a year).

Institutul Naţional de Medicină Veterinară Pasteur (Pasteur National Institute of Veterinary Medicine): Calea Giuleşti 333, 77826 Bucharest; tel. (21) 220-64-86; fax (21) 220-69-15; f. 1909; attached to Acad. of Agricultural and Forestry Sciences; library of 30,000 vols; Dir Dr C. ŞTIRBU; publ. *Studies and Research in Veterinary Medicine* (1 a year).

Institutul Naţional de Cercetări-Dezvoltare pentru Protectia Mediului (National Institute for Research and Development of Environmental Protection): Splaiul Independenţei 294, 060031 Bucharest; tel. (21) 318-20-57; fax (21) 318-20-01; e-mail icim@icim.ro; internet www.icim.ro; f. 1952; library of 5,000 vols; Dir Gen. Prof. Dr NECULAI MIHAILESCU.

Institutul Naţional de Cercetare-Dezvoltare pentru Biologie şi Nutriţie Animala (National Research Development Institute for Animal Biology and Nutrition): Judet Ilfov, 077015 Baloteşti; tel. (21) 351-20-81; fax (21) 351-20-80; e-mail secretariat@ibna.ro; internet www.ibna.ro; f. 1970; attached to Acad. of Agricultural and Forestry Sciences; library of 5,000 vols; Gen. Man. Prof. Dr HORIA GROSU; Dir of Science Dr CATALIN DRAGOMIR; publs *Anale* (1 a year), *Archiva Zootechnica* (in English, 4 a year).

Societatea Comerciala Romsuintest Periş SA (Trade Society Romsuintest Periş SA): Judeţul Ilfov, 077150 Periş; tel. (21) 796-07-05; fax (21) 796-07-01; f. 1970; attached to Acad. of Agricultural and Forestry Sciences; research into pig-breeding; library of 8,000 vols; Dir Dr ŞTEFAN MANTEA; publ. *Lucrări ştiinţifice* (Scientific Work, 1 a year).

Centrul de Cercetare—Dezvotare pentru Combaterea Eroziunii Solului Perieni (Research and Development Centre for Soil Erosion Control Perieni): Perieni, 737405 Judetul Vaslui; tel. and fax (235) 55-01-55; e-mail office@cesperieni.ro; internet cesperieni.ro; f. 1954; attached to Acad. of Agricultural and Forestry Sciences, Bucharest; study on soil erosion by means of standard runoff check plots, determinations of optimal doses of fertilizers, establishing species and mixtures of perennial herbs necessary to rehabilitate deteriorated pastures, experimental studies on forestal shelter belts, research on soil erosion control by agrotechnical methods (conservation agriculture), studies on types of crop rotation on sloping land, establishing crops range (sorts) on sloping land, chemical weed control, water balance on agricultural land deteriorated by gullies and/or landslides; Dir Dr DUMITRU NISTOR.

Staţiunea Centrală de Cercetări pentru Cultura şi Industrializarea Tutunului (Central Research Station for Tobacco Growing and Industrialization): Str. Gârlei 1, 013721 Bucharest; tel. (21) 230-45-75; fax (21) 230-51-58; f. 1929; attached to Acad. of Agricultural and Forestry Sciences; Dir MARIANA TIGĂU; publ. *Buletinul tutunului* (1 a year).

Staţiunea de Cercetăre-Dezvoltare Agricola Brăila (Brăila Agricultural Research and Development Station): Şoseaua Vizirului km. 9, Judeţul Brăila, 810008 Brăila; tel. (239) 68-46-95; fax (239) 68-47-44; f. 1954; attached to Acad. of Agricultural and Forestry Sciences; 12 mems; Dir Dr Ing. MARCEL BULARDA; Scientific Sec. Dr Ing. VISINESCU IOAN; publ. *Scientific Works* (1 a year).

ARCHITECTURE AND TOWN PLANNING

Centrul pentru Noi Arhitecturei Electronice (Centre for New Electronic Architecture): Bdul Armata Poporului 1–3, Bucharest; tel. (21) 631-78-00; attached to Romanian Acad.; Dir ŞTEFAN GHEORGHE.

Prodomus SA—Institut de Studii şi Proiectare pentru Construcţii Civile (Institute of Research and Design for Civil Engineering Works): Str. Nicolae Filipescu 53–55, 020961 Bucharest; tel. (21) 211-78-40; f. 1949; housing, social bldgs; Dir Eng. CORNELIU VELICU; publs *Prodomus—SA*, *'bdi'* (bulletin of documentation and information).

Proed SA—Institut de Studii şi Proiectare pentru Lucrări Tehnico-Edilitare (Studies and Design Institute for Public Works): Str. Tudor Arghezi 21, 020943 Bucharest; tel. (21) 211-55-10; fax (21) 210-18-01, f. 1949; water, sewerage and other public facilities, traffic organization and public transport; Man. Dir Gen. CONSTANTIN HOTULETE; publ. *'bdi'* (bulletin of documentation and information, 4 a year).

ECONOMICS, LAW AND POLITICS

Institutul 'Gheorghe Zane' de Cercetări Economice şi Sociale (Gheorghe Zane Institute for Economic Research): Str. Theodor Codrescu 2, 700481 Iaşi; tel. and fax (332) 10-65-07; e-mail magdalena_lazar15@yahoo.com; internet www.ices.ro; f. 1992; attached to Romanian Acad.; library of 40,000 vols; Dir Prof. TEODOR DIMA; publs *Anuarul de Cercetări Economice*, *Anuarul Idei şi Valori Perene*, *Symposion*.

Institutul de Cercetări Juridice 'Acad. Andrei Rădulescu' (Institute of Judicial Research of the Academy Andrei Rădulescu): Calea 13 Septembrie 13, Sector 5, 050711 Bucharest; tel. (21) 318-81-30; fax (21) 318-24-53; e-mail icj_juridic@yahoo.com; internet www.icj.ro; f. 1954; attached to Romanian Acad.; research in all branches of law; library of 7,120 vols, 2,210 periodicals; Pres. Prof. EMIL GHEORGHE MOROIANU; Sec. Dr BOGDAN PĂTRAŞCU; publ. *Studii de Drept Românesc* (4 a year).

Institutul Naţional de Cercetări Economice 'Costin C. Kiritescu' (National Institute of Economic Research 'Costin C. Kiritescu'): Calea 13 Septembrie 13, 050711 Bucharest; tel. and fax (21) 318-81-06; e-mail ciumara@zappmobile.ro; internet www.ince.ro; f. 1990; attached to Romanian Acad.; Dir-Gen. Prof. Dr MIRCEA CIUMARA; Dirs-Gen. Adjunct Prof. Dr CONSTANTIN CIUTACU, Prof. Dr NAPOLEON POP, Prof. Dr VALERIU IOAN-FRANCE; Scientific Sec. Dr LUMINITA CHIVU; publs *Analele INCE* (4 a year), *Probleme economice* (47 a year), *Româna de Economie* (2 a year), *Romanian Economic Research Observer* (6 a year), *Romanian Economic Review* (2 a year), *Studii şi cercetări economice* (12 a year).

Attached Institutes:

Centrul de Cercetări Financiare şi Monetare 'Victor Slăvescu' (Centre of Financial and Monetary Research 'Victor Slăvescu'):tel. and fax (21) 318-24-19; e-mail icfm01@icfm.ro; internet www.icfm.ro; f. 1967 as Centrul de Finanţe, Preţuri şi Probleme Valutare 'Victor Slăvescu', present name and status 2001; attached to Romanian Acad.; library of 700 vols; Dir Dr NAPOLEON POP; publ. *Studii Financiare* (Financial Studies, 4 a year).

Centrul de Economia Industriei şi a Serviciilor (Centre for the Industrial and Service Economy):tel. and fax (21) 318-24-18; e-mail office@iei.ro; internet www.iei.ro; f. 1977; attached to Romanian Acad.; Dir Dr MIHAI-SABIN MUSCALU; Dir Adjunct Dr MARIUS BULEARCA; publs *Probleme economice* (Economic Problems, 47 a year), *Revista de Economie Industriala* (1 a year).

Centrul Român de Economie Comparată şi Consens:tel. (21) 411-60-75; fax (21) 411-54-86; internet www.ince.ro/ecc.htm; f. 1999; attached to Romanian Acad.; Dir TUDOREL POSTOLACHE.

Institutul de Economie Mondială 'Costin Murgescu' (Institute of World Economy 'Costin Murgescu'):; tel. (21) 318-24-60; fax (21) 318-24-54; e-mail office@iem.ro; internet www.iem.ro; f. 1967; attached to Romanian Acad.; library of 21,500 vols, 320 periodicals, World Bank depository library; Dir Dr CONSTANTIN CIUPEGEA; Scientific Sec Dr VIRGINIA CÎMPEAN; publs *Conjunctura economiei mondiale* (1 a year), *Evoluţia preţurilor internaţionale* (2 a year), *Piaţa internaţională* (96 a year), *Buletin de preţuri şi cotaţii pe piaţa internaţională* (144 a year), *Eurolex* (4 a year), *Euroinfo* (2 a year).

Institutul de Economie Naţională (Institute of National Economy):tel. and fax (21) 318-24-67; e-mail office@ien.ro; internet www.ien.ro; f. 1953 as Institute for Economic Research of the Romanian Academy, present status 1990; attached to Romanian Acad.; Dir GHEORGHE ZAMAN; Dir Adjunct CONSTANTIN CIUTACU; publ. *Revista Româna de Economie* (Romanian Economic Review, in English, 2 a year).

Institutul de Prognoză Economică (Institute for Economic Forecasting):tel. and fax (21) 318-81-48; e-mail ipe@ipe.ro; internet www.ipe.ro; f. 1970 as Centre of Planning Studies and Research (attached to State Planning Cttee); reorg. as Institute for Planning and Forecasting (attached to State Planning Cttee and National Institute for Economic Research) 1977; present status 1990; attached to Romanian Acad.; Dir Prof. Dr LUCIAN-LIVIU ALBU; Dir Adjunct Dr MARIOARA IORDAN; publ. *Romanian Journal for Economic Forecasting* (4 a year).

EDUCATION

Institutul de Cercetări pentru Inteligenţă Artificială (Research Institute for

Artificial Intelligence): Calea 13 Septembrie 13, 050711 Bucharest; tel. (21) 318-81-03; fax (21) 318-81-42; e-mail office@racai.ro; internet www.racai.ro; f. 1994 as Centrul de Cercetări Avansate în Învăţarea Automată, Prelucrarea Limbajului Natural şi Modelarea Conceptuală, present name 2002; attached to Romanian Acad.; researches in areas of natural language processing, machine learning, knowledge acquisition, computer-aided instruction, structural-phenomenological modelling; Dir Prof. Dr IOAN DAN TUFIS; Scientific Dir Dr ANGELA IONITA; Hon. Dir GHEORGHE TECUCI.

FINE AND PERFORMING ARTS

Institutul de Arheologie şi Istoria Artei al Academiei Române (Institute of Archaeology and History of Art of the Romanian Academy): Str. M. Kogălniceanu 12–14, 400084 Cluj-Napoca; tel. (264) 59-11-25; fax (264) 59-44-70; e-mail iaiacluj@yahoo.com; internet www.institutarheologie-istoriaarteicj.ro; f. 1990; attached to Romanian Acad.; library of 20,874 vols; Dir Dr MARIUS PORUMB; Dir Adjunct Dr CORIOLAN OPREAN; publs *Ephemeris Napocensis* (1 a year), *Ars Transsilvaniae* (1 a year).

Institutul de Istoria Artei 'G. Oprescu' (G. Oprescu Institute of the History): 196 Calea Victoriei, Sector 1, 010098 Bucharest; tel. and fax (21) 314-40-70; e-mail istartro@yahoo.com; internet www.istoria-artei.ro; f. 1949; attached to Romanian Acad.; Romanian medieval art, Byzantine art, creative folk, modern art, architecture, theatre, music, cinema; library of 72,000 vols, 108,000 photographs and 21,000 video cliches; Dir Dr ADRIAN-SILVIU IONESCU; Scientific Sec. Dr MARINA SABADOS; publs *Revue Roumaine d'Histoire de l'Art: Série Beaux-Arts* (1 a year with 2 series, on fine arts and on theatre, music and cinema), *Studii şi Cercetări de Istoria Artei: Teatru, Muzică, Cinematografie* (1 a year).

HISTORY, GEOGRAPHY AND ARCHAEOLOGY

Centrul de Istorie şi Civilizaţie Europeană (Centre for History and European Civilization): Aleea M. Sadoveanu 3, parter, 700490 Iaşi; tel. (232) 21-24-41; fax (232) 21-24-41; f. 1992; attached to Romanian Acad.; Dir GHEORGHE BUZATU; publ. *Europa XXI* (every 2 years).

Centrul pentru Studiul Istoriei Evreilor din România (Centre for the Study of the History of Jews in Romania): Str. Mămulari 4, 1st Fl., Apt. 1, 030772 Bucharest; tel. and fax (21) 315-10-45; e-mail csier_fcer@yahoo.com; f. 1977; attached to the Fed. of Jewish Communities in Romania; Dir Dr LIVIU ROTMAN; publ. *Buletinul* (bulletin, 2 a year).

Institutul de Arheologie 'Vasile Pârvan' (Vasile Pârvan Institute of Archaeology): Str. Henri Coandă 11, 010667 Bucharest; tel. and fax (21) 212-88-62; e-mail ionmotzoichicideanu@archaeology.ro; internet www.instarhparvan.ro; f. 1956; attached to Romanian Acad.; library of 200,000 vols; Dir Prof. Dr ALEXANDRU VULPE; publs *Dacia—Revue d'Archéologie et d'Histoire Ancienne* (1 a year), *Materiale şi cercetări arheologice* (1 a year), *Studii şi cercetări de istorie veche* (4 a year), *Studii şi cercetări de numismatică* (every 2 years), *Thraco-Dacica*.

Institutul de Arheologie (Institute of Archaeology): Str. Lascăr Catargi 18, 700107 Iaşi; e-mail vspin@uaic.ro; internet www.arheo.ro; tel. and fax (332) 10-61-73; f. 1990; attached to Romanian Acad.; Dir Prof. Dr VICTOR SPINEI; Asst Dir VIRGIL MIHAILESCU-BÎRLIBA; publs *Arheologia Moldovei* (1 a year), *Bibliotheca Archaeologica Iassiensis* (irregular), *Bibliotheca Archaeologica Moldaviae* (irregular), *Honoraria* (irregular), *Studia Et Acta Historiae Iudaeorum Romaniae*.

Institutul de Geografie (Institute of Geography): Str. Dimitrie Racoviţă 12, 023993 Bucharest; tel. (21) 313-59-90; fax (21) 311-12-42; e-mail geoinst@fx.ro; f. 1944; attached to Romanian Acad.; library of 50,000 vols, 200 periodicals, 1,900 atlases and maps; Dir Prof. DAN BĂLTEANU; publ. *Revista Geografică* (1 a year).

Institutul de Istorie 'A. D. Xenopol' (A. D. Xenopol Institute of History): Str. Lascăr Catargi 15, 700107 Iaşi; tel. and fax (332) 10-61-72; e-mail institut@xenopol.iasi.astral.ro; internet www.academiaromana-is.ro/adxenopol; f. 1941; attached to Romanian Acad.; Romanian and world history; 27 mems; library of 55,000 vols, 900 titles; Dir Prof. Dr GHEORGHE CLIVETI; Dir Adjunct Prof. Dr GHEORGHE CLIVETI; Sec. MIHAELA CAZACU; publs *Anuarul Institutului de Istorie A. D. Xenopol* (1 a year), *Studia et Acta Historiae Iudaeorum Romaniae* (1 a year), *Xenopoliana. Buletinul Fundaţiei Academice A. D. Xenopol* (4 a year).

Institutul de Istorie 'Nicolae Iorga' (Nicolae Iorga Institute of History): Bdul Aviatorilor 1, 011851 Bucharest; tel. (21) 212-53-37; fax (21) 311-03-71; e-mail institutul.iorga@email.ro; internet www.iini.ro; f. 1937; attached to Romanian Acad.; historical research (middle ages to 20th century); library of 130,000 vols; Dir Dr OVIDIU CRISTEA; Scientific Sec. Dr ILEANA CAZAN; publs *Historical Yearbook* (1 a year), *Revista Istorică* (6 a year), *Revue Roumaine d'histoire* (4 a year), *Studii şi Materiale de Istorie Contemporana* (1 a year), *Studii şi Materiale de Istorie Medie* (1 a year), *Studii şi Materiale de Istorie Modernă* (1 a year).

University '1 December 1918' Alba Iulia Systemic Archaeology Institute: Str. Mihai Viteazul 12, 510010 Alba Iulia; tel. (258) 81-70-71; fax (258) 81-84-59; e-mail arhsis@uab.ro; internet www.bcum.uab.ro; f. 2001; attached to Universitatea '1 Decembrie 1918' din Alba Iulia; archaeology; preservation and restoration of archaeological sites; Dir Dr MIHAI GLIGOR.

LANGUAGE AND LITERATURE

Institutul de Filologie Română 'Al. Philippide' (Al. Philippide Institute of Romanian Philology): Str. Theodor Codrescu 2, 700481 Iaşi; tel. and fax (332) 10-65-08; e-mail secretariat_philippide@yahoo.com; internet www.academiaromana-is.ro/philippide; f. 1927; attached to Romanian Acad.; depts of lexicology and lexicography, dialectology, toponymy, literature, ethnology; 41 mems; library of 60,000 vols; Dir Prof. Dr EUGEN MUNTEANU; publs *Anuar de Lingvistică şi Istorie Literară*, *Buletinul* (4 a year), *Philologica Jassyensia* (2 a year).

Institutul de Istorie şi Teorie Literară 'G. Călinescu' (G. Călinescu Institute of Literary History and Theory): Calea 13 Septembrie 13, 050711 Bucharest; tel. and fax (21) 318-81-06 ext. 2023; e-mail instcalinescu@yahoo.com; internet www.institutulcalinescu.ro; f. 1949; attached to Romanian Acad.; library of 15,000 vols; Dir Prof. Dr EUGEN SIMION; publs *Revista de Istorie şi Teorie Literară* (4 a year), *Synthesis* (1 a year).

Institutul de Lingvistica 'Iorgu Iordan–Al. Rosetti' (Iorgu Iordan–Al. Rosetti Institute of Linguistics): Calea 13 Septembrie 13, 050711 Bucharest; tel. and fax (21) 318-24-52; e-mail inst@lingv.ro; internet www.lingv.ro; f. 1949; attached to Romanian Acad.; Dir MARIUS SALA; publs *Fonetică şi Dialectologie* (1 a year), *Limba Română* (6 a year), *Revue Roumaine de Linguistique* (4 a year), *Studii şi Cercetări Lingvistice* (2 a year).

MEDICINE

Centrul de Sănătate Publică (Public Health Centre): Str. Gh. Marinescu 40, 540136 Târgu-Mureş; tel. (265) 21-83-60; fax (265) 21-93-20; e-mail secretariat@cspmures.ro; internet www.cspmures.ro; f. 1956 as Scientific Research Base, present name and status 2001; attached to Acad. of Medical Sciences; library of 12,000 vols; Dir Prof. Dr FRANCISC JESZENSZKY.

Centre for Drug Research: 1 Mai Ave 66, 200638 Craiova; tel. (251) 523929; attached to Universitatea de Medicină şi Farmacie din Craiova.

Centrul Metodologic dc Parodontologie (Paradontology Methodological Centre): Str. 11 Iunie 10, 040172 Bucharest; tel. (21) 641-20-79; f. 1968; library of 326 vols; Dir Dr THEODORA GUŢU.

Institutul de Fonoaudiologie şi Chirurgie Funcţională ORL 'Prof. Dr. D. Hociotă' (Prof. Dr. D. Hociotă Institute of Phono-Audiology and ENT Surgery): Str. Mihai Cioranu 21, 050751 Bucharest; tel. (21) 410-21-70; fax (21) 410-02-78; e-mail secretariat@ifacforl.ro; internet ifacforl.ro; f. 1972 as Centrul Medical de Fonoaudiologie şi Chirurgie Funcţională O.R.L.; attached to Acad. of Medical Sciences; library of 2,000 vols; Man. MARINESCU ANDREEA; Admin. Dir BANGIU MIHAIL-ADRIAN; Finance Dir SUE MIHAELA-CRISTINA; Medical Dir STANESCU RALUCA DANIELA.

Institutul de Endocrinologie 'C.I. Parhon' (C. I. Parhon Institute of Endocrinology): Bdul Aviatorilor 34–36, 011863 Bucharest; tel. (21) 317-20-41; fax (21) 317-06-07; e-mail contact@parhon.ro; internet www.instparhon.ro; f. 1946; attached to Acad. of Medical Sciences; library of 65,800 vols; Man Dr PAUN DIANA LORETA; Dir Medical Dr GRIGORIE DANIEL; Dir Admin. Ing. SIMION MARIETA; publ. *Romanian Journal of Endocrinology* (4 a year).

Institutul de Fiziologie Normală şi Patologică 'D. Danielopolu' (D. Danielopolu Institute of Normal and Pathological Physiology): Bdul Ion Mihalache 11A, 011171 Bucharest; tel. (21) 312-89-38; fax (21) 312-59-37; e-mail ifnp@cmb.ro; f. 1949; attached to Acad. of Medical Sciences; library of 49,000 vols; Dir Prof. Dr GR. BENETATO; publ. *Romanian Journal of Physiology* (4 a year).

Institutul de Medicină Internă 'Nicolae Gh. Lupu' (Nicolae Gh. Lupu Institute of Internal Medicine): Şoseaua Ştefan cel Mare 19–21, 020125 Bucharest; tel. (21) 611-13-70; e-mail cbaicus@clicknet.ro; f. 1949; attached to Acad. of Medical Sciences; library of 72,000 vols; Dir Prof. C. TANASESCU; publ. *Romanian Journal of Internal Medicine* (4 a year).

Institutul de Neurologie şi Psihiatrie (Institute of Neurology and Psychiatry): Şoseaua Berceni 10–12, 041915 Bucharest; tel. (21) 683-78-31; f. 1950; attached to Acad. of Medical Sciences; library of 7,957 vols; Dir Prof. V. VOICULESCU; publ. *Neurologie et Psychiatrie* (series of *Revue Roumaine de Médecine*, 4 a year).

Institutul de Patologie şi Genetică Medicală 'V. Babeş' (V. Babeş Institute of Pathology and Medical Genetics): Splaiul Independenţei 99–101, 050096 Bucharest; tel. (21) 411-51-52; fax (21) 411-51-05; f. 1887; attached to Acad. of Medical Sciences; genetics, immunology, pathology and ultrastructure; library of 20,000 vols; Dir Prof. Dr

L. M. Popescu; publ. *Romanian Journal of Morphology and Embryology* (4 a year).

Institutul de Sănătate Publică (National Institute of Public Health): Str. Dr V. Babeş 14, 700465 Iaşi; tel. (232) 26-18-40; fax (232) 21-03-99; e-mail ispiasi@yahoo.com; internet www.pub-health-iasi.ro; f. 1930; attached to Min. of Health; library of 17,000 vols; Dir Prof. Dr Luminiţa Smaranda Iancu; Dir Adjunct Dr Oana Iacob; publ. *Journal of Preventive Medicine* (4 a year).

Institutul de Sănătate Publică, Bucureşti (Institute of Public Health, Bucharest): Str. Dr Leonte 1–3, 050463 Bucharest; tel. (21) 318-36-20; fax (21) 312-34-26; e-mail directie@ispb.ro; internet ispb.ro; f. 1927; attached to Min. of Health; library of 36,000 vols; separate medical history library of 41,000 vols; Dir Gen. Dr Mihai Marius Dan; publ. *Sănătate şi Prevenţie* (4 a year).

Institutul de Sănătate Publică 'Prof. Dr Iuliu Moldovan' (Prof. Dr Iuliu Moldovan Institute of Public Health): Str. Louis Pasteur 6, 400349 Cluj-Napoca; tel. (264) 59-42-52; fax (264) 59-98-91; e-mail inst@ispcj.ro; internet www.ispcj.ro; f. 1930; monitors public health in 11 Transylvanian counties, provides technical assistance, continuing education, field applied scientific research, public health services; library of 30,150 vols; Dir Prof. Dr Ioan Stelian Bocşan.

Institutul de Sănătate Publică 'Prof. Dr Leonida Georgescu', Timişoara (Prof. Dr Leonida Georgescu Institute of Public Health, Timişoara): Bdul Dr Victor Babeş 16, 300226 Timişoara; tel. and fax (256) 49-21-01; e-mail rox_mol@yahoo.com; internet www.ispt.ro; f. 1946; attached to Acad. of Medical Sciences; library of 14,966 vols; Dir Prof. Dr Roxana Moldovan; publs *Annals of the Institute of Public Health, Timişoara* (1 a year), *Documentary Booklet* (1 a year).

Institutul de Virusologie 'Ştefan S. Nicolau' (IVN) (Ştefan S. Nicolau Institute of Virology): Şoseaua Mihai Bravu 285, 030304 Bucharest; tel. and fax (21) 324-25-90; e-mail ivngripa@b.astral.ro; internet www.virology.ro; f. 1949; attached to Romanian Acad.; WHO Virus Collaborating Centre; research on respiratory viral infections, arboviral infections, viral hepatitis, AIDS; 60 mems; library of 60,000 vols, 200 periodicals; Dir Dr Mihai Stoian; Hon. Dir Dr Costin Cernescu; Scientific Sec. C.N. Zaharia; publs *Proceedings of the Romanian Academy, series B, Science and Life* (in English, 2 a year), *Studii şi Cercetări de Virusologie* (in Romanian, 2 a year).

Institutul Cantacuzino (Cantacuzino Institute): Spl. Independenţei 103, CP 1-525, 050096 Bucharest; tel. (21) 306-91-00; fax (21) 306-93-07; e-mail office@cantacuzino.ro; internet www.cantacuzino.ro; f. 1921; attached to Acad. of Medical Sciences; microbiology, immunology and epidemiology of communicable diseases, biotechnology; library of 119,714 vols; Gen. Dir Dr Radu Iordachel; Sec. Gen. Felicia Mardale; publ. *Romanian Archives of Microbiology and Immunology* (4 a year).

Institutul Naţional de Medicină Legală 'Mina Minovici' (Mina Minovici National Institute for Legal Medicine): Şoseaua Vitan-Bârzeşti 9, 042122 Bucharest; tel. (21) 332-11-56; fax (21) 334-62-60; e-mail danderme@legmed.ro; internet www.legmed.ro; f. 1892; forensic genetics, forensic toxicology, forensic pathology, clinical forensic medicine, forensic psychiatry, forensic anthropology; library of 20,000 vols; Dir Prof. Dr Dan Dermengiu; publ. *Romanian Journal of Legal Medicine* (online at www.rjlm.ro, 4 a year).

Institutul Oncologic 'Al. Trestioreanu' (Al. Trestioreanu Institute of Oncology): Şoseaua Fundeni 252, 022338 Bucharest; tel. (21) 227-1400; fax (21) 318-3262; e-mail secretariat@iob.ro; internet www.iob.ro; f. 1949; attached to Acad. of Medical Sciences; research; teaching; methodology; training of specialized personnel; library of 41,144 vols; Man. Prof. Dr Rodica Anghel; Medical Dir Dr Ileana Condrea; Admin. Dir Elena Iliescu; publ. *Oncologia* (4 a year).

Institutul pentru Controlul de Stat al Medicamentului şi Cercetări Farmaceutice 'Petre Ionescu-Stoian' (Petre Ionescu-Stoian State Institute for Drug Control and Pharmaceutical Research): Str. Aviator Sănătescu 48, 011478 Bucharest; tel. (21) 224-10-79; fax (21) 230-50-83; e-mail dd@ns.icsmcf.ro; f. 1929; Dir Prof. Dr Dumitru Dobrescu; publ. *Farmaco-vigilenţa* (Drug Monitoring, 4 a year).

Research Centre of Gastroenterology and Hepatology: 1 Mai Ave 66, 200638 Craiova; tel. (251) 310287; e-mail ccgh@umfcv.ro; attached to Universitatea de Medicină şi Farmacie din Craiova; Dir Tudorel Ciurea.

Research Centre for Microscopic Morphology and Immunology: Str. Petru Rareş 2, 200349 Craiova; tel. and fax (351) 46-14-58; e-mail cmi@umfcv.ro; internet www.umfcv.ro; attached to Universitatea de Medicină şi Farmacie din Craiova.

NATURAL SCIENCES

Biological Sciences

Institutul de Biochimie (Institute of Biochemistry): Spl Independenţei 296, 060031 Bucharest; tel. (21) 223-90-69; fax (21) 223-90-68; internet www.biochim.ro; f. 1990; attached to Romanian Acad.; research into protein science, particularly the biosynthesis and function of proteins and glycoproteins; 47 mems; Dir Dr Stefana M. Petrescu; publ. *Romanian Journal of Biochemistry* (2 a year).

Institutul de Biologie (Institute of Biology): Splaiul Independenţei 296, 060031 Bucharest; tel. (21) 221-92-02; fax (21) 221-90-71; e-mail biologie@ibiol.ro; internet www.ibiol.ro; f. 1957 as Biological Research Centre, present name and status 1990; attached to Romanian Acad.; library of 200,000 vols; Dir Dr Madalin Enache; Scientific Sec. Dr Zamfir Medana; publ. *Romanian Journal of Biology* (2 a year).

Institutul de Biologie şi Patologie Celulară 'Nicolae Simionescu' (Institute of Cellular Biology and Pathology 'Nicolae Simionescu'): Bogdan Petriceicu Haşdeu 8, POB 35-14, 050568 Bucharest; tel. (21) 319-45-18; fax (21) 319-45-19; internet www.icbp.ro; f. 1979; attached to Romanian Acad.; Dir Maya Simionescu.

Institutul de Cercetări Biologice Cluj-Napoca (Biological Research Institute of Cluj-Napoca): Str. Republicii 48, 400015 Cluj-Napoca; tel. and fax (264) 19-12-38; e-mail icb@mail.dntcj.ro; internet www.icb.dntcj.ro; f. 1958; attached to Institutul Naţional de Cercetare-Dezvoltare pentru Ştiinţe Biologice; biology, biotechnology, plant and animal ecology, molecular taxonomy, physiology; library of 13,019 vols, 25,120 periodicals; Dir Dr Gheorghe Coldea; Scientific Dir Dr M. Keul; Scientific Sec. Dr V. V. Pop; publ. *Contribuţii Botanice* (1 a year).

Institutul de Cercetări Biologice Iaşi (Iaşi Biological Research Institute): Bdul Carol I 20A, 700505 Iaşi; tel. (232) 21-82-03; fax (232) 21-81-21; internet www.icb-iasi.ro; f. 1964 as Institute of General and Applied Biology, present name 1996; attached to Institutul Naţional de Cercetare-Dezvoltare pentru Ştiinţe Biologice; library of 35,000 vols; Dir Dr Alexandru Manoliu.

Institutul de Cercetări Eco-Muzeale Tulcea (Institute of Eco-Museal Research Tulcea): Str. 14 Noiembrie 1, 820009 Tulcea; tel. and fax (240) 51-32-31; e-mail icemtl@icemtl.ro; internet www.icemtl.ro; f. 1950, present status 1993; attached to Tulcea County Council; archaeology, natural history, history, ethnography, art; library of 50,000 vols; Dir Florin George Topoleanu; publ. *Peuce* (1 a year).

Institutul Naţional de Cercetare-Dezvoltare pentru Ştiinţe Biologice (National Institute of Research and Development for Biological Sciences): Splaiul Independentei 296, sector 6, C.P. 17–16, 060031 Bucharest; tel. (21) 220-77-80; fax (21) 220-76-95; e-mail office@dbio.ro; internet www.dbioro.eu; f. 1996; research in the life sciences; devt of organisms in specific environmental conditions, biodiversity and preservation of the nat. geno-fund.

Mathematical Sciences

Institutul de Matematică 'Octav Mayer' (Octav Mayer Institute of Mathematics): Bdul Carol I 8, 700501 Iaşi; tel. and fax (232) 21-11-50; f. 1948; attached to Romanian Acad.; library of 20,000 vols; Dir Viorel Barbu; publ. *Studii şi Cercetări Ştiinţifice.*

Institutul de Matematică 'Simion Stoilow' (Simion Stoilow Institute of Mathematics): POB 1-764, 014700 Bucharest; Str. Calea Grivitei 21, 010702 Bucharest; tel. (21) 319-65-06; fax (21) 319-65-05; e-mail vasile.brinzanescu@imar.ro; internet www.imar.ro; f. 1949, re-f. 1990; 128 mems; attached to Romanian Acad.; library of 35,000 vols, 121,000 journals; Dir Prof. Dr Şerban A. Basarab; publs *Revue Roumaine de Mathématiques Pures et Appliquées* (6 a year), *Mathematical Reports* (4 a year).

Institutul de Statistică Matematică şi Matematică Aplicată 'Gheorghe Mihoc-Caius Iacob' (Gheorghe Mihoc-Caius Iacob Institute of Mathematical Statistics and Applied Mathematics): Calea 13 Septembrie 13, Casa Academiei Române, 050711 Bucharest; tel. (21) 318-24-33; fax (21) 318-24-39; e-mail miosifes@acad.ro; internet www.csm.ro; f. 1964; attached to Romanian Acad.; Dir Marius Iosifescu; publs *Mathematical Reports* (1 a year), *Revue Roumaine de Mathématiques Pures et Appliquées* (Romanian Journal of Pure and Applied Mathematics, 1 a year).

Physical Sciences

Institutul Astronomic (Institute of Astronomy): Str. Cuţitul de Argint 5, 040557 Bucharest; tel. (21) 335-68-92; fax (21) 337-33-89; e-mail vmioc@aira.astro.ro; internet www.astro.ro; f. 1908, re-f. 1990; attached to Romanian Acad.; library of 10,000 vols; Dir Dr Vasile Mioc; Deputy Dir Dr Nedelia Antonia Popescu; publs *Romanian Astronomical Journal* (2 a year), *Anuarul Astronomic* (Astronomical Yearbook, 1 a year).

Institutul de Cercetări Chimice (Institute of Chemical Research): Splaiul Independenţei 202, 060021 Bucharest; tel. (21) 315-32-99; fax (21) 312-34-93; f. 1950; natural and bioactive products, technological engineering, chemical products and technologies; Gen. Man. Sever Şerban.

Institutul de Chimie Fizică 'Ilie Murgulescu' (Ilie Murgulescu Institute of Physical Chemistry): Splaiul Independenţei 202, 060021 Bucharest; tel. (21) 316-79-12; fax (21) 312-11-47; e-mail mpopa@icf.ro; internet www.icf.ro; f. 1963; attached to Romanian Acad.; Dir Mihai Vasile Popa; Deputy Dir Dr Vlad T. Popa; Scientific Sec. Dr Mircea

OLTEANU; publs *Revue Roumaine de Chimie* (12 a year), *Roumanian Chemical Quarterly Review*.

Institutul de Chimie Macromoleculară 'Petru Poni' al Academiei Romane ('Petru Poni' Institute of Macromolecular Chemistry of the Romanian Academy): Str. Aleea Grigore Ghica Vodă 41A, 700487 Iaşi; tel. (232) 21-74-54; fax (232) 21-12-99; e-mail bcsimion@icmpp.ro; internet www.icmpp.ro; f. 1949; attached to Romanian Acad.; research in polymer chemistry, polymer physics and material science; library of 100,000 vols; Dir Acad. Dr BOGDAN CRISTOFOR SIMIONESCU; Deputy Dir Dr ANTON AIRINEI; Deputy Dir Dr VALERIA HARABAGIU.

Institutul de Chimie Organică 'Costin D. Neniţescu' (Costin D. Neniţescu Institute of Organic Chemistry): Splaiul Independenţei 202B, 060023 Bucharest; tel. (21) 316-79-00; fax (21) 312-16-01; e-mail pfilip@cco.ro; internet www.cco.ro; f. 1949; attached to Romanian Acad.; basic research in organic chemistry, fine organic synthesis and structural analysis of organic compounds; Dir Dr Ing. PETRU IVAN FILIP.

Institutul de Chimie Timişoara (Timişoara Institute of Chemistry): Bdul Mihai Viteazul 24, 300223 Timişoara; tel. (256) 49-18-18; fax (256) 49-18-24; e-mail ocostisor@acad-icht.tm.edu.ro; internet acad-icht.tm.edu.ro; f. 1967; attached to Romanian Acad.; library of 10,000 vols; Dir Dr OTILIA COSTISOR; Hon. Dir ZENO SIMON; Dir Adjunct Scientific Dr LUDOVIC SAYTI; Scientific Sec Dr RAMONA TUDOSE; publ. *Annals of the West University of Timişoara, Chemistry Series* (2 or 3 a year).

Institutul Naţional pentru Fizică şi Inginerie Nucleară 'Horia Hulubei' (Horia Hulubei National Institute of Physics and Nuclear Engineering): St. Reactorului 30, 077125 Bucharest-Măgurele; tel. (21) 404-23-00; fax (21) 404-44-40; e-mail dirgen@ifin.nipne.ro; internet www.ifin.ro; f. 1949; research and devt in physical and natural sciences; library of 385,000 vols; Dir-Gen. Prof. Dr NICOLAE VICTOR ZAMFIR; Scientific Sec Dr IOAN URSU; publs *Conference Proceedings*, *IFA-Preprints*, *Romanian Journal of Physics* (12 a year), *Romanian Reports in Physics* (12 a year).

Institutul de Geodinamică 'Sabba S. Ştefănescu' ('Sabba S. Ştefănescu' Institute of Geodynamics): Str. Jean Louis Calderon 19–21, 020032 Bucharest; tel. (21) 317-21-26; fax (21) 317-21-20; internet inst_geodin@geodin.ro; internet www.geodin.ro; f. 1990; attached to Romanian Acad.; geophysical research; study of space-time variations; monitoring of space-time variations of gravitational, geomagnetic, geoelectric fields of, modelling of the thermo-mechanical evolution of the lithosphere, non-linear analysis of geodynamic systems, studies of endogeneous processes in the geodynamic evolution of the Romanian territory, study of heliosphere/geomagnetic field; organizes PhD programmes; Dir Dr CRISAN DEMETRESCU; Deputy Dir Dr Ing. DUMITRU STANICA; Hon. Dir Dr Ing. DOREL ZUGRAVESCU; publs *Revue Roumaine de Géophysique* (1 a year), *Studii si Cercetari de Geofizica* (1 a year).

Institutul de Speologie 'Emil Racoviţă' (Emil Racoviţă Institute of Speleology): Calea 13 Septembrie 13, 050711 Bucharest; tel. (21) 311-08-29; fax (21) 318-81-32; e-mail iser_b@yahoo.com; internet www.iser.ro; f. 1920; attached to Romanian Acad.; biospeleology, phreatobiology, edaphobiology, paleobiology, sedimentology, geohydrochemistry, karstology, geospeleology, paleoclimatology, karst protection, arheometry; br. in Cluj-Napoca; library of 5,600 vols, 770 periodicals; Dir IOAN POVARA; Deputy Dir CRISTIAN GORAN; publs *Travaux* (1 a year), *Theoretical and Applied Karstology* (1 a year).

Institutul Geologic al României (Romanian Geological Institute): Str. Caransebeş 1, 012271 Bucharest; tel. (21) 318-13-28; fax (21) 318-13-26; e-mail geol@igr.ro; internet igr.ro; f. 1906; library of 270,000 vols; conservation and recovery of drilling cores; colln of minerals, rocks, flowers; monitoring of mining areas; fundamental and applied research; technological devt; studying and forecasting; deciphering geological composition and evolution of the country; defining areas of useful minerals; preparation and editing of geological, hydrogeological, geophysical and geochemical maps; fundamental and basic research in areas of mineralogy, paleontology, stratigraphy, geochemistry, regional geology, hydrogeology, geotechnics, magnetometry, gravimetry, geoelectricity, seismics; studies on impact of human activities on groundwater pollution; studies on devt of earth sciences according to int. economic situation; expertise in mine flowers, precious stones; research and analysis of geomagnetic field distribution; gravitational, geothermal, electromagnetic fields in Romania; geoinformational system (GIS); geoid; analysis of satellite images; Dir-Gen. Dr STEFAN MARINCEA; publs Romanian journals of mineralogy, petrology, mineral deposits and environmental geochemistry, stratigraphy, palaeontology, tectonics and regional geology, geophysics (1 a year), *Memorii* (irregular).

Institutul National de Cercetare-Dezvoltare 'Delta Dunarii' (Danube Delta National Institute for Research and Development): Str. Babadag 165, 820112 Tulcea; tel. (240) 53-15-20; fax (240) 53-35-47; e-mail office@indd.tim.ro; internet www.indd.tim.ro; f. 1970; attached to Min. of Environment; promotes the conservation of biodiversity and the sustainable devt of wetlands in Romania and the Danube Delta area; library of 40,000 vols; Gen. Dir Eng. ROMULUS ŞTIUCĂ; Scientific Dir Dr MIRCEA STARAS; Technical Dir Eng. DAN DAVID; Financial Dir ANA BULETE; publs *Annals*, *Review of Ecological Restoration in the Danube Delta Biosphere Reserve*.

Institutul Naţional de Cercetare Dezvoltare pentru Chimie si Petrochimie (National Institute of Research and Development for Chemistry and Petrochemistry): Spl. Independentei 202, sector 6, O.P. 35, 060021 Bucharest; tel. (21) 316-30-72; fax (21) 312-34-93; e-mail general.manager@icechim.ro; internet www.icechim.ro; f. 2004; scientific research and technological devt; depts of biotechnology, chemical and petrochemical technology; Dir-Gen. Ing. SANDA VELEA.

Institutul Naţional de Cercetare-Dezvoltare pentru Fizică Tehnică—IFT Iaşi (National Institute of Research and Development for Technical Physics): Bdul Dimitrie Mangeron 47, 700050 Iaşi; tel. (232) 43-06-80; fax (232) 23-11-32; e-mail hchiriac@phys-iasi.ro; internet www.phys-iasi.ro; f. 1951; fundamental and applied research activities in field of magnetism and magnetic materials; design and fabrication of new sensors for biomedical applications, sensors and actuators based on magnetoelastic phenomena, magnetic field sensors and spin-valve devices; devt of medicine and biotechnology, design and fabrication of non-destructive control sensors; 91 mems; library of 5,548 vols; Dir-Gen Prof. Dr HORIA CHIRIAC; publ. *Proceedings* (every 2 years).

Institutul Naţional de Meteorologie şi Hidrologie (National Institute of Meteorology and Hydrology): Şoseaua Bucureşti-Ploieşti 97, 013686 Bucharest; tel. (21) 318-32-40; fax (21) 316-31-43; e-mail relatii@meteo.inmh.ro; internet www.meteoromania.ro; f. 1884 as Meteorological Service of Romania, present name and status 1970; climatology; physics of atmosphere; agrometeorology; meteorological methodology; numeric modelling; long-range forecasting; remote sensing and GIS laboratory; Dir Gen. Dr ION SANDU; publs daily weather reports, *Studii şi Cercetări* (in 2 parts: Meteorology, Hydrology; 1 vol. a year), *Meteorology Journal* (2 a year), *Hydrology Journal* (2 a year), *Bibliografia hidrologică* (1 a year), *Bibliografia meteorologică* (1 a year).

Institutul Naţional de Metrologie (National Institute of Metrology): Şoseaua Vitan-Bîrzeşti 11, 042122 Bucharest; tel. (21) 334-55-20; fax (21) 334-55-33; e-mail boiciuc@inm.ro; internet www.inm.ro; f. 1951; attached to Romanian Bureau of Legal Metrology; devt, maintenance, utilization of nat. measurement standards; providing traceability to the SI; dissemination of units of measurement at nat. level; library of 15,000 vols; Dir Eng. DRAGOŞ BOICIUC; Scientific Dir Eng. MIRELLA BUZOIANU; publ. *Metrologie* (4 a year).

PHILOSOPHY AND PSYCHOLOGY

Institutul de Filosofie şi Psihologie 'C. Rădulescu-Motru' (C. Rădulescu-Motru Institute of Philosophy and Psychology): Calea 13 Septembrie 13, POB 15-137, 050711 Bucharest; tel. and fax (21) 410-56-59; e-mail ifilosofie@yahoo.com; internet ifilosofie.uv.ro; f. 1948; attached to Romanian Acad.; Dir Prof. ALEXANDRU SURDU; Academic Sec. BOGDAN DANCIU; publs *Cercetări Filosofico-Psihologice* (2 a year), *Probleme de Logică* (1 a year), *Revista de Filosofie* (3 a year), *Revista de Psihologie* (4 a year), *Revue Roumaine de Philosophie* (2 a year), *Studii de Istorie a Filosofiei Româneşti* (1 a year), *Studii de Istorie a Filosofiei Universale* (1 a year).

Institutul de Psihologie (Institute of Psychology): Calea 13 Septembrie 13, O.P. 5, POB 5-8, 050711 Bucharest; tel. (21) 318-81-06; fax (21) 318-24-42; e-mail lili.preda@gmail.com; internet ipsihologie.uv.ro; attached to Romanian Acad.; Dir ALEXANDRU SURDU; Scientific Sec. Dr BOGDAN DANCIU; publs *Revista de Psihologie* (4 a year), *Revue Roumaine de Psychologie* (2 a year).

RELIGION, SOCIOLOGY AND ANTHROPOLOGY

Institutul de Antropologie Francisc I. Rainer (Francisc Rainer Institute of Anthropology): Bdul Eroilor Sanitari 8, POB 35-13, 050474 Bucharest; tel. (21) 317-50-71; fax (21) 317-50-72; e-mail franciscrainer@yahoo.com; internet www.antroplogia.ro; f. 1937; attached to Romanian Acad.; library of 7,000 vols, 25 periodicals; Dir Dr CRISTIANA GLAVCE; Scientific Sec. Dr MATEI STIRCEA-CRACIUN; publ. *Annuaire d'Etudes Anthropologiques* (1 a year).

Institutul de Cercetări Socio-Umane (Institute for Studies in Social Sciences and Humanities from Sibiu): Bdul Victoriei 40, 550024 Sibiu; tel. (269) 21-26-04; fax (269) 21-66-05; e-mail secretariat@icsusib.ro; internet www.icsusib.ro; f. 1956; attached to Romanian Acad.; history and culture of Transylvanian Saxons; their relationship to history and culture of Romanians in the immediate environment and in Transylvania; Transylvanian Saxon dialect; urban history; ethnology; library of 7,850 vols, 10,200 periodicals; Man. Dr PAUL NIEDERMAIER; publs *Anuarul (Yearbook)* (1 a year), *For-*

schungen zur Volks- und Landeskunde (2 a year), *Historia Urbana* (2 a year), *Studii şi Comunicări de Etnologie* (1 a year).

Institutul de Studii Banatice 'Titu Maiorescu' (Titu Maiorescu Institute for Research): Str. Mihai Viteazul 24, 300223 Timişoara; tel. and fax (256) 49-18-23; e-mail icsutm@acad-tim.tm.edu.ro; f. 1970; attached to Romanian Acad.; library of 8,000 vols; Dir Prof. Dr CRISU DASCĂLU; publs *Caietul Cercului de Studii* (2 a year), *Dialectologie* (1 a year), *Limbăliterară* (1 a year), *Poetică* (1 a year), *Revista de studii banatice* (2 a year), *Studii de istorie a Banatului* (1 a year), *Toponimie* (1 a year).

Institutul de Cercetări Socio-Umane 'Gheorghe Şincai' al Academiei Române (Gheorghe Şincai Institute for Social Sciences and Humanities): Str. Al. Papiu Ilarian 10A, 540074 Târgu-Mureş; tel. and fax (265) 26-02-38; e-mail icsu_ms@clicknet.ro; internet icsu-ms.tripod.com; f. 1957; attached to Romanian Acad.; history, history of literature, folklore, sociology; library of 338,290 vols; Dir Dr CORNEL SIGMIREAN; publ. *Anuarul Institutului de Cercetari Socio-Umane Gheorghe Şincai* (1 a year).

Institutul de Cercetări Socio-Umane 'C. S. Nicolaescu-Plopsor' (C. S. Nicolaescu-Plopsor Institute for Research in Social and Human Sciences): Str. Unirii 68, 200345 Craiova; tel. (251) 52-33-30; fax (251) 52-57-02; e-mail avramcezar@yahoo.com; internet cis01.ucv.ro/academiaromana; f. 1965; attached to Romanian Acad.; library of 300,000 vols; Dir Prof. Dr AVRAM CEZAR GABRIEL; publs *Arhivele Olteniei* (1 a year), *Anuarul* (1 a year).

Institutul de Etnografie şi Folclor 'Constantin Brăiloiu' (Constantin Brăiloiu Institute of Ethnography and Folklore): Str. Tache Ionescu 25, 010353 Bucharest; tel. (21) 318-39-00; fax (21) 318-39-01; e-mail ief .brailoiu@gmail.com; internet www.acad.ro/ ief; f. 1949; library of 50,000 vols; Nat. Folk Archives of sound, image and MSS; Dir Dr SABINA ISPAS; Scientific Sec. Dr ION GHINOIU; publ. *Revista de etnografie şi folclor* (Journal of Ethnography and Folklore, 2 a year).

Institutul de Sociologie 'Dimitrie Gusti' (Dimitrie Gusti Institute of Sociology): Calea 13 Septembrie 13, 050711 Bucharest; tel. (21) 411-85-32; e-mail insoc@insoc.ro; f. 1965; attached to Romanian Acad.; Man. Dir Prof. Dr ILIE BĂDESCU,; publs *Revue Roumaine des Sciences Sociales—série de Sociologie* (4 a year, English edn 2 a year), *Sociologie Românească* (6 a year).

Institutul de Ştiinţe Politice şi Relaţii Internaţionale (Institute of Political Sciences and International Relations): Bdul Iuliu Maniu 1–3, Corp A, etaj 7, 061071 Bucharest; tel. and fax (21) 316-96-61; e-mail ispri@ispri.ro; internet www.ispri.ro; f. 1990, as Institute of Social Theory and Political Science; attached to Romanian Acad.; library of 1,000,000 vols; Dir Prof. Dr ION BULEI; publs *Revista de Ştiinţe Politice şi Relaţii Internaţionale* (4 a year), *Revista Romana de Teorie Socială* (4 a year), *Revue Roumaine de Teorie Sociale* (3 a year), *Romanian Journal of Political Science and International Relations* (2 a year).

Institutul de Ştiinţe Socio-Umane (Institute of Social and Human Sciences): Str. T. Codrescu 2, 700481 Iaşi; tel. (232) 11-59-87; f. 1969; attached to Romanian Acad.; library of 35,000 vols; Dir TUDOREL DIMA; publs *Anuar de Ştiinţe Socio-Umane*, *Revista Romana de Sociologie* (2 a year), *Romanian Journal of Sociology*.

International Association for South-East European Studies: Str. Nicolae Racota 12–14, Apt. 18, Bucharest 011393; tel. (21) 224-29-65; fax (21) 224-29-64; e-mail aiesee@rdslink.ro; f. 1963; attached to ICPHS, UNESCO; social sciences; promotes the study of the civilizations spread over the Balkans and South-East Europe; 29 mems; library of 40,000 vols; Pres. LUAN OMARI; Gen.-Sec. RAZVAN THEODORESCU; publ. *Revue de l'AIESEE* (1 a year).

TECHNOLOGY

Institutul de Informatică Teoretică (Institute of Computer Science): Str. Gh. Asachi 2, 700481 Iaşi; tel. (332) 10-65-05; e-mail vapopei@iit.tuiasi.ro; internet www.iit .tuiasi.ro; f. 1984; attached to Romanian Acad.; Dir Prof. H. N. TEODORESCU; Scientific Sec. VASILE APOPEI.

Institutul de Mecanica Solidelor (Institute of Solids Mechanics): Str. Constantin Mille 15, 10141 Bucharest; tel. and fax (21) 312-67-36; e-mail siret@imsar.bu.edu.ro; internet www.imsar.ro; f. 1949 as Institute of Applied Mechanics 'Traian Vuia', present name 1990; attached to Romanian Acad.; control of dynamic systems, mechanics of deformable media, ultrasonics, tribology, mechatronics and robotics; control strategies based on artificial intelligence methods; wave propagation techniques for characterization of mechanical properties; dynamics of elastic structures; direct and inverse methods for biomechanic systems; ultrasonic methods for improvement of non-destructive testing; mechanical and tribological properties investigation for classical and unconventional materials; bio-tribology; methods, strategies for robotics and mechatronics; Dir Dr TUDOR SIRETEANU; Deputy Dir Dr Ing. LUCIAN CAPITANU; Scientific Sec. Dr ARON IAROVICI; publ. *Revue Roumaine des Sciences Techniques Série de Mécanique appliquée* (Romanian Journal of Technical Sciences—Applied Mechanics, 3 a year).

Institutul National De Cercetare Dezvoltare Pentru Metale Neferoase Şi Rare (National Institute of Research And Development for Non-Ferrous and Rare Metals): Bdul Biruinţei 102, Pantaleon; tel. and fax (21) 352-20-48; e-mail imnr@imnr.ro; internet www.imnr.ro; f. 1966; research in nanostructured materials; ecotechnologies and environment protection; Dir Dr Ing. TEODOR VELEA; Scientific Dir Dr Ing. ROXANA PITICESCU.

Institutul Naţional de Cercetare-Dezvoltare pentru Protecţia Mediului (ICIM Bucureşti) (National Research and Development Institute for Environmental Protection (ICIM Bucharest)): Splaiul Independenţei 294, 060031 Bucharest; tel. (21) 318-20-57; fax (21) 318-20-01; e-mail icim@ icim.ro; internet www.icim.ro; f. 1952; attached to Min. of Environment; management, control of water, land and air quality; integrated monitoring of environmental factors; control of water pollution; water technologies; technologies and equipment for cleaning sewage; sludge-processing; aquatic ecosystems; biodiversity; fluid mechanics; dispersion of pollutants; noise pollution and vibrations; solid waste management; environmental impact of construction; library of 20,000 vols and journals; Dir-Gen. Prof. Dr Ing. NECULAI MIHAILESCU; Scientific Dir Dr VASILICA DAESCU; publs *The Environment* (4 a year), *An Environment for the Future* (1 a year).

Institutul Naţional de Informare şi Documentare (National Institute for Information and Documentation): Str. I. D. Mendeleev 21–25, 010362 Bucharest; tel. (21) 315-87-65; fax (21) 312-67-34; e-mail inid@iniduw.inid.ro; internet www.inid.ro; f. 1949; promotes the use of modern equipment for automatic data processing in the area of documentary information; library: see Libraries and Archives; Dir-Gen. TIBERIUS IGNAT; publs *Asigurerea şi Promovarea Calităţii* (4 a year), *Informarea şi Documentarea Modernă* (4 a year), *Management şi Marketing Coentemporan* (4 a year).

Libraries and Archives

Alba Iulia

Biblioteca Judeţeană 'Lucian Blaga' Alba (Alba 'Lucian Blaga' District Library): Str. Dr Camil Velican 22, 510113 Alba Iulia; tel. (258) 81-14-43; fax (258) 81-72-04; e-mail bjalba@gmail.com; internet www.bjalba.ro; f. 1943; 250,000 vols; Dir MIOARA POP.

Biblioteca Naţională a României, Filiala Batthyaneum (National Library of Romania, Batthyaneum Branch): Str. Gabriel Bethlen 1, 510009 Alba Iulia; tel. and fax (258) 81-19-39; e-mail ileana.darja@bibnat .ro; internet www.bibnat.ro/ filiala-batthyaneum-s75-ro.htm; f. 1798; attached to Biblioteca Naţională; 71,149 vols, 4,327 periodicals; spec. collns of 1,778 MSS since 9th century, 571 incunabula, documents, rare books, ex-libris; mineralogical and numismatic colln; scientific instruments, clocks; religious art; 18th-century astronomical observatory; Dir-Gen. Dr ELENA TÎRZIMAN.

Alexandria

Biblioteca Judeţeană 'Marin Preda' Teleorman (Teleorman 'Marin Preda' District Library): Str. Mitiţă Filipescu 9, 140056 Alexandria; tel. (247) 32-28-94; fax (247) 32-28-94; e-mail alexandria@mymail.ro; internet www.bjmarinpreda.ro; f. 1949; 130,000 vols; Dir NICOLETA-LILIANA ALEXE.

Arad

Biblioteca Judeţeană 'A. D. Xenopol' Arad (Arad 'A. D. Xenopol' District Library): Str. Gheorghe Popa de Teiuş 2–4, 310022 Arad; tel. and fax (257) 25-65-10; e-mail bja-director@aradlibrary.org; internet www .aradlibrary.org; f. 1913; 21,522 vols; Dir FLORIN DIDILESCU; Sec CRISTINA TEIUŞANU.

Bacău

Biblioteca Judeţeană 'Costache Sturdza' Bacău (Bacău 'Costache Sturdza' District Library): Str. Aleea Parcului 9, 688843 Bacău; tel. (234) 51-31-26; fax (334) 40-51-74; e-mail g.muraru@bjbc.ro; internet www.bjbc.ro:8080/bjbc; f. 1893; 430,000 vols and periodicals; Dir GABRIELA MURARU; Economic Dir MARIA TUDORACHE; publs *Bibliografia Judeţului Bacău*, *Cartea*, *Ex-Libris*.

Baia Mare

Biblioteca Judeţeană 'Petre Dulfu' Maramureş (Maramureş 'Petre Dulfu' District Library): Bdul Independenţei 4B, 430123 Baia Mare; tel. (262) 27-55-83; fax (262) 27-58-99; e-mail biblioteca@bibliotecamm.ro; internet www.bibliotecamm.ro; f. 1951; 433,828 vols; Dir-Gen. TEODOR ARDELEAN.

Bistriţa

Biblioteca Judeţeană Bistriţa-Năsăud (Bistriţa-Năsăud District Library): Str. Gării 2, 420041 Bistriţa; tel. and fax (263) 23-70-03; e-mail pia_olimpia@yahoo.com; internet www.bjbn.ro; f. 1951; 28 mems; 209,530 vols; Dir OLIMPIA POP; publs *Labirint*, *Specialty Journal* (1 a year).

Blaj

Biblioteca Documentară 'Timotei Cipariu' ('Timotei Cipariu' Documentary

Library): Str. Petru Pavel Aron 2–4, 515400 Blaj; tel. (258) 71-01-10; f. 1754; attached to Cluj-Napoca br. library of Romanian Academy; 30,000 vols in humanities and sciences; spec. colln of rare and ancient books on history of the Romanian people.

Botoşani

Biblioteca Judeţeană 'Mihai Eminescu' Botoşani (Botosani County Library): Str. Calea Naţională 64, 710028 Botoşani; tel. (231) 51-46-86; fax (231) 53-33-34; e-mail biblioteca@petar.ro; internet www.bibliotecabotosani.ro; f. 1882; 500,000 vols; Dir Prof. CORNELIA VIZITEU; publs *Studii eminescologice / Études sur Eminescu / Eminescu Studies / Eminescu Studien* (1 a year), *Catalogul Fondului Documentar 'Mihai Eminescu', Catalogul Fondului Documentar*.

Brăila

Biblioteca Judeţeană 'Panait Istrati' Brăila (Brăila 'Panait Istrati' County Library): Calea Călăraşilor 52, 810010 Brăila; tel. (239) 61-12-92; fax (239) 61-95-90; e-mail bjpi@bjbraila.ro; internet www.bjbraila.ro; f. 1881; 388,968 vols, 4 brs; coordinates activity of 3 city libraries and 39 village libraries; Dir DRAGOS ADRIAN NEAGU; publ. *Ex-libris* (1 a year).

Braşov

Biblioteca Judeţeană 'George Bariţiu' Braşov ('George Bariţiu' County Library Braşov): Bdul Eroilor 33–35, 500036 Braşov; tel. (268) 41-93-38; fax (268) 41-50-79; e-mail biblgb@rdsbv.ro; internet www.bjbv.ro; f. 1835; 800,000 vols; reading and loan services; cultural and social activities, courses, lectures, conferences and workshops; Man. Dr DANIEL NAZARE.

Biblioteca Universităţii 'Transilvania' din Braşov (Transylvania University of Braşov Central Library): Str. Iuliu Maniu 41, 500091 Braşov; tel. (268) 47-60-50; fax (268) 47-60-51; e-mail biblioteca@unitbv.ro; internet www.unitbv.ro/biblio; f. 1948; 790,000 vols; Dir Prof. Dr Eng. ELENA HELEREA.

Bucharest

Arhivele Naţionale ale României (National Archives): Bdul Regina Elisabeta 49, 050013 Bucharest; tel. (21) 312-67-10; fax (21) 312-58-41; e-mail secretariat.an@mai.gov.ro; internet www.arhivelenationale.ro; f. 1831; 1,221,500 medieval documents, 22,000 seals, 12,820 MSS, 816,929 ft modern documents, 735,680 vols of plans and maps; documentary libraries; Dir Dr DORIN DOBRINCU; publ. *Revista Arhivelor* (1 a year).

Attached Library:

Biblioteca Documentară a Arhivelor Naţionale (Documentary Library of the National Archives): Bdul Regina Elisabeta 49, 050013 Bucharest; tel. (21) 303-70-80; fax (21) 312-58-41; e-mail publicatii.an@mira.gov.ro; internet www.arhivelenationale.ro; f. 1862; 70,000 vols, 50,000 periodicals; Dir Dr DORIN DOBRINCU; Library Coordinator CAMELIA COJOCARU; Librarian VALENTINA DINU; publ. *Revista Arhivelor* (Archives Review).

Biblioteca Academiei Române (Library of the Romanian Academy): Calea Victoriei 125, 010071 Bucharest; tel. (21) 212-82-84; fax (21) 212-58-56; e-mail biblacad@biblacad.ro; internet www.biblacad.ro; f. 1867; legal nat. deposit for Romanian and UN publs; produces Romanian nat. bibliography of books and serials; 11,500,000 vols, 3.6m. monographs, 5.3m. serials, 500,000 historical documents, 350,000 photographs; spec. collns incl. Romanian, Greek, Slavonic, Oriental and Latin MSS; drawings, engravings, photographs, music MSS, maps; numismatic colln; Dir Gen. FLORIN FILIP; Dir Adjunct CORNEL LEPADATU; publs *Cărţi intrate în reţeaua bibliotecilor Academiei Române* (1 a year), *Periodice intrate în reţeaua bibliotecilor Academiei Române* (1 a year), *Publicaţii Periodice Româneşti*.

Biblioteca Centrală a Academiei de Ştiinţe Agricole şi Silvice 'Gheorghe Ionescu-Şişeşti' (Central Library of the Gheorghe Ionescu-Sişeşti Academy of Agricultural and Forestry Sciences): Bdul Mărăşti 61, 011464 Bucharest; f. 1928; 136,000 vols; Chief Librarian N. FLORESCU; publs *Bibliografia agricolă curentă română* (4 a year), *Noutăţi documentare FAO* (12 a year), *Cărţi străine intrate in bibliotecile din România—seria Agricultură* (12 a year).

Biblioteca Centrală Academiei de Studii Economice (Central Library of the Academy of Economic Studies): Piaţa Romană 6, 010374 Bucharest; tel. (21) 319-19-00; fax (21) 319-18-99; e-mail biblioteca@ase.ro; internet www.biblioteca.ase.ro; f. 1913; 900,000 vols; Dir LIVIU BOGDAN VLAD.

Biblioteca Centrală a Universităţii 'Politehnica' din Bucureşti (Central Library of Politehnica University of Bucharest): Calea Grivitei 132, 060042 Bucharest; tel. (21) 402-39-82; fax (21) 312-70-44; e-mail c_albu@library.pub.ro; internet www.library.pub.ro; f. 1868; 1,094,360 vols and periodicals; Dir Ing. CRISTINA ALBU; publ. *Scientific Bulletin* (4 series: mechanical engineering, electrical engineering, chemistry and materials science, applied mathematics and physics).

Biblioteca Centrală Universitară 'Carol I' (Central University Library 'Carol I'): Str. Boteanu 1, Sector 1, 010027 Bucharest; tel. and fax (21) 313-16-05; fax (21) 312-01-08; e-mail mireille.radoi@bcub.ro; internet www.bcub.ro; f. 1891; 1,896,288 vols; Dir-Gen. Dr MIRELLE CARMEN RADOI; Librarian GETA COSTACHE; publs *Ghidul lucrărilor de referinţe în colecţiile Bibliotecii Centrale Universitare 'Carol I' din Bucureşti* (Guide to Reference Works in the Collections of the Library of Bucharest University, 2 a year), *Informaţie şi Formaţie* (12 a year), *UniBib* (online).

Biblioteca de Documentare Medicală 'Dr Dimitrie Nanu' (Dr Dimitrie Nanu Medical Documentation Library): Str. Pitar Moş 7–15, 010451 Bucharest; tel. (21) 211-04-30; fax (21) 211-11-45; f. 1951; attached to Centrul de Calcul, Statistică Sanitară şi Documentare Medicală; 310,556 vols; Dir FELICIA-IOANA DOBRESCU.

Biblioteca Documentară de Istorie a Medicinei (Documentary Library of the History of Medicine): Str. Dr Leonte 1–3, 050463 Bucharest; tel. (21) 638-40-10; fax (21) 312-34-26; f. 1953; 50,200 vols, 1,100 periodicals, 3,500 MSS and documents, 5,200 museum pieces; Dir Prof. MARIOARA GEORGESCU.

Biblioteca Institutului Naţional de Informare şi Documentare (Library of the National Institute for Information and Documentation): Str. I. D. Mendeleev 21–25, 010362 Bucharest; tel. (21) 313-40-10; fax (21) 312-67-34; e-mail inid_bucuresti@home.ro; internet www.inid.ro; f. 1949; 743,000 vols incl. 135,000 periodicals; Chief Librarian DACIA CRISTIANA STATIE.

Biblioteca Metropolitană Bucureşti (Bucharest Metropolitan Library): Str. Tache Ionescu 4, 010354 Bucharest; tel. (21) 316-83-00; fax (21) 316-36-25; e-mail biblioteca@bmms.ro; internet www.bmms.ro; f. 1831; 1,337,078 vols, periodicals, newspapers, musical scores; Dir Gen. Dr FLORIN ROTARU; publs *Bibliografia oraşului Bucureşti* (1 a year), *Biblioteca Bucureştilor* (12 a year), *Buletinul Bibliotecilor din Franţa* (12 a year).

Biblioteca Naţională a României (National Library of Romania): Str. Ion Ghica 4, 030046 Bucharest; tel. (21) 314-24-34; fax (21) 312-33-81; e-mail biblioteca@bibnat.ro; internet www.bibnat.ro; f. 1838; 12,000,000 vols; acts as copyright deposit library and nat. bibliographic agency; incorporates research centre for librarianship and book pathology and restoration; spec. collns of MSS, old and rare books, musical scores, photographs, maps, prints, old illustrated postcards and drawings; Dir-Gen. Dr ELENA TÎRZIMAN; publs *ABSI—Abstracte în bibliologie şi ştiinţa informării* (4 a year), *Aniversări culturale* (2 a year), *Bibliografia Naţională Română* (6 series), *Biblioteconomie—Culegere de traduceri prelucrate* (4 a year), *Catalogul colectiv al cărţilor străine intrate în bibliotecile din România* (4 a year), *Repertoriul periodicelor străine intrate în bibliotecile din România* (1 a year), *Revista Bibliotecii Naţionale a României* (2 a year), *Revista Biblioteca* (12 a year), *Revista Română de Conservare şi Restaurare* (1 a year), *Revista Română de Istorie a Cărţii* (1 a year).

Biblioteca Pedagogică Naţională 'I. C. Petrescu' ('I. C. Petrescu' National Education Library): Str. Zalomit 12, 010151 Bucharest; tel. and fax (40) 311-03-23; e-mail director@bpn.ro; internet www.bpn.ro; f. 1880; 480,000 educational vols and periodicals; methodological centre for the nat. network of school libraries; Dir-Gen. Dr GEORGE ANCA; Librarian MANUELA POPA; publs *Education en Roumanie* (Education in Romania, 1 a year), *Modernizarea învăţământului* (1 a year), *Informare tematică* (1 a year), *Bibliografia pedagogică* (1 a year), *LIBER. Revistă pentru bibliotecile pedagogice şi şcolare* (4 a year), *Studii de biblioteconomie şi informare documentară* (irregular).

Biblioteca Universităţii de Arte Bucureşti (Library of the Bucharest University of Fine Arts): Str. Gen. Budişteanu 19, 010773 Bucharest; tel. (21) 314-32-11; f. 1864; 60,000 vols, 261,262 slides and photographs; spec. colln: 19th- and 20th-century European fine-art periodicals; Dir GABRIELA BĂJENARU.

Biblioteca Universităţii de Ştiinţe Agronomice şi Medicina Veterinară (Library of the University of Agronomic Sciences and Veterinary Medicine): Bdul Mărăşti 59, 011464 Bucharest; tel. (21) 318-25-67; fax (21) 318-28-88; e-mail biblioteca_usamv@yahoo.com; f. 1868; 480,000 350,000 vols; Dir CARMEN CONSTANTIN; publs *Agronomy*, *Biotechnology*, *Horticulture*, *Land Reclamation*, *Veterinary Medicine*, *Zootechnics*.

Biblioteca Universităţii Naţionale de Muzică din Bucureşti (Library of the Bucharest University of Music): Str. Ştirbei Vodă 33, 010102 Bucharest; tel. (21) 314-26-10; e-mail biblioteca@unmb.ro; f. 1864; 41,962 vols, 82,190 scores, 16,545 recordings, 7,200 tapes, 14,465 periodicals, 3,083 theses, 521 MSS; Head CIOPONEA MARIA.

Centrul de Documentare pentru Construcţii, Arhitectură, Urbanism şi Amenajarea Teritoriului (Documentation Centre for Building, Architecture, Urban Studies and Town Planning): Şoseaua Pantelimon 266, 021613 Bucharest; tel. (21) 255-50-22; fax (31) 405-58-40; e-mail office@cdcas.ro; internet www.cdcas.ro; f. 1957; 350,000 vols, 200 current periodicals; Dir-Gen. Dr SIMONA BARA; publs *Buletin tehnic informativ* (2 a year), *Revista sumarelor* (4 a year), *Semnalari bibliografice* (4 a year).

Centrul de Informare şi Documentare Economică (Centre of Economic Information and Documentation): Casa Academiei Române, Calea 13 Septembrie 13, 050711 Bucharest; tel. (21) 318-24-38; fax (21) 318-24-32; e-mail cide@zappmobile.ro; internet www.ince.ro; f. 1990; attached to Romanian Acad.; Dir IOAN-FRANC VALERIU; publs *Probleme Economice* (48 a year), *Studii şi Cercetări Economice* (12 a year), *Romanian Economic Research Observer* (12 a year), *Analele INCE* (4 a year), *Marketing Management* (6 a year), *Caiete Critice* (12 a year), *Romanian Journal of Economic Forecasting* (4 a year), *Revista Română de Economie* (2 a year).

S. C. Biblioteca Chimiei SA (S. C. Chemistry Library SA): Calea Plevnei 139B, 060011 Bucharest; tel. and fax (21) 314-24-47; e-mail biblioteca_de_chimie@syscom18.com; internet www.bch.ro; f. 1956; provides access to nat. and foreign scientific and technical literature; 46,000 vols, 141,000 vols of periodicals; Gen. Man. Ing. ION ANDRONACHE; publs *Materiale Plastice* (4 a year), *Revista de Chimie* (Chemistry magazine, 12 a year).

Serviciul de Documentare al Ministerului Învăţământului (Documentation Service of the Ministry of Education): Str. Spiru Haret 12, 010716 Bucharest; tel. (21) 614-26-80; fax (21) 312-47-53; f. 1971; information and documentation on teaching and educational management abroad; Romanian legislation on education; Head EUGENIU TOMA; publs *Educaţie-Învăţământ* (2 a year), *Buletinul Ministerului Invăţământului* (4 a year).

Serviciul de Informare, Documentare şi Informatizare al Academiei de Ştiinţe Agricole şi Silvice 'Gheorghe Ionescu-Şişeşti' (Information, Documentation and Electronic Information Service of the Gheorghe Ionescu-Şişteşti Academy of Agricultural and Forestry Sciences): Bdul Mărăşti 61, 011464 Bucharest; tel. (21) 618-25-54; fax (21) 617-01-55; f. 1928; attached to Acad. of Agricultural and Forestry Sciences; 147,000 vols and CD-ROMs; Head Dr C. KEVORCHIAN; publ. *Curierul ASAS* (4 a year).

Buzău

Biblioteca Judeţeană 'V. Voiculescu' Buzău (Buzău 'V. Volcalescu' District Library): Bdul Unirii 140, 120360 Buzău; tel. (238) 72-15-09; fax (238) 71-72-83; e-mail sorin.burlacu@bjvvbuzau.ro; internet bjvvbuzau.ro; f. 1873; 290,000 vols; Dir SORIN BURLACU.

Călăraşi

Biblioteca Judeţeană 'Al. Odobescu' Călăraşi (Călăraşi 'Al. Odobescu' District Library): Str. Bucureşti 102, 910161 Călăraşi; tel. (242) 31-67-57; fax (242) 31-67-57; f. 1883; 265,254 vols; Dir GHIŢĂ DUMITRU.

Cluj-Napoca

Biblioteca Centrală Universitară 'Lucian Blaga' ('Lucian Blaga' University Central Library): Str. Clinicilor 2, 400006 Cluj-Napoca; tel. (264) 59-70-92; fax (264) 59-76-33; e-mail informatii@bcucluj.ro; internet bcu.ubbcluj.ro; f. 1872; 3,553,596 vols; Dir DORU RADOSAV.

Biblioteca Filialei Cluj-Napoca a Academiei Române (Library of the Cluj-Napoca Branch of the Romanian Academy): Str. M. Kogălniceanu 12–14, 400084 Cluj-Napoca; tel. (264) 59-50-27; e-mail biblacadcj@yahoo.com; internet www.bibacadcj.ro; f. 1950; 760,000 vols and periodicals on the humanities and science, 179 incunabula, 2m. documents; spec. collns incl. Romanian, Latin, Hungarian, Slavonic MSS; Dir Prof. Dr IOAN CHINDRIS; publ. *Biblioteca si Cercetarea*.

Biblioteca Judeţeană 'Octavian Goga' Cluj ('Octavian Goga' Cluj County Library): Calea Dorobanţilor 104, 400691 Cluj-Napoca; tel. (264) 43-03-23; fax (264) 59-54-28; e-mail bjc@bjc.ro; internet www.bjc.ro; f. 1921; 3 br. libraries; 97 mems; 765,700 vols; Dir SORINA STANCA; Deputy Dir FLOAREA ELENA MOŞOIU; publs *Anul editorial clujean*, *Buletin UE-INFO* (1 a year), *Calendarul evenimentelor şi manifestărilor culturale* (1 a year).

Biblioteca Centrala 'Valeriu Bologa' (Central Library): Victor Babes 8, 400012 Cluj-Napoca; tel. and fax (264) 59-72-56; e-mail irobu@umfcluj.ro; internet www.umfcluj.ro/lista.aspx?t=biblioteca-prezentare; f. 1949; attached to Univ. of Medicine and Pharmacy; 321,000 vols and periodicals, online collns; Dir IOANA ROBU; publ. *Clujul Medical* (4 a year).

Biblioteca Universităţii Tehnice din Cluj-Napoca (Library of Cluj-Napoca Technical University): Str. Republicii 107, 400020 Cluj-Napoca; tel. (264) 40-19-99; fax (264) 43-04-08; e-mail calin.campean@biblio.utcluj.ro; internet www.utcluj.ro/biblioteca; f. 1884, reorganized in 1948; 700,000 vols and 3,000 periodicals; Dir Dipl. Eng. CĂLIN CÂMPEAN; publ. *Acta Technica Napocensis* (in English, 1 a year).

Constanţa

Biblioteca Judeţeană 'Ioan N. Roman' Constanţa ('Ioan N. Roman' Constanţa County Library): Str. Mircea cel Bătrân 104A, 900663 Constanţa; tel. and fax (241) 61-62-44; fax (241) 61-44-82; e-mail bjc@biblioteca.ct.ro; internet www.biblioteca.ct.ro; f. 1931; 650,000 vols; Dir Dr LILIANA LAZIA; publs *Bibliografia Dobrogei* (1 a year), *Biblion* (2 a year).

Craiova

Biblioteca Judeţeană 'Alexandru şi Aristia Aman' Dolj (Public Library 'Alexandru and Aristia Aman' County Dolj): Str. M. Kogălniceanu 9, 200390 Craiova; tel. (251) 53-22-67; fax (251) 52-31-77; e-mail lucian.dindirica@aman.ro; internet www.aman.ro; f. 1908; 466,000 vols; Dir LUCIAN DINDIRICĂ.

Biblioteca Universităţii din Craiova (University of Craiova Library): Str. A. I. Cuza 13, 200585 Craiova; tel. and fax (251) 41-24-79; e-mail bib@central.ucv.ro; internet biblio.central.ucv.ro; f. 1966, by merger of Agronomic Institute Library (f. 1948) and Pedagogical Institute Library (f. 1959); 1,026,950 vols; Dir Dr MIHAI COŞOVEANU.

Deva

Biblioteca Judeţeană 'Ovid Densusianu' Hunedoara-Deva (Hunedoara-Deva 'Ovid Densusianu' District Library): Str. 1 Decembrie 26, 330025 Deva; tel. and fax (254) 21-64-57; e-mail bibliotecadeva@upcmail.ro; internet www.bibliotecadeva.ro; f. 1951; 330,000 vols, periodicals and audiovisual items; Dir GABRIELA MARCU; publ. *Vox Libri* (4 a year).

Drobeta-Turnu Severin

Biblioteca Judeţeaňa 'I. G. Bibicescu' Mehedinţi (Mehedinţi 'I. G. Bibicescu' District Library): Str. Traian 115, 220134 Drobeta-Turnu Severin; tel. and fax (252) 31-56-82; f. 1921; 450,000 vols; Dir RALUCA ŞTEFANIA GRAF.

Focşani

Biblioteca Judeţeană 'Duiliu Zamfirescu' Vrancea (Vrancea 'Duiliu Zamfirescu' District Library): Str. M. Kogălniceanu 12–13, 620036 Focşani; tel. and fax (237) 21-45-62; e-mail bjfocsani@vrancea.info; internet www.bjvrancea.ro; f. 1910; 198,000 vols; Dir TEODORA FÎNTÎNARU.

Galaţi

Biblioteca Judeţeană 'V. A. Urechia' Galaţi (Galaţi 'V. A. Urechia' County Library): Str. Mihai Bravu 16, 800208 Galaţi; tel. (236) 41-10-37; fax (236) 31-10-60; e-mail bvau@bvau.ro; internet www.bvau.ro; f. 1890; 709,434 vols; Man. Prof. ZANFIR ILIE; Dir Adjunct LETIŢIA BURUIANĂ; Dir Adjunct GETA EFTIMIE; publs *Buletinul Fundaţiei Urechia* (2 a year), *Revista trimestrială de Cultură: Axis Libri* (4 a year), *Asociaţia* (4 a year).

Biblioteca Universităţii 'Dunarea de Jos' din Galaţi (University of Galaţi 'Dunarea de Jos' Library): Str. Domnească 47, 800008 Galaţi; tel. (236) 41-41-12; fax (236) 46-13-53; e-mail biblioteca@ugal.ro; internet www.lib.ugal.ro; f. 1948; 480,000 vols mainly on science, technology and engineering, food industry, history, theology, languages and literature, economics; Dir MIOARA VONCILĂ.

Giurgiu

Biblioteca Judeţeană 'I. A. Bassarabescu' Giurgiu (Giurgiu District 'I. A. Bassarabescu' Library): Soseaua Bucuresti 53, 080033 Giurgiu; tel. and fax (246) 21-23-46; e-mail bibliotecagr@pscomp.ro; internet www.bjgiurgiu.info; f. 1951; 199,178 vols and periodicals; Dir Prof. ION GAGHII; publ. *Libris*.

Iaşi

Biblioteca Centrală a Universităţii de Medicină şi Farmacie 'Gr. T. Popa' Iaşi (Central Library of the Gr. T. Popa University of Medicine and Pharmacy in Iaşi): Str. Vasile Alecsandri 7, 700054 Iaşi; tel. (232) 21-37-01; fax (232) 21-82-24; e-mail vscutariu@biblio.umfiasi.ro; internet biblio.umfiasi.ro; f. 1882; central library with 90 brs; 264,243 vols; Dir Prof. VIORICA SCUTARIU.

Biblioteca Centrală Universitară 'Mihai Eminescu' Iaşi (University 'Mihai Eminescu' Central Library Iaşi): Str. Păcurari 4, 700511 Iaşi; tel. (232) 26-42-45; fax (232) 26-17-96; e-mail bcuis@bcu-iasi.ro; internet www.bcu-iasi.ro; f. 1835; 2,456,909 vols; Dir-Gen. Prof. Dr ALEXANDRU CĂLINESCU; Dir Gen. Adjunct NICOLETA POPESCU; Economic Dir VLADIMIR PETREA.

Biblioteca Judeţeană 'Gh. Asachi' Iaşi (Iaşi 'Gh. Asachi' District Library): Str. Palat 1, 700019 Iaşi; tel. (232) 21-33-53; fax (232) 21-21-70; e-mail bibiasi@hotmail.com; internet www.bjiasi.ro; f. 1920; 600,000 vols, 12,000 records; Dir Prof. Dr CĂTĂLIN BORDEIANU; Dir Adjunct VALERIU STANCU; publ. *Bibliographical Annual of the Iaşi District*.

Biblioteca Universităţii Tehnice 'Gheorghe Asachi' Iaşi (Library of the Iaşi Gheorghe Asachi Technical University): Bdul Carol I 11, 700506 Iaşi; tel. and fax (232) 21-27-73; e-mail mstirbu@library.tuiasi.ro; internet www.library.tuiasi.ro; f. 1937; 1m. vols; Library Man. MIHAELA STIRBU; publ. *Iaşi Polytechnic Magazine* (1 a year).

Miercurea-Ciuc

Biblioteca Judeţeană Kájoni János: Piaţa Libertăţii 16, 530100 Miercurea-Ciuc; tel. (266) 37-17-90; fax (266) 37-19-88; e-mail info@bibliohr.topnet.ro; internet bibliohr.topnet.ro; f. 1950; 242,000 vols; Dir KATALIN-MARIA KOPACZ.

Năsăud

Biblioteca Documentară Năsăud (Năsăud Documentary Library): Str. Grănicerilor 41, 425200 Năsăud; tel. (263) 36-20-02; f. 1931; attached to Cluj-Napoca br. library of Romanian Academy; 53,323 vols; Dir MARIA ŞUTEU.

Oradea

Biblioteca Judeţeană 'Gheorghe Şincai' Bihor Oradea ('Gheorghe Şincai' Bihor Oradea District Library): Str. Armatei Române 1A, 410100 Oradea; tel. (359) 80-03-68; fax (259) 43-12-57; e-mail bibliobihor@yahoo.com; internet www.bibliobihor.ro; f. 1911; public county library; 700,000 vols; Dir Man. Prof. LIGIA-ANTONIA MIRIŞAN.

Piatra-Neamţ

Biblioteca Judeţeană 'G. T. Kirileanu' Neamţ (Neamţ 'G. T. Kirileanu' District Library): Bdul Republicii 15, 610005 Piatra-Neamţ; tel. (233) 21-15-24; fax (233) 21-03-79; e-mail bib_gtk_neamt@yahoo.com; internet www.bibgtkneamt.ro; f. 1956; 286,424 vols and periodicals; Dir CONSTANTIN BOSTAN.

Piteşti

Biblioteca Judeţeană Argeş 'Dinicu Golescu' (Argeş District Library 'Dinicu Golescu'): Str. Victoriei 18, 110017 Piteşti; tel. (248) 22-30-30; fax (248) 22-34-16; e-mail bjdgarges@gmail.com; internet www.bjarges.ro; f. 1880; 404,849 vols and periodicals, 2,018 audiovisual items, 120 electronic documents; Dir Dr MIHAIL OCTAVIAN SACHELARIE.

Ploieşti

Biblioteca Centrală a Universităţii 'Petrol-Gaze' din Ploieşti (Central Library of Petroleum Gas University of Ploiesti): Bdul Bucureşti 39, 100680 Ploieşti; tel. (244) 57-31-71; fax (244) 57-58-47; e-mail biblioteca@upg-ploiesti.ro; internet www.upg-ploiesti.ro; f. 1948; 296,231 vols; Dir Prof. DAN EMIL; Librarian NICOLAE MADALINA.

Biblioteca 'Nicolae Iorga' Prahova ('Nicolae Iorga' Library): Str. Sublocotenent Erou Călin Cătălin 1, 100066 Ploieşti; tel. (244) 12-19-00; fax (244) 51-83-43; e-mail bjprahova@yahoo.com; internet bni.asesoft.ro; f. 1921; 550,000 vols; Dir Prof. NICOLAE BOARU.

Râmnicu Vâlcea

Biblioteca Judeţeană 'Antim Ivireanul' Râmnicu Vâlcea (Vâlcea 'Antim Ivireanul' District Library): Str. Carol I 26, 240591 Râmnicu Vâlcea; tel. (350) 40-17-94; fax (250) 73-92-21; e-mail biblioteca_antim@bjai.ro; internet www.bjai.ro; f. 1950; 400,000 vols; Dir SANDA CONSTANTINESCU; publ. *Biblioteca Vâlceană—Revista de Cultură a Bibliotecii Judeţene 'Antim Ivireanul'*.

Reşiţa

Biblioteca Judeţeană 'Paul Iorgovici' Reşiţa (Reşiţa 'Paul Iorgovici' District Library): Str. Paul Iorgovici 50, 320026 Reşiţa; tel. (55) 21-25-35; fax (55) 21-16-87; e-mail bjpi_resita@yahoo.com; internet bjpiresita.blogspot.com; f. 1952; 287,000 vols; Dir NICOLAE SÂRBU; publ. *Revista Noastră*.

Satu Mare

Biblioteca Judeţeană Satu Mare (Satu Mare District Library): Str. Decebal 2, 440006 Satu Mare; tel. (261) 71-58-60; fax (261) 71-11-99; e-mail santa@p5net.ro; internet www.bibliotecasatumare.ro; f. 1951; 379,553 vols; Dir VOICU D. RUSU.

Sf. Gheorghe

Biblioteca Judeţeană 'Bod Péter' Megyei Könyvtár (Covasna County Public Library): Gábor Áron 14, 520008 Sfantu Gheorghe; tel. and fax (267) 35-16-09; e-mail biblio@kmkt.ro; internet www.kmkt.ro; f. 1880; 220,000 vols; Man. Dr SZABOLCS SZONDA.

Sibiu

Biblioteca Judeţeană 'Astra' Sibiu (Sibiu 'Astra' District Library): Str. Gh. Bariţiu 5–7, 550178 Sibiu; tel. (269) 21-05-51; fax (269) 21-57-75; e-mail bjastrasibiu@yahoo.com; internet www.bjastrasibiu.ro; f. 1861; 688,377 vols; 4 brs; Dir ONUC NEMEŞ-VINTILĂ; publs *DeLiriKoN* (4 a year), *Mlădite* (4 a year).

Biblioteca Muzeului Brukenthal (Library of Brukenthal Museum): Piaţa Mare 4, 550163 Sibiu; tel. (269) 21-16-99; fax (269) 21-15-45; e-mail info@brukenthalmuseum.ro; internet www.brukenthalmuseum.ro; f. 1817; 280,000 vols; Dir-Gen. Prof. Dr SABIN ADRIAN LUCA; Head of Library CONSTANTIN ITTU.

Slatina

Biblioteca Judeţeană 'Ion Minulescu' Olt (Olt 'Ion Minulescu' District Library): Bdul A.I. Cuza 3B, 230025 Slatina; tel. and fax (349) 40-75-17; e-mail bibljolt@yahoo.com; internet www.bibliotecaslatina.ro; f. 1931; 231,667 vols and periodicals; Dir Dr PAUL MATIU.

Slobozia

Biblioteca Judeţeană 'Ştefan Bănulescu' Ialomiţa (Ialomiţa 'Ştefan Bănulescu' District Library): Bdul Matei Basarab 26, 920031 Slobozia; tel. and fax (243) 23-00-55; e-mail biblioteca_ialomita@bji.ro; internet www.bji.ro; f. 1933; 132,242 vols and periodicals; Dir MIHAELA RACOVIŢEANU; publ. *Salonul Anual de Carte* (1 a year).

Suceava

Biblioteca Bucovinei 'I. G. Sbierea' ('I. G. Sbierea' Library of Bucovina): Str. Mitropoliei 4, 720035 Suceava; tel. (30) 21-31-90; fax (30) 53-07-98; internet www.biblioteca.suceava.ro; f. 1923; 342,509 vols and periodicals; Dir GHEORGHE-GABRIEL CĂRĂBUŞ.

Târgovişte

Biblioteca Judeţeană 'Ion Heliade Rădulescu' Dâmboviţa (Dâmboviţa 'Ion Heliade Rădulescu' District Library): Str. Stelea 2, 130018 Târgovişte; tel. (245) 61-23-16; fax (372) 87-04-42; e-mail office@bjdb.ro; internet www.bjdb.ro; f. 1944; 273,000 vols and periodicals; Dir Prof. VĂDAN CARMEN; publ. *Curier*.

Târgu Jiu

Biblioteca Judeţeană 'Christian Tell' Gorj (Gorj 'Christian Tell' District Library): Str. Calea Eroilor 23, 210135 Târgu Jiu; tel. and fax (253) 21-49-04; e-mail bjgorj@bibliotell.ro; internet www.bibliotell.ro; f. 1934; 273,542 vols; Dir ALEXANDRA ANDREI.

Târgu Mureş

Biblioteca Documentară 'Teleki-Bolyai' ('Teleki-Bolyai' Documentary Library): Str. Bolyai 17, 540067 Târgu Mureş; tel. (265) 16-18-57; f. 1962, by the merger of Teleki library (f. 1802) and Bolyai library (f. 1557); books in the natural and social sciences before 19th century; maps, incunabula and MSS; 200,000 vols; Dir DIMITRIE POPTĂMAŞ.

Biblioteca Judeţeană Mureş (Mureş County Library): Str. Georges Enescu 2, 540052 Târgu Mureş; tel. (265) 26-26-31; fax (265) 26-43-84; internet www.bjmures.ro; f. 1913; 900,000 vols; Dir MONICA AVRAM; publs *Biblitheca Marisiana*, *Libraria*.

Timişoara

Biblioteca Centrală Universitară 'Eugen Todoran' (Central University Library 'Eugen Todoran'): Bdul V. Pârvan 4A, 300223 Timişoara; tel. (256) 49-03-53; fax (256) 49-40-04; e-mail dostafe@bcut.ro; internet www.bcut.ro; f. 1948 as Biblioteca Universităţii Timişoara, present name 2000; 991,673 vols and periodicals; Gen. Man. Prof. Dr VASILE DOCEA; Deputy Gen. Man Ing. DELIA PÂRŞAN; Deputy Gen. Man. Dr Ing. DOINA OSTAFE.

Biblioteca Judeţeană Timiş (Timiş District Library): Piaţa Libertăţii 3, 300077 Timişoara; tel. (256) 43-07-46; fax (256) 43-39-98; e-mail secretariat@bjt.ro; internet www.bjt.ro; f. 1904; 750,000 vols; Dir PAUL EUGEN BANCIU.

Tulcea

Biblioteca Judeţeană 'Panait Cerna' Tulcea (Tulcea County Library 'Panait Cerna'): Str. Isaccei 20, 820241 Tulcea; tel. and fax (240) 51-38-33; e-mail bjt@tulcealibrary.ro; internet www.tulcealibrary.ro; f. 1879; 303,795 vols, 7,472 audiovisual materials and 17,045 periodicals; Man. OVIDIU GHIONU.

Vaslui

Biblioteca Judeţeană 'Nicolae Milescu Spătarul' Vaslui (Vaslui 'Nicolae Milescu Spătarul' County Library): Str. Hagi Chiriac 2, 730129 Vaslui; tel. and fax (35) 31-37-67; e-mail office@bjvaslui.ro; internet www.bjvaslui.ro; f. 1951; organizes exhibitions and cultural events; 250,000 vols; Man. Prof. GELU VOICU BICHINEŢ.

Zalău

Biblioteca Judeţeană 'Ioniţă Scipione Bădescu' Sălaj (Sălaj 'Ioniţă Scipione Bădescu' District Library): Str. Iuliu Maniu 13, 450016 Zalău; tel. (360) 56-69-19; fax (260) 63-20-07; e-mail biblio@bjs.ro; internet www.bjs.ro; f. 1950; 196,894 vols; Dir Prof. FLORICA POP; publ. *Revista I.D.E.I.*

Museums and Art Galleries

Aiud

Muzeul de Istorie Aiud (Aiud Museum of History): Piaţa Consiliul Europei 24, Judeţul Alba, 515200 Aiud; tel. (258) 86-54-59; fax (258) 86-12-80; e-mail paulscrobota@gmail.com; internet muzeu-aiud.cimec.ro; f. 1796; 30,000 museum objects; archaeology of the primitive commune, the Dacian-Roman period and the pre-feudal period; library of 1,800 vols; Dir PAUL VASILE SCROBOTĂ.

Muzeul de Ştiinţele Naturii Aiud (Aiud Natural Sciences Museum): Str. Bethlen Gabor 1, 515200 Aiud; tel. (258) 86-25-69; e-mail paulscrobota@gmail.com; internet muzeu-aiud.cimec.ro; f. 1796; collns of geology, mineralogy, palaeontology, botany, zoology; library of 500 vols; Dir PAUL VASILE SCROBOTĂ.

Alba Iulia

Muzeul Naţional al Unirii (National Museum of Union): Str. Mihai Viteazul 12–14, 510010 Alba Iulia; tel. (258) 81-33-00; fax (258) 81-18-53; e-mail muzeulalba_relatiipublice@yahoo.com; internet www.mnuai.ro; f. 1888; exhibits relating to prehistoric and Roman archaeology, medieval era, ecclesiastical history, ethnography and Romanian Union; library of 70,000 vols; Dir Dr GABRIEL TIBERIU RUSTOIU; publs

Apulum—Acta Musei Apulensis (1 a year), *Bibliotheca Musei Apulensis* (1 a year).

Alexandria

Muzeul Judeţean Teleorman (Teleorman District Museum): Str. 1848 1, 140033 Alexandria; tel. and fax (247) 31-47-61; e-mail muzjudteleorman@yahoo.com; internet www.muzeulteleorman.ro; f. 1952 as Alexandria Museum of History; archeology, art, ethnography, history, numismatics, palaeontology; Dir Dr ECATERINA ŢÂNŢĂREANU; publ. *Buletinul Muzeului Judetean Teleorman Seria Arheologie* (1 a year).

Arad

Complexul Muzeal Arad (Arad Museum Complex): Piaţa George Enescu 1, 310131 Arad; tel. (257) 28-18-47; fax (257) 28-01-14; e-mail office@museumarad.ro; internet www.museumarad.ro; f. 1893; archaeology, history, ethnology, natural sciences, fine and applied art; Man. Dr PETER HÜGEL; publs *Armonii Naturale* (natural history, every 2 years), *Studii şi Comunicări* (studies and communications of art and architecture, every 2 years), *Zarandul* (ethnology, every 2 years), *Ziridava* (archaeology and history, every 2 years).

Bacău

Complexul Muzeul 'Iulian Antonescu' Bacău (Bacău 'Iulian Antonescu' Museum Complex): Str. 9 Mai 7, 600037 Bacău; tel. and fax (234) 51-24-44; e-mail muzeuistorie_bacau@yahoo.com; internet www.cmiabc.ro; f. 1957; history, art, archaeology, ethnography, literature; library of 9,000 vols; Dir Prof. SILVIA IACOBESCU; publ. *Carpica* (1 a year).

Complexul Muzeul de Ştiinţele Naturii 'Ion Borcea' Bacău ('Ion Borcea' Natural Sciences Museum Complex of Bacău): Str. Aleea Parcului 9, 600033 Bacău; tel. and fax (234) 51-20-06; e-mail muzstnatbc@yahoo.com; internet www.adslexpress.ro/muzstnat; f. 1964; botany, geology, mineralogy, palaeontology, zoology; incl. Natural Sciences Museum of Bacău, vivarium of Bacău, Astronomic Observatory and Ion Borcea Memorial House, Racova, Bacău county; education, research; library of 23,000 vols; Dir Dr GABRIELA GURĂU; Deputy Dir Dr ORTANSA JIGAU; publ. *Studii şi Comunicări* (1 a year).

Baia Mare

Muzeul Judeţean Maramureş (Maramureş District Museum): Str. Monetăriei 1–3, 430406 Baia Mare; tel. and fax (262) 21-19-27; e-mail muzeumm@rdslink.ro; internet www.muzeumm.baiamare.rdsnet.ro; f. 1899; archeology, ethnography, history, planetary, Romanian art; library of 20,000 vols; Dir Gen. Prof. GRIGORE MAN; publ. *Marmaţia* (1 a year).

Associated Museum:

Muzeul de Mineralogie Baia Mare (Baia Mare Mineralogical Museum): Bdul Traian 8, 430212 Baia Mare; tel. and fax (262) 22-75-17; e-mail muzmin@rdslink.ro; internet www.muzeuminbm.ro; f. 1989; exhibition of rocks; minerals; mineralogical and crystallographic research; library of 900 vols; Man. IOAN BOB.

Bistriţa

Muzeul Judeţean Bistriţa (Bistriţa County Museum): Str. Gen. Grigore Bălan 19, 420016 Bistriţa; tel. and fax (263) 21-10-63; f. 1950; Dir Dr IOAN CHINTAUAN; publs *Studii şi Cercetări Etnoculturale*, *Revista Bistriţei* (history), *Studii şi Cercetări Ştiinţele Naturii*.

Botoşani

Muzeul Judeţean Botoşani (Botoşani District Museum): Str. Unirii 15, 710221 Botoşani; tel. (231) 51-34-46; fax (231) 53-69-89; e-mail istorie@muzeubt.ro; internet www.muzeubt.hhe.ro; f. 1955; history, archaeology, ethnography, fine arts; incl. 'Nicolae Iorga' and 'George Enescu' memorial houses; library of 10,000 vols; Man. Prof. LUCICA PÂRVAN.

Brad

Muzeul de Istorie şi Etnografie Brad (Brad History and Ethnography Museum): 335200 Brad; f. 1987; traditional arts and crafts, spec. colln of wooden objects; Curator MIHAI DAVID.

Brăila

Muzeul Brăilei (Brăila Museum): Piaţa Traian 3, 810153 Brăila; tel. (339) 40-10-02; fax (339) 40-10-03; e-mail sediu@muzeulbrailei.ro; internet www.muzeulbrailei.ro; f. 1881; archaeology, history, fine arts, ethnography, natural sciences; library of 26,000 vols and periodicals; Dir Dr IONEL CÂNDEA; Dir Adjunct VALERIU SÎRBU; Dir Adjunct ZAMFIR BĂLAN; publs *ISTROS* (every 2 years), *Analele Brăilei* (every 2 years).

Bran

Muzeul Bran (Bran Museum): Str. Traian Mosoiu 495–498, 507025 Bran; tel. (268) 23-83-33; fax (268) 47-56-07; e-mail contact@muzeul-bran.ro; internet www.muzeul-bran.ro; f. 1957; Bran castle, history, ethnography, feudal art; Dir NARCIS DORIN ION.

Braşov

Muzeul, Biblioteca şi Arhiva Istorică a Primei Şcoli Româneşti din Şcheii Braşovului (Museum, Library and Historical Archive of First Romanian School of Braşov): Piaţa Unirii 1, 500123 Braşov; tel. (268) 14-38-79; f. 1933; historical museum in building of first Romanian school (15th century); Dir Dr VASILE OLTEANU.

Muzeul de Artă (Art Museum): Bdul Eroilor 21, 500030 Braşov; tel. (268) 47-72-86; fax (268) 47-51-72; e-mail contact@muzeulartabv.ro; internet www.muzeulartabv.ro; f. 1949; decorative arts, Romanian fine arts; Dir BARTHA ÁRPÁD.

Muzeul de Etnografie (Ethnographical Museum): Bdul Eroilor 21A, 500030 Braşov; tel. (268) 47-62-43; fax (268) 47-55-62; e-mail muzeu@etnobrasov.ro; internet www.etnobrasov.ro; Dir Dr LIGIA FULGA.

Muzeul Judeţean de Istorie Braşov (Braşov District History Museum): Nicolae Bălcescu 67, 500019 Braşov; tel. and fax (268) 47-23-50; internet istoriebv.ro; f. 1908; library of 23,000 vols; Dir Dr RADU ŞTEFĂNESCU; publ. *Cumidava*.

Bucharest

Muzeul Căilor Ferate Române (Romanian Railway Museum): Calea Griviţei 193A, 010711 Bucharest; tel. (21) 223-06-60; f. 1939; attached to Min. of Transport; materials, parts, documentary illustrating the evolution of rail transport.

Muzeul de Istorie al Evreilor din România 'Dr Moses Rosen' (Dr Moses Rosen History Museum of the Jews in Romania): Str. Mămulari 3, 030771 Bucharest; tel. (21) 311-08-70; e-mail bucharestjewmuseum@gmail.com; f. 1978; Dir Dr E. MAXIM.

Muzeul Literaturii Române (Museum of Romanian Literature): Bdul Dacia 12, 010412 Bucharest; tel. (21) 212-58-45; fax (21) 212-58-46; internet www.mlr.ro; f. 1957; library of 80,000 vols and periodicals and 46,000 MSS and photographs; historical documents; old and rare books; art objects; periodicals; photographs; audio/video colln; publ. *Manuscriptum* (4 a year).

Muzeul Municipiului Bucureşti (Bucharest Municipality Museum): Bdul I. C. Brătianu 2, 030174 Bucharest; tel. (21) 315-68-58; fax (21) 310-25-62; e-mail mmb@muzeulbucurestiului.ro; internet www.muzeulbucurestiului.ro; f. 1921; 10 affiliated museums; library of 53,700 vols; Dir Dr IONEL IONITA; publ. *Bucuresti: Materiale de Istorie si Muzeografie*.

Muzeul Naţional Cotroceni (Cotroceni National Museum): Bdul Geniului 1, 060116 Bucharest; tel. (21) 317-31-06; fax (21) 312-16-18; e-mail vizitare@aim.com; internet www.muzeulcotroceni.ro; f. 1991; Romanian art, medieval architecture, decorative art, history; museum pedagogy; tours and visits; organizes confs, exhibits and workshops; Dir ADINA RENŢEA.

Muzeul Naţional de Artă al României (National Museum of Art of Romania): Calea Victoriei 49–53, 010063 Bucharest; tel. (21) 314-81-19; fax (21) 312-47-27; e-mail national.art@art.museum.ro; internet www.mnar.arts.ro; f. 1950; European art since 14th century, Romanian religious and secular works of art from 14th–18th centuries, Romanian modern art since 19th century; also administers Arts Collns Museum, Theodor Pallady Museum and K. H. Zambaccian Museum; library of 40,000 vols; Gen. Dir ROXANA THEODORESCU.

Muzeul Naţional de Istorie a României (National History Museum of Romania): Calea Victoriei 12, 030026 Bucharest; tel. (21) 315-82-07; fax (21) 311-33-56; e-mail direct@mnir.ro; internet www.mnir.ro; f. 1972; library of 45,000 vols; Dir Dr CRIŞAN MUŞEŢEANU; publs *Muzeul Naţional*, *Cercetări arheologice*, *Cercetări numismatice*.

Muzeul Naţional de Istorie Naturală 'Grigore Antipa' ('Grigore Antipa' National Natural History Museum): Şoseaua Kiseleff 1, 011341 Bucharest; tel. (21) 312-88-26; fax (21) 312-88-63; e-mail imatache@antipa.ro; internet www.antipa.ro; f. 1834; zoology, hydrobiology, anatomy, oceanography, ecology, zoogeography, ethnography, anthropology; library of 30,200 vols, 20,000 periodicals; Dir-Gen. Adjunct IOANA MATACHE; publ. *Travaux* (1 a year).

Muzeul Naţional 'George Enescu' ('George Enescu' National Museum): Calea Victoriei 141, 010071 Bucharest; tel. (21) 318-14-50; fax (21) 312-91-82; e-mail office@georgeenescu.ro; internet www.georgeenescu.ro; f. 1956; Dir ILINCA DUMITRESCU.

Muzeul National al Satului 'Dimitrie Gusti' (National Village Museum 'Dimitrie Gusti'): Şoseaua Kiseleff 28–30, 011347 Bucharest; tel. (21) 317-91-03; fax (21) 317-90-68; e-mail contact@muzeul-satului.ro; internet www.muzeul-satului.ro; f. 1936; open-air nat. museum of village life since 17th century; library of 30,000 vols, 130,000 photographs; Dir-Gen. Dr PAULA POPOIU; publ. *Ethnos* (ethnographical and ethnological studies).

Muzeul National Filatelic: Calea Victoriei 12, sector 3, Bucharest; tel. (12) 312-74-99; fax (21) 312-55-85; internet www.muzeulfilatelic.ro; f. 1990; history of stamps and post; exhibits.

Muzeul Poliţiei Române: c/o Poliţia Română, Str. Mihai Voda 6, sector 5, Bucharest; tel. (21) 208-25-25; internet www.politiaromana.ro; f. 2000.

Muzeul National al Ţăranului Român (National Museum of the Romanian Peasant): Şoseaua Kiseleff 3, 011341 Bucharest;

tel. (21) 317-96-61; fax (21) 317-96-60; e-mail info@muzeultaranuluiroman.ro; internet www.muzeultaranuluiroman.ro; f. 1906; colln of 100,000 items on peasant art and traditions; research in field of ethnology and anthropology; Dir Gen. Dr VIRGIL STEFAN NITULESCU; publ. *MARTOR* (review, in French and English, 1 a year).

Muzeul Tehnic 'Prof. Ing. Dimitrie Leonida' (Prof. Eng. Dimitrie Leonida Museum of Technology): Str. Candiano Popescu 2, 040583 Bucharest; tel. and fax (21) 336-77-77; e-mail muztech@fdeb.rdsnet; f. 1909; library of 25,000 vols; Dir Dipl. Eng. NICOLAE DIACONESCU; publ. *Anuar*.

Buzău

Muzeul Judeţean Buzău (Buzău District Museum): N. Balcescu 50, 120360 Buzău; tel. (238) 71-05-61; fax (238) 71-06-38; e-mail home@muzeubuzau.ro; internet www.muzeubuzau.ro; f. 1951; history, folk art, contemporary decorative arts; Dir DOINA CIOBANU; publ. *Musaios* (1 a year).

Călăraşi

Muzeul Dunării de Jos (Museum of the Lower Danube): Str. 1 December 1918 1, 910019 Călăraşi; tel. (242) 31-13-01; fax (242) 33-16-09; e-mail cjcalarasi@calarasi.ro; internet www.calarasi.ro; f. 1951; archaeology, numismatics, medieval history, modern arts, natural history, ethnography of the area; Dir Dr MARIAN NEAGU; Pres. GEORGE RADUCU FILIPESCU; Vice-Pres. DANIEL STEPHEN DRAGULIN; Sec. ALAN VIRTEJANU.

Câmpulung

Muzeul Zonal Câmpulung (Câmpulung Zonal Museum): Str. Negru Vodă 119, 115100 Câmpulung; tel. (248) 11737; f. 1880; history, arts, natural science, ethnography, folk art; Dir ŞTEFAN TRĂMBACIU; publs *Studii şi comunicări*, *Istoria Câmpulungului şi a zonei Muscel*.

Câmpulung Moldovenesc

Muzeul Artei Lemnului (Wooden Art Museum): Calea Transilvaniei 10, 725100 Câmpulung Moldovenesc; tel. (230) 31-13-78; f. 1936; ethnography, history, arts, folk art; Dir MARCEL ZAHANICIUC.

Caracal

Muzeul Romanaţiului Caracal (Caracal Museum of the Romanaţi): Str. Libertăţii 26, 235200 Caracal; tel. (249) 51-13-44; f. 1951; history, ethnography, art, lapidarium; Dir PAUL LICĂ.

Caransebeş

Muzeul Judeţean de Etnografie şi a Regimentului de Graniţă-Caransebeş (Caransebeş Border District Ethnographic and Regimental Museum): Piaţa Gen. Ion Dragalina 2, 325400 Caransebeş; tel. (255) 51-41-73; fax (255) 51-21-93; f. 1929; history, ethnography, folk-art; incl. Tibiscum archaeological site; Dir Prof. Dr NICOLETA GUMĂ; publs *Tibiscum*, *Studii şi Comunicări de Etnografie şi Istorie*.

Cluj-Napoca

Grădina Botanică Alexandru Borza (The Alexandru Borza Botanical Garden): Republicii St 42, 400015 Cluj-Napoca; tel. (264) 59-76-04; fax (264) 43-18-58; e-mail grbot@grbot.ubbcluj.ro; internet www.ubbcluj.ro; f. 1920; attached to Babes-Bolyai Univ.; ornamental, phytogeographic, systematic, economic and medicinal sections; 51 mems; library of 25,000 vols; Dir Dr VASILE CRISTEA; publs *Contribuţii botanice* (1 a year), *Flora Romaniae Exsiccata*, *Delectus seminum* (1 a year), *The Seeds Catalogue and the Botanical Contributions review*.

Muzeul Etnografic al Transilvaniei (Transylvanian Museum of Ethnography): Memorandum St 21, 400114 Cluj-Napoca; tel. (264) 59-23-44; fax (264) 59-21-48; e-mail contact@muzeul-etnografic.ro; internet www.muzeul-etnografic.ro; f. 1922; incl. open-air nat. ethnographic park; Dir SIMONA MUNTEANU.

Muzeul Naţional de Artă Cluj: Piaţa Unirii 30, 400098 Cluj-Napoca; tel. (264) 59-69-52; e-mail macn@cluj.astral.ro; internet www.macluj.ro; f. 1951; Romanian and foreign art from 16th to 21st centuries; library of 9,000 vols; Dir Dr LIVIA DRĂGOI.

Muzeul Naţional de Istorie a Transilvaniei (National History Museum of Transylvania): Str. Constantin Daicoviciu 2, 400020 Cluj-Napoca; tel. (264) 19-56-77; fax (264) 19-17-18; internet www.museum.utcluj.ro; f. 1859; library of 28,000 vols; Dir IOAN PISO; publ. *Acta Musei Napocensis* (1 a year).

Muzeul Zoologic al Universităţii 'Babeş Bolyai' Cluj-Napoca (Zoological Museum of the Cluj-Napoca 'Babeş Bolyai' University): Str. Clinicilor 5–7, 400006 Cluj-Napoca; tel. (264) 59-57-39; e-mail dceuca@hasdeu.ubbcluj.ro; internet www.ubbcluj.ro; f. 1859; integrated in the Faculty of Biology and Geology; incl. exhibits, scientific collns, museum reserve; Dir Dr IION COROIU; publ. *Studia* (1 a year).

Constanţa

Complexul Muzeal de Ştiinţe ale Naturii (Natural History Museum Complex): Bdul Mamaia 255, 900522 Constanţa; tel. (241) 54-70-55; fax (241) 48-12-36; e-mail office@delfinariu.ro; internet www.delfinariu.ro; f. 1958; aquarium, dolphinarium, planetarium, astronomical observatory, micro-reservation; Dir GABRIELA PLOTOAGĂ; publ. *Pontus Euxinus*.

Muzeul de Artă (Art Museum): Bdul Tomis 84, 900657 Constanţa; tel. (241) 61-70-12; f. 1961; Romanian paintings and other works of art; Dir DOINA PAULEANU.

Muzeul de Artă Populară (Folk Art Museum): Bdul Tomis 32, 900742 Constanţa; tel. (241) 61-61-33; fax (241) 61-61-33; e-mail muzeuetno@yahoo.com; internet muzeuetno.blogspot.com; Dir Dr MARIA MAGIRU.

Muzeul de Istorie Naţională şi Arheologie Constanţa (Constanţa Museum for National History and Archaeology): Piaţa Ovidiu 12, 900745 Constanţa; tel. (241) 61-87-63; e-mail minaconstanta@gmail.com; internet www.minac.ro; f. 1879; educational, archaeological activities, affiliated archaeological museums of Histria, Tropaeum Traiani and Capidava; library of 40,000 vols; 103 mems; Dir Dr GABRIEL CUSTUREA; publs *Pontica* (archaeology, ancient and medieval history, numismatic; 1 a year), *Analele Dobrogei* (modern and contemporary history; 1 a year).

Muzeul Marinei Române (Romanian Naval Museum): Str. Traian 53, 900725 Constanţa; tel. (241) 61-90-35; fax (241) 61-90-35; e-mail naval.museum@yahoo.com; internet www.navy.ro; f. 1969; history of Romanian navy and merchant fleet; Dir Cmdr Dr GLODARENCO OLIMPIU MANUEL.

Corabia

Muzeul de Arheologie şi Etnografie Corabia (Corabia Archaeological and Ethnographical Museum): Str. Cuza Vodă 65, 235300 Corabia; tel. (249) 56-13-64; Dir FLOREA BÂCIU.

Craiova

Muzeul Regional al Olteniei (Regional Museum of Oltenia): Madona Dudu St. 14, 200410 Craiova; tel. (251) 41-77-56; fax (251) 41-94-35; e-mail office@muzeulolteniei.ro; internet www.muzeulolteniei.ro; f. 1915; incorporates museums of art, ethnography, natural history, and archaeology and history; library of 12,000 vols; Gen. Man. Prof. Dr MIHAI VIOREL FIFOR; publ. *Oltenia—Studii şi cercetări*.

Curtea de Argeş

Muzeul de Istorie şi Etnografie (History and Ethnography Museum): Str. Negru Vodă 2, 115300 Curtea de Argeş; tel. (248) 1-14-46; Dir N. MOISESCU.

Deva

Muzeul Civilizaţiei Dacice şi Romane Deva (Deva Museum of Dacian and Roman Civilization): Bdul 1 Decembrie 1918 nr. 39, 2700 Deva, Hunedoara; tel. (254) 21-22-00; fax (254) 21-22-00; e-mail museum@worldwidesam.net; internet museum.worldwidesam.net; f. 1882; archaeology, history, natural sciences, numismatics, art, ethnography; incorporates museum of Roman archaeology at Sarmizegetusa and the ethnographical museums at Orăştie and Brad; library of 30,980 vols; Dir ADRIANA RUSU-PESCARU; publ. *Sargetia. Acta Musei Devensis*.

Drobeta-Turnu Severin

Muzeul Regiunii 'Porţile de Fier' ('Iron Gates' Regional Museum): Str. Independenţei 2, 220171 Drobeta-Turnu Severin; tel. (52) 31-21-77; fax (52) 32-00-27; f. 1882; natural history, ethnography, archaeology and Roman ruins; aquarium; Dir Dr ION KNOWNGA; Deputy Dir GABRIEL CRACIUNESCU; publ. *Drobeta* (1 a year).

Focşani

Muzeul Vrancei (Vrancea Museum): Bdul Gării 5, 620012 Focşani; tel. (237) 22-28-90; f. 1951; incorporates museums of ethnography (open-air), natural history, and history and archaeology; Dir HORIA DUMITRESCU.

Galaţi

Muzeul Judeţean de Istorie (District Museum of History): Str. Maior Iancu Fotea 2, 800017 Galaţi; tel. (236) 41-42-28; f. 1939; library of 8,000 vols; Dir ŞTEFAN STANCIU; publ. *Danubius*.

Attached Museums:

Complexul Muzeal de Ştiinţele Naturii (Natural Science Museum Complex): Str. Regiment 11 Siret, 800340 Galaţi; tel. (236) 41-18-98; fax (236) 41-44-75; e-mail contact@cmsngl.ro; f. 1956; flora and fauna of the region, botanical and zoological gardens, aquarium; Dir Ing. CAMELIA GROSU.

Muzeul de Arta Vizuala (Visual Art Museum): Str. Domnească 141, 800163 Galaţi; tel. (236) 41-34-52; fax (236)-31-25-02; e-mail contact@mavgl.ro; internet www.mavgl.ro; f. 1956; Dir DAN BASARAB NANU.

Gherla

Muzeul de Istorie Gherla: Str. Mihai Viteazul 6, Judeţul Cluj, 405300 Gherla; tel. (264) 24-19-47; fax (264) 24-16-66; e-mail mihaimester@personal.ro; f. 1881; Daco-Roman archaeology, ethnography, local history; library of 4,221 vols; Dir RODICA PINTEA.

Giurgiu

Muzeul Judeţean 'Teohari Antonescu' (Giurgiu District Museum): Str. Constantin Dobrogeanu Gherea nr 3, 080024 Giurgiu;

tel. (246) 21-68-01; e-mail muzeuljudeteangiurgiu@gmail.com; internet muzulgiurgiu.ro; f. 1934; history, ethnography; medieval archaeology, prehistoric archaeology, memorial history; Dir TRAIAN POPA; publ. *File de istorie*.

Goleşti

Muzeul Viticulturii şi Pomiculturii Goleşti (Viticulture and Tree Growing Museum from Goleşti): Ştefăneşti Commune, Judeţul Argeş, 117715 Goleşti; tel. and fax (248) 26-63-64; e-mail cmngolesti@yahoo.com; internet www.muzeulgolesti.ro; f. 1939; history of fruit- and vine-growing; library of 13,000 vols; Dir Dr FILOFTEIA PALLY.

Gura Humorului

Muzeul Obiceiurilor Populare din Bucovina (Museum of Bucovinean Folk Traditions): Piaţa Republicii 2, 725300 Gura Humorului; tel. (230) 23-11-08; fax (230) 23-50-51; e-mail muzeulhumor@gmail.com; f. 1958; ethnographic colln; colln of numismatics; colln of songs, historic and natural sciences; library of 2,415 vols; Dir ELVIRA ROMANIUC.

Iaşi

Complexul Naţional Muzeal 'Moldova' Iaşi ('Moldova' Iaşi National Museum Complex): Piaţa Ştefan cel Mare şi Sfânt 1, 700028 Iaşi; tel. and fax (232) 21-83-83; internet www.palatulculturii.ro; f. 1992; closed for renovation during 2011; Dir VAL CONDURACHE; publs *Cercetări istorice* (1 a year), *Buletinul Ioan Neculce* (1 a year), *Anuarul Muzeului Etnografic al Moldovei* (1 a year), *Buletinul Centrului de Restaurare-Conservare* (2 a year).

Selected Constituent Museums:

Muzeul de Artă din Iaşi (Iaşi Art Museum): Piaţa Ştefan cel Mare şi Sfânt 1, 700028 Iaşi; tel. (232) 31-41-36 ext. 124; fax (232) 21-83-83; internet www.palatulculturii.ro; f. 1860; Curator IVONA ARAMĂ.

Muzeul Etnografic al Moldovei (Ethnographic Museum of Moldavia): Piaţa Ştefan cel Mare şi Sfânt 1, 700028 Iaşi; tel. (232) 31 41 36 ext. 144, fax (232) 21-83-83; internet www.palatulculturii.ro; f. 1943; Curator VASILE MUNTEANU.

Muzeul de Istorie a Moldovei (History Museum of Moldavia): Piaţa Ştefan cel Mare şi Sfânt 1, 700028 Iaşi; tel. (232) 31-41-36 ext. 135; fax (232) 21-83-83; internet www.palatulculturii.ro; f. 1916; incl. Al. I. Cuza Memorial Museum, in Ruginoasa, Mihail Kogalniceanu Memorial Museum in Iaşi, Museum of the Union in Iaşi (dedicated to the period of creating and maintaining the union of the Romanian lands), History Museums in Hârlău and Paşcani, and archaeological sites at Cucuteni and Cotnari; Curator SENICA TURCANU.

Muzeul Ştiinţei şi Tehnicii 'Ştefan Procopiu' (Museum of Science and Technology 'Stefan Procopiu'): Piaţa Ştefan cel Mare şi Sfânt 1, 700028 Iaşi; tel. (232) 31-41-36 ext. 145; fax (232) 21-83-83; internet www.palatulculturii.ro; f. 1955; incl. Iaşi Memorial Museum 'Poni-Cernatescu'; Curator LENUŢA CHIRIŢĂ.

Muzeul de Istorie Naturală Iaşi (Iaşi Natural History Museum): Str. Română 40, 700312 Iaşi; f. 1834; attached to Alexandru Ioan Cuza Univ.; geology, palaeontology, zoology; Dir Dr ION COJOCARU.

Muzeul Literaturii Române Iaşi: Str. Vasile Pogor 4, Iaşi; tel. (232) 41-03-40; fax (232) 21-32-10; e-mail contact@muzeulliteraturiiiasi.ro; internet www.muzeulliteraturiiiasi.ro; f. 1918; organizes exhibits, confs; modern and contemporary Romanian literature; publ. *Dacia literară*.

Mangalia

Muzeul de Arheologie 'Callatis' Mangalia (Callatis Archaeological Museum of Mangalia): Şoseaua Constanţei 23, 905500 Mangalia; tel. (241) 75-35-80; e-mail sorinmarcelcolesniuc@yahoo.com; internet www.muzeulcallatis.ro; f. 1924; prehistory, Greek and Roman periods, ancient Greek colony of Callatis; library of 2,800 vols; Dir Dr SORIN MARCEL COLESNIUC; publ. *Studia Callatiana*.

Mediaş

Muzeul Municipal Mediaş (Mediaş Municipal Museum): Str. M. Viteazu 46, 551034 Mediaş; tel. (269) 84-12-99; fax (269) 84-12-29; f. 1950; history, natural history, ethnography, incl. classical and contemporary arts; Dir Dr PETER WEBER.

Miercurea Ciuc

Muzeul Secuiesc al Ciucului/Csíki Székely Múzeum (Szekler Museum of Ciuc): Piaţa Cetăţii 2, Judeţul Harghita, 530132 Miercurea Ciuc; tel. (266) 37-20-24; fax (266) 31-17-27; e-mail info@csikimuzeum.ro; internet www.csikimuzeum.ro; f. 1930; history, ethnography, archaeology, 20th-century art history, old books; library of 9,000 vols; Dir ZSOLT GYARMATI; publ. *Yearbook*.

Mogoşoaia

Centrul Naţional de Cultura Mogoşoaia (Mogoşoaia National Cultural Centre): Brâncoveanu Palace, Ilfov, Str. Valea Parcului 1, Com., 077135 Mogoşoaia; tel. (21) 490-40-22; fax (21) 225-66-90; e-mail pbpb@xnet.ro; f. 1702; medieval Romanian art; Dir DOINA MANDRU.

Năsăud

Muzeul Năsăudean (Năsăud Museum): Str. Grănicerilor 19, 425200 Năsăud; tel. (263) 36-29-67; history, ethnography; Dir IOAN RADU NISTOR.

Negresti Oas

Muzeul Ţării Oaşului: Str. Victoriei 140, Negresti Oas, Satu Mare; tel. and fax (261) 85-48-39; internet www.oasmuseum.ro; colln of ethnography and folk art.

Oradea

Muzeul Ţării Crişurilor (Criş County Museum): Bdul Dacia 1–3, 410464 Oradea; tel. (259) 41-27-24; fax (259) 41-27-25; e-mail contact@mtariicrisurilor.ro; internet www.mtariicrisurilor.ro; f. 1971; history, art, ethnography and natural science; library of 30,000 vols; Gen. Man. Prof. Dr AUREL CHIRIAC; publs *Biharea* (ethnography and art, 1 a year), *Crisia* (history and archaeology, 1 a year), *Nymphaea* (natural sciences, 1 a year).

Orăştie

Sectia de Etnografie şi Artă Populară Orăştie (Dept of Ethnography and Folk Art Orăştie): Piata Aurel Vlaicu 1, 335700 Orăştie; tel. and fax (254) 24-73-00; f. 1952; Curator COSMA AURELIAN.

Petroşani

Muzeul Mineritului (Mining Museum): Str. N. Bălcescu 12, 332026 Petroşani; tel. (254) 54-17-44; f. 1961; history of mining in the Jiu Valley; Dir DUMITRU PELIGRAD.

Piatra-Neamţ

Complexul Muzeal Judeţean Neamţ (Neamţ District Museums Complex): Bdul Mihai Eminescu 10, 610029 Piatra-Neamţ; tel. (233) 21-74-96; e-mail muzeupn@yahoo.com; internet www.neamt.ro; f. 1978; archaeology, history, arts, memoirs, ethnography, natural sciences colln; Dir GHEORGHE DUMITROAIA.

Selected Affiliated Museums:

Muzeul de Artă Piatra-Neamţ (Piatra-Neamţ Art Museum): Piaţa Libertăţii 1, 610100 Piatra-Neamţ; tel. (233) 21-68-08; internet www.neamt.ro; f. 1980; Romanian art; Curator VIOLETA DINU.

Muzeul de Etnografie Piatra-Neamţ (Piatra-Neamţ Ethnography Museum): Piaţa Libertăţii 1, 610100 Piatra-Neamţ; tel. (233) 21-68-08; internet www.neamt.ro; Curator FLORENTINA BUZENSCHI.

Muzeul de Istorie şi Arheologie Piatra-Neamţ (Piatra-Neamţ History and Archaeology Museum): Bdul Mihai Eminescu 10, 610029 Piatra-Neamţ; tel. (233) 21-81-08; e-mail muzeupn@yahoo.com; internet www.neamt.ro; f. 1934; archaeological colln; Curator GHEORGHE DUMITROAIA; publ. *Memoria Antiquitatis* (1 a year).

Muzeul de Ştiinţele Naturii Piatra-Neamţ (Piatra-Neamţ Natural History Museum): Str. Petru Rareş 26, 610119 Piatra-Neamţ; tel. (233) 22-42-11; internet www.neamt.ro; f. 1960; colln of fossil fish; Curator NICOLETA LĂCĂTUS; publ. *Studii şi comunicări* (1 a year).

Piteşti

Muzeul Judeţean Argeş (Argeş County Museum): Str. Armand Călinescu 44, 110047 Piteşti; tel. and fax (248) 21-25-61; e-mail muzeuarges@yahoo.com; internet www.muzeul-judetean-arges.ro; f. 1928; history, art, natural history, archaeology, numismatics, fine arts, planetarium, museum of sports, editorial house (Editura Ordessos); organizes nat. and int. exhibits; library of 22,000 vols; Gen. Dir Dr SPIRIDON CRISTOCEA; Dir Adjunct Dr DRAGOS MANDESCU; publs *Argessis—Studii şi comunicări* (Studies and Reports), *Argessis—Studii şi comunicări* (history series and natural science series, 1 a year), *Naturalia* (ecology, 1 a year).

Ploieşti

Muzeul Judetean de Stiintele Naturii Prahova (Prahova County Natural Sciences Museum): Erou Calin Catalin 1, 100066 Ploieşti; tel. (244) 59-78-96; fax (244) 51-19-70; e-mail office@muzbioph.ro; internet www.muzbioph.ro; f. 1956; Dir Gen. Prof. Dr EMILIA IANCU; Dir PETRESCU VICTOR; publ. *Comunicări şi referate*.

Muzeul Judeţean de Artă Prahova: Bdul Independenţei 1, 100028 Ploieşti; tel. (244) 52-22-64; fax (244) 51-13-75; e-mail office@artmuseum.ro; internet www.artmuseum.ro; f. 1931; present name 1955; Dir FLORIN SICOIE; Deputy Dir ALICE NECULEA.

Muzeul Judeţean de Istorie şi Arheologie Prahova (Prahova District Museum of History and Archaeology): Str. Toma Caragiu 10, 100042 Ploieşti; tel. and fax (244) 51-44-37; e-mail histmuseumph@yahoo.com; internet www.histmuseumph.ro; f. 1953; library of 60,247 vols; Dir-Gen. LIA MARIA VOICU; Deputy Dir EUGEN STANESCU; Deputy Dir MARINELA PENEŞ; Dir VALERIA ANGHEL; publs *Studii şi comunicări* (1 a year), *Yearbook Museum of History and Archaeology Prahova*.

Muzeul Naţional al Petrolului (National Oil Museum): Str. Dr Bagdazar 8, 100575 Ploieşti; tel. (244) 59-75-85; fax (244) 51-95-42; e-mail muzeu.petrol@petrom.com; f. 1961; history of the Romanian oil industry;

library of 3,000 vols; Dir GABRIELA TĂNĂSESCU.

Rădăuţi

Muzeul Etnografic Rădăuţi (Rădăuţi Ethnographic Museum): Piaţa Unirii 63, 725400 Rădăuţi; tel. (230) 46-25-65; internet www.muzeulradauti.ro; f. 1920; Dir TRAJAN POSTOLACHE.

Râmnicu Vâlcea

Muzeul Judeţean Vâlcea: Calea Traian 143, Râmnicu Vâlcea; tel. (250) 73-81-21; e-mail mjv@avansoft.ro; internet www.muzee-valcea.ro; f. 1955; cultural institution specialized in research, conservation, restoration and cultural heritage.

Attached Museums:

Muzeul de Istorie a Judetului Valcea: Calea lui Traian 143, Râmnicu Vâlcea; tel. and fax (250) 73-81-21; e-mail mjv@avansoft.ro; collns of Paleolithic, Neolithic and Bronze ages.

Muzeul de Arta Casa Simian: Strada Carol I 25, Râmnicu Vâlcea; tel. and fax (250) 73-81-21; painting and sculpture from 18th, 19th and 20th centuries.

Complexul Muzeal Maldaresti: comuna Maldaresti, la aprox. 3 km de orasul Horezu; tel. and fax (250) 86-15-10.

Casa Memoriala Anton Pann: Str. Stirbei Voda 4, Râmnicu Vâlcea; tel. and fax (250) 73-80-26.

Muzeul de arheologie si arta religioasa Gh. Petre-Govora: Baile Govora, judetul Valcea; tel. and fax (250) 73-81-21; archeological colln, incl. material, coins, works of art and rare books.

Colectia de arta plastica Alexandru Balintescu: comuna Costesti, la aprox. 5 km de orasul Horezu, drumul spre m-rea Bistrita, Judeţul Valcea; tel. and fax (250) 73-81-21; Colln of fine arts.

Muzeul Satului Valcean: Comuna Bujoreni, Judeţul Valcea; tel. (250) 74-68-69; images of traditional rural settlements.

Reghin

Muzeul Etnografic Reghin (Reghin Ethnographic Museum): Str. Vînătorilor 51, Judeţul Mureş, 545300 Reghin; tel. (265) 51-25-71; e-mail muzeureghin@yahoo.com; internet muzeureghin.xhost.ro; f. 1960; folk art, textiles, wood icons, costumes; library of 2,336 vols, 3,186 slides, 128 ethnological films; Dir MARIA BORZAN; Librarian ADRIAN BUGNAR.

Reşiţa

Muzeul Banatului Montan (Museum of the Mountainous Banat): Bdul Republicii 10, 320151 Reşiţa; tel. (355) 40-12-19; fax (355) 40-12-20; e-mail office@muzeulbanatuluimontan.ro; internet www.muzeulbanatuluimontan.ro; f. 1959; culture; research; museography; museology; archaeology; library of 27,000 vols; Dir Dr DUMITRU ŢEICU; publs *Arheologia Medievală*, *Banatica*, *Yearbook*.

Roman

Muzeul de Istorie Roman (Museum of Roman History): Str. Cuza Vodă 19, 611009 Roman; tel. (233) 72-77-26; fax (233) 72-77-26; f. 1957; Curator Dr VASILE URSACHI.

Satu Mare

Muzeul Judeţean Satu Mare (Satu Mare District Museum): Bdul Vasile Lucaciu 21, 440031 Satu Mare; tel. (261) 73-75-26; fax (261) 76-87-61; e-mail muzeusm@gmail.com; internet www.muzeusm.ro; f. 1891; history, ethnography, paintings by Aurel Popp; library of 60,000 vols; Man. VIOREL CIUBOTA; publs *Studii şi Comunicări*, *Satu Mare*.

Sf. Gheorghe

Muzeul Naţional Secuiesc (National Szekler Museum): Str. Kos Karoly 10, jud. Covasna, 520055 Sfântu Gheorghe; tel. and fax (267) 31-24-42; e-mail office.sznm@gmail.com; internet www.szekelynemzetimuzeum.ro; f. 1875; history, ethnography, archaeology, natural history, icons, classical and modern Hungarian art; library of 110,000 vols; Dir MIHÁLY VARGHA; Sec. TÜNDE TAMÁS; publs *Acta Margitensia* (1 a year), *Acta Siculica* (1 a year).

Sibiu

Complexul Naţional Muzeal 'ASTRA' (ASTRA National Museum Complex): Piaţa Mică 11, jud. Sibiu, 550182 Sibiu; tel. (269) 21-81-95; fax (269) 21-80-60; e-mail office@muzeulastra.ro; internet www.muzeulastra.ro; f. 1963; present name 2001; incl. Muzeul de Etnografie Universală 'Franz Binder'; Muzeul Civilizaţiei Populare Tradiţionale ASTRA; Muzeul Civilizaţiei Transilvane Astra; Muzeul de Etnografie şi Artă Populară Săsească 'Emil Sigerus'; Proiectul unui Muzeu al Culturii şi Civilizaţiei Rromilor; library of 16,428 vols; Dir VALERIU ION OLARU; publ. *Cibinium* (Romanian museology and the history of traditional folk civilization, every 2 years).

Muzeul Naţional Brukenthal (Brukenthal National Museum): Piaţa Mare 4–5, Sibiu; tel. (269) 21-76-91; fax (269) 21-15-45; e-mail info@brukenthalmuseum.ro; internet www.brukenthalmuseum.ro; f. 1817; history, ethnography, 15th- to 18th-century European painting; library: see Libraries and Archives; Dir-Gen. SABIN ADRIAN LUCA; Scientific Dir GHEORGHE BAN; publs *Cibinium*, *Studii şi Comunicări*.

Affiliated Museums:

Muzeul de Istorie Naturală din Sibiu (Sibiu Natural History Museum): Str. Cetăţii 1, 550160 Sibiu; tel. (369) 10-17-82; e-mail rodica.ciobanu@brukenthalmuseum.ro; f. 1849; library of 65,000 vols; Dir Dr RODICA CIOBANU; publ. *Studii şi Comunicări de Ştiinţe Naturale*.

Muzeul de Istorie 'Casa Altemberger': Str. Mitropoliei 2, Sibiu; tel. (269) 21-81-43; e-mail dragos.diaconescu@brukenthalmuseum.ro; Dir Dr DRAGOŞ DIACONESCU.

Muzeul de Istorie a Farmaciei: Piata Mica 26, Sibiu; tel. (269) 21-81-91; f. 1972.

Muzeul de Vânătoare 'August Von Spiess': Str. Şcoala de Înot 4, Sibiu; tel. (369) 10-17-84; f. 1966.

Sighetu Marmaţiei

Muzeul Maramureşului, Sighetul Marmaţiei (Sighetul Marmaţiei Maramureş Museum): Str. Libertăţii 15, 435500 Sighetul Marmaţiei; tel. and fax (262) 31-15-21; e-mail muzeulmaramureşului@yahoo.com; f. 1873; history, ethnography, natural history, open-air museum, memorial houses (Elie Wiesel's memorial house, Dr Ioan Mihaly de Apşa's memorial house, etc., traditional houses preserved in situ); Dir Dr MIHAI DĂNCUŞ; publs *Acta Musei Maramorosiensis* (1 a year), *Tradiţii şi Patrimoniu* (Traditions and Patrimoniu, 2 a year).

Sighişoara

Muzeul de Istorie Sighişoara (Sighişoara History Museum): Piaţa Muzeului 1, 545400 Sighişoara; tel. and fax (265) 77-11-08; e-mail info@muzeusighisoara.com; internet www.muzeusighisoara.com; f. 1899; weapon colln; Dir Dr NICOLAE TESCULA.

Slatina

Muzeul Judeţean Olt (Olt District Museum): Str. Ana Ipătescu 1, 230079 Slatina; tel. and fax (249) 41-52-79; e-mail muzeu_olt@yahoo.com; internet www.mjolt.ro; f. 1951; archaeology collns; Dir LAURENTIU GUTICA-FLORESCU.

Slobozia

Muzeul Judeţean Ialomiţa (Ialomiţa District Museum): Bdul Matei Basarab 30, 920055 Slobozia; tel. (243) 23-00-54; e-mail office@mjialomita.ro; internet www.cicnet.ro; history, ethnography, archaeology, and plastic art; painting, graphics, sculpture; Dir FLORIN VLAD.

Suceava

Muzeul Naţional al Bucovinei (Bucovina National Museum): Str. Ştefan cel Mare 33, 720003 Suceava; tel. (230) 71-64-39; f. 1900; folk art, history, natural history, astronomical observatory, planetarium, Romanian fine arts; library of 91,000 vols; Dir PAVEL BLAJ; publ. *Suceava—Anuarul Muzeului judeţean* (history and natural sciences sections).

Târgovişte

Complexul National Muzeal 'Curtea Domneasca' (The National Museum Complex 'The Royal Court'): Str. Justiţiei 7, 130014 Târgovişte, jud. Dambovita; tel. and fax (245) 61-28-77; e-mail contact@muzee-dambovitene.ro; internet www.muzee-dambovitene.ro; f. 1940; archaeology, ethnography, fine arts, history of books and printing in Romania; Dir GH. BULEI; publ. *Vallachica*.

Târgu Jiu

Muzeul Judeţean Gorj (Gorj District Museum): c/o Muzeul de Istorie şi Arheologie, Str. Geneva 8, 210136 Târgu Jiu; tel. (253) 21-20-44; fax (253) 21-20-44; Dir Prof. VASILE MARINOIU.

Constituent Museums:

Muzeul Arhitecturii Populare din Gorj (Gorj Museum of Folk Architecture): open-air Curtişoara village, 215101 Bumbeşti-Jiu; f. 1968; Curator Prof. VASILE PETRE.

Muzeul de Artă (Art Museum): Parcul Central, 210132 Târgu Jiu; tel. (253) 21-85-50; f. 1982; Romanian contemporary art; sculptures by Brâncuşi; Curator CARMEN SILVIA ŞOCU.

Muzeul de Istorie şi Arheologie (History and Archaeology Museum): Str. Geneva 8, Jud. Gorj, 210136 Târgu Jiu; tel. (253) 21-20-44; f. 1894; library of 10,000 vols.

Târgu Mureş

Muzeul Judeţean Mureş (Mureş District Museum): Str. Horea 24, 540036 Târgu Mureş; tel. (265) 42-56-34; Dir VALER POP; publ. *Marisia* (1 a year).

Attached Museums:

Muzeul de Arheologie şi Istorie (Archaeology and History Museum): Str. George Enescu 2, 540052 Târgu Mureş; tel. (265) 43-25-12.

Muzeul de Artă (Art Museum): Str. George Enescu 2, 540052 Târgu Mureş; tel. (265) 43-21-79; f. 1913; art of the 19th and 20th centuries.

Timişoara

Muzeul Banatului Timişoara (Timiş Museum of the Banat): Piaţa Huniade nr. 1, în clădirea monument istoric, Castelul Huniazilor, 300002 Timişoara, Timiş; tel. (256) 49-13-39; fax (256) 20-13-21; e-mail muzeul.banatului@yahoo.com; internet www

.muzeulbanatului.ro; f. 1872; archaeology, natural history, ethnography, art; Dir DAN LEOPOLD CIOBOTARU; publ. *Analele Banatului* (1 a year).

Vaslui

Muzeul Judeţean 'Ştefan cel Mare' Vaslui (Vaslui District 'Stephen the Great' Museum): Piaţa Independenţei 1, 730240 Vaslui; tel. (235) 31-16-26; e-mail museumvs@yahoo.com; f. 1975; ancient history and archaeology, ethnography and folk art, modern Romanian art; library of 5,000 vols; Dir IOAN MANCAŞ; publ. *Acta Moldaviae Meridionalis* (5–10 a year).

Zalău

Muzeul Judeţean de Istorie şi Artă Sălaj (Sălaj District Museum of History and Art): Str. Unirii 9, 450042 Zalău; tel. (260) 61-22-23; fax (260) 66-17-06; e-mail muzeu@zalau.astral.ro; f. 1951; library of 14,975 vols; Dir DUMITRU GHEORGHE TAMBA; publ. *Acta Musei Porolissensis* (1 a year).

Universities

UNIVERSITATEA '1 DECEMBRIE 1918' DIN ALBA IULIA (1 December 1918 University, Alba Iulia)

Str. Gabriel Bethlen 5, 510009 Alba Iulia
Telephone: (258) 80-61-30
Fax: (258) 81-26-30
E-mail: cond@uab.ro
Internet: www.uab.ro

Founded 1991
State control
Languages of instruction: Romanian, English, French
Academic year: October to July

Rector: Prof. Dr Eng. MOISE IOAN ACHIM
Vice-Rector for Education and Institutional Strategy: Assoc. Prof. Dr LUCIA CABULEA
Vice-Rector for Financing, Human Resources and Investments: Prof. Dr NICOLAE TODEA
Vice-Rector for Scientific Research and Int. Relations: Prof. Dr IOAN ILEANA
Gen.-Man. Dir: Eng. VASILE MARCULET
Chief Accountant: SOFIA MIHALACHE
Sec.-in-Chief: CRISTINA HAVA
Library Dir: CORINA TOTAR

Library of 63,000 vols, 17,000 periodicals
Number of teachers: 175
Number of students: 6,022

Publication: *Bulletin of Medical Students*

Publications: *Acta Universitatis Apulensis* (1 a year), *RevCad* (1 a year), *Revista Annales Universitatis Apulensis*, *Pro Cont* (every 2 years)

DEANS

Faculty of History and Philology: Prof. Dr ILEANA VOICHITA GHEMES
Faculty of Law and Social Sciences: Assoc. Prof. Dr IOAN GANFALEAN
Faculty of Orthodox Theology: Prof. Dr ANDREICUT IOAN ANDREI
Faculty of Sciences: Prof. Dr SORIN BRICIU

UNIVERSITATEA 'ALEXANDRU IOAN CUZA' IAŞI

Bdul Carol I 11, 700506 Iaşi
Telephone: (232) 20-10-00
Fax: (232) 20-11-21
E-mail: contact@uaic.ro
Internet: www.uaic.ro

Founded 1860
State control
Academic year: October to July

Rector: Prof. Dr VASILE IŞAN
Vice-Rector for Alumni and Graduate Affairs: Prof. Dr CARMEN CREŢU
Vice-Rector for Institutional Devt: Prof. Dr Rev. GHEORGHE POPA
Vice-Rector for Int. Relations: Prof. Dr HENRI LUCHIAN
Vice-Rector for MA and PhD Studies: Prof. Dr GHEORGHE IACOB
Vice-Rector for Research and Innovation: Prof. Dr GHEORGHE POPA
Vice-Rector for Undergraduate Studies: Prof. Dr CONSTANTIN SĂLĂVĂSTRU
Univ. Chancellor: Prof. Dr CĂTĂLIN TĂNASE
Univ. Chief Sec.: OANA CONSTANDACHE
Gen. Admin. Man.: BOGDAN-EDUARD PLEŞCAN
Int. Relations Officer: LIVIA VRĂNESCU
Dir of Central Univ. Library: Prof. Dr ALEXANDRU CĂLINESCU

Library: see Libraries and Archives
Number of teachers: 838
Number of students: 38,000

Publication: *Analele Universităţii*

DEANS

Faculty of Biology: Prof. Dr ION MOGLAN
Faculty of Chemistry: Prof. Dr DUMITRU GÂNJU
Faculty of Computer Science: Prof. Dr GHEORGHE GRIGORAŞ
Faculty of Economics: Prof. Dr DINU AIRINEI
Faculty of Geography and Geology: Prof. Dr OVIDIU GABRIEL IANCU
Faculty of History: Prof. Dr ALEXANDRU FLORIN PLATON
Faculty of Law: Prof. Dr TUDOREL TOADER
Faculty of Letters: Prof. Dr ŞTEFAN AVĂDANEI
Faculty of Mathematics: Prof. Dr OVIDIU CÂRJĂ
Faculty of Orthodox Theology: Rev. Prof. Dr VIOREL SAVA
Faculty of Philosophy: Prof. Dr NICU GAVRILUŢĂ
Faculty of Physical Education and Sport: Assoc. Prof. MARIN CHIRAZI
Faculty of Physics: Prof. Dr MIHAI TOMA
Faculty of Psychology and Education Sciences: Prof. Dr ION DAFINOIU
Faculty of Roman Catholic Theology: Rev. Assoc. Prof. EMIL DUMEA

PROFESSORS

Faculty of Biology (Bdul Carol I 20, A, 700505 Iaşi; tel. (232) 20-10-72; fax (232) 20-14-72; e-mail admbio@uaic.ro; internet www.bio.uaic.ro):

AILIESEI, O., Microbiology, Immunology
ARTENIE, V., Biochemistry
CHIFU, T., Environmental Protection and Nature Preservation, Environmental Biodiversity, Phylogenesis
COJOCARU, D., Enzymology, Biochemistry
ION, I., Vertebrate Zoology
MIRON, I., Aquaculture, Limnology
MISĂILĂ, C., Animal Physiology
MITITIUC, M., Phytopathology, Biogeography
MOGLAN, I., Invertebrate Zoology
MURARIU, A., Vegetal Physiology, Basis of Environment Protection
MUSTAŢĂ, GH., Evolutionary Biology
NEACŞU, I., Biophysics, Molecular Biology
ŞTEFAN, N., Vegetal Taxonomy, Phytosociology, Phytocenology
TĂNASE, C., Micology, Botany
TOMA, C., Plant Anatomy, Vegetal Cytology, Phylogenesis
TOMA, O., Structural Organization of Proteins and Nucleic Acids
ZAMFIRACHE, M. M., Vegetal Physiology

Faculty of Chemistry (Bdul Carol I 11, 700506 Iaşi; tel. (232) 20-13-63; fax (232) 20-13-13; e-mail infochem@uaic.ro; internet www.chem.uaic.ro):

BÎCU, E., Organic Chemistry
BOURCEANU, G., Physical Chemistry
CONSTANTINESCU, M., Physical Chemistry
DROCHIOIU, G., Biochemistry
DULMAN, V., Analytical Chemistry
IORDAN, A., Inorganic Chemistry
MANGALAGIU, I., Organic Chemistry
NEMŢOI, G., Electrochemistry
PALAMARU, M., Inorganic Chemistry
POPOVICI, E., Material Sciences
PUI, A., Inorganic Chemistry
VASILE, A., Chemical Technology

Faculty of Computer Science (Str. G. Berthelot 16, 700483 Iaşi; tel. (232) 20-10-90; fax (232) 20-14-90; e-mail secretariat@info.uaic.ro; internet www.infoiasi.ro):

CRISTEA, D., Artificial Intelligence, Natural Language Processing
CROITORU, C., Algorithms, Combinatorial Optimization
FELEA, V., Data Bases, Logic Programming
GRIGORAS, GH., Programming, Computer Construction
JUCAN, T., Formal Languages, Petri Nets
LUCANU, D., Formal Methods in Software Engineering, Semantic Web
LUCHIAN, H., Meta-heuristics
MASALAGIU, C., Logic in Computer Science
ŢIPLEA, F. L., Algebraic Foundations of Computer Science, Coding Theory and Cryptography, Computability, Decidability and Complexity, Security Protocols, Programme Analysis

Faculty of Economics (Bdul Carol I nr. 22, 700505 Iaşi; tel. (232) 20-10-70; fax (232) 21-70-00; e-mail feaa@uaic.ro; internet www.feaa.uaic.ro):

AIRINEI, D., Data Warehouses, Business Information Technologies, End-User Computing
ANDONE, I., Accounting Information Systems and Expert Systems in Accounting
ASANDULUI, L., Demography
BEDRULE-GRIGORUŢĂ, V., Public Services Management
BRĂILEAN, T., Economic Politics
BUCĂTARU, D., Business Finances
BUDUGAN, D., Managerial Accounting
CIOBANU, I., Management
COCRIŞ, V., Money and Credit, Risk Management in Banking
DUMITREAN, E., Financial Accounting
DUMITRIU, F., Information Systems Design
FĂTU, T., Business Information Technologies
FILIP, G., Public Finances
FILIP, M., Business Information Technologies, End-User Computing
FOTACHE, D., Groupware, Enterprise Resource Planning, Business Information Technologies
FOTACHE, M., Databases, Information and Knowledge Management
GEORGESCU, I., Fundamentals of Accounting, Managerial Accounting
GEORGESCU, M., Office Information Systems, Business Information Technologies
GRAMA, A., End-User Computing, Business Information Technologies
HOROMNEA, E., Fundamentals of Accounting
IGNAT, I., Macroeconomics
IŞAN, V., Economics
JABA, E., Statistics
JABA, O., Management
LUTAC, G., Political Economics
MAXIM, E., Management and Marketing
MEŞNIŢĂ, G., Project Management, Information Systems Analysis
MIHĂESCU, S., Finances, Finance and Banking Control
MIRONIUC, M., Financial and Accounting Management of the Company
MUNTEANU, A., Information Systems Audit

MUNTEANU, C., Marketing
NECHITA, V., Political Economy
NICA, P., Management
NIȚĂ, V., Merchandising, Hotel Management
ONOFREI, M., Financial Management, Decision in Public Administration
OPREA, D., Information Systems Design, Project Management
PASCARIU, G., European Economics
PEKAR, V., Agricultural Economics
PETRESCU, S., Economic Analysis, Evaluation Concepts and Theories in Business
PINTILESCU, C., Multivariate Statistics, Data Analysis
POHOAȚĂ, I., Economic Doctrines
PRALEA, S., International Economics
PRISACARIU, M., Capital Markets, Modern Management of the Portofolio
PRODAN, A., Human Resource Managements
PRUTIANU, S., Business Communication and Negotiations
SASU, C., Marketing
SCORȚESCU, GH., Public Accounting
STOICA, O., European Financial and Monetary Integration, European Financial Markets
STEFURA, G., Public Budgetary Process
TABĂRĂ, N., Fundamentals of Accounting, Compared Accounting Systems
ȚARCĂ, M., Economic Statistics
TOFAN, A., Management
ȚUGUI, A., End-User Computing, Expert Systems
VOINEA, G., International Foreign Exchange and Financial Relations, Local Finances
ZAIT, A., Direct Marketing, Public Relations
ZAIȚ, D., Intercultural Management

Faculty of Geography and Geology (Bdul Carol I nr. 20A, 700505 Iași; tel. (232) 20-10-74; fax (232) 20-14-74; e-mail geoiasi@uaic.ro; internet www.geo.uaic.ro):

APOSTOL, L., Human Geography
BRÂNZILĂ, M., Geology and Palaeontology
GROZA, O., Human Geography
IANCU, O. G., Geochemistry
IAȚU, C., Human Geography
IONIȚĂ, I., Geomorphology
LĂCĂTUȘU, R., Physical Geography
MUNTELE, I., Human Geography
ROMANESCU, GH., Physical Geography
RUSU, C., Physical Geography of Romania
RUSU, E., Human Geography

Faculty of History (tel. (232) 20-10-56; fax (232) 20-11-56; e-mail istorie@uaic.ro; internet www.history.uaic.ro):

BĂDĂRĂU, G., Modern History
BÎRLIBA, L., Ancient History
BOUNEGRU, O., Ancient History
CIUPERCĂ, I., Contemporary World History
CLIVETTI, G., Modern History
CRISTIAN, V., Modern World History
GOROVEI, S., Medieval History
IACOB, G., Contemporary History
LÁSZLÓ, A., Ancient History
PLATON, F., Medieval History
PUNGĂ, G., Medieval History
SOLCANU, I., Medeival History
SPINEI, V., Ancient History
SZEKELY, M., Medieval History
URSULESCU, N., Ancient History
ZAHARIUC, P., Medieval History
ZUGRAVU, N., Ancient History

Faculty of Law (Bdul Carol I nr. 11, 700506 Iași; tel. (232) 20-10-58; fax (232) 20-11-58; e-mail drept@uaic.ro; internet www.laws.uaic.ro):

CIUCĂ, V., Roman Law
DURAC, G., Civil Procedure
MACOVEI, I., International Trade Law
THEODORU, G., Criminal Procedure
TOADER, T., Criminal Law, Special Part

Faculty of Letters (Bdul Carol I nr. 11, 700506 Iași; tel. (232) 20-10-52; fax (232) 20-11-52; e-mail letters@uaic.ro; internet www.letters.uaic.ro):

ALBU, R., English Language
AVĂDANEI, ST., American Literature
BLUMENFELD, O., English Language and Literature
CĂLINESCU, A., French Literature
CĂRĂUȘU, M. L., Romanian Language
CERNĂUȚI GORODEȚCHI, M., Comparative Literature
CIUBOTARU, M., Romanian Language
CUȚITARU, L. C., English and American Literature
COTORCEA, L., Russian Literature
DIACONU, D., Spanish Literature
DIMITRIU, R., English Language
DOROBĂȚ, D., English Literature
GAFTON, A., Romanian Language
GOGĂLNICEANU, C. L., English Language
HOIȘIE, A., German Literature
JEANRENAUD, M., French Literature
LĂCĂTUȘU, T., English Language
MUNTEANU, E., Romanian Language
MUREȘANU, M., French Literature
PETRESCU, M., French Language
PIRVU, S., English Literature
POPESCU, I., French Literature
PORUCIUC, A., English Language
PRICOP, C., Romanian Literature
SECRIERU, M. L., Romanian Language

Faculty of Mathematics (Bd. Carol I nr. 11, 700506 Iași; tel. and fax (232) 20-10-60; e-mail admmath@uaic.ro; internet www.math.uaic.ro):

ANASTASIEI, M., Geometry
ANICULĂESEI, GH., Applied Mathematics
ANIȚA, S., Applied Mathematics
ARNĂUTU, V., Applied Mathematics
BARBU, V., Applied Mathematics
BRÂNZEI, D., Geometry
CÂRJĂ, O., Mathematical Analysis
CHIRIȚĂ, S., Applied Mathematics
FLORESCU, L., Mathematical Analysis
HĂVÂRNEANU, T. D., Applied Mathematics
IEȘAN, D., Applied Mathematics
ILIOI, C., Applied Mathematics
LEFTER, C. G., Applied Mathematics
MIRON, R., Applied Mathematics
OPROIU, V., Geometry
POP, I., Geometry
POPA, C. G., Applied Mathematics
POPA, E., Mathematical Analysis
PRECUPANU, A., Mathematical Analysis
PRECUPANU, T., Mathematical Analysis
RĂȘCANU, A., Applied Mathematics
TOFAN, I., Algebra
TURINICI, M., Applied Mathematics
VRABIE, I., Applied Mathematics
ZĂLINESCU, C., Mathematical Analysis

Faculty of Orthodox Theology (Str. Cloșca 9, 700066 Iași; tel. (232) 25-84-30; e-mail contact@teo.uaic.ro; internet www.teologie.uaic.ro):

ACHIMESCU, N., History and Philosophy of Religions
PETRARU, GH., Missiology and Ecumenism
POPA, GH., Christian Morals and Orthodox Morals
SANDU, I., Branch Orthodox Theology, Cultural Inheritance
SAVA, V., Liturgical Theology and Practice
SEMEN, P., Study and Biblical Exegesis of the Old Testament
TEȘU, I. C., Orthodox Spirituality

Faculty of Philosophy (Bdul Carol I nr. 11, 700506 Iași; tel. (232) 20-10-54; fax (232) 20-11-54; e-mail alexandru.durnea@uaic.ro; internet philosophy.uaic.ro):

ADĂMUȚ, A., History of Philosophy
AFLOROAEI, ST., Ontology, Hermeneutics, Metaphysics
BACIU, M., Sociology
BALAHUR, D., Sociology
BEJAN, P., Hermeneutics
CARPINSCHI, A., Political Science
COZMA, C., Ethics
DIMA, T., Logic and Epistemology
DUMITRESCU, P., History of Philosophy
GAVRILUȚĂ, N., Sociology
GHIDEANU, T., History of Philosophy
IOAN, P., Logic
IONESCU, I., Sociology
MARIN, C., History of Philosophy
MIFTODE, V., Sociology, Social Anthropology
NISTOR, M., Aesthetics, History and Philosophy of Religions
POEDE, G., Political Sciences
RÂMBU, N., Philosophy of Culture and Hermeneutics
SĂLĂVĂSTRU, C., Logic and Semiology
STĂNCIULESCU, T. D., Semiotics and Philosophy of Creation
TEODORESCU, G., Sociology

Faculty of Physical Education and Sport (Str. Toma Cozma nr. 3, 700554 Iași; tel. (232) 20-10-26; fax (232) 20-11-26; e-mail admefs@uaic.ro; internet www.sport.uaic.ro):

BĂLTEANU, V., Massage
DROSESCU, P., Anatomy
IACOB, I., Sports Management

Faculty of Physics (tel. (232) 20-10-50; fax (232) 20-11-50; e-mail admphys@uaic.ro; internet www.physics.uaic.ro):

BIBOROSCH, L., Plasma Physics
CĂLȚUN, O. F., Electricity and Magnetism
CREANGĂ, D. E., Biophysics
DARIESCU, C., Quantum Mechanics
DARIESCU, M. A., Quantum Mechanics
DOROHOI, O. D., Optics and Spectroscopy
DUMITRAȘCU, N. V., Plasma Physics
GEORGESCU, V., Solid State Physics
IACOMI, F. D., Solid State Physics
IGNAT, E. M., Theoretical Physics
LOZNEANU, E., Plasma Physics
LUCA, D., Solid State Physics
LUCHIAN, T., Biophysics
MARDARE, D., Biophysics
MELNIG, V., Biophysics
MERCHEȘ, I., Theoretical Physics
MITOȘERIU, L., Electricity and Magnetism
POPA, G., Plasma Physics
RUSU, G., Solid State Physics
RUSU, M., Solid State Physics
SANDULOVICIU, M., Plasma Physics
SINGUREL, G., Spectroscopy and Quantum Optics
STANCU, A., Electricity and Magnetism
STRAT, M., Optics and Spectroscopy
TOMA, M., Plasma Physics

Faculty of Psychology and Education (Str. Toma Cozma 3, 700554 Iași; tel. (232) 20-10-28; fax (232) 21-06-60; e-mail secretariat@psih.uaic.ro; internet www.psychology.uaic.ro):

ANTONESEI, L., Pedagogy
CONSTANTIN, A., Psychology
CONSTANTIN, T., Psychology
COZMA, T., General Education
CREȚU, C., Psycho-pedagogy of Excellence and Creativity
CUCOȘ, C., Pedagogy
DAFINOIU, I., Medical Psychology
GHEORGHIU, M. D., Psychology
HAVARNEANU, E., Psychology
IACOB, L., Psychology
NECULAU, A., Social Psychology
ȘOITU, L., Pedagogy
TURLIUC, N., Medical Psychology and Special Psycho-pedagogy

Faculty of Roman Catholic Theology (Bdul Carol I 11, 700506 Iași; tel. (232) 20-11-15; fax (232) 20-11-14; e-mail ftrc@uaic.ro; internet www.ftrc.uaic.ro):

DUMEA, E., Church History

UNIVERSITATEA 'ANDREI ŞAGUNA' DIN CONSTANŢA
(Andrei Saguna University of Constanţa)

Bdul Alexandru Lapusneanu 13, 900196 Constanţa
Telephone and fax (241) 66-25-20
E-mail: contact@andreisaguna.ro
Internet: www.andreisaguna.ro

Founded 1992
Private Control

Rector: Prof. Dr AUREL PAPARI
Dir-Gen.: Dr ADRIAN PAPARI
Chancellor: Prof. Dr LEFTER CHIRICA

DEANS

Department of Shipping and Maritime and Inland Waterway Transport: Prof. Dr TĂNASE SUSANU
Faculty of Economics: Dr GEORGE PAPARI
Faculty of Law and Administrative Sciences: Dr GABRIEL NAGHI
Faculty of Mass Communication and Political Science: Dr IOAN DAMASCHIN
Faculty of Psychosociology: Dr LIVICA FRATIMAN

UNIVERSITATEA 'ATHENAEUM' DIN BUCUREŞTI
(Athenaeum University of Bucharest)

Str. Giuseppe Garibaldi 2A, Sector 2, Bucharest
Telephone: (21) 230-57-38
Fax: (21) 231-74-18
E-mail: secretariat@univath.ro
Internet: www.univath.ro

Founded 1990
Private control
Languages of instruction: Romanian, English
Academic year: October to June

Rector: Prof. Dr EMILIA VASILE

Library of 20,925
Number of teachers: 85
Number of students: 1,500

Publication: *Internal Auditing & Risk Management*

DEANS

Faculty of Economics: Dr ION NITU
Faculty of Public Administration: Dr ARON LIVIU DEAC

UNIVERSITATEA 'AUREL VLAICU' DIN ARAD

Bdul Revoluţiei 7, POB 2/158, 310130 Arad
Telephone: (257) 28-30-10
Fax: (257) 28-00-70
E-mail: rectorat@uav.ro
Internet: www.uav.ro
State control
Academic year: October to July

Rector: Prof. Dr LIZICA MIHUT
Pres.: Prof. Dr ANTON ILICA
Vice-Rectors: Prof. Dr Ing. IOAN RADU, Prof. Dr FLORENTINA MUNTEANU, Prof. Dr ALINA ZAMFIR
Scientific Sec.: Dr Ing. GHEORGHE SIMA

Publications: *Educatia Plus* (2 a year), *Revista AGORA*, *Scientific and Technical Bulletin*

DEANS

Faculty of Design: Prof. Dr FLOREA LUCACI
Faculty of Educational Sciences, Psychology and Social Sciences: Prof. Dr ANTHON ILICA
Faculty of Economic Sciences: Assoc. Prof. Dr SPÎNU MARIAN-NICU
Faculty of Engineering: Dr Eng Prof. DOINA MORTOIU
Faculty of Exact Sciences: Assoc. Prof. Dr SORIN NĂDĂBAN
Faculty of Food Engineering, Tourism and Environmental Protection: Prof. Dr Ing. BUJOR PANCAN
Faculty of Humanities and Social Sciences: Prof. Dr FLOREA LUCACI, Prof. Dr IONEL FUNERIU
Faculty of Physical Education and Sport: Assoc. Prof. DAN BANCIU
Faculty of Theology: Prof. Dr IOAN TULCAN

UNIVERSITATEA 'BABEŞ-BOLYAI' CLUJ-NAPOCA

Str. M. Kogălniceanu 1, 400084 Cluj-Napoca
Telephone: (264) 19-43-15
Fax: (264) 19-19-06
Internet: www.ubbcluj.ro

Founded 1919
Languages of instruction: Romanian, Hungarian, German
Academic year: October to July (2 semesters)

Rector: Prof. Dr ANDREI MARGA
Vice-Rector for Devt: NICOLAE BOCŞAN
Vice-Rector for Economic Cooperation, Financing and Admin.: Assoc. Prof. CRISTINA CIUMAŞ
Vice-Rector for Human Resources and Staff Securement; Alumni Cooperation: Prof. POMPEI COCEAN
Vice-Rector for Int. Affirmation and Cooperation: Prof. TOADER NICOARĂ
Sec.-Gen.: BATIZ ENIKŐ
Librarian: Prof. Dr DORU RADOSAV

Library: see Libraries and Archives
Number of teachers: 1,700
Number of students: 53,000

Publications: *Studia Universitatis Babeş-Bolyai*, *Judaic Library Collection*, *Colloquia: Journal of Central European History*, *Studi Italo-Romeni*, *Brain and Cognition and Behaviour*, *Botanical Contributions*, *Papers of Transition*

DEANS

Department of Theatre and Television: LIVIU MALITA
Faculty of Biology and Geology: V. CRISTEA
Faculty of Business: Assoc. Prof JOHN CHRISTIAN CHIFU
Faculty of Chemistry and Chemical Engineering: Assoc. Prof. MAJDIK CORNELIA
Faculty of Economics: D. RACOVIŢAN
Faculty of European Studies: Prof. Dr LADISLAU GYÉMÁNT
Faculty of Geography: Prof. PETREA MAHO
Faculty of Greek Catholic Theology: A. GOŢIA
Faculty of History and Philosophy: Dr OVIDIU GHITTA
Faculty of Law: Prof. Dr PAUL DOE
Faculty of Letters: I. POP
Faculty of Mathematics and Computer Science: Prof. Dr LEON ŢÂMBULEA
Faculty of Orthodox Theology: Rev. JOHN CHIRILA
Faculty of Physical Education and Sports: M. ALEXEI
Faculty of Physics: Prof. Dr ONUC COZAR
Faculty of Political Science and Public Administration: V. BOARI
Faculty of Protestant Theology: Z. GÁLFI
Faculty of Psychology and Education: Prof. Dr CALIN FELEZEU
Faculty of Roman Catholic Theology: J. MARTON
Faculty of Sociology and Social Work: DAN CHIRIBUCĂ

PROFESSORS

Faculty of Biology and Geology:

BALINTONI, I. C., Geotectonics
BEDELEAN, I., Mineralogy
BUCUR, I., Palaeontology
COMAN, N., Genetics
CRISTEA, V., Botany
DRĂGAN BULARDA, M., Microbiology
MUREŞAN, I., Mineralogy
PÉTERFI, L. S., Botany
PETRESCU, I., Palaeobotany
POPESCU, O., Cell Biology
TARBA, C., Biophysics
TOMESCU, N., Zoology
TRIFU, M., Plant Physiology
TUDORANCEA, C., Ecology
VLAD, Ş. N., Petrology

Faculty of Business:

GIURGIU, A., Finance
VORZSÁK, M., Micro and Macroeconomics

Faculty of Chemistry and Chemical Engineering:

AGACHI, P. Ş., Chemical Engineering
BÂLDEA, I., Physical Chemistry
CORDOŞ, E., Analytical Chemistry
DIUDEA, M., Organic Chemistry
GROSU, I., Organic Chemistry
HOROVITZ, O., Physical Chemistry
MAGER, S., Organic Chemistry
POPESCU, C., Physical Chemistry
SILAGHI-DUMITRESCU, I., Inorganic Chemistry
SILBERG, I. A., Organic Chemistry
SILVESTRU, C., Inorganic Chemistry
VLASSA, M., Organic Chemistry

Faculty of Economics:

AVORNICULUI, C., Data Processing in Economics
AVRAM-NIŢCHI, R., Data Processing in Economics
BĂTRÎNCEA, I., Economic Analysis
BEJU, V., Finance
CĂINAP, I., Economic Analysis
CISTELECAN, L., Finance
DIŢU, G., Political Economy
DRĂGOESCU, A., Political Economy
DRĂGOESCU, E., Finance
DUMBRAVĂ, P., Accountancy
FLOREA, I., Statistics
FRĂŢILĂ, R., Manufacture and Marketing of Products
GHIŞOIU, N., Data Processing in Economics
GORON, S., Data Processing in Economics
ILIEŞ, L., Transport Management
IONESCU, T., Political Economy
LAZĂR, D., Marketing
LAZĂR, I., Agricultural Management
MIHUŢ, I., Management
NAGHI, M., Management
NISTOR, I., Finance
NISTOR, L. I., Macroeconomic Forecasting
NIŢCHI, I. Ş., Data Processing in Economics
OPREAN, D., Data Processing in Economics
OPREAN, I., Accountancy
OPREAN, V., Data Processing in Economics
PAINA, N., Marketing
PÂNTEA, P., Accountancy
PLĂIAŞ, I., Marketing
POP, S. I., Management
POPESCU, G., Political Economy
POSTELNICU, G., Political Economy
PURDEA, D., Management
RACOVIŢAN, D., Data Processing in Economics
ROŞCA, T., Finance
STĂNEANU, G., Finance
TEMEŞ, I., Accountancy
TULAI, C., Finance
VINCZE, M., Agricultural Economics
VORZSÁK, A., Marketing

Faculty of European Studies:

BÎRSAN, M., Management of European Institutions
GYEMANT, L., European Studies
MARGA, A., Philosophy
PĂUN, N., Management of European Institutions

Faculty of Geography:

CIANGĂ, N., Human Geography
COCEAN, P., Regional Geography

GÂRBACEA, V., Regional Geography
MAC, I., Physical Geography
POP, G., Human Geography
RABOCA, N., Economic Geography
SOROCOVSCHI, V. E., Hydrology
SURD, V., Rural Geography

Faculty of Greek Catholic Theology:

GOŢIA, A., Catechetical Theology
GUDEA, N., History of the Greek Catholic Church

Faculty of History and Philosophy:

BĂRBULESCU, M., Ancient History and Archaeology
BOCŞAN, N., Modern History
CIPĂIANU, G. A., Contemporary History
CODOBAN, A. T., Philosophy
CSUCSUJA, Ş., Contemporary History
EDROIU, N., Medieval History of Romania
GLODARIU, I., Ancient History
ILUŢ, P., Sociology
MAGYARI, A., Modern History
MUSCĂ, V., History of Philosophy
PAVEL, T., Modern History
PISO, I., Ancient History and Archaeology
POP, I. A., Medieval History
PUŞCAŞ, V., Contemporary History
ROTARIU, T., Sociology
TEODOR, P., Medieval History of Romania
ŢOCA, M., History of Art
VESE, V., Contemporary History

Faculty of Law:

COSTIN, M. N., Commercial Law
POP, L., Civil Law
URSA, V., Criminal Law
ZĂPÎRŢAN, L., Political Science

Faculty of Letters:

BACIU, I., French Language
BORCILĂ, M., General Linguistics
CĂPUŞAN, M., French Literature
CSEKE, E., Hungarian Literature and Society
DRAGOŞ, E., History of the Romanian Language
FANACHE, V., History of Romanian Literature
GRUIŢĂ, G., Contemporary Romanian Language
KOZMA, D., Hungarian Literature
MUTHU, M., Theory of Literature and Aesthetics
OLTEAN, Ş., History of the English Language
PAPAHAGI, M. D., Italian Literature
PÉNTEK, J., General Linguistics
PETRESCU, I., History of Romanian Literature
POP, I., History of Romanian Literature
POP, R., French Literature
ŞEULEAN, I., Folklore and Cultural Anthropology
STANCIU, V., English Literature
VARTIC, I., Comparative Literature and Theory of Drama
ZDRENGHEA, M., Contemporary English Literature

Faculty of Mathematics and Computer Science:

ANDRICA, D., Geometry
BLAGA, P., Numerical Analysis
BOIAN, F. M., Informatics
BOTH, N., Algebra
BRECKNER, W. W., Functional Analysis and Optimization
CĂLUGĂREANU, G., Algebra
COBZAŞ, Ş., Functional Analysis
COMAN, G., Numerical Analysis
DUCA, D., Mathematical Analysis
DUMITRESCU, D., Informatics
FRENŢIU, M., Informatics
KOLUMBÁN, I., Mathematical Analysis
MICULA, G., Differential Equations
MIHOC, I., Probability Theory
MOCANU, P., Mathematical Analysis
MOLDOVAN, G., Informatics
MUNTEAN, E., Informatics
MUREŞAN, A., Applied Mathematics
NÉMETH, A., Mathematical Analysis
PÂRV, B., Informatics
PETRILA, T., Fluid Mechanics
POP, M. I., Fluid Mechanics
POP, V., Astronomy
PURDEA, I., Algebra
RUS, A. I., Differential Equations
SĂLĂGEAN, G. Ş., Mathematical Analysis
SZILÁGYI, P., Differential Equations
TÂMBULEA, L., Informatics
TRIF, D., Differential Equations
URECHE, V., Astronomy
VASIU, A., Geometry

Faculty of Orthodox Theology:

ICĂ, I., Fundamental Theology
MORARU, A., History of the Orthodox Church

Faculty of Physical Education and Sport:

BENGEANU, C., Volleyball
BRĂTUCU, L. S., Anatomy and Physiology
MAROLICARU, M., Methodology of Scientific Research
NETA, G., Football

Faculty of Physics:

ARDELEAN, I., Materials Science
BARBUR, I., Solid State Physics
BURZO, E., Solid State Physics
COLDEA, M., Solid State Physics
COSMA, C., Physics of Radiation
COZAR, O., Atomic and Molecular Physics
CRIŞAN, M., Theoretical Physics
CRIŞAN, V., Solid State Physics
CRISTEA, G., Solid State Physics
ILIESCU, T., Optics and Spectroscopy
ILONCA, G., Solid State Physics
POP, I., Solid State Physics
ŞIMON, S., Solid State Physics
TATARU, E., Electronics
ZNAMIROVSCHI, V., Atomic and Nuclear Physics

Faculty of Political Science and Public Administration:

BOARI, V., Political Ideology
STEGĂROIU, D. C., Management of Human Resources

Faculty of Psychology and Education:

GOIA, V., Methodology
IONESCU, M., Education
LĂSCUŞ, V., Education
MICLEA, M., Psychology
PITARIU, H., Psychology
PREDA, V., Psychology for Teaching

Faculty of Roman Catholic Theology:

MARTON, J., Ecclesiastical History

UNIVERSITATEA BIOTERRA DIN BUCURESTI
(Bioterra University of Bucharest)

Str. Garlei 81, Sector 1, Bucharest
Telephone: (21) 269-34-47
Fax: (21) 269-34-38
E-mail: nicolaebio@yahoo.com
Internet: www.bioterra.ro

Founded 1994
Private control

Rector: Prof. Dr FLOAREA NICOLAE
Rector for Scientific Activity and International Relations: Prof. Dr STAN PETRESCU
Rector for Teaching: Prof. Dr ION CHIPAILA
Scientific Sec.: Dr DANIELA MIHAILA

Library of 20,547 vols, 3,196 titles

DEANS

Faculty of Agrotourism: Prof. Dr Ing. MIHAI MARES
Faculty of Food Engineering: Prof. Dr Ing. ATUDOSIEI NICOLE

UNIVERSITATEA 'BOGDAN-VODĂ' DIN CLUJ-NAPOCA
(Bogdan-Vodă University of Cluj-Napoca)

Str.Grigore Alexandrescu 26A, Cluj-Napoca
Telephone: (264) 59-87-87
Fax: (264) 59-18-30
E-mail: ubv@ubv.ro
Internet: www.ubv.ro

Founded 1992
Private control

Pres.: Prof. JARADAT MOHAMMAD
Rector: Prof. PURDEA DUMITRU
Vice-Rector: RACOVITAN DAN

DEANS

Faculty of Economics: Prof. Dr PAŞÕCA NICOLAE
Faculty of Law: Dr MOCUŢA GHEORGHE
Faculty of Physical Education and Sports: Prof. NEŢA GHEORGHE

UNIVERSITATEA 'CONSTANTIN BRANCOVEANU' DIN PITEŞTI
(Constantin Brancoveanu University of Piteşti)

Calea Bascovului 2A, Piteşti
Telephone: (248) 21-26-27
Fax: (248) 21-64-27
E-mail: pitesti@univcb.ro
Internet: www.univcb.ro

Founded 1991
Private control

Rector: Prof. Dr ALEXANDRU PUIU
Pro-Rector for Economic Activity: Prof. Dr OVIDIU PUIU
Pro-Rector for Didactic Activity: Prof. Dr MARIUS GUST
Pro-Rector for Scientific Activity: Prof. Dr ION SCURTU
Scientific Sec.: Dr MIHAELA DUTU

Publication: *Strategii manageriale* (magazine)

DEANS

Department of Finance and Accounting, Piteşti: Prof. Dr SILVIA DUGAN
Faculty of Legal, Administrative and Communication sciences, Piteşti: Dr MIHAELA ASANDEI
Faculty of Management Marketing in Business Economics, Piteşti: Prof. Dr RADU GABRIEL PARVU
Department of Administrative and Communication Sciences, Braila: Dr DORIAN RAIS
Faculty of Management Marketing in Business Economics, Braila: Dr ELENA ENACHE
Faculty of Management Marketing in Business Economics, Ramnicu-Valcea: Prof. Dr IULIANA CIOCHINA

UNIVERSITATEA 'CONSTANTIN BRÂNCUSI' DIN TÂRGU JIU

Bdul Republicii 1, Târgu Jiu
Telephone: (253) 21-43-07
Fax: (253) 21-57-94
E-mail: univ@utgjiu.ro
Internet: www.utgjiu.ro

State control
Language of instruction: English
Academic year: October to June

Rector: Prof. Dr ADRIAN GORUN
Pro-Rector: Prof. Dr Ing STEFAN GHIMISI
Pro-Rector: Prof. Dr MIHAI CRUCERU
Pro-Rector: Dr LIVIU NEAMTU

Library of 120,000 vols
Number of teachers: 154
Number of students: 6,000

Publications: *Revista de mecanică*, *Revista de matematică*, *Analele UCB*.

UNIVERSITATEA CRESTINA 'DIMITRIE CANTEMIR' ('Dimitrie Cantemir' Christian University)

Splaiul Unirii 176, Sector 4, Bucharest
Telephone: (21) 330-79-00
Fax: (21) 330-87-74
E-mail: office@ucdc.ro
Internet: www.ucdc.ro
Founded 2002
Private control
Pres.: Prof. Dr MOMCILO LUBURICI
Rector: Prof. Dr CORINA DUMITRESCU ADRIANA
Pro-Rector: Prof. Dr CRISTIANA CRISTUREANU
Pro-Rector: Prof. Dr VELCEA ION
Scientific Sec.: Prof. Dr BIJI ELENA
Number of students: 20,000

DEANS

Faculty of Foreign Languages and Literatures: Assoc. Prof. GABRIELA LUPCHIAN
Faculty of International Business and Economics: Prof. Dr VIRGIL ADASCĂLIȚEI
Faculty of Juridical and Administrative Sciences: Assoc. Prof. PETRICA TRUSCA
Faculty of Tourism and Commercial Management: Prof. Dr CAPRARESCU GHEORGHITA

UNIVERSITATEA DANUBIUS DIN GALAȚI (Danubius University of Galați)

Bdul Galați 3, 800654 Galați
Telephone: (372) 36-12-07
Fax: (372) 36-12-92
E-mail: rectorat@univ-danubius.ro
Internet: www.univ-danubius.ro
Founded 1992
Private control
Rector: Prof. Dr BENONE PUSCA
Pro-Rector for Scientific Research: Prof. Dr VIOREL ARITON
Pro-Rector for Teaching: Dr ANDY CORNELIU PUSCA
Dir-Gen.: Prof. Dr DRAGOMIR GEORGETA
Scientific Sec.: Prof. Dr DOINITA ARITON
Library of 30,000 vols, 2,000 periodicals

DEANS

Faculty of Communication Sciences: DUMITRU TIUTIUCA
Faculty of Economic Sciences: Dr RODICA PRIPOAIE
Faculty of Law: Prof. Dr VASILICA NEGRUȚ
Faculty of International Relations and European Studies: Dr ANIȘOARA POPA

UNIVERSITATEA DE ARTĂ ȘI DESIGN DIN CLUJ-NAPOCA

Pta. Unirii 31, 400098 Cluj-Napoca
Telephone and fax (264) 59-81-90
E-mail: secretarsef@uad.ro
Internet: www.uartdcluj.ro
Founded 1925
Pres.: Prof. Dr IOAN SBÂRCIU
Rector: Prof. Dr RADU SOLOVASTRU
Gen Sec.: ANAMARIA BOCEAN

DEANS

Faculty of Applied Arts and Design: Dr ALEXANDRU ALAMOREANU
Faculty of Fine Arts: Dr RADU SOLOVASTRU

DIRECTORS

Dept for Teacher Training: Prof. MARIOARA PETCU
Fine and Decorative Arts Colleges: Dr DOREL MOISE

UNIVERSITATEA DE ARTĂ TEATRALĂ ȘI CINEMATOGRAFICĂ 'I. L. CARAGIALE' (I. L. Caragiale University of Drama and Cinematography)

Str. Matei Voievod 75–77, 021452 Bucharest
Telephone: (21) 252-74-57
Fax: (21) 252-58-81
E-mail: rector1@unatc.ro
Internet: www.unatc.ro
Founded 1950
Rector: Prof. Dr GELU COLCEAG
Scientific Sec.: Prof. Dr DAN VASILIU
Library of 95,000 vols (incl. English theatre library of 5,000 vols)
Number of teachers: 190
Number of students: 680

UNIVERSITATEA DE ARTĂ TEATRALĂ TÂRGU-MUREȘ (University of Dramatic Art of Târgu-Mureș)

Str. Köteles Sámuel nr. 6, 540057 Târgu Mureș
Telephone and fax (265) 26-62-81
E-mail: uat@uat.ro
Internet: www.uat.ro
Founded 1954 as Institutul de Teatru 'Szentgyörgyi István'
Rector: Dr GÁSPÁRIK ATTILA
Chancellor: Dr OANA LEAHU
Chief Sec.: ALÍZ BORDI
Library of 40,000 vols
Number of teachers: 81
Number of students: 130
Faculties of arts, music, theatre.

UNIVERSITATEA DE ARTE 'GEORGE ENESCU'

Str. Horia 7–9, 700126 Iași
Telephone: (232) 21-25-49
Fax: (232) 21-25-51
E-mail: enescu@arteiasi.ro
Internet: www.arteiasi.ro
Founded 1860, renamed 1960
Academic year: October to May
Rector: Prof. Dr VIOREL MUNTEANU
Vice-Rector for Scientific Activities: Assoc. Prof. Dr FLORIN GRIGORAS
Vice-Rector for Teaching Activities: Assoc. Prof. Dr DORU ALBU
Chancellor: Assoc. Prof. Dr ANCO CIOBOTARU
Sec.: Eng. TANIA SCAFARU
Librarian: IOAN BĂDULEȚ
Library of 190,000 vols, incl. books and periodicals; 7,000 records, 1,500 cassette tapes
Number of teachers: 134
Number of students: 1,279
Publication: *Byzantion* (Byzantine studies)

DEANS

Faculty of Composition, Musicology and Musical and Theatrical Education: Dr LAURA OTILIA VASILIU
Faculty of Fine and Decorative Arts and Design: Prof. Dr ATENA ELENA SIMIONESCU
Faculty of Musical Interpretation: Dr TATIANA LAURA POCINOC

UNIVERSITATEA DE NORD, BAIA MARE (North University of Baia Mare)

Str. Victor Babes 62A, 430083 Baia Mare, Maramureș
Telephone: (262) 21-89-22
Fax: (262) 27-61-53
E-mail: dan.calin.peter@ubm.ro
Internet: www.ubm.ro
Founded 1961, as Institute of Higher Education; univ. status 1990
State control
Academic year: October to June
Rector: Prof. Dr Ing DAN CALIN PETER
Vice-Rector: Prof. Dr VASILE VIMAN
Vice-Rector: GEORGETA CORNITA
Scientific Sec.: Prof. Dr Ing GHEORGHE DAMIAN
Chief Librarian: LAURA VARGA
Library of 2,000,000 vols
Number of teachers: 198
Number of students: 5,520
Publications: *Scientific Bulletin of Philology*, *Scientific Bulletin of Foreign Languages*, *Scientific Bulletin of Pedagogy, Psychology and Methodology*, *Scientific Bulletin of Philosophy and Theology*, *The Maramureș Orthodoxy*, *Scientific Bulletin of Economics*, *Scientific Bulletin of Mathematics and Informatics*, *Proceedings of the Mathematical Creativity Seminar*, *Scientific Bulletin of Chemistry and Biology*, *Physics Journal*, *Scientific Bulletin of Electrotechnology, Electronics, Automation*, *Scientific Bulletin of Tribology and Machine Construction Technology*

DEANS

Faculty of Engineering: Prof. Dr RADU COTETIU
Faculty of Letters: Prof. Dr PETRU DUNCA
Faculty of Mineral Resources and Environment: Prof. Dr VASILE OROS
Faculty of Sciences: Assoc. Prof. Dr NICOLAE POP

PROFESSORS

Faculty of Engineering (Str. Dr V. Babeș 62A, 430083 Baia Mare; tel. (362) 40-12-65; fax (262) 27-61-53):

COTETIU, A.
COTETIU, R.
FILIP, D.
LOBONTIU, M.
NASUI, V.
OPREA, C.
PETER, D. C.
PEREAN, L.
TIPLEA, V.
TISAN, V.
TOADER, C.
UNGUREANU, N.

Faculty of Letters (Str. Victoriei 76, 430122 Baia Mare; tel. (262) 27-63-05; fax (262) 27-54-36):

CORNITA, C.
CORNITA, G.
DUNCA, P.
GLODEANU, G.
ISTRATE, A.
MUNTEANU, C.

Faculty of Mineral Resources and Environment (Str. Dr V. Babeș 62A, 430083 Baia Mare; tel. (362) 40-12-66; fax (262) 27-61-53):

BANCILA-AFRIM, N.
BUD, I.
DAMIAN, F.
OROS, V.

Faculty of Sciences (Str. Victoriei 76, 430122 Baia Mare; tel. (262) 27-60-59; fax (262) 27-53-68):

ARDELEAN, G.
BERINDE, V.
HUTIRA, T.
MICU, C.
MIHALY-COZMUTH, A.
MODORAN, D.
MORAR, G.
POP, I.
VIMAN, V.

UNIVERSITATEA DE VEST DIN TIMIŞOARA
(West University of Timişoara)

Bdul V. Pârvan 4, 300223 Timişoara, Timiş
Telephone: (256) 59-21-11
Fax: (256) 59-23-10
E-mail: secretariat@rectorat.uvt.ro
Internet: www.uvt.ro

Founded 1944
State control
Academic year: October to June

Rector: Prof. Dr IOAN TALPOS
Vice-Rector for International Relations: Prof. Dr FLORIN FOLTEAN
Vice-Rector for Administrative Affairs: Prof. Dr PETRU STEFEA
Vice-Rector for Research Affairs: Prof. Dr VASILE OSTAFE
Vice-Rector for Student Affairs: Prof. DOREL JULEAN
Chief Sec.: MIHAELA RĂDUŢĂ
Chancellor and Scientific Sec.: Prof. Dr DAN MOGA
Librarian: Prof. VASILE ŢÂRA

Number of teachers: 719
Number of students: 18,603

Publications: *Analele Universităţii de Vest Din Timişoara, Seria Fizica, Analele Universităţii de Vest din Timişoara, Seria Drept, Analele Universităţii de Vest din Timişoara, Seria Geografie, Analele Universităţii de Vest din Timişoara, Seria Teologie, Analele Universităţii de Vest din Timişoara-Seria Sociologie, Psihologie, Pedagogie şi Asistenta Sociala, Analele Universităţii de Vest Timişoara, Seria Matematica–Informatica, Analele Universităţii de Vest din Timişoara, Seria Stiinte Filologice, Annals of West University Of Timişoara* (Series of Chemistry), *B. A. S. British and American Studies, BHAUT* (Bibliotheca Historica et Archaeologica Universitatis Timisiensis), *Caiet de Semiotica, Copiii de azi sunt parintii de mâine, Dialogues Francophones, Geographica Timisiensis, Gender Studies, Journal of Social Informatics—Revista de informatică socială, Paradigme, Probleme de Filologie Slavă, Revart* (Specialized Review of Theory and Critique of Art), *Revista de Ştiinţe ale Educatie, Review of Historical Geography and Toponomastics, Romanian Journal of Applied Psychology, Romanian Journal of English Studies, Studii de Istorie a Banatului, Studii de Literatură Romana şi Comparată, Studii de Slavistică, Temeswarer Beiträge zur Germanistik, Timişoara Physical Education and Rehabilitation Journal, Translationes*

DEANS

Faculty of Arts and Design: Assoc. Prof. ADRIANA LUCACIU
Faculty of Chemistry, Biology and Geography: Assoc. Prof. Dr GHEORGHE IANOŞ
Faculty of Economics and Business Administration: Prof. Dr MARILEN PIRTEA
Faculty of Letters, History and Theology: Prof. Dr OTILIA HEDESAN
Faculty of Mathematics and Informatics: Prof. Dr VIOREL NEGRU
Faculty of Law and Administrative Sciences: Prof. Dr RADU I. MOTICA
Faculty of Music: Prof. Dr WALTER KINDL
Faculty of Physics: Prof. Dr VULCANOV DUMITRU
Faculty of Political Sciences and Communication: GEORGE CLITAN
Faculty of Physical Education and Sports: Prof. DORU CIOSICI
Faculty of Sociology and Psychology: Prof. Dr ANCA MUNTEANU

PROFESSORS

Faculty of Mathematics (Bdul V. Pârvan 4, 300223 Timişoara, Timiş; tel. and fax (256) 59-23-16; e-mail secretariat@info.uvt.ro; internet www.math.uvt.ro.):

ALBU, A., Differential Geometry
BALINT, Ş., Mathematical Equations
BOROŞ, E., Algebra
CONSTANTIN, GH., Probability Theory
CRAIOVEANU, M., Spectral Geometry
GAŞPAR, D., Functional Analysis, Spectral Theory
IVAN, GH., Algebra
MĂRUŞTER, Ş., Non-Linear Optimization and Computer Science
MEGAN, M., Mathematical Analysis
OBĂDEANU, V., Theoretical Mechanics and Differential Geometry, Operational Research
OPRIŞ, D., Operational Research
PAPUC, D. I., Differential Geometry
PREDA, P., Mathematical Analysis
PUTA, M., Differential Equations in Geometry
RADU, V., Stochastic Analysis and Probability Theory
REGHIŞ, M., Differential Equations
SCHWAB, E., Homological Algebra
STRĂTILĂ, Ş., Mathematical Analysis and Operator Algebras
SUCIU, N., Complex Analysis

Faculty of Physics (Bdul V. Pârvan 4, 300223 Timişoara, Timiş; tel. and fax (256) 59-21-08; e-mail secretary@physics.uvt.ro; internet www.physics.uvt.ro):

AVRAM, N., Atomic and Molecular Physics and Spectroscopy
BIRĂU, O., Thermodynamics and Molecular Physics
HRIANCA, I., Electricity and Magnetism
MUSCUTARIU, I., Electricity and Magnetism, Solid State and Semiconductor Physics
NICOARĂ, I., Laser Crystals
SCHLETT, Z., Plasma Physics, Semiconductor Materials and Devices

Faculty of Chemistry, Biology and Geography (Str. I. Pestalozzi 16, 300115 Timişoara; tel. (256) 59-26-22; fax (256) 59-26-20; e-mail cbg@cbg.uvt.ro; internet www.cbg.uvt.ro):

CHIRIAC, A., Physical Chemistry
DOCA, N., Chemical Engineering
MRACEC, M., Physical Chemistry
NUŢIU, R., Organic Chemistry
TRUŢI, S., Geography

Faculty of Letters, History and Theology (Bdul V. Pârvan 4, 300223 Timişoara, Timiş; tel. and fax (256) 59-21-64; e-mail litere@litere.uvt.ro; internet www.litere.uvt.ro):

BENEA, D., Ancient History
BIRIŞ, I., History of Culture and Civilization
BUCA, M., Russian Language
CHEIE, I., Romanian Literature
CIOCÂRLIE, L., French Literature
EVSEEV, I., Russian Language
FRĂŢILĂ, V., Dialectology
GRECU, C., Philosophy of Logic
GYURCSIK, M., French Literature
HARANGUŞ, C., Ontology
MIOC, S., Romanian Literature
MUNTEANU, I., Modern Romanian History
OANCEA, I., Romance Philology
PÂRLOG, H., English Linguistics
SÂRBU, R., Russian Language
ŢÂRA, V., History of the Romanian Language

Faculty of Economics and Business Administration (Bdul Pestalozzi 16, 300115 Timişoara; tel. (256) 59-25-05; fax (256) 59-25-00; e-mail secretariat@feaa.uvt.ro; internet www.feaa.uvt.ro):

BĂBĂIŢĂ, I., Political Economy
BĂBĂIŢĂ, V., Accounting
BĂILEŞTEANU, GH., Business Economics
BURTICĂ, M., Macroeconomic Forecasting
CĂTINIANU, FL., Prices and Tariffs
CERNA, S., Currency and Credits
CRĂCIUNESCU, V., Management
CRISTEA, H., Business Finance
DĂNĂIAŢĂ, I., Management
EPURAN, M., Accounting
FALNIŢĂ, E., Science of Commodities
GOIAN, M., Management
IONESCU, GH., Marketing
IVAN, ŞT., Informatics
LĂDAR, L., Marketing
LUPULESCU, M., Computer Programming
MARTIN, I., Microeconomic Analysis
MIHAI, I., Financial Analysis
NEGRUT, C., Agrarian Economics and Policy
OPRIŞ, L., Agrarian Policies in the World
POPOVICI, AL., Programming of Production
PUTZ, E., Transport in Tourism
ROTARIU, I., Management of Foreign Trade
SILAŞI, GR., Regional and World Economy
ŞOŞDEANU, A., Accounting
TALPOŞ, I., Public Finance
TRANDAFIR, N., Political Economy
VÂRLAN, GH., Economic Forecasting

Faculty of Sociology and Psychology (Bdul V. Pârvan 4, 300223 Timişoara, Timiş; tel. and fax (256) 59-23-20; e-mail steb@socio.uvt.ro; internet www.socio.uvt.ro):

DABU, R., Sociology
POENARU, R., Pedagogy, Deontology
VINTILESCU, D., Educational Theory

Faculty of Law and Administrative Sciences (Bdul Eroilor 9A, 300575 Timişoara; tel. (256) 592400; fax (256) 592442; e-mail drept@drept.uvt.ro; internet www.drept.uvt.ro):

DRESSLER, M., Forensic Medicine
MIHAI, GH., Philosophy of Law
MOTICA, R. I., Law
POPA, V., Roman Law, Labour Law

Faculty of Arts (Str. Oituz 4, 300086, Timişoara; tel. and fax (256) 59-26-51; e-mail arte@arte.uvt.ro; internet www.arte.uvt.ro):

FÂNTÂNARIU, S., Graphic Arts
FLONDOR, C., Painting
JECZA, P., Sculpture
NUŢIU, R., Painting
SULEA, I., Painting
ZIMAN, M., Textile Arts

Faculty of Music (Bdul V. Piaţa Libertatii 1, 300077 Timişoara, Timiş; tel. and fax (256) 59-26-54; e-mail muzica@muzica.uvt.ro; internet www.muzica.uvt.ro):

STANCOVICI, F., Piano
VULPE, D., Choral Conducting

Faculty of Political Sciences Philosophy and Communication (Bdul V. Pârvan 4, 300223 Timişoara, Timiş; tel. (256) 59-21-32; fax (256) 59-23-07; e-mail secr_polsci@polsci.uvt .ro; internet www.polsci.uvt.ro):

COLTESCU, G., Political Sciences

Faculty of Physical Education and Sport (Bdul V. Pârvan 4, 300223 Timişoara, Timiş; tel. and fax (256) 59-22-07; e-mail secr_sport@sport.uvt.ro; internet www.sport.uvt.ro):

GÖNCZI-RAICU, M., Gymnastics
IONESCU, I., Football

UNIVERSITATEA DE VEST 'VASILE GOLDIŞ' DIN ARAD
(Vasile Goldis Western University of Arad)

Bdul Revolutiei 94, Arad
Telephone: (257) 28-03-35
E-mail: rectorat@uvvg.ro
Internet: www.uvvg.ro

Founded 1990
Private control

Rector: Prof. Dr AUREL ARDELEAN
Pro-Rectors: Prof. Dr MARTIAN IOVAN, Prof. Dr DELIA PODEA, Prof. Dr GAVRIL ARDELEAN, Prof. Dr CALIN POP, Prof. Dr CORNEL SOMESAN
Library: 1m. vols

DEANS

Faculty of Economics: Prof. Dr FLORIN DUMESCU
Faculty of Legal Sciences: Prof. Dr IOAN TRIFA
Faculty of Medicine, Pharmacy and Dentistry
Prof. Dr LIANA MOŞ
Faculty of Natural SciencesProf. DORINA CACHIĂŢ
Faculty of InformaticsAssoc. Prof. ANTOANELA NAAJI

UNIVERSITATEA 'DIMITRIE CANTEMIR' DIN TÂRGU-MUREŞ (Dimitrie Cantemir University of Târgu-Mureş)

Str. Bodoni Sandor 3–5, Târgu-Mureş
Telephone: (365) 40-11-27
Fax: (365) 40-11-25
E-mail: universitate@cantemir.ro
Internet: www.cantemir.ro

Founded 1991
Private control
Number of teachers: 130
Faculties of law, economic sciences, psychology and educational sciences and geography.

UNIVERSITATEA DIN BUCUREŞTI

Bdul Mihail Kogălniceanu 34–46, sector 5, 050107 Bucharest
Telephone: (21) 307-73-00
Fax: (21) 313-17-60
E-mail: secretariat@unibuc.ro
Internet: www.unibuc.ro

Founded 1864
State control
Academic year: October to July

Rector: Prof. JOHN PANZARU
Dir: MARIA PRUNĂ
Pro-Rectors: Prof. Dr CONSTANTIN BUŞE, Prof. Dr DANA MARINESCU, Prof. Dr IOAN MIHĂILESCU, Prof. Dr ION MUNTEANU
Librarian: Prof. Dr MIRCEA REGNEALĂ
Library: see Libraries and Archives
Number of teachers: 1,490
Number of students: 24,650
Publications: *Analele Universităţii din Bucureşti* (Chemistry, Law, Geology, Geography, History, Romanian Language and Literature, Physics, 1 a year), *Euroatlantic Studies* (in English, 2 a year), *Geography Communications* (in French and English, 1 a year), *Revue Roumaine d'Egyptologie*, *Science and Technology of Environmental Protection*

DEANS

Faculty of Baptist Theology: Prof. Dr OTNIEL IOAN BUNACIU
Faculty of Biology: Prof. Dr TATIANA VASSU DIMOV
Faculty of Chemistry: Prof. Dr DIMITRU OANCEA
Faculty of Foreign Languages and Literature: Prof. Dr ALEXANDRA CORNILESCU
Faculty of Geography: Prof. Dr MIHAI IELENICZ
Faculty of Geology and Geophysics: Prof. Dr Eng VICTOR MOCANU
Faculty of History: Prof. Dr ALEXANDRU BARNEA
Faculty of Political Sciences and Admin.: Prof. Dr CRISTIAN PREDA
Faculty of Journalism and Communication Sciences: Prof. Dr MIHAI COMAN
Faculty of Law: Prof. Dr VIOREL MIHAI CIOBANU
Faculty of Letters: Prof. Dr DAN HORIA MAZILU
Faculty of Mathematics: Prof. Dr VICTOR TIGOIU
Faculty of Orthodox Theology: Prof. Dr NICOLAE NECULA
Faculty of Philosophy: Assist Dr VASILE ROMULUS
Faculty of Physics: Prof. Dr STEFAN ANTOHE
Faculty of Psychology and Education: Prof. Dr DAN POTOLEA
Faculty of Public Admin.: Dr MAGDALENA PLATIS
Faculty of Roman Catholic Theology and Social Work: Prof. Dr ISIDOR MARTINCA
Faculty of Sociology and Social Work: Prof. Dr CATALIN BASARAB ZAMFIR
Dept of Open and Distance Education: Dr BOGDAN LOGOFĂTU

PROFESSORS

Faculty of Baptist Theology (Str. Berzei 29, Bucharest; tel. and fax (21) 224-88-49; e-mail bbts@fx.ro; internet www.unibuc.ro/en/fac_ftb_en):

BUNACIU, I., New Testament
TALPOŞ, V., Old Testament

Faculty of Biology (Splaiul Independenţei 91–95, Sector 5, 76201 Bucharest; tel. (21) 411-52-07; fax (21) 411-23-10; e-mail web@bio.bio.unibuc.ro; internet www.bio.unibuc.ro):

BOTNARIUC, N., Ecology
COSTACHE, M., Biochemistry
CRISTUREAN, I., Botany
DINISCHIOTY, A., Biochemistry
FLONTA, M. L., Animal Physiology and Biophysics
GAVRILĂ, L., Plant Genetics
GEORGESCU, D., Anatomy
IGA, D. P., Anatomy
IORDĂCHESCU, D., Biochemistry
LAZĂR, V., Microbiology
MAILAT, I. E., Anatomy
MANOLACHE, V., Animal Biology
MARIN, A., Botany
MEŞTER, L. E., Animal Biology
MIHĂESCU, G., Microbiology
MIŞCALENCU, D., Anatomy
NĂSTĂSESCU, M., Animal Biology
SÂRBU, A., Botany
SESAN, T., Botany
STOIAN, V., Genetics
TEODORESCU, I., Ecology
TESIO, C., Animal Biology
TOMA, N., Botany
VĂDINEANU, A., Ecology
VASSU, T., Genetics
VOICA, C., Plant Physiology
ZĂRNESCU, O., Histology

Faculty of Chemistry (Bdul Regina Elisabeta 4–12, Sector 1, Bucharest; tel. and fax (21) 315-92-49; e-mail chimie_secretariat@yahoo.com; internet www.chimie.unibuc.ro):

ANDRUH, M., Inorganic Chemistry
ANGELESCU, E., Chemical Technology and Catalysis
BACIU, I., Organic Chemistry
BALA, C., Analytical Chemistry
BĂIULESCU, G.-E., Analytical Chemistry
BREZEANU, M., Inorganic Chemistry
CENUŞE, A., Physical Chemistry
CERCASOV, C., Organic Chemistry
CIOACĂ, C., Physics
CIOBANU, A., Organic Chemistry
CIOCĂZANU, I., Physical Chemistry
CIUCU, A., Analytical Chemistry
CONSTANTINESCU, E., Physical Chemistry
CONTINEANU, M., Physical Chemistry
CRISTUREAN, E., Inorganic Chemistry
DĂNEŢ, A. F., Analytical Chemistry
DAVID, V., Analytical Chemistry
DUMITRESCU, V., Analytical Chemistry
FIFIRIG, M., Physics
GĂINAR, I., Physical Chemistry
HILLEBRAND, M., Physical Chemistry
IVAN, L., Organic Chemistry
KRIZA, A., Inorganic Chemistry
LECA, M., Physical Chemistry
MAGEARU, V., Analytical Chemistry
MANDRAVEL, L. C., Physical Chemistry
MARIAN, P., Physics
MARINESCU, D., Inorganic Chemistry
MEDVEDOVICI, A., Analytical Chemistry
MELTZER, V., Physical Chemistry
MIHALCEA, I., Physical Chemistry
MUTIHAC, L., Analytical Chemistry
NEGOIU, D., Inorganic Chemistry
NEGOIU, M., Inorganic Chemistry
NICOLAE, A., Organic Chemistry
OANCEA, D., Physical Chemistry
OLTEANU, M. V., Physical Chemistry
ONCESCU, T., Physical Chemistry
PÂRVULESCU, V., Chemical Technology and Catalysis
PATROESCU, C., Analytical Chemistry
PAULINA, M., Physics
POPA, N., Inorganic Chemistry
ROŞU, T., Inorganic Chemistry
SAHINI, V., Physical Chemistry
SĂNDULESCU, I., Chemical Technology and Catalysis
SEGAL, E., Physical Chemistry
SZABÓ, A., Chemical Technology and Catalysis
TĂNASE, I., Analytical Chemistry
UDREA, I., Organic Chemistry
VÂLCU, R., Physical Chemistry
VLĂDESCU, L., Analytical Chemistry
VOLANSCHI, E., Physical Chemistry

Faculty of Foreign Languages and Literature (Str. Edgar Quinet 5–7, Sector 1, 70106 Bucharest; tel. and fax (21) 312-13-13; e-mail office@limbi-straine.ro; internet www.limbi-straine.ro):

ANGHELESCU, N., Oriental Languages
BACIU, I., English
BĂDESCU, I., French
BĂLUŢĂ-SKULTETY, M., Classical Languages
BARBORICĂ, C., Slovak Language
CĂLIN, G., Slavic Languages
CIZEK, E. A., Classical Languages
CORNILESCU, A., English
CREŢIA, G., Classical Languages
CUNIŢĂ, A., French
DERER, D., Italian
DOBREA, A., Russian
DOBRIŞAN, N., Oriental Languages
DUMITRIU, G., English
GĂMULESCU, D., Serbo-Croat Language
GUŢU, G., German
HOGEA-VELISCU, I., Oriental Languages
IONESCU, A.-I., Slavic Languages
IRIMIA, M. L., English
MICLĂU, P., French
MIHĂILĂ, GH., Slavic Languages
MIHĂILĂ, R., American Literature
MITU, M., Slavic Languages
MOLNAR, S., Hungarian
MURVAI, O., Hungarian
NICOLAESCU, M., English
NICOLESCU, A., English
PANĂ, I., English
PÂNZARU, I., French
PETRICĂ, I., Slavic Languages
REBUŞAPCĂ, I., Slavic Languages
RÎPEANU, S., Romance Languages
ROŞIANU, N., Russian
SANDU, D., German
SĂULESCU, M., English
SLUŞANSCHI, D. M., Classical Languages

ŞOPTEREANU, V., Russian
STĂNESCU, C., German
SURDULESCU, R., English
SZOBOLCS, A., Hungarian
TOMA, D., French
TOMA, R., French
TUPAN, M., English
TUŢESCU, M., French
VIANU, L., English
VISAN, F., Oriental Languages
VIŞAN, V., French
WALD, L., Classical Languages

Faculty of Geography (Bdul Nicolae Bălcescu 1, Sector 1, Bucharest; tel. (21) 315-30-74; fax (21) 315-35-08; e-mail secretariat@geo.unibuc.ro; internet www.geo.unibuc.ro):

BĂLTEANU, D., Geomorphology
CÂNDEA, M., Human and Economic Geography
CIULACHE, S., Meteorology and Hydrology
ERDELI, G., Human and Economic Geography
GEANANĂ, M., Geomorphology and Pedology
GRECU, F., Geomorphology and Pedology
GRIGORE, M., Geomorphology and Pedology
IANOŞ, I., Human and Economic Geography
IELENICZ, M., Geomorphology and Pedology
MARIN, I., Regional Geography
POPESCU, N., Geomorphology and Pedology
VESPREMEANU, E., Meteorology and Hydrology

Faculty of Geology and Geophysics (Str. Traian Vuia 6, Sector 6, Bucharest; tel. (21) 211-31-20; fax (21) 211-73-90; e-mail secr@gg.unibuc.ro; internet www.gg.unibuc.ro):

ANASTASIU, N., Mineralogy
CONSTANTINESCU, E., Mineralogy
DANCHIV, A., Geological Engineering
DINU, C., Geology and Palaeontology
DRĂGĂSTAN, O., Geology and Palaeontology
GEORGESCU, P., Geophysics
GRIGORESCU, D., Geology and Palaeontology
IVAN, M., Geophysics
MĂRUNŢEANU, C., Geological Engineering
MATEI, L., Mineralogy
POPESCU, R., Mineralogy
SCRĂDEANU, D., Geological Engineering
ZAMFIRESCU, F., Geological Engineering

Faculty of History (Bdul Regina Elisabeta 4–12, Sector 5, Bucharest; tel. (21) 314-53-89; fax (21) 310-06-80; e-mail historybucharest@hotmail.com; internet www.unibuc.ro/ro/fac_fistr_ro):

BABEŞ, M., Prehistory and Archaeology
BARNEA, A., Ancient History, Archaeology and Epigraphy
BOIA, I., Historiography and Modern History
BREZEANU, S., Byzantine History
BULEI, I., Modern Romanian History
BUŞE, C., Contemporary History, Euro-Atlantic Studies
CIUCĂ, M., Medieval Romanian History
GIURESCU, D. C., Contemporary Romanian History
ISAR, N., Modern Romanian History
LUKACZ, A., Medieval History
MAIOR, L., Modern Romanian History
MAXIM, M., Ottoman History
MURGESCU, B., Modern and Economic History
NISTOR, V., Ancient Roman History
PANAITE, V., Ottoman History
PETOLESCU, C. C., Ancient Roman History and Epigraphy
PETRE, Z., Ancient Greek History
PIPPIDI, A., Medieval History
RETEGAN, M., Contemporary Romanian History
SCURTU, I., Contemporary Romanian History
ŞTEFĂNESCU, ŞT., Medieval Romanian History
TEOTEOI, T., Medieval Romanian and Byzantine History
VULPE, A., Prehistory and Archaeology
ZBUCHEA, GH., South-east European History

Faculty of Journalism and Communication Sciences (Bdul Iuliu Maniu 1–3, A Building, 6th Floor, Sector 5 Bucharest; tel. (21) 318-15-55; fax (21) 410-06-43; e-mail mcoman53@yahoo.com; internet www.fjsc.unibuc.ro):

COMAN, M., Journalism
FRUMUŞANI, D., Journalism
ZOLTAN, R., Communications

Faculty of Law (Bdul Mihail Kogălniceanu 36–46, Sector 5, 70709 Bucharest; tel. (21) 315-71-87; fax (21) 312-07-19; internet www.drept.unibuc.ro):

ATHANASIU, A., Private Law
BÂRSAN, C., Private Law
BESTELIU, R., Public Law
BIZIM, A., Sports
BUCUR, I., Economic Sciences
CĂRPENARU, ST., Private Law
CIOBANU, V., Private Law
CIOCLEI, V., Criminal Law
CORNESCU, V., Economic Sciences
CREŢOIU, GH., Economic Sciences
FILIPAŞ, A., Criminal Law
IORGOVAN, A., Constitutional Law
MARINESCU, D., Private Law
MITRACHE, C., Criminal Law
MOLCUŢ, E., Public Law
MURARU, I., Public Law
NĂSTASE, A., Public Law
NEAGU, I., Public Law
POPA, N., Public Law
ŞAGUNA, D., Public Law
SITARU, D., Private Law
STANCIU, S., Economic Sciences
STANCU, E., Criminal Law
VOLONCIU, N. D., Criminal Law

Faculty of Letters (Str. Edgar Quinet 5–7, Sector 1, Bucharest; tel. (21) 314-35-08; fax (21) 313-43-36; internet www.lit.unibuc.ro):

ANGELESCU, S., Folklore
ANGHELESCU, M., Romanian Literature
BĂLTĂCEANU, I., Hebrew Studies
BANCIU, D., Communication and Public Relations
BERCIU, A., College of Administration
BIDU VRÂNCEANU, A., Romanian Language
BRÎNCUŞI, GR., Romanian Language
CAZIMIR, ŞT., Romanian Literature
CHIVU, GH., Romanian Language
CONSTANTINESCU, N., Folklore
CORNEA, L. P., Romanian Literature
DINDELEGAN, G., Romanian Language
DINU, M. C., Communication and Public Relations
DOCA, GH., Romanian Language
DOMINTE, C., Romanian Language
FILIPAŞ, E., Romanian Literature
FORASCU, N., Romanian Language
GANĂ, G., Romanian Literature
GRIGORESCU, D., Comparative Literature
GUŢU ROMALO, V., Romanian Language
HANŢĂ, A., Romanian Literature
HRISTEA, TH., Romanian Language
MANOLESCU, N. A., Romanian Literature
MANZAS, Z., Romanian Language
MARTIN, M. A., Theory of Literature
MAZILU, D. H., Romanian Literature
MELIAN, A., Romanian Literature
MICU, D., Romanian Literature
MIHĂILESCU, F., Romanian Literature
MORARU, M., Romanian Language
MUNTEANU, R., Comparative Literature
NEGRICI, E., Romanian Literature
NICULESCU, F., Romanian Language
REGNEALA, M., Communication and Public Relations
RUXANDOIU, L., Romanian Language
SARAMANDU, N., Romanian Language
ŞERBAN, I. V., European Studies
SIMION, E., Romanian Literature
SLAMA CAZACU, T., Romanian Language
SPIRIDON, M., Communication and Public Relations
STOICA, I., Library and Information Science
TĂNĂSESCU, A., Theory of Literature
VRÂNCEANU, A., Romanian Language
ZAMFIR, M., Romanian Literature

Faculty of Mathematics and Informatics (Str. Academiei 14, Sector 1, Bucharest; tel. (21) 314-28-63; fax (21) 315-69-90; e-mail secretariat@fmi.unibuc.ro; internet www.fmi.unibuc.ro):

ALBU, T., Algebra
ATANASIU, A., Theoretical Computer Science
BĂDESCU, L., Geometry
BOBOC, N., Mathematical Analysis
BUCUR, GH., Mathematical Analysis
CAMENSCHI, G., Mechanics and Equations
CĂZĂNESCU, V., Theoretical Computer Science
CHIŢESCU, I., Mathematical Analysis
CRISTEA, M., Mathematical Analysis
CUCULESCU, I., Probability Theory, Statistics and Operational Research
DĂSCĂLESCU, S., Algebra
DINCĂ, G. I., Mechanics and Equations
DUMITRESCU, M., Probability Theory, Statistics and Operational Research
GEORGESCU, G., Theoretical Computer Science
GEORGESCU, H., Computer Science
IANUŞ, S., Geometry
IFTIMIE, V., Mechanics and Equations
ION, I., Algebra
IONESCU, P., Algebraic Geometry
MIHĂILĂ, I., Mechanics and Equations
MILITARU, G., Algebra
MIRICĂ, S., Mechanics and Equations
MITRANA, V., Theoretical Computer Science
NĂSTĂSESCU, C., Algebra
NICOLESCU, L., Geometry
NIŢĂ, C., Algebra
POPA, N., Mathematical Analysis
POPESCU, D., Algebra
POPESCU, I., Information Technology
POPESCU, L., Informatics
PREDA, V., Probability Theory, Statistics and Operational Research
PROPOAIE, G., Geometry
RUDEANU, S. A., Computer Science
SABAC, M., Mathematical Analysis
ŞANDRU, N., Mechanics and Equations
ŞTEFĂNESCU, A., Probability Theory, Statistics and Operational Research
ŞTEFĂNESCU, GH., Computer Science
STRĂTILĂ ŞERBAN, V., Mathematical Analysis
ŢIGOIU, S., Mechanics and Equations
TOMESCU, I., Computer Science
TUDOR, C., Probability Theory, Statistics and Operational Research
VĂDUVA, I., Statistics and Stochastic Models

Faculty of Orthodox Theology (Str. Sfânta Ecaterina 2, Sector 4, 040155 Bucharest; tel. (21) 335-61-17; fax (21) 335-41-83; internet www.unibuc.ro/ro/fac_fto_ro):

CORNIŢESCU, C., Biblical Theology, Cultural Heritage and Church Painting
CORNIŢESCU, E., Biblical Theology, Cultural Heritage and Church Painting
DAVID, P., Systematic Theology
DURA, N., Practical Theology
IONIŢĂ, V., Church History
MOLDOVEANU, N., Practical Theology
NECULA, N., Practical Theology
RĂDUCĂ, P., Systematic Theology
RUS, R., Systematic Theology

Faculty of Philosophy (Splaiul Independenţei 204, Sector 5, 70609 Bucharest; tel. (21) 410-

29-74; fax (21) 411-52-89; e-mail matei@fil.unibuc.ro; internet filosofie.unibuc.ro):

BĂNŞOIU, I., History of Philosophy and Philosophy of Culture
DUMITRU, M., Logic and Theoretical Philosophy
FLONTA, M., Logic and Theoretical Philosophy
IANOŞI, I., History of Philosophy and Philosophy of Culture
ILIESCU, A., Political and Moral Philosophy
MORAR, V., History of Philosophy and Philosophy of Culture
MUREŞAN, V., Political and Moral Philosophy
PÂRVU, I., Logic and Theoretical Philosophy
STOIANOVICI, D., Logic and Theoretical Philosophy
SURDU, A., History of Philosophy and Philosophy of Culture
TONOIU, V., Logic and Theoretical Philosophy
ŢURLEA, M., Logic and Theoretical Philosophy
VIERU, S., Political and Moral Philosophy
VLĂDUŢESCU, GH., History of Philosophy and Philosophy of Culture

Faculty of Physics (Str. Atomistilor 405, 077125 Platforma Magurele, Bucharest; tel. (21) 457-44-19; fax (21) 457-45-21; e-mail secretariat@fizic.unibuc.ro; internet www.fizica.unibuc.ro):

ALEXANDRU, H., Solid State Physics
ANGELESCU, T., Nuclear Physics and Particle Physics
ANTOHE, ST., Electricity, Solid State Physics
ARMEANU, I., Mathematical Physics
BEŞLIU, C., Nuclear Physics
BORŞAN, D., Atmospheric Physics
BRÂNCUŞ, D., Solid State Physics
CIOBANU, GH., Statistical Physics and Thermodynamics
CONSTANTINESCU, A., Nuclear Physics, Computational Physics
CONSTANTINESCU, L. M., Physics of Polymers
COSTESCU, A., Theoretical Physics
COTFAS, N., Mathematical Physics
DOLOCAN, V., Solid State Physics, Electrophysics
DRAGOMAN, D., Solid State Physics
DULIU, O., Nuclear Physics
FLORESCU, V., Quantum Mechanics
GEORGESCU, L., Polymer Physics
GHIORDĂNESCU, N., Nuclear Physics
GHEORGHE, V., Biophysics
GRECU, V., Atomic Physics
IONESCU, A., Atomic Physics
IOVA, I., Optics, Spectroscopy
JIPA, A., Relativistic Nuclear Physics
LAZANU, I., Nuclear Physics
LICEA, I., Solid State Physics
MARIAN, T., Quantum Mechanics
MIHUL, A., Nuclear Physics
MUNTEANU, I., Solid State Physics
MUTIHAC, R., Electricity
NENCIU, GH., Quantum Mechanics
PĂTRAŞCU, ŞT., Earth Physics
PLĂVIŢU, C., Molecular Physics, Polymers
POPA-NIŢĂ, V., Polymer Physics
POPESCU, A., Biophysics
POPESCU, F., Atomic Physics
POPESCU, I., Optics, Spectroscopy, Plasma, Lasers
RĂDUŢĂ, A., Theoretical Physics
REVEICA, I. M., Nuclear Physics
RUXANDRA, V., Electricity
SIMA, O., Nuclear Physics
ŞTEFĂNESCU, D., Mathematical Physics
TOADER, E., Optics, Plasma Physics
TUDOR, T., Optics, Lasers, Holography
TURCU, G., Biophysics
TURBATU, S., Mathematical Physics
VLĂDUCĂ, G., Nuclear Physics

Faculty of Political Sciences (Str. Sfântul Ştefan 24, Sector 2, Bucharest; tel. (21) 313-90-07; fax (21) 312-53-78; e-mail fspub@fspub.ro; internet www.fspub.ro):

ANDREESCU, Ş., International Relations
BARBU, D., Political Sciences
FIDULU, P., International Relations
MELEŞCANU, T., International Relations
MOTOC, I., International Relations
PREDA, C., Political Sciences
STOICA, G., Political Sciences
VLAD, L., International Relations

Faculty of Psychology and Education (Bdul Iuliu Maniu 1–3, A Building, 5th Fl., Sector 6, Bucharest; tel. (314) 25-34-52; fax (21) 411-68-90; internet www.fpse.ro):

CREŢU, T., Psychology
CRISTEA, S., Teacher Training
ENĂCHESCU, S., Special Education
FĂTU, S., Teacher Training
LERGHIT, I., Education
MITROFAN, I., Psychology
MITROFAN, N., Psychology
NEACŞU, I., Education
NICOLESCU, V., Education
PĂUN, E., Education
POPESCU, E., Education
POTOLEA, D., Education
RĂŞCANU, R., Psychology
ROCO, M., Psychology
SCHIOPU, U., Psychology
STANCIU, I., Education
TOMŞA, G., Education
VERZA, E., Special Education
ZLATE, M., Psychology

Faculty of Public Administration (tel. (21) 312-49-31; fax (21) 312-16-50; e-mail mihaela.dutulescu@drept.unibuc.ro):

BUCUR, I., Public Administration
CORNESCU, V., Public Administration

Faculty of Roman Catholic Theology and Social Work (Str. General Berthelot 19, Sector 1, Bucharest; tel. and fax (21) 314-86-10; internet www.unibuc.ro/ro/fac_ftrcas_ro):

FERENŢ, E., Theology
MĂRTINCĂ, I., Theology
PETERCĂ, V., Theology
ROBU, I., Theology

Faculty of Sociology and Social Work (Str. Schitu Magureanu 9, Sector 5, Bucharest; tel. and fax (21) 315-83-91; e-mail secretar@sas.unibuc.ro; internet www.sas.swork.unibuc.ro):

ABRAHAM, P., Social Work
ANGHEL, P., Social Work
BĂDESCU, I., Sociology
CHELCEA, S., Sociology
DRĂGAN, I., Sociology
GEANĂ, GH., Sociology
GHEŢĂU, V., Sociology
LARIONESCU, M., Sociology
MĂRGINEAN, I., Sociology
MIHĂILESCU, I., Sociology
SANDU, D., Sociology
VOINEA, M., Sociology
ZAMFIR, C., Sociology
ZAMFIR, E., Social Work

UNIVERSITATEA DIN CRAIOVA

Str. A. I. Cuza 13, 200585 Craiova
Telephone: (251) 41-43-98
Fax: (251) 41-16-88
E-mail: relint@central.ucv.ro
Internet: www.central.ucv.ro

Founded 1947
State control
Academic year: October to July

Rector: ION VLADIMIRESCU
Vice-Rectors: NICU PANEA, DUMITRU TOPAN, DAN POPESCU, MARCEL DRACEA, COSTEL PETCU
Scientific Sec.: EDMOND-GABRIEL OLTEANU
Gen. Sec.: MIRCEA ZĂVĂLEANU
Librarian: MIHAI COSOVEANU

Library: see Libraries and Archives
Number of teachers: 1,084
Number of students: 32,000

Publications: *University Bulletin* (1 a year, in 16 series according to subject), *Revista de Ştiinţe Juridice*, *Studii si Cercetari de Onomastica*, *Viitorul*, *Revista Forum Geografic—Studii şi Cercetari de Geografie şi Protectia Mediului*, *Revista Arhivele Olteniei*

DEANS

Faculty of Agriculture: MARIN SOARE
Faculty of Automatics, Computers and Electronics: EUGEN BOBAŞU
Faculty of Chemistry: CEZAR SPÎNU
Faculty of Economic Sciences and Business Administration: LUCIAN BUSE
Faculty of Electrotechnology: ELEONOR STOENESCU
Faculty of Engineering and Management of Technological Systems: ION CIUPITU
Faculty of Engineering for Electromechanics, Environment and Industrial Informatics: SORIN ENACHE
Faculty of Horticulture: ION MITREA
Faculty of Law and Administration: DAN CLAUDIU DANISOR
Faculty of Letters: GABRIEL COSOVEANU
Faculty of Mathematics and Computer Science: NICOLAE ŢANDAREANU
Faculty of Mechanics: NICOLAE DUMITRU
Faculty of Physical Education and Sports: MARIAN DRAGOMIR
Faculty of Physics: DAN RADU CONSTANTINESCU
Faculty of Socio-Human Sciences: DUMITRU OTOVESCU
Faculty of Theology: IRINEU IOAN POPA

PROFESSORS

Faculty of Agriculture:

GĂNGIOVEANU, I., Agrotechnology
IONESCU, I., Meadow Cultivation
MARIN, N., Agrochemistry
MATEI, I., Agrotechnics
MOCANU, R., Agrochemistry
NICOLESCU, M., Phytotechnics
PANĂ, D., Management
POP, L., Agrotechnics
ŞOROP, G., Pedology
VASILE, D., Pedology
VOICA, N., Genetics

Faculty of Automatics, Computers and Electronics:

BĂDICĂ, C., Computers and Information Technology
BÎZDOACĂ, N., Mechatronics and Robotics
BOBASU, E., Automatics
BREZOVAN, M., Computers and Information Technology
BURDESCU, D., Computers and Information Technology
COJOCARU, D., Mechatronics and Robotics
DIACONU, I., Mechatronics and Robotics
IANCU, E., Automatics
IONETE, C., Automatics
IVANESCU, M., Mechatronics and Robotics
LUNGU, M., Computers and Information Technology
MARIAN, G., Computers and Information Technology
MARIN, C., Automatics
MOCANU, M., Computers and Information Technology
NICULESCU, E., Simulation
NITULESCU, M., Mechatronics and Robotics
PETRE, E., Automatics

POPESCU, D., Automatics
POPESCU, D., Mechatronics and Robotics
PURCARU, D., Electronic Structures for Measuring and Monitoring
RASVAN, V., Automatics
SELISTEANU, D., Automatics
STANESCU, L., Computers and Information Technology
STOIAN, Mechatronics and Robotics
VÎNATORU, M., Automatics

Faculty of Chemistry (Calea Bucureşti 107, 200479 Craiova; tel. (251) 54-46-21; fax (251) 44-66-30; e-mail negrum@mecanica.ucv.ro; internet chimie.ucv.ro):
BRĂTULESCU, G., Organic Chemistry
POPESCU, A., Analytical Chemistry
PREDA, M., Physical Chemistry
SPÎNU, C., Inorganic Chemistry

Faculty of Economic Sciences and Business Administration (tel. and fax (251) 41-13-17; e-mail stec@central.ucv.ro; internet stec.central.ucv.ro):
AVRAM, M., Accounting
AVRAM, V., Currency and Credits
BĂNDOI, A., Price and Competitiveness
BERCEANU, D., Corporate Finance
BURLEA-SCHIOPOIU, A., Management
BUSE, L., Economic and Financial Analysis
CONSTANTINESCU, D., Management
CRĂCIUN, L., Marketing
DOMNISORU, S., Accounting
DRĂCEA, M., Public Finance
GEORGESCU, V., Statistics
GIURGITEANU, N., Informatics
GRUESCU, R., Economics
IACOB, C., Accounting
IONASCU, C., Statistics
LITOIU, V., Informatics
LOLESCU, E., Economics
MIHAI, M., Accounting
NETOIU, L., Currency and Credits
NISTORESCU, T., Marketing
OPRITESCU, M., Currency and Credits
PETCU, C., Economics
PIRVU, C., Accounting
PÎRVU, G., Economics
POPA, S., Informatics
SICHIGEA, N., Corporate Finance
SIMINICĂ, M., Economic and Financial Analysis
SITNIKOV, C., Management
SOAVĂ, G., Informatics
SPULBĂR, C., Banking Management
ZAHARIA, C., Management

Faculty of Electrotechnology (Bdul Decebal 107, Craiova; tel. and fax (251) 43-64-47; e-mail decanat@elth.ucv.ro; internet elth.ucv.ro):
BROJBOIU, M., Electrical Engineering
CIONTU, M., Energetic Engineering
DIGĂ, S., Energetic Engineering
GOSEA, I., Energetic Engineering
LUNGU, R., Aerospace Engineering
MĂNESCU, L., Energetic Engineering
MIRCEA, I., Energetic Engineering
NICOLAE, P., Electrical Engineering
PASĂRE, S., Electrical Engineering
POPA, I., Electrical Engineering
TOPAN, D., Electrical Engineering
TUSALIU, P., Electrical Engineering

Faculty of Engineering for Electromechanics, Environment and Industrial Informatics:
BITOLEANU, A., Electrotechnics
IVANOV, S., Electrotechnics
MANOLEA, G., Electromechanics
MIHAI, D., Electrotechnics
NICOLA, A., Electrotechnics
POPESCU, M., Electrotechnics
ROSCA, D., Mechanics
VLAD, I., Electrotechnics

Faculty of Horticulture (Str. A. I. Cuza 13, 200585 Craiova; tel. and fax (251) 41-45-41; e-mail horticultura@central.ucv.ro; internet cis01.central.ucv.ro/facultatea_horticultura):
ACHIM, G., Fruit Farming
ANTON, D., Floriculture
BACIU, A., Fruit Farming
BOTU, I., Amelioration
BOTU, M., Fruit Farming
CHILOM, P., Vegetable Farming
CORNEANU, G., Genetics
DINCĂ, F., Biology
GAVRILESCU, E., Pollution and Pollutants
GHEORGHIŢĂ, M., Oenology
GIUGEA, N., Viticulture
IACOBESCU, F., Geometry
MITREA, I., Entomology
MITREA, R., Phytopathology
NOUR, V., Food Production
OLTEANU, I., Viticulture
PARASCHIVU, M., Phytopathology
POPA, A., Microbiology
POPA, D., Microbiology

Faculty of Law and Administration (e-mail secretariat@drept.ucv.ro; internet drept.ucv.ro):
CERCEL, S., Civil Law
DĂNIŞOR, D., Political Institutions, Constitutional Law
GĂINĂ, V., Commercial Law
NICULEANU, C., General Criminal Law
OLTEANU, G., Intellectual Property Law
SÂMBRIAN, T., Roman Law
SANDU, A., Political Economy
SCURTU, S., International Commercial Law
TURCULEANU, I., Civil Law Succession

Faculty of Letters (tel. (251) 41-44-68; fax (251) 41-66-88; e-mail litere@central.ucv.ro; internet www.ucv.ro):
AFANA, E., Stylistics, Poetics, Semiotics, Theory of Communication
BUCIU, M., Romanian Literature
BURDESCU, F., English Literature
COSTĂCHESCU, A., French Linguistics, Pragmatics
MURAR, I., English Linguistics
PANEA, N., Anthropology, Romanian Literature
RĂDULESCU, A., French Linguistics, Theory of Translation
SCURTU, G., French Linguistics, General Linguistics
SÎRBULESCU, E., English Literature
TEODORESCU, C., French Linguistics, Theory of Communication
TROCAN, L., French Literature

Faculty of Mathematics and Computer Science (tel. (251) 41-37-28; fax (251) 41-26-73; e-mail facmatinf@central.ro; internet inf.ucv.ro):
BUSNEAG, D., Algebra
DINCĂ, A., Algebra
IANCU, I., Artificial Intelligence
MICU, S., Numarical Analysis
NICULESCU, C., Mathematical Analysis
RĂDULESCU, V., Partial Differential Equations
ŢĂNDĂREANU, N., Artificial Intelligence
VLADIMIRESCU, I., Probability and Statistics

Faculty of Mechanics:
ASTEFANEI, I., Fluid Mechanics
BĂGNARU, D., Mechanics
BICĂ, M., Thermotechnics and Thermic Machines
CĂTĂNEANU, A., Machineries
CERNĂIANU, A., Advanced Production Systems
CHERGHINA, G., Technical Drawing and Infografics
CIOLACU, F., Chip Tooling Theory
CREŢU, S., Machineries
DUMITRU, N., Machine Elements
DUMITRU, C., Engineering and Design of Products
GEORGESCU, I., Steel Armed Concrete Buildings
ILINCIOIU, D., Materials Resistance
MARIN, M., Materials Resistance
NANU, G., Mechanics
OŢĂT, V., Automotive Dynamics
RINDERU, P., Mechanical Vibrations
ROŞCA, V., Materials Resistance
STANIMIR, A., Technology of Machine Construction
TĂRÂŢĂ, D., Material Science
TARNIŢĂ, D., Statistics
VINTILĂ, D., Mechanics
ZAMFIRACHE, M., Mechanicals Works

Faculty of Physical Education and Sports (Str. Brestei 156, Craiova; tel. and fax (251) 42-27-43; e-mail efs_kineto@sport.ucv.ro; internet cis01.central.ucv.ro/educatie_fizica-kineto/):
AVRAMESCU, T., Sport Medicine
CĂTĂNEANU, S., Physical Education and Sports
DĂNOIU, M., Sport Medicine
DRAGOMIR, M., Physical Education and Sports
DRAGOMIR, M., Physical Education and Sports
ORTĂNESCU, C., Physical Education and Sports
ORTĂNESCU, D., Physical Education and Sports
RUSU, L., Sport Medicine

Faculty of Physics (tel. and fax (251) 41-50-77; e-mail fizica@central.ucv.ro; internet fizica.ucv.ro):
BIZDADEA, C., Classical Mechanics
CONSTANTINESCU, R., Electrodynamics
SALIU, S., Constained Dynamics
SOCACIU, M., Liquid Crystals, Dielectrics
URSACHE, M., Optics

Faculty of Socio-Human Sciences (tel. and fax (251) 41-85-15; e-mail ifgcraiova@yahoo.com; internet www.ucv.ro):
AVRAM, C., History
CIOBOTEA, D., History
DEACONESCU, I., Philology
GHERGHE, P., History
LUNGU, M., History
OSIAC, V., History
OTOVESCU, D., Sociology
PITURCĂ, A., History-Philosophy
TOMESCU, V., Geography

Faculty of Technological System Managements and Engineering 'Dr Tr. Severin':
BENGA, G., Fundamentals of Cutting Technologies, Machining Technologies
CIUPITU, I., Cold Plastic Deformation
GÎNGU, O., Material Science and Engineering
MANGRA, M., Material Science and Engineering

Faculty of Theology:
CHIRILĂ, P., Pastoral Medicine and Bioethics
ISVORANU, A., Old Testament Study
PĂTULESCU, C., Universal Church History
POPA, I., Orthodox Dogmatics
RESCEANU, Ş., Religions History

UNIVERSITATEA DIN ORADEA
(University of Oradea)

CP 114, Oficiul Postal 1, Str. Universităţii 1, Oradea
Telephone: (259) 40-81-05
Fax: (259) 43-27-89
E-mail: rectorat@uoradea.ro
Internet: www.uoradea.ro
Founded 1990
State control
Academic year: October to July
Rector: Prof. Dr Eng. CORNEL ANTAL

Vice-Rectors: Prof. Dr Teodor Jurcut, Prof. Dr Elena Bonchiş, Prof. Dr Eng Ioan Felea, Prof. Dr Iacob Hantiu, Prof. Dr Barbu Ştefănescu
Scientific Sec.: Prof. Dr. Sorin Curilă
Gen. Admin. Dir: Prof. Dr Mircea Gordan

Number of teachers: 1,287
Number of students: 24,600

DEANS

Faculty of Architecture and Construction: Prof. Dr Aurora Mancia
Faculty of Economics: Prof. Dr Anca Dodescu
Faculty of Electrical Engineering and Informatics: Prof. Dr Ing. Teodor Leuca
Faculty of Energy Engineering: Prof. Dr. Marcel Roşca
Faculty of Environmental Protection: Prof. Dr Vasile Bara
Faculty of History, Geography and International Relations: Prof. Dr Ioan Horga
Faculty of Law and Jurisprudence: Prof. Dr Valentin Mirişan
Faculty of Letters: Prof. Dr Ion Simuţ
Faculty of Management and Technological Engineering: Ing. Negrau Maria
Faculty of Medicine and Pharmacy: Prof. Dr Gheorghe Bumbu
Faculty of Music: Prof. Dr Agneta Marcu
Faculty of Orthodox Theology: Prof. Dr Nicu Dumitraşcu
Faculty of Physical Education and Sport: Prof. Dr Octavian Băc
Faculty of Political Science and Communication Sciences: Prof. Dr Lia Pop
Faculty of Science: Prof. Dr Sanda Monica Filip
Faculty of Social Humanistic Science: Prof. Dr Floare Chipea
Faculty of Technological and Management Engineering: Prof. Dr Constantin Bungău
Faculty of Textiles and Leatherwork: Prof. Dr Ing. Vasile Anton
Faculty of Textile and Leatherware: Prof. Dr Vasile Anton
Faculty of Visual Arts: Prof. Dr Ioan Pantea
Univ. College of Education: Dr Ioan Sabău
Univ. College of Technology, Economics and Administration: Prof. Dr Ing. Dinu Mircea Fodor
Univ. Medical College: Prof. Dr Mircea Ifrim
Teacher Training Dept: Prof. Dr Vasile Marcu

UNIVERSITATEA DIN PETROŞANI (University of Petroşani)

Str. Universităţii 20, 332006 Petroşani, Hunedoara
Telephone: (254) 54-25-80
Fax: (254) 54-34-91
E-mail: m_georgescu@upet.ro
Internet: www.upet.ro

Founded 1864; became Coal Institute 1948, Mining Institute 1957 and Technical Univ. of Petroşani 1991; present name 1995
State control
Academic year: October to July

Rector: Prof. Dr Ing. Emil Pop
Vice-Rectors: Ing. Ilie Mitran, Prof. Dr Ing. Viorel Voin, Dr Ilie Rascolean
Chancellor: Dr Ing. Marius Marcu
Scientific Sec.: Assoc. Prof. Dr Eng. Ec. Ioan Cucu
Chief Registrar: Maria Zapartan
Librarian: Eng. Luminiţa Danciu

Library of 305,172 vols
Number of teachers: 215
Number of students: 6,341

Publications: *Annals of Economics* (1 a year), *Annals of Electrical Engineering* (1 a year), *Annals of Mechanical Engineering* (1 a year), *Annals of Mining Engineering* (1 a year), *Annals of Physics* (1 a year), *Annals of Social Sciences* (1 a year), *Informative Gazette* (12 a year), *Library's Informative Gazette* (4 a year), *Mining Magazine* (12 a year)

DEANS

Faculty of Machine and Electrical Engineering: Prof. Dr Eng. Aron Poanta
Faculty of Mining: Prof. Dr Eng. Ioan Dumitrescu
Faculty of Science: Assoc. Prof. Dr Eng. Ilie Mitran
Univ. College: Prof. Dr Eng. Mihai Pasculescu (Dir)

UNIVERSITATEA DIN PITEŞTI

Piteşti Str. Targu din Vale 1, 110040 Arges
Telephone: (348) 45-31-00
Fax: (348) 45-31-23
E-mail: info@upit.ro
Internet: www.upit.ro

Founded 1962, present name and status 1991
State control

Rector: Barbu Gheorghe
Rector of Social Affairs and Students: Crivac Gheorghe
Rector of Int. Relations and European Integration: Chirlesan Dumitru
Vice-Rector for Scientific Research: Serban Gheorghe
Rector of Quality Education and Investment: Tabacu Ion

DEANS

Faculty of Economics Sciences: Prof. Dr Constantin Draghici
Faculty of Educational Sciences: Prof. Dr Constantin Tibrian
Faculty of Electronics, Communications and Computers: Prof. Dr Ing. Silviu Ionita
Faculty of Law and Administrative Sciences: Prof. Dr Eugene Chelaru
Faculty of Letters: Prof. Dr Alexandrina Mustatea
Faculty of Mathematics and Computer Science: Dr Paul-Corneliu Radovici-Marculescu
Faculty of Mechanics and Technology: Prof. Dr Viorel Nicolae
Faculty of Orthodox Theology: Prof. Dr Ion Popescu
Faculty of Physical Education and Sport: Prof. Dr Niculescu Mugurel
Faculty of Sciences: Dr Aurel Popescu
Faculty of Social Sciences: Prof. Dr Geanina Cucu-Ciuhan

UNIVERSITATEA 'DUNAREA DE JOS' DIN GALAŢI

Str. Domnească 47, 800008 Galaţi
Telephone: (336) 13-01-09
Fax: (236) 46-13-53
Internet: www.ugal.ro

Founded 1948, Univ. status 1974
State control
Languages of instruction: Romanian, English, French
Academic year: October to July

Rector: Viorel Minzu
Pro-Rectors: Toader Munteanu, Mirela Praisler, Iulian Gabriel Birsan, Victor Cristea, Daniela Ancuta Sarpe
Registrar: Dana Mioara Rotaru
Librarian: Mioara Voncila

Number of teachers: 679
Number of students: 15,164

DEANS

Faculty of Arts: Toader Nita
Faculty of Computer Science: Adrian Filipescu
Faculty of Economic Sciences: Costel Nistor
Faculty of Electronics and Electrical Engineering: Dorel Aiordachioaie
Faculty of Engineering in Brăila: Adrian Goanta
Faculty of Food Science and Engineering: Petru Alexe
Faculty of History, Philosophy and Theology: Ivlampie Ivan
Faculty of Legal, Social and Political Sciences: Oprea Raducan
Faculty of Letters: Nicolae Ioana
Faculty of Mechanical Engineering: Catalin Fetecau
Faculty of Medicine and Pharmacy: Aurel Nichita
Faculty of Metallurgy and Materials Science: Nicolae Cananau
Faculty of Naval Architecture: Adrian Lungu
Faculty of Physical Education and Sport: Alexandru Pacuraru
Faculty of Sciences: Puiu Lucian Georgescu

PROFESSORS

Faculty of Arts:

- Bulancea, G., History of Music, Aesthetics, Folklore
- Dumitriu, M., History of Theatre
- Nita, T., Vocal Interpretation

Faculty of Computer Science:

- Dumitriu, L., Applied IT and Computer Science
- Filipescu, A., Industrial IT and Automation
- Puscasu, G., Industrial IT and Automation
- Segal, C., Applied IT and Computer Science

Faculty of Economic Sciences:

- Buhociu, F., Finances
- Puscasu, V., Economy
- Nistor, C., Business Communication
- Sarpe, D., Economy

Faculty of Electronics and Electrical Engineering:

- Aiordachioaie, D., Data Compression and Signals
- Badea, N., Electrical Equipment
- Minzu, V., Automatic control systems
- Munteanu, T., Electrotechnical Materials

Faculty of Engineering (in Brăila):

- Ciurea, A., Technical Equipment
- Goanta, A., Computer-aided Graphics
- Oproescu, Gh., Technical Equipment
- Picu, M., Fundamental Sciences

Faculty of Food Science and Engineering:

- Alexe, P., Biochemistry
- Bahrim, G., Bioengineering
- Cristea, V., Fishery
- Nicolae, A., Bioengineering
- Vizireanu, C., Biochemistry

Faculty of History, Philosophy and Theology:

- Ivan, I., History of Contemporary Philosophy
- Lica, V., History
- Siscanu, I., History
- Tofan, S., Philosophy

Faculty of Legal, Social and Political Sciences:

- Raducan, O., Law of Internal Combustion Engines
- Victor, I., Public Administration

Faculty of Letters:

- Croitoru, E., Law of Internal Combustion Engines
- Gata, A., Public Administration
- Ioana, N., Law of Internal Combustion Engines
- Milea, D., Law of Internal Combustion Engines
- Praisler, M., Law of Internal Combustion Engines

Faculty of Mechanical Engineering:
- ANDREI, G., Machine-parts Design and Graphics
- BIRSAN, I., Machine-parts Design
- CHIRICA, I., Structures Strength
- FETECAU, C., Machine Manufacturing and Robotics
- MEREUTA, E., Applied Mechanics

Faculty of Medicine and Pharmacy:
- FIRESCU, D., General Surgery, Low-invasive Surgery
- MUSAT, C., Physiology and Sports Medicine
- NICHITA, A., Pediatrics, Phisiology

Faculty of Metallurgy and Materials Science:
- BENEA, L., Environmental and Materials Engineering
- CANANAU, N., Plastic Deformation and Heat Treatment
- MUSAT, V., Plastic Deformation and Heat Treatment
- RADU, T., Environmental and Materials Engineering
- VLAD, M., Environmental and Materials Engineering

Faculty of Naval Architecture:
- DOMNISORU, L., Naval Structures
- LUNGU, A., Naval Structures
- OBREJA, C., Naval Hydrodynamics

Faculty of Physical Education and Sport:
- LIUSNEA, S., Body Building
- NICOLAE, P., Athletics
- PACURARU, A., Sport Games and Physical Education

Faculty of Sciences:
- CARAC, G., Chemistry
- GEORGESCU, L., Chemistry
- GEORGHIES, C., Physics
- MORARU, L., Physics
- PRAISLER, M., Physics

UNIVERSITATEA ECOLOGICA DIN BUCURESTI
(Ecological University of Bucharest)

Bdul Vasile Milea 1G, Sector 6, 061341 Bucharest
Telephone: (21) 316-79-32
Fax: (21) 316-63-37
E-mail: ecoueb@gmail.com
Internet: www.ueb.ro

Founded 1990
Private control

Rector: Prof. Dr ALEXANDRU TICLEA
Pro-Rectors: CAMELIA CAMASOIU, VLADIMIR ROJANSCHI, NICOLAE GALDEAN
Chancellor: CONSTANTIN DANCIULESCU

Library of 9,820 vols.

UNIVERSITATEA 'EFTIMIE MURGU' REŞIŢA

Piaţa Traian Vuia 1–4, 320085 Reşiţa
Telephone: (255) 21-02-27
Fax: (255) 21-02-30
E-mail: rector@uem.ro
Internet: www.uem.ro

Founded 1992
State control

Rector: Prof. Eng. DOINA FRUNZAVERDE
Rector for Education: Prof. Eng. GILBERT-RAINER GILLICH
Rector for Image and Communication: Prof. Dr MARIAN MICHAEL
Pres.: Prof. Dr Eng. ION VELA
Scientific Sec.: Prof. Eng. VIOREL CAMPIAN

DEANS

Faculty of Engineering: Prof. Dr Eng. SAVA IANICI
Faculty of Economics and Administrative Sciences: Prof. Dr GHEORGHE POPOVICI

UNIVERSITATEA 'EMANUEL' DIN ORADEA
(Emanuel University of Oradea)

Str. Nufarului 87, 410597 Oradea
Telephone and fax (259) 42-66-92
E-mail: contact@emanuel.ro
Internet: www.emanuel.ro

Founded 1986
Private control

Rector: Prof. Dr PAUL NEGRUŢ
Pro-Rector: Prof. Dr NICOLAE BICA
Chancellor: Dr IOAN GH. POP

Library of 61,000 vols

Publication: *Revista de teologie Perichoresis* (4 a year)

DEANS

Faculty of Theology: Dr MARIUS CRUCERU
Faculty of Management: Dr SEBASTIAN VĂDUVA

UNIVERŞITATEA EUROPEANĂ 'DRAGAN' DIN LUGOJ
(Dragan European University of Lugoj)

Str. Ion Huniade 2, 305500 Lugoj, Timiş
Telephone: (256) 35-91-98
E-mail: rectorat@deu.ro
Internet: www.universitateaeuropeanadragan.ro

Founded 1991
Private control
Academic year: October to September

Rector: Prof. Dr NICU TRANDAFIR
Pro-Rector: Prof. Dr PERSIDA CECHIN-CRISTA
Chancellor: Prof. Dr LIVIUS BERCEA
Dir: FLORIN MIHAI

DEANS

Faculty of Economics: Prof. Dr DĂNUŢ RADA
Faculty of Law: Dr DUMITRU CORNEAN

UNIVERSITATEA 'GEORGE BACOVIA' DIN BACĂU
(George Bacovia University of Bacău)

Str. Pictor Aman 96, 600164 Bacău
Telephone: (234) 56-26-00
Fax: (234) 51-64-48
E-mail: rectorat@ugb.ro
Internet: www.ugb.ro

Founded 1992
Private control

Rector: Prof. Dr TOADER GHERASIM
Pro-Rector: Prof. Dr DUMITRU BONTAS
Chancellor: Prof. Dr LIVIU DRUGUS

DEANS

Faculty of Accounting and Business Data Processing: Prof. CONSTANTIN COJOCARU
Faculty of Business Administration: Assoc. Prof. ANDREIA MELNIC
Faculty of Management: Prof. TATIANA PUIU

UNIVERSITATEA 'LUCIAN BLAGA' SIBIU
(Lucian Blaga University of Sibiu)

Bdul Victoriei 10, 550024 Sibiu
Telephone: (269) 21-60-62
Fax: (269) 21-04-92
E-mail: ccom@ulbsibiu.ro
Internet: www.ulbsibiu.ro

Founded 1990
State control
Academic year: October to June

Rector: Prof. Eng. CONSTANTIN OPREAN CIOCOI-POP
Vice-Rector: Assoc. Prof. RODICA MICLEA
Vice-Rector: Prof. LUIGI DUMITRESCU
Vice-Rector: Prof. DAN-MANIU DUSE
Vice-Rector: Prof. ALEXANDRU BACACI
Vice-Rector: Prof. MIHAI LEONIDA NEAMTU
Scientific Sec.: Prof. DORIN STOICESCU
Dir-Gen.: Econ. VASILE MOŢOC
Scientific Sec. to the Senate: Prof. Dr GHEORGHE DORIN STOICESCU

Library of 600,000 vols, 14,000 periodicals
Number of teachers: 486
Number of students: 20,000 (8,573 undergraduate, 367 postgraduate)

DEANS

Faculty of Agriculture, Food Industry and Environmental Protection: IOAN DANCIU
Faculty of Economics: Prof. Dr CARMEN COMĂNICIU
Faculty of Engineering 'Hermann Oberth': Prof. Dr IOAN BONDREA
Faculty of Food and Textile Processing Technology: Prof. Dr VASILE JĂŞCANU
Faculty of History and Patrimony 'Nicolae Lupu': Dr SORIN RADU
Faculty of Journalism: ION DUR
Faculty of Law 'Simion Bărnuţiu': Prof. Dr IOAN LEAŞ
Faculty of Letters, and Arts: Prof. Dr ALEXANDRA MITREA
Faculty of Medicine 'Victor Papilian': Prof. Dr MANUELA MIHALACHE
Faculty of Political Science, International Relations and European Studies: VASILE TABĂRĂ
Faculty of Sciences: Prof. Dr DUMITRU BATÂR
Faculty of Theology 'Andrei Şaguna': Prof. Dr LAURENŢIU STREZA
Univ. College: Prof. Dr NICOLAE TODERICIU (Dir)

UNIVERSITATEA 'MIHAIL KOGALNICEANU' DIN IAŞI
(Mihail Kogalniceanu University of Iaşi)

Str. Băluşescu 2, 700309 Iaşi
Telephone: (232) 21-24-16
Fax: (232) 27-98-21
E-mail: secretariat@umk.ro
Internet: www.umk.ro

Founded 1990
Private control
Language of instruction: Romanian
Academic year: October to July

Rector: Prof. Dr GENOVEVA VRABIE
Chancellor: Dr CRISTIAN SANDACHE

Library of 12,300
Number of teachers: 40
Number of students: 1,000

Publication: *B+ category*

DEANS

Faculty of Law: Prof. Dr AURORA CIUCA

UNIVERSITATEA NATIONALA DE ARTE BUCUREŞTI
(National University of Arts Bucharest)

Str. Gen. Budişteanu 19, 010773 Bucharest 1
Telephone and fax (21) 312-54-29
E-mail: rectorat@unarte.ro
Internet: www.unarte.ro

Founded 1864 as Scoala Naţionala de Arte Frumoase
Academic year: October to June
State control

Rector: Dr RUXANDRA DEMETRESCU
Chancellor: Dr CATALIN BALESCU

Library: see Libraries and Archives
Number of teachers: 274
Number of students: 1,000

Depts of ceramics, glass and metal, design (industrial and graphic), graphic fine art, history and theory of art, mural art, painting, pedagogy of art, photography, video and new media, sculpture, stage design and scenography, textile arts, work of art restoration

DEANS

Faculty of Fine Arts: MIHAIL MANESCU
Faculty of Applied Arts and Design: ALEXANDRU GHILDUS
Faculty of Art History and Theory: CORINA POPA

UNIVERSITATEA NAŢIONALĂ DE EDUCAŢIE FIZICĂ ŞI SPORT
(National University of Physical Education and Sport)

Str. Constantin Noica 140, Sector 6, 060057 Bucharest
Telephone: (21) 316-41-07
Fax: (21) 312-04-00
E-mail: rector@anefs.edu.ro
Internet: www.anefs-edu.ro

Founded 1922
State control

Rector: Prof. Dr VIOREL COJOCARU
Pro-Rector: Prof. Dr CORINA TIFREA
Pro-Rector: Dr TUDOR VIRGIL

Library of 102,222 vols, 3,963 titles
Number of teachers: 99
Number of students: 887

Publication: *Discobolul*

DEANS

Faculty of Physical Education and Sport: SORIN SERBĂNOIU
Faculty of Physical Therapy: ANTOINETTE CRETU

UNIVERSITATEA NAŢIONALĂ DE MUZICĂ DIN BUCUREŞTI

Str. Ştirbei Vodă 33, Sector 1, 010102 Bucharest
Telephone and fax (21) 314-63-41
E-mail: international@unmb.ro
Internet: www.unmb.ro

Founded 1864
State control
Languages of instruction: Romanian, English, French, German
Academic year: October to June

Rector: Prof. Dr DAN DEDIU
Chair.: Prof. Dr DOREL PAŞCU RĂDULESCU
Pro-Rectors: Prof. Dr DANA BORŞAN, Prof. Dr TEODOR ŢUŢUIANU

Library of 249,000
Number of teachers: 210
Number of students: 1,250 (full-time)

Publication: *Musicology Today*

DEANS

Faculty of Composition, Musicology and Musical Education: Prof. Dr SMARANDA MURGAN
Faculty of Performing Arts: Assoc. Prof. Dr BIANCA LUIGIA MANOLEANU

PROFESSORS

Musicology: Prof. Dr LIVIU DANCEANU
Composition: Prof. Dr DOINA ROTARU
Music Theory: Assoc. Prof. Dr MAGDA BUCIU
Byzantine Music: Prof. Dr SEBASTIAN BARBU BUCUR
Conducting: Prof. Dr DOREL PASCU-RADULESCU
Piano: Prof. Dr DANA BORSAN
Violin: Prof. Dr OCTAVIAN RATIU
Chamber Music: Assoc. Prof. Dr RALUCA VOICU-ARNAUTOIU
Wind Instruments: Assoc. Prof. Dr FLORENEL IONOAIA
Singing: Assoc. Prof. Dr ELEONORA ENACHESCU

UNIVERSITATEA 'NICOLAE TITULESCU' DIN BUCUREŞTI
(Nicolae Titulescu University of Bucharest)

Calea Văcăreşti 185, Sector 4, 040051 Bucharest
Telephone: (21) 330-90-32
Fax: (21) 330-86-06
E-mail: office@univnt.ro
Internet: www.univnt.ro

Founded 1990
Private control

Rector: Prof. Dr ION NEAGU

Faculties of banking and finance, law, public administration, sociolology

Publications: *Lex et Scientia magazine B plus*, *Romanian Journal of Intellectual Property Law*.

UNIVERSITATEA OVIDIUS CONSTANŢA

Bdul Mamaia 124, 900527 Constanţa
Telephone and fax (241) 60-64-65
Fax: (241) 51-15-12
E-mail: rectorat@univ-ovidius.ro
Internet: www.univ-ovidius.ro

Founded 1990
State control

Rector: Prof. Dr VICTOR CIUPINĂ
Vice-Rector for Institutional Devt Issues and Regional Cooperation: Prof. VICTOR PLOAE
Vice-Rector for Admin. and Students' Social Problems: Prof. NICULAE PERIDE
Scientific Sec.: Assoc. Prof. LUCIAN CRISTIAN PETCU

Number of teachers: 857
Number of students: 16,702

DEANS

Faculty of Arts: Prof. Dr CARMEN CRISTESCU
Faculty of Dental Medicine: Prof. Dr AMARIEI CORNELIU
Faculty of Economic Sciences: Prof. Dr EPURE DĂNUŢ TIBERIUS
Faculty of General Medicine: VIRGIL BREABAN
Faculty of History and Political Science: Dr DANIEL FLAUT
Faculty of Law and Public Admin.: Prof. Dr ANA RODICA STĂICULESCU
Faculty of Letters: Prof. Dr ADINA CIUGUREANU
Faculty of Mathematics and Informatics: MACEDON TEODOSIE
Faculty of Mechanical Engineering, Industrial and Maritime: Prof. Dr PETRU BORDEI
Faculty of Medicine: Prof. Dr Ing ZAGAN REMUS
Faculty of Natural and Agricultural Sciences: Prof. Dr DRAGOMIR COPREAN
Faculty of Pedagogy: FLORENTA MARINESCU
Faculty of Petroleum Technology: MARIAN COJOC
Faculty of Pharmacy: Prof. Dr GHEORGHE ŢARĂLUNGĂ
Faculty of Physics, Chemistry, Electronics and Oil Technology: MIHAI GÎRŢU
Faculty of Psychology and Educational Sciences: Prof. Dr ANCA DRAGU
Faculty of Sports: IONEL NICOLAE
Faculty of Theology: Prof. Dr TEODOSIE PETRESCU
School of Construction: Prof. Dr Ing VIRGIL BREABĂN

UNIVERSITATEA 'PETRE ANDREI' DIN IAŞI
(Petre Andrei University of Iaşi)

Str. Grigore Ghica Voda 13, 700400 Iaşi
Telephone and fax (232) 21-59-22
E-mail: facultateadeeconomie@yhaoo.com
Internet: www.upaiasi.ro

Private control

Rector: Prof. Dr N. NICULESCU

DEANS

Faculty of Communication Sciences: Prof. Dr ODETTE ARHIP
Faculty of Economics: Prof. Dr BOGDAN CONSTANTIN ANDRONIC
Faculty of Medicine: Prof. Dr CARMEN STADOLEANU
Law School: Prof. Dr CONSTANTIN ANDRONOVICI

UNIVERSITATEA 'PETROL-GAZE' DIN PLOIEŞTI

Bdul Bucureşti 39, POB 52, 100680 Ploieşti
Telephone: (244) 57-31-71
Fax: (244) 57-58-47
E-mail: rectorat@upg-ploiesti.ro
Internet: www.upg-ploiesti.ro

Founded 1948 as Institutul de Petrol şi Gaze; present name 1994
State control
Academic year: October to July

Pres.: Prof. Dr Ing. VLAD ULMANU
Vice-Rector for Scientific Research: Prof. Dr Ing. ION BOLOCAN
Vice-Rector for Academic Affairs: Prof. Dr Ing. DRAGOS CIUPARU
Vice-Pres. for Admin. Affairs: Prof. Dr Ing. MIHAI PASCU COLOJA
Vice-Rector for Int. Relations: Prof. Dr Ing. LIVIU DUMITRAŞCU
Scientific Sec.: Prof. Dr IONUT LAMBRESCU

Library of 259,542 vols, 2,879 periodicals
Number of teachers: 726
Number of students: 11,544

Publication: *Bulletin of Petroleum Gas University of Ploiesti* (series on Philology, Mathematics-Informatics, Physics, Economics, Educational Sciences, Law and Social Sciences)

DEANS

Faculty of Petroluem and Gas Engineering: Prof. Dr Ing. IULIAN NISTOR
Faculty of Petroleum Technology and Petrochemistry: Assoc. Prof. Dr Ing. PAUL ROSCA
Faculty of Mechanical and Electrical Engineering: Prof. Dr Ing. MIHAIL MINESCU
Faculty of Letters and Sciences: Assoc. Prof. Dr CHRISTIAN MARINOIU
Faculty of Economical Sciences: Prof. Dr ION IARCA

PROFESSORS

ANGHEL, A.
ANTONESCU, L.
ANTONESCU, N. N.
AVRAM, L.
BADOIU, D.
BALU, I.
BOLOCAN, I.
BUCUR, C.
CARTOAJE, V.
COLOJA, M. P.
CUTU, I.
DUDA, G.
DUMITRASCU, L.
FRUZESCU, D.
GEORGESCU, D.
GEORGESCU, O.
GHEORGHITOIU, M.
GRIGORE, N.
IARCA, I.
IONESCU, M.
IORDACHE, G.
MALUREANU, I.
MARIN, C.
MINESCU, F.
MINESCU, M.
NISTOR, I.
OPREA, M.

PANAIT, G.
PARASCHIV, N.
PATARLAGEANU, M.
PETCU, A.
POPA, C.
ROSCA, P.
SIRO, B.
SOARE, A.
STEFAN, G.
STOICESCU, C. C.
STRATULA, C.
TALLE, V.
TOMESCU, D.
TUDOR, I.
ULMANU, V.
VASILESCU, S.
VOICU, I.
ZECHERU, G.

UNIVERSITAȚEA 'PETRU MAIOR' DIN TÂRGU-MUREȘ
(Petru Maior University of Târgu-Mureș)

Str. Nicolae Iorga 1, 4300 Târgu-Mureș, Mureș
Telephone and fax (265) 16-22-75
E-mail: rectorat08@upm.ro
Internet: www.upm.ro

Founded 1960
State control
Academic year: October to July

Rector: Prof. Dr. Eng. LIVIU MARIAN
Vice-Rectors: Prof. Dr. Eng. VASILE BOLOS, Assoc. Prof. Dr CĂLIN ENĂCHESCU
Chancellor: Assoc. Prof. Dr CORNEL SIGMIREAN

Library of 120,000 vols
Number of teachers: 333 (133 full-time, 200 part-time)
Number of students: 6,200
Publications: *Buletinul Ştiinţific* (1 a year), *Studia Universitatis—Filologia* (1 a year), *Studia Universitatis—Istoria* (1 a year)

DEANS

Faculty of Economics and Admin. Sciences: Assoc. Prof. ZSUZANNA SZABO
Faculty of Engineering: Prof. Dr. Eng. DIANA-SIMONA ROTAR
Faculty of Sciences and Letters: Prof. Dr MARCELA COJOC
Univ. College: Assoc. Prof. Dr MARIA GEORGESCU

UNIVERSITATEA ROMANO-AMERICANA DIN BUCUREȘTI
(Romanian-American University of Bucharest)

Bdul Expozitiei 1B, Sector 1, 012101 Bucharest
Telephone: (21) 202-95-18
Fax: (21) 318-35-66
Internet: www.rau.ro

Founded 1991
Private control

Rector: Prof. Dr ION SMEDESCU.

UNIVERSITATEA ROMÂNĂ DE ȘTIINȚE ȘI ARTE 'GHEORGHE CRISTEA'
(Gheorghe Cristea Romanian University of Sciences and Arts)

Bdul Energeticienilor 9E, bloc M1, et. 1, Sector 3, Bucharest
E-mail: ugc_rei@ugc.ro
Internet: www.ugc.ro

Founded 1990
Private control

Rector: Prof. Dr Ing. LIDIA CRISTEA

Faculties of arts and sciences, business, legal and administration
Library of 60,000 vols.

UNIVERSITATEA 'ȘTEFAN CEL MARE'
(Ștefan Cel Mare University)

Str. Universităţii 13, 720229 Suceava
Telephone: (230) 52-00-81
Fax: (230) 52-00-80
E-mail: rectorat@usv.ro
Internet: www.usv.ro

Founded 1963 as Pedagogical Institute, became Institute of Higher Education 1976, univ. status 1990
State control
Academic year: October to July

Rector: Prof. ADRIAN GRAUR
Vice-Rector for Academic Services: Prof. EMANUEL DIACONESCU
Vice-Rector for Int. Relations: Prof. SANDA-MARIA ARDELEANU
Vice-Rector for Material Resources: Prof. AUREL BURCIU
Gen. Admin. Dir: Ing. EMIL NECHIFOR
Registrar: Ing. MARIA MUSCĂ
Library Dir: Prof. VASILE DOSPINESCU

Library of 233,640 vols, 3,207 periodicals
Number of teachers: 360
Number of students: 13,300 vols
Publications: *Acta Tribologica* (1 a year), *Annals* (philosophy and socio-human disciplines, geography, philology (literature), philology (linguistics), mechanics, electrical engineering, forestry, economic sciences and public admin., education; annals of univ. college, 1 a year), *Atelier de Traduction* (2 a year), *ISTECFILO* (2 a year), *La Lettre 'R'* (2 a year)

DEANS

Faculty of Economic Sciences and Public Administration: Prof. Dr ELENA HLACIUC
Faculty of Education Sciences: Dr RODICA NAGY
Faculty of Electrical Engineering and Computer Science: Prof. Dr STEFAN-GHEORGHE PENTIUC
Faculty of Food Engineering: Prof. Dr SONIA GUTT
Faculty of Forestry: Assoc. Prof. SERGIU ANDREI HORODNIC
Faculty of History and Geography: Prof. Dr STEFAN PURICI
Faculty of Letters and Communication Sciences: Prof. Dr MIRCEA A. DIACONU
Faculty of Mechanical Engineering, Mecatronics and Management: Prof. Dr IOAN MIHAI
Faculty of Physical Education and Sport: Assoc. Prof. PETRU GHERVAN

PROFESSORS

Faculty of Economic Sciences and Public Administration (tel. (230) 52-29-78; fax (230) 52-02-73; e-mail secretariat@seap.usv.ro; internet www.seap.usv.r):

BOSTON, I., Financial Control
BURCIU, A., Management
HAPENCIUC, C.-V., Entreprise Economy, Economic Statistics
HLACIUC, E., Accounting, Accounting Expertise
IFTIME, E., Law
LUPU, V., Informatics
PAVALEANU, V., Law
PETRIS, R., Accounting, Financial-Accounting Audit
PRELIPCEAN, G., Management, Capital Markets
PRISACARIU, G., Management
SANDU, G., Finance

Faculty of Education Sciences (tel. and fax (230) 52-04-65):

NAGY, R., Contemporary Romanian Language, History of Literary Language

Faculty of Electrical Engineering and Computer Science (Str. Universităţii 13, 720229 Suceava; tel. and fax (230) 52-48-01; e-mail secretariat@eed.usv.ro; internet www.eed.usv.ro):

CERNOMAZU, D., Inventics and Design
GAITAN, V., Computer Networks; Operating Systems; Computing Systems Architecture
GRAUR, A., Electonics; Electronic Devices
PENTIUC, GH., Computer Programming and Programming Languages; Programming of Distributed Systems
PENTIUC, R., Industrial Consumers' Power Alimentation
POPA, V., Applied Electronics; System Input/Output; Identification Systems
POTORAC, A., Computer Networks; Digital Integrated Circuits
TURCU, C., Systems Theory; Intelligent Systems; Theory of Automatic Regulation

Faculty of Food Engineering (Str. Universităţii 9, 720225 Suceava; tel. (230) 21-61-47; fax (230) 52-02-67; e-mail gutts@usv.ro; internet www.fia.usv.ro):

GUTT, G., Materials Engineering
GUTT, S., Food Engineering
SOLOMON, N., Equipment for Food Industry, Refrigeration Machinery, Operations and Devices in Food Industry

Faculty of Forestry (Str. Universităţii 13, 720229 Suceava; tel. and fax (230) 52-29-78; fax (230) 52-16-64; e-mail silvic@usv.ro; internet www.silvic.usv.ro):

CENUSA, R., Forestry
GIURGIU, V., Dendrometry
HOREANU, C., Botanics
MILESCU, I., Forest Economy, Law and Forest Legislation

Faculty of History and Geography (Str. Universităţii 13, 720229 Suceava; tel. (230) 21-61-47; fax (230) 52-37-42; e-mail stefanp@atlas.usv.ro; internet atlas.usv.ro):

BRANDUS, C., Regional Geography of Romania, Geomorphology
EFROS, N., Economic Geography, Geography of Tourism, Geography of Industry, Transport and Trade
GULICIUC, E., History of Contemporary Philosophy
GULICIUC, V., Theory and Practice of Communication, Semiotics
IACOBESCU, M., Contemporary History, History of Bucovina
MAXIM, T., Moral and Political Philosophy, History of Romanian Philosophy
PURICI, S., Slav History, History of Basarabia, European and Euroatlantic Integration
RADOANE, M., Geomorphology, Modern Methods in Geomorphology
RADOANE, N., Physical Geography of Romania, Geomorphology
SANDRU, D., Contemporary History, International Relations in the 20th Century

Faculty of Letters and Communication Sciences (Str. Universităţii 13, 720229 Suceava; tel. (230) 21-61-47; fax (230) 52-40-97; e-mail secretariat@litere.usv.ro; internet www.litere.usv.ro):

ARDELEANU, S.-M., Discourse Analysis, Language Semiotics
BARLEANU, I.-H., History of Communication, Actual Publishing Language, Introduction in Communication Sciences
CONSTANTINESCU, M., History of French Literature, Translation

DIACONU, M., Ideology and Exile, Romanian Post-war Poetry, Modernism after Modernism
DOSPINESCU, V., Contemporary French Language, Didactic Semiotics
OPREA, I., European Culture and Languages, Fundamentals of Lexical Theory
STEICIUC, E.-B., Translation, French Literature

Faculty of Mechanical Engineering, Mecatronics and Management (Str. Universităţii 9, 720225 Suceava; tel. and fax (230) 52-37-43; e-mail secretariat@fim.usv.ro; internet www.fim.usv.ro):

AMARANDEI, D., Manufacturing Technologies
BANCESCU, N., Materials Technology, Thermic Treatments
CEFRANOV, E., Quality Management, Manufacturing Technologies
CIOBANU, M., Metalworking, Quality Assurance
DIACONESCU, E., Tribology; Mechanical Contact
FRUNZA, G., Equipment Maintenance and Repair, Machines Manufacturing Technology
GRAMATICU, M., Materials Science, Thermic Treatments
GLOVNEA, M., Mechanical Contact, Elasticity and Strength of Materials
IACOB, D., Statistics, Quality Statistic Control
IONESCU, R., Robots and Flexible Systems, Industrial Automations
MIHAI, I., Thermodynamics and Thermic Machines
MUSCA, I., Numerical Analysis, Mechanisms and Machines Design, Tribology
RATA, V., Machines Manufacturing Technology, Equipment Maintenance and Repair
SEVERIN, L., Cold Plastic Deformation, Management

UNIVERSITATEA 'SPIRU HARET' DIN BUCURESTI
(Spiru Haret University of Bucharest)

Str. Ion Ghica 13, Sector 3, 030045 Bucharest
Telephone: (21) 314-00-75
Fax: (21) 314-39-08
E-mail: info@spiruharet.ro
Internet: www.spiruharet.ro

Founded 1991
Private control
Language of instruction: Romanian
Academic year: October to July

Rector: Prof. Dr AURELIAN A. BONDREA
Vice-Rector: Prof. Dr GHEORGHE BICA, Prof. Dr DOINEL DINUICA, Prof. Dr IOAN GAF-DEAC, Prof. Dr ELENA DOVAL, Assoc. Prof. Dr MANUELA EPURE, Assoc. Prof. Dr EDUARD IONESCU

Number of teachers: 1,264
Number of students: 90,565

Library of 675,464 vols, 4,738 journals

Publications: *Annals of Spiru Haret, Economic Series, Annals of Spiru Haret University, Filology Series—Foreign Languages, Annals of Spiru Haret University, Geography Series, Annals of Spiru Haret University, Journalism Studies, Annals of Spiru Haret University, Mathematics-Informatics Series, Annals of Spiru Haret University, Music Series, Annals of Spiru Haret University,Veterinary Medicine Series*

DEANS

Department of Finance and Banking: Prof. Dr GHEORGHE PISTOL
Department of Marketing and International Business: Prof. Dr LUMINITA PISTOL
Department of Theatre: Prof. Dr LUCIA MUREŞAN
Faculty of Arts: Assoc. Prof. Dr GEORGE GRIGORE
Faculty of Accounting and Finance, Câmpulung-Muscel: Assoc. Prof. Dr ODI MIHAELA ZARNESCU
Faculty of Accounting and Finance, Râmnicu-Vâlcea: Assoc. Prof. Dr LUMINITA IONESCU
Faculty of Architecture: Prof. Dr EMIL CREANGĂ
Faculty of Economic Sciences, Blaj: Prof. Dr EMIL POPA
Faculty of Financial and Accounting Management, Constanţa: Assoc. Prof. Dr DRAGOS MIHAI IPATE
Faculty of Financial and Accounting Management, Craiova: Assoc. Prof. Dr ION VIOREL MATEI
Faculty of Financial and Accounting Management, Constanţa: Assoc. Prof. Dr DRAGOS MIHAI IPATE
Faculty of Foreign Languages and Literatures: Prof. Dr ELENA BĂLAN
Faculty of Geography: Dr GHEORGHE HERISANU
Faculty of Geography and Tourism: Dr CORNELIA MARIN
Faculty of History, Museology and Archival Science: Prof. Dr DUŢU ALEXANDRU
Faculty of Journalism, Communication and Public Relations: Assoc. Prof. Dr SOFIA BRATU
Faculty of Law and Public Administration: Prof. Dr LAZĂR CARJAN
Faculty of Law and Public Administration, Constanta: Assoc. Prof. Dr GHEORGHE DINU
Faculty of Law and Public Administration, Craiova: Assoc. Prof. Dr BUJOR FLORESCU
Faculty of Law and Public Administration, Ramnicu Valcea: Assoc. Prof. Dr CONSTANTIN PLETEA
Faculty of Legal and Administrative Sciences, Braşov: Prof. Dr ALEXANDRU IONAS
Faculty of Letters: Dr TAMARA CEBAN
Faculty of Management, Braşov: Prof. Dr STELIAN PANZARU
Faculty of Mathematics and Informatics: Prof. Dr GRIGORE ALBEANU
Faculty of Music: Prof. Dr PETRU STOIANOV
Faculty of International Relations, History and Philosophy: Prof. Dr GHEORGHE ONIŞORU
Faculty of Physical Education and Sport: Assoc. Prof. Dr GEORGETA NICULESCU
Faculty of Philosophy, Political Science and Cultural Studies: Prof. Dr IOAN N. ROŞCA
Faculty of Psychology and Pedagogy, Braşov: Prof. Dr PETRE LISIEVICI
Faculty of Romanian Language and Literature: Dr VALERIU MARINESCU
Faculty of Sociology - Psychology: Prof. Dr FLORIN TUDOSE
Faculty of Veterinary Medicine: Assoc. Prof. Dr DANUT TURCU
Financial and Accounting Management Faculty: Assoc. Dr EUGEN GHIORGHIŢĂ

UNIVERSITATEA 'TIBISCUS' DIN TIMIŞOARA
(Tibiscus University of Timişoara)

Str. Lascăr Catargiu 4–6, 300559 Timişoara
Telephone and fax (256) 22-06-89
E-mail: rectorat@tibiscus.ro
Internet: www.tibiscus.ro
Private control

Rector: Prof. Dr CORNEL HARANGUŞ
Pro-Rector: Prof. Dr CRĂCIUN SABĂU
Chancellor: DAN LACRĂMĂ
Library of 135,000 vols

DEANS

Faculty of Computer Science and Applied Information Technology: Dr LUCIAN LUCA
Faculty of Design, Music: Dr TIBERIU MARIUS KARNYANSZKY
Faculty of Economics: Prof. Dr ADRIAN COJOCARIU
Faculty of Education and Sports: Dr CORINA MUŞUROI
Faculty of Law and Public Administration: Dr DUMITRU VLĂDUŢ
Department of Psychology: Prof. Dr RADU RĂDUCAN

UNIVERSITATEA 'TITU MAIORESCU'
(Titu Maiorescu University)

Str. Dâmbovnicului 22, Sector 4, 040441 Bucharest
Telephone and fax (213) 16-16-43
E-mail: rectorat@utm.ro
Internet: www.utm.ro

Founded 1990
Private control

Rector: Prof. IOSIF R. URS
Pro-Rectors: Prof. VALENTIN CORNELIU PAU, Prof. Dr DUMITRU GHEORGHIU, Prof. Dr MAGDALENA NEGRUŢIU
Scientific Sec. of the Senate: Prof. ANA LUCIA RADULESCU

Library of 1,500,000 vols (central library; there are also separate faculty libraries)

DEANS

Faculty of Dental Medicine: Prof. DAN FLORIN UNGUREANU
Faculty of Economic Sciences: Dr FLORIN VĂDUVA
Faculty of Economics, Târgu. Jiu: Prof. Dr ION PÂRGARU
Faculty of Information Sciences and Technology: Prof. EMIL CRETU
Faculty of Law: Dr DAN VOINEA
Faculty of Medicine: Prof. DAN FLORIN UNGUREANU
Faculty of Psychology: Prof. VIOREL IULIAN TANASE

UNIVERSITATEA 'TRANSILVANIA' DIN BRAŞOV

Bdul Eroilor 29, 500036 Braşov
Telephone: (268) 41-20-88
Fax: (268) 41-05-25
E-mail: rectorat@unitbv.ro
Internet: www.unitbv.ro

Founded 1971, by merger of Polytechnical and Pedagogical Institutes of Braşov
State control
Languages of instruction: Romanian, English, German, French
Academic year: October to July

Rector: Prof. Dr Ing. ION VISA
Vice-Rector for Research and IT: Prof. Dr Ing. MIHAI ROMANCA
Vice-Rector for Liaison with Economic, Social and Cultural Environment: Prof. Dr EMIL STOICA
Vice-Rector for Quality Assurance and Int. Evaluation: Prof. Dr Ing. SIMONA LACHE
Vice-Rector for Student Activities: Assoc. Prof. Dr CONSTANTIN DUGULEANA
Vice-Rector for Int. and Nat. Relations: Prof. Dr Ing. MARINA CIONCA
Chancellor: Prof. Dr LILIANA ROGOZEA
Registrar: Ing. ALINA POPESCU
Library Dir: Prof. Dr Ing. ELENA HELEREA

Library: see Libraries and Archives
Number of teachers: 815
Number of students: 22,399

Publication: *Buletinul Universităţii 'Transilvania' din Braşov*

DEANS

Faculty of Civil Engineering: Prof. Dr Eng. IOAN TUNS
Faculty of Economic Sciences and Business Administration: Prof. Dr GABRIEL BRATUCU
Faculty of Electrical Engineering and Computer Science: Prof. Dr Eng. SORIN MORARU
Faculty of Food and Tourism: Prof. Dr Eng. ROMULUS GRUIA
Faculty of Silviculture and Forest Engineering: Prof. Dr Eng. IOAN ABRUDAN
Faculty of Law: Prof. Dr CRISTINEL MURZEA
Faculty of Languages and Literatures: Prof. Dr ANDREI BODIU
Faculty of Materials Science and Engineering: Prof. Dr Eng. MIRCEA TIEREAN
Faculty of Mathematics and Computer Science: Assoc. Prof. Dr EUGEN PALTANEA
Faculty of Mechanical Engineering: Prof. Dr Eng. ANGHEL CHIRU
Faculty of Medicine: Prof. Dr LAZĂR ONISAI
Faculty of Music: Prof. Dr STELA DRAGULIN
Faculty of Physical Education and Mountain Sports: Assoc. Prof. Dr RAZVAN ENOIU
Faculty of Product Design and Environment: Prof. Dr Eng. CODRUTA JALIU
Faculty of Psychology and Educational Sciences: Assoc. Prof. Dr MARIELA PAVALACHE-ILIE
Faculty of Sociology and Communication: Prof. Dr SILVIU COPOSESCU
Faculty of Technological Engineering and Industrial Management: Prof. Dr Eng. NOURAS-BARBU LUPULESCU
Faculty of Wood Engineering: Prof. Dr Eng. GAVRIL BUDAU

PROFESSORS

Faculty of Economic Sciences (Colina Universității 1, 500036 Brașov; tel. (268) 41-93-04; fax (268) 41-93-04; e-mail f8-economic@unitbv.ro; internet econ.unitbv.ro):

BĂCANU, V. B., Finance, Accounting and Economic Theory
BRÂNZAN, I., Management and Computing
BRĂTUCU, G., Marketing and Tourism
DUGULEANĂ, L., Management and Computing
FORIȘ, T., Management and Computing
LEFTER, C., Marketing and Tourism
LIXĂNDROIU, D. I., Management and Computing
OPREI, I., Management and Computing
POPA, M., Management and Computing
POPESCU, M., Management and Computing
SAON, S., Finance, Accounting and Economic Theory

Faculty of Electrical Engineering (Str. Politehnicii 1, 500024 Brașov; tel. (268) 47-47-18; fax (268) 47-47-18; e-mail f4-electro@unitbv.ro; internet www.vega.unitbv.ro):

ANDONIE, R., Electronics
BIDIAN, D. Ș., Electrical Engineering
BORZA, P. N., Electronics
CERNAT, M., Electrical Engineering
DAN, ȘT., Automation
FRATU, A., Automation
GEORGESCU, M., Electrical Engineering
GOGIOIU, A., Electrical Engineering
HELEREA, E., Electrical Engineering
MĂRGINEANU, I., Automation
MARINESCU, C., Electrical Engineering
MATLAC, I. V., Electrical Engineering
NICOLAIDE, A. C., Electrical Engineering
OLTEAN, I. D., Electronics
PEȘTEANU, O., Electrical Engineering
SCUTARU, GH., Electrical Engineering
SISAK, F., Automation
STOIA, D. D., Electrical Engineering
SZABO, W., Electronics
SZEKELY, I., Electronics
ȚAȚA, M. S., Electrical Engineering
TOACȘE, GH., Electronics
TOPA, I., Automation

Faculty of Forestry and Forest Exploitation (Șirul Beethoven 1, 500123 Brașov; tel. (268) 47-57-05; fax (268) 47-57-05; e-mail f5-silvic@unitbv.ro; internet www.unitbv.ro/silvic):

ALEXANDRU, V. M., Forest Exploitation
BELDEANU, E., Forest Exploitation
BOȘ, N.
CHIȚEA, GH., Biostatistics
CIORTUZ, I., Silviculture
CIUBOTARU, A., Forest Exploitation
CLINCIU, I., Flood Control
COSTEA, C.
DANCIU, M. A., Silviculture
FLORESCU, I. I., Silviculture
IONAȘCU, GH., Forest Exploitation
KISS, A., Topography
LEAHU, I., Dendrometry
MARCU, M., Silviculture
MARCU, O., Silviculture
NEGRUȚIU, A., Silviculture
NEGRUȚIU, F., Silviculture
OLTEANU, N., Forest Exploitation
OPREA, I., Forest Exploitation
PARASCAN, D., Silviculture
POPESCU, I., Forest Exploitation
RUSU, A.
SIMON, D., Silviculture
ȘOFLETEA, N., Silviculture
SPÂRCHEZ, GH., Silviculture
TAMAȘ, Ș., Operations Research
TÂRZIU, D., Silviculture
UNGUREANU, ȘT., Forest Exploitation

Faculty of Law and Sociology (Bdul Eroilor 25, 500030 Brașov; tel. and fax (268) 47-40-17):

BUJDOIU, N., Sociology, Philosophy and Law
CHIRIȚĂ, R., Sociology, Philosophy and Law
POENARU, E., Sociology, Philosophy and Law

Faculty of Materials Science and Engineering (Colina Universității 1, 500068 Brașov; tel. and fax (268) 47-16-26; fax (268) 47-16-26; e-mail f3-simat@unitbv.ro; internet www.unitbv.ro):

ANDREESCU, F. G., Welding Equipment
BEJAN, V., Technology of Fabrication and Maintenance of Equipment
BOT, D., Heating Equipment, Foundry Technology
CÂNDEA, V. N., Welding Technology
CHICHERNEA, F., Technological Equipment and Materials Science
CIOBANU, I., Fundamentals of Foundry
CONSTANTINESCU, A., Foundry Equipment
CRIȘAN, A., Technological Equipment and Materials Science
DUȚĂ-CAPRĂ, A., Chemistry
EFTIMIE, L., Welding Technology
ENE, V., Special Proceedings for Foundry
FĂTU, S., Study of Metals
FLOREA, R. G., Welding Technology
GEAMĂN, V., Technological Equipment and Materials Science
GIACOMELLI, I., Equipment and Technologies for Thermal Treatments
IOVANĂȘ, R., Technology of Welding by Pressing
LUCA, V., Study of Metals
MACHEDON, T., Welding Equipment, Non-Destructive Testing, Hydraulic and Pneumatic Engines
MARKOS, Z., Welding Technology
MILOȘAN, I.
MUNTEANU, A., Thermal Treatments and Heat Processing
NOVAC, GH., Welding Equipment
PAȚACHIA, S., Chemistry
POPA, A., Technology of Plastic Deformation
POPESCU, R. M., Welding Technology
SAMOILĂ, C., Furnaces and Equipment for Heating
SCOROBEȚIU, L., Fundamentals of Welding Processes
ȘERBAN, C., Study of Metals
ȚICĂ, E.-R., Chemistry
ȚIEREAN, M., Welding Technology
TRIF, N., Mechanization, Automation and Robots for Welding Processing
TUDORAN, P., Study of Metals
VARGA, B., Technological Equipment
VEȚELEANU, A.

Faculty of Mathematics and Computing (Str. Iuliu Maniu 50, 500091 Brașov; tel. and fax (268) 41-40-16; e-mail f-mate-info@unitbv.ro; internet cs.unitbv.ro):

ATANASIU, GH., Geometry
CIUREA, E., Computing
COCAN, M., Computing
LUPU, M., Differential Equations
MARIN, M., Differential Equations
MARINESCU, C., Differential Equations
MUNTEANU, GH., Differenctial Equations
ORMAN, G., Mathematical Analysis and Probability
OVESEA, H., Mathematical Analysis and Probability
PASCU, N., Mathematical Analysis and Probability
PESCAR, V., Geometry
PITIȘ, GH., Differential Equations
RADOMIR, I., Mathematical Analysis and Probability
SCHEIBER, E., Computing
TIȚA, N., Mathematical Analysis and Probability

Faculty of Mechanics (Str. Politehnicii 1, 500036 Brașov; tel. and fax (268) 47-47-61; e-mail f-mecanica@unitbv.ro; internet mecanica.unitbv.ro):

ABĂITĂNCEI, D., Automotive Technology
BĂCANU, GH., Physics
BALCU, I., Strength of Materials and Vibration
BENCHE, V., Heat Engineering and Fluid Mechanics
BIȚ, C. S., Strength of Materials and Vibration
BOBESCU, GH., Automotive Technology
BOLFA, T. E., Strength of Materials and Vibration
BRĂTUCU, GH., Agricultural and Food-processing Machinery
CÂMPIAN, V., Automotive Technology
CÂNDEA, I., Mechanics
CHIRIACESCU, T. S., Strength of Materials and Vibration
CHIRU, A., Automotive Technology
CIOFOAIA, V., Strength of Materials and Vibration
CIOLAN, GH., Automotive Technology
COFARU, C., Automotive Technology
CONSTANTIN, F., Mechanics
CRISTEA, L., Precision Engineering and Mechatronics
CURTU, T. I., Strength of Materials and Vibration
DELIU, GH., Mechanics
DUMITRIU, A., Precision Engineering and Mechatronics
FETCU, D., Heat Engineering and Fluid Mechanics
GOIA, A.I, Strength of Materials and Vibration
IONESCU, EMIL GH., Precision Engineering and Mechatronics
IONESCU, ENACHE, Agricultural and Food-processing Machinery
MUNTEANU, GH. M., Strength of Materials and Vibration
MUREȘAN, M., Heat Engineering and Fluid Mechanics
NAGY, T., Automotive Technology
NĂSTĂSOIU, S., Automotive Technology
OLTEANU, C., Precision Engineering and Mechatronics

POPA, V. A., Strength of Materials and Vibration
POPARAD, H., Precision Engineering and Mechatronics
POPESCU, S., Agricultural and Food-processing Machinery
POSTELNICU, A., Heat Engineering and Fluid Mechanics
PREDA, I., Automotive Technology
RADU, GH. A., Automotive Technology
RADU, N. GH., Strength of Materials and Vibration
ROŞCA, ILEANA C., Strength of Materials and Vibration
ROŞCA, IOAN C., Precision Mechanics and Mechatronics
RUS, F., Agricultural and Food-processing Machinery
SĂLĂJAN, C., Automotive Technology
SECARA, E. M., Mechanics
SEITZ, N., Automotive Technology
ŞERBĂNOIU, N., Heat Engineering and Fluid Mechanics
SOARE, I., Automotive Technology
ŞOVA, M., Heat Engineering and Fluid Mechanics
ŞOVA, V., Heat Engineering and Fluid Mechanics
SZÁVA, I., Strength of Materials and Vibration
ŢANE, N., Agricultural and Food-processing Machinery
TOFAN, M., Mechanics
ŢUREA, N., Automotive Technology
ULEA, M., Strength of Materials and Vibration
UNGUREANU, V. B., Heat Engineering and Fluid Mechanics
VEŞTEMEAN, N., Heat Engineering and Fluid Mechanics
VLASE, S., Mechanics

Faculty of Medicine (Str. N. Bălcescu 56, 500019 Braşov; tel. and fax (268) 41-21-85; e-mail f-medicina@unitbv.ro; internet www .unitbv.ro/faculties/medicina):

COMAN, GH., Preclinical Medicine
LEAŞU, T., Specialized Medicine
RĂDOI, M., Internal Medicine
RADU, I., Preclinical Medicine

Faculty of Music (Str. Andrei Saguna 2, Braşov; tel. (268) 47-88-84; fax (268) 41-05-25; e-mail f-muzica@unitbv.ro; internet www .unitbv.ro/muzica):

BICA, N., Teaching Music
DRĂGULIN, S. D., Instrumental Interpretation
IACOBESCU, L., Instrumental Interpretation

Faculty of Technical Engineering (Str. Colina Universităţii 1, 500036 Braşov; tel. and fax (268) 41-46-90; e-mail f2-itehn@unitbv.ro; internet www.unitbv.ro/tech):

ALEXANDRU, P., Mechanisms
BOBANCU, Ş., Mechanisms
BONCOI, GH., Automatic Machine Tools
BRANA, M. A., Descriptive Geometry and Technical Drawing
BUZATU, C., Automation of Technological Processes
CALEFARIU, G.
CHIŞU, E., Machine Components
CIOBOTĂ, M., Precision Mechanics
CRUCIAT, P., Technical Measurements
DAJ, I., Machine Components
DEACONESCU, T.
DELIU, M.
DIACONESCU, D. V., Mechanisms
DIŢU, V., Car Construction Technology
DUDIŢĂ, F., Mechanisms
DUMITRU, S., Physics
GAGIONEA, E. L., Descriptive Geometry and Technical Drawing
INŢA, I., Physics
IVAN, M., Machine Tools and Dimensional Control
IVAN, N. V., Machine Engineering Technology
JULA, A., Machine Elements
LUPULESCU, N.-B., Car Construction Technology
MĂNIUŢ, P.
MĂRĂSCU KLEIN, V., Unconventional Materials, Computer-Aided Production Systems Design
MARTINESCU, I., Technology of Cold-pressing
MOGAN, GH. L., Machine Elements
MOLDOVEAN, GH., Machine Elements
NEDELCU, A.
OBACIU, GH., Electric Drive and Machine Tools
PĂUNESCU, T., Car Construction Technology
POPESCU, I., Technical Measurement and Tolerance
ROŞCA, D. M., Metal-cutting Theory
SĂVESCU, D., Machine Elements
SECARĂ, GH., Metal Cutting, Tool Design
SOFONEA, L., Physics
STAREŢU, I., Machine Components
STROE, I., Machine Components
TALABĂ, D., Machine Components
TĂNĂSESCU, I., Machine Elements and Mechanisms
TUREAC, I., Machines for Processing by Deformation
URSUŢIU, D., Physics
VĂSÎI-ROŞCULEŢ, S., Design of Devices
VELICU, D., Descriptive Geometry and Technical Drawing
VIŞA, I., Mechanisms

Faculty of Wood Technology (Str. Colina Universităţii 1, 500068 Braşov; tel. (268) 41-53-15; fax (268) 41-53-15; e-mail f-ilemn@unitbv.ro; internet www.unitbv.ro/il):

BĂDESCU, L. A.-M., Wood-processing Machinery
BARBU, M. C., Wood Technology
BUDĂU, G., Wood-processing Machinery
CISMARU, I., Wood Technology
DOGARU, V., Wood-processing Machinery
ISTRATE, V., Wood Technology
LĂZĂRESCU, C., Wood-processing Machinery
MIHAI, D., Wood Technology
MITIŞOR, A., Wood Technology
NĂSTASE, V., Wood Technology
PETROVICI, V., Wood Technology
ŢĂRAN, N., Wood-processing Machinery
TUDOR, E., Wood-processing Machinery
ZLATE, GH., Wood Technology

UNIVERSITATEA 'VALAHIA' DIN TÂRGOVIŞTE

Bdul Regele Carol I 2, 130024 Târgovişte
Telephone: (245) 20-61-01
Fax: (245) 21-76-92
E-mail: rectorat@valahia.ro
Internet: www.valahia.ro

Founded 1989

Rector: Prof. Dr ION CUCUI
Pro-Rectors: Prof. Dr MARIN CIRCIUMARU, Prof. Dr CONSTANTIN GHITA, Prof. Dr GHEORGHE IONITA
Librarian: Prof. AGNES ERICH

Number of teachers: 400
Number of students: 10,000

DEANS

Faculty of Arts and Sciences: Dr LAURA MONICA GORGHIU
Faculty of Economic Sciences: Dr LEONARDO BADEA
Faculty of Environmental Engineering and Biotechnology: Prof. Dr STEFANIA IORDACHE
Faculty of Electrical Engineering: Dr Ing. HENRI GEORGE COANDA
Faculty of Humanities: Prof. Dr CONSTANTIN PEHOIU
Faculty of Law: Dr LIVIA MOCANU
Faculty of Material Sciences, Mechatronic Engineering and Robotics: Prof. Dr VASILE BRATU
Faculty of Theology: Prof. Dr MIHAITA NIFON

DIRECTORS OF COLLEGES

Univ. College of Economics and Admin.: Dr VIRGIL POPA
Univ. College of Education: (vacant)
Univ. College of Technology: Dr CORNEL MARIN

UNIVERSITATEA 'VASILE ALECSANDRI' DIN BACĂU ('Vasile Alecsandri' University Of Bacău)

Calea Mărăşeşti 157, 600115 Bacău
Telephone: (234) 54-24-11
Fax: (234) 54-57-53
E-mail: rector@ub.ro
Internet: www.ub.ro

Founded 1961 as Pedagogical Institute; became Bacău Institute of Higher Education 1974; 1990 became Univ. of Bacău; present name and status 2009
State control
Languages of instruction: Romanian, French, English
Academic year: October to July

Rector: Prof. VALENTIN NEDEFF
Vice-Rector for Economical and Quality Strategies: Prof. GHEORGHE PINTILIE
Vice- Rector for Educational Programmes and Student activities: Assoc. Prof. Dr GABRIELA RAVEICA
Vice-Rector for Research Programmes and Int. Relations: Prof. GABRIEL LAZĂR
Chancellor: Prof. CĂTĂLINA ABABEI
Gen.-Man.: Eng. IOAN-CIPRIAN DRUGĂ
Registrar and Chief Sec.: Eng. ADRIAN APĂVĂLOAIE
Head of Int. Relations: SILVIA LEONTE
Chief Libarian: Eng. CECILIA ANGHEL

Library of 175,400 vols, 56,120 periodicals
Number of teachers: 243
Number of students: 6,857

Publications: *Actes du Colloque Franco-Roumain de Chimie Appliquée, Cultural Perspectives—Journal for Literary and British Cultural Studies in Romania* (1 a year), *Gymnasium* (2 a year), *Interstudia* (2 a year), *Journal of Engineering Studies and Research* (4 a year), *Junimea studenţească băcăuană, Kinetostud, Reste a voir, Ro-Brit, Scientific Study & Research—Chemistry and Chemical Engineering, Biotechnology, Food Industry* (4 a year), *Scientific Studies and Research—Series Mathematics and Informatics* (2 a year), *Scientific Studies and Research—Mathematics* (12 a year), *Studenţimea băcăuană, Studii şi Cercetări—Seria Biologie* (2 a year), *Voxstud*

DEANS

Faculty of Economic Sciences: Prof. Dr Ing. OVIDIU-LEONARD TURCU
Faculty of Engineering: Prof. Dr Ing. CAROL SCHNAKOVSZKY
Faculty of Letters: Prof. Dr ADRIANA-GERTRUDA ROMEDEA
Faculty of Movement, Sport and Health Sciences: Assoc. Prof. Dr DĂNUŢ NICU MÂRZA DĂNILĂ
Faculty of Sciences: Prof. Dr MIHAI TĂLMACIU

UNIVERSITATEA ROMÂNO-GERMANĂ DIN SIBIU (Romanian-German University of Sibiu)

Calea Dumbravii 28–32, 550324 Sibiu
Telephone: (269) 23-35-68
Fax: (269) 23-35-76
E-mail: rectorat@roger-univ.ro
Internet: www.roger-univ.ro

Founded 1998
Private control
Rector: Prof. Dr HORTENSIA GORSKI
Pro-Rector: Prof. Dr GHEORGHE BICHICEAN
Scientific Sec.: Prof. Dr IOAN CONSTANTIN PETCA
Library of 18,000 vols, 11,500 Romanian, 5,000 German, 1,280 English, 220 other languages

DEANS
Faculty of Economics: Dr Ing. ELENA SIMA
Faculty of Law and Administrative Science: Dr TITUS SEREDIUC

Technological Universities

IULIU HAŢIEGANU UNIVERSITY OF MEDICINE AND PHARMACY CLUJ-NAPOCA

Str. Emil Isac 13, 400023 Cluj-Napoca
Telephone: (264) 59-72-56
Fax: (264) 59-72-57
E-mail: rectoratumf@umfcluj.ro
Internet: www.umfcluj.ro

Founded 1872
Public control
Languages of instruction: Romanian, English, French
Academic year: October to July (2 semesters)
Rector: Prof. Dr CONSTANTIN CIUCE
Pres.: Prof. Dr MARIUS BOJIŢĂ
Vice-Rector for Academic Affairs: Prof. Dr SORIN DUDEA
Vice-Rector for Management and Academic Development: Assoc. Prof. Dr DORIN FARCĂU
Vice-Rector for Scientific Affairs: Assoc. Prof. Dr ALEXANDRU IRIMIE
Vice-Rector for Academic Evaluation and Quality Assurance: Prof. RADU OPREAN
Vice-Rector for Postgraduate Studies: Prof. Dr GRIGORE BACIUT
Gen. Man.: IOAN POP
Registrar in Chief: MIHAI GUDEA
Library Dir: IOANA ROBU
Library of 270,850 vols
Number of teachers: 750
Number of students: 9,000
Publications: *Acta Dermatologica Transilvanica, Acta Neurologica Transilvanicae, Anuarul Universităţii, Applied Medical Informatics, Biology and Therapy of Cancer Cell, Cosmetic Dentistry—Beauty and Science, Chirurgia, Clujul Medical, Diabetes Management, Diabet, Nutritie, Risc Cardiometabolic, Jurnalul de Diabet, Journal of Clinical Oncology, Journal of Clinical Anatomy and Embriology, Journal of Gastrointestinal and Livers Diseases, Journal of Radiotherapy & Medical Oncology, Jurnalul Roman de Anestezie şi Terapie Intensiva, Jurnalul Roman de Pediatrie, Minimally Invasive Surgery, Medical Ultrasonography, Obstetrica si Ginecologia, Pediatria.ro, Palestrica Mileniului III—Civilizatie si sport, Quo Vadis, Radiology and Medical Oncology, Revista de Recuperare, Medicina Fizica si Balneologie, Revista Romana de Chirurgie Rinosinusala, Romanian Journal of Angiology and Vascular Surgery, Romanian Journal of Gastroenterology, Romanian Journal of Pathology, Romanian Journal of Hand and Reconstructive Microsurgery, The Heart, Transilvania Stomatologica*

DEANS
Faculty of Dental Medicine: Prof. Dr ALIN SERBANESCU
Faculty of Medicine: Prof. Dr ANCA DANA BUZOIANU
Faculty of Pharmacy: Prof. Dr FELICIA LOGHIN

PROFESSORS
Faculty of Medicine:
ACALOVSCHI, I., Anaesthesiology and Intensive Care
ANDERCOU, A., Surgery
BADEA, R., Medical Imaging
BÂRSAN, M., Cardiology
BENGA, G., Cellular and Molecular Biology
BENGA, I., Paediatric Neurology
BOCŞAN, I., Epidemiology
BOLOSIU, H. D., Internal Medicine
CĂLUGĂRU, M., Ophthalmology
CĂPÂLNEANU, R., Cardiology
CÂRSTINA, D., Infectious Diseases
COCÂRLĂ, A., Occupational Health
COSTIN, N., Gynaecology
DEJICA, D., Clinical Immunology
DRAGHICI, A., Internal Medicine
DUNCEA, C., Internal Medicine
FUNARIU, GH., Surgery
GHERMAN, M., Nephrology
GHILEZAN, N., Oncology
GRIGORESCU-SIDO, F., Anatomy
GRIGORESCU-SIDO, P., Paediatrics
HANCU, N., Nutrition and Metabolic Diseases
IONUT, C., Hygiene
JEBELEANU, GH., Biochemistry
KORY, S., Neurology
LAZĂR, L., Oncology
LUCAN, M., Urology
MACREA, R., Paediatric Psychiatry
MAIER, N., Dermatology
MIU, N., Paediatrics
MUREŞAN, A., Physiology
NANULESCU, M., Paediatrics
OLINIC, N., Internal Medicine
OLINICI, C., Morphopathology
PARAIAN, N., Paediatric Surgery
PASCU, O., Gastroenterology
PLESCA-MANEA, L., Physiopathology
POPESCU, A., Neonatology
SANDOR, V., Pharmacology
SASCA, C., Microbiology
SURCEL, I. V., Gynaecology
ŢIGAN, S., Medical Informatics
TOADER RADU, M., Histology
TOMESCU, E., Otorhinolaryngology
TURDEANU, N., Surgery
VLAD, L., Surgery
ZAMORA, C., Pneumophthisiology
ZDRENGHEA, D., Cardiology

Faculty of Pharmacy:
BOJIŢĂ, M., Drug Control
COMAN, M., Drug Industry
LEUCUŢA, S., Pharmaceutical Technology
MOLDOVAN, M., Dermatopharmacy and Cosmeticology
ONIGA, I., Pharmacognosy
ONIGA, O., Pharmaceutical Chemistry
OPREAN, L., Inorganic Chemistry
POLICINENCU, C., Pharmaceutical Legislation, Marketing and Management
PRODAN, A., Informatics
SĂNDULESCU, R., Analytical Chemistry
TĂMAŞ, M., Pharmaceutical Botany
TĂRMURE, C., Biochemistry

Faculty of Stomatology:
BĂCUIŢ, G., Oral and Maxillofacial Surgery
BORZEA, D., Stomatological Propaedeutics
COCÂRLĂ, E., Orthodontics, Pedodontics
FILDAN, F., Oral Radiology
NEGUCIOIU, M., Dental Propaedeutics
POPA, S., Dental Propaedeutics
ROTARU, A., Oral and Maxillofacial Surgery

UNIVERSITATEA DE ARHITECTURA ŞI URBANISM 'ION MINCU'

Str. Academiei 18–20, 010014 Bucharest
Telephone: (21) 307-71-12
Fax: (21) 307-71-09
E-mail: rectorat.uauim@gmail.com
Internet: www.uauim.ro

Founded 1892 by the Romanian Soc. of Architects as a private school of architecture, present name and status 2000
State control
Academic year: October to July
Chair.: Prof. Dr EMIL BARBU POPESCU
Rector: Prof. Dr ŞTEFAN SCAFA UDRISTE
Rector for Professional Issues: Prof. Dr RODICA CRIŞAN
Rector for Students: Prof. Dr DAN CORNELIUS ŞERBAN
Chancellor: Prof. Dr NICOLAE LASCU
Dir of Library: GABRIELA TABACU
Library of 170,000 vols, 50 Periodicals
Number of teachers: 267 (incl. 150 part-time)
Number of students: 3,280
Publications: *Analele Arhitecturii, Arhitext Design*

DEANS
Faculty of Architecture: Prof. Dr ZENO BOGDĂNESCU
Faculty of Interior Architecture: Dr IULIUS IONESCU
Faculty of Urbanism: Prof. Dr ALEXANDRU M. SANDU

DIRECTORS
Univ. College: Prof. Dr NICULAE GRAMA
School of Advanced Studies: Prof. Dr HANNA DERER

UNIVERSITATEA DE MEDICINĂ ŞI FARMACIE 'CAROL DAVILA' (Carol Davila University of Medicine and Pharmacy)

Str. Dionisie Lupu 37, Bucharest
Telephone: (21) 318-07-18
Fax: (21) 318-07-19
Internet: www.univermed-cdgm.ro

Founded 1857 (fmrly Institutul de Medicina şi Farmacie, renamed 1990)
Rector: Prof. Dr FLORIAN POPA
Pro-Rectors: Prof. Dr CONSTANTIN VIRGILIU ARION, Prof. Dr ION FULGA, Prof. Dr IOAN LASCAR, Prof. Dr MONICA DANIELA POP, Prof. Dr IOANEL SINESCU
Library of 388,614 vols, 1,690 periodicals
Number of teachers: 2,323
Number of students: 8,436

DEANS
Faculty of Dentistry: Prof. Dr DRAGOŞ STANCIU
Faculty of Medicine: Prof. Dr VICTOR STOICA
Faculty of Pharmacy: Prof. Dr DUMITRU LUPULIASA

UNIVERSITATEA DE MEDICINĂ ŞI FARMACIE DIN CRAIOVA

Str. No Petru Rares 2, 200349 Craiova
Telephone: (251) 52-24-58
Fax: (251) 59-30-77
E-mail: rectorship@umfcv.ro
Internet: www.umfcv.ro

Academic year: October to July
Founded 1998
Rector: Prof. Dr ADRIAN SAFTOIU

Vice-Rectors for Academic and Scientific Affairs: TUDOREL CIUREA, Prof. Dr AUGUSTIN CUPSA ION GEORGESCU
Vice-Rector for Student Affairs: Prof. Dr TUDOR UDRISTOIU
Scientific Sec.: Prof. Dr FLORINEL BĂDULESCU
Head of Library Services: Prof. ALINA CROITORU

Library of 70,000 vols, 59 periodicals
Number of teachers: 453
Number of students: 4,478

Publications: *Craiova Medicala* (4 a year), *Journal of Pharmacology* (4 a year), *Romanian Journal of Morphology and Embriology*

DEANS

Faculty of Medicine: Prof. Dr ION ROGOVEANU
Faculty of Dentistry: Prof. Dr VERONICA MERCUT
Faculty of Midwifery and Nursing: Assoc. Prof. IULIANA NICOLESCU
Faculty of Pharmacy: Prof. Dr JOHNY NEAMTU

PROFESSORS

Faculty of Medicine:

ANUŞCA, D.
BADEA, M.
BĂDULESCU, F.
BISTRICEANU, M.
BRĂILA, M.
BUTEICĂ, E.
CÂRSTEA, D.
CERNEA, N.
CIUREA, P.
CIUREA, T.
CRĂIŢOIU, S.
CUPŞA, A.
DINCĂ, M.
ENĂCHESCU, V.
GĂMAN, G.
GEORGESCU, E.
GEORGESCU, I.
IANCĂU, M.
IONESCU, D.
IONIŢA, E.
MARINESCU, D.
MIXICH, F.
MOGOANTĂ, L.
MOGOŞ, D.
MOŢA, E.
MOŢA, M.
NOVAC, L.
PLEŞEA, I.
POPESCU, R.
PREJBEANU, I.
ROGOVEANU, I.
ROŞU, A.
ROŞU, L.
SABETAY, C.
SĂFTOIU, A.
SBÂRCEA, V.
SIMIONESCU, C.
STANCIU, P.
STOICA, Z.
TĂRÂŢĂ, M.
TOMA, I.
UDRIŞTOIU, T.
VASILE, I.
VRABETE, M.
ZAHARIA, C.
ZĂVOI, R.

Faculty of Dentistry:

BANIŢĂ, I.
CALOTĂ, F.
MANOLESCU, I.
MERCUŢ, V.
PETCU, P.
STOICESCU, I.
SURPĂTEANU, M.

Faculty of Midwifery and Nursing:

MERCUŢ, D.
NICOLESCU, I.
TRAŞCĂ, E.

Faculty of Pharmacy:

BĂNICERU, M.
GOFIŢA, E.
PISOSCHI, C.
RADU, S.
AVRAMESCU, C.
GORUNESCU, F.
NEAMŢU, J.
TIŢA, I.

UNIVERSITATEA DE MEDICINĂ ŞI FARMACIE 'GR. T. POPA'

Str. Universităţii 16, 700115 Iaşi
Telephone: (232) 30-16-00
Fax: (232) 21-18-20
E-mail: rectorat@umfiasi.ro
Internet: www.umfiasi.ro

Founded 1879
State control
Languages of instruction: Romanian, English, French
Academic year: October to July

Rector: Prof. Dr VASILE ASTARASTOAE
Vice-Rector: Prof. TRAIAN MIHAESCU
Vice-Rector: Prof. IOAN COSTEA
Vice-Rector: Prof. MARIA STAMATIN
Vice-Rector: Prof. DRAGOS PIEPTU
Registrar: GEANINA CARMEN UNGUREANU
Library Man.: Prof. VIORICA SCUTARU

Library of 264,243 vols
Number of teachers: 900
Number of students: 9,824

DEANS

Faculty of Dentistry: Prof. Dr NORINA FORNA
Faculty of Medical Bioengineering: Dr DAN ZAHARIA
Faculty of Medicine: Prof. Dr DOINA AZOICAI
Faculty of Pharmacy: Prof. Dr MONICA HANCIANU

PROFESSORS

Faculty of Medical Bioengineering (Str. Kogalniceanu 9–13, Iaşi; tel. and fax (232) 21-35-73; e-mail pflocea@bioing.umfiasi.ro; internet www.umfiasi.ro):

APOSTOL, I., Clinical Physiology
BALTAG, O., Exact, Metrological and Informatics Sciences
CHIRIAC, H., Biomedical Engineering
DIACONU, I., Exact, Metrological and Informatics Sciences
GROSU, I., General and Applied Physics
PETRESCU, GH., General Management and Marketing
POEATA, I., Biomaterials and Techniques of Prosthetic Systems
UGLEA, C., Applied Chemistry and Physical Chemistry
UNGUREANU, M., Synthetic and Bioactive Substances

Faculty of Medicine (Str. Universitatii 16, 700115 Iaşi; tel. (232) 30-16-15; fax (232) 30-16-33; e-mail gcuciureanu@medgen.umfiasi.ro; internet www.umfiasi.ro):

ALDEA, A. S., Thoracic Surgery
ANTOHE, D. S., Anatomy
ARSENESCU, C., Internal Medicine
ASTARASTOAIE, V., Forensic Medicine
BĂDESCU, A., Histology
BĂDESCU, M., Physiopathology
BALAN, G., Internal Medicine
BILD, E., Oncology and Radiotherapy
BOISTEANU, P., Psychiatry
BRĂNIŞTEANU, D., Physiology
BRUMARU, O., Paediatrics
BUIUC, D., Microbiology
CARASIEVICI, E., Immunology
CHIRIAC, R. M., Rheumatology and Balneophysiotherapy
CHIRIŢA, V., Psychiatry
CHISĂLIŢA, D., Ophthalmology
CIORNIA, T., Forensic Medicine
COLEV, V., Physiopathology
COMAN, G., Microbiology
COSOVANU, A., Internal Medicine
COSTĂCHESCU, GH., Obstetrics and Gynaecology
COSTINESCU, V., Otorhinolaryngology
COTRUTZ, C., Cell Biology
COTUŢIU, C., Histology
COVIC, M., Genetics
COVIC, M., Internal Medicine
DANIIL, C., Radiology
DATCU, G., Internal Medicine
DATCU, M. D., Internal Medicine
DIACONU, C., Surgery
DIMITRIU, A. G., Paediatrics
DRAGOMIR, C., Infant Care
DRAGOMIR, C., Surgery
DRAGOMIR, D., Obstetrics and Gynaecology
FRÎNCU, D. L., Anatomy
FRÎNCU, D. L., Physical Education
GAVĂT, V., Hygiene
GEORGESCU, G., Internal Medicine
GEORGESCU, N. M., Orthopaedics and Traumatology
GHEORGHIŢĂ, N., Biochemistry
GOŢIA, D. G., Paediatric Surgery
GOŢIA, S., Paediatrics
IANOVICI, N., Neurosurgery
IONESCU, C., History of Medicine
IVAN, A., Epidemiology
LUCA, M., Parasitology and Mycoses
LUCA, V., Infectious Diseases
LUCA, V., Physiopathology
MĂTĂSARU, S., Paediatrics
MIHAILOVICI, M. S., Pathological Anatomy
MIHAIESCU, T., Pneumopthisiology
MIHALACHE, C., Occupational Medicine
MIHALACHE, ST., Surgery
MOGOŞ, V., Endocrinology
MORARU, D., Paediatrics
MORARU, E., Paediatrics
MUNGIU, C. O., Pharmacology
PANDELE, G. I., Internal Medicine
PETRESCU, GH., Physiology
PETRESCU, Z., Dermatology
PETROVANU, R., Family Practice Medicine
PLAHTEANU, M., Forensic Medicine
PLEŞA, C., Surgery
POPESCU, D. C., Neurobiology
PRELIPCEAN, C., Internal Medicine
PRICOP, F., Obstetrics and Gynaecology
PRICOP, M., Obstetrics and Gynaecology
RADULESCU, D., Pathological Anatomy
RUSU, V., Biophysics
SINIŢCHI, G., Family Practice Medicine
SLĂTINEANU, S., Physiology
STAN, M., Internal Medicine
STANCIU, C., Internal Medicine
ŞTEFANACHE, F., Neurology
STOIAN, M., Surgery
STRATONE, A., Exploration Physiology
TÎRCOVEANU, E., Surgery
TOPOLICEANU, F., Exploration Physiology
UNGUREANU, G., Internal Medicine
ZAMFIR, M., Anatomy
ZBRANCA, E., Endocrinology

Faculty of Pharmacy (Str. Universitati 16, 700115 Iaşi; tel. (232) 30-16-23; fax (232) 21-18-20; e-mail eonica@farmacie.umfiasi.ro; internet www.umfiasi.ro):

CARAMAN, C., Inorganic Chemistry
CUCIUREANU, R., Environmental Chemistry
DĂNILĂ, GH., Pharmaceutical Chemistry
DORNEANU, M., Organic Chemistry
DORNEANU, V., Analytical Chemistry
GAFIŢEANU, E., Pharmaceutical Technology
HRISCU, A., Pharmacodynamics
LAZAR, M., Drug Control
PĂDURARU, I., Pharmaceutical Biochemistry
PAVELESCU, M. D. G., Pharmacology
POPOVICI, I., Pharmaceutical Technology
PROCA, M., Toxicology
SCUTARIU, M. D., Anatomy and Physiology
STAN, M., Analytical Chemistry

STĂNESCU, U. H., Pharmacognosy
ŞTEFĂNESCU, E., Organic Chemistry

UNIVERSITATEA DE MEDICINĂ ŞI FARMACIE TÂRGU MUREŞ

Gh. Marinescu 38, 540000 Târgu Mureş
Telephone: (265) 21-55-51
Fax: (265) 21-04-07
E-mail: rectorat@umftgm.ro
Internet: www.umftgm.ro

Founded 1948
State control
Languages of instruction: Romanian, Hungarian, English
Academic year: October to September

Rector: Prof. Dr CONSTANTIN COPOTOIU
Vice-Rectors: Assoc. Prof. Dr KLARA BRÎNZANIUC, Prof. Dr ÖRS ŞTEFAN NAGY
Chief Sec.: ELENA NISTOR
Scientific Sec.: Prof. Dr AUREL NIREŞTEAN
Int. Relations Officer: ANNAMÁRIA GYÖRFI
Librarian: FLORIN DAMIAN

Library of 184,600 vols
Number of teachers: 422
Number of students: 3,530

Publication: *Revista de Medicină şi Farmacie / Orvosi és Gyógyszerészeti Szemle* (4 a year)

DEANS

Faculty of Dentistry: Prof. Dr MIRCEA SUCIU
Faculty of General Medicine: Dr DAN DOBREANU
Faculty of Pharmacy: Prof. Dr DANIELA-LUCIA MUNTEAN

PROFESSORS

Faculty of Dentistry (tel. (265) 21-55-51 ext. 130; fax (265) 21-04-07; e-mail decanatstoma@umftgm.ro):

KOVÁCS, D.
PĂCURAR, M., Pedodontics and Orthodontics
POPŞOR, S.
SZEKELY, M., Teeth and Dental Arches Morphology

Faculty of General Medicine (tel. (265) 21-55-51 ext. 110; fax (265) 21-04-07; e-mail decanatmg@umftgm.ro):

ABRAM, Z., Hygiene
AZAMFIREI, L., Intensive Care
BANCU, S., Surgery
BOJA, R., Urology
BORDA, A., Histology
BRASSAI, Z., Internal Medicine
BRATU, D., Internal Medicine
BURIAN, M., Radiology
CARASCA, E., Internal Medicine
COPOTOIU, C., Surgery
DEAC, R., Cardiac Surgery
DRAŞOVEANU, C., Otorhinolaryngology
EGYED, Z., Pathomorphology
GEORGESCU, C., Internal Medcine
GEORGESCU, L., Physiotherapy
HOBAI, S., Biochemistry
INCZE, A., Internal Medicine
JUNG, I., Pathology
KIKELI, P. I., Family Medicine
KUN, I. Z., Endocrinology
MATHE, I., Biochemistry
MONEA, M., Pharmacology
MUNTEANU, I., Paediatrics
NAGY, Ö., Orthopaedics
NICOLAESCU, I., Biophysics
NIRESTEAN, A., Psychiatry
OLTEANU, G., Internal Medicine
SABĂU, M., Epidemiology
TOGĂNEL, R., Paediatrics

Faculty of Pharmacy (tel. (265) 21-55-51 ext. 111; fax (265) 21-04-07; e-mail rectorat@umftgm.ro):

DOGARU, M. T.
DUDUCZ, G., Medicinal Biotechnology
GYÉRESI, A., Pharmaceutical Chemistry
IMRE, S., Drugs Analysis
KINCSES-AJTAI, M., Toxicology
MUNTEAN, D. L., Drugs Analysis
OROIAN, S.

UNIVERSITATEA DE MEDICINĂ ŞI FARMACIE 'VICTOR BABEŞ'

Piăta Eftimie Murgu 2, 300041 Timişoara
Telephone: (256) 20-44-00
Fax: (256) 49-06-26
E-mail: rectorat@umft.ro
Internet: www.umft.ro

Founded 1945 as Institutul de Medicină
Academic year: October to July

Rector: Prof. Dr STEFAN IOSIF DRAGULESCU
Pro-Rector: Prof. Dr POMPILIA DEHELEAN
Pro-Rector: Prof. Dr MARIUS RAICA
Pro-Rector: Prof. Dr DAN V. POENARU
Scientific Sec. of the Senate: Prof. Dr DAN GAIŢA

Library of 195,000 vols, 31,000 journals
Number of teachers: 963
Number of students: 4,028

Publications: *Cercetări Medico-Chirurgicale* (4 a year), *Fiziologia-Physiology* (4 a year), *Timişoara Medicală* (4 a year)

DEANS

Dental Medicine: Prof. Dr VIRGIL CARLIGERIU
Medicine: Prof. Dr DORU ANASTASIU
Pharmacy: Prof. Dr CARMEN CRISTESCU

UNIVERSITATEA DE ŞTIINŢE AGRICOLE ŞI MEDICINĂ VETERINARĂ A BANATULUI DIN TIMIŞOARA

(Banat University of Agricultural Sciences and Veterinary Medicine, Timişoara)

Calea Aradului 119, 300645 Timişoara
Telephone: (256) 49-40-23
Fax: (256) 20-02-96
E-mail: usabtm@mail.dnttm.ro
Internet: www.usab-tm.ro

Founded 1945
State control
Academic year: September to September
Languages of instruction: English, Romanian

Rector: Acad. Prof. Dr Dr H. C. ALEXANDRU MOISUC
Vice-Rector for Economic and Social Problems: Prof. Dr STELIAN ACATINCAI
Vice-Rector for Educational Issues, Int. Relations and Quality Management: Prof. Dr HORIA CERNESCU
Gen. Admin. Dir: Ing. TRAINA BERAR
Admin. Officer: ENIKO NĂDĂŞAN
Scientific Advisor: Prof. Dr FLORIN SALA
Head of Int. Relations Office: Prof. Dr H.C. HORIA CERNESCU
Librarian: Prof. GHEORGHE NISTOR

Library of 368,307 vols, 45 periodicals
Number of teachers: 332
Number of students: 7,040

Publications: *Didactica*, *Journal of Agroalimentary Processes and Technologies*, *Journal of Horticulture, Forestry and Biotechnology*, *Journal of Linguistic Studies*, *Research Journal of Agricultural Science*, *Scientific Papers: Animal Sciences and Biotechnologies*, *Scientific Papers: Farm Management*, *Scientific Papers: Veterinary Medicine*, *Scientific Papers of Young Researchers*

DEANS

Faculty of Agriculture: Prof. Dr PAUL PÎRŞAN
Faculty of Animal Husbandry and Biotechnologies: Prof. Dr NICOLAE PACALA
Faculty of Farm Management: Prof. Dr VASILE GOSA
Faculty of Food Processing Technologies: Prof. Dr TEODOR TRASCA
Faculty of Horticulture and Forestry: Prof. Dr AUREL LAZUREANU
Faculty of Veterinary Medicine: Prof. Dr GHEORGHE DĂRĂBUŞ

PROFESSORS

Faculty of Agriculture (Calea Aradului 119, 300645 Timişoara, Timiş; tel. (256) 27-70-07; fax (256) 27-71-26; internet www.agricultura.usab-tm.ro):

ADRIAN, B., Phytopathology
DORIN, A., Land Evaluation
DORU, P., Entomology
FLORIAN, B., Biodiversity
GICU GABRIEL, A., Botanics
HORTENSIA, R., Policies and Environmental Depopulation Techniques
IACOB, B., General Ecology and Environmental Protection
IOANA, G., Entomology
RADU, P., Comparative Anatomy and Etology
SILVICA, O., Land Improvement
VALERIA, C., Topography

Faculty of Animal Husbandry and Biotechnologies (Calea Aradului 119, 300645 Timişoara, Timiş; tel. and fax (256) 27-71-10; e-mail info@animalsci-tm.ro; internet www.animalsci-tm.ro):

ADRIAN, G., Aquaculture
BENONI, L., Animal Hygiene
CORNELIA, V., Processing and Animal Products Control
DAN, D., Biotechnologies in Animal Nutrition
EUGENIE, G., Management
GHORGHE, N., Animal Husbandry and Nutrition
IOAN, P., Sheep Breeding Technologies
LAVINIA, A., Animal Nutrition
MARIAN, B., Breeding of Fur-Bearing Animals, Bees and Small Animals
NECULAI, D., Fodder Production and Preservation
NICOLAE, P., Animal Reproduction
STELIAN, A., Bovine Breeding Technologies

Faculty of Farm Management:

CORNELIA, P., Growth of Products through Processing
IOAN, C., Rural Services
IOAN, P., Production Systems Modulation and Simulation
LIVIU, S., Production Management
NICOLETA, M., Agricultural Policies
PĂUN ION, O., Durable Development Management
VASILE, G., Financial Management

Faculty of Food Processing Technologies (Calea Aradului 119, 300645 Timisoara; tel. (256) 27-70-04; fax (256) 27-73-26; e-mail secretariattpa@yahoo.com; internet tpa.usab-tm.ro):

ADRIAN, C., Organic Chemistry
ADRIAN, R., Food Contaminants
CONSTANTIN, M., Applied Physics
DOREL, P., Physical and Coloidal Chemistry
ERSILIA, A., Vegetable Origins Food Technologies
IONEL-VASILE, J., Food Industry General Technologies
IOSIF-IOAN, G., Agro-alimentary Products Analysis
MIHAI, D., Food Quality Control
TEODOR-IOAN, T., Food Industry Machines

Faculty of Horticulture and Forestry (Calea Aradului 119, 300645 Timişoara, Timiş; tel. (256) 27-70-06; internet www.horticultura.usab-tm.ro):

ALIN, D., Viticulture
ARSENIE, H., Special Vegetable Crops
AUREL, L., Agrotechnology
DAGMAR, V., Dendrology
DORICA, B., Industrial Biotechnologies
EMILIAM, M., Plant Improvement
GHORGHE, C., Soil Work Management
IRINA, P., Genetics
MARIA, B., Floriculture
MIHAELA, C., Genetics
OLIMPIA, I., Fruit Growing
RADU, A., Vegetable Physiology
SIMION, A., Soil Work Maintenance and Preparation Techniques
SORIN, C., Experimental Techniques
VIOREL, B., General Vegetable Crops

Faculty of Veterinary Medicine (Calea Aradului 119, 300645 Timişoara, Timiş; tel. (256) 27-71-18; fax (256) 27-70-08; e-mail office@fmvt.ro; internet usab-tm.ro):

ALEXANDRA, T., Toxicology
CARMEN, G., Anatomy
CORNEL, I., Surgery Diseases
EMIL, T., Immunology
EUGENIU, C., Nutrition and Fodder Control
GHEORGHE, D., Parasitology
GHORGHE, B., Medical Genetics
HOREA, S., Physiology
HORIA, C., Reproduction, Obstetrics, Gynecology
IOAN, O., Forensics
IOAN, A., Entomology
ION, O., Animal Biology and Ecology
MARIAN, C., Pathological Anatomy
MIHAI, D., Animal Protection
NICOLAE, C., Infectious Diseases
ROMEO, C., Pharmacology
TEODOR, M., Medical Pathology
VASILE, A., Reproduction, Obstetrics, Gynaecology
VIOREL, H., Infectious Diseases

UNIVERSITATEA DE ŞTIINŢE AGRICOLE ŞI MEDICINĂ VETERINARĂ CLUJ-NAPOCA

Calea Mănăştur 3–5, 400372 Cluj-Napoca
Telephone: (264) 59-63-84
Fax: (264) 59-37-92
E-mail: contact@usamvcluj.ro
Internet: www.usamvcluj.ro

Founded 1869 as Institutul Agronomic; present name and status 1992

Rector: Prof. Dr DORU PAMFIL
Pres.: Prof. Dr LIVIU AL. MĂRGHITAŞ
Vice-Rector for Academic Affairs: Prof. Dr CORNEL CATOI
Vice-Rector for Admin. Affairs: Prof. Dr SEVASTIŢA MUSTE
Vice-Rector for Scientific Research: Prof. Dr AUGUSTIN VLAIC
Gen. Dir: VIOREL PORUŢIU

Library of 170,000 vols, 10,000 documents
Number of teachers: 267
Number of students: 6,202

Publications: *Notulae Botanicae Horti Agrobotanici Cluj Napoca (ISI)*, *Bulletin of USAMV Cluj Napoca, Agriculture series (B+)*, *Bulletin of USAMV Cluj Napoca, Horticulture series (B+)*, *Bulletin of USAMV Cluj Napoca, Animal Science and Biotechnology series (B+)*, *Bulletin of USAMV Cluj Napoca, Veterinary Medicine series (B+)*, *Agriculture* (magazine), *Hops and Medical Plants* (magazine), *Index Seminum*, *Scientia parasitological*, *Clujul Medical Veterinar*

DEANS

Faculty of Agriculture: Prof. Dr IOAN ROTAR
Faculty of Animal Science and Biotechnology: Prof. Dr VIOARA MIRESAN
Faculty of Horticulture: Prof. Dr RADU SESTRAS
Faculty of Veterinary Medicine: Prof. Dr IOAN STEFAN GROZA

UNIVERSITATEA DE ŞTIINŢE AGRICOLE ŞI MEDICINĂ VETERINARĂ 'ION IONESCU DE LA BRAD' DIN IAŞI

Aleea Mihail Sadoveanu 3, 700490 Iaşi
Telephone: (232) 27-49-33
Fax: (232) 26-06-50
E-mail: rectorat@univagro-iasi.ro
Internet: www.univagro-iasi.ro

Founded 1912; present name 1990

Rector: Prof. Dr GERARD JITĂREANU
Vice-Rector for Didactic Activity: Prof. Dr VASILE VÎNTU
Vice-Rector for Social and Students' Issues): Prof. Dr GHEORGHE SAVUŢA
Vice-Rector for Scientific Activity: Prof. Dr VALERIU V. COTEA

Library of 112,597 vols, incl. 105,942 books and 6,655 periodicals

Publications: *Cercetari Agronomice in Moldova*, *Lucrări Ştiinţifice Editura* (1 a year)

DEANS

Faculty of Agriculture: Prof. Dr CONSTANTIN LEONTE
Faculty of Animal Science: Prof. Dr BENONE PĂSĂRIN
Faculty of Horticulture: Prof. Dr GICĂ GRĂDINARIU
Faculty of Veterinary Medicine: Prof. Dr OCTAVIAN ZAHARIE OPREAN

UNIVERSITATEA DE ŞTIINŢE AGRONOMICE ŞI MEDICINĂ VETERINARĂ DIN BUCUREŞTI (University of Agricultural Sciences and Veterinary Medicine in Bucharest)

Bdul Mărăşti 59, 011464 Bucharest
Telephone: (21) 318-22-66
Fax: (21) 318-28-88
E-mail: post@info.usamv.ro
Internet: www.usab.ro

Founded 1852 as Institutul Agronomic 'N. Bălcescu'

Rector: Prof. Dr STEFAN DIACONESCU
Pres.: Prof. Dr IOAN-NICULAE ALECU

Library: see Libraries and Archives
Number of teachers: 495
Number of students: 4,573 (4,298 undergraduate, 275 postgraduate)

Publication: *Lucrări Ştiinţifice* (1 a year)

DEANS

Department of Land Improvement and Environmental Engineering: SORIN CÎMPEANU
Faculty of Agriculture: Prof. Dr COSTICĂ CIONTU
Faculty of Horticulture: Prof. Dr DOREL HOZA
Faculty of Zoology: Prof. Dr VAN ILIE
Faculty of Veterinary Medicine: Prof. Dr GABRIEL PREDOI
Faculty of Biotechnology: Prof. Dr PETRU NICULIŢĂ

UNIVERSITATEA MARITIMĂ DIN CONSTANŢA

Str. Mircea cel Bătrân 104, 900663 Constanţa
Telephone: (241) 66-47-40
Fax: (241) 61-72-60
E-mail: info@imc.ro
Internet: www.cmu-edu.eu

Founded 1972
State control
Languages of instruction: Romanian, English
Academic year: October to June

Rector: Prof. Dr Ing. CORNEL PANAIT
Vice-Rector for Scientific Research and Int. Cooperation: Assoc. Prof. Dr EUGEN BARSAN
Rector for Academic and Devt Issues: Dr Ing. EMIL OANŢĂ
Scientific Sec.: Dr Ing. VIOLETA CIUCUR
Librarian: TANASE RALUCA

Library of 71,000 vols, 20 periodicals
Number of teachers: 95
Number of students: 6,407

Publications: *Constanta Maritime University Annals*, *Journal of Maritime Technology*, *Journal of Maritime Transport*

DEANS

Faculty of Naval Electromechanics: Prof. Dr CARUNTU GEORGE
Faculty of Navigation and Naval Transport: Assoc. Prof. Dr GHIORGHE BATRANCA

UNIVERSITATEA 'POLITEHNICA' DIN BUCUREŞTI

Splaiul Independenţei 313, 060042 Bucharest
Telephone: (21) 402-91-00
Fax: (21) 318-10-01
E-mail: relatii.publice@upb.ro
Internet: www.pub.ro

Founded 1818
State control
Academic year: October to July (2 semesters)

Rector: Prof. Dr Eng. ECATERINA ANDRONESCU
Vice-Rector for Financial Affairs: Prof. Dr MIHAI OCTAVIAN POPESCU
Vice-Rector for Graduate Education: Prof. Dr MARIN DRAGULINESCU
Vice-Rector for Int. Relations, European Integration and Partnership: Prof. Dr MARIAN GHEORGHE
Vice-Rector for Scientific Research: Prof. Dr SERBAN RAICU
Vice-Rector for Undergraduate Education: Prof. Dr DUMITRU CEZAR IONESCU
Scientific Sec.: Prof. Dr IULIAN RIPOSAN
Chief Admin. Officer: Prof. Dr GABRIEL IACOBESCU
Dir of the Int. Cooperation Dept: (vacant)
Librarian: Dr DUMITRU RADU POPESCU

Library: see Libraries and Archives
Number of teachers: 1,590
Number of students: 22,000

DEANS

Faculty of Aerospace Engineering: Prof. VIRGIL STANCIU
Faculty of Applied Sciences: Prof. CONSTANTIN UDRISTE
Faculty of Automatic Control and Computer Science: Prof. Dr DUMITRU POPESCU
Faculty of Biotechnical Systems Engineering: Prof. Dr GIGEL PARASCHIV
Faculty of Electrical Engineering: Prof. CLAUDIA POPESCU
Faculty of Electronics and Telecommunications: Prof. Dr TEODOR PETRESCU
Faculty of Engineering and Management of Technological Systems: Prof. Dr Ing. GHEORGHE AMZA
Faculty of Engineering Sciences Taught in Modern Languages: Prof. Dr Ing. ADRIAN VOLCEANOV
Faculty of Industrial Chemistry: Prof. Dr HORIA IOVU
Faculty of Materials Science and Engineering: Prof. Dr RAMI SABAN
Faculty of Mechanical Engineering: Prof. Dr Ing. TUDOR PRISECARU
Faculty of Power Engineering: Prof. GEORGE DARIE
Faculty of Transport Engineering: Prof. Dr CORNELIU MIHAIL ALEXANDRESCU

DIRECTORS

Technical College No. 1 (Mechanical College): Prof. Dr GHEORGHE SOLOMON

Technical College No. 2 (Electrical College): Dr ISTVAN SZTOJANOV

PROFESSORS

Faculty of Aerospace Engineering (Str. George Polizu, nr. 1, sector 1, 011061 Bucharest; tel. and fax 402-38-14; e-mail s_galetuse@aero.pub.ro; internet www.aero.pub.ro):

BERBENTE, C., Aircraft Engineering
GĂLETUŞE, S., Aircraft Engineering
STANCIU, V., Aircraft Engineering

Faculty of Automatic Control and Computer Science (Splaiul Independenţei 313, Sector 6, 060042 Bucharest; tel. (21) 402-94-94; fax (21) 410-10-14; e-mail dpopescu@indinf.pub.ro; internet www.acs.pub.ro):

ATHANASIU, I., Computer Sciencc
BORANGIU, T., Robotics
CRISTEA, V., Computer Science
CUPCEA, N., Computer Science
DUMITRACHE, I., Control Engineering
GIUMALE, C., Computer Science
ILIESCU, S., Control Engineering
IONESCU, T., Control Engineering
IORGA, V., Computer Science
MOISA, T., Computer Science
NIŢU, C., Control Engineering
PETRESCU, A., Computer Science
POPEEA, C., Control Engineering
POPESCU, D., Control Engineering
STANESCU, A., Control Engineering
TĂPUŞ, N., Computer Science

Faculty of Biotechnical Systems Engineering (Splaiul Independenţei 313, Sector 6, 060042 Bucharest; tel. (21) 402-96-49; fax (21) 318-10-18; e-mail paraschiv2005@yahoo.com; internet www.isb.pub.ro):

DAVID, L., Agricultural Machines
MURAD, E., Agricultural Machines
PAUNESCU, I., Agricultural Machines

Faculty of Electrical Engineering (Splaiul Independenţei 313, Sector 6, body EA 123, 060042 Bucharest; tel. (21) 402-91-49; fax (21) 410-43-55; e-mail elth@electro.pub.ro; internet www.upb.ro):

CRĂCIUNESCU, A., Drive Systems
CRISTEA, P., Basic Electrical Engineering
FLUERAŞU, C., Basic Electrical Engineering
GALAN, N., Electrical Machines
GAVRILĂ, H., Basic Electrical Engineering
GOLOVANOV, C., Theory and Design of Electrical Apparatus
HĂNŢILĂ, I. F., Basic Electrical Engineering
IOAN, C. D., Basic Electrical Engineering
IONESCU, F., Theory and Design of Electrical Apparatus
MĂGUREANU, R., Micromachines and Drive Systems
MOREGA, AL., Electrical Materials
NOŢINGHER, P., Electrical Materials
POPESCU, M. O., Theory and Design of Electrical Apparatus
SPINEI, F., Basic Electrical Engineering
TĂNĂSESCU, F., Electrical Engineering
TOMESCU, F., Basic Electrical Engineering
TRUŞCĂ, V., Theory and Design of Electrical Apparatus

Faculty of Electronics and Telecommunications (Bdul Iuliu Maniu 1–3, Sector 6, 061071 Bucharest; tel. (21) 402-46-18; fax (21) 411-33-73; e-mail decanat@electronica.pub.ro; internet www.electronica.pub.ro):

BĂNICĂ, I., Telecommunications
BODEA, M., Electronic Devices and Circuits
BORCOCI, E., Telecommunications
BREZEANU, GH., Electronic Devices and Circuits
BURILEANU, L., Telecommunications
BUZULOIU, V., Information Theory
CONSTANTIN, I., Telecommunications
DASCĂLU, D., Electronic Devices and Circuits
DRAGULANESCU, N., Reliability
DRAGULIMISCU, M., Reliability
IANCU, O., Reliability
LĂZĂRESCU, V., Information Theory
MANOLESCU, A., Electronic Devices and Circuits
MANOLESCU, A. M., Electronic Devices and Circuits
PROFIRESCU, M., Electronic Devices and Circuits
RUSU, A., Electronic Devices and Circuits
STRUNGARU, R., Medical Engineering
SVASTA, P., Reliability

Faculty of Engineering and Management of Technological Systems (Splaiul Independenţei 313, Sector 6, 060042 Bucharest; tel. (21) 402-95-20; fax (21) 411-42-67; e-mail amza@camis.pub.ro; internet www.imst.pub.ro):

ANTONESCU, P., Mechanism Theory
AURITE, T., Machine Tools
CONSTANTINESCU, I., Strength of Materials
DORIN, A., Machine Tools
GHEORGHE, M., Machine-Building Technology
ILIESCU, N., Strength of Materials
ISPAS, C., Machine Tools
MINCIU, C., Machine Tools
NEAGU, C., Machine-Building Technology
POPESCU, I., Machine-Building Technology
RADEŞ, M., Strength of Materials
ZGURĂ, GH., Technology of Materials

Faculty of Industrial Chemistry (Str. Polizu 1, Bucharest; tel. and fax (21) 223-09-03):

ANDRONESCU, E., Silicate and Oxide Compounds Chemistry
BANCIU, M., Organic Chemistry
BOZGA, GH., Chemical Reactors
CONSTANTINESCU, I., Inorganic Chemical Technology
DIMONIE, M., Polymer Science
FILIPESCU, L., Inorganic Chemical Technology
GEANĂ, D., Physical Chemistry
GEORGESCU, M., Silicate and Oxide Compounds Chemistry
GURAN, C., Inorganic Chemistry
JINESCU, GH., Chemical Engineering
JITARU, I., Inorganic Chemistry
MEGHEA, A., Physical Chemistry
MUNTEAN, M., Silicate and Oxide Compounds Chemistry
RADU, C., Management in the Chemical Industry
RADU, D., Silicate and Oxide Compounds Chemistry
ROŞCA, S., Organic Chemistry
TARABAŞANU, C., Dyes
VASILESCU, D. S., Polymer Science
VIŞAN, T., Physical Chemistry and Electrochemical Technology
WOINAROSCHY, E. A., Chemical Engineering

Faculty of Materials Science and Engineering (Splaiul Independenţei 313, Sector 6, 060042 Bucharest; tel. (21) 402-96-24; fax (21) 410-39-85; e-mail decanat@sim.pub.ro; internet www.sim.pub.ro):

BOJIN, D., Metallurgy of Non-Ferrous Metals
BRATU, C., Forge and Foundry Technology
BUNEA, D., Forge and Foundry Technology
COJOCARU, M., Metallurgy of Non-Ferrous Metals
MOLDOVAN, P., Metallurgy of Non-Ferrous Metals
PANAIT, N., Metallurgy of Non-Ferrous Metals
RIPOŞAN, I., Forge and Foundary Technology
TALOI, D., Metallurgy of Non-Ferrous Metals
ZAMFIR, S., Metallurgy of Non-Ferrous Metals

Faculty of Mechanical Engineering (Splaiul Independenţei 313, Sector 6, 060042 Bucharest; tel. (21) 402-94-35; fax (21) 410-42-51; e-mail tudor.prisecaru@upb.ro; internet www.mecanica.home.ro):

ALEXANDRESCU, N., Fine Mechanics
BRĂTIANU, C., Thermomechanical Equipment
JINESCU, V., Thermomechanical Equipment
MARINESCU, M., Thermodynamics
MICU, C., Fine Mechanics
MIHAIESCU, L., Thermomechanical Equipment
PANA, C., Internal Combustion Engines
PASCOVICI, M., Machine Elements
PASCU, A., Fine Mechanics
PETRESCU, S., Thermodynamics
TUDOR, A., Machine Elements

Faculty of Power Engineering (Splaiul Independenţei 313, Sector 6, 060042 Bucharest; tel. (21) 402-94-33; fax (21) 410-43-50; e-mail facultatea.energetica@gmail.com; internet www.energ.pub.ro):

ATHANASOVICI, V., Electric Power Plants
BADEA, A., Electric Power Plants
COATU, S., High Voltage Technology
CRISTESCU, D., High Voltage Technology
EREMIA, M., High Voltage Technology
GOLOVANOV, N., High Voltage Technology
HURDUBETIU, S., High Voltage Technology
IONESCU, D. C., Reliability
ISBĂŞOIU, E., Hydraulics
NISTREANU, V., Hydraulics
PANAITESCU, V., Hydraulics
POSTOLACHE, P., High Voltage Technology
ROBESCU, D. N., Hydraulics
SETEANU, I., Hydraulics
VASILIU, N., Hydraulics

Faculty of Transport Engineering (Splaiul Independenţei 313, Sector 6, 060042 Bucharest; tel. (21) 402-95-68; fax (21) 411-16-59; e-mail cma@eltrans.pub.ro):

ALEXANDRESCU, C., Remote Controls and Electronics
FRĂŢILĂ, GH., Automotive Engineering
NEGRUŞ, E., Automotive Engineering
RAICU, Ş., Transport Engineering
SEBEŞAN, I., Railway Vehicles
STOICESCU, A., Automotive Engineering
TANASUICA, I., Transport Engineering

UNESCO Department (tel. (21) 402-94-75; fax (21) 402-93-87; e-mail leca@eeee.unesco.pub.ro):

LECA, A., Environment

Basic Training:

BLANDU, M., Modern Languages
CRAIU, M., Mathematical Analysis
ENESCU, N., Mechanics
FLONDOR, P., Mathematical Analysis
STAICU, M., Mechanics
STĂNĂŞILĂ, O., Algebra, Mathematical Analysis
UDRIŞTE, C., Special Mathematics

UNIVERSITATEA 'POLITEHNICA' DIN TIMIŞOARA

Piaţa Victoriei 2, 300006 Timişoara
Telephone: (256) 40-30-00
Fax: (256) 40-30-21
E-mail: rector@rectorat.upt.ro
Internet: www.upt.ro

Founded 1920; attached to The Romanian Agency for Quality Assurance in Higher Education

Public control

Languages of instruction: Romanian, English, German, French

Academic year: October to July
Rector: Prof. Dr Eng. NICOLAE ROBU
Vice-Rector: Prof. Dr Eng. VIOREL-AUREL SERBAN
Vice-Rector: Prof. Dr Eng. CORNELIU DAVIDESCU
Vice-Rector: Prof. Dr Eng. SEVASTEAN IANCA
Scientific Sec.: Prof. Dr Eng. RADU VASIU
Chief Sec.: Prof. A. GASPAR
Admin. Dir: Dr Eng. FLORENTIU STAICU
Dir of the Library: ERICA OTESTEANU

Number of teachers: 887
Number of students: 15,000

Library of 500,000 vols

Publications: *Research Report* (1 a year), *Scientific and Technical Bulletins* (2 to 4 a year)

DEANS

Department of Communications and Foreign Languages: Prof. Dr RODICA SUPERCEANU

Department for Continuing Education: VASILE RUSET

Department for Distance Education: Dr DIANA ANDONE

Department of Mathematics: Prof. Dr OCTAVIAN LIPOVAN

Department of Physical Foundations of Engineering: Prof. Dr DUMITRU TOADER

Faculty of Architecture: Prof. Dr SMARANDA BICA

Faculty of Civil Engineering: GHEORGHE LUCACI

Faculty of Computers and Automatization: Prof. Dr Eng. OCTAVIAN PROŞTEAN

Faculty of Electronics and Telecommunications: Prof. Dr Eng. MARIUS OTEŞTEANU

Faculty of Electrotechnical Engineering: Prof. Dr Eng. PETRU ANDEA

Faculty of Engineering (in Hunedoara): TEODOR HEPUT

Faculty of Hydrotechnical Engineering: Prof. Dr Eng. TEODOR EUGEN MAN

Faculty of Industrial Chemistry and Environmental Engineering: Prof. Dr Eng. LUCIAN RUSNAC

Faculty of Management in Production and Transport: Prof. Dr Ing. MONICA IZVERCIANU

Faculty of Mechanical Engineering: Prof. Dr Eng. LIVIU BERETEU

PROFESSORS

Faculty of Civil Engineering:

BĂNCILĂ, R., Steel Structures
BOB, C., Chemistry and Construction Materials
BOTICI, A., Statics, Stability and Dynamics of Constructions
CADAR, I., Reinforced Concrete Structures
CARABA, I., Steel Structures
CIOBANU, G., English
CLIPII, T., Reinforced Concrete Structures
COSTESCU, I., Road Design and Construction
CUTEANU, E., Strength of Materials
DIMOIU, I., Earthquake Engineering
DUBINA, D., Construction
FURDUI, C., Civil Construction
GĂDIANU, L., Steel Structures
GAVRA, C. S., History of Architecture
GHEORGHIU, T., Urbanism, Architecture Design
GIONCU, V. M., Structures
GRUIA, A., Soil Mechanics and Foundation Engineering
HAIDA, V., Soil Mechanics and Foundation Engineering
IANCA, S., Civil Engineering, Architecture and Urbanism
IVAN, M., Statics, Stability and Dynamics
JIVA, C., Concrete Bridges
MARIN, M., Soil Mechanics and Foundation Engineering
MERCEA, G., Steel Structures
NEAMŢU, M., Topography
PATCAS, I., Steel Structures
PODRUMAR, D. G., Heating Installations
REGEP, Z., Steel Structures
RETEZAN, A., Installations
SÂRBU, I., Numerical Methods in Installations Optimization
SCHEIN, T., Soil Mechanics and Foundation Engineering
STOIAN, V., Civil Construction
TOMA, A., Technologies and Mechanization in Civil Engineering
TUDOR, D., Civil Construction

Faculty of Computers and Automatization (Bdul Vasile Pârvan 2, 300223 Timişoara; tel. (256) 40-32-11; fax (256) 40-32-14; e-mail secretariat@ac.upt.ro; internet www.ac.upt.ro):

BREABAN, F., Biomedical Engineering
CIOCARLIE, H., Numerical Processing of Signals
CRETU, V., Advanced Data Structures and Programming Techniques
CRIŞAN, M., Artificial Intelligence
DRAGOMIR, T.-L., Systems Theory
ELES, P., Programming Techniques
HOLBAN, S., Basis of Artificial Intelligence
JIAN, I., Database Design and Use
JURCĂ, I., Operating Systems Design
PREITL, S., Automatic Adjustment Engineering
PROSTEAN, O., System Identification
ROBU, N., Neuronal Networks
STRATULAT, M., Creation of Interfaces, Circuits
STRUGARU, C., Peripheral Devices and Data Transmission
VLĂDUTIU, M., Computer Reliability

Faculty of Electronics and Telecommunications (Bdul Vasile Pârvan 2, 300223 Timişoara; tel. (256) 40-32-91; fax (256) 40-32-95; internet www.etc.upt.ro):

BOGDANOV, I., Robotics
CARSTEA, H., Electronic Equipment Testing and Control
CHIVU, M., Electric and Electronic Measurements
CIUGUDEAN, M., Integrated Circuits and Electronics
CRISAN, S., Electronic Measurements
IGNEA, A., Electric and Electronic Measurements
IONEL, S., Statistics Processing of Signals
ISAR, A., Signals, Circuits, Systems
MUREŞAN, T., Integrated Circuits and Electronics
NAFORNITĂ, I., Signals Processing
NAFORNIŢA, M., Data Transfer, Modern Communications Networks
OTESTEANU, M., Television
POLICEC, A., Communications Systems and Techniques
POPESCU, V., Power Electronics
TĂNASE, M., Electronics
TIPONUT, V., Electronic Devices
TOMA, C., Television
TOMA, L., Data Acquisition Systems

Faculty of Electrotechnical Engineering (Bdul V. Pârvan 2, 300223 Timişoara; tel. (256) 40-33-81; fax (256) 40-33-84; e-mail decanat@et.upt.ro; internet www.et.upt.ro):

ANDEA, P., Electrical Apparatus Technology
ATANASIU, G., Special Electrical Machines
BABESCU, M., Electrical Machines
BANZAR, T., Mathematics
BARTZER, S., Technology of Electrical Products
BIRIESCU, M., Electromechanical Systems Testing
BOJA, N., Mathematics
BOLDEA, I., Electrical Machines
BUTTA, A., Power Delivery
CONSTANTIN, I., Mathematics
CRĂCIUN, P., Physics
CRISTEA, M., Physics
DABA, D., Theoretical Electrotechnics
DELESEGA, I., Electrical Apparatus and Equipment Testing
DOBRE, S., Electrotechnics
DUŞA, V., Optimization Techniques in Industrial Energetics
GHEJU, P., Industrial Power Systems and Networks
HEINRICH, I., Stations and Transformation Posts
HELER, A., Electrotechnics and Electric Machines
IVASCU, C., Automation and Power Systems Protection
KILYENI, S., Numerical Methods in Engineering
LIPOVAN, O., Mathematics
LUSTREA, B., Basis of Energetics and Energy Conversion
MARCU, C., Physics
MIHALCA, I., Physics
MOGA, B., Microprocessors in Electroenergetics
MOLDOVAN, L., Electric Equipment
NEAGU, M., Mathematics
NEGRU, V., High-Voltage Engineering
NEMEŞ, M., Electrical Power Systems
NICA, E., Electrical Machines
POPOVICI, D., Electrical Drives
RADU, D., Non-linear Electrotechnics
SORA, I., Electroheat, Electrotechnology, Electrical Lighting
TOADER, D., Electromechanical Engineering
VASILIEVICI, A., Electrical Equipment
VELICESCU, C., Power Systems and Network Viability
VETRES, I., Basis of Electrotechnics

Faculty of Engineering (Hunedoara) (Str. Revoluţiei 5, 331128 Hunedoara; tel. (254) 20-75-02; fax (254) 20-75-01; e-mail decan@fih.upt.ro; internet www.fih.upt.ro):

ILCA, I., Technology of Plastic Deformation
SAIMAC, A., Electrotechnics

Faculty of Hydrotechnical Engineering (George Enescu St 1A. 300022 Timişoara; tel. (256) 40-40-81; fax (256) 40-40-83; e-mail decan@hidro.upt.ro; internet www.hidro.upt.ro):

CIOMOCOS, F., Strength of Materials
CRETU, G., Hydrology, Water Resources Supply
DANILESCU, A., Statics, Stability and Dynamics of Construction
DAVID, A., Hydraulics, Transport, Groundwater Pollution Modelling
DOANDES, V., Topography, Road Topography
ION, M., Hydrotechnical Construction
IONESCU, N., Machines for Construction, Irrigation and Drainage
MAN, E. T., Irrigation and Drainage
MARTON, A., Ecology, Ecotoxicology
MIREL, I., Water Supply and Town Drainage
NICOARĂ, T., Hydraulics
POPA, G., Hydrotechnical Construction
PRELUSCHEK, E., Hydrotechnical Construction
ROGOBETE, G., Improvement of Soils and Polluted Areas
WEHRY, A., Irrigation and Drainage

Faculty of Industrial Chemistry and Environmental Engineering (Piaţa Victoriei 2, 300006 Timişoara; tel. (256) 40-30-63; fax (256) 40-30-60; e-mail secretar.sef@chim.upt.ro; internet www.chim.upt.ro):

BURTICA, G., Mineral Salts Technology
CSUNDERLIK, C., Organic Chemistry

DAESCU, C., Pharmaceutical Products
IOVI, A., Technology of Mineral Fertilizers
LAZĂU, I., Physical Chemistry
LUPEA, A. X., Pharmaceutical Products
NUŢIU, M., Organic Chemistry
OPRESCU, D., General Chemistry
PERJU, D., Process Modelling
PETCA, G., Technology of General Chemistry, Water and Waste Water Technology
PUGNA, I., Chemical Industry

Faculty of Management in Production and Transport (Str. Remus 14, 300289 Timişoara; tel. (256) 40-42-84; fax (256) 40-42-87; e-mail office@mpt.upt.ro; internet www.mpt.upt.ro):

DĂNILĂ, C., Harvesting Machines
DUMITRESCU, C., Ergonomics, Quality Engineering
GLĂVAN, S., Agrobiological Basis of Agricultural Mechanics
IZVERCIAN, M., Management
NICA, C., Zootechnical Machines
POCINOG, G., Modelling, Simulation and Study of Production
POPA, H., Management and Industrial Engineering
SABAU, C., Finances, Accounting, Ergonomic Analysis, Management
ŞTEFAN, C., Agricultural Engineering
TAROATA, A., Marketing, Industrial Engineering

Faculty of Mechanical Engineering (Bdul Mihai Viteazu 1, 300222 Timişoara; tel. (256) 40-35-21; fax (256) 40-35-23; e-mail cab_robu@rectorat.upt.ro; internet www.mec.upt.ro):

ANCUSA, V., Fluid Mechanics, Transport Phenomena
BABEU, T., Theory of Elasticity and Strength of Materials
BACRIA, V., Mechanics
BAGIU, L., Electromechanical Engineering
BALAŞOIU, V., Hydropneumatic Equipment
BALEKICS, M., Machine Elements
BĂRGLĂZAN, M., Hydraulic Turbines
BRESTIN, A., Technology of Materials
BRÎNDEU, L., Mechanics and Vibration
BUDĂU, V., Materials, Quality Control
CARTE, I., Hydraulic Machines
CARTIS, I., Heat Treatment
CHIRIAC, A., Robotics and Automation in the Textile Industry
CRISTUINEA, C., Theory of Elasticity
CRUDU, M., Mechanisms
CUCURUZ, L., Materials, Casting
DAVID, I., Tolerances
DOBRE, I., Theory of Elasticity and Strength of Materials
DOLGA, V., Mechanical Engineering
DRĂGHICI, G., Manufacturing Engineering
DRĂGULESCU, D., Mechanical Engineering
DUMITRU, I., Technical Mechanics, Strength of Materials
DUNGAN, M., Calculus and Construction of Weight-bearing Structures of Railway Rolling Stock
FAUR, N., Elasticity and Strength of Materials
FLESER, T., Quality Control
GHEORGHIU, M., Mechanics of Fluids and Hydraulic Machines
GLIGOR, O., Components for Precision Mechanics Devices
GLIGOR, T., Mechanics
GLITA, G., Non-Conventional Welding Technologies
HEGEDUS, A., Mechanics
HERMAN, R., Technology Systems and Adjustments
HOANCĂ, V., Thermal Engines
ICLĂNZAN, T., Plastics Manufacturing
IONEL, I., Combustion and Environmental Impact of Stationary Combustion Facilities
IONESCU, N., Mechanisms
IORGA, D., Internal Combustion Engines
JADANEANŢ, M., Thermotechnics
KOVACS, A., Mathematics
LĂNCRĂNGEAN, Z., Technology of Materials
MĂDĂRAS, L., Machine Elements
MANIU, I., Dynamics, Construction and Design of Robotic Systems
MARCUSANU, A., Tolerances
MARINA, M., Mechanisms
MARINCA, V., Mechanics
MESAROŞ, A., Mechatronics, Mechanics
MILOŞ, L., Welding
MITELEA, I., Materials Science
NAGI, M., Thermic Devices, Heat and Mass Transfer
NEGREA, V. D., Internal Combustion Engines
NEGUT, N., Elasticity and Strength of Materials
NICA, C. M., Basic Experimental Research
NICHICI, A., Technology of Materials
NICOARĂ, I., Optical Devices
OPREA, M., Anti-Corrosive Protection Technologies, Materials Technology
PERJU, D., Mechanisms
POMMERSHEIM, A., Programming Languages
POPOVICI, I., Technology of Materials
POPOVICI, V., Welding Equipment
RADULESCU, C., Robotics, Industrial Robots
SAFTA, V., Welding Control and Welded Constructions
SANTĂU, I., Pumping Services
SAVII, G., Computer-Aided Design
SERBAN, V., Materials and Primary Technologies
SMICALĂ, I., Mechanics
SPOREA, I., Materials Technology
SURU, P., Management and Marketing, Computer-Aided Design
TOADER, M., Mechanics
TUCU, D., Technologies and Machines for the Food Industry
URDEA, G., Machine Tools
VACARESCU, I., Biomedical Apparatus

UNIVERSITATEA TEHNICA DIN CLUJ-NAPOCA

Str. Constantin Daicoviciu 15, 400020 Cluj-Napoca
Telephone: (264) 40-12-00
Fax: (264) 59-20-55
E-mail: int.rel.office@staff.utcluj.ro
Internet: www.utcluj.ro

Founded 1948
Academic year: October to July

Rector: Prof. Dr Eng. RADU MUNTEANU
Deputy-Rectors: Prof. Dr Eng. MIRCEA PETRINA, Prof. Dr Eng. AUREL VLAICU, Prof. Dr Eng. IOAN ABRUDAN
Registrar: ELENA FĂRĂGĂU

Library: see Libraries and Archives
Number of teachers: 660
Number of students: 13,000

Publications: *ACAM-Automation, Computer Science and Applied Mathematics*, *Acta Technica Napocensis*, *Logi A*, *Scientific Bulletin of the Cluj-Napoca Technical University* (1 a year)

DEANS

Faculty of Architecture and Urban Planning: Prof. Dr Eng. MIRCEA SERGIU MOLDOVAN
Faculty of Automation and Computer Science: Prof. Dr Eng. SERGIU NEDEVSCHI
Faculty of Civil Engineering: Prof. Dr Eng. MIHAI ILIESCU
Faculty of Electrical Engineering: Prof. Dr Ing. RADU CIUPA
Faculty of Electronics and Telecommunications: Prof. Dr MARINA TOPA
Faculty of Machine Building: Prof. Dr Eng. GHEORGHE ACHIMAS
Faculty of Materials Science: Prof. Dr Eng. TIBERIU RUSU
Faculty of Mechanical Engineering: Prof. Dr Eng. NICOLAE CORDOŞ
College for Technical, Economic and Business Administration Studies: Dr Eng. SORIN GROZAV

PROFESSORS

Faculty of Architecture and Urban Planning (Str. Observator 72–76, 3400 Cluj-Napoca; tel. (264) 59-18-12; fax (264) 59-09-13; e-mail moldovanms@hotmail.com; internet www.utcluj.ro/utcn/arch):

MATEI, A., Architectural Composition
MOLDOVAN, M., History of World Architecture, Aesthetics, History of Arts
MURADIN, C., Styles of Furniture
SZABO, B., Theory of Structures and Renovation of Constructions

Faculty of Automation and Computer Science (Str. G. Bariţiu 26–28, 400027 Cluj-Napoca; tel. (264) 40-12-18; fax (264) 19-48-35; internet ac.utcluj.ro):

CĂMPEANU, V., Mathematical Analysis
COLOSI, T., Theory of Systems, Automation
COROVEI, I., Algebra, Special Mathematics
CRIVEI, I., Algebra, Mathematical Analysis
DĂDÂRLAT, T., Digital Circuits
FEŞTILĂ, C., Control Structures and Algorithms
GANSCA, I., Mathematical Analysis
GAVREA, I., Calculus
GORGAN, D., Fundamentals of Computer Graphics
IGNAT, I., Operating Systems
IVAN, D. M., Numerical Analysis, Mathematical Analysis
LAZEA, GH., Theory of Robot Control
LEŢIA, I. A., Real Time Control
LUNG, N., Special Mathematics
NEDEVSCHI, S., Design with Microchips
OPRIŞ, GH., Special Mathematics, Differential Equations
PUSZTAI, K., Computer Networks
RASA, I., Numerical Mathematics
SALOMIE, I., Design Techniques
TOADER, GH., Mathematical Analysis
VORNICESCU, N., Differential Equations, Mathematical Analysis

Faculty of Civil Engineering (Str. G. Baritiu 25, 400027 Cluj-Napoca; tel. (264) 40-12-49; fax (264) 59-49-67; internet constructii.utcluj.ro):

ALEXA, P., Theoretical Mechanics, Structural Dynamics, Structural Stability
ANDREICA, H., Timber Structures
BADEA, G., Water Supplies and Sewerage
BÂRSAN, G., Theoretical Mechanics, Structural Dynamics, Structural Stability
BIA, C., Strength of Materials, Theory of Elasticity
BORŞ, I., Theoretical Mechanics, Numerical Methods
BRUMARU, M., Buildings
BUCUR, I., Reinforced Concrete Structures
CĂTĂRIG, A., Structural Analysis
CHIOREAN, T., Economics of the Construction Industry, Management and Organization
CHISĂLIŢĂ, A., Theoretical Mechanics, Numerical Methods, Cable and Hinged Structures, Non-Linear Analysis
COMŞA, E., Buildings
CORDOŞ, GH., Sociology
DOMŞA, J., Construction Technology
DUMITRAŞ, M., Buildings
HOSSU, T., Management in Civil Engineering
ILIESCU, M., Road Engineering
IOANI, A., Strength of Materials, Theory of Elasticity
IONESCU, A., Reinforced Concrete Structures

JURCĂU, N., Psychology
KOPENETZ, L., Computer-Aided Engineering and Design, Structural Analysis, Lightweight Structures
MĂGUREANU, C., Reinforced and Prestressed Concrete
MARȚIAN, I., Strength of Materials, Theory of Elasticity
MOGA, A., Construction Technology
MOGA, I., Thermotechnology
MOGA, P., Metal Bridges
NISTOR, I., History of Culture and Civilization
OLARIU, I., Structural Analysis
ONEȚ, T., Reinforced and Prestressed Concrete
OPRIȚOIU, A., Heat Engineering
PĂCURAR, V., Steel Structures
PANȚEL, E., Strength of Materials, Theory of Elasticity, Numerical Methods
PETRINA, M., Structural Analysis, Computer Programming
POP, F., Electric Installation
POP, I., Seismic Engineering
POPA, A., Soil Mechanics and Foundations
VERDEȘ, D., Agricultural Buildings, Physics of Construction
VIOREL, G., Concrete Bridges

Faculty of Electrical Engineering (Str. G. Barițiu 26–28, 400027 Cluj-Napoca; tel. (264) 40-12-28; e-mail decanatet@utcluj.ro; internet ie.utcluj.ro):

BĂLAN, H., Electrical Equipment
BIRO, K., Electrical Machines
CATANĂ, D., Marketing
CATANĂ, GH., Marketing
CHINDRIȘ, M., Technological Design of Management Systems
CIUPA, R., Principles of Electronics
DARIE, S., Electrical Power Stations, Electrical Apparatus
DRAGOMIR, N., Electrical Measuring
IANCU, V., Electrical Machines
IMECS, M., Theory of Automatic Control Systems
IUGA, A., Electrotechnical Engineering
MAIER, V., Electrothermics
MAN, E., Elements of Electrotechnics
MARSCHALKO, R., Electronics
MICU, D., Electrical Engineering
MUNTEANU, R., Data Acquisition, Sensors and Control
RĂDULESCU, M., Electrical Drives
SIMION, E., Non-linear Circuits, Basic Electrical Engineering
TÂRNOVAN, I. G., Electronic Measurements
TODORAN, GH., Electrical Measurements
TRIFA, V., Applied Informatics and Microprocessor Systems
VIOREL, A., Electrical Machines

Faculty of Electronics and Telecommunications (Str. G. Barițiu 26–28, 400027 Cluj-Napoca; tel. and fax (264) 59-16-89; e-mail aurel.vlaicu@com.utcluj.ro; internet www.utcluj.ro/utcn/eltc):

BORDA, M., Information Theory
DOBROTĂ, V., Telecommunications
FEȘTILĂ, L., Analogical Integrated Circuits
LUNGU, Ș., Electronics
MIRON, C., Electronics
PITICĂ, D., Applied Electronics
RUSU, C., Signal Processing
TODEREAN, G., Communications Engineering
VAIDA, M., Informatics
VLAICU, A., Multimedia Systems
VOICULESCU, E., Optoelectronics
ZĂHAN, S., Telecommunications

Faculty of Machine Building (Bdul Muncii 103–105, 3400 Cluj-Napoca; tel. (264) 41-50-51; fax (264) 41-50-54; e-mail gheorghe.achimas@tcm.utcluj.ro; internet zeus.east.utcluj.ro/mb):

ABRUDAN, I., Production Systems
ACHIMAȘ, GH., Metal Forming
ANTAL, A., Machine Components
ARGHIR, M., Computer Programming
BANABIC, D., Manufacturing Technologies
BERCE, P., Manufacturing Technologies
BLEBEA, I., Industrial Robots
BOJAN, I., Management Information Systems
CÂNDEA, D., Industrial Management
CĂZILĂ, A., Machine Components
CREȚU, M., Machine Tools and Industrial Robots
DEACU, L., Hydraulics
GALIȘ, M., Design of Machine Tools
GYENGE, CS., Manufacturing Technologies
IANCĂU, H., Plastics
ISPAS, V., Mechanics, Robotics
ITU, T., Technical Measurements
MORAR, L., Numerical Control
NEGREAN, L., Mechanics
OLTEANU, R., Manufacturing Technology
PLITEA, N., Mechanics
POP, D., Machine Components
POP, I., Hydraulics
POPA, M., Unconventional Technologies
POPESCU, S., Mechanics
PRUNEA, P., Economics
ROȘ, O., Manufacturing Technologies
SUCALĂ, F., Machine Components
URSU-FISCHER, N., Computer Programming

Faculty of Materials Science (Bdul Muncii 103–105, 400641 Cluj-Napoca; tel. (264) 41-50-51; fax (264) 41-50-54; e-mail trusu@sim.east.utcluj.ro; internet www.utcluj.ro/utcn/facsim):

ARGHIR, G., Crystallography
BICSAK, E., Science of Materials, Welded Constructions Technology
BIRIȘ, I., Heat Processes in Metallurgical Furnaces
CÂNDEA, V., Materials Science
CANTA, T., Plastic Deformation Theory
COMAN, S., Mechanical Engineering, Mechanical Technology
COSMA, I., Physics
CULEA, E., Physics
DEMCO, D., Physics
DOMȘA, S., Materials Technology
IANCU, D., Heat and Thermochemical Treatment Technologies
LUCACI, P., Physics
LUPȘA, I., Physics
MILEA, I., Physics
MILITARU, V., Physics
NAGY, E., Steel Casting
NAȘCU, H., Chemistry
ORBAN, R., Materials Technology
PICĂ, M., Chemistry
POP, O., Physics
RUSU, T., Quality Management, Environmental Protection
SOPORAN, V., Technology for Casting Alloys
SPÂRCHEZ, Z., Composite Materials, Metallurgical Physics
VERMEȘAN, G., Heat and Thermochemical Treatment Technologies
VIDA, S., Materials Manufacturing Technology

Faculty of Mechanical Engineering (Bdul Muncii 103–105, 400641 Cluj-Napoca; tel. (264) 41-50-51; fax (264) 41-54-90; e-mail cordos_n@yahoo.fr; internet www.east.utcluj.ro/mec):

APAHIDEAN, B., Thermodynamics
BĂȚAGĂ, N., Heat Machines
BEJAN, M., Strength of Materials
BRÂNZAȘ, P., Management and Marketing
BURNETE, N., Automobiles and Tractors
CORDOȘ, N., Vehicle Dynamics
CREȚU, A., Strength of Materials
HĂRDĂU, M., Strength of Materials
MĂDĂRĂȘAN, T., Thermodynamics and Thermal Machines
MĂTIEȘ, V., Mechanics
ROȘ, V., Forming Machines

UNIVERSITATEA TEHNICĂ DE CONSTRUCȚII BUCUREȘTI (Bucharest Technical University of Civil Engineering)

Bdul Lacul Tei 122–124, Sector 2, 020396 Bucharest

Telephone: (21) 242-12-08
Fax: (21) 242-07-81
E-mail: secretariat@utcb.ro
Internet: www.utcb.ro

Founded 1864

Rector: Prof. Dr Ing. JOHAN NEUNER
Pro-Rectors: Prof. Dr Ing. ANTHONY CHIRITA, Prof. Dr Ing. ANTON ANTON, Prof. Dr Ing. MICHAEL TOMA
Scientific Sec.: Prof. Dr RADU DROBOT

Library of 560,000 vols
Number of teachers: 530
Number of students: 6,964

Publication: *Ştiinţific Journal* (Scientific Bulletin, 4 a year)

DEANS

Faculty of Bridges, Roads and Railways: Prof. Dr Ing. MIHAI DICU
Faculty of Civil, Industrial and Agricultural Buildings: Prof. Dr Ing. DANIELA PREDA
Faculty of Engineering in Foreign Languages: Prof. Dr Ing. NICOLETA RADULESCU
Faculty of Geodesy: Prof. Dr Ing. DUMITRU ONOSE
Faculty of Hydrotechnic: Prof. Dr Ing. IOAN BICA
Faculty of School Equipment: Prof. Eng. SERBAN LAZAR
Faculty of Technological Equipment: Prof. Dr Ing. ION DAVID

UNIVERSITATEA TEHNICĂ 'GHEORGHE ASACHI' DIN IAŞI ('Gheorghe Asachi' Technical University of Iaşi)

Strada Prof. Dr. Docent Dimitrie Mangeron, 700050 Iaşi

Telephone: (232) 27-86-83
Fax: (232) 21-16-67
E-mail: international@tuiasi.ro
Internet: www.tuiasi.ro

Founded 1937, present name and status 1993
State control
Languages of instruction: Romanian, English, French
Academic year: October to October

Rector: Prof. Dr Ing. ION GIURMA
Vice-Rector for Academic Affairs: Prof. Dr MIRCEA DAN GUŞĂ
Vice-Rector for Scientific Research: Prof. Dr CARMEN TEODOSIU
Vice-Rector for International Relations and University Image: Prof. Dr HORIA-NICOLAI TEODORESCU
Scientific Sec.: Prof. Dr DAN GELU GALUŞĂ
Registrar: GABRIELA IURCAN
Librarian: MIHAELA ŞTIRBU

Library: see Libraries and Archives
Number of teachers: 1,164
Number of students: 10,117

Publications: *Environmental Engineering and Management Journal*, *Review Magazine* (2 a year), *Scientific Bulletin* (2 a year), *The Bulletin of the Polytechnic Institute of Iaşi*

DEANS

Cross-Border Faculty of Engineering (in collaboration with Technical University of Moldova): Prof. GH. NISTOR
Faculty of Architecture: Prof. Dr Arch. VIRGILIU CAŞCAVAL

Faculty of Automatic Control and Computer Engineering: Prof. Dr Ing. VASILE MANTA
Faculty of Chemical Engineering and Environmental Protection: Prof. Dr Ing. DAN CAŞCAVA
Faculty of Civil Engineering and Building Services: Prof. Dr Ing. NICOLAE ŢĂRANU
Faculty of Electrical Engineering: Prof. Dr Ing. ALEXANDRU SALCEANU
Faculty of Electronics, Telecommunications and Information Technology: Prof. Dr Ing. ION BOGDAN
Faculty of Hydrotechnical Engineering, Geodesy and Environmental Engineering: Prof. Dr Ing. DORIN COTIUSCA
Faculty of Machine Manufacturing and Industrial Management: Prof. Dr Ing. GHEORGHE NAGÎŢ
Faculty of Materials Science and Engineering: Prof. Dr Ing. IULIAN IONIĂŢ
Faculty of Mechanical Engineering: Prof. Dr Ing. VIOREL CHIRILĂ
Faculty of Textiles and Leather Engineering and Industrial Management: Prof. Dr Ing. CARMEN LOGHIN

PROFESSORS

Faculty of Architecture 'G. M. Cantacuzino' (Bdul Dimitrie Mangeron 43, 700050 Iaşi; tel. (232) 27-86-80; fax (232) 21-15-95; e-mail arhitect@ce.tuiasi.ro; internet www.tuiasi.ro):

BLIUC, I., Building Elements
ONOFREI, V., Architectural Theory

Faculty of Chemical Engineering and Environmental Protection (Bdul Dimitrie Mangeron 73, 700050 Iaşi; tel. (232) 27-86-83; fax (232) 27-13-11; e-mail decanat@ch.tuiasi.ro; internet www.ch.tuiasi.ro):

AELENEI, N., Physical Chemistry
APOSTOLESCU, M., Mineralogy
BALASANIAN, I., Technology of Inorganic Substances
BEZDADEA, M., General Chemistry
BOBU, E., Equipment in the Pulp and Paper Industry
BULACOVSCHI, V., Macromolecular Chemistry
CIOVICĂ, S., Paper Technology
CRISTIAN, GH., Equipment for Organic Industry
DĂRÂNGĂ, M., Physical Chemistry of Polymers
DUMITRIU, E., Organic Technology
GAVRILESCU, D., Pulp and Paper Technology
GORDUZA, V., Technology of Dyes
GRIGORIU, I., Equipment for Inorganic Technology
IVĂNOIU, M., Physical Chemistry of Polymers
LAZĂR, D., Electrochemistry
LUCA, C., General Chemistry
LUNGU, M., Rheology of Polymers
MACOVEANU, M., General Technology
MIHĂILESCU, C., Physico-Chemistry of Polymers
NICU, M., Technology of Polymers
NICU, V., General Technology
OBROCEA, P., Pulp and Paper Technology
ONISCU, C., Technology of Synthetic and Biosynthetic Drugs
ONU, P., General Chemistry
OPREA, CL., Mechano-chemistry of Polymers, Monomers and Polymer Technology
OPREA, SP., Chemical Organic Technology
PETRESCU, S., Materials Science
POPA, I. M., Physical Chemistry
POPA, M., Polymer Technology
POPA, V., Wood Chemistry
ROŞCA, I., Inorganic Chemistry
RUSU, M., Rubber and Plastic Materials Processing
SCUTARU, D., Organic Chemistry
SIMINICEANU, I., Technology of Inorganic Substances
SIMIONESCU, B., Physical Chemistry of Polymers
SÎRGHIE, I., Analytical Chemistry
STANCU, A., Transport Phenomena in the Chemical Industry
SZEP, A., Technology of Inorganic Substances
UNGUREANU, ŞT., Automation in the Chemical Industry
VÂTĂ, M., Organic Chemistry

Faculty of Civil Engineering and Building Services (Bdul Dimitrie Mangeron 43, 700050 Iaşi; tel. (232) 27-86-83; fax (232) 23-33-68; e-mail decanat@ce.tuiasi.ro; internet www.ce.tuiasi.ro):

AMARIEI, C., Structural Mechanics, Plastic Design
ANDREI, R., Transport Infrastructure
ATANASIU, M. G., Structural Mechanics, Computer-Aided Design, Earthquake Engineering
AXINTE, E., Steel Structures
BOBOC, V., Road Engineering
BROŞTEANU, M., Buildings
BUDESCU, M., Structural Mechanics, Computer-Aided Design, Earthquake Engineering
CIONGRADI, I., Structural Mechanics, Computer-Aided Design, Earthquake Engineering
CIORNEI, AL., Buildings
COROBCEANU, S., Concrete and Reinforced Concrete Construction
COSOSCHI, B., Road Engineering
DUMITRAŞ, A., Structural Mechanics
FLOREA, N., Hydrotechnical Structures
GAVRILAŞ, I., Construction
GIUŞCĂ, N., Construction Technology
GORBĂNESCU, D., Strength of Materials, Theory of Elasticity and Plasticity
GRECU, V., Soil Mechanics and Foundation Engineering
GROLL, L., Building Materials
GUGIUMAN, G., Road Engineering
HAGIU, V., Management of Construction Works
HIRHUI, I., Building Materials
IGNAT, J., Electrical Installations
IONESCU, C., Structural Mechanics, Earthquake Engineering
ISOPESCU, D., Wooden Constructions, Composite Structures
JANTEA, C., Bridge Engineering
MATEESCU, TH., Water Supply and Sewerage Installations, Installations for Buildings
MIHALACHE, N., Strength of Materials, Theory of Elasticity and Plasticity, Numerical Methods
MUŞAT, V., Soil Mechanics and Foundation
NOUR, S., Concrete and Reinforced Concrete Constructions
PESCARU, V., Steel Structures
POPOVICI, D., Highways
PRECUPANU, D., Strength of Materials, Theory of Elasticity and Plasticity
RĂILEANU, P., Soil Mechanics and Foundations
SECU, AL., Industrial and Agricultural Constructions
ŞERBANOIU, I., Managerial Analysis of the Building Process, Management of Construction Work
STANCIU, A., Soil Mechanics and Foundations
ŞTEFĂNESCU, D., Buildings
ŢĂRANU, N., Industrial Buildings and Composite Structures, Steel Structures
UNGUREANU, N., Strength of Materials, Theory of Elasticity and Plasticity, Numerical Methods
VARLAM, F., Concrete Bridge Engineering
VELICU, C., Thermal Engineering, Rehabilitation of Buildings
VEREŞ, AL., Buildings and Architectural Acoustics
VLAD, I., Strength of Materials, Theory of Elasticity and Plasticity
VLAD, N., Road Technology Engineering

Faculty of Control Systems and Computer Engineering (Bdul Dimitrie Mangeron 53A, 700050 Iaşi; tel. (232) 23-13-43; fax (232) 21-42-90; e-mail decanat@ac.tuiasi.ro):

BALABAN, E., Digital Control Systems, Control of Electrical Drives
BOŢAN, C., Optimization Techniques, Optimal Control
BOTEZ, C., Databases and Computer Programming, Software Engineering
GÂLEA, D., Artificial Intelligence
GANCIU, T., Systems Identification, Data Processing
HOZA, F., Digital Computers, Microcontrollers
HUŢANU, C., Multiprocessor Systems, Microprocessor Systems
ILINCA, M., Computer Programming
LAZĂR, C., Control Engineering, Data Transmission
OLAH, I., Electrical and Electronic Control Equipment, Servomechanisms
PAL, C., Robot Control Systems
PĂNESCU, A. D., Knowledge-Based Systems, Robot Control Systems
PĂSTRĂVANU, O. C., Discrete Event Systems, Neural Networks in Control Engineering
VALACHI, A., Digital Logic Design, Digital Systems Design
VOICU, M., Systems Theory, Principles of Feedback Control

Faculty of Electrical Engineering (Bdul Dimitrie Mangeron 51–53, 700050 Iaşi; tel. and fax (232) 27-86-83; fax (232) 23-76-27; e-mail secretariat@ee.tuiasi.ro; internet www.ee.tuiasi.ro):

ADAM, M., Electrical Equipment
ALEXANDRESCU, V., Power Systems
ANDRONE, C., Principles of Electrical Engineering
ASAFTEI, C., Power Plants
ASANDEI, D., Power Plants
BALAN, T., Electrical Materials
BALUTA, GH., Principles of Electrical Engineering
BARABOI, A., Electrical Equipment, EMC, Power Electronics
CANTEMIR, L., Electric Traction, Uses of Electrical Energy in Modelling, Electrical Drives, Systems Theory, Intelligent Control
CÂRŢÎNĂ, GH., Optimal Control and Computer Applications in Energetics
CIOBANU, L., Electrical Drives of Robots, Reliability
CIOBANU, R. C., Electrical Materials
CREŢU, A., Electrical Engineering
CREŢU, M., Electrical Measurements and Transducers
DIACONESCU, M., Electrical Drives, Electronics and Power Electronics
GAVRILAŞ, M., Power Plants
GEORGESCU, GH., Power Networks
GRAUR, I., Power Electronics, Vector Control of AC Drives
GUŞĂ, M., High-Voltage Engineering
HNATIUC, E., Electrical Apparatus Design, Environmental Protection
IVAS, D., Power Systems Reliability
LEONTE, P., Electrical Equipment
LIVINŢ, GH., Systems Theory, Automatic Control
MITREA, S., Principles of Electrical Engineering
MUNTEANU, F., Power Systems Reliability
NEMESCU, M., Systems Theory and Industrial Automation

OLAH, R., Overvoltages and Insulation Engineering
OLARU, R., Industrial Automation
POPESCU, I., Fundamentals of Electrical Engineering
SIMION, A., Electrical Machines
SUCHAR, I., Electrical Engineering and Electronics
TEODORU, E., Electrical Machines and Drives

Faculty of Electronics Telecommunications and Information Technology (Bdul Carol I 11, 700506 Iaşi; tel. (232) 21-37-37; fax (232) 21-77-20; e-mail decanat@etc.tuiasi.ro; internet www.tuiasi.ro):

ALEXA, D., Microwave Engineering, Power Electronics
ALEXANDRU, D. N., Telecommunications, Communications Systems
BÂRSAN, T., Mathematics
BEJANCU, A., Mathematics
BOGDAN, I., Mobile Communications, Antennas
CASSIAN, I., Fibre-optic Communications, Microwave Technology
CEHAN, V., Radio Transmitters, Satellite Communications
CIOBANU, GH., Mathematics
CORDUNEANU, A., Mathematics
COTAE, P., Digital Communication
CRĂCIUN, I., Mathematics
DIMITRIU, L., Electronic Measurement and Control Apparatus, Automotive Electronics
DUMA, P., Microprocessors, Microcontrollers, Electronic Telephone Exchanges
FETECĂU, C., Mathematics
GORAS, L., Signals, Circuits and Systems
GRIGORAS, V., Signals, Circuits and Systems
LUCANU, M., Industrial Electronics, PWM Techniques for Converters
MUNTEANU, V., Information Theory
NEAGU, AL., Mathematics
NEGOESCU, N., Mathematics
PAPAGHIUC, N., Mathematics
SAVA, V., Mathematics
SÎRBU, A., Software Engineering, Computer-Aided Design
STIURCĂ, D., Analogue Integrated Circuits
TALPALARU, P., Mathematics
TARNICERIU, D., Signal Processing
TEODORESCU, H., Medical Electronics, Image Processing, Neural Networks and Fuzzy Systems

Faculty of Hydrotechnical Engineering, Geodesy and Environmental Engineering (Bdul Dimitrie Mangeron 65, 700050 Iaşi; tel. and fax (232) 27-08-04; e-mail decanat@hidro.tuaisi.ro; internet www.tuiasi.ro):

ALEXANDRESCU, O., Pumping Installations
AXINTE, S., Ameliorative Agriculture
BÂRSAN, E., Water Supply
BARTHA, I., Hydraulics
BLĂGOI, O., Hydraulics
CISMARU, C., Irrigation and Drainage
COJOCARU, I., Irrigation and Drainage
DIMA, M., Sewerage, Waste Water Treatment
GIURMĂ, I., Hydrology and Water Management
HOBJILĂ, V., Construction Technology
LUCA, M., Hydraulics
MANOLOVICI, M., Hydrotechnical Constructions
NISTOR, GH., Surveying
NIŢESCU, E., Work Technology and Mechanization in Land Reclamation
PATRAŞ, M., Reinforced Concrete
POPESCU, ST., Numerical Methodology, Dispersion
POPOVICI, N., Soil Erosion Control, Regulation and Management of Watercourses
STĂTESCU, F., Soil Science

Faculty of Machine Building (Bdul Dimitrie Mangeron 63, 700050 Iaşi; tel. (232) 24-21-09; fax (232) 21-16-67; e-mail secretariat@tcm.tuiasi.ro):

AGOP, M., Physics
BOHOSIEVICI, C., Technology of Machine Building
BRAHA, V., Mechanical Engineering
CĂLUGĂRU, GH., Physics
CARATA, E., Machine Tools
CHIRILĂ, V., Technology of Machine Building
CIUBOTARIU, C., Physics
CONSTANTINESCU, C., Machine Tools
COZMÎNCĂ, M., Metal Cutting
DUSA, P.
FETECĂU, C., Theoretical Mechanics
GHERGHEL, N., Design of Mechanical Devices
GRĂMESCU, TR., Technology of Machine Building
IBĂNESCU, I., Theoretical Mechanics
LUNGU, GH., Machine Tools
MUSCĂ, G., Computer-Aided Manufacturing
NEAGU, E., Physics
NEAGU, R., Physics
PANAIT, S., Metal Cutting
PARASCHIV, DR., Machine Repairing Technology
PLĂHTEANU, B., Machine Tools
RUSU, E., Theoretical Mechanics
SLĂTINEANU, L., Machine Building Technology
UNGUREANU, GH., Computer-Aided Design
URSU, D., Physics
ZET, GH., Physics
ZETU, D., Design of Automatic Machine Tools

Faculty of Materials Science and Engineering (Bdul Dimitrie Mangeron 61A, 700050 Iaşi; tel. and fax (232) 23-00-09; e-mail decanat@sim.tuiasi.ro):

ALEXANDRU, I., Technology of Materials
BACIU, C., Technology of Materials
BULANCEA, V., Rolling
CARCEA, I., Composites
COJOCARU FILIPIUC, V., Metallurgy
DIMA, A., Technology and Applied Metallurgy
FLORESCU, A., Materials Technology
GĂLUSCĂ, D. G., Technology of Thermal Treatment
MĂLUREANU, I., Technology of Metals
MUNTEANU, C., Materials Technology
PETRUŞ, O., Computational Metallurgy
SUSAN, M., Applied Metallurgy

Faculty of Mechanical Engineering and Industrial Management (Bdul Dimitrie Mangeron 59A, Et. 1, 700050 Iaşi; tel. and fax (232) 24-21-09; e-mail secretariat@tcm.tuiasi.ro):

AMARIEI, N., Strength of Materials
ATANASIU, V., Mechanical Transmissions
BÂRSĂNESCU, P., Strength of Materials
BERCEA, M., Machine Design
COMANDAR, C., Strength of Materials
COZMA, D., Agricultural Machines
CRĂCIUN, V., Agricultural Machines
CREŢU, SP., Machine Design, Tribology and Vibration
DĂSCĂLESCU, D., Internal Combustion Engines
DRĂGAN, B., Machine Vibrations
DUCA, C., Mechanisms
DUMITRAŞCU, GH., Thermotechnics and Heat Engines
GAFIŢANU, M., Machine Design, Tribology and Vibration
GAIGINSCHI, R., Internal Combustion Engines
GRIGORAS, S., Machine Design and Reliability
HAGIU, GH., Machine Design and Vibration
HORBANIUC, G., Thermotechnology and Heat Engines
HOSTIUC, L., Machine Design
LEON, D., Strength of Materials
LOZONSCHI, GH., Thermotechnics and Heat Engines
MERTICARU, V., Machine Dynamics
MOCANU, F., Strength of Materials
NECULĂIASA, V., Agricultural Machines
OLARU, D., Tribology and Machine Design
OPRIŞAN, C., Mechanisms
PALIHOVICI, VAL., Strength of Materials
POPOVICI, A., Mechanisms
RACOCEA, C., Machine Design
RECEANU, D., Mechanisms
ŢENU, I., Equipment for the Food Industry
ŽUBCU, V., Gas and Steam Turbines

Faculty of Textiles and Leather Engineering and Industrial Management (Bdul Dimitrie Mangeron 29, 700050 Iaşi; tel. and fax (232) 23-04-91; e-mail decanat@tex.tuiasi.ro; internet www.tuiasi.ro/facultati/tex):

ANTONIU, GH., Textile Raw Materials
AVRAM, D., Structure of Textile Yarns
BADEA, N., Leather and Furs Chemistry and Technology
BORDEIANU, D., Technology and Equipment for Spinning Mills
BRUDARU, O., Fuzzy Systems
BUCEVSCHI, D., Technology of Leather Substitutes
BUDULAN, C., Equipment and Automation in the Knitwear Industry
BUTNARU, R., Chemistry and Technology of Textile Materials
CIOCOIU, M., Weaving Process and Machinery, Statistical Methods in Textiles
CONDUCARCHE, GH., Management
DRĂGOI, L., Weaving Machinery Design and Automation
GRIBINCEA, V., Textile Raw Materials
GRIGORIU, A., Special Technologies of Textile Products Finishing
ILIESCU, E., Principles of Chemical Technology
IRIMIA, M., Economics and Accountability
LEONTE, R., Marketing
LIUŢE, D., Preparatory Weaving Processes, Weaving Technology
LUCA, G., Management
MĂLUREANU, G., Footwear Design
MITU, S., Clothing
MUNTEANU, A., Marketing and Economics
MUNTEANU, V., Marketing
MUREŞAN, A., Equipment for Textile Finishing
MUSTAŢĂ, A., Bast Fibre Spinning
NECULĂIASA, M., Textile Metrology, Textile Quality Control
PINTILIE, E., Computer-Aided Design in Ready-Made Clothing, Design of Ready-Made Clothing Machinery
RUSU, C., Total Quality Management, Human Resources Management
VÎLCU, M., Theoretical Bases of Spinning
VITAN, F., Transfer Phenomena and Equipment
VOICU, M., Interpersonal Communication

Other Institutes of Higher Education

Academia de Arte Vizuale 'Ioan Andreescu' (Academy of Visual Arts 'Ioan Andreescu'): Piaţa Unirii 31, 400098 Cluj-Napoca; tel. (264) 19-15-77; fax (264) 19-28-90; f. 1950; faculties of fine arts, decorative arts and design; library: 52,000 vols; 75 teachers; 553 students; Rector IOACHIM NICA.

Academia de Muzică 'Gheorghe Dima': Str. Ion. C. Brătianu 25, 400079 Cluj-Napoca; tel. (264) 59-12-41; fax (264) 59-38-

79; e-mail conscluj@gmail.com; internet www.amgd.ro; f. 1819, reorganized 1919, present name 1990; faculties of instrumental performance, music theory, singing and stage art; library: 188,000 vols; 250 teachers; 1,182 students; Rector Prof. Dr ADRIAN POP; Pro-rector Prof. Dr GABRIEL BANCIU; Scientific Sec. Dr ELENA CHIRCEV; publs *Intermezzo* (magazine), *Lucrări de Muzicologie* (Musicology Articles, 1 a year).

Academia de Studii Economice (Academy of Economic Studies): Piaţa Română 6, sector 1, 010374 Bucharest; tel. (21) 319-19-00; fax (21) 319-18-99; e-mail rectorat@ase.ro; internet www.ase.ro; f. 1913; faculties of management, economics, agricultural and food production, economy and administration, finance and banking, administration and accounting, cybernetics, statistics and computer science for economics, trade, international economic relations, economic studies in foreign languages; college of economics at Buzău; library: see Libraries and Archives; 765 teachers; 49,000 students; Rector Prof. Dr ION GH. ROSCA; Vice-Rector for Bachelors and Masters programmes Prof. NICOLAE DARDAC; Vice-Rector for Int. Relations and European Integration Prof. VIOREL LEFTER; Vice-Rector for Scientific Research and PhD programmes Prof. ION STANCU; Scientific Sec. Prof. RAZVAN ZAHARIA; publs *Economic Journal* (in Romanian and English, 4 a year), *Informatica Economică* (4 a year).

Attached Centre:

Bulgaria–Romania Interuniversity Europe Centre/BRIE–Giurgiu: Str. Mircea cel Batran 36, 080036 Giurgiu; tel. (21) (246)21-91-61; fax (21) 312-95-49; e-mail brie@ase.ro; internet www.brie.ase.ro; f. 2001; operates through collaboration between Rusenski Universitet 'Angel Kanchev' (see Bulgaria chapter) and the Academia de Studii Economice; Dir Prof. Dr CONSTANTIN APOSTOL.

Academiei Naţionale de Informaţii 'Mihai Viteazul': Şoseaua Odăi 20, sector 1, Bucharest; tel. (21) 410-65-60; fax 31-04-750; e-mail ani@sri.ro; internet www.sri.ro; training intelligence officers; offers bachelors, masters and doctoral courses.

Institutul Teologic Baptist din Bucureşti: Str. Berzei, 29, sector 1, 010251 Bucharest; tel. (21) 315-91-08; fax (21) 318-15-93; e-mail bbtseminary@yahoo.com; internet www.itb.ro; f. 1921; Rector Prof. Dr VASILE TALPOS.

Institutul Teologic Protestant Cluj: Piaţa Avram Iancu 13, 400124 Cluj-Napoca; tel. and fax (264) 59-13-68; internet proteo.cj.edu.ro; f. 1568; offers bachelors, masters and doctoral courses.

Institutul Teologic Romano-Catolic 'Sf. Losif' Iaşi: Str. Th. Văscăuţeanu 6, 700462 Iaşi; tel. (232) 41-04-19; fax (232)21-14-76; e-mail decan@itrc.ro; internet www.itrc.ro; f. 1886; Rector Dr WILHELM DANCĂ; Vice-Rector Dr ŞTEFAN LUPU; Dean Dr MIHAI PATRAŞCU; publs *Dialog Teologic*, *Drumuri Deschise*, *Educatorul Creştin*, *Lasati Copiii Sa Vina La Mine*.

RUSSIA

The Higher Education System

In March 1917 the last Tsar of the Romanov dynasty, which had ruled Russia as an autocracy since 1613, was forced to abdicate and a liberal Provisional Government took power. The Bolsheviks overthrew the Provisional Government in November of the same year and the Russian Soviet Federative Socialist Republic (RSFSR) was proclaimed. In 1922 the RSFSR joined the Union of Soviet Socialist Republics (USSR), which disintegrated in 1991, when the Russian Federation, as the RSFSR was formally renamed, was founded. The oldest current institutions of higher education date from the 18th century, notably St Petersburg State University (founded 1724) and Moscow State University 'M. V. Lomonsov' (founded 1755). Several specialist institutions were founded during the reign of Catherine the Great (1762–96). Major institutions founded during the 19th century include Moscow Agricultural Academy 'K. A. Tirmiyazev' (founded 1865), Tomsk Polytechnic University (founded 1896) and Nizhnii Novgorod State Technical University (founded 1898 in Warsaw, Poland). Universal education was a fundamental Bolshevik principle, and during the period of Soviet rule (1917–91) more than 340 institutions of higher education were founded. In 2008/09 there were 7,543,000 students enrolled in 1,134 institutions of higher education. Under Soviet rule all educational institutions were state-owned but a wide range of independent schools and colleges were created in the early 1990s. In 2008/09 there were 474 independent higher education institutions.

Higher education institutions are categorized as Academies, Universities, Institutes and Conservatories. Universities are sub-divided by subject area: Agriculture, Humanities and Sciences, Medical, Pedagogical and Technical. The Ministry of Education and Science has overall responsibility for higher education, particularly the licensing and accreditation of institutions. Russia participates in the Bologna Process to establish a European Higher Education Area, the first phase of which is to adopt a credit-based system of comparable degrees with two main cycles (undergraduate and graduate). In 2007 Russia enacted a law that replaced the traditional five-year model of education with a two-tiered approach: a four-year Bachelors degree followed by a two-year Masters. This system was to be fully implemented by 2010.

Admission was formerly made on the joint basis of the Certificate of Secondary Education (Attestat o srednem obrazovanii) and performance in a competitive entrance examination. However, a system of Single Entry University Examinations was gradually adopted by the administrative regions (48 by 2003), testing students in a range of compulsory and designated subjects (the latter depending on the institution's requirements). In 2007 the Unified State Examination (USE), a standardized common university admission examination replacing the state final school attestation and entrance examinations, was introduced by law. Since 2009 the USE has been adopted nationwide and is compulsory for all graduates. However in 2009, 24 universities received the right to administer their own entrance exams and in 2010 a further 11 Russian universities were allowed to do this as well. The undergraduate degree is the Bachelors (Baklavr), a four-year programme of study divided into two years of general studies and two years of specialized studies. Graduates holding the Bachelors are eligible to study for the Masters (Magistr), the first postgraduate degree, which is either a one-year taught course or a two-year period of research. Doctoral-level studies consist of Aspirantura and Doktorantura. Aspirantura is a period of study following the Masters lasting a minimum of three years and culminating with the defence of a thesis and the award of the title Candidate of Sciences (Kandidat Nauk). Following Aspirantura, Doktorantura lasts for an unspecified period of time that, upon completion, results in the title Doctor of Sciences (Doktor Nauk).

Technical and vocational education is largely offered by specialist institutions and technical colleges at the upper secondary level. The primary qualifications are the Diploma of Completed Specialized Secondary Education (advanced level) and Diploma of Completed Specialized Secondary Education (basic level).

The Federal Service for Supervision in Education and Science carries out quality control, licensing, certification and state accreditation of educational institutions.

Regulatory and Representative Bodies

GOVERNMENT

Ministry of Culture and the Mass Media: 109074 Moscow, Kitaigorodskii proyezd 7; tel. (495) 625-11-95; internet www.mkmk.ru; Minister ALEKSANDR S. SOKOLOV.

Ministry of Education and Science: 125993 Moscow, ul. Tverskaya 11; tel. (495) 629-70-62; internet www.mon.gov.ru; Min. ANDREI A. FURSENKO.

ACCREDITATION

Agency for Higher Education Quality Assurance and Career Development (AQA): 101000 Moscow, Myasnitskaya ul., 24, Bldg 1, Office 79; tel. (495) 628-05-09; fax (495) 628-47-79; e-mail akkork@akkork.ru; internet www.akkork.ru; f. 2005; carries out ind. analysis, evaluation and assurance of the quality of education provided by higher education instns; Dir-Gen. Dr VYACHESLAV SAMOILOV.

ENIC Russia: 117198 Moscow, Nat. Information Centre for Academic Recognition and Mobility, Mikluho-Maklaya St 6, RUDN; Moscow, Ordzhonikidze St 3; tel. (495) 958-28-81; fax (495) 433-15-11; e-mail russianenic@sci.pfu.edu.ru; internet www.russianenic.ru; f. 1999; Dir Dr GENNADY LUKICHEV.

Federal Service for Supervision in Education and Science: 115998 Moscow, ul. Shabolovka 33; tel. (495) 208-68-38; internet www.obrnadzor.gov.ru; provides supervision and guidance in the sphere of education and science; monitors the quality of education in instns; organizes licensing, attestation and accreditation of educational instns; Head VIKTOR ALEXANDROVICH BOLOTOV.

National Accreditation Agency: 424000 Yoshkar-Ola, 3 Lenin Sq.; tel. (8362) 41-61-94; fax (8362) 41-38-84; e-mail umo@nica.ru; internet www.nica.ru; f. 1995; supports higher-education instns, vocational-training establishments and the educational authorities in carrying out their state accreditation procedures; Dir Prof. VLADIMIR NAVODNOV.

NATIONAL BODIES

Association of Non-State Higher Education Establishments: 107005 Moscow, Radio St 22; tel. (495) 105-03-83; fax (495) 105-03-81; e-mail va_zernov@mtu-net.ru; Pres. VLADIMIR ZERNOV.

Association of Russian Higher Education Institutions: 105064 Moscow, 4 Gorokhovsky per.; tel. (499) 261-31-52; fax (499) 267-46-81; e-mail svp@miigaik.ru; Pres. VIKTOR SAVINYKH.

Federal Agency for Education: 115998 Moscow, Lyusinovskaya ul. 51; tel. (495) 237-97-63; fax (495) 236-01-71; e-mail bicab@ed.gov.ru; internet www.ed.gov.ru; manages state property, implements education and training policies, funds higher-education instns; Head NIKOLAI IVANOVICH BULAEV.

Russian Academy of Education: 119121 Moscow, Pogodinskaya ul. 8; tel. (495) 245-16-41; fax (495) 246-81-77; f. 1943; br. depts of philosophy of education and theoretical pedagogy, psychology and physiology in education, general secondary education, culture and education, basic vocational training, higher education; regional depts: Northwest (St Petersburg), Siberia (Krasnoyarsk), Southern (Rostov-on-Don), Central (Moscow), Povolzhskoe (Kazan), Urals (Ekaterinburg); 4 experimental schools, 30 research institutes; see Research Institutes; library:

see Libraries and Archives; Pres. Prof. Dr N. D. NIKANDROV; Chief Learned Sec. Prof. Dr I. V. ROBERT; publs *Defektologiya* (Defectology, 6 a year), *Izvestiya RAO* (News, 4 a year), *Pedagogika* (Pedagogics, 12 a year), *Voprosy Psikhologii* (Problems of Psychology, 12 a year).

Russian Rectors' Union: 119991 Moscow, V-234, Vorobievy Gory, Lomonosov Moscow State Univ., Glavnoe Zdanie, Rooms 1001–1003; tel. and fax (495) 939-20-32; e-mail office@rsr-online.ru; internet rsr-online.ru/english; f. 1992; c. 1,000 mems; Pres. VIKTOR A. SADOVNICHY; Sec. Gen. OLGA V. KASHIRINA.

Learned Societies

GENERAL

Russian Academy of Natural Sciences: 113105 Moscow, Varshavskoye shosse 8; tel. (495) 954-26-11; fax (495) 954-73-05; e-mail presidium@raen.ru; internet www.raen.ru; f. 1990; organizes and coordinates pure and applied research; sections: Mathematics; Physics; Chemistry; Earth Sciences; Mining and Metallurgy; Issues in Education; Informatics; Biomedicine; Biology and Ecology; Russian Encyclopedia; Economics and Sociology; Issues in Macroeconomics; Geopolitics and Security; Noosphere Knowledge and Technology; Humanities and Creative Work; Interbranch Ecological and Economic Systems Research; Environmental Sciences; depts: St Petersburg Branch for Education and Science Development; Oil and Gas; Forest Sciences; Eurasia Concept and Culture; Ecology, Hydrogeology, Engineering Geology and Geocryology; Applied Mathematics and Mathematical Physics; Class and National Traditions; 2,500 mems (incl. 100 hon., 250 foreign); Pres. Prof. Dr OLEG L. KUZNETSOV; Chief Scientific Sec. LIDA V. IVANITSKAYA.

Russian Academy of Sciences: 119991 Moscow, Leninsky pr. 14; tel. (495) 954-29-05; fax (495) 954-33-20; e-mail uvs@pran.ru; internet www.pran.ru; f. 1724; depts of mathematics (Academician-Sec. L. D. FADEYEV), physics (Academician-Sec. A. F. ANDREEV), power engineering, mechanics and control processes (Academician-Sec. V. E. FORTOV), information science and computer technology (Academician-Sec. E. P. VELIKHOV), chemistry and materials (Academician-Sec. V. A. KABANOV), biology (Academician-Sec. A. I. GRIGORIEV), earth sciences (Academician-Sec. O. A. BOGATIKOV), social sciences (Academician-Sec. V. L. MAKAROV), history and philology (Academician-Sec. A. P. DEREVYANKO); Siberian division (Pr. Akademika Lavrenteva 17, 630090 Novosibirsk; tel. 30-05-67; Chair. N. L. DOBRETSOV), incl. centres in Krasnoyarsk, Irkutsk, Kemerovo, Omsk, Tomsk and Tumen; Far Eastern division (Svetlanskaya 50, 690600 Vladivostok; tel. 2-25-28; Chair. V. J. SERGIENKO); Urals division (Pervomaiskaya 91, 620219 Ekaterinburg; tel. 74-02-23; Chair. V. A. CHERESHNEV), incl. centres in Perm and Komi; additional centres in Makhachkala, Petrozavodsk, Kazan, Nalchik, Ufa and Apatity; attached research institutes: see Research Institutes; libraries and archive: see Libraries and Archives; 1,429 mems (501 academicians, 720 corresp. mems, 208 foreign mems); Pres. YU. S. OSIPOV; Chief Learned Sec. V. V. KOSTYUK; publs *Izvestiya Rossiiskoi Akademii Nauk* (Bulletin of the Russian Academy of Sciences, in 16 series: Biology, Geography, Literature and Language, Mathematics, Metals, Economics and Society, Mechanics of Liquids and Gases, Solid State Mechanics, Technical Cybernetics, Energy and Transport (6 a year); Geology, Inorganic Materials, Physics of Atmosphere and Ocean, Earth Physics, Physics, Chemistry (12 a year)), *Doklady Rossiiskoi Akademii Nauk* (Proceedings of the Academy, 36 a year), *Izvestiya Sibirskogo otdeleniya Rossiiskoi Akademii Nauk* (Bulletin of the Siberian Branch of the Russian Academy of Sciences, in 5 series: Biological and Medical Sciences, History, Philology and Philosophy, Economics and Applied Sociology (4 a year); Technical Sciences, Chemical Sciences (6 a year)), *Nauka v Rossii* (Science in Russia, in Russian and English, 6 a year), *Vestnik Rossiiskoi Akademii Nauk* (Journal of the Russian Academy of Sciences, 12 a year), *Vestnik Dalnevostochnogo otdeleniya RAN* (Journal of the Far Eastern Division of the Russian Academy of Sciences).

UNESCO Office Moscow: 119331 Moscow, ul. Mytnaya 1; tel. (495) 230-10-65; fax (495) 238-60-85; e-mail moscow@unesco.org; internet www.unesco.ru; designated Cluster Office for Armenia, Azerbaijan, Belarus, Moldova and Russia; Dir BADARCH DENDEV.

Union of Scientific and Engineering Associations: 119034 Moscow, Kursovoi per. 17; tel. (495) 290-62-86; fax (495) 291-85-06; Pres. Acad. I. GULIAEV; Learned Sec. S. V. PRYANISHNIKOV; Sec.-Gen. V. SITSEV.

AGRICULTURE, FISHERIES AND VETERINARY SCIENCE

Russian Academy of Agricultural Sciences: 107814 Moscow, Bolshoi Kharitonevsky per. 21; tel. (495) 207-39-42; f. 1992; depts of plant breeding and genetics (Academician-Sec. V. S. SHEVELUKHA), arable farming and the use of agricultural chemicals (Academician-Sec. I. P. MAKAROV), feed and fodder crops production (Academician-Sec. (vacant)), plant protection (Academician-Sec. N. M. GOLYTSIN), livestock production (Academician-Sec. (vacant)), veterinary science (Academician-Sec. V. P. SHISHKOV), mechanization, electrification and automation in farming (Academician-Sec. G. E. LISTOPAD), forestry (Academician-Sec. V. N. VINOGRADOV), the Economics and Management of agricultural production (Academician-Sec. (vacant)), land reform and the organization of land use (Academician-Sec. (vacant)), land reclamation and water resources (Academician-Sec. B. B. SHUMAKOV), the storage and processing of agricultural products (Academician-Sec. (vacant)); regional depts in St Petersburg (Non Black Soil Zone), Novosibirsk (Siberia), Khabarovsk (Far East); 150 mems; 128 corresp. mems; 73 foreign corresp. mems; attached research institutes: see Research Institutes; library: see Libraries and Archives; Pres. A. A. NIKONOV; Chief Learned Sec. V. P. SHISHKOV; publs *Doklady* (Proceedings), *Mekhanizatsiya i elektrificatsiya selskogo khozyaistva* (Mechanization and Electrification of Agriculture), *Selektsiya i Semenovodstvo* (Selection and Seed Science), *Selskokhozyaistvennaya biologiya* (Agricultural Biology), *Sibirskii vestnik selskokhozyaistvennoi nauki* (Siberian Agricultural Science Journal), *Vestnik selskokhozyaistvennoi nauki* (Agricultural Science Journal).

Society of the Timber and Forestry Industry: 103062 Moscow, Ul. Chernyshevskogo 29; tel. (495) 923-95-70; Chair. YU. A. YAGODNIKOV.

Soil Science Society: 109017 Moscow, Pyzhevskii per. 7; tel. (495) 231-43-59; attached to Russian Acad. of Sciences; Pres. G. V. DOBROVOLSKY.

ARCHITECTURE AND TOWN PLANNING

Union of Russian Architects: 123001 Moscow, Granatni per. 22; tel. (495) 291-55-78; fax (495) 202-81-01; e-mail sarrus@rambler.ru; f. 1981; 12,000 mems; Pres. YU. P. GNEDOVSKIY; publ. *Vesti SAR* (4 a year).

ECONOMICS, LAW AND POLITICS

Association of International Law: 119841 Moscow, ul. Frunze 10; attached to Russian Acad. of Sciences; Chair. Prof. G. I. TUNKIN.

Association of Orientalists: 103753 Moscow, ul. Rozhdestvenka 12; tel. (495) 928-57-64; attached to Russian Acad. of Sciences; Chair. M. S. KAPITSA.

Association of Political Sciences: 118941 Moscow, ul. Znamenka 10; attached to Russian Acad. of Sciences; Pres. Dr G. K. SHAKHNAZAROV.

Economics Society: 117259 Moscow, B. Cheremushkinskaya ul. 34; tel. (495) 120-13-21; Chair. V. S. PAVLOV.

Municipal Economy and Services Society: 103001 Moscow, Trekhprudny per. 11/13; tel. (495) 299-83-00; Chair. A. F. PORYADIN.

Russian Association of Sinologists: 117218 Moscow, Nakhimovsky pr. 32; tel. (495) 124-08-35; fax (495) 310-70-56; e-mail ifes@cemi.rssi.ru; f. 1992; 700 mems; attached to Russian Acad. of Sciences; Pres. V. S. MYASNIKOV.

EDUCATION

All-Russia 'Znanie' Society: 101990 Moscow, Novaya pl. 3/4; tel. (495) 621-90-58; fax (495) 625-42-49; e-mail znanie@znanie.org; internet www.znanie.org; f. 1947; co-founder of 30 non-govt instns of higher education and 40 instns or centres of additional education; publishes science-popular brochures and books, educational and methodical literature books for children and parents (incl. those on problems of prevention of drug addiction and AIDS), magazines; 120,000 mems; Pres. Prof. OLEG N. SMOLIN; publ. *New Knowledge* (online, 4 a year).

FINE AND PERFORMING ARTS

Russian Academy of Arts: 119034 Moscow, Ul. Prechistenka 21; tel. and fax (495) 201-39-71; f. 1757; depts of Painting (Academician-Sec. E. N. MAXIMOV), Sculpture (Academician-Sec. A. A. BICHUKOV), Graphic Art (Academician-Sec. M. P. MITURICH-KHLEBNIKOV), Decorative Arts (Academician-Sec. L. A. SOKOLOVA), Architecture and Monumental Art (Academician-Sec. M. M. POSOKHIN); attached research institutes: see Research Institutes; 218 mems (100 ordinary, 118 corresp.); library: see Libraries and Archives; Pres. Z. K. TSERETELY; Chief Learned Sec. M. M. KURILKO-RYUMIN; publ. *Informatsionny Byulleten* (Information Bulletin, 4 a year).

Russian Union of Composers: 125009 Moscow, per. Bryusova 8/10; tel. (495) 629-52-18; fax (495) 629-08-67; e-mail ubioncomposers@mail.ru; internet www.soyuzkompozitorov.ru; f. 1960; organizes music competitions and festivals; 1,600 mems; Chair. VLADISLAV KAZENIN; publs *Musical Life*, *Muzikalnaya Akademia*.

Theatre Union of the Russian Federation: 103009 Moscow, ul. Gorkogo 16/2; tel. (495) 229-91-52; 30,124 mems; library of 300,000 vols; Chair. M. A. ULYANOV; publ. *Problems of Contemporary Theatre*.

Union of Arts of the Russian Federation: 103062 Moscow, ul. Pokrovka 37.

Union of Russian Filmmakers: 123056 Moscow, Vasilevskaya 13; tel. (495) 251-53-

70; e-mail unikino3@aha.ru; internet www.unikino.ru; Chair. Nikita Mikhalkov.

HISTORY, GEOGRAPHY AND ARCHAEOLOGY

Russian Geographical Society: 190000 St Petersburg, tsentr, per. Grivtsova 10; tel. (812) 315-85-35; fax (812) 315-63-12; e-mail rgo@spb.org.ru; internet spb.org.ru/rgo; f. 1845; attached to Russian Acad. of Sciences; 20,000 mems; library of 470,000 vols, archive of 600,000 units; Pres. Prof. Sergei B. Lavrov; publ. *Izvestiya RGS* (6 a year).

LANGUAGE AND LITERATURE

Alliance Française: 191186 St Petersburg, ul. Zhukovskogo 16; tel. (812) 272-08-60; e-mail info@af.spb.ru; internet www.af.spb.ru; offers courses and exams in French language and culture and promotes cultural exchange with France; attached offices in Ekaterinburg, Irkutsk, Kazan, Nizhnii Novgorod, Novosibirsk, Rostov-on-Don, Samara and Yakutsk; Dir of School Galina Dragan.

British Council: 109189 Moscow, ul. Nikoloyamskaya 1; tel. (495) 782-02-00; fax (495) 782-02-01; e-mail bc.moscow@britishcouncil.ru; internet www.britishcouncil.ru; teaching centre; offers courses and exams in English language and British culture and promotes cultural exchange with the UK; attached centres in Ekaterinburg, Irkutsk, Krasnoyarsk, Nizhnii Novgorod, Novosibirsk, Rostov-on-Don, Samara, Sochi, Tomsk, Yaroslavl and Yuzhno-Sakhalinsk; Dir Adrian Greer; Training Centre Man. Clare Jeffs.

Instituto Cervantes: 121069 Moscow, Novinski bul. 20 bl. 1–2; tel. (495) 937-19-52; fax (495) 937-19-51; e-mail cenmos@cervantes.es; internet moscu.cervantes.es; offers courses and exams in Spanish language and culture and promotes cultural exchange with Spain and Spanish-speaking Latin and Central America; library of 12,000 vols; Dir Juan Carlos Vidal García.

International Community of Writers' Unions: 121825 Moscow, Povarskaya ul. 52; tel. (495) 291-63-07; f. 1992; 7,000 mems; Chair. G. M. Markov; First Sec. Timur Pulatov; publs *Inostrannaya Literatura* (12 a year), *Literaturnaya Gazeta* (52 a year), *Novyi Mir* (12 a year).

Press Society: 103051 Moscow, Petrovka 26; tel. (495) 921-82-98; Chair. B. A. Kuzmin.

Russian Association for Comparative Literature: 121069 Moscow, ul. Vorovskogo 25A; tel. (495) 290-17-09; attached to Russian Acad. of Sciences; Chair. Acad. Yu. B. Vipper.

Russian Linguistics Society: 103009 Moscow, ul. Semashko 1/12; attached to Russian Acad. of Sciences; Chair. Acad. T. V. Gamkrelidze.

Russian PEN Centre: 107031 Moscow, ul. Neglinnaya 18/1, str. 2; tel. (495) 625-27-18; fax (495) 625-35-73; e-mail penrussian@mail.ru; internet www.penrussia.org; f. 1989; protection of freedom of expression, int. exchange; writers in prison cttee; 355 mems; Pres. Andrei Bitov; Dir Mikhail Demchenkov; Deputy Dir Ekaterina Turchaninova.

Union of Writers of the Russian Federation: 119087 Moscow, Komsomolsky pr. 13; tel. (495) 246-43-50.

MEDICINE

Federation of Anaesthesiologists and Reanimatologists: 125284 Moscow, POB 87, Botkin Hospital K. 14; tel. and fax (495) 945-97-25; e-mail admin@far.org.ru; internet far.org.ru; f. 1991 (fmrly All-Union Society, f. 1959); 600 mems; Chair. I. Molchanov.

International Society for Pathophysiology: 125315 Moscow, ul. Baltiiskaya 8; tel. (095) 151-17-56; fax (095) 151-95-40; e-mail 4909.g23@g23.relcom.ru; internet home.ptt.ru/pathophysiology; f. 1991; 1,200 mems; Pres. Prof. Osmo Hänninen; Sec.-Gen. L. Szollar; publ. *Pathophysiology* (4 a year).

National Immunological Society: 115478 Moscow, Kashirskoe shosse 24/2; tel. (499) 611-83-33; fax (499) 616-10-27; f. 1983; 500 mems; Chair. R. V. Petrov; Gen. Sec. S. Yu. Sidorovich; publ. *Immunologiya* (6 a year).

National Medical and Technical Scientific Society: 129301 Moscow, ul. Kasatkina 3; tel. (495) 283-97-84; fax (495) 187-37-34; f. 1968; 55,000 mems and 512 orgs; library: Central State Scientific Medical Library of 3m. vols; Pres. B. I. Leonov; Chief Learned Sec. B. E. Belousov; publ. *Biomedical Engineering* (6 a year).

National Ophthalmological Society: 103064 Moscow, ul. Sadovo-Chernogryazskaya 14/19; Chair. E. S. Avetisov; Chief Learned Sec. T. I. Forofonofa; publ. *Vestnik oftalmologii* (6 a year).

National Pharmaceutical Society: 117418 Moscow, ul. Krasikova 34; Chair. M. T. Alyushin; Chief Learned Sec. R. S. Skulkova.

National Scientific Medical Society of Anatomists, Histologists and Embryologists: 117869 Moscow, ul. Ostrovityanova 1; Chair. V. V. Kupriyanov; Chief Learned Sec. V. V. Korolev.

National Scientific Medical Society of Endocrinologists: 117036 Moscow, ul. Dm. Ulyanova 11; Chair. V. G. Baranov; Chief Learned Sec. N. T. Starkova.

National Scientific Medical Society of Haematologists and Transfusiologists: 125167 Moscow, Novozykovskii pr. 4-a; Chair. V. N. Shabalin; Chief Learned Sec. M. P. Khokhlova.

National Scientific Medical Society of the History of Medicine: 101838 Moscow, Petrovirigskii per. 6/8; Chair. Yu. P. Lisitsyn; Chief Learned Sec. I. V. Vengrova.

National Scientific Medical Society of Hygienists: 103064 Moscow, Mechnikova per. 5; Chair. G. N. Serdyukovskaya; Chief Learned Sec. A. G. Sukharev.

National Scientific Medical Society of Infectionists: 125284 Moscow, 1 Botkinskii pr. 3; Chair. V. N. Nikiforov; Chief Learned Sec. N. M. Belyaeva.

National Scientific Medical Society of Nephrologists: 119021 Moscow, ul. Rossolimo 11-A; tel. (495) 248-53-33; f. 1969; holding of conferences, congresses, symposia; 1,200 mems; Chair. N. A. Mukhin; Chief Learned Sec. S. O. Androsova.

Serbsky National Research Centre for Social and Forensic Psychiatry: 119992 Moscow, Kropotkinsky per. 23; tel. (495) 637-52-62; fax (495) 637-72-31; e-mail international@serbsky.ru; internet serbsky.ru; Dir Prof. Zurab I. Kekelidze (acting).

National Scientific Medical Society of Obstetricians and Gynaecologists: 113163 Moscow, ul. Shabolovka 57; Chair. G. M. Saveleva; Chief Learned Sec. T. V. Chervakova.

National Scientific Medical Society of Oto-Rhino-Laryngologists: 119435 Moscow, Bol. Pirogovskaya 6; Chair. N. A. Preobrazhenskii; Chief Learned Sec. N. P. Konstantinova.

National Scientific Medical Society of Paediatricians: 117963 Moscow, Lomonosovskii pr. 2/62; Chair M. Yu. Studenikin; Chief Learned Sec. G. V. Yatsyk.

National Scientific Medical Society of Phthisiologists: 107564 Moscow, platforma Yauza, ul. 6 km Severnoi Zheleznoi Dorogi; Chair. A. G. Khomenko; Chief Learned Sec. V. V. Erokhin.

National Scientific Medical Society of Physical Therapists and Health-Resort Physicians: 121099 Moscow, Kalinina pr. 50; Chair. A. N. Obrosov; Chief Learned Sec. V. D. Grigoreva.

National Scientific Medical Society of Physicians-Analysts: 123242 Moscow, ul. Sadovaya-Kudrinskaya 3; Chair. B. F. Korovkin; Chief Learned Sec. R. L. Martsishevskaya.

National Scientific Medical Society of Physicians in Curative Physical Culture and Sports Medicine: 117963 Moscow, Lomonosovskii pr. 2/62; Chair. S. V. Kruzshev; Chief Learned Sec. A. V. Sokova.

National Scientific Medical Society of Roentgenologists and Radiologists: 117837 Moscow, ul. Profsoyuznaya 86; Chair. A. S. Pavlov; Chief Learned Sec. V. Z. Agranat.

National Scientific Medical Society of Stomatologists: 119435 Moscow, ul. Pogodinskaya 5; Chair. N. N. Bazhanov; Chief Learned Sec. V. M. Bezrukov.

National Scientific Medical Society of Surgeons: 119874 Moscow, Abrikosovskii per. 2; Chair. B. V. Petrovskii; Chief Learned Sec. M. I. Perelman.

National Scientific Medical Society of Therapists: 121500 Moscow, 3 Cherepkovskaya 15; Chair. A. S. Smetnev; Chief Learned Sec. B. A. Sidorenko.

National Scientific Medical Society of Traumatic Surgeons and Orthopaedists: 125299 Moscow, ul. Priorova 10; tel. (495) 450-24-72; fax (495) 154-31-39; f. 1921; Chair. S. P. Mironov; Chief Learned Sec. V. V. Trotsenko; publ. *N. N. Priorov Journal of Traumatology and Orthopaedics* (4 a year).

National Scientific Medical Society of Urological Surgeons: 105483 Moscow, ul. 3-ya Parkovaya 51; tel. (495) 367-62-62; fax (495) 164-76-60; e-mail urology@cdromclub.ru; f. 1925; 5,506 mems; Chair. N. A. Lopatkin; Chief Learned Sec. L. M. Gorilovski; publ. *Urology and Nephrology* (6 a year).

National Scientific Medical Society of Venereologists and Dermatologists: 107076 Moscow, Korolenko str. 3, bldg 6; tel. and fax (495) 964-26-20; e-mail info@cnikvi.ru; f. 1921; Chair. A. A. Kubanova; Chief Learned Sec. I. N. Lesnaya.

Russian Academy of Medical Sciences: 109801 Moscow, ul. Solyanka 14; tel. (095) 298-21-37; fax (095) 921-56-15; e-mail orlov@ramn.ru; f. 1944; depts of Preventive Medicine (Academician-Sec. N. F. Izmerov), Clinical Medicine (Academician-Sec. E. I. Gusev), Medical and Biological Sciences (Academician-Sec. K. V. Sudakov); Siberian dept (Academician-Sec. V. A. Trufakin), Northwest dept (Academician-Sec. B. I. Tkachenko); 496 mems (191 ordinary, 232 corresp., 73 foreign); 60 specialist research ccls; attached research institutes: see Research Institutes; library: see Libraries and Archives; Pres. V. I. Pokrovsky; Gen. Sec. V. A. Tutelian; publs *Vesti Meditsyny* (Medical News), *Vestnik Rossiiskoi Akademii Meditsinskikh Nauk* (Journal of the Russian Academy of Medical Sciences), *Arkhiv Patologii* (Pathology Archive), *Byulleten Eksperimentalnoi Biologii i Meditsiny* (Bulletin of Experimental Biology and Medicine), *Voprosy Virusologii* (Problems in Virology), *Voprosy Meditsinskoi Khimii* (Problems in Medical Chemistry), *Immunologiya* (Immunology), *Meditsinskaya Radiologiya* (Medical Radiology and Radiation Safety), *Morfologia* (Morphology), *Patologicheskaya Fiziologiya i Eksperimentalnaya Terapiya* (Pathological Physiology and Experimental Therapy), *Eksperimentalnaya i Klinicheskaya Pharmakologiya* (Experimental and Clinical Pharmacology), *Byulleten Sibirskogo Otdeleniya Rossiiskoi AMN* (Bulletin of the Siberian Division of the Russian Academy of Medical Sciences).

Russian Gastroenterological Association: 119881 Moscow, ul. Pogodinskaya 5; tel. (495) 248-38-00; fax (495) 248-36-10; f. 1995; 2,500 mems; Pres. Prof. Dr V. T. IVASHKIN; Sec. Dr A. S. TRUKHMANOV; publs *Journal of Gastroenterology, Hepatology and Coloproctology* (6 a year).

Russian Medical Association: 125315 Moscow, ul. Baltiskaya 10/3; tel. (495) 151-27-67; fax (495) 151-55-25; e-mail rmass@online.ru; internet www.rmass.ru; f. 1993; 262,000 mems; Chair. Prof. A. G. SARKISIAN; Learned Sec. Dr LEV MALYSHEV; publ. *Vrachebnaya Gazeta* (12 a month).

Russian Neurosurgical Association: 603600 Nizhnii Novgorod, Verkhne-Volskaya nab. 18; tel. (8312) 46-36-48; fax (8312) 36-05-95; Pres. A. P. FRAERMAN; Sec. S. N. KOLESOV.

Russian Oncological Society (St Petersburg branch): 197758 St Petersburg, pos. Pesochnyi-2, ul. Leningradskaya 68; tel. (812) 596-86-54; fax (812) 596-89-47; f. 1954; 460 mems; Chair. Prof. Dr VLADIMIR F. SEMIGLAZOV; Sec.-Gen. Dr EVGENIA V. TSYRLINA; publ. *Voprosi oncologii* (6 a year).

Russian Pharmacology Society: 125315 Moscow, ul. Baltiyskaya 8; tel. (495) 151-18-81; fax (495) 151-12-61; f. 1958 (fmrly All-Union Scientific Medical Soc. of Pharmacologists); 295 mems; library of 10,000 vols; Chair. SERGEY SEREDENIN; Sec.-Gen. ELENA VALDMAN; publ. *Russian Journal of Experimental and Clinical Pharmacology* (in Russian).

Russian Rheumatological Association: 115522 Moscow, Kashirskoye shosse 34A; tel. (495) 114-44-90; fax (495) 114-44-68; e-mail sokrat@irramn.ru; internet www.rheumatolog.ru; f. 1928; 1,860 mems; library of 102,000 vols; Chair. E. NASONOV; Gen. Sec. I. ALEXEEVA; publ. *Clinical-practical Rheumatology* (6 a year).

Russian Society of Medical Genetics: 115478 Moscow, Moskvorechie ul. 1; tel. (499) 612-86-07; fax (495) 324-07-02; e-mail mgnc@med-gen.ru; internet www.med-gen.ru; f. 1993; human genome project, human genetics, cytogenetics, clinical genetics, genetic counselling, experimental genetics, ecogenetics and human molecular genetics; 500 mems; Chair. E. K. GINTER; Chief Learned Sec. V. L. IZHEVSKAYA; publ. *Medical Genetics* (12 a year).

Russian Society of Toxicologists: 117105 Moscow, 19A, Varshavskoye shosse; tel. (495) 633-95-90; fax (495) 633-16-84; e-mail khalidiya@yandex.ru; internet www.rpohv.ru; f. 1996; represents Russian toxicologists in int. orgs; contributes information on advanced studies and achievements among toxicologists in Russia; 200 mems; Chair. Dr B. A. KURLYANDSKIY; Exec. Sec. Dr KHALIDYA KHAMIDULINA; publ. *Toxicological Review*.

Scientific Medical Society of Anatomists-Pathologists: 109801 Moscow, ul. Bolshaya Serpuhovskaya 27; Chair. D. S. SARKISOV.

Society of Cardiology: 101953 Moscow, Petroverigskii ul. 10; tel. (495) 623-86-36; e-mail info@cardiosite.ru; internet www.cardiosite.ru; f. 1963; cardiology, diagnosis, treatment and prevention of cardiovascular disease; training courses; 188 mems; Pres. Dr RAFAEL OGANOV; Sec.-Gen. Prof. SVETLANA A. SHALNOVA; publs *Cardiovascular Therapy and Prevention* (6 a year), *Russian Journal of Cardiology* (6 a year).

NATURAL SCIENCES

General

Moscow House of Scientists: 119821 Moscow, Kropotkinskaya ul. 16; tel. (495) 201-45-55; attached to Russian Acad. of Sciences; Dir A. I. DERGACHEV.

St Petersburg M. Gorky House of Scientists: 191065 St Petersburg, Dvortsovaya nab. 26; tel. (812) 315-88-14; attached to Russian Acad. of Sciences; Dir L. M. ANISIMOVA.

Biological Sciences

Biochemical Society: c/o Prof. M. B. Agalarova, Ovchinnikov Institute of Bio-organic Chemistry, 117871 Moscow, Miklukho-Maklaya 16/10; tel. and fax (495) 724-81-44; e-mail biosoc@mail.ibch.ru; f. 1959; attached to Russian Acad. of Sciences; 6,500 mems; Pres. Acad. A. G. GABIBOV; Sec. Gen. MARIA B. AGALAROVA.

Biotechnology Society: 109044 Moscow, Bol. Kommunisticheskaya ul. 27; tel. (495) 272-67-49; Chair. V. E. MATVEYEV.

Hydrobiological Society: 103050 Moscow, Tverskaya ul. 27; tel. (495) 299-65-04; attached to Russian Acad. of Sciences; Pres. L. M. SUSHCHENYA.

Interregional Russian Microbiological Society: 117312 Moscow, pr. 60-letiya Oktyabrya 7, korp. 2; tel. (499) 135-01-80; fax (499) 135-65-30; e-mail microbsociety@inmi.host.ru; internet www.inmi.ru/microbsociety/news.htm; f. 2004; attached to Russian Acad. of Sciences; 580 mems; Pres. V. F. GALCHENKO.

Moscow Society of Naturalists: 103009 Moscow, ul. Gertsena 6; tel. (495) 203-67-04; f. 1805; sections for zoology, botany, geology, hydrobiology, geography, biophysics, palaeontology, histology, experimental morphology, genetics, etc.; 2,700 mems; library of 500,000 vols; Chair A. L. YANSHIN; publ. *Byulleten Moskovskogo Obshchestva Ispytatelei prirody* (6 a year).

Palaeontological Society: 199106 St Petersburg, Sredny Prospect 74; tel. (812) 328-91-56; fax (812) 321-30-23; e-mail po_ran@vsegei.ru; f. 1916; attached to Russian Acad. of Sciences; 720 mems; Pres. Acad. B. S. SOKOLOV.

Russian Botanical Society: 197376 St Petersburg, ul. Prof. Popova 2; tel. (812) 346-47-53; fax (812) 234-45-12; attached to Russian Acad. of Sciences; Pres. R. V. KAMELIN.

Russian Entomological Society: 199034 St Petersburg, Universitetskaya nab. 1; tel. (812) 328-12-12; fax (812) 114-04-14; e-mail reo@zisp.spb.su; f. 1859; attached to Russian Acad. of Sciences; 2,000 mems; library of 80,000 vols; Pres. G. S. MEDVEDEV; publs *Chtenia pamyati N.A. Kholodkovskogo* (1 a year), *Entomologicheskoe obozrenie* (4 a year), *Trudy Russkogo Entomologicheskogo Obschestva* (irregular).

Russian Society of Geneticists and Breeders: 117312 Moscow, ul. Fersmana 11, korp. 2; tel. (495) 124-59-52; attached to Russian Acad. of Sciences; Pres. Acad. V. A. STRUNNIKOV.

Society of Helminthologists: 117259 Moscow, Bol. Cheremushkinskaya 28; attached to Russian Acad. of Sciences; Pres. A. S. BESSONOV.

Society of Ornithologists: c/o Russian Academy of Sciences, 117901 Moscow, Leninsky pr. 14; attached to Russian Acad. of Sciences; Pres. V. D. ILICHEV.

Society of Protozoologists: 194064 St Petersburg, Tikhoretsky pr. 4; tel. (812) 247-18-36; fax (812) 247-03-41; e-mail tamara@tb10336.spb.edu; f. 1968 as All-Union Society of Protozoologists; present name 1991; attached to Russian Acad. of Sciences; 200 mems; Pres. (vacant); Sec.-Gen. Prof. Dr TAMARA V. BEYER; publs *Protistology* (4 a year), *Tsitologiya* (Cytology, in Russian with English summaries, 12 a year).

Physical Sciences

Astronomical and Geodesical Society: 103001 Moscow, Sadovo-Kudrinskaya ul. 24; attached to Russian Acad. of Sciences; Pres. YU. D. BULANZHE.

Ferrous Metallurgy Society: 129812 Moscow, pr. Mira 101; tel. (495) 287-83-80; Chair. N. I. DROZDOV.

Gubkin, Acad. I. M., Petroleum and Gas Society: 117876 Moscow, 12-ya Parkovaya ul. 5; tel. (495) 463-93-72; Chair. S. T. TOPLOV.

Mendeleev, D. I., Chemical Society: 101907 Moscow, Krivokolennyi per. 12; tel. (495) 928-43-51; fax (495) 928-43-54; f. 1868; 45 regional orgs; 1,800 mems; Sec.-Gen. NATATYA KOSSINOVA; publs *Chemistry in Russia* (12 a year bulletin), *Russian Chemical Journal* (6 a year).

Russian Geological Society: 113191 Moscow, 2-aya Roshinskaya ul. 10; tel. (495) 954-96-34; fax (495) 954-96-22; f. 1988; 1,025 mems; Pres. V. P. ORLOV.

Russian Mineralogical Society: 199026 St Petersburg, 21st line 2; tel. and fax (812) 328-86-40; e-mail rmo@minsoc.ru; internet www.minsoc.ru; f. 1817; attached to Russian Acad. of Sciences; mineralogy and adjacent sciences; 1,200 mems; library of 85,000 vols; Pres. Prof. DMITRY RUNDQVIST; Vice-Pres. Prof. YURI MARIN; publ. *Zapiski RMO (Proceedings of the Russian Mineralogical Society)*.

Society of Non-Ferrous Metallurgy: 103001 Moscow, Sadovaya-Kudrinskaya ul. 18; tel. (495) 291-29-87; Chair. V. S. LOBANOV.

PHILOSOPHY AND PSYCHOLOGY

Russian Philosophical Society: 119991 Moscow, ul. Volhonka 14, Room 102; tel. (495) 609-90-76; e-mail rphs@iph.ras.ru; internet www.dialog21.ru; f. 1971; attached to Russian Acad. of Sciences; 6,131 mems; Pres. V. S. STEPIN; Vice-Pres. A. N. CHUMAKOV; publ. *Bulletin of the Russian Philosophical Society*.

Society of Psychologists: 129366 Moscow, Yaroslavskaya ul. 13; tel. (495) 282-45-03; attached to Russian Acad. of Sciences; Chair. E. V. SHOROKHOVA.

RELIGION, SOCIOLOGY AND ANTHROPOLOGY

Russian Society of Sociologists: 117259 Moscow, ul. Krzhizhanovskogo 24/35 str. 5; tel. (495) 719-09-71; fax (495) 719-07-40; e-mail mansurov@isras.rssi.ru; internet www.isras.rssi.ru; f. 1989; attached to Russian Acad. of Sciences; 1,350 mems; Chair. VALERY A. MANSUROV.

TECHNOLOGY

Aircraft Building Society: 125040 Moscow, Leningradskii pr. 24a; tel. (495) 214-22-88; Chair. A. M. BATKOV.

Civil Engineering Society: 103062 Moscow, Podsosensky per. 25; tel. (495) 297-07-29; Chair. I. I. ISHENKO.

Computers and Informatics Society: 127486 Moscow, Deguninskaya ul. 1, korp. 4; tel. (495) 487-31-61; Chair. I. N. BUKREYEV.

Mapping and Prospecting Engineering Society: 117801 Moscow, ul. Krzhizhanovskogo 14, korp. 2; tel. (495) 124-35-60; Chair. A. A. DRAZHNYUK.

Mechanical Engineering Society: 109004 Moscow, ul. Zemlyanoi Val 64, korp. 1; tel. (495) 297-93-00; Chair. B. N. SOKOLOV.

Mining Engineers' Society: 103006 Moscow, Karetnyi ryad 10/18; tel. (495) 299-88-15; Chair. A. P. FISUN.

Popov, A. S., Radio Engineering, Electronics and Telecommunications Society: 103897 Moscow, Kuznetskii Most 20/6; tel. (495) 921-71-08; Chair. YU. V. GULYAEV.

Power and Electrical Power Engineering Society: 191025 St Petersburg, Stremyannaya ul. 10; tel. (812) 311-32-77; Chair. N. N. TIKHODEYEV.

Scientific-Technical Association: 198103 St Petersburg, pr. Ogorodnikova 26; tel. (812) 251-28-50; attached to Russian Acad. of Sciences; General Dir M. L. ALEKSANDROV.

Shipbuilding Engineering Society: 191011 St Petersburg, Nevskii pr. 44; tel. (495) 315-50-27; Chair. I. V. GORYNIN.

Society of the Food Industry: 103031 Moscow, Kuznetskii Most 19, pod. 2; tel. (495) 924-49-30; Chair. A. N. BOGATYREV.

Society of the Instrument Manufacturing Industry and Metrologists: 103009 Moscow, Tverskaya ul. 12, str. 2; tel. (495) 209-47-98; Chair. G. I. KAVALEROV.

Society of Light Industry: 117846 Moscow, ul. Vavilova 69; tel. (495) 134-90-01; Chair. R. A. CHAYANOV.

Vavilov, S. I., Society of Instrument Manufacturers: 121019 Moscow, Mokhovaya ul. 17, str. 2; tel. (495) 203-34-65.

Water Transport Society: 103012 Moscow, Staropansky per. 3; tel. (495) 921-18-12; Chair. (vacant).

Research Institutes

AGRICULTURE, FISHERIES AND VETERINARY SCIENCE

Adygea Agricultural Research Institute: 352764 Krasnodar krai, Maikop, Podgornoe; attached to Russian Acad. of Agricultural Sciences.

Afanasev, V. A., Research Institute of Fur-Bearing Animals and Rabbits: 140143 Moscow oblast, Ramensky raion, p/o Rodniki; tel. (495) 501-53-55; fax (495) 501-53-55; f. 1932; attached to Russian Acad. of Agricultural Sciences; Dir N. A. BALAKIREV.

Agrarian Institute: 103064 Moscow, Bol. Kharitonevskaya per. 21, korp. 2, POB 34; tel. (495) 207-70-75; fax (495) 928-22-90; e-mail agrin@glas.apc.org; f. 1990; attached to Russian Acad. of Agricultural Sciences; Dir Dr A. V. PETRIKOV.

Agricultural Research Institute for the Central Areas of the Non-Black Soil (Nechernozem) Zone: 143104 Moscow oblast, Odintsovsky raion, Nemchinovka, ul. Agrokhimikov 6; tel. (495) 591-83-91; attached to Russian Acad. of Agricultural Sciences.

Agrophysical Research Institute: 195220 St Petersburg, Grazhdanskii Pr.14; tel. (495) 543-46-30; attached to Russian Acad. of Agricultural Sciences; Dir I. B. USKOV.

All-Russia Horticulture Institute for Breeding, Agrotechnology and Nursery: 115598 Moscow, Birulevo-Zagorie, ul. Zagorievskogo; tel. and fax (495) 329-51-66; e-mail vstisp@vstisp.org; internet www.vstisp.org; attached to Russian Acad. of Agricultural Sciences; Dir IVAN KULIKOV; publ. *Fruit Trees and Small Fruits of Russia* (2 a year).

All-Russia Institute of Plant Protection: 196608 St Petersburg, Pushkin, shosse Podbelskogo 3; tel. (812) 470-43-84; fax (812) 470-51-10; e-mail vizrspb@mail333.com; internet www.vizrspb.chat.ru; f. 1929; attached to Russian Acad. of Agricultural Sciences; Dir V. A. PAVLYUSHIN; publ. *Plant Protection News* (3 a year).

All-Russia Legumes and Pulse Crops Research Institute: 302502 Orel, P/O Streletskoe; tel. (0862) 403-224; fax (0862) 403-130; e-mail office@vniizbk.orel.ru; attached to Russian Acad. of Agricultural Sciences; Dir Prof. V. I. ZOTIKOV.

All-Russia Maize Research Institute: 860022 Nalchik, ul. Mechnikova 130A; tel. (86622) 5-03-16; attached to Russian Acad. of Agricultural Sciences.

All-Russia Meat Research Institute: 109316 Moscow, ul. Talilikhina 26; tel. (495) 276-95-11; fax (495) 276-95-51; e-mail vniimp@glasnet.ru; f. 1930; attached to Russian Acad. of Agricultural Sciences; Dir L. A. BORISOVICH.

All-Russia Potato Research Institute: 140052 Moscow oblast, Lyuberetsky raion, pos. Korenevo, ul. Lorkha; tel. (495) 557-10-11; fax (495) 557-10-11; f. 1930; attached to Russian Acad. of Agricultural Sciences; library of 500,000 vols; Dir Prof. A. V. KORSHUNOV.

All-Russia Poultry Research and Technology Institute: Moscow oblast, Sergiev pos.; attached to Russian Acad. of Agricultural Sciences.

All-Russia Rapeseed Research and Technological Institute: 398037 Lipetsk, Boevoi pr. 26, kod 074; tel. (0742) 26-08-64; attached to Russian Acad. of Agricultural Sciences.

All-Russia Research and Technological Institute for Chemical Land Reclamation: 189520 St Petersburg, Pushkin, ul. Lermontova 9; tel. (812) 465-58-75; attached to Russian Acad. of Agricultural Sciences.

All-Russia Research and Technological Institute for Chemicalization in Agriculture: 143013 Moscow oblast, Odinstsovsky raion, Nemchinovka, ul. Agrokhimikov 6; tel. (495) 591-91-73; attached to Russian Acad. of Agricultural Sciences.

All-Russia Research and Technological Institute for Mechanization in Livestock Raising: 142004 Moscow oblast, Podolsky raion, p/o Znamya Oktyabrya; 31; tel. (495) 119-74-97; fax (495) 119-75-17; f. 1969; attached to Russian Acad. of Agricultural Sciences; Dir N. M. MOROZOV; publ. *Scientific Research Problems of Mechanization and Automation of Livestock Farming.*

All-Russia Research and Technological Institute for Organic Fertilizers: 601242 Vladimir oblast, Vyatkino; attached to Russian Acad. of Agricultural Sciences.

All-Russia Research Institute for Agricultural Biotechnology: 127550 Moscow, Timiryazevskaya ul. 42; tel. (495) 976-65-44; fax (495) 977-09-47; e-mail iab@iab.ac.ru; internet www.agrobiotech.ru; f. 1974; attached to Russian Acad. of Agricultural Sciences; Dir P. N. KHARCHENKO.

All-Russia Research Institute for Agricultural Economics and Standards and Norms: 344006 Rostov on Don, pr. Sokolova 52; tel. (8632) 65-31-81; fax (8632) 64-89-61; f. 1980; attached to Russian Acad. of Agricultural Sciences; Dir Dr VLADIMIR V. KUZNETSOV.

All-Russia Research Institute for Beef Cattle Breeding and Production: Orenburg, Yanvarskaya ul. 29; attached to Russian Acad. of Agricultural Sciences.

All-Russia Research Institute for Biological Control: 350039 Krasnodar, a/ya 39; tel. (8612) 50-81-91; attached to Russian Acad. of Agricultural Sciences.

All-Russia Research Institute for Cybernetics in the Agro-industrial Complex: 117218 Moscow, ul. Krzhizhanovskogo 14/1; tel. (495) 124-76-02; attached to Russian Acad. of Agricultural Sciences.

All-Russia Research Institute for Economics, Labour and Management in Agriculture: 111621 Moscow, Orenburgskaya ul. 15; tel. (495) 550-06-71; attached to Russian Acad. of Agricultural Sciences.

All-Russia Research Institute for Electrification in Agriculture: 109456 Moscow, 1-i Veshnyakovskii pr. 2; tel. (499) 171-19-20; fax (499) 170-51-01; e-mail viesh@dol.ru; internet www.viesh.ru; f. 1930; attached to Russian Acad. of Agricultural Sciences; rural energy and electrification, solar energy biomass and wind energy; library of 135,000 vols; Dir Acad. D. S. STREBKOV; publ. *Scientific Proceedings* (2 a year).

All-Russia Research Institute for Farm Animal Genetics and Breeding: 196600 St Petersburg-Pushkin, Moskovskoye shosse 55a; tel. (812) 470-76-63; fax (812) 465-99-89; e-mail spbvniigen@mail.ru; attached to Russian Acad. of Agricultural Sciences; Dir Acad. P.N. PROCHORENKO.

All-Russia Research Institute for Floriculture and Subtropical Crops: 354002 Sochi, Jan Fabriziusa str. 2/28; tel. (8622) 96-40-21; fax (8622) 46-80-16; e-mail subplod@mail.ru; f. 1894; attached to Russian Acad. of Agricultural Sciences; library of 77,000 vols.

All-Russia Research Institute for Horse Breeding: 391105 Ryazan oblast, Rybnoyek raion; tel. (0912) 24-02-65; fax (0912) 24-02-65; internet www.ruhorses.ru; f. 1930; attached to Russian Acad. of Agricultural Sciences; library of 47,000 vols; Dir Prof. Dr V. V. KALASHNIKOV; publs *Stud Book* (every 4 years, with 1 a year supplement), *Scientific Works* (1 a year).

All-Russia Research Institute for Irrigated Arable Farming: 400002 Volgograd, Timiryazevskaya ul. 9; tel. (8442) 43-49-79; fax (8442) 43-34-75; e-mail vniioz@avtlg.ru; f. 1967; attached to Russian Acad. of Agricultural Sciences; library of 138,000 vols; Dir Dr V. V. MELIKHOV.

All-Russia Research Institute for Irrigated Horticulture and Vegetable Crops Production: 416300 Astrakhan oblast, Kamyziak, ul. Lubicha 13; attached to Russian Acad. of Agricultural Sciences.

All-Russia Research Institute for Mechanization in Agriculture: 109389 Moscow, 1-i Institutskii pr. 5; tel. (495) 171-19-33; attached to Russian Acad. of Agricultural Sciences; Dir Acad. V. A. KUIBYSHEV.

All-Russia Research Institute for Sheep and Goat Breeding: 355014 Stavropol, Zootekhnichesky per. 15; tel. (8652) 34-76-88; fax (8652) 34-76-88; f. 1932; attached to Russian Acad. of Agricultural Sciences; Dir. Prof. VASILY MOROZ.

All-Russia Research Institute for the Agricultural Use of Reclaimed and Improved Land: 170530 Tver oblast, Emmaus; tel. (0822) 37-15-46; fax (0822) 36-

07-63; e-mail vniimz@mail.ru; internet www.vniimz.newmail; f. 1977; attached to Russian Acad. of Agricultural Sciences; library of 20,000 vols; Dir Dr N. KOVALEV.

All-Russia Research Institute for the Biosynthesis of Protein Substances: 109004 Moscow, Bol. Kommunisticheskaya 27; tel. (495) 912-70-09; fax (495) 911-39-23; e-mail belok@rutenia.ru; attached to Russian Acad. of Agricultural Sciences; Dir Dr ALEXANDER P. ZAKHARYCHEV.

All-Russia Research Institute for Vegetable Breeding and Seed Production: 143080 Moscow oblast, Odintsovsky raion, Lesnoi gorodok; tel. (495) 599-24-42; fax (495) 599-22-77; e-mail vniissok@cea.ru; f. 1920; attached to Russian Acad. of Agricultural Sciences; Dir. Prof. VICTOR F. PIVOVAROV.

All-Russia Research Institute for Veterinary Sanitation, Hygiene and Ecology: 123022 Moscow, Zvenigorodskoe shosse 5; tel. (495) 256-35-81; attached to Russian Acad. of Agricultural Sciences.

All-Russia Research Institute of Agricultural Microbiology: 189620 St Petersburg, Pushkin 8, shosse Podbelskogo 3; tel. (812) 470-51-00; fax (812) 470-43-62; f. 1930; attached to Russian Acad. of Agricultural Sciences; Dir Prof. I. A. TIKHONOVICH.

All-Russia Research Institute of Animal Husbandry: 142023 Moscow oblast, Podolskii raion, pos. Dubrovitsy; tel. (495) 546-63-35; attached to Russian Acad. of Agricultural Sciences; Dir Acad. A. P. KALASHNIKOV.

All-Russia Research Institute of Arable Farming and Soil Erosion Control: 305021 Kursk, ul. Karla Marksa 70B; tel. (0712) 53-42-56; fax (0712) 53-67-29; e-mail vnizem@kursknet.ru; f. 1970; attached to Russian Acad. of Agricultural Sciences; library of 20,000 vols, 40 periodicals; Dir G. N. CHERKASOV.

All-Russia Research Institute of Economics in Agriculture: 123007 Moscow, Khoroshevskoe shosse 35, korp 3; tel. (495) 195-60-16; attached to Russian Acad. of Agricultural Sciences; Dir I. G. USHCHACHEV.

All-Russia Research Institute of Information, Technological and Economic Research on the Agro-Industrial Complex: c/o Russian Academy of Agricultural Sciences, 107814 Moscow, Bolshoi Kharitonevsky per. 21; attached to Russian Acad. of Agricultural Sciences; Dir Acad. V. I. NAZARENKO.

All-Russia Research Institute of Marine Fisheries and Oceanography: 107140 Moscow, Verkhnyaya Krasnoselskaya 17; tel. (495) 264-93-87; Dir A. S. BOGDANOV.

All-Russia Research Institute of Medicinal and Aromatic Plants: 113628 Moscow, ul. Grina 7; tel. (495) 382-83-18; attached to Russian Acad. of Agricultural Sciences.

All-Russia Research Institute of Phytopathology: 143050 Moscow oblast, Vyazemy; tel. (495) 592-92-87; attached to Russian Acad. of Agricultural Sciences.

All-Russia Research Institute of Pond Fishery: 141821 Moscow oblast, Dmitrovsky raion, p/o Rubnoe; tel. (495) 587-21-98; attached to Russian Acad. of Agricultural Sciences.

All-Russia Research Institute of Tobacco, Makhorka and Tobacco Products: 350072 Krasnodar, Moskovskaya ul. 42; tel. (861) 252-08-82; attached to Russian Acad. of Agricultural Sciences; Dir V. A. SALOMATIN.

All-Russia Rice Research Institute: 353204 Krasnodar krai, Dinskoi raion, pos. Belozernoe; tel. (8612) 56-65-96; fax (8612) 50-91-24; attached to Russian Min. of Agriculture; Dir Prof. E. P. ALESHIN.

All-Russia Vegetable Production Research Institute: 141018 Moscow oblast, Mytishchi, Novomytishchinsky pr. 82; tel. (495) 582-00-15; attached to Russian Acad. of Agricultural Sciences.

All-Russia Veterinary Research Institute for Poultry Diseases: St Petersburg, Moskovsky pr. 99; attached to Russian Acad. of Agricultural Sciences.

All-Russian Plant Quarantine Centre: 140150 Moscow oblast, Ramensky raion, pos. Bykovo, Pogranichnaya 32; tel. (499) 271-38-24; fax (495) 785-76-13; e-mail vniikr@mail.ru; internet www.vniikr.ru; f. 1979; plant quarantine research and diagnostics; library of 10,000 vols; Dir Dr ULLUBY MAGOMEDOV; Deputy Dir Dr NATALYA SHEROKOLAVA; Deputy Dir Dr MUZAFAR ABASOV; Deputy Dir Dr VERA IAKOVLEVA; publ. *Problems of Plant Quarantine*.

Altai Experimental Farm: 659739 Altai krai, Gorno-Altaisky autonomous oblast, Shebalinsky raion, selo Cherga; attached to Russian Acad. of Sciences; Dir YU. S. ZEMIROV.

Bashkir Research and Technological Institute for Animal Husbandry and Feed Production: Bashkortostan, 450025 Ufa, Pushkinskaya ul. 86; tel. (3472) 22-17-23; attached to Russian Acad. of Agricultural Sciences.

Bashkir Research Institute for Arable Farming and Field Crops Breeding: 450059 Ufa, ul. Zorge 19; tel. (3472) 24-07-08; attached to Russian Acad. of Agricultural Sciences.

Caspian Research Institute for Arid Arable Farming: 431213 Astrakhan, Solenoe zaimishche; tel. (851) 24-38-36; fax (851) 192-17-00; f. 1991; attached to Russian Acad. of Agricultural Sciences; library of 30,000 vols.

Chelyabinsk Agricultural Research Institute: 436404 Chelyabinsk oblast, Chebarkulsky raion, Timiryazevsky; tel. (35168) 33-23-16; attached to Russian Acad. of Agricultural Sciences.

Dagestan Agricultural Research Institute: 367014 Makhachkala, pr. K. Marksa, Nauchnyi park; tel. (8722) 3-66-60; attached to Russian Acad. of Agricultural Sciences.

Don Zone Agricultural Research Institute: 346714 Rostov oblast, Aksai raion, Rassvet; attached to Russian Acad. of Agricultural Sciences.

Flax Research Institute: 172060 Tverskii raion, Torzhok, ul. Lunacharskogo 35; tel. (08251) 5-16-45; fax (08251) 5-44-58; e-mail vniil@tver.dep.ru; f. 1930; library of 50,000 vols; Dir ANATOLI N. MARCHENKOV; publ. *Trudy VNIL* (1 a year).

Forest Research Institute of the Karelian Research Centre: 185910 Petrozavodsk, Pushkinskaya ul. 11; tel. and fax (8142) 76-81-60; e-mail forest@krc.karelia.ru; internet forestry.krc.karelia.ru; f. 1957; attached to Russian Acad. of Sciences; Dir Dr VITALY KRUTOV.

Institute of Forest Research: 143030 Moscow oblast, Odintsovsky raion, p/o Uspenskoe; tel. (495) 419-52-57; fax (495) 419-52-57; f. 1958; attached to Russian Acad. of Sciences; library of 51,400 vols; Dir Prof. S. E. VOMPERSKY; publ. *Lesovedenie* (Russian Forest Science, 6 a year).

Institute of Forestry: 620134 Ekaterinburg, Bilimbaevskaya ul. 32A; tel. (3432) 52-08-80; attached to Russian Acad. of Sciences; Dir. S. A. MAMAEV.

Institute of Soil Science and Agrochemistry: 630099 Novosibirsk, Sovetskaya St. 18; tel. (3832) 22-50-88; fax (3832) 22-76-52; e-mail go2siberia@gmail.com; internet www.siberia-eco.org; f. 1968; attached to Russian Acad. of Sciences; education and research soil science, plant nutrition, pedology, soil chemistry, soil microbiology, int. field courses, summer schools in Siberia, int. annual soil-ecological excursions in Siberia; Dir Dr KONSTANTIN S. BAYKOV; Scientific Sec. for Int. Cooperation Dr PAVEL A. BARSUKOV.

Kovalenko, Ya. R., All-Russia Institute of Experimental Veterinary Science: 109472 Moscow, Kuzminki; tel. (495) 377-29-79; attached to Russian Acad. of Agricultural Sciences; Dir G. F. KOROMYSLOV.

Krasnodar Scientific Research Institute of the Storage and Processing of Agricultural Produce: 350072 Krasnodar, Topolinskaya ul. 2; tel. (8612) 57-95-93; fax (8612) 57-98-44; e-mail kisp@kubannet.ru; attached to Russian Acad. of Agricultural Sciences.

Krasnodar Scientific Research Institute of Vegetable and Potato Production: 350921 Krasnodar Belozerny; tel. (8612) 229-54-90; f. 1931; attached to Russian Acad. of Agricultural Sciences; library of 10,000 vols.

Kursk Research Institute of the Agro-industrial Complex: 307026 Kursk oblast, Cheremushki; attached to Russian Acad. of Agricultural Sciences.

Lukianenko, P. P., Krasnodar Agricultural Research Institute: 350012 Krasnodar; tel. (8612) 56-28-15; attached to Russian Acad. of Agricultural Sciences.

Michurin, I. V., All-Russia Research Institute for Genetics and Breeding in Horticulture: 393740 Tambov oblast, Michurinsk; tel. (47545) 5-78-87; fax (47545) 5-79-29; e-mail cglm@rambler.ru; attached to Russian Acad. of Agricultural Sciences; Dir SAVELYEV NIKOLAI IVANOVICH.

Michurin, I. V., All-Russia Research Institute for Horticulture: 393740 Tambov oblast, Michurinsk, ul. Michurina 30; tel. and fax (47545) 2-07-61; e-mail vniis@pochta.ru; f. 1931; attached to Russian Acad. of Agricultural Sciences; Dir Prof. Dr YURI TRUNOV.

Nizhne-Volzhsky Agricultural Research Institute: 404013 Volgograd oblast, Nizheznensky; attached to Russian Acad. of Agricultural Sciences.

North Caucasus Mountains and Foothills Agricultural Research Institute: 363110 North Ossetia, Prigorny raion, Mikhailovskoe; attached to Russian Acad. of Agricultural Sciences.

North Caucasus Research Institute for Horticulture and Viticulture: 350029 Krasnodar, ul. 40-letiya Pobedy 9; tel. (8612) 54-06-74; attached to Russian Acad. of Agricultural Sciences.

Orenburg Agricultural Research Institute: 460051 Orenburg, ul. Gagarina 27/1; tel. (3532) 3-86-94; attached to Russian Acad. of Agricultural Sciences.

Pacific Fisheries Research Centre (TINRO): 690950 Vladivostok, ul. Shevchenko 4; tel. (4232) 400921; fax (4232) 300752; e-mail tinro@tinro.ru; f. 1925; ichthyology, oceanography, commercial invertebrates, commercial marine algae, parasitology of marine animals, commercial fisheries, mechanization of fish processing, technology of fish and marine production, aquaculture (marine and freshwater), study of marine pollution; brs at Amur (Khabarovsk) and Chukotka; library of 61,500 vols,

11,000 MSS; Dir Dr L. N. BOCHAROV; publ. *Izvestiya TINRO* (1–3 a year).

Potapenko, Ya. I., All-Russia Research Institute for Viticulture and Winemaking: Rostovsky raion, 346421 Novocherkassk, pr. Baklanovsky 166; tel. (86352) 6-70-88; fax (86352) 6-64-59; fax ruswine@yandex.ru; internet www.rusvine.com; f. 1936; attached to Russian Acad. of Agricultural Sciences; Dir Dr LEONID VASILIEVICH KRAVCHENKO.

Povolzhsky Research Institute for the Economics and Development of the Agro-industrial Complex: 410020 Saratov, ul. Shekhurdina 12; tel. (8452) 64-06-47; attached to Russian Acad. of Agricultural Sciences.

Pryanishnikov, D. N., All-Russia Research Institute of Agrochemistry: 127550 Moscow, ul. Pryanishnikova 31A; tel. (495) 976-37-50; fax (495) 976-37-39; e-mail info@vniia-pr.ru; internet www.vniia-pr.ru; f. 1931; attached to Russian Acad. of Agricultural Sciences; coordination of field experiments with Fertilizers Network, Scientific and Methodical Center of Agrochemical Service, Official Registration Agency for Chemicals and Soils; theory of crop nutrition, soil fertility monitoring of agricultural lands, strategy of fertilizers and chemicals application, geographical principles of fertilizers efficiency, new fertilizers; updating of agrochemical service, integration of agrochemical data; Dir V. G. SYCHEV.

Pustovoit, V. S., All-Russia Research Institute of Oil Crops: 350038 Krasnodar, ul. Filatova 17; tel. (861) 255-59-33; fax (861) 254-27-80; e-mail vniimk-center@mail.ru; internet www.vniimk.ru; f. 1912; attached to Russian Acad. of Agricultural Sciences; breeding and seed growing of oil crops: sunflower, soybean, flax, mustard, rapeseed; library of 100,300 vols; Dir-Gen. Dr VYACHESLAV M. LUKOMETS; publ. *Oil Crops Scientific Bulletin* (2 a year).

Research and Technological Institute for Agricultural Biotechnology: 410020 Saratov, ul. Tulaikova 7; tel. (8452) 64-04-31; attached to Russian Acad. of Agricultural Sciences.

Research Institute for Animal Nutrition: Moscow oblast, Dmitrovsky raion, pos. Ermolovo.

Research Institute for Breeding and Diversity in Horticulture: 303130 Orel, Zhilina; attached to Russian Acad. of Agricultural Sciences.

Research Institute of Agricultural Forest Reclamation: 400062 Volgograd, Universitetsky pr. 97; tel. (8442) 46-25-67; fax (8442) 46-25-10; e-mail vnialmi@avtlg.ru; internet www.vnialmi.ru; f. 1931; attached to Russian Acad. of Agricultural Sciences; researches on reclamation of agricultural lands by methods of forest and phytomelioration; combats desertification processes; ecological investigations; library of 93,700 vols; Dir Acad. KONSTANTIN N. KULIK; publ. *Scientific Papers* (2 a year).

Research Institute of Chemical Means of Plant Protection: 109088 Moscow, Ugreshskaya 31; tel. (495) 679-55-40; Dir B. P. VASILENKOV.

Research Institute of Farm Animal Physiology, Biochemistry and Nutrition: 249010 Kaluzhskaya oblast, Borovsk; tel. (495) 996-34-15; fax (48438) 42088; e-mail bifip@kaluga.ru; internet bifip2006.narod.ru; f. 1960; attached to Russian Acad. of Agricultural Sciences; library of 55,000 vols; Dir Dr A. SH. USHAKOV; publ. *Problems of Productive Animal Biology* (4 a year).

Research Institute of Non-infectious Animal Diseases: Moscow oblast, Istrinsky raion.

Research Institute of Technological Studies in Agricultural Cybernetics: c/o Russian Academy of Agricultural Sciences, 107814 Moscow, Bolshoi Kharitonevsky per. 21; attached to Russian Acad. of Agricultural Sciences.

Research Institute of the Economics and Development of the Agro-industrial Complex in the Central Black Soil (Chernozem) Zone: 394042 Voronezh, ul. Sarafimovicha 26A; tel. and fax (4732) 22-99-40; e-mail niieoapk@mail.ru; internet niieoapk.ru; f. 1930; attached to Russian Acad. of Agricultural Sciences; Dir I. HITSKOV.

Research Institute of Veterinary Entomology and Arachnology: 625010 Tyumen, Institutskaya ul. 2; attached to Russian Acad. of Agricultural Sciences; Dir V. Z. YAMOV.

Russian Institute of Agricultural Radiology and Agroecology: 249032 Kaluga oblast, Obninsk, Kievskoe shosse 109 km; tel. (48439) 6-48-02; fax (48439) 6-80-66; e-mail riarae@riar.obninsk.org; f. 1971; attached to Russian Acad. of Agricultural Sciences; library of 70,000 vols; Dir RUDOLF M. ALEXAKHIN; Deputy Dir NATALYA I. SANZHAROVA.

St Petersburg Forestry Research Institute: 194021 St Petersburg, Institutsky pr. 21; tel. (812) 552-80-21; fax (812) 552-80-42; e-mail spbfriin@nm10043.spb.edu; internet www.spbniilh.ru; f. 1929; 130 mems; library of 90,000 vols; Dir ALEXANDER B. EGOROV (acting).

State Scientific Institution Voronezh Scientific Research Institute of Agriculture: 397463 Voronezh, p/o Institute Dokuchaev, oblast, Talovya raion; e-mail niishi1c@mail.ru; internet www.niidokuchaeva.ru; attached to Russian Acad. of Agricultural Sciences.

Samoilov, Ya. V., Research Institute of Fertilizers and Insectofungicides: 119333 Moscow, Leninsky pr. 55/1, bld. 1; tel. (495) 232-96-89; fax (495) 956-19-02; e-mail info@niui.ru; internet www.niuif.ru; f. 1919; technology for production of phosphate fertilisers, sulphuric, phosphoric and nitric acid, and feed phosphates; Gen. Dir V. V. DAVYDENKO; publ. *Mir Sery i NPK (The World of Sulphur & NPK)*.

Skryabin, K. I., All-Russia Institute of Helminthology: 117259 Moscow, Bol. Cheremushkinskaya, 28; tel. (495) 124-56-55; attached to Russian Acad. of Agricultural Sciences; Dir Acad. V. S. ERSHOV.

South-East Agricultural Research Institute: 410020 Saratov, ul. Tulaykova 7; tel. (8452) 64-76-88; fax (8452) 64-76-88; f. 1910; attached to Russian Acad. of Agricultural Sciences; library of 350,000 vols; Dir NIKOLAI I. KOMAROV.

South Urals Agricultural Research Institute: 454002 Chelyabinsk, Shershni; tel. (3512) 42-42-01; attached to Russian Acad. of Agricultural Sciences.

Stavropol Agricultural Research Institute: 356200 Stavropol krai, Shpakovskoe; attached to Russian Acad. of Agricultural Sciences.

Sukachev, V. N., Institute of Forestry: 660036 Krasnoyarsk, Akademgorodok 50, Bldg 28; tel. and fax (3912) 43-36-86; f. 1944; attached to Russian Acad. of Sciences; library of 200,000 vols; Dir ALEXANDER A. ONUCHIN.

Tula Agricultural Research Institute: 301053 Tula oblast, Molochnye dvory; tel. (08752) 5-23-41; fax (08752) 2-30-15; f. 1956; attached to Russian Acad. of Agricultural Sciences; Dir Prof. V. I. SEVEROV.

Tulaikov, M. M., Samara Agricultural Research Institute: 446080 Samara oblast, Bezenchuk, ul. K. Marksa 41; attached to Russian Acad. of Agricultural Sciences.

Ulyanovsk Agricultural Research Institute: 433115 Ulyanovsk oblast, Timiryazevskoe; tel. (8422) 31-78-58; attached to Russian Acad. of Agricultural Sciences.

N.I. Vavilov All Russian Research Institute of the Plant Industry: 190000 St Petersburg Bolshaya Morskaya St42–44; tel. (812) 315-50-93; fax (812) 311-87-62; internet vir.nw.ru; f. 1894; attached to Russian Acad. of Agricultural Sciences; departments: computerized information systems; plant biochemistry and molecular biology; laboratory for long-term storage of seeds; rye, barley and oats; fruit crops; industrial crops; experimental stations: Astrakhan, Daghestan, Far East, Krymsk, Kuban, Maikop, Moscow, Pavlovsk, Polar, Volgograd, Yekaterinino, Zeya; herbarium of 250,000 specimens; Dir Prof. Dr NIKOLAI I. DZYUBENKO.

All-Russian Williams Fodder Research Institute: 141055 Moscow oblast, Lobnia Nauchniy gorodok; tel. (495) 577-73-37; fax (495) 577-71-07; e-mail vniicormov@nm.ru; internet www.vniikormov.ru; f. 1922; attached to Russian Acad. of Agricultural Sciences; scientific researches in field of agriculture, biology, genetics, breeding and seed multiplication of forage crops; devts in meadow management, fodder production, fodder preservation and utilization; library of 15,000 vols of books, scientific journals, methodological recommendations, brochures, patents, dissertations; Dir Prof. Dr VLADIMIR KOSOLAPOV; publ. *Adaptive Fodder Production (AFP)* (4 a year, online).

V. V. Dokuchaev Soil Science Institute: 109017 Moscow, Pyzhevsky per. 7; tel. (495) 951-50-37; e-mail khitrov@agro.geonet.ru; internet www.esoil.ru; f. 1927; attached to Russian Acad. of Agricultural Sciences; research in field of soil science; Dir N. B. KHITROV.

ARCHITECTURE AND TOWN PLANNING

Central Research and Design Institute of Dwellings: 127434 Moscow, Dmitrovskoe shosse 9, korp. 8; tel. (495) 976-28-19; fax (495) 976-37-82; f. 1962; Dir STANISLAV V. NIKOLAEV.

Central Research and Design Institute of Town Planning: 117944 Moscow, pr. Vernadskogo 29; tel. (495) 138-28-06; fax (495) 133-11-29; f. 1963; library of 25,000 vols; Dir YU. N. MAXIMOV.

Kucherenko, V. A., State Central Research and Experimental Design Institute for Complex Problems of Civil Engineering and Building Structures: 109428 Moscow, 2-ya Institutskaya 6; tel. (495) 171-26-50; fax (495) 171-28-58; f. 1927; Dir VASIL GORPINCHENKO; publs *Earthquake Engineering* (6 a year), *Investigation into Building Structures* (1 a year), *Investigations into Structural Earthquake Resistance* (every 2 years), *Large-Panel and Masonry Structures* (every 3 years), *New Forms and Strength of Metal Structures* (very 3 years), *Numerical Methods of Analysis and Optimization of Building Structures* (every 2 years), *Phosphate Materials* (1 a year), *Strength and Reliability of Structures* (every 2 years), *Structural Dynamics* (every 2 years), *Timber Structures* (every 2 years).

Panfilov, K. D., Academy of Municipal Economics: 123371 Moscow, Volokolamskoe shosse 116; tel. (495) 490-31-66; fax (495)

490-36-00; f. 1931; depts of scientific-technical co-ordination, municipal electrical supply, urban electric transport, anti-corrosion protection of underground metal structures, urban roads maintenance, municipal sanitation, urban landscaping, housing and municipal buildings, information, automation of technological processes, ecology; 5 research institutes (Moscow, St Petersburg, Rostov on Don, Tomsk, Ekaterinburg); 2 experimental factories (Moscow, St Petersburg); library of 740,000 vols; Dir V. F. Pivovarov; Scientific Sec. A. N. Prokhorov.

Research Institute of Foundations and Underground Structures: 109428 Moscow, 2-ya Institutskaya 6; tel. (495) 171-22-40; fax (495) 171-37-01; f. 1931; Dir Prof. V. A. Ilyichev; publ. *Soil Mechanics and Foundation Engineering* (6 a year).

Scientific and Research Institute for Architecture and Town Planning Theory: 121019 Moscow, pr. Vozdvizhenka 5; tel. (495) 290-36-80; fax (495) 290-36-80.

BIBLIOGRAPHY, LIBRARY SCIENCE AND MUSEOLOGY

All-Russia Research Institute of Restoration: 109172 Moscow, Krestyanskaya ul. 10; tel. (495) 276-99-90.

Book Research Institute: 103473 Moscow, 2-i Volkonsky per. 10; tel. (495) 281-72-58; Dir A. I. Solovev.

Library Association of Dagestan: 367026 Dagestan, ul. Batyraya 1; tel. (8722) 68-02-74; Pres. Kazim Omarov.

ECONOMICS, LAW AND POLITICS

All-Russia Research and Design Institute of the Statistical Information System: 127486 Moscow, Deguninskaya ul. 1/3; tel. (495) 488-14-04.

All-Russia Research Institute of Economic Problems in Development of Science and Technology: 111024 Moscow, Aviamotornaya ul. 26/5; tel. (495) 273-52-31; f. 1986; library of 15,000 vols.

Bank Credit and Finance Research Institute: 103016 Moscow, ul. Alekseya Tolstogo 30/1; tel. (495) 925-61-18.

Central Economics and Mathematics Institute: 117418 Moscow, Nakhimovsky pr. 47; tel. (495) 129-16-44; fax (495) 310-70-15; e-mail director@cemi.rssi.ru; internet www.cemi.rssi.ru; f. 1963; attached to Russian Acad. of Sciences; Dir V. L. Makarov; publs *Economics and Mathematical Methods* (4 a year), *Economics of Contemporary Russia* (4 a year).

Central Economics Research Institute: 119898 Moscow, Smolensky bul. 3/5; tel. (495) 246-84-63.

Central Laboratory of Socio-Economic Measurements: c/o Russian Academy of Sciences, 117418 Moscow, ul. Krasikova 32; attached to Russian Acad. of Sciences; Dir A. Yu. Shevyakov.

Centre for the Study of Nationality Problems: 117036 Moscow, ul. Dm. Ulyanova 19; tel. (495) 123-90-61; attached to Russian Acad. of Sciences; Head M. N. Guboglo.

Federal Service of State Statistics: 107450 Moscow, ul. Myasnitskaya 39; tel. (495) 207-49-02; fax (495) 207-40-87; e-mail stat@gks.ru; internet www.gks.ru; f. 1918 as Central Statistical Board; present name 1991; provides demographic and economic statistical information and analysis to state authorities, the scientific community and commercial and international organizations; Dir Vladimir Sokolin.

Financial Research Institute: 103006 Moscow, Nastasinsky per. 3 korp. 2; tel. (495) 299-74-14; fax (495) 299-31-69; f. 1937.

Institute for African Studies: 123001 Moscow, ul. Spiridonovka 30/1; tel. (495) 290-27-52; fax (495) 202-07-86; e-mail dir@inafr.ru; f. 1959; attached to Russian Acad. of Sciences; Dir A. M. Vasiliev; publs *Asia and Africa Today* (jtly with Institute of Oriental Studies, 12 a year), *Vostok-Orience* (jointly with Institute of Oriental Studies, 6 a year).

Institute for Comparative Political Studies: 101831 Moscow, Kolpachnyi per. 9a; tel. (495) 916-37-03; fax (495) 916-03-01; f. 1966; attached to Russian Acad. of Sciences; library of 50,000 vols; Dir T. T. Timofeev; publs *Forum* (1 a year), *Polis* (6 a year).

Institute for Economics and Mathematics at St Petersburg: Tchaikovski ul. 1, St Petersburg 191187; tel. and fax (812) 273-7953; e-mail emi@emi.spb.ru; internet www.spbrc.nw.ru; f. 1990; attached to Russian Acad. of Sciences; Dir Prof. Leonid A. Rukhovets.

Institute for International Economic and Political Studies: 117418 Moscow, Novocheremushkinskaya 46; tel. (495) 128-91-57; fax (495) 120-83-71; internet www.transecon.ru; f. 1960; attached to Russian Acad. of Sciences; Dir Prof. Dr Ruslan Grinberg; publ. *The World of Transformations* (4 a year).

Institute for Legislation and Comparative Law: 103728 Moscow, Vozdvizhenka 4/22; tel. (495) 291-02-07; fax (495) 290-58-56; f. 1925 (fmrly All-Union Research Institute of Soviet Legislation); library of 180,000 vols; Dir Lev A. Okunkov; publs *Commentary on New Russian Legislation* (1 a year), *Legislation of Foreign Countries* (6 or 7 a year), *Materials of Foreign Legislation and International Private Law* (1 a year), *Problems of Perfecting Legislation* (3 a year).

Institute for Socio-Economic Studies of Population: 117218 Moscow, Nakhimovsky pr. 32; tel. (495) 129-04-00; fax (495) 129-08-01; e-mail isesp_ras@mtu-net.ru; internet www.cemi.rssi.ru/isesp; f. 1988; attached to Russian Acad. of Sciences; Dir Natalia Rimashevskaya; publ. *Population* (4 a year).

Institute of Economic and Social Problems of the North: 167610 Syktyvkar, Kommunisticheskaya ul. 26; tel. (8212) 42-42-67; fax (8212) 42-42-67; attached to Russian Acad. of Sciences; Dir V. N. Lazhentsev.

Institute for Economic Studies: 184209 Murmansk oblast, Apatity, ul. Fersmana 24a; tel. (81555) 7-64-72; fax (81555) 7-48-44; e-mail iep@iep.kolasc.net.ru; internet www.ksc.ru; f. 1986; attached to Kola Science Centre (Russian Acad. of Sciences); Dir Prof. Fiodor D. Larichkin; publ. *Sever i rynok* (The North and the Market, in Russian, 3 a year).

Institute of Economic Research: 680042 Khabarovsk, Tikhookeanskaya ul. 153; tel. (421) 272-48-88; fax (421) 272-48-07; e-mail minakir@ecrin.ru; internet www.ecrin.ru; f. 1976; attached to Russian Acad. of Sciences; Dir Acad. P. A. Minakir; publ. *Spatial Economics* (4 a year).

Institute of Economics: 620219 Ekaterinburg, Moskovskaya ul. 29; tel. (3432) 51-45-36; fax (3432) 51-45-36; e-mail green@uran.ru; f. 1971; attached to Russian Acad. of Sciences; Dir A. I. Tatarkin.

Institute of Economics: 119991 Moscow, Leninskii Av. 14; tel. (495) 938-03-09; fax (495) 954-33-20; attached to Russian Acad. of Sciences; Dir Acad. Ruslan S. Grinberg.

Institute of Europe: 103873 Moscow, Mokhovaya 8–3; tel. (495) 203-73-43; fax (495) 200-42-98; f. 1988; attached to Russian Acad. of Sciences; library of 3,000 vols; Dir Vitaly V. Zhurkin.

Institute of Far Eastern Studies: 117218 Moscow, Nakhimovsky pr. 32; tel. (495) 124-01-17; fax (495) 310-70-56; e-mail ifes@cemi.rssi.ru; f. 1966; attached to Russian Acad. of Sciences; Dir M. L. Titarenko; publ. *Far Eastern Affairs* (6 a year).

Institute of Foreign Economic Research: c/o Russian Academy of Sciences, 117418 Moscow, ul. Krasikova 32; attached to Russian Acad. of Sciences; Dir S. A. Sitaryan.

Institute of National Economic Forecasting: 117418 Moscow, Nakhimovsky pr. 47; tel. (495) 129-34-33; fax (495) 718-97-71; e-mail office@ecfor.ru; internet www.ecfor.ru; f. 1986; attached to Russian Acad. of Sciences; undertakes macroeconomic analysis; short-, medium-, and long-term forecasting of the Russian economy; Dir Prof. Victor V. Ivanter; publs *Problemy Prognozirovaniya* (in Russian, 6 a year), *Studies on Russian Economic Development* (in English, 6 a year).

Institute of Philosophy and Law: 620144 Ekaterinburg, ul. 8 Marta 68; tel. (3432) 22-23-46; attached to Russian Acad. of Sciences; Dir S. S. Alekseev.

Institute of Problems of Assimilation of the North: 625003 Tyumen, a/ya 2774; tel. (3452) 7-82-76; attached to Russian Acad. of Sciences; Dir V. P. Melnikov.

Institute of Problems of the Marketplace: 117418 Moscow, Nakhimovsky pr. 47; tel. (495) 129-10-00; attached to Russian Acad. of Sciences; Dir N. Ya. Petrakov.

Institute of Social Sciences: 670042 Ulan-Ude, ul. Marii Sakhyanovoi 6; tel. (3012) 3-66-25; attached to Russian Acad. of Sciences; Dir V. T. Naidakov.

Institute of Socio-Economic Problems of the Development of the Agroindustrial Complex: 401600 Saratov, pr. Lenina 94; tel. (8452) 24-25-38; attached to Russian Acad. of Sciences; Dir V. B. Ostrovsky.

Institute of Socio-Political Research: 119991 Moscow, Leninsky pr. 32a; tel. and fax (495) 938-53-70; e-mail ispr@ras.ru; internet www.ispr.ru; f. 1991; attached to Russian Acad. of Sciences; Dir Prof. Dr Gennady Osipov; publs *Eurasia* (1 a year), *Science, Culture, Society* (4 a year), *Social and Demographic Policies*.

Institute of State and Law: 119841 Moscow, ul. Znamenka 10; tel. (495) 291-33-81; attached to Russian Acad. of Sciences; Dir B. N. Topornin.

Institute of the Economics of the Comprehensive Assimilation of the Natural Resources of the North: 677891 Yakutsk, ul. Petrovskogo 2; tel. (4112) 3-52-46; attached to Russian Acad. of Sciences; Dir N. V. Igoshin.

Institute of USA and Canada Studies: 121814 Moscow, Khlebnyi per. 2/3; tel. (495) 291-20-52; fax (495) 200-12-07; e-mail iskran@glasnet.ru; attached to Russian Acad. of Sciences; Dir Sergei Rogov; publs *Ideology* (12 a year), *Policy*, *US: Economy*.

Institute of World Economics and International Relations: 117957 Moscow, Profsoyuznaya 23; tel. (495) 120-43-32; fax (495) 120-65-75; e-mail imemoran@imemo.ru; internet www.imemo.ru; attached to Russian Acad. of Sciences; 545 mems; Dir Prof. Simonia A. Nodari (acting); publs *World Economics and International Relations* (12 a year, in Russian), *Russian Economic Barometer* (4 a year, in English).

International Research Institute for Management Sciences: 117312 Moscow, Pr. 60-letiya Oktyabrya 9; tel. (495) 137-28-57.

Latin America Institute: 115035 Moscow, Bol. Ordynka 21; tel. (495) 951-53-23; fax (495) 953-40-70; e-mail ilac-zan@mtu-net.ru; internet www.mtu-net.ru/ilaran; f. 1961; attached to Russian Acad. of Sciences; Dir Dr V. M. DAVYDOV; publ. *Iberoamerica* (in Spanish, 4 a year).

Peace Research Center of IMEMO: 117859 Moscow, ul. Profsoyuznaya 23; tel. (495) 128-93-89; fax (495) 120-65-75; e-mail imemoran@online.ru; attached to Russian Acad. of Sciences; Dir A. K. KISLOV; publ. *Ways to Security* (in Russian, 2 or 3 a year).

Pricing Research Institute: 107078 Moscow, Kirovsky pr-d 4/3; tel. (495) 925-50-56.

Research Institute for the Strengthening of the Legal System and Law and Order: 123805 Moscow, GSP 2-ya Zvenigorodskaya ul. 15; tel. (495) 256-54-63.

Research Institute of Planning and Normatives: 125319 Moscow, Kochnovsky pr. 3; tel. (495) 152-45-91; attached to Russian Acad. of Sciences; Dir B. V. GUBIN (acting).

Sochi Research Centre: 354000 Sochi, Teatralnaya 8a; tel. (862) 92-37-71; fax (862) 292-44-11; e-mail snic@sochi.ru; f. 1988; attached to Russian Acad. of Sciences; research into management of the development of recreational areas and tourism; Dir M. M. AMIRKHANOV.

Survey Technique and Applied Research (STAR) Centre of the Institute of Sociology: 117259 Moscow, ul. Krzhizhanovskogo 24/35, str. 5; tel. (495) 719-09-71; fax (495) 719-07-40; e-mail valman@socio.msk.su; f. 1983; attached to Russian Acad. of Sciences; opinion survey design, data collection; Dir Prof. V. MANSUROV.

EDUCATION

Central Sports Research Institute: 107005 Moscow, Elizavetinsky per. 10; tel. (499) 261-50-76.

Centre for Pre-School Education: 113035 Moscow, ul. Osipenko 21; tel. (495) 231-49-28; attached to Russian Acad. of Education; Dir A. S. SPIVAKOVSKAYA.

Centre for Social Pedagogics: 119905 Moscow, Pogodinskaya ul. 8; tel. (495) 246-44-58; attached to Russian Acad. of Education; Dir V. G. BOCHAROVA.

Institute for Advanced Training: 109180 Moscow, ul. Bol. Polyanka 58; tel. (095) 237-31-51; attached to Russian Acad. of Education; Dir Y. A. ROODIE.

Institute for Educational Innovation: 117449 Moscow, ul. Vinokurova 3-B; tel. (095) 126-26-30; attached to Russian Acad. of Education; Dir V. I. SLOBODCHIKOV.

Institute for School Development in Siberia, the Far East and the North: 634050 Tomsk, ul. Gertsena 68; tel. (3822) 21-28-21; attached to Russian Acad. of Education; Dir G. V. ZALEVSKY.

Institute for the Occupational Training of Youth: 119903 Moscow, Pogodinskaya ul. 8; tel. (495) 245-05-13; attached to Russian Acad. of Education; Dir V. A. POLYAKOV.

Institute of Developmental Physiology: 119869 Moscow, ul. Pogodinskaya 8, korp. 2; tel. (495) 245-04-33; attached to Russian Acad. of Education; Dir Dr M. M. BEZRUKIKH.

Institute of Higher Education: 111024 Moscow, Tretya Kabelynaya ul. 1; tel. (495) 273-48-19; e-mail sav@niivo.hetnet.ru; attached to Russian Acad. of Education; Dir ALEXANDER SAVELIEV.

Institute of National Problems of Education: 105077 Moscow, Pervomayskaya 101; tel. (495) 461-92-45; fax (495) 461-92-45; f. 1991; (fmrly Research Institute of National Schools, f. 1949); Dir Prof. M. N. KOUZMIN; publ. *Uchenye Zapiski* (1 a year).

Institute of Secondary Education: 119906 Moscow, ul. Pogodinskaya 8; tel. (495) 245-37-33; attached to Russian Acad. of Education; Dir. V. S. LEDNEV.

Institute of Secondary Specialized Education: Tatarstan, 420039 Kazan, ul. Isayeva 12; tel. (8432) 42-63-24; fax (8432) 42-46-80; f. 1976; attached to Russian Acad. of Education; Dir G. V. MUKHAMETZYANOVA; publ. *Professional Education* (4 a year).

Institute of Teaching and Learning Resources: 119903 Moscow, ul. Pogodinskaya 8; tel. (495) 246-35-90; attached to Russian Acad. of Education; Dir T. S. NAZAROVA.

Institute of Theoretical Pedagogics and International Research in Education: 129278 Moscow, ul. Pavla Korchagina 7; tel. (495) 283-09-55; attached to Russian Acad. of Education; Dir B. S. GERSHUNSKY.

Institute of Vocational Education: 119186 St Petersburg, nab. Moiki 48; tel. (812) 311-60-88; attached to Russian Acad. of Education; Dir A. P. BELYAEVA.

Psychological Institute: 125009 Moscow, Mokhovaya ul. 9, Bldg 4; tel. (495) 695-88-76; fax (495) 695-81-28; e-mail pirao@list.ru; internet www.pirao.ru; f. 1912; attached to Russian Acad. of Education; library of 60,000 vols; Dir Prof. VITALY V. RUBTSOV; Vice-Dir for science Prof. SERGEY MALYKH; publs *New trends in Psychology* (4 a year, in Russian), *Theoretical and Experimental Psychology* (4 a year, in Russian).

Research Centre for Aesthetic Education: 119034 Moscow, Kropotkinskaya nab. 15; tel. (495) 202-25-97; attached to Russian Acad. of Education; Dir B. P. YUSOV.

Research Centre for the Teaching of Russian: 119903 Moscow, Pogodinskaya ul. 8; tel. (495) 246-05-59; attached to Russian Acad. of Education; Dir E. A. BYSTROVA.

Research Institute of Remedial Education: 119869 Moscow, ul. Pogodinskaya 8, korp. 1; tel. (495) 245-04-52; attached to Russian Acad. of Education; Dir N. N. MALOFEEV.

Siberian Institute of Educational Technologies: 630098 Novosibirsk, Primorskaya ul. 22; tel. (3832) 45-18-32; fax (3832) 45-87-51; f. 1985; attached to Russian Acad. of Education; Dir I. M. BOBKO; publ. *Information Technologies in Education* (2 a year).

Family and Education Institute: 119121 Moscow, ul. Pogodinskaya 8; tel. (499) 255-26-06; fax (499) 255-24-77; e-mail niisv@mail.ru; internet www.niisv.ru; f. 1998; attached to Russian Acad. of Education; Dir Acad. SERGEI VLADIMIROVICH DARMODECHIN.

FINE AND PERFORMING ARTS

Scientific-Research Museum of the Russian Academy of Fine arts: St Petersburg, Universitetskaya nab. 17; tel. (812) 328-27-19; fax (812) 323-61-69; e-mail sekretar@nimrah.ru; internet www.nimrah.ru; f. 1758; attached to Russian Acad. of Arts; casts, masterpieces of antique sculpture and models of antique architecture monuments made in 18th century of cork in workshop of Chichi, Roman patternmaker and sculptor; history of Russian artistic school; works of Losenko, Borovikovsky, Bryullov, P.P. Chistyakov, Kustodiyev, Brodsky, A.P. Ostroumova-Lebedeva, sculptors Shubin, Kozlovsky, Shchedrin, Prokofyev, Antokolsky; Saint Petersburg architecture of the 18th–19th centuries in patterns, paintings and drawings; Dir LUDMILA KONDRATENKO.

Research Institute of Film Art: 125009 Moscow, Degtyarny per. 8; tel. and fax (095) 299-56-79; e-mail cineaste@mail.ru; f. 1974; research in the field of history and theory of film and monitoring of the situation in Russian and world cinema; 65 mems; library of 60,000 vols; still photos archive; Dir LIUDMILA BUDYAK; Deputy Dirs DMITRY KARAVAEV, MARK ZAK; publs *Kinograph* (almanac), *Kinovedcheskie Zapisky* (Film Notebooks, 4 a year).

Research Institute of the Theory and History of Fine Arts: 119034 Moscow, ul. Prechistenka 21; tel. (495) 201-42-91; attached to Russian Acad. of Arts; Dir V. V. VANSLOV.

State Institute for Art Studies: 125000 Moscow, Kozitsky per. 5; tel. (495) 200-03-71; fax (495) 785-24-06; e-mail institut@sias.ru; internet www.sias.ru; f. 1944; research in fine art, theatre, music, architecture, folklore, mass media; studies in sociology, economics and the politics of culture; library of 70,000 vols; Dir Dr A. I. KOMECH; publs *Cultural Transactions* (every 2 years), *Occidental Art of the 20th Century* (every 2 years), *Theory of Culture* (1 a year), *World of Arts* (1 a year).

HISTORY, GEOGRAPHY AND ARCHAEOLOGY

Institute of Archaeology: 117036 Moscow, ul. Dm. Ulyanova 19; tel. (495) 126-47-98; fax (495) 126-06-30; e-mail ia.ras@mail.ru; internet archaeolog.ru; f. 1919; attached to Russian Acad. of Sciences; Dir N. A. MAKAROV; publ. *Russiyskaya Archeologia* (4 a year).

V. B. Sochava Institute of Geography: 664033 Irkutsk, Ulanbatorskaya 1; tel. (3952) 42-61-00; fax (3952) 42-27-17; e-mail postman@irigs.irk.ru; internet www.irigs.irk.ru; f. 1957; attached to Russian Acad. of Sciences; the state and devt of Siberia's regions; landscape science; devt of the geographical framework for territorial org. of production, and population formation; systemic mapping; creation of the theoretical foundation for forecasting, monitoring and controlling the geosystem; library of 52 vols; Dir Dr VICTOR M. PLYUSNIN.

Institute of Geography: 109017 Moscow, Staromonetnii per. 29; tel. (495) 959-00-32; fax (495) 959-00-33; e-mail igras@igras.geonet.ru; internet www.igras.ru; f. 1918; attached to Russian Acad. of Sciences; research on interaction between nature and society at global, regional, and national scales; evolutionary analysis of environment and its components for forecast of global and regional changes; monitors and evaluates efficiency of natural resource utilization; elaboration of ecological and geographical bases of sustainable devt at global, regional, and nat. levels; library of 10,000 vols; Dir Acad. V. M. KOTLYAKOV; publs *Ekologicheskoe Planirovanie i Upravlenie* (6 a year), *Geomorphology* (4 a year), *Izvestiya Akademii Nauk – Seriya Geograficheskaya* (6 a year), *Lyod i Sneg* (2 a year), *Problemy regionalnoi Ekologii* (6 a year).

Institute of History and Archaeology: 620219 Ekaterinburg, ul. R. Lyuksemburg 56; tel. (3432) 22-14-02; fax (3432) 22-42-30; e-mail istor@uran.ru; internet www.uran.ru/structure/institutions/history/index.htm; f. 1988; attached to Russian Acad. of Sciences; Dir Prof. V. V. ALEKSEEV; publ. *Ural Historical Journal* (1 a year).

Institute of History, Language and Literature: 450054 Ufa, pr. Oktyabrya 71; tel. (3472) 35-60-50; fax (3472) 35-60-77; e-mail rihll@anrb.ru; internet rihll.ru; f. 1932; attached to Russian Acad. of Sciences; Dir Prof. Dr FIRDAUS G. KHISAMITDINOVA.

Institute of History, Philology and Philosophy: 630090 Novosibirsk, pr. Akad. Lavrenteva 17; tel. (3832) 35-05-37; fax (3832) 35-77-91; attached to Russian Acad. of Sciences; Dir Acad. A. P. DEREVYANKO.

Institute of Language, Literature and Arts: 367025 Makhachkala 25, ul. Magomeda Gadjieva 45; tel. (872) 267-06-21; fax (872) 267-06-21; f. 1924; attached to Russian Acad. of Sciences; library of 160,000 vols; Dir M. I. MAGOMEDOV.

Institute of Language, Literature and History: 167610 Syktyvkar, Kommunisticheskaya ul. 26; tel. (8212) 24-55-64; fax (8212) 44-21-97; e-mail smetanin@mail.komisc.ru; internet www.komisc.ru/illh; f. 1970; attached to Russian Acad. of Sciences; Dir ALEXANDR F. SMETANIN.

Institute of Linguistics, Literature and History: 185610 Petrozavodsk, Pushkinskaya ul. 11; tel. (8142) 77-44-96; attached to Russian Acad. of Sciences; Dir YU. A. SAVVATEEV.

Institute of Military History: 117330 Moscow, Universitetskii pr. 14; tel. (495) 147-45-65; attached to Russian Acad. of Sciences; Dir A. N. BAZHENOV.

Institute of Oriental Manuscripts: 191186 St Petersburg, Dvortsovaya 18; tel. (812) 315-87-28; fax (812) 312-14-65; e-mail iom@orientalstudies.ru; internet www.orientalstudies.ru; f. 1818; attached to Russian Acad. of Sciences; specialized collns of MSS and early printed books of countries of East; archive of Orientalists; Dir IRINA F. POPOVA; publ. *Pismennye pamyatniki Vostoka* (2 a year).

Institute of Research in the Humanities: 677007 Sakha Republic, Yakutsk, Petrovskaya ul. 1; tel. and fax (4112) 35-49-96; f. 1935; attached to Acad. of Sciences of the Sakha Republic; history, language and culture of the peoples of the Sakha Republic; Dir VASILY N. IVANOV; publ. *Yakutsky arkhiv* (12 a year).

Institute of Russian History: 117036 Moscow, ul. Dm. Ulyanova 19; tel. (495) 126-94-49; fax (495) 126-39-55 br. at St Petersburg: 197110 St Petersburg, Petrozavodskaya 7; tel. (812) 235-41-98; fax (812) 235-64-85; attached to Russian Acad. of Sciences; Dir A. N. SAKHAROV.

Institute of Slavonic Studies: 117334 Moscow, Leninsky pr. 32A; tel. (495) 938-17-80; fax (495) 938-00-96; e-mail ritlen@mail.ru; f. 1947; attached to Russian Acad. of Sciences; Dir V. K. VOLKOV; publ. *Slavyanovedeniye* (4 a year).

Institute of the History, Archaeology and Ethnography of the Peoples of the Far East: 690950 Vladivostok, ul. Pushkinskaya 89; tel. (4232) 22-05-07; fax (4232) 26-82-11; internet www.febras.ru/~ihae; f. 1971; attached to Russian Acad. of Sciences; Dir Dr V. L. LARIN; publ. *Russia and the Pacific* (in Russian, 4 a year).

Institute of the History of Material Culture: 191065 St Petersburg, Dvortsovaya nab. 18; tel. (812) 312-14-84; attached to Russian Acad. of Sciences.

Institute of World History: 117036 Moscow, ul. Dm. Ulyanova 19; tel. (495) 126-94-21; attached to Russian Acad. of Sciences; Dir A. O. CHUBARYAN.

Krasovsky, F. N., Central Research Institute for Geodesy, Aerial Photography, and Cartography: 125413 Moscow, Onezhskaya 26; tel. (495) 456-95-31.

Oceanography Research Institute: 190121 St Petersburg, nab. Moiki 120; Dir I. S. GRAMBERG.

Pacific Institute of Geography: 690041 Vladivostok, ul. Radio 7; tel. (4232) 32-06-72; fax (4232) 31-21-59; f. 1971; attached to Russian Acad. of Sciences; library of 28,000 vols; Dir Prof. P. YA. BAKLANOV; publ. *Zov Taigi*.

State Oceanography Institute: 119838 Moscow, Kropotkinskii per. 6; tel. (095) 246-72-88 199026 St. Petersburg, V.O., 23-ya liniya 2-a; tel. (812) 218-81-23; Dir F. S. TERZIEV.

Udmurt Institute of History, Language and Literature: 426004 Izhevsk, ul. Lomonosova 4; tel. (3412) 75-53-21; fax (3412) 75-39-94; f. 1931; attached to Russian Acad. of Sciences; library of 60,000 vols; Dir KUZMA I. KULIKOV.

LANGUAGE AND LITERATURE

Gorky, A. M., Institute of World Literature: 121069 Moscow, ul. Vorovskogo 25A; tel. (495) 290-50-30; attached to Russian Acad. of Sciences; Dir F. F. KUZNETSOV.

Ibragimov, G., Institute of Language, Literature and Art: 420503 Kazan, ul. Lobachevskogo 2/31; tel. (8432) 38-70-59; fax (8432) 38-74-79; attached to Acad. of Sciences of the Republic of Tatarstan; Dir M. Z. ZAKIEV.

Institute of Linguistic Research: 199053 St Petersburg, Tuchkov per. 9; tel. (812) 328-16-11; fax (812) 328-46-11; f. 1921; attached to Russian Acad. of Sciences; Dir Prof. Dr ANATOLY DOMASHNEV.

Institute of Linguistics: 125009 Moscow, ul. Bol. Kislovsky per. 1, st. 1; tel. (495) 690-35-85; fax (495) 690-05-28; e-mail iling@iling-ran.ru; internet www.iling-ran.ru; f. 1950; attached to Russian Acad. of Sciences; Dir V. A. VINOGRADOV; Vice-Dir M. ALEKSEYEV; publs *Ural-Altaic Studies* (2 a year), *Voprosy Filologii* (3 a year), *Voprosy Psikholingvistiki* (2 a year).

Institute of Russian Literature (Pushkin House): 199034 St Petersburg, nab. Makarova 4; tel. (812) 328-19-01; fax (812) 328-11-40; e-mail irli@mail.ru; f. 1905; attached to Russian Acad. of Sciences; Dir N. N. SKATOV; publ. *Russian Literature* (4 a year).

Russian Institute for Cultural Research: 119072 Moscow, Bersenevskaya nab. 20; tel. (495) 959-09-08; fax (495) 959-10-17; e-mail riku@dol.ru; internet www.ricur.ru; f. 1932; attached to Min. of Culture and the Mass Media; research in theory and history of culture, humanities, applied cultural research; organizes conferences, publs, workshops and festivals; br. in Omsk; library: library of 67,000 books and periodicals; Dir Prof. KIRILL E. RAZLOGOV; Deputy Dir Prof. ELEONORA A. SHOULEPOVA; Deputy Dir Assoc. Prof. ALEXEI G. VASILIEV; Deputy Dir Prof. YURI M. REZNIK; publ. *Journal of Cultural Research* (online).

Vinogradov Institute of the Russian Language: 121019 Moscow, Volkhonka 18/2; tel. (495) 202-65-40; fax (495) 291-23-17; f. 1944; attached to Russian Acad. of Sciences; library of 110,000 vols; Dir Dr A. M. MOLDOVAN; publs *Rusistics Today* (4 a year), *Russian Speech* (6 a year).

MEDICINE

All-Russia Antibiotics Research Institute: 113105 Moscow, Nagatinskaya ul. 3a; tel. (499) 611-42-38; fax (495) 118-93-66; f. 1947; library of 65,000 vols; br. in Penza; Dir Prof. S. M. NAVASHIN; publ. *Antibiotics and Chemotherapy*.

All-Russia Research Institute of Eye Diseases: 119021 Moscow, ul. Rossolimo 11; tel. (495) 248-01-25; f. 1973; micro-surgery of the eye, therapeutic ophthalmology, laser ophthalmology, new technical equipment in ophthalmology; Chief Officers ALEKSEEV, KRASNOV, KUZNETSOVA, MUSTAEV; publ. *Vestnik Oftalmologii* (6 a year).

All-Russia Research Institute of Pharmaceutical Plants: 113628 Moscow, ul. Grina 7; tel. (495) 382-83-18; Dir P. T. KONDRATENKO.

All-Russia Research Institute of the Technology of Blood Substitutes and Hormonal Preparations: 109044 Moscow, per. Lavrov 6; tel. (495) 276-43-60.

Allergen State Unitary Enterprise: 355019 Stavropol, Biologicheskaya ul. 20; tel. (8652) 24-40-84; fax (8652) 25-31-46; f. 1918; vaccines and sera, allergens, nutrient media, pharmaceuticals; library of 39,500 vols and periodicals; Dir-Gen. V. V. ERMELOV.

Anokhin, P. K., Institute of Normal Physiology: 103009 Moscow, ul. Bolshaya Nikitskaya 6; tel. (495) 203-66-70; fax (495) 203-54-32; attached to Russian Acad. of Medical Sciences; Dir K. V. SUDAKOV.

Bakulev Scientific and Research Centre for Cardiovascular Surgery: 117049 Moscow, Leninskii pr. 8; tel. (495) 236-13-61; fax (495) 237-21-72; e-mail leoan@online.ru; internet www.bakoulev.sovintel.ru; f. 1956; attached to Russian Acad. of Medical Sciences; Head Acad. L. A. BOCERIA; publs *Journal of Thoracic and Cardiovascular Surgery* (in Russian, 6 a year), *Annals of Surgery* (in Russian, 6 a year), *Annals of Arrhythmology* (in Russian, 6 a year).

Blokhin, N. N., Cancer Research Center: Kashirskoe shosse 24, 115478 Moscow; tel. (495) 324-11-14; fax (495) 323-53-55; e-mail info@eso.ru; internet www.cancercenter.ru; f. 1951; attached to Russian Acad. of Medical Sciences; Dir MIKHAIL V. DAVYDOV; publs *Herald of Moscow Cancer Society* (12 a year), *Journal* (4 a year), *Journal of Biotherapy* (24 a year), *Pediatric Oncology* (24 a year).

Attached Institutes:

Research Institute of Carcinogenesis: Kashirskoe shosse 24, 115478 Moscow; tel. (495) 324-14-70; attached to Russian Acad. of Medical Sciences; Dir DAVID G. ZARIDZE.

Research Institute of Experimental Therapy and Tumour Diagnosis: Kashirskoe shosse 24, 115478 Moscow; tel. (495) 324-22-74; attached to Russian Acad. of Medical Sciences; Dir ANATOLY Y. BARYSHNIKOV.

Research Institute of Pediatric Oncology: Kashirskoe shosse 24, 115478 Moscow; tel. (495) 324-43-09; attached to Russian Acad. of Medical Sciences; Dir LEV A. DURNOV.

Russian Institute of Clinical Oncology: Kashirskoe shosse 24, 115478 Moscow; tel. (495) 324-44-16; attached to Russian Acad. of Medical Sciences; Dir MIKHAIL I. DAVYDOV.

Blood Transfusion Research Institute: 125167 Moscow, Novozykovsky pr-d 4A; tel. (495) 212-45-51; fax (495) 212-42-52.

Burdenko Neurosurgical Institute: 125047 Moscow, ul. Fadeeva 5; tel. (0495) 251-65-26; fax (495) 250-93-51; attached to Russian Acad. of Medical Sciences; Dir A. N. KONOVALOV.

Cardiological Research Centre: 121552 Moscow, 3°, Cherepkovskaya ul. 15; tel. (495)

415-13-47; fax (495) 415-29-62; attached to Russian Acad. of Medical Sciences; Dir E. I. CHAZOV.

Attached Institutes:

Institute of Experimental Cardiology: 121552 Moscow, 3 Cherepkovskaya ul. 15A; tel. (495) 415-00-35; attached to Russian Acad. of Medical Sciences; Dir V. N. SMIRNOV.

Myasnikov, A. L., Institute of Cardiology: 12155 2 Moscow, 3°, Cherepkovskaya ul. 15; tel. (495) 415-52-05; attached to Russian Acad. of Medical Sciences; Dir YU. N. BELENKOV.

Central Institute of Traumatology and Orthopaedics: 125299 Moscow, ul. Priorova 10; tel. (495) 450-24-72; fax (495) 154-31-39; f. 1921; 12 clinics; library of 40,000 vols; Dir Prof. S. P. MIRONOV; publ. *N. N. Priorov Journal of Traumatology and Orthopaedics* (4 a year).

Central Research Institute for the Evaluation of Working Capacity and Vocational Assistance to Disabled Persons: 127486 Moscow, ul. Susanina 3; tel. (495) 906-18-31; fax (495) 906-18-32; f. 1930; library of 50,000 vols; Dir D. I. LAVROVA.

Central Research Institute of Dermatology and Venereal Diseases: 107076 Moscow, ul. Korolenko 3; tel. (495) 964-26-20; fax (495) 964-43-22; e-mail info@cnikvi.ru; internet www.cnikvi.ru; f. 1921; attached to Federal Agency for High Technology Medical Care; Dir Prof. ALEXEI KUBANOV; publ. *Vestnik Dermatologii i Venerologii* (Journal of Dermatology and Venereology, 6 a year).

Central Research Institute of Epidemiology: 111123 Moscow, Novogireevskaya 3-a; tel. (495) 176-02-19; Dir A. SUMAROKOV.

Central Research Institute of Gastroenterology: 111123 Moscow, shosse Enthuziastov 86; tel. and fax (495) 304-19-42; e-mail gastroenter@rambler.ru; internet www.gastro-online.ru; f. 1973; Dir Prof. LEONID LAZEBNIK; publ. *Experimental and Clinical Gastroenterology* (12 a year).

Central Research Institute of Roentgenology and Radiology: 197758 St Petersburg, Pesochny, ul. Leningradskaya 70/4; tel. (812) 596-84-62; fax (812) 596-67-05; e-mail crirr@peterlink.ru; internet www.private.peterlink.ru/crirr; f. 1918; Dir Prof. ANATOLY M. GRANOV; publ. *Volume of Conference Reports* (1 a year).

Central Tuberculosis Research Institute: 107564 Moscow, Yauzskaya alleya 2; tel. (499) 785-90-19; fax (499) 785-91-08; e-mail cniit@cniitramn.ru; internet www.cniitramn.ru; f. 1921; attached to Russian Acad. of Medical Sciences; Dir Prof. V. V. EROKHIN.

Centre for the Chemistry of Drugs—All-Russia Chemical and Pharmaceutical Research Institute: 119815 Moscow, ul. Zubovskaya 7; tel. (495) 246-97-68; fax (495) 246-78-05; f. 1920; research on drugs; library of 150,000 items; Dir R. G. GLUSHKOV; publ. *Collection of Proceedings* (1 a year).

Chumakov, M. P., Institute of Poliomyelitis and Virus Encephalitis: 142782 Moscow oblast, Kievskoe shosse, 27 km; tel. (495) 439-90-07; attached to Russian Acad. of Medical Sciences; Dir S. G. DROZDOV.

Chuvash Eye Diseases Research Institute: 428028 Cheboksary, Traktorostroitelei 10; tel. (8350) 26-05-75; fax (8350) 26-52-13; f. 1987; Dir Dr NIKOLAI PASHTAEV.

Dagestan Medical Research Centre: 367020 Makhachkala, ul. Gorikogo 53; tel. (87200) 7-49-97; attached to Russian Acad. of Medical Sciences; Dir S.-M. A. OMAROV.

Eastern Siberian Research Centre: 664003 Irkutsk, ul. Timiryazeva 16; tel. (3952) 27-54-48; fax (3952) 27-48-13; e-mail scippnw@sbamsr.irk.ru; attached to Russian Acad. of Medical Sciences; Chair. of Presidium Acad. S. I. KOLESNIKOV.

Attached Institutes:

Institute of Epidemiology and Microbiology: 664000 Irkutsk, ul. Karla Marksa 3; tel. (3952) 33-34-23; fax (3952) 33-34-45; attached to Russian Acad. of Medical Sciences; Dir Prof. V. I. ZLOBIN.

Institute of Industrial Medicine and Human Ecology: 665827 Irkutskaya oblast, Angarsk 27, a/ya 1170; tel. (218) 55-90-70; fax (218) 55-40-77; e-mail rvc@iimhe.irk.ru; attached to Russian Acad. of Medical Sciences; Dir V. S. RUKAVISHNIKOV.

Institute of Paediatrics and Human Reproduction: 664003 Irkutsk, ul. Timiryazeva 16; tel. (3952) 34-73-67; fax (3952) 27-48-13; e-mail scippnw@sbamsr.irk.ru; attached to Russian Acad. of Medical Sciences; Dir Acad. S. I. KOLESNIKOV.

Institute of Surgery: 664047 Irkutsk, Yubileiny mikroraion 100; tel. and fax (3952) 38-53-31; attached to Russian Acad. of Medical Sciences; Dir Prof. E. G. GRIGOREV.

Institute of Traumatology and Orthopaedics: 664003 Irkutsk, ul. Bortsov Revolyutsii 1; tel. and fax (3952) 27-54-30; attached to Russian Acad. of Medical Sciences; Dir Prof. A. P. BARABASH.

Ekaterinburg Institute of Restorative Surgery, Traumatology and Orthopaedics: Ekaterinburg, Bankovsky per. 7.

Ekaterinburg Region Institute of Dermatology and Venereal Diseases: Ekaterinburg, ul. K. Libknekhta 9.

Ekaterinburg Viral Infections Research Institute: 620030 Ekaterinburg, Letnyaya ul. 23; tel. (3432) 61-99-60; e-mail virus@etel.ru; f. 1920; Dir Prof. NINA P. GLINSKIKH; publ. *Viral Infections: Urgent Problems* (1 a year).

Endocrinology Research Centre: 117036 Moscow, ul. Dm. Ulyanova 11; tel. (495) 500-00-90; fax (495) 718-05-22; e-mail science@endocrincentr.ru; internet www.endocrincentr.ru; f. 1925; attached to Russian Acad. of Medical Sciences; Dir I. I. DEDOV; publ. *Diabetes Mellitus* (in Russian, 4 a year).

Attached Institutes:

Institute of Clinical Endocrinology: Institute of Clinical Endocrinology: Moscow; tel. (495) 129-01-24; fax (495) 718-05-22; e-mail endocrin@endocrincentr.ru; f. 1988; Dir J. A. MELNICHENKO.

Institute of Experimental Endocrinology: 112255 Moscow, ul. Moskvorechie 1; tel. (495) 324-93-25; f. 1965; Dir V. N. BABICHEV.

Institute of Diabetes: Moscow; tel. (495) 1244500; fax (495) 7180522; f. 1988; Dir M. I. BALABOLKIN.

Ersman Hygiene Research Institute: 141000 Mytishchi, ul. Semashko 2; tel. (495) 583-82-14.

Far Eastern Scientific Center of Physiology and Pathology of Respiration: 675000 Blagoveshchensk, ul. Kalinina 22; tel. and fax (4162) 53-35-45; e-mail cfpd@amur.ru; internet www.people.amursu.ru/cfpd/win; f. 1981; attached to Russian Acad. of Medical Sciences; Dir Prof. Dr VICTOR P. KOLOSOV; Vice-Dir Prof. Dr YULIY M. PERELMAN; publ. *Bulletin Physiology and Pathology of Respiration*.

Federal Bureau for Medical and Social Expertise: 127486 Moscow, ul. Ivana Susanina 3; tel. (495) 487-57-11; fax (495) 487-81-81; e-mail fbmse@inbox.ru; f. 2000 as Federal Scientific and Practical Centre for Medico-Social Expertise and Rehabilitation of Invalids (formed by merger of Central Research Institute of Prosthetics and Prosthesis Design and Central Research Institute for the Evaluation of Working Capacity and Vocational Assistance to Disabled Persons); present name 2005; library of 45,000 vols; Dir Prof. Dr S. N. PUZIN; publ. *Journal of Medical and Social Expertise and Rehabilitation* (4 a year).

Federal Research Institute for Health Education and Health Promotion: 103101 Moscow, ul. A. Mitskevicha 3; tel. (495) 202-18-13; fax (495) 202-54-08; f. 1927; library of 10,000 vols; Dir Dr V. A. POLESKY.

Federal Research Institute of Paediatric Gastroenterology: 603950 Nizhnii Novgorod, ul. Semashko 22; tel. (8312) 36-66-35; fax (8312) 36-56-59; e-mail niidegastro@mail.ru; f. 1929; Dir Prof. Dr ANATOLY I. VOLKOV.

Gamalei, N. F., Institute of Epidemiology and Microbiology: 123098 Moscow, ul. Gamalei 18; tel. (495) 193-30-01; fax (495) 305-67-38; attached to Russian Acad. of Medical Sciences; Dir S. V. PROZOROVSKII.

Haematological Research Centre: 125167 Moscow, Novozykovsky pr-d 4A; tel. (495) 212-21-23; fax (495) 212-42-52; attached to Russian Acad. of Medical Sciences; Dir A. I. VOROBIEV.

Herzen, P. A., Moscow Cancer Research Institute: 125284 Moscow, 2-i Botkinsky pr-d 3; tel. (495) 945-19-35; f. 1903; library of 19,336 vols; Dir Prof. V. I. CHISSOV.

Mother and Child Care Institute: 680022 Khabarovsk, ul.Voronezgskaya, 49, bldg 1; tel. (4212) 98-02-15; fax (4212) 98-03-35; e-mail zdorovye@mail.redcom.ru; f. 1986 collaboration with Far-Eastern State Medical Univ. and other medical instns of the whole Russia and foreign countries (USA, Japan, China, Germany and others); attached to Russian Acad. of Medical Sciences; scientific activities incl. ecological-medical, molecular mechanisms investigations in aspects of the children and adolescents healthcare in the Far-Eastern region of Russia, estimation of viral and bacterial infections influence for the reproductive function and foetus formation and infants loss; the formation and support of tissue homeostasis at the early stages of ontogenesis; investigations of the immune-dependent peculiarities for pathologic states among children and adolescents at the Far-Eastern region of Russia; Dir V. K. KOZLOV.

Scientific Research Institute of Biochemistry: 630117 Novosibirsk, Academician Timakov St. 2; tel. (383) 332-27-35; fax (383) 333-67-58; e-mail ibch@soramn.ru; internet www.ibch.soramn.ru; f. 1988; attached to Russian Acad. of Medical Sciences; Dir L. E. PANIN.

Institute of Biomedical Chemistry: 119121 Moscow, ul. Pogodinskaya 10; tel. (495) 246-69-80; fax (495) 245-08-57; internet www.ibmc.msk.ru; f. 1944; attached to Russian Acad. of Medical Sciences; library of 136,000 vols; Dir Prof. ALEXANDER IVANOVICH ARCHAKOV; publ. *Voprosy meditsinskoy khimii* (6 a year).

Institute of Biomedical Problems: 123007 Moscow, Khoroshevskoe shosse 76A; tel. (495) 195-23-63; fax (495) 195-22-53; f. 1963; environmental effects on the human body, with emphasis on the effect of space flights; library of 80,000 vols; Dir ANATOLY I.

GRIGORIEV; publ. *Aerospatial and Environmental Medicine* (6 a year).

Institute of Biomedical Research and Therapy: 113149 Moscow, Simferopolsky bul. 8; tel. (495) 113-23-51; Dir A. V. KARAULOV.

Institute of Clinical and Experimental Lymphology: 630117 Novosibirsk, ul. Timakova 2; tel. (383) 333-64-09; fax (383) 333-51-22; f. 1991; attached to Russian Acad. of Medical Sciences; library of 1,000 vols; Dir V. I. KONENKOV.

Institute of Clinical and Preventive Cardiology: 625026 Tyumen, ul. Melnikaite 111, POB 4312; tel. (3452) 22-76-08; fax (3452) 22-53-49; f. 1985; attached to Russian Acad. of Medical Sciences; Dir V. A. KUZNETSOV.

Institute of Clinical Immunology: 630091 Novosibirsk, ul. Yadrintsovskaya 14; fax (3832) 22-70-28; attached to Russian Acad. of Medical Sciences; Dir V. A. KOZLOV.

Institute of Epidemiology and Microbiology: 690028 Vladivostok, ul. Selskaya 1; tel. (4232) 29-43-03; attached to Russian Acad. of Medical Sciences; Dir N. N. BESEDNOVA.

Institute of Experimental Medicine: 197376 St Petersburg, ul. Akad. Pavlova 12; tel. (812) 234-54-01; fax (812) 234-94-89; e-mail iem@iemrams.ru; internet www.iemrams.spb.ru; f. 1890; attached to Russian Acad. of Medical Sciences; library of 500,000 vols; Dir GENRIKH A. SOFRONOV; Librarian ARINA DZENISKEVICH.

Institute of Eye Diseases: 119021 Moscow, ul. Rossolimo 11; tel. (495) 248-78-92; fax (495) 248-01-25; attached to Russian Acad. of Medical Sciences; Dir M. M. KRASNOV.

Institute of General Pathology and Pathological Physiology: 125315 Moscow, ul. Baltiiskaya 8; tel. (495) 151-17-56; fax (495) 151-95-40; attached to Russian Acad. of Medical Sciences; Dir G. N. KRYZHANOVSKII.

Institute of Human Morphology: 117418 Moscow, ul. Tsyuryupy 3; tel. (495) 120-80-65; fax (495) 120-14-56; attached to Russian Acad. of Medical Sciences; Dir N. K. PERMYAKOV.

Institute of Immunology: 142380 Moscow oblast, Chekhovsky raion, Lyubuchany; tel. (495) 546-15-55; fax (495) 546-15-55; f. 1980; library of 2,800 vols; Dir V. P. ZAVYALOV.

Institute of Immunology: 115478 Moscow, Kashirskoe shosse 24, korp. 2; tel. (499) 611-83-01; fax (499) 616-10-27; Dir R. M. KHAITOV.

Institute of Influenza: 197022 St Petersburg, ul. Prof. Popova 15/17; tel. (812) 234-58-75; fax (812) 234-01-50; attached to Russian Acad. of Medical Sciences; Dir O. I. KISELEV.

Institute of Internal Medicine: 630089 Novosibirsk, ul. Bogatkova 175/1; tel. and fax (3832) 64-25-16; e-mail office@iimed.ru; f. 1981; attached to Russian Acad. of Medical Sciences; Dir Prof. M. I. VOEVODA; publ. *Interpress* (4 a year).

Institute of Medical and Biological Cybernetics: 630117 Novosibirsk, ul. Akad. Timakova 2; tel. (3832) 32-12-56; fax (3832) 32-55-58; f. 1992; attached to Russian Acad. of Medical Sciences; Dir M. B. SHTARK; publ. *Biofeedback* (every 3 years).

Institute of Medical Climatology and Rehabilitation: 690025 Vladivostok, Sadgorod 25; tel. (4232) 33-05-22; fax (4232) 25-11-83; f. 1984; attached to Russian Acad. of Medical Sciences; library of 20,000 vols; Dir Prof. Dr E. M. IVANOV.

State Scientific Research Institute on Medical Problems of the Far North of Russian Academy of Medical Sciences: 629730 Tyumen oblast, Yamalo-Nenets Autonomous Okrug, Nadym, km 107; tel. (34995) 3-03-20; fax (34995) 9-74-53; e-mail nii-mpks@mail.ru; internet mpks.ptline.ru; f. 1994; attached to Russian Acad. of Medical Sciences; health service and scientific researches in cardiology, pulmonology, pediatrics, gastroenterology, immunology, genetics, ecology and some other biological and medical brs taking into account the unfavourable conditions of the Far North and influence of extreme northern factors upon people's health; library of 2,000 vols on medical and biological sciences; Dir Prof. A. A. BUGANOV; publ. *Questions of Polar Medicine* (2 a year).

Institute of Medical Problems of the North: 660022 Krasnoyarsk, ul. Partizana Zheleznyaka 3G; fax (3912) 23-19-63; f. 1976; attached to Russian Acad. of Medical Sciences; Dir VALERY T. MANCHUK.

Institute of Nutrition: 109240 Moscow, Ustinskii pr-d 2/14; tel. (495) 917-44-85; attached to Russian Acad. of Medical Sciences; Dir M. N. VOLGAREV.

Institute of Occupational Health: 105275 Moscow, pr. Budennogo 31; tel. (495) 365-02-09; fax (495) 366-05-83; attached to Russian Acad. of Medical Sciences; Dir Prof. N. F. IZMEROV.

Institute of Paediatrics: 117296 Moscow, Lomonsovskii pr. 2/62; tel. (495) 134-03-61; fax (495) 134-13-08; attached to Russian Acad. of Medical Sciences; Dir M. YA. STUDENIKIN.

Institute of Paediatrics and Child Surgery of the Ministry of Public Health of the Russian Federation: 127412 Moscow, Taldomskaya ul. 2; tel. (495) 484-02-92; fax (495) 438-62-32; Dir Prof. YURI E. VELTISCHEV; publ. *Vestnik* (Annals of Perinatology and Paediatrics).

Institute of Pharmacology: 125315 Moscow, ul. Baltiiskaya 8; tel. (495) 151-18-41; fax (495) 151-12-61; attached to Russian Acad. of Medical Sciences; Dir S. B. SEREDENIN.

Institute of Physiology: 630117 Novosibirsk, ul. Akad. Timakova 4; fax (3832) 32-42-54; attached to Russian Acad. of Medical Sciences; Dir V. A. TRUFAKIN.

Institute of Regional Pathology and Pathomorphology: 630117 Novosibirsk, ul. Timakova 2; tel. (3833) 34-84-38; fax (3833) 33-48-45; e-mail pathol@soramn.ru; internet www.pathomorphology.soramn.ru; f. 1992; attached to Russian Acad. of Medical Sciences; diagnostic and training centre; diagnostics of viral hepatitis, tumours, lung, heart, kidney, gastrointestinal chronic diseases; Dir L. M. NEPOMNYASHCHIKH; Deputy Dir for Science and Research ELENA L. LUSHNIKOVA.

Institute of Rheumatology: 115552 Moscow, Kashirskoe shosse 34-a; tel. (495) 114-44-90; fax (495) 114-44-68; f. 1959; attached to Russian Acad. of Medical Sciences; br. at Volgograd; Dir V. A. NASONOVA; publ. *Revmatologia* (6 a year).

Institute of the Brain: 107120 Moscow, per. Obukha 5; tel. (495) 917-80-07; fax (495) 916-05-95; attached to Russian Acad. of Medical Sciences; Dir N. N. BOGOLEPOV.

Institute of the Molecular Pathology and Biochemistry of Ecology: 630117 Novosibirsk, ul. Akad. Timakova 2; fax (3832) 32-31-47; attached to Russian Acad. of Medical Sciences; Dir V. V. LYAKHOVICH.

Institute of Viral Preparations: 109088 Moscow, 1 Dubrovskaya ul. 15; tel. (495) 274-81-45; fax (495) 274-57-10; attached to Russian Acad. of Medical Sciences; Dir O. G. ANDZHAPARIDZE.

Irkutsk Antiplague Research Institute of Siberia and the Far East: 664047 Irkutsk, ul. Trilissera 78; tel. (3952) 22-01-35; fax (3952) 22-01-40; e-mail adm@chumin.irkutsk.ru; internet www.irkutsk.ru/chumin; f. 1934; library of 55,000 vols; Dir Prof. E. P. GOLUBINSKY.

Irkutsk Institute of Orthopaedics and Traumatology: 664003 Irkutsk, ul. Bortzov Revoliutsii 1; tel. (3952) 27-54-30; f. 1946; diseases of the skeleton and bone tissue regeneration; library of 32,000 vols; Dir Prof. A. P. BARABASH.

Irkutsk Research Institute of Epidemiology and Microbiology: 664000 Irkutsk, ul. Karla Marksa 3; tel. (3952) 24-42-30; Dir V. I. ZLOBIN.

Ivanovskii, D. I., Institute of Virology: 123098 Moscow, ul. Gamalei 16; tel. (499) 190-28-74; fax (499) 190-28-67; attached to Russian Acad. of Medical Sciences; Dir Acad. DMITRY K. LVOV.

Kazan Institute of Epidemiology, Microbiology and Hygiene: 420015 Kazan, Bol. Krasnaya ul. 67; tel. (8432) 32-25-80; Dir F. Z. KAMALOV.

Kazan State Institute of Orthopaedics and Traumatology: 420015 Kazan, ul. Gorkogo 3; tel. (8432) 38-59-05; f. 1945; library: 13,500 units; publ. *Transactions* (1 a year).

Khabarovsk Research Institute of Epidemiology and Microbiology Rospotrebnadzor: Khabarovsk, Shevchenko 2; tel. and fax (4212) 32-54-13; e-mail bovlad@email.kht.ru; internet www.hniiem.rospotrebnadzor.ru; f. 1925; Head of Institute OLGA E. TROTSENKO; publ. *The Far Eastern Journal of Infectious Pathology*.

Laboratory of Experimental Biological Models: 143412 Moscow oblast, PO Otradnoe, pos. Svetlye Gory; tel. (495) 561-53-70; attached to Russian Acad. of Medical Sciences; Dir T. I. ZAITSEV.

Laboratory of Polar Medicine: 663310 Norilsk 10, ul. Talnakhskaya 7A, p/ya 625; fax (3919) 34-47-19; attached to Russian Acad. of Medical Sciences; Dir L. A. NADTOCHII.

Martsinovsky, I. E., Institute of Medical Parasitology and Tropical Medicine: 119435 Moscow, Mal. Pirogovskaya ul. 20; tel. (495) 246-80-49; fax (495) 246-90-47; f. 1920; library of 70,000 vols; Dir Prof. V. P. SERGIEV; publ. *Medical Parasitology and Parasitic Diseases* (4 a year).

Mechnikov I. I., Institute of Vaccines and Sera: 103064 Moscow, Mal. Kazenny per. 5A; tel. (495) 917-49-00; fax (495) 917-54-60; f. 1919; attached to Russian Acad. of Medical Sciences; Dir B.F. SEMENOV.

Medical Research Centre for Preventive Medicine and the Protection of the Health of Industrial Workers: 620014 Ekaterinburg, ul. Popova 30; tel. (3432) 71-87-54; fax (3432) 71-87-40; e-mail mrc@etel.ru; f. 1929; Dir SERGEY V. KUZMIN; publs *Balneology and Physiotherapy* (1 a year), *Urgent Issues of Preventive Medicine in the Urals* (1 a year).

Moscow G. N. Gabrichevskii Institute of Epidemiology and Microbiology: 125212 Moscow, ul. Admirala Makharova 10; tel. (495) 452-18-16; fax (495) 452-18-30; f. 1895; library of 8,922 vols; Dir Prof. BORIS A. SHENDEROV; publ. *Medical Aspects of Microecology* (1 a year).

Moscow Helmholtz Research Institute of Eye Diseases: 103064 Moscow, ul. Sadovaya-Chernogryazskaya 14/19; tel. (495) 207-

23-19; fax (495) 975-24-00; f. 1900; library of 69,445 vols; Dir ALEXANDER M. YUZHAKOV.

Moscow Municipal Research First Aid Institute: 129010 Moscow, Sukharevskaya pl. 3; tel. (495) 925-38-97; f. 1923; library of 30,000 vols; Dir Prof. B. D. KOMAROV.

Moscow Research Institute of Psychiatry: 107076 Moscow, Poteshnaya ul. 3; tel. (495) 963-76-26; fax (495) 963-09-97; e-mail krasnov@mtu-net.ru; internet www.mniip.org; f. 1920; social and biological psychiatry; treats mental illness, alcohol and drug addiction; Dir VALERY KRASNOV; publ. *Social and Clinical Psychiatry* (in Russian, 4 a year).

Nizhnii Novgorod Institute for Skin and Venereal Diseases: Nizhnii Novgorod, ul. Kovalikhinskaya 49; f. 1930; library of 10,000 vols; Dir Prof. T. A. GLAVINSKAYA.

Nizhnii Novgorod Institute of Industrial Hygiene and Occupational Diseases: Nizhnii Novgorod, ul. Semashko 20.

Nizhnii Novgorod Research Institute of Traumatology and Orthopaedics: 603155 Nizhnii Novgorod, V. Volzhskaya nab. 18; tel. (8312) 36-01-60; fax (8312) 36-05-91; e-mail gito@pop.sci-nnov.ru; internet www.nniito.ru; f. 1945; 222 mems; library of 38,035 vols; Dir Prof. V. AZOLOV.

Novosibirsk Institute of Tuberculosis: Novosibirsk, ul. Chaplygina 75.

Omsk Research Institute of Naturally Occurring Infections: 644080 Omsk 80, pr. Mira 7; tel. (3812) 65-06-33; Dir A. A. MATUSHENKO.

Ott, D. O., Research Institute of Obstetrics and Gynaecology: 199034 St Petersburg, Mendeleevskaya liniya 3; tel. (812) 328-14-02; fax (812) 328-23-61; f. 1797; attached to Russian Acad. of Medical Sciences; Dir Prof. EDWARD K. AILAMAZYAN.

Pharmacy Research Institute: 117418 Moscow, ul. Krasikova 34; tel. (495) 128-57-88; Dir A. I. TENTSOVA.

Plague Prevention Research Institute for the Caucasus and Transcaucasia: 355106 Stavropol, Sovetskaya ul. 13; tel. (8652) 3-13-12; Dir V. I. EFREMENKO.

Research Centre for Medical Genetics: 115478 Moscow, Moskvorechie 1; tel. (499) 612-86-07; fax (495) 324-07-02; e-mail ekginter@mail.ru; internet www.med-gen.ru; f. 1969; attached to Russian Acad. of Medical Sciences; medical genetics, molecular genetics, cytogenetics, genetics of populations, clinical genetics, genetic counselling, hereditary metabolic diseases, prenatal diagnostics; library of 37,500 vols; Dir Prof. EVGENY K. GINTER; publ. *Medical Genetics* (12 a year).

Attached Institutes:

Institute of Clinical Genetics: Moscow; tel. (499) 611-85-94; attached to Russian Acad. of Medical Sciences; Dir Prof. EVGENY K. GINTER.

Institute of Human Genetics: Moscow; tel. (499) 611-85-87; attached to Russian Acad. of Medical Sciences; Dir S. S. SHISHKIN.

Research Centre for Molecular Diagnostics and Therapy: 117638 Moscow, Simferopolsky bul. 8; tel. (495) 113-23-51; fax (495) 113-26-33; e-mail e.severin@mtu-net.ru; f. 1985; Dir E. S. SEVERIN; publs *Molecular Medicine* (4 a year), *Problems of Biological, Medical and Pharmaceutical Chemistry* (4 a year).

Research Centre for Obstetrics, Gynaecology and Perinatology: 117815 Moscow, GSP-7, ul. Akademika Oparina; tel. (495) 438-51-71; internet www.pregnancy.ru; Dir Prof. VLADIMIR I. KULAKOV; Scientific Sec. Dr TATYANA V. LEOPATINA.

Research Centre of Medical Radiology: 249020 Kaluga oblast, Obninsk, ul. Koroleva 4; tel. (495) 956-14-39; fax (495) 956-14-40; f. 1958; attached to Russian Acad. of Medical Sciences; library of 121,000 vols; Dir A. F. TSYB; publ. *Radiation and Risk* (2 a year).

Research Centre of Mental Health: 115552 Moscow, Kashirskoe shosse 34; tel. (499) 616-61-83; fax (495) 952-89-40; attached to Russian Acad. of Medical Sciences; Dir A. S. TIGANOV.

Research Centre of Neurology: 125367 Moscow, Volokolamskoe shosse 80; tel. (495) 490-20-02; fax (495) 490-22-10; e-mail center@neurology.ru; internet www.neurology.ru; f. 1945; attached to Russian Acad. of Medical Sciences; Dir Z. A. SUSLINA.

Research Centre of Obstetrics, Gynaecology and Perinatology: 117815 Moscow, ul. Akad. Oparina 4; tel. (495) 438-18-00; fax (495) 438-18-00; attached to Russian Acad. of Medical Sciences; Dir VLADIMIR KULAKOV.

Research Centre of Surgery: 119991 Moscow, Abrikosovski per. 2; tel. (499) 246-95-63; fax (499) 246-89-88; e-mail nrcs@med.ru; internet med.ru; attached to Russian Acad. of Medical Sciences; Dir SERGEY L. DZEMESHKEVICH.

Research Institute for Complex Problems of Hygiene and Occupational Diseases: 654041 Novokuznetsk, ul. Kutuzova 23; tel. (3843) 79-69-79; fax (3843) 79-66-69; e-mail zacharenkov@nvkz.kuzbass.net; internet www.ni-kpg.ru; f. 1976; attached to Russian Acad. of Medical Sciences; Dir Dr V. V. ZAKHARENKOV.

Research Institute of Children's Infections: 197022 St Petersburg, ul. Prof. Popova 9; tel. (812) 234-18-62; f. 1927; library of 25,000 vols; Dir V. V. IVANOVA; publ. *Infectious Diseases of Childhood* (1 or 2 a year).

Research Institute of Epidemiology and Microbiology: 603600 Nizhnii Novgorod, Gruzinskaya ul. 44; tel. (8312) 33-40-07; fax (8312) 35-64-80; f. 1929; library of 10,000 vols; Dir I. N. BLOKHINA; publ. *Annual Collection of Research Articles*.

Research Institute of Forensic Medicine: 123242 Moscow, ul. Sadovaya-Kudrinskaya 3, Korp. 2; tel. (495) 254-32-49; Dir Prof. V. I. PROZOROVSKY.

Research Institute of Haematology and Intensive Therapy: 125167 Moscow, Novozykovsky pr-d 4A; tel. (495) 212-45-51; fax (495) 212-42-52; f. 1926; library of 50,000 vols; publ. *Sovremennye Problemy Gematologii i Perelivaniya Krovi* (12 a year).

Research Institute of Laser Medicine: 121165 Moscow, Studencheskaya ul. 40; tel. (495) 249-39-05.

Research Institute of Medical Primatology: 354376 Sochi-Adler, Veseloye 1; tel. (8622) 41-68-62; fax (8622) 41-62-39; e-mail iprim@mail.sochi.ru; f. 1927; attached to Russian Acad. of Medical Sciences; principal research programmes: primatology, maintaining and breeding primates, primate models of human diseases, endocrinology, immunology and cell biology, pathomorphology, comparative pathology, infectious pathology, infectious virology; library of 2,000 vols; Dir Prof. Acad. BORIS ARKADIEVICH LAPIN.

Research Institute of Occupational Safety under the auspices of the Independent Russian Trade Unions: 191187 St Petersburg, ul. Gagarinskaya 3; tel. (812) 279-08-13; fax (812) 275-42-48; f. 1927; noise control, respiratory protection, air conditioning, ventilation, air pollution analysis, hygiene and VDUs, certification of personal protective equipment and workplaces; library of 47,000 vols; Dir E. A. KOLODIN.

Research Institute of Radiation Hygiene: 197101 St Petersburg, ul. Mira 8; tel. (812) 233-53-63; fax (812) 233-26-12; e-mail irii@ek6663.spb.edu; f. 1956.

Research Institute of the Technology and Safety of Medicines: 142450 Moscow oblast, Noginsky raion, pos. Staraya Kupavna, ul. Kirova 23; tel. (495) 524-09-36; attached to Russian Acad. of Sciences; Dir YU. V. BUROV.

Research Institute of Traditional Methods of Treatment: 103051 Moscow, Petrovsky bul. 8; tel. (495) 200-27-91.

Research Institute of Transplants and Artificial Organs: 123436 Moscow, Shchukinskaya ul. 1; tel. (495) 190-29-71.

Research Institute of Vaccines and Sera: 614089 Perm, GSP, NIIVS.

Research Institute of Vaccines and Sera: 634004 Tomsk, ul. Lenina 32; tel. (3822) 22-45-12; Dir N. B. CHERNY.

Rostov Institute of Radiology and Oncology: Rostov-on-Don, Voroshilovsky pr. 119; affiliated to the Chelyabinsk Radiation Hygiene Institute.

Rostov Region Paediatric Research Institute: Rostov-on-Don, Dolomanovsky per. 142.

Rostov Research Institute for Plague Control: 344007 Rostov on Don, ul. M. Gorkogo 117; tel. (8632) 66-57-03; fax (8632) 34-13-76; f. 1934; library of 52,300 vols; Dir Prof. YU. M. LOMOV.

Russian Anti-plague Research Institute 'Microbe': 410005 Saratov, ul. Universitetskaya 46; tel. (8452) 26-21-31; fax (8452) 51-52-12; e-mail microbe@san.ru; internet www.microbe.ru; f. 1918; library of 100,000 vols; Dir Dr Prof. V. V. KUTYREV; publ. *Problems of Particularly Dangerous Infections* (4 a year).

Russian Institute of Medical Parasitology: Rostov-on-Don, Moskovskaya 67.

Russian Polenov, A. L., Neurosurgical Institute: 191104 St Petersburg, ul. Mayakovskogo 12; tel. (812) 272-98-79; fax (812) 275-56-03; f. 1926; library of 36,000 vols; Dir V. P. BERSNEV; publ. *Neurosurgery* (1 a year).

Russian Research Centre of Rehabilitation and Physiotherapy: 121099 Moscow, Novy Arbat 32; tel. (495) 252-18-83; fax (495) 292-65-11; f. 1920; library of 73,500 vols; Dir Dr V. M. BOGOLYUBOV; publs *Problems of Health Resorts, Physiotherapy and Exercise Therapy* (6 a year).

Russian Research Institute of Haematology and Transfusiology: 191024 St Petersburg, 2-a Sovetskaya ul. 16; tel. (812) 274-56-50; fax (812) 274-92-27; e-mail bloodscience@mail.ru; internet www.bloodscience.ru; f. 1932; Dir Dr E. A. SELIVANOV.

Research Institute of Phthisiopulmonology of the First Moscow Sechenov Medical University: 127994 Moscow, ul. Dostoevskogo 4; tel. (495) 281-84-22; fax (495) 281-59-88; e-mail tbcripp@mail.ru; f. 1918; research in area of identification, diagnostics, treatment of pulmonary and extrapulmonary tuberculosis and sarcoidosis in children, adolescents and adults; epidemiological surveys and assistance in organization of anti-tuberculosis aid; library of 54,517 vols; Dir Dr SERGEY V. SMERDIN; publ. *Tuberculosis and Ecology* (6 a year).

Russian Research Institute of Traumatology and Orthopaedics 'Vreden, R. R.': 195427 St Petersburg, ul. Akademika Baykova, dom 8; tel. (812) 670-89-05; fax (812) 670-95-68; e-mail info@rniito.org; internet www.rniito.org; f. 1906; orthopaedic clinical research centre; postgraduate training; library of 57,000 vols; Dir Prof. RASHID

TIKHILOV; publ. *Travmatologia i Ortopedia Rossii* (Traumatology and Orthopaedics of Russia, 4 a year).

Russian Scientific Centre of Roentgen-oradiology: 117837 Moscow, ul. Profsoyuznaya 86; tel. (495) 333-94-39; fax (495) 334-79-24; e-mail mailbox@rncrr.rssi.ru; internet www.space.ru/rncrr; f. 1924; laser diagnosis and treatment of malignant tumours; library of 51,700 vols; Dir Prof. V.P. KHARCHENKO.

St Petersburg Artificial Limb Research Institute: St Petersburg, pr. K. Marxa 9/12.

St Petersburg Institute of Ear, Throat, Nose and Speech: St Petersburg, Bronnitskaya 9; tel. (812) 292-54-29; f. 1930; library of 45,000 vols; Dir A. A. LANTSOV.

St Petersburg Institute of Eye Diseases: St Petersburg, Mokhovaya 38.

St Petersburg Institute of Phthisiopulmonology: 193036 St Petersburg, Ligovsky pr. 2–4; tel. (812) 279-25-54; fax (812) 279-25-73; f. 1923; library of 26,000 vols; Dir Prof. ALEXANDR V. VASILEV.

St Petersburg Institute of Tuberculosis: 193130 St Petersburg, Ligovsky pr. 2/4.

St Petersburg Institute of Vaccines and Sera: 198320 Krasnoe Selo, ul. Svobody 52; tel. (812) 741-19-78; fax (812) 741-10-53; e-mail reception@spbniivs.ru; internet www.spbniivs.ru; Dir R. N. RODIONOVA.

St Petersburg Pasteur Institute of Epidemiology and Microbiology: 197101 St Petersburg, ul. Mira 14; tel. (812) 233-20-92; fax (812) 232-92-17; e-mail intdeppi@ok7368.spb.edu; internet www.pasteur-nii.spb.ru; f. 1923; library of 60,000 vols; Dir Prof. ANATOLY ZHEBRUN.

St Petersburg Petrov, N. N., Research Institute of Oncology: 188646 St Petersburg, Pesochny 2, St Petersburgskaya ul. 68; tel. (812) 237-89-94.

St Petersburg Research Institute of Industrial Hygiene and Occupational Diseases: 193036 St Petersburg, 2-a Sovetskaya ul. 4; tel. (812) 279-40-11; f. 1924.

Samara Institute of Epidemiology, Microbiology and Hygiene: Samara, Chapaevskaya 87.

Saratov Institute of Restorative Surgery, Traumatology and Orthopaedics: Saratov, ul. Chernyshevskogo 148.

Scientific Centre of Clinical and Experimental Medicine: ul. Akad. Timakova 2, 630117 Novosibirsk; tel. (3832) 33-64-56; fax (3832) 33-64-56; e-mail sck@cyber.ma.nsc.ru; f. 1970; attached to Russian Acad. of Medical Sciences; Dir Dr V. A. SHKURUPY; publ. *Siberian Consilium* (medical pharmaceuticals, 6 a year).

Scientific Research Institute for General Reanimatology: 103031 Moscow, ul. Petrovka 25; tel. (495) 200-27-08; fax (495) 209-96-77; e-mail miiorramn@mediann.ru; f. 1936; attached to Russian Acad. of Medical Sciences; Dir Prof. V. V. MOROZ; br. at Novokuznetsk.

Scientific Research Institute for the Investigation of New Antibiotics: 119867 Moscow, Bol. Pirogovskaya 11; tel. (495) 246-99-80; fax (495) 245-02-95; attached to Russian Acad. of Medical Sciences; Dir YU. V. DUDNIK.

Semashko, N. A., Research Institute of Social Hygiene, Health Service Economics and Management: 103064 Moscow, ul. Vorontsovo Pole 12; tel. (495) 917-48-86; fax (495) 916-03-98; f. 1944; attached to Russian Acad. of Medical Sciences; Dir O. P. SHCHEPIN; publ. *Journal of Social Hygiene and the History of Medicine*.

Serbsky National Research Centre for Social and Forensic Psychiatry: 119034 Moscow, Kropotkinsky per. 23; tel. (495) 201-52-62; fax (495) 201-72-31; internet www.psi.med.ru/sspcen.htm; f. 1921; forensic psychiatry, social and clinical issues of psychiatry; library of 74,000 vols; Dir T. B. DMITRIEVA; publ. *Russian Psychiatric Journal* (contents and summaries in English, 6 a year).

Sochi Health Research Institute: Sochi, Kurortny pr. 110.

State Institute of Natural Curative Factors: 357500 Pyatigorsk, pr. Kirova 30; tel. (87933) 50-050; fax (87933) 55-618; f. 1920; neurology, rheumatology, pain assessment and management, behavioural therapy; library of 120,000 vols; Dir Prof. KRIVOBOROV.

State Research Institute for the Standardization and Control of Drugs: 117246 Moscow, Nauchni pr-d 14A; tel. (495) 128-26-32; Dir Prof. YU. F. KRYLOV.

State Scientific Research Institute of Medical Polymers: 117246 Moscow, Nauchni pr-d 10; tel. (495) 120-21-62; fax (495) 120-05-61; internet www.medpol.ru; f. 1966; library of 15,000 vols; Dir Prof. G. A. MATJUSHIN.

Sysin, A. N., Institute of Human Ecology and Environmental Hygiene: 119833 Moscow, ul. Pogodinskaya 10; tel. (495) 246-58-24; fax (495) 247-04-28; f. 1931; attached to Russian Acad. of Medical Sciences; Dir G. I. SIDORENKO.

Tarasevich, L. A., State Research Institute for the Standardization and Control of Medical Biological Preparations: 121002 Moscow, Sivtsev-Vrazhek 41; tel. (495) 241-39-22; fax (495) 241-39-22; e-mail gisk@glasnet.ru; f. 1919; library of 20,000 vols; Dir Prof. N. V. MEDUNTSIN.

Technological Research Institute for Antibiotics and Medical Enzymes: 198020 St Petersburg, Ogorodnikov pr. 41; tel. (812) 251-19-44; f. 1956; antifungal antibiotics, enzymes for medical use, nucleoside preparation of cardiovascular action; library of 55,000 vols; Dir Dr B. V. MOSKVICHEV.

Tomsk Institute of Physiotherapy and Spa Treatment: Tomsk, ul. Rosa Luxembourg 1.

Tomsk Research Centre: 634012 Tomsk, Kievskaya ul. 111/2; fax (3822) 44-50-57; attached to Russian Acad. of Medical Sciences; Chair. of the Presidium R. S. KARPOV.

Attached Institutes:

Institute of Cardiology: 634012 Tomsk, Kievskaya ul. 111/2; tel. (3822) 44-33-97; attached to Russian Acad. of Medical Sciences; Dir R. S. KARPOV.

Institute of Medical Genetics: 634050 Tomsk, pos. Sputnik, nab. Ushaika 10; tel. (3822) 22-22-28; attached to Russian Acad. of Medical Sciences; Dir V. P. PUZYREV.

Cancer Research Institute: 634050 Tomsk, Kooperativnyi st 5; tel. (3822) 51-10-39; fax (3822) 51-40-97; e-mail nii@oncology.tomsk.ru; internet www.oncology.tomsk.ru; f. 1979; attached to Siberian Br. Russian Acad. of Medical Sciences; studies on cancer prevalence and carcinogenesis on the territory of Siberia and the Russian Far E; detects endogenous and exogenous factors in tumour devt; investigates biochemical and molecular-genetic factors reflecting the mechanisms of carcinogenesis and tumour progression for assessing cancer risk and disease prognosis; develops new efficient programmes of the combined modality treatment for cancer patients using high-technology approaches; improves reconstructive plastic and organ-preserving surgeries and approaches for medical-social rehabilitation; Dir EVGENY L. CHOYNZONOV; publ. *Siberian Journal of Oncology* (6 a year).

Institute of Pharmacology: 634028 Tomsk, pr. Lenina 3; fax (3822) 41-83-79; attached to Russian Acad. of Medical Sciences; Dir E. D. GOLDBERG.

Laboratory of Experimental Biomedical Models: 634009 Tomsk, Kooperativny per. 7B; tel. (3822) 22-36-26; attached to Russian Acad. of Medical Sciences; Dir S. A. KUSMARTSEV.

Mental Health Research Institute: 634014 Tomsk, Sosnovy Bor, Aleutskaya St, 4; tel. (3822) 72-43-79; fax (3822) 72-44-25; e-mail redo@mail.tomsknet.ru; internet tomskinstitute.mental-health.ru; f. 1981; attached to Siberian Br., Russian Acad. of Medical Sciences; library of 8,120 vols; Dir Acad. VALENTIN SEMKE; Deputy Dir Prof. NIKOLAYF BOKHAN; publ. *Siberian Journal of Psychiatry and Addiction Psychiatry* (6 a year).

Institute of Toxicology: 192019 St Petersburg Bekhtereva St 1; tel. (812) 365-06-80; fax (812) 365-06-80; e-mail info@toxicology.ru; internet www.toxicology.ru; f. 1935; attached to Federal Medico-Biological Agency of Russia Federal State Scientific Institution; Dir SERGEY P. NECHIPORENKO; Deputy Dir for Research Affairs EVGENY YU. BONITENKO.

Turner Scientific Research Institute of Child Orthopaedics and Traumatology: 189620 St Petersburg, ul. Parkovaya 64–68; tel. (812) 465-28-57; f. 1932; library of 33,600 vols; Dir Prof. V. L. ANDRIANOV; publ. scientific papers (2–3 a year).

Ufa Eye Research Institute: 450077 Ufa, 90 Pushkin str.; tel. (347) 272-37-75; fax (347) 272-08-52; e-mail eye@academy.bashnet.ru; f. 1926; Dir Prof. M. M. BIKBOV; publ. *Collected Articles* (1 a year).

Ufa Research Institute of Occupational Health and Human Ecology: 450106 Ufa, ul. Kuvykina 94; tel. (3472) 28-53-19; fax (3472) 28-49-16; f. 1955; complex development of scientific fundamentals of labour hygiene and physiology, industrial toxicology, occupational pathology, environmental hygiene and aspects of hygiene in juvenile vocational training and the workplace in the oil, petrochemical, gas and microbiological industries; library of 63,000 vols; Dir A. B. BAKIROV; publ. *Production and Environmental Hygiene: Workers' Health Care in Oil and Gas Extracting and Petrochemical Industries* (1 a year).

Ufa Skin and Venereal Diseases Institute: Ufa, ul. Frunze 43.

Urals Research Institute of Maternity and Childhood Care: 620028 Ekaterinburg, ul. Repina 1; tel. (3432) 51-42-02; fax (3432) 51-22-12; f. 1877; library of 30,000 vols; Dir Dr G. A. CHERDANTSEVA.

Urals Research Institute of Phthisiopulmonology: 620039 Ekaterinburg, ul. 22 Partsezda 50; tel. (3432) 32-72-20; fax (3432) 31-80-41; e-mail urniif@mail.ur.ru; internet www.urniif.okb1.mplik.ru; f. 1931; library of 5,000 vols; Dir V. A. SOKOLOV.

Urology Research Institute: 105425 Moscow, 3-ya Parkovaya ul. 51; tel. (495) 367-62-62; fax (495) 367-62-62; e-mail urology@cdromclub.ru; f. 1979; Dir Acad. NIKOLAI A. LOPATKIN.

Vishnevsky, A. V., Institute of Surgery: 113811 Moscow, Bol. Serpukhovskaya 27; tel. (495) 236-72-90; fax (495) 237-08-14; attached to Russian Acad. of Medical Sciences; Dir V. D. FEDOROV.

Volgograd Plague Prevention Research Institute: 400131 Volgograd, Golubinskaya ul. 7; tel. (8442) 37-37-74; fax (8442) 32-33-36; e-mail vari2@sprint-v.com.ru; f. 1970; library of 13,320 vols; Dir V. V. ALEKSEEV.

Voronezh Region Radiological and Oncological Institute: Voronezh, ul. Kalyaeva 2.

NATURAL SCIENCES

General

Arctic and Antarctic Research Institute: 199397 St Petersburg, ul. Beringa 38; tel. (812) 352-00-96; fax (812) 352-26-88; Dir I. YE. FROLOV.

Institute of Economic and International Problems of the Assimilation of the Ocean: 690600 Vladivostok, ul. Sukhanova 5-a; tel. (4232) 5-77-31; attached to Russian Acad. of Sciences; Dir. R. SH.-A. ALIEV.

Institute of Global Climate and Ecology: 107258 Moscow, Glebovskaya 20B; tel. (495) 169-01-43; attached to Russian Acad. of Sciences; Dir YU. A. IZRAEL.

Institute of Limnology: 196199 St Petersburg, ul. Sevastyanova 9; tel. (812) 297-22-97; attached to Russian Acad. of Sciences; Dir V. A. RUMYANTSEV.

Institute of Natural Sciences: 670042 Ulan-Ude, ul. M. Sakhyanovoi 6; tel. (3012) 3-01-62; attached to Russian Acad. of Sciences; Dir K. A. NIKIFOROV.

Institute of the History of Science and Technology 'S. I. Vavilov': 109012 Moscow, Staropanskii per. 1/5; tel. and fax (495) 925-22-80; e-mail postmaster@ihst.ru; internet www.ihst.ru; f. 1953; attached to Russian Acad. of Sciences; research in history of natural sciences and technology (history of maths, physics, mechanics, biology, chemistry, social studies, Earth sciences, ecology and history of space); library of 70,000 vols; Dir Dr YURY M. BATURIN; publ. *Voprosy istorii estestvoznaniya i tekhniki* (4 a year).

Branch:

Institute for the History of Science and Technology – St Petersburg Branch: Universitetskaya nab. 5, 199034 St Petersburg; tel. (812) 328-47-12; fax (812) 328-46-67; e-mail ihst@ihst.nw.ru; internet ihst.nw.ru; Dir Prof. E. I. KOLCHINSKY.

Limnological Institute: 664033 Irkutsk, Ulan-Batorskaya ul. 3; tel. (3952) 42-65-04; fax (3952) 42-54-05; e-mail info@lin.irk.ru; internet www.lin.irk.ru; attached to Siberian Br., Russian Acad. of Sciences; Dir M. A. GRACHEV.

Mountain Taiga Station: 692533 Primorskii krai, Ussuriisky raion, pos. Gornotaezhnoe; tel. (42341) 9-11-10; attached to Russian Acad. of Sciences; Dir P. S. ZORIKOV.

North-East Interdisciplinary Science Research Institute FEB RAS: 685000 Magadan, Portovaya 16; tel. and fax (4132) 63-00-51; e-mail secretary@neisri.ru; internet www.neisri.ru; f. 1960; attached to Russian Acad. of Sciences; geology, geophysics, metallogeny, history, archaeology, economics; library of 450,000 vols; Dir Prof. Dr NIKOLAI ANATOLYEVICH GORYACHEV; Scientific Sec. PLYASHKEVICH ANNA ALEKSEEVNA; publ. *Vestnik NESC* (4 a year).

Pacific Oceanological Institute: 690041 Vladivostok, Baltiiskaya ul. 43; tel. (4232) 31-14-00; fax (4232) 31-25-73; attached to Russian Acad. of Sciences; Dir Prof. V. A. AKULICHEV.

Pushchino Scientific Centre: 142290 Moscow oblast, Pushchino, pr. Nauki 3; tel. and fax (495) 923-80-03; e-mail nazarova@psn.ru; internet www.psn.ru; f. 1963; attached to Russian Acad. of Sciences; Dir VLADIMIR A. SHUVALOV.

Shirshov, P. P., Institute of Oceanology: 117997 Moscow, Nakhimovsky pr. 36; tel. (495) 124-59-96; fax (495) 124-59-83; e-mail office@ocean.ru; internet www.ocean.ru; f. 1946; attached to Russian Acad. of Sciences; brs in Kaliningrad, Gelendzhik, St Petersburg; Dir Prof. S. S. LAPPO.

Biological Sciences

All-Russia Research Institute for Nature Conservation: 113628 Moscow, Znamenskoe-Sadki, VNII Priroda; tel. (495) 423-03-22; fax (495) 423-23-22; f. 1981; research, general methodology, environmental protection strategy and coordination at home and internationally; 5 depts: animal protection, plant protection, ecosystem protection and recovery (incl. aquatic ecosystems), utilization of natural resources and nature reserves; library (books, journals, theses); Dir Prof. V. A. KRASILOV.

All-Russia Research Institute of Applied Microbiology: 142279 Moscow oblast, Serpukhovsky raion, Obolensk; tel. (0967) 2-77-61; Dir N. N. URAKOV.

Bakh, A. N., Institute of Biochemistry: Leninsky Pr. 33, 119071 Moscow; tel. (495) 952-34-41; fax (495) 952-27-32; e-mail inbi@inbi.ras.ru; internet www.inbi.ras.ru; attached to Russian Acad. of Sciences; 255 mems; Dir Prof. V. O. POPOV; Vice-Dir Prof. B. B. DZANTIEV; publs *Applied Biochemistry and Microbiology* (6 a year), *Uspekhi Biologicheskoi Khimii* (Progress of Biological Chemistry, in Russian, 1 a year).

Bioengineering Research Centre: 117984 Moscow, ul. Vavilova 34/5; tel. (495) 135-73-19; fax (495) 135-05-71; attached to Russian Acad. of Sciences; Dir K. G. SKRYABIN.

Biotechnical Research Institute: 119034 Moscow, ul. Prechistenka 38; tel. (495) 246-16-56; Dir A. M. KARPOV.

Biotechnologia JSC: 117246 Moscow, Nauchny pr-d 8; tel. (495) 332-34-20; fax (495) 331-01-01; f. 1993 as private company (fmrly state enterprise, f. 1986); biotechnology, pharmaceuticals; Gen. Dir RAIF G. VASILOV.

Borissiak Palaeontological Institute of Russian (PIN RAS): 117647 Moscow, Profsoyuznaya 123; tel. (495) 339-05-77; fax (495) 339-12-66; e-mail admin@paleo.ru; internet www.paleo.ru; f. 1930; attached to Russian Acad. of Sciences; library of 20,000 vols; attached museum: see Museums and Art Galleries; Dirs Acad. A. YU. ROZANOV, Prof. S. V. ROZHNOV, Prof. A. V. LOPATIN; publs *Paleontological Journal* (6 a year, in English and Russian), *Transactions* (3 or 4 a year).

Engelhardt Institute of Molecular Biology: 117984 Moscow, ul. Vavilova 32; tel. (495) 135-23-11; fax (495) 135-14-05; attached to Russian Acad. of Sciences; Dir Acad. A. D. MIRZABEKOV.

Institute of Bio-organic Chemistry: 630090 Novosibirsk, pr. Akad. Lavrenteva 8; tel. (3832) 35-64-41; fax (3832) 35-16-65; attached to Russian Acad. of Sciences; Dir Prof. V. V. VLASOV.

Institute of Biological Problems of the North: 685000 Magadan, pr. K. Marksa 24; tel. (41322) 2-47-30; fax (41322) 2-01-66; f. 1972; attached to Russian Acad. of Sciences; Dir Prof. F. B. CHERNYAVSKY.

Institute of Biology: 630091 Novosibirsk, ul. Frunze 11; tel. (3832) 20-96-14; attached to Russian Acad. of Sciences; Dir V. I. EVSIKOV.

Institute of Biology: 185610 Petrozavodsk, Pushkinskaya ul. 11; tel. (8142) 7-36-15; attached to Russian Acad. of Sciences; Dir S. N. DROZDOV.

Institute of Biology: 167610 Syktyvkar, Kommunisticheskaya ul. 28; tel. (8212) 42-52-02; fax (8212) 42-01-63; f. 1962; attached to Russian Acad. of Sciences; Dir Dr A. I. TASKAEV.

Institute of Biology: 450054 Ufa, 25, pr. Oktyabrya 69; tel. (3472) 34-34-01; attached to Russian Acad. of Sciences; Dir V. M. KORSUNOV.

Institute of Biology: 670047 Ulan-Ude, ul. M. Sakhyanovoi 6; tel. (3012) 43-45-75; attached to Russian Acad. of Sciences; Dir L. L. UBUGUNOV.

Institute of Biology: 677891 Yakutsk, pr. Lenina 41; tel. (4112) 2-77-81; attached to Russian Acad. of Sciences; Dir. N. G. SOLOMONOV.

Institute of Biology and Soil Science: 690022 Vladivostok, pr. Stoletiya Vladivostoka 159; tel. (4232) 31-04-10; fax (4232) 31-01-93; internet www.ibss.febras.ru; f. 1962; attached to Russian Acad. of Sciences; library of 80,000 vols; Dir Prof. YU. N. ZHURAVLEV; publ. *Proceedings* (in Russian, 1 a year).

Institute of Biophysics: 660036 Krasnoyarsk, Akademgorodok; tel. (3912) 43-15-79; fax (3912) 43-34-00; internet www.ibp.ru; f. 1981; attached to Russian Acad. of Sciences; Dir Dr A. G. DEGERMENDZHY; Scientific Sec. Dr EGOR ZADEREEV.

Institute of Biophysics: 123182 Moscow, Zhivopisnaya ul. 46; tel. (495) 190-56-51; fax (495) 190-35-90; e-mail ibphgen@rcibph.dol.ru; f. 1946; radiobiology, radiation protection, health physics, medical radiology, non-ionizing radiation; Dir L. A. ILYIN.

Institute of Cell Biophysics: 142290 Moscow oblast, Pushchino, Institutskaya ul. 3; tel. (495) 625-59-84; fax (496) 733-05-09; f. 1991; attached to Russian Acad. of Sciences; Dir Prof. EVGENII FESENKO.

Institute of Cytology: 194064 St Petersburg, Tikhoretsky pr. 4; tel. (812) 247-18-29; fax (812) 247-03-41; attached to the Soc. of Protozoologists, affiliated with the Russian Acad. of Sciences; Dir Prof. Dr VLADIMIR N. PARFENOV.

Institute of Cytology and Genetics: 630090 Novosibirsk, pr. Akad. Lavrenteva 10; tel. (3832) 363-49-80; fax (3832) 333-12-78; internet www.bionet.nsc.ru; f. 1957; attached to Russian Acad. of Sciences; Dir Acad. N. A. KOLCHANOV; Scientific Sec. G. V. ORLOVA.

Institute of Food Substances: c/o Russian Academy of Sciences, 117901 Moscow, Leninsky pr. 14; attached to Russian Acad. of Sciences; Dir M. N. MANAKOV.

Institute of Higher Nervous Activity and Neurophysiology: 117865 Moscow, ul. Butlerova 5a; tel. (495) 334-70-00; attached to Russian Acad. of Sciences; Dir Acad. P. V. SIMONOV.

Institute of Marine Biology: Petropavlovsk-Kamchatskii; attached to Russian Acad. of Sciences; Dir (vacant).

Institute of Marine Biology: 690041 Vladivostok, ul. Palchevskogo 17; tel. (4232) 31-09-05; fax (4232) 31-09-00; e-mail inmarbio@mail.primorye.ru; internet www.imb.dvo.ru; f. 1970; attached to Russian Acad. of Sciences; library of 40,000 vols; Dir Prof. VLADIMIR L. KASYANOV; publs *Biologiya morya* (6 a year), *Russian Journal of Marine Biology* (online, 7 a year).

Institute of Microbiology: 117811 Moscow, pr. 60-letiya Oktyabrya 7, korp. 2; tel. (495) 135-45-66; attached to Russian Acad. of Sciences; Dir Acad. M. V. IVANOV.

Institute of Molecular Biology of the Gene: 117333 Moscow, ul. Vavilova 34/5; tel. (495) 135-60-89; attached to Russian Acad. of Sciences; Dir Acad. G. P. GEORGIEV.

Institute of Molecular Genetics: 123182 Moscow, pl. Kurchatova 2; tel. (499) 196-00-00; fax (499) 196-02-21; e-mail img@img.ras.ru; internet www.img.ras.ru; f. 1978; attached to Russian Acad. of Sciences; Dir Prof. SERGEY V. KOSTROV.

Institute of Parasitology: 117071 Moscow, Leninskii pr. 33; tel. (495) 952-57-46; attached to Russian Acad. of Sciences; Dir M. D. SONIN.

Institute of Physicochemical and Biological Problems in Soil Science: 142290 Moscow oblast, Serpukhovskii raion, Pushchino; tel. (0967) 73-36-34; fax (0967) 33-05-95; e-mail soil@issp.serpukhov.su; internet www.issp.serpukhov.su; f. 1999; attached to Russian Acad. of Sciences; Dir Prof. V. N. KUDEYAROV.

Institute of Physiologically Active Substances: 142432 Moscow oblast, Noginskii raion, p/o Chernogolovka; tel. (096) 524-50-62; attached to Russian Acad. of Sciences; Dir Acad. N. S. ZEFIROV.

Institute of Physiology: c/o Russian Academy of Sciences, 117901 Moscow, Leninsky pr. 14; attached to Russian Acad. of Sciences; Dir O. G. GAZENKO.

Institute of Physiology: 167982 Syktyvkar, Pervomayskaya str. 50; tel. and fax (8212) 24-10-01; e-mail ovoys@physiol.komisc.ru; internet www.physiol.komisc.ru; f. 1988; attached to Russian Acad. of Sciences; Urals br. of the Russian Acad. of Sciences; Dir Prof. Dr Y. S. OVODOV.

Institute of Plant and Animal Ecology, Ural Division of Russian Academy of Sciences: 620144 Ekaterinburg, 8 Marta St 202; tel. (343) 260-82-55; fax (343) 260-65-00; e-mail common@ipae.uran.ru; internet www.ipae.uran.ru; f. 1944; attached to Russian Acad. of Sciences; investigations on regularities of org., functioning, dynamics and stability of living systems on population, community and ecosystem levels incl. palaeoreconstructions of late quaternary ecosystems of the Urals mountains and adjacent territories (N Eurasia); elaboration of theoretical foundations of rational nature management ecological regulation, bio-indication, ecotoxicology and radioecology; library of 150,000 vols; Dir Acad. VLADIMIR N. BOLSHAKOV; Deputy Dir VLADIMIR D. BOGDANOV; Deputy Dir EUGENE L. VOROBEICHIK; publ. *Russian Journal of Ecology* (6 a year).

Institute of Problems of the Industrial Ecology in the North (INEP KSC): 184209 Murmansk region, Apatity Fersman St, 14; tel. (81555) 6-10-93; fax (81555) 7-49-64; e-mail vandysh@inep.ksc.ru; internet inep.ksc.ru; f. 1989; attached to Kola Science Centre, Russian Acad. of Sciences; library of 400,000 vols; Dir Prof. Dr VLADIMIR A. MASLOBOEV.

Institute of Protein Research: 142292 Moscow oblast, Serpukhovskii raion, Pushchino; tel. (495) 924-04-93; fax (495) 924-04-93; e-mail protres@sun.ipr.serpukhov.su; attached to Russian Acad. of Sciences; Dir Prof. A. S. SPIRIN.

Institute of the Biochemistry and Physiology of Micro-organisms: 142292 Moscow oblast, Serpukhovskii raion, Pushchino; tel. (277) 3-05-26; attached to Russian Acad. of Sciences; Dir A. M. BORONIN.

Institute of the Biochemistry and Physiology of Plants and Micro-organisms: 410049 Saratov, pr. Entuziastov 13; tel. (8452) 97-04-44; fax (8452) 97-03-83; e-mail institute@ibppm.sgu.ru; internet www.ibppm.saratov.ru; f. 1980; attached to Russian Acad. of Sciences; library of 30,000 vols; Dir V. V. IGNATOV.

Institute of the Biology of Inland Waters: 152742 Yaroslavskaya oblast, Nekouzsky raion, p/o Borok; tel. (08547) 24-042; fax (08547) 24-042; e-mail ibiw@mail.ru; internet www.ibiw.yaroslavl.ru; f. 1956; attached to Russian Acad. of Sciences; Dir Dr SERGEI I. GENKAL; publ. *Biology of Inland Waters* (3 a year).

Institute of the Ecology and Genetics of Micro-organisms: 614081 Perm, ul. Goleva 13; tel. (3422) 44-67-12; fax (3422) 44-67-11; internet www.ecology.psu.ru; f. 1988; attached to Russian Acad. of Sciences; library of 3,000 vols; Dir V. A. CHERESHNEV; publ. *Proceedings of Scientific Research* (1 a year).

Institute of the Ecology of the Volga Basin: 445003 Togliatti; tel. (8469) 23-54-78; fax (8469) 48-95-04; attached to Russian Acad. of Sciences; Dir G. S. ROZENBERG.

Institute of Theoretical and Experimental Biophysics: 142290 Moscow oblast, Serpukhovsky raion, Pushchino; tel. (495) 632-78-69; fax (496) 733-05-53; e-mail office@iteb.ru; attached to Russian Acad. of Sciences; Dir Prof. G. R. IVANITSKY; Asst Dir A. NAUMOV.

Institute of Water and Ecological Problems: 680063 Khabarovsk, ul. Kim Yu Chena 65; tel. (4212) 22-75-73; fax (4212) 22-70-85; f. 1968; attached to Russian Acad. of Sciences; Dir Dr B. A. VORONOV; publ. *Biogeochemical and Hydroecological Peculiarities of the Amur River Watershed Ecosystems* (1 a year).

Institute for Water and Environmental Problems: 656038 Barnaul, Molodyozhnaya ul. 1; tel. (3852) 66-64-60; fax (3852) 24-03-96; e-mail iwep@iwep.asu.ru; internet www.iwep.asu.ru; f. 1987; research into hydrology, physical geography, cartography, biogeochemistry, geomorphology, limnology, air and water quality, mathematical modelling of contaminant transport in the environment; attached to Russian Acad. of Sciences; library of 37,000 vols; Dir Prof. YURI I. VINOKUROV; publ. *Polzunovsky Vestnik* (in Russian, 6 a year).

Kazan Institute of Biology: 420111 Kazan, ul. Lobachevskogo 2/31; tel. (8432) 32-64-91; attached to Russian Acad. of Sciences; Dir Dr A. I. TARCHEVSKY.

Koltsov, A. N., Institute of Developmental Biology: 117808 Moscow, ul. Vavilova 26; tel. (495) 135-64-83; attached to Russian Acad. of Sciences; Dir N. G. KHRUSHCHOV.

Komarov, V. L., Botanical Institute: 197376 St Petersburg, ul. Prof. Popova 2; tel. (812) 234-12-37; fax (812) 234-45-12; e-mail binadmin@ok3277.spb.edu; internet www.binran.spb.ru; f. 1713; attached to Russian Acad. of Sciences; 460 mems; Dir V. T. YARMISHKO; publs *Botanichesky Zhurnal* (12 a year), *Rastitelnost Rossii* (2 or 3 a year).

Murmansk Marine Biological Institute: 183010 Murmansk, Vladimirskaya ul. 17; tel. (8152) 25-39-63; fax (8152) 25-39-94; e-mail mmbi@mmbi.info; internet www.mmbi.info; f. 1935; attached to Russian Acad. of Sciences; oldest instn of the Kola Scientific Centre of the Russian Acad. of Sciences; conducts complex investigations of Nordic seas from Iceland to the Laptev Sea; studies southern seas: the Barents Sea and the Sea of Azov are the focus of ecosystem investigations; addresses problems of climate, marine peri-glacial, quaternary and current ecology, aquaculture, bioresources and environmental safety; monitors the ecosystem of the northern sea route, atomic fleet bases, and other water areas exposed to anthropogenic impacts; develops marine biotechnologies and prediction models for oceanologic processes, and environmental and engineering strategies to be applied to Arctic and southern sea; library of 70,000 vols; Dir Acad. GENNADY MATISHOV.

Pacific Institute of Bio-organic Chemistry: 690022 Vladivostok, pr. 100-letiya Vladivostoka 159; tel. (4232) 31-14-30; fax (4232) 31-40-50; f. 1964; attached to Russian Acad. of Sciences; Dir Prof. A. STONIK.

Pavlov Institute of Physiology: 199034 St Petersburg, nab. Makarova 6; tel. (812) 328-07-01; fax (812) 328-05-01; e-mail krylov@infran.ru; internet www.infran.ru; f. 1925; attached to Russian Acad. of Sciences; Dir Prof. D. P. DVORETSKY.

Research Institute for Monitoring Land and Ecosystems: 101000 Moscow, Bolshevistaky per. 11; tel. (495) 924-55-52.

Research Institute for the Biological Testing of Chemical Compounds: Moscow oblast, Kupavna, ul. Kirova 23; Dir L. A. PIRUZYAN.

Research Institute for the Genetics and Selection of Industrial Micro-organisms: 113545 Moscow, 1-i Dorozhnyi per. 1; tel. (495) 315-37-47; Dir V. G. DEBABOV.

Research Institute of Food Biotechnology: 109033 Moscow, Samokatnaya 4B; tel. (495) 362-44-95.

Scientific Centre of Biological Research: Moscow oblast, Serpukhovskii raion, Pushchino; attached to Russian Acad. of Sciences; Dir E. L. GOLOVLEV.

Sechenov, I. M., Institute of Evolutionary Physiology and Biochemistry: 194223 St Petersburg, pr. M. Toreza 44; tel. (812) 552-79-01; attached to Russian Acad. of Sciences; Dir Acad. V. L. SVIDERSKY.

Severtsov, A. N., Institute of Ecology and Evolution: 119071 Moscow, Leninskii pr. 33; tel. (495) 952-20-88; fax (495) 954-55-34; e-mail admin@sevin.ru; attached to Russian Acad. of Sciences; Dir Acad. DMITRI S. PAVLOV; publs *Russian Journal of Aquatic Ecology* (2 a year), *Lutreola* (2 a year).

Shemyakin-Ovchinnikov Institute of Bio-organic Chemistry: 117871 Moscow, ul. Miklukho-Maklaya 16/10; tel. (495) 335-01-00; fax (495) 310-70-07; f. 1959; attached to Russian Acad. of Sciences; library of 250,000 vols; br. at Pushchino; Dir Prof. V. T. IVANOV; publ. *Journal of Bio-organic Chemistry* (in Russian and English, monthly).

Siberian Institute of Plant Physiology and Biochemistry: 664033 Irkutsk 33, POB 317; tel. (3952) 42-67-21; fax (3952) 51-07-54; e-mail matmod@sifibr.irk.ru; internet sifibr.irk.ru; f. 1961; attached to Russian Acad. of Sciences; researches on plant physiology and biochemistry, microbiology and soil science, entomology, botany, geobotany and forestry; Dir Dr VICTOR VOINIKOV; publ. *Journal of Stress Physiology & Biochemistry*.

State Research Centre of Virology and Biotechnology (Vector): 630559 Novosibirsk oblast, Koltsovo; tel. (3832) 36-60-10; fax (3832) 36-74-09; internet www.vector.nsc.ru; f. 1974; library of 90,000 vols; Dir Acad. LEV S. SANDAKHCHIEV.

State Research Institute of Highly Pure Biopreparations (IHPB): 197110 St Petersburg, Pudozhskaya St 7; tel. (812) 235-12-25; fax (812) 230-49-48; e-mail onir@hpb-spb.com; internet www.hpb.-spb.com; f. 1974; basic research and applied activities using the latest advances in molecular biology, microbiology, virology, and biotechnology; Dir Prof. VALERIY DOBRITSA.

Timiryazev, K. A., Institute of Plant Physiology: 127276 Moscow, Botanicheskaya 35; tel. (495) 977-80-22; fax (495) 977-80-18; e-mail ifr@ippras.ru; internet www.ippras.ru; f. 1890; attached to Russian Acad. of Sciences; library of 83,000 vols; Dir Prof. VL. V. KUZNETSOV; publ. *Russian Journal of Plant Physiology* (6 a year).

Vavilov Institute of General Genetics: 119991 Moscow, ul. Gubkina 3; tel. (495) 135-62-13; fax (495) 135-12-89; e-mail iogen@vigg.ru; internet www.vigg.ru; f. 1966; attached to Russian Acad. of Sciences; library of 5,000 vols; Dir Prof. YU. P. ALTUKHOV; publs *Russian Journal of Genetics* (12 a year), *Advances in Current Biology* (6 a year).

Zoological Institute: 199034 St. Petersburg, Universitetskaya nab. 1; tel. (812) 218-02-11; attached to Russian Acad. of Sciences; Dir O. A. SKARLATO.

Mathematical Sciences

Euler, L., International Institute of Mathematics: 197022 St Petersburg, Pesochnaya nab. 10; tel. (812) 234-05-74; fax (812) 234-58-19; internet www.pdmi.ras.ru/eimi; f. 1988; attached to Russian Acad. of Sciences; Dir Acad. L. D. FADDEEV.

Institute of Mathematics: 450057 Ufa, ul. Tukaeva 50; tel. (3472) 22-59-36; attached to Russian Acad. of Sciences; Dir V. V. NAPALKOV.

Sobolev Institute of Mathematics: 630090 Novosibirsk, pr. Akad. Koptyuga 4; tel. (3833) 33-28-92; fax (3833) 33-25-98; e-mail im@math.nsc.ru; internet www.math.nsc.ru; f. 1957; attached to Russian Acad. of Sciences; library of 120,000 vols; Dir Acad. YU. L. ERSHOV; Scientific Sec. YURIY VOLKOV; publs *Diskretny Analiz i Issledovanie Operatsii* (6 a year), *Matematicheskie Trudy* (2 a year), *Siberian Electronic Mathematical Reports*, *Sibirsky Matematichesky Zhurnal* (6 a year), *Sibirsky Zhurnal Industrialnoy Matematiki* (4 a year).

Steklov, V. A., Institute of Mathematics: 119991 Moscow, ul. Gubkina 8; tel. (495) 135-22-91; fax (495) 135-05-55; e-mail steklov@mi.ras.ru; internet www.mi.ras.ru; attached to Russian Acad. of Sciences; Dir Acad. YU. S. OSIPOV.

St Petersburg Department of V. A. Steklov Mathematical Institute: 191023 St Petersburg, nab. Fontanki 27; tel. (812) 312-40-58; fax (812) 310-53-77; e-mail admin@pdmi.ras.ru; internet www.pdmi.ras.ru; f. 1940, ind. instn; attached to Russian Acad. of Sciences; Dir Acad. S. V. KISLYAKOV; Exec. Academic Sec. Dr MAXIM VSEMIRNOV; publs *Journal of Mathematical Sciences* (11 a year), *St Petersburg Math Journal* (24 a year).

Physical Sciences

All-Russia Geological Oil Research Institute (VNIGNI): 105819 Moscow, shosse Entuziastov 36; tel. (495) 273-26-51; fax (495) 273-55-38; f. 1953; library of 80,000 vols; Dir Dr K. A. KLESCHEV; publs *Geology of Oil and Gas* (1 a year), *Proceedings* (6 a year).

All-Russia Research Institute for the Geology and Mineral Resources of the World's Oceans: 190121 St Petersburg, Angliisky 1; tel. (812) 113-83-79; fax (812) 114-14-70; f. 1948; library of 60,500 vols; Dir Prof. I. S. GRAMBERG.

All-Russia Research Institute of Chemical Technology: 115409 Moscow, Kashirskoe shosse 33; tel. (495) 324-61-55.

All-Russian Research Institute of Geological, Geophysical and Geochemical Systems (VNIIgeosystem): 117105 Moscow, Varshavskoe shosse 8; tel. (495) 954-53-50; fax (495) 958-37-11; e-mail geosys@geosys.ru; internet www.geosys.ru; f. 1961; fundamental and applied scientific research; experimental design and technological research in earth sciences and geological exploration; library of 38,000 vols; Dir LEONID E. CHESALOV; publ. *Geoinformatika* (6 a year).

All-Russia Research Institute of Hydrolysis: 198099 St Petersburg, ul. Kalinina 13; tel. (812) 186-29-22; Dir O. I. SHAPOVALOV.

All-Russia Research Institute of Natural Gases and Gas Technology: 142717 Moscow oblast, Leninsky raion, pos. Razvilka; tel. (495) 355-92-06; fax (495) 399-16-77; e-mail samsr@gazprom.ru; f. 1948; library of 100,000 vols.

All-Russia Research Institute of Optical and Physical Measurements: 103031 Moscow, ul. Rozhdestvenka 27; tel. (495) 208-41-83; attached to Russian Acad. of Sciences; Gen. Dir I. G. BARANNIK.

All-Russia Research Institute of Physical-Technical and Radiotechnical Measurements: 147570 Moscow oblast, Solnechnogorsky raion, p/o Mendeleevo; tel. (495) 535-92-78; attached to Russian Acad. of Sciences; Dir B. I. ALSKIN.

All-Russia Scientific Research Institute of Mineral Resources: 109017 Moscow, Staromonetni per. 31; tel. (495) 231-50-43; fax (495) 238-19-21; f. 1918; prospecting for and estimating ore deposits, research in processing; library of 345,000 vols; Dir Prof. A. N. EREMEEV.

Amur Complex Research Institute: 675000 Amur oblast, Blagoveshchensk, per. Relochnyi 1; tel. (4162) 42-72-32; fax (4162) 42-59-31; f. 1980; attached to Russian Acad. of Sciences; geology, minerals; library of 26,000 vols; Dir V. G. MOISEENKO.

Andreev Acoustics Institute: 117036 Moscow, ul. Shvernika 4; tel. (495) 126-74-01; fax (495) 126-84-11; e-mail dubrov@akin.ru; internet www.akin.ru; f. 1953; attached to Russian Acad. of Sciences; Dir N. A. DUBROVSKY.

Arbuzov, A. E., Institute of Organic and Physical Chemistry: 420088 Kazan, ul. Akad. Arbuzova 8; tel. (8432) 73-93-65; fax (8432) 73-22-53; e-mail arbuzov@iopc.kcn.ru; internet www.iopc.kcn.ru; f. 1965; attached to Russian Acad. of Sciences; Dir O. G. SINYASHIN.

Baikov, A. A., Institute of Metallurgy: 117911 Moscow, Leninskii pr. 49; tel. (495) 135-86-11; attached to Russian Acad. of Sciences; Dir Acad. N. P. LYAKISHEV.

Bardin, I. P., Central Research Institute of Ferrous Metallurgy: 107005 Moscow, 2-ya Baumanskaya 9/23; tel. (495) 265-72-04; fax (499) 267-48-27; e-mail ferrum.sc@online.ru; f. 1944; library of 65,000 vols; Dir-Gen. VLADIMIR I. MATORIN.

Bochvar, A. A., All-Russia Research Institute of Inorganic Materials: 123060 Moscow, ul. Rugova 5a; tel. (495) 190-82-97; fax (495) 196-41-68; e-mail post@bochvar.ru; internet www.bochvar.ru; f. 1945; Dir-Gen. ALEKSANDR VIKTOROVICH VATULIN; publ. *Materialovedeniye i Novye Materialy* (Materials Science and New Materials, 1 a year).

Boreskov Institute of Catalysis: 630090 Novosibirsk, pr. Akad. Lavrenteva 5; tel. (383) 330-82-69; fax (383) 330-47-19; e-mail bic@catalysis.ru; internet www.catalysis.ru; attached to Russian Acad. of Sciences; Dir V. N. PARMON.

Central Aerological Observatory: 141700 Moscow, 3 Pervomayskaya St., Dolgoprudny; tel. (495) 408-61-48; fax (495) 575-33-27; e-mail caohead@cao-rhms.ru; internet www.cao-rhms.ru; f. 1941; atmospheric physics and chemistry up to 100 km, study and monitoring of ozone layer, cloud physics, applied meteorology, weather modification; use of aircraft, rockets, satellites and radar for atmospheric studies.; library of 61,000 vols; Dir A. A. IVANOV; publ. *CAO Proceedings*.

Central Seismological Observatory: Obninsk; attached to Russian Acad. of Sciences.

Chita Institute of Natural Resources: 672014 Chita, ul. Nedorezova 16, POB 147; tel. (302) 221-25-82; fax (302) 221-25-82; internet www.chita.ru/public_htm/cinr/cinr.htm; f. 1981; attached to Russian Acad. of Sciences; library of 6,000 vols; Dir A. B. PTITSYN; publ. *Report on Environmental Conditions in Zabailkalye* (1 a year).

Far Eastern Institute of Geology: 690022 Vladivostok, pr. Stoletiya Vladivostoka 159; tel. (4232) 31-87-50; fax (4232) 31-78-47; e-mail fegi@online.marine.su; f. 1959; attached to Russian Acad. of Sciences; Dir A. I. KHANCHUK.

General Physics Institute: 119991 Moscow, ul. Vavilova 38; tel. (495) 135-82-96; fax (495) 234-31-96; e-mail director@gpi.ru; internet www.gpi.ru; f. 1983; attached to Russian Acad. of Sciences; brs in Tarusa and Troitsk; Dir Prof. IVAN A. SHCHERBAKOV.

Geological Institute: 670047 Ulan-Ude, ul. Sakhyanova 6A; tel. (3012) 43-30-24; fax (3012) 43-30-24; e-mail gin@gin.bscnet.ru; internet geo.stbur.ru; f. 1973; attached to Siberian Br., Russian Acad. of Sciences; study of structure, history of development and matter composition of earth crust in the Buryatia and Chita regions by geological, geophysical and geochemical methods; Dir GENNADI TATKOV.

Geological Institute of Kola Science Centre: 184209 Murmansk oblast, Apatity, ul. Fersmana 14; tel. (81555) 79656; fax (81555) 76481; e-mail geoksc@geoksc.apatity.ru; internet geoksc.apatity.ru; f. 1951; attached to Russian Acad. of Sciences; Dir YURY L. VOYTEKHOVSKY.

Graphite Research Institute: 111524 Moscow, Elektrodnaya 2; tel. (495) 176-13-06; fax (495) 176-12-63; Dir V. I. KOSTIKOV.

Grebenshchikov, I. V., Institute of Silicate Chemistry: 199155 St Petersburg, ul. Odoevskogo 24, korp. 2; tel. (812) 350-65-16; fax (812) 328-54-01; e-mail ichsran@isc.nw.ru; attached to Russian Acad. of Sciences; Dir Acad. V. J. SHEVCHENKO.

High-Mountain Geophysical Institute: 360030 Nalchik, pr. Lenina 2; tel. (866) 247-00-31; fax (866) 247-00-24; e-mail vgikbr@rambler.ru; f. 1963; meteorology, climatology, glaciology, geophysics, ecology; library of 17,230 vols, 26,288 periodicals; Dir Dr VALERY O. TAPASKHANOV.

Institute for Geothermal Research: 367030 Makhachkala, pr. Shamila 39-A; tel. and fax (8722) 62-93-57; e-mail geoterm@mail.ru; internet www.ipgdncran.ru; f. 1980; attached to Russian Acad. of Sciences; fundamental scientific research on heat physics, hydrodynamics and heat exchange in geothermal systems, mathematical and information models in geothermy, renewable energy; Dir Prof. A. B. ALKHASOV; publ. *Proceedings of the Scientific Training 'Actual problems of renewable energy resources development'* (2 a year).

Institute for High-Energy Physics: 142281 Moscow oblast, Protvino; tel. (4967) 74-04-56; fax (4967) 74-49-37; e-mail yury.ryabov@ihep.ru; internet www.ihep.ru; f.

1963; library of 300,000 vols; Dir N. E. TYURIN.

Institute for Metals Superplasticity Problems of RAS: 450001 Ufa, 39 St Khalturina; tel. (347) 223-64-07; fax (347) 282-37-59; e-mail imsp@anrb.ru; f. 1985; attached to Russian Acad. of Sciences; library of 8,700 vols; Dir R. R. MYLYUKOV.

Institute of Applied Astronomy: 197110 St Petersburg, ul. Zhdanovskaya 8; tel. (812) 275-11-18; fax (812) 275-11-19; e-mail ipa@ipa.rssi.ru; internet www.ipa.rssi.ru; f. 1988; attached to Russian Acad. of Sciences; Dir Dr A. M. FINKELSTEIN; publs *Trudy IPA RAN* (in Russian, 2 a year), *Communications* (in Russian and English, 10 a year).

Institute of Applied Physics: 603600 Nizhny Novgorod, ul. Ulyanova 46; tel. (831) 436-58-10; attached to Russian Acad. of Sciences; Dir Acad. A. G. LITVAK.

Institute of Astronomy: 109017 Moscow, Pyatnitskaya ul. 48; tel. (495) 951-54-61; fax (495) 951-55-57; e-mail admin@inasan.rssi.ru; internet www.inasan.rssi.ru; f. 1936; attached to Russian Acad. of Sciences; Dir Prof. BORIS M. SHUSTOV.

Institute of Atmospheric Optics: 634055 Tomsk, Akademicheskii pr. 1; tel. (382) 249-27-38; fax (382) 249-20-86; e-mail mgg@iao.ru; internet www.iao.ru; f. 1969; research and development in physics, laser engineering, aerosol technology and ozone; attached to Siberian br. of the Russian Acad. of Sciences; Dir Prof. GENNADY GRIGOREVICH MATVIENKO.

Institute of Atmospheric Physics: 119017 Moscow, Pyzhevskii per. 3; tel. (495) 951-55-65; fax (495) 953-16-52; e-mail mail_adm@omega.ifaran.ru; f. 1956; attached to Russian Acad. of Sciences; library of 4,000 vols, 40 periodicals; Dir Acad. G. S. GOLITSYN; publ. *Izvestiya—Atmospheric and Oceanic Physics* (6 a year).

Institute of Chemical Kinetics and Combustion: 630090 Novosibirsk, Institutskaya 3; tel. (3832) 34-41-50; fax (3832) 34-23-50; f. 1957; attached to Russian Acad. of Sciences; library of 88,000 vols; Dir Prof. YU. D. TSVETKOV.

Institute of Chemistry: 690022 Vladivostok, pr. Stoletiya Vladivostoka 159; tel. (4232) 31-25-90; fax (4232) 31-18-89; e-mail chemi@online.ru; f. 1971; attached to Russian Acad. of Sciences; library of 5,000 vols; Dir Prof. Dr V. YU. GLUSHCHENKO.

Institute of Coal and Coal Chemistry: 650610 Kemerovo GSP, ul. Rukavishnikova 21; tel. (3842) 28-14-33; fax (3842) 21-18-38; e-mail pvp@kemsc.ru; internet www.kemsc.ru; f. 1983; attached to Russian Acad. of Sciences; library of 40,000 vols; Dir G. I. GRITSKO; publ. *Coalbed Methane* (4 a year).

Yu. G. Shafer Institute of Cosmophysical Research and Aeronomy: 677980 Yakutsk, pr. Lenina 31; tel. (4112) 39-04-00; fax (4112) 39-04-50; e-mail ikfia@ysn.ru; internet ikfia.ysn.ru; f. 1962; attached to Russian Acad. of Sciences; scientific research in field cosmic ray physics and solar-terrestrial physics incl. upper atmosphere physics; library of 40,000 vols; Dir Dr EVGENY G. BEREZHKO.

Institute of Electrophysics: 620219 Ekaterinburg, Amundsena ul. 106; tel. (3432) 67-87-96; fax (3432) 67-87-94; attached to Russian Acad. of Sciences; Dir V.G. SHPAK; Scientific Sec. E. E. KOKORINA.

Institute of Energy Problems of Chemical Physics: 117829 Moscow, Leninskii pr. 38, korp. 2; tel. (495) 137-34-79; attached to Russian Acad. of Sciences; Dir V. L. TALROZE.

Institute of Experimental Meteorology: Obninsk; Dir M. A. PETROSYANTS.

Institute of Experimental Mineralogy: 142432 Moscow oblast, Noginskii raion, Chernogolovka, Institutskaya ul. 4; tel. (496) 524-44-25; fax (496) 524-96-87; e-mail shap@iem.ac.ru; internet www.iem.ac.ru; f. 1969; attached to Russian Acad. of Sciences; 206 mems; Dir YURI B. SHAPOVALOV; publ. *Experiments in Geosciences* (1 a year).

Institute of Geochemistry: 664033 Irkutsk, ul. Favorskogo 1a; tel. (3952) 46-05-00; attached to Russian Acad. of Sciences; Dir M. I. KUZMIN.

Institute of Geology: 367025 Makhachkala, ul. Gadzhieva 45; attached to Russian Acad. of Sciences; Dir V. V. SUETNOV.

Institute of Geology: 109017 Moscow, Pyzhevskii per. 7; tel. (495) 230-80-29; fax (495) 231-04-43; f. 1930; attached to Russian Acad. of Sciences; Dir Y. G. LEONOV.

Institute of Geology of Karelian Research Centre: 185910 Petrozavodsk, Pushkinskaya ul. 11; tel. (8142) 78-06-02; fax (8142) 77-06-02; e-mail geology@krc.karelia.ru; internet geoserv.krc.karelia.ru; f. 1946; attached to Russian Acad. of Sciences; Dir V. V. SHCHIPTSOV (acting).

Institute of Geology: 167982 Syktyvkar, Pervomaiskaya ul. 54; tel. (8212) 24-00-37; fax (8212) 24-09-70; f. 1958; attached to Russian Acad. of Sciences; Dir A. M. ASKHABOV; publs *Vestnik* (12 a year), *Proceedings* (4 a year).

Institute of Geology: 450000 Ufa 25, ul. K. Marksa 16/2; tel. (3472) 22-82-56; fax (3472) 23-03-68; attached to Russian Acad. of Sciences; Dir V. N. PUCHKOV.

Diamond and Precious Metal Geology Institute of the Siberian Branch of the Russian Academy of Sciences (DPMGI SB RAS): 677890 Yakutsk, pr. Lenina 39; tel. (4112) 33-58-64; fax (4112) 33-57-08; e-mail geo@yakutia.ru; internet www.diamond.ysn.ru; f. 1957; attached to Russian Acad. of Sciences; tectonics and geodynamics of Siberian platform and Verkhoyansk-Kolyma folded region; kimberlite magmatism, formation and disposition laws for deposits of diamond, gold, silver, MPG and other; investigation of diamonds; paleontology and stratigraphy of Phanerozoic era; Dir Dr ALEXANDER P. SMELOV.

Institute of Precambrian Geology and Geochronology: 199034 St Petersburg, 2 nab. Makarova; tel. (812) 328-47-01; fax (812) 328-48-01; e-mail a.b.vrevsky@ipgg.ru; internet www.ipgg.ru; f. 1967; attached to Russian Acad. of Sciences; Dir Dr A. B. VREVSKY; Sec. for Science S. G. SKUBLOV.

Institute of Geomechanics: c/o Russian Academy of Sciences, 117333 Moscow, ul. Vavilova 44 (korp. 2, komn. 86); attached to Russian Acad. of Sciences.

Institute of Geophysics: 620016 Ekaterinburg, ul. Amundsena 100; tel. (343) 267-88-68; attached to Russian Acad. of Sciences; Dir P. S. MARTYSHKO.

Institute of High-Pressure Physics: 142092 Moscow oblast, Troitsk; tel. (495) 334-00-10; fax (495) 334-00-12; internet www.hppi.troitsk.ru; f. 1958; attached to Russian Acad. of Sciences; Dir Prof. S. M. STISHOV.

Institute of High-Temperature Electrochemistry: 620219 Ekaterinburg, S. Kovalevskaya 22; tel. (343) 374-50-89; fax (343) 374-59-92; e-mail head@ihte.uran.ru; internet www.ihte.uran.ru; f. 1958; attached to Russian Acad. of Sciences; Dir Prof. V. A. KHOKHLOV.

Institute of High-Temperature Physics: 127412 Moscow, Izhorskaya 13/19; tel. (495) 485-83-45; attached to Russian Acad. of Sciences; Dir V. M. BATENIN.

Institute of Hydrodynamics: 630090 Novosibirsk, pr. Akad. Lavrenteva 15; tel. and fax (383) 333-16-12; e-mail igil@hydro.nsc.ru; internet www.hydro.nsc.ru; f. 1957; attached to Russian Acad. of Sciences; library of 87,000 vols; Dir Prof. ANATOLY VASILYEV; publs *Combustion Explosions and Shock Waves* (6 a year), *Continuum Dynamics* (1 or 2 a year), *Journal of Applied Mechanics and Technical Physics* (6 a year).

Institute of Macro-Molecular Compounds: 199004 St Petersburg, Bolshoi pr. 31; tel. (812) 213-10-70; fax (812) 218-68-69; attached to Russian Acad. of Sciences; Dir E. F. PANARIN.

Institute of Marine Geology and Geophysics: 693002 Yuzhno-Sakhalinsk, ul. Nauki 5; tel. (4242) 2-21-28; attached to Russian Acad. of Sciences; Dir K. F. SERGEEV.

Institute of Metal Physics: 620041 Ekaterinburg, GSP-170, ul. Sofia Kovalevskaya 18; tel. (343) 374-02-30; fax (343) 374-52-44; e-mail physics@imp.uran.ru; internet www.imp.uran.ru; f. 1932; attached to Russian Acad. of Sciences; library of 18,000 vols, 92,000 periodicals; Dir Prof. Dr V. V. USTINOV; publs *Fizika metallov i metallovedenie* (Physics of Metals and Metallography, 12 a year), *Defectoscopiya* (Journal of Non-Destructive Testing, 12 a year).

Institute of Metallo-organic Chemistry: 603600 Nizhnii Novgorod, ul. Tropinina 49; tel. (8312) 66-27-09; fax (8312) 66-14-97; f. 1989; attached to Russian Acad. of Sciences; library of 50,000 vols; Dir G. A. ABAKUMOV.

Institute of Metallurgy: Ural Div., 620016 Ekaterinburg, ul. Amundsen 101; tel. (343) 2679-124; fax (343) 2679-186; e-mail admin@imet.mplik.ru; internet www.imet-uran.ru; f. 1955; attached to Russian Acad. of Sciences; Devt of physicochemical principles of high temperature processes in ferrous and non-ferrous metallurgy; library of 35,000 vols; Dir Acad. L. I. LEONTIEV; publ. *Melts* (6 a year).

Institute of Mineralogy: 456301 Chelyabinsk oblast, Miass; tel. (35135) 5-35-62; attached to Russian Acad. of Sciences; Dir V. N. ANFILOGOV.

Institute of New Chemical Problems: 142432 Moscow oblast, Noginsky raion, Chernogolovka; tel. (495) 524-50-24; attached to Russian Acad. of Sciences; Dir V. N. TROITSKII.

Institute of Nuclear Physics: 630090 Novosibirsk, pr. Akad. Lavrenteva 11; tel. (3832) 35-97-77; fax (3832) 35-21-63 br. in Protvin; attached to Russian Acad. of Sciences; Dir Acad. A. N. SKRINSKY.

Institute of Nuclear Research: 117312 Moscow, pr. 60-letiya Oktyabrya 7A; tel. (499) 135-77-60; attached to Russian Acad. of Sciences; Dir Dr V. A. MATVEEV.

Institute of Organic Chemistry: 630090 Novosibirsk, Akademgorodok, pr. Akad. Lavrenteva 9; tel. (3832) 35-16-52; attached to Russian Acad. of Sciences; Dir Acad. G. A. TOLSTIKOV.

Institute of Organic Chemistry: 450054 Ufa, pr. Oktyabrya 71; tel. and fax (347) 235-60-66; e-mail valeev@anrb.ru; internet w3.chem.anrb.ru; attached to Russian Acad. of Sciences; Dir Acad. M. S. YUNUSOV.

Institute of Organic Synthesis: 620219 Ekaterinburg, ul. S. Kovalevskoi 20; tel. (3432) 74-11-89; fax (3432) 74-11-89; e-mail chupakhin@ios.uran.ru; f. 1993; attached to Russian Acad. of Sciences; Dir Prof. OLEG N. CHUPAKHIN.

Institute of Petroleum Chemistry: 634021 Tomsk, Akademicheskii pr. 4; tel. (3822) 49-16-23; fax (3822) 49-14-57; e-mail canc@ipc.tsc.ru; internet www.ipc.tsc.ru; f. 1970; attached to Siberian Br., Russian Acad. of Sciences; chemistry of Russian oils, physicochemical fundamentals of enhanced oil recovery, transformations of oils and their natural components; Dir Prof. Dr LYUBOV K. ALTUNINA; publs *Journal Russian Chemical Reviews*, *Kinetics and Catalysis*.

Institute of Physical Chemistry: 117915 Moscow, Leninskii pr. 31; tel. (495) 955-46-36; attached to Russian Acad. of Sciences; Dir YU. M. POLUKAROV.

Institute of Physics: 367003 Makhachkala 3, ul. 26 Bakinskikh Komissarov 94; tel. (8722) 2-51-60; attached to Russian Acad. of Sciences; Dir I. K. KAMILOV.

Institute of Problems of the Geology and Extraction of Oil and Gas: 117917 Moscow, Leninskii pr. 65; tel. (495) 135-75-66; attached to Russian Acad. of Sciences; Dir V. N. VINOGRADOV.

Institute of Problems of Chemical Physics: Chernogolovka; tel. (495) 993-57-07; fax (496) 524-96-76; e-mail sma@icp.ac.ru; internet www.icp.ac.ru; attached to Russian Acad. of Sciences; fundamental research in chemistry, chemical physics, biology, applied research; Dir SERGEY ALDOSHIN.

Institute of Semiconductor Physics: 630090 Novosibirsk, pr. Akad. Lavrenteva 13; tel. (383) 333-39-50; fax (383) 333-27-71; f. 1962; attached to Russian Acad. of Sciences; Dir Prof. A. L. ASEEV.

Institute of Solid State Chemistry: 620219 Ekaterinburg, ul. Pervomaiskaya 91; tel. (3432) 74-52-19; fax (3432) 74-44-95; e-mail server@ihim.uran.ru; internet www.uran.ru/structure/institutions/chimtt/issc.htm; f. 1932; attached to Russian Acad. of Sciences; Dir V. G. BAMBUROV.

Institute of Solid State Physics: 142432 Moscow oblast, Chernogolovka; tel. (495) 962-80-54; fax (496) 524-97-01; e-mail adm@issp.ac.ru; internet www.issp.ac.ru; f. 1963; attached to Russian Acad. of Sciences; Dir Prof. V. V. KVEDER.

Institute of Solution Chemistry: 153045 Ivanovo, Akademicheskaya ul. 1; tel. (0932) 37-85-21; fax (0932) 37-85-09; e-mail adm@isc-ras.ru; internet www.isc-ras.ru; f. 1981; attached to Russian Acad. of Sciences; library of 70,000 vols; Dir Prof. ANATOLY ZAKHAROV; publs *Chemical Thermodynamics and Thermochemistry* (2 a year), *Problems of Solution Chemistry* (4 a year), *Proceedings* (1 a year), *Textile Chemistry* (2 a year).

Institute of Space Physics Research and the Diffusion of Radio Waves: 684034 Kamchatka obl., Elizovsky raion, Paratunka, Mirnaya ul. 7; tel. (41531) 9-31-93; attached to Russian Acad. of Sciences; Dir I. N. AMIANTOV.

Institute of Space Research: 117997 Moscow, Profsoyuznaya 84/32; tel. (495) 333-20-88; fax (495) 310-12-48; internet www.iki.rssi.ru; f. 1965; attached to Russian Acad. of Sciences; Dir Prof. Dr L. M. ZELENYI.

Institute of Spectroscopy: 142092 Moscow oblast, Troitsk; tel. (495) 334-05-79; fax (495) 334-08-86; attached to Russian Acad. of Sciences; Dir E. A. VINOGRADOV.

Institute of Strength Physics and Materials Science: 634021 Tomsk, Akademicheskii pr. 2/1; tel. (3822) 25-94-81; fax (3822) 25-95-76; internet www.ispms.tsc.ru; f. 1984; attached to Russian Acad. of Sciences; Dir Acad. V. E. PANIN; publ. *Physical Mesomechanics* (6 a year).

Institute of Structural Macrokinetics and Materials Science: 142342 Moscow oblast, Chernogolovka, Institutsky 8; tel. (495) 962-80-01; fax (495) 962-80-70; e-mail director@ism.ac.ru; internet www.ism.ac.ru; f. 1988; attached to Russian Acad. of Sciences; studies on macroscopic kinetics of chemical reactions; Dir Prof. YURI GORDOPOLOV.

Institute of Tectonics and Geophysics: 680022 Khabarovsk, ul. Kim Yu Chena 65; tel. (4212) 22-71-89; fax (4212) 22-76-84; attached to Russian Acad. of Sciences; Dir N. P. ROMANOVSKY; publ. *Tikhookeanskaya Geologiya* (in Russian and English, 6 a year).

Institute of Terrestrial Magnetism, the Ionosphere and Radio Wave Propagation: 142092 Moscow oblast, Troitsk; tel. (495) 334-01-20; fax (495) 334-01-24; f. 1940; attached to Russian Acad. of Sciences; library of 100,000 vols; br. in St Petersburg; Dir Prof. VICTOR N. ORAEVSKY.

Institute of the Chemistry and Technology of Rare Elements and Mineral Raw Materials: 184200 Apatity, ul. Fersmana 26a; tel. (81555) 7-95-49; fax (81555) 7-94-14; e-mail office@chemy.kolasc.net.ru; internet www.kolasc.net.ru/chemy; f. 1957; attached to Russian Acad. of Sciences; Dir V. T. KALINNIKOV.

Institute of the Chemistry of High-Purity Substances: 603950 Nizhnii Novgorod, ul. Tropinina 49; tel. (831) 462-56-70; fax (831) 462-56-66; e-mail victor@ihps.nnov.ru; internet www.ihps.nnov.ru; f. 1988; attached to Russian Acad. of Sciences; fundamental and applied research of high-purity substances; production of zinc selenide, quartz and chalcogenide optical fibres; Dir Prof. MIKHAIL CHURBANOV; publs *Journal of Optoelectronics and Advanced Materials*, *Optical Letters*.

Institute of the Earth's Crust: 664033 Irkutsk, ul. Lermontova 128; tel. (3952) 42-70-00; fax (3952) 46-69-00; e-mail drf@crust.irk.ru; internet www.crust.irk.ru; f. 1949; attached to Russian Acad. of Sciences; library of 318,000 vols; Corresp. Mem. of the Russian Acad. of Science EUGENE V. SKLYAROV; publ. *Geodynamics & Tectonophysics*.

Institute of the Geology of Ore Deposits, Petrography, Mineralogy and Geochemistry: 119017 Moscow, Staromonetnyi per. 35; tel. (495) 951-45-79; fax (495) 230-21-79; e-mail director@igem.ru; internet www.igem.ru; f. 1955; attached to Russian Acad. of Sciences; Dir NIKOLAY BORTNIKOV.

Institute of the Mineralogy, Geochemistry and Crystal Chemistry of Rare Elements: 121357 Moscow, ul. Veresaeva 15; tel. (495) 443-84-28; fax (495) 443-90-43; f. 1956; attached to Russian Acad. of Sciences and Min. of Natural Resources; Dir A. A. KREMENETSKY; publ. *Applied Geochemistry* (1 a year).

Institute of Theoretical and Experimental Physics: 117218 Moscow, Bol. Cheremushkinskaya ul. 25; tel. (495) 123-02-88; fax (495) 123-30-28; e-mail director@itep.ru; internet www.itep.ru; f. 1945; Dir M. V. DANILOV.

Institute of Theoretical Astronomy: 191187 St Petersburg, nab. Kutuzova 10; tel. (812) 279-06-67; e-mail ita@ita.spb.su; attached to Russian Acad. of Sciences; Dir A. G. SOKOLSKII.

Institute of Thermal Physics: 620016 Ekaterinburg, Amundsena 106; tel. (3432) 67-88-01; fax (3432) 67-88-00; e-mail itp@itp.uran.ru; f. 1988; attached to Russian Acad. of Sciences; Dir V. G. BAIDAKOV.

Institute of Thermophysics: 630090 Novosibirsk, pr. Akad. Lavrenteva 1; tel. (3833) 30-70-50; fax (3833) 30-84-80; e-mail web@itp.nsc.ru; internet www.itp.nsc.ru; f. 1957; attached to Russian Acad. of Sciences; undertakes research in the fields of heat and mass transfer, physical hydrodynamics and gas dynamics, thermal physics of ionized gases and physics of low-temperature plasma; library of 100,000 vols; Dir Dr S. V. ALEKSEENKO; publs *Thermophysics and Aeromechanics* (4 a year), *Journal of Engineering Thermophysics* (4 a year).

Institute of Volcanology and Seismology: 683006 Petropavlovsk-Kamchatsky, bul. Piipa 9; tel. (4152) 25-95-13; fax (4152) 25-47-23; e-mail volcan@kcs.iks.ru; internet www.kcs.iks.ru; 130 mems; attached to Russian Acad. of Sciences; Dir EVGENY I. GORDEEV.

Institute of Water Problems: 107078 Moscow, Novaya Basmannaya ul. 10, POB 231; tel. (495) 265-97-57; fax (495) 265-18-87; e-mail iwapr@iwapr.msk.su; f. 1968; attached to Russian Acad. of Sciences; library of 35,000 vols; Dir M. G. KHUBLARYAN; publ. *Water Resources* (6 a year).

Institute of Water Problems of the North: Petrozavodsk, pr. Uritskogo 50; tel. (8142) 5-34-71; attached to Russian Acad. of Sciences; Head N. N. FILATOV (acting).

International Institute of Earthquake Prediction Theory and Mathematical Geophysics: 117997 Moscow, Profsoyuznaya ul. 84/32; tel. (495) 333-45-13; fax (495) 333-12-55; e-mail mitpan@mitp.ru; internet www.mitp.ru; f. 1990; attached to Russian Acad. of Sciences; Dir A. A. SOLOVIEV; publ. *Computational Seismology* (1 a year).

Irkutsk Institute of Chemistry 'A. E. Favorsky': 664033 Irkutsk, 1 Favorsky Stu; tel. (3952) 51-14-31; fax (3952) 41-93-46; e-mail irk_inst_chem@irioch.irk.ru; internet www.inchemistry.irk.ru; f. 1957; attached to Russian Acad. of Sciences; research and devt in organic chemistry; elemento-organic chemistry; chemistry of polymers; wood chemistry; library of 10,000 vols, 55,000 periodicals; Dir Prof. BORIS A. TROFIMOV.

Joint Institute for Nuclear Research: 141980 Moscow oblast, Dubna; tel. (9621) 65-059; fax (9621) 65-599; e-mail post@jinr.ru; internet www.jinr.ru; f. 1956; conducts studies on the structure of matter, high- and low-energy physics, condensed matter, heavy ion and neutron physics; education programme; languages of instruction: Russian, English; library of 422,000 vols; Dir V. G. KADYSHEVSKY; publs *Journal of Elementary Particles and the Atomic Nucleus* (6 a year), *Particles and Nuclei—Letters* (6 a year).

Kapitza, P. L., Institute of Physical Problems: 117973 Moscow, GSP-1, ul. A. N. Kosygina 2; tel. (495) 137-32-48; fax (495) 938-20-30; e-mail andreev@kapitza.ras.ru; attached to Russian Acad. of Sciences; Dir Acad. A. F. ANDREEV.

Karpinsky, A. P., All-Russia Geological Research Institute: 199106 St Petersburg, Vasilevsky ostrov, Sredny pr. 74; tel. (812) 321-57-06; fax (812) 321-30-23; e-mail vsegei@vsegei.ru; internet www.vsegei.ru; f. 1882; Dir O. V. PETROV; publ. *Regional Geology and Metallogeny* (2 a year).

Karpov Institute of Physical Chemistry: ul. Vorontsovo Pole 10, 105064 Moscow; tel. (495) 917-32-57; fax (495) 975-24-50; e-mail center@cc.nifhi.ac.ru; internet www.nifhi.ac.ru; f. 1918; 900 mems; library of 38,000 vols; Exec. Dir Prof. ALEXANDER PAVLOVICH SIMONOV.

Khlopin, V. G., Radium Institute: 194021 St Petersburg, 2-i Murinskiy pr. 28; tel. (812)

247-56-41; fax (812) 247-57-81; e-mail moshkov@atom.nw.ru; f. 1922; radiochemistry, nuclear physics; library of 170,000 vols; Dir Dr ALEXANDER A. RIMSKY-KORSAKOV; publ. *Radiochemistry* (in Russian, 6 a year).

Kirensky Institute of Physics: 660036 Krasnoyarsk; tel. (3912) 43-26-35; fax (3912) 43-89-23; e-mail dir@iph.krasn.ru; internet www.kirensky.ru; f. 1956; attached to Russian Acad. of Sciences; 300 mems; main fields of activity: physics, magnetic phenomena and magnetic materials; condensed matter physics and materials for electronics; design and engineering of new active elements; components and devices for radio-electronics, acousto-electronics, optoelectronics and quantum electronics; training of higher level material science specialists; Dir Acad. Prof. VASILY F. SHABANOV; Scientific Sec. Dr KIRILL A. SHAIKHUTDINOV.

Konstantinov, B. P., St Petersburg Institute of Nuclear Physics: 188350 Leningrad oblast, Gatchina, Orlova Roscha; tel. (812) 297-91-25; fax (812) 713-71-96; attached to Russian Acad. of Sciences; Dir ANSELM.

Krylov, A. P., All-Russia Oil and Gas Research Institute: 125422 Moscow, Dmitrovsky pr. 10; tel. (495) 976-83-01.

Kurchatov, I. V., Institute of Atomic Energy: 123182 Moscow, ul. Kurchatova 46; tel. (495) 196-61-07; fax (495) 943-00-74; Dir Acad. EVGENII P. VELIKHOV.

Kurnakov, N. S., Institute of General and Inorganic Chemistry: 117907 Moscow, Leninskii pr. 31; tel. (495) 952-07-87; fax (495) 954-12-79; f. 1918; attached to Russian Acad. of Sciences; Dir Acad. NIKOLAI T. KUZNETSOV.

Landau, L. D., Institute of Theoretical Physics: 117940 Moscow V-234, ul. A. N. Kosygina 2; tel. (495) 137-32-44; fax (495) 938-20-77; attached to Russian Acad. of Sciences; Dir Acad. I. M. KHALATNIKOV.

Lebedev, P. N., Physics Institute: 117924 Moscow, Leninskii pr. 53; tel. (495) 135-14-29; fax (495) 135-85-33; attached to Russian Acad. of Sciences; br. in Kuibyshev; Dir Acad. L. V. KELDYSH.

Lithosphere Institute: 109180 Moscow, Staromonetnyi per. 22; tel. (495) 233-55-88; attached to Russian Acad. of Sciences; Dir N. A. BOGDANOV.

Main Astronomical Observatory: 196140 St Petersburg, Pulkovo; tel. (812) 297-98-41; attached to Russian Acad. of Sciences; br. in Nikolaev oblast; Dir V. K. ABALAKIN.

Melnikov Permafrost Institute: 677010 Yakutsk, ul. Merzlotnaya 36; tel. and fax (4112) 33-44-76; e-mail mpi@ysn.ru; internet mpi.ysn.ru; f. 1961; attached to Russian Acad. of Sciences, Siberian Br.; library of 40,000 vols; Dir RUDOLF V. ZHANG.

D. I. Mendeleyev Institute of Metrology (VNIIM), Scientific and Research Centre of the Russian Federation: 190005 St Petersburg, Moskovskii pr. 19; tel. (812) 251-76-01; fax (812) 713-01-14; f. 1842; attached to Rosstandart of Russian Fed.; library of 80,000 vols; Dir Dr N. I. KHANOV.

Moscow Radiotechnical Institute: 117519 Moscow, Varshavskoe shosse 132; tel. (495) 315-31-11; fax (495) 314-10-53; e-mail mrti@mrtiran.ru; internet www.mrtiran.ru; f. 1946; attached to Russian Acad. of Sciences; devt of particle accelerators for industrial and medical applications; high-power SHF and x-ray technologies and installations; plasma technologies and installations; computer control and data-processing systems for applications such as accelerators, medicine, ecology and safety; Dir Dr BORIS ALEKSANDROVICH.

Nesmeyanov, A. N., Institute of Elementary Organic Compounds: 119991 Moscow V-334, GSP 1, Vavilova str. 28, INEOS; tel. (495) 135-61-66; fax (495) 135-50-85; e-mail larina@ineos.ac.ru; f. 1954; attached to Russian Acad. of Sciences; Dir Prof. YU. N. BUBNOV.

Nikolaev Institute of Inorganic Chemistry: 630090 Novosibirsk, pr. Akad. Lavrenteva 3; tel. (3832) 34-44-90; fax (3832) 34-44-89; e-mail sam@she.nsk.su; internet www.che.nsk.su; f. 1958; attached to Russian Acad. of Sciences; Dir Acad. F. A. KUZNETSOV; publ. *Journal of Structural Chemistry* (6 a year).

Noginsk Research Centre: c/o Institute of Solid State Physics, 142342 Moscow oblast, Chernogolovka; attached to Russian Acad. of Sciences; Chair. Acad. YU. A. OSIPYAN.

Polar Geospace Physics Observatory 'Tiksi': 678400 Bulunsky raion, Tiksi, Leninskaya ul. 25; tel. (41167) 2-17-89; fax (41167) 5-39-94; e-mail common@pgo.ysn.ru; attached to Russian Acad. of Sciences; Dir V. N. MEDVEDEV.

Polar Institute of Geophysics: 183023 Murmansk, ul. Khalturina 15; tel. (8152) 6-58-29; attached to Russian Acad. of Sciences; br. in Apatity; Dir V. G. PIVOVAROV.

Radiophysics Research Institute: 603950 Nizhnii Novgorod, Bol. Pecherskaya ul. 25/12a; tel. (831) 436-72-94; fax (831) 436-99-02; e-mail sneg@nirfi.sci-nnov.ru; internet www.nirfi.sci-nnov.ru; f. 1956; library of 250,000 vols; Dir Dr S. D. SNEGIREV; Acad. Sec VLADMIR FRIDMAN; publ. *Izvestiya vysshikh uchebnykh zavedenii—Radiofizika* (12 a year).

Research Centre for the Study of Properties of Surfaces and Vacuums: c/o Russian Academy of Sciences, 117901 Moscow, Leninsky pr. 14; attached to Russian Acad. of Sciences; Dir L. E. LAPIDUS.

Research Institute of Experimental Physics: 607190 Nizhegorodskaya oblast, Sarov, pr. Mira 37; tel. (83130) 4-44-68; fax (83130) 5-38-08; e-mail osv@dc.vniief.ru; f. 1946; Dir Dr RADY I. ILKAEV; publs *Questions of Atomic Science and Technics* (4 a year), *Atom* (4 a year).

Research Institute of Geophysical Research on Exploration Wells: Bashkortostan, 452620 Oktyabrsky, ul. Gorkogo 1; tel. (34767) 5-30-24; fax (34767) 5-50-16; e-mail vniigis@poikc.bashnet.ru; internet www.vniigis.bashnet.ru; f. 1956; geophysical well logging; library of 177,000 vols; Dir A. P. POLIAKOV.

Research Institute of Geophysical Shock Waves: Moscow oblast, Ramenskoe, Pryamolineinaya ul. 26.

Research Institute of Gold and Rare Metals: Magadan, ul. Gagarina 2.

Research Institute of the Geochemistry of the Biosphere: 353918 Novorossiisk, Leninsky pr. 54; tel. (8617) 23-03-03; fax (8617) 23-03-03; e-mail niigb@mail.kubtelecom.ru; f. 1992; attached to Rostov on Don State University; Dir V. A. ALEKSEENKO; publs *Ecology: Experience, Problems* (irregular), *Geochemistry of the Biosphere* (1 a year).

Russian Research Institute for Integrated Water Management and Protection: 620062 Ekaterinburg, ul. Mira 23; tel. and fax (343) 374-26-79; e-mail wrm@wrm.ru; internet www.wrm.ru; f. 1969; 98 mems; library of 30,000 vols; Dir Prof. Dr N. B. PROKHOROVA; Deputy Dir Y. A. PODZINA; publs *Water of Russia* (12 a year), *Water Sector of Russia* (6 a year).

Semenov, N. N., Institute of Chemical Physics: 117977 Moscow, ul. A. N. Kosygina 4; tel. (495) 939-72-00; fax (495) 651-21-91; e-mail icp@chph.ras.ru; internet www.chph.ras.ru; f. 1931; attached to Russian Acad. of Sciences; Dir A. A. BERLIN; publ. *Khimicheskaya fizika* (12 a year).

Shmidt Institute of Earth Physics: 123995 Moscow, Bol. Gruzinskaya ul. 10; tel. (495) 252-07-26; fax (495) 255-60-40; e-mail ifz@ifz.ru; internet www.ifz.ru; f. 1928; attached to Russian Acad. of Sciences; fundamental and applied research in internal structure and physical processes in the Earth's interior; global and regional geodynamics, stresses in the Earth's crust and mantle; seismisity, seismic risk assessment and earthquake prediction; magnetic, electromagnetic, gravity and other measurements and analysis of the Earth's physical fields; mathematical geophysics and geoinformatics; Dir ALEXANDER GLIKO.

Shubnikov, A. V., Institute of Crystallography: 117333 Moscow, Leninskii pr. 59; tel. (495) 135-63-11; fax (495) 135-10-11; attached to Russian Acad. of Sciences; br. in Kaluga; Dir V. I. SIMONOV (acting).

Siberian Research Institute of Geology, Geophysics and Mineral Raw Materials: 630104 Novosibirsk, Krasny pr. 67; tel. (3832) 22-45-03.

Special Astrophysical Observatory: 369167 Karachai-Cherkessian Republic, pos. Nizhnii Arkhyz; tel. (901) 498-29-31; fax (901) 498-29-31; e-mail adm@sao.ru; internet www.sao.ru; f. 1966; attached to Russian Acad. of Sciences; library of 205,247 vols; Dir YU. YU. BALEGA.

State Hydrological Institute: 199053 St Petersburg, V.O., 2-ya liniya 23; tel. (812) 213-89-16; Dir I. A. SHIKLOMANOV.

State Research Institute of Non-ferrous Metals: 129515 Moscow, ul. Akad. Koroleva 13; tel. (495) 215-61-73; fax (495) 215-34-53; e-mail gin@gintsvet.msk.ru; f. 1918; library of 500,000 vols; Dir ANDREI TARASOV; publ. *Gintsvetmet Proceedings* (1 a year).

The Institute of Solar-Terrestrial Physics: 664033 Irkutsk, ul. Lermontova 126A; tel. (3952) 42-82-65; fax (3952) 42-55-57; e-mail uzel@iszf.irk.ru; internet www.iszf.irk.ru; f. 1960; attached to Siberian Br., Russian Acad. of Sciences; current problems in astronomy, astrophysics, and research into outer space, incl. solar physics, physics of interplanetary medium, near-Earth environment, ionosphere, and atmosphere; research into solar-terrestrial rels, devt of methods and facilities for investigations in the field of astrophysics and geophysics; library of 115,000 books, brochures, periodicals, MSS; Dir Acad. GELIY ZHEREBTSOV.

Titanium Research Institute: 117393 Moscow, ul. Obrucheva 52; tel. (495) 332-95-55.

Troitsk Research Centre: 142092 Moscow oblast, Troitsk, Yubileinaya 3; tel. (495) 334-06-35; fax (495) 334-06-32; e-mail laptev@inr.troitsk.ru; attached to Russian Acad. of Sciences; Chair. Acad. VICTOR A. MATVEEV.

United Institute of Geology, Geophysics and Mineralogy: 630090 Novosibirsk, pr. Akad. Koptyuga 3; tel. (3832) 33-26-00; fax (3832) 33-27-92; attached to Russian Acad. of Sciences; Dir-Gen. Acad. N. L. DOBRETSOV.

Vernadsky, V. I., Institute of Geochemistry and Analytical Chemistry: 119991 Moscow, ul. A. N. Kosygina 19; tel. (495) 137-14-84; fax (495) 938-20-54; e-mail geokhi.ras@relcom.ru; internet www.geokhi.ru; f. 1947; attached to Russian Acad. of Sciences; library of 33,000 vols, 230 periodicals; Dir Prof. ERIC M. GALIMOV; publs *Geochemical*

International (12 a year), *Journal of Analytical Chemistry* (12 a year).

Voeikov, A. I., Main Geophysical Observatory: 194018 St Petersburg, ul. Karbysheva 7; tel. (812) 297-01-03; fax (812) 297-86-61; f. 1849; climatology, atmospheric physics, air pollution; library of 380,000 vols; Dir Dr V. M. KATTSOV; publ. *Trudy GGO*.

A. N. Zavaritzky Institute of Geology and Geochemistry: 620075 Ekaterinburg, Pochtovy per. 7; tel. (343) 371-19-97; fax (343) 371-52-52; e-mail director@igg.uran.ru; internet www.igg.uran.ru; f. 1939; attached to Russian Acad. of Sciences; scientific research and applications in geology, geochemistry and geo-ecology; library of 90,000 vols; Dir SERGEY L. VOTYUAKOV; Deputy Dir ELENA V. ANIKINA; publ. *Lithosphere* (6 a year).

Zelinsky, N. D., Institute of Organic Chemistry: 119991 Moscow, Leninsky pr. 47; tel. (499) 137-29-44; fax (499) 135-53-28; e-mail secretary@ioc.ac.ru; internet www.ioc.ac.ru; f. 1934; attached to Russian Acad. of Sciences; fundamental research in organic chemistry; library of 213,300 vols; Dir Prof. MIKHAIL P. EGOROV; publs *Mendeleev Communication* (6 a year), *Russian Chemical Bulletin* (12 a year), *Russian Chemical Reviews* (12 a year).

PHILOSOPHY AND PSYCHOLOGY

Institute of Philosophy: 119991 Moscow, Volkhonka ul. 14; tel. (495) 697-92-17; fax (495) 609-93-50; e-mail iph@iph.ras.ru; internet www.iph.ras.ru; f. 1929; attached to Russian Acad. of Sciences; 300 mems; library of 89,500 vols; Dir A. A. GUSEINOV; Acad. Sec. B. O. NIKOLAICHEV; publs *Epistemology and Philosophy of Science* (4 a year), *Personality, Culture, Society* (4 a year), *Philosophical journal* (2 a year).

Institute of Psychology: 129366 Moscow, Yaroslavskaya ul. 13; tel. (495) 282-51-49; attached to Russian Acad. of Sciences; Dir A. V. BRUSHLINSKY.

RELIGION, SOCIOLOGY AND ANTHROPOLOGY

Institute of Sociology: 117259 Moscow, ul. Krzhizhanovskogo 24/35, korp. 5; tel. (495) 128-91-09 br. in St Petersburg: 198147 St Petersburg, ul. Serpukhovskaya 38; tel. (812) 292-27-65; fax (812) 292-29-29; attached to Russian Acad. of Sciences; Dir V. A. YADOV.

Miklukho-Maklai, N. N., Institute of Ethnology and Anthropology: 117334 Moscow, Leninsky pr. 32A; tel. (495) 938-17-47; fax (495) 938-06-00; e-mail anthpub@iea.ras.ru; internet www.iea.ras.ru; f. 1933; attached to Russian Acad. of Sciences; library of 60,000 vols; Dir V. A. TISHKOV; publs *Etnograficheskoe obozrenie* (Ethnographic Review, 6 a year), *Bulletin of Ethnological Monitoring* (6 a year).

Research and Training Centre for Problems of Human Activity: 117279 Moscow, ul. Profsoyuznaya 83B; tel. (495) 333-01-02; attached to Russian Acad. of Sciences; Gen. Dir V. A. SHESTAKOV.

TECHNOLOGY

Accounting Machine Building Research Institute: 115230 Moscow, Varshavskoe shosse 42; tel. (499) 611-51-61.

All-Russia Electrotechnical Institute (VEI): 111250 Moscow, Krasnokazarmennaya ul. 12; tel. (495) 362-55-08; fax (495) 362-56-17; e-mail vkozlov@online.ru.

All-Russia Logachev Scientific Research Institute of Exploration Geophysics (VIRG-Rudgeofizika): 193019 St Petersburg, Fayansovaya ul. 20; tel. (812) 567-68-03; fax (812) 567-87-41; internet www.virg.spb.ru; f. 1945; devt of instruments and technology for predicting, exploring, evaluating and mining ores and diamonds, drilling for oil and gas; solving environmental problems; provision of services in these areas; library of 54,000 vols; Dir G. N. MIKHAILOV; publs *Geophysical Instruments* (2 a year), *Russian Journal of Geophysics* (2 a year).

All-Russia Oil Geological Prospecting Institute: 191104 St Petersburg, Liteinyi pr. 39; tel. (812) 273-43-83; fax (812) 273-73-87.

All-Russia Railway Transport Research Institute: 107996 Moscow, 3-ya Mytishchinskaya str. 10; tel. (495) 687-64-23; fax (495) 687-65-48; e-mail mnts@vniizht.ru; internet www.vniizht.ru; f. 1917; Dir-Gen. Dr BORIS LAPIDUS; Deputy Dir-Gen. ALEXANDER KASSAY; publ. *Vestnik VNIIZhT* (12 a year).

All-Russia Research and Design Institute for Atomic Power Station Equipment: 125171 Moscow, ul. Volkova Kosmonavta 6A; tel. (495) 150-83-55.

All-Russia Research and Design Institute for Problems of the Development of Oil and Gas Resources on the Continental Shelf: 107078 Moscow, Kalanchevskaya ul. 11; tel. (495) 971-51-03; fax (495) 280-23-57; Dir I. B. DUBIN.

All-Russia Research and Design Institute of Electroceramics: 111024 Moscow, shosse Entuziastov 17; tel. (495) 273-13-34.

All-Russia Research and Design Institute of Metallurgical Engineering: 109428 Moscow, Ryazansky pr. 8A; tel. (495) 174-37-00; attached to Russian Acad. of Sciences; Gen. Dir V. M. SINITSKY.

All-Russia Research and Design Institute of the Oil-Refining and Petrochemical Industry: 107005 Moscow, ul. Fridrikha Engelsa 32; tel. (499) 261-96-26; fax (499) 261-66 44; e-mail vnipineft@vnipineft.ru; internet www.vnipineft.ru; f. 1929; Dir V. M. NIKITIN.

All-Russia Research, Design and Technological Institute of Lighting Technology: 129626 Moscow, pr. Mira 106; tel. (495) 287-13-52; fax (495) 287-08-91; f. 1953.

All-Russia Research Institute for Nuclear Power Plant Operation: 109507 Moscow, Ferganskaya 25; tel. (495) 376-15-43; fax (495) 376-83-33; f. 1979; Dir-Gen. Prof. A. A. ABAGYAN.

All-Russia Research Institute for Oil Refining JSC: 111116 Moscow, Aviamotornaya ul. 6; tel. (499) 261-52-02; fax (499) 261-02-95; f. 1933; Dir E. F. KAMINSKY; publ. *Mir Nefteproduktov* (The World of Oil Products, 4 a year).

All-Russia Research Institute for the Canned and Vegetable Dry Products Industry: 142703 Moscow oblast, Vidnoe, Shkolnaya 78; tel. (495) 541-08-72; attached to Russian Acad. of Agricultural Sciences.

All-Russia Research Institute for the Dairy Industry: 113093 Moscow, Lyusinovskaya 35; tel. (495) 236-31-64; attached to Russian Acad. of Agricultural Sciences.

All-Russia Research Institute for the Protection of Metals from Corrosion: 125209 Moscow, Baltiiskaya ul. 14; tel. (495) 151-55-01.

All-Russia Research Institute for the Refrigeration Industry: 125422 Moscow, ul. Kostyakova 12; tel. (495) 216-00-04; attached to Russian Acad. of Agricultural Sciences; Dir V. F. LEBEDEV.

All-Russia Research Institute of Electrical Insulating Materials and Foiled Dielectrics: 111250 Moscow, Krasnokazarmennaya ul. 12; tel. (495) 273-24-78.

All-Russia Research Institute of Electromechanics (VNIIEM): 101000 Moscow, Glavpochtamt Box 496 VNIIEM, Khoromny Tupik 4; tel. (495) 208-84-67; fax (495) 207-49-62; f. 1941; research and devt in space technology, monitoring and control systems for nuclear reactors, electromechanical systems, devices and materials; library of 200,000 vols; Dir Dr S. A. STOMA; publ. *Trudy VNIIEM* (proceedings, 3 a year).

All-Russia Research Institute of Exploration Geophysics: 101000 Moscow, ul. Pokrovka 22; tel. (495) 925-45-13; fax (495) 956-39-38; f. 1944; library of 50,000 vols; Dir A. V. MIKHALTSEV; publs *Prikladnaya Geofizika* (2 a year), *Razvedochnaya Geofizika*.

All-Russia Research Institute of Fibre-Optic Systems of Communication and Data Processing: 107066 Moscow, Khiznyaya Krasnoselskaya ul. 13, korp. 1; tel. (499) 267-20-31.

All-Russia Research Institute of Food Biotechnology: 109033 Moscow, Samokatnaya ul. 4B; tel. (495) 362-44-95; attached to Russian Acad. of Agricultural Sciences.

All-Russia Research Institute of Fuel and Energy Problems (VNIIKTEP): 117259 Moscow, Bol. Cheremushkinskaya 34; tel. (495) 128-90-14; fax (495) 128-85-91; f. 1975; library of 63,000 vols; Dir N. K. PRAVEDNIKOV; publ. *The Fuel and Energy Complex of Russia* (1 a year).

All-Russia Research Institute of Helium Technology: 119270 Moscow, Luzhnetskaya nab. 10A; tel. (495) 242-50-77; fax (495) 234-91-11.

All-Russia Research Institute of Mineral Resources and the Use of the Subsurface: 123007 Moscow, 3-ya Magistralnaya 38; tel. (495) 259-69-88; fax (495) 259-91-25; e-mail info@viems.ru; internet www.viems.ru; f. 1964, attached to Russian Acad. of Sciences and Russian Min. of Natural Resources; Dir-Gen. M. A. KOMAROV.

All-Russia Research Institute of Organic Synthesis (VNIIOS): 105005 Moscow, ul. Radio 12; tel. (499) 261-96-88; fax (499) 261-07-77; e-mail vniios@aha.ru; internet www.vniios.ru; f. 1949; Dir-Gen. V. K. S. CHERNYKH.

All-Russia Research Institute of Problems of Computer Technology and Information Science: 113114 Moscow, 2-i Kozhevnichesky per. 4/6; tel. (495) 235-58-09; Dir V. ZAKHAROV.

All-Russia Research Institute of Radiotechnology: 107055 Moscow, Bol. Pochtovaya ul. 55–59; tel. (499) 267-66-04.

All-Russia Research Institute of Refractory Metals and Hard Alloys: 115430 Moscow, Varshavskoe shosse 56; tel. (495) 113-55-72.

All-Russia Research Institute of Starch Products: 140052 Moscow oblast, pos. Korenevo, ul. Nekrasova; tel. (495) 557-15-00; attached to Russian Acad. of Agricultural Sciences.

All-Russia Research Institute of Television and Radio Broadcasting JSC: 123298 Moscow, 3-ya Khoroshevskaya ul. 12; tel. (495) 192-90-02; fax (495) 943-00-06; e-mail vniitr@online.ru; internet www.vniitr.com; f. 1934; Gen. Dir ALEXANDER S. MKRTUMOV; publ. *Teleraidoveshchaniye* (4 a year).

All-Russia Research Institute of the Cable Industry: 111112 Moscow, shosse Entuziastov 5; tel. (495) 278-02-16.

All-Russia Research Institute of Trunk Pipeline Construction: 105058 Moscow, Okruzhnoi pr-d 19; tel. (495) 366-68-39.

All-Russia Scientific Research Institute for Exploration Methods and Engineering: 199106 St Petersburg, Veselnaya ul. 6; tel. (812) 322-78-53; fax (812) 322-79-37; e-mail vitr@spb.cityline.ru; f. 1955; drilling equipment and techniques for minerals and water; library of 30,000 vols, patents; Dir IVAN S. AFANASYEV; publ. *Collection of Scientific Works* (4–6 a year).

All-Russian Scientific Research Institute of Aviation Materials (VIAM): 105005 Moscow, ul. Radio 17; tel. (499) 261-86-77; fax (499) 267-86-09; e-mail admin@viam.ru; internet www.viam.ru; f. 1932; Dir-Gen. EVGENY N. KABLOV; publ. *Aircraft Materials and Technology* (1 a year).

All-Russia Scientific Research Institute of Fats: 191119 St Petersburg, ul. Chernyakovskogo 10; tel. (812) 164-15-24; fax (812) 112-25-74; e-mail wniig@peterlink.ru; f. 1933; attached to Russian Acad. of Agricultural Sciences; Dir ALEXANDER N. LISITSYN; publ. *Trudy* (works, irregular).

All-Russia Scientific Research Institute of Natural and Synthetic Diamonds and Tools: 129110 Moscow, ul. Giliarovskogo 65; tel. (495) 281-59-07; fax (495) 288-99-42; f. 1948; library of 25,000 vols; Dir N. A. KOLCHEMANOV; publ. *Works of VNIIALMAZ* (1 a year).

All-Russian Scientific Research Institute of Technical Physics and Automation: 115230 Moscow, Varshavskoe shosse 46; tel. (499) 611-2522; fax (499) 611-5344; e-mail kancelaria@vniitfa.ru; internet www.vniitfa.ru; f. 1960 as Research Institute of Radiation Technology; Dir NIKOLAY KUZELEV.

Blagonravov, A. A., Institute of Machine Science: 101830 Moscow, ul. Griboedova 4; tel. (495) 924-98-00; attached to Russian Acad. of Sciences; brs in St Petersburg, Samara, Saratov, Nizhnii Novgorod; Dir Acad. K. V. FROLOV.

Budnikov, P. P., All-Russia Research Institute of Construction Materials and Structures: 140080 Moscow, pos. Kraskovo, ul. Karla Marksa 117; tel. (495) 557-30-66; fax (495) 557-30-09; f. 1931; library of 180,000 vols; Dir YU. GUDKOV; publs *Autoclaved Materials* (1 a year), *Ceramic Materials* (1 a year), *Gypsum Binders and Products* (1 a year).

Burenie Scientific and Production Co.: 350624 Krasnodar, ul. Mira 34; tel. (8612) 62-23-34; fax (8612) 62-23-34; f. 1970; drilling and maintenance of wells; library of 100,000 vols; Gen. Dir Dr SERGEI A. RYABOKON.

Central Boiler and Turbine Institute: 194021 St Petersburg, Politekhnicheskaya ul. 24; tel. (812) 277-95-64; fax (812) 277-40-95; e-mail ckti@neva.spb.ru; internet www.ckti.ru; f. 1927; Dir-Gen E. K. CHAVCHANIDZE.

Central Design and Research Institute of the Standard and Experimental Design of Livestock Units for the Production of Milk, Beef and Pork: 121002 Moscow, Maly Mogiltsevsky per. 3; tel. (495) 241-36-82.

Central Diesels Research and Development Institute: 196158 St Petersburg, Moskovskoe shosse 25, korp. 1; tel. (812) 291-65-81; fax (812) 291-22-73; f. 1924; library of 62,000 vols; Dir V. BORDUKOV; publ. *Dvigatelestroynie* (4 a year).

Central Electronics Research Institute: 117415 Moscow, pr. Vernadskogo 39; tel. (495) 432-93-30; fax (495) 431-58-86; f. 1964; Dir B. N. AVDONIN.

Central Institute of Aviation Engines: 111116 Moscow, Aviamotornaya ul. 2; tel. (495) 361-64-81; fax (499) 267-13-54; f. 1930; Dir V. SKIBIN.

Central Marine Research and Design Institute Ltd (CNIIMF): 193015 St Petersburg, Kavalergardskaya ul. 6; tel. (812) 271-12-83; fax (812) 274-38-64; f. 1929; shipbuilding, marine equipment, navigation, transport technology; library of 312,000 vols; Dir VSEVOLOD I. PERESYPKIN; publ. *Transactions*.

Central Paper Research Institute: 141290 Moscow oblast, Pushkinsky raion, pos. Pravdinsky, ul. Lenina 15/1; tel. (495) 584-36-23; fax (495) 292-65-11; f. 1918; library of 90,000 vols; Dir B. V. OREKHOV; publs *Board* (12 a year), *Paper, Pulp, Research Papers of ZNIIB* (1 a year).

Central Research and Design Institute of Fuel Apparatus and Vehicle and Tractor Engines and Stationary Engines: 192102 St Petersburg, Volkovskii pr-d 102; tel. (812) 166-91-11.

Central Research Institute for Machine Building: 141070 Moscow oblast, Korolev, Pionyerskaya ul. 4; tel. (495) 513-50-00; fax (495) 187-03-22; f. 1946; spacecraft and rocket engineering, aero and gas dynamics, heat and mass exchange, strength of materials, reliability, mission control for spacecraft and space stations; library of 100,000 vols; Dir NIKOLAI A. ANFIMOV; publs *Astronautics and Rocket Engineering* (3 or 4 a year), *Rocketry and Space Technology* (52 a year).

Central Research Institute of Coating Materials and Artificial Leathers: 113184 Moscow, ul. Bakhrushina 11; tel. (495) 953-23-55; fax (495) 951-39-27; e-mail cniipik@mail.ru; Dir Dr C. N. KOZLOV.

Central Research Institute of Engineering Technology: 109088 Moscow, Sharikopodshipnikovskaya ul. 4; tel. (495) 275-83-00.

Central Research Institute of Geological Prospecting for Base and Precious Metals: 117545 Moscow, Varshovskoe shosse 129B; tel. and fax (495) 313-18-18; e-mail tsnigri@tsnigri.ru; internet www.tsnigri.ru; f. 1935; forecasting, prospecting, exploration and assessment of deposits of base and precious metals; library of 200,000 vols; Dir Dr IGOR MIGACHEV; publs *Otechestvennaya Geologia* (6 a year, in Russian with English abstracts), *Rudy i Metally* (6 a year, in Russian with English abstracts).

Central Research Institute of Telecommunications: 111141 Moscow, 1-i pr-d Perova Polya 8; tel. (495) 304-57-97; fax (495) 274-00-67.

Central Research Institute of the Ministry of Defence: 141090 Moscow oblast, Bolshevo, V/Ch 25840; tel. (495) 472-92-12; Dir L. I. VOLKOV.

Central Research Laboratory for the Introduction of Personal Computers: c/o Russian Academy of Sciences, 117901 Moscow, Leninsky pr. 14; attached to Russian Acad. of Sciences; Dir A. N. ILIN.

Central Scientific Research and Design Institute of the Wood Chemical Industry: 603603 Nizhnii Novgorod, Moskovskoe shosse 85, GSP 703; tel. (8312) 41-36-98; fax (8312) 41-36-90; f. 1932; library of 146,000 vols; Dir VICTOR YA. BONDAREV; publ. *Scientific Works* (1 a year).

Concrete and Reinforced Concrete Research Design and Technological Institute: 109428 Moscow, Vtoraya Institutskaya ul. 6; tel. (495) 171-26-69; fax (495) 174-77-24; e-mail niizhb@niizhb.ru; internet www.niizhb.ru; f. 1927; devt of standards and norms for concrete construction and design; certification testing; postgraduate courses; 400 mems; library of 200,000 vols; Dir Dr A. I. ZVEZDOV; Deputy Dir Dr V. FALIKMAN; Scientific Dir Dr T. MOUKHAMEDIEV; publs *Beton i Zhelezobeton* (Concrete and Reinforced Concrete, 6 a year), *Proceedings of NIIZLB* (1 a year).

Design and Research Institute of the Synthetic Rubber Industry: 105318 Moscow, ul. Ibragimova 15; tel. (495) 366-43-44; fax (495) 369-52-55; Dir S. I. KARTASHOV.

Design and Technological Institute of Monocrystals: 630058 Novosibirsk, Russkaya ul. 43; tel. (3832) 33-22-39; fax (3832) 33-22-59; f. 1978; attached to Russian Acad. of Sciences; Head ANATOLY I. CHEPUROV.

Dollezhal, N. A. Research and Development Institute of Power Engineering: 101000 Moscow, POB 788; tel. (499) 263-73-88; fax (499) 788-20-52; e-mail nikiet@nikiet.ru; internet www.nikiet.ru; f. 1952; nuclear power, thermal physics and hydrodynamics; radiation, nuclear and environmental safety of nuclear reactors; strength, reliability and material science; conversion of nuclear technologies; library of 200,000 vols; Dir B. A. GABARAEV.

Dorodnicyn Computing Centre of the Russian Academy of Sciences (CC RAS): 119333 Moscow, ul. Vavilova 40; tel. (499) 135-24-89; e-mail wcan@ccas.ru; internet www.ccas.ru; f. 1955; attached to Russian Acad. of Sciences; scientific divs: mechanics and mathematical physics, informatics and mathematical cybernetics, mathematical systems and decisions modelling, mathematical and programming software, computational technique; Dir Prof. YU. G. EVTUSHENKO; Scientific Sec. SHURSHALOV LEV.

Efremov, D. V., Institute of Electrophysical Apparatus: 196641 St Petersburg, Sovetsky pr. 1; tel. (812) 464-89-63; fax (812) 464-79-79; e-mail glukhikh@niiefa.spb.su; internet www.niiefa.spb.su; f. 1945; Dir V. A. GLUKHIKH; publ. *Plasma Devices and Operations*.

Electronic Control Machines Research Institute: 117812 Moscow, ul. Vavilova 24; tel. (495) 135-32-21; Dir N. L. PROKHOROV.

Energy Systems Institute: 664033 Irkutsk, Lermontova ul. 130; tel. (3952) 42-47-00; fax (3952) 42-44-44; e-mail root@isem.sei.irk.ru; internet www.sei.irk.ru; f. 1960; attached to Russian Acad. of Sciences; Dir N. I. VOROPAI.

Ershov, A. P., Institute of Informatics Systems: 630090 Novosibirsk, pr. Akad. Lavrenteva 6; tel. (3832) 35-56-52; fax (3832) 32-34-94; f. 1990; attached to Russian Acad. of Sciences; library of 100,000 vols; Dir Prof. ALEXANDER G. MARCHUK; publ. *Systems Informatics* (1 a year).

Experimental Factory for Analytical Instrumentation: 198510 St Petersburg, Lomonosov, ul. Fedyuninskogo 3; tel. (812) 473-06-48; attached to Russian Acad. of Sciences; Dir V. I. STEPANOV.

Experimental Factory for Scientific Instrumentation: 142342 Moscow oblast, Noginsk raion, p/o Chernogolovka; tel. (495) 524-50-05; attached to Russian Acad. of Sciences; Dir L. P. KOKURIN.

Experimental Research Institute of Metal-Cutting Machine Tools: 117419 Moscow, 5-i Donskoi pr-d 21B; tel. (495) 952-39-63; Dir V. S. BELOV.

Far Eastern Research Institute of Mineral Raw Materials: 680005 Khabarovsk, ul. Gerasimova 31; tel. (4212) 34-28-43; Dir YU. I. BAKULIN.

Federal State Unitary Enterprise Central Scientific Research Automobile and Engine Institute of the Russian Federation: 125438 Moscow, Avtomotornaya st. 2;

tel. (495) 456-30-81; fax (495) 456-31-32; e-mail admin@nami.ru; internet www.nami.ru; national automobile manufacturing and testing; f. 1918; library of 106,000 vols, spec. colln 93,600 vols; Gen. Dir Prof. A. IPATOV; publ. various journals.

Fedorov, E. K., Institute of Applied Geophysics: 129128 Moscow, Rostokinskaya ul. 9; tel. (495) 181-37-14; Dir S. I. AVDYUSHIN.

Gubkin Russian State University of Oil and Gas: 119991 Moscow, Leninsky pr. 65; tel. (499) 233-92-25; fax (499) 135-88-95; e-mail com@gubkin.ru; internet www.gubkin.ru; f. 1930, present status 2010; educational and research and devt programmes through the full process chain of petroleum engineering, 330 journals; library: 1.5m. vols incl. rare monographs, MSS theses and specialized journals; Rector Prof. VICTOR G. MARTYNOV; publs *Chemistry & Technology of Fuels and Oils*, *Oil, Gas & Business*.

High-Technology Ceramics Research Centre: 119361 Moscow, Ozernaya ul. 48; tel. (495) 430-77-70; fax (495) 437-98-93; attached to Russian Acad. of Sciences; Dir V. YA. SHEVCHENKO.

Hydrochemical Institute: 344090 Rostov on Don, pr. Stachki 198; tel. (8632) 22-44-70; fax (8632) 22-44-70; e-mail ghi@aaanet.ru; f. 1920; library of 40,000 vols; Dir A. M. NIKANOROV; publ. *Gidrokhimicheskiye Materialy* (3 a year).

Image Processing Systems Institute: 443001 Samara, ul. Molodogvardeiskaya 151; tel. (846) 332-56-20; fax (846) 332-27-63; e-mail ipsi@smr.ru; internet www.ipsi.smr.ru; f. 1988; attached to Russian Acad. of Sciences; diffractive optics, nanophotonics, image processing and pattern recognition; library of 1,000 vols; Dir Prof. V. A. SOIFER; publ. *Computer Optics* (in Russian, 4 a year).

Institute for Systems Analysis: 117312 Moscow, pr. 60-letia Oktyabrya 9; tel. (495) 135-42-22; fax (495) 938-22-09; e-mail isa@isa.ru; internet www.isa.ru; f. 1976; attached to Russian Acad. of Sciences; Dir YU. S. POPKOV.

Institute of Analytical Instrumentation: 190103 St Petersburg, Rizhsky pr. 26; tel. (812) 251-86-00; fax (812) 251-70-38; e-mail iap@ianin.spb.su; internet www.iai.rssi.ru; f. 1977; attached to Russian Acad. of Sciences; fundamental and applied research aimed at development of new methods, instruments and technologies in the areas of elemental phase and structural analysis; nanotechnology and surface diagnostics; biotechnology, ecology and medicine; Dir Prof. V. E. KUROCHKIN; publ. *Scientific Instrumentation* (4 a year).

Institute of Applied Mathematics: 690041 Vladivostok, ul. Radio 7; tel. (4232) 31-33-30; fax (4232) 31-18-56; f. 1988; attached to Russian Acad. of Sciences; library of 21,000 vols; Dir Prof. N. V. KUZNETSOV.

Institute of Applied Mechanics: c/o Russian Academy of Sciences, 119991 Moscow, Leninsky pr.; tel. (495) 938-18-45; fax (495) 938-07-11; attached to Russian Acad. of Sciences; Dir YU G. YANOVSKY; publ. *Journal on Composite Materials and Design* (4 a year).

Institute of Applied Mechanics: 426067 Izhevsk, T. Baramzinoy 34; tel. (3412) 50-88-10; fax (3412) 50-79-59; e-mail foipm@udm.ru; internet www.udman.ru; f. 1989; attached to Russian Acad. of Sciences; physics and mechanics of heterogenous media; problems of mechanics of deformed solid and material tribo-technology; new materials; Dir Acad. ALEXEY LIPANOV; publ. *Chemical Physics and Mezoscopy* (4 a year).

Institute of Automation and Control Processes: 690041 Vladivostok, ul. Radio 5; tel. (4232) 31-04-39; fax (4232) 31-04-52; e-mail director@iacp.vl.ru; internet www.dvo.ru/iacp; f. 1971; attached to Russian Acad. of Sciences; Dir V. P. MYASNIKOV.

Institute of Automation and Electrometry: 630090 Novosibirsk, Universitetskii pr. 1; tel. (3832) 35-10-52; fax (3832) 35-48-51; e-mail malinovsky@iae.nsk.su; attached to Russian Acad. of Sciences; Dir Prof. S. T. VASKOV.

Institute of Biological Instrumentation: 123373 Moscow, Volokalamskoe shosse 91; tel. (495) 491-73-72; Dir V. N. ZLOBIN.

Institute of Chemistry and Chemical Technology: 660049 Krasnoyarsk, ul. K. Marksa 42; tel. (3912) 27-38-31; fax (3912) 23-86-58; e-mail chem@krsk.info; internet krsk.info/icct; f. 1981; attached to Russian Acad. of Sciences; Dir Prof. G. L. PASHKOV; publs *Proceedings of Workshops* (every 3 years), *Siberian Gold* (symposium proceedings, every 2 years).

Institute of Computational Technologies: 630090 Novosibirsk, pr. Akad. Lavrenteva 6; tel. (383) 330-61-50; fax (383) 330-63-42; e-mail shokin@ict.nsc.ru; internet www.ict.nsc.ru; f. 1990; attached to Russian Acad. of Sciences, Siberian br.; designs and implements informational-telecommunication technologies in decision-making problems; applies mathematical modelling and computational algorithm devt to a wide range of problems arising in mechanics of continuous media, physics and ecology; Head YURI SHOKIN; publ. *Journal of Computational Technologies* (6 a year).

Institute of Continuous Media Mechanics: 614013 Perm, ul. Akad. Koroleva 1; tel. (3422) 33-07-21; fax (3422) 33-69-57; e-mail mvp@admin.icmm.perm.su; f. 1971; attached to Russian Acad. of Sciences; Dir V. P. MATVEYENKO.

Institute of Control Sciences, Automation and Telemechanics: 117806 Moscow, ul. Profsoyuznaya 65; tel. (495) 334-89-10; fax (495) 334-93-40; e-mail vasmac@ipu.rssi.ru; attached to Russian Acad. of Sciences; Dir Acad. I. V. PRANGISHVILI.

Institute of Electronic Measurement 'Kvarz': 603009 Nizhnii Novgorod, pr. Gagarina 176; tel. (8312) 66-70-93; fax (8312) 66-55-62; e-mail nnipi_kvarz@sinn.ru; internet www.kvarz.ru; f. 1949; research, development and manufacture of electronic measurement equipment; 1,200 mems; Dir-Gen. A. M. KUDRIAVTSEV; publ. *Electronic Measurements* (in Russian, 1 a year).

Institute of Energy Research: 117333 Moscow, ul. Vavilova 44, korp. 2; tel. (495) 127-48-34; attached to Russian Acad. of Sciences; Dir A. A. MAKAROV.

Institute of Engineering Science: 620219 Ekaterinburg, Komsomolskaya ul. 34, GSP-207; tel. (343) 374-47-25; fax (343) 374-53-30; e-mail ges@imach.uran.ru; internet www.imach.uran.ru; f. 1986; attached to Russian Acad. of Sciences; research into mechanics of solids and structures, advanced materials and technologies; automated systems of measurements, nondestructive testing and diagnostics of machine life; mechanics and control of transportation and traction machines; creation of basic algorithms, software and hardware for systems of automated control of compound objects; library of 16,700 vols; Dir Prof. E. S. GORKUNOV.

Institute of High Current Electronics: 634055 Tomsk, pr. Akademichesky 2–3; tel. (3822) 49-15-44; fax (3822) 49-24-10; e-mail contact@hcei.tsc.ru; internet www.hcei.tsc.ru; f. 1977; attached to Russian Acad. of Sciences; library of 50,000 vols; Dir Acad. SERGEI D. KOROVIN.

Institute of Informatics and Mathematical Modelling of Technological Processes: 184200 Murmansk oblast, Apatity, ul. Fersmana 24A; tel. (81555) 7-40-50; fax (81555) 7-42-26; e-mail putilov@iimm.kolasc.net.ru; f. 1989; attached to Russian Acad. of Sciences; Dir Dr V. A. PUTILOV; publ. *Computer-Aided Simulation*.

Institute of Informatics Problems of the Russian Academy of Sciences (IPIRAN): 119333 Moscow, ul. Vavilova 44-2; tel. (499) 137-34-94; fax (495) 930-45-05; e-mail sshorgin@ipiran.ru; internet www.ipiran.ru; f. 1983; attached to Russian Acad. of Sciences; fundamental and applied research and devt in integrated information-telecommunication networks and systems and stochastic systems; theoretical problems and applied technologies in accumulation, processing and representation of information; creation of computerized information systems; Dir Acad. IGOR SOKOLOV; Deputy Dir SERGEY SHORGIN; publs *Informatics and Applications* (4 a year), *Systems and Methods of Informatics* (1 a year).

Institute of Information Science and Automation: 199178 St Petersburg, 14 liniya 39; tel. (812) 218-03-82; attached to Russian Acad. of Sciences; Dir V. M. PONOMAREV.

Institute of Information Transmission Problems (Kharkevich Institute): 127994 Moscow 19/1, Bol. Karetny per.; tel. (495) 650-42-25; fax (495) 650-05-79; e-mail director@iitp.ru; internet www.iitp.ru; f. 1961; attached to Russian Acad. of Sciences; Dir ALEXANDER KULESHOV; publs *Automation and Remote Control* (12 a year), *Information Processes*, *Problems of Information Transmission* (4 a year).

Institute of Laser and Information Technology: 140700 Moscow oblast, Shatura, Svyatoozerskaya ul. 1; tel. (496) 452-59-95; fax (496) 452-25-32; e-mail center@laser.ru; internet www.laser.ru, f. 1979; attached to Russian Acad. of Sciences; library of 35,000 vols; Dir Prof. V. YA. PANCHENKO.

Institute of Mathematics and Mechanics: 620219 Ekaterinburg, ul. S. Kovalevskoi 16; tel. (3432) 374-83-32; fax (3432) 374-25-81; e-mail bvi@imm.uran.ru; internet www.imm.uran.ru; f. 1956; attached to Ural Branch of the Russian Acad. of Sciences; Dir Prof. V. I. BERDYSHEV.

Institute of Medical Instrument Making: 125422 Moscow, Timiryazevskaya ul. 1; tel. (495) 211-09-65; fax (495) 200-22-13; attached to Russian Acad. of Medical Sciences; Dir V. A. VIKTOROV.

Institute of Mining, Khabarovsk: 680000 Khabarovsk, ul. Turgeneva 51; tel. (4212) 33-79-27; attached to Russian Acad. of Sciences; Dir G. V. SEKISOV.

Institute of Mining, Novosibirsk: 630091 Novosibirsk, Krasny pr. 54; tel. (3832) 17-05-36; fax (3832) 17-06-78; e-mail admin@misd.nsc.ru; internet www.misd.nsc.ru; f. 1944; attached to Russian Acad. of Sciences; library of 40,000 vols; Dir OPARIN VICTOR NIKOLAEVICH; Academic Sec. TARASIK T. MIKHAILOVNA; publ. *Journal of Mining Science* (6 a year).

Institute of Mining of the North: 677018 Yakutsk, ul. Lenina 43; tel. (4112) 44-59-30; fax (4112) 44-59-30; f. 1980; attached to Russian Acad. of Sciences; Dir Dr M. D. NOVOPASHIN.

Institute of Mining, Perm: 614007 Perm, Sibirskaya ul. 78A; tel. (3422) 16-75-02; fax (3422) 16-09-69; e-mail arc@mi-perm.ru; f. 1988; attached to Russian Acad. of Sciences; library of 3,000 vols; Dir Prof. ARKADI E.

KRASNO-SHTEIN; publs *Collection of Scientific and Research Works* (1 a year), *Mining Echo* (4 a year), *Proceedings* (1 a year).

Institute of Monitoring of Climatic and Ecological Systems: 634055 Tomsk, Akademicheskii pr. 10/3; tel. (3822) 492265; fax (3822) 491950; e-mail post@imces.ru; internet www.imces.ru; f. 1972, fmrly the Institute of Optical Monitoring; attached to Russian Acad. of Sciences; scientific and technological basis for monitoring and modelling climatic and ecosystem changes under impact of natural and anthropogenic factors; Dir V. A. KRUTIKOV; Scientific Sec. for Foreign Relations ELENA YURIEVNA GENINA.

Institute of Petrochemistry and Catalysis: 450075 Bashkortostan, Ufa, pr. Oktyabrya 141; tel. and fax (3472) 31-27-50; e-mail ink@anrb.ru; internet www.anrb.ru/ink/index.html; f. 1992; Dir USAIN M. DZHEMILEV.

Institute of Petroleum Refining and Petrochemistry: 450065 Bashkortostan, Ufa, Initsiativnaya ul. 12; tel. (3472) 43-31-17; fax (3472) 43-31-17; f. 1956; Dir E. G. TELIASHEV.

Institute of Physical and Technical Problems of the North: 677891 Yakutsk, Oktyabrskaya ul. 1; tel. (4112) 44-66-65; fax (4112) 44-66-65; attached to Russian Acad. of Sciences; f. 1970; Dir Acad. V. P. LARIONOV.

Institute of Physics and Power Engineering: Bondarenko pl. 1, 249033 Kaluga oblast, Obninsk; tel. (08439) 98250; fax (08439) 58545; e-mail avzrod@ippe.obninsk.ru; internet www.ippe.ru; f. 1946; nuclear systems for civil and defence purposes; nuclear, laser and reactor physics; thermal physics, hydro-, gas and plasma-dynamics, liquid-metal coolant technologies; radiation material science; 3,800 mems; library of 320,000 vols; Dir-Gen. ANATOLY V. ZRODNIKOV.

Institute of Problems in Cybernetics: 117312 Moscow, ul. Vavilova 37; tel. (495) 124-77-67; attached to Russian Acad. of Sciences; Dir (vacant).

Institute of Problems in the Complex Utilization of Mineral Resources: 111020 Moscow, Kryukovskii tupik 4; tel. and fax (495) 360-89-60; e-mail info@ipkonran.ru; internet www.ipkonran.ru; f. 1977; attached to Russian Acad. of Sciences; Dir V. A. CHANTURIA.

Institute of Problems in the Safe Development of Nuclear Energy: 115191 Moscow, Bol. Tulskaya; tel. (495) 952-24-21; attached to Russian Acad. of Sciences; Dir L. A. BOLSHOV.

Institute of Problems of Marine Technology: 690600 Vladivostok, ul. Sukhanova 5A; tel. (4232) 22-64-16; fax (4232) 22-64-51; f. 1988; attached to Russian Acad. of Sciences; Dir M. D. AGEEV.

Institute of Problems of Mechanics: 119526 Moscow, pr. Vernadskogo 101; tel. (495) 434-32-38; fax (495) 938-20-48; f. 1965; attached to Russian Acad. of Sciences; library of 150,000 vols; Dir Prof. F. L. CHERNOUSKO.

Institute of Programmable Systems: 152140 Pereslavl-Zalesskii; tel. (08535) 9-81-21; attached to Russian Acad. of Sciences; Dir A. K. AILAMAZYAN.

Institute of Radio Engineering and Electronics: 103907 Moscow, Mokhovaya ul. 8; pr. K. Marksa 18; tel. (495) 203-52-93; fax (495) 200-52-58; attached to Russian Acad. of Sciences; br. in Saratov; Dir Acad. YU. V. GULYAEV.

Institute of Regional Systems Research: Birobidzhan; attached to Russian Acad. of Sciences; (in process of formation).

Institute of Remote Sensing Methods for Geology (VNIIKAM): 199034 St Petersburg, Birzhevoi pr-d 6; tel. (812) 218-28-01; fax (812) 218-39-16; Dir ALEXEI V. PERTSOV.

Institute of Solid State Chemistry and Mechanochemistry: 630128 Novosibirsk, Kutateladze ul. 18; tel. (383) 332-96-00; fax (383) 332-28-47; e-mail root@solid.nsc.ru; internet www.solid.nsc.ru; f. 1944; attached to Russian Acad. of Sciences; topo-chemical, radiation chemical and mechano-chemical methods of the control of the reactivity of solids; chemistry of supramolecular systems; reactions of intercalation; transport properties of composite materials; processes of electro-deposition and electro-dissolution of solid metallic electrodes in water solutions; devt of methods for nano-sized and high-dispersed materials preparation; mechanical alloying and mechano-chemical interaction in organic systems; synthesis of bismuth compounds of high purity and reactivity; library of 50,000 vols; Dir Prof. N. Z. LYAKHOV; publ. *Chemistry for Sustainable Development* (6 a year).

Institute of Synthetic Polymer Materials: 117393 Moscow, Profsoyuznaya 70; tel. (495) 335-91-00; attached to Russian Acad. of Sciences; Dir (vacant).

Institute of Technical Chemistry: 614013 Perm, ul. ak. Koroleva; tel. and fax (342) 237-82-90; e-mail techem@permonline.ru; internet www.itch.permonline.ru; f. 1985; attached to Russian Acad. of Sciences; Dir Dr V. N. STRELNIKOV.

Institute of the Automation of Design: 123056 Moscow, 2-ya Brestskaya; tel. (495) 250-02-62; attached to Russian Acad. of Sciences; Dir O. M. BELOTSERKOVSKY.

Institute of the Economics and Organization of Industrial Production: 630090 Novosibirsk, pr. Akad. Lavrenteva 17; tel. (3832) 35-05-36; fax (3832) 35-55-80; attached to Russian Acad. of Sciences; Dir (vacant).

Institute of the Geology and Exploitation of Fossil Fuels: 117312 Moscow, ul. Fersmana 50; tel. (495) 124-91-55; attached to Russian Acad. of Sciences; Dir N. KRYLOV.

Institute of Theoretical and Applied Mechanics: 630090 Novosibirsk, Institutskaya ul. 4/1; tel. (3832) 33-35-34; fax (3832) 34-22-68; e-mail fomin@itam.nsc.ru; internet www.itam.nsc.ru; f. 1957; attached to Russian Acad. of Sciences; library of 87,000 vols; Dir Prof. V. M. FOMIN; publs *Combustion, Explosion and Shock Waves* (6 a year), *Journal of Applied Mechanics and Technical Physics* (6 a year), *Physical Mesomechanics* (4 a year), *Thermophysics and Aeromechanics* (4 a year).

Institute of Trade Machinery: 127521 Moscow, Scheremetevskaya ul. 47; tel. (495) 218-51-47; fax (495) 219-73-21; f. 1961; Dir VYACHESLAV LVOVICH UMANSKY.

Ioffe, Acad. A. F., Physical-Technical Institute: 194021 St Petersburg, Politeckhnicheskaya ul. 26; tel. (812) 247-21-45; fax (812) 247-10-17; attached to Russian Acad. of Sciences; br. in Shuvalovo; Dir Acad. ZH. I. ALFEROV.

Joint Russian-Vietnamese Tropical Research and Technological Centre: 117071 Moscow, Leninsky pr. 33; tel. (495) 954-12-19; f. 1987; attached to Russian Acad. of Sciences; long-term health consequences of Agent Orange, ecology, tropical resistance of materials and equipment; Head Acad. D. S. PAVLOV.

Kargin, V. A., Polymer Research Institute: 606006 Nizhegorodskaya oblast, Dzerzhinsk; tel. (8313) 25-50-00; fax (8313) 33-13-18; e-mail niip@kis.ru; internet www.advtech.ru/nipolymer/nipolymer1.htm; f. 1949; library of 142,000 vols; Gen. Dir Prof. V. V. GUZEEV.

Kazan Physical-Technical Institute: 420029 Kazan, ul. Sibirskii trakt 10/7; tel. (8432) 76-50-44; attached to Russian Acad. of Sciences; Dir K. M. SALIKHOV.

Keldysh, M.V., Institute of Applied Mathematics: 125047 Moscow, Miusskaya pl. 4; tel. (495) 972-37-14; attached to Russian Acad. of Sciences; Dir S. P. KURDYUMOV.

Kostyakov, A. N., All-Russian Research Institute of Hydraulic Engineering and Land Reclamation: 127550 Moscow, Bol. Akademicheskaya 44; tel. (499) 153-72-70; fax (499) 729-35-00; library of 8,000 vols; Dir Prof. Dr B. M. KIZYAEV (acting); publ. *Transactions* (1 or 2 a year).

Krylov Shipbuilding Research Institute: 196158 St Petersburg, Moskovskoe shosse 44; tel. (812) 727-93-48; fax (812) 727-93-49; e-mail krylov@krylov.spb.ru; internet www.krylov.com.ru; f. 1894; Science Prin. and Dir V. M. PASHIN; publ. *Proceedings* (1 a year).

Krzhizhanovsky, G. M., State Energy Research Institute: 117927 Moscow, Leninsky pr. 19; tel. (495) 954-37-32; attached to Russian Acad. of Sciences; Dir E. P. VOLKOV.

Lebedev, S. A., Institute of Precision Mechanics and Computing Technology: 117333 Moscow, Leninsky pr. 51; tel. (495) 137-15-67; attached to Russian Acad. of Sciences; Dir G. G. RYABOV.

Lebedev, S. V., All-Russia Synthetic Rubber Research Institute: 198035 St Petersburg, Gapsalskaya ul. 1; tel. (812) 251-40-28; fax (812) 251-48-13; f. 1928; synthetic elastomeric materials, production processes, applications; Dir Prof. VITALY A. KORMER.

Mining Institute: 184209 Murmansk oblast, Apatity, ul. Fersmana 24; tel. (81555) 7-43-42; fax (81555) 7-46-25; e-mail root@goi.kolasc.net.ru; internet www.goikolasc.ru; attached to Russian Acad. of Sciences; Dir Acad. N. N. MELNIKOV.

Mints, Acad. A. L., Institute of Radio Technology JSC: 127083 Moscow, ul. 8 Marta 10/1; tel. (495) 214-04-51; fax (495) 214-06-62; e-mail spz@newmail.ru; Gen. Dir V. I. SHUSTOV.

Moscow Scientific-Industrial Association 'Spektr': 119048 Moscow, ul. Usacheva 35; tel. (495) 245-56-56; fax (495) 246-88-88; f. 1964; attached to Russian Acad. of Sciences; research, devt and manufacture of non-destructive-testing equipment and instruments; Gen. Dir V. V. KLYUEV.

National Institute of Aviation Technology: 127051 Moscow, Petrovka 24; tel. (495) 311-05-41; fax (495) 311-03-23; e-mail info@niat.ru; internet www.niat.ru; f. 1920; Dir. O. S. SIROTKIN; publ. *Aviation Industry* (in Russian and English).

Paper Research Institute: 194018 St Petersburg, pr. Shvernika 49; tel. (812) 247-17-03; Dir A. IVANOV.

Pechora Research and Design Institute for the Oil Industry: 169400 Komi, Ukhta, Oktyabrskaya ul. 11; tel. (82147) 6-16-63; fax (82147) 6-03-36; Dir A. N. ILIN.

Physical-Technical Institute: 42600 Izhevsk, ul. Kirova 132; tel. (3142) 43-02-03; fax (3142) 25-06-14; e-mail fti@fti.udm.ru; internet fti.udm.ru; attached to Russian Acad. of Sciences; Dir Dr VLADIMIR LADYANOV.

Plastics Research Institute: 111112 Moscow, Perovskii pr. 35; tel. (495) 361-64-21; Dir V. I. ILICH.

Polymer Plastics Research Institute: St Petersburg, Polyustrovskii pr. 32; Dir Z. N. POLYAKOV.

Polzunov, I. I., Scientific and Development Association for Research and Design of Power Equipment JSC: 191167 St Petersburg, Atamanskaya str. 3/6; tel. (812) 578-87-13; fax (812) 717-43-00; e-mail general@ckti.ru; f. 1927; attached to Russian Acad. of Sciences; Dir YU. K. PETRENYA; publ. *Proceedings*.

Republic Engineering-Technical Centre for the Restoration and Strengthening of Components of Machines and Mechanisms: 634067 Tomsk, Khim ploshchadka; tel. (3822) 1-45-04 br. at Novosibirsk: 630055 Novosibirsk, ul. Musy Dzhalilya 9; tel. (3832) 32-12-49; attached to Russian Acad. of Sciences; Dir V. F. PINKIN (Tomsk); Dir V. M. NEZAMUTDINOV (Novosibirsk).

Research and Design Institute for the Mechanical Processing of Minerals: 199026 St Petersburg, V. O., 21-ya liniya 8A; tel. (812) 321-97-29; fax (812) 325-62-02; f. 1920; Dir VASILY ARSENTIEV; publ. *Obogashcheniye Rud* (Mineral Processing Journal, 6 a year).

Research and Design Institute of Artificial Fibres: 141009 Moscow oblast, Mytishchi, ul. Kolontsova 5; tel. (495) 284-44-78; Dir V. SMIRNOV.

Research and Design Institute of Autogenous Engineering: 109004 Moscow, Shelaputinsky per. 1; tel. and fax (495) 915-09-60; e-mail vniiautogen@newmail.ru; f. 1944; equipment for thermal cutting and spraying; Dir NIKOLAI I. NIKIFOROV; publ. *Research Work* (irregular).

Research and Design Institute of Chemical Engineering: 125015 Moscow, Bol. Novodmitrovskaya 14; tel. (495) 685-56-74; fax (495) 685-29-23; e-mail info@niichimmash.ru; internet niichimmash.ru; f. 1943; Gen. Dir A. TSYGANKOV.

Research and Design Institute of Management Information Technology: 125083 Moscow, ul. Yunnatov 18; tel. (495) 212-60-60.

Research and Design Institute of Metallurgical Engineering: 109428 Moscow, Ryazanskii pr. 8A; tel. (495) 174-37-00.

Research and Design Institute of Polymer Construction Materials: 117419 Moscow, 2-i Verkhny Mikhailovsky pr. 9; tel. (495) 952-30-68; fax (495) 954-40-91; attached to Polymerstroymateriali JSC; Dir ALEXANDER V. POGORELOV.

Research and Design Institute of the Bearings Industry: 109088 Moscow, 2-ya ul. Mashinostroeniya 27; tel. (495) 275-11-59.

Research and Design Institute of Woodworking Machinery: 107082 Moscow, Rubtsovskaya nab. 3; tel. (495) 261-16-73; f. 1948; library of 50,000 vols; publ. *Catalogue of Woodworking Machines* (1 a year).

Research and Design Technological Institute of Heavy Engineering: Ekaterinburg, pl. 1-i Pyatiletki.

Research and Experimental Design Institute of Machinery for the Food Industry: 123308 Moscow, pr. Marshala Zhukova 1.

Research Centre for Fundamental Problems of Computer Technology and Control Systems: 117218 Moscow, ul. Krasikova 25A; tel. (495) 125-77-09; attached to Russian Acad. of Sciences; Chair. of Presidium K. A. VALIEV.

Attached Institutes:

Institute of Computer Technology Problems: 150007 Yaroslavl, Universitetskaya 21; tel. (0852) 35-52-83; attached to Russian Acad. of Sciences; Dir YU. A. MAMATOV.

Institute of Microelectronics Technology and High-purity Materials: 142432 Moscow oblast, Chernogolovka vul. Institutskay 6; tel. (495) 962-80-74; fax (495) 962-80-47; e-mail general@iptm.ru; internet www.iptm.ru; attached to Russian Acad. of Sciences; Dir V. A. TULIN.

Microelectronics Institute: 150007 Yaroslavl, Universitetskaya 21; tel. (0852) 11-65-52; attached to Russian Acad. of Sciences; Dir V. A. KURCHIDIS.

Physical Technological Institute: 117218 Moscow, ul. Krasikova 25-A; tel. (495) 125-77-09; attached to Russian Acad. of Sciences; Dir K. A. VALIEV.

Research Institute of Systems of Automated Designing of Radioelectronic Apparatus and Very Large Scale Integrated Circuits: 103681 Moscow, Zelenograd, ul. Sovetskaya 3; tel. (495) 531-56-45; attached to Russian Acad. of Sciences; Dir A. L. STEMPKOVSKY.

Special Design Bureau for Microelectronics and Computer Technology: 15007 Yaroslavl, Universitetskaya 21; tel. (0852) 11-81-73; attached to Russian Acad. of Sciences; Dir A. M. GLUSHKOV.

Research Centre for Space Probes: 117810 Moscow, Profsoyuznaya ul. 84/32; attached to Russian Acad. of Sciences; Head N. A. DOLGIKH (acting).

Research, Design and Technological Institute of Electrothermic Equipment: 109052 Moscow, Nizhegorodskaya 29; tel. (495) 278-75-09.

Research Design-Technological Institute for Coal Machinery: 109193 Moscow, ul. Petra Romanova 7; tel. (495) 279-47-66.

Research Institute for Food Concentrates and Food Technologies and Special Food Technology: 117279 Moscow, Miklukho-Maklaya ul. 32; tel. and fax (495) 429-04-11; e-mail niispt@yandex.ru; internet www.niippspt.ru; f. 1981; attached to Russian Acad. of Agricultural Sciences; develops food concentrates, cereal snacks; food rations for Armed Forces and cosmonauts; tea and coffee products, infant foods; library of 7,000 vols; Dir Dr VICTOR F. DOBROVOLSKY; publ. *Tea and Coffee in Russia* (4 a year).

Research Institute for Instrumentation: 125124 Moscow, ul. Raskovoi 20; tel. (495) 214-55-88.

Research Institute for Systems Research: 109280 Moscow, Avtozavodskaya 23; tel. (495) 277-87-31; attached to Russian Acad. of Sciences; Dir V. B. BETELIN.

Research Institute for the Bakery and Confectionery Industry: 107553 Moscow, Bol. Cherkizovskaya ul. 26A; tel. (495) 161-41-44; attached to Russian Acad. of Agricultural Sciences.

Research Institute for the Beer, Soft Drinks and Wine Industry: 119021 Moscow, ul. Rossolimo 7; tel. (495) 246-67-69; attached to Russian Acad. of Agricultural Sciences.

Research Institute for the Organization, Management and Economics of the Oil and Gas Industry: 117420 Moscow, ul. Nametkina 14; tel. (495) 332-00-22.

Research Institute for the Processing of Casing Head Gas: 350550 Krasnodar, Krasnaya ul. 118; tel. (8612) 55-85-52; Dir N. I. KORSAKOV.

Research Institute of Abrasives and Grinding: 197342 St Petersburg, Beloostrovskaya ul. 17; tel. (812) 245-33-05; fax (812) 245-47-90; f. 1931; library of 62,000 vols; Dir S. MOLCHANOV.

Research Institute of Agricultural Engineering: 127427 Moscow, Dmitrovskoe shosse 107; tel. (495) 485-55-81.

Research Institute of Applied Automated Systems: 103009 Moscow, ul. Nezhdanovoi 2A; tel. (495) 229-78-46; attached to Russian Acad. of Sciences; Dir O. L. SMIRNOV.

Research Institute of Atomic Reactors: Ulyanovsk oblast, 433510 Dimitrovgrad; tel. (84235) 3-20-21; fax (84235) 3-56-48; e-mail adm@niiar.ru; internet www.niiar.ru; f. 1956; library of 150,000 vols; Dir Dr A. V. BYCHKOV.

Research Institute of Automobile Electronics and Electrical Equipment: 105187 Moscow, Kirpichnaya 39–41; tel. (495) 365-25-66.

Research Institute of Automobile Industry Technology: 115333 Moscow, pr. Andropova 22/30; tel. (495) 118-20-00; Dir S. V. PODOBLYAEV.

Research Institute of Building Ceramics: 143980 Moscow oblast, Zheleznodorozhnyi-1; tel. (495) 527-73-73.

Research Institute of Chemical Fibres and Composite Materials: 195030 St Petersburg, ul. Khimikov 28; tel. (812) 227-61-48; Dir P. E. MIKHAILOV.

Research Institute of Chemical Reagents and Ultrapure Chemical Substances: 107258 Moscow, Bogorodskii val 3; tel. (495) 963-70-70; Dir E. A. RYABENKO.

Research Institute of Chemicals for Polymer Materials: 392680 Tambov, ul. Montazhnikov 3; tel. (0752) 29-51-52; attached to Syntez joint-stock company; Dir B. N. GORBUNOV.

Research Institute of Construction and Road Machinery: 123424 Moscow, Volokolamskoe shosse 73; tel. (495) 491-10-33.

Research Institute of Construction Physics: 127238 Moscow, Lokomotivny pr. 21; tel. (495) 482-40-76; fax (495) 482-40-60; e-mail niisf@ipc.ru; f. 1956; library of 2,000 vols; Dir G. L. OSIPOV.

Research Institute of Current Sources: 129626 Moscow; tel. (495) 287-97-42; attached to Russian Acad. of Sciences; Dir YU. V. SKOKOV.

Research Institute of Drilling Technology: 117957 Moscow, Leninsky pr. 6; tel. (495) 236-01-70; Dir A. V. MNASHCHAKOV.

Research Institute of Earthmoving Machinery: c/o VNIIZEMMASH, 198005 St Petersburg, Petrovskii pr. 2; tel. (812) 235-57-84; fax (812) 235-57-84; attached to VNIIZEMMASH; Dir V. P. KORNEEV.

Research Institute of Elastic Materials and Products: 119048 Moscow, Mal. Trubetskaya ul. 28; tel. (495) 242-53-42; fax (495) 245-62-10; Dir S. V. REZNICHENKO.

Research Institute of Electrical Engineering: 191186 St Petersburg, Dvortsovaya nab. 18; tel. and fax (812) 387-55-22; e-mail jandan@peterlink.ru; f. 1992; attached to Russian Acad. of Sciences; Dir Acad. Y. B. DANILEVICH; publs *Electrichestvo* (12 a year), *Energetics News of RAS* (6 a year).

Research Institute of Electro-welding Technology: 194100 St Petersburg, Litovskaya ul. 10; tel. (812) 245-40-95; Dir V. V. SMIRNOV.

Research Institute of Electromeasuring Equipment: 195267 St Petersburg, pr. Prosveshcheniya 85; tel. (812) 559-51-41.

Research Institute of Foundry Machinery and the Technology and Automation of Foundry Production: 123557 Moscow, Presnenskii val 14; tel. (495) 252-27-25; Dir E. KRAKOVSKII.

Research Institute of Gas Use in the Economy and Underground Storage of Oil, Oil Products and Liquefied Gases: 123298 Moscow, ul. Berzarina 12; tel. (499) 946-89-11.

Research Institute of Hydrogeology and Engineering Geology (VSEGINGEO): 142452 Moscow oblast, Noginskii raion, p/o Kupavna, pos. Zelenyi; tel. (495) 521-20-00; fax (495) 913-51-26; e-mail gvartany@online.ru; f. 1939; Dir Acad. G.S. VARTANYAN.

Research Institute of Instrumentation Technology: 113191 Moscow, Gamsonovskii per. 9; tel. (495) 232-10-41.

Research Institute of Light Alloys: Moscow, ul. Gorbanova 20; Dir N. I. KORYAGINA.

Research Institute of Light and Textile Machinery: 113105 Moscow, Varshavskoe shosse 33; tel. (499) 611-00-30; fax (495) 958-58-41; e-mail vniiltek@mail.magelan.ru; internet www.vimi.ru/vniiltekmash; f. 1932; library of 30,000 vols; Dir Prof. Dr R. M. MALAFEYEV.

Research Institute of Organizational Technology: 119146 Moscow, Komsomolskii pr. 9A; tel. (495) 246-41-21.

Research Institute of Road Traffic Safety: 109389 Moscow, Mal. Lubyanka 16/4.

Research Institute of Rubber and Latex Products: 107564 Moscow, Krasnobogatyrskaya ul. 42; tel. (495) 161-02-92; fax (495) 963-49-11; Dir V. A. BERESTENEV.

Research Institute of Rubber Technical Products: 141300 Moscow oblast, Sergievsky Posad; tel. (496) 544-57-59; fax (0496) 544-10-52; f. 1960; library of 15,000 vols; Dir V. V. SHVARTS.

Research Institute of Special Engineering: 107082 Moscow, Cheshikhinsky pr-d 18/20; tel. (499) 261-50-76.

Research Institute of Synthetic Fibres: 170613 Tver, ul. Pashi Savelevoi 45; tel. (08222) 5-36-10; Dir V. F. LOSKUTOV.

Research Institute of Technical Physics: 454070 Chelyabinsk oblast, Chelyabinsk 70; Dir V. Z. NECHAI.

Research Institute of the Cement Industry OJSC (NIICement): 107014 Moscow, 3-i Luchevoy prosek 12; tel. (495) 268-27-21; fax (495) 268-27-26; e-mail riicement@mtu-net.ru; f. 1947; formerly State Research Institute of the Cement Industry; Dir-Gen. Prof. Dr V.I. SHUBIN.

Research Institute of the Chemistry and Technology of Organoelement Compounds: 105118 Moscow, shosse Entuziastov 38; tel. (495) 673-49-53; fax (495) 913-25-38; e-mail eos2004@inbox.ru; internet www.eos.su; f. 1945; Gen.-Dir P. A. STOROZHENKO.

Research Institute of the Clock and Watch Industry: 125315 Moscow, Chasovaya 24/1; tel. (495) 151-15-01.

Research Institute of the Factory Technology of Prefabricated Reinforced Concrete Structures and Items: 111524 Moscow, ul. Plekhanova 7; tel. (495) 176-27-04.

Research Institute of the Gas Industry: 142700 Moscow oblast, Vidnoe.

Research Institute of the Metrology Service: 119361 Moscow, G-361, Ozernaya ul. 46; tel. (495) 437-55-77; fax (495) 437-56-66; e-mail office.vniims@relcom.ru; attached to Russian Acad. of Sciences; Dir V. V. SAZHIN.

Research Institute of the Tyre Industry: 105118 Moscow, ul. Burakova 27; tel. (495) 273-69-01; fax (495) 176-37-42; Dir A. A. VOLNOV.

Research Institute of Tooling: 105023 Moscow, Bol. Semenovskaya 49; tel. (495) 366-94-11.

Research Institute of Transport Construction: 129329 Moscow, Kolskaya 1; tel. (495) 180-20-42; fax (495) 189-72-53; e-mail mail@tsniis.com; internet www.tsniis.com; f. 1935; research on bridges, tunnels, railways and associated structures, and development of standards and codes of practice; Dir-Gen. ANATOLY SYCHEV.

Research Institute of Vehicle and Tractor Materials: 113184 Moscow, Ozerkovskaya nab. 22/24; tel. (495) 230-94-59.

Research-Training Centre 'Robototekhnika': 105037 Moscow, Izmailovskaya pl. 7; tel. (495) 165-17-01; fax (495) 367-06-36; e-mail robot@bmstu.ru; internet www.robot.bmstu.ru; f. 1983; attached to Russian Acad. of Sciences and Bauman Moscow State Technical University; Head Prof. A. S. YUSCHENKO.

Russian Research, Design and Technological Institute for Crane and Traction Electrical Equipment: 109280 Moscow, ul. Masterkova 4; tel. (495) 275-61-66; fax (495) 275-49-03; f. 1960; library of 160,000 vols; Dir ANATOLY D. MASHIKHIN.

Russian Research Institute of Industrial Design: 129223 Moscow, pr. Mira, VVTs, korp. 312; tel. (495) 216-90-10; fax (495) 216-88-10; f. 1962; Dir LEV A. KUZMICHEV; publs *Tekhnicheskaya Estetika* (2 a year), *Designer's Library* (2 a year).

Russian Research Institute of Information Technology and Automated Design Systems: 129090 Moscow, ul. Shchepkina 22; tel. (495) 288-19-24.

Russian Scientific Centre of Applied Chemistry: 197198 St Petersburg, pr. Dobrolyubova 14; tel. (812) 325-66-45; fax (812) 325-66-48; f. 1919; library of 500,000 vols; Gen. Dir Prof. G. F. TERESHCHENKO; publ. *Annual Proceedings*.

Science Production Association 'Orgstankinprom': 105264 Moscow, 5-ya Parkovaya 37, korp. 2; tel. (495) 164-56-53.

Scientific and Engineering Centre 'SNIIP': 123060 Moscow, ul. Raspletina 5; tel. (499) 198-97-64; fax (499) 943-00-63; e-mail support@sniip.ru; internet www.sniip.ru; attached to Rosatom (State Atomic Energy Corporation); systems and instrumentation connected with nuclear power production, electronics and space research; library of 83,000 research vols; Dir-Gen. Dr ALEXANDER F. PELEVIN; publ. *Proceedings* (1 a year).

Scientific and Research Institute for Standardization and Certification in the Engineering Industry: 123007 Moscow, ul. Shenogina 4; tel. (495) 256-04-49; fax (495) 943-00-78; f. 1957; standardization, certification of products.

Scientific and Research Institute of Motor Transport: 123514 Moscow, ul. Geroev-Panfilovtsev 24; tel. (495) 496-55-23; fax (495) 496-61-36; e-mail niiat@niiat.ru; internet www.niiat.ru; f. 1930; research and devt in field of motor transport operation, incl. transport and traffic management, traffic safety, urban transport, transport and the environment, transport economy; library of 250,000 vols.

Scientific and Technical Complex 'Progress': 119034 Moscow, Kropotkinskaya ul. 13/7; tel. (495) 301-23-25; attached to Russian Acad. of Sciences; Gen. Dir L. N. LUPICHEV.

Scientific Centre of Complex Transportation Problems: 113035 Moscow, Sofiiskaya nab. 34, korp. V; tel. (495) 233-89-13; fax (495) 231-14-54; f. 1955; Dir V. ARSENOV.

Scientific-Experimental Centre for the Automation of Air Traffic Control: 123182 Moscow, Volokolamskoe shosse 26; tel. (495) 190-42-18; attached to Russian Acad. of Sciences; Head T. G. ANODINA.

Scientific Research Institute for Systems Studies: 117218 Moscow, pr. Nakhimovsky 36, korp. 1; tel. (495) 719-76-51; fax (495) 719-76-81; e-mail betelin@sistyd.msk.su; internet www.niisi.ru; f. 1989; attached to Russian Acad. of Sciences; Dir V. B. BETELIN; publs *Issues in Cybernetics* (1 a year), *Issues of SRISA* (2 a year).

Scientific Research Institute of Comprehensive Engineering Problems in Animal Husbandry and Fodder Production (VNIIKOMZH): 101509 Moscow, Lesnaya 43; tel. (495) 250-37-90; fax (495) 978-91-38; f. 1974; library of 40,000 vols; Dir-Gen. I. V. ILIN; publ. *Scientific Research Works of VNIIKOMZH* (1 a year).

Scientific Research Institute of Multiprocessor Computer Systems of the Taganrog State University of Radio Engineering: 347928 Taganrog, ul. Chekhova 2; tel. (86344) 36-07-57; fax (86344) 36-03-76; internet www.mvs.tsure.ru; f. 1972; attached to Russian Acad. of Sciences; Dir I. A. KALIAEV; publ. *Multiprocessor Computer Structures* (1 a year).

Scientific-Technical Co-operative 'Problems of Mechanics and Technology': 109180 Moscow, ul. Bol. Polyanka 2/10; tel. (495) 251-52-08; attached to Russian Acad. of Sciences; Chair. Acad. V. V. STRUMINSKY.

Siberian Research Institute of the Oil Industry: 625016 Tyumen, ul. 50-let Oktyabrya 118; tel. (3452) 21-19-16; Dir R. I. KUZOVATKIN.

Skochinsky Institute of Mining: 140004 Moscow, Lyubertsy 4; tel. (495) 554-85-13; fax (495) 554-52-47; e-mail igd@igd.ru; internet www.igd.ru; f. 1927; attached to Russian Acad. of Sciences; technology of opencast and underground coal mining; certification of mine electrical equipment and explosion-proof equipment; library of 40,000 vols; Dir ANATOLY DMITRIEVICH RUBAN; publs *Economics of the Coal Industry* (1 or 2 a year), *Technology of Opencast and Underground Coal Mining* (4 a year).

Special Design Bureau for Applied Geophysics: 630058 Novosibirsk, Russkaya ul. 35; tel. (3832) 32-36-45; e-mail geophys@hydromet.ru; attached to Russian Acad. of Sciences; Head N. P. RASHENTSEV.

Special Design Bureau for Automation of Marine Research: 693023 Yuzhno-Sakhalinsk, ul. Gorkogo 25; tel. and fax (424) 255-49-66; e-mail skb-sami@sakhalin.ru; f. 1972; attached to Russian Acad. of Sciences; Head ANATOLY E. MALASHENKO.

Special Design Bureau for High Capacity Electronics: 634055 Tomsk, Akademicheskii pr. 4; tel. (3822) 1-84-59; attached to Russian Acad. of Sciences; Head A. P. KHUZEEV.

Special Design Bureau for Hydroimpulse Technology: 630090 Novosibirsk, ul. Tereshkovoi 29; tel. (3832) 35-72-91; attached to Russian Acad. of Sciences; Head A. A. DERIBAS.

Special Design Bureau for Scientific Instruments: 630058 Novosibirsk, Russkaya ul. 41; tel. (3832) 35-30-41; attached to Russian Acad. of Sciences; Head YU. V. CHUGUI.

Special Design-Technological Bureau for Special Electronics and Analytical Instrumentation: 630090 Novosibirsk, ul.

Akad. Nikolaeva 8; tel. (3832) 32-24-40; attached to Russian Acad. of Sciences; Head K. K. SVITASHCHEV.

Special Design-Technological Bureau 'Nauka': 66049 Krasnoyarsk, pr. Mira 53; tel. (3912) 27-29-12; attached to Russian Acad. of Sciences; Head V. V. MOSKVICHEV.

State Design and Research Institute for the Design of Research Institutes, Laboratories and Research Centres of the Academy of Sciences: 117971 Moscow, ul. Gubkina 3; tel. (495) 135-73-01; fax (495) 135-02-20; e-mail gp@gpran.msk.ru; f. 1938; attached to Russian Acad. of Sciences; Dir A. S. PANFIL.

State Design and Research Institute of Power Systems and Electricity Networks: 107884 Moscow, 2-ya Baumanskaya 7; tel. (499) 261-98-21.

State Institute of Mined Chemical Raw Materials: 140000 Moscow oblast, Lyubertsy, Oktyabrsky pr. 259; tel. (495) 554-42-46.

State Research and Project Development Institute of Maritime Transport: 125319 Moscow, Bol. Koptevsky pr-d 6; tel. (495) 152-36-51; fax (495) 152-09-16; f. 1939; design of port structures and ship repair yards; economic problems of maritime transport; maritime law; Dir FELIX G. ARAKELOV.

State Research Institute for the Nitrogen Industry and the Products of Organic Synthesis: 109815 Moscow, Zemlyanoi val 50; tel. (495) 227-00-04; Dir N. D. ZAICHKO.

State Research Institute for the Operation and Repair of Civil Aviation Equipment: Moscow, ul. Krzhizhanovskogo 7.

State Research Institute of Civil Aviation: 103340 Moscow oblast, Sheremetevo Airport; tel. (495) 578-48-01.

State Research Institute of the Rare Metals Industry: 109017 Moscow, Bol. Tolmachevsky per. 5; tel. (495) 239-90-66.

'Submicron' Research Institute: 103482 Moscow, Zelenograd, korp. 331A; tel. (495) 536-26-17.

Topchiev, A. V., Institute of Petro-Chemical Synthesis: 117912 Moscow, Leninskii pr. 29; tel. (495) 954-22-92; attached to Russian Acad. of Sciences; Dir Acad. N. A. PLATE.

Tractor Research and Development Institute: 125040 Moscow, Verkhnyaya 34; tel. (495) 257-01-10; fax (495) 973-20-23; e-mail nati@ccas.ru; f. 1925; Dir NIKOLAI A. SHCHELTSIN.

Vavilov State Optical Institute: 199034 St Petersburg, Birzhevaya Liniya 12; tel. (812) 328-48-92; fax (812) 328-37-20; e-mail leader@soi.spb.ru; internet soi.srv.pu.ru; f. 1918; library of 600,000 vols; Dir Dr G. PETROVSKY; publ. *Journal of Optical Technology* (12 a year).

'VNIPIenergoprom' Association JSC: 105094 Moscow, Semenovskaya nab. 2/1; tel. (495) 360-76-40; fax (495) 366-36-25; internet www.vnipiep.ru; f. 1942; design, research and devt of energy transmission systems, combined heating and power plants, project management, devt of heat and power-supply schemes for municipal areas, principally Moscow.

Vologdin, V. P., Research Institute of High-Frequency Currents: 197376 St Petersburg, ul. L. Tolstogo 7; tel. (812) 594-81-23; fax (812) 594-81-27; e-mail vniitvch@mail.ru; internet www.vniitvch.spb.ru; f. 1947; Dir F. V. BEZMENOV.

Zhukovsky, N. E., Central Aero- and Hydro-dynamics Institute: 140160 Moscow oblast, Zhukovsky 3; tel. (495) 556-41-79; Dir G. P. SVISHCHEV.

Libraries and Archives

Arkhangelsk

Dobroliubov Arkhangelsk Regional Research Library: 163061 Arkhangelsk, ul. Loginova 2; tel. (8182) 65-11-28; fax (8182) 43-97-39; internet www.dvinalend.ru; Dir OLGA STIUPINA.

Barnaul

Altai State University Library: 656099 Barnaul, Sotsialisticheskii pr. 68; 159,000 vols; Dir GALINA TRUSHNIKOVA.

Cheboksary

Chuvash State University Library: 428034 Cheboksary, Universitetskaya 38; tel. (8835) 49-79-88; e-mail library@chuvsu.ru; internet library.chuvsu.ru; 1,703,091 vols; Dir NINA D. NIKITINA.

Ekaterinburg

Scientific Library of Ural State University 'M. Gorky': 620083 Ekaterinburg, 51, Lenina ave; tel. and fax (343) 350-75-65; e-mail library@usu.ru; internet lib.usu.ru; f. 1920; incl. rare book dept; institutional repository; 1,261,687 vols; Dir K. P. KUZNETSOVA.

Elista

Kalmyk State University Library: Elista, ul. R. Luksemburg 4; c. 350,000 vols; Dir P. A. DOLINA.

Grozny

Chechen State University Library: 364907 Grozny, ul. N. Buachidze 34/96; 460,000 vols; Dir R. M. NAZARETYANI.

Ingushetia

National Library of Ingushetia: 366700 Ingushetia, Sunezhsky district, ul. Lunacharskogo 106; Dir RADIMA GAZDIEVA.

Irkutsk

Irkutsk State University Library: 664695 Irkutsk, bul. Gagarina 24; 3,200,000 vols; Dir R. V. PODGAICHENKO.

Ivanovo

Ivanovo State University Library: 153377 Ivanovo, ul. Ermaka 37; 410,000 vols; Dir A. N. KRUPPA.

Library of Ivanovo State Chemistry and Technology University: 153460 Ivanovo, ul. Fridrikha Engelsa 7; tel. (0932) 32-73-54; fax (0932) 32-95-02; Dir VERA DMITRIEVA.

Izhevsk

Udmurt State University Library: 426034 Izhevsk, Universitetskaya ul. 1; tel. (3412) 52-60-89; fax (3412) 75-58-66; e-mail admin@lib.udsu.ru; internet lib.udsu.ru; f. 1932; 970,647 vols; Librarian L. P. BESKLINSKAYA.

Kaliningrad

Immanuel Kant State University of Russia Library: 236040 Kaliningrad, Universitetskaya ul. 2; tel. (4012) 53-31-29; fax (4012) 53-36-08; e-mail eafilippova@kantiana.ru; internet lib.albertina.ru; f. 1968; 624,212 vols; Dir A. N. CHERNYAKOV; Deputy Dir FILIPPOVA ELENA.

Kazan

Kazan Federal University N. I. Lobachevsky Library: 420008 Kazan, Kremlevskaya 35; tel. (843) 264-47-54; e-mail lsl@ksu.ru; internet www.lsl.ksu.ru; f. 1804; 4,922,313 vols; Dir Dr ZAVDAT S. MINNULLIN; Chief Librarian ZHANNA SHCHELYVANOVA; publs *Opisaniya rukopisei*, *Retrospektivnye bibliograficheskie ukazately*.

Kemerovo

Kemerovo State University Library: 650043 Kemerovo, Krasnaya ul. 6; tel. (3842) 23-14-26; f. 1928; 350,000 vols; Librarian N. P. KONOVALOVA.

Krasnodar

Kuban State University Library: 350049 Krasnodar, Stavropolskaya ul. 149; tel. (8612) 69-95-52; fax (8612) 69-95-17; e-mail gsol@pop.kubsu.ru; internet www.library.kubsu.ru; f. 1920; 1,253,824 vols; Dir G. V. SOLOVEVA.

Krasnoyarsk

Krasnoyarsk State University Library: 660049 Krasnoyarsk, ul. Maerchaka 6; tel. (3912) 21-03-17; 166,000 vols; Librarian E. G. KRIVONOSOVA.

Makhachkala

Dagestan State University Library: 367008 Makhachkala, Batir ul. 1; tel. (8722) 68-02-74; e-mail alieva_li@mail.ru; internet elib.dgu.ru; 780,000 vols; Dir A. M. SHAKHSHAEVA.

Moscow

'All-Russia Patent and Technical Library' of Federal Institute of Industrial Property of Federal Service for Intellectual Property, Patents and Trademarks (Rospatent): 123995 Moscow, Berezhkovskaya nab. 24; tel. (499) 240-64-25; fax (499) 240-44-37; e-mail omobp@rupto.ru; internet www1.fips.ru/wps/wcm/connect/content_ru/ru/activity_lines/fonds; f. 1896; the only Russian library which receives Russian and all foreign patents; copies of 117,986,700 patent documents; Dir V. I. AMELKINA; publs *Guidebook to funds of Division 'All-Russia Patent and Technical Library'*, *Thematic bibliographic indexes of the literature*.

All-Russia Scientific and Research Institute of Patent Information (VNIIPI): 113035 Moscow, Raushskaya nab. 4; tel. (495) 959-33-13; fax (495) 959-33-04; f. 1964; Dir V. D. ZINOVIEV; publs *Inventions* (36 a year), *Service Marks. Appellations of Origin of Goods* (12 a year), *Trademarks, Utility Models. Industrial Designs* (12 a year).

Archives of the Russian Academy of Sciences: 117218 Moscow, Novocheremushkinskaya ul. 34; tel. (499) 129-19-10; fax (499) 129-19-66; e-mail academ_archive@mail.ru; f. 1728; 9,000 vols; Dir V.Y. AFIANI; publs *Proceedings*, *Scientific Heritage*.

Central Library of the Academy of Medical Sciences: 125874 Moscow, Baltiiskaya ul. 8; tel. (495) 155-47-93; f. 1935; 640,000 vols; acts as an enquiry, loan, research and guide centre for 42 libraries in the institutes and laboratories of the Academy of Medical Sciences; Dir G. I. BAKHEREVA.

Central Scientific Agricultural Library of the Russian Academy of Agricultural Sciences: 107139 Moscow, Orlikov per. 3, korp. V; tel. (495) 207-54-48; fax (495) 207-89-72; e-mail dir@cnshb.msk.ru; f. 1930; centre for bibliographical information on national and foreign agricultural literature, and for scientific and methodological work of agricultural libraries in Russia; 3m. vols, 3,300 periodicals; Dir V. POZDNYAKOV; publs *Bibliographic Information* (52 a year), *Selskoe khozyaistvo* (12 a year), *Selskokhozyaistvennaya literatura* (12 a year), *Subject Bibliographic Lists* (15 a year).

Central State Archives: 125212 Moscow, Vyborgskaya 3; tel. (495) 159-73-83; Dir A. PROKOPENKO.

Centre for the Preservation of Historical Documentary Collections: Moscow, Vyborgskaya ul. 3; tel. (495) 159-74-71; Dir V. BONDAREV; formerly Central State Archive of the USSR (TsGA SSSR) Special Archive.

Federal Archival Agency: 103132 Moscow, ul. Ilyinka 12; tel. (495) 606-35-31; fax (495) 606-55-87; e-mail rosarhiv@archives.ru; internet www.rusarchives.ru; f. 1991; Head ANDREY ARTIZOV; publ. *Otechestvenniye archivy* (6 a year).

Gorky, A. M., Archives: 121069 Moscow, ul. Vorovskogo 25A; tel. (495) 291-19-23; fax (495) 200-32-16; f. 1937; Dir VLADIMIR S. BARAKHOV.

Institute for Scientific Information on the Social Sciences of the Russian Academy of Sciences: 117418 Moscow, ul. Krasikova 28/21; tel. (495) 128-88-81; fax (495) 420-22-61; f. 1969; sections on philosophy, history, economics, sociology, politology, culturology, global problems and international relations, law, science of sciences, linguistics, theory of literature; 13,500,000 vols; Dir V. A. VINOGRADOV; publs *The Human Being: Image and Essence* (1 a year), *Theory and Practice of Information in Social Sciences* (1 a year), various periodicals on social sciences and other subjects.

Institute of Scientific and Technical Information: 125219 Moscow, ul. Usievicha 20A; tel. (495) 155-43-96; attached to Russian Acad. of Sciences; Dir P. V. NESTEROV.

International Centre for Scientific and Technical Information: 125252 Moscow, ul. Kuusinena 21 B; tel. (495) 198-70-21; fax (495) 943-00-89; e-mail alsor@icsti.su; internet www.icsti.su; f. 1969; Dir Dr ZURAB A. YAKOBASHVILI.

Library for Natural Sciences of the Russian Academy of Sciences: 119992 Moscow GSP-2, ul. Znamenka 11/11; tel. (495) 291-22-89; fax (495) 291-91-93; e-mail osiat@benran.ru; internet www.benran.ru/ben_ne2.htm; f. 1973; 12,549,000 items in main and associated libraries; Dir Prof. Dr N. E. KALENOV; publ. *Libraries of Academies of Sciences* (in Russian, 1 a year).

Library of the State A. S. Pushkin Museum of Fine Arts: 121019 Moscow, ul. Volkhonka 12; tel. (495) 697-97-28; fax (495) 697-32-08; e-mail bib@artsmuseum.ru; f. 1898; mem of Russian Library Asscn; holds encyclopaedic colins, European art, Egyptian, Greek and Roman art, numismatic, archaeology; art education, architecture, world history, museology; supports research activities; 250,000 vols of books (17th–21st centuries), 400,000 periodicals of 19th–21st centuries, 100,000 reproductions on paper and canvas, 120,000 negatives and photographs, 70,000 slides; Dir OLGA B. MALINKOVSKAYA; publ. *Bulletin of the New Acquisitions* (2 a year, spec. issue for researchers).

Library of the State Central Museum of the Contemporary History of Russia: 103050 Moscow, Tverskaya ul. 21; tel. (495) 299-52-17; fax (495) 299-85-15; e-mail sovrhistory@mtu-net.ru; internet www.sovr.ru; f. 1917 as Museum of the Russian Revolution; 360,000 vols, 825,000 periodicals; Chief Librarian TATYANA N. EREMEEVA.

Library of the State Literature Museum: Moscow, Rozhdestvenskii bul. 16; f. 1926; collection of 180,000 books, 27,644 periodicals; Russian and foreign works from 16th to 20th centuries; letters and autographed works; folklore works; periodical collection; Dir ANNA IVANOVNA NIKULINA.

Library of the State Museum of Oriental Arts: 103064 Moscow, Vorontsovo pole 16A; tel. and fax (495) 916-34-29; e-mail dinagnw@rambler.ru; f. 1918; 75,000 vols; Dir DIANA VAKHTANGOVA; publ. *Scientific Reports* (1 a year).

Library (Book Fund Department) of the State Theatrical A. A. Bakhrushin Museum: 115054 Moscow, Bakhrushin St. 31/12; tel. (495) 953-48-48; fax (495) 953-54-48; e-mail gctm@gctm.ru; internet www.gctm.ru; f. 1894; colln of 1.5m. objects reflecting history of theatre in Russia from 17th century until present day; 120,000 vols on theatrical art; Head TITANIA BONILYA; Gen. Dir RODIONOV DMITRY.

Library of the Tolstoy State Museum: 119034 Moscow, ul. Prechistenka 11; tel. (495) 202-78-51; fax (495) 202-93-38; f. 1911; 76,000 vols, 86,000 newspaper cuttings; Dir L. M. LUBIMOVA.

The M. I. Rudomino, All-Russia State Library for Foreign Literature: 109189 Moscow, Nikoloyamskaya St 1; tel. (495) 915-36-21; fax (495) 915-36-37; e-mail vgbil@libfl.ru; internet www.libfl.ru; f. 1922; research and public library; cultural centre; exchange arrangements with 500 libraries, publishing houses and univs in 90 countries; 4,428,000 vols in 140 foreign languages; Dir E. YU. GENIEVA; publ. *'Otkrytyj Dostup: Biblioteki za rubezhom'* (Open Access: Libraries around the World).

Moscow State University Scientific Library: 103009 Moscow, Mokhovaya 10.

Russian National Public Library for Science and Technology: 103031 Moscow, Kuznetskii Most 12; tel. (495) 925-92-88; fax (495) 921-98-62; e-mail root@gpntb.ru; internet www.gpntb.ru; f. 1958; permanent contacts with 7,000 enterprises in Russia and other republics of the former USSR; 8m. books, periodicals and documents on natural sciences, technology, agriculture and medicine; special collection of domestic literature of limited distribution; 24 original databases; Dir Dr A. I. ZEMSKOV; publs *Journal of Research, Scientific and Technical Libraries, Proceedings of Crimea Conferences*.

Russian Peoples' Friendship University Library: 117198 Moscow, Miklukho-Maklaia 6; tel. (495) 434-86-32; fax (495) 433-15-11; e-mail lib.rudn@gmail.com; internet lib.rudn.ru; f. 1960, present status 2008; organizes Russian language programme, books and art exhibitions; 1.8m. vols, 280 periodicals; Dir ELENA LOTOVA.

Russian State Archive of Modern History: 103132 Moscow, ul. Ilinka 12; tel. (495) 206-50-06; fax (495) 206-23-21; f. 1991; based on the Archive of the General Department of the Communist Party of the fmr USSR; Dir N. G. TOMILINA.

Russian State Archives of Old Documents: 119992 GSP-2 Moscow, G-435, Bolshaya Pirogovskaya ul. 17; tel. (495) 580-87-23; fax (8) 499-30-98; e-mail rgada@archives.ru; annals, charts of grand dukes and independent princes, legal documents of Early Russia (11th–18th centuries), documents of central and patrimonial archives of nobility and gentry, archives of church establishments and the largest monasteries of Russia; Dir MIKHAIL R. RYZHENKOV.

Russian State Archive of Social-Political History: 109999 Moscow, Bol. Dmitrovka 15; tel. (495) 629-97-26; fax (495) 692-90-17; e-mail rgaspi@inbox.ru; internet www.rgaspi.ru; f. 1920s; 10,000 vols; incl. colln from Central Archive of Komsomol; Dir Dr OLEG VLADIMIROVICH NAUMOV; publ. *Scientific Information Bulletin* (1 a year).

Russian State Archives of Sound Recording: 107005 Moscow, 2-ya Baumanskaya ul. 3; tel. (495) 261-13-00; f. 1932; sound recordings from 1902 of artistic and documentary nature; Dir V. A. KOLIADA.

Russian State Archives of the National Economy: 119435 Moscow, Bol. Pirogovskaya ul. 17; tel. (495) 245-26-64; documents of the state bodies in charge of management of industries, agriculture, transportation, communication, construction and of central bodies of financing, planning and statistics (1917–); Dir E. A. TYURINA.

Russian State Army Archives: 125212 Moscow, ul. Admirala Makarova 29; tel. (495) 159-80-91; documents of military authorities of the RSFSR and the USSR, of the military areas, detachments, units and establishments of the Soviet Army and Frontier Guards (1918–40); Dir V. D. ZAPOROZHNICHENKO.

Russian State Art Library: 107031 Moscow, Bol. Dmitrovka 8/1; tel. (495) 692-06-53; fax (495) 692-06-53; e-mail bisk@liart.ru; internet www.liart.ru; f. 1922; 1,701,000 items (books, periodicals, press cuttings, engravings, sketches, postcards, photographs, posters); Dir A. A. KOLGANOVA.

Russian State Library for the Blind: 129090 Moscow, Protopopovsky per. 9; tel. and fax (495) 680-26-14; e-mail admin@rgbs.ru; internet www.rgbs.ru; f. 1920; acts as methodical, coordinating and resources centre for special libraries throughout Russia; 1,320,000 vols; Dir T. N. ELFIMOVA; publs *The Visually-impaired and Society* (12 a year), *Correspondence School for the Parents* (2 a year).

Russian State Literature and Art Archives: 125212 Moscow, Vyborgskaya 3, korp. 2; tel. (495) 150-78-10; fax (495) 159-73-81; e-mail rgali@satel.ru; f. 1941; documents of prominent Russian and Soviet writers, composers, artists, theatrical and cinema workers; documents of state and public organizations concerned with the arts (mid-18th century–present day); 1,154,000 vols; Dir T. M. GORYAEVA; publ. *Vstrechi s proshlym* (irregular).

Russian State Military Historical Archives: 107005 Moscow, ul. 2-ya Baumanskaya 3; tel. (495) 261-20-70; fax (495) 267-18-66; f. 1797; documents of central and district military administrations and establishments of the Russian Army, private collections of prominent generals, military leaders and historians (end 17th century–1918); Dir I. O. GARKUSHA.

Scientific Library of the State Tretyakov Gallery: 113035 Moscow, 1-i Kadashevskii per. 14; tel. (495) 953-41-85; fax (495) 953-10-51; f. 1899; stock relating to Russian and Soviet art; 400,000 vols; Dir Z. P. SHERGINA.

Scientific S. I. Taneev Library of the Moscow P. I. Tchaikovsky State Conservatoire: 125009 Moscow, ul. B. Nikitskaya 13/6; tel. and fax (495) 629 6062; e-mail rassina@lib.mosconsv.ru; internet www.taneevlib.ru; f. 1866; Russian and foreign music and books on music; complete files of many Russian and foreign musical periodicals; 1,250,941 vols; Dir E. B. RASSINA.

State Archives of the Russian Federation: 119992 Moscow, Bol. Pirogovskaya ul. 17; tel. (495) 245-12-87; fax (495) 245-12-87; e-mail garf@online.ru; internet www.garf.narod.ru; f. 1992; 5,513,107 items; Dir SERGEY V. MIRONENKO; publ. *Archive of Contemporary Russian History* (3 series: catalogues, documents, research).

State Central Polytechnic Library: 101000 Moscow, Politekhnicheskii pr-d 2;

tel. (495) 928-64-65; f. 1964; 3m. vols, incl. periodicals; Dir N. G. REINBERG.

State Medical Library of Russia: 117418 Moscow, Nakhimovskaya ul. 49; tel. (495) 128-33-46; fax (495) 128-87-39; e-mail loginov@server.scsml.rssi.ru; f. 1919; 3m. vols; Dir Dr B. R. LOGINOV; publs *Medicine and Public Health* (bibliographical index), *New Medical Books*.

State Public Historical Library of Russia: 101990 Moscow, Starosadskii per. 9; tel. (495) 925-65-14; fax (495) 928-02-84; e-mail maf@shpl.ru; internet www.shpl.ru; f. 1938; 3,229,696 vols, including 74,695 in the Department of Rare Books, 1,107,604 items in the Serials Department; special collection of 10,119 unofficial publications; Dir Dr MIKHAIL AFANASIEV.

Turgenev Library No. 13: 101000 Moscow, Bobrov per. 6, str. 2; tel. (495) 921-00-52; fax (495) 921-99-17; e-mail biblioteka@turgenev.ru; Dir TATYANA KOROBKINA.

Institution of Russian Academy of Education Ushinsky State Pedagogical Library: 119017 Moscow, Bol. Tolmachevskii per. 3; tel. (495) 951-05-85; fax (495) 953-22-61; e-mail gnpbu@gnpbu.ru; internet www.gnpbu.ru; f. 1925; 2,000,000 units; Dir TAMARA S. MARKAROVA (acting); publ. *Literatura po pedagogicheskim naukam i narodnomu obrazovaniyu* (4 a year).

Nalchik

Kabardino-Balkar State University Library: 360004 Nalchik, ul. Chernyshevskogo 173; 738,000 vols; Dir E. D. MIGUCHKINA.

Nizhnii Novgorod

Nizhnii Novgorod N. I. Lobachevsky State University Central Library: 603091 Nizhnii Novgorod, pr. Gagarina 23; tel. (8312) 31-11-54; 1,210,470 vols; Dir A. I. SAVENKOV.

Novosibirsk

Novosibirsk State University Library: 630090 Novosibirsk, Akademgorodok; tel. (3832) 65-62-60; 450,000 vols; Dir L. G. TORSHENOVA.

Scientific-Technical Centre for Chemical Information: 630090 Novosibirsk, pr. Akad. Lavrenteva 9; tel. (3832) 35-64-40; attached to Russian Acad. of Sciences; Head Acad. V. A. KOPTYUG.

State Public Scientific and Technical Library of the Siberian Department of the Russian Academy of Sciences: 630200 Novosibirsk, Voskhod 15; tel. (3832) 66-18-60; fax (3832) 66-33-65; e-mail office@spsl.nsc.ru; internet www.spsl.nsc.ru; f. 1918; acts as reference, loan, research and coordinating centre for 65 academic institutes located in Siberia and the Far East; 14,000,000 vols; Dir Prof. B. S. ELEPOV.

Omsk

Omsk State University Library: 644077 Omsk, pr. Mira 55A; 182,000 vols; Dir L. A. BALAKINA.

Perm

Perm State University Scientific Library: 614990 Perm, ul. Bukireva 15; tel. (3422) 39-64-80; e-mail library@psu.ru; internet www.library.psu.ru; f. 1916; 1,467,000 vols; Dir NATALIA YAKSHINA.

Petrozavodsk

Petrozavodsk State University Library: 185640 Petrozavodsk, pr. Lenina 33; tel. (8142) 71-10-44; 850,000 vols; Dir MARINA P. OTLIVANCHIK.

Rostov-on-Don

'Yu. A. Zhdanov' Zone Scientific Library at Southern Federal University: 344049 Rostov-on-Don, Pushkinskaya 148; tel. and fax (8632) 64-08-56; e-mail fld@lib.rsu.ru; internet www.library.sfedu.ru; f. 1915; attached Museum of the History of Books; 2,496,621 vols; Dir SVETLANA A. BONDARENKO; publ. *Donskaya Speech*.

St Petersburg

All-Russian Geological Library: 199106 St Petersburg, Srednii pr. 74; tel. and fax (812) 321-72-12; e-mail vgb@vsegei.ru; f. 1882; scientific and technical literature; 1m. books, monographs, periodicals and special maps; Dir O. K. ERMILOVA; publ. *Geologicheskaya literatura* (Geological Literature, 1 a year).

Central Music Library attached to the S. M. Kirov State Academic Theatre of Opera and Ballet: 190000 St Petersburg, Teatralnaya pl., 1; tel. (12) 326-4164; e-mail cml@mariinsky.ru; contains one of the largest collections in the world of Russian music in MSS, single copies, first editions, etc, 1,500 copies of Russian vaudeville scores, 200 MSS of ballet scores, and a large collection of opera scores including 1,000 foreign operas; Dir Prof. Dr MARIA N. SHCHERBAKOVA.

Department of the Art and Museum Book Collections of the State Russian Museum: 191186 St Petersburg, Inzhenernaya ul. 4; tel. (812) 595-42-08; fax (812) 314-41-53; e-mail library@rusmuseum.ru; internet library.rusmuseum.ru; f. 1898; 185,000 vols; Dir YULIA JURKINA.

Library of the National Pushkin Museum: 191186 St Petersburg, nab. Moiki 12; tel. (812) 571-06-19; fax (812) 315-73-79; e-mail vmp@mail.admiral.ru; internet www.museumpushkin.ru; f. 1953; collections of works by Russian authors incl. Pushkin, V. A. Krylov and S. Mazkov; 80,000 vols; Dir M. V. BOKARIUS.

Library of the Russian Academy of Sciences: 199034 St Petersburg, Birzhevaya liniya 1; tel. (812) 328-35-92; fax (812) 328-74-36; e-mail ban@rasl.nw.ru; internet www.ban.ru; f. 1714, 20,353,000 vols; collection of 19,000 MSS, 250,000 rare books, including 834 incunabula; 123,000 maps, 1.8m. publications of the Russian Academy of Sciences; acts as inter-library loan and reference service, exchange centre and book publisher; conducts research in library science, bibliography, palaeography and conservation; coordinates network of 31 specialized libraries in the Academy's research institutes; Dir Dr VALERII P. LEONOV; publs *Bibliography of Publications of the Russian Academy of Sciences* (1 a year), *Book in Russia* (1 a year), *Quarterly Bibliography*.

Library of the State Hermitage Museum: St Petersburg, Dvortsovaya nab. 34; f. 1762; over 500,000 vols; on painting, sculpture and all branches of graphic arts throughout the centuries; Dir MAKAROVA.

Music Library of the St Petersburg Conservatoire: St Petersburg, Teatralnaya pl. 3; fax (812) 312-89-74; e-mail admlib@conservatory.ru; internet biblio.conservatory.ru; f. 1862; 500,000 vols, incl. 180,000 Russian and foreign works on music, 306,000 scores, 7,600 MSS, 490 incunabula; Dir E. NEKRASOVA; publs *Musicus* (4 a year), *Opera Musicologica* (4 a year).

Music Library of the St Petersburg Dmitri Shostakovich State Philharmonic Society: 191011 St Petersburg, Mikhailovskaya ul. 2; f. 1882; 200,000 scores and books on music, 40,000 engravings, lithographs and paintings of musicians, composers, etc; 1,000,000 newspaper cuttings; Dir G. L. RETROVSKAYA.

National Library of Russia: 191069 St Petersburg, Sadovaya ul. 18; tel. (812) 310-98-50; fax (812) 310-61-48; internet www.nlr.ru; f. 1795; 32,064,000 items, including a large collection of incunabula and MSS; Dir VLADIMIR N. ZAITSEV; publ. *PNB-Informazia* (12 a year).

Russian State Historical Archives: 190000 St Petersburg, Angliiskaya nab. 4; tel. (812) 311-09-26; fax (812) 311-22-52; f. 1918; documents of central state bodies of the Russian Empire, state and private banks, railways, industrial, trade and other companies; private collections of prominent political and public figures, etc. (18th century–1917); 350,000 vols; Dir A. R. SOKOLOV; publ. *Herald* (irregular).

Russian State Naval Archives: St Petersburg, Millionnaya ul. 36; tel. (812) 315-90-54; f. 1724; documents of central institutions of the Russian pre-revolutionary and Soviet Navy and prominent naval officers (17th century–1940); 1,219,454 vols; Dir V. G. MISHANOV.

St Petersburg State University M. Gorky Scientific Library: 199034 St Petersburg, Universitetskaya nab. 7/9; tel. (812) 328-27-41; fax (812) 328-27-41; e-mail marina@lib.pu.ru; internet www.lib.pu.ru; f. 1783; 7m., 100,000 rare books, 1,000 MSS; Dir N. A. SHESHINA; publs *Pravovedenie* (6 a year), *Vestnik St. Petersburg* (24 a year).

St Petersburg Theatrical Library: St Petersburg, ul. Zodchego Rossi 2; f. 1756; 800,000 vols of plays and works on theatrical subjects, department of French works with first editions of Corneille; MSS and letters by Chekhov, Turgenev, Diaghilev, Fokine; department of stage designs by Bakst, Benoit, etc; department of classical and contemporary fiction; Dir ANASTASIYA G. GAI.

Scientific Library attached to the Russian Institute for the History of Arts: 190000 St Petersburg, Isaakievskaya pl. 5; tel. (812) 315-55-87; fax (812) 315-72-02; f. 1912; 300,000 books and periodicals on theatre, music, cinematography, history of literature and art, fiction, philosophy, aesthetics, folklore; Chief Librarian I. V. KYTMANOVA.

Scientific Library of the Russian Academy of Arts: 199034 St Petersburg, Universitetskaya nab. 17; Moscow Branch: 119034 Moscow, ul. Prechistenka 21; f. 1757; 471,445 vols on art, architecture, applied and folk arts, including rare 16th- and 17th-century vols and a notable collection of 18th-century works on architecture; Dir L. S. POLAYKOVA; Dir N. V. KOMAROVA.

Samara

Russian State Scientific and Technical Archives: 443096 Samara, ul. Michurina 58; tel. (846) 336-17-81; fax (846) 336-17-85 also: Moscow, Profsoyuznaya ul. 82; tel. (495) 335-00-95; f. 1964; documentation of research and devt projects in industry, construction, transport and communications; invention applications; Dir IRINA N. DAVYDOVA.

Samara State University Library: 443086 Samara, ul. Potapova 64/163; 245,000 vols; Dir N. I. PARANINA.

Saransk

Mordovian N. P. Ogarev State University Library: 430000 Saransk, Bolshevistskaya ul. 68; tel. (8342) 4-49-91; f. 1931; 1,954,861 vols; Dir Doc. A. V. SMOLYANOV.

Saratov

V. A. Artisevich Zonal Scientific Library: 410000 Saratov, Universitetskaya ul. 42; tel.

(845) 227-14-80; fax (845) 251-40-00; e-mail library@sgu.ru; internet library.sgu.ru/nbsgu; f. 1909; 2,861,763 vols; Dir IRINA V. LEBEDEVA.

Syktyvkar

Syktyvkar State University Library: 167001 Syktyvkar, Oktyabrskii pr. 55; tel. (8212) 43-94-51; fax (8212) 43-72-86; f. 1972; 560,980 vols; 812 MSS and books published in Russia before the 18th century; 22 personal archives of scientists; Dir NONNA F. AKOPOVA; publs *Rubezh* (4 a year), *Vestnik* (1 a year).

Tomsk

Russian State Historical Archive of the Far East: Tomsk, ul. K. Marksa 26; tel. (3822) 2-29-15; formerly Central State Archive of the RSFSR of the Far East (TsGA RSFSR DV).

Tomsk State University Library: 634010 Tomsk, Leninskii pr. 34A; tel. (3822) 2-44-69; 3,320,000 vols; Dir E. SYNTIN.

Tver

Tver State Medical Academy Library: 170000 Tver, ul. Sovetskaya 4; tel. (822) 33-27-26; fax (822) 33-43-09; f. 1954; 468 vols; Dir O. V. TULTSEVA.

Tyumen

Tyumen State University Library: 625036 Tyumen, ul. Volodarskogo 38; 382,000 vols; Dir L. P. KRYUKOVA.

Ufa

Bashkir State University Library: 450074 Ufa, ul. Zaki Validi 32; tel. (3472) 73-66-26; fax (3472) 73-67-78; e-mail jane@ic.bashedu.ru; internet www.bashlib.ru; f. 1909; 1,405,779 vols; Dir E. G. GELVANOVSKAYA.

National Library of Bashkortostan: 450000 Ufa, ul. Lenina 4; tel. and fax (3472) 22-04-89; e-mail bashnl@mail.ru; internet bashnl.ru; f. 1836; collecting, processing, storage, use of information resources; 3.3m. vols; Dir AZAT IBRAGIMOV.

Vladikavkaz

North-Ossetian State University Library: 362000 Vladikavkaz, ul. Vatutina 46; 76,000 vols; Dir K. L. KOCHISOV.

Vladimir

Central State Archives of the Nation's Documentary Films and Photographs: Vladimir, Letneperevozinskaya ul. 9; tel. (0922) 2-79-95 also: Moscow oblast, Krasnogorsk, Rechnaya ul. 1; tel. (495) 563-08-45; topical films, newsreels and historical material which was not included in finished films, negatives of documentary photographs (1854–); Dir L. P. ZAPRYAGAEVA.

Vladivostok

Far Eastern State University Central Library: 690652 Vladivostok, Okeanskii pr. 37/41; 700,000 vols; Dir A. G. TRETYAKOVA.

Voronezh

Scientific Library of Voronezh State University: 394000 Voronezh, pr. Revolyutsii 24; tel. (4732) 55-35-59; fax (4732) 20-82-58; e-mail minakov@lib.vsu.ru; internet www.lib.vsu.ru; f. 1918; 3,156,723 vols; Dir ARKADY MINAKOV; Chief Librarian LYUBOV KATZ.

Yakutsk

Scientific Library of Yakutsk State University: 677018 Yakutsk, Belinsky St 58; tel. (4112) 36-38-82; fax (4112) 35-62-95; e-mail libr@sitc.ru; internet www.ysu.ru/library; f. 1934; compiles and publishes bibliographic indexes; 1,235,006 vols; Dir SEMENOV ANATOLY PETROVICH; Deputy Dir SIVTSEVA VALENTINA SERAFIMOVNA.

Yalutorovsk

Centre for the Preservation of the Reserve Collection: Tyumen oblast, Yalutorovsk, Ishimskaya ul. 136; tel. (34535) 2-29-87; formed from Central State Archive Reserve Collection of Documents of the State Archive Collection of the USSR (TsGA SF SSSR).

Yaroslavl

P. G. Demidov Yaroslavl State University Library: 150000 Yaroslavl, ul. Sovetskaya 14; tel. (4852) 79-16-34; internet www.uniyar.ac.ru; 774,324 vols; Dir I. V. DENEZHKINA.

Museums and Art Galleries

Arkhangelsk

Arkhangelsk State Museum: 163061 Arkhangelsk, pl. V. I. Lenina 2; tel. (8182) 3-66-79; f. 1737; contains 150,000 items featuring the history of the North coast area of Russia, since ancient times; large collection of archaeology, ethnography, documents and photographs; library of 30,000 vols; Dir YU. P. PROKOPEV.

Arkhangelsk State Museum of Fine Arts: 163061 Arkhangelsk, nab. Lenina 79; tel. (8182) 3-26-73; e-mail m1444@mail.museum.ru; internet www.museum.ru/m1444; contains over 150,000 items of ancient North and Western European art; library of 30,000 vols; Dir M. V. MITKEVICH.

Ashaga-stal

Stalsky Memorial Museum: 368765 Dagestan, Suleiman-Stalskii raion, Ashaga-stal; internet www.museum.ru/m1802; f. 1950; exhibits on the history of Dagestan literature, former home of poet Suleiman Stalskii; library of 20,000 vols; Dir LIDIYA M. STALSKAYA.

Astrakhan

Astrakhan State B. M. Kustodiev Gallery: Astrakhan, ul. Sverdlova 81; tel. (8512) 22-66-65; fax (8512) 22-66-65; f. 1918; fine arts; library of 15,000 vols; Dir L. J. ILINA.

Barnaul

State Art Museum of Altai Territory: Barnaul, pr. Lenina 88; tel. (3852) 61-25-10; fax (3852) 61-06-70; e-mail muzei@ab.ru; internet muzei.ab.ru; f. 1959; large collection since 16th century, of icons, paintings, sculptures, wood carvings, ceramics, national costumes; library of 13,526 vols; Dir I. K. GALKINA.

Belinsky

Belinsky, V. G., State Museum: Penza oblast, Belinsky, ul. Belinskogo 11; f. 1938; 31,280 exhibits on the life and work of the literary critic V. G. Belinsky; Curator I. A. GERASEKIN.

Borodino

Borodino State War and History Museum: 143240 Moscow oblast, Mozhaisk, selo Borodino; tel. (09638) 6-32-23; fax (09638) 6-32-22; e-mail pr@borodino.ru; internet www.borodino.ru; f. 1839; researches into 1812 campaign, the Battle of Borodino and the 1941–45 war; 60,000 exhibits incl. material on the Battle of Borodino; library of 12,100 vols; Dir MIKHAIL R CHEREPASHENETS; Curator GALINA N. NEVSKAYA.

Bryansk

Bryansk State Museum of Soviet Fine Arts: Bryansk, ul. Gagarina 19; Dir B. F. FAENKOV.

Cheboksary

Chuvash Art Museum: 428008 Cheboksary, Kalinina 60; tel. (8352) 22-07-04; f. 1939; 12,000 exhibits, mainly modern Russian, Soviet and Chuvash artists and traditional Chuvash decorative art; library of 15,000 vols; Dir N. SADYUKOV.

Chelyabinsk

Chelyabinsk State Picture Gallery: Chelyabinsk, ul. Truda 92A; 5,000 items; Dir I. F. TKACHENKO.

Ekaterinburg

Ekaterinburg Picture Gallery: Ekaterinburg, ul. Vainera 11; f. 1746; Western European, Russian and Soviet artists and objects from the Kishisk foundries; Dir E. V. KHAMTSOV.

State Amalgamated Museum of the Writers of the Urals: 620075 Ekaterinburg, Tolmacheva ul. 41; tel. (343) 371-46-52; f. 1940 (amalgamated 1980); study and popularization of the heritage of the writers of the Urals, collns incl. the personal belongings and archives of Mamin-Sibiryak, Bazhov and other Ural writers, illustrations to edns of their works and various other artworks, 34,723 items in all; incorporates the House of D. N. Mamin-Sibiryak in Ekaterinburg, the House of P. P. Bazhov, the House of F. M. Reshetnikov; library of 37,700 vols; Dir V. P. PLOTNIKOV.

Ural Geological Museum: 620144 Ekaterinburg, ul. Kuibysheva 30; tel. (343) 257-31-09; fax (343) 257-48-38; f. 1937; Dir YURI A. POLENOV.

Gagarin

Yurii Gagarin Memorial Museum: 215010 Gagarin, ul. Gerzena 7; tel. (08135) 4-88-37; fax (08135) 4-88-37; f. 1970; exhibits depicting the life and career of Yurii Alekseevich Gagarin (the first man in space) and other early Soviet cosmonauts, and the designers of the spaceships; Dir MARIA STEPANOVA.

Ivanovo

Ivanovo Museum of Art: 153002 Ivanovo, pr. Lenina 33; tel. (0932) 32-65-04; f. 1960; Greek, Roman and Ancient Egyptian art, icons, 18th–20th-century Russian art; library of 7,500 vols; Dir L. W. WOLOWENSKAYA.

Kaluga

Kaluga Museum of Art: Kaluga, ul. Lenina 104; 2,700 exhibits; Dir. A. V. KAZAK.

Tsiolkovsky, K. E., State Museum of the History of Cosmonautics: Kaluga, ul. Koroleva 2; tel. (842) 57-43-33; fax (842) 57-43-33; e-mail director@mkosmos.kaluga.ru; internet www.museum.ru/gmik; f. 1967; contains K. E. Tsiolkovsky's scientific works, history of rocket technique and cosmonautics, large collection of objects relating to astronautics and rocket technology, including the first experimental rocket launched in 1933, the *Sputniks* and *Luniks*, models of orbital stations; library of 35,600 vols; Dir EVGENY KOUZIN.

Kazan

Kazan State A. M. Gorky Memorial Museum: Kazan, ul. Gorkogo 10; exhibits illustrating Gorky's life in the flat where he lived and wrote.

National Museum of the Republic of Tatarstan: Tatarstan, 420111 Kazan, Kremlevskaya ul. 2; tel. (8432) 92-71-62; fax (8432) 92-14-84; e-mail tatar_museum@mail.ru; internet www.tatar.museum.ru; f. 1894; history, archaeology, ethnography, natural resources and decorative applied art of Tatarstan, Russia and other countries; library of 12,000 vols; 54 brs; Gen. Man. G. S. MYKHANOV.

State Museum of Fine Arts of the Republic of Tatarstan: 420015 Kazan, ul. K. Marksa 64; tel. (8432) 36-69-21; fax (8432) 36-18-65; internet www.kcn.ru/tat_en/culture/art_museum/home.htm; f. 1958; large collections of Russian, Western European and Soviet paintings; 10,000 exhibits; Dir ANATOLIY A. SLASTUNIN.

Tatar Historical Museum (House of V. I. Lenin): Tatarstan, Kazan, ul. Ulyanova 58; 10,000 exhibits including documents, photographs, works of art and other exhibits relating to Lenin's life.

Kirov

Kirov Victor and Apollinaris Vasnetsov Museum: 610000 Kirov, ul. K. Marksa 70; tel. (8332) 62-26-46; f. 1910; Russian and Western European sculpture, paintings, engravings and decorative arts; library of 14,000 vols; Dir ALLA A. NOSKOVA.

Kirovsk

Polar Alpine Botanical Garden Institute: 184230 Murmansk region, Kirovsk; tel. (81555) 63350; fax (81555) 79448; e-mail pabgi@aprec.ru; attached to Russian Acad. of Sciences; Dir Prof. VLADIMIR K. ZHIROV.

Klin

Tchaikovsky House-Museum: 141600 Klin, ul. Tchaikovskogo 48; tel. (49624) 5-81-96; fax (49624) 5-84-67; e-mail gdmch@dol.ru; internet www.russianmuseums.info/m443; f. 1894; composer's last residence and first Russian musical museum; contains 211,452 documents and museum treasures associated with the life and work of Tchaikovsky and other Russian musicians; library of 57,053 vols; Dir GALINA I. BELONOVICH.

Komsomolsk-on-Amur

Komsomolsk-on-Amur Museum of Soviet Fine Arts: Komsomolsk-on-Amur, pr. Mira 50; 5,000 exhibits; Dir E. Y. TURCHINSKAYA.

Konchanskoe-Suvorovskoe

Suvorov Museum: 174435 Novogorodskaya oblast, Borovichskii raion, selo Konchanskoe-Suvorovskoe; tel. (81664) 9-85-33; internet www.museum.ru/m669; the museum features the main periods in the life of General A. V. Suvorov; Dir V. P. MALYSHEVA.

Kostroma

Kostroma Museum of Fine Arts: Kostroma, pr. Mira 5; f. 1913; 5,700 items; collecting, exhibitions, sales, scientific and historical Russian art research, art restoration; library of 6,410 vols; special collections of Ancient Russian religious books and the work of Y. Chestnyakov; Dir V. Y. IGNATEV.

Krasnoyarsk

Krasnoyarsk Arts Museum: 660097 Krasnoyarsk, Parizhskoi Kommuny ul. 20; tel. (3912) 27-25-58; f. 1958; Russian art (including icons), Russian pre-revolutionary applied art, Siberian folk art and Soviet art; painting, sculpture, graphic art, applied arts; library of 7,700 vols; Dir A. F. EFIMOVSKII; publ. *Surikov Readings* (2 a year).

Krasnoyarsk Museum and Historical Centre: Krasnoyarsk, pl. Mira 1; tel. (3912) 23-82-02; f. 1987; Dir MIKHAIL SHUBSKY.

Kursk

Kursk Art Gallery: 305016 Kursk, ul. Sovetskaya 3; tel. and fax (4712) 54-87-21; e-mail gallery@sovtest.ru; internet www.kursk.amr-museum.ru; f. 1935; Russian, Soviet and European painting and sculpture; library of 50,000 vols; Dir I. A. PRIPACHKIN.

Lermontovo

Lermontov State Museum 'Tarkhany': 442280 Penza oblast, Belinskii raion, Lermontovo; tel. and fax (84153) 2-07-99; e-mail muslerm@sura.ru; internet www.tarhany.ru; f. 1939; life and work of M. Yu. Lermontov; library of 15,000 vols; Dir TAMARA MIKHAILOVNA MELNIKOVA; publ. *Tarkhansky vestnik* (bulletin, 1 a year).

Makhachkala

Dagestan Museum of Fine Arts: Makhachkala, ul. Markova 45; 7,000 exhibits.

Maloyaroslavets

Maloyaroslavets Museum of Military History of 1812: 249050 Maloyaroslavets, Moskovskaya ul. 27; tel. (08431) 2-27-11; f. 1939; collection and study of exhibits of the 1812 war; library of 1,100 vols; Dir N. V. KOTLYAKOVA; publ. *Nashe Nasledie* (Our Heritage, 6 a year).

Melikhovo

Chekhov, A. P. State Literature and Memorial Museum-Reserve: 142326 Melikhovo, Chekhovsky region, Moscow oblast; tel. (49672) 2-36-10; fax (49927) 0-79-91; e-mail melikhovo@mail.ru; internet www.chekhov-melikhovo.com; f. 1944; the house where the writer lived and worked during 1892–1899; library of 28,514 vols; Dir K. V. BOBKOV.

Miass

Natural Science Museum of the Ilmen State Reserve: 456301 Chelyabinsk oblast, Miass 1; tel. (35135) 5-48-90; fax (35135) 5-02-86; e-mail founds@imin.urc.ac.ru; f. 1930; the museum shows the mineralogical resources of the Ilmen State Reserve, the grounds of which contain more than 250 minerals; library of 17,000 vols; Dir Dr S. N. NIKANDROV; publs *Trudy Ilmenskogo Zapovednika, Uralsky mineralogichesky Sbornik*.

Moscow

'All-Russia Patent and Technical Library' of Federal Institute of Industrial Property of Federal Service for Intellectual Property, Patents and Trademarks (Rospatent): 123995 Moscow, Berezhkovskaya nab. 24; tel. (499) 240-64-25; fax (499) 240-44-37; e-mail omobp@rupto.ru; internet www1.fips.ru/wps/wcm/connect/content_ru/ru/activity_lines/fonds; f. 1896; the only Russian library which receives Russian and all foreign patents; copies of 117,986,700 patent documents; Dir V. I. AMELKINA; publs *Guidebook to funds of Division 'All-Russia Patent and Technical Library', Thematic bibliographic indexes of the literature*.

Anuchin Institute and Museum of Anthropology of Moscow State University: 125009 Moscow Mokhovaya str. 11; tel. (495) 629-44-49; fax (495) 629-75-21; e-mail anthropos.msu@mail.ru; internet www.antropos.msu.ru; f. 1879; 5 depts: laboratories of anthropogenesis, human diversity, anthropo-ecology, human auxology, human morphology and the Museum of Anthropology; about 470,000 items; anthropology and archaeology of the Stone Age; collns from outstanding Russian explorers; Mousterian Man from Teshik-Tash and Staroseliye; Mesolithic burials from the Dnieper Region in the Ukraine; library of 30,000 vols; Dir Prof. Dr ALEXANDRA BUZHILOVA; publs *Antropologia, Vestnik MGU*.

Central Museum of Aviation and Cosmonautics: 125167 Moscow, Krasnoarmeiskaya 4; tel. (495) 212-73-01; f. 1924; to record the national development of aeronautics and astronautics; contains original full-size aircraft, spacecraft, recovered space exploration vehicles, instruments, flight clothing, accessories of technical, historical and biographical interest; library of 15,800 vols; Dir P. F. VYALIKOV.

Central Museum of the Armed Forces: 129110 Moscow, I-110, ul. Sovetskoi Armii 2, a/ya 125; tel. and fax (495) 681-18-80; e-mail cmvs-secretariat@mail.ru; internet www.cmaf.ru; f. 1919; military exhibits; library of 90,000 vols; Dir ALEXANDER K. NIKONOV.

Chekhov, A. P., House-Museum: 103001 Moscow, Sadovaya-Kudrinskaya 6; tel. (495) 291-61-54; f. 1954; flat where the writer lived from 1886–1890; branch of the State Literature Museum.

Dostoevsky, F. M., Museum: 127473 Moscow, ul. Dostoyevskogo 2; tel. (495) 681-10-85; fax (495) 680-30-17; e-mail litmuz@arc.ru; f. 1928; affiliated to the State Literature Museum; exhibits illustrating Dostoyevsky's life, organized in the flat where he lived until sixteen years old; Dir GALINA B. PONOMAREVA.

Fersman Mineralogical Museum: 119071 Moscow, Leninsky pr. 18, korp. 2; tel. (495) 954-39-00; fax (495) 952-48-50; e-mail mineral@fmm.ru; internet www.fmm.ru; f. 1716; attached to Russian Acad. of Sciences; 150,000 mineral samples from throughout the world; library of 16,700 vols; Dir Prof. M. I. NOVGORODOVA; publ. *New Data on Minerals* (1 a year).

'Glinka, M. I.', State Central Museum of Musical Culture: 125047 Moscow, ul. Fadeeva 4; tel. (495) 972-32-37; fax (495) 972-32-55; internet www.museum.ru/glinka; f. 1943; based on the Museum of the Moscow Conservatoire; collects archives, MSS and memorabilia; musical instruments; musical iconography; records and tape recordings; music, books, posters, programmes—in all, 800,000 items; exhibits: musical instruments of the world; Russian musical culture; Dir-Gen. A. D. PANIUSHKIN.

Gogol, N. V., House-Museum and Gogol Study Centre: 121019 Moscow, Nikitsky bul. 7; tel. (495) 291-15-50; fax (495) 291-15-50; e-mail vik@systel.ru; f. 1974; library of 200,000 vols, Gogol spec. colln of 600 vols and manuscript room; also exhibits illustrating life and work of Gogol; Dir VERA P. VIKULOVA.

Gorky, A. M., Memorial Museum: Moscow 121069, Malaya Nikitskaya ul. 6/2; tel. (495) 290-05-35; f. 1965 in the house where the author lived; contains Gorky's private library of 10,000 vols, and his collection of Oriental arts (ivory); Dir L. P. BYKOVTSEVA.

Gorky, A. M., Museum: 121069 Moscow, ul. Povarskaya 25A; tel. (495) 291-51-30; f. 1937; 44,500 items, including literary and photographic documents, works of art, memorabilia; Dir L. P. BYKOVTSEVA.

Moscow Kremlin Museums: 103073 Moscow, Kremlin; tel. (495) 695-89-23; fax (495) 621-63-23; e-mail head@kremlin.museum.ru; internet www.kreml.ru; f. 1806; monuments built from late 15th to 20th centuries; incl. cathedrals-museums: Assumption Cathedral, Archangel Cathedral, Annunciation Cathedral, Church of Deposition of Robe of the Holy Virgin, Palace of Patriarch of 17th century with Church of Twelve Apostles, bell tower of Ivan the Great with the belfry and the State Armoury Chamber-treasury; collns of State Historical and Cultural Museum-Preserve comprise over than 60,000 historical, cultural and artistic monuments; library of 49,000 vols; Dir YELENA GAGARINA.

Attached Sites:

Armoury: 103073 Moscow, Kremlin; f. 1857; Museum since 1806; 3,500 artworks: ancient state regalia, diplomatic gifts to Russian Tsars, vestments of Russian Church hierarchs of 14th–18th centuries, coronation suits of Russian Emperors and dresses of Empresses, artworks by Russian gold and silversmiths of 12th–20th centuries, monuments of Byzantine and Western European art of 15th–19th centuries, ceremonial weapons, and ancient carriages.

Kremlin Cathedrals: 103073 Moscow, Kremlin; The cathedrals around the Cathedral Square (Sobornaya ploshchad) include, among others, the following: Cathedral of the Assumption (f. 1479); icons of the 14th–17th centuries; throne of Ivan the Terrible; Cathedral of the Annunciation (f. 1489); iconostasis by leading artists of the 14th–15th centuries. Archangel Cathedral (1508); tombs of Ivan Kalita and other Russian Grand Dukes and Czars. Rizpolozhenskii Cathedral (f. 1485). Cathedral of the Twelve Apostles and Patriarch's Palace; 17th-century items of applied decorative art.

Main Botanical Garden 'N. V. Tsitsin': 127276 Moscow, Botanicheskaya ul. 4; tel. (495) 977-90-44; fax (495) 977-91-72; e-mail info@gbsad.ru; internet www.gbsad.ru; f. 1945; attached to Russian Acad. of Sciences; br. in Cheboksary; Dir Dr ALEXANDER S. DEMIDOV; publs *Bulletin* (2 a year), *Newsletter* (2 a year).

Marx-Engels Museum: c/o Russian State Archive of Modern History, 103132 Moscow, ul. Ilinka 12; f. 1962; 2,000 exhibits descriptive of the lives of Marx and Engels; Dir V. N. KUZNETSOV.

Moscow Arts Theatre Museum: 103009 Moscow, pr-d Khudozhestvennogo Teatra 3A; tel. (495) 229-00-80; f. 1923; Dir V. S. DAVIDOV.

Attached Museums:

Nemirovich-Danchenko, V., Flat-Museum: 103009 Moscow, Ul. Nemirovicha-Danchenko 5/7, kv. 52; tel. (495) 209-53-91; f. 1944; illustrating career of Nemirovich-Danchenko.

Stanislavsky, K. S., House-Museum: 103009 Moscow, Ul. Stanislavskogo 6; tel. (495) 229-28-55; f. 1948; attached to Theatre Museum; deals with Stanislavsky's work and the theatrical career of People's Artist, M. P. Lilina.

Moscow State University Museum of Zoology: 125009 Moscow, ul. Bol. Nikitskaya 6; tel. (495) 203-64-93; fax (495) 203-27-17; e-mail zmmu@zmmu.msu.ru; internet zmmu.msu.ru; f. 1791; systematics, speciation, zoogeography, fauna research, phylogenetics; library of 190,000 vols; Dir Dr OLGA L. ROSSOLIMO; publs *Archives* (1 a year), *Zoologicheskie Issledovania (Zoological Research)*.

The Earth Science Museum of the Moscow State M. V. Lomonosov University: 119992 Moscow, GSP-2, MGU; tel. (495) 939-14-15; fax (495) 939-29-76; e-mail info@mes.msu.ru; internet www.museum.msu.ru; f. 1955; includes material on the origin of the face of the earth, its geospheres, surface and underwater landscapes, earth crust, climates, waters, soils, plants, animals, economic resources; on the conservation, utilization and reconstruction of nature; complex geological and geographical characteristics of Russia and of the earth; science-teaching museum for students of the geological, geographical, biological soil science et al depts of Moscow University; 48000 samples; library of 5,000 vols in library; Dir Prof. A. V. SMUROV; publ. *Zhizn Zemli* (The Life of the Earth, 1 vol. every 1–2 years).

Museum of Frontier Guards: Moscow, ul. Bol. Bronnaya 23; 110,000 exhibits featuring the history of Soviet frontier guards.

Museum of the History of the City of Moscow: 103012 Moscow, Novaya pl. 12; tel. (495) 924-31-45; fax (495) 924-31-45; f. 1896; Dir G. I. VEDEZNIKOVA.

Museum of the Palaeontological Institute: 117647 Moscow, Profsoyuznaya ul. 123; tel. (495) 339-05-77; fax (495) 339-12-66; e-mail admin@paleo.ru; internet www.paleo.ru; f. 1930; attached to Russian Acad. of Sciences; library of 20,000 vols; Dir A. YU. ROZANOV.

Museum of the State Academic Malyi Theatre: 103009 Moscow, Malyi teatr, Teatralnaya pl. 1/6; tel. (495) 921-85-48; f. 1932, being developed out of 1927 exhibition; illustrates and studies history of the Theatre; Dir YU. M. STRUTINSKAYA.

Nikolai Rubinstein Museum: 125009 Moscow, Bol. Nikitskaya 13; tel. and fax (495) 629-90-98; e-mail museumrub@mail.ru; internet www.mosconsv.ru; f. 1995; colln incl. musical instruments and portraits and sculptures of Russian composers; documents, photographs, phonographs, antique furniture; Dir. Dr EVGENIA GUREVICH.

Novodevichii Monastery Museum: 119435 Moscow, Novodevichii pr. 1; tel. (495) 246-22-01; fax (495) 246-85-26; e-mail m337@mail.museum.ru; internet www.shm.ru/filials/novodev/fil_nov.htm; Smolensky Cathedral (1524) and other monuments of Russian architecture form the architectural ensemble of the monastery; Russian fine and decorative art (16th and 17th centuries); Dir IRINA G. BORISENKO.

Obraztsov Puppet Museum of the Central State Academic Puppet Theatre: 123473 Moscow Sadovaya-Samotechnaya ul. 3; tel. (495) 699-55-53; fax (495) 699-89-10; e-mail museum@obraztsov.ru; internet www.puppet.ru/museum; f. 1937; Central Puppet Theatre; 5,600 dolls from 50 countries; puppet theatres of the fmr USSR and many other countries; colln of cartoons, sketches, MSS and other documents; library of 15,000 books; Vice-Dir Dr BORIS GOLDOVSKY.

Permanent Tchaikovsky Exhibition in the Tchaikovsky Concert Hall: 125047 Moscow, pl. Triumfalnaya 4/31; exhibits of the composer's life and works.

Petrographic Museum: 109017 Moscow, Staromonetnyi per. 35; tel. (495) 230-82-92; fax (495) 230-21-79; internet www.museum.ru/m417; f. 1934; Dir V. A. PAVLOV.

Pharmaceutical Museum of the Central Drug Research Institute: 117418 Moscow, ul. Krasikova 34; tel. (495) 120-91-51; unique collection of about 6,000 items on the history of pharmacy in Russia and the fmr USSR; Dir B. M. SALO.

Polytechnical Museum: 101000 Moscow, Polytekhnicheskii pr-d 2; tel. (495) 928-64-65; fax (495) 923-51-60; e-mail cpb@polymus.ru; internet www.polymus.ru; f. 1864; over 100,000 exhibits; features history and latest developments in science and technology; belongs to the Ministry of Culture; library of 3m. vols; Dir Prof. G. G. GRIGORIAN.

Rublev, Andrei, Central Museum of Ancient Russian Culture and Art: 107120 Moscow, Andronevskaya pl. 10; tel. (495) 678-14-67; fax (495) 678-50-55; e-mail rublevmuseum@aha.ru; internet www.rublev-museum.ru; f. 1947; Russian art, icons, applied art, manuscripts, old printed books; library of 23,000 vols; Dir Dr G. V. POPOV.

Shchukin, B. V., Museum-Room: Moscow, Flat 11, ul. Shchukina 8; contains material he had about him during his lifetime as a great actor at the Vakhtangov Theatre.

Shchusev, A. V., State Research Architectural Museum: 121019 Moscow, ul. Vozdvizhenka 5/25; tel. (495) 291-21-09; fax (495) 291-21-09; e-mail schusev@muar.ru; internet www.muar.ru; f. 1934; objects: study, collection, care and popularization of historical architecture, outstanding contemporary work, monumental sculpture and painting; collection and care of documents on architecture and town planning; over 70,000 sheets of architectural drawings; over 300,000 negatives and 400,000 photographs of architectural monuments throughout the world; library of 50,000 vols; Dir I. M. KOROBINA; Curator I. V. SEDOVA.

Skryabin, A. N., Museum: 121002 Moscow, ul. Vakhtangova 11; tel. (495) 241-19-01; f. 1919, opened in 1922 in flat where the composer lived and died; MSS, letters, Skryabin's personal library and magnetic-tape archive of Skryabin's compositions performed by the composer and famous artists; excursions, lectures and concerts; library of 287 vols in Skryabin's personal library, 2,149 vols in scientific library; Dir RYBAKOVA.

State Academic Bolshoi Theatre Museum: 103009 Moscow, Bolshoi Teatr, Okhotnyi Ryad 8/2; tel. (495) 292-00-25; f. 1920; objects: documentation of the work of the Bolshoi Theatre, collection of materials and documents on its history and work, study of history of the theatre; Dir V. I. ZARUBIN.

State Central Museum of Contemporary Russian History: 125009 Moscow, Tverskaya ul. 21; tel. (495) 299-52-17; fax (495) 299-85-15; e-mail 9055.g23@g23.relcom.ru; internet www.sovr.ru; f. 1917; social and political history of Russia since 1850; library of 360,000 vols and 825,000 periodicals; Dir Dr TAMARA SHUMNAYA; publ. *Trudy* (Proceedings).

State Central Theatrical Museum 'A. A. Bakhrushin': 115054 Moscow, ul. Bakhrushina 31/12; tel. (495) 953-48-48; fax (495) 953-54-48; e-mail gctm@gctm.ru; internet www.gctm.ru; f. 1894; collects, houses, studies and exhibits varied materials on history and theory of theatre; approx. 1.5m. exhibits; archives of original MSS of Ostrovsky, Lensky, Stanislavsky, Meyerhold, etc.; library of 120,000 vols; Dir-Gen. DMITRY V. RODIONOV.

State Darwin Museum: 117292 Moscow, Vavilova 57; tel. (495) 135-33-76; fax (495) 135-33-84; e-mail darwin@museum.ru; internet www.darwin.museum.ru; f. 1907; natural history and evolution; total holdings of 360,065 items; library of 30,000 vols; Dir A. I. KLUKINA.

State Historical Museum: 103012 Moscow, Krasnaya pl. 1/2; tel. (495) 924-45-29; fax (495) 925-95-27; e-mail shkurko@shm.ru; internet www.shm.ru; f. 1872; 4.5m. exhibits covering Russian history from pre-history to the present; colln of birch-bark writings; library of 229,000 vols, 29,000 MSS, 25,000 rare books; Dir-Gen. ALEXANDER SHKURKO; publs *Ezhegodnik GIM*, *Numizmaticheskii sbornik* (irregular), *Trudy GIM*.

State Literature Museum: 103051 Moscow, Petrovka ul. 28; tel. (495) 921-38-57; fax (495) 923-30-22; f. 1934; the museum is a research and educational centre which collects, studies and publishes material on the history of Russian and Soviet literature; br. (museums of Lermontov, Herzen, Dostoevsky, Chekhov, Tolstoy, Pasternak, Prishvin, Aksakov and Bryusov); library of 250,000 vols; Gen. Dir NATALYA V. SHAKHALOVA.

State Museum of Ceramics (country-seat Kuskovo): 111402 Moscow Yunosti ul. 2; tel. (495) 370-01-50; fax (495) 918-65-40; internet www.kuskovo.ru; large collection of Russian art: paintings, furniture, porcelain, pottery; collection of Western European art, tapestries, furniture, paintings, porcelain, pottery, etc.; Dir YELENA S. YERITSYAN.

State Museum of Oriental Art: 107120 Moscow, Nikitsky bul. 12A; tel. (495) 291-96-14; fax (495) 202-48-46; internet www.orientalart.ru; f. 1918; large collection of Middle and Far Eastern art, art of the fmr Soviet Central Asian Republics and Transcaucasia, carpets, fabrics, ceramics, etc.; Dir-Gen. V. A. NABACHIKOV.

State Pushkin Museum: 119034 Moscow, ul. Prechistenka 12/2; tel. (495) 202-43-54; fax (495) 202-43-54; f. 1958; 200,000 exhibits; library of 51,000 vols; maintains br. in Pushkin's former home (Arbat 53); Dir E. BOGATYREV.

State Pushkin Museum of Fine Arts: 121019 Moscow, Volkhonka 12; tel. (495) 203-58-09; fax (495) 203-46-74; e-mail finearts@gmii.museum.ru; internet www.museum.ru/gmii; f. 1912; about 558,000 items of ancient Eastern, Graeco-Roman, Byzantine, European and American art; numismatic colln of 200,000 items; library of 200,000 vols; Dir I. A. ANTONOVA; Chief Conservator GALINA ERSHOVA.

State Tretyakov Gallery: 117049 Moscow, Lavrushinskii per. 10; tel. (495) 230-77-88; fax (495) 231-10-51; e-mail tretyakov@tretyakov.ru; internet www.tretyakov.ru; f. 1856; collection of 130,000 Russian icons and works of Russian and Soviet painters, sculptors and graphic artists since 11th century; also 3,200 items from the former Pyotr Zakharov Fine Arts Museum in Grozny; new building at Krymskiy Val houses an exhibition of Russian art from 20th century; Dir VALENTIN A. RODIONOV.

State V. V. Mayakovsky Museum: 101000 Moscow, pr. Serova 3/6; tel. (095) 921-93-87; f. 1974 in the building where Mayakovsky lived 1919–30; manuscripts, documentary material, notebooks, memorial items; library and reading room with c. 200,000 vols, including periodicals; Dir S. E. STRIZHNIKOVA.

S. T. Morozov Folk-Art Museum: 103009 Moscow, Leontyevskii per. 7; tel. (495) 290-52-22; f. 1885; three sections devoted to (a) handicrafts connected with peasant daily life; (b) applied arts both ancient and contemporary; (c) experimental decorative applied art; about 800,000 exhibits; under the jurisdiction of the Russian Council of Local Industries; Dir G. A. YAKOVLEVA.

Timiryazev, K. A., Apartment Museum: 103009 Moscow, Romanovski per. 2, str. 2, kv. 29; tel. (495) 202-80-64; fax (495) 976-29-10; f. 1942; cultural and historical memorial to K. A. Timiryazev; 7,545 exhibits and archives on his life and work; library: personal library of 4,871 vols; Dir A. A. DRUCHEK.

Timiryazev State Museum of Biology: 123242 Moscow, Mal. Gruzinskaya 15; tel. (499) 252-55-42; fax (499) 255-63-21; e-mail gbmt@gbmt.ru; internet www.gbmt.ru; f. 1922; origin and evolution of life on earth; library of 70,000 vols; Dir E. A. CHUSOVA.

Tolstoy Residence Museum: 119021 Moscow, ul. Lva Tolstogo 21; tel. (495) 246-94-44; rooms arranged as they were when the author lived there; 4,200 exhibits; Dir A. V. SALOMATIN.

Leo Tolstoy State Museum: 119021 Moscow, ul. Prechistenka 11/8; tel. (499) 766-93-28; e-mail tolstoy@museum.comsat.ru; internet www.tolstoymuseum.ru; f. 1911; MSS section contains 400,000 items of Tolstoy's writings and nearly 600,000 MSS and archive material on Tolstoy and his circle; library of 76,800 works by or about Tolstoy; nearly 87,000 newspaper cuttings, and over 42,000 exhibits in the form of painting, sculpture, photographs, etc.; 4 brs: Literary Museum, urban estate 'Khamovniki', exhibition hall and Leo Tolstoy museum 'Astapovo'; Dir VITALY REMIZOV.

Vakhtangov Theatre Museum: Moscow; history of the Vakhtangov Theatre; Dir I. L. SERGEEVA.

Vernadsky State Geological Museum: 103009 Moscow, Mokhovaya ul. 11, korp. 2; tel. (495) 203-52-87; fax (495) 203-47-98; e-mail info@sgm.ru; internet www.sgm.ru; f. 1755; Dir Prof. D. V. RUNDQVIST.

Zhukovskii, N. E., Memorial Museum: 107005 Moscow, ul. Radio 17; tel. (495) 267-50-54; 25,000 items feature the work of N. E. Zhukovskii, and Soviet contributions to aviation and astronautics; Dir V. I. MASLOV.

Nalchik

Kabarda-Balkar Art Museum: Nalchik, pr. V. I. Lenina 35; 3,500 exhibits; Dir I. Z. BATASHOV.

Nizhnii Novgorod

Nizhnii Novgorod Historical Museum: Nizhnii Novgorod, nab. Zhdanova 7; 160,000 exhibits including collections of archaeology, featuring the history of the Central Volga area since ancient times.

Nizhnii Novgorod State Museum of Art: 603082 Nizhnii Novgorod, korp. 3 Kremlya; tel. (8312) 39-08-55; fax (8312) 19-20-85; e-mail art@museum.nnov.ru; internet www.museum.nnov.ru/art; f. 1896; Dir VALENTINA N. KRIVOVA.

State A. M. Gorky Museum of Literature: 603155 Nizhnii Novgorod, ul. Minina 26; tel. and fax (8312) 36-15-29; e-mail danco6@yandex.ru; internet www.museum.nnov.ru/danco; f. 1928; 102,000 exhibits, illustrating the life and work of the writer; library of 40,000 vols; Dir T. A. RIZHOVA.

Novocherkassk

Novocherkassk Museum of the History of the Don Cossacks: 346430 Rostov oblast, Novocherkassk, Atamanskaya ul. 38; tel. (86352) 4-80-59; e-mail m838@mail.museum.ru; internet www.doncossacks.ru; f. 1899; deals with the traditions and exploits of the Don Cossacks; collections of porcelain and painting; library of 17,000 vols; Dir SVETLANA A. SEDINKO.

Novosibirsk

Central Siberian Botanical Garden: 630090 Novosibirsk, Zolotodolinskaya ul. 101; tel. (3832) 30-41-01; fax (3832) 30-19-86; e-mail root@botgard.nsk.su; internet www.cbsg.narod.ru; f. 1946; attached to Russian Acad. of Sciences; Dir Prof. V. P. SEDELNIKOV.

Omsk

Omsk Fine Art Museum: Omsk, ul. Lenina 23; 3,780 exhibits; Dir A. A. GERZON.

Orel

Turgenev, I. S., State Literary Museum: 302000 Orel, ul. Turgeneva 11; tel. (08622) 6-27-37; f. 1918; library of 60,000 vols; Dir V. V. SAFRONOVA.

Branch museums:

Andreev Leonid, House Museum: Orel, Pushkarnaya 41; tel. (4862) 76-48-24; f. 1991; Man. O. V. VOLOGINA.

Bunin Museum: 302000 Orel, Oktyabrsky pr. 1; tel. (08622) 6-07-74; f. 1991; Man. I. A. KOSTOMAROVA.

Granovsky, T. N., Museum: Orel, ul. 7 Noyabrya 24; tel. (08622) 6-34-65; f. 1985; devoted to public figures born in Orel; Man. E. A. IVUSHKINA.

Leskov, N. S., House Museum: 301028 Orel, ul. Oktyabrskaya 9; tel. (08622) 6-33-04; f. 1974; Man. L. S. KAMYSHALOVA.

Literary Museum: 302000 Orel, ul. Turgeneva 11; tel. (08622) 6-35-28; f. 1957; devoted to writers born in Orel; Man. L. E. URAKOVA.

Orenburg

Orenburg Fine Art Museum: Orenburg, ul. Pravdy 6; 3,500 items; Dir L. B. POPOVA.

Palekh

State Museum of Palekh Art: 155620 Ivanovo oblast, Palekh ul. Bakanova 50; tel. (49334) 2-20-54; fax (49334) 2-26-41; e-mail m1571@mail.museum.ru; internet www.museum.ru/m1571; f. 1934; library of 16,000 books, photographs and film docs; Dir ALEVTINA G. STRAKHOVA.

Pavlovsk

The State Museum 'Pavlovsk': 196621 St. Peterburg Pavlovsk, ul. Sadovaya 20; tel. (812) 452-21-55; fax (812) 465-11-04; e-mail palace@pavlovskmuseum.ru; internet www.pavlovskmuseum.ru; f. 1918; many examples of Russian garden architecture, antique sculpture and sculpture by 18th-century Italian and French masters; European paintings of the 16th to 19th centuries, Russian portraits of the 18th century, Russian decorative art of the 18th and 19th centuries; furniture, porcelain, bronzes and textiles; library of 17,000 vols; Dir N. S. TRETYAKOV.

Penza

Penza Picture Gallery: 660026 Penza, Sovetskaya ul. 3; tel. (8412) 66-64-00; f. 1892; library of 3,200 vols; 7,700 exhibits; also 3 memorial museums; Dir VALERYI SAZONOV.

Perm

Perm State Art Gallery: 614045 Perm, Komsomolskyi Ave 4; tel. (342) 212-95-24; fax (342) 212-22-50; e-mail pghg@mail.ru; internet www.gallery.permonline.ru; f. 1922; colln management (conservation, restoration, art expertise); academic work (research, exhibitions, confs, seminars, publs, scholarly exchange); adult and children education (guide tours, programmers, actions); information technologies; devt and fund raising, PR support; colln stocks 50,000 works of art of the 15th–21st centuries; Russian and foreign art: paintings, graphic, decorative and applied art objects; the Stroganovs school icons and Perm wood carving cult sculptures; library of 28,900 vols; Dir NADEZHDA V. BELYAEVA.

Petrodvorets

Peterhof State Museum Reserve: 198516 St Petersburg, Petrodvorets, ul. Rasvodnaya 2; tel. (812) 427-74-25; fax (812) 427-93-30; e-mail admin@peterhof.org; internet www

.peterhof.org; f. 1918; 18th- to 20th-century architecture, painting and landscape gardening; 18th- and 19th-century sculpture, furniture, porcelain, clocks and jewellery; library of 21,000 books, special collection of 2,000 rare books, 7,000 Russian book-plates, 1,300 printed graphics; Dir V. V. ZNAMENOV.

Petrozavodsk

Karelian Museum of Fine Arts: 185035 Republic of Karelia, Petrozavodsk, pr. K. Marksa 8; tel. (8142) 77-98-60; fax (8142) 78-25-78; e-mail pictures@sampo.ru; internet artmuseum.karelia.ru; f. 1960; Karelian iconic paintings from 15th–19th centuries, Karelian folk art, modern Karelian art, Russian art from the 18th century to present, western European art; library of 21,000 vols; Dir NATALIA I. VAVILOVA.

Karelian State Regional Museum: 185035 Republic of Karelia, Petrozavodsk, pl. Lenina 1; tel. (8142) 78-02-40; fax (8142) 78-02-40; e-mail kgkm@karelia.ru; internet karelia.ru/~kgkm; f. 1871; history, economy, science, culture, and natural history of the area; 3 brs; library of 25,700 vols; Dir ELENA ZARINA; publs *Museum Herald* (1 a year), *Museums of Karelia* (4 a year), *Vestnik* (1 a year).

Kizhi State Open-Air Museum of History, Architecture and Ethnography: 185610 Republic of Karelia, Petrozavodsk, Neglinskaya nab. 23; tel. (8142) 76-57-66; e-mail olga@kizhi.karelia.ru; f. 1961; wooden architecture, history, ethnography, early Russian and Karelian painting and folklore; library of 8,500 vols; Dir O. A. NABOKOVA.

Pushkin

Tsarskoe Selo State Museum: 189690 Leningrad oblast, Tsarskoe Selo, Sadovaya ul. 7; tel. (812) 466-66-69; fax (812) 465-21-96; e-mail tzar@spb.cityline.ru; internet www.tzar.ru; f. 1918; former imperial summer residence, incl. Catherine and Alexander Palaces; park and garden architecture and 100 architectural ornaments from 18th to 20th centuries, esp. in Baroque and Classical styles; library of 18,041 vols including collection of rare books of 2,375 vols; Dir I. P. SAUTOV.

Pushkinskie Gory

State Memorial Museum-Reserve of A. S. Pushkin 'Mikhailovskoye': 181370 Pskovskaya oblast, Pushkinskie Gory, Novorzhevskaya 21; tel. and fax (81146) 2-19-50; e-mail pgmuseum@ellink.ru; internet www.pushkin.ellink.ru; f. 1922; 33,000 exhibits on the life in exile of the poet, Aleksandr Pushkin (1799–1837); the preserve incl. the family lands at Mikhailovskoe, Trigorskoe and Petrovskoe, the ancient towns of Voronich and Savkina Gorka, and the grave of Pushkin; library of 21,000 vols; Dir G. N. VASILEVICH.

Pyatigorsk

State Lermontov Literary Memorial Museum: Pyatigorsk, Lermontovskaya ul. 4; tel. (87933) 5-27-10; f. 1912; exhibits feature the life and work of M. Yu. Lermontov in the Caucasus; library of 14,000 vols; Dir L. MOROZOVA.

Roslavl

Roslavl Historical Museum: Roslavl, ul. Proletarskaya 63; tel. (08134) 3-18-49; f. 1920; collection tracing the history, economy and culture of Russian people from the earliest times; library of 1,300 vols; Dir M. I. IVANOVA.

Rostov-on-Don

Rostov Museum of Fine Art: 344002 Rostov-on-Don, ul. Pushkinskaya 115; tel. and fax (8632) 69-10-88; e-mail romii@mail.ru; f. 1938; old Russian, Soviet and foreign descriptive art; library of 16,697 vols; Dir KRUZE SVETLANA VALEREVNA; publ. *Khudozhnik.*

Ryazan

Ryazan Kremlin Historical and Architectural Museum Reserve: Ryazan, Kreml 118; tel. (0912) 27-60-65; fax (0912) 21-56-70; e-mail root@riamz.ryazan.ru; internet www.ryazankreml.ru; f. 1884; over 220,000 items describing the history, culture and art of the peoples of Russia; Dir LUDMILA MAKSIMOVA; publs *Yakhontovsky's Readings* (every 2 years), *Scientific Works* (every 5 years).

Ryazan Regional Art Museum: Ryazan, Svoboda st. 57; tel. and fax (4912) 28-04-24; f. 1913; old Russian (15th–20th centuries), European (16th–19th centuries) and Soviet art; library of 17,000 vols; Dir M. A. KOTOVA.

St Petersburg

Acad. F. N. Chernyshev Central Scientific Research Geological and Prospecting Museum (CNIGR museum): 199106 St Petersburg, Vasilevskii ostrov, Srednii pr. 74; tel. and fax (812) 321-53-99; e-mail cnigr_museum@vsegei.ru; internet www.vsegei.com; f. 1882, opened 1930; attached to A. P. Karpinsky Russia Geological Research Institute (VSEGEI); c. 1m. geological specimens incl. examples of mineral deposits from all over the fmr USSR; monographic and palaeontological collns; popularization of geological knowledge; Dir Dr ALEKSEY SOKOLOV.

Botanical Museum: 197022 St Petersburg, ul. Prof. Popova 2; tel. (812) 234-84-39; f. 1823; over 60,000 specimens; br. of V. L. Komarov Botanical Institute of Academy of Sciences; Dir L. YU. BUDANTSEV.

Central Museum of Railway Transport of Russia: St Petersburg, Sadovaya ul. 50; fax (812) 315-14-76; e-mail cmrt1813@yandex.ru; internet www.railroad.ru/cmrt; f. 1813; traces the history of railway transport in Russia; incl. unique colln of miniature models of engines and carriages; Dir G. ZAKREVSKAYA.

Central Naval Museum: 199034 St Petersburg, Birzhevaya pl. 4; tel. (812) 328-27-02; fax (812) 328-27-01; internet www.museum.navy.ru; f. 1709; relics and other materials from the Russian and Soviet Navies; departments of history of the Russian Navy, history of the Soviet Navy, history of the Navy in the 1941–45 period, history of the Navy in the post-war period; responsible for Kronstadt Fortress, cruiser Aurora and submarine Narodovolets; library of 16,000 vols; Dir E. N. KORCHAGIN.

Dokuchaev Central Soil Museum: St Petersburg, Birzhevoi pr-d 6; tel. (812) 328-54-02; fax (812) 328-56-02; e-mail soilmuseum@bk.ru; internet www.soil-museum.ru; f. 1904; about 5,000 specimens of soil from nearly every soil zone in the world; library of 14,000 vols (Dokuchaev personal library); Dir Dr B. F. APARIN.

Dostoevsky Memorial Museum: 191002 St Petersburg, Kuznechnyi per. 5/2; tel. (812) 571-40-31; e-mail ashimbaeva@md.spb.ru; internet www.md.spb.ru; f. 1971; the house where the author lived 1878–81; MSS, documentary material, memorial items; library of 23,000 vols; Dir Dr NATALIA ASHIMBAEVA.

Literary Museum of the Institute of Russian Literature: 199034 St Petersburg, Pushkinskii Dom, nab. Makarova 4; tel. (812) 328-05-02; fax (812) 328-11-40; e-mail irliran@mail.ru; internet www.pushkinhouse.spb.ru; f. 1905; based on the material of the Pushkin Anniversary Exhibition of 1899; contains 95,000 exhibits and over 120,000 items of reference material; 7 halls containing permanent exhibitions devoted to G. R. Derzhavin, A. S. Pushkin, M. Y. Lermontov, N. V. Gogol, F. M. Dostoevsky, I. S. Turgenev, L. N. Tolstoy and other Russian writers and poets; Dir L. G. AGAMALIAN.

Lomonosov, M. V., Museum: 199164 St Petersburg, Universitetskaya nab. 3; tel. (812) 328-10-11; internet www.kunstkamera.ru/en/museums_structure/research_departments/mv_lomonosov_museum; f. 1947; attached to Museum of Anthropology and Ethnography (Kunstkamera); 3,000 exhibits; Head MARGARITA F. KHARTONOVICH.

Military Medical Museum: 191180 St Petersburg, Lazaretny per. 2; tel. (812) 315-53-58; fax (812) 310-20-25; e-mail m170@mail.museum.ru; internet www.museum.ru/m170; f. 1942; history of Russian and Soviet military medicine; library: research library of 50,000 vols, also collections of rare books; 60m. archive docs on citizens of 45 countries in Europe, Asia, America and Africa; Dir Prof. Dr A. A. BUDKO; publs *History of Medicine in St Petersburg* (1 a year), *History of Military Medicine in Russia* (1 a year), *Memorial Dates of Military Medicine* (1 a year), *Military Medicine Abroad* (6 a year), *Review of the History of Military Medicine* (1 a year).

Mining Museum of the St Petersburg State Mining Institute (Technical University): 199106 St Petersburg, 21-ya liniya 2; tel. (812) 328-84-29; fax (812) 327-73-59; e-mail rectorat@spmi.ru; internet www.gorny-ins.ru; f. 1773; specimens of minerals, rocks, ores, fossils, meteorites; historical mining techniques illustrated by models of the 19th and early 20th century; colln of edged weapons from the Zlatoust Arms Factory; Dir J. POLYARNAYA.

Museum of Artillery, Engineers and Signal Corps: 197046 St Petersburg, Aleksandrovsky park 7; tel. (812) 238-47-04; fax (812) 238-47-04; f. 1703; library of 115,000 vols; Dir Col V. M. KRYLOV.

Museum of Sculpture: St Petersburg, pl. A. Nevskogo 1; largest collection of Russian sculpture, collection and care of documents on architecture and town planning; over 150,000 sheets of architectural drawings; Dir N. H. BELOVA.

Museum of the Gorky Bolshoi Drama Theatre: St Petersburg, ul. Fontanka 65.

Museum of the History of Religion: 191186 St Petersburg, Kazanskaya pl. 2; fax (812) 311-94-83; f. 1932; 186,000 exhibits on Russian Orthodox Church, Roman Catholic and other Christian churches, Judaism, Islam and Buddhism; library of 170,000 vols; Dir S. A. KUCHINSKY; publ. *Theses* (1 a year).

Library of the Mariinsky State Academic Theatre of Opera and Ballet: 190000 St Petersburg, ul. Zodchego Rossi 2, Teatralnaya pl. 1; tel. (812) 326-41-64; e-mail cml@mariinsky.ru; library: consists of repertoire and archive sections; Dir Prof. Dr MARIYA N. SHCHERBAKOVA.

Museum of the St Petersburg Mussorgsky Academic Opera and Ballet Theatre: St Petersburg, pl. Iskusstv 1; tel. (812) 595-43-13; fax (812) 314-36-53; internet www.reserve.sp.ru; f. 1935; colln of materials (sketches, posters, photographs, costumes) depicting the history of the theatre and its work; Dir M. KORTUNOVA.

Museum of Zoology: 199034 St Petersburg, Universitetskaya nab. 1; tel. (812) 328-01-12; fax (812) 328-29-41; e-mail museum@zin.ru; internet www.zin.ru; f. 1832; over 30,000 items describe the origin and evolution of the animal world; attached to Zoological Institute of the Russian Acad. of Sciences (see under Research Institutes); Chief ALEXEI TIKHONOV; publ. *Proceedings of the Zoological Institute*.

National Pushkin Museum: 191186 St Petersburg, nab. Moiki 12; tel. (812) 571-38-01; fax (812) 315-73-79; e-mail vmp@mail.admiral.ru; internet www.museumpushkin.ru; f. 1879; under supervision of Ministry of Culture; exhibits illustrating the life and work of the poet and his epoch; Dir S. M. NEKRASOV.

Annexes:

Lyceum Museum: 196600 Pushkin, Sadovaya 2; tel. (812) 476-64-11; fax (812) 315-73-79; e-mail vmp@mail.admiral.ru; internet www.museumpushkin.ru; f. 1949; Chief Curator M. N. PETAI.

Main Literary Exposition–Life and Creative Work of Alexander Pushkin: 191186 St Petersburg, nab. Moiki 12; tel. (812) 314-00-07; fax (812) 315-73-79; e-mail vmp@mail.admiral.ru; internet www.museumpushkin.ru; f. 1999; Chief Curator N. L. PETROVA.

Museum of Derzhavin and Russian Literature of the 18th Century: 198005 St Petersburg, nab. Fontanki 118; tel. (812) 713-07-17; fax (812) 315-73-79; e-mail vmp@mail.admiral.ru; internet www.museumpushkin.ru; f. 2003; Chief Curator N. P. MOROZOVA.

Nekrasov Apartment Museum: 191104 St Petersburg, Liteiny pr. 36; tel. (812) 272-01-65; fax (812) 315-73-79; e-mail vmp@mail.admiral.ru; internet www.museumpushkin.ru; f. 1946; Chief Curator E. YU. GLEVENKO.

Pushkin Apartment Museum: 191186 St Petersburg, nab. Moiki 12; tel. (812) 117-35-31; fax (812) 315-73-79; e-mail vmp@mail.admiral.ru; internet www.museumpushkin.ru; f. 1925; Chief Curator G. M. SEDOVA.

Pushkin Country House Museum: 196607 Pushkin, Pushkinskaya ul. 2; tel. (812) 476-69-90; tel. (812) 315-73-79; e-mail vmp@mail.admiral.ru; internet www.museumpushkin.ru; f. 1958; Chief Curator T. I. GALKINA.

Permanent Exhibition of Musical Instruments: St Petersburg, 5 Isaakievskaya pl.; about 3,000 exhibits, including a large collection of instruments made by outstanding Russian and foreign craftsmen: Batov, Leman, Nalimov, Krasnoshchekov, Fedorov, Amati, Villaume, Tilke and Denner.

Peter the Great Museum of Anthropology and Ethnography (Kunstkamera): 199034 St Petersburg, Universitetskaya nab. 3; tel. (812) 328-07-12; fax (812) 328-08-11; e-mail info@kunstkamera.ru; internet www.kunstkamera.ru; f. 1714; attached to Russian Acad. of Sciences; ethnographical, archaeological, and anthropological material on the native peoples of all continents; anatomical colln; scientific instruments; Dir Prof. YURI K. CHISTOV; publs *Etnograficheskiye tetradi* (1 a year), *Forum for Anthropology and Culture* (2 in Russian, 1 in English and 2 online), *Kuryer* (2 a year), *Mauscripta Orientalia* (4 a year), *Sbornik MAE* (1 a year).

Popov, A. S., Central Museum of Communications: 190000 St Petersburg, Pochtamtskaya ul. 7; tel. and fax (812) 315-48-73; e-mail bakayutova@telecommuseum.sp.ru; internet www.rustelecom-museum.ru; f. 1872; over 8m. items representing the development of all types of communication used in Russia and the former USSR; includes the national postage stamp collection; Dir L. BAKAYUTOVA.

Russian Ethnographic Museum: St Petersburg, Inzhenernaya ul. 4/1; tel. (812) 210-47-68; fax (812) 315-85-02; e-mail rme@infopro.spb.ru; internet www.ethnomuseum.ru; f. 1902; 150,000 photographs; library of 105,000 vols; Dir V. M. GRUSMAN; publ. *Collected Articles* (2 a year).

Russian State Museum of the Arctic and the Antarctic: 191040 St Petersburg, ul. Marata 24A; tel. (812) 713-19-98; fax (812) 764-68-18; e-mail boyarsky@norpolex.com; internet www.polarmuseum.ru; f. 1930; exploration, history and environment of polar regions; library of 6,362 vols; Dir Dr VICTOR I. BOYARSKY; Scientific Deputy Dir Dr M. V. DUKALSKAYA.

St Petersburg State Museum of Theatre and Music: 191011 St Petersburg, pl. Ostrovskogo 6; tel. (812) 315-52-43; fax (812) 314-77-46; e-mail theatre@museums.org.ru; internet www.theatremuseum.ru; f. 1918; over 440,000 exhibits depicting the history of Russian, Soviet and foreign theatre; 31,000 stage designs, 7,000 prints, 900 sculptures, 240,000 photographs, 24,000 MSS and documents, 62,000 posters and programmes, 4,000 theatre costumes; library of 5,000 vols; museum branches: *Rimsky-Korsakov Museum:* f. 1971; memorial museum in house where the composer lived; *F. I. Chaliapin Museum:* f. 1975; museum of history of Russian opera, in former house of Chaliapin; *Music Museum at the Sheremetev Palace*: f. 1991; museum of music incl. 3,000 instruments, and international music centre; *Samoilov Family Museum:* f. 1994; museum of a dynasty of Russian actors; Dir IRINA V. YEVSTIGNEYEVA.

State Circus Museum: 191011 St Petersburg, ul. Fontanka 3; tel. (812) 313-44-13; fax (812) 314-80-59; e-mail circusmuseum@aport.ru; internet www.circus.spb.ru; f. 1928; 80,000 exhibits of plans, sketches, paintings; section on the circus in Western Europe since 18th century and on Russian and fmr Soviet state circus; library of 4,000 items, Russian and foreign works; 300 videocassettes of circus material; Dir NATALIA KUZNETSOVA.

State Hermitage Museum: 190000 St Petersburg, Dvortsovaya nab. 34; tel. (812) 110-90-79; e-mail chancery@hermitage.ru; internet www.hermitagemuseum.org; f. 1764 as a court museum; opened to public 1852; richest collection in fmr USSR of the art of pre-historic, ancient Eastern, Graeco-Roman and medieval times; preserves 2.8m. *objets d'art*, including 600,000 drawings and engravings; works by Leonardo da Vinci, Raphael, Titian, Rubens and Rembrandt; collection of coins, weapons and applied art; Dir MIKHAIL PETROVSKY.

State Museum of the History of St Petersburg: 197046 St Petersburg, Petropavlovskaya krepost 3; tel. (812) 498-05-11; fax (812) 498-02-43; internet www.spbmuseum.ru; f. 1957; more than 1.5m. exhibits; shows history and architectural devt of St Petersburg; 7 brs: Peter and Paul Fortress, 'Oreshek' Fortress, Alexander Blok Museum, Museum of Printing, Sergey. Kirov Museum, Monument to Heroic Defenders of Leningrad, Rumyantsev Mansion; Dir ALEXANDER KOLYAKIN.

State Museum of the Political History of Russia: 197046 St Petersburg, ul. Kuybysheva 2–4; tel. (812) 233-70-48; fax (812) 233-73-00; e-mail polithist@cards.lanck.net; internet www.museum.ru/museum/polit_hist; f. 1919; history of Russia in the 19th and 20th centuries with particular reference to political and social development; Dir E. G. ARTEMOV.

State Russian Museum: 191186 St Petersburg, Inzhenernaya ul. 4; tel. (812) 595-42-40; fax (812) 314-41-53; e-mail info@rusmuseum.ru; internet www.rusmuseum.ru; f. 1895; Russian icons, folk and applied arts, painting, sculpture, 10th–21st-century drawings; Dir Dr V. A. GUSEV.

Summer Garden and Museum Palace of Peter the Great: 191186 St Petersburg, Letny Sad; tel. (812) 312-77-15; fax (812) 312-96-66; e-mail m126@mail.museum.ru; f. 1934; 18th-century architecture and sculpture; Dir T. D. KOZLOVA.

Samara

Samara A. M. Gorky Memorial Museum: Samara, ul. S. Razina 126; f. 1946; literary museum devoted to the life and work of Gorky; exhibits in the house and furniture which belonged to him; Chief Curator YELENA KOTELNIKOVA.

Samara Art Museum: 443001 Samara 10, pl. Kuibysheva, Palace of Culture; f. 1897; fine arts museum with 11,000 exhibits; library of 7,000 vols; Dir ANNETA YU. BASS.

Saransk

Mordovian Republic S. D. Erzi Museum of Fine Arts: 430000 Mordoviya Saransk, Kommunisticheskaya ul. 61; tel. (8342) 17-56-38; fax (8342) 17-56-38; e-mail m1451@mail.museum.ru; internet www.museum.ru/m1451; f. 1960; painting, sculpture, prints, decorative arts; library of 10,000 vols; Dir M. N. BARANOVA.

Saratov

Chernyshevsky Memorial Museum: 410002 Saratov, ul. Chernyshevskogo 142; tel. (8452) 26-35-83; fax (8452) 26-33-67; f. 1920; study of N. G. Chernyshevsky's life, times and literary inheritance; library of 14,232 vols; Dir GALINA P. MURENONA; publs *Propagandist Velikovo Naslediya* (Publicist of the Great Inheritance, every 5 years), *N. G. Chernyshevsky Articles, Investigations and Materials* (every 3 years).

Saratov A. N. Radishchev State Art Museum: 410031 Saratov, Pervomaiskaya 75; tel. and fax (8452) 26-12-09; e-mail radmuseumart@radmuseumart.ru; internet www.radmuseumart.ru; f. 1885; library of 34,000 vols; brs: Victor Borisov-Musatov and Pavel Kuznetsov memorial museums (Saratov), Kuzma Petrov-Vodkin memorial museum (Khvalynsk, Saratov region), Balakovo art gallery (Balakovo, Saratov region), A. A. Mylnikov Engels Art Gallery (Engels, Saratov region); Dir T. V. GRODSKOVA.

Sergievsky Posad

Sergiev Posad State History and Art Museum: 141300 Moscow oblast, Sergiev Posad, pr. Krasnoi Armii 144; tel. (09654) 4-13-58; fax (09654) 4-13-58; e-mail sergiev@divo.ru; internet www.musobl.divo.ru; f. 1920; items dealing with the development of Russian art from the 14th century to the present; icons, embroidery, jewellery, porcelain, glass, vestments; secular applied arts, folk arts; library of 17,000 vols; Dir FELIKS KH. MAKOYEV; Scientific Sec. Dr S. V. NIKOLAEVA.

Starki

Far Eastern State Marine Reserve: 690601 Vladivostok, o. Popova, pos. Starki, Olkhovaya 11; tel. (4232) 9-66-82; attached to Russian Acad. of Sciences; Head V. V. GORLACH.

Stavropol

Stavropol Museum of Fine Arts: Stavropol, ul. Dzerzhinskogo 115–119; tel. (8652) 26-54-78; fax (8652) 26-54-78; e-mail izomuz@iskra.stavropol.ru; internet www.museum.ru/m1608; f. 1962; Dir Z. A. BELAYA.

Syktyvkar

National Gallery of the Komi Republic: 167981 Komi Republic, Syktyvkar, ul. Kirova 44; tel. and fax (8212) 42-60-66; e-mail nrgk@online.ru; internet www.komi.com/ngall; f. 1943; Komi, Russian, Soviet and Western European fine art; Dir SVETLANA BELYAEVA.

Taganrog

Chekhov, A. P., Museum: Taganrog, ul. Oktyabrskaya 9; tel. (86344) 6-27-45; rooms arranged as they were when Chekhov lived there in his childhood.

Tambov

Tambov Picture Gallery: 392000 Tambov, Sovetskaya ul. 97; tel. (0752) 2-36-95; f. 1960; 3,500 exhibits; library of 7,000 vols; Dir T. N. SHESTAKOVA.

Tikhvin

Rimsky-Korsakov House-Museum: 187500 Leningrad oblast, Tikhvin, ul Rimskogo Korsakova 12; tel. (81267) 1-15-09; f. 1944 in house where composer was born; main exhibition devoted to composer's childhood; also material on his later life; special collections: original scores, etc.

Tobolsk

Tobolsk Picture Gallery: Tobolsk, Krasnaya pl. 2; 1,800 items.

Tula

Tula Art Museum: 300012 Tula, ul. Engelsa 64; tel. (0872) 35-42-72; fax (0872) 35-42-72; f. 1919; library: specialist art library of 15,000 vols; Dir M. N. KUSINA.

Tula Museum of Regional Studies: Tula, ul. Sovetskaya 68; tel. (0872) 36-22-08; f. 1919; natural sciences, archaeology, literature, architecture, art, history of Tula region; library of 10,806 vols; Dir N. B. NEMOVA.

Tver

Tver Art Gallery: 170640 Tver, ul. Sovetskaya 3; tel. and fax (822) 33-25-61; e-mail art@tversu.ru; internet www.gallery.tversu.ru; f. 1937; library of 33,000 vols; Dir TATYANA S. KUYUKINA.

Tyumen

Tyumen Picture Gallery: Tyumen, ul. Respubliki 29; Dir I. S. TERENTEV.

Uglich

Uglich Historical Museum: Uglich, Kreml 3; tel. (08532) 5-17-57; fax (08532) 5-36-78; e-mail uglmus@yaroslavl.ru; f. 1892; exhibits on the history of the Russian people; Dir VALERY DENISOV.

Vladikavkaz

North-Ossetian K. L. Khetagurov Memorial Museum: Vladikavkaz, Butirina 19; tel. (86722) 3-62-22; f. 1979; collection of materials on Caucasian poetry and literature; Dir E. A. KESAYEVA.

Vladivostok

Botanical Garden FEB RAS: 690024 Vladivostok, ul. Makovskogo 142; tel. (4232) 38-80-41; fax (4232) 38-80-41; e-mail gardens@yandex.ru; internet botsad.ru; f. 1949; attached to Russian Acad. of Sciences; research in botany, plant ecology, plant cultivation, plant resources, investigation of biological diversity of the Russian Far East; environmental education; maintaining exhibits of living plants; landscaping and design; library of 22,000 vols, attached to FEB RAS Central Academical Library, Vladivostok; Dir Dr PAVEL KRESTOV; Deputy Dir Dr OLGA KHRAPKO; publ. *Bulletin of Botanical Garden FEB RAS* (online at botsad.ru/journal).

Oceanarium of the Pacific Research Fisheries Centre: 690950 Vladivostok, Batareinaya ul. 4; tel. (4232) 40-19-65; fax (4232) 30-07-52; e-mail oceanariumtinro@mail.ru; internet www.tinro-center.ru; f. 1991; freshwater aquarium; 2,500 exhibits of flora and fauna of the Pacific Ocean; marine museum, 1,950 exhibits; study of hydrobiology and aquaculture; maintenance of zoological colln; library of 3,242 rare vols; Dir B. K. RAZUVAEV.

Voeikovo

Meteorological Museum of the Central Geophysical Observatory: Leningrad oblast, Vsevolozhskii raion, Voeikovo; Dir A. A. VASILIEV.

Volgograd

Volgograd State Museum and Panorama of the Battle of Stalingrad: 400053 Volgograd, ul. Marshal Chuykov 47; tel. (8442) 34-72-72; fax (8442) 34-72-41; e-mail panorama@volgadmin.ru; internet www.volgadmin.ru/panorama; f. 1937; exhibits feature the defence of the city during the Civil War (1918–20) and the Battle of Stalingrad (1942–43); library of 14,450 vols; Dir B. G. USIK.

Vologda

Vologda Historical, Architectural and Artistic Museum Reserve: 160035 Vologda, Orlov 15; tel. (8172) 72-22-83; f. 1885; history, archaeology, ethnography, nature, literature, handicrafts, folk art, decorative and applied art, old Russian painting, modern art of the Vologda region, architecture; library of 40,000 vols; Dir SUVOROV ALEXANDR VALERYEVICH; publ. catalogues.

Vologda Picture Gallery: Vologda, Kremlevskaya pl.; 6,500 exhibits; Dir S. G. IVENSKII.

Voronezh

Voronezh Art Museum: Voronezh, pr. Revolyutsii 18; tel. (0732) 55-28-43; f. 1933; 22,065 exhibits; library of 18,800 vols; Dir VLADIMIR Y. USTINOV.

Yakutsk

Yakutsk Museum of Fine Arts: 677000 Yakutsk, ul. Khabarova 27; tel. (4112) 2-77-98; f. 1928; folk art, Western European, Russian and Soviet art of 17th to 20th centuries; Dir N. M. VASILEVA.

Yaroslavl

Yaroslavl Historical and Architectural Museum: 150000 Yaroslavl, pl. Bogoyavlenskaya 25; tel. (0852) 30-56-30; fax (0852) 30-57-55; e-mail mp@yarmp.yar.ru; internet www.yarmp.yar.ru; f. 1865; over 370,000 exhibits on the history of the Russian people from ancient times to the present; library of 42,000 vols; Dir YELENA A. ANKUDINOVA; publ. *Kraevedcheskiye Zapiski* (irregular).

Yasnaya Polyana

Leo Tolstoy Museum and Estate: 301214 Tula Region, Shchekino Dist., Yasnaya Polyana; tel. (4872) 38-67-10; fax (4872) 38-67-10; e-mail yaspol@tula.net; internet yasnayapolyana.ru; f. 1921; memorial house and estate belonging to L. N. Tolstoy; over 33,000 original objects in the Tolstoy House; literary museum devoted to his life and work; estate with park and forest; library of 22,000 vols in Tolstoy's personal library (in the Tolstoy House); c. 60,000 vols in museum library; Dir VLADIMIR I. TOLSTOY; publ. *Yasnaya Polyana* (Writers' Meetings, 1 a year).

Universities

AGRICULTURAL UNIVERSITIES

ALTAI STATE AGRARIAN UNIVERSITY

656099 Barnaul, Krasnoarmeisky pr. 98
Telephone and fax (3852) 62-83-96
E-mail: rector@asau.ru
Internet: www.asau.ru

Founded 1943 as Altai Agricultural Institute, present name and status 1991

Depts: accounting, agronomy, animal production, economics, irrigation and land reclamation, management, mechanization, veterinary, zoology

Rector: Prof. SERGEI V. ZOLOTAREV

Library of 360,430 vols
Number of teachers: 508
Number of students: 10,010

BASHKIR STATE AGRARIAN UNIVERSITY

450001 Ufa, 50 let Oktyabrya ul. 34
Telephone: (3472) 28-08-98
Fax: (3472) 28-08-98
E-mail: bgau@ufanet.ru
Internet: www.bsau.ru

Rector: Prof. VLADIMIR D. NEDOREZKOV

Number of teachers: 685

CHELYABINSK STATE AGRO-ENGINEERING UNIVERSITY

454080 Chelyabinsk, Lenina Ave 75
Telephone: (3512) 66-65-30
Fax: (3512) 66-65-35
E-mail: kbv@agroun.urc.ac.ru
Internet: www.csaa.ru

Founded 1930

Training of engineers, economists, agronomists, teachers and agroecologists for state and private farms and businesses; bachelors and masters for agro-engineering

Rector: YURY B. CHETYRKIN

Library of 550,000 vols
Number of teachers: 350
Number of students: 5,600

Publications: *Trudy Chimeskh*, *Vestnik Akademii*, *Vestnik Universiteta*.

DON STATE AGRARIAN UNIVERSITY

346493 Rostov oblast, Oktyabrsky r-n, pos. Persianovsky
Telephone and fax (86360) 35-150
E-mail: dgau-web@mail.ru
Internet: www.dongau.ru

Founded 1840
State control
Language of instruction: Russian

Rector: Prof. ANATOLY I. BARANIKOV

Library of 540,000 vols
Number of teachers: 414
Number of students: 3,152

Fields of study: agronomy, animal husbandry, biotechnology, economy, processing of agricultural products, veterinary science.

FAR EAST STATE AGRARIAN UNIVERSITY

675005 Blagoveshchensk, Politekhnicheskaya ul. 86

Telephone: (4162) 42-32-06
Fax: (4162) 42-31-79
E-mail: dgu@inbox.ru

Founded 1950

Institutes of agronomy, mechanization, finance and economics, civil engineering, technology, veterinary science and animal husbandry, electrification and the automation of agriculture, forestry, humanities; research institutes of stockbreeding, selection and technology in plant breeding, construction, systems of machinery, technology of the processing of agricultural production

Rector: BORIS I. KASHPURA

Library of 398,000 vols
Number of teachers: 570
Number of students: 8,000

Publications: *Amur Researcher* (2 a year), *Collection of Scientific Publications* (separate series published by each of 14 institutes, each 1 or 2 a year), *Science to Production* (conference report, 1 a year), *Students' Research to Production* (1 a year).

GORSKY STATE AGRICULTURAL UNIVERSITY

362040 Vladikavkaz, ul. Kirova 37

Telephone: (8672) 3-23-04
Fax: (8672) 53-90-04

Library of 208,000 vols

Rector: BORIS B. BASAEV

Number of teachers: 412
Number of students: 6,500

Fields of study: agronomy, animal husbandry, mechanization, economics and management, accounting.

KRASNOYARSK STATE AGRARIAN UNIVERSITY

660049 Krasnoyarsk, pr. Mira 88

Telephone: (3912) 27-36-09
Fax: (3912) 27-03-86
E-mail: info@kgau.ru
Internet: www.kgau.ru

Founded 1953
Language of instruction: Russian
Academic year: September to June

Rector: Prof. Dr NIKOLAY V. TSUGLENOK

Library of 360,442 vols
Number of teachers: 636
Number of students: 7,020

DEANS

Institute of Agro-Business of Food and Processing Industry: Prof. Dr NADEZHDA VELICHKO
Institute of Agroecological Management: Prof. Dr VLADIMIR IVCHENKO
Institute of Applied Biotechnology And Veterinary Medicine: Prof. Dr TAMARA LEFLER
Institute of Economy and Finance of Agro-Industrial Complex: Doc. MARIYA OZEROVA
Institute of Engineering Systems Management: NIKITA DEMSKY
Institute of Int. Management And Business: Doc. NATALYA ANTONOVA
Institute of Land Utilization, Land-Survey and Nature Management: Prof. Dr NIKOLAI CHEPELEV
Institute of Legal Examination and Law: Doc. NATALYA TSUGLENOK
Institute of Management and Agro-Business: Doc. ZINAIDA SHAPOROVA
Institute of Power Engineering and Energy Resource Management of Agro-Industrial Complex: Doc. SERGEY SHAKHMATOV
Law institute: Doc. ALEXANDRA ZENKINA

KUBAN STATE AGRARIAN UNIVERSITY

350044 Krasnodar, ul. Kalinina 13

Telephone: (8612) 56-49-42
Fax: (8612) 50-29-35
E-mail: inform@kubagro.ru
Internet: www.kubagro.ru

Founded 1922

Library of 635,000 vols
Number of teachers: 1,070
Number of students: 17,496

Rector: Dr IVAN T. TRUBILIN

Fields of study: agrochemistry and soil science, agronomy, tropical and sub-tropical agriculture, veterinary, horticulture and viticulture, animal husbandry, mechanization, plant protection, electrification, construction, law, economics and management, accountancy.

MICHURINSK STATE AGRARIAN UNIVERSITY

393760 Tambov oblast, Michurinsk Internationalnaya 101

Telephone and fax (47545) 5-26-35
E-mail: info@mgau.ru
Internet: www.mgau.ru

Founded 1931
Language of instruction: Russian

Rector: ALEXANDR V. NIKITIN

Library of 300,000 vols
Number of teachers: 395
Number of students: 7,000

Fields of study: fruit and vegetable production, viticulture, agronomy, selection and genetics of crops, storing and processing of agricultural produce, agroecology, commodity research, horticulture, economics and management of agricultural enterprises, livestock production, commerce, accounting and auditing, banking and finance, catering technologies, municipal management, landscape design

Publication: *Herald of Michurinsk State Agrarian University*.

MOSCOW STATE AGRO-ENGINEERING UNIVERSITY, V. P. GORYACHKIN

127540 Moscow, ul. Timiryazevskaya 58

Telephone: (495) 976-36-40
Fax: (495) 976-78-74
E-mail: rkt@mail.msau.ru
Internet: www.msau.ru

Founded 1930

Faculties of agricultural mechanization, agricultural technical services, engineering, economics, farm electrification

Rector: MIKHAIL N. EROKHIN

Library: 1m. vols
Number of teachers: 400
Number of students: 5,500

MOSCOW STATE UNIVERSITY OF LAND MANAGEMENT

105064 Moscow, ul. Kazakova 15

Telephone: (495) 261-31-46
Internet: www.guz.ru

Founded 1779

Faculties of architecture, correspondence, further training, land management, land tenure, law, municipal land tenure, retraining

Rector: Prof. SERGEI N. VOLKOV

Library of 220,000 vols

Publications: *Land Boundary Register* (1 a year), *Rural Architecture* (1 a year).

NOVOSIBIRSK STATE AGRARIAN UNIVERSITY

630039 Novosibirsk, ul. Dobrolyubova 160

Telephone: (3832) 67-38-11
Fax: (3832) 67-39-22
E-mail: public@nsau.edu.ru
Internet: www.nsau.edu.ru

Rector: Prof. ANATOLY F. KONDRATOV

Library of 252,000 vols
Number of teachers: 437
Number of students: 9,400

Fields of study: agronomy, plant protection, mechanization, economics and management, accounting.

OMSK STATE AGRARIAN UNIVERSITY

644008 Omsk, Institutskaya pl. 2

Telephone: (3812) 65-17-72
Fax: (3812) 65-10-72
E-mail: adm@omgau.ru
Internet: www.omgau.ru

Founded 1918

Faculties of agricultural engineering, agrochemistry, agronomy, dairy production technology, mathematics and social studies, soil science and environment, water resource engineering, humanities; institute of economics and finance, institute of land use planning and tenure, institute of veterinary medicine institute of part-time and continued education

Rector: NIKOLAI M. KOLYCHEV

Library of 622,000 vols
Number of teachers: 979
Number of students: 10,357

Publications: *Kirovets* (12 a year), *Vestnik OmGAU* (4 a year).

OREL STATE AGRARIAN UNIVERSITY

302019 Orel, ul. Generala Rodina 69

Telephone: (0862) 29-40-50
Fax: (0862) 29-40-79
E-mail: pnv@orel.ru
Internet: www.orelsau.ru

Founded 1975 as Orel Agricultural Institute; present name and status 1999

Rector: Prof. NIKOLAI V. PARAKHIN.

ORENBURG STATE AGRARIAN UNIVERSITY

460014 Orenburg, ul. Leninskaya 59

Telephone and fax (3532) 77-52-30
E-mail: orensau@mail.ru
Internet: www.orensau.ru

Founded 1930

Faculties of agronomy, biotechnology, economics and law, forestry, information technology, mechanization of agriculture, veterinary medicine

Rector: VLADIMIR V. KARAKULEV

Library of 842,127 vols
Number of teachers: 601
Number of students: 8,210

Publication: *Works*.

ST PETERSBURG STATE AGRARIAN UNIVERSITY

189620 St Petersburg, Pushkin, Peterburgskoe shosse 2

Telephone: (812) 470-04-22

Fax: (812) 465-05-05

Founded 1904

Br. in Polessk; depts of agroecology and soil science, agronomy, animal husbandry, economics, engineering, farm electrification, law, plant protection, vegetable growing

Rector: VLADIMIR S. SHKRABAK

Library of 782,700 vols

Number of teachers: 473

Number of students: 7,865

Publication: *Collection of Scientific Research Works* (8 a year).

SARATOV STATE AGRARIAN UNIVERSITY, N. I. VAVILOV

410034 Saratov, Teatralnaya pl. 1

Telephone: (8452) 26-32-92

Fax: (8452) 72-30-42

E-mail: rector@ssau.saratov.ru

Internet: www.ssau.saratov.ru

Founded 1997

Fields of study: agricultural electrification and automation, agricultural mechanization, agronomy, amelioration and village arrangement, biotechnology, economics, forestry, mechanization of farm production processing, plant protection, technical service, technology, veterinary

Rector: NIKOLAI I. KUZNETSOV

Library of 1,500,000 vols

Number of teachers: 1,189

Number of students: 19,036

STAVROPOL STATE AGRARIAN UNIVERSITY

355017 Stavropol, Zootekhnichesky per. 12

Telephone: (8652) 35-22-82

Fax: (8652) 34-58-70

E-mail: rector@stgau.ru

Internet: www.stgau.ru

Founded 1930

Languages of instruction: English, Russian

Academic year: September to June

Rector: Prof. VLADIMIR IV. TRUKHACHEV

Vice-Rector for Education: SVETLANA IV. TARASOVA

Library: 3m. vols

Number of teachers: 1,500

Number of students: 17,500

Publication: *Collection of Scientific Works* (1 a year)

DEANS

Accounting and Audit: Prof. YURY SKLYAROV

Agricultural Mechanization: Dr VICTOR BUDKOV

Agronomy and Plant Protection: Prof. ALEXANDER ESAULKO

Economics: Prof. OLGA KUSAKINA

Electrical Engineering: Dr IVAN ATANOV

Finance and Banking: Dr NATALIA KULISH

Technological Management: Prof. MARINA SELIONOVA

Veterinarian Medicine: Dr VALERY BELYAEV

VORONEZH STATE AGRARIAN UNIVERSITY, K. D. GLINKA

394087 Voronezh, ul. Michurina 1

Telephone: (0732) 52-86-31

Fax: (0732) 52-86-31

E-mail: an@vsau.ru

Internet: www.vsau.ru

Founded 1913

Rector: VLADIMIR E. SHEVCHENKO

Library of 870,000 vols

Number of teachers: 528

Number of students: 8,663

Publication: *Zapiski* (Notes)

Fields of study: agribusiness, agricultural economics, agricultural engineering, agrochemistry and soil science, agronomy, animal sciences, food-processing technology, land surveying, veterinary science.

HUMANITIES AND SCIENCES UNIVERSITIES

ADYGHE STATE UNIVERSITY

352700 Republic of Adygheya, Maykop, ul. Universitetskaya 208

Telephone: (87722) 7-02-73

Fax: (87722) 7-02-73

E-mail: adsu@adygnet.ru

Internet: www.adygnet.ru

State control

Founded 1941; present name and status 1993

Rector: Prof. RASHID D. KHUNAGOV

Library of 529,000 vols

Number of teachers: 550

Number of students: 7,547

Brs in Apsheronsk, Belorechensk, Eisk, Novokubansk, Sochi and Koshekhabl.

DEANS

Faculty of Economics: RAMAZAN M. TESHEV

Faculty of Foreign Languages: SUSANNA K. BEDANOKOVA

Faculty of Law: AZAMAT M. SHADZHE

Faculty of Pedagogy: FATIMA P. KHAKNOVA

Faculty of Philology: UCHUZHUK M. PANESH

DIRECTORS

Institute of Arts: NATALYA L. CHEPNIYAN

Institute of Physical Culture and Judo: YAKUB K. KOBLEV

ALTAI STATE UNIVERSITY

656049 Altai Krai, Barnaul, pr. Lenina 61

Telephone: (3852) 66-75-84

Fax: (3852) 66-76-26

E-mail: rector@dcn-asu.ru

Internet: www.asu.ru

Founded 1973

State control

Language of instruction: Russian

Academic year: September to June

Rector: YURI KIRUSHIN

Vice-Rector for Academic Affairs: GENNADY LAVRENTIEV

Vice-Rector for Finance: VITALY MISHCHENKO

Vice-Rector for Int. Affairs: VALERY NEVINSKY

Vice-Rector for Science: NIKOLAI MIKHAILOV

Librarian: GALINA TRUSHNIKOVA

Library: 1m. vols, 1,400 periodicals; 6 museums; art gallery

Number of teachers: 750

Number of students: 18,000

Publications: *Chemistry of Vegetative Raw Materials* (online, 4 a year), *Proceedings* (4 a year), *Turchaninovia* (online, 4 a year)

DEANS

Faculty of Arts: T. STEPANSKAYA

Faculty of Biology: G. SOKOLOVA

Faculty of Chemistry: N. BAZARNOVA

Faculty of Distance Learning: D. RUDER

Faculty of Economics: O. MAMCHENKO

Faculty of Geography: V. REVYAKIN

Faculty of History: V. VLADIMIROV

Faculty of Journalism: V. MANSUROVA

Faculty of Law: V. MUZYUKIN

Faculty of Mathematics: S. KUZIKOV

Faculty of Pedagogical Education: G. SPITSKAYA

Faculty of Philology: N. KUZNETSOVA

Faculty of Physics: A. SHATOKHIN

Faculty of Political Science: E. PRITCHINA

Faculty of Preliminary Training: N. YAKOVLEVA

Faculty of Psychology and Philosophy: L. DEMINA

Faculty of Sociology: S. GRIGORIEV

PROFESSORS

ALGAZIN, G., Mathematical Methods in Sociology
BARUSHNIKOV, G., Geography
BAZARNOVA, N., Chemistry
BELYAEV, V., Marketing
BEZNOSUK, S., General Physics
BOBROV, M., Sociology
BUDKIN, A., Algebra and Mathematical Logic
BUKATY, V., General Physics
BURDASOV, V., Biology
CHERNUSHOV, Y., Ancient History
CHERVYAKOV, V., Economic Geography
CHUVAKIN, A., Philology
DEMCHIK, E., Sociology
DEMINA, L., Psychology and Philosophy
ELCHANINOV, V., Philosophy
FEDYUKIN, V., Philosophy
GAVLO, V., Criminology
GLUSHANIN, E., History
GOLEV, N., Russian Language
GRIGORYEV, S., Sociology
GUBAR, A., Economics
GUSLYAKOVA, L., Social Work
IVANOV, A., Philosophy
IVOLGIN, A., Political Science
KHALINA, N., Linguistics
KIRUSHIN, Y., Archaeology
KISELEV, V., Human and Animal Physiology
KOMAROV, S., Radio Physics
KOZLOVA, S., Philology
KUPRIYANOV, A., Biology
LAGUTIN, A., Theoretical Physics
LAVRENTIEV, G., Education
MALOLETKO, A., Nature Management
MALTSEV, Y., Algebra and Mathematical Logic
MAMCHENKO, O., Information Systems
MEDVEDEV, N., Algebra and Mathematical Logic
MELNIKOV, A., Philosophy
MELNIKOVA, L., Regional Economics
MIRONOV, V., Radiophysics
MISCHENKO, V., Regional Economics
MOISEEV, V., Oriental History
NEVINSKY, V., Constitutional Law
NOVOZHENOV, ., Constitutional Law
OSKORBIN, N., Cybernetics and Applied Mathematics
PETROV, B., Analytical Chemistry
POLYAKOV, V., Applied Physics
RASTOV, Y., Empiric Sociology
RAZGON, V., History
REVYAKIN, V., Geography
REVYAKINA, N., Geography
ROGOVSKY, E., Management
SAGALAKOV, A., Experimental Physics
SEMILET, T., Psychology
SENKO, Y., Education
SHAIDUK, A., General Physics
SHELEPOVA, L., Philology
SKUBNEVSKY, V., History
STARTSEV, O., Applied Physics
STEPANSKAYA, T., Art
TROTSKOVSKY, A., Theory of Economics
TRUKHINA, V., Art
TSUB, S., History
USHAKOVA, E., Philosophy
VASILYEV, V., Biochemistry
YELCHANINOV, V., Philosophy
ZEMLYUKOV, S., Criminal Law

AMUR STATE UNIVERSITY

675027 Amur Region, Blagoveshchensk, Ignatevskoye shosse 21
Telephone: (4162) 39-46-86
Fax: (4162) 39-45-25
E-mail: master@amursu.ru
Internet: www.amursu.ru

Founded 1975
State control
Language of instruction: Russian
Academic year: September to July

Pres.: ELENA S. ASTAPOVA
Vice-Pres.: VICTOR V. PROKAZIN
Pro-Rectors: LUDMILA N. GERASIMOVA, ANDREW P. ZABEAKO
Chief Admin. Officer: TATYANA V. ASTAFUROVA
Librarian: LUDMILA A. PROKAZINA

Library of 232,000 vols
Number of teachers: 600
Number of students: 8,500

Publication: *Bulletin* (3 a year)

DEANS

Applied Arts: ALEXANDER M. MEDVEDEV
Economics: NATALIA A. BABKINA
Engineering and Physics: VERA F. ULYANYCHEVA
International Relations: SVETLANA S. KOSIKHINA
Law: SERGEY V. CHERDAKOV
Mathematics and Computer Science: SVETLANA G. SAMOKHVALOVA
Philology: IRINA I. LEIFA
Power Engineering: NATALIA V. SAVINA
Social Sciences: NELLE K. SCHEPKINA

BASHKIR STATE UNIVERSITY

450074 Bashkortostan, Ufa, Z. Validie 32
Telephone: (3472) 72-63-70
Fax: (3472) 73-66-80
E-mail: interdpt@bsu.bashedu.ru
Internet: www.bsunet.ru

Founded 1909
State Control
Language of instruction: Russian
Academic year: September to June

Rector: Prof. AHAT G. MUSTAFIN
Vice-Rector for Education: Prof. YAUDAT T. SULTANAEV
Vice-Rector for Academic Affairs: Prof. NIKOLAI D. MOROZKIN
Vice Rector for Science: Prof. RIFKAT TALIPOV
Vice-Rector for Int. Cooperation: ALEXANDR I. SHABRIN
Univ. Library Dir: EVGENIYA GELVANOVSKAYA

Library of 2,000,000 vols
Number of teachers: 1,325
Number of students: 22,300

DEANS

Faculty of Biology: Prof. RINAT I. IBRAHIMOV
Faculty of Chemistry: Prof. RINAT M. AHMETHANOV
Faculty of Economics: Prof. FANIYA S. ISKHAKOVA
Faculty of Geography: Prof. INBER M. YAPPAROV,
Faculty of History: Prof. MARAT M. KULSHARIPOV
Faculty of Mathematics: Prof. TAGIR G. AMALGILDIN
Faculty of Philology: Prof. ALEXANDER A. FEDOROV
Faculty of Philosophy and Sociology: Prof. DAMIR A NURIEV
Faculty of Physics: Prof. ROBERT A. YAKSHIBAEV
Faculty of Romance and Germanic Philology: Prof. RAKHIM Z. MURYASSOV

BELGOROD STATE UNIVERSITY

308015 Belgorod, ul. Pobedy 30
Telephone: (0722) 30-12-11
Fax: (0722) 30-10-12
E-mail: info@bsu.edu.ru
Internet: www.bsu.edu.ru
State control

Founded 1876 as Belgorod Teaching Institute; 1939–1957 as Belgorod State Teaching Institute; 1957–1994 as Belgorod State Pedagogical Institute; as Belgorod State Pedagogical Univ. 1994–1996; present name and status 1996

Rector: Prof. LEONID YA. DYATCHENKO
First Pro-Rector for Admin., Finance and Security: MIKHAIL V. KOSTROV
First Pro-Rector and Pro-Rector for Science: TATYANA M. DAVYDENKO
Pro-Rector for Academic Affairs: VIKTOR N. TKACHEV
Pro-Rector for Distance and Evening Education: VLADIMIR A. SHAPOVALOV
Chief Accountant: NATALYA P. KOZYREVA

Brs in Alekseevka and Stary Oskol, both f. 1999.

Library of 987,987 vols
Number of teachers: 717
Number of students: 13,015

DEANS

Faculty of Biology and Chemistry: GENNADY M. FOFANOV
Faculty of Computer Science and Telecommunications: EVGENY G. ZHILYAKOV
Faculty of Economics: VLADIMIR I. BOLTENKOV
Faculty of Geology and Geography: ALEXANDER N. PETIN
Faculty of History: ELENA YU. PROKOFIEVA
Faculty of Law: EVGENY E. TONKOV
Faculty of Management and Business: VIKTORIA B. TARABAEVA
Faculty of Medicine: YURI I. AFANASEV
Faculty of Pedagogy: NIKOLAI V. PODDUBNY
Faculty of Philology: SVETLANA P. GRINEVA
Faculty of Physical Culture: VASILY V. SOKOREV
Faculty of Physics and Mathematics: OLEG M. PENKIN
Faculty of Psychology: NADEZHDA I. ISAEVA
Faculty of Romance and Germanic Philology: OLGA N. PROKHOROVA
Faculty of Socio-Theology: SERGEI A. KOLESNIKOV
International Faculty: MIKHAIL A. TRUBITSYN

BELGOROD UNIVERSITY OF CONSUMER CO-OPERATIVES

308023 Belgorod, ul. Sadovaya 116A
Telephone: (0722) 6-08-48
Fax: (0722) 6-49-65
E-mail: bupk@intbel.ru
Internet: www.bupk.ru

Faculties of economics, trade management; br. in Stavropol

Rector: VITALY I. TEPLOV

Number of teachers: 326
Number of students: 8,030

BRATSK STATE UNIVERSITY

665709 Bratsk, Makarenko ul. 40
Telephone: (3953) 33-20-08
Fax: (3953) 33-20-08
E-mail: rector@brstu.ru
Internet: www.brstu.ru

Founded 1980 as Bratsk Industrial Institute; 1994–1999 as Bratsk State Technical Univ.; present name and status 2004

Faculties of construction, distance learning, economics, forestry engineering, humanities, international education, mechanics, power

Rector: Prof. SERGEI V. BELOKOBYLSKY

Library of 448,851 vols
Number of teachers: 337
Number of students: 9,823

BRYANSK STATE UNIVERSITY

241036 Bryansk, Bezhitskaya ul. 14
Telephone: (083) 246-65-38
Fax: (083) 246-63-53
Internet: www.bgunet.com
State control

Founded 1974

Rector: Prof. ANDREI V. ANTYUKHOV
Pro-Rector of Academic Affairs: Prof. VLADIMIR V. SHLYK

Number of teachers: 515
Number of students: 15,712

BURYAT STATE UNIVERSITY

670000 Ulan-Ude, ul. Smolina 24A
Telephone: (3012) 21-15-80
Fax: (3012) 21-05-88
E-mail: univer@bsu.ru
Internet: www.bsu.ru

Founded 1995 following the merger of State Teachers-Training Institute and the Ulan-Ude Branch of Novosibirsk State Univ.
Public control
Languages of instruction: Buryat, Russian
Academic year: August to June

Rector: Prof. STEPAN V. KALMYKOV
Pro-Rector for Research: Prof. Dr ALEXANDER S. BULDAEV
Pro-Rector for Academic Affairs: IRINA S. BATUEVA
Pro-Rector for Social Policy and Extra-Curricular Activities: Assoc. Prof. GALINA I. ROGALEVA
Pro-Rector for Admin.: Assoc. Prof. ALEXANDER G. SHARGAEV
Academic Council's Sec.: Asoc. Prof. TATIANA V. PALIKOVA

Library of 1,150,000 vols
Number of teachers: 612
Number of students: 10,000

DEANS

Faculty of Biology and Geography: ERDENI N. ELAEV
Faculty of Chemistry: GALINA N. BATOROVA
Faculty of Eastern Studies: EDUARD K. SHOHOEV
Faculty of Economics and Management: MARIYA V. BADMAEVA
Faculty of Foreign Languages: NINA A. BOKHACH
Faculty of History: ANNA A. BURKINA
Faculty of Law: JAMILYA K. CHIMITOVA
Faculty of Medicine: VLADIMIR E. KHITRIKHEEV
Faculty of Physics and Technology: VALENTINA M. KHALTANOVA
Faculty of Socio-Psychology: TATIYANA S. BAZAROVA
Faculty of Philology: VERA V. BASHKEEVA
Faculty of Physical Culture, Sport and Tourism: GENNADY P. PETRENKO
Institute of Mathematics and Computer Science: VLADIMIR V. KIBIREV
National Institute: BATOR B. ZANDARAEV
Pedagogical Institute: NINA Z. DAGBAEVA

CHELYABINSK STATE UNIVERSITY

454021 Chelyabinsk, ul. Bratev Kashirinykh 129
Telephone: (3512) 42-05-31
Fax: (3512) 42-09-25
E-mail: postmaster@csu.ru
Internet: www.csu.ru

Founded 1976

Academic year: September to July
Rector: Prof. V. D. BATUKHTIN
Registrar: A. YU. SHATIN
Librarian: L. M. KISELYOVA
Number of teachers: 1,760 (1,410 full-time, 350 part-time)
Number of students: 14,369 (7,800 full-time, 6,569 correspondence)
Publication: *Vestnik*

DEANS

Faculty of Access to Higher Education: E. A. MARTYNOVA
Faculty of Biology: A. L. BURMISTROVA
Faculty of Chemistry: A. V. BELIK
Faculty of Continuing Education: V. A. BURMISTROV
Faculty of Ecology: S. G. AGEEV
Faculty of Economics: T. A. VERESHCHAGINA
Faculty of Eurasia and the East: G. V. SACHKO
Faculty of History: G. A. GONCHAROV
Faculty of Journalism: B. N. KIRSHIN
Faculty of Law: V. A. LEBEDEV
Faculty of Linguistics and Translation: L. A. NEFYODOVA
Faculty of Management: L. A. KUZNETSOVA
Faculty of Mathematics: O. N. DEMENTIEV
Faculty of Original Professions: T. M. KUYASHEVA
Faculty of Philology: I. YU. KARTASHOVA
Faculty of Physics: V. D. BUCHELNIKOV
Institute of Psychology and Pedagogics: S. A. REPIN

PROFESSORS

ABRAMOVSKY, A. P., History
AKHMEDZIANOV, M. G., Physical Education
ALEEV, Physics and Mathematics
ALEVRAS, N. N., History
AZNACHEEVA, E. N., Linguistics
BALYKIN, V. P., Chemistry
BATUKHTIN, V. D., Mathematical Theory of Optimization and Control
BELANKOV, Physics and Mathematics
BELIK, A. V., Chemistry
BENT, M. I., Philology
BLUDENOV, A. F., Economics
BUCHELNIKOV, V. D., Physics and Mathematics
BURMISTROV, V. A., Physics and Mathematics
BURMISTROVA, A. L., Biology
BYCHKOV, I. V., Physics and Mathematics
CHERNETSOV, P. I., Education
DARANKOV, A. Y., Economics
DEMENTIEV, O. N., Physics and Mathematics
DUDOROV, A. Y., Physics and Mathematics
GALIULINA, G. S., History
GOLIKOV, A. A., Economics
GOLOVANOV, V. I., Technology
GORSHKOV, A. V., Economics
GRUDZINSKY, V. V., History
ILYIN, A. M., Physics and Mathematics
JEYT, Physics and Mathematics
KOLOSOVA, O. S., Medicine
KORNEV, N. I., Economics
LAPPA, A. V., Physics and Mathematics
LEBEDEV, V. A., Law
LEZHNEVA, Pedagogics
MARTYNOVA, Pedagogics
MATUSHKIN, S. I., Didactics
MATVEEV, S. V., Topology
MIKHNUKEVICH, V. A., Philology
NARSKY, I. V., History
NEFYODOVA, L. A., Linguistics
NEVELEV, A. B., Philosophy
PAVLENKO, V. N., Physics and Mathematics
PISCHCLIULIN, Pedagogics
PITINA, S. A., Linguistics
PLOKHIKH, N. A., Geology and Mineralogy
POPOV, V. I., Law
POPOVA, N. B., Philology
PRIVEZENTSEV, A. P., Physics and Mathematics
RATANOV, N. E., Physics and Mathematics
REPIN, S. A., Didactics
ROZKOV, A. V., Physics and Mathematics
SABITOV, P. A., Law
SEDOV, V. V., Political Economy
SHATIN, A. YU., Economics
SHISHMARENKOVA, G. YA., Education
SHKATOVA, L. A., Russian Language
SINYAVSKY, V. A., Geology and Mineralogy
SMIRNOV, S. S., History
SOLOVIEV, A. A., Physics and Mathematics
SUKHANOV, K. N., Philosophy
SUROV, Physics and Mathematics
SVIRIDUK, G. A., Physics and Mathematics
TANANA, V. P., Mathematics
TYUMENTSEV, V. A., Physics and Mathematics
UCHOBOTOV, V. I., Physics
YALOVETS, A. P., Physics
YARTSEV, V. M., Physics and Mathematics
ZAGIDULLINA, M. V., Linguistics

CHECHEN STATE UNIVERSITY

Chechnya, 364907 Groznyi, ul. Sheripova 32
Telephone: (87322) 23-40-89
Founded 1972
Faculties of chemistry and biology, economics, geography, history, mathematics, philology, physics, romance and Germanic philology
Rector: ADNAN D. KHAMZAYEV
Number of teachers: 620
Number of students: 8,000

CHEREPOVETS STATE UNIVERSITY

162600 Cherepovets, ul. Lunacharskogo 5
Telephone: (8202) 55-65-97
Fax: (8202) 55-70-49
E-mail: chsu@chsu.ru
Internet: www.chsu.ru
Founded 1919
Rector: Prof. VLADIMIR S. GRYZLOV
First Pro-Rector: Prof. EVGENY V. ERSHOV
Library of 437,168 vols.

CHITA STATE UNIVERSITY

672039 Chita, Aleksandro-Zavodskaya ul. 30
Telephone and fax (3022) 41-64-44
E-mail: root@chitgu.ru
Internet: www.chitgu.ru
Founded 1966 as a br. of Irkutsk State Polytechnic Institute
State control
Languages of instruction: Russian, English, French, Chinese
Academic year: September to June (two semesters)
Rector: Prof. YURI N. REZNIK
Vice-Rector: Prof. SERGEY A. IVANOV
Librarian: NINA V. OKUNEVA
Library of 828,057 vols
Number of teachers: 845
Number of students: 12,377
Publications: *ChSU Journal* (Scientific, 6 a year), *Science: XX1 Century* (Scientific, 1 a year), *Social Anthropology of North-East Asia* (SCANEA journal, Scientific, 4 a year)

DEANS

Automobile Transportation: SERGEI P. OZORNIN
Civil Engineering: A.V. KUYDIN
Computer Science and Economics: TATYANA A. PLYUSNINA
Ecology: VLADIMIR V. ZVYAGINTSEV
Economics: S. V. VASILIEVA
Geology: SERGEI V. SMOLICH
Law: V. V. BESSONOVA
International Law: D. S. LUKONIN
Management: N. P. KALASHNIKOVA
Mining: LUDMILA G. NIKITINA
Power Technology: YURI V. ERMOLAEV
Professional Development: M. G. MELKOYAN
Social Policy and Cultural Studies: E. E. KOVALENOK
Social Systems and Regional Forecasting: A. A. RUSANOVA
Technology: VITALY V. GRUSHEV

PROFESSORS

ABAKUMOV, Y., Mathematics
ABRAMOV, V., Philosophy
ABRAMOVA, N., Oriental Studies
BALANDIN, O., Constructing Engineering
BEIDINA, T., Political Studies
BERNUKEVICH, T., Social Philosophy
BORODIN, V., Law
BUKIN, A., Anthropology
CHERKASOV, V., Mining
ERDYNEEVA, K., Psychology
FATIANOV, A., Mining Engineering
FOMINA, M., Philosophy
GARMAEV, Y., Law
GERASIMOV, V., Geotechnology
GLAZYRINA, I., Economy
IMETINOV, N., Civil Engineering
IVANOV, S., Power Engineering
KARASEV, K., Chemistry
KOGAN, E., Mathematics
KONDRATIEV, V., Geocryology
KOSTROMIN, M., Mining Engineering
KUZNETSOV, O., Ethnography
LETUNOV, V., Chemistry
LIZUNKIN, V., Geotechnology
LUBIMOVA, L., Linguistic
MAKAROV, A., Law
MALYSHEV, E., Economy
MYAZIN, V., Mining Engineering
OVESHNIKOV, Y., Geoecology
OVSEYCHUK, V., Geotechnology
POLUTOVA, M., Pedagogy
REZNIK, Y., Geotechnology
ROMANOVA, N., Sociology
SEKISOV, G., Geotechnology
SHVETSOV, M., Pedagogy
SUVOROV, I., Engineering
SVININ, V., Engineering
TEREKHOVA, T., Pedagogy
TRUBACHEV, A., Mining Engineering
VASILIEVA, K., Philosophy
VORONOV, E., Geotechnology
ZASLONOVSKY, V., Hydrology

CHUVASH STATE UNIVERSITY

428015 Chuvash Autonomous Republic, Cheboksary, Moskovsky pr. 15
Telephone: (8352) 24-03-79
Fax: (8352) 42-80-90
E-mail: office@chuvsu.ru
Internet: www.chuvsu.ru
Founded 1967
State control
Languages of instruction: Chuvash, Russian
Academic year: September to July
Rector: Prof. Dr LEV P. KURAKOV
First Vice-Rector: NIKOLAI F. GRIGORIEV
Vice-Rector for Academic Affairs: VSEVOLOD G. AGAKOV
Librarian: NINA D. NIKITINA
Library: see Libraries and Archives
Number of teachers: 1,270
Number of students: 19,391
Publications: *Chuvash segodny*, *Ulyanovets* (52 a year)

DEANS

Faculty of Arts: M. N. YACLASHKYN
Faculty of Chemistry: O. Y. NOSAKIN
Faculty of Chuvash Philology and Culture: V. G. RODIONOV
Faculty of Construction: Y. V. CHERNOV
Faculty of Economics: A. E. YAKOVLEV
Faculty of Electrical and Power Engineering: N. A. KOKOREV

Faculty of Electrical Engineering: N. A. KOKOREV
Faculty of Geography: I. N. SHIROKOV
Faculty of History: A. V. ARSENTEVA
Faculty of Journalism: A. P. DANILOV
Faculty of Law: N. V. IVANZOVA
Faculty of Mathematics: V. G. AGAKOV
Faculty of Medicine: V. E. VOLKOV
Faculty of Philology: G. E. KORNILOV
Faculty of Physics: L. K. MYTRUCHIN
Faculty of Psychology and Administration: E. N. KADISHEV
Faculty of Stomatology and Pediatrics: E. V. BUSHUEVA
Higher Business School: L. P. KURAKOV (Dir)
Higher School For Training Engineers: V. A. CHEDRIN (Dir)

DAGESTAN STATE UNIVERSITY

Dagestan, 367025 Makhachkala, Gadzhiyeva ul. 8
Telephone: (87200) 68-23-26
Fax: (87200) 67-06-33
E-mail: dgu@dgu.ru
Internet: www.dgu.ru

Founded 1931
State control
Language of instruction: Russian
Academic year: September to July

Rector: Prof. O. A. OMAROV
Vice-Rector: Prof. E. Z. EMIRBEKOV
Registrar: Prof. M. I. ABAKAROV
Librarian: L. I. ALIEVA

Number of teachers: 1,000
Number of students: 20,000

Publication: *Transactions*

DEANS

Faculty of Biology: Dr KH. M. RAMAZANOV
Faculty of Chemistry: Dr K. M. YUNUSOV
Faculty of Culture: Dr M. A. ISRAFILOV
Faculty of Dagestan Philology: Dr Z. A. MAGOMEDOV
Faculty of Finance and Economics: Dr R. K. KADIEV
Faculty of History: Dr B. B. BULATOV
Faculty of Law: Dr A. R. OMAROV
Faculty of Management in Economics: Dr M. M. MAGOMAEV
Faculty of Mathematics: Dr M. G. MEKHTIEV
Faculty of Physics: Dr KH. A. MAGOMEDOV
Faculty of Romance and Germanic Philology: Dr M. M. ABDULSALAMOV
Faculty of Russian Language and Literature: Dr SH. A. MAZANAEV

ELETS STATE UNIVERSITY 'I. A. BUNIN'

399770 Lipetsk Region, Elets, ul. Kommunarov 28
Telephone: (07467) 2-21-93
Fax: (07467) 2-04-63
E-mail: main@elsu.ru
Internet: www.elsu.ru
State control

Founded 1939

Rector: VALERY P. KUZOVLEV
First Pro-Rector for Academic Affairs: TATYANA A. POZNYAK
Second Pro-Rector for Academic Affairs: OLGA N. SARYCHEVA
Pro-Rector for Admin. and Finance: STANISLAV A. KLEIMENOV

DEANS

Faculty of Design: NADEZHDA P. LOGINOVA
Faculty of Economics: SVETLANA A. VOROTYNTSEVA
Faculty of Engineering and Physics: NATALYA A. FORTUNOVA
Faculty of Foreign Languages: ALEXANDER S. ERENKOV
Faculty of Further Pedagogic Training: EKATERINA V. CHERNYKH
Faculty of History: OLEG A. POZDNYAKOV
Faculty of Law: ELENA V. SAFRONOVA
Faculty of Pedagogy and Primary Education: VIKTORIA YU. BABAITSEVA
Faculty of Pedagogy and Psychology: IRINA D. EMELYANOVA
Faculty of Philology: IRINA M. KURNOSOVA
Faculty of Physics and Mathematics: OLGA A. SAVVINA
Faculty of Sport: ALEXANDER I. PROKOFIEV

FAR EASTERN STATE UNIVERSITY

690600 Vladivostok, ul. Sukhanova 8
Telephone: (4232) 26-12-80
Fax: (4232) 25-72-00
E-mail: office@dip.dvgu.ru
Internet: www.dvgu.ru

Founded 1899
State control
Language of instruction: Russian
Academic year: September to June

Rector: V. I. KURILOV
Pro-Rectors: V. P. DIKAREV, N. M. PESTEREVA, B. L. REZNIK, R. M. SAMIGULIN, R. P. SHEPELEVA, G. S. VOROPAYEV
Librarian: N. N. GAIDARENKO

Library: see Libraries

Number of teachers: 993
Number of students: 16,000

Publications: *News of the Institute of International Studies* (4 a year), *News of the Institute of Oriental Studies* (1 a year), *The Russian Far East* (4 a year)

DEANS

Chemistry and Chemical Ecology: A. A. KAPUSTINA
Correspondence Programme: L. I. ROMANOVA
Economics: R. V. SABITOVA
Entrepreneurial Law: A. S. SHEVCHENKO
German Philology: L. P. BONDARENKO
History and Philosophy: O. V. SIDORENKO
Information Technology: I. V. SOPPA
International Economic Relations and Management: A. A. KHAMATOVA
International Law: V. V. GAVRILOV
International Relations: T. D. KHUZIYATOV
Investigation and Public Prosecution: A. F. REKHOVSKY
Japanese Studies: A. G. SHNYRKO
Journalism: V. V. BAKSHIN
Jurisprudence: A. G. KORCHAGIN
Law (in Petropavlovsk-Kamchatsky): L. A. ZAKHOZHY
Law (in Yuzhno-Sakhalinsk): M. G. SEREBRENNIKOV
Management and Business: S. B. GOLOVACHEV
Mathematics and Computer Science: V. B. OSIPOV
Physics: P. N. KORNYUSHIN
Physics and Engineering: V. G. LIFSHITS
Political Science and Public Administration: A. M. KUZNETSOV
Psychology and Social Work: A. V. STETSIV
Romance Philology: N. S. MOREVA
Russian Philology: V. I. SHESTOPALOVA
Sinology: O. V. KUCHUK
State Law: V. F. SHEKHOVTSOV
Academy of Ecology, Marine Biology and Biotechnology: V. A. KUDRYASHOV
Higher College of Korean Studies: V. V. VERKHOLYAK (Dir)
Institute of Environment: YU. B. ZONOV (Dir)
Institute of Foreign Languages: L. P. BONDARENKO (Dir)
Institute of International Tourism and Hospitality: N. M. PESTEREVA (Dir)
Institute of Law: V. I. KURILOV (Dir)
Institute of Management and Business: A. A. BELUSOV (Dir)
Institute of Military Programmes: S. A. BOGATYRENKO (Dir)
Institute of Oriental Studies: A. A. KHAMATOVA (Dir)
Institute of Physics and Information Technology: V. I. BELOKON (Dir)
Institute of Pre-University Training: N. A. SMAL (Dir)
Institute of Professional Development and In-Service Training: E. M. CHUKHRAYEV (Dir)
Institute for Training Highly Qualified Specialists: B. L. REZNIK (Dir)
Pacific Institute of Distance Education and Technology: V. I. VOVNA (Dir)
Research Institute of Chemistry: N. P. SHAPKIN (Dir)
Research Institute of Regional Studies: B. K. STAROSTIN (Dir)
Vladivostok Institute for International Studies of the Asia-Pacific Region: M. YU. SHINKOVSKY (Dir)
FESU branch in Artem: P. V. KHARITONSKY (Dir)
FESU branch in Hakodate: S. N. ILYIN (Dir)
FESU branch in Nakhodka: A. I. RAZGONOV (Dir)

PROFESSORS

ABAKUMOV, A. I., Mathematics
ABRAMOVA, L. A., Economics
AFINOGENOV, YU. A., Law
AKIMOVA, L. V., Economics
AKIMOVA, T. I., Chemistry
ALEXANDROVSKAYA, L. V., Economics
ALEXEYEV, G. V., Mathematics
ANIKONOV, D. S., Mathematics
ANISIMOV, A. P., Biology
ANISIMOV, N. A., Mathematics
ASHCHEPKOV, L. T., Mathematics
BAKLANOV, P. YA., Physical Geography
BAKSHIN, V. V., Journalism
BELOKON, V. I., Physics
BELOUSOV, A. A., Economics
BEREZNIKOV, K. P., Geophysics
BESSONOVA, V. I., Chemistry
BINDER, A. I., Economics
BINEVSKY, A. A., Philosophy
BONDARENKO, L. P., English Philology
BRESLAVETS, T. I., Japanese Philology
BRODYANSKY, D. L., History
BROVKO, P. F., Geography
BUKIN, O. A., Physics
CHEBOTKEVICH, L. A., Physics
CHIZHOV, L. N., Management
CHUVAKIN, A. A., Russian Philology
DASHKO, N. A., Geophysics
DERBENTSEVA, A. M., Biology
DROZDOV, A. L., Chemistry
DUBININ, V. N., Mathematics
DYUZHIKOVA, E. A., English
EFIMENKO, V. F., Physics
ELANTSEVA, O. P., History
ELYAKOV, G. B., Chemistry
FISENKO, A. I., Economics
FROLOV, N. N., Mathematics
GALKINA, L. V., Korean Philology
GAVRILOVA, T. L., Mathematics
GERASIMENKO, M. D., Physics
GLUSHCHENKO, I. I., History
GRAMM-OSIPOV, L. M., Chemistry
GRAMM-OSIPOVA, V. N., Chemistry
IGNATYUK, V. A., Physics
ILYUSHIN, I. A., Journalism
ISAYEVA, T. S., Law
ISAYEVA, V. V., Biology
IVANKOV, V. N., Biology
IVLEV, A. M., Biology
KAMINSKY, V. A., Chemistry
KAPUSTINA, A. A., Chemistry
KARTAVTSEV, YU. F., Biology
KHAMATOVA, A. A., International Economic Relations and Management
KHRISTOFOROVA, N. K., Biology
KILMATOV, T. R., Oceanology
KLESHCHEV, A. S., Mathematics

KNYAZEV, S. D., Law
KOCHETKOV, V. P., English Language
KOGAN, B. I., Mathematics
KOMAROVA, T. A., Biology
KONDRIKOV, N. B., Chemistry
KORNYUSHIN, P. N., Physics
KOROBEYEV, A. I., Law
KOROTKY, A. M., Physical Geography
KOSTETSKY, E. YA., Biology
KRIVSHENKO, S. F., Russian Philology
KUDRYASHOV, V. A., Biology
KULEBYAKIN, YE. V., Social Work
KULESHOV, YE. L., Physics
KURILOV, V. I., Law
KUSAKIN, O. G., Biology
KUZNETSOV, A. M., Political Science
KUZNETSOV, N. V., Mathematics
KUZNETSOVA, N. V., Economy and Finance of Asian Pacific Countries
LEBEDKO, M. G., English
LIFSHITS, V. G., Physics
MEDVEDEVA, E. S., Economics
MEDVEDEVA, K. A., Russian Philology
MEGRABOVA, E. G., English
MELNIKOVA, T. N., English
MIKHAILOV, V. S., International Law
MIKHEEV, R. I., Law
MIRONETS, YU. A., English
NEDOLUZHKO, A. V., Biology
NELEZIN, A. D., Oceanology
NEMOV, R. S., Psychology
NESTERENKO, A. D., Economics
NOMOKONOV, V. A., Law
NURMINSKY, YE. A., Mathematics
OSIPOV, V. B., Mathematics
OSTANIN, V. A., Economics
OVRAKH, G. P., Political Science
PAK, G. K., Mathematics
PECHERITSA, V. F., International Relations
PESTEREVA, N. M., Geophysics
PRIYATKINA, A. F., Russian Philology
PROSHINA, Z. G., English
PSCHENICHNIKOV, B. F., Biology
RAGULIN, P. G., Economics
REZNICHENKO, I. M., Law
REZNIK, B. L., Physics
ROMANOVA, L. I., Law
SABITOVA, R. G., Economics
SAMIGULIN, R. M., History
SARANIN, A. A., Physics
SAZONOV, V. G., International Economics
SEROV, V. M., Japanese Studies
SHAKHOV, V. N., Economics
SHAPKIN, N. P., Chemistry
SHASHKOV, N. I., Philosophy
SHAVKUNOV, E. V., History
SHCHETINNIKOV, P. S., Economics
SHEKHOVTSOV, V. A., Law
SHEPELEVA, R. P., Mathematics
SHEVCHENKO, A. S., Law
SHEVCHENKO, D. K., Mathematics
SHISHMARYOV, YU. E., Mathematics
SHLYK, V. A., Mathematics
SHNYRKO, A. A., Japanese Studies
SOLONITSYNA, A. A., Sociocultural Service and Tourism
SONIN, V. V., Law
SOVASTEEV, V. V., History
STARODUMOVA, YE. A., Russian Philology
STONIK, V. A., Chemistry
SUKHANOV, V. V., Biology
SVYATETSKAYA, T. K., Law
TEREKHOVA, E. V., Foreign Languages
TITOV, A. I., Physics
TKACHEV, V. A., Journalism
TSITSIASHVILI, G. SH., Mathematics
TURCHIN, D. A., Law
VANEEVA, L. A., Law
VASKOVSKY, V. E., Chemistry
VELIKAYA, N. I., Russian Philology
VERISOTSKAYA, YE. V., Japanese Studies
VOLOSHIN, G. YA., Mathematics
VOVNA, V. I., Physics
VYSOTSKY, V. I., Chemistry
YACHIN, S. E., Philosophy
YAKUNIN, L. P., Oceanology
YAROVENKO, V. V., Law
YELANTSEVA, O. P., Economics
YERMAKOVA, E. V., History
YUDIN, V. V., Physics
YUDINA, L. A., Physics
ZAKHOZHY, L. A., Law
ZAYATS, T. S., Chinese Philology
ZHARIKOV, E. P., International Economics
ZHIRMUNSKY, A. V., Biology
ZHURAVLEV, YU. N., Biology
ZOLOTAR, G. YA., Chemistry
ZONOV, YU. B., Geophysics
ZUS, L. B., Law

GORNO-ALTAISK STATE UNIVERSITY

Altai Republic, 649000 Gorno-Altaisk, Lenkina ul. 1
Telephone: (38822) 2-64-39
Fax: (38822) 2-67-35
E-mail: office@gasu.ru
Internet: www.gasu.ru

Founded 1949, present name and status 1993
State control
Academic year: September to January
Academic year: February to June

Rector: Prof. VALERY G. BABIN
Vice-Rector for Academic Affairs: EUGENIY E. SHVAKOV
Vice-Rector for Educational Work: Prof. BORIS V. PAKHAYEV
Vice-Rector for Science and Innovations: Prof. YURY V. TABAKAYEV
Librarian: NATALYA N. VAKHRENEVA

Library of 345,763 vols 312 periodicals
Number of teachers: 353
Number of students: 5,147 , of whom 1,663 external

DEANS

Faculty of Agriculture: LUDMILA I. SURTAEVA
Faculty of Biology and Chemistry: VERA N. ALEYNIKOVA
Faculty of Economics: JULIA G. GAZUKINA
Faculty of Foreign Languages: TATYANA V. DERBENEVA
Faculty of Geography: ALEXEI V. BONDARENKO
Faculty of History: TATYANA S. PUSTOGACHEVA
Faculty of Law: VERA S. KRASHENININA
Faculty of Philology: TATYANA N. NIKONOVA
Faculty of Physics and Mathematics: IVAN B. DAVYDKIN
Faculty of Psychology and Pedagogy: OLGA V. OSTAPOVICH
College of Agriculture: YELENA V. PIVOVAROVA

INGUSH STATE UNIVERSITY

Republic of Ingushetia, 366700 Magas, Aleksandro-Zavodskaya ul. 30
Telephone: (87345) 5-12-64
Fax: (87345) 5-12-64

Founded 1994

Rector: ARSAMAK MARTAZANOV
First Pro-Rector: AKHMED MATIYEV
Pro-Rector for Int. Relations: ZAHIDAT SULTYGOVA

Number of teachers: 316
Number of students: 2,752

IRKUTSK STATE UNIVERSITY

664003 Irkutsk, 3, K. Marksa ul. 1
Telephone: (3952) 24-34-53
Fax: (3952) 24-22-38
E-mail: rector@isu.ru
Internet: www.isu.ru

Founded 1918
State control
Language of instruction: Russian
Academic year: September to May

Rector: Prof. ALEXANDER I. SMIRNOV
Vice-Rector for Academic Affairs: I. GUTNIK
Vice-Rector for Devt: V. SAUNIN
Vice-Rector for Finance and Gen. Affairs: V. I. GLEBETS
Vice-Rector for Scientific Research: A. V. ARGUCHINTSEV
Librarian: R. V. PODGAICHENKO

Library: 3m. vols
Number of teachers: 900
Number of students: 17,230

Publications: *Collected Short Scientific Papers, Proceedings of the Applied Physics Research Institute, Proceedings of the Biological Research Institute, Proceedings of the Oil and Coal Products Research Institute, Transactions*

DEANS

Baikal School of International Business: V. N. SAUNIN
Faculty of Biology and Soil Sciences: Asst Prof. A. N. MATVEYEV
Faculty of Chemistry: Prof. Dr A. YU. SAFRONOV
Faculty of Geography: Asst Prof. A. V. ARGUCHINTSOVA
Faculty of Geology: Asst Prof. S. P. PRIMINA
Faculty of History: Prof. YU. A. ZULYAR
Institute of Law: Assoc. Prof. O. P. LICHICHAN
Faculty of Philology: Prof. A. S. SOBENNIKOV
Faculty of Physics: Prof. YU. V. AGRAPHONOV
Faculty of Psychology: Asst Prof. I. A. KOPONAK
Faculty of Service and Advertisment: Asst Prof. V. K. KARNAUKHOVA
Siberian-American Faculty of Management: Asst Prof. A. V. DIOGENOV
Institute of Social Sciences: Prof. V. A. RASHETNIKOV
Institute of Mathematics, Economics and Information Science: Prof. YU. D. KOROLKOV
International Institute of Economics and Linguistics: Asst Prof. V. YA. ANDRUKHOVA

IVANOVO STATE UNIVERSITY

153025 Ivanovo, ul. Ermaka 39
Telephone: (932) 32-62-10
Fax: (932) 32-46-77
E-mail: rector@ivanovo.ac.ru
Internet: www.ivanovo.ac.ru

Founded 1974
State control

Faculties of biology and chemistry, economics, history, law, mathematics, philology, physics, romance and Germanic philology

Number of teachers: 429
Number of students: 7,919 (4,452 full-time and 3,467 by correspondence)

Rector: Prof. VLADIMIR N. YEGOROV
Pro-Rectors: ALEXEY I. SCHEGLOV (Academic), Dr. VLADIMIR S. RADNYUK (Admin. and Finance), Dr VLADIMIR I. NAZAROV (Distance Learning and Further Education), Dr NADEZHDA V. USOLTSEVA (Int. Affairs), Dr OLGA M. KARPOVA (Public Relations), Dr DMITRY I. POLYVYANNY (Scientific).

KABARDINO-BALKARIAN STATE UNIVERSITY

360004 Kabardino-Balkar Republic, Nalchik, ul. Chernyshevskogo 173
Telephone and fax (095) 337-99-55
E-mail: bsk@ns.kbsu.ru
Internet: www.kbsu.ru

Founded 1932
State control
Language of instruction: Russian
Academic year: September to June

Rector: BARASBI S. KARAMURZOV

Vice-Rector for Extramural Studies and Postgraduate Studies: SVETLANA K. BASHIEVA
Vice-Rector for Foreign Affairs: HAZESHA T. TAOV
Vice-Rector for Scientific Studies: ALEKSEY P. SAVINTSEV
Registrar: I. SHOMAKHOVA
Librarian: ROSA N. UNACHEVA

Library: see Libraries
Number of teachers: 950
Number of students: 20,635

DEANS

Faculty of Biology: A. M. PARITOV
Faculty of Chemistry: T. KH. LYGIDOV
Faculty of Computer Science and Systems Control: A. S. KSENOFONTOV
Faculty of Economics: R. V. GURFOVA
Faculty of Law: M. KH. GUKEPSHOKOV
Faculty of Mathematics: M. ABREGOV
Faculty of Mechanical Engineering: V. D. BATYROV
Faculty of Medicine: R. M. ZAKHOKHOV
Faculty of Microelectronics: R. SH. TESHEV
Faculty of Pedagogy and Methods of Primary Education: A. ZH. NASIPOV
Institute of Philology: L. A. KHARAEVA
Faculty of Physical Education and Sport: A. TKHAZEPLOV
Faculty of Physics: A. A. AKHUBEKOV
Institute of Social Sciences and Humanities: KH. B. MAMSIROV

KALININGRAD STATE UNIVERSITY 'IMMANUEL KANT'

236041 Kaliningrad, ul. A. Nevskogo 14
Telephone: (112) 46-59-17
Fax: (112) 46-58-13
E-mail: rector@admin.albertina.ru
Internet: www.albertina.ru

Founded 1967
Academic year: September to June

Faculties of biology, chemistry, English, German and French philology, economics, geography, history, mathematics, physical training and sport, physics, law, Russian philology, teacher training

Rector: Dr A. P. KLEMESHEV
Pro-Rector: Dr V. N. KHUDENKO
Librarian: A. D. SHKITSKAYA

Library: see Libraries and Archives
Number of teachers: 807
Number of students: 10,821
Publication: *Proceedings*.

KALMYK STATE UNIVERSITY

358000 Elista, ul. Pushkina 11
Telephone: (84722) 5-34-31
Fax: (84722) 5-37-29
E-mail: uni@kalmsu.ru
Internet: www.kalmsu.ru

Founded 1970

Faculties of general engineering, philology, biology, physics, mathematics, oriental studies and agriculture

Rector: G. M. MANDZHIYEVICH
Vice-Rector for Academic Affairs: Prof. ANATOLY V. RUDENKO
Vice-Rector for Admin. and Finance: Prof. VLADIMIR V. UCHUROV
Vice-Rector for Scientific Affairs: Prof. ALEKSANDR A. SOLOVEV
Vice-Rector for Social-Economic Affairs: Prof. VALERY U. MANDZHIEV
Vice-Rector for Univ.–Industry Liaison: Prof. ARKADY K. NATYROV
Number of students: 5,000

KAZAN (VOLGA REGION) FEDERAL UNIVERSITY

420008 Tatarstan, Kazan, ul. Kremlyovskaya 18
Telephone: (843) 292-76-00
Fax: (843) 292-74-18
E-mail: public.mail@ksu.ru
Internet: www.ksu.ru

Founded 1804
State control
Languages of instruction: Russian, Tatar, English
Academic year: September to June

Rector: Prof. ILSHAT R. GAFUROV
Councillor: ANDREY N. KHASHOV
Pres.: Prof. MYAKZYUM KH. SALAKHOV
Pro-Rector: Prof. DANIS K. NURGALIEV
Pro-Rector: MARAT R. SAFIULLIN
Pro-Rector: Prof. NAIL F. KASHAPOV
Pro-Rector: Prof. ARIF M. MEZHVEDILOV
Pro-Rector: Prof. RIYAZ G. MINZARIPOV
Pro-Rector: LENAR S. SAFIULLIN
Pro-Rector: RAISA R. MULLAKAEVA
Librarian: ZHANNA V. SHCHELYVANOVA

Library of 4,920,000 vols
Number of teachers: 4,000
Number of students: 40,000
Publication: *Mathematics*

DEANS

Faculty of Biology and Soil: Prof. RUSHAN M. SABIROV
Faculty of Computer Science and Cybernetics: Prof. RUSTAM KH. LATYPOV
Faculty of Economics and Management: Prof. GALINA A. SULDINA
Faculty of Geography and Ecology: Prof. OLEG P. ERMOLAEV
Faculty of Geology: Prof. ANATOLIY S. BORISOV
Faculty of History: Prof. EVGENIY A. CHIGLINTSEV
Faculty of Journalism and Sociology: Prof. VASIL Z. GARIFULLIN
Faculty of Law: Prof. ILDAR A. TARKHANOV
Faculty of Mathematics and Mechanics: Prof. SEMEN R. NASYROV
Faculty of Philology: Prof. KAMIL R. GALIULLIN
Faculty of Philosophy: Prof. MIKHAIL D. SCHELKUNOV
Faculty of Physics: Prof. ALBERT V. AGANOV
Faculty of Psychology: Prof. BULAT S. ALISHEV
Faculty of Tatar Philology and History: Prof. ISKANDER A. GILYAZOV
Institute of Chemistry: Prof. VLADIMIR I. GALKIN
Institute of Oriental Studies: Prof. DZHAMIL G. ZAINULLIN

PROFESSORS

AGANOV, A. V., Physics
AKHMADULLIN, A. G., Philology
ALATYREV, V. I., Physiology
ANDRAMONOVA, N. A., Russian Philology
ANDREEV, V. I., Education
ARSLANOV, M. M., Mathematics
BAKHTIN, A. I., Mineralogy
BALALYKINA, E. A., Philology
BARABANSHIKOV, B. I., Genetics
BASHKIROV, SH. SH., Physics
BUDNIKOV, G. K., Chemistry
BUKHARAEV, R. G., Cybernetics
BUROV, B. V., Lithology
BUSYGIN, E. P., History
BUTAKOV, G. P., Geomorphology
CHERKASOV, R. A., Chemistry
ERMOLAEV, I. P., History
FARUKSHIN, M. H., Sociology
GABDULKHAEV, B. G., Mathematics
GALIULLIN, T. N., Philology
GOLUBEV, A. I., Zoology
KAIGORODOV, V. R., Physics
KHAIRUTDINOV, R. G., History
KHAKOV, V. H., Turkic Languages
KHALYMBADYA, V. G., Palaeontology
KHOKHLOVA, L. P., Plant Physiology
KOCHELAEV, B. I., Physics
KONOPLEV, YU. G., Mechanics
KOPOSOV, G. F., Soil Studies
KURDYUKOV, G. I., Law
KUZNETSOV, V. A., Ichthyology
LESHCHINSKAYA, I. B., Microbiology
LIASHKO, A. D., Computing Mathematics
LITVIN, A. L., History
LYUBARSKI, E. L., Botany
MAKLAKOV, A. I., Physics
MALKOV, V. P., Law
NAFIGOV, R. I., History
NEPRIMEROV, N. N., Electronics
NIKOLAEV, G. A., Philology
PEREVEDENTSEV, YU. P., Meteorology
RAKHMATULLIN, E. S., Sociology
RESHETOV, YU. S., Law
RYABOV, A. A., Law
SADYKOV, M. B., Philosophy
SAKHIBULLIN, N. A., Astrophysics
SALNIKOV, YU. I., Chemistry
SEMENOV, V. F., Political Economy
SHARIFYANOV, I. I., History
SHERSTNEV, A. N., Mathematics
SHIROKOV, A. P., Geometry
SIDOROV, V. V., Radiophysics
TAGIROV, I. R., History
TEPLOV, M. A., Physics
TEPTIN, G. M., Meteorology
TORSUEV, N. P., Geomorphology
TROFIMOV, A. M., Geomorphology
TUMASHEVA, D. G., Turkic Languages
USMANOV, M. A., History
YEGALOV, V. I., Differential Equations
YIGUNIN, V. D., History
ZABOTIN, YA. I., Computing Mathematics

KEMEROVO STATE UNIVERSITY

650043 Kemerovo, Krasnaya ul. 6
Telephone: (3842) 23-12-26
Fax: (3842) 23-30-34
E-mail: rector@kemsu.ru
Internet: www.kemsu.ru

Founded 1974
State control
Language of instruction: Russian
Academic year: September to July

Faculties of biology, chemistry, economics, foreign languages, history, law, mathematics, philology, physics, social sciences and sport

Rector: YU. A. ZAKHAROV
Pro-Rectors: K. E. AFANASIEV, T. M. CHUREKOVA, B. P. NEVZOROV, T. M. PANINA, B. A. SECHKARYOV, V. A. VOLCHEK
Librarian: N. P. KONOVALOVA

Number of teachers: 780
Number of students: 8,834

KHAKASSIA STATE UNIVERSITY 'N. F. KATANOV'

Khakassia Republic, 655000 Abakan, Lenina pr. 90
Telephone: (3902) 24-53-29
Fax: (3902) 24-33-64
E-mail: univer@khsu.ru
Internet: www.khsu.ru
State control

Founded 1994

Accredited by Fed. Service of Supervision in Education and Science of Nat. Accreditation Agency of Russia

Rector: Prof. GENNADY STANISLAVOVICH SURVILLO
First Vice-Rector, Vice-Rector of Scientific Work: ANDREY ANATOLYEVICH POPOV
Vice-Rector of Quality Control and Devt: VASILY VASILJEVICH ANJUSHIN

Vice-Rector of Teaching and Organizational Work: SVETLANA MIKHAILOVNA KUBRINA
Vice-Rector of Pedagogical Work: SVETLANA AFANASYEVNA SUBRAKOVA
Vice-Rector of Admin. Work: YURY VASILYEVICH RYBALCHENKO

Library: more than 1m. vols in 9 libraries and 15 reading-halls; more than 700 periodicals
Number of teachers: 591
Number of students: 17,459 , of whom 7,501 external
Publications: *Herald of Katanov State University of Khakassia*, *Yearbook of the Institute of Sajan-Altay Turkology*

DEANS AND DIRECTORS

Agrarian Dept: ALEXEY NIKOLAEVICH KADYCHEGOV
Centre of Socio-Political and Humanitarian Education: TATYANA SERGEEVNA TCHIVERSKAJA
College of Agriculture: GALINA ALEKSANDROVNA MINYUHINA
College of Medicine: OLGA VLADIMIROVNA SHTYGASHEVA
College of Music: NINA NIKOLAEVNA KUSHNIR
College of Pedagogical Education, Computer Science and Law: NADEZHDA VIKTOROVNA NADEEVA
College of Service Technologies: NINA VIKTOROVNA SLICHNAYA
Dept of Physical Training: ALEXANDER VICTOROVICH FOMINYKH
Engineering and Technical Dept: OLEG NICOLAEVICH KHEGAY
Institute of Arts: NINA NIKOLAEVNA KUSHNIR
Institute of Computer Science and Telematics: SERGEY VIKTOROVICH SHWETZ
Institute of Continuing Pedagogical Education: LYUDMILA ANATOLJEVNA MINDIBEKOVA
Institute of Economics and Management: NINA FEDOTOVNA DITZ
Institute of History and Law: VLADIMIR GEORGEVICH KICHEEV
Institute of Medicine, Psychology and Social Sciences: OLGA VLADIMIROVNA SHTYGASHEVA
Institute of Natural Sciences and Mathematics: IRINA VICTOROVNA KARPUKHINA
Institute of Philology: IVAN IVANOVICH KREMICH
Institute of Sajan-Altay Turkology: TAMARA GERASIMOVNA BORGOYAKOVA
Institute of Service and Design Technologies: MARINA VICTOROVNA KHORTOVA
Institute of Upgrading Skills and Staff Retraining: LIDIA NIKOLAEVNA CHAIRKINA
Veterinary Medicine Dept: VICTOR YURYEVICH TCHUMAKOV

KOSTROMA STATE NEKRASSOV UNIVERSITY

156961 Kostroma, ul. Pervogo Maya 14
Telephone: (4942) 31-82-91
Fax: (4942) 31-65-61
E-mail: rgc@ksu.edu.ru
Internet: www.ksu.edu.ru

Founded 1918
State control

Rector: Prof. NIKOLAI M. RASSADIN
First Pro-Rector: SERGEI N. NIKOLAEV
Pro-Rector for Academic Affairs: IRINA G. ASADULINA
Pro-Rector for Computerisation: VLADIMIR N. ERSHOV
Pro-Rector for Household Affairs: VYACHESLAV V. ROGACHEV
Pro-Rector for Int. Relations: LIDIA N. VAULINA
Pro-Rector for Science: ANATOLY G. KIRPICHNIK
Pro-Rector for Social Affairs: ALEXEI E. PODOBIN
Librarian: NATALIA A. SMIRNOVA

Library of 584,000 vols
Number of teachers: 700
Number of students: 7,000
Publications: *Educational economic*, *Vestnik KSU*

DEANS

Faculty of Art: MARINA A. ALEKSEEVA
Faculty of Foreign Languages: MARGARITA M. KAPLINA
Faculty of History: ANDREI M. BELOV
Faculty of Music: ANDREI I. SAKHAROV
Faculty of Natural Science: IGOR G. KRINITSIN
Faculty of Philology: MADINA A. FOKINA
Faculty of Physical Education: LILIA M. BOCHKOVA
Faculty of Physics and Mathematics: DMITRI E. POPOV
Faculty of Service and Technologies: NATALIA B. TARASOVA
Institute of Economics: SINAIDA V. BRAGINA
Institute of Pedagogics and Psychology: ANDREI I. TIMONIN

KUBAN STATE UNIVERSITY

350040 Krasnodar, ul. Stavropolskaya 149
Telephone: (8612) 69-95-02
Fax: (8612) 69-95-17
E-mail: rector@kubsu.ru
Internet: www.kubsu.ru

Founded 1924
State control
Languages of instruction: Russian, English
Academic year: September to July

Pres.: VLADIMIR A. BABESHKO
Chief Vice-Pres. and Vice-Pres. for Information: ALEXANDER G. IVANOV
Vice-Pres. for Academic Affairs: NATALYA V. KRASNOVA
Vice-Pres. for Additional Education: ELENA A. ZHURAVLEVA
Vice-Pres. for Capital Construction and Repairs: ELENA N. SAVENKO
Vice-Pres. for Distance Education: IGOR D. BREGEDA
Vice-Pres. for Science and Research: ALEXANDER A. GAVRILOV
Vice-Pres. for Social Affairs: VIKTOR V. MOMOTOV
Sec. of the Univ. Academic Ccl: TATYANA M. BELOKON
Librarian: G. V. SOLOVIEVA

Number of teachers: 1,000 (incl. 144 professors and 506 associate professors)
Number of students: 16,770
Publications: *Ekologichesky vestnik nauchnykh tsentrov TchES* (Letters of BSEC Research centres, 4 a year), *Ekonomika* (1 a year), *Filologiya* (Philology, 2 a year), *Golos Minuvshego* (The Voice of the Past, 4 a year), *Obshchestvo i Chelovek* (Society and Mankind, 4 a year), *Priroda* (Nature, 4 a year), *Terra Incognita* (2 a year), *Upravleniye* (Management, 1 a year)

DEANS

Faculty of Applied Mathematics: YU. V. KOLTSOV
Faculty of Architecture and Design: S. YU KOCHETKOVA
Faculty of Biology: V. YA. NAGALEVSKY
Faculty of Chemistry: V. D. BUYKLISKY
Faculty of Economics: I. V. SHEVCHENKO
Faculty of Geography: M. YU. BELIKOV
Faculty of Graphic Art: YU. V. KOROBKO
Faculty of History, Sociology and International Relations: G. M. ACHAGU
Faculty of Journalism: V. V. ROUNOV
Faculty of Law: I. A. NIKOLAYCHUK
Faculty of Management: A. M. ZHDANOVSKY
Faculty of Mathematics: G. F. SOKOL
Faculty of Philology: V. P. ABRAMOV
Faculty of Physics and Technics: N. A. YAKOVENKO
Faculty of Romano-Germanic Philology: V. I. TKHORIK

KURGAN STATE UNIVERSITY

640669 Kurgan, ul. Gogolya 25
Telephone: (3522) 43-26-52
Fax: (3522) 43-20-51
E-mail: rektor@kgsu.ru
Internet: www.kgsu.ru

Founded 1952

Faculties of mathematics and information technology, natural sciences, history, law, philology, economics, health protection, psychology and sport, pedagogy, technology, transport systems

Rector: Prof. OLEG I. BUKHTOYAROV

Library of 1,000,000 vols
Number of teachers: 700
Number of students: 8,000

KURSK STATE UNIVERSITY

305000 Kursk, ul. Radischeva 33
Telephone: (4712) 70-05-38
Fax: (4712) 51-36-49
E-mail: kurskgu@kursk-uni.ru
Internet: www.kursksu.ru

Public control
Language of instruction: Russian
Academic year: September to June

Founded 1934 as Kursk State Pedagogical Institute

Rector: Prof. VYACHESLAV V. GVOZDEV
First Vice-Rector: NIKOLAI N. GREBENKOV
Vice-Rector for Academic Affairs: Dr VLADIMIR V. ZAKHAROV
Vice-Rector for Int. Relations: Dr ELENA I. MIKHAILINA
Vice-Rector for Science and Research: Dr VITALIY A. KUDINOV
Vice-Rector for Technical Support: IGOR O. SHULGIN
Chief Accountant: GALINA E. KLOCHKOVA

Library of 65,000 vols
Number of teachers: 900
Number of students: 12,000 (of which 9,000 internal and 3,000 external students)

DEANS

Faculty of Art and Design: VIKTOR I. ZHILIN
Faculty of Computer Science: Dr VITALIY A. KUDINOV
Faculty of Economy and Management: Dr VIKTOR A. KRIULIN
Faculty of Foreign Languages: NIKOLAI A. SMAKHTIN
Faculty of Geography: IRINA P. BALABINA
Faculty of History: PLAKSIN
Faculty of Law: Dr VLADIMIR V. ZAKHAROV
Faculty of Philology: YURI L. PHILIPPOV
Faculty of Physics and Mathematics: VYACHESLAV V. MELENTYEV
Faculty of Psychology and Pedagogics: MARINA A. LUKINA
Faculty of Sport and Physical Education: Dr TATYANA V. SKOBLIKOVA
Faculty of Theology and Religion Studies: ANATOLIY A. KORZINKIN

LENINGRAD STATE UNIVERSITY 'A. S. PUSHKIN'

196605 St Petersburg, Pushkin, Peterburgskoe shosse 10
Telephone: (812) 466-65-58
Fax: (812) 466-49-99
E-mail: pushkin@infos.ru
Internet: www.lgu-edu.spb.ru

State control
Founded 1992 as Leningrad Regional Pedagogical Institute; as Leningrad State Regional Univ. 1996–1999; as A. S. Pushkin Leningrad State Regional Univ. 1999–2003; present name and status 2003
Rector: Prof. VYACHESLAV N. SKVORTSOV
First Pro-Rector: Prof. GALINA P. CHEPURENKO
Pro-Rector for Academic Affairs: Prof. TATYANA V. MALTSEVA
Pro-Rector for Economic and Int. Affairs: Dr LEONID L. BUKIN
Pro-Rector for External and Further Professional Education: Prof. TATYANA S. KOMISSAROVA
Pro-Rector for Science: Dr EKATERINA S. NERYSHKINA
Number of teachers: 361
Number of students: 13,403

DEANS
Faculty of Arts: Dr SVETLANA I. NAZAROVA
Faculty of Foreign Languages: Prof. SVYATOSLAV I. ALATORTSEV
Faculty of Law: Prof. GALINA P. CHEPURENKO
Faculty of Mathematics, Physics and Information Science: Dr SERGEI D. BORONENKO
Faculty of Natural Sciences, Geography and Tourism: Dr ANATOLY M. MAKARSKY
Faculty of Philology: Prof. TATYANA V. MALTSEVA

MAGNITOGORSK STATE UNIVERSITY

455043 Magnitogorsk, Lenina pr. 114
Telephone: (3511) 35-15-32
Fax: (3511) 35-15-32
E-mail: masu@masu.ru
Internet: www.masu.ru
State control
Founded 1932
Rector: Prof. VALENTIN F. ROMANOV
First Pro-Rector: Prof. VLADIMIR P. SEMENOV
Librarian: LUDMILA V. KOTELNIKOVA
Library of 443,335 vols

DEANS
Faculty of Advancement of Qualifications and Training of Specialists: Prof. LUDMILA A. MIROSHNICHENKO
Faculty of Art and Design: Prof. VLADIMIR M. BELY
Faculty of History: Prof. MIKHAIL G. ABRAMZON
Faculty of Information Technology: Prof. ELMIRA R. IPATOVA
Faculty of Linguistics and Translation: Prof. GALINA I. VASINA
Faculty of Pedagogy and Methods of Primary Education: Prof. YURI D. KOROBKOV
Faculty of Philology: Prof. LYUBOV D. PONOMAREVA
Faculty of Physics and Mathematics: Prof. VIKTOR A. KUZNETSOV
Faculty of Pre-School Education: Prof. BORIS D. KULANIN
Faculty of Psychology: Prof. ELENA D. PETROVA
Faculty of Social Work: Prof. FLYURA A. MUSTAEVA

MARI STATE UNIVERSITY

424001 Mari-El Republic, Yoshkar-Ola, pl. Lenina 1
Telephone: (8362) 12-59-20
Fax: (8362) 45-45-81
E-mail: postmaster@marsu.ru
Internet: www.marsu.ru
Founded 1972
State control
Academic year: September to July
Rector: V. I. MAKAROV
Vice-Rector: V. I. CHEMODANOV
Chief Admin. Officer: L. N. STRELNIKOVA
Number of teachers: 384
Number of students: 4,055
Publication: *Arkheograficheskу vestnik* (Archaeological News, 2 a year)

DEANS
Faculty of Agriculture: G. S. YUNUSOV
Faculty of Biology and Chemistry: M. G. GRIGORIEV
Faculty of Culture and Arts: R. L. YASHMETOVA
Faculty of Economics: K. V. SHAKIROV
Faculty of Electric Power Technology: L. M. RIBAKOV
Faculty of History and Philology: A. N. CHIMAEV
Faculty of Law: A. M. LOMONOSOV
Faculty of Linguistics and Intercultural Communication: Z. G. ZORINA
Faculty of Physics and Mathematics: G. A. SITNIKOV

MORDOVIAN STATE UNIVERSITY

430005 Mordovia, Saransk, Bolshevistskaya ul. 68
Telephone: (8342) 24-48-88
Fax: (8342) 32-75-27
E-mail: vice-rector@adm.mrsu.ru
Internet: www.mrsu.ru
Founded 1957
State control
Academic year: September to June
Rector: Prof. SERGEY M. VDOVIN
First Vice-Rector for Academic Studies: Prof. N. E. FOMIN
Vice-Rector for Extracurricular Activities: Prof. MARINA D. MARTYNOVA
Vice-Rector for Financial Admin.: Prof. N. D. KULIKOV
Vice-Rector for Further Training and Professional Devt Programmes: ANTONINA M. AKHMETOVA
Vice-Rector for Innovative Research and Devt Activities: PETR V. SENIN
Vice-Rector for Logistics Accomplishment: Prof. SERGEI V. KARGIN
Vice-Rector for Major Construction Work: STEPAN P. GUDOZHNIKOV
Vice-Rector for Science and Research: Prof. V. D. CHERKASOV
Vice-Rector for Security: Prof. ALEKSANDR I. EKIMOV
Registrar: MIKHAIL M. GOUDOV
Librarian: I. V. OTSTAVNOVA
Library of 2,196,381 vols, 731 periodicals
Number of teachers: 1,689
Number of students: 39,787
Publications: *Integration of Education* (4 a year), *Regionologiya* (4 a year), *Vestnik Mordovskogo Universiteta* (4 a year)

DEANS
Faculty of Biology: Prof. V. W. REVIN
Faculty of Economics: Prof. N. D. GUSKOVA
Faculty of Electronics: I. V. GULAYEV
Faculty of Foreign Languages: Prof. NATALIA V. BURENINA
Faculty of Geography: ANATOLY A. YAMASHKIN
Faculty of Industrial and Civil Construction: Prof. V. T. EROFEYEV
Faculty of Law: Prof. YULIA N. SUSHKOVA
Faculty of Mathematics: Prof. I. I. CHUCHAYEV
Faculty of Medicine: Prof. ANNA A. USANOVA
Faculty of National Culture: B. S. BRYZHINSKY
Faculty of Philology: Prof. M. V. MOSIN
Faculty of Lighting Engineering: Prof. OLGA E. ZHELEZNIKOVA
Folk Culture Institute: TATYANA N. SIDORKINA

DIRECTORS
Institute of Agrocomplex: SAMIL I. AKHMETOV
Institute of Economics: NIKOLAI P. MAKARKIN
Institute of Man and Light: LUDMILA V. ABRAMOVA
Science and Research Institute of Ecology: VICTOR N. MASKAIKIN
Science and Research Institute of Industrial and Civil Construction: VLADIMIR P. SELYAYEV
Science and Research Institute of Mathematics: EVGENY V. VOSKRESENSKY
Science and Research Institute of Regional Studies: ALEXANDR I. SUKHAREV

MOSCOW STATE REGIONAL UNIVERSITY

107005 Moscow, ul. Radio 10A
Telephone and fax (495) 261-22-28
E-mail: mgou@mgou.ru
Internet: www.mgou.ru
State control
Founded 1923 as Moscow State Pedagogical Technical College
Faculties of business and technology, decorative arts, economics, further education for higher education specialists, law, linguistics, mathematics and physics, military education, pedagogy, physical education and philology, politics, translation; 73 depts
Rector: Prof. VLADIMIR V. PASECHNIK
First Pro-Rector for Academic Affairs: Dr SERGEI G. DEMBITSKY
Pro-Rector for Admin. and Finance: Dr MIKHAIL V. YUDIN
Pro-Rector for Distance Learning: Prof. NINA G. GOLTSOVA
Pro-Rector for Education and Youth Politics: Dr MIKHAIL V. YUDIN
Pro-Rector for Scientific and Int. Cooperation: Prof. YURI I. YAMALOV
Number of teachers: 586

MOSCOW STATE UNIVERSITY 'M. V. LOMONOSOV'

119991 Moscow, GSP-1, Leninskie Gory
Telephone: (495) 939-10-00
Fax: (495) 939-01-26
E-mail: info@rector.msu.ru
Internet: www.msu.ru
Founded 1755
Academic year: September to June
Rector: Acad. VIKTOR SADOVNICHY
Vice-Rector for Academic Policy and Degree Programs Man.: PYOTR VRZHESHCH
Vice-Rector for Educational Standards, Curricula and Syllabi: IGOR KOTLOBOVSKY
Vice-Rector for Innovations, Informatization and Int. Scientific Cooperation: ALEXEI KHOKHLOV
Vice-Rector for Int. Cooperation: NIKOLAY SYOMIN
Vice-Rector for Research Policy and Research Man.: VLADIMIR BELOKUROV
Vice-Rector for Social Services and Facilities Devt: ALEXANDER CHERNYAEV
Vice-Rector: NIKITA ANISSIMOV (acting)
Vice-Rector: YURI BELENKOV
Vice-Rector: ALEXEY REYMERS (acting)
Vice-Rector: VICTOR TROFIMOV
Number of teachers: 10,441
Number of students: 40,756
Publications: *Moscow State University* (52 a year), *Vestnik MGU* (20 series, 2 a year)

DEANS
Faculty of Bioengineering and Bioinformatics: VLADIMIR SKULACHEV

Faculty of Biology: MIKHAIL KIRPICHNIKOV
Faculty of Chemistry: VALERY LUNIN
Faculty of Computational Mathematics and Cybernetics: YEVGENY MOISEEV
Faculty of Economics: VASSILI KOLESOV
Faculty of Educational Studies: NIKOLAI ROZOV
Faculty of Fine and Performing Arts: ALEXANDER LOBODANOV
Faculty of Foreign Languages and Area Studies: SVETLANA TER-MINASOVA
Faculty of Fundamental Medicine: VSEVOLOD TKACHUK
Faculty of Geography: NIKOLAI KASIMOV
Faculty of Geology: DMITRY PUSHCHAROVSKY
Faculty of Global Processes: V. I. ILIYIN (acting)
Faculty of History: SERGEY KARPOV
Faculty of Journalism: YASEN ZASURSKY
Faculty of Law: ALEXANDER GOLICHENKOV
Faculty of Material Sciences: YURI TRETYAKOV
Faculty of Mechanics and Mathematics: VLADIMIR CHUBARIKOV (acting)
Faculty of Philology: MARINA REMNYOVA
Faculty of Philosophy: VLADIMIR MIRONOV
Faculty of Physical Chemistry: SERGEY ALDOSHIN
Faculty of Physics: VLADIMIR TRUKHIN
Faculty of Political Science: A. YU. SHUTOV (acting)
Faculty of Psychology: YURI ZINCHENKO
Faculty of Public Administration: (vacant)
Faculty of Sociology: VLADIMIR DOBRENKOV
Faculty of Soil Science: SERGEY SHOBA
Faculty of World Politics: ANDREI KOKOSHIN
Graduate School of Innovative Business: DMITRY KOSHUG
Graduate School of Management and Innovation: VLADIMIR VASSILIEV
School of Business Administration: OLEG VIKHANSKY
School of Comtemporary Social Sciences: G. V. OSIPOV
Moscow School of Economics: ALEXANDER NEKIPELOV (Dir)
School of Television: VITALY TRETYAKOV
School of Translation and Interpretation: NIKOLAI GARBOVSKY
Institute of Asian and African Studies: MIKHAIL MEYER

MOSCOW UNIVERSITY OF CONSUMER COOPERATIVES

141014 Moscow oblast, Mytischi, ul. V. Voloshinoi 12
Telephone: (495) 582-97-37
Fax: (495) 582-93-10
E-mail: muller@mupk.ru
Internet: www.mupk.ru

Founded 1913

Areas of study: accounting and auditing, commerce, commodity science, economics, economic information systems, finance and credit, global economics, jurisprudence, management, marketing

Pres. and Rector: Prof. MARIA V. SEROSHTAN

Number of teachers: 500
Number of students: 12,000

NIZHNII NOVGOROD STATE UNIVERSITY 'N. I. LOBACHEVSKY'

603950 Nizhnii Novgorod, pr. Gagarina 23
Telephone: (831) 462-30-90
Fax: (831) 462-30-85
E-mail: unn@unn.ru
Internet: www.unn.ru

Founded 1916
State control
Language of instruction: Russian
Academic year: September to June

Rector: Prof. EVGENY V. CHUPRUNOV
Vice-Rector for Academic Affairs: Assoc. Prof. ALEXANDER V. PETROV
Vice-Rector for Research: Prof. SERGEI N. GURBATOV
Vice-Rector Int. Relations and Innovations in Education: Prof. ALEXANDER O. GRUDZINSKY
Pres.: Prof. ROMAN G. STRONGIN
Librarian: Dr YURI M. SOROKIN

Number of teachers: 1,350
Number of students: 40,000

Publication: *Vestnik of the Nizhnii Novgorod University*

DEANS

Faculty of Biology: Dr A. P. VESELOV
Faculty of Business and Management: Dr A. O. GRUDZINSKY
Faculty of Chemistry: Dr A. V. GUSHCHIN
Faculty of Computer Science and Cybernetics: Dr V. P. GERGEL
Faculty of Economics: Dr YU. V. TRIFONOV
Faculty of Finance: Dr V. N. YASENEV
Faculty of History: Dr E. A. MOLEV
Faculty of International Relations: Dr O. A. KOLOBOV
Faculty of Law: Dr V I. TSYGANOV
Faculty of Mechanics and Mathematics: Dr A. K. LYUBIMOV
Faculty of Philology: Dr L. I. RUCHINA
Faculty of Physical Training and Sport: Dr V. G. KUZMIN
Faculty of Physics: Dr K. A. MARKOV
Faculty of Radiophysics: Dr A. V. YAKIMOV
Faculty of Social Sciences: Dr V. A. BLONIN
Advanced School of General and Applied Physics: Dr M. D. TOKMAN

NORTH OSSETIAN STATE UNIVERSITY

362025 Vladikavkaz, ul. Vatutina 46
Telephone: (8672) 53-09-04
Fax: (8672) 74-05-79
E-mail: webmaster@nosu.ru
Internet: www.nosu.ru

Founded 1969
Language of instruction: Russian
Academic year: September to June

Rector: AKHURBEK M. MAGOMETOV
First Pro-Rector, Pro-Rector for Academic Affairs: ANATOLY V. RAITSEV
Pro-Rector for Int. Affairs: OLEG S. KHATSAYEV
Pro-Rector for Science: VALERY G. SOZNANOV
Librarian: KLARA K. KOKAYEVA

Number of teachers: 833
Number of students: 11,718

DEANS

Faculty of Arts and Design: V. N. TSALAGOV
Faculty of Biology and Soil Studies: R. G. ZANGIONOVA
Faculty of Chemistry and Technology: N. I. KALOYEV
Faculty of Economics: Z. G. TEDEEV
Faculty of Education and Elementary Education: V. K. KOCHISOV
Faculty of Foreign Languages: T. T. KAMBOLOV
Faculty of Geography: B. M. BEROYEV
Faculty of History: A. I. ABAYEV
Faculty of Law: E. G. PLIYEV
Faculty of Management: V. G. TSOGOYEV
Faculty of Mathematics: A. A. AZIYEV
Faculty of Ossetian Philology: R. Z. KOMAYEVA
Faculty of Philology: L. M. BESOLOV
Faculty of Physical Education and Sports: F. G. KHAMIKOYEV
Faculty of Physics: A. P. BLIYEV

NORTHERN INTERNATIONAL UNIVERSITY

685014 Magadan, ul. Portovaya 13
Telephone: (41322) 3-00-21
Fax: (41322) 3-42-37
Internet: www.niu.ru.

NOVGOROD STATE UNIVERSITY

173003 Veliky Novgorod, St Petersburgskaya ul. 41
Telephone: (8162) 62-72-44
Fax: (8162) 62-41-10
E-mail: novsu@novsu.ru
Internet: www.novsu.ru

Founded 1993
Academic year: September to June

Faculties of administration, agricultural engineering, agricultural production technology, architecture, arts and design, arts and technology, biology, chemistry and environmental science, child education and psychology, economics, engineering and technology, finance, foreign languages, higher nursing education, history, law, medicine, pharmacy, philosophy, physics and technology, stomatology

Rector: Prof. Dr VIKTOR VEBER

Number of teachers: 896
Number of students: 14,000

Publications: *Chelo* (History and Literature, 4 a year), *Vestnik Novgorodskogo Gosudarstvennogo Universiteta* (Research, 4 a year).

NOVOSIBIRSK STATE UNIVERSITY

630090 Novosibirsk, ul. Pirogova 2
Telephone: and fax (3832) 39-73-78
E-mail: inter@nsu.ru
Internet: www.nsu.ru

Founded 1959
State control
Language of instruction: Russian
Academic year: September to June

Rector: Prof. NIKOLAY S. DIKANSKY
Vice-Rector for Int. Activities: ELENA M. LISMAN
Vice-Rector for Research: Prof. GENNADY YU. SHVEDENKOV
Vice-Rector for Studies: Prof. NATALIA V. DULEPOVA
Registrar: N. I. BOIKOVA
Librarian: L. A. LYAGUSHINA

Library of 815,051 vols
Number of teachers: 2,226
Number of students: 6,038

Publications: *Algebra and Logics* (6 a year), *Critics and Semiotics* (1 a year), *Philosophy of Science* (4 a year), *Siberian Philological Journal* (2 a year), *Vestnik NGU* (3 a year)

DEANS

Department of Economics (tel. (3832) 39-72-42; e-mail dekeko@lab.nsu.ru; f. 1967):
Prof. GAGIK M. MKRTCHAN
Department of Foreign Languages:
Prof. G. G. KURKINA
Department of Geology and Geophysics (tel. (3832) 39-72-18; e-mail shatsky@uiggm.nsu.ru; internet ggd.nsu.ru; f. 1962):
Prof. VLADISLAV S. SHATSKY
Department of the Humanities (tel. (3832) 30-08-62; e-mail info@gf.nsu.ru; internet www.gf.nsu.ru; f. 1962):
Prof. LEONID G. PANIN

Department of Information Technologies (tel. (3832) 39-77-95; e-mail dekanat@ccfit.nsu.ru; internet www.fit.nsu.ru; f. 2000):

Dr MIKHAIL M. LAVRENTIEV

Department of Mechanics and Mathematics (tel. (3832) 39-75-81; e-mail mmf@msu.ru; internet mmfd.nsu.ru):

Prof. SERGEY S. GONCHAROV

Department of Natural Sciences (tel. (3832) 39-74-30; e-mail decan@fen.nsu.ru; internet www.fen.nsu.ru; f. 1959):

Prof. VLADIMIR A. REZNIKOV

Department of Physics (tel. (3832) 39-78-00; e-mail dean@phys.nsu.ru; internet www .phys.nsu.ru; f. 1961):

Prof. ANDREY V. ARZHANNIKOV

OMSK STATE UNIVERSITY

644077 Omsk, pr. Mira 55A
Telephone: (3812) 67-01-04
Internet: www.omsu.ru
Founded 1974
State control
Language of instruction: Russian
Academic year: September to June

Rector: Prof. GENNADY I. GERING
Pro-Rectors: Dr MIKHAIL V. KHOROSHEVSKY, Dr VALERY V. DUBITSKY (Academic), Dr VLADIMIR P. AVILOV (Finance and Admin.), Dr VLADIMIR I. STRUNIN (Scientific)
Librarian: LYUDMILA A. BALAKINA

Number of teachers: 640
Number of students: 10,000

Publications: *Omsky Universitet* (28 a year), *Vestnik Omskogo Universiteta* (4 a year)

DEANS

Faculty of Arts and Culture: NINA M. GENOVA
Faculty of Chemistry: IRINA V. VLASOVA
Faculty of Economics: LYUDMILA N. IVANOVA
Faculty of Foreign Languages: NATALYA G. GICHEVA
Faculty of History: ALEXEY V. YAKUB
Faculty of International Business: YURI P. DRUS
Faculty of Law: MAXIM S. FOKIN
Faculty of Mathematics: VLADIMIR B. NIKOLAEV
Faculty of Philology: NIKOLAI N. MISYUROV
Faculty of Physics: KLIMENTY N. YUGAI
Faculty of Psychology: LYUDMILA I. DEMENTY
Faculty of Theology and World Culture: DMITRY P. SINELNIKOV

PROFESSORS

ADEEV, G. D., Theoretical Nuclear Physics
AKELKINA, E. A., Literature
AZAROV, V. A., Law
BAOURIN, S. N., Law
BORBAT, V. F., Chemistry and Technology of Non-ferrous and Noble Metals
DUBENSKY, U. P., Pedagogics
ELOVIKOV, L. A., Methodology of Local Labour Management
FAIZULLIN, R. T., Mathematics
FISYUK, A. S., Chemistry
FOMENKO, S. V., History
GERING, G. I., Physics
GOOTS, A. K., Geometry
GRIN, A. G., Mathematics
GRINBERG, M. S., Criminal Law
GRISHKOV, A. N., Mathematics
ISSERS, O. S., Linguistics
KASANNIK, A. I., Ecological Law
KLEIMENOV, M. P., Law
KUKIN, G. P., Algebra
KUZMINA, N. A., Linguistics
LAVROV, E. I., Political Economy
MATYUSCHENKO, V. I., Archaeology
MILLER, A. E., Economy
NOVATOROV, V. E., Pedagogics
OSIPOV, B. I., Linguistics
OSTROVSKY, N. M., Chemistry
OVSIANNIKOVA, I. N., Philosophy
PERTSEV, N. V., Mathematics
POSDNIAKOV, N. K., Politology
PRUDNIKOV, V. V., Physics
RAZUMOV, V. I., Philosophy
REMNEV, A. V., History
ROMANKOV, V. A., Mathematics
ROY, O. M., Sociology
SAGITULLIN, R. S., Chemistry of Heterocyclic Compounds
SEMIKOLENOVA, N. A., Physics
SHIROKOV, I. V., Physics
SKOBELKIN, V. V., Labour Law
SOROKIN, U. A., History
STRUGOV, U. F., Mathematics
TIPUKHIN, V. N., Philosophy
TOLOCHKO, A. P., Pre-Revolutionary Native History
TOMILOV, N. A., Ethnography
VERSHININ, V. I., Analytical Chemistry
YUGAI, K. N., Physics
ZOLOTARYOV, I. D., Physics

OREL STATE UNIVERSITY

302015 Orel, Komsomolskaya ul. 95
Telephone: (0862) 77-73-18
Fax: (0862) 77-73-32
Internet: www.osu.edu.ru
State control
Founded 1974

Rector: Prof. FEDOR S. AVDEEV
Pro-Rector for Academic Affairs: Prof. NADEZHDA A. ILYINA
Pro-Rector for External Education and Int. Relations: Prof. NADEZHDA A. ILYINA
Pro-Rector for Science: Prof. GENNADY P. VERKEENKO

Number of teachers: 668
Number of students: 11,203

ORENBURG STATE UNIVERSITY

460018 Orenburg, pr. Pobedy 13
Telephone: (3532) 77-67-70
Fax: (3532) 72-37-01
E-mail: oms@mail.osu.ru
Internet: www.osu.ru
Founded 1971
Public control
Language of instruction: Russian
Academic year: September to July

Rector: Dr VLADIMIR KOVALEVSKIY
Pro-Rector for Scientific Research: Dr SERGEY N. LETUTA
Pro-Rector for Academic Affairs: ALEXANDER D. PROSKURIN
Pro-Rector for Academic Methodology: TATYANA P. PETUKHOVA
Pro-Rector for Admin. Maintenance and Capital Construction: VLADIMIR P. KOLGANOV
Pro-Rector for Int. Students Affairs: BALAZHAN M. KARCHAEVA
Pro-Rector for Social and Educational Affairs: TATYANA A. NOSOVA
Pro-Rector for Informatization and Security: VICTOR V. BIKOVSKY

Library of 1,000,000 vols
Number of teachers: 2,659
Number of students: 39,865

PACIFIC STATE UNIVERSITY

680035 Khabarovsk, ul. Tikhookeanskaya 136
Telephone: (4212) 72-07-12
Fax: (4212) 72-07-12
E-mail: info@khstu.ru
Internet: www.khstu.ru
Founded 2005, fmrly Khabarovsk State Univ. (f. 1958)
Academic year: September to June

Faculties of economics and management, architecture and civil engineering, law, information technologies, highways, forestry, international studies, mathematical modelling and modelling of management processes

Rector: SERGEI N. IVANCHENKO

Library: 1m. vols
Number of teachers: 800
Number of students: 19,000

PACIFIC STATE UNIVERSITY OF ECONOMICS

690950 Vladivostok, Okeansky pr. 19
Telephone: (4232) 26-62-21
E-mail: web@psue.ru
Internet: www.psue.ru
State control
Founded 1964

Rector: Prof. VIKTOR G. BELKIN.

PENZA STATE UNIVERSITY

440026 Penza, Krasnaya ul. 40
Telephone: (8412) 66-29-27
Fax: (8412) 66-29-27
E-mail: cnit@stup.ac.ru
Internet: www.stup.ac.ru
State control
Founded 1943; present name and status 1998

Rector: Prof. VLADIMIR VOLCHIKHIN
First Pro-Rector: VICTOR A. MESCHERYAKOV
Pro-Rector for Academic Affairs: VICTOR B. MEKHANOV
Pro-Rector for Admin. and Finance: BORIS V. MALSANOV
Pro-Rector for Governance and Personnel: YURI V. KLOCHKOV
Pro-Rector for Science: MIKHAIL A. SCHERBAKOV

Number of teachers: 725
Number of students: 13,895.

UNIVERSITY BRANCH

Serdobsk Branch: Penza Region, 442890 Serdobsk, Lenina ul. 285A; Dir IVAN I. IVANOV.

PEOPLES' FRIENDSHIP UNIVERSITY OF RUSSIA

117198 Moscow, Miklukho-Maklaya ul. 6
Telephone: (095) 434-70-27
Fax: (095) 433-15-11
E-mail: druzhba@rudn.ru
Internet: www.rudn.ru

Founded 1960 as Patrice Lumumba Peoples' Friendship Univ.

Self-governing
Language of instruction: Russian
Academic year: September to July

Rector: Prof. VLADIMIR M. FILIPPOV (acting)
Vice-Rectors: N. A. CHICHULIN, A. D. GLADUSH, V. F. PONYKA, V. D. PROTSENKO, E. L. SHESHNYAK, G. G. SOKOLOV, N. V. VENSKOVSKY, A. P. YEFREMOV
Librarian: A. N. SHUMILOV

Number of teachers: 2,112
Number of students: 4,000

Publications: *Druzhba* (52 a year, university newspaper), *Vestnik Rossiiskogo Universiteta Druzhby Narodov* (4 a year)

DEANS

Faculty of Agriculture: Prof. V. V. GORCHAKOV
Faculty of Ecology: Prof. S. N. SIDORENKO
Faculty of Economics: Prof. N. P. GUSAKOV
Faculty of Engineering: Prof. N. K. PONOMAREV

Faculty of Foreign Languages and General Educational Disciplines: Prof. V. V. YAKUSHEV
Faculty of Humanities and Social Sciences: Prof. N. S. KIRABAEV
Faculty of Law: Prof. A. Y. KAPUSTIN
Faculty of Medicine: Prof. V. A. FROLOV
Faculty of Philology: Prof. V. N. DENISENKO
Faculty of Physical, Mathematical and Natural Sciences: Prof. V. V. DAVYDOV
Academic and Scientific Institute of Information Technology in Physics and Chemistry: Prof. S. N. SIDORENKO
Institute of Distance Learning: Prof. G. A. KRASNOVA
Institute of Foreign Languages: Prof. N. L. SOKOLOVA
Institute of Hotel Business and Tourism: Prof. S. V. DIKHTYAR
Institute of World Economy and Business (International School of Business): Prof. N. P. GUSAKOV

PERM STATE UNIVERSITY

614600 Perm, GSP, ul. Bukireva 15
Telephone: 33-61-83
Fax: 33-80-14
Internet: www.psu.ru
Founded 1916
State control
Language of instruction: Russian
Academic year: September to June
Faculties of biology, chemistry, economics, geology, geography, history, law, mechanics and mathematics, philology, physics
Rector: V. V. MALANIN
Vice-Rectors: Prof. V. I. KACHEVROVSKY, Prof. V. I. KOSTYTSIN, Prof. B. M. OSOVETSKY
Librarian: R. N. ROGALNIKOVA
Number of teachers: 683
Number of students: 9,167
Publications: *Caves Research Problems* (1 a year), *Computer Systems and Processes Modelling* (1 a year), *Geophysical Methods of Oil and Gas Exploration* (1 a year), *Mechanics of Controlled Movement Problems* (1 a year), *Radiospectroscopy* (1 a year), *Statistical Methods of Verifying and Estimating Hypotheses* (1 a year), *Uchenye Zapiski* (Transactions).

PETROZAVODSK STATE UNIVERSITY

185640 Republic of Karelia, Petrozavodsk, pr. Lenina 33
Telephone: (8142) 78-51-40
Fax: (8142) 71-10-00
E-mail: rectorat@psu.karelia.ru
Internet: petrsu.ru
Founded 1940
State control
Languages of instruction: Russian, English
Academic year: September to June
Rector: Prof. ANATOLY VORONIN
Pres.: Prof. VICTOR VASILYEV
Vice-Rector for Admin. and Economic Work: LJUDMILA BEZLATNAYA
Vice-Rector for Education: Prof. VLADIMIR SYUNEV
Vice-Rector for Innovation and Production Activities: Prof. ILYA SHEGELMAN
Vice-Rector for Organizational Work: Prof. SERGEY KORZHOV
Vice-Rector for Pre-Univ. Training and Career Guidance: Assoc. Prof. ANATOLY LOPUHA
Vice-Rector for Research: Prof. NATALIA DORSHAKOVA
Head of Directorate for Int. Cooperation: LYUDMILA KULIKOVSKAYA
Librarian: MARINA OTLIVANCHIK
Library of 1,179,042 vols
Number of teachers: 905
Number of students: 18,616
Publications: *Trudy* (Works, 1 a year), *Ucheniye Zapiski* (1 a year)

DEANS

Faculty of Agriculture: NIKITA ONISCHENKO
Faculty of Baltic and Finnish Philology and Culture: TAMARA STARSHOVA
Faculty of Ecology and Biology: ERNEST IVANTER
Faculty of Economics: VLADIMIR AKULOV
Faculty of Forest Engineering: ALEXANDER PITUKHIN
Faculty of History: SERGEY VERIGIN
Faculty of Improvement of Professional Skills: TATYANA AGARKOVA
Faculty of Industrial and Civil Engineering: YURY MARKADANOV
Faculty of Law: SERGEY CHERNOV
Faculty of Mathematics: VLADIMIR SHESTAKOV
Faculty of Medicine: YURY LUPANDIN
Faculty of Mining and Geology: VLADIMIR AMINOV
Faculty of Philology: ANDREY KUNILSKY
Faculty of Physical Engineering: VALERY SYSUN
Faculty of Political and Social Sciences: VALENTINA MAKSIMOVA

POMORSKY STATE UNIVERSITY 'M. V. LOMONSOV'

163002 Arkhangelsk, Lomosova pr. 4
Telephone: (8182) 28-07-80
Fax: (8182) 28-07-80
E-mail: dit@pomorsu.ru
Internet: www.pomorsu.ru
State control
Founded 1991; present name and status 1996
Rector: Prof. VLADIMIR N. BULATOV
First Pro-Rector: YURI V. KUDRYASHOV
Pro-Rectors for Academic Affairs: IRINA R. LUGOVSKAYA, LEONID N. SHESTAKOV
Pro-Rector for Admin. and Finance: ALEXANDER G. LESCHIKOV
Pro-Rector for External Academic Affairs: ANATOLY A. SEMIN
Pro-Rector for Int. Affairs: ALEXANDER S. KRYLOV
Pro-Rector for Science: VLADISLAV I. GOLDIN
Library of 700,000 vols
Number of students: 12,419

ROSTOV STATE UNIVERSITY OF ECONOMICS (RINKH)

344007 Rostov-on-Don, Bol. Sadovaya ul. 69
Telephone: (8632) 66-51-23
Fax: (8632) 65-45-21
E-mail: rector@rseu.ru
Internet: www.rseu.ru
Founded 1931
Rector: VLADIMIR S. ZOLOTAREV
Library of 750,000 vols
Number of teachers: 400
Number of students: 15,830
Publications: *Bulletin* (4 a year), *Scientific Notes* (4 a year).

RUSSIAN STATE SOCIAL UNIVERSITY

107150 Moscow, ul. Losinoostrovskaya 24
Moscow, ul. Vilgelma Pika ul., korp. 1
Telephone: (495) 187-60-25
Fax: (495) 783-71-25
E-mail: info@mgsu.info
Internet: www.rgsu.net
Founded 1991 as Russian State Social Institute; accredited with univ. status as Moscow State Social Univ. 1994; present name 2004
Rector: Prof. VASILY I. ZHUKOV
Vice-Rector: GENNADY V. SAENKO

DEANS

Faculty of Foreign Languages: IRINA N. TUPITSYNA
Faculty of Further Education: TAMARA S. SUMSKAYA
Faculty of Humanities: LEONID G. LAPTEV
Faculty of Law: DIMITRY V. ILYAKOV
Faculty of Personnel Training and Qualification Improvement: TATYANA V. SHELYAG
Faculty of Socioeconomics: NIKOLAI N. PILIPENKO
Faculty of Social Information Technologies: VITALY M. ARISTOV
Faculty of Social Insurance and Finance: ALEXANDER A. GRUNIN
Faculty of Social Management: OLGA A. URZHA
Faculty of Social Medicine and Rehabilitation Technologies: VALENTINA V. CHESHIKHINA
Faculty of Sociology: DINA T. KABDULLINOVA
Faculty of Social Work, Pedagogy and Psychology: VLADISLAV A. NIKITIN
Faculty of Work and Employment Security: YURI G. SOROKIN

RUSSIAN STATE TRADE AND ECONOMICS UNIVERSITY

125993 Moscow, ul. Smolnaya 36
Telephone: (495) 458-94-79
Fax: (495) 458-72-47
E-mail: mail@rsute.ru
Internet: www.rsute.ru
Founded 1930
Language of instruction: Russian
Academic year: September to July
Rector: Prof. Dr SERGEY N. BABURIN
Library of 900,239 vols
Number of students: 75,000
Publications: *Caucasian research notes* (scientific journal), *Science Horizons*, *Vestnik of RSUTE* (scientific journal)

DEANS

Faculty of Computing Technologies: Prof. DMITRY NECHAEV
Faculty of Commerce and Marketing: Prof. TATYANA PARAMONOVA
Faculty of Finance and Economics: Prof. ALEKSANDR LITVINYUK
Faculty of Hospitality, Restaurant Business and Services: Prof. SERGEY DRUGANOV
Faculty of Law: Prof. OLEG SAULYAK
Faculty of Social Technologies: Prof. NIKOLAY MASLOV
Faculty of Tax and Taxation: Prof. DMITRY RAZUMOVSKY
Faculty of Management: Prof. LYUDMILA NIKITINA
Faculty of World Economics and Trade: Prof. ELENA VAVILOVA

RUSSIAN STATE UNIVERSITY FOR THE HUMANITIES

125267 Moscow, Miusskaya pl. 6
Telephone: (495) 250-61-18
Fax: (495) 250-51-09
E-mail: afn@rggu.msk.su
Internet: www.rsuh.ru
Founded 1991
Rector: Prof. YURI N. AFANASYEV
Library of 1,500,000 vols
Number of teachers: 484
Number of students: 4,120

ST PETERSBURG STATE UNIVERSITY

199034 St Petersburg, Universitetskaya nab. 7/9
Telephone: (812) 328-20-00
Fax: (812) 328-04-02
E-mail: office@inform.pu.ru
Internet: www.spbu.ru
Founded 1724
State control
Academic year: September to June (2 terms)
Rector: Prof. NIKOLAY M. KROPACHEV
Vice-Rector: I. A DEMENTYEV
Vice-Rector for Academics: Prof. IGOR A. GORLINSKY
Vice-Rector for Academic Affairs: Prof. NIKOLAY V. KALEDIN
Vice-Rector for Admission: Prof. VALERY S. KATKALO
Vice-Rector for Economics: Prof. IVAN I. BOYKO
Vice-Rector for Economy and Social Devt: Prof. STANISLAV G. EREMEEV
Vice-Rector for Innovative Devt Projects: ILYA A. DEMENTYEV
Vice-Rector for Int. Affairs: Prof. KONSTANTIN K. KHUDOLEY
Vice-Rector for Legal Issues: MIKHAIL N. KUDILINSKY
Vice-Rector for Philology and Arts: Prof. SERGEY I. BOGDANOV
Vice-Rector for Research: Prof. NIKOLAY G. SKVORTSOV
Librarian: MAXIM GORKY
Library: see Libraries and Archives
Number of teachers: 6,000
Number of students: 32,400
Publications: *Jurisprudence*, *Vestnik St. Petersburg University* (Journal, in 7 series)

DEANS

Faculty of Applied Mathematics: Dr LEON A. PETROSIAN
Faculty of Arts: VALERY A. GERGIEV
Faculty of Asian and African Studies: Prof. EVGENIY I. ZENELEV
Faculty of Biology and Soil Science: Prof. IGOR A. GORLINSKY
Faculty of Chemistry: Prof. ALEXANDER YU. BILIBIN
Faculty of Economics: Prof. IVAN P. BOYKO
Faculty of Geography and Geo-Ecology: Prof. NIKOLAY V. KALDENIN
Faculty of Geology: Prof. IGOR V. BULDAKOV
Faculty of History: Prof. ANDREY YU. DVORNICHENKO
Faculty of International Relations: Prof. KONSTANTIN K. KHUDOLEY
Faculty of Journalism: Prof. ANATOLY S. PUYU
Faculty of Law: Prof. NIKOLAY. M. KROPACHEV
Faculty of Management: Prof. VALERY S. KATKALO
Faculty of Mathematics and Mechanics: Prof. GENNADY. A. LEONOV
Faculty of Medicine: Prof. PETR K. YABLONSKY
Faculty of Oriental Studies: Dr I. M. STEBLIN-KAMENSKY
Faculty of Philology: Prof. LUDMILA A. VERBITSKAYA
Faculty of Philosophy: Prof. YURY N. SOLONIN
Faculty of Physics: Dr ALEXANDER S. CHIRTSOV
Faculty of Political Science: Prof. STANISLAV G. EREMEEV
Faculty of Psychology: Dr LARISSA A. TSVETKOVA
Faculty of Sociology: Dr NIKOLAY G. SKVORTSOV

ATTACHED INSTITUTES

Institute of Astronomy: Dir Dr V. V. VITYAZEV.
Botanical Gardens: Dir V. N. NIKITINA.
Institute of Applied Mathematics: Dir Dr D. A. OVSIANNIKOV.
Institute of Biology: Dir Dr D. V. OSIPOV.
Institute of Chemistry: Dir Dr YU. E. ERMOLENKO.
Institute of Complex Social Research: Dir Dr V. E. SEMENOV.
Institute of Geography: Dir Dr A. I. CHISTOBAEV.
Institute of the Earth's Crust: Dir Dr V. V. KURILENKO.
Institute of Mathematics and Mechanics: Dir Dr G. A. LEONOV.
Institute of Physics: Dir Dr YE. I. RYUMTSEV.
Institute of Physiology: Dir Dr I. YE. KANUNIKOV.
Institute of Radiophysics: Dir O. V. SOLOVIEV.
Institute of Information Technology: Dir Dr A. N. TEREKHOV.
Institute of Laser Research: Dir Dr YU. S. TVERIANOVICH.

ST PETERSBURG STATE UNIVERSITY OF CINEMA AND TELEVISION

191126 St Petersburg, ul. Pravdy 13
Telephone: (812) 315-74-83
E-mail: info@gukit.ru
Internet: www.gukit.ru
Founded 1918
Study areas incl. art of cinema and television, economics, electrical engineering, film equipment, film and photographic materials
Rector: Prof. ALEXANDER A. BELUSOV
Library of 500,000 vols
Number of students: 4,500
Publication: *Proceedings*.

ST PETERSBURG STATE UNIVERSITY OF ECONOMICS AND FINANCE

191023 St Petersburg, ul. Sadovaya 21
Telephone: (812) 310-38-23
Fax: (812) 110-56-74
E mail: rector@finec.ru
Internet: www.finec.ru
Founded 1930, present name and status 1997
Faculties of accounting, banking, economic theory, finance, industrial economics, international economic relations, management, marketing, statistics; also comprises a Higher Economics School
Rector: LEONID S. TARASEVICH
Number of teachers: 2,000
Number of students: 12,000
Library: 1m. vols.

SAKHALIN STATE UNIVERSITY

693008 Yuzhno-Sakhalinsk, ul. Lenina 290
Telephone: (424) 42-43-57
E-mail: admin@sakhgu.sakhalin.ru
Internet: www.sakhgu.ru
State control
Founded 1949 as teacher training institute, reorganized into Yuzhno-Sakhalinsk State Pedagogical Institute in 1954; present name and status 1998
Rector: Dr BORIS R. MISIKOV
Library of 613,099 vols
Number of teachers: 350
Number of students: 7,483
Publications: *Law Journal*, *Maymanovsky Readings*, *Philological Journal*, *Regional Studies Bulletin*.

SAMARA STATE UNIVERSITY

443011 Samara, ul. Akademika Pavlova 1
Telephone: (8462) 34-54-02
Fax: (8462) 34-54-17
E-mail: avn@ssu.samara.ru
Internet: www.ssu.samara.ru
Founded 1969
State control
Language of instruction: Russian, English
Academic year: September to June
Rector: GENNADY P. YAROVOY
First Pro-Rector: PETR S. KABYTOV
Pro-Rector for Education: VITALY P. GARKIN
Pro-Rector for Science: YURI N. GORELOV
Chief Librarian: GALINA A. BARSUKOVA
Library of 900,000 vols
Number of teachers: 820
Number of students: 14,000
Publications: *Bulletin* (8 a year), *Physics of Wave Processes and Radio-Technical Systems* (4 a year), *Samara Zemsky Collection* (4 a year)

DEANS

Faculty of Biology: G. L. RYTOV
Faculty of Chemistry: S. V. KURBATOVA
Faculty of History: U. N. SMIRNOV
Faculty of Languages and Literature: A. A. BEZRUKOVA
Faculty of Law: A. A. NAPREENKO
Faculty of Mathematics and Mechanics: V. M. KLIMKIN
Faculty of Physics: V. V. IVAKHNIK
Faculty of Psychology: K. S. LISETSKY
Faculty of Sociology: V. YA. MACHNEV

PROFESSORS

ASTAFIEV, V. I., Mechanics
BLATOV, V. A., Inorganic Chemistry
BREUSOV, Y. G., Economics
BULANOVA, A. V., General Chemistry and Chromatography
FILATOV, O. P., Equations of Mathematical Physics
GIZATULLIN, M. H., Physics and Mathematics
GOLUBKOV, S. A., Russian and Foreign Literature
GORELOV, Y. N., Differential Equations
KABYTOV, P. S., History of Russia
KHRAMKOV, I. V., History of Russia
KLIMKIN, V. M., Functional Analysis
KOMOV, A. N., Electronics
KONEV, V. A., Philosophy of the Humanities Faculties
KOZENKO, B. D., World History
KOZHEVNIKOV, Y. N., Physics and Mathematics
LEONOV, M. I., Russian History
LOBACHEV, A. L., Chemistry and Chromatography
MATVEEV, N. M., Ecology, Botany and Environmental Protection
MERKULOVA, N. A., Human and Animal Physiology
MOLEVICH, E. F., Sociology and Political Science
PLAKSINA, T. I., Ecology, Botany and Environmental Protection
PODKOVKIN, V. G., Biochemistry
PURYGIN, P. P., Organic Chemistry
RUDNEVA, T. I., Education
RYMAR, N. T., Russian and Foreign Literature
SARAEV, L. A., Mathematics and Computers
SEREZHKIN, V. N., Inorganic Chemistry
SEREZHKINA, L. B., Inorganic Chemistry
SHEIFER, S. A., Criminal Court Proceedings and Investigation
SHESTAKOV, A. A., Philosophy
SIKORA, P. E., State and Administrative Law
SKOBELEV, V. P., Russian and Foreign Literature
SKOBLIKOVA, Y. S., Philology, Russian Language

SOBOLEV, V. A., Differential Equations
SOLODYANNIKOV, Y. V., Functional Analysis and Theory of Functions
VOSKRESENSKY, V. E., Algebra and Geometry
YAROVOY, G. P., Radiophysics and Computers
ZAGUZOV, I. S., Mechanics

SARATOV STATE UNIVERSITY 'N. G. CHERNYSHEVSKY'

410012 Saratov, Astrakhanskaya ul. 83
Telephone: (2) 26-16-96
Fax: (2) 27-85-29
E-mail: rector@sgu.ru
Internet: www.sgu.ru
Founded 1909
State control
Academic year: September to July

Br. in Astrakhan; colleges and institutes: College of Radioelectronics, P. N. Yablochkov; Geological College; College of Management and Service; Pedagogical Institute in Balashov.

Rector: LEONID YU. KOSSOVICH
Vice-Rector for Academic Affairs: IRINA YU. IVANYUSHINA
Vice-Rector for Int. Affairs: DIMITRY V. PROKHOROV
Vice-Rector for Science: DIMITRY A. USANOV
Registrars: YURI SKLYAROV, SVETLANA MUSHTAKOVA
Librarian: VERA A. ARTISEVICH

Library: 3m. vols
Number of teachers: 1,951
Number of students: 28,075

Publications: *Applied Nonlinear Dynamics, Contemporary Herpertology, Differential Equations and Functions Theory, Electrochemical Energetics, Entomological and Parasitological Research in the Volga Region, Mechanics of Deformable Environments, News of Higher Educational Institutions, News of Saratov University, Numbers Theory Research, Problems of Applied Physics*

DEANS

Biology: Dr GENNADIY V. SHLYAKHTIN
Chemistry: Dr OLGA V. FEDOROVA
Computer Sciences and Information Technologies: Dr DMITRY V. SPERANSKY
Geography: Dr ALEXEY N. CHUMACHENKO
Geology: Dr EVGENY M. PERVUSHOV
History: Dr VELIKHAN S. MIRZEKHANOV
Humanities and Social Sciences: Dr YURI P. SUSLOV
Mechanics and Mathematics: Dr ANDREY M. ZAKHAROV
Non-Linear Processes: Dr YURIY I. LEVIN
Philology: Dr VALERY V. PROZOROV
Philosophy: Dr VLADIMIR N. BELOV
Physics: Dr IGOR N. SALY
Sociology: Dr GENNADIY V. DYLNOV

SOUTH URAL STATE UNIVERSITY

454080 Chelyabinsk, pr. Lenina 76
Telephone: (3512) 65-65-04
Fax: (3512) 65-38-04
E-mail: iao@susu.ac.ru
Internet: www.susu.ac.ru

Founded 1943, fmrly Chelyabinsk State Technical Univ., present name and status 1997
State control
Academic year: September to June

Consists of 33 faculties, 13 branches and 8 regional campuses

Rector: Prof. GERMAN P. VYATKIN
First Vice-Rector for Academics: Prof. GENNADY G. MIKHAILOV
Vice-Rector for Academics: Prof. SERGEY Y. GUREVICH
Vice-Rector for Admin. and Finance: Prof. VADIM A. TROFIMYCHEV
Vice-Rector for Scientific Affairs: Prof. ALEXANDER L. SHESTAKOV
Registrar: IGOR V. SIDOROV
Dir of Int. Relations Dept: SERGEY G. BARYSHNIKOV
Dir of Library: IRINA P. BERGER

Number of teachers: 5,000
Number of students: 55,000

Publication: *Bulletin* (12 a year)

DEANS

Architecture Faculty: SALAVAT G. SHABIEV
Architecture and Construction Faculty: VLADIMIR V. SPASIBOZHKO
Automobile and Tractor Faculty: YURI V. ROZHDESTVENSKY
Commerce Faculty: VALENTINA Y. LOPATINA
Economics and Business Faculty: VALENTINA A. KISELEVA
Economics and Management Faculty: VICTOR I. BARHATOV
Electronics Faculty: LEV S. KAZARINOV
International Faculty: VLADIMIR P. GORSHENIN
Law Faculty: VLADIMIR I. MAYOROV
Law and Finance Faculty: BORIS I. ROVNY
Linguistics Faculty: TAMARA N. KHOMUTOVA
Mechanical-Mathematical Faculty: ALEXANDR D. DROZIN
Mechanical-Technological Faculty: ALEXANDR I. SIDOROV
Physical Faculty: NATALIA D. KUNDIKOVA
Physical and Metallurgical Faculty: YURI D. KORIAGIN
Power Engineering Faculty: YURI I. KHOKHLOV
Faculty of Psychology: NIKOLAY A. BATURIN
Service and Light Industry Faculty: VICTOR A. LIVSHITS
Social and Humanitarian Faculty: VICTOR S. BALAKIN
Rocket Space Technology Faculty: YURI S. PAVLYUK
Valeology, Physical Training and Sports Faculty: YURI M. CHERNETSKY

SOUTHERN FEDERAL UNIVERSITY

344006 Rostov-on-Don, ul. Bolshaya Sadovaya 105/42
Telephone: (863) 263-31-58
Fax: (863) 263-84-98
E-mail: info@sfedu.ru
Internet: www.sfedu.ru

Founded 2006 by merger of Rostov State Acad. of Architecture and Arts, Rostov State Pedagogical Univ. and Taganrog State Radio Engineering Univ. to the Rostov State Univ.
State Control

37 Faculties, 16 research institutes and design centres, 15 education and research centres

Rector: Dr Sc. Prof. VLADISLAV G. ZAKHAREVICH
Sr Vice-Rectors for Academic Affairs: Prof. IGOR M. UZNARODOV
Sr Vice-Rector for Research and Innovations: EVGENY K. AYDARKIN
Vice-Rector for Curriculum and Staff Devt: Prof. IRINA V. MOSTOVAYA
Vice-Rector for Economics: ALEKSEY Y. ARHIPOV
Vice-Rector for Int. Relations: Assoc. Prof. SERGEY A. DUZHIKOV
Vice-Rector for Human Resources: ANATOLY G. MISNIK
Academic Sec.: Dr VALENTINA N. CHYBAROVA

Library of 2,411,520 vols, 2.3m. books, 180,000 books in European and Arabic languages, 600,000 periodicals, 8,000 rare items (incl. MSS, W European publs from 16th–18th centuries, traditional Cyrillic type books, rare and banned edns of the works of Karl Marx, Lenin and other political figures)
Number of teachers: 3,508
Number of students: 44,889

DEANS

Faculty of Biology and Soils: VITOLD G. PARSHIN
Faculty of Chemistry: EVGENY B. TSUPAK
Faculty of Economics: Prof. VALERY A. ALESHIN
Faculty of Geology and Geography: Prof. NIKOLAY I. BOYKO
Faculty of High Technologies: ANATOLY E. PANICH
Faculty of History: NIKOLAI A. TRAPSH
Faculty of Information Security: SVETLANA M. LYAH
Faculty of Law: Assoc. Prof. SVETLANA M. LYAKH
Faculty of Mathematics, Mechanics and Computer Science: Prof. MIKHAIL I. KARYAKIN
Faculty of Military Instruction
Faculty of Philology and Journalism: Assoc. Prof. ELENA V. GRIGORYEVA
Faculty of Philosophy and Culture Studies: Prof. GENNADY V. DRACH
Faculty of Physics: VYACHESLAV S. MALYSHEVSKY
Faculty of Psychology: Prof. PAVEL N. ERMAKOV
Faculty of Regional Studies: NATALYA I. CHERNOBROVKINA
Faculty of Social and Political Science: VIKTOR I. FILONENKO

SFU INSTITUTES

Institute of Architecture and Art

344082 Rostov-on-Don, Budennovsky pr. 39
Telephone: (8632) 39-09-62
E-mail: rai@aaanet.ru
Founded 1988

Architecture, environmental design, arts and crafts, history of art, fashion design, management in architecture

Library of 300,000 vols
Number of teachers: 181
Number of students: 1,091

Rector: V. A. KOLESNIK

Publication: *Problems of Architectural Education* (1 a year)

SFU Pedagogical Institute

Rostov oblast, 347928 Taganrog, GSP-17a, Nekrasovsky pr. 44
Telephone: (863) 4431-05-98
Fax: (863) 446-05-19
E-mail: rspu@rspu.edu.ru
Internet: www.rspu.edu.ru

Founded 1869 as Rostov State Pedagogical Univ.
Academic year: September to June

Dir: Dr Sc. Prof. VLADIMIR I. MAREEV
Number of students: 1,746

Taganrog Institute of Technology

Rostov oblast, 347928 Taganrog, GSP-17a, Nekrasovsky pr. 44
Telephone: (863) 439-30-29
Fax: (863) 431-05-98
E-mail: rector@tsure.ru
Internet: www.tsure.ru

Founded 1952 as Taganrog Institute of Radio Engineering, renamed Taganrog State Univ. of Radio Engineering 1993, present status 2006
Academic year: September to June

Head: ALEKSANDER IVANOVICH SUKHINOV

First Deputy Head: VICTOR ALEKSANDROVICH OBUKHOVETS
Deputy Head for Int. Relations: VADIM P. POPOV
Library of 980,000 vols
Number of teachers: 804
Number of students: 11,300

ACADEMIC INSTITUTES AND RESEARCH INSTITUTES

Institute of Economics and Foreign Economic Relations: 344002 Rostov-on-Don, Soborny 26; tel. and fax (863) 244-15-02; e-mail iecier@sfedu.ru.

Inter-regional Institute of Social Science: 344006 Rostov-on-Don, Bol. Sadovaya 105; e-mail narezhni@mis.sfedu.ru; internet www.rostov.iriss.ru; Acad. Dir ANATOLY IVANOVICH NAREZHNY.

Institute of Law and Management.

Independent Russian—Germany Institute of Journalism.

ATTACHED RESEARCH CENTRES

Research and Educational Centre 'Nanotechnologies': integration of education and research as well as improvement of cooperation with scientific orgs and institutes of South Federal Dist.

Research Centre for Nanoscale structure of Matter: 344090 Rostov-on-Don, Sorge 5; tel. (8632) 97-53-26; e-mail asoldatov@phys.rsu.ru; internet www.nano.sfedu.ru; study of 3D local atomic nanoscale geometry and electronic structure in various types of advanced novel materials; Dir Prof. ALEXANDER V SOLDATOV.

14 attached research institutes.

STATE UNIVERSITY FOR THE HUMANITIES

119334 Moscow, Leninsky pr-t, 32A
Telephone: (495) 938-10-09
Fax: (495) 938-22-88
E-mail: gugn@gugn.info
Internet: www.gugn.ru
State control
Founded 1992 as the Republican Centre for Humanities Education; present name 1998
Institutes of advancement of qualifications and teacher training, economics, culture, history, law, literary culture and management, philosophy, politology, psychology, sociology, world politics
Rector: Prof. ALEXANDER O. CHUBARYAN
First Pro-Rector: Prof. NATALYA N. NIKITINA
Pro-Rector for Gen. Affairs: GEORGY N. KRASNOV
Pro-Rector for Science: Prof. MIKHAIL V. BIBIKOV
Academic Sec.: DENIS V. FOMIN-NILOV.

STATE UNIVERSITY OF MANAGEMENT

109542 Moscow, Ryazansky pr. 99
Telephone: (495) 371-13-22
Fax: (495) 174-62-81
E-mail: rectorat@guu.ru
Internet: www.guu.ru
Founded 1919
Rector: ANATOLY G. PORSHNEV
Library of 280,000 vols
Number of teachers: 700
Number of students: 10,000

STAVROPOL STATE UNIVERSITY

355009 Stavropol, ul. Pushkina 1
Telephone: (8652) 35-72-65
Fax: (8652) 35-40-33
E-mail: stavsu@stavsu.ru
Internet: www.stavsu.ru
State control
Founded 1930 as Stavropol Agro-Pedagogical Institute; 1932–1994 as Stavropol Pedagogical Institute, 1994–1996 as Stavropol State Pedagogical Univ., present name 1996
Academic year: September to June
Rector: Prof. VLADIMIR ALEXANDROVICH
Vice-Rector for Capital Construction: LUBENETS YURIY PETROVICH
Vice-Rector for Curriculum: Prof. BELOZEROV VITALY SEMENOVICH
Vice-Rector for Economic Issues and Additional Educational Programmes: Prof. EROKHIN ALEKSEY MIKHAILOVICH
Vice-Rector for Maintenance: VASILENKO ANATOLIY KUZMICH
Vice-Rector for Research: Prof. LIKHOVID ANDREY ALEXANDROVICH
Vice-Rector for Security: Assoc. Prof. TERESCHENKO NIKOLAY VIKTOROVICH
Dean of Extra Mural and Externship Dept: Prof. TARANOVA TATYANA NIKOLAEVNA
Dir for Studies: Assoc. Prof. VOLKOVA VALENTINA IVANOVNA
Dir for Univ. Scientific Library: KUZMINA ELENA ANATOLIEVNA
Library: 1.2m. vols, 382 periodicals
Number of teachers: 900
Number of students: 15,000
Publication: *Stavropol State University Vestnik*

DEANS

Advanced Training: Prof. GUROV VALERIY NIKOLAEVICH
Arts: Assoc. Prof. MARKOV ALEKSANDR IVANOVICH
Economics: Prof. AKININ PETR VIKTOROVICH
Geography: Prof. SCHITOVA NATALYA ALEKSANDROVNA
History: Prof. KUDRYAVSTEV ALEXANDER ABAKAROVICH
Law: Assoc. Prof. SCHERBAKOVA LUDMILA MIKHAILOVNA
Medicine Biology and Chemistry: Prof. IVANOV ALEXANDER LVOVICH
Philology and Journalism: Assoc. Prof. SERBRYAKOV ANATOLY ALEKSEEVICH
Physical Education: Prof. MAGIN VLADIMIR ALEKSEEVICH
Physics and Mathematics: Assoc. Prof. AGIBOVA IRINA MARKOVNA
Psychology: Prof. AKHVERDOVA OLGA ALBERTOVNA
Romance and Germanic Languages: Prof. LOMTEVA TATYANA NIKOLAEVNA

SURGUT STATE UNIVERSITY

628400 Tyumen oblast, Surgut, ul. Energetikov 30
Telephone: (3462) 52-47-00
Fax: (3462) 52-47-29
E-mail: info@inao.surgu.ru
Internet: www.surgu.ru
Founded 1993
Private control
Rector: Prof. GEORGY I. NAZIN
Vice-Rector for Academic Affairs: Prof. YURI V. KUZNETSOV
Vice-Rector for Admin. and Finance: Dr BORIS U. SERAZETDINOV
Vice-Rector for Capital Construction: KONSTANTIN S. MOKHOV
Vice-Rector for Distance Learning: Prof. SERGEI F. KOZHUKOV
Vice-Rector for Economic and Social Affairs: VIKTOR I. LYUTY
Vice-Rector for Information Resources: Dr NIKOLAI G. SHEVCHENKO
Vice-Rector for Science: Dr VIKTOR P. SAMSONOV
Vice-Rector for Student Affairs: Dr BORIS U. SERAZETDINOV
Librarian: VALENTINA N. SHEVCHENKO
Library of 282,354 vols

DEANS

Biology: VLADIMIR P. STARIKOV
Economics: LEONID A. AVDEEV
Engineering and Physics: NIKOLAI N. BADULIN
History: ALEXANDER I. PRISCHEPA
Information Technology: FEDOR F. IVANOV
Law: VLADIMIR V. CHERUSHEV
Linguistics: SVETLANA G. KULAGINA
Medicine: LUDMILA V. KOVALENKO
Physical Culture: SERGEI M. OBUKHOV
Psychology: IRINA P. GREKHOVA

SYKTYVKAR STATE UNIVERSITY

167001 Syktyvkar, Oktyabrskii pr. 55
Telephone: (8212) 43-68-20
Fax: (8212) 43-68-20
E-mail: ssu@syktsu.ru
Internet: www.syktsu.ru
Founded 1972
State control
Languages of instruction: Russian, Komi
Academic year: September to July
Rector: VASILY N. ZADOROZHNY
Vice-Rector: NIKOLAI A. TIKHONOV
Chief Admin. Officer: OLGA P. ZBOROVSKAYA
Librarian: V. PROKURATOVA
Number of teachers: 330
Number of students: 4,250
Publications: *Rubezh* (4 a year), *Vestnik* (1 a year)

DEANS

Faculty of Arts: LUDMILA V. GURLENOVA
Faculty of Chemistry and Biology: IRINA V. PIYR
Faculty of Finance and Economics: EVGENIA A. BADOKINA
Faculty of History: LUBOV A. MAKSIMOVA
Faculty of Humanities: ELENA G. TONKOVA
Faculty of Information Systems and Technologies: DMITRIY A. BELYAEV
Faculty of Law: DMITRIY I. PINAEVSKIY
Faculty of Mathematics: VYACHESLAV G. ANTONOV
Faculty of Management: LUDMILA I BUSHUEVA
Faculty of Philology: MIKHAIL V. MELIKHOV
Faculty of Physics and Engineering: YURIY N. BELYAEV
Faculty of Physical Training and Sports: SERGEI A. SOKOLOV
Faculty of Psychology and Social Work: LUDMILA I. BYKOVSKAYA

PROFESSORS

ARAPOV, N., Jurisprudence
BOLOTOV, S., Management
BRACH, B., Chemistry
IRZHAK, L., Physiology
KNJAZEVA, G., Finance
MIKHAILOVSKY, E., Computer Science
NAGAEV, V., Psychology
NIKETENKOV, V., Mathematics
NOVIKOV, Y., Management
POROSHKIN, A., Mathematical Analysis
SEMENOV, V., History
TIKHOMIROV, A., Mathematics
VITYAZEVA, V., Economics
ZADOROZHNIY, V., Economics
ZOLOTAREV, V., History

TAMBOV STATE UNIVERSITY 'G. R. DERZHAVIN'

392000 Tambov, Internatsionalnaya ul. 33
Telephone: (0752) 72-12-29
Fax: (0752) 72-36-31

E-mail: priem1@tsu.tmb.ru
Internet: tsutmb.ru

Founded 1994, on the basis of Tambov State Pedagogical Institute and Tambov State Institute of Culture
State control
Languages of instruction: English, French, Russian
Academic year: September to June

Rector: Prof. VLADISLAV YURIEV
Vice-Rector for Int. Relations: Prof. TATIANA OSADCHAYA
Vice-Rector for Academic Affairs: Prof. VLADIMIR MAMONTOV
Pro-Rector for Research: Prof. NIKOLAY BOLDYREV
Vice-Rector for Educational Policy and Innovation: Prof. MARINA CHVANOVA

Library: 1.5m. vols
Number of teachers: 900
Number of students: 15,000

Publications: *Issues of Cognitive Linguistics*, *Social-Economic Phenomena and Processes*, *Vestnik Tambovskogo Universiteta (Tambov University Reports)* (Series: Natural and Technical Sciences; the Humanities).

TOGLIATTI STATE UNIVERSITY

445667 Togliatti, Belorusskaya ul. 14
Telephone: (8482) 54-63-99
Fax: (8482) 53-95-22
E-mail: office@tltsu.ru
Internet: www.tltsu.ru

Founded 1951, as Togliatti Polytechnic Institute; present name and status 2001 following merger with Togliatti State Pedagogical Univ. (f. 1988)
Public conrol
Language of instruction: Russian
Academic year: September to June

Rector: Prof. Dr MIKHAIL M. KRISHTAL
First Vice-Rector: Assoc Prof. Dr NADEZHDA G. PUDOVKINA

Library of 1,093,941 vols
Number of teachers: 570
Number of students: 13,000

Publications: *Herald of the Humanities*, *Vector of Science*

DEANS

Faculty of Electrical Engineering: Assoc. Prof. Dr VLADIMIR SHAPOVALOV
Faculty of Fine, Decorative and Applied Arts: Assoc. Prof. Dr ALEXANDER KOZLYAKOV
Faculty of Mathematics and Informatics: Prof. Dr PETR ZYBROV
Faculty of Physical Education and Sport: Assoc. Prof. Dr VALENTINA BALASHOVA
Law Faculty: Prof. Dr RUDOLF KHACHATUROV
Teachers Training Faculty: Prof. Dr IRINA NEPROKINA

TOMSK STATE UNIVERSITY

634050 Tomsk, pr. Lenina 36
Telephone: (3822) 52-95-58
Fax: (3822) 52-95-85
E-mail: rector@tsu.ru
Internet: www.tsu.ru

Founded 1878
State control
Academic year: September to June

Faculties of applied mathematics and cybernetics, biology and soil science, chemistry, computer science, economics, foreign languages, geology and geography, history and international relations, journalism, law, mechanics and mathematics, philology, philosophy, physics, political science, psychology, sociology and radio-physics, technical physics; Institute of Culture; International Faculty of Public and Business Administration

Rector: Prof. GEORGY V. MAYER
Sr Vice-Rector: Dr MIKHAIL D. BABANSKY
Vice-Rector for Academic Affairs: Prof. ALEXANDER S. REVUSHKIN
Vice-Rector for Int. Affairs: Dr SERGEY N. KIRPOTIN
Vice-Rector For Research and Postgraduate Studies: Prof. GRIGORY E. DUNAEVSKY
Registrar: N. BUROVA
Librarian: EVGENY N. SYNTIN

Library: see Libraries and Archives
Number of teachers: 1,410
Number of students: 14,000 (10,000 full-time, 4,000 part-time)

Publications: *Krylovia: Siberian Botanical Journal* (2 a year), *Physics* (4 a year), *Vestnik* (4 a year).

TVER STATE UNIVERSITY

170100 Tver, ul. Zhelyabova 33
Telephone: (4822) 33-11-95
Fax: (4822) 33-12-74
E-mail: rector@tversu.ru
Internet: university.tversu.ru

Founded 1971
Academic year: September to June

Rector: ANDREY VKADLENOVICH BELOTSERKOVSKY
Pro-Rector: LIUDMILA NIKOLAEVNA SKAKOVSKAYA
Librarian: OLGA V. VERSHININA

Number of teachers: 720
Number of students: 10,000

TYUMEN STATE UNIVERSITY

625003 Tyumen, ul. Semakova 10
Telephone: (3452) 46-01-41
Fax: (3452) 46-19-30
E-mail: international@utmn.ru
Internet: www.utmn.ru

Founded 1930 as Tyumen Pedagogical Institute, present name 1973

Faculties of chemistry and biology, economics, geography, history, philology, physics and mathematics, romance and Germanic philology

Rector: Prof. Dr CHEBOTAREV GENNADY NIKOLAEVITCH
Pres.: Prof. Dr KUTSEV GENNADY PHILIPOVITCH

Number of teachers: 929
Number of students: 40,000

Publications: *Philological Discourse*, *Siberian Historical Journal*, *The Journal of Tyumen State University*.

UDMURT STATE UNIVERSITY

426034 Udmurt, Izhevsk, Universitetskaya ul. 1
Telephone: (3412) 68-16-10
Fax: (3412) 68-58-66
E-mail: adm@uni.udm.ru
Internet: www.udsu.ru

Founded 1931
State control
Language of instruction: Russian
Academic year: September to June

Rector: Prof. SEMEN D. BUNTOV
Chief Vice-Rector for Academic Affairs: Dr GALINA V. MERZLYAKOVA
Vice-Rector for Finance and Economics: GERMAN S. SERGEEV
Vice-Rector for Int. Relations: MARIA I. BESNOSOVA
Vice-Rector for Public Relations: Assoc. Prof. VLADIMIR A. BAYMETOV
Vice-Rector for Research and Devt, Business and Manufacturing Integration: Prof. NIKOLAY I. LEONOV
Vice-Rector for Strategic Planning and Devt of Territorial Division: Assoc. Prof. MICHAEL Y. MALYSHEV
Vice-Rector for Quality Assurance: Assoc. Prof. IGOR V. MENSHIKOV
Vice-Rector for Social and Educational Work and Extra Curricular Activities: SERGEY V. VOSTROKUTNOV
Dir of the Univ. Library: LYUDMILA P. BESKLINSKAYA

Library of 1,000,000 vols, 40 periodicals, 50 newspapers
Number of teachers: 1,000
Number of students: 25,000

Publications: *Management: Theory and Practice* (4 a year), *Nonlinear Dynamics* (4 a year), *Problems of Regional Economics* (4 a year), *Quantum, Computers and Computing* (1 a year), *Regular and Chaotic Dynamics)* (English version, 6 series a year), *Udmurt University* (12 a year), *Univer.ru* (12 a year), *Vestnik UdSU* (6 series, 2 a year)

DEANS

Faculty of Biology and Chemistry: NIKOLAY E. ZUBTSOVSKY
Faculty of Geography: IVAN I. RYSSIN
Faculty of History: NADEZHA YU. STARKOVA
Faculty of Journalism: VLADIMIR A. BAYMETOV
Faculty of Mathematics: NIKOLAY N. PETROV
Faculty of Medical Biotechnology: ALEXEY K. BARSUKOV
Faculty of Oil and Gas: ALEXEY YA. VOLKOV
Faculty of Philosophy and Sociology: Prof. MARINA N. MAKAROVA
Faculty of Physics and Energetics: VLADIMIR P. BOVIN
Faculty of Professional Foreign Language Study: RAISA G. SHISHKINA
Faculty of Psychology, Pedagogics and Social Technology: Prof. ALEXANDER A. BARANOV
Faculty of Russian Philology: ELENA A. PODSHIVALOVA
Faculty of Udmurt Philology: LUBOV P. FYODOROVA
Pedagogical Faculty of Physical Training: ALEXANDER E. ALABUZHEV
Institute of Arts and Design: MARINA V. BOTYA
Institute of Civil Defence: VLADIMIR M. KOLODKIN
Institute of Economics and Management: ANATOLY A. ANOSHIN
Institute of Foreign Languages and Literature: Prof. TAMARA E. ZELENINA
Institute of Law, Social Management and Security: VLADIMIR G. IVSHIN
Institute of Social Communications: LARISA V. BATALOVA

PROFESSORS

Faculty of Biology and Chemistry (tel. (3412) 75-56-48; fax (3412) 75-58-66; e-mail bhf@uni.udm.ru):

BARANOVA, O., Botany and Plant Ecology
KORNEV, V., Inorganic and Analytic Chemistry
MAKAROVA, L., Physical and Organic Chemistry
PRONICHEV, I., Anatomy and Human and Animal's Physiology
TUGANAEV, V., General Ecology

Faculty of Geography (tel. (3412) 916070; e-mail rvsin@uni.udm.ru):

RYSSIN, I. I., Physical Geography and Landscape Ecology
STURMAN, V. I., Natural Use and Geo-Ecological Cartography

Faculty of History (tel. (3412) 916184; e-mail history@udsu.ru):

EFREMOVA, T., Native History of newer time
GOLDINA, R., Archeology and the History of Primitive Society
SANNIKOV, N., New History and International Relations
SHISHKINA, N., Ancient World and the Middle Ages
VLADYKIN, V. E., Ethnology and Regional Study

Faculty of Information Technology and Computer Engineering (tel. (3412) 916131; e-mail rodionov@uni.udm.ru):

BELTYUKOV, A., Theoretical and Informatic Basis
ISLAMOV, G., Computation and Parallel Programming
KOLODKIN, V., Mathematical Modelling and Forecasting
NIKOLAY, N., Theory and Methodology of Informatics

Faculty of Mathematics (tel. (3412) 916086; e-mail dekanmf@udsu.ru):

BELTYUKOV, A., Mathematical Provision for Computers and Software
DERR, V., Mathematical Analysis
GRYZLOV, A., Algebra and Topology
ISLAMOV, G., Calculus Mathematics
KARPOV, A., Computer Techniques
KONDRATYEV, B., Astronomy and Topology
TONKOV, E., Differential Equation

Faculty of Physics and Energetics (tel. (3412) 916129; e-mail bovin@uni.udm.ru):

TARPEZNIKOV, V., Surface Physics

Faculty of Philology (tel. (3412) 916154; e-mail ktl@udm.ru):

DONETSKIK, L., Contemporary Russian Language and History
PODSHIVOLAVA, E., Russian Literature of the 20th Century and Folklore
SHEIDAEVA, S., Language Theory and Speech
VOROZHTSOVA, I., Lingual Didactics

Faculty of Professional Foreign Languages (tel. (3412) 685557; e-mail profin@udm.ru):

MERZLYAKOVA, A., Romance Languages

Faculty of Sociology and Philosophy (tel. (3412) 916020):

KRUTKIN, V., Philosophy and Sociology of CultureLADYZHETZ, N., Sociology

Faculty of Udmurt Philology (tel. (3412) 755920):

KELMAKOV, V. K., General and Finno-Ugric Linguistics
SHUTOV, A. F., Udmurt Language and Pedagogy
TARAKANOV, I. V., Udmurt Language and Pedagogy
VLADIKINA, T. G., Russian Philology

Institute of Economics and Management (tel. (3412) 916062; e-mail ier@inem.uni.udm.ru):

BOTKIN, O. I., Economic Theory
LETCHIKOV, A. V., Mathematical Methods in Economics
MATVEEV, V. V., Business Economics
PEREVOSCHIKOV, YU. S., Business Economics

Institute of Foreign Languages and Literature (tel. (3412) 916179; e-mail ifl@pils.uni.udm.ru):

PUSHINA, N. I., Grammar and History of English
UTEKHINA, A. N., German Philology

Institute of Law, Social Management and Security (tel. (3412) 916002; e-mail lawfak@uni.udm.ru; internet www.ipsub.udsu.ru):

IAKOVLEV, V., Ecological and Agrarian Law and Law of Natural Resources
KAMINSKY, M. K., Criminology and Court Examination
POSKONINA, O. V., Philosophy and Sociology of Law
VOYTOVICH, V. YU., Legal Basis of State and Municipal Services
ZINATULLIN, Z. Z., Criminal Procedure

Institute of Pedagogic Philosophy and Social Technology (tel. (3412) 916119; e-mail baranov@ppf.uni.udm.ru):

BARANOV, A., Developmental Psychology and Differential Psychology
KHOTINETS, U., General Psychology
LEONOV, N., Social Psychology

Institute of Social Communications (tel. (3412) 916035; e-mail pr@udsu.ru):

RODIONOV, B., Sociology of Communications
YEROHIN, A., Publishing and Book Studies

ULYANOVSK STATE UNIVERSITY

432700 Ulyanovsk, ul. L. Tolstogo 42
Telephone: (8422) 41-20-88
Fax: (8422) 41-23-40
E-mail: contact@ulsu.ru
Internet: www.ulsu.ru
State control

Founded 1974

Rector: Prof. YURI V. POLYANSKOV
First Pro-Rector and Pro-Rector for Academic Affairs: TOFIK Z. BIKTIMINOV
Pro-Rector for Admin. and Finance: VALERY V. NEFEDKIN
Pro-Rector for Economic and Legal Affairs: NATALYA N. LOMOVYEVA
Pro-Rector for New Information and Teaching Technologies: DIMITRY YU. SHABALKIN
Pro-Rector for Pre-Univ. Education: SERGEI N. MITIN
Pro-Rector for Research: SERGEI V. BULYARSKY
Pro-Rector for Social Devt, Internal Communication and Marketing: TATYANA E. NIKITINA

Number of teachers: 635
Number of students: 10,695

URALS STATE UNIVERSITY

620083 Ekaterinburg, pr. Lenina 51
Telephone: (3432) 55-74-20
Fax: (3432) 55-59-64
E-mail: doc_office@usu.ru
Internet: www.usu.ru

Founded 1920
State control
Language of instruction: Russian
Academic year: September to July

Rector: Prof. VLADIMIR E. TRETYAKOV
Vice-Rector for Academics: Prof. VITALY P. PROKOPEV
Vice-Rector for Research: Prof. EVGENY A. PAMYATNYKH
Vice-Rector for Social Affairs: ANATOLY N. YAKOVLEV
Librarian: KLAVDIYA P. KUZNETSOVA

Library of 1,064,789 vols
Number of teachers: 900
Number of students: 12,400

DEANS

Faculty of Art Criticism and Culture: Asst Prof. T. A. RUNEVA
Faculty of Biology: Asst Prof. N. N. FIRSOV
Faculty of Chemistry: Assoc. Prof. A. A. VSHIVKOV
Faculty of Economics: Prof. D. V. NESTEROVA
Faculty of History: Asst Prof. D. V. BUGROV
Faculty of Journalism: Asst Prof. B. N. LOZOVSKY
Faculty of Mathematics and Mechanics: Assoc. Prof. M. O. ASANOV
Faculty of Philology: Prof. V. V. BLAZHES
Faculty of Philosophy: Prof. A. V. PERTSEV
Faculty of Physics: Prof. A. N. BABUSHKIN
Faculty of Psychology: Prof. G. A. GLOTOVA
Faculty of Sociology and Politics: Asst Prof. B. B. BAGIROV

PROFESSORS

Faculty of Art Criticism and Culture:

GOLINETS, S. V., History of Art
MIKHAILOV, S. A., Cultural Studies
PIVOVAROV, D. V., History and Philosophy of Religion
TROSHINA, T. M., Museology

Faculty of Biology:

BIBIN, I. A., Human and Animal Physiology
MUKHIN, V. A., Botany
NOVOZHENOV, Y. I., Zoology
PYANKOV, V. I., Plant Physiology

Faculty of Chemistry:

NEUCHADINA, L. N., Analytical Chemistry
NEYMAN, A. YA., Inorganic Chemistry
PETROV, A. N., Physical Chemistry
SUVOROVA, A. I., Higher Molecular Compounds
VSHIVKOV, A. A., Organic Chemistry

Faculty of Economics:

AKBERDINA, R. A., Economics
GREBENKIN, A. V., History and Theory of Management
IVANTSOV, G. B., Theory of Economics
MAZUROV, V. D., Economic Models and Information
NESTEROVA, D. V., Economic History and World Economics
SEMYAKIN, M. N., Economics and Law

Faculty of History:

CHERNUKHOV, A. V., Archives
CHEVTAEV, A. G., Modern History
MIKHAILENKO, V. I., Theory and History of Foreign Affairs
MINENKO, N. A., Ethnology and Special Historical Sciences
POLYAKOVSKAYA, M. A., Ancient and Medieval History
ROMANCHUK, A. I., Archaeology
SHASHKOV, A. G., Russian History

Faculty of Journalism:

BRODSKY, I. S., Television, Radio and Technical Methods of Journalism
KOVALEVA, M. M., History of the Press
LAZAREVA, E. H., Stylistics and Russian Language
OLESHKO, V. F., Periodical Press

Faculty of Mathematics and Mechanics:

ALBREKHT, E. G., Applied Mathematics
ARESTOV, V. V., Mathematical Analysis and Theory of Functions
ASANOV, M. O., Mathematics for Economics
IVANOV, A. O., Mathematical Physics
PROKOPIEV, V. P., Theoretical Mechanics
RYASHKO, L. V., Computational Mathematics
SHEVRIN, L. N., Algebra of Discrete Mathematics
TRETYAKOV, V. E., Computer Information Science and Management Processes

Faculty of Philology:

BABENKO, L. G., Modern Russian Language
BLAZHES, V. V., Folklore
BIKOV, L. P., Criticism of 20th-century Literary Theory
MATVEEV, A. V., General Linguistics
MIKHAILOVA, O. A., Rhetoric and Stylistics of Russian Language
PAVERMAN, V. M., Foreign Literature
SIDOROVA, O. G., Romance and Germanic Philology

Faculty of Philosophy:

BRYANIK, N. V., Ontology and Theory of Cognition

EREMEEV, A. P., Ethics, Aesthetics, History and Theory of Culture
KEMEROV, V. E., Social Philosophy
LYUBUTIN, K. N., History of Philosophy

Faculty of Physics:
BABUSHKIN, A. N., Low-Temperature Physics
BARANOV, N. V., Condensed Matter
BORISOV, S. F., General and Molecular Physics
GULYAEV, S. A., Astronomy and Geodesy
IVANOV, O. A., Magnetic Phenomena
MOSKVIN, A. S., Theoretical Physics
ZVEREV, L. P., Semiconductor Physics, Radiospectroscopy

Faculty of Psychology:
GLOTOVA, G. A., General Psychology and Psychology of Personality
LUPANDIN, V. I., Psychophysiology

Faculty of Sociology and Politics:
BAGIROV, B. B., Social Politics
BARAZGOVA, E. S., Theory and History of Sociology
MERENKOV, A. V., Sociology
MIRONOV, D. A., History of Politics

URAL STATE UNIVERSITY OF ECONOMICS

620219 Yekaterinburg, ul. 8 Marta 62
Telephone: (343) 257-96-15
Fax: (343) 257-71-47
E-mail: start@usue.ru
Internet: www.usue.ru

Founded 1967
Academic year: September to June
Rector: MIKHAIL FEDOROV
Library of 624,800 vols, 9000 periodicals
Number of teachers: 542
Number of students: 24,000

STOLETOV VLADIMIR STATE UNIVERSITY

600000 Vladimir, Gorkogo St. 87
Telephone: (4922) 47-77-79
Fax: (4922) 47-97-79
E-mail: prorms@vlsu.ru
Internet: www.vlsu.ru

Founded 1958
Public control
Languages of instruction: English, Russian
Academic year: September to June

Rector: Prof. VALENTIN V. MOROZOV
First Vice-Rector: Dr VALERIY G. PROKOSHEV
Vice-Rector for Methodological Work and Int. Cooperation: Prof. VLADIMIR A. NEMONTOV
Vice-Rector for Capital Building and Material Resources: Dr IGOR A. GANDELSMAN
Vice-Rector for Economics: Prof. SVETLANA M. BASHARINA
Vice-Rector for Education and Social Policy: Dr ANZOR M. SARALIDZE
Vice-Rector for Gen. Affairs: Dr ALEXANDER V. CHUB
Vice-Rector for Innovations and Strategic Devt: Prof. SERGEY M. ARAKELYAN
Vice-Rector for Research: Prof. VLADIMIR N. LANTSOV

Number of teachers: 756
Number of students: 22,000

DEANS

Faculty of Architecture and Building: Prof. SERGEY N. AVDEEV
Faculty of Automobile Transport: Prof. YURI V. BAZHENOV
Faculty of Chemistry and Ecology: Prof. JURI T. PANOV
Faculty of Economics: Prof. SERGEY A. MAXIMOV
Faculty of History: Dr MICHAEL A. BARASHEV
Faculty of Information Technologies: Dr ALEXANDER A. GALKIN
Faculty of Mechanical Engineering: Dr ELENA A. NOVIKOVA
Faculty of Philosophy and Social Sciences: NATALYA M. MARKOVA
Faculty of Physics and Applied Mathematics: NIKOLAI D. DAVIDOV
Faculty of Radiophysics, Electronics and Medical Engineering: Prof. ALEXANDER G. SAMOILOV
Faculty of Correspondence and Distance Learning: Prof. ILYA E. ZHIGALOV
Institute of Law and Psychology: Dr OKSANA V. BOGATOVA
Institute of Small and Medium Business: Dr OLGA P. POLOTSKAYA
Institute of Staff Development and Re-training: Prof. VLADIMIR P. LEGAEV

VLADIVOSTOK STATE UNIVERSITY OF ECONOMICS

690600 Vladivostok, ul. Gogolya 41
Telephone: (4232) 25-08-53
Fax: (4232) 25-09-54
E-mail: international@vvsu.ru
Internet: www.vvsu.ru

Founded 1967
Fields of study: business administration, culture, fashion and design, information technology and technical systems, politics and law of Asian-Pacific countries, service, social and political studies, tourism and hospitality
Rector: Prof. GENNADY I. LAZAREV
Library of 258,170 vols
Number of teachers: 410
Number of students: 5,986
Publication: *Russia—21st Century* (4 a year).

VOLGOGRAD STATE UNIVERSITY

400062 Volgograd, Pr. Universitetsky 100
Telephone: (8442) 43-81-24
Fax: (8442) 43-81-24
E-mail: oms@volsu.ru
Internet: www.volsu.ru

Founded 1980
Public control
Languages of instruction: Russian, English, French
Academic year: September to June

Rector: Prof. Dr OLEG V. INSHAKOV
Deputy Rector: Dr VASILY V. TARAKANOV
Vice-Rector for Academic Affairs: Dr SERGEI G. SIDOROV
First Vice-Rector: Dr BORIS N. SIPLIVY
Chief Admin. Officer: SERGEI G. SIDOROV
Librarian: LARISA E. YAKOVLEVA

Library of 900,000 vols
Number of teachers: 612
Number of students: 13,545

Publications: *Archaeological Vestnik of the Lower Volga* (1 a year), *Economic History of Russia* (1 a year), *Junior Faculty and Students' Papers and Reports* (1 a year), *Proceedings of the Annual Scientific Conference* (1 a year), *Proceedings of International Conferences* (5 a year), *Strezhen* (1 a year), *The Region's Economic Development: Problems, Searches, Prospects* (2 a year), *Vestnik VolGU* (10 series, 1 a year)

DEANS

Faculty of Continuing Education: Dr ELLA V. ISKRENKO
Faculty of History and Int. Relations: Dr ANDREW V. LUNOCHKHIN
Faculty of Information Technology and Telecommunications: Dr IGOR V. SHARKEVICH
Faculty of Int. Economics and Finance: Dr ELENA G. RUSSKOVA
Faculty of Law: Dr IRINA N. FALALEEVA
Faculty of Linguistics and Intercultural Communication: Dr NIKOLAI L. SHAMNE
Faculty of Mathematics and Informational Technologies: Dr ALEXANDER G. LOSEV
Faculty of Natural Sciences: Prof. Dr ALEXANDR B. MULIK
Faculty of Philology and Journalism: Dr DMITRY YU. ILYIN
Faculty of Philosophy and Social Technology: Dr NIKOLAI V. OMELCHENKO
Faculty of Philosophy, History, Int. Relations and Social Technologies: Prof. Dr OLGA U. REDKINA
Faculty of Physics: Dr VALERY V. YATSYSHEN
Institute of Philology and Intercultural Communication: Prof. Dr NIKOLAI L. SHAMNE
Institute of Physics and Telecommunications: Prof. Dr KONSTANTIN M. FIRSOV
Institute of World Economy and Finances: Prof. Dr ELENA G. RUSSKOVA
Faculty of Regional Economics and Management: Dr VICTOR O. MOSEYKO

VORONEZH STATE UNIVERSITY

394006 Voronezh, Universitetskaya pl. 1
Telephone: (0732) 20-75-22
Fax: (0732) 20-87-55
E-mail: office@main.vsu.ru
Internet: www.vsu.ru

Founded 1918
State control
Academic year: September to July

Rector: Prof. IVAN I. BORISOV
First Vice-Rector: SERGEY A. ZAPRYAGAEV
Vice-Rector: VLADIMIR T. TITOV
Vice-Rector for Admin. and Finance: ANATOLY N. PODOBEDOV
Vice-Rector for Information Services: ALEXANDER P. TOLSTOBROV
Vice-Rector for Major Construction Projects: ANATOLY I. BIRYUKOV
Vice-Rector for Organizational and Legal Matters: VALERY P. TROFIMOV
Vice-Rector for Pre-Univ. Training: VLADIMIR N. GLAZYEV
Vice-Rector for Research: ALEXANDER S. SIDORKIN
Librarian: SVETLANA V. YANTS

Library: 3m. vols
Number of teachers: 1,300
Number of students: 21,000

Publication: *Vestnik Voronezhskogo Universiteta*

DEANS

Faculty of Applied Mathematics and Mechanics: A. I. SHASHKIN
Faculty of Biology and Soil Science: V. G. ARTYUKHOV
Faculty of Chemistry: YU. P. AFINOGENOV
Faculty of Computer Science: E. A. ALGAZINOV
Faculty of Economics: V. P. BOCHAROV
Faculty of Geography and Geo-Ecology: V. I. FEDOTOV
Faculty of Geology: V. M. NENAKHOV
Faculty of History: A. Z. VINNIKOV
Faculty of Journalism: V. V. TULUPOV
Faculty of Law: V. A. PANYUSHKIN
Faculty of Mathematics: V. A. KOSTIN
Faculty of Pharmaceutics: A. I. SLIVKIN
Faculty of Philology: V. M. AKATKIN
Faculty of Philosophy and Psychology: YU A. BUBNOV
Faculty of Physics: A. M. VOROBEV
Faculty of Romance and Germanic Philology: N. A. FENENKO

YAKUTSK STATE UNIVERSITY

Republic of Sakha (Yakutia), 677000 Yakutsk, ul. Belinskogo 58
Telephone: (4112) 26-33-44
Fax: (4112) 26-14-53
E-mail: oip@sitc.ru
Founded 1956
State control
Languages of instruction: Russian, Yakut
Academic year: September to July
Chancellor: ANATOLY N. ALEXEEV
Vice-Chancellor: EGOR E. PETROV
Librarian: ANATOLY P. SEMENOV
Number of teachers: 950
Number of students: 10,000
Publication: *Nauka i obrazovaniye* (4 a year)

DEANS

Faculty of Biology and Geography: BORIS M. PESTRYAKOV
Faculty of Engineering Technology: ANATOLY T. KOPYLOV
Faculty of Foreign Languages: LUDMILA S. ZAMORSHIKOVA
Faculty of Geology: IGOR I. KOLODEZNIKOV
Faculty of History: YURI D. PETROV
Faculty of Law: ALBINA A. STEPANOVA
Faculty of Philology: VLADIMIR M. PEREVERZIN
Faculty of Yakut Philology and Native Culture: GAVRIL G. FILIPPOV
Institute of Applied Mathematics and Computer Science: VASILY I. VASILIEV
Institute of Economics: ANATOLY A. POPOV
Institute of Education: INNOKENTY A. GOLIKOV
Institute of Medicine: PALMIRA G. PETROVA
Institute of Physics and Technology: INNOKENTY A. GOGOLEV
Teacher-Training Institute: RAISA E. TIMOFEEVA
Mirny Polytechnic Institute: ALBINA A. GOLDMAN
Neryungri Technical Institute: ANATOLY M. SAMOKHIN

PROFESSORS

ALEXEEV, A. N., History
ANDREEV, V. S., Engineering
ANISIMOV, V. M., Education
ANTONOV, N. K., Philosophy
BASHARIN, K. G., Medicine
BEGIEV, V. G., Medicine
BLOKHIN, I. P., Biology
BURTSEV, A. A., Philology
BURYANINA, N. S., Geology
BUSHKOV, P. N., Surgery
CHEMEZOV, E. N., Geology
DANILOV, D. A., Pedagogics
DIACHKOVSKY, N. D., Yakut Language and Literature
DOBROVOLSKY, G. N., Engineering
EGOROV, I. E., Mathematics
FEDOROV, M. M., Law
FOMIN, M. M., Pedagogics
FRIDOVSKY, V. Y., Geology
GOGOLEV, A. I., General History
GOGOLEV, M. P., Medicine
ILLARIONOV, V. V., Philology
IVANOV, A. I., Medicine
IVANOVA, A. V., Education
IZAKSON, V. Y., Mathematics
KERSHENGOLTS, B. M., Biology
KHANDY, M. V., Medicine
KHATYLAEV, M. M., History
KOCHNEV, V. P., Education
KOLODEZNIKOV, I. I., Geology and Mineralology
KORNILOVA, A. G., Education
KOZHEVNIKOV, N. N., Philosophy
KYCHKIN, I. S., Theoretical Physics
KYLACHANOV, A. P., Engineering
LUKOVTSEV, V. S., Philosophy
MAKAROV, V. M., Medicine
MAKHAROV, Y. M., Philosophy
MAKSIMOV, G. N., Philosophy
MIKHAILOV, V. D., Philosophy
MISHLIMOVICH, M. Y., Philology
MORDOSOV, I. I., Biology
NEUSTROEV, N. D., Education
NIKOLAEV, N. S., Engineering
NOVIKOV, A. G., Philosophy
OKONESHNIKOVA, A. P., Psychology
PETROV, E. E., Mathematics
PETROV, N. E., Philology
PETROVA, P. G., Medicine
PETROVA, S. M., Education
POPOV, A. A., Economics
POPOV, B. N., Philosophy
PROKOPIEVA, S. M., Philology
SAMOKHIN, A. V., Mining
SAMSONOV, N. G., Philology
SHAMAEV, N. R., Education
SHEPELEV, V. S., Geology
SIVTSEV, I. S., History
SLASTENA, YU. L., Geology
SMIRNOV, V. P., Engineering
SOLOMONOV, N. G., Biology
STOGNY, V. V., Geology
TAZLOVA, R. S., Psychiatry
TIKHONOV, D. G., Medicine
TOBUROKOV, N. N., Linguistics
TOLSTIKHIN, O. N., Permafrost
TOMSKY, I. E., Economics
TYRLYGIN, M. A., Medicine
VASILIEV, E. P., Medicine
VASILIEV, V. I., Mathematics
VASILIEVA-KRALINA, I. I., Biology
VIKULOV, M. A., Engineering
VINOGRADOV, A. V., Chemistry
YAKIMOV, O. D., Journalism
ZAROVNYAEV, B. N., Geology

YAROSLAVL STATE UNIVERSITY

150000 Yaroslavl, ul. Sovetskaya 14
Telephone: (0852) 72-51-38
Fax: (0852) 30-75-15
E-mail: depint@uniyar.ac.ru
Internet: www.uniyar.ac.ru
Founded 1970
Academic year: September to July
Rector: Prof. G. S. MIRONOV
First Vice-Rector: A. I. RUSAKOV
Vice-Rector (Economy): R. P. USATYUK
Vice-Rector (Education): I. M. LOKHANINA
Vice-Rector (Innovation): S. A. KASHCHENKO
Vice-Rector (Science): Y. A. BRUKHANOV
Registrar: V. P. ISAYEVA
Librarian: I. V. DENEZHKINA
Number of teachers: 530
Number of students: 6,500
Publications: *Aktualnye Problemy Fiziki* (Current Problems of Physics, 1 a year), *Ekonomichesky Vestnik* (Bulletin on Economics, 1 a year), *Modelirovaniye i Analiz Informatsionnykh System* (Modelling and Analysis of Information Systems, 1 or 2 a year), *Ocherki po Torgovomy Pravu* (Sketches on Trade Law, 1 or 2 a year), *Problemy Novoi i Noveishei Istorii* (Issues of Modern and Contemporary History), *Put v Nauku* (Road to Science, 1 a year), *Sovremennye Problemy Matematiki i Informatiki* (Modern Problems of Mathematics and Informatics, 1 a year), *Yuridicheskiye zapiski* (Judicial Notes, 1 a year)

DEANS

Faculty of Biology: A. V. EREMEISHVILI
Faculty of Economics: L. B. PARFIONOVA
Faculty of History: N. P. RYAZANTSEV
Faculty of Information Science and Computing Technology: A. V. ZAFIEVSKY
Faculty of Law: N. N. TARUSINA
Faculty of Mathematics: V. G. DURNEV
Faculty of Physics: V. P. ALEKSEYEV
Faculty of Psychology: A. V. KARPOV
Faculty of Social Sciences: G. M. NAZHMUTDINOV

YUGORSKY STATE UNIVERSITY

628012 Khanty-Mansiysk, ul. Chekhova 16
Telephone: (34671) 35-77-13
E-mail: ugrasu@ugrasu.ru
Internet: www.ugrasu.ru
State control
Founded 2001
Rector: Prof. YURI I. REUTOV
First Pro-Rector: TATIANA D. KARMINSKAYA
Pro-Rector for Academic Affairs: OLGA F. SHAPKINA
Pro-Rector for Research: VLADIMIR Z. KOVALEV (acting)
Librarian: NINA I. SMIRNOVA
Library of 170,000 vols, 248 periodicals
Number of teachers: 521
Number of students: 5,138
Publication: *Vestnik of YuSU* (scientific journal)

DEANS

Applied Mathematics, Computer Science and Control: YURIY V. KOLOKOLOV
Economics and Finance: ALEXEY P. ERMILOV
Engineering: VLADIMIR Z. KOVALEV
Further Education: ARKADY V. KRASILNIKOV
Geology, Oil and Gas: TATIANA I. ROMANOVA
Humanities: VLADIMIR A. MISHCHENKO
Language, History and Culture of the Peoples of Yugra: VICTORIA I. SPODINA
Law: STANISLAV V. ROZENKO
Sports and Tourism: SERGEY V. BARBASHOV

MEDICAL UNIVERSITIES

ALTAI STATE MEDICAL UNIVERSITY

656038 Barnaul, pr. Lenina 40
Telephone: (3852) 36-88-48
Fax: (3852) 36-60-91
E-mail: rector@mail.ru
Internet: www.agmu.ru
Founded 1954
Language of instruction: Russian
Rector: VALERY M. BRYUKHANOV
Library of 542,000 vols
Number of teachers: 536
Number of students: 5,079

DEANS

Faculty of General Medicine: Prof. V. G. LICHEV
Faculty of Paediatrics: Prof. G. E. VYKHODTCEVA
Faculty of Pharmaceuticals: Prof. Y. F. ZVEREV
High Qualified Nurses' Education: Assoc. Prof. I. E. GOSSEN
Medico—Preventive Faculty: Prof. E. L. BOBROVSKY

BASHKIR STATE MEDICAL UNIVERSITY

450092 Bashkortostan, Ufa, ul. Lenina 3
Telephone: (3472) 22-41-73
Fax: (3472) 22-37-51
E-mail: admin@bsmu.anrb.ru
Internet: www.bsmu.anrb.ru
Founded 1932
Rector: VIL M. TIMERBULATOV
Library of 600,000 vols
Number of teachers: 650
Number of students: 4,175

IRKUTSK STATE MEDICAL UNIVERSITY

664003 Irkutsk, ul. Krasnogo Vosstaniya 1
Telephone: (3952) 24-38-25
Fax: (3952) 340336
E-mail: rector_ismu@bk.ru
Internet: www.ismu.baikal.ru

Founded 1919

Rector: Prof. ASKOLD A. MAIBORODA.

KAZAN STATE MEDICAL UNIVERSITY

420012 Kazan, ul. Butlerova 49
Telephone: (8432) 36-06-52
Fax: (8432) 36-03-93
E-mail: office@intdept.kcn.ru
Internet: www.kgmu.kcn.ru

Founded 1814

Faculties of dentistry, graduate nursing, medicine, paediatrics, pharmaceutics, prophylactic medicine, management, social work

Rector: Prof. NAIL KH. AMIROV

Library of 10,000 vols
Number of teachers: 500
Number of students: 4,500

Publication: *Kazan Medical Journal* (6 a year).

KURSK STATE MEDICAL UNIVERSITY

305041 Kursk, ul. Karla Marksa 3
Telephone: (0712) 58-81-32
Fax: (0712) 56-73-99
E-mail: main@kgmu.kursknet.ru
Internet: www.kgmu.kursknet.ru

Founded 1935

Rector: Prof. A. LAZAREVA

Library of 320,214 vols.

MOSCOW STATE MEDICAL-STOMATOLOGICAL UNIVERSITY

127473 Moscow, ul. Delegatskaya 20/1
Telephone: (495) 631-25-44
Fax: (495) 973-37-26
E-mail: mmsi@online.ru
Internet: www.msmsu.ru

Founded 1922
Academic year: September to June

Faculties of advanced training in dentistry, clinical psychology, general medicine, postgraduate education, stomatology; Institute of Orthodontics, State Stomatological Research Institute

Rector: Prof. NIKOLAI D. YUSHCHUK

Library of 549,979 vols
Number of teachers: 1,147
Number of students: 6,000

NORTHERN STATE MEDICAL UNIVERSITY

163001 Arkhangelsk, Troitsky pr. 51
Telephone: (8182) 21-00-00
E-mail: info@nsmu.ru
Internet: www.nsmu.ru

Founded 1932 as Arkhangelsk State Medical Institute, present name and status 2000

Faculties of adaptive physical training, ecology, general practice, medical clinical psychology, medical management, paediatrics, pharmaceutics, prophylactic medicine, social work, stomatology; institutes: management, medical education, information technology

Rector: PAVEL I. SIDOROV

Library of 400,000 vols
Number of students: 5,500

Publications: *Human Ecology* (4 a year), *Medik Severa* (12 a year).

ROSTOV STATE MEDICAL UNIVERSITY

344022 Rostov-on-Don, Nakhichevansky per. 29
Telephone: (863) 265-23-91
Fax: (863) 253-06-11
Internet: www.rgmu.al.ru

Founded 1931

Rector: Prof. VIKTOR N. CHERNYSHOV

Library of 340,000 vols.

RUSSIAN STATE MEDICAL UNIVERSITY

117869 Moscow, ul. Ostrovityanova 1
Telephone: (495) 434-03-29
Fax: (495) 434-47-87
E-mail: rgmu@rsmu.ru
Internet: www.rsmu.ru

Founded 1906, present name and status 1991

Faculties of biomedicine, medicine, paediatrics

Rector: Prof. Dr VLADIMIR N. YARYGIN

Library of 900,000 vols
Number of teachers: 1,200
Number of students: 6,300

Publication: *Vestnik* (4 a year).

ST PETERSBURG STATE MEDICAL UNIVERSITY 'ACAD. I. P. PAVLOV'

197022 St Petersburg, ul. L. Tolstogo 6/8
Telephone: (812) 238-71-12
Fax: (812) 234-08-97
E-mail: admission@spmu.rssi.ru
Internet: www.spmu.runnet.ru

Founded 1897

Areas of study: basic sciences, dentistry, medicine, sports medicine

Rector: Prof. NIKOLAI A. YAITSKY
Vice-Rector for Academic Affairs: Prof. U. D. IGNATOV
Vice-Rector for Int. Affairs: Prof. S. H. AL-SHUKRI
Vice-Rector for Research: Prof. E. E. ZVARTAU
Dean of Faculty of Gen. Medicine: Prof. N. N. PETRISHEV
Dean of Foreign Students Affairs: Prof. M. SH. VAKHITOV

Library: 1m. vols

Publications: *Arterial Hypertension* (4 a year), *Nephrology* (4 a year), *Scientific Items* (4 a year), *St Petersburg Medical News* (6 a year).

SAMARA STATE MEDICAL UNIVERSITY

443099 Samara, ul. Chapaevskaya 89
Telephone: (8462) 32-16-34
Fax: (8462) 33-29-76
E-mail: info@samsmu.ru
Internet: samsmu.ru

Founded 1919

Fields of study: cardiology, dentistry, general medicine, gerontology, healthcare, ionizing radiation, medical management, medical prophylactics, military medicine, nursing, paediatrics, pharmaceutics, psychology, surgery, therapy, traumatology; tissue bank

Rector: Prof. Dr GENNADY P. KOTELNIKOV

Library of 570,183 vols
Number of teachers: 700
Number of students: 6,500

Publications: *Annals of Traumatology and Orthopaedics* (6 a year), *Aspirant Herald of Volga Region* (12 a year), *Older Generation* (12 a year), *Samara Medical Archive* (6 a year), *Transregional Association 'Povolzhye Healthcare' Herald* (12 a year).

SARATOV STATE MEDICAL UNIVERSITY

410012 Saratov, Bol. Kazachya 112
Telephone: (8452) 27-33-70
Fax: (8452) 51-15-34
E-mail: meduniv@sgmu.ru
Internet: www.sgmu.ru

Founded 1909

Rector: Dr PETR V. GLYBOCHKO

Library of 950,000 vols.

SIBERIAN STATE MEDICAL UNIVERSITY

534050 Tomsk, Moskovsky Trakt 2
Telephone: (3822) 53-04-23
Fax: (3822) 53-33-09
E-mail: office@ssmu.net.ru
Internet: www.ssmu.ru

Founded 1888

Faculties of biological medicine, medicine, military medicine, nursing, paediatrics, pharmaceutics, postgraduate education, preparatory education; institutes: cardiology, genetics, oncology, pharmacology, psychiatric health; attached hospital

Pres.: Prof. Dr VYACHESLAV V. NOVITSKY

Library of 500,000 vols
Number of teachers: 676
Number of students: 3,445

Publications: *Bulletin of Siberian Healthcare* (4 a year), *Questions of Reconstructive and Plastic Surgery* (4 a year), *Siberian Magazine of Gastroenterology and Haematology* (4 a year).

VLADIVOSTOK STATE MEDICAL UNIVERSITY

690600 Vladivostok, pr. Ostryakova 2
Telephone: (4232) 45-16-24
Fax: (4232) 45-17-19
E-mail: webadmin@vgmu.ru
Internet: www.vgmu.ru

Founded 1958

Faculties of therapeutics, medicine and prophylaxis, paediatrics, qualification improvement

Rector: Prof. YURI V. KAMINSKY

Number of teachers: 400
Number of students: 2,717

VOLGOGRAD STATE MEDICAL UNIVERSITY

400066 Volgograd, pl. Pavshikh Bortsov 1
Telephone and fax (8442) 38-50-05
E-mail: cved@volgmed.ru
Internet: www.volgmed.ru

Founded 1935

Colleges of advanced and continuing education, clinical psychology, general medicine, dentistry, medical biology, paediatrics, pharmacy, social work

Rector: Prof. VLADIMIR I. PETROV

Number of teachers: 657
Number of students: 5,070

PEDAGOGICAL AND LINGUISTIC UNIVERSITIES

BARNAUL STATE PEDAGOGICAL UNIVERSITY

656031 Altai Region, Barnaul, ul. Molodezhnaya 55
Telephone: (3852) 22-85-52

Fax: (3852) 26-08-36
E-mail: rector@bspu.secna.ru
Internet: www.bspu.secna.ru

Rector: Prof. VLADIMIR N. LOPATKIN

Number of teachers: 563
Number of students: 8,534

BLAGOVESHCHENSK STATE PEDAGOGICAL UNIVERSITY

675000 Blagoveshchensk, Amur oblast, ul. Lenina 104

Telephone: (4162) 52-41-64
Fax: (4162) 52-41-64
E-mail: rektorat@bgpu.ru
Internet: www.bgpu.ru
State control
Language of instruction: Russian
Academic year: September to July

Founded 1930, present status 1996

Rector: Prof. YURI P. SERGIENKO
First Vice-Rector: YURY MALINOVSKY
Dir of the Foreign Affairs Office: NIKOLAY KUKHARENKO

Library of 700,000 vols
Number of teachers: 449
Number of students: 6,200

Publications: *Geographical Aspects of Upper Amur Area*, *Salut! Cava?*, *Za Pedkadry!* (official univ. newspaper)

DEANS

Dept of Foreign Languages: ELENA IVASHCHIK
Dept of History and Philology: DMITRY BOLOTIN
Dept of Industry and Pedagogics: IRINA KIYASHKO
Dept of Natural Sciences and Geography: IRINA TROFIMOVA
Dept of Pedagogics and Elementary Education: TATIANA PLOTNIKOVA
Dept of Physical Culture and Sports: NIKOLAY DARYIN
Dept of Physics and Mathematics: VALENTINA NEMILOSTEVYKH
Dept of Psychology and Pedagogics: SVETLANA ZUEVA
Int. Dept: VERA PIRKO

IRKUTSK STATE LINGUISTIC UNIVERSITY

664000 Irkutsk, ul. Lenina 8

Telephone: (3952) 20-03-61
E-mail: islu@islu.irk.ru
Internet: www.islu.ru

Founded 1948

Faculties of eastern languages, English language, foreign languages and social science, German language, Romance languages, training of foreign students and advancement of qualifications; external faculty

Rector: Prof. GRIGORY D. VOSKOBOYNIK.

MOSCOW STATE LINGUISTICS UNIVERSITY

119837 Moscow, ul. Ostozhenka 38

Telephone: (495) 246-86-03
Fax: (495) 246-83-66
E-mail: info@linguanet.ru
Internet: www.linguanet.ru

Founded 1930, present name and status 1990

Fields of study: humanities and applied science, English, German and French teaching, interpretation and translation, international economics, management, law, international relations, political studies, public relations, cultural studies, regional studies; in-service training for foreign-language teachers and advanced training for interpreters; Interdisciplinary In-Service Training Institute; Foreign Language Methodology Centre for Non-Philological Universities; Russian language programmes.

Rector: Prof. IRINA I. KHALEEVA

Library: 1m. vols
Number of teachers: 1,500
Number of students: 10,000

NIZHNII NOVGOROD STATE LINGUISTICS UNIVERSITY 'N. A. DOBROLYUBOV'

603155 Nizhnii Novgorod, ul. Minina 31A

Telephone: (8312) 36-15-75
Fax: (8312) 36-20-49
E-mail: admdep@lunn.sci-nnov.ru
Internet: www.lunn.sci-nnov.ru

Founded 1937

Faculties of business administration, economics, hotel and tourism management, journalism, international relations, law, office management, pedagogy, philology, public relations, translation and interpretation

Rector: Prof. GENNADY P. RYABOV

Library of 400,000 vols
Number of teachers: 400
Number of students: 4,000

PYATIGORSK STATE LINGUISTIC UNIVERSITY

357532 Pyatigorsk, pr. Kalinina 9

Telephone: (8793) 400-505
Fax: (8793) 400-527
E-mail: ums@pglu.ru
Internet: www.pglu.ru

Founded 1939
State control
Academic year: September to June

Educational programmes: English, French, German, Spanish, Arabic and Chinese languages, Russian as a second language, govt and public admin., business admin., hospitality and tourism management, int. relations, public relations, journalism, psychology, theology, customs management

Rector: Prof. ALEXANDER P. GORBUNOV
Vice-Rector: Prof. YURI Y. GRANKIN
Dir for Int. Office: Dr VICTOR E. MISHIN
Chief Librarian: SVETLANA A. CHERNOMORDOVA

Library of 850,000 vols
Number of teachers: 562
Number of students: 5,500

Publications: *PSLU Bulletin*, *PSLU Herald* (4 a year, research journal).

RUSSIAN STATE VOCATIONAL PEDAGOGICAL UNIVERSITY

620012 Ekaterinburg, ul. Mashinostroitelei 11

Telephone: (343) 338-44-47
Fax: (343) 338-44-42
E-mail: mail@rsvpu.ru
Internet: www.rsvpu.ru

Founded 1979

Rector: GENNADY M. ROMANTSEV

Library of 333,800 vols
Number of teachers: 441
Number of students: 18,124

Publications: *Bulletin of Teaching Research* (2 a year), *Bulletin of the Association of Russian Educational Institutions on Vocational Pedagogics* (1 a year), *Improvement of Educational Processes in Vocational Schools* (1 a year), *Innovations in Industry and Education* (1 a year), *Integrational Processes in Pedagogical Theory and Practice* (1 a year), *Problems of Public Development in the Fields of Sociology and Economics*.

SIBERIAN FEDERAL UNIVERSITY

660041 Karsnoyarsk, Svobodny pr. 79,

Telephone: (391) 244-82-13
Fax: (391) 244-86-24
E-mail: rector@sfu-kras.ru
Internet: www.sfu-kras.ru

Founded 2006, reorganised Karsnoyarsk State Univ., Karsnoyarsk State technical Univ., Karsnoyarsk State Academy of Architecture and Civil Construction, State Univ. of Non-Ferrous Metals and Gold
State Control
Language of instruction: Russian
Academic year: September to July

Rector: EVGENY A. VAGANOV
Vice-Rector: SERGEY V. VERKHOVETS
Vice-Rector: VLADIMIR I. KOLMAKOV
Vice-Rector: PAVEL M VCHERASHINY
Vice-Rector: SERGEY A. PODLESNYI
Vice-Rector: VLADISLAV YU. PANCHENKO
Vice-Rector: VALENTIN M. ZURAVLEV
Vice-Rector: NIKOLAY N. DOVZHENKO
Librarian: EVEGINYA G. KRIVONOSOVA

Library: 3.7m.
Number of teachers: 3,300
Number of students: 43,000

Publications: *New University Life* (48 a year), *Scientific Journal of Siberian Federal University* (5 series, 4 a year).

URALS STATE PEDAGOGICAL UNIVERSITY

620219 Ekaterinburg, GSP 135, pr. Kosmonavtov 26

Telephone: (343) 34-12-59
Fax: (343) 34-97-71
E-mail: root@uspu.ru
Internet: www.uspu.ru

Founded 1930 as Urals Industrial Pedagogical Institute; as Urals State Pedagogical Institute 1932–1993; present name and status 1994
State control

Rector: Prof. VLADIMIR D. ZHAVORONKOV

Number of teachers: 720
Number of students: 7,600

VOLGOGRAD STATE PEDAGOGICAL UNIVERSITY

400013 Volgograd 13, pr. V. I. Lenina 104

Telephone: (8442) 30-28-12
Fax: (8442) 24-13-68
E-mail: vspu@vspu.ru
Internet: www.vspu.ru
State control

Rector: VALERY I. DANILCHUK

Number of teachers: 596
Number of students: 6,455

VORONEZH STATE PEDAGOGICAL UNIVERSITY

394043 Voronezh, ul. Lenina 86

Telephone: (0732) 55-19-49
Fax: (0732) 55-17-50
E-mail: rector@vspu.ac.ru
Internet: www.vspu.ac.ru

Founded 1930
State control

Rector: Prof. VYACHESLAV V. PODKOLZIN

Library of 600,000 vols
Number of teachers: 473

TECHNICAL UNIVERSITIES

ARKHANGELSK STATE TECHNICAL UNIVERSITY

163002 Arkhangelsk, Severnaya Dvina nab. 17
Telephone: (8182) 28-76-14
Fax: (8182) 28-76-14
E-mail: public@agtu.ru
Internet: www.agtu.ru
Founded 1929
Academic year: September to June
Faculties of chemical technology, construction, distance learning, forestry, industrial power engineering, law, mechanical engineering, mechanical wood technology, natural resources, re-training and preparatory studies; institutes of chemical technology, economics, finance and business, information technology, law and entrepreneurship, oil and gas; colleges of business, information technology, law; centres of innovative technologies and information science; brs in Naryan-Mar, Kotlas, Velsk, Novodvinsk and Mirny
Rector: ALEXANDER L. NEVZOROV
Library of 720,000 vols, 380 periodicals
Number of teachers: 515
Number of students: 12,040
Publication: *Lesnoi Zhurnal* (Forestry Journal, 6 a year).

ASTRAKHAN STATE TECHNICAL UNIVERSITY

414025 Astrakhan, ul. Tatishcheva 16
Telephone: (8512) 25-09-23
Fax: (8512) 25-73-68
E-mail: astu@astu.org
Internet: www.astu.org
Founded 1930
Public control
Language of instruction: Russian
Academic year: September to June
Rector: Prof. Y. T. PIMENOV (acting)
Library of 700,000 vols
Number of teachers: 450
Number of students: 12,000
Publications: *ASTU Herald* (1 a year), *Proceedings*

DEANS
Construction Faculty: Prof. Dr RAMAZAM ABDULMUMINOVICH NABIEV
Faculty of Law: Prof. Dr IVAN VLADIMIROVICH MAKSIMOV
Institute of Economics: Assoc. Prof. TAMARA FEDOROVNA LOKTEVA
Institute of Fisheries, Biology and Nature Management: Prof. Dr ALEXANDR NIKOLAEVICH NEVALENNYI
Institute of Humanities: Dr ELVIRA ZELETDINOVA
Institute of Information Technologies and Communications: Dr IRINA YURIEVNA KVYATKOVSKAYA
Institute of Oil and Gas: Assoc. Prof. NATALIA NIKOLAEVNA LETICHEVSKAYA
Institute of Marine Sciences, Energy And Transport: SERGEY VLADIMIROVICH VINOGRADOV
Institute of Mechanics And Engineering: Prof. ANATOLY VIKTOROVICH KARABLIN
Preparatory Faculty for Foreign Citizens: NATALIA VITALIEVNA SHTEINIKOVA

BALTIC STATE TECHNICAL UNIVERSITY 'D. F. USTINOV' (VOENMEKH)

198005 St Petersburg, ul. 1-ya Krasnoarmeiskaya 1/21
Telephone: (812) 316-26-13
E-mail: zag@insu.ru
Internet: www.insu.ru
Founded 1930
Depts of aerospace, applied mechanics and automation, guidance systems, humanities, international industrial management, natural sciences, rocketry and aircraft
Rector: Prof. YURI V. ZAGASHVILI
Library of 1,100,000 vols
Number of teachers: 600
Number of students: 5,300

BELGOROD STATE TECHNOLOGICAL UNIVERSITY 'V. G. SHUKOV'

308012 Belgorod, ul. Kostyukova 46
Telephone: (722) 54-20-87
Fax: (722) 25-71-39
E-mail: rektor@intbel.ru
Internet: www.bstu.ru
Founded 1970
Academic year: September to June
Institutes of building materials, economics and management, mechanical equipment in the building industry; depts: architecture and building technologies, civil engineering, engineering and ecology, highways, machine building, production automation and information technologies; 4 brs across Russia
Rector: Prof. ANATOLY M. GRIDCHIN
Library of 600,000 vols
Number of teachers: 540
Number of students: 9,152
Publication: *Tekhnolog* (newspaper, 6 a year).

BRYANSK STATE TECHNICAL UNIVERSITY

241035 Bryansk, bul. 50-let. Oktyabrya 7
Telephone: (4832) 56-09-05
Fax: (4832) 56-24-08
E-mail: rector@tu-bryansk.ru
Internet: www.tu-bryansk.ru
Founded 1929
Rector: Prof. ALEXANDER V. LAGEREV
Library of 705,668 vols
Number of teachers: 1,131
Number of students: 8,859
Publication: *Vestnik BGTU*.

DAGHESTAN STATE TECHNICAL UNIVERSITY

367015 Makhachkala, 70 Imama Shamil pr.
Telephone and fax (8722) 62-37-61
E-mail: dstu@dstu.ru
Internet: www.dstu.ru
Founded 1960 as Daghestan Polytechnic Institute
Academic year: September to July
Rector: Prof. TAGIR A. ISMAILOV
Vice-Rector for Academics: Prof. KADI A. GASANOV
Vice-Rector for Humanities and Educational work: Prof. YUSUP N. ABDULKADYROV
Vice-Rector for Economy: Prof. NURMAGOMED S. SURAKATOV
Vice-Rector for Science: SHIRALIE A. YUSUFOV
Vice-Rector for Administration: ALIMAGOMED G. MIRZEMAGOMEDOV
Head Librarian: TAMILA A. RAGHIMOVA
Library of 818,231 vols, 68,725 periodicals
Number of teachers: 800
Number of students: 14,000
Publications: *Herald of DSTU* (technical sciences, humanities), *Thematic Collected Scientific Papers*

DEANS
Architecture and Construction: Prof. GADGIMAGOMED N. KHADGISHALAPOV
Engineering and Economics: Prof. ELENA I. PAVLYUCHENKO
Finance and Audit: Prof. AMMAKADI R. RABADANOV
Humanities and Social Science: Prof. GYULNARA ALIEVA
Informatics and Management: Assoc. Prof. ARSLAN MUSTAFAEV
Information Systems: Prof. TADZHIDIN E. SARKAROV
Law and Customs Affairs: Assoc. Prof. NADIR K. SANAEV
Oil, Gas and Environmental Devt: Assoc. Prof. MARINA KOTENKO
Public and Municipal Management: Assoc. Prof. KHADGIMURAD KHALIMBEKOV
Radio Engineering: Assoc. Prof. GAMID IRZAEV
Skill Improvement and Personnel Retraining: Asst Prof. AISHAT R. SHAKHMAEVA
Technology: Assoc. Prof. MAGOMED AKHMEDOV
Transport: Asst Prof. GUSEIN M. MAGOMEDOV

DON STATE TECHNICAL UNIVERSITY

344010 Rostov-on-Don, pl. Gagarina 1
Telephone: (822) 38-15-25
Fax: (822) 32-79-53
E-mail: root@sintez.rud.su
Founded 1930 as Rostov Institute of Agricultural Engineering, present name 1992
Rector: Prof. Dr ANATOLY A. RYZHKIN
Library of 837,000 vols
Number of teachers: 650
Number of students: 6,000

EASTERN SIBERIAN STATE UNIVERSITY OF TECHNOLOGY

670013 Ulan-Ude, ul. Klyuchevskaya 40B
Telephone: (3012) 37-56-00
Fax: (3012) 44-14-15
E-mail: office@esstu.ru
Internet: www.esstu.ru
Founded 1962
Fields of study: mechanics and technology of light industry, construction, mechanical engineering, electrical engineering, power engineering, preparatory faculty; institutes: sustainable development, economics and law, food industry and biotechnology; postgraduate courses, Russian language courses, Russian language summer school, pre-university training courses
Rector: Prof. VLADIMIR E. SAKTOYEV
Library of 715,246 vols
Number of teachers: 868
Number of students: 10,640

FAR EASTERN NATIONAL TECHNICAL UNIVERSITY

690990 Vladivostok, ul. Pushkinskaya 10
Telephone: (4232) 26-51-18
Fax: (4232) 26-69-88
E-mail: festu@festu.ru
Internet: www.festu.ru
Founded 1899
Institutes of architecture, automatics and advanced technologies, civil engineering, continuing and distance education, economics and management, engineering, humanities, information science, maritime engineering, mechanics, mining engineering, natural sciences, oriental studies, politics and law, radioelectronics and electrical engineering, social ecology; brs in Nakhodka, Arseniev, Petropavlovsk-Kamchatsky, Dalnegorsk, Dalnerechensk, Bolshoi Kamen,

Artyom, Lesozavodsk, Yuzhno-Sakhalinsk and Kirovsky

Pres.: ANVIR A. FATKULIN

Library of 2,328,000 vols, 300 periodicals
Number of teachers: 109
Number of students: 25,000

Publications: *Pacific Science Review* (jtly with Kangnam Univ., Republic of Korea, annual), *Proceedings* (1 a year).

FAR EASTERN STATE TECHNICAL FISHERIES UNIVERSITY

690600 Vladivostok, ul. Lugovaya 52B
Telephone: (4232) 44-03-06
Fax: (4232) 44-24-32
E-mail: support@dalrybvtuz.ru
Internet: www.dalrybvtuz.ru

Founded 1930

Rector: Prof. GEORGY N. KIM

Library of 450,000 vols
Number of teachers: 266
Number of students: 6,264

Publications: *Dalrybvtuz* (2 a year), *Scientific Papers* (2 a year).

FAR EASTERN STATE TRANSPORT UNIVERSITY

680021 Khabarovsk, ul. Serysheva 47
Telephone: (4212) 40-72-00
Fax: (4212) 40-73-21
E-mail: root@festu.khv.ru
Internet: www.festu.khv.ru

Founded 1937
Public control
Languages of instruction: English, Russian
Academic year: September to July

Rector: Prof. BORIS E. DYNKIN
Vice-Rector: ANDREY N. GANUS

Library of 960,000 vols
Number of teachers: 520
Number of students: 25,000

IRKUTSK STATE TECHNICAL UNIVERSITY

664074 Irkutsk, ul. Lermontova 83
Telephone: (3952) 40-52-00
Fax: (3952) 40-51-00
E-mail: oms@istu.edu
Internet: www.istu.edu

Founded 1930
State control
Language of instruction: Russian
Academic year: September to June

Rector: Prof. Dr IVAN GOLOVNYKH
Vice-Rector for Int. Relations: Prof. Dr ALEXANDER AFANASYEV

Library: 1.5m. vols
Number of teachers: 1,450
Number of students: 31,000

Publications: *Geology, Search and Prospecting for Oil and Mineral Deposits, Higher Educational Institutes' News: Geoscience, ISTU Bulletin, Ore Dressing, Problems of the Development of Eastern Siberia's Mineral Base*

DEANS

Faculty of Applied Linguistics: Prof. Dr OLGA DEMENTIEVA
Faculty of Business and Management: Prof. GENNADIY DYKUSOV
Faculty of Chemical Engineering and Metallurgy: Prof. SVETLANA DYACHKOVA
Faculty of Civil Engineering and Municipal Economy: Prof. VIKTOR R. CHUPIN
Faculty of Computer Sciences: Prof. ALEXANDER PETROV
Faculty of Fine Arts: Dr OLGA IGNATIEVA
Faculty of Geology, Geoinformatics and Geoecology: Prof. IVAN I. VERKHOZIN
Faculty of Law, Sociology and Mass Media: Prof. ARTUR KHARINSKIY
Faculty of Mining Engineering: Prof. BORIS L. TALGAMER
Faculty of Power Engineering: Dr VADIM FEDCHISHIN
Faculty of Technology and Computerization of Mechanical Engineering: Prof. VLADIMIR P. KOLTSOV
Faculty of Transportation: Prof. IGOR N. GUSEV
Institute of Architecture and Civil Engineering: Prof. VIKTOR CHUPIN
Institute of Aviation Mechanical Engineering and Transport: Dr. RASHID AKHATOV
Institute of Nature Resources: Prof. BORIS TALGAMER
Int. Faculty: Dr VITALIY EFREMOV
Physical and Engineering Institute: Prof. KONSTANTIN KAZAKOV

IVANOVO STATE ENERGY UNIVERSITY

153548 Ivanovo, ul. Rabfakovskaya 34
Telephone: (0932) 32-72-43
Fax: (0932) 38-57-01
E-mail: nvn@ispu.ru
Internet: www.ispu.ru

Faculties of electrical engineering, heat and power engineering, industrial heat and power engineering, power engineering

Rector: VLADIMIR N. NUZHDIN

Number of teachers: 1,500
Number of students: 8,000

IVANOVO STATE UNIVERSITY OF CHEMISTRY AND TECHNOLOGY

153460 Ivanovo, pr. F. Engelsa 7
Telephone: (0932) 32-92-41
Fax: (0932) 41-79-95
E-mail: rektor@isuct.ru
Internet: www.isuct.ru

Founded 1918 as Ivanovo-Vosnessensk Polytechnic Institute, Ivanovo Institute of Chemistry and Technology 1930–92, as Ivanovo State Acad. of Chemistry and Technology 1992–98, present name and status 1998

Faculties of inorganic chemistry technology, organic chemistry, silicates and engineering

Rector: OSCAR I. KOIFMAN.

IZHEVSK STATE TECHNICAL UNIVERSITY

426069 Izhevsk, ul. Studencheskaya 7
Telephone: (3412) 59-25-55
Fax: (3412) 58-88-52
E-mail: info@istu.ru
Internet: www.istu.ru

Founded 1952

Faculties of civil engineering, mechanical engineering, robotics engineering, quality management, instrumentation engineering, computer science, management and marketing, education, humanities, applied mathematics and mechanics, sport; brs in Votkinsk, Glazov, Tchaikovsky and Sarapul

Rector: Prof. IVAN V. ABRAMOV

Library of 700,000 vols
Number of teachers: 760
Number of students: 11,300

KALININGRAD STATE TECHNICAL UNIVERSITY

236000 Kaliningrad, Sovietsky pr. 1
Telephone: (0112) 27-22-55
Fax: (0112) 27-95-11
E-mail: ivanov@klgtu.ru
Internet: www.klgtu.ru

Founded 1930
Academic year: September to June

Faculties of biological resources and water usage, commercial fisheries, economics and humanities, mechanics and technology, naval and power engineering, production automation and control

Rector: Prof. VICTOR E. IVANOV

Library of 530,000 vols
Number of teachers: 560
Number of students: 7,000

Publication: *Izvestiya KGTU* (12 a year).

KAZAN STATE TECHNICAL UNIVERSITY 'A. N. TUPOLEV'

420111 Kazan, ul. K. Marksa 10
Telephone and fax (8432) 31-02-44
E-mail: icd@kai.ru
Internet: www.kai.ru

Founded 1932, present name and status 1992

Rector: Prof. YURIY GORTYSHOV

Library: 3m. vols
Number of teachers: 1,800
Number of students: 24,000

Publications: *Aviatsionaya Tekchnika: Izvestia VUZov* (Russian Aeronautics, in Russian and English, 4 a year), *Non-Linear Analysis Problems in Engineering Systems* (in English, 2 a year), *Problemy Nelineinogo Analiza v Inzhenernykh Sistemakh* (Non-Linear Analysis Problems in Engineering Systems, in Russian and English, 2 a year), *Russian Aeronautics* (in English, 4 a year), *Radioelectronnye Ustroistva* (Radioengineering Devices, in Russian, 2 a year), *Vestnik KGTU* (Proceedings of KSTU, in Russian, 4 a year).

KAZAN STATE TECHNOLOGICAL UNIVERSITY

420015 Kazan, ul. K. Marksa 68
Telephone: (8432) 38-56-94
Fax: (8432) 19-42-16
E-mail: office@kstu.ru
Internet: www.kstu.ru

Founded 1919

Faculties of light industry engineering, mechanics, chemical engineering, oil and oil refining, polymers, chemical technology, energy engineering and technological engineering, power machinery construction and process equipment, management and automation, humanities and food technology; br. at Nizhnekamsk

Rector: SERGEI G. DYAKONOV

Library: 1.6m. vols
Number of teachers: 950
Number of students: 25,000

Publications: *Economy of Industrial Production, Heat and Mass Transfer in Chemical Engineering*.

KAZAN STATE UNIVERSITY OF ARCHITECTURE AND CIVIL ENGINEERING

420043 Kazan, ul. Zelenaya 1
Telephone: (843) 510-46-10
Fax: (843) 238-79-72
E-mail: rector@kgasu.ru
Internet: www.kgasu.ru

Founded 1930 as Kazan Engineering and Civil Engineering Institute; later Kazan State Acad. of Architecture and Civil Engineering; present name 2005
Academic year: September to June

Rector: RASHIT K. NIZAMOV

Vice-Rector: ILFAC E. VILDANOV
Vice-Rector for Academic Affairs: DAMIR K. SHARAFUTDINOV

Library of 583,000 vols
Number of teachers: 540
Number of students: 6,799

DEANS

Architecture: ALEXANDER D. KULIKOV
Building Science Engineering: VLADIMIR S. AGAFONKIN
Construction Technologies: DMITRIY A. SOLDATOV
Design: SERGEY M. MIKHAILOV
Economics: GUZEL M. HARISOVA
Engineering: MUNIR A. VALIULLIN
Engineering Basics: NAIL K. TUKTAMISHEV
Engineering Systems and Ecology: RAIS S. SAFIN
General Architectural and Art Training: HANIFA G. NADIROVA
Part-time and Extended Studies: VICTOR YA. ORLOV
Transport Engineering: ILVERA N. HABIBULLINA

KOMSOMOLSK-ON-AMUR STATE TECHNICAL UNIVERSITY

681013 Komsomolsk-on-Amur, pr. Lenina 27
Telephone: (4217) 53-23-04
Fax: (4217) 53-61-50
E-mail: office@knastu.ru
Internet: www.knastu.ru

Founded 1955

Rector: Prof. YURI KABALDIN
Number of students: 3,500

KOSTROMA STATE TECHNOLOGICAL UNIVERSITY

156005 Kostroma, ul. Dzerzhinskogo 17
Telephone: (4942) 31-48-14
Fax: (4942) 31-70-08
E-mail: info@kstu.edu.ru
Internet: www.kstu.edu.ru

Founded 1932, as Kostroma Textile Institute, as Kostroma Technological Institute 1962, present name and status 1995

Rector: ANDREI P. BOLOTNY
Vice-Rector for International Links: VICTOR P. KALASHNIK

Library of 608,000 vols
Number of teachers: 430
Number of students: 6,520

KUBAN STATE TECHNICAL UNIVERSITY

350072 Krasnodar, ul. Moskovskaya 2
Telephone: (861) 255-84-01
Fax: (861) 257-65-92
E-mail: adm@kgtu.kuban.ru
Internet: www.kubstu.ru

Founded 1918

Faculties of chemical engineering, civil engineering, computer technology and automated systems, economics, food technology, gas and power engineering, highway engineering, oil, mechanical engineering, technology of grain products; Institute of Mechanical Engineering in Armavir, br. in Novorossiisk

Rector: Prof. A. A. PETRIK

Library of 720,000 vols
Number of teachers: 800
Number of students: 13,000

Publications: *Izvestiya Vuzov, Pishevaya Teckhnologiya* (Food Technology, 6 a year).

KURSK STATE TECHNICAL UNIVERSITY

305040 Kursk, ul. 50-letiya Oktyabrya 94
Telephone: (0712) 22-57-43
Fax: (0712) 56-18-85
E-mail: rector@kstu.kursk.ru
Internet: www.kstu.kursk.ru

Founded 1964

Faculties of civil and industrial construction engineering, computer engineering and automation systems, economics, environmental protection, finance and auditing, law, management, machine-building, textile technology

Rector: Prof. IVAN S. ZAKHAROV

Library of 536,000 vols
Number of teachers: 530
Number of students: 4,400

Publication: *Izvestia* (2 a year).

KUZBASS STATE TECHNICAL UNIVERSITY

650026 Kemerovo, ul. Vesennyaya 28
Telephone: (3842) 23-33-80
Fax: (3842) 36-16-87
E-mail: rector@kuzstu.ru
Internet: www.kuzstu.ru

Founded 1950

Faculties of biotechnology, chemical engineering, construction, economics, electrical, humanities, mechanical engineering, mine construction, mining engineering

Rector: VALERY I. NESTEROV

Library of 611,057 vols
Number of teachers: 678
Number of students: 20,078

LIPETSK STATE TECHNICAL UNIVERSITY

398055 Lipetsk, ul. Moskovskaya 30
Telephone: (0742) 25-00-61
Fax: (0742) 31-04-73
E-mail: mailbox@stu.lipetsk.su
Internet: www.stu.lipetsk.ru

Founded 1956

Rector: Prof. MIKHAIL P. KUPRYANOV

Number of teachers: 500
Number of students: 5,000

MAGNITOGORSK STATE TECHNICAL UNIVERSITY 'G. I. NOSOV'

455000 Magnitogorsk, pr. Lenina 38
Telephone: (3519) 22-12-87
Fax: (3519) 29-84-26
E-mail: mgtu@magtu.ru
Internet: www.magtu.ru

Founded 1932

Rector: Dr BORIS A. NIKIFOROV

Library of 846,656 vols
Br. in Beloretsk.

MARI STATE TECHNICAL UNIVERSITY

424024 Yoshkar-Ola, 3 Lenin pl.
Telephone: (8362) 41-08-72
E-mail: rector@marstu.net
Internet: www.marstu.net

Founded 1932

Rector: EVGENY M. ROMANOV

Library: 1m. vols
Number of teachers: 591
Number of students: 12,406

MOSCOW AVIATION INSTITUTE (STATE TECHNICAL UNIVERSITY)

125993 Moscow, A-80, GSP-3, Volokolamskoe shosse 4
Telephone: (495) 158-04-65
Fax: (495) 158-29-77
E-mail: aet@mai.ru
Internet: www.mai.ru

Founded 1930

Schools of aerospace engineering, aircraft engineering, applied mathematics and physics, applied mechanics, control systems, economics and management, flight vehicle engines, humanities and preparatory studies, informatics and electric power engineering, robotics and intelligent systems, vehicle flight radioelectronics

Rector: Prof. Dr ALEXANDR M. MATVEENKO

Library of 909,000 vols
Number of teachers: 2,000
Number of students: 14,000

MOSCOW ENGINEERING PHYSICS INSTITUTE (STATE UNIVERSITY)

115409 Moscow, Kashirskoe shosse 31
Telephone: (495) 324-74-91
Fax: (495) 324-85-20
E-mail: degnn@mephi.ru
Internet: www.mephi.ru

Founded 1942

Rector: Prof. BORIS N. ONYKY

Library of 1,000,000 vols
Number of teachers: 880
Number of students: 6,000

MOSCOW INSTITUTE OF ELECTRONIC TECHNOLOGY (TECHNICAL UNIVERSITY)

124498 Moscow, Zelenograd, pr-d 4806, 5
Telephone: (499) 720-8933
Fax: (499) 734-3453
E-mail: netadm@miee.ru
Internet: www.miet.ru

Founded 1965
Public control
Language of instruction: Russian
Academic year: September to June

Rector: Prof. YURI A. CHAPLYGIN
Dean of Computer Science and Telecommunications: Prof. Dr ALEXANDER GUREEV

Library of 680,000 vols
Number of teachers: 530
Number of students: 6,400

Publication: *Collection of Research Work* (12 a year).

MOSCOW INSTITUTE OF PHYSICS AND TECHNOLOGY (STATE UNIVERSITY)

141700 Moscow oblast, Dolgoprudny, Institutsky per. 9
Telephone: (495) 408-57-00
Fax: (495) 408-68-69
E-mail: rector@mipt.ru
Internet: www.mipt.ru

Founded 1951

Depts of aeromechanics and flight engineering (located in Zhukovsky), aerophysics and space research, applied mathematics and economics and problems of physics and power engineering, general and applied physics, molecular and biological physics, physical and quantum electronics, radio engineering and cybernetics

Rector: Prof. NIKOLAY N. KUDRYAVTSEV

Library of 733,000 vols
Number of teachers: 470 full-time, 1,090 part-time

Number of students: 3,500

MOSCOW POWER ENGINEERING INSTITUTE (TECHNICAL UNIVERSITY)

111250 Moscow, ul. Krasnokazarmennaya 14
Telephone: (495) 362-56-45
Fax: (495) 362-89-18
E-mail: uvs@mpei.ru
Internet: www.mpei.ru
Founded 1930
Public control
Languages of instruction: English, Russian
Academic year: September to June
Rector: Prof. SERGEY SEREBRIANNIKOV
Vice-Rector for Int. relations: Prof. IGOR ZHELBAKOV
Library: 2m. vols
Number of teachers: 1,500
Number of students: 15,000
Publication: *Vestnik MPEI* (6 a year).

MOSCOW STATE ACADEMY OF FINE CHEMICAL TECHNOLOGY 'M. V. LOMONOSOV'

117571 Moscow, pr. Vernadskogo 86
Telephone: (495) 434-71-55
Fax: (495) 434-87-11
E-mail: mitht@mitht.ru
Internet: www.mitht.ru
Founded 1930
Rector: Prof. ALLA K. FROLKOVA
Library of 220,000 vols

DEANS

Faculty of Biotechnology and Organic Synthesis: Prof. A. F. MIRONOV
Faculty of Chemistry and Technology Polymer Processing: Prof. E. E. POTAPOV
Faculty of Chemistry and Technology of Rare Elements and Materials for Electronic Technology: Prof. D. V. DROBOT
Faculty of Engineering: Prof. G. I. LAPSHENKOV
Faculty of Management, Ecology and Economics: Doc. I. H. ROZDIN
Faculty of Natural Sciences: Prof. E. M. KARTASHOV
Preparatory Faculty: V. B. MARGULIS
Evening Classes: Doc. A. P. PETRUSENKO

MOSCOW STATE AUTOMOBILE AND ROAD TECHNICAL UNIVERSITY

125829 Moscow, Leningradsky pr. 64
Telephone: (495) 151-03-71
E-mail: info@madi.ru
Internet: www.madi.ru
Founded 1930
Faculties of building and technological machines, correspondence learning, economics, energy and ecology, design and mechanical engineering, foreign citizen preparation, humanities, management, military training, motor transport, natural sciences, pre-admission preparation, road, road building; institute for the improvement of professional skills and retraining of personnel in the transport and road infrastructure; Moscow Transport Institute; Centre of Engineering Pedagogy; Centre of Innovations in Engineering Education
Rector: Prof. VYACHESLAV M. PRIKHODKO
Library of 1,000,000 vols
Number of teachers: 850
Number of students: 10,000

MOSCOW STATE FORESTRY UNIVERSITY

141005 Moscow oblast, Mytischi, 1-ya Institutskaya ul. 1
Telephone: (495) 588-55-78
E-mail: mgul@mgul.ac.ru
Internet: www.mgul.ac.ru
Founded 1919
Faculties of forestry, mechanical and chemical wood technology, electronics and technical systems, economics and foreign relations, humanities, landscape architecture, International School of Business and Management
Rector: Prof. VIKTOR G. SANAEV
Library of 550,000 vols
Number of teachers: 627
Number of students: 10,000

MOSCOW STATE INDUSTRIAL UNIVERSITY

115280 Moscow, ul. Avtozavodskaya 16
Telephone: (495) 675-52-37
Fax: (495) 674-63-92
Internet: www.msiu.ru
Founded 1960
Faculties of applied mathematics and engineering physics, automotive engineering, information technology and law, management
Rector: Prof. VIKTOR DEMIN
Number of teachers: 790
Number of students: 7,000

MOSCOW STATE INSTITUTE OF ELECTRONICS AND MATHEMATICS (TECHNICAL UNIVERSITY)

109028 Moscow, Bolshoi Trekhsvyatitelsky per. 1-3/12
Telephone: (495) 917-90-89
Fax: (495) 916-28-07
E-mail: lenor@miem.edu.ru
Internet: www.miem.edu.ru
Founded 1962
Rector: Dr DMITRY V. BYKOV
Library of 600,000 vols
Number of students: 5,000

MOSCOW STATE INSTITUTE OF RADIO ENGINEERING, ELECTRONICS AND AUTOMATION (TECHNICAL UNIVERSITY)

119454 Moscow, pr. Vernadskogo 78
Telephone: (495) 433-00-44
Fax: (495) 434-86-65
E-mail: rector@mirea.ru
Internet: www.mirea.ru
Founded 1947
Academic year: September to June
Languages of instruction: Russian, English
Rector: ALEXANDER S. SIGOV
Library of 1,500,000 vols
Number of teachers: 1,200
Number of students: 16,000
Publication: *Proceedings of MIREA* (irregular)

DEANS

Faculty of Cybernetics: Prof. MIKHAIL ROMANOV
Faculty of Economy and Management: Prof. ALEXANDER BOLSHAKOV
Faculty of Electronics: Prof. YURI FETISOV
Faculty of Information Technologies: Prof. ANDREY PETROV
Facultyof Radioengineering: Prof. GENNADY KULIKOV
International Faculty of Informatics: Prof. ALEKSEY LOBUZOV

MOSCOW STATE MINING UNIVERSITY

117049 Moscow, Leninsky pr. 6
Telephone: (495) 236-94-80
Fax: (495) 237-31-63
Internet: www.msmu.ru
Founded 1918
Faculties of applied physics, coal mining and underground construction, mining automation and control, mining electrification and mechanization, mining of mineral and non-mineral deposits
Rector: Prof. Dr LEV A. PUCHKOV
Library of 800,000 vols
Number of teachers: 540
Number of students: 5,270
Publications: *Gornyatskaya Smena* (52 a year), *Scientific Papers* (2 a year).

MOSCOW STATE TECHNICAL UNIVERSITY 'MAMI'

107023 Moscow, ul. Bol. Semenovskaya 38
Telephone: (495) 369-91-53
Fax: (495) 918-29-75
E-mail: decinter@mami.ru
Founded 1865
Faculties of automation and control, design and technology, economics and engineering economics, machine-building, mechanical engineering, motor vehicles and tractors, power engineering
Rector: Prof. ANATOLY L. KARUNIN
Library: 1m. vols
Number of teachers: 800
Number of students: 7,500

MOSCOW STATE TECHNICAL UNIVERSITY OF CIVIL AVIATION

125838 Moscow, GSP-47, Kronshtadtsky bul. 20
Telephone: (495) 459-07-07
Fax: (495) 457-12-01
E-mail: rectorat@mail.mstuca.ru
Internet: www.mstuca.ru
Founded 1971 as Moscow Institute of Civil Aviation Engineers, present name and status 1992
Faculties of applied mathematics, computer systems and networks, maintenance of aircraft and engines, maintenance of aircraft electrical systems and avionics, maintenance of transport radio equipment, management, technological processes and safety in the aviation industry
Rector: Prof. VLADIMIR G. VOROBIEV
Library: 1.1m. vols
Number of teachers: 300
Number of students: 5,300
Publication: *Proceedings* (1 a year).

MOSCOW STATE TECHNICAL UNIVERSITY 'N. E. BAUMAN'

107005 Moscow, 2-ya Baumanskaya ul. 5
Telephone: (495) 261-40-55
Fax: (495) 267-98-93
E-mail: irina@interd.bmstu.ru
Founded 1830
Faculties of basic sciences, electronics and laser technology, engineering business, humanities, informatics and control systems, management, materials and technology, power engineering, robotics and complex automation, special machinery; br. in Kaluga
Rector: Prof. IGOR B. FEDOROV

Library: 3m. vols
Number of teachers: 2,500
Number of students: 18,000
Publications: *Izvestiya Vuzov* (mechanical engineering), *Vestnik MGTU* (issues each on instrumental engineering and mechanical engineering).

MOSCOW STATE TECHNOLOGICAL UNIVERSITY, STANKIN

101472 Moscow, Vadkovsky per. 3-a
Telephone: (495) 973-30-66
Fax: (495) 973-38-85
E-mail: rector@stankin.ru
Internet: www.stankin.ru
Founded 1930
Faculties of economics, information technology, innovation technology management, mechanics and control, metrological informatics, technology
Rector: Prof. YURY M. SOLOMENTSEV
Library of 700,000 vols
Number of teachers: 677
Number of students: 5,873

MOSCOW STATE TEXTILE UNIVERSITY

119991 Moscow, ul. Malaya Kaluzhskaya 1
Telephone: (495) 954-70-73
Fax: (495) 952-14-40
E-mail: office@msta.ac.ru
Internet: www.msta.ac.ru
Founded 1919
Faculties of mechanical technology, textile machinery, chemical technology, applied arts, economics and management, information, automation and energetics
Rector: SERGEI D. NIKOLAEV
Library of 780,000 vols
Number of teachers: 530
Number of students: 5,000
Publication: *Vestnik MGTU* (2 a year).

MOSCOW STATE UNIVERSITY OF CIVIL ENGINEERING

129337 Moscow, Yaroslavskoe shosse 26
Telephone: (495) 183-44-38
Fax: (495) 183-48-01
E-mail: kanz@mgsu.ru
Internet: www.mgsu.ru
Founded 1921
Faculties of constructional technology, economics organization and management of construction, heat and power construction, heat and ventilation, hydraulic engineering, industrial and civil construction, mechanization and automation of construction, urban construction and services, water and sewerage
Rector: Prof. VALERY I. TELICHENKO
Library of 1,600,000 vols
Number of teachers: 1,300
Number of students: 11,000
Publication: *Proceedings of MSUCE* (4 a year).

MOSCOW STATE UNIVERSITY OF ENGINEERING ECOLOGY

105066 Moscow, ul. Staraya Basmannaya 21/4
Telephone: (495) 267-07-01
Fax: (495) 261-49-61
Internet: www.msuie.ru
Founded 1920 as Moscow State Acad. of Chemical Engineering; present name and status 1997
Faculties of chemical and biological engineering and economics, chemical apparatus manufacture, chemical machine building, cryogenic technology, technical cybernetics and automation of technological processes
Rector: Prof. MIKHAIL B. GENERALOV
Library of 650,000 vols
Number of teachers: 400
Number of students: 3,000

MOSCOW STATE UNIVERSITY OF ENVIRONMENTAL ENGINEERING

127550 Moscow, ul. Pryanishnikova 19
Telephone and fax (495) 976-10-46
E-mail: mailbox@msuee.ru
Internet: www.msuee.ru
Founded 1930
Rector: Prof. DMITRY V. KOZLOV
Vice-Rector for Academic Affairs: VLADIMIR F. STORCHEVOY
Vice-Rector for Int. Affairs: ANDREI SOROKIN
Vice-Rector for Research: VALENTIN N. KRASNOSHCHEOKOV
Number of teachers: 400
Number of students: 3,700
Publication: *Environmental Engineering* (in Russian).

MOSCOW STATE UNIVERSITY OF GEODESY AND CARTOGRAPHY

105064 Moscow, Gorokhovsky per. 4
Telephone: (495) 261-31-52
Fax: (495) 267-46-81
E-mail: rector@miigaik.ru
Internet: www.miigaik.ru
Founded 1779
Academic year: September to June
Faculties of applied cosmonautics, cartography, geodesy, humanities, optical instrument manufacture, space surveying and photogrammetry, territorial economics and land management
Rector: Prof. VIKTOR P. SAVINYKH
Library of 800,000 vols
Number of teachers: 400
Number of students: 5,000
Publication: *Geodeziya i Aerofotosiomka* (6 a year).

MOSCOW STATE UNIVERSITY OF RAILWAY ENGINEERING

103055 Moscow, ul. Obraztsova 15
Telephone: (495) 681-31-77
Fax: (495) 681-13-40
E-mail: mgups@online.ru
Internet: www.miit.ru
Founded 1896, present name and status 1993
Faculties of mechanical engineering, mechanical engineering technology, railway automation, telemechanics and communication, technical cybernetics, industrial and civil construction, traffic management, electrification of railways, railway construction, bridges and tunnels engineering and economics
Rector: Prof. BORIS A. LEVIN
Library: 2m. vols
Number of teachers: 1,300
Number of students: 12,000
Publications: *Inzhener Transporta*, *MREI* (colln of works).

MOSCOW TECHNICAL UNIVERSITY OF COMMUNICATION AND INFORMATICS

111024 Moscow, ul. Aviamotornaya 8A
Telephone: (495) 957-77-09
Fax: (495) 274-00-32
E-mail: mtuci@mtuci.ru
Internet: www.mtuci.ru
Founded 1921 as Moscow Institute of Electrical Engineering and Communications; present name and status 1992
Faculties of radio communication and radio and television broadcasting, multi-channel communications, postal services automation, automatic telecommunications and engineering and economics; brs in Rostov-on-Don, Nizhnii Novgorod
Rector: Prof. VAGAN V. SHAKHGILDYAN
Library: 1.3m. vols
Number of teachers: 850
Number of students: 14,000

MURMANSK STATE TECHNICAL UNIVERSITY

183010 Murmansk, Sportivnaya ul. 13
Telephone: (8152) 45-46-09
E-mail: webmaster@mstu.edu.ru
Internet: www.mstu.edu.ru
Founded 1950
Rector: Dr ALEXANDER ERSHOV
Library of 350,000
Number of teachers: 394
Number of students: 4,458

NATIONAL RESEARCH UNIVERSITY

119991 Moscow, Leninsky pr. 65
Telephone: (4959) 137-81-08
Fax: (499) 135-88-95
E-mail: com@gubkin.ru
Internet: www.gubkin.ru
Founded 1930
Academic year: September to June
Faculties of automation and computer science, construction and operation, chemical and environmental engineering, economics and management and law, liberal arts and humanities, mechanical engineering, natural science studies, oil and gas fields devt, petroleum geology and geophysics, pipeline network design, reservoir engineering; brs in Ashgabat, Orenburg, Tashkent
Rector: ALBERT I. VLADIMIROV
Vice-Rector for Academic Affairs: MIKHAIL A. SILIN
Vice-Rector for Int. Affairs: ANATOLY B. ZOLOTUKHIN
Library: 1.5m. vols
Number of teachers: 900
Number of students: 8,500

NIZHNII NOVGOROD STATE TECHNICAL UNIVERSITY

603600 GSP 41, Nizhnii Novgorod, ul. Minina 24
Telephone: (8312) 36-23-25
Fax: (8312) 36-05-69
E-mail: nntu@nntu.nnov.ru
Internet: www.nntu.nnov.ru
Founded 1898 in Warsaw as Warsaw Polytechnic Institute; relocated to Moscow 1916, then Nizhnii Novgorod in 1917; re-established as Nizhnii Novgorod Polytechnic Institute; present name and status 1992
Rector: VLADIMIR P. KIRIENKO
Number of teachers: 1,166
Number of students: 12,310

NIZHNII NOVGOROD STATE UNIVERSITY OF ARCHITECTURE AND CIVIL ENGINEERING

603950 Nizhnii Novgorod, ul. Ilyinskaya 65
Telephone: (8312) 33-82-47

Fax: (8312) 33-73-66
E-mail: srec@nngasu.ru
Internet: www.nngasu.ru

Founded 1930
State control
Academic year: September to June

Fields of study: architecture, design, urban development, environmental engineering, economics, law, industrial management, environmental management and occupational safety; distance learning programmes

Rector: Prof. VALENTIN V. NAIDENKO
Vice-Rector for Int. Relations: Dr ALEXANDER PALEEV

Library of 800,000 vols
Number of teachers: 890
Number of students: 8,000

Publication: *Collected Papers and Proceedings of Scientific Conferences* (2 a year).

NORTH CAUCASIAN INSTITUTE OF MINING AND METALLURGICAL (STATE TECHNOLOGICAL UNIVERSITY)

362021 North-Ossetian Republic, Vladikavkaz, ul. Kosmonavta Nikolaeva 44
Telephone: (8672) 74-93-79
Fax: (8672) 74-99-45
E-mail: skgtu@skgtu.ru
Internet: www.skgtu.ru

Founded 1931 as the North Caucasian Institute of Non-Ferrous Metals

Faculties of construction, electromechanical, electronic engineering, metallurgical, mining, management

Rector: Dr VLADIMIR S. VAGIN

Library of 520,000 vols
Number of teachers: 500
Number of students: 4,000

Publications: *Izvestiya Vuzov, Tsvetnaya Metallurgia* (6 a year).

NORTH CAUCASIAN STATE TECHNICAL UNIVERSITY

362021 Stavropol, pr. Kulakova 2
Telephone: (8652) 95-68-08
Fax: (8652) 95-68-08
E-mail: info@ncstu.ru
Internet: www.ncstu.ru

Founded 1958

Rector: Prof. BORIS M. SINELNIKOV.

NORTH-WEST STATE TECHNICAL UNIVERSITY

191186 St Petersburg, ul. Millionnaya 5
Telephone: (812) 312-94-84
Fax: (812) 312-94-84
E-mail: office@nwpi.ru
Internet: www.nwpi.ru

Founded 1930

Rector: ALEXANDER A. KONDRATYEV

Library of 1,544,698 vols
Number of teachers: 400

NOVOSIBIRSK STATE TECHNICAL UNIVERSITY

630092 Novosibirsk, pr. Karla Marksa 20
Telephone: (3832) 46-50-01
Fax: (3832) 46-02-09
Internet: www.nstu.ru

Founded 1953

11 Faculties; 80 depts

Rector: Prof. NIKOLAI V. PUSTOVOI

Number of teachers: 1,105
Number of students: 9,354

NOVOSIBIRSK STATE UNIVERSITY OF ARCHITECTURE AND CIVIL ENGINEERING

630008 Novosibirsk-8, ul. Leningradskaya 113
Telephone: (3832) 66-41-25
Fax: (3832) 16-11-07
E-mail: uungas@sibstrin.ru
Internet: www.sibstrin.ru

Founded 1930

Faculties of architecture and construction, building specialists refresher programmes and further training, construction technology, environmental engineering, first stage of higher education, part-time and correspondence education, preliminary training, training of overseas students; institutes: architecture and civil engineering, economics and management, general and basic education, humanities

Rector: Prof. ARKADY P. YANENKO

Library of 553,000 vols
Number of teachers: 580
Number of students: 6,700

Publication: *Izvestiya vuzov—Stroitelstvo* (Higher School News—Civil Engineering, 12 a year).

OBNINSK STATE TECHNICAL UNIVERSITY FOR NUCLEAR POWER ENGINEERING (TECHNICAL UNIVERSITY)

249020 Kaluga oblast, Obninsk, Studgorodok 1
Telephone: (08439) 7-01-31
Fax: (08439) 7-08-22
E-mail: priem@iate.obninsk.ru
Internet: www.iate.obninsk.ru

Founded 1953 as a br. of Moscow Engineering and Physics Institute; as Obninsk Institute for Nuclear Power Engineering 1985–2002, present name and status 2002

Faculties of advanced education, cybernetics, distance education, economics, evening education, natural science, physics and power engineering

Rector: Prof. NIKOLAI L. SALNIKOV

Library of 140,000 vols
Number of teachers: 340
Number of students: 2,100

OMSK STATE TECHNICAL UNIVERSITY

644050 Omsk, Mira pr. 11
Telephone: (3812) 65-33-89
Fax: (3812) 65-26-98
E-mail: info@omgtu.ru
Internet: inter.omgtu.ru

Founded 1942
Public control
Academic year: September to June

Rector: Prof. VICTOR SHALAY
Vice-Rector for Education: Prof. ALEXANDER MYSHLYAVTSEV
Vice-Rector for Research: Prof. ANATOLY KOSYKH

Library of 1,281,294 vols
Number of teachers: 1,000
Number of students: 17,000 (incl. 500 int. students)

Publications: *Analysis and Synthesis of Mechanical Systems* (1 a year), *International conference: Dynamics of Machines and Mechanisms* (every 2 years), *Omsk Scientific Bulletin* (12 a year)

DEANS

Economics and Management Faculty: Prof. VERA POTUDANSKAYA
Energy Institute: Prof. VLADIMIR GORYUNOV
Humanitarian Education Faculty: Prof. MIKHAIL MASHKARIN
Information Technologies and Computer Systems Faculty: Prof. ANNA ZYKINA
Mechanical Engineering Institute: Prof. EVGENIY EREMIN
Petrochemical Institute: Prof. VLADIMIR YUSHA
Radio Engineering Faculty: Prof. VALERIY LEVCHENKO
Transport, Oil and Gas Faculty: Prof. VALENTIN BELKOV

OMSK STATE TRANSPORT UNIVERSITY

644046 Omsk, pr. Karla Marksa 35
Telephone and fax (3812) 31-42-13
E-mail: omgups@omgups.ru
Internet: www.omgups.ru

Founded 1930

Faculties of locomotives, railway rolling stock, electric transport, power supply for railways, automation, telemechanics and communication facilities for railway vehicles, technology of machine-building, heat and power engineering, control and information technology in technical systems, information systems, world economy, management, marketing, finance and credit, quality control

Rector: Prof. ILKHAM I. GALIEV

Library of 700,000 vols
Number of teachers: 310
Number of students: 6,000

PENZA STATE UNIVERSITY OF ARCHITECTURE AND CONSTRUCTION

440028 Penza, ul. Titova 28
Telephone: (8412) 48-74-76
Fax: (8412) 48-27-77
E-mail: relay@gasa.penza.com.ru
Internet: www.gasa.penza.com.ru

Founded 1958

Faculties of architecture, automotive engineering, construction, economics and management, engineering ecology, technology

Rector: ALEXANDER I. EREMKIN

Library of 370,000 vols
Number of teachers: 395
Number of students: 5,735

PERM STATE TECHNICAL UNIVERSITY

614600 Perm, Komsomolsky pr. 29A
Telephone: (3422) 12-87-53
Fax: (3422) 12-11-47
E-mail: rector@pstu.ac.ru
Internet: www.pstu.ac.ru

Founded 1953 as Perm Mining Institute

Faculties of aerospace technology, applied mathematics and mechanics, chemical technology, construction, electrical engineering, humanities, mining, road transport

Rector: VASILY YU. PETROV

Library: 1.4m. vols
Number of teachers: 932
Number of students: 12,500

PETERSBURG STATE TRANSPORT UNIVERSITY

190031 St Petersburg, Moskovsky pr. 9
Telephone: (812) 310-25-21
Internet: www.pgups.ru

Founded 1809

Faculties of bridge and tunnel construction, construction, electrical engineering, electrification, mechanics, traffic management; br. in Velikie Luki

Rector: Prof. VALERY I. KOVALEV

Library: 1.5m. vols

Number of teachers: 700

Publication: *Proceedings* (1 a year).

POLZUNOV ALTAI STATE TECHNICAL UNIVERSITY

656038 Barnaul, Lenina pr. 46

Telephone: (3852) 26-05-42

Fax: (3852) 36-78-64

E-mail: nikonov@mail.altstu.ru

Internet: www.altstu.ru

Founded 1942

Language of instruction: Russian

Rector: Prof. LEV A. KORSHUNOV

Vice-Rector: Prof. OLEG I. KHOMUTOV

Library of 992,456 vols

Number of teachers: 1,500

Number of students: 21,000

Publication: *Polzunovsky Vestnik*

Faculties of automotive, part-time studies, humanities, natural science, extramural education, innovation technologies in machine building, information technologies, second degree education, food and chemical engineering, social science and tourism, civil engineering, power engineering, military training; institutes of architecture and design, intensive education, further professional education development, textile and light industry, economics and management; brs: Biysk Technological Institute, Rubtsovsk Industrial Institute.

ROSTOV STATE UNIVERSITY OF CIVIL ENGINEERING

344022 Rostov-on-Don, Sotsialisticheskaya ul. 162

Telephone: (8632) 65-50-76

Fax: (8632) 65-57-31

E-mail: rgsu@jeo.ru

Internet: www.rgsu.ru

Founded 1943

Institutes of civil engineering technology and materials, economics, environmental engineering, highways and transport, industrial and civil engineering, management

Rector: VIKTOR I. SHUMEIKO

Library of 710,000 vols

Publication: *Izvestiya* (4 a year).

ROSTOV STATE UNIVERSITY FOR RAILWAY TRANSPORTATION

344038 Rostov-on-Don, pl. Narodnogo Opolcheniya 2

Telephone: (8632) 45-06-13

Fax: (8632) 45-06-13

E-mail: rek@rgups.ru

Internet: www.rgups.ru

Founded 1929

Rector: VLADIMIR I. KOLESNIKOV

Library of 980,000 vols

Number of teachers: 550

Number of students: 5,000

Fields of study: automation and telemechanics, power engineering, electromechanical engineering, railway construction, traffic and transport management, road building machinery, humanities; Institute of Management and Law.

RUSSIAN STATE HYDROMETEOROLOGICAL UNIVERSITY

195196 St Petersburg, Malookhtinsky pr. 98

Telephone: (812) 444-41-63

Fax: (812) 444-60-90

E-mail: rector@rshu.ru

Internet: www.rshu.ru

Founded 1930

Library of 300,000 vols

Number of teachers: 250

Number of students: 5,500

Rector: Prof. LEV N. KARLIN

Vice-Rectors: Prof. ANDREI V. BELOTSERKOVSKY (Academic Asscns), Dr ANATOLY I. BOGUSH (Int. Relations), VLADIMIR N. VOROBYEV (Research), Dr VLADIMIR M. SAKOVICH (Undergraduate and Graduate Education)

Publication: *Proceedings* (4 a year)

DEANS

Faculty of Ecology and Natural Physics: Dr ANNA L. SKOBLIKOVA

Economic and Social-Humanitarian Faculty: Prof. MIKHAIL M. GLAZOV

Hydrological Faculty: Dr ARKADY DOGANOVSKY

Meteorological Faculty: Prof. LEONID DIVINSKY

Oceanological Faculty: Dr ALEXANDER S. AVERKIYEV

Correspondence Education: Prof. VADIM G. ORLOV

BRANCHES

RSHU Aleksin: 301351, Tula oblast, Aleksin District, Kolosovo; tel. (8753) 7-34-17; Dir VALERY M. BORTYAKOV.

RSHU Rostov-on-Don: 344025 Rostov-on-Don, 31-aya Liniya 4; tel. (8632) 91-41-05; Dir SERGEY S. ANDREEV.

RSHU Tuapse: 352800 Krasnodar oblast, Tuapse, ul. Morskaya 4; tel. (8616) 72-37- 63; Dir YARVANT O. YAILY.

RUSSIAN STATE OPEN TECHNICAL UNIVERSITY OF RAILWAY TRANSPORT

125993 Moscow, ul. Chasovaya 22/2

Telephone: (495) 151-14-51

Fax: (495) 151-18-37

E-mail: org@rgotups.ru

Internet: www.rgotups.ru

Founded 1951

Faculties of Railway Traffic and Management, Railway Construction and Civil Engineering, Economics and General Technology; brs in Nizhnii Novgorod, Voronezh, Yaroslavl, Smolensk, Saratov, Bryansk, Tula, Novomoskovsk, Ryazan, Murom, Elets, Vologda, Vladimir, Kirov, Izhevsk, Lisky, Kotlas, Kaliningrad, Orel, Rtitshevo, Labytnangy, Astrakhan, Volgograd, Uhta

Rector: Prof. Dr A. T. DEMCHENKO

Vice-Rector: Prof. Dr V. I. APATZEV

Library of 930,453 vols

Number of teachers: 508

Number of students: 21,573

RUSSIAN STATE TECHNOLOGICAL UNIVERSITY 'K. E. TSIOLKOVSKY' (MATI)

103767 Moscow, ul. Orshanskaya 3

Telephone: (495) 141-18-40

Fax: (495) 141-19-50

E-mail: intdep@intedu.mati.msk.ru

Internet: www.mati.ru

Founded 1932

Faculties of aerospace engineering and technology, applied mathematics and mechanics, avionics, computer science, economics and business, ecology, materials science and technology, satellite communications and technology

Rector: ANATOLY P. PETROV

Library of 800,000 vols

Number of teachers: 1,103

Number of students: 9,000

RUSSIAN UNIVERSITY OF CHEMICAL TECHNOLOGY 'D. MENDELEEV'

125047 Moscow, Miusskaya pl. 9

Telephone: (495) 978-87-33

Fax: (495) 200-42-04

E-mail: rector@muctr.edu.ru

Internet: www.muctr.edu.ru

Founded 1920

Faculties of chemical technology of inorganic substances, chemical technology of organic substances, chemical technology engineering, chemical technology of polymers, cybernetics of chemical technological processes, ecological engineering, physical chemistry engineering, general engineering and economics; br. in Novomoskovsk

Rector: Dr PAVEL D. SARKISOV

Library of 1,700,000 vols

Number of teachers: 1,003

Number of students: 8,416

Publication: *Trudy* (6 a year).

ST PETERSBURG ELECTROTECHNICAL UNIVERSITY 'LETI' (ETU)

197376 St Petersburg, ul. Prof. Popova 5

Telephone: (812) 346-44-87

Fax: (812) 234-54-05

E-mail: intdep@eltech.ru

Internet: www.eltech.ru

Founded 1886

Schools of biomedical and ecological engineering, computer technology and informatics, economics and management, electrical engineering and automation, electronics, humanities, instrumentation, radio engineering and telecommunications

Rector: DIMITRY V. PUZANKOV

Library of 1,063,000 vols

Number of teachers: 1,000

Number of students: 8,000

Publications: *Izvestiya ETU* (14 a year), *Izvestiya Vuzov Rossii—Radioelektronika*.

ST PETERSBURG STATE MARINE TECHNICAL UNIVERSITY

190008 St Petersburg, ul. Lotsmanskaya 3

Telephone: (812) 114-41-68

Fax: (812) 318-52-27

E-mail: inter@smtu.ru

Internet: www.smtu.ru

Founded 1930

Faculties of natural and social sciences and humanities, naval architecture and ocean engineering, marine engineering, marine electronics and control systems, business and management

Rector: Dr KONSTANTIN P. BORISENKO

Library of 862,380 vols

Number of teachers: 600

Number of students: 5,500

ST PETERSBURG STATE MINING INSTITUTE (TECHNICAL UNIVERSITY)

199026 St Petersburg, Vasilevskii ostrov, 21-ya Liniya 2
Telephone: (812) 213-60-78
Fax: (812) 327-73-59
E-mail: rectorat@spmi.ru
Internet: www.spmi.ru

Founded 1773

Rector: Prof. VLADIMIR S. LITVINENKO

Library of 1,209,266 vols
Number of students: 8,000

ST PETERSBURG STATE POLYTECHNICAL UNIVERSITY

195251 St Petersburg, Politekhnicheskaya ul. 29
Telephone: (812) 247-1616
Fax: (812) 552-6080
E-mail: rector@stu.neva.ru
Internet: www.spbstu.ru

Founded 1899
State control
Languages of instruction: Russian, English
Academic year: September to July

Faculties of computer science and engineering, biomedical engineering, electrical engineering, economics and management, humanities, hydraulic engineering, industrial engineering, mechanical engineering, physical science and engineering, physics and mechanical sciences, power engineering, radiophysical science and engineering, technology and materials science; brs at Pskov, Cherboksary and Orsk

Pres.: Prof. MIKHAIL P. FIODOROV

Library: 2.5m. vols
Number of teachers: 2,000
Number of students: 16,000

Publications: *Scientific and Engineering News*, *Transactions*.

ST PETERSBURG STATE TECHNOLOGICAL UNIVERSITY OF PLANT POLYMERS

198095 St Petersburg, ul. Ivan Chernykh 4
Telephone: (812) 786-57-44
Fax: (812) 786-86-00
E-mail: zsv@gturp.spb.ru
Internet: www.gturp.spb.ru

Founded 1931, present name and status 1993
Academic year: September to June

Integrated training of specialists for enterprises in the pulp and paper industry and the fuel and power sector; depts of automated control systems, chemical engineering, economics and management, environmental engineering, heat and power engineering, mechanical, part-time studies

Rector: VYACHESLAV A. SUSLOV (acting)
Vice-Rector for Economics and Devt: ALEXANDER L. ASHKALUNIN
Vice-Rector for Innovations: ALEXANDER N. IVANOV
Vice Rector for Int. Relations: NADEZHDA V. KHODYREVA
Vice-Rector for Research: VICTOR S. KUROV
Vice-Rector for Studies: PAVEL V. LUKANIN

Library of 740,000 vols
Number of teachers: 300
Number of students: 5,000

Publications: *JPPS*, *Pulp Paper Board Magazine*, *TAPPI*.

ST PETERSBURG STATE UNIVERSITY OF ARCHITECTURE AND CIVIL ENGINEERING

190005 St Petersburg, 2nd Krasnoarmeiskaya ul., 4
Telephone: (812) 316-58-72
Fax: (812) 575-05-34
E-mail: rector@spbgasu.ru
Internet: www.spbgasu.ru

Founded 1832

Advanced training and retraining institute; faculties of architecture, civil engineering, automobile and road building, environment engineering, economics and management, urban construction and public utilities, correspondence faculty

Rector: Prof. YEVGENY I. RYBNOV

Library of 855,000 vols
Number of teachers: 870
Number of students: 8,775

Publications: *Masterok* (4 a year), *Za stroitel'nye kadry* (12 a year).

ST PETERSBURG STATE UNIVERSITY OF INFORMATION TECHNOLOGY, MECHANICS AND OPTICS

197101 St Petersburg, ul. Sablinskaya 14
Telephone: (812) 233-00-89
Fax: (812) 232-23-07
E-mail: rector@mail.ifmo.ru
Internet: www.ifmo.ru

Founded 1900

Rector: Prof. VLADIMIR N. VASILEV

Library of 900,000 vols
Number of teachers: 500
Number of students: 4,000

Publication: *Izvestiya Vuzov (Priborostroenie)* (4 a year).

ST PETERSBURG STATE UNIVERSITY OF REFRIGERATION AND FOOD ENGINEERING

191002 St Petersburg, ul. Lomonosova 9
Telephone and fax (812) 315-36-17
E-mail: refr@gunipt.spb.ru
Internet: www.gunipt.edu.ru

Founded 1931
Academic year: September to June

Rector: ALEXANDER V. BARANENKO
Vice-Rector for Int. Contacts: OLGA N. RUMYANTSEVA

Library: 1m. vols
Number of teachers: 337
Number of students: 6,344

DEANS

Faculty of Correspondence and Extramural: Prof. DMITRY P. MALYAVKO
Faculty of Cryogenics and Conditioning Systems: Dr IGOR V. BARANOV
Faculty of Economics and Environmental Management: Dr VICTOR L. VASILYONOK
Faculty of Food Manufacturing Facilities: Prof. ELENA V. VERBOLOZ
Faculty of Food Technologies: Dr ALEXANDER L. ISHEVSKY
Faculty of Refrigeration Engineering: Prof. VLADIMIR A. KOROTKOV

ST PETERSBURG STATE UNIVERSITY OF TECHNOLOGY AND DESIGN

191186 St Petersburg, Bol. Morskaya ul. 18
Telephone and fax (812) 315-12-10
E-mail: international@sutd.ru
Internet: www.sutd.ru

Founded 1828, present name and status 1992
Academic year: September to June

Rector: Prof. ALEXEY V. DEMIDOV
Head of Library: O. TEROVA

Library of 1,245,684 vols
Number of teachers: 900
Number of students: 11,000 (incl. 6,500 full-time)

DEANS

Faculty of Applied Chemistry and Ecology: Prof. N. NOVOSELOV
Faculty of Information Technologies and Machine Science: Prof. V. ENTIN
Faculty of Natural Sciences and Humanities: S. IVANOVA
Faculty of Textiles and Clothing: Prof. E. SURZHENKO

ST PETERSBURG STATE UNIVERSITY OF TELECOMMUNICATIONS 'PROF. M. A. BONCH-BRUYEV'

191065 St Petersburg, nab. Moiki 61
Telephone: (812) 315-01-18
Fax: (812) 315-32-27
E-mail: rector@sut.ru
Internet: www.sut.ru

Founded 1930

Faculties of biomedical electronics, economics and management, multi-channel telecommunication systems, radio broadcasting and television, radio communication, switching systems and computer technology, telecommunication networks, telecommunication technologies

Rector: Prof. ALEXANDER A. GOGOL

Library of 90,000 vols.

ST PETERSBURG STATE UNIVERSITY OF WATER COMMUNICATIONS

198035 St Petersburg, ul. Dvinskaya 5/7
Telephone: (812) 251-12-21
Fax: (812) 251-01-14
E-mail: rector@spbuwc.ru
Internet: www.spbuwc.ru

Founded 1809

Rector: Prof. SERGEY O. BARYSHNIKOV

Library of 950,663 vols
Number of teachers: 376
Number of students: 7,353 (3,953 full-time, 3,400 correspondence)

DEANS

Evening and Correspondence Study: Dr YURI E. EZHOV
Faculty of Arts and Social Sciences: OLEG A. CHULKOV
Faculty of Economics and Finance: Dr IGOR E. RASTORGUEV
Faculty of Information Technologies: Dr EVGENIY G. BARSCHEVSKIY
Faculty of Law: Prof. OLEG G. KARATAEV
Faculty of Navigation: Dr KIRILL V. SLATIN
Hydrotechnical Engineering Faculty: SERGEY A. GOLOVKOV
Marine Engineering: Dr YURI K. LOPAREV
Port Facilities and Electrical Engineering: Dr EVGENIY N. ANDRIANOV
Regional and Distant Learning: Dr LARISA V. ALPEEVA

SAMARA STATE AEROSPACE UNIVERSITY 'S. P. KOROLEV'

443086 Samara, Moskovskoye shosse 34
Telephone: (8462) 35-18-51
Fax: (8462) 35-18-36
E-mail: ssau@ssau.ru
Internet: www.ssau.ru

Founded 1942

Faculties of aircraft construction, flying-vehicle engines, air transport engineers, plastic working of metals, radio engineering, information science, economics and management, aircraft engines (evenings), aircraft production technology and organization (evenings), correspondence education, information science and pre-university training

Rector: VICTOR A. SOIFER

Library of 1,092,955 vols
Number of teachers: 750
Number of students: 10,500

SAMARA STATE TECHNICAL UNIVERSITY

443010 Samara, ul. Molodogvardeiskaya 244

Telephone: (8462) 78-43-00
Fax: (8462) 78-44-00
E-mail: postman@samgtu.ru
Internet: www.samgtu.ru

Founded 1914

Faculties of automation and information technology, chemical technology, economics and humanities, electrotechnology, engineering technology, machine building, oil technology, physical technology, thermal power

Rector: VLADIMIR V. KALASHNIKOV
Number of students: 10,000

SAMARA STATE UNIVERSITY OF ARCHITECTURE AND CIVIL ENGINEERING

443001 Samara, Molodogvardeiskaya ul. 194

Telephone: (8462) 42-17-84
Fax: (8462) 32-19-65
E-mail: sgasu@sgasu.smr.ru
Internet: www.sgasu.smr.ru
State control
Languages of instruction: Russian, English
Academic year: September to June

Founded 1930 as Samara State Acad. of Architecture and Civil Engineering, present name and status 2004

Rector: Prof. MIKHAIL I. BALZANNIKOV
Pres.: VSEVOLOD A. SHABANOV
Vice-Rector: NATALYA G. CHUMACHENKO
Library Dir: LYUDMILA I. KORYTINA

Library of 1,000,000 vols, incl. 300,000 specialist books
Number of teachers: 420
Number of students: 8,000

DEANS

Centre for Linguistic Training and Translation/Interpretation: Prof. EUPHYM G. VYSHKIN
Construction Institute: Prof IGOR S. KHOLOPOV
Faculty of Architecture: Assoc. Prof ELINA V. DANILOVA
Faculty of Construction Engineering: Assoc. Prof. KONSTANTIN S. GALITSKOV
Faculty of Design: Assoc. Prof SVETLANA G. MALYSHEVA
Faculty of Engineering Economics: Assoc. Prof VALERY A. PROTSENKO
Faculty of Engineering Systems and Environment Protection Construction: Assoc. Prof. MIKHAIL V. SHUVALOV
Faculty of Industrial and Civil Engineering: Assoc. Prof VALERY M. KAZAKOV
Faculty of Information Systems and Technologies: Prof. SEMYON A. PIYAVSKIY
Faculty of Transport and Town Development: Assoc. Prof. TATYANA E. GORDEYEVA
Institute of Architecture and Design: Prof. YELENA A. AKHMEDOVA
Institute of Ecology and Engineering Life Support Systems: Prof. ALEKSANDR K. STRELKOV
Institute of Economics and Management: Prof IRINA P. SCHEGOLEVA

SARATOV STATE TECHNICAL UNIVERSITY

410054 Saratov, ul. Politekhnicheskaya 77

Telephone: (8452) 50-77-40
Fax: (8452) 50-75-40
E-mail: sstu_office@sstu.saratov.su
Internet: www.sstu.ru

Founded 1930

Faculties of electronics and instrument-making, power engineering, motor vehicles, architecture and construction, mechanical engineering, highways and transport construction, social work, business and social systems management; Computer Training Centre

Rector: Prof. YURI V. CHEBOTAREVSKY

Library: 2m. vols
Number of teachers: 1,100
Number of students: 13,000

SIBERIAN STATE AEROSPACE UNIVERSITY 'M. F. RESHETNEV'

660014 Krasnoyarsk, 31 Krasnoyarsky Rabochy pr.

Telephone: (391) 264-00-14
Fax: (391) 264-47-09
E-mail: info@sibsau.ru
Internet: www.sibsau.ru

Founded 1959
State control
Languages of instruction: Russian, English
Academic year: September to June

Rector: Prof. IGOR V. KOVALEV
Vice-Rector for Academic Affairs: ANNA A. LUKIANOVA
Vice-Rector for Devt: VLADIMIR A. KURESHOV
Vice-Rector for Research and Innovations: YURIY Y. LOGINOV
Vice-Rector for Pre-univ. Training and Educational work: VADIM V. KOLGA
Vice-Rector for General Affairs and Public Relations: BORIS V. VERBENKO
Vice-Rector for Int. Cooperation and Additional Education: ANNA A. VOROSHILOVA
Vice-Rector for Admin. and Social Affairs: SERGEY N. SKOTNIKOV

Library of 858,424 vols, 427 titles
Number of teachers: 808
Number of students: 11,403
Publication: *Vestnik Sibsau*

DEANS

Faculty of Distance and Additional Learning: LILIYA V. ERYGINA
Faculty of Economics and Finance: YURIY V. ERYGIN
Faculty of Humanities: SVETLANA Y. PISKORSKAYA
Faculty of Physical Education and Sport: IGOR A. TOLSTOPYATOV
Faculty of Professional Devt of Teaching Staff: VALERIY A. LEVKO
Faculty of Retraining and Professional Devt of Specialists: GRIGORIY B. DOBRETSOV
Institute of Civil Aviation: VLADIMIR L. MEDVEDEV
Institute of Information Science and Telecommunication: ALEKSEY M. POPOV
Institute of Machine Science and Innovation: EVGENIY V. SUGAK
Institute of Space Technology: NIKOLAY A. TEREKHIN
Institute of Space Research and High Technologies: VASILIY F. SHABANOV
Int. Higher School of Innovating Business and Admin.: OLGA E. PODVERBNYKH
Military Institute: EVGENIY I. DOBRYAKOV

SIBERIAN STATE TECHNOLOGICAL UNIVERSITY

660049 Krasnoyarsk, pr. Mira 82

Telephone: (3912) 276382
Fax: (3912) 274440
E-mail: repyakh@sibstu.kts.ru
Internet: www.sibstu.kts.ru

Founded 1930

Faculties of automation and robot technology, chemical technology, engineering economics, engineering for chemical technology, forestry, humanities and mechanics, woodworking technology, timber technology and equipment; brs in Lesosibirsk and 5 representative offices in major Siberian cities

Rector: Prof. EDUARD S. BUKA

Library of 243,000 vols
Number of teachers: 682
Number of students: 12,912

SIBERIAN STATE UNIVERSITY OF TELECOMMUNICATIONS AND INFORMATICS

630102 Novosibirsk, ul. Kirova 86

Telephone: (3832) 66-10-38
Fax: (3832) 66-10-39
E-mail: rectorat@neic.nsk.ru
Internet: www.sibsutis.ru

Founded 1953

Faculties of automatic electrical communication, engineering economics and informatics, multi-channel electrical communication, radio communication and broadcasting; brs in Khabarovsk, Ekaterinburg, Ulan-Ude

Rector: Prof. VALERY P. BAKALOV

Library of 463,638 vols
Number of teachers: 650
Number of students: 10,000

SIBERIAN TRANSPORT UNIVERSITY

630023 Novosibirsk, ul. D. Kovalchuk 191

Telephone: (3832) 28-74-70
Fax: (3832) 26-79-78

Founded 1932

Faculties of accounting and auditing, bridges and tunnels, civil engineering, construction and track machinery, economics and building management, economics and transport management, management and world economics, railway construction, railway traffic management, water supply and sewerage

Rector: Dr VLADIMIR D. VERESKUN

Library of 773,000 vols
Number of teachers: 600
Number of students: 12,000
Publication: *Proceedings* (5 or 6 a year).

SOUTH RUSSIA STATE TECHNICAL UNIVERSITY (NOVOCHERKASSK POLYTECHNIC INSTITUTE)

346428 Novocherkassk, ul. Prosveshcheniya 132

Telephone: (8635) 25-55-14
Fax: (8635) 22-72-69
E-mail: ngtu@novoch.ru
Internet: www.npi-tu.ru

Founded 1907
State control

Faculties of chemical technology, civil engineering, computer systems and robotics, electrical engineering, humanities and social economic education, manufacturing machines and robots, mechanics, mining and geology prospecting, power

Pres.: Prof. VALENTIN E. SHUKSHUNOV
Rector: Prof. VLADIMIR G. PEREDERIY
Dir: LUBOV D. KUINDZHY

Library of 3,162,689 vols, 300 periodical titles
Number of teachers: 2,111
Number of students: 24,616

Publications: *Izvestiya SK NC Visshey Shkoly* (4 a year), *Izvestiya Vuzov Severo-Cavkazskogo regiona: Elektromekhanika* (12 a year).

STATE EDUCATIONAL INSTITUTION OF HIGHER PROFESSIONAL EDUCATION ULYANOVSK STATE TECHNICAL UNIVERSITY

432027 Ulyanovsk, ul. Severny Venets 32
Telephone: (8422) 43-06-43
Fax: (8422) 43-02-37
E-mail: rector@ulstu.ru
Internet: www.ulstu.ru

Founded 1957 as Ulyanovsk Evening Polytechnic Institute; reorganized into Ulyanovsk Polytechnic Institute 1962, renamed Ulyanovsk State Technical University 1994, present name and status 2002

Rector: Prof. Dr ALEXANDER D. GORBOKONENKO
Vice-Rector: N. YARUSHKINA
Librarian: TAMARA M. SMIRNOVA

Library of 1,411,507 vols
Number of teachers: 637
Number of students: 13,318

Publication: *Vestnik Ulyanovsk State Technical University* (4 a year)

Faculties of information systems and technology, radio engineering, power engineering, civil engineering, mechanical engineering, aircraft engineering, humanities, economics, mathematics, correspondent (evening) studies, open education centres and distance education; open business school at Dimitrovgrad.

TAMBOV STATE TECHNICAL UNIVERSITY

392000 Tambov, Sovetskaya ul. 106
Telephone: (4752) 63-10-19
Fax: (4752) 63-02-16
E-mail: tstu@admin.tstu.ru
Internet: www.tstu.ru

Founded 1958
Public control
Language of instruction: Russian
Academic year: September to July

Rector: Prof. Dr SERGEY V. MISCHENKO
Vice-Rector: Dr VYACHESLAV F. KALININ
Vice-Rector: Dr NIKOLAY S. POPOV
Librarian: IRINA V. SCHUKINA

Library of 1,500,000 vols
Number of teachers: 700
Number of students: 12,000

Publications: *Problems of Contemporary Science and Practice* (4 a year), *TSTU Transactions* (4 a year)

DEANS

Architecture and Civil Engineering: PAVEL MONASTYREV
Correspondence Study and External Studies: VALERIY ODNOLKO
Economics: BORIS GERASIMOV
Information Technologies: YURIY GROMOV
International Education: MAXIM PROMOTOV
Motor Transport: OLEG DMITRIEV
Nanotechnologies: ALEXANDER MAYSTRENKO
Noosphere Safety and Law: SERGEY YESIKIV
Power Engineering: TATYANA CHERNYSHEVA
Pre-University Training: VLADIMIR PLOTNIKOV

PROFESSORS

BELYAEV, P.
BRUSENTOV, Y.
BYKOVSKIY, V.
CHERNYSHEVA, T.
CHERNYSHEV, V. N.
DEMIN, O. B.
DMITRIEV, O.
DVORETSKIY, S. I.
DZUBA, S.
FROLOV, S.
GATAPOVA, N. T.
GERASIMOV, B. I.
GROMOV, Y.
KALININ, V. F.
KILIMNIK, A.
KLIMOV, A. M.
KLINKOV, A.
KONOVALOV, V.
KULIKOV, G.
KULIKOV, N.
KUROCHKIN, I. M.
LAZAREV, S.
LEDENEV, V.
LEONTYEVA, A. I.
MAKEEVA, M.
MALYGYN, E.
MARTEMYANOV, Y. F.
MATVEYKIN, V.
MOLOTKOVA, N
MILOVANOV, I. V.
MISCHENKO, S. V.
MOLOTKOV, N.
NIKULIN, V. V.
ODNOLKO, V. G.
PARKHOMENKO, L.
PENKOV, V.
PERSHIN, V.
PODOLSKIY, V. Y.
POPOVA, I.
POPOV, N. S.
PROMTOV, M. A.
PUCHKOV, N. P.
PUDOVKIN, A.
ROMANOV, A. P.
SHAMKIN, V. N.
SLEZIN, A.
TKACHEV, A.
VANIN, V.
VOROBYEV, Y.
VORONKOVA, O.
YESIKOV, S. A.
ZHARIKOV, V.
ZHUKOV, N. P.

TOMSK POLYTECHNIC UNIVERSITY

634050 Tomsk, pr. Lenina 30
Telephone: (3822) 56-34-70
Fax: (3822) 56-38-65
E-mail: tpu@tpu.ru
Internet: www.tpu.ru

Founded 1896

Faculties of applied physics and engineering, chemistry and chemical engineering, economics and management, electrophysics and electronic equipment, humanities, mechanical engineering, thermal power engineering, natural science and mathematics; institutes of continuing education of specialists, cybernetics, distance learning, electrical engineering, engineering education, geology and oil and gas industries, international education, languages and communication

Rector: YURI P. POKHOLKOV

Library: 2.7m. vols
Number of teachers: 1,924
Number of students: 22,876

TOMSK STATE UNIVERSITY OF CONTROL SYSTEMS AND RADIOELECTRONICS

634050 Tomsk, pr. Lenina 40
Telephone: (3822) 51-05-30
Fax: (3822) 51-32-62
E-mail: office@tusur.ru
Internet: www.tusur.ru

Founded 1962

Faculties of computing systems, control systems, electronic engineering, economics, humanities, radio design, radio engineering; Institute of Innovation and Higher College of Informatics, Electronics and Management

Rector: YURY A. SHURYGIN
Dir: ANATOLY V. KOBZEV

Library of 601,000 vols
Number of teachers: 600
Number of students: 14,000

TULA STATE UNIVERSITY

300600 Tula, pr. Lenina 92
Telephone: (0872) 35-21-55
Fax: (0872) 33-13-05
E-mail: info@tsu.tula.ru
Internet: www.tsu.tula.ru

Founded 1930

Faculties of mechanics and control systems, mechanics and mathematics, applied physics, engineering, cybernetics, mining and construction, medicine, natural sciences, humanities, economics and law, technological, physical culture, sport and tourism, int. students' faculty

Rector: Prof. MIKHAIL V. GRYAZEV

Library: 1m. vols
Number of teachers: 1,386
Number of students: 17,000

Publication: *Izvestiya* (4 a year).

TVER STATE TECHNICAL UNIVERSITY

170026 Tver, nab. A. Nikitina 22
Telephone: (0822) 31-15-09
Fax: (0822) 31-43-07
E-mail: common@tstu.tver.ru
Internet: www.tstu.tver.ru

Founded 1922

Faculties of machine building, automatic control systems, civil and industrial engineering, environmental engineering, humanities, postgraduate, evening and distance education

Rector: Prof. VYACHESLAV A. MIRONOV

Library: 2m. vols.

TYUMEN STATE OIL AND GAS UNIVERSITY

625000 Tyumen, ul. Volodarskogo 38
Telephone: (3452) 25-08-61
Fax: (3452) 25-08-25
E-mail: general@tgngu.tyumen.ru
Internet: www.tgngu.tyumen.ru

Founded 1963

Faculties of geology and geoinformatics, oil and gas fields, pipeline engineering, transport, technical cybernetics, oil and gas refining, management, drilling and mechanical engineering

Rector: NIKOLAI N. KARNAUKHOV

Library of 677,000 vols
Number of teachers: 1,230
Number of students: 30,000

UFA STATE AVIATION TECHNICAL UNIVERSITY

450000 Bashkortostan, Ufa, ul. K. Marksa 12
Telephone: (3472) 56-96-93
Fax: (3472) 56-96-93
E-mail: root@admin.ugatu.ac.ru
Internet: www.ugatu.ac.ru

Founded 1932

Faculties of aircraft engines, aircraft machine building technology, aircraft technological systems, general sciences, informatics and robotics, economics, management and finance, social sciences

Rector: Prof. MURAT B. GUZAIROV

Library of 700,000 vols

Publications: *Higher School Collections on Research* (irregular), newspaper (52 a year).

UFA STATE PETROLEUM TECHNOLOGICAL UNIVERSITY

450062 Bashkortostan, Ufa, ul. Kosmonavtov 1

Telephone: (3472) 42-03-70
Fax: (3472) 43-14-19
E-mail: info@rusoil.net
Internet: www.ugntu.ru

Founded 1941

Faculties of oil and mining, pipeline transport, petrochemical, oil equipment, construction, technology, economics and management, automation of production processes, humanities, military studies; brs in Oktyabrsky, Salavat, Sterlitamak

Rector: AYRAT M. SHAMMAZOV

Library of 1,031,930 vols
Number of teachers: 802
Number of students: 14,000

URALSKIY GOSUDARSTVENNYY LESOTEHNICHESKIY UNIVERSITET (Ural State Forest Engineering University)

260100 Ekaterinburg, ul. Sibirsky Trakt 37

Telephone: (343) 254-65-06
Fax: (343) 254-62-25
E-mail: general@usfeu.ru
Internet: www.usfeu.ru

Founded 1930
State control
Language of instruction: Russian
Academic year: September to June

Rector: Prof. VASILY A. AZARENOK
Pro-Rector for Educational Work: Prof. SERGEY I. BULDAKOV
Pro-Rector for Scientific Work: Prof. SERGEY V. ZALESOV
Pro-Rector for Personnel: Prof. VLADIMIR G. NOVOSELOV
Librarian: LUDMILA K. BUKVAREVA

Library of 826,000 vols, 230 periodical titles
Number of teachers: 489
Number of students: 9,500

DEANS

Faculty of Complementary Education: Prof. LEO G. SHVAMM
Faculty of Correspondence: Prof. ANATOLY V. KAPRALOV
Faculty of Ecological Engineering: Prof. ALESJA V. VURASKO
Faculty of Economics and Management: Prof. VICTOR P. CHASOVSKIH
Faculty of Forestry: Prof. ZUFAR YA. NAGIMOV
Faculty of Forestry Engineering: Prof. EDWARD F. GUERZ
Faculty of Humanities: IRINA G. SVETLOVA
Faculty of Mechanical Engineering: Prof. VALERY P. SIVAKOV
Faculty of Professional Education: OLGA A. UDACHINA
Faculty of Wood Technology: Prof. YURY I. TRAKALO

URALS STATE MINING UNIVERSITY

620144 Ekaterinburg, ul. Kuibysheva 30

Telephone: (3432) 22-25-47
Fax: (3432) 29-48-38
E-mail: office@usmga.ru
Internet: www.usmga.ru

Founded 1914 as Ekaterinburg Mining Institute; as Sverdlovsk Mining Institute 1934–1993; as Urals State Acad. of Mining and Geology 1993–2004; present name and status 2004

Faculties of economics, environmental engineering, geology, geophysics, mining engineering, mining technology

Rector: Prof. NIKOLAI P. KOSAREV

Library of 800,000 vols
Number of teachers: 1,500
Number of students: 6,000

URALS STATE TECHNICAL UNIVERSITY

620002 Ekaterinburg, ul. Mira 19

Telephone: (343) 374-54-34
Fax: (343) 374-38-84
E-mail: inter@inter.ustu.ru
Internet: www.ustu.ru

Founded 1920

Faculties of chemical technology, civil engineering, construction materials, economics and management, electrical engineering, heat and power engineering, mechanical engineering, metallurgy, physical engineering, humanities, physical training and sport, radio engineering

Rector: Prof. STANISLAV S. NABOICHENKO

Library: 2m. vols
Number of teachers: 2,233
Number of students: 35,000

URALS STATE UNIVERSITY OF RAILWAY TRANSPORT

620034 Ekaterinburg, ul. Kolmogorova 66

Telephone and fax (343) 245-34-67
E-mail: rector@usart.ru
Internet: www.usart.ru

Founded 1956
State control; attached to the Min. of Transport of the Russian Federation
Academic year: September to June

Faculties of construction, economics, electrical engineering, electrification, mechanics, traffic management

Rector: Prof. ALEXANDER V. EFIMOV
Vice-Rector for Int. Affairs: BORIS M. GOTLIB

Library of 600,000 vols
Number of teachers: 580
Number of students: 10,186 ; 6,000 full-time, 4,186 correspondence

Publication: *Research Reviews* (every 2 years).

VOLGOGRAD STATE TECHNICAL UNIVERSITY

400131 Volgograd, pr. Lenina 28

Telephone: (8442) 23-66-35
Fax: (8442) 23-41-21
E-mail: rector@vstu.ru
Internet: www.vstu.ru

Founded 1930
Academic year: September to June

Faculties: automobile transport, chemical technology, construction materials technology, economics and business administration, electronics and computer science, evening faculty (Kirovsky district), machine building, preparatory faculty for foreign students, preparatory training faculty, training and retraining evening faculty (Traktorzavodsky district)

Rector: Prof. IVAN A. NOVAKOV
Vice-Rector for Int. Relations and Cooperation: Prof. ALEXANDER A. CHUGUNOV

Library of 1,235,810 vols
Number of teachers: 1,112
Number of students: 18,000

Publication: *Polytekhnik* (26 a year)

DEANS

A. V. BELOV
A. E. GODENKO
V. F. KABLOV
VASILIY G. KARABAN
YURI Y. KOMAROV
OLEG D. KOSOV
S. M. LEDENEV
A. P. MANTOROSHIN
YURI P. MUKHA
YURI I. OSADSHY
O. P. OTCHENASHEV
A. N. SAVKIN
N. I. ZUBAN

VOLGOGRAD STATE UNIVERSITY OF ARCHITECTURE AND CIVIL ENGINEERING

400074 Volgograd, Akademicheskaya ul. 1

Telephone: (8442) 97-48-72
Fax: (8442) 97-49-33
E-mail: info@vgasu.ru
Internet: www.vgasu.ru

Founded 1952, present name and status 2003

5 Br. institutes: Institute of Architecture and Civil Engineering, Institute of Traffic Engineering, Institute of Economics and Law, Institute of Ecology, Institute of Distance Education; attached institute: Volzhsky Institute of Civil Engineering and Technologies

Rector: SERGEY YU. KALASHNIKOV

Library: 1.1m. vols
Number of teachers: 879
Number of students: 12,026

VOLOGDA STATE TECHNICAL UNIVERSITY

160000 Vologda, ul. Lenina 15

Telephone: (8172) 72-46-45
E-mail: rector_s@mh.vstu.edu.ru
Internet: www.vstu.edu.ru

Founded 1975 as Vologda Polytechnic Institute

Brs in Cherepovets and Veliky Ostyug

Rector: Prof. RUSLAN V. DERYAGIN

Library: 1.2m. vols.

VORONEZH STATE TECHNICAL UNIVERSITY

394026 Voronezh, Moskovsky pr. 14

Telephone: (0732) 21-09-19
Fax: (0732) 78-38-91
E-mail: rector@vorstu.ru
Internet: www.vorstu.ru

Faculties of automation and mechanization of engineering, aviation, automation and electrical engineering, engineering economics, radio engineering, physical engineering

Rector: Prof. VADIM N. FROPOV

Library of 700,000 vols.

VYATKA STATE TECHNICAL UNIVERSITY

610601 Kirov, GSP (Centre), Moskovskaya ul. 36

Telephone and fax (8332) 62-65-71
E-mail: root@kpicnit.vyatka.su

Founded 1963

Faculties of electrical engineering, automation and computer technology, chemical technology, construction engineering, socioeconomics and machine engineering

Rector: Prof. VASILY M. KONDRATOV

Library: 1m. vols

Publication: *Transactions.*

YAROSLAVL STATE TECHNICAL UNIVERSITY

150053 Yaroslavl, Moskovsky pr. 88

Telephone: (0852) 44-15-19

E-mail: webmaster@ystu.ru

Internet: www.ystu.ru

Founded 1944; present name and status 1994

Rector: Prof. YURI A. MOSKVICHEV

Number of students: 5,000

Academies

ARCHITECTURE AND CIVIL ENGINEERING

Ivanovo Academy of Civil Engineering and Architecture: 153002 Ivanovo, ul. 8 Marta 20; tel. (0932) 32-85-40; fax (0932) 30-00-74; e-mail post@iisi.asinet.ivanovo.su; f. 1981; facilities: construction technology, economics, architecture; library: 250,000 vols; Rector Prof. Dr S. V. FEDOSOV.

Tomsk State Academy of Civil Engineering: 634003 Tomsk, Solyanaya pl. 2; tel. 75-39-30; fax 75-33-58; f. 1952; faculties: architecture, civil and industrial construction engineering, road building, mechanical engineering, technology; library: 638,000 vols; 458 teachers; 5,086 students; Rector G. M. ROGOV.

Tyumen Civil Engineering and Architectural Academy: 625001 Tyumen, ul. Lunacharskogo 2; tel. (3452) 46-10-10; fax (3452) 46-23-90; e-mail tumgasa@sbtx.tmn.ru; internet www.tumgasa.ru; f. 1971; faculties: construction, engineering networks and systems, road building, economics and management; 360 teachers; 5,000 students; Rector Dr TCHIKICHEV.

Ural State Academy of Architecture and Arts: 620075 Ekaterinburg, ul. Karla Libknekhta 23; tel. (3432) 51-33-69; fax (3432) 51-95-32; e-mail vgafurov@usaaa.ru; internet www.usaaa.ru; f. 1972 (fmrly Sverdlovsk Architectural Institute); depts of architecture, applied decorative art, design, fashion design, monumental decorative art, urban planning; library: 80,000 vols; 1,100 students; Rector A. A. STARIKOV; publ. *Architecton* (4 a year).

Voronezh State University of Architecture and Civil Engineering: 394006 Voronezh, 20-Letiya Oktyabrya ul. 84; tel. (0732) 71-52-68; fax (0732) 71-58-54; e-mail rectorat@vgasu.vrn.ru; internet www.vgasu.vrn.ru; f. 1930; academic year September to July; faculties of arts, automation and information systems, architecture, construction, construction technology, engineering economics, engineering systems and buildings, mechanical engineering and highway construction; distance learning courses available; Rector IGOR S. SUROVTSEV; library: 500,000 vols; 485 teachers; 7,981 students; publ. *Scientific Bulletin* (colln of scientific articles, 1 a year).

AGRICULTURE AND VETERINARY SCIENCE

Belgorod State Agricultural Academy: 309103 Belgorod oblast, pos. Maiskii, Vavilova ul. 1; tel. (0722) 39-21-79; fax (0722) 39-11-74; e-mail bsaa@csn.ru; internet www.bsaa.edu.ru; f. 1978; 490 teachers; 4,500 students; Rector ALEXANDR V. TURIANSKY.

Bryansk State Agricultural Academy: 243365 Bryansk oblast, Vygonichesky r-n, pos. Kokino; tel. (8341) 2-43-21; e-mail bgsha@bitmcnit.bryansk.su; internet www.bgsha.com; f. 1980; library: 385,000 vols, 150 periodicals; Rector Prof. NIKOLAI M. BELUS; publ. *Collection of Scientific Papers* (1 a year).

Buryat State Agricultural Academy: 670024 Ulan-Ude, Pushkina ul. 8; tel. (3012) 34-26-11; fax (3012) 34-22-54; e-mail bgsha@eastsib.ru; f. 1932; depts: animal husbandry, agronomy, veterinary medicine, economics, farm mechanization, land tenure regulations, accounting, management; library: 582,000 vols; 325 teachers; 4,800 students; Rector Prof. ALEXANDER P. POPOV.

Chuvash State Agricultural Academy: 428000 Cheboksary, K. Marksa ul. 29; tel. (8352) 22-23-34; depts: agronomy, mechanization, animal husbandry; library: 83,000 vols; Rector NIKOLAI K. KIRILLOV.

Dagestan State Agricultural Academy: 367032 Makhachkala, M. Gadzhieva ul. 180; tel. (8722) 68-24-70; f. 1932; Rector MAGOMED M. DZHAMBULATOV; library: 200,000 vols; publ. *Works*; fields of study: zootechnics, veterinary, fruit and vegetable growing, accountancy.

Irkutsk State Agricultural Academy: 664038 Irkutsk, pos. Molodozhny; tel. (3952) 39-93-30; fax (3952) 39-94-18; e-mail rector@ishi.baikal.ru; internet www.irgsha.narod.ru; f. 1934; depts at main campus: economics, accounting, computer engineering, agronomy, agroecology, soil management, energy engineering, mechanization, zoological engineering, veterinary science, wildlife management; Chita campus: economics, accounting, agronomy, mechanization, zoological engineering; library: 504,814 vols; 357 teachers; 7,736 students; br. in Chita; Rector ALEXANDER A. DOLGOPOLOV.

Ivanovo Agricultural Academy: 153012 Ivanovo, Sovetskaya ul. 45; tel. and fax (0932) 32-81-44; e-mail ivgsha@tpi.ru; f. 1918; depts: agronomy, zootechnics, veterinary medicine, mechanization in agriculture, service and exploitation of farm machines and equipment, land use and land distribution, economics and management in rural production, agroecology; library: 260,364 vols; 211 teachers; 3,328 students; Rector V.F. TSARYOV.

Izhevsk State Agricultural Academy: Udmurt Republic, 426069 Izhevsk, Studencheskaya ul. 11; tel. (3412) 58-99-48; fax (3412) 58-99-47; e-mail root@isa.udm.ru; internet isa.udm.ru; f. 1954; depts: agronomy, animal husbandry, veterinary science, forestry, mechanization, bookkeeping and agricultural analysis, economics, mechanization of the processing of farm produce; library: 500,000 vols; 357 teachers; 6,038 students; extra-mural faculty; Pres. Prof. V. V. FOKIN.

Kazan State Academy of Veterinary Medicine 'N. E. Bauman': Tatarstan, 420074 Kazan, Sibirsky trakt ul.; tel. (8432) 76-15-05; f. 1873; advanced training of veterinary and animal husbandry specialists; library: 410,000 vols; 230 teachers; 3,700 students; Rector Acad. G. Z. IDRISOV; publ. *Nauchnye Trudy* (4–5 a year).

Kazan State Agricultural Academy: 420015 Kazan, Karla Marksa ul. 65; tel. (8432) 36-65-22; fax (8432) 36-66-51; internet www.ksha.ru; fields of study: agronomy, mechanization, economics and management, accounting; library: 135,000 vols; Rector Prof. DZHAUDAT I. FAIZRAKHMANOV.

Kostroma State Agricultural Academy: 156530 Kostroma, P/O Karavaevo; tel. (0942) 54-12-63; fax (0942) 54-34-23; e-mail mobot@ksaa.edu.ru; internet www.ksaa.edu.ru; f. 1949; depts: agronomy, zootechnics, veterinary science, farm mechanization, automobiles and automobile facilities, service and operation of vehicles and machines, electrification and automation of agricultural production, application of computers, architecture, industrial and civil engineering, economics and management, accountancy and auditing, finance and credit, fundamentals of law in agriculture, agricultural management; library: 510,000 vols; 370 teachers; 5,100 students; Rector V. I. VOROBEV.

Kursk State Agricultural Academy 'I. I. Ivanov': 305034 Kursk, Karla Marksa ul. 70; tel. (0712) 33-06-05; fax (0712) 23-13-30; e-mail academy@kgsha.ru; internet www.kgsha.ru; f. 1956; fields of study: agronomy, plant protection, zootechnics, mechanization, economics and management, accounting, agroecology, veterinary medicine, seed processing and storage; library: 130,000 vols; Rector VLADIMIR D. FLOUR.

Moscow Agricultural Academy 'K. A. Timiryazev': 127550 Moscow, Timiryazevskaya ul. 49; tel. (495) 976-04-80; fax (495) 976-29-10; e-mail info@timacad.ru; internet www.timacad.ru; f. 1865; faculties of agricultural chemistry, agronomy, agropedagogy, horticulture, economics, soil science and ecology, zootechnics; 33 attached research stations and 5 experimental and instructional farms; br. in Kaluga; library: 1.5m. vols; 650 teachers; 10,000 students; Rector Prof VLADIMIR M. BAUTIM; publs *Papers of TSHA* (1 a year), *Proceedings of TSHA* (6 a year).

Moscow State Academy of Veterinary Medicine and Biotechnology 'K. I. Skryabin': 100472 Moscow, Akad. K. I. Skryabina 23 ul.; tel. (495) 377-91-17; f. 1919; faculties: veterinary biological science, animal husbandry, pedagogical, animal products; library: 500,000 vols, 300 teachers; 3,500 students; Rector Acad. A. D. BELOV.

Nizhnii Novgorod State Agricultural Academy: 603078 Nizhnii Novgorod pr. Gagarina 97; tel. (8312) 66-07-30; fax (8312) 66-06-84; f. 1930; fields of study: accounting, agrochemistry, agronomy, animal husbandry, mechanization, veterinary medicine; library: 500,000 vols; 5,000 students; Rector ALEZEY GALKIN; publ. *Scientific Works* (1 a year).

Penza State Agricultural Academy: 440014 Penza, Botanicheskaya ul. 30; tel. (8412) 59-63-54; fax (8412) 59-63-54; e-mail psaca@penza.com.ru; internet pgsha.penza.com.ru; f. 1951; fields of study: agronomy, agroecology, animal husbandry, mechanization of agriculture, machine repairing, bookkeeping and auditing, economics, administration, farm production technology, motor vehicles and motor vehicle management; library: 264,000 vols; 264 teachers; 3,500 students; Rector Prof. VLADIMIR D. KOROTNEV.

Perm Agricultural Academy 'Acad. D. N. Pryanishnikov': 614600 Perm, Kommunisticheskaya ul. 23; tel. and fax (3422) 12-53-94; e-mail pgsha@permregion.ru; f. 1918; depts: agrochemistry and soil science, agronomy, animal husbandry, mechanization, economics and management, accounting, forestry, food technology, applied informatics; library: 320,000 vols; 376 teachers; 9,000 students; Rector YU. N. ZUBAREV.

Primorsky State Agricultural Academy: 692510 Ussuriisk, pr. Blyukhera 44; tel. (42341) 6-33-91; fax (42341) 6-03-13; e-mail agracad@hotbox.ru; internet www.primacad.ru; institutes: land management and farming, animal husbandry and veterinary medicine, forestry, economics and business, farm mechanization, staff upgrading and retraining for the agro-industrial complex; f. 1957; library: 380,000 vols; 500 teachers; 5,000 students; Rector A. A. DYOMIN.

Ryazan State Agricultural Academy: 390044 Ryazan, Kostycheva ul. 1; tel. (0912) 55-35-01; fax (0912) 55-10-70; e-mail rsaa@narod.ru; internet www.rsaa.narod.ru; fields of study: agronomy, animal husbandry, mechanization, economics and management, accounting; library: 94,000 vols; Rector GENNADY M. TUNIKOV.

St Petersburg Academy of Forestry Technology: 194018 St Petersburg, Institutsky per. 5; tel. (812) 550-07-00; fax (812) 550-08-15; f. 1803; faculties: chemical technology, engineering economics, forest machinery, forestry, forestry engineering, mechanical technology of timber; library: 1,400,000 vols; 613 teachers; 9,000 students; br. in Syktyvkar; Rector Prof. V. I. ONEGIN; publ. *Nauchnye trudy* (1 a year).

Tyumen State Agricultural Academy: 625003 Tyumen, Respubliki ul. 7; tel. (3452) 46-16-50; fax (3452) 46-16-50; e-mail acadagro@tmn.ru; internet www.tgsha.ru; f. 1879; attached Institutes of Agronomy and Ecology, Finance and Management, Veterinary Medicine and Aquaculture; library: 700,000 vols; 250 teachers; 5,000 students; Rector Dr NIKOLAI V. ABRAMOV.

Ulyanovsk State Agricultural Academy: 432601 Ulyanovsk, bul. Novy Venets 1; tel. (88422) 31-42-72; fax (88422) 31-42-72; e-mail academy@mv.ru; internet www.academy.mv.ru; f. 1943; depts: agronomy, animal husbandry, mechanization, veterinary, medicine, economics; library: 452,000 vols; 312 teachers; 4,248 students; Rector B. I. ZOTOV.

Urals State Academy of Veterinary Medicine: 457100 Chelyabinsk oblast, Troitsk, Gagarina ul. 13; tel. (3516) 32-00-10; fax (3516) 32-04-72; internet www.ugavm.boom.ru; f. 1929; library: 200,000 vols; 180 teachers; 1,434 students; Rector Prof. V. LAZARENKO.

Urals State Agricultural Academy: 620219 Ekaterinburg, K. Libknekhta ul. 42; tel. (3432) 51-33-63; fax (3432) 51-24-80; e-mail academy@usaca.ru; internet www.usaca.ru; f. 1940; library: 450,000 vols; 700 teachers; 2,500 students; Rector ALEXANDER N. SEMIN.

Velikie Luki State Agricultural Academy: 182100 Pskov oblast, Velikie Luki, pl. V. I. Lenina 1; tel. (81153) 3-77-28; fax (81153) 3-26-73; e-mail vgsha@mart.ru; f. 1958; depts: agronomy and ecology, economics, animal husbandry, engineering; library: 390,000 vols; 291 teachers; 4,114 students; Rector Prof. V. P. SPASOV; publ. *Works* (1 a year).

Volgograd State Agricultural Academy: 400041 Volgograd, Institutskaya ul. 8; tel. (8442) 43-08-45; fax (8442) 43-18-07; f. 1944; depts: agronomy, animal husbandry, farm mechanization, farm electrification, ecology and land reclamation, accounting; library: 568,000 vols; 4,000 students; Rector Acad. A. M. GAVRILOV; publ. *Scientific Information* (2 a year).

Vologda State Dairy Academy 'N. V. Vereschagin': 160555 Vologda pos. Molochnoe, Shmidta ul. 2; tel. (8172) 76-17-30; fax (8172) 76-10-69; e-mail rector@molochnoe.ru; internet www.molochnoe.ru; f. 1911; library: 420,000 vols; 270 teachers; 4,000 students; Rector Dr VLADIMIR N. OSTRETSOV; publ. *Works*.

Voronezh State Academy of Forestry Engineering: 394613 Voronezh, Timiryazeva ul. 8; tel. (0732) 53-74-98; fax (0732) 53-86-10; e-mail postmaster@julygb.vsi.ru; internet vglta.vrn.ru; f. 1918; faculties: forest engineering, forestry, wood-processing technology, motor-vehicle engineering, forest industry economics and management, furniture design, forest machinery and equipment, safety traffic regulation, landscape gardening, gamekeeping and national parks management, international wood trade, industrial process automation; library: 568,000 vols; 397 teachers; 5,500 students; Rector Prof. V. K. POPOV.

Vyatka State Agricultural Academy: 610017 Kirov, Oktyabrsky pr. 133; tel. (8332) 62-97-19; fax (8332) 62-23-17; e-mail vsaa@vit.kirov.ru; f. 1930; depts: agronomy, biology, economics, veterinary medicine, mechanization; library: 407,000 vols; Rector A. K. BOLOTOV.

ECONOMICS, LAW AND POLITICS

Academy of Social Sciences: 117606 Moscow, pr. Vernadskogo 84; tel. (95) 436-93-30; f. 1946; library: 2m. vols; Rector R. G. YUNOVSKII.

Finance Academy under the Government of the Russian Federation: 125468 Moscow, Leningradsky pr. 49; tel. (495) 943-98-55; fax (495) 157-70-70; e-mail academy@fa.ru; internet www.fa.ru; f. 1918; institutes and depts: finance, credit, financial management, insurance, taxes and taxation, accounting and audit, international economic relations, mathematical methods in economics and crisis management, tax police, evening school, distance learning, short-term retraining and skill development; 21st-Century International Finance University; MBA Business School; 650 teachers; 10,000 students; Rector A. G. GRYAZNOVA.

Irkutsk State Academy of Economics: 664015 Irkutsk, ul. Lenina 11; tel. (3952) 24-10-55; fax (3952) 24-28-38; e-mail kvm@cc.isea.baikal.ru; f. 1930; faculties: law, world economics, finance, economics of mining industry and construction, economics of engineering and road transport, accounting, information systems, labour economics, public administration, management, economics of using natural resources; library: 530,000 vols; Rector M. A. VINOKUROV.

Khabarovsk State Academy of Economics and Law: 680042 Khabarovsk, Tikhookeanskaya ul. 134; tel. (4212) 35-87-37; fax (4212) 72-79-14; auditing and accounting, finance, management, commerce, law, foreign economic relations; library: 400,000 vols; 220 teachers; 7,000 students; Rector Prof. V. A. LIKHOBABIN.

Polar Academy: 192007 St Petersburg, Voronezhskaya ul. 79, A/Ya 533; tel. (812) 167-04-52; fax (812) 167-08-50; f. 1992; Master-level training of students from native Siberian peoples, who are expected to be appointed to high administrative posts in northern and far eastern Siberia; 60 teachers; 100 students; Rector AZURGET CHAUKENVAEVA; publ. *Polarnaya Akademia* (2 a year).

Russian Academy of Economics 'G. V. Plekhanov': 115998 Moscow M-54, Stremyannyi per. 36; tel. (095) 237-85-17; fax (095) 237-95-18; e-mail inter@rea.ru; internet www.rea.ru; f. 1907; faculties: general economics, finance, taxation, national economy, trade in commodities, economics and mathematics, economics and engineering, international economic relations; graduate school; library: 815,000 vols; 1,000 teachers; 12,000 students; Rector V. I. VIDYAPIN.

St Petersburg State Academy of Engineering and Economics: 191002 St Petersburg, ul. Marata 27; tel. (812) 112-06-33; fax (812) 112-06-07; e-mail oms@engec.ru; internet www.engec.ru; f. 1930; institutes: industrial economics and management, regional economics and management, transport economics and management, management information systems, general management of business and finance, tourism and hotel management; library: 370,000 vols; 310 teachers; 3,540 students; Rector A. I. MIKHAILUSHKIN; publ. *Scientific Proceedings of the Institute* (1 a year).

Samara State Academy of Economics: 443090 Samara, ul. Sovetskoi Armii 141; tel. (8462) 22-15-42; fax (8462) 22-09-53; f. 1931; faculties: finance, industrial economics, commerce and marketing, agribusiness, law, management, accounting; library: 596,000 vols; Rector Prof. A. I. NOSKOV.

Saratov State Academy of Law: 410720 Saratov, GSP, Chernyshevskogo ul. 104; tel. (8452) 25-04-86; fax (8452) 25-32-78; e-mail post@sgap.ru; internet www.sgap.ru; f. 1931; library: 500,000 vols; 300 teachers; 3,000 students; Rector FEDOR A. GRIGORYEV; publ. *Vestnik Saratovskoi gosudarstvennoi akademii prava*.

Urals State Academy of Law: 620066 Ekaterinburg, Komsomolskaya ul. 21; tel. (3432) 74-43-63; fax (3432) 74-50-34; e-mail rektorat@usla.ru; internet www.usla.ru; f. 1931; library: 850,000 vols; 327 teachers; 7,310 students; Rector Prof. VIKTOR D. PEREVALOV; publ. *Russian Law Journal* (4 a year).

Volgograd Academy of Public Administration: 400131 Volgograd Gagarina ul. 8; tel. (8442) 33-58-39; fax (8442) 36-29-51; e-mail rector@vags.ru; internet www.vags.ru; f. 1992 to prepare and develop qualified administrators for government and non-profit positions; br. in Astrakhan; 250 teachers; 3,000 students; Rector MIKHAIL A. SUKIASYAN.

ENGINEERING AND INDUSTRY

Ivanovo State Textile Academy: 153000 Ivanovo, pr. F. Engels 21; tel. (0932) 32-85-45; fax (0932) 41-21-08; e-mail rector@igta.ru; internet www.igta.ru; f. 1918; Rector Prof. VLADIMIR V. ZRYUKIN; Vice-Rectors Prof. ALEXANDER A. TUVIN (Complementary Education), Prof. ALEXANDER N. SMIRNOV (Information and Int. Relations), Prof. GRIGORY I. CHRISTOBORODOV (Scientific and Industrial Activity), Prof. VLADIMIR V. LYUBIMTSEV (Studies); library 740,911 vols; 388 teachers (incl. 51 professors); 8,488 students; publ. *Technology of Textile Industry* (6 a year).

Moscow State Academy of Light Industry: 113127 Moscow, ul. Osipenko 33; tel. (495) 231-58-01; faculties: chemical technology, sewn goods technology, mechanical, leather goods technology, engineering economics; br. in Novosibirsk; library: 392,000 vols; Rector V. A. FUKIN.

Siberian State Academy of Mining and Metallurgy: 654007 Kemerovo oblast, Novokuznetsk, pr. Kirova 42; tel. (3843) 46-35-02; fax (3843) 46-57-92; faculties: mining, metallurgy, electrometallurgy, foundry work, mechanical, technology, construction; library: 1,010,000 vols; 620 teachers; 6,000 students; Rector N. M. KULAGIN.

MEDICINE

Astrakhan State Medical Academy: 414000 Astrakhan, Bakinskaya ul. 121; tel. (8512) 22-70-16; fax (8512) 39-41-30; e-mail agma@astranet.ru; internet www.agma.astranet.ru; f. 1918; library: 700,000 vols; 520 teachers; 3,500 students; Rector Prof. VALENTIN M. MIROSHNIKOV.

Blagoveshchensk State Medical Academy: 675006 Blagoveshchensk, Gorkogo ul. 95; tel. (4162) 2-27-13; tel. (4162) 2-28-68; 264 teachers; 1,681 students.

Chelyabinsk State Medical Academy: 454092 Chelyabinsk, Vorovskogo ul. 64; tel. (3512) 34-16-86; fax (3512) 34-03-36; internet www.vita.chel.su; library: 500,000 vols; 3,000 students; Rector Prof. YURI S. SHAMUROV.

Chita State Medical Academy: 672090 Chita, Gorkogo ul. 39A; tel. (3022) 23-41-63; fax (3022) 32-30-58; e-mail macadem@mail.chita.ru; f. 1953; library: 387,000 vols; 311 teachers; 2,400 students; Rector VLADIMIR N. IVANOV.

Dagestan State Medical Academy: 367025 Dagestan Autonomous Republic, Makhachkala, pl. Lenina 6; tel. (8722) 67-07-94; fax (8722) 68-12-80; e-mail dgma@iwt.ru; internet www.dgma.ru; Rector ABDURAKHMAN O. OSMANOV.

Ivanovo State Medical Academy: 153462 Ivanovo, pr. F. Engelsa 8; tel. (0932) 30-17 66; fax (0932) 32-66-04; e-mail adm@isma.ivanovo.ru; internet www.isma.ivanovo.ru; f. 1930; library: 545,059 vols; 578 teachers; 2,084 students; Rector Prof. RUDOLF R. SHILYAEV.

Izhevsk State Medical Academy: 426034 Udmurt Republic, Izhevsk, Revolyutsionnaya ul. 199; tel. (3412) 52-62-01; fax (3412) 65-81-67; e-mail rector@igma.udm.ru; internet www.igma.udm.ru; f. 1933; library: 402,000 vols; 387 teachers; 2,500 students; Rector Prof. NIKOLAI S. STRELKOV.

Kemerovo State Medical Academy: 650029 Kemerovo, Voroshilova ul. 22A; tel. (3842) 73 48-55; fax (3842) 73-48-55; e-mail ksma@ksma.kuzstu.ac.ru; internet ksma.kuzstu.ac.ru; f. 1956; library: 390,681 vols; 461 teachers; 3,573 students; Rector ALEXANDER YA. EVTUSHENKO.

Krasnoyarsk State Medical Academy: 660022 Krasnoyarsk, Partizana Zheleznyaka ul. 1; tel. (3912) 27-49-24; fax (3912) 23-78-35; e-mail onmpi@krsk.infotel.ru; internet www.krasgma.ru; f. 1942; library: 472,000 vols; 609 teachers; 3,270 students; Rector Prof. VICTOR I. PROKHORENKOV; publ. *Medical Man* (12 a year).

Kuban State Medical Academy: 350614 Krasnodar, Sedina ul. 4; tel. (8612) 68-34-57; fax (8612) 68-34-57; e-mail corpus@ksma.kubannet.ru; internet www.ksma.ru; f. 1920; present name and status 1994; library: 560,000 vols; 600 teachers; 5,000 students; Rector BORIS G. ERMOSHENKO.

Nizhnii Novgorod State Medical Academy: 603005 Nizhnii Novgorod, pl. Minina i Pozharskogo 10/1; tel. and fax (8312) 39-06-43; e-mail nnsma@sandy.ru; internet www.n-nov.mednet.com; f. 1920; 645 teachers; 3,542 students; library: 480,000 vols; publ. *Zhurnal* (4 a year); Rector Prof. VYACHESLAV V. SHKARIN.

North Ossetia State Medical Academy: 362019 North Ossetia, Vladikavkaz, Pushkinskaya ul. 40; tel. (8672) 53-42-21; fax (8672) 53-03-97; e-mail nosma@dol.ru; f. 1796; 278 teachers; library: 265,000 vols; Rector Prof. KAZBEK D. SALBIEV.

Novosibirsk State Medical Academy: 630091 Novosibirsk, Krasnyi pr., 52; tel. and fax (3832) 22-32-04; e-mail rector@medin.nsc.ru; internet www.medin.nsc.ru; f. 1935; academic year September to June (2 semesters); faculties of clinical psychology, ecology, international physicians, laboratory medicine, medicine, paediatrics, physicians' and professors' improving and retraining and preparatory studies, nurses' training, pharmaceutical science, social activity, stomatology, traditional medicine; evening lyceum, institute of public health economics and management; library: 400,000 specialized vols and periodicals; 784 teachers; 4,500 students; Rector Prof. ANATOLY V. EFREMOV; publs *Eksperimentalnaya klinicheskaya medicina* (Experimental Clinical Medicine, 4 a year), *Meditsinskaya Gazeta* (Medical Newspaper, 26 a year).

Omsk State Medical Academy: 644099 Omsk, Lenina ul. 12; tel. (3812) 23-32-89; fax (3812) 23-14-57; e-mail osma@omsk-osma.ru; internet www.omsk-osma.ru; f. 1921; faculties: therapeutic and preventive medicine, paediatrics, stomatology; library: 573,199 vols; Rector Prof. ALEXANDER I. NOVIKOV.

Orenburg State Medical Academy: 460014 Orenburg, Sovetskaya ul. 6; tel. (3532) 77-61-03; fax (3532) 77-94-08; library: 160,000 vols; Rector SERGEI A. PAVLOVICHEV.

Perm State Medical Academy: 614600 Perm, Kuybyshevskaya ul. 39; tel. (3422) 90-44 53; fax (3422) 33-84-55; e-mail med@psma.ru; internet www.psma.ru; library: 541,000 vols; Rector Prof. VLADIMIR A. CHERKASSOV.

St Petersburg State Academy of Paediatric Medicine: 194100 St Petersburg, Litovskaya ul. 2; tel. (812) 245-06-46; fax (812) 245-40-85; f. 1925; library: 600,000 vols; Rector V. V. LEVANOVICH.

St Petersburg State Chemical-Pharmaceutical Academy: 197376 St Petersburg, ul. Professora Popova 14; tel. (812) 234-57-29; fax (812) 234-60-44; e-mail rector@spcpa.ru; internet www.spcpa.ru; f. 1919; faculties: drug industry technology, pharmacy, further education; library: 334,200 vols; 250 teachers; 2,000 students; Rector G.P. YAKOVLEV.

St Petersburg State Medical Academy 'I. I. Mechnikov': 195067 St Petersburg, Piskarovsky pr. 47; tel. (812) 543-50-14; fax (812) 140-15-24; e-mail mechnik@westcall.net; internet www.mechnik.spb.ru; f. 1907; faculties: pre-medical training, general medical, preventative medicine, advanced nursing, foreign students, further training, advanced training; library: 556,000 vols; 361 teachers; 4,500 students; Rector Prof. ALEXANDER V. SHABROV.

Smolensk State Medical Academy: 214019 Smolensk, Krupskoi ul. 28; tel. (0812) 55-26-92; fax (0812) 55-26-92; e-mail admsgma@sci.smolensk.ru; internet www.sgma.ru; library: 207,000 vols; Rector Prof. VLADIMIR G. PLESHKOV.

Stavropol State Medical Academy: 355017 Stavropol, Mira ul. 310; tel. (8652) 37-06-92; fax (8652) 37-06-42; e-mail sgma@statel.stavropol.ru; internet www.stgma.ru; f. 1937; languages of instruction: English, Russian; academic year September to July; Faculties: General Medicine, Stomatology, Paediatrics, Medical College Teaching Skills, Nursing, Postgraduate Studies; 2 attached museums; clinics of ophthalmology, neurology and vertebraneurology; library: 345,000 vols; 525 teachers; 3,500 students; Rector Prof. B. D. MINAEV; publ. *South Russia Medical Magazine* (6 a year).

Tver Medical Academy: 170642 Tver, Sovetskaya ul. 4; tel. (0822) 33-17-79; fax (0822) 33-57-59; library: 446,000 vols; Rector BORIS N. DAVYDOV.

Tyumen Medical Academy: 625023 Tyumen, Odesskaya ul. 54; tel. (3452) 22-62-00; fax (3452) 25-23-19; e-mail tgma@tgma.info; internet www.tgma.info; f. 1963; 515 teachers; 3,256 students.

Urals State Medical Academy: 620219 Ekaterinburg, Repina ul. 3; tel. (3432) 51-14-90; fax (3432) 51-64-00; e-mail info@usma.ru; internet www.usma.ru; f. 1931; areas of study: anaesthesiology, dentistry, epidemiology, gynaecology, obstetrics, ophthalmology, otolaryngology, paediatric surgery, pathology, surgery paediatrics, therapeutics; library: 600,000 vols; Rector Prof. ANATOLY P. YASTREBOV; publ. *Herald* (12 a year).

Voronezh State Medical Academy 'N. N. Burdenko': 394036 Voronezh, Studencheskaya ul. 10; tel. and fax (0732) 53-03-98; e-mail foreign@vsma.ac.ru; internet www.vsma.ac.ru; f. 1918; academic year September to June (two semesters); library: 500,000 vols; 1,105 teachers; 3,850 students; Rector Prof. Dr I. E. YESAULENKO; publs *Applied Informational Aspects in Medicine* (4 a year), *Medical Staff* (12 a year).

Yaroslavl State Medical Academy: 150000 Yaroslavl, Revolutsionnaya ul. 5; tel. (0852) 30-56-41; fax (0852) 30-50-13; e-mail rector@yma.ac.ru; internet www.yma.ac.ru; Rector YURI V. NOVIKOV.

SCIENCE AND TECHNOLOGY

Moscow State Academy of Applied Biotechnology: 109029 Moscow, ul. Talalikhina 33; tel. (495) 276-19-10; fax (495) 276-14-23; f. 1931; faculties: dairy industry technology, meat industry technology, food production, automation, plastics processing, low-temperature technology, veterinary sanitation, book-keeping, management; library: 611,000 vols; Rector IOSIF A. ROGOV.

Moscow State Academy of Food Industry: 125080 Moscow, Volokolamskoe shosse 11; tel. (495) 158-03-71; fax (495) 158-03-71; f. 1931; food technology, chemical engineering and biotechnology, information systems in economics, management and marketing, machinery, informatics, power engineering, agricultural engineering; 500 teaching staff; library: 1,000,000 vols; 6,000 students; Pres. Prof. V. I. TUZHILKIN.

Moscow State Academy of Instrumentation and Informatics: 107076 Moscow, ul. Stromynka 20; tel. (495) 268-01-01; faculties: automation in instrument making, engineering, transport and power machine building; library: 250,000 vols; Rector Prof. BORIS M. MIKHAILOV.

Moscow State Geological Prospecting Academy: 117873 Moscow, ul. Miklukho-Maklaya 23; tel. (495) 433-62-56; fax (495) 433-56-33; faculties: geology, geophysics, hydrogeology, prospecting engineering and mining, economics; library: 410,335 vols; 439 teachers; 3,964 students; Rector L. G. GRABCHAK; publ. *Geology and Prospecting* (6 a year).

Ryazan State Radio Engineering Academy: 390005 Ryazan, ul. Gagarina 59/1; tel. (0912) 72-18-44; fax (0912) 72-22-15; f. 1951; faculties: automation and telemechanics, computer technology, electronics, engineering economics, humanities, radio engineering, radio equipment design; library: 720,000 vols; Rector V. K. ZLOBIN.

Rybinsk State Academy of Aviation Technology: 152934 Rybinsk, ul. Pushkina 53; tel. (0855) 52-09-90; fax (0855) 21-39-64; e-mail root@rgata.adm.yar.ru; internet www.rgata.yaroslavl.ru; f. 1955; faculties: aerotechnology, informatics, radioelectronics, rocket technology; library: c. 500,000 vols; 230 teachers; 4,000 students; Rector Prof. V.

F. BEZYAZICHNY; publs *Scientific Notes* (1 a year), *Vestnik* (1 a year).

St Petersburg Academy of Civil Aviation: 196210 St Petersburg, ul. Pilotov 38; tel. (812) 291-28-43; faculty: air traffic control; Rector P. V. KARTAMYSHEV.

St Petersburg State Academy of Aerospace Instrumentation: 190000 St Petersburg, Bol. Morskaya ul. 67; tel. (812) 117-15-22; fax (812) 313-70-18; e-mail common@aanet.ru; internet www.suai.ru; fields of study: automation, informatics and computer systems, information systems in economics, instrumentation, law, management, radio engineering; Rector Prof. ANATOLY A. OVODENKO; library: 1,000,000 vols; publ. *V polet* (12 a year).

St Petersburg State Academy of Refrigeration and Food Technology: 191002 St Petersburg, ul. Lomonosova 9; tel. (812) 315-36-17; fax (812) 315-05-35; depts of refrigeration engineering, equipment for food manufacturing and commerce, cryogenics and conditioning systems; faculties: refrigeration equipment, equipment for food industry, trade and public catering, cryogenic technology and conditioning; library: 850,000 vols; Rector A. V. BARANENKO.

Siberian State Academy of Geodesy: 630108 Novosibirsk, Plakhotnogo ul. 10; tel. (3832) 43-39-37; fax (3832) 44-30-60; e-mail rektorat@ssga.ru; internet www.ssga.ru; f. 1932; faculties: geodesy and economics, aerial phototopography, cadastre and regional planning, management and regulation of land relations, optics and optoelectronic instruments, correspondence, evening, preliminary training; institutes: surveying and management, cadastre and geographic information systems, remote sensing and natural resources management, optics and optical technologies, distance education; library: 267,000 vols; 345 teachers; 9,500 students; Rector Prof. IVAN V. LESNYKH.

Volga Region State Academy of Telecommunications and Informatics: 443010 Samara, ul. L. Tolstogo 23; tel. and fax (8462) 33-58-56; internet www.psati.ru; f. 1956; faculties: radio engineering, radio communication and television, general engineering, economics, telecommunications and informatics, electrical communication, continuing education, extra-mural; Telecom College of PSATI, regional telecommunications training centre; brs in Stavropol and Orenburg; library: 461,000 vols; 298 teachers; 4,100 students; Rector VLADIMIR A. ANDREEV.

Voronezh State Technological Academy: 394000 Voronezh, pr. Revolyutsii 19; tel. and fax (732) 55-42-67; e-mail rector@vgta.vrn.ru; internet www.vgta.vrn.ru; f. 1930, present name and status 1994; faculties: mechanical, automation, chemical, technological, technology of meat and dairy products; library: 850,000 vols; 491 teachers; 4,800 students; Rector VITALY K. BITYUKOV.

TRANSPORT

Admiral Makarov State Maritime Academy: 199026 St Petersburg, Vasilevskii ostrov, Kosaya Liniya 15A; tel. (812) 217-19-34; fax (812) 217-07-82; f. 1876; faculties: arctic, navigation, radio engineering, international transport management, electrical engineering, marine engineering; brs in Arkhangelsk, Murmansk; library: 762,000 vols; 380 teachers; 4,400 students; Pres. IVAN I. KOSTYLEV.

Baltic Fishing Fleet State Academy: 236029 Kaliningrad oblast, Molodezhnaya ul. 6; tel. (0112) 21-72-04; fax (0112) 51-66-90; e-mail rector@bga.gazinter.net; f. 1966; faculties: economics, marine engineering, navigation, radio engineering; library: 165,426 vols; 253 teachers; 3,000 students; Dir Prof. A. PIMOSHENKO; publ. *Research Work* (1 a year).

Far-Eastern State Maritime Academy: Vladivostok, Verkhneportovaya ul. 50A; tel. (4232) 22-49-58; fmrly Far Eastern Higher School of Marine Engineering; faculties: navigation, ship engineering, management of marine transport, electrical engineering, practical psychology; library: 360,000 vols; Rector V. I. SEDYKH.

Kamchatka State Fishing Fleet Academy: 683003 Petropavlovsk-Kamchatsky, Klyuchevskaya ul. 35; tel. and fax (41500) 22-45-38; e-mail rektor@marine.kamchatka.su; f. 1987; trains specialists for the fishing industry, navigators, marine engineers, electrical engineers, radio engineers, technologists and refrigeration engineers; library: 70,000 vols; 250 teachers; 2,000 students; Rector BORIS I. OLEINIKOV; publ. *Conference Papers* (1 a year).

Moscow State Academy of Water Transport: 115407 Moscow, ul. Sudostroitelnaya 46; tel. (495) 116-30-88; fax (495) 118-31-11; f. 1980; faculties: marine engineering, operations, navigation, mechanization and automation of ports, hydrotechnical construction, engineering economics, legislation, international economic management for water wransport; library: 106,000 vols; 5,000 students; Rector Prof. N. P. GARANIN.

Novorossiisk State Maritime Academy: 353918 Novorossiisk, pr. Lenina 93; tel. (8617) 23-03-93; fax (8617) 23-22-95; f. 1975; trains specialists in navigation, ship power plant operation, ship electrical and automated equipment operation, ship radio equipment operation, economics and management for the merchant marine; library: 267,000 vols; Dir VASILY GUTSULYAK.

Novosibirsk State Academy of Water Transport: 630099 Novosibirsk, Ul. Shchetinkina 33; tel. (3832) 22-24-28; fax (3832) 22-49-76; e-mail vyacheslavh@mail.ru; f. 1951; faculties: hydroengineering for waterways and ports, navigation and operation of water transport, ship engineers, electrical engineering, water transport management and economics; library: 450,000 vols; 380 teachers; 10,000 students; Dir I. A. RAGULIN.

Volga State Academy of Water Transport: 603600 Nizhnii Novgorod, ul. Nesterova 5; tel. (8312) 36-37-80; fax (8312) 32-17-91; courses in: transport operation and navigation, shipbuilding and ocean technology, land transport systems, electromechanics, electrical engineering, hydrotechnical construction, economics, business management, law; library: 500,000 vols.

Institutes of Higher Education

ARCHITECTURE AND CIVIL ENGINEERING

Moscow Architectural Institute: 103754 Moscow Centre GSP, ul. Rozhdestvenka 11; tel. (495) 924-79-90; fax (495) 921-12-40; e-mail marhi@marhi.ru; internet www.miarch.ru; f. 1866; library: 400,000 vols; 400 teachers; 2,000 students; Pres. ALEKSANDR P. KUDRYAVTSEV.

Moscow Institute of Municipal Economy and Construction: 109807 Moscow, Srednyaya Kalitnikovskaya ul. 30; tel. (495) 278-32-05; fax (495) 278-15-10; f. 1944; faculties: construction, technology, mechanical engineering, urban construction, ecology and sanitary engineering, engineering, management and economic, commerce; 500 teachers; 13,000 students; library: 600,000 vols; Rector N. V. KOLKUNOV.

Novosibirsk Architectural Institute: 630008 Novosibirsk, Belinskogo 151; tel. and fax (3832) 66-42-64; f. 1989; architecture, design; library: 50,000 vols.

AGRICULTURE AND VETERINARY SCIENCE

All-Russian Extra-Mural Agricultural Institute: 143900 Moscow oblast, Balashikha 8; tel. (095) 521-24-64; fax (095) 521-24-56; f. 1930; depts: agriculture, economics and management, electrification, information technology in economics and law, mechanization, zoological engineering; library: 517,000 vols; Rector L. Y. KISELEV; publ. collections of scientific works of the institute (1 a year).

Azov-Black Sea Institute of Agricultural Mechanization: 347720 Rostov oblast, Zernograd, ul. Lenina 21; tel. (08536) 3-18-31; library: 192,000 vols; Rector B. M. TITOV.

Kabardino-Balkar Land Improvement Institute: 360004 Nalchik, ul. L. Tolstogo 185; tel. (86600) 5-69-43.

Kurgan Agricultural Institute: 641311 Kurgan oblast, Ketovskii raion, selo Lesnikovo; tel. (35222) 9-41-40; f. 1944; depts: agronomy, zootechnics, economics, mechanization, industrial and civil construction; library: 358,600 vols; Rector V. D. PAVLOV.

Omsk Veterinary Institute: 664007 Omsk, Oktyabrskaya ul 92; tel. and fax (3812) 24-15-35; f. 1918; library: 205,000 vols; 229 teachers; 2,600 students; Dir Prof. GENNADY A. KHONIN.

St Petersburg Veterinary Institute: 196006 St Petersburg, Moskovskii pr. 112; tel. (812) 298-36-31; f. 1919; library: 194,000 vols; 140 teachers; 1,340 students; Rector G. S. KUZNETSOV; publ. *Trudy* (Works).

Samara Agricultural Institute: 446400 Kinel, Poselok Ust-Kinelskii; tel. (8462) 4-68-72; f. 1919; depts: agronomy, animal husbandry, mechanization; library: 215,000 vols; 210 teachers; 3,500 students; Rector N. S. SHIBRAEV.

Saratov Animal Husbandry and Veterinary Institute: 410071 Saratov, Bol. Sadovaya 220; tel. (8452) 24-45-32; f. 1918; library: 376,500 vols; 213 teachers; 4,500 students; Rector V. I. VOROBYEV.

Saratov Institute of Agricultural Engineering: 410740 Saratov, Sovetskaya ul. 60; tel. (8452) 24-37-66; f. 1932; library: 550,000 vols; 320 teachers; 3,500 students; Rector A. G. RYBALKO.

Tver Agricultural Institute: 171314 Tver, P/O Sakharovo; tel. (0822) 39-92-32.

Yakutsk Agricultural Institute: 677891 Yakutsk, ul. P. Morozova 2; tel. (41122) 2-23-20.

ECONOMICS, LAW AND POLITICS

All-Russian Distance Institute of Finance and Economics: 121807 Moscow, ul. Oleko Dundicha 23; tel. (95) 144-85-19; fax (95) 144-86-19; faculties: finance and credit, accounting, management, marketing; depts and brs in 21 Russian cities; library: 1.5m. vols.

Far Eastern Institute of Trade: 690600 Vladivostok, Okeanskii pr. 19; tel. (4232) 2-50-89; f. 1964; faculties: economics, accounting, foodstuffs and non-foodstuffs sciences, technology, organization of public catering;

library: 220,000 vols; 572 teachers; 2,760 students; Rector Prof. L. S. PUZYREVSKY.

Institute of Business Studies: 117571 Moscow, pr. Vernadskogo 82; tel. (495) 434-92-53; fax (495) 434-11-48; e-mail ibs@ane.ru; f. 1989; independent; library: 10,500 vols; 182 teachers (32 full-time, 150 part-time); 1,500 students; Pres. Dr SERGEI MIASOEDEV.

Kazan Finance and Economics Institute: 420012 Tatarstan, Kazan, ul. Butlerova 4; tel. (8432) 36-54-41; fax (8432) 38-30-54; e-mail rector@kfei.kcn.ru; internet kfei.kcn.ru; f. 1932; faculties: general economics, business economics, finance and credit, distance learning, advanced training for professionals; 240 teachers; 5,000 students; library: 330,000 vols; Rector N. G. KHAIRULLIN.

Krasnoyarsk Institute of Commerce: 660049 Krasnoyarsk, ul. L. Prushinskoi 14; tel. (3912) 21-93-33; f. 1989; library: 205,835 vols; Chief Officers Y. L. ALEXANDROV, B. K. GUSEV.

Moscow Institute of Economics, Statistics and Informatics: 119501 Moscow, Nezhinskaya ul. 7; tel. (495) 442-65-77; fax (495) 442-65-88; e-mail office@rector.mesi.ru; internet www.mesi.ru; f. 1932; faculties: economics and finance, management, law and humanities, statistics and economics, computer technology, Masters programmes; MBA; Open Education and Distance Learning Systems, Institute of Professional Development; library: 269,000 vols; 6,110 teachers (425 in Moscow, 5,685 in Russian regions); 65,000 students (10,000 in Moscow, 55,000 in Russian regions); Rector Prof. VLADIMIR P. TIKHOMIROV.

Moscow State Institute of International Relations: 117454 Moscow, pr. Vernadskogo 76; tel. (495) 434-91-74; fax (495) 434-90-66; internet www.mgimo.ru; f. 1944; faculties: international relations, international economic relations, international law, international business and business administration, international journalism, political science; library: 750,000 vols; 974 teachers; 2,848 students; Rector A. V. TORKUNOV.

Novosibirsk Institute of Commerce: 630087 Novosibirsk, pr. K. Marksa 26; tel. (3832) 46-58-52; f. 1956; faculties: trade economics, trade, accounting, technology; library: 197,000 vols; 240 teachers; 7,500 students; br. in Chita; Rector N. N. PROTOPOPOV.

Novosibirsk Institute of National Economy: 630070 Novosibirsk, Kamennaya ul. 56; tel. (3832) 24-27-22; f. 1968; faculties of industrial economics, economics and planning of supply, financial economics, accounting and statistics; library: 250,000 vols; 4,800 students; Rector V. N. SHCHUKIN.

St Petersburg Institute of Trade and Economics: 194018 St Petersburg, Novorossiiskaya 50; tel. (812) 247-78-06; f. 1930; faculties: trade economics, accounting, trade in industrial goods, trade in foodstuffs, technology; library: 595,300 vols; br. in Krasnoyarsk; Rector V. A. GULIAEV.

Saratov Institute of Economics: 410760 Saratov, ul. Radishcheva 89; tel. (8452) 26-38-50; f. 1918; faculties: industry, agriculture, credit and economics, accounting; library: 255,000 vols; 160 teachers; 4,000 students; Rector K. I. BABAYTSEV.

ENGINEERING AND INDUSTRY

Grozny State Oil Institute: 364051 Grozny, pl. Ordzhonikidze 100; tel. and fax (8712) 22-31-20; f. 1920; faculties: geology, petroleum technology, mechanical engineering, construction engineering, automation and applied informatics; library: 175,864 vols; 340 teachers; 5,565 students; Rector I. A. KERIMOV.

Moscow Institute of Printing: 127550 Moscow, ul. Pryanishnikova 2A; tel. (495) 216-07-46; faculties: printing equipment, printing technology, engineering economics, book trade, layout; br. in St Petersburg.

Norilsk Industrial Institute: 663310 Norilsk, ul. 50-let Oktyabrya 7; tel. (3919) 42-16-31; fax (3919) 42-17-41; f. 1961; faculties: mining, metallurgy, economics, mechanical technology, civil and electrical engineering; library: 300,000 vols; 500 teachers; 3,500 students; Rector A. A. KOLEGOV.

Novocherkassk Institute of Engineering Amelioration: 346409 Novocherkassk, Pushkinskaya 111; tel. (86352) 5-57-56; f. 1907; depts: irrigation and land reclamation, forestry; library: 170,000 vols; 250 teachers; 5,100 students.

Rostov-on-Don Automation and Mechanical Engineering Institute: 344023 Rostov-on-Don, pl. Strany Sovetov 2; tel. (8632) 52-93-51; fax (8632) 54-84-11; f. 1960; faculties: agricultural engineering, mechanical engineering, automation and robotics; library: 237,424 vols; 565 teachers; 1,730 students; Rector N. G. CHEREDNICHENKO; publ. *Economics and Industrial Management*.

Rubtsovsk Industrial Institute: 658207 Rubtsovsk, Traktornaya ul. 2/6; tel. (38557) 3-26-29; fax (38557) 3-54-22; e-mail rii@inst.rubtsovsk.ru; f. 1946; br. of Altai State Technical University; machine technology, motor car and tractor construction, motor vehicles and vehicle equipment, foundry machinery and technology, applied mathematics, management, industrial and civil engineering; library: 130,000 vols; 193 teachers; 1,950 students; Rector S. A. GURCHENKOV.

St Petersburg Institute of Engineering (LMZ-VTUZ): 195197 St Petersburg, Polyustrovsky pr. 14; tel. (812) 540-01-54; fax (812) 540-01-59; f. 1930; faculties: mechanical engineering, Nuclear power engineering, turbine manufacture, management; library: 185,000 vols; 350 teachers; 5,000 students; Rector Prof. M. A. MARTYNOV.

Ukhta Industrial Institute: 169400 Komi Autonomous Republic, Ukhta, Pervomaiskaya ul. 13; tel. (82147) 6-06-10.

MEDICINE

Khabarovsk State Pharmaceutical Institute: 680000 Khabarovsk, ul. K. Marksa 30; tel. (4210) 34-68-26.

Perm Pharmaceutical Institute: 614600 Perm, GSP-277, ul. Lenina 48; tel. (3422) 12-34-45; fax (3422) 12-94-76; e-mail pfa@degacom.ru; f. 1937; library: 80,000 vols; 220 teachers; 3,500 students; Rector Prof. Y. OLESHKO.

Pyatigorsk Pharmaceutical Institute: 357533 Pyatigorsk, pr. Kalinina 11; tel. (8790) 9-44-74; f. 1943; library: 370,000 vols; 308 teachers; 2,300 students; Rector V. G. BELIKOV.

SCIENCE AND TECHNOLOGY

Bryansk Technological Institute: 241037 Bryansk, ul. Stanke Dimitrova 3; tel. (0832) 1-19-12; faculties: forestry engineering, forestry machinery, forestry management, timber technology.

Kemerovo Institute of Food Science and Technology: 650056 Kemerovo, bul. Stroitelei 47; tel. (3842) 73-40-40; fax (3842) 73-41-03; e-mail office@kemtipp.ru; internet www.kemtipp.ru; f. 1972; divs: mechanics, refrigeration machines, food products technology, meat and dairy products, technology and organisation of public catering; 480 teachers; 10,000 students; Rector VLADIMIR PETROVITCH YUSTRATOV.

Moscow State Food Institute: 109803 Moscow, Zemlynoi Val 73; tel. (495) 915-03-40; fax (495) 915-08-77; f. 1953; faculties: bread products, fish breeding and biotechnology, industrial economics, mechanical engineering; brs in Krasnoyarsk, Vyazma and Rostov; 211 teachers; library: 380,000 vols; Rector O. K. FILATOV.

Moscow Technological Institute: 141220 Moscow oblast, Pushkinskii raion, pos. Cherkizovo 1, Glavnaya ul. 99; tel. (495) 584-30-86; faculties: art and technology, chemical technology, engineering economics, mechanical and radio engineering; brs in St Petersburg, Ufa and Tolyatti.

Omsk Technological Institute for Service Industries: 644099 Omsk, Krasnogvardeiskaya 9; tel. (3812) 24-16-93; faculties: Art and Technology, Engineering Economics.

Penza Technological Institute: 440600 Penza, pr. Baidukova 1A; tel. (8412) 55-60-86; e-mail rector@vmis.pti.ac.ru; faculties: mechanical engineering, computer science, economics; library: 140,000 vols; Rector Prof. V. B. MOISEEV.

Russian Extra-Mural Institute of the Textile and Light Industries: 123298 Moscow, ul. Narodnogo Opolcheniya 38, korp. 2; tel. (095) 943-63-59; f. 1932; faculties: textile industry technology, light industry technology, chemical technology, electrical engineering, engineering economics; brs in Barnaul, Ufa, Kemerovo and Omsk; library: 780,000 vols; 350 teachers; 13,000 students; Rector V. S. STRELYAEV.

Shakhty Technological Institute for Service Industries: 346500 Rostov oblast, Shakhty, ul. Shevchenko 147; tel. (08536) 2-20-37; f. 1969; courses in fields of municipal finance and planning, light industry, service industries,; library: 370,000 vols, 250,000 patent documents; 300 teachers; 2,000 full-time students; Rector Prof. VICTOR ROMANOV; publ. *Sbornik rabot instituta* (collected works, 1 a year).

TRANSPORT

Irkutsk Institute of Railway Engineers: 664074 Irkutsk, ul. Chernyshevskogo 15; tel. (3952) 28-27-12; faculties: electromechanical, construction, traffic management; library: 116,000 vols; 497 teachers; Rector L. P. SURKOV.

Samara Institute of Railway Engineers: 443066 Samara 9, Pervyi Bezymyannyi per. 18; tel. (8462) 51-75-09; fax (8462) 51-77-90; faculties: construction, electromechanical, electrotechnical, operating; library: 260,000 vols; 6,000 students; Rector Prof. V. V. IVANOVICH.

Siberian Motor and Highway Institute: 644080 Omsk, pr. Mira 5; tel. (38112) 65-03-02; fax (38112) 65-03-23; e-mail info@sibadi.omsk.ru; internet www.sibadi.omsk.ru; f. 1930; faculties: road-building machinery, highway and airport building, bridges and tunnels, industrial and civil engineering, vehicles and vehicle services, traffic organization and services management, road transport economics and management; library: 747,000 vols; 500 teachers; 5,000 students; Rector V. A. SALNIKOV.

Schools of Art and Music

CONSERVATOIRES AND SCHOOLS OF MUSIC

Astrakhan State Conservatoire: 414000 Astrakhan, Sovetskaya ul. 23; tel. (8510) 2-93-11; f. 1969; courses: choral conducting, orchestral instruments, piano, folk instruments, singing, musicology; 450 students; Rector GEORGI I. SLAVNIKOV.

Kazan State Conservatoire: 420015 Tatarstan, Kazan, Bol. Krasnaya ul. 38; tel. (8432) 36-55-33; fax (8432) 36-56-41; f. 1945; piano, organ, orchestral and folk instruments, composition, singing, choral conducting, musicology; library: 223,000 vols; 178 teachers; 659 students; Rector R. K. ABDULLIN.

Moscow State Conservatoire 'P. I. Tchaikovsky': 103871 Moscow, ul. Bolshaya Nikitskaya 13; tel. (495) 229-06-41; fax (495) 229-96-59; internet www.mosconsv.ru; f. 1866; faculties: piano, orchestral instruments, singing, operatic and symphonic conducting, choral conducting, composition, musicology; 386 teachers; 865 students; library: 1,244,412 vols; Rector M. A. OVCHINNIKOV (acting).

Nizhnii Novgorod State Conservatoire 'M. I. Glinka': 603600 Nizhnii Novgorod GSP-30, ul. Piskunova 40; tel. (8312) 36-45-27; fax (8312) 36-42-37; f. 1946; piano, orchestral and folk instruments, singing, choral conducting, opera and symphony conducting, composition, musicology; library: 130,000 vols; 170 teachers; 700 students; Rector E. B. FERTELMEISTER.

Novosibirsk State Conservatoire 'M. I. Glinka': 630099 Novosibirsk, Sovetskaya ul. 31; tel. (3832) 22-25-22; fax (3832) 23-95-37; f. 1956; piano, orchestral and folk instruments, singing, symphony and choral conducting, composition, musicology; library: 104,000 vols; Rector Prof. Dr E. G. GURENKO.

Rostov State Conservatoire 'S. V. Rakhmaninov': 344008 Rostov-on-Don, Budennovsky pr. 23; tel. (8632) 62-36-14; fax (8632) 62-35-84; e-mail rostcons@aaanet.ru; internet www.rostcons.aaanet.ru; f. 1967 (fmrly Rostov Musical Pedagogical Institute, present name 1992); courses: piano, orchestral instruments, folk instruments, singing, choral conducting, orchestral conducting, composition, musicology, jazz; library: 204,000 vols; 124 teachers; 630 students; Prin. Prof. A. S. DANILOV.

Russian State Academy of Music 'Gnesins': 121069 Moscow, Povarskaya ul. 30–36; tel. (495) 291-15-54; fax (495) 290-17-65; f. 1944; 476 teachers; 1,337 students; Prin. Prof. S. M. KOLOBKOV.

St Petersburg State Conservatoire 'N. A. Rimsky-Korsakov': 190000 St Petersburg, Teatralnaya pl. 3; tel. (812) 314-96-93; fax (812) 311-82-88; e-mail info@conservatory.ru; internet www.conservatory.ru; f. 1862; piano, orchestral instruments, singing, operatic, symphonic and choral conducting, composition, musicology, opera and ballet direction, musical comedy, folk instruments; library: 462,000 vols, 2,431 incunabula, 7,000 MSS of Russian and European composers; 266 teachers; 1,000 students; Rector S. P. ROLDUGIN; publ. *Teatralnaya ploshchad* (6 a year).

Saratov State Conservatoire 'L. V. Sobinov': 410600 Saratov, pr. Kirova 1; tel. (8452) 26-06-38; fax (095) 975-09-33; piano, orchestral and folk instruments, choral conducting, singing, composition, musicology, theatre and cinema acting, musical comedy acting; library: 54,065 vols; Rector Prof. VALERY P. LOMAKO.

Urals State Conservatoire 'M. P. Mussorgsky': 620014 Ekaterinburg, pr. Lenina 26; tel. (3432) 71-21-80; fax (3432) 71-21-80; e-mail mail@uscon.ru; internet www.uscon.ru; f. 1934; piano, orchestral and folk instruments, singing, choral conducting, composition, musicology, sound production; library: 130,000 vols; 190 teachers; 700 students; Rector Prof. MIKHAIL V. ANDRIANOV.

SCHOOLS OF ARTS AND CULTURE

Altai State Institute of Culture: 656055 Barnaul, ul. Yurina 277; tel. (3852) 44-57-09; tel. (3852) 44-54-57; librarianship, cultural and educational work; br. in Omsk.

Chelyabinsk State Institute of Art and Culture: 454091 Chelyabinsk, ul. Ordzhonikidze 36A; tel. (3512) 33-89-32; f. 1968; training in theatre direction, choreography, ballet, conducting, library science; library: 301,000 vols; 508 teachers; 2,700 students; Rector A. P. GRAI.

Eastern Siberian State Institute of Culture: 670005 Buryat Autonomous Republic, Ulan-Ude, ul. Tereshkovoi 1; tel. (31022) 3-33-22; f. 1960; faculties: library science, bibliography; library: 420,000 vols.

Far-Eastern State Academy of Arts: 690600 Vladivostock, Petr Veliky 3; tel. (4232) 26-49-22; fax (4232) 26-44-88; e-mail dvgii@fastmail.vladivostock.ru; f. 1962; piano, orchestral instruments, folk instruments, singing, choral conducting, musicology, drama, painting, directing; library: 102,000 vols; 100 teachers; 450 students.

Kazan State Institute of Culture: 420059 Kazan, Orenburgskii trakt 3A; tel. (8432) 37-31-27; librarianship, cultural and educational work.

Kemerovo State Academy of Culture and Arts: 650029 Kemerovo, ul. Voroshilova 17; tel. (3842) 73-29-67; fax (3842) 73-28-08; e-mail kemgaki@mail.ru; internet www.art.kemerovonet.ru; f. 1969; library sciences, information technology, social education, music, theatre, video art, design, art management, worldwide art studies; library: 249,000 vols; 210 teachers; 3,000 students; Rector Prof. EKATERINA L. KUDRINA.

Khabarovsk State Institute of Culture: 680045 Khabarovsk, Krasnorechenskaya ul. 112; tel. (4210) 36-30-39; dept: library science.

Krasnodar State Institute of Culture and Art: 350072 Krasnodar, ul. 40-letiya Pobedy 33; tel. (8612) 55-30-63; f. 1967; depts: library science, folk culture; library: 152,500 vols; 267 teachers; 2,800 students; Dir IRINA I. GORLOVA.

Krasnoyarsk State Institute of Fine Arts: 660049 Krasnoyarsk, ul. Lenina 22; tel. (3912) 23-35-02; courses: piano, orchestral instruments, folk instruments, singing, choral conducting, musicology, theatre and cinema acting.

Moscow Higher School of Industrial Art: 125080 Moscow A-80, Volokolamskoe shosse 9; tel. (495) 158-01-33; f. 1825; refounded 1945; faculties: industrial arts, decorative and applied art, interior design, monumental art; library: 50,000 vols; 1,300 students; Rector A. S. KVASOV.

Moscow Literary Institute of the Union of Writers 'M. Gorky': 103104 Moscow, Tverskoi bul. 25; tel. (495) 291-22-66; library: 106,000 vols.

Moscow State Art Institute 'V. I. Surikov': 109004 Moscow, Tovarishchesky per. 30; tel. (495) 912-39-32; fax (495) 912-18-75; e-mail artinst@online.ru; f. 1843; depts: architecture, graphic arts, painting, sculpture, theory and history of art; library: 154,000 vols; 103 teachers; 450 students; Dir A. A. BICHUKOV.

Moscow State Institute of Culture: 141400 Moscow oblast, Khimki 6, Bibliotechnaya ul. 7; tel. (495) 570-31-33; f. 1930; librarianship, bibliography, information science, cultural studies, museum studies; library: 786,814 vols; 6,000 students; Rector L. P. BOGDANOV.

Perm State Institute for Arts and Culture: 614000 Perm, ul. Gazety 'Zvezda' 18; tel. (3422) 12-45-93; fax (3422) 12-45-93; f. 1975; educational and cultural work; 156 teachers; 1,814 students; library: 170,000 vols; Rector Y. A. MALYANOV.

Samara State Institute of Culture: 443010 Samara, ul. Frunze 167; tel. (8462) 32-76-54; f. 1971; librarianship, educational and cultural work; library: 239,100 vols; 200 teachers; Dir Prof. I. M. KUZMIN; publs *Culture, Creative Activity, Humanity*.

St Petersburg Academy of Art and Design: 191028 St Petersburg, Solyanoi per. 13; tel. (812) 273-38-04; fax (812) 272-84-46; f. 1876 (fmrly St Petersburg V. I. Mukhina Higher Industrial Art School, present name 1992); faculties: decorative and applied art, monumental arts, design; library: 140,000 vols; 230 teachers; 1,100 students; Rector Prof. A. Y. TALASCHUK.

St Petersburg Institute of Painting, Sculpture and Architecture 'I. E. Repin': 199034 St Petersburg, Universitetskaya nab. 17; tel. (812) 213-61-89; fax (812) 213-65-48; f. 1757; attached to the Acad. of Arts of Russia; depts: painting, sculpture, graphic art, architecture, theory and history of art; library: 500,000 vols; 160 teachers; 1,370 students; Rector Prof. O. A. YEREMEYEV.

St Petersburg State Institute of Culture: 191065 St Petersburg, Dvortsovaya nab. 4; tel. (812) 314-11-21; f. 1918; librarianship, cultural, musical and theatrical studies, cinema and television; library: 600,000 vols; 492 teachers; 5,000 students; Rector Prof. P. A. PODBOLOTOV; publ. *Trudy Instituta* (Proceedings).

Ufa State Institute of Fine Arts: 450025 Bashkortostan, Ufa, ul. Lenina 14; tel. (3472) 23-49-56; depts: piano, orchestral instruments, folk instruments, choral conducting, singing, composition, musicology, theatre and cinema acting, folk theatre, painting; Rector Prof. Z. A. NURGALIN.

Voronezh State Institute of Fine Arts: 394088 Voronezh, ul. Lizyukova 42; tel. (0732) 13-14-81; tel. (0732) 13-08-90; piano, orchestral instruments, folk instruments, singing, choral conducting.

SCHOOLS OF FILM AND THEATRE

Drama School attached to the E. B. Vakhtangov State Theatre 'B. V. Shchukin': 121002 Moscow, ul. Vakhtangova 12a; tel. (495) 241-56-44; theatre and cinema acting.

Drama School attached to the Maly Theatre 'M. S. Shchepkin': 103012 Moscow, Pushechnaya ul. 2/6; tel. (495) 923-18-80; tel. (495) 924-38-89; theatre and cinema acting.

Ekaterinburg State Theatrical Institute: 620151 Ekaterinburg, ul. K. Libknechta 38; tel. (3432) 51-36-90; f. 1985; 350 students; Rector Prof. V. BABENKO.

Moscow Choreographic Institute: 119146 Moscow, 2-ya Frunzenskaya ul. 5; tel. (495) 247-37-80.

Russian Academy of Theatre Arts: 103888 Moscow, Mal. Kislovsky per. 6; tel. (495) 291-91-92; fax (495) 290-05-97; e-mail info@gitis.net; internet www.gitis.net; f.

1878; faculties and depts: acting, directing (directing dramatic theatre, circus direction), musical theatre (musical theatre direction and acting), theatre history and criticism (world theatre history, Russian theatre history), ballet-master faculty (choreography), variety theatre (variety arts), theatre management and production (performing arts management), set design; inter-faculty deps: voice and speech training, vocal training, dance training, movement training, history of the arts, history and theory of music and musical performance, history, philosophy and literature, foreign languages, Russian as a foreign language; Rector Prof. MARINA KHMELNITSKAYA.

St Petersburg State Theatre Arts Academy: 192028 St Petersburg, ul. Mokhovaya 34; tel. (812) 273-15-81; fax (812) 272-17-89; e-mail international@tart.spb.ru; internet www.tart.spb.ru; f. 1779; drama and cinema acting, rock opera acting, puppet theatre, stage directing, theatre planning and organization, theatrical equipment and stage planning; research dept; library: 350,000 vols; 150 teachers; 1,160 students; Rector Prof. Dr L. G. SOUNDSTREM.

State Institute of Cinematography: 129226 Moscow, ul. Vilgelma Pika 3; tel. (495) 181-38-68; f. 1919; direction, shooting, screen play and script writing, cinema studies, economics of cinematography, arts; library: 300,000 vols; 200 teachers; 1,550 students; Rector ALEXANDER NOVIKOV; publs *Tvorchestvo Molodykh* (Creations of Young Artists), etc.

Studio-School of the Moscow Arts Theatre 'V. I. Nemirovich-Danchenko': 103009 Moscow, Tverskaya ul. 6, str. 7; tel. (495) 229-39-36; fax (495) 200-42-41; f. 1943; drama and cinema acting, theatre directing, theatre technology, set and costume design, theatre management; library: 20,000 vols; 80 teachers; 230 students; Rector Prof. O. P. TABAKOV.

Yaroslavl State Theatre Institute: 150000 Yaroslavl, Pervomaiskaya ul. 43; tel. and fax (0852) 22-23-11; f. 1980; theatrical art; library: 25,300 vols; 300 students; Rector Prof. STANISLAV KLITIN.

RWANDA

The Higher Education System

In 1962 Rwanda became independent from Belgium, and in 1963 the Université Nationale du Rwanda, its oldest institution of higher education, was founded. In 2004/05 there were 26,378 students enrolled in tertiary education; there are six public and 14 private higher education institutions. The Ministry of Education is the national coordinating body for higher education. The Minister of Education is the Chairman of the Governing Council of the Université Nationale du Rwanda. The Council's leading officers, including the Rector and Vice-Rectors, are government appointees. The Higher Education Law was passed in 2005. It defines the operating environment for all higher education institutions, both public and private. The National Council of Higher Education plans to develop a National Strategic Planning Framework which will establish a National Quality System and a National Qualification Framework. It will also have the power to accredit and approve the operations of all higher education providers.

The secondary school Diplôme des Humanités Complètes is required for admission to higher education. University degrees are divided into two cycles: the first cycle lasts two years and leads to the award of the Baccalauréat in most subjects (engineering lasts three years); the second cycle is between two and four years in duration, following the award of the Baccalauréat, and leads to the award of either the Licence or a professional title. Students studying medicine are awarded the title of Docteur en Médecine after seven years.

The universities and specialist institutes offer post-secondary technical and vocational education. Courses last two years and students receive (usually) the Diplôme de Technicien Supérieur or Ingénieur Technicien.

Regulatory Bodies

GOVERNMENT

Ministry of Education: BP 622, Kigali; tel. 583051; fax 582161; e-mail info@mineduc.gov.rw; internet www.mineduc.gov.rw; Minister DAPHROSE GAHAKWA.

Ministry of Youth, Sports and Culture: BP 1044, Kigali; tel. 583527; fax 583518; e-mail minicult@rwanda1.com; internet www.mijespoc.gov.rw; Minister JOSEPH HABINEZA.

Learned Society

GENERAL

UNESCO Office Kigali: BP 2502, Kigali; MINEDUC Compound, Kigali; tel. 513845; fax 513844; e-mail kigali@unesco.org; Programme Specialist CONSTANTINO CONSTATINI.

Research Institutes

GENERAL

Institut de Recherche Scientifique et Technologique: BP 227, Butare; tel. 530395; fax 530939; f. 1989; pharmacology, energy, social sciences; library of 9,500 vols; Dir-Gen. Prof. Dr CHRYSOLOGUÉ KOURANGUIÉ; Dir of Pharmacology Centre POLYCARPE NYETERO; Dir of Energy Centre DÉO NKRORUMZIZA; Dir of Centre for Rwanda Studies JEAN MARARA.

AGRICULTURE, FISHERIES AND VETERINARY SCIENCE

Institut des Sciences Agronomiques du Rwanda (ISAR): BP 138, Butare; tel. 530145; fax 530642; internet www.isar.cgiar.org; f. 1962; attached to Min. of Agriculture; 1,000 personnel; library of 2,500 vols; Dir Dr ELIE MUGUNGA MUHINDA; publ. *Technical Letters*.

Attached Research Stations:

Agricultural Research Institute of Rwanda–Ruhande Station: BP 617, Butare; forestry; Dir ATHANASE MUKURARINDA.

Centre de Sélection Bovine de Songa: BP 138, Butare; stockbreeding (cattle, sheep, poultry); Dir (vacant).

Station ISAR/PNAP: BP 73, Ruhengeri; Dir GERVAIS NGERERO.

Station Karama: BP 121, Kigali; plant breeding (living plants, irrigation), stockbreeding (cattle, goats); Dir Ir LAMBERT MAYALA.

Station Rubona: BP 138, Butare; laboratories (chemistry, technology, phytopathology), environmental studies, phytotechnics (living plants, cash crops: coffee, tobacco), zootechnics.

Station Rwerere: BP 73, Ruhengeri; high-altitude cultures (wheat, peas, potatoes); Dir C. SEHENE.

Station Tamira: BP 69, Gisenyi; high-altitude cultures (pyrethrum); Dir C. NTAMBABAZI.

TECHNOLOGY

Direction des Mines et de la Géologie: Ministère de l'Energie, de l'Eau et des Ressources Naturelles, BP 447, Kigali; tel. 570496; f. 1962; geological services to the Government and private industry; to prepare a geological map of Rwanda; prospecting; library of 6,000 vols; Dir EMMANUEL BIZIMANA; publ. *Bulletin du Service Géologique* (1 a year).

Libraries and Archives

Butare

Bibliothèque Universitaire: Université Nationale du Rwanda, BP 117, Butare; tel. 530330; fax 530210; internet www.lib.nur.ac.rw; f. 1964; 206,000 vols; Dir EMMANUEL SERUGENDO.

Kigali

Archives Nationales du Rwanda: BP 1044, Kigali; tel. 83525; fax 83518; f. 1979; 7 staff; 600 vols; Dir ELIAS KIZARI; publ. *Presidential Speeches* (1 a year).

Bibliothèque Nationale du Rwanda: BP 1044, Kigali; tel. 572730; fax 83518; f. 1989; 6,000 vols; Dir SÉVERIM SEKUBUMBA.

Universities

INSTITUT DES SCIENCES, TECHNOLOGIE ET DE GESTION DE KIGALI (KIST)
(Kigali Institute of Science, Technology and Management (KIST))

Ave de l'Armée, BP 3900, Kigali

Telephone: 574696
Fax: 571924
E-mail: info@kist.ac.rw
Internet: www.kist.ac.rw

Founded 1997
Academic year: February to November

Rector: Prof. Dr SILAS LWAKABAMBA
Vice-Rector for Academic Affairs: Ing. ALBERT BUTARE
Vice-Rector for Finance and Admin.: Dr NELSON LUJARA
Dir of Academic Services: Prof. ELIPHAZ BISANDA
Dir of Admin.: ANSELME SANO
Dir of Finance: CALISTUS OBIERO
Chief Librarian: ALPHONSE NGABONZIZA

Number of teachers: 165
Number of students: 2,416

DEANS

Centre for Continuing Education: ANTONIA MUTORO NSANGANO
Faculty of Management: Dr IBRAHIM MUSOBO
Faculty of Science: Dr DESIRÉ KARANGWA
Faculty of Technology: Prof. GRANT MONNEY
School of Language Studies: TEMBWE Z. WA OLOLO

UNIVERSITÉ NATIONALE DU RWANDA

BP 56, Butare

Telephone: 530122
Fax: 530121
E-mail: rector@nur.ac.rw
Internet: www.nur.ac.rw

Founded 1963
Languages of instruction: French, English
State control
Academic year: January to October (two semesters)

Rector: Dr EMILE RWAMASIRABO
Vice-Rector for Academic Affairs: Prof. SILAS MURERAMANZI

Vice-Rector for Admin. and Finance: CANISIUS KARURANGA

Library: see Libraries

Number of teachers: 384

Number of students: 7,240

Publications: *Etudes Rwandaises* (2 a year), *Annuaire*, *Revue Juridique*

DEANS

Faculty of Agriculture: Dr CANISIUS KANANGIRE

Faculty of Arts and Humanities: DÉO BYANAFASHE

Faculty of Economics, Social Sciences, and Management: Dr JEAN BOSCO MUTAJOGIRE

Faculty of Education: Dr JEAN-PIERRE DUSINGIZEMUNGU

Faculty of Law: Dr NGAGI ALPHONSE

Faculty of Medicine: Dr ALEXIS NYAKAYIRO

School of Journalism: JEAN-PIERRE GATSINZI

School of Modern Languages: DEO HODARI

School of Public Health and Nutrition: Dr JOSEPH NTAGANIRA

Colleges

Institut Africain et Mauricien de Statistique et d'Economie Appliquée: BP 109, Kigali; tel. 84989; f. 1975 by the OCAM states; 3-year diploma course; library: 9,184 vols; 7 teachers; 38 students; Dir SÉRIGNE T. DIASSE; publ. *Rapport d'enquête* (1 a year).

Institut Supérieur des Finances Publiques (ISFP): BP 1514, Kigali; tel. 574302; f. 1987; attached to the Ministry of Finance; offers 2-year courses in the financial aspects of public administration; library; Dir JEAN-BAPTISTE BYILINGIRO.

SAINT CHRISTOPHER AND NEVIS

The Higher Education System

The islands of St Christopher and Nevis were settled by the British in the 1620s and remained under British control until 1983, when they jointly became an independent state and joined the Commonwealth as a full member. The College of Further Education was founded in 1988 as an amalgamation of previously existing institutions and was renamed Clarence Fitzroy Bryant College in 1996. In 2000 a privately financed 'offshore' medical college, the Medical University of the Americas, opened in Nevis. There is also a branch campus of the University of the West Indies located in Basseterre. In 2003/04 there were 751 students in tertiary education. One national and four private institutions offer a number of degree programmes recognized and accredited by the Accreditation Board of the Ministry of Education and Youth.

Admission to Bachelors degree courses requires sufficient passes in the Caribbean Examinations Council Secondary Education Certificate or GCE A-Level. The Bachelors degree at the University of the West Indies lasts three to four years while the Masters degree takes two years and is mostly coursework based. Following completion of the Masters, the Doctorate requires two to four years of further study, culminating in the submission and defence of a thesis.

Clarence Fitzroy Bryant College and other colleges offer post-secondary vocational and technical education, leading to the award of qualifications such as Diplomas, Technician Diplomas and Associate Degrees.

Regulatory and Representative Bodies

GOVERNMENT

Ministry of Education and Youth: Church St, POB 333, Basseterre; tel. 465-2521; Minister SAM TERRENCE CONDOR.

Ministry of Tourism, Culture and Sport: POB 878, Port Zante, Basseterre; tel. 465-2521; fax 465-7075; e-mail culture@sisterisles.kn; Minister Dr DENZIL LLEWELLYN DOUGLAS.

ACCREDITATION

Accreditation Board: Min. of Education and Youth, POB 333, Lockhart St, Basseterre; tel. 466-8610; fax 466-3322; e-mail board_acc@hotmail.com; Chair. Dr HERMIA MORTON-ANTHONY; Sec. EVAN HARVEY.

Accreditation Commission on Colleges of Medicine (ACCM): see under Ireland.

Learned Societies

HISTORY, GEOGRAPHY AND ARCHAEOLOGY

Nevis Historical and Conservation Society: POB 563, Charlestown, Nevis; tel. 469-5786; fax 469-0274; e-mail museums@nevis-nhcs.org; internet www.nevis-nhcs.org; f. 1980; administers Nevis Field Study Centre, Museum of Nevis History (birthplace of Alexander Hamilton), Horatio Nelson Museum; 650 mems; library: materials on history and culture of Nevis, St Kitts and West Indies, Alexander Hamilton, Horatio Nelson, and Amerindians; Archives of Nevis, newspapers, and civil, parish and government records, maps; Pres. HALSTEAD BYRON; Sec. SUZANNE GORDON; Exec. Dir JOHN GUILBERT.

LANGUAGE AND LITERATURE

Alliance Française: 1 Orchid St, Greenlands, POB 93, Basseterre, St Kitts; tel. 465-9415; fax 465-0478; e-mail allfrskn@caribsurf.com; offers courses and exams in French language and culture and promotes cultural exchange with France.

Library

Charlestown

Nevis Public Library: Prince William St, Charlestown, Nevis; tel. 469-0421; fax 469-1207; e-mail nepublib@caribsurf.com; Librarian HAZEL FRANCIS (acting).

Universities and Colleges

Clarence Fitzroy Bryant College: Burdon St Campus, POB 268, Basseterre, St Kitts; tel. 465-2856; fax 465-8279; e-mail info@cfbc.edu.kn; internet www.cfbc.edu.kn; f. 1988 as College of Further Education by merger of 4 instns; present name 1996; Prin. MARILYN ROGERS (acting); Registrar VENETTA MILLS; Librarians LORREL BRADSHAW, LEAH LIBURD.

Medical University of the Americas: POB 701, Charlestown, Nevis; tel. 469-9177; fax 469-9180; e-mail admissions@mua.edu; internet www.mua.edu; f. 1998; Private control; library: 2,950 books, 110 periodicals; 80 teachers; 600 students (postgraduate); Pres. Dr DAVID L. FREDRICK; Exec. Dean Dr SEWELL DIXON; Dean, Basic Sciences Dr RAY LASH.

University of the West Indies Branch: Basseterre; tel. 465-6583; fax 465-2190; e-mail ewiskn@caribsurf.com; Dir OLIVIA EDGECOMBE-HOWELL.

SAINT LUCIA

The Higher Education System

The island became a British colony in 1814 and remained under British rule until 1979, when it became independent (but remaining within the Commonwealth). Tertiary education is principally offered by a branch campus of the University of the West Indies. In 2000/01 there were 1,403 students enrolled in tertiary education and 729 students in adult education. The Ministry of Education and Culture is the government agency responsible for higher education.

Sir Arthur Lewis Community College offers qualifications at the upper-secondary and tertiary levels. The Associate degree is a two- or three-year programme of study, depending on the subject. Undergraduate Bachelors and postgraduate Masters degrees are available at the University of the West Indies.

Regulatory Body

GOVERNMENT

Ministry of Education and Culture: Francis Compton Bldg, Waterfront, Castries; tel. 468-5203; fax 453-2299; e-mail mineduc@candw.lc; internet www.education.gov.lc; Minister Arsene Vigil James.

Learned Societies

EDUCATION

National Research and Development Foundation: La Clery, POB 3067, Castries; tel. 452-4253; fax 453-6389; e-mail info@nrdf.org.lc; internet www.nrdf.org.lc; f. 1983 to promote research and the expansion of economic devt in St Lucia; provides technical assistance, training and consultancy; offers short courses in business management and admin.; Exec. Dir Gerald Morris.

HISTORY, GEOGRAPHY AND ARCHAEOLOGY

St Lucia Archaeological and Historical Society: Vigie, POB 3060, La Clery, Castries; tel. 453-2519; f. 1954; organizes public lectures, exhibitions and educational activities; Pres. Fortuna Anthony; Admin. Sec. Eric Branford.

LANGUAGE AND LITERATURE

Alliance Française: La Pyramide, Pointe Séraphine, POB 898, Castries; tel. 452-6602; fax 452-1871; e-mail alliancefrancaise@candw.lc; internet www.af-antilles.org; f. 1994; offers courses and examinations in French language and culture, and promotes cultural exchange with France; library of 3,792 vols; Dir Claude Gonin.

NATURAL SCIENCES

Biological Sciences

St Lucia Naturalists' Society: POB 783, Castries; tel. 451-6957; conservation and educational activities; Chair. Crispin d'Auvergne.

RELIGION, SOCIOLOGY AND ANTHROPOLOGY

Folk Research Centre: Mount Pleasant, POB 514, Castries; tel. 453-1477; fax 451-9365; e-mail frc@candw.lc; internet www.stluciafolk.org; f. 1973 to preserve and promote the cultural heritage of St Lucia; Chair. Victor Poyotte; Exec. Dir Kennedy Samuel.

Libraries and Archives

Castries

Central Library of St Lucia: POB 103, Castries; tel. 452-2875; internet www.educ.gov.lc; f. 1847; dept of Min. of Education and Culture; government public library; 160,000 vols; Dir of Library Services John Robert Lee.

National Archives of St Lucia: POB 3060, La Clery, Castries; tel. 452-1654; fax 453-1405; e-mail stlunatarch_mt@candw.lc; internet www.stluciaarchives.org; f. 1995; 6,000 vols; unselected govt records; spec. historical collns, multimedia; Archivist Margot Thomas.

Museum

Castries

St Lucia National Trust: POB 595, Castries; tel. 452-5005; fax 453-2791; internet www.slunatrust.org; f. 1975; responsible for the protected areas of Pigeon Island (history, archaeology, geology, natural history), Fregate Islands Nature Reserve and the proposed Praslin Protected Landscape (archaeology, history, coastal resources, geology, flora and fauna), the Anse Galet Nature Reserve (flora and fauna, history) and several offshore islands (bird nesting sites) and other sites; 600 mems; Dir Bishnu Tulsie; publ. *Conservation News* (4 a year).

College

University of the West Indies, School of Continuing Studies: University Centre, POB 306, The Morne, Castries; tel. 452-3866; fax 452-4080; e-mail uwislu@candw.lc; f. 1948; continuing education; houses the University's Distance Education Centre (UWIDEC) linking the university campuses with eight university centres; Resident Tutor and Head Matthew Vernon Roberts.

SAINT VINCENT AND THE GRENADINES

The Higher Education System

From the 18th century the islands were under British control until they became fully independent, within the Commonwealth, as Saint Vincent and the Grenadines in 1978. The Vincentian education system is modelled on the British system. Post-secondary education is provided through the Kingstown Medical College, a campus of St George's University (Grenada), located near Kingstown. The University maintains affiliations with hospitals in the USA, the UK and the Caribbean for clinical programmes. There are also teacher-training, technical, nursing and community colleges, with total enrolment in 2000 of 904 students. The Ministry of Education is the national body responsible for higher education.

Regulatory Bodies

GOVERNMENT

Ministry of Education: Halifax St, Kingstown; tel. 456-1877; fax 457-1114; Minister GIRLYN MIGUEL.

Ministry of Urban Development, Labour, Culture and Electoral Matters: Marion House Bldg, Ground Floor, Murray's Rd, Kingstown; tel. 457-1789; fax 485-6737; e-mail office.elections@mail.gov.vc; Minister RENEÉ MERCEDES BAPTISTE.

Learned Societies

ARCHITECTURE AND TOWN PLANNING

Saint Vincent and the Grenadines National Trust: POB 1538, Heritage Hall, Carnegie Bldg, Kingstown; tel. 451-2921; e-mail svgntrust@vincysurf.com; f. 1969; concerned with the preservation of the architectural, cultural and environmental heritage of St Vincent and the Grenadines; educational workshops on conservation and preservation values and skills; advises govt and private sector on sustainable devt policies and legislation; restores and preserves bldgs and objects of archaeological, architectural, artistic, historic, scientific or traditional merit; lists historical bldgs, sites, flora and fauna; maintains photographic inventories of historical and natural sites; 200 mems; Man. Dir RACHEL MOSES.

FINE AND PERFORMING ARTS

Saint Vincent and the Grenadines Visual Arts Society: POB 2303, Kingstown; tel. 457-4454; f. 2003 to encourage the local devt of the visual arts; organizes exhibitions and other events; Sec. CÉCILE COMBLEN.

LANGUAGE AND LITERATURE

Alliance Française: POB 560, Kingstown; Old Public Library Bldg, Kingstown; tel. and fax 456-2095; e-mail afsvg@vincysurf.com; f. 1969; organizes French classes, confs, exhibitions, seminars, films and lectures; Dir VANESSA DEMIRCIYAN.

Libraries and Archives

Kingstown

Department of Libraries, Archives and Documentation Services: Richmond Hill, Kingstown; tel. and fax 457-2022; e-mail publiclibrary@vincysurf.com; f. 1893; attached to Min. of Education; oversees 20 br. libraries containing 262,000 vols; Dir JOAN L. JOB MOSES (acting); Librarian DANA NEVERSON.

Principal Attached Centres:

Documentation Centre: Richmond Hill, Kingstown; tel. 456-1689; e-mail document@caribsurf.com; f. 1982; 15,000 vols; Librarian TRISHA-ANN MOSES.

Kingstown Public Library: Richmond Hill, Kingstown; tel. and fax 457-2022; e-mail publiclibrary@vincysurf.com; f. 1893; 48,216 vols; 6,209 mems; Librarian DONNA MCLEAN.

National Archives: Richmond Hill, Kingstown; tel. 450-0485; e-mail archives@vincysurf.com; f. 1990; 15,000 vols; Archivist TRISHA-ANN JOB.

Museums and Galleries

Kingstown

Botanical Gardens: New Montrose, Kingstown; tel. 457-1003; f. 1763; the oldest botanical gardens in the western hemisphere; conservation of rare species of plants; aviary containing St Vincent parrots; Dir EMMETT DOYLE.

Dr Cecil Cyrus Museum: Montrose, Kingstown; tel. 457-8981; fax 457-0812; e-mail cyrusclinic@caribsurf.com; f. 2002; colln of medical exhibits, 1,000 pathological specimens, 3,000 photographs; memorabilia of Vincentian life and history, historical maps; Keeper Dr A. CECIL CYRUS.

Fort Charlotte: Berkshire Hill, Kingstown; f. 1806; contains a museum depicting the history of the Black Caribs.

College

Kingstown Medical College: POB 585, Ratho Mill, Kingstown; tel. 456-4832; fax 456-9670; e-mail sgu_info@mssl.com; internet www.sgu.edu; f. 1979; preclinical school affiliated to St George's Univ., Grenada; Dean Dr EDWARD S. JOHNSON.

SAMOA

The Higher Education System

In 1962 Western Samoa (as it was then known) gained independence, having been governed by New Zealand since 1919, first as a League of Nations mandate and then as a UN Trust Territory. The current name was adopted in 1997. The National University of Samoa was founded in 1988, and other institutions of higher education include a branch campus of the University of the South Pacific. In 2001 some 1,179 students were enrolled in higher education.

Admission to non-university-level higher education is on the basis of the Samoa School Certificate, while admission to university-level higher education requires completion of Senior Secondary school and award of the Pacific Senior Secondary School Certificate. The National University of Samoa and the University of the South Pacific also offer one-year pre-university preparation and foundation courses. Sub-degree level qualifications include one-year Certificates and one- or two-year Diplomas. Undergraduate Bachelors degrees at the National University of Samoa and the University of the South Pacific last three years and qualify students for the postgraduate Masters, which follows a two-year programme of study.

Regulatory Body

GOVERNMENT

Ministry of Education, Sports and Culture: POB 1869, Apia; tel. 21911; fax 21917; e-mail samoamesc@lesamoa.net; Minister TOOMATA ALAPATI POESE TOOMATA.

Learned Society

GENERAL

UNESCO Office Apia: POB 5766, Mata'utu-Uta Post Office, Apia; tel. 24276; fax 22253; e-mail apia@unesco.org; f. 1984; designated Cluster Office for Australia, Cook Islands, Fiji, Kiribati, Marshall Islands, Federated States of Micronesia, Nauru, New Zealand, Niue, Palau, Papua New Guinea, Samoa, Solomon Islands, Tonga, Tuvalu and Vanuatu; documentation centre; Dir VISESIO PONGI.

Libraries and Archives

Apia

Avele College Library: POB 45, Apia; tel. 20831; 5,000 vols serving 520 students.

Nelson Memorial Public Library: POB 598, Apia; tel. and fax 21208; e-mail jpgodinet@lesamoa.net; f. 1959; 92,000 vols; 1 br. library on Savaii island; 1 bookmobile; spec. collns: R. L. Stevenson, Samoa and Pacific; Sr Librarian JACINTA P. GODINET.

Museum

Apia

Robert Louis Stevenson Museum: POB 850, Apia; tel. 20798; fax 25428; e-mail rlsm@ipasifika.net; f. 1990; writer Robert Louis Stevenson's (1850–1894) restored house and estate; Manager SOLOIA M. FRITZ.

University

IUNIVESITE AOAO O SAMOA (National University of Samoa)

POB 1622, Apia
Telephone: 20072
Fax: 25489
E-mail: secretariat@nus.edu.ws
Internet: www.nus.edu.ws

Founded 1984
Languages of instruction: English, Samoan
Academic year: February to November

Vice-Chancellor and Pres.: Prof. LE'APAI TU'UA 'ILAOA ASOFOU SO'O
Deputy Vice Chancellor: Dr EMMA KRUSE VAAI
Registrar: LUAGALAU FOISAGAASINA ETEUATI SHON
Univ. Librarian: AVALOGO TOGI TUNUPOPO

Number of teachers: 140
Number of students: 2,500

Publications: *Jafnus* (arts, 1 a year), *Journal of Samoan Studies*, *Prismcs* (science, 1 a year)

DEANS

Centre for Samoan Studies: Prof. IUPATI LAFITAI FUATAI (Dir)
Faculty of Arts: MARIA KERSLAKE
Faculty of Business and Entrepreneurship: Dr WOOD SALELE
Faculty of Education: EPENESA LAFI ESERA
Faculty of Nursing: FULISIA PITA-UO AIAVAO
Faculty of Science: Dr IOANA CHAN MOW
Oloamanu Centre for Professional Devt and Continuing Education: GATOLOAIFA'ANA TILIANAMUA AFAMASAGA (Dir)

Colleges

Avele College: POB 45, Apia; tel. 20831; f. 1924, under Min. of Education, Sports and Culture 1966; 5-year courses; 520 students, incl. students from the Tokelau Islands; Prin. L. A. SANERIVI.

University of the South Pacific, Alafua Campus: PMB, Apia; tel. 21671; fax 22933; e-mail enquiries@samoa.usp.ac.fj; internet www.usp.ac.fj/soa; f. 1977; academic year February to December; diploma, degree and higher degree courses; library: 15,000 vols, 1,000 periodicals; 19 teachers; 200 students; Head Dr DAVID HUNTER (acting); publs *IRETA South Pacific Agriculture News* (12 a year), *Journal of South Pacific Agriculture* (4 a year), *South Pacific Agricultural Teacher* (4 a year); (see also Fiji chapter).

SAN MARINO

The Higher Education System

San Marino evolved as a city-state in the early Middle Ages and is the sole survivor of the numerous independent states that existed in Italy before its unification in the 19th century. A treaty of friendship and cooperation with Italy was signed in 1862, renewed in March 1939 and revised in September 1971. The only institution of higher education is the Università degli Studi della Repubblica di San Marino (founded 1985). In 2008/09 42 students attended the Università, and another 832 students were attending courses outside San Marino.

The Rector is the university's senior administrative and academic officer and is responsible for its internal affairs and external relations. The Departments, Centres and Schools constitute the university's academic division, while the Administrative Directorate deals with its financial affairs.

Regulatory and Representative Bodies

GOVERNMENT

Secretariat of State for Education, Culture and the University: Contrada Omerelli, 47890 San Marino; tel. 0549-882548; fax 0549-882301; e-mail segreteria.ic@gov.sm; internet www.educazione.sm; Secretary of State Dott. ROMEO MORRI.

ACCREDITATION

ENIC/NARIC San Marino: Dipartimento Pubblica Istruzione, Contrada Omerelli 23, 47890 San Marino; tel. 0549-882550; fax 0549-882301; e-mail segr.pub-istr@omniway.sm; Coordinator FILIBERTO BERNARDI.

Learned Society

LANGUAGE AND LITERATURE

Alliance Française: Centro Social Dogana, Piazza Tini, 47891 Dogana, San Marino; e-mail alliancefrsm@yahoo.fr; internet www.alliancefrancaise.sm; offers courses and exams in French language and culture and promotes cultural exchange with France.

Library

San Marino

Biblioteca di Stato: Palazzo Valloni 13, Contrada Omerelli, 47890 San Marino; tel. 0549-882248; fax 0549-882295; e-mail biblioteca@omniway.sm; internet www.bibliotecadistato.sm; f. 1839; 120,000 vols, 77 periodicals, collns of posters, photographs and MSS; Dir ELISABETTA RIGHI IWANEJKO.

Museums

San Marino

Museo delle Curiosità: Salita all Rocca 26, Centro Storico, 47890 San Marino; tel. 0549-992437; fax 0549-991075; e-mail info@museodellecuriosita.sm; internet www.museodellecuriosita.sm; colln of curiosities and highly unusual objects.

Museo di San Francesco: Via Basilicius, 47890 San Marino; tel. 0549-885132; internet www.museidistato.sm/museo_trad/msf; f. 1966; exhibits of the artistic heritage of the monastery and other Franciscan churches; panel paintings, canvases, vestments, furnishings, sculptures.

Museo di Stato: Sede Espositiva, Piazzetta del Titano 1, 47890 San Marino; tel. 0549-882670; fax 0549-882679; e-mail info@museidistato.sm; internet www.museidistato.sm; f. 1899; reorganized as autonomous entity 1982; 5,000 objects; archaeological finds from the Neolithic to early Middle Ages; architectural remains of the ancient Basilica; paintings and objects from the 17th-century convent of the Clarisse; works of art of the Republic; San Marino coins and medals (1865–1938); Egyptian, Etruscan and Roman archaeological finds donated to the State; Dir Dott. FRANCESCA MICHELOTTI.

University

UNIVERSITÀ DEGLI STUDI DELLA REPUBBLICA DI SAN MARINO

Antico Monastero Santa Chiara, Contrada Omerelli 20, 47890 San Marino

Telephone: 378-882541
Fax: 378-882545
E-mail: rettorato@unirsm.sm
Internet: www.unirsm.sm

Founded 1985
State control

Rector: Prof. GIORGIO PETRONI
Admin. Dir: Avv. MARIA SCIARRINO
Librarian: Dott. GABRIELLA LORENZI

Library of 45,000 vols, 500 periodicals

Publication: *L'Ateneo del Citano* (1 a year)

DEANS

Department of Biomedical Studies: Prof. VINCENZO GASBARRO

Department of Communication: Prof. PATRIZIA VIOLI

Department of Economics and Technology: Prof. ANGELO MARCELLO TARANTINO

Department of Education and Training: Prof. LUIGI GUERRA

Department of Historical Studies: Prof. LUCIANO CANFORA

Department of Law Studies: Prof. PIER GIORGIO PERUZZI

SÃO TOMÉ E PRÍNCIPE

The Higher Education System

The Democratic Republic of São Tomé and Príncipe is a group of islands lying in the Gulf of Guinea, off the west coast of Africa, which achieved independence from Portugal in 1975. The Government has made higher education a national priority; however São Tomé e Príncipe is a small, poor and isolated nation, and as such faces many challenges in progressing towards its strategic goals. The Instituto Superior Politécnico de São Tomé e Príncipe was founded in 1997 and is administered by the Government. It offers Bachelors degrees, particularly in teacher training although its curriculum has recently expanded to include areas such as business administration, languages, literature and technology. In 2001 117 students were enrolled at the polytechnic. The country's first university, Universidade Lusíada, was inaugurated in 2006.

Regulatory Body

GOVERNMENT

Ministry of Education, Culture and Sport: Rua Misericórdia, CP 41, São Tomé; tel. 222861; fax 221466; e-mail mineducal@cstome.net; internet www.minecjdesportos.gov.st; Minister MARIANA RUTE LEAL.

Learned Society

LANGUAGE AND LITERATURE

Alliance Française: CP 974, São Tomé; tel. 242300; fax 242309; e-mail alliancefr@cstome.ne.

Libraries and Archives

São Tomé

Arquivo Histórico de São Tomé e Príncipe: CP 87, São Tomé; tel. 222306; fax 224201; e-mail ahstp@cstome.net; f. 1969; 60,000 boxes of documents; 5,000 vols of bibliography; Dir MARIA NAZARÉ DE CEITA.

Biblioteca do Ministério de Agricultura e Pesca: CP 47, São Tomé; tel. 224657; f. 1973; 1,750 vols; Librarian TOMÉ DE SOUSA DA COSTA.

Biblioteca Municipal: São Tomé.

Centro de Documentação Técnica e Científica: São Tomé; 45,000 vols of specialized documents on agriculture, fisheries, economics; 2,000 periodicals; Dir MARIA ROSÁRIO ASSUNÇÃO.

Museum

São Tomé

Museu Nacional: CP 87, São Tomé; tel. 221874; history, ethnography, religious art.

College

Instituto Superior Politécnico de São Tomé e Príncipe: Endereço Ministério da Educação, Quinta de Santo António, CP 41, Príncipe; tel. and fax 223896; e-mail isptsp@cstome.net; internet www.stome.net/educa/isp.htm; f. 1997; Dir LÚCIO LIMA VIEGAS PINTO.

SAUDI ARABIA

The Higher Education System

The Kingdom of Saudi Arabia was proclaimed in 1932 following the unification of the central Najd (Nejd) and western Hedjaz regions of the Arabian peninsula under the rule of Ibn Sa'ud, who also established the current ruling Saudi dynasty. The oldest existing institution of higher education is the Madrasat Ahl al-Hadith (founded 1933), a school of Islamic studies. King Saud University (founded 1957; current name 1982) was the first university-level institution, and by 2008 there were an estimated 659,887 students enrolled in higher education. Universities mostly consist of colleges and male and female students are often segregated; there are three single-sex institutions. Tertiary institutions in 2006 included 110 university colleges and 87 colleges exclusively for women. Construction of the first private university, King Faisal University, in partnership with a US technology institute, commenced in 2006. The Council for Higher Education is the supreme national body of post-secondary, non-military education. Quality assurance and accreditation is undertaken by the National Commission for Academic Accreditation and Assessment (founded 2002).

Admission to higher education is based on the award of the General Secondary Education Certificate (Tawjihiyah) and performance in the General Aptitude Tests. The Associate degree and undergraduate Diploma are pre-university qualifications offered by community colleges (the undergraduate Diploma is also offered by universities) and are four-semester (two-year) programmes of study. Saudi degrees are awarded on a 'credit–semester' system, whereby students are required to accrue a specified number of credits each semester in order to graduate. Both the Associate degree and the undergraduate Diploma require 48–70 credits for graduation. The undergraduate Bachelors degree is often a four-year programme of study, although degrees in professional fields of study such as medicine, pharmacy, engineering and architecture last upwards of five years. The minimum number of credits required for graduation is 120. Graduates holding the Bachelors degree are eligible for admission to the postgraduate Diploma or Masters degree. The postgraduate Diploma lasts one year (30 credits) and the Masters degree is a two-year course (42 credits), including submission of a dissertation. The highest university degree is the Doctorate, which requires a minimum of three years of study and research, culminating in the public defence of a dissertation.

Post-secondary technical and vocational education is supervised by the General Organization for Technical Education and Vocational Training, and the admission criteria are the same as for university education. Institutions offering technical and vocational education include Colleges of Technology, Higher Technical Institutes, Pre-Vocational and Vocational Training Centres, Trade Schools and Junior Health Colleges. Colleges of Technology provide two-year courses of education leading to the award of the Technical College Certificate; Higher Technical Institutes offers a Diploma programme; Trade Schools specialize in programmes of study relating to trades and professions; and Junior Health Colleges train technicians for the health services profession. In 2008 a total of 83,347 students attended 101 technical and vocational institutes.

Regulatory and Representative Bodies

GOVERNMENT

Ministry of Education: Riyadh 11148; tel. (1) 404-2888; fax (1) 401-2365; internet moe .gov.sa; Minister ABDULLAH AL-OBAID.

Ministry of Higher Education: King Faisal Hospital St, Riyadh 11153; tel. (1) 441-5555; fax (1) 441-9004; e-mail contact@mohe .gov.sa; internet www.mohe.gov.sa; Minister Dr KHALID AL-ANGARI; Gen. Superintendent and Legal Dir ABDULLAH BIN HAMAD AL-RASHED.

Ministry of Culture and Information: Nasseriya St, Riyadh 11161; tel. (1) 401-4440; fax (1) 402-3570; e-mail samirad@ saudinf.com; internet www.saudinf.com; Min. Dr ABDUL AZIZ BIN MUHIYUDDIN KHOJA.

ACCREDITATION

National Commission for Academic Accreditation and Assessment: POB 8252, Riyadh 11482; fax (1) 212-0666; internet www.ncaaa.org.sa; 17 mems; Chair. THE MINISTER OF HIGHER EDUCATION.

Learned Societies

BIBLIOGRAPHY, LIBRARY SCIENCE AND MUSEOLOGY

Arab Regional Branch of the International Council on Archives (ARBICA): Institute of Public Administration, POB 205, Riyadh 11141; tel. (1) 476-1600, ext. 462; close collaboration with ICA, UNESCO and other int. orgs; mems: 20 Arab countries; Pres. A. TAMINI (Tunisia); Sec.-Gen. FAHD AL-ASKAR (Saudi Arabia); publ. *Arab Archives Journal* (1 a year).

LANGUAGE AND LITERATURE

British Council: C-14, Third Fl., Al-Fazari Sq., Diplomatic Quarter, POB 58012, Riyadh 11594; tel. (1) 483-1818; fax (1) 483-1717; e-mail enquiry.riyadh@sa.britishcouncil.org; internet www.britishcouncil.org/saudiarabia; teaching centre (men's and women's sections); offers courses and examinations in English language and British culture and promotes cultural exchange with the UK; attached teaching centres in Jeddah and Dammam; Country Dir ALAN SMART; Teaching Centre Man. (Men's section) MALCOLM JARDINE; Teaching Centre Man. (Women's section) HELEN GLENN.

NATURAL SCIENCES

Biological Sciences

Saudi Biological Society: King Saud University, POB 2455, Riyadh 11451; tel. (1) 467-5835; fax (1) 467-5833; f. 1975; 350 mems; Pres. Dr I. A. IRIF; Sec.-Gen. Dr F. AL-MANA; publ. *Journal of the Saudi Biological Society*.

Geographical Sciences

Saudi Geographical Society: POB 2456, Riyadh 11451; tel. (1) 467-8798; fax (1) 467-7732; e-mail sgs@ksu.edu.sa; internet www .saudigs.org; Chair. Prof. MOHAMMAD MAKKI; Sec.-Gen. Dr ABDALLAH H. AL-SOLAI.

Research Institutes

GENERAL

King Faisal Centre for Research and Islamic Studies: POB 51049, Riyadh 11543; tel. (1) 465-2255; fax (1) 465-9993; e-mail kfcrisinfo@kff.com; internet www.kfcris.com; f. 1983; part of King Faisal Foundation; research in various fields of Islamic civilization; library of 85,000 books, 2,400 periodicals, 23,833 original MSS, 13,000 microfilm and microfiche; audiovisual library of 10,000 vols; children's library of 17,000 vols; Chair. HRH Prince TURKI AL-FAISAL; Sec.-Gen. Dr YAHYA MAHMOUD AL-JUNAID; publs *Al-Faisal* (12 a year), *Journal of Linguistic Studies* (in Arabic, 6 a year).

ECONOMICS, LAW AND POLITICS

Islamic Research and Training Institute: POB 9201, Jeddah 21413; tel. (2) 636-1400; fax (2) 637-8927; e-mail irti@isdb.org; internet www.irti.org; f. 1982; part of Islamic Development Bank; research to enable the economic and financial activities of the IDB's mem. countries to conform to the Islamic Sharia; research into all aspects of mem. countries' economic and financial systems; training of personnel (but no formal teaching courses); language of instruction: Arabic; library of 9,000 vols; Dir Prof. Dr MABID ALI AL-JARHI.

EDUCATION

Centre for Research in Islamic Education: POB 1034, Mecca; tel. (2) 556-5677; fax (2) 558-6707; f. 1980 by the Organization of the Islamic Conference, affiliated 1982 to

Umm Al-Qura University; aims to promote Islamic values in education through research, devt and training; Dir Dr ABDUR-RAZZAK AHMED ZAFAR.

HISTORY, GEOGRAPHY AND ARCHAEOLOGY

King Abdulaziz Research Centre: POB 2945, Riyadh 11461; tel. (1) 441-2316; fax (1) 441-7020; f. 1972 in memory of the late King; historical research, preservation of historical documents, photographs and other cultural material; library of 28,000 vols, 200 periodicals; also the private library of the late King (2,000 vols); historical archive incl. documents in various languages, esp. Turkish and English, and Arabic MSS; King Abdulaziz Memorial Hall shows events in the late King's life, esp. his military battles; Sec.-Gen. Dr FAHD AL-SEMMARI.

MEDICINE

Saudi–German Institute for Nursing and Allied Health Sciences: POB 2550, Jeddah 21461; e-mail webmaster@sgnursing.com; internet www.sgna-sa.com; Pres. Dr SOBHI IBRAHIM BATTERJEE.

TECHNOLOGY

Bureau de Recherches Géologiques et Minières (BRGM): POB 1492, Jeddah 21431; tel. (2) 665-1104; (see main entry under France).

King Abdulaziz City for Science and Technology: POB 6086, Riyadh 11442; tel. (1) 481-4329; fax (1) 481-6730; internet www.kacst.edu.sa; nat. science agency; Pres. Dr MOHAMMAD IBN IBRAHIM AL-SUWAIYEL.

Libraries and Archives

Jeddah

Educational Library: General Directorate of Broadcasting, Press and Publications, Jeddah.

Mecca

Abbas Kattan Library: Mecca; 7,800 vols, 200 MSS.

Library of Alharam: Mecca; 6,000 vols.

Madrasat Ahl Al-Hadith Library: Mecca.

Medina

Islamic University Library: POB 170, Medina; tel. (4) 847-4080; fax (4) 847-4560; f. 1961; consists of a central library and 11 brs; 143,000 vols, 27,772 MSS, 8,761 microfilms, 3,247 theses.

King Abdulaziz Library: Medina; tel. (4) 823-2134; fax (4) 823-2126; f. 1983; 120,000 vols and MSS; Dir D. ABDULRAHMAN BIN SULIMAN ALMUZINY.

Riyadh

Institute of Public Administration Library: POB 205, Riyadh 11141; tel. (1) 476-8888; fax (1) 479-2136; e-mail library@ipa.edu.sa; internet www.ipa.edu.sa; f. 1961; 240,000 vols in Arabic, English and French, 1,088 periodical titles, 55,000 Saudi public records, 4,953 official publs., 33,420 microforms, 712 CD-ROMs; Dir-Gen. EN MOSTAFA SADHAN.

King Abdulaziz Public Library: POB 86486, Riyadh 11622; tel. (1) 491-1300; fax (1) 491-1949; internet www.kapl.org.sa; f. 1985; 275,000 vols (Arabic and non-Arabic), 1,100 current periodicals, 2,500 MSS, 53,000 historic documents on microform, 5,000 audiovisual items, doctoral dissertations; equestrian information; Supervisor-Gen. FAISAL A. AL-MUAAMMAR.

King Saud University Libraries: POB 22480, Riyadh 11495; tel. (1) 467-3404; fax (1) 467-6127; e-mail itlibrary@ksu.edu.sa; internet www.ksu.edu.sa; f. 1957; central library and 7 brs; 1.1 m. vols, 3,500 periodicals, 20,000 MSS, 90,100 govt publs, 22,000 microfilm items, 4,000 microfiche items, 16,000 audiovisual items; br. libraries incl. Prince Salman Central Library, Central Library for Girls (Malaz), Univ. Studies Centre for girls (Ulayshah), The Faculty of Medicine, King Abdulaziz Univ. Hospital, College of Dentistry, College of Applied Medical Sciences, College of Community Services; Dean Dr AHMAD ABDULLAH BIN KHUDAIR; Vice-Dean Dr ABDUL RAHMAN A. AL-SHAMMARI; publ. journals.

King Abdulaziz City for Science and Technology Library: POB 6086, Riyadh 11442; tel. (1) 488-3555; fax (1) 488-3118; 50,000 vols, 75,000 technical reports; Dir of Information Systems HAMAD AL-SADOUN.

King Fahad National Library: POB 7572, Riyadh 11472; tel. (1) 462-4888; fax (1) 464-5341; e-mail headoffice@kfnl.gov.sa; internet www.kfnl.gov.sa; f. 1968; 37,000 vols in Arabic, English, French; 150 MSS; Dir ABDUR RAHMAN AL-SARRA.

Saudi Arabian Standards Organization Information Centre: POB 3437, Riyadh 11471; tel. (1) 452-0000; fax (1) 452-0086; f. 1972; 10,000 vols, 650,000 nat., int. and foreign standards; Dir MOHAMMAD ALMESHARI.

Museums

Al-Ahsa

Al-Hafouf Museum: Al-Ahsa; tel. (3) 580-2639; f. 1991; regional folklore and archaeological collns.

Al-Baha

Al-Baha Museum: Al-Baha; tel. (7) 725 5251; fax (7) 725-5212; f. 2003; regional archaeological and heritage collns.

Al-Jouf

Al-Jouf Museum: Al-Jouf; tel. (4) 622 2151; f. 2004; regional archaeological collns; next to ancient Mraid Castle.

Al-Ola

Museum of Al-Ola Antiquities: Medina Al-Munwarrah, Al-Ola; tel. (4) 884-1536; fax (4) 884-1536; f. 1991; archaeological colln.

Dammam

Dammam Museum: Dammam 31158; tel. (3) 826-6056; e-mail offica18@school.adst.net; f. 1985; antiquities and heritage collns.

Hail

Al Qushlah Museum: Hail; tel. (6) 533-1684; f. 2004; regional archaeological collns.

Jazan

Jazan Museum: Jazan province, Subia; tel. (7) 326-1193; f. 1991; regional archaeological collns; next to Al-Adareisa archaeological site.

Jeddah

Al-Khozam Palace Museum: Jeddah; tel. (2) 636-4271; fax (2) 636-4271; f. 1995; Saudi history from Stone Age to Islamic Age; folklore colln.

Najran

Najran Museum: Al-Okhdood; f. 1995; housed on archaeological site of ancient city of Najran; regional folklore and archaeological collns; restoration laboratory.

Riyadh

National Museum, Riyadh: POB 3734 Riyadh 11481; tel. (1) 403-0104; fax (1) 404-1391; f. 1999; Saudi history, archaeology, geology, trade, social life and ethnography, and man's relationship with the Universe; Dir-Gen. Dr ALI SALEH AL-MOGHANNAM.

Taif

Shobrah Palace Museum: Taif; tel. (2) 732-1033; f. 1995; Saudi history from Stone Age to Islamic Age.

Universities

AL-FAISAL UNIVERSITY

POB 50927, Riyadh 11533
Telephone: (1) 440-2000
Fax: (1) 462-3508
E-mail: info@alfaisal.edu
Internet: www.alfaisal.edu
Founded 2004
Private control
Academic year: September to July

Provost: Dr FAISAL ALMUBARAK (acting)
Vice-Pres. for Research and Graduate Studies: Dr MATHEUS GOOSEN
Vice-Pres. for Advancement: Prof. AHMED AL OBAID (acting)
Dean for Student Affairs: Dr MOHAMMED ALOWAYED
Vice-Provost for Accreditation and Quality Assurance: Prof. ALA AL-BAKRI
Librarian: Prof. THOMAS L. WILLIAMS

DEANS

College of Business: Dr EARL NAUMANN
College of Engineering: Dr ABDULMAJEED MOHAMMED
College of Medicine: Prof. KHALED AL-KATTAN
College of Science and General Studies: Dr NORMAN SWAZO

AL-IMAM MUHAMMAD IBN SAUD ISLAMIC UNIVERSITY

POB 5701, Riyadh 11432
Telephone: (1) 258-0812
Fax: (1) 259-0271
E-mail: admission@imamu.edu.sa
Internet: www.imamu.edu.sa
Founded 1953, Univ. status 1974
State control
Language of instruction: Arabic
Academic year: August to June

Rector: HE Prof. Dr SULIMAN A. ABA AL-KHAIL
Vice-Rector: Dr ABDULLAH ASH-SHETHRY
Vice-Rector for Sharia Institute Affairs: Dr BANDAR F. AS-SUWAILAM
Vice-Rector for Higher Studies and Scientific Research: Dr ABDULLAH H. AL-KHALAF
Vice-Rector for Studies, Devt, and Academic Accreditation: Dr ABDUR-RAHMAN H. AD-DAWUD
Vice-Rector for Community Service and Continuing Education: AHMAD Y. A. AD-DRIWEESH (acting)
Vice-Rector for Female Student Affairs: Dr KHALID SAAD AL-MEGREN
Dean of Academic Research: Dr ABDULLAH IBN ABDULLRAHMAN AL-RABEE
Dean of Admissions and Registrations: Dr SAAD A. AL-GUSAIBY
Dean of Admissions and Students Affairs in Qassim: Dr MEZAYAD IBN IBRAHIM AL-MEZAYAD
Dean of Admissions and Students Affairs in the South: Dr SAAD IBN HUSAIN OTHMAN
Dean of Higher Studies: Dr KHALID A. AL-MESHAL
Dean of Institute Affairs Abroad: Dr IBRAHIM A. AS-SAADAN

Dean of Libraries: Dr MUSAED S. AT-TAIYAR
Dean of Students: Dr MEGREN S. AL-MEGREN
Dean of Univ. Centre for Community Service and Continuing Education: Dr ABDULLAH M. AR-REZAIN
Number of teachers: 1,648
Number of students: 39,938

DEANS AND DIRECTORS

Arabic Language Teaching Institute (Riyadh): Dr ABDULAZIZ I. AL-ESAILY
College of Arabic Language: Dr MOHAMMED A. AS-SEHABEAIN
College of Arabic and Social Sciences (Qassim): Dr MOHAMMAD IBN SULAIMAN-RAJHI
College of Arabic and Social Sciences (in the South): Dr ALI IBN MUHAMMAD ARISH
College of Computer and Information: Dr ABDULLAH A. AT-TAMIM (acting)
College of Dawa and Mass Communication: Dr ABDULLAH AL-MAJALY
College of Economics and Administrative Sciences: Dr KHALID AL-MEGREN
College of Fundamentals of Religion: Dr FAHD S. AL-FUHAID
College of Islamic Law and Fundamentals of Religion (in the South): Dr ABDULAZIZ IBN ALI AL-GHAMDI
College of Islamic Call Dawa (Medina): Dr MOSTAFA IBN OMAR HALABI
College of Islamic Law and Fundamentals of Religion (Al-Qassim): Dr ABDUL RAHMAN AL-MEZAINI (acting)
College of Language and Translation: Dr MOHAMMED S. AL-ALAM
College of Medicine: Prof. Dr KHALID A. AL-ABDUL-RAHMAN
College of Science: Dr MOHAMMED A. AL-QADI (acting)
College of Sharia and Islamic Studies (Al-Ihsa): Dr MOHAMMED A. AL-JABR
College of Social Science: Dr FAWZAN A. AL-FAWAZAN
Female University Study Centre: Dr MOHAMMED I. AL-AJLAN
Sharia College: Dr ABDULLAH E. AL-ESA
Supreme Jurisdiction Institute: Dr ABDULLAH AS-SELAMAY (acting)

AL-YAMAMAH UNIVERSITY

POB 45180, Riyadh 11512
Telephone: (1) 224-2222
Fax: (1) 224-1111
E-mail: info@alyamamah.edu.sa
Internet: www.yu.edu.sa

Founded 2001 as Al-Yamamah College; Univ. status in 2008
Private control

Accredited by Saudi Ministry of Higher Education

Pres.: Dr AHMED M. AL-EISA (acting)
Vice-Pres. for Academic Affairs: Dr OWEN F. CARGOL
Dean of Women's College: Dr HESSAH M. AL-SHEIK
Dir of Student Affairs: RAMI AL-SHARAFEEN
Dir of Library: MOHAMMAD ASSIM

Colleges of Business Admin., Computing and IT.

ISLAMIC UNIVERSITY IN MEDINA

POB 170, Medina
Telephone: (1) 847-4080
Fax: (1) 827-4560
Internet: www.iu.edu.sa

Founded 1961
State control
Language of instruction: Arabic

Chancellor: Dr ABDULLAH BIN SALAH AL-ABID
Vice-Rector: ABDUL MUHSIN BEN HAMAD AL-ABBAD
Number of teachers: 620
Number of students: 3,140

DEANS

College of Prophet Sayings (Hadeith) and Islamic Studies: (vacant)
College of the Holy Koran and Islamic Studies: (vacant)
Faculty of Arabic Language: A. D. ABDUL RAZAK BIN FARRAJ ALSAIDI
Faculty of Dawa and the Fundamentals of Islam: (vacant)
Faculty of Islamic Law (Sharia): D. AHMED ABDULLAH

JAZAN UNIVERSITY

POB 114, Jazan
Telephone: (7) 321-0869
Fax: (7) 321-1052
Internet: www.jazanu.edu.sa

Founded 2006
State control

Pres.: Prof. MOHAMMED A. AL-HAYAZA (acting)

Faculties of applied medical science, architecture and design, arts and humanities, business administration, computer and information systems, dentistry, education, engineering, health sciences, medicine, pharmacy, science, science and arts (in Al-Darb, Farasan, Samtah); Girls faculty of health sciences, Community college.

KING ABDULAZIZ UNIVERSITY

POB 1026, Jeddah 21441
Telephone: (2) 695-1995
Fax: (2) 640-5974
Internet: www.kau.edu.sa

Founded 1967
State control
Languages of instruction: Arabic, English
Academic year: September to June

Pres.: Prof. USAMA SADIQ TAYEB
Vice-Pres.: (vacant)
Vice-Pres. for Graduate Studies and Academic Research: Prof. FOUAD M. GHAZALI
Vice-Pres. for Post-Graduate Studies and Scientific Research: Prof. ABDULLA OMAR BAFAIL
Supervisor-Gen. for Admin. and Financial Affairs: Dr SAMIR A. MURSHID
Librarian: Dr MOFAKHAR H. KHAN

Library of 500,000 vols
Number of teachers: 1,145
Number of students: 30,773

Publication: research publs, bulletins

DEANS

Faculty of Applied Medical Sciences: Prof. GHAZI DAMANHOURI
Faculty of Arts and Humanities: Dr M. A. ABOZEID
Faculty of Computing and Information Technology: A. D. KHALID BIN ABDULLAH FAKIH
Faculty of Dentistry: Prof. TAREK LOUTFI AL-KHATEEB
Faculty of Earth Sciences: Prof. MOHAMMED R. MOUFTI
Faculty of Economics and Administration: Prof. HUSSAM A. AL-ANGARI
Faculty of Education: Dr A. I. HAFIZ
Faculty of Engineering: Dr FAISAL ISKANDERANI
Faculty of Marine Sciences: Dr O. A. HASHIM
Faculty of Medicine: Dr ADNAN ABDULLA ALMAZROA
Faculty of Meteorology, Environment and Arid Land Agriculture: Dr ABDUL REHMAN KHALAF M. AL-KHALAF
Faculty of Pharmacy: Dr HISHAM A. M. MOSLI
Faculty of Science: Prof. ABDULLAH YOUSIF ABDULLAH OBAID

PROFESSORS

Faculty of Arts and Humanities:
AL-BAGHDADI, M. M., Arabic Literature
AL-DIGS, K. S., Islamic Literature
AL-JERASH, M. A., Climatology and Quantitative Methods
AL-KHERIJI, A. M., Social Development
AL-ZEID, I. M., History
ANQAWI, A. A., Medieval Islamic History
BAGADER, A. A., Social Changes
OMER, M. Z., Modern History
TASHKANDI, A. S., Arabic Manuscripts

Faculty of Dentistry:
ABDULRAHMAN, A., Paediatric Dentistry
AL-JEYAR, I. L., Operative
AL-KHATEB, M. M., Fixed Prosthodontics
AL-SABBAGH, A. M., Oral Surgery
FARGHALY, M. M., Dental Public Health
KAMAR, A. A., Dental Biomaterials
KATALDO, A., Oral Pathology
MASOUD, A. J., Endodontics
MOHAMED, M. A., Operative
MOUSTAFA, M. A., Removable Prosthodontics, Partial Dentures
NADA, A. M., Removable Prosthodontics, Partial Dentures
OMAR, T. A., Oral Pathology
SAMAH, A., Paediatric Dentistry
SHARQAWI, M. M., Operative
SHOUKRY, M. M. S., Periodontics

Faculty of Earth Sciences:
ALLOUSH, M. A., Building Materials
AL-MAHDI, O. R., Mineral Resources
AL-NASSER, H. S., Geophysics
AL-SHANTI, A. M., Mineralogy
BASAHEL, A. N., Structural Geology
MARZOUKI, M. H., Petrology and Mineralogy
NASSIEF, A. O., Petrology and Mineralogy
RADEEN, A. A., Petrology and Mineralogy
SHAREEF, F. A., Petroleum and Stratigraphy
SHEHATA, W. M., Engineering Geology

Faculty of Economics and Administration:
AL-AMRI, B. O., Civil Law
AL-SOBIANI, A. A., Administration and Management Planning
ALAKI, M. A., Administration and Management Relations
AL-JEFRI, Y. A., Business Administration
ALSABBAB, A. A., Administration and Management Relations
BAIOUMI, A. M., Cost and Management Accounting
BAMOKHRAMA, A. S., Economics
FADEL, S. Y., International Relations
HASANAIN, O. S., Cost Accounting
MADANI, G. O., Finance and Investment
OMRAN, O. A., Law
SOFI, A. A., Financial Administration
ZA'ED, M. E., Cost Accounting
ZOBAIR, M. O., Monetary Theory

Faculty of Education:
ABDULRADHI, H. M., Physics and Theory
AL-MOJADDADI, M. H. M., Shariah and Legal System
AL-OQABI, A. H., Modern History
AL-SHATAIRI, B. A., Chemistry
BADAWI, A. A., History
BADAWI, F. A., Ancient History
BAMASHMOOS, S. M., Educational Planning
BEDAIR, A. H. M., Biochemistry
HAMID, M. A. I., Weaving
HASSAN, N. M. A., Psychology
JALLOON, A. D., Archery
KHALIL, M. S. M., Fish Anatomy
KHATIR, K. I. M., Tradition of the Prophet
KHOGALI, M. M., Human Geography
MADBROOK, N. A., Principles of Language
REDWAN, M. N., Wrestling
SHAIKH, A. A., English Language Teaching Methods
SHEHATAH, M. N., Entomology

Faculty of Engineering:
- ABD. EL-LATIF, A. K., Mechanical Design and Stress Analysis
- ABDEL RAHMAN, M. M., Aerodynamics
- ABDIN, M. F., Metrology and Advanced Manufacturing Technology
- ABDUL-MAJID, S., Nuclear Instrumentation
- ABOKHASHABA, A., Metal Cutting and Spare Parts
- ABOLANIN, G. M., Heat and Energy Transfer
- ABOLFARAJ, W. H., Industrial Engineering
- ABORAZIZAH, O. S., Civil Engineering
- AHMED, K. M., Structure and Construction
- AKYURT, M., Mechanisms and Robotics
- AL-IDRISI, M. M., Operational Research
- AL-NOURY, S. I., Structure
- ALP, T. Y., Physical Metallurgy
- ALY, S. E., Desalination Technology and Two-Phase Flow
- AWAD, A. E., Biotechnology, Floriculture
- DARWISH, M. A., Rock Blasting
- ELGILLANI, D. A., Mineral Processing and Metallurgy
- EL-NAGGAR, M. M., Extractive Metallurgy
- FATHALAH, K., Heat and Mass Transfer
- FATTAH, A. A., Nuclear Reactor Safety and Nuclear Desalination
- FOUAD, A. A., Nuclear Desalination
- GHAZALI, F. M., Geotechnics
- HAQUE, M. Z., Mine Management and Mining Law
- KUTBI, I. I., Nuclear Desalination
- MOHAMED, S. E., Electrical Power Engineering
- NAHHAS, M. N., Aviation Engineering
- MOUSSA, H. A., Electrical Power Engineering
- NAHHAS, M. N., Aviation Engineering
- NAJJAR, Y., Gas Turbines, Engines and Energy Systems
- NAWAIR, M. H., Human Factors
- RAIH, M. A., Aviation Engineering
- RUSHDI, A. M., Computer Engineering and Electrical Communication
- SABBAGH, J. A., Heat and Energy Transfer
- WAFA, F. F., Structural Engineering
- WANAS, M. A., Electronics
- YORULMAZ, Y. K., Petroleum Refining and Petrochemicals

Faculty of Marine Sciences:
- AHMAD, F., Residual and Tidal Currents
- BEHAIRY, A. K. A., Modern Marine Sediments
- EL-NAKKADI, A. N., Biochemistry
- KHAFAJI, A. K., Marine Plant Physiology
- NIAZ, G. R., Marine Biochemistry

Faculty of Medicine and Allied Sciences:
- ABDULMONAM, N. A., Community Medicine
- AHMAD, A. O., Haematology
- AJABNOOR, M. A., Biochemistry
- AL-ARDAWI, M. S., Biochemistry
- AL-AWWAD, A. M., Chemistry
- AL-BADWI, A. A., Surgery
- AL-JOHARI, K. M., Anatomy
- AL-KHATEEB, A. M., Physics
- AL-MATRAWI, U. M., Parasitology
- AL-QADASI, A. A., Biochemistry
- AL-SHAIKH, S. A., Paediatrics
- ALI, F. M., Medical Technology
- ATTALLAH, A. A., Physiology
- BASALAMAH, A. H., Obstetrics and Gynaecology
- FATANI, H. H., Medicine
- ISLAM, S. I., Pharmacology
- KHAN, N. M., Anatomy
- MATIX, F. A., Microbiology
- MUKHTAR, A. M., Surgery
- OSMAN, O. O., Pharmacology
- RAFFAH, H. M., Surgery
- RAZIK, S. M., Surgery
- SAJINEE, S. A., Haematology
- SALAMA, H. S., Biology
- SALMAN, KH. M., Surgery
- SHARIF, M. A., Radiology
- SHARIF, M. T., Anatomy
- SHOBOKSHI, O. A., Medicine
- SIRAJ, A. A., E.N.T.
- SOLIMAN, S. A., Chemistry
- SUKKAR, M. Y., Physiology
- SULAIMAN, N. K., Community Medicine
- TAYEB, O. S., Pharmacology
- TILMISANY, A. M., Pharmacology
- YOUSIF, K. M., Surgery
- ZAFAR, M. N., Radiology
- ZAHRAN, F. M., E.N.T.

Faculty of Meteorology, Environment and Arid Land Agriculture:
- ABDURAZZAK, M. G., Water Resources
- ABOHASSAN, A. A., Forest Management
- AL-HASHIM, G. M., Environmental Toxicology and Health
- AL-HIFNY, A. M., Entomology (Bees)
- ARAFA, A. S., Environmental Health
- EL-AGAMY, S. A., Horticulture
- GOKNIL, M. H., Air Pollution
- SAMARRAI, S. M., Genetics and Plant Breeding
- SHAHEEN, M. A., Genetics and Fruit Breeding

Faculty of Science:
- ABOU-ZAID, A. A., Fermentation
- AHMAD, I., Theoretical Nuclear Physics
- AL-DESSOUKI, T. A., Laser Optics
- ALHARBI, M. A., Theoretical Nuclear Physics
- AL-SAYAD, G. M., Statistics
- BAESHIN, N. A., Genetics
- BANAGAH, A. A., Parasitology
- BAGHLAF, A. O., Chemistry
- BASAHEL, S. N., Chemistry
- ELDIN, H. M., Environmental Microbiology
- EL-MASHAK, E. M., Biophysics
- EZMIRLI, T. S., Chemistry
- FARAG, A. A., Vertebrate Zoology
- GHANEM, K. M., Biotechnology
- KHOJA, S. M., Enzymes and Metabolic Regulation
- MAGHRABI, Y. M., Plant Physiology
- MELIBARI, A. A., Biology
- RAFI, M., Experimental Molecular Physics
- SABBAK, O. A., Chemistry
- SAHAB, S. M., Mathematics
- SEJINI, M. J., Plant Pathology
- SHAHAB, F., Theoretical Particle Physics
- SOLEIMAN, A. H., Chemistry
- TAHER, M. O., Entomology (Bionomics)
- TAWFIK, K. A., Plant Pathology

ATTACHED RESEARCH INSTITUTES

Centre of Excellence in Environmental Studies: POB 80216, Jeddah 21589; tel. (2) 640-0200; fax (2) 640-2000; e-mail cees@kau.edu.sa; Dir GHAZI A. JAMJOOM.

Centre of Excellence In Genomic Medicine Research: POB 80216, Jeddah 21589; tel. (2) 640-1000; fax (2) 695-2521; e-mail cegmr.info@kau.edu.sa; internet www.kau.edu.sa/centers/cegmr; Exec. Dir Dr MOHAMMED H. ALQAHTANI.

Centre for Nanotechnology: POB 80216, Jeddah 21589; tel. (2) 695-1399; fax (2) 695-1566; e-mail cnt@kau.edu.sa; Dir Dr SAMI S. HABIB.

FAH Research Centre: POB 80202, Jeddah 21589; tel. (2) 695-2353; fax (2) 695-1732; e-mail rca_kaau@hotmail.com; internet www.kau.edu.sa/rca/rca; Pres. Dr AYMAN BIN ABDULLAH HABIS.

Islamic Economics Research Centre: POB 80214, Jeddah 21589; tel. (2) 695-2751; fax (2) 695-2404; e-mail cn-crie@kau.edu.sa; Dir Dr M. A. ELGARI.

King Fahd Medical Research Centre: POB 80216, Jeddah 21589; tel. (2) 640-0000; fax (2) 695-2076; e-mail kfmrc@kau.edu.sa; internet www.kau.edu.sa/kfmrc; Dir GHAZI A. JAMJOOM (acting).

Water Research Centre: POB 80160, Jeddah 21589; tel. (2) 695-2507; fax (2) 695-1403; e-mail wrc@kau.edu.sa; internet wrc.kau.edu.sa; Dir Dr ABDULLAH S. AL-GHAMDI.

KING ABDULLAH UNIVERSITY OF SCIENCE AND TECHNOLOGY

POB 55455, 4700 KAUST Thuwal 23955-6900

Internet: www.kaust.edu.sa

Founded 2009

Pres.: CHOON FONG SHIH
Provost: BRIAN MORAN
Dir of Libraries: JOSEPH J. BRANIN

Library of 25,000 books, 2,000 journals (incl. 1,500 e-journals), 10 online research databases

DEANS

Chemical and Life Sciences and Engineering: KEN MINNEMAN
Mathematical and Computer Sciences and Engineering: DAVID KEYES
Physical Sciences and Engineering: (vacant):

KING FAHD UNIVERSITY OF PETROLEUM AND MINERALS

POB 5082, Dhahran 31261
Telephone: (3) 860-0000
Fax: (3) 860-3018
E-mail: registrar@kfupm.edu.sa
Internet: www.kfupm.edu.sa

Founded 1963, Univ. status 1975
State control with semi-autonomous operation under a Board of the Univ.
Languages of instruction: English, Arabic
Academic year: September to June (summer semester: June to August)

Chair. of Board of Trustees: HE The Minister of Higher Education Dr KHALID M. AL-ANGARY
Rector: HE Dr KHALID S. AL-SULTAN
Vice-Rectors: Dr ABDULAZIZ A. AL-SUWAYAN (Academic Affairs), Dr SALEH N. ABDULJAUWAD (Applied Research and Scientific Research and Graduate Studies), Dr FALEH ABDULLAH AL-SULAIMAN (Technology Devt and Industrial Relations)
Dean, Admissions and Registration: Dr MAMDOUH M. NAJJAR
Dean of Library Affairs: Dr IBRAHIM M. AL-JABRI

Library of 355,700 vols
Number of teachers: 950
Number of students: 8,155

Publication: *Arabian Journal for Science and Engineering* (6 a year)

DEANS

Computer Science and Engineering: Dr UMAR AL-TURKI
Dammam Community College: TARIQ AL-JUFRI
Educational Services: Dr MUHAMMAD S. AL-MULHEM
Engineering Sciences and Applied Engineering: Dr SAMIR A. AL-BAIYAT
Environmental Design: Dr ABDULAZIZ BUBSHAIT
Industrial Management: Dr AREF A. AL-ASHBAN
Sciences: Dr WALID S. AL-SABAHI
Scientific Research: Dr OSAMA A. JANNADI
Graduate Studies: Dr OSAMA A. JANNADI

KING FAISAL UNIVERSITY

POB 380, Al-Hassa 31982
and POB 1982, Dammam 31441
Telephone: (Dammam) (3) 587-7000

Fax: (Dammam) (3) 587-6748
Telephone: (Al-Hassa) (3) 850-0000
Fax: (Al-Hassa) (3) 580-1243
Internet: www.kfu.edu.sa

Founded 1975
State control
Languages of instruction: Arabic, English
Academic year: September to June

Pres.: Prof. Dr YUSSUF M. AL-GINDAN
Vice-Pres.: Dr ABDULAZIZ AL-SAATI (Dammam)
Vice-Pres. for Academic Affairs: Dr SAAD M. AL-HAREKY (Al-Hassa)
Vice-Pres. for Graduate Studies and Scientific Research: Dr ABDULLAH I. AL-SAADAT (Al-Hassa)
Sec.-Gen.: Dr SAAD MUHAMMAD AL-HAREKY
Librarian: Dr FADEL M. HOUSAWI (Al-Hassa)

Number of teachers: 717
Number of students: 12,880

Publications: *Basic and Applied Sciences* (2 a year), *Humanities and Management Sciences* (2 a year)

DEANS

College of Agricultural and Food Sciences (Al-Hassa): Dr ABDULLAH S. AL-GAMDI
College of Applied and Community Service (Al-Hassa): Dr ADNAN AL-MULHIM
College of Applied Medical Sciences (Dammam): Dr BASIL A. AL-SHIAKH
College of Architecture and Planning (Dammam): Dr MOHAMMAD MASOUD AL-ABDULLAH
College of Clinical Pharmacy (Al-Hassa): Dr AHMED A. AL-SHAOIBY
College of Computer Science and Information Tecnology (Al-Hassa): Dr BADIR AL-GOHAR
College of Dentistry (Dammam): Dr ABDULSALAM A. AL-SULIAMAN
College of Education (Al-Hassa): Dr MOHAMMAD AL-OMARE
College of Management Sciences and Planning (Al-Hassa): Dr HASSAN AL-HAJHOOJ
College of Medicine (Al-Hassa): Dr ALI AL-SULTAN
College of Medicine (Dammam): Dr ABDULLAH M. AL-ROBIASH
College of Nursing (Dammam): Dr NAIF I. AL-AWAAD
College of Science (Al-Hassa): Dr SHAR A. AL-SHIHRY
College of Veterinary Medicine and Animal Resources (Al-Hassa): Dr ABDULLAH AL-AZRAGY

KING KHALID UNIVERSITY

Abha 418, Asir Province
Telephone: (7) 339-0641
Fax: (7) 339-0531
E-mail: kku@kku.edu.sa
Internet: www.kku.edu.sa

Founded 1998
State control

Rector: Dr ABDULLAH AL-RASHID

Faculties of Arabic Language, Computer Science, Dentistry, Engineering, Science and Sharia Law; Colleges of Education, Medicine and Medicinal Science and Pharmacy; Institute of English and Translation.

KING SAUD UNIVERSITY

POB 2454, Riyadh 11451
Telephone: (1) 467-0000
Fax: (1) 467-8301
E-mail: rectoroffice@ksu.edu.sa
Internet: www.ksu.edu.sa

Founded 1957 as Riyadh Univ., present name 1982
State control
Language of instruction: Arabic (English in Medicine and Engineering)
Academic year: October to June

Rector: Prof. ABDULLAH A. AL-OTHMAN
Vice-Rector: Prof. ABDULAZIZ SALEM AL-RUWAIS
Dean of Admissions and Registrations: Dr ABDULLAH AL-SALMAN
Dean of Student Affairs: Dr FAHED ABDULMUHSEN AL-MISNED (acting)
Dean of Library Affairs: Dr SULIMAN SALEH AL-AQLAA

Library: see Libraries and Archives
Number of teachers: 2,768
Number of students: 37,324

Publications: *Journal of King Saud University*, *Statistical Yearbook*

DEANS

Arabic Language Institute: Dr NASSER A. ALGHALI
College of Administrative Sciences: Dr ABDULLAH BIN MOHAMMAD AL-FAISAL
College of Agriculture and Veterinary Medicine: Dr AHMED BIN ALI AL-RUGEIBAH
College of Applied Medical Sciences: Dr ABDULLAH Z. AL-OTAIBI
College of Applied Studies and Community Service: Dr FAHAD N. AL-FAHAD
College of Architecture and Planning: Prof. ABDUL AZIZ S. H. AL MOGREN
College of Arts: Dr FAHAD M. AL-KOLIBI
College of Arts and Sciences in Wady Addwaser: Dr MUBARAK MOHAMMED EL HAMAD
College of Business Administration: Dr AHMED BIN SALEM AL AMERI
Centre of Female Scientific and Medical Colleges: Dr AMAL JAMIL FATANI
College of Computer and Information Sciences: Dr SAMI SALEH AL-WAKEEL
College of Dentistry: Prof. ABDULLAH S. AL-YAHYA
College of Education: KAHID BIN FAHAD AL-HUTHAIFI
College of Engineering: Prof. ABDULAZIZ A.AL-HMAID
College of Engineering in Al-Kharj: Dr AWAD KH. AL-ASMARI
College of Food and Agricultural Sciences: Dr HASSAN A. AL-KAHTANI
College of Languages: Dr SAAD ALHASHASH
College of Law and Political Science: Dr FAHAD HAMOUD ALANAZI
College of Medicine: Prof. MUSSAAD AL-SALMAN
College of Medicine in Al-Kharj: Prof. ABDULLAH M. AL-BEKAIRI
College of Nursing: Dr MOHAMMED S. AL-NAIF
College of Pharmacy: Dr YOSEF A. ASIRI
College of Pharmacy in Al-Kharj: Dr SALEH I. ALQASOUMI
College of Science: Prof. AWAD BIN MUTAIRIK AL-JOHANI
College of Science and Humanitarian Studies in Al-Kharj: Dr ABDULRAHMAN AL-KHEDHAIRI
College of Higher Studies: Dr AHMAD SULAIMAN AL-OBAID
College of Teaching: Prof. ALI ABDULLAH AL-AFNAN
College of Tourism and Archaeology: Prof. SAID AL-SAID
Community College in Al-Afalj: Dr RASHED BEN MUBARAK AL-RUSHOUD
Community College in Al-Majma'ah: Dr ABDULLAH ALDAHASH
Community College of Al-Quawyiyah: Dr NASER OREIFI
Community College in Al-Riyadh: Prof. SAAD M. ALSHEHRI
Olyashah Centre for Girls: Dr JAZI BINT MOHAMMED BIN FAHD ALCBIKI

KING SAUD UNIVERSITY FOR HEALTH SCIENCES

Riyadh
Telephone: (1) 252-0088
Internet: www.ksau-hs.edu.sa

Founded 2008
Campuses in Jeddah and Al-Hassa

Pres.: Dr BANDAR ABDULMOHSEN AL-KNAWY (acting)
Vice-Pres. for Academic Affairs: Prof. YOUSEF ABDULLAH AL-EISSA
Vice-Pres. for Postgraduate Education: Prof. RASHED SULAIMAN AL-RASHED
Dean of Student Affairs: Prof. ALI SULAIMAN AL-TUWAIJRI

DEANS

College of Applied Medical Sciences: MOHAMMAD ABDULLAH AL-KHAZIM
College of Medicine (Jeddah): Dr HASSAN SAEED BA'AQEEL
College of Nursing (Al-Hassa): Dr ABDULATIF ABDULLAH AL-FARAID
College of Nursing (Jeddah): Dr WAFIKA ABDULRAHEM SULAIMAN
College of Nursing (Riyadh): Dr HAYA MOHAMMAD AL-FOZAN
College of Public Health and Health Informatics: Dr MAJID MOHAMMED AL-TUWAIJRI

NAIF ARAB UNIVERSITY FOR SECURITY SCIENCES

POB 6830, Riyadh 11452
Telephone: (1) 246-3444
Fax: (1) 246-4713
E-mail: info@nauss.edu.sa
Internet: www.nauss.edu.sa.

PRINCE MOHAMMAD BIN FAHD UNIVERSITY

POB 1664, Al-Khobar 31952
E-mail: info@pmu.edu.sa
Internet: www.pmu.edu.sa

Founded 2006
Private control

Rector: Dr ISSA AL-ANSARI (acting)
Vice-Rector for Academic Affairs: Dr NASSAR M. SHAIKH
Vice-Rector for Business Devt: Dr MASHARY AL-NAIM
Dir of Libraries: Dr JAMIL AHMAD QURESHY

BSc and Masters degree level; Colleges of Business, Engineering, IT.

PRINCE SULTAN UNIVERSITY

POB 66833, Riyadh 11586
Telephone: (1) 494-8000
Fax: (1) 454-8317
E-mail: info@psu.edu.sa
Internet: www.psu.edu.sa

Founded 1999 as Prince Sultan Private College; Univ. status in 2003
Private control

Rector: Dr AHMED AL-YAMANI (acting)
Vice-Rector for Academic Affairs: Dr ABDUL HAFEEZ FEDA
Vice-Rector for Admin. and Financial Affairs: Dr SAAD SALEH AL-RWAITA
Dean of College for Women: Dr FADIA SAUD ALSALEH
Dir of Libraries: Prof. Dr FOUAD H. R. FARSUNI

DEANS

College of Business Admin.: Dr YAHYA N. AL-SERHAN
College of Computer and Information Sciences: Dr ELTAYEB SALIH ABUELYAMAN

QASSIM UNIVERSITY

POB 6677, Buraydah, Qassim 51452
Telephone: (6) 380-3373
Fax: (6) 380-1152
E-mail: syhya@qec.edu.sa
Internet: www.qu.edu.sa

Founded 2004

Number of students: 40,000

Colleges of Agricultural and Veterinary Sciences, Applied Medical Sciences, Arabic and Social Sciences, Computer Science, Dentistry, Economics, Engineering, Medicine, Pharmacy, Science, Sharia; Community Colleges, Girls' Education Colleges.

TAIBAH UNIVERSITY

Madinah
Telephone: (4) 846-0008
Fax: (4) 846-0020
E-mail: dar@taibahu.edu.sa
Internet: www.taibahu.edu.sa

Pres.: Prof. MANSOUR BIN MOHAMMED AL-NOUZHA (acting)

Vice-Pres. for Academic Affairs: Dr OSAMAH BIN ISMAEL ABDULAZIZ

Vice-Pres. for Graduate Studies and Research: Prof. TALA BIN OMAR HALAWANI

Colleges of Applied Medical Sciences, Computer Science and Engineering, Dentistry, Education, Engineering, Finance and Admin., Medicine, Pharmacy, Science.

UMM AL-QURA UNIVERSITY

POB 715, Mecca
Telephone: (2) 557-4644
Fax: (2) 556-4560
E-mail: info@uqu.edu.sa
Internet: www.uqu.edu.sa

Founded 1979 from existing faculties of King Abdulaziz Univ.

Rector: Prof. WALEED HUSSAIN ABULFARAJ

Deputy Rector: Dr HASHIM BAKR MOHAMMED HARIRI

Deputy Rector for Graduate Studies and Scientific Research: Prof. HASHIM BAKR MOHAMMED HARIRI

Dean of Admission and Registration: Dr ABDULLAH AHMED ABDULLAH

Dean of Graduate Studies: Dr THAMIR HAMDAN JABIR AL-HARBI

Dean of Libraries Affairs: Dr ADNAN MOHAMMED FAIZ AL-HARTHI

Dean of Students Affairs: Dr SALIH HASAN AL-MAB'UTH

Library of 450,000 vols

Number of teachers: 1,408

Number of students: 32,000

Publications: *Journal of Arabic Language and Sharia Sciences*, *Journal of Engineering, Medicine and Applied Sciences*, *Journal of Social Sciences and Education*

DEANS

Faculty of Applied Sciences: Dr AHMED ALI AL-KHAMMASH

Faculty of Arabic Language and Literature: Dr ABDULLAH NASIR AL-GARNI

Faculty of Dawa: Dr ABDULLAH OMAR AL-DUMEIGI

Faculty of Education (Makkah): Dr ZOHAIR AHMED ALI AL-KADMI

Faculty of Education (Taif): Dr SUBHI ABDUL-HAFEEZ QADI

Faculty of Engineering and Islamic Architecture: Dr TARIG MOHAMMAD AHMED NAHAAS

Faculty of Medicine and Medical Studies: Prof. ABDUL-RAZZAG MOHAMMED NUR SULTAN

Faculty of Science (Taif): Dr BAKHIT NAFIE AL-MATRAFI

Faculty of Sharia and Islamic Studies: Dr SAUD IBRAHIM AL- SHEREAM

Faculty of Social Sciences: Dr AHMED YAHIA AL-GHAMDI

Institute of the Custodian of the Two Holy Mosques for Haj Research: Dr USAMA FADL AL-BAR

Institute of Scientific Research and Revival of Islamic Heritage: MOHAMMED HAMZA AL-SULEIMANI

Institute of Teaching Arabic for Non-native Speakers: Dr SALIH KHAILD DERRI

ATTACHED CAMPUS

Umm Al-Qura University, Taif Campus

Al-Saddad Rd, Shihar, Taif
Telephone: (2) 749-1917
Fax: (2) 746-3008

Founded 1981

Pres.: Dr RASHID BIN RAJIH

Vice-Pres.: Dr MUHAMMAD IBRAHIM AHMED ALI, Higher Studies and Research: Dr SAAD AL-SOBAI, Finance and Admin.

Registrar: ALI F. AL-FAER

Librarian: MOHD ADIL USMANI

Library of 50,000 vols

Number of teachers: 90

Number of students: 2,000

DEANS

Faculty of Education: Dr ABDULLAH ABDUL KARIM AL-ABBADI

Faculty of Library Studies: Dr HAMMAD MUHAMMAD AL-SOMALI

UNIVERSITY OF HA'IL

Ha'il City
Telephone: (6) 531-2500
Fax: (6) 531-0900
E-mail: al-ghazi@uoh.edu.sa
Internet: www.uoh.edu.sa

Founded 1998 as Ha'il Community College; Univ. status in 2005

Rector: Dr AHMED M. AL-SAIF (acting)

Vice-Rector for Academic Affairs: Dr MOHAMMAD A. AL-NAAFA

Dir of Admissions: SAUD ABDULLAH AL-GAHZI

Number of students: 16,000

DEANS

College of Computer Science and Engineering: Dr SALAH A. ZUGAIL

College of Engineering: Dr MOHAMMAD A. AL-NAAFA

College of Sciences: Dr ALI A. AL-QARAWI

Institutes of Higher Education

College of Business Administration: POB 110200, Jeddah 21361; tel. (2) 215-9000; fax (2) 656-3175; e-mail info@cba.edu.sa; internet www.cba.edu.sa; Private control; degree level; Dean Prof. HUSSEIN AL-ALAWI.

Dar Al-Hekma College: POB 34801, Jeddah 21478; tel. (2) 630-3333; e-mail officeofthedean@dah.edu.sa; internet www.daralhekma.edu.sa; private control; f. 1999; accredited by Accrediting Ccl for Ind. Colleges and Schools; to Bachelor degree level; Dean Dr SUHAIR HASSAN AL-QURASHI.

Dr Soliman Fakeeh College for Nursing and Medical Science: POB 2537, Jeddah 21461; tel. (2) 665-5000; fax (2) 660-4332; e-mail college@drfakeehhospital.com; internet www.dsf-nursingcollege.com; private control; f. 2003; women's nursing college to Bachelor degree level; Chair. Dr MAZIN FAKEEH.

Effat College: POB 34689, Jeddah 21478; tel. (2) 636-4300; fax (2) 637-7447; e-mail admissions@effatcollege.edu.sa; internet www.effatcollege.edu.sa; private control; degree level; colleges of business, engineering, humanities and social sciences; Dean Dr HAIFA JAMAL AL-LAIL.

English Language Teaching Institute: POB 58012, Al Mousa Bldg, Olaya Main Rd, Riyadh 11594; tel. (1) 462-1818; fax (1) 462-0663; f. 1969 by Min. of Education and directed by the British Ccl; brs in Jeddah and Dammam; Direct Teaching Operations Man. KEVIN SMITH.

Ibn Sina National College for Medical Studies: Jeddah; tel. (2) 637-4566; fax (2) 637-6630; internet www.ibnsina.edu.sa; private control; under supervision of Ministry of Higher Education; MMS, BDS and Pharm-D qualifications; medicine, dentistry, pharmacy; Dean Dr RASHID HASSAN HABIBULLA KASHGARI.

Institute of Public Administration: POB 205, Riyadh 11141; tel. (1) 476-7305; fax (1) 479-2136; e-mail esl@ipa.edu.sa; internet www.ipa.edu.sa; f. 1961; conducts training courses for govt and private-sector employees; researches into and offers advice on admin. problems; Dir-Gen. HAMAD I. AL-SALLOOM; publ. *PA Journal* (4 a year, in Arabic).

Jeddah College of Technology: King Khaled St, Jeddah 17608; tel. (2) 637-0387; fax (2) 637-8376; internet www.jct.edu.sa.

Jeddah Health Institute: Jeddah; provides basic medical training; similar Institutes at Riyadh and Hofouf.

Jubail Industrial College: POB 10099, Jubail Industrial City 31961; tel. (3) 340-2000; fax (3) 341-1258; internet www.jic.edu.sa; f. 1982; private control; BSc degrees in chemical, electrical, mechanical engineering.

King Abdulaziz Military Academy: POB 5969, Riyadh; tel. (1) 465-4244; f. 1955; courses given in modern languages, incl. English, French and Hebrew, science and military subjects; library: 20,000 vols; 1,300 students; publ. *Journal*.

King Fahd Security College: POB 2511, Riyadh 11461; tel. (1) 246-4444; fax (1) 246-4320; internet www.kfsc.edu.sa.

Madrasat Ahl Al-Hadith: Mecca; f. 1933; the institute provides instruction in the Hadith, Koran, Fiqh, Tawheed and other Islamic religious studies; Prin. Sheikh MUHAMMAD ABDUL RAZZAQ; Sec. MUHAMMAD OMAR ABDULHADI.

Prince Sultan College of Tourism and Business: POB 7307, Jeddah 21462; tel. (2) 667-0110; fax (2) 668-5977; internet www.pscabha.edu.sa; private control, King Faisal Foundation; accredited by Ministry of Higher Education; BSc degrees in business admin., hospitality management, management information systems, travel and tourism.

Saad College of Nursing and Allied Health Sciences: POB 30353, Al-Khobar 31952; tel. (3) 801-3555; fax (3) 801-1940; e-mail college@saad.com.sa; internet www.saadcollege.com; private control, Saad Group; attached to Univ. of Ulster; Bachelor of Science nursing degree.

Technical Institute: Riyadh; f. 1964; 1,000 students.

Yanbu Industrial College: POB 30436, Madinat Yanbu Al-Sinaiyah; tel. (4) 394-6111; fax (4) 392-0213; e-mail yic.dir@rc-ynb.com; internet www.yic.edu.sa; f. 1989; engineering technology; library: 11,570 vols; 127 teachers; 1,400 students; Man. Dir BASSAM ABDULLAH YAMANI; Registrar HAMZA ATIK.

SENEGAL

The Higher Education System

Senegal was a French colony from the 17th century until independence was achieved in 1960. The first institution of higher education, a school of medicine, was founded in 1915; this later became an institute of higher education in 1950 and was incorporated into the new Université Cheikh Anta Diop de Dakar in 1957. Université Cheikh Anta Diop de Dakar is one of the three public universities, the others being Université de Saint-Louis (or Université de Gaston-Berger—founded 1990) and Université du Sahel (founded 1998). Other institutions of higher education, which mirror the French system, include schools of science and veterinary medicine, agriculture and health. In 2004/05 there were 59,100 students in tertiary education. Higher education is largely state funded, although some funding is provided by major international organizations such as USAID, the EU and the World Bank.

The secondary school Baccalauréat is the main qualification required for admission to higher education, although applicants without the Baccalauréat can sit an alternative entrance examination. University degrees are divided into three cycles, in accordance with the old French system. The first cycle is an undergraduate course of study lasting two years and leading to the award of one of the following diplomas, depending on the subject area: Diplôme Universitaire d'Études Littéraires (humanities), Diplôme Universitaire d'Études Scientifiques (sciences), Diplôme d'Études Juridiques Générales (law) and Diplôme d'Études Économiques Générales (economics). Alternatively, the École Nationale Supérieure de Technologie offers a two-year Diplôme Universitaire de Technologie. The second cycle follows the award of the Diplômes and is, first, a one-year programme of study culminating in the award of the Licence degree and, second, another year of study after the Licence leading to the award of the Maîtrise. In law and economics the Maîtrise is an integrated second-cycle degree awarded after two years, while in pharmacy, dentistry and medicine the first degrees are, respectively, Diplôme de Pharmacien, Diplôme de Docteur en Chirurgie Dentaire and Diplôme d'État de Docteur en Médecine. Finally, the third cycle consists of doctoral-level studies, leading to the award of Diplôme d'Études Approfondies after one year and Doctorat de Troisième Cycle after an additional two years. The highest doctoral-level degree is the Doctorat d'État, which is awarded following a minimum of two years research in law, economics, pharmacy, arts or science after the award of Doctorat de Troisième Cycle.

The primary qualification for post-secondary technical and vocational education is currently the Brevet de Technicien Supérieur en Maintenance.

Regulatory Bodies

GOVERNMENT

Ministry of Culture, Protected National Heritage, National Languages and Francophone Affairs: Bldg Administratif, ave Léopold Sédar Senghor, BP 4001, Dakar; tel. 33-822-4303; fax 33-822-1638; internet www.culture.gouv.sn; Minister MAME BIRAME DIOUF; Office Dir PAPE MASSÈNE SENE.

Ministry of Education: rue Docteur Calmette, BP 4025, Dakar; tel. 33-849-5454; fax 33-822-1463; internet www.education.gouv.sn; Minister Prof. MOUSTAPHA SOURANG.

Learned Societies

BIBLIOGRAPHY, LIBRARY SCIENCE AND MUSEOLOGY

Association Sénégalaise de Bibliothécaires, Archivistes et Documentalistes: ASBAD, BP 3252, Dakar; tel. 33-864-2773; fax 33-824-2379; internet www.ebad.ucad.sn/asbad; f. 1988; 200 mems; Pres. DJIBRIL NDIAYE; Sec. BERNARD DIONE; publ. *Canal I. S. T.* (3 a year).

EDUCATION

UNESCO Office Dakar and Regional Bureau for Education in Africa: BP 3311, Dakar; 12 ave L. S. Senghor, Dakar; tel. 33-823-8393; fax 33-849-2323; e-mail dakar@unesco.org; internet www.dakar.unesco.org; f. 1970; designated Cluster Office for Cape Verde, Gambia, Guinea, Guinea-Bissau, Liberia, Senegal and Sierra Leone; Dir ARMOOGUM PARSURAMEN.

LANGUAGE AND LITERATURE

Alliance Française: 3, Rue Parchappe, BP 1777, Dakar; tel. 33-821-0822; fax 33-822-1225; e-mail alliancefg@gamtel.gm; internet www.alliancefr-senegalgambie.org; offers courses and exams in French language and culture and promotes cultural exchange with France; attached teaching centres in Kaolack, St Louis, Tambacounda and Ziguinchor; also responsible for operations in Gambia; Dir of Office and of Operations in Senegal and Gambia SERGE AYASSE.

British Council: 34–36 Blvd de la République, Immeuble Sonatel, BP 6232, Dakar; tel. 33-822-2015; fax 33-821-8136; e-mail postmaster@britishcouncil.sn; internet www.britishcouncil.org/senegal; teaching centre; offers courses and examinations in English language and British culture and promotes cultural exchange with the UK; library of 3,500 vols; Dir ANDREW MCNAB.

Goethe-Institut: Rue de Diourbel angle Piscine Olympique, Dakar; tel. 33-869-8880; fax 33-825-1371; e-mail prog@dakar.goethe.org; internet www.goethe.de/dakar; f. 1978; offers courses and examinations in German language and culture and promotes cultural exchange with Germany; Dir UWE RIEKEN.

Research Institutes

GENERAL

Institut de Recherche pour le Développement, Centre de Dakar (IRD): BP 1386, Route des Pères Maristes, Dakar; tel. 33-832-3480; fax 33-832-4307; e-mail durand@orstom.sn; internet www.ird.sn; f. 1950; soil biology, pedology, medical entomology, hydrology, geology, nematology, demography, economics, zoology, botany, agronomy, geography, sociology, nutrition, marine fisheries, public health, tree viruses, vegetal ecology, geophysics, microbiology; library of 10,000 vols; Dir J. R. DURAND; (see main entry under France).

Institut Fondamental d'Afrique Noire Cheikh Anta Diop: BP 206, Université Cheikh Anta Diop de Dakar, Dakar; tel. 33-824-1652; fax 33-824-4918; e-mail bifan@ucad.sn; internet www.refer.sn; f. 1936, reconstituted 1959; scientific and humanistic studies on Black Africa; library and museums (see below); Dir DJIBRIL SAMB; publs *Bulletin de l'IFAN, Série A—Sciences Naturelles, Série B—Sciences Humaines, Notes Africaines* (4 a year), *Mémoires de l'IFAN, Initiations et Etudes Africaines*.

AGRICULTURE, FISHERIES AND VETERINARY SCIENCE

Institut Sénégalais de Recherches Agricoles (ISRA): BP 3120, Route des Hydrocarbures, Bel-Air, Dakar; tel. 33-832-2420; e-mail dgisra@isra.sn; internet www.isra.sn; f. 1974; research in all fields of agriculture, forestry and pisciculture; Dir Dr MOUSSA BAKHAYOKHU.

Attached Centres:

Centre de Recherche Agronomique de Djibélor: BP 34, Ziguinchor; tel. 33-991-1205; fax 33-991-1293; Dir SAMBA SALL.

Centre de Recherche Agronomique de Kaolack: BP 199, Kaolack; tel. 33-941-2916; fax 33-941-2902; Dir Dr MODOU SENE.

Centre de Recherche Agronomique de Saint-Louis: BP 240, Richard-Toll; tel. 33-961-1751; fax 33-961-1891; Dir Dr SIDY SECK.

Centre de Recherches Océanographiques de Dakar-Thiaroye (CRODT): BP 2241, Dakar; tel. 33-834-0536; f. 1956 for the study of oceanographic physics and biology; 67 scientists; library of 450 vols and 74 periodicals; Dir DIAFARA TOURE.

Centre de Recherches Zootechniques de Dahra-Djoloff: BP 01, Dahra-Djoloff; tel. 33-968-6111; fax 33-968-6271; f. 1950;

amelioration of local bovine and ovine breeds, rearing and cross-breeding; Dir TAMSIR DIOP.

Centre de Recherches Zootechniques de Kolda: BP 53, Kolda; tel. 33-996-1152; fax 33-996-1152; f. 1972; amelioration of local bovine and ovine breeds; fodder cultivation; Dir Dr DEMBA FARBA MBAYE.

Centre National de Recherches Agronomiques (CNRA): BP 53, Bambey; tel. 33-973-6050; fax 33-973-6052; f. 1921; applied agricultural research; stations at Louga and Thilmakha; 45 research mems; library of 6,700 vols; Dir Dr DOGO SECK; publs *Rapport de synthèse*, *Annuaire analytique des travaux de l'IRAT au Sénégal*.

Centre pour le Développement de l'Horticulture (CDH): BP 2619, Dakar; tel. 33-835-0610; fax 33-835-1075; f. 1972; market garden research; Dir Dr ALAIN MBAYE.

Direction des Recherches sur les Productions Forestières: BP 2313, Route des Pères Maristes, Dakar-Hann; tel. 33-832-3219; fax 33-832-9617; Dir Dr PAPE NDIENGOU SALL.

ECONOMICS, LAW AND POLITICS

Institut Africain de Développement Economique et de Planification des Nations Unies (United Nations African Institute for Economic Development and Planning): BP 3186, Dakar; tel. 33-823-1020; fax 33-822-2964; f. 1962 under the aegis of the Economic Comm. for Africa; financed jointly by African states, the UN, and bilateral and multilateral partners; provides training through the org. of courses, seminars, etc., and undertakes research; library of 25,000 vols, 1,400 periodicals; Dir Dr JEGGAN C. SENGHOR.

MEDICINE

Institut d'Hygiène Sociale: Ave Blaise-Diagne, Dakar.

Institut Pasteur: BP 220, Dakar; tel. 33-839-9200; fax 33-839-9210; e-mail pasteur .dakar@pasteur.sn; internet www.pasteur .sn; f. 1896; medical research, microbiology, virology, immunology; library of 2,030 vols, 88 periodicals; Dir Dr PHILIPPE MAUCLERE; Exec. Sec. CAMILLE ABBEY.

Organisme de Recherches sur l'Alimentation et la Nutrition Africaines (ORANA): BP 2089, 39 ave Pasteur, Dakar; tel. 33-822-5892; f. 1956; research into African foods and nutritional values, investigations, documentation, teaching; 30 mems; Dir Dr AMADOU MAKHTAR NDIAYE.

TECHNOLOGY

African Regional Centre for Technology/Centre Régional Africain de Technologie: BP 2435, Dakar; tel. 33-823-7712; fax 33-823-7713; f. 1977 as an intergovernmental institution under the auspices of the OAU and UNECA; aims to promote the use of technology to improve the socio-economic development of Africa; advises and sets up national institutions, holds training seminars and workshops; activities include food science and technology, energy technology, technological consulting and advisory services, training and information and documentation; 31 mem. states; library of 6,000 vols, patents, microfiches, video cassettes; Exec. Dir Dr OUSMANE KANE; publs *African Technodevelopment Bulletin* (English and French, 2 a year), *Alert Africa Newsletter* (4 a year), *Infonet* (irregular).

Bureau de Recherches Géologiques et Minières (BRGM): BP 268, Dakar; tel. 33-822-7219; mining, hydrogeology, irrigation; also directs research in Mali and Mauritania; Dir D. FOHLEN.

Libraries and Archives

Dakar

Archives du Sénégal: Immeuble administratif, Ave Léopold Sédar Senghor, Dakar; tel. 33-823-5072; fax 33-822-5126; e-mail pmarchi@primature.sn; f. 1913; 26,000 vols, 1,500 periodicals, 8,000 official publs, 12 km of documents; Dir SALIOU MBAYE; publ. *Bibliographie du Sénégal* (2 a year).

Bibliothèque Centrale, Université Cheikh Anta Diop de Dakar: BP 2006, Dakar; tel. 33-824-6981; fax 33-824-2379; e-mail hsene@ucad.sn; internet www.bu .ucad.sn; f. 1952; higher education, human and social sciences, law and economics, medicine and pharmacy, science and technology, veterinary science, information science; 353,000 vols, 5,000 periodicals (of which 1,000 are current); Dir HENRI SENE.

Bibliothèque de l'Alliance Française: BP 1777, 2 rue Assane Ndoye, Dakar; tel. 33-821-0822; f. 1948; 12,000 vols; Dir PATRICK MANDRILLY.

Bibliothèque de l'Institut Fondamental d'Afrique Noire: BP 206, Dakar; tel. 33-825-0090; f. 1936; research in humanities and natural sciences; 70,000 vols, 8,200 brochures, 4,036 collections of periodicals, 1,600 microfilms, 2,566 maps, 32,000 photographs, 2,100 slides, 12,200 files of documents; Librarian GORA DIA.

Centre National de Documentation Scientifique et Technique (CNDST): Ministère de la Recherche Scientifique et de la Technologie (MRST), 61 Blvd Djily Mbaye, BP 3218, Dakar; tel. 33-822-9619; fax 33-822-6144; f. 1977; maintains a database each of research institutions, researchers, research projects and research results, and a socio-economic databank on Senegal; Dir MOHAMED FADHEL DIAGNE; publs *Répertoire des sources d'information sur l'environnement*, *Répertoire des organismes de documentation au Sénégal*, *Répertoire des textes législatifs et réglementaires dans le domaine de l'environnement au Sénégal* (1 a year), *Répertoire des textes législatifs et réglementaires au Sénégal* (1 a year).

Centre Régional de Recherche et de Documentation pour le Développement Culturel (CREDEC) (Regional Research and Documentation Centre for Cultural Development): 13 ave du Pdt Bourguiba, Dakar; tel. 33-827-8059; fax 33-821-7515; f. 1976; mems: 20 African states; part of African Cultural Institute (see under International); 3,200 vols, spec. collns on African crafts; Coordinator FALILOU DIALLO; publ. *ICA-Information* (4 a year).

Museums and Art Galleries

Dakar

Musée d'Art Africain de Dakar: BP 6167, Dakar-Étoile; f. 1936; administered by Institut Fondamental d'Afrique Noire; ethnography and African art; Curator Dr TAHIROU DIAW.

Gorée

Musée de la Mer: Gorée; f. 1959; administered by Institut Fondamental d'Afrique Noire; sea sciences, oceanography, fishing; Curator Dr SECK.

Musée Historique: Gorée; administered by Institut Fondamental d'Afrique Noire; Curator Dr ABDOULAYE CAMARA.

Universities

UNIVERSITÉ CHEIKH ANTA DIOP DE DAKAR

BP 5005, Dakar-Fann
Telephone: 33-825-7528
Fax: 33-825-3724
E-mail: info@ucad.sn
Internet: www.ucad.sn

Founded 1915 as École de Médecine, became Institut des Hautes Études 1950; univ. status 1957
State control
Language of instruction: French
Academic year: October to July

Rector: ABDEL KADER BOYE
Vice-Pres.: MOUSTAPHA SOURANG
Sec.-Gen.: ALIOUNE BADARA DIAGNE
Librarian: HENRI SENE

Library: see Libraries and Archives
Number of teachers: 700
Number of students: 22,000

Publications: *Annuaire* (periodical), *Bulletin de l'IFAN* (periodical, 3 a year), *Dakar médical* (periodical, 3 a year), *Journal de la Faculté des Sciences et Techniques* (periodical, 2 a year), *Notes Africaines* (periodical), *Revue de l'Ecole Normale Supérieure* (periodical, 2 a year), *Revue de la Faculté des Lettres* (periodical)

DEANS

Faculty of Arts and Humanities: MAMADOU KANDJI
Faculty of Economics and Management: MOUSTAPHA KASSE
Faculty of Law and Political Science: MOUSTAPHA SOURANG
Faculty of Medicine, Pharmacy and Odonto-Stomatology: RENÉ NDOYE
Faculty of Science and Technology: LIBASSE DIOP

UNIVERSITÉ DU SAHEL

BP 5355 33, Sotrac-Mermoz, Dakar
Telephone: 33-860-9975
Fax: 33-860-9975
E-mail: unis@refer.sn
Internet: www.unis.sn

Founded 1998
State control

Pres.: ISSA SALL

Number of teachers: 80
Number of students: 400

Publications: *Les Annales du Sahel*, *Le Sahalien* (12 a year)

DIRECTORS

School of Economics and Administration: MOUSTAPHA THIOUINE
School of Educational Sciences: BADARA SALL
School of Humanities and Civilization: BADARA SALL
School of Law and Political Science: MARIE-PIERRE TRAORÉ SARR
School of Science, Engineering and Technology: KHADIR DIOP
School of Social Sciences: MAME DEMBA THIAM

UNIVERSITÉ DE SAINT-LOUIS (Université Gaston-Berger)

BP 234, Saint-Louis
Telephone: 33-961-1906
Fax: 33-961-1884

E-mail: webmaster@ugb.sn
Internet: www.ugb.sn

Founded 1990
State control
Language of instruction: French
Academic year: October to July

Rector: Prof. NDIAWAR SARR
Sec.-Gen.: PAPA SÉKOU SONKO
Librarian: MAMADOU LAMINE NDOYE

Library of 18,500 vols
Number of teachers: 237
Number of students: 2,663

HEADS OF TEACHING AND RESEARCH UNITS

Applied Mathematics and Computer Science: MARY TEUW NIANE
Arts and Humanities: GORA MBODJ
Economics and Management: ADAMA DIAW
Law: SAMBA TRAORÉ

Colleges

Ecole Inter-Etats des Sciences et Médecine Vétérinaires (EISMV): BP 5077, Dakar; tel. 33-865-1008; fax 33-825-4283; e-mail mariamd@eismv.refer.sn; internet www.refer.sn/sngal_ct/edu/eismv/eismv.htm; f. 1968; representing 13 French-speaking African countries; 36 teachers (17 full-time, 19 part-time); 232 students; Dir Prof. FRANÇOIS ADÉBAYO ABIOLA.

Ecole Nationale d'Administration du Sénégal: BP 5209, Dakar; f. 1959; Dir A. N'DENE N'DIAYE.

Ecole Nationale d'Economie Appliquée: BP 5084, Dakar/Fann; tel. 33-824-7928; f. 1963; library: 4,500 vols; 147 students; Dir SAMBA DIONE; publ. *Bulletin de Recherche Appliquée*.

Ecole Nationale Supérieure d'Agriculture: BP A 296, Thiès; tel. 33-951-1257; fax 33-951-1551; e-mail ensath@sentoo.sn; internet www.refer.sn/ensa/accueil.htm; f. 1980; 5-year courses in agricultural engineering; training for mems of the agricultural sector; library: 6,000 vols; 10 full-time teachers; 132 students; Dir Prof. PAPA IBRA SAMB.

Ecole Supérieure Polytechnique: BP 5085, Dakar; tel. 33-825-0879; fax 33-825-5594; e-mail esp@ucad.sn; internet www.esp.sn; 2nd campus in Thiès; f. 1994; 5-year diploma courses in engineering; library: 22,378 vols; 116 teachers; 2,105 students, (913 undergraduate, 1192 postgraduate); Dir ABIB NGOUM; Registrar MARIE NOËLLE MBENGUE; Vice-Dean MAMADOU ADJ; Librarians PHILOMÈNE FAYE, EMMANUEL CABOU.

Institut de Technologie Alimentaire: BP 2765, Hann, Dakar; tel. 33-832-0070; fax 33-832-3295; e-mail ita@metissacana.sn; internet www.ita.sn; f. 1963; Dir Dr AMADOU TIDIANE GUIRO.

SERBIA

The Higher Education System

Following the dissolution of the Socialist Federal Republic of Yugoslavia in 1992, Serbia became part of the Federal Republic of Yugoslavia, which was renamed the State Union of Serbia and Montenegro in 2003. In 2006 Montenegro declared independence from the State Union of Serbia and Montenegro. There are seven state universities in Serbia, the oldest of which is Univerzitet u Beogradu (University of Belgrade – founded 1865), and seven private universities. Serbian is the main language of instruction, but Hungarian is also used at Univerzitet u Novum Sadu (University of Novi Sad). In addition to the universities, higher education is offered by university faculties, specialist institutes and high schools. The New University Law (2002) initiated several new reforms, including adoption of the European Credit Transfer System (ECTS) and increased autonomy for universities; additionally, Serbia participates in the Bologna Process to establish a European Higher Education Area, the first phase of which was to adopt a credit-based system of comparable degrees with two main cycles (undergraduate and graduate). The practical implementation of the Bologna Process formally began in 2006/2007, including changes to quality assurance in higher education and the introduction of a three-cycle structure, which involved a complete redesign of university curricula. In 2003 the Commission for Accreditation and Quality Assessment was established. With further changes to the law in 2005, there were more developments regarding accreditation and quality assurance processes which apply to all higher education institutions and all programmes. The Law also introduced the mandatory use of the ECTS. In 2006/07 an estimated 238,710 students were enrolled in 272 institutes of higher education.

Under the old system, admission to higher education was based on completion of general secondary education or four-year vocational certificate programmes and award of the Secondary School Leaving Diploma. Universities also set their own entrance examinations. Quotas for admissions were set by the Government. The new undergraduate Bachelors degree (four years) replaces the old-style awards of Diplom Višeg Obrazovanje (two to three years) and Diplom Visokog Obrazovanja (four to six years). The Masters degree (Magistarska Dimploma) is a one-year programme of study following the Bachelors. Finally, the Doctorate (Doktorat Nauka) is the highest university-level degree and is awarded after a period of research culminating with defence of a thesis.

Technical and vocational education has undergone recent reforms. The aims of the reforms, started in 2002, included creating a centre to develop occupational standards and profiles, teacher training initiatives and new qualifications. Previously two- to three-year post-secondary vocational schools offered vocational qualifications, regarded as final qualifications, with the potential to allow access to second- or third-year university undergraduate education. Through reforms along Bologna lines, post-secondary vocational schools have now been transformed into higher education professional (vocational) colleges, offering higher education courses that combine theoretical knowledge with occupational skills.

Regulatory and Representative Bodies

GOVERNMENT

Ministry of Culture: Vlajkovićeva 3, 11000 Belgrade; tel. and fax (11) 303-2112; e-mail kabinet@kultura.gov.rs; internet www.kultura.sr.gov.yu; Min. NEBOJS BRADIC.

Ministry of Education: Nemanjina 24, 11000 Belgrade; tel. (11) 361-6489; fax (11) 361-6491; e-mail kabinet@mp.gov.rs; internet www.mps.sr.gov.rs; Min. Dr ŽARKO OBRADOVIĆ.

ACCREDITATION

ENIC/NARIC Serbia: ENIC Centre of Serbia, Ministry of Education, Nemanjina 22–26, 1000 Belgrade; tel. (11) 361-6607; fax (11) 361-6514; e-mail enic@mps.sr.gov.rs; internet www.mps.sr.gov.rs; Contact MILENA DAMJANOVIC.

Learned Societies

GENERAL

Matica srpska (Serbian Cultural and Scientific Association): Matice Srpske 1, 21000 Novi Sad; tel. (21) 527-622; fax (21) 528-901; e-mail ms@maticasrpska.org.rs; internet www.maticasrpska.org.rs; f. 1826; literary, scientific, cultural and publishing soc.; 2,830 mems; library of 3,000,000 vols; Pres. BOŽIDAR KOVAČEK; Sec. DRAGAN STANIĆ; publs *Letopis Matice srpske* (literary magazine), *Proceedings* (in the following series: natural sciences, history, social sciences, literature and language, philology and linguistics, art, Slavonic studies, theatre and music, classical studies).

Srpska Akademija Nauka i Umetnosti (Serbian Academy of Sciences and Arts): Knez Mihailova 35, 11001 Belgrade; tel. (11) 2027-200; fax (11) 219-2825; e-mail sasadir@sanu.ac.rs; internet www.sanu.ac.rs; f. 1886; sections of mathematics, physics and geosciences (Sec. ZORAN MAKSIMOVIĆ), chemical and biological sciences (Sec. MIROSLAV GAŠIĆ), technical sciences (Sec. PETAR MILJANIĆ), medical sciences (Sec. VESELINKA ŠUŠIĆ), literature and language (Sec. PREDRAG PALAVESTRA), social sciences (Sec. MIHAILO ĐURIĆ), historical Sciences (Sec. VASILIJE KRESTIĆ), fine arts and music (Sec. DEJAN DESPIĆ); 143 mems (111 ordinary, 32 corresp.); library of 1,200,000 vols (incl. 650,000 vols of periodicals); Pres. NIKOLA HAJDIN; Gen. Sec. DIMITRIJE STEFANOVIĆ; Exec. Dir DRAGANA PETROVIC RADJENOVIC; publs *Bulletin*, *Ekonomski zbornik* (Collection of Economic Works), *Galerija* (Gallery), *Godišnjak* (Yearbook), *Glas* (Review), *Iz teorije prava* (Theory of Law), *Naučni skupovi* (Scientific Conferences), *Muzička izdanja* (Musical Editions), *Posebna izdanja* (Monographs), *Spomenik* (Monument), *Srpski dijalektološki zbornik* (Serbian Dialectology Collection), *Srpski etnografski zbornik* (Serbian Ethnographic Collection).

BIBLIOGRAPHY, LIBRARY SCIENCE AND MUSEOLOGY

Bibliotekarsko društvo Srbije (Serbian Library Association): Skerlićeva 1, 11000 Belgrade; tel. (11) 451-242; fax (11) 452-952; e-mail milun67@gmail.com; internet www.bds.rs; f. 1947 as Society of Library Workers of Serbia; 2,000 mems; Pres. Dr ŽELJKO VUČKOVIĆ; Sec. VESNA CRNOGORAC; publ. *Bibliotekar* (The Librarian, 2 a year).

ECONOMICS, LAW AND POLITICS

Association of Jurists of Serbia: Proleterskih brigada 74, Belgrade; f. 1946; Pres Prof. Dr MIODRAG ORLIĆ; publ. *Pravni život*.

Drustva sudija Srbije (Judges' Association of Serbia): Alekse Nenadovća 24, Belgrade; tel. (11) 344-3132; fax (11) 344-3505; e-mail jaserbia@verat.net; internet www.sudije.rs; f. 1997; non-govt, non-profit org.; works towards advancement of regulations, strengthening respect, professional ethics; dignity of judges; Pres. DRAGANA BOLJEVIC; Pres. MARKO SARIC; Pres. DUSKO MARTIC; publ. *Informator*.

Economists' Society of Serbia: Nusićeva 6/III, POB 490, Belgrade; f. 1944; Pres. BOGOLJUB STOJANOVIĆ; publ. *Ekonomika preduzeća* (12 a year).

EDUCATION

Pedagoško društvo Srbije (Pedagogical Society of Serbia): Terazije 26, 11000 Belgrade; tel. and fax (11) 268-7749; e-mail drustvo@pedagog.rs; internet www.pedagog.rs; f. 1924, reorganized 1949 and 1977; training programmes; devt and project planning; 2,000 mems; Pres. SONJA ŽARKOVIĆ; Sec. MILENA DJOKIĆ; publs *Nastava i vaspitanje* (Teaching and Education, 5 a year), *Pedagoška Biblioteka* (Pedagogical Library, irregular).

FINE AND PERFORMING ARTS

Akademija umetnosti (Academy of Arts): Nemanjina 28, Belgrade; tel. and fax (11) 361-8715; fax (11) 361-8716; e-mail info@

akademijaumetnosti.edu.rs; internet www.akademijaumetnosti.edu.rs; f. 1998; offers undergraduate, graduate academic, specialist academic and doctoral studies in drama and audiovisual arts, music and performing arts, arts, applied art and design; library of 4,000 vols; Dean Prof. MIRJANA KARANOVIC; Pres. DUŠAN ĐOKOVIĆ.

HISTORY, GEOGRAPHY AND ARCHAEOLOGY

Historical Society of Serbia: Faculty of Philosophy, Čika Ljubina 18–20, Belgrade; f. 1948; 1,500 mems; Pres. Prof. Dr LJUBOMIR MAKSIMOVIĆ; publ. *Istoriski glasnik* (2 a year).

Srpsko geografsko drustvo (Serbian Geographical Society): Studenski trg 3/III, Belgrade; tel. (11) 2184-065; fax (11) 2184-065; e-mail info@sgd.org.rs; internet www.sgd.org.rs; f. 1910; 1,500 mems; library of 4,500 vols; Pres. Prof. Dr STEVAN M. STANKOVIĆ; Sec. DUSAN KIĆOVIĆ; publs *Bulletin* (2 a year), *Editions Spéciales* (1 or 2 a year), *Géographique Actualité*, *Globus* (1 a year), *Glasnik* (4 a year), *Mémoires*, *Terre et Hommes* (1 a year).

LANGUAGE AND LITERATURE

British Council: Terazije 8/II, 11000 Belgrade; tel. (11) 302-3800; fax (11) 302-3898; e-mail info@britishcouncil.rs; internet www.britishcouncil.rs; f. 1940 as Yugoslav–British Institute, present name 2001; teaching centre; offers courses and exams in English language and British culture; conducts seminars and workshops; promotes cultural exchange with the UK; attached centres in Priština and Podgorica (Montenegro); library of 9,000 vols, 30 periodicals; Dir ANDREW GLASS.

Društvo za Srpski Jezik i Književnost (Society of Serbian Srpski Language and Literature): University, Studenski trg 1, Belgrade; f. 1910; Pres. P. STEVANOVIĆ; Sec. D. PAVLOVIĆ; publ. *Pritozi za knjizevnost, jezik, istorija i folklor*.

Goethe-Institut: Knez Mihailova 50, POB 491, 11000 Belgrade; tel. (11) 262-2823; fax (11) 263-6746; e-mail info@belgrad.goethe.org; internet www.goethe.de/belgrad; f. 1970; offers courses and exams in German language and culture; promotes cultural exchange with Germany; organizes exhibitions and seminars; library of 12,000 vols; Dir VOLKER MARWITZ.

Serbian PEN Centre: 29/II Terazije St, 11000 Belgrade; tel. (11) 334-4607; fax (11) 334-4427; e-mail pencent@bitsyu.net; f. 1926, re-f. 1962; 83 mems; Pres. VIDA OGNJENOVIC; Sec. NEDA BOBIC; publ. *Relations* (4 a year, in English, with Asscn of Serbian Writers).

Srpska književna zadruga (Serbian Literary Association): Kralja Milana 19, 11000 Belgrade; tel. (11) 3230-305; e-mail skz@beotel.rs; internet www.srpskaknjizevnazadruga.com; f. 1892; publishing of literary, historical and other learned works; 2,500 mems; library of 12,000 vols; spec. colln of 19th-century periodicals; Pres. SLOBODAN RAKITIC; Sec.-Gen. RADIVOJE KONSTANTINOVIĆ; publ. *Glasnik* (1 a year).

MEDICINE

Serbian Society for Fight against Cancer: Pasterova 14 St, 11000 Belgrade; tel. (11) 2656-386; fax (11) 2656-386; e-mail serbca@ncrc.ac.yu; internet www.serbiancancer.org; f. 1927; voluntary non-profit org.; raises awareness; supports health professionals and orgs; 30,000 mems; Chair. Prof. Dr SLOBODAN CIKARIĆ; Vice-Chair. Dr PREDRAG BRZAKOVIĆ; Sec. Dr ANA JOVICEVIC; Sec. Dr VESNA LUKIC; publ. *Bolje Sprečiti nego Lečiti* (The Best Cure is Prevention, 4 a year).

NATURAL SCIENCES

Mathematical Sciences

Society of Mathematicians of Serbia: Knez Mihailova 35, POB 791, Belgrade; tel. (11) 638-263; f. 1948; Pres. Dr DJORDJE KARAPANDŽIĆ; publ. *Matematički Vesnik* (4 a year).

Physical Sciences

Serbian Chemical Society: Karnegijeva 4, 11120 Belgrade; tel. and fax (11) 337-0467; e-mail shd@shd.org.rs; internet www.shd.org.rs; f. 1897; promotes chemical research and education; 850 mems; library of 23,000 vols; Pres. Prof. Dr IVANKA POPOVIC; Vice-Pres Prof. Dr ŽIVOSLAV TEŠIC; Vice-Pres. Prof. Dr VERA DONDUR; Sec. Prof. Dr SLAVICA RAŽIC; Sec. Prof. Dr RADA BAOŠIĆ; publs *Journal of the Serbian Chemical Society* (in English, 12 a year), *Hemijski Pregled* (in Serbian, 6 a year).

Srpsko Geološko Društvo (Serbian Geological Society): Kamenička 6, POB 227, 11000 Belgrade; e-mail nsgd@verat.net; internet www.nsgd.org; f. 1891; sections for history of geology; stratigraphy, palaeontology and tectonics; mineralogy, petrology, geochemistry and sedimentology; hydrogeology; engineering geology; oil geology and geophysics; economic geology and the study of ore deposits; organizes symposia and other scientific and professional meetings; 300 mems (active and inactive); library of 3,500 vols; Pres. Dr NENAD BANJAC; Vice-Pres. MIODRAG BANJEŠEVIĆ; Sec. ALEKSANDRA MARAN; Treas. LJUBINKO SAVIĆ; publ. *Zapisnici srpskog geološkog društva* (reports, 1 a year).

TECHNOLOGY

Nikola Tesla Society: POB 359, Belgrade; e-mail boris@tesla-society.org; internet www.tesla-society.org; f. 1936 reorg. 1993; organizes int. festival of scientific and technical films, held every 2 years; conducts study tours and scientific meetings; publishing.

Savez inženjera i tehničara Srbije (Union of Engineers and Technicians of Serbia): Kneza Miloša 7, 11000 Belgrade; tel. and fax (11) 323-0067; e-mail office@sits.rs; internet www.sits.org.rs; f. 1868; voluntary, non-govt, non-profit, professional, scientific org.; 44 mem. orgs; Pres. Prof. Dr ČASLAV LAČNJEVAC; Vice-Pres. Dr IGOR MARIĆ; Sec.Gen. BRANISLAV VUJINOVIĆ; publ. *Tehnika* (scientific and technical magazine).

Research Institutes

GENERAL

Ethnographic institute of the Serbian Academy of Sciences and Arts: Knez Mihailova 36 /IV, 11000 Belgrade; tel. (11) 263-6804; e-mail eisanu@ei.sanu.ac.rs; internet www.etno-institut.co.rs; promotes theoretical and methodological knowledge in the field of ethnology; organizes ethnological research, scientific conferences, lectures, study visits; cooperates with related cultural institutions in the country and abroad; Dir DRAGANA RADOJIČIĆ; Sec. NEVENKA SPASOJEVIC; publ. *Proceedings of the EI SASA* (bulletin, 1 a year).

Matematički Institut SANU (Mathematical Institute SANU): Kneza Mihaila 36, 11001 Belgrade; tel. (11) 263-0170; fax (11) 218-6105; e-mail office@mi.sanu.ac.rs; internet www.mi.sanu.ac.rs; f. 1961; organizes seminars and colloquiums; int. collaborations; Dir Dr ZORAN MARKOVI; Deputy Dir Dr ZORAN OGNJANOVIĆ; Pres. MILAN BOŽIĆ; publs *Publications de l'Institut Mathématique* (2 a year), *Visual Mathematics* (4 a year, online).

AGRICULTURE, FISHERIES AND VETERINARY SCIENCE

Institute for Agricultural Mechanization: Zemun, POB 41, Belgrade; f. 1947; 30 mems; library of 6,000 vols; Dir DJORDJE DJURDJEVIĆ; publ. *Poljoprivredna Tehnika* (Agricultural Engineering, 1 a year).

Institute for Plant Protection and the Environment: T. Drajzera 9, POB 936, 11000 Belgrade; tel. (11) 266-9860; fax (11) 266-9860; e-mail izbisfu@beotel.yu; f. 1945; depts of biological control, environmental protection, phytopathology, phytopharmacy, toxicology; library of 7,000 books, 12,650 periodicals; Dir Dr DIMITRIJE MATIJEVIĆ; publ. *Zaštita bilja* (Plant Protection, 4 a year).

BIBLIOGRAPHY, LIBRARY SCIENCE AND MUSEOLOGY

Republički zavod za zaštitu spomenika kulture (Institute for the Protection of Cultural Monuments of Serbia): Božidara Adžije 11, 11118 Belgrade; tel. (11) 454-786; fax (11) 344-14-30; e-mail rzzsk@eunet.yu; f. 1947; research, documentation, conservation and restoration, legal protection and maintenance of central registers of immovable cultural property; specialized training of personnel; publication of books and periodicals; Dir MILETA MILIĆ; Head, Architecture Dept BRANA STOJKOVIĆ PAVELKA; Head, Paintings Dept RADIŠA ŽIKIĆ; Head, Physical and Chemical Laboratory (vacant); Head of Dept of History of Art, Ethnology and Archaeology RADOJKA ZARIĆ; depts of law, documentation, photographic laboratory; library of 21,000 vols; publ. *Saopštenja* (Communications).

ECONOMICS, LAW AND POLITICS

Institute of International Politics and Economics: POB 750, Makedonska 25, 11000 Belgrade; tel. (11) 337-3824; fax (11) 337-3835; e-mail iipe@diplomacy.bg.ac.yu; internet www.diplomacy.bg.ac.yu; f. 1947; int. relations; world economy; int. law; social, economic and political devt in all countries; library of 150,000 vols; Dir DUŠKO DIMITRIJEVIĆ; publs *International Problems* (4 a year), *Medjunarodna Politika* (4 a year), *Pregled evropskog zakonodavstva* (Survey of European Legislations, 6 a year), *Review of International Affairs* (4 a year).

FINE AND PERFORMING ARTS

Institute of Musicology of the Serbian Academy of Sciences and Arts: Knez Mihailova 35, 11000 Belgrade; tel. (11) 639-033; fax (11) 182-825; e-mail music.inst@bib.sanu.ac.yu; f. 1948; history of Serbian and Yugoslav music, Balkan folk music, medieval and traditional Orthodox church music, music theory and aesthetics; library of 5,500 vols; Dir Prof. Dr DANICA PETROVIĆ; publs *Musicology* (1 a year), *Sources for the History of Serbian Music* (1 a year).

HISTORY, GEOGRAPHY AND ARCHAEOLOGY

Arheološki Institut (Archaeological Institute): Knez Mihailova 35/IV, Belgrade; tel. (11) 637-191; fax (11) 180-189; e-mail institut@ai.sanu.ac.yu; internet www.ai.sanu.ac.rs; f. 1947; study of prehistoric, classical and medieval archaeology in the

Central Balkan area; library of 13,000 books, 23,000 vols of periodicals; Dir Dr MILOJE VASIĆ; Admin. Sec. OLIVERA ILIĆ; publs *Djerdapske sveske – Cahiers des Portes de Fer*, *Singidunum* (irregular), *Starinar* (1 a year).

Geographical Institute 'Jovan Cvijić': Đure Jakšića 9, 11000 Belgrade; tel. (11) 263-6276; fax (11) 263-7597; e-mail general@gi.sanu.ac.rs; internet www.gi.sanu.ac.rs; f. 1947; physical geography; social geography; regional geography; cartography with GIS; environmental studies; spatial planning; Head Dr MILAN RADOVANOVIĆ; publ. *Journal of the Geographical Institute* (1 a year).

Institute For Balkan Studies Serbian Academy Of Sciences And Arts: Knez Mihailova 35/IV, 11000 Belgrade; tel. (11) 263-9830; fax (11) 263-8756; e-mail balkinst@bi.sanu.ac.rs; internet www.balkaninstitut.com; f. 1934 started as Institut des Études Balkaniques; present name 1969; Balkans studies from prehistory to the modern age; incl. archaeology, ethnography, anthropology, history, culture, art, literature, law; multidisciplinary approach; Dir Acad. NIKOLA TASIĆ; Vice-Dir DUŠAN T. BATAKOVIĆ; Librarian VALENTINA BABIC; publ. *Balcanica*.

Institute for Byzantine Studies of the Serbian Academy of Sciences and Arts: Knez-Mihailova 35, 11000 Belgrade; tel. (11) 263-7095; fax (11) 328 8441; e-mail inst.byz@vi.sanu.ac.rs; internet www.vi.sanu.ac.rs; f. 1948; research in modern Byzantine studies; int. cooperation; library of 21,000 vol; Dir Prof. LJUBOMIR MAKSIMOVIĆ; Deputy Dir BOJANA KRSMANOVIĆ; publ. *Zbornik radova Vizantoloskog instituta (ZRVI)*.

LANGUAGE AND LITERATURE

Institute For Serbian Language SASA: Đure Jaksic 9, 11000 Belgrade; tel. (11) 218-1383; fax (11) 218-3175; e-mail isj@isj.sanu.ac.yu; internet www.isj.sanu.ac.rs; f. 1947, present name 1992; processing old Serbian written monuments; etymological research dialectological research; description and Serbian language standardization; scientific meetings; lectures; Pres. PREDRAG PIPER.

MEDICINE

Institut za javno zdravlje Srbije (Institute of Public Health of Serbia): Dr Subotića 5, 11000 Belgrade; tel. (11) 268-4566; fax (11) 268-5735; e-mail info@batut.org.rs; internet www.batut.org.rs; f. 1924 as Central Institute of Hygiene, present name 2006; epidemiology, microbiology, hygiene and human ecology, social medicine; health care orgs and services; health education; library of 40,000 vols; Dir Dr TANJA KNEZEVIC; publ. *Glasnik* (2 a year).

NATURAL SCIENCES

Biological Sciences

Botanical Institute and Garden of the University of Belgrade: Takovska 43, 11000 Belgrade; tel. (11) 767-988; fax (11) 638-500; f. 1874; library of 7,000 vols; Dir Prof. Dr JELENA BLAŽENČIĆ; publ. *Bulletin* (1 a year).

Physical Sciences

Astronomska Opservatorija (Astronomical Observatory): Volgina 7, 11060 Belgrade; tel. and fax (11) 241-9553; e-mail contact@aob.rs; internet www.aob.rs; f. 1887, reformed 1932; astrometry, astrophysics, astrodynamics, cosmology, astrobiology, astronomy and planetology; library of 15,000 vols; Dir Dr ZORAN KNEŽEVIĆ; Chief Officer SRETEN STEPANOVIĆ; publs *Publications of the Astronomical Observatory of Belgrade* (irregular), *Serbian Astronomical Journal* (2 a year).

Hidrometeorološki Zavod Republike Srbije (Hydrometeorological Service of Serbia): Kneza Višeslava 66, 11000 Belgrade; tel. (11) 3050-923; fax (11) 3050-847; e-mail office@hidmet.gov.rs; internet www.hidmet.gov.rs; f. 1888; forecasts weather and issues severe weather warnings; Dir MILAN DACIĆ; Deputy Dir. DANICA SPASOVA.

Attached observatory:

Meteorološka opservatorija Beograd (Belgrade Meteorological Observatory): Bul. JNA 8, 11000 Belgrade; tel. (11) 685-770; fax (11) 685-840; f. 1887; Chief Officer SLOBODAN HADŽIVUKOVIĆ; publ. *Observations Météorologiques à Belgrade*.

Seismological Institute: Tasmajdanski park bb, POB 16, 11120 Belgrade; tel. (11) 322-7013; e-mail seismo@seismo.sr.gov.yu; internet www.seismo.gov.rs; f. 1906; Dirs Dr B. A. SIKOŠEK, Dr M. N. VUKAŠINOVIČ; Gen.-Man. SLAVITZA RADOVANOVITCH; Sec. SLADYANA MAKSIN-JOKSIMOVITCH; 12 mems; publs *Annuaire macroséismique et microséismique*, *Bulletin mensuel*, *Studies*.

TECHNOLOGY

Institut za nuklearne nauke 'Vinča' (Vinča Institute of Nuclear Sciences): Mike Petrovića Alasa 12–14, Belgrade; tel. (11) 243-8906; fax (11) 344-2420; e-mail office@vin.bg.ac.rs; internet www.vin.bg.ac.rs; f. 1948; multidisciplinary scientific research; basic and applied research in natural, technological and nuclear sciences; consulting and research programmes in physics, chemistry, physical chemistry, biology, technical sciences, nuclear energy, electronics, computing, material sciences; production and application of radio isotopes; information systems and data processing; library of 30,000 vols; Dir Dr JOVAN NEDELJKOVIĆ; Pres. Prof. Dr DRAGAN MITRAKOVIC; Exec. Sec. MAJA MILANOV.

Institut za Tehnologiju Nuklearnih i Drugih Mineralnih Sirovina (Institute for Technology of Nuclear and Other Mineral Raw Materials): Franše D'Epere 86, POB 390, 11000 Belgrade; tel. (11) 3691-581; fax (11) 3691-583; e-mail itnms@itnms.ac.rs; internet www.itnms.ac.rs; f. 1948; research and application of technology in the field of processing nuclear, metallic and non-metallic mineral raw materials; environmental protection; training; 168 staff; library of 4,000 vols, 40,000 periodicals; Dir-Gen. Prof. ZVONKO GULISIJA.

Institute of Technical Sciences of The Serbian Academy of Sciences and Arts: Knez-Mihailova 35/IV, POB 377, 11000 Belgrade; tel. (11) 218-5437; fax (11) 218-5263; e-mail its@itn.sanu.ac.rs; internet www.itn.sanu.ac.rs; f. 1947; centres for fine particles processing and nanotechnologies; metallic constructions in civil engineering; scientific and research programmes; publishing and conferences; int. cooperation; Dir Dr DRAGAN P. USKOKOVIĆ; Sec. ALEKSANDRA STOJIČIĆ.

Libraries and Archives

Belgrade

Arhiv Jugoslavije: Vase Pelagića 33, POB 65, 11000 Belgrade; tel. (11) 369-0252; fax (11) 306-6635; e-mail arhivyu@arhivyu.rs; internet www.arhivyu.rs; f. 1950; documents regarding Yugoslav history; offers professional training in archival theory and practice; archival literature; exhibits; 26,621 vols, 17,810 reference books and 8,811 periodicals; Dir MILOŠEVIĆ MILADIN (acting); publ. *Arhiv* (1 a year).

Arhiv Srbije (Archives of Serbia): Karnegijeva 2, 11000 Belgrade; tel. (11) 337-0781; fax (11) 337-0246; e-mail office@archives.org.rs; internet www.archives.org.rs; f. 1900, present name 1969; history of Serbia; protection of cultural heritage, professional guidance and education; assignment of professional titles; devt and promotion of archival activities; 75,000 vols; Dir MIROSLAV PERIŠIĆ; publ. *Arhivski pregled* (1 a year).

Biblioteka grada Beograda (Belgrade City Library): Knez Mihailova 56, Belgrade; tel. (11) 202-4000; internet www.bgb.rs; f. 1929, present bldg 1986; 2m. vols; depts of arts, children's periodicals, cultural programmes, local history; Dir JOVAN RADULOVIC.

Biblioteka Srpske akademije nauka i umetnosti (Library of the Serbian Academy of Sciences and Arts): Knez Mihailova 35, 11000 Belgrade; tel. (11) 2639-120; fax (11) 2639-120; e-mail katalog@bib.sanu.ac.rs; internet www.sanu.ac.rs; f. 1842 by the Serbian Learned Society; present name 1960; information service, inter-library loan scheme; prepares bibliographies and edits spec. publs; primarily for mems; 1,200,000 vols (incl. 550,000 books and 650,000 vols of periodicals); Dir NIKŠA STIPČEVIĆ; publ. *Izdanja biblioteke*.

Narodna biblioteka Srbije (National Library of Serbia): Skerlićeva 1, 11000 Belgrade; tel. (11) 245-1242; fax (11) 245-1289; e-mail nbs@nb.rs; internet www.nb.rs; f. 1832; large fed. copyright and deposit library; nat. agency for CIP, ISBN, ISSN, ISMN, DOI numbers; centre for nat. current bibliography; nat. centre for conservation and preservation; nat. digital library centre; 5,500,000 vols, incl. electronic titles; large colln of medieval Cyrillic MSS; Dir SRETEN UGRIČIĆ; publs *Arheografski prilozi* (1 a year), *Glasnik narodne biblioteke Srbije* (Herald of the Nat. Library of Serbia, 1 a year), *Srpska bibliografija* (Serbian nat. bibliography, 17 volumes).

Univerzitetska biblioteka 'Svetozar Marković' (University Library 'Svetozar Marković'): Bulvr Kralja Aleksandra 71, 11000 Belgrade; tel. (11) 337-0512; fax (11) 337-0354; e-mail pitajbibliotekara@unilib.bg.ac.rs; internet www.unilib.bg.ac.rs; f. 1921 as successor to the library of the Serbian Lyceum (1838); centre of the network of univ. libraries in Serbia; exhibits; inter-library loan scheme; 1,448,245 vols (books, periodicals, newspapers), 548 Serbian and other MSS 12th–18th century, 5,000 old documents; Dir Dr STELA FILIPI MATUTINOVIĆ; Deputy Dir BOGOLJUB MAZIĆ; publ. *Infoteka* (2 a year).

Cacak

Gradska biblioteka Vladislav Petković Dis (Public library 'Vladislav Petkovic Dis'): Gospodar Jovanova 6, 32000 Cacak; tel. (32) 340-960; fax (32) 223-608; e-mail biblioteka@cacak-dis.rs; internet www.cacak-dis.rs; f. 1848 as Assn for Reading Serbian–Slavonic Newspapers in Čačak, present name 1998; incl. scientific dept; depts for adults, children; inter-library loans; 150,000 vols; Dir DANICA OTAŠEVIĆ.

Kragujevac

Narodna biblioteka (Public Library): Kragujevac; f. 1866; 50,000 vols.

Niš

Narodna Biblioteka 'Stevan Sremac' (National Library 'Stevan Sremac'): Borivoje Gojkovic no. 9, 18000 Niš; tel. (18) 511-410;

fax (18) 250-188; e-mail n.vasic09@yahoo.com; internet www.nbss.rs; f. 1879; collns of the Serbian Acad. of Science and Art and Serbian graphics; depts of ancient and rare books; local history; 250,000 vols, 950 titles, 200 original graphic prints; Dir NEBOJŠA VASIĆ; Sec. SONJA SUKOVIĆ; Librarian SLAVICA KRIVOKUĆA.

Novi Sad

Arhiv Vojvodine (Archives of Vojvodina): Dunavska 35, 21000 Novi Sad; tel. (21) 489-1800; fax (21) 522-332; e-mail info@arhivvojvodine.org.rs; internet www.arhivvojvodine.org.rs; f. 1926 as State archives in Novi Sad, present name 1970; 30,000 vols; Dir STEVAN RAJČEVIĆ; publs *Izveštaji o naučno-istraživačkom radu u inostranstvu* (Research reports from archives abroad), *Naučno-informativna sredstva o arhivskoj gradji u arhivima Vojvodine* (Scientific information on the Vojvodina archives, 4 a year).

Biblioteka Matice srpske (Matica Srpska Library): Ul. Matice srpske 1, 21000 Novi Sad; tel. (21) 420-199; fax (21) 528-574; e-mail bms@bms.ns.ac.rs; internet www.bms.rs; f. 1826 in Budapest, opened 1838, present location 1864; copyright and deposit library for Serbia; regional information centre of Science and Technology Information Network; depository library for FAO and UNESCO; 3m. books and periodicals, 17 incunabula, 671 MSS, 500 paleotype, 35,000 old and rare books, 700,000 units of spec. library material (maps, posters, leaflets, music records, cassettes, etc.); Dir MIRO VUKSANOVIĆ.

Požarevac

Narodna biblioteka (Public Library): Drinska 2, 12000 Požarevac; tel. (12) 221-957; fax (12) 221-029; e-mail bibliotekapo@ptt.yu; f. 1847; 112,000 vols.

Sabac

Narodna biblioteka 'Žika Popovič' (Public Library 'Zika Popović'): Masarikova 18, 15000 Sabac; f. 1847; 200,000 vols.

Museums and Art Galleries

Belgrade

Etnografski muzej u Beogradu (Ethnographical Museum of Belgrade): Studentski trg. 13, p.p. 357, Belgrade; tel. (11) 328-1888; fax (11) 328-2944; e-mail etnografski.muzej@nadlanu.com; internet www.etnografskimuzej.rs; f. 1901; permanent and temporary exhibits; collns incl. nat. costumes, jewellery, embroidery and lace, textile household items, devices and contrivances for productions of textile, elements of nat. architecture, rural household, urban architecture, urban household, agriculture, crafts, pottery, traffic and transport of goods, hunting and fishing, music instruments, custom items, folk knowledge and belief, warriors' equipment, measures and tally, glass, tuxedo outfits, children's toys, photographs and negatives, art, video records, items of European and other cultures, archives; library of 60,000 vols; Deputy Dir VILMA NIŠKANOVIĆ; Sec. MIROSLAV TASIC; publ. *Glasnik etnografskog muzeja* (1 a year).

Istorijski muzej Srbije (Historical Museum of Serbia): Đure Jaksic 9, Belgrade; tel. (11) 328-7242; fax (11) 328-7243; e-mail istorijskimuzej@imus.org.yu; internet www.imus.org.rs; f. 1844 as National Museum, present name and status 1963; Dir Dr ANA STOLIĆ; Sr Curator ANDREJ VUJNOVIĆ; publs *Zbornik* (1 a year), *Proceedings of the Historical Museum of Serbia*.

Museum of Contemporary Art: Ušće 10, blok 15, 11070 Belgrade; tel. (11) 367-6288; fax (11) 367-6291; e-mail msub@msub.org.rs; internet www.msub.org.rs; f. 1958; opened 1965, exhibits Serbian and foreign art; library of 5,200 vols, 25,500 catalogues; Dir BRANISLAVA ANDJELKOVIC DIMITRIJEVIC; Exec. Dir SLOBODAN NAKARADA; publ. *World Art Critics* (1 a year).

Muzej istorije Jugoslavije (Museum of Yugoslav History): Botićeva 6, 11000 Belgrade; tel. (11) 367-1485; fax (11) 266-0170; e-mail info@mij.rs; internet www.mij.rs; f. 1996 by merger of Josip Broz Tito Memorial Centre and Museum of Revolution of Nations and Nationalities of Yugoslavia; history of the people of the fmr Yugoslavia; the life and work of Josip Tito (1892–1980), Pres. of Yugoslavia 1953–80; research, art and educational programmes; library of 200,000 items; Dir KATARINA ZIVANOVIC (acting); Curator ANA PANIC.

Muzej afričke umetnosti (Museum of African Art): Andre Nikolića 14, 11000 Belgrade; tel. and fax (11) 265-1654; fax (11) 265-1269; e-mail office@museumofafricanart.org; internet www.museumofafricanart.org; f. 1977; displays traditional arts of W Africa; collns incl. masks, sculptures in wood and bronze, gold weights, ceramics, musical instruments, textiles, jewellery, objects of everyday use; organizes exhibitions, workshops, lectures; Dir and Curator NARCISA KNEŽEVIĆ ŠIJAN; Chair. Dr MIROSLAVA LUKIĆ KRSTANOVIĆ.

Muzej grada Beograda (Belgrade City Museum): Zmaj Jovina St 1, 11000 Belgrade; tel. (11) 263-8744; fax (11) 328-3504; e-mail office@mgb.org.rs; internet www.mgb.org.rs; f. 1903; Belgrade from prehistory to the present; depts of archaeology, art, history, literature, numismatics, science; documentation centre; conservation laboratory; library of 21,060 vols, 305 rare books; Dir DANICA JOVOVIC PRODANOVIC; publ. *Godišnjak Grada Beograda* (1 a year).

Muzej Nikole Tesle (Nikola Tesla Museum): Krunska 51, 11000 Belgrade; tel. (11) 243-3886; fax (11) 243-6408; e-mail info@tesla-museum.org; internet www.tesla-museum.org; f. 1952; preserves legacy of the engineer and inventor, Nikola Tesla (1856–1943); contains biographical and scientific works; library of 786 vols, 323 magazines, 155,000 pages of Nikola Tesla's original documents and 1,000 of his personal items; Dir VLADIMIR JELENKOVIĆ; Curators BRATISLAV STOJILJKOVIĆ, IVANA ZORIĆ.

Muzej Pozorišne Umetnosti Srbije (Serbian Museum of Theatre): Gospodar Jevremova 19, 11000 Belgrade; tel. (11) 262-6630; fax (11) 262-8920; e-mail office@mpus.org.rs; internet www.mpus.org.rs; f. 1950; documents, photographs, newspaper cuttings on the theatre, costumes, decorations, audiovisual documentation; colln of art and memorial objects, theatrical programmes and posters; archives; library of 7,500 vols; Dir KSENIJA RADULOVIĆ; Sec.-Treas. LJILJANA BANOVIC; Sr Curator MIRJANA ODAVIĆ; publ. *Teatron* (4 a year, print and online).

Muzej primenjene umetnosti (Museum of Applied Art): Vuka Karadžića 18, 11000 Belgrade; tel. (11) 262-6841; fax (11) 262-9121; e-mail info@mpu.rs; internet www.mpu.rs; f. 1950; collects, conserves, studies, publishes works of applied art; exhibits incl. ceramics, porcelain, glass, metalwork, jewellery, period furniture, woodwork, textiles and costume, photography, book layout, modern architecture and design, contemporary applied art, fashion and clothing; library: 2m. books, 960 periodicals; Dir IVANKA ZORIĆ; Sec. SLAĐANA TOMIĆ; Sr Curator MILICA CUKIĆ; publ. *Journal* (1 a year).

Narodni muzej u Beogradu (National Museum in Belgrade): Trg Republike 1A, 11000 Belgrade; tel. (11) 330-6000; fax (11) 262-7721; e-mail pr@narodnimuzej.rs; internet www.narodnimuzej.rs; f. 1844 as Museum Serbski, present name and bldg 1952; archaeological and historical art collns (medieval, Yugoslav and foreign collns), numismatics; conducts exhibitions; library of 85,000 vols; Dir TATJANA CVJETIĆANIN; publs *Glasnik društva prijatelja Narodnog muzeja*, *Kovčežić*, *Numizmatičar*, *Zbornik Narodnog muzeja*.

Prirodnjački muzej u Beogradu (Natural History Museum Belgrade): Njegoševa 51, POB 401, 11000 Belgrade; tel. (11) 344-2147; fax (11) 344-6580; e-mail nhmbeo@nhmbeo.rs; internet www.nhmbeo.rs; f. 1895 as Jestastvenički Museum of Serbian Land; botanical, environmental, geological, mineralogical, palaeontological, petrological and zoological studies and collns; library: 21,554 books, 1,183 journal titles, 1,005 maps and 226 MSS; Dir Dr SLAVKO SPASIĆ; Sec. for Admin. and Technical affairs MARIJA VUCETIC; publ. *Bulletin* (separate series on biology and geology).

Vojni Muzej (Military Museum): Kalemegdan bb, 11000 Belgrade; tel. (11) 334-3441; fax (11) 334-3915; e-mail vojnimuzej@mod.gov.rs; internet www.muzej.mod.gov.rs; f. 1878; military history of Serbia, incl. collns of arms, medals, flags, uniforms; archaeological and art colln; archive of 100,000 photographs; 30,000 objects in 12 collns; library of 15,000 vols, 5,000 magazines; Chief Col MIROSLAV KNEŽEVIĆ; publ. *Vesnik* (1 a year).

Zeljeznicki Muzej (Railway Museum of Serbia): 6 Nemanjina ul., 11000 Belgrade; tel. (11) 361-4811; fax (11) 361-6722; e-mail medijacentar@srbrail.rs; internet www.zeleznicesrbije.com; f. 1950; library of 20,000 vols; Dir MILAN RADIVOJEVIĆ.

Novi Sad

Galerija Matice Srpska (Art Gallery of Matica Srpska): Trg Galerija 1, 21000 Novi Sad; tel. (21) 489-9000; fax (21) 489-9000; e-mail ms@maticasrpska.org.rs; internet www.maticasrpska.org.rs; f. 1847; fine art; paintings, graphics, sculptures and drawings from the 16th to 20th centuries; Dir LEPOSAVA ŠELMIĆ.

Muzej Vojvodine (Museum of Vojvodina): Dunavska 35–37, 21000 Novi Sad; tel. (21) 420-566; fax (21) 520-135; e-mail muzejvojvodine1@nscable.net; internet www.muzejvojvodine.org.rs; f. 1947; sections: archaeology, ethnology, history, applied art; organizes lectures, workshops, exhibits; library of 80,000 vols; Dir Prof. Dr VLADMIR MITROVIĆ; publs *Posebna izdanja* (irregular), *Rad Muzeja Vojvodine* (1 a year).

Subotica

Gradski muzej—Városi Múzeum (Municipal Museum of Subotica): Trg Sinagoge 3, 24000 Subotica; tel. (24) 555-128; fax (24) 555-228; e-mail olivera.p.v@arhivyu.rs; internet www.gradskimuzej.subotica.rs; f. 1892; sections: archaeology, local history, art, ethnology (collns from Africa and SE Asia and Oceania), biology, coins (Hungarian and Roman); library of 12,000 vols; Dir HULLÓ ISTVÁN.

Universities

DRŽAVNI UNIVERZITET U NOVOM PAZARU
(State University in Novi Pazar)

Vuk Karadzic bb, Novi Pazar
Telephone: (20) 317-754
Fax: (20) 337-669
E-mail: rektorat@np.ac.rs
Internet: www.np.ac.rs

Founded 2006
State Control

Rector: Prof. ĆEMAL DOLIĆANIN (acting)

Offers Bachelors, Masters and Doctoral courses in depts of arts; biochemical and medical sciences; legal and economic sciences; mathematical, physical and information sciences; philosophical-philological sciences; technical and technological sciences.

MEGATREND UNIVERZITET
(Megatrend University)

8 Goce Delceva, 11070 Belgrade
Telephone: (11) 220-3029
E-mail: info@megatrend.edu.rs
Internet: www.megatrend-edu.net

Founded 1989
Private Control

Rector: Prof. Dr MICA JOVANOVIC
Pres.: WALTER SCHWIMMER
Vice Rector for Teaching and Internal Organization: Prof. Dr VESNA MILANOVIC
Int. Cooperation: Prof. SLOBODAN PAJOVIC
Vice Rector for Research Work: Prof. DRAGANA GNJATOVIĆ

Number of students: 26,000

Publication: *Megatrend Review* (applied economics)

DEANS

Faculty of Biofarming in Backa Topola: Prof. JELENA BOŠKOVIĆ
Faculty of Business Studies: Prof. Dr GORDANA KOMAZEC
Faculty of Culture and Media: Prof. Dr MILIVOJE PAVLOVIC
Faculty of Management in Zajecar: Prof. Dr NEDELJKO MAGDALINOVIĆ
Faculty of Public Administration: Prof. Dr MILOMIR MINIĆ
Geoeconomic Faculty: Prof. Dr BRANISLAV PELEVIĆ
Graduate School of Arts and Design, Belgrade: Prof. MILOS SOBAJIC
Graduate School of Bio-farming, Backa Topola: Prof. JELENA BOSKOVIC
Graduate School of Business Economy, Valjevo: Prof. MILAN GRUJIC
Graduate School of Business Studies, Belgrade: Prof. ANA LANGOVIC
Graduate School of Business Studies, Pozarevac: Prof. DRAGAN KOSTIC
Graduate School of Business Studies, Vrsac: Prof. MILAN MILANOVIC
Graduate School of Computer Science, Belgrade: Prof. MILAN TUBA
Graduate School of Culture and Media, Belgrade: Prof. MILIVOJE PAVLOVIC
Graduate School of International Economy, Belgrade: BRANISLAV PELEVIC
Graduate School of Management, Zajecar: Prof. NEDELJKO MAGDALINOVIC
Graduate School of Public Admin.: Prof. MILOMIR MINIC
Management and Business College, Professional Studies, Zajecar: DRAGAN MIHAJLOVIC (Dir)
Megatrend Basketball College Borislav Stankovic: Prof. TOMISLAV OBRADOVIC
Megatrend Business College, Professional Studies, Belgrade: NATASA SIMIC (Dir)
Megatrend Virtual Univ., MTVU: Prof. VELJKO SPASIC

UNIVERZITET SINGIDUNUM
(Singidunum University)

Danijelova 32, Belgrade
Telephone: (11) 309-3220
Fax: (11) 309-3294
E-mail: mstanisic@singidunum.ac.rs
Internet: www.singidunum.ac.rs

Founded 2005
Private Control

Rector: Prof. Dr MILOVAN STANIŠIĆ
Sec.-Gen.: LJILJANA STANCIC-BUKVIC

Publication: *Singidunum Show* (Journal of Theory and Practice)

DEANS

Faculty of Applied Ecology: Prof. Dr GORDANA DRAZIC
Faculty of Business in Belgrade: Prof. Dr DANIJEL CVJETICANIN
Faculty of Business in Valjevo: Prof. Dr OLIVERA NIKOLIC
Faculty of Economics, Finance and Administration: Prof. Dr MIHAILO CRNOBRNJA
Faculty for European law, Political studies: Prof. Dr ILIJA BABIC
Faculty of Informatics and Computing: Prof. Dr MLADEN VEINOVIĆ
Faculty of Management: Prof. Dr BRANISLAV MASIC
Faculty of Media and Communications: NADA POPOVIC-PERISIC
Faculty of Tourism and Hospitality Management: Prof. Dr KRUNOSLAV ČAČIĆ

UNIVERZITET U BEOGRADU
(University of Belgrade)

Studentski trg 1, 11000 Belgrade 6
Telephone: (11) 263-5153
Fax: (11) 263-8912
E-mail: officebu@rect.bg.ac.rs
Internet: www.bg.ac.rs

Founded 1808 as the College of Velika škola, reorganized 1905 and 1954
State Control
Academic year: October to September

Rector: Dr BRANKO KOVAČEVIĆ
Vice-Rector for Education: Dr NEDA BOKAN
Vice-Rector for Finances and Organization: Dr NEVENKA ŽARKIĆ-JOKSIMOVIĆ
Vice-Rector for International Relations: Dr VOJISLAV LEKOVIĆ
Vice-Rector for Science: Dr MARKO IVETIĆ
Sec.-Gen.: SLAVICA KAPETANOVIĆ
Librarian: DEJAN AJDAČIĆ

Library of 700,000 vols, 10,000 periodicals
Number of teachers: 2,552
Number of students: 92,652 (90,152 undergraduate, 2,500 postgraduate)

Publications: *Acta Veterinaria*, *Annals of the Faculty of Law* (in Serbian), *Annals of the Faculty of Philology*, *Bulletin Astronomique de Belgrade*, *Collection of Works of the Faculty of Mining and Geology* (in Serbian), *Collection of Works of the International Slavistics Centre*, *Contemporary Research in Physics* (in Serbian), *Contributions to Language, Literature and Folklore*, *Economic Annals* (in Serbian, 4 a year), *Education – the Theory and the Practice* (in English, Russian and Serbian), *Gazette of the Faculty of Forestry* (2 a year), *Geological Annals of the Balkan Peninsula* (in Serbian), *Germanica Belgradensia*, *Headmaster* (in Serbian), *Information Bulletin* (Faculty of Agriculture, in Serbian, 12 a year), *Innovations in the Field of Instruction* (in Serbian), *Italica Belgradensia*, *Journal of Automatic Control* (in English), *Journal of Mining and Metallurgy* (in Serbian), *Lectures in Physical Sciences*, *Management*, *Mathematics* (in Serbian), *Medical Research* (in Serbian), *Medical Students*, *Miscellaneous Studies of the Faculty of Philosophy* (series A: culture and history; series B: social sciences), *October Symposium of Miners and Metallurgists* (1 a year, colln of works, in Serbian), *Philosophical Yearbook* (in Serbian), *Philosophy and Society* (in Serbian), *Physical Education*, *Physical Engineering* (in English), *Population*, *Power Engineering* (in English), *Problems of Ethnology and Anthropology*, *Psychological Research*, *Review of Research Work at the Faculty of Agriculture* (in English), *Sociological Review*, *Studies of Adult Education Topics*, *Transactions* (mechanical engineering, in Serbian and English, 2 a year), *Transport and Traffic in Cities* (in Serbian), *Underground Works* (in Serbian), *The Veterinary Herald* (in Serbian), *Yugoslav Journal of Operations Research* (in English), *Zograf* (iconography)

DEANS

Faculty of Agriculture: Dr NEBOJŠA RALEVIĆ
Faculty of Architecture: Dr VLADIMIR MAKO
Faculty of Biology: Dr JELENA KNEŽEVIĆ-VUKČEVIĆ
Faculty of Chemistry: Dr BRANIMIR JOVANČIĆEVIĆ
Faculty of Civil Engineering: Dr ĐORĐE VUKSANOVIĆ
Faculty of Defectology: Dr JASMINA KOVAČEVIĆ
Faculty of Economics: Dr MARKO BACKOVIĆ
Faculty of Forestry: Dr MILAN MEDAREVIĆ
Faculty of Geography: Dr SRBOLJUB STAMENKOVIĆ
Faculty of Law: Dr MIRKO VASILJEVIĆ
Faculty of Mathematics: Dr MIODRAG MATELJEVIĆ
Faculty of Mechanical Engineering: Dr MILORAD MILOVANČEVIĆ
Faculty of Mining and Geology: Dr VLADICA CVETKOVIĆ
Faculty of Organizational Sciences: Dr MILAN MARTIĆ
Faculty of Pharmacy: Dr NADA KOVAČEVIĆ
Faculty of Philology: Dr SLOBODAN GRUBAČIĆ
Faculty of Philosophy: Dr VESNA DIMITRIJEVIĆ
Faculty of Physical Chemistry: Dr ŠĆEPAN ŠĆEPAN
Faculty of Physics: Dr LJUBIŠA ZEKOVIĆ
Faculty of Political Sciences: Dr ILIJA VUJAČIĆ
Faculty of Security Studies: Dr VLADIMIR CVETKOVIĆ
Faculty of Sports and Physical Education: Dr DUŠAN MITIĆ
Faculty of Stomatology: Dr DRAGOSLAV STAMENKOVIĆ
Faculty of Teacher Training: Dr ALEKSANDAR JOVANOVIĆ
Faculty of Technology and Metallurgy: Dr IVANKA POPOVIĆ
Faculty of Transport and Traffic Engineering: Dr SLOBODAN SLOBODAN
Faculty of Veterinary Medicine: Dr VELIBOR STOJIĆ
School of Electrical Engineering: Dr MIODRAG POPOVIĆ
School of Medicine: Dr VLADIMIR BUMBAŠIREVIĆ
Technical Faculty in Bor: Dr MILAN ANTONIJEVIĆ

PROFESSORS

Faculty of Agriculture (Nemanjina 6, 11080 Belgrade-Zemun; tel. (11) 261-5315; fax (11) 219-3659; e-mail office@agrif.bg.ac.rs; internet www.agrifaculty.bg.ac.rs):

BLAGOJEVIĆ, S., Agricultural Chemistry
ČANAK, M., Mathematics
COROVIĆ, M., Market and Turnover of Agricultural and Agroindustrial Products
ELEZOVIĆ, I., General Phytopharmacy
ERCEGOVIĆ, Đ., Elements and Agricultural Machinery Mechanics
GLAMOČLIJA, Đ., Crop Farming
GRUBIĆ, G., Ruminant Nutrition
IVANOVIĆ, M., Plant Mycosis
JAKOVLJEVIĆ, M. D., Soil and Water Chemistry
JANKOVIĆ, M., Cooling Technology
JELIĆ, M. P., Mathematics
KOSI, F., Thermodynamics and Thermotechnics
KOSTIĆ, N. M., Agrogeology
KOVAČEVIĆ, D., General Crop Farming
LATINOVIĆ, D., Population Genetics and Fertilization of Domestic Animals
LESKOŠEK CUKALOVIĆ, I., Malt and Beer Technology
MAČEJ, O., Milk Proficiency and Preparation
MITROVIĆ, S., Zootechnics
MRATINIĆ, E., Special Fruit Growing
NEDIĆ, M. J., Special Crop Farming
OBRADOVIĆ, D. B., Technological Microbiology
OSTOJIĆ, M., Milk Production
PAVASOVIĆ, V. L., Technological Operations
PEKIĆ, S., Botany
PERIĆ, V. T., Meat Proficiency and Preparation
PEŠIĆ, R., Macroeconomic Analysis
PETANOVIĆ, R., Acarology
PETKOVIĆ, S., Hydraulics
PETROVIĆ, M., Cattle Breeding
RADOVANOVIĆ, R. M., Meat Industry Follow-Up Products Technology
RAIČEVIĆ, D., Agricultural Machinery
RALEVIĆ, N., Statistics
RALEVIĆ LJUBANOVIĆ, I., Statistics and Operational Research
RISTIĆ, N., Organic Chemistry
RUDIĆ, D. V., Drainage
SKALICKI, Z., Zootechnics
SPALEVIĆ, B., Soil and Water Conservation
SPASIĆ, R., Special Entomology
STEVANOVIĆ, Đ., Sociology
STEVANOVIĆ, D. R., Agrochemistry
ŠTIKIĆ, R., Plant Physiology
ŠESTOVIĆ, M. B., Special Phytopharmacy
ŠEVRALIĆ, M., Field and Cooperative Movement Economics
ŠINŽAR, B. C., Botany
ŠURLAN MOMIROVIĆ, G., Genetics
TODOROVIĆ, M. S., Thermodynamics
VASIĆ, G., Reclamation Systems Production and Maintenance
VELIČKOVIĆ, M., General Fruit Growing
VEREŠ, M., Plant Products Technology
VITOROVIĆ, S. L., Agricultural Toxicology
VUKIĆ, Đ., Agricultural Electrical Technology
VUKŠA, P., Plant Protection Technology
ŽEŽELJ, M., Wheat and Flour Technology

Faculty of Architecture (Blvr Kralja Aleksandra 73/II, 11000 Belgrade; tel. (11) 322-5254; fax (11) 337-0193; e-mail fakultet@arh.bg.ac.rs; internet www.arh.bg.ac.rs):

BADOVINC, P., Urban Functions
BAJIĆ BRKOVIĆ, M., Urban and Regional Planning
CAGIĆ, P. R., Architectural Design, Design Studio
ĐORDEVIĆ, D., Construction Management and Utilities Management in Architecture
JOVANOVIĆ POPOVIĆ, M., Architectural Construction and Principles of Bioclimatic Design
KRUNIĆ, S., Design Studio
KUJUNDŽIĆ, V. B., Wood and Metal Structures
KURTOVIĆ FOLIĆ, N., History of Architecture and Settlements
LAZAREVIĆ BAJEC, N., Urban Structures and Zoning
LOJANICA, M. M., Design Studio, Process in Architectural Design
MARUŠIĆ, D. M., Architectural Design, Design Studio
MIHAJLOVIĆ, M., Physics and Materials in Architectural Building Physics
MIHALJEVIĆ, G. P., Built Environment Economics
MITROVIĆ, B., Architectural Design, Design Studio
NESTOROVIĆ, M., Structural Systems, Spatial Structures
PEROVIĆ, M. R., History of Modern Architecture and Town Planning
RAJIĆ, D., Mechanics and Strength of Materials
RAJOVIĆ, S., Architectural and Urban Design
RAKOČEVIĆ, M., Architectural Design
RIBAR, M., Architectural Design, Specific Design Problems
RISTIĆ, M., Analysis of Metal Structures

Faculty of Biology (Studentski trg 16, 11000 Belgrade; tel. (11) 218-6635; fax (11) 263-8500; e-mail dekanat@bio.bg.ac.rs; internet www.bio.bg.ac.rs):

ANĐELKOVIĆ, M. L., Population Genetics
ĆURČIĆ, B., Pedology and Pedobiology with Soil Protection
CVIJIĆ, G., Experimental Physiology
KALEZIĆ, M., Vertebrate Comparative Morphology
KEKIĆ, V., Behavioural Genetics
KONJEVIĆ, R., Plant Physiology
PETKOVIĆ, B., Plant Morphology, General Botany, Botany with Mycology
RADOVIĆ, I., Principles of Ecology
ROMAC, S., Eucariote Molecular Biology
SIMIĆ, D., Microbiology, Microbiology and Microbial Ecology Genotoxicology, Water Microbiology
STEVANOVIĆ, B., Plant Ecology and Phytogeography, Plant Ecology, Physiology and Physiological Ecology of Plants, Plant Adaptive Types, Physiological Ecology of Plants, Aquatic Botany
STEVANOVIĆ, V., Plant Ecology and Phytogeography, Principles of Ecology, Biogeography, Biodiversity Protection and Revival, Ecosystems of Yugoslavia and the Balkan Peninsula
TOPISIROVIĆ, LJ., Biochemistry
TUČIĆ, N., Organic Evolution Theory

Faculty of Chemistry (Studentski trg 12–16, 11000 Belgrade; tel. (11) 328-2111; fax (11) 638-785; e-mail dekan@chem.bg.ac.rs; internet www.chem.bg.ac.rs):

BOJOVIĆ, S., Chemical Education
DOŠEN-MIĆOVIĆ, L., Organic Chemistry
GRŽETIĆ, I., Applied Chemistry
JANKOV, R., Biochemistry
JOVANČIĆEVIĆ, B., Applied Chemistry
JURANIĆ, I., Organic Chemistry
MARKOVIĆ, R., Organic Chemistry
MILOSAVLJEVIĆ, S., Organic Chemistry
NIKETIĆ, S., Inorganic Chemistry
NIKETIĆ, V., Biochemistry
PAVLOVIĆ, V., Organic Chemistry
ŠAIČIĆ, R., Organic Chemistry
SOLAJA, B., Organic Chemistry
SOVILJ, S., Inorganic Chemistry
TEŠIĆ, Ž., Analytical Chemistry
VRVIĆ, M., Biochemistry
VUČKOVIĆ, G., Inorganic Chemistry

Faculty of Civil Engineering (Blvr Kralja Aleksandra 73/I, 11000 Belgrade; tel. (11) 321-8524; fax (11) 337-0223; e-mail lilja@grf.bg.ac.rs; internet www.grf.bg.ac.rs):

ANĐUS, V., Road Design
BAJIĆ, D., Concrete Structures
BRČIĆ, S., Engineering Mechanics and Strength of Materials
BUĐEVAČ, D., Metal Structures
ČORIĆ, B., Theory of Structures
CVETANOVIĆ, A., Elements of Transportation, Roads
ĐORDJEVIĆ, B., Water Power Engineering, Water Resource Systems
DUNICA, S., Engineering Mechanics and Strength of Materials
GEORGIJEVIĆ, V., Technical Physics, Building Physics, Introduction to Electronics
IVKOVIĆ, B., Construction Management and Technology, Construction Project Management
JOKSIĆ, D., Geodesy, Geodesy on Roads and Railways, Engineering, Geodesy in City Infrastructure Systems, Photogrammetry, Remote Sensing
JOVANOVIĆ, M., River Engineering, Waterways and Ports
KLEM, N., Automatic Data Processing in Geodesy
KOLUNDŽIJA, B., Structural Theory
LJUBISAVLJEVIĆ, D., Municipal Hydraulic Engineering, Water Quality
MAKSIMOVIĆ, Č., Fluid Mechanics, Hydraulic Measurement, Engineering
MAKSIMOVIĆ, M., Soil Mechanics
MALETIN, M., Urban Streets
MURAVLJOV, M., Building Materials
NADJANOVIĆ, D., Concrete Structures
OPRICOVIĆ, S., Systems Optimization
PEROVIĆ, G., Calculus, Congruence Theory
PRAŠĆEVIĆ, Ž., Construction Management and Technology, Special Construction Problems
ŠEKULOVIĆ, M., Structural Theory
ŠUMARAC, D., Engineering Mechanics and Strength of Materials
VRAČARIĆ, K., Geodesy
VUKSANOVIĆ, Đ., Structural Theory

Faculty of Defectology (Visokog Stevana 5, 11000 Belgrade; tel. (11) 218-3036; fax (11) 218-3081; e-mail info@fasper.bg.ac.rs; internet www.fasper.bg.ac.rs):

ANDREJEVIĆ, I., Professional and Occupational Training of Persons with Mental Retardation, Professional Training of Deaf and Hard of Hearing Persons
ANIČIĆ, L., Pedagogy of Mentally Retarded Persons, Methodology of Preschool Work with Mentally Retarded Persons
GOLOBOVIĆ, S., Clinical Logopaedia
ILANKOVIĆ, V., Basics of Kinesitherapy
ISPANOVIĆ RADOJKOVIĆ, V., Neurology and Psychiatry, Neuropsychiatry with Re-educational Methods
JOVANOVIĆ, T., Medical Psychology with Basics of Anatomy
KAŠIĆ, Z., Phonetics, Linguistics
KRAJGER GUZINA, A., Neurology and Psychiatry
MATEJIĆ ĆURIČIĆ, Ž., Developmental Psychology, Psychology of Blind and Low Vision Persons
MILANDINOVIĆ, V., Serbian Language Methodology for Children with Mental Retardation, Mathematical Methodology for Children with Mental Retardation
POPOVIĆ KANDIĆ, Z., Criminal Law
RADOMAN, V., Psychology of Deaf and Hard of Hearing Persons, Psychology of Persons with Speech Disturbances
RADOVANOVIĆ, D., Psychology of Persons with Behavioural Disturbances
RADULOVIĆ, K., Psychology of Persons with Mental Retardation, Psychology of Physically Challenged Persons
RAPAIĆ, D., Clinical Somatopaedia
STANKOV, B., Basics of Strabology with Orthoptics and Pleoptics

TREBJEŠANIN, Ž., General Psychology with Personality Psychology

Faculty of Economics (Kamenička 6, 11000 Belgrade; tel. (11) 302-1240; fax (11) 263-9560; e-mail ekof@ekof.bg.ac.rs; internet www.ekof.bg.ac.rs):

ANIČIĆ, R. M., Methods of Economic Analysis
ARSENIĆ, Ž., Vehicle Design, Experimental Methods
BABIĆ, S. L., Price Theory, Industrial Organization
BAJEC, J. M., Contemporary Economic Systems, Public Sector Economy
BAKIĆ, O., Tourism Marketing, Tourist Organization Business Operations
BORIČIĆ, B., Mathematics, Program Languages
BOŽIĆ, V. S., Transport Economics, Marketing Logisitics
ČAČIĆ, K. T., Tourism and Catering Business Management, Tourism Economics, Tourism Marketing
CEROVIĆ, B. D., Transition Economics
CVIJETIĆANIN, D., Operational Research, Economic and Mathematical Methods and Models
DEVETAKOVIĆ, S. R., National Economy, Technological Development and Policy, Agrarian Policy
ĐOLEVIĆ, V. R., Economic Statistics, Bases of Statistical Analysis
ĐUKIĆ, Đ., Banking, Securities Trading
ĐURIČIN, D., Strategic Management
EREMIĆ, M. B., Market Research, Bases of Statistical Analysis, Theoretical Statistics
ILIĆ, B. B., Political Economy
IVANIŠEVIĆ, M., Business Finance, Business Financial Restructuring
JAKŠIĆ, M. P., Development and Contemporary Economic Thought, Macroeconomic Analysis
JOKSIMOVIĆ, L., Contemporary Economic Systems, Public Sector Economics
JOVANOVIĆ GAVRILOVIĆ, B., National Economy, Development Theory and Planning, Industrial Economics
JOVANOVIC GAVRILOVIĆ, P. R., Yugoslav Economic Relations with Foreign Countries, International Business Finance, International Financing
JOVIČIĆ, M. M., Econometry, Times Series Analysis
KOČOVIĆ, J., Financial and Actuary Mathematics, Insurance, Insurance Tariffs
KOVAČ, O., International Finances, Yugoslav Economic Relations with Foreign Countries, European Union Economics
LOVRETA, S. M., Trade and Sales Management, Trade Economics
LOVRIĆ, M., Bases of Statistical Analysis
MALENOVIĆ, N., Business Economics
MARIČIĆ, B. R., Marketing, Consumer Behaviour
MEDOJEVIĆ, B. V., Political Economy
MILOVANOVIĆ, M. R., Price Theory, Macroeconomic Analysis
NIKOLIĆ, M. M., Business Economic, Energy Economics
PAVLIČIĆ, D., Bases of Statistical Analysis, Decision Making Theory
PETKOVIĆ, M., Business Organization, Human Resources Management, Organizational Development
PETKOVIĆ, V. V., Sociology with Labour Sociology, Tourism Sociology
PETROVIĆ, L., Samples Theory and Experiment Planning, Mathematics, Theoretical Statistics
PETROVIĆ, P. D., Econometry, Open Economy Macroeconomics
RIKALOVIĆ, G., National Economy, Agrarian Economics, Transport Economics
ŠKARIĆ JOVANOVIĆ, K. I., Financial Accounting, Balance Theory and Policy, Special Balances
STANIŠIĆ, M., Accounting Information Systems, Auditing Theory, Auditing
STEVANOVIĆ, N., Cost Accounting Systems, Management Accounting
ŠUVAKOVIĆ, DJ. M., Price Theory, Production Theory
TODOROVIĆ, J. B., Marketing Research and Marketing Information Systems, Management Information Systems, Price Theory
ZARIĆ, S., Economic Analysis Methods, Market and Market Institutions

Faculty of Forestry (Kneza Višeslava 1, 11000 Belgrade; tel. (11) 305-3990; fax (11) 254-5485; e-mail sf.bg@sezampro.rs; internet www.sfb.bg.ac.rs):

BAJIĆ, V., Forest Utilization, Forestry Mechanization
BANKOVIĆ, S. V., Dendrometry, Geodesy
DANON, G., Basics of Mechanical Engineering, Wood Processing Tool Machinery
ĐOROVIĆ, M., Agricultural Field Improvement
ISAJEV, V., Seed Production, Nursery Practice and Afforestation, Genetics with Plant Breeding
JAIĆ, M., Surface Wood Processing
JOKSIMOVIĆ, V., Erosion Control Agroecosystems
KARADŽIĆ, D., Forest Phytopathology, Ornamental Plant Diseases
KOLIN, B., Hydrothermic Wood Processing, Veneers and Composite Boards
KOSTADINOV, S., Torrents and Erosion
KOSTADINOVIĆ, A., Sociology
KRSTIĆ, M., Silviculture, Forest Improvement
LETIĆ, L., Woodland Water Exploitation, Forest Hydrology
MARJANOV, M., Engineering Mechanics
MATIĆ, V., Materials in Erosion Control Works, Ecological Materials
MIHAJLOVIĆ, L., Forest Protection, Forest Entomology
MILJKOVIĆ, J. P., Chipboards, Particle Boards and Wood-Based Materials
NEŠIĆ, M., Wood Processing Production Management, Change Control, Wood Processing Management
PETKOVIĆ, S. D., Hydraulics with Hydrology, Water Management Basics
RANKOVIĆ, N., Forest Economics, Forest Organization and Management, Timber Trade, Forest Economic Geography
SKAKIĆ, D., Final Wood Processing, Timber Construction
SOKOLOVIĆ, S., Design, Furniture Design
STOJANOVIĆ, L., Silviculture, Forest Improvement
ŠOŠKIĆ, B. M., Wood Properties, Mill Conversion of Wood
ŠULETIĆ, R., Wood Processing Enterprise Design, Project and Investment Management, Enterprise Development Management
TODOROVIĆ, P. S., Wood Industry Control System Technology, Engineering Physics
TODOROVIĆ, T. N., Geotechnics in Flood Control, Geodynamics, Hydrogeology with Geomorphology
TOMIĆ, Z. S., Dendrology, Forest Phytocenology
VUČKOVIĆ, M., Increment Study
VOJKOVIĆ, L., Landscape Design, History of Landscape Architecture
VUKIĆEVIĆ, M., Wood Processing Production Organization, Operational Research

Faculty of Geography (Studentski trg 3/III, 11000 Belgrade; tel. (11) 218-3537; fax (11) 218-2889; e-mail dekanat@gef.bg.ac.rs; internet www.gef.bg.ac.rs):

DERIĆ, B., Regional Planning
GRČIĆ, M., Political Geography, Industrial and Transport Geography
KUKRIKA, M., Computing, Information Technology
LJEŠEVIĆ, M., Environment
MANOJLOVIĆ, P., Geomorphology, Mathematical Geography
PAVLOVIĆ, M., Yugoslav Geography, Yugoslav Regional Geography
SPASOVSKI, M., Population Geography, Demography
STAMENKOVIĆ, S., Urban Geography, Applied Urban Geography
STANKOVIĆ, S. M., Tourism Geography, World Tourism Geography
STOJKOV, B., Spatial Planning Analysis and Synthesis Methods, Urban and Rural Spatial Planning
ŽIVKOVIĆ, D., Cartography, Topical Mapping

Faculty of Law (Blvr Kralja Aleksandra 67, 11000 Belgrade; tel. (11) 302-7600; fax (11) 322-1299; e-mail pravni@ius.bg.ac.rs; internet www.ius.bg.ac.rs):

ANTIĆ, O., Succession Law
AVRAMOVIĆ, S. D., General History of Law
BASTA, D. N., Legal Philosophy
BESAROVIĆ, V. M., Commercial Law, Copyright and Intellectual Property Law
BRAJIĆ, V. M., Labour Law
ČAVOŠKI, K. S., Introduction to Law
ĐUKIĆ VELJOVIĆ, Z., Constitutional Law
IGNJATOVIĆ, Đ., Criminology and Penology
JANJIĆ KOMAR, M., Family Law
JEKIĆ, Z. M., Criminal Procedure
KOŠUTIĆ, B. P., Introduction to Law
KREĆA, M. D., International Public Law
LABUS, M. Z., Political Economy
LILIĆ, S., Administrative Law and Governance
MARKOVIĆ, R. Č., Constitutional Law, Administrative Law
MARKOVIĆ, S., Copyright and Intellectual Property Law
MILIĆ, V. B., Sociology
MITROVIĆ, D., Introduction to Law, Autonomy Law
MITROVIĆ, M., Sociology
ORLIĆ, M. V., Introduction to Civil Law, Real Law
POPOVIĆ, D. M., Public Finances and Financial Law
POPOVIĆ, D. M., General History of Law
STOJANOVIĆ, Z., Criminal Law
ŠUNDEROVIĆ, B., Labour Law
TABOROŠI, S. A., Law of the Economic System
TODOROVIĆ, M., Sociology
TRKULJA, J., Political Systems
VASILJEVIĆ, M. S., Commercial Law and Traffic Law
VUKADIN, E., Economic Policy

Faculty of Mathematics (Studentski trg 16, 11000 Belgrade; tel. (11) 202-7801; fax (11) 263-0151; e-mail matf@matf.bg.ac.rs; internet www.matf.bg.ac.rs):

ANGELOV, T., Stellar Astronomy, Stellar Structure and Evolution
BOKAN, N., Differential Geometry
JARIĆ, J. P., Continuum Mechanics, Tensor Calculus
JEVTIĆ, M. J., Complex Analysis
JOVANOVIĆ, B. S., Numerical Analysis
KADELBURG, Z. L., Analysis
KNEŽEVIĆ, J., Differential Equations
KUZMANOVSKI, M., Positional Astronomy
LAŽETIĆ, N., Analysis
MATELJEVIĆ, M. S., Complex Analysis
MIJAJLOVIĆ, Ž. D., Algebra, Mathematical Logic
PAVLOVIĆ, M., Complex and Functional Analysis
RADOJČIĆ, M., Algebra, Mathematical Logic
VREĆICA, S., Topology

Faculty of Mechanical Engineering (K. M. Arias Raljić 1, 11120 Belgrade; tel. (11) 337-0266; fax (11) 337-0364; e-mail dekan@mas.bg.ac.rs; internet www.mas.bg.ac.rs):

ADŽIĆ, M., Fuels, Industrial Water, Lubricants, Combustion
BENIŠEK, M. H., Hydraulic Machinery, Measurement Techniques
BLAGOJEVIĆ, Đ., Rocket Propulsion, Flight Dynamics with Aerodynamics
BOGNER, M. G., Process Equipment Mechanical Design and Selection
BOJANIĆ, P. O., Computer Graphics
BRKIĆ, L. D., Steam Boilers, Thermal Power
ČANTRAK, S., Hydraulics and Pneumatics, Hydromechanics
ČOVIĆ, V. M., Mechanics
DEBELJKOVIĆ, D. L., Linear System Design, Object and Process Dynamics
ĐORĐEVIĆ, S., Mechanism Design
ĐORDJEVIĆ, V. D., Fluid Mechanics
DUBOKA, Č. V., Vehicle Maintenance Technology, Experimental Methods
DUBONJIĆ, R. R., Economy
GAJIĆ, A., Turbomachinery, Hydraulic Torque Converters
GEORGIJEVIĆ, D., Mathematics
GOLUBOVIĆ, Z., Mechanics
HOFMAN, M., Ship Theory, Ship Behaviour in Waves
IVANOVIĆ, G., Theory of Vehicle Motion, Theory of Effectiveness
JAĆIMOVIĆ, B., Process Planning, Heat and Mass Transfer Equipment
JANKES, G., Industrial Furnaces and Boilers, Furnace Design
JANKOVIĆ, J., Aircraft Equipment and Systems
JANKOVIĆ, M., Fundamentals of Machine Design
JARAMAZ, S., Interior Ballistics, Projectile Design
JOJIĆ, B. Ž., Aircraft Propulsion, Rocket Propulsion
KALAJDŽIĆ, M. J., Production Process Automation
KLARIN, M. M., Production Organization, Terotechnology
KORUGA, D., Bioautomatic Control
KOZIĆ, Đ., Thermodynamics, Heat and Mass Transfer
KRIVOŠIĆ, I. N., Aircraft Structure
KUBUROVIĆ, M., Environmental Engineering, Drying Equipment
MAJSTOROVIĆ, V., Quality Management
MARKOSKI, M. J., Cooling Devices, Pipelines
MARKOVIĆ, D., Agricultural Machines
MILINOVIĆ, M., Rocket and Launcher Design, Fire Control Systems
MILOSAAVLJEVIĆ, A., Engineering Materials
MILUTINOVIĆ, D., Manufacturing Technology, Industrial Robots
MLADENOVIĆ, N., Mechanics
NEDELJKOVIĆ, M., Hydraulic Machinery, Pumps and Fans
OGNJANOVIĆ, M., Machine Elements, Machine Design
PAVLOVIĆ, M., Fluid Mechanics, Gas Dynamics
PEŠIĆ, S., Aerodynamics, Propellers and Rotors
PETKOVIĆ, Z., Material Handling Machines, Steel Structures
PETROVIĆ, S. V., Internal Combustion Engine Theory and Design
PETROVIĆ, Z., Computer-Aided Design, Aircraft Armament
PILIPOVIĆ, M., Manufacturing Systems, Production Process Automation
PLAVŠIĆ, N. I., Machine Elements, Fundamentals of Machine Design
POKRAJAC, S., Sociology, Industrial Management
RAC, A. A., Tribology
RADENOVIĆ, S., Mathematics
RADOJČIĆ, D., Resistance, Propulsion Steering of Ships
RADOVANOVIĆ, M. R., Fuels, Industrial Water, Lubricants
RAŠUO, B., Aircraft Maintenance, Flight Mechanics
RIBAR, Z., Pneumoelectric Control Systems, Hydroelectric Control Systems
RUŽIĆ, D. B., Strength of Materials
SAVIĆ, B., Heat Turbomachines, Thermal Power Plants
SEDMAK, A., Engineering Materials
SEKULIĆ, A., Mechanism Design, Technical Drawing with Engineering Design Graphics
ŠIJAČKI ŽERAVČIĆ, V., Engineering Materials
SPASIĆ, Ž., Computer-Integrated Manufacturing
STEFANOVIĆ, Z., Aerodynamic Construction
STUPAR, S., Computer-Aided Design, Aircraft Armament
TANOVIĆ, L., Tools and Tooling, Manufacturing Technology
TOMIĆ, M., Internal Combustion Engines, Internal Combustion Engine Equipment
TOPIĆ, R., Agricultural Machinery Design and Construction
TOŠIĆ, S., Conveyors and Lifting Devices, Material Handling System Design
VELJIĆ, M., Agricultural Machinery Design and Construction
VUKOVIĆ, J. U., Mechanics
ZEKOVIĆ, D., Mechanics
ŽIVANOVIĆ, T., Power Steam Boilers, Plant Boilers

Faculty of Mining and Geology (7 Djušina Str., 11000 Belgrade; tel. (11) 323-8832; fax (11) 323-5539; e-mail dean@rgf.bg.ac.rs; internet www.rgf.bg.ac.rs):

BABIĆ, D., Genetic Mineralogy, Mineralogy, Technical Mineralogy
BATALOVIĆ, V., Hydraulic and Pneumatic Machines in Mining, Boring Machines and Equipment, Exploitation and Oil and Gas Transport
BLEČIĆ, N., Coal Deposits, Mining Geology
ĆALIĆ, N. M., Theoretical Bases of Mineral Processing, Mineral Processing
ČOKORILO, V., Underground Mining Mechanization
ĆORIĆ, S., Geostatic Calculation
CVETKOVIĆ MRKIĆ, S., Ground Improvement Methods and Engineering Geology
ĐAJIĆ, N., Thermodynamics, Heat Engines and Energy Plants, Automation and Process Control
DANGIĆ, A. V., Geochemistry, Mineral Raw Material Deposits, Geology and Environmental Protection
DEUŠIĆ, S., Mineral Processing Machinery and Equipment
DIMITRIJEVIĆ, S., Surveying, Mining Photogrammetry
ĐOKOVIĆ, I. M., Geological Mapping, Environmental Geology
DRAGIŠIĆ, V., Mineral Deposit Hydrogeology, General Hydrogeology
GAGIĆ, D., Methods and Technology for Underground Excavation of Bedded Deposits, Underground Excavation Methods
GRUBOR, D., Physics
GRUJIĆ, M., Mine Transport and Hoisting
GRŽETIĆ, I., Physical Chemistry of Ore Deposits, Geology and Environmental Protection, Laboratory Investigation of Mineral Resources
ILIĆ, M. M., Exploration of Building Material Deposits, Nonmetallic Mineral Deposits
IVIĆ, A. P., Mathematics
IVKOVIĆ, S. Ž., Elements of Machines, Machine Design, Metalworking
JANIČEVIĆ, D., Historical Geology, Geology of Yugoslavia
JELENKOVIĆ, R., Metallic Mineral Deposits, Mineral Deposits
JEVREMOVIĆ, D., Engineering Geological Investigation, Geological Construction Materials
KARANOVIĆ, L., X-Ray Structural Analysis, Applied Crystallography
KNEŽEVIĆ, S., Historical Geology, Quaternary Geology, Stratigraphy of Yugoslavia
KOSTIĆ PULEK, A., Chemistry
LAZIĆ, M., Special Hydrogeology, Exploratory Drilling
LILIĆ, N., Mine Ventilation, Mine Safety, Environmental Impact of Surface Drilling
LOGAR, M., Silicate Classification, Industrial Product Mineralogy, Geology and Environmental Protection, Mineral Raw Materials in Technology
LOKIN, P. M., Principles of Geotechnics, Geotechnical Investigation Methods
MARINKOVIĆ, S., Chemistry, Oil Chemistry with Basic Refining
MAROVIĆ, M. S., Neotectonics, Geotectonics, Geology of Yugoslavia
MIHAJLOVIĆ, Đ., Palaeobotany, Palaeoecology, Evolutionary Palaeontology, Fossil Organism Comparative Morphology, Micropalaeontology
MILIČIĆ, M., Mathematics, Numerical Analysis
MILOVANOVIĆ, D. J., Metamorphic Rock Petrology, Technical Petrology, Yugoslav Rock Formation Geology
MITROVIĆ, V., Reservoir Physics, Fluid Mechanics, Oil and Gas Reservoir Engineering
PAVLOVIĆ, V., Open Pit Exploitation Technology, Open Pit Exploration Technology, Removal of Water in Open Pit Mining
PEŠIĆ, L., Essentials of Geology, Principles of Geology
PETKOVIĆ, Z., Basics of Deposit Exploitation, Mineral Resource Deposit Exploitation
POHARAC LOGAR, V., Instrumental Mineralogy, Mineralogy
POPOV, S. R., Physical Chemistry, Fundamentals of Inorganic Chemistry
PROHASKA, S. J., Hydrogeology
PURTIĆ, N. M., Drilling and Blasting
PUŠIĆ, M., Ground Water Dynamics and Hydrology
RABRENOVIĆ, D., Historical Geology, Palaeogeography
RADOJEVIĆ, J. R., Rock Mechanics, Geomechanics, Rock and Soil Mechanics
SIMEUNOVIĆ, D. M., Underground Mine Design, Mine Organization, Underground Excavation Methods
SIMIĆ, R., Surface Mining Methods, Removal of Water in Open Pit Mining
STAJEVIĆ, B., Solid Mineral Deposit Prospecting and Exploration, Geological and Geochemical Prospecting
STARČEVIĆ, M., Gravity Methods for Investigation, Geophysical Investigation Methodology, Seismology, Geophysical Electronic Instruments, Geophysics
STEVANOVIĆ, Z., Hydrogeological Investigation Methods, Hydrogeological Investigation
SUDAR, M., Micropalaeontology, Palaeontological and Biostratigraphic Research Methodology
SUNARIĆ, D., Engineering Geology, Engineering Geodynamics
TANSKOVIĆ, T., Mining Equipment Maintenance, Thermodynamic Machinery

TOMANEC, R., Raw Material Testing Methods for Mineral Processing Technology
TOMIĆ, V., Hydrogeological Mapping
TRIFUNOVIĆ, P., Mining Materials Technology
VUJASINOVIĆ, S. O., Ground Water Protection, Geology and Environmental Protection
VUJIĆ, S. B., Application of Computers in Mining, Programming
ZAJIĆ, B., Hoisting Equipment

Faculty of Organizational Sciences (Jove Ilića 154, 11040 Belgrade; tel. (11) 395-0893; fax (11) 461-221; e-mail dekanat@fon.bg.ac.rs; internet www.fon.bg.ac.rs):

ĆAMILOVIĆ, S. V., Human Resources Management
ČANGALOVIĆ, M., Operations Research, Discrete Mathematics
ĆIRIĆ, V. V., Computer Program Design Principles
ČUPIĆ, M. E., Decision Making Theory, Decision Support Systems
DABIĆ, S., Stock Exchanges and Shareholding
DAJOVIĆ, S. V., Mathematics
DRAKULIĆ, M., Information Systems and Law, Business Law
DULANOVIĆ, Ž., Basics of Organization, Organization Projects
FILIPOVIĆ, V., Marketing, Strategic Marketing
JOVANOV, Đ., Mathematics, Numerical Analysis
KOSTIĆ, K., Management Systems
KRČEVINAC, S. B., Operations Research, Econometric Methods
LAZAREVIĆ, B. J., Information System Design
LEVI JAKŠIĆ, M. I., Technology Management
MILIĆEVIĆ, V., Management Economics and Business Planning, International Management
MITROVIĆ, Ž. V., Quality Management, Quality Control
PEŠALJEVIĆ, M., Quality Management, Standardization Systems, Metrology Systems
PETROVIĆ, B. M., Work Studies
PETROVIC, M. M., Manpower Planning
RADENKOVIĆ, B., Simulation and Simulation Languages
RADOVIĆ, M. K., Fundamentals of Production Systems, Production Systems
STARČEVIĆ, D., Distributed Information Systems
TODOROVIĆ, J. M., Production Management
VUČIĆ, V. V., Mathematics, Operations Research
VUJOŠEVIĆ, M., Optimization Methods
VUKOVIĆ, N. A., Probability and Statistics
ŽARKIĆ JOKSIMOVIĆ, N., Financial Management and Accounting, Management Accounting

Faculty of Pharmacy (Vojvode Stepe 450, 11221 Belgrade; tel. (11) 247-3224; fax (11) 397-2840; e-mail info@pharmacy.bg.ac.rs; internet www.pharmacy.bg.ac.rs):

AGBABA, D., Pharmaceutical Chemistry
DIMITRIJEVIĆ, M., Immunology
ĐURIĆ, Z., Pharmaceutical Technology with Biopharmacy, Industrial Pharmacy with Cosmetology
JANČIĆ, R., Botany
JELIĆ IVANOVIĆ, Z., Medicinal Biochemistry and Clinical Chemistry
JELIKIĆ STANKOV, M., Analytical Chemistry
JOVANOVIĆ, M., Pharmaceutical Technology with Biopharmacy, Industrial Pharmacy with Cosmetology
JOVANOVIĆ, T., General and Inorganic Chemistry
KORIĆANAC, Z, General and Inorganic Chemistry
KRSTIĆ, S., Pharmacology
LEPOSAVIĆ, G., Pathophysiology
MAJKIĆ SINGH, N., Medicinal Biochemistry and Clinical Enzymology
MALEŠEV, D., Physical Chemistry, Instrumental Methods, Chemical Laboratory Methods
MEDENICA, M., Physical Chemistry, Instrumental Methods, Chemical Laboratory Methods
MILETIĆ, I., Bromatology, Quality and Food Safety Control
POKRAJAC, M., Analytical Chemistry
RISTOVSKI, L., Physics
SPASIĆ, S., Medical Biochemistry, Statistics in Pharmacy
SPASOJEVIĆ KALIMANOVSKA, V., Medicinal Biochemistry and Clinical Enzymology
STOJANOV, M., General Biochemistry and Medicinal Biochemistry
STUPAR, M., Pharmaceutical Technology with Biopharmacy, Industrial Pharmacy with Cosmetology
UGREŠIĆ, N., Pharmacology
VLADIMIROV, S., Pharmaceutical Chemistry
VULETA, G., Industrial Pharmacy with Cosmetology
ŽIVANOVIĆ, L., Drugs Analysis

Faculty of Philology (Studentski trg 3, 11000 Belgrade; tel. (11) 263-8622; fax (11) 263-0039; e-mail info@fil.bg.ac.rs; internet www.fil.bg.ac.rs):

BOGOSAVLJEVIĆ, S., German Literature
BOJOVIĆ, Z., Yugoslav Literature from the Renaissance to Romanticism
BOZOVIĆ, R. N., Arabic Language and Literature
BOZOVIĆ, Z. N., Russian Literature
ĆORIĆ, B., History of the Serbian Language
DERETIĆ, J. R., Serbian and South-Slav Literature
DESIĆ, M. P., Serbo-Croat Language Teaching Methodology
DJINDJIĆ, S. M., Albanian Studies
GRUBAČIĆ, S. K., German Language
HLEBEC, B., English Language
IVANIĆ, D., Modern Serbian Literature
JANIĆEVIĆ, J., Cultural Studies
JANKOVIĆ, V. D., Literary Theory
JEREMIĆ, L., World Literature and Literary Theory
JOVANOVIĆ, G. M., Polish Literature
KOJEN, L., Aesthetics and Literary Theory
MAROJEVIĆ, R. N., Russian Literature
NESKOVIĆ, R. R., Philosophical Fundamentals of Marxism
NIKOLIĆ, M., Contemporary Serbian Language
NOVAKOVIĆ, J. R., French Literature
PETKOVIĆ, N. B., Modern Yugoslav Literature, Twentieth Century Literature
PETROVIĆ, S. D., Sociology of Culture and Art
PIPER, P. J., Russian Literature
POLOVINA, V., General Linguistics
RADIĆ DUGONJIĆ, M., Russian Language
SIMIĆ, R. D., Contemporary Serbo-Croatian Language with Stylistics
STANKOVIĆ, B. D., Russian Language
STOJANOVIĆ, D. S., World Literature with Literary Theory
TANASKOVIĆ, D. R., Arabic Language and Literature
TRNAVCI, H. I., Albanian Language and Literature
VUKOBRAT, S., English Literature

Faculty of Philosophy (Čika Ljubina 18–20, 11000 Belgrade; tel. (11) 263-9119; fax (11) 263-9356; e-mail info@f.bg.ac.rs; internet www.f.bg.ac.rs):

ALIBABIĆ, Š., Theory of Educational Organization
BANDIĆ, D. I., Ethnology of Yugoslavia (Spiritual Culture)
BOGDANOVIĆ, M. I., Social Research Methodology
BOGOSAVLJEVIĆ, S., Statistics in Psychology
BOJANOVIĆ, R. Z., Psychology of Interpersonal Relations
BOLČIĆ, S. I., Sociology of Work
BULATOVIĆ, R. N., Andragogy of Work
ČUPURDIJA, B., Social Anthropology
DENEGRI, J., History of Modern Art
DIMIĆ, L., Yugoslav History
DOŠEN, K., Philosophy
DUŠANIĆ, S. S., Ancient History
ELAKOVIĆ, S., History of Philosophy
HRNJICA, S., General Psychology with Personality Psychology
JELIĆ, V., History of Greek Literature
KAČAVENDA RADIĆ, N., Andragogy of Free Time
KOCIĆ, L. P., General Pedagogy
KOVAČEVIĆ, I., Methodology of Ethnology and Anthropology
KULJIĆ, T., Political Sociology
KUZMANOVIĆ, B., Social Psychology
LAZIĆ, M., Sociology
LJUSIĆ, R., National History of the New Age
LOMA, A., Historical Grammar of the Greek Language
MAKSIMOVIĆ, L. M., Byzantine History
MEDIĆ, S., Family Andragogy
MIKIĆ, Ž. M., Physical Anthropology
MILIĆ, A., Family Sociology
MILIN, M., Introduction to the Classics
MIMICA, A., History of Social Theory
MITROVIĆ, A., General History of the New Age
OPALIĆ, P., Social Pathology
PAJEVIĆ, D., Work Psychology
PEŠIĆ, M., Preschool Pedagogy
RADOŠ, K., Educational Psychology
RICL, M., Ancient History
RISTOVIĆ, M., General Modern History
ŠARANOVIĆ BOŽANOVIĆ, N., General Pedagogy
SPREMIĆ, M. M., General History of the Middle Ages
STANKOVIĆ, DJ. DJ., Yugoslav History
SUPUT, M., History of Architecture
TODIĆ, B., Introduction to Art History
TRNAVAC, N., School Pedagogy
VOJVODIĆ, M. S., General History of the New Age
VUJOVIĆ, S., Urban Sociology
ZEC, M., Introduction to Economics
ZUROVAC, M. M., Aesthetics

Faculty of Physical Chemistry (Studentski trg 12–16, 11000 Belgrade; tel. (11) 218-7133; fax (11) 218-7133; e-mail ffh@ffh.bg.ac.rs; internet www.ffh.bg.ac.rs):

ANIĆ, S., Physical Chemistry
BAČIĆ, G., Physical Chemistry of Fluids, Nuclear Spectrometry
DONDUR, V., Chemical Kinetics, Catalysis
HOLCLAJTNER ANTUNOVIĆ, I., General Physical Chemistry, Plasma Physical Chemistry
JEREMIĆ, M., Physical Chemistry
MARKOVĆ, D., Physical Chemistry, Physical Chemistry in Environmental Protection
MENTUS, S. V., Electrochemistry, Physical Chemistry of Solid Electrolytes
MILJANIĆ, Š., Radiochemistry and Nuclear Chemistry
MIOČ, U., Physico-Chemical Analysis, Applied Spectroscopy
PERIĆ, M. N., Quantum Chemistry and Molecular Structures, Spectra and Structures

Faculty of Physics (Studentski trg 12, 11000 Belgrade; tel. (11) 263-0152; fax (11) 328-2619; e-mail dekanat@ff.bg.ac.rs; internet www.ff.bg.ac.rs):

ANIČIN, I., Nuclear Physics

BELIĆ, D. S., Atomic and Molecular Physics, Applied Physics
ĆURIĆ, M. B., Dynamic Meteorology, Cloud Physics
DAMNJANOVIĆ, M., Quantum and Mathematical Physics, Condensed Matter Physics
ĐENIŽE, S. I., Ionized Gas and Plasma Physics, Atomic and Molecular Physics
DRNDAREVIĆ, S., Nuclear Physics, Particle and Field Physics
JANJIĆ, Z. I., Dynamic Meteorology
KNEŽEVIĆ, M., Statistical Physics
KONJEVIĆ, N., Classical and Quantum Optics, Lasers
KRPIĆ, D., Nuclear Physics, Particle and Field Physics
MILOŠEVIĆ, S., Statistical Phsyics
PURIĆ, J. M., Ionized Gas and Plasma Physics
SAVIĆ, I., Nuclear Physics, Condensed Matter Physics
SREKOVIĆ, A., Ionized Gas and Plasma Physics
STAMATOVIĆ, A. S., Applied Physics, Atomic and Molecular Physics
ZEKOVIĆ, L., Applied Physics, Condensed Matter Physics

Faculty of Political Sciences (Jove Ilića 165, 11000 Belgrade; tel. (11) 397-6422; fax (11) 249-1501; e-mail fpn@fpn.bg.ac.rs; internet www.fpn.bg.ac.rs):

DAMJANOVIĆ, M. D., Organization and Management Studies
JEVTIĆ, M., Religious and Political Studies
KECMANOVIĆ, N., Family Sociology
LAKIČEVIĆ, M., Social Development and Planning
MILOSAVLJEVIĆ, M. V., Social Pathology
PAVLOVIĆ, V. D., Political Sociology of Modern Society
PEŠIĆ, M. D., General Sociology
PODUNAVAC, M. L., Theory of Political Systems
RADOJKOVIĆ, M. J., Communication Studies
SAMARDŽIĆ, S., European Relations and European Union Studies
SIMEUNOVIĆ, D., Foundations of Political Science
SIMIĆ, M., Rehabilitation of Disabled Persons, Public Health
SLAVUJEVIĆ, Z., Political Marketing and Public Relations
SOKIĆ, S. R., Yugoslav Economy, National Economic Studies
ŠTAMBUK, V. Z., Cybernetics and Informatics
TRGOVČEVIĆ, L., Contemporary Political History
VASILJEVIĆ, B., Contemporary Political Economy
VESELINOV, D. S., Political Ecomony
VIDANOVIĆ, I., Social Case Work
VUKOVIĆ, D., Systems of Social Welfare

Faculty of Security Studies (Gospodara Vučića 50, 11000 Belgrade; tel. (11) 645-1843; fax (11) 645-7-685; e-mail dekanat@fb.bg.ac.rs; internet www.fb.bg.ac.rs):

CVETKOVIĆ, M., Contemporary Combat Systems and Devices
KANDIĆ, D., Introduction to Philosophy and Ethics, Ethics
MILAŠINOVIĆ, R., Conflict Theory
MIŠOVIĆ, S., Violent Conflict Theory
PLAVŠIĆ, M., Macroeconomics

Faculty of Sports and Physical Education (Blagoja Parovića 156, 11000 Belgrade; tel. (11) 353-1000; fax (11) 353-1100; e-mail dekanat@dif.bg.ac.rs; internet www.dif.bg.ac.rs):

ALEXSIĆ, V., Football
BOKAN, B., Physical Culture Theory
ĆIRKOVIĆ, Z., Martial Arts
ILIĆ, N., Physiology
JOVANOVIĆ, S., Martial Arts
KARALEJIĆ, M., Basketball
KUKOLJ, M., General Anthropology
LAZAREVIĆ, L., Psychology
NIKOLIĆ, Z., Physiology
PETROVIĆ, Z., Physical Culture Facilities
RADISAVIJEVIĆ, L., Rhythmic-Sports Gymnastics
RADISAVIJEVIĆ, M., Corrective Gymnastics
RADOJEVIĆ, J., Sports Gymnastics
ŠTAKIĆ, Đ., General Sociology and Physical Culture Sociology
STEFANOVIĆ, Đ., Athletics
UGARKOVIĆ, D., Human Development Biology with Elements of Sports Medicine

Faculty of Stomatology (Dr Subotića 8, 11000 Belgrade; tel. (11) 268-5288; fax (11) 685-361; e-mail dekan@stomf.bg.ac.rs; internet www.stomf.bg.ac.rs):

BELOICA, D. Ć., Paediatrics, Preventive Dentistry
DAPČEVIĆ, B., Internal Medicine
DERGENC, R, Otorhinolarnygology
DIMITRIJEVIĆ, B. B., Periodontology, Oral Medicine
DIMITRIJEVIĆ, B. R., Maxillofacial Surgery
GAVRIĆ, M. M., Maxillofacial Surgery
IVANOVIĆ, V., Conservation Dentistry Endodontics
JANKOVIĆ, L., Periodontology, Oral Medicine
KONTIĆ, M., General Surgery
LEKOVIĆ, V. M., Periodontology, Oral Mechine
MIJANOVIĆ, B., General Surgery
MIKOVIĆ, M. D., Forensic Medicine
MILENKOVIĆ, P. B., Pathophysiology
NIKODIJEVIĆ, M., General Surgery
NIKOLIĆ, L., Ophthalmology
PAP, K., Conservation Dentistry Endodontics
POTIĆ, J. B., Neurology and Psychiatry
SJEROBABIN, I., Maxillofacial Surgery
STAMENKOVIĆ, D., Prosthodontics
STANIŠIĆ-SINOBAD, D. N., Prosthodontics
STOJIĆ, D., Pharmacology, Toxicology
TODOROVIĆ, L. M., Oral Surgery
URSU MAGIDU, I., Periodontology, Oral Medicine
VRANJEŠ, D., Neurology and Psychiatry
VULOVIĆ, M. D., Paediatric Preventive Dentistry
ZELIĆ, O. B., Periodontology, Oral Medicine

Faculty of Teacher Training (Narodnog frontna 43, 11000 Belgrade; tel. (11) 361-5225; fax (11) 264-1060; e-mail dekanat@uf.bg.ac.rs; internet www.uf.bg.ac.rs):

BANDJUR, V. B., Didactics
JOVANOVIĆ, A., Literature
KECMANOVIĆ, N., Sociology

Faculty of Technology and Metallurgy (Karnegijeva 4, 11000 Belgrade; tel. (11) 337-0460; fax (11) 337-0387; e-mail tmf@tmf.bg.ac.rs; internet www.tmf.bg.ac.rs):

IVANIĆ, L., Casting, Theory of Casting
MAGADALINOVIĆ, D., Comminution and Classification
MARKOVIĆ, D., Materials Testing
MILIĆEVIĆ, Ž., Underground Mining Technology
MILJKOVIĆ, M., Mine Ventilation, Technical Safety Precautions
RAJČIĆ VUJASINOVIĆ, M., Hydro- and Electrometallurgical Process Theory
STANKOVIĆ, R., Transport and Haulage, Transport in Mineral Technologies
STANKOVIĆ, V., Metallurgical Operations
STANKOVIĆ, Z., Physical Chemistry
STANOJLOVIĆ, R., Physical Methods of Concentration, Mineral Processing
STAVRIĆ, B. J., Economics and Production Organization
ŽIVKOVIĆ, Ž., Nonferrous Metal and Alloy Metallurgy, Pyrometallurgical Process Theory

Faculty of Transport and Traffic Engineering (Vojvode Stepe 305, 11000 Belgrade; tel. (11) 309-1234; fax (11) 246-6294; e-mail dean@sf.bg.ac.rs; internet www.sf.bg.ac.rs):

BABIĆ, O., Air Traffic Control, Air Cargo Transport
BAKMAZ, M. R., Telecommunications Switching Technology, Telecommunications Traffic and Networks
BOJKOVIĆ, Z. S., Electrical Engineering, Basic Telecommunications Technology, Telecommunications Traffic Exploitation
BUKUMIROVIĆ, M. M., Cybernetics, Cybernetics in Transport and Traffic, Computer Simulation, System Modelling on Computer, Programming Languages in Postal and Telecommunications Traffic
ČOLIĆ, V., Ships and Vessels, Ship Resistance and Propulsion, Basics of Water Transport
CVETKOVIĆ, P. A., Fluid Mechanics, Mechanics, Materials Strength
KUZMANOVIĆ, D., Mechanics
LAZOVIĆ, S. M., Telecommunication Systems
MANDIĆ, D., Railway Traction, Urban Rail Systems, Rail Traffic Operation, Application of Telematics and Process Automation in Railway Traffic
MILORADOVIĆ, S., Mathematics
PANTELIĆ VUJANIĆ, S., Sociology, Traffic and Transport Engineering Law, Navigable Waterways Law, Air Transport Law, Traffic Law, Postal and Telecommunications Law, Railway Transport Law
PAPIĆ, V., Motor Vehicle Maintenance, Transport Vehicles and Maintenance
POPOVIĆ, J., Probability and Statistics, Operations Research
PUTNIK, N. D., Terminals
RADMILOVIĆ, Z., Port Planning and Design, Fleet Operation and Management, Water Transport Basics
RADOJKOVIĆ, Z., Roads, Civil Engineering Basics
ŠELMIĆ, R. R., Elements of Transport Devices and Installations, Thermodynamics
SRETENOVIĆ, M., Materials Handling, Fundamentals in Materials Handling
TOŠIĆ, V. S., Airports
VEŠOVIĆ, V. B., Transport and Traffic Organization and Manangement, Transport and Traffic, Transport and Traffic Work Organization, Postal and Telecommunications Organization and Management
VUJANIĆ, M., Traffic Safety, Accident Prevention, Accident Reconstruction
VUKANOVIĆ, S. V., Traffic Management and Control, Intelligent Transport Systems
VUKOBRAT, M. D., Mechanics
ŽEŽELJ, S., Motor Vehicles

Faculty of Veterinary Medicine (Blv Oslobođenja 18, 11000 Belgrade; tel. (11) 361-5436; fax (11) 268-5936; e-mail podrska@vet.bg.ac.rs; internet www.vet.bg.ac.rs):

ALEKSIĆ, Z., Forensic Veterinary Medicine
AŠANIN, R. M., Microbiology and Immunology
BALTIĆ, M., Fish, Crab and Shellfish Food Quality and Hygiene
BALGOJEVIĆ, Z., Anatomy
BOŽIĆ, T., Pathophysiology
BUNIČIĆ, O., Meat Hygiene and Meat Technology
DJURIČIĆ, B., Infectious Diseases of Domestic Animals
DOBRIĆ, Đ., Infectious Diseases of Domestic Animals
DREKIĆ, D. M., Anatomy

GLEDIĆ, D. S., Histology and Embryology
IVANOV, I., Ruminant and Swine Diseases, Clinical Diagnostics
JEZDIMIROVIĆ, M., Pharmacology and Toxicology
JOVANOVIĆ, M., General Pathology and Pathological Morphology
JOVANOVIĆ, S. J., Animal Breeding
KATIĆ, V., Dairy Product Hygiene
KATIĆ RADIVOJEVIĆ, S., Parasitology
KNEŽEVIĆ, M. A., General Pathology and Pathological Morphology
KULIŠIĆ, Z., Parasitology
LAZAREVIĆ, M., Physiology
MIJAČEVIĆ, Z. M., Dairy Product Technology
NIKOLIĆ, Z., Anatomy
NIKOLOVSKI STEFANOVIĆ, Z., Equine and Small Animal Disease, Clinical Propedeutics
PALIĆ, T. D., Avian Diseases, Equine and Small Animal Diseases
PAVLOVIĆ, V., Domestic Animal Reproduction, Artificial Insemination
PEJIN, I., Statistics
PETRUJKIĆ, T., Domestic Animal Reproduction, Artificial Insemination
POPOVIĆ, D., Biophysics
POPOVIĆ, N., Wild Animal Diseases, Equine and Small Animal Diseases
RADENKOVIĆ DAMNJANOVIĆ, B., Animal Hygiene and General Hygiene
ŠAMANC, H., Ruminant and Swine Diseases
ŠĆEPANOVIĆ, D., Sociology and Ethics
SIMIĆ, M., Histology and Embryology
SINOVEC, Z., Animal Nutrition Physiology and Pathology
SMILJANIĆ, D., Unit Operations
STOJANOVIĆ, L. V., Dairy Product Hygiene
STOJIĆ, V., Physiology
TRAILOVIĆ, D., Cattle Production Economics and Organization, Health Care, Cattle and Food Marketing and Transfer, Equine and Small Animal Diseases, Clinical Propedeutics
VASIĆ, J., Surgery, Orthopaedics, Ophthalmology
VICKOVIĆ, D., Forensic Veterinary Medicine
VUKOVIĆ, I., Meat Technology

School of Electrical Engineering (Blvr Kralja Aleksandra 73, 11120 Belgrade; tel. (11) 324-8464; fax (11) 324-8681; e-mail dekanat@etf.rs; internet www.etf.bg.ac.rs):

CVETKOVIĆ, D. M., Mathematics
ĐORDJEVIĆ, A. R., Microwave Technology, Electromagnetics, Fundamentals of Electrical Engineering
DRAJIĆ, D. B., Statistical Telecommunication Theory, Computer Telecommuncations, Digital Transfer Techniques, Transfer and Recording Codes
DUKIĆ, M., Signal Processing and Transfer, Telecommunications, Radio Systems
ĐURIĆ, M., Power System Components, Power Engineering System Regulation, Replay Protection, Power Stations and Distribution Plants
KOSTIĆ, M., Electrical Lighting, Electrical Installations with Lighting
KOVAČEVIĆ, B. D., Automatic Control, Stochastic Systems and Estimation
LACKOVIĆ, I. B., Mathematics
LAZIĆ, B., Fundamentals of Computer Technology, Computer Architecture, Operating Systems
MARJANOVIĆ, S. N., Electronics
MATAUŠEK, M. R., Optimal Process Control, Automatic Control Systems, Process Control, Process Identification
MERKELE, M., Mathematics, Probability and Statistics
MIKIČIĆ, D. J., Technical Mechanics with Hydraulics, Fundamentals of Mechanical Engineering
MILANOVIĆ, V., Quantum Mechanics, Electronic Device Components, Solid State Physical Electronics, Semiconducting Microstructures
MILUTINOVIĆ, V., Microprocessing Systems, Computer VLSI Systems
OSMOKROVIĆ, P., Electrical Engineering Materials, Dosimetry and Radiation Protection, Nuclear Physics
PAUNOVIĆ, Đ., Radio Systems, Telecommunication Electronics, Radio Relay Systems, Design and Simulation Methods, Radiotechnics
PETROVIĆ, D., A.C. Electrical Machinery, Electromechanical Power Conversion
PETROVIĆ, G., Digital Telecommunications, Digital Telephone Exchange Design, Telecommunication Networks, Digital Transfer Technology, Communication System Simulation, Computational Systems
PETROVIĆ, T., Simulation and Modelling, Non-linear Control Systems, Automatic Control Robust Systems Regulation
PETROVIĆ, Z., Satellite Systems, Fundamentals of Telecommunications, Integrated Telecommunications Networks
POPOVIĆ, B. D., Electrical Measurements, Biomedical Engineering, Biomedical Instrumentation
POTKONJAK, V. N., Robots and Automation
PRAVICA, P. B., Telecommunications
RADUNOVIĆ, J. B., Materials Physics, Optoelectronic Devices and Systems, Optoelectronic and Laser Systems, Electro-optics, Statistical Physics
RAJAKOVIĆ, N., Distributive and Industrial Networks, Power Systems Analysis, Power Systems Exploitation, Power Systems Analysis
RAKOVIĆ, D., Materials Physics, Biophysics
RAMOVIĆ, R., Microelectronics, Electronic Device Components, Semiconductor Analysis and Modelling
REIJIN, B., Electrical Circuit Theory, Medical Informatics, Digital Information Processing, Electrical Circuit Theory
SAVIĆ, M. S., High Voltage Technology, High Voltage Equipment
ŠIMIĆ, S. K., Mathematics
ŠKOKLJEV, I., General Power Engineering, Power Engineering System Planning
SREĆKOVIĆ, M., Laser Technics, Quantum Electronics
STANKOVIĆ, D. K., Sensors and Converters, Physico-Technical Measurement, Sensors and Actuators
STANKOVIĆ, S. S., Stochastic Signal Processing, Artificial Intelligence and Neural Networks, Automatic Control Systems, Digital Signal Processing
STOJIĆ, M. R., Automatic Control, Digital Control Systems
VASILJEVIĆ, D. M., Digital System Design
VELAŠEVIĆ, D. M., Programming Compilers, Expert Systems, Digital Programming
ŽIVKOVIĆ, D. B., Computer System Control, Pulse and Digital Electronics
ZLATANOVIĆ, M. D., Sensors and Convertors, Atomic and Molecular Spectroscopy, Fundamentals of Mechanical Engineering

School of Medicine (Dr Subotica 8, 11000 Belgrade; tel. (11) 363-6368; fax (11) 363-6368; e-mail boca@med.bg.ac.rs; internet www.med.bg.ac.rs):

ALEKSANDRIĆ, B., Forensic Medicine
ANTUNOVIĆ, V., Surgery
APOSTOLSKI, S., Neurology
ARSOV, V. J., Surgery
ASIĆ RADOSAVLJEVIĆ, G., Internal Medicine
AVRAMOVIĆ, D. M., Internal Medicine
BACETIĆ, D., Pathological Anatomy
BANIĆEVIĆ, M., Paediatrics
BLAGOTIĆ, M. Ž., Anatomy
BOGDANOVIĆ, R., Paediatrics
BOŠKOVIĆ, D., Internal Medicine
BOŠNJAK, V. I., Internal Medicine
BOŽANIĆ, M., Internal Medicine
BOŽIĆ, M., Infectious Diseases
BRKIĆ POPOVIĆ, V., Internal Medicine
BULAJIĆ, M., Internal Medicine
BUMBAŠIREVIĆ, V., Histology and Embryology
BUNJEVAČKI, G., Paediatrics
ȘUTKOVIĆ, I., Surgery
ÇEBEŠEK, R., Internal Medicine
ÇEMERIKIĆ, D. A., Pathological Physiology
ÇOLOVIĆ, M., Internal Medicine
ČOLOVIĆ, R., Surgery
CUCIĆ, V. S., Social Medicine
CVEJIĆ, V., Biochemistry
CVETKOVIĆ, D. H., Pathological Anatomy
CVETKOVIĆ, M., Gynaecology and Obstetrics
DENIĆ DJORDJEVIĆ, G., Pathological Physiology
ĐERIĆ, D., Otolaryngology and Maxillofacial Surgery
DJORDJEVIĆ, L. V., Anatomy
DJURIČIĆ, B., Biochemistry
ĐORĐEVIĆ, M., Surgery
ĐORĐEVIĆ, P., Internal Medicine
DOTLIĆ, R., Statistics and Informatics in Medicine
DRAŠKOVIĆ MAŠIREVIĆ, G., Physiology
DREZGIĆ, M., Internal Medicine
ĐUKIĆ, P., Surgery
ĐUKIĆ, V., Surgery
DUNJIĆ, D., Forensic Medicine
ERIĆ MARINKOVIĆ, J., Statistics and Informatics in Medicine
GANOVIĆ, R., Gynaecology and Obstetrics
GLEDOVIĆ, Z., Epidemiology
GLIŠIĆ, S., Surgery
GOLUBOVIĆ, G., Internal Medicine
GOLUBOVIĆ, S., Ophthalmology
GRBOVIĆ, L. Č., Pharmacology and Toxicology
GRUJIĆ, M., Internal Medicine
HADŽI ĐOKIĆ, J. B., Surgery
HAN, R., Nuclear Medicine
HAVELKA, M., Pathological Anatomy
IGNAJČEV, M., Ophthalmology
ILANKOVIĆ, N., Psychiatry
ILIĆ, A. B., Anatomy
JAKOVIĆ, M., Surgery
JANIĆIJEVIĆ, M., Surgery
JANKOVIĆ, S., Epidemiology
JANOŠEVIĆ, L., Otolaryngology and Maxillofacial Surgery
JANOŠEVIĆ, S., Statistics and Informatics in Medicine
JAREBINSKI, M. S., Epidemiology
JAŠOVIĆ, M., Psychiatry
JEVREMOVIĆ, I., Epidemiology
JORGA, I., Physiology
JORGA, V., Hygiene and Medical Ecology
JOVANOVIĆ, T. M., Physiology
JOVANOVIĆ, T. P., Microbiology and Immunology
KALEZIĆ, V., Surgery
KAŽIĆ, T. M., Pharmacology and Toxicology
KOCIJANČIĆ, M., Internal Medicine
KOCIJANČIĆ, R., Hygiene and Medical Ecology
KONTIĆ, Đ., Ophthalmology
KOSTIĆ, V., Neurology
KOVAČEVIĆ, N., Internal Medicine
KOVAČEVIĆ, S. J., Forensic Medicine
LABAN, A. I., Pathological Anatomy
LAČKOVIĆ, V. B., Histology and Embryology
LASTIĆ, S. S., Anatomical Pathology
LATKOVIĆ, Z., Ophthalmology
LONČAR STEVANOVIĆ, H., Physiology
LOTINA, S., Surgery
LUKIĆ, V. S., Neurology
MAGLAJIĆ, S., Paediatrics
MAKSIMOVIĆ, Ž., Surgery
MANČIĆ, J., Paediatrics

MARIĆ, J., Psychiatry
MARINKOVIĆ, S. V., Anatomy
MARŠEVALSKI, A., Physical Medicine and Rehabilitation
MARTINOVIĆ, Ž., Neurology
MATIĆ, M., Internal Medicine
MICIĆ, D., Internal Medicine
MICIĆ, S., Surgery
MIJAĆ, M., Anatomy
MILENKOVIĆ, S., Ophthalmology
MILIČEVIĆ, N., Histology and Embryology
MILIČEVIĆ, R., Surgery
MILIČEVIĆ, Ž., Histology and Embryology
MILIKIĆ MITIĆ, M., Internal Medicine
MILOVIĆ, I., Surgery
MILUTINOVIĆ, D., Surgery
MIMIĆ OKA, J. I., Biochemistry
MISITA, V., Ophthalmology
MITROVIĆ, M. M., Surgery
MUJOVIĆ, V. M., Physiology
MUNJIZA, M., Psychiatry
NEDELKJOV, V., Pathological Physiology
NEŠIĆ, V., Internal Medicine
NIKOLIĆ, G., Physical Medicine and Rehabilitation
NIKOLIĆ, S., Infectious Diseases
NIKOLIĆ, P. L., Infectious Diseases
OBRADOVIC, M., Forensic Medicine
OBRADOVIĆ, V., Nuclear Medicine
OCIĆ, G., Neurology
OSTOJIĆ, M., Internal Medicine
OŠTRIĆ, V., Internal Medicine
PANTELIĆ ATANACKOVIĆ, M., Pathological Anatomy
PANTIĆ, S., Histology and Embryology
PAOVIĆ STANOJEVIĆ, A., Ophthalmology
PAPOVIĆ, R., Biology and Human Genetics
PAUNOVIĆ, V., Psychiatry
PAVLOVIĆ, M. D., Infectious Diseases
PAVLOVIĆ, M. R., Physiology
PAVLOVIĆ, M. Ž., Occupational Medicine
PAVLOVIĆ, S., Nuclear Medicine
PEJOVIĆ, M., Psychiatry
PERIŠIĆ, M., Internal Medicine
PERIŠIĆ, V., Paediatrics
PEŠIĆ, B., Pathological Physiology
PETKOVIĆ, S., Gynaecology and Obstetrics
PILIPOVIĆ, N., Internal Medicine
PLEĆAŠ, D., Hygiene and Medical Ecology
POPOVIĆ, G., Physical Medicine and Rehabilitation
POPOVIĆ, M. R., Surgery
POTIĆ VESOVIĆ, V., Physical Medicine and Rehabilitation
PROSTRAN, M., Anatomy
PROSTRAN, M., Pharmacology and Toxicology
RADEVIĆ, B., Surgery
RADONJIĆ, V., Anatomy
RADULOVIĆ, N., Paediatrics
RADULOVIĆ, R., Otolaryngology and Maxillofacial Surgery
RAMIĆ, Z., Microbiology and Immunology
RANKOVIĆ, A., Anatomy
REBIĆ, P., Internal Medicine
REPAC, R. M., Surgery
RISTIĆ, M., Surgery
RUNIĆ, S., Gynaecology and Obstetrics
SAMARDŽIĆ, M., Surgery
SAMARDŽIĆ, R. G., Pharmacology and Toxicology
ŠAŠIC, M., Infectious Diseases
SAVIČ DJURKOVIĆ, R. M., Biochemistry
ŞEFEROVIĆ, P., Internal Medicine
ŠIKIĆ, B., Pathological Physiology
SIMEUNOVIĆ, S. D., Paediatrics
SIMIĆ, S., Social Medicine
SINĐELIĆ, R., Surgery
SKENDER, M., Pathological Anatomy
SLAVKOVIĆ, S., Surgery
STANIMIROVIĆ, B., Gynaecology and Obstetrics
STARČEVIĆ, V., Physiology
STAROVIĆ, D., Surgery
STEFANOVIĆ, B., Histology and Embryology
STEVOVIĆ, D. M., Surgery
STOJKOVIĆ MOSTARICA, M., Microbiology and Immunology
SUBOTIĆ, S. L., Surgery
SUZIĆ, S., Physiology
TALIĆ, B. S., Surgery
TEOFILOVSKID, G. E., Anatomy
TIMOTIJEVIĆ, I., Psychiatry
TODOROVIĆ, S., Neurology
TRPINAC, D., Histology and Embryology
VASILJEVIĆ, J., Pathological Anatomy
VASILJEVIĆ, Z., Internal Medicine
VELIMIROVIĆ, D., Surgery
VELIMIROVIĆ, D., Pathological Anatomy
VELJKOVIĆ, S. D., Forensic Medicine
VIDAKOVIĆ, A. R., Occupational Medicine
VLAHOVIĆ ŠVABIĆ, M., Microbiology and Immunology
VLAJINAC, H. D., Epidemiology
VUČKOVIĆ, V., Physiology
VUČOVIĆ, D., Surgery
VULOVIĆ, D. M., Pathological Physiology
VULOVIĆ, Z., Chemistry in Medicine
ZAMAKLAR, D., Surgery
ZEC KRANJČIĆ, I., Microbiology and Immunology
ŽIVKOVIĆ, S., Surgery

Technical Faculty in Bor (Vojske Jugoslavije 12, 19210 Bor; tel. (30) 424-555; fax (30) 421-078; e-mail office@tf.bor.ac.rs; internet www.tf.bor.ac.rs):

IVANIĆ, L., Casting, Theory of Casting
MAGDALINOVIĆ, N. M., Comminution and Classification
MARKOVIĆ, D., Metals Testing
MILIĆEVIĆ, Ž. M., Underground Mining Technology
MILJKOVIĆ, M. A., Mine Ventilation, Technical Safety Precautions
RAJČIĆ VUJASINOVIĆ, M., Theory of Hydro- and Electrometallurgical Processes
STANKOVIĆ, R., Transport and Haulage, Transport in Mineral Technologies
STANKOVIĆ, V., Metallurgical Operations
STANKOVIĆ, Z. D., Physical Chemistry
STANOJLOVIĆ, R. D., Physical Concentration Methods, Mineral Processing
ŽIVKOVIĆ, Ž. D., Metallurgy of Non-Ferrous Metals and Alloys, Pyrometallurgical Process Theory

UNIVERZITET U KRAGUJEVCU
(University of Kragujevac)

Jovana Cvijica bb, 34000 Kragujevac
Telephone: (34) 370-270
Fax: (34) 370-168
E-mail: unikg@kg.ac.rs
Internet: www.kg.ac.rs

Founded 1976
State control
Academic year: October to June

Rector: Prof. Dr SLOBODAN ARSENIJEVIC
Vice-Rector for Finance: Prof. Dr BRANISLAV JEREMIC
Vice-Rector for Education: Prof. Dr ZORA ARSOVSKI
Vice-Rector for Science and Research: Prof. Dr ZIVADIN BUGARCIC
Gen.-Sec.: ZORICA AVRAMOVIC
Librarian: RUŽICA IGNJATOVIĆ

Library of 100,000 vols
Number of teachers: 1,000
Number of students: 14,000

Publication: *LIPAR* (cultural and literary themes, 4 a year)

DEANS

Faculty of Agriculture in Čačak: Prof. Dr MIROSLAV SPASODEVIĆ
Faculty of Economics in Kragujevac: Prof. Dr SLOBODAN MALINIĆ
Faculty of Law in Kragujevac: Prof. Dr PREDRAG STOJANOVIC
Faculty of Mechanical Engineering in Kragujevac: Prof. Dr MIROSLAV BABIĆ
Faculty of Mechanical Engineering in Kraljevo: Dr NOVAK NEDIĆ
Faculty of Medicine in Kragujevac: Dr NEBOJSA ARSENIJEVIĆ
Faculty of Philology and Arts in Kragujevac: Prof. FREE ŠTETIĆ
Faculty of Science and Mathematics in Kragujevac: Assoc. Prof. Dr DRAGOSLAV NIKEZIĆ
Faculty of Technology in Čačak: Prof. Dr JEROSLAV ŽIVANIĆ
Teacher-Training Faculty in Jagodina: Prof. SRETKO DIVLJAN
Teacher-Training Faculty in Užice: Prof. Dr KRSTIVOJE ŠPIJUNOVIĆ

UNIVERZITET U NIŠU
(University of Niš)

Univerzitetski trg 2, 18000 Niš
Telephone: (18) 257-970
Fax: (18) 257-950
E-mail: uniuni@ni.ac.rs
Internet: www.ni.ac.rs

Founded 1965
State control

Rector: Prof. Dr DAGAN ANTIC (acting)
Vice-Rector for Teaching: Prof. Dr VLASTIMIR DJOKIC (acting)
Vice-Rector for Scientific Work: Prof. Dr DRAGAN DÖNITZ (acting)
Vice-Rector for International Cooperation: Prof. Dr VESNA LOPICIC (acting)
Vice-Rector for Finance: Prof. Dr SLOBODAN ANTIC (acting)
Sec.-Gen.: DRAGOSLAV DJOKIĆ

Number of teachers: 1,514
Number of students: 25,844

Publications: *Facta Universitatis* (scientific journal, irregular), *Teme* (journal for social theory and practice, 4 a year)

DEANS

Faculty of Arts: Prof. DRAGOSLAV ACIMOVIC (acting)
Faculty of Civil Engineering and Architecture: Prof. Dr DRAGAN ARANDJELOVIĆ
Faculty of Economics: Dr EVICA PETROVID
Faculty of Electronic Engineering: Prof. Dr DRAGAN ANTIĆ
Faculty of Law: Prof. Dr NEVENA PETRUSIC
Faculty of Mechanical Engineering: Prof. Dr VLASTIMIR NIKOLIĆ
Faculty of Medicine: Prof. Dr MILAN VIŠNJIĆ
Faculty of Occupational Safety: Prof. Dr LJILJANA ŽIVKOVIĆ
Faculty of Philosophy: Prof. Dr MOMCILO STOJKOVIC
Faculty of Science and Mathematics: Prof. Dr DRAGAN S. ĐORĐEVIĆ
Faculty of Sports and Physical Education: Prof. Dr DOBRICA ŽIVKOVIČ
Faculty of Technology in Leskovac: Prof. Dr JAKOV STAMENKOVIĆ
Teacher-Training Faculty in Vranje: Prof. Dr STANA SMILJKOVIĆ

PROFESSORS

Faculty of Arts (Knjeginje Ljubice 10, 18000 Niš; tel. and fax (18) 522-396; fax (18) 513-272; e-mail info@artf.ni.ac.rs; internet www.artf.ni.ac.rs):

CEKIĆ, N., Forms Design

Faculty of Civil Engineering and Architecture (Aleksandra Medvedeva 14, 18000 Niš; tel. (18) 588-200; fax (18) 588-200; e-mail gaf@gaf.ni.ac.rs; internet www.gaf.ni.ac.rs):

ANDJELKOVIĆ, H., Descriptive Geometry
ANDJELKOVIĆ, M., Industrial Facilities Design, Public Facilities Design
ARANDJELOVIĆ, D., Hydraulic Engineering
CEKIĆ, N., Public Facilities Design, Essential Designing
DAMNJANOVIĆ, M., Architectural Structures, Metal Structures, Metal Structures in Buildings
DRENIĆ, D., Structure Testing, Coupled and Special Structures
IGIĆ, T., Strength of Materials, Structure Plasticity and Limitation Analysis
ILIĆ, C., Railway Engineering, Superstructures and Stations
ILIĆ, D., Housing Design, Project Development
MARKOVIĆ, M., Descriptive Geometry
MARKOVIĆ, V., Dams and Water Potential Utilization
MILENKOVIĆ, S., Urban Water Supply and Sewerage Systems Engineering
MITKOVIĆ, P., Urbanism, Area Planning
PETKOVIĆ, D., Concrete Structures, Concrete Bridges
POPOVIĆ, B., Structure Plasticity and Limitation Analysis, Structure Statics
PROLOVIĆ, V., Foundation Engineering
PROTIĆ, P., Mathematics
RADIVOJEVIĆ, G., Statics of Architectural Structures, Construction Systems
SPASOJEVIĆ, N., Concrete Bridges, Concrete Structures
STOJIĆ, D., Timber Structures and Scaffolds, Timber and Masonry Structures
TRAJKOVIĆ, D., Organization of Construction Works
VELIČKOVIĆ, D., Metal Structures
ZDRAVKOVIĆ, S., Structural Stability and Dynamics, Theory of Surface Girders
ŽIVKOVIĆ, D., Hydrotechnical Structures
ZLATANOVIĆ, M., Organization of Construction Works, Elements of Road Engineering

Faculty of Economics (Trg Kralja Aleksandra Ujedinitelja 11, 18000 Niš; tel. (18) 528-601; fax (18) 523-859; e-mail ekonomski@eknfak.ni.ac.rs; internet www.eknfak.ni.ac.rs):

ARANDJELOVIĆ, Z., Yugoslav Economy, Economic Policy
BARAC, N., Business Logistics Management
BOGDANOVIĆ, S., Mathematics
CVETANOVIĆ, S., Theory and Policy of Economic Development
ĆUZOVIĆ, S., Trade Economics, Trade Management
DJEKIĆ, S., Agricultural Economics, Agricultural Management
FIGAR, N., Business Economics
GLIGORIJEVIĆ, Ž., Industrial Economics, Industrial Management
GROZDANOVIĆ, D., Business Economics
HAFNER, P., Sociology
JOVANOVIĆ, R., Informatics
KITANOVIĆ, D., Political Economy
KOSTIĆ, V., Russian Language
KRSTIĆ, B., Banking, Banking Management
KRSTIĆ, J., Financial Accounting, Auditing
NIKOLIĆ, S., Business Organization
NOVIĆEVIĆ, B., Managerial Accounting
PREDIĆ, B., Business Planning and Development Policy
SEKULOVIĆ, M., Economic Doctrines, Transition Economics
STANKOVIĆ, L., Marketing, International Marketing
TODOROVIĆ, E., Business Finance
TODOROVIĆ, O., Operations Research, Financial Mathematics
ZDRAVKOVIĆ, D., Theory of Prices and Pricing Policy

Faculty of Electronic Engineering (Aleksandra Medvedeva 14, 18000 Niš; tel. (18) 529-105; fax (18) 588-399; e-mail efinfo@elfak.ni.ac.rs; internet www.elfak.ni.ac.rs):

ARSIĆ, M., Measurements in Electronics, Telemetry
DAMNJANOVIĆ, M., VLSI Design, Electronic System Design
DANKOVIĆ, B., Methods of Intelligent Control, Process Control, Process Identification
DELETIĆ, S., Theory of Social Development
DIMITRIJEVIĆ, B., Electrical Measurement, Intelligent Instrumentation, Measurement in Microelectronics
DJORDJEVIĆ, B., Digital Electronics, Electronic Circuits
DJORDJEVIĆ KAJAN, S., Computer Graphics, Systems Software, Data Structures and Databases, Software Engineering
GMITROVIĆ, M., Network Synthesis and Signal Processing
JANKOVIĆ, N., Power Components and Circuits, Sensors and Convertors
KOCIĆ, LJ., Mathematics, Numerical Mathematics
KOVAČEVIĆ, M., Mathematics, Numerical Mathematics
KRSTIĆ, D., Wireless Engineering, High-Frequency Electronics
LITOVSKI, V., Electronics, Neural Networks, Electronic Circuit Design
MARKOVIĆ, V., Microwave Electronics, Satellite Communications
MILOSAVLJEVIĆ, Č., Elements of Automatic Control, EMP Regulation
MILOŠEVIĆ, M., Electroacoustics, Audiotechnics
MILOVANOVIĆ, B., Microwave Technology, Microwave Systems, Mobile Telecommunications
MILOVANOVIĆ, D., Electronics, Analogue Electronics
MILOVANOVIĆ, G., Mathematics, Mathematical Methods, Numerical Mathematics
MILOVANOVIĆ, I., Mathematics, Discrete Mathematics
MITIĆ, D., Elements of Electrical Engineering, Electromagnetics
NAUMOVIĆ, M., SAU Design, Automatic Control Theory, Intelligent Control Methods
NIKOLIĆ, Z., Quality and Reliability
NIKOLIĆ, Z., Mobile Telecommunications, Basic Telecommunications, Telecommunications in Electronic Power Engineering
PEJČIĆ, M., Philosophy and Sociology
PEJOVIĆ, M., Physics
PETKOVIĆ, M., Mathematics
PETKOVIĆ, P., Computer-Aided Design, Electronics Circuit Design, Integrated Circuit Design
RADENKOVIĆ, V., Electrical Measurement, Measurement in Electric Power Engineering
RANČIĆ, P., Electrical Installations and Illumination, Special Electrical Installations
RISTIĆ, S., Electronic Components, Semiconducting Components, Power Components and Circuits
STANKOVIĆ, M., Basic Computer Technology, Programming Languages, Assemblers
STANKOVIĆ, R., Logic Design, Pattern Recognition
STEFANOVIĆ, D., Optoelectronics
STEFANOVIĆ, M., Optic Telecommunications, Telecommunication Theory, Digital Telecommunications, Telecommunication System Design, Radar Systems and Radiolocation
STOJADINOVIĆ, N., Quality and Reliability, Physical Electronics, Failure Physics and Diagnostics, Components Characterization, Basic Microelectronics
STOJANOVIĆ, V., Circuit Theory, Television Systems, Television, Digital Picture Processing
STOJČEV, M., Microprocessing Technology, Microprocessing Systems
STOJILKOVIĆ, S., Low Temperature Electronics
TOKIĆ, T., Microcomputers and Programming, Microcomputer Systems and I/O Devices
VELIČKOVIĆ, D., Electromagnetics, Basic Electrical Engineering
ŽIVKOVIĆ, LJ., Materials for Electronics

Faculty of Law (Trg Kralja Aleksandra 11, 18000 Niš; tel. (18) 500-201; fax (18) 4523-747; e-mail pravni@prafak.ni.ac.rs; internet www.prafak.ni.ac.rs):

BOŽIĆ, M., Economic Policy
ĆIRIĆ, A., International Trade Law
DJURDJIĆ, V., Criminal Procedural Law with Crime Investigation and Law Enforcement
GORČIĆ, J., Financial Law
KONSTANTINOVIĆ-VILIĆ, S., Criminology, Penology
KOVAČEVIĆ-KUŠTRIMOVIĆ, R., Introduction to Civil and Property Law
MIJAČIĆ, M., Law of Obligation
MILENOVIĆ, D., Trade Law
NIKOLIĆ, D., General Legal History
PETROVIČ, M., Administrative Law, Management Science with Legal Informatics
RADIVOJEVIĆ, Z., Public International Law
ROČKOMANOVIĆ, M., Private International Law
SERJEVIĆ, V., Political Economy
SIMIĆ, M., Introduction to Law
STANIMIROVIĆ, D., Sociology
STANKOVIĆ, G., Civil Procedural Law, Arbitration Law
STOJANOVIČ, D., Constitutional Law
STOJIČIĆ, S., National Legal History

Faculty of Mechanical Engineering (ul. Aleksandra Medvedeva 14, 18000 Niš; tel. (18) 588-229; fax (18) 588-244; e-mail info@masfak.ni.ac.rs; internet www.masfak.ni.ac.rs):

BLAGOJEVIĆ, B., Aeration and Ventilators, Cooling Techniques
BOGDANOVIĆ, B., Hydro-Power Transmitters, Compressors and Ventilators, Piping
BORIČIĆ, Z., Fluid Mechanics, Hydraulic and Pneumatic Systems of Automatic Control
ĆOJBAŠIĆ, LJ., Basic Processing Technology, Prime Materials
DJOKIĆ, V., Theory and Methods of Mechanical Systems Design, Elements of Construction Theory, Construction Methods, Welded Constructions, Rubber Construction Machines
DJORDJEVIĆ, D., Sociology and Philosophy of Natural Sciences, Basic Labour Sociology and Economics
DJURDJANOVIĆ, M., Welding, Welding Technology, Machine Systems Tribology
DOMAZET, D., Modelling and Optimization of Production Systems, Computer-Aided Production Design
HEDRIH, K., Elastodynamics
ILIĆ, G., Measurement Technology, Thermodynamics
JEVTIĆ, V., Technical Logistics, Mining and Building Machinery, Continuous Transport Machinery, Mining Mechanization, Driving System Dynamics, Fundamentals of Technical Logisitics
JOVANOVIĆ, M., Computer-Aided Design, Information Technologies, Structure Analysis, Geometric Modelling, Metal Construction
LAKOVIĆ, S., Thermal Plants, Thermal Power Plants, Boilers

LAZAREVIĆ, D., Tools, Non-Conventional Methods, Polymer Modelling Tools
MARINKOVIĆ, V., Machining, Processing Tribology
MILENKOVIĆ, D., Turbomachine Theory and Fundamentals, Hydraulic Machines, Special Pumps
MILOVANČEVIĆ, D., Mathematics
MILTENOVIĆ, V., Machine Parts, Reliability of Machine Systems, Integral Product Development, Machine System Supervision and Protection
NIKODIJEVIĆ, D., Fluid Mechanics, Oil Hydraulics and Pneumatics, Hydraulic Components, Hydro-Pneumatic Elements in Mechatronics, Physics
NIKOLIĆ, V., Automatic Control, Automatic Control Discrete Systems, Systems of Control in Mechatronics, Optimal Control, Nonlinear Control Systems, Neural and Fuzzy Modelling and Control
PAVLOVIĆ, N., Mechanisms in Mechatronics, Micromechanics, Elements of Fine Mechanics, Optical Elements in Mechatronics
PAVLOVIĆ, R., Mechanics, Plate and Shell Theory
PETKOVIĆ, LJ., Mathematics, Numerical Mathematics and Programming
PETROVIĆ, T., Measurement Techniques, Basic Mechatronics, Mechanical Elements in Mechatronics, Mechatronic System Design, Special Design Methods
RADOJKOVIĆ, N., Thermodynamics, Thermal and Diffusing Apparatus
STEFANOVIĆ, A., Internal Combustion Engines
STOJILJKOVIĆ, M., Automation of Production, Packing Machines, Pneumatic and Hydraulic Components, Assembling and Packing Technology, Digital Control Techniques
STOJILJKOVIĆ, V., Production Management, Processing by Plastic Deformation, Management in Mechanical Engineering, Production Process Statistical Control
TASIĆ, Ž., Electrical Engineering and Electronics, Basic Mechatronics
TEMELJKOVSKI, D., Machines for Processing by Deformation
VULIĆ, A., Power Conveyors, Quality of Machine Systems, Technical Diagnostics, Special-Purpose Machines, Agricultural Machines
ŽIVKOVIĆ, D., Hydromechanics of Mixtures, Thermal Turbomachines
ŽIVKOVIĆ, Ž., Theory of Machines and Mechanisms, Technical Drawing, Mechatronic System Modelling

Faculty of Medicine (Blvr Dr Zorana Đinđića 81, 18000 Niš; tel. (18) 457-0029; fax (18) 423-8770; e-mail contact@medfak.ni.ac.rs; internet www.medfak.ni.ac.rs):

ANTIĆ, M., Medical Sociology
BABIĆ, M., Neurosurgery
BAŠIĆ, H., Pathological Anatomy
BJELAKOVIĆ, G., Biochemistry
BOGIĆEVIĆ, M., Nuclear Medicine
BOŠNAKOVIĆ, P., Radiology
BURAZOR, M., Internal Medicine, Cardiology
DAČIĆ-SIMONOVIĆ, D., Dental Pathology
DENOVIĆ, B., Forensic Medicine
DIMOV, D., Pathological Anatomy
DJORDJEVIĆ, D., Internal Medicine, Pneumophysiology
DJORDJEVIĆ, V., Biochemistry
DJORDJEVIĆ, V., Internal Medicine, Nephrology
FILIPOVIĆ, S., Elements of Clinical Oncology
IGIĆ, A., Prosthodontics
IGIĆ, S., Prosthodontics
ILIĆ, R., Pathological Anatomy
ILIĆ, S., Internal Medicine, Cardiology
ILIĆ, SL., Nuclear Medicine
JEREMIĆ, M., Surgery, General Surgery
JOVANOVIĆ, D., Physiology
JOVČIĆ, S., Paediatric Surgery
KAMENOV, B., Paediatrics
KATIĆ, V., Pathological Anatomy
KOCIĆ, B., Microbiology and Immunology
KOJOVIĆ, Z., Physical Medicine and Rehabilitation
KONSTANTINOVIĆ, LJ., Infectology
KOSTIĆ, V., Infectology
KOSTIĆ, Z., Hygiene and Medical Ecology
KRSTIĆ, M., Infectology
KUTLEŠIĆ, Č., Pathological Anatomy
LOVIĆ, B., Internal Medicine, Cardiology
MALOBABIĆ, Z., Pharmacology and Toxicology
MARKOVIĆ, V., Internal Medicine, Cardiology
MARKOVIĆ, Z., Internal Medicine, Rheumatology
MIHAJLOVIĆ, D., Pathological Anatomy
MIHAJLOVIĆ, M., Physiology
MIHAJLOVIĆ, P., Physics
MILADINOVIĆ, P., Gynaecology and Obstetrics
MILATOVIĆ, S., Radiology
MILENKOVIĆ, Z., Surgery, Neurosurgery
MILIĆEVIĆ, R., Paediatric Surgery
MILOSAVLJEVIĆ, LJ., Otorhinolaryngology
MILOSAVLJEVIĆ, M., Gynaecology and Obstetrics
MILJKOVIĆ, S., Psychiatry with Medical Psychology
MIRKOVIĆ, B., Oral and Periodontal Diseases
MITIĆ, N., Dental Pathology
MITIĆ, S., Dental Pathology
MITROVIĆ, M., Surgery, Orthopaedics
MITROVIĆ, R., Hygiene, Medical Ecology
NIKOLIĆ, J., Biochemistry
NOVAK, D., Paediatrics
ORLOV, S., Oral and Periodontal Diseases
PARAVINA, M., Dermatovenereology
PAVLOVIĆ, D., Biochemistry
PEROVIĆ, M., Histology and Embryology
POP-TRAJKOVIĆ, Ž., Gynaecology and Obstetrics
RADENKOVIĆ, S., Pathological Physiology
RADIĆ, S., Pathological Physiology
RAIČEVIĆ, R., Internal Medicine, Nephrology
RANKOVIĆ, Ž., Infectology
SAVIĆ, M., Paedodontics and Preventive Stomatology
SAVIĆ, V., Pathological Anatomy
SKOČAJIĆ, S., Dental Pathology
SPALEVIĆ, M., Forensic Medicine
SPASIĆ, M., Epidemiology
STAMENKOVIĆ, I., Internal Medicine, Gastroenterology
STANIŠIĆ, V., Medical Statistics and Informatics
STANKOVIĆ, A., Internal Medicine, Rheumatology
STANKOVIĆ, D., Prosthodontics
STEFANOVIĆ, N., Anatomy
STEFANOVIĆ, V., Internal Medicine, Nephrology
STOJILJKOVIĆ, M., General Surgery
STOJILJKOVIĆ, S., Pathological Physiology
TIODOROVIĆ, B., Epidemiology
VELJKOVIĆ, S., Physiology
VIŠNJIĆ, M., Plastic Surgery
VUČETIĆ, D., Gynaecology and Obstetrics
VUČETIĆ, R., Anatomy
VUJIČIĆ, B., Oral Surgery
ZLATANOVIĆ, G., Opthalmology
ŽIVKOVIĆ, DJ., Internal Medicine, Pneumophysiology

Faculty of Occupational Safety (Čarnojevića 10A, 18000 Niš; tel. (18) 529-701; fax (18) 249-962; e-mail dekanat@znrfak.ni.ac.rs; internet www.znrfak.ni.ac.rs):

ANDJELKOVIĆ, B., Protection against Fire in Technical Processes, Introduction to Working and Living Environment Protection, Technological Processes in the Living Environment
CVETKOVIĆ, D., Noise and Vibrations, Noise in the Living Environment
DJORDJEVIĆ, J., Sociology, Social Ecology
IVANJAC, M., Labour Law
JANKOVIĆ, Ž., Safety at Work with Machines and Devices, Fire Extinguishing Processes and Methods
JOVANOVIĆ, D., Protection against Fire and Explosions, Uncontrolled Combustion Processes
MITIĆ, D., Ignition and Combustion Theory, Engineering Materials
NEDELJKOVIĆ, V., Ventilation and Air-Conditioning Systems, Energy and Living Environment
SPASIĆ, D., Economics of Occupational Safety, Economics of Environmental Protection
STANKOVIĆ, M., Mathematics, Mathematical Modelling
ŽIVKOVIĆ, LJ., Safety at Work with Thermal Plants
ŽIVKOVIĆ, N., Systems and Equipment for Industrial Waste Treatment, Air Protection

Faculty of Philosophy (Ćirila i Metodija 2, 18000 Niš; tel. (18) 514-312; fax (18) 514-310; internet www.filfak.ni.ac.rs):

BOGDANOVIĆ, N., History of Serbian Language, Dialectology
BUTIGAN, Z., Sociology of Politics
DJORDJEVIĆ, Z., Introduction to History with Methodology
DJUROVIĆ, R., Serbian Language (Phonology with Accentology)
IVKOVIĆ, M., Sociology of Education, Social Sciences Teaching Methods
MAŠOVIĆ, D., Introduction to American Studies, American Literature
MILOSAVLJEVIĆ, LJ., History of Social Theories, Introduction to Philosophy
MITROVIĆ, LJ., General Sociology
NAUMOVIĆ, M., Sociology of Rural Areas, Sociology of Urban Areas
NEŠIĆ, B., Pedagogical Psychology
NEŠIĆ, V., Social Psychology
PETROVIĆ, Č., Political Economy with Elements of Economic Systems
RISTIĆ, R., Introduction to Canadian and Australian Studies
STOJADINOVIĆ, M., Yugoslav Literature
STOJANOVIĆ, M., Yugoslav Literature
STOJKOVIĆ, M., Sociology of Morals, Labour Sociology
VELIČKOVIĆ, D., Russian Language
VIDANOVIĆ, DJ., English Morphology and Teaching Methods
ŽUNIĆ, D., Sociology of Art, Sociology of Culture and Arts with Serbian Cultural History

Faculty of Sciences and Mathematics (Višegradska 33, 18000 Niš; tel. (18) 223-430; fax (18) 533-014; e-mail dragan@pmf.ni.ac.rs; internet www.pmf.ni.ac.rs):

ĆIRIĆ, M., Mathematical Logic, Computer Technology Teaching Methods, Philosophy and History of Mathematics
DIMITRIJEVIĆ, P., Electromagnetism and Optics, Physics
JANKOVIĆ, S., Differential and Integral Equations, Theory of Probability and Random Processes
KOČINAC, LJ., Linear Algebra and Analytical Geometry, Topology
MILETIĆ, G., Instrumental Analytical Chemistry
MILJKOVIĆ, LJ., Solid State Physics, Physics of Materials
NIKOLIĆ, R., Higher Inorganic Chemistry
NOVAKOVIĆ, N., Physics, Plasma Physics

OBRADOVIĆ, M., Physical Chemistry
PALIĆ, R., Organic Chemistry
PAVLOTIĆ, T., Mechanics and Thermodynamics, Physics of Surfaces and Thin Layers
PECEV, T., Analytical Chemistry
PREMOVIĆ, P., General and Inorganic Chemistry
PURENOVIĆ, M., Industrial Chemistry
RADOVANOVIĆ, B., Instrumental Methods of Structural Analysis, Mechanisms of Organic Reactions
RAKOČEVIĆ, V., Functional Analysis, Theory of Measures and Integrals
STANIMIROVIĆ, P., Programming Languages, Mathematical Programming
URSIĆ-JANKOVIĆ, J., Biochemistry

Faculty of Sports and Physical Education (Čarnojevića 10A, 18000 Niš; tel. (18) 510-900; fax (18) 42-482; e-mail info@ffk.ni.ac.rs; e-mail faksfiz@ni.ac.rs):

BUBANJ, R., Biomechanics
DJURAŠKOVIĆ, R., Biology of Human Development with Sports Medicine
JOKSIMOVIĆ, S., Football, Skiing
KOSTIĆ, R., Dancing
KOSTIĆ, R., Volleyball
PETKOVIĆ, D., Sports Gymnastics
POPOVIĆ, R., Rhythmical and Sports Gymnastics
VUČKOVIĆ, S., Recreation Theory and Teaching Methods, Activities in Nature
ŽIVANOVIĆ, N., Theory and History of Physical Education
ŽIVKOVIĆ, D., Theory of Corrective Gymnastics, Corrective Gymnastics Teaching Methods

Faculty of Technology in Leskovac (Blvr oslobodjenja 124, 16000 Leskovac; tel. (16) 247-203; fax (16) 242-859; e-mail info@tehfin.tehfak.ni.ac.rs):

CAKIĆ, M., Physical Chemistry, Instrumental Analysis
CVETKOVIĆ, D., Organic Chemistry, Organo-Chemical Technology
CVETKOVIĆ, LJ., Production Management and Basic Marketing, Product Management
DJORDJEVIĆ, G., Mathematics
DJORDJEVIĆ, S., Organic Chemistry
GLIGORIJEVIĆ, V., Planning of Textile Processes, Knitting Technology
ILIĆ, P., General Chemistry
KOCIĆ, M., Physics
MARKOVIĆ, D., Instrumental Analysis, Organic Analysis, Chemical-Engineering Thermodynamics
NOVAKOVIĆ, M., Dyeing and Printing Technology
STANKOVIĆ, M., Biochemistry, Technology of Natural Organic Products
STANKOVIĆ, S., Analytical Chemistry
STOJILJKOVIĆ, D., Elements of Equipment in Processing Industry, Engineering Drawing, Mechanics
STOJILJKOVIĆ, S., Thermodynamics and Thermotechnics, Construction Materials, Process Analysis and Simulation, Chemical-Engineering Thermodynamics
TRAJKOVIĆ, C., Clothing Production Technology, Textile Quality Control and Testing
VELJKOVIĆ, V., Unit Operations in Chemical Engineering

Teacher-Training Faculty in Vranje (Partizanska 14, 17500 Vranje; tel. (17) 431-960; fax (17) 421-633; e-mail ucfaxvranje@yahoo.com; internet www.ucfak.ni.ac.rs):

CENIĆ, S., General Pedagogy, History of Pedagogy
MALINOVIĆ, T., Mathematics, Mathematical Teaching Methods

UNIVERZITET U NOVOM PAZARU
(University of Novi Pazar)

Demetrius Tucovića bb, 36300 Novi Pazar
Telephone: (20) 316-634
Fax: (20) 337-322
E-mail: info@uninp.edu.rs
Internet: www.uninp.edu.rs

Founded 2002
Private Control

Pres.: MUFTI MUAMER EF. ZUKORLIĆ
Rector: Prof. Dr MEVLUD DUDIC

Library of 10,000 vols

DEANS

Dept of Art: Prof. Dr FEHIM HUSKOVIĆ
Dept of Economics: Prof. Dr BEĆIR KALAC
Dept of Legal Science: Prof. Dr MUAMMER NICEVIĆ
Dept of Natural and Technical Sciences: Prof. Dr CAMIL SUKIĆ
Dept of Pedagogical and Psychological science: Prof. Dr ADMIR MURATOVIĆ
Dept of Philological Sciences: Dr SAMINA DAZDAREVIĆ

UNIVERZITET U NOVOM SADU
(University of Novi Sad)

Trg Dositeja Obradovića 5, 21000 Novi Sad
Telephone: (21) 6350-622
Fax: (21) 450-418
E-mail: rektorat@uns.ac.rs
Internet: www.uns.ac.rs

Founded 1960
State control
Languages of instruction: Serbian, Hungarian
Academic year: October to July

Rector: Prof. MIROSLAV VESKOVIĆ
Vice-Rector for Education: Prof. MILAN SIMIĆ
Vice-Rector for Finance: Prof. RADOVAN PEJANOVIĆ
Vice-Rector for International Relations and Science: Prof. PAVLE SEKERUŠ
Vice-Rector for Students: GORAN RADIĆ
Gen.-Sec.: ANĐELKA STANOJEVIĆ

Library of 15,000 vols, 450 theses, 400 Periodicals
Number of teachers: 3,297
Number of students: 48,415
Publication: *Glas Univerziteta* (newspaper, 12 a year)

DEANS

Academy of Arts: Prof. ZORAN TODOVIĆ
Faculty of Agriculture: Prof. Dr MILAN KRAJINOVIĆ
Faculty of Civil Engineering: Prof. Dr DRAGAN MILAŠINOVIĆ
Faculty of Economics: Prof. Dr NENAD VUNJAK
Faculty of Education: Prof. Dr ALEKSANDAR PETOJEVIĆ
Faculty of Law: Prof. Dr RANKO KEČA
Faculty of Mathematics, Natural Sciences: Prof. Dr NEDA MIMICA-DUKIĆ
Faculty of Medicine: Prof. Dr NIKOLA GRUJIĆ
Faculty of Philosophy: Prof. Dr LJILJANA SUBOTIĆ
Faculty of Sport and Physical Education: Prof. Dr MILENA MIKALAČKI
Faculty of Technical Sciences: Prof. Dr ILIJA ĆOSIĆ
Faculty of Technology: Prof. Dr ZOLTAN ZAVARGO
'Mihajlo Pupin' Technical Faculty: Prof. Dr MILAN PAVLOVIĆ
Teacher Training Faculty in Hungarian: Prof. Dr KATALIN KAIĆ

PROFESSORS

Academy of Arts (Akademija Umetnosti, Djure Jakšića 7, 21000 Novi Sad; tel. (21) 422-177; fax (21) 420-187; e-mail aofarts@uns.ac.rs; internet www.akademija.uns.ac.rs):

BLANUŠA, M., Painting and Painting Technology
ČERNOGUBOV, B., Choir
DENKOVIĆ, LJ., Sculpture
DOBANOVAČKI, B., Poster Arts
DRAŠKOVIĆ, B., Acting, Directing
DJAK, Ž., Graphics and Graphic Technology
GILIĆ, V., Directing
HORVAT, L., Viola
JANKETIĆ, M., Acting
JOVANOVIĆ, V., Elements of Vocal Technique
JOVANOVIĆ, Z., Chamber Music
KATUNAC, D., History of Music, History of Performing
KINKA, R., Piano
KLEMENC, I., Stage Movement
KNEŽEVIĆ, S., Graphics and Graphic Technology
LAZIĆ, R., History and Aesthetics of Directing
MARINKOVIĆ, O., Diction
MIŠIĆ, LJ., Dance
OGNJENOVIĆ, V., Acting
OSTOJIĆ, N., Tone Syllable
OSTOJIĆ, T., Conducting
PREDOJEVIĆ-MILOVANOVIĆ, V., Voice Technique
RAKIDŽIĆ, J., Painting and Painting Technology
RNJAK, D., History of World Drama and Theatre
SIMONOVIĆ, M., Voice Technique
SRDIĆ, N., Clarinet
STANOJEV, M., Graphics and Graphic Technology
STAŠEVIĆ, M., Drawing and Drawing Technology
SUBOTIĆ, I., History of Art
STATKIĆ, M., Composition
TODOROVIĆ, D., Painting and Painting Technology
UZELAC, M., Aesthetics
VARGA, I., Cello

Faculty of Agriculture (Poljoprivredni Fakultet, Trg Dositeja Obradvića 8, 21000 Novi Sad; tel. (21) 485-3500; fax (21) 459-761; e-mail dean@polj.ns.ac.rs; internet polj.uns.ac.rs):

ALMAŠI, R., Special Entomology
ANTOV, G., Cattle Breeding, Animal Husbandry
BABIĆ, LJ., Drying and Storage, Basic Agricultural Engineering
BAJKIN, A., Agricultural Machinery
BALAŽ, F., Mycoses of Plants, Plant Protection
BALAŽ, J., Mycoses and Bacterioses of Plants
BELIĆ, S., Water Management, Irrigation and Drainage Engineeering
BOGDANOVIĆ, D., Agrochemistry
BOŠNJAK, DJ., Crop Irrigation
BOŽIDAREVIĆ, D., Marketing of Agricultural and Food Products
BRKIĆ, M., Elements of Agricultural Technology, Thermotechnology in Agriculture
ĆINDRIĆ, P., Fruit Growing and Viticulture
ĆOBANOVIĆ, K., Statistics, Statistical Methods
DJUKIĆ, D., Forage Crop Production
DJUKIĆ, NI., Agricultural Machinery
DJUROVKA, M., Vegetable Crop Production
ERIĆ, P., Forage Crops
GOVEDARICA, M., Microbiology
GVOZDENOVIĆ, D., Pomology, Picking and Storage of Fruit
HADŽIĆ, V., Pedology

JARAK, M., Microbiology
JASNIĆ, S., Plant Pathology, Plant Viruses
JOVANOVIĆ, M., Economics of Agricultural Estates, Economics of Agricultural Engineering
KEVREŠAN, S., Chemistry
KNEŽEVIĆ, A., Botany
KONSTANTINOVIĆ, B., Special Phytopharmacy, Control of Weeds
KORAĆ, M., Pomology, Viticulture
KOVČIN, S., Nutrition of Nonruminant Animals
KRAJINOVIĆ, M., Animal Husbandry
KRALJEVIĆ-BALALIĆ, M., Genetics
LAZIĆ, B., Vegetable Crop Production
LAZIĆ, V., Agricultural Machinery
MALETIN, S., Agricultural Zoology
MALINOVIĆ, N., Agricultural Machinery
MARINKOVIĆ, B., Arable Crop Production, Agronomy
MARKOVIĆ, V., Vegetable Crop Production
MIHAILOVIĆ, D., Meteorology
MIHAJLOVIĆ, L., Agricultural Cooperative Economics, Agrarian Policy
MIHALJEV, I., Seed Production
MILIĆ, D., Organization of Fruit and Vine Production, Business Organization and Economics
MOLNAR, I., Agronomy
NIKOLIĆ, R., Agricultural Tractors, Agricultural Machinery
NOVKOVIĆ, N., Planning Theory and Methodology of Organization
OBRENOVIĆ, D., Business Analysis, Bookkeeping
PAPRIĆ, DJ., General Viticulture
PEJANOVIĆ, R., Economy
PEJIĆ, N., Nutrition of Ruminant Animals
PEKANOVIĆ, V., Botany
PETRIĆ, D., General Entomology
PETROVIĆ, N., Plant Physiology, Protection of Ecosystems
PETROVIĆ, S., Genetics
POKRIĆ, V., Land Reclamation
POPOVIĆ, M., Plant Biochemistry, Biochemistry of Farm Animals
POTKONJAK, S., Economics of Melioration and Mechanization, Economics of Water Resources
POTKONJAK, V., Mechanization in Animal Breeding, Means of Transportation in Agriculture
RATAJAC, R., Agricultural Zoology, Ecology
SAVIĆ, S., Fodder, Feeding Technology
SRDJEVIĆ, B., Informatics
STANČIĆ, B., Breeding of Farm Animals
STARČEVIĆ, LJ., Arable Crop Production
STEVANOVIĆ, M., Agronomy
STOJANOVIĆ, S., Botany
SUPIĆ, B., Poultry Production, Animal Husbandry
ŠTAJNER, D., Chemistry
ŠTRBAC, P., Special Entomology, Plant Protection
TEODOROVIĆ, M., Pig Breeding
UBAVIĆ, M., Agrochemistry
VIDOVIĆ, V., Improvement of Farm Animals
ŽIVANOVIĆ, M., Special Phytopharmacy

Faculty of Civil Engineering (Gradjevinski Fakultet, Kozaračka 2A, 24000 Subotica; tel. (24) 554-300; fax (24) 554-580; e-mail dekanat@gf.su.ac.rs; internet www.gf.uns.ac.rs):

BENAK, J., Water Refinement and Water Quality
ĆULIBRK, R., Earthworks, Elements of Traffic Arteries
DELEVIĆ, K., Organization in Building
GOSTOVIĆ, M., Engineering Geodesy
KLEIN, R., Architecture
MEŠTER, DJ., Technical Mechanics
MIHAILOVIĆ, V., Concrete Structures
MILAŠINOVIĆ, D., Resistance of Materials, Theory of Surface Bearers
SAM, A., Social Sciences
STOJKOVIĆ, S., Watercourses, Flood Management
VLAJIĆ, LJ., Experimental Analysis of Construction
ZELENHASIĆ, E., Hydrology and Elements of Hydrotechnology

Faculty of Economics (Ekonomski Fakultet, Segedinski put 9–11, 24000 Subotica; tel. (24) 628-000; fax (24) 546-486; e-mail dekanat@ef.uns.ac.rs; internet www.ef.uns.ac.rs):

ACIN, DJ., International Economic Relations
ACIN SIGULINSKI, S., International Trade, Management in International Trade
ADŽIĆ, S., Economic System and Economic Policy, National Economy
AHMETAGIĆ, E., Theory of an Organization
ANDRIĆ, M., Accountancy and Revision, Financial Control and Revision
BALABAN, N., Principles of Informatics, Support Systems in Decision Making
BALJ, B., Philosophy
BANDIN, J., Accountancy and Bookkeeping
BANDIN, T., Business Economics
ČILEG, M., Operational Research
DJURKOVIĆ, J., Principles of Informatics, Analysis and Planning of Information Systems
DMITROVIĆ, LJ., Management Accounting
GABRIĆ MOLNAR, I., Sociology
JAKOVČEVIĆ, K., Business Economics
JOSIFIDIS, K., Macroeconomics
KALINIĆ, V., Trade Company Management, Marketing in Trade
KIŠ, T., Econometrics
KONČAR, J., Economics of Domestic Commerce and Commercial Politics
KRMPOTIĆ, T., Agrotechnology
LEKIĆ, T., Development of Technology and Commercial Recognition of Goods
LEKOVIĆ, B., Principles of Management
LJUBOJEVIĆ, Č., Marketing Services
LOVRE, K., Programming of Agricultural Development
MALEŠEVIĆ, DJ., Analysis of Business Enterprise Operations
MESAROŠ, K., Mathematics for Economists
SALAI, S., Marketing of Research, Market Communications
STOJKOVIĆ, M., Statistics
ŠAGI, A., Microeconomics
SUŠNJAR, G., Human Resources Management
ŠUVAKOV, T., Microeconomics
TODOSIJEVIĆ, R., Strategic Management, Investments
TOT, A., History of Economic Thought
VASILJEV, S., Marketing
VUGDELIJA, D., Mathematics for Economists
VUNJAK, N., Finance, Banking

Faculty of Education (Pedagoški Fakultet, Podgorička 4, 25000 Sombor; tel. (25) 460-595; fax (25) 26461; e-mail dekanat@pef.uns.ac.rs; internet www.pef.uns.ac.rs):

BERBER, S., School Hygiene with Ecology
DJURIĆ, DJ., Social Psychology, Educational Psychology
ERAKOVIĆ, T., Defectology
GRHOVAC, S., Teaching Methods in Serbian Language and Literature, Performing Arts
JANKOVIĆ, P., General Pedagogy
LIPOVAC, M., Pedagogy, Didactics
LJUBOJEV, P., Mass Communication, Film and Television Culture
MALEŠEVIĆ, J., Elements of Natural Sciences
NENADIĆ, M., General Sociology, Sociology of Education
PETROVIĆ, N., Mathematics and Teaching Methods in Mathematics
PINTER, J., Teaching Methods in Mathematics, Informatics in Education

Faculty of Law (Pravni Fakultet, Trg Dositeja Obradovića 1, 21000 Novi Sad; tel. (21) 485-3040; fax (21) 450-427; e-mail dekanat@pf.ns.ac.rs; internet www.pf.uns.ac.rs):

ARSIĆ, Z., Economic Law
BOŠKOVIĆ, M., Criminology, Penology
CARIĆ, S., Economic Law
CVEJIĆ-JANČIĆ, O., Family Law, Inheritance Law
DJURDJEV, A., Constitutional Law
DJURDJEV, D., International Public Law
ETINSKI, R., International Public Law
GRUBAČ, M., Criminal Procedural Law
JOVANOVIĆ, PA., Contemporary Political Systems
JOVANOVIĆ, PR., Labour Law
KEČA, R., Civil Procedural Law
KRKLJUŠ, LJ., History of Yugoslav State and Law
MALENICA, A., Roman Law
MARJANOVIĆ, M., Sociology
MILKOV, D., Administrative Law
PAJVANČIĆ, M., Constitutional Law
PERIĆ, O., Criminal Law
PIHLER, S., Criminal Law
POPOV, DJ., Principles of Economics
POPOVIĆ, M., Theory of State and Law
SALMA, J., Law of Obligation
STANKOVIĆ, F., Principles of Economics
ŠARKIĆ, S., History of State and Law
SOGOROV, S., Economic Law
VRANJEŠ, M., Financial Law
VUČKOVIĆ, M., Law of Obligation
VUKADINOVIĆ, G., Theory of State and Law
VUKIĆEVIĆ, M., Introductory Economics

Faculty of Medicine (Medicinski Fakultet, Hajduk Veljkova 3, 21000 Novi Sad; tel. (21) 420-677; fax (21) 662-4153; e-mail dekanmf@uns.ac.rs; internet www.medical.uns.ac.rs):

ALEKSIĆ, S., Gynaecology and Obstetrics
AVRAMOV, S., Surgery
BABIĆ, LJ., Pathology
BALTIĆ, V., Internal Medicine
BUDAKOV, P., Pathology
BUJAS, M., Gynaecology and Obstetrics
BORIŠEV, V., Surgery
BOROTA, J., Biochemistry
ČVEJANOV, M., Surgery
ČIKOŠ, J., Internal Medicine
ČURIĆ, S., Internal Medicine
DJAKOVIĆ-ŠVARCER, K., Pharmacology and Toxicology
DJILAS-TODOROVIĆ, LJ., Internal Medicine
DOKMANOVIĆ-DJORDJEVIĆ, M., Gynaecology and Obstetrics
DŽOLEV, A., Maxillofacial Surgery
ERI, Ž., Pathology
FILIPOVIĆ, D., Physiology
GEBAUER, E., Paediatrics
GRUJIĆ, N., Physiology
GRUJIĆ, V., Social Medicine
GUDOVIĆ, R., Anatomy
GUDURIĆ, B., Surgery
HADŽIĆ, B., Pathology
HADŽIĆ, M., Pathology
IVETIĆ, V., Physiology
IVKOVIĆ-LAZAR, T., Internal Medicine
JANJIĆ, DJ., Surgery
JERANT-PATIĆ, V., Microbiology with Parasitology and Immunology
JEŠIĆ-VINDIŠ, M., Internal Medicine
JOVANOVIĆ, J., Infectious Diseases
KNEŽEVIĆ, A., Psychiatry and Medical Psychology
KOVAČEVIĆ, Z., Biochemistry
KRISTIFOROVIĆ-ILIĆ, M., Hygiene
KRSTIĆ, A., Paediatrics
KRSTIĆ-BOŽIĆ, V., Biology
KULAUZOV, M., Pathological Physiology
KULAUZOV, M., Microbiology with Parasitology and Immunology
LATINOVIĆ, S., Ophthalmology
LAŽETIĆ, B., Physiology
LUČIĆ, A., Pathological Physiology
LUČIĆ, Z., Radiology

LUKAČ, I., Radiology
MAČVANIN, N., Occupational Medicine
MARTINOV-CVEJIN, M., Social Medicine
MIHALJ, M., Anatomy
MIHALJEV-MARTINOV, J., Neurology
MIKOV, M., Pharmacology and Toxicology
MILIČIĆ, A., Surgery
MIROSAVLJEV, M., Hygiene
MILOŠEVIĆ, D., Otorhinolaryngology
MILUTINOVIĆ, B., Physiology
MIRKOVIĆ, M., Surgery
MIROSAVLJEV, M., Hygiene
OBRADOVIĆ, D., Anatomy
PAVLOV-MIRKOVIĆ, M., Gynaecology and Obstetrics
PAVLOVIĆ, S., Internal Medicine
PEJIN, D., Internal Medicine
PJEVIĆ, M., Gynaecology and Obstetrics
PJEVIĆ, M., Surgery
POLZOVIĆ, A., Anatomy
POPOV, I., Psychiatry, Medical Psychology
POPOVIĆ, D., Forensic Medicine
POPOVIĆ, J., Pharmacology and Toxicology
POPOVIĆ, LJ., Surgery
POPOVIĆ, M., Chemistry
RISTIĆ, J., Maxillofacial Surgery
RONČEVIĆ, N., Paediatrics
SABO, A., Pharmacology and Toxicology
SAVIĆ, K., Medical Rehabilitation
SAVIĆ, M., Occupational Medicine
SEDLAK-VADOC, V., Pathological Physiology
SEGEDI, D., Obstetrics and Gynaecology
SIMIČ, M., Forensic Medicine
SOMER, LJ., Histology and Embryology
SOMER, T., Surgery
STANKOVIĆ, S., Biophysics
STANULOVIĆ, M., Pharmacology and Toxicology
STOJANOVIĆ, S., Surgery
STOJKOV, J., Surgery
STOJŠIĆ, DJ., Internal Medicine
ŠĆEKIĆ, V., Internal Medicine
ŠEGULJEV, Z., Epidemiology
ŠLJAPIĆ, N., Pathology
TASIĆ, M., Forensic Medicine
TOPALOV, V., Internal Medicine
VADOC-SEDLAK, V., Pathological Physiology
VOJINOVIĆ-MILORADOV, M., Chemistry
VUKADINOVIĆ, S., Surgery
VUKOVIĆ, B., Epidemiology
ZAMUROVIĆ, A., Medical Rehabilitation
ŽIKIĆ, M., Neurology
ZORIČIĆ, D., Surgery

Faculty of Natural Sciences and Mathematics (Prirodno-Matematički Fakultet, Trg Dositeja Obradovića 3, 21000 Novi Sad; tel. (21) 455-630; fax (21) 455-662; e-mail dekanpmf@uns.ac.rs; internet www.pmf.uns.ac.rs):

ABRAMOVIĆ, B., Microanalysis
ACKETA, D., Informatics and Numerical Mathematics
BIKIT, I., Nuclear Physics
BJELICA, L., Physical Chemistry
BOGDANOVIĆ, Ž., Physical Geography
BOŽIĆ-KRSTIĆ, V., Biology with Human Genetics
BUDIMAC, Z., Informatics and Numerical Mathematics
BUDINČEVIĆ, M., Analysis and Geometry
BUGARSKI, D., Geography
CRVENKOVIĆ, S., Mathematics
CVETKOVIĆ, LJ., Informatics and Numerical Mathematics
ĆURČIĆ, S., Social Geography
DALMACIJA, B., Chemical Technology and Environmental Protection
DAVIDOVIĆ, R., Regional Geography
DIVJAKOVIĆ, V., Physics of Condensed Matter
DJURDJEV, B., Social Geography
DJUROVIĆ, S., Atomic Physics, Physical Electronics
GAAL, F., Analytical Chemistry
GAJIĆ, LJ., Analysis and Probability
GAJIN, S., Microbiology
GRUBOR-LAJŠIĆ, G., Biochemistry, Physiology, Histology
HADŽIĆ, O., Probability and Statistics, Mathematics
HALAŠI, R., Organic Analysis
HERCEG, D., Numerical Mathematics
JANJIĆ, J., Physics
JOVANOVIĆ, LJ., Chemistry
KAPOR, A., Physics of Condensed Matter
KAPOR, D., Theoretical Physics
KARLOVIĆ, E., Chemical Technology and Environmental Protection
KOSANIĆ, M., General Chemistry
KOVAČEVIĆ, R., Biochemistry
KUHAJDA, K., Chemistry of Natural Products
KRSTIĆ, B., Plant Physiology
LEOVAC, V., Inorganic Chemistry
LOZANOV-CRVENKOVIĆ, Z., Analysis and Probability
MADARASZ-SZILAGYI, R., Algebra and Mathematics
MAŠKOVIĆ, LJ., Classical Theoretical Mechanics
MATAVULJ, M., Microbiology
MERKULOV, LJ., Botany, Plant Anatomy and Morphology
MILJKOVIĆ, LJ., Physical Geography
MILJKOVIĆ, N., Physical Geography
NIKOLIĆ, A., Physical Chemistry
OBADOVIĆ, D., Physics, Physics of Liquid Crystals
PAP, E., Mathematics, Analysis and Geometry
PAUNIĆ, DJ., Informatics and Numerical Mathematics
PENOV-GAŠI, O., Organic Chemistry
PERIŠIĆ-JANJIĆ, N., General and Inorganic Chemistry
PETROVIĆ, D., Biophysics, Medical Physics
PETROVIĆ, J., Organic Chemistry
PETROVIĆ, O., Microbiology, Bacteriology
PETROVIĆ, V., Algebra and Mathematics
PILIPOVIĆ, S., Analysis and Probability
POPSAVIN, V., Chemistry of Natural Products
STANKOVIĆ, Š., Biophysics, Medical Physics
STANKOVIĆ, Ž., Plant Physiology
STEVANOVIĆ, D., Morphology and Taxonomy of Invertebrates
STOJAKOVIĆ, Z., Linear Algebra
STOJANOVIĆ, S., Theoretical Mechanics and Electrodynamics
SURLA, D., Computer Science
ŠURLA, K., Numerical Mathematics
ŠEŠELJA, B., Mathematical Logic and Algebra, Mathematical Elements of Informatics
ŠETRAJČIĆ, J., Theoretical Physics
ŠIMIĆ, S., Biology, Zoology
ŠKRINJAR, M., Theoretical Physics
ŠURANJI, T., Analytical Chemistry
TAKAČI, A., Mathematics
TAKAČI, DJ., Mathematics, Analysis and Geometry
TERZIĆ, M., Atomic and Isotopic Molecular Spectroscopy
TOMIĆ, P., Geography
TOŠIĆ, B., Theoretical Physics
TOŠIĆ, R., Combinatorics
VAPA, LJ., Biochemistry, Physiology, Histology, Genetics
VOJINOVIĆ-MILORADOV, M., General Chemistry
VOJVODIĆ, G., Algebra and Logic
VRBAŠKI, Ž., Chemical Technology
VUČKOVIĆ, M., Botany, Plant Ecology, Ecology of Medicinal Herbs
VUJIČIĆ, B., Physical Electronics
ŽDERIĆ, M., Biology
ŽIGRAI, I., Analytical Chemistry

Faculty of Philosophy (Filozofski Fakultet, Dr Zorana Đinđića 2, 21000 Novi Sad; tel. (21) 450-690; fax (21) 450-929; e-mail dekanat@unsff.ns.ac.rs; internet www.ff.uns.ac.rs):

BANJAI, J., Literary Theory
BEKIĆ, T., German Literature
BERIĆ, V., History of German Language
BIRO, M., Elements of Clinical Psychology, Elements of Psychotherapy and Consulting
BOŠNJAK, I., Hungarian Literature
BURZAN, M., Serbian Language
ČAKI, P., Introduction to Expert and Scientific Work, Library Science
ČELOVSKI, S., Slovak Studies
ĆOVIĆ, B., Russian Literature
DINIĆ-KNEŽEVIĆ, D., Medieval History of Yugoslav Nations
DJOŠIĆ, D., Demography with Statistics
DUDOK, D., History of Slovak Language and Literature
EGERIĆ, M., Modern Serbian Literature
GADJANSKI-MARICKI, K., Classical Languages, Ancient History
GENC, L., Genetics and Educational Psychology
GEROLD, L., Hungarian Literature
GORDIĆ, S., Serbian and Yugoslav Literature, Serbian Critics
GRANDIĆ, R., Theory of Education, Family Pedagogy
GRKOVIĆ, M., History of Serbian and Comparative Grammar of Slavic Languages
HARPANJI, M., Slovak Literature, Literary Theory
IGNJATOVIĆ, I., General Psychology, Psychology of Personality
IVANOVIĆ, R., History of Yugoslav Literature
JUKIĆ, S., Elements of Pedagogy, Methodical Bases of Educational Work
JUNG, K., Ethnology, Hungarian Folk Literature
KAIĆ, K., History of Hungarian Culture
KAMENOV, E., Pre-School Education
KAPOR-STANULOVIĆ, P., Development of Psychology, Mental Health
KARANOVIĆ, Z., Serbian Folk Literature
KLEUT, M., Serbian Literature
KOKOVIĆ, D., Sociology and Sociology of Culture
KOSANOVIĆ, B., Russian Literature
KULIĆ, M., Philosophy
LANC, I., Introduction to General and Hungarian Linguistics
MATIĆ, LJ., French Literature
MATIJAŠEVIĆ, J., Modern Russian Language
MILOSAVLJEVIĆ, P., Methodology of Literary Studies
MILOŠEVIĆ, B., Introduction to Sociology, Occupational Sociology
MLADENOVIĆ, U., Pedagogic Psychology, Genetic and Pedagogic Psychology
MOLNAR-ČIKOŠ, L., Syntax of Hungarian Language, Phonetics of Hungarian Language
MOMČILOVIĆ, B., English Literature
OLJAČA, M., Educational System
PEROVIĆ, M., Philosophy
PETROVIĆ, D., Dialectology of Serbian and Standard Serbian Language
PIŽURICA, M., History of Serbian Language
POPOV, Č., Modern History
PUŠIĆ, LJ., Urban Sociology
RADOVANOVIĆ, M., General Linguistics
RADOVIĆ, M., Comparative Literature
RAMAČ, J., Ruthenian Language, Ukrainian Language
REDJEP, J., Medieval Literature
RISTIĆ, Ž., Methodology of Psychology
RODIĆ, R., School Education
ROKAI, P., Medieval History
SAVIĆ, S., Sociolinguistics and Discourse Analysis
SIMEUNOVIĆ, V., Philosophy

STEFANOVIĆ, M., Literary Theory, Serbian Literature
STEPANOV, R., Theory of Law and Politics
STOJAKOV, S., Introduction to Education Science
STRAJNIĆ, N., Comparative Literature
ŠIPKA, M., Statistical Psychology
TAMAŠ, J., Ruthenian Literature, Ukrainian Literature
TOČANAC, D., Modern French Language
TRIPKOVIĆ, M., Sociology and Sociological Theories
UTAŠI, Č., History of Hungarian Literature
VUKOVIĆ, G., Modern Serbian Language

Faculty of Sport and Physical Education (Fakultet sporta i fizičkog vaspitanja, Lovćenska 16, 21000 Novi Sad; tel. (21) 450-188; fax (21) 450-199; e-mail admin@fsfv.ac.rs; internet www.fsfvns.rs):

BALA, G., Kinesiology of Individual Sports
BJELICA, S., Sociological and Psychological Elements of Kinesiology
DIMOVA, K., Kinesiology of Individual Sports
DUNDJEROVIĆ, R., Kinesiology of Individual Sports
KALAJDŽIĆ, J., Kinesiology of Sports Games
KRSMANOVIĆ, B., Theory and Methods of Physical Education
LUKAČ, D., Sports Medicine
MALACKO, J., Kinesiology of Sports
NIĆIN, DJ., Kinesiology
RADOSAV, M., Football
RAIČ, A., Economical and Political Elements of Kinesiology
SAVIĆ, M., Martial Sports
TONČEV, I., Kinesiology of Individual Sports
ULIĆ, D., Kinesitherapy

Faculty of Technical Sciences (Fakultet Tehničkih Nauka, Trg Dositeja Obradovića 6, 21000 Novi Sad; tel. (21) 485-2055; fax (21) 458-133; e-mail ftndean@uns.ac.rs; internet www.ftn.uns.ac.rs):

ATANACKOVIĆ, T., Material Resistance
BABIN, N., Transport Machines
BAČLIĆ, B., Mechanics and Thermodynamics of Continuum
BANJANIN, M., Theory of Communications
BAŠIĆ, DJ., Thermoprocessing Systems
BOROVAC, B., Industrial Robots
BUKUROV, Ž., Fluid Mechanics
ČASNJI, F., Motor Vehicles
ĆIRIĆ, D., Physics
ĆOMIĆ, I., Mathematics
COSIĆ, I., Planning of Production Systems
CVETIĆANIN, L., Mechanics
DIMIĆ, M., Mass Transfer, Heat Apparatus
DJORDJEVIĆ, R., Construction Theory
DJORDJEVIĆ, T., Theory of Traffic Flow and Capacity
DJUKIĆ, DJ., Mechanics
DOROSLOVAČKI, R., Discrete Mathematics
DOVNIKOVIĆ, L., Descriptive Geometry
FOLIĆ, R., Concrete Structures and Structural Theory
GAJIĆ, V., Logistics of Enterprise
GALOGAŽA, M., Technology of Prediction, Marketing and Enterprise
GATALO, R., Machine Tools, Flexible Technological Systems
GEORGIJEVIĆ, M., Storage, Equipment and Simulations
GERIĆ, LJ., Distributive Installations
GRKOVIĆ, V., Turbines
GVOZDENAC, D., Thermal Energy and Measurement in Thermal Engineering
HAJDUKOVIĆ, M., Architecture of Computer Systems
HODOLIĆ, J., Productive Engineering Equipment
INIĆ, M., Traffic Safety
KAKAŠ, D., Heat Treatment
KISIN, S., Metal Constructions
KLINAR, I., Motor Equipment
KOPIĆ, DJ., Technology of Railway Transport
KOVAČ, P., Welding
KOVAČ, R., Casting Technology
KOVAČEVIĆ, I., Mathematics
KOVAČEVIĆ, V., Logical Planning of Computing Systems
KOZIMIDIS-LUBURIĆ, U., Physics
KOZIMIDIS-PETROVIĆ, A., Physics
KUZMANOVIĆ, S., Mechanical Elements
LIČEN, H., Automation of Measuring Processes
LUKIĆ, S., Elements of Building Planning
MALBAŠA, V., Electronic Systems and Communication Networks
MALBAŠKI, D., Elements of Computer Programming and Programme Languages
MARIĆ, M., Heat Science, Drying Technology
MARINIĆ, I., Sociology and Economy
MARTINOV, M., Agricultural Machines
MILIDRAG, S., Motor Vehicles
MILIKIĆ, D., Treatment Methods by Material Removal
MILINSKI, N., Physics
MILOŠEVIĆ, V., Digital Telecommunication
MOGIN, P., Databases
NIKIĆ, J., Mathematics
NOVAK, L., Circuit and Systems Theory
OBRADOVIĆ, D., Digital Communications
OBRADOVIĆ, M., Intercomputer Communications
PEKARIĆ-NADJ, N., Principles of Electrical Engineering
PERUNOVIĆ, P., Boilers
PEŠALJEVIĆ, M., Engineering Communications and Logistic Control
PETROVAČKI, D., Automatic Control
PLANČAK, M., Technology of Plasticity and Cold Extrusion
POPOVIĆ, D., Synthesis of Complex Systems in Automatic Control
PRODANOVIĆ, M., City and Spatial Planning
RADIVOJEVIĆ, R., Sociology, Sociology of Work
RADOVIĆ, R., Urban Planning, Contemporary Architecture
SABO, B., Welding Technology
SATARIĆ, M., Physics
SAVIĆ, V., Logistic Technical Systems
SEŠIĆ, Ž., Internal Combustion Engines
SIDJANIN, L., Materials Science, Engineering Materials
SOVILJ, B., Technoeconomic Optimization
STANIVUKOVIĆ, D., Reliability of Mechanical Systems
STOJAKOVIĆ, M., Mathematics, Statistical Methods in Planning
STREZOSKI, V., Elements of Electroenergetics
TEŠIĆ, M., Agricultural Machinery
TODIĆ, V., Technological Processes
TOROVIĆ, T., Internal Combustion Engine
UZELAC, Z., Mathematical Methods
VILOTIĆ, D., Plasticity Technology
VLADIĆ, J., Uninterrupted and Automatic Transport
VLAHOVIĆ, M., Recognition of Goods in Transport
VUKOVIĆ, S., Architectural Construction
VUKOVIĆ, V., Fluid Mechanics
ŽIVANOV, LJ., Microelectronics, Principles of Electronics
ZLOKOLICA, M., Theory of Mechanisms and Machines
ŽUPUNSKI, I., Electrical Measurements

Faculty of Technology (Tehnološki Fakultet, Blvr Cara Lazara 1, 21000 Novi Sad; tel. (21) 485-3600; fax (21) 450-413; e-mail deantf@uns.ac.rs; internet www.tf.uns.ac.rs):

CARIĆ, M., Milk and Dairy Technology
CURAKOVIĆ, M., Wrapping and Packaging
DOKIĆ, P., Chemistry and Technology of Emulsions and Cosmetics, Colloid Chemistry
DJILAS, S., Organic Chemistry
DJURIĆ, M., Engineering Thermodynamics
GRUJIĆ-IVKOV, O., Malt and Beer Technology
JAKOVLJEVIĆ, J., Starch Technology
KIŠ, E., Physical Chemistry Catalysis
LOMIĆ, G., Physical Chemistry, Catalysis
MARINKOVIĆ-NEDUČIN, R., Physical Chemistry, Catalysis
MARJANOVIĆ, N., Food Analysis
PAUNOVIĆ, R., Mathematical Modelling in Industrial Processes
PEJIN, D., Yeast and Alcohol Technology, Industrial Microbiology
PERIČIN, D., Biochemistry, Industrial Enzymology
PERUNIČIĆ, M., Process Dynamics and Control, Process Control Systems
PETROVIĆ, LJ., Meat Processing Technology
POPOV-RALJIĆ, J., Ready-Made Food Technology
PRIBIŠ, V., Meat Processing Technology, Sensory Evaluation of Food
RADONJIĆ, LJ., Construction Materials, Inorganic Materials
RANOGAJEC, J., Ceramics Technology, Inorganic Raw Materials and Products
RAZMOVSKA, R., Yeast and Alcohol Technology
RUŽIĆ, N., Technology of Wine Production
SOKOLOVIĆ, S., Petroleum Refining Technology, Petrochemical Products Applications
SOVILJ, M., Unit Operations, Measurement Techniques
SOVILJ, V., Colloid Chemistry, Physical Chemistry of Macromolecules
STOILJKOVIĆ, D., Physical Chemistry of Polymer Materials, Plastics Materials Technology
ŠEĆEROV-SOKOLOVIĆ, R., Industrial Processes Design, Environmental Protection in the Chemical Industry
ŠKRBIĆ, B., Natural Gas Engineering
ŠKRINJAR, M., Food Microbiology
TEKIĆ, M., Design of Equipment for the Chemical Industry, Separation Processes
TOJAGIĆ, S., Ready-Made Food Technology

'Mihajlo Pupin' Faculty of Technical Engineering (Tehnički Fakultet 'Mihajlo Pupin', Djure Djakovića bb, 23000 Zrenjanin; tel. (23) 550-515; fax (23) 550-520; e-mail dekanat@tf.zr.ac.rs; internet www.tfzr.uns.ac.rs):

ADAMOVIĆ, Ž., Mechanics, Maintenance, Hydraulics and Pneumatics
ČERNIČEK, I., Theory of Systems, Theory of Management and Decision Making
DJARMATI, Z., Chemistry with Chemical Technology, Chemistry and Biochemistry
HOTOMSKI, P., Informatics
LAMBIĆ, M., Mechanical Engineering, Energetics
MITROVIĆ, Ž., Mathematics
SOTIROVIĆ, V., Informatics
STOJADINOVIĆ, V., Industrial Engineering
ŠUNJKA, S., Textile Technology

There are research institutes attached to each faculty

UNIVERZITET UMETNOSTI U BEOGRADU
(University of Arts in Belgrade)

Kosančićev venac 29, 11000 Belgrade
Telephone: (11) 262-5166
Fax: (11) 262-9785
E-mail: rektorat@arts.bg.ac.rs
Internet: www.arts.bg.ac.rs

Founded 1957 as Acad. of Arts, present status 1973
Academic year: October to September
Rector: Prof. Dr LJILJANA MRKIĆ POPOVIĆ
Pres.: Prof. SLAVENKO SALETOVIC
Vice-Pres.: Prof. Dr DIMITRIJE GOLEMOVIĆ
Vice-Pres.: Prof. ANDJELKA BOJOVIĆ
Vice-Pres.: Prof. MARINA NAKIĆENOVIĆ
Sec.-Gen.: OLGA STANKOVIĆ
Library of 200,000 vols
Number of teachers: 500
Number of students: 2,500
Publication: *Bilten INFO* (dramatic arts, 12 a year)

DEANS

Faculty of Applied Arts: Prof. VLADIMIR KOSTIĆ DIVAĆ
Faculty of Dramatic Arts: ZORAN S. POPOVIĆ
Faculty of Fine Arts: Prof. SLOBODAN ROKSANDIĆ
Faculty of Music: Prof. Dr DUBRAVKA JOVIČIĆ (acting)

PROFESSORS

Faculty of Applied Arts (Kralja Petra 4, 11000 Belgrade; tel. and fax (11) 218-2047; e-mail fpu@eunet.rs; internet www.fpu.edu.rs):

ANĐELKOVIĆ, M.
BAJIĆ, M.
BLAŽINA, Z.
BOČINA, R.
BOŽOVIĆ, N.
BULAJIĆ, Z.
ÇVIJANOVIĆ, S.
ÇIRIĆ, R.
ĆIRIĆ-KRSTIĆ, G.
DENIĆ, D.
DIMITRIJEVIĆ, D.
DRAGOVIĆ, J.
DRAGUTINOVIĆ, A.
DRAGUTINOVIĆ, M.
DRAGUTINOVIĆ-KOMATINA, S.
DRAMIĆANIN, M.
ĐOLIĆ, S.
ĐULIZAREVIĆ, S.
ĐURIČKOVIĆ, S.
FULGOSI, D.
GAVRIĆ, Z.
GLOGOVAC, M.
HULJEV, I.
IVANOVIĆ, Z.
IZVONAR, D.
JANKOVIĆ, Z.
JANKOVIĆ-NEDELKOV, T.
KAJTEZ, S.
KARANOVIĆ, B.
KNEŽEVIĆ, I.
KNEŽEVIĆ, N.
KOMAD-ARSENIJEVIĆ, G.
KOSTIĆ, M.
KOSTIĆ, V.
KRSMANOVIĆ, K.
KUZMANOVIĆ, B.
KUZMANOVIĆ-NOVOVIĆ, I.
LAĐUŠIĆ, M.
LALIĆ, R.
LAZIĆ, T.
LAZOVIĆ, M.
LUKOVIĆ, M.
MANOJLOVIĆ, D.
MANOJLOVIĆ, S.
MANOJLOVIĆ, T.
MARCIKIĆ, I.
MIĆANOVIĆ, Z.
MIJATOVIĆ, A.
MILIĆEVIĆ, I.
NAKIĆENOVIĆ, M.
NANOVIĆ, B.
NEŠIĆ, D.
NIKOLIĆ, S.
NINČIĆ, O.
NOVAKOVIĆ, M.
OGNJANOVIĆ, M.
PETKOVIĆ, Z.
PETROVIĆ, G.
PETROVIĆ, L.
PETROVIĆ, M.
POPOVIĆ, Z.
RAKIĆ, I.
RUSALIĆ, D.
SAMARDŽIĆ, R.
SAVIĆ, S.
SEKULIĆ, T.
SIMONOVIĆ, J.
STAMENKOVIĆ, M.
STOJADINOVIĆ, O.
ŞTOJANOVIĆ, D.
ŠĆEPANOVIĆ, V.
ŠTRBAC, V.
TATAREVIĆ, V.
TIKVEŠA, L.
TODIĆ, M.
TOMAŠEVIĆ, M.
TRNINIĆ, M.
VELJOVIĆ, I.
VIĆENTIĆ, N.
VLAHOVIĆ, J.
VUČKOVIĆ, M.
VUJOVIĆ-STOJANOVIĆ, M.
VUKIĆEVIĆ, V.
VUKSAN, D.
ZARIĆ, G.
ZEČEVIĆ, S.
ŽIKIĆ, S.
ŽIVKOVIĆ, M.

Faculty of Dramatic Arts (Blvr umetnosti 20, 11070 Belgrade; tel. (11) 214-0419; fax (11) 213-0862; e-mail fduinfo@eunet.rs; internet www.fdubg.com):

ALEKSIC, B.
BAJIC, D.
BOGOEVA SEDLAR, LJ.
COLAKOVIC, M.
COLIC BILJANOVSKI, D.
DAKOVIC, N.
DAUTOVIC, F.
DEJANOVIC, V.
DESPOT, B.
DIMITRIJEVIC, A.
DRAGICEVIC SESIC, M.
DJOKIC, J.
DJUKIC, A.
DJUKIC, V.
GADJANSKI, M.
GLUSICA, M.
IMAMI, P.
IVANOVIC, S.
JEVTIC, N.
JEVTOVIC, V.
JEZERKIC, V.
JOVANOVIC, D.
JOVIĆEVIC, A.
KARAJICA, F.
KARANOVIC, S.
KNEZEVIC, R.
MANDIC, A.
MANDIC, T.
MARICIC, N.
MARIC, G.
MARKOVIC, G.
MARKOVIC, M.
MILETIN, M.
MRKIC POPOVIC, L.
PAJKIC, N.
PAVLOVIC, M.
PEKOVIC, G.
POPOV, D.
POPOVIC, Z.
PROKIC, N.
RANKOVIC, R.
SALETOVIC, S.
SAVIN, E.
SAVKOVIC, M.
SIMJANOVIC, Z.
SIJAN, S.
TABACKI, M.
TERZIC, G.
TODOROVIC, R.
VESELINOVIC, D.
VOLK, M.
VUJIC, I.

Faculty of Fine Arts (Pariska br. 16, 11000 Belgrade; tel. (11) 263-0635; fax (11) 218-1214; e-mail dekanat@flu.bg.ac.rs; internet www.flu.bg.ac.rs):

ANTONIJEVIĆ, R.
BAJIĆ, M.
BISENIĆ, D.
BOJOVIĆ, A.
DIMOVSKI, Z.
DRAGOJLOVIĆ, M.
DRAGOJLOVIĆ, M.
GRAOVAC, Z.
GRBA, D.
ILIĆ, D.
JOKSIMOVIĆ, A.
JOKSIMOVIĆ, Z.
JOVANOVIĆ, D.
KAĆIĆ, D.
KALIĆ-KUMANUDI, J.
KNEŽEVIĆ, R.
KNEŽEVIĆ, V.
KRSTIĆ, V.
LALIĆ, V.
MILINKOVIĆ, Z.
MLADENOVIĆ, A.
MLAĐOVIĆ, M.
MOMIROV, D.
NIKOLIĆ, G
NOVAKOVIĆ, Z.
PANTIĆ, A.
PECIĆ, D.
PETROVIĆ, D.
POPTSIS, M.
PRODANOVIĆ, M.
RADOJEV, N.
RAJČEVIĆ, S.
RAKOVIĆ, B
ROKSANDIĆ, S.
SIMEONOVIĆ ČELIĆ, I.
SIVAČKI, J.
SMILJANIĆ, Z.
ŞTANAĆEV, D.
ŠKORC, B.
ŠUICA, N.
TODOROVIĆ, J.
TODOROVIĆ, Z.
VASIĆ, C.
VELJAŠEVIĆ, V.
VUKOSAVLJEVIĆ, N.
VUKOVIĆ, B.
VUKOVIĆ, Z.
ZARIĆ, K.
ŽIVKOVIĆ, V.

Faculty of Music (Kralja Milana 50, 11000 Belgrade; tel. (11) 265-9466; fax (11) 264-3598; e-mail fmuinfo@fmu.bg.ac.rs; internet www.fmu.bg.ac.rs):

BELIĆ, S.
BOŽIĆ, S.
ČETKOVIĆ, Z.
ĐORĐEVIĆ, M.
ERIĆ, Z.
GOLEMOVIĆ, D.
GRGIN, A.
HOFMAN, S.
IGNJATOVIĆ, N.
ISAESKI, M.
JOVIČIĆ, D.
JOVANOVIĆ, L.
JOKANOVIĆ, M.
KARLOVIĆ, M.
KOSANOVIĆ, M.
KRŠIĆ-SEKULIĆ, V.
MAKSIMOVIĆ-VESELINOV, J.
MARINKOVIĆ, S.
MEZEI, L.
MIHAILOVIĆ, J.
MILANKOVIĆ, V.
MLAĐENOVIĆ, D.
NIKOLIĆ, M.
OGRIZOVIĆ, V.
PERIĆ, D.

PETROVIĆ, M.
POPOVIĆ, N.
POPOVIĆ, L.
RAŠKOVIĆ, F.
SERDAR, A.
SINADINOVIĆ, D.
ŠUĐIĆ, B.
ŠUVAKOVIĆ, M.
TOŠIĆ, S.
TOŠIĆ, V.
TRAJKOVIĆ, V.
VASIĆ, O.
VESELINOVIĆ-HOFMAN, M.
VUJIĆ, A.
ŽIVKOVIĆ, N.

College

Belgrade Business School: Kraljice Marije 73 (27 Marta 149), 11000 Belgrade; tel. (11) 240-1888; fax (11) 242-4069; e-mail info@bbs.edu.rs; internet www.bbs.edu.rs; f. 1956 as Junior Commercial-Business College, present name and status 2002; offers three-year diploma courses in finance, accounting, marketing, foreign and domestic trade, commerce, management, business informatics and computers, banking and insurance, customs, taxes and budget; int. studies programme; distance studies; library: 20,000 vols; 90 teachers (60 full-time, 30 part-time); 2,000 students; Dir Prof. Dr ILIJA SAMARDŽIĆ (acting).

SEYCHELLES

The Higher Education System

The Republic of Seychelles comprises some 115 islands in the western Indian Ocean. Seychelles achieved full independence from Britain, as a sovereign republic within the Commonwealth, in 1976. There are no university-level institutions of higher education in the Seychelles apart from the University of Seychelles—American Institute of Medicine. However the Seychelles Polytechnic (founded 1983) offers one- to three-year Diploma and Certificate courses, and the National College of the Arts (founded 1997) offers one- and two-year programmes of study. There are several professional institutes of training and an Adult Learning and Distance Education Centre. The Ministry of Education and Youth is responsible for post-secondary, tertiary and adult education. The Ministry offers scholarships for students wishing to pursue tertiary education overseas. There were 2,130 students in post-secondary (non-tertiary) education in 2008.

Under the Higher Education Act, the Ministry of Education and Youth has instigated reforms in the education system in five priority areas to increase its effectiveness. In 2009 a number of reforms were carried out and more were to be implemented in 2010. Given their nature and complexity, some may not be implemented before 2011.

Regulatory Bodies

GOVERNMENT

Ministry of Community Development, Youth, Sports and Culture: Oceangate House, POB 731, Victoria; tel. 225477; fax 225254; e-mail frevet@seychelles.net; Minister VINCENT MERITON.

Ministry of Education and Youth: POB 48, Mont Fleuri; tel. 283283; fax 224859; e-mail pamedu@seychelles.net; internet www.education.gov.sc; Min. BERNARD SHAMLAYE.

Learned Societies

LANGUAGE AND LITERATURE

Alliance Française: Ave Bois de Rose, BP 210, Victoria; tel. 282424; fax 225172; internet www.alliancefr.sc; offers courses and exams in French language and culture and promotes cultural exchange with France.

British Council: see chapter on Mauritius.

Research Institute

GENERAL

National Heritage: POB 573, Victoria, Mahé; tel. 321333; fax 322531; e-mail heritage@seychelles.net; f. 1987; controlled by Culture Division of the Min. of Education and Youth; carries out research into the cultural heritage of Seychelles; Advisor MARCEL BARRY ROSALIE.

Libraries and Archives

Victoria

Seychelles National Archives: POB 720, 5th June Ave, Victoria, Mahé; tel. 321333; fax 322481; e-mail archives@seychelles.net; internet www.sna.gov.sc; Dir ALAIN LUCAS.

Seychelles National Library: POB 45, Francis Rachel St, Victoria, Mahé; tel. and fax 321333; e-mail natlib@seychelles.net; internet www.national-library.edu.sc; f. 1910 as Carnegie Library; 75,000 vols (incl. 3 br. libraries & 2 regional reading centres); 3 brs; spec. collns: documents on Indian Ocean region, FAO, UNESCO, IMO and ILO publs; Prin. Librarian ANNE-MARY ROBERT; Sr Librarian CHRISTIANE ADELINE.

Museum

Victoria

National Museum: POB 720, La Bastille, Victoria, Mahé; tel. (248) 321333; e-mail mizenasyonal@gmail.com; f. 1964; Dir CECILLE KALEBI.

Polytechnic

SEYCHELLES POLYTECHNIC

POB 77, Anse Royale, Victoria
Telephone: 371188
Fax: 371545
E-mail: info@seypoly.edu.sc
Internet: www.seypoly.edu.sc

Founded 1983
State control
Language of instruction: English
Academic year: January to December

Dir: JEAN RASSOOL
Asst Dir (Admin.: HELENE BELMONT
Asst Dir (Studies): AUDREY NANON
Sr Librarian: MARIE-FRANCE LOZÉ

Library of 9,500 vols
Number of teachers: 56
Number of students: 578

HEADS OF PROGRAMMES

Academic Studies: SHELLA MOHIDEEN
Business and Secretarial Studies: ALPHONSO RODRIGUES
Technical Studies: JAYAH HARRIS
Manchester Training Programme: LIAM CAMPLING

School of Music

National College of the Arts: Ministry of Youth and Culture, POB 1383, Mahé; tel. 224777; fax 321591; e-mail acollart@hotmail.com; f. 1997; depts of music, dance, visual arts, drama; 33 teachers (28 full-time, 5 part-time); 720 students (120 full-time, 600 part-time); Dir DAVID CHETTY.

SIERRA LEONE

The Higher Education System

Formerly a British colony and protectorate, Sierra Leone gained independence from the United Kingdom in 1961. Fourah Bay College (founded 1827), a constituent college of the University of Sierra Leone (founded 1967), is the oldest current institution of higher education. Before joining the University, degrees from Fourah Bay College were awarded by the University of Durham (United Kingdom). The University of Sierra Leone is the only university, and consists of six colleges and institutes. In 2001/02 a total of 9,041 students were enrolled in tertiary education. The Ministry of Education, Youth and Sports is responsible for higher education.

Admission to the University is on the basis of the Senior School Certificate examination. The University offers two- and three-year Certificate and Diploma courses in mostly professional fields of study, such as agriculture, engineering and marine biology. The undergraduate Bachelors is either a three-year 'General' degree or a four-year 'Honours' degree. At postgraduate level, students first take the Masters degree, which is awarded after one year following the Bachelors (Honours) or two years following the Bachelors (General). After the award of the Masters the Doctor of Philosophy is the highest university degree, requiring three years of research leading to submission of a thesis.

Technical and vocational education at the post-secondary level is available from technical institutes in Kenema and Freetown and the Institute of Public Administration and Management attached to the University of Sierra Leone. The technical institutes offer a range of British-accredited qualifications, including City and Guilds certificates, London Chamber of Commerce and Industry examinations and Royal Society of Arts secretarial examinations. The Institute of Public Administration and Management (founded 1980) specializes in continuing education and workplace-based training.

Regulatory Bodies

GOVERNMENT

Ministry of Education, Youths and Sports: New England, Freetown; tel. (22) 240881; fax (22) 240137; Minister Dr MINKAILU BAH.

Ministry of Tourism and Cultural Affairs: Ministerial Bldg, George St, Freetown; tel. (22) 222588; Minister HINDOLO TRYE.

Learned Societies

BIBLIOGRAPHY, LIBRARY SCIENCE AND MUSEOLOGY

Sierra Leone Association of Archivists, Librarians and Information Scientists: 7 Percival St, Freetown; f. 1970; 90 mems; Pres. OLATUNGIE CAMPBELL; Sec. AGNES MOROVIA; publ. *SLAALIS Bulletin* (4 a year).

HISTORY, GEOGRAPHY AND ARCHAEOLOGY

Historical Society of Sierra Leone: c/o Dept of History, Fourah Bay College, University of Sierra Leone, Freetown; f. 1975; 30 mems; Pres. G. S. ANTHONY; publ. *Journal* (2 a year).

LANGUAGE AND LITERATURE

Alliance Française: 30 Howe St, POB 510, Freetown; tel. (76) 683523; e-mail alliancefreetown@yahoo.fr; offers courses and exams in French language and culture and promotes cultural exchange with France.

British Council: Tower Hill, POB 124, Freetown; tel. (22) 222223; fax (22) 224123; e-mail info.enquiry@sl.britishcouncil.org; internet www.britishcouncil.org/sierraleone; offers courses and exams in English language and British culture and promotes cultural exchange with the UK; Dir RAJIV BENDRE.

MEDICINE

Sierra Leone Medical and Dental Association: POB 850, Freetown; tel. (22) 229825; fax (22) 228430; f. 1961; 220 mems; library of 3,000 vols (shared with main hospital); Pres. Dr S. U. M. JAH; Sec. Dr DESMOND WRIGHT; publ. *Journal* (1 a year).

NATURAL SCIENCES

General

Sierra Leone Science Association: c/o Dept of Physics, Fourah Bay College, University of Sierra Leone, Freetown; tel. (22) 231617; fax (22) 224439; f. 1960; Hon. Pres. Prof. Dr ERNEST H. WRIGHT; Hon. Sec. (vacant).

Research Institutes

GENERAL

Institute of African Studies: c/o University of Sierra Leone, Fourah Bay College, Freetown; f. 1962; undertakes research in sociology, history and culture of Sierra Leone; offers undergraduate and postgraduate courses in cultural studies; Dir Dr ARTHUR ABRAHAM; publ. *Africana Research Bulletin* (2 a year).

NATURAL SCIENCES

Biological Sciences

Institute of Marine Biology and Oceanography: Fourah Bay College, University of Sierra Leone, Freetown; tel. (22) 250775; f. 1966; 4-year degree programme in marine science, undergraduate diploma in aquatic biology and fisheries; research and training in oceanography, marine algae and ecology, fishery biology and management, aquaculture, marine pollution, estuarine dynamics, and coastal processes; Dir Dr I. W. O. FINDLAY; publ. *Annual Bulletin*.

Physical Sciences

Geological Survey Division: Ministry of Mines, Youyi Bldg, Brookfields, Freetown; f. 1918 to locate mineral deposits and to advise on all matters relating to the Earth; library of 16,000 vols including periodicals; Dir A. H. GABISI; publs *Bulletin* (1 a year), *Short Papers* (1 a year).

Libraries and Archives

Freetown

Fourah Bay College Library: Univ. of Sierra Leone, Freetown; tel. (22) 229471; e-mail fbclibrary2005@yahoo.com; internet www.daco-sl.org/encyclopedia/1_gov/1_7fourahbay.htm; f. 1827; 200,000 vols, 300 current periodicals; Sr Librarian OLIVER HARDING.

Public Archives of Sierra Leone: c/o Fourah Bay College, Freetown; f. 1965; 63,000 linear ft of records; Sr Archivist ALBERT MOORE.

Sierra Leone Library Board: POB 326, Rokel St, Freetown; tel. (22) 223848; e-mail sielib2002@yahoo.com; f. 1959; nationwide public library service; also acts as a nat. library (legal deposit); 5 central libraries (HQs), 3 regional libraries, 14 brs of district libraries; 110,000 vols; Chief Librarian ISAAC D.B. JOHN (acting); publs *Children's magazine*, *Golden Jubilee Souvenir*, *Sierra Leone Publications* (1 a year).

Museum

Freetown

Sierra Leone National Museum: Cotton Tree Building, POB 908, Freetown; tel. (22) 223555; fax (22) 224439; e-mail cabnicol70@yahoo.co.uk; historical, ethnographical and archaeological collection; Curator CELIA NICOL.

University

UNIVERSITY OF SIERRA LEONE

PMB, Freetown

Telephone: (22) 226859

Founded 1967

State control

Language of instruction: English

Academic year: October to June

Chancellor: THE PRESIDENT OF THE REPUBLIC OF SIERRA LEONE

Vice-Chancellor: Prof. ERNEST H. WRIGHT

Pro-Chancellor: Dr ARTHUR PORTER

Pro-Vice-Chancellor: Prof. A. M. ALGHALI
Sec. and Registrar: J. A. G. THOMAS
Librarian: GLADYS JUSU-SHERIFF

Number of teachers: 301
Number of students: 4,310 (full-time)

Publications: *African Research Bulletin* (2 a year), *Calendar and Prospectus* (1 a yearl), *Varsity Update* (12 a year).

CONSTITUENT COLLEGES

Fourah Bay College

POB 87, Mount Aureol, Freetown

Telephone: (22) 227924
Internet: fbcusl.8k.com

Founded by the Church Missionary Society in 1827, it was affiliated to the Univ. of Durham in 1876 and became a constituent college of the Univ. in 1966

Prin.: Prof. V. E. H. STRASSER-KING
Vice-Prin.: Prof. A. J. G. WYSE

DEANS

Faculty of Arts: Rev. Dr L. E. T. SHYLLON
Faculty of Economic and Social Sciences: Prof. A. ABRAHAM
Faculty of Engineering: Prof. O. R. DAVIDSON
Faculty of Law: Prof. H. M. JOKO-SMART
Faculty of Pure and Applied Science: Prof. V. E. GODWIN
Postgraduate Studies: Prof. A. J. G. WYSE

PROFESSORS

Faculty of Arts:

WYSE, A. J. G., History

Faculty of Economic and Social Sciences:

ABRAHAM, A., Institute of African Studies

Faculty of Engineering:

DAVIDSON, O. R., Mechanical Engineering

Faculty of Law:

JOKO-SMART, H. M.

Faculty of Pure and Applied Science:

AWUNOR-RENNER, E. R. T., Physics
COLE, N. H. A., Botany
STRASSER-KING, V. E. H., Geology
WILLIAMS, M. O., Zoology

DIRECTORS

Institute of Adult Education and Extra-Mural Studies: E. D. A. TURAY
Institute of African Studies: Prof. A. ABRAHAM
Institute of Marine Biology and Oceanography: Dr I. W. O. FINDLAY
Institute of Population Studies: Dr A. C. THOMAS

College of Medicine and Allied Health Sciences

Telephone: (22) 240884
Founded 1987

Prin.: Prof. A. M. TAQI
Vice-Prin.: Assoc. Prof. F. D. R. LISK

DEANS

Faculty of Basic Medical Sciences: Dr J. K. GEORGE
Faculty of Clinical Sciences: Dr L. GORDON-HARRIS
Faculty of Pharmaceutical Sciences: Prof. E. AYITEY-SMITH

PROFESSORS

Faculty of Basic Medical Sciences:

GEORGE, J. K., Anatomy

Faculty of Clinical Sciences:

TAQI, A. M., Paediatrics

Faculty of Pharmaceutical Sciences:

AYITEY-SMITH, E., Pharmacology

Njala University College

Telephone: (22) 228788
E-mail: nuc@sierratel.sl
Internet: www.nuc-online.com

Founded 1964

Prin.: Prof. A. M. ALGHALI
Vice-Prin.: P. K. SAIDU

DEANS

Faculty of Agriculture: Prof. E. R. RHODES
Faculty of Education: Dr T. M. DUGBA
Faculty of Environmental Sciences: Dr G. M. T. ROBERT

PROFESSORS

Faculty of Agriculture:

KOROMA, J. P. C., Crop Science
RHODES, E. R., Soil Science

Faculty of Education:

BOMAH, A. K., Geography and Rural Development.

OFF-CAMPUS INSTITUTES

Institute Of Education: PMB, Tower Hill, Freetown; tel. (22) 226874; Dir MELISSA F. JONAH (acting).

Institute Of Library Studies: Mount Aureol, Freetown; tel. (22) 240290; Dir GLADYS JUSU-SHERIFF.

Institute Of Public Administration And Management: PMB, Tower Hill, Freetown; tel. (22) 224801; Dir I. I. MAY-PARKER.

Colleges

Milton Margai College of Education and Technology: Goderich, nr Freetown; f. 1960; trains secondary school teachers; library: 23,000 vols; 55 teachers; 624 students; Prin. Dr DENIS KARGBO; Registrar J. U. WRIGHT (acting).

Paramedical School: POB 50, Bo; f. 1979 with funds from the Govt and the EEC; trains primary health workers; Prin. Dr V. O. COLE.

Technical Institute: Congo Cross, Freetown; tel. (22) 231368; fax (22) 231368; f. 1952; 80 teachers; 980 students; City and Guilds Craft and Technical Courses and Commercial Education; certificate, diploma and higher diploma courses in engineering, business, secretarial work and education; focal point for the UNEVOC project; Prin. MOHAMED A. JALLOH.

Technical Institute: Kenema; vocational courses.

SINGAPORE

The Higher Education System

In 1826 the East India Company formed the Straits Settlements by the union of Singapore and the dependencies of Penang and Malacca on the Malay Peninsula. They came under British rule in 1867. In 1946 Singapore became a separate crown colony, and in 1959 achieved complete internal self-government. After seceding from the Federation of Malaysia in 1965, Singapore became an independent republic. There are four universities, the oldest of which is National University of Singapore (founded 1980). In 2005 the Open University Centre (founded 1992), affiliated with the Open University (United Kingdom), was elevated to university status and renamed SIM University; it specializes in adult education and correspondence courses. All the universities are publicly funded, but the Singapore Management University (founded 2000) is under private management. In 2007 the total number of students enrolled in university-level education was 65,746 (excluding SIM University), with a further 72,379 students enrolled at the country's five polytechnics.

Admission to university undergraduate degrees is on the basis of results in A-Level examinations. The undergraduate Bachelors degree lasts three years at 'Pass' level and four years at 'Honours' level. Degrees in professional fields of study, such as dentistry, law, engineering and construction, last longer. Both postgraduate Diplomas and Masters degrees are one- or two-year programmes of study, and the Doctor of Philosophy, the highest university degree, lasts three years.

Post-secondary technical and vocational education is offered by the polytechnics and the Institute of Technical Education. The five polytechnics offer three levels of qualification, Certificate, Diploma and Advanced Diploma, in a range of professional fields of study. The Institute of Technical Education (founded 1992) replaced the former Vocational and Industrial Training Board and consists of 10 centres on two campuses; it specializes in full- and part-time training, work-place-based traineeships and continuing education. Qualifications offered include the Industrial Technician Certificate and National Technical Certificate.

In the late 2000s the number of higher education institutions increased with the opening of, among others, the Singapore University of Technology and Design and the Singapore Institute of Technology. There were also several private institutions operating in conjunction with universities overseas—in particular in Germany and the USA.

Regulatory Body

GOVERNMENT

Ministry of Education: 1 North Buona Vista Drive, MOE Bldg, Singapore 138675; tel. 68722220; fax 67755826; e-mail contact@moe.edu.sg; internet www.moe.gov.sg; Minister NG ENG HEN; Permanent Sec. TAN CHING YEE.

Learned Societies

GENERAL

Singapore National Academy of Science: 1st Floor, Singapore Science Centre Building, off Jurong Town Hall Rd, Singapore 2260; established to promote the advancement of science and technology and to represent the mem. societies, institutes and other founder/affiliate mems of the Academy; Pres. Prof. LEO TAN WEE HIN; Sec. Dr CHIA WOON KIM.

Singapore Society of Asian Studies: Kent Ridge, POB 1076, Singapore 9111; f. 1982 to promote the study of Asian culture and heritage, with special emphasis on the South-East Asian region; 130 mems; Pres. LIM GUAN HOCK; Sec. Dr YEO MANG THONG; publ. *Asian Culture* (1 a year).

ARCHITECTURE AND TOWN PLANNING

Singapore Institute of Architects: 79 Neil Rd, Singapore 088904; tel. 62262668; fax 62262663; e-mail info@sia.org.sg; internet www.sia.org.sg; f. 1923; 1,000 mems; Pres. EDWARD D'SILVA; Hon. Sec. JOHNNY TAN; publs *Singapore Architect* (4 a year), *SIA Year Book*.

BIBLIOGRAPHY, LIBRARY SCIENCE AND MUSEOLOGY

Library Association of Singapore: Bukit Merah Central, POB 0693, Singapore 9115; internet www.las.org.sg; f. 1955; 328 mems; Pres. CHOY FATT CHEONG; Hon. Sec. LIM-YEO PIN PIN; publs *Singapore Libraries* (2 a year), *Singapore Libraries Bulletin* (4 a year).

ECONOMICS, LAW AND POLITICS

Singapore Institute of International Affairs: 2 Nassim Rd, Singapore 258370; tel. 67349600; fax 67336217; e-mail research@siiaonline.org; f. 1961; organizes talks, conferences etc.; commissions research on East-Asian economic integration, sustainable development and governance issues, and peace and development in South-East Asia; 379 mems; Chair. Assoc. Prof. SIMON TAY; Dir YEO LAY HWEE.

FINE AND PERFORMING ARTS

Singapore Art Society: 6001 Beach Rd, No. 18–08, Golden Mile Tower, Singapore 0719; tel. 62924244; f. 1949 to foster the practice and appreciation of art in Singapore; 325 mems; Pres. HO KOK HOE; Hon. Sec. QUEK KIAN GUAN.

LANGUAGE AND LITERATURE

Alliance Française: 1 Sarkies Rd, Singapore 258130; tel. 67378422; fax 67333023; e-mail afsing@alliancefrancaise.org.sg; internet www.alliancefrancaise.org.sg; offers courses and examinations in French language and culture and promotes cultural exchange with France; Exec. Dir YVES CORBEL.

British Council: 30 Napier Rd, Singapore 258509; tel. 64731111; fax 64721010; e-mail enquiries@britishcouncil.org.sg; internet www.britishcouncil.org.sg; f. 1947; teaching centre; offers courses and exams in English language and British culture and promotes cultural exchange with the UK; attached teaching centres in Holland Village, Marsiling and Tampines; Dir LES DANGERFIELD; Dir, Teaching Centre MARTIN HOPE.

Goethe-Institut: 163 Penang Rd 05-01, Winsland House II, Singapore 238463; tel. 67354555; fax 67354666; internet www.goethe.de/so/sin/deindex.htm; offers courses and examinations in German language and culture and promotes cultural exchange with Germany; library of 8,000 vols; Dir Dr ULRICH NOWAK.

MEDICINE

Academy of Medicine, Singapore: College of Medicine Bldg, Level 1, Left Wing, 16 College Rd, Singapore 0316; tel. 62238968; fax 62255155; f. 1957; professional corporate body of medical and dental specialists; also involved in the postgraduate training of doctors; Master Dr N. C. TAN; Chief Administrator Y. L. LAM; publ. *Annals* (4 a year).

Singapore Medical Association: Level 2, 2 College Rd, Alumni Medical Centre, Singapore 169850; tel. 62231264; fax 62247827; e-mail sma@sma.org.sg; internet www.sma.org.sg; f. 1959; 3,900 mems; Pres. Prof. C. H. LOW; Hon. Sec. Dr W. M. YUE; publ. *Singapore Medical Journal* (12 a year).

NATURAL SCIENCES

General

Singapore Association for the Advancement of Science: 1st Floor, Singapore Science Centre Bldg, off Jurong Town Hall Rd, Singapore 2260; f. 1976 for the dissemination of science and technology; Pres. Prof. ANG KOK PENG; Sec. Dr LEO TAN WEE HIN.

Mathematical Sciences

Singapore Mathematical Society: Mathematics Dept, National University of Singapore, Kent Ridge, Singapore 119260; tel. 68742394; fax 67795452; e-mail smsuser@math.nus.edu.sg; internet sms.math.nus.edu.sg; f. 1952; aims to maintain the status and advance the interests of the profession of mathematics, to improve the teaching of mathematics, and to provide means of interaction between students, teachers and others interested in mathematics; 620 mems; Pres. Prof. TAN ENG CHYE; Sec. Prof. TANG WEE KEE; publ. *Mathematical Medley* (2 a year).

Physical Sciences

Institute of Physics, Singapore: c/o Dept of Physics, National University of Singapore, Kent Ridge, Singapore 119260; tel. 67722604; fax 67776126; f. 1973 to promote study of and research in physics in Singapore; organizes conferences, talks, seminars, exhibitions, visits to industrial and commercial establishments and educational tours abroad; 180 mems; Pres. Prof. BERNARD TAN; Sec. Assoc. Prof. ANDREW T. S. WEE; publs *Singapore Journal of Physics* (2 a year), *Physics Update* (2 a year).

Research Institutes

ECONOMICS, LAW AND POLITICS

Asian Media Information and Communication Centre: Jurong Point, POB 360, Singapore 916412; tel. 67927570; fax 67927129; e-mail enquiries@amic.org.sg; internet www.amic.org.sg; f. 1971; non-profit regional documentation centre; works in cooperation with UNESCO and other int. orgs to promote the understanding and devt of communication and its application in the Asia-Pacific region with regard to economic, social and cultural progress; publishes media journals and books; organizes seminars, capacity building workshops; convenes confs; conducts communication research; library of 35,000 records in databases, 350 journals; regional centre for Japan Prize Circulating Library; Sec.-Gen. Prof. SUNDEEP R. MUPPIDI; publs *AMCB* (6 a year), *Asian Communication Handbook* (every 3-4 years), *Asian Journal of Communication* (6 a year), *Media Asia* (4 a year).

Institute of Southeast Asian Studies: Heng Mui Keng Terrace, Pasir Panjang, Singapore 119614; f. 1968 to undertake research on SE Asia, especially problems of devt, modernization, political and social change; library of 400,000 vols; Dir K. KESAVAPANY; Head of Admin. Y. L. LEE; Librarian CH'NG KIM SEE; publs *Contemporary Southeast Asia* (3 a year), *Regional Outlook*, *Southeast Asian Affairs* (1 a year), *SOJOURN, Social Issues in Southeast Asia* (2 a year), *ASEAN Economic Bulletin* (3 a year).

EDUCATION

East Asian Institute: 469 A Bukit Timah Rd, Tower Block, 06–01, Singapore 259770; tel. 65163715; fax 67793409; e-mail eaizyn@nus.edu.sg; internet www.eai.nus.edu.sg; f. 1997; attached to Nat. Univ. of Singapore; promotes study of China's political, economic and social devt; Dir Prof. YONGNIAN ZHENG.

Institute of Technical Education (ITE): 10 Dover Drive, Singapore 138683; tel. 67757800; fax 67762172; e-mail itehq@ite.edu.sg; internet www.ite.edu.sg; Chair. ERIC GWEE TECK HAI; Dir Dr LAW SONG SENG; publ. *The Quality Workforce* (6 a year).

Libraries and Archives

Singapore

National Archives of Singapore: National Heritage Board, 1 Canning Rise, Singapore 179868; fax 63393583; f. 1968; 3,400 vols, 43 current periodicals, 1.5m. photographs, 128,200 building plans, 6,630 maps, 66,427 microfilm rolls, 18,000 tapes of recorded interviews; Senior Dir LILY TAN.

National Library Board: 100 Victoria St, 14-01, Nat. Library Bldg, Singapore 188064; tel. 63323133; fax 63323332; e-mail helpdesk@nlb.gov.sg; internet www.nlb.gov.sg; f. 1995; 1.2m. vols collns by languages consist of about 66% in English, 17% in Chinese, 5% in Malay, 2% in Tamil; 119,838 serial titles; 115,977 spec. materials such as microfilm, audiovisuals and 1.2m. book titles available in Malay, Chinese, Tamil and English colln; oversees management of Nat. Library and network of public libraries, also 1 community children's library and 17 libraries belonging to govt agencies, schools and instns; Chief Exec. Dr N. VARAPRASAD; publs *Singapore Periodicals Index* (1 a year), *Books about Singapore* (online), *Singapore National Bibliography* (CD-ROM, 2 a year).

National University of Singapore Libraries: 12 Kent Ridge Crescent, Singapore 119275; tel. 65162069; fax 67771272; e-mail clbsec@nus.edu.sg; internet www.lib.nus.edu.sg; f. 1905; 2.4m. vols (Central Library 1.1m. vols; Japanese Resources 51,955 vols; Chinese Library 465,644 vols; C. J. Koh Law Library 157,087 vols; Hon Sui Sen Memorial Library 90,992 vols; Medical Library 170,040 vols; Science Library 286,221 vols), 23,844 electronic titles, 27,423 audiovisual items, 24,266 microforms; Dir., NUS Libraries SYLVIA YAP; publ. *Guide to NUS Libraries* (1 a year).

Museums and Art Galleries

Singapore

National Heritage Board: 93 Stamford Rd, Singapore 78897; tel. 63361460; fax 63323568; f. 1849; consists of Asian Civilizations Museum, Singapore History Museum, Singapore Art Museum, Children's Discovery Gallery; library of 25,000 vols; history and oral history archives; CEO LIM SIAM KIM.

Singapore Art Museum: 71 Bras Basah Rd, Singapore 189555; tel. 63323222; fax 63347919; internet www.museum.org.sg/sam/sam.shtml; f. 1996; modern and contemporary South-East Asian art.

Singapore Botanic Gardens: National Parks Board, Cluny Rd, Singapore 259569; tel. 64717361; fax 64674832; internet www.nparks.gov.sg; f. 1859; botanical and horticultural research with particular reference to South-East Asia and the tropics; library of 30,000 vols; CEO N. G. LANG; Dir of Gardens Dr CHIN SEE CHUNG; Keeper of Herbarium and Library Dr BENITO TAN; publ. *The Gardens Bulletin Singapore* (2 a year).

Universities

NANYANG TECHNOLOGICAL UNIVERSITY

50 Nanyang Ave, Singapore 639798
Telephone: 67911744
Fax: 67911604
E-mail: adm_intnl@ntu.edu.sg
Internet: www.ntu.edu.sg

Founded 1981 as Nanyang Technological Institute; present name and status 1991
Academic year: July to July

Pres.: Dr SU GUANING
Provost: Prof. BERTIL ANDERSSON
Sr Assoc. Provost: Prof. ER MENG HWA
Assoc. Provost for Graduate Education and Special Projects: Prof. LAM KHIN YONG
Assoc. Provost for Innovation: JEFFREY NADISON
Assoc. Provost for Research: Prof. MICHAEL KHOR
Sec.: ANTHONY TEO
Chief Planning Officer and Registrar: CHAN KWONG LOK
Chief Financial Officer: GOH BOON HUAT
Chief Human Resource Officer: ANGELA LIM SAU TING
Chief Univ. Advancement Officer: CHEW KHENG CHUAN
Dir of Corporate Communications: Dr VIVIEN CHIONG
Librarian: CHOY FATT CHEONG

Number of teachers: 1,635
Number of students: 33,087

Publications: *Asian Journal of Communication* (3 a year), *Media Asia* (4 a year), *Asian Mass Communication Bulletin* (6 a year), *Electrical and Electronic Engineering Bulletin* (1 a year), *Nanyang Business Review* (2 a year), *Asian Business Law Review* (4 a year), *Mechanical and Aerospace Engineering Research Bulletin* (1 a year), *Asia Pacific Journal of Education* (2 a year), *Pedagogies: An International Journal* (2 a year), *Singteach* (4 a year), *Teaching Education* (4 a year), *Technical Reports* (12 a year), *School of Computer Engineering Research Report* (1 a year)

DEANS

College of Engineering: Prof. PAN TSO-CHIEN
College of Humanities, Arts and Social Sciences: Prof. ALAN CHAN KAM-LEUNG
College of Science: Prof. MARK FEATHERSTONE
Nanyang Business School: Prof. GILLIAN YEO HIAN HENG
School of Art, Design and Media: Prof. VIBEKE SORENSEN
School of Biological Sciences: Prof. ALEX LAW SAI KIT (acting)
School of Chemical and Biomedical Engineering: Prof. CHING CHI BUN
School of Civil and Environmental Engineering: Assoc. Prof. EDMOND LO YAT-MAN
Wee Kim Wee School of Communication and Information: Assoc. Prof. BENJAMIN HILL DETENBER
School of Computer Engineering: Prof. THAMBIPILLAI SRIKANTHAN
School of Electrical and Electronic Engineering: Prof. KAM CHAN HIN
School of Humanities and Social Sciences: Prof. EUSTON QUAH (acting)
S. Rajaratnam School of Int. Studies: Ambassador BARRY DESKER
School of Materials Science and Engineering: Prof. FREDDY BOEY YING CHIANG (acting)
School of Mechanical and Aerospace Engineering: Prof. LING SHIH FU (acting)
School of Physical and Mathematical Sciences: Prof. LING SAN
Cornell-Nanyang Institute of Hospitality Management: Dr RUSSELL ARTHUR SMITH

DIRECTORS

Confucius Institute: Assoc. Prof. KOH HOCK KIAT
Earth Observatory of Singapore: Prof. KERRY SIEH
Institute of Advanced Studies: Adjunct Prof. PHUA KOK KHOO
National Institute of Education: Prof. LEE SING KONG

PROFESSORS

College of Engineering (Block S3.2, Level B1, 50 Nanyang Ave, Singapore 639798; tel. 67906706; fax 67912523; e-mail d-coe@ntu.edu.sg; internet www.ntu.edu.sg/coe):

LIM, E. N.
LIM, M. K.

Nanyang Business School (Block S3, 50 Nanyang Ave, Singapore 639798; tel. 67904636; fax 67913697; e-mail wwwnbs@ntu.edu.sg; internet www.nbs.ntu.edu.sg):

ANG, S., Strategy, Management and Organization
DUFEY, G., Banking and Finance
HONG, H.
NEO, B. S.
SETHI, V., Information Technology and Operations Management
SIGUAW, J. A., Cornell-Nanyang Institute of Hospitality Management
TAN, H. T., Accounting
WEE, C. H., Strategy, Management and Organization
WILLIAMS, J. J., Accounting
YEO, F. H. H., Accounting

National Institute of Education (1 Nanyang Walk, Singapore 637616; tel. 67903888; fax 68968874; e-mail niepr@nie.edu.sg; internet www.nie.edu.sg):

CHEW, C. H.
GAN, L. H.
GOH, K. C.
GOPINATHAN, S.
HOGAN, D. J.
LEE, S. K.
LUKE, A. A. J.
MATTHEWS, J. S.
TAN, L. W. H.
XU, S. Y.

School of Biological Sciences (60 Nanyang Dr., SBS-01n-21, Singapore 637551; tel. 63162800; fax 67913856; e-mail d-sbs@ntu.edu.sg; internet www.ntu.edu.sg/sbs):

LAW, A. S. K., Molecular and Cell Biology
LUN, K. C., Structural and Computational Biology
NORDENSKIÖLD, L., Structural and Computational Biology
TAM, J. P. K.

School of Chemical and Biomedical Engineering (Block 1 Innovation Centre, 16 Nanying Dr., Unit 100, Level 1, Singapore 637722; tel. 67906743; fax 67947553; e-mail cbe@ntu.edu.sg; internet www.ntu.edu.sg/cbme):

CHING, C. B.

School of Civil and Environmental Engineering (Block N1, 50 Nanyang Ave, Singapore 639798; tel. 67905265; fax 67910676; e-mail d-cee@ntu.edu.sg; internet www.ntu.edu.sg/cee):

CHIEW, Y. M., Environmental and Water Resources Engineering
CHOA, V. C. E., Geotechnical Engineering
CHOI, E. C. C., Construction Technology and Management
FAN, H. S. L., Transportation Engineering
FAN, S. C., Structures and Mechanics
PAN, T. C., Structures and Mechanics
RAHARDJO, H., Geotechnical and Transportation Engineering
SOH, C. K., Structures and Mechanics
TAY, J. H., Environmental and Water Resources Engineering

School of Communication and Information (31 Nanyang Link, Singapore 637718; tel. 67904577; fax 67943662; e-mail wwwsci@ntu.edu.sg; internet www.ntu.edu.sg/sci):

FOO S. B., Information Studies
KUO C. Y. E., Communication Research

School of Computer Engineering (Block N4, 2A-32, Nanyang Ave, Singapore 639798; tel. 67905786; fax 67926559; e-mail wwwsce@ntu.edu.sg; internet www.ntu.edu.sg/sce):

GOH, A. E. S., Information Systems

School of Electrical and Electronic Engineering (Block S2.1, 50 Nanyang Ave, Singapore 639798; tel. 67905367; fax 67912687; e-mail wwweee@ntu.edu.sg; internet www.ntu.edu.sg/eee):

CHOI, S. S., Power Engineering
DO, M. A., Circuits and Systems
ER, M. H.
GAY, R. K. L., Information Communication Institute of Singapore
KAM, C. H., Microelectronics
KOH, S. N., Communication Engineering
KOT, C. C., Information Engineering
LIM, Y. C., Information Engineering
SOH, Y. C., Control and Instrumentation
SUNDARARAJAN, N., Control and Instrumentation
XIE, L. H., Control and Administration
YOON, S. F., Microelectronics
ZHU, W. G., Microelectronics

School of Humanities and Social Sciences (Block S3.2, Level B2, 50 Nanyang Ave, Singapore 639798; tel. 67906983; fax 67942830; e-mail d-hss@ntu.edu.sg; internet www.hss.ntu.edu.sg):

CHEW, S. B., Economics
KOH, T. A., English
KUO, C. O. E., Sociology
LIM, C. Y., Economics
REISMAN, D. A., Economics

School of Materials Science and Engineering (Block N4.1, #01-30, Nanyang Ave, Singapore 639798; tel. 67904142; fax 67909081; e-mail wwwsme@ntu.edu.sg; internet www.ntu.edu.sg/sme):

BOEY, F. Y. C.

School of Mechanical and Production Engineering (Block N3, 50 Nanyang Ave, Singapore 639798; tel. 67905486; fax 67911859; e-mail wwwmae@ntu.edu.sg; internet www.ntu.edu.sg/mae):

ASUNDI, A. K., Engineering Mechanics
HELANDER, M. E. G., Systems and Engineering Management
KHOO, L. P., Mechatronics and Design
KHOR, K. A., Manufacturing Engineering
LAM, Y. C., Manufacturing Engineering
LIEW, K. M., Engineering Mechanics
LIM, L. E. N., Manufacturing Engineering
LIM, M. K., Engineering Mechanics
LING, S. F., Engineering Mechanics
LYE, S. W., Manufacturing Engineering
MEGUID, S. A., Engineering Mechanics
SHANG, H. M., Engineering Mechanics
TAM, K. C., Manufacturing Engineering
YUE, C. Y.

School of Physical and Mathematical Sciences (Block 5, Level 3, 1 Nanyang Walk, Singapore 637616; tel. 67903754; fax 67906984; e-mail spms-v1@ntu.edu.sg; internet www.ntu.edu.sg/spms/home):

LEE, S. Y.
LEUNG, P. H., Physical and Mathematical Sciences
LING, S., Mathematical Sciences
LOH, T. P., Chemistry and Biological Chemistry

ATTACHED RESEARCH INSTITUTES

Advanced Materials Research Centre: tel. 67904626; fax 67909081; e-mail d-amrc@ntu.edu.sg; Dir Assoc. Prof. SUBODH MHAISALKAR.

Bioinformatics Research Centre: tel. 63162957; fax 67912274; internet www.ntu.edu.sg; Dir Assoc. Prof. SUBBU S. VENKATRAMAN.

BioMedical Engineering Research Centre: Dir Assoc. Prof. LIM CHU SING DANIEL.

Centre for Advanced Numerical Engineering Simulations: Dir Prof. LIEW KIM MEOW.

Centre for Financial Engineering: tel. 67904758; fax 67937440; e-mail mfe@ntu.edu.sg; Dir Assoc. Prof. BUEN SIN LOW.

Centre for Graphics and Imaging Technology: Dir Assoc. Prof. WONG KOK CHEONG.

Centre for High-Performance Embedded Systems: tel. 67906638; fax 67920774; e-mail chipes@ntu.edu; internet www.chipes.ntu.edu.sg; Dir Prof. THAMBIPILLAI SRIKANTHAN.

Environmental Engineering Research Centre: Dir Assoc. Prof. STEPHEN TAY TIONG LEE.

Maritime Research Centre: tel. 67905321; fax 67906620; e-mail d-mrc@ntu.edu.sg; Dir Assoc. Prof. TAN SOON KEAT.

Nanyang Technopreneurship Centre: tel. 67906675; fax 67920467; e-mail ntc@ntu.edu.sg; Dir Assoc. Prof. TAN TENG KEE.

Network Technology Research Centre: tel. 67905019; fax 67904685; e-mail ntrc@ntu.edu.sg; internet www.ntu.edu.sg/ntrc; Dir Assoc. Prof. PING SHUM.

NTU-BCA Centre for Advanced Construction Studies: Dir Assoc. Prof. TING SENG KIONG.

NTU-MINDEF Protective Technology Research Centre: tel. 67905285; fax 67910046; e-mail ptrc@ntu.edu.sg; internet www.ntu.edu.sg/ptrc; Dir Prof. TSO-CHIEN PAN.

Positioning and Wireless Technology Centre: tel. 67917326; fax 6793318; e-mail d-pwtc@ntu.edu.sg; internet www.ntu.edu.sg/centre/pwtc; Dir Assoc. Prof. CHOI LOOK LAW.

Robotics Research Centre: tel. 67905568; e-mail d-rrc@ntu.edu.sg; internet www.ntu.edu.sg/mae/centres/rrc; Dir Assoc. Prof. GERALD SEET.

NATIONAL UNIVERSITY OF SINGAPORE

21 Lower Kent Ridge Rd, Singapore 119077
Telephone: 65166666
Internet: www.nus.edu.sg

Founded 1980 by merger of fmr Univ. of Singapore and Nanyang Univ.
State control
Language of instruction: English
Academic year: July to June (2 semesters)

Pres.: Prof. TAN CHORH CHUAN
Deputy Pres. for Acad. Affairs and Provost: Prof. TAN ENG CHYE
Deputy Pres. for Research and Technology: Prof. BARRY HALLIWELL
Deputy Pres. for Admin.: JOSEPH P. MULLINIX
Vice-Pres. for Campus Infrastructure: Prof. YONG KWET YEW
Vice-Pres. for Human Resources: DANIEL CHO KWONG CHOW
Vice-Pres. for Univ. and Global Relations: Prof. LILY KONG
Vice-Pres. for Research Strategy: Prof. SEERAM RAMAKRISHNA
Vice-Pres. for Endowment and Institutional Devt: WEE SIN THO
Vice-Provost for Academic Personnel: Prof. LAI CHOY HENG
Vice-Provost for Education: Prof. TAN THIAM SOON
Vice-Provost for Student Life: Prof. TAN TAI YONG
CEO: Dr LILY CHAN
Registrar: CHRISTINE CHEN (acting)
Librarian: JILL QUAH

Library: see Libraries and Archives
Number of teachers: 2,207
Number of students: 33,741
Publication: *Knowledge Enterprise* (10 year)

DEANS

Faculty of Arts and Social Sciences: Prof. BRENDA YEOH
Faculty of Dentistry: Assoc. Prof. GRACE ONG HUI LIAN
Faculty of Engineering: Prof. CHAN ENG SOON
Faculty of Law: Prof. TAN CHENG HAN

Faculty of Science: Prof. ANDREW WEE
NUS Business School: Prof. BERNARD YEUNG
School of Computing: Prof. BENG CHIN OOI
School of Design and Environment: Prof. HENG CHYE KIANG
Yong Loo Lin School of Medicine: Prof. JOHN WONG
Lee Kwan Yew School of Public Policy: Prof. KISHORE MAHBUBANI
NUS Graduate School for Integrative Sciences and Engineering: Prof. LI BAOWEN (Exec. Dir)
Duke-NUS Graduate Medical School Singapore: TONY CHEW (Chair.)
Yong Siew Toh Conservatory of Music: Prof. BERNARD LANSKEY (Dir)

PROFESSORS

Faculty of Arts and Social Sciences:

CHAN, H. C., Political Science
KAPUR, B. K., Economics
MOHANAN, K. P., English Language and Literature
MUKUL, A., Public Policy
NG, C. K., History
QUAH, S. T. J., Political Science
SIDLE, R. C., Geography
SINGH, R., Social Work and Psychology
SURYADINATA, L., Political Science
WANG, G. W., East Asian Institute
WONG, K. L. C. A., Sociology
WONG, Y. W., Chinese Studies

Faculty of Business Administration:

KAU, A. K., Marketing
LEONG, S. M., Marketing
TAN, C. H., Management and Organization
WONG, K. A., Finance and Accounting

Faculty of Dentistry:

CHEW, C. L., Restorative Dentistry
LOH, H. S., Oral and Maxillofacial Surgery

Faculty of Engineering:

ANG, B. W., Industrial and Systems Engineering
ARUN, S. M., Mechanical Engineering
CHAN, S. H. D., Electrical and Computer Engineering
CHEONG, H. F., Civil Engineering
CHEW, Y. T., Mechanical Engineering
CHING, C. B., Chemical and Environmental Engineering
CHOW, Y. K., Civil Engineering
CHUA, S. J., Electrical and Computer Engineering
CHUNG, T. S. N., Chemical and Environmental Engineering
FWA, T. F., Civil Engineering
GOH, T. N., Industrial and Systems Engineering
HANG, C. C., Electrical and Computer Engineering
KAM, P. Y., Electrical and Computer Engineering
KANG, E. T., Chemical and Environmental Engineering
KOOI, P. S., Electrical and Computer Engineering
LAM, K. Y., Mechanical Engineering
LEE, T. H., Electrical and Computer Engineering
LEONG, M. S., Electrical and Computer Engineering
LI, M. F., Electrical and Computer Engineering
LIEW, A. C., Electrical and Computer Engineering
LIM, S. C., Mechanical Engineering
LIM, Y. C., Electrical and Computer Engineering
LING, C. H., Electrical and Computer Engineering
LOW, T. S., Electrical and Computer Engineering
LYE, K. M., Electrical and Computer Engineering
NEE, Y. C. A., Mechanical Engineering
NEOH, K. G., Chemical and Environmental Engineering
NG, W. J., Civil Engineering
NHAN, P. T., Mechanical Engineering
PARAMASIVAM, P., Civil Engineering
PHANG, C. H. J., Electrical and Computer Engineering
POO, A. N., Mechanical Engineering
SHANG, H. M., Mechanical Engineering
SHANKAR, N. J., Civil Engineering
SHANMUGAM, N. E., Civil Engineering
SHIH, C. F., Engineering
TAN, T. C., Chemical and Environmental Engineering
TAY, A. O. A., Electrical and Computer Engineering
TOYOAKI, N., Civil Engineering
VISWANADHAM, N., Mechanical Engineering
WIJEYSUNDERA, N. E., Mechanical Engineering
WONG, L., Electrical and Computer Engineering
YAP, M., Chemical and Environmental Engineering
YEO, S. P., Electrical and Computer Engineering
YONG, K. Y., Civil Engineering

Faculty of Law:

JAYAKUMAR, S.
KOH, T. B. T.
PINSLER, J.
SORNARAJAH, M.
TAN, Y. L.
WOON, C. M. W.

Faculty of Medicine:

AW, T. C., Pathology
BOSE, K., Orthopaedic Surgery
CHAN, H. L., Medicine
CHAN, S. H., Microbiology
CHIEW, Y. C., Medicine
GOPALAKRISHNAKONE, P., Anatomy
GWEE, M., Pharmacology
HALLIWELL, B., Biochemistry
HWANG, L. H. P., Physiology
KOH, S. Q. D., Community, Occupational and Family Medicine
KUA, E. H., Psychological Medicine
LEE, E. H., Orthopaedic Surgery
LEE, H. P., Community, Occupational and Family Medicine
LEE, J. D. E., Pharmacology
LEE, T. L., Anaesthesia
LEE, Y. S., Pathology
LIM, P., Medicine
LING, E. A., Anatomy
LIU, E., Medicine
LOW, P. S., Paediatrics
NG, S. C., Obstetrics and Gynaecology
OH, M. S. V., Medicine
ONG, C. N., Community, Occupational and Family Medicine
PHO, W. H. R., Orthopaedic Surgery
PRASAD, R. N. V., Obstetrics and Gynaecology
SATKUNANANTHAM, K., Orthopaedic Surgery
SHAMAL, D. D., Orthopaedic Surgery
SIT, K. H., Anatomy
SIT, K. P., Biochemistry
TAN, C. C., Medicine
TAN, K. A. L., Diagnostic Radiology
TAN, W. C., Medicine
TAN, Y. H., Medicine
WEE, A., Pathology
WONG, E. L. J., Medicine
YAP, H. K., Paediatrics

Faculty of Science:

BAI, Z., Statistics and Applied Probability
BERRICK, A. J., Mathematics
CHAN, S. O. H., Chemistry
CHEN, H. Y. L., Mathematics
CHONG, C. T., Mathematics
CHOU, L. M., Biological Sciences
CHOW, S. N., Mathematics
DING, J. L., Biological Sciences
GOH, S. H., Chemistry
HEW, C. L., Biological Sciences
HOR, T. S. A., Chemistry
IP, Y. K. A., Biological Sciences
KOH, K. M., Mathematics
LAI, C. H., Physics
LAM, T. J., Biological Sciences
LEE, C. K., Chemistry
LEE, S. L., Mathematics
LEE, S. Y., Chemistry
LI, F. Y. S., Chemistry
LIM, C. S., Mathematics
LIM, H., Physics
NIEDERREITER, H., Mathematics
OH, C. H., Physics
ONG, C. K., Physics
ONG, P. P. P., Physics
PHILPOTT, M. R., Materials Science
SY, H. K., Physics
TANG, S. H., Physics
TANG, S. M., Physics
TRUONG, Y. K.-N., Statistics and Applied Probability
WATT, F., Physics

School of Computing:

JAFFAR, J., Computer Science
LING, T. W., Computer Science
LU, H. J., Computer Science
OOI, B. C., Computer Science
PNG, P. L. I., Information Systems
WEI, K. K., Information Systems
YUEN, C. K., Computer Science

School of Design and Environment:

BROWN, G. R., Real Estate
OFORI, G., Building

SIM UNIVERSITY

461 Clementi Rd, Singapore 599491
Telephone: 62489777
Fax: 67639077
E-mail: student_recruitment@unisim.edu.sg
Internet: www.unisim.edu.sg

Founded 1992, present name and status 2005
Private control

Chair.: Prof. CHAM TAO SOON
Pres.: CHEONG HEE KIAT
Registrar: Assoc. Prof YIP WOON KWONG

DEANS

School of Arts and Social Sciences: Dr GENICE NGG (acting)
School of Business: Prof. TAN NGOH TIONG
School of Human Development and Social Services: Prof. TAN NGOH TIONG
School of Science and Technology: Assoc. Prof. PHILIP CHEANG HONG NING (acting)

SINGAPORE INSTITUTE OF TECHNOLOGY

25 N Bridge Rd, EFG Bank Bldg 03–01, Singapore 179104
Telephone: 65921189
E-mail: adm.intl@singaporetech.edu.sg
Internet: www.singaporetech.edu.sg

Founded 2009
State control

Chair.: NG YAT CHUNG
Deputy Chair.: NG CHER PONG
Pres.: Prof. TAN CHIN TIONG
Deputy Pres. for Academics: Dr TING SENG KIONG
Deputy Pres. for Operations: TAN CHEK MING.

SINGAPORE MANAGEMENT UNIVERSITY

Tanglin, POB 257, Singapore 912409
Bukit Timah Campus, 469 Bukit Timah Rd, Oei Tiong Ham Bldg, Singapore 259756
Telephone: 68220100
Fax: 68220101
E-mail: enquire@smu.edu.sg
Internet: www.smu.edu.sg

Founded 2000
Private control

Pres.: HOWARD HUNTER
Provost: Prof. CHIN TIONG TAN
Registrar: TAN LEE CHUAN
Chief Librarian: KOH BEE CHIN

DEANS

School of Accountancy: Assoc. Prof. PANG YANG HOONG
Lee Kong Chian School of Business: Prof. DAVID B. MONTGOMERY
School of Economics and Social Sciences: Prof. ROBERTO S. MARIANO
School of Information Systems: STEVEN MILLER

PROFESSORS

School of Accountancy (Accountancy Bldg, 469 Bukit Timah Rd, Singapore 259756; tel. 68220610; fax 68220600; e-mail adelineheng@smu.edu.sg; internet www.accountancy.smu.edu.sg):

TAN, T. M.
YOUNG, K. K.

Lee Kong Chian School of Business (Business Bldg, 469 Bukit Timah Rd, Singapore 259756; e-mail dmontgomery@smu.edu.sg; internet www.business.smu.edu.sg):

LIM, K. G.
MONTGOMERY, D.
PANG, E. F.
PHANG, A.
TAN, C. T.
YANG, K. K.

School of Economics and Social Sciences (The Federal Bldg, 469 Bukit Timah Rd, Singapore 259756; tel. 68220832; fax 68220833; e-mail sess@smu.edu.sg; internet www.sess.smu.edu.sg):

KUEN, T. S.
MARIANO, R. S.

School of Information Systems (Raffles Bldg, 469 Bukit Timah Rd, Singapore 259756; tel. 68220903; fax 68220919; e-mail sis@smu.edu.sg; internet www.sis.smu.edu.sg):

DENG, R. H.
LEE, J. K.

SINGAPORE UNIVERSITY OF TECHNOLOGY & DESIGN (SUTD)

287 Ghim Moh Rd, 04-00, Singapore 279623
Telephone: 63036600
E-mail: enquiry@sutd.edu.sg
Internet: www.su.edu.sg

Offers courses in architecture and sustainable design, engineering product development, engineering systems and design, information systems technology and design

Chair.: PHILIP NG
Pres.: TOM MAGNANTI
Provost: Prof. CHONG TOW CHONG
Assoc. Provost: Prof. PEY KIN LEONG.

Polytechnics

NANYANG POLYTECHNIC

180 Ang Mo Kio Ave 8, Singapore 569830
Telephone: 64515115
Internet: www.nyp.edu.sg

Founded 1992

Pres.: TAN PHENG HOCK
Prin. and CEO: LIN CHENG TON
Deputy Prin. for Academic Affairs and Registrar: CHAN LEE MUN
Deputy Prin. for Devt: BRUCE POH GEOK HUAT
Deputy Prin. for Technology: EDWARD HO SZE LEUNG
Chief Librarian: WONG CHIEW AUN

DIRECTORS

School of Business Management: V. SESHAMANI
School of Chemical and Life Sciences: Dr JOEL LEE
School of Engineering: CHAN YEW MENG
School of Health Sciences: LONG CHOOI FONG
School of Information Technology: JOHN TAN

NGEE ANN POLYTECHNIC

535 Clementi Rd, Singapore 599489
Telephone: 64666555
Fax: 64687326
E-mail: dept-cc@np.edu.sg
Internet: www.np.edu.sg

Founded 1963
State control
Language of instruction: English
Academic year: April to March

Chair.: TAN HUP FOI
Prin.: CHIA MIA CHIANG
Deputy Prin.: FOO SEE MENG
Registrar: ROSALIND GOH CHWEE NEO
Dir of Library: CAROLINE PHUA CHOON KHENG

Library of 207,000 vols, 1,100 periodicals, 10,000 online books, 45 databases, 45,000 audiovisual items, 2,500 application software titles
Number of teachers: 850
Number of students: 14,687

Publications: *NP News*, *eXtra* (online magazine), *Urban Wire*

DIRECTORS

School of Business and Accountancy: PHILIP LAU TIONG LIP
School of Film and Media Studies: ANITA HWAI MIN KUAN
Health Sciences: Dr CHIEW HUN PHANG
School of Infocomm Technology: ANGELA WEE LI KWANG
School of Interdisciplinary Studies: JACINTHA JOHN
School of Life Sciences and Chemical Technology: TANG-LIM GUEK IM
Building and Environment Division (School of Engineering): GRACE QUA-OON GEK NEO
Electrical Engineering Division (School of Engineering): KOH WEE HIONG
Electronic and Computer Engineering Division (School of Engineering): Dr LIM CHOO MIN
Multidisciplinary Engineering: ANDREW SABARATNAM
Technology Devt and External Liaison: HANG KIM YAM
Centre for Professional Devt: YOLA CHUAN YUNG LIM

REPUBLIC POLYTECHNIC

1 Kay Siang Rd, Singapore 248922
Telephone: 63768000
Fax: 64151310
E-mail: gsm@rp.edu.sg
Internet: www.rp.edu.sg

Founded 2002

Prin. and Chief Exec.: Prof. LOW TECK SENG
Deputy Registrar: SEAN TAY
Library Man.: YEE WAI FUN

DIRECTORS

School of Applied Science: Dr TERENCE CHONG
School of Engineering: FONG YEW CHAN
School of Information Technology and Communications Technology: TAY KHENG TIONG
Centre for Culture and Communication: GAN SU-LIN
Centre for Educational Development: GLEN O'GRADY
Centre for Innovation and Enterprise: CHANG YORK BOON (Man.)

SINGAPORE POLYTECHNIC

500 Dover Rd, Singapore 139651
Telephone: 67751133
Fax: 67806189
E-mail: info@sp.edu.sg
Internet: www.sp.edu.sg

Founded 1954
Language of instruction: English
Academic year: April to February (four terms)

Chair.: TAN KAY YONG
Prin.: TAN HANG CHEONG
Deputy Prin. for Admin.: EDWARD QUAH KOK WAH
Deputy Prin. for Corporate Devt: HEE JOH LIANG
Registrar: TAN PENG ANN
Librarian: FANG SIN GUEK

Library of 266,000 vols, periodicals and multimedia and 60,000 electronic resources
Number of teachers: 857
Number of students: 17,443 (15,523 full-time, 1,920 part-time)

Publications: *fullstop* (8 a year), *inSPire* (1 a year), *RIOT* (1 a year)

DIRECTORS

School of Architecture and the Built Environment: LIM CHER YAM
School of Business: V. MAHEANTHARAN
School of Chemical and Life Sciences: Dr CHAI MIN SEN
School of Communication, Arts and Social Sciences: LAM YOKE
School of Design and the Environment: JEFFREY HO KIAT
School of Electrical and Electronic Engineering: NG WENG LAM
School of Info-communications Technology: TIMOTHY CHAN WAI KUEN
School of Mechanical and Manufacturing Engineering: NG ENG HONG
Singapore Maritime Academy: ROLAND TAN

TEMASEK POLYTECHNIC

21 Tampines Ave 1, Singapore 529757
Telephone: 67882000
Fax: 67898220
E-mail: corpcomm@tp.edu.sg
Internet: www.tp.edu.sg

Founded 1990

Prin.: BOO KHENG HUA
Registrar: SOH ENG KHIM
Library Dir: ESTHER ONG

Library of 218,000 vols, 1,900 periodicals
Number of teachers: 775
Number of students: 15,933

Publications: *In Tempo* (online, 4 a year), *Temasek Journal*, *T's* (2 a year)

DIRECTORS

Applied Science School: SOON-ONG MENG WAN
Business School: DANIEL YEOW AIK LIANG
Design School: MOSES WONG CHIAT CHANG
Engineering School: LAY-TAN SIOK LEE

Humanities and Social Sciences School: BEN LIM ENG KIAT
Informatics and IT School: LIM SOK KEOW

Institutes of Technical Education

DIGIPEN INSTITUTE OF TECHNOLOGY—SINGAPORE

PIXEL Bldg, 10 Central Exchange Green, 01-01, Singapore 138649
Telephone: 65771900
Fax: 65771908
E-mail: singapore@digipen.edu
Internet: singapore.digipen.edu

Founded 2008
Private control

Bachelors in arts (game design), fine arts (production animation), science (game design, real-time interactive simulation).

GERMAN INSTITUTE OF SCIENCE AND TECHNOLOGY—TUM ASIA (GIST-TUM ASIA)

10 Central Exchange Green, 03-01, Pixel Bldg, Singapore 138649
Telephone: 67777407
Fax: 67777236
E-mail: admin@gist.edu.sg
Internet: www.gist.edu.sg
Private control

Offers Bachelors and Masters programmes in aerospace engineering, electrical engineering and information technology, industrial chemistry, integrated circuit design, microelectronics, transport and logistics; br. of Technische Universität München, Germany

Publication: *GIST-TUM Asia Digest*.

INSTITUTE OF TECHNICAL EDUCATION

10 Dover Dr., Singapore 138683
Telephone: 65902288
Fax: 65902578
E-mail: itehq@ite.edu.sg
Internet: www.ite.edu.sg

Founded 1992 as Post-Secondary Technical Education Institution
State control

3 Colleges: ITE College Central, ITE College East, ITE College West; courses in applied and health sciences, automotive engineering, business and services, design and media, electronics and info-comm technology, engineering, machine technology
State control
Chair.: BOB TAN BENG HAI
Deputy Chair.: HENG CHIANG GNEE
Dir and CEO: BRUCE POH GEOK HUAT
Publications: *ignITE* (2 a year), *iLink*, *infinITE*, *Transforming Lives—The ITE Story*.

Schools of Art and Music

LASALLE College of the Arts: 1 McNally St, Singapore 187940; tel. 64965000; fax 64965353; e-mail enquiries@lasalle.edu.sg; internet www.lasalle.edu.sg; f. 1984 as St Patrick's Arts Centre, present status 2004, present name and location 2007; attached to LASALLE Foundation Limited; design, fine art, media, performing arts; 2,300 students; Pres. Prof. ALASTAIR PEARCE; Provost and Chief Academic Officer VENKA PURUSHOTHAMAN; Chair. PETER SEAH.

Nanyang Academy of Fine Arts: 80 Bencoolen St, Singapore 189655; tel. 65124000; fax 63373920; e-mail president@nafa.edu.sg; internet www.nafa.edu.sg; f. 1938 as Nanyang Fine Arts College, present name 1990; offers diploma, Bachelors and Masters degrees; depts of 3D design, arts management and education, dance, design and media, fashion studies, fine art, music, theatre; library: 80,000 vols of books and journals; 2,200 students; Chair. Prof. CHAM TAO SOON; Vice-Chair. POH CHOON ANN; Vice-Chair. Prof. PHUA KOK KHOO; Pres. CHOO THIAM SIEW; Vice-Pres. LIEW CHIN CHOY.

New York University Tisch School of Arts Asia: 3 Kay Siang Rd, Singapore 248923; tel. 65001700; fax 65001719; e-mail tisch.asia@nyu.edu; internet www.tischasia.nyu.edu.sg; f. 2007; offers Masters degree in animation and digital arts, dramatic writing, film production; Dean and Chair. MARY SCHMIDT CAMPBELL; Artistic Dir OLIVER STONE; Pres. PARI SARA SHIRAZI; Chair. of Graduate Dept of Dramatic Writing RICHARD WESLEY; Chair. of Graduate Dept of Film DAVID K. IRVING; Exec. Dir ANNIE STANTON; Exec. Dir GERARD I. BUENO; Dir of Admin. JASON SETH BECKERMAN; Dir for Graduate Dept of Animation and Digital Arts JEAN MARC GAUTHIER; Dir of Public Affairs and Marketing TIMOTHY TAN.

Colleges

ESSEC Business School: 100 Victoria St, 13-02, Nat. Library Bldg, Singapore; tel. 68849780; fax 68849781; e-mail mailtaxe@nullessec.fr; internet www.essec.edu; f. 2006; offers Bachelors, Masters and PhD; courses in business administration, finance and asset management, financial techniques, hospitality management, information systems and telecommunication networks, international business law and management, international food industry management, international luxury brand management, international supply chain management, logistics and supply chain management, management, management of technological projects, marketing management, strategy and management of international business, urban environmental and services management, executive MBA, executive education; Dean JEAN-MARC XUEREB.

INSEAD: 1 Ayer Rajah Ave, Singapore 138676; tel. 67995388; fax 67995399; internet www.insead.edu; f. 2000; offers MBA, Exec. MBA, PhD programmes; Dean FRANK BROWN.

S P Jain Center of Management: 10 Hyderabad Rd, off Alexandra Rd, Singapore 119579; tel. 62704748; fax 68385406; e-mail admissionssg@spjain.org; internet www.spjain.org; f. 2006; banking and international finance, business strategy, communications, economics, entrepreneurship, financial management, human resource management, information technology management, international business, international management, leadership, logistics, marketing management, mergers and acquisitions, operations management, organizational behaviour, portfolio management, quantitative methods, services management, supply chain management; Head Prof. SUBBARAMAN IYER; Dean Dr MICHAEL J. BARNES; Deputy Dean Dr PARVINDER ARORA; Dean for Global Bachelor of Business Admin. Programme Dr DAWN DEKLE.

The University of Chicago Booth School of Business: 101 Penang Rd, Singapore 238466; tel. 68356482; fax 68356483; e-mail asia.inquiries@chicagobooth.edu; internet www.chicagobooth.edu; f. 2000; offers Exec. MBA programmes; Dean (vacant); publ. *Chicago Booth Magazine* (3 a year).

William F. Harrah College of Hotel Administration: 100 Victoria St, Fl. 11–02, Nat. Library Bldg 11–02, Singapore 188064; tel. 63329538; fax 63329531; e-mail admissions@unlv.edu.sg; internet www.unlv.edu.sg; f. 2006; attached to University. of Nevada, Las Vegas; Dean STUART H. MANN.

SLOVAKIA

The Higher Education System

Many of Slovakia's higher education institutions predate the foundation of the former Czechoslovakia in 1918, with the oldest being the Univerzita Komenského v Bratislave (Comenius University in Bratislava—founded 1465). The next oldest university is the Univerzita Pavla Jozefa šafárika v Košiciach (šafárik University of Košice—the history of which can be traced back to the foundation of Academia Cassoviensis by Benedikt Kishdy, Bishop of Eger, in 1657). In 1990, following the removal of the communist Government which had been in power since 1948, Czechoslovakia was replaced by the Czech and Slovak Federative Republic (CzSFR). In turn, the CzSFR was dissolved in 1993 and the Czech Republic and Slovakia became independent sovereign states. In addition to the universities, higher education is offered by academies of art, military and police academies, technical universities, universities of economics and universities of pedagogy.

Higher education is administered according to the Higher Education Act (No. 172) of 1990, and following ratification of later legislation in 2002 Slovakia now participates in the Bologna Process to establish a European Higher Education Area, the first phase of which is to adopt a credit-based system of comparable degrees with two main cycles (undergraduate and postgraduate). Since 2005/2006 the use of European Credit Transfer and Accumulation System (ECTS) has been obligatory in all higher education institutions, although some had already begun the implementation before then. Since 2008/2009 Diploma Supplements have been issued automatically to all graduates. In 2007 there were 30 institutions of higher education, with a total enrolment of 132,499 students. There has been a marked increase in postgraduate students and in 2008/2009 there were 10,417 Slovak and 754 foreign students studying for a PhD in the Slovak Republic.

The Secondary School Leaving Certificate (Vysvedcenie o Maturitnej Skúške) is the main requirement for admission to higher education; additionally, many institutions administer entrance examinations. The Bachelors (Bakalár) is the undergraduate degree and is awarded after three years' study. Graduates holding the Bakalár are eligible for admission to the first postgraduate degree, the Masters (Magister), which lasts between one and three years depending on the subject. Professional titles awarded at this level include Inzinier (Engineer), Doktor Medicíny (Doctor of Medicine) and Doktor Veterinárnej Medicíny (Doctor of Veterinary Medicine). Doctoral-level studies last at least three years and lead to the award of the Doctorate (Doktor).

Regulatory and Representative Bodies

GOVERNMENT

Ministry of Culture: nám. SNP 33, 813 31 Bratislava; tel. (2) 59-39-11-55; fax (2) 59-39-11-74; e-mail mksr@culture.gov.sk; internet www.culture.gov.sk; Minister Mgr MAREK MAĎARIČ; State Secs Mgr IVAN SEČÍK, Dr AUGUSTÍN JOZEF LANG.

Ministry of Education: Stromová 1, 813 30 Bratislava; tel. (2) 59-37-41-11; fax (2) 59-37-43-35; e-mail kancmin@minedu.sk; internet www.minedu.sk; Minister Prof. Ing. JÁN MIKOLAJ; State Secs Mgr BIBIÁNA OBRIMČÁKOVÁ, Dr Ing. JOZEF HABÁNIK.

ACCREDITATION

Akreditacná komisia (Accreditation Commission): Stromová 1, 813 30 Bratislava; tel. (2) 59-23-81-19; fax (2) 59-23-81-18; e-mail contact@akredkom.sk; internet www.akredkom.sk; f. 1990; ind. body set up to monitor and evaluate the quality of education, research and other activities in Slovak univs; 21 mems; Chair. Prof. PAVOL NÁVRAT.

ENIC/NARIC Slovakia: Centre for the Recognition of Diplomas, Ministry of Education, Stromová 1, 813 30 Bratislava 1; tel. (2) 59-23-81-21; fax (2) 59-23-81-24; e-mail naric@minedu.sk; Dir Prof. PETER PLAVCAN.

NATIONAL BODIES

Slovenská akademická asociácia pre medzinárodnú spoluprácu (Slovak Academic Association for International Co-operation): Staré grunty 52, 842 44 Bratislava 4; tel. (2) 65-42-43-83; fax (2) 65-42-44-83; e-mail tajomnik@saaic.sk; internet www.saaic.sk/saaic/eng; f. 1992; ind. NGO providing information to univs and other instns about participation in educational and research activities through int. programmes; Pres. Doc. PhDr JANA LENGHARDTOVÁ.

Slovenská akademická informačná agentúra (Slovak Academic Information Agency): Nám. slobody 23, 812 20 Bratislava 1; tel. (2) 54-41-14-26; fax (2) 54-41-14-29; e-mail saia@saia.sk; internet www.saia.sk; f. 1990; ind. NGO assisting in internationalization of education and research in Slovakia; supports the mobility of students, university teachers and researchers from public and private research orgs; nat. scholarship programme; Chair. PhDr HELENA WOLEKOVÁ; Exec. Dir KATARÍNA KOŠŤÁLOVÁ.

Slovenská rektorská konferencia (Slovak Rectors' Conference): Inštitút Slovenskej rektorskej konferencie, Konventná 1, 812 02 Bratislava; tel. (2) 57-29-45-21; fax (2) 57-29-45-22; e-mail srk@srk.sk; internet www.srk.sk; f. 1993; Pres. Prof. Dr LIBOR VOZÁR; Gen. Sec. Ing. DENISA VOKÁROVÁ.

Learned Societies

GENERAL

Slovenská Akadémia Vied (Slovak Academy of Sciences): Štefánikova 49, 814 38 Bratislava; tel. (2) 52-49-56-34; fax (2) 52-44-49-28; internet www.savba.sk; f. 1953; depts of exact and technical sciences, natural sciences and chemistry, social sciences; attached research institutes: see Research Institutes; library: see Libraries and Archives; Pres. ŠTEFAN LUBY; publs *Acta Hydrologica* (2 a year), *Acta Montanistica Slovaca* (4 a year), *Acta Physica Slovaca* (6 a year), *Acta Virologica* (4 a year), *Architektúra a urbanizmus* (4 a year), *ARS* (3 a year), *Asian and African Studies* (2 a year), *Biologia* (6 a year), *Building Research Journal* (4 a year), *Computing and Informatics* (6 a year), *Contributions of the Astronomical Observatory Skalnaté Pleso* (4 a year), *Contributions to Geodesy and Geophysics* (4 a year), *Časopis pre Politické Vedy* (2 a year), *Človek a Spoločnosť* (e-journal), *Ekológia* (4 a year), *Ekonomický časopis* (10 a year), *Endocrine Regulations* (4 a year), *Entomological Problems* (6 a year), *Filozofia* (10 a year), *Folia Œcologica* (2 a year), *General Physiology and Biophysics* (4 a year), *Geografický časopis* (4 a year), *Geographia Slovaca* (1–2 a year), *Geologica Carpathica* (6 a year), *Geologica Carpatica Clays* (2 a year), *Helminthologia* (4 a year), *Historický časopis* (4 a year), *Human Affairs* (2 a year), *Chemical Papers* (6 a year), *Jazykovedný časopis* (2 a year), *Journal of Electrical Engineering* (12 a year), *Journal of Hydrology and Hydromechanics* (4 a year), *Kovové materiály* (6 a year), *Kultúra slova* (6 a year), *Mathematica Slovaca* (5 a year), *Neoplasma* (6 a year), *Organon F* (4 a year), *Power Metallurgy Progress* (4 a year), *Právny obzor* (6 a year), *Slavica Slovaca* (2 a year), *Slovak Review* (2 a year), *Slovenská archeológia* (2 a year), *Slovenská literatúra* (6 a year), *Slovenská reč* (6 a year), *Slovenské divadlo* (4 a year), *Slovenské štúdie* (2 a year), *Slovenský národopis* (4 a year), *Sociológia* (6 a year), *Studia Psychologica* (4 a year), *Sytematische Musikwissenschaften* (2 a year), *Tatra Mountains—Mathematical Publications* (3 a year), *Životné prostredie* (6 a year).

AGRICULTURE, FISHERIES AND VETERINARY SCIENCE

Slovenská spoločnosť pre polnohospodárske, lesnícke a potravinárske vedy (Slovak Society for Agriculture, Forestry and Food): Radlinskeho 9, 812 37 Bratislava; tel. (2) 52-92-60-55; fax (2) 52-49-31-89; f. 1968; 564 mems; Pres. Prof. Dr A. DANDAR; Sec. Assoc. Prof. Dr M. TAKÁCSOVA.

ARCHITECTURE AND TOWN PLANNING

Spolok architektov Slovenska (Slovak Architects' Society): Panská 15, 811 01 Bratislava; tel. (2) 54-43-14-31; fax (2) 54-43-57-44; e-mail sas@euroweb.sk; internet www.archinet.sk; 1,900 mems; library of 2,700 vols; Pres. Prof. Dr Ing. Arch. ŠTEFAN

ŠLACHTA; Dir Dr FRANTIŠEK KYSELICA; publs *Projekt* (review of Slovak architecture, 6 a year), *Fórum architektúry* (12 a year).

EDUCATION

Slovenská pedagogická spoločnosť (Slovak Education Society): Filozofická fakulta UPJŠ, 080 01 Prešov; internet www.ucm.sk/ff/slovensky/sps; f. 1965; 365 mems; Pres. Prof. Mgr LADISLAV MACHÁČEK; Sec. Doc. PhDr JÁN DANEK.

FINE AND PERFORMING ARTS

Slovenská výtvarná únia (Slovak Union for the Visual Arts): Dostojevskeho rad 2, 811 09 Bratislava; tel. (2) 52-96-24-02; e-mail svu@svu.sk; internet www.svu.sk; f. 1990; 1,800 mems; Pres. PAVOL KRAL; publs *Profil*, *Výtvarný život*.

HISTORY, GEOGRAPHY AND ARCHAEOLOGY

Slovenská archeologická spoločnosť (Slovak Archaeological Society): Akademická 2, 949 21 Nitra; tel. (37) 733-57-38; fax (37) 733-56-18; e-mail nrauklku@savba.savba.sk; f. 1956; 300 mems; library of 860 vols; Pres. Dr JAN RAJTÁR; Sec. Dr KLÁRA KUZMOVÁ; publs *Bibliografia Slovensky Archeologie* (irregular), *Informator* (2 a year).

Slovenská geografická spoločnosť pri SAV (Slovak Geographical Society): Štefánikova 49, 814 73 Bratislava; tel. (2) 57-51-02-09; e-mail geognovo@savba.sk; internet www.sgs.sav.sk; f. 1945; 250 mems; Pres. Prof. RENÉ MATLOVIČ; Treas. Dr JÁN NOVOTNÝ; Sec. FRANTIŠEK KRIŽAN.

Slovenská historická spoločnosť pri SAV (Slovak Historical Society): Klemensova 19, 813 64 Bratislava 1; tel. (2) 52-92-57-53; fax (2) 52-96-16-45; e-mail viliam.cicaj@savba.sk; internet www.shs.sav.sk; f. 1946; sections devoted to modern history, economic history, urban history, military history, gender studies, literature, history of religion; regional divisions in Trenčín, Topoľčany, Košice, Banská Bystrica and Prešov; 280 mems; Pres. PhDr VILIAM ČICAJ; Sec. PhDr KATARÍNA HRADSKÁ.

LANGUAGE AND LITERATURE

Alliance Française: 812 83 Bratislava 1, Palais Kutscherfeld, Sedlarska 7, POB 152; tel. (2) 59-34-77-77; fax (2) 59-34-77-05; internet slovaquie.alliance.free.fr; offers courses and exams in French language and culture and promotes cultural exchange with France; Dir JEAN-PIERRE MEULLENET.

British Council: 814 99 Bratislava, Panská 17, POB 68; tel. (2) 54-43-10-74; fax (2) 54-43-47-05; e-mail info.bratislava@britishcouncil.sk; internet www.britishcouncil.org/slovakia; teaching centre; offers courses and exams in English language and British culture and promotes cultural exchange with the UK; attached centres in Banská Bystrica and Košice; Dir HUW JONES.

Goethe-Institut: Panenská 33, 814 82 Bratislava; tel. (2) 54-43-31-30; fax (2) 54-43-31-34; e-mail info@bratislava.goethe.org; internet www.goethe.de/bratislava; offers courses and exams in German language and culture and promotes cultural exchange with Germany; library of 12,500 vols; Dir Dr WOLFGANG FRANZ.

Slovenská jazykovedná spoločnosť (Slovak Linguistics Society): Panská 26, 813 64 Bratislava; tel. (2) 54-33-17-61; fax (2) 54-33-17-56; e-mail mirod@juls.savba.sk; f. 1957; 266 mems; Pres. Prof. PhDr MIROSLAV DUDOK; Sec. Mgr GABRIELA MÚCSKOVÁ; publs *Spisy SJS*, *Varia*, *Zápisník slovenského jazykovedca*.

Spoločnosť učiteľov nemeckého jazyka a germanistov Slovenska (SUNG) (Verband der Deutschlehrer und Germanisten der Slowakei/Union of German Teachers and Germanists of Slovakia): Tomášikova 4, POB 14, 820 09 Bratislava 29; tel. (2) 43-42-22-53; fax (2) 48-20-94-28; internet www.sung.sk; f. 1991 as the successor organization to Krúžok moderných filológov (Union of Modern Philology); Pres. Prof. Dr HELENA HANULJAKOVÁ; Gen. Sec. NADEŽDA ZEMANÍKOVÁ; publs *Begegnungen* (1 or 2 a year), *Zeitschrift für Germanistische Sprach- Literaturwissenschaft in der Slowakei*, *Zeitschrift Mosaik* (1 a year).

Spolok slovenských spisovateľov (Slovak Writers' Society): Laurinská 2, 815 84 Bratislava 1; tel. (2) 54-41-86-70; fax (2) 54-43-53-71; e-mail spolspis@stonline.sk; f. 1923; 350 mems; Pres. Mgr art. PAVOL JANÍK; Sec. JOZEF ZAVARSKÝ; publs *Dotyky* (literature by young writers), *Literárny týždenník* (Literary Weekly).

MEDICINE

Slovenská parazitologická spoločnosť (Slovak Society for Parasitology): Hlinkova 3, 040 01 Košice; tel. (55) 633-44-55; fax (55) 633-14-14; e-mail pausav@saske.sk; internet www.saske.sk/~pauwww/helminth.htm; f. 1993; 92 mems; Pres. Prof. Dr P. DUBINSKÝ, Sec. Prof. Dr V. LETKOVÁ; publ. *Správy slovenskej parazitologickej spoločnosti* (irregular).

NATURAL SCIENCES

General

Rada vedeckých spoločností (Council of Scientific Societies): Štefánikova 49, 814 38 Bratislava; tel. (2) 52-49-61-48; fax (2) 52-49-61-48; f. 1990; 45 Slovak mem. socs; Pres. Dr Dipl. Ing. JAN KNOPP.

Biological Sciences

Slovenská biologická spoločnosť (Slovak Biological Society): Sasinkova 4, 811 08 Bratislava; f. 1967; 180 mems; Pres. Asst Prof. Dr IGOR M. TOMO; publ. *Bulletin* (2 a year).

Slovenská botanická spoločnosť pri SAV (Slovak Botanical Society): Dúbravská cesta 14, 841 01 Bratislava 4; fax (2) 54-77-19-48; e-mail pavol.mereda@savba.sk; internet www.sbs.sav.sk; f. 1955; attached to Slovac Acad. of Sciences; 390 mems; Pres. Doc. RNDr IGOR MISTRÍK; Sec. RNDr PAVOL MEREDA.

Slovenská ekologická spoločnosť (Slovak Ecological Society): c/o Institute of Botany, Dúbravská cesta 14, 845 23 Bratislava; tel. (25) 477-35-07; fax (25) 477-19-48; e-mail viera.vitekova@savba.sk; internet ibot.sav.sk; f. 1992; 192 mems; Pres. Prof. Ing. IVAN VOLOŠČUK; Sec. Ing. BRANISLAV OLAH; publs *Ekologické Štúdie* (Ecological Studies, 1 a year), *SEKOS Bulletin* (2 a year).

Slovenská entomologická spoločnosť (Slovak Entomology Society): c/o Dept of Zoology, Univerzita Komenského, Mlynská dolina, 842 15 Bratislava 4; tel. (2) 60-29-62-49; internet www.ses.sav.sk; f. 1957; 235 mems; Pres. Dr STANISLAV KALUZ; Sec. Dr LADISLAV ROLLER; publs *Entomofauna carpathica* (4 a year), *Entomological Problems* (2 a year).

Slovenská spoločnosť pre biochémiu a molekulárnu biológiu (Slovak Society for Biochemistry and Molecular Biology): Vlárska 3, 833 06 Bratislava 3; internet www.ssbmb.sav.sk; f. 1959; 220 mems; Pres. Dr JÁN TURŇA; Sec. Ing. Dr ALBERT BREIER.

Slovenská zoologická spoločnosť pri SAV (Slovak Zoological Society): Mlynská dolina B-2, 842 15 Bratislava; tel. (2) 60-29-66-80; e-mail talka@zoznam.sk; internet www.szs.sav.sk; f. 1956; 200 mems; Pres. Mgr JÁN KAUTMAN; Sec. Dr LUCIA KRŠKOVÁ; publ. *Správy Slovenskej zoologickej spoločnosti* (1 a year).

Mathematical Sciences

Jednota slovenských matematikov a fyzikov (Union of Slovak Mathematicians and Physicists): Faculty of Mathematics, Physics and Informatics, Univerzita Komenského, Mlynská dolina F2, 842 48 Bratislava; tel. (2) 60-29-51-111; fax (2) 65-41-23-05; e-mail sd@fmph.uniba.sk; internet www.fmph.uniba.sk/index.php?id=1743; f. 1969; 1,500 mems; Pres. Assoc. Prof. MARTIN KALINA; Sec. Dr MAREK HYČKO; publ. *Obzory matematiky, fyziky a informatiky* (4 a year).

Physical Sciences

Slovenská astronomická spoločnosť (Slovak Astronomical Society): 059 60 Tatranská Lomnica; tel. (52) 787-91-48; fax (52) 446-76-56; e-mail sas@ta3.sk; internet www.ta3.sk/sas; f. 1959; 160 mems; Pres. RNDr JURAJ ZVERKO; Sec. RNDr LADISLAV HRIC.

Slovenská chemická spoločnosť (Slovak Chemical Society): Radlinského 9, 812 37 Bratislava; tel. (2) 59-32-52-99; fax (2) 52-49-52-05; e-mail schs@chtf.stuba.sk; internet www.schems.sk; f. 1929; 874 mems; Pres. Dr MILAN DRÁBIK; Sec. Dr DALMA GYEPESOVÁ; publ. *Chemti* (2 a year).

Slovenská geologická spoločnosť (Slovak Geological Society): Mlynská dolina 1, 817 04 Bratislava; tel. (2) 59-37-53-78; fax (2) 54-19-40; e-mail iglarova@gssr.sk; internet dionysos.gssr.sk/sgs; f. 1965; 350 mems; Pres. Dr P. REICHWALDER; Sec. Dr M. ELEČKO; publ. *Mineralia slovaca* (4 a year).

Slovenská meteorologická spoločnosť (Slovak Meteorological Society): c/o Slovenský hydrometeorologický ústav, Jeséniova 17, 833 15 Bratislava; tel. (2) 54-77-20-04; fax (2) 54-77-20-34; f. 1960; 175 mems; Pres. PAVEL ŠŤASTNÝ; Sec. MARIAN OSTROŽLÍK.

PHILOSOPHY AND PSYCHOLOGY

Slovenské filozofické združenie (Slovak Philosophical Association): Klemensova 19, 813 64 Bratislava; tel. (2) 52-92-64-48; fax (2) 52-92-12-15; e-mail sfz@sfz.sk; internet www.sfz.sk; f. 1990; 292 mems; Pres. Mgr Dr SLAVOMÍR GÁLIK; Sec. Mgr PhDr ERIKA LALÍKOVÁ.

RELIGION, SOCIOLOGY AND ANTHROPOLOGY

Národopisná spoločnosť Slovenska (Slovak Ethnography Society): Klemensova 19, 813 64 Bratislava; tel. and fax (2) 52-96-47-07; e-mail nss@savba.sk; internet net.sav.sk/nss; f. 1958; 250 mems; Chair. Dr HANA HLOSKOVA; Scientific Sec. Dr KATANRA NOVAKOVA; publ. *Etnologické rozpravy* (Ethnological Review, 2 a year).

Slovenská antropologická spoločnosť (Slovak Anthropological Society): Mlynská dolina B2, 842 15 Bratislava; e-mail benus@fns.uniba.sk; f. 1965; 117 mems; Pres. Doc. RNDr MILAN THURZO; Sec. Prof. RNDr DANIELA SIVAKOVA; Sec. Doc. RNDr RADOSLAV BENUS; Treas. RADOSLAV BENUS; publ. *Slovenska Antropologia*.

Slovenská orientalistická spoločnosť (Slovak Society for Oriental Studies): Klemensova 19, 813 64 Bratislava; tel. (2) 52-92-63-26; fax (2) 52-92-63-26; e-mail koholla@klemens.savba.sk; f. 1960; 42 mems; Pres. Doc. Dr KAROL SORBY; Sec. Dr GABRIEL PIRICKÝ; publs *Asian and African Studies* (2 a year), *Human Affairs* (2 a year).

Slovenská sociologická spoločnost' (Slovak Sociological Association): Klemensova 19, 813 64 Bratislava; tel. (2) 52-96-43-55; fax (2) 52-96-23-15; e-mail bednarik@sspr.gov.sk; internet www.sociologia.eu.sk; f. 1964; 270 mems; Pres. Dr RASTISLAV BEDNÁRIK; Scientific Sec. Dr MARGITA MINICHOVÁ; publs *Sociologicky Zapisník* (4 a year), *Spravodajca SSS* (2 a year).

TECHNOLOGY

Slovenská spoločnost' pre mechaniku (Slovak Society for Mechanics): Dúbravská cesta 9, 845 03 Bratislava; tel. (2) 54-78-86-62; fax (2) 54-77-35-48; e-mail usarslad@savba.sk; internet mppserv.utc.sk; f. 1967; 252 mems; Pres. Dr J. SLADEK; Sec. Ing. O. IVANKOVA.

Research Institutes

ARCHITECTURE AND TOWN PLANNING

Institute of Construction and Architecture: Dúbravská cesta 9, 845 03 Bratislava; tel. and fax (2) 54-77-35-48; e-mail usarslad@savba.sk; f. 1953; attached to Slovak Acad. of Sciences; Dir Dr JAN SLADEK; publs *Architektura a urbanizmus* (4 a year), *Building Research Journal* (4 a year).

ECONOMICS, LAW AND POLITICS

Ekonomický ústav SAV (Institute of Economic Research): Šancova 56, 811 05 Bratislava; tel. (2) 52-49-82-14; fax (2) 52-49-51-06; e-mail milan.sikula@savba.sk; internet www.ekonom.sav.sk; f. 1953; attached to Slovak Acad. of Sciences; library of 32,000 vols, 1,400 periodicals; Dir Prof. Ing. Dr MILAN ŠIKULA; publ. *Ekonomický Časopis* (Journal of Economics, 10 a year).

Institute of Political Science: Dúbravská cesta 9, 813 64 Bratislava; tel. (2) 54-78-97-24; fax (2) 54-78-97-26; internet nic.savba.sk/sav/inst/poli; f. 1990; attached to Slovak Acad. of Sciences; Dirs PhDr JOZEF JABLONICKÝ, PhDr MIROSLAV PEKNÍK; publ. *Politické vedy* (Political Sciences, 4 a year).

Institute of State and Law: Klemensova 19, 813 64 Bratislava; tel. (2) 52-96-18-33; fax (2) 52-96-23-25; e-mail usap@klemens.savba.sk; internet klemens.savba.sk/usap; f. 1953; attached to Slovak Acad. of Sciences; Dir JUDr EDUARD BARÁNY; publ. *Právny odbor* (6 a year).

Prognostického ústavu Slovenskej akadémie vied (Institute of Forecasting of the Slovak Academy of Sciences): Šancova 56, 811 05 Bratislava; tel. (2) 52-49-51-14; fax (2) 52-49-50-29; e-mail progasis@savba.sk; internet www.prog.sav.sk; f. 1989; attached to Slovak Acad. of Sciences; behavioural economy, physical and space planning, prognostics environmental economy; Dir Dr EDITA NEMCOVÁ; Deputy Dir Dr Mgr TATIANA KLUVÁNKOVÁ-ORAVSKÁ; Scientific Sec. Dr Ing. DUŠAN BEVILAQUA; publs *Ekonomický časopis / Economic Magazin*, *Prognostické práce / Forecasting Papers*.

EDUCATION

Ústav informácií a prognóz školstva (Institute of Information and Prognoses of Education): Staré grunty 52, 842 44 Bratislava 4; tel. (2) 69-29-51-01; fax (2) 65-42-61-80; e-mail uips@uips.sk; internet www.uips.sk; f. 1976; library of 4,691 vols; Dir ROMAN BARANOVIČ; Librarian VIEROSLAVA CHUDIKOVÁ; publs *Academia* (4 a year), *Mládež a spoločnost'* (Youth and Society, 4 a year), *Informatika v škole* (Informatics in Education, 2 a year), *Prevencia* (Prevention, 4 a year).

FINE AND PERFORMING ARTS

Institute of Art History: Dúbravská cesta 9, 841 04 Bratislava; tel. and fax (2) 54-79-38-95; e-mail dejusekr@savba.sk; internet www.dejum.sav.sk; f. 1953, as Dept for Theory and History of Art of the Institute of History of the Slovak Acad. of Sciences, present name 1990; attached to Slovak Acad. of Sciences; researches into history of Slovak art and architecture since Middle Ages; Dir Dr IVAN GERÁT; Sec. ERIKA OKRUHLICOVA; publ. *ARS* (2 a year).

Institute of Musicology: Dúbravská cesta 9, 841 04 Bratislava; tel. and fax (2) 54-77-35-89; e-mail musicology@savba.sk; internet www.uhv.sav.sk; f. 1943; attached to Slovak Acad. of Sciences; Dir Prof. PhDr ArtD JURAJ LEXMANN; publs *Musicologica Slovaca et Europaea* (irregular), *Ethnomusicologicum* (irregular).

Institute of Theatre and Film (Kabinet divadla a filmu SAV): Dúbravská cesta 9, 841 04 Bratislava; tel. (2) 54-77-71-93; fax (2) 54-77-35-67; internet www.kadf.sav.sk; f. 1953; attached to Slovak Acad. of Sciences; Dir PhDr MILOŠ MISTRIK; publ. *Slovenské divadlo* (4 a year).

HISTORY, GEOGRAPHY AND ARCHAEOLOGY

Institute of Archaeology: Akademická 2, 949 21 Nitra; tel. (37) 733-56-17; fax (37) 733-56-18; e-mail nraurut@savba.sk; internet www.sav.sk; attached to Slovak Acad. of Sciences; Dir Prof. PhDr ALEXANDER RUTTKAY; publs *AVANS* (1 a year), *Slovenská archeológia* (2 a year), *Študijné zvesti AÚ SAV* (6 a year), *Východoslovenský pravek* (irregular), *Slovenská numizmatika* (jtly with Nat. Numismatic Cttee, every 2 years).

Institute of Geography: Štefánikova 49, 814 73 Bratislava; tel. (2) 57-51-01-87; fax (2) 52-49-13-40; e-mail geogsekr@savba.sk; internet www.geography.sav.sk; f. 1943; attached to Slovak Acad. of Sciences; basic and strategic applied research in human geography, regional geography, physical geography and geoinformatics; library of 15,570 vols, 118 series of journals; Dir Prof. Dr VLADIMÍR IRA; publs *Cartographic Letters* (yearbook), *Geografický časopis (Geographical Journal)* (yearbook), *Geographia Slovaca* (1 a year).

Institute of Historical Studies: Klemensova 19, 813 64 Bratislava; tel. (2) 52-92-63-21; fax (2) 52-96-16-45; e-mail histor@klemens.savba.sk; internet klemens.savba.sk/husav/prac.htm; f. 1942; attached to Slovak Acad. of Sciences; library of 75,000 vols; Dir PhDr VALERIAN BYSTRICKÝ; publs *Forum Historiae* (www.forumhistoriae.sk; 2 a year), *Historický časopis* (Journal of History, 4 a year), *Historické štúdie* (Historical Studies, 1 a year), *Human Affairs* (2 a year), *Slovanské štúdie* (Slavonic Studies, 2 a year), *Studia Historica Slovaca* (1 a year), *Z dejín vied a techniky* (Studies in the History of Science and Technology, 1 a year).

LANGUAGE AND LITERATURE

Institute of Slovak Literature: Konventná 13, 813 64 Bratislava; tel. and fax (2) 54-41-60-25; e-mail usllnada@savba.sk; internet www.uslit.sav.sk; f. 1943; attached to Slovak Acad. of Sciences; library of 50,000 vols; Dir Doc. PhDr JELENA PASTEKOVA; Sec. Doc. PhDr NADEŽDA BUGÁROVÁ; publ. *Slovenská literatúra* (6 a year).

Institute of World Literature: Konventná 13, 813 64 Bratislava; tel. (2) 54-41-33-91; fax (2) 54-43-19-95; e-mail usvlust@savba.sk; internet www.usvl.sav.sk; f. 1991; attached to Slovak Acad. of Sciences; basic research of phenomena and processes of world literature in these major fields: developmental tendencies of modern literary movements, theoretical and methodological questions of general literary process, history of literary translation in Slovakia, theoretical and methodological questions of translation, interdisciplinary research of major cultural epochs; 29 mems; library of 52,866 vols; Dir ADAM BŽOCH; publs *Slovak Review of World Literature Research* (2 a year), *World Literature Studies* (4 a year).

Ľudovít Štúr Institute of Linguistics: Panská 26, 813 64 Bratislava; tel. (2) 54-43-17-61; fax (2) 54-43-17-56; e-mail slavoo@juls.savba.sk; f. 1943; attached to Slovak Acad. of Sciences; library of 22,000 vols; Dir PhDr SLAVO ONDREJOVIČ; publs *Jazykovedný časopis* (2 a year), *Kultúra slova* (6 a year), *Slovenská reč* (6 a year).

MEDICINE

Cancer Research Institute: Vlárska 7, 833 91 Bratislava; tel. (2) 59-32-72-60; fax (2) 59-32-72-50; e-mail exonalt@savba.sk; internet www.exon.sav.sk; f. 1946; attached to Slovak Acad. of Sciences; Dir Doc. Ing. ČESTMÍR ALTANER; Scientific Sec. Dr ALENA GABELOVA; publ. *Neoplazma* (6 a year).

Institute of Experimental Endocrinology: Vlárska 3, 833 06 Bratislava; tel. (2) 54-77-28-00; fax (2) 54-77-42-47; e-mail ueenregu@savba.sk; internet www.elis.sk; f. 1969; attached to Slovak Acad. of Sciences; Dir RNDr RICHARD KVETŇANSKÝ; publ. *Endocrine Regulations* (4 a year).

Institute of Experimental Pharmacology: Dúbravská cesta 9, 842 16 Bratislava; tel. (2) 54-77-35-86; fax (2) 54-77-59-28; e-mail exfastol@savba.sk; internet nic.savba.sk/sav/insl/exfa/index.htm; f. 1969; attached to Slovak Acad. of Sciences; Scientific Sec. Ing. MÁRIA ĎURIŠOVÁ.

Institute for Heart Research: Dúbravská cesta 9, 842 33 Bratislava; tel. (2) 54-77-44-05; fax (2) 54-77-66-37; e-mail usrdsekr@savba.sk; internet www.usrd.sav.sk; attached to Slovak Acad. of Sciences; Dir Dr JAN STYK; Scientific Sec. Dr MIROSLAV BARANČÍK.

Institute of Neurobiology: Šoltésovej 4, 040 01 Košice; tel. (55) 678-50-69; fax (55) 678-50-74; internet www.saske.sk/inb; f. 1977; attached to Slovak Acad. of Sciences; Dir Dr IVO VANICKÝ.

Institute of Normal and Pathological Physiology: Sienkiewiczova 1, 813 71 Bratislava; tel. (2) 52-92-66-18; fax (2) 52-96-85-16; e-mail postmast@unpf.savba.sk; internet nic.savba.sk/sav/inst/unpf/index.html; f. 1953; attached to Slovak Acad. of Sciences; Dir MUDr FEDOR JAGLA.

Institute of Parasitology: Hlinkova 3, 040 01 Košice; tel. (55) 633-44-55; fax (55) 633-14-14; e-mail pausav@saske.sk; internet www.saske.sk/~pauwww/helminth.htm; f. 1953; attached to Slovak Acad. of Sciences; library of 8,000 vols; Dir Assoc. Prof. Dr B. PEŤKO; publ. *Helminthologia* (4 a year).

Institute of Virology: Dúbravská cesta 9, 842 46 Bratislava; tel. (2) 54-77-42-68; fax (2) 54-77-42-84; e-mail virufcem@savba.savba.sk; internet www.nic.savba.sk/sav/ins/viru; f. 1953; attached to Slovak Acad. of Sciences; Dir Doc. MUDr FEDOR ČIAMPOR; publ. *Acta Virologia* (6 a year).

NATURAL SCIENCES

Biological Sciences

Institute of Animal Biochemistry and Genetics: Moyzesova 61, 900 28 Ivanka pri Dunaji; tel. (2) 45-94-30-52; fax (2) 45-94-39-

23; e-mail greksak@ubgz.savba.sk; f. 1990; attached to Slovak Acad. of Sciences; Dir Doc. RNDr MILOSLAV GREKSÁK.

Institute of Animal Physiology: Šoltésovej 4, 040 01 Košice; tel. (55) 728-78-41; fax (55) 728-78-42; e-mail ufhzsav@saske.sk; internet www2.saske.sk/iap; f. 1964; attached to Slovak Acad. of Sciences; Dir MVDr JURAJ KOPPEL.

Institute of Botany: Dúbravská cesta 9, 845 23 Bratislava; tel. (2) 54-77-35-07; fax (2) 54-77-19-48; e-mail botuinst@savba.sk; internet ibot.sav.sk; f. 1963 by merger of the Laboratory of Geobotany and Floristics and Laboratory of Plant Biology; attached to Slovak Acad. of Sciences; strategic and applied research in biological and ecological sciences; nat. nature protection and environment management; library of 22,000 vols; Dir IVAN JAROLÍMEK; publ. *Biologia* (6 a year).

Institute of Experimental Phytopathology and Entomology: Nádražná 52, 900 28 Ivanka pri Dunaji; tel. (2) 45-94-33-31; fax (2) 45-94-34-31; internet nic.savba.sk/sav/inst/uefe/informatclip.htm; f. 1953; attached to Slovak Acad. of Sciences; Dir Doc. Ing. ANTON JANITOR; publ. *Entomological Problems* (2 a year).

Institute of Forest Ecology: Štúrova 2, 960 53 Zvolen; tel. (45) 533-09-14; fax (45) 547-94-85; internet www.savzv.sk; f. 1983; attached to Slovak Acad. of Sciences; Dir Prof. Ing. JOZEF VAĽKA; publ. *Folia Oecologica*.

Institute of Landscape Ecology: Štefánikova 3, POB 254, 814 99 Bratislava; tel. (2) 52-49-38-82; fax (2) 52-49-45-08; e-mail director@uke.savba.sk; attached to Slovak Acad. of Sciences; Dir Ing. JÚLIUS OSZLÁNYI; publs *Ecology* (4 a year), *Životné postredie* (6 a year).

Institute of Molecular Biology: Dúbravská cesta 9, 842 51 Bratislava; tel. (2) 59-30-74-11; fax (2) 59-30-74-16; internet imb.savba.sk; f. 1976; incorporated Institute of Microbiology 2000; attached to Slovak Acad. of Sciences; Dir Prof. Ing. Dr JOZEF TIMKO; Scientific Sec. RNDr GABRIELA BUKOVSKA; publ. *Biologia*.

Institute of Molecular Physiology and Genetics: Vlárska 5, 833 34 Bratislava; tel. (2) 54-77-52-66; fax (2) 54-77-36-66; e-mail usrdtylo@savba.savba.sk; internet nic.savba.sk/sav/inst/umfg; f. 1990; attached to Slovak Acad. of Sciences; library of 1,000 vols; Dir Dr ALBERT BREIER; publ. *General Physiology and Biophysics* (4 a year).

Institute of Plant Genetics and Biotechnology: Akademická 2, POB 39A, 950 07 Nitra; tel. (37) 733-66-59; fax (37) 733-66-60; internet pribina.savba.sk/ugbr/sk; f. 1990, present name 1998; attached to Slovak Acad. of Sciences; research activities are focused on plant reproduction and breeding, as well as molecular biology and biotechnology of plant processes; Dir Dr JÁN SALAJ; Scientific Sec. ILDIKÓ MATUŠÍKOVÁ.

Institute of Zoology: Dúbravská cesta 9, 842 06 Bratislava; tel. (2) 59-30-26-01; fax (2) 59-30-26-46; internet www.zoo.sav.sk; attached to Slovak Acad. of Sciences; Dir RNDr MILAN LABUDA; publs *Biologia* (6 a year), *Entomological Problems* (2 a year).

Mathematical Sciences

Institute of Mathematics: ul. Štefánikova 49, 814 73 Bratislava; tel. (2) 57-51-04-14; fax (2) 52-49-73-16; internet www.mat.savba.sk; f. 1959; attached to Slovak Acad. of Sciences; research in mathematics, applied mathematics, computer science; undergraduate and graduate studies; cooperation with home and foreign scientific and research instns; publishing of scientific journals and books; scientific information providing for the institutes and citizens of Slovakia; cooperation with univs and supporting education on univs; science popularization; brs in Košice, Banská Bystrica; library of 25,589 vols; Dir Prof. RNDr ANATOLIJ DVUREČENSKIJ; Scientific Sec. KAROL NEMOGA; publs *Mathematica Slovaca* (6 a year), *Tatra Mountains Mathematical Publications*, *Uniform Distribution Theory*.

Physical Sciences

Astronomical Institute: Slovak Acad. of Sciences, 059 60 Tatranská Lomnica; tel. (52) 787-91-57; fax (52) 446-76-56; e-mail astrinst@astro.sk; internet www.astro.sk; f. 1943; attached to Slovak Acad. of Sciences; astronomical and astrophysical research, incl. sun, interplanetary matter, star systems, exoplanets; library of 9,000 vols, 6,000 vols of periodicals; Dir Dr ALEŠ KUČERA; Deputy Dir Assoc. Prof. JÁN SVOREŇ; Scientific Sec. Dr DRAHOMÍR CHOCHOL; publ. *Contributions of the Skalnaté Pleso Observatory* (2 a year).

Institute of Chemistry: Dúbravská cesta 9, 845 38 Bratislava; tel. (2) 54-77-20-80; fax (2) 59-41-02-22; e-mail chemsekr@savba.sk; internet chem.sav.sk; f. 1953; attached to Slovak Acad. of Sciences; Dir Dr JÁN HIRSCH; publ. *Chemical Papers* (6 a year).

Institute of Experimental Physics: Watsonova 47, 040 41 Košice; tel. (55) 792-22-01; fax (55) 633-62-92; e-mail sekr@saske.sk; internet www.saske.sk/uef/index.php; f. 1969; attached to Slovak Acad. of Sciences; research into the fields of sub-nuclear physics, condensed-matter physics, space physics, theoretical physics and biophysics; Dir Doc. RNDr PETER KOPČANSKÝ.

Institute of Geology: Dúbravská cesta 9, 842 26 Bratislava; tel. (2) 54-77-39-41; fax (2) 54-77-70-97; e-mail geolinst@savba.savba.sk; internet nic.savba.sk/sav/inst/geol/index.html; f. 1952; attached to Slovak Acad. of Sciences; Dir Dr JOZEF MICHALÍK; publ. *Geologica Carpathica* (6 a year).

Institute of Geophysics: Dúbravská cesta 9, 845 28 Bratislava; tel. (2) 59-41-06-26; fax (2) 59-41-06-26; e-mail geofiabi@savba.sk; internet gpi.savba.sk; f. 1953; attached to Slovak Acad. of Sciences; Dir Dr IGOR TUNYI; publ. *Contributions to Geophysics and Geodesy* (4 a year).

Institute of Geotechnics: Watsonova 45, 043 53 Košice; tel. (55) 633-40-49; fax (55) 632-34-02; e-mail ugtsekr@saske.sk; f. 1957; attached to Slovak Acad. of Sciences; Dir Dr VITÁZOSLAV KRÚPA.

Institute of Hydrology: Račianská 75, 831 02 Bratislava 3; tel. and fax (2) 44-25-94-04; e-mail supervisor@uh.savba.sk; internet www.ih.savba.sk; f. 1955 as Water Management Laboratory; present name 1989; attached to Slovak Acad. of Sciences; Dir Dr V. STEKAUEROVA; publ. *Journal of Hydrology and Hydromechanics* (produced jtly with the Institute of Hydrodynamics of the Academy of Sciences of the Czech Republic, 6 a year).

Institute of Inorganic Chemistry: Dúbravská cesta 9, 845 36 Bratislava; tel. (2) 59-41-04-01; fax (2) 59-41-04-44; e-mail uachsekr@savba.sk; internet www.uach.sav.sk; f. 1953; attached to Slovak Acad. of Sciences; Dir Prof. PAVOL ŠAJGALÍK.

Institute of Materials Research: Watsonova 47, 040 01 Košice; tel. (55) 792-24-02; fax (55) 792-24-08; internet www.imr.saske.sk; f. 1955; attached to Slovak Acad. of Sciences; develops new materials and technologies; conducts research on the nature of transformations and transport processes that occur within the structures of materials of varying chemical character (metals, ceramics, plastics, etc.) and internal composition (crystalline, amorphous, composite, etc.); also conducts research on the mechanical and physical properties of materials; Dir Dr PETER ŠEVC; Scientific Sec. ĽUBOMÍR MEDVECKÝ; publs *Acta Metallurgica Slovaca* (4 a year), *Kovové materiály* (Metallic Materials, 6 a year), *Powder Metallurgy Progress* (4 a year).

Institute of Measurement Science: Dúbravská cesta 9, 841 04 Bratislava; tel. (2) 54-77-40-33; fax (2) 54-77-59-43; e-mail umersekr@savba.sk; internet www.um.savba.sk; f. 1953; attached to Slovak Acad. of Sciences; scientific departments: optoelectronic measuring methods, magnetometry, theoretical methods, imaging methods, biomeasurements; 76 mems; library of 8,000 vols; Dir Assoc. Prof. MILAN TYSLER; Scientific Board Chair. Assoc. Prof. VIKTOR WITKOVSKÝ; publ. *Measurement Science Review* (online, www.measurement.sk).

Institute of Physics: Dúbravská cesta 9, 845 11 Bratislava; tel. (2) 59-41-05-00; fax (2) 54-77-60-85; e-mail fyzihaso@nic.savba.sk; internet www.fu.sav.sk; f. 1955; attached to Slovak Acad. of Sciences; Dir Prof. Ing. IVAN STICH; publ. *Acta Physica Slovaca* (6 a year).

Institute of Polymer Research: Dúbravská cesta 9, 842 36 Bratislava; tel. (2) 54-77-34-48; fax (2) 54-77-59-23; e-mail upolsekr@savba.sk; internet www.savba.sk/polymer; f. 1963; attached to Slovak Acad. of Sciences; Dir RNDr PAVOL HRDLOVIČ.

PHILOSOPHY AND PSYCHOLOGY

Institute of Experimental Psychology: Dúbravska cesta 9, 813 64 Bratislava; tel. (2) 54-77-56-25; fax (2) 54-77-55-84; e-mail ida.prokopcakova@savba.sk; internet www.psychologia.sav.sk; f. 1955; attached to Slovak Acad. of Sciences; Dir Prof. Dr VIERA BAČOVÁ; publ. *Studia Psychologica* (4 a year).

Institute of Philosophy: Klemensova 19, 813 64 Bratislava; tel. (2) 52-96-15-27; fax (2) 52-92-12-15; e-mail filosekr@savba.sk; internet sav.sk; f. 1946; attached to Slovak Acad. of Sciences; Dir Prof. TIBOR PICHLER; publs *Filozofia* (10 a year), *Organon F* (4 a year).

RELIGION, SOCIOLOGY AND ANTHROPOLOGY

Department of Social and Biological Communication: Klemensova 19, 813 64 Bratislava; tel. (2) 54-77-56-83; fax (2) 54-77-34-42; e-mail kvsbk@savba.sk; internet kvsbk.sav.sk; f. 1990; attached to Slovak Acad. of Sciences; Dirs Assoc. Prof. PhDr GABRIEL BIANCHI, Assoc. Prof. PhDr OLGA ZAPOTOCNA; publs *Human Affairs* (2 a year), *Human Communication Studies* (1 a year).

Institute of Ethnology: Klemensova 19, 813 64 Bratislava; tel. (2) 52-96-47-07; fax (2) 52-96-47-07; e-mail gabriela.kilianova@savba.sk; internet www.uet.sav.sk/en/index.htm; f. 1946; attached to Slovak Acad. of Sciences; library of 10,000 vols, 63 periodicals; Dir Dr GABRIELA KILIÁNOVÁ; publs *Etnologické rozpravy* (2 a year), *Slovenský národopis* (5 a year).

Institute of Oriental Studies: Klemensova 19, 813 64 Bratislava; tel. (2) 52-92-63-26; fax (2) 52-92-63-26; e-mail kaoreast@savba.sk; internet www.orient.sav.sk; f. 1960; attached to Slovak Acad. of Sciences; history, linguistics, literature, religion, ethnography, philosophy; library of 13,500 vols; 18 mems; Dir Dr DUŠAN MAGDOLEN; publ. *Asian and African Studies* (2 a year).

Institute of Social Sciences: Karpatská 5, 040 00 Košice; tel. (55) 625-58-56; fax (55)

625-58-56; e-mail gajdosm@saske.sk; f. 1975; attached to Slovak Acad. of Sciences; library of 7,000 vols; Dir Dr MARIÁN GAJDOŠ; publ. *International Journal of Transdisciplinary Studies* (4 a year).

Institute of Sociology: Klemensova 19, 813 64 Bratislava; tel. (2) 52-96-43-55; fax (2) 52-96-23-15; e-mail sociolog@savba.sk; internet www.sociologia.sav.sk; f. 1990; attached to Slovak Acad. of Sciences; Dir Dr ĽUBOMIR FALŤAN; publ. *Sociológia* (6 a year).

TECHNOLOGY

Institute of Electrical Engineering: Dúbravská cesta 9, 842 39 Bratislava; tel. (2) 54-77-58-06; fax (2) 54-77-58-16; e-mail elusav@savba.sk; internet www.elu.sav.sk; f. 1963; attached to Slovak Acad. of Sciences; Dir Dr KAROL FROHLICH; publ. *Journal of Electrical Engineering* (12 a year).

Institute of Informatics: Dúbravská cesta 9, 845 07 Bratislava; tel. (2) 54-77-10-04; fax (2) 54-77-10-04; e-mail upsysekr@savba.sk; internet www.ui.sav.sk; f. 1991; attached to Slovak Acad. of Sciences; research and education in informatics, nano- and micro-technology, cybernetics; Dir Dr LADISLAV HLUCHÝ; publ. *Computing and Informatics* (6 a year).

Institute of Materials and Machine Mechanics: Račianska 75, 831 02 Bratislava 3; tel. (2) 44-25-47-51; fax (2) 44-25-33-01; e-mail ummjerz@savba.sk; internet www.immm.sav.sk; f. 1980; attached to Slovak Acad. of Sciences; library of 13,000 vols; Dir Dr FRANTIŠEK SIMANČÍK; publs *Kovové materiály* (Metallic Materials, 6 a year), *Strojnícky časopis* (Journal of Mechanical Engineering, 6 a year).

Transport Research Institute, Inc.: Veľký Diel 3323, 010 08 Žilina; tel. (41) 565-28-19; fax (41) 565-28-83; e-mail management@vud.sk; internet www.vud.sk; f. 1954; Man. Dir Ing. LUBOMIR PALČÁK; publ. *Horizonty dopravy* (4 a year).

Vúje Trnava Inc.: Okružná 5, 918 64 Trnava; tel. (33) 599-13-56; fax (33) 599-11-93; e-mail vuje@vuje.sk; internet www.vuje.sk; f. 1977; library: of 23,000 items; engineering design and research; Man. Dir Ing. MATEJ KOREC; publ. *Spravodajca VÚJE* (1 a year).

Libraries and Archives

Banská Bystrica

Štátna vedecká knižnica (State Scientific Library): Lazovná 9, POB 205, 975 58 Banská Bystrica; tel. (48) 415-51-11; fax (48) 412-40-96; e-mail svkbb@svkbb.sk; internet www.svkbb.sk; f. 1924; 2m. vols; Dir Mgr Dr OĽGA LAUKOVÁ.

Bratislava

Archív hlavného mesta SR Bratislavy (Archives of the Capital of the Slovak Republic, Bratislava): Markova 1, 850 05 Bratislava; POB 40, 850 05 Bratislava; tel. (2) 54-43-32-48; fax (2) 54-43-08-48; e-mail archiv@samb.vs.sk; f. 13th century (archives); 1923 (library); attached to Min. of Interior; 95,000 vols; Dir Dr ANNA BUZINKAYOVÁ.

Centrum vedecko-technických informácií Slovenskej republiky (Slovak Centre for Scientific and Technical Information): Nám. Slobody 19, 812 23 Bratislava; tel. (2) 36-24-19; fax (2) 32-35-27; e-mail cvti@cvtisr.sk; internet www.cvtisr.sk; f. 1938; 362,000 books, 144,000 vols of periodicals, 28,000 trade publs, 239,000 patents, 90,000 standards; Dir ULRICH KOLOMAN; publs *Bulletin Centra VTI SR* (4 a year), *Euro-Info* (10 a year), *Infotrend* (4 a year), *Signálne informácie* (12 a year).

Mestská knižnica Bratislava (Bratislava Municipal Library): Klariská 16, 814 79 Bratislava; tel. (2) 54-43-32-44; fax (2) 54-43-51-48; e-mail bratislava@mestskakniznica.sk; internet www.mestskakniznica.sk; f. 1900; 310,000 vols; Dir PhDr ELENA VEĽASOVÁ.

Slovenská ekonomická knižnica Ekonomickej univerzity v Bratislave (Slovak Economic Library): Dolnozemská cesta 1/a, 852 35 Bratislava; tel. (2) 67-29-14-14; fax (2) 67-29-11-61; e-mail sek@sekba.euba.sk; internet www.sek.euba.sk; f. 1948, present name 1993; specialized material in field of economic sciences and interdisciplinary sciences; 364,757 vols, 297 periodicals; Dir JITKA KMEŤOVÁ.

Slovenská pedagogická knižnica (Slovak Education Library): Hálova 16, 851 01 Bratislava 5; tel. (2) 62-41-09-92; fax (2) 62-41-09-92; e-mail postmast@spgk.sk; internet www.spgk.sk; f. 1956; 296,000 vols; Dir PhDr HELENA PANGRÁCOVÁ.

Univerzitná knižnica v Bratislave (University Library of Bratislava): Michalská 1, 814 17 Bratislava 1; tel. (2) 59-80-42-22; fax (2) 54-43-42-46; e-mail ukb@ulib.sk; internet www.ulib.sk; f. 1919; 2.4m. vols; Dir PhDr TIBOR TRGIŇA.

Ústredná knižnica Slovenskej akadémie vied (Central Library of the Slovak Academy of Sciences): Klemensova 19, 814 67 Bratislava; tel. (2) 52-92-17-33; fax (2) 52-92-17-33; e-mail andrea.doktorova@savba.sk; internet www.uk.sav.sk; f. 1953; 520,000 vols; Dir Mgr ANDREA DOKTOROVÁ.

Košice

Štátna vedecká knižnica (State Scientific Library): Hlavná 10, 042 30 Košice; tel. (55) 622-67-24; fax (55) 622-23-31; e-mail svkk@ke.sanet.sk; f. 1657; 3.4m. vols; Dir Mgr DANIELA DŽUGANOVÁ; publs *Zoznam zahraničných časopisov objednaných na východné Slovensko* (1 a year), *Súpis bibliografií a rešerší vypracovaných v ŠVK Košice* (1 a year).

Verejná knižnica Jána Bocatia (Ján Bocatius Public Library): Hlavná 48, 042 61 Košice; tel. (55) 622-32-91; fax (55) 622-32-92; f. 1924; 476,000 vols; Dir Dr KLÁRA KERNEROVÁ.

Martin

Matica slovenská (Slovak National Library): Nám. J. C. Hronskeho 1, 036 52 Martin; tel. (43) 430-18-03; fax (43) 430-18-02; e-mail snk@snk.sk; internet www.snk.sk; f. 1863; 4.5m. vols; literary archives and museum documents, and complete Slovak printed production; Dir Dr DUŠAN KATUŠČÁK; publs *Biografické štúdie* (1 a year), *Genealogicko-heraldický hlas* (2 a year), *Inventar rukopisov ALU MS* (1 a year), *Knižnica* (Library, 12 a year), *Slovenská národná bibliografia* (CD-ROM, 4 a year; print, 1 a year).

Nitra

Slovenská poľnohospodárska knižnica (Slovak Agricultural Library): Štúrova 51, POB 20B, 949 59 Nitra; tel. (37) 651-77-43; fax (37) 651-77-43; e-mail slpk@uniag.sk; internet www.slpk.sk; f. 1946; 530,000 vols; Dir BEÁTA BELLÉROVÁ.

Prešov

Štátna vedecká (State Scientific Library): Hlavná ul. 99, 081 89 Prešov; tel. (51) 772-49-60; fax (51) 772-49-60; e-mail kniznica@svkpo.sk; internet www.svkpo.sk; f. 1952; 450,000 vols; Dir PhDr ANNA HUDÁKOVÁ.

Zvolen

Slovenská lesnícka a drevárska knižnica (Slovak Library for Forestry and Wood Technology): Masarykova 20, 961 02 Zvolen; tel. (45) 520-66-41; fax (45) 547-99-42; e-mail sldk@sldk.tuzvo.sk; internet sldk.tuzvo.sk; f. 1952; attached to the Technical Univ. in Zvolen; 360,000 vols; Dir Ing. ALENA POLÁČIKOVÁ; publs *Bibliography of the Technical University in Zvolen* (1 a year), *Ecology Bulletin* (6 a year), *Forestry Bulletin* (12 a year), *Wood Sciences Bulletin* (12 a year).

Museums and Art Galleries

Banská Bystrica

Múzeum Slovenského národného povstania (Slovak National Uprising Museum): Kapitulská č. 23, 974 00 Banská Bystrica; tel. (48) 415-20-70; fax (48) 412-37-16; e-mail muzeumsnp@isternet.sk; internet www.muzeumsnp.sk; f. 1955; anti-fascist struggle of the Slovak people during the Second World War; library of 17,000 vols; Dir Dr JÁN STANISLAV.

Stredoslovenské múzeum (Central Slovakia Museum): Nám. Slovenského národného povstania 4, 974 00 Banská Bystrica; tel. (48) 412-58-97; fax (48) 415-50-77; e-mail smbb@stonline.sk; internet www.stredoslovenskemuzeum.sk; f. 1889; natural sciences, history, ethnography; library of 12,000 vols; Dir Dr ZUZANA DRUGOVÁ; publs *Katalog chladných zbraní*, *Katalog fajky a fajčiarske potreby*, *Stredné Slovensko* (1 a year).

Banská Štiavnica

Slovenské banské múzeum (Slovak Mining Museum): Kammerhofská 2, 969 01 Banská Štiavnica; tel. (45) 694-94-22; e-mail sbm@muzeumbs.sk; internet www.muzeumbs.sk; f. 1900; library of 21,000 vols; Dir Dr JOZEF LABUDA; publ. *Zborník SBM* (bulletin).

Bratislava

Galéria mesta Bratislavy (Municipal Gallery of Bratislava): Mirbachov palác, Františkánske nám. 11, 815 35 Bratislava; tel. (2) 54-43-51-02; fax (2) 54-43-26-11; e-mail gmb@gmb.sk; internet www.gmb.sk; f. 1961; Slovak and Central European art; library of 12,000 vols; Dir Dr IVAN JANČÁR.

Mestské muzeum v Bratislave (Bratislava City Museum): Primaciálne nám. 3, 815 18 Bratislava; tel. (2) 54-43-47-42; fax (2) 54-43-46-31; e-mail mmba@bratislava.sk; f. 1868; archaeology, history, art history, applied arts, numismatics, history of pharmacy, ethnography; library of 21,000 vols; Dir PhDr PETER HYROSS.

Slovenská národná galéria (Slovak National Gallery): Riečna 1, 815 13 Bratislava; tel. (2) 54-43-20-81; fax (2) 54-43-39-71; e-mail info@sng.sk; internet www.sng.sk; f. 1948; art, applied art; library of 100,710 vols, 80,000 documents; Dir-Gen. Dr ALEXANDRA KUSÁ; publ. *Yearbook*.

Slovenské národné múzeum (Slovak National Museum): Vajanského nábrežie č 2, POB 13, 810 06 Bratislava 16; tel. (2) 59-34-91-11; fax (2) 52-92-43-44; e-mail riaditel@snm.sk; internet www.snm.sk; f. 1893; history, natural history, art, archaeology; Dir PhDr PETER MARÁKY; publs *História* (1 a year), *Prírodné vedy* (1 a year), *Etnografia* (1 a year), *Archeológia* (1 a year), *Annotationes Zoologicae et Botanicae*, *Pamiatky a múzeá* (Cultural Heritage Review, 4 a year),

Múzeum (guidance for museum and art gallery workers, 4 a year).

Košice

Východoslovenské múzeum (Museum of Eastern Slovakiá): Hviezdoslavová 3, 041 36 Košice; tel. (55) 622-03-09; fax (55) 622-86-96; f. 1872; history, natural sciences, art, ethnography; library of 53,000 vols; Dir PhDr RÓBERT POLLÁK; publs *Historica Carpatica* (1 a year), *Natura Carpatica* (1 a year).

Kremnica

NBS—Múzeum mincí a medailí (National Bank of Slovakia—Museum of Coins and Medals): Štefánikovo nám. 11/21, 967 01 Kremnica; tel. (45) 678-03-01; fax (45) 674-21-21; e-mail muzeum@nbs.sk; internet www.nbs.sk/en/museum-of-coins-and-medals; f. 1890; Dir MARIANA NOVOTNÁ.

Piešťany

Balneologické múzeum (Museum of Balneology): Beethovenova 5, 921 01 Piešťany; tel. and fax (33) 772-28-75; e-mail krupa.vladimir@zupa-tt.sk; internet www.balneomuzeum.sk; f. 1928; history of Slovak spas, regional history; Dir PhDr VLADIMÍR KRUPA.

Svidník

Múzeum ukrajinsko-rusínskej kultúry (Museum of Ukrainian-Ruthenian Culture): Centrálna 258, 089 01 Svidník; tel. (54) 752-13-65; fax (54) 752-15-69; f. 1956; history and culture of the Ukrainians and Ruthenians in Slovakia; library of 44,354 vols; Dir PhDr MIRÓSLAV SOPÓLIGA.

Vojenské historické múzeum (Military Historical Museum): Bardejovská 14, 089 01 Svidník; tel. (54) 752-13-98; f. 1965; history of the military in eastern Slovakia 1914-1945; library of 3,225 vols; Dir Dr JOZEF RODÁK.

Tatranská Lomnica

Múzeum Tatranského národného parku (Tatras National Park Museum): 059 60 Tatranská Lomnica; tel. (52) 446-79-51; fax (52) 446-79-58; e-mail sl@tanap.sk; f. 1957; geology, botany, zoology, natural history; ethnography, history; library of 19,520 vols; Dir Ing. MIKULÁŠ MICHELČIK.

Universities

EKONOMICKÁ UNIVERZITA V BRATISLAVE
(University of Economics in Bratislava)

Dolnozemská cesta 1/B, 852 35 Bratislava 5

Telephone: (2) 62-41-14-78
Fax: (2) 62-24-73-48
E-mail: komunikacia@euba.sk
Internet: www.euba.sk

Founded 1940, became State School 1945
State control
Languages of instruction: Slovak, English, French, German
Academic year: September to June,

Rector: Prof. Dr Ing. RUDOLF SIVÁK
Vice-Rectors: Assoc. Prof. Ing. FERDINAND DAŇO, Assoc. Prof. Ing. JANA MIKOCZIOVÁ, Assoc. Prof. Ing. ĽUBOMÍR STRIEŠKA, Assoc. Prof. Ing. JANA LENGHARTOVÁ, Assoc. Prof. Ing. ANETTA ČAPLÁNOVÁ
Registrar: Dr MÁRIA DZIUROVÁ
Librarian: Dr JITKA KMEŤOVÁ

Number of teachers: 658
Number of students: 12,243

Publications: *Acta oeconomica Cassoviensia* (2 a year), *Almanac: current issues of World Economics and Politics* (2 a year), *Business review* (2 a year), *Economic Review* (4 a year), *Economics and Management* (3 a year), *Economics and Informatics* (2 a year), *Economics of Tourism and Business* (4 a year), *Ekonóm* (5 a year), *International relations*, *Nová ekonomika* (4 a year), *Studia commercialita Bratislavensia* (4 a year)

DEANS

Faculty of Applied Language: Prof. Ing. LÍVIA ADAMCOVÁ
Faculty of Business Economics (in Košice): Prof. Dr MICHAL TKÁČ
Faculty of Business Management: Prof. Ing. ĽUBOSLAV SZABO
Faculty of Commerce: Ing. ŠTEFAN ŽÁK
Faculty of Economic Informatics: Prof. Dr MICHAL FENDEK
Faculty of International Relations: Assoc. Prof. Dr Ing. ĽUDMILA LIPKOVÁ
Faculty of National Economy: Prof. Ing. JÁN LISÝ

KATOLÍCKA UNIVERZITA V RUŽOMBERKU
(Catholic University in Ružomberok)

Nám. Andreja Hlinku 60, 034 01 Ružomberok

Telephone: (44) 431-62-00
Fax: (44) 431-62-07
E-mail: rektorat@ku.sk
Internet: www.ku.sk

Founded 2000
Jt control of Slovak state and the Catholic Church
Language of instruction: Slovak

Rector: Prof. Dr BORIS BANÁRY
Vice-Rectors: Prof. Dr JÁN KURUCZ, Prof. Dr DALIBOR MIKULÁS, Prof. Dr ĽUBOMÍR STANČEK
Librarian: Mag. PETER DVORSKÝ

Library of 17,000 vols
Number of teachers: 300
Number of students: 3,000

Publication: *Disputationes Scientificae Universitatis Catholicae in Ružomberok*

DEANS

Faculty of Health Service: Dr ANTON LACKO
Faculty of Pedagogy: Prof. Dr AMANTIUS AKIMJAK
Faculty of Philosophy: Prof. Dr IMRICH VAŠKO
Faculty of Theology: ANTON KONEČNY

PREŠOVSKÁ UNIVERZITA
(University of Prešov)

Nám. Legionárov 3, 080 01 Prešov

Telephone: (51) 756-31-10
Fax: (51) 756-31-47
E-mail: erasmus@unipo.sk
Internet: www.unipo.sk

Founded 1997
State control
Academic year: September to June

Rector: Prof. RENÉ MATLOVIČ
Vice-Rector for Academic Affairs: Prof. Dr IVANA CIMERMANOVÁ
Vice-Rector for Devt: Doc. Ing. JANA BURGEROVÁ
Vice-Rector for Int. Relations: Doc. PhDr IVETA KOVALČÍKOVÁ
Vice-Rector for Science and Research: Prof. PhDr PETER KÓNYA

Library of 300,000 vols
Number of students: 12,000

DEANS

Faculty of Arts (ul. 17 novembra 1, 080 78 Prešov; tel. (51) 773-10-64):

Prof. PhDr RUDOLF DUPKALA

Faculty of Education (ul. 17 novembra 1, 081 16 Prešov; tel. (51) 747-05-50; fax (51) 747-05-51):

Doc. PhDr MILAN PORTIK

Faculty of Greek Catholic Theology (ul. bisbupa Gojdića 2, 080 01 Prešov; tel. (51) 772-51-66; fax (51) 773-38-40; e-mail gkbfpu@unipo.sk):

Prof. PETER ŠTURÁK

Faculty of Health (ul. Sládkovićova 36, 080 24 Prešov; tel. (51) 773-33-04; fax (51) 773-37-06; e-mail lackovak@unipo.sk):

Dr EVA KOVAĽOVÁ

Faculty of Humanities and Natural Sciences (ul. 17 novembra 1, 081 16 Prešov; tel. (51) 772-53-62; fax (51) 772-53-61):

Prof. RnDr IVAN BERNASOVSKÝ

Faculty of Orthodox Theology (Masarykova 15, POB 60 , 081 60 Prešov; tel. (51) 772-47-29; fax (51) 773-26-77):

Prof. ThDr JÁN ZOZUĽÁK

SLOVENSKÁ POL'NOHOSPODÁRSKA UNIVERZITA V NITRE
(Slovak University of Agriculture in Nitra)

Tr. A. Hlinku 2, 949 76 Nitra

Telephone: (37) 641-55-33
Fax: (37) 653-43-93
E-mail: verejnost@uniag.sk
Internet: www.uniag.sk

Founded 1946 as Vysoká Škola Pol'nohospodárska; new name c. 1996
Public control
Languages of instruction: Slovak, English
Academic year: September to June

Rector: Prof. Dr Ing. PETER BIELIK
Vice-Rectors: Prof. ZDENKA GÁLOVÁ, Prof. Ing. MARIÁN BRESTIČ, Prof. Dr Ing. ELENA HORSKÁ, Dr Ing. ZUZANA PALKOVÁ
Chancellor: Ing. ANNA BOŽIKOVÁ
Bursar: Dr Ing. OĽGA ROHÁČIKOVÁ

Library: see 'Slovenská pol'nohospodárská knižnica', under Libraries and Archives
Number of teachers: 474
Number of students: 10,300

Publications: *Acta fytotechnica et zootechnica* (4 a year), *Acta Horticulturae et regioecturae* (4 a year), *Acta regionalia et envirormentalica* (4 a year), *Acta oeconomica et informatica* (4 a year), *Acta Zootechnica* (1 a year)

DEANS

Faculty of Agricultural Engineering: Assoc. Prof. Dr Ing. ZDENKO TKÁČ
Faculty of Agrobiology and Food Resources: Prof. Dr Ing. DANIEL BÍRO
Faculty of Biotechnology and Food Sciences: Prof. Ing. JÁN TOMÁŠ
Faculty of Economics and Management: Prof. Dr Ing. IVETA ZENTKOVÁ
Faculty of European Studies and Regional Devt: Prof. Dr ANNA BANDLEROVÁ
Faculty of Horticulture and Landscape Engineering: Assoc. Prof. Ing. KAROL KALÚZ

PROFESSORS

Faculty of Agricultural Engineering (tel. (37) 651-32-44; fax (37) 741-70-03; e-mail dekmf@uniag.sk):

BALLA, J., Agricultural Engineering
JECH, J., Technology and Mechanization of Agriculture
LOBOTKA, J., Technology and Mechanization of Agriculture
PÁLTIK, J., Technology and Mechanization of Agriculture
PETRANSKÝ, I., Technology and Mechanization of Agriculture

SEMETKO, J., Technology and Mechanization
ŠESTÁK, J., Technology and Mechanization of Agriculture
ŢOLNAI, R., Agricultural Engineering
ŽIKLA, A., Technology and Mechanization

Faculty of Agronomy (tel. (37) 651-12-44; fax (37) 741-14-51; e-mail dekaf@uniag.sk):

BEŽO, M., Plant Genetics
BULLA, J., Fundamental Zootechnics
FECENKO, J., Special Plant Production
GÁLIK, R., Fundamental Zootechnics
HALAJ, M., Special Zootechnics
HANES, J., Pedology
HOLÚBEK, R., Special Plant Production
KOVÁČ, L., Fundamental Zootechnics
KOVÁČIK, J., General Zootechnics
KÚBEK, A., Fundamental Zootechnics
KULICH, J., Plant Production
LÍŠKA, E., General Plant Production
MICHALÍK, I., Plant Production
MICHALÍKOVÁ, A., Plant Protection
PAJTÁŠ, M., General Zootechnics
PAŠKA, I., Special Zootechnics
PIVKO, J., General Zootechnics
POLÁČEK, Š., Plant Production
PRASLIČKA, J., Plant Protection
ŠŤASTNÝ, P., Fundamental Zootechnics

Faculty of Economics and Management (tel. (37) 651-11-51; fax (37) 651-15-89; e-mail dekfem@uniag.sk):

BANDLEROVÁ, A., Economics and Management
BIELIK, P., Food Industry Management
GOZORA, V., Economics and Management
HRONEC, O., Management
HRUBÝ, J., Economics
HUDÁK, J., Sectorial Economics
KABÁT, L., Economics
KUZMA, F., Economics
OKENKA, I., Economics and Management
PODOLÁK, A., Economics
ŖEPKA, I., Economics
ŠIMO, D., Economics
VIŠŇOVSKÝ, J., Economics
ZOBORSKÝ, I. M., Economics

Faculty of Gardening and Landscape Engineering (Ul. Tulipanová 7, 949 76 Nitra; tel. (37) 652-27-41; fax (37) 652-27-41; e-mail dekfzki@uniag.sk):

ANTAL, J., Land Improvement
DEMO, M., Plant Production
HRICOVSKY, I., Plant Production
HRUBÍK, P., Horticulture
HUSKA, D., Land Improvement
MACHOVEC, J., Horticulture
ŠPÁNIK, F., Special Plant Production
STRED'ANSKY, J., Land Improvement
SUPUKA, J., Phytopathology
VREŠTIAK, P., Special Plant Production

SLOVENSKÁ TECHNICKÁ UNIVERZITA V BRATISLAVE (Slovak University of Technology in Bratislava)

Vazovova 5, 812 43 Bratislava
Telephone: (2) 52-49-71-96
Fax: (2) 57-29-43-33
E-mail: rector@stuba.sk
Internet: www.stuba.sk

Founded 1938
State control
Languages of instruction: Slovak, English
Academic year: September to September

Rector: Assoc. Prof. Dr ROBERT REDHAMMER
Vice-Rector for Economy and Devt: Prof. Dr MILAN SOKOL
Vice-Rector for Education: Prof. JÁN KALUŽNÝ
Vice-Rector for Int. Relations: Prof. Dr. MARIÁN PECIAR
Vice-Rector for Science and Research: Prof. Dr STANISLAV BISKUPIČ
Bursar: Ing. HELENA ZIDEKOVA
Librarian: VIERA POLČÍKOVÁ

Number of teachers: 1,170
Number of students: 18,900

Publications: *Almanach Znalca* (in Slovak, 4 a year), *ALFA—Architektonické listy FA STU* (in Slovak with summary in English, 4 a year), *Acta Chimica Slovaca* (in English, 4 a year), *AT & P Journal* (in Slovak with summary in English, 12 a year), *Computing and Informatics* (in English, 4 a year), *EE–Journal for Electrical and Power Engineering* (in Slovak with summary in English, 6 a year), *Formation Sciences and Technologies- Bulletin of the ACM Slovakia* (2–4 a year), *Journal of Electrical Engineering* (in English, 6 a year), *Journal of Cybernetics and Informatics* (e-journal for control community, in English), *Kovové materiály* (in Slovak, 12 a year), *Mathematical Publications* (in English, 2–3 a year), *Scientific Proceedings of FME STU in Bratislava* (in English), *Slovak Journal of Civil Engineering* (in English, 4 a year), *Spektrum-Informative Journal of STU* (in Slovak, 10 a year), *Tatra Mountains*

DEANS

Faculty of Architecture: Assoc. Prof. Ing. Dr LUBICA VITKOVA
Faculty of and Food Technology: Prof. Dr JAN SAJBIDOR
Faculty of Civil Engineering: Prof. Ing. ALOJZ KOPACIK
Faculty of Electrical Engineering and Information Technology: Assoc. Prof. Dr GABRIEL JUHAS
Faculty of Informatics and Information Technology: Prof. Dr LUDOVIT MOLNAR
Faculty of Materials Science and Technology: Prof. Dr Ing. OLIVER MORAVCIK
Faculty of Mechanical Engineering: Prof. Ing. LUBOMIR SOOS

PROFESSORS

Faculty of Architecture:

DULLA, M., Architecture
KEPPL, J., Architecture
KOVÁČ, B., Town Planning
PETELEN, I., Industrial Design
PETRÁNSKÝ, L'., Theory and History of Art Design
ŠPAČEK, R., Architecture
VODRÁŽKA, P., Architecture

Faculty of Chemical and Food Technology:

BAJUS, M., Fuel Technology
BAKOŠ, D., Macromolecular Chemistry and Engineering
BÁLEŠ, V., Chemical Engineering and Process Control
BOČA, R., Inorganic Chemistry
BOSKUPIČ, S., Physical Chemistry and Chemical Physics
BREZOVA, V., Chemical Physics
BUSTIN, D., Analytical Chemistry
CIK, G., Technology of Macromolecular Substances
FELLNER, P., Technology of Inorganic Chemistry
FIŠERA, L., Organic Chemistry
GRACZA, T., Organic Chemistry
HIVES, J., Technology of Inorganic Chemistry and Materials
HRONEC, M., Organic Technology
KOMAN, M., Inorganic Chemistry
KRUPČÍK, J., Analytical Chemistry
LABUDA, J., Analytical Chemistry
LEHOTAY, J., Analytical Chemistry
LOKAJ, J., Material Engineering
MALÍK, F., Biochemical Technology
MARCHALIN, S., Organic Chemistry
MARKOS, J., Chemical Engineering and Process Control
MESZAROS, A., Chemical Engineering and Process Control
MIKLEŠ, J., Technical Cybernetics
MOCÁK, J., Analytical Chemistry
MRAVEC, D., Organic Technology and Fuel Technology
ŠAJBIDOR, J., Biochemical Technology
SCHMIDT, S., Food Chemistry and Technology
ŞIMA, J., Inorganic Chemistry
ŠIMON, P., Physical Chemistry
STASKO, A., Physical Chemistry
VALACH, F., Physical Chemistry and Chemical Physics
VALKO, L., Physical Chemistry
VARECKA, L., Biochemistry

Faculty of Civil Engineering:

AGÓCS, Z., Steel and Timber Structures
BAJZA, A., Non-Metallic Materials and Construction Materials
BALÁŽ, I., Construction Engineering
BALIAK, F., Construction Engineering
BANÍK, I., Physics
BARTOŠ, P., Geodesy and Cartography
BEDNÁROVÁ, E., Hydraulic Engineering
BETKO, B., Engineering Theory and Construction Engineering
BEZÁK, B., Transport Engineering
BIELEK, M., Building Construction
BILČÍK, J., Construction Engineering
CHMÚRNY, I., Engineering Theory and Construction Engineering
DUŠIČKA, P., Hydraulic Engineering
FILLO, L., Construction Engineering
GAŠPARÍK, J., Construction Technology
GSCHWENDT, I., Transport Engineering
HEFTY, J., Geodesy and Cartography
HRAŠKA, J., Engineering Theory and Construction Engineering
HULLA, J., Geotechnology
KLEPSATEL, F., Building Construction
KOMORNÍKOVÁ, M., Applied Mathematics
KOPÁČIK, A., Geodesy and Cartography
KRIŠ, J., Construction in Health-care Sector
LAPOS, J., Construction Engineering
LOVIŠEK, J., Mechanics of Solid and Pliable Bodies
MACURA, V., Landscaping
MAJDÚCH, D., Concrete Structures and Bridges
MELICHER, J., Geodesy and Cartography
MESIAR, R., Applied Mathematics
MIKULA, K., Applied Mathematics
MUDRONČÍK, M., Bulding Structures and Architecture
OHRABLO, F., Building Construction
OLÁH, J., Building Construction
PETRÁŠ, D., Engineering Theory and Construction Engineering
PUŠKÁR, A., Engineering Theory and Construction Engineering
RAVINGER, J., Applied Mechanics
ROUSEKOVÁ, I., Non-Metallic Materials and Construction Materials
ŠIRÁŇ, J., Applied Mathematics
SOKOL, M., Applied Mechanics
ŞOKOL, Š., Geodesy and Cartography
ŠOLTÉSZ, A., Hydraulic Engineering
STANĚK, V., Geodesy and Cartography
ŞUMEC, J., Building Construction
ŠVEDA, M., Non-Metallic Materials and Construction Materials
SZOLGAY, J., Hydrology and Water Management
TOMAŠOVIČ, P., Engineering Theory and Construction Engineering
TURČEK, P., Building Construction
VALÁŠEK, J., Building Construction
ZAJAC, J., Building Construction
ZAPLETAL, I., Technology and Materials Engineering

Faculty of Electrical Engineering and Information Technology:

BALLO, I., Physical Engineering

BAROŇÁK, I., Telecommunication
BOCK, I., Applied Mathematics
BREZA, J., Electronics
CIRÁK, J., Physical Engineering
DONOVAL, D., Electronics
ĎURAČKOVÁ, D., Electronics
DURNÝ, R., Solid State Physics
FARKAŠ, P., Telecommunication
GROŠEK, O., Applied Informatics
HUBA, M., Automation
JANÍČEK, F., Electrical Energy
JASENEK, J., Theory of Electromagnetism
JURIŠICA, L., Technical Cybernetics
KOVÁČ, J., Electronics
KOZÁK, Š., Automation and Control
MIGLIERINI, M., Solid State Physics
MURGAŠ, J., Cybernetics
MURÍN, J., Applied Mechanics
NEČAS, V., Nuclear Energy
PODHRADSKÝ, P., Telecommunications
POLEC, J., Telecommunications
SITEK, J., Condensed Matter Physics and Acoustics
SLUGEŇ, V., Nuclear Energy
SMIEŠKO, V., Measurement Engineering
SMOLA, A., Electrical Energy
STOPJAKOVÁ, V., Electronics
TVAROŽEK, V., Electronics
UHEREK, F., Electronics
ŽALMAN, M., Automation and Control

Faculty of Informatics and Information Technology:
BIELIKOVA, M., Software Engineering
HORVATH, P., Applied Informatics
KOLESAR, M., Computer Engineering
KVASNICKA, V., Artificial Intelligence
MOLNAR, L., Informatics
NAVRAT, P., Information Systems
POSPICHAL, J., Applied Informatics
SAFARIK, J., Informatics

Faculty of Materials Science and Technology in Trnava:
BAČA, J., Mechanical Engineering Technology
BALOG, K., Occupational Health and Safety
BARÁNEK, I., Production Technologies, Machine Technologies and Materials
BLAŠKOVITŠ, P., Mechanical Engineering Technology
BLEHA, T., Materials
ČAMBÁL, M., Industrial Engineering
ČAUS, A., Production Technologies, Machine Technologies and Materials
CYRUS, P., Teacher Training of Vocational Subjects and Practical Training for Didactics
DRIENSKY, D., Engineering Education
DUSZA, J., Materials
GRGAČ, P., Materials Engineering
HRIVŇÁK, I., Physical Metallurgy and Materials Engineering
HRIVŇÁKOVÁ, D., Physical Metallurgy
HUSAR, P., Automation, Applied Informatics
JAHNÁTEK, L., Industrial Engineering
JANAČ, A., Machinery
JANOVEC, J., Materials
JOEHNK, P., Industrial Engineering
KALUŽNÝ, J., Materials Engineering
KIPS, M., Teacher Training of Vocational Subjects and Practical Training
KOLITSCH, A., Materials
KOŠTURIAK, J., Quality of Production
KOVÁČ, J., Physics
KOZÍK, T., Teacher Training of Vocational Subjects and Practical Training for Didactics
KUPČA, L., Materials
LINCZÉNYI, A., Quality of Production
LIPA, Z., Production Technologies
LOKAJ, J., Materials
MORAVČÍK, O., Applied Information Science and Automation in Industry
MUDRONČÍK, D., Automation and Applied Information Science
MURGAŠ, M., Industrial Engineering
OŽVOLD, M., Materials
PETERKA, J., Production Technologies, Machine Technologies and Materials
POKUSA, A., Production Technologies
RICHTER, V., Automation
SABLIIK, J., Quality of Production
SAKÁL, P., Industrial Engineering
SCHREIBER, P., Automation and Applied Informatics
ŠVRČEK, D., Production Technology
TURŇA, M., Welding and Welding Machines
ULRICH, K., Production Technologies, Machine Technologies and Materials
URBAN, M., Materials
VELÍŠEK, K., Production Technology
VRBAN, A., Applied Information Science and Automation

Faculty of Mechanical Engineering:
BENKO, B., Production Technology and Materials
BUKOVECZKY, J., Transportation Machines and Equipments
DEDIK, L., Instrumentation, Informatics and Automation Technology
ELESZTOS, P., Applied Mechanics
GODNAR, E., Production Technology and Materials
GULAN, L., Machines and Equipments for Building, Processing and Agriculture
HAVELSKY, V., Thermal Power Engineering and Environmental Technology
HEKELOVA, E., Production Quality and Technological Systems Safety
HULKO, G., Instrumentation, Informatics and Automation Technology
KRESEK, A., Manufacturing Systems with Industrial Robots and Manipulators
MOLNAR, V., Power Engineering
PALENCAR, R., Instrumentation, Informatics and Automation Technology
PECIAR, M., Machines and Equipment for Chemical and Food Industries
ROHLA-ILKIV, B., Instrumentation, Informatics, Mechatronic and Automation Technology
SKAKALA, J., Instrumentation, Informatics and Automation Technology
SLADEK, J., Applied Mechanics
SOOS, L., Production Machines
STAREL, L., Applied Mechanics
TICHY, J., Transport Technology
TOLNAY, M., Mechanical Engineering Technologies
URBAN, J., Transport Technology
VALCUHA, Š., Construction of Manufacturing Machines
VARCHOLA, M., Hydraulic and Pneumatic Machines and Equipment
VAVRO, K., Power Engineering
VERES, M., Machine Parts and Mechanisms
ZAHOREC, O., Applied Mechanics

Institute of Engineering Studies:
MESZAROS, A., Chemical Engineering and Process Control

Institute of Management:
FINKA, M., Spatial Planning
IVANICKA, K., Management
ROCH, I., Spatial Planning
SCHOLICH, D., Spatial Planning

SLOVENSKÁ ZDRAVOTNÍCKA UNIVERZITA
(Slovak Medical University)

Limbová 12, 883 03 Bratislava
Telephone: (2) 59-37-01-11
E-mail: info@szu.sk
Internet: www.szu.sk

Founded 2002
State control
Language of instruction: Slovak
Rector: Prof. JÁN ŠTENCL
First Pro-Rector and Pro-Rector for Educational Affairs: Prof. Dr DANA FARKAŠOVÁ
Pro-Rector for Int. Relations: Prof. Dr JURAJ ŠVEC
Vice-Rector for Pedagogical and Academic Affairs: Assoc. Prof. Dr JAROSLAV HINŠT
Pro-Rector for Curative and Preventive Activity: Prof. Dr JÁN BREZA
Pro-Rector for Public Relations: Prof. Dr VILIAM FISCHER
Pro-Rector for Research: Assoc. Prof. Dr KATARÍNA ŠEBEKOVÁ
Bursar: Ing. MILAN CAGÁŇ
Librarian: ZUZANA ONDEROVÁ

Library of 19,311 vols, 150 periodicals
Number of teachers: 397
Number of students: 16,535

DEANS

Faculty of Nursing and Health Professional Studies: Prof. Dr DANA FARKAŠOVÁ
Faculty of Public Health: Assoc. Prof. ROMAN KOVÁČ
Faculty of Health Care (Banskej Bystrici): Prof. Dr SVETOZÁR DLUHOLUCKÝ
Faculty of Medical Specialization Studies: Prof. TIBOR ŠAGÁT

PROFESSORS

Faculty of Health Care:
DLUHOLUCKÝ, S., Paediatrics
KRALINSKÝ, K., Urgent Medical Care

Faculty of Medical Specialization Studies:
BREZA, J., Urology
ČERNÁK, A., Ophthalmology
FISCHER, V., Cardiosurgery
GÚTH, A., Physiology, Balneology, and Medical Rehabilitation
HARUŠTIAK, S., Surgery and Thoracic Surgery
HATALA, R., Cardiology
HOLOMÁŇ, J., Clinical Pharmacology
KOTHAJ, P., Gastroenterological Surgery
KOVÁČ, G., Clinical Biochemistry and Laboratory Medicine
KOZA, I., Clinical Oncology
KRAJČÍK, S., Geriatrics
KRESÁNEK, J., Adolescent Medicine
KRISTÚFEK, P., Functional Diagnostics
KUKUMBERG, P., Neuropsychiatry
LECHTA, V., Logopaedia
LISÝ, L., Neurology
MASARIK, J., Biophysics
PECHAN, J., Surgery
RIEČANSKÝ, I., Cardiology and Angiology
ROVENSKÝ, J., Rheumatology
ŠABÓ, A., Biology
ŠAGÁT, T., Paediatric Anaesthiology and Intensive Medicine
ŠAKALOVÁ, A., Haematology
ŠEFRÁNEK, V., Vascular Surgery
ŠIMKO, P., Injury-related Surgery
ŠTENCL, J., Obstetrics and Gynaecology
ŠTEŇO, J., Neurosurgery
TÓTH, K., Medical Law
VAVREČKA, A., Gastroenterology
VOJTAŠŠÁK, J., Orthopaedics

Faculty of Nursing and Health Professional Studies:
FARKAŠOVÁ, D., Nursing
MALÝ, M., Physiotherapy
ŠVEC, J., Oncology

Faculty of Public Health:
HEGYI, L., Medical Teaching
ŠAJTER, V., Theoretical Science
ŠULCOVÁ, M., Health in the Workplace

TECHNICKÁ UNIVERZITA V KOŠICIACH
(Technical University of Košice)

Letná 9, 042 00 Košice
Telephone: (55) 602-11-11

Fax: (55) 633-27-48
E-mail: rektor@tuke.sk
Internet: www.tuke.sk

Founded 1952
State control
Languages of instruction: Slovak, English
Academic year: September to August

Rector: Prof. Dr JURAJ SINAY
Vice-Rector for Devt: Prof. Dr DUŠAN MALINDŽÁK
Vice-Rector for Education: Assoc. Prof. Dr VLADIMÍR PENJAK
Vice-Rector for Informatics: Prof. Dr ANTON ČIŽMÁR
Vice-Rector for Science, Research and Int. Relations: Prof. Dr KAROL FLÓRIÁN
Questor: Ing. GABRIEL FISCHER
Librarian: Dr VALÉRIA KROKAVCOVÁ

Number of teachers: 850 (820 full-time, 30 part-time)
Number of students: 13,351
Publications: *Acta Electrotechnica et Informatica* (4 a year), *Acta Mechanica Slovaca* (4 a year), *Acta Metallurgica Slovaca* (4 a year), *Acta Montanistica Slovaca* (4 a year), *Halo TU* (12 a year)

DEANS

Faculty of Arts: Assoc. Prof. Dr JAROSLAV JAREMA
Faculty of Civil Engineering: Prof. Dr STANISLAV KMEŤ
Faculty of Economics: Prof. Dr TOMÁŠ SABOL SOLTÉS
Faculty of Electrical Engineering and Informatics: Assoc. Prof. Dr DUŠAN KOCUR
Faculty of Mechanical Engineering: Prof. Dr MIROSLAV BADIDA
Faculty of Metallurgy: Prof. Dr KAREL TOMÁŠEK
Faculty of Mining, Ecology, Control and Geotechnology: Prof. Dr PAVOL RYBÁR
Faculty of Production Technology: Assoc. Prof. Dr SLAVKO PAVLENKO

PROFESSORS

Faculty of Arts (tel. and fax (55) 602-21-77; e-mail dekan.fuu@tuke.sk; internet www.fu.tuke.sk):

BARTUSZ, J., Fine Art

Faculty of Civil Engineering (Vysokoškolská 4, 042 00 Košice; tel. (55) 633-53-11; fax (55) 623-32-19; e-mail stanislav.kmet@tuke.sk; internet svfweb.tuke.sk):

HORNIAKOVÁ, L., Theory of Construction of Overground Buildings
HUDÁK, J., Theory of Construction of Engineering Structures
JUHÁS, P., Theory of Construction of Engineering Structures
KMEŤ, S., Theory of Construction of Engineering Structures
ŠTEVULOVÁ, N., Environmental Studies
TKÁČOVÁ, K., Mineralogy and Ecotechnology

Faculty of Economics (B. Němcovej 32, 040 01 Košice; tel. and fax (55) 633-09-83; e-mail ekfdec@tuke.sk; internet www.tuke.sk/ekf/ekf.html):

ŠAMSON, Š., Economic Theory
SOLTÉS, V., Mathematics

Faculty of Electrical Engineering and Informatics (tel. (55) 632-24-83; fax (55) 633-01-15; e-mail dusan.kocur@tuke.sk):

BANSKÝ, J., Radio Electronics, Electronic Technology
ČIŽMÁR, A., Electronics and Telecommunications Engineering
HUDÁK, Š., Computers and Informatics
JELŠINA, M., Electronic Computers
KOLCUM, M., Energetics, High Voltage Engineering
KOVÁČ, D., Energetics, High Voltage Engineering
KROKAVEC, D., Technology and Automation
KROKAVEC, M., Computers and Informatics
LEVICKÝ, D., Radio Electronics
MADARÁSZ, L., Technical Cybernetics
MARCHEVSKÝ, S., Electronics and Telecommunications Engineering
MARTON, K., Energetics, High Voltage Engineering
MICHAELI, L., Radio Electronics
MIHALÍK, J., Electronics and Telecommunications Engineering
SARNOVSKÝ, J., Technical Cybernetics
SINČÁK, P., Artificial Intelligence
ŠOMORA, M., Materials Engineering
ŠPÁNY, V., Radio Electronics
TIMKO, J., Electrical Engineering
TURÁN, J., Radio Electronics
ZBORAY, L., Electrical Engineering

Faculty of Mechanical Engineering (tel. (55) 625-78-25; fax (55) 633-47-38; e-mail miroslav.badida@tuke.sk; internet www.sjf.tuke.sk):

BADIDA, M., Environmental Protection
BIGOŠ, P., Construction of Transport Machinery
ČOP, V., Robots and Manipulators
HAJDUK, M., Manufacturing Systems with Robots and Manipulators
HRIVŇÁK, A., Technology of Mechanical Engineering
IMRIŠ, I., Non-Ferrous Metallurgy
KAŽIMÍR, I., Technology of Mechanical Engineering
KLIMO, V., Machine Parts
KNIEWALD, D., Technology of Mechanical Engineering
KOVÁČ, J., Automation and Management
KOVÁČ, M., Robots and Manipulation Devices
LACHVÁČ, J., Production Machines and Equipment
LIBERKO, I., Industrial Engineering and Management
MAJERNÍK, M., Environmental Studies
POLLÁK, L., Technology of Mechanical Engineering
RITÓK, Z., Machine Parts
SALOKY, T., Automation and Control in Mechanical Engineering
ŠIMSÍK, D., Automation and Management
SINAY, J., Transport and Manipulation
SMRČEK, J., Manufacturing Systems with Robots and Manipulators
SPIŠÁK, E., Engineering Technology and Materials
TAKÁČ, K., Technology of Mechanical Engineering
TREBUŇA, F., Mechanics

Faculty of Metallurgy (tel. (55) 633-18-14; fax (55) 633-70-48; e-mail dhf@hfnov.tuke.sk; internet www.tuke.sk/tu/hf):

BURŠÁK, M., Physical Metallurgy and Materials Science
FLÓRIÁN, K., General and Analytical Chemistry
HAVLIK, T., Non-Ferrous Metallurgy
HOLOUBEK, D., Thermal Power Engineering
KRAKOVSKÁ, E., Analytical Chemistry
KVAČKAJ, T., Ferrous Metallurgy
LUKÁČ, I., Physical Metallurgy and Materials Science
MICHEL', J., Materials Science
MIHOK, L., Ferrous Metallurgy
ŠTOFKO, M., Non-Ferrous Metallurgy
TOMÁŠEK, K., Non-Ferrous Metallurgy
VARGA, A., Thermal Power Engineering
VIRČÍKOVÁ, E., Non-Ferrous Metallurgy
ZRNÍK, J., Physical Metallurgy and Materials Science

Faculty of Mining, Ecology, Control and Geotechnology (tel. (55) 633-00-18; fax (55) 633-66-18; e-mail pavol.rybar@tuke.sk; internet www.tuke.sk/fberg):

BOROŠKA, J., Mining, Mechanization, Transport and Deep Well Drilling
DOJČÁR, O., Mining
FABIÁN, J., Mining
FARYAD, S. W., Mining Geology and Geological Prospecting
JACKO, S., Geological Prospecting, Geological Engineering
KOŠTIAL', I., Production Control
KOSTÚR, K., Control of the Acquiring and Processing of Raw Materials
KUNÁK, L., Mining Surveying and Geodesy
LEŠKO, M., Minerals Processing
MALINDŽÁK, D., Control of Acquiring and Processing of Raw Materials
PINKA, J., Mining, Mechanization, Transport and Deep Well Drilling
PODLUBNÝ, I., Control of Acquiring and Processing of Raw Materials
RYBÁR, P., Mining and Geotechnology
SASVÁRI, T., Mining Geology and Geological Prospecting
ŠEKULA, F., Mining
ŠTROFFEK, E., Mining, Mining Mechanization
ŠÜTTI, J., Three-Dimensional Geodesy
VODZINSKÝ, V., Economy and Management
WEISS, G., Mining Surveying and Geodesy
ZÁBRANSKÝ, F., Petrology

Faculty of Production Technology (Plzenská 10, 080 01 Prešov; tel. (51) 772-30-12; fax (51) 773-34-53; e-mail pavlenko.slavko@fvt.sk; internet www.tuke.sk/fvtpo):

NOVÁK-MARCINČIN, P., Production Engineering
RAGAN, E., Mechanical Technology
VASILKO, K., Mechanical Technology

TECHNICKÁ UNIVERZITA VO ZVOLENE
(Technical University in Zvolen)

T. G. Masaryka 24, 960 53 Zvolen
Telephone: (45) 520-61-03
Fax: (45) 533-00-27
E-mail: rektor@vsld.tuzvo.sk
Internet: www.tuzvo.sk

Founded 1807, reorganized 1952 as Univ. of Forestry and Wood Technology, renamed 1991
State control
Languages of instruction: Slovak, Czech; for graduate studies, also English, German and Russian
Academic year: September to June

Rector: Prof. Ing. JÁN TUČEK
Vice-Rectors: Assoc. Prof. JURAJ MAHÚT, Assoc. Prof. JÁN ŠIMKO, Prof. ŠTEFAN ŽÍHLAVNÍK
Questor: Dr MÁRIA BÍZIKOVÁ
Librarian: Dr ĽUBICA LUDVIGHOVÁ

Library of 359,000 vols
Number of teachers: 243
Number of students: 2,200
Publications: *Acta Facultatis Forestalis* (1 a year), *Acta Facultatis Xylologiae* (1 a year), *Proceedings of Research Works of the Faculty of Ecology and Environmental Sciences* (1 a year), *Scientific and Pedagogical News* (1 a year)

DEANS

Faculty of Ecology and Environmental Science: Assoc. Prof. Dr IMRICH BESEDA
Faculty of Environmental and Manufacturing Technology: Assoc. Prof. JÁN ZELENÝ
Faculty of Forestry: Assoc. Prof. MILAN HLADÍK

Faculty of Wood Sciences and Technology: Assoc. Prof. MIKULÁŠ ŠUPÍN

PROFESSORS

Faculty of Ecology and Environmental Science:

CHRAPAN, J., Radioecology
KOŠTÁLIK, J., Physical Geography
MIDRIAK, R., Landscape Ecology
MIKLOS, L., Landscape Ecology
SUPUKA, J., Landscape Ecology

Faculty of Environmental and Manufacturing Technology:

DANKO, M., Processes and Technology of Forest Production
MIKLEŠ, M., Processes and Technology of Forest Production

Faculty of Forestry:

BUBLINEC, E., Nature and Environment
GARAJ, P., Forest Protection and Game Management
HLADÍK, M., Forest Management
KODRÍK, J., Forest Protection and Game Management
KOLENKA, I., Forest Economics
PAGAN, J., Silviculture
PAULE, L., Forest Genetics
SANIGA, M., Silviculture
ŠMELKO, Š., Biometry and Forest Management
VALTÝNI, J., Forest Hydrology—Torrent Control
ŽIHLAVNÍK, S., Geodesy and Photogrammetry

Faculty of Wood Sciences and Technology:

BOROTA, J., Management of Tropical Forests
BUČKO, J., Chemistry and Chemical Technology
DEKRÉT, A., Mathematics
DUBOVSKÁ, R., Metal Processing Technology
HORSKÝ, D., Mechanical Technology of Wood
KURJATKO, S., Wood Science
LIPTÁKOVÁ, E., Wood Products Manufacturing
MARCOK, M., Physics and Applied Mechanics
OSVALD, A., Fire Protection
PETRANSKY, L., Design
RAJČAN, E., Physics and Applied Mechanics
REINPRECHT, L., Wood Technology Engineering
ŠUPÍN, M., Forestry Policy, Trade, Marketing
TREBULA, P., Technology of Wood
VINCÚR, P., Economics

TRENČIANSKA UNIVERZITA ALEXANDRA DUBČEKA (Alexander Dubček University in Trenčín)

Študentská 2, 911 50 Trenčín
Telephone: (32) 740-01-08
Fax: (32) 740-01-02
E-mail: slabeycius@tnuni.sk
Internet: www.tnuni.sk

Founded 1997
State control
Academic year: September to June

Rector: IVAN KNEPPO
Vice-Rector for Education: Dr ERNEST BROSKA
Vice-Rector for Investment and Devt: Assoc. Prof. IGNÁC PRNO
Vice-Rector for Science, Research and Int. Cooperation: Prof. JURAJ SLABEYCIUS
Vice-Rector for Social Care: Dr ERNEST BROSKA
Chief Librarian: Mgr MÁRIA REHUŠOVÁ

Library of 13,663 vols
Number of teachers: 245
Number of students: 5,393
Publications: *Socialno-ekonomicka Revue* (4 a year), *TnU Trendy* (4 a year)

DEANS

Faculty of Industrial Technology: Assoc. Prof. Dr ONDREJ NEMČOK
Faculty of Mechatronics: Prof. Dr DUŠAN MAGA
Faculty of Social and Economic Relations: Prof. Dr MIROSLAV MEČÁR
Faculty of Special Technologies: Prof. BOHUMIL BÁTORA

PROFESSORS

Faculty of Industrial Technology:

CAPEK, I.
JAMBRICKY, M.
KOPECKY, M.
KOSTIAL, P.
LETKO, I.
MACKO, V.
SLABEYCIUS, J.
STEFANIK, J.
YONA, E.

Faculty of Mechatronics:

BORSC, M.
KNEPPO, I.
KNEPPO, P.
PLANDER, I.
RACEK, V.
TKAC, M.
WAGNER, J.

Faculty of Social and Economic Relations:

ALEXY, J.
BARÁNIK, M.
BARTAK, P.
BENCO, J.
BLAZEJ, A.
CAMPAI, O.
LIPTAK, J.
STRAZOVSKA, H.
VOJTOVIC, S.

Faculty of Special Technologies:

BATORA, B.
DUBOVSKA, R.
VARKOLY, L.

TRNAVSKÁ UNIVERZITA (Trnava University)

Hornopotočná 23, 918 43 Trnava
Telephone: (33) 593-92-03
Fax: (33) 551-11-29
E-mail: rektor@truni.sk
Internet: www.truni.sk

Founded 1992
State control
Academic year: October to August

Rector: Prof. JUDr PETER BLAHO
Vice-Rector for Academic Affairs: Doc. ThDr ANDREJ FILIPEK
Vice-Rector for Devt and Foreign Relations: Prof. MVDr ALEXANDER SABÓ
Vice-Rector for External Relations and Continuing Education: Doc. PhDr Dr Prof. JANA BÉREŠOVÁ
Vice-Rector for Information Systems and Publishing: Doc. PhDr Dr MILAN KATUNINEC
Vice-Rector for Science and Research: Prof. JUDR. IVAN ŠIMOVČEK
Librarian: Ing. ZUZANA MARTINKOVIČOVÁ

Library of 68,073 books, 241 periodicals
Number of teachers: 350
Number of students: 7,677

DEANS

Faculty of Arts: Doc. PhDr MARTA DOBROTKOVÁ
Faculty of Education: Doc. RNDr PAVEL HÍC
Faculty of Health and Social Work: Prof. MUDr FRANTIŠEK MATEIČKA
Faculty of Law: Prof. JUDr HELENA BARANCOVÁ
Faculty of Theology: Doc. PhDr ThLic. JURAJ DOLINSKÝ

UNIVERZITA J. SELYEHO V KOMÁRNE/SELYE JÁNOS EGYETEM, KOMÁROM (University of J. Selyeho in Komárno)

Bratislavská cesta 3322, 945 01 Komárno
Telephone: (35) 773-30-73
Fax: (35) 773-30-72
E-mail: info@selyeuni.sk
Internet: www.selyeuni.sk

Founded 2004
State control
Language of instruction: Hungarian

Rector: Dr. JÁNOS TÓTH
Vice-Rector: Dr MELINDA NAGY
Vice-Rector: Dr PETER CSIBA
Vice-Rector: Prof. Ing. VERONIKA STOFFOVA

Library of 150,000 vols, 40 periodicals
Number of teachers: 86
Number of students: 3,000

DEANS

Faculty of Economy: Prof. Dr habil SIKOS T. TAMÁS
Faculty of Pedagogy: Dr MARGITY ERDÉLYI
Faculty of Reformed Theology: Dr JÁNOS MOLNÁR

UNIVERZITA KOMENSKÉHO V BRATISLAVE (Comenius University in Bratislava)

Šafárikovo nám. 6, 818 06 Bratislava 16
Telephone: (2) 52-92-15-94
Fax: (2) 52-96-38-36
E-mail: kr@rec.uniba.sk
Internet: www.uniba.sk

Founded 1465 as Academia Istropolitana; reopened with present name 1919
State control
Languages of instruction: Slovak, English
Academic year: October to June

Rector: Prof. PhDr FRANTIŠEK GAHÉR
Vice-Rector for Devt: Assoc. Prof. RNDr IVAN OSTROVSKÝ
Vice-Rector for Education: Prof. RNDr PAVEL SÚRA
Vice-Rector for Int. Relations: MUDr PETER OSUSKÝ
Vice-Rector for Legislation and Public Relations: JUDr MÁRIA DURAČINSKÁ
Vice-Rector for Science: Prof. RNDr DUŠAN MLYNARČÍK
Bursar: Ing. ZORA DOBRÍKOVÁ

Number of teachers: 2,092
Number of students: 27,000

Publication: numerous faculty publications

DEANS

Faculty of Education: Prof. RNDr OTO MAJZLAN
Faculty of Law: Assoc. Prof. JUDr MARIÁN VRABKO
Faculty of Management: Prof. RNDr JOZEF KOMORNIK
Faculty of Mathematics, Physics and Informatics: Assoc. Prof. RNDr JÁN BOĎA
Faculty of Medicine in Bratislava: Prof. MUDr PAVEL TRAUBNER
Jessenius Faculty of Medicine in Martin: Prof. MUDr JÁN DANKO
Faculty of Natural Sciences: Assoc. Prof. RNDr ANTON GÁPLOVSKÝ
Faculty of Pharmacy: Assoc. Prof. RNDr JOZEF SEGINKO
Faculty of Philosophy: Assoc. Prof. PhDr ANTON ELIÁŠ
Faculty of Physical Education and Sport: Assoc. Prof. PedDr DUŠAN KUTLÍK

Faculty of Protestant Theology: Prof. ThDr IGOR KIŠŠ
Faculty of Roman Catholic Theology: Prof. ThDr VILIAM JUDÁK
Faculty of Social and Economic Sciences: Prof. Ing. LADISLAV KABÁT

PROFESSORS

Faculty of Education (Račianska 59, 813 34 Bratislava; tel. (2) 44-25-49-60; fax (2) 44-25-49-56; e-mail sd@fedu.uniba.sk; internet www.fedu.uniba.sk):

BLANÁR, V., Slovak Language
CIŽMÁR, J., Teaching of Mathematics
CVRKAL, I., Modern Non-Slavonic Philology, German Literature
KAČALA, J., Slovak Language
KOVÁČ, D., Educational Psychology
KUSIN, V., Philosophy
LECHTA, V., Special Education
MAJZLAN, O., Ecology
MARČOK, V., Theory and History of Slovak Literature
MISTRÍK, E., Synthetic Philosophy
OBDRŽÁLEK, Z., Education
ONDREIČKA, K., Graphics
PAŽITKA, M., Modern Non-Slavonic Philology
PIKÁLEK, Š., Social Work
POVCHANIČ, Š., Modern Non-Slavonic Philology
POŽÁR, L., Psychology
RANINEC, J., Music Education
REPKA, R., Linguistics of Concrete Language Groups
ŠEDIVÝ, O., Descriptive Geometry
SLIACKY, O., Theory and History of Slovak Literature
ŠTRAUS, F., Theory and History of Slovak Literature
ŠULKA, R., Descriptive Geometry
ŠUPŠÁKOVÁ, B., Arts and Crafts
ŠVEC, M., Mathematics
TRUP, L., Modern Non-Slavonic Philology
VAŠEK, Š., Special Education
VIETOROVÁ, N., Modern Non-Slavonic Philology
ZELINA, M., Education

Faculty of Law (tel. (2) 59-24-41-03; fax (2) 59-24-42-16; e-mail sd@flaw.uniba.sk; internet www.flaw.uniba.sk):

CÚTH, J., International Law
HUSÁR, E., Penal Law
KLIMKO, J., History of State and Law
MAMOJKA, M., Commercial Law
MATHERN, V., Penal Law
OVEČKOVÁ, O., Economic and Financial Law
PLANKOVÁ, O., Civil Law
POSLUCH, M., State Law
ŠKULTÉTY, P., Administrative Law
STRAKA, J., Czechoslovak History

Faculty of Management (POB 95, Odbojárov 10, 820 05 Bratislava; tel. (2) 55-56-67-02; fax (2) 55-56-67-03; e-mail sd@fm.uniba.sk; internet www.fm.uniba.sk):

HLAVATÁ, I., Finance
KOMORNÍK, J., Probability and Mathematical Statistics
KORČEK, L'., Economics
PIŠKANIN, A., Economics and Industrial Management
RALBOVSKÝ, M., Finance
RUDY, J., Business Management
ZAPLETAL, V., Economics

Faculty of Mathematics, Physics and Informatics (Mlynská dolina, 842 48 Bratislava; tel. (2) 65-42-67-20; fax (2) 65-42-58-82; e-mail sd@fmph.uniba.sk; internet www.fmph.uniba.sk):

BEZÁK, V., Condensed Matter Physics
BRUNOVSKÝ, P., Mathematics
CHORVÁT, D., Biophysics
CIŽMÁR, J., Teaching Mathematics
DUBNIČKOVÁ, A., Physics
GRUSKA, J., Informatics
HIANÍK, T., Biophysics
HUBAČ, I., Biophysics
KABÁT, L., Economics
KAČUR, J., Mathematics
KATRIŇÁK, T., Mathematics
KODNÁR, R., Mathematics
KOSTYRKO, P., Mathematics
LUKÁČ, P., Plasma Physics
MASARIK, J., Physics
MEDVEĎ, M., Mathematics
MOCZO, P., Physics
NOGA, M., Theoretical Physics
PÁZMÁN, A., Mathematics
PIŠÚT, J., Theoretical Physics
PLESNÍK, J., Mathematics
POVINEC, P., Physics
PREŠNAJDER, P., Physics
ROVAN, B., Informatics
RUŽIČKA, J., Physics
ŠALÁT, T., Mathematics
ŠÁRO, S., Nuclear Physics
SITÁR, B., Physics
ŠKALNÝ, J., Physics
ŠTRBA, A., Experimental Physics
TOMLAIN, J., Meteorology and Climatology

Faculty of Medicine in Bratislava (Špitálska 24, 813 72 Bratislava; tel. (2) 52-96-17-36; fax (2) 59-35-72-70; e-mail sd@fmed.uniba.sk; internet ww.fmed.uniba.sk):

ÁGHOVÁ, L'., Public Health
BADA, V., Internal Medicine
BAKOSS, P., Epidemiology
BALAŽOVJECH, I., Internal Medicine
BÁLINT, O., Infectious Diseases
BENIAK, M., Social Medicine
BEŇUŠKA, J., Normal Anatomy, Histology and Embryology
BERGENDI, L'., Biochemistry
BILICKÝ, J., Radiology
BOROVSKÝ, M., Gynaecology and Obstetrics
BREZA, J., Urology
BUC, M., Immunology
BUCHVALD, J., Dermatovenereology
ČÁRSKY, J., Medicinal Chemistry and Biochemistry
DANIHEL, L'., Pathological Anatomy and Forensic Medicine
ĎURAČKOVÁ, Z., Biochemistry
ĎURIŠ, I., Internal Medicine
FERENČÍK, M., Immunology and Immunochemistry
GERINEC, A., Ophthalmology
HOLOMÁŇ, K., Gynaecology and Obstetrics
HORŇÁK, M., Urology
HULÍN, L., Normal and Pathological Anatomy
JAKUBOVSKÝ, J., Pathological Anatomy and Forensic Medicine
KAPELLEROVÁ, A., Paediatrics
KOTULOVÁ, D., Microbiology
KOVÁCS, L., Paediatrics
KRIŠKA, M., Pharmacology
MAKAI, F., Orthopaedics and Traumatology
MICHALKOVÁ, D., Paediatrics
MIKEŠ, Z., Internal Medicine, Cardiology
MRÁZ, P., Anatomy
OLÁH, Z., Ophthalmology
ONDRUŠ, D., Oncology
PONŤUCH, P., Internal Medicine
PROFANT, M., Otorhinolaryngology
REDHAMMER, R., Internal Medicine
REMKOVÁ, A., Internal Medicine
SATKO, I., Stomatology
ŠIMAN, J., Surgery
ŠIMKO, F., Normal and Pathological Physiology
ŠTRMEŇ, P., Ophthalmology
ŠTVRTINOVÁ, V., Internal Medicine
ŠUŠKA, P., Gynaecology and Obstetrics
ŠVEC, J., Oncology
TRAUBNER, P., Neurology
TURČÁNI, M., Normal and Pathological Physiology
TURČÁNI, P., Neurology
VARSÍK, P., Neurology
VAŠKO, J., Stomatology
VOJTASSAK, J., Surgery
ZAVIAČIČ, M., Pathological Anatomy and Forensic Medicine
ZLATOŠ, J., Normal Anatomy, Histology and Embryology
ZLATOŠ, L., Normal and Pathological Physiology
ŽUCHA, L., Psychiatry

Jessenius Faculty of Medicine in Martin (POB 34, Záborského 2, 036 45 Martin; tel. (43) 413-33-05; fax (43) 413-63-32; e-mail sd@jfmed.uniba.sk; internet www.jfmed.uniba.sk):

BÁNOVČIN, P., Paediatrics
BUCHANCOVÁ, J., Internal Medicine
BUCHANEC, J., Paediatrics
DANKO, J., Gynaecology and Obstetrics
DROBNÝ, M., Neurology
HAJTMAN, A., Otorhinolaryngology
HANÁČEK, J., Physiology and Pathophysiology
JAKUŠ, J., Pathophysiology
JAVORKA, K., Physiology and Pathophysiology
JURKO, A., Paediatrics
KLIMENT, J., Urology
KORPÁŠ, J., Pathological Physiology
KUBISZ, P., Internal Medicine
LEHOTSKÝ, J., Biochemistry
MAZÚCH, J., Surgery
MEŠKO, D., Internal Medicine
MÉZEŠ, V., Medicinal Biochemistry
MOKÁŇ, D. M., Internal Medicine
NOSÁĽOVÁ, G., Pharmacology
NOVOMESKÝ, F., Forensic Medicine
PÉČ, J., Dermatovenereology
PLANK, L., Pathological Anatomy
SÁMEL, M., Epidemiology
STRAKA, S., Epidemiology
STRÁNSKY, A., Physiology and Pathophysiology
TATÁR, M., Normal and Pathological Physiology
ZIBOLEN, M., Paediatrics

Faculty of Natural Sciences (Mlynská dolina, 842 15 Bratislava; tel. (2) 60-29-66-71; fax (2) 65-42-90-64; e-mail sd@fns.uniba.sk; internet www.fns.uniba.sk):

ADAMČÍKOVÁ, L'., Physical Chemistry and Chemical Physics
EBRINGER, L., Microbiology
GROLMUS, J., Genetics
HENSEL, K., Zoology
HOLBA, V., Physical Chemistry
HOVORKA, D., Petrology
HUDÁK, J., Plant Physiology
JEDLIČKA, L., Zoology
JURÁNI, B., Pedology
KELLÖ, V., Physical Chemistry and Chemical Physics
KETTNER, M., Microbiology
KMINIAK, M., Ecology
KOLAROV, J., Biochemistry
KOLLÁROVÁ, M., Biochemistry and Molecular Biology
KOVÁČ, L., Biochemistry
KOVÁČ, M., Stratum Geology, Geology and Palaeontology, Applied Geophysics
KRAUS, I., Applied Geophysics
KRCHO, J., Cartography
MACÁŠEK, F., Nuclear Chemistry
MASAROVIČOVÁ, E., Plant Physiology
MATYS, M., Engineering Geology
MIADOKOVÁ, E., Genetics
MLÁDEK, J., Human and Regional Geography
ONDRÁŠIK, R., Hydrology and Engineering Geology
ORSZÁGH, L., Zoology
PAULOV, J., Human and Regional Geography

ROJKOVIČ, I., Stratum Geology, Geology and Palaeontology, Applied Geophysics
SCHWENDT, P., Inorganic Chemistry
ŠEFARA, J., Stratum Geology, Geology and Palaeontology, Applied Geophysics
ŠEVČÍK, P., Physical Chemistry
SILNÝ, P., Theory of Teaching Chemistry
SOJÁK, L., Analytical Chemistry
SOMŠÁK, L., Botany
ŠUBÍK, J., Biochemistry
SUCHA, V., Stratum Geology
TOMA, Š., Organic Chemistry
URBAN, M., Chemical Physics
VLČEK, D., Genetics
VOZÁROVÁ, A., Mineralogy, Petrology and Geochemistry
ZAŤKO, M., Geography
ŽÚRKOVÁ, L., Inorganic Chemistry

Faculty of Pharmacy (Odbojárov 10, 832 32 Bratislava; tel. (2) 55-57-20-22; fax (2) 55-57-20-65; e-mail sd@fpharm.uniba.sk; internet www.fpharm.uniba.sk):

BALGAVÝ, P., Physics
ČIŽMÁRIK, J., Pharmaceutical Chemistry
DEVÍNSKY, F., Pharmaceutical Chemistry
FOLTÁN, V., Public Health
GRANČAI, D., Pharmacognosis
HAVRÁNEK, E., Pharmaceutical Chemistry
KOVÁCS, P., Biochemistry
MLYNARČÍK, D., Galenic Pharmacy
PŠENÁK, M., Biochemistry
RAK, J., Galenic Pharmacy
REMKO, M., Physical Chemistry and Chemical Physics
SARKA, K., Physical Chemistry and Chemical Physics
ŠPRINGER, V., Social Pharmacy
ŠVEC, P., Pharmacology

Faculty of Philosophy (Gondova 2, 818 01 Bratislava; tel. (2) 52-92-10-78; fax (2) 52-96-60-16; e-mail sd@fphil.uniba.sk; internet www.fphil.uniba.sk):

BAĎURÍK, J., History
BAJZÍKOVÁ, E., Slovak Language
BAKOŠ, J., Fine Art
CHALUPKA, L., Music
DOLNÍK, J., General Linguistics
DUDOK, M., Slavonic Philology
HERETÍK, A., Psychology
HOLEC, R., History
HRČKOVÁ, N., Music
HVIŠČ, J., Slavonic Philology
KIMLIČKA, Š., Librarianship and Information Science
KOLLÁRIK, T., Psychology
KREKOVIČ, E., Archaeology
KUKLICA, P., Classical Philology
KUSÝ, M., Philosophy
MARCELLI, M., Philosophy
MÉSZÁROS, O., Modern Non-Slavonic Philology
MICHÁLEK, J., Ethnography
MIKULA, V., Slovak Literature
MLACEK, J., Slovak Language
PAULÍNY, J., Modern Non-Slavonic Philology
PERHÁCS, J., Pedagogy
POTZLOVÁ-MALIKOVÁ, M., Fine Art
POVCHANIČ, Š., Modern Non-Slavonic Philology
PŠENÁK, J., Pedagogy
SCHENK, J., Sociology
SOKOLOVSKÝ, L., History
ŠVEC, Š., Pedagogy
SZOMOLÁNYIOVÁ, S., Political Science
TANDLICHOVÁ, E., Theory of English Language Teaching
TUŠER, A., Journalism
VOJTEK, J., General History
ZAMBOR, M., Philosophy
ŽIGO, M., Philosophy
ŽIGO, P., Slovak Language
ŽILINEK, M., Pedagogy

Faculty of Physical Education and Sport (Nábrežie arm. generála L. Sobodu, 814 69 Bratislava; tel. (2) 54-41-19-09; fax (2) 54-41-33-27; e-mail sd@fsport.uniba.sk; internet www.fsport.uniba.sk):

GREXA, J., History
HAMAR, D., Sport Kinanthropology
HELLEBRANDT, V., Sport Kinanthropology
KAMPMILLER, T., Sport Kinanthropology
KASA, J., Sport Kinanthropology
LABUDOVÁ, J.
MORAVEC, R., Sport Kinanthropology
ŠTULRAJTER, V., Physiology

Faculty of Protestant Theology (Bartókova 8, 811 02 Bratislava; tel. (2) 67-28-82-50; fax (2) 62-80-39-51; e-mail sd@fevth.uniba.sk; internet www.fevth.uniba.sk):

BÁNDY, J., Protestant Theology
KIŠŠ, L., Protestant Theology

Faculty of Roman Catholic Theology (Kapitulska 26, 814 58 Bratislava; tel. (2) 54-43-51-09; fax (2) 54-43-51-09; e-mail sd@frcth.uniba.sk; internet www.frcth.uniba.sk):

BOŠMÁNSKY, K., Catholic Theology
ĎURICA, M., Catholic Theology
JUDÁK, V., Catholic Theology
KUTARŇA, J., Theology
VRAGAŠ, Š., Catholic Theology

Faculty of Social and Economic Sciences (Odbojárov 10A, 820 05 Bratislava; tel. (2) 55-56-67 18; fax (2) 55-42-36-02; e-mail sd@fses.uniba.sk; internet www.fses.uniba.sk):

KABÁT, L., Economics
KLEIN, F., Therapeutics and Special Education
KOLLÁRIK, T., Psychology
KUSÝ, M., Philosophy
KVASNIČKA, V., Informatics

UNIVERZITA KONŠTANTÍNA FILOZOFA V NITRE
(Constantine the Philosopher University in Nitra)

Trieda A. Hlinku 1, 949 74 Nitra
Telephone: (37) 640-80-01
Fax: (37) 640-80-20
E-mail: ukf@ukf.sk
Internet: www.ukf.sk

Founded 1959 as Pedagogical Institute, Univ. status 1992, present name 1996
State control
Languages of instruction: Slovak, English, German, Russian, French, Italian, Spanish, Hungarian
Academic year: September to August

Rector: Prof. RNDr LIBOR VOZÁR
Vice-Rector for Academic Affairs: Doc. Dr RUŽENA ŽILOVÁ
Vice-Rector for Implementation of Information Technology: Mgr JÁN SKALKA
Vice-Rector for Int. Relations: Prof. Dr EVA MALÁ
Vice-Rector for Public Relations and Social Affairs: Doc. Dr MIROSLAV TVRDOŇ
Vice-Rector for Science and Research: Prof. Dr MÁRIA BAUEROVÁ
Bursar: Ing. ĽUBICA EHRENHOLDOVÁ

Library of 231,469 vols, 429 periodical titles
Number of teachers: 584
Number of students: 12,428

DEANS

Faculty of Arts: Prof. Dr ZDENKA GADUŠOVÁ
Faculty of Central European Studies: Dr ATTILA KOMZSÍK
Faculty of Education: Prof. Dr EVA SZÓRÁDOVÁ
Faculty of Natural Sciences: Prof. Dr ĽUBOMÍR ZELENICKÝ
Faculty of Social Sciences and Health Care: Prof. Dr EVA SOLLÁROVÁ

PROFESSORS

Faculty of Arts (Štefánikova 67, 949 74 Nitra; tel. (37) 640-84-44; fax (37) 640-85-00; e-mail dekanatff@ukf.sk; internet www.ff.ukf.sk):

BOTÍK, J.
BUJNA, J.
ČAHOJOVÁ, B.
ČUKAN, J.
DIATKA, C.
FARKAŠ, P.
FEGLOVÁ, V.
GADUŠOVÁ, Z.
GARAJ, B.
GERO, Š.
GROMOVÁ, E.
HAJKO, D.
HEČKOVÁ, J.
INŠTITORISOVÁ, D.
KAPSOVÁ, E.
KERUĽOVÁ, M.
KOLI, F.
KOPRDA, P.
LEIKERT, J.
LIBA, P.
MEŠŤAN, P.
MIŠŠÍKOVÁ, G.
ONDREJKOVIČ, P.
PAVELKA, J.
PLESNÍK, Ľ.
RADIČOVÁ, I.
ROMSAUER, P.
RUTTKAY, A.
SOKOLOVÁ, J.
SWIATKIEWICZ, W.
TUČNÁ, E.
VAŇKO, J.
WIEDERMANN, E.
ŽBIRKOVÁ, V.
ZELENICKÁ, E.
ŽILKOVÁ, M.

Faculty of Central European Studies (Dražovská 2, 949 74 Nitra; tel. and fax (37) 640-88-53; e-mail dkss@ukf.sk; internet www.fss.ukf.sk):

KÁRPÁTI, A.
LÁSZLÓ, B.
MÉSZÁROS, O.
NAGY, G.
PUSZTAY, J.
ZELENKA, M.
ŽILKA, T.

Faculty of Education (Dražovská 2, 949 74 Nitra; tel. (37) 640-82-18; fax (37) 640-82-61; e-mail dpf@ukf.sk; internet www.pf.ukf.sk):

BOHONY, P.
FELIX, K.
HAŠKOVÁ, A.
KOMLÓSI, L.
KOZÍK, T.
KURINCOVÁ, V.
LONGAUER, Ľ.
MALÁ, E.
OBDRŽÁLEK, Z.
PERHÁCS, J.
PETLÁK, E.
PLAVČAN, P.
PORUBSKÁ, G.
SEIDLER, P.
ŠIMONEK, J.
SZÓRÁDOVÁ, E.

Faculty of Natural Sciences (Tr. A. Hlinku 1, 949 74 Nitra; tel. (37) 640-85-55; fax (37) 640-85-56; e-mail dfpv@ukf.sk; internet www.fpv.ukf.sk):

BAUEROVÁ, M.
BÍLEK, M.
CHALUPA, P.
FULIER, J.
HETÉNYI, L.
HOVORKA, D.
HRAŠKA, Š.
HREŠKO, J.
KECSKÉS, A.
KLUVANEC, D.

KMEŤ, T.
KOREC, P.
KRAUS, I.
KYSEĽ, O.
LAUKO, V.
LAURINČÍK, J.
MAZÚREK, J.
PRASLIČKA, J.
RÓZOVÁ, Z.
RUŽIČKA, M.
ŠEDIVÝ, O.
STEHLÍKOVÁ, B.
TIRPÁKOVÁ, A.
TURČÁNI, M.
VOZÁR, L.
ZELENICKÝ, L.

Faculty of Social Sciences and Health Care (Kraskova 1, 949 74 Nitra; tel. (37) 640-87-51; fax (37) 640-87-63; e-mail dekanatfsv@ukf.sk; internet www.fsv.ukf.sk):

LIŠKOVÁ, A.
LOHNERT, J.
MAZUR, S.
MILOVSKÝ, V.
MLYNČEK, M.
RUISEL, I.
SOLLÁROVÁ, E.
SVAČINA, S.
TKÁČ, V.

UNIVERZITA MATEJA BEL
(Matej Bel University)

Národná 12, 974 01 Banská Bystrica
Telephone: (48) 446-11-52
Fax: (48) 415-31-80
Internet: www.umb.sk
Founded 1992 following merger of Pedagogic Faculty and School of Economics
Academic year: September to June
Rector: Doc. Ing. MILAN MURGAŠ
Vice-Rector for Education and Devt: Prof. Ing. JOZEF BENČO
Vice-Rector for Research and Int. Relations: Doc. PaedDr PAVOL ODALOŠ
Number of students: 7,500

DEANS

Faculty of Economics: Prof. Ing. MILOTA VETRÁKOVÁ
Faculty of Finance: Prof. Ing. JURAJ NEMEC
Faculty of Humanities: Doc. PhDr VLADIMÍR VARINSKÝ
Faculty of Law: Prof. JuDR MOJMÍR MAMOJKA
Faculty of Natural Sciences: Doc. RnDR STANISLAV HOLEC
Faculty of Pedagogy: Prof. PhDr BEATA KOSOVÁ
Faculty of Philology: Doc. PhDr FRANTIŠEK ALABÁN
Faculty of Political Sciences and International Relations: Doc. PhDr PETER KULAŠIK

UNIVERZITA PAVLA JOZEFA ŠAFÁRIKA V KOŠICIACH
(Šafárik University of Košice)

Šrobárova 2, 041 80 Košice
Telephone: (55) 622-26-08
Fax: (55) 622-81-09
E-mail: zahrodd@kosice.upjs.sk
Internet: www.upjs.sk
Founded 1657 as Academia Cassoviensis by Benedikt Kishdy, bishop of Eger, present name and status 1959
State control
Languages of instruction: Slovak, English
Academic year: September to July
Rector: Prof. Dr DUŠAN PODHRADSKÝ
Pro-Rectors: Prof. Dr IGOR PALÚŠ, Doc. Dr PAVOL PETROVIČ, Doc. Dr LEONARD SIEGFRIED, Prof. Dr JÚLIUS VAJÓ
Registrar: Dr Ing. JOZEF LOKŠA
Librarian: Dr DARINA KOŽUCHOVÁ
Number of teachers: 400
Number of students: 4,100
Publications: *Acta iuridica Cassoviensia*, *Folia Facultatis Medicae Universitatis Šafarikianae Cassoviensia*, *Thaiszia*

DEANS

Faculty of Law: Doc. Dr PETER VOJČÍK
Faculty of Medicine: Doc. Dr LADISLAV MIROSSAY
Faculty of Natural Sciences: Prof. Dr ALEXANDER FEHER
Faculty of Public Administration: Doc. Dr LADISLAV LOVAŠ

PROFESSORS

Faculty of Law:

GAŠPAR, M., Administrative Law
PALÚŠ, I., Administrative Law

Faculty of Medicine:

JURKOVIČ, I., Pathology
KAFKA, J., Psychiatry
KALINA, I., General Biology
KOHÚT, A., Pharmacology
MYDLÍK, M., Internal Medicine
PAČIN, J., Gynaecology and Obstetrics
ŠAŠINKA, A., Paediatrics
SULLA, I., Neurosurgery
TOMORI, Z., Physiology
VAJÓ, J., Surgery

Faculty of Natural Sciences:

AHLERS, I., General Biology
AHLERSOVÁ, E., Animal Physiology
BUKOVSKÝ, L., Mathematics
CHALUPKA, S., Theoretical Physics
FEHER, A., Physics
GÁLOVÁ, M., Analytical Chemistry
GYÖRYOVÁ, K., Inorganic Chemistry
HONČARIV, R., Genetics
JENDROĽ, S., Mathematics
KRISTIÁN, F., Organic Chemistry
MIŠUROVÁ, E., General Biology
PODHRADSKÝ, D., Biochemistry
SÍLEŠ, E., Physics

Department of Languages:

RYBÁK, J., Slavonic Languages

UNIVERZITA SV. CYRILA A METODA V TRNAVA
(University of Saints Cyril and Methodius in Trnava)

Námestie Jozefa Herdu 2, 917 01 Trnava
Telephone: (33) 556-51-11
Fax: (33) 556-51-20
E-mail: info@ucm.sk
Internet: www.ucm.sk
Founded 1997
State control
Academic year: October to June
Rector: Assoc. Prof. Dr EDUARD KOSTOLANSKÝ
Vice-Rector for Education: Dr DAGMAR VALENTOVIČOVÁ
Vice-Rector for Int. Relations: Assoc. Prof. Dr JÁN DANEK
Vice-Rector for Investment and Devt: Assoc. Prof. Ing. ERNEST ŠTURDÍK
Vice-Rector for Research: Prof. Dr RASTISLAV TOTH
Number of teachers: 221
Number of students: 3,130

DEANS

Faculty of Mass Media and Communications: Doc. Dr VIERA GAŽOVÁ
Faculty of Natural Sciences: Prof. Dr Ing. JOZEF OBOŇA
Faculty of Philosophy: Assoc. Prof. Dr RUŽENA KOZMOVÁ

UNIVERZITA VETERINÁRSKEHO LEKÁRSTVA A FARMÁCIE V KOŠICIACH
(University of Veterinary Medicine and Pharmacy in Košice)

Komenského 73, 041 81 Košice
Telephone and fax (55) 632-52-93
E-mail: rektor@uvlf.sk
Internet: www.uvlf.sk
Founded 1949
State control
Languages of instruction: Slovak, English
Academic year: September to June
Chancellor: Mgr ĽUDMILA KUNDRÍKOVÁ
Rector: Prof. Dr EMIL PILIPČINEC
Vice-Rector: Prof. Dr JANA MOJŽIŠOVÁ
Vice-Rector: Prof. Dr Ing. OĽGA ONDRAŠOVIČOVÁ
Vice-Rector: Prof. Dr JAROSLAV
Vice-Rector: Assoc. Prof. Dr PETER KORIM
Chief Admin. Officer: SILVIA ROLFOVÁ
Librarian: Assoc. Prof. Dr LIBUŠA BODNÁROVÁ
Library of 91,133 vols, 114 periodicals
Number of teachers: 201
Number of students: 1,800
Publications: *Folia Veterinaria* (4 a year), *Slovenský veterinársky časopis* (6 a year)

PROFESSORS

BAJOVÁ, V., Infectious Diseases
BÍREŠ, J., Internal Diseases of Ruminants and Swine
BLAHOVEC, J., Biochemistry
CABADAJ, R., Food Hygiene and Food Technology
DANKO, J., Anatomy and Histology
KAČMÁRIK, J., Obstetrics and Gynaecology
KOVÁČ, G., Internal Diseases of Ruminants and Swine
LEGÁTH, J., Toxicology
LENARTOVÁ, V., Chemistry and Biophysics
LEŠNÍK, F., Biology
LEVKUT, M., Pathological Anatomy
MARÁČEK, I., Physiology
MARETTA, M., Anatomy and Histology
MESÁROŠ, P., Andrology
MIKULA, I., Microbiology and Immunology
PAULÍK, Š., Infectious Diseases
VAJDA, V., Nutrition and Veterinary Dietetics
VÁRADY, J., Comparative Physiology
ZIBRÍN, M., Anatomy and Histology

ŽILINSKÁ UNIVERZITA
(University of Žilina)

Univerzitná 1, 010 26 Žilina
Telephone: (41) 513-51-30
Fax: (41) 513-50-56
E-mail: peter.fabian@rekt.utc.sk
Internet: www.utc.sk
Founded 1953 as Vysoká Škola Dopravy a Spojov; present title 1996
Public control
Languages of instruction: Slovak, English
Academic year: September to June
Rector: Prof. Ing. Dr TATIANA ČOREJOVÁ
Vice-Rector for Devt: Prof. Ing. Dr MILAN MALCHO
Vice-Rector for Education: Assoc. Prof. Ing. Dr MILAN TRUNKVALTER
Vice-Rector for Foreign and Public Relations: Assoc. Prof. Ing. Dr PETER FABIÁN
Vice-Rector for Science and Research: Prof. Ing. Dr JÁN ČELKO
Registrar: MSc. LADISLAV CIMERÁK
Dir of Univ. Library: PhDr MARTA SAKALOVÁ
Library of 216,025 vols
Number of teachers: 696
Number of students: 10,154
Publications: *Komunikácie – vedecké listy ŽU* (Communications – Scientific Letters, 4 a year), *Krizový Manažment* (Crisis Management), *Materiálové inžinierstvo* (Materials

Engineering, 1 a year), *Pokrok v Elektrikom a Elektromikrom Inžinigrstve* (Advances in Electrical and Electronic Engineering), *Práce a štúdie ŽU* (Works and Studies, 1 a year), *Zborník z konferencie TRANSCOM* (Proceedings of the TRANSCOM Conference, every 2 years), *Zborník z vedeckých konferencií ŽU* (Proceedings of the Scientific Conferences, every 5 years), *Znalectvo-Cestná doprava, elektrotechnika, strojarstvo* (Expertise in Road Traffic, Electrotechnology and Mechanical Engineering, 4 a year), *Znalectvo-Stavebnictvo a Podnikové Hospodárstvo* (Expertise in Civil Engineering and Economics of Enterprise, 4 a year)

DEANS

Faculty of Civil Engineering: Prof. Ing. Dr JÁN VIČAN
Faculty of Electrical Engineering: Prof. Ing. Dr MILAN DADO
Faculty of Management Science and Informatics: Prof. Ing. Dr KAROL MATIAŠKO
Faculty of Mechanical Engineering: Prof. Ing. Dr ŠTEFAN MEDVECKÝ
Faculty of Operation and Economics of Transport and Communications: Assoc. Prof. Dr ANNA KRIŽANOVÁ
Faculty of Human Sciences: Assoc. Prof. Dr ZDENA KRALOVA
Faculty of Special Engineering: Prof. Ing. Dr LADISLAV SIMÁK

PROFESSORS

Faculty of Civil Engineering (Komenského 52, 010 26 Žilina; tel. (41) 513-55-01; fax (41) 723-35-02; e-mail education@fstav.utc.sk; internet svf.utc.sk):

BENČAT, J., Structural Mechanics
BUJŇÁK, J., Theory and Construction of Engineering Structures
ČELKO, J., Theory and Construction of Engineering Structures
ČOREJ, J., Theory and Construction of Engineering Structures
KOVAŘÍK, K., Theory and Construction of Engineering Structures
MELCER, J., Structural Mechanics
MIKOLAJ, J., Theory and Construction of Engineering Structures
MORAVČÍK, M., Applied Mechanics
SCHLOSSER, F., Theory and Construction of Engineering Structures
VIČAN, J., Theory and Construction of Engineering Structures

Faculty of Electrical Engineering (Univerzitná 1, 010 26 Žilina; tel. (41) 513-20-51; fax (41) 513-15-15; e-mail education@fel.utc.sk; internet fel.utc.sk):

BLUNÁR, K., Communications Engineering
BURY, P., Physics of Condensed Matter and Acoustics
ČÁPOVÁ, K., Theoretical Electrotechnology
DADO, M., Telecommunications
DOBRUCKÝ, B., Electric Traction and Electric Drives
HRABOVCOVÁ, V., Electric Traction and Electric Drives
NEVESELÝ, M., Theoretical Electrotechnology
TRSTENSKÝ, D., Communications Engineering
VITTEK, J., Electric Traction and Electric Drives

Faculty of Management Science and Informatics (Univerzitná 1, 010 26 Žilina; tel. (41) 513-40-51; fax (41) 565-20-44; e-mail education@fri.utc.sk; internet www.fri.utc.sk):

ALEXÍK, M., Information and Control Systems
CENEK, P., Transport and Communications Technology
HITTMÁR, Š., Management in Transport
JANÁČEK, J., Transport and Communications Technology
MANULIAK, I., Information and Control Systems
MARČEK, D., Management
SKÝVA, L., Technical Cybernetics

Faculty of Mechanical Engineering (Univerzitná 1, 010 26 Žilina; tel. (41) 513-25-00; fax (41) 565-29-40; e-mail education@dsjf.utc.sk; internet fstroj.utc.sk):

BOKUVKA, O., Materials Engineering
DZIMKO, M., Machine Elements and Mechanisms
GREGOR, M., Industrial Engineering and Management
HLAVŇA, V., Transportation and Handling Technologies
HONNER, K., Workplace Arrangement
KONEČNÁ, R., Material Engineering
KOŠTURIAK, J., Industrial Engineering and Management
KUKUČA, P., Transportation and Handling Technologies
KURIC, I., Mechanical Engineering
MÁLIK, L., Machine Elements and Mechanisms
MEDVECKÝ, Š., Machine Elements and Mechanisms
MEŠKO, J., Mechanical Engineering
MIČIETA, B., Industrial Management
OBMAŠČÍK, M., Mechanical Engineering
PALČEK, P., Materials Engineering
SKOČOVSKÝ, P., Materials Engineering
SLÁDEK, G., Mechanical Engineering
ZVOLENSKÝ, P., Transport and Handling Technologies

Faculty of Operation and Economics of Transport and Communications (Univerzitná 1, 010 26 Žilina; tel. (41) 513-30-50; fax (41) 565-14-99; e-mail education@fpedas.utc.sk; internet fpedas.utc.sk):

ČISKO, Š., Economics
ČOREJOVÁ, T., Transport and Communications Technology
GNAP, J., Economics
HAVEL, K., Transport and Communications Technology
HOLLAREK, T., Transport Engineering
KAZDA, A., Transport and Communications Technology
KEVICKÝ, D., Transport and Communications Technology
KRÁLOVENSKÝ, J., Economics
KŘÍŽ, J., Transport and Communications Technology
LIŠČÁK, Š., Transport and Communications Technology
NEDELKA, M., Transport and Communications Technology
ŠEDLÁČEK, B., Economics
ŠTOFKOVÁ, J., Economics
SUROVEC, P., Transport and Communications Technology
VOLESKÝ, K., Transport and Communications Technology

Faculty of Science (Hurbanova 15, 010 26 Žilina; tel. (41) 513-61-01; fax (41) 564-30-85; e-mail education@fpv.utc.sk; internet www.fpv.utc.sk):

BAJÁK, I., Physics
BOICHUK, O., Mathematics
ČÁP, I., Physics
DIBLÍK, J., Applied Mathematics
KONVIT, M., Transport and Communications Technology
KURCZ, J., Musicology
OBERUČ, J., Education and Psychology
POLONSKÝ, D., Education and Psychology
VOLF, I., Teaching of Physics

Faculty of Special Engineering (Ul. 1. mája 32, 011 17 Žilina; tel. (41) 513-66-01; fax (41) 513-66-20; e-mail education@fsi.utc.sk; internet www.utc.sk/fsi):

MACA, J., Operational Research, Stochastic Dynamics of Systems
MIKOLAJ, J., Transport Economics
POLEDŇÁK, P., Fire Protection
ŠEIDL, M., Logistics, Transport Technology
ŠIMÁK, L., Crisis Management

Schools of Art and Music

VYSOKÁ ŠKOLA MÚZICKÝCH UMENÍ (Academy of Music and Dramatic Arts)

Ventúrska 3, 813 01 Bratislava
Telephone: (2) 54-43-21-72
Fax: (2) 54-43-01-25
E-mail: rektorat@vsmu.sk
Internet: www.vsmu.sk
Founded 1949
Academic year: September to June
Rector: Prof. ONDREJ ŠULAJ
Library of 65,000 vols
Number of teachers: 220
Number of students: 880

DEANS

Faculty of Drama and Puppetry: Assoc. Prof. JURAJ LETENAY
Faculty of Film and Television: Prof. STANISLAV PÁRNICKÝ
Faculty of Music and Dance: Prof. JÁN VLADIMÍR MICHALKO

VYSOKÁ ŠKOLA VÝTVARNÝCH UMENÍ V BRATISLAVE (Academy of Fine Arts and Design Bratislava)

Hviezdoslavovo nám. 18, 814 37 Bratislava
Telephone: (2) 59-42-85-02
Fax: (2) 59-42-85-03
E-mail: rektor@vsvu.sk
Internet: www.afad.sk
Founded 1949
Public control
Language of instruction: Slovak
Academic year: October to July
Rector: Prof. STANISLAV STANKOCI
Vice-Chancellor for Academic Affairs: Asst Prof. JOZEF KOVALČÍK
Vice-Chancellor for Foreign Relations: Asst Prof. SILVIA SENEŠI LUTHEROVÁ
Vice-Chancellor for Devt, Science and Research: Prof. IVAN CSUDAI
Registrar: Ing. LÝDIA MACUROVÁ
Library of 37,300 vols
Number of teachers: 108
Number of students: 667

Konzervatórium: Timonova 2, 042 03 Košice; tel. (55) 622-19-67; fax (55) 622-20-92; e-mail kon-ke@stonline.sk; internet www.cassovia.sk/konzervatorium; f. 1951; library: 20,185 vols, 3,079 records; 103 teachers; 262 students; Dir Mag. BARTOLOMEJ BURÁŠ.

SLOVENIA

The Higher Education System

Slovenia's higher education institutions predate the foundation of the former Yugoslavia in 1918, with the oldest being Univerza v Ljubljani (University of Ljubljana), which was founded in 1595. In 1991 Slovenia declared independence from the Socialist Federal Republic of Yugoslavia. There are four universities and in 2006/07 91,229 undergraduates were enrolled in tertiary education.

Higher education is organized according to the terms of the Higher Education Act (1994, amended 2004 and 2006) and in addition to the universities, other institutions of higher education include university faculties (fakultet), art academies (urnetniske akademije), high schools (visoke skole) and professional institutes. The Council for Higher Education was founded in 1993 as the main accreditation body and since 2006 has been responsible for quality assurance. In 1998 a 'credit' system for awarding postgraduate degrees was introduced and extended to undergraduate degrees in 2002. Following amendments to the Higher Education Act in 2004, Slovenia now participates in the Bologna Process to establish a European Higher Education Area, the first phase of which is to adopt a credit-based system of comparable degrees with two main cycles (undergraduate and graduate). The Professional and Scientific Titles Act (2006) laid out the new system of degrees and titles to be awarded in accordance with the principles of the Bologna Process. However from 2009/10, all offerings will be Bologna-style programmes

The secondary school leavers' diploma (Matura) is the main requirement for admission to higher education. University places are offered on a quota basis (numerus clausus). Higher education degrees are now divided into three cycles. The first cycle consists of either academic or professional undergraduate degrees, equivalent to Bachelors, requiring 180–240 credits during two to four years of study. The second cycle degree is the Masters (Magister), lasting up to two years and requiring 60–120 credits. Doctoral studies (Doctorat) constitute the third cycle of university degrees and usually last three years.

Post-secondary technical and vocational education is provided by vocational colleges (visje strokovne sole). The primary qualification is the Post-Secondary Diploma. Quality standards are set by the national accreditation bodies, but higher vocational education is administered by the Ministry of Education and Sport and regulated by the Higher Vocational Education Act (2004).

Regulatory and Representative Bodies

GOVERNMENT

Ministry of Culture: Maistrova ul. 10, 1000 Ljubljana; tel. (1) 369-59-00; fax (1) 369-59-01; e-mail gp.mk@gov.si; internet www.mk.gov.si; Minister MAJDA ŠIRCA; State Sec. Dr STOJAN PELKO.

Ministry of Education and Sport: Masarykova 16, 1000 Ljubljana; tel. (1) 400-54-00; fax (1) 400-53-29; e-mail gp.mss@gov.si; internet www.mss.gov.si; Minister Dr IGOR LUKŠIČ; State Sec. ALENKA KOVŠCA.

Ministry of Higher Education, Science and Technology: Kotnikova 38, 1000 Ljubljana; tel. (1) 478-46-00; fax (1) 478-47-19; e-mail gp.mvzt@gov.si; internet www.mvzt.gov.si; Minister GREGOR GOLOBIČ; State Sec. Dr JÓZSEF GYÖRKÖS.

ACCREDITATION

Council for Higher Education: trg OF 13, 1000 Ljubljana; tel. (1) 400-57-71; fax (1) 400-57-79; e-mail gp.svs@gov.si; internet www.svs.gov.si; f. 1993; approves higher education study programmes and assesses teaching and research quality; Min. GREGOR GOLOBIČ.

ENIC/NARIC Slovenia: Min. of Higher Education, Science and Technology, Education Recognition Office, ENIC-NARIC, Kotnikova 38, 1000 Ljubljana; tel. (1) 478-46-00; fax (1) 478-47-19; e-mail naric.mvzt@gov.si; internet www.mvzt.gov.si/si/delovna_podrocja/priznavanje_izobrazevanja_enicnaric; Head Mag. ALENKA LISEC.

NATIONAL BODY

Association of Rectors of Slovenia: University of Nova Gorica, 5000 Nova Gorica; tel. (5) 331-52-61; fax (5) 331-52-24; internet www.ung.si; Pres. Prof. Dr DANILO ZAVRTANIK.

Learned Societies

GENERAL

Slavistično društvo Slovenije (The Society for Slavic Studies of Slovenia): Aškerčeva 2/II, 1000 Ljubljana; internet www.ff.uni-lj.si/slovjez/sds/sds.html; f. 1935; a forum for professional Slavists, to provide a link between research and professional practice, to nurture cultural values regarding Slovene language and literature and awareness of Slovene history; to organize support for and publish Slavic research in academic and popular books and periodicals; 900 mems; Chair. IRENA NOVAK POPOV; Sec. MATJAŽ ZAPLOTNIK; publs *Jezik in slovstvo* (Language and Literature, 6 a year), *Kronike Slavističnega Društva* (12 a year, online), *Slavistična revija* (Slavonic Review, 4 a year).

Slovenska Akademija Znanosti in Umetnosti (Slovenian Academy of Sciences and Arts): Novi trg 3, 1000 Ljubljana; tel. (1) 470-61-00; fax (1) 425-34-23; e-mail sazu@sazu.si; internet www.sazu.si; f. 1938; promotes and contributes to the devt of scientific thought and artistic creativity; 70 full mems, 30 assoc. mems; library: see Libraries and Archives; Pres. Prof. Dr JOŽE TRONTELJ; Vice-Pres. TADEJ BAJD; Vice-Pres. MARKO MARIJAN MUŠIČ; Sec.-Gen. Prof. Dr ANDREJ KRANJC; publs *Acta Archaeologica*, *Acta Carsologica*, *Acta Geographica*, *Opera*, *Traditiones*.

BIBLIOGRAPHY, LIBRARY SCIENCE AND MUSEOLOGY

Zveza bibliotekarskih društev Slovenije (Union of Associations of Slovene Librarians): Turjaška 1, 1000 Ljubljana; tel. (1) 200-11-93; fax (1) 251-30-52; e-mail zveza-biblio.ds-nuk@guest.arnes.si; internet www.zbds-zveza.si; f. 1947; 1,000 mems, coordinates activities with 8 regional library assocs; Pres. MELITA AMBROŽIČ; Vice-Pres. MARTINA KEREC; Sec. LILI HUBEJ; Treas. ZDENKA RUDOLF; publ. *Knjižnica* (Library, 4 a year).

ECONOMICS, LAW AND POLITICS

Society of Jurists of Slovenia: Dalmatinova 4, Ljubljana; f. 1947; 1,073 mems; Pres. JOŽE PAVLIČIČ; publ. *Jurist*.

FINE AND PERFORMING ARTS

Društvo slovenskih skladateljev (Society of Slovene Composers): trg francoske revolucije 6, 1000 Ljubljana; tel. (1) 241-56-60; fax (1) 241-56-66; e-mail info@dss.si; internet www.dss.si; f. 1945; represents and promotes Slovene composers; promotes the creation of new Slovene music; organizes concerts of contemporary Slovene music; 114 mems; Pres. NENAD FIRST; publ. *Edicije DSS* (printed scores, etc., of its mems).

Slovensko umetnostnozgodovinsko društvo (Slovenian Art History Society): Aškerčeva cesta 2, 1000 Ljubljana; tel. (1) 241-12-10; fax (1) 241-12-11; e-mail suzd@suzd.si; internet www.suzd.si; f. 1921; excursions, symposia, congresses; 300 mems; library of 22,000 vols; Chair. Assoc. Prof MATEJ KLEMENCIC; Vice-Pres. Dr MATEJA KOS; Sec. METKA DOLENEC ŠOBA; publs *Bilten SUZD* (5 a year, online), *Zbornik za umetnostno zgodovino* (Art History Journal, 1 a year, print and online).

HISTORY, GEOGRAPHY AND ARCHAEOLOGY

Zveza geografov Slovenije (Association of Slovenian Geographers): Filozofska fakulteta, Aškerčeva 2, 1000 Ljubljana; tel. (1) 241-12-1248; fax (1) 425-77-93; e-mail matej@zrc-sazu.si; internet zgs.zrc-sazu.si; f. 1922; supports professional research, stimulates and directs modernization of teaching; organizes professional confs, lectures, publs and field works;; 700 mems; Pres. MATEJ GABROVEC; Vice-Pres. STANKO PELC; Sec. LUCIJA MIKLIČ CVEK; publs *Geografski obzornik* (4 a year), *Geografski vestnik* (2 a year).

Zveza zgodovinskih društev Slovenije (Slovenian Historical Association): Aškerčeva 2, 1000 Ljubljana; tel. (1) 241-12-01;

fax (1) 241-11-97; e-mail zzds@ff.uni-lj.si; internet www.ff.uni-lj.si/drustva/zzds; f. 1839; 1,649 mems; library of 5,215 vols; Pres. Dr EGON PELIKAN; Vice-Pres. Dr NEVENKA TROHA; Vice-Pres. BORUT BATAGELJ; publs *Časopis za zgodovino in narodopisje* (2 a year), *Kronika* (3 a year), *Prispevki za novejšo zgodovino* (Contributions to Contemporary History, 1 a year), *Zgodovinski časopis* (Historical Review, 4 a year).

LANGUAGE AND LITERATURE

Goethe-Institut: Tivolska 30, 1000 Ljubljana; tel. (1) 300-00-11; fax (1) 300-03-19; e-mail info@ljubljana.goethe.org; internet www.goethe.de/ins/si/lju/deindex.htm; offers courses and exams in German language and culture; promotes cultural exchange with Germany; Dir HENDRIK KLONINGER.

Slovenska Matica (Slovenian Society): Kongresni trg 8, 1000 Ljubljana; tel. (1) 422-43-40; fax (1) 422-43-44; e-mail drago.jancar@siol.net; internet www.slovenska-matica.si; f. 1864; literary and publishing soc.; 2,800 mems; library of 10,000 vols; Pres. Prof. Dr MILČEK KOMELJ; Sec. DRAGO JANČAR.

NATURAL SCIENCES

General

Društvo matematikov, fizikov in astronomov Slovenije (Society of Mathematicians, Physicists and Astronomers of Slovenia): Jadranska ul. 19, 1000 Ljubljana; tel. (1) 476-65-59; fax (1) 251-72-81; e-mail tajnik@dmfa.si; internet www.dmfa.si; f. 1949; 1,130 mems; Chair. Prof. Dr SANDI KLAVŽAR; Vice-Pres. NADA RAZPET; publs *Obzornik mat. fiz.* (6 a year), *Presek* (6 a year).

Prirodoslovno Društvo Slovenije (Natural History Society of Slovenia): Salendrova ul. 4, 1573, 1001 Ljubljana; tel. (1) 252-19-14; fax (1) 421-21-21; e-mail prirodoslovno.drustvo@guest.arnes.si; internet www.proteus.si; f. 1934; 2,500 mems; Pres. RADOVAN KOMEL; Sec.-Gen. JANJA BENEDIK; publ. *Proteus* (10 a year).

Physical Sciences

Jamarska zveza Slovenije (Speleological Association of Slovenia): Lepi pot 6, POB 2544, 1109 Ljubljana; tel. and fax (1) 428 34 44; e-mail predsedstvo@jamarska-zveza.si; internet www.jamarska-zveza.si; f. 1889; 43 caving socs and research groups with a total of 1,000 mems; Pres. VIDKO KREGAR; Sec IRENA STRAŽAR; publs *Jamar* (1 a year), *Naše jame* (2 a year).

Research Institutes

GENERAL

Inštitut za Antropološke in Prostorske Študije ZRC SAZU (Institute of Anthropological and Spatial Studies ZRC SAZU): Novi trg 2, 1000 Ljubljana; tel. (1) 470-64-95; fax (1) 425-77-95; e-mail iaps@zrc-sazu.si; internet iaps.zrc-sazu.si; f. 1994; attached to Scientific Research Centre of SASA (ZRC SAZU); Dir Dr IVAN ŠPRAJC.

Kmetijski inštitut Slovenije (Agricultural Institute of Slovenia): Hacquetova ul. 17, 1000 Ljubljana; tel. (1) 280-52-62; fax (1) 280-52-55; e-mail info@kis.si; internet www.kis.si; f. 1898; library of 32,000 vols; Dir Dr ANDREJ SIMONČIČ; publ. *Raziskave in Študije* (Research and Studies).

Zavod za gradbeništvo Slovenije (Slovenian National Building and Civil Engineering Institute): Dimičeva 12, 1000 Ljubljana; tel. (1) 280-42-50; fax (1) 280- 44-84; e-mail info@zag.si; internet www.zag.si; f. 1949; research and devt in the field of building and civil engineering; Dir Dr ANDRAŽ LEGAT.

Znanstvenoraziskovalni Center SAZU (ZRC SAZU) (Scientific Research Centre of SASA): Novi trg 2, 1000 Ljubljana; tel. (1) 425-52-26; fax (1) 425-52-53; e-mail zrc@zrc-sazu.si; internet odmev.zrc-sazu.si/zrc; f. 1981 by Slovenian Acad. of Sciences and Arts; now an independent body with a network of research institutes (listed individually in this section of Research Institutes) in the humanities and natural sciences; Dir Dr OTO LUTHAR.

BIBLIOGRAPHY, LIBRARY SCIENCE AND MUSEOLOGY

Inštitut za Kulturno zgodovino ZRC SAZU (Institute for Cultural History at ZRC SAZU): Novi trg 5, 1000 Ljubljana; tel. (1) 470-61-00; fax (1) 425-52-53; e-mail ibb@zrc-sazu.si; internet odmev.zrc-sazu.si/instituti/ikz; f. 1999, as Inštitut za Biografiko in Bibliografijo (Institute of Biographical and Bibliographical Studies), current name 2007; attached to Scientific Research Centre of SASA (ZRC SAZU); biographical research and studies; research of modern Slovenian and European history; Head Prof. IGOR GRDINA; publ. *Življenja in dela-Lives and Works* (book series).

FINE AND PERFORMING ARTS

Glasbenonarodopisni Inštitut ZRC SAZU (Institute of Ethnomusicology ZRC SAZU): Novi trg 2, 1000 Ljubljana; tel. (1) 470-62-65; fax (1) 425-77-53; e-mail gni@zrc-sazu.si; internet gni.zrc-sazu.si; f. 1934; attached to Scientific Research Centre of SASA (ZRC SAZU); Dir Dr MARJETKA GOLEŽ KAUČIČ; publ. *Traditiones* (1 a year).

Muzikološki inštitut ZRC SAZU (Institute of Musicology at ZRC SAZU): Novi trg 2, 1000 Ljubljana; tel. (1) 470-61-96; fax (1) 425-77-99; internet mi.zrc-sazu.si; f. 1972; attached to Scientific Research Centre of SASA (ZRC SAZU); library of 7,000 vols; Head Dr METODA KOKOLE; publs *De Musica Disserenda* (2 a year), *Monumenta Artis Musicae Sloveniae* (2 a year).

Umetnostnozgodovinski inštitut Franceta Steleta ZRC SAZU (France Stele Institute of Art History at ZRC SAZU): Novi trg 2, POB 306, 1001 Ljubljana; tel. (1) 470-61-00; fax (1) 425-78-00; e-mail umzg@zrc-sazu.si; internet uifs.zrc-sazu.si; f. 1972; attached to Scientific Research Centre of SASA (ZRC SAZU); library of 17,000 vols; Dir Dr BARBARA MUROVEC (acting); Sec. ROMANA ZAJC; publs *Acta historiae artis Slovenica* (1 a year), *Umetnosta Kronika* (4 a year).

HISTORY, GEOGRAPHY AND ARCHAEOLOGY

Geografski inštitut Antona Melika ZRC SAZU (Anton Melik Geographical Institute at ZRC SAZU): Gosposka ul. 13, 1000 Ljubljana; tel. (1) 470-63-54; fax (1) 425-77-93; e-mail gi@zrc-sazu.si; internet giam.zrc-sazu.si; f. 1946; attached to Scientific Research Centre of Slovenian Acad. of Sciences and Arts (ZRC SAZU); depts of physical, social, regional geography, natural disasters, geographical information system, thematic cartography, environmental protection; geographical museum and library; also houses a cartographic colln and 3 spec. geographical collns: Landscapes of Slovenia, Settlements of Slovenia and Glaciers of Slovenia; HQ of the Comm. for the Standardization of Geographical Names; library of 42,000 vols and periodicals; Dir Dr DRAGO PERKO; Asst Dir Dr MATIJA ZORN; Asst Dir Dr. MIMI URBANC; publs , *Geografija Slovenije* (Geography of Slovenian, book series, in Slovene, 2 a year), *Geografski zbornik* (Acta Geographica Slovenica, scientific journal, in English and Slovenian, 2 a year), *Georithem* (in Slovene, 2 to 5 a year), *GIS v Sloveniji* (GIS in Slovenia, book series, in Slovene, every 2 years), *Naravne nesreče* (Natural Disasters, book series, in Slovene, every 3 years), *Regionalni razvoj* (Regional Devt, book series, in Slovene, every 2 years).

Inštitut za arheologijo ZRC SAZU (Institute of Archaeology at ZRC SAZU): Novi Trg 2, 1000 Ljubljana; tel. (1) 470-63-80; fax (1) 425-77-57; e-mail iza@zrc-sazu.si; internet iza.zrc-sazu.si; f. 1947; attached to Scientific Research Centre of SASA (ZRC SAZU); library of 50,000 vols; Dir Dr JANA HORVAT; publs *Arheološki vestnik* (Acta Archaeologica, 1 a year), *Opera Instituti archaeologici Sloveniae*.

Uprava Republike Slovenije za kulturno dediščino (Cultural Heritage Office of the Republic of Slovenia): Plečnikov trg 2, 1000 Ljubljana; tel. (1) 251-32-87; fax (1) 425-54-71; e-mail urskd@gov.si; f. 1913; preserves and studies historical and archaeological monuments, and sites of historical, artistic, scientific, ethnological and sociological interest; maintains complete register of historical monuments in Slovenia; library of 13,500 books; Dir STANE MRVIČ; publs *Kulturni in naravni spomeniki Slovenije* (series of guides to the historical and natural monuments of Slovenia, 10 a year), *Varstvo spomenikov* (Preservation of Monuments, 1 a year), *Vestnik* (Bulletin).

Zgodovinski inštitut Milka Kosa ZRC SAZU (Milko Kos Historical Institute at ZRC SAZU): Novi trg 2, 1000 Ljubljana; tel. (1) 470-62-00; fax (1) 425-78-01; e-mail zi@zrc-sazu.si; internet zimk.zrc-sazu.si; f. 1947; attached to Scientific Research Centre of SASA (ZRC SAZU); Head Prof. Dr PETRA SVOLJŠAK.

LANGUAGE AND LITERATURE

Inštitut za slovenski jezik Frana Ramovša ZRC SAZU (Fran Ramovš Institute of the Slovenian Language at ZRC SAZU): Novi trg 4, p.p. 306, 1001 Ljubljana; tel. (1) 470-61-60; fax (1) 425-77-96; e-mail isj@zrc-sazu.si; internet isjfr.zrc-sazu.si; f. 1945; attached to Scientific Research Centre at SASA (ZRC SAZU); Slovenian lexicography; library of 25,000 vols; 45 mems; Head Dr MARKO SNOJ; Sec. ALENKA LAP; publs *Jezikoslovni zapiski* (2 a year), *Slovenski jezik* (Slovene Linguistic Studies, every 2 years).

Inštitut za slovensko literaturo in literarne vede ZRC SAZU (Institute of Slovenian Literature and Literary Studies at ZRC SAZU): Novi trg 2, 1000 Ljubljana; tel. (1) 470-63-00; fax (1) 425-77-54; e-mail lit@zrc-sazu.si; internet lit.zrc-sazu.si; f. 1947; attached to Research Centre of the Slovenian Academy of Sciences and Arts (ZRC SAZU); research on Slovenian literature and literary studies and related artistic, aesthetictic, cultural, and historical issues; library of 37,000 vols; Dir Dr MARKO JUVAN; Sec. ALENKA MAČEK; publs *CLCWeb: Comparative Literature and Culture.* (4 a year), *Primerjalna književnost* (Comparative Literature, 3 a year), *Slavistična revija* (Slavic Review, 4 a year).

MEDICINE

Družbenomedicinski inštitut ZRC SAZU (Sociomedical Institute at ZRC SAZU): Novi trg 2, 1000 Ljubljana; tel. (1) 470-61-00; fax (1) 426-14-93; e-mail imv@zrc-sazu.si;

internet dmi.zrc-sazu.si; f. 1981 as Inštitut za medicinske vede; social sciences, humanities and medical sciences; sociological and social-anthropological interpretation of classical demographic models and concepts, social-anthropological theory of ethnicity and nationalism, personality, psychosocial, neuropsychological and neurobiological theories of social behaviour; attached to Scientific Research Centre of SASA (ZRC SAZU); Dir Dr DUŠKA KNEŽEVIĆ HOČEVAR.

NATURAL SCIENCES

Biological Sciences

Biološki inštitut Jovana Hadžija ZRC SAZU (Jovan Hadži Institute of Biology at ZRC SAZU): Novi trg 5, 1000 Ljubljana; tel. (1) 470-63-10; fax (1) 425-77-97; e-mail bio@zrc-sazu.si; internet bijh.zrc-sazu.si; f. 1950; attached to Scientific Research Centre of SASA (ZRC SAZU); Chair. Dr MATJAŽ KUNTNER.

Paleontološki inštitut Ivana Rakovca ZRC SAZU (Ivan Rakovec Institute of Palaeontology at ZRC SAZU): Novi trg 2, p.p. 306, 1001 Ljubljana; tel. (1) 470-63-71; fax (1) 425-77-55; e-mail spela@zrc-sazu.si; internet piir .zrc-sazu.si; f. 1949; attached to Scientific Research Centre of the Slovenian Acad. of Sciences and Arts (ZRC SASA); Dir Dr ŠPELA GORIČAN.

Physical Sciences

Inštitut za matematiko, fiziko in mehaniko Jezik (Institute of Mathematics, Physics and Mechanics): Jadranska 19, 1000 Ljubljana; tel. (1) 426-71-77; fax (1) 426-71-78; internet www.imfm.si; f. 1960; research and technical activities in fields of Mathematics, Physics, Mechanics and Theoretical Computer Science; Dir Prof. Dr JERNEJ KOZAK; Deputy Dir TANJA CVEK; publ. *Ars Mathematica Contemporanea* (2 a year).

Institut Jožef Stefan (Jožef Stefan Institute): Jamova 39, 1000 Ljubljana; tel. (1) 477-39-00; fax (1) 251-93-85; e-mail info@ijs.si; internet www.ijs.si; f. 1949; basic and applied research in the fields of natural sciences and technology; Dir Prof. Dr JADRAN LENARČIČ.

Geološki Zavod Slovenije (Geological Survey of Slovenia): Dimičeva ul. 14, 1000 Ljubljana; tel. (1) 280-97-00; fax (1) 280-97-53; e-mail www@geo-zs.si; internet www .geo-zs.si; f. 1946; geology, geotechnology, geophysics, mining, soil and rock mechanics, drilling and blasting, manufacturing and maintenance of drilling equipment; 1,300 mems; library of 15,000 vols, 300 periodicals, 30,000 reports; Dir Dr MARKO KOMAC; publ. *Geologija* (2 a year).

Inštitut za raziskovanje krasa ZRC SAZU (Karst Research Institute at ZRC SAZU): Titov trg 2, 6230 Postojna; tel. (5) 700-19-00; fax (5) 700-19-99; e-mail izrk@zrc-sazu.si; internet kras.zrc-sazu.si; f. 1947; karstology and speleology; attached to Scientific Research Centre of SASA (SRC SAZU); Dir Dr TADEJ SLABE; Sec. SONJA STAMENKOVIĆ; publs *Acta Carsologica* (2 a year), *Annotated Bibliography of Karst Publications* (1 a year).

PHILOSOPHY AND PSYCHOLOGY

Filozofski inštitut ZRC SAZU (Institute of Philosophy at ZRC SAZU): Novi trg 2, POB 306, 1001 Ljubljana; tel. (1) 470-64-70; fax (1) 425-77-92; e-mail fi@zrc-sazu.si; internet fi .zrc-sazu.si; f. 1979; attached to Scientific Research Centre at SASA (ZRC SAZU); research on encounters between philosophy and psychoanalysis, science, politics, and art; library of 5,000 vols; Head Dr RADO RIHA; Sec. MATEJ AŽMAN; publ. *Filozofski vestnik* (3 a year).

RELIGION, SOCIOLOGY AND ANTHROPOLOGY

Inštitut za narodnostna vprašanja (Institute for Ethnic Studies): Erjavčeva 26, 1000 Ljubljana; tel. (1) 200-18-72; fax (1) 251-09-64; e-mail inv@inv.si; internet www.inv.si; f. 1925; study of inter-ethnic relations in Slovenia and abroad and of Slovene ethnic minorities in neighbouring countries; sociolinguistics, human rights, migration, general ethnic issues; library of 38,000 vols; Pres. ŽARKO BOGUNOVIČ; Dir SONJA NOVAK LUKANOVIC; publ. *Razprave in gradivo* (Treatises and Documents, 3 a year).

Inštitut za slovensko izseljenstvo in migracije ZRC SAZU (Slovenian Migration Institute ZRC SAZU): Novi trg 2, 1000 Ljubljana; tel. (1) 470-64-85; fax (1) 425-78-02; e-mail izi@zrc-sazu.si; internet isi .zrc-sazu.si; f. 1986; attached to Scientific Research Centre of SASA (ZRC SAZU); interdisciplinary research of migration processes in Slovenia and in the international environment; Head Dr MARINA LUKŠIČ-HACIN; publs *Bilten* (Newsletter, 1 a year), *Dve Domovini* (Two Homelands, 2 a year).

Inštitut za slovensko narodopisje ZRC SAZU (Institute of Slovenian Ethnology at ZRC SAZU): Novi trg 2, 1000 Ljubljana; tel. (1) 470-62-80; fax (1) 425-77-52; e-mail ngrid .slavec-gradisnik@zrc-sazu.si; internet isn .zrc-sazu.si; f. 1951; attached to Scientific Research Centre of SASA (ZRC SAZU); research in ethnology and folklore studies; library of 19,000 vols; 16 mems; Sec. BOZENA GABRIJELČIČ; Documentarian, Archivist STANKA DRNOVŠEK, MIHA PECE; Librarian VANJA HUZJAN; publs *Studia Mythologica Slavica* (1 a year), *Traditiones* (2 a year).

Libraries and Archives

Celje

Osrednja knjižnica Celje (Public Library of Celje): Muzejski trg 1A, 3000 Celje; tel. (3) 426-17-10; e-mail sikce@knjiznica-celje.si; internet www.ce.sik.si; f. 1946; 365,000 vols; Librarian BRANKO GOROPEVŠEK; Deputy Librarian MARTINA ROZMAN SALOBIR.

Koper

Osrednja knjižnica Srečka Vilharja (Srečko Vilhar Public Library): trg Brolo 1, 6000 Koper; tel. (5) 663-26-00; fax (5) 663-26-15; e-mail info@kp.sik.si; internet www.kp .sik.si; f. 1951; 300,000 vols; Librarian Prof. IVAN MARKOVIĆ.

Ljubljana

Arhiv Republike Slovenije (Archives of the Republic of Slovenia): Zvezdarska 1, p.p. 21, 1127 Ljubljana; tel. (1) 241-42-00; fax (1) 241-42-69; e-mail ars@gov.si; internet www .arhiv.gov.si; f. 1887; colln of important archives, esp. those connected with the territory populated by Slovenes since 12th century; archive of Slovene film production since 1905; Dir Dr DRAGAN MATIĆ.

Biblioteka Slovenske akademije znanosti in umetnosti (Library of the Slovenian Academy of Sciences and Arts): Novi trg 3–5, POB 323, 1000 Ljubljana; tel. (1) 470-62-46; fax (1) 425-34-62; e-mail sazu-biblioteka@sazu.si; internet www.sazu.si/biblioteka .html; f. 1938; 520 vols; Librarian MARIJA FABJANČIČ; publs *Kratko poročilo o delu v letu* (1 a year), *Mesečni seznam novosti* (12 a year), *Objave* (irregular).

British Library: 1000 Ljubljana, Center Tivoli, Tivolska 30; tel. (1) 300-20-30; fax (1) 300-20-44; e-mail info@britishcouncil.si; internet www.britishcouncil.si; offers courses and exams in English language and British culture and promotes cultural exchange with the UK; 400 vols; Dir STEVE GREEN.

Centralna ekonomska knjižnica (Central Economic Library): Kardeljeva ploščad 17, 1000 Ljubljana; tel. (1) 589-25-91; fax (1) 589-26-98; e-mail cek@ef.uni-lj.si; internet www .ef.uni-lj.si/cek; f. 1946; library and information centre for business, economics and related sciences; European documentation centre; 242,000 vols; 301 current periodicals (print), 11,000 e-journals; 9,000 mems; Head IVAN KANIČ; publ. *Mesečni pregled novih knjig* (12 a year).

Centralna medicinska knjižnica, Medicinska fakulteta (Central Medical Library, Faculty of Medicine): Vrazov trg 2, 1000 Ljubljana; tel. (1) 543-77-35; fax (1) 543-77-45; e-mail infocmk@mf.uni-lj.si; internet www.mf.uni-lj.si/cmk; f. 1945; central library for the Faculty of Medicine, Slovene healthcare orgs and biomedical research instns; literature of biomedicine; 210,000 books and periodicals, 1,100 e-journals and 150 ebooks; Dir Dr ANAMARIJA ROŽIĆ-HRISTOVSKI.

Centralna tehniška knjižnica Univerze v Ljubljani (Central Technical Library of the University of Ljubljana): trg republike 3, 1000 Ljubljana; tel. (1) 200-34-00; fax (1) 425-66-67; e-mail post@ctk.uni-lj.si; internet www.ctk.uni-lj.si; f. 1949; central technical library for the university; specialized information centre for engineering, civil engineering and standards; information and referral centre for science and technology; inter-library loan centre; 230,000 vols, research papers, standards, regulations; Dir Dr MIRO PUŠNIK; publ. *New Books Accession List* (4 a year).

Knjižnica Narodnega Muzeja Slovenije (Library of the National Museum of Slovenia): Prešernova 20, POB 1967, 1000 Ljubljana; tel. (1) 241-44-68; fax (1) 241-44-00; e-mail anja-dular@nms.si; internet www .nms.si/anj/odd/knj/knj.html; f. 1821; 200,000 vols; spec. colln of Slovene prints from 16th century; Librarian Doc. Dr ANJA DULAR; publs *ARGO* (journal on museology), *Viri – monograph series* (Topics in Slovenian Material Culture).

Knjižnica Pravne fakultete (Library of the Faculty of Law): Poljanski Nasip 2, 1000 Ljubljana; tel. (1) 420-32-31; fax (1) 420-32-82; e-mail knjiznica@pf.uni-lj.si; internet www.pf.uni-lj.si/knjiznica-in-zalozba; f. 1920; 123,000 vols; Head Librarian MARIJAN PAVČNIK.

Narodna in univerzitetna knjižnica (National and University Library): Turjaška 1, POB 259, 1000 Ljubljana; tel. (1) 200-11-88; fax (1) 425-72-93; e-mail uprava@nuk .uni-lj.si; internet www.nuk.uni-lj.si; f. 1774; incorporates state copyright and deposit library, Nat. Slovene library, Univ. of Ljubljana library, library promotion and consultancy centre, permanent education centre and library research centre; UNESCO deposit library; Information and Documentation Centre on the Council of Europe, and EU Colln; 2,500,000 vols, incl. 1.2m. books, 324,000 serials, 80,000 printed music items, 23,700 sound recordings, 13,800 audiovisual items, 7,400 MSS (incl. 85 parchments and 508 incunabula), 74,000 maps, 170,000 pictorial items, 3,800 microforms; Dir MATEJA KOMEL SNOJ; publs *Knjižničarske novice* (print, 12 a year; online), *Novice NUK* (newsletter, 2 a year), *Signalne informacije* (print, 12 a year; online), *Slovenska bibliografija* (print, 4 a year; also online).

Mestna knjižnica Ljubljana (Ljubljana City Library): Kersnikova ul. 2, 1000 Ljubljana; tel. (1) 600-13-00; fax (1) 600-13-32; e-mail info@mklj.si; internet www.mklj.si; f. 2008, as Slovanska knjižnica Ljubljana (Slavic Library); language, literature, history and culture of the Slavs; 1,613,357 vols; Dir Mag. JELKA GAZVODA.

Maribor

Univerzitetna knjižnica Maribor (University of Maribor Library): Gospejna ul. 10, 2000 Maribor; tel. (2) 250-74-00; fax (2) 252-60-87; e-mail ukm-tajnistvo@uni-mb.si; internet www.ukm.si; f. 1903; 960,000 vols; Dir Dr. ZDENKA PETERMANEC (acting); publ. *Časopis za zgodovino in narodopisje* (Journal of History and Ethnology, 1 a year).

Novo Mesto

Knjižnica Mirana Jarca ('Milan Jarc' Regional Library): Rozmanova ul. 28, 8000 Novo Mesto; tel. (7) 393-46-00; fax (7) 393-46-01; e-mail infosiknm@nm.sik.si; internet www.nm.sik.si; f. 1946; 5200000 vols; Dir CLAUDIA JERINA MESTNIK.

Museums and Art Galleries

Brežice

Posavski muzej (Regional Museum): Cesta prvih borcev 1, 8250 Brežice; tel. (7) 496-12-71; fax (7) 466-05-16; e-mail ivan.kastelic@guest.arnes.si; internet www.posavski-muzej.si; f. 1949; colln of archaeological exhibits from Neolithic times to the early Middle Ages; also ethnographical colln; historical section: from Slovene-Croat peasants' revolt of 1573 to the present; Baroque festival hall with frescoes (1703) and Baroque gallery; memorial room of painter Franjo Stiplovšek; library of 7,350 vols, 35 periodicals; Dir Dr. TOM TEROPŠIČ; Curator IVAN KASTELIČ.

Celje

Pokrajinski muzej Celje (Celje Regional Museum): trg Celjskih knezov 8, 3000 Celje; tel. (3) 428-09-50; fax (3) 428-09-66; e-mail info@pokmuz-ce.si; internet www.pokmuz-ce.si; f. 1882 as City Museum; present status 1965; collns of archaeology, art and cultural history, ethnography and history; library of 8,456 vols; Dir DARJA PIRKMAJER.

Ljubljana

Mednarodni Grafični Likovni Center (MGLC) (International Centre of Graphic Arts): Grad Tivoli, Pod turnom 3, 1000 Ljubljana; tel. (1) 241-38-00; fax (1) 241-38-21; e-mail lili.sturm@mglc-lj.si; internet www.mglc-lj.si; f. 1986; permanent colln of contemporary int. graphics, artist's books and printed ephemera; organizes the int. Biennial of Graphic Arts; exhibitions of prints, drawings, artists' books and printed ephemera; print workshop; Dir Dr BARBARA SAVENC.

Mestni muzej Ljubljana (City Museum of Ljubljana): Gosposka 15, 1000 Ljubljana; tel. (1) 241-25-00; fax (1) 241-25-40; e-mail info@mgml.si; internet www.mgml.si; f. 1935; cultural history museum of Ljubljana; collns incl. archaeological dept, containing articles from lake dwellings of the chalcolithic period, cemeteries of the Illyrian-Celtic period and of Roman domination (Emona), and from the Old Slavic period; cultural historical colln; modern history; also fine arts exhibitions; information centre about the cultural and natural heritage in the Ljubljana area; publs various guides; library of 9,324 vols; Dir BLAŽ PERŠIN.

Moderna galerija (Museum of Modern Art): Tomšičeva 14, 1000 Ljubljana; tel. (1) 241-68-00; fax (1) 251-41-20; e-mail info@mg-lj.si; internet www.mg-lj.si; f. 1948; permanent colln of contemporary Slovene art from the Impressionists to the present day and worldwide modern art; organizes regular art exhibitions; photographic archive; library: art library of 50,000 vols; Dir ZDENKA BADOVINAC.

Muzej novejše zgodovine slovenije (National Museum of Contemporary History): Celovška c. 23, 1001 Ljubljana; tel. (1) 300-96-10; fax (1) 433-82-44; e-mail uprava@muzej-nz.si; internet www.muzej-nz.si; f. 1948; important archives, museum objects and library material of Slovene history since 1914; Dir Dr JOŽE DEŽMAN.

Narodna galerija (National Gallery): Puharjeva 9, 1000 Ljubljana; tel. (1) 241-54-34; fax (1) 241-54-03; e-mail info@ng-slo.si; internet www.ng-slo.si; f. 1918; colln of Gothic sculptural arts, medieval frescoes and copies of Gothic frescoes from Slovenia; colln of Slovenian Renaissance, Baroque and 19th-century paintings and sculptures; paintings by Slovenian impressionists; European painters since the 14th century; colln of Slovenian graphic arts from the 18th to the early 20th centuries; photo-documentation of works of art from Slovenia; library of 34,000 vols; Dir Dr BARBARA JAKI.

Narodni muzej Slovenije (National Museum of Slovenia): Prešernova ul. 20, POB 1967, 1000 Ljubljana; tel. (1) 241-44-00; fax (1) 241-44-22; e-mail info@nms.si; internet www.nms.si; f. 1821; depts of archaeology; history and applied arts; coins and medals; graphic arts; conservation and restoration; library of 220,000 vols; brs: National Museum of Slovenia (Metelkova); Sneznik Castle Museum; Museum of Bled (medieval castle); Dir Prof. Dr PETER KOS; publs *Argo* (2 a year), *Catalogi et Monographiae* (1 a year), *Situla* (1 a year), *Viri* (irregular).

Prirodoslovni muzej Slovenije (Slovenian Museum of Natural History): Prešernova 20, POB 290, 1001 Ljubljana; tel. (1) 241-09-40; fax (1) 241-09-53; e-mail uprava@pms-lj.si; internet www2.pms-lj.si; f. 1821; zoology, botany, geology; library of 12,500 books and periodicals; Dir BREDA CINC JUHANT; publs *Acta Entomologica Slovenica* (2 a year), *Illiesia – International Journal of Stonefly Research* (print and online, 1 a year;), *Scopolia* (3 a year).

Slovenski etnografski muzej (Slovenian Ethnographical Museum): Metelkova 2, 1000 Ljubljana; tel. (1) 300-87-00; fax (1) 300-87-36; e-mail etnomuz@etno-muzej.si; internet www.etno-muzej.si; f. 1923; Slovenian and non-European ethnographic collns; library of 30,000 vols; Dir Dr BOJANA ROGELJ ŠKAFAR; publs *Etnolog* (1 a year), *Knjižnica Slovenskega etnografskega muzeja* (library newsletter, 1 or 2 a year).

Slovenski šolski muzej (Slovenian School Museum): trg Plečnikov 1, 1000 Ljubljana; tel. and fax (1) 251-30-24; e-mail solski.muzej@guest.arnes.si; internet www.ssolski-muzej.si; f. 1898; school documents and educational books since 16th century; exhibition about the devt of schools in Slovenia; library of 59,000 vols, 542 fascicules; 17,084 documents for all schools in Slovenia; Dir Mag. STANKO OKOLIŠ; publ. *Šolska kronika* (School Chronicle, 2 a year).

Zemljepisni muzej Geografskega inštituta Antona Melika ZRC SAZU (Geographical Museum of the Anton Melik Geographical Institute at ZRC SAZU): Gosposka ul. 13, 1000 Ljubljana; tel. (1) 470-63-58; e-mail zm@zrc-sazu.si; internet giam.zrc-sazu.si; f. 1946; attached to the Anton Melik Geographical Institute at ZRC SAZU; maps and atlases of Slovenia, geographical collns; Head PRIMOŽ GAŠPERIČ; Dir Dr DRAGO PERKO.

Maribor

Pokrajinski muzej Maribor (Regional Museum of Maribor): Grajska ul. 2, 2000 Maribor; tel. (2) 228-35-51; fax (2) 252-77-77; e-mail info@pmuzej-mb.si; internet www.pmuzej-mb.si; f. 1903 from collns of the Maribor Museum, the historical socs and the Episcopal Museum; archaeological, ethnological, historical, fine and applied art, costume colln exhibits; library of 12,000 vols; Dir MIRJANA KOREN.

Piran

Obalne Galerije Piran (Coastal Galleries of Piran): Tartinijev trg 3, 6330 Piran; tel. (5) 671-20-80; fax (5) 671-20-90; internet www.obalne-galerije.si; f. 1975; group of galleries; display contemporary art of Slovenian coast; Dir TONI BILOSLAV.

Pomorski Muzej Sergej Mašera (Maritime Museum Sergej Masera): Cankarjevo nabrežje 3 p.p. 103, 6330 Piran; tel. (5) 671-00-40; fax (5) 671-00-50; e-mail muzej@pommuz-pi.si; internet www2.arnes.si/~kppomm; f. 1954 as the Civic Museum of Piran, present name 1967; colln and study of the maritime past of the Slovene coast, Slovene naval history and related economic activities; archaeological, maritime and art-history collns; an anthropological study and colln of items used in salt-making and fishing; library of 14,000 vols; Dir MARTINA GAMBOZ.

Ptuj

Pokrajinski muzej Ptuj (Ptuj Regional Museum): Muzejski trg 1, 2250 Ptuj; tel. (2) 787-92-30; fax (2) 787-92-45; e-mail muzej-ptuj.uprava@siol.net; internet www.pok-muzej-ptuj.si; f. 1893; history, archaeology, art, ethnography, numismatics, musical instruments, lapidary; reconstructions of 4 temples of Mithras; library of 17,000 vols; Dir Prof. ALEŠ ARIH; publs *Archaeologia Poetovionensis*, *Zbornik*.

Škofja Loka

Loški Muzej (Loški Museum): Grajska pot 13, 4220 Škofja Loka; tel. (4) 517-04-00; fax (4) 517-04-12; e-mail loski.muzej@guest.arnes.si; internet www.loski-muzej.si; f. 1939 by the Museum Asscn of Škofja Loka; special colln of exhibits relating to the Freising dominion (973–1803); ethnographic, topographic, natural history and historical exhibits; records of altars since 17th century, exhibits of medieval guilds; relics of the struggle for national liberation; art gallery; open-air museum; library of 18,000 vols; Pres. JANA MLAKAR; publ. *Loški razgledi*.

Universities

UNIVERZA NA PRIMORSKEM
(University of Primorska)

Titov trg 4, 6000 Koper
Telephone: (5) 611-75-00
Fax: (5) 611-75-30
E-mail: info@upr.si
Internet: www.upr.si

Founded 2003
State control
Languages of instruction: Slovenian, English
Academic year: October to September

Rector: Prof. RADO BOHINC
Vice-Rector for Education: Prof. ROBERTO BILOSLAVO
Vice-Rector for Science and Research: Prof. RADO PIŠOT
Sec.-Gen.: ASTRID PRAŠNIKAR
Library of 40,000 vols, 400 periodicals across 5 libraries
Number of teachers: 260 , 81 research staff
Number of students: 5,338

DEANS

College of Health Care (Izola): Dr NADJA PLAZAR
College of Tourism—Touristica (Portoroz): Dr ALEKSANDRA BREZOVEC
Faculty of Education (Koper): Dr MARA COTIČ
Faculty of Humanities (Koper): Dr VESNA MIKOLIĆ
Faculty of Management (Koper): Dr ANITA TRNAVČEVIČ
Faculty of Mathematics, Science and Information Technology: Dr. DRAGAN MARUSIC

UNIVERZA V LJUBLJANI
(University of Ljubljana)

Kongresni trg 12, 1000 Ljubljana
Telephone: (1) 241-85-00
Fax: (1) 241-86-60
E-mail: rektorat@uni-lj.si
Internet: www.uni-lj.si
Founded 1595, reconstituted 1809, reopened 1919
State control
Languages of instruction: Slovene, English
Academic year: October to September (two terms)
Rector: Prof. Dr RADOVAN STANISLAV PEJOVNIK
Vice-Rector: Prof. Dr JULIJANA KRISTL
Vice-Rector: Prof. Dr MIHA JUHART
Vice-Rector: Prof. Dr ANDREJ KOVAČIČ
Vice-Rector: Prof. Dr ALEŠ VALIC
Sec.-Gen.: ANDREJA KERT
Librarians: MIRO PUŠNIK (Central and Technical Library), MATEJA KOMEL SNOJ (Nat. and Univ. Library)
Library of 2,998,433 vols
Number of teachers: 4,088
Number of students: 66,000
Publications: *Seznam predavanj* (1 a year), *University of Ljubljana, Welcome*

DEANS

Academy of Fine Arts: Prof. BOJAN GORENC
Academy of Music: Prof. ANDREJ GRAFENAUER
Academy of Theatre, Radio, Film, Television: Prof. ALEŠ VALIČ
Faculty of Architecture: Prof. PETER GABRIJELČIČ
Faculty of Arts: Prof. Dr VALENTIN BUCIK
Faculty of Biotechnology: Prof. Dr MIHAEL JOŽEF TOMAN
Faculty of Chemistry,Chemical Technology: Prof. Dr ANTON MEDEN
Faculty of Civil and Geodetic Engineering: Prof. Dr MATJAŽ ,. MIKOŠ
Faculty of Computer, Information Science: Prof. Dr NIKOLAI ZIMIC
Faculty of Economics: Prof. DUSAN MRAMOR
Faculty of Education: Prof. JANEZ KREK
Faculty of Electrical Engineering: Prof. Dr JANEZ NASTRAN
Faculty of Health Sciences: Prof. Dr FRANCE SEVŠEK
Faculty of Law: Prof. Dr PETER GRILC
Faculty of Maritime Studies, Transport: Prof. ELEN TWRDY
Faculty of Mathematics, Physics: Prof. ANDREJ LIKAR
Faculty of Mechanical Engineering: Prof. Dr JOŽE DUHOVNIK
Faculty of Medicine: Prof. Dr DUŠAN ŠUPUT
Faculty of Natural Sciences, Engineering: Prof. JAKOB LIKAR
Faculty of Pharmacy: Prof. Dr STANISLAV GOBEC
Faculty of Public Admin.: Prof. Dr STANKA SETNIKAR CANKAR
Faculty of Social Sciences: Prof. Dr ANTON GRIZOLD
Faculty of Social Work: Prof. Dr BOGDAN LEŠNIK
Faculty of Sports: Prof. Dr MILAN ŽVAN
Faculty of Theology: Prof. Dr STANKO GERJOLJ
Faculty of Veterinary Medicine: Prof. Dr MARJAN KOSEC

UNIVERZA V MARIBORU
(University of Maribor)

Slomškov trg 15, 2000 Maribor
Telephone: (2) 235-52-80
Fax: (2) 235-52-11
E-mail: rektorat@uni-mb.si
Internet: www.uni-mb.si
Founded 1975
State control
Language of instruction: Slovene
Academic year: October to September
Rector: Prof. Dr IVAN ROZMAN
Vice-Rector for Int. and Inter-Univ. Cooperation: Assoc. Prof. Dr MARKO MARHL
Vice-Rector for Scientific Research and Business Cooperation: Prof. Dr MILAN MARČIČ
Vice-Rector for Legal and General Affairs: Prof. Dr BOJAN ŠKOF
Vice-Rector for Students: DANIEL VUK
Sec.-Gen.: BOŠTJAN BRUMEN
Librarian: Dr ZDENKA PETERMANEC
Number of teachers: 1,800
Number of students: 24,600
Publications: *Časopis za zgodovino in narodopisje*, *Naše gospodarstvo* (published by the Faculty of Business and Economics, 6 a year), *Organizacija in Kadri* (published by the Faculty of Organizational Sciences, 10 a year), *Univerzitetna revija*, *Znanstvena revija*

DEANS

Faculty of Agricultural Sciences and biosystems: Dr JERNEJ TURK
Faculty of Arts: Prof. Dr MARKO JESENŠEK
Faculty of Business and Economics: Prof. Dr SAMO BOBEK
Faculty of Chemistry and Chemical Engineering: Prof. Dr ŽELJKO KNEZ
Faculty of Civil Engineering: Prof. Dr MIROSLAV PREMROV
Faculty of Criminal Justice: Prof. Dr GORAZD MESKO
Faculty of Education: Prof. Dr SAMO FOŠNARIČ
Faculty of Electrical Engineering,Computer Science: Prof. Dr IGOR TIČAR
Faculty of Energy: Prof. Dr ANDREJ PREDIN
Faculty of Health Sciences: Prof. Dr PETER KOKOL
Faculty of Law: Prof. Dr RAJKO KNEZ
Faculty of Logistics: Prof. Dr MARTIN LIPIČNIK
Faculty of Mechanical Engineering: Prof. Dr NIKO SAMEC
Faculty of Medicine: Prof. Dr IVAN KRAJNC
Faculty of Natural Sciences and Mathematics: Prof. Dr NATAŠA VAUPOTIČ
Faculty of Organizational Sciences: Dr FERJAN MARKO

PROFESSORS

Faculty of Agriculture (Pivola 10, 2311 Maribor; tel. (2) 320-90-00; fax (2) 616-11-58; e-mail fk@uni-mb.si; internet fk.uni-mb .si):

BAVEC, F., Organic Farming, Crops, Vegetables and Ornamental Plants
CENCIČ, A., Microbiology, Biochemistry, Molecular Biology and Biotechnology
IVANCIC, A., Genetics and Breeding of Plants
KRAJNČIČ, B., Plant Physiology, Biology, Botany
KRAMBERGER, B., Grass and Fodder Production
LAKOTA, M., Engineering biosystems
LEŠNIK, M., Phytomedicine
LEŠNIK, M., Foreign Languages Expert
NEMEC, J., Mathematical Methods, Informatics and Statistics in agriculture
ŠKORJANC, D., Animal Genetics and Breeding
SLEKOVEC, M., Chemistry, Agrochemistry and Pedology
TOJNKO, S., Fruit and Fruit Processing
TURK, J, Agricultural Economics and Rural Devt
VOLK, M., Physiology, Anatomy and Animal Health
VRŠIC, S., Viticulture and Enology

Faculty of Business and Economics (Razlagova 14, 2000 Maribor; tel. (2) 229-00-00; fax (2) 229-02-17; e-mail epf@uni-mb.si; internet www.epf.uni-mb.si):

BOBEK, D., Business Administration in Banking
BELAK, J., Economics
FILIPIČ, D., Finance
GUSEL, L., Yugoslav Import-Export System
HAUC, A., Project Management
INDIHAR, S., Mathematics
KENDA, V., International Trade
KOKOTEC-NOVAK, M., Economics
KOLETNIK, F., Accounting, Auditing
MULEJ, M., Dialectical Theory of Systems
MUSIL, V., Polymeric Materials
OVIN, R., Economic Policy
PAUKO, F., Tourism
PIVKA, H., Business Law
RADONJIČ, D., Market Research
SAVIN, D., Political Economy
SRUK, V., Sociology, Philosophy and Political Science
ŽIŽMOND, E., Economic Policy

Faculty of Chemistry and Chemical Engineering (Smetanova ul. 17, 2000 Maribor; tel. (2) 229-44-01; fax (2) 252-77-74; e-mail fkkt@ uni-mb.si; internet www.atom.uni-mb.si):

DOBČNIK, D., Analytical Chemistry
DOLEČEK, V., Physical Chemistry
DROFENIK, M., Inorganic Chemistry
GLAVIČ, P., Inorganic Technology
KNEZ, Ž, Separation Process
KROPE, J., Thermoenergetics

Faculty of Civil Engineering (Smetanova ul. 17, 2000 Maribor; tel. (2) 229-43-02; fax (2) 252-41-79; e-mail fg@uni-mb.si; internet kamen.uni-mb.si):

CVIKL, B., Physics
LEP, J., Mathematics
PŠUNDER, M., Building Economics
ŠKRABL, S., Materials
TRAUNER, L., Soil Mechanics, Geotechnics
UMEK, A., Earthquake Engineering

Faculty of Education (Koroska 160, 2000 Maribor; tel. (2) 229-36-00; fax (2) 251-81-80; internet www.pfmb.uni-mb.si):

BELEC, B., Geography
BOKOR, J., Hungarian Linguistics
BREŠAR, M., Mathematics
BRUMEN, M., Physics
FLERE, S., Sociology
JAUŠOVEC, N., Psychology
JUTRONIĆ-TIHOMIROVIĆ, D., English Linguistics
KLAVŽAR, S., Mathematics
KLEMENČIČ, M., Contemporary History
MIŠČEVIĆ, N., History of Philosophy
MLINARIČ, J., History of Middle Ages

PANDUR, L., Painting Design
ROZMAN, F., History of Southeast Europe
VAUHNIK, J., Special Didactics of Sports Education
VUKMAN, J., Mathematics
ZORKO, Z., History of Language, Dialectology

Faculty of Electrical Engineering and Computer Science (Smetanova ul. 17, 2000 Maribor; tel. (2) 220-70-00; fax (2) 251-11-78; e-mail feri@uni-mb.si; internet www.feri.uni-mb.si):

BREŠAR, F., Mathematics
DOLINAR, D., Electro-Mechanical Control Systems
GRČAR, B., Control and Regulation Systems
GUID, N., Computer Graphics
HORVAT, B., Computing and Microcomputer Systems
JEZERNIK, K., Robotics
KUMPERŠČAK, V., Physics
ROZMAN, I., Information Systems
ZAGRADIŠNIK, I., Electrical Machines
ZAZULA, D., Systems Software
ŽUMER, V., Programming Languages

Faculty of Law (Mladinska 9, 2000 Maribor; tel. (2) 250-42-00; fax (2) 252-32-45; e-mail info.pf@uni-mb.si; internet www.pf.uni-mb.si):

DEVETAK, S., Public International Law
FLERE, S., Sociology
GEČ-KOROŠEC, M., Family Law
IVANJKO, Š., Company Law, Insurance Law
KRANJC, J., Roman Law
OJNIK, S., History of Law
PERNEK, F., Financial Law
RUPNIK, J., Constitutional Law
TOPLAK, L., International Business Law

Faculty of Mechanical Engineering (Smetanova ul. 17, 2000 Maribor; tel. (2) 220-75-00; fax (2) 220-79-90; e-mail fs@uni-mb.si; internet www.fs.uni-mb.si/en):

ALUJEVIĆ, A., Mechanics, Thermodynamics
BALIČ, J., Manufacturing Technologies, Theory of Systems, Computer Integrated Manufacturing, Manufacturing Systems
FLAŠKER, J., Machine Elements II, Mechanical Design of Devices I, Technical Regulations
JEZERNIK, A., CAD/CAM
KRIŽMAN, A., Industrial Engineering, Metal Heat Processing
MAJCEN LE MARECHAL, A., Chemistry, Organic Chemistry I
OBLAK, M., Mechanics and Hydrodynamics
POLAJNAR, A., Work Study and Manufacturing Systems Planning
ŠKERGET, L., Fluid Mechanics and Heat Transfer, Transport Phenomena, Eco-Engineering in Manufacturing
ŠOSTAR, A., Technological Measurements

Faculty of Organizational Sciences (Kidričeva cesta 55A, 4000 Kranj; tel. (4) 237-42-00; fax (4) 237-42-99; e-mail dekanat@fov.uni-mb.si; internet www.fov.uni-mb.si):

FLORJANČIČ, J., Personnel Administration
GRIČAR, J., Analysis and Design of Organizational Systems
JEREB, J., Human Resources Management
JESENKO, J., Quantitative Methods
JUG, J., Andragogy and Human Relations, Human Resources
KLJAJIČ, M., Systems Theory
RAJKOVIČ, V., Management Information Systems
VILA, A., Production Process Management
VRŠEC, E., Production Systems

Faculty of Health Sciences (Zitna 15, 2000 Maribor; tel. (2) 300-47-00; fax (2) 300-47-47; e-mail vzs@uni-mb.si; internet sola.vzdr.uni-mb.si):

BERVAR, M., Surgery
BORKO, E., Gynaecology and Obstetrics
BRUMEC, V., Physiology
GOLOUH, R., Pathology
HREN-VENCELJ, H., Microbiology, Parasitology
KAJZER, Š., Elements of Administration and Management
KRAJNC-SIMONETTI, S., Social Medicine and Statistics in Health Care
MULEJ, M., Anaesthesiology and Reanimatology
POKORN, D., Medical Dietetics
RAIŠP, I., Internal Medicine

UNIVERZA V NOVI GORICI
(University of Nova Gorica)

Vipavska 13, Rožna Dolina, 5000 Nova Gorica
Telephone: (5) 331-53-97
Fax: (5) 331-53-81
E-mail: info@ung.si
Internet: www.ung.si

Founded 1995
Autonomous

Pres.: Prof. Dr DANILO ZAVRTANIK
Vice-Pres. for Research: Prof. Dr GVIDO BRATINA
Vice-Pres. for Education: Prof. Dr MLADEN FRANKO
Sec.: ERICA GOJKOVIĆ

Library of 10,000 vols, 100 periodicals, 200 non-book materials and e-edition of scientific journals
Number of students: 800

DEANS

Business School of Engineering: Prof. Dr TANJA URBANČIČ
College of Arts: BOŠTJAN POTOKAR
College of Viticulture, Enology: Prof. DANILO ZAVRTANIK
Faculty of Applied Sciences: Prof. Dr GVIDO BRATINA
Faculty of Environmental Sciences: Prof. Dr POLONCA TREBŠE
Faculty of Humanities: Dr FRANC MARUŠIČ
Faculty of Postgraduate studies: Prof. IZTOK ARCON

SOLOMON ISLANDS

The Higher Education System

Formerly a British protectorate since 1900, the Solomon Islands became independent within the Commonwealth in 1978. The Solomon Islands College of Higher Education (founded 1984) and the University of the South Pacific Solomon Islands Centre (founded 1971) are the principal institutions of higher education. Scholarships are available for higher education at various universities overseas. Higher education is the responsibility of the Ministry of Education and Human Resources Development.

The Pacific Senior Secondary Certificate or the Solomon Islands School Certificate is the main requirement for admission to the University of the South Pacific (and also to the University of Papua New Guinea). Preliminary and Foundation programmes are available to prepare students for admission to degree courses. The Bachelors is the main undergraduate degree, and lasts for three years in most subjects except medicine, which lasts four years and is taught at the Fiji School of Medicine. After the Bachelors, the first postgraduate degree is the one- to two-year Masters, which is followed by the two-year Doctorate, the highest university degree.

Solomon Islands College of Higher Education is principally an institution of technical and vocational education offering certificate and diploma courses.

Regulatory Body

GOVERNMENT

Ministry of Education and Human Resources Development: POB G28, Honiara; tel. 23900; fax 20485; Minister MATTHEW WALE.

Libraries and Archives

Honiara

Solomon Islands College of Higher Education Library: Kukum Campus, Prince Philip Highway, Honiara; tel. 39016; fax 30390; internet www.siche.edu.sb/library.html; attached to Solomon Islands College of Higher Education; 80,000 vols, 26 serial titles, 20 current serial titles; Dir NELSON B. MANERARA.

Solomon Islands National Archives: Ministry of Education and Human Resources Development, POB 781, Honiara; tel. 21426; f. 1979; British Solomon Islands Protectorate records 1900–78, Solomon Islands Government records since 1978; collections of records, microfilm, film and sound recordings on Solomon Islands and Western Pacific; Government Archivist JOSEPH P. WALE.

Solomon Islands National Library: POB 165, Ministry of Education and Human Resources Development, Watts St, Honiara; tel. 21601; fax 25366; e-mail nls@welkam.solomon.comb.sb; f. 1974; 120,000 vols; Solomon Islands colln and central reference colln; 2 br. libraries at Solomon Islands Centre of the University of the South Pacific and Solomon Islands National Museum and Cultural Centre; Dir EDDIE MARAHARE.

Museum

Honiara

Solomon Islands National Museum and Cultural Centre: POB 313, Honiara; tel. 24896; fax 23492; e-mail loafoa@yahoo.com; f. 1969; part of Dept of Culture, Tourism and Aviation; colln began in 1950s, permanent site 1969; research into all aspects of Solomons culture (prehistory, language, oral tradition, music, dance, architecture, etc.); promotes traditional crafts, music and dance; art, heritage, photography, archaeology, natural history (animal specimens, wet and dry), contemporary, technology, audiovisual material, books, journals, posters, pamphlets, documents, outdoor sculptures, art, monuments; also houses relics of Second World War; Dir LAWRENCE FOANA'OTA; publs *Journal*, *Custom Stories*.

Colleges

Solomon Islands College of Higher Education: POB R113, Honiara; tel. 30111; fax 30390; e-mail siche@solomon.com.sb; internet www.siche.edu.sb; f. 1984; library: see Libraries and Archives; 135 teachers; 1,200 students; Dir GABRIEL TALOIKWAI.

University of the South Pacific Solomon Islands Centre: POB 460, Honiara; tel. 21307; fax 24024; e-mail usuramo_j@usp.ac.fj; internet www.usp.ac.fj; f. 1971; responsible for providing USP courses through extension; developing nat. continuing education courses; promoting research on subjects of nat. interest; library: 6,000 vols; 4 teachers; 600 students (mostly distance-learning); Dir GLYNN GALO.

SOMALIA

The Higher Education System

The union of former British and Italian Somaliland took effect in 1960, when the independent Somali Republic (Somalia) was proclaimed. In 1954 the Italian Government established institutes of law, economics and social studies, and in 1969 these institutions were incorporated into the National University of Somalia. In 1990 there were an estimated 10,400 students enrolled in higher education and in 1991 there were 4,640 university students. However, in the early 1990s the campus of the National University of Somalia in Mogadishu was largely destroyed during civil war. In 1997 Mogadishu University was established as a private institution due to lack of government funding. Until mid-2005 the Somali Government was based in Nairobi, Kenya, for security reasons; hence there was no direct government control over higher education prior to this. Since 2004 several new private universities have been founded including Benadir University, Kismayo University, the University of Gedo, Puntland State University, Amoud University, the University of Hargeisa, Somaliland University of Technology and Burao University.

The Secondary School Certificate is the main requirement for admission to higher education; other criteria include two years' national youth service and a competitive entrance examination. The Bachelors (Laurea) is the main undergraduate degree, and lasts four years. The University of Somalia is in the process of introducing Masters degrees. There are numerous institutions of professional education offering post-secondary vocational and technical qualifications.

Research Institutes

MEDICINE

Institute for the Preparation of Serums and Vaccines: Mogadishu.

Laboratory of Hygiene and Prophylaxis: Mogadishu; sections of medicine and chemistry.

NATURAL SCIENCES

Physical Sciences

Geological Survey Department: Ministry of Water Development and Mineral Resources, POB 744, Mogadishu; library of 500 vols; Dir V. N. KOZERENKO.

Libraries and Archives

Mogadishu

National Library of Somalia: POB 1754, Mogadishu; tel. (1) 22758; f. 1970; research, legal deposit; 30,000 vols, 75 periodicals; training in library science; Dir HASSAN NOOR FARAH.

Somali Institute of Public Administration Library: Mogadishu.

Museum

Mogadishu

Somali National Museum: Corso Repubblica, POB 6917, Mogadishu; tel. 21041; f. 1934; ethnographical, historical and natural science collections; library of 3,000 vols; Dir AHMED FARAH.

Universities

AMOUD UNIVERSITY

Borama, Awdal
Internet: www.amoud-university.borama.ac.so
Private control
Pres.: Prof. SULEIMAN AHMED GULAID
Vice Pres. for External Affairs: Prof. ABDILLAHI HASHI ABIB
1st Vice-Pres. for Planning and Registrar: Prof. AHMED HASHI ABIB
2nd Vice-Pres. for Academic Affairs and Students: Prof. AHMED A. BOQORE
Librarian: QABUL NUH ALI
Library: main campus library: 65,000 vols, all subjects; Borama City campus: 30,000 vols, all subjects; medical and allied health sciences library of 20,000 vols

DEANS

Faculty of Agriculture and Environmental Sciences: Prof. ABUBAKAR SH. ABDI
Faculty of Business and Public Administration: Prof. HASSAN OMAR HALAS
Faculty of Education: Prof. FARAH ABDILLAHI FARID
Faculty of Medicine and Allied Health Sciences: Dr SAEED WALHAD

NATIONAL UNIVERSITY OF SOMALIA

POB 15, Mogadishu
Telephone: (1) 80404
Founded 1954, Univ. status 1969
Languages of instruction: Somali, Arabic, Italian, English
Rector: MOHAMED GANNI MOHAMED
Vice-Rector for Academic Affairs: MOHAMED ELMI BULLALE
Registrar: NUREYN SHEIKH ABRAR
Librarian: Mrs SIRAD YUSUF ISMAIL
Number of teachers: 549
Number of students: 4,640

DEANS

Faculty of Agriculture: MOHAMED ALI MOHAMED
Faculty of Economics: MOHAMED ISMAIL SHEIKH
Faculty of Education: HUSSEIN MUSA ALI
Faculty of Engineering: ABDULLAHI JIMALE MOHAMED
Faculty of Geology: MOHAMMOUD ABDI ARUSH
Faculty of Industrial Chemistry: AHMED MAYE ABDURAHMAN
Faculty of Islamic and Arabic Studies: SHARIF MOHAMED ALI ISAAK
Faculty of Journalism: MOHAMOUD ISMAIL ABDIRAHMAN
Faculty of Languages: (vacant)
Faculty of Law: ABUD MUSAD ABUD
Faculty of Medicine: ABDI AHMED FARAH
Faculty of Political Science: ADEN ABDULLAHI NUR
Faculty of Technical Teacher Education: ABDULLAHI MOHAMUD WARSAMME
Faculty of Veterinary Medicine: ABDULHAMID HAJI MOHAMED
Somali Institute of Development Administration and Management: IBRAHIM MOHAMUD ABYAN

UNIVERSITY OF HARGEISA

University Ave Rd, Hargeisa
Telephone: (2) 422166
E-mail: contact@hargeisauniversity.net
Internet: www.hargeisauniversity.net
Founded 2000
Private control
Academic year: September to July, two semesters
Vice-Pres. for Admin.: MOHAMED MOHAMOUD FARAH
Registrar: YUSUF AINAB
Library of 15,000 vols.

Colleges

School of Industrial Studies: Mogadishu; depts of radio, carpentry, mechanics, electricity, building construction.

School of Islamic Disciplines: Mogadishu; incl. a faculty of law.

School of Public Health: Mogadishu.

School of Seamanship and Fishing: Mogadishu; 170 students.

Technical College: Burgo; f. 1965; 4-year courses.

Veterinary College: Mogadishu; 10 teachers; 30 students; Projects Dir Dr J. NEILSEN.

SOUTH AFRICA

The Higher Education System

Higher education institutions predate the formation of the Union of South Africa in 1910, with the oldest being the University of Cape Town (formerly South African College), which was founded in 1829. The development of the higher education system in the 20th century was affected by the 'apartheid' (segregation) laws imposed by the National Party in the period 1948–91, which resulted in the emergence of historically 'white' and 'black' universities and technikons (tertiary education institutions offering technological and commercial vocational training). In 1986 the 'quota clause' of the governing Universities Act was abolished and institutions were free to admit students regardless of race or ethnicity; by 1991 all the apartheid laws had been repealed. In 1999 there were 21 universities and 15 technikons. In 2002 it was announced that the number of universities was to be reduced to 11, the number of technikons reduced to six, and that four comprehensive institutions and two national higher education institutes would be created. These changes were implemented during 2004–05. In 2004 there were 744,488 students enrolled in 29 public institutions of higher education and 394,027 in further education and training.

Higher education is principally funded by the Government and administered by the Ministry of Higher Education and Training (formed when the Ministry of Education was controversially split in two in 2009), under the terms of the Higher Education Act (1997). The government of a University is the duty of the Council, which comprises senior officers, such as the Vice-Chancellor, staff representatives, students, alumni and local government officials, among others. The Senate is the supreme academic body, and is made up of Heads of Department and Professors. Faculty Boards are subordinate to the Senate. The Vice-Chancellor, Rector or Principal is the chief executive officer. The government budget and students' tuition fees are the main sources of higher education funding.

The Senior Certificate was gradually phased out in favour of the National School Certificate as the main criterion for admission to higher education and this process was completed by 2009. Undergraduate admissions are administered by the Matriculation Board of the Higher Education South Africa (formed in 2005 from the amalgamation of the South African Universities Vice-Chancellors Association and the Committee of Technikon Principals). The main undergraduate degree is the 'Ordinary' or 'Honours' Bachelors, which is often a three-year programme of study, although some professionally related fields of study, such as architecture, dentistry and medicine, last upwards of five years. A Bachelors with 'Honours' is required for admission to the postgraduate Masters degree, a one- or two-year course of research. Finally, the Doctorate is the highest university degree, and requires a minimum research period of two years after the award of the Masters.

Tertiary-level technical and vocational education is principally offered by the technikons. In addition to non-university Certificates and Diplomas, the technikons offer university-level degrees with a professional or technical focus. The Bachelor of Technology is a four-year undergraduate degree, the Master of Technology is a one-year postgraduate research degree and the Doctor of Technology is a two-year research project following the award of the Master of Technology.

The Council on Higher Education (CHE) has been established in terms of the Higher Education Act, 1997 (Act 101 of 1997) and is responsible for quality assurance in higher education and training by accrediting private providers and programmes. Standard-setting has been added as a core function of the CHE and new structures and regulations were expected to be drafted in 2008.

Regulatory and Representative Bodies

GOVERNMENT

Ministry of Arts and Culture: Private Bag X899, Pretoria 0001; 481 Church St, 10th Floor, cnr Church and Beatrix Sts, Kingsley Centre, Arcadia, Pretoria; tel. (12) 441-3709; fax (12) 440-4485; e-mail sandile.memela@dac.gov.za; internet www.dac.gov.za; Minister Dr Z. PALLO JORDAN; Dir-Gen. THEMBINKOSI PHILEMON WAKASHE.

Ministry of Education: Private Bag X895, Pretoria, 0001; Sol Plaatje House, 123 Schoeman St, Pretoria 0002; tel. (12) 312-5911; fax (12) 321-6770; e-mail webmaster@doe.gov.za; internet www.education.gov.za; Minister G. NALEDI PANDOR; Dir-Gen. DUNCAN HINDLE.

ACCREDITATION

Council for Quality Assurance in General and Further Education and Training: Post Net Suite 102, Private Bag X 1, Queenswood, Pretoria 0121; 37 General Van Ryneveld St, Persequor Techno Park, Pretoria; tel. (12) 349-1510; fax (12) 349-1511; e-mail info@umalusi.org.za; internet www.umalusi.org.za; monitors and improves the quality of gen. and further education and training in SA; Chair. Prof. JOHN D. VOLMINK; CEO Dr PELIWE LOLWANA.

Higher Education Quality Committee (HEQC): POB 13354, The Tramshed, Pretoria 0126; Didacta Bldg, 211 Skinner St, Pretoria 0001; tel. (12) 392-9100; fax (12) 392-9110; e-mail admin@che.ac.za; internet www.che.ac.za/heqc/heqc.php; the HEQC is in the process of implementing new audit and accreditation systems as well as supporting capacity devt in a number of areas; CEO Prof. CHERYL DE LA REY.

NATIONAL BODIES

Council on Higher Education: POB 13354, The Tramshed, Pretoria 0126; Didacta Bldg, 211 Skinner St, Pretoria 0001; tel. (12) 392-9100; fax (12) 392-9110; e-mail admin@che.ac.za; internet www.che.ac.za; f. 1998; aims to contribute to the devt of a higher education system characterized by quality and excellence, equity, responsiveness to economic and social devt needs, and effective and efficient provision, governance and management; CEO Prof. CHERYL DE LA REY.

Higher Education South Africa: POB 27392, Sunnyside, Pretoria 0132; UNISA Sunnyside Campus, Bldg 3, Level 1, cnr Rissik and Mears St, Sunnyside, Pretoria; tel. (12) 481-2842; fax (12) 481-2843; e-mail admin@hesa.org.za; internet www.hesa.org.za; f. 2005; works to enhance the role and contribution of higher education in society; aims to contribute to nat. devt goals through critical enquiry, and scholarly and intellectual leadership; 23 mems (public univs and univs of technology); Chair. Dr T. ELOFF; CEO Prof. DUMA MALAZA.

International Education Association of South Africa: POB 27394, Sunnyside, Pretoria 0132; Room 2–11, Level 1, Bldg 3, UNISA Sunnyside Campus Cnr. Rissik & Mears Sts, Sunnyside, Pretoria 0002; tel. (12) 481-2908; fax (12) 649-1247; e-mail admin@ieasa.studysa.org; internet www.ieasa.studysa.org; f. 1997; advocates, promotes and supports internationalization of higher education by providing a professional forum for instns and individuals to address challenges and develop opportunities in int. education; Pres. MERLE HODGES; Exec. Dir Dr ROSHEN KISHUN.

Matriculation Board: POB 3854, Pretoria 0001; Ground Fl., Bldg 3, Unisa Sunnyside North Campus, cnr Rissik and Mears St, Sunnyside, Pretoria; tel. (12) 481-2848; fax (12) 481-2922; e-mail exemption@hesa-enrol.ac.za; internet www.hesa-enrol.ac.za/mb; f. 1997; advisory cttee on minimum gen. univ. admission requirements to Higher Education South Africa; Chair. HUGH AMOORE (acting).

National Association of Distance Education and Open Learning in South Africa (NADEOSA): POB 31822, Braamfontein, Johannesburg 2017; tel. (11) 403-2813; fax (11) 403-2814; e-mail info@saide.org.za; internet www.nadeosa.org.za; f. 1996; 55 mem. orgs; Pres. RACHEL PRINSLOO.

Learned Societies

GENERAL

Royal Society of South Africa: P. D. Hahn Bldg, POB 594, Cape Town 8000; tel. (21) 650-2543; fax (21) 650-2710; e-mail roysoc@science.uct.ac.za; internet www.rssa.uct.ac.za; f. 1877 to advance all aspects of science; Royal Charter 1908; 490 mems (193 fellows, 40 hon. foreign fellows, 257 ordinary mems); library of 33,000 vols of scientific periodicals; Pres. Prof. D. E. Rawlings; Gen. Sec. Prof. R. L. Christie; Foreign Sec. Prof. M. N. Bruton; publ. *Transactions* (1 a year).

South African Academy of Science and Arts/Suid-Afrikaanse Akademie vir Wetenskap en Kuns: Private Bag X11, Arcadia, Pretoria 0007; tel. (12) 328-5082; fax (12) 328-5091; e-mail akademie@akademie.co.za; internet www.akademie.co.za; f. 1909 for the promotion of science, technology, arts and the Afrikaans language; 1,000 mems; Chair. Prof. T. Erasmus; Sec. Prof. L. R. McFarlane; publs *Nuusbrief* (2 a year), *SA Tydskrif vir Natuurwetenskappe en Tegnologie* (4 a year), *Tydskrif vir Geesteswetenskappe* (4 a year).

AGRICULTURE, FISHERIES AND VETERINARY SCIENCE

South African Society for Animal Science/Suid-Afrikaanse Vereniging vir Veekunde: POB 13884, Hatfield, Pretoria 0028; tel. (12) 420-5017; fax (12) 420-3290; e-mail secretary@sasas.co.za; internet www.sasas.co.za; f. 1961; advances animal science and promotes viable animal production systems; 400 mems; Pres. E. C. Webb; Sec. Prof. J. B. J. van Ryssen; publs *Applied Animal Husbandry & Rural Development*, *South African Journal of Animal Science* (4 a year).

South African Society of Dairy Technology: POB 1853, Silverton 01217; tel. (12) 804-0818; fax (12) 804-9692; e-mail dairy-foundation@pixie.co.za; f. 1967; 400 mems; Pres. A. P. De Klerk; Sec. Y. E. Steyn.

Southern African Institute of Forestry/Suider-Afrikaanse Instituut van Bosswese: Postnet Suite 329, P/Bag X4, Menlo Park 0102; tel. (12) 348-1745; fax (12) 348-1745; e-mail forestry@mweb.co.za; internet www.saif.org.za; f. 1937; aims to collect and publish information on all aspects of forestry, to conserve the forest estate, to encourage the practice of scientific forestry, to create a forum for discussion of topics related to forestry; 560 mems; Chair. G. Marais; Sec.-Treas. C. Viljoen; publ. *Southern African Forestry Journal* (3 a year).

ARCHITECTURE AND TOWN PLANNING

South African Institute of Architects: Private Bag X10063, Randburg 2125; Bouhof, 31 Robin Hood Rd, Robindale, Randburg; tel. (11) 782-1315; fax (11) 782-8771; e-mail admin@saia.org.za; internet www.saia.org.za; f. 1996 by merger of existing organizations; professional voluntary association of architects; 2,600 mems; Exec. Officer S. Linning; publs *Architecture South Africa* (6 a year), *Digest of South African Architecture* (1 a year).

BIBLIOGRAPHY, LIBRARY SCIENCE AND MUSEOLOGY

Library and Information Association of South Africa (LIASA): POB 1598, Pretoria 0001; LIASA House, 228 Proes St, Pretoria Central; tel. (12) 323-4912; fax (12) 323-1033; e-mail liasa@liasa.org.za; internet www.liasa.org.za; f. 1997; advocates, supports and promotes the provision of efficient, user-orientated library and information services; develops library and information services profession; offers networking, education, training and devt and professional recognition opportunities; 3,000 mems; Pres. Naomi Haasbroek; Pres.-Elect Ujala Satgoor; publ. *South African Journal of Libraries and Information Science* (2 a year).

South African Museums Association: POB 12413, Central Hill, Port Elizabeth 6006; tel. (11) 936-7754; fax (86) 503-4521; e-mail sama@futurserve.co.za; internet www.samaweb.org.za; f. 1936; membership-based professional nat. museums asscn; 400 mems incl. 150 institutional mems; Pres. Ishmael Mbhokodo; publs *Samab Conference Bulletin* (1 a year), *Samantics* (Newsletter, 4 a year).

ECONOMICS, LAW AND POLITICS

Economic Society of South Africa: Department of Economics, University of South Africa, POB 302, Pretoria 0001; tel. (11) 429-4878; internet www.essa.org.za; f. 1925 to promote the thorough discussion of and research into economic questions, in particular those affecting South Africa; 550 mems, incl. 6 honorary mems, 14 life members, 22 foreign members; brs in Bloemfontein, Cape Town, Eastern Cape, Johannesburg, Kwazulu-Natal, Limpopo, North-West, Pretoria and Stellenbosch; Pres. Prof. Elsabé Loots; publ. *The South African Journal of Economics* (4 a year).

Institute of Bankers in South Africa: POB 61420, Marshalltown 2107; 1st Fl., Sunnyside Ridge Bldg, Sunnyside Office Park, 32 Princess of Wales Terrace, Parktown; tel. (11) 481-7000; fax (11) 484-8716; e-mail iobinfo@iob.co.za; internet www.iob.co.za; f. 1904; 20,000 mems; Chief Exec. Phil Mnisi; Pres. T. A. Boardman; publ. *South African Banker* (4 a year).

South African Institute of International Affairs: POB 31596, Braamfontein, Johannesburg 2017; Jan Smuts House, East Campus, University of the Witwatersrand, Johannesburg; tel. (11) 339-2021; fax (11) 339-2154; e-mail saiiagen@global.co.za; internet www.saiia.org.za; f. 1934 to promote understanding of international issues among South Africans; 3,500 mems; library: Jan Smuts Library; 10,000 books, 2,000 journals; spec. collns incl. UN depository colln, World Bank regional depository library, Martin Edmonds colln; Chair. of the Nat. Ccl Fred Phaswana; Nat. Dir Elizabeth Sidiropoulos; publs *eAfrica* (online, 12 a year), *SADC Barometer* (online, 12 a year), *South African Foreign Policy Monitor* (online, 6 a year), *South African Journal of International Affairs* (2 a year), *South African Yearbook of International Affairs*.

FINE AND PERFORMING ARTS

Federasie van Afrikaanse Kultuurvereniginge (Association of Afrikaans Cultural Societies): POB 73169, Lynnwoodrif 0040; Gerard Moerdyk-huis, Voortrekkermonumentterrein Eeufeesweg, Pretoria; tel. (12) 326-8646; fax (12) 326-9171; e-mail fak@mweb.co.za; internet www.fak.org.za; f. 1929; 2,300 affiliated socs; Chair. Prof. Danie Goosen; Dir Dr Carel Stander; publ. *Handhaaf Newsletter* (3 a year).

South African National Association for the Visual Arts (SANAVA): POB 6188, Pretoria 0001; tel. (12) 460-5862; fax (12) 323-1275; f. 1851 as the Cape Fine Arts Society; became the South African Fine Arts Asscn in 1871; became the South African Asscn of Arts in 1945; mem. of Int. Asscn of Art; present name 1998; encourages visual arts nationally and internationally; 23 autonomous brs with individual galleries, management cttees, as well as 22 affiliated orgs; 5,500 mems; Nat. Pres. Anton Loubser; Vice-Pres Lynette den Krooden, Helen Weldrick; Hon. Consultant for Social Devt Avitha Sooful; Treas. Basie Botha.

HISTORY, GEOGRAPHY AND ARCHAEOLOGY

Genealogical Society of South Africa: Suite 143, Postnet X2600, Houghton 2041; e-mail tesourier@ggsa.info; internet www.ggsa.info; tel. (86) 672-2412; f. 1964; promotes and facilitates interest in genealogy and family history; brs in Pretoria, Cape Town, Johannesburg, Western Gauteng, Vanderbijlpark, Bloemfontein, Durban, Pietermaritzburg, Port Elizabeth, Potchefstroom; 900 mems; Pres. Johann Janse Van Vuuren; Sec. Marilyn Coetzee; publ. *Familia* (4 a year).

Nederlands Cultuurhistorisch Instituut: University of Pretoria, Pretoria 0002; tel. (12) 420-2808; fax (12) 362-5100; e-mail pieter.vandermerwe@up.ac.za; internet www.up.ac.za; f. 1931; offers books and information on Dutch culture, history and art; 250 mems; library of 32,000 vols; Dir Robert Moropa.

Society of South African Geographers: Dept of Geography (53), POB 339, Univ. of the Free State, Bloemfontein 9301; tel. (51) 401-2184; fax (51) 401-3816; e-mail britss@ufs.ac.za; internet www.ssag.co.za; f. 1994 by merger of existing orgs; 400 mems; Pres. Prof. Cecil Seethal; Hon. Sec. Lt-Col J. A. Jacobs; publ. *South African Geographical Journal* (2 a year).

South African Archaeological Society: POB 15700, Vlaeberg 8018; tel. (21) 481-3886; fax (21) 481-3993; e-mail archsoc@iziko.org.za; internet www.archaeology.org.za; f. 1945; 1,000 mems; library of 1,000 vols, 5,000 periodicals; Hon. Sec. J. Deacon; publs *The Digging Stick* (3 a year), *Goodwin Series* (irregular), *South African Archaeological Bulletin* (2 a year).

Van Riebeeck Society: POB 15151, Vlaeberg 8018; Centre for the Book, 62, Queen Victoria St, Cape Town 8000; tel. (21) 423-8424; fax (86) 670-9828; e-mail vanriebk@mweb.co.za; internet www.vanriebeecksociety.co.za; f. 1918; publishes and republishes original and rare documents, books and pamphlets relating to the history of Southern Africa; 1,075 mems; Chair. Prof. H. Phillips; Sec. P. E. Westra; Sec. Dr Cora Ovens.

LANGUAGE AND LITERATURE

Alliance Française: POB 72067, Parkview 2122; 17 Lower Park Dr., Cnr Kerry Rd, Johannesburg; tel. (11) 646-1169; fax (11) 646-4521; e-mail info@alliance.org.za; internet www.alliance.org.za; f. 1936; offers courses and exams in French language and culture and promotes cultural exchange with France; attached teaching centres in Bloemfontein, Bosmont, Cape Town, Diepkloof, Durban, East London, Florida Hills, Klerksdorp, Lowveld, Mitchell's Plain, Nelspruit, Parkview, Pietermaritzburg, Port Elizabeth, Potchefstroom, Pretoria, Somerset West, Soweto, Stellenbosch, Vaal Triangle, Vanderbijlpark, Vlaeberg and Welkom; also responsible for Alliance Française operations in Botswana, Lesotho and Swaziland.

British Council: Ground Fl., Forum 1, Braampark, 33 Hoofd St, Braamfontein, Johannesburg; tel. (11) 718-4300; fax (11) 718-4400; e-mail information@britishcouncil.org.za; internet www.britishcouncil.org/africa-south-africa.htm; offers courses and exams in English language and British culture and promotes cultural exchange with the UK; attached offices in Johannesburg (teaching centre), Cape Town and Durban; responsible for British Council activities in Botswana, Lesotho, Malawi, Mauritius, Mozambique, Namibia, Swaziland, Zambia and Zimbabwe; Regional Dir, Southern Africa ROSEMARY ARNOTT; Dir of Operations, South Africa DAVID HIGGS.

Classical Association of South Africa: c/o Academia Latina, Univ. of Pretoria, Pretoria 0002; tel. (12) 420-2368; fax (12) 420-4008; internet www.casa-kvsa.org.za; f. 1965 to promote the study and appreciation of classical antiquity; 350 mems; Chair. J. L. HILTON; Sec. M. R. DIRCKSEN; publs *Acta Classica* (1 a year), *Akroterion* (1 a year).

English Academy of Southern Africa: POB 124, WITS, Johannesburg 2050; tel. (11) 717-9339; fax (11) 717-9339; e-mail englishacademy@societies.wits.ac.za; internet www.englishacademy.co.za; f. 1961; concerned with all forms and uses of English; promotes education, research and debate; organizes lectures and promotes creative, critical and scholarly talents of users of English in Southern Africa; awards the English Academy Medal, the Olive Schreiner Prize, the Thomas Pringle Awards, the Percy FitzPatrick Prize, and the Sol Plaatje Prize for Translation for translation; over 300 mems; Pres. Prof STANLEY RIDGE; Hon. Sec. DAVID ROBINSON; publ. *The English Academy Review: Southern African Journal of English Studies* (2 a year, online).

Goethe-Institut: 119 Jan Smuts Ave, Parkwood 2193, Johannesburg; tel. (11) 442-3232; fax (11) 442-3738; e-mail info@johannesburg .goethe.org; internet www.goethe.de/ johannesburg; offers courses and exams in German language and culture and promotes cultural exchange with Germany; attached centre in Cape Town; library of 7,600 vols, incl. books, magazines, newspapers, audio and video tapes and DVDs; Regional Dir for Sub-Saharan Africa Dr KATHARINA VON RUCKTESCHELL-KATTE.

South African PEN Centre: POB 732, Constantia 7848; e-mail rudebs@icon.co.za; internet www.sapen.co.za; f. 1960; 165 mems (155 full, 10 assoc.); Sec. DEBORAH HORN-BOTHA.

MEDICINE

Association of Surgeons of South Africa/ Chirurgiese Vereniging van Suid-Africa: POB 1105, Johannesburg, Cramerview 2132; tel. (11) 706-4815; fax (11) 463-1041; e-mail surgicom@worldonline.co.za; internet www.surgeon.co.za; f. 1945; 250 mems; Pres. Prof. M. R. Q. DAVIES; Chair. Dr S. S. PILLAY; publ. *South African Journal of Surgery*.

Colleges of Medicine of South Africa: 17 Milner Rd, Rondebosch 7700; tel. (21) 689-9533; fax (21) 685-3766; e-mail admin@ colmedsa.co.za; internet www.collegemedsa .ac.za; f. 1954; provides postgraduate examinations in all branches of medicine for all doctors and dentists in South Africa; 9,000 mems; library: small archive and reference library; CEO and Sec. BERNISE BOTHMA; publ. *Transactions* (2 a year).

Nutrition Society of Southern Africa: POB 1697, Brits 0250; tel. (82) 667-4723; fax (12) 521-3510; internet www .nutritionsociety.co.za; f. 1955 to advance the scientific study of nutrition; 235 mems; Pres. Prof. ESTÉ VORSTER; Chair. Dr MARIUS SMUTS; Sec. P. M. N. KUZWAYO; publ. *The South African Journal of Food Science and Nutrition*.

South African Medical Association: Private Bag X1, Pinelands 7430, Cape Town; Block F, Castle Walk, Office Park, Nossob St, Erasmuskloof Ext. 3, Pretoria; tel. (21) 481-2000; fax (21) 481-2100; e-mail online@ samedical.org; internet www.samedical.org; f. 1998 from existing organizations; 16,000 mems; professional org. for medical practitioners in South Africa; Pres. Prof. RALPH KIRSCH; Chair. (vacant); publs *Continued Medical Education* (12 a year), *South African Medical Journal* (12 a year).

South African Pharmacology Society: Box 16, Pharmacology, North-West Univ., Potchefstroom 2520; tel. (18) 299-2304; fax (18) 299-2447; e-mail office@sapharmacol.co .za; internet www.sapharmacol.co.za; f. 1966; promotes and develops interest in teaching and research in basic and clinical pharmacology; promotes communication and cooperation between socs and industry representing pharmacology and related disciplines; creates forums to present and exchange ideas with state and provincial depts, local and other authorities; 154 mems; Pres. Prof. WIM DU PLOOY; Vice-Pres. CHRISTIAAN BRINK; Sec. Prof. VANESSA STEENKAMP.

South African Society of Obstetricians and Gynaecologists: POB 363, Tongaat 4400; tel. (83) 944-1308; e-mail biggles@ ispace.co.za; internet www.sasog.co.za; f. 1946; 571 mems; Pres. Dr A. B. KOLLER; Sec. Dr M. PILLAY.

NATURAL SCIENCES

General

Associated Scientific and Technical Societies of South Africa: POB 93480, Yeoville 2143; located at: 18A Gill St, Observatory 2198; tel. (11) 487-1512; fax (11) 648-1876; f. 1920; to promote the interests of scientific, professional and technical societies; to advance the knowledge of scientific and technical subjects; to assist in raising the standard of mathematics and science for underprivileged scholars; to raise awareness of career prospects in technology; and to provide secretarial, liaison, and meeting facilities, etc., for its member societies; 60,000 mems in 51 mem. socs; Pres. A. S. MEYER; Man. ERROL H. VAN ROOY.

Southern Africa Association for the Advancement of Science: POB 366, Irene 0062; tel. and fax (12) 667-2544; e-mail s2a3@ global.co.za; internet s2a3.up.ac.za; f. 1902; 83 mems; Pres. Dr I. RAPER; Hon. Sec. S. A. KORSMAN.

Biological Sciences

BirdLife South Africa: POB 515, Randburg 2125, Johannesburg; 239 Barkston Dr., Blairgowrie, Johannesburg; tel. (11) 789-1122; fax (11) 789-5188; e-mail info@birdlife .org.za; internet www.birdlife.org.za; f. 1930; 6,000 mems; Pres. Prof. PETER RYAN; Dir M. D. ANDERSON; publs *Africa Birds and Birding* (6 a year), *Ostrich* (4 a year).

Botanical Society of South Africa: Private Bag X10, Claremont 7735; tel. (21) 797-2090; fax (21) 797-2376; e-mail info@ botanicalsociety.org.za; internet www .botanicalsociety.org.za; f. 1913; 15,000 mems; promotes the conservation, cultivation, wise use and study of the indigenous flora of Southern Africa; Pres. Adv. A. B. MEIRING; Dir ZAITOON RABANEY; publ. *Veld and Flora* (4 a year).

Herpetological Association of Africa: Dept of Herpetology, National Museum, POB 266, Bloemfontein 9300; e-mail herp@ nasmus.co.za; internet www.wits.ac.za/haa; promotes the study and conservation of reptiles and amphibians, especially African species; Chair. MICHAEL F. BATES; Sec. ROSE SEPHTON-POULTNEY; publs *African Herp News*, *African Journal of Herpetology*.

South African National Biodiversity Institute: Head Office: Private Bag X101, Pretoria 0001; tel. (12) 843-5000; fax (12) 804-3200; e-mail info@sanbi.org; internet www.sanbi.org; f. 1913 as the Nat. Botanical Institute; present name 2004; promotes the conservation, sustainable use and appreciation of South Africa's biodiversity; library: libraries at Pretoria and Kirstenbosch with 15,500 vols; Chief Exec. SUNJIT SINGH (acting); publs *Bothalia* (2 a year), *Strelitzia* (irregular), *Flowering Plants of Africa* (2 a year).

Southern African Society of Aquatic Scientists: c/o Dr Nico Smit, Centre for Aquatic Research, Department of Zoology, University of Johannesburg, POB 524, Auckland Park 2006; tel. (11) 559-2457; fax (11) 559-2286; e-mail nicos@uj.ac.za; internet www.riv.co.za/sasaqs; f. 1964 as Limnological Society of South Africa; holds annual congresses and general meetings; 250 mems; Pres. Prof. WYNAND VLOK; Hon. Sec. and Treas. Dr PAUL FOUCHE; Vice-Pres. Dr JAN ROOS; publ. *African Journal of Aquatic Science* (3 a year).

South African Society of Biochemistry and Molecular Biology: c/o Dept of Biochemistry, Microbiology and Biotechnology, Rhodes Univ,. Grahamstown 6140; tel. (46) 603-8262; fax (46) 622-3984; e-mail g.blatch@ ru.ac.za; internet www.sasbmb.org.za; f. 1973; 450 mems; Pres. Prof. GREG BLATCH; Sec. FOURIE JOUBERT.

South African Society for Microbiology: Dept of Biotechnology, University of the Free State, POB 339, Bloemfontein 9300; tel. (51) 401-2223; fax (51) 444-3219; internet www .sasm.za.net; 420 mems; Pres. Dr KOOS ALBERTYN; Sec. Dr EVODIA SETATI.

Southern African Wildlife Management Association: POB 217, Bloubergstrand 7436; tel. (21) 554-1297; fax (86) 672-9882; e-mail elma@mweb.co.za; internet www .sawma.co.za; f. 1970; 370 mems; Pres. Dr CHRISTO MARAIS; Vice-Pres. and Treasurer JULIUS KOEN; publ. *South African Journal of Wildlife Research*.

WESSA – Wildlife and Environment Society of South Africa: 1 Karkloof Rd, POB 394, Howick 3290; tel. (33) 330-3931; fax (33) 330-4576; e-mail marketing@wessa .co.za; internet www.wessa.org.za; f. 1926; 5,500 mems; Chair. Dr RICHARD LEWIS; Hon. Treas. JAMES PINNELL; publs *EnviroKids* (in English, 4 a year), *Environment*.

Physical Sciences

Astronomical Society of Southern Africa: POB 9, Observatory 7935; tel. (21) 447-0025; e-mail assa@saao.ac.za; internet assa.saao.ac.za; f. 1922; 250 mems; Pres. MICHAEL POLL; Hon. Sec. LAURIE SIMONE; publs *Monthly Notes* (6 a year), *SkyGuide Africa South* (1 a year).

Geological Society of South Africa: POB 61809, Marshalltown 2107; Chamber of Mines Bldg, 5th Fl., 5 Hollard St, Marshalltown; tel. (11) 492-3370; fax (11) 492-3371; e-mail info@gssa.org.za; internet www.gssa .org.za; f. 1895; promotes the study of the earth sciences, facilitates the professional devt of its members, and advances the use of geoscience in the academic, professional, and public sectors; 2,700 mems, incl. 500 student mems; Exec. Man. CRAIG SMITH; publs *Geobulletin* (4 a year), *South African Journal of Geology* (4 a year).

South African Chemical Institute: POB 407, Witwatersrand 2050; Humphrey Raikes Bldg, Rm 500, Wits Campus, Witwatersrand; tel. (11) 717-6741; fax (11) 717-6779; e-mail saci@aurum.wits.ac.za; internet www.saci.co.za; f. 1912; promotes chemistry and chemical industry in South Africa; 755 mems; Pres. Prof. IVAN GREEN; Vice-Pres. Prof. JAMES DARKWA; publ. *South African Journal of Chemistry* (4 a year).

South African Institute of Physics: Postnet Suite 165, Private Bag X025, Lynnwood Ridge 0040; tel. (12) 841-2627; fax (86) 648-8474; e-mail secretary@saip.org.za; internet www.saip.org.za; f. 1955; 540 mems; Pres. Dr PETER MARTINEZ; Council Sec. Dr JACKIE NEL; Exec. Officer BRIAN MASARA.

RELIGION, SOCIOLOGY AND ANTHROPOLOGY

South African Institute of Race Relations: Private Bag X13, Marshalltown, 2107 Johannesburg; tel. (11) 492-0600; fax (11) 492-0588; e-mail sairr@sairr.org.za; internet www.sairr.org.za; f. 1929; research, publishing, bursary admin.; library: J. H. Hofmeyer Library specializing in South African current affairs incl. 120 journals, historical documents, statistics, biographies; Pres. J. D. JANSEN; Chief Exec J. S. KANE-BERMAN; publs *Fast Facts* (12 a year), *South Africa Survey* (1 a year).

TECHNOLOGY

Aeronautical Society of South Africa (AeSSA): POB 14717, Sinoville 0129; tel. and fax (12) 808-1359; internet www.aessa.org.za; f. 1911 to advance the growth and scientific study of aeronautics; merged with South African Institute of Aerospace Engineering and the Royal Division of AeSSA 2001, to form Royal Aeronautical Society of South Africa (RAeSSA); present name 2005 (while retaining Royal Division status); theoretical and practical research; offers advice, instruction and facilities for those studying the subject; organizes meetings, lectures, etc.; 20,000 mems; Chair. Dr ROB HURLIN; Hon. Sec. Dr C. LAW.

Chartered Institute of Transport in Southern Africa: POB 95327, Grant Park 2051; tel. (11) 888-1813; fax (11) 782-8265; e-mail citsa@global.co.za; f. 1993; 700 mems; Pres. MALCOLM F. MITCHELL; Exec. Man. C. LARKIN; publs *CITSA Handbook* (1 a year), *Pegasus* (4 a year).

Institution of Certificated Mechanical and Electrical Engineers, South Africa: POB 93480, Yeoville 2143; 18A Gill St, Observatory, Johannesburg 2198; tel. (11) 487-1683; fax (8667) 18533; e-mail icmee@pixie.co.za; internet www.icmeesa.com; f. 1912; 1,444 mems; Pres. CHRIS SCHNEHAGE; Hon. Treas. ROBBY HOLMWOOD; publ. *Vector Magazine* (12 a year).

South African Institute of Agricultural Engineers/Suid-Afrikaanse Instituut van Landbou-Ingenieurs: POB 912-719, Silverton 0127; tel. (12) 804-1540; fax (12) 804-0753; f. 1964; 500 mems; meetings, lectures, symposia, etc.; awards study bursaries; Pres. Prof. P. W. L. LYNE; Sec. F. B. REINDERS; publ. *Agricultural Engineering in South Africa* (1 a year).

South African Chemical Institute: The Secretary, South African Chemical Institute, POB 407, Witwatersrand 2050; e-mail saci.chem@wits.ac.za; f. 1919; upholds the status and interests of the profession of assaying in all its brs; 900 mems; Administrator L SMITH; publ. *South African Journal of Chemistry* (online).

South African Institute of Electrical Engineers: POB 751253, Gardenview 2047; Innes House, 18A Gill St, Observatory, Johannesburg; tel. (11) 487-3003; fax (11) 487-3002; e-mail info@saiee.org.za; internet www.saiee.org.za; f. 1909; 5,000 mems; Pres. ANDRIES TSHABALALA; Sr Sec. GERDA GEYER; Dir STAN BRIDGENS; publs *SAIEE Africa Research Journal* (4 a year), *WATTnow* (12 a year).

South African Institute of Mining and Metallurgy: POB 61127, Marshalltown 2107; 5th Fl., Chamber of Mines Bldg, 5 Hollard St, Johannesburg; tel. (11) 834-1273; fax (11) 838-5923; e-mail carina@saimm.co.za; internet www.saimm.co.za; f. 1884; 3,000 mems; Pres. Dr WILLEM VAN NIEKERK; Man. CARINA REYNDERS; publ. *Journal* (6 a year).

South African Institution of Civil Engineering (SAICE): Private Bag X200, Halfway House 1685; Building 19, Thornhill Office Park, Bekker St, Vorna Valley, Midrand; tel. (11) 805-5947; fax (11) 805-5971; e-mail civilinfo@saice.org.za; internet www.civils.org.za; f. 1903; represents the civil engineering profession in South Africa; 6,571 mems; Exec. Dir D. B. BOTHA; publs *Civil Engineering* (magazine, 11 a year), *Journal* (technical journal for research papers, 4 a year).

South African Institution of Mechanical Engineering: POB 511, Bruma 2026; tel. (11) 615-5660; fax (11) 388-5356; e-mail saimeche@iafrica.com; internet www.saimeche.org.za; f. 1892; 4,500 mems; Pres. Prof. H. L. T. JEFFERY; Hon. Treasurer G. BARBIC; publs *R&D Journal* (4 a year), *SA Mechanical Engineer* (12 a year).

Research Institutes

GENERAL

Africa Institute of South Africa: POB 630, Pretoria 0001; Embassy House, cnr of Edmond St and Bailey Lane, Arcadia, Pretoria; tel. (12) 304-9760; fax (12) 323-8153; e-mail ai@ai.org.za; internet www.ai.org.za; f. 1960; applied research and the colln of information in the fields of politics, socio-economics, devt and int. relations on the African continent and its diaspora; CEO Dr MATLOTLENG P. MATLOU; publs *Africa Insight* (4 a year), *Inside AISA* (newsletter, 6 a year).

Council for Scientific and Industrial Research (CSIR): POB 395, Pretoria 0001; Meiring Naudé Rd, Brummeria, Pretoria; tel. (12) 841-2911; fax (12) 841-4326; e-mail callcentre@csir.co.za; internet www.csir.co.za; f. 1945; directed and multi-disciplinary research in areas of biosciences, built environment, natural resources and the environment, defence, peace, safety and security, materials science and manufacturing; and in emerging research areas of nanotechnology, synthetic biology, and mobile autonomous intelligent systems; provides consulting and analytical services incl. forensic fire investigations, food and beverage analysis, environmental testing, engineering forensics, wire rope testing, mechanical testing, fires and explosion testing, sports technology and analysis, and project management; library: see Libraries and Archives; Pres. and CEO Dr SIBUSISO SIBISI; Chief Financial Officer EBIE MAYET; Group Exec. for Operations HOFFIE MAREE; Exec. Dir Services RAYNOLD ZONDO; Group Exec. for Research and Devt Outcomes and Strategic Human Capital Devt KHUNGEKA NJOBE; publs *CSIR eNews* (electronic newsletter, 6 a year), *ScienceScope* (4 a year), research reports.

AGRICULTURE, FISHERIES AND VETERINARY SCIENCE

Agricultural Research Council: POB 8783, Pretoria 0001; 1134 Park St, Hatfield, Pretoria; tel. (12) 427-9700; fax (12) 342-3948; e-mail nkami@arc.agric.za; internet www.arc.agric.za; f. 1992; Pres. and CEO Dr N. TAU-MZAMANE.

Attached Research Institutes:

Agrimetrics Institute: Private Bag X5013, Stellenbosch 7599; tel. (12) 342-9968; fax (12) 342-9969; interdisciplinary service of biometrical and datametrical input to all institutes of the Agricultural Research Ccl; planning of scientific experiments, analysis and interpretation of research results; datametric service for devt and application of scientific data and management of computer systems; Dir Dr PIET JOOSTE.

Animal Improvement Institute, Irene: ARC Livestock Division, Private Bag X2, Irene 0062; tel. (12) 672-9055; fax (12) 665-1550; e-mail andrew@arc.agric.za; internet www.arc.agric.za; research and devt in animal breeding and genetics; nutrition and food science; library of 10,000 vols; Dir Dr M. A. MAGADLELA.

Animal Nutrition and Animal Products Institute, Irene: Private Bag X2, Irene 1675; tel. (12) 672-9111; fax (12) 665-1609; research and devt in animal nutrition, meat and dairy products; Dir Dr HEINZ MEISSNER.

ARC Institute for Industrial Crops: Private Bag X82075, Rustenburg 0300; tel. (14) 5363150; fax (14) 5363113; e-mail infoiic@arc.agric.za; internet www.arc.agric.za; basic and applied research on tobacco cotton and industrial crops; Sr Man. Dr GRAHAM THOMPSON; Sr Sec. KAREN SMOOK.

ARC Infruitec-Nietvoorbij: Private Bag X5026, Stellenbosch 7599; tel. (21) 809-3100; fax (21) 809-3400; e-mail breedtk@arc.agric.za; internet www.arc.agric.za; f. 1960; research on the cultivation and post-harvest technology of deciduous fruit, on all aspects of cultivation of table, raisin and wine grapes, and on production of wine and brandy; library of 5,000 vols; Research Man. Dr JOHAN VAN ZYL.

Grain Crops Institute: Private Bag X1251, Potchefstroom 2520; tel. (18) 299-6100; fax (18) 294-7146; f. 1981; research on grain crops and oil and protein seeds; Dir Dr P. J. A. VAN DER MERWE.

Institute for Agricultural Engineering: Private Bag X519, Silverton 0127; tel. (12) 842-4000; fax (12) 804-0753; f. 1961; research on agricultural mechanization, farm structures, irrigation, resource conservation, energy, aquaculture and product processing; Dir Prof. TIMOTHY SIMALONGA.

Institute for Soil, Climate and Water: Private Bag X79, Pretoria 0001; tel. (12) 310-2500; fax (12) 323-1157; e-mail iscwinfo@arc.agric.za; f. 1902; soil science, agrometeorology, water utilization, remote sensing, analytical services; library of 10,000 vols; Research and Technology Man. Dr M. MAILA; Librarian REJAENE VAN DYK.

Institute of Tropical and Subtropical Crops: Private Bag X11208, Nelspruit 1200; tel. (13) 753-2071; fax (13) 752-3854; f. 1926; research on fruit, cocoa, and exotic crops; Dir Dr JOHANN VAN ZYL.

Onderstepoort Veterinary Institute: Private Bag X5, Onderstepoort 0110, Pretoria; tel. (12) 529-9111; fax (12) 565-6573; e-mail ovi-info@arc.agric.za; internet www.arc.agric.za; f. 1908; research on animal diseases; production of vaccines; diagnostic service; library of 96,000 vols; Dir Dr DAAN VERWOERD; Research Institute Man. Prof.

TONY MUSOKE; publ. *Onderstepoort Journal of Veterinary Research* (4 a year).

Plant Protection Research Institute: Private Bag X134, Pretoria 0001; tel. (12) 808-0952; fax (12) 808-1489; promotes economically and environmentally acceptable pest control and sustainable farming; research on invertebrates, fungi, bacteria and viruses; advisory service on aspects of biological control; library of 9,000 vols; Dir MIKE WALTERS.

Range and Forage Institute: Private Bag X05, Lynn East, Pretoria 0039; tel. (12) 841-9611; fax (12) 808-2155; research on sustainable livestock and rangeland management systems; Head Dr AIMIE AUCAMP.

Roodeplaat Vegetable and Ornamental Plant Institute: Private Bag X293, Pretoria 0001; tel. (12) 841-9611; fax (12) 808-0844; f. 1949; research on vegetables, and on cut flowers, pot plants and other ornamental plants; Dir Dr SONJA VENTER; publ. *Roodeplaat Bulletin*.

Small Grain Institute: Private Bag X29, Bethlehem 9700; tel. (58) 307-3400; fax (58) 307-3519; e-mail kilianj@arc.agric.za; internet www.arc.agric.za; f. 1947; research on improvement and cultivation of small grain crops; Man. Dr COBUS LE ROUX.

Attached Unit:

Plant Genetic Resources Unit: c/o The Division Manager, Private Bag X05, Lynn East 0039; tel. (12) 841-9716; fax (12) 808-1001; centralizes and co-ordinates plant genetic resources activities within the plant science institutes and liaises with regional and int. agencies; responsible for documenting Agricultural Research Council germplasm and for arranging safety base collection facilities; Man. Dr ROGER ELLIS.

MEDICINE

National Health Laboratory Service: POB 1038, Johannesburg 2000; 1 Modderfontein Rd, Sandringham, Johannesburg; tel. (11) 386-6000; fax (11) 386-6002; e-mail info@nhls.ac.za; internet www.nhls.ac.za; f. 1912, formerly South African Institute for Medical Research; national network of approx 250 regional pathology laboratories, situated in all provinces except KwaZulu-Natal; co-ordinates diagnostic pathology services, research, teaching, training and production of anti-snake sera, reagents and media; member institutions include the pathology departments and laboratories of the medical schools of the universities of the Witwatersrand, Pretoria, Cape Town, Free State and Transkei and the Medical University of South Africa; library of 17,500 vols, 250 periodical titles, 5,000 reprint titles of staff papers; Chair. of Board of Management SESI BALOYI; CEO JOHN ROBERTSON; Head of Dept of Anatomical Pathology Prof. A. PATTERSON; Head of Dept of Chemical Pathology (vacant); Head of Dept of Clinical Microbiology and Infectious Diseases Prof. A. DUSE; Head of Dept of Haematology Prof. WENDY STEVENS; Head of Dept of Human Genetics Prof. D. VILJOEN; Head of Dept of Immunology Prof. A. A. WADEE; Head of Dept of Medical Entomology Prof. M. COETZEE; publ. *South African Journal of Epidemiology and Infection*.

South African Brain Research Institute: 6 Campbell St, Waverley, Johannesburg 2090; tel. (11) 786-2912; fax (11) 786-1766; e-mail mag@iafrica.com; internet www.sabri.org.za; f. 1981; all aspects of pure and applied brain research; library of 10,000 vols; CEO Prof. M. A. GILLMAN.

South African Medical Research Council: POB 19070, Tygerberg 7505; located at: Francie van Zijl Drive, Parowvallei, Western Cape; tel. (21) 938-0911; fax (21) 938-0200; e-mail info@mrc.ac.za; internet www.mrc.ac.za; f. 1969; nat. research programmes: environment and development, health systems and policy, infection and immunity, molecules to disease, non-communicable diseases, and women and child health; Pres. Prof. ANTHONY MBEWU.

NATURAL SCIENCES

Biological Sciences

Municipal Botanic Gardens: 70 St Thomas Rd, Durban, KwaZulu-Natal; tel. (31) 201-1303; fax (31) 201-7382; e-mail sandig@prcsu.durban.gov.za; internet www.durbanbotanicgardens.org.za; f. 1849, for the propagation, display and landscape of ornamental, exotic and Southern African indigenous flora, and as a place for the study of and instruction in botany and horticulture and potential agricultural crops; extensive collections of orchids, cycads, palms and bromeliads; herb garden; garden for the blind; water lily pond, fern garden; indigenous medicinal plants; Chair. Prof. DONAL MCCRACKEN; Curator, Durban Botanic Gardens C. G. M. DALZELL.

National Zoological Gardens of South Africa: POB 754, Pretoria 0001; located at: 232 Boom St, Pretoria 0001; tel. (12) 328-3265; fax (12) 323-4540; e-mail zoologic@cis.co.za; internet www.zoo.ac.za; f. 1899; attached to National Research Foundation; library of 4,000 vols, 40 periodicals; CEO WILLIE LABUSCHAGNE; publ. *Zoön*.

Physical Sciences

Council for Geoscience: Private Bag X112, Pretoria 0001; 280 Pretoria St, Silverton, Pretoria 0001; tel. (12) 841-1911; fax (12) 841-1221; internet www.geoscience.org.za; f. 1912; applied and fundamental geological research, mapping; library of 200,000 books, 10,000 maps; CEO THIBEDI RAMONTJA; publs bulletins, biographies, handbooks, *Groundwater Series*, *Memoirs*, *Seismological Series*.

Hartebeesthoek Radio Astronomy Observatory: POB 443, Krugersdorp 1740; tel. (12) 326-0742; fax (12) 326-0756; e-mail info@hartrao.ac.za; internet www.hartrao.ac.za; f. 1961, since 1988 a national facility under Foundation for Research Development (now National Research Foundation); radio telescope 26 m in diameter used for observations of Local Galaxy, spectroscopy of interstellar and circumstellar atoms and molecules, masers, pulsars, quasars and active galaxies; collaborates in global VLBI Networks; library of 1,000 vols, 75 periodicals; Dir Prof. ROY BOOTH.

NECSA (South African Nuclear Energy Corporation): POB 582, Pretoria 0001; located at: Church St W Extension, Pelindaba, Brits District; tel. (12) 305-4911; fax (12) 305-3111; e-mail webmaster@necsa.co.za; internet www.necsa.co.za; f. 1982 as Atomic Energy Corporation of South Africa Ltd (AEC); 10 mems; operates UF6 conversion, fuel fabrication facilities, isotope production centre, hot cell facility and food radurization plant; enrichment research; operates 20- MW ORR type research reactor (SAFARI-1); 3.75- MV Van der Graaff accelerator; CEO Dr ROB ADAM.

Satellite Applications Centre: Division of Microelectronics and Communications Technology, CSIR, POB 395, Pretoria 0001; tel. (12) 841-9211; fax (12) 349-1153; e-mail callcentre@csir.co.za; internet www.csir.co.za/sac; f. 1961 as part of US Satellite Tracking and Data Network; since 1975 part of CSIR; receives, archives and processes METEOSAT, LANDSAT, NOAA and SPOT data; online LANDSAT data catalogue; 45 staff; library of 500 vols, 30 periodicals; Operations Man. RAOUL HODGES.

South African Astronomical Observatory: POB 9, Observatory 7935; POB 25, Sutherland 6920; tel. (21) 447-0025; fax (21) 447-3639; e-mail enquiries@saao.ac.za; internet www.saao.ac.za; f. 1972 by a merger of Royal Observatory Cape of Good Hope and Republic Observatory, Johannesburg; equipment incl. 11-, 1.9-, 1.0-, 0.75- and 0.5-m reflectors; library of 30,000 vols; Dir Prof. P. A. CHARLES; Librarian SHIREEN DAVIS.

RELIGION, SOCIOLOGY AND ANTHROPOLOGY

Human Sciences Research Council (HSRC): Private Bag X41, Pretoria 0001; 134 Pretorius St, Pretoria 0002; tel. (12) 302-2000; fax (12) 302-2001; e-mail helpdesk@hsrc.ac.za; internet www.hsrc.ac.za; f. 1969; promotes, supports and coordinates research in the human and social sciences; advises the govt on research priorities; disseminates research findings; promotes the training of people for research work and makes available to all South Africans the full range of disciplines in the human sciences; library of 60,000 vols, 700 current periodicals; Pres. and CEO Dr OLIVE SHISANA; publ. *HSRC Review* (4 a year).

Institute for the Study of Mankind in Africa: School of Anatomical Sciences, University of the Witwatersrand Medical School, 7 York Rd, Parktown 2193; tel. (11) 717-2405; e-mail science.pg@wits.ac.za; f. 1960 to perpetuate the work of Prof. Raymond A. Dart on the study of mankind in Africa, past and present, in health and disease; serves as a centre of anthropological and medical field work; it functions partly through the auspices of the University of the Witwatersrand; Pres. Prof. J. N. MAINA.

TECHNOLOGY

MINTEK: PMB X3015, Randburg 2125; tel. (11) 709-4111; fax (11) 793-2413; e-mail info@mintek.ac.za; internet www.mintek.co.za; f. 1934; research, devt and technology transfer to promote mineral technology and to foster the establishment and expansion of industries in the fields of minerals and mineral products; investigates all aspects of mineral beneficiation, especially areas such as new alloys and chemical products; divs specializing in mineralogy, minerals eng., hydrometallurgy, pyrometallurgy, measurement and control, analytical science, physical metallurgy, analytical and process chemistry; sponsors univ. research groups; library of 30,000 vols; CEO Dr PAUL JOURDAN; publs *Mintek Bulletin* (12 a year), *Research Reports* (irregular).

South African Bureau of Standards: Private Bag X191, 1 Dr Lategan Rd, Groenkloof, Pretoria 0001; tel. (12) 428-7911; fax (12) 344-1568; e-mail info@sabs.co.za; internet www.sabs.co.za; f. 1945; draws up national standards, administers the SABS mark and listing schemes; Pres. M. J. KUSCUS (acting); publ. *Standards Bulletin: Official information* (online).

Libraries and Archives

Alice

University of Fort Hare Library: Private Bag X1322, Alice 5700; tel. (40) 602-2612; fax

(40) 653-1423; f. 1916; 165,000 vols; contains the Howard Pim Library of Rare Books; University Librarian YOLISA K. SOUL.

Bloemfontein

Free State Library and Information Services: Private Bag X20606, Bloemfontein 9300; tel. (51) 405-4680; fax (51) 403-3567; e-mail jacomien@majuba.ofs.gov.za; internet mangaung.ofs.gov.za; f. 1948; 3m. books; serves 135 public libraries; Dir T. A. LUBBE; publ. *Free State Libraries* (4 a year).

Mangaung Library Services: POB 1029, Bloemfontein 9301; tel. (51) 405-8241; fax (51) 405-8604; f. 1875; Legal Deposit, National Drama Library, and Public Library; 500,000 vols, 65,000 plays; Man., Education, Library, Arts and Culture N. L. MOHLAODI; publ. *Catalogue of the National Drama Library*.

University of the Free State Library and Information Services: POB 301, Blomfontein 9300; tel. (51) 401-3488; fax (51) 444-6343; e-mail eisterkb@ufs.ac.za; internet www.ufs.ac.za; f. 1904; colln incl. rare pamphlets and other early South African publs of Dreyer-Africana Colln and items on South African War; 576,000 vols (3,000 periodicals); Dir K. B. EISTER.

Cape Town

Cape Town City Libraries: POB 4728, Cape Town 8000; tel. (21) 462-4400; fax (21) 461-5981; f. 1952; free municipal public library service; central library and 32 suburban brs, travelling, hospital, old age homes, homebound library services; 1.5m. vols; special art, music and business collections; Librarian H. C. F. HEYMANN.

Library and Information Unit of Parliament: POB 18, Cape Town 8000; located at: Ground Fl., NCOP Wing, Parliament St, Cape Town 8000; tel. (21) 403-2140; fax (21) 461-4331; e-mail library@parliament.gov.za; internet www.parliament.gov.za; f. 1857; provides general and legislative reference services and a press-cutting service to members and officers of Parliament; legal deposit library and depository for UN publs; 350,000 items, including the Mendelssohn Africana Collection; 2,700 current periodicals; local and foreign government and parliamentary publs; Librarian ALBERT NTUNJA.

Royal Society of South Africa Library: 4.17 P D Hahn Bldg, c/o Univ. of Cape Town, Rhodes Gift 7700; tel. (21) 650-2543; e-mail royalsociety@uct.ac.za; internet www.royalsocietysa.org.za; f. 1877, Royal Charter 1908; 33,000 vols of scientific periodicals, held by Univ. of Cape Town Library; Hon. Librarian Prof. J. R. E. LUTJEHARMS; publ. *Transactions of the Royal Society of South Africa* (3 a year).

South African Library: POB 496, Cape Town 8000; 5 Queen Victoria St, POB 496, Cape Town 8000; tel. (21) 424-6320; fax (21) 423-3359; internet www.nlsa.ac.za; f. 1818; national reference and preservation library with legal deposit privileges; 750,000 books and official publs, 200,000 bound periodicals, 8,000 current periodicals, 45,000 bound newspapers, 300 current newspapers, 20,000 maps, 100,000 iconographic items; MS collections of Cape and early SA; comprehensive Africana collection pertaining to South Africa, with materials on neighbouring Southern African countries; UN and World Bank depository library; special collections incl. Grey Collection of 115 medieval MSS, 5,000 vols incl. incunabula and early South African imprints; Dessinian (17th–18th century); Nourse Cromwelliana (17th century); Fairbridge (19th century); reference room for research; regular exhibitions of library material; microfilming, photographic and copying services; Dir JOHN KGWALE TSEBE; publs *Grey Bibliographies*, *Quarterly Bulletin*.

University of Cape Town Libraries: Private Bag X3, Rondebosch, Cape Town 7701; tel. (21) 650-3134; fax (21) 650-2965; e-mail libraries@uct.ac.za; internet www.lib.uct.ac.za; f. 1905; comprises Chancellor Oppenheimer Library and brs: African Studies Library; Bolus Herbarium Library; Brand van Zyl Law Library; Built Environment Library; Health Sciences Library; Hiddingh Hall Library (fine arts and drama); Institute of Child Health Library; Jewish Studies Library; WH Bell Music Library; spec. collns incl. Rare Books (some with fore-edge paintings); Kipling Colln; African Studies (incl. pre-1925 Africana, local imprints, and grey literature); Bolus Colln (antiquarian botanical works); Medical History Colln; Van Zyl Colln (antiquarian legal works); MSS and Archives (incl. original material relating to South African history with a strong focus on the W Cape; Bleek and Lloyd Colln; the papers of Jack and Ray Simons, C. Louis Leipoldt, Pauline Smith, and Olive Schreiner; African language collns; archives of the Black Sash (Cape Western Region); collns of Victorian and late 20th-century architects; records of the Jewish community in the W Cape; and MSS music scores of South African composers; 1.2m. print vols, 91,400 journal titles, of which 63,166 are electronic journals, 201 online databases; Exec. Dir JOAN RAPP; Head Librarian FIONA JONES.

Western Cape Education Library and Information Service (EDULIS): Private Bag X9099, Cape Town 8000; tel. (21) 957-9618; fax (21) 948-0748; e-mail edulis@pgwc.gov.za; internet edulis.pgwc.gov.za; f. 1859; 8,000 mems; 60,000 vols, 150 current periodicals; Head LYNE MCLENNAN.

Western Cape Provincial Library Service: POB 2108, Cape Town 8000; cnr of Chiappinni and Hospital Sts, Cape Town 8001; tel. (21) 483-2273; fax (21) 483-2031; e-mail capelib@pgwc.gov.za; internet www.capegateway.gov.za/library; f. 1945; 15 regional libraries, 316 affiliated libraries; library promotion; training of public librarians; selection, buying and distribution of library material; central reference service; computerized library and information system; 5.7m. vols; collns of art prints, phonographic records, CDs, audio cassettes, 16mm films, video cassettes, DVDs; Dir, Library and Archival Services NOMAZA DINGAYO; publ. *Cape Librarian / Kaapse Bibliotekaris* (6 a year).

Durban

eThekwini Municipal Library Service: City Hall, Smith St, POB 917, Durban 4000; tel. (31) 311-2444; fax (31) 311-2410; e-mail masingat@durban.gov.za; internet www.durban.gov.za; f. 1853; spec. collns of African Studies and Shakespearean; 89 brs; 1.5m. vols; Dir R. NYONGWANA (acting); Dir TREVOR MASINGA (acting).

University of KwaZulu-Natal Library: King George V Ave, Glenwood, Durban 4041; tel. (31) 260-2317; fax (31) 260-1084; e-mail buchanan@ukzn.ac.za; internet www.library.und.ac.za; f. 2004; five main libraries in two centres, four in Durban and one in Pietermaritzburg and several br. libraries; 1,321,971 vols; Dir of Library Services NORA BUCHANAN.

East London

Buffalo City Municipal Library Service: Gladstone St, POB 652, East London; tel. (43) 722-4991; fax (43) 743-1729; f. 1876; 30,000 mems; 225,000 vols; Librarian Mrs M. M. DAVIDSON.

Grahamstown

Grahamstown Public Library: POB 180, Grahamstown 6140; tel. (46) 603-6040; fax (46) 622-9488; e-mail library@makana.gov.za; internet www.makana.gov.za; f. 1842; 81,053 vols; Librarian P. VUBELA.

National English Literary Museum: Private Bag 1019, Grahamstown 6140; tel. (46) 622-7042; fax (46) 622-2582; e-mail nelm@ru.ac.za; internet www.rhodes.ac.za/nelm; f. 1972; research collns of books, literary MSS, photographs, journal articles, academic theses and press cuttings; conducts environmental literary camps, exhibitions, lectures, poetry readings, book launches; 27,000 vols; Dir BEVERLEY THOMAS; Head Librarian DEBBIE LANDMAN; Head Archivist ANN TORLESSE; publ. *NELM News* (2 a year).

Rhodes University Library: Rhodes Univ., POB 184, Grahamstown 6140; tel. (46) 603-8436; fax (46) 603-7310; e-mail library@ru.ac.za; internet www.ru.ac.za/library; f. 1904; 400,000 vols; Dir for Library Services GWENDA THOMAS.

Johannesburg

City of Johannesburg Library and Information Services: Central Reference Library, Market Sq., Johannesburg; tel. (11) 870-1227; e-mail joburgconnect@joburg.org.za; f. 1890; 1.9m. vols; Regional Man. (vacant); publ. *Local Government Library Bulletin* (12 a year).

Library of the South African Institute of Race Relations: POB 291722, Melville 2109; 2 Clamart Road Richmond, Johannesburg 2092; tel. (11) 482 7221; fax (11) 482 7690; e-mail prisca@sairr.org.za; internet www.sairr.org.za; f. 1929; 7,030 vols; valuable archival and documentary material; newspaper clippings from 1930 on race relations, politics, labour and economics; bibliographies on race relations; Information Dir T. DIMANT.

University of the Witwatersrand Library: Private Bag XI, PO Wits, 2050; tel. (11) 717-1901; fax (11) 717-1946; e-mail felix.ubogu@library.wits.ac.za; internet www.wits.ac.za/library; f. 1922; 1.2m. vols, access to 46,000 e-journal titles; 2 central libraries (undergraduate and research), also br. libraries: architecture, biological and physical sciences, management, geological and mathematical sciences, education and commerce, engineering, law, health sciences, nuclear sciences; spec. collns incl. Africana, Hebraica and Judaica, Portuguese, Archaeology and Egyptology, Historical and Literary Papers (incl. Church of the Province of South Africa), Early Printed Books; Librarian FELIX N. UBOGU.

Kimberley

Kimberley Public Library: POB 627, Kimberley 8300; tel. (53) 830-6241; fax (53) 833-1954; internet home.global.co.za/~afrilib; f. 1882; 127,000 vols; Africana Library of 20,000 vols, 545 MSS, 1,145 photographs (North Cape and Diamond Fields); Judy Scott Library of 43,000 vols; Librarian F. VAN DYK.

Mmabatho

North-West Provincial Library Services: Private Bag X2044, Mmabatho 2735; tel. (18) 392-2060; f. 1978; under Dept of Arts, Culture and Sport; 75 public libraries, 7 college libraries, 1,000 school libraries, 7 govt dept libraries; 1.6m. vols; Deputy Dir N. B. NOMNGA.

Pietermaritzburg

KwaZulu-Natal Provincial Library Service: Private Bag X9016, Pietermaritzburg; tel. (33) 341-3000; fax (33) 394-2237; e-mail frenchl@plho.kzntl.gov.za; f. 1952; consists of central org. and reference library at Pietermaritzburg; 4 regional offices for Coast, S Coast, Midlands and N areas, serving 172 public libraries; 3.4m. vols, 21,000 CDs, 32,000 video cassettes, 6,500 DVDs; Man. CAROL SLATER; Asst Man., Central Reference Library LINDY FRENCH; publ. *KZN Librarian* (4 a year).

Natal Society Library: Churchill Sq., Church St, Pietermaritzburg 3200, Natal; tel. (33) 345-2383; fax (33) 394-0095; f. 1851; lending, children's, reference, legal deposit, school assignments, music, special collections, map collns, Africana colln; 6 brs, hospital, housebound and travelling library services; 600,000 vols; 6,332 current legal deposit periodicals and newspapers, 122 current overseas periodicals, numerous bound legal deposit and overseas periodicals and newspapers; Dir J. C. MORRISON; publs *Natalia* (1 a year), *AIDS Bibliography*.

University of KwaZulu-Natal Library, Pietermaritzburg Campus: Private Bag X014, Scottsville 3209; tel. (33) 260-6194; fax (33) 260-5260; e-mail sukram@ukzn.ac.za; internet www.library.unp.ac.za; f. 1909; 375,000 vols; Librarian PRAVERSH SUKRAM (acting).

Port Elizabeth

Nelson Mandela Metropolitan Libraries: POB 66, Port Elizabeth 6000; tel. (41) 506-1373; fax (41) 506-1390; e-mail kdeklerk@mandelametro.gov.za; f. 1901; public library with extensive Africana, genealogical and maritime collns; research and orientation workshops for scholars; 500,000 vols; Head of Libraries BONGIWE CHIGUMBU.

Nelson Mandela Metropolitan University Library and Information Services: POB 77700, Port Elizabeth 6000; tel. (41) 504-2281; fax (41) 504-2280; internet www.nmmu.ac.za; f. 1964; 507,356 vols; L. C. Steyn Collection of Roman Dutch Law; Director MARJORY EALES.

Potchefstroom

Ferdinand Postma Library, North-West University: Private Bag X05, Noordbrug 2522; tel. (18) 299-2000; fax (18) 299-2999; e-mail fpbalg@nwu.ac.za; internet www.nwu.ac.za/library; f. 1869; 547,035 vols, 1,694 current periodicals; Main Library (Ferdinand Postma Library), Library of the Theological School of the Reformed Churches in South Africa (Jan Lion Cachet Library), Music Library, Natural Sciences Library, Vaal Triangle Campus Library at Vanderbijlpark; special collections: Carney Africana Collection, Hertzog Law Collection, Collection of the Institute for Research in Children's Literature; Dir TOM LARNEY.

Pretoria

Council for Scientific and Industrial Research (CSIR) Information Services: POB 395, Pretoria 0001; tel. (12) 841-2911; fax (12) 841-4405; internet www.csir.co.za; f. 1945; 90,000 bound vols, 4,000 serial titles and 22,000 pamphlets; provides scientific, technical and business management information services to CSIR research staff and to external clients; Man. Dr MARTIE VAN DEVENTER; publ. *Technobrief*.

Department of Agriculture, Fisheries & Forestry Information Centre: Private Bag X388, Pretoria 0001; tel. (12) 319-6872; fax (12) 319-7245; e-mail daleenk@daff.gov.za; internet www.daff.gov.za; f. 1910; library services, distribution of departmental publs; 40,000 vols, 50 current periodicals, 140,000 pamphlets; Asst Dir DALEEN KOEN.

Department of Arts, Culture, Science and Technology Library: Private Bag X894, Pretoria 0001; tel. (12) 314-6033; fax (12) 323-2720; special collections: library science, science planning, state language services, national terminology services; 42,000 vols; 153 current periodicals; Librarian D. E. MOHLAKWANA.

Department of Education Library: Private Bag X895, Pretoria 0001; tel. (12) 312-5265; fax (12) 325-1475; f. 1994; Asst Dir REGINAH BAMUZA.

Gauteng Library Information Policy and Archiving Services: Private Bag X33, Marshalltown 2000; tel. (11) 355-2500; fax (11) 355-2565; e-mail koekie.meyer@gpg.gov.za; internet www.srac.gpg.gov.za; f. 1995; consists of Head Office in Johannesburg, and 4 Regional Libraries; provides library and information service to 324 public and community libraries and depots in Gauteng Province; 3.5m. vols; Dir J. M. MEYER (acting).

Mary Gunn Library, South African National Biodiversity Institute: Private Bag X101, Pretoria 0001; tel. (12) 843-5042; fax (12) 804-8740; e-mail potgietere@sanbi.org; internet www.sanbi.org; f. 1916; 17,642 vols; Chief Exec. Dr T. ABRAHAMSE.

National Archives and Heraldic Services: Private Bag X236, Pretoria 0001; tel. (12) 323-5300; fax (12) 323-5287; e-mail arg02@dacst4.pwv.gov.za; provides a comprehensive archives service to all government offices and local authorities; processes and stores archive material; makes archives and facilities available to researchers; National Archivist for the Republic of South Africa Dr G. A. DOMINY.

State Library: POB 397, Pretoria 0001; tel. (12) 321-8931; fax (12) 325-5984; f. 1887; national and legal depository library, and depository library for US Government and UN publications; 684,000 vols, 9,600 current serials; responsible for compiling the national bibliography; international and national interlending centre; Southern African Book Exchange Centre; ISBN and ISSN centre for South Africa; Dir Dr PETER J. LOR; publs *South African National Bibliography* (quarterly and annual cumulations, paper and machine-readable format), *Index to South African Periodicals* (CD-ROM and machine-readable format), *RSA Government Gazette* (microfiche, quarterly), *South African Newspapers on Microfilm*, *Bibliography of the Xhosa Language*, *Northern Sotho Bibliography*, *Directory of South African Publishers*.

Transvaal Education Department, Education Media Service: 328 Van der Walt St, Private Bag X290, Pretoria 0001; tel. (12) 322-7685; fax (12) 322-7699; f. 1951; 385,000 vols, 600 periodicals, 3,000 video cassettes; Dir J. A. BIERMAN.

University of Pretoria Libraries: Academic Information Service, University of Pretoria, Pretoria 0002; tel. (12) 420-4111; fax (12) 362-5182; e-mail jaboon@up.ac.za; internet www.up.ac.za/asservices/ais/ais.htm; f. 1908; 1.2m. vols, pamphlets, govt publs, 5,698 periodicals, etc., 8,000 gramophone records, 26,000 items of sheet-music, 2,250 CDs; Dir J. A. BOON.

University of South Africa Library: POB 392, UNISA 0003; tel. (12) 429-3131; fax (12) 429-2925; e-mail mbambtb@unisa.ac.za; internet www.unisa.ac.za/library; f. 1947; 2m. vols, 335,000 bound serials; science library and law colln specializing in foreign and comparative law; brs in Cape Town, Durban, Pretoria Johannesburg, Rustenburg, Addis Ababa and Polokwane; Exec. Dir Dr MBAMBO-THATA; publ. *Mousaion* (irregular).

Sovenga

University of Limpopo Library: Private Bag X1112, Sovenga, Limpopo 0727; tel. (15) 268-2656; fax (15) 268-2198; internet www.ul.ac.za/library; 80,000 vols, 581 periodicals; Exec. Dir. MAKGABELA CHUENE; Librarian PATEKA MATSHAYA.

Stellenbosch

Stellenbosch University Library and Information Service: Stellenbosch University, Private Bag X5036, Stellenbosch 7599; tel. (21) 808-4876; fax (21) 808-3723; e-mail etise@sun.ac.za; internet www.sun.ac.za/library; f. 1895; 701,853 books; Sr Dir ELLEN TISE.

Museums and Art Galleries

Bloemfontein

National Museum: POB 266, Bloemfontein 9300; 36 Aliwal St, Bloemfontein 9301; tel. (51) 447-9609; fax (51) 447-6273; e-mail ornito@nasmus.co.za; internet www.nasmus.co.za; f. 1877; main focus is on natural history (incl. Florisbad human fossil skull); also social and local history; library of 11,600 vols, 1,730 serial titles, 11,200 pamphlets; Dir R. J. NUTTALL; publs *CULNA*, *Navorsinge van die Nasionale Museum / Researches of the National Museum*, *Praktikum*.

Cape Town

Iziko Museums of Cape Town: POB 61, Cape Town 8000; tel. (21) 481-3800; fax (21) 481-3993; internet www.iziko.org.za; f. 1999; CEO Prof. H. C. BREDEKAMP.

Art Sites:

Iziko–Michaelis Collection: POB 61, Cape Town 8000; The Old Town House, Greenmarket Sq., Cape Town; tel. (21) 481-3933; fax (21) 424-6441; internet www.iziko.org.za/michaelis; f. 1916; Dutch and Flemish paintings, drawings and prints of the 16th century to the early 20th century; Dutch and colonial furniture; library of 1,500 vols; Dir, Art Collns M. H. MARTIN.

Iziko–Natale Labia Museum: POB 61, Cape Town 8000; 192 Main Rd, Muizenberg, Cape Town 7945; tel. (21) 788-4106; fax (21) 788-3908; internet www.iziko.org.za/natale; f. 1988; built 1929 as residence of first Italian Minister Plenipotentiary in SA, Prince Natale Labia; elaborate Italianate furnishings with 18th- and 19th-century British and European art; Dir for Art Collns M. H. MARTIN.

Iziko–South African National Gallery Library: POB 61, Cape Town 8001; tel. (21) 467-4660; fax (21) 467-4680; e-mail info@iziko.org.za; internet www.iziko.org.za/sang; f. 1871; collns of South African, African, British, French, Dutch and Flemish art; also photography, sculpture, beadwork, textiles and architecture; library of 10,000 vols, journals and pamphlets; public access by appointment; Dir for Art Collns RAISON NAIDOO; Librarian MAUREEN CHIWARE.

Natural History Sites:

Iziko–Planetarium: 25 Queen Victoria St, Cape Town 8000; tel. (21) 481-3900; fax (21) 481-3990; e-mail tferreira@iziko.org.za; internet www.iziko.org.za/

planetarium; f. 1987; organizes shows; holiday workshops and astronomy courses; Man. THEO FERREIRA.

Iziko–South African Museum: 25 Queen Victoria St, Cape Town 8000; tel. (21) 481-3900; fax (21) 481-3990; internet www.iziko.org.za/sam; f. 1825; collns incl. ethnography, applied arts, philately, transport, weaponry, toys; library of 12,000 vols, 4,000 periodicals; Dir, Natural History Collns Dr H. ROBERTSON; publ. *African Natural History* (1 a year).

Iziko–West Coast Fossil Park: POB 42, Langebaanweg, Cape Town 7375; R27 Langebaanweg, Cape Town 7375; tel. (22) 766-1606; fax (22) 766-1765; e-mail info@iziko.org.za; internet www.iziko.org.za/iziko/partners/wcfp.html; f. 1998; Dir for Natural History Collns Dr P. HAARHOFF.

Social History Sites:

Iziko–Bertram House: Hiddingh Campus, Orange St, Cape Town 8000; tel. (21) 481-3940; fax (21) 481-3941; internet www.iziko.org.za/bertram; f. 1984; early 19th-century Georgian townhouse; displays of Georgian furniture, Chinese and English porcelain, and English silver and kitchenware; Dir for Social History Collns Dr P. J. DAVISON.

Iziko–Bo-Kaap Museum: 71 Wale St, Cape Town 8000; tel. (21) 481-3939; fax (21) 481-3938; internet www.iziko.org.za/bokaap; f. 1978; focuses on the social history of the local community; Dir for Social History Collns Dr P. J. DAVISON.

Iziko–Groot Constantia: Groot Constantia Estate, Constantia, Cape Town 8000; tel. (21) 795-5140; fax (21) 795-5150; internet www.iziko.org.za/grootcon; f. 1927; 17th-century wine estate and manor house; art colln; wine museum; Dir for Social History Collns Dr P. J. DAVISON.

Iziko–Koopmans-De Wet House: 35 Strand St, Cape Town 8000; tel. (21) 481-3935; fax (21) 424-6441; internet www.iziko.org.za/koopmans; f. 1914; early 18th-century townhouse; colln of Cape furniture, Chinese and Japanese ceramics, Dutch Delft ware, paintings, glass and silverware; Dir for Social History Collns Dr P. J. DAVISON.

Iziko–Rust-en-Vreugd: 78 Buitenkant St, Cape Town 8000; tel. (21) 464-3280; fax (21) 461-9620; internet www.iziko.org.za/rustvreugd; f. 1965; 18th-century Cape Dutch house with colln of African watercolours and prints from the William Fehr Colln; Dir for Art Collns M. H. MARTIN.

Iziko–Slave Lodge: 49 Adderley St, Cape Town 8000; tel. (21) 467-7229; fax (21) 461-2960; internet www.iziko.org.za/slavelodge; f. 1966 as South African Cultural History Museum, present name 1998; slavery, human rights, nat. and local history, illustrating life in 18th and 19th centuries; library of 14,000 vols; Dir for Social History Collns J. L. MELTZER; Curator for Social History Collns F. H. CLAYTON.

Iziko–South African Maritime Museum: Victoria and Albert Waterfront, Table Bay Harbour, Cape Town 8000; tel. (21) 405-2880; fax (21) 405-2882; internet www.iziko.org.za/maritime; f. 1990; focuses on fishing and shipping industry; colln of ships; floating exhibition: SAS *Somerset*, boom defence vessel built in 1942; Dir for Social History Collns Dr P. J. DAVISON.

Iziko–William Fehr Collection: POB 61, Cape Town 8000; The Castle of Good Hope, Buitenkant St, Cape Town 8000; tel. (21) 464-1260; fax (21) 464-1280; internet www.iziko.org.za/castle; f. 1965; colln of paintings and decorative arts of relevance to Cape region; Dir for Social History Collns P. J. DAVISON.

Museum of Coast and Anti-Aircraft Artillery: Fort Wynyard, POB 14068, Green Point 8051; tel. (21) 419-1765; internet www.museum.com/jb/museum?id=24015; f. 1987; coast and anti-aircraft guns and relics displayed in a restored coast artillery battery.

Durban

Durban Museums: City Hall, POB 4085, Durban 4000; tel. (31) 300-6911; fax (31) 300-6308; e-mail mnikathib@prcsu.durban.gov.za; internet www.durban.gov.za; f. 1887; South African fauna, flora, ethnography, archaeology, paintings, graphic art, porcelain, sculptures, local history; Dir of Durban Art Gallery C. BROWN; Dir of Local History Museums R. OMAR; Dir of Natural Science Museum Q. B. HENDEY; publ. *Novitates* (1 a year).

Local History Museums: Old Court House Museum, Aliwal St, Durban; tel. (31) 311-2223; fax (31) 311-2224; f. 1966; local and KwaZulu Natal historical collns, restored Natal colonial public building; Dir M. NGUBANE.

Attached Museums:

Bergtheil Museum: c/o Old Court House Museum, Aliwal St, Durban; e-mail mnikathib@prcsu.durban.gov.za; collections related to local communities, particularly early German settlers.

Cato Manor Heritage Centre: c/o Old Court House Museum, Aliwal St, Durban; e-mail mnikathib@prcsu.durban.gov.za; interpretative centre featuring the history of Cato Manor, including aspects related to forced removals and the Apartheid era.

Kwa Muhle Museum: 130–132 Ordnance Rd, Durban; tel. (31) 311-1111; fax (31) 311-2224; f. 1994; urban life in the Apartheid era, with emphasis on the 'Durban System' of administering the African population 1908–1986.

Old House Museum: c/o Old Court House Museum, Aliwal St, Durban; e-mail mnikathib@prcsu.durban.gov.za; a replica of the Robinson Home, a house belonging to the founder of the city's first morning newspaper; contains displays of early domestic life.

Pinetown Museum: c/o Old Court House Museum, Aliwal St, Durban; e-mail mnikathib@prcsu.durban.gov.za; collections related to the Pinetown area.

Port Natal Maritime Museum: c/o Old Court House Museum, Aliwal St, Durban; f. 1988; Natal and Durban maritime history, two tugs and a minesweeper.

East London

East London Museum: POB 11021, Southernwood, East London 5213; 319 Oxford St, Southernwood, East London 5201; tel. (43) 743-0686; fax (43) 743-3127; e-mail rachel@tsamail.co.za; f. 1931; collns of conchology, ichthyology, ornithology of the Eastern Cape Province, cultural history of the Border region and ethnography of the Southern Nguni peoples; houses specimen of Coelacanth (primitive fish) and world's only dodo egg; administers Victorian house museum; library: library holds books, journals, video cassettes, cartographic material, microfiches, microfilms, photographs, reprints, slides; Museum Dir MCEBISI MAGADLA (acting); Museum Librarian RACHEL WILLIAMS; publ. *Annals of the Eastern Cape Museums* (jtly with 4 other museums).

Franschhoek

Huguenot Memorial Museum and Monument: Lambrechts St, POB 37, Franschhoek 7690; tel. (21) 876-2532; fax (21) 876-3649; e-mail hugenoot@museum.co.za; internet www.museum.co.za; f. 1967; research into Cape Huguenot history, exhibition of over 400 Huguenot artefacts and documents; Chair. L. CYSTER; Curator E. A. JOHANNES; publ. *Bulletin of the Huguenot Society of South Africa*.

Grahamstown

Albany Museum: Somerset St, Grahamstown 6139; tel. (46) 622-2312; fax (46) 622-2398; e-mail l.webley@ru.ac.za; internet www.ru.ac.za/albany-museum; f. 1855; archaeology, terrestrial entomology, freshwater ichthyology, freshwater invertebrates, botany, palaeontology, ornithology, history and material cultures of the peoples of the Eastern Cape Province; library of 2,000 vols, 1,400 periodicals; Librarian A. PANTSI; publs *Annals of the Eastern Cape Provincial Museums* (jtly with 3 other museums, irregular), *Southern African Field Archaeology* (1 a year).

Johannesburg

Apartheid Museum: POB 82283, Southdale, 2135 Johannesburg; Northern Parkway and Gold Reef Rd, Ormonde 2001; tel. (11) 309-4700; fax (11) 309-4726; e-mail info@apartheidmuseum.org; internet www.apartheidmuseum.org; f. 2001; film footage, photographs and artefacts illustrating the rise and decline of the apartheid system; Chair. Dr JOHN KANI.

City of Johannesburg Museums and Galleries:; internet www.joburg.org.za/arts/arts_heritage.stm#museums; Dir of Arts, Culture and Heritage Services STEVEN SHACK.

Branch Museums:

Adler Museum of Medicine: Faculty of Health Sciences, Univ. of the Witwatersrand, 7 York Rd, Parktown, Johannesburg 2193; tel. (11) 717-2081; fax (86) 553-2484; e-mail adler.museum@wits.ac.za; internet www.wits.ac.za/health/adlermuseum; f. 1962; history of medicine, dentistry, optometry and pharmacy; colln of medical, dental and surgical instruments and equipment; reconstructions of early 20th-century pharmacy, doctor's and dentist's surgeries, herbalist shop and traditional medicine display, incl. unani/tibb, ayurveda, western herbal medicine and homoeopathy, traditional healing; guided tours exhibits and public lectures; facilities of medical historical research; library of 10,000 vols; Curator ROCHELLE KEENE; publ. *Adler Museum Bulletin* (2 a year).

Bensusan Museum of Photography and Library: MuseuMAfricA, 121 Bree St, Newtown, Johannesburg; tel. (11) 833-5624; fax (11) 833-5636; e-mail photographiclibrary@joburg.org.za; f. 1968; colln incl. rare and valuable precision-made photographic equipment, incl. early Daguerre camera bought in 1839; Collector's Gallery; colln of pictures from the earliest wet-plate prints to digital images and experiments in 3 dimensions, such as stereoscopic views and holograms; specializes in preserving the work of South African photographers; Curator JONATHAN FROST.

Bernberg Fashion Museum: c/o Museum Africa, POB 517, Newtown 2113, Johannesburg; 121 Bree St, Newtown, Johannesburg; tel. (11) 833-5624; fax (11) 833-5636; e-mail museumafrica@joburg.org.za; internet www.joburg.org.za/

culture/museums-galleries/museumafrica; f. 1973; costume and accessories since the 17th century; collns housed in Museum Africa and displayed in temporary exhibitions; Man. DIANA WALL; Costume and Textile Curator (vacant).

Hector Pieterson Museum: 8288 Maseko St, Orlando West 1804; tel. and fax (11) 536-0611; named after one of the first fatalities of the march through Soweto on 16 June 1976, when police were ordered to shoot at a crowd of demonstrating students; commemorates the day's events, incl. television footage of the uprising and coverage of the anti-apartheid struggle generally; museum is next to the Pieterson Memorial, and the area has been declared a nat. heritage site; Curator ALI HLONGWANE.

James Hall Museum of Transport: Pioneers' Park, Rosettenville Rd, La Rochelle 2190, Johannesburg; tel. (11) 435-9485; fax (11) 435-9821; e-mail curator@jhmt.org.za; internet www.jhmt.org.za; f. 1964; largest and most comprehensive land transport museum in South Africa; land transport in all its forms: ox-wagons, coaches and carts, bicycles, motorbikes, tractors, fire engines, buses, trams, trains, and cars from the Model T Ford to electric cars; Curator PETER HALL.

Johannesburg Art Gallery: POB 30951, Braamfontein 2017, Johannesburg; tel. (11) 725-3130; fax (11) 720-6000; e-mail job@joburg.org.za; internet www.joburg.org.za; f. 1910; colln of 9,000 artworks comprising contemporary S African art; traditional Southern African art and modern int. art; print colln and historical European paintings and sculptures; extensive public programmes; library of 9,500 vols; Dir CLIVE KELLNER.

MuseuMAfricA: 121 Bree St, Newtown, Johannesburg; tel. (11) 833-5624; fax (11) 833-5636; e-mail museumafrica@joburg.org.za; permanent displays show urban life in Johannesburg and its place in South Africa's history; themes incl. the gold miner, life in a shack and township jazz; coverage of Mahatma Gandhi's and Nelson Mandela's time in the city; displays on early man, stone-age and iron-age communities, San rock art in a reconstructed shelter, lifestyle of the first white settlers in the Johannesburg area; Chief Curator DAWN ROBERTSON.

Roodepoort Museum: Civic Centre, Christiaan de Wet Rd, Florida Park 1709; tel. (11) 761-0225; fax (11) 674-4043; e-mail annes@joburg.org.za; internet www.joburg.org.za; f. 1963; permanent displays illustrate the changes brought about by the discovery of gold in the area, incl. reconstructed 19th-century farmhouse, late Victorian home, 1920s and 1930s interiors; exhibition of decorative arts; guided tours; curriculum-based school programme; open by appointment only; Curator ANNE SMART.

Kimberley

McGregor Museum: Atlas St, POB 316, Kimberley 8300; tel. (53) 839-2700; fax (53) 842-1433; e-mail cfortune@museumsnc.co.za; internet www.museumsnc.co.za; f. 1907; archaeology and rock art, history (incl. Anglo-Boer War of 1899–1902), geology, zoology and herbarium of N Cape; ethnological collection housed in Duggan-Cronin Gallery, incorporates Magersfontein Battlefield Museum, Rudd House, Dunluce and Memorial to the Pioneers of Aviation; Dir C. FORTUNE.

King William's Town

Amathole Museum: Cnr Albert Rd and Alexandra Rd, POB 1434, King William's Town 5600; tel. (43) 642-4506; fax (43) 642-1569; e-mail fred.k@museum.za.net; internet www.museum.za.net/content/view/1/1; f. 1884 as a naturalist soc.; studies, collects, houses and exhibits Southern Africa mammalogy, Xhosa ethnography, local history, Eastern Cape missionary history and Eastern Cape German settler history; library of 8,200 vols, 150 current periodicals; spec. collns incl. Kitton Colln of Africana; Dir FRED KIGOZI; publ. *Cape Provincial Museums Annals* (jtly with 4 other museums).

Attached Museum:

Missionary Museum: Berkeley St, POB 1434, King William's Town 5600; tel. (43) 642-4506; fax (43) 642-1569; e-mail stephanie.v@museum.za.net; internet www.museum.za.net; f. 1972; satellite museum; missionary history in E Cape; missionary library; Dir FRED KIGOZI; Curator of History STEPHANIE VICTOR; publ. *Imvubu*.

Pietermaritzburg

Natal Museum: Private Bag 9070, Pietermaritzburg 3200; 237 Ndlovu St, Pietermaritzburg 3201; tel. (33) 345-1404; fax (33) 345-0561; internet www.nmsa.org.za; f. 1904; collns incl. entomology, mollusca, archaeology, historical anthropology, mammals, arachnology, earthworms, herpetology, palaentology, local history; library of 12,000 books, 2,500 periodicals, 61,000 pamphlets, 8,000 photographs, 900 maps, 8,000 slides; Dir (vacant); publs *Annals*, *Natal Museum Journal of Humanities* (1 a year).

Tatham Art Gallery (Municipal): Commercial Rd, opp. City Hall, Pietermaritzburg; tel. (33) 342-1804; e-mail bell@tatham.org.za; f. 1903; British and French painting since 19th century, sculpture and graphics, Southern African painting, sculpture, ceramics, prints and ethnic objets d'art; library: public reference library of 2,300 vols; Dir BRENDAN BELL.

Port Elizabeth

Bayworld (incorporating Port Elizabeth Museum, Snake Park, Oceanarium and No. 7 Castle Hill Historical Museum): POB 13147, Humewood, Port Elizabeth 6013; tel. (41) 584-0650; fax (41) 584-0661; e-mail pr@bayworld.co.za; internet www.bayworld.co.za; f. 1856; research on maritime history, marine biology, marine mammalogy, herpetology, marine ornithology and local history; Museum: marine life, maritime history, birds, dinosaurs, costume and local history; Snake Park: African colln of reptiles; library of 20,000 vols; Dir SYLVIA VAN ZYL.

Nelson Mandela Metropolitan Art Museum: 1 Park Drive, Port Elizabeth; tel. (41) 586-1030; fax (41) 586-3234; e-mail artmuseum@artmuseum.co.za; internet www.artmuseum.co.za; f. 1956 as King George VI Art Gallery; municipal art museum; collections of South African and British art, Indian miniatures, international graphics, Chinese textiles; library of 5,460 vols; Dir Dr MELANIE HILLEBRAND.

Pretoria

National Cultural History Museum: POB 28088, Sunnyside 0132; tel. and fax (12) 328-5173; e-mail nchm@nfi.org.za; internet www.nfi.org.za; f. 1892; exhibitions; research, education and conservation; library; special collns: Jansen, ethnography, archaeological, furniture and ceramics; library of 17,500 vols, 200 periodicals; Man. NEO MALAO; publ. *Nasko Navorsing* (research by the museum, 1 a year).

Pretoria Art Museum (Municipal Art Museum): POB 40925, Arcadia Park, Pretoria 0007; Arcadia Park (Cnr Schoeman and Wessels Sts), Arcadia, Pretoria 0083; tel. (12) 344-1807; fax (12) 344-1809; e-mail art.museum@tshwane.gov.za; internet www.pretoriaartmuseum.co.za; f. 1964; South African art, small colln of European graphic art, some 17th-century Dutch art, colln of traditional and contemporary African art; Head D. OEGEMA (acting).

Transvaal Museum: Paul Kruger St, POB 413, Pretoria; tel. (12) 322-7632; fax (12) 322-7939; e-mail perregil@nfi.museum; f. 1893, from 1964 a natural history museum only; taxonomy, ecology, zoo-geography and evolutionary studies with main emphasis on Southern Africa; mammals, birds, herpetology, palaeontology (incl. mammal-like reptiles and early hominids), Coleoptera, Lepidoptera, Orthoptera, invertebrates, archaeo-zoology and education; library of 11,000 vols, 2,000 periodicals and 80,000 reprints; rare book collection; Dir Dr MARTIN KRÜGER; publs *Annals of the Transvaal Museum* (1 a year), *Transvaal Museum Monographs* (irregular).

Stellenbosch

Stellenbosch Museum: Private Bag X5048, Stellenbosch 7599; Erfurthuis, Ryneveld St 37, Stellenbosch 7600; tel. (21) 887-2948; e-mail stelmus@mweb.co.za; internet www.stelmus.co.za; f. 1962; comprises 18th-century powder magazine (weaponry, Stellenbosch military history); Village Museum (bldgs illustrating life from 1690–1890), Toy and Miniature Museum; reference library; Man. W. SCHOLTZ.

Universities and Colleges

CAPE PENINSULA UNIVERSITY OF TECHNOLOGY

POB 1906, Belleville 7535

Telephone: (21) 959-6911

Fax: (21) 959-6069

E-mail: info@cput.ac.za

Internet: www.cput.ac.za

Founded 2005 by merger of Cape Technikon and Peninsula Technikon

Vice-Chancellor: Prof. L. VUYISA MAZWI-TANGA

Campuses at Cape Town, Granger Bay, Mowbray, Wellington

DEANS

Faculty of Applied Sciences: Prof. O. FATOKI

Faculty of Business: Prof. S. BAYAT

Faculty of Education and Social Sciences: Prof. M. ROBINSON

Faculty of Engineering: Dr O. FRANKS

Faculty of Health and Wellness Sciences: Dr D. GIHWALA

Faculty of Informatics and Design: Prof. J. CRONJE

RESEARCH CENTRES

Centre for Instrumentation Research: POB 652, Cape Town 8000; tel. (21) 460-4281; fax (21) 460-3705; e-mail cir@cput.ac.za; Dir Prof. JEVON DAVIES.

Fundani Centre for Higher Education Development: Dir Dr NOMATHAMSANQA TISANI.

Water Supply and Sanitation Unit (WSSU): tel. (21) 959-6111; fax (21) 959-6786; e-mail brandc@cput.ac.za; Dir Prof. ALVIN LAGARDIEN.

CENTRAL UNIVERSITY OF TECHNOLOGY, FREE STATE

PMB X20539, Bloemfontein 9300
Pres. Brand St 20, Bloemfontein 9301

Telephone: (51) 507-3911
Fax: (51) 507-3019
E-mail: cajvr@cut.ac.za
Internet: www.cut.ac.za

Founded 1981
Academic year: January to December

Vice-Chancellor and Prin.: Prof. T. Z. MTHEMBU
Deputy Vice-Chancellor for Academic Affairs: Prof. M. D. R. RALEBIPI-SIMELA
Deputy Vice-Chancellor for Resources and Operations: Prof. M. E. RALEKHETHO (acting)
Deputy Vice-Chancellor for Institutional Planning, Partnerships and Communications: Prof. T. G. SCHULTZ
Registrar: Dr M. J. G. VINGER
Welkom Campus Man.: Dr S. MAKOLA
Dir of Library: J. M. KABAMBA

Library of 143,354 vols
Number of teachers: 1,500
Number of students: 12,000

DEANS

Faculty of Engineering and Information-Technology: Prof. Y. E. WOYESSA (acting)
Faculty of Health and Environmental Sciences: Prof. L. DE JAGER
Faculty of Humanities: Prof. D. NGIDI
Faculty of Management Sciences: Prof. A. STRYDOM

DURBAN UNIVERSITY OF TECHNOLOGY

41–43 Centenary Rd, Durban 4001
E-mail: webmaster@dit.ac.za
Internet: www.dit.ac.za

Founded 2002 following merger of M. L. Sultan Technikon (f. 1946) and Technikon Natal (f. 1907); incorporated Umlazi Campus of University of Zululand 2004; univ. status and incorporated Mangosuthu Technikon 2006

Chancellor: PATRICIA DE LILLE
Vice-Chancellor: Prof. DAN J. NCAYIYANA
Chief Librarian: ROY RAJU.

CAMPUSES

M. L. Sultan Campus

41–43 Centenary Rd, Durban 4001

Telephone: (31) 308-5111
Fax: (31) 308-5194
E-mail: info@mlsultan.ac.za
Internet: www.mlsultan.ac.za

Deputy Vice-Chancellor: UJEN PURMASIR
Library Man.: SIZA RODABE

Library: B. M. Patel Memorial Library of 55,000 books, 900 journals, 4,000 video- and audiotapes

Faculties of Arts, Commerce, Engineering, Science.

Steve Biko Campus

(formerly Technikon Natal)

70 Mansfield Rd, Berea, Durban 4001

Telephone: (31) 204-2111
Fax: (31) 204-2663
E-mail: postmaster@ntech.ac.za
Internet: www.ntech.ac.za

Vice-Chancellor and Prin.: Prof. B. KHOAPA
Vice-Prin. for Academic Affairs: Prof. LOUIS DU PREEZ
Vice-Prin. for Admin.: Dr REGINALD THABEDE
Vice-Prin. for Student Affairs and Devt: Adv. REAGAN JACOBUS
Asst Vice-Prin. for Undergraduate Studies: Prof. NQABOMZI GAWE
Academic Registrar: DAVID HELLINGER
Registrar (Pietermaritzburg): Prof. SAM ZOND

Library of 81,000 vols, 1,001 periodical titles

DEANS

Faculty of Arts: A. R. STARKEY
Faculty of Commerce: T. DAGNALL-QUINN
Faculty of Engineering and Science: M. STEWART
Faculty of Health: A. MILNE

MANGOSUTHU TECHNIKON

POB 12363, Jacobs 4026
Mangosuthu Highway, Umlazi, Durban

Telephone: (31) 907-7111
Fax: (31) 907-2892
E-mail: miken@julian.mantec.ac.za
Internet: www.mantec.ac.za

Founded 1978
Academic year: January to December

Prin. and Vice-Chancellor: Prof. A. M. NDLOVU
Vice-Prin. for Academic Affairs: Prof. E. C. ZINGU
Vice-Prin. for Admin.: Dr Y. L. MBELE
Academic Registrar: S. NAIDOO

Library of 54,454 vols
Number of teachers: 150
Number of students: 10,000

DEANS

Faculty of Engineering: S. MALINGA
Faculty of Management Sciences: Prof. E. C. ZINGU
Faculty of Natural Sciences: Prof. ALLAN FEMI LANA

NELSON MANDELA METROPOLITAN UNIVERSITY

POB 77000, Port Elizabeth 6031

Telephone: (41) 504-1111
Fax: (41) 583-1558
E-mail: info@nmmu.ac.za
Internet: www.nmmu.ac.za

Founded 2005 by merger of Univ. of Port Elizabeth, PE Technikon and the Port Elizabeth Campus of Vista Univ.
Public control
Language of instruction: English
Academic year: February to November

Vice-Chancellor and CEO: Prof. DERRICK SWARTZ
Deputy Vice-Chancellors: Prof. CHRISTO VAN LOGGERENBERG
Deputy Vice-Chancellor: Dr SIBONGILE MUTHWA
Deputy Vice-Chancellor: Prof. MOHAMMED JEENAH
Campus Prin. for George Campus: Prof. CHRISTO FABRICIUS
Campus Prin. for Missionvale Campus: KHAYA MATISO
Campus Prin. for Vista Campus: Prof. M. STRUWIG
Dean of Students: THOBEKO SOGA

Library: see Libraries and Archives
Number of teachers: 1,500
Number of students: 25,000

DEANS

Faculty of Arts: Prof. VELILE NOTSHULWANA
Faculty of Business and Economic Sciences: Prof. NIEKIE DORFLING
Faculty of Education: Prof. DENISE ZINN
Faculty of Engineering: Prof. HENK DE JAGER
Faculty of Health Sciences: Prof. RAJ NAIDOO
Faculty of Law: Prof. VIVIENNE LAWACK-DAVIDS
Faculty of Science: Prof. ANDREW LEITCH

NORTH-WEST UNIVERSITY

Mafikeng Campus, PMB X2046, Mmabatho 2735

Telephone: (18) 389-2111
Fax: (18) 392-5775
E-mail: motabogis@uniwest.ac.za
Internet: www.uniwest.ac.za

Founded 1980 as Univ. of North-West; merged with Potchefstroom Univ. and incorporated Sebokeng Campus of Vista Univ. 2004
Autonomous control
Languages of instruction: Afrikaans, English
Academic year: February to November

Chancellor: Dr POPO MOLEFE
Vice-Chancellor: Dr THEUNS ELOFF
Chair. of the Ccl: L. NYHONYA
Vice-Prin.: Dr M. N. TAKALO
Registrar: Prof. C. F. C. VAN DER WALT
Librarian: DUDU NKOSI

Library of 90,000 vols
Number of teachers: 588 (Potchefstroom and Vaal Triangle Campus 226 full-time, 7 part-time (incl. 99 professors); Mafikeng Campus 172 full-time, 183 part-time)
Number of students: 40,702 (Potchefstroom Campus 28,390; Vaal Triangle Campus 2,836; Mafikeng Campus 9,476)

Publications: *Didaktikom* (4 a year), *Fokus* (4 a year), *In die Skriflig* (4 a year), *Koers* (4 a year), *Literator* (3 a year), *Woord en Daad* (4 a year)

DEANS

Mafikeng Campus:
- Faculty of Agriculture, Science and Technology: Dr S. H. TAOLE
- Faculty of Commerce and Admin.: G. D. STESETSE
- Faculty of Education: L. M. E. M. SEHLARE
- Faculty of Human and Social Sciences: Dr R. M. MANYANE
- Faculty of Law: R. L. KETTLES

Potchefstroom Campus:
- Faculty of Arts: Prof. A. L. COMBRINK
- Faculty of Economic and Management Sciences: Prof. G. J. DE KLERK
- Faculty of Educational Sciences: Prof. H. J. STEYN
- Faculty of Engineering: Prof. J. I. J. FICK
- Faculty of Health Sciences: Prof. H. A. KOELEMAN
- Faculty of Law: Prof. F. VENTER
- Faculty of Natural Sciences: Prof. D. J. VAN WYK
- Faculty of Theology: Prof. A. LE R. DU PLOOY

Vaal Triangle Campus:
- Vaal Triangle Faculty: Prof. A. M. C. THERON

PROFESSORS

Mafikeng Campus (Private Bag X2046, Mmabatho 2735; tel. (18) 389-2111; fax (18) 392-5575; e-mail travisk@uniwest.ac.za; internet www.uniwest.ac.za):

Faculty of Agriculture, Science and Technology:

BEIGHLE, D. E., Animal Health
FUNNAH, S. M., Plant Production
KHALIQUE, C. M., Mathematical Sciences
TAOLO, S. H., Mathematical Sciences

Faculty of Human and Social Sciences:

CHIKULO, B. C., Development Studies
KALULE-SABITI, I., Population Training and Research Unit
MANSON, A., History
MOGEKWU, M., Communication

Faculty of Law:

MBAO, M. L. M., Public Law and Legal Philosophy

Potchefstroom Campus (Private Bag X6001, Potchefstroom 2520; tel. (18) 299-1111; fax (18) 299-2799; internet www.puk.ac.za):

Faculty of Arts:

CARSTENS, W. A. M., School of Languages (Dir)
COMBRINK, A. L., Dean
DE LANGE, A. M., English and Literature
DU PISANI, J. A., History
DU PLESSIS, H. G. W., ATKV Writing School
DU PLOOY, H. J. G., Afrikaans and Dutch
JOOSTE, S. J., Music
MOLLER, P. H., Sociology
SCHUTTE, P. J., Communication Studies
VAN DER WALT, J. L., English and Literature
VAN WYK, W. J., School of Social Studies (Dir)
VENTER, J. J., Philosophy

Faculty of Economic and Management Sciences:

BISSCHOFF, C. A., Potchefstroom Business School
COETSEE, L. D., Potchefstroom Business School
COETZEE, K., Chartered Accountant Training
COETZEE, W. N., Potchefstroom Business School
DE KLERK, G. J., Dean
DU PLESSIS, J. L., Potchefstroom Business School
DU TOIT, A., Chartered Accountant Training
ELOFF, T., School of Accounting Sciences (Dir)
GERICKE, J. S., Chartered Accountant Training
JANSEN VAN RENSBURG, L. R., Entrepreneurship, Marketing and Tourism Management
JORDAAN, K., Chartered Accountant Training
KOTZE, J. G., Potchefstroom Business School
KROON, J., Entrepreneurship, Marketing and Tourism Management
NAUDE, W. A., Decision-making and Management for Economic Development
PRETORIUS, J. P. S., Potchefstroom Business School
RADEMEYER, A., Chartered Accountant Training
ROTHMAN, S., Industrial Psychology
SAAYMAN, M., Tourism
SCHOLTZ, P. E., School of Human Resource Sciences (Dir)
VAN HEERDEN, J. H. P., School of Economics, Risk Management and International Trade (Dir)
VISSER, S. S., Management Accountant Training
VIVIERS, W., Economics, Risk Management and International Trade

Faculty of Educational Sciences:

DREYER, C., Postgraduate School of Education
MENTZ, P. J., Education and Training
MONTEITH, J. L. D. K., Postgraduate School of Education
SPAMER, E. J., Teachers' Centre
STEYN, H. J., Dean
VAN DER WESTHUIZEN, P. C., Postgraduate School of Education

Faculty of Engineering:

DE KOCK, J. A., Electrical and Electronic Engineering
DU TOIT, C. G. D. K., Mechanical and Material Engineering
FICK, J. I. J., Dean
GREYVENSTEIN, G. P., Mechanical and Material Engineering
HELBERG, A. S. J., Electrical and Electronic Engineering
HOFFMAN, A. J., Electrical and Electronic Engineering
MATHEWS, E. H., Centre for Research and Commercialization
ROUSSEAU, P. G., Energy Systems
WAANDERS, F. B., Chemical and Mineral Engineering

Faculty of Health Sciences:

BERGH, J. J., Pharmaceutical Chemistry
BONESCHANS, B., CENQAM
BREYTENBACH, J. C., Pharmaceutical Chemistry
DE RIDDER, J. H., Human Movement Studies
DEKKER, T. G., Industrial Pharmacy
DU PLESSIS, J., Drug Research and Development
GREEF, M., Nursing
HARVEY, B. H., Pharmacy
KOELEMAN, H. A., Dean
KOTZÉ, A. F., Pharmaceutics
KOTZE, G. J., Social Work
LIEBENBERG, W., Institute for Industrial Pharmacy
MALAN, D. D. J., Human Movement Studies
MALAN, N. T., Physiology, Nutrition and Consumer Sciences
OLIVER, D. W., Pharmacy
STRYDOM, H., Social Work
THOMAS, A. J., Pharmacy
VENTER, C. A., Physiology
VENTER, D. P., Pharmacology
WISSING, M. P., Psycho-social Behavioural Science

Faculty of Law:

DU PLESSIS, W., Legal Pluralism and Legal History
FERREIRA, G. M., Public Law and Legal Philosophy
PIENAAR, G. J., Private Law
ROBINSON, J. A., Private Law
STANDER, A. L., Private Law
VENTER, F., Dean

Faculty of Natural Sciences:

BOUWMAN, H., Zoology
BREET, E. L. J., Chemistry
BRUINSMA, O. S. L., Separation Sciences and Technology
BURGER, R. A., Space Physics
DE JAGER, O. C., Physics
DE JONGH, D. C. J., Centre for Business Mathematics and Informatics
DE JONGH, P. J., Centre for Business Mathematics and Informatics
DE KLERK, J. H., Mathematics
DE VILLIERS, A. B., Geography and Environmental Studies
DU TOIT, G. J., Environment Sciences and Management
FOURIE, J. H., Computer, Statistical and Mathematical Sciences
GEYSER, H. S., Town and Regional Planning
GROBLER, J. J., Business Mathematics and Informatics
KOTZÉ, H. F., Biochemistry
MORAAL, H., Physics
PETERSEN, M. A., Mathematics
PIENAAR, J. J., Chemistry and Biochemistry
PIETERSE, A. J. H., Life Sciences
POTGIETER, M. S., Physics
RAUBENHEIMER, B. C., Space Physics
RIEDEL, K. J., Microbiology
STEYN, T., Computer Sciences and Information
STYGER, P., Centre for Business Mathematics and Informatics
SWANEPOEL, J. W. H., Statistics and Operational Research
THERON, P. D., Zoology
VAN DER WALT, D. J., Physics
VAN HAMBURG, H., Environment Sciences and Development
VAN WYK, D. J., Dean
VOSLOO, H. C. M., Chemistry

Faculty of Theology:

DE KLERK, B. J., Practical Theology
DU PLOOY, A. LE R., Dean
JANSE VAN RENSBURG, J. J., New Testament
JORDAAN, G. J. C., New Testament
LOTTER, G. A., Practical Theology
VAN ROOY, H. F., Theology and the Development of the South African Society
VENTER, J. M., Practical Theology
VORSTER, J. M., Ecclesiology

Vaal Triangle Campus (Private Bag X6001, Potchefstroom 2520; tel. (16) 910-3710; fax (16) 910-3103; e-mail dvdamct@puknet.puk.ac.za; internet www.puk.ac.za):

Faculty of the Vaal Triangle:

DE KLERK, P., History
JORDAAN, D. B., Modelling Sciences
LUCOUW, P., Economic Sciences
PRETORIUS, J. B., Business Management
THERON, A. M. C., Dean
VERHOEF, M. M., Languages

RHODES UNIVERSITY

POB 94, Grahamstown 6140
Telephone: (46) 603-8101
Fax: (46) 603-8127
E-mail: registrar@ru.ac.za
Internet: www.ru.ac.za

Founded 1904; East London Campus incorporated into Univ. of Fort Hare 2004
State control
Language of instruction: English
Academic year: February to November (4 terms)

Chancellor: Prof. G. J. GERWEL
Chair. of the Ccl: Hon. Mr Justice R. J. W. JONES
Prin. and Vice-Chancellor: D. R. WOODS
Vice-Prin. and Pro-Vice-Chancellor: C. T. JOHNSON
Dean of Research: J. R. DUNCAN
Dean of Students: M. A. MOTARA
Registrar: S. FOURIE
Librarian: M. A. E. KENYON

Library: see Libraries and Archives
Number of teachers: 305
Number of students: 6,155

Publications: *English in Africa* (1 a year), *Journal of Contemporary African Studies* (2 a year), *New Coin Poetry* (2 a year), *Philosophical Papers* (2 a year), *Rhodes Journalism Review* (irregular)

DEANS

Faculty of Commerce: A. C. M. WEBB
Faculty of Education: G. J. EUVRARD
Faculty of Humanities: F. T. HENDRICKS
Faculty of Law: J. R. MIDGLEY
Faculty of Pharmacy: I. KANFER
Faculty of Science: P. D. TERRY

PROFESSORS

ADENDORFF, R., English Language and Linguistics
ADESINA, J. O. T., Sociology and Industrial Sociology
ANTROBUS, G. G., Economics
BERGER, G. J. E. G., Journalism and Media Studies
BERNARD, R. T. F., Zoology
BLATCH, G. L., Biochemistry, Microbiology and Biotechnology
BOTHA, C. E. J., Botany
CHARTERIS, J., Human Kinetics and Ergonomics
CLAYTON, P. G., Computer Science
COETZEE, J. K., Sociology and Industrial Sociology

CRAIG, A. T. F., Zoology and Entomology
DAVIES-COLEMAN, M. T., Chemistry
DAYA, S., Pharmacy
DE KLERK, V. A., Linguistics and English Language
DE WET, C. J., Anthropology
DUNCAN, J. R., Biochemistry
EDWARDS, D. J. A., Psychology
EUVRARD, G. J., Education
FABRICIUS, C., Environmental Science
FAURE, P., Economics
FOX, R. C., Geography
GORDON, G. E., Drama
GOUWS, J. S., English
HAIGH, J. M., Pharmacy
HARVEY, N., Management
HENDRICKS, F. T., Sociology and Industrial Sociology
HEPBURN, H. R., Entomology
HODGSON, A. N., Zoology and Entomology
HUGHES, D. A., Water Research
IRWIN, P. R., Education
JACOB, R. E., Geology
JAQUES, F. E., School of Languages
JONAS, J. L., Physics and Electronics
KANFER, I., Pharmaceutics
KAYE, P. T., Organic Chemistry
LEWIS, C. A., Geography
MABIZELA, S. G., Pure and Applied Mathematics
MARSH, J. S., Geology
MAYLAM, P. R., History
MCQUAID, C. D., Zoology
MIDGLEY, J. R., Law
MØLLER, V., Social and Economic Research
MOORE, J. M., Exploration Geology
MQEKE, R. B., Law
NEL, E. L., Geography
NEL, H., Economics
NYOKONG, T., Chemistry
RADLOFF, S. E., Statistics
ROSE, P. D., Biotechnology
ROWNTREE, K. M., Geography
SCARR, D. T., Music and Musicology
SCHMAHMANN, B. L., Fine Art
SCOTT, P. A., Human Kinetics and Ergonomics
SEWRY, D. A., Information Systems
SKELTON, P., Aquatic Biodiversity
STACK, E. M., Accounting
STAUDE, G. E., Management
STONES, C. R., Psychology
TERRY, P. D., Computer Science
VALE, P. C. J., Political and International Studies
WALTERS, P. S., English
WEBB, A. C. M., Economics
WENTWORTH, E. P., Computer Science
WRIGHT, L. S., Study of English in Africa

TSHWANE UNIVERSITY OF TECHNOLOGY

PMB X 680, Pretoria 0001
Telephone: (12) 318-5911
Fax: (12) 318-5114
E-mail: general@tut.ac.za
Internet: www.techpta.ac.za

Founded 2004 by merger of Technikon Pretoria, Technikon North Gauteng and Technikon North West

Vice-Chancellor and Rector: Prof. REGGIE NGCOBO
Exec. Mans and Deputy Vice-Chancellors: Prof. N. P. DU PREEZ, Prof. H. H. DÜRRHEIM, Prof. J. G. PRETORIUS
Registrar: N. J. V. D. M. STOFBERG
Library Dir: Dr A. SWANEPOEL

Library of 70,000 vols
Number of students: 40,000

Publication: *Peritus* (4 a year)

DEANS

Faculty of Agriculture, Horticulture and Nature Conservation: Prof. J. J. BOTHA
Faculty of Arts: E. R. DINKELMANN
Faculty of Economic Sciences: Prof. M. J. VAN DER MERWE
Faculty of Engineering: Prof. F. OTIENO
Faculty of Health Sciences: Prof. M. M. J. LOWES
Faculty of Information and Communication Technology: Dr J. ZAAIMAN
Faculty of Natural Sciences: Prof P. J. J. G. MARAIS
Faculty of Social Development Sciences: Prof. S. N. IMENDA

UNIVERSITY OF CAPE TOWN

Private Bag X3, Rondebosch 7701
Telephone: (21) 650-9111
Fax: (21) 650-2138
E-mail: int-iapo@uct.ac.za
Internet: www.uct.ac.za

Founded 1829 as South African College; univ. status 1918
Autonomous, state-subsidized
Language of instruction: English
Academic year: February to December (2 semesters)

Chancellor: GRAÇA MACHEL
Vice-Chancellor: Dr MAX PRICE
Deputy Vice-Chancellors: Prof. T. NHLAPO, Prof. J. BEALL, Prof. C. SOUDIEN, Prof. D. VISSER
Registrar: HUGH AMOORE
Librarian: JOAN RAPP

Library: see Libraries and Archives
Number of teachers: 1,980
Number of students: 23,500

Publications: *Acta Juridica* (1 a year), *Contributions from the Bolus Herbarium* (irregular), *Journal of Energy in Southern Africa* (4 a year), *Pretexts* (4 a year), *Responsa Meridiana* (1 a year), *Sea Changes* (2 a year), *Selected Energy Statistics: Southern Africa* (4 a year), *Social Dynamics* (2 a year), *UCT Research Report* (1 a year)

DEANS

Faculty of Commerce: Prof. DON ROSS
Faculty of Engineering and the Built Environment: Prof. FRANCIS PETERSEN
Faculty of Health Sciences: Prof. MARIAN JACOBS
Faculty of Humanities: Prof. PAULA ENSOR
Faculty of Law: Prof. PAMELA JANE SCHWIKKARD
Faculty of Science: Prof. KATHY DRIVER
Graduate School of Business: Prof. WALTER BAETS
Centre for Higher Education Devt: Prof. NAN YELD

PROFESSORS

Faculty of Commerce (tel. (21) 650-2694; fax (21) 650-2696; e-mail comsec@commerce.uct.ac.za):

ABEDIAN, I., Economics
BARR, G. D. I., Statistical Sciences
BRADFIELD, D., Statistical Sciences
DORRINGTON, R. E., Management Studies
EVERINGHAM, G. K., Accounting
FAULL, N. H. B., Graduate School of Business
HORWITZ, F., Graduate School of Business
KAHN, S. B., Economics
KANTOR, B. S., Economics
KAPLAN, D., Economics
LICKER, P. S., Information Systems
NATTRASS, N., Economics
SIMPSON, J. D., Business Science
SMITH, D. C., Information Systems
SULCAS, P., Graduate School of Business
TROSKIE, C. G., Statistical Sciences
UNDERHILL, L. G., Statistical Sciences
WILSON, F. A. H., Economics

Faculty of Engineering and the Built Environment (tel. (21) 650-2699; fax (21) 650-3782; e-mail engsec@eng.uct.ac.za):

ABBOTT, J., Civil Engineering
ALEXANDER, M. G., Civil Engineering
ALLEN, C., Mechanical Engineering
BALL, A., Mechanical Engineering
BENNETT, K. F., Mechanical Engineering
BOWEN, P. A., Construction Economics and Management
BRAAE, M., Electrical Engineering
DE JAGER, G., Electrical Engineering
DEWAR, D., School of Architecture and Planning
DOWNING, B. J., Electrical Engineering
EKAMA, G. A., Civil Engineering
GRYZAGORIDAS, T., Mechanical Engineering
HANSFORD, G. S., Chemical Engineering
NURICK, G. N., Mechanical Engineering
O'CONNOR, C. T., Chemical Engineering
REDDY, B. D., Centre for Research in Computational and Applied Mechanics
REINECK, K. M., Electrical Engineering
RÜTHER, H., Geomatics
STEVENS, A. J., Construction Economics and Management

Faculty of Health Sciences (tel. (21) 406-6346; fax (21) 447-8955; e-mail medfac@curie.uct.ac.za):

BAQWA, D., Primary Health Care
BATEMAN, E. D., Medicine
BEATTY, D. W., Paediatrics and Child Health
BENATAR, S. R., Medicine
BENINGFIELD, S. J., Radiology
BONNICI, F., Medicine
BORNMAN, P. C., Surgery
COMMERFORD, P. J., Medicine
CRUSE, J. P., Anatomical Pathology
DAVIDSON, J., Chemical Pathology
DENT, D. M., Surgery
ELS, W. J., Anatomy and Cell Biology
FOLB, P. I., Pharmacology
GEVERS, W., Medical Biochemistry
HALL, P., Anatomical Pathology
HARLEY, E. H., Chemical Pathology
JACOBS, M. E., Paediatrics and Child Health
JAMES, M. F. M., Anaesthetics
KIRSCH, R. E., Medicine
KNOBEL, G. J., Forensic Medicine and Toxicology
LOUW, J., Medicine
MOLTENO, C. D., Psychiatry
MURRAY, A. D. N., Ophthalmology
MYERS, J. E., Community Health
NOAKES, T. D., Physiology
NOVITZKY, N., Haematology
PADAYACHEE, G. N.
PARKER, M. I., Medical Biochemistry
PETER, J. C., Neurosurgery
POWER, D. J., Paediatrics and Child Health
RAMESAR, R., Human Genetics
ROBERTSON, B. A., Psychiatry
RODE, H., Paediatric Surgery
SEGGIE, J., Medicine
SELLARS, S. L., Otorhinolaryngology
STEYN, L. M., Medical Microbiology
VAN DER SPUY, Z. M., Obstetrics and Gynaecology
VAN NIEKERK, J. P., Medicine
VAUGHAN, C. L., Biomedical Engineering
VILJOEN, J. F., Anaesthesia
VON OPPEL, U., Cardiothoracic Surgery
WALTERS, J., Orthopaedic Surgery
WERNER, I. D., Radiation Oncology
WILSON, E. L., Immunology
ZILLA, P., Cardiovascular Research

Faculty of Humanities (tel. (21) 650-4216; fax (21) 686-9840; e-mail artsec@beattie.uct.ac.za):

BRINK, A., English Language and Literature
BUNTING, I., Philosophy

CHIDESTER, D. S., Religious Studies
COCHRANE, J. R., Religious Studies
COETZEE, J. M., English Language and Literature
COOPER, B., Centre for African Studies
CORNILLE, J.-L., French Language and Literature
DE GRUCHY, J., Religious Studies (Graduate School of Humanities)
DU TOIT, A. B., Political Studies
FOSTER, D. H., Psychology
GITAY, Y., Hebrew and Jewish Studies
GODBY, M. A. P., Historical Studies
HAYNES, D. J., Drama
KLATZOW, P., Music
LASS, R. G., Linguistics
LOUW, J., Psychology
MAMA, A., African Gender Institute
MAREE, J., Sociology
MAY, J., South African College of Music
MESTHRIE, R., Linguistics and Southern African Languages
MULLER, J. P., Education
NASSON, W., History
NOYES, J., German Language and Literature
REYNOLDS, P. F., Social Anthropology
SALAZAR, PH.-J., French Language and Literature (Graduate School of Humanities)
SATYO, S. C., African Languages
SAUNDERS, C. C., Historical Studies
SCHRIRE, R. A., Political Studies
SEEGERS, A., Political Studies
SHAIN, M., Hebrew and Jewish Studies
SKOTNES, P., Fine Art
SNYMAN, H. J., Afrikaans and Netherlandic Studies (Graduate School of Humanities)
TAYOB, A. I., Religious Studies
UNDERWOOD, P. G., School of Librarianship
VAN HEERDEN, E. R., Afrikaans and Netherlandic Studies
WEST, M., Social Anthropology
WHITAKER, R. A., Classics
WORDEN, N. A., Historical Studies
YOUNG, D. N., Education
YOUNGE, G., Fine Art

Faculty of Law (tel. (21) 650-3086; fax (21) 686-2577; e-mail lawnv@law.uct.ac.za):

BENNETT, T. W., Public Law
BLACKMAN, M. S., Commercial Law
BURMAN, S. B., Private Law
CHEADLE, M. H., Public Law
CORDER, H. M., Public Law
DEVINE, D. J., Public Law
HUTCHISON, D. B., Private Law
JOOSTE, R. D., Commercial Law
MALUWA, T., Public Law
MURRAY, C. M., Public Law
VAN BUEREN, G., Law
VISSER, D. P., Private Law

Faculty of Science (tel. (21) 650-2712; fax (21) 650-2710; e-mail scifac@psipsy.uct.ac.za):

ASCHMAN, D. G., Physics
BARR, G. D. I., Statistical Sciences
BECKER, R. I., Mathematics and Applied Mathematics
BOND, W., Botany
BRADFIELD, D., Statistical Sciences
BRANCH, G. M., Zoology
BRUNDRIT, G. B., Oceanography
BULL, J., Chemistry
BUTTERWORTH, D. S., Mathematics and Applied Mathematics
CLEYMANS, J. W. A., Physics
DE WIT, M. J., Geological Sciences
DOMINGUEZ, C. A., Physics
DU PLESSIS, M., Zoology
ELLIS, G. F. R., Mathematics and Applied Mathematics
FAIRALL, A. P., Astronomy
FIELD, J. G., Zoology
FUGGLE, R. F., Environmental and Geographical Science
GÄDE, G., Zoology
GURNEY, J. J., Geological Sciences
HALL, M. J., Archaeology
KHAM, M. J., Mathematics, Science and Technology Education
KLUMP, H. H., Biochemistry
KRITZINGER, P. S., Computer Science
KURTZ, D. W., Astronomy
LE ROEX, A. P., Geological Sciences
LUTJEHARMS, J. R. E., Oceanography
MACGREGOR, K. J., Computer Science
MOSS, J. R., Chemistry
NASSIMBENI, L. R., Chemistry
PARKINGTON, J. E., Archaeology
PEREZ, S. M., Physics
REDDY, B. D., Mathematics and Applied Mathematics
SILLEN, A., Archaeology
STEWART, T. J., Statistical Sciences
THOMSON, J. A., Microbiology
TROSKIE, C. G., Statistical Sciences
UNDERHILL, L. G., Statistical Sciences
VAN DER MERWE, N. J., Archaeology
VIOLLIER, R. D., Physics
WARNER, B., Astronomy
WEBB, J. H., Mathematics and Applied Mathematics

UNIVERSITY OF FORT HARE

Private Bag X1314, Alice 5700
Telephone: (40) 602-22011
Fax: (40) 653-1023
E-mail: dmc@ufh.ac.za
Internet: www.ufh.ac.za

Founded as 'South African Native College' in 1916 by the United Free Church of Scotland; transferred to the Dept of Bantu Education in 1960 to cater specifically for the Xhosa ethnic group; present name 1970; incorporated Medical School of Univ. of Transkei and East London Campus of Rhodes Univ. 2004
Language of instruction: English
Academic year: February to December

Chancellor: Prof. S. M. BHENGU
Vice-Chancellor and Rector: Prof. DERRICK SWARTZ
Deputy Vice-Chancellor for Admin. and Finance: R. OLANDER
Dean of Students: N. MORRISON
Librarian: Y. K. SOUL

Library: see Libraries
Number of teachers: 239
Number of students: 2,869

Publications: *Ardrinews*, *Fort Hare Papers*, *The Fort Harian*

DEANS

Faculty of Agricultural and Environmental Studies: Prof. J. RAATS
Faculty of Arts: Prof. C. R. BOTHA
Faculty of Economic Sciences: Prof. T. M. JORDAN
Faculty of Education: Prof. P. M. FIHLA
Faculty of Law: Prof. J. ROBBERTSON
Faculty of Medicine and Health Sciences: Prof. E. L. MAZWAI
Faculty of Science and Technology: Dr D. O. OKEYO
Faculty of Social Sciences: Prof. SOBAHLE
Faculty of Theology: Prof. S. P. ABRAHAMS

PROFESSORS

Faculty of Agricultural and Environmental Studies:

BESTER, B. J., Agricultural Economics
IGODAN, C. O., Agricultural Extension and Rural Development
MNKENI, P. N. S., Crop Science
MZAMANE, N., Agronomy
RAATS, J. G., Livestock and Pasture Science
TROLLOPE, W. S. W., Livestock and Pasture Science

Faculty of Arts:

AUCAMP, J. C., History
BOTHA, C. R., African Languages
BROUWER, P., Political Science and Public Administration
DE WET, G., Communication
ELS, J. M., Classical Languages
ETSIAH, A. K., Political Science and Public Administration
HALLIER, M. G. T., Fine Arts
LOSAMBE, L., English
LOUW, T. J. G., Philosophy
PRINS, M. J., Afrikaans and Dutch
SIRAYI, G. T., Centre for Cultural Studies
VERHAGE, H. M., Psychology

Faculty of Economic Sciences:

JORDAN, T. M., Accountancy
SWARTZ, D. I., Intergovernmental Relations
VAN DAALEN, H. J., Industrial Psychology

Faculty of Education:

DARGIE, D. J., Music
DREYER, J. N., Foundations of Education
FILHA, P. M., Educational Psychology
JIYA, M. A. Y., Curriculum Studies and Didactics
LINDEQUE, B. R. G., Curriculum Studies and Didactics

Faculty of Law:

DU PLESSIS, P. A., Mercantile Law
IYA, P. F., African and Comparative Law
LABUSCHAGNE, J., Constitutional and Public International Law
REMBE, N. S., Oliver Tambo Chair of Human Rights

Faculty of Scienceand Technology:

BRAND, J. M., Biochemistry and Microbiology
FATOKI, O. S., Chemistry
MAKUNGA, O. H. D., Plant Sciences
SADIMENKO, A., Chemistry
SANYAL, D. K., Chemistry
SERETIO, J. R., Physics
TYLER, J. C., Statistics
VAN DYK, T. J., Mathematics
VAN HEERDEN, J. W. A., Zoology
WAGENER, P. C., Applied Mathematics

Faculty of Theology:

ABRAHAMS, S. P., Old Testament and Hebrew
THOM, G., Historical and Contextual Theology

UNIVERSITY OF JOHANNESBURG

POB 524, Auckland Park, Johannesburg 2092
Telephone: (11) 559-4555
Fax: (11) 559-2191
Internet: www.uj.ac.za

Founded 2005 by merger of Rand Afrikaans Univ. and Technikon Witwatersrand
State control
Languages of instruction: Afrikaans, English
Academic year: January to November

Chancellor: WENDY LUHABE
Vice-Chancellor: Prof. IHRON RENSBURG
Pro-Vice-Chancellor: Prof. DEREK VAN DER MERWE
Deputy Vice-Chancellor for Academic: Prof. ANGINA PAREKH
Deputy Vice-Chancellor for Research, Innovation and Advancement: Prof. ADAM HABIB
Deputy Vice-Chancellor for Finance: Prof. HENK KRIEK

Library of 452,273 vols
Number of teachers: 350
Number of students: 49,000

DEANS

Faculty of Art, Design and Architecture: MARIAN SAUTHOFF

Faculty of Economic and Financial Science: Prof. AMANDA DEMPSEY
Faculty of Education: Prof. SARAH GRAVETT
Faculty of Engineering and the Built Environment: Prof. TSHILIDZI MARWALA
Faculty of Health: Prof. ANDRE SWART
Faculty of Humanities: Prof. RORY RYAN
Faculty of Law: Prof. PATRICK O'BRIEN
Faculty of Management: Prof. STEPHEN KRUGER
Faculty of Natural Science: Prof. KINTA BURGER

PROFESSORS

ABRAHAMSE, H., Biomedical Technology
ALBERTS, V., Physics
ALEXANDER, P., Centre for Sociological Research
AMORY, A., Mathematics, Science, Technology and Computer Education
ANKIEWICZ, P., Mathematics, Science, Technology and Computer Education
ANNEGARN, H., Geography and Environmental Management and Energy Studies
AURIACOMBE, C., Public Governance
BERNDT, A., Marketing Management
BEUKES, N., Geology
BOESSENKOOL, A., Business Management
BROERE, I., Mathematics
BUHLUNGU, S., Sociology
BURGER, W., Afrikaans
BURNETT-LOUW, C., Sport and Movement Studies
CAIRNCROSS, B., Geology
CASE, M., Power and Control Engineering Technology
CHABELI, M., Professional Nursing Practice
CLOETE, G., Public Governance
COETSEE, D., Accountancy
COETZEE, J., Biblical and Religious Studies
COETZEE, J., Industrial Psychology and People Management
COETZEE, P., Chemistry
CONNELL, S., Geography and Environmental Management and Energy Studies
CONRADIE, C., Afrikaans
CONRADIE, W., APB Entrepreneurship
CORNELIUS, S., Private Law
CROUS, F., Industrial Psychology and People Management
DARKWA, J., Chemistry
DE BRUIN, G., Industrial Psychology and People Management
DE BRUYN, H., Business Management
DE KLERK, N., Communication
DE VILLIERS, D., Criminal Law and Procedure
DE WET, D., Humanities Dean's Office
DEMPSEY, A., Economic and Financial Sciences Dean's Office
DU RAND, J., Biblical and Religious Studies
DU TOIT, A., Information and Knowledge Management
DU TOIT, S., Mercantile Law
DUBERY, I., Biochemistry
EHLERS, E., Academy for Information Technology
ESACK, F., Psychology
FERREIRA, H., Electrical and Electronic Engineering Science
FERREIRA, J., Optometry
FRANGOS, C., Statistics
GELDENHUYS, D., Politics
GREYLING, L., Economics and Econometrics
GRUNDLINGH, L., Historical Studies
HAARHOFF, J., Civil Engineering Science
HAMILTON, L., Politics
HARRIS, W., Optometry
HOLLANDER, W., Sport
JACOBS, G., Division for Institutional Planning and Quality Promotions
JANSE VAN RENSBURG, J., Semitic Languages
JANSE VAN VUREN, J., Zoology
JOHL, C., Linguistics and Literary Theory
JOOSTE, C., Marketing Management
JOOSTE, K., Professional Nursing Practice
KATZ, Z., Mechanical Engineering Science
KRUGER, G., Chemistry
KRUGER, S., Management Dean's Office
LANDSBERG, C., Politics
LOMBARD, F., Statistics
LOTTER, H., Philosophy
MACKENZIE, C., English
MAINA, J., SWC Chemistry
MALHERBE, E., Public Law
MANS, K., Accountancy
MARWALA, T., Engineering and the Built Environment Dean's Office
MARX, B., Accountancy
METZ, T., Philosophy
MOORE, D., Anthropology and Development Studies
MYBURGH, C., Educational Psychology
NEELS, J., Private Law
NEL, A., Mechanical Engineering Science
NIEUWENHUIZEN, C., Business Management
NOLTE, A., Maternal and Child Nursing
NURICK, A., Mechanical Engineering Science
O'BRIEN, P., Law Dean's Office
OLDEWAGE, A., Zoology
OLIVIER, L., Accountancy
OTTO, J., Private Law
PATEL, L., Social Work
PIENAAR, M., Afrikaans
PILLAY, J., Educational Psychology
POGGENPOEL, M., Psychiatric Nursing
POSTHUMUS, L., African Languages
PRETORIUS, J., Electrical and Electronic Engineering Science
PRINSLOO, G., Transport and Supply Chain Management
RAUBENHEIMER, H., Mathematics
RAUTENBACH, I., Law Dean's Office
RENSLEIGH, C., Information and Knowledge Management
ROODT, G., Industrial Psychology and People Management
RUTTKAMP, E., Philosophy
SADIE, A., Politics
SAUTHOFF, M., APB Art, Design and Architecture Dean's Office
SCHERZINGER, K., English
SMIT, N., Mercantile Law
SMITH, D., Industrial Psychology and People Management
SNYMAN, J., Philosophy
SONNEKUS, J., Private Law
STEEB, W., Applied Mathematics
STONES, C., Psychology
STRYDOM, A., Physics
STRYDOM, H., Public Law
THOMAS, A., Business Management
TRIEGAARDT, J., Social Work
UYS, J., Industrial Psychology and People Management
UYS, J., Sociology
VAN DER BANK, F., Zoology
VAN DER LINDE, K., Mercantile Law
VAN DER WESTHUIZEN, D., Mathematics, Science, Technology and Computer Education
VAN LILL, D., Tourism and Hospitality Management
VAN ROOYEN, H., Curriculum and Instruction
VAN TONDER, C., Industrial Psychology and People Management
VAN VUUREN, L., Industrial Psychology and People Management
VAN WYK, B., Botany and Plant Biotechnology
VAN ZYL, G., Economics and Econometrics
VELDSMAN, T., Industrial Psychology and People Management
VENTER, A., Politics
VERHOEF, G., Accountancy
VERWEY, S., Communication
VILJOEN, K., Geology
VILLET, C., Applied Mathematics
VIVIERS, H., Biblical and Religious Studies
VON SOLMS, S., Academy for Information Technology
VOOGT, T., Accountancy
WALTERS, J., Transport and Supply Chain Management
WATNEY, M., Criminal Law and Procedure
WEPENER, V., Zoology
WHITEHEAD, C., Botany and Plant Biotechnology
WILLIAMS, D., Chemistry
WINKLER, H., Physics
WOLMARANS, J., Greek and Latin Studies
ZIMPER, A., Economics and Econometrics

UNIVERSITY OF KWAZULU-NATAL

Westville Campus, PMB X54001, Durban 4000
Telephone: (31) 260-7111
Fax: (31) 204-4383
E-mail: enquiries@ukzn.ac.za
Internet: www.ukzn.ac.za

Founded 2004 by merger of Univ. of Natal and Univ. of Durban-Westville
Language of instruction: English
Autonomous control
Academic year: February to December (4 terms)

Chancellor: Judge ZAC M. YACOOB
Vice-Chancellor and Prin.: Prof. M. W. MAKGOBA
Deputy Vice-Chancellor for Finance and Admin.: Prof. HILTON STANILAND
Deputy Vice-Chancellor for Research and Devt: Prof. SALIM S. ABDOOL KARIM

Publication: *Con-text* (irregular)

DEANS

Faculty of Education: Prof. TUNTUFYE MWAMWENDA
Faculty of Engineering: Prof. DENYS SCHREINER
Faculty of Health Sciences: Prof. LEANA UYS
Faculty of Humanities, Devt and Social Science: (vacant)
Faculty of Law: Prof. L. GERING
Faculty of Management Studies: Prof. KANTILAL BHOWAN (Asst Dean)
Faculty of Nursing: Prof. OLUYINKA ADEJUMO (Head of School)
Faculty of Science and Agriculture: Prof. P. J. K. ZACHARIAS

BRANCH CAMPUSES

Edgewood Campus: cnr Richmond Rd and Marionhill Rd, Pinetown 3605; tel. (31) 260-3414; e-mail connawayn@ukzn.ac.za.

Howard College Campus: University KZN, Durban 4041; tel. (31) 260-2212.

Medical School Campus: Umbilo Rd, Durban 4013; tel. (31) 260-4248; e-mail undergrad@ukzn.ac.za.

Pietermaritzburg Campus: King Edward Ave, Scottsville, Pietermaritzburg 3209; tel. (33) 260-5212; e-mail naidoo@ukzn.ac.za.

UNIVERSITY OF LIMPOPO

PMB X1106, Sovenga 0727
Telephone: (15) 268-3061
Fax: (15) 268-3567
Internet: www.ul.ac.za

Founded 2005 by the merger of Medical University of Southern Africa and Univ. of the North
Academic year: January to December

Vice-Chancellor: Prof. MOKGALONG (acting)
Campus Prin.: K. NHLANE (acting)
Registrar: Prof. P. FRANKS (acting)

Library: see Libraries and Archives
Number of teachers: 400
Number of students: 12,000.

CONSTITUENT CAMPUSES

Medunsa Campus

POB 189, Medunsa 0204
Telephone: (12) 521-4111

DEANS

Faculty of Dentistry: Prof. T. S. GUGUSHE
Faculty of Medicine: Prof. C. F. VAN DER MERWE (acting)
Faculty of Sciences: Prof. J. V. GROENEWALD
National School of Public Health: Prof. A. A. HERMAN

Turfloop Campus

PMB X1106, Sovenga, Limpopo 0727
Telephone: (15) 268-9111
Fax: (15) 267-0152

DEANS

Faculty of Humanities: Prof. L. J. TEFFO
Faculty of Management Sciences and Law: Prof. P. E. FRANKS
Faculty of Sciences, Health and Agriculture: Dr N. M. MOKGALONG

DIRECTORS

Faculty of Humanities:
- School of Education: Prof. J. KUIPER
- School of Languages and Communication Studies: Prof. S. LOUW
- School of Social Sciences: Dr N. C. KIRK

Faculty of Management Sciences and Law:
- School of Economics and Management: Prof. A. DE VILLIERS
- School of Law: Prof. M. C. OKBPALUBA
- Graduate School of Leadership: Prof. L. G. BUBERWA

Faculty of Sciences, Health and Agriculture:
- School of Agricultural and Environmental Sciences: Prof. N. M. MOLLEL
- School of Computational and Mathematical Sciences: Prof. B. W. BECKER
- School of Health Sciences: Prof. P. A. VENTER
- School of Physical and Mineral Sciences: Dr W. P. MASHELA (acting)

UNIVERSITY OF PRETORIA

Pretoria 0002
Telephone: (12) 420-4111
Fax: (12) 362-5168
E-mail: csc@up.ac.za
Internet: www.up.ac.za
Founded 1908 as Transvaal Univ. College; granted Charter as Univ. of Pretoria 1930
Private control
Languages of instruction: Afrikaans, English
Academic year: February to December (two semesters)

Chancellor: Dr C. L. STALS
Vice-Chancellor and Prin.: Prof. C. W. I. PISTORIUS
Advisor to the Prin.: Prof. A. P. MELCK
Vice-Prins: Prof. C. R. DE BEER, Prof. R. M. CREWE, Prof. N. C. MANGANYI, Prof. R. A. MOGOTLANE
Exec. Dirs: Prof. A. M. DE KLERK, J. S. J. NEL, Prof. S. VIL-NKOMO
Head of the Secretariat: M. G. VILJOEN
Registrar: Prof. N. J. GROVÉ
Dir for Academic Admin.: Dr D. D. MARAIS
Dir of Academic Information Service: Prof. J. A. BOON
Dir of Client Services Centre: Dr K. LAZENBY
Dir for Corporate Communication and Marketing: Dr K. LAZENBY
Dir of Facilities Planning and Services: D. MOKOTEDI
Dir of Financial Admin.: T. G. KRUGER
Dir of Human Resources: Prof. A. VAN ASWEGEN
Dir of Dept of Information Technology: Dr J. A. PRETORIUS
Dir of Institutional Research and Planning: Prof. P. J. VERMEULEN
Dir of Mamelodi Campus: E. SMITH
Dir of Management Services: Prof. Q. VORSTER
Dir of Telematic Learning and Education Innovation: Prof. J. A. BOON
Dir of TuksSport: J. K. VAN DER WALT
Dean of Students: Prof. M. T. SPECKMAN

Library: see Libraries and Archives

Number of teachers: 1,385
Number of students: 39,000

Publications: *Ad Destinatum: Gedenkboek van die Universiteit van Pretoria*, *Huldigingsbundels* (irregular), *Openbare Fakulteitslesings* (irregular), *Opvoedkundige Studies* (Educational Studies, 3 or 4 a year), *Publikasies van die Universiteit van Pretoria–Nuwe Reeks* (Publications of the University of Pretoria—New Series (I) Research, 1 a year), *Tukkie-Werf* (4 a year)

DEANS

Faculty of Economic and Management Sciences: Prof. C. KOORNHOF
Faculty of Education: Prof. J. D. JANSEN
Faculty of Engineering, Built Environment and Information Technology: Prof. R. F. SANDENBERGH
Faculty of Health Sciences: Prof. T. J. MARIBA
Faculty of Humanities: Prof. M. E. MULLER
Faculty of Law: Prof. D. G. KLEYN
Faculty of Natural and Agricultural Sciences: Prof. A. STRÖH
Faculty of Theology: Prof. C. A. VOS
Faculty of Veterinary Science: Prof. N. P. J. KRIEK
School of Dentistry: Prof. A. J. LIGTHELM (Chair.)

PROFESSORS

Faculty of Economic and Management Sciences:
- ALBERTS, N. F., Tourism Management
- BASSON, J. S., Human Resources Management
- BLIGNAUT, J. N., Economics
- BRAND, H. E., Human Resources Management
- BRYNARD, P. A., School of Public Management and Administration
- DE BEER, J. J., Human Resources Management
- DE JAGER, H., Auditing
- DE LA REY, J. H., Financial Management
- DE VILLIERS, C. J., Financial Management
- DE WET, J. M., Marketing and Communication Management
- DE WIT, P. W. C., Business Management
- DU PLESSIS, P. J., Marketing and Communication Management
- FOURIE, D. J., School of Public Management and Administration
- GLOECK, J. D., Auditing
- GOUWS, D. G., Financial Management
- HALL, J. H., Financial Management
- HARMSE, C., Economics
- HEATH, E. T., Tourism Management
- HOOLE, C. R., Human Resources Management
- KOORNHOFF, C., Accounting
- KUYE, J. O., School of Public Management and Administration
- LAMBRECHTS, H. A., Financial Management
- MAASDORP, E. F. DE V., Business Management
- MARX, A. E., Business Management
- OOST, E. J., Financial Management
- SCHOEMAN, N. J., Economics
- STEYN, F. G., Economics
- THORNHILL, C., School of Public Management and Administration
- VAN DER SCHYF, D. B., Auditing
- VAN HEERDEN, J. H., Economics
- VERMEULEN, L. P., Human Resources Management

Faculty of Education:
- ALANT, E., Augmentative and Alternative Communication
- BECKMANN, J. L., Education Management and Policy Studies
- BOUWER, A. C., Educational Psychology
- CRONJÉ, J. C., Curriculum Studies
- FRASER, W. J., Curriculum Studies
- MAREE, J. G., Curriculum Studies
- NKOMO, M., Educational Management and Policy Studies
- ONWU, G. O. M., Science, Mathematics and Technology Education
- VAN ROOYEN, L., Curriculum Studies

Faculty of Engineering, Built Environment and Information Technology (University of Pretoria, Pretoria 0002; tel. (12) 420-2005; fax (12) 362-5173; e-mail dean@eng.up.ac.za; internet www.up.ac.za/ebit):
- BOTHMA, T. J. D., Information Science
- BRÜMMER, D. G., Construction Economics
- CLAASEN, S. J., Industrial and Systems Engineering
- CRIMSEHL, U. H. J., Chemical Engineering
- DE VILLIERS, C., Informatics
- ELOFF, J. H. P., Computer Science
- FISHER, R. C., Architecture
- GRIMSEHL, U. H. J., Chemical Engineering
- HORAK, E., Civil and Biosystems Engineering
- LEUSCHNER, F. W., Electrical, Electronic and Computer Engineering
- MEYER, J. P., Mechanical and Aeronautical Engineering
- ORANJE, M. C., Town and Regional Planning
- PISTORIUS, P. C., Materials Science and Metallurgical Engineering
- POURIS, A., Institute for Technological Innovation
- PRETORIUS, M. W., Engineering and Technology Management
- VAN DER MERWE, J. N., Mining Engineering

Faculty of Health Sciences:
- ANDERSON, R., Immunology
- BARTEL, P. R., Neurology
- BECKER, J. H. R., Surgery
- BLITZ-LINDEQUE, J. J., Family Medicine
- BUCH, E., School of Health Systems and Public Health
- DIPPENAAR, N. G., Physiology
- DREYER, L., Anatomical Pathology
- DU PLESSIS, D. J., Cardiothoracic Surgery
- GREY, S. V., Health Sciences General
- KER, J. A., Internal Medicine
- KRUGER, M., Paediatrics
- LEVINSON, I. P., Urology
- LINDEQUE, B. G., Obstetrics and Gynaecology
- MAFOJANE, N. A., Neurology
- MARITZ, N. G. J., Orthopaedics
- MATHIVHA, T. M., Cardiology
- MEDLEN, C. E., Pharmacology
- MEIRING, J. H., Anatomy
- MEYER, H. P., Internal Medicine
- MOKOENA, T. R., Surgery
- MULDER, A. A. H., Ear, Nose and Throat Medicine
- MWANTEMBE, O., Internal Medicine
- PATTINSON, R. C., Obstetrics and Gynaecology
- RANTLOANE, J. L. A., Anaesthesiology
- REIF, S., Urology
- RHEEDER, P., Clinical Epidemiology
- ROOS, J. L., Psychiatry
- ROUX, P., Ophthalmology
- SAAYMAN, G., Forensic Medicine
- SCHOLTZ, M. E., Radiology
- SCHUTTE, C.-M., Neurology
- SNYMAN, J. R., Pharmacology
- STEYN, M., Anatomy
- SWART, J. G., Otorhinolaryngology
- VAN GELDER, A. L., Internal Medicine
- VAN PAPENDORP, D. H., Physiology

VAN WYK, N. C., Nursing Science
VERMAAK, W. J. H., Chemical Pathology
VILJOEN, M., Physiology
WITTENBERG, D. F., Paediatrics

Faculty of Humanities:

ANTONITES, A., Philosophy
BERGH, J. S., Historical and Heritage Studies
BOTHA, P. J., Ancient Languages
CARSTENS, A., Afrikaans
DU PLESSIS, A., Political Sciences
FOURIE, E., Music
GOSLIN, A. E., Biokinetics
GRAY, R. A., English
GROBBELAAR, J., Sociology
HAGEMANN, F. R., Drama
HARRIS, K. L., Historical and Heritage Studies
HOUGH, M., Political Sciences
KRUGER, P. E., Biokinetics, Sport and Leisure Sciences
LOMBARD, A., Social Work
LOUW, B., Communication Pathology
MARCHETTI-MERCER, M. C., Psychology
MAREE, D. J. F., Pyschology
MEDALIE, D., English
MITI, K. N., Political Science
MLAMBO, A. S., Historical and Heritage Studies
NEOCOSMOS, M., Sociology
NIEHAUS, I. A., Anthropology and Archaeology
NZEWI, M. E., Music
OHLHOFF, C. H. F., Afrikaans
PEETERS, L. F. H. M. C., Modern European Languages
POTGIETER, J. H., Ancient Languages
PRETORIUS, F., Historical and Heritage Studies
PRETORIUS, R., Criminology
PRINSLOO, D. J., African Languages
PRINSLOO, G. T. M., Ancient Languages
ROODT, P. H., Afrikaans
SAUTHOFF, M. D., Visual Arts
SCHOEMAN, J. B., Psychology
SCHOEMAN, M. M. E., Political Sciences
SHARP, J. S., Anthropology and Archaeology
STANDER, H. F., Ancient Languages
STANFORD, H. J., Music
STEYN, B. J. M., Biokinetics
VAN DER MERWE, A., Communication Pathology
VAN DER MESCHT, H., Music
VAN NIEKERK, C., Music
VAN WYK, G. J., Biokinetics, Sport and Leisure Sciences
VILJOEN, W. D., Music
WALTON, C. R., Music
WEBB, V. N., Afrikaans
WEIDEMAN, A. J., Unit for Language Skills Development
WESSELS, J. A., English
WILLEMSE, H. S. S., Afrikaans

Faculty of Law (tel. (12) 420-2412; fax (12) 362-5184; e-mail duard.kleyn@up.ac.za):

BORAINE, A., Procedural Law
BOTHA, C. J., Public Law
BURDETTE, D. A., Centre for Practical and Continuing Legal Education
CARSTENS, P. A.,, Public Law
DAVEL, C. J., Private Law and Centre for Child Law
DELPORT, P. A., Mercantile and Labour Law
HANSUNQULE, K. M., Centre for Human Rights
HAUPT, F. S., Law Clinic
HEYNS, C. H., Centre for Human Rights
KLOPPER, H. B., Mercantile and Labour Law
KOTZE, D. J. L., Procedural Law
LOTZ, D. J., Mercantile Law
MAITHUFI, I. P., Private Law
NAGEL, C. J., Mercantile Law
NICHOLSON, C. M. A., Legal History, Comparative Law and Legal Philosophy
SCHOEMAN, M. C., Private Law
SCOTT, T. J., Private Law
THOMAS, P. J., Legal History, Comparative Law and Legal Philosophy
VAN ECK, B. P. S., Mercantile Law
VAN JAARSVELD, S. R., Mercantile Law
VAN MARLE, K., Legal History, Comparative Law and Legal Philosophy
VAN SCHALKWYK, L. N., Private Law
VILJOEN, F. J., Legal History, Comparative Law and Legal Philosophy
VISSER, P. J., Private Law

Faculty of Natural and Agricultural Sciences (Room 2-32, Agricultural Sciences Building, University of Pretoria, Pretoria 0002; tel. (12) 420-3201; fax (12) 420-3890; internet www.up.ac.za/science):

ALBERTS, H. W., Physics
AURET, F. D., Physics
BEAVON, K. S. O., Geography and Geoinformatics
BENNETT, N. C., Zoology and Entomology
BESTER, M. N., Zoology and Entomology
BRAUN, M. W. H., Physics
BREDENKAMP, G. J., Botany
BRINK, D. J., Physics
CASEY, N. H., Animal and Wildlife Sciences
CLOETE, T. E., Microbiology and Plant Pathology
COUTINHO, T. A., Microbiology and Plant Pathology
CROWTHER, N. A. S., Statistics
DE KLERK, H. M., Consumer Science
DE WAAL, S. A., Geology
HUISMANS, H., Genetics
KIRSTEN, J. F., Agricultural Economics, Extension and Rural Development
KUNERT, K. J., Botany
LOTZ, S., Chemistry
LOUW, A. I., Biochemistry
MALHERBE, J. B., Physics
MEYER, J. J. M., Botany
MILLER, H. G., Physics
MINNAAR, A., Food Sciences
NEITZ, A. W. H., Biochemistry
NICOLSON, S. W., Zoology and Entomology
PLASTINO, A. R., Physics
REINHARDT, C. F., Plant Production and Soil Science
ROHWER, E. R., Chemistry
SCHOLTZ, C. H., Zoology and Entomology
STRÖH, A., Mathematics and Applied Mathematics
VAN AARDE, R. J., Zoology and Entomology
VAN ROOYEN, C. J., Agricultural Economics, Extension and Rural Development
VAN WYK, A. E., Botany
VERSCHOOR, J. A., Biochemistry
VLEGGAAR, R., Chemistry

Faculty of Theology:

DE VILLIERS, D. E., Dogmatics and Christian Ethics
DREYER, Y., Practical Theology
HOFMEYR, J. W., Church History and Church Policy
HUMAN, D. J., Old Testament Studies
LE ROUX, J. H., Old Testament Studies
MEIRING, P. G. J., Science of Religion and Missiology
MÜLLER, J. C., Practical Theology
VAN AARDE, A. G., New Testament
VAN DER MERWE, P. J., Science of Religion and Missiology
VAN DER WATT, J. G., New Testament Studies
VENTER, P. M., Old Testament Studies
WETHMAR, C. J., Dogmatics and Christian Ethics

Faculty of Veterinary Science (Private Bag X04, Ondestepoort 0110; tel. (12) 529-8000; fax (12) 529-8300; e-mail dean@op.up.ac.za; internet www.up.ac.za/academic/veterinary):

BERTSCHINGER, H. J., Wildlife Unit
BOOMKER, J. D. F., Veterinary Tropical Diseases
BOOTH, K. K., Anatomy and Physiology
COETZER, J. A. W., Veterinary Tropical Diseases
GROENEWALD, H. B., Anatomy and Physiology
GUTHRIE, A. J., Centre for Equine Research
KIRBERGER, R. M., Companion Animal Clinical Studies
LOURENS, D. C., Production Animal Studies
MCCRINDLE, C. M., Paraclinical Sciences
PENZHORN, B. L., Veterinary Tropical Diseases
RAUTENBACH, G. H., Production Animal Studies
STADLER, P., Companion Animal Clinical Studies
SWAN, G. E., Paraclinical Sciences
TERBLANCHE, W. M., Deputy Dean

School of Dentistry:

BOTHA, S. J., Centre for Stomatological Research
BUCH, B., Diagnostics and Röntgenology
BÜTOW, K. W., Maxillofacial and Oral Surgery
DE WET, F. A., Prosthetics and Dental Mechanics
JACOBS, F. J. (acting), Maxillofacial and Oral Surgery
KEMP, P. L., Prosthetics and Dental Mechanics
VAN HEERDEN, W. F. P., Oral Pathology and Oral Biology
VAN WYK, P. J., Community Dentistry
VERWAYEN, F. D., Periodontics and Oral Medicine

UNIVERSITY OF SOUTH AFRICA

POB 392, Unisa 0003
Telephone: (12) 429-3111
Fax: (12) 429-3221
E-mail: artes@unisa.ac.za
Internet: www.unisa.ac.za

Founded 1873, Royal Charter 1877; merged with Technikon Southern Africa and incorporated Vista Univ. 2004
Languages of instruction: Afrikaans, English
Academic year: February to November

Chancellor: Justice BERNARD MAKGABO NGOEPE
Vice-Chancellor: Prof. BARNEY PITYANA
Chair. of the Ccl: Dr MATTHEWS PHOSA
Pro-Vice-Chancellor: Prof. NEO MATHABE
Deputy Vice-Chancellor and Vice-Prin. for Operations: Prof. D. L. MOSOMA (acting)
Vice-Prin. for Academic Affairs: Prof. C. F. SWANEPOEL
Vice-Prin. for Finance: Prof. G. J. DE J. CRONJE (acting)
Vice-Prin. for Learner Support: Prof. A. H. LOUW
Vice-Prin. for Research and Planning: Prof. N. BAIJNATH
Vice-Prin. for Student and Alumni Affairs: Prof. R. C. BODIBE
Registrar: Prof. T. H. LINKS
Academic Registrar: Prof. L. MOLAMU (acting)
Librarian: Prof. J. WILLEMSE

Number of teachers: 1,074
Number of students: 200,000

Publications: *Africanus* (2 a year), *Ars Nova* (1 a year), *Codicillus* (2 a year), *Communicatio* (2 a year), *De Arte* (2 a year), *Educare* (1 a year), *Kleio* (1 a year), *Language Matters* (1 a year), *Mousaion* (2 a year), *Musicus* (2 a year), *Politeia* (3 a year), *Scrutiny*[2] (2 a year), *Unisa Bulletin* (5 a year), *Unisa News* (4 a year), *Unisa Psychologia* (2 a year)

DEANS

College of Agriculture and Environment Sciences: (vacant)
College of Economics and Management Sciences: Prof. MRAD SHAHIA
College of Human Sciences: Prof. M. S. MAKHANYA
College of Law: Prof. RITA MARE'
College of Science, Engineering and Technology: Prof. G. J. SUMMERS
Graduate School of Business Leadership: Prof. H. C. NGAMBI (Executive Director)

PROFESSORS

ABRIE, A., Accounting
ACKERMANN, P. L. S., Graduate School of Business Leadership
ADLEM, W. L. J., Public Administration
AILOLA, D. A., Mercantile Law
BADENHORST, J. A., Business Management
BARROW, J. E., Computer Science
BEATY, D. T., Graduate School of Business Leadership
BECKER, H. M. R., Applied Accountancy
BEGEMANN, E., Business Management
BEKKER, P. M., Criminal and Procedural Law
BESTER, G., Educational Studies
BEYERS, E., Psychology
BISHOP, N. T., Mathematics, Applied Mathematics and Astronomy
BODENSTEIN, H. C. A., Educational Studies
BOOT, G., Accounting
BOOYENS, S. W., Advanced Nursing Sciences
BOOYSE, J. J., Further Teacher Training
BOOYSEN, H., Constitutional and International Law
BORNMAN, C. H., Computer Science
BOTHA, J. E., New Testament
BOTHA, N. J., Constitutional and International Law
BOTHA, P. J. J., New Testament
BRITS, J. P., History
BRYNARD, D. J., Public Administration
BURNS, Y. M., Constitutional and International Law
CALITZ, E., Economics
CANT, M. C., Business Management
CARPENTER, G., Constitutional and International Law
CHURCH, J., Jurisprudence
CILLIERS, C. H., Criminology
CILLIERS, F. VAN N., Industrial Psychology
COETZER, I. A., Educational Studies
CONRADIE, H., Criminology
CRONJE, D. S. P., Private Law
CRONJE, G. J. DE J., Business Management
CRONJE, P. M., Accounting
CROUS, S. F. M., Educational Studies
DADOO, Y., Semitics
DE BEER, C. S., Information Science
DE BEER, F. C., Anthropology and Archaeology
DE BEER, F. C., Development Administration
DE JONGH, M., Anthropology and Archaeology
DEMBETEMBE, N. C., African Languages
DICK, A. L., Information Science
DREECKMEYER, M., Secondary School Education
DREYER, J. M., Advanced Nursing Sciences
DU PISANIE, J. A., Economics
DU PLESSIS, I. J., New Testament
DU PLESSIS, P. J., Graduate School of Business Leadership
DU TOIT, C. W., Research Institute for Theology and Religion
DU TOIT, G. S., Business Management
ENGELBRECHT, J., New Testament
ERASMUS, B. J., Business Management
FARIS, J. A., Criminal and Procedural Law
FAURE, A. M., Political Sciences
FINLAYSON, R., African Languages
FOURIE, D. P., Psychology
FOURIE, L. J., Economics
FOURIE, P. J., Communication
FRANZSEN, R. C. D., Mercantile Law
GELDENHUYS, D. G., Musicology
GHYOOT, V. G., Business Management
GRÄBE, R. C., Theory of Literature
GROBBELAAR, A. F., Accounting
GROBBELAAR, J. I., Sociology
GROBLER, G. M. M., African Languages
GROBLER, P. A., Business Management
GRUNDLINGH, A. M., History
HAVENGA, M. K., Mercantile Law
HAVENGA, P. H., Mercantile Law
HAWTHORNE, L., Private Law
HEIDEMA, J., Mathematics, Applied Mathematics and Astronomy
HENDRIKSE, A. P., Linguistics
HIGGS, P., Educational Studies
HOFMEYR, K. B., Graduate School of Business Leadership
HOUGH, J., Business Management
HUBBARD, E. H., Linguistics
HUGO, P. J., Political Sciences
HUGO, W. M. J., Graduate School of Business Leadership
JANSE VAN RENSBURG, J. B., Applied Accountancy
JORDAAN, W. J., Psychology
JOUBERT, J. J., Criminal and Procedural Law
JULYAN, F. W., Accounting
KATKOVNIK, V., Statistics
KLERCK, W. G., Graduate School of Business Leadership
KRIEK, D. J., Political Science
KRITZINGER, J. N. J., Missiology
KRUGER, E. G., Secondary School Teacher Education
KRÜGER, J. S., Religious Studies
LANDMAN, A. A., Mercantile Law
LEMMER, E. M., Further Teacher Training
LESSING, A. C., Educational Studies
LIEBENBERG, E. C., Geography
LIGTHELM, A. A., Bureau for Market Research
LOMBARD, D. B., Classics
LÖTTER, S., Criminal and Procedural Law
LOUWRENS, L. J., African Languages
LÜBBE, J. C., Semitics
LUCAS, G. H. A., Business Management
MCKAY, V. I., Institute for Adult Basic Education and Training
MCLEARY, F., Graduate School of Business Leadership
MADER, G. J., Classics
MARAIS, A. DE K., Business Management
MARE, E. A., History of Art, Fine Art
MARÉ, M. C., Criminal and Procedural Law
MAREE, M. C., Romance Languages
MARKHAM, R., Statistics
MARTINS, J. A., Bureau for Market Research
MARX, J., Business Management
MISCH, M. K. E., German
MOHR, P. J., Economics
MOTLHABI, M. B. G., Systematic Theology and Theological Ethics
MSIMANG, C. T., African Languages
MYNHARDT, C. M., Mathematics, Applied Mathematics and Astronomy
NAUDE, C. M. B., Criminology
NELL, V., Social and Health Sciences
NESER, J. J., Criminology
NTULI, D. B., African Languages
OBERHOLZER, M. O., Educational Studies
OLIVIER, A., Primary School Education
ORR, M. A., English
PALMER, P. N., Business Management
PAUL, S. O., Chemistry
PAUW, J. C., Public Administration
PELSER, G. P. J., Graduate School of Business Leadership
PIETERSE, H. J. C., Practical Theology
PLUG, C., Psychology
POTGIETER, C., Further Teacher Education
POTGIETER, J. M., Private Law
POTGIETER, T. J. E., Graduate School of Business Leadership
POULOS, G., African Languages
PRETORIUS, E. A. C., New Testament
PRETORIUS, J. T., Mercantile Law
PRETORIUS, L., Sociology
PRINSLOO, E. D., Philosophy
RABINOWITZ, I. A., English
RADEMEYER, G., Psychology
REYNHARDT, E. C., Physics
ROELOFSE, J. J., Communication
ROOS, H. M., Afrikaans
RUTHERFORD, B. R., Mercantile Law
RYAN, P. D., English
SADLER, E., Applied Accountancy
SALBANY, S. DE O., Applied Mathematics, Mathematics and Astronomy
SCHEFFLER, E. H., Old Testament
SCOTT, S. J., Private Law
SEBOTHOMA, W. A., New Testament
SERUDU, S. M., African Languages
SHAHIA, M., Transport Economics and Logistics
SMIT, B. F., Criminology
SMIT, P. J., Business Management
SMITH, J. DU P., Economics
SMITH, K. W., History
SMUTS, C. A., Transport Economics and Logistics
SNYDERS, F. J. A., Psychology
SNYMAN, C. R., Criminal and Procedural Law
SNYMAN, J. W., African Languages
SOFIANOS, S. A., Physics
SÖHNGE, W. F., Educational Studies
STEENEKAMP, T. J., Economics
STEFFENS, F. E., Statistics
STEYN, B. L., Accounting
STRIKE, W. N., Romance Languages
STRYDOM, J. W., Business Management
SUMMERS, G. J., Chemistry
SWANEPOEL, C. F., African Languages
SWANEPOEL, C. H., Institute for Educational Research
SWANEPOEL, C. J., Quantitative Management
SWANEPOEL, F. A., C. B. Powell Bible Centre
SWANEPOEL, P. H., Afrikaans
SWANEVELDER, J. J., Accounting
SWART, G. J., Mercantile Law
SWEMMER, P. N., Auditing
TERBLANCHE, S. S., Criminal and Procedural Law
THOMASHAUSEN, A. E. A. M., Institute for Foreign and Comparative Law
TORR, C. S. W., Economics
TROSKIE, R., Advanced Nursing Sciences
VAKALISA, N. C. G., Secondary School Education
VAN ASWEGEN, A., Private Law
VAN BILJON, R. C. W., Social Work
VAN BLERK, A. E., Jurisprudence
VAN DELFT, W. F., Social Work
VAN DEN BERG, P. H., Graduate School of Business Leadership
VAN DER MERWE, C. A., Quantitative Management
VAN DER MERWE, D. P., Criminal and Procedural Law
VAN DER WALT, A. J., Private Law
VAN DYK, P. J., Old Testament
VAN HEERDEN, B., Auditing
VAN NIEKERK, E., Systematic Theology, Theological Ethics
VAN NIEKERK, J. P., Mercantile Law
VAN ROOY, M. P., Educational Studies
VAN WYK, A. M. A., Private Law
VAN WYK, C. W., Jurisprudence
VAN WYK, D. H., Constitutional and International Law
VAN WYK, H. DE J., Bureau for Market Research
VAN ZYL, A. E., Educational Studies
VILJOEN, H. G., Psychology
VISSER, C. J., Mercantile Law
VISSER, P. S., Educational Studies
VORSTER, H. J. S., Auditing
VORSTER, J. N., New Testament
VORSTER, L. P., Indigenous Law
VORSTER, S. J. R., Mathematics, Applied Mathematics and Astronomy
WATKINS, M. L., Industrial Psychology
WEINBERG, A. M., English

WESSELS, W. J., Old Testament
WHELPTON, F. P. VAN R., Indigenous Law
WIECHERS, E., Educational Studies
WIECHERS, N. J., Private Law
WILLIAMS, G., Applied Accountancy
WOLFAARDT, J. A., Practical Theology
WOLFAARDT, J. B., Industrial Psychology
WOLVAARDT, J. S., Quantitative Management
YADAVALLI, V. S. S., Statistics

UNIVERSITY OF STELLENBOSCH

PMB X1, Matieland 7602, Cape Province
Telephone: (21) 808-9111
Fax: (21) 808-4499
E-mail: webinfo@maties.sun.ac.za
Internet: www.sun.ac.za

Founded 1918; dental faculty incorporated into Univ. of the Western Cape 2004
Language of instruction: Afrikaans
Academic year: February to December (four terms)

Chancellor: Prof. ELIZE BOTHA
Prin. and Vice-Chancellor: Prof. C. H. BRINK
Vice-Prin. for Academic Affairs: Prof. H. R. BOTMAN
Vice-Prin. for Operations: Prof. J. F. SMITH
Vice-Prin. for Research: Prof. W. T. CLAASSEN
Registrar: J. A. ASPELING
Sr Dir of Library Services: ELLEN TISE

Number of teachers: 745
Number of students: 22,000

Publications: *Maatskaplike Werk* (Social Work, 4 a year), *Matieland*, *Opinion Survey Report* (Bureau of Economic Research, 4 a year), *Research Report* (1 a year), *Survey of Contemporary Economic Conditions and Prospects* (1 a year)

DEANS

Faculty of Agriculture and Forestry: Prof. L. VAN HUYSTEEN
Faculty of Arts: Prof. H. J. KOTZÉ
Faculty of Economic and Management Sciences: Prof. J. U. DE VILLIERS
Faculty of Education: Prof. T. PARK
Faculty of Engineering: Prof. A. SCHOONWINKEL
Faculty of Health Sciences: Prof. W. L. VAN DER MERWE
Faculty of Law: (vacant)
Faculty of Military Science: Prof. D. J. MALAN
Faculty of Science: Prof. A. S. VAN JAARSVELD
Faculty of Theology: Prof. A. E. J. MOUTON

PROFESSORS

Faculty of Agriculture and Forestry (tel. (21) 808-4792; fax (21) 808-2001; e-mail lvh@maties.sun.ac.za; internet www.sun.ac.za/agric):

AGENBAG, G. A., Agronomy and Pastures
BREDENKAMP, B. V., Forestry Science
BRITZ, T., Food Science
FEY, M. V., Soil Science
GOUSSARD, P. G., Oenology and Viticulture
HOLZ, G., Plant Pathology
MARAIS, G. F., Genetics
SAMWAYS, M. J., Entomology
THERON, K. I., Horticulture
VAN HUYSSTEEN, L., Soil Science
VAN WYK, G., Forestry Science
VINK, N., Agricultural Economics
WARNICH, L., Genetics

Faculty of Arts (tel. (21) 808-2138; fax (21) 808-2123; e-mail hjk@maties.sun.ac.za; internet www.sun.ac.za/arts):

BEKKER, S. B., Sociology
BOTHA, R. P., Linguistics
CILLIERS, F. P., Philosophy
CORNELIUS, I., Ancient Studies
DU TOIT, P. V. D. P., Political Science
GAGIANO, A. H., English
GOUWS, A., Political Science
GOUWS, R. H., Afrikaans and Dutch
GREEN, S., Social Work
GROVÉ, I. J., Music
GRUNDLINGH, A. M., History
HATTINGH, J. P., Philosophy
HAUPTFLEISCH, T., Drama
KAGEE, S. A., Psychology
KINGHORN, J., Biblical Studies
KLOPPER, D. C., English
KLOPPER, S., Fine Arts
KOTZE, H. J., Political Science
KRITZINGER, A. S., Sociology
MOUTON, J., Sociology
NAIDOO, A. V., Psychology
RABE, L., Journalism
ROOSENSCHOON, H., Music
SWARTZ, L. P., Psychology
THOM, J. C., Ancient Studies
VAN DER MERWE, W. L., Philosophy
VAN DER WAAL, C. S., Sociology
VAN NIEKERK, A. A., Philosophy
VILJOEN, L., Afrikaans and Dutch
VON MALTZAN, C. H., Modern Foreign Languages
ZIETSMAN, H. L., Geography and Environmental Studies
ZULU, N. S., African Languages

Faculty of Economic and Management Sciences (tel. (21) 808-2225; fax (21) 808-2409; e-mail calitz@maties.sun.ac.za; internet www.sun.ac.za/economy):

AUGUSTYN, J. C. D., Industrial Psychology
BIEKPE, N. B., Business Administration
BROWN, W., Accounting
BURGER, A. P., Public and Development Management
CLOETE, G. S., Public and Development Management
DE VILLIERS, J. U., Business Management
DE WET, T., Statistics and Actuarial Science
GEVERS, W. R., Business Management and Administration
HOUGH, J., Business Management
LEIBOLD, M., Business Management
MOSTERT, F. J., Business Management
OLIVIER, P., Accounting
OOSTHUIZEN, H., Business Administration
PIENAAR, W. J., Logistics
SCHOOMBEE, G. A., Economics
SCHWELLA, E., Public and Development Management
SLATTERY, P. G., Statistics and Actuarial Science
SMIT, B. W., Economics
SMIT, E. VAN DER M., Business Management and Administration
STEEL, S. J., Statistics and Actuarial Science
SWILLING, M., Public and Development Management
TERBLANCHE, N. S., Business Management
VAN DER BERG, S., Economics
VAN SCHALKWYK, C. J., Accounting

Faculty of Education (tel. (21) 808-2258; fax (21) 808-2269; e-mail tp@maties.sun.ac.za; internet www.sun.ac.za/education):

BERKHOUT, S. J., Educational Policy Studies
BITZER, E. M., Didactics
CARL, A. E., Didactics
KAPP, C. A., Centre for Higher and Adult Education
LE GRANGE, L. L. L., Didactics
PARK, T., Didactics
SCHREUDER, D. R., Didactics
SWART, R. E., Educational Psychology
WAGHID, Y., Educational Policy Studies

Faculty of Engineering (tel. (21) 808-4203; fax (21) 808-4206; e-mail schoonwinkel@maties.sun.ac.za; internet www.sun.ac.za/eng):

ALDRICH, C., Chemical Engineering
BASSON, A. H., Mechanical Engineering
BASSON, G. R., Civil Engineering
BESTER, C. J., Civil Engineering
BRADSHAW, S. M., Chemical Engineering
BURGER, A. J., Chemical Engineering
CLOETE, J. H., Electrical and Electronic Engineering
DAVIDSON, D. B., Electrical and Electronic Engineering
DUNAISKI, P. E., Civil Engineering
DU PLESSIS, J. P., Applied Mathematics
DU PREEZ, N. D., Industrial Engineering
HERBST, B. M., Applied Mathematics
JENKINS, K. J., Civil Engineering
KAMPER, M. J., Electrical and Electronic Engineering
KNOETZE, J. H., Chemical Engineering
LORENZEN, L., Chemical Engineering
LOURENS, J. G., Electrical and Electronic Engineering
MEYER, P., Electrical and Electronic Engineering
PEROLD, W. J., Electrical and Electronic Engineering
READER, H. C., Electrical and Electronic Engineering
SCHOONWINKEL, A., Electrical and Electronic Engineering
STEYN, W. H., Electrical and Electronic Engineering
VAN NIEKERK, J. L., Mechanical Engineering
VON BACKSTRÖM, T. W., Mechanical Engineering
WEIDEMAN, J. A. C., Applied Mathematics

Faculty of Health Sciences (tel. (21) 938-9200; fax (21) 938-9558; e-mail wvdmerwe@maties.sun.ac.za; internet www.sun.ac.za/med.fac):

BEYERS, N., Paediatrics and Child Health
BRINK, P. A., Internal Medicine
CHIKTE, U. M. E., Associate Dean
COETZEE, A. R., Anaesthesiology
DE VILLIERS, B., Associate Dean
DE VILLIERS, M. R., Family Medicine and Primary Care
DE VILLIERS, P. J. T., Family Medicine and Primary Care
DOUBELL, A. F., Internal Medicine
DU TOIT, D., Anatomy and Histology
EMSLEY, R. A., Psychiatry
ERASMUS, R. T., Chemical Pathology
HEYNS, C. F., Urology
HOUGH, F. S., Internal Medicine
KOESLAG, J. H., Medical Physiology and Biochemistry
KRUGER, T. F., Obstetrics and Gynaecology
LABADARIOS, D., Human Nutrition
LIEBOWITZ, L. D., Medical Microbiology
LOOCK, J. W., Otorhinolaryngology
MANSVELT, E. P., Haematology
MEYER, D., Ophthalmology
MOORE, S. W., Surgery
ROSSOUW, G. J., Cardiothoracic Surgery
SCHER, A. T., Radiation Oncology
SCHNEIDER, J. W., Anatomical Pathology
SEEDAT, S., Psychiatry
THERON, G. B., Obstetrics and Gynaecology
VAN DER BIJL, P., Pharmacology
VAN DER MERWE, W. L., Medical Physiology and Biochemistry
VAN HEERDEN, B. B., Head of School of Medicine
VERNIMMEN, F. J. A. I., Radiation Oncology
VLOK, G. J., Orthopaedic Surgery
WARREN, B. L., Surgery
WELMANN, E. B., Nursing Science
WRIGHT, C. A., Anatomical Pathology

Faculty of Law (tel. (21) 808-4853; fax (21) 886-6235; e-mail jsaf@maties.sun.ac.za; internet www.sun.ac.za/law):

BUTLER, D. W., Mercantile Law
DE VOS, W., Private Law and Roman Law
DE WAAL, M. J., Private Law and Roman Law
DU PLESSIS, J. E., Private Law and Roman Law

Du Plessis, L. M., Public Law
Erasmus, M. G., Public Law
Hugo, C. F., Mercantile Law
Human, C. S., Private Law and Roman Law
Liebenberg, S., Public Law
Loubser, M. M., Private Law and Roman Law
Lubbe, G. F., Private Law and Roman Law
Pienaar, J. M., Private Law and Roman Law
Sutherland, P. J., Mercantile Law
Van der Merwe, S. E., Public Law
Van der Walt, A. J., Public Law

Faculty of Science (tel. (21) 808-3072; fax (21) 808-3608; e-mail asvanj@maties.sun.ac.za; internet www.sun.ac.za/science):

Chown, S. L., Plant and Animal Science
Crouch, A. M., Chemistry
De Villiers, J. M., Mathematics
Dicks, L. M. T, Microbiology
Dillen, J. L. M., Chemistry
Eggers, H. C., Chemistry
Geyer, H. B., Physics
Green, B. W., Mathematics
Hapgood, J. P., Biochemistry
Hofmeyr, J. H. S., Biochemistry
Koch, K. R., Chemistry
Kossmann, J. M., Zoology
Krzesinski, A. E., Computer Science
Laurie, D. P., Mathematics
Mucina, L., Plant and Animal Science
Myburgh, K. H., Physiological Sciences
Prior, B. A., Microbiology
Prodinger, H., Mathematics
Raubenheimer, H. G., Chemistry
Rawlings, D. E., Microbiology
Reinecke, A. J., Plant and Animal Science
Richardson, D. M., Plant and Animal Science
Robinson, T. J., Plant and Animal Science
Rozendaal, A., Geology
Sanderson, R. D., Polymer Science
Scholtz, F. G., Physics
Smith, V. R., Plant and Animal Science
Snoep, J. L., Biochemistry
Stevens, G., Geology
Swart, P., Biochemistry
Van Jaarsveld, A. S., Plant and Animal Science
Van Wyk, L., Mathematics
Van Zyl, W. H., Microbiology
Von Bergmann, H. M., Physics

Faculty of Theology (tel. (21) 808-3255; fax (21) 808-3251; e-mail djl@maties.sun.ac.za; internet www.sun.ac.za/theology):

Bosman, H. L., Old and New Testament
Hendriks, H. J., Practical Theology and Missiology
Mouton, A. E. J., Old and New Testament
Smit, D. J., Systematic Theology

UNIVERSITY OF THE FREE STATE

POB 339, Bloemfontein 9300
Telephone: (51) 401-9111
Fax: (51) 401-2117
E-mail: info@stiq.ufs.ac.za
Internet: www.uovs.ac.za

Founded 1855, fmrly a constituent college of the Univ. of South Africa, became ind. as Univ. of the Orange Free State 1950, present name 2003, incorporated Bloemfontein Campus of Vista Univ. 2004
Languages of instruction: Afrikaans, English
Academic year: February to November

Chancellor: Dr Franklin Sonn
Vice-Chancellor and Rector: Prof. Jonathan Jansen
Vice-Rector for Academic Operations: Prof. Teuns Verschoor
Vice-Rector for Academic Planning: Prof. Magda Fourie
Vice-Rector for Student Affairs: Dr Raletsatsi Ezekiel Moraka
Dean of Students: Dr Natie Luyt
Registrar: Prof. Izak Steyn
Dir of Library and Information Services: Clemence Namponya

Number of teachers: 476
Number of students: 20,000

DEANS

Faculty of Economic and Management Sciences: Prof. Tienie Crous
Faculty of Health Sciences: Prof. Letticia Moja
Faculty of Humanities: Prof. Gerhardt de Klerk
Faculty of Law: Prof. Johan Henning
Faculty of Natural and Agricultural Sciences: Prof. Herman van Schalkwyk
Faculty of Theology: Prof. Hermie van Zyl

ATTACHED CAMPUS

University of the Free State, Qwaqwa Campus

PMB X13, Phuthaditjhaba 9866
Telephone: (58) 713-0211
Fax: (58) 713-0158
Founded 1982
Chancellor: Dr N. R. Mandela
Vice-Chancellor and Prin.: Prof. N. Ndebele
Vice-Prin.: Prof. Dr W. Mödinger
Registrars: A. T. Kgabo, T. P. Masihleho, N. T. Mosia
Librarian: C. J. Kok
Library of 30,000 vols
Number of teachers: 85
Number of students: 2,500

DEANS

Faculty of Arts: Prof. L. J. Ferreira
Faculty of Education: L. E. Mofokeng
Faculty of Management Sciences: P. C. Mojet
Faculty of Mathematics and Natural Sciences: Prof. Dr P. C. Keulder
Faculty of Theology: Dr S. P. Botha

PROFESSORS

Faculty of Arts:

Ferreira, L. J., Political Science
Jones, H. J., Afrikaans
Moolman, J. P. F., History

Faculty of Education:

Moletsane, R. I. M., Comparative Education

Faculty of Management Sciences:

Cloete, N., Commercial Law
Jonker, L. J. G., Business Economics
Venter, A. P., Industrial Psychology
Webster, S. A., Accounting

Faculty of Mathematics and Natural Sciences:

De Haas, W., Physics
Den Heyer, J., Zoology
Jordaan, D. B., Computer Science
Keulder, P. C., Botany
Luyt, A. S., Chemistry
Moffett, R. O., Botany
Mthembu, T. Z., Mathematics

UNIVERSITY OF THE WESTERN CAPE

Private Bag X17, Bellville 7535
Telephone: (21) 959-2911
Fax: (21) 959-3627
Internet: www.uwc.ac.za

Founded 1960
Languages of instruction: Afrikaans, English
Academic year: February to December

Chancellor: (vacant)
Vice-Chancellor and Rector: Prof. Brian O'Connell
Vice-Rector for Academic Affairs: Prof. Ramesh Bharuthram (acting)
Deputy Vice-Chancellor and Vice-Rector for Student Affairs: Prof. L. Tshiwula
Registrar: Dr Ingrid Miller
Librarian: P. P. Ntshuntshe-Matshaya

Library of 297,756 vols, 1,280 journals, 41,333 electronic journals
Number of teachers: 910
Number of students: 17,500

Publications: *Journal of Community Health* (staff research publication, 1 a year), *KRONOS: Journal of Cape History, Law, Democracy and Development* (4 a year)

DEANS

Faculty of Arts: Prof. Duncan Brown (acting)
Faculty of Community and Health Sciences: Prof. Ratie Mpofu
Faculty of Dentistry: Prof. Y. Osman
Faculty of Economics and Management Sciences: Prof. Chris Tapscott
Faculty of Education: Prof. Zubeida Desai
Faculty of Law: Prof. Julia Sloth-Nielsen
Faculty of Natural Science: Prof. Jan van Beverdonker

UNIVERSITY OF THE WITWATERSRAND, JOHANNESBURG

PMB X3, Wits 2050
Telephone: (11) 717-1054
Fax: (11) 717-1059
E-mail: studysa.international@wits.ac.za
Internet: www.wits.ac.za

Founded 1922
State-subsidized, but functions under its own charter
Language of instruction: English
Academic year: February to November

Chancellor: Dep. Chief Justice Dikgang Moseneke
Vice-Chancellor and Prin.: Prof. Loyiso Nongxa
Vice-Prin. and Deputy Vice-Chancellor for Academic Affairs: Prof. Yunus Ballim
Deputy Vice-Chancellor for Partnerships and Advancement: Prof. Rob Moore
Deputy Vice-Chancellor for Research: Prof. Belinda Bozzoli
Registrar: Dr Derek Swemmer
Exec. Dir: Rev. Lulamile Mbete (acting)
Univ. Librarian: Felix Obogu

Library: see Libraries
Number of teachers: 1,766
Number of students: 27,722

Publications: *African Studies* (2 a year), *English Studies in Africa* (2 a year), *Palaeontologia Africana* (1 a year), *Perspectives in Education* (4 a year), *Philosophical Papers* (3 a year), *The Industrial Law Journal* (6 a year), *The Research Report* (1 a year)

DEANS

Faculty of Commerce, Law and Management: Prof. Katherine Munro (acting)
Faculty of Engineering and the Built Environment: Prof. Beatrys Lacquet
Faculty of Health Sciences: Prof. Helen Laburn
Faculty of Humanities: Prof. Tawana Kupe
Faculty of Science: Prof. Andrew Crouch

PROFESSORS

Faculty of Arts and Faculty of Science:

Adler, J., Mathematics Education Development
Alexander, J. J., Microbiology
Anhaeusser, C. R., Geology
Asher, A., Statistics and Actuarial Science

BEICHELT, F., Statistics and Actuarial Science
BONNER, P. L., History
BOZZOLI, B., Sociology
BRADLEY, J. D., Chemistry
BUNN, D., History of Art
CAWTHORN, R. G., Geology
COCK, J., Sociology
COMINS, J. D., Physics
COPLAN, D. B., Social Anthropology
COVILLE, N. J., Organo-Metallic Chemistry
CRUMP, A., Fine Arts
DABBS, E., Genetics
DELIUS, P. S., History
DIRR, H. W., Biochemistry
DRIVER, K., Mathematics
DU PLESSIS, P., Physics
EVERY, A. G., Physics
FABIAN, B. C., Zoology
FATTI, L. P., Statistics
FISHER, J., Psychology
GLASSER, L., Physical Chemistry
HEISS, W. D., Theoretical Physics
HOCH, M. J. R., Solid State Physics
HOFMEYR, I., African Literature
HUFFMAN, T. N., Archaeology
HUNT, J. H. V., Mathematics
LODGE, T., Political Studies
LOWTHER, J. E., Physics
LUBINSKY, D. S., Mathematics
MAAKE, N. P., African Languages
MASON, D. P., Applied Mathematics
MARQUES, H., Chemistry
MCCARTHY, T. S., Geology
MCKENDRICK, B. W., Social Work
MCLACHLAN, D. S., Electronic Properties of Solids
MICHAEL, J. P., Organic Chemistry
MOYS, M., School of Process and Materials Engineering
MURRAY, B. K., Edwardian British History
OLIVIER, G., Afrikaans and Dutch
OWEN-SMITH, N., Zoology
PENDLEBURY, M., Philosophy
PENN, C., Speech Pathology and Audiology
PIENAAR, R. N., Botany
PRODINGER, H., Mathematics
ROBB, L. J., Geology
RODRIGUES, J. A. P., Physics
ROGERS, K. H., Botany
ROGERSON, C. M., Geography
ROLLNICK, M., College of Science
RUBIDGE, B. S., Palaeontology
SCURRELL, M. S., Chemistry
STADLER, A. W., Political Studies
STREMLAU, J. J., International Relations
TAYLOR, J., Dramatic Art
TYSON, P. D., Climatology
VILJOEN, M. J., Mining Geology
VON HOLY, A., Microbiology
WEBSTER, E. C., Sociology
WRIGHT, C., Geophysics
WRIGHT, C. J., Computational and Applied Mathematics

Faculty of Commerce:
DAGUT, M., Economics
DE KOKER, A. P., Accounting
NEGASH, M., Accounting
REEKIE, W. D., Business Economics
SIMKINS, C., Economics
VIVIAN, R., Insurance and Risk Management

Faculty of Education:
ENSLIN, P. A.
PENDLEBURY, S. A.
SKUY, M. S.

Faculty of Engineering:
BRYSON, A. W., Chemical Engineering
ERIC, R. H., Metallurgy and Materials Engineering
FOURIE, A., Civil Engineering
GLASSER, D., Chemical Engineering
HANRAHAN, H. E., Electrical Engineering
HILDEBRANDT, D., Process and Materials Engineering
IWANKIEWICZ, R. M., Applied Mathematics
LANDY, C. F., Electrical Engineering
MACLEOD, I. M., Control Engineering
MCCUTCHEON, R. T., Project and Construction Management
ONSONGO, W. M., Undergraduate Engineering Education
PHILLIPS, H. R., Mining Engineering
REYNDERS, J. P., Electrical Engineering
SHEER, T. J., Mechanical Engineering
SKEWS, B. W., Mechanical Engineering
STEPHENSON, D., Hydraulic Engineering

Faculty of Engineering and the Built Environment:
BREMNER, L., Architecture
MULLER, J. G., Town and Regional Planning
SCHLOSS, R. I., Construction Economics and Management

Faculty of Health Sciences:
ALLWOOD, C., Psychiatry
ALTINI, M., Oral Pathology
CARMICHAEL, T., Ophthalmology
CARR, L., Prosthetic Dentistry
CLEATON-JONES, P. E., Experimental Odontology
COOPER, P. A., Paediatrics
CREWE-BROWN, H., Medical Microbiology
CRONJE, S. L., Cardiothoracic Surgery
DAVIES, M. R. Q., Paediatric Surgery
ERKEN, E. H. W., Orthopaedic Surgery
EVANS, W. G., Orthodontics
FELDMAN, C., Medicine
FRITZ, V. U., Neurology
GEORGE, J. A., Orthopaedic Surgery
GRAY, I. P., Chemical Pathology
HAVLIK, I., Pharmacology
HOFMEYR, G. J., Obstetrics and Gynaecology
HUDDLE, K., Medicine
JOFFE, B. I., Medicine
KALK, W. J., Clinical Endocrinology
KEW, M. C., Medicine
KLUGMAN, K. P., Clinical Microbiology
KRAMER, B., Anatomical Sciences
LABURN, H. P., Physiology
LOWNIE, J. F., Maxillofacial and Oral Surgery
MACPHAIL, A. P., Medicine
MAINA, J. N., Anatomical Sciences
MANGA, P., Cardiology
MCINTOSH, W., Ear, Nose and Throat Surgery
MEYERS, A. M., Nephrology
MILNE, F. J., Medicine
MITCHELL, D., Physiology
MITCHELL, G., Physiology
OWEN, P., Prosthetic Dentistry
PANTANOWITZ, D., Surgery
PATERSON, A. C., Anatomical Pathology
PETIT, J.-C., Oral Medicine and Periodontology
PETTIFOR, J. M., Paediatrics
PICK, W., Community Health
RAMSAY, M., Human Genetics
REES, D., Occupational Health
RUDOLPH, M. J., Community Medicine
SARELI, P., Cardiology
SCHOUB, B. D., Virology
SHIPTON, E. A., Anaesthesia
SPARKS, B. L. W., Family Health
SUR, R., Radiation Oncology
VAN GELDEREN, C. J., Obstetrics and Gynaecology
VILJOEN, D., Human Genetics
WADEE, A. A., Immunology

Faculty of Law:
COCKRELL, A. H. P.
HOEXTER, C.
ITZIKOWITZ, A.
LARKIN, M. P.
LEWIS, C. H.
MOSIKATSANA, T.
PAIZES, A. P.
PANTAZIS, A.
SKEEN, A. ST A.

Faculty of Management:
ABRATT, R., Business Administration
AHWIRENG-OBENG, F., Business Administration
CAWTHRA, G., Defence and Security Management
DE CONING, C., Development Management
KLEIN, S., International Business
MABIN, A. S., Public and Development Management
MHONE, G. C. Z., Public and Development Management

UNIVERSITY OF VENDA FOR SCIENCE AND TECHNOLOGY

PMB X5050, Thohoyandou 0950, Limpopo
Telephone: (15) 962-8000
Fax: (15) 962-4749
E-mail: prd@univen.ac.za
Internet: www.univen.ac.za

Founded 1982 as Univ. of Venda by Venda Parliament; nat. status as Univ. of Venda 1996; non-statutory name Univ. of Venda for Science and Technology
State control

Schools: agriculture, environmental sciences and engineering; health sciences; human and social sciences; management sciences and law; mathematics and natural sciences; postgraduate and integrated studies; rural development and forestry

Prin. and Vice-Chancellor: Prof. G. M. NKONDO

Library of 90,871 vols, 823 periodicals
Number of teachers: 301
Number of students: 9,500

Publication: *Journal of Educational Studies* (2 a year)

EXECUTIVE DEANS

Faculty of Health, Agriculture and Rural Development: Prof. N. S. MAHOKO
Faculty of Human and Social Sciences, Management Sciences and Law: Prof. M. D. R. RALEBIPI-SIMELA
Faculty of Natural and Applied Sciences: Prof. P. H. OMARA-OJUNGU

PROFESSORS

Faculty of Human and Social Sciences, Management Sciences and Law:
AKINNUSI, D. M.
AYURU, R. N.
BAYONA, E. L. M.
GYEKE, A. B.
LUKHAIMANE, E. K.
MIREKU, O.
SIMUKONDA, H. P. M.
SPENCER, J. P.
STEYN, J. N.

Faculty of Natural and Applied Sciences:
AGBONJINMI, A. P.
AMUSA, L. O.
DU TOIT, P. J.
KHOZA, L. B.
KIRUNDA, E. F.
MAKINDE, M. O.
MBHENYANE, X. G.
OGOLA, J. S.
OLE-MEILUDI, R. E.
OLORUNDA, A. O.
OMARA-OJUNGU, P. H.
ONI, S. A.
SHAI-MAHOKO, N. S.
SIMALENGA, T. E.
VAN DER WAAL, B. C. W.
VAN REE, T.

UNIVERSITY OF ZULULAND

PMB X1001, KwaDlangezwa, KwaZulu-Natal 3886
Telephone: (35) 902-6000
Fax: (35) 793-3735
Internet: www.uzulu.ac.za

Founded 1960; Umlazi Campus incorporated into Durban Institute of Technology 2004
State control
Language of instruction: English
Academic year: February to December

Chancellor: Dr JACOB ZUMA
Vice-Chancellor and Rector: Prof. RACHEL GUMBI
Vice-Rector for Academic Affairs and Research: Prof. L. M. MAGI
Chief Financial Officer: M. GOUINDSAMY
Dean of Students: M. M. HLONGWANE
Registrar: G. S. MAPHISA
Librarian: L. VAHED

Number of teachers: 293
Number of students: 7,978

Publications: *Journal of Psychology*, *Paidonomia*, *Unizul*

DEANS

Faculty of Arts: Prof. L. Z. M. KHUMALO
Faculty of Commerce and Administration: Prof. T. R. SABELA
Faculty of Education: Prof. R. V. GABELA
Faculty of Law: Prof. R. SONI
Faculty of Science and Agriculture: Prof. M. F. COETSEE
Faculty of Theology and Religious Studies: Prof. J. A. LOUBSER

PROFESSORS

Faculty of Arts (tel. (35) 902-6087; e-mail bbishop@pan.uzulu.ac.za):

BUIJS, G. C. U., Anthropology
DALRYMPLE, L. I., Drama
DE VILLIERS, J., History
EDWARDS, S. D., Psychology
GLASS, H. G. L., Sociology
GUMBI, T. A. P., Social Work
HOOPER, M. J., English
KHUMALO, L. Z. M., African Languages
KLOPPER, R. M., Afrikaans
MAKHANYA, E. M., Geography
MEIHUIZEN, N. C. T., English
MERSHAM, G. M., Communication Science
NZIMAKWE, D. P., Nursing Science
OCHOLLA, D. N., Library and Information Science
POTGIETER, P. J., Criminal Justice
WAIT, E. C., Philosophy
ZUNGU, B. M., Nursing Science

Faculty of Commerce and Administration (tel. (35) 902-6173; fax (35) 793-3583; e-mail sbooysen@pan.uzulu.ac.za):

CLOETE, J., Business Management
LIVINGSTONE, M., Accountancy and Auditing
NAIDOO, I. U., Accountancy and Auditing
SABELA, T. R., Public Administration and Political Science
SHRESTHA, B. C., Economics

Faculty of Education (tel. (35) 902-6258; fax (35) 793-3149; e-mail rvgabela@pan.uzulu.ac.za):

COETSEE, M. F., Human Movement Science
DLAMINI, E. T., History of Education and Comparative Education
GABELA, R. V., Educational Planning and Administration
JACOBS, M., Didactics
SIBAYA, P. T., Educational Psychology
URBANI, G., Educational Psychology

Faculty of Law (tel. (35) 902-6212; fax (35) 793-3529; e-mail sjclarke@pan.uzulu.ac.za):

SONI, R., Constitutional Law

Faculty of Science and Agriculture (tel. (35) 902-6649; fax (35) 793-3162; e-mail lorraine@pan.uzulu.ac.za):

BEESHAM, A., Mathematical Sciences
BERMANSEDER, N., Engineering
COETSEE, M. F., Human Movement Science
CYRUS, D. P., Zoology
DAVIDSON, A. T., Physics
DJAVOVA, T., Biochemistry
FERREIRA, D. P., Botany
JURY, M. R., Geography
KELBE, B. E. M.-L., Hydrology
KOLAWOLE, G. A., Chemistry
NDWANDWE, M. O., Physics

Faculty of Theology and Religious Studies (tel. (35) 902-6716; fax (35) 793-3159; e-mail asong@uzulu.ac.za; internet www.uzulu.ac.za/the/the.html):

LOUBSER, J. A., Bibliological Studies
SONG, A., Missiology, Religious Studies and Practical Theology

VAAL UNIVERSITY OF TECHNOLOGY

PMB X021, Vanderbijlpark, 1900 Gauteng
Telephone: (16) 950-9000
Fax: (16) 950-9787
E-mail: international@vut.ac.za
Internet: www.vut.ac.za

Founded 1966, present name 1979

Vice-Chancellor and Rector: Prof. A. T. MOKADI
Vice-Rector for Academic Affairs: Prof. ROY DU PRÉ
Vice-Rector for Admin.: Dr PRAKASH NAIDOO
Librarian: A. J. GOZO

Library of 42,000 vols, 4,480 periodicals
Number of teachers: 311 full-time, 551 part-time
Number of students: 12,434

Publications: *Sediba sa Thuto* (academic journal, 1 a year), *Tempo* (communications journal, 2 a year)

Faculties of applied and computer sciences, engineering and technology, humanities and management sciences.

WALTER SISULU UNIVERSITY FOR TECHNOLOGY AND SCIENCE, EASTERN CAPE

Founded 2005 by merger of Eastern Cape Technikon, Border Technikon and Univ. of Transkei.

CONSTITUENT INSTITUTION

University of Transkei

PMB X1, Unitra
Telephone: (47) 502-2111
Fax: (47) 532-6820
E-mail: postmaster@getafix.utr.ac.za
Internet: www.utr.ac.za

Founded 1976 as br. of Fort Hare Univ., ind. 1977
State control
Language of instruction: English
Academic year: January to December

Chancellor (vacant)
Administrator: Prof. N. I. MORGAN
Vice-Prin.: Prof. J. M. NORUWANA
Registrar: Prof. P. N. LUSWAZI
Chief Librarian: P. E. OFORI

Number of teachers: 357
Number of students: 4,551

Publications: *Journal of Humanities* (2 a year), *Perspectives in Education* (1 a year)

DEANS

Faculty of Arts: Prof. N. MIJERE
Faculty of Economic Sciences: Prof. M. MAHABIR
Faculty of Education: Prof. S. V. S. NGUBENTOMBI
Faculty of Law: Prof. V. DLOVA
Faculty of Medicine and Health Sciences: Prof. E. L. MAZWAI
Faculty of Natural Sciences: Prof. B. S. NAKANI

PROFESSORS

Faculty of Arts:

ALABI, G. A., Information Science
COETSER, A., Afrikaans
MIJERE, N., Sociology

Faculty of Economic Sciences:

MAHABIR, M., Business Management

Faculty of Education:

LWANGA-LUKWAGO, J., Social Studies Education
NGUBENTOMBI, S. V. S., Educational Foundations

Faculty of Law:

DLOVA, V., Mercantile Law

Faculty of Medicine and Health Sciences:

ERASMUS, R. T., Chemical Pathology
IPUTO, J. E., Physiology
MAZWAI, E. L., Surgery
MEISSNER, O., Pharmacology
MFENYANA, K., Family and Community Medicine
NGANWA-BAGUMAH, A. B., Anatomy
STEPHEN, A., Pathology

Faculty of Natural Sciences:

EMMERSON, W., Zoology
FANIRAN, J. A., Science Foundation Year Programme
JACOBS, T. V., Botany
MISHRA, S. N., Mathematics

SPAIN

The Higher Education System

Institutions of higher education pre-date the consolidation of the Kingdom of Spain within the Iberian peninsula in the early 16th century, with the oldest being Universidad Pontificia de Salamanca, which was founded in 1134. The Ministry of Education has overall responsibility for higher education, although much of the administration has been devolved to the 17 Autonomous Communities. Universities were granted autonomy under the law on University Reform (1983), which was supplemented by further reforms enacted following the Spanish Universities Act (2001), covering university governance, entrance examinations, quality assurance, accreditation and staff recruitment. Spain participates in the Bologna Process to establish a European Higher Education Area, the first phase of which is to adopt a credit-based system of comparable degrees with two main cycles (undergraduate and graduate). Little progress was made until 2005, when a royal decree was passed establishing the new degree structure. Higher education is provided by public and private universities, higher technical colleges (escuelas técnicas superiores), university colleges (colegios universitarios), university faculties (facultades universitarias) and university schools (escuelas universitarias). An estimated 1,381,749 students were attending university in 2007/08. In that year there were 72 universities, including the open university (UNED), established in 1972.

The main requirements for admission to higher education are the secondary school certificate (Bachillerato) and the university entrance examination (Prueba de Acceso Universidad). University degrees are divided into three cycles. The first cycle lasts three years and is equivalent to a Bachelors; the main qualifications are the Diplomado (offered in the four subject areas of experimental and health science, humanities, social sciences and law, and technical education) and Diplomatura. Professional titles such as Arquitecto Técnico and Ingeniero Técnico are also awarded. The second cycle lasts two years and is equivalent to the Masters; the main degrees awarded are the Licenciado, Licenciatura or professional title. Finally, the third cycle constitutes the highest level of university degree, namely the Título de Doctorado, which requires three years of classwork and research, culminating with the submission and defence of a thesis.

The main qualification offered in vocational and technical education is the Técnico Superior, awarded after one-and-a-half to two years of study. Occupational training is also available; students are awarded the Certificados de Profesionalidad.

The National Agency for Quality Assessment and Accreditation was founded in 2002 following the Spanish Universities Act and is responsible for accrediting programmes of study, providing quality assurance and acting as the inter-agency coordinating body for Spanish higher education.

Regulatory and Representative Bodies

GOVERNMENT

Ministry of Culture: Plaza del Rey 1, 28004 Madrid; tel. (91) 7017000; fax (91) 7017352; e-mail contacte@mcu.es; internet www.mcu.es; Minister ÁNGELES GONZÁLEZ-SINDE REIG.

Ministry of Education: Alcalá 36, 28071 Madrid; tel. (91) 7018098; fax (91) 7018648; e-mail prensa@educacion.es; internet www.educacion.es; Minister ÁNGEL GABILONDO PUJOL.

Ministry of Science and Innovation: Albacete 5, 28027 Madrid; tel. (91) 4959554; e-mail informa@micinn.es; internet www.micinn.es; Minister CRISTINA GARMENDIA MENDIZÁBA.

ACCREDITATION

Agencia Nacional de Evaluación de la Calidad y Acreditación (National Agency for Quality Assessment and Accreditation): Calle Orense 11, 7°, 28020 Madrid; tel. (91) 4178230; e-mail informacion@aneca.es; internet www.aneca.es; f. 2002; contributes to the quality improvement of the higher education system through the assessment, certification and accreditation of univ. degrees, programmes, teaching staff and instns; Dir ZULIMA FERNÁNDEZ.

ENIC/NARIC Spain: NARIC Centre of Spain, Subdirección General de Títulos y Reconocimiento de Cualificaciones, Paseo del Prado 28, 28014 Madrid; tel. (91) 5065593; fax (91) 5065706; e-mail naric@educacion.es; internet www.educacion.es; Technical Assessor ISABEL BARRIOS.

FUNDING

Fundación Juan March: Castelló 77, 28006 Madrid; tel. (91) 4354240; fax (91) 5763420; e-mail info@march.es; internet www.march.es; f. 1955; awards scholarships and research grants to Spanish profs and scholars in molecular biology and other fields; organizes cultural, artistic and musical activities; library dealing with modern Spanish theatre and contemporary Spanish music; Pres. JUAN MARCH DELGADO; Dir JAVIER GOMÁ LANZÓN; publ. *Revista de la Fundación Juan March* (9 a year).

NATIONAL BODIES

Asociación Iberoamericana de Educación Superior a Distancia (Ibero-American Association for Open and Distance Higher Education): Calle Bravo Murillo 38, 7°, 28015 Madrid; tel. (91) 3986549; fax (91) 3986587; e-mail aiesad@adm.uned.es; internet www.aiesad.org; f. 1981; network for the devt of distance education in Spanish-speaking Latin America; biannual int. seminars, joint projects and electronic newsletter; 43 mems; library of 50 vols; bibliography of distance- and open-education in Spanish-speaking Latin America; Pres. Dr JUAN A. GIMENO ULLASTRES; Permanent Sec. Dra MARÍA TERESA AGUADO ODINA; publ. *Revista Iberoamericana de Educación a Distancia (RIED)* (scientific review, available electronically).

Conferencia de Rectores de las Universidades Españolas (CRUE) (Spanish Universities' Rectors' Conference): Plaza de las Cortes 2, 7°, 28014 Madrid; tel. (91) 3601200; fax (91) 3601201; e-mail info@crue.org; internet www.crue.org; f. 1994; fosters links between the univs, studies and analyses univ. problems, acts as link between the Univ. Council and the state univs; 74 mems; Pres. FEDERICO GUTIÉRREZ-SOLANA SALCEDO; Gen. Sec. MARÍA TERESA LOZANO MELLADO.

Conferencia General de Política Universitaria (National Conference of University Policy): c/o Alcalá 36, 28071 Madrid; f. 2007, together with Consejo de Universidades (*q.v.*), to replace Consejo de Coordinación Universitaria (f. 1983); coordinating, cooperative and consultative body for matters concerning higher education policy; chaired by the Min. of Education.

Consejo de Universidades (University Council): c/o Alcalá 36, 28071 Madrid; f. 2007, together with Conferencia General de Política Universitaria (*q.v.*), to replace Consejo de Coordinación Universitaria (f. 1983); advises and promotes coordination in the univ. system; chaired by the Min. of Education; mems incl. (among others) the Rectors of the state univs.

Consejo General de Colegios Oficiales de Doctores y Licenciados en Filosofía y Letras y en Ciencias (National Council of Official Colleges of Doctors and Licentiates in Arts and Science): Bolsa 11, 28012 Madrid; tel. and fax (91) 5224597; e-mail secretaria@consejogeneralcdl.es; internet www.consejogeneralcdl.es; f. 1945; protects and represents education professionals, and seeks to promote initiatives that contribute to improving the quality of education in Spain; 60,000 mems; Pres. JOSEFINA CAMBRA GINÉ; Gen. Sec. JESÚS BONALS CODINA; publ. *Trivium* (4 a year).

Learned Societies

GENERAL

Agencia Española de Cooperación Internacional para el Desarrollo (AECID)

(Spanish Agency for International Development Cooperation): Avda Reyes Católicos 4, Ciudad Universitaria, 28040 Madrid; tel. (91) 5838100; fax (91) 5838310; internet www.aecid.es; f. 1946; aims to contribute to peace, freedom, human security and the eradication of poverty; to promote respect for human rights and development of democratic systems; and to promote the role of culture and knowledge in development; Pres. MARIA SORAYA RODRÍGUEZ RAMOS; Dir ELENA MADRAZO HEGEWISCH; publ. *Cooperación Española* (4 a year).

Attached Institutes:

Instituto de Cooperación con el Mundo Arabe, Mediterráneo y Países en Desarrollo (Institute for Cooperation with the Arab World, the Mediterranean and Developing Countries): Avda Reyes Católicos 4, Ciudad Universitaria, 28040 Madrid; tel. (91) 5838565; fax (91) 5838219; technical assistance, economic cooperation, cultural activities, research grants, scholarships; library of 65,000 vols, 800 periodicals; Dir SENÉN FLORENSA PALAU; publs *Arabismo* (4 a year), *Awraq* (1 a year).

Instituto de Cooperación Iberoamericana (Institute for Ibero-American Co-operation): Avda Reyes Católicos 4, Ciudad Universitaria, 28040 Madrid; tel. (91) 5838100; fax (91) 5838310; f. 1946; promotes cultural understanding between Spain and the USA by organizing conferences, congresses, cultural exhibitions and university exchanges, scholarships for students; finances programmes of cultural, scientific, economic and technical cooperation; information department; Centre for Advanced Hispanic Studies; organizes programmes to diffuse the Spanish language and culture in the USA; radio, cinema and theatre unit; large library open to students; Spanish Library: see Libraries; Pres. FERNANDO VILLALONGA; Dir-Gen. JESÚS MANUEL GRACIA ALDAZ; publs *Cuadernos Hispanoamericanos* (12 a year), *Pensamiento Iberoamericano* (2 a year).

Casa de Velázquez: Calle Paul Guinard 3, Ciudad Universitaria, 28040 Madrid; tel. (91) 4551580; fax (91) 5446879; e-mail info@casadevelazquez.org; internet www.casadevelazquez.org; f. 1928; French school for research into all aspects of Iberia; grants sr fellowships to French artists or scholars to work in Spain; 34 mems; library of 100,000 vols, 1,700 current periodicals; Dir JEAN-PIERRE ÉTIENVRE; Sec.-Gen. DOMINIQUE DUMAS; publ. *Mélanges de la Casa de Velázquez* (4 a year).

Dirección General de Relaciones Culturales y Científicas (Cultural and Scientific Relations Department): Agencia Española de Cooperación Internacional, Avda Reyes Católicos 4, 28040 Madrid; tel. (91) 5838100; internet www.maec.es; f. 1926; promotes Spanish culture and science in foreign countries; int. cultural and scientific agreements, exchange of professors and lecturers, scholarships, etc.; Dir-Gen. ANTONIO NICOLUA MARTÍ.

Fundación Instituto de Estudios Norteamericanos (Institute of North American Studies): Vía Augusta 123, 08006 Barcelona; tel. (93) 2405110; fax (93) 2020690; e-mail ien@ien.es; internet www.ien.es; f. 1951; cultural exchange programmes, lectures, discussions, musical events, theatre, cinema, art exhibitions, seminars, etc.; courses in English and in American Studies; runs an academic counselling service and is the official centre for examinations for students entering US universities; 400 mems; 18,000 students; library of 10,000 vols, 100 periodicals; Pres. ROBERT M. MANSON; Exec. Dir CARLES DOMINGO.

Institut d'Estudis Catalans (Institute of Catalan Studies): Carrer del Carme 47, 08001 Barcelona; tel. (93) 2701620; fax (93) 2701180; e-mail informacio@iec.cat; internet www.iec.cat; f. 1907; incorporates sections on history and archaeology, science and technology, philology, philosophy and social sciences, biology; 183 mems (125 ordinary, 58 corresp.), 28 affiliated scientific socs; Pres. SALVADOR GINER DE SAN JULIÁN; Sec.-Gen. ROMÀ ESCALAS I LLIMONA; publs *Acta Numismàtica, Anuari de la Societat Catalana d'Economia, Anuari de la Societat Catalana de Filosofia, Anuari de la Societat Catalana d'Estudis Jurídics, Arxiu de Textos Catalans Antics, Butlletí de la Institució Catalana d'Història Natural, Butlletí de la Societat Catalana d'Estudis Històrics, Butlletí de la Societat Catalana de Matemàtiques, Butlletí de la Societat Catalana de Musicologia, Butlletí de la Societat Catalana de Pedagogia, Cinematògraf, Dossiers Agraris, Educació i Història: Revista d'Història de l'Educació, Estudis Romànics, Gazeta, Lambard, Llengua i Literatura, Memòria, Miscel·lània Litúrgica Catalana, Notícies de la Societat Catalana de Matemàtiques, Quaderns Agraris, Periodística, Recursos de Física, Revista Catalan de Dret Privat, Revista Catalan de Física, Revista Catalana de Micologia, Revista Catalan de Musicologia, Revista Catalan de Pedagogia, Revista Catalan de Sociologia, Revista de Dret Històrica Català, Revista de la Societat Catalana de Química, Sessió Conjunta d'Entomologia, Tamid, Tecnologia i Ciència dels Aliments (TECA), Trabades d'Història de la Ciència i la Tècnica, Treballs de Comunicació, Treballs de Física, Treballs de la Societat Catalana de Biologia, Treballs de la Societat Catalana de Geografia, Treballs de Sociolingüística Catalana*.

Instituto Cervantes: Alcalá 49, 28014 Madrid; tel. (91) 4367600; fax (91) 4367691; e-mail informa@cervantes.es; internet www.cervantes.es; f. 1991; promotes Spanish language and the culture of Spain and Spanish-speaking Latin and Central America globally; operates in 26 countries; maintains teaching centres in Sofia (Bulgaria), Zagreb (Croatia), Belgrade (Serbia) and Hanoi (Viet Nam); Dir CARMEN CAFFAREL SERRA; Gen. Sec. CARMEN PÉREZ-FRAGERO RODRÍGUEZ DE TEMBLEQUE.

Instituto de España (Institute of Spain): San Bernardo 49, 28015 Madrid; tel. (91) 5224885; fax (91) 5210654; e-mail secretaria@insde.es; internet www.insde.es; f. 1938; the Institute's constituent academies form a 'Senado de la Cultura Española'; Pres. VÍCTOR GARCÍA DE LA CONCHA; Sec.-Gen. PEDRO GARCÍA BARRENO.

Constituent Academies:

Real Academia de Bellas Artes de San Fernando (San Fernando Royal Academy of Fine Arts): Calle Alcalá 13, 28014 Madrid; tel. (91) 5240864; fax (91) 5231599; e-mail director@rabasf.org; internet rabasf.insde.es; f. 1752; attached museum: see Museums and Art Galleries; 57 mems; library of 40,000 vols, 1,100 periodicals; Dir ANTONIO BONET CORREA; Vice-Dir ISMAEL FERNÁNDEZ DE LA CUESTA; Sec.-Gen. FERNANDO DE TERÁN TROYANO.

Real Academia de Ciencias Exactas, Físicas y Naturales (Royal Academy of Exact, Physical and Natural Sciences): Valverde 22 y 24, 28004 Madrid; tel. (91) 7014230; fax (91) 7014232; e-mail secretaria@rac.es; internet www.rac.es; f. 1847; sections of exact sciences (Pres. DARÍO MARAVALL CASENOVES), natural sciences (Pres. LUIS FRANCO VERA), physical and chemical sciences (Pres. ANTONIO HERNANDO GRANDE); 43 mems, 90 Spanish corresp. mems; Pres. MIGUEL ÁNGEL ALARIO FRANCO; publs *Revista* (4 a year), *Serie A: Matemáticas* (4 a year).

Real Academia de Ciencias Morales y Políticas (Royal Academy of Moral and Political Sciences): Casa de los Lujanes, Plaza de la Villa 2, 28005 Madrid; tel. (91) 5481330; fax (91) 5481975; e-mail biblioteca@racmyp.es; internet www.racmyp.es; f. 1857; 89 mems (44 ordinary, 14 Spanish corresp., 35 foreign corresp.); library of 125,000 vols, 340 periodicals; Pres. MARCELINO OREJA AGUIRRE; Sec. FERNANDO SUÁREZ GONZÁLEZ; publs *Anales* (1 a year), *Papeles y Memorias* (4 a year).

Real Academia de Jurisprudencia y Legislación (Royal Academy of Jurisprudence and Law): Calle Marqués de Cubas 13, 28014 Madrid; tel. (91) 5222069; fax (91) 5234021; e-mail secretaria.rajyl@insde.es; internet rajyl.insde.es; f. 1730; 38 mems; library of 40,000 vols; Pres. LANDELINO LAVILLA ALSINA; Sec.-Gen. RAFAEL NAVARRO-VALLS; publ. *Anales*.

Real Academia de la Historia (Royal Academy of History): Calle León 21, 28014 Madrid; tel. (91) 4290611; fax (91) 3694636; e-mail direccion@rah.es; internet www.rah.es; f. 1738; 33 mems, 370 corresp. mems; library of 350,000 vols, 180,000 MSS; Dir GONZALO ANES Y ÁLVAREZ DE CASTRILLÓN; Permanent Sec. ELOY BENITO RUANO.

Real Academia Española (Royal Spanish Academy): Calle de Felipe IV 4, 28014 Madrid; tel. (91) 4201478; fax (91) 4200079; e-mail secretaria@rae.es; internet www.rae.es; f. 1713; 40 ordinary mems, 3 elected mems; Dir VICTOR GARCÍA DE LA CONCHA; Sec. DARÍO VILLANUEVA.

Real Academia Nacional de Farmacia (Royal National Academy of Pharmacy): Calle de la Farmacia 9–11, 28004 Madrid; tel. (91) 5310307; fax (91) 5310306; e-mail secretaria@ranf.com; internet www.ranf.com; f. 1589; 44 mems; library of 30,000 vols; Pres. MARIA TERESA MIRAS PORTUGAL; Permanent Sec. LUIS ANTONIO DOADRIO VILLAREJO; publ. *Anales* (4 a year).

Real Academia Nacional de Medicina (Royal National Academy of Medicine): Calle Arrieta 12, 28013 Madrid; tel. (91) 5470318; fax (91) 5470320; internet www.ranm.es; f. 1733; 46 mems; 81 Spanish corresp. mems; 82 foreign corresp. mems; library of 100,000 vols; Pres. MANUEL DÍAZ-RUBIO GARCÍA; Sec.-Gen. MIGUEL LUCAS TOMÁS; publ. *Anales* (4 a year).

Instituto Egipcio de Estudios Islámicos (Egyptian Institute of Islamic Studies): Calle Francisco de Asís Méndez Casariego 1, 28002 Madrid; tel. (91) 5639468; fax (91) 5638640; e-mail secretaria@institutoegipcio.com; internet www.institutoegipcio.com; f. 1950; 14 mems; library of 38,000 vols, 1,200 periodicals; Dir Dr ELSAYED IBRAHIM SOHEIM; Sec. ALMUDENA GARCÍA; publ. *Revista* (1 a year).

Real Academia de Bellas Artes y Ciencias Históricas de Toledo (Toledo Royal Academy of Fine Arts and Historical Sciences): Calle Esteban Illán 9, 45002 Toledo; tel. and fax (92) 5214322; internet www.realacademiatoledo.es; f. 1916; 24 mems, 26 corresp. mems; library of 4,000 vols; Dir RAMÓN SÁNCHEZ GONZÁLEZ; Sec. JOSÉ LUIS ISABEL SÁNCHEZ; publ. *Toletum*.

Real Academia de Ciencias y Artes de Barcelona (Barcelona Royal Academy of Science and Arts): Rambla de los Estudios

115, 08002 Barcelona; tel. (93) 3170536; fax (93) 3011656; e-mail info@racab.es; internet www.racab.es; f. 1764; 75 mems; attached observatory: see Research Institutes; library of 150,000 vols; Pres. Dr RAFAEL FOGUET I AMBRÓS; Sec.-Gen. JOAN JOFRE I TORROELLA; publ. *Memòries*.

Real Academia de Doctores (Royal Academy of Doctors): Calle de San Bernardo 49, 28015 Madrid; tel. (91) 5319522; fax (91) 5240027; e-mail rad@radoctores.es; internet www.radoctores.es; f. 1920; sections of architechture, commerce, economics, engineering, law, literature, medicine, pharmacy, philosophy, politics, veterinary science, sciences; 4 hon. mems, 100 mems, 110 national corresp., 90 foreign corresp. mems; Pres. Dr LUIS MARDONES SEVILLA; Sec.-Gen. Dra ROSA MARÍA GARCERÁN PIQUERAS; publs *Anales* (irregular), *Anuario*.

Real Academia Galega (Royal Galician Academy): Rúa Tabernas 11, 15001 A Coruña; tel. (981) 207308; fax (981) 216467; e-mail secretaria@realacademiagalega.org; internet www.realacademiagalega.org; f. 1905; promotes Galician language and literature; 29 mems; library of 65,000 vols, incl. valuable colln of books on Galicia; Pres. MÉNDEZ FERRÍN XOSÉ LUÍS; Sec. AXEITOS AGRELO XOSÉ LUÍS; publs *Boletín da Real Academia Galega* (Galician literature and history), *Cadernos de Lingua* (Galician language: grammar, phonetics, lexicography, sociolinguistics).

Real Academia Hispano-Americana (Royal Spanish-American Academy): Paseo Carlos III 9, 1°, 11003 Cadiz; tel. (95) 6221680; fax (95) 6221224; e-mail raha@raha.es; internet www.raha.es; f. 1910; library of 120,000 vols; 25 mems, 6 hon. mems; Dir MARÍA DEL CARMEN CÓZAR NAVARRO; Sec.-Gen. FERNANDO SÁNCHEZ GARCIA; publ. *Anuario*.

AGRICULTURE, FISHERIES AND VETERINARY SCIENCE

Institut Agrícola (Agricultural Institute): Plaça Sant Josep Oriol 4, 08002 Barcelona; tel. (93) 3011636; fax (93) 3173005; e-mail info@institutagricola.org; internet www.institutagricola.org; f. 1851; 2,000 mems; library of 16,000 vols, 200 periodicals; Pres. BALDIRI ROS I PRAT; Sec. MATEU COMALRENA DE SOBREGRAU; publ. *La Drecera* (6 a year).

Real Academia de Ciencias Veterinarias (Royal Academy of Veterinary Sciences): c/o Prof. Dr Mariano Illera Martín, Maestro Ripoll 8, 28006 Madrid; tel. (91) 5611799; fax (91) 3943864; e-mail info@racve.es; internet www.racve.es; f. 1975; 38 mems, 5 hon. mems, 32 corresp. mems in Spain, 81 corresp. mems abroad; Pres. CARLOS LUIS DE CUENCA Y ESTEBAN; Sec.-Gen. JULIO SALVIO JIMÉNEZ PÉREZ; publ. *Anales* (1 a year).

ARCHITECTURE AND TOWN PLANNING

Col·legi d'Arquitectes de Catalunya (Association of Catalan Architects): Plaça Nova 5, 08002 Barcelona; tel. (93) 3015000; fax (93) 3186029; e-mail coac@coac.net; internet www.coac.net; f. 1931; 9,000 mems; library of 80,000 vols; Dean LUÍS-XAVIER COMERÓN I GRAUPERA; Sec. ASSUMPCIÓ PUIG I HORS; publ. *Quaderns d'Arquitectura i Urbanisme*.

BIBLIOGRAPHY, LIBRARY SCIENCE AND MUSEOLOGY

Amics dels Museus de Catalunya (Friends of the Catalan Museums): Palau de la Virreina, La Rambla 99, 08002 Barcelona; tel. (93) 3014379; fax (93) 3189421; e-mail amics@amicsdelsmuseus.org; internet www.amicsdelsmuseus.org; f. 1933; 800 mems, 6 hon., 81 associates, 52 others; Pres. FAUSTO SERRA DE DALMASES; Sec.-Gen. MARINA GÓMEZ CASAS.

Federación Española de Asociaciones de Archiveros, Bibliotecarios, Arqueólogos, Museólogos y Documentalistas (Spanish Federation of Associations of Archivists, Librarians, Archaeologist, Museums and Archives): Calle Recoletos 5, 3°, 28001 Madrid; tel. (91) 5751727; fax (91) 5781615; e-mail anabad@anabad.org; internet www.anabad.org; f. 1949; more than 1,500 mems; groups all specialists working in the country's archive services, libraries, museums and documentation services; has regional branches in Aragón, Castilla-La Mancha, Galicia, La Rioja and Murcia; Pres. ANTONIO CASADO POYALES; Sec. RAMÓN VILLA GONZÁLEZ.

ECONOMICS, LAW AND POLITICS

Centro de Estudios Políticos y Constitucionales (Centre for Political and Constitutional Studies): Plaza de la Marina Española 9, 28071 Madrid; tel. (91) 5401950; fax (91) 5419574; e-mail cepc@cepc.es; internet www.cepc.es; f. 1977, by merger with Instituto de Estudios Políticos; organizes courses and seminars on politics and constitutional law; 100 mems; library of 85,500 vols; Dir Dra PALOMA BIGLINO CAMPOS; Man. JOSÉ ÁNGEL MANZANO GARCÍA; publs *Anuario Iberoamericano de Justicia Constitucional* (1 a year), *Derecho Privado y Constitución* (1 a year), *Historia y Política* (2 a year), *Revista de Administración Pública* (3 a year), *Revista de Derecho Comunitario Europeo* (3 a year), *Revista de Estudios Políticos* (4 a year), *Revista Española de Derecho Constitucional* (3 a year).

Col·legi de Notaris de Catalunya (College of Catalan Notaries): Carrer Notariat 4, Barcelona; tel. (93) 3174800; fax (93) 3026331; e-mail info@catalunya.notariado.org; internet www.colnotcat.es; f. 1932; 500 mems; Dir ÁNGEL SERRANO DE NICOLÁS; Sec. ESTEBAN CUYAS HENCHE; publ. *La Notaría*.

Il·lustre Col·legi d'Advocats de Barcelona (Barcelona Bar Association): Calle Mallorca 283, 08037 Barcelona; tel. (93) 4961880; fax (93) 4871589; e-mail icab@icab.es; internet www.icab.es; f. 1832; 20,000 mems; library: see Libraries and Archives; Dean PEDRO L.YÚFERA SALES; Sec. LUIS ANTONIO SALES CAMPRODON; publs *Món Jurídic* (12 a year), *Revista Jurídica de Catalunya* (8 a year).

Instituto Nacional de Administración Pública (National Institute of Public Administration): Atocha 106, 28012 Madrid; tel. (91) 2739281; fax (91) 2739287; e-mail direccion@inap.es; internet www.inap.map.es; f. 1940; library of 150,000 vols, 3,000 periodicals; Sec.-Gen. MARÍA SOL SERRANO ALONSO; Dir ÁNGEL MANUEL MORENO MOLINA; publs *Cuadernos de Derecho Publico* (3 a year), *Documentación Administrativa* (3 a year), *Gestión y Análysis de Políticas Públicas* (3 a year), *Revista de Estudios de Administración Local* (3 a year), *Revista Internacional de Administrativas* (4 a year).

Instituto Nacional de Estadística (National Statistical Office): Paseo de la Castellana 183, 28071 Madrid; tel. (91) 5839100; fax (91) 5839158; e-mail biblioteca@ine.es; internet www.ine.es; f. 1945; library of 170,000 vols, 125,000 microfiches; Pres. JAUME GARCÍA VILLAR; Sec.-Gen. NATIVIDAD DOMÍNGUEZ CALAVERAS; publs *Anuario Estadístico de España* (1 a year), *Boletín Mensual de Estadística* (data on short-term indicators, 12 a year), *Boletín Trimestral de Coyuntura* (national accounts and other indicators, 4 a year), *Censos de la Población y de la Vivienda* (every 10 years), *Dirce* (number of enterprises by sector and breakdown by number of workers and activity), *Encuesta Anual de Comercio* (data on trade, 1 a year), *Epa* (employment), *España en Cifras* (main statistical indicators and data, in Spanish or English), *Estadística Española* (statistical theory and methodology, 3 a year), *Estadística Industrial* (data on production and business turnover, 1 a year), *Nomenclaturas y Metodología*.

Real Sociedad Económica de Amigos del País de Tenerife (Royal Economic Society of Friends of Tenerife): Calle San Agustín 23, 38201 San Cristóbal de La Laguna, Tenerife, Canary Islands; tel. (922) 250010; fax (922) 257735; e-mail secretaria@rseapt.com; internet www.rseapt.com; f. 1777; 500 mems; library of 12,000 vols; Dir ANDRÉS M. DE SOUZA IGLESIAS; Sec. MARÍA LUISA DE CÓRDOVA SANTANA.

EDUCATION

Fundación José Ortega y Gasset: Calle Fortuny 53, 28010, Madrid; tel. (91) 7004100; fax (91) 7003530; e-mail comunicacion@fog.es; internet www.ortegaygasset.edu; f. 1978; organizes cultural activities and undertakes debate and research in the fields of the social sciences and humanities; attached institute in Toledo offers courses in Hispanic, Latin American and European Studies (incl. anthropology, archaeology, politics, economics, geography, history, art, Spanish language, literature), designed specifically for foreign students; Pres. JOSÉ VARELA ORTEGA; Dir-Gen. JESÚS SÁNCHEZ LAMBÁS; publs *Revista de Estudios Orteguianos* (2 a year), *Revista de Occidente* (12 a year).

FINE AND PERFORMING ARTS

Asociación Española de Pintores y Escultores (Association of Spanish Artists and Sculptors): Calle Infantas 30, 2°, 28004 Madrid; tel. (91) 5224961; fax (91) 5225508; e-mail administracion@aepe.e.telefonica.net; internet www.apintoresyescultores.es; f. 1910; 1,000 mems; Pres. ROSA MARTÍNEZ DE LAHIDALGA; Sec. MARÍA ISABEL MORENO GONZÁLEZ; publ. *Gaceta de las Bellas Artes* (12 a year).

Ateneo Científico, Literario y Artístico (Scientific, Literary and Artistic Athenaeum): Sa Rovellada de Dalt 25, 07703 Mahón, Minorca, Balearic Islands; tel. 971-36-05-53; f. 1905; library of 15,000 vols; 630 mems; Pres. JOSÉ ANTONIO FAYAS JANER; Sec. CATALINA SEGUI DE VIDAL; publ. *Revista de Menorca* (4 a year).

Ateneo Científico, Literario y Artístico de Madrid (Scientific, Literary and Artistic Athenaeum in Madrid): Calle Prado 21, 28014 Madrid; tel. (91) 4291750; fax (91) 4297901; e-mail admonateneo@telefonica.net; internet www.ateneodemadrid.com; f. 1820; 7,000 mems; library of 500,000 vols; Pres. CARLOS PARÍS AMADOR; Sec. CARLOS GARCÍA; publ. *El Ateneno* (1 a year).

Ateneu Barcelonès (Barcelona Athenaeum): Calle de la Canuda 6, 08002 Barcelona; tel. (93) 3436121; fax (93) 3171525; e-mail info@ateneubcn.org; internet www.ateneubcn.org; f. 1860; library: see Libraries; 4,000 mems; Pres. ORIOL BOHIGAS GUARDIOLA; Sec. MERCÈ ÀLVAREZ.

Consejo General de la Música (General Council on Music): Calle Davallada 12, Planta Baixa, 08870 Sitges; tel. (93) 8949990; fax (93) 8948996; e-mail consejo@musicae.org; mem. of Int. Music Council (*q.v.*); Pres. MANUEL VALLRIBERA I MIR.

Institut Amatller d'Art Hispànic (Amatller Institute of Hispanic Art): Passeig de Gràcia 41, 08007 Barcelona; tel. (93) 2160175; fax (93) 4670194; e-mail administracio@amatller.org; internet www.amatller.org; f. 1941; library of 26,000 vols; colln of 350,000 photographs; Pres. MONTSERRAT BLANCH ALMUZARA; Sec. JACINT BERENGUER I CASAL.

Institut del Teatre (Theatrical Institute): Plaça Margarida Xirgu, s/n, 08004 Barcelona; tel. (93) 2273900; fax (93) 2273939; e-mail i.teatre@diba.es; internet www.institutdelteatre.org; f. 1913; drama and dance school; documentation and research information centre; library of 150,000 vols; Dir JORDI FONT I CARDONA.

Real Academia de Bellas Artes de la Purísima Concepción (Royal Academy of Fine Arts): Casa de Cervantes, Calle del Rastro, s/n, 47001 Valladolid; tel. (983) 398004; fax (983) 390703; e-mail info@realacademiaconcepcion.net; internet www.realacademiaconcepcion.net; f. 1779; 32 mems; Pres. JOAQUÍN DÍAZ GONZÁLEZ; Sec. JESÚS URREA FERNÁNDEZ.

Real Academia de Bellas Artes de San Telmo (Royal Academy of Fine Arts, San Telmo): Málaga; internet www.realacademiasantelmo.org; f. 1849 as Academia de Bellas Artes de Málaga; present name adopted 1883; 34 mems; Pres. MANUEL DEL CAMPO Y DEL CAMPO; Sec. FRANCISCO CABRERA PABLOS; publ. *Anuario*.

Real Academia de Bellas Artes de Santa Isabel de Hungría (Royal Academy of Fine Arts, Santa Isabel de Hungría): Abades 14, Casa de los Pinelo, 41004 Seville; tel. and fax (95) 4221198; e-mail rabasih@insacan.org; internet www.insacan.org/rabasih/rabasihsede.html; f. 1660; research, courses and exhibitions; 40 mems; library of 3,900 vols; Pres. ISABEL DE LEÓN BORRERO; Gen. Sec. FERNANDO FERNÁNDEZ GÓMEZ; publs *Boletín de Bellas Artes* (1 a year), *Temas de Estética y Arte* (1 a year).

Real Academia de Nobles y Bellas Artes de San Luis (Royal Academy of Fine Arts, San Luis): Plaza de los Sitios 6, 50001 Zaragoza; tel. (97) 6217969; fax (97) 6222378; e-mail rasanluis@rasanluis.es; internet www.rasanluis.es; f. 1792; comprises 5 sections (architecture, sculpture, painting, music, literature) and 3 permanent cttees; 38 mems; library of 5,500 vols; Pres. DOMINGO JESÚS BUESA CONDE; Sec.-Gen. JAVIER SAURAS VIÑUALES.

Real Sociedad Fotográfica (Royal Photographic Society): Apdo 7238, 28080 Madrid; Calle de los Tres Peces 2, 28012 Madrid; tel. (91) 5397579; e-mail info@rsf.es; internet www.rsf.es; f. 1899; 1,400 mems; library of 3,800 vols; Pres. ENRIQUE SANZ RAMÍREZ; Sec.-Gen. MARIA ANTONIA GARCÍA DE LA VEGA; publ. *Boletín* (4 a year).

HISTORY, GEOGRAPHY AND ARCHAEOLOGY

Arxiu Històric de la Ciutat de Barcelona: Casa de l'Ardiaca, Carrer Santa Llúcia 1, 08002 Barcelona; tel. (93) 3181195; fax (93) 3178327; e-mail arxiuhistoric@bcn.cat; internet www.bcn.es/arxiu/arxiuhistoric; f. 1917; archives of municipal records and local press; the Archives undertake historical research on Barcelona, organize courses, lectures, exhibitions; library: see Libraries and Archives; Dir XAVIER TARRAUBELLA MIRABET; publs *Barcelona Quaderns d'Història* (2 a year), *História, Antropología, y Fuentes Orales* (2 a year), *Quaderns del Seminari d'Història de Barcelona* (irregular).

Deutsches Archaeologisches Institut (German Archaeological Institute): Serrano 159, 28002 Madrid; tel. (91) 4110163; fax (91) 5640054; e-mail sekretariat@madrid.dainst.org; internet www.dainst.de; f. 1943; library of 65,000 vols; archive of photographs; Dir Prof. Dr HANS-JOACHIM GEHRKE; publs *Hispania Antiqua, Iberia Archaeologica, Madrider Beiträge, Madrider Forschungen, Madrider Mitteilungen* (1 a year), *Studien über frühe Tierknochenfunde von der Iberischen Halbinsel*.

Instituto de Historia y Cultura Naval (Institute of Naval History and Culture): Calle Juan de Mena 1, 28014 Madrid; tel. (91) 3795050; fax (91) 3795945; f. 1942 as Instituto Histoórico de la Marina; present name adopted 1976; associated with the Consejo Superior de Investigaciones Científicas; for library see entry under Museo Naval; Dir Contralmirante TEODORO DE LESTE CONTRERAS.

Instituto Geográfico Nacional (National Geographical Institute): Calle del General Ibáñez de Ibero 3, 28003 Madrid; tel. (91) 5979453; fax (91) 5532913; e-mail ign@mfom.es; internet www.mfom.es/ign; f. 1870; 1,200 mems; library of 28,000 vols; geodesy and geophysics, cartography, map printing, seismology, astronomy, runs the Nat. Astronomical Observatory (see under Research Institutes); Dir-Gen. ALBERTO SERENO ÁLVAREZ; publs *Boletín Astronómico, Anuario del Observatorio Astronómico, Anuario de Geomagnetismo, Boletines Sísmicos*.

Real Sociedad Geográfica (Royal Geographic Society): Calle Monte Esquinza 41, 28010 Madrid; tel. (91) 3082477; fax (91) 3082478; e-mail secretaria@realsociedadgeografica.com; internet www.realsociedadgeografica.com; f. 1876; geography and earth sciences; 450 mems; library of 11,000 vols, 12,700 booklets, 110 periodicals; Pres. JUAN VELARDE FUERTES; Perm. Sec. Dr JOAQUÍN BOSQUE MAUREL.

Reial Societat Arqueològica Tarraconense (Royal Archaeological Society in Tarragona): POB 573, 43080 Tarragona; Carrer Major 35, 43003 Tarragona; tel. and fax (977) 23-37-89; e-mail informacio@arqueologica.org; internet www.arqueologica.org; f. 1844; Iberian, Roman and early Christian archaeology; ancient, medieval, modern and contemporary history of Tarragona; 600 mems; library of 4,000 vols, 18,000 vols of periodicals; Pres. RAFAEL GABRIEL COSTA; Sec. JORDI ROVIRA SORIANO; publ. *Butlletí Arqueològic* (4 a year).

Servicio de Investigación Prehistórica de la Excelentísima Diputación Provincial (Prehistoric Research Society of the Province of Valencia): Calle de la Corona 36, 46003 Valencia; tel. (96) 3883587; fax (96) 3883536; e-mail sip@dival.es; internet www.museoprehistoriavalencia.es; f. 1927; palaeolithic, neolithic, Bronze and Iron Ages, Iberian and colonial exhibits, prehistoric Americana; 30 mems; library of 60,000 vols; Curator MARÍA JESÚS DE PEDRO MICHÓ; publs *Serie de Trabajos Varios, Archivo de Prehistoria Levantina*.

Societat Arqueològica Lul·liana (Lulliana Archaeological Society): Calle Monti-Sion 9, 07001 Palma de Mallorca, Balearic Islands; tel. (971) 713912; e-mail info@arqueologicaluliana.com; internet www.arqueologicaluliana.com; f. 1880; 600 mems; library of 20,000 vols; museum; Pres. MARIA BARCELÓ CRESPÍ; Sec. MARIA ANTÒNIA SEGURA BONNÍN; publ. *Bolletí de la Societat Arqueològica Lul·liana: Revista d'estudis històrics* (1 a year).

LANGUAGE AND LITERATURE

Alliance Française: Calle Marqués de la Ensenada 10, 28004 Madrid; tel. (91) 7007736; fax (91) 7007707; e-mail secaf@alliancefrancaise.es; internet www.alliancefrancaise.es; offers courses and exams in French language and culture and promotes cultural exchange with France; attached offices in Alicante, Burgos, Cartagena, Gijon, Girona, Granada, Granollers, La Coruña, Las Palmas, Lerida, Lleida, Malaga, Oviedo, Palma de Mallorca, Sabadell, Sama de Langreo, Santa Cruz de Tenerife, Santander, Santiago de Compostela, Valladolid, Vigo and Vitoria.

Asociación de Escritores y Artistas Españoles (Spanish Writers' and Artists' Association): Calle de Leganitos 10, 1° Derecha, 28013 Madrid; tel. (91) 5599067; fax (91) 5424467; e-mail secretaria@aeae.es; internet www.aeae.es; f. 1871; 527 mems; library of 3,000 vols; Pres. JUAN VAN-HALEN; Dir and Sec.-Gen. JOSÉ LÓPEZ MARTÍNEZ.

British Council: Paseo del General Martinez, Campos 31, 28010 Madrid; tel. 91-337-35-00; fax 91-337-35-73; e-mail prensa@britishcouncil.es; internet www.britishcouncil.es; offers courses and examinations in English language and British culture and promotes cultural exchange with the United Kingdom in 13 centres across Spain (7 in Madrid, 2 in Barcelona, and 1 each in Bilbao, Valencia, Segovia and Plama de Mallorca); Dir CHRIS HICKEY.

Euskaltzaindia/Real Academia de la Lengua Vasca (Royal Academy of the Basque Language): Plaza Barria 15, 48005 Bilbao; tel. (94) 4158155; fax (94) 4158144; e-mail info@euskaltzaindia.net; internet www.euskaltzaindia.net; f. 1919; research into and conservation of the Basque language; 30 full mems, 33 hon. mems, 135 assoc. academic mems; library of 70,000 vols specializing in philology and linguistics, principally of the Basque language; Pres. ANDRÉS URRUTIA BADIOLA; Vice-Pres. AURELIA ARKOTXA MORTALENA; Sec. XABIER KINTANA URTIAGA; Treas. JOSE LUIS LIZUNDIA ASKONDO; publs *Erlea, Euskera* (3 a year), *Euskaltzainak Bilduma* (irregular), *Euskaltzaindiaren Arauak* (3 a year), *Euskararen Lekukoak, Iker, Jagon, Mendaur bilduma* (irregular), *Onomasticon Vasconiae, Plazaberri* (irregular).

Goethe-Institut: Calle Zurbarán 21, 28010 Madrid; tel. (91) 3913944; fax (91) 3913945; e-mail info@madrid.goethe.org; internet www.goethe.de/madrid; offers courses and exams in German language and culture and promotes cultural exchange with Germany; attached centres in Alcalá de Henares, Colmenarejo, Colmenar Viejo, Getafe, Leganés, Villanueva de la Cañada, Granada and San Sebastián; library of 15,000 vols; Dir MARGARETA HAUSCHILD; Sec. REBECA CASTELLANO.

Real Academia Sevillana de Buenas Letras (Seville Royal Academy of Belles Lettres): Calle Abades 14, 41004 Seville; tel. (95) 4225200; e-mail secretariarasbl@infonegocio.com; internet www.academiasevillanadebuenasletras.org; f. 1751; 29 mems, 7 hon., 100 corresp.; library of 20,000 vols; Dir MANUEL GONZÁLEZ JIMÉNEZ; Sec. ENRIQUETA VILA VILAR; publ. *Boletín* (1 a year).

Reial Acadèmia de Bones Lletres (Royal Academy of Belles Lettres): Carrer del Bisbe

Caçador 3, 08002 Barcelona; tel. and fax (93) 3102349; e-mail bones-lletres@boneslletres .cat; internet www.bonesl1etres.cat; f. 1700; 36 mems; Pres. EDUARD RIPOLL; Sec. ALBERT CORBETO LÓPEZ; publ. *Boletín*.

Sociedad General de Autores y Editores (General Society of Authors and Publishers): Fernando VI 4, 28004 Madrid; tel. (91) 3499550; internet www.sgae.es; f. 1932; 95,000 mems; library of 25,000 vols, relating to the theatre, music (scores) and cinema only; Pres. JOSÉ LUIS BORAU MORADELL; publ. *Boletín* (4 a year).

MEDICINE

Academia de Ciencias Médicas de Bilbao (Academy of Medical Sciences, Bilbao): Lersundi 9, 5°, 48009 Bilbao; tel. (94) 4233768; fax (94) 4232161; e-mail academiacmb@gruponahise.com; internet www.icombi.org/academiacm.htm; f. 1895; more than 1,200 mems; library of 10,000 vols; Pres. Dr JUAN IGNACIO GOIRIA ORMAZABAL; Sec.-Gen. Prof. Dr RICARDO FRANCO VICARIO; publ. *Gaceta Médica de Bilbao* (4 a year).

Acadèmia de Ciències Mèdiques de Catalunya i de Balears (Academy of Medical Sciences and Health of Catalonia and the Balearic Islands): Paseo de la Bonanova 51, 08017 Barcelona; tel. (93) 4188729; e-mail academia@academia.cat; internet www .acmcb.es; f. 1872; 20,000 mems; Pres. JOSEP ANTONI BOMBÍ LATORRE; publ. *Annals de Medicina* (4 a year).

Academia Española de Dermatología y Venereología (Spanish Academy of Dermatology and Venereology): Calle Ferraz 100, 1° izq, 28008 Madrid; tel. (91) 5446284; fax (91) 5494145; e-mail contacto@aedv.es; internet www.aedv.es; f. 1909; brs: Andalusia; Asturias, Cantabria and Castille Leon; Balearic Islands; Canary Islands; Catalonia; Centro; Euskadi, Navarre, La Rioja and Aragon; Galicia; Murcia; Valencia; 450 mems, 50 hon., 3 corresp.; library of 1,000 vols; Pres. Dr JOSÉ CARLOS MORENO GIMÉNEZ; Sec. Dr HUGO ALBERTO VÁZQUEZ VEIGA; publ. *Actas Dermosifiliográficas* (12 a year).

Academia Médico-Quirúrgica Española (Spanish Academy of Medicine and Surgery): Calle Villanueva 11, 28001 Madrid; f. 1844; 500 mems; Pres. Prof. LUIS ORTIZ QUINTANA; Sec. Dr JULIO MÚÑIZ GONZÁLEZ; publ. *Anales*.

Consejo General de Colegios Oficiales de Farmacéuticos (General Council of Official Colleges of Pharmacists): Calle Villanueva 11, 7°, 28001 Madrid; e-mail buzon@ redfarma.org; internet www.portalfarma .com; f. 1942; 13,500 mems; Pres. ERNESTO MARCO CAÑIZARES; publ. *Farmacéuticos* (9–12 a year).

Organización Médica Colegial—Consejo General de Colegios Oficiales de Médicos de España (Spanish General Council of Official Medical Colleges): Plaza de las Cortes 11, 28014 Madrid; tel. (91) 4317780; fax (91) 4319620; e-mail administrador@ cgcom.org; internet www.cgcom.org; f. 1930; 52 mems; Pres. Dr JUAN JOSÉ RODRÍGUEZ SENDÍN; Sec.-Gen. Dr SERAFÍN ROMERO AGÜIT; publs *Europa al Día* (26 a year), *Periódico OMC* (12 a year).

Real Academia de Medicina y Cirugía de Palma de Mallorca (Royal Academy of Medicine and Surgery, Palma de Mallorca): Calle Morey 8, 07001 Palma de Mallorca; tel. (971) 721230; f. 1831; 19 mems; Pres. JOSÉ TOMÁS MONSERRAT; Sec. SANTIAGO FORTEZA FORTEZA.

Sociedad de Pediatría de Madrid y Castilla-La Mancha (Paediatrics Society of Madrid and Castilla La Mancha): Calle Cea Bermúdez 39, Bajo, 28003 Madrid; tel. (91) 4358031; e-mail spmycm@mcmpediatria .org; internet www.mcmpediatria.org; f. 1913; 750 mems; Pres. Dr JOSÉ GARCIA-SICILIA LÓPEZ; Sec.-Gen. Dr JUAN JOSÉ JIMÉNEZ GARCÍA; publ. *MCM—Pediatría* (3 a year).

Sociedad Española de Patología Digestiva (Society of Digestive Diseases): Francisco Silvela 69, 2° C, 28028 Madrid; tel. (91) 4021353; fax (91) 4027691; e-mail sepd@sepd .es; internet www.sepd.es; f. 1933; 800 mems; Pres. Dr JUAN ENRIQUE DOMÍNGUEZ MUÑOZ; Sec. Dr FEDERICO ARGÜELLES ARIAS; publs *G.I. & Hepatology News*, *Revista Española de las Enfermedades Digestivas* (12 a year).

Sociedad Española de Radiología Médica (Spanish Society of Medical Radiology): Gran Vía 1, 28013 Madrid; tel. (91) 5752613; fax (91) 5763279; e-mail secretaria@seram .es; internet www.seram.es; f. 1946; 3,500 mems; 200 founder mems; Pres. Dr EDUARDO FRAILE MORENO; Sec.-Gen. Dr MIGUEL ANGEL LÓPEZ PINO; publs *Diagnóstico por la Imagen* (4 a year), *Radiología* (6 a year).

NATURAL SCIENCES

General

Real Academia de Ciencias Exactas, Físicas, Químicas y Naturales de Zaragoza (Royal Academy of Exact, Physical, Chemical and Natural Sciences in Zaragoza): Facultad de Ciencias, Calle Pedro Cerbuna 12, 50009 Zaragoza; tel. (976) 761128; fax (976) 761125; e-mail acz@posta.unizar.es; internet www.unizar.es/acz; f. 1916; comprises sections on Exact Sciences, Physics and Chemistry, and Natural Sciences; Pres. LUIS JOAQUÍN BOYA BALET; Sec. JOSÉ F. CARIÑENA MARZO; 40 mems, 44 corresp. mems; publ. *Revista* (1 a year).

Sociedad de Ciencias 'Aranzadi' Zientzia Elkartea (Aranzadi Society of Sciences): Calle del Alto de Zorroaga 11, 20014 San Sebastián; tel. (943) 466142; fax (943) 455811; e-mail idazkaritza@ aranzadi-zientziak.org; internet www .aranzadi-zientziak.org; f. 1947; encourages interest in various brs of natural science, prehistory and ethnology; 1,540 mems; library of 28,000 vols, 2,181 periodicals; Pres. FRANCISCO ETXEBERRIA; Sec. JAVIER CANTERA; publs *Aranzadiana* (1 a year), *Aranzadi Berriak*, *Boletín de Astronomía* (4 a year), *Munibe Antropologia—Arkeologia* (1 a year), *Munibe Ciencias Naturales—Natur Zientziak* (1 a year).

Biological Sciences

Asociación Española de Entomología (Spanish Entomological Association): c/o Dr Eduardo Galante Patiño, Centro Iberoamericano de Biodiversidad, Universidad de Alicante, Apdo 99, 03080 Alicante; e-mail galante@ua.es; internet www.entomologica .es; f. 1977; Pres. Dr EDUARDO GALANTE PATIÑO; Sec. Dr JOSÉ MARÍA HERNÁNDEZ DE MIGUEL; publ. *Boletín* (2 a year).

Real Sociedad Española de Historia Natural (Royal Spanish Natural History Society): Facultades de Biología y Geología, Universidad Complutense de Madrid, 28040 Madrid; tel. and fax (91) 3945000; e-mail rsehno@bio.ucm.es; internet rshn.geo.ucm .es; f. 1871; biological and geological sciences; 800 mems; library of 10,000 vols, 2,500 current periodicals; Pres. Dr JOSÉ LUIS VIEJO MONTESINOS; Sec.-Gen. Dr ALFREDO BARATAS DÍAZ; publs *Boletín: Sección Biológica* (4 a year), *Boletín: Sección Geológica* (4 a year).

Sociedad Española de Etología (Spanish Ethological Society): Museu Ciències Naturals, P° Picasso, s/n, Parc Ciutadella, 08003 Barcelona; tel. (93) 2562217; fax (93) 3104999; e-mail larroyo@bcn.cat; internet www.etologia.org; f. 1984; 450 mems; Pres. JUAN CARRANZA; Sec. JUAN CARLOS SENAR; publs *Etología* (1 a year), *EtoloGUÍA* (2 a year).

Mathematical Sciences

Real Sociedad Matemática Española (Royal Spanish Mathematical Society): Despacho 525, Facultad de Matemáticas, Universidad Complutense, 28040 Madrid; tel. (91) 3944937; fax (91) 3945027; e-mail secretaria@rsme.es; internet www.rsme.es; f. 1911; 1,500 mems; Pres. ANTONIO CAMPILLO LÓPEZ; Sec. HENAR HERRERO SANZ; publs *La Gaceta* (3 a year), *Revista Matemática Iberoamericana* (4 a year).

Physical Sciences

Asociación Nacional de Químicos de España (Spanish National Association of Chemists): Calle Lagasca 27, 28001 Madrid; tel. (91) 4310703; fax (91) 5765279; e-mail anquejg@mail.ddnet.es; internet www.anque .es; f. 1945; 10,000 mems; mem. of the int. Fed. of Mediterranean Asscns and of the European Fed. of Chemical Engineering; Pres. BALDOMERO LÓPEZ PÉREZ; Sec. IGNACIO RAMÍREZ CUESTA; publ. *Química e Industria* (12 a year).

Real Sociedad Española de Física (Royal Spanish Society of Physics): Facultad de Ciencias Físicas, Universidad Complutense, Ciudad Universitaria, s/n, 28040 Madrid; tel. (91) 3944350; fax (91) 3944362; e-mail rsef@ fis.ucm.es; internet www.rsef.org; f. 1903; 800 mems; Pres. Prof. MARÍA ROSARIO HERAS CELEMÍN; Sec.-Gen. Prof. CARMEN MARÍA PEREÑA FERNÁNDEZ; publs *Revista Iberoamericana de Física* (1 a year), *Revista Española de Física* (4 a year).

Real Sociedad Española de Química (Royal Spanish Society of Chemistry): Facultad de Ciencias Químicas, Universidad Complutense, Ciudad Universitaria, s/n, 28040 Madrid; tel. (91) 3944361; fax (91) 5433879; e-mail secretario.general@rseq.org; internet www.rseq.org; f. 1903; 3,578 mems; Pres. Prof. NAZARIO MARTÍN LEÓN; Sec.-Gen. JESÚS JIMÉNEZ BARBERO; publ. *Anales* (4 a year).

Sociedad Española de Astronomía (Spanish Astronomical Society): Universitat de Barcelona, Facultad de Física, Avda Martí Franquès 1, 08028 Barcelona; tel. (93) 4034986; fax (93) 4021133; e-mail secretaria@sea.am.ub.es; internet www .sea-astronomia.es; f. 1991; lectures, courses, etc.; 500 mems; library of 3,000 vols; Pres. EMILIO ALFARO; Sec. RUTH CARBALLO FIDALGO.

Sociedad Geológica de España (Geological Society of Spain): Facultad de Ciencias, Universidad de Salamanca, Plaza de la Merced, s/n, 37008 Salamanca; tel. (923) 294752; e-mail sge@usal.es; internet www .sociedadgeologica.es; f. 1985; 1,000 mems; Pres. ANA CRESPO BLANCSORANDO; Sec. JOSÉ EUGENIO ORTIZ MENÉNDEZ; Treas. GABRIEL GUTIERREZ-ALONSO; publs *Geogaceta* (2 a year), *Geo-Temas* (irregular), *Revista* (4 a year).

RELIGION, SOCIOLOGY AND ANTHROPOLOGY

Federación Española de Religiosos de Enseñanza—Centres Catholiques (FERE-CECA)/Escuelas Católicas (Spanish Federation of Religious Institutions in Education—Catholic Centres): Calle Hacienda de Pavones 5, 1°, 28030 Madrid; tel. (91) 3288000; fax (91) 3288001; e-mail escuelascatolicas@escuelascatolicas.es; internet www.escuelascatolicas.es; f. 1957 as Federación Española de Religiosos de Enseñanza (FERE); groups all the centres of elementary, secondary and higher education of the Catholic Church; 2,635 centres; library of 7,000 vols, 150 periodicals; Pres. INMACULADA TUSET GARÍN; Sec.-Gen. JUAN ANTONIO OJEDA ORTIZ; publs *Educadores* (Teachers' Review, 4 a year), *Revista EC* (6 a year).

Institución 'Fernando el Católico', Excma Diputación Provincial de Zaragoza (Institution of Ferdinando the Catholic): Plaza de España 2, 50071 Zaragoza; tel. (976) 288878; fax (976) 288869; e-mail ifc@dpz.es; internet www.ifc.dpz.es; f. 1943 as Institución 'Fernando el Católico'; present name adopted 2006; part of CSIC; sections: linguistics and literature, Aragonese art, history, geography and ecology, economic and social studies, law, music for young people, ancient music; Council of 12 representing the univ. and municipality; library of 83,000 vols; Pres. JAVIER LAMBÁN MONTAÑÉS; Sec. JESÚS COLÁS TENAS; publs *Archivo de Filología Aragonesa, Caesaraugusta: Revista de Arqueología, Prehistoria e Historia Antigua, Ciencia Forense: Revista Aragonesa de Medicina Legal, Cuadernos de Aragón, Emblemata, IVS FVGIT: Revista de Estudios Histórico-Jurídicos de la Corona de Aragón, Nassarre: Revista Aragonesa de Musicología, Palaeohispanica: Revista sobre Lenguas y Culturas de la Hispania Antigua, Poesía en el Campus: Editado por Ibercaja y la Universidad de Zaragoza, Revista de Derecho Civil Aragonés, Revista de Historia 'Jerónimo Zurita', Seminario de Arte Aragonés.*

Real Instituto de Estudios Asturianos (Institute of Asturian Studies): Palacio Conde de Toreno, Plaza Porlier 9, 1°, 33003 Oviedo; tel. (98) 4182801; fax (98) 4283391; e-mail ridea@asturias.org; internet ridea.org; f. 1946; 50 mems, 4 hon. mems, 77 corresp. mems; library of 27,000 vols, 250 periodicals; Asturian studies (literature, history, folklore, language); historical archive, archive of 3,000 photographs; Dir JUAN IGNACIO RUIZ DE LA PEÑA SOLAR; Sec. OLGA CASARES ABELLA; publ. *Boletín de Ciencias de la Naturaleza* (1 a year).

Real Sociedad Bascongada de los Amigos del País (Royal Society of Friends of the Basque Country): Calle General Alava 5, 01005 Vitoria-Gasteiz; tel. (945) 147770; fax (945) 155015; e-mail info@bascongada.org; internet www.bascongada.org; f. 1764, the first of such societies in Spain; 25 mems; organized Museo de San Telmo and Museo Naval, also Conservatorio Municipal de Música; f. Editorial Guipuzcoana de Ediciones y Publicaciones, Books in Basque and Biblioteca Vascongada de los Amigos del País, collaborated in archaeological exploration of the prehistoric cave dwellings of the district; the Guipuzcoan Office of the Consejo Superior de Investigaciones Científicas, Madrid (see below); Pres. MIREN SANCHEZ ERAUSKIN; Sec. JOSÉ IGNACIO VEGAS; publs *Anuario de Eusko-Folklore Aranzadiana Orria, Boletín* (4 a year), *Boletín de la Cofradía Vasca de Gastronomía, Boletín de Estudios Históricos sobre San Sebastián* (1 a year), *Egan* (literary supplement), *Munibe* (natural sciences supplement).

TECHNOLOGY

Col·legi Oficial d'Enginyers Industrials de Catalunya: Via Laietana 39, 08003 Barcelona; tel. (93) 5572049; fax (93) 3100681; e-mail atencioeic@eic.cat; internet www.eic.cat; f. 1950; 8,000 mems; asscn of engineering graduates of the Schools of Industrial Engineers of Spain; library of 22,000 vols; Dean JOAN VALLVÉ I RIBERA; Sec. JOSEP M. ROVIRA I RAGUÉ; publs *Agenda Dels Enginyers* (24 a year), *Full Dels Enginyers* (12 a year).

Instituto de la Ingeniería de España (Spanish Institute of Engineering): Calle General Arrando 38, 28010 Madrid; tel. (91) 3197417; fax (91) 3103380; e-mail iie@iies.es; internet www.iies.es; f. 1905; 100,000 mems; comprises 10 asscns of higher engineers and the *Aula de Ingeniería* (training centre), offering courses, seminars, etc. for postgraduate students; Pres. MANUEL ACERO GARCÍA; Gen. Sec. ASIS MARTÍN-OAR FERNÁNDEZ DE HEREDIA.

Sociedad Española de Cerámica y Vidrio (Spanish Ceramic and Glass Society): Calle Kelsen 5, 28049 Madrid; tel. (91) 7357860; fax (91) 7355843; e-mail secv@icv.csic.es; internet www.secv.es; f. 1960; promotes technical progress in ceramic and glass work and disseminates info. about manufacture and devts within the field; 750 mems; library of 500 vols; Pres. JORGE J. BAKALI BAKALI; Sec.-Gen. EMILIO CRIADO; publ. *Boletín* (6 a year).

Research Institutes

GENERAL

Consejo Superior de Investigaciones Científicas (CSIC) (Council for Scientific Research): Serrano 117, 28006 Madrid; tel. (91) 5681400; fax (91) 4113077; internet www.csic.es; f. 1940; largest multidisciplinary research body in Spain to serve cultural and technological devt; acts as a creative instrument and forum for Spanish science; has 100 research centres distributed throughout Spain, incl. institutes directly governed by CSIC, those operated jtly by CSIC and univs, and others in association with regional govt or other instns; more than 7,500 employees, 2,000 scientists, 1,500 trainees, 3,300 researchers and technicians, 700 admin. staff; maintains office for transfer of technology in cooperation with Spanish supervisory agencies for technological devt; library and two centres for documentation and information comprising more than 100,000 vols, journals published by the institutes, scientific and cultural dissemination, scientific publishing house, technical facilities and installations; Pres. RAFAEL RODRIGO MONTERO; Sec.-Gen. EUSEBIO CARLOS JIMÉNEZ ARROYO; publ. *Arbor* (12 a year).

Attached Research Institutes in the Field of Humanities and Social Sciences:

Centro de Ciencias Humanas y Sociales (Centre for Humanities and Social Sciences): Calle Albasanz 26–28, 28037 Madrid; tel. (91) 6022300; fax (91) 6022971; e-mail director.cchs@csic.es; internet www.cchs.csic.es; f. 2006; research on field of humanities and social sciences; library: 1m. vols; Dir EDUARDO MANZANO MORENO; publs *Al-Qantara* (2 a year), *Anales Cervantinos* (1 a year), *Archivo Español de Arqueología* (1 a year), *Archivo Español de Arte* (4 a year), *Asclepio* (2 a year), *Emerita* (2 a year), *Estudios Geográficos* (2 a year), *Gladius* (1 a year), *Hispania* (3 a year), *Hispania Sacra* (2 a year), *Isegoría* (2 a year), *Revista de Dialectología y Tradiciones Populares* (2 a year, Spanish), *Revista de Filología Española* (2 a year), *Revista de Indias* (3 a year), *Revista de Literatura* (2 a year), *Revista Española de Documentación Científica* (4 a year), *Sefarad* (2 a year), *Trabajos de Prehistoria* (1 a year).

Escuela de Estudios Árabes (School of Arabic Studies): Cuesta del Chapiz 22, 18010 Granada; tel. (958) 222290; fax (958) 224754; e-mail director.eeh@csic.es; internet www.eea.csic.es; Dir JUAN BRACERS CASTILLA.

Escuela de Estudios Hispano Americanos (School of Hispanic-American Studies): Calle Alfonso XII 16, 41002 Seville; tel. (95) 4501120; fax (95) 4500954; e-mail director.eeha@csic.es; internet www.eeha.csic.es; Dir SALVADOR BERNABÉU ALBERT; publ. *Anuario de Estudios Americanos* (2 a year).

Escuela Española de Historia y Arqueología en Roma (CSIC) (Spanish School of Roman History and Archeology): Via di Torre Argentina 18, 00186 Rome, Italy; tel. (06) 68100021; fax (06) 68309047; e-mail escuela@csic.it; internet www.eehar.csic.es; f. 1910; library of 22,000 vols; Dir RICARDO OLMOS ROMERA.

Institución Milá y Fontanals: Calle Egipciaques 15, 08001 Barcelona; tel. (93) 4423489; fax (93) 4430071; e-mail director.imf@csic.es; internet www.imf.csic.es; f. 1968; research activities: anthropology, archaeology, medieval studies, ethnography, history of science, musicology and sociology; Dir LUIS CALVO CALVO; library of 60,000 monographs, 2,250 periodicals; publs *Anuario de Estudios Medievales* (2 a year), *Anuario Musical* (12 a year).

Instituto de Análisis Económico (Institute of Economic Analysis): Universitad-tAutònoma, 08193 Bellaterra (Barcelona); tel. (93) 5806612; fax (93) 5801452; e-mail director.iae@csic.es; internet www.iae.csic.es; f. 1985; econometrics; experimental economics; game theory; industrial org. and regulation; growth and devt; macroeconomics; monetary economics; political economics and public economics; Dir Dr CLARA PONSATI OBIOLS.

Instituto de Economía, Geografía y Demografía: Calle Albasanz 26–28, 28037 Madrid; tel. (91) 6022674; fax (91) 6022971; e-mail director.ieg@csic.es; internet www.cchs.csic.es; f. 1986; Dir Prof. RICARDO MENDEZ GUITÉRREZ DEL VALLE; publ. *Estudios Geográficos* (4 a year).

Instituto de Estudios Documentales sobre Ciencia y Tecnología: Calle Albasanz 26–28, 28037 Madrid; tel. (91) 6022883; fax (91) 3045710; e-mail director.cindoc@csic.es; internet www.cindoc.csic.es; f. 1992, as Centro de Información y Documentación Científica (CINDOC), following merger between Instituto de Información y Documentación en Ciencia y Tecnología (ICYT) and Instituto de Información y Documentación en Ciencias Sociales y Humanidades (ISOC); mainly devoted to the analysis of science, technology and knowledge transfer; Dir Dr LUIS PLAZA; publ. *Revista Española de Documentación Científica* (4 a year).

Instituto de Estudios Gallegos 'Padre Sarmiento': San Roque 2, 15704 Santiago de Compostela (La Coruña); tel. (981) 540220; fax (981) 540222; e-mail director.iegps@csic.es; internet www.iegps.csic.es; f. 1943; library of 35,000 vols; Dir Prof. EDUARDO PARDO DE GUEVARA Y VALDÉS; publs *Cuadernos de Estudios Gallegos* (1 a year), *Serie de 'Anejos' de Cuadernos de Estudios Gallegos* (1 a year).

Instituto de Estudios Sociales Avanzados: Calle Campo Santo de los Mártires 7, 14004 Córdoba; tel. (957) 760625; fax (957) 760153; e-mail contacto@iesa.csic.es; internet www.iesa.csic.es; Dir EDUARDO MOYANO ESTRADA; publ. *Revista Internacional de Sociología* (3 a year).

Instituto de Filosofía (Institute of Philosophy): Calle Pinar 25, 28006 Madrid; tel.

(91) 4117005; fax (91) 5645252; e-mail director.ifs@csic.es; internet www.ifs.csic.es; library of 50,000 vols; Dir José María González García; publs *Isegoria* (2 a year), *SORITES: Electronic Magazine of Analytical Philosophy* (online).

Instituto de Historia (Institute for History): Calle Albasanz 26–28, 28037 Madrid; tel. (91) 6022300; fax (91) 6022971; e-mail mercedes.aguilar@cchs.csic.es; internet www.ih.csic.es; Dir Dr Leoncio López-Ocón Cabrera; publs *Archivo Español de Arqueología* (1 a year), *Archivo Español de Arte* (4 a year), *Asclepio* (2 a year), *Gladius* (1 a year), *Hispania* (3 a year), *Hispania Sacra* (2 a year), *Revista de Indias* (3 a year), *Trabajos de Prehistoria* (2 a year).

Instituto de Historia de la Ciencia y Documentación López Piñero: Palacio Cerveró, Plaza Cisneros 4, 46003 Valencia; tel. (96) 3926229; fax (96) 3919691; internet www.ihmc.uv-csic.es; Dir José Antonio Díaz Rojo.

Instituto de Lengua, Literatura y Antropología: Calle Albasanz 26–28, 28037 Madrid; tel. (91) 6022300; fax (91) 3692971; e-mail director.ile@csic.es; internet www.cchs.csic.es; f. 2007; Dir Violeta Demonte Barreto; publs *Anales Cervantinos* (1 a year), *Revista de Dialectología y Tradiciones Populares* (2 a year), *Revista de Filología Española* (2 a year), *Revista de Literatura* (2 a year).

Instituto de Lenguas y Culturas del Mediterráneo y Oriente Próximo: Calle Albasanz 26–28, 28037 Madrid; tel. (91) 6022430; fax (91) 6022970; e-mail maite.ortega@cchs.csic.es; internet www.ilc.csic.es; f. 1984 as Instituto de Filologia, integrated within Centro de Ciencias Humanas y Sociales (CCHS) 2008; studies and edns of texts in ancient languages: Arabic, Hebrew, Latin and Greek; studies in Near Eastern cultures, cuneiform studies, Egyptology, MSS in oriental languages (Hebrew, Greek, Coptic, Arabic and Latin); library: 1m. vols; Dir Dr María Teresa Ortega Monasterio; publs *Al-Qantara* (2 a year), *Emerita* (2 a year), *Sefarad* (2 a year).

Instituto Histórico Hoffmeyer: Avda de la Constitución 114, 10400 Jaraiz de la Vera (Cáceres); tel. (927) 170646; fax (927) 170645; e-mail hoffmeyer@iam.csic.es; internet www.hoffmeyer.iam.csic.es; Dir Pedro Mateos Cruz; publ. *Gladius* (1 a year).

Unidad de Políticas Comparadas: Alfonso XII 18, 5°, 28014 Madrid; tel. (91) 5219160; fax (91) 5218103; e-mail director.upc@csic.es; internet www.iesam.csic.es; Dir Luis Sanz Menéndez.

Attached Research Institutes in the Field of Biology and Biomedicine:

Centro Andaluz de Biología del Desarrollo: CSIC-Universidad Pablo de Olavide, Carretera de Utrera, Km 1, 41013 Seville; tel. (954) 349399; fax (954) 349376; internet www.cabd.es; Dir Acaimo González-Reyes.

Centro Biológica Molecular Severo Ochoa: Calle Nicolás Cabrera 1, Campus de la Universidad Autónoma, 28049 Madrid; tel. 91-1964401; fax 91-1964420; e-mail institucional@cbm.uam.es; internet www.cbm.uam.es; Dir Manuel Fresno Escudero.

Centro de Investigación y Desarrollo: Carrer de Jordi Girona 18–26, 08034 Barcelona; tel. (93) 4006100; fax (93) 2045904; e-mail director@cid.csic.es; internet www.cid.csic.es; f. 1967; library of 30,000 vols; Dir Angel Messeguer Peypoch.

Centro de Investigaciones Biológicas: Ramiro de Maeztu 9, 28040 Madrid; tel. (91) 8373112; fax (91) 5360432; e-mail vlarraga@cib.csic.es; internet www.cib.csic.es; Dir Vicente Larraga Rodríguez de Vera.

Centro de Investigaciones Científicas Isla de la Cartuja: Avda Americo Vespucio 49, Isla de la Cartuja, 41092 Seville; tel. (95) 4489501; fax (95) 4460165; e-mail ciccartuja@ciccartuja.es; internet www.ciccartuja.es; Dir Miguel Angel de la Rosa Acosta.

Centro Nacional de Biotecnología: UAM, Campus del Cantoblanco, 28049 Cantoblanco (Madrid); tel. (91) 5854500; fax (91) 5854506; e-mail director.cnb@csic.es; internet www.cnb.uam.es; Dir José María Valpuesta.

Instituto Biomedicina de Valencia: Jaime Roig 11, 46010 Valencia; tel. (96) 3391760; fax (96) 3690800; e-mail director.ibv@csic.es; internet www.ibv.csic.es; f. 1998; research into structural biology (X-ray crystallography), human molecular genetics, molecular/cell biology related to human disease, venomics, inborn errors of urea cycle, signalling cascades related to AMP kinase and to esteroids, molecular biology, genetics and signalling in type 2 diabetes; Dir Prof. Vicente Rubio Zamora.

Instituto Cajal: Avda Dr Arce 37, 28002 Madrid; tel. (91) 5854750; fax (91) 5854754; e-mail director.incr@csic.es; internet www.cajal.csic.es; f. 1906; neurobiological research; library of 36,000 vols; Dir Ignacio Torres Alemán.

Instituto de Biología Molecular 'Eladio Viñuela': c/o Nicolás Cabrera 1, 28049 Cantoblanco (Madrid); tel. (91) 1964401; fax (91) 1964420; e-mail director.ibm@csic.es; internet www.uam.es/institutos/bmolecular; f. 1975; Dir César de Haro Castella.

Instituto de Biología Molecular de Barcelona: Calle Baldiri Reixac 10–12, 08028 Barcelona; tel. (93) 4034668; fax (93) 4034979; e-mail lcabmc@ibmb.csic.es; internet www.ibmb.csic.es; Dir Martí Aldea.

Instituto de Biología Molecular y Celular de Plantas 'Eduardo Primo Yúfera': Ingeniero Fausto Elio, s/n, 46022 Valencia; tel. (96) 3877856; fax (96) 3877859; e-mail director.ibmcp@csic.es; internet www.ibmcp.upv.es; f. 1994; Dir Prof. Vicente Pallás Benet.

Instituto de Biología Molecular y Celular del Cáncer (CSIC-USAL): Campus Miguel de Unamuno, Universidad de Salamanca, 37007 Salamanca; tel. (923) 294720; fax (923) 294743; e-mail cicancer@usal.es; internet www.cicancer.org; f. 1997; basic, clinical and translational cancer research; Dir Dr Eugenio Santos.

Instituto de Biología y Genética Molecular: Calle Sanz y Fores, s/n, esq. Real de Burgos, 47003 Valladolid; tel. (983) 184801; fax (983) 184800; e-mail director.ibgm@csic.es; internet www.ibgm.med.uva.es; f. 1998; Dir José Ramón López López.

Instituto de Bioquímica Vegetal y Fotosíntesis: Avda Americo Vespucio, s/n, Isla de la Cartuja, 41092 Seville; tel. (95) 4489506; fax (95) 4460065; e-mail director@ibvf.csic.es; internet www.ibvf.csic.es; Dir Luis Carlos Romero González.

Instituto de Farmacología y Toxicología: CSIC-Universidad Complutense, Faculted de Medicina, Ciudad Universitaria, 28040 Madrid; tel. (91) 3941469; fax (91) 3941470; e-mail director.ift@csic.es; internet www.csic.es; Dir Juan Tamargo Menéndez.

Instituto de Investigaciones Biomédicas 'Alberto Sols': Calle Arturo Duperier 4, 28029 Madrid; tel. (91) 5854400; fax (91) 5854401; e-mail info@iib.csic.es; internet www.iib.uam.es; f. 1973; Dir Dr Lisardo Boscá Gomar.

Instituto de Investigaciones Biomédicas de Barcelona: Calle Roselló 161, 6–7°, 08036 Barcelona; tel. (93) 3638300; fax (93) 3638301; e-mail director.iibb@csic.es; internet www.iibb.csic.es; f. 1995; multidisciplinary biomedical research in biochemistry, cell biology, neurosciences, with spec. emphasis on translational research; Dir Dr Cristina Suñol Esquirol.

Instituto de Microbiología Bioquímica: Campus Miguel de Unamuno, Universidad de Salamanca, Edif. Departmental, Avda Campo Charro, s/n, 37007 Salamanca; tel. (923) 294462; fax (923) 224876; e-mail directorimb@usal.csic.es; internet www.imb.usal-csic.es; Dir Dr Dr. Angel Durán Bravo.

Instituto de Neurociencias: Apdo de Correos 18, 03550 San Juan (Alicante); tel. (96) 5233700; fax (96) 5919561; e-mail in@umh.es; internet in.umh.es; Dir Juan Lerma Gómez.

Instituto de Parasitología y Biomedicina 'López Neyra': Parque Tecnológico de Ciencias de la Salud, Avda del Conocimiento, s/n, 18100 Armilla (Granada); tel. (958) 181621; fax (958) 181632; e-mail director.ipbln@csic.es; internet www.ipb.csic.es; Dir Alfredo Berzal Herranz.

Unidad de Biofísica: Apdo 644, 48080 Bilbao; tel. (94) 6012625; fax (94) 6013360; e-mail biofisica@lg.ehu.es; internet www.unidaddebiofisica.org; f. 1999; joint centre of the CSIC and the Univ. of the Basque Country; basic research and graduate teaching in biophysics; Dir Félix M. Goñi.

Attached Research Institutes in the Field of Natural Resources:

Centro de Ciencias Medioambientales: Calle Serrano 115 bis, 28006 Madrid; tel. (91) 7452500; fax (91) 5640800; e-mail director.ccma@csic.es; internet www.ccma.csic.es; Dir Alberto Fereres Castiel.

Centro de Edafología y Biología Aplicada del Segura: Campus Universitario de Espinardo, 30100 Murcia; tel. (968) 396200; fax (968) 396213; e-mail director.cebas@csic.es; internet www.cebas.csic.es; Dir Dr Francisco Tomás Barberán.

Centro de Estudios Avanzados de Blanes: Cala St Francesc 14, 17300 Blanes (Gerona); tel. (972) 336101; fax (972) 337806; e-mail director.ceab@csic.es; internet www.ceab.csic.es; Dir Daniel Martín Sintes.

Centro de Investigaciones sobre Desertificación: Camí de la Marjal, s/n, 46470 Albal (Valencia); tel. (96) 1220540; fax (96) 1270967; e-mail cide@uv.es; internet www.uv.es/cide; f. 1996; Dir Dr Patricio Garcia-Fayos.

Estación Biológica de Doñana: Apdo 1056, 41013 Seville; tel. (95) 4232340; fax (95) 4621125; e-mail director.ebd@csic.es; internet www.ebd.csic.es; f. 1964; wetland ecology, evolutionary and molecular ecology, ecological synthesis, conservation biology (incl. biological invasions), and plant–animal interactions; library of 10,000 vols; Dir Prof. Fernando Hiraldo Cano; publ. *Doñana. Acta Vertebrata* (2 a year).

Estacíon Experimental de Zonas Áridas: Cuetra de Sacramento, s/n, La Cañada de San Urbano, 04120 Almería; tel. (950) 281045; fax (950) 277100; e-mail director.eeza@csic.es; internet www.eeza.csic.es; Dir FRANCISCO VALERA HERNÁNDEZ.

Instituto Agroquímica y Tecnología Alimentos: Apdo 73, 46100 Burjassot (Valencia); tel. (96) 3900022; fax (96) 3636301; e-mail info@iata.csic.es; internet www.iata.csic.es; Dir LORENZO ZACARIAS; publ. *Food Science and Technology International* (6 a year).

Instituto Andaluz de Ciencias de la Tierra: CSIC-Universidad de Granada, Facultad de Ciencias, Avda Fuentenueva, s/n, 18002 Granada; tel. (958) 243158; fax (958) 243384; e-mail director.iact@csic.es; internet www.iact.csic.es; Dir ALBERTO LÓPEZ GALINDO.

Instituto Botánico de Barcelona: Passeig del Migdia, Parque de Monjuïc, 08038 Barcelona; tel. (93) 2890611; fax (93) 2890614; e-mail biblioteca@ibb.csic.es; internet www.institutbotanic.bcn.es; f. 1917; affiliated to the Botanic Garden of Barcelona, Montjuïc Park; library of 30,000 vols, 80,000 herbarium sheets; Man. JOAN LAMBEA CASTRO; publ. *Collectanea Botanica* (1 a year).

Instituto de Acuicultura de Torre de la Sal: Calle Ribera de Cabanes, s/n, Cabanes, 12595 Castellón; tel. (964) 319500; fax (964) 319509; e-mail director.iats@csic.es; internet www.iats.csic.es; Dir JAUME PÉREZ SÁNCHEZ.

Instituto de Astronomía y Geodesia: Facultad de Matemáticas, Universidad Complutense, Plaza de Ciencias 3, 28040 Madrid; tel. (91) 3944585; fax (91) 3944615; e-mail director.iag@csic.es; internet www.iag.csic.es; Dir JOSÉ FERNÁNDEZ TORRES.

Instituto de Ciencias de la Tierra 'Jaime Almera': Calle Lluis Solé Sabarís, s/n, Apdo 30102, 08028 Barcelona; tel. (93) 4095410; fax (93) 4110012; e-mail director.ictja@csic.es; internet www.ija.csic.es; library of 16,500 vols, 1,050 periodicals; Dir MANEL FERNANDEZ I ORTIGA.

Instituto de Ciencias del Mar: Passeig Marítim de la Barceloneta 37–49, 08003 Barcelona; tel. (93) 2309500; fax (93) 2309555; e-mail icmdir@icm.csic.es; internet www.icm.csic.es; Dir ALBERT PALANQUES MONTEYS; publ. *Scientia Marina* (4 a year).

Instituto de Ciencias Marinas de Andalucía: Calle República Saharaui 2, Campus Universitario Río San Pedro, 11519 Puerto Real (Cádiz); tel. (956) 832612; fax (956) 834701; e-mail director.icman@csic.es; internet www.csic.es; f. 1955; Dir MARÍA DEL CARMEN SARASQUETE REIRIZ.

Instituto de Geología Económica: Calle José Antonio Novais 2, Facultad de Ciencias Geólogicas, Universidad Complutense, 28040 Madrid; tel. (91) 3944813; fax (91) 3944808; e-mail ige.mixto@geo.ucm.es; internet www.ige.csic.es; f. 1971; Dir RAFAEL FORT GONZÁLEZ.

Instituto de Investigación en Recursos Cinegéticos: Ronda de Toledo, s/n, 13071 Ciudad Real; tel. (926) 295450; fax (926) 295451; e-mail irec@irec.uclm.es; internet www.uclm.es/irec; Dir JAVIER VIÑUELA MADURA.

Instituto de Investigaciones Marinas: Calle Eduardo Cabello, 36208 Vigo (Pontevedra); tel. (986) 231930; fax (986) 292762; e-mail direccion@iim.csic.es; internet www.iim.csic.es; f. 1951 as Instituto de Investigaciones Pesqueras de Barcelona, present name adopted 1986; Dir AIDA FERNÁNDEZ RÍOS.

Instituto de Productos Naturales y Agrobiología: Astrofísico Francisco Sánchez 3, 38206 La Laguna (Tenerife); tel. (922) 256847; fax (922) 260135; e-mail director.ipna@csic.es; internet www.ipna.csic.es; f. 1956 as Centro de Edafología y Biología Aplicada de Tenerife, present name 1990; Dir Dr COSME GARCIA FRANCISCO.

Instituto de Recursos Naturales y Agrobiología de Salamanca: Apdo 257, 37071 Salamanca; Cordel de Merinas 40–52, 37008 Salamanca; tel. (923) 219606; fax (923) 219609; e-mail secretaria@irnasa.csic.es; internet www.csic.es; f. 1957 as Centro de Edafología y Biología Aplicada de Salamanca, present name 1988; scientific research on agriculture and natural resources; incl. sustainable devt of agri-forest systems, animal pathology, environmental degradation and recovery, and plant abiotic stress; Dir Dr RAFAEL MARTINEZ-CARRASCO TABUENCA.

Instituto de Recursos Naturales y Agrobiología de Sevilla: Apdo 1052, Estafeta-Puerto, 41080 Seville; Avda Reina Mercedes 10, 41012 Seville; tel. (954) 624711; fax (954) 624002; e-mail director.irnas@csic.es; internet www.irnase.csic.es; Dir LUIS CLEMENTE SALAS.

Instituto Mediterraneo de Estudios Avanzados: Calle Miquel Marquès 21, 07190 Esporles, Mallorca; tel. (971) 611716; fax (971) 611761; e-mail director.imdea@csic.es; internet www.imedea.uib-csic.es; Dir JOAQUÍN TINTORÉ SUBIRANA.

Instituto Pirenaico de Ecología: Avda Montañana 1005, 50059 Zaragoza; tel. (976) 716034; fax (976) 716019; e-mail director.ipe@csic.es; internet www.ipe.csic.es; f. 1983; Dir BLAS LORENZO VALERO GARCÉS; publ. *Pirineos* (1 a year).

Museo Nacional de Ciencias Naturales:see under Museums and Art Galleries.

Real Jardín Botánico:see under Museums and Art Galleries.

Attached Research Institutes in the Field of Agricultural Sciences:

Instituto de Ganadería de Montaña: Finca Marzanas, s/n, 24346 Grulleros, (León); tel. (987) 317064; fax (987) 317161; e-mail director.eae@csic.es; internet www.csic.es; Dir Dr FRANCISCO JAVIER GIRÁLDEZ GARCÍA.

Estación Experimental de Aula Dei: Avda Montañana 1005, 50059 Zaragoza; tel. (976) 716100; fax (976) 716145; e-mail director.eead@csic.es; internet www.eead.csic.es; f. 1944; library of 9,802 vols of book titles, 190,000 e-books, 1,804 journals, 13,000 electronic journals; Dir JESÚS VAL FALCÓN.

Estación Experimental del Zaidín: Apdo 419, 18008 Granada; Calle Professor Albareda 1, 18008 Granada; tel. (958) 181600; fax (958) 129600; e-mail director.eez@csic.es; internet www.eez.csic.es; library of 4,000 vols, 300 periodicals; Dir NICOLÁS TORO GARCÍA.

Estación Experimental 'La Mayora': 29760 Algarrobo-Costa, (Málaga); tel. (952) 548990; fax (952) 552677; e-mail director.eelm@csic.es; internet www.eelm.csic.es; f. 1968; agronomy, horticulture, pomology, virology, mycology, plant tissue culture; library of 3,000 vols; Dir ENRIQUE MORIONES ALONSO.

Instituto de Agricultura Sostenible: Alameda del Obispo, s/n, Apdo 4084, 14080 Córdoba; tel. (957) 499200; fax (957) 499252; e-mail gerente.ias@csic.es; internet www.ias.csic.es; Dir PABLO J. ZARCO TEJADAL.

Instituto de Agrobiotecnología: Universidad Publica de Navarra, Campus de Arrosadia, 31192 Navarra; tel. (948) 168000; fax (948) 232191; e-mail info@agrobiotechnologia.es; internet www.agrobiotechnologia.es; f. 1999 as Instituto de Agrobiotecnología y Recursos Naturales, present name 2004; Dir PEDRO APARICIO TEJO.

Instituto de Investigaciones Agrobiológicas de Galicia: Avda de Vigo, s/n, Apdo 122, 15780 Santiago de Compostela (La Coruña); tel. (981) 590958; fax (981) 592504; e-mail director.iiag@csic.es; internet www.iiag.csic.es; library of 3,000 vols, 279 periodicals; Dir MARÍA TARSY CARBALLAS FERNÁNDEZ.

Misión Biológica de Galicia: Apdo 28, 36080 Pontevedra; El Palacio, Salcedo, 36143 Pontevedra; tel. (986) 854800; fax (986) 841362; e-mail director.mbg@csic.es; internet www.mbg.csic.es; Dir ROSA ANA MALVAR PINTOS.

Attached Research Institutes in the Field of the Science and Technology of Physics:

Centro de Tecnologías Físicas 'Leonardo Torres Quevedo': Calle Serrano 144, 28006 Madrid; tel. (91) 5618806; fax (91) 4117651; e-mail director.cetef@csic.es; internet www.cetef.csic.es; Dir JUAN ANTONIO GALLEGO JUAREZ.

Centro Física 'Miguel A. Catalán': Calle Serrano 121, 28006 Madrid; tel. (91) 5616800; fax (91) 5645557; e-mail gerente.cfmac@csic.es; internet www.cfmac.csic.es; Dir FRANCISCO JOSE BALTA CALLEJA.

Centro Nacional de Microelectrónica: Campus Universidad Autonoma, 08193 Bellaterra (Barcelona); tel. (93) 5947700; fax (93) 5801496; e-mail info@cnm.es; internet www.cnm.es; f. 1986; research and devt of micro- and nanoelectronics; Dir FRANCISCO SERRA MESTRES.

Centro Técnico de Informática: Calle Pinar 19, 28006 Madrid; tel. (91) 5642963; fax (91) 5616193; e-mail director.cti@csic.es; internet www.cti.csic.es; Dir JOSÉ CARRERO VIVAS.

Instituto de Acústica: Calle Serrano 144, 28006 Madrid; tel. (91) 5618806; fax (91) 4117651; e-mail director.ia@csic.es; internet www.ia.csic.es; Dir Dr CARLOS RANZ GUERRA; publs *ACUSTICA* (12 a year), *Ferroelectrics* (12 a year), *IEEE Transactions on Ultrasonics, Ferroelectrics and Frequency Control* (12 a year), *Journal of Sound and Vibration* (12 a year), *Journal of the Acoustical Society of America, JASA* (12 a year), *Ultrasonics* (12 a year).

Instituto de Astrofísica de Andalucía: Apdo 3004, 18080 Granada; Glorieta de la Astronomía, s/n, 18008 Granada; tel. (958) 121311; fax (958) 814530; e-mail director.iaa@csic.es; internet www.iaa.es/index.html; Dir MATILDE FERNÁNDEZ HERNÁNDEZ.

Instituto de Automática Industrial: Carretera de Campo Real, Km 0.200, 28500 Arganda del Rey (Madrid); tel. (91) 8711900; fax (91) 8717050; e-mail director.iai@csic.es; internet www.iai.csic.es; Dir Dr MANUEL ANGEL ARMADA RODRÍGUEZ (acting).

Instituto de Estructura de la Materia: Calle Serrano 121, 28006 Madrid; tel. (91) 5616800; fax (91) 5645557; e-mail director.iem@csic.es; internet www.iem.csic.es; f.

1976; Dir Dr GUILLERMO ANTONIO MENA MARUGÁN.

Instituto de Física Aplicada: Calle Serrano 144, 28006 Madrid; tel. (91) 5618806; fax (91) 4117651; e-mail director .ifa@csic.es; internet www.ifa.csic.es; Dir FRANCISCO JAVIER GUTIÉRREZ MONREAL.

Instituto de Física Corpuscular: Edificio Institutos de Investigación, Apdo 22085, 46071 Valencia; tel. (96) 3543473; fax (96) 3543488; e-mail director.ific@csic .es; internet ific.uv.es; Dir FRANCISCO J. BOTELLA OLCINA.

Instituto de Física de Cantabria: Edificio Juan Jorda, Avda de los Castros, s/n, 39005 Santander; tel. (94) 2201459; fax (94) 2200935; e-mail info@ifca.unican.es; internet www.ifca.es; Dir FRANCISCO MATORRAS.

Instituto de Física Fundamental: Calle Serrano 113–123, 28006 Madrid; tel. (91) 5616800; fax (91) 5854894; e-mail director .iff@csic.es; internet www.iff.csic.es; f. 1992, present name 2009; scientific research in basic physics: theoretical physics of molecules, cluster and extended media, quantum information, dark energy, probabilistic logical inference, physical modelling and entropy, radiation–matter interactions; Dir Dr GERARDO DELGADO BARRIO.

Instituto de Investigación de Inteligencia Artificial: Universidad Autónoma, 08193 Bellaterra (Barcelona); tel. (93) 5809570; fax (93) 5809661; e-mail director.iiia@csic.es; internet www.iiia.csic .es; Dir RAMÓN LÓPEZ DE MÁNTARAS.

Instituto de Microelectrónica de Barcelona: Universidad Autónoma, 08193 Cerdanyola del Valles, (Barcelona); tel. (93) 5947700; fax (93) 5801496; e-mail director.imb-cnm@csic.es; internet www .imb-cnm.csic.es; Dir Prof. EMILIO LORA-TAMAYO.

Instituto de Microelectrónica de Madrid: Calle Isaac Newton 8, Tres Cantos, 28760 Madrid; tel. (91) 8060700; fax (91) 8060701; e-mail director .imm-cnm@csic.es; internet www.imm-cnm .csic.es; Dir Prof. LUIS GONZÁLEZ SOTOS.

Instituto de Microelectrónica de Sevilla: Calle Américo Vespucio s/n, 41092 Seville; tel. (95) 4466666; fax (95) 4466690; e-mail director.ims-cnm@csic.es; internet www.imse-cnm.csic.es; f. 1996; Dir Prof. JOSÉ LUIS HUERTAS DÍAZ.

Instituto de Óptica 'Daza de Valdés': Calle Serrano 121, 28006 Madrid; tel. (91) 5616800; fax (91) 5645557; e-mail director .io@csic.es; internet www.io.csic.es; f. 1946; research in visual optics, biophotonics, image science, non-linear dynamics, fiber optics, nanophotonics, plasmonics, photonics with high energy ions, photonics and nanostructures and ultrafast science; Dir JAVIER SOLÍS CÉSPEDES.

Instituto de Robótica e Informática Industrial: Calle Llorens i Artiges 4–6, 2°, Parc Tecnològic de Barcelona, 08028 Barcelona; tel. (93) 4015751; fax (93) 4015750; e-mail admin-iri@iri.upc.edu; internet www.iri.upc.es; Dir ALBERTO SANFELIU.

Observatorio Física Cósmica de l'Ebro: Horta Alta 38, Apdo 10, 43520 Roquetas (Tarragona); tel. (977) 500511; fax (977) 504660; e-mail biblioteca@ obsebre.es; internet www.obsebre.es; f. 1904; 4 sections: geomagnetism; ionosphere; seismology; meteorology, climate and solar activity; library of 50,000 vols, 2,100 periodicals; Dir Dr JUAN JOSÉ CURTO.

Attached Research Institutes in the Field of Materials Science and Technology:

Centro de Física de Materiales: P. Manuel de Lardizabal 5, 20018 Donostia, San Sebastián; tel. (94) 3018000; fax (94) 3015800; e-mail wapetalap@sq.ehu.es; internet cfm.ehu.es; Dir Prof. JUAN COLMENERO DE LEON.

Centro Nacional de Investigaciones Metalúrgicas: Avda Gregorio del Amo 8, 28040 Madrid; tel. (91) 5538900; fax (91) 5347425; e-mail director.cenim@csic.es; internet www.cenim.csic.es; f. 1964; metallurgical research, steel research, new materials, composites, recycling of metals; library of 20,000 vols; Dir MANUEL CARSÍ CEBRIÁN; publ. *Revista de Metalurgia* (6 a year).

Instituto de Cerámica y Vidrio: Campus de UAM, 28049 Madrid; tel. (91) 7355840; fax (91) 7355843; e-mail director .icv@csic.es; internet www.icv.csic.es; Dir Dr JUAN E. IGLESIAS PÉREZ.

Instituto de Ciencia de Materiales de Aragón, CSIC—Universidad de Zaragoza: Facultad San Ciencias, CSIC—Universidad de Zaragoza, Pl. de San Francisco, s/n, 50009 Zaragoza; tel. (97) 6761231; fax (97) 6762453; e-mail director .icma@csic.es; internet www.icma .unizar-csic.es/webicma; f. 1985; Dir Dr RAMÓN BURRIEL LAHOZ.

Instituto de Ciencia de Materiales de Barcelona: Campus Universidad Autónoma, 08193 Cerdanyola del Valles, (Barcelona); tel. (93) 5801853; fax (93) 5805729; e-mail info@icmab.es; internet www.icmab .es; Dir XAVIER OBRADORS.

Instituto de Ciencia de Materiales de Madrid: Cantoblanco, 28049 Madrid; tel. (91) 3349000; fax (91) 3720623; e-mail director.icmm@csic.es; internet www.icmm .csic.es; f. 1986, by merger of 3 centres: Institute of Materials Physics, Solid State Physics Institute, and Mineral Physics-Chemistry Institute; personnel from the Inorganic Chemistry 'Elhuyar' Institute joined the ICMM 1987; attached to the Consejo Superior de Investigaciones Científicas (CSIC) (Spanish Nat. Research Ccl); research in material science, aiming at multidisciplinary character and covering theoretical and experimental, basic and applied aspects; Dir Prof. FEDERICO JESÚS SORIA GALLEGO.

Instituto de Ciencia de Materiales de Sevilla: CSIC—Universidad de Sevilla, Americo Vespucio, s/n, Isla de la Cartuja, 41092 Seville; tel. (95) 4489527; fax (95) 4460665; e-mail buzon@icmse.csic.es; internet www.icmse.cartuja.csic.es; Dir ALFONSO CABALLERO MARTÍNEZ.

Instituto de Ciencia y Tecnología de Polímeros: Calle Juan de la Cierva 3, 28006 Madrid; tel. (91) 5622900; fax (91) 5644853; e-mail director.ictp@csic.es; internet www.ictp.csic.es; library of 2,000 vols, 40 periodicals; Dir Dra PAULA BOSCH SAROBE.

Instituto de Ciencias de la Construcción 'Eduardo Torroja': Calle Serrano Galvache 4, 28033 Madrid; tel. (91) 3020440; fax (91) 3020700; e-mail director .ietcc@csic.es; internet www.ietcc.csic.es; Dir VÍCTOR RAMÓN VELASCO RODRÍGUEZ; publs *Informes de la Construcción* (6 a year), *Materiales de la Construcción* (4 a year).

Attached Research Institutes in the Field of Foodstuff Science and Technology:

Instituto de Fermentaciones Industriales: Calle Juan de la Cierva 3, 28006 Madrid; tel. (91) 5622900; fax (91) 5644853; e-mail director.ifi@csic.es; internet www.ifi.csic.es; f. 1967; research in food science and technology; participation in research projects and contracts with companies, nat. and int. confs, scientific symposia; teaching doctorate courses in univs, undergraduate and dipl. courses, masters courses and training teachers for technical college; Dir Dra LOURDES AMIGO GARRIDO.

Instituto de la Grasa: Avda Padre García Tejero 4, 41012 Seville; tel. (95) 4611550; fax (95) 4616790; e-mail director.ig@csic .es; internet www.ig.csic.es; Dir FRANCISCO JAVIER HIDALGO HUERTAS; publ. *Grasas y Aceites* (6 a year).

Instituto de Nutrición y Bromatología: CSIC—Universidad Complutense, Facultad de Farmacia, Cdad Universitaria, 28040 Madrid; tel. (91) 5490038; fax (91) 5495079; e-mail director.inb@csic.es; internet www.csic.es; Dir ASCENSIÓN MARCOS SÁNCHEZ.

Instituto de Productos Lácteos de Asturias: Ctra de Infiesto, s/n, Apdo 85, 33300 Villaviciosa (Oviedo); tel. (98) 5892131; fax (98) 5892233; e-mail director .ipla@csic.es; internet www.ipla.csic.es; Dir JUAN CARLOS BADA GANCEDO.

Instituto del Frío: Calle José Antonio Novais 10, 28040 Madrid; tel. (91) 5492300; fax (91) 5493627; e-mail director .if@csic.es; internet www.if.csic.es; Dir M. P. MONTERO GARCÍA.

Attached Research Institutes in the Field of Chemical Science and Technology:

Centro de Química Orgánica Lora Tamayo: Juan de la Cierva 3, 28006 Madrid; tel. (91) 5622900; fax (91) 5644853; e-mail director.cenquior@csic.es; internet www.cenquior.csic.es; Dir BERNARDO HERRADÓN GARCÍA.

Instituto de Carboquímica: Miguel Luesma Castán 5, 50018 Zaragoza; tel. (97) 6733977; fax (97) 6733318; e-mail director@icb.csic.es; internet www.icb.csic .es; Dir RAFAEL MOLINER ALVAREZ; publ. *Memoria Cientifica* (every 2 years).

Instituto de Catálisis y Petroleoquímica: Calle Marie Curie 2, 28049 Cantoblanco (Madrid); tel. (91) 5854800; fax (91) 5854760; e-mail director.icp@csic .es; internet www.icp.csic.es; Dir JAVIER SORIA RUIZ.

Instituto de Investigaciones Químicas: Calle Americo Vespucio 49, Isla de la Cartuaja, 41092 Seville; tel. (95) 4489553; fax (95) 4460565; e-mail director .iiq@csic.es; internet www.iiq.cartuja.csic .es; Dir JOSÉ MANUEL GARCÍA FERNÁNDEZ.

Institut de Química Avançada de Catalunya: Calle Jordi Girona 18–26, 08034 Barcelona; tel. (93) 4006100; fax (93) 2045904; e-mail director.cid@csic.es; internet www.iqac.csic.es; Dir Prof. ANGEL MESSEGUER PEYPOCH.

Instituto de Química Física Rocasolano: Calle Serrano 119, 28006 Madrid; tel. (91) 5619400; fax (91) 5642431; e-mail director.iqfr@csic.es; internet www.iqfr .csic.es; Dir JOSÉ ANTONIO GARCÍA DOMÍNGUEZ.

Instituto de Química Médica: Calle Juan de la Cierva 3, 28006 Madrid; tel. (91) 5622900; fax (91) 5644853; e-mail director.iqm@csic.es; internet www.iqm .csic.es; Dir PILAR GOYA LAZA.

Instituto de Química Orgánica General: Calle Juan de la Cierva 3, 28006 Madrid; tel. (91) 5622900; fax (91) 5644853; e-mail director.iqog@csic.es; internet www.iqog.csic.es; f. 1966; research in organic chemistry and related fields, incl. organic synthesis, inhibitors of proteases, physical organic chemistry, environmental chemistry, analytical chemistry of organic compounds, natural products, bio-organic chemistry, peptides, proteins, computational chemistry, computational toxicology; library of 3,000 vols; Dir Dr EDUARDO GARCÍA-JUNCEDA.

Instituto de Tecnología Química: CSIC-Universidad Politécnica, Avda de los Naranjos, s/n, 46022 Valencia; tel. (96) 3877800; fax (96) 3879444; e-mail director.itq@csic.es; internet itq.webs.upv.es; Dir AVELINO CORMA CANÓS.

Instituto Nacional del Carbón: Calle Francisco Pintado Fe 26, 33080 Oviedo; tel. (98) 5119090; fax (98) 5297662; e-mail director.incar@csic.es; internet www.incar.csic.es; Dir JESÚS A. PAJARES SOMOANO.

Laboratorio de Investigación en Tecnologías de la Combustión (Laboratory for Research in Combustion Technologies): Calle María de Luna 10, 50018 Zaragoza; tel. (976) 506520; fax (976) 506644; e-mail litec@litec.csic.es; internet www.litec.csic.es; f. 1991; research in combustion and fluid mechanics; Dir Dr ANTONIO LOZANO FANTOBA.

Fundació Catalana per a la Recerca i la Innovació (FCRI) (Catalan Foundation for Research and Innovation): Pg Lluís Companys 23, 08010 Barcelona; tel. (93) 2687700; fax (93) 2683768; e-mail fcri@fcri.es; internet www.fcr.es; f. 1986; promotes scientific, sociological and technological research; Pres. JOSEP HUGUET I BIOSCA; Sec. XAVIER QUERALT I BLANCH; publ. *Tecno 2000* (6 a year).

Institut d'Estudis Internacionals i Interculturals (Institute for International and Intercultural Studies): Edifici E1, 08193 Bellaterra, Barcelona; tel. (93) 5812111; fax (93) 5813266; e-mail ce.internacionals@uab.es; internet www.uab.es/ceii; attached to Universitat Autònoma de Barcelona; Dir SEÁN GOLDEN.

Instituto CEU de Humanidades Ángel Ayala: Calle Juan XXIII 8, 28040 Madrid; tel. (91) 4568406; e-mail ihuman@ceu.es; internet www.angelayala.ceu.es; attached to Universidad CEU San Pablo; research within the field of the humanities, specifically in the areas of art, history, literature, social doctrine of the Church, thought and philosophy, and the humanistic aspects of the natural sciences; Dir JUAN JOSÉ SANZ JARQUE.

Instituto de Relaciones Europeo-Latinoamericanas (IRELA) (Institute for European-Latin American Relations): Apdo 2600, 28002 Madrid; Pedro de Valdivia 10, 28006 Madrid; tel. (91) 5617200; fax (91) 5626499; e-mail info@irela.org; f. 1984; organization of conferences, etc., for European and Latin American officials, diplomats, journalists, politicians, businessmen, trade unionists and academics on different aspects of European-Latin American relations; collection and systematization of information on relations between the two regions; advisory activities for regional instns in Europe and Latin America; promotion, coordination and pursuit of specific research on relations between the two regions; Dir WOLF GRABENDORFF.

Instituto Interuniversitario de Estudios de Iberoamérica y Portugal (Inter-University Institute of Latin American and Portuguese Studies): Casa del Tratado, 47100 Tordesillas; tel. (98) 3771806; fax (98) 3796338; e-mail ieip@uva.es; internet www3.uva.es/ieip; attached to Universidad de Valladolid; Dir FELIPE CANO TORRES.

AGRICULTURE, FISHERIES AND VETERINARY SCIENCE

Centro de Investigación Ecológica y Aplicaciones Forestales (Ecological Research and Forestry Centre): Edifici C, Campus de Bellaterra, 08193 Cerdañola del Vallés; tel. (93) 5811312; fax (93) 5814151; e-mail ibec0@uab.es; internet www.creaf.uab.es; f. 1987; attached to Universidad Autónoma de Barcelona; Dir JAVIER RETANA.

Instituto Nacional de Investigación y Tecnología Agraria y Alimentaria (INIA) (National Institute for Food and Agricultural Research and Technology): Carretera de la Coruña, Km 7.5, 28040 Madrid; tel. (91) 3473930; fax (91) 3473931; e-mail direccion@inia.es; internet www.inia.es; f. 1971; library of 30,000 vols, 5,000 periodicals; Sec.-Gen. MARÍA ALARCÓN ALARCÓN; Dir MANUEL NÚÑEZ GUTIÉRREZ; publs *Spanish Journal of Agricultural Research* (4 a year, in English), *Forest Systems* (3 a year, in English).

ECONOMICS, LAW AND POLITICS

Centro de Investigaciones Sociológicas: Montalbán 8, 28014 Madrid; tel. (91) 5807600; e-mail cis@cis.es; internet www.cis.es; f. 1977; attached to govt Min. of the Presidency; promotes research in social sciences, arranges courses and seminars, collaborates with similar nat. and int. orgs, and creates databases for relevant material; library of 30,000 vols; Pres. RAMÓN RAMOS TORRE; Sec.-Gen. MARÍA FERNÁNDEZ SÁNCHEZ; publs *Clásicos Contemporáneos*, *Clásicos del Pensamiento Social*, *Cuadernos Metodológicos* (4 a year), *Revista Española de Investigaciones Sociológicas* (4 a year).

Instituto de Estudios de la Democracia (Institute of Democratic Studies): Calle Julián Romea 23, 28003 Madrid; tel. (91) 4566311; fax (91) 5140141; e-mail id@ceu.es; attached to Universidad CEU San Pablo; Dir LUIS NÚÑEZ LADEVÉZE.

Instituto de Estudios Fiscales (Institute of Fiscal Studies): Avda Cardenal Herrera Oria 378, 28035 Madrid; tel. (91) 3398800; fax (91) 3398964; e-mail informacion@ief.meh.es; internet www.ief.es; f. 1960; public finance; library of 80,000 vols; Dir-Gen. JOSÉ MARÍA LABEAGA AZCONA; publs *Crónica Tributaria* (4 a year), *Hacienda Pública Española* (4 a year), *Presupuesto y Gasto Público* (3 a year).

Instituto Valenciano de Investigaciones Económicas (Valencian Institute of Economic Research): Calle Guardia Civil 22 esc. 2, 1°, 46020 Valencia; tel. (96) 3190050; fax (96) 3190055; e-mail ivie@ivie.es; internet www.ivie.es; f. 1990; attached to Universidad de Alicante; Dir of Research Prof. Dr FRANCISCO PÉREZ GARCÍA; Man. Dir GERMÁN MOLINA PARDO.

'L. R. Klein' Instituto de Predicción Económica ('L. R. Klein' Institute of Economic Forecasting): Facultad de CC EE. y EE, Módulo E-XIV, 28049 Madrid; tel. and fax (91) 3978670; internet www.uam.es/otroscentros/klein; f. 1999; Dirs JOSÉ VICÉNS, ANTONIO PULIDO.

EDUCATION

Centro de Investigación y Documentación Educativa (CIDE) (Centre for Educational Research and Documentation): Calle General Oraá 55, 28006 Madrid; tel. (91) 7459400; fax (91) 7459438; internet www.educacion.es/cide; f. 1983; conducts and coordinates educational research; manages the library, archive and documentation centre of the Min. of Education and Science; library of 85,000 vols; publ. *Boletín*.

Institut de l'Educació (Institute of Education): Edifici del Rectorat, 08193 Bellaterra; tel. (93) 5811708; fax (93) 5812000; e-mail ice@uab.cat; internet www.uab.es/ice; attached to Universitat Autònoma de Barcelona; Dir NEUS SANMARTÍ PUIG.

Institut de Ciències de l'Educació (Institute of Education Sciences): Edifici Ventura i Gassol, Carretera de Valls, s/n, 43007 Tarragona; tel. (97) 7558071; fax (97) 7558072; e-mail gesice@urv.es; internet www.ice.urv.es; f. 1991; attached to Universitat Rovira i Virgili; Dir ANGEL-PÍO GONZÁLEZ SOTO.

Institut de Ciències de l'Educació Josep Pallach (Josep Pallach Institute of Education): Castell de Peralada, 14 Baixos, 17003 Gerona; tel. (972) 418702; fax (972) 484212; e-mail ice@udg.edu; internet www.udg.edu/ice; attached to Universitat de Girona; Dir MERITXELL ESTEBANELL MINGUELL.

Institut de Creativitat i Innovació Educatives (Institute of Creativity and Educational Innovation): Facultat de Filologia, Traducció i Interpretació, Universidad de Valencia, Avda Blasco Ibáñez 32, 46010 Valencia; tel. (96) 3864132; fax (96) 3983085; e-mail iucie@uv.es; internet www.uv.es/icie; f. 1978; attached to Universidad de Valencia; Dir MARÍA PETRA PÉREZ ALONSO-GETA.

FINE AND PERFORMING ARTS

Instituto del Patrimonio Cultural de España (Institute of Cultural Heritage of Spain): Calle Pintor el Greco 4, Ciudad Universitaria, 28040 Madrid; tel. (91) 5504400; fax (91) 5504444; internet www.mcu.es/patrimonio/mc/iphe; f. 1985 as Instituto de Conservación y Restauración de Bienes Culturales; name subsequently changed to Instituto del Patrimonio Histórico; present name adopted 2008; attached to Min. of Culture; library of 40,000 vols, 1.600 periodicals; archive of 800,000 photographs; publs *Revista Bienes Culturales*, *Revista Patrimonio Cultural de España*.

HISTORY, GEOGRAPHY AND ARCHAEOLOGY

Centro de Documentación y Estudios para la Historia de Madrid (Centre of Documentation and Studies on the History of Madrid): Facultad de Formación del Profesorado, Despachos 305–306, Campus de Cantoblanco, 28049 Madrid; tel. (91) 3974201; fax (91) 3974123; e-mail director.cdhm@uam.es; internet www.uam.es/otroscentros/historiamadrid; f. 1989; attached to Universidad Autónoma de Madrid; Dir VIRGILIO PINTO CRESPO.

Centro de Estudios del Patrimonio Arqueológico de la Prehistoria (Centre for Studies on the Archaeological Heritage of Prehistory): Edifici B, 08193 Bellaterra, (Barcelona); tel. (93) 5813705; fax (93) 5811140; e-mail cepap@uab.es; internet www.uab.es/cepap; attached to Universitat Autònoma de Barcelona; Dir RAFAEL MORA TORCAL.

Instituto Feijoo del Siglo XVIII (Feijoo Institute of Eighteenth-Century Studies): Facultad de Filología, Universidad de Oviedo, Campus de Humanidades, Calle Teniente Alfonso Martínez, s/n, 33011 Oviedo; tel. (98) 5104671; fax (98) 5104670; e-mail admifes@uniovi.es; internet www.ifesxviii.es; attached to Universidad De Oviedo; Dir ÁLVARO RUIZ DE LA PEÑA SOLAR.

Instituto Universitario de Historia Simancas (Simancas Institute of History): Calle Real de Burgos, s/n, 47011 Valladolid; tel. and fax (98) 3423527; e-mail simancas@uva.es; internet www3.uva.es/simancas; f.

1997; attached to Universidad de Valladolid; Dir MARÍA ISABEL DEL VAL VALDIVIESO.

LANGUAGE AND LITERATURE

Centro de Investigaciones Lingüísticas (Linguistics Research Centre): Casa Dorado Montero, Paseo del Rector Esperabé 47, 37008 Salamanca; tel. (92) 3294400; fax (92) 3294655; e-mail cilus@usal.es; internet www.usal.es/cilus; f. 1995; attached to Universidad de Salamanca; Dir MARÍA JESÚS MANCHO DUQUE.

Instituto de Lengua y Cultura Catalanas (Institute of Catalan Language and Culture): Plaça Ferrater Mora 1, 17071 Gerona; tel. (97) 2418231; fax (97) 2418230; e-mail ilcc@udg.edu; internet www.udg.edu/ilcc; attached to Universitat de Girona; Dir ALBERT ROSSICH ESTRAGÓ.

MEDICINE

Centro de Investigación del Cáncer: Campus Miguel de Unamuno, 37007 Salamanca; tel. (92) 3294720; fax (92) 3294743; e-mail cicancer@usal.es; internet www.cicancer.es; attached to Universidad de Salamanca; Dir EUGENIO SANTOS.

Centro Público de Educación Especial María Soriano (Public Centre For Special Educational Needs): Avda de la Peseta 30, 28054 Madrid; tel. (91) 4624600; fax (91) 4628444; e-mail cpee.mariasoriano.madrid@educa.madrid.org; internet www.educa.madrid.org/cpee.mariasoriano.madrid; f. 1922; Dir JULIÁN PALACIOS SÁNCHEZ; Sec. RAQUEL GARZÓN ALONSO.

Escuela Nacional de Medicina del Trabajo (National School of Occupational Medicine): Pabellón 8, Facultad de Medicina, Ciudad Universitaria, 28040 Madrid; tel. (91) 8224012; fax (91) 5437271; e-mail direccion.enmt@isciii.es; internet www.isciii.es; f. 1948; Dir Prof. MANUEL DOMINGUEZ CARMONA; publ. *Medicina y Seguridad del Trabajo* (4 a year, in print and online).

Institut Universitari d'Investigació en Ciències de la Salut (Institute for Research in Health Sciences): Edif. Cientificotècnic, Campus Universitari, Univ. de les Illes Balears, Carretera de Valldemossa, Km 7.5, 07122 Palma, Mallorca; tel. (97) 1173257; e-mail fgrases@uib.es; internet www.iunics.es; attached to Universitat de les Illes Balears; Dir Dr FELIX GRASES.

NATURAL SCIENCES

General

Instituto Español de Oceanografía (Spanish Institute of Oceanography): Avda de Brasil 31, 28020 Madrid; tel. (91) 5974443; fax (91) 5974770; e-mail ieo@md.ieo.es; internet www.ieo.es; f. 1914; comprises physics, chemistry, pollution, geology, fishery biology and marine biology sections in Madrid; coastal laboratories at Cádiz, Gijón, La Coruña, Málaga, Palma de Mallorca, San Pedro del Pinatar, Santa Cruz de Tenerife, Santander and Vigo; 6 research vessels; library of 12,500 vols, 3,200 periodicals; Dir EDUARDO BALGUERÍAS GUERRA; Sec.-Gen. JOSÉ LUIS DE OSSORNO ALMÉCIJA; publ. *IEO* (4 a year).

Physical Sciences

Agencia Estatal de Meteorología (State Meteorological Agency): Calle Leonardo Prieto Castro 8, Ciudad Universitaria, 28071 Madrid; tel. (91) 5819810; fax (91) 5819811; internet www.aemet.es; f. 2006 to replace Instituto Nacional de Meteorología (f. 1887); 17 meteorological centres, 4,500 stations, 90 observatories; library of 20,000 vols.

Fundación Galileo Galilei (Galileo Galilei Foundation): Rambla José Ana Fernández Pérez 7, Apdo 565, 38712 San Antonio de Breña Baja, La Palma, Canary Islands; tel. (92) 2433666; fax (92) 2420508; e-mail oliva@tng.iac.es; internet www.tng.iac.es; f. 1979; attached to Istituto Nazionale di Astrofisica, Italy; promotes astrophysical research by managing and running the Telescopio Nazionale Galileo (TNG), a 3.58 m optical/infrared telescope located on La Palma; Dir EMILIO MOLINARI.

Instituto de Astrofísica de Canarias (IAC) (Canaries Institute of Astrophysics): Calle Vía Láctea, s/n, 38205 La Laguna, Tenerife, Canary Islands; tel. (92) 2605200; fax (92) 2605210; e-mail secadm@iac.es; internet www.iac.es; f. 1982; incl. int. observatories on Tenerife and La Palma; library of 13,000 vols, 360 periodicals; Dir Prof. FRANCISCO SÁNCHEZ MARTÍNEZ; Head. of Admin. RAFAEL ARNAY.

Attached 0bservatories:

Observatorio del Roque de los Muchachos: Apdo 50, Calle Cuesta de San José, s/n, 38712 Santa Cruz de La Palma, Canary Islands; tel. (92) 2405500; fax (92) 2405501; e-mail orm@iac.es; internet www.iac.es; f. 1985; European Northern Observatory; Site Man. Dr JUAN CARLOS PÉREZ ARENCIBIA.

Observatorio del Teide: Calle Vía Láctea, s/n, 38205 La Laguna, Tenerife, Canary Islands; tel. (92) 2329100; fax (92) 2329117; e-mail ot@iac.es; internet www.iac.es; f. 1985; European Northern Observatory; Site Man. Dr MIQUEL SERRA RICART.

Observatorio Astronómico Nacional (National Astronomical Observatory): Campus de la Universidad de Alcalá, 28801 Madrid; tel. (91) 5270107; fax (91) 5271935; e-mail spider@oan.es; internet www.oan.es; f. 1790; attached to Instituto Geográfico Nacional; library of 12,000 vols; Dir Dr RAFAEL BACHILLER; publ. *Anuario* (1 a year).

Observatorio Fabra: Camí de l'Observatori, s/n, 08035 Barcelona; tel. (93) 4175736; internet www.fabra.cat; f. 1905; attached to Real Academia de Ciencias y Artes de Barcelona; astronomy, meteorology and seismology; Dir Dr JOSEP MARIA CODINA I VIDAL.

Real Instituto y Observatorio de la Armada (Royal Naval Institute and Observatory): Cecilio Pujazón, s/n, 11110 San Fernando, (Cádiz); tel. (95) 6545590; fax (95) 6599366; e-mail secretaria@roa.es; internet www.roa.es; f. 1753; positional astronomy, ephemerides, time, geophysics and satellite geodesy; collaborates with the British and the American Nautical Almanac Offices, Centre Nat. d'Etudes Spatiales, Le Bureau des Longitudes and Das Astronomische Rechen Institut; library of 29,900 vols, 3,500 maps and plans; Dir Dr FERNANDO BELIZÓN RODRÍGUEZ; publs *Almanaque Náutico* (1 a year), *Anales, Observaciones Meteorológicas, Magnéticas y Sísmicas, Efemérides Astronómicas* (1 a year), *Fenómenos Astronómicos* (2 a year).

RELIGION, SOCIOLOGY AND ANTHROPOLOGY

Centro de Investigación en Contabilidad Social y Medioambiental (Centre for Research in Social and Environmental Accounting): Edificio 10, 2°, Despacho 24, Universidad Pablo de Olavide, Ctra de Utrera, Km 1, 41013 Seville; tel. (95) 4349278; fax (95) 4349339; e-mail cicsma@upo.es; internet www.upo.es/cicsma; f. 2003; attached to Universidad Pablo de Olavide; Dir FRANCISCO CARRASCO FENECH.

Instituto Universitario de Estudios de la Mujer (University Institute of Women's Studies): Calle Francisco Tomás y Valiente 5, Edificio de Ciencias Económicas y Empresariales, Módulo VI, Planta Baja, Campus Cantoblanco, 28049 Madrid; tel. (91) 4970034; fax (91) 4975553; e-mail documentacion.iuem@uam.es; internet iuem.jimdo.com; f. 1993; attached to Universidad Autónoma de Madrid; Dir YOLANDA GUERRERO NAVARRETE.

Instituto Universitario de Investigación Ortega y Gasset (Ortega y Gasset University Research Institute): Calle Fortuny 53, 28010, Madrid; tel. (91) 7004149; fax (91) 7003530; e-mail jefatura.estudios@fog.es; internet www.ortegaygasset.edu; f. 1986; attached to Fundación José Ortega y Gasset; affiliated to Universidad Complutense de Madrid; graduate degree programmes and research in social sciences and humanities; library of 50,000 vols, 300 periodicals.

TECHNOLOGY

Centro de Estudios e Investigaciones Técnicas de Gipuzkoa (Centre for Technical Studies and Research, Gipuzkoa): Paseo de Manuel Lardizabal 15, 20018 San Sebastián; tel. (94) 3212800; fax (94) 3213076; e-mail comunicacion@ceit.es; internet www.ceit.es; f. 1982; attached to Universidad de Navarra; areas of research incl. applied mechanics, electronics and communications, environmental engineering, microelectronics and microsystems; Gen. Dir ALEJO AVELLO ITURRIAGAGOITIA.

Centro de Investigaciones Energéticas, Medioambientales y Tecnológicas (Centre for Energy, Environmental and Technological Research): Avda Complutense 22, 28040 Madrid; tel. (91) 3466000; fax (91) 3466005; e-mail contacto@ciemat.es; internet www.ciemat.es; f. 1951; controls and directs research and study of nuclear and new and renewable energies, environmental policy and several advanced technologies; library of 32,000 vols, 300,000 reports, 750,000 microcards, 2,000 periodicals; Dir-Gen. CAYETANO LÓPEZ MARTÍNEZ.

Instituto Científico y Tecnológico de Navarra (Scientific and Technological Institute, Navarre): Avda Pío XII 53, 31008 Pamplona; tel. (94) 8176748; fax (94) 8425223; e-mail ict@unav.es; internet www.unav.es/ict; f. 1986; attached to Universidad de Navarra; Dir GUILLERMO GARCÍA DEL BARRIO.

Instituto de Biocomputación y Física de Sistemas Complejos (Institute of Biocomputation and Physics of Complex Systems): Edif. I+D, Calle Mariano Esquillor, 50018 Zaragoza; tel. (97) 6762989; fax (97) 6762990; e-mail info@bifi.es; internet bifi.es; attached to Universidad de Zaragoza; aims to develop competitive research in the areas of computing applied to the physics of complex systems and biological models; Dir JOSÉ FÉLIX SÁENZ LORENZO.

Instituto de Investigación en Ingeniería de Aragón (Aragón Engineering Research Institute): I3A Edif. I+D+i, Calle Mariano Esquillor, s/n, 50018 Zaragoza; tel. (97) 6762707; fax (97) 6762043; e-mail i3a@unizar.es; internet i3a.unizar.es; f. 2002; attached to Universidad de Zaragoza; aims to contribute to the economic devt of Aragon through the creation, and exploitation by industry, of new knowledge and technology; Dir RAFAEL BILBAO.

Instituto de Robótica (Institute of Robotics): Avda 2085, 46071 Valencia; Parc Científic Polígono de La Coma, s/n, 46980 Paterna, Valencia; tel. (9) 63543475; fax (9) 63543550; internet www.robotica.uv.es; f.

1991; attached to Universitat de València; research within the fields of transport and traffic telematics, computer graphics and virtual reality simulation of civil equipment, network services and computer security, control of robotic devices and digital image processing; Dir JUAN JOSÉ MARTÍNEZ DURÁ.

Instituto Geológico y Minero de España (Spanish Geological and Mining Institute): Calle Ríos Rosas 23, 28003 Madrid; tel. (91) 3495700; fax (91) 4426216; e-mail igme@igme.es; internet www.igme.es; f. 1849; attached to Min. of Science and Innovation; documentation centre of 20,000 items in microfilm; sections: geology, geophysics, mineral resources, subterranean hydrology, laboratories, museum; library of 45,000 vols; Pres. FELIPE PÉTRIZ CALVO; Dir ROSA DE VIDANIA MUÑOZ; Gen. Sec. AMOR SUÁREZ MUÑOZ; publs *Boletín Geológico y Minero* (4 a year), *Revista Española de Micropaleontología* (3 a year), geological, metallogenic and hydrogeological maps.

Libraries and Archives

Barcelona

Archivo Capitular de la Santa Iglesia Catedral de Barcelona (Archive of the Holy Church of the Cathedral of Barcelona): Catedral de Barcelona, Pla de la Seu s/n, 08002 Barcelona; tel. (93) 3153156; fax (93) 3100797; f. 9th century; documents since 9th century; treatises on Holy Scripture, ecclesiastical history and law; religious and economic history; 255 MSS, 200 incunabula and various printed books from the original Biblioteca Capitular; 41,000 parchment documents, 20,000 vols; Archives Prefect JOSEP BAUCELLS REIG.

Archivo de la Corona de Aragón (Royal Archives of Aragon): Calle Almogávars 77, 08018 Barcelona; tel. (93) 4854285; fax (93) 3001252; e-mail aca@mcu.es; internet www.mcu.es/archivos/mc/aca; f. 14th century; auxiliary 21,000 vols, 870 periodicals; Dir CARLOS LÓPEZ RODRÍGUEZ.

Arxiu Diocesà de Barcelona (Diocesan Archives, Barcelona): Palacio Arzobispal, Calle Obispo Irurita 5, 08002 Barcelona; tel. (93) 2701017; e-mail dpcarqbcn@filnet.es; f. 11th century; registers (1,200) from 1302; Diocesan Archivist Dr JOSÉ MA MARTI BONET; publ. *El Archivo Diocesano d' Barcelona*.

Biblioteca Balmes (Balmes Library): Duran i Bas 9, 08002 Barcelona; tel. (93) 3177284; fax (93) 3170498; e-mail biblioteca@balmesiana.org; internet www.balmesiana.org; f. 1923; specializes in church studies; 40,000 vols, 345 periodicals; Dir Dr RAMÓN CORTS BLAY.

Biblioteca de la Universitat de Barcelona (Barcelona University Library): Baldiri Reixac 2, 08028 Barcelona; tel. (93) 4035715; fax (93) 4034592; internet www.bib.ub.es/biblioteques; f. 1835; network of 19 libraries attached to the univ.; 1.2m. vols, of which 5,000 date from 16th century, 1,000 incunabula, 2,500 MSS; Dir DOLORS LAMARCA MORELL.

Biblioteca de l'Arxiu Històric de la Ciutat de Barcelona: Carrer Santa Llúcia 1, 08002 Barcelona; tel. (93) 3181195; fax (93) 3178327; e-mail bibliotecaarxiuhistoric@bcn.cat; internet www.bcn.cat/arxiu/arxiuhistoric; f. 1921; gen. works, books published in Barcelona since the 15th century; the Massana Library, containing works on iconography and the history of costume; other libraries donated by private donors, e.g. Eduardo Toda (British and gen. books); 150,000 vols, divided into several sections; Dir XAVIER TARRAUBELLA MIRABET.

Biblioteca de l'Associació d'Enginyers Industrials de Catalunya (Library of the Association of Industrial Engineers of Catalonia): Via Laietana 39, 08003 Barcelona; tel. (93) 3192366; fax (93) 3198811; e-mail biblioteca@eic.cat; internet www.eic.cat; f. 1863; 21,200 vols; Librarian FERRAN PUERTA I SALES.

Biblioteca del Centre Excursionista de Catalunya (Library of the Catalonia Mountaineering Centre): Calle Paradís 10, 08002 Barcelona; tel. (93) 3152311; fax (93) 3151408; e-mail biblioteca@cec.cat; internet biblioteca.cec.cat; f. 1876; 39,000 vols, 7,000 maps, 300 periodicals; Dir FRANCESC OLIVÉ; publs *Espeleòleg* (irregular), *Muntanya* (6 a year).

Biblioteca del Collegi de Notaris i Arxiu Històric de Protocols de Barcelona (Library of College of Notaries, Barcelona): Notariat 4, 08001 Barcelona; tel. (93) 3174800; e-mail info@catalunya.notariado.org; internet www.colnotcat.es; f. 1862; specializes in law and the medieval history of Catalonia; 25,000 vols, 50,000 protocols since 13th century; Archivist LAUREÀ PAGAROLAS SABATÉ; Librarian MONTSERRAT GÓMEZ; publs *Estudios Històrics i Documents dels Arxius de Protocols*, *La Notaría*.

Biblioteca del Foment del Treball Nacional (Library of Department of Trade Development): Vía Laietana 32, 08003 Barcelona; tel. (93) 4841200; fax (93) 4841230; e-mail foment@foment.com; internet www.foment.com; f. 1889; 90,000 vols, 2,500 periodicals; Librarian NURIA SARDÁ; publ. *Horizonte Empresarial* (12 a year).

Ilustre Collegi d'Advocats de Barcelona, Biblioteca (Barcelona Bar Association Library): Mallorca 283, 08037 Barcelona; tel. (93) 4961880; fax (93) 4871128; e-mail direcciobiblioteca@icab.cat; internet www.icab.cat; f. 1833; renewing and reservation; interlibrary loan; document supply; online resources; selective dissemination of information; Wi-Fi expositions; more than 300,000 vols, 1,500 periodicals; Head PATRICIA SANPERA; publs *Revista Jurídica de Catalunya* (4 a year), *Món Jurídic* (10 a year).

Reial Acadèmia Catalana de Belles Arts de Sant Jordi (Royal Catalan Academy of Fine Arts, Sant Jordi): Casa Llotja, 2°, Passeig d'Isabel II 1, 08003 Barcelona; tel. (93) 3192432; fax (93) 3190216; e-mail biblioteca@racba.org; internet www.racba.org; f. 1849; 10,000 vols; Pres. JORDI BONET ARMENGOL; Sec. LEOPOLDO GIL NEBOT; publ. *Annuari* (every 2 years).

Bilbao

Biblioteca Universitaria de Deusto: Ramón Rubial 1, 48009 Bilbao; tel. (94) 4139419; fax (94) 4139424; e-mail biblioteca@deusto.es; internet www.biblioteca.deusto.es; f. 1886; 1m. vols, 10,000 periodicals; Dir NIEVES TARANCO DEL BARRIO.

Granada

Archivo de la Real Chancillería de Granada (Archives of the Royal Chancery of Granada): Plaza del Padre Suárez 1, 18009 Granada; tel. (95) 8575757; fax (95) 8575756; e-mail informacion.arch.gr.ccul@juntadeaudalucia.es; internet www.juntadeandalucia.es/cultura/archivos; f. 1494; 13,000 linear metres of conventional archive material, incl. lawsuits settled by the Tribunal de la Real Chancillería from 1490 to 1834; also holds documents issued by the Audiencia Territorial de Granada from 1834 to 1989; Dir DAVID TORRES IBÁÑEZ.

Jerez de la Frontera

Biblioteca del Museo Arqueológico Municipal de Jerez (Jerez Archaeological Museum Town Library): Plaza del Mercado, s/n, 11408 Jerez de la Frontera; tel. (95) 6149560; fax (95) 6322975; e-mail museoarq@aytojerez.es; internet www.museoarqueologico.webjerez.com; f. 1873 (library), 1933 (museum); incunabula, important collns from 17th–18th centuries, local collns on horses, bullfighting, flamenco; documents dating back to the reconquest of Jerez by Alfonso El Sabio, documents on the discovery of America; 100,000 vols; Dirs RAMON CLAVIJO PROVENCIO, CRISTOBAL ORELLANA; Librarians CARLA PUERTO CASTRILLON, AMPARO GOMEZ MARTIN.

Biblioteca del Campus de Jerez: Avda. de la Universidad, s/n, 11405 Jerez de la Frontera; tel. (95) 6037015; fax (95) 6037077; e-mail biblioteca.campusjerez@uca.es; internet biblioteca.uca.es/sbuca/bibcjer.htm; f. 1979; 75,000 vols, 1,500 periodicals; Head Librarian ROSA MARÍA TORIBIO RUIZ.

La Coruña

Arquivo do Reino de Galicia (Archive of the Kingdom of Galicia): Jardín de San Carlos, s/n, 15001 La Coruña; tel. (98) 1209251; fax (98) 1227094; e-mail arq.reino.galicia@xunta.es; internet www.xunta.es; f. 1775; comprises a total of 150,926 bundles of documents dating back to AD 867, the most important since the 16th century, concerning disputes and lawsuits of the 'Real Audiencia de Galicia' and the 'Audiencia Territorial' relative to the clergy, the nobility, villages and private persons; 18th- and 19th-century documents of 'Real Intendencia', concerning govt and admin. of Galicia; documents 1808–14 of the 'Junta Superior de Armamento y Defensa' relative to the Peninsular War; documents of Provincial Administration of La Coruña since the 19th century, concerning the govt, police, education, economy, tourism, finance, health; records of families, labour unions and churches since the 12th century; colln of parchment 867–1586; 7,686 maps, plans and drawings since the 16th century; 101,847 photographs and postcards, 1,298 microforms; 25,475 vols, 1,551 periodicals (incl. 23 current) and 929 pamphlets closely related to the archives and of special interest for research; Dir MARÍA CARMEN PRIETO RAMOS.

Lérida (Lleida)

Arxiu Històric de Lleida (Historical Archive of Lleida): Carrer Governador Montcada, s/n, 25002 Lleida; tel. (97) 3288250; fax (97) 3288525; e-mail ahll.cultura@gencat.cat; internet cultura.gencat.cat/arxius/ahl; f. 1952; 9,817 linear metres of documents dating from 14th to 21st century; incl. records from Administració de la Generalitat de Catalunya; Dir GLÒRIA VILELLA.

Madrid

Archivo Central del Ministerio de Trabajo e Inmigración (Central Archive of the Ministry of Labour and Immigration): Calle Agustín de Bethencourt 4, 28003 Madrid; tel. (91) 3630921; e-mail archivocentral@mtin.es; internet www.mtin.es; Head CARMEN CONCEPCIÓN SAIZ GÓMEZ; publ. *Revista del Ministerio de Trabajo e Inmigración* (12 a year).

Archivo General de la Administración Civil del Estado: Paseo de Aguadores 2, 28804 Alcalá de Henares, Madrid; tel. (91) 8892950; fax (91) 8822435; e-mail alfonso.davila@mcu.es; internet www.mcu.es/archivos/mc/aga; f. 1969; preserves and makes available for information or scientific research documents on public admin. that are no longer of current admin. relevance; 3,000 vols; Dir ALFONSO DÁVILA OLIVEDA.

Archivo Histórico Nacional (National Historical Archives): Calle Serrano 115, 28006 Madrid; tel. (91) 7688500; fax (91) 5631199; e-mail ahn@mcu.es; internet www.mcu.es/archivos/mc/ahn; f. 1866; 400,000 archival items and 30,000 library items, 4,000 ancient monographs and 400 periodicals; Dir CARMEN SIERRA BÁRCENA.

Biblioteca Central de Marina (Central Naval Library): Calle Montalbán 2, 28014 Madrid; tel. and fax (91) 3796024; e-mail bca@fn.mde.es; internet www.portalcultura.mde.es/cultural/bibliotecas/madrid/biblioteca_121.html; f. 1874; 90,000 vols; Dir MARÍA EUGENIA MOREU ABOAL.

Biblioteca Central del Ministerio de Economía y Hacienda (Central Library of the Ministry of Economy and Finance): Calle Alcalá 9, Planta Baja, 28071 Madrid; tel. (91) 5958342; fax (91) 5958431; e-mail biblioteca.alcala@minhac.es; internet www.meh.es/es-es/publicaciones/bibliotecas; f. 1852; 82,000 vols on economics, finance and government legislation; Librarian ESPERANZA SALÁN PANIAGUA.

Biblioteca Central Militar (Central Military Library): Paseo de Moret 3, , 28008 Madrid; tel. (91) 7808700; fax (91) 3796024; e-mail ftorra@et.mde.es; internet www.portalcultura.mde.es/cultural/bibliotecas/madrid/biblioteca_107.html; f. 1932; 300,000 vols on military history, civil and military engineering, architecture, science; 1,000 periodicals; rare books, engravings, photographs, maps and plans, microforms; Dir FERNANDO TORRA PÉREZ.

Biblioteca de la Escuela Técnica Superior de Ingenieros de Caminos, Canales y Puertos (Library of the Higher School for Road, Canal and Port Engineers): Ciudad Universitaria, 28040 Madrid; tel. (91) 3366739; internet www.caminos.upm.es; f. 1834; 64,269 vols, 1,384 periodicals (123 current), 3,501 maps, 13,779 microfiches, 587 theses; Head CONCEPCIÓN GARCÍA VIÑUELA.

Biblioteca de la Escuela Técnica Superior de Ingenieros Industriales (Library of the Higher School for Industrial Engineers): Calle José Gutiérrez Abascal 2, 28006 Madrid; tel. (91) 3363076; e-mail biblioteca.industriales@upm.es; internet www.etsii.upm.es/inforgen/biblioteca; f. 1905; 40,000 vols; Dir ISABEL INÉS MENDOZA GARCÍA.

Biblioteca de la Universidad Complutense de Madrid (Complutense University of Madrid Library): Edificio Multiusos 1, Calle Professor Aranguren s/n, 28040 Madrid; tel. (91) 3947985; fax (91) 3947849; e-mail buc@buc.ucm.es; internet www.ucm.es/bucm; f. 1499; 2.7m. vols, 72,879 MSS, 727 incunabula, 181,066 special materials, 50,750 periodicals; Dir JOSÉ ANTONIO MAGÁN WALS.

Biblioteca del Ministerio de Asuntos Exteriores y de Cooperación (Library of the Ministry of Foreign Affairs and Cooperation): Plaza de la Provincia 1, 28012 Madrid; tel. (91) 3799219; fax (91) 3666026; f. 1943; 52,341 vols, 293 periodicals; works on history, geography, international law, political and civil law, and international relations; Dir MARÍA JOSÉ ALBO ALVAREZ.

Biblioteca Hispánica (de la Agencia Española de Cooperación Internacional para el Desarrollo) (Hispanic Library): Avda de los Reyes Católicos 4, Ciudad Universitaria, 28040 Madrid; tel. (91) 5838175; fax (91) 5838525; e-mail biblioteca.hispanica@aecid.es; internet www.aecid.es/bibliotecas; f. 1947; 550,000 vols and 11,600 periodicals; spec. colln: Latin American incunabula; Dir Dra CARMEN DIEZ HOYO.

Biblioteca Nacional de España (National Library of Spain): Paseo de Recoletos 20, 28071 Madrid; tel. (91) 5807800; fax (91) 5775634; e-mail info@bne.es; internet www.bne.es; f. 1712 as Royal Library; 3.7m. vols, 2.6m. monographs, 152,604 periodicals, 148,320 drawings and photographs, 309,662 audio recordings, 171,725 musical scores, 90,427 video cassettes, 70,156 maps and charts, 28,494 MSS; deposit library; ISSN nat. centre; Dir GLÒRIA PÉREZ-SALMERÓN.

Biblioteca San Dámaso: Calle San Buenaventura 9, 28005 Madrid; tel. and fax (91) 3644010; e-mail biblioteca@fsandamaso.es; internet www.fsandamaso.es/facultad/biblioteca.htm; f. 1929; comprises sections on theology and philosophy; auxiliary libraries incl. Biblioteca Alemana Görres (studies on German-Spanish cultural relations); 40,000 vols, 672 periodicals; Dir Prof. NICOLÁS ÁLVAREZ DE LAS ASTURIAS; Librarian REGINE BAUMEISTER.

Centro de Información Documental de Archivos Subdirección General de Archivos Estatales Ministerio de Cultura: Paseo de Aguadores, 2-pl. baja , 28871 Madrid; tel. (91) 8838539; fax (91) 8829470; e-mail biblioteca.cida@mcu.es; internet www.mcu.es/archivos/mc/cida/index.html; f. 1979; Dir JOSEFA VILLANUEVA TOLEDO; publ. *Boletín de Información Bibliográfica*.

Hemeroteca Municipal de Madrid (Periodicals Library of the Corporation of Madrid): Calle Conde Duque 9–11, 28015 Madrid; tel. (91) 5885775; fax (91) 5885909; e-mail hemeroteca@munimadrid.es; internet www.madrid.es/hemeroteca; f. 1918; 250,000 vols spanning more than 20,000 titles; the library maintains a microfilm service; Dir CARLOS DORADO FERNÁNDEZ.

Real Biblioteca (Royal Library): Palacio Real, Calle Bailén, s/n, 28071 Madrid; tel. (91) 4548700; fax (91) 4548867; e-mail realbiblioteca@patrimonionacional.es; internet www.realbiblioteca.es; f. early 18th century; 250,000 printed vols; fine collns of MSS, incunabula, music, rare editions since 16th century, maps, engravings and drawings; colln of bookbindings; research library; Dir Dr MARÍA LUISA LÓPEZ-VIDRIERO; publ. *Avisos: Noticias de la Real Biblioteca* (4 a year).

Palma de Mallorca

Arxiu del Regne de Mallorca (Archives of the Kingdom of Mallorca): Cuerta de Valldemossa, km 7, Edifici Adduno, Calle de Blaise Pascal, Parc Bit, 07121 Palma de Mallorca, Balearic Islands; tel. (97) 1725999; fax (97) 1177357; e-mail arm@arxregne.caib.es; internet arxregne.caib.es/web/default.htm; f. 1851; 11,000 linear m of documents; public and private archives since 13th century; 15,000 vols, 265 periodicals; Dir RICARD URGELL HERNÁNDEZ.

Peralada

Biblioteca del Palacio de Peralada (Palace of Peralada Library): Plaça del Carmen s/n, 17491 Peralada (Girona); tel. (97) 2538125; fax (97) 2538087; e-mail inespadrosa@castilloperalada.com; f. 1882, by the Count of Peralada; confs; exhibitions; lends books for exhibitions; 80,000 vols, 1,200 MSS, 200 incunabula, 10,000 photographs, 20,000 pamphlets and parchments on history; Librarian INÉS PADROSA; Archivist JOSEP CLAVAGUERA.

Sabadell

Arxiu Històric de Sabadell (Historical Archives, Sabadell): Carrer Indústria 32–34, 08202 Sabadell; tel. (93) 7268777; fax (93) 7275703; e-mail ahs@ajsabadell.es; internet www.sabadell.net/websajsab/arxiu; f. 14th century; documents since 1111; MSS of *Arxius Privats* (private records) since 1247, *Fons eclesiàstics* (ecclesiastical archives) since 1334, *Corts Senyorials* (Court of Justice) since 1347, *Escrivania* (notarial archives) since 1400, *Actes* (Proceedings of local council meetings) since 1449, *Hemeroteca oficial* since 1570, *Fons d'empresa* (records of 30 companies) from 19th century; collection of local journals and reviews since 1855; 10,000 vols, 100,000 photographs and 625 audiovisual records; Dir JOAN COMASÒLIVAS I FONT; publ. *Arraona* (1 a year).

San Lorenzo de El Escorial

Real Biblioteca del Monasterio de San Lorenzo de El Escorial (Royal Library of the Monastery of San Lorenzo de El Escorial): 28200 San Lorenzo de El Escorial, Madrid; tel. (91) 8903889; fax (91) 8908369; e-mail real.biblioteca@ctv.es; f. 1575; 75,000 vols, 650 incunabula, 10,000 engravings and prints; MSS: 2,000 Arabic, 2,090 Latin and vernacular, 72 Hebrew, 580 Greek; many rare and unique edns, incl. complete copy of the *Biblia Poliglota Complutensis* and of the *Biblia Poliglota* of Antwerp on parchment, and the *Epítome de Anatomía*, by Vesalius, also on parchment; Dir P. JOSÉ LUIS DEL VALLE MERINO.

Santander

Biblioteca Central de Cantabria (Central Library of Cantabria): Ruiz de Alda 19, 39009 Santander; tel. (94) 2241550; fax (94) 2241551; e-mail bcc@gobcantabria.es; internet bcc.cantabria.es; f. 1839 as Biblioteca del Instituto Cántabro para la Enseñanza de la Náutica y el Comercio; present name adopted 1999; present site 2010; Dir JUAN JOSÉ AMADO FERNÁNDEZ.

Biblioteca de Menéndez Pelayo (Menéndez Pelayo Library): Calle Rubio 6, 39001 Santander; tel. (94) 2234534; fax (94) 2373766; e-mail biblioteca-mp@ayto-santander.es; internet www.bibliotecademenendezpelayo.org; the private library of this writer, 45,000 vols, not to be increased in number, left by him to the town; opened to the public 1915; inaugurated 1923 by Alfonso XIII; Dir ROSA FERNÁNDEZ-LERA; publ. *De re Bibliographica* (1 a year).

Seville

Archivo Ducal de Medinaceli (Medinaceli Archives): Plaza de Pilatos 1, Seville; tel. (95) 4225055; fax (95) 4224677; e-mail casapilatos@infonegocio.com; internet www.fundacionmedinaceli.org/archivo; archives of 9th to 20th centuries; more than 5,000 vols; Dir JUAN MANUEL ALBENDEA SOLÍS; publ. *Histórica*.

Archivo General de Indias (Archives of the Indies): Avda de la Constitución 3, Edificio de La Cilla, Calle Santo Tomás 5, 41071 Seville; tel. (95) 4500528; fax (95) 4219485; e-mail isabel.simo@mcu.es; internet www.mcu.es/archivos/mc/agi; f. 1785; documents relating to Spanish colonial administration in America and the Philippines; 36,000 vols, 43,000 files; Dir ISABEL SIMÓ RODRIGUEZ; publs incl. *Catálogos de Pasajeros a Indias*, *Catálogos de Mapas y Planos*, *CD-ROM Tesoros del Archivo General de Indias*.

Biblioteca Capitular y Colombina: Institución Colombina, Calle Alemanes, s/n, 41004 Seville; tel. (95) 4560769; fax (95) 4211876; e-mail bibliotecaic@institucioncolombina.org; f. 13th century; 60,000 vols; incl. the 3,500-vol. library of Hernando Colón, son of the explorer, Cristóbal; Dir NURIA CASQUETE DE PRADO SAGRERA.

Simancas

Archivo General de Simancas (Simancas General Archives): Calle Miravete 8, 47130 Simancas (Valladolid); tel. (98) 3590750; fax (98) 3590311; e-mail eduardo.pedruelo@mcu.es; internet www.mcu.es/archivos/mc/ags; f. 1540; 70,000 filed documents and 5,000 vols of documents; 20,000 vols on history; Dir EDUARDO MARTÍN PEDRUEL.

Toledo

Archivo y Biblioteca Capitulares (Archives and Library of the Cathedral Chapter): Catedral de Toledo, Hombre de Palo 2, Apdo 295, 45001 Toledo; tel. and fax (92) 5212423; e-mail archivocapitular@architoledo.org; internet www.architoledo.org/catedral/archivos/textoarchivo.htm; f. 1085; the *Archivo Capitular* contains 11,000 documents (mostly medieval) since 1085; the library (f. 1383) contains 2,521 MSS, 1,200 printed books; Dirs Dr ÁNGEL FERNÁNDEZ COLLADO, Dr RAMON GONZÁLVEZ RUIZ.

Biblioteca de Castilla—La Mancha (Library of Castilla—La Mancha): Cuesta de Carlos V, s/n, 45001 Toledo; tel. (92) 5256680; fax (92) 5253642; e-mail biblioclm@jccm.es; internet www.jccm.es/biblioclm; f. 1998; 380,000 vols, 4,000 periodicals; spec. collns incl. Borbón-Lorenzana (more than 100,000 vols 16th–19th centuries, 700 MSS, 414 incunabula), Fondo Regional; Dirs PALOMA FERNÁNDEZ DE AVILÉS, CARMEN MORALES MATEO.

Valencia

Archivo del Reino de Valencia (Archive of United Kingdom of Valencia): Paseo de la Alameda 22, 46010 Valencia; tel. (96) 3184550; fax (96) 3184527; e-mail arv@gva.es; internet dglab.cult.gva.es/arxiuregne; f. 1419; 100,000 MSS books (13th century to present), 50,000 files of MSS, 61,483 charters, deeds, etc., since 13th century; auxiliary library comprises 13,500 vols, 4,190 pamphlets and 250 periodicals; Dir FRANCESC TORRES FAUS.

Zaragoza

Biblioteca Ibercaja 'José Sinues': Fernando el Católico 1–3, 50006 Zaragoza; tel. (97) 6359887; e-mail bjsinues@ibercajaobrasocial.org; f. 1975; owned by the Ibercaja credit company; open only to mems; 64,152 vols, 50 periodicals, 250 audiovisual items; spec. colln: Biblioteca Moncayo of 15,000 vols by Aragonese authors or on the subject of Aragón.

Museums and Art Galleries

Barcelona

Museu d'Art Contemporani de Barcelona (Barcelona Museum of Contemporary Art): Plaça dels Àngels 1, 08001 Barcelona; tel. (93) 4120810; fax (93) 4124602; e-mail administracio@macba.es; internet www.macba.es; f. 1995; modern Catalan and int. art; Dir BARTOMEU MARÍ.

Museu d'Arqueologia de Catalunya (Archaeological Museum of Catalonia): Passeig de Santa Madrona 39–41, Parc de Montjuïc, 08038 Barcelona; tel. (93) 4232149; fax (93) 4254244; e-mail mac.cultura@gencat.cat; internet www.mac.cat; f. 1935; collns of prehistoric, Greek, Phoenician, Visigothic and Roman art; library of 40,000 vols; Dir XAVIER LLOVERA MASSANA; publs *Cypsela* (every 2 years), *Empúries* (every 2 years).

Museu d'Història de Barcelona: Plaça del Rei, s/n, 08002 Barcelona; tel. (93) 3151111; fax (93) 3150957; e-mail museuhistoria@bcn.es; internet www.museuhistoria.bcn.es; f. 1943; 15th-century mansion containing Roman remains in situ (1st- to 4th-century Roman wall), 11th- to 15th-century Royal Palace; documentation centre, information service; Dir ANTONI NICOLAU MARTÍ; publ. *Quaderns d'Arqueologia i Història de la Ciutat de Barcelona*.

Subordinate institutions:

Casa Museu Verdaguer: Carrer Major 7, 08519 Folgueroles; tel. and fax (93) 8122157; e-mail info@verdaguer.cat; internet www.verdaguer.cat; 18th-century farmhouse, former home of the poet Jacint Verdaguer; Dir CARME TORRENTS I BUXÓ.

Centre d'Interpretació del Park Güell: Pavelló de Consergia, Park Güell, Carrer Olot, s/n, 08024 Barcelona; tel. (93) 2856899; fax (93) 2856900; e-mail museuhistoria@bcn.cat; internet www.bcn.cat/museuhistoriaciutat/ca/park_guell.html; information centre; incl. maps, models, photographs and audiovisual items.

Conjunto Monumental de la Plaça del Rei: Plaça del Rei, s/n, 08002 Barcelona; tel. (93) 2562100; fax (93) 2680454; e-mail museuhistoria@bcn.es; internet www.bcn.cat/museuhistoriaciutat/es/placa_del_rei.html; 11th-century Count's Palace, later the residence of the kings of Catalonia and Aragón; Padellàs House, a Gothic palace; Roman remains in situ (1st century BC–8th century AD); Chief Curator JULIA BELTRÁN DE HEREDIA.

Espai Santa Caterina, Centro de Interpretación Arqueológica: Plaça Joan Capri, Mercat de Santa Caterina, 08003 Barcelona; tel. (93) 2562100; fax (93) 2680454; e-mail museuhistoria@bcn.cat; internet www.bcn.cat/museuhistoriaciutat/es/santa_caterina.html; depicts the archaeological history of the city of Barcelona, from the Bronze Age to the latest examples of contemporary architecture.

Museu-Monestir de Pedralbes: Baixada del Monestir 9, 08034 Barcelona; tel. (93) 2039282; fax (93) 2039408; e-mail monestirpedralbes@bcn.es; f. 1326; opened to public 1983; Gothic church and monastery; Chief Curator ANNA CASTELLANO I TRESSERRA.

Museu de Ciències Naturals de Barcelona (Natural History Museum of Barcelona): Passeig Picasso, s/n, 08003 Barcelona; tel. (93) 3196912; fax (93) 3199312; e-mail museuciencies@bcn.cat; internet www.bcn.es/museuciencies; f. 1878; permanent exhibitions on classification of the animal kingdom; honey bees; urban birds; minerals, rocks and fossils; large collns of coleoptera, mollusca, fossils and minerals; 2–4 temporary exhibitions annually; research areas incl. evolutionary ecology, biospeleology, palaeontology, petrology and the history of science; library of 20,150 vols, 3,000 periodicals, 3,600 maps; Dir ANNA OMEDES; publs *Animal Biodiversity and Conservation* (2 a year), *Arxius de Miscelània Zoològica* (online), *Collectanea Botanica*, *Treballs del Museu de Geologia* (1 a year).

Subordinate Institution:

Museu de Ciències Naturals de Barcelona—Edifici de Geologia (Natural History Museum of Barcelona, Geology Building): Parc de la Ciutadella, s/n, 08003 Barcelona; tel. (93) 3196912; fax (93) 3199312; e-mail museuciencies@bcn.cat; f. 1882; library: geology library; publ. *Treballs del Museu de Geologia de Barcelona* (1 a year).

Museu de la Música (Museum of Music): L'Auditori, Calle Lepant 150, 2°, 08013 Barcelona; tel. (93) 2563650; fax (93) 2650102; e-mail museumusica@bcn.cat; internet www.museumusica.bcn.cat; f. 1946; valuable collns of antique instruments; phonographs and gramophones, historical early recordings; archives of Albéniz, Granados and other Catalan composers; library of 12,000 vols; Dir ROMÀ ESCALAS.

Museu Etnològic (Museum of Ethnology): Passeig de Sta Madrona 16–22, Parc de Montjuïc, 08038 Barcelona; tel. (93) 4246807; fax (93) 4237364; e-mail metno@intercom.es; internet www.museuetnologic.bcn.es; f. 1948; more than 70,000 artefacts pertaining to African, Asiatic, American, Oceanic, and Spanish ethnography and American archaeology; library of 40,000 vols, more than 1,000 periodicals; Dir JOSEP FORNÉS I GARCÍA.

Museu Geològic del Seminari de Barcelona (Geological Museum of Barcelona Seminary): Diputació 231, 08007 Barcelona; tel. (93) 4541600; e-mail mgsb@almeracomas.e.telefonica.net; internet www.bcn.es/medciencies/mgsb; f. 1874; palaeontology of invertebrates, colln of nearly 70,000 fossils; library of 13,000 vols; Dir Dr S. CALZADA; publs *Batalleria* (1 a year), *Scripta Musei Geologici Seminarii* (irregular).

Museu Marítim de Barcelona (Barcelona Maritime Museum): Avda de les Drassanes, s/n, 08001 Barcelona; tel. (93) 3429920; fax (93) 3187876; e-mail m.maritim@diba.cat; internet www.mmb.cat; f. 1941; library of 15,000 vols; photographic, cartographic and documental archives; colln of 158 objects of weaponry; restoration workshop; Dir ROGER MARCET I BARBÉ.

Museu Nacional d'Art de Catalunya (National Art Museum of Catalonia): Palau Nacional, Parc de Montjuïc, 08038 Barcelona; tel. (93) 6220360; fax (93) 6220369; e-mail mnac@mnac.es; internet www.mnac.cat; f. 1934; incl., on various sites, National Art Museum of Catalonia; educational programmes, debates, lectures and seminars, guided tours; library of 154,000 vols, 2,465 periodicals; Pres. NARCÍS SERRA I SERRA; Dir MARÍA TERESA OCAÑA GOMÀ; publs *Butlletí*, *Revista*.

Museu Picasso (Picasso Museum): Carrer Montcada 15–23, 08003 Barcelona; tel. (93) 2563000; fax (93) 3150102; e-mail museupicasso@bcn.cat; internet www.museupicasso.bcn.cat; f. 1963; comprises more than 4,000 paintings, pottery, drawings and engravings by Pablo Picasso (1881–1973), incl. the series 'Las Meninas' and the artist's donation, in 1970, of 940 works of art; library of 4,000 vols; Dir PEPE SERRA.

Bilbao

Guggenheim Bilbao Museoa (Guggenheim Museum, Bilbao): Abandoibarra 2, 48001 Bilbao; tel. (94) 4359000; fax (94) 4359010; e-mail infomacion@guggenheim-bilbao.es; internet www.guggenheim-bilbao.es; f. 1997; modern American and European art; Dir-Gen. JUAN IGNACIO VIDARTE.

Museo de Bellas Artes de Bilbao (Bilbao Museum of Fine Arts): Plaza del Museo 2, 48009 Bilbao; tel. (94) 4396060; fax (94) 4396145; e-mail info@museobilbao.com; internet www.museobilbao.com; f. 1908, opened to public 1914; colln incl. major works by Bermejo, Benson, Mandijn, Vredeman de Vries, De Vos, Moro, Sánchez Coello, El Greco, Pourbus, Gentileschi, Ribera, Zurbarán, Van Dyck, Murillo, Arellano, Meléndez, Bellotto, Goya, Paret, Villamil, Ribot, Zamacois, Madrazo, Gauguin, Cassatt, Sorolla, Guiard, Ensor, Regoyos, Romero de Torres, Zuloaga, Sunyer, Arteta, Gutiérrez Solana, Vázquez Díaz, Lipchitz, Delaunay, González, Gargallo, Bacon, Palazuelo, Oteiza, Chillida, Caro, Millares, Tàpies, Saura, Lüpertz, Kitaj, Blake, Arroyo and Barceló; library of 33,000 vols, 300 periodicals; Dir JAVIER VIAR.

Burgos

Museo de Burgos: Calle Miranda 13, 09002 Burgos; tel. (94) 7265875; fax (94) 7276792; e-mail museo.burgos@jcyl.es; internet www.museodeburgos.com; f. 1871; Casa Miranda: archaeological collns (from Palaeolithic to Visigothic); Casa Angulo: fine arts collns (from Mozarabic to contemporary painting), enamels, ivories, tomb of Juan de Padilla, Tablas Flamencas (Ecce Homo) and 15th- to 20th-century painting, sculpture, altarpieces; library of 3,000 vols, specializing in archaeology and art; Dir Dr J. C. ELORZA Y GUINEA; publ. *Anales*.

Cartagena

Museo Arqueológico Municipal (Archaeological Museum): Calle Ramón y Cajal 45, 30205 Cartagena; tel. (96) 8539027; fax (96) 8515449; e-mail informacionmuseo@ayto-cartagena.es; internet www.museoarqueologicocartagena.es; f. 1943; important collns of Roman remains found in the area, incl. mining, architecture, sculpture, industrial arts exhibits; model sites; Dir Dra ELENA RUIZ VALDERAS.

Chipiona

Museo Misional de Nuestra Señora de Regla: Colegio de Misioneros Franciscanos, 11550 Chipiona; f. 1939; about 600 exhibits of early Roman Christian relics, ancient Egyptian and other North African objects, antique coins, etc.; Dir R. P. RECTOR DEL COLEGIO.

Córdoba

Museo Arqueológico Provincial de Córdoba: Plaza de Jerónimo Páez 7, 14003 Córdoba; tel. (95) 7355517; fax (95) 7355534; e-mail museoarqueologicocordoba.ccul@juntadeandalucia.es; internet www.juntadeandalucia.es/cultura/museos/maeco; f. 1867; 33,500 exhibits; archaeological, prehistoric and local finds, Roman and medieval collns; library of 13,500 vols; Dir MARÍA DOLORES BAENA ALCANTARA.

Figueres

Teatre-Museu Dalí (Dali Museum): Plaça Gala Dalí 5, 17600 Figueres; tel. (97) 2677500; fax (97) 2501666; e-mail t-mgrups@dali-estate.org; internet www.salvador-dali.org; f. 1974; comprises 1,500 paintings, sculptures and other works by Salvador Dalí, and his private colln of works by other artists; Dir ANTONI PITXOT I SOLER.

Granada

Museo de Bellas Artes (Museum of Fine Arts): Palacio de Carlos V, 18009 Granada; tel. (95) 8575450; fax (95) 8575451; e-mail portaldemuseos@juntadeandalucia.es; internet www.juntadeandalucia.es/cultura/museos/mbagr; f. 1958 (present site); paintings and sculpture by local artists from 16th century to mid-20th century; library of 5,000 vols; Dir RICARDO TENORIO VERA.

Ibiza

Museo Arqueológico dEivissa i Formentera: Via Romana 31, 07800 Ibiza, Balearic Islands; tel. (97) 1301771; fax (97) 1303263; e-mail maef@telefonica.net; internet www.aamaef.org; f. 1907; Phoenician, Carthaginian and Roman remains from the necropolis of Puig des Molins (nat. monument and World Heritage Property); Dir JORGE H. FERNÁNDEZ GÓMEZ; publ. *Treballs del Museu Arqueològic d'Eivissa I Formentera* (2 a year).

Attached Museum:

Museo Monográfico y Necrópolis del Puig des Molins: Via Romana 31, Eivissa (Ibiza); tel. (97) 1301771; fax (97) 1303263; e-mail mmpm@telefonica.net; f. 1966; Phoenicean, Punic and Roman remains from the nat. monument of Puig des Molins, declared as a World Heritage Site by UNESCO in 1999; annual program of activities incl. lectures, courses about archaeology and Phoenicean-Punic archaeology, guided visits to the necropolis for school groups, and activities for children; library of 21,586 vols; Dir and Curator JORGE H. FERNÁNDEZ GÓMEZ; publ. *Treballs del Museu Arqueològic d'Eivissa I Formentera*.

La Escala

Museu d'Arqueologia de Cataluyna—Empúries: Calle Puig i Cadafalch, s/n, 17130 L'Escala; tel. (97) 2770208; fax (97) 2775975; e-mail macempuries.cultura@gencat.cat; internet www.mac.cat/cat/seus/empuries; f. 1908; colln of excavations of Graeco-Roman city Empúries; library of 3,500 vols; Dir XAVIER LLOVERA.

Las Palmas

Museo Canario (Canarian Museum): Dr Verneu 2, Vegueta, 35001 Las Palmas de Gran Canaria; tel. (92) 3336800; fax (92) 3336801; e-mail info@elmuseocanario.com; internet www.elmuseocanario.com; f. 1879; local archaeology and anthropology, ethnography and natural sciences; library of 65,000 vols; Dir-Gen. DIEGO LÓPEZ DÍAZ; publ. *El Museo Canario* (1 a year).

Lérida (Lleida)

Gabinet Numismàtic: Institut d'Estudis Ilerdencs, Plaça de la Catedral, s/n, 25002 Lérida; tel. (97) 3271500; e-mail iei@fpiei.es; Roman, Iberian, Ibero-Roman, medieval and modern exhibits; local collns.

Museo de la Paeria: Plaça Paeria 1, 25007 Lérida; tel. (90) 2250050; fax (97) 3238953; f. 1963; historical documents and objects belonging to the municipality; archaeological finds of Lérida.

Museu d'Art Jaume Morera: Carrer Major 31, Edifici Casino, 25007 Lérida; tel. (97) 3700419; fax (97) 3700487; e-mail mmorera@paeria.cat; internet www.paeria.cat/mmorera; f. 1917; museum of modern paintings mainly by Catalan artists, incl. works by Morera, C. Haes and others; Dir JESÚS NAVARRO I GUITART.

Museu de Lleida: diocesà i comarcal: Carrer Sant Crist 1, 25002 Lérida; tel. (97) 3283075; fax (97) 3261582; e-mail museu@museudelleida.cat; internet www.museudelleida.cat; f. 1997; medieval sculptures; also sub-section at Rambla de Aragón containing religious paintings, metalwork and vestments; Dir MONTSERRAT MACIÀ I GOU.

Servei d'Arqueologia de la Fundació Pública Institut d'Estudis Ilerdencs (Archaeological Services of the Public Foundation the Institute of Lleida Studies): Apartat de Correus 79, 25080 Lérida; Plaça Catedral, s/n, 25002 Lérida; tel. (97) 3271500 ext. 307; fax (97) 3274538; e-mail arqueolo@diputaciolleida.cat; internet www.fpiei.cat; f. 1954; archaeology, excavation; first Trinitarian house of Iberian Peninsula; audiovisual teaching aids; Dir JOAN RAMON GONZÁLEZ PÉREZ.

Madrid

Fundación Lázaro Galdiano (Lázaro Galdiano Foundation): Calle Serrano 122, 28006 Madrid; tel. (91) 5616084; fax (91) 5617793; e-mail secretaria.fundacion@flg.es; internet www.flg.es; f. 1948; 13,000 items: Italian, Spanish and Flemish Renaissance paintings; Primitives; Golden Age, 18th- and 19th-century Spanish paintings; 16th- and 17th-century Dutch paintings; English 18th- and 19th-century colln; Golden Age MSS and incunabula; collns of ivory, enamels, watches, jewellery, furniture, weapons and armour, oriental and Spanish tapestries and cloth; library of 40,000 vols, 1,000 periodicals; Dir ELENA HERNANDO GONZALO; publ. *Goya. Revista de Arte* (3 a year).

Instituto de Valencia de Don Juan (Don Juan Institute of Valencia): Calle Fortuny 43, 28010 Madrid; tel. (91) 3081848; f. 1916; historical archives; museum of ancient Spanish industrial arts; illuminated MS *Les Statuts de la Toison d'Or* with miniatures; library of 10,000 historical and art vols; Dir BALBINA MARTÍNEZ CAVIRO.

Museo Arqueológico Nacional (National Archaeological Museum): Calle Serrano 13, 28001 Madrid; tel. (91) 5777912; fax (91) 4316840; e-mail sugerencias.man@mcu.es; internet man.mcu.es; f. 1867; 16th-century miniatures; collns relating to Egyptian, Cypriot, Greek and Etruscan antiquities and to national prehistory, Iron Age, Iberian and Hispano-Roman art; from medieval and modern times: ivory carvings, Spanish pottery, Islamic pottery, brocades, tapestries, porcelain, furniture, textiles and a numismatic colln; library of 140,000 vols, 3,000 serial titles; medieval MSS incl. Huesca Bible of 12th century, *Beato de Liébana*, *Comentarios al Apocalipsis* (12th–13th century), *Martirologio y Regla de S. Benito* (13th century), *Cantorales* (15th century); Dir ROSA CHUMILLAS ZAMORA; publ. *Boletín* (irregular).

Museo Cerralbo: Ventura Rodríguez 17, 28008 Madrid; tel. (91) 5473646; fax (91) 5591171; e-mail mudeo@mcerralbo.mcu.es; internet museocerralbo.mcu.es; f. 1924; the 17th Marquis of Cerralbo left his house to the nation as a museum, together with his colln of 50,000 paintings, drawings, engravings, porcelain, arms, carpets, coins, furniture; incl. paintings by El Greco, Ribera, Titian, Van Dyck, Tintoretto; library of 13,000 vols; Dir LURDES VAQUERO ARGÜELLES.

Museo de Historia (Historical Museum): Calle Fuencarral 78, 28004 Madrid; tel. (91) 7011863; fax (91) 7011686; e-mail smuseosm@munimadrid.es; internet www.munimadrid.es/museodehistoria; f. 1929, fmrly Museo Municipal de Madrid; historical and artistic evolution of Madrid since 16th century; portraits, paintings, designs, engravings, sculptures, plans, silversmiths' work, coins, ceramics, porcelain; paintings by Berruguete, Maella, Luca Giordano, Bayeu, Castillo, Goya and other contemporary artists, 1830 Madrid scale model, Ramón de Mesonero Romanos and Ramón Gómez de la Serna studies; Dir CARMEN PRIEGO FERNÁNDEZ DEL CAMPO.

Museo de la Farmacia Hispana (Museum of Sapnish Medicine): Facultad de Farmacia, Universidad Complutense Madrid, Plaza de Ramón y Cajal, s/n, 28040 Madrid; tel. and fax (91) 3941797; e-mail museofar@farm.ucm.es; internet www.ucm.es/info/mhfarhis; f. 1951; library of 10,000 vols; Dir FRANCISCO JAVIER PUERTO SARMIENTO.

Museo de la Real Academia de Bellas Artes de San Fernando (Royal Academy of Fine Arts, San Fernando): Calle Alcalá 13, 28014 Madrid; tel. (91) 5240864; fax (91)

5241034; e-mail museo@rabasf.org; internet rabasf.insde.es; f. 1744; Spanish paintings since 16th century (incl. works by Goya, Zurbarán, Murillo, Ribera and Pereda), European paintings from 16th–18th centuries, Spanish sculpture since 17th century; Dir JOSÉ MARTA LUZOŃ NOGUÉ.

Museo del Ejército (Army Museum): Calle Méndez Núñez 1, 28071 Madrid; tel. (91) 5228977; fax (91) 5314624; internet www.ejercito.mde.es/unidades/madrid/ihycm/museos/ejercito; f. 1803 as Real Museo Militar; 30,000 exhibits; collns of arms, war trophies, flags and tin soldiers; br. museum in Toledo; library of 10,000 vols; Dir-Gen. JOSÉ A. RIVAS OCTAVIO.

Museo del Ferrocarril (Railway Museum): Paseo Delicias 61, 28045 Madrid; tel. (90) 2228822; fax (91) 5068478; e-mail museodelicias@ffe.es; internet www.museodelferrocarril.org; f. 1984; steam, diesel and electric trains, models, exhibitions; photographic archive; Dir/Curator Dr MIGUEL MUÑOZ; publs *Cuadernos del Archivo Histórico Ferroviario*, *Cuadernos del Museo* (12 a year), *Railway Museum Bulletin*, *TST (Transports, Services and Telecommunications)*.

Museo Nacional Centro de Arte Reina Sofía: Plaza Santa Isabel 52, 28012 Madrid; tel. (91) 7741000; fax (91) 7741056; e-mail quejas.mncars@mcu.es; internet www.museoreinasofia.es; f. 1986 in a refurbished 18th-century bldg; contemporary art; library of 120,000 vols, 1,700 periodicals; Dir ANA MARTINEZ DE AGUILAR; publ. *Carta* (2 a year).

Museo Nacional de Antropología (National Museum of Anthropology): Calle Alfonso XII 68, 28014 Madrid; tel. (91) 5306418; fax (91) 4677098; e-mail antropologico@mcu.es; internet mnantropologia.mcu.es; f. 1910, fmrly a section of the Nat. Museum of Natural Science; colln formed by 30,000 objects and documents from Europe, Asia, the Philippines, Micronesia, Melanesia, Central and S America, the Sahara, Morocco, W and Central Africa, and the fmr Spanish Guinea; organizes temporary exhibitions, workshops for children, families and adults, concerts, lectures; library of 14,000 vols and anthropological periodicals; closed for renovations from Oct. 2010; Dir PILAR ROMERO DE TEJADA Y PICATOSTE; publ. *Anales* (1 a year).

Museo Nacional de Artes Decorativas (National Museum of Decorative Arts): Calle Montalbán 12, 28014 Madrid; tel. (91) 5326845; fax (91) 5232086; e-mail mnad@mnad.mcu.es; internet mnartesdecorativas.mcu.es; f. 1912; collns of interior decorative arts, especially Spanish from 15th–19th centuries, incl. carpets, furniture, leatherwork, jewellery, tapestries, ceramics, glass, porcelain, textiles; library of 20,000 vols, 500 periodicals; Dir Dr ALBERTO BARTOLOMÉ ARRAIZA.

Museo Nacional de Ciencia y Tecnología (National Museum of Science and Technology): Paseo de las Delicias 61, 28045 Madrid; tel. (91) 5303001; fax (91) 4675119; e-mail museo.mnct@mec.es; internet www.micinn.es/mnct; f. 1980; library of 11,000 vols, 900 periodicals; Dir RAMÓN NÚÑEZ CENTELLA.

Museo Nacional de Ciencias Naturales (Natural Science Museum): José Gutiérrez Abascal 2, 28006 Madrid; tel. (91) 4111328; fax (91) 5645078; e-mail director.mncn@csic.es; internet www.mncn.csic.es; f. 1771 as Gabinete de Historia Natural by Carlos III; attached to CSIC; valuable natural history and scientific collections, mainly from Iberia, Central and S America, the Philippines and N Africa; library of 63,000 vols, incl. over 2,000 volumes from 15th–18th centuries and 1 incunabulum; 4,300 periodicals, since 1790; Dir ESTEBAN MANRIQUE REOL; publs *Graellsia* (1 a year), *Estudios Geológicos* (3 a year).

Museo Nacional de Reproducciones Artísticas (National Museum of Art Reproductions): Avda Juan de Herrera 2, 28040 Madrid; tel. (91) 5497150; fax (91) 5448004; internet mnreproduccionesartisticas.mcu.es; f. 1877; library of 10,000 vols; more than 3,000 reproductions of Oriental, Greek, Roman and Hispano-Roman statuary, medieval and Renaissance art, classical and medieval sculpture and decorative arts; Dir MARÍA JOSÉ ALMAGRO GORBEA.

Museo Nacional del Prado (National Prado Museum): Paseo del Prado, s/n, 28014 Madrid; tel. (91) 3302800; fax (91) 3302856; e-mail museo.nacional@museodelprado.es; internet www.museoprado.es; f. 1819; paintings by Botticelli, Rembrandt, Velázquez, El Greco, Goya, Murillo, Raphael, Bosch, Van der Weyden, Zurbarán, Van Dyck, Tiepolo, Ribalta, Rubens, Titian, Veronese, Tintoretto, Moro, Juanes, Meléndez, Poussin, Ribera; Classical and Renaissance sculpture; jewels and medals; library of 60,000 vols, 700 periodicals; Dir MIGUEL ZUGAZA; publ. *Boletín* (1 a year).

Museo Naval (Naval Museum): Paseo del Prado 5, 28014 Madrid; tel. (91) 5238789; fax (91) 3795056; internet www.museonavalmadrid.com; f. 1843; engravings of sea battles, portraits, nautical instruments and armaments; models of ships since 14th century; more than 6,000 original maps, charts, prints and drawings of many countries since 1600; 70,000 photographs (of which 27,000 are catalogued); library of 20,000 vols, 3,500 vols of MSS; Dir GONZALO RODRÍGUEZ GONZÁLEZ-ALLER; publ. *Revista de Historia Naval* (4 a year).

Museo del Romanticismo (Museum of the Romantic Period): San Mateo 13, 28004 Madrid; tel. (91) 4481045; fax (91) 4456940; e-mail informacion.romanticismo@mcu.es; internet museoromantico.mcu.es; f. 1924 as Museo Romántico, closed 2001, reopened under present name 2009; paintings, furniture, books and decorations of Spanish romantic period; concerts, meetings, family and school programmes, lectures; library of 13,000 vols, 300 periodicals; Dir Dra ASUNCIÓN CARDONA.

Museo de los Orígenes, Casa de San Isidro (Museum of Origins, House of St Isidro): Plaza San Andrés 2, 28005 Madrid; tel. (91) 3667415; fax (91) 3541719; e-mail museodelosorigenes@munimadrid.es; internet www.munimadrid.es/museodelosorigenes; f. 2000; fmrly Museo de San Isidro; archaeology and history of Madrid and environs; library of 12,000 vols; Dir EDUARDO SALAS VÁZQUEZ; publ. *Estudios de Prehistoria y Arqueología Madrileñas* (1 a year).

Museo Sorolla (Sorolla Museum): General Martínez Campos 37, 28010 Madrid; tel. (91) 3101584; fax (91) 3085925; e-mail museo@msorolla.mcu.es; internet museosorolla.mcu.es; f. 1931; permanent exhibition of some 350 of the artist's works, incl. drawings, watercolours, portraits, and his own art collns; library of 7,000 vols; Dir FLORENCIO DE SANTA-ANA Y ALVAREZ OSSORIO.

Museo Thyssen-Bornemisza: Palacio de Villahermosa, Paseo del Prado 8, 28014 Madrid; tel. (91) 3690151; fax (91) 4202780; e-mail mtb@museothyssen.org; internet www.museothyssen.org; f. 1992; paintings and sculpture from 13th–20th centuries; Man. Dir MIGUEL ÁNGEL RECIO CRESPO.

Patrimonio Nacional (National Heritage): Palacio Real, Calle Bailen, s/n, 28071 Madrid; tel. (91) 4548700; fax (91) 5426947; e-mail info@patrimonionacional.es; internet www.patrimonionacional.es; f. 1940; state instn responsible for all the museums situated in royal palaces and properties; governed by Admin. Council; Dir MIGUEL ANGEL RECIO CRESPO; publ. *Reales Sitios* (4 a year).

Subordinate Institutions:

Abadía Benedictina de la Santa Cruz del Valle de los Caídos: Carretera de Guadarrama-El Escorial, 28209 Valle de Cuelgamuros, (Madrid); tel. (91) 8905611; fax (91) 8905544; internet www.patrimonionacional.es; f. 1957; monument to the fallen, commissioned by Gen. Franco.

Monasterio de las Descalzas Reales: Plaza de las Descalzas, s/n, 28013 Madrid; tel. (91) 4548800; fax (91) 5426947; internet www.patrimonionacional.es; f. 1557; combined museum and enclosed convent; 16th- and 17th-century paintings and artefacts.

Monasterio de Santa Maria la Real de las Huelgas: Calle Los Compases, s/n, 09001 Burgos; tel. (94) 7201630; fax (94) 7279729; internet www.patrimonionacional.es; f. 1187 by Alfonso VIII.

Monasterio de Yuste: 10430 Cuacos de Yuste, (Cáceres); tel. (92) 7172197; fax (92) 7172347; internet www.patrimonionacional.es; f. 1402.

Palacio Real de Aranjuez: Plaza de Parejas, 28300 Aranjuez, (Madrid); tel. (91) 8910740; fax (91) 8921532; internet www.patrimonionacional.es; former royal palace rich in 18th-century art.

Palacio Real de El Pardo: Calle Manuel Alonso, s/n, 28048 El Pardo (Madrid); tel. (91) 3761500; fax (91) 3760452; internet www.patrimonionacional.es; f. built for Henry IV in 15th century; rebuilt for Carlos I in 1553 and enlarged in the 18th century by Sabatini; 18th-century tapestries, some by Goya.

Palacio Real de la Almudaina: Palau Reial, s/n, 07001 Palma de Mallorca, Balearic Islands; tel. (97) 1214134; fax (97) 1719145; internet www.patrimonionacional.es; built in the middle ages; royal palace; Gothic chapel of St Anne; Arab baths.

Palacio Real de La Granja de San Ildefonso: Plaza de España 17, 40100 La Granja de San Ildefonso (Segovia); tel. (92) 1470019; fax (92) 1471895; internet www.patrimonionacional.es; f. 18th century; built for Philip V; gardens and fountains; colln of furniture and artefacts from the 18th and 19th centuries; tapestry museum.

Palacio Real de Madrid: Calle Bailen, s/n, 28071 Madrid; tel. (91) 4548800; fax (91) 5426947; internet www.patrimonionacional.es; f. 18th century; rooms devoted to 16th- to 18th-century tapestries, clocks, painting and porcelain from the royal palaces and pharmacy; Royal Armoury; rooms with original 18th-century decor; colln of furniture, paintings and porcelain from the 18th and 19th centuries; library: see Libraries and Archives; archives since the 12th century.

Palacio Real de Riofrío: Bosque de Riofrío, 40420 Navas de Riofrío (Segovia); tel. (92) 1470020; fax (92) 1471895; internet www.patrimonionacional.es; built in 1752.

Real Monasterio de la Encarnación: Plaza de la Encarnación 1, 28013 Madrid; tel. (91) 4548800; fax (91) 5426947; internet www.patrimonionacional.es; f. 1611; combined museum and enclosed convent; 17th- and 18th-century paintings and sculptures; colln of 700 bronze, coral, ivory and fine timber artefacts from Spain, Germany, Italy and the Netherlands.

Real Monasterio de Santa Clara de Tordesillas: 47100 Tordesillas (Valladolid); tel. (98) 3770071; internet www.patrimonionacional.es; f. 1363.

Real Monasterio de Santa Isabel: Calle de Santa Isabel 48, 28012 Madrid; internet www.patrimonionacional.es; f. 16th century by Philip II; 17th- and 18th-century paintings.

Planetario de Madrid (Planetarium of Madrid): Avda del Planetario, 28045 Madrid; tel. (91) 4673461; fax (91) 4681154; e-mail buzon@planetmad.es; internet www.planetmad.es; f. 1986; exhibition and projection room seating 250 people; Dir ASUNCIÓN SÁNCHEZ JUSTE.

Real Jardín Botánico (Royal Botanical Garden): Plaza de Murillo 2, 28014 Madrid; tel. (91) 4203017; fax (91) 4200157; e-mail director.rjb@csic.es; internet www.rjb.csic.es; f. 1755; attached to CSIC (*q.v.*); botanical research; herbarium with more than 1m. specimens; library of 34,000 vols, 2,094 periodicals, 20,000 historical documents, 10,000 botanical drawings; Dir GONZALO NIETO FELINER; publ. *Anales* (2 a year).

Mérida

Museo Nacional de Arte Romano (National Museum of Roman Art): Calle José Ramón Mélida, s/n, 06800 Mérida Badajoz; tel. (92) 4311690; fax (92) 4302006; e-mail mnar@mnar.es; internet www.museoarteromano.mcu.es; f. 1838, present site 1986; 37,000 artefacts; Roman, Visigoth archaeology; library of 16,000 specialized vols, 695 periodicals; Dir Dr JOSÉ MARÍA ALVAREZ MARTÍNEZ; publs *Anas* (1 a year), *Cuadernos Emeritenses* (irregular), *Studia Lusitana*.

Palma de Mallorca

Museo de Mallorca: Calle Portella 5, 07001 Palma; tel. (97) 1717540; fax (97) 1710483; internet www.museudemallorca.es; f. 1961; history, ethnology, fine arts, prehistory; Dir GUILLERMO ROSSELLÓ BORDOY.

Pontevedra

Museo de Pontevedra: Calle Pasantería 2–12, 36002 Pontevedra; tel. (98) 6851455; fax (98) 6840693; internet www.museo.depo.es; f. 1927; pottery and ancient industrial and naval history of Galicia; prehistoric jewellery and jet ornaments; Spanish paintings since 15th century; library of 150,000 vols on literature, art and archaeology of Galicia, 6,000 periodicals, 500 maps; Dir Dr JOSÉ CARLOS VALLE PÉREZ; publ. *El Museo de Pontevedra* (1 a year).

Sabadell

Museu d'Art de Sabadell: Carrer Dr Puig 16, 08202 Sabadell; tel. (93) 7278555; fax (93) 7275507; e-mail mas@ajsabadell.cat; f. 1981; painting, ceramics, photography from early 19th century to 1960s; Dir JOSEP SERRANO; publ. *Arraona*.

Museu d'Història de Sabadell: Carrer Sant Antoni 13, 08201 Sabadell; tel. (93) 7278555; fax (93) 7266042; e-mail mhs@ajsabadell.es; f. 1931 as Museu de la Ciutat; present name adopted 1970; prehistoric archaeological, numismatic collections, native handicrafts; Iberico-Roman section, sections on textiles and mineralogy; Dir GENÍS RIBÉ MONGÉ; publ. *Arraona* (1 a year).

Sabiñánigo

Museo de Dibujo 'Castillo de Larrés': Apdo 25, 22612 Sabiñánigo (Huesca); tel. (97) 4482981; e-mail serrablo@serrablo.org; internet www.serrablo.org/museodibujo; f. 1986 by 'Amigos de Serrablo', a cultural asscn specializing entirely in contemporary Spanish and Spanish-American design; Pres. ALFREDO GAVÍN.

San Roque

Museo Monográfico Municipal de Carteia: Palacio de los Gobernadores, Calle Rubín de Celis 1, 11360 San Roque (Cádiz); tel. (95) 6781587; e-mail prensasanroque@airtel.net; f. 2001; explains the history of excavations in the town and the historical devt of the ancient settlement of Carteia; Dir RAFAEL CALDELA LÓPEZ.

San Sebastián

Palacio del Mar—Aquarium (Sea Museum and Aquarium): Sociedad de Oceanografía de Guipúzcoa, Plaza Jacques Cousteau 1, 20003 Donostia, San Sebastián; tel. (94) 3440099; fax (94) 3430092; e-mail sog@aquariumss.com; internet www.aquariumss.com; f. 1928; history of seafaring since 13th century, models of historical ships, portraits of navigators and local fishing tackle; oceanographic museum and marine laboratory; aquarium with Atlantic and tropical fishes; Dir CARMEN ARRAZOLA.

San Telmo Museoa: Andereño Elbira Zipitria 1, 20003 Donostia, San Sebastián; tel. (94) 3481580; fax (94) 3481581; e-mail santelmo@donostia.org; internet www.santelmomuseoa.com; f. 1902; reopened in 2011 to the public as a museum on the Basque Soc. housed in the former Dominican convent of San Telmo, built in the 16th century, and inaugurated 1932 by Alfonso XIII; library of 11,000 vols; Dir SUSANA SOTO.

Santander

Museo de Prehistoria y Arqueología de Cantabria (Prehistoric and Archaeological Museum): Avda Los Castros 65–67, 39005 Santander; tel. (94) 2207106; fax (94) 2207106; internet www.museosdecantabria.com/preh/museo.htm; f. 1941; palaeolithic to Middle Ages in Cantabria; library of 62,000 vols; Curator AMPARO LÓPEZ ORTIZ.

Santiago de Compostela

Museo das Peregrinacións (Pilgrimage Museum): San Miguel 4, 'Casa Gotica', 15704 Santiago de Compostela; tel. (98) 1581558; fax (98) 1581955; e-mail difusion.mdperegrinacions@xunta.es; internet www.mdperegrinacions.com; f. 1951, inaugurated 1965; relics and items related to St James and the Pilgrimages; medieval art and history of the 'Camino de Santiago'; library of 8,246 vols, 350 periodicals; Dir BIEITO PÉREZ OUTEIRIÑO.

Seville

Museo Arqueológico de Sevilla (Archaeological Museum of Sevilla): Plaza de América (Parque de María Luisa), s/n, 41013 Seville; tel. (95) 4786474; fax (95) 4786478; e-mail museoarqueologicosevilla.ccul@juntadeandalucia.es; internet www.juntadeandalucia.es/cultura/museos/muse; f. 1880; 60,000 exhibits; Roman statues, mosaics; incorporates municipal collns; treasures of Tarshish; Dir CONCEPCIÓN SAN MARTÍN MONTILLA.

Museo de Bellas Artes de Sevilla (Museum of Fine Arts of Sevilla): Plaza del Museo 9, 41001 Seville; tel. (95) 4786500; fax (95) 4786490; e-mail museobellasartessevilla.ccul@juntadeandalucia.es; internet www.juntadeandalucia.es/cultura/museos/mbase; f. 1835; paintings by local artists from 15th to 20th centuries; Baroque art (esp. Murillo, Zurbarán and Valdés Leal); library of 12,000 vols, 450 periodicals; Dir MARÍA DEL VALME MUÑOZ RUBIO; Curator VIRGINIA MARQUÉS.

Sitges

Museu Cau Ferrat: Calle Fonollar, s/n, 08870 Sitges; tel. (93) 8940364; fax (93) 8948529; e-mail m.sitges@diba.es; internet www.diba.cat/museuslocals/nouwebmuseus/buscar/cercador_generic.asp; f. 1933; closed for renovations from 2010; house and studio of the painter and writer Santiago Rusiñol; contains drawings and paintings by Rusiñol and his friends and contemporaries, (Casas, Picasso, Utrillo); also woodcarving, sculpture, paintings (El Greco), ceramics (since 14th century), furniture, ironwork (13th–19th centuries), glass (16th–19th centuries); Dir MARIA-NADAL SAU I GIRALT.

Soria

Museo Numantino: Paseo del Espolón 8, 42001 Soria; tel. (97) 5221397; fax (97) 5229872; f. 1916; prehistoric, ethnological, Roman and medieval archaeological collections, comprising 180,000 objects; library of 10,000 vols; Dir ELÍAS TERÉS NAVARRO.

Tarragona

Museu i Necròpolis Paleocristians:; tel. (97) 7211175; fax (97) 7252286; e-mail mnat@mnat.cat; internet www.mnat.es/cat/mnat/necr; f. 1930; objects discovered during excavation of the Roman-Christian necropolis; Dir FRANCESC TARRATS-BOU.

Museu Nacional Arqueològic de Tarragona (National Museum of Archaeology of Tarragona): Plaça del Rei 5, 43003 Tarragona; tel. (97) 7251515; fax (97) 7252286; e-mail mnat@mnat.es; internet www.mnat.es; f. 1834; archaeological, historical, local Roman exhibits; library of 12,000 vols; Dir FRANCESC TARRATS-BOU.

Toledo

Museo del Greco (El Greco Museum): Calle Samuel Leví, s/n, 45002 Toledo; tel. (92) 5224405; fax (92) 5224559; e-mail secretaria.greco@telefonica.net; f. 1911; the artist's house; contains important later works by El Greco; works from the Spanish schools of the 17th century; furniture of the 16th–17th century and ceramics from the Talaverana factory; colln of paintings by Spanish artists incl. Francisco de Zurbarán and Bartolomé Esteban Murillo; Dir ANA CARMEN LAVÍN BERDONCES.

Museo de Santa Cruz: Calle Cervantes 3, 45001 Toledo; tel. (92) 5221036; fax (92) 5225862; f. 1958; archaeology, fine arts, industrial and decorative arts; library of 13,000 vols; Dir RAFAEL GARCÍA SERRANO; publ. *Memoria del Museo de Santa Cruz* (irregular).

Affiliated Museums:

Museo Casa de Dulcinea en El Toboso: Calle Don Quijote 1, 45820 El Toboso; tel. (92) 5197288; fax (92) 5225862; f. 1967; ethnography of La Mancha area and period reconstruction in the 17th-century Casa Solariega.

Museo de Arte Contemporáneo: Calle de las Bulas, s/n, 45002 Toledo; tel. (92) 5227871; f. 1973; closed for renovation until further notice.

Museo de Cerámica 'Ruíz de Luna': Plaça de San Agustín, s/n, 45600 Talavera de la Reina; tel. and fax (92) 580-01-49; f. 1963; local ceramics.

Museo de los Concilios y de la Cultura Visigoda: Calle San Román, s/n, 45002 Toledo; tel. (92) 5227872; fax (92) 5225862; f. 1969; Visigothic art and archaeology.

Museo Taller del Moro: Calle Taller del Moro 4, 45002 Toledo; tel. (92) 5224500; fax (92) 5225862; f. 1961; Mudejar art and archaeology.

Museo Sefardi-Sinagoga del Tránsito: Calle Samuel Leví, s/n, 45002 Toledo; tel. (92) 5223665; fax (92) 5215831; e-mail museo.msefardi@mcu.es; internet www.museosefardi.net; f. 1964; Jewish synagogue built in the 14th century by Samuel Ha-Levi, treasurer to King Don Pedro I, 'The Cruel'; given to the Military Order of Calatrava in 1494 by Ferdinand and Isabella; in 18th century became church of Sta María del Tránsito; nat. monument; created Sephardic Museum 1964; archaeology, life and costumes of Sephardic Jews; library of 20,000 vols on Judaism, Hebraism, Sephardism, Museology, Restauration; Dir SANTIAGO PALOMERO PLAZA.

Valencia

Museo de Bellas Artes de Valencia (Museum of Fine Arts of Valencia): Calle de San Pío V 9, 46010 Valencia; tel. (96) 3870300; fax (96) 3870301; e-mail museobellasartesvalencia@gva.es; internet museobellasartesvalencia.gva.es; f. 1839; temporary exhibitions; more than 3,000 paintings; also sculpture, archaeology, drawing and print sections; library of 24,043 vols on art, 840 periodicals, 7,892 photographs; Dir FERNANDO BENITO DOMÉNECH.

Museo Nacional de Cerámica 'González Martí': Poeta Querol 2, 46002 Valencia; tel. (96) 3516392; fax (96) 3513512; e-mail difusion.mceramica@mcu.es; internet mnceramica.mcu.es; f. 1947; 26,200 exhibits; a nat. museum of ceramics and decorative arts, set in the Palace of the Marquis of Dos Aguas; library of 25,000 vols; Dir Dr JAUME COLL CONESA; publ. *Materiales y Documentos*.

Museu de Prehistòria de València: Corona 36, 46003 Valencia; tel. (96) 3 883565; fax (96) 3 883536; e-mail sip@dival.es; internet www.museuprehistoriavalencia.es; f. 1927; prehistoric art and culture; Roman era; Iberian culture and coin collns; Valencian archaeology; intense field work in archaeological sites; educational activities, guided tours and workshops; temporary exhibits; courses, confs and workshops; library of 60,000 vols, 1,380 periodicals; Dir HELENA BONET ROSADO; publs *Archivo de Prehistoria Levantina*, *Serie de Trabajos Varios del S.I.P.*

Valladolid

Museo Casa de Cervantes, Valladolid (Cervantes' House Museum, Valladolid): Calle del Rastro, s/n, 47001 Valladolid; tel. (98) 3308810; fax (98) 3390703; e-mail informacion@mcervantes.mcu.es; internet museocasacervantes.mcu.es; f. 1948; furniture and possessions of the writer; library of 10,000 vols; Dir AMPARO MAGDALENO DE LA CRUZ.

Museo de Valladolid (Valladolid Museum): Palacio de Fabio Nelli, Plaza de Fabio Nelli, s/n, 47003 Valladolid; tel. (98) 3351389; fax (98) 3350422; e-mail museo.valladolid@jcyl.es; f. 1879; archaeology and fine art, articles from palaeolithic times to the 18th century; library: specialized library of more than 15,000 vols, restricted access; Dir ELOISA WATTENBERG GARCÍA.

Museo Nacional Colegio de San Gregorio: Cadenas de San Gregorio 1–3, 47011 Valladolid; tel. (98) 3250375; fax (98) 3259300; e-mail museosangregorio@mcu.es; internet www.museosangregorio.mcu.es; f. 1933 as Museo Nacional de Escultura; present name adopted 2008; housed in the old Colegio de San Gregorio, since late 15th century; works by Alonso Berruguete, Juan de Juni, Gregorio Fernández, Alonso Cano, Felipe Vigarny and others; library of 20,000 vols; Dir MARÍA BOLAÑOS ATIENZA; publ. *Boletín*.

Vic

Museu Episcopal de Vic (Episcopal Museum of Vic): Plaça Bisbe Oliba 3, 08500 Vic; tel. (93) 869360; fax (93) 8869361; e-mail informacio@museuepiscopalvic.com; internet www.museuepiscopalvic.com; f. 1891; medieval arts, provincial Romanesque, Gothic precious metalwork, textiles, embroideries, liturgical vestments, forged iron, etc.; Dir MIQUEL TRESSERRAS.

Zamora

Museo de Zamora (Museum of Zamora): Palacio del Cordón, Plaza de Sta Lucía 2, 49002 Zamora; tel. (98) 0516150; fax (98) 0535064; e-mail museo.zamora@jcyl.es; internet www.museoscastillayleon.jcyl.es/museodezamora; f. 1877; housed in 16th-century palace; collns (300,000 items): palaeontology, prehistory and archaeology, fine arts, ethnography; library of 8,766 vols, 227 periodicals; Dir ROSARIO GARCÍA ROZAS.

Zaragoza

Museo de Zaragoza (Museum of Zaragoza): Plaza de los Sitios 6, 50001 Zaragoza; tel. (97) 6222181; fax (97) 6222378; e-mail museoza@aragob.es; internet www.aragob.es/edycul/patrimo/museos/zaragoza.htm; f. 1848; archaeological; prehistory, Roman, Arab, Gothic, Moorish, Romanesque and Renaissance exhibits; primitive arts and crafts, paintings from 14th–19th centuries, contemporary Aragonese artists; ethnology and ceramics sections are located at Parque Primo de Rivera; library of 31,000 vols; Dir Dr MIGUEL BELTRÁN LLORIS; publs *Boletín* (1 a year), *Guías Didácticas* (2 or 3 a year), *Catálogos Exposiciones*.

Museo Pablo Gargallo: Plaza de San Felipe 3, 50003 Zaragoza; tel. (97) 6392524; fax (97) 6395597; e-mail museogargallo-oficinas@ayto-zaragoza.es; internet www.zaragoza.es/ciudad/museos/es/gargallo; f. 1982; important colln of sculpture, designs and cartoons by Gargallo; research on his life and works, and modern art in gen.; library of 9,000 vols on Gargallo and sculpture in gen.; Dir MARÍA CRISTINA GIL IMAZ.

Universities

ASOCIACIÓN UNIVERSITARIA IBEROAMERICANA DE POSTGRADO

Colegio Arzobispo Fonseca, Calle Fonseca 4, 37002 Salamanca
Telephone: (92) 3210039
Fax: (93) 3214949
E-mail: auip@auip.org
Internet: www.auip.org

Some 100 universities offer 1,500 postgraduate courses under the aegis of the AUIP

Pres.: FRANCISCO GONZÁLEZ LODEIRO
Dir-Gen.: VICTOR CRUZ CARDONA
Deputy Dir-Gen.: FRANCISCO MARTOS PERALES.

I. E. UNIVERSIDAD

Campus de Santa Cruz la Real, 40003 Segovia
Telephone: (92) 1412410
Fax: (92) 1445593
E-mail: university@ie.edu
Internet: www.ie.es

Founded 1992
Private control
Academic year: September to June

Rector: Dr JUAN LUIS MARTÍNEZ SÁNCHEZ
Vice-Rector for Planning: Dr SAMUEL GONZÁLEZ MANCEBO
Vice-Rector for Research and Teaching Staff: SALVADOR CARMONA MORENO
Vice-Rector for Students: Dr MIGUEL LARRAÑAGA ZULUETA
Registrar: Dr ROBERTO RUIZ SALCES
Dir of Academic Org.: ANTONIO DE CASTRO CARPEÑO
Man.: IGNACIO SOTOMAYOR SAEZ
Library Dir: AMADA MARCOS BLÁZQUEZ

Library of 36,000 vols, 4,500 periodicals
Number of teachers: 190
Number of students: 1,400

DEANS

Faculty of Experimental Sciences: JESÚS A. GÓMEZ OCHOA DE ALDA
Faculty of Human, Social and Communication Sciences: SANTIAGO LÓPEZ NAVIA

MONDRAGON UNIBERTSITATEA

Loramendi 4, Apdo 23, 20500 Mondragón
Telephone: (94) 3712185
Fax: (94) 3712193
E-mail: info@mondragon.edu
Internet: www.mondragon.edu

Founded 1997
Private control
Languages of instruction: Basque, Spanish, English
Academic year: September to July

Rector: IOSU ZABALA
Vice-Rector: JOSE MARI AIZEAGA ZUBILLAGA
Registrar and Financial Dir: IDOIA PEÑACOBA ETXEBARRIA
Librarian: OBDULIA VELEZ

Library of 80,000 vols, 800 periodicals
Number of teachers: 250
Number of students: 4,000

DEANS

Faculty of Business Studies: LANDER BELOKI
Faculty of Humanities and Education: NEKANE ARRATIBEL
Higher Polytechnic School: VICENTE ATXA (Dir)

UNIVERSIDAD ALFONSO X EL SABIO

Campus de Villanueva de la Cañada, Avda Universidad 1, 28691, Madrid
Telephone: (90) 2100868
Fax: (91) 8109101
E-mail: info@uax.es
Internet: www.uax.es

Founded 1993
Academic year: October to June

Pres.: JESÚS NÚÑEZ VELÁZQUEZ

Library of 15,000 vols
Number of teachers: 1,000
Number of students: 10,000

Publications: *A x A* (art and architecture, online), *Linguax* (applied languages, online), *Revista Electrónica Biociencias* (life sciences, online), *Saberes* (law, economics and social sciences, online), *Tecnología y Desarrollo* (science, technology and environment, online)

DEANS

Faculty of Applied Languages: Dr JOAQUÍN GONZÁLEZ IBÁÑEZ
Faculty of Health Sciences: Dr ALFREDO ENTRALA BUENO
Faculty of Social Studies: Dr ANDRÉS TAGLIAVIA LÓPEZ

Polytechnic School: Dr JUAN HERRANZ ARRIBAS

UNIVERSIDAD ANTONIO DE NEBRIJA

Campus de la Berzosa, Hoyo de Manzanares, 28249 Madrid
Telephone: (91) 4521101
E-mail: informa@nebrija.es
Internet: www.nebrija.com

Founded 1995
Private control

Rector: Profa Dra PILAR VÉLEZ MELÓN
Vice-Rector for Academic Affairs: ALBERTO LÓPEZ ROSADO
Vice-Rector for Int. Rels and Registrar: JUAN CAYÓN PEÑA
Vice-Rector for Research: JUAN ANTONIO MAESTRO DE LA CUERDA

Library of 44,000 vols, 300 periodicals
Number of students: 3,500

DEANS

Faculty of Arts and Letters: PABLO ÁLVAREZ DE TOLEDO MÜLLER (Vice-Dean)
Faculty of Communications Science: FERNANDO GONZÁLEZ URBANEJA
Faculty of Social Science: CARLOS CUERVO-ARANGO MARTÍNEZ

UNIVERSIDAD AUTÓNOMA DE MADRID

Ciudad Universitaria de Cantoblanco, Carretera de Colmenar, Km 15, 28049 Madrid
Telephone: (91) 4975100
Fax: (91) 3974123
E-mail: informacion.general@uam.es
Internet: www.uam.es

Founded 1968
State control
Language of instruction: Spanish
Academic year: October to June

Rector: JOSÉ MARÍA SANZ MARTÍNEZ
Vice-Rector for Campus and Environmental Quality: MARÍA ÁNGELES ESPINOSA BAYAL
Vice-Rector for Infrastructure and Technological Devt: JOSÉ MARÍA SANZ MARTÍNEZ
Vice-Rector for Innovation and Technology: JOSÉ RAMÓN DORRONSORO IBERO
Vice-Rector for Institutional Relations and Cooperation: MARGARITA ALFARO AMIEIRO
Vice-Rector for Int. Relations: ASUNCIÓN MARTÍNEZ CEBRIÁN
Vice-Rector for Postgraduate Studies: ÁNGEL RODRÍGUEZ GARCÍA-BRAZALES
Vice-Rector for Research: RAFAEL GARESSE ALARCÓN
Vice-Rector for Students and Continuing Education: ANTONIO ÁLVAREZ-OSSORIO ALVARIÑO
Vice-Rector for Teaching and Research Staff: CARLOS GARCÍA DE LA VEGA
Vice-Rector for Undergraduate Studies: JUAN ANTONIO HUERTAS MARTÍNEZ
Vice-Rector for Univ. Extension and Outreach: VALERIA CAMPORESI
Registrar: JUAN DAMIÁN MORENO
Man.: PEDRO GARCÍA MORENO
Librarian: MIGUEL JIMÉNEZ ALEIXANDRE

Library of 840,000 vols, 18,000 periodicals
Number of teachers: 2,250
Number of students: 35,000

Publications: *Al Sur* (4 a year), *Anuario del Departamento de Filosofía* (4 a year), *Anuario del Departamento de Historia de la Filosofía* (1 a year), *Anuario del Departamento de Historia y Teoría del Arte* (1 a year), *Apuntes de la Autónoma* (irregular), *Boletín del Instituto de Ciencias de la Educación* (irregular), *Boletín Geográfico* (3 a year), *Coyuntura Trimestral* (journal of the Laurence R. Klein Institute of Economic Forecasting, 4 a year), *Cuaderno Gris* (3 a year), *Cuadernos de Prehistoria y Arqueología* (1 a year), *Edad de Oro* (1 a year), *Encuentros Multidisciplinares* (multidisciplinary research and debate, 3 a year), *Journal of Human Ecology* (irregular), *La Ecoalternativa* (4 a year), *Manuscrit. CAO* (1 a year), *Narria* (4 a year), *Revista de Cantoblanco* (12 a year), *Revista de Lengua y Literatura Catalana, Gallega y Vasca* (1 a year), *Tarbiya* (educational research and innovation, 3 a year)

DEANS

Faculty of Economics and Business Studies: ANA MARÍA LÓPEZ GARCÍA
Faculty of Law: FERNANDO MOLINA FERNÁNDEZ
Faculty of Medicine: Dr JOSÉ ANTONIO RODRÍGUEZ MONTES
Faculty of Philosophy and Letters: ANTONIO CASCÓN DORADO
Faculty of Psychology: ÁNGELA LOECHES ALONSO
Faculty of Science: ISABEL CASTRO PARGA
Faculty of Teacher Training and Education: ROSALÍA ARANDA REDRUELLO

ATTACHED CENTRES

Escuela Universitaria de Enfermería de la Comunidad de Madrid: Avda Orellana, s/n, Recinto Hospital Severo Ochoa, 28911 Leganés, (Madrid); tel. (91) 6931511; e-mail e.u.enfermeria@salud.madrid.org; internet www.eulasalle.com; f. 1948 as teaching institute; courses in educational science, health sciences and management and technology.

Escuela Universitaria de Fisioterapia de la Organización Nacional de Ciegos Españoles: Calle Nuria 42, 28034 Madrid; tel. (91) 5894500; fax (91) 5894498; e-mail euf@once.es; internet euf.once.es; Dir JAVIER SAINZ DE MURIETA Y RODEYRO.

La Salle Centro Universitario: Calle La Salle 10, 28023 Madrid; tel. (91) 7401980; fax (91) 3571730; e-mail sia@lasallecampus.es; internet www.eulasalle.com; f. 1948 as teaching institute; courses in educational science, health sciences and management and technology.

UNIVERSIDAD CAMILO JOSÉ CELA

Castillo de Alarcón 49, Villafranca del Castillo Urb, 28692 Madrid
Telephone: (91) 8153131
Fax: (91) 8153130
E-mail: info@ucjc.edu
Internet: www.ucjc.edu

Founded 2000
Private control

Rector: Dr RAFAEL CORTÉS ELVIRA
Vice-Rector for Academic Affairs and Teaching: ENRIQUE FERNÁNDEZ REDONDO
Vice-Rector for Research and Graduate Affairs
Registrar: JOSÉ LUIS DELSO MARTÍNEZ-TREVIJANO
Dir-Gen.: CONCHA CANOYRA
Library Dir: BELÉN PALOMERO
Number of students: 5,000

Publication: *Revista Edupsykhé* (1 a year)

DEANS

Faculty of Communications: JULIO CÉSAR HERRERO
Faculty of Health Sciences: MIGUEL ÁNGEL PÉREZ NIETO
Faculty of Law and Economics: JESÚS GRACIA SANZ
Faculty of Social Sciences and Education: ESTHER ROBLES SASTRE

UNIVERSIDAD CARLOS III DE MADRID

Calle Madrid 126, 28903 Getafe, Madrid
Telephone: (91) 6246000
Internet: www.uc3m.es

Founded 1989
State control
Language of instruction: Spanish, English
Academic year: September to June

Rector: Prof. DANIEL PEÑA SANCHEZ DE RIVERA
Vice-Rector of Communication, Culture and Sports, and Continuing Education: MONTSERRAT IGLESIAS SANTOS
Vice-Rector of Equality and Cooperation: PILAR AZCÁRATE AGUILAR-AMAT
Vice-Rector of Graduate Programmes and Quality: CARMEN VÁZQUEZ GARCÍA
Vice-Rector of Infrastructure and Environmental Matters: PEDRO ISASI VIÑUELA
Vice-Rector of Int. Relations: ÁLVARO ESCRIBANO SÁEZ
Vice-Rector of Research: CARLOS BALAGUER BERNALDO DE QUIRÓS
Vice-Rector of Student Affairs and Residence Halls: HENAR MIGUÉLEZ GARRIDO
Vice-Rector of Teaching Staff and Depts: JUAN JOSÉ ROMO URROZ
Vice-Rector of the Colmenarejo Campus: MIKEL TAPIA TORRES
Vice-Rector of Undergraduate Studies: ISABEL GUTIÉRREZ CALDERÓN
Registrar: JESÚS RAFAEL MERCADER UGUINA
Man.: JUAN MANUEL MORENO ÁLVAREZ
Library Dir: MARGARITA TALADRIZ MÁS

Number of teachers: 1,666
Number of students: 17,929

Publications: *Boletín Inflación y Análisis Macroeconómico (BIAM)*, *Bulletin EU & US Inflation and Macroeconomic analysis (BIMA)*, *Cuadernos del Instituto Antonio de Nebrija de estudios sobre la Universidad (CIAN)*, *Derechos y libertades : Revista del Instituto Bartolomé de las Casas*, *Forinf@ Online. Revista Iberoamericana Sobre Servicios de Información*, *Litterae: Cuadernos Sobre Cultura Escrita*, *Revista de Historia Económica—Journal of Iberian and Latin American Economic History*, *Revista de Historiografía*, *Semanal 3*, *Universitas: revista de filosofía, derecho y política*

DEANS

Faculty of Social Sciences and Law: Prof. MANUEL ÁNGEL BERMEJO CASTRILLO
Higher Polytechnical School: Prof. EMILIO OLÍAS RUIZ
School of Humanities, Communications and Documentation: JOSÉ MANUEL PALACIO ARRANZ

ATTACHED INSTITUTES

Instituto Alonso Martínez de Justicia y Litigación ('Alonso Martinez' Institute of Justice and Litigation): Calle Madrid 126, 28903 Getafe, Madrid; tel. (91) 6249718; e-mail iam@listserv.uc3m.es; internet www.turan.uc3m.es/uc3m/inst/amj/home.htm; Dir VÍCTOR MORENO CATENA.

Instituto Antonio de Nebrija de Estudios sobre la Universidad ('Antonio de Nebrija' Institute of University Studies): Calle Madrid 126, Despacho 11.0.10, 28903 Getafe, Madrid; tel. (91) 6249797; fax (91) 6249517; e-mail anebrija@der-pu.uc3m.es; internet turan.uc3m.es/uc3m/inst/an/anebrija.html; Dir Profa Dra ADELA MORA CAÑADA.

Instituto Agustín Millares de Documentación ('Agustin Millares' Institute for Documentation and Information Management): Calle Madrid 126, Edif. 14, Oficina 14.2.52, 28903 Getafe, Madrid; tel. (91) 6249252; fax

(91) 6249212; e-mail instituto-millares@bib.uc3m.es; internet iamc.uc3m.es; Dir Profa. Dra MERCEDES CARIDAD SEBASTIÁN.

Instituto 'Conde de Campomanes' de Iniciativas Empresariales y Empresa Familiar ('Conde de Campomanes' Institute of Entrepreneurship and Family Business): Calle Madrid 126, 28903 Getafe, Madrid; tel. (91) 6249345; fax (91) 6245707; e-mail organizaciondeempresas@uc3m.es; internet www.uc3m.es/portal/page/portal/instituto_iniciativas_emp_empresa_familiar/conde_-camp_institute; Dir ZULIMA FERNÁNDEZ RODRÍGUEZ.

Instituto de Cultura y Tecnología 'Miguel de Unamuno' ('Miguel de Unamuno' Institute of Culture and Technology): Calle Madrid 126, Edif. Concepción Arena, 28903 Getafe, Madrid; tel. (91) 6249258; fax (91) 6249212; e-mail buforn@pa.uc3m.es; internet turan.uc3m.es/uc3m/inst/mu/dpmu.html; Dir Prof. Dr ANTONIO RODRÍGUEZ DE LAS HERAS.

Instituto de Derechos Humanos 'Bartolomé de las Casas' ('Bartolomé de las Casas' Institute of Human Rights): Calle Madrid 126, Despacho 11.1.03. CP, 28903 Getafe, Madrid; tel. (91) 6249834; fax (91) 6248923; e-mail idhbc@pa.uc3m.es; internet turan.uc3m.es/uc3m/inst/bc; Dir Prof. Dr RAFAEL DE ASIS ROIG.

Instituto de Derecho y Economía (Institute of Law and Economics): Calle Madrid 126, 28903 Getafe, Madrid; tel. (91) 6249846; fax (91) 6249802; e-mail iudec@eco.uc3m.es; internet turan.uc3m.es/uc3m/inst/de; Dir DAVID CAMINO BLASCO.

Instituto de Estudios Internacionales y Europeos 'Francisco de Vitoria' ('Francisco de Vitoria' Institute of International and European Studies): Calle Madrid 126, 28903 Getafe, Madrid; tel. (91) 6249843; fax (91) 6249517; e-mail fvitoria@der-pu.uc3m.es; internet turan.uc3m.es/uc3m/inst/fv/dpfv.html; Dir Prof. Dr FERNANDO MARIÑO MENÉNDEZ.

Instituto de Historiografía 'Julio Caro Baroja' (The 'Julio Caro Baroja' Institute for Histography): Calle Madrid 126, 28903 Getafe, Madrid; e-mail ijcarobaro@uc3m.es; internet turan.uc3m.es/uc3m/inst/jcb; Dir JAIME ALVAR EZQUERRA.

Instituto de Política y Gobernanza 'Fermín Caballero' ('Fermin Caballero' Institute of Politics and Government): Calle Madrid 126, 28903 Getafe, Madrid; tel. (91) 6245728; fax (91) 6245848; e-mail ipoliticagobernanza@uc3m.es; internet www.uc3m.es/portal/page/portal/inst_pol_gob_fermin_caballero; Dir ANTONIO NATERA PERAL.

Instituto de Público Derecho Comparado ('Manuel García Pelayo' Institute of Comparative Public Law): Calle Madrid 126, Despacho 11.07, 28903 Getafe, Madrid; tel. (91) 6249714; fax (91) 6249517; e-mail imgp@der-pu.uc3m.es; internet turan.uc3m.es/uc3m/inst/mgp/portada.htm; Dir Prof. Dr MIGUEL REVENGA SÁNCHEZ.

Instituto de Seguridad de los Vehículos Automóviles (Institute of Automotive Vehicle Safety): Avda de la Universidad 30, Edif. Agustín de Betancourt, Despacho 1.1.C.05, 28911 Leganés, Madrid; tel. (91) 6249460; e-mail celtia@pa.uc3m.es; internet turan.uc3m.es/uc3m/inst/isva/home.htm; Dir Prof. Dr VICENTE DÍAZ LÓPEZ.

Instituto de Seguridad Social 'Juan Luis Vives' ('Juan Luis Vives' Institute of Social Security): Calle Madrid 126, Edif. Luis Vives, Despacho 11.07, 28903 Getafe, Madrid; tel. (91) 6249371; fax (91) 6249517; e-mail ijlv@pa.uc3m.es; internet turan.uc3m.es/uc3m/inst/iuss/dpiuss.html; Dir Prof. Dr SANTIAGO GONZÁLEZ ORTEGA.

Instituto 'Flores de Lemus' ('Flores de Lemus' Institute of Advanced Studies in Economics): Calle Madrid 126, Laboratorio Predicción y Análisis Macroeconómico, 28903 Getafe, Madrid; tel. (91) 6249889; fax (91) 6249305; e-mail laborat@est-econ.uc3m.es; internet turan.uc3m.es/uc3m/inst/fl; Dir Prof. Dr ANTONI ESPASA TERRADES.

Instituto Interuniversitario para la Comunicación Cultural (Interuniversity Institute for Cultural Communication): Calle Madrid 126, Despacho 15.1.5.9, 28903 Getafe, Madrid; tel. (91) 6245781; fax (91) 6249517; e-mail icultura@pa.uc3m.es; internet turan.uc3m.es/uc3m/inst/iudc; Dir Prof. Dr JESÚS PRIETO DE PEDRO.

Instituto 'Juan Velazquez de Velasco' de Investigación en inteligencia para la Seguridad y la Defensa ('Juan Velazquez de Velasco' Institute for Research and Intelligence for Security and Defence): Avda de la Universidad Carlos III 22, Edif. Miguel de Unamuno, 1.2.B10, 28270 Colmenarejo, Madrid; tel. (91) 8561275; fax (91) 6249212; e-mail institutodeinteligencia@uc3m.es; internet www.institutodeinteligencia.uc3m.es; Dir DIEGO NAVARRO BONILLA.

Instituto 'Laureano Figuerola' de Historia Económica e Instituciones ('Laureano Figueroa' Institute of Economic History and Institutions): Calle Madrid 126, 28903 Getafe, Madrid; tel. (91) 6249620; fax (91) 6249574; e-mail laureano_figuerola@uc3m.es; internet turan.uc3m.es/uc3m/inst/lf; Dir JUAN CARMONA PIDAL.

Instituto 'Lucio Anneo Séneca' de Estudios Clásicos sobre la Sociedad y la Política ('Lucio Anneo Seneca' Institute for Classic Studies on Society and Politics): Calle Madrid 133, Edif. 17 Ortega y Gasset, Despacho 17.02.43, 28903 Getafe, Madrid; tel. (91) 6245868; fax (91) 6249212; e-mail seneca@hum.uc3m.es; internet turan.uc3m.es/uc3m/inst/ls/home.htm; Dir FRANCISCO LISI BERETERBIDE.

Instituto 'Pascual Madoz' del Territorio, Urbanismo y Medio Ambiente ('Pascual Madoz' Institute of Territorial, Urban and Environmental Studies): Calle Madrid 126, Edif. Luis Vives, 28903 Getafe, Madrid; tel. (91) 6249838; fax (91) 6249212; e-mail cruiz@pa.uc3m.es; internet turan.uc3m.es/uc3m/inst/pm/dppm.html; Dir Prof. Dr LUCIANO JOSÉ PAREJO ALFONSO.

Instituto sobre Desarrollo Empresarial 'Carmen Vidal Ballester' ('Carmen Vidal Ballester' Institute of Business Development): internet turan.uc3m.es/uc3m/inst/cvb.

Instituto Tecnológico de Química y Materiales 'Álvaro Alonso Barba' ('Álvaro Alonso Barba' Technological Institute of Chemistry and Materials): Avda de la Universidad 30, Edif. Agustín de Betancourt, 28911 Leganés, Madrid; tel. (91) 6249990; e-mail fvelasco@ing.uc3m.es; internet turan.uc3m.es/uc3m/inst/aab/principal.html; Dir Prof. Dr FRANCISCO JAVIER VELASCO LÓPEZ.

Instituto Universitario 'Pedro Juan de Lastanosa' de Desarrollo Tecnológico y Promoción de la Innovación ('Pedro Juan de Lastanosa' Institute of Technological Development and the Promotion of Innovation): Avda de la Universidad 30, 28911 Leganés, Madrid; e-mail lastanosa@uc3m.es; internet turan.uc3m.es/uc3m/inst/pl; Dir Prof. Dr FERNANDO LÓPEZ MARTÍNEZ.

UNIVERSIDAD CEU CARDENAL HERRERA

Edificio Seminario, Avda Seminario s/n, 46113 Moncada (Valencia)
Telephone: (96) 1369000
Fax: (96) 1395272
E-mail: informa@uch.ceu.es
Internet: www.uch.ceu.es

Founded 1999
Private control

Rector: JOSÉ MARÍA DÍAZ Y PÉREZ DE LA LASTRA
Vice-Rector for Academic Affairs and Teaching Staff: FRANCISCO BOSCH MORELL
Vice-Rector for Centre at Elche: CÉSAR CASIMIRO ELENA
Vice-Rector for Institutional Relations: Dr PILAR PARICIO ESTEBAN
Vice-Rector for Research: JUAN MANUEL CORPA ARENAS
Vice-Rector for Strategic Action Plan Coordination: HIGINIO MARÍN PEDREÑO
Vice-Rector for Student Affairs and Univ. Extension: RAFAEL FAYOS FEBRER
Registrar: ROSA VISIEDO CLAVEROL
Man.: BARTOLOMÉ SERRA MARQUÉS
Library Dir: ELENA SAURÍ RODRIGO

Library of 90,000 vols, 2,019 periodicals

DEANS

Faculty of Communication Science: ELIAS DURÁN DE PORRAS
Faculty of Health Sciences: FRANCISCO JAVIER ROMERO GÓMEZ
Faculty of Law, Business and Politics: ROSA PASCUAL SERRATS (acting)
Faculty of Veterinary Science: SANTIAGO VEGA GARCÍA

ATTACHED SCHOOL

San Pablo Business School: Palacio de Colomina, Calle Almudín 1, 46003 Valencia; tel. (96) 3156306; fax (96) 3918684; e-mail env@env.ceu.es; internet www.env.ceu.es; Dir CARMEN MARCILLA CUBELLS.

UNIVERSIDAD CEU SAN PABLO

Julián Romea 23, 28003 Madrid
Telephone: (91) 4566300
E-mail: ceu.sec.vrrii@ceu.es
Internet: www.uspceu.com

Founded 1993
Private control
Languages of instruction: Spanish, English
Academic year: September to June

Rector: RAFAEL SÁNCHEZ SAUS
Vice-Rector for Academic and Graduate Affairs: AGUSTÍN PROBANZA LOBO
Vice-Rector for Int. Relations: ALFONSO MARTÍNEZ-ECHEVARRÍA Y GARCÍA DE DUEÑAS
Vice-Rector for Research: ELENA POSTIGO SOLANA
Vice-Rector for Student Affairs: CARMEN FERNÁNDEZ DE LA CIGOÑA CANTERO
Vice-Rector for Teaching Staff: MANUEL ALEJANDRO RODRÍGUEZ DE LA PEÑA
Registrar: MARTA VILLAR EZCURRA
Man.: EUGENIO UBIETA BRAVO
Library Dir: JOSÉ MORILLO-VELARDE SERRANO

Library of 230,000 vols
Number of teachers: 923
Number of students: 7,998

DEANS

Faculty of Business and Economics: Dra CRISTINA ELORZA ARANZÁBAL
Faculty of Humanities and Communication Sciences: Dr JOSÉ FRANCISCO SERRANO OCEJA
Faculty of Law: Dr JUAN MANUEL BLANCH NOUGUÉS
Faculty of Medicine: Dra INMACULADA CASTILLA DE CORTÁZAR LARREA

Faculty of Pharmacy: BEATRIZ DE PASCUAL-TERESA FERNÁNDEZ
Higher Polytechnic School: FELIX HERNANDO MANSILLA (Dir)

UNIVERSIDAD COMPLUTENSE DE MADRID

Ciudad Universitaria, Avda Seneca 2, 28040 Madrid
Telephone: (91) 4520400
Fax: (91) 3943400
E-mail: infocom@ucm.es
Internet: www.ucm.es

Founded 1508

Rector: Prof. CARLOS BERZOSA ALONSO-MARTÍNEZ
Vice-Rector for Academic Policy and Teaching Staff: CARLOS ANDRADAS HERANZ
Vice-Rector for Aranjuez Campus Org. and Integration: MERCEDES ELICES LÓPEZ
Vice-Rector for Culture and Sport: JUAN MANUEL ÁLVAREZ JUNCO
Vice-Rector for Doctorate and Diploma Studies: MANUEL RODRÍGUEZ SÁNCHEZ
Vice-Rector for Depts and Centres: MARÍA JESÚS SUÁREZ GARCÍA
Vice-Rector for Devt and Teaching Quality: MATILDE AZCÁRATE LUXÁN
Vice-Rector for Economic Affairs: MARÍA DEL CARMEN NOVERTO LABORDA
Vice-Rector for European Higher Education Convergence: COVADONGA LÓPEZ ALONSO
Vice-Rector for Information and Communication Technology: MARÍA DEL CARMEN FERNÁNDEZ CHAMIZO
Vice-Rector for Institutional Relations and Cooperation: RAFAEL HERNÁNDEZ TRISTÁN
Vice-Rector for Int. Relations: LUCILA GONZÁLEZ PAZOS
Vice-Rector for Research and Science Policy: CARMEN ACEBAL SARABIA
Vice-Rector for Student Affairs: MARGARITA BARÁNANO CID
Registrar: JULIO VICTOR GONZÁLEZ GARCÍA
Man.: FRANCISCO JAVIER SEVILLANO MARTÍN
Library Dir: JOSÉ ANTONIO MAGÁN WALS
Library: see under Libraries and Archives
Number of teachers: 6,206
Number of students: 75,601
Publications: *Memoria de la UCM*, *Gaceta Complutense*

DEANS

Faculty of Biological Sciences: ANTONIO TORMO GARRIDO
Faculty of Chemical Sciences: REYES JIMÉNEZ APARICIO
Faculty of Computer Science: DANIEL MOZOS MUÑOZ
Faculty of Dentistry: MARIANO SANZ ALONSO
Faculty of Economics and Business: LUIS PERDICES DE BLAS
Faculty of Education: MARÍA JOSÉ FERNÁNDEZ DÍAZ
Faculty of Fine Arts: JOSU LARRAÑAGA ALTUNA
Faculty of Geography and History: LUIS ENRIQUE OTERO CARVAJAL
Faculty of Geological Sciences: EUMENIO ANCOCHEA SOTO
Faculty of Information Science: LUIS FERNANDO RAMOS SIMÓN
Faculty of Law: RAÚL LEOPOLDO CANOSA USERA
Faculty of Mathematics: FRANCISCO JAVIER MONTERO DE JUAN
Faculty of Medicine: JOSÉ LUIS ÁLVAREZ-SALA WALTHER
Faculty of Pharmacy: RAFAEL LOZANO FERNÁNDEZ
Faculty of Physical Sciences: MARÍA LUISA LUCÍA MULAS
Faculty of Philology: DÁMASO LÓPEZ GARCÍA
Faculty of Philosophy: RAFAEL VALERIANO ORDEN JIMÉNEZ
Faculty of Politics and Sociology: HERIBERTO CAIRO CAROU
Faculty of Psychology: CARLOS GALLEGO LÓPEZ
Faculty of Veterinary Science: JOAQUÍN GOYACHE GOÑI

DIRECTORS

University School of Business Studies: MIGUEL ÁNGEL SASTRE CASTILLO
University School of Nursing, Physiotherapy and Podiatry: ENRIQUE PACHECO DEL CERRO
University School of Optics: FRANCISCO JAVIER ALDA SERRANO
University School of Social Work: ANDRÉS ARIAS ASTRAY
University School of Statistics: CARMEN NIETO ZAYAS

ATTACHED INSTITUTES

Complutense Institute of Administrative Science: Facultad de Ciencias Políticas y Sociología, Departamento de Derecho Aministrativo II, 3°, Martillo 5°, Campus de Somosaguas, 28223 Pozuelo de Alarcón (Madrid); tel. (91) 3942893; fax (91) 3942620; Dir JOSÉ VICENTE GÓMEZ RIVAS.

Complutense Institute of Economic Analysis: Facultad de Ciencias Económicas y Empresariales, Pabellón prefabricado, 1°, ala Norte, Campus de Somosaguas, 28223 Pozuelo de Alarcón (Madrid); tel. (91) 3942611; fax (91) 3942613; e-mail icaesec@ccee.ucm.es; internet www.ucm.es/icae; Dir ANTONIO ABADÍA CASELLES.

Complutense Institute of Industrial and Financial Analysis: Facultad de Ciencias Económicas y Empresariales, Pabellón Central, 1°, Campus de Somosaguas, 28223 Pozuelo de Alarcón (Madrid); tel. and fax (91) 3942456; e-mail joost@ccee.ucm.es; internet www.ucm.es/bucm/cee/iaif; Dir MIKEL BUESA BLANCO.

Complutense Institute of Morphofunctional and Sport Sciences: Facultad de Medicina, Pabellón 6, Plantas Baja, Ciudad Universitaria, 28040 Madrid; tel. (91) 3941339; fax (91) 3941342; Dir JOSÉ RAMÓN MÉRIDA VELASCO.

Higher Centre for Studies on Management, Analysis and Evaluation: Finca Mas Ferré, Edificio B, Campus de Somosaguas, 28223 Pozuelo de Alarcón (Madrid); tel. (91) 3942958; fax (91) 3942956; e-mail csegae05@cseg.ucm.es; internet www.ucm.es/info/csegae; Dir JUAN GÓMEZ CASTAÑEDA.

Institute of Bromatology and Nutrition: Facultad de Farmacia, 2°, Ciudad Universitaria, 28040 Madrid; tel. (91) 3941799; fax (91) 3941732; Dir ESPERANZA TORIJA ISASA.

Institute of Education: Calle Santísima Trinidad 37, 28010 Madrid; tel. (91) 3946707; fax (91)3946695; e-mail captutor@edu.ucm.es; internet www.ice.ucm.es; Dir MARÍA DEL CARMEN CHAMORRO PLAZA.

Institute of Environmental Science: Manuel Bartolomé Cossio, s/n, 1°, 28040 Madrid; tel. and fax (91) 5491075; e-mail lopezal@pdi.ucm.es; internet www.ucm.es/info/iuca; Dir ALEJANDRO LÓPEZ LÓPEZ.

Institute of Meat Science and Technology: Facultad de Veterinaria, 2°, Ciudad Universitaria, 28040 Madrid; tel. (91) 3943749; fax (91) 3943743; e-mail icamber@vet.ucm.es; Dir ISABEL CAMBERO RODRÍGUEZ.

Instituto Universitario de Investigación Ortega y Gasset (Ortega y Gasset University Research Institute): see under Learned Societies—Education.

UNIVERSIDAD DE ALCALÁ

Plaza de San Diego, s/n, 28801 Alcalá de Henares (Madrid)
Telephone: (91) 8854000
Fax: (91) 8854095
E-mail: ciu@uah.es
Internet: www.uah.es
Founded 1977
State control
Language of instruction: Spanish
Academic year: September to June

Rector: FERNANDO GALVÁN REULA
Vice-Rector for Academic Organization and Teaching Staff: JOSÉ VICENTE SAZ PÉREZ
Vice-Rector for Coordination and Communication: JOSÉ SANTIAGO FERNÁNDEZ VÁZQUEZ
Vice-Rector for Guadalajara Campus: NAZARETH PÉREZ DE CASTRO
Vice-Rector for Innovation and New Technology: JOSÉ ANTONIO GUTIÉRREZ DE MESA
Vice-Rector for Int. Relations: ELENA LÓPEZ DÍAZ-DELGADO
Vice-Rector for Postgraduate and Continuing Education: JUAN RAMÓN VELASCO PÉREZ
Vice-Rector for Research: MARÍA LUISA MARINA ALEGRE
Vice-Rector for Students and Sports: CARMELO PÉREZ GARCÍA
Vice-Rector for Teaching Quality and Innovation: LEONOR MARGALEF GARCÍA
Vice-Rector for Univ. Extension and Institutional Relations: JAVIER RIVERA BLANCO
Registrar: MIGUEL RODRÍGUEZ BLANCO
Gen. Man.: RUBÉN GARRIDO YSERTE
Library Dir: CARMEN FERNÁNDEZ-GALIANO PEYROLÓN

Number of teachers: 1,762 (947 full-time, 815 part-time)
Number of students: 28,909

Publications: *Barataria*, *Cairón*, *Encuentro*, *Estudios de Historia Económica y Social de América*, *Henares*, *Idagación*, *Las Comarcas Agrarias de España*, *Polis*, *Quodlibelt*, *Quórum Revista de Pensamiento Iberoamericano*, *Reale*, *Reden*, *Revista*, *Signo*, *Teatre*

DEANS

Faculty of Biology: CARMEN BARTOLOMÉ ESTEBAN
Faculty of Chemistry: MELIA RODRIGO LÓPEZ
Faculty of Documentation: M. PILAR LACASA DÍAZ
Faculty of Economics and Business: EMMA CASTELLÓ TALIANI
Faculty of Environmental Sciences: ROSA VICENTE LAPUENTE
Faculty of Law: ALFONSO CARLOS GARCÍA-MONCÓ MARTÍNEZ
Faculty of Medicine: M. JULIA BUJÁN VARELA
Faculty of Pharmacy: JULIO ÁLVAREZ-BUILLA GÓMEZ
Faculty of Philosophy and Arts: JOSÉ IGNACIO RUIZ RODRÍGUEZ

UNIVERSIDAD DE ALICANTE

Carretera San Vicente del Raspeig, s/n, 03690 Alicante
Telephone: (96) 5903400
Fax: (96) 5903464
E-mail: informacio@ua.es
Internet: www.ua.es
Founded 1979
State control
Languages of instruction: Spanish, Valenciano
Academic year: October to July

Pres.: Dr IGNACIO JIMÉNEZ RANEDA
Vice-Pres. for Academic Org. and Teaching Staff: Dr JESÚS PRADELLS NADAL
Vice-Pres. for Economic Planning: Dr MARÍA BEGOÑA SUBIZA MARTINEZ

Vice-Pres. for Extracurricular Activities: Dra Josefina Bueno Alonso
Vice-Pres. for Infrastructure, Space Management and Environment: Dr Vicente Montiel Leguey
Vice-Pres. for Institutional Relations: Dr Aránzazu Calzada González
Vice-Pres. for Int. Relations and Cooperation: Dr María Begoña San Miguel del Hoyo
Vice-Pres. for Research, Devt and Innovation: Dr Manuel Palomar Sanz
Vice-Pres. for Strategical Planning and Quality: Dra Cecilia Gómez Lucas
Vice-Pres. for Students: Dr José Vicente Cabezuelo Pliego
Vice-Pres. for Technology and Educational Innovation: Dr Faraón Llorens Largo
Registrar: Nuria Fernandez Perez
Man.: Álvaro A. Berenguer Berenguer
Library Dir: Remedios Blanes

Number of teachers: 1,600
Number of students: 30,000

Publication: *Anales* (all faculties)

DEANS

Faculty of Arts: Jorge Olcina Cantos
Faculty of Economics and Business Administration: Juan Llopis Taverner
Faculty of Education: María Ángles Martinez Ruiz
Faculty of Law: África García Moreno
Faculty of Sciences: Nuria Grané Teruel

DIRECTORS

Polytechnic University College: Fernando Llopis Pascual
University College of Nursing: Ana Laguna Pérez

UNIVERSIDAD DE ALMERÍA

Ctra Sacramento, s/n, La Cañada de San Urbano, 04120 Almería
Telephone: (95) 0015000
E-mail: aagg@ual.es
Internet: www.ual.es

Founded 1993
State control

Rector: Pedro Roque Molina García
Vice-Rector for Academic Org. and Teaching Staff: José Juan Carrión Martínez
Vice-Rector for Culture, Sport and Univ. Extension: José Antonio Guerrero Villalba
Vice-Rector for Graduate Affairs and Continuing Education: María Trinidad Angosto Trillo
Vice-Rector for Information and Communication Technology: Manuel Berenguel Soria
Vice-Rector for Infrastructure and Campus Sustainability: Juan Francisco Pérez Cano
Vice-Rector for Int. Relations and Devt Cooperation: María Sagrario Salaberri Ramiro
Vice-Rector for Planning, Quality and Social Participation: Luís Francisco Fernández-Revuelta Pérez
Vice-Rector for Research, Devt and Innovation: José Luís Martínez Vidal
Vice-Rector for Students and Employment: Rafael Quirosa-Cheyrouze Muñoz
Registrar: María Luisa Trinidad García
Man.: Antonio Miguel Posadas Chinchilla
Library Dir: Encarnación Fuentes Melero

Publications: *Nimbus* (climatology and meteorology, 2 a year), *Odisea* (English studies, 1 a year)

DEANS

Faculty of Economics and Business: José Joaquín Céspedes Lorente
Faculty of Education: Juan Fernández Sierra
Faculty of Experimental Sciences: Enrique de Amo Artero
Faculty of Health Sciences: Genoveva Granados Gámez
Faculty of Humanities: Manuel López Muñoz
Faculty of Law: Fernando Fernández Marín
Faculty of Psychology: Juan García García
Higher Technical School of Engineering: Francisco Javier Lozano Cantero (Dir)

UNIVERSIDAD DE BURGOS

Hospital del Rey, s/n, 09001 Burgos
Telephone and fax (94) 7258736
E-mail: intl@ubu.es
Internet: www.ubu.es

Founded 1994

Rector: Alfonso Murillo Villar
Vice-Rector for Academic Affairs: Manuel Pérez Mateos
Vice-Rector for Finance, Planning and Technological Innovation: José Luis Peña Alonso
Vice-Rector for Infrastructure: Jesús Ángel Meneses Villagrá
Vice-Rector for Int. Relations and Cooperation: Inés Praga Terente
Vice-Rector for Quality and Accreditation: Arázazu Mendía Jalón
Vice-Rector for Research: Jordi Rovira Carballido
Vice-Rector for Student Affairs, Employment and Univ. Extension: René Jesús Payo Hernanz
Registrar: José María García-Moreno Gonzalo
Man.: Enrique de Simón García-Vicente
Library Dir: Fernando Martín Rodríguez

Library of 100,000 vols, 1,500 periodicals
Number of teachers: 700
Number of students: 9,000

DEANS

Faculty of Economics and Business: María Begoña Prieto Moreno
Faculty of Humanities and Education: Raquel de la Fuente Anuncibay
Faculty of Law: Amable Corcuera Torres
Faculty of Sciences: José Miguel García Pérez

UNIVERSIDAD DE CÁDIZ

Calle Ancha 16, 11001 Cádiz
Telephone: (956) 015000
E-mail: jose.palao@uca.es
Internet: www.uca.es

Founded 1979
Academic year: October to July

Rector: Diego Sales Márquez
Deputy Rector: Francisco Alvarez González
Vice-Rector for Bahía de Algeciras Campus: Francisco Trujillo Espinosa
Vice-Rector for Graduate and Continuing Education: María Luisa González de Canales García
Vice-Rector for Information Technology and Educational Innovation: Eduardo Blanco Ollero
Vice-Rector for Int. Relations and Cooperation: Alejandro del Valle Gálvez
Vice-Rector for Planning and Quality: José María Rodríguez-Izquierdo Gil
Vice-Rector for Research, Technological Devt and Innovation: Francisco Antonio Macías Domínguez
Vice-Rector for Students: David Almorza Gomar
Vice-Rector for Teaching and Academic Management: María José Rodríguez Mesa
Vice-Rector for Univ. Extension: Marieta Cantos Casenave
Sec.-Gen.: Ana María Rodríguez Tirado
Man.: Antonio Vadillo Iglesias (acting)
Library Dir: Miguel Duarte Barrionuevo (acting)

Number of teachers: 1,052
Number of students: 18,202

DEANS

Faculty of Economics and Business: Fernando Martín Alcázar
Faculty of Educational Science: José María Mariscal Chicano
Faculty of Labour Sciences: Francisca Fuentes Rodríguez
Faculty of Law: Rocío Domínguez Bartolomé
Faculty of Marine and Environmental Sciences: Rafael Mañanes Salinas
Faculty of Medicine: María Felicidad Rodríguez Sánchez
Faculty of Nautical Science: Juan Moreno Gutiérrez
Faculty of Nursing: Ángeles Martelo Baro
Faculty of Philosophy and Letters: Manuel Arcila Garrido
Faculty of Science: Manuel García Basallote

DIRECTORS

Higher Polytechnic School: Ignacio Turias Domínguez
School of Engineering: Mariano Marcos Barcena
School of Naval and Oceanic Engineering: Francisco José Pacheco Romero
School of Physical Education and Sport Medicine: Manuel Rosety Plaza

UNIVERSIDAD DE CANTABRIA

Avda de los Castros, s/n, 39005 Santander
Telephone: (94) 2201500
Fax: (94) 2201103
E-mail: informacion.general@unican.es
Internet: www.unican.es

Founded 1972 as Universidad de Santander
State control
Language of instruction: Spanish
Academic year: September to July

Rector: Federico Gutiérrez-Solana Salcedo
Deputy Rector for Governance, Coordination and Planning: José Manuel Revuelta Soba
Vice-Rector for Academic Affairs: Concepción López Fernández
Vice-Rector for Coordination of the Campus of Excellence: Gonzalo Capellán de Miguel
Vice-Rector for Educational Quality and Innovation: José Luis Ramírez Sádaba
Vice-Rector for Int. Relations: Miguel Ángel Serna Oliveira
Vice-Rector for Knowledge Dissemination and Social Participation: José Carlos Gómez Sal
Vice-Rector for Research and Knowledge Transfer: José Carlos Gómez Sal
Vice-Rector for Student Affairs: Emilio Eguía López
Vice-Rector for Teaching: Fernando Cañizal Berini
Registrar: Luis Gaspar Vega Argüelles
Man.: Enrique Alonso Díaz
Sec.-Gen.: Luis Gaspar Vega Argüelles
Library Dir: María Jesús Sáiz

Library of 399,372 vols, 7,036 online magazines, 4,034 electronic books, 23,764 electronic magazines
Number of teachers: 1,218
Number of students: 12,489

DEANS

Faculty of Economics and Business Studies: BEGOÑA TORRE OLMO
Faculty of Education: JOSÉ MANUEL OSORO SIERRA
Faculty of Humanities: FIDEL GÓMEZ OCHOA
Faculty of Law: JUAN BARÓ PAZOS
Faculty of Medicine: FRANCISCO JAVIER LLORCA DÍAZ
Faculty of Sciences: ERNESTO ANABITARTE CANO

UNIVERSIDAD DE CASTILLA-LA MANCHA

Calle Altagracia 50, 13071 Ciudad Real
Telephone: (902) 204100
Fax: (902) 204130
E-mail: informacion@uclm.es
Internet: www.uclm.es
Founded 1982
State control
Language of instruction: Spanish
Academic year: October to June
Rector: Prof Dr ERNESTO MARTÍNEZ ATAZ
Vice-Rector for Academic Affairs and Continuing Education: Profa Dra FÁTIMA GUADAMILLAS GÓMEZ
Vice-Rector for Coordination and Communication: Prof. Dr FRANCISCO ALÍA MIRANDA
Vice-Rector for Cultural Cooperation and Ciudad Real Campus: Profa Dra MAIRENA MARTÍN LÓPEZ
Vice-Rector for Entrepreneurial Projects and Albacete Campus: Prof. Dr ANTONIO RONCERO SÁNCHEZ
Vice-Rector for Finance and Planning: Prof. Dr JESÚS FERNANDO SANTOS PEÑALVER
Vice-Rector for Infrastructure and Corporate Relations: Prof. Dr JUAN JOSÉ HERNÁNDEZ ADROVER
Vice-Rector for Institutional Relations and Toledo Campus: Profa Dra EVANGELINA ARANDA GARCÍA
Vice-Rector for Int. Relations and Devt Cooperation: Prof. Dr JUAN JOSÉ RUBIO GUERRERO
Vice-Rector for Research: Prof. Dr FRANCISCO JOSÉ QUILES FLOR
Vice-Rector for Students: Profa Dra CARMEN LÓPEZ BALBOA
Vice-Rector for Studies and Programmes: Prof. Dr MIGUEL ÁNGEL COLLADO YURRITA
Vice-Rector for Teaching Staff: Prof. Dr PABLO CAÑIZARES CAÑIZARES
Vice-Rector for Univ. Extension and Cuenca Campus: Prof. Dr JOSÉ IGNACIO ALBENTOSA HERNÁNDEZ
Registrar: Profa Dra MARÍA CÁNDIDA GUTIÉRREZ GARCÍA
Man.: JOSÉ LUIS MORAGA ALCAZAR
Librarian: FRANCISCO ALIA MIRANDA
Library of 952,268 vols, 22,252 periodicals
Number of teachers: 2,396
Number of students: 28,026
Publication: *Info-Campus* (12 a year)

DEANS

Faculty of Arts (Ciudad Real): MATIAS BARCHINO PÉREZ
Faculty of Chemical Sciences (Ciudad Real): ÁNGEL RÍOS CASTRO
Faculty of Economics and Business Sciences (Albacete): ÁNGEL TEJADA PONCE
Faculty of Education (Albacete: PEDRO LOSA SERRANO
Faculty of Education (Ciudad Real: EMILIO NIETO LÓPEZ
Faculty of Education (Cuenca: MARTÍN MUELAS HERRAÍZ
Faculty of Education (Toledo: ERNESTO GARCÍA SANZ
Faculty of Education Sciences and Humanities (Cuenca): MARIA DEL CARMEN POYATO HOLGADO
Faculty of Environmental Sciences and Biochemistry (Toledo): MARÍA JOSÉ RUIZ GARCÍA
Faculty of Fine Arts (Cuenca): ANA NAVARRETE TUDELA
Faculty of Humanities (Albacete): FRANCISCO CEBRIÁN ABELLÁN
Faculty of Humanities (Toledo): RICARDO IZQUIERDO BENITO
Faculty of Law (Albacete): DIEGO JOSÉ GÓMEZ INIESTA
Faculty of Law and Social Sciences (Ciudad Real): JUAN RAMÓN DE PÁRAMO ARGÜELLES
Faculty of Law and Social Sciences (Toledo): PEDRO J. CARRASCO PARRILLA
Faculty of Medicine (Albacete): JOSÉ MARTÍNEZ PÉREZ
Faculty of Medicine (Ciudad Real): EMILIO FELIU ALBIÑANA
Faculty of Nursing (Albacete): ANGEL LÓPEZ GONZÁLEZ
Faculty of Nursing (Ciudad Real): CARMEN PRADO LAGUNA
Faculty of Nursing (Cuenca): MARÍA ROSARIO OLMO GASCÓN
Faculty of Pharmacy (Albacete): JORGE DE LAS HERAS IBAÑEZ
Faculty of Social Sciences (Cuenca): MARÍA ÁNGELES ZURILLA CARIÑANA
Faculty of Sport Sciences (Toledo): SUSANA MENDIZABAL ALBIZU

UNIVERSIDAD DE CÓRDOBA

Alfonso XIII 13, 14071 Córdoba
Telephone: (95) 7218000
Fax: (95) 7218030
E-mail: secretaria.rector@uco.es
Internet: www.uco.es
Founded 1972
Language of instruction: Spanish
Academic year: October to June
Rector: JOSÉ MANUEL ROLDÁN NOGUERAS
Vice-Rector for Academic Affairs and Teaching Staff: JOSÉ NARANJO RAMÍREZ
Vice-Rector for Communication and Institutional Coordination: MANUEL TORRALBO RODRÍGUEZ
Vice-Rector for Information Technology and Communications: JUAN ANTONIO CABALLERO MOLINA
Vice-Rector for Infrastructure: MARÍA DEL PILAR DORADO PÉREZ
Vice-Rector for Innovation and Educational Quality: MARÍA TERESA SÁNCHEZ PINEDA DE LAS INFANTAS
Vice-Rector for Int. Relations and Cooperation: CARMEN GALÁN SOLDEVILLA
Vice-Rector for Policy Development: PEDRO GÓMEZ CABALLERO
Vice-Rector for Postgraduate and Continuing Education: JOSÉ CARLOS GÓMEZ VILLAMANDOS
Vice-Rector for Science Policy: ENRIQUE AGUILAR BENÍTEZ DE LUGO
Vice-Rector for Students and Culture: MANUEL TORRES AGUILAR
Registrar: JULIA ANGULO ROMERO
Man.: ANTONIO CUBERO ATIENZA
Librarian: MARÍA DEL CARMEN LIÑÁN MAZA
Library of 460,000 vols, 10,000 periodicals
Number of teachers: 1,250
Number of students: 20,000

DEANS

Faculty of Education: FRANCISCO VILLAMANDOS DE LA TORRE
Faculty of Labour Relations: Prof. Dr FEDERICO NAVARRO NIETO
Faculty of Law and Economics: Prof. Dr MIGUEL J. AGUDO ZAMORA
Faculty of Medicine: Prof. Dr RAFAEL SOLANA LARA
Faculty of Philosophy and Letters: Prof. Dr EULALIO FERNÁNDEZ SÁNCHEZ
Faculty of Science: Prof. Dr MANUEL BLÁZQUEZ RUIZ
Faculty of Veterinary Science: Prof. Dr LIBRADO CARRASCO OTERO

UNIVERSIDAD DE DEUSTO

Apdo 1, 48080 Bilbao
Avda de las Universidades 24, 48007 Bilbao
Telephone: (94) 4139000
Fax: (94) 4139098
E-mail: secretaria.general@deusto.es
Internet: www.deusto.es
Founded 1886
Private control, directed by the Jesuits
Languages of instruction: Spanish, Basque
Academic year: October to June
Chancellor: R. P. ADOLFO NICOLÁS PACHÓN
Deputy-Chancellor: R. P. JUAN JOSÉ ETXEBERRIA SAGASTUME
Vice-Chancellor: R. P. JAVIER LÓPEZ ARÍZTEGUI
Rector: R. P. JAIME ORAÁ ORAÁ
Vice-Rector for Academic Organization and Educational Innovation: MARÍA BEGOÑA ARRIETA HERAS
Vice-Rector for Communication, Multilingualism and Social Affairs: ROBERTO SAN SALVADOR DEL VALLE DOISTUA
Vice-Rector for Int. Relations: JULIA GONZÁLEZ FERRERAS
Vice-Rector for Research, Innovation and Knowledge Transfer: JOSÉ LUIS DEL VAL ROMAN
Vice-Rector for Research: JOSÉ LUIS AVILA ORIVE
Vice-Rector for San Sebastián Campus and Univ. Community and Identity: R. P. JOSÉ JAVIER PARDO IZAL
Registrar: MARÍA BEGOÑA ARRIETA HERAS
Librarian: NIEVES TARANCO
Library: see Libraries and Archives
Number of teachers: 1,818
Number of students: 13,173
Publications: *ADOZ Boletín del Centro de Documentación en Ocio* (4 a year), *Anuario de Estudios Cooperativos* (1 a year), *Anuario del Instituto Ignacio de Loyola* (1 a year), *Boletín Asociación Internacional de Derecho Cooperativo* (6 a year), *Boletín de Estudios Económicos* (3 a year), *Cuadernos Europeos de Deusto* (2 a year), *Enseiukarrean* (1 a year), *ESIDE* (1 a year), *Estudios de Deusto* (2 a year), *Estudios Empresariales* (3 a year), *Letras de Deusto* (4 a year), *Mundaiz* (2 a year), *Revista de Derecho y Genoma Humano* (2 a year), *Revista Noticias UD Berriak* (4 a year), *RAS* (2 a year)

DEANS

Faculty of Economics and Business Studies (Bilbao): ANTONIO YABAR MAISTERRENA
Faculty of Economics and Business Studies (San Sebastián): VÍCTOR URCELAY YARZA
Faculty of Law: JOSÉ LUIS AVILA ORIVE
Faculty of Psychology and Education: JOSU SOLABARRIETA
Faculty of Social and Human Sciences: JOSÉ ANGEL ACHÓN INSAUSTI
Faculty of Theology: VICENTE VIDE RODRIGUEZ

UNIVERSIDAD DE EXTREMADURA

Avda de Elvas, s/n, 06071 Badajoz
Plaza de los Caldereros 1, 10071 Cáceres
Telephone: (924) 289369 (Badajoz); (927) 257040 (Cáceres)
Fax: (924) 276367 (Badajoz); (927) 257002 (Cáceres)

E-mail: rector@unex.es
Internet: www.unex.es
Founded 1973
State control
Language of instruction: Spanish
Academic year: October to June

Rector: Prof. Dr JUAN FRANCISCO DUQUE CARRILLO
Vice-Rector for Academic Planning: Prof. JAVIER GRANDE QUEJIGO
Vice-Rector for Economic Planning: AGUSTÍN GARCÍA GARCÍA
Vice-Rector for Information and Communications Technology: JUAN MANUEL MURILLO RODRÍGUEZ
Vice-Rector for Institutional Relations and Cultural Outreach: Prof. FERNANDO SÁNCHEZ FIGUEROA
Vice-Rector for Quality and Continuing Education: Dra MARÍA JOSÉ MARTÍN DELGADO
Vice-Rector for Research, Devt and Infrastructure: Prof. JUAN MANUEL SÁNCHEZ GUZMÁN
Vice-Rector for Student Affairs and Employment: ANTONIO JAVIER FRANCO RUBIO
Vice-Rector for Teaching Staff: ANTONIO HIDALGO GARCÍA
Registrar: Prof. FRANCISCO ÁLVAREZ ARROYO
Man.: LUCIANO CORDERO SAAVEDRA

Number of teachers: 1,995
Number of students: 23,862

Publication: *Boletín*

DEANS

Faculty of Business Studies and Tourism (Cáceres): JOSÉ ANTONIO PÉREZ RUBIO
Faculty of Economics and Business (Badajoz): ANTONIO FERNÁNDEZ FERNÁNDEZ
Faculty of Education (Badajoz): MA. ROSA LUENGO GONZÁLEZ
Faculty of Law (Cáceres): EMILIO CORTÉS BECHIARELLI
Faculty of Library Science (Badajoz): ANTONIO PULGARÍN GUERRERO
Faculty of Medicine (Badajoz): PEDRO BUREO DACAL
Faculty of Philosophy and Letters (Cáceres): LUIS MERINO JEREZ
Faculty of Science (Badajoz): MANUEL GONZÁLEZ LENA
Faculty of Sports Science (Cáceres): FERNANDO DEL VILLAR ÁLVAREZ
Faculty of Teacher Training (Cáceres): BEATRIZ MARTÍN MARÍN
Faculty of Veterinary Science (Cáceres): PEDRO LUIS RODRÍGUEZ MEDINA

UNIVERSIDAD DE GRANADA

Avda del Hospicio, s/n, 18071 Granada

Telephone: (95) 8243000
Fax: (95) 8243066
E-mail: informa@ugr.es
Internet: www.ugr.es

Founded 1526, charter granted 1531, est. 1536
State control
Language of instruction: Spanish
Academic year: October to May

Rector: FRANCISCO GONZÁLEZ LODEIRO
Vice-Chancellor for Academic Organization and Teaching Staff: LUIS M. JIMÉNEZ DEL BARCO JALDO
Vice-Chancellor for Campus Infrastructure: BEGOÑA MORENO ESCOBAR
Vice-Chancellor for Environmental Quality, Welfare and Sport: PEDRO ESPINOSA HIDALGO
Vice-Chancellor for Int. Relations: DOROTHY KELLY
Vice-Chancellor for Quality Assurance: MARÍA JOSÉ LEÓN GUERRERO
Vice-Chancellor for Undergraduate and Postgraduate Teaching: LOLA FERRE CANO
Vice-Rector for Science Policy and Research: MARÍA DOLORES SUÁREZ ORTEGA
Vice-Chancellor for Student Affairs: INMACULADA MARRERO ROCHA
Vice-Chancellor for the Health Sciences Technoogical Park: MOLINA PINEDA DE LAS INFANTAS
Vice-Chancellor for Univ. Extension and Devt: MIGUEL GÓMEZ OLIVER
Registrar: ROSSANA GONZÁLEZ GONZÁLEZ
Man.: ANDRÉS NAVARRO GALERA
Librarian: JOSE ARIZA RUBIO

Library of 686,300 vols, 15,338 periodicals, 35 incunabula
Number of teachers: 3,650
Number of students: 60,000

Publications: *Anales de la Cátedra Francisco Suarez, Arenal: Revista de Historia de Mujeres, Chronica Nova: Revista de Historia Moderna, Cuadernos de Arte, Cuadernos de Estudios Medievales, Cuadernos de Estudios Medievales y Ciencias y Técnicas Historiográficas, Cuadernos de Prehistoria, Cuadernos Geográficos, Dynamis: Acta Hispanica ad Medicinae: Scientiarumque Historiam Ilustrandam, Florentia Iliberritana, Miscelánea de Estudios Arabes y Hebraicos, Revista de Educación, Revista de la Facultad de Derecho de la Universidad de Granada, Sendebar: Boletín de la Facultad de Traducción e Interpretación, Zoologica Baetica*

DEANS

Faculty of Communication and Documentation: ANTONIO ÁNGEL RUIZ RODRÍGUEZ
Faculty of Dentistry: Dr ALBERTO RODRÍGUEZ ARCHILLA
Faculty of Economic and Business Administration: Dra MARÍA DEL MAR HOLGADO MOLINA
Faculty of Education and Humanities (Ceuta): RAMÓN GALINDO MORALES
Faculty of Education and Humanities (Melilla): JUAN GRANDA VERA ROMERO
Faculty of Educational Sciences: Dr JOSÉ ANTONIO NARANJO RODRÍGUEZ
Faculty of Fine Arts: Dr VÍCTOR MEDINA FLÓREZ
Faculty of Health Sciences (Ceuta): Dr RAFAEL GUISADO BARRILAO
Faculty of Labour Sciences: Dr ANTONIO DELGADO PADIAL
Faculty of Law: Prof. Dr JUAN LÓPEZ MARTÍNEZ
Faculty of Nursing (Melilla): Dra BIBINHA BENBUNAN BENTATA
Faculty of Medicine: Dr RAMÓN GALINDO MORALES
Faculty of Pharmacy: LUÍS RECALDE MANRIQUE
Faculty of Philosophy and Literature: Dra MARIA ELENA MARTIN-VIVALDI CABALLERO
Faculty of Physical Education and Sports Sciences: AURELIO UREÑA ESPA
Faculty of Political Science and Sociology: Dra SUSANA CORZO FERNÁNDEZ
Faculty of Psychology: Dr ANTONIO MALDONADO LÓPEZ
Faculty of Sciences: Dr ANTONIO RÍOS GUADIX
Faculty of Translation and Interpretation: Dra EVA MUÑOZ RAYA

AFFILIATED INSTITUTIONS

Institute of Nutrition and Food Technology: Edif. Fray Luís de Granada, C/ Ramón y Cajal 4, 18071 Granada; tel. (95) 8244174; fax (95) (8248326); internet www.ugr.es/%7ewinyta; Dir EMILIO MARTÍNEZ DE VICTORIA MUÑOZ.

Andalusian Institute of Earth Sciences: Facultad de Ciencias, Universidad de Granada, Campus Fuentenueva s/n, 18002 Granada; tel. (95) 8243158; fax (95) 8243384; e-mail offiact@ugr.es; internet www.iact.csic.es; Dir ANDRES MALDONALDO LOPEZ.

Andalusian Institute of Geophysics and Prevention of Seismic Disasters: Campus Universitario de Cartuja s/n, 18071 Granada; tel. (95) 8243557; fax (95) 8160907; e-mail morales@iag.ugr.es; internet www.ugr.es/%7eiag; Dir JOSÉ MORALES SOTO.

Biotechnology Institute: Facultad de Ciencias, Universidad de Granada, Campus Fuentenueva, s/n, 18002 Granada; tel. (95) 8200686; e-mail info@biotec.ugr.es; internet biotec.conzepto.com/index.asp; Dir Dr ANTONIO OSUNA CARRILLO DE ALBORNOZ.

'Carlos I' Institute of Theoretical and Computational Physics: Facultad de Ciencias, Universidad de Granada, Campus de Fuentenueva, 18071 Granada; tel. (95) 8242860; fax (95) 8242862; e-mail carlos1@ugr.es; internet www.ugr.es/%7ecarlos1; Dir PEDRO L. GARRIDO GALERA.

'Federico Oloriz' Institute of Neurosciences: C/o Avda de Madrid, s/n, Facultad de Medicina, Universidad de Granada, Granada; tel. (95) 8244033; fax (95) 8246187; e-mail ifeolo@andalusi.ugr.es; internet www.ugr.es/%7einsneuro; Dir Dr JOSÉ MANUEL BAEYENS CABRERA.

Interuniversity Andalusian Institute of Criminology: Sección Universidad de Granada, Edificio Centro de Documentación Científica, C/ Rector López Argüeta, s/n, 18071 Granada; tel. (95) 8243150; fax (95) 8243095; e-mail criminol@ugr.es; internet www.ugr.es/%7ecriminol; Dir Prof. Dr JESÚS BARQUÍN SANZ.

'La Inmaculada' University College of Teacher Training: Carretera de Murcia s/n, 18010 Granada; tel. (95) 8205861; fax (95) 8287469; internet www.lainmaculada.com; Pres. and Dir ANTONIO ALMENDROS GALLEGO.

Regional Development Institute: Universidad de Granada, Edificio Centro de Documentación Científica, C/ Rector López Argüeta s/n, 18071 Granada; tel. (95) 8243083; fax (95) 8248967; e-mail idesareg@azahar.ugr.es; internet www.ugr.es/%7eidr; Dir Dr FRANCISCO RODRÍGUEZ MARTÍNEZ.

University Institute of Peace and Conflict: Edificio de Documentación Científica, C/ Rector López Argüeta s/n, 18071 Granada; tel. (95) 8244142; fax (95) 8248974; e-mail eirene@ugr.es; internet www.ugr.es/%7eeirene; Dir Prof. MARIO LÓPEZ MARTÍNEZ.

University Institute of Studies on Women: Edificio de Documentación Científica, C/ Rector López Argüeta s/n, 18071 Granada; tel. (95) 8248366; fax (95) 8242828; e-mail insmujer@azahar.ugr.es; internet www.ugr.es/%7eiem; Dir Dra MARIA EUGENIA FERNÁNDEZ FRAILE.

Water Institute: Edif. Fray Luis de Granada, C/ Ramon y Cajal 4, 18071 Granada; tel. (95) 8243093; fax (95) 8243094; e-mail javicruz@instagua.ugr.es; internet www.ugr.es/%7ejjcruz/instagua.htm; Dir LUIS CRUZ PIZARRO.

UNIVERSIDAD DE HUELVA

Calle Dr Cantero Cuadrado 6, 21071 Huelva

Telephone: (95) 9218001
Fax: (95) 9218080
E-mail: rector@uhu.es
Internet: www.uhu.es

Founded 1993
State control

Rector: Prof. Dr FRANCISCO JOSÉ MARTÍNEZ LÓPEZ
Vice-Rector for Academic Organization and Teaching Staff: Prof. Dr JUAN JOSÉ GARCÍA DEL HOYO

Vice-Rector for Infrastructure and Services: Prof. Dr EMILIO MANUEL ROMERO MACÍAS
Vice-Rector for Int. Relations: Prof. Dr ENRIQUE BONSÓN PONTE
Vice-Rector for Lifelong Learning and Innovation: Profa Dra MARÍA CARMEN FONSECA MORA
Vice-Rector for Research: Prof. Dr JESÚS DAMIÁN DE LA ROSA DÍAZ
Vice-Rector for Student Affairs, Employment and Business Administration: Profa Dra ISABEL MARÍA RODRÍGUEZ GARCÍA
Vice-Rector for Technology and Quality: Prof. Dr JOSÉ IGNACIO AGUADED GÓMEZ
Vice-Rector for Univ. Extension: Prof. Dr MANUEL JOSÉ DE LARA RÓDENAS
Registrar: Profa Dra MARÍA LUISA PÉREZ GUERRERO
Man.: ANTONIO MORILLA FRÍAS
Librarian: MARÍA ANTONIA ÁLVAREZ ÁLVAREZ

Library of 259,839 vols, 4,755 periodicals
Number of teachers: 700
Number of students: 14,500

DEANS

Faculty of Business Studies: Profa Dra MARÍA ASUNCIÓN GRÁVALOS GASTAMINZA
Faculty of Education: FRANCISCO JOSÉ MORALES GIL
Faculty of Experimental Sciences: GABRIEL RUIZ DE ALMODÓVAR SEL
Faculty of Humanities: Prof. Dr ZENÓN LUIS MARTÍNEZ
Faculty of Labour Relations: Prof. Dr AGUSTÍN GALÁN GARCÍA
Faculty of Law: Prof. Dr SALVADOR RAMÍREZ GÓMEZ

UNIVERSIDAD DE JAÉN

Campus Las Lagunillas, 23071 Jaén
Telephone: (95) 3012121
Fax: (95) 3012239
E-mail: info@ujaen.es
Internet: www.ujaen.es

Founded 1993
State control

Rector: MANUEL PARRAS ROSA
Vice-Rector for Academic Org., Educational Innovation and Teaching Staff: JUAN CARLOS CASTILLO ARMENTEROS
Vice-Rector for European Convergence, Postgraduate Studies and Life Long Learning: JOAQUÍN TOVAR PESCADOR
Vice-Rector for Information and Communication Technology: FRANCISCO ROCA RODRÍGUEZ
Vice-Rector for Infrastructure and Campus Devt: NICOLAS RUÍZ REYEZ
Vice-Rector for Institutional Relations and Communication: ESTHER LÓPEZ ZAFRA
Vice-Rector for Int. Relations and Cooperation: VICTORIA LÓPEZ RAMÓN
Vice-Rector for Research, Technological Devt and Innovation: MARIA ANGELES PEINADO HERREROS
Vice-Rector for Strategic Planning and Quality Management: JORGE DELGADO GARCÍA
Vice-Rector for Student and Labour Orientation: MOZAS MORAL
Vice-Rector for Univ. Extension: ANA ORTIZ COLÓN
Registrar: JOSÉ CUESTA REVILLA
Man.: ARMANDO MORENO CASTRO
Library Dir: SEBASTIÁN JARILLO CALVARRO

Library of 205,000 vols, 4,356 periodicals
Number of teachers: 1,000
Number of students: 16,000

DEANS

Faculty of Experimental Sciences: Dr MARÍA ISABEL TORRES LÓPEZ
Faculty of Health Sciences: MANUEL LINARES ABAD
Faculty of Humanities and Education: Dr ANTONIO BUENO GONZÁLEZ
Faculty of Law and Social Sciences: Dr JORGE LOZANO MIRALLES
Faculty of Social Work: Dra YOLANDA DE LA FUENTE ROBLES

ATTACHED INSTITUTIONS

Andalusian Centre of Iberian Archaeology: Paraje las Lagunillas, s/n, 23071 Jaén; tel. (95) 3012132; fax (95) 3012287; e-mail caai@ujaen.es; internet www.ujaen.es/centros/caai; Dir Dr ARTURO CARLOS RUIZ RODRÍGUEZ.

University School of Teacher Training in Úbeda: Avda Cristo Rey 25, 23400 Úbeda (Jaén); tel. (95) 3796102; e-mail magisterio@safa.edu; internet magisterio.safa.edu; Dir FRANCISCO JAVIER MUÑOZ DELGADO.

UNIVERSIDAD DE LA LAGUNA

Pabellón de Gobierno, Calle Molinos de Agua, s/n, 38207 La Laguna, Tenerife, Canary Islands
Telephone: (92) 2319000
Fax: (92) 2319544
E-mail: ccti@ull.es
Internet: www.ull.es

Founded 1792
State control
Language of instruction: Spanish
Academic year: October to June

Rector: EDUARDO DOMÉNECH MARTÍNEZ
Vice-Rector for Academic Affairs: JOSÉ MARÍA PALAZÓN LÓPEZ
Vice-Rector for Cultural Affairs and Infrastructure: PABLO GONZÁLEZ VERA
Vice-Rector for Economic Planning: LILIBETH FUENTES MEDINA
Vice-Rector for Int. Relations: MARÍA GRACIA RODRÍGUEZ BRITO
Vice-Rector for Institutional Quality and Educational Innovation: JUSTO ROBERTO PÉREZ CRUZ
Vice-Rector for Research, Technological Devt and Innovation: LORENZO MORENO RUIZ
Vice-Rector for Student Affairs: ROBERTO RODRÍGUEZ GUERRA
Vice-Rector for Teaching Staff: CARMEN DOLORES SOSA CASTILLA
Vice-Rector for Univ. and Society Relations: MARÍA NÉLIDA RANCEL TORRES
Vice-Rector for Univ. Services: ROSA MARÍA AGUILAR CHINEA
Man.: FRANCISCO CALERO GARCÍA
Registrar: FERNANDO ROSA GONZÁLEZ
Librarian: FERNANDO RODRIGUEZ JUNCO

Library of 637,202 vols, 12,025 periodicals
Number of teachers: 1,794
Number of students: 23,167

Publications: *Anales de la Facultad de Derecho* (1 a year), *Clepsidra* (1 a year), *Cuadernos de Cemyr* (1 a year), *Latente* (1 a year), *Revista Canaria de Estudios Ingleses* (2 a year), *Revista de Bellas Artes* (1 a year), *Revista de Filología* (1 a year), *Revista de Historia Canaria* (1 a year), *Revista Fortunatae* (1 a year), *Revista Laguna* (2 a year), *Tempora* (1 a year)

DEANS

Faculty of Biology: JUAN FELIPE PÉREZ FRANCÉS
Faculty of Chemistry: ANA MARÍA AFONSO PERERA
Faculty of Economics and Business Administration: CARLOS RODRÍGUEZ FUENTES
Faculty of Education: OLGA MARÍA ALEGRE DE LA ROSA
Faculty of Fine Arts: ALFONSO RUIZ RALLO
Faculty of Geography and History: MANUEL DE PAZ SÁNCHEZ
Faculty of Information Science: CARMEN RODRÍGUEZ WANGÜEMERT
Faculty of Law: MARCEL MANUEL BONNET ESCUELA
Faculty of Mathematics: ANTONIO MARTINÓN CEJAS
Faculty of Medicine: EMILIO SANZ ÁLVAREZ
Faculty of Pharmacy: ENRIQUE MARTÍNEZ CARRETERO
Faculty of Philology: JUAN IGNACIO OLIVA CRUZ
Faculty of Philosophy: ÁNGELA SIERRA GONZÁLEZ
Faculty of Physics: TEODORO ROCA CORTÉS
Faculty of Political and Social Sciences: CARMEN MARINA BARRETO VARGAS
Faculty of Psychology: PEDRO AVERO DELGADO

ATTACHED INSTITUTES

Andrés Bello Institute of Linguistics: C/ Juan de Vera 13, La Laguna; Dir MANUEL ALMEIDA SUÁREZ.

Antonio González University Institute of Bio-Organics: Avda Astrofísico Fco. Sánchez 2, La Laguna; tel. (92) 231-85-70; fax (92) 231-85-71; e-mail iubo@ull.es; internet www.iubo.ull.es; Dir VÍCTOR SOTERO MARTÍN GARCÍA.

Astrophysics Institute of the Canary Islands: Avda Astrofísico Francisco Sánchez, s/n, 38206 La Laguna; tel. (92) 2318121; fax (92) 2318123; e-mail mcv@ll .iac.es; internet www.ull.es/departamento; Dirs MANUEL MAS GARCÍA, ANTONIO APARICIO JUAN.

University Business Institute: Avda 25 de Julio 9, 38004 Santa Cruz de Tenerife; tel. (92) 2319708; fax (92) 2319709; e-mail iude@ull.es; Dir Dr JOSÉ ANTONIO LASTRES SEGRET.

University Institute of Political and Social Sciences: Facultad de Derecho, módulo D-02, Campus de Guajara, 38071 La Laguna; tel. (92) 2317306; fax (92) 2317308; e-mail inucps@ull.es; Dir MA. TERESA GONZÁLEZ DE LA FE.

University Institute of Regional Development: Facultad de Económicas, Campus de Guajara s/n, 38071 La Laguna; tel. (92) 2317112; Dir ROSA MARINA GONZÁLEZ MARRERO.

University Institute of Tropical Diseases and Public Health of the Canaries: Unidad de Parasitología, Facultad de Farmacia, Avda Astrofísico Fco. Sánchez s/n, 38071 La Laguna; tel. (92) 2318486; e-mail jcastilo@ull.es; Dir JOSÉ ANTONIO DEL CASTILLO REMIRO.

UNIVERSIDAD DE LA RIOJA

Calle Avda de La Paz 93–103, 26006 Logroño
Telephone: (94) 1299100
Fax: (94) 1299120
E-mail: informacion@unirioja.es
Internet: www.unirioja.es

Founded 1992
State control
Academic year: September to July

Rector: JOSÉ MARÍA MARTÍNEZ DE PISÓN CAVERO
Vice-Rector for Academic Org. and Teaching Staff: JOSÉ IGNACIO EXTREMIANA ALDANA
Vice-Rector for Infrastructure and Technology: ELISEO VERGARA GONZÁLEZ
Vice-Rector for Int. and Institutional Relations: SYLVIA SASTRE I RIBA
Vice-Rector for Planning and Quality: RODOLFO SALINAS ZÁRATE
Vice-Rector for Research: EDUARDO J. FERNÁNDEZ GARBAYO
Vice-Rector for Student Affairs: MARÍA DEL MAR ASENSIO AROSTEGUI

Registrar: ISABEL MARTINEZ NAVAS
Man.: GUILLERMO BRAVO MENÉNDEZ-RIVAS
Librarian: MARTA MAGRIÑÁ CONTRERAS

Library of 250,000 vols, 6,000 periodicals
Number of teachers: 430
Number of students: 7,500

Publications: *Anuario Jurídico de La Rioja* (1 a year), *Brocar: Cuadernos de Investigación Histórica* (1 a year), *Contextos Educativos* (education review, 1 a year), *Cuadernos de Gestión* (2 a year), *Cuadernos de Investigación Filológica* (1 a year), *Cuadernos de Investigación Geográfica* (1 a year), *Iberia: Revista de la Antigüedad* (1 a year), *Journal of English Studies* (1 a year)

DEANS

Faculty of Arts and Education: JOSÉ ANTONIO CABALLERO LÓPEZ
Faculty of Business Sciences: EDUARDO RODRÍGUEZ OSÉS
Faculty of Law and Social Sciences: MARIOLA URREA CORRES
Faculty of Sciences, Agriculture Studies and Computer Engineering: SUSANA CABREDO PINILLOS
Higher School of Industrial Engineering: JOSÉ IGNACIO CASTRESANA RUIZ-CARRILLO (Dir)

ATTACHED INSTITUTIONS

University School of Labour Relations: Edificio Quintiliano, La Cigüeña 60, 26004 Logroño; tel. (94) 1299100; fax (94) 1299259; internet www.unirioja.es/facultades_escuelas/relaciones_laborales.shtml; Dir MANUEL GARCIA-MIGUEL GARCIA-ROSADO.

University School of Nursing: Calle Donantes de Sangre, s/n, 26004 Logroño; tel. and fax (94) 1261443; internet www.unirioja.es/facultades_escuelas/enfermeria.shtml; Dir ROSARIO ARÉJULA BENITO.

University School of Tourism: Calle Quintiliano 5–7, 26005 Logroño; tel. (94) 1257372; fax (94) 1248506; internet www.escuela-turismo-larioja.com; Gen. Dir YOLANDA MONFORTE MORÚA; Academic Dir MERCEDES GONZÁLEZ MARIJUÁN.

UNIVERSIDAD DE LAS PALMAS DE GRAN CANARIA

Calle Juan de Quesada 30, 35001, Las Palmas de Gran Canaria, Canary Islands
Telephone: (92) 8451000
Fax: (92) 8451022
E-mail: universidad@ulpgc.es
Internet: www.ulpgc.es

Founded 1980
State control
Language of instruction: Spanish
Academic year: October to September

Rector: Dr JOSÉ REGIDOR GARCÍA
Vice-Rector for Academic Org. and European Higher Education Convergence: Dr LUIS ÁLVAREZ ÁLVAREZ
Vice-Rector for Culture and Sport: Dra ISABEL PASCUA FEBLES
Vice-Rector for Int. and Institutional Relations: Dra ROSARIO BERRIEL MARTÍNEZ
Vice-Rector for Quality and Educational Innovation: Dra RAQUEL ESPINO ESPINO
Vice-Rector for Research, Devt and Innovation: Dr FERNANDO REAL VALCÁRCEL
Vice-Rector for Student Affairs and Univ. Extension: Dr NICOLÁS DÍAZ DE LEZCANO SEVILLANO
Vice-Rector for Teaching Staff: Dr GUSTAVO MONTERO GARCÍA
Registrar: CARMEN SALINERO ALONSO
Man.: CONRADO DOMÍNGUEZ TRUJILLO
Library Dir: MARÍA DEL CARMEN MARTÍN MARICHAL

Library of 477,251 vols, 9,634 periodicals
Number of teachers: 1,500
Number of students: 25,000

DEANS

Faculty of Computer Science: MANUEL GONZÁLEZ RODRÍGUEZ
Faculty of Economics and Business: SERGIO J. MARTÍN MACHÍN
Faculty of Geography and History: JOSEFA DOMÍNGUEZ MUJICA
Faculty of Health Sciences: JUAN CABRERA CABRERA
Faculty of Law and Social Sciences: IGNACIO DÍAZ DE LEZCANO SEVILLANO
Faculty of Marine Sciences: JOSÉ MIGUEL PACHECO CASTELAO
Faculty of Philology: EUGENIO PADORAO NAVARRO
Faculty of Physical Activity Science and Sport: FERNANDO AMADOR RAMÍREZ
Faculty of Teacher Training: GERMÁN HERNÁNDEZ RODRÍGUEZ
Faculty of Translating and Interpreting: MA. JESÚS GARCÍA DOMÍNGUEZ
Faculty of Veterinary Science: ANSELMO GRACIA MOLINA

ATTACHED INSTITUTES

Innovation Centre for the Information Society: Edificio Central del Parque Científico y Tecnológico, Campus Universitario de Tafira, 35017 Las Palmas de Gran Canaria; tel. (92) 8451045; fax (92) 8451492; e-mail info@cicei.com; internet www.cicei.com; Dir Prof. Dr ENRIQUE RUBIO ROYO.

Institute for Cybernetic Science and Technology: Campus Universitario de Tafira, 35017 Las Palmas de Gran Canaria; tel. (92) 8457100; e-mail mperez@ciber.ulpgc.es; internet www.iuctc.ulpgc.es.

Institute of Applied Microelectronics: Edificio de Electrónica y Telecomunicación, Campus Universitario de Tafira, 35017 Las Palmas de Gran Canaria; tel. (92) 8451233; fax (92) 8451243; e-mail carballo@iuma.ulpgc.es; internet www.iuma.ulpgc.es; Dir ANTONIO NÚÑEZ ORDÓÑEZ.

Marine Biotechnology Centre: Muelle de Taliarte, s/n, 35214 Telde, Las Palmas de Gran Canaria; tel. (98) 72912581; fax (98) 72912671; e-mail ggarcia@dbio.ulpgc.es; internet www.cbm.ulpgc.es; Dir Prof. GUILLERMO GARCÍA REINA.

UNIVERSIDAD DE LEÓN

Edif. Rectorado, Pabellón de Gobierno, Avda de la Facultad 25, 24004 León
Telephone: (98) 7291607
Fax: (98) 7291939
E-mail: rectorado@unileon.es
Internet: www.unileon.es

Founded 1979
State control
Language of instruction: Spanish
Academic year: October to September

Rector: JOSÉ ÁNGEL HERMIDA ALONSO
Vice-Rector for Academic Org.: MATILDE SIERRA VEGA
Vice-Rector for Campus Infrastructure: MARÍA VICTORIA SECO FERNÁNDEZ
Vice-Rector for Economic Affairs: ÁNGELES MARÍN RIVERO
Vice-Rector for Int. and Institutional Relations: JOSÉ LUIS CHAMOSA GONZÁLEZ
Vice-Rector for Ponferrada Campus: VICTORIA SECO FERNÁNDEZ
Vice-Rector for Quality and Accreditation: JUAN CARLOS REDONDO CASTÁN
Vice-Rector for Research: ALBERTO JOSÉ VILLENA CORTÉS
Vice-Rector for Student Affairs: JOSÉ MANUEL GONZALO ORDEN
Vice-Rector for Teaching Staff: JOSÉ LUIS FANJUL SUÁREZ
Registrar: PIEDAD GONZÁLEZ GRANDA
Man.: JOSÉ LUIS MARTÍNEZ JUAN
Library Dir: MARÍA MARSÁ VILA

Library of 458,170 vols, 13,815 periodicals
Number of teachers: 898
Number of students: 15,072

Publications: *Contextos*, *De Arte*, *Estudios Humanísticos:Filología*, *Estudios Humanísticos:Historia*, *Lancia: Revista de Arqueología, Prehistoria e Historia Antigüa*, *Polígonos*, *Silva: Estudios de Humanismo y Tradicción Clásica*

DEANS

Faculty of Biology and Environmental Sciences: BLANCA RAZQUÍN PERALTA
Faculty of Economics and Business: MARÍA JESÚS MURES QUINTANA
Faculty of Education: JOSÉ MARÍA SANTAMARTA LUENGOS
Faculty of Labour Studies: GERMÁN BARREIRO GONZÁLEZ
Faculty of Law: Dr TOMÁS QUINTANA LÓPEZ
Faculty of Philosophy and Letters: CARLOS FERNÁNDEZ RODRÍGUEZ
Faculty of Physical Education and Sport: Dra MARTA ZUBIAUR GONZÁLEZ
Faculty of Veterinary Science: JOSÉ GABRIEL FERNÁNDEZ ÁLVAREZ

ATTACHED INSTITUTES

Institute of Automation and Manufacturing: Dir for Automation Section DAVID MARCOS MARTÍNEZ; Dir for Automation Section MANUEL DOMÍNGUEZ GONZÁLEZ; Dir for Imaging Section ÁNGEL ALONSO ÁLVAREZ; Dir for Manufacturing Engineering Section JULIO LABARGA.

Institute of Biomedical Research: Departamento de Fisiología, Campus de Veganaza, 24071 León; tel. (98) 7291258; fax (98) 7291267; e-mail dfijgg@unileon.es; Dir Dr JAVIER GONZÁLEZ GALLEGO.

Institute of Biotechnology: Avda Real 1, 24006 León; tel. (98) 7210308; fax (98) 7210388; e-mail inbiotec@inbiotec.com; internet www.inbiotec.com; Dir Dr JUAN FRANCISCO MARTÍN MARTÍN.

Institute of Cattle Development: Campus de Veganaza, 24071 León; tel. (98) 7291928; fax (98) 7291638; e-mail dbbmfg@unileon.es; Dir (vacant).

Institute of Food Science and Technology: Calle La Serna 56, 24007 León; tel. (98) 7243123; e-mail dhtjfb@unileon.es; Dir Dr JOSÉ MARÍA FRESNO BARO.

Institute of Natural Resources: Campus de la Escuela T y S de Agrónomos, Avda de Portugal 42, 24071 León; tel. (98) 7291844; fax (98) 7291839; e-mail dfqamp@unileon.es; Dir Dr ANTONIO MORÁN PALAO.

Institute of the Environment: Calle La Serna 56, 24007 León; tel. (98) 7291568; e-mail degelc@unileon.es; Dir Dr ESTANISLAO LUIS CALABUIG.

Institute of Toxicology: Avda Real 1, 24006 León; tel. (98) 7210083; fax (98) 7210091; e-mail dftdoe@unileon.es; Dir Dr DAVID ORDÓÑEZ ESCUDERO.

UNIVERSIDAD DE MÁLAGA

El Ejido, s/n, 29071 Málaga
Telephone: (95) 2131000
Fax: (95) 2263858
E-mail: informacion@uma.es
Internet: www.uma.es

Founded 1972
State control
Language of instruction: Spanish
Academic year: October to July

Rector: ADELAIDA DE LA CALLE MARTÍN
Vice-Rector for Academic Affairs: ANA LOZANO VIVAS
Vice-Rector for Academic Org.: ANA CAÑIZARES LASO
Vice-Rector for Culture and Institutional Relations: ANA MARÍA SÁNCHEZ TEJEDA
Vice-Rector for Infrastructure and Sustainability: RAFAEL MORALES BUENO
Vice-Rector for Int. Relations: MARÍA DEL ROSARIO CABELLO PORRAS
Vice-Rector for Quality, Strategic Planning and Social Responsibility: CARLOS A. BENAVIDES VELASCO
Vice-Rector for Research: JOSÉ ÁNGEL NARVÁEZ BUENO
Vice-Rector for Student Affairs: JUAN ANTONIO PERLES ROCHEL
Vice-Rector for Teaching, Training and Coordination: ENRIQUE CARO GUERRA
Vice-Rector for Technological Devt and Innovation: MARÍA VALPUESTA FERNÁNDEZ
Vice-Rector for Univ. Business Relations: ANA MARÍA SÁNCHEZ TEJEDA
Vice-Rector for Welfare and Equality: MARÍA TERESA PRIETO RUZ
Registrar: MIGUEL PORRAS FERNÁNDEZ
Manager: JOSÉ ANTONIO MOLINA RUIZ
Library Coordinator: GREGORIO GARCÍA RECHE

Library of 921,364 vols, 23,706 periodicals
Number of teachers: 1,600
Number of students: 36,000

Publications: *Boletín de Arte* (1 a year), *Filosofía Malacitana* (1 a year), *Histología Médica* (2 a year)

DEANS

Faculty of Communication: JUAN ANTONIO GARCÍA GALINDO
Faculty of Economic and Business Studies: Dr EUGENIO JOSÉ LUQUE DOMÍNGUEZ
Faculty of Education: JOSÉ FRANCISCO MURILLO MAS
Faculty of Fine Arts: CARMEN OSUNA LUQUE
Faculty of Law: ALEJANDRO J. RODRÍGUEZ CARRIÓN
Faculty of Medicine: ALFREDO BLANES BERENGUEL
Faculty of Philosophy and Letters: SEBASTIÁN FERNÁNDEZ LÓPEZ
Faculty of Psychology: JULIÁN ALMARAZ CARRETERO
Faculty of Science: JOSÉ JOAQUÍN QUIRANTE SÁNCHEZ

PROFESSORS

Faculty of Economic and Business Studies:
AGUIRRE SADABA, A., Economics and Business Administration
GARCÍA LIZANA, A., Applied Economics (Political)
GONZÁLEZ PAREJA, A., Applied Economics (Mathematics)
MOCHON MORCILLO, F., Economic Analysis
OTERO MORENO, J. M., Applied Economics (Statistics and Econometrics)
PINO ARTACHO, J. DEL, State Law and Sociology
REQUENA RODRÍGUEZ, J. M., Financial Economics and Accountancy
SANCHEZ MALDONADO, J., Applied Economics (Structure and Public Finance)

Faculty of Law:
AURIOLES MARTIN, A., Private Law
CARRETERO LESTON, J. L., Public Law
ORTEGA CARILLO DE ALBÓRNOZ, A., Civil, Ecclesiastical and State Law
ROBLES GARZON, J. A., Political Science, International Law

Faculty of Medicine:
BROTAT ESTER, M., Radiology, Physical and Psychiatric Medicine
CASTILLA GONZALO, J., Normal and Pathological Morphology
FERNÁNDEZ-CREHUET NAVAJAS, J., Preventative Medicine and Public Health
OCAÑA SIERRA, J., Medicine
SÁNCHEZ DE LA CUESTA Y ALARCÓN, F., Physiology, Pharmacology and Paediatrics
SÁNCHEZ DEL CURA, G., Surgery, Obstetrics and Gynaecology

Faculty of Philosophy and Letters:
ALVAR EZQUERRA, M., Spanish and Romance Philology
CUEVAS GARCÍA, C., Spanish Philology and Theory of Literature
ESTEVE ZARAZAGA, J. M., Theory and History of Education
GARCÍA DE LA FUENTE, O., Classical Philology and Arabic and Islamic Studies
LAVIN CAMACHO, E., English and French Philology
MARTÍNEZ FREIRE, P., Philosophy
MORALES FOLGUERAS, J. M., History of Art
NADAL SANCHEZ, A., Modern History
OCANA OCANA, M. C., Geography
PEREZ GOMEZ, A., Didactics
RODRIGUEZ OLIVA, P., Prehistory and Science of Antiquity and Middle Ages
TRAINES TORRES, M. V., Psychology

Faculty of Science:
ARENAS ROSADO, J. F., Physical Chemistry
CABEZUDO ARTERO, B., Plant Biology
CANO PAVÓN, J. M., Analytical Chemistry
CUENCA MIRA, J. A., Algebra, Geometry and Topology
FERNÁNDEZ-FIGARES PEREZ, J. M., Cellular and Genetic Biology
FERNÁNDEZ JIMENEZ, C., Applied Physics
GARCÍA RASO, E., Animal Biology
JIMÉNEZ LÓPEZ, A., Inorganic Chemistry, Crystalography and Mineralogy
RODRÍGUEZ JIMENEZ, J. J., Chemical Engineering
RODRÍGUEZ ORTIZ, C., Applied Mathematics and Statistics
SERRANO LOZANO, L., Ecology and Geology
SUAU SUÁREZ, R., Biochemistry, Molecular Biology and Organic Chemistry

University School of Teacher Training:
DEL CAMPO Y DEL CAMPO, M., Didactics of Expression, Music
GARCÍA ESPAÑA, J., Didactics, Social Science, Experimental Science
MANTECON RAMIREZ, B., Didactics of Language and Literature

University Polytechnic:
OLLERO BATURONE, A., Systems Engineering, Information Science, Electronics
RUIZ MUNOZ, J. M., Electrical Engineering, Electronic Technology
SIMON MATA, A., Mechanical Engineering, Engineering Graphics
TROYA LINERO, J. M., Language and Science of Computing

UNIVERSIDAD DE MURCIA

Avda Teniente Flomesta 5, 30003 Murcia
Telephone: (96) 8363000
Fax: (96) 8363603
E-mail: siu@um.es
Internet: www.um.es

Founded 1915
State control
Language of instruction: Spanish
Academic year: September to June

Rector: JOSÉ ANTONIO COBACHO GÓMEZ
Vice-Rector for Academic Staff: JOSÉ MARÍA RUIZ GÓMEZ
Vice Rector for Coordination and Communication: MARIA ANGELES ESTEBAN ABAD
Vice-Rector for Finance and Infrastructure: ANTONIO CALVO-FLORES SEGURA
Vice-Rector for Int. Relations and Innovation: PILAR ARNAIZ SÁNCHEZ
Vice-Rector for Research: JUAN MARÍA VÁZQUEZ ROJAS
Vice Rector for Strategic Devt and Training: FERNANDO MARTÍN RUBIO
Vice-Rector for Students and Employment: MARÍA ISABEL SÁNCHEZ-MORA MOLINA
Vice-Rector for Studies: CONCEPCIÓN R. PALACIOS BERNAL
Vice Rector for Univ. Extension: GUILLERMO DÍAZ BAÑOS
Registrar: NATALIA EGEA DÍAZ
Man.: JORGE NAVARRO OLIVARES
Library Dir: LOURDES COBACHO GÓMEZ

Library of 718,276 vols, 9,416periodicals, 14,625 electronic journals
Number of teachers: 2,101
Number of students: 34,483

Publications: *Anales de Biología* (1 a year), *Antigüedad y Cristianismo* (1 a year), *Daimon* (philosophy, 2 a year), *Historia Agraria* (4 a year), *Myrtia* (classical philology, 2 a year), *Papeles de Geografía* (2 a year)

DEANS

Faculty of Arts: JOSÉ MARÍA JIMÉNEZ CANO
Faculty of Biology: JOSÉ MESEGUER PEÑALVER
Faculty of Chemistry: M. GLORIA SÁNCHEZ GÓMEZ
Faculty of Communication and Documentation: JOSÉ VICENTE RODRÍGUEZ MUÑOZ
Faculty of Computer Science: JOSÉ MANUEL GARCÍA CARRASCO
Faculty of Economics and Business Studies: MARÍA PILAR MONTANER SALAS
Faculty of Education: CONCEPCIÓN MARTÍN SÁNCHEZ
Faculty of Fine Arts: JUAN ROMERA AGULLÓ
Faculty of Labour Relations: DOMINGO A. MANZANARES MARTÍNEZ
Faculty of Law: FAUSTINO CAVAS MARTÍNEZ
Faculty of Mathematics: FRANCISCO ESQUEMBRE MARTÍNEZ
Faculty of Medicine: JOAQUÍN GARCÍA-ESTAÑ LÓPEZ
Faculty of Optometry: PALOMA SOBRADO CALVO
Faculty of Philosophy: ANTONIO CAMPILLO MESEGUER
Faculty of Psychology: JUAN JOSÉ LÓPEZ GARCÍA
Faculty of Social Work: ENRIQUE PASTOR SELLER
Faculty of Veterinary Studies: ANTONIO ROUCO YÁÑEZ

ATTACHED INSTITUTIONS

Institute of Ageing: Campus Universitario de Espinardo, 30100 Espinardo (Murcia); tel. (96) 8363499; e-mail maemedina@um.es; internet www.um.es/estructura/institutos/iupe; Dir MANUEL E. MEDINA TORNERO.

Institute of Education: Edificio D, 3°, Campus de Espinardo, 30100 Murcia; tel. (96) 8363926; fax (96) 8363925; e-mail ice@um.es; internet www.um.es/ice; Dir JUAN MANUEL ESCUDERO MUÑOZ.

Institute of Financial and Fiscal Studies: Dept Hacienda y Economía del Sector Público, Despacho B109, Campus de Espinardo, 30100 Murcia; tel. (96) 8367798; e-mail inueff@um.es; internet www.um.es/inueff; Dir GLORIA ALARCÓN GARCÍA.

Institute of Sport Science: Facultad de Educación, Campus Universitario de Espinardo, 30100 Espinardo (Murcia); tel. (96) 8364052; fax (96) 8364146; e-mail icd@um.es; internet www.um.es/icd; Dir ARTURO DÍAZ SUÁREZ.

Institute of University Teaching: Calle Real 80, Cartagena (Murcia); tel. (96)

8505313; internet www.um.es/isen; Dir MA. DOLORES FONTES BASTOS.

Institute of Water and the Environment: Edificio D, Campus de Espinardo, 30100 Murcia; tel. (96) 8364910; fax (96) 8363389; e-mail inuama@um.es; internet www.um.es/inuama; Dir ALBERTO BARBA NAVARRO.

Inter-university Institute of the Ancient Near East: Antigua Escuela de Empresariales, Calle Actor Isidoro Máiquez 8, Vistalegre, 30007 Murcia; tel. and fax (96) 8363890; e-mail ipoa@um.es; internet www.um.es/ipoa.

University School of Nursing in Cartagena: Plaza San Agustín 3, 30201 Cartagena (Murcia); tel. (96) 8326696; fax (96) 8326695; internet www.um.es/eu-enfermeria-ct; Dir CARMEN SÁNCHEZ TRIGUEROS.

University School of Tourism: Paseo de Malecón 5, 30004 Murcia; tel. (96) 8293624; fax (96) 8291096; e-mail eutm@um.es; Academic Dir BERNARDINO BENITO LÓPEZ.

UNIVERSIDAD DE NAVARRA

Campus Universitario, 31080 Pamplona

Telephone: (94) 8425600
Fax: (94) 8425619
E-mail: relint@unav.es
Internet: www.unav.es

Founded 1952
Private control
Languages of instruction: Spanish, English
Academic year: September to June

Chancellor: JAVIER ECHEVARRÍA
Vice-Chancellor: Mgr RAMÓN HERRANDO
Rector: Prof. ÁNGEL JOSÉ GÓMEZ MONTORO
Vice-Rector for Academic Org. and Educational Innovation: Prof. BORJA LOPEZ-JURADO
Vice-Rector for Academic Staff: Prof. CONCEPCION NAVAL-DURAN
Vice-Rector for Corporate Communication: Prof. JUAN MANUEL MORA
Vice-Rector for Int. Relations: Prof. ALFONSO SANCHEZ-TABERNERO
Vice-Rector for Research: Prof. LUIS MONTUENGA-BADIA
Vice-Rector for Student Affairs and Univ. Extension: Prof. MARIA IRABURU-ELIZALDE
Registrar: Dr GONZALO ROBLES GONZÁLEZ
Man.: XABIER AIZPURUA TELLERÍA
Admin. Dir: IGOR ERRASTI
Library Dir: VÍCTOR SANZ SANTACRUZ

Library of 1,200,000 vols, 60,000 journals
Number of teachers: 900 full-time, 891 part-time
Number of students: 11,198 full-time, 1,999 part-time

Publications: *Anuario de Derecho Internacional* (1 a year), *Anuario Filosófico* (3 a year), *Comunicación y Sociedad* (2 a year), *Ius Canonicum* (2 a year), *Nuestro Tiempo* (12 a year), *Persona y Derecho* (2 a year), *Redacción* (4 a year), *Revista de Edificación* (4 a year), *Revista de Medicina* (4 a year), *RILCE* (2 a year), *Scripta Theologica* (4 a year)

DEANS

Faculty of Architecture: MARIANO GONZALEZ-PRESENCIO
Faculty of Canon Law: JORGE MIRAS POUSO
Faculty of Communication: MONICA HERRERO
Faculty of Economics: REYES CALDERÓN
Faculty of Engineering: ALEJO AVELLO
Faculty of Humanities and Social Sciences: JAUME AURELL
Faculty of Law: PABLO SANCHEZ-OSTIZ
Faculty of Medicine: JORGE IRIARTE
School of Nursing: MERCEDES PEREZ-DIEZ DEL CORRAL
Faculty of Pharmacy: ADELA LOPEZ DE CERAIN
Faculty of Sciences: IGNACIO LÓPEZ GOÑI
Faculty of Theology: JUAN CHAPA
IESE School of Business Administration.: Professor JORDI CANALS-MARGALEF
Univ. Hospital: JOSE A. GOMEZ-CANTERO

PROFESSORS

Faculty of Canon Law:
BAÑARES PARERA, J. I., Family Law
CALVO-ÁLVAREZ, J., Administrative Canon Law
FUENTES ALSONSO, J. A., Administrative Canon Law
GÓMEZ-IGLESIAS, V., Constitutional Canon Law
MIRAS POUSO, J. M., Administrative Canon Law
MOLANO GRAGERA, E., Constitutional Canon Law
OTADUY, J., Ecclesiastical Law
OTADUY GUERIN, J., General and Personal Law
RINCÓN, T., Administrative Canon Law
RODRÍGUEZ-OCAÑA, R., Procedural Canon Law
VIANA TOMÉ, A., Ecclesiastical Organization
VILADRICH BATALLER, P. J., Canon Law

Faculty of Communication:
AMOEDO CASAIS, A., Journalistic Projects
ARRESE RECA, A., Media Business
ARTÁZCOZ LÓPEZ, M. A., Journalistic Projects
AZURMENDI ADARRAGA, A., Public Communication
BARRERA DEL BARRIO, C., Public Communication
BRINGUÉ SALA, J., Media Business
CODINA BLASCO, M., Public Communication
CUEVAS ÁLVAREZ, E., Audiovisual Communication
DE LA RICA ARANGUREN, A., Audiovisual Communication
DE LOS ÁNGELES VILLENA, J., Media Business
ECHART ORÚS, P., Audiovisual Communication
ETAYO PÉREZ, C., Media Business
FAUS BELAU, A., Audiovisual Communication
GARCÍA AVILÉS, J. A., Journalistic Projects
GARCÍA-NOBLEJAS LINIERS, J. J., Audiovisual Communication
JIMENO LÓPEZ, M. A., Journalistic Projects
LA PORTE FERNÁNDEZ-ALFARO, M. T., Public Communication
LATORRE IZQUIERDO, J., Audiovisual Communication
LEÓN ANGUIANO, B., Journalistic Projects
LÓPEZ PAN, F., Journalistic Projects
LÓPEZ-ESCOBAR FERNÁNDEZ, E., Public Communication
LOZANO BARTOLOZZI, P., Public Communication
MARTÍNEZ COSTA, M. P., Journalistic Projects
MEDINA, M., Media Business
MONTERO DÍAZ, M., Public Communication
MORENO MORENO, E., Journalistic Projects
NAVAS GARCÍA, A., Public Communication
ORIHUELA COLLIVA, J. L., Audiovisual Communication
PARDO FERNÁNDEZ, A., Audiovisual Communication
PÉREZ LATRE, F. J., Media Business
PIQUE I FERNÁNDEZ, A. M., Journalistic Projects
PORTILLA MANJÓN, I., Media Business
REDONDO GÁLVEZ, G., History
SÁDABA CHALEZQUER, R., Media Business
SÁDABA GARRAZA, M. T., Public Communication
SALAVERRÍA ALIAGA, R., Journalistic Projects
SÁNCHEZ ARANDA, J. J., Public Communication
SÁNCHEZ-TABERNERO SÁNCHEZ, A., Media Business
VARA MIGUEL, A., Media Business
VERDERA ALBIÑANA, F., Public Communication
ZORRILLA RUIZ, J., Journalistic Projects

Faculty of Economics and Business:
ABBRITTI, M., Economics
ALFARO TANCO, J. A., Business Admin.
ALVAREZ ARCE, J. L., Economics
ARANDA LEÓN, C., Business Admin.
ARELLANO GIL, J., Business Admin.
BLANCO, B., Business Economics and Quantitative Methods
BLAZSEK, S., Economics
CALDERÓN CUADRADO, R., Business Admin.
CORGNET, B., Economics
CUÑADO EIZAGUIRRE, J., Applied Economics
ELIZALDE, J., Applied Economics
GALERA PERAL, F., Applied Economics
GAVLE, S., Business Economics and Quantitative Methods
GIL ALAÑA, L., Economics
GONZÁLEZ ENCISO, A., Economics
KINATEDEE, M., Economics
LEIVA, R., Business
MARTÍNEZ-ECHEVARRÍA, M. A., Economics
MATEO DUEÑAS, R., Business
MATHEW, A. J., Economics
MENDI GÜEMES, P., Economics
MOLERO GARCÍA, J. C., Applied Economics
MORENO ALMÁRCEGUI, A., Economics
MORENO IBÁÑEZ, A., EconomicsPÉREZ DE GRACIA HIDALGO, F., Applied Economics
PUJOL TORRAS, F., Economics
RÁBADE Y HERRERO, L. A., Business
RAVINA BOHORQUEZ, L., Economics
RODRÍGUEZ CARREÑO, I., Economics
RODRÍGUEZ CHACÓN, V., Business
SALVATIERRA, S. M., Quantitative Methods
SAN MARTÍN ECHAURI, C., Quantitative Methods
SEBREK, S., Business
TOLSA MAJÓS, A., Applied Economics
TORRES SÁNCHEZ, R., Economics
ZARATIEGUI LAVIANO, J. M., Economics
ZARCO JASSO, H., Business Admin.

Faculty of Law:
APARISI MIRALLES, A., Philosophy of Law
ARECHEDERRA ARANZADI, L., Civil Law
BLANCO FERNÁNDEZ, M., Canon Law
DOMINGO OSLÉ, R., Roman Law
GÓMEZ MONTORO, A., Constitutional Law
LÓPEZ SÁNCHEZ, M. A., Commercial Law
LÓPEZ-JURADO, B., Administrative Law
MUERZA ESPARZA, J., Procedural Law
SÁNCHEZ-OSTIZ GUTIÉRREZ, P., Criminal Law
SIMÓN ACOSTA, E., Financial Law
VALPUESTA GASTAMINZA, E., Commercial Law

Faculty of Medicine:
ALBEROLA GÓMEZ-ESCOLAR, I., Internal Medicine
ALCÁZAR ZAMBRANO, J. L., Obstetrics and Gynaecology
ALEGRÍA EZQUERRA, E., Cardiology
ÁLVAREZ-CIENFUEGOS SUÁREZ, J., General Surgery
ALZINA DE AGUILAR, V., Paediatrics
AMILLO GARAYOA, S., Orthopaedics Surgery
AQUERRETA BEOLA, A., Radiology
ARTIEDA GONZÁLEZ-GRANDA, J., Neurology
AYMERICH SOLER, M. S., Neurology
AZANZA PEREA, J. R., Pharmacology
AZCONA SAN JULIÁN, C., Paediatrics
BARBA ÇOSIALS, J., Cardiology
BAZÁN ÁLVAREZ, A., Plastic Surgery
BEGUIRISTAIN GÚRPIDE, J. L., Orthopaedics Surgery
BELOQUI RUIZ, Ó., Internal Medicine
BERIÁN POLO, J. M., Urology

Bilbao Jaureguizar, I., Radiology
Bodegas Frías, M. E., Histology
Borrás Cuesta, F., Biochemistry
Burrell Bustos, M. A., Pathological Anatomy
Calabuig Nogués, J., Cardiology
Calvo González, A., Histology
Carrascosa Moreno, F., Anaesthesiology and Resuscitation
Casado Casado, M., Radiology
Cenarruzbeitia Sagarminaga, E., Physiology
Cervera Enguix, S., Psychiatry
Civeira Murillo, M. P., Medical Secretaryship
Colina Lorda, I., Internal Medicine
Coma Canella, I., Cardiology
Corrales Izquierdo, J., Internal Medicine
Cuesta Palomera, B., Haematology
de Castro, P., Neurology
de Miguel Vázquez, C., Biochemistry
Del Pozo León, J. L., Microbiology
Díaz García, R., Microbiology
Diéguez López, I., Allergology
Diez Goñi, N., Physiology
Díez Martínez, J., Internal Medicine
Echarte Alonso, L., Biomedicine
Fernández Alonso, M., Microbiology
Forriol Campos, F., Laboratory Medicine
Frechilla Manso, D., Pharmacology
García-Morato, J. R., Anthropology
Gil Sotres, P., Biomedicine
Honorato Pérez, J., Pharmacology
Hontanilla Catalay, B., Plastic Surgery
Idoate Gastearena, M., Pathological Anatomy
Iraburu Elizalde, M., Biochemistry
Irala Estevez, J. de, Preventive Medicine
Lahortiga Ramos, F., Psychiatry
Lasheras Aldaz, B., Pharmacology
Lázaro Cantero, R., Anthropology
León Sanz, M. P., Biomedicine
López Garacía, M. P., Psychiatry
Lozano Escario, M. D., Pathological Anatomy
Lucas Ros, I., Internal Medicine
Luquin Pulido, M. R., Neurology
Maldonado López, M., Ophthalmology
Manrique Rodríguez, M., Otolaryngology
Manrique Smela, M., Neurology
Martín Algarra, S., Oncology
Martín Trenor, A., General Surgery
Martínez de Tejada de Garaizabal, G., Microbiology
Martínez González, M. A., Epidemiology and Public Health
Martínez Irujo, J. J., Biochemistry
Martínez Lage, M., Neurology
Martínez Monge, R., Radiology
Martínez Regueira, F., General Surgery
Martínez Vila, E., Neurology
Masdeu Puche, J., Neurology
Medina Cabrera, J. F., Internal Medicine
Melero Bermejo, I., Immunology
Mengual Poza, E., Anatomy
Merino Roncal, J., Immunology
Monedero Rodríguez, P., Anaesthesiology and Resuscitation
Montuenga Badia, L., Histology
Moreno Montañés, J., Ophthalmology
Moriyón Uría, I., Microbiology
Muñoz Navas, M. A., General Surgery
Narbona García, J., Paediatrics
Novo Villaverde, J., Genetics
Obeso Inchausti, J., Neurology
Odero de Dios, L., Genetics
Olavide Goya, I., Anaesthesiology
Páramo Fernández, J. A., Haematology
Pardo Caballos, A., Biomedicine
Pardo Mindán, J., Pathological Anatomy
Pastor Muñoz, M. A., Neurology
Peñuelas Sánchez, I., Biochemistry
Pérez Fernández, N., Otolaryngology
Pérez Mediavilla, L. A., Biochemistry
Prensa Sepúlveda, L., Anatomy
Prieto Valtueña, J., Internal Medicine
Prósper, F., Haematology
Purroy Unanua, A., Nephrology
Qian, C., Internal Medicine
Quiroga Vilas, J., Internal Medicine
Redondo, P., Dermatology
Richter Echevarría, J. A., Nuclear Medicine
Rio Zambrana, J., Pharmacology
Robles García, J. E., Urology
Rocha Hernando, E., Haematology
Rodríguez Ortigosa, C., Biochemistry
Rosell Costa, D., Urology
Rouzaut Subirá, A., Biochemistry
Rubio Vallejo, M., Microbiology
Ruiz-Canela López, M., Biomedicine
Salvador Rodríguez, F. J., Endocrinology
Sánchez Ibarrola, A., Immunology
Sangro Gómez-Acebo, B., Internal Medicine
Santidrian Alegre, S., Physiology
Sanz Larruga, M. L., Allergology
Seguí Gómez, M., Internal Medicine
Serrano Martínez, M., Internal Medicine
Sesma Egozcue, P., Pathological Anatomy
Sierrasesúmaga Ariznavarreta, L., Paediatrics
Sola Gallego, J. J., Pathological Anatomy
Torre Buxalleu, W., General Surgery
Ullán Serrano, J., Anatomy
Valentí Nin, J. R., Orthopaedic Surgery
Velayos Jorge, J. L., Anatomy
Villaro Gumpert, A. C., Histology
Villas Tomé, C., Orthopaedic Surgery
Viteri Torres, C., Neurology
Zapata García, R., Psychiatry
Zornoza Celaya, G., General Surgery
Zubieta Zarraga, J. L., Radiology
Zudaire Bergara, J. J., Urology

Faculty of Pharmacy

(Some professors also serve in the Faculty of Sciences)

Aguirre García, N., Pharmacology
Aldana Moraza, I., Organic Chemistry
Aldaz Pastor, A., Pharmacy and Pharmaceutical Technology
Ansorena, D., Bromatology and Toxicology
Aquerreta González, I., Pharmacy and Pharmaceutical Technology
Astiasarán Anchía, I., Bromatology and Toxicology
Barber Cárcamo, A., Physiology and Nutrition
Beitia Berrotarán, G.
Berjón San Juan, A., Physiology and Nutrition
Blanco, M. J., Pharmacy and Pharmaceutical Technology
Calvo, I., Pharmacy and Pharmaceutical Technology
Cid Canda, C., Bromatology and Toxicology
de Peña Fariza, M. P., Bromatology
Díaz García, J. M., Pharmacy and Pharmaceutical Technology
Dios Viéitez, C., Pharmacy and Pharmaceutical Technology
Espuelas, S., Pharmacy and Pharmaceutical Technology
Idoate García, A., Pharmacy and Pharmaceutical Technology
Fernández de Trocóniz, I., Pharmacy and Pharmaceutical Technology
Font Arellano, M., Organic Chemistry
García del Barrio, G., Pharmacy and Pharmaceutical Technology
Garrido, M. J., Pharmacy and Pharmaceutical Technology
Gil Royo, A. G., Bromatology and Toxicology
Giráldez Deiró, J., Pharmacy and Pharmaceutical Technology
Goñi Leza, M. del M., Pharmacy and Pharmaceutical Technology
Lacasa Arregui, C., Pharmacy and Pharmaceutical Technology
Lasheras Aldaz, B., Pharmacology
Lizarraga Pérez, E., Organic Chemistry
Lobo, J. M., Pharmacy and Pharmaceutical Technology
López de Ceráin, A., Bromatology and Toxicology
López Guzmán, J., Biomedicine
Lostao Crespo, P., Physiology and Nutrition
Manuel Irache Garreta, J. M., Pharmacy and Pharmaceutical Technology
Martí del Moral, A., Physiology and Nutrition
Martínez Hernández, A., Physiology and Nutrition
Mohino Sánchez, A., Bromatology and Toxicology
Monge Vega, A., Organic Chemistry
Moreno Aliaga, M. J., Physiology and Nutrition
Muñoz Hornillos, M., Physiology and Nutrition
Ortega Eslava, A., Pharmacy and Pharmaceutical Technology
Palop Cubillo, J. A., Organic Chemistry
Ramírez Gil, M. J., Pharmacology
Recarte Flamarique, F., Pharmacy and Pharmaceutical Technology
Renedo Omaechevarría, M. J., Pharmacy and Pharmaceutical Technology
Romero Cuevas, M., Organic Chemistry
Ruiz de la Heras, A., Bromatology and Toxicology
Sanmartín Grijalba, C., Organic Chemistry
Tros de Ilarduya, C., Pharmacy and Pharmaceutical Technology
Ygartua Ayerra, P., Pharmacy and Pharmaceutical Technology
Zamarreño Arregui, A. M., Pharmacy and Pharmaceutical Technology
Zapelena Íñiguez, M. J., Bromatology and Toxicology
Zulet Alzórriz, M. A., Physiology

Faculty of Sciences:

Aguirreola Morales, J., Plant Physiology
Alvarez Calviño, R., Botany
Alvarez Galindo, J. I., Chemistry and Pedology
Álvarez Jaurrieta, M. L., Chemistry and Edaphology
Antolín Bellver, C., Plant Physiology
Aquerreta Molina, S., Botany
Ardanza-Trevijano, S., Physics and Applied Mathematics
Ariño Plana, A., Zoology and Ecology
Azcárate Iriarte, R., Chemistry and Edaphology
Baquero Martín, E., Zoology and Ecology
Bragard, J., Physics and Applied Mathematics
Burguete Más, F. J., Physics and Applied Mathematics
Calasanz Abinzano, M. J., Genetics
Cavero, Y., Chemistry and Pedology
Chasco Ugarte, M. J., Physics and Applied Mathematics
Clavería Iracheta, V., Botany
de Miguel Velasco, A., Botany
Díaz Calavia, E. J., Physics
Ederra Indurain, A., Botany
Escala Urdapilleta, C., Zoology and Ecology
Fernández Alvarez, J. M., Chemistry and Pedology
Fernández Asenjo, L., Chemistry and Pedology
Garayoa Poyo, R., Economy
García Casado, P., Chemistry and Pedology
García Delgado, M., Genetics
García Unciti, M. S., Dietetics

GARCÍA ZAMORA, J. M., Chemistry and Pedology
GARCÍA-MINA FREIRE, J. M., Chemistry and Pedology
GARCIMARTÍN, A., Physics and Applied Mathematics
GARDE GARDE, J. M., Zoology and Ecology
GARRIGÓ I REIXACH, J., Chemistry and Pedology
GOICOECHEA PREBOSTE, N., Plant Physiology
GONZÁLEZ, W., Physics and Applied Mathematics
GONZÁLEZ GAITANO, G., Chemistry and Pedology
GUERRERO SETAS, D., Edaphology
HERNÁNDEZ MINGUILLÓN, M. A., Zoology and Ecology
HERRERA MESA, L., Zoology and Ecology
IBÁÑEZ GASTÓN, R., Botany
IRIGOYEN IPARREA, J. J., Plant Physiology
ISASI ALLICA, J. R., Chemistry and Pedology
JORDANA BUTTICAZ, R., Zoology and Ecology
JUARISTI IRANZU, R., Botany
LABAT AYERRA, A., Chemistry and Pedology
LARRAZ AZCÁRATE, M., Zoology and Ecology
LÓPEZ FERNÁNDEZ, M. L., Botany
LÓPEZ GOÑI, I., Microbiology
LÓPEZ MORATALLA, N., Biochemistry
LÓPEZ ZABALZA, M. J., Biochemistry
MANCINI, H., Physics and Applied Mathematics
MARTÍN BACHILLER, C., Chemistry and Pedology
MARTÍNEZ OHARRIZ, C., Chemistry and Pedology
MARTÍNEZ REMÍREZ, M., Physiology
MAZA OZCOIDI, D., Physics and Applied Mathematics
MIRANDA FERREIRO, R., Zoology and Ecology
MORAZA ZORRILLA, L., Zoology and Ecology
NAVARRO BLASCO, I., Chemistry and Pedology
NOVO VILLAVERDE, J., Genetics
ODERO DE DIOS, M. D., Genetics
PALACIOS, C., Physics and Applied Mathematics
PELAEZ LÓPEZ, A., Physics and Applied Mathematics
PEÑAS, F. J., Chemistry and Pedology
PÉREZ GARCÍA, C., Physics and Applied Mathematics
PIUDO AINZINENA, M. J., Botany
PUIG BAGUER, J., Zoology and Ecology
RODÉS NAVARRO, D., Zoology and Ecology
RODRÍGUEZ GARCÍA, J. A., Genetics
RUILOPE PINEDA, R., Chemistry and Pedology
SÁNCHEZ CARPINTERO, I., Chemistry and Pedology
SÁNCHEZ DÍAZ, M., Plant Physiology
SÁNCHEZ GONZÁLEZ, M., Chemistry and Pedology
SÁNCHEZ MONGE, J. M., Chemistry and Pedology
SANTAMARÍA ELOLA, C., Chemistry and Pedology
SANTAMARÍA ULECIA, J. M., Chemistry and Pedology
SERRANO MARTÍNEZ, M., Zoology and Ecology
SIRERA BEJARANO, R., Chemistry and Pedology
VELAZ RIVAS, I., Chemistry and Pedology
VIZMANOS, J. L., Genetics
ZORNOZA CEBEIRO, A., Chemistry and Pedology
ZUDAIRE RIPA, I., Genetics

Faculty of Theology:
ARANDA LOMEÑA, A., Dogmatic Theology
ARANDA PÉREZ, G., Sacred Scripture: New Testament
BASTERO ELEIZALDE, J. L., Dogmatic Theology
IZQUIERDO URBINA, C., Fundamental Theology
MERINO RODRÍGUEZ, M., Patristics
SARANYANA CLOSA, J. I., History of Theology
SARMIENTO FRANCO, A., Moral Theology
VARO PINEDA, F., Sacred Scripture: New Testament

School of Engineering:
ALVAREZ SÁNCHEZ-ARJONA, M. J., Industrial Organization
ARCELUS ALONSO, M., Organization
ARIZTI URQUIJO, F., Fundamental Electronics
AVELLO ITURRIAGAGOITIA, A., Theory of Machines
BAGUER ALCALÁ, A., Organization of Work
BASTERO DE ELEIZALDE, C., Mathematical Methods
BASTERO DE ELEIZALDE, J. M., Mechanics
BERENGUER PÉREZ, R., Electronics
BISTUÉ GARCÍA, G., Electricity
BLANCO DEL PRADO, C., Calculus
BUSTAMENTE MERINO, P., Informatics
CAMPOS CAPELASTEGUI, J., Mechanics
CELIGÜETA LIZARZA, J. T., Computational Mechanics
DE LOS MOZOS VILLAR, L., Mechanics
DE MIGUEL SICILIA, J. J., Anthropology
DE NO LENGARÁN, J., Electricity
FERNÁNDEZ DÍEZ, J., Mechanical Technology
FLAQUER FUSTER, J., Linear Algebra
FLÓREZ ESNAL, J., Robotics
FONTAN AGORRETA, L., Fundamentals of Electronics
FUENTES PÉREZ, M., Metallurgy
GARCÍA RICO, A., Electrical Machines
GARCÍA-ALONSO MONTOYA, A., Electrical Engineering
GARCÍA-ROSALES VÁZQUEZ, C., Materials
GIL NOBAJAS, J. J., Electricity and Electronics
GIL SEVILLANO, J., Metallurgy
GIMÉNEZ ORTIZ, G., Mechanical Technology
GÓMEZ-ACEBO TEMES, T., Thermodynamics
GRACIA GAUDÓ, J., Electronics
GURRUCHAGA VÁZQUEZ, J. M., Technical Drawing
IZU BELLOSO, P., Materials
JIMÉNEZ CONDE, M., General Physics
LÓPEZ DE ARANCIBIA, A., Mechanics
LÓPEZ SORIA, B., Materials
MARTÍN ABREU, F., Mechanics
MARTÍNEZ ESNAOLA, J. M., Mechanics of Continua
MUÑOZ EMPARAN, A., Telecommunications
PARGADA GIL, M., Advanced Mathematics
PÉREZ TOCA, M., Electricity
PUENTE URRUZMENDI, I., Mechanics
RAMOS GONZÁLEZ, J. C., Mechanics
RIVAS NIETO, A., Fluids
RODRÍGUEZ IBABE, J. M., Materials
RUBIO DÍAZ-CORDOVÉS, A. R., Electricity
SANCHO SEUMA, J. I., Electricity
SANTOS GARCÍA, J., Organization
SARRIEGUI DOMÍNGUEZ, J. M., Organization
SERNA OLIVEIRA, M. A., Mechanics
SERRANO BÁRCENA, N., Organization
VERA RODRÍGUEZ, E., Steel Structures
VILES DÍEZ, E., Statistics
VIÑOLAS PRAT, J., Mechanics

ATTACHED INSTITUTES AND SCHOOLS

Higher Institute of Religious Studies: Universidad de Navarra, Edificio de Facultades Eclesiásticas, 31080 Pamplona, (Navarra); tel. (94) 8425716; fax (94) 8425633; e-mail iscr@unav.es; internet www.unav.es/iscr; Dir ENRIQUE MOLINA.

Institute of Advanced Business Studies (IESE): Avda Pearson 21, 08034 Barcelona; tel. (93) 2534200; fax (93) 2534343; e-mail info@iese.edu; internet www.iese.edu*also at:* Camino del Cerro del Águila 3 (Ctra. de Castilla km 5.180), 28023 Madrid; tel. (91) 3570809; fax (91) 3572913; f. 1958; business administration; 98 full-time teachers; 1,500 students; library of 31,784 vols, 7,700 periodicals; Dean Prof. Dr JORDI CANALS.

Institute of Anthropology and Ethics: Universidad de Navarra, Edificio Central, 31009 Pamplona; tel. (94) 8425600 ext. 2047; e-mail iae@unav.es; internet www.unav.es/iae; Dir SERGIO SÁNCHEZ-MIGALLÓN.

Institute of Enterprise and Humanism: Edificio de Bibliotecas, Campus Universitario s/n, 31080 Pamplona; tel. (94) 8425600; e-mail cosinaga@unav.es; internet www.unav.es/empresayhumanismo; Dir RAFAEL ALVIRA.

Institute of Family Studies: Edificio Los Nogales, Universidad de Navarra, 31080 Pamplona; tel. (94) 8425600; fax (94) 8425640; e-mail icf@unav.es; internet www.unav.es/icf; Dir PEDRO-JUAN VILADRICH BATALLER.

Institute of Food Sciences: Edificio de Ciencias, Universidad de Navarra, C/ Irunlarrea 1, 31008 Pamplona; tel. (94) 8425600; fax (94) 8425649; e-mail icaun@unav.es; internet www.unav.es/icaun.

Institute of Human Rights: Despacho 1731, Edificio de Bibliotecas, Campus Universitario s/n, 31080 Pamplona; tel. (94) 8425600; fax (94) 8425621; e-mail idh@unav.es; internet www.unav.es/idh/default.html; Dir ÁNGELA APARISI MIRALLES.

Institute of Medieval Studies: e-mail saurell@unav.es; internet www.unav.es/iestmedie; Dir JAUME AURELL.

Institute of Physics: Universidad de Navarra, Irunlarrea, s/n, 31080 Pamplona; e-mail hmancini@fisica.unav.es; internet instituto.fisica.unav.es; Dir HÉCTOR L. MANCINI.

Martín Azpilcueta Institute: Edificio de Bibliotecas, Campus Universitario, s/n, 31080 Pamplona; tel. (94) 8425631; fax (94) 8425636; e-mail ima@unav.es; internet www.unav.es/ima; Dir Prof. JORGE OTADUY.

Professional School of Clinical Biochemistry: Dir (vacant).

Professional School of Internal Medicine: Facultad de Medicina; Dir JESÚS PRIETO.

Professional School of Medical-Surgical Dermatology and Venereology: Dir (vacant).

Professional School of Psychiatry: Dir SALVADOR CERVERA.

Professional School of the Digestive Apparatus: Dir FEDERICO CONCHILLO.

School of Legal Practice: Dir FAUSTINO CORDON.

Urban Ecology Studies Centre: Dir MANUEL FERRER.

University Clinic: Avda Pío XII 36, 31008 Pamplona; tel. (94) 8255400; fax (94) 8296500; internet www.cun.es; Gen. Dir AMADOR SOSA LORA; Medical Dir Dr JAVIER ÁLVAREZ-CIENFUEGOS SUÁREZ.

UNIVERSIDAD DE OVIEDO

Calle San Francisco 3, 33003 Oviedo
Telephone: (98) 5104058
Fax: (98) 5104085
E-mail: causi@uniovi.es
Internet: www.uniovi.es

Founded 1608
Language of instruction: Spanish
State control
Language of instruction: English

Academic year: September to July
Rector: Prof. VICENTE GOTOR SANTAMARÍA
Vice-Rector for Campus: Prof. MARÍA PAZ SUÁREZ RENDUELES
Vice-Rector for Economic Planning: SANTIAGO ÁLVAREZ GARCÍA
Vice-Rector for Infrastructure, Campus and Sustainability: Prof. JOSÉ CARLOS RICO FERNÁNDEZ
Vice-Rector for Int. Relations and Devt Cooperation: Prof. ANA MARÍA FERNÁNDEZ GARCÍA
Vice-Rector for IT and Communications: Prof. VÍCTOR GUILLERMO GARCÍA GARCÍA
Vice-Rector for Research: Prof. SANTIAGO GARCÍA GRANDA
Vice-Rector for Students and Employment: Prof. SUSANA LÓPEZ ARES
Vice-Rector for Studies and New Degrees: Prof. COVADONGA BETEGÓN BIEMPICA
Vice-Rector for Teaching Staff, Depts and Centres: Prof. JULIO ANTONIO GONZÁLEZ GARCÍA
Vice-Rector for Univ. Extension, Culture and Sport: Prof. VICENTE JESÚS DOMÍNGUEZ GARCÍA
Gen. Sec.: Prof. JOSÉ FRANCISCO FERNÁNDEZ GARCÍA
Man.: EUSEBIO GONZÁLEZ GARCÍA
Librarian: Dr. RAMÓN RODRÍGUEZ ÁLVAREZ

Library of 1,000,000 vols, 14,000 periodicals
Number of teachers: 2,154
Number of students: 29,000

Publications: *Aljamía, Archivos de la Facultad de Medicina, Asturiensia Medievalía, Brevoria Geológica Astúrica, Ería, Archivum, Liño, Memorias de Historia Antigua y Territorio, Revista de Biología, Revista de Ciencias, Revista de Minas, Sociedad y Poder, Trabajos de Geología*

DEANS

Faculty of Biology: TOMÁS EMILIO DÍAZ GONZÁLEZ
Faculty of Chemistry: JOSÉ MANUEL FERNÁNDEZ COLINAS
Faculty of Commerce, Tourism and Social Sciences 'Jovellanos': (vacant)
Faculty of Economics and Business Studies: Prof. MANUEL GONZALEZ DÍAZ
Faculty of Geology: LOPEZ CALLEJA ESCUDERO
Faculty of Law: RAMÓN DURÁN RIVACOBA
Faculty of Medicine and Health Sciences: ANTONIO CUETO ESPINAR
Faculty of Philology: JESÚS MENÉNDEZ PELÁEZ
Faculty of Philosophy and Letters: CRISTINA VALDÉS RODRÍQUEZ
Faculty of Psychology: MARCELINO CUESTA IZQUIERDO
Faculty of Science: NORBERTO CORRAL BLANCO
Faculty of Teaching Training and Education: JUAN CARLOS SAN PEDRO VELEDO
Faculty of Trade, Tourism and Social Sciences 'Jovellanos': RAFAEL PÉREZ LORENZO
Higher School of Civil Navy: Prof. RAFAEL GARCÍA MÉNDEZ
Higher Technical School of Mine Engineering: Prof. MARIO MENÉNDEZ ÁLVAREZ
IT Engineering School: Prof. JOSÉ EMILIO LABRA GAYO
Polytechnic School (Mieres): Prof. ANTONIO BERNARDO SÁNCHEZ
Polytechnic School of Egineering (Gijón): Prof. HILARIO LÓPEZ GARCÍA

ATTACHED SCHOOLS AND CENTRES

'Padre Enrique de Ossó' University School of Teacher Training: Calle Prau Picon, s/n, 33008 Oviedo; e-mail informa@eupo.es; internet www.eupo.es; Dir FERNANDO PENDAS FERNÁNDEZ.

University School of Industrial Relations: Avda Manuel Llaneza 75, 33208 Gijón; e-mail eurlgijo@correo.uniovi.es; internet www.uniovied.es/relacioneslaboralesgijon; Dir JULIO RODRÍGUEZ SUAREZ.

University School of Nursing: Calle Hospital de Cabueñes s/n, 33294 Gijón; e-mail escuelaenfermeria.gae5@sespa.princast.es; Dir CRISTINA FERNÁNDEZ ÁLVAREZ.

University School of Social Work: Calle Fortuna Balnearia 1, 33207 Gijón; e-mail admon@eutsgijon.com; internet www.unioviedo.es/eutsg; Dir MARÍA JOSÉ CAPELLÍN CORRADA.

University School of Tourism in Asturias: Avda de los Monumentos 11, 33012 Oviedo; e-mail escuastur@fade.es; internet www.escuastur.com; Dir COVADONGA VIGIL ÁLVAREZ.

UNIVERSIDAD DE SALAMANCA

Patio de Escuelas Mayores 1, Apdo 20, 37008 Salamanca
Telephone: (92) 3294400
Fax: (92) 3294502
E-mail: informacion@usal.es
Internet: www.usal.es

Founded 1218 by Alfonso IX of León and reorganized 1254 by Alfonso X of Castile
State control
Language of instruction: Spanish
Academic year: October to July

Rector: DANIEL HERNÁNDEZ RUIPÉREZ
Vice-Rector for Economics and Management: RICARDO LÓPEZ FERNÁNDEZ
Vice-Rector for Innovation and Infrastructure: PASTORA VEGA CRUZ
Vice-Rector for Int. and Institutional Relations: NOEMÍ DOMÍNGUEZ GARCÍA
Vice-Rector for Research: MARÍA DE LOS ÁNGELES SERRANO GARCÍA
Vice-Rector for Strategic Planning and Evaluation: MIGUEL PÉREZ FERNÁNDEZ
Vice-Rector for Student Affairs: CRISTINA PITA YAÑEZ
Vice-Rector for Teaching: JOSÉ ÁNGEL DOMÍNGUEZ PÉREZ
Vice-Rector for Teaching Staff: MARIANO ESTEBAN DE VEGA
Registrar: ANA CUEVAS BADALLO
Man.: LUIS J. MEDIERO OSLÉ

Library: 1.05m. vols, 22,706 periodicals
Number of teachers: 2,200
Number of students: 32,000

DEANS

Faculty of Agricultural and Environmental Sciences: FERNANDO SANTOS FRANCÉS
Faculty of Biology: MANUEL ANTONIO MANSO MARTÍN
Faculty of Chemistry: CARMEN MARÍA DEL HOYO MARTÍNEZ
Faculty of Economics and Business: ALBERTO DE MIGUEL HIDALGO
Faculty of Education: MARÍA ESPERANZA HERRERA GARCÍA
Faculty of Fine Arts: JOSÉ MANUEL PRADA VEGA
Faculty of Geography and History: VALENTÍN CABERO DIÉGUEZ
Faculty of Law: RAFAEL DE AGAPITO SERRANO
Faculty of Medicine: JOSÉ CARRETERO GONZÁLEZ
Faculty of Pharmacy: JULIÁN C. RIVAS GONZALO
Faculty of Philology: ROMÁN ÁLVAREZ RODRÍGUEZ
Faculty of Philosophy: PABLO GARCÍA CASTILLO
Faculty of Psychology: JOSÉ CARLOS SÁNCHEZ GARCÍA
Faculty of Sciences: JUAN MANUEL CORCHADO RODRÍGUEZ
Faculty of Social Sciences: PEDRO ANTONIO CORDERO QUIÑONES
Faculty of Translation and Documentation: CARLOS FORTEA GIL

ATTACHED CENTRES AND COLLEGES

Centro de Historia Universitaria Alfonso IX: Colegio Mayor San Bartolomé, Plaza de Fray Luis de León 1–8, 37008 Salamanca; tel. (92) 3294500; fax (92) 3294779; e-mail chuaix@usal.es; internet campus.usal.es/~alfonix; Dir LUIS E. RODRÍGUEZ-SAN PEDRO BEZARES.

College of Industrial Relations: Calle San Torcuato 43, 49014 Zamora; tel. (98) 0531549; fax (98) 0533623; Dir JOSÉ MARÍA GARCÍA SÁNCHEZ.

College of Nursing at Ávila: Calle Canteros, s/n, 05005 Ávila; tel. (92) 0253889; fax (92) 0200164; Dir MARÍA DEL PILAR GONZÁLEZ ARRIETA.

College of Nursing at Zamora: Avda de Requejo 21, 1°, 49014 Zamora; tel. (98) 0519343; fax (98) 0519462; Dir MARÍA SOLEDAD SÁNCHEZ ARNOSI.

UNIVERSIDAD DE SEVILLA

Calle de San Fernando 4, 41004 Seville
Telephone: (95) 4551000
Fax: (95) 4212803
E-mail: rector@us.es
Internet: www.us.es

Founded 1505
State control
Language of instruction: Spanish
Academic year: October to July

Rector: Dr JOAQUÍN LUQUE RODRÍGUEZ
Vice-Rector for Academic Affairs: Dr MIGUEL ÁNGEL CASTRO ARROYO
Vice-Rector for Infrastructure: Dr ANTONIO RAMÍREZ DE ARELLANO LÓPEZ
Vice-Rector for Institutional Relations: Dr TERESA GARCÍA GUTIÉRREZ VENTOSA UCERO
Vice-Rector for Int. Relations: Dra LOURDES MUNDUATE JACA
Vice-Rector for Research: Dr MANUEL GARCÍA LEÓ
Vice-Rector for Students: Dra ROSARIO RODRÍGUEZ DÍAZ
Vice-Rector for Teaching: Dra JULIA DE LA FUENTE FERIA
Vice-Rector for Teaching Staff: Dra MARÍA ELENA CANO BAZAGA
Vice-Rector for Technology Transfer: Dr RAMÓN GONZÁLEZ CARVAJALI
Registrar: Dra CONCEPCIÓN HORGUÉ BAENA
Man.: JUAN IGNACIO FERRARO GARCÍA
Library Dir: SONSOLES CELESTINO ANGULO

Number of teachers: 4,478
Number of students: 75,250

Publication: *Anales de la Universidad Hispalense* (1 a year)

DEANS

Faculty of Biology: FRANCISCO JAVIER MORENO ONORATO
Faculty of Chemistry: MARÍA PILAR MALET MAENNER
Faculty of Communication: ANTONIO CHECA GODOY
Faculty of Economics and Business: CARMEN NUÑEZ GARCIA
Faculty of Education: JUAN DE PABLOS PONS
Faculty of Fine Arts: MARÍA TERESA CARRASCO GIMENA
Faculty of Geography and History: ANTONIO JOSÉ ALBARDONEDO FREIRE
Faculty of Labour Science: MARÍA MILAGRO MARTIN LÓPEZ (acting)
Faculty of Law: ANTONIO MERCHAN ALVAREZ
Faculty of Mathematics: ANTONIO BEATO MORENO
Faculty of Medicine: JUAN RAMON LACALLE REMIGIO

Faculty of Nursing, Physical Therapy and Podiatry: JUAN PABLO SOBRINO TOBO
Faculty of Odontology: PEDRO BULLON FERNANDEZ
Faculty of Pharmacy: JOSÉ MANUEL VEGA PEREZ
Faculty of Philology: RAFAEL DE LA CRUZ LÓPEZ-CAMPOS BODINEAU
Faculty of Philosophy: MANUEL BARRIOS CASARES
Faculty of Physics: JOSÉ GOMEZ ORDONEZ
Faculty of Psychology: ANTONIO AGUILERA JIMENEZ
Faculty of Tourism and Finance: JOSÉ LUIS CABALLERO JIMENEZ

DIRECTORS

Higher Technical School of Agronomical Engineering: CARLOS AVILLA HERNÁNDEZ
Higher Technical School of Architecture: NARCISO JESUS VAZQUEZ CARRETERO
Higher Technical School of Computer Engineering: JESUS TORRES VALDERRAMA
Higher Technical School of Industrial Engineering: JOSÉ MARÍA CALAMA RODRÍGUEZ
University Polytechnic School: JORGE JESUS LOPEZ VAZQUEZ

ATTACHED CENTRES

Andalusian Inter-university Institute of Criminology (Seville Branch): Escuela Técnica Superior de Ingeniería Informática, Avda Reina Mercedes, s/n, 41012 Seville; tel. (95) 4551396; fax (95) 4551397; e-mail iaic@us.es; internet www.iaic.us.es; Dir BORJA MAPELLI CAFFARENA.

'Cardenal Spinola' Centre for Advanced Studies: Campus Universitário, 41930 Bormujos (Seville); tel. (95) 4488000; fax (95) 4488010; e-mail info@ceuandalucia.com; internet www.ceuandalucia.com/indice.html; education and educational psychology; Dir MANUEL GÓMEZ GUILLÉN.

'Cruz Roja Española' University College of Nursing: Avda de la Cruz Roja 1, 41009 Seville; tel. and fax (95) 4350997; e-mail creseue@creseue.infonegocio.com; internet www.infonegocio.com/creseue; Dir FÉLIX JULIO JARA FERNÁNDEZ.

'Francisco Maldonado' University College: Campo de Cipreses 1, (Edif. Antigua Universidad), 41640 Osuna; tel. (95) 5820292; fax (95) 5820289; internet www.euosuna.org; Dir JAVIER MUÑOZ RANGEL.

García Oviedo Institute: Facultad de Derecho, Avda del Cid s/n, 41004 Seville; tel. (95) 4551226; fax (95) 4557899; e-mail instgarciaov@us.es; internet www.us.es/iugo; administrative law; Dir FRANCISCO LÓPEZ MENUDO.

National Accelerators Centre: Parque Tecnológico Cartuja 93, Avda Thomas A. Edison s/n, 41092 Seville; tel. (95) 4460553; fax (95) 4460145; e-mail respaldiza@us.es; internet www.us.es/cna; Dir MIGUEL ÁNGEL RESPALDIZA GALISTEO.

University College of Tourism: Calle Isabela 1, 41013 Seville; tel. (95) 4238797; fax (95) 4238942; e-mail cpino@eusa.cenp.es; internet www.eusa.cenp.es/turismo.htm; Dir FRANCISCO GUERRERO DÍAZ.

'Virgen del Rocío' University College of Nursing: Avda Manuel Siurot, s/n, Edificio de Gobierno, 41013 Seville; tel. (95) 5013434; fax (95) 5013473; e-mail eu.hvr.sspa@juntadeandalucia.es; Dir MERCEDES BUENO FERRÁN.

UNIVERSIDAD DE VALLADOLID

Plaza de Santa Cruz 8, 47002 Valladolid
Telephone: (98) 423283
Fax: (98) 423234
E-mail: relint@uva.es
Internet: www.uva.es
Founded 13th century
Academic year: October to June
Rector: MARCOS SACRISTÁN REPRESA
Vice-Rector for Academic Affairs: LUIS MIGUEL NIETO CALZADA
Vice-Rector for Culture and Infrastructure: ANTONIO ORDUÑA DOMINGO
Vice-Rector for Economy: GUIOMAR MARTÍN HERRÁN
Vice-Rector for Int. Relations: LUIS ANTONIO SANTOS DOMÍNGUEZ
Vice-Rector for Research and Scientific Policy: JOSÉ MANUEL LÓPEZ RODRÍGUEZ
Vice-Rector for Segovia Campus: JOSÉ VICENTE ÁLVAREZ BRAVO
Vice-Rector for Soria Campus: AMELIA RUTH MOYANO GARDINI
Vice-Rector for Students: ROCÍO ANGUITA MARTÍNEZ
Vice-Rector for Teaching: JOSÉ MARÍA MARBÁN PRIETO
Vice-Rector for Teaching and Training: JOSÉ MARÍA MARBÁN PRIETO
Registrar: MIGUEL ÁNGEL GONZÁLEZ REBOLLO
Man.: JOSÉ ANTONIO ANTONA MONTORO
Library Dir: MERCEDES ARRANZ SOMBRÍA
Library of 958,343 vols, 15,725 periodicals and 5,907 audiovisual
Number of teachers: 2,618
Number of students: 26,370

DEANS

Faculty of Arts: MILAGROS ESTILITA ALARIO TRIGUEROS
Faculty of Economics and Business: JOSEFA EUGENIA FERNÁNDEZ ARUFE
Faculty of Education and Social Work: JOSÉ SIXTO OLIVAR PARRA
Faculty of Labour Science (Palencia): JOSÉ ANTONIO OREJAS CASAS
Faculty of Law: LUIS ANTONIO VELASCO SAN PEDRO
Faculty of Medicine: RICARDO JAIME RIGUAL BONASTRE
Faculty of Science: FERNANDO VILLAFAÑE GONZÁLEZ
Faculty of Social, Legal and Communication Sciences (Segovia): JUAN JOSÉ GARCILLÁN GARCÍA
Faculty of Translation and Interpretation (Soria): ANTONIO BUENO GARCÍA

UNIVERSIDAD DE ZARAGOZA

Calle Pedro Cerbuna 12, 50009 Zaragoza
Telephone: (97) 6761001
Fax: (97) 6761009
E-mail: rector@unizar.es
Internet: www.unizar.es
Founded in 1542 by the Emperor Charles V
State control
Language of instruction: Spanish
Academic year: October to June
Rector: MANUEL JOSÉ LÓPEZ PÉREZ
Vice-Rector for Academic Affairs: MIGUEL ÁNGEL RUIZ CARNICER
Vice-Rector for Academic Staff: JOSÉ ANTONIO MAYORAL MURILLO
Vice-Rector for Cultural and Social Projection: CONCEPCIÓN LOMBA SERRANO
Vice-Rector for Economic Affairs: FRANCISCO JAVIER TRÍVEZ BIELSA
Vice-Rector for Health Sciences: JOSÉ LUIS OLIVARES LÓPEZ
Vice-Rector for Huesca Campus: PILAR BOLEA CATALÁN
Vice-Rector for Int. Relations: REGINA LÁZARO GISTAU
Vice-Rector for Research: JOSÉ RAMÓN BELTRÁN BLÁZQUEZ
Vice-Rector for Student Affairs and Employment: FERNANDO ZULAICA PALACIOS
Vice-Rector for Teruel Campus: MARÍA ALEXIA SANZ HERNÁNDEZ
Registrar: JUAN FRANCISCO HERRERO PEREZAGUA
Man.: ROSA CISNEROS LARRODÉ
Librarian: RAMÓN ABAD HIRALDO
Library: more than 1m. vols, 20,000 periodicals
Number of teachers: 3,006
Number of students: 35,886

Publications: *Ager: Revista de Estudios sobre Despoblación Rural* (rural depopulation, 1 a year), *Anales de la Facultad de Veterinaria, Antigrama: Revista del Departamento de Historia del Arte* (1 a year), *Anuario de pedagogía* (1 a year), *Aragón en la Edad Media, Archivos de la Facultad de Medicina, Arqueología Espacial: Revista del Seminario de Arqueología y Etnología Turolense, Boletín de la Asociación de Demografía Histórica* (2 a year), *Boletín Informativo, Cuadernos Aragoneses de Economía* (2 a year), *Cuadernos de Bioestadística y sus Aplicaciones Informáticas* (2 a year), *El Gnomo: Boletín de Estudios Becquerianos, European Journal of Psychiatry, Geographicalia, Geórgica, Guía, Kalathos: Revista del Seminario de Arqueología y Etnología Turolense* (1 a year), *Llull: Revista de la Sociedad Española de Historia de la Ciencia y de las Técnicas* (3 a year), *Medicina Naturista: Revista Internacional de Difusión Biomédica* (4 a year), *Miscelánea* (1 a year), *Naturaleza Aragonesa: Revista de la Sociedad de Amigos del Museo Paleontológico* (2 a year), *Organización del Conocimiento en Sistemas de Información y Documentación* (2 a year), *Resúmenes de Tesis Doctorales, Revista Aquatic, Revista de Demografía Histórica* (2 a year), *Revista de Desarrollo Rural y Cooperativismo Agrario, Revista de Gestión Pública y Privada* (1 a year), *Revista Española de Filosofía Medieval* (1 a year), *Revista Interuniversitaria de Formación del Profesorado* (3 a year), *Revista Universidad, Riff-Raff: Revista de Pensamiento y Cultura* (3 a year), *Saldvie: Estudios de Prehistoria y Archeología* (1 a year), *Scire: Representación y Organización del Conocimiento* (2 a year), *Stvdivm: Revista de Humanidades* (2 a year), *Tropelías: Revista de Teoría de la Literatura y Literatura Comparada* (1 a year), *Temas*

DEANS

Faculty of Arts: Dr SEVERINO ESCOLANO UTRILLA
Faculty of Economics and Business Studies: Dr JOSÉ ALBERTO MOLINA CHUECA
Faculty of Education: Dr ENRIQUE GARCÍA PASCUAL
Faculty of Health Sciences and Sport, Huesca: Dr MIGUEL TOMÁS CHIVITE IZCO
Faculty of Humanities and Education, Huesca: Dr JOSÉ DOMINGO DUENA LORENTE
Faculty of Law: Dr JUAN GARCÍA BLASCO
Faculty of Medicine: Dr FRANCISCO JAVIER CASTILLO GARCÌA
Faculty of Sciences: Dra ANA ISABEL ELDUQUE PALOMO
Faculty of Social Sciences and Labour: Dr MIGUEL MIRANDA ARANDA
Faculty of Veterinary Science: Dr JESÚS GARCÍA SÁNCHEZ

ATTACHED SCHOOLS

Polytechnic University School, La Almunia: Calle Mayor, s/n, 50100 La Almunia de Doña Godina (Zaragoza); tel. (97) 6600813; engineering, architecture; Dir ANTONIO ORZEGA TELLO.

University College of Nursing, Teruel: Avda América 15, 44002 Teruel; tel. (97)

8620648; fax (97) 8620954; internet www.teruel.unizar.es/enfermeria/enfermeria.html; Dir MARÍA CARMEN GÓRRIZ GONZÁLEZ.

UNIVERSIDAD DEL PAÍS VASCO/ EUSKAL HERRIKO UNIBERTSITATEA (University of the Basque Country)

Apdo 1397, 48080 Bilbao

Telephone: (94) 6012000
Fax: (94) 4801590
E-mail: internacional@ehu.es
Internet: www.ehu.es

Founded 1968, reorganized 1980

3 Campuses: Bizkaia Campus, Araba Campus, Gipuzkoa Campus
Basque Regional Govt control
Languages of instruction: Spanish, Basque
Academic year: September to July

Rector: IÑAKI GOIRIZELAIA ORDORIKA
Vice-Rector for Academic Org.: CARMEN GONZÁLEZ MURUA
Vice-Rector for Araba Campus: EUGENIO RUIZ URRESTARAZU
Vice-Rector for Basque Language and Multilingualism: JON IRAZUSTA
Vice-Rector for Bizkaia Campus: CARMELO GARITAONANDIA
Vice-Rector for Coordination and Planning: ITSASO IBÁÑEZ FERNÁNDEZ
Vice-Rector for Economic Affairs: EVA FERREIRA GARCÍA
Vice-Rector for Gipuzkoa Campus: CRISTINA URIARTE TOLEDO
Vice-Rector for Int. Relations: MIRIAM PEÑALBA
Vice-Rector for Quality and Educational Innovation: ITZIAR ALKORTA
Vice-Rector for Research: MIGUEL ÁNGEL GUTIÉRREZ ORTIZ
Vice-Rector for Science and Technology Devt: JOAN SALLÉS
Vice-Rector for Social Responsibility and Community Relations: AMAIA MASEDA
Vice-Rector for Student Affairs: ELENA BERNARAS
Vice-Rector for Teaching Staff: JUAN JOSÉ UNCILLA GALÁN
Vice-Rector for Univ. Extension: AMAIA MASEDA
Registrar: EVA FERREIRA
Admin. Dir: XABIER AIZPURUA TELLERÍA
Librarian: CARMEN GUERRA

Library: 1m. vols, 17,800 periodicals
Number of teachers: 5,000
Number of students: 45,000

Publications: *Acto de Investidura* (1 a year), *Anuario del Seminario de Filología Vasca 'Julio de Urquijo'* (International Journal of Basque Linguistics and Philology, 1 a year), *Memoria de Actividades* (1 a year), *Memoria Estadística* (1 a year), *Psicodidactics* (The International Journal of Development Biology, 8–10 a year), *Recursos Científicos y Líneas de Investigación* (1 a year), *Resúmenes de Tesis Doctorales* (1 a year)

DEANS

(The letters A, B, G refer to the Araba, Bizkaia and Gipuzkoa campuses)

Faculty of Chemistry (G): IÑIGO LEGORBURU FAUS
Faculty of Computer Science (G): ARANTZA ILLARRAMENDI ECHAVE
Faculty of Economics and Business Administration (B): ARTURO RODRÍGUEZ CASTELLANOS
Faculty of Fine Arts (B): JOSU REKALDE IZAGIRRE
Faculty of Law (G): FRANCISCO JAVIER QUEL LÓPEZ
Faculty of Letters (A): FERNANDO GARCÍA MURGA
Faculty of Medicine and Dentistry (B): AGUSTÍN MARTÍNEZ IBARGÜEN
Faculty of Pharmacy (A): AURORA FERNÁNDEZ ASTORGA
Faculty of Philosophy and Education Science (G): IÑAKI ZABALETA IMAZ
Faculty of Physical Activities and Sport Science (A): INÉS GARCÍA AZKOAGA
Faculty of Psychology (G): ARANTZA AZPIROZ SÁNCHEZ
Faculty of Sciences and Technology (B): ESTHER DOMÍNGUEZ PÉREZ
Faculty of Social and Communication Sciences (B): ALFONSO UNCETA SATRÚSTEGUI

DIRECTORS

(The letters A, B, G refer to the Araba, Bizkaia and Gipuzkoa campuses)

College of Business Studies (A): MIREN ARTARAZ
College of Business Studies (B): XABIER RENTERÍA
College of Business Studies (G): IÑAKI HERAS
College of Industrial and Topographical Engineering (A): LUIS MIGUEL CAMARERO ESTELA
College of Industrial Engineering (B): FRANCISCO JOSÉ SAINZ ALVES
College of Industrial Engineering (G): ÁNGEL FRANCO
College of Industrial Relations (B): (vacant)
College of Nursing (B): TERESA FEITO
College of Nursing (G): PILAR TAZON ANSOLA
College of Social Work (A): CHARO OVEJAS
College of Technical Mining Engineering (B): ITZIAR ARANGUIZ
Donostia Polytechnic Univ. College (G): CARLOS OCHOA
Higher Technical School of Architecture (G): ALBERTO ZULUETA
Higher Technical School of Industrial Engineering and Telecommunications (B): JAVIER MUNIOZGUREN COLINDRES
Higher Technical School of Navigation and Naval Engineering (B): FERNANDO CAYUELA CAMARERO
Teacher Training College (A): TERESA VIZCARRA
Teacher Training College (B): GURUTZE EZKURDIA
Teacher Training College (G): PELLO URKIDI
Univ. College of the Labour Relations Studies (B): ÁNGEL ELÍAS

UNIVERSIDAD EUROPEA DE MADRID (CEES)

Calle Tajo, s/n, Urbanización el Bosque, 28670 Villaviciosa de Odón, Madrid

Telephone: (91) 2115200
E-mail: uem@uem.es
Internet: www.uem.es

Founded 1995

Rector: Dra ÁGUEDA BENITO
Vice-Rector for Academic Quality and Innovation: Dr PEDRO JOSÉ LARA
Vice-Rector for Students and Employment: Dra MARTA ARROYO
Vice-Rector for Teaching and Research: Dra MARÍA ADELAIDA PORTELA
Registrar: ELENA DE LA FUENTE
Librarian: ISABEL RICO RODRÍGUEZ

DEANS

Faculty of Biomedical Sciences: Dr JUAN PÉREZ-MIRANDA
Faculty of Communication and Humanities: Dr LUIS CALANDRE
Faculty of Health Sciences: Dr ELENA GAZAPO
Faculty of Physical Education and Sport: Dr JUAN MAYORGA GARCÍA
Faculty of Social Sciences: Dr JOSÉ RAMOS

UNIVERSIDAD INTERNACIONAL DE ANDALUCÍA

Rectorado de la Universidad, Sede de la Cartuja, Monasterio Santa María de las Cuevas, Calle Americo Vespucio 2, Isla de la Cartuja, 41092 Seville

Telephone: (95) 4462299
Fax: (95) 4462288
E-mail: sevilla@unia.es
Internet: www.unia.es

Founded 1994

Rector: JUAN MANUEL SUÁREZ JAPÓN
Vice-Rector for Academic Affairs and Graduate Studies: PLÁCIDO NAVAS LLORET
Vice-Rector for Int. Relations and Cooperation: MARÍA ANTONIA PEÑA GUERRERO
Vice-Rector for Planning and Quality: JULIO TERRADOS CEPEDA
Vice-Rector for Research and Communication Technologies: LLANOS MORA LÓPEZ
Vice-Rector for Univ. Extension and Participation: MARÍA DEL ROSARIO GARCÍ A-DONCEL HERNÁNDEZ
Registrar: MARÍA JESÚS GUERRERO LEBRÓN
Man.: LUISA MARGARITA RANCAÑO MARTÍN.

CAMPUSES OF THE UNIVERSITY

Sede Antonio Machado

Palacio de Jabalquinto, Plaza de Santa Cruz, s/n, 23440 Baeza (Jaén)

Telephone: (95) 3742775
Fax: (95) 3742975
E-mail: baeza@unia.es

Dir: MARÍA ALCAZAR CRUZ RODRÍGUEZ.

Sede Iberoamericano Santa María de La Rábida

Paraje La Rábida, s/n, 21819 Palos de la Frontera (Huelva)

Telephone: (95) 9350452
Fax: (95) 9350158
E-mail: larabida@unia.es

Dir: YOLANDA PELAYO DÍAZ.

Sede de Málaga

Avda Severo Ochoa 16–20, Málaga Business-Park, Edificio Estepona, Parque Tecnológico de Andalucía, 20590 Málaga

Telephone: (95) 2028411
Fax: (95) 2028419
E-mail: malaga@unia.es

Dir: ANTONIO SÁNCHEZ SÁNCHEZ.

UNIVERSIDAD JAUME I DE CASTELLÓN

Campus de Riu Sec, Avda de Vicent Sos Baynat, s/n, 12071 Castellón

Telephone: (96) 4728000
Fax: (96)4 729016
E-mail: info@uji.es
Internet: www.uji.es

Founded 1991
State control

Rector: FRANCISCO TOLEDO LOBO
Vice-Rector for Academic Org. and Teaching Staff: Prof. SERAFÍ BERNAT MARTÍ
Vice-Rector for Culture: Profa MARGARITA PORCAR MIRALLES
Vice-Rector for Economic Affairs and Online Services: Prof. MODESTO FABRA VALLÉS
Vice-Rector for Educational Quality and European Harmonization: Profa ROSA MARÍA GRAU GUMBAU
Vice-Rector for Infrastructure and Admin. Services: Prof. VICENTE CERVERA MATEU
Vice-Rector for Institutional Relations and Social Welfare: Prof. MANUEL CHUST CALERO

Vice-Rector for Int. Cooperation and Solidarity: Profa EVA SOLER ALCÓN
Vice-Rector for Postgraduate Studies: Prof. JUAN ANTONIO BARBA
Vice-Rector for Research: Profa ROSA LLUSAR BARELLES
Vice-Rector for Scientific and Technological Promotion: Prof. VICENTE ORTS RÍOS
Vice-Rector for Students and Employment: Profa LEONOR LAPEÑA
Registrar: MARÍA VICTORIA PETIT LAVALL
Library Dir: VICENT FALOMIR DEL CAMPO

Library of 274,444 vols
Number of teachers: 1,022
Number of students: 12,677

DEANS

Faculty of Humanities and Social Sciences: Prof. MANUEL ROSAS ARTOLA
Faculty of Law and Economics: Prof. GERMÁN ORÓN MORATAL
Higher School of Technology and Experimental Sciences: Prof. FERNANDO RAJADELL VICIANO (Dir)

UNIVERSIDAD MIGUEL HERNÁNDEZ DE ELCHE

Edificio Torrevaillo, Avda de la Universidad, s/n, 03202 Elche (Alicante)
Telephone: (96) 6658604
Fax: (96) 6658602
E-mail: gerente@umh.es
Internet: www.umh.es
State control

Rector: JESÚS RODRÍGUEZ MARÍN
Vice-Rector for Academic Planning and Studies: JOSÉ NAVARRO PEDREÑO
Vice-Rector for Coordination and Scheduling: CARMEN VICTORIA ESCOLANO ASENSI
Vice-Rector for Economic Affairs, Employment and Relations with Business: JOSÉ MARÍA GÓMEZ GRAS
Vice-Rector for Int. Relations: JUSTO MEDRANO HEREDIA
Vice-Rector for Material Resources and Equipment: JOAQUÍN JULIÁN PASTOR PÉREZ
Vice-Rector for Personnel: JOSÉ FRANCISCO GONZÁLEZ CARBONELL
Vice-Rector for Research and Technological Devt: SALVADOR VINIEGRA BOVER
Vice-Rector for Student Affairs: FERNANDO BORRÁS ROCHER
Vice-Rector for Univ. Planning and Continuing Education: JUANA GALLAR MARTÍNEZ
Registrar: FERMÍN CAMACHO DE LOS RÍOS
Manager: RAFAEL GANDÍA BALAGUER

DEANS

Faculty of Experimental Sciences: MARÍA DOLORES ESTEBAN LEFLER
Faculty of Fine Arts: RAMÓN DE SOTO ARANDIGA
Faculty of Medicine: JUAN MANUEL CATURLA SUCH
Faculty of Pharmacy: MARÍA DEL CARMEN DE FELIPE FERNÁNDEZ
Faculty of Social and Juridical Sciences at Elche: JOSÉ ANTONIO TRIGUEROS PINA
Faculty of Social and Juridical Sciences at Orihuela: JAVIER REIG MULLOR

ATTACHED INSTITUTES

Institute of Bioengineering: Edificio Vinalopó, Avda del Ferrocarril s/n, 03202 Elche; tel. (96) 6658510; fax (96) 6658511; internet bioengenieria.umh.es; Dir BERNAT SORIA ESCOMS.

Institute of Molecular and Cell Biology: Edificio Torregaitán, Avda de la Universidad s/n, 03202 Elche; tel. (96) 6658759; fax (96) 6658758; e-mail biomolcel@umh.es; internet ibmc.umh.es; Dir JOSÉ MANUEL GONZÁLEZ ROS.

Institute of Research into Drug Addiction: Facultad de Medicina, Campus de San Juan, Ctra Alicante-Valencia, Km 87, Apdo no. 18, 03550 San Juan de Alicante; tel. (96) 5919319; fax (96) 5919566; e-mail inid@umh.es; internet inid.umh.es; Dir JOSÉ ANTONIO GARCÍA DEL CASTILLO RODRÍGUEZ.

Neurosciences Institute: Apdo 18, 03550 San Joan d'Alacant; tel. (96) 5919487; fax (96) 5919561; e-mail in@umh.es; internet in.umh.es/index2.htm; Dir CARLOS BELMONTE MARTÍNEZ.

Operational Research Centre: Campus de Elche, Edificio Torretamarit, Avda del Ferrocarril s/n, 03202 Elche; tel. (96) 6658752; fax (96) 6658715; e-mail cio@umh.es; internet cio.umh.es; Dir JESÚS TADEO PASTOR CIURANA.

UNIVERSIDAD NACIONAL DE EDUCACIÓN A DISTANCIA (Open University)

Ciudad Universitaria, s/n, 28040 Madrid
Telephone: (91) 3986600
Fax: (91) 3986037
E-mail: infouned@adm.uned.es
Internet: www.uned.es

Founded 1972
State control
Language of instruction: Spanish
Academic year: October to July

Rector: JUAN A. GIMENO ULLASTRES
Vice-Rector for Academic Affairs: ENCARNACIÓN SARRIÁ SÁNCHEZ
Vice-Rector for Associated Centres: ANTONIO FERNÁNDEZ FERNÁNDEZ
Vice-Rector for Continuing Education: JULIO BORDAS MARTÍNEZ
Vice-Rector for Innovation and Teaching Support: MIGUEL SANTAMARÍA LANCHO
Vice-Rector for Int. and Institutional Relations: MARÍA TERESA AGUADO ODINA
Vice-Rector for Planning and Economic Affairs: ANA ISABEL SEGOVIA SAN JUAN
Vice-Rector for Print and Audiovisual Media: IRENE DELGADO SOTILLOS
Vice-Rector for Research: PALOMA COLLADO GUIRAO
Vice-Rector for Student Life, Employment and Culture: ALVARO JARILLO ALDEANUEVA
Vice-Rector for Teaching Staff: MIGUEL ÁNGEL RUBIO ÁLVAREZ
Vice-Rector for Technology: COVADONGA RODRIGO SAN JUAN
Registrar: ANA MARÍA MARCOS DEL CANO
Chief of Admin.: JORDI MONTSERRAT GARROCHO
Librarian: ISABEL BELMONTE MARTÍNEZ

Library: 1.2m. vols
Number of teachers: 1,496
Number of students: 205,931 (incl. 111,310 enrolled on degree and diploma courses)

DEANS

Faculty of Economics and Business Administration: AMELIA PÉREZ ZABALETA
Faculty of Education: LORENZO GARCÍA ARETIO
Faculty of Geography and History: ENRIQUE CANTERA MONTENEGRO
Faculty of Law: ANA ROSA MARTÍN MINGUIJÓN
Faculty of Philology: Dr ANTONIO MORENO HERNÁNDEZ
Faculty of Philosophy: Dr MANUEL FRAIJÓ NIETO
Faculty of Politics and Sociology: MARÍA ELISA CHULIÁ RODRIGO
Faculty of Psychology: Dr MIGUEL ÁNGEL SANTED GERMÁN
Faculty of Sciences: Dr ANTONIO ZAPARDIEL PALENZUELA
Technical School of Industrial Engineering: JOSÉ IGNACIO PEDRERO MOYA (Dir)
Technical School of Computer Science: ROBERTO HERNANDEZ BERLINCHES (Dir)

UNIVERSIDAD PABLO DE OLAVIDE

Carretera de Utrera, Km 1, 41013 Seville
Telephone: (95) 4349200
Fax: (95) 4349204
Internet: www.upo.es

Founded 1997
State control
Language of instruction: Spanish
Academic year: September to July

Rector: Dr JUAN JIMÉNEZ MARTÍNEZ
Vice-Rector for Graduate Studies: LINA GÁLVEZ MUÑOZ
Vice-Rector for Information Technologies and Communication: Dr ANDRÉS GARZÓN VILLAR
Vice-Rector for International and Institutional Relations: Dr LUIS PÉREZ-PRAT DURBÁN
Vice-Rector for Quality and Planning: Dra ALICIA TRONCOSO LORA
Vice-Rector for Research and Technology Transfer: Dr MANUEL HERRERO SÁNCHEZ
Vice-Rector for Social Participation: Dra ROSALÍA MARTÍNEZ GARCÍA
Vice-Rector for Student Affairs and Sports: Dr FRANCISCO BEDOYA BERGUA
Vice-Rector for Teaching and European Convergence: Dr JUAN MANUEL CORTÉS COPETE
Vice-Rector for Teaching Staff: Dr JOSÉ ANTONIO SÁNCHEZ MEDINA
Registrar: Dr FRANCISCO OLIVA BLÁZQUEZ
Man.: RAFAEL SERRANO AGUILAR

Library of 347,577 vols, 25,284 periodicals, 12,763 audiovisual items
Number of teachers: 1,100
Number of students: 11,500

DEANS

Faculty of Business Sciences: Dr FRANCISCO CARRASCO FENECH
Faculty of Experimental Sciences: Dr ANTONIO GALLARDO CORREA
Faculty of Humanities: Dr GONZALO MALVÁREZ GARCÍA
Faculty of Law: Dr ANDRÉS RODRÍGUEZ BENOT
Faculty of Social Sciences: Dr GUILLERMO DOMÍNGUEZ FERNÁNDEZ
Faculty of Sports: Dr JUAN JOSÉ GONZÁLEZ BADILLO
Polytechnic School: JESÚS SALVADOR AGUILAR RUIZ (Dir)
School of Engineering: Dr JESÚS AGUILAR RUIZ

UNIVERSIDAD PONTIFICIA 'COMILLAS'

Calle Alberto Aguilera 23, 28015 Madrid
Telephone: (91) 5422800
Fax: (91) 5596569
E-mail: oia@oia.upcomillas.es
Internet: www.upcomillas.es

Founded by Pope Leo XIII; classes commencing at Comillas, Santander, in 1890; the right to confer degrees was granted in 1904; moved to Madrid in 1960
Private control (Soc. of Jesus)
Language of instruction: Spanish
Academic year: October to June

Grand Chancellor: ADOLFO NICOLÁS PACHÓN
Rector: Dr JOSÉ RAMÓN BUSTO SAIZ
Vice-Rector for Academic Affairs and Teaching Staff: Dr ANTONIO OBREGÓN GARCÍA
Vice-Rector for Economic Affairs: Dr CECILIO MORAL BELLO
Vice-Rector for Int. Relations and Services to the Univ. Community: Dr ROMANO GIANNETTI
Vice-Rector for Research, Devt and Innovation: Dr JULIO LUIS MARTÍNEZ MARTÍNEZ

Registrar: Dra CLARA MARTÍNEZ GARCÍA
Librarian: EUSEBIO GIL CORIA

Library of 550,000 vols
Number of teachers: 962
Number of students: 9,804

Publications: *Estudios Eclesiásticos* (4 a year), *ICADE* (4 a year), *Migraciones* (2 a year), *Miscelánea Comillas* (3 a year), *Pensamiento* (3 a year)

DEANS

Faculty of Canon Law and Theology: Dr GABINO URÍBARRI BILBAO
Faculty of Economics and Business: Dra ALFREDO ARAHUETES GARCÍA
Faculty of Human and Social Sciences: Dra BELÉN MERCEDES UROSA SANZ
Faculty of Law: Dra MARÍA CONCEPCIÓN MOLINA BLÁZQUEZ

ATTACHED CENTRES AND INSTITUTES

Centro Teológico de Las Palmas de Gran Canaria: Seminario Mayor, 35001 Las Palmas de Gran Canaria.

Estudio Teológico Agustiniano: Paseo de Filipinos 7, 47007 Valladolid.

Estudio Teológico Claretiano: Juan Alvarez Mendizal 65 Duplicado, 1°, 28008 Madrid.

Estudio Teológico del Seminario Mayor de Córdoba: Amador de los Ríos 1, 14004 Córdoba.

Estudio Teológico del Seminario Mayor de Logroño: Seminario Mayor, Apdo de Correos 150, 26080 Logroño.

Estudio Teológico del Seminario Mayor Diocesano: Carretera de Porzuna s/n, 13002 Ciudad Real.

Estudio Teológico del Seminario Mayor 'Tagaste': Padres Agustinos, Santa Emilia 10, 28409 Los Negrales (Madrid).

Estudio Teológico Monseñor Romero: Apdo Postal (01) 168, San Salvador, El Salvador (Central America).

Instituto Fe y Secularidad: Diego de León 33, 28006 Madrid.

Instituto Internacional de Teología a Distancia: José Ortega y Gasset 62, 1°, 28006 Madrid.

Instituto Superior de Ciencias Morales: Calle Félix Boix 13, 28016 Madrid.

Instituto Superior de Ciencias Religiosas 'San Agustín': José Ortega y Gasset 62, 1°, 28006 Madrid.

ASSOCIATED INSTITUTIONS

There are other Theological and Philosophical Faculties in Spain conferring degrees, which are partly associated with the Pontifical Universities, as follows:

Facultad de Teología de Granada (Institución Universitaria de la Compañía de Jesús)

Apdo 2002, 18080 Granada
Telephone: (95) 8185252
Fax: (95) 8162559
E-mail: info@teol-granada.com
Internet: www.teol-granada.com

Founded 1939
Academic year: October to July

Grand Chancellor: R. P. ADOLFO NICOLÁS PACHÓN
Vice-Grand Chancellor: R. P. FRANCISCO JOSÉ RUIZ PÉREZ
Rector: R. P. ILDEFONSO CAMACHO LARAÑA
Vice-Rector for Academic Affairs: Prof. JOSÉ LUIS SÁNCHEZ NOGALES
Registrar and Man.: CARLOS JAVIER PALOMEQUE BAENA
Librarian: R. P. GABRIEL VERD CONRADI

Library of 350,000 vols
Number of teachers: 27
Number of students: 250

Publications: *Archivo Teológico Granadino* (Post-Tridentine theology, 1 a year), *Proyección* (4 a year)

PROFESSORS

ALARCOS MARTÍNEZ, F., Moral Theology
BÉJAR BACAS, J. S., Dogmatic Theology
BERDUGO VILLENA, T., Latin
CAMACHO LARAÑA, I., Moral Theology
CASTÓN BOYER, P., Sociology
DOMÍNGUEZ MORANO, C., Psychology
GRANADO BELLIDO, C., Patrology and Dogmatic Theology
GUEVARA LLAGUNO, M., Scripture
HERNÁNDEZ MARTÍNEZ, J., Dogmatic Theology
JIMÉNEZ ORTIZ, A., Fundamental Theology
LÓPEZ AZPITARTE, E., Moral Theology
LÓPEZ CUERVO, T., Greek
MARTÍN MORILLAS, A., Philosophy
MARTÍNEZ MEDINA, J., Ecclesiastical Art
MOLINA MOLINA, D., Dogmatic Theology
NAVAS GUTIÉRREZ, A., Ecclesiastical History
RODRÍGUEZ CARMONA, A., Scripture
RODRÍGUEZ IZQUIERDO GAVALA, J. M., Liturgy
ROJAS GÁLVEZ, I., Scripture
ROMÁN MARTÍNEZ, M. C., Scripture
RUIZ LOZANO, P., Philosophy
SÁNCHEZ NOGALES, J. L., Philosophy
SICRE DIAZ, J. L., Scripture
VOLO PÉREZ, R., Scripture
YUBERO SOTO, J., Dogmatic Theology

ATTACHED INSTITUTES

Centro de Estudios Teológicos: Avda Cardenal Buenomonreal 43, 41012 Seville; Rector LUIS F. ALVAREZ.

Centro de Estudios Teológicos: Juan Montilla 1, 23002 Jaén; Rector MANUEL RUIZ CARRERO.

Centro de Estudios Teológicos: Compañía s/n, 11005 Cádiz; Rector JESÚS J. GARCÍA CORNEJO.

Centro de Estudios Teológicos: Carretera de Nijar 61, 04009 Almería; Rector JUAN A. MOYA SÁNCHEZ.

Centro Diocesano de Teología de Málaga: Calle Toquero 20, 29013 Málaga; Rector (vacant).

Instituto Superior de Ciencias Religiosas 'San Pablo': Santa María 20, 29015 Málaga; Rector ILDEFONSO CAMACHO LARAÑA.

Instituto Superior de Ciencias Religiosas 'Tomás Sánchez': Apdo 2002, 18080 Granada; Rector ANTONIO M. NAVAS GUTIÉRREZ.

Institut de Teologia Fonamental

Calle Llaceres 30, Sant Cugat del Vallés Barcelona
Telephone: (93) 6741150
Fax: (93) 6752461
E-mail: itf@jesuites.net

Founded 1964

Jesuit College forming part of the Faculty of Theology of Cataluña; open to non-Jesuit students

Chancellor: Dr LLUÍS MARÍA SISTACH (Archbishop of Barcelona)
General Moderator: LLUÍS MAGRIÑÀ VECIANA
Dir: JOSEP BOADA
Registrar: JORDI ESCUDE
Librarian: JORDI ESCUDE

Library of 350,000 vols, 800 periodicals
Number of teachers: 14
Number of students: 150

Publications: *Actualidad Bibliográfica*, *Cuadernos de Teología Fundamental*, *Selecciones de Teología*

PROFESSORS

ALEGRE, X., New Testament Scripture
BOADA, J., Fundamental Theology
CARRERA, J., Fundamental Moral Theology
COLL, J. MA., Fundamental Theology
FLAQUER, J., Fundamental Theology
GARCÍA DONCEL, M., Philosophy of Sciences
GIMÉNEZ, J., Fundamental Theology
GONZÁLEZ FAUS, J. I., Systematic Theology
MANRESA, F., Fundamental Theology
MELLONI, X., Fundamental Theology
PUIG, LL., Fundamental Theology
RAMBLA, J. MA., Spiritual Theology
SALVAT, I., Fundamental Social Morality
TUÑÍ, O., New Testament Scripture

UNIVERSIDAD PONTIFICIA DE SALAMANCA

Calle Compañía 5, Apdo 541, 37002 Salamanca
Telephone: (92) 3277100
Fax: (92) 3277123
E-mail: gabi.com@upsa.es
Internet: www.upsa.es

Founded 1134 as the Ecclesiastical School of Salamanca Cathedral; named a univ. by Alfonso IX of León in 1219; had ceased to function by the end of the 18th century, but restored in 1940 by Pope Pius XII
Private control
Language of instruction: Spanish
Academic year: October to June

Grand Chancellor: Dr RICARDO BLÁZQUEZ PÉREZ
Rector: Dr MARCELIANO ARRANZ RODRIGO
Vice-Rector for Academic Org. and Economy: Dra MA. FRANCISCA MARTÍN TABERNERO
Vice-Rector for Pastoral Affairs, Research and Quality: Dr SANTIAGO GUIJARRO OPORTO
Vice-Rector for Teaching Staff, Student Affairs, Communication and Services: Dra ROSA PINTO LOBO
Registrar: Dr LUIS MIGUEL PEDRERO ESTEBAN
Admin. Coordinator: Lic. MA. TERESA GÓMEZ MARCOS
Dir of Library: Dr ANTONIO GARCÍA MADRID

Library of 500,000 vols and numerous MSS
Number of teachers: 351
Number of students: 8,500

Publications: *Cuadernos Salmantinos de Filosofía*, *Comunicación y Pluralismo*, *Diálogo Ecuménico*, *Familia*, *Helmántica*, *Papeles Salmantinos de Educación*, *Revista Española de Derecho Canónico*, *Salmanticensis*, *Sociedad y Utopía*

DEANS

Faculty of Canon Law: Dr FEDERICO RAFAEL AZNAR GIL
Faculty of Communication: Dr ÁNGEL LOSADA VÁZQUEZ
Faculty of Computer Sciences (Madrid): Dr LUIS JOYANES AGUILAR
Faculty of Education: Dr ANTONIO GARCÍA MADRID
Faculty of Insurance, Law and Management (Madrid): Dr ANTONIO GUARDIOLA LOZANO
Faculty of Philosophy: Dr LEONARDO RODRÍGUEZ DUPLÁ
Faculty of Political and Social Sciences (Madrid): Dr JUAN MANUEL DÍAZ SÁNCHEZ
Faculty of Psychology: Dr MA. PAZ QUEVEDO AGUADO
Faculty of Theology: Dr JOSÉ-RAMÓN FLECHA ANDRÉS

ATTACHED CENTRES

Institute of Biblical Archaeology: tel. (92) 3277143; fax (92) 3277101; e-mail casadesantiago@upsa.es; internet www.ipi.upsa.es; Dir Dr MARCELIANO ARRANZ RODRIGO.

Institute of Education Science: tel. (92) 3277140; fax (92) 3277101; e-mail ice@upsa.es; internet www.ice.upsa.es; Dir Dra MARÍA JESÚS GARCÍA ARROYO.

Institute of European Studies and Human Rights: tel. (92) 3277142; fax (92) 3277101; e-mail europa@upsa.es; internet www.europa.upsa.es; Dir Dr JOSÉ-ROMÁN FLECHA ANDRÉS.

Institute of Family Studies: tel. (92)3 277141; fax (92) 3277101; e-mail cc.familia@upsa.es; Dir Dr ÁNGEL GALINDO GARCÍA.

Institute of Iberoamerican Thought: tel. (92) 3277143; fax (92) 3277101; e-mail ipi@upsa.es; internet www.ipi.upsa.es; Dir Prof. Dr ILDEFONSO MURILLO MURILLO.

UNIVERSIDAD PÚBLICA DE NAVARRA

Campus de Arrosadía, 31006 Pamplona (Navarre)

Telephone: (94) 8169000
Fax: (94) 8169169
E-mail: infoweb@unavarra.es
Internet: www.unavarra.es

Founded 1987
State control ended Sept. 1993
Languages of instruction: Spanish, Basque, English
Academic year: September to June

Rector: JULIO LAFUENTE LÓPEZ
Vice-Rector for Economic Affairs, Planning and Forecasting: KATRIN SIMON ELORZ
Vice-Rector for Research: ALFONSO CARLOSENA GARCÍA
Vice-Rector for Social and Cultural Projection: CAMINO OSLÉ GUERENDIÁIN
Vice-Rector for Student Affairs and Int. Relations: JAVIER CASALÍ SARASÍBAR
Vice-Rector for Teaching: JESÚS MARÍA PINTOR BOROBIA
Vice-Rector for Teaching Staff: JOSÉ ASIÁIN OLLO
Vice-Rector for Tudela Campus: JOSÉ ASIÁIN OLLO
Registrar: SOLEDAD BARBER BURUSCO
Man.: PEDRO IRAIZOZ MUNÁRRIZ
Library Dir: GUILLERMO SÁNCHEZ MARTÍNEZ

Library of 339,160 vols, 9,309 periodicals
Number of teachers: 800
Number of students: 9,000

Publications: *Anales de Derecho* (1 a year), *Filología y Didáctica de la Lengua*, *Geografía e Historia* (1 a year), *Psicología y Pedagogía* (1 a year)

DEANS

Faculty of Economics and Business: JOSEBA DE LA TORRE CAMPO
Faculty of Humanities and Social Sciences: MARÍA JESÚS GOIKOETXEA TABAR
Faculty of Law: JOSÉ LUIS GOÑI SEIN

ATTACHED INSTITUTIONS

'Estanislao de Aranzadi' School of Practice in Law: Edificio de El Sario, Módulo 2, 2°, Campus de Arrosadía, 31006 Pamplona; tel. (948) 8169814; e-mail escuela.practica.juridica@unavarra.es; Dir PEDRO CHARRO AYESTARÁN.

Institute of Agrobiotechnology and Natural Resources: Campus de Arrosadía, 31192 Mutilva Baja (Navarra); tel. (94) 8242834; fax (94) 8232191; Dir JAVIER POZUETA ROMERO.

UNIVERSIDAD REY JUAN CARLOS

Calle Tulipán, s/n, 28933 Móstoles (Madrid)

Telephone: (91) 6655060
Fax: (91) 6147120
E-mail: info@urjc.es
Internet: www.urjc.es

Founded 1997
State control
Academic year: October to June

Rector: PEDRO GONZÁLEZ-TREVIJANO SÁNCHEZ
Vice-Rector for Academic Affairs, Teaching Staff and Campus Coordination: FERNANDO SUÁREZ BILBAO
Vice-Rector for European Harmonization and Alignment: JOSÉ MARÍA ÁLVAREZ MONZONCILLO
Vice-Rector for Information and Communication: FRANCISCO JOSÉ BLANCO JIMÉNEZ
Vice-Rector for Int. Relations, Employment and Devt Cooperation: ANA MARÍA SALAZAR DE LA GUERRA
Vice-Rector for Research: RAFAEL VAN GRIEKEN SALVADOR
Vice-Rector for Student Affairs: MARÍA ANGUSTIAS PALOMAR GALLEGO
Vice-Rector for Univ. Extension and Affiliated Centres: JOSÉ MANUEL VERA SANTOS
Registrar: ANDRÉS GAMBRA GUTIÉRREZ
Gen. Man.: JOSÉ MARÍA BETHENCOURT FONTENLA
Library Dir: RICARDO GONZÁLEZ CASTRILLO

Number of teachers: 900
Number of students: 15,000

DEANS

Faculty of Communication Science: ANTONIO GARCÍA JIMÉNEZ
Faculty of Health Sciences: RAFAEL LINARES GARCÍA-VALDECASAS
Faculty of Law and Social Sciences: CAMILO PRADO FREIRE
Faculty of Tourism: CATALINA VACAS GUERRERO

ATTACHED CENTRES

Higher College of Business Management and Marketing (ESIC): Avda Valdenigrales, s/n, 28223 Pozuelo de Alarcón (Madrid); tel. (91) 4524100; fax (91) 3528534; internet www.esic.es; Gen. Dir SIMÓN REYES MARTÍNEZ CÓRDOVA.

Institute of Public Law: Facultad de Ciencias Jurídicas y Sociales, Despacho 2, Campus de Vicálvaro, Paseo de Artilleros s/n, 28032 Vicálvaro (Madrid); tel. (91) 4887792; fax (91) 3718885; e-mail idp@fcjs.urjc.es; Dir Prof. Dr ENRIQUE ÁLVAREZ CONDE.

UNIVERSIDAD VIC

Calle Sagrada Família 7, 08500 Vic, (Barcelona)

Telephone: (93) 8861222
Fax: (93) 8891063
E-mail: relin@uvic.es
Internet: www.uvic.es

Founded 1977, present status since 1997

Pres.: JORDI MONTAÑA
Rector: JORDI MONTAÑA I MATOSAS
Vice-Rector for Academic Org. and Teaching Staff: PERE QUER
Vice-Rector for Research and Knowledge Transfer: JOSEP M. SERRAT
Registrar: MONTSERRAT VILALTA
Gen. Man.: PILAR SOLDEVILA
Library Dir: ANNA ANDREU MOLINA

Library of 63,284 vols, 68,000 docs, 1,484 periodicals, 5,170 electronic journals
Number of teachers: 544
Number of students: 4,597

DEANS

Faculty of Business and Communication: Dra ANTÒNIA PUJOL
Faculty of Education: FRANCESC CODINA
Faculty of Humanities, Translation and Documentation: CARME SANMARTÍ

ATTACHED CENTRE

BAU College of Design: Calle Pujades 118, 08005 Barcelona; tel. (93) 4153474; fax (93) 3001552; e-mail info@bau.cat; internet www.bau.cat; Academic Dir HUMBERT PLANTADA.

UNIVERSIDADE DA CORUÑA

A Maestranza, s/n, 15001 A Coruña

Telephone: (98) 1167000
Fax: (98) 1167011
E-mail: rede@udc.es
Internet: www.udc.es

Founded 1989
Languages of instruction: Spanish, Galician

Rector: JOSÉ MARÍA BARJA PÉREZ
Vice-Rector for Academic Organization: ANA DOROTEA TARRÍO TOBAR
Vice-Rector for Campus at Ferrol and University-Business Relations: LUIS FERNANDO BARRAL LOSADA
Vice-Rector for Culture and Communication: LUÍS CAPARRÓS ESPERANTE
Vice-Rector for Infrastructure and Environmental Management: JOSÉ LUIS MARTÍNEZ SUÁREZ
Vice-Rector for Quality and New Technology: MARÍA ELENA SIERRA PALMEIRO
Vice-Rector for Research: MARÍA CONCEPCIÓN HERRERO LÓPEZ
Vice-Rector for Strategy and Economic Planning: ÁNGEL FERNÁNDEZ CASTRO
Vice-Rector for Student Affairs and Int. Relations: MARÍA JOSÉ MARTÍNEZ LÓPEZ
Vice-Rector for Teaching Staff: XOSSÉ LUIS ARMESTO BARBEITO
Registrar: CARLOS AMOEDO SOUTO
Man.: MARIA JESÚS GRELA BARREIRO
Head Librarian: ÁNGELES CAMPOS RODRÍGUEZ

Library of 670,000 vols, 7,600 periodicals
Number of teachers: 1,250
Number of students: 25,000

DEANS

Faculty of Business and Economics: GUSTAVO REGO VEIGA
Faculty of Communication Science: JOSÉ JUANANTONI VIDELA RODRIGUEZ
Faculty of Computing: ALBERTO VALDERRUTEN VIDAL
Faculty of Economics and Business: GUSTAVO REGO VEIGA
Faculty of Education: NARCISO DE GABRIEL FERNÁNDEZ
Faculty of Health Sciences: SERGIO EDUARDO SANTOS DEL RIEGO
Faculty of Humanities: JOSÉ MANUEL RECUERO ASTRAY
Faculty of Labour Relations: MOISES ALBERTO GARCIA NUÑEZ
Faculty of Law: JOSÉ MARÍA PENA LÓPEZ
Faculty of Philology: MARÍA TERESA LÓPEZ FERNANDEZ
Faculty of Sciences: HORACIO NAVEIRA FACHAL
Faculty of Sociology: ANTONIO ALVAREZ SOUSA
Faculty of Sports and Physical Education Science: RAFAEL MARTIN ACERO

ATTACHED INSTITUTES

Centre of Educational Training and Innovation: Edificio Facultade de Socioloxía, 1° andar, Campus de Elviña, s/n, 15071 A Coruña; tel. (98) 1167189; fax (98) 1167188; e-mail administracion.cufie@udc.es; internet www.udc.es/cufie; Dir ENRIQUE DE LA TORRE FERNÁNDEZ.

Institute of European Studies: Casa de Galería, Campus de Elviña, s/n, 15071 A Coruña; tel. (98) 1167000 ext. 1966; fax (98) 1167013; e-mail iuee@udc.es; internet www.udc.es/iuee; Dir JOSÉ MANUEL SOBRINO HEREDIA.

Institute of Geology: Edificio de Servicios Centrales de Investigación, Campus de Elviña, 15071 A Coruña; tel. (98) 1167000 ext. 2910; fax (98) 1167172; e-mail xeoloxia@udc.es; internet www.iux.es; Dir JUAN RAMÓN VIDAL ROMANÍ.

Institute of Health Sciences: Hospital Marítimo de Oza, Area Jubias de Arriba, A Coruña; tel. (98) 1171360; fax (98) 1138714; e-mail iucs@udc.es; internet www.udc.es/cisaude/homepage.html; Dir Dr ALFONSO CASTRO BEIRAS.

Institute of Irish Studies: Edificio Servicios Centrais de Investigación, Campus de Elviña, s/n, 15071 A Coruña; tel. (98) 1167000 ext. 2686; fax (98) 1167172; e-mail amergin@udc.es; internet www.udc.es/amergin; Dir Dr ANTONIO RAÚL DE TORO SANTOS.

Institute of Maritime Studies: Universidade da Coruña, Campus de Elviña, 15071 A Coruña; tel. (98) 1167000 ext. 2463; fax (98) 1167125; e-mail iuem@udc.es; internet www.udc.es/iuem; Dir FERNANDO GONZÁLEZ LAXE.

Institute of the Environment: Pazo de Lóngora 29, Santa Eulalia de Liáns, 15179 Oleiros; tel. (98) 1648569; fax (98) 1648568; e-mail iuma@udc.es; internet www.udc.es/iuma; Dir Prof. Dr DARÍO PRADA RODRÍGUEZ.

Technological Institute of Communication: Paseo de Ronda 47, 15011 A Coruña; tel. (98) 1150100; e-mail info@telematica.org; internet www.telematica.org; Dir Dr ANGEL VIÑA.

UNIVERSIDADE DE SANTIAGO DE COMPOSTELA

Colexio de San Xerome, Praza do Obradoiro, s/n, 15782 Santiago de Compostela

Telephone: (98) 1547111
Fax: (98) 1588522
E-mail: reitor@usc.es
Internet: www.usc.es

Founded 1495
State control
Languages of instruction: Spanish, Galician

Rector: JUAN J. CASARES LONG
Vice-Rectors: BENITA SILVA HERMO, CARMEN FERNÁNDEZ MORANTE, EVA CASTRO CARIDAD, FRANCISCO GONZÁLEZ GARCÍA, FRANCISCO RAMÓN DURÁN VILLA, JAVIER GARBAYO MONTABES, MARÍA ISABEL GONZÁLEZ REY, MERCEDES PINTOS BARRAL, PEDRO GARCÍA HERRADÓN, SARA CANTORNA AGRA
Registrar: LOURDES NOYA FERREIRO
Man.: MARÍA LOURDES BATÁN AIRA
Librarian: CONCEPCIÓN VARELA OROL

Gen. Library of 1.5m. vols, more than 140 incunabula, prayer book of Fernando I of Castile (11th century); other special libraries in the faculties

Number of teachers: 2,177
Number of students: 29,709

Publications: *Acta Científica Compostelana, Anejos de la revista Verba, Anuario Gallego de Filología, Cursos y Congresos de la Universidad de Santiago de Compostela, Memoria, Trabajos Compostelanos de Biología, Verba*

DEANS

Faculty of Biology: MARÍA LUZ GONZALEZ CAAMAÑO
Faculty of Chemistry: JOSÉ RAMON CABANAS ESTEVEZ
Faculty of Communication Science: JOSÉ FARIÑA PEREIRA
Faculty of Economic and Business Science: MARÍA EMILIA VÁZQUEZ ROZAS
Faculty of Geography and History: JUAN M. MONTERROSO MONTERO
Faculty of Humanities (in Lugo): ALEJANDRO S. VEIGA RODRIGUEZ
Faculty of Law: LUIS MIGUEZ MACHO
Faculty of Mathematics: VICTORIA M. OTERO ESPINAR
Faculty of Medicine and Dentistry: JOSÉ M. FRAGA BERMUDEZ
Faculty of Philosophy and Education: JUAN VÁZQUEZ SÁNCHEZ
Faculty of Pharmacy: ISABEL M. SANDEZ MACHO
Faculty of Philology: ERNESTO XOSÉ GONZALEZ SEOANE
Faculty of Philosophy: LUIS MODESTO GARCÍA SOTO
Faculty of Physics: JOSÉ M. FDEZ. DE LABASTIDA Y DEL OLMO
Faculty of Political and Social Sciences: JOSÉ VILAS NOGUEIRA
Faculty of Psychology: CAROLINA TINAJERO VACAS
Faculty of Sciences (in Lugo): FRANCISCO FRAGA LOPEZ
Faculty of Veterinary Medicine (in Lugo): ANNA M. BRAVO MORAL

UNIVERSIDADE DE VIGO

Campus as Lagoas, Marcosende, 36310 Vigo

Telephone: (98) 6812000
Fax: (98) 6813559
E-mail: informacion@uvigo.es
Internet: www.uvigo.es

Founded 1990
State control
Academic year: October to July

Rector: Prof. SALUSTIANO MATO DE LA IGLESIA
Vice-Rector for Academic Org., Teaching Staff and Degrees: Prof. MARGARITA ESTÉVEZ TORANZO
Vice-Rector for Economy and Planning: Prof. JOSÉ MANUEL GARCÍA VÁZQUEZ
Vice-Rector for Int. Relations: Prof. MANUEL FERNÁNDEZ IGLESIAS
Vice-Rector for Knowledge Transfer: Prof. JOSÉ ANTONIO VILÁN VILÁN
Vice-Rector for Orense Campus: Profa MARÍA LAMEIRAS FERNÁNDEZ
Vice-Rector for Pontevedra Campus: Profa ANTONIA BLANCO PESQUEIRA
Vice-Rector for Research: Profa MARÍA ASUNCIÓN LONGO GONZÁLEZ
Vice-Rector for Student Affairs, Teaching and Quality: Prof. IGNACIO BARCIA RODRÍGUEZ
Vice-Rector for Univ. Extension: Prof. XOSÉ HENRIQUE COSTAS GONZÁLEZ
Registrar: Profa INMACULADA VALEIJE ALVAREZ
Man.: AUGUSTO VISO ALONSO
Librarian: MARÍA DEL CARMEN PÉREZ PAIS

Library of 180,000 vols
Number of teachers: 1,200
Number of students: 30,000

Publication: *DUVI* (online newspaper, daily)

DEANS

Orense Campus

Faculty of Business and Tourism: Profa MARÍA ELISA ALÉN GONZÁLEZ
Faculty of Education: Profa MERCEDES SUÁREZ PAZOS
Faculty of History: Profa Dra MARÍA MILAGROS CAVADA NIETO
Faculty of Law: Prof. Dr MIGUEL MICHINEL ÁLVAREZ
Faculty of Science: Prof. PEDRO ARAÚJO NESPEREIRA
Higher School of Computer Engineering: Prof. ENRIQUE BARREIRO ALONSO (Dir)
University School of Nursing: ESTRELLA PORTELA ATRIO (Dir)

Pontevedra Campus

Faculty of Science Education and Sport: Profa FRANCISCA FARIÑA RIVERA
Faculty of Fine Arts: Prof. JUAN CARLOS MEANA MARTÍNEZ
Faculty of Social Sciences and Communication: Prof. FORTUNATO RODRÍGUEZ FERNÁNDEZ (acting)
University School of Forestry Engineering: LUIS ORTIZ TORRES (Dir)
University School of Physiotherapy: MANUEL GUTIÉRREZ NIETO (Dir)

Vigo Campus (Lagoas-Marcosende)

Faculty of Biology: Profa MARÍA CRISTINA ARIAS FERNÁNDEZ
Faculty of Chemistry: LUIS MUÑOZ LOPEZ
Faculty of Economics and Business: SANTIAGO GÓMEZ FRAIZ
Faculty of Law and Labour Science: ANA MARÍA PITA GRANDAL
Faculty of Naval Science: JESÚS SOUZA TRONCOSO
Faculty of Philology and Translation: LUIS DOMÍNGUEZ CASTRO
Higher Technical School of Industrial Engineering: Prof. LUIS GONZÁLEZ PIÑEIRO (Dir)
Higher Technical School of Mining Engineering: Prof. PEDRO ARIAS SÁNCHEZ (Dir)
Higher Technical School of Telecommunications Engineering: Prof. MARÍA EDITA DE LORENZO RODRÍGUEZ (Dir)

Vigo City Campus

University Business School: Prof. PATRICIO SÁNCHEZ BELLO (Dir)
University School of Nursing (Meixoeiro): LUIS MORANO AMADO (Dir)
University School of Nursing (Povisa): ALFONSO GARCÍA SUÁREZ (Dir)
University School of Technical Industrial Engineering: Prof. CARLOS VIVAS MARTÍNEZ (Dir)
University Teacher Training School: MARÍA JESÚS AYUSO MANSO (Dir)

UNIVERSITAT ABAT OLIBA CEU

Calle Bellesguard 30, 08022 Barcelona

Telephone: (93) 2540900
Fax: (93) 4189380
E-mail: info@uao.es
Internet: www.uao.es

Founded 2003
Private control
Languages of instruction: Spanish, English, Catalan

Rector: Dr CARLOS PÉREZ DEL VALLE
Vice-Rector for Research, Graduate Affairs and Quality Control: Dr ENRIQUE MARTÍNEZ
Vice-Rector for Student Affairs: Dr MARCIN KAZMIERCZAK
Gen.-Sec.: Dr CARMEN PARRA
Man.: JUAN ÁLVAREZ

Library of 20,000 vols, 100 periodicals
Number of students: 2,000

Courses in advertising, business admin. and management economics, computer engineering, higher education management, journalism, law, politics, public management, publicity, public relations, psychology

HEADS OF DIVISION

JOAN A. ROCHA, Communication Sciences
FERRAN PORTA, Economic and Social Sciences
MIGUEL A. BELMONTE, Humanities
JOSÉ A. ROZAS, Legal and Political Sciences
MARTÍN ECHAVARRÍA, Psychology

UNIVERSITAT AUTÒNOMA DE BARCELONA

Campus Universitari, 08193 Bellaterra (Barcelona)
Telephone: (93) 5811111
Fax: (93) 5812000
E-mail: informacio@uab.es
Internet: www.uab.es
Founded 1968
Regional govt control
Languages of instruction: Spanish, Catalan
Academic year: September to June
Rector: ANA RIPOLL ARACIL MISSATGE
Vice-Rector for Academic Staff: MIQUEL ÀNGEL SENAR ROSELL
Vice-Rector for Academic Policy: MONTSERRAT FARELL FERRER
Vice-Rector for Economic Policy and Org.: JOSEP ENRIC LLEBOT RABAGLIATI,
Vice-Rector for Institutional Relations and Communication: MARÍA JOSÉ RECODER SELLARÈS
Vice-Rector for Int. Relations: MERCEDES UNZETA LÓPEZ
Vice-Rector for Research: JOAN GÓMEZ PALLARÈS
Vice-Rector for Social and Cultural Transfer: BONAVENTURA BASSEGODA HUGAS
Vice-Rector for Strategic Projects and Planning: CARLES JAIME CARDIEL
Registrar: ISABEL PONT CASTEJÓN
Man.: SANTIAGO GUERRERO BONED
Librarian: JOAN RAMÓN GÓMEZ ESCOFET
Library of 1,114,509 vols, 39,000 periodicals
Number of teachers: 3,566
Number of students: 53,232
Publications: *Anàlisi: Quaderns de Comunicació i Cultura, Anuari d'Anglès, Cuadernos de Psicología, Cuadernos de Traducción e Interpretación, Documents d'Anàlisi Geogràfica, Educar, Enrahonar: Quaderns de Filosofia, Estudios de la Antigüedad, Faventia, Medievalia, Orsis: Organismes i Sistemes, Papers: Revista de Sociologia, Quaderns de Música Històrica Catalana, Quaderns de Treball, Recerca Musicològica*

DEANS

Faculty of Communication Science: JOSEP M. CATALÀ
Faculty of Economics and Business: JOAN CLAVERA
Faculty of Educational Sciences: ROSA MARÍA PUJOL
Faculty of Law: JOSEP M. DE DIOS MARCER
Faculty of Medicine: JOAQUIM COLL I DAROCA
Faculty of Philosophy and Letters: TERESA CABRÉ MONNÉ
Faculty of Political Sciences and Sociology: SALVADOR CARDÚS I ROS
Faculty of Psychology: MAITE MARTÍNEZ GONZÁLEZ
Faculty of Science: JORDI BARBÉ GARCIA
Faculty of Translation and Interpretation: FRANCESC PARCERISAS I VÁZQUEZ
Faculty of Veterinary Medicine: MANEL LÓPEZ BÉJAR

UNIVERSITAT DE BARCELONA

Gran Via de les Corts Catalanes 585, 08007 Barcelona
Telephone: (93) 4021100
Fax: (93) 3025947
E-mail: comunicacio@ub.edu
Internet: www.ub.es
Founded 1450
State control
Languages of instruction: Catalan, Castilian
Academic year: October to September
Rector: Dr DÍDAC RAMÍREZ I SARRIÓ
Vice-Rector for Admin.: CARME PANCHÓN IGLESIAS
Vice-Rector for Arts, Culture and Heritage: LOURDES CIRLOT VALENZUELA
Vice-Rector for Financial Resources: GONZALO BERNARDOS DOMÍNGUEZ
Vice-Rector for Information and Communication: PERE QUETGLAS NICOLAU
Vice-Rector for Innovation and Knowledge Transfer: SÍLVIA ATRIÁN VENTURA
Vice-Rector for Int. Relations and Deputy Rector: Dr CARLES CARRERAS VERDAGUER
Vice-Rector for Research: Dr JORDI ALBERCH VIÉ
Vice-Rector for Students and Language Policy: GEMMA FONRODONA BALDAJOS
Vice-Rector for Teaching and Science Policy: MARÍA TERESA ANGUERA ARGILAGA (acting)
Vice-Rector for Teaching Staff: MANUEL VILADEVALL SOLÉ
Registrar: JORDI GARCIA VIÑA
Gen. Man.: VÍCTOR GÓMEZ GÓMEZ
Library Dir: DOLORS LAMARCA MARGALEF
Library: 1.65m. vols
Number of teachers: 3,808
Number of students: 91,138

DEANS

Faculty of Biology: JOAQUÍN GUTIÉRREZ FRUITÓS
Faculty of Chemistry: PERE LLUÍS CABOT JULIÀ
Faculty of Dentistry: SÍLVIA SÁNCHEZ GONZÁLEZ (acting)
Faculty of Economics and Business: ELISENDA PALUZIE HERNÁNDEZ
Faculty of Education: ANA MARÍA ESCOFET ROIG
Faculty of Fine Arts: SALVADOR GARCÍA FORTES
Faculty of Geography and History: M. ÁNGELES DEL RINCÓN MARTÍNEZ
Faculty of Geology: LUIS CABRERA PÉREZ
Faculty of Law: ENOCH ALBERTÍ ROVIRA
Faculty of Library Science and Documentation: CRISTÓBAL URBANO SALIDO
Faculty of Mathematics: MARIA CARMEN CASCANTE CANUT
Faculty of Medicine: FRANCESC CARDELLACH LÓPEZ
Faculty of Pharmacy: JUAN ESTEVA DE SAGRERA
Faculty of Philology: ADOLFO SOTELO VÁZQUEZ
Faculty of Philosophy: AGUSTÍN GONZÁLEZ GALLEGO
Faculty of Physics: JOAN ÀNGEL PADRÓ CÀRDENAS
Faculty of Psychology: MANEL VIADER JUNYENT
Faculty of Teacher Training: ALBERTO BATALLA FLORES
School of Nursing: ANA MARÍA PULPON SEGURA (Dir)

UNIVERSITAT DE GIRONA

Edifici Les Àligues, Pl. Sant Domènec 3, 17071 Gerona
Telephone: (97) 2418028
Fax: (97) 2418031
E-mail: informacio@udg.es
Internet: www.udg.es
Founded 1992
State control
Academic year: September to June
Rector: Dra ANNA M. GELI
Vice-Rector for Academic Policy: Dr FRANCESC FELIU TORRENT
Vice-Rector for Campus Infrastructure: LLUÍS ALBÓ RIGAU
Vice-Rector for Int. Policy: Dra MARIA LLUÏSA PÉREZ CABANÍ
Vice-Rector for Personnel and Social Policy: Dr TEODOR M. JOVÉ LAGUNAS
Vice-Rector for Planning and Quality: Dr MARTÍ CASADESÚS FA
Vice-Rector for Regulation Devt: Dr SUSANNA OROMÍ VALL-LLOVERA
Vice-Rector for Research and Knowledge Transfer: Dr JOSEP CALBÓ ANGRILL
Vice-Rector for Strategic Projects and Finance: Dr LIBRADO JESÚS GARCÍA GIL
Vice-Rector for Student Affairs, Cooperation and Equality: MARIA ROSA TERRADELLAS PIFERRER
Registrar: Dr CARLES ABELLÀ AMETLLER
Man.: JOSEP M. GÓMEZ PALLARÈS
Librarian: ANTÒNIA BOIX
Library of 372,144 vols, 6,793 periodicals
Number of teachers: 804
Number of students: 12,952

DEANS

Faculty of Arts: JOSÉ LUIS VILLANOVA VALERO
Faculty of Economics and Business Studies: ANNA GARRIGA RIPOLL
Faculty of Education and Psychology: FRANCISCO JIMENEZ MARTINEZ
Faculty of Law: GUILLERMO ORMAZABAL SANCHEZ
Faculty of Medicine: RAMON BRUGADA
Faculty of Science: VICTORIA DE LOS ANGELES SALVADO MARTIN
Faculty of Tourism: LLUIS MUNDET I CERDAN

ATTACHED SCHOOLS

CETA University School of Tourism: C/ Pàdua 11–13, 08023 Barcelona; tel. (93) 2118074; e-mail informacio@cetaturisme.com; internet www.cetaturismo.com; Dir Dr RAMÓN BOSCH.

ESMA University School of Tourism: Consell de Cent 42, 08014 Barcelona; tel. (93) 4269988; fax (93) 4267621; e-mail esma@esma.es; internet www.esma.es; Man. Dir JOAN B. RENART I MONTALAT.

Euroaula University School of Tourism: C/ Aragó 208–210, 08011 Barcelona; tel. (93) 451-03-06; e-mail turisme@euroaula.com; internet www.euroaula.com.

Garbí University School of Physiotherapy: C/ Ángel Guimerà 108, 17190 Salt, Gerona; tel. (97) 2405130; e-mail garbi.girona@udg.es; internet www.fisiogarbi.org; Dir ANTONIO NARBONA JIMÉNEZ.

Sant Pol de Mar University School of Hotel Business and Tourism: Carretera N-II s/n, 08395 Sant Pol de Mar, Barcelona; tel. (93) 7600212; fax (93) 7600985; e-mail %20mail@euht-santpol.org; internet www.euht-santpol.org; President RAMON SERRA.

School of Audiovisual and Multimedia Production: Crta Santa Coloma 115, 17005 Gerona; tel. (97) 2401300; e-mail escola@ege.es; internet www.ege.es/eram.

Terrassa University School of Tourism: Vapor Universitari, Colom 114, 08222 Terrassa; tel. (93) 7311869; fax (93) 7843706; e-mail info-turisme@fundaciofiac.com; internet www.fundaciofiac.com.

University School of Communication Sciences: Campus de Montilivi s/n, 17071 Gerona; tel. (97) 2418904; fax (97) 2418732; e-mail iolanda.vila@pas.udg.es; internet www.eucc-udg.org; Dir Dra CARMEN ECHAZARRETA SOLER.

UNIVERSITAT DE LES ILLES BALEARS

Campus Universitari, Cra de Valldemossa, Km 7.5, 07122 Palma, Mallorca
Telephone: (97) 1173000
Fax: (97) 1172852
E-mail: informacio@uib.es
Internet: www.uib.es
Founded 1978

State control
Languages of instruction: Catalan, Spanish, English
Academic year: October to September
Rector: Dra MONTSERRAT CASAS AMETLLER
First Vice-Rector for Univ. Planning and Coordination: Dr MARTÍ X. MARCH CERDÀ
Vice-Rector for Academic Regulation and European Convergence: Dr MATEU SERVERA BARCELÓ
Vice-Rector for Academic Staff and Pedagogical Innovation: Dr JOSEP LLUÍS FERRER GOMILA
Vice-Rector for Cultural Projection: Dr PATRÍCIA TRAPERO LLOBERA
Vice-Rector for Economic and Admin. Planning: Dr ANTONI LLULL GILET
Vice-Rector for Int. Relations and Mobility Programmes: Dra CATALINA NATIVITAT JUANEDA SAMPOL
Vice-Rector for Research: Dr JORDI LALUCAT JO
Vice-Rector for Student and Campus Affairs: Dr CELSO GARCÍA GARCÍA
Vice-Rector for Univ. Infrastructure: Dra RAQUEL HERRANZ BASCONES
Registrar: Dr FEDERICO F. GARAU SOBRINO
Man.: BEGOÑA MOREY AGUIRRE
Librarian: MIQUEL PASTOR TOUS
Number of teachers: 1,202
Number of students: 14,739
Publications: *Annuals of Tourism Research, Educació i Cultura, Mayurqa, Psicologia del Deporte, Taula, Treballs de Geografia*

DEANS

Faculty of Economics and Business: MARGALIDA PAYERAS LLODRÀ
Faculty of Education: JOSÉ LUIS OLIVER TORELLÓ
Faculty of Humanities: PERE JOAN BRUNET ESTARELLAS
Faculty of Law: SANTIAGO JOSÉ CAVANILLAS MÚJICA
Faculty of Psychology: ALBERT JOSÉ SESÉ ABAD
Faculty of Sciences: ANTONI MIRALLES SOCÍAS
Faculty of Tourism: MARCO ANTONIO ROBLEDO CAMACHO
Higher Polytechnic University School: GABRIEL OLIVER CODINA
University School of Nursing and Physiotherapy: MARGALIDA MIRÓ BONET

ATTACHED CENTRES

Alberta Giménez University School: Calle de Saragossa 16, Palma, Mallorca; tel. (97) 1792818; fax (97) 1798078; internet www.cesag.org; Dir MARC CARBONELL HUGUET.

Balearic Islands College of Hotel Management: Edif. Arxiduc Lluís Salvador, Campus Universitari, Cra. de Valldemossa, Km 7.5, 07702 Palma, Mallorca; tel. (97) 1172608; fax (97) 1172617; e-mail escola.hoteleria@uib.es; internet www.ehib.es/nova; Dir FRANCESC SASTRE ALBERTÍ.

College of Industrial Relations: Via Alemanya 7, 2n dreta, 07003 Palma, Mallorca; tel. (97) 1723268; Dir MARGARITA TARABINI-CASTELLANI AZNAR.

College of Tourism of the Island Council of Ibiza-Formentera: Edif. Polivalent, Cas Serres s/n, 07800 Ibiza; tel. (97) 1392762; fax (97) 1307255; internet euroibiza.org; Dir JOAN B. GARAU VADELL.

Felipe Moreno University School of Tourism (Mahón): Avda Sant Ferran 17, 07702 Mahón, Menorca, Islas Baleares; tel. and fax (97) 1350508; internet www.etb-baleares.es; Dir ONOFRE MARTORELL CUNILL.

Felipe Moreno University School of Tourism (Palma): Calle Sol 1, 07001 Palma, Mallorca; tel. (97 1721473; fax (97) 1714988; e-mail acapo@etb-baleares.es; internet www.etb-baleares.es; Dir ONOFRE MARTORELL CUNILL.

UNIVERSITAT DE LLEIDA

Plaça de Víctor Siurana 1, 25003 Lleida
Telephone: (97) 3702000
Fax: (97) 3702062
E-mail: pdi@seu.udl.cat
Internet: www.udl.cat
Founded 1991
State control
Language of instruction: Catalan, Spanish, English
Academic year: September to July
Rector: Dr JOAN VIÑAS SALAS
Vice-Rector for Cultural Activities and Univ. Outreach: Dr JAUME BARULL PELEGRÍ
Vice-Rector for Education: Dr ISABEL DEL ARCO
Vice-Rector for Infrastructure and Information Technology: PERE SOLÀ SOLÉ
Vice-Rector for Int. Relations and Cooperation: Dra CARMEN FIGUEROLA CABROL
Vice-Rector for Quality and Strategic Planning: RAMON SALADRIGUES SOLÉ
Vice-Rector for Research: ANA PELACHO
Vice-Rector for Scientific Policy and Technology: RAMON CANELA GARAYOA
Vice-Rector for Students: XAVIER GÓMEZ ARBONÉS
Vice-Rector for Teaching Staff: JOAN RAMON ROSELL POLO
Registrar: Dra ANA MARÍA ROMERO BURILLO
Man.: JOSEP MARIA SENTÍS SUÑÉ
Library Dir: LOLI MANCIÑEIRAS VAZ-ROMERO
Library of 320,341 vols, 4,861 periodicals, 18,747 e-publs
Number of teachers: 1,000
Number of students: 9,500
Publications: *Arrabal* (1 a Year), *Qualitative Theory of Dynamic Systems* (2 a year), *Revista d'Arqueologia de Ponent* (1 a year), *Sintagma* (1 a year), *Ull Crític* (1 a year)

DEANS

Faculty of Arts: JOAN J. BUSQUETA RIU
Faculty of Educational Sciences: MARI-PAU CORNADÓ TEIXIDO
Faculty of Law and Economics: Dra JOAN PERE ENCISO RODRÍGUEZ
Faculty of Medicine: JOAN RIBERA CALVET
Institute of Education: ISABEL DEL ARCO BRAVO
School of Agricultural Engineering: M. ROSA TEIRA ESMATGES
University Polytechnic School: FERRAN BADIA PASCUAL
University School of Nursing: Mª LUISA GUITARD SEIN-ECHALUBE

ATTACHED CENTRES

National Institute of Physical Education of Catalonia: Pda de la Caparrella, s/n, 25192 Lleida; tel. (97) 3272022; fax (97) 3275941; e-mail inefclleida@inefc.es; internet www.inefc.cat/inefc; Dir CRISTÒFOL SALAS.

University School of Labour Relations: Gran Passeig de Ronda 55–57, 25006 Lleida; tel. (97) 3248993; fax (97) 3221818; e-mail capadministracio@eurl.es; internet www.eurl.es; Dir Dra MARIA JOSÉ PUYALTO FRANCO.

UNIVERSITAT DE VALÈNCIA

Avda Blasco Ibáñez 13, 46010 Valencia
Telephone: (96) 3864100
Fax: (96) 3864885
E-mail: rectorado@uv.es
Internet: www.uv.es
Founded 1499
State control
Language of instruction: English, Spanish, Valencian (specific programmes)
Academic year: October to September
Rector: Prof. Dr ESTEBAN MORCILLO SÁNCHEZ
Vice-Rector for Academic Org.: Dra MARÍA VICENTA MESTRE ESCRIVÁ
Vice-Rector for Arts, Culture and Heritage: Dr JOSEP LLUÍS SIRERA TURÓ
Vice-Rector for Communications and Institutional Relations: Dra SILVIA BARONA VILAR
Vice-Rector for Community Participation and Outreach: Dr JORGE HERMOSILLA PLA
Vice-Rector for Continuing Education: (vacant)
Vice-Rector for Economics: MÁXIMO FERRANDO BOLADO
Vice-Rector for Infrastructure and Sustainability: Dra CLARA MARTÍNEZ FUENTES
Vice-Rector for Int. Relations and Cooperation: Dra OLGA GIL MEDRANO
Vice-Rector for Planning and Equality: Dr ANTONIO ARIÑO VILLARROYA
Vice-Rector for Postgraduate Studies: Dra ROSA MARÍN SÁEZ
Vice-Rector for Research and Scientific Policy: Dr PEDRO M. CARRASCO SORLI
Vice-Rector for Studies and Language Policy: Dra ISABEL VÁZQUEZ NAVARRO
Registrar: MARÍA JOSÉ AÑÓN ROIG
Man.: JOAN OLTRA VIDAL
Library Dir: JOSEP LLUÍS SIRERA TURÓ
Library of 1,484,000 vols, 17,600 periodicals
Number of teachers: 3,347
Number of students: 46,480 (undergraduates), 4,000 (masters and doctorates)

DEANS

Faculty of Biology: VICENTE ROCA VELASCO
Faculty of Chemistry: PILAR CAMPINS FALCÓ
Faculty of Economics: TRINIDAD CASASÚS ESTELLÉS
Faculty of Geography and History: ELENA GRAU ALMERO
Faculty of Law: SALVADOR MONTESINOS OLTRA
Faculty of Mathematics: RAFAEL CRESPO GARCÍA
Faculty of Medicine and Odontology: ANTONIO PELLICER MARTÍNEZ
Faculty of Pharmacy: MARÍA TERESA BARBER SANCHIS
Faculty of Philology, Translation and Communication: MARÍA JOSÉ COPERÍAS AGUILAR
Faculty of Philosophy and Education: RAMÓN LÓPEZ MARTÍN
Faculty of Physical Activity and Sport: VICTOR TELLA MUÑOZ
Faculty of Physics: JOSÉ ANTONIO PEÑARROCHA GANTES
Faculty of Psychology: JOSÉ RAMOS LÓPEZ
Faculty of Social Sciences: IGNASI LERMA MONTERO

UNIVERSITAT OBERTA DE CATALUNYA

Avda Tibidabo 39–43, 08035 Barcelona
Telephone: (93) 2532300
Fax: (93) 4716495
E-mail: queries@uoc.edu
Internet: www.uoc.edu
Founded 1995
Rector: IMMA TUBELLA CASADEVALL
Vice-Rector for Academic Policy and Teaching Staff: PERE FABRA ABAT
Vice-Rector for Postgraduate and Continuing Education: JOSEP MARIA DUART MONTOLIU
Vice-Rector for Research and Innovation: BEGOÑA GROS SALVAT
Vice-Rector for Technology: LLORENÇ VALVERDE GARCIA
Gen. Man.: ÓSCAR AGUER BAYARRI
Librarian: PEP TORN POCH
Library of 18,000 vols

Number of teachers: 2,346
Number of students: 54,378

DIRECTORS

Arts and Humanities: AGUSTÍ COLOMINES COMPANYS
Business Administration and Economics: JORDI VILASECA REQUENA
Communication: LLUÍS PASTOR PÉREZ
Computer Engineering: RAFAEL NADAL MACAU
Information and Documentation: LLUÍS PASTOR PÉREZ
Law and Political Science: AGUSTÍ CERRILLO MARTÍNEZ
Psychology and Educational Sciences: JOSEP MARIA MOMINÓ DE LA IGLESIA

UNIVERSITAT POMPEU FABRA

Plaça de la Mercè 10–12, 08002 Barcelona
Telephone: (93) 5422000
Fax: (93) 5422002
E-mail: premsa@upf.edu
Internet: www.upf.edu

Founded 1990
Regional govt control
Languages of instruction: Catalan, Spanish
Academic year: September to June

Rector: Dr JOSEP JOAN MORESO MATEOS
Vice-Rector for Academic Org. and Teaching: Dr JOSEP ELADI BAÑOS DÍEZ
Vice-Rector for Economics, Information Resources and Institutional Relations: Dr DANIEL SERRA DE LA FIGUERA
Vice-Rector for Institutional Quality and Strategy: Dr MIQUEL OLIVER RIERA
Vice-Rector for Int. Relations: Dr JOSEP FERRER RIBA
Vice-Rector for Postgraduate and Doctorate Studies: Dra OLGA VALVERDE GRANADOS
Vice-Rector for Research: LOUISE ELIZABETH MCNALLY SEIFERT
Vice-Rector for Science Policy: Dra TERESA GARCIA-MILÀ LLOVERAS
Vice-Rector for Student Affairs: Dr EMMA RODERO ANTÓN
Vice-Rector for Teaching Staff: Dr JOSEP M. MICÓ JUAN
Registrar: JOSEP FARGAS FERNÁNDEZ
Man.: RICARD BOIX I JUNQUERA
Librarian: MERCÈ CABO

Library of 500,000 vols, 8,600 periodicals
Number of teachers: 1,197
Number of students: 9,522

Publication: *Línia 14* (4 a year)

DEANS

Faculty of Communication: Dr JOSEP M. CASASÚS I GURI
Faculty of Economics and Business: Dr ALBERT CARRERAS DE ODRIOZOLA
Faculty of Health and Life Sciences: Dr JORDI PÉREZ
Faculty of Humanities: Dr MIREIA TRENCHS PARERA
Faculty of Law: Dr JOSEP M. VILAJOSANA RUBIO
Faculty of Political and Social Sciences: Dr JORDI GUIUPAYÀ
Faculty of Translation and Interpreting: Dra CRISTINA GELPÍ ARROYO
Polytechnic College: ALEJANDRO FEDERICO FRANGI CAREGNATO
University School of Business Studies: Dr JOAQUÍN TENA

UNIVERSITAT RAMÓN LLULL

Claravall 1–3, 08022 Barcelona
Telephone: (93) 6022200
Fax: (93) 6022249
E-mail: info@url.edu
Internet: www.url.es

Founded 1990
Private control
Academic year: September to June

Rector: Dra ESTHER GIMÉNEZ-SALINAS
Vice-Rector for Academic Affairs, Educational Innovation and Quality: Dr JORDI RIERA ROMANÍ
Vice-Rector for Research and Innovation: Dra ANNA BERGA TIMONEDA
Vice-Rector for Students and Int. Relations: Dra ANNA BERGA TIMONEDA
Vice-Rector for Univ. Policy and Registrar: Dr JOSEP M. GARRELL I GUIU

Library: 1.2m. vols, 14,000 periodicals
Number of teachers: 1,494
Number of students: 18,543

Publications: *La URL Informa, Signes*

DEANS

Blanquerna Faculty of Communication Sciences: Dr MIQUEL TRESSERRAS MAJÓ
Blanquerna Faculty of Psychology, Educational Sciences and Sport Science: Dr CLIMENT GINÉ I GINÉ
Blanquerna Faculty of Health Sciences: Dr MÀRIUS DURAN HORTOLÀ
Faculty of Economics: Dr JESÚS TRICÀS PRECKLER
Faculty of Law at the Higher School of Business Administration and Management (ESADE): Dr ENRIC BARTLETT CASTELLA
Faculty of Philosophy and Humanities: Dr JOAN MARTÍNEZ PORCELL
Higher School of Business Administration and Management (ESADE): Dr ALFONS SAUQUET ROVIRA
Higher Technical School: Dra ROSA NOMEN RIBÉ
Pere Tarrés Faculty of Social Education and Social Work: FRANCISCO JOSÉ LÓPEZ JIMÉNEZ

UNIVERSITAT ROVIRA I VIRGILI

Calle de l'Escorxador, s/n, 43003 Tarragona
Telephone: (90) 2337878
Fax: (97) 7558022
E-mail: contacteu@urv.cat
Internet: www.urv.cat

Founded 1991
State control
Academic year: September to July

Rector: Prof. FRANCESC XAVIER GRAU VIDAL
Vice-Rector for Academic and Scientific Policy: Dr JOSEP MANEL RICART PLA
Vice-Rector for Institutional Relations and Society: Dra ENCARNACIÓ RICART MARTÍ
Vice-Rector for Innovation and Transfer: Dra MISERICÒRDIA CARLES LAVILA
Vice-Rector for Int. Relations: Dra ANNA ARDÈVOL GRAU
Vice-Rector for Org. and Resources: Dr XAVIER FARRIOL ROIGÉS
Vice-Rector for Postgraduate and Continuing Education: Prof. AURORA RUIZ MANRIQUE
Vice-Rector for Research and Health Instns: Prof. ROSA SOLÀ I ALBERICH
Vice-Rector for Students and Univ. Community: Dra MARIA BARGALLÓ ESCRIVÀ
Vice-Rector for Teaching and European Higher Education Convergence: Dra MARIA MARQUÈS I BANQUÉ
Vice-Rector for Teaching Staff and Research Staff: Prof JOSEP PALLARÈS MARZAL
Sec. Gen.: Dr ANTONI GONZÀLEZ SENMARTÍ
Man.: MANUEL MOLINA CLAVERO

Library of 270,000 vols
Number of teachers: 931
Number of students: 11,344 undergraduate, 1,100 postgraduate

Publications: *Indicador Universitari* (12 a year), *Rovira i Virgili* (4 a year)

DEANS

Faculty of Arts: Dr JOHN STYLE
Faculty of Chemistry: Dr JOAN IGUAL RIPOLLÈS
Faculty of Economics and Business Studies: Dra MARÍA GLÒRIA BARBERÀ MARINÉ
Faculty of Educational Sciences and Psychology: Dra MONTSERRAT GUASCH GARCIA
Faculty of Legal Sciences: Dr FREDERIC ADÁN DOMÈNECH
Faculty of Medicine and Health Sciences: Dra MONTSERRAT GIRALT BATISTA
Faculty of Oenology: Prof. ALBERT BORDONS DE PORRATA-DORIA

ATTACHED CENTRE

Centre for Advanced Studies in Aviation (CESDA): Carretera del Aeropuerto s/n, Apdo 481, 43206 Reus (Tarragona); tel. (97) 7300027; fax (97) 7300028; e-mail cesda@cesda.com; internet www.cesda.com; Dir FRANCESC DÍAZ GONZÁLEZ.

Polytechnics

UNIVERSIDAD POLITÉCNICA DE CARTAGENA

Plaza del Cronista Isidoro Valverde, Edif. La Milagrosa, 30202 Cartagena (Murcia)
Telephone: (96) 8325400
Fax: (96) 8325972
E-mail: gestion.academic@upct.es
Internet: www.upct.es

Founded 1998
State control
Language of instruction: Spanish
Academic year: September to July

Rector: FÉLIX FAURA MATEU
Vice-Rector for Academic Affairs: JOSEFINA GARCÍA LEÓN
Vice-Rector for Academic Staff: ANTONIO VIGUERAS CAMPUZANO
Vice-Rector for Doctorate and Graduate Affairs: PEDRO SÁNCHEZ PALMA
Vice-Rector for Infrastructure: JUAN PATRICIO CASTRO VALDIVIA
Vice-Rector for New Technology: BÁRBARA ÁLVAREZ TORRES
Vice-Rector for Planning and Coordination: JOSÉ ANTONIO CASCALES PUJALTE
Vice-Rector for Research and Innovation: JOSÉ ANTONIO FRANCO LEEMHUIS
Vice-Rector for Student Affairs and Univ. Extension: FRANCISCO MARTÍNEZ GONZÁLEZ
Registrar: JOSÉ LUJÁN ALCARAZ
Man.: ESTHER NATIVIDAD DULCE
Librarian: MA. ÁNGELES GARCÍA DEL TORO

Library of 50,000 books, 2,528 periodicals
Number of teachers: 500
Number of students: 7,000.

CONSTITUENT SCHOOLS

Escuela de Arquitectura e Ingeniería de Edificación (School of Architecture and Engineering): Paseo Alfonso XIII 50, 30203 Cartagena; tel. and fax (86) 8071223; e-mail eaie@upct.es; internet www.arquide.upct.es; Dir JOSÉ CALVO LÓPEZ.

Escuela de Ingeniería de Caminos y de Minas (School of Civil Engineering and Mining): Calle Paseo Alfonso XIII 52, 30203 Cartagena; tel. and fax (96) 8325425; fax (96) 8327066; e-mail direccion@euitc.upct.es; internet www.upct.es/~euitc; Dir ANTONIO GARCÍA MARTÍN.

Escuela Técnica Superior de Ingeniería Agronómica (Higher Technical School of Agricultural Engineering): Paseo Alfonso XIII 48, 30203 Cartagena; tel. (96) 8325419; fax (96) 8325793; e-mail direccion@etsia.upct

.es; internet www.etsia.upct.es; Dir DON PABLO BIELZA LINO.

Escuela Técnica Superior de Ingeniería Industrial (Higher Technical School of Industrial Engineering): Campus Muralla del Mar, Calle Doctor Fleming, s/n, 30202 Cartagena; tel. (96) 8325417; fax (96) 8325420; e-mail etsii@etsii.upct.es; internet www.industriales.upct.es; Dir LUIS JAVIER LOZANO BLANCO.

Escuela Técnica Superior de Ingeniería de Telecomunicación (Higher Technical School of Telecommunications Engineering): Campus Muralla del Mar, Calle Doctor Fleming, s/n, 30202 Cartagena; tel. (96) 8338919; fax (96) 8325338; e-mail etsit@etsit.upct.es; internet www.teleco.upct.es; Dir LEANDRO JUAN LLÁCER.

Escuela Técnica Superior de Ingeniería Naval y Oceánica (Higher Technical School of Naval and Oceanic Engineering): Paseo Alfonso XIII 52, 30203 Cartagena; tel. and fax (96) 8325422; e-mail secretaria@etsino.upct.es; internet www.upct.es/~etsino; Dir DOMINGO L. GARCÍA LÓPEZ.

Facultad de Ciencias de la Empresa (Faculty of Business Science): Calle Real 3, 30201 Cartagena; tel. (96) 8325569; fax (96) 8325577; e-mail decanato@fce.upct.es; internet www.upct.es/~fcee; Dean ANTONIO GARCÍA SÁNCHEZ.

ATTACHED INSTITUTES

Academia General del Aire (General Air Academy): Calle Coronel López Peña, s/n, 30729 Santiago de la Ribera, (Murcia); tel. and fax (96) 8189921; e-mail contacto@cud.upct.es; internet www.cud.upct.es; Dir JOAQUÍN ROCA DORDA.

Escuela Universitaria de Turismo (University School of Tourism): Calle Ingeniero de la Cierva, s/n, Edificio UNED 4°, 30203 Cartagena; tel. and fax (96) 8528027; e-mail escuela.turismo@upct.es; internet www.eutcartagena.es; Dir MARÍA DEL MAR ANDREU MARTÍ.

UNIVERSITAT POLITÈCNICA DE CATALUNYA BARCELONATECH

Calle Jordi Girona 31, 08034 Barcelona
Telephone: (93) 4016200
Fax: (93) 4016210
E-mail: international@barcelonatech.upc.edu
Internet: www.barcelonatech.upc.edu

Founded 1971
Regional govt control
Languages of instruction: Spanish, Catalan, English
Academic year: September to June

Rector: ANTONI GIRÓ ROCA
Vice-Rector for Academic Policy: ANNA SASTRE REQUENA
Vice-Rector for Academic Staff: ENRIQUE GARCÍA-BERRO MONTILLA
Vice-Rector for Infrastructure: JOSEP BOSCH ESPELTA
Vice-Rector for Institutional Relations: MARISOL MARQUÉS CALVO
Vice-Rector for Int. Policy: PEDRO DÍEZ MEJÍA
Vice-Rector for Science Policy: FRANCESC XAVIER GIL MUR
Vice-Rector for Teaching and Students: XAVIER COLOM FAJULA
Sec.-Gen.: ANA ABELAIRA TATO
Head of Admin.: CARME LÓPEZ POL
Man.: CARME LÓPEZ I POL

Library: each constituent school has an attached library
Number of teachers: 2,750
Number of students: 30,000
Publications: *Informacions*, *The Mag* (4 a year).

CONSTITUENT SCHOOLS

Faculty of Mathematics and Statistics: Calle Pau Gargallo 5, 08028 Barcelona; tel. (93) 4017298; fax (93) 4015881; internet www-fme.upc.es; Dean SEBASTIÀ XAMBÓ DESCAMPS.

Faculty of Nautical Studies, Barcelona: Pl. de Palau 18, 08003 Barcelona; tel. (93) 4017936; fax (93) 4017910; internet www.fnb.upc.es; Dean ALEXANDRE MONFERRER DE LA PEÑA.

Higher Polytechnic School, Castelldefels: Avda del Canal Olímpic s/n, 08860 Castelldefels; tel. (93) 4137000; fax (93) 4137007; e-mail info@epsc.upc.es; internet www-epsc.upc.es; Dir MIGUEL VALERO GARCIA.

Higher Polytechnic School of Building, Barcelona: Avda Doctor Marañon 44–50, 08028 Barcelona; tel. (93) 4016300; fax (93) 4017700; internet www.epseb.upc.edu; Dir FRANCISCO JAVIER LLOVERA SÁEZ.

Higher Polytechnic School of Engineering, Vilanova i la Geltrú: Avda Víctor Balaguer s/n, 08800 Vilanova i la Geltrú; tel. (93) 8967701; fax (93) 8967700; internet www.upc.edu/epsevg; Dir ANDREU CATALÀ MALLOFRÉ.

Higher Technical School of Architecture, Barcelona: Avda Diagonal 649, 08028 Barcelona; tel. (93) 4016359; fax (93) 4015871; internet www.upc.es/etsab; Dir JAUME SANMARTÍ VERDAGUER.

Higher Technical School of Architecture, Vallès: Calle Pere Serra 1–15, 08190 St Cugat del Vallès; tel. (93) 4017900; fax (93) 4017901; e-mail pilar@etsavdaupc.es; internet www.etsavdaupc.es; Dir RAMON SASTRE SASTRE.

Higher Technical School of Civil Engineering, Barcelona: Calle Jordi Girona 1–3, Campus Norte, Edif. C2, 08034 Barcelona; tel. (93) 4016900; fax (93) 4016504; internet www.camins.upc.es; Dir FRANCESC ROBUSTÉ I ANTON.

Higher Technical School of Industrial Engineering, Barcelona: Avda Diagonal 647, 08028 Barcelona; tel. (93) 4016700; fax (93) 4016600; e-mail punt inf@etseib.upc.es; internet www.etseib.upc.es; Dir FERRAN PUERTA SALES.

Higher Technical School of Industrial Engineering, Terrassa: Calle Colom 11, 08222 Terrassa; tel. (93) 7398102; fax (93) 7398101; internet etseit-ct.upc.es; Dir JAUME GIBERT PEDROSA.

Higher Technical School of Telecommunications Engineering, Barcelona: Calle Jordi Girona 1–3, Campus Norte, Edif. B3, 08034 Barcelona; tel. (93) 4016800; fax (93) 4016801; e-mail infoteleco@etsetb.upc.es; internet www.etsetb.upc.es; Dir JUAN ANTONIO FERNÁNDEZ RUBIO.

School of Informatics, Barcelona: Calle Jordi Girona 1–3, Campus Norte, Edif. B6, 08034 Barcelona; tel. (93) 4017000; fax (93) 4017113; e-mail informacio@fib.upc.es; internet www.fib.upc.es; Dean MARIA RIBERA SANCHO.

University Polytechnic School, Manresa: Avda de les Bases de Manresa 61–73, 08240 Manresa; tel. (93) 8777200; fax (93) 8777202; e-mail eupm@eupm.upc.es; internet www.eupm.upc.es; Dir JUAN JORGE SÁNCHEZ.

University School of Industrial Engineering, Terrassa: Calle Colom 1, 08222 Terrassa; tel. (93) 7398132; fax (93) 7398225; internet euetit-ct.upc.es; Dir JUAN ANTONIO GALLARDO LEÓN.

University School of Optics and Optometry, Terrassa: Calle Violinista Vellsolà 37, 08222 Terrassa; tel. (93) 7398300; fax (93) 7398301; internet euoot-ct.upc.es; Dir NÚRIA LUPÓN BAS.

ATTACHED INSTITUTES

Caixa Terrassa Business College: Ctra de Terrassa, Km 3, 08227 Terrassa; tel. (93) 7301900; fax (93) 7301901; internet www.euncet.com; Dir JORDI BALCELLS GENÉ.

Catalan Technical Foundation School of Photography: Calle de la Igualtat 33, 08222 Terrassa; tel. (93) 7398312; fax (93) 7398365; internet www.citm.upc.es; Dir of Centre of the Image and Multimedia Technology MIQUEL MORÓN TARIFA.

College of Agricultural Engineering: Comte d'Urgell 187, 08036 Barcelona; tel. (93) 4137500; fax (93) 4137501; internet www.esab.upc.es; Dir F. XAVIER MARTÍNEZ FARRÉ.

College of Industrial Engineering, Barcelona: Comte d'Urgell 187, 08036 Barcelona; tel. (93) 4137400; fax (93) 4137401; internet www.euetib.upc.es; Dir MARTÍ LLORENS MORRAJA.

College of Industrial Engineering, Igualada: Plaça del Rei 15, 08700 Igualada; tel. (93) 8035300; fax (93) 8031589; internet www.euetii.upc.es; Deputy Dir RITA PUIG I VIDAL.

College of Knitted Fabric Engineering: Plaça de la Indústria 1, 08360 Canet de Mar; tel. (93) 7940150; fax (93) 7954817; internet www.diba.es/canet; Dir MIQUEL SOLER LUQUE.

Institute of Education: Calle Jordi Girona 29, Edif. Nexus II, Despatx OD, 08034 Barcelona; tel. (93) 4137643; e-mail info.ice@upc.es; internet www.ice.upc.es; Dir RAFAEL PINDADO RICO.

Institute of Industrial Systems Organization and Control: Avda Diagonal 647, 11°, Edif. H, 08028 Barcelona; tel. (93) 4016653; fax (93) 4016605; e-mail enric.fossas@upc.es; internet www.ioc.upc.es; Dir ENRIC FOSSAS COLET.

Institute of Power Engineering: Avda Diagonal 647, 08028 Barcelona; tel. (93) 4016692; fax (93) 4017149; e-mail ortega@inte.upc.es; internet www.upc.es/inte/index.html; Dir XAVIER ORTEGA ARAMBURU.

Institute of Textile Research and Industrial Cooperation, Terrassa: Calle Colom 15, 08222 Terrasa; tel. (93) 7398270; fax (93) 7398272; e-mail director-ins@intexter.upc.es; internet www.ct.upc.es/intexter; Dir LLIBERT COLL TORTOSA.

Mataró Technical College: Avda Puig i Cadafalch 101–111, 08303 Mataró; tel. (93) 7574404; fax (93) 7570524; internet www.eupmt.es; Dir JOAN GIL LÓPEZ.

School of Business Administration: Aragó 55, 08015 Barcelona; tel. (93) 2278090; fax (93) 3194436; e-mail eae@eae.es; internet www.eae.es; Dir FERNANDO CASADO JUAN.

School of Multimedia of the UPC Foundation: Calle de la Igualtat 33, 08222 Terrassa.

School of Occupational Hazard Prevention: Calle Dulcet 2–10, 08034 Barcelona; tel. (93) 2804542; fax (93) 2803642; e-mail neus.guardiola@fpc.upc.es; internet www.escuela-prevencion.com.

UNIVERSIDAD POLITÉCNICA DE MADRID

Calle Ramiro de Maeztu 7, 28040 Madrid
Telephone: (91) 3366000
Fax: (91) 3366173
Internet: www.upm.es

Founded 1971
State control

Language of instruction: Spanish
Academic year: October to July
Rector: JAVIER UCEDA ANTOLÍN
Vice-Rector for Academic Administration and Teaching Staff: EMILIO MÍNGUEZ TORRES
Vice-Rector for Academic Affairs and Strategic Planning: CARLOS CONDE LÁZARO
Vice-Rector for Doctorate and Postgraduate Studies: ERNESTINA MENASALVAS RUÍZ
Vice-Rector for Economic Planning: ADOLFO CAZORLA MONTERO
Vice-Rector for Information and Communication: JOSÉ MANUEL PERALES PERALES
Vice-Rector for Int. Relations: JOSÉ MANUEL PÁEZ BORRALLO
Vice-Rector for Research: GONZALO LEÓN SERRANO
Vice-Rector for Student Affairs: LUIS GARCÍA ESTEBAN
Registrar: CRISTINA PÉREZ GARCIA
Chief Admin. Officer: SIXTO GARCIA ALONSO

Library: each constituent school has an attached library; 775,000 vols, 11,800 periodicals
Number of teachers: 3,414
Number of students: 41,374.

CONSTITUENT SCHOOLS

Faculty of Computer Science: Campus Montegancedo, Boadilla del Monte, 28660 Madrid; tel. (91) 3367399; fax (91) 3367412; internet www.fi.upm.es; Dean FRANCISCO JAVIER SEGOVIA PÉREZ.

Faculty of Physical Activity and Sport: C/ Martín Fierro, s/n, Ciudad Universitaria, 28040 Madrid; tel. (91) 3364000; fax (91) 5441331; internet www.inef.upm.es; Dir JAVIER SAMPEDRO MOLINUEVO.

Higher Technical School of Aeronautical Engineering: Pza Cardenal Cisneros 3, Ciudad Universitaria, 28040 Madrid; tel. (91) 3366300; fax (91) 5439859; internet www.aero.upm.es; Dir MIGUEL ANGEL GÓMEZ TIERNO.

Higher Technical School of Agronomy: Avda Complutense, s/n, Ciudad Universitaria, 28040 Madrid; tel. (91) 3365600; fax (91) 5434879; internet www.etsia.upm.es; Dir JESÚS VÁZQUEZ MINGUELA.

Higher Technical School of Architecture: Avda Juan de Herrera 4, Ciudad Universitaria, 28040 Madrid; tel. (91) 3366524; fax (91) 5442481; internet www.aq.upm.es; Dir LUIS MALDONADO RAMOS.

Higher Technical School of Civil Engineering: Ciudad Universitaria, 28040 Madrid; tel. (91) 3363800; fax (91) 5492289; internet www.caminos.upm.es; Dir JUAN ANTONIO SANTAMERA SÁNCHEZ.

Higher Technical School of Forestry: Ciudad Universitaria, 28040 Madrid; tel. (91) 3367073; fax (91) 5439557; internet www.montes.upm.es; Dir ANTONIO NOTARIO GÓMEZ.

Higher Technical School of Industrial Engineering: Calle José Gutiérrez Abascal 2, 28006 Madrid; tel. (91) 3363060; internet www.etsii.upm.es; Dir JESÚS FÉLEZ MINDÁN.

Higher Technical School of Mining Engineering: Ríos Rosas 21, 28003 Madrid; tel. (91) 3367071; internet www.minas.upm.es; Dir BENJAMÍN CALVO PÉREZ.

Higher Technical School of Shipbuilding: Avda Arco de la Victoria s/n, Ciudad Universitaria, 28020 Madrid; tel. (91) 3367140; fax (91) 3367511; internet www.etsin.upm.es; Dir JESÚS PANADERO PASTRANA.

Higher Technical School of Telecommunications Engineering: Ciudad Universitaria, 28040 Madrid; tel. (91) 3367234; fax (91) 5439652; internet www.etsit.upm.es; Dir GUILLERMO CISNEROS PÉREZ.

Polytechnic School of Higher Education: C/ Ramiro de Maeztu 7, 28040 Madrid; tel. (91) 3365912; fax (91) 3365912; Dir JOSÉ LUIS ENRÍQUEZ ESCUDERO.

University School of Aeronautical Engineering: Pza Cardenal Cisneros, s/n, Ciudad Universitaria, 28040 Madrid; tel. (91) 3364166; fax (91) 3367511; internet www.euita.upm.es; Dir MIGUEL ÁNGEL BARCALA MONTEJANO.

University School of Agricultural Engineering: Ciudad Universitaria, 28040 Madrid; tel. (91) 3365400; internet www.agricolas.upm.es; Dir FRANCISCO GONZÁLEZ TORRES.

University School of Architecture: Avda Juan de Herrera, 6, Ciudad Universitaria, 28040 Madrid; tel. (91) 336-7636; fax (91) 3367644; internet www.euatm.upm.es; Dir MERCEDES DEL RIO MERINO.

University School of Computer Science: Camino de la Arboleda, s/n, Campus Sur, 28031 Madrid; tel. (91) 3367903; internet www.eui.upm.es; Dir JESÚS GARCIA LÓPEZ DELACALLE.

University School of Forestry: Avda Ramiro de Maeztu, s/n, Ciudad Universitaria, 28040 Madrid; tel. (91) 3367652; internet www.forestales.upm.es; Dir GERMÁN GLARIA GALCERÁN.

University School of Industrial Engineering: Ronda de Valencia, 3, 28012 Madrid; tel. (91) 3367699; internet www.euiti.upm.es; Dir SARA GÓMEZ MARTÍN.

University School of Public Works: Alfonso XII 3, 28014 Madrid; tel. (91) 3367743; fax (91) 3367958; internet www.op.upm.es; Dir CARLOS DELGADO ALONSO-MARTIRENA.

University School of Telecommunications Engineering: Camino de la Arboleda, s/n, Campus Sur, 28031 Madrid; tel. (91) 3367780; fax (91) 3319229; internet www.euitt.upm.es; Dir CESAR SANZ ÁLVARO (acting).

Higher Technical School of Topography, Geodesy and Cartography: Camino de la Arboleda, s/n, Campus Sur, 28031 Madrid; tel. (91) 3367915; internet www.euitto.upm.es; Dir ROSA MARIANA CHUECA CASTELO.

ATTACHED INSTITUTES

Higher Centre of Fashion Design: Camino de la Arboleda, s/n, Campus Sur, 28031 Madrid; tel. (91) 3310126; fax (91) 3321767; internet www.csdmm.upm.es; Dir DIANA FERNÁNDEZ GONZÁLEZ.

Higher School of Brewing: E. T. S. de Ingenieros Industriales, Laboratorio deTecnología Química, Calle José Gutiérrez Abascal 2, 28006 Madrid; tel. (91) 3363190; fax (91) 3363009; e-mail eroche@etsii.upm.es; internet www.aetcm.es/escuela.htm#inicio; Dir ERCARNACIÓN RODRIGUEZ HURTADO.

Institute of Automobile Research: Ctra de Valencia Km 7, Campus Sur UPM, 28031 Madrid; tel. (91) 3365300; fax (91) 3365302; e-mail insia@insia.upm.es; internet www.insia.upm.es; Dir FRANCISCO APARICIO IZQUIERDO.

Institute of Education: C/ Profesor Aranguren, s/n, Ciudad Universitaria, 28040 Madrid; tel. (91) 3366815; fax (91) 3366812; e-mail ice@ice.upm.es; internet www.ice.upm.es; Dir ROSA MARIA GONZÁLEZ TIRADOS.

Institute of Microgravity 'Ignacio Da Riva': UPM, ETSI Aeronáuticos, 28040 Madrid; tel. (91) 3366353; fax (91) 3366363; e-mail idr@idr.upm.es; internet www.idr.upm.es; Dir JOSÉ MESEGUER RUÍZ.

Institute of Nuclear Fusion: E. T. S. de Ingenieros Industriales, Calle José Gutiérrez Abascal 2, 28006 Madrid; tel. (91) 3363108; Dir JOSÉ MANUEL PERLADO.

Institute of Optoelectronic Systems and Microtechnology: ETSI Telecomunicación (UPM), Ciudad Universitaria, 28040 Madrid; tel. (91) 3367321; fax (91) 5490909; e-mail montse.isom@die.upm.es; internet www.isom.upm.es; Dir ENRIQUE CALLEJA PARDO.

Institute of Solar Energy: E. T. S. de Ingenieros de Telecomunicación, Ciudad Universitaria, 28040 Madrid; tel. (91) 5441060; fax (91) 5446341; e-mail info@ies-def.upm.es; internet www.ies.upm.es; Dir CARLOS DE CAÑIZO NADAL.

Laser Centre: Edif. Tecnológico 'La Arboleda', Campus Sur UPM, Carretera de Valencia Km 7,300, 28031 Madrid; tel. (91) 3324280; fax (91) 33-6906; e-mail jlocana@faii.ctsii.upm.es; internet www.upmlaser.upm.es; Dir JOSÉ LUIS OCAÑA MORENO.

UNIVERSIDAD POLITÉCNICA DE VALENCIA

Camino de Vera, s/n, 46022 Valencia
Telephone: (96) 3877000
Fax: (96) 3879009
E-mail: informacion@upv.es
Internet: www.upv.es

Founded 1968
State control
Languages of instruction: Spanish, Valencian
Academic year: October to June

Rector: JUAN JULIÁ IGUAL
Vice-Rector for Campus and Infrastructure: SALVADOR LÓPEZ GALARZA
Vice-Rector for Culture, Communication and Institutional Image: JUAN BAUTISTA PEIRÓ LÓPEZ
Vice-Rector for Devt of ITC Technologies: VICENT J. BOTTI NAVARRO
Vice-Rector for Faculty and Academic Planning: JOSÉ LUIS BERNÉ VALERO
Vice-Rector for Int. Relations and Cooperation: JUAN MIGUEL MARTÍNEZ RUBIO
Vice-Rector for Planning and Innovation: FRANCISCO JOSÉ MORA MÁS
Vice-Rector for Quality and Academic Assessment: JUAN JAIME CANO HURTADO
Vice-Rector for Research: AMPARO CHIRALT BOIX
Vice-Rector for Social Affairs and Corporate Social Responsibility: MARÍA PILAR SANTAMARINA SIURANA
Vice-Rector for Sport: ÁNGEL FRANCISCO BENITO BEORLEGUI
Vice-Rector for Student Affairs: VICTORIA VIVANCOS RAMÓN
Vice-Rector for Studies and European Convergence: MIGUEL ÁNGEL FERNÁNDEZ PRADA
Registrar: VICENT CASTELLANO I CERVERA
Man.: JOSÉ ANTONIO PÉREZ GARCÍA
Librarian: JOSÉ LLORENS SÁNCHEZ

Library of 52,000 vols, 10,000 periodicals
Number of teachers: 2,500
Number of students: 37,500.

CONSTITUENT SCHOOLS

Higher Technical School of Agronomy: Edificio 3H, Camino de Vera, s/n, 46022 Valencia; tel. (96) 3877130; fax (96) 3877139; e-mail etsia@etsia.upvnet.upv.es; internet www.etsia.upv.es; Dir NEMESIO FERNÁNDEZ MARTÍNEZ.

Higher Technical School of Architecture: Edificio 2I, Camino de Vera, s/n, 46022 Valencia; tel. (96) 3877110; fax (96) 3877119; e-mail etsa@upvnet.upv.es; internet www.arq.upv.es; Dir IGNACIO BOSCH REIG.

Higher Technical School of Applied Computer Science: Edificio 1G, Camino de Vera, s/n, 46022 Valencia; tel. (96) 3877210; fax (96) 3877219; e-mail einf_ei@upvnet.upv.es; internet www.eui.upv.es; Dir ANTONIO ROBLES MARTÍNEZ.

Higher Technical School of Building Management: Edificio 1B, Camino de Vera, s/n, 46022 Valencia; tel. (96) 3877120; fax (96) 3877943; e-mail euat@upvnet.upv.es; internet www.arq.upv.es; Dir RAFAEL CAPUZ LLADRÓ.

Higher Technical School of Civil Engineering: Edificio 4H, Camino de Vera s/n, 46022 Valencia; tel. (96) 3877150; fax (96) 3877159; e-mail etsiccp@upvnet.upv.es; internet www.iccp.upv.es; Dir JOSÉ AGUILAR HERRANDO.

Higher Technical School of Design Engineering: Edificio 7B, Camino de Vera, s/n, 46022 Valencia; tel. (96) 3877180; fax (96) 3877189; e-mail info@etsid.upv.es; internet www.etsid.upv.es; Dir ENRIQUE BALLESTER SARRIAS.

Higher Technical School of Geodesic, Cartographic and Topographic Engineering: Edificio 7E, Camino de Vera, s/n, 46022 Valencia; tel. (96) 3877160; fax (96) 3877169; e-mail etsigct@upvnet.upv.es; internet www.top.upv.es; Dir MANUEL CHUECA PAZOS.

Higher Technical School of Industrial Engineering: Edificio 5F, Camino de Vera, s/n, 46022 Valencia; tel. (96) 3877170; fax (96) 3877179; e-mail etsii@upvnet.upv.es; internet www.etsii.upv.es; Dir JUAN JAIME CANO HURTADO.

Higher Technical School of Telecommunications Engineering: Edificio 4D, Camino de Vera, s/n, 46022 Valencia; tel. (96) 3877190; fax (96) 3877199; e-mail etsitv@upvnet.upv.es; internet www.etsit.upv.es; Dir ELÍAS DE LOS REYES DAVÓ.

Higher Technical School of the Rural Environment and Oenology: Avda Blasco Ibáñez 21, 46010 Valencia; tel. (96) 3877140; fax (96) 3877149; e-mail euita@upvnet.upv.es; internet www.euita.upv.es; Dir SANTIAGO GUILLEM PICÓ.

Faculty of Business Administration and Management: Edificio 8H, Camino de Vera, s/n, 46022 Valencia; tel. (96) 3879270; fax (96) 3879279; e-mail ade@upv.es; internet www.upv.es/ade; Dean ENRIQUE DE MIGUEL FERNÁNDEZ.

Faculty of Computer Science: Edificio 1E, Camino de Vera, s/n, 46022 Valencia; tel. (96) 3877200; fax (96) 3877924; e-mail finfv@upvnet.upv.es; internet www.fiv.upv.es; Dean EMILIO SANCHÍS ARNAL.

Faculty of Fine Arts: Edificio 3L, Camino de Vera, s/n, 46022 Valencia; tel. (96) 3877220; fax (96) 3879229; e-mail fbbaa@upvnet.upv.es; internet www.bbaa.upv.es; Dean ELÍAS MIGUEL PÉREZ GARCÍA.

Higher Polytechnic School, Alcoy: Pl. Ferrándiz Carbonell, s/n, 08301 Alcoy (Alicante); tel. (96) 6528400; fax (96) 6528409; e-mail epsa@upvnet.upv.es; internet www.epsa.upv.es; Dir ENRIQUE JUAN MASIÁ BUADES.

Higher Polytechnic School, Gandía: Carretera Nazaret-Oliva, s/n, 46730 Gandía (Valencia); tel. (96) 2849300; fax (96) 2849309; e-mail epsg@upvnet.upv.es; internet www.epsg.upv.es; Dir MARÍA MANUELA FERNÁNDEZ MÉNDEZ.

ATTACHED INSTITUTIONS

Escuela Universitaria Ford España: 46440 Almussafes, (Valencia); tel. (96) 1792246; fax (96) 1792255; e-mail asanramo@ford.com; internet www.escuelaford.com; areas of study: mechanical engineering.

Florida Training Centre: Calle Rei En Jaume I 2, Apdo 15, 46470 Catarroja (Valencia); tel. (96) 1220380; fax (96) 1269933; e-mail info.general@florida-uni.es; internet www.florida.es; aeas of study: mechanics, industrial electronics; Gen. Dir EMPAR MARTÍNEZ BONAFÉ.

Colleges

GENERAL

Schiller International University—Madrid: (For general information, see entry for Schiller International University in Germany chapter) Calle Serrano 156, Plaza de la Republica Argentina, 28002 Madrid; tel. (91) 4482488; fax (91) 4452110; e-mail mad_admissions@schiller.edu; internet www.schiller.edu/campuses/madrid-spain; f. 1967; Dir L. BURGUNDE.

Universidad Internacional Menéndez Pelayo: Calle Isaac Peral 23, 28040 Madrid; tel. (94) 2298800; fax (94) 2298820; internet www.uimp.es; f. 1932; offers long-vacation courses to Spanish and foreign students, and grants fellowships for scientific research; campuses in Santander, Barcelona, Cuenca, Santa Cruz de Tenerife, La Coruña, Seville, Valencia, Formigal (Huesca); library: 16,000 vols; 700 teachers; 15,000 students; Rector SALVADOR ORDÓÑEZ DELGADO.

ECONOMICS AND LAW

ESADE (Escuela Superior de Administración y Dirección de Empresas) (Higher School of Administration and Business Management): Avda Pedralbes 60–62, 08034 Barcelona; tel. (93) 2806162; fax (93) 2048105; e-mail info@esade.edu; internet www.esade.edu; f. 1958; schools of business, law, languages, tourism; 4 campuses: 2 in Barcelona, and 1 each in Madrid and Buenos Aires, Argentina.; Dir-Gen. EUGENIA BIETO.

EuroArab Management School (EAMS): Calle Cárcel Baja 3, 18001 Granada; tel. (95) 8805050; fax (95) 8800152; f. 1995, jtly by the EU and the League of Arab States, with support of Spanish Govt; management devt; Dir-Gen. JOAQUÍN ABÓS.

Institut Universitari d'Estudis Europeus: Universitat Autonoma de Barcelona, Edif. E1, 08193 Bellaterra (Barcelona); tel. (93) 5812016; fax (93) 5813063; internet www.iuee.eu; f. 1985; studies in political, economic, cultural, scientific and judicial aspects of modern Europe; participates in conferences on European issues throughout Spain; Dir Dr BLANCA VILÀ.

Instituto de Empresa (Business School): María de Molina 11, 28006 Madrid; tel. (91) 5689600; fax (91) 4115503; e-mail admissions@ie.edu; internet www.ie.edu; f. 1973; 500 teachers; 7,800 students; Dean SANTIAGO IÑIGUEZ DE OZOÑO.

Real Centro Universitario 'Escorial—María Cristina': Paseo de los Alamillos 2, 28200 San Lorenzo del Escorial, (Madrid); tel. (91) 8904545; fax (91) 8906609; e-mail contacto@rcumariacristina.com; internet www.rcumariacristina.com; f. 1892; private college of the Augustinian Fathers accredited by Universidad Complutense de Madrid; library: 57,000 vols, 500 periodicals; 60 teachers; 1,200 students; Rector EDELMIRO MATEOS MATEOS; publs *Anuario jurídico y económico escurialense* (1 a year), *La Ciudad de Dios* (4 a year), *Nueva Etapa* (1 a year).

MEDICINE

Escuela Andaluza de Salud Pública (Andalusian School of Public Health): Cuesta del Observatorio 4, 18080 Granada; tel. (95) 8027400; fax (95) 8027503; e-mail comunicacion@easp.es; internet www.easp.es; f. 1985; affiliated with Universidad de Granada; Masters degree and other courses in public health management and services; drug information centre; cancer registry; library: 56,000 vols, 1,229 current periodicals; 50 teachers; 2,000 students; Dir HERMINIA MUÑOZ.

MILITARY SCIENCE

Escuela de Guerra del Ejército (Army War College): Santa Cruz de Marcenado 25, 28015 Madrid; tel. (91) 5242000; fax (91) 5425509; f. 1842; library: 140,000 vols; 60 teachers; 180 students; Dir Brig.-Gen. RICARDO MARTÍNEZ ISIDORO.

TECHNOLOGY

Escuela Técnica Superior de Ingenieros Industriales (Higher School for Industrial Engineers): José Gutiérrez Abascal 2, 28006 Madrid; tel. (91) 3363060; fax (91) 5618618; e-mail administrador.industriales@upm.es; internet www.etsii.upm.es; f. 1850; library: see Libraries; 350 teachers; 3,500 students; Dir JESUS FÉLEZ MINDÁN.

ETEA—Institución Universitaria de la Compañía de Jesús: Escritor Castilla Aguayo 4, Apdo 439, 14004 Córdoba; tel. (95) 7222100; fax (95) 7222101; e-mail comunica@etea.com; internet www.etea.com; f. 1963; undergraduate and postgraduate courses in business administration; research institute; extension courses in management; management consultancy services; 150 teachers; library: 50,000 vols; Dir GABRIEL PÉREZ ALCALÁ.

Institut Químic de Sarrià (Sarrià Institute of Chemistry): Universitat Ramon Llull, Calle Via Augusta 390, 08017 Barcelona; tel. (93) 2672000; fax (93) 2056266; e-mail secre@iqs.edu; internet www.iqs.edu; f. 1916; library: 55,000 vols, 780 periodicals; 125 teachers; 1,500 students; Dir-Gen. Dr ENRIC JULIÀ; publs *Afinidad* (6 a year), *IQS* (1 a year).

Schools of Art, Architecture and Music

Conservatori Municipal de Música de Barcelona: Bruc 110–112, 08009 Barcelona; tel. (93) 4584302; fax (93) 4593104; e-mail conservatori@cmmb.cat; internet www.cmmb.cat; f. 1886; library: 27,400 vols and scores, 7,250 items of audio material; 102 teachers; 1,815 students; Pres. ALBERT LLANAS.

Conservatorio Superior de Música de Málaga: Plaza Maestro Artola 2, 29013 Málaga; tel. (95) 1298340; fax (95) 1298341; e-mail info@conserv-sup-malaga.com; internet www.conserv-sup-malaga.com; f. 1880; Dir MARIANO TRIVIÑO ARREBOLA; publ. *Hoquet* (1 a year).

Conservatorio Superior de Música de Valencia: Calle del Cineasta Ricardo Muñoz Suay, s/n, 46013, Valencia; tel. (96) 3605316; fax (96) 3605701; e-mail 46013129@centres.cult.gua.es; internet www.csmvalencia.es; f. 1879; library: 12,000 vols; 40 teachers; 900 students; Pres. and Dir EDUARDO MONTESINOS COMAS; publ. *Memoria* (1 a year).

Conservatorio Superior de Música 'Rafael Orozco' de Córdoba: Calle Angel

Saavedra 1, 14003 Córdoba; tel. (95) 7379647; fax (95) 7379653; e-mail oficina@csmcordoba.com; internet www.csmcordoba.com; f. 1902; library: 15,000 vols; 95 teachers; 3,000 students; Dir MANUEL ABELLA FÉRRIZ; publ. *Musicalia*.

Conservatorio Superior de Música 'Manuel Castillo': Calle Baños 48, 41002 Seville; tel. (95) 4915630; fax (95) 4374373; e-mail secretaria@consev.es; internet www.csmsev.es; f. 1933; library: 25,000 books and scores; 120 teachers; 2,400 students; Dir LUIS IGNACIO MARÍN GARCÍA; publ. *Diferencias*.

Conservatorio Superior de Música de Murcia: Paseo del Malecón 9, 30004 Murcia; tel. (96) 8294758; fax (96) 8294756; e-mail info@csmmurcia.com; internet www.csmmurcia.com; f. 1916; library: 1,546 vols, 52 periodicals, 3,914 musical scores, 1,704 audio materials; 85 teachers; 3,000 students; Dir MIGUEL BARÓ BO; publ. *Cadencia* (3 a year).

Subordinate Institute:

Escuela Superior de Arte Dramático de Murcia: Plaza de los Apóstoles, 30001 Murcia; tel. (96) 8214629; fax (96) 8217636; internet www.esad-murcia.com; f. 1918 as Conservatorio Provincial de Música y Declamación; changed name to Escuela Superior de Arte Dramático y Danza 1982; present name adopted 1993; Dir JUAN ÁNGEL SERRANO MASEGOSO.

Escuela Superior de Bellas Artes de San Carlos (San Carlos School of Fine Arts): Calle San Pio V 9, 46010 Valencia; f. 1756; library: 5,100 vols; 30 teachers; 300 students; Dir DANIEL DE NUEDA LLISIONA.

Escuela Superior de Música Reina Sofía (Reina Sofía Higher School of Music): Plaza de Oriente, s/n, 28013 Madrid; tel. (91) 5230419; fax (91) 5329661; e-mail esmrs@albeniz.com; internet www.escuelasuperiordemusicareinasofia.es; f. 1991; depts of performance, academic studies, artistic studies, and complementary training; library: 1,200 books, 3,600 musical scores, 2,400 CDs, 2,500 LPs, 2,500 video and audio cassettes; Pres. PALOMA O'SHEA.

Escuela Técnica Superior de Arquitectura de Sevilla (Seville School of Architecture): Avda Reina Mercedes 2, 41012 Seville; tel. (95) 4556501; fax (95) 4556534; e-mail directoretsa@us.es; internet www.etsa.us.es; f. 1964; library: 18,000 vols; 160 teachers; 2,200 students; Dir Dr NARCISO-JESÚS VÁZQUEZ CARRETERO.

IES 'Islas Filipinas': Calle Jesús Maestro 3, 28003 Madrid; tel. (91) 5344349; fax (91) 5537592; e-mail ies.islasfilipinas.madrid@educa.madrid.org; internet www.islasfilipinas.com; f. 1968 as Escuela Nacional de Artes Gráfica; name changed to Instituto de Formación Profesional 'Islas Filipinas' 1985; present name subsequently adopted; building and civil engineering, delineation, graphic arts, information technology; library: 15,000 vols; 110 teachers; 2,000 students; Dir JUSTA ACEDO BARTOLOMÉ.

Musikene—Euskal Herriko Goi-Mailako Musika Ikastegia/Conservatorio Superior de Música del País Vasco: Palacio Miramar, Mirakontxa 48, 20007 Donostia-San Sebastián; tel. (94) 3316778; fax (94) 3316916; e-mail info@musikene.net; internet www.musikene.net; f. 2001; 150 teachers; Gen. Coordinator CARMEN RODRÍGUEZ SUSO; publ. *Ahaire*.

Real Conservatorio Profesional de Música 'Manuel de Falla': Calle Marqués del Real Tesoro 10, 11001 Cádiz; tel. (95) 6243106; fax (95) 6243109; internet www.conservatoriomanueldefalla.es; f. 1860 as Academia Santa Cecilia; 60 professors; 1,000 students; Dir MIGUEL GARRIDO ALDOMAR.

Real Conservatorio Superior de Música de Madrid (Royal Academy of Music, Madrid): Calle Santa Isabel 53, Planta Baja, 28012 Madrid; tel. (91) 5392901; fax (91) 5275822; e-mail secretario.rcsmm@telefonica.net; internet www.educa.madrid.org/web/csm.realconservatorio.madrid; f. 1830; library: 135,000 vols, incl. 10,000 original 18th- and 19th-century musical scores; 150 teachers; 700 students; Dir ANSELMO IGNACIO DE LA CAMPA DÍAZ; publ. *Musica* (1 a year).

Real Escuela Superior de Arte Dramático (Royal School of Dramatic Art): Avda de Nazaret 2, 28009 Madrid; tel. (91) 5042151; fax (91) 5741138; e-mail secretaria@resad.es; internet www.resad.es; f. 1831; library: 28,300 vols; 50 teachers; 350 students; Dir ÁNGEL MARTÍNEZ ROGER; publ. *Acotaciones* (2 a year).

SRI LANKA

The Higher Education System

Institutions of higher education pre-date the independence of Sri Lanka (formerly Ceylon) from the United Kingdom in 1948, with the oldest being the University of Colombo, which was founded in 1921 (present name 1979). In 1978 an Act of Parliament created the current university system, following which several existing colleges were promoted to university status. There are 26 teacher-training colleges, 12 universities, 13 polytechnic institutes, eight junior technical colleges and an open university. In 2003 there were 59,734 students enrolled at the 12 universities (not including the Open University). The governing body of the universities is the University Grants Commission. The universities are mostly government funded, and although students do not pay tuition fees they are required to pay registration and examination fees. Private higher education institutions are not recognized by the state in Sri Lanka. They are not quality assured by the University Grants Commission or other Sri Lankan authorities as they are not considered to offer legal degrees. Consequently they cannot issue Sri Lankan degrees but operate in conjunction with overseas universities, including British institutions. There are private colleges that award post-secondary qualifications but not degrees.

In 2000 new regulations regarding university entrance requirements came into effect. Students must now complete a minimum of three subjects at GCE A-Level in addition to sitting a Common General Paper and a General English Paper, although the Open University (established in 1980) does not have formal entrance requirements. The undergraduate Bachelors degree is classified as either 'General' or 'Special': the former lasts three years and covers three subjects in equal depth, while the latter lasts four years and is a subject-specific programme of study, culminating in a dissertation. Professional degrees last four years and are offered in technical or practical disciplines such as medicine, engineering and architecture. Graduates with the Bachelors degree are eligible for the one-year Postgraduate Diploma or the two-year Masters degree. Finally, the Doctorate (mostly PhD) is awarded after a two- or three-year period of research following the award of the Masters.

Post-secondary technical and vocational education comprises: short-term training courses of up to six months offered to all school-leavers by the Ministry of Vocational and Technical Training and the National Apprenticeship Board; and courses of two to four years leading to the award of, variously, the National Certificate, National Diploma and Higher National Diploma. The National Vocational Qualifications Framework of Sri Lanka was introduced in 2005 in a bid to unify Technical and Vocational Education and Training (TVET). The framework and skill standards are based on the New Zealand Qualifications Framework. The Tertiary and Vocational Education Commission is the national lead body for the implementation of TVET in Sri Lanka.

Regulatory and Representative Bodies

GOVERNMENT

Ministry of Cultural Affairs: 'Sethsiripaya', 8th Floor, Battaramulla, Colombo; tel. (11) 2872001; fax (11) 2872021; e-mail mcasec@sltnet.lk; Minister MAHINDA YAPA ABEYWARDENA.

Ministry of Education: 'Isurupaya', Pelawatte, Battaramulla, Colombo; tel. (11) 2785141; fax (11) 2785162; e-mail minedu@moe.gov.lk; internet www.moe.gov.lk; Minister SUSIL PREMAJAYANTHA.

Ministry of Higher Education: 18 Ward Place, Colombo 7; tel. (11) 2694486; fax (11) 2697239; e-mail mioh.hied@sltnet.lk; internet www.mohe.gov.lk; Minister Prof. WISWA WARNAPALA.

FUNDING

University Grants Commission: 20 Ward Pl., Colombo 7; tel. (11) 2695301; fax (11) 2688045; e-mail secretary@ugc.ac.lk; internet www.ugc.ac.lk; f. 1979; allocates funds to the univs and univ. institutes, serves as the central admissions agency for undergraduate studies; plans, coordinates and monitors the activities of the univ. system to maintain academic standards; 8 mems; Chair. Prof. S. V. D. G. SAMARANAYAKE; Sec. TISSA NANDASENA.

Learned Societies

GENERAL

Institute of Sinhala Culture: 375 Bauddhaloka Mawatha, Colombo 7; tel. (11) 4687979; f. 1954 for the preservation and development of Sinhala culture: art and architecture, drama, dance, music, folklore, arts and crafts, film, research, traditional embroidery, puppetry; presents cultural programmes; holds seminars and workshops; 680 mems; Pres. L. STANLEY JAYEWARDANE; Hon. Sec. Mrs R. G. SENANAYAKE.

National Academy of Sciences of Sri Lanka: 120/10 Wijerama Mawatha, Colombo 7; f. 1976; 104 mems; Pres. Prof. M. U. S. SULTANBAWA; Gen. Sec. Prof. ERIC H. KARUNANAYAKE; Sec. for Foreign Relations Dr U. PETHIYAGODA.

Royal Asiatic Society of Sri Lanka: Royal Asiatic Society Bldg, 96 Ananda Coomaraswamy Mawatha, Colombo 7; tel. and fax (11) 2699249; e-mail rassrilanka@gmail.com; internet www.royalasiaticsociety.lk; f. 1845; promotes inquiries into the history, religions, languages, literature, arts, sciences and social conditions of the present and fmr inhabitants of Sri Lanka, and connected cultures; library contains one of the largest collns of books on Sri Lanka, and others on Indian and Eastern culture in gen.; library of 1,100 vols, 350 titles; 950 mems; Pres. Dr SUSANTHA GOONATILAKE; Hon. Secs MALINI DIAS, PADMA EDIRISINGHE; Admin. Sec. B. E. WIJESURIYA; publ. *Journal of the Royal Asiatic Society of Sri Lanka* (1 a year).

BIBLIOGRAPHY, LIBRARY SCIENCE AND MUSEOLOGY

Sri Lanka Library Association: The Professional Centre, 275/75 Bauddhaloka Mawatha, Colombo 7; tel. (11) 4589103; f. 1960; 415 mems; Pres. H. U. YAPA; Gen. Sec. DEEPDI TALAGALA; publs *Sri Lanka Library Review* (1 a year), *SLLA Newsletter* (4 a year).

ECONOMICS, LAW AND POLITICS

Ceylon Institute of World Affairs: c/o Mervyn de Silva, 82B Ward Place, Colombo 7; f. 1957; Pres. Maj.-Gen. ANTON MUTTUKUMARU.

EDUCATION

National Education Society of Sri Lanka: Faculty of Education, University of Colombo, Colombo 3; 75 mems; publ. *Education.*

FINE AND PERFORMING ARTS

Arts Council of Sri Lanka: 8th Fl., Sethsiripaya, Battaramulla; tel. (11) 4872031; fax (11) 4872035; f. 1952 to promote art projects in Sri Lanka; the Council carries out projects in all fields of arts, incl. painting, drama, music, literature, ballet, dancing, folk song, folklore; Pres. K. JAYATILAKA; Sec. RAJENDRA BANDARA; publ. *Kala Magazine* (4 a year).

Ceylon Society of Arts: Art Gallery, Ananda Coomarassamy Mawatha, Colombo 7; tel. (11) 4693067; f. 1887; Pres. KALAPATHI-P. SUNIL; Hon. Gen. Sec. M. D. S. GUNATHILAKE.

HISTORY, GEOGRAPHY AND ARCHAEOLOGY

Archaeological Society of Sri Lanka: c/o Dept of Archaeology, Sir Marcus Fernando Mawatha, Colombo 7; f. 1966; Pres. Prof. CHANDRA WIKKRAMAGAMAGE; Co-Secs S. LAKDUSINGHE, W. H. WIJAYAPALA.

Ceylon Geographical Society: 61 Abdul Caffoor Mawatha, Colombo 3; f. 1938; 100 mems; Pres. Prof. K. KULARATNAM; Secs Dr W. P. T. SILVA, Dr K. U. SIRINANDA; publ. *The Ceylon Geographer* (1 a year).

LANGUAGE AND LITERATURE

Alliance Française: 11 Barnes Pl., Colombo 7; tel. (11) 2693467; fax (11) 2688735; e-mail info@alliancefr.lk; internet www.alliancefr.lk; f. 1955; offers courses and exams in French language and culture and promotes cultural exchange with France; attached teaching centres in Kandy and Matara; 600 mems; Dir JEAN-PHILIPPE ROY; publ. *Rendez-vous* (12 a year).

British Council: 49 Alfred House Gardens, POB 753, Colombo 3; tel. (11) 2581171; fax (11) 2587079; internet www.britishcouncil.lk; teaching centre; offers courses and exams in English language and British culture and promotes cultural exchange with the UK; responsible for British Council work in the Maldives; attached teaching centre in Kandy; Dir TONY O'BRIEN; Teaching Centre Man. RICHARD LUNT.

English Speaking Union of Sri Lanka: 14A, 16K Lane Galle Rd, Colombo 3; tel. (11) 4575843; f. 1981; library of 3,000 vols; includes an English Language School; Pres. Dr TERENCE AMERASINGHE; publ. *Open Mind* (4 a year).

Goethe-Institut: 39 Gregory's Rd, Colombo; tel. (11) 2694562; fax (11) 2693351; internet www.goethe.de/colombo; f. 1957; offers courses and examinations in German language and culture and promotes cultural exchange with Germany; library of 6,000 vols; Dir RICHARD LANG.

MEDICINE

Sri Lanka Medical Association: Wijerama House, 6 Wijerama Mawatha, Colombo 7; tel. (11) 2693324; fax (11) 2698802; e-mail slma@eureka.lk; f. 1887; 1,200 mems; Pres. Dr NARADA WARNASURIYA; Hon. Sec. Dr INDIKA KARUNATHILKE; publs *Abstracts of Anniversary Academic Sessions* (1 a year), *Ceylon Medical Journal* (4 a year), *Newsletter* (12 a year).

NATURAL SCIENCES

General

Sri Lanka Association for the Advancement of Science: 120/10 Vidya Mandiraya, Vidya Mawatha, Colombo 7; tel. and fax (11) 2691681; internet www.nsf.ac.lk/slaas; f. 1944 to provide for systematic direction of scientific enquiry in the interests of the country, to promote contact among scientific workers, and to disseminate scientific knowledge, etc.; holds annual session; seven sections; 6,000 mems; Gen. Pres. Dr T. SOMASERKARAM; Gen. Secs Prof. JAYANTHA WELIHINDA, Dr SUDARSHINI WASALATANTHRI; publs *Proceedings*, *Vidya Viyapthi*, *Vingnana Murusu*.

PHILOSOPHY AND PSYCHOLOGY

Ceylon Humanist Society: Rutnam Inst. Bldg, University Lane, Jaffna; Pres. J. T. RUTNAM; Sec. O. M. DE ALWIS.

RELIGION, SOCIOLOGY AND ANTHROPOLOGY

Buddhist Academy of Ceylon: 109 Rosmead Place, Colombo.

Maha Bodhi Society of Sri Lanka: 130 Rev. Hikkaduwe Sri Sumangala Nahimi Mawatha, Colombo 10; tel. and fax (11) 2677626; e-mail banagalaupatissa@gmail.com; f. 1891; propagates Buddhism throughout the world; 900 mems; Pres. BANAGALA UPATISSA NAYAKA THERO; Hon. Sec. VASANTHA DE SILVA; publ. *Sinhala Bauddhaya* (12 a year).

TECHNOLOGY

Institution of Engineers, Sri Lanka: 120/15 Wijerama Mawatha, Colombo 7; tel. (11) 4698426; fax (11) 4699202; e-mail iesl@slt.lk; internet www.iesl.slt.lk; f. 1906; 7,273 mems; library of 12,000 vols; Pres. Eng. Prof. L. RATNAYAKE; Exec. Sec. Eng. RUSSEL DE ZILVA; publs *Engineer* (3 a year), *Sri Lanka Engineering News* (12 a year), *Transactions* (1 a year).

Research Institutes

AGRICULTURE, FISHERIES AND VETERINARY SCIENCE

Coconut Research Institute: Bandirippuwa Estate, Lunuwila 61150; tel. (31) 2255300; fax (31) 2257391; e-mail director@cri.lk; internet www.cri.lk; f. 1929; quasi-governmental research institute serving coconut industry of Sri Lanka; library: see Libraries and Archives; Chair. Dr NIMAL WEERASINGHE; Dir Dr C. JAYASEKARE; publs *COCOS* (4 a year), *Coconut Bulletin* (4 a year), *Coco News* (3 a year).

Hector Kobbekaduwa Agrarian Research and Training Institute: POB 1522, 114 Wijerama Mawatha, Colombo 7; tel. (11) 4696981; fax (11) 4692423; e-mail harti@slt.lk; internet www.harti.slt.lk; f. 1972; research into and policy analysis on agrarian structures and the economic, social and institutional aspects of agricultural development; operates training programmes; library: see Libraries; Dir Dr S. G. SAMARASINGHE; publ. *Sri Lanka Journal of Agrarian Studies* (in English and Sinhala, 2 a year).

Horticultural Research and Development Institute: Gannoruwa, Peradeniya; tel. (81) 2288011; f. 1965; research on fruit, vegetables, roots and tubers and other horticultural crops, and soya processing; library of 16,500 vols; Dir Dr S. D. B. G. JAYAWARDANE; publ. *Tropical Agriculturist* (1 a year).

National Aquatic Resources Research and Development Agency: Crow Island, Colombo 15; tel. (11) 4522000; fax (11) 4522932; e-mail postmast@nara.ac.lk; internet www.nara.ac.lk; f. 1982; library of 350 vols; Dir-Gen. NILMINI DIYABEDANAGE; publ. *Journal* (1 a year).

Rice Research and Development Institute: Batalagoda, Ibbagamuwa; tel. (37) 2222681; fax (37) 2222681; e-mail rice@rrdi.ac.lk; f. 1994; Dir S. ABEYSIRIWARDENE.

Rubber Research Institute of Sri Lanka: Dartonfield, Agalawatta; tel. (34) 2247426; fax (34) 2247427; e-mail dirrri@slt.lk; f. 1909; Colombo office and laboratories: Telawala Rd, Ratmalana, Mt Lavinia; research and advisory services on rubber planting and manufacture; comprises ten research depts, biometry section, adaptive research unit, extension dept and economic research unit, specification unit and estate dept; about 500 staff; Dir Dr L. M. K. TILLEKERATNE; publs *Annual Review*, journals, bulletins and advisory circulars, audio-visuals.

Tea Research Institute of Sri Lanka: St Coombs, Talawakelle; tel. (52) 2222601; fax (52) 2258229; e-mail postmaster@tri.ac.lk; internet www.tri.gov.lk; f. 1925; library: see Libraries; Dir I. S. B. ABESINGHE; publs *Sri Lanka Journal of Tea Science* (2 a year), *Tea Bulletin* (2 a year), *TRI Update* (2 a year).

Veterinary Research Institute: POB 28, Gannoruwa, Peradeniya; tel. (81) 2288311; fax (81) 2288125; f. 1967; concerned with research and investigations into health and production problems of livestock and poultry; veterinary vaccine production; Head Dr RANJITH WICKRAMASINGHE; publ. *Sri Lanka Veterinary Journal* (4 a year).

ECONOMICS, LAW AND POLITICS

Economic Research Unit: Business Intelligence Dept, Bank of Ceylon, Colombo; Business Intelligence Officer S. E. A. JAYAWICKREMA.

Marga Institute Centre for Development Studies: 941/1 Jayanthi Mawatha, Kotte Rd, Ethul Kotte 10100; tel. (11) 2888790; fax (11) 2888794; e-mail library@margasrilanka.org; internet www.margasrilanka.org; f. 1972; non-profit multi-disciplinary research org. undertaking critical, non-partisan study of devt issues in Sri Lanka and the wider Asian region; library of 24,000 vols, 150 periodicals; Chair. Dr MANGALA MOONESINGHE; Chair. Emeritus Dr GODFREY GUNATILLEKE; Vice-Chair. MYRTLE PERERA; Head of Library and Information Service DEEPALI TALAGALA; publs *Marga Monograph Series on Ethnic Reconciliation*, *The Marga Quarterly Journal*.

Wiros Lokh Institute: 81-1A Isipatana Mawatha, Colombo 5; tel. and fax (11) 2580817; e-mail wiroshermes@yahoo.com; internet www.socialreit.org; f. 1981, operationally merged with Capital Markets for the Marginalized Inc. (USA) and Capital for the Marginalized Ltd (Singapore); private research and training foundation; promotes awareness of globalization in the region; spec. projects: innovation in social housing and financing, urban regeneration and sports recreation for urban areas; capital markets, spices, silks and other traditional crafts; library of 20,000 vols; 75 mems; Chair. Dr DARIN GUNESEKERA; Dir of Child Rights Div. CHANDRIKA GUNESEKERA; Exec. ABHEYAPALA DE SILVA.

HISTORY, GEOGRAPHY AND ARCHAEOLOGY

Archaeological Survey Department of Sri Lanka: Sir Marcus Fernando Rd, Colombo 7; tel. (11) 4694727; fax (11) 4696250; e-mail arch@diamond.lanka.net; f. 1890; library of 15,000 vols; Dir-Gen. S. U. DERANIYAGALA; publs *Administration Report* (1 a year), *Ancient Ceylon* (1 a year), *Memoirs*.

MEDICINE

Medical Research Institute: Baseline Rd, Colombo 8; tel. (11) 4677715; e-mail medrisit@slt.lk; f. 1900; comprising deps of bacteriology, biochemistry, chemistry of natural products, entomology, food and water bacteriology, leptospira, media, mycology, clinical pathology, parasitology, nutrition, pharmacology, salmonella, serology, vaccines, virology, animal centre, school of medical laboratory technology; Dir Dr G. S. S. K. COLOMBAGE.

NATURAL SCIENCES

Biological Sciences

Department of Wild Life Conservation: 18 Gregory's Rd, Colombo 7; tel. (11) 4698086; fax (11) 4698556; f. 1950; library of 1,962 vols; Dir N. W. DISSANAYAKE; publs *Sri Lanka Wild Life*, *Vana Divi* (1 a year), *National Parks of Sri Lanka*.

Physical Sciences

Department of Meteorology: 383 Bauddhaloka, Mawatha, Colombo 7; tel. (11) 2694104; fax (11) 2698311; e-mail meteo@slt.lk; internet www.meteo.gov.lk; f. 1948; climatological data for Sri Lanka; time service; astronomical service; weather forecasting; agrometeorological service; weather services to the gen. public, the agricultural, aviation, energy sectors, fisheries, shipping sectors; research in meteorology, climatology, climate change and allied subjects; library of 18,000 vols; Dir Dr G. B. SAMARASINGHE; publs *Agrometeorological Bulletin* (4 a year), *Monthly Weather Review* (12 a year), *Report of the Department of Meteorology* (1 a year).

TECHNOLOGY

Geological Survey and Mines Bureau: Senanayake Bldg, 4 Galle Rd, Dehiwala; tel. (11) 2725745; fax (11) 2735752; e-mail gsmb@slt.lk; internet www.gsmb.sit.lk; f. 1903; systematic geological mapping of Sri Lanka;

identification and assessment of its mineral resources; issues licences to regulate exploration, mining, processing, transport, trading in and export of minerals; Chair. Prof. P. G. R. DHARMARATNE (acting); Dir S. WEERAWARNAKULA; publs *Memoirs*, *Mineral Year Book*.

Industrial Technology Institute: 363 Bauddhaloka Mawatha, Colombo 7; tel. (11) 4693807; fax (11) 4686567; e-mail info@iti.lk; internet www.iti.lk; f. 1955 as Ceylon Institute of Scientific and Industrial Research; present name 1998; applied technical research in several industrial sectors for government agencies and the public; process research, resource studies, waste material utilization, product testing, standards, calibration and repair of instruments, technical consultation; industrial devt; information services centre: see Libraries and Archives; Chair Prof. VIJAYA KUMAR; publ. *Bulletin* (4 a year).

National Science Foundation: 47/5 Maitland Pl., Colombo 7; tel. (11) 2696771; fax (11) 2691691; e-mail info@nsf.ac.lk; internet www.nsf.ac.lk; f. 1968 as Nat. Science Ccl; initiates, facilitates and supports basic and applied scientific research by univs, scientific and technological institutions and scientists; fosters the interchange of scientific information among scientists in Sri Lanka and foreign countries; awards scholarships and fellowships for scientific study or work at appropriate institutions; provides a central clearing house for the colln and analysis of data on the scientific and technical resources in Sri Lanka; provides information for policy formulation on science and technology; promotes the popularization of science; documentation and publications unit; acts as National Research Reports Depository on science and technology; library of 7,123 vols; Dir Dr SARATH ABAYAWARDANA; publs *Journal of the National Science Foundation* (4 a year), *Sri Lanka Journal of Social Sciences* (2 a year).

Sri Lanka Water Resources Board: 2A Gregory's Ave, Colombo 7; established 1966; advises the Govt on all matters concerning the conservation and utilization of water resources; library of 4,620 vols, 60 periodicals; Chair. K. YOGANATHAN.

Libraries and Archives

Agalawatta

Rubber Research Institute of Sri Lanka Library: Dartonfield, Agalawatta; br. library: Telawala Rd, Ratmalana; tel. (34) 2247426; fax (34) 2247427; f. 1953; 10,000 vols, 255 periodical titles; Dir Dr R. C. W. M. R. A. NUGAWELA; publs *Annual Review*, *Bulletin* (1 a year), *Journal* (1 a year), *Rubber Puwath* (1 a year).

Colombo

Centre for Development Information: National Planning Dept, Min. of Finance and Planning, POB 1547, Galleface Secretariat, Colombo 1; tel. (11) 2484609; fax (11) 2448063; e-mail npdedi@yahoo.com; f. 1979; participates in regional information networks, and maintains an int. exchange programme; nat. focal point for SAARC Documentation Centre, New Delhi, India; coordinates and collates socio-economic information; 25,000 vols, unpublished report colln; Sr Librarian I. HENDAVITHARANA; publs *Bibliography of Economic and Social Development in Sri Lanka*, *Current Acquisitions* (4 a year), *Guide to current periodical literature in economic and social development* (4 a year), *Register of Development Research in Sri Lanka*.

Colombo National Museum Library: POB 854, Colombo 7; f. 1877 (incorporating collection of Government Oriental Library, f. 1870); depository for Sri Lanka publications since 1885; 618,221 items (including 141,703 monographs, 4,500 periodical titles, 3,772 palm leaf MSS in Sinhala and Sanskrit, Pali, Burmese and Cambodian); publs *Sri Lanka Periodicals Index*, *NML Acquisitions Bulletin*, *Sri Lanka Periodicals Directory*, *Bibliographical Series*.

Department of National Archives: POB 1414, 7 Reid Ave, Colombo 7; tel. (11) 4694523; f. 1902; contains official records of the Dutch Administration from 1640 to 1796, British Administration from 1796 to 1948; official records of Independent Sri Lanka since 1948; a few codices of Portuguese Administration prior to 1656 and some documents in French, Sinhalese and Tamil; operates a Presidential Archival Depository and a Reference Service; operates Hon. J. R. Jayewardene Research Centre; deals with documents in private possession; is the legal depository for all printed material in the country, effects the registration of printing presses, printed publications, and newspapers; holds copies of books printed since 1885 and newspapers since 1832; Dir Dr SAROPA WEPPASINGHE; publs *Administration Report of The National Archives*, *Catalogue of Newspapers* (1 a year), *Catalogue of Printing Presses* (1 a year), *Sri Lanka Archives* (1 a year), *Quarterly Statement of Books printed in Sri Lanka*.

Hector Kobbekaduwa Agrarian Research and Training Institute Library: POB 1522, 114 Wijerama Mawatha, Colombo 7; tel. (11) 4696981; fax (11) 4692423; e-mail harti@slt.lk; internet www.harti.slt.lk; f. 1972; 18,000 vols and 62 periodicals; several hundred reports and reprints; special collection on Sri Lanka; part of Nat. Centre for Information on Agrarian Development; Librarian G. H. KARUNARATNE.

Industrial Technology Institute Information Services Centre: 363 Bauddhaloka Mawatha, Colombo 7; tel. (11) 4698624; f. 1955; 35,000 vols, 300 journals; several thousand reports, reprints, standards; information service to scientists, industrialists and engineers; computer database of books and articles in periodicals; national centre of Asian and Pacific Information Network on Medicinal and Aromatic Plants; Man. Information Services Centre D. S. T. WARNASURIYA; publs *Bibliographical Series*, *State of the Art surveys on spices and essential oilbearing plants*, *News Digest*, *Food Digest*, *CISIR News Bulletin*, *S & T News*, *Management Thought*.

Law Library: Hultsdorp, Colombo 12; tel. (11) 4324676; f. 1855; Dir A. COOREY.

Municipal Council Public Library: 15 Sir Marcus Fernando Mawatha, Colombo 7; tel. (11) 4691968; f. 1925; 15 brs; five mobile libraries; 794,088 vols, 2,000 periodical titles; special collections: Sri Lanka, Buddhism, FAO Depository, fine arts, Braille, Japan, Theo Auer collection; Chief Librarian M. D. H. JAYAWARDHANA; publ. *Administration Report* (1 a year).

National Library and Documentation Centre: 14 Independence Ave, Colombo 7; tel. (11) 2687581; fax (11) 2685201; e-mail nldc@mail.natlib.lk; internet www.natlib.lk; f. 1990; 257,000 vols (incl. govt publs), 500 periodical titles, 6,000 microforms, 1,800 maps, audiovisual items, electronic media; special collections: Ola Leaf collection, drama MS collection, library and information science collection, Martin Wickramasinghe collection, folklore collection; ISBN, ISMN and ISSN national centres; compiles National Union Catalogue and Online Public Access Catalogue (OPAC); Dir M. S. UPALI AMARASIRI; publs *Directory of Government Publications*, *Devolution of Power and Ethnic Problems* (database), *Library News* (4 a year), *Index to Postgraduate Theses*, *ISBN Publishers Directory*, *Natnet Lanka Newsletter*, *Periodical Article Index* (4 a year), *Sri Lanka National Bibliography* (12 a year), *Sri Lanka Newspaper Index*.

University of Colombo Library: Colombo 3; tel. and fax (11) 4583043; e-mail scj@cmb.ac.lk; f. 1967; 240,000 vols; Librarian S. C. JAYASURIYA; publs *Ceylon Journal of Medical Science* (2 a year), *Colombo Law Review* (1 a year), *Sri Lanka Journal of International Law* (1 a year), *University of Colombo Review* (1 a year).

Lunuwila

Coconut Research Institute Library: Lunuwila; tel. (31) 2253795; fax (31) 2257391; e-mail library@cri.lk; internet www.cri.lk; f. 1929; houses the Int. Coconut Information Centre; special colln of world literature on the coconut available in hard copy; microfiches, diskettes; 35,000 vols; 75 mems; Librarian P. D. U. C. DHARMAPALA (acting); publs *Cocos*, *Coconut Bulletin*.

Moratuwa

Centre for Industrial Technology Information Services: I. D. B., 615 Galle Rd, Katubedda, 10400 Moratuwa; tel. (11) 2605372; fax (11) 2607002; e-mail idb@sltnet.lk; internet www.idb.lk; f. 1969; acquisition, processing and dissemination of technology information, reference and enquiry services, networking; 19,000 vols, 25 current periodicals; Deputy Dir T. C. PEIRIS; publs *Karmantha Bulletin* (4 a year), *New Arrivals* (12 a year).

Peradeniya

University of Peradeniya Library: POB 35, Peradeniya; tel. and fax (81) 2388678; e-mail librarian@pdn.ac.lk; internet www.pdn.ac.lk; f. 1921; 670,062 vols; collns incl. deposit materials obtained under printers' and publishers' ordinance since 1955, reference colln on Sri Lanka, palm-leaf manuscripts and rare materials on Sri Lanka, and collns on environmental and religious studies; Librarian P. E. HARRISON PERERA; publs *Ceylon Journal of Science—Biological Sciences*, *Ceylon Journal of Science—Physical Sciences*, *Sri Lanka Journal of the Humanities*, *Modern Sri Lanka Studies*.

Talawakele

Tea Research Institute Library: St Coombs, Talawakelle; tel. (52) 2258201; fax (52) 2258311; e-mail info@tri.lk; internet www.tri.lk; f. 1925; collects and disseminates information on tea and allied subjects; 25,000 vols and 250 periodicals for reference and loan, incl. spec. reference section dealing with tea and allied subjects; Librarian (vacant); publ. *Sri Lanka Journal of Tea Science* (2 a year).

Museums and Art Galleries

Anuradhapura

Anuradhapura Folk Museum: Anuradhapura; tel. (25) 2252589; f. 1971; regional museum for North Central Province.

Colombo

Colombo Dutch Period Museum: Pettah, Colombo; tel. (11) 4448466; f. 1982; period museum depicting life and times during Dutch rule 1656–1796.

National Museum (Cultural): Sir Marcus Fernando Mawatha, Colombo 7; tel. (11) 2697467; e-mail nmdep@slt.lk; f. 1877; national collection of art, antiquities and folk culture; research centre; Dir YASANTHA MAPATUNA.

National Museum (Natural History): Ananda Coomaraswamy Mawatha, Colombo 7; tel. (11) 2694767; f. 1985; national collection of natural sciences.

Galle

Galle National Museum: Church St, Galle; tel. (91) 2232051; f. 1986; regional museum for Galle District.

Kandy

Kandy National Museum: Dharmapala Mawatha, Kandy; tel. (81) 2223867; f. 1942; regional museum for the Central Province; 17th- to 18th-century Kandyan history.

Peradeniya

Royal Botanic Gardens: Peradeniya; tel. and fax (81) 2388238; e-mail dirnbg@sltnet.lk; f. 1821; 62 ha of gardens; botanical survey of Sri Lanka, floriculture research and development; education, training and extension; Supt Dr D. S. A. WIJESUNDARA.

Ratnapura

Ratnapura National Museum: Ehelapola Walauwa, Colombo Rd, Ratnapura; tel. (45) 2252451; f. 1942; regional museum for the Sabaragamuwa Province; prehistory of the region and exhibits on gem-mining.

Universities

UNIVERSITY OF COLOMBO

94 Cumaratunga Munidasa Mawatha, Colombo 3
Telephone: (11) 2581835
Fax: (11) 2583810
Internet: www.cmb.ac.lk

Founded 1921, present name 1979
State control
Languages of instruction: Sinhala, Tamil, English
Academic year: October to September

Chancellor: Rev. Bishop OSWALD GOMIS
Vice-Chancellor: Prof. T. HETHARACHCHY
Registrar: V. S. SIVALINGAM (acting)
Rector of Sripalee Campus: W. N. WILSON
Librarian: S. C. JAYASURIYA

Number of teachers: 448
Number of students: 9,158

Publications: *The Ceylon Journal of Medical Science* (2 a year), *University of Colombo Review* (1 a year), *University Calendar* (every 3 years)

DEANS

Faculty of Arts: Prof. S. M. P. SENANAYAKE
Faculty of Education: Prof. L. S. PERERA
Faculty of Law: N. SELVAKKUMARAN
Faculty of Management and Finance: M. G. S. P. RANDIWELA
Faculty of Medicine: Prof. S. P. LAMABADUSURIYA
Faculty of Science: Prof. R. L. C. WIJESUNDERA
Faculty of Graduate Studies: Prof. D. M. S. S. L. DISSANAYAKE

ATTACHED RESEARCH INSTITUTES

Institute of Biochemistry, Molecular Biology and Biotechnology: Dir Prof. U. P. E. H. KARUNANAYAKE.

Institute of Indigenous Medicine: Nawala, Rajagiriya; Dir Dr H. JAYAWARDENA.

Institute of Workers' Education: 275 Bauddhaloka Mawatha, Colombo 7; Dir Prof. H. P. R. GUNAWARDENA.

National Institute of Library and Information Science: Dir PRADEEPA WIJETUNGA.

Postgraduate Institute of Medicine: 160 Norris Canal Rd, Colombo 8; Dir Prof. LALITHA MENDIS.

University of Colombo School of Computing: UCSC Building Complex No. 35, Reid Ave, Colombo 7; Dir Dr A. R. WEERASINGHE.

EASTERN UNIVERSITY

Vantharumoolai, Chenkaladi
Telephone: (65) 2240490
Fax: (65) 2240585
E-mail: aradmin@esn.ac.lk
Internet: www.esn.ac.lk

Founded 1981 as Batticaloa Univ. College, present name 1986
State control
Languages of instruction: English, Tamil
Academic year: January to December

Chancellor: Dr T. VARAGUNAM
Vice-Chancellor: Prof. M. S. MOOKIAH
Registrar: A. D. HARRIS (acting)
Sr Asst Librarian: T. ARULNANDHY

Library of 60,000 vols
Number of teachers: 105
Number of students: 2,423 (1,514 internal, 909 external)

DEANS

Faculty of Agriculture: S. RAVEENDRANATH
Faculty of Arts and Culture: A. MURUGATHAS (acting)
Faculty of Commerce and Management: S. SENTHILNATHAN
Faculty of Science: Dr J. C. N. RAJENDRA

UNIVERSITY OF JAFFNA

Thirunelvely, Jaffna
Telephone: (21) 2222483
Fax: (21) 2222006
E-mail: ujvc@mail.ewisl.net

Founded 1974, present name 1978
State control
Languages of instruction: Tamil, English
Academic year: October to July

Chancellor: Prof. M. SIVASURIYA
Vice-Chancellor: Prof. N. SHANMUGALINGAM
Registrar: V. KANDEEPAN
Librarian: (vacant)

Library of 165,000 vols
Number of teachers: 242
Number of students: 5,946

Publications: *Cintanai* (4 a year), *Journal of Science* (2 a year), *Sri Lanka Journal of South Asian Studies* (1 a year), *Vingnanam*

DEANS

Faculty of Agriculture: S. SIVACHANDRAN
Faculty of Arts: Prof. S. KRISHNARAJAH
Faculty of Management Studies and Commerce: Prof. K. THEVARAJAH
Faculty of Medicine: Dr K. SIVAPALAN
Faculty of Science: Prof. R. KUMARAVADIVEL
Faculty of Graduate Studies: Prof. S. SATHIASEELAN

UNIVERSITY OF KELANIYA

Dalugama, Kelaniya
Telephone: (11) 24914474
Fax: (11) 24911485

Fmrly Vidayalankara Pirivena; Univ. status 1959; reorganized 1972 as a campus of Univ. of Sri Lanka; present name 1978
State control
Languages of instruction: English, Sinhala

Chancellor: Ven. Welamitiyawe Dharmakeerthi Sri KUSALADHAMMA THERO
Vice-Chancellor: Prof. SARATH AMUNUGAMA (acting)
Deputy Vice-Chancellor: (vacant)
Registrar: W. M. KARUNARATNE
Librarian: Dr L. A. JAYATISSA

Number of teachers: 480
Number of students: 8,423

Publications: *Journal of the Faculty of Humanities* (1 a year), *Journal of the Faculty of Social Science* (1 a year), *Kalyani* (1 a year)

DEANS

Faculty of Commerce And Management Studies: A. PATABENDIGE
Faculty of Humanities: Prof. K. KUMARASINGHE
Faculty of Medicine: Prof. A. PATABENDIGE
Faculty of Science: Prof. L. N. DE SILVA
Faculty of Social Science: Y. M. S. MADDUMA BANDARA

PROFESSORS

CHANDRASENA, L., Biochemistry and Clinical Chemistry
DANGALLE, N., Geography
DE SILVA, H., Medicine
EDIRISINGHE, D., Philosophy
JAYASEKARA, L., Botany
KARUNANANDA, U., History
KUMARASINGHE, K., Sinhala
PATHIRATNE, A., Zoology
SIRIPALA, W., Physics
SUMANAPALA, G., Pali and Buddhist Studies
TILLEKERATNE, K., Mathematics
WIDANAPATHIRANA, S., Microbiology
WIJEYARATNE, M., Zoology

UNIVERSITY OF MORATUWA

Katubedda, Moratuwa
Telephone: (11) 2650441
Fax: (11) 2650622
E-mail: info@mrt.ac.lk
Internet: www.mrt.ac.lk

Founded 1966 as Ceylon College of Technology, present name 1978
State control
Language of instruction: English
Academic year: October to September

Chancellor: Dr ROLAND SILVA
Vice-Chancellor: Prof. K. A. M. K. RANASINGHE
Registrar: A. L. JOUFER SADIQUE
Librarian: R. C. KODIKARA

Number of teachers: 280
Number of students: 4,700

Publications: *Ambalama*, *Development Planning Review* (4 a year), *Tampitavihara*

DEANS

Faculty of Architecture: Prof. P. K. S. MAHANAMA
Faculty of Engineering: Prof. U. G. A. PUSWEWALA
Faculty of Information Technology: Prof. A. S. KARUNANANDA (acting)
Institute of Technology: Dr T. A. G. GUNASEKERA (Dir)

OPEN UNIVERSITY OF SRI LANKA

POB 21, Nawala, Nugegoda
Telephone: (11) 2822712

Founded 1980
State control
Languages of instruction: Sinhala, Tamil, English

Chancellor: Dr GAMINI COREA
Vice-Chancellor: Prof. U. COOMARASWAMY
Registrar: S. J. JAYASOORIYA
Librarian: S. R. KORALE

Number of teachers: 306
Number of students: 19,287
Publication: *Open University Review of Engineering Technology*

DEANS

Faculty of Engineering Technology: Dr H. D. GOONETILLEKE
Faculty of Humanities and Social Sciences: Prof. G. I. C. GUNAWARDENA
Faculty of Natural Sciences: Prof. E. M. JAYASINGHE

UNIVERSITY OF PERADENIYA

University Park, Peradeniya
Telephone: (81) 2388151
Fax: (81) 2389164
E-mail: vc@pdn.ac.lk
Internet: www.pdn.ac.lk

Founded 1942 by the incorporation of the Ceylon Medical College (f. 1870) and the Ceylon Univ. College (f. 1921); reorganized 1972, present name 1978
State control
Languages of instruction: Sinhala, Tamil, English
Academic year: October to September

Chancellor: Deshamanya. R. K. W. GOONESEKERA
Vice-Chancellor: Prof. K. G. A. GOONESEKERE
Registrar: M. S. M. MUSTHAFA (acting)
Librarian: P. E. HARRISON PERERA

Number of teachers: 745
Number of students: 9,500

Publications: *Modern Sri Lanka Studies*, *Sri Lanka Journal of Biological Science*, *Sri Lanka Journal of Humanities*, *Sri Lanka Journal of Physical Science*

DEANS

Faculty of Agriculture: Prof. P. W. M. B. B. MARAMBE
Faculty of Arts: Prof. Y. R. AMARASINGHE
Faculty of Dental Sciences: Prof. R. L. WIJEYEWEERA
Faculty of Engineering: Dr S. D. PATHIRANA
Faculty of Medicine: Dr A. S. B. WIJEKOON
Faculty of Science: Prof. V. KUMAR
Faculty of Veterinary Medicine and Animal Science: Dr H. ABEYGUNAWARDENA

PROFESSORS

Faculty of Agriculture (tel. (81) 2388041; fax (81) 2388041; e-mail nimalgun@mail.pdn.ac.lk; internet www.pdn.ac.lk/agri/home/homepage/agricindex.html):

BANDARA, J. M. R. S., Agricultural Biology
BOGAHAWATTA, C., Agricultural Economics
CYRIL, H. W., Animal Science
DE COSTA, W. A. J. M., Crop Science
GOONASEKERE, K. G. A., Agricultural Engineering
GUNATHILAKA, H. M., Agricultural Economics
GUNAWARDENA, E. R. N., Agricultural Engineering
IBRAHIM, M. N. M., Animal Science
ILLEPERUMA, D. C. K., Food Science and Technology
JAYAKODY, A. N., Agricultural Soil Science
KUMARAGAMAGE, D., Agricultural Soil Science
MAPA, R. B., Soil Science
PEIRIS, B. C. N., Agricultural Crop Science
PERERA, A. L. T., Agricultural Biology
PERERA, A. N. F., Animal Science
PERERA, E. R. K., Animal Science
SAMARAJEEWA, U., Food Science and Technology
SANGAKKARA, U. R., Agricultural Crop Science
SIVAYOGANATHAN, C., Agricultural Extension
THATTIL, R. O., Crop Science

Faculty of Arts (tel. (81) 2388345; fax (81) 2388933; e-mail dean@arts.pdn.ac.lk; internet www.pdn.ac.lk/arts):

AMARASINGHE, Y. R., Political Science
DE SILVA, M. W. A., Sociology
GUNATHILAKE, W. M., Sinhala
HENNAYAKE, H. M. S. K., Geography
KARUNATILAKE, P. V. B., History
LIYANAGE, K., Political Science
MADDEGAMA, U. P., Sinhala
MADDUMA BANDARA, C. M., Geography
NUHUMAN, M. A. M., Tamil
PATHMANATHAN, S., History
PERERA, S. W., English
PREMASIRI, P. D., Pali and Buddhist Studies
SAMARANAYAKE, S. V. D. G., Political Science
SENADHEERA, S., Education
SENEVIRATNE, S. D. S., Archaeology
SILVA, K. T., Sociology
SIRISENA, W. M., Sociology
SIRIWEERA, W. S., History
SIVARAJAH, A., Political Science
WEERAKKODY, D. P. M., Classical Languages
WICKRAMASINGHE, A., Geography

Faculty of Dental Sciences (tel. (81) 2388948; fax (81) 2388948; e-mail deandental@pdn.ac.lk; internet www.pdn.ac.lk/dental):

AMARATUNGE, N. A. DE S., Oral Surgery
EKANAYAKE, A. N. I., Community Dentistry
EKANAYAKE, S. L., Community Dentistry
MENDIS, B. R. R. N., Oral Pathology
NANAYAKKARA, C. D., Basic Science
WIJEYEWEERA, R. L., Community Dentistry

Faculty of Engineering (tel. (81) 2388322; fax (81) 2388158; e-mail deaneng@pdn.ac.lk; internet www.pdn.ac.lk/eng):

AMIRTHANATHAM, G. E., Chemical Engineering
EKANAYAKE, E. M. N., Electrical and Electronic Engineering
HOOLE, S. R. H., Electrical and Electronic Engineering
RANAWEERA, M. P., Civil Engineering
SAMUEL, T. D. M. A., Engineering Mathematics
SENEVIRATNE, K. G. H. C. N., Civil Engineering
SIVASEGARAM, S., Mechanical Engineering

Faculty of Medicine (tel. (81) 2388315; fax (81) 2389106; e-mail dean@med.pdn.ac.lk; internet www.pdn.ac.lk/med):

AMARASINGHE, W. I., Obstetrics and Gynaecology
CHANDRASEKERA, M. S., Anatomy
EDIRISINGHE, J. S., Parasitology
NUGEGODA, D. B., Community Medicine
PERERA, P. A. J., Biochemistry
RATNATUNGE, N. V. I., Pathology
RATNARUNGE, P. C. A., Surgery
SENANAYAKE, N., Medicine
THEVANESAN, V., Microbiology
UDUPIHILLE, M., Physiology
WELGAMA, D. J., Parasitology
WIJESUNDARA, M. K. DE S., Parasitology

Faculty of Science (tel. (81) 2389126; fax (81) 2388018; e-mail dean@sci.pdn.ac.lk; internet www.pdn.ac.lk/sci):

ADIKARAM, N. K. B., Botany
BANDARA, B. M. R., Chemistry
BANDARA, H. M. N., Chemistry
CAREEM, M. A., Physics
DAHANAYAKE, K. G. A., Geology
DE SILVA, K. H. G. M., Zoology
DE SILVA, P. K., Chemistry
DISSANAYAKE, C. B., Geology
DISSANAYAKE, M. A. K. L., Physics
EDIRISINGHE, J. P., Zoology
GUNATILLAKE, C. V. S., Botany
GUNATILLAKE, I. A. U. N., Botany
GUNAWARDANA, R. P., Chemistry
ILLEPERUMA, O. A., Chemistry
KARUNARATHNA, N. L. V. V., Chemistry
KARUNARATNE, B. S. B., Physics
KARUNARATNE, S. H. P. P., Zoology
KULASOORIYA, S. A., Botany
KUMAR, N. S., Chemistry
KUMAR, V., Chemistry
NAMAL PRIYANTHA, Chemistry
RAJAPAKSHE, R. M. G., Chemistry
SENEVIRATNE, H. H. G., Mathematics
TENNAKOON, D. T. B., Chemistry

Faculty of Veterinary Medicine and Animal Science (tel. (81) 2388205; fax (81) 2388205; e-mail dean@vet.pdn.ac.lk; internet www.pdn.ac.lk/vet):

ABEYGUNAWARDENA, H., Farm Animal Production and Health
ABEYNAYAKE, P., Veterinary Pathological Biology
GUNAWARDENA, V. K., Veterinary Basic Science
KURUWITA, V. Y., Veterinary Clinical Science
SILVA, I. D., Veterinary Clinical Science

Postgraduate Institute of Agriculture (tel. (81) 2389205; fax (81) 2388318; e-mail congress@pgia.pdn.ac.lk; internet www.pgia.ac.lk):

THATTIL, R. O. (Dir)

Postgraduate Institute of Science (tel. (81) 2387218; fax (81) 2389029; e-mail director@pgis.lk; internet www.pgis.lk):

DISSANAYAKE, M. (Dir)

RAJARATA UNIVERSITY OF SRI LANKA

Mihintale, Anuradhapura
Telephone: (25) 2266650
Fax: (25) 2266511
E-mail: rajalib@sltnet.lk

Founded 1996
State control
Languages of instruction: Sinhala, English

Chancellor: Dr J. B. KELEGAMA
Vice-Chancellor: Prof. W. I. SIRIWEERA
Registrar: A. G. KARUNARATNE
Librarian: K. J. SIRISENA

Library of 43,000 vols
Number of teachers: 60
Number of students: 418

DEANS

Faculty of Applied Sciences: Dr J. L. RATNASEKARA
Faculty of Management Studies: T. B. ANDARAWEWA
Faculty of Social Sciences and Humanities: Prof. K. WIJERATNE

UNIVERSITY OF RUHUNA

Matara
Telephone: (41) 2222681
Fax: (41) 2222683
E-mail: vc@ruh.ac.lk
Internet: www.ruh.ac.lk

Founded 1978 as Ruhuna Univ. College, present name 1984
State control
Languages of instruction: Sinhala, English
Academic year: October to September

Chancellor: Ven. Dr Sri ATHTHUDAWE RAHULA THERO
Vice-Chancellor: Prof. R. SENARATNE
Registrar: K. D. DUMINDUSENA
Librarian: K. J. SIRISENA

Library of 140,000 vols
Number of teachers: 550
Number of students: 5,500

DEANS

Faculty of Agriculture: Prof. K. D. N. WEERASINGHE
Faculty of Engineering: Prof. C. L. V. JAYATHILLAKE
Faculty of Humanities and Social Sciences: S. WAWWAGE
Faculty of Medicine: Prof. A. L. S. MENDIS
Faculty of Science: Prof. R. N. PATHIRANA

SABARAGAMUWA UNIVERSITY OF SRI LANKA

POB 02, Belihuloya, Ratnapura
Telephone and fax (45) 2280045
E-mail: library@sab.ac.lk
Internet: www.sab.ac.lk

Founded 1996
Semi-government control
Language of instruction: English

Chancellor: Dr C. R. PANABOKKE
Vice-Chancellor: Prof. MAHINDA S. RUPASINGHE
Registrar: T. K. W. T. THALAGUNE
Librarian: T. N. NEIGHSOOREI

Library of 116,070 vols, 262 periodical titles

DEANS

Faculty of Agricultural Sciences: Dr A. A. Y. AMARASINGHE
Faculty of Applied Sciences: Prof. K. B. PALIPANA
Faculty of Geomatics: K. R. M. U. BANDARA
Faculty of Management Studies: D. A. I. DAYARATHNE
Faculty of Social Sciences and Languages: Prof. H. M. S. PRIYANATH

SOUTH EASTERN UNIVERSITY OF SRI LANKA

University Park, Oluvil 32360
Telephone and fax (67) 2255168
E-mail: seusl@seu.ac.lk
Internet: www.seu.ac.lk

Founded 1995 at Addalaichenai as South Eastern Univ. College; present name, status and location 1996
State control
Languages of instruction: English, Tamil

Vice-Chancellor: Dr A. G. HUSSAIN ISMAIL
Registrar: M. F. HIBATHUL CAREEM (acting)
Bursar: A. GULAM RASHEED
Librarian: M. M. RIFAUDEEN (acting)

Library of 45,000 books, 20 periodicals
Number of teachers: 118
Number of students: 1,270

Publication: *Journal of Management* (1 a year)

DEANS

Faculty of Applied Sciences: A. N. AHMED (acting)
Faculty of Arts and Culture: M. I. M. KALEEL
Faculty of Islamic Studies and Arabic Language: M. S. M. JALALDEEN
Faculty of Management and Commerce: HANSIYA RAUFF

UNIVERSITY OF SRI JAYEWARDENEPURA

Gangodawila, Nugegoda
Telephone: (11) 2802695
Fax: (11) 2801604
E-mail: unisjay@sjp.ac.lk
Internet: www.sjp.ac.lk

Founded 1959 as Vidyodaya University of Ceylon; reorganized 1972 as campus of University of Sri Lanka; present name and status 1978
Languages of instruction: Sinhala, English

Chancellor: Rev. Dr MEDAGODA SUMANATISSA THERO
Vice-Chancellor: Prof. NARADA WARNASURIYA
Registrar: D. P. ATHULATHMUDALI
Librarian: P. VIDANAPATHIRANA

Number of teachers: 410
Number of students: 8,400

Publications: *Vidyodaya Journal of Sciences*, *Vidyodaya Journal of Social Sciences*

DEANS

Faculty of Applied Sciences: Prof. W. S. FERNANDO
Faculty of Arts: Prof. CHANDIMA WIJEBANDARA
Faculty of Management Studies and Commerce: W. H. E. SILVA
Faculty of Medical Sciences: Prof. D. P. A. FERNANDO
Faculty of Graduate Studies: Prof. D. A. THANTHIRIGODA

PROFESSORS

ABEYSEKARA, A. M., Chemistry
ARIYARATNE, S., Sinhala
BAMUNUARACHCHI, A., Chemistry
DAYANANDA, R. A., Statistics
DE SILVA, W. M. M., Surgery
DERANIYAGALA, S. P., Chemistry
ENDAGAMA, M., History and Archaeology
FERNANDO, D. J. S., Medicine
FERNANDO, D. P. A., Surgery
FERNANDO, G. H., Pharmacology
FERNANDO, S., Microbiology
FERNANDO, W. S., Chemistry
HETTIARATCHI, S. B., History and Archaeology
JANSZ, E. R., Biochemistry
JAYATISSA, W. A., Social Statistics
JAYAWARDENA, M. A. J., Obstetrics and Gynaecology
JIFFRY, M. T. M., Physiology
JINADASA, J., Zoology
KARIYAWASAM, T., Sinhala
KARUNANAYAKE, M. M., Geography
NANDADASA, H. G., Botany
PERERA, B. A. T., Sociology and Anthropology
PERERA, G. A., Pali and Buddhist Studies
PIYASIRI, S., Zoology
RANASINGHE, D. M. S. H. K., Forestry and Environmental Science
TANTRIGODA, D. A., Physics
WARNASOORIYA, N. D., Paediatrics
WEERAKOON, S., Mathematics
WEERASEKARA, D. S., Obstetrics and Gynaecology
WICKRAMASINGHE, S. M. D. N., Biochemistry
WIJAYARATNE, M. W. W., Sinhula
WIJEBANDARA, W. D. C., Pali and Buddhist Studies
WIJEWARDENA, K. A. K. K., Community Medicine and Family Medicine
WITHANA, R. J., Pathology
YAPA, P. A. J., Botany

WAYAMBA UNIVERSITY OF SRI LANKA

Kuliyapitiya
Telephone: (37) 81392
Fax: (37) 81392
E-mail: appliedadd@slt.lk

Founded 1999

Chancellor: W. D. AMARADEVA
Vice-Chancellor: Prof. V. Y. KURUWITA
Registrar: R. M. B. MUTHUBANDA (acting)
Librarian: K. J. SIRISENA

Number of students: 1,309

DEANS

Faculty of Agriculture and Plantation Management: S. J. JAYASEKERA
Faculty of Applied Sciences: Dr E. M. P. EKANAVAKE
Faculty of Business Studies and Finance: E. S. WICKRAMASINGHE
Faculty of Livestock, Fisheries and Nutrition: Prof. T. S. G. FONSEKA

Colleges

Aquinas College of Higher Studies: Colombo 8; tel. (11) 2694014; fax (11) 2678463; e-mail aqrector@pan.lanka.net; internet www.webstation.lk/aquinas; f. 1954; courses for the external examinations of Universities in Sri Lanka and abroad, for the Aquinas Diplomas and Certificates, and for examinations conducted by professional institutions in Sri Lanka and abroad; faculties of arts and science; institute of technology; schools of agriculture, English, computer studies, psychology and counselling; experimental farm at Ragama; library: 43,000 vols; 150 teachers; 7,500 students; Rector Rev. Fr W. D. G. CHRISPIN LEO; Vice-Rector Rev. Fr NAMAL FERNANDO; Registrar M. L. FERNANDO; publ. *Aquinas Journal* (1 a year).

Ceylon College of Physicians: 6 Wijerama Mawatha, Colombo 7; tel. (11) 671842; fax (11) 695418; e-mail ccp@eureka.lk; f. 1967; 360 mems; Pres. Prof. SAMAN GUNATILAKE; Joint Secs Dr UDAYA RANAWAKA, Dr NAOMALI AMAVASENA; publ. *Ceylon College of Physicians Journal* (1 a year).

In-Service Training Institute: Gannoruwa, POB 21, Peradeniya; tel. (81) 2288146; f. 1965; agricultural education and training; 22 staff; Dir HENRY GAMAGE.

Institute of Aesthetic Studies: 21 Albert Crescent, Colombo 7; tel. and fax (11) 2686071; f. 1974; attached to Univ. of Kelaniya; dancing, music, art and sculpture; 78 teachers; 8,057 students; library: 23,000 vols; Dir H. M. K. HERATH.

Jaffna College: Vaddukoddai; tel. (70) 2212531; f. 1823, renamed 1872; provides primary, secondary, tertiary and technical education; library: 60,000 vols; 55 teachers; 1,172 students; Prin. Rev. ANTHONY A. PAUL; publ. *Jaffna College Miscellany*.

Attached Institutes:

Christian Institute for the Study of Religion and Society: c/o Christian Theological Seminary, Maruthanarmadam, Chunnakam; Dir C. V. SELLIAH.

Evelyn Rutnam Institute for Inter-Cultural Studies: University Lane, Thirunelvely, Jaffna; Dir Rev. ANTHONY A. PAUL.

Institute of Agriculture: Maruthanamadam; 5 teachers; 40 students; Prin. T. KUGATHASAN.

Institute of Technology: Vaddukoddai; 11 teachers; 150 students; Dir H. R. G. HOOLE (acting).

School of Agriculture: Kundasale; tel. (81) 2420485; f. 1916; library: 5,500 vols; 20 teachers; 253 students; Prin. P. K. K. R. PERERA; publ. *Progress Report* (1 a year).

Sri Lanka Law College: 244 Hulftsdorp St, Colombo 12; tel. (11) 4323759; fax (11) 4436040; f. 1900; run by Ccl of Legal Education; prepares students for admission to the Bar, and conducts the examinations; 1,500 students; library: 11,462 vols; Prin. Dr H. J. F. SILVA.

Sri Lanka Technical College: Colombo 10; f. 1893; courses in trades and commerce; 4,525 students; Prin. B. P. H. S. MENDIS; Registrar H. V. S. BREMADASA; Librarian A. A. WIJERATNE.

SUDAN

The Higher Education System

Higher education institutions pre-date the independence of Sudan (formerly The Sudan) from the United Kingdom in 1956, with the oldest being Omdurman Islamic University, which was founded in 1912. Gordon Memorial College (founded 1902) has offered degrees since 1945, under the supervision of University of London (United Kingdom), and from 1956 became known as University of Khartoum. In 2000 there were an estimated 200,538 students enrolled in universities (of which 26 were public) and other institutions of higher education.

There is a Ministry of Education, and higher education is governed by the Higher Education Act (1990) and the Higher Education Regulatory Act (2005). The National Council of Higher Education, which consists of the Minister of Education, university vice-chancellors and prominent academic figures, is responsible for implementing government policies on higher education; this body is also responsible for quality assurance. In 2007 the Arab Network for Quality Assurance in Higher Education was established as a non-profit non-governmental organization, working with the International Network of Quality Assurance Agencies in Higher Education and the Association of Arab Universities. Its member organizations include the Evaluation and Accreditation Commission, part of the Sudanese Ministry of Higher Education. The President of Sudan is the Chancellor of every university and is also responsible for appointing most of the other senior officers. Each university is operated by a University Council.

Results in the Sudan School Certificate are the main criterion for admission to higher education: students are required to achieve a pass-mark of 50% or higher in seven subjects to be admitted to university, and 50% or higher in five subjects to be admitted to non-university courses. Non-university courses consist principally of Intermediate or General Diplomas and are offered by several public and private institutions. Courses last for three years. The Bachelors is the undergraduate qualification, and may be awarded as either a 'General' (four years) or an 'Honours' (five years) degree. Professional areas of study, such as medicine, dentistry and engineering, may last longer (up to six years). Graduates with either of the Bachelors degrees may be admitted to programmes of study leading to the award of the Postgraduate Diploma, a one-year course, but only graduates with the Bachelors (Honours) degree may be admitted to the postgraduate Masters degree, a two- to three-year programme of study. The highest university-level degree is the Doctor of Philosophy, a three-year research degree.

Technical and vocational education is principally offered at secondary level, but the Sudan University of Science and Technology and the Sudan Open University (founded 2002) provide correspondence courses and continuing education.

Regulatory Bodies

GOVERNMENT

Ministry of Culture, Youth and Sport: Khartoum; Minister MUHAMMAD YUSSUF ABDALLAH.

Ministry of Education: Khartoum; tel. (183) 772808; e-mail moe-sd@moe-sd.com; internet www.moe-sd.com; Minister HAMID MUHAMAD IBRAHIM.

ACCREDITATION

Evaluation and Accreditation Commission: Ministry of Education, Khartoum; tel. (91) 23126; fax (83) 765986; e-mail evacsud@yahoo.com; f. 2003; Pres. MUHAMMAD SALIM.

Learned Societies

LANGUAGE AND LITERATURE

Alliance Française: POB 465, El Obeid; tel. (183) 23617; e-mail haidaro2000@yahoo.fr; offers courses and exams in French language and culture and promotes cultural exchange with France; attached teaching centre in Wad Medani.

British Council: 14 Abu Sin St, POB 1253, Central Khartoum; tel. (183) 780817; fax (183) 774935; e-mail info@sd.britishcouncil.org; internet www.britishcouncil.org/sudan; offers courses and exams in English language and British culture and promotes cultural exchange with the UK; library of 10,000 vols, 90 periodicals; Dir DAVID CODLING.

Research Institutes

GENERAL

National Centre for Research: POB 2404, Khartoum; tel. (183) 779040; fax (183) 770701; e-mail profsalih@hotmail.com; f. 1991; conducts pure and applied scientific research for the realization of Sudan's economic and social development; incorporates research institutes in renewable energy, environment and natural resources, technology, tropical medicine, medicinal and aromatic plants, economic and social studies, remote sensing, biotechnology and biological engineering; Dir Prof. ABDEL KARIM MOHAMED SALIH.

AGRICULTURE, FISHERIES AND VETERINARY SCIENCE

Agricultural Research Corporation: POB 126, Wad Medani; tel. (511) 842226; fax (511) 843213; e-mail arcdg@sudanmail.net; internet www.arcsudan.sd; f. 1904; part of Ministry of Science and Technology; research centres: Food Research Centre, Land and Water Research Centre, Crop Protection Research Centre, Forestry Research Centre, Date Palm Research Centre; 16 research stations; library: see Libraries; Dir-Gen. Prof. AZHARI ABDELAZIM HAMADA; publ. *Sudan Journal of Agricultural Research* (2 a year).

Animal Production Corporation, Research Division: POB 624, Khartoum; Dir of Research Dr MUHAMMAD EL TAHIR ABDEL RAZIG; Senior Veterinary Research Officer Dr AMIN MAHMOUD EISA.

Forestry Research Centre: POB 7089, Khartoum; f. 1962; Dir Prof. HASSAN A. MUSNAD.

ECONOMICS, LAW AND POLITICS

Sudan Academy for Administrative Sciences: POB 2003, Khartoum; f. 1980; provides post-service training for government officials; conducts studies on current administrative problems; Dir-Gen. Dr OSMAN ELZUBERI AHMED; publ. *Journal of Administration and Development*.

MEDICINE

Sudan Medical Research Laboratories: POB 287, Khartoum; f. 1935; Dir MAHMOUD ABDEL RAHMAN ZIADA.

NATURAL SCIENCES

Physical Sciences

Geological Research Authority: POB 410, Khartoum; tel. (183) 777939; fax (183) 776681; e-mail gras@sudanmail.net; internet www.gras-sd.com; f. 1905; attached to Min. of Energy and Mining; applied research and surveys; library: see Libraries and Archives; Dir-Gen. Dr ABDELRAZIG O. M. AHMED.

TECHNOLOGY

Industrial Research and Consultancy Centre: POB 268, Khartoum; tel. (183) 613225; f. 1965 by the Government with assistance from the UN Development Programme; performs tests, investigations, analysis, research and surveys; offers advice and consultation services to industry; General Dir Dr IBRAHIM HASSAN M. EL AMIN.

Libraries and Archives

Juba

University of Juba Library: POB 82, Juba; f. 1977; 38,700 vols, 664 periodicals;

acts as a depository library for UN, UNESCO, WHO, FAO and World Bank; Librarian OKENY A. ADALA (acting).

Khartoum

Antiquities Service Library: POB 178, Khartoum; tel. (183) 780935; fax (183) 786784; f. 1946; 7,200 vols excluding periodicals; Librarian AWATIF AMIN BEDAWI.

Educational Documentation Centre: POB 2490, Khartoum; tel. (183) 71898; f. 1967; 7 mems; 20,000 vols; Dir IBRAHIM M. S. SHATIR; publs *Al-Tawitheq El Tarbawi* (Educational Documentation, 2 a year), annual reports and educational researches.

Flinders Petrie Library: Sudan Antiquities Service, POB 178, Khartoum; tel. (183) 780935; fax (183) 786784; f. 1946; 6,000 vols.

Geological Research Authority of the Sudan Library: POB 410, Khartoum; tel. (183) 770934; f. 1904; 2,200 vols, 63 periodicals; special collection: geology of the Sudan; Chief Librarian SALAH ABDEL GADIR MOHMED; publ. *Bulletin*.

Library of the Sudan University of Science and Technology: POB 407, Khartoum; tel. (183) 778922; fax (183) 774559; f. 1950; 14 libraries on 9 sites; 55,000 vols; Chief Librarian GAWAHIR SIDAHMED EL HASSAN.

National Chemical Laboratories Library: National Chemical Laboratories, Ministry of Health, POB 287, Khartoum; f. 1904; 2,500 vols, 1,600 pamphlets.

National Records Office: POB 1914, Khartoum; f. 1953; 20,000,000 documents covering Sudanese history since 1870; 12,820 vols; Sec.-Gen. Dr M. I. ABU SALEEM; publ. *Majallatal Wathaiq* (Archives Magazine).

Sudan Medical Research Laboratories Library: POB 287, Khartoum; f. 1904 (as part of Wellcome Tropical Research Laboratories); 7,000 pamphlets, 6,000 vols.

University of Khartoum Library: POB 321, Khartoum; f. 1945; 333,000 vols, 4,200 periodicals; includes a special Sudan and African collection; acts as a depository library for UN, FAO, ILO, WHO and UNESCO publications; both are under the general charge of the University Librarian Dr EL-HIBIR YOUSIF.

Omdurman

Omdurman Central Public Library: Omdurman; f. 1951; 17,650 vols.

Wad Medani

Agricultural Research Corporation, Central Library: POB 126, Wad Medani; tel. (511) 842226; fax (511) 843213; e-mail arc .library@arcsudan.sd; internet www .arcsudan.sd; f. 1930; 15,000 vols, 20,000 pamphlets, 250 periodicals, set of *The Essential Electronic Agricultural Library* (TEEAL) on CD-ROM and LAN version (LanTEEAL); Head Librarian AHLAM ISMAIL MUSA; publs *Sudan Journal of Agricultural Research (SJAR)* (online), *Annual Reports of the ARC research programs, Proceedings of the ARC research programs*.

Gezira Research Station Library: Wad Medani; 6,500 vols on agricultural topics.

Museums and Art Galleries

Khartoum

Sudan National Museum: POB 178, Khartoum; tel. (183) 70680; f. 1971; depts of antiquities, ethnology and Sudanese modern history; Dir HASSAN HUSSEIN IDRIS; Curator SIDDIG M. GASM AL-SID; publ. *Report on the Antiquities Service and Museums, Kush* (1 a year).

Attached Museums:

Ethnographical Museum: POB 178, Khartoum; tel. (183) 77052; f. 1956; collection and preservation of ethnographical objects; Curator MOHAMMED HAMED.

Khalifa's House: Omdurman.

Merowe Museum: Merowe, Northern Province; antiquities and general.

Sheikan Museum: El Obeid; archaeological and ethnographic museum.

Sultan Ali Dinar Museum: El Fasher.

Sudan Natural History Museum: University of Khartoum, POB 321, Khartoum; tel. (183) 81873; f. 1920; library of 801 vols; Dir Dr DAWI MUSA HAMED.

Universities

AL-FASHIR UNIVERSITY

POB 125, Al-Fashir, North Darfur
Telephone: (527) 43394
Fax: (527) 52111
Founded 1975
Vice-Chancellor: ABD ELBAGI MOHAMMED KABIR

Faculties of Education, Environmental Studies and Natural Resources and Medicine and Health Sciences; Centres of Scientific Research and Documentation and Societal Development and Extramural Studies.

AL-NEELAIN UNIVERSITY

POB 12702, Khartoum 12702
Founded 1955 as Khartoum br. of Cairo Univ.; ind. status and present name 1993
State control
Language of instruction: Arabic
Vice-Chancellor: AWAD HAJ ALI AHMED
Number of teachers: 270
Number of students: 36,000

Faculties of agriculture, animal production and fisheries, arts, commerce and socio-economic studies, engineering, graduate studies, law, medicine, optometry and visual sciences, science and technology and statistics, population studies and information technology; Nile Basin Studies Research Centre.

AL-ZAIEM AL-AZHARI UNIVERSITY

POB 1933, Omdurman
Telephone: (15) 560501
Fax: (15) 562536
E-mail: qurashi@sudanmail.net
Founded 1993
State control
Number of teachers: 350
Number of students: 5,109

BAHR AL-GHAZAL UNIVERSITY

POB 10739, Khartoum, West Bahr Al-Ghazal
Telephone: (183) 224629
Fax: (183) 223015
E-mail: ubgzal@sudanmail.net
Founded 1991
State Control
Languages of instruction: Arabic, English
Vice-Chancellor: ADUOL MATHEW ATEM
Number of teachers: 273
Number of students: 1,513
Publication: *The Pioneer* (2 a year)

DEANS

College of Economics and Rural Studies: MADUT ABALLIAAK THEM
College of Education: ALAMIN ALFATEH MUSTAFA
College of Medicine and Health Sciences: ABDEL LATIF JUBARA MAHMOUD
College of Veterinary Science: ALI HASSAN AHMED

BAKHET EL-RUDDA UNIVERSITY

POB 1311, Khartoum, Eldewaym
Telephone: (531) 22440
Fax: (531) 20548
Founded 1997
State control
Languages of instruction: Arabic, English
Vice-Chancellor: ANAAS A. EL-HAFEEZ
Number of teachers: 198
Number of students: 4,035

DEANS

Faculty of Agriculture and Natural Resources: GHANIM SABIH
Faculty of Economics and Administration: ILHAM SAADALLAH
Faculty of Education: SALIH NOURIN
Faculty of Medicine: YOUSIF SULTAN
Faculty of Postgraduate Studies: MAHMOUD HASSAN

BLUE NILE UNIVERSITY

POB 143, Damazeen, Blue Nile
Telephone: (183) 785614
Vice-Chancellor: MOHAMMED EL-HASSAN ABDUL EL-RAHMAN
Founded 1995

Faculties of education and engineering; centres of extramural studies and continuing education.

UNIVERSITY OF DONGOLA

POB 47, Dongola
Telephone: (241) 21515
Fax: (241) 21514
Founded 1994
State control
Vice-Chancellor: MOHAMMED OSMAN AHMED

Faculties of agriculture, arts, education, law and Islamic law, medicine, mining and earth sciences.

EL-DALANG UNIVERSITY

El-Dalang, South Kordofan
Telephone: (183) 785614
Founded 1990
State control
Vice-Chancellor: KAMESS KAGO KUNDA

Faculties of agriculture, education, social development, teacher training; centres of computer science, peace studies.

EL-GADARIF UNIVERSITY

POB 449, El-Gadarif 32211
Telephone: (441) 43668
Fax: (441) 43120
E-mail: unged@sudanmail.net
Founded 1990; univ. status 1994
State control
Languages of instruction: Arabic, English
Vice-Chancellor: OMER KURDI
Number of teachers: 154
Number of students: 3,845

DEANS

Faculty of Agricultural and Environmental Sciences: ABDEL-AZIZA TAHA
Faculty of Economics and Administrative Science: EL-GUZOLI MOHAMAD
Faculty of Education: SULTAN NOUR
Faculty of Medicine and Medical Sciences: EL-DIRDIRY SALAH

EL-IMAM EL-MAHDI UNIVERSITY

POB 209, Kosti 11588
Telephone: (571) 22545
Fax: (571) 22222
E-mail: abdosm@sudanmail.net
Founded 1993
State control
Vice-Chancellor: ABDELRAHIM OSMAN MOHAMED
Faculties of Arabic and Islamic sciences, arts, engineering and technical studies, law and Islamic law, medicine and health sciences; centres for computer studies, extramural studies.

UNIVERSITY OF GEZIRA

POB 20, Wad Medani, 2667 Khartoum
Founded 1975
Language of instruction: English
Vice-Chancellor: (vacant)
Sec.-Gen.: Dr MAHMOUD ABDALLA IBRAHIM
Librarian: ABUEL GAITH SANHOURI
Number of teachers: 140
Number of students: 1,000

DEANS

Faculty of Agriculture: Dr OSMAN ALI SID AHMED
Faculty of Economics and Rural Development: Dr EL TAHIR MOHAMED NUR
Faculty of Education: Prof. ABDEL SALAM MAHMOUD ABDALLA
Faculty of Medicine: Prof. SALAH ELDIN TAHA SALIH
Faculty of Science and Technology: Dr ELNUR KAMAL EL DIN ABU SABAH
Graduate Studies and Academic Affairs: ISAM ABDEL RAHMAN AHMED
Preparatory College: Prof. FAYSAL AWAD
Dean of Students: Dr ABD EL-MUTAAL GIRSHAB

UNIVERSITY OF HOLY QU'RAN AND ISLAMIC SCIENCES

POB 1459, Omdurman
Telephone: (15) 559594
Fax: (15) 559175
Founded 1990 by merger of Holy Qu'ran College and Omdurman Higher Institute
State control
Vice-Chancellor: AHMED KHALID BABIKER
Faculties of Arabic language, community development, media studies, education, educational sciences, the Holy Qu'ran and Islamic law, law; centre for women's studies.

UNIVERSITY OF JUBA

POB 82, Juba
Telephone: 2113
Founded 1975 with financial help from the EEC; first student admission 1977
Language of instruction: English
Academic year: March to December (two semesters)
Chancellor: (vacant)
Vice-Chancellor: Prof. MAHMOUD MUSA MAHMOUD
Sec.-Gen.: Prof. MOSES MACAR KACUOL
Librarian: ALFRED D. LADO (acting)
Number of teachers: 220
Number of students: 1,200
Publications: *Juvarsity* (12 a year), *Library News* (12 a year)

DEANS

College of Adult Education and Training: GEORGE ISMAIL GABRA
College of Education: Dr ABDEL MONIEM MOHAMED OSMAN
College of Medicine: Dr MATHEW ATEM ADUOL
College of Natural Resources and Environmental Studies: Prof. JOSEPH AWAD MORGAN
College of Social and Economic Studies: Dr VENANSIO TOMBE MULUDIANG
Dean of Students: AJANG BIOR DUOT

PROFESSORS

College of Medicine:
SUBBARAO, V. V., Physiology

College of Natural Resources and Environmental Studies:
ASHRAF, M., Crop Breeding
MORGAN, J. A., Animal Production
TINGWA, P. O., Horticulture

KASSALA UNIVERSITY

Kassala 266
Telephone: (411) 22095
Fax: (411) 23501
Founded 1990
State control
Vice-Chancellor: MUSTAFA ALI ABASHER
Faculties of agriculture and natural resources, economics and administration, education, medicine and health sciences.

UNIVERSITY OF KHARTOUM

POB 321, 11115 Khartoum
Telephone: (83) 772601
Fax: (83) 780295
E-mail: vc@uofk.edu
Internet: www.uofk.edu
Founded 1956; fmrly Univ. College of Khartoum
State control
Languages of instruction: Arabic, English
Academic year: July to April
Vice-Chancellor: Prof. MOHAMED AHMED ALI EL SHEIKH
Deputy Vice-Chancellor: Prof. EL SIDDIG AHMED EL MUSTAFA EL SHEIKH
Prin.: Prof. MOHAMED NOURI EL AMIN
Academic Sec.: Dr MUSTAFA MOHAMED ALI EL BALLA
Personnel Sec.: Ustaz EL TAHIR OMER KHALID
Librarian: Prof. MONA MAHJOUB MOHAMED AHMED
Library: see Libraries and Archives
Number of teachers: 1,560
Number of students: 19,814

DEANS

Faculty of Agriculture: Dr SIDDIG MOHAMED EL HASSAN
Faculty of Animal Production: Dr OSMAN ALI OSMAN ELOUMIE
Faculty of Arts: Dr MOHAMED A. HALIM MOHAMED
Faculty of Dentistry: Dr AHMED MOHAMED SULEIMAN
Faculty of Economic and Social Studies: Dr AHMED EL SHEIKH MOHAMED AHMED
Faculty of Education: Dr ABDALLA EL KHIDIER MADANI
Faculty of Engineering and Architecture: Dr ABDALLA KHOJALI AHMED
Faculty of Forestry: Dr ABDEL AZIM YASSIN ABDEL GADIR
Faculty of Law: Dr MOHAMED IBRAHIM EL TAHER
Faculty of Mathematical Sciences: Dr MOHSIN HASSAN ABDALLA HASHIM
Faculty of Medical Laboratory Sciences: Dr SAYDA HASSAN EL-SAFI
Faculty of Medicine: Prof. ABDEL GADIR MOHAMED YOUSIF EL KADAROU
Faculty of Nursing Sciences: Dr NIEMA MIRGHANI IBRAHIM
Faculty of Pharmacy: Prof. KAMAL EL DIN EL TAYIB IBRAHIM
Faculty of Public Health and Environmental Hygiene: Dr ABDEL WAHAB MOHAMED EL MAKIE
Faculty of Science: Dr OSMAN IBRAHIM OSMAN ABDEL KARIM
Faculty of Technological and Developmental Studies: Dr ABDALLA GUMAA FRWA
Faculty of Veterinary Medicine: Prof. SULIMAN MOHAMED ELSONOSI
Graduate College: Prof. ZEN EL ABDEEN A. RAHEEM KARAR
School of Management Studies: Dr AHMED OSMAN HAMZA

UNIVERSITY OF KORDOFAN

POB 160, El Obeid, North Kordofan 517
Telephone: (611) 23119
Fax: (611) 23108
E-mail: info@uni-kordofan.com
Internet: www.uni-kordofan.com
Founded 1990
State control
Vice-Chancellor: OSMAN ADAM OSMAN
Faculties of commercial studies and business administration; education, engineering and technical science, medicine and health sciences, natural resources, science and humanities, Gum Arabic Research Centre; Institute of Accounting, Banking and Information Systems; Centre for Intermediate Technology in Agriculture.

NILE VALLEY UNIVERSITY

POB 52, Addamer
Telephone: (216) 24433
Fax: (216) 24106
Internet: www.nile-vunv.net
Founded 1990
State control
Language of instruction: Arabic
Academic year: October to June
Vice-Chancellor: Prof. FASIAL A. EL-HAG
Prin.: Dr ATTA A. FADLALLA
Academic Sec.: Prof. MAHMOUD Y. OSMAN
Library of 31,143 books, 76 periodicals
Number of teachers: 240
Number of students: 6,886 (6,796 undergraduate, 90 postgraduate)

DEANS

Faculty of Agriculture: Dr SAIFELDIN M. AL-AMIN
Faculty of Commerce and Business Administration: HAMZA A. HAMZA
Faculty of Education: Dr MOHMED A. MOHAMED
Faculty of Engineering and Technology: IZZELDIN A. ABDALLA
Faculty of Islamic and Arabic Studies: ABDELNABI A. EL-TAYEB
Faculty of Medicine: (vacant)
Teaching-Training College: ABDELGADIR S. HAMAD

NYALA UNIVERSITY

POB 155, Nyala, South Darfur
Telephone: (711) 33122
Fax: (711) 33123
E-mail: nyalauni@yahoo.com

Internet: www.nyalauniversity.net
Founded 1994
State control
Academic year: April to December
Vice-Chancellor
Number of teachers: 151
Number of students: 6,301
Faculties of community development, economics and commerce, education, engineering, law, nursing, technology, veterinary science; Centre for Peace Studies.

OMDURMAN ISLAMIC UNIVERSITY

POB 382, Omdurman
Telephone: (187) 511525
Fax: (187) 511525
Internet: www.oiu.edu
Founded 1912; univ. status 1965
State control
Language of instruction: Arabic
Academic year: October to June
Chair. of Univ. Ccl: Sheikh M. M. SADIQ AL-KAMMOURI
Vice-Chancellor: Prof. MOHAMMED OSMAN SALIH
Sec.-Gen.: Dr HASSAN AHMED HASSAN
Academy Sec.: Prof. HASSAN AHMED EL-HASSAN
Librarian: ABDUL SEED OSMAN
Library of 172,858 vols
Number of teachers: 854
Number of students: 51,636 (47,636 undergraduate, 4,000 postgraduate)
Publications: *Faculty of Arts Magazine*, *Faculty of Islamic Studies Magazine*

DEANS

Faculty of Agriculture: Dr M. AL-H. SIDDEEG
Faculty of Arabic Language: Prof. BABEKIR AL-ZACOULT
Faculty of Arts: Prof. H. ABDUL-RAHMAN
Faculty of Basic Medical Sciences: Dr M. SALAH ELDIN
Faculty of Computer Sciences: M. S. MOHAMMED
Faculty of Economics: Dr S. M. MOHAMED
Faculty of Education: Prof. AL-H. OMER HAJ
Faculty of Engineering: Dr H. AL-TAYEB
Faculty of Higher Studies: Dr H. AL-ABBASSI
Faculty of Human Development: Dr IBRAHEEM A. M. AHMED
Faculty of Management Science: Dr A. ABDELRAIID
Faculty of Medicine: Prof. A. I. YOUSSIF
Faculty of Pharmacy: Dr M. AL-H. ABDULLAH
Faculty of Sharia and Law: Dr A. IBRAHEEM

RED SEA UNIVERSITY

POB 24, Port Sudan
Telephone: (311) 27878
Fax: (311) 27778
Founded 1994
State control
Vice-Chancellor: ABDEL GADIR DAFALLA ELHAG
Number of teachers: 80
Number of students: 800
Faculties of applied sciences, earth sciences, economics and administration, education, engineering, marine science and fisheries, maritime transport economics, medicine and health sciences, teacher training; Institute of Oceanography.

SHENDI UNIVERSITY

POB 142, Shendi
Telephone: (261) 72184
Fax: (261) 72509
Founded 1990 as Faculty of Nile Valley Univ.; present status and title 1994
State control
Vice-Chancellor and Pres.: ALI ABDEL ABDEL RAHMAN BARRI
Number of teachers: 215
Number of students: 3,700
Publication: *Journal of Shendi University* (scientific, cultural and social topics, 2 a year)
Faculties of arts, community development, economics, commerce and business administration, law (incl. Sharia law), medicine and health sciences, primary school teacher training; centres for adult education and extramural studies, agricultural irrigation, animal production and crop research, educational development and continuing education; Al-Faith Islamic Studies Centre.

SINAR UNIVERSITY

Sinar
Telephone: (561) 785614
Fax: (561) 730697
Founded 1977; present status 1995
Prin.: MOHAMMED AWAD SALIH
Faculties of agriculture, Arabic and Islamic studies, education, engineering, medicine, natural resources and environment; centre for extramural studies; Da'wah Centre.

SUDAN UNIVERSITY OF SCIENCE AND TECHNOLOGY

POB 407, Khartoum
Telephone: (183) 772508
Fax: (183) 774559
E-mail: sust@sudanet.net
Internet: www.sustech.edu
Founded 1950
State control
Academic year: September to May
Vice-Chancellor: Prof. Dr AHMED ELTAYEB AHMED
Deputy Vice-Chancellor: Prof. Dr GADALLA ABDALLA ELHASSAN
Sec.-Gen.: Dr HASHIM ALI SALIM
Number of teachers: 977
Number of students: 55,924
Publication: *Science and Technology* (2 a year)

DEANS

College of Agricultural Studies: Dr YOUSIF MOHAMED AHMED
College of Animal Production Science and Technology: Dr HASSAN MOHAMED ADAM
College of Business Studies: Dr MUSA HASAB ELRASOUL KHIER ELSIED
College of Communication Science: Prof. MUKHTAR OSMAN ELSIDDIQ
College of Computer Science and Information Technology: Dr MOHAMED ELHAFIZ MUSTAFA
College of Education: Dr ABDEL RAZEG ABDALLAH ELBONI
College of Engineering: Prof. SHAMBUOL ADLAN MOHAMED
College of Fine and Applied Arts: Dr OMER MOHAMED ELHASSAN
College of Forestry and Range Science: Dr ALI KHALID ALI
College of Graduate Studies: Prof. Dr OSMAN SAAD ALI
College of Languages: Dr SAADIA MOSA OMER
College of Medical Laboratory Science: Dr HUMODI AHMED SAEED
College of Music and Drama: Dr SAAD YOUSIF OBEID
College of Petroleum Engineering and Technology: Dr RASHID AHMED MOHAMMED
College of Physical Education and Sports: Dr HAMID ELSAYED DAFALLAH
College of Medical Radiologic Sciences: Dr ALSAFI AHMED ABD ALLA
College of Sciences: Dr ELFATIH AHMED HASSAN
College of Technology: Dr MUBARAK EL MAHAL AHMED
College of Veterinary Medicine: Prof. Dr AMEL OMER BAKHEIT
College of Water and Environmental Engineering: Dr YOUSIF ALI YOUSIF

UPPER NILE UNIVERSITY

POB 1660, Khartoum
Telephone: (183) 220825
Founded 1991
State control
Language of instruction: Arabic
Academic year: November to June
Vice-Chancellor: Prof. MOSES MACAR KACUOL
Deputy Vice-Chancellor (Academic): Dr JOSHUA OTOR AKOL
Prin. (Admin.): NATHANIEL GANY GAI
Librarian: ABDEL BAGI MOHAMED EL-FAHAL (acting)
Library of 23,000 vols
Number of teachers: 92
Number of students: 1,167

DEANS

College of Agriculture: SAYED BUNDUKI BOLLO
College of Animal Production: ZEINAB MOHAMED TOM
College of Education: AKOY DUAL AKOY
College of Forestry: MASIMO KALISTO MOILINGA
College of Medicine: Dr OSMAN AHMED EL-BAKHIT
School of Nursing: NAHID KHALIL EL-FAKI (Director)
School of Public and Environmental Health: HATIM RAHAMTALLA ALALAWI (Director)

UNIVERSITY OF WEST KORDOFAN

POB 16722, Khartoum, El-Foula, West Kordofan
Telephone: (183) 785614
Founded 1997
State control
Vice-Chancellor: IBRAHIM MUSA TIBIN
Faculties of economics and community development, education, Islamic and Arabic sciences, natural resources and environmental studies.

UNIVERSITY OF ZALENGEI

Zalengei, West Darfur 6
Telephone: (713) 22013
Fax: (713) 22013
E-mail: uzal@student.net
Founded 1994
State control
Language of instruction: Arabic
Vice-Chancellor: AHMED MOHAMED ABAKER
Number of teachers: 105
Number of students: 1,249

DEANS

Faculty of Agriculture: KUMAL IBRAHIM ADAM
Faculty of Education: ABDUL MUTALIB MOHAMED KHATIR
Holy Koran and Islamic Studies Institute: ABDOUL MUTALIB MOHAMED KHATIR

Colleges and Institutes

Faculty of Hygiene and Environmental Studies: POB 205, Khartoum; tel. 72690; f. 1933; 26 staff; 4 depts; awards BSc and MSc in Environmental Health; Librarian M. MOHD. SALIH; Dean B. M. EL-HASSAN.

Khartoum Nursing College: POB 1063, Khartoum; 3-year diploma course; Prin. A. M. OSMAN.

Yambio Institute of Agriculture: Sud 82/002, c/o UNDP POB 913, Khartoum; f. 1972; library: 5,000 vols; 15 staff; 130 students; two-year diploma courses; Prin. CHRISTOPHER LADO GALE.

SURINAME

The Higher Education System

Higher education institutions predate the independence of Suriname (formerly Dutch Guiana) from the Netherlands in 1975, with the oldest being Anton de Kom Universiteit van Suriname, which was founded in 1968. In addition to the university, higher education is offered by technical and vocational schools. The Ministry of Education and Community Development is the government agency responsible for higher education. In 2001/02 there were 3,250 students enrolled at the university, with a further 1,936 students enrolled in other institutions of higher education.

The Dutch-style secondary school certificate (VWO) is the main criterion for admission to higher education. The Bachelors is the undergraduate degree at the University and the course lasts four years, including a practicum. Bachelors degrees are also offered by the Academie voor Hoger Kunst en Cultuuronderwijs, and take four years. The University does not offer Masters degrees.

Regulatory Body

GOVERNMENT

Ministry of Education and Community Development: Dr Samuel Kafiluddistraat 117–123, Paramaribo; tel. 498383; fax 495083; e-mail minond@sr.net; Minister EDWIN TOEKIDJAN WOLF.

Learned Society

LANGUAGE AND LITERATURE

Alliance Française: Prins Hendrikstraat 8, POB 9209, Paramaribo; tel. 4211305; offers courses and exams in French language and culture and promotes cultural exchange with France.

Research Institutes

AGRICULTURE, FISHERIES AND VETERINARY SCIENCE

Centre for Agricultural Research in Suriname: POB 1914, Paramaribo; tel. 490128; fax 498069; e-mail celos@sr.net; internet www.celos.sr.org; f. 1965; a branch of the University of Suriname; research in tropical agriculture; Dir R. O. RAVENSWAAY; publ. *Celos Bulletins*.

Landbouwproefstation (Agricultural Experiment Station): POB 160, Paramaribo; tel. 472442; fax 420152; internet odlb.ond@sr.net; f. 1903; attached to Min. of Agriculture, Animal Husbandry and Fisheries; agricultural research; library of 28,502 vols, incl. bound periodicals and pamphlets; Dir Drs ELVIS GOEDHART (acting); Librarian R. CHOTOE; publs *Bulletins* (irregular), *Suriname Agriculture* (2 to 3 a year).

TECHNOLOGY

Geologisch Mijnbouwkundige Dienst (Geological Mining Service): Lachmonstr. 181, Paramaribo; tel. 434187; fax 434252; f. 1943; publs contributions in *Mededelingen*, geological maps.; library of 20,000 vols; Head M. AUTAR (acting).

Library

Paramaribo

Bibliotheek van het Cultureel Centrum Suriname (Library of the Suriname Cultural Centre): POB 1241, Paramaribo; tel. 473309; fax 476519; e-mail stgccs@yahoo.com; internet www.ccs-suriname.com; f. 1948; 7 brs, 2 book-mobiles; 50,000 vols; Librarian MARCELLA AUGUSTUSZOON; Dir Dr ELVIERA SANDIE.

Museum

Paramaribo

Stichting Surinaams Museum: POB 2306, Abraham Crijnssenweg 1, Paramaribo; tel. 425871; fax 425881; e-mail museum@cq-link.sr; internet www.surinaamsmuseum.net; f. 1947; archaeology, art, history, ethnology; library of 35,000 vols; Dir Drs J. H. J. VAN PUTTEN; publ. *Libri Musei Surinamensis*.

University

ANTON DE KOM UNIVERSITEIT VAN SURINAME (Anton de Kom University of Suriname)

Universiteitscomplex Leysweg 86, POB 9212, Paramaribo

Telephone: 465558
Fax: 462291
E-mail: info@uvs.edu
Internet: www.uvs.edu

Founded 1968
Language of instruction: Dutch
Academic year: October to September

Pres.: Dr G. A. RUSLAND
Vice-Pres.: Dr A. LI FO SJOE
Sec.: Drs J. C. PAWIROREDJO

Number of teachers: 316
Number of students: 3,857

Publications: *Journal of Social Sciences* (2 a year), *Suriname Medical Bulletin* (4 a year)

DEANS

Faculty of Medicine: Drs G. OEHLERS
Faculty of Social Sciences: Drs L. BEEK
Faculty of Technology: Ir J. MARTINUS

SWAZILAND

The Higher Education System

Higher education institutions pre-date the independence of Swaziland from the United Kingdom in 1968, with the oldest being the University of Swaziland (formerly the University of Botswana, Lesotho and Swaziland), which was founded in 1964. In 2005/06 5,692 students were enrolled at the University of Swaziland, which has campuses at Luyengo and Kwaluseni; there are also a number of other institutions of higher education.

GCE A-Levels, the Cambridge Overseas School Certificate or the Cambridge Overseas Higher School Certificate can be used to gain admission to undergraduate courses at the University. The undergraduate Bachelors degree is divided into Part 1 and Part 2, lasting four years overall. Postgraduate Masters degrees are awarded in a restricted number of fields, including arts, sciences and education. Masters degrees are usually one-year programmes of full-time study (or two years part-time).

Post-secondary technical and vocational education is offered by a number of institutions, including Swaziland College of Technology, the Institute of Health Sciences and Swaziland Institute of Management and Public Administration.

Regulatory Body

GOVERNMENT

Ministry of Education: POB 39, Mbabane; tel. 4042491; fax 4043880; Minister THEMBA MSIBI.

Learned Societies

GENERAL

Royal Swaziland Society of Science and Technology: c/o The University, Private Bag, Kwaluseni; tel. 5284011; fax 5285276; f. 1977 to promote science and technology and relevant research; organizes meetings, seminars, etc.; 100 mems; Pres. Prof. L. P. MAKHUBU; Sec. R. MARTIN; publ. *Swaziland Journal of Science and Technology* (2 a year).

BIBLIOGRAPHY, LIBRARY SCIENCE AND MUSEOLOGY

Swaziland Library Association: POB 2309, Mbabane H100; Elwatini Bldg, cnr Market and Warner Sts, Mbabane; tel. 4042633; fax 4043863; e-mail fmkhonta@uniswacc.uniswa.sz; internet www.swala.sz; f. 1984; 120 mems; Chair. FAITH MKHONTA; Sec. JABULILE DLAMINI; publ. *SWALA Journal* (2 a year).

FINE AND PERFORMING ARTS

Swaziland Art Society: POB 812, Mbabane; tel. 4044136; e-mail artsociety@mailfly.com; internet www.swazilandartsociety.org.sz; f. 1970; classes, workshops, exhibitions, films, discussions, etc.; 60 mems; Chairs HELEN MOIR, ANS VRIEND.

LANGUAGE AND LITERATURE

Alliance Française: Swazi Plaza, POB A266, Mbabane; tel. 4043667; fax 4048340; e-mail mbabane@alliance.org.za; internet www.swaziplace.com/alliancefrancaise/index.html; offers courses and exams in French language and culture and promotes cultural exchange with France.

Research Institutes

AGRICULTURE, FISHERIES AND VETERINARY SCIENCE

Lowveld Experiment Station: POB 11, L312 Matata; tel. 3636311; fax 5283360; f. 1964; agricultural research, cotton breeding, cotton entomology; Chief Research Officer P. MKHATSHWA.

Malkerns Research Station: POB 4, Malkerns; tel. 5283306; fax 5283306; f. 1959; general research on crops, vegetables, fruits and farming systems; 14 research sections, library of 5,000 vols; Chief Research Officer P. D. MKHATSHWA.

Mpisi Cattle Breeding Experimental Station: Mpisi; aims to improve indigenous Nguni cattle; to provide multiplication studs of Brahman, Simmentaler and Friesland cattle for beef, milk and cross breeding; Dir R. A. JOHN; Man. I. A. MORLEY HEWITT.

TECHNOLOGY

Geological Survey and Mines Department: POB 9, Mbabane; tel. 4042411; fax 4045215; e-mail geo.director@swazi.net; f. 1944; activities: mapping of the territory (published at a scale of 1:25,000 and 1:50,000), the investigation of mineral occurrences by prospecting, detailed mapping and diamond drilling, mine and quarry inspections, control of explosives and prospecting; 18 mems; small library; Dir Dr M. MAPHALALA; publ. *Bulletins*.

Libraries and Archives

Mbabane

Swaziland National Archives: POB 946, Mbabane; tel. 4161196; fax 4161241; e-mail kholekilemthethwa@gmail.com; f. 1970; 5,600 vols; govt records since 1880s; colln of historical photographs, newspapers, maps, reports; oral history and biographies of prominent Swazis; Dir D. F. K. MTHETHWA (acting).

Swaziland National Library Service: POB 1461, Mbabane; tel. 4042633; fax 4043863; e-mail snlssz@snls.gov.sz; internet www.gov.sz; f. 1971; operates a public library service throughout the country with branch libraries at Manzini, Mpaka, Lomahasha, Nhlangano, Siteki, Pigg's Peak, Big Bend, Bhunya, Tshaneni, Mankayana, Lavumisa, Hlatikulu and Mhlume; mobile library visits; libraries at secondary schools; 80,000 vols, 150 periodicals; a national library was est. in 1986, which will eventually function as the focal point in Swaziland's documentation and information system; Dir D. J. KUNENE; publs *Accessions List* (irregular), *Index to Swaziland Collection* (irregular).

Museum

Lobamba

Swaziland National Museum: POB 100, Lobamba; tel. 4161178; fax 4161875; f. 1972, under the patronage of the Swaziland National Trust Commission; museum with extra-mural functions, giving information about Swazi culture as well as other Southern African Bantu groups; reference library; Curator ROSEMARY ANDRADE; publ. *Museum Occasional Paper*.

University

UNIVERSITY OF SWAZILAND

Private Bag 4, M201 Kwaluseni
Telephone: 5184011
Fax: 5185276
E-mail: registrar@admin.uniswa.sz
Internet: www.uniswa.sz

Founded 1964 as part of Univ. of Botswana, Lesotho and Swaziland, present name 1982
Language of instruction: English
Academic year: August to May

Chancellor: HM KING MSWATI III
Vice-Chancellor: (vacant)
Pro-Vice-Chancellor: Prof. C. M. MAGAGULA
Registrar: S. S. VILAKATI
Librarian: M. R. MAVUSO

Library of 178,000 vols, 1,500 periodicals
Number of teachers: 303
Number of students: 4,198

Publications: *UNISWA Journal of Agriculture, Science and Health Sciences* (2 a year), *UNISWA Journal of Social Science, Humanities and Education* (2 a year)

DEANS

Faculty of Agriculture: Dr G. N. SHONGWE
Faculty of Commerce: Prof. M. A. KHAN
Faculty of Education: Prof. J. C. B. BIGALA
Faculty of Health Sciences: Dr P. S. DLAMINI
Faculty of Humanities: Dr H. L. NDLOVU
Faculty of Postgraduate Studies: Prof. E. C. L. KUNENE
Faculty of Science: Prof. V. S. B. MTETWA
Faculty of Social Sciences: Prof. A. A. AL-TERAIFI

There is also an Institute of Distance Education

Colleges

Swaziland College of Technology: POB 69, H100 Mbabane; tel. 4042681; fax 4044521; e-mail scot@africaonline.co.sz; f. 1946 as Trade School, present name 1968; diploma courses in mechanical engineering, electrical and electronics engineering, telecommunications engineering, building and civil engineering, hotel and catering, secretarial studies, commercial and technical teaching; certificate courses in accounting, plumbing, block- and bricklaying, carpentry; library: 18,000 vols; 60 teachers; 700 students; Prin. HEBRON T. SUKATI; Registrar ATWELL GULE.

Swaziland Institute of Management and Public Administration: POB 495, Mbabane; tel. 4220740; fax 4220742; e-mail simpa@realnet.co.sz; f. 1965; 21 teachers (15 full-time, 6 part-time); 900 students; Prin. M. N. KHOZA.

SWEDEN

The Higher Education System

The oldest institution of higher education is Uppsala Universitet (Uppsala University), which was founded in 1477; the next oldest is Lunds Universitet (Lunds University), which was founded in 1666. Several institutions date from the 19th century, among them Kungliga Tekniska Högskolan (Royal Institute of Technology—founded 1827), Stockholms Universitet (Stockholm University—founded 1878) and Göteborgs Universitet (Gothenburg University—founded 1891).

In 1977 the Higher Education Act classified 100 programmes of undergraduate education by five subject areas (administrative, economic and social science; health; information, communication and fine arts; teacher training; and technical); however, in 1989 responsibility for curriculum planning was handed over to the universities, and further reforms in 1993 delineated undergraduate programmes into general or professional fields of study. Also in that year higher education was decentralized and a new degree system was introduced. Sweden participates in the Bologna Process to establish a European Higher Education Area, the first phase of which is to adopt a credit-based system of comparable degrees with two main cycles (undergraduate and graduate). In 2002 the Ministry of Education and Research established a working group to assess the feasibility of introducing a new degree system to correspond with the criteria of the Bologna Process, and subsequently a new system (see below) was fully implemented in 2007. The Swedish National Agency for Higher Education quality-assured all professional degree programmes in the period 2001–2006. The new six-year cycle of programme evaluations started in 2007, covering all degrees at first, second and third level. Higher education is offered by universities (universitet), university colleges or institutes of higher education (högskola). In 2003/04 there were 397,679 students enrolled in higher education.

The main requirement for admission to higher education is completion of secondary education and award of the Upper Secondary School Leaving Certificate (Avgångsbetyg or Slutbetyg från Gymnasieskola). Alternatively, applicants can be admitted upon completion of adult secondary school (komvux), completion of folk high school (folkhögskola) or at least four years of professional experience before the age of 25. Specialist programmes of study may have additional criteria. Furthermore, applicants sit either a special aptitude test (Högskoleprov) or National University Aptitude Test (Högskoleprovet). The newly established university degree system comprises three cycles, each subdivided into two parts; degrees are awarded on a 'credit' basis, and Sweden has adopted the European Credit Transfer System (ECTS). The undergraduate Bachelors degrees are the Högskoleexamen, which requires 80 credits over two years, and the Kandidatexamen, which requires 120 credits over three years. Professional degrees (Yrkesexamen) may last longer. The Masters-equivalent degrees are the Magisterexamen, lasting one year, and the Masterexamen, which lasts two years. Finally, doctoral-level studies consist of the Licentiatexamen, a two-year research degree, and the Doktorsexamen, a research degree culminating with submission and defence of a thesis; the Doktorsexamen requires a minimum of 160 credits in at least four years.

In 2002 legislation was enacted establishing a new form of post-secondary technical and vocational education called Advanced Vocational Education (Kvalificerad Yrkesutbildning). This primarily consists of programmes of study jointly organized by employers and institutions of tertiary education; the main Government provider is the Swedish Agency for Advanced Vocational Education (Myndigheten för kvalificerad yrkesutbildning).

Regulatory and Representative Bodies

GOVERNMENT

Ministry of Culture: Drottninggatan 16, SE-103 33 Stockholm; tel. (8) 405-10-00; fax (8) 21-68-13; e-mail registrator@culture.ministry.se; internet www.sweden.gov.se/sb/d/8371; Min. of Culture and Sport LENA ADELSOHN LILJEROTH.

Ministry of Education and Research: Drottninggatan 16, SE-103 33 Stockholm; tel. (8) 405-10-00; fax (8) 723-11-92; e-mail registrator@education.ministry.se; internet www.sweden.gov.se/sb/d/2063; Min. of Education JAN BJÖRKLUND; Deputy Min. of Education NYAMKO SABUNI; Min. of Higher Education and Research TOBIAS KRANTZ.

ACCREDITATION

ENIC/NARIC Sweden: Swedish Nat. Agency for Higher Education, POB 7851, SE-103 99 Stockholm; Luntmakargatan 13, SE-111 37 Stockholm; tel. (8) 563-085-00; fax (8) 563-086-50; e-mail hsv@hsv.se; internet www.hsv.se; f. 1995; Head LARS HAIKOLA.

NATIONAL BODIES

Folkhögskolornas informationstjänst (Information Service of the Swedish Folk High Schools): Box 380 74, SE-100 64 Stockholm; Rosenlundsgatan 50, Stockholm; tel. (8) 796-00-50; fax (8) 21-88-26; e-mail info@folkhogskola.nu; internet www.folkhogskola.nu; Coordinator AGNETA WALLIN.

Myndigheten för Yrkeshögskolan (Swedish National Agency for Higher Vocational Education): Box 145, SE-721 05 Västerås; Ingenjör Bååths gata 19, SE-722 12 Västerås; tel. (10) 209-01-00; fax (21) 13-20-16; e-mail info@yhmyndigheten.se; internet www.yhmyndigheten.se; f. 2009; Gen. Dir PIA ENOCHSSON.

Myndigheten för Nätverk och Samarbete inom Högre Utbildning (Swedish Agency for Networks and Cooperation in Higher Education): POB 194, SE-871 24 Härnösand; Brunnshusgatan 6, SE-871 33 Härnösand; tel. (611) 34-95-00; fax (611) 34-95-05; e-mail info@nshu.se; internet www.nshu.se; Dir-Gen. HÅKAN LARSSON (acting).

Rådet för högre utbildning (Council for the Renewal of Higher Education): POB 7285, SE-103 89 Stockholm; Luntmakargatan 13, Stockholm; tel. (8) 56-30-88-61; fax (8) 56-30-88-50; e-mail rhu@rhu.se; internet www.rhu.se; f. 1990; Chair. Prof. LARS HAIKOLA.

Skolverket (Swedish National Agency for Education): SE-106 20 Stockholm; Alströmergatan 12, Stockholm; tel. (8) 52-73-32-00; fax (8) 24-44-20; e-mail skolverket@skolverket.se; internet www.skolverket.se; Dir HELÉN ÅNGMO.

Styrelsen för Internationellt Utvecklingssamarbete (Swedish International Development Cooperation Agency): Valhallavägen 199, SE-105 25 Stockholm; tel. (8) 698-50-00; fax (8) 20-88-64; e-mail sida@sida.se; internet www.sida.se; attached to Min. for Foreign Affairs; Dir-Gen. CHARLOTTE PETRI GORNITZKA (acting); Deputy Dir-Gen. BO NETZ.

Svenska institutet (Swedish Institute): Slottsbacken 10, Box 7434, SE-103 91 Stockholm; tel. (8) 453-78-00; fax (8) 20-72-48; e-mail si@si.se; internet www.si.se; Dir-Gen. ANNIKA REMBE.

Sveriges universitets- och högskoleförbund (SUHF) (Association of Swedish Higher Education): Tryckerigatan 8, SE-111 28 Stockholm; tel. (8) 32-13-88; fax (8) 32-93-70; e-mail jennie.reponen@suhf.se; internet www.suhf.se; f. 1995; 40 mems; Chair. PAM FREDMAN; Vice-Chair. AGNETA STARK; Sec.-Gen. DR BENGT KARLSSON.

Learned Societies

GENERAL

Finlandsinstitutet (Finnish Cultural Centre): POB 1355, SE-111 83 Stockholm; Snickarbacken 2–4 (vid Birger Jarlsgatan 35), SE-111 83, Stockholm; tel. (8) 54-52-12-00; fax (8) 54-52-12-10; e-mail info@

finlandsinstitutet.se; internet www.finlandsinstitutet.se; f. 1995; one of 16 Finnish cultural instns worldwide; organizes cultural events, seminars, concerts, art exhibitions, language courses; library of 16,000 vols; cassette books, CDs, video cassettes; Dir BENGT PACKALÉN.

Kungl. Humanistiska Vetenskaps-Samfundet i Uppsala (Royal Society of Humanities at Uppsala): c/o Prof. Staffan Fridell, Dept of Scandinavian Languages, POB 527, SE-751 20 Uppsala; tel. (18) 471-12-73; fax (18) 471-12-72; e-mail info@khvsu.se; internet www.khvsu.se; f. 1889; promotes study of humanities; 5 meetings a year, with lectures and discussion; distributes awards and scholarships; 120 mems (100 Swedish, 20 foreign); Pres. Prof. HANS KRONNING; Gen. Sec. Prof. STAFFAN FRIDELL; publs *Acta Westiniana*, *Årsböcker* (Yearbook), *Skrifter* (Proceedings, irregular), *Uppländska domböcker*.

Kungl. Vetenskapsakademien (Royal Swedish Academy of Sciences): POB 50005, SE-104 05 Stockholm; Lilla Frescativägen 4A, SE-114 18 Stockholm; tel. (8) 673-95-00; fax (8) 15-56-70; e-mail info@kva.se; internet kva.se; f. 1739; acts as a forum where researchers can meet across subject borders; offers unique research environments; supports young researchers; rewards prominent contributions to research; arranges int. scientific contacts; acts as a voice of science and influences research policy priorities; stimulates interest in mathematics and natural sciences in schools; disseminates scientific and popular-scientific information in various forms; 595 mems (420 Swedish, 175 foreign); library: see Libraries and Archives; Pres. Prof. SVANTE LINDQVIST; Vice-Pres. STEFAN CLAESSON; Vice-Pres. CHRISTINA MOBERG; Vice-Pres. ULF PETTERSSON; Permanent Sec. Prof. STAMMAN NORMARK; publs *Acta Mathematica*, *Acta Zoologica*, *Ambio*, *Arkiv för Matematik*, *ETAI*, *Physica Scripta*, *Zoologica Scripta*.

Kungl. Vetenskaps- och Vitterhets-Samhället i Göteborg (KVVS) (Royal Society of Arts and Sciences in Göthenburg): POB 222, SE-405 30 Gothenburg; tel. (31) 786-14-00; fax (31) 786-55-50; e-mail info@kvvs.se; internet www.kvvs.se; f. 1778; scientific lectures, confs, symposia; cooperation with other scientific academies, domestic and foreign support to long-term scientific research programmes; publs, exchange of publs nationally and internationally; stipends to jr and sr researchers; 331 mems (256 Swedish, 75 foreign); Pres. BIRGITTA SKARIN FRYKMAN; Vice-Pres. BJÖRN RYDEVIK; Sec.-Gen. Prof. BIRGER KARLSSON; Treas. MARTIN FRITZ; Librarian Prof. BO LINDBERG; publs *Acta Regiae Societatis Scientiarum et Litterarum Gothoburgensis* (monographs), *Årsbok*.

Kungl. Vetenskaps-Societeten i Uppsala (Royal Society of Sciences of Uppsala): St Larsgatan 1, SE-753 10 Uppsala; tel. and fax (18) 13-12-70; e-mail kansli@vetenskapssocietetenuppsala.se; internet www.vetenskapssocietetenuppsala.se; f. 1710, charter 1728; promotes research principally in mathematics, natural sciences, medicine, Swedish antiquities and topography by publishing scholarly works, awarding grants, collecting and making available relevant publs, lectures; 230 mems (130 full mems, 100 foreign mems); library of 600 periodicals; Pres. HM KING CARL XVI GUSTAF; Chair. Prof. LARS ENGWALL; Vice-Chair. Prof. LENNART DENCKER; Sec. Prof. LARS-OLOF SUNDELÖF; Treas. ARNE FORSELL; publs *Matrikel* (1 a year), *Nova Acta Regia Societatis Scientiarum Upsaliensis* (irregular).

Kungl. Vitterhets Historie och Antikvitets Akademien (Royal Swedish Academy of Letters, History and Antiquities): Kungl. Vitterhetsakademien, POB 5622, SE-114 86 Stockholm; tel. (8) 440-42-80; fax (8) 440-42-90; e-mail kansli@vitterhetsakad.se; internet www.vitterhetsakad.se; f. 1753, present name 1786; promotes research and other activities in the fields of humanities, social sciences, religion, law; 161 mems (121 Swedish, 40 foreign); library: see Libraries and Archives; Pres. Prof. GUNNEL ENGWALL; Vice-Pres. Prof. DAN BRÄNDSTRÖM; Sec.-Gen. Dr ERIK NORBERG; Deputy Sec. Prof. BENGT LANDGREN; publs *Arkiv* (archives), *Fornvännen* (journal), *Handlingar* (proceedings).

AGRICULTURE, FISHERIES AND VETERINARY SCIENCE

Kungl. Skogs- och Lantbruksakademien (Royal Swedish Academy of Agriculture and Forestry): POB 6806, SE-113 86 Stockholm; Drottninggatan 95B, SE-113 86 Stockholm; tel. (8) 545-477-00; fax (8) 545-477-10; e-mail akademien@ksla.se; internet www.ksla.se; f. 1869; promotes sustainable devt, agriculture, forestry, horticulture, animal husbandry, hunting, fishing and water management; 545 mems (20 hon., 400 working, 125 foreign); library: see Libraries and Archives; Pres. Prof. SARA VON ARNOLD; Vice-Pres. Prof. ÅKE BRUCE; Sec. Gen. ÅKE BARKLUND; Chief Information Officer YLVA NORDIN; publ. *Kungl. Skogs och Lantbruksakademiens Tidskrift (KSLAT)* (4 a year).

ARCHITECTURE AND TOWN PLANNING

Svenska Teknik & Designföretagen (Swedish Federation of Consulting Engineers and Architects): POB 555 45, SE-102 04 Stockholm; Sturegatan 11, SE-102 04 Stockholm; tel. (8) 762-67-00; fax (8) 762-67-10; e-mail std@std.se; internet www.std.se; f. 2001; focuses to improve the environment for mem. cos that operate both as a commercial party and employer; 740 mem cos; Chair. BENT JOHANNESSON; Man. Dir LENA WÄSTFELT; publ. *Sector Review* (1 a year).

ECONOMICS, LAW AND POLITICS

Centre for the Study of International Relations: Hagtornsvägen 9, Enebyberg, SE-182 47 Stockholm; tel. (8) 612-33-62; fax (8) 758-30-39; e-mail info@cintrel.org; f. 1971; studies social sciences, int. politics, law and economy; ind. of any political party; organizes lectures and confs, research seminars; library; Pres. CLÄES PALME; Vice-Pres. and Dir Prof. Dr RICHARD K. T. HSIEH; Sec. Prof. Dr JACOB W. F. SUNDBERG; Sec. Prof. Dr LARS HJERNER; publ. *Review*.

International Law Association, Swedish Branch: c/o Attorney John Kadelburger AB, Engelbrektsgatan 9–11, SE-114 32 Stockholm; tel. (8) 120-66-132; fax (8) 120-661-10; e-mail sekretariat@ilasweden.se; internet www.ilasweden.se; f. 1922; studies and develops int. law (private and procedural); promotes studies in comparative law; draws up proposals for conflict resolution and unification of measures in int. law; fosters int. understanding and goodwill; Pres. Prof. OVE BRING; Sec. and Treas. JOHN KADELBURGER.

Kungl Krigsvetenskapsakademien (Royal Swedish Academy of War Sciences): Teatergatan 3, 5 tr, SE-111 48 Stockholm; tel. (8) 611-14-00; fax (8) 667-22-53; e-mail info@kkrva.se; internet www.kkrva.se; f. 1796 as Swedish Military Asscn, present status 1805; promotes military sciences, incl. civil defence, economic defence and psychological defence, security and defence policy; 400 mems; Pres. Prof. BO HULDT; Vice-Pres. ERIK ROSSANDER; Sec. BJÖRN ANDERSON; publ. *Kungl Krigsvetenskapsakademiens Handlingar och Tidskrift* (4 a year).

Nationalekonomiska Föreningen (Swedish Economic Association): c/o SOFI, Stockholm Univ., SE-106 91 Stockholm; tel. (8) 16-25-13; fax (8) 15-46-70; e-mail anders.bohlmark@sofi.su.se; f. 1877; study of economics; 1,200 mems; Chair. Dr PEHR WISSÉN; Vice-Chair. Prof. MÅRTEN PALME; Sec. ANDERS BÖHLMARK; publ. *Ekonomisk Debatt* (8 a year).

Utrikespolitiska Institutet (Swedish Institute of International Affairs): POB 27035, SE-102 51 Stockholm; Drottning Kristinas väg 37, SE-102 51 Stockholm; tel. (8) 511-768-00; fax (8) 511-768-99; e-mail info@ui.se; internet www.ui.se; f. 1938; researches on int. affairs; enhances public understanding of current int. affairs; confs, seminars and other events; 250 mems; library of 40,000 vols, 400 periodicals; Pres. MATS BERGQUIST; Dir ANNA JARDFELT; Dir for Admin LARS ÅMAN (acting); Research Dir Dr HANNA OJANEN; publs *Internationella studier*, *Länder i fickformat*, *Research Report*, *UI Papers*, *Världens Fakta*, *Världspolitikens dagsfrågor*.

FINE AND PERFORMING ARTS

Föreningen Svenska Tonsättare (Society of Swedish Composers): POB 27327, SE-102 54 Stockholm; tel. (8) 783-95-90; fax (8) 783-95-40; e-mail katarina.widell@fst.se; internet www.fst.se; f. 1918; promotes contemporary classical music composition; 329 mems; Pres. MARTIN Q. LARSSON; Vice-Pres. CHRICHAN LARSON.

Fylkingen (Society of Contemporary Music and Intermedia Art): Söder Mälarstrand 27, SE-118 25 Stockholm; Torkel Knutssonsgatan 2, Münchenbryggeriet, Stockholm; tel. (8) 84-54-43; fax (8) 669-38-68; e-mail intermedia@fylkingen.se; internet www.fylkingen.se; f. 1933 as a chamber music society; promotes new music and intermedia art; 248 mems; Chair. JOHANNES BERGMARK; publ. *Hz* (online, 2 a year).

Kungliga Akademien för de fria Konsterna (Konstakademien) (Royal Swedish Academy of Fine Arts): POB 16317, SE-103 26 Stockholm; Fredsgatan 12, Jakobsgatan 27C, SE-103 26 Stockholm; tel. (8) 23-29-25; fax (8) 790-59-24; e-mail susanna.sloor@konstakademien.se; internet www.konstakademien.se; f. 1735; promotes devt of painting, sculpture, architecture and allied arts; 145 mems (102 Swedish, 24 foreign, 19 hon.); library of 60,000 vols; Pres. ULLA FRIES; Vice-Pres. LAR STURE KOINBERG; Permanent Sec. SUSANNA SLÖÖR; Curator EVA-LENA BENGTSSON; Librarian ULF NORDQVIST.

Kungl. Musikaliska Akademien (Royal Swedish Academy of Music): Blasieholmstorg 8, SE-111 48 Stockholm; tel. (8) 407-18-00; fax (8) 611-87-18; e-mail adm@musakad.se; internet www.musakad.se; f. 1771; promotes and protects the art and science of music; awards Rolf Schock Prize, Christ Johnson Prize and Royal Swedish Acad. of Music Jazz Prize; 170 Swedish mems; 60 foreign mems; Pres. Prof. KJELL INGEBRETSEN; Vice-Pres. THOMAS JENNEFELT; Vice-Pres. ANNA LINDAL; Permanent Sec. Dr ÅKE HOLMQUIST; publs *Årsskrift* (yearbook), *Musica Sveciae* (record anthology).

Musikaliska Konstföreningen (Swedish Art Music Society): Sveavägen 12, Saltsjöbaden, SE-111 48 Stockholm; tel. (709) 20-61-96; e-mail sheetmusic@musikaliskakonstforeningen.se; internet www.musikaliskakonstforeningen.se; f. 1859; publishes and sells works of ancient and contemporary composers; promotes

Swedish music; Chair. ERIK LUNDKVIST; Sec. HANS ENFLO; Treas. ALF WESTELIUS.

Kulturrådet (Swedish Arts Council): POB 27215, SE-102 53 Stockholm; tel. (8) 519-264-00; fax (8) 519-264-99; e-mail kulturradet@kulturradet.se; internet www.kulturradet.se; f. 1974; funding, advisory and investigatory body responsible for implementing nat. cultural policy; covers theatre, dance, music, literature, cultural journals, public libraries, art, museums and exhibitions; Chair. KERSTIN BRUNNBERG; Dir-Gen. KENNET JOHANSSON; publ. *Kulturrådet*.

Svenska Samfundet för Musikforskning (Swedish Society for Musicology): POB 7448, SE-103 91 Stockholm; tel. (46) 121-027; e-mail jacob.derkert@music.su.se; internet musikforskning.se; f. 1919; unifying forum for musicologists; disseminates knowledge of musicological research in and about Sweden; 87 mems; Chair. JACOB DERKERT; Vice-Chair. EVA GEORGII-HEMMING; Sec. MATTIAS LUNDBERG; Treas. EVA KJELLANDER; publs *Monumenta Musicae Sveciae, Svensk Tidskrift för Musikforskning* (Swedish Journal of Musicology, 1 a year).

Svensk Form (Swedish Society of Crafts and Design): POB 204, SE-101 24 Stockholm; Skeppsholmen, Svensksundsvägen 13, SE-111 49 Stockholm; tel. (8) 463-31-30; fax (8) 644-22-85; e-mail info@svenskform.se; internet www.svenskform.se; f. 1845 as Swedish Society for Industrial Design; promotes Swedish designs; 8,000 mems; Chair. ERIKA LAGERBIELKE; publ. *Form* (6 a year).

Sveriges Allmänna Konstförening (Swedish General Art Association): POB 5343, SE-102 47 Stockholm; Liljevalchs konsthall, Djurgårdsv 60, Stockholm; tel. (8) 10-46-77; fax (8) 20-14-57; e-mail info@konstforeningen.se; internet www.konstforeningen.se; f. 1832; promotes Swedish contemporary art; organises exhibitions; 8,000 mems; Pres. EVA SCHÖLD; Vice-Pres. MÅRTEN CASTENFORS; Treas. JAN-ERIK SÖDERHIELM; publ. *Sveriges Allmänna Konstförenings årspublikation* (Swedish General Art Association's annual publication).

HISTORY, GEOGRAPHY AND ARCHAEOLOGY

Karolinska Förbundet: c/o Gidlöf, Hildebergsvägen 16, SE-117 62 Stockholm; tel. (8) 727-02-15; e-mail info@karolinska-forbundet.org; internet www.karolinska-forbundet.org; f. 1910; promotes research and dissemination of knowledge on Caroline era; 1,000 mem companies; Pres. Dr ÅSA KARLSSON; Vice-Pres. Col BERTIL WENNERHOLM; Sec. LEIF GIDLÖF; publ. *Karolinska Förbundets Årsbok*.

Kartografiska Sällskapet (Swedish Cartographic Society): c/o Lantmäteriet, SE-801 82 Gävle; tel. (26) 63-32-37; e-mail ks@kartografiska.se; internet www.kartografiska.se; f. 1908; promotes and develops cartography and other topics related to mapping or use of maps in Sweden in areas such as photogrammetry, remote sensing, geodesy, geographical information systems, geographic information technology, historical cartography and cartography; 2,000 mems; Pres. PETER WASSTRÖM; Vice-Pres. ANN ERIKSSON; Sec. KARIN GRÅNÄS; Treas. TORBJÖRN OHLSSON; publs *Kart & Bildteknik* (4 a year), *National Report* (mapping activities, in English, every 4 years), *Sveriges Kartläggning* (mapping of Sweden, every 10 years).

Svenska Museiföreningen (Swedish Museums Association): Åsögatan 90, 118 29 Stockholm; tel. (8) 640-43-72; e-mail per.kaks@telia.com; f. 1906; asscn of Swedish museums and mems of staff; debates, etc., concerning practical devt and museum policy issues; mem of Network of European Museum Organizations (NEMO); 1,000 individual mems, 200 institutional mems; Pres. LARS AMREUS; Sec.-Gen. MATS PERSSON; publ. *Svenska Museer* (5 a year).

Svenska Sällskapet för Antropologi och Geografi (Swedish Society for Anthropology and Geography): c/o Fil dr Mattias Viktorin, Sunnerstavägen 102, SE-186 70 Brottby; tel. (73) 646-60-95; fax (8) 16-48-18; e-mail ssagmail@yahoo.se; internet www.ssag.se; f. 1873 as Asscn for Anthropology, present name 1877; forwards the devt of anthropology and geography in Sweden, communicates with foreign socs with the same objectives, and supports investigations into anthropology and geography; 900 mems; library of 10,000 vols; Pres. Prof. GUNHILD ROSQVIST; Vice-Pres. Doc. BRITA HERMELIN; Sec. Dr MATTIAS VIKTORIN; Treas. Dr THOMAS BORÉN; publs *Årsboken Ymer* (1 a year), *Geografiska Annaler A—Physical Geography* (4 a year), *Geografiska Annaler B—Human Geography* (4 a year), *Ymir* (1 a year).

LANGUAGE AND LITERATURE

Alliance Française: c/o Diana Schwarcz, Sandhamnsgatan 12, SE-11 540 Stockholm; tel. (8) 662-27-35; e-mail info@alliancefrancaisesthlm.com; internet www.alliancefrancaise-se.com; f. 1889; offers courses and exams in French language and culture and promotes cultural exchange with France; attached offices in Borås, Falun, Gothenburg, Halmstad, Helsingborg, Höglandet, Jönköping, Kalmar, Kristianstad, Linköping, Lund, Norrköping, Nyköping, Örebro, Ornskoldsvik, Östersund, Skaraborg, Skelleftea and Uppsala; Pres. JOHAN STENBERG; Vice-Pres. DANIÈLE BERENHOLT; Sec. DIANA SCHWARCZ; Treas. AKE NILSSON.

British Council: c/o British Embassy, Skarpögatan 6–8, POB 27819, SE-115 93 Stockholm; tel. (70) 671-02-28; e-mail elin.svensson@britishcouncil.se; internet www.britishcouncil.org/sweden; offers courses and exams in English language and British culture and promotes cultural exchange with the UK; Country Man. ELIN SVENSSON.

Goethe-Institut: Bryggargatan 12A, SE-111 21 Stockholm; tel. (8) 459-12-00; fax (8) 459-12-15; e-mail info@stockholm.goethe.org; internet www.goethe.de/stockholm; offers courses and exams in German language and culture and promotes cultural exchange with Germany; attached teaching centre in Gothenburg; library of 3,500 vols, 45 periodicals; Dir and Head of Program Work HEIKE FRIESEL; Dir and Head of Program Work RAINER HAUSWIRTH; Deputy Dir and Head of Language Work BERND ZABEL.

Instituto Cervantes: Bryggargatan 12A, SE-111 21 Stockholm; tel. (8) 440-17-60; fax (8) 21-04-31; e-mail info.stockholm@cervantes.es; internet www.cervantes.se; f. 2005; offers courses and exams in Spanish language and culture and promotes cultural exchange with Spain and Spanish-speaking Latin and Central America; library of 10,000 vols (books, magazines, CDs, DVDs); Dir JOAN M. ALVAREZ VALENCIA; Librarian JOHNNY PETTERSSON.

Samfundet de Nio (Academy of the Nine): Villagatan 14, SE-114 32 Stockholm; tel. (8) 70-573-44-08; fax (8) 611-22-03; internet www.samfundetdenio.se; f. 1913; Pres. Prof. INGE JONSSON; Sec.and Treas. ANDERS R. ÖHMAN; publ. *De Nios litterära kalender* (1 a year).

Språkrådet (Language Council): POB 20057, SE-104 60 Stockholm; Bjurholmsgatan 10, Stockholm; tel. (8) 442-42-00; fax (8) 455-42-26; e-mail sprakradet@sprakradet.se; internet www.sprakradet.se; f. 2006 by merger of Swedish Language Council, Sweden Finnish Language Council and Plain group in the Cabinet Office; attached to Institute for Language and Folklore; official language planning agency; provides advice on language issues and follows language devt in Sweden; engaged in linguistic research and promotes Swedish and Nordic language of cooperation; Head LENA EKBERG; publs *Kieliviesti* (4 a year), *Klarspråk–bulletin från Språkrådet* (4 a year).

Svenska Akademien (Swedish Academy): POB 2118, SE-103 13 Stockholm; Källargränd 4, Gamla Stan, Stockholm; tel. (8) 555-125-00; fax (8) 555-125-49; e-mail sekretariat@svenskaakademien.se; internet www.svenskaakademien.se; f. 1786; Swedish language and literature; awards Nobel Prize for Literature; 18 mems; library: see Libraries and Archives; Permanent Sec. Prof. PETER ENGLUND; publ. *Svenska Akademiens Handlingar* (1 a year).

Svenska PEN (Swedish PEN): POB 3159, SE-103 63 Stockholm; c/o Albert Bonniers Förlag, Sveavägen 56, SE-103 63 Stockholm; tel. (8) 736-19-40; e-mail ola@larsmo.se; internet www.svenskapen.se; f. 1922; promotes literature; discussion, debates, communication among writers; 600 mems; Chair. BJÖRN LINNELL; Vice-Chair. BIRGITTA ÖHMAN; Pres. OLA LARSMO; Sec. MARTIN KAUNITZ.

Svenska Vitterhetssamfundet: POB 2118, SE-103 13 Stockholm; tel. (8) 10-19-69; fax (8) 765-57-71; e-mail barbro@sjonell.se; internet www.svenskavitterhetssamfundet.se; publishes classics by Swedish authors; 410 mems; Sec. PETRA SÖDERLUND.

Sveriges Författarförbund (Swedish Writers' Union): POB 3157, Drottninggatan 88B, SE-103 63 Stockholm; tel. (8) 545-132-00; fax (8) 545-132-10; e-mail sff@forfattarforbundet.se; internet www.forfattarforbundet.se; f. 1893 as Swedish Asscn of Authors, present name and status 1970; protects intellectual and economic interests of writers and translators; 2,400 mems; Pres. BUNNY RAGNERSTAM; Dir HELENA NELSON-BÜLOW; publ. *Författaren* (6 a year).

MEDICINE

Socialstyrelsen (National Board of Health and Welfare): SE-106 30 Stockholm; Rålambsvägen 3, Stockholm; tel. (8) 75-247-30-00; fax (8) 75-247-32-52; e-mail socialstyrelsen@socialstyrelsen.se; internet www.socialstyrelsen.se; f. 1968 by the merger of Royal Medical Board and Royal Board of Social Affairs; attached to Min. of Health and Social Affairs; public health, medical and social services admin.; Dir-Gen. LARS-ERIK HOLM; Deputy Dir-Gen. HÅKAN CEDER.

Svenska Läkaresällskapet (Swedish Society of Medicine): POB 738, SE-101 35 Stockholm; Klara Östra Kyrkogata 10, SE-101 35 Stockholm; tel. (8) 440-88-60; fax (8) 440-88-99; e-mail sls@sls.se; internet www.sls.se; f. 1808, present bldg 1906; promotes research, education and devt in health care sector; 17,000 mems; Chair. MARGARETA TROEIN TÖLLBORN; Vice-Chair. PETER FRIBERG; Sec. BRITT NORDLANDER; publ. *Svenska Läkaresällskapets Handlingar Hygiea*.

NATURAL SCIENCES

General

Wenner-Gren Stiftelserna (Wenner-Gren Foundations): Sveavägen 164, 23rd Fl., SE-113 46 Stockholm; tel. (8) 736-98-11; fax (8) 31-33-17; e-mail susanne.falck@swgc.org; internet www.swgc.org; f. 1962; residence and meeting place for foreign and visiting scientists; Chair. Prof. INGE JONSSON; Vice-

Chair. KERSTIN ELIASSON; Scientific Sec. Prof. BERTIL DANEHOLT.

Kungl. Skytteanska Samfundet (Royal Skytte Society): Humanisthuset, SE-901 87 Umeå; tel. (90) 14-14-28; e-mail skytteanska@adm.umu.se; internet www.skytteanskasamfundet.se; f. 1956; promotes and supports scientific research, particularly that of Norrland interest; Pres. LARS-ERIK EDLUND; Vice-Pres. ERIK LUNDGREN; Sec. ULF WIBERG; publs *Journal of Northern Studies* (2 a year), *THULE* (1 a year).

Svenska Linnésällskapet (Swedish Linnaeus Society): POB 15093, SE-750 15 Uppsala; tel. (18) 471-62-71; fax (18) 471-62-70; e-mail info@linnaeus.se; internet www.linnaeus.se; f. 1917; expands knowledge about Carl Linnaeus and his work; encourages interest in nature and scientific culture; publish writings by and about Carl Linnaeus and his disciples; attached museum; Pres. Doc. ROLAND MOBERG; Sec. EVA NYSTRÖM; publ. *Swedish Linnaeus Society Yearbook (SLÅ)*.

Biological Sciences

Kungl. Fysiografiska Sällskapet i Lund (Royal Physiographic Society of Lund): Stortorget 6, SE-222 23 Lund; tel. (46) 13-25-28; fax (46) 13-19-44; e-mail kansli@fysiografen.se; internet www.fysiografen.se; f. 1772 as Acad. of Natural Sciences, Medicine and Technology, present name and status 1778; science, medicine and technology; 500 mems, 100 foreign corresps; Pres. Prof. CHARLOTTE ERLANSON-ALBERTSSON; Vice-Pres. TORBJÖRN FREJD; Dir ULF KÖRNER; Sec.and Treas. PER ALM; publ. *Årsbok* (every 2 years).

Svenska Bioenergiföreningen (Svebio) (Swedish Bioenergy Association (Svebio)): Torsgatan 12 plan 3, SE-111 23 Stockholm; tel. (8) 441-70-80; fax (8) 441-70-89; e-mail info@svebio.se; internet www.svebio.se; f. 1980; devt of bioenergy in Sweden; 300 mems; Chair. LENA SÖDERBERG; Pres. GUSTAV MELIN.

Naturskyddsföreningen (Swedish Society for Nature Conservation): POB 4625, Åsögatan 115, 2 tr., SE-116 91 Stockholm; tel. (8) 702-65-00; fax (8) 702-08-55; e-mail medlem@naturskyddsforeningen.se; internet www.naturskyddsforeningen.se; f. 1909; deals with environmental issues; areas of work incl. climate, oceans, forests, pollution, agriculture; mem. of IUCN; 181,000 mems; Pres. MIKAEL KARLSSON; Vice-Pres. LENA ERIKSSON; Vice-Pres. KARIN ÅSTRÖM; Treas. BO JÖNSON; publ. *Sveriges Natur* (6 a year).

Mathematical Sciences

Lunds Matematiska Sällskap (Lund Mathematical Society): c/o Matematiska Institutionen, POB 118, SE-221 00 Lund; fax (46) 222-40-10; internet www.matematik.lu.se/lms; f. 1923; promotes greater interest in mathematics and related subjects, both among the gen. public and students; 150 mems; Pres. Prof. NILS DENCKER; Vice-Pres. ANDERS HOLST; Sec. and Treas. THOMAS EDLUND.

Matematiska Föreningen i Uppsala (Mathematical Society of Uppsala): Dept of Mathematics, Uppsala Univ., POB 480, SE-751 06 Uppsala; tel. (18) 471-32-00; fax (18) 471-32-01; e-mail mans.eriksson@math.uu.se; f. 1853, present name and status 1889; 50 mems; Chair. Dr MÅNS ERIKSSON; Sec. Dr DANIEL STRÖMBOM.

Svenska Matematikersamfundet (Swedish Mathematical Society): c/o Tobias Ekholm, Dept of Mathematics, Uppsala Univ., POB 480, SE-751 06 Uppsala; tel. (46) 471-63-99; fax (46) 471-32-01; e-mail president@swe-math-soc.se; internet www.swe-math-soc.se; f. 1950; meetings, journals, education of mathematics teachers, mathematics competition for students, travel grants for PhD students, research prizes for young mathematicians; 540 mems; Chair. Prof. TOBIAS EKHOLM; Vice-Chair. MIKAEL PASSARE; Sec. Dr WARWICK TUCKER; Treas. MILAGROS IZQUIERDO BARRIOS; publs *Mathematica Scandinavia* (with other Scandinavian mathematical socs), *Nordisk Matematisk Tidskrift* (with other Scandinavian mathematical socs).

Svenska Statistikfrämjandet (Swedish Statistics Promotion): Arenavägen 7, SE-121 88 Stockholm; tel. (8) 688-76-66; e-mail sekrfram@gmail.com; internet www.statistikframjandet.se; f. 2008 by merger of Statistical Society and Swedish Statistician Community; promotes research, devt, education in statistics; provides a forum for its mems; Pres. BERNHARD HUITFELDT; Vice-Pres. SUNE KARLSSON; Sec. ANNA JOHANSSON.

Physical Sciences

Geologiska Föreningen (Geological Society of Sweden): c/o Dept of Geology and Geochemistry, Stockholm Univ., SE-106 91 Stockholm; tel. (8) 674-77-27; fax (8) 674-78-97; e-mail gff@geologiskaforeningen.nu; internet www.geologiskaforeningen.nu; f. 1871 as Geological Society in Stockholm; promotes geology and earth science; 600 mems; Chair. and Sec. Assoc. Prof. VIVI VAJDA (acting); Treas. KARI NIIRANEN; publs *Geologiskt forum* (in Swedish, 4 a year), *GFF* (in English, 4 a year).

Kungl. Örlogsmannasällskapet (Royal Swedish Society of Naval Sciences): Teatergatan 3, 5 tr, SE-111 48 Stockholm; tel. (8) 664-70-18; e-mail akademien@koms.se; internet www.koms.se; f. 1771, reorganised 1777; promote devts in naval sciences and maritime sciences; library of 15,000 vols, maps, charts, archival records; 400 mems; Pres. THOMAS ENGEVALL; Vice-Pres. Col PER JENVALD; Sec. Gen. BO RASK; publ. *Tidskrift i Sjöväsendet* (4 a year).

Svenska Fysikersamfundet (Swedish Physical Society): Dept of Physics and Astronomy, POB 516, SE-751 20 Uppsala; tel. (13) 28-12-03; fax (13) 13-22-85; e-mail kansliet@fysikersamfundet.se; internet www.fysikersamfundet.se; f. 1920; promotes physics research and applications; spreads knowledge about physics and physics education; stimulates public interest in physics and natural sciences in gen.; 800 mems; Chair. KARL-FREDRIK BERGGREN; Sec. Dr RAIMUND FEIFEL; Treas. LAGE HEDIN; publs *Fysikaktuellt* (4 a year), *Kosmos* (1 a year).

RELIGION, SOCIOLOGY AND ANTHROPOLOGY

Kungl. Gustav Adolfs Akademien för svensk folkkultur (Royal Gustavus Adolphus Academy for Swedish Folk Culture): Klostergatan 2, SE-753 21 Uppsala; tel. (18) 71-16-38; fax (18) 54-87-83; e-mail info@kgaa.nu; internet www.kgaa.nu; f. 1932; promotes research on Swedish folk culture; 220 mems (incl. honorary); Pres. Prof. LENNART ELMEVIK; Vice-Pres. Prof. BIRGITTA SKARIN FRYKMAN; Sec. Doc. MAJ REINHAMMAR; Treas. INGEMAR ANDERSÉN; publs *Acta Academiae Regiae Gustavi Adolphi*, *Arv. Nordic Yearbook of Folklore* (1 a year), *Ethnologia Scandinavica* (1 a year), *Namn och bygd* (1 a year), *Saga och Sed* (1 a year), *Studia Anthroponymica Scandinavica* (1 a year), *Svenska landsmål och svenskt folkliv* (1 a year).

TECHNOLOGY

Kungl. Ingenjörsvetenskapsakademien—IVA (Royal Swedish Academy of Engineering Sciences): POB 5073, SE-102 42 Stockholm; Grev Turegatan 16, SE-102 42 Stockholm; tel. (8) 791-29-00; fax (8) 611-56-23; e-mail info@iva.se; internet www.iva.se; f. 1919; promotes engineering and economic science; acts as a clearing house for scientific information; establishes contacts with foreign research orgs by means of lectures and confs, trade research orgs and research agreements with East European countries, China and the Republic of Korea; library of 10,000 vols; 1,000 Swedish and foreign mems; Pres. Prof. BJÖRN O. NILSSON; Chair. Prof. LENA TRESCHOW TORELL; Vice-Chair. CHARLOTTE BROGREN; Vice-Chair. Assoc. Prof. KARL-OLOF HAMMARKVIST; Vice-Chair. PETER GUDMUNDSON; Vice-Chair. Prof. STAFFAN JOSEPHSON; Sec. PER ÖDLING; publs *IVA-Aktuellt*, *Meddelanden*, *Rapporter*.

Svenska Geotekniska Föreningen (Swedish Geotechnical Society): c/o Swedish Geotechnical Institute, SE-581 93 Linköping; tel. (13) 20-18-00; fax (13) 20-19-09; e-mail info@sgf.net; internet www.sgf.net; f. 1950; soil mechanics, geotechnical engineering, environmental geotechnics; 900 individual mems, 25 corporate mems; Chair. STEFAN ARONSSON; Vice-Chair. ANDERS DAHLBERG; Sec. SARA BLOMBERG; Treas. MATTIAS GUSTAVSSON.

Sveriges Ingenjörer (Swedish Association of Graduate Engineers): POB 1419, SE-111 84 Stockholm; Malmskillnadsgatan 48, Stockholm; tel. (8) 613-80-00; fax (8) 796-71-02; e-mail info@sverigesingenjorer.se; internet www.sverigesingenjorer.se; f. 2007, merger of Civil Engineers and Professional Engineers; mem. of European Metalworker's Fed.; makes employing engineers easier for small and mid-size cos; ensures that engineers receive better salaries; 125,684 mems; Pres. ULF BENGTSSON; Man. Dir RICHARD MALMBORG; publs *Civilingenjören* (9 a year), *Ny Teknik-Teknisk Tidskrift* (52 a year).

Research Institutes

GENERAL

Entrepreneurship and Small Business Research Institute: Saltmätargatan 9, SE-113 59 Stockholm; tel. (8) 458-78-00; e-mail info@esbri.se; internet www.esbri.se; f. 1996; research on entrepreneurship and small and medium enterprises; founded award for entrepreneurship; Chair. ANDERS FLODSTRÖM; Man. Dir MAGNUS ARONSSON.

Forskningsrådet Formas (Swedish Research Council Formas): POB 1206, SE-111 82 Stockholm; Kungsbron 21, Stockholm; tel. (8) 775-40-00; fax (8) 775-40-10; e-mail registrator@formas.se; internet www.formas.se; f. 2001; govt research funding agency; encourages and supports research related to sustainable devt; programme areas: environment, agriculture (incl. horticulture, fisheries and reindeer husbandry), forestry and the natural environment, the built environment, urban and regional planning; Chair. LARS-ERIK LILJELUND; Dir-Gen. ROLF ANNERBERG; Sec.-Gen. Prof. ANNA LEDIN; publs *Miljöforskning* (6 a year, print and online), *Sustainability* (in English, 4 a year, online).

Life & Peace Institute: Sysslomansgatan 7, 1st Fl., SE-753 11 Uppsala; tel. (18) 16-95-00; fax (18) 69-30-59; e-mail info@life-peace.org; internet www.life-peace.org; f. 1985; deals with non-violent conflict transformation and research about role of religion in peace and conflict as well as traditional conflict resolution mechanisms; offices in

Congo, Kenya, Sudan, Sweden; Pres. GUSTAF ÖDQVIST; Exec. Dir PETER KARLSSON SJÖGREN; publ. *New Routes* (4 a year).

Stockholm International Water Institute: Drottninggatan 33, SE-111 51 Stockholm; tel. (8) 522-139-60; fax (8) 522-139-61; e-mail siwi@siwi.org; internet www.siwi.org; f. 1997; policy institute on world water crisis; organizes World Water Week; Exec. Dir ANDERS BERNTELL; Deputy Exec. Dir PER BERTILSSON.

Stockholm Resilience Centre: Stockholm Univ., Kräftriket 2B, SE-106 91 Stockholm; tel. (8) 674-70-70; fax (8) 674-70-20; e-mail info@stockholmresilience.su.se; internet www.stockholmresilience.org; f. 2007; transdisciplinary research of social-ecological systems; joint initiative between Stockholm Univ., Stockholm Environment Institute and the Beijer International Institute of Ecological Economics; Exec. Dir JOHAN ROCKSTRÖM; Science Dir CARL FOLKE.

Vetenskapsrådet (Swedish Research Council): POB 1035, SE-101 38 Stockholm; Klarabergsviadukten 82, Stockholm; tel. (8) 546-440-00; fax (8) 546-441-80; e-mail vr@vr.se; internet www.vr.se; f. 2001; attached to Dept of Education and Culture; provides support for basic research of highest academic quality within all areas of knowledge; assumed duties of fmr Swedish Ccl for Planning and Co-ordination of Research, Swedish Ccl for Research in the Humanities and Social Sciences, Swedish Medical Research Ccl, Swedish Natural Science Research Ccl, and Swedish Research Ccl for Engineering Sciences; cttees for Culture and the Social Sciences (First Sec. BENGT HANSSON), Medicine (First Sec. OLLE STENDAHL), Natural and Engineering Sciences (First Sec. KÅRE BREMER); Chair. LARS ANELL; Vice-Chair. BRITT-MARIE SJÖBERG; Dir-Gen. Prof. PÄR OMLING.

AGRICULTURE, FISHERIES AND VETERINARY SCIENCE

AgriFood Economics Centre: POB 730, Scheelevägen 15D, SE-220 07 Lund; e-mail info@agrifood.lu.se; internet www.agrifood.se; f. 2009; cooperative venture between Swedish Univ. of Agricultural Sciences (SLU) and Lund Univ.; economic analysis of food, agriculture, fishing and rural devt.

JTI–Institutet för jordbruks- och miljöteknik (JTI—Swedish Institute of Agricultural and Environmental Engineering): POB 7033, SE-750 07 Uppsala; tel. (10) 516-69-00; fax (18) 30-09-56; e-mail info@jti.se; internet www.jti.se; f. 1945, present status 2009; attached to SP Technical Research Institute of Sweden; focuses on research, devt and information in areas of agricultural engineering and environmental technology; Man. Dir KLAS HESSELMAN (acting); Sec. MARI ENGVALL; publ. *JTI Informerar* (8 a year).

Skogforsk (Forestry Research Institute of Sweden): Dag Hammarskjölds Väg 36A, Uppsala Science Park, SE-751 83 Uppsala; tel. (18) 18-85-00; fax (18) 18-86-00; e-mail skogforsk@skogforsk.se; internet www.skogforsk.se; central research body for the Swedish forestry sector; Exec. Dir. JAN FRYK; Deputy Dir. KAJ ROSÉN; publ. *Skogforsks Redogörelser* (6 a year).

Statens Veterinärmedicinska Anstalt (National Veterinary Institute): Ulls Väg 2B, SE-751 89 Uppsala; tel. (18) 67-40-00; fax (18) 30-91-62; e-mail sva@sva.se; internet www.sva.se; f. 1911; research, diagnostic work, consultative work concerning control and prophylaxis of animal diseases; nat. veterinary laboratory; org.: central laboratory, epizootiology unit, animal diseases specialists unit, admin.; library of 27,000 vols; Dir-Gen. ANDERS ENGVALL; Personnel. Dir HÅKAN PALLIN; Dir. for Planning STAFFAN ROS; Sec. GUNILLA LINDGREN; publ. *SVA Vet* (irregular).

Wallenberg Wood Science Centre: Teknikringen 56–58, KTH, Campus Valhallavägen, SE-100 44 Stockholm; tel. (8) 790-81-18; e-mail blund@kth.se; f. 2009; joint research centre at KTH and Chalmers; focus on new materials from trees; Dir LARS BERGLUND; Sec. EWA WAERN-MORATH.

ARCHITECTURE AND TOWN PLANNING

European Network for Housing Research: ENHR, Institute for Housing and Urban Research, Uppsala University, POB 785, SE-801 29 Gavle; tel. (26) 420-65-00; fax (26) 420-65-01; e-mail enhr@ibf.uu.se; internet www.enhr.ibf.uu.se; f. 1988; major int. conferences; 20 working groups; smaller conferences; active group of PhD students; Chair. PETER BOELHOUWER; Vice-Chair. IVÁN TOSICS.

Nordregio (Nordic Centre for Spatial Development): POB 1658, SE-111 86 Stockholm; Skeppsholmen, Holmamiralens väg 10, Stockholm; tel. (8) 463-54-00; fax (8) 463-54-01; e-mail nordregio@nordregio.se; internet www.nordregio.se; f. 1997, present status 2000; administered by Nordic Ccl of Mins; demography, global climate change and local adaptation, governance and gender, innovation and knowledge, int. energy policy, regional devt, urban and rural systems; Chair. KIRSTEN VINTERSBORG; Vice-Chair. SVERKER LINDBLAD; Dir OLE DAMSGAARD; publs *Journal of Nordregio* (4 a year), *European Journal of Spatial Development* (online at www.nordregio.se/ejsd).

ECONOMICS, LAW AND POLITICS

Beijerinstitutet för Ekologisk Ekonomi (Beijer Institute of Ecological Economics): Lilla Frescativägen 4A, POB 50005, SE-104 05 Stockholm; tel. (8) 673-95-00; fax (8) 15-24-64; e-mail beijer@beijer.kva.se; internet www.beijer.kva.se; f. 1977; attached to Royal Swedish Academy of Sciences; collaborative research between economists and ecologists and related disciplines; Dir CARL FOLKE; Deputy Dir ANNE-SOPHIE CRÉPIN; publs *Ecology and Society* (e-journals, 2 a year), *Environment and Development Economics* (e-journal).

Ekonomiska Forskningsinstitutet (Economic Research Institute): EFI, The Economic Research Institute at the Stockholm School of Economics, POB 6501, SE-113 83 Stockholm; tel. (8) 736-90-00; fax (8) 31-62-70; e-mail efi@hhs.se; internet www.hhs.se/efi; f. 1929; attached to Stockholm School of Economics; research in economics, business administration, finance and law; 20 centres; library of 150,000 vols, 15,000 e-journals, 60 databases; Dir FILIP WIJKSTRÖM; Chair. CARIN HOLMQUIST; publ. *Forskning i Fickformat* (4 a year).

Entrepreneurship and Small Business Research Institute: Saltmätargatan 9, SE-113 59 Stockholm; tel. (8) 458-78-00; e-mail info@esbri.se; internet www.esbri.se; f. 1996; research on entrepreneurship and small and medium enterprises; founded award for entrepreneurship; Chair. ANDERS FLODSTRÖM; Man. Dir MAGNUS ARONSSON.

Humanistisk-samhällsvetenskapliga (Swedish Council for Humanities and Social Sciences): POB 7120, SE-103 78 Stockholm; tel. (8) 454-43-10; fax (8) 454-43-20; f. 1977; 11 mems; Chair. Dr JANE CEDERQVIST; Sec.-Gen. Prof. ANDERS JEFFNER; Dir BJÖRN THOMASSON.

Institute for International Economic Studies: A-building, 8th Fl., Södra Huset, Univ. of Stockholm, SE-104 05 Stockholm; tel. (8) 16-20-00; fax (8) 16-14-43; internet www.iies.su.se; Dir HARRY FLAM; Deputy Dir JAKOB SVENSSON; publ. *The Review of Economic Studies* (4 a year).

Institute for Security and Development Policy: Västra Finnbodavägen 2, SE-131 30 Nacka; tel. (8) 410-569-60; fax (8) 640-33-70; e-mail info@isdp.eu; internet www.isdp.eu; f. 2007; research on int. conflict, security and devt; especially Eurasia; Dir SVANTE CORNELL; Deputy Dir JOHANNA POPJANEVSKI; publ. *The Central Asia-Caucasus Analyst* (web journal); publs *The China and Eurasia Forum Quarterly* (4 a year), *The Turkey Analyst* (52 a week).

Institutet för Näringslivsforskning (Research Institute of Industrial Economics): POB 55665, SE-102 15 Stockholm; Grevgatan 34, 2nd Fl., SE-102 15 Stockholm; tel. (8) 665-45-00; fax (8) 665-45-99; e-mail info@ifn.se; internet www.ifn.se; f. 1939 as Research Institute of Industries, present name 2006; conducts research on economic and social issues with relevance for industrial devt; 23 research fellows; Chair. Dr BJÖRN HÄGGLUND; Dir Prof. MAGNUS HENREKSON; Deputy Dir Assoc. Prof. LARS PERSSON; publ. *Årsbok* (yearbook).

Latinamerika-institutet i Stockholm (Institute of Latin American Studies, University of Stockholm): Universitetsvägen 10B, SE-106 91 Stockholm; tel. (8) 16-34-36; fax (8) 15-85-78; e-mail secretaria@isp.su.se; internet www.lai.su.se; f. 1951, present name and status 1969; research on Latin American economic, social and political development; information, seminars, courses; library of 40,000 vols; Dir Prof. MONA ROSENDAHL; Librarian MARGARETA BJÖRLING; publ. *Ibero-Americana: Nordic Journal of Latin American Studies*.

Nordiska Afrikainstitutet (Nordic Africa Institute): POB 1703, SE-751 47 Uppsala; Kungsgatan 38, Uppsala; tel. (18) 56-22-00; fax (18) 56-22-90; e-mail nai@nai.uu.se; internet www.nai.uu.se; f. 1962; documentation, information and research centre for current African affairs; publ. work, lectures and seminars; library of 68,000 vols, 230 electronic books, 450 print periodicals, 127 online databases (incl. electronic periodicals); Dir CARIN NORBERG; Chief Librarian ÅSA LUND MOBERG; publs *Africa Now*, *Current African Issues*, *Discussion Paper*, *Policy Dialogue*, *Policy Notes*.

Raoul Wallenberg Institute of Human Rights and Humanitarian Law: Stora Gråbrödersg. 17B, POB 1155, SE-221 05 Lund; tel. (46) 222-12-00; fax (46) 222-12-22; e-mail marie.tuma@rwi.lu.se; internet www.rwi.lu.se; f. 1984; independent academic instn. for human rights promotion through research, training and education; Dir MARIE TUMA; publs *Baltic Yearbook of International Law*, *Chinese Yearbook of Human Rights*, *International Journal on Minority and Group Rights* (4 a year), *Nordic Journal of International Law* (4 a year).

Ratio Institute: Sveavägen 59, 4 tr., POB 3203, SE-103 64 Stockholm; tel. (8) 441-59-00; e-mail info@ratio.se; internet www.ratio.se; f. 2002; researches enterprise and entrepreneurship; conducts research-seminar series; Pres. NILS KARLSON; Vice-Pres. NICLAS BERGGREN.

Statistiska Centralbyrån (Statistics Sweden): POB 24300, SE-104 51 Stockholm; Karlavägen 100, Stockholm; tel. (8) 506-940-00; fax (8) 661-52-61; e-mail scb@scb.se; internet www.scb.se; f. 1858; supplies customers (govt and private sector) with statistics for decision making, debate and research; br. in Örerbo; library: see Libraries and Archives; Dir.-Gen. STEFAN LUNDGREN; publs *Företag—Tidning för Uppgiftslämnare* (1 a year), *Journal of Official Statistics*, *SCB—Kundtidning* (4 a year), *Statistical Abstract of Sweden*, *Statistical Reports*, *Statistical Yearbook of Sweden*, *Survey of Living Conditions*.

Stiftelsen Företagsadministrativ Forskning (Scandinavian Institutes for Administrative Research): c/o Edqvist, Sigtunagatan 5, SE-113 22 Stockholm; tel. (70) 94-44-74; e-mail j.edqvist@gmail.com; internet www.siar.a.se; f. 1966; provides financial support for research in business administration and business economics; Dir CHRISTIAN JUNNELIUS; Sec. JOHAN EDQVIST.

Stockholm Institute for Scandinavian Law: Stockholm Institute for Scandinavian Law, Faculty of Law, University of Stockholm, SE-106 91 Stockholm; tel. (8) 16-25-48; fax (8) 612-90-72; e-mail sisl@juridicum.su.se; internet www.scandinavianlaw.se; f. 1956; attached to Faculty of Law, Stockholm Univ.; spreads knowledge about Scandinavian law and jurisprudence abroad.

Stockholm Institute of Transitional Economics: Sveavägen 65, 9th Fl., A, POB 6501, SE-113 83 Stockholm; tel. (8) 736-96-70; fax (8) 31-64-22; e-mail site@hhs.se; internet www.hhs.se/site; f. 1989; attached to Stockholm School of Economics; research and policy centre on transition in former USSR and Eastern Europe; Chair. MICHAEL SOHLMAN; Dir TORBJÖRN BECKER.

Stockholm International Peace Research Institute: Signalistgatan 9, SE-169 70 Solna; tel. (8) 655-97-00; fax (8) 655-97-33; e-mail cloo@sipri.org; internet www.sipri.org; f. 1966; research in conflict, armaments, arms control and disarmament; library of 50,000 vols; 600 journals; Chair. GÖRAN LENNMARKER; Dir BATES GILL; publ. *SIPRI Yearbook*.

Swedish Collegium for Advanced Study (SCAS): Linneanum, Thunbergsvägen 2, SE-752 38 Uppsala; tel. (18) 55-70-85; fax (18) 52-11-09; e-mail info@swedishcollegium.se; internet www.swedishcollegium.se; f. 1985; offers 14 fellowships for study at the Collegium each semester; Chair. Prof. LARS MAGNUSSON; Prin. Prof. BJÖRN WITTROCK.

LANGUAGE AND LITERATURE

Institutet för Språk och Folkminnen (Institute for Language and Folklore): POB 135, SE-751 04 Uppsala; von Kraemers allé 2, Arkivcentrum, Uppsala; tel. (18) 65-21-60; fax (18) 65-21-65; internet www.sofi.se; f. 2006; collects, preserves and researches on dialects, place names, personal names and folklore; works on language planning and language policy; Gen.-Dir INGRID JOHANSSON LIND.

MEDICINE

Livsmedelsverket (National Food Administration): POB 622, SE-751 26 Uppsala; Hamnesplanaden 5, Uppsala; tel. (18) 17-55-00; fax (18) 10-58-48; e-mail livsmedelsverket@slv.se; internet www.slv.se; f. 1972; attached to Min. of Agriculture, Food and Fisheries; central admin. agency in Sweden for foodstuffs and handling of foodstuffs in accordance with the Food Act; library of 11,000 vols; Dir-Gen. INGER ANDERSSON; Deputy Dir-Gen. JAN MOVITZ; publs *Livsmedelsverkets författningar* (The National Food Administration's Regulations), *Livstecknet* (Newsletter), *Vår Föda* (popular scientific).

Ludwig Institute for Cancer Research Ltd: Biomedical Centre, Husargatan 3, Entrance C11, 3rd Fl., POB 595, SE-751 24 Uppsala; tel. (18) 16-04-00; fax (18) 16-04-20; e-mail ludwig@licr.uu.se; internet www.licr.uu.se; f. 1986; non-profit research org. for cancer control; 10 research centres worldwide; in Sweden in Stockholm (Karolinska Institutet) and Uppsala; Dir CARL-HENRIK HELDIN; Sec. INGEGÄRD SCHILLER.

Molecular Infection Medicine Sweden: Laboratory for Molecular Infection Medicine Sweden, University of Umeå, SE-901 87 Umeå; tel. (90) 785-67-60; fax (90) 786-66-76; e-mail eva-maria.diehl@mims.umu.se; internet www.mims.umu.se; f. 2007; Swedish node of the Nordic EMBL Partnership for Molecular Medicine; joint venture between the European Molecular Biology Laboratory (EMBL) and the Univ. of Helsinki, Finland, Univ. of Oslo, Norway and Univ. of Umeå, Sweden; Dir BERNT ERIC UHLIN; Sec. ÅKE FORSBERG.

Statens Folkhälsoinstitut (Swedish National Institute of Public Health): Forskarens väg 3, SE-831 40 Östersund; tel. (63) 19-96-00; fax (63) 19-96-02; e-mail info@fhi.se; internet www.fhi.se; state agency under the Ministry of Health and Social Affairs; Dir Gen. Dr SARAH WAMALA.

Stockholm Brain Institute: Karolinska Institutet, SE-171 77 Stockholm; tel. (8) 517-77-341; e-mail none-marie.kemp@ki.se; internet www.stockholmbrain.se; research on neuroscience; consortium of Karolinska Institutet, Royal Institute of Technology and Stockholm University; Dir HANS FORSSBERG; Sec. NONE-MARIE KEMP.

Structural Genomics Consortium, Karolinska Institutet: Karolinska Institutet MBB/SGC, SE-171 77 Stockholm; e-mail sgcinfo@mbb.ki.se; internet sgc.ki.se; f. 2005; non-profit org. to determine the 3D structure of proteins and place them in public domain; operates out of the Univ. of Oxford, Univ. of Toronto and Karolinska Institutet; Dir. Dr JOHAN WEIGELT.

NATURAL SCIENCES

General

Abisko naturvetenskapliga station (Abisko Scientific Research Station): SE-981 07 Abisko; tel. (980) 400-21; fax (980) 401-71; e-mail ans@ans.kiruna.se; internet www.linnea.com/~ans; f. 1903, present status 1935; attached to Royal Swedish Acad. of Sciences; researches mainly on sub-arctic biology and earth sciences; hosts the Climate Impacts Research Centre (CIRC); Dir Prof. TERENCE V. CALLAGHAN; Deputy Dir CHRISTER JONASSON.

Stockholm Environment Institute: Kräftriket 2B, SE-106 91 Stockholm; tel. (8) 674-70-70; e-mail info@sei-international.org; internet sei-international.org; f. 1989; governed by an international Board; policy-related research on international environmental technology and management issues, incl. acidic deposition co-ordinated abatement strategies, climatic change assessment, energy futures, economics and environmental value, water, sanitation and integrated waste-management, urban environment, common property, energy and development, biotechnology, risk assessment, atmospheric environment, cleaner production, sustainable devt planning and computer tools for integrated management risk and vulnerability; centres in Stockholm, Tallinn (Estonia), Dar Es Salaam (Tanzania), Bangkok (Thailand), York (UK), Oxford (UK), and Boston (USA); Chair. KERSTIN NIBLAEUS; Exec. Dir Adjunct Prof. JOHAN ROCKSTRÖM; publ. *Renewable Energy for Development* (4 a year).

Sven Lovén Centrum för Marina Vetenskaper (Sven Lovén Centre for Marine Sciences): Kristineberg 566, SE-450 34 Fiskebäckskil; tel. (523) 185-00; fax (523) 185-02; e-mail katarina.abrahamsson@loven.gu.se; internet www.loven.gu.se; f. 1877 as Kristineberg Marine Research Station, present name and status 2008; attached to Gothenburg Univ.; marine ecology, taxonomic, systematics and biodiversity, morphological, molecular and physiological research on marine animals and plants; laboratory at Tjärnö; Dir KATARINA ABRAHAMSSON.

Biological Sciences

Bergianska stiftelsen (Bergius Foundation): POB 50017, SE-104 05 Stockholm; tel. (8) 545-917-00; fax (8) 612-90-05; e-mail birgitta.bremer@bergianska.se; internet www.bergianska.se/forskning.php; f. 1791; attached to Royal Swedish Acad. of Sciences; botanical and horticultural research; biodiversity projects: Rubiaceae, Rosaleae; Dir Prof. Bergianus BIRGITTA BREMER.

IVL Svenska Miljöinstitutet (IVL Swedish Environmental Research Institute): POB 210 60, SE-100 31 Stockholm; tel. (8) 598-563-00; fax (8) 598-563-90; e-mail info@ivl.se; internet www.ivl.se; f. 1966; Chair. ANNIKA LUNDSTRÖM; Pres. TORD SVEDBERG.

Science for Life Laboratory: Karolinska Institutet Science Park, Tomtebodavägen 23A, SE-171 65 Solna; tel. (70) 326-29-11; fax (85) 248-14-25; e-mail fredrik.sterky@scilifelab.se; internet www.scilifelab.se; national resource centre; research in molecular biosciences and medicine; org. divided into SciLifeLab Stockholm and SciLifeLab Uppsala; SciLifeLab Stockholm between three univs: KTH, KI, SU; SciLifeLab Uppsala organized by Uppsala University; Dir (Stockholm) FREDRIK STERKY.

Mathematical Sciences

Institut Mittag-Leffler (Mittag-Leffler Institute): Auravägen 17, SE-182 60 Djursholm; tel. (8) 622-05-60; fax (8) 622-05-89; e-mail info@mittag-leffler.se; internet www.mittag-leffler.se; f. 1916, present status 1919; attached to Royal Swedish Acad. of Sciences; research and postdoctoral training in mathematical sciences; library of 60,000 vols; Chair. JAN-ERIK ROOS; Vice-Chair. BJÖRN JAHREN; Dir Prof. ANDERS BJÖRNER; Deputy Dir Prof. MIKAEL PASSARE; publs *Acta Mathematica* (4 a year), *Arkiv för matematik* (2 a year).

Physical Sciences

Institutet för rymdfysik (Swedish Institute of Space Physics): POB 812, SE-981 28 Kiruna; Rymdcampus 1, SE-981 92 Kiruna; tel. (980) 790-00; fax (980) 790-50; e-mail irf@irf.se; internet www.irf.se; f. 1957 as Kiruna Geophysical Observatory, present status 1973, present name 1987; research, education and associated observatory activities in space physics, space technology and atmospheric physics; library of 7,000 books, 200 journals; Dir Dr LARS ELIASSON; publs *IRF Scientific Report*, *Kiruna Geophysical Data* (4 a year).

Kungl. Vetenskapsakademiens Institut för Solfysik (Institute for Solar Physics of the Royal Swedish Academy of Sciences): AlbaNova Univ. Centre, Roslagstullsbacken 21 SE-106 91 Stockholm; tel. (8) 16-20-00; fax (8) 553-785-20; e-mail scharmer@astro.su.se;

internet www.solarphysics.kva.se; f. 1951 as Research Station for Astrophysics in Italy, reorganized 1978; attached to Royal Swedish Acad. of Sciences; associated with Stockholm Univ.; solar research; operates Swedish 1-m Solar Telescope (SST) at La Palma; Dir Prof. GÖRAN SCHARMER.

Manne Siegbahnlaboratoriet (MSL) (Manne Siegbahn Laboratory (MSL)): Frescativägen 26, SE-114 18 Stockholm; tel. (8) 16-20-00; fax (8) 16-11-12; internet www.msi.se; f. 1937 as Nobel Institute of Physics, present name 1993, present status 2004; attached to Stockholm Univ.; research in atomic, molecular and surface physics; low-energy ion accelerators (ion sources), accelerator-storage ring for highly charged ions; computer, electronics, and mechanical workshop divs; library of 10,000 vols; Dir SVEN MANNERVIK; Deputy Dir ANDERS KÄLLBERG.

Nordiska Institutet för Teoretisk Fysik (Nordic Institute for Theoretical Physics): Nordita, AlbaNova Univ. Centre, Roslagstullsbacken 23, SE-106 91 Stockholm; tel. (8) 553-784-36; fax (8) 553-784-04; e-mail info@nordita.org; internet www.nordita.org; f. 1957; run by Royal Institute of Technology and Stockholm University; has centres in all Nordic countries; main research in astrophysics and astrobiology, condensed matter, statistical and biological physics, high energy and nuclear physics; Dir LÁRUS THORLACIUS; Deputy Dir AXEL BRANDENBURG.

Stockholms Observatorium (Stockholm Observatory): SE-106 91 Stockholm; tel. (8) 553-785-01; fax (8) 553-785-10; internet www.astro.su.se; f. 1753; attached to Institutionen för Astronomi, Stockholms Univ.; Dir Prof. GÖRAN ÖSTLIN.

Sveriges Geologiska Undersökning (Geological Survey of Sweden): POB 670, SE-751 28 Uppsala; Villavägen 18, Uppsala; tel. (18) 17-90-00; fax (18) 17-92-10; e-mail sgu@sgu.se; internet www.sgu.se; f. 1858; attached to Min. of Enterprise, Energy and Communications; nat. authority responsible for matters relating to Sweden's geological characteristics and mineral resources management; library of 100,000 vols; Dir.-Gen. JAN MAGNUSSON.

Swedish Meteorological and Hydrological Institute: Folkborgsvägen 1, SE-601 76 Norrköping; tel. (11) 495-80-00; fax (11) 495-80-01; e-mail smhi@smhi.se; internet www.smhi.se; under Min. of Environment; manages and develops information on weather, water and climate; Dir Gen. LENA HÄLL ERIKSSON; Deputy Dir Gen. TORD KVICK.

RELIGION, SOCIOLOGY AND ANTHROPOLOGY

Institutet för Social Forskning (Swedish Institute for Social Research): Universitetsvägen 10F, University of Stockholm, SE-106 91 Stockholm; tel. (8) 16-20-00; fax (8) 15-46-70; internet www.sofi.su.se; f. 1972; attached to Stockholm Univ.; research on social policy, welfare, inequality and labour market; Chair. KÅRE BREMER; Dir ANDERS BJÖRKLUND.

Institute of International Sociology: c/o The Swedish Collegium for Advanced Study, Linneanum, Thunbergsvägen 2, SE-752 38 Uppsala; tel. (18) 55-70-85; fax (18) 52-11-09; e-mail info@iisoc.org; internet www.iisoc.org; f. 1893; oldest continuous sociological asscn; organizes world congress in sociology; Pres. BJÖRN WITTROCK; Sec. Gen. PETER HEDSTRÖM; publs *Annals of the International Institute of Sociology*, *International Review of Sociology* (3 a year; oldest sociology journal).

TECHNOLOGY

CBI Betonginstitutet AB (Swedish Cement and Concrete Research Institute): SE-100 44 Stockholm; Drottning Kristinas väg 26, SE-114 28 Stockholm; tel. (10) 516-68-00; fax (8) 24-31-37; e-mail cbi@cbi.se; internet www.cbi.se; f. 1942, present status 2008; conducts research into and acts as a consultancy for engineering materials based on cement and concrete and allied materials; library of 10,000 vols; Dir Prof. JOHAN SILFWERBRAND; Chair. INGVAR BÖRTEMARK; Deputy Chair. PER-ERIK PETERSSON; Librarian TUULA OJALA; publs *CBI-nytt* (2 a year), *CBI rapporter / report*.

FOI Totalförsvarets Forskningsinstitut (FOI Swedish Defence Research Agency): SE-164 90 Stockholm; Gullfossgatan 6, Stockholm; tel. (8) 555-030-00; fax (8) 555-031-00; e-mail registrator@foi.se; internet www.foi.se; f. 2001; attached to Min. of Defence; conducts research into security-policy studies and analyses of defence and security; systems for control and management of crises; protection against and management of hazardous substances, IT security; brs in Grindsjön, Linköping, Umeå; Chair. SÖREN MELLSTIG; Dir-Gen. JAN-OLOF LIND.

Glafo (Swedish Glass Research Institute): Vejdes Plats 3, SE-352 52 Växjö; tel. (10) 516-63-50; e-mail info@glafo.se; internet www.glafo.se; attached to Technical Research Institute of Sweden; conducts research for the glass industry; Man. Dir MARIANNE GRAUERS.

Mobile Life Centre: Electrum Bldg, 6th Fl., Kistagången 16/Isafjordsgatan 22, SE-164 26 Kista; tel. (703) 79-39-64; e-mail oskar@mobilelifecentre.org; internet www.mobilelifecentre.org; research in mobile services and ubiquitous computing; Chair. MARTIN KÖRLING; Dir OSKAR JUHLIN.

SIK—Institutet för Livsmedel och Bioteknik AB (SIK—Swedish Institute for Food and Biotechnology): POB 5401, SE-402 29 Gothenburg; Frans Perssons väg 6, Delsjömotet; tel. (10) 516-66-00; fax (31) 83-37-82; e-mail webmaster@sik.se; internet www.sik.se; f. 1946; research and devt, documentation and education on production, preservation, food safety, biotechnology, structure and rheology, packaging, information and marketing; library of 7,000 vols; Chair. CHRISTER ÅBERG; Pres. KLAS HESSELMAN; Vice-Pres. HANS LINGNERT; Sec. TINA PETERSSON; publs *SIK-Dokument*, *SIK-Infood* (in English), *SIK-Publikation*, *SIK-Rapport*.

SP Sveriges Tekniska Forskningsinstitut (SP Technical Research Institute of Sweden): POB 857, SE-501 15 Borås; Brinellgatan 4, SE-504 62 Borås; tel. (10) 516-50-00; fax (33) 13-55-02; e-mail info@sp.se; internet www.sp.se; f. 1920, fmrly Testing Institute of the Royal Institute of Technology (f. 1896); focuses on calibration, testing, inspection and certification of products and management systems; undertakes applied research and services in technical evaluation, measurement methods, research and devt; library of 17,000 vols; CEO MARIA KHORSAND.

Stålbyggnadinstitutet (Swedish Institute of Steel Construction): Vasagatan 52, 4th Fl., SE-111 20 Stockholm; tel. (8) 661-02-80; fax (8) 24-54-64; e-mail info@sbi.se; internet www.sbi.se; f. 1967; steel construction research; organizes annual steel construction conference; instituted steel industry award; Chair. JOHAN ANDERSSON; publ. *Stålbyggnad* (4 a year).

Statens Geotekniska Institut (Swedish Geotechnical Institute): Olaus Magnus Väg 35, SE-581 93 Linköping; tel. (13) 20-18-00; fax (13) 20-19-14; e-mail info@swedgeo.se; internet www.swedgeo.se; f. 1944; govt agency responsible for safety issues relating to landslides and coastal erosion; research, information and consulting work in soil mechanics and foundation engineering, environment and energy geotechnology; computerized library retrieval system; brs in Borlänge, Gothenburg, Malmö, Stockholm, Sundsvall; library of 100,000 bibliographic records, 10,000 books, 1,600 journals; Dir-Gen. BIRGITTA BOSTRÖM; Deputy Dir ELVIN OTTOSSON; Sec. KERSTIN CARLSSON; publs *SGI Information*, *SGI Report*, *SGI Varia*.

Innventia AB: POB 5604, SE-114 86 Stockholm; Drottning Kristinas väg 61, Stockholm; tel. (8) 676-70-00; fax (8) 411-55-18; e-mail info@innventia.com; internet www.innventia.com; f. 1942 as STFI-Packforsk, present name 2009; research into pulp, paper, graphic media, packaging and logistics; activities range from basic research to projects into packaging, graphic media and environmentally friendly energy and chemicals; library of 15,000 vols, 500 periodicals; Chair. MATS NORDLANDER; Pres. BIRGITTA SUNDBLAD; Exec. Vice-Pres. ANDERS ENGSTRÖM; publ. *Beyond* (4 a year).

Swedish ICT: Electrum 233, Isafjordsgatan 22/Kistagången 16, SE-164 40 Kista; tel. (8) 632-78-90; e-mail info@swedish-ict.se; internet www.swedish-ict.se; research and devt on information, communication, technology; group of instns includes Acreo, SICS, Interactive Institute, Imego, Viktoria Institute, Santa Anna IT Research Institute; Chair. ULF WAHLBERG; CEO HANS HENTZELL.

Swerea IVF AB: POB 104, SE-431 22 Mölndal; Argongatan 30, SE-431 53 Mölndal; tel. (31) 706-60-00; fax (31) 27-61-30; e-mail ivf@swerea.se; internet www.swerea.se/ivf; attached to Swerea Group; production engineering, materials applications, textiles, polymers, ceramics; CEO MATS LUNDIN; Sec. INGRID CHRISTOFFERSON; publ. *Teknik & Tillväxt* (Technology & Growth, 6 a year).

Swerea KIMAB AB (Swerea Corrosion and Metals Research Institute AB): POB 55970, SE-102 16 Stockholm; Drottning Kristinas väg 48, SE-114 28 Stockholm; tel. (8) 440-48-00; fax (8) 440-45-35; e-mail kimab@swerea.se; internet www.swereakimab.se; f. 1921, present status 2005; attached to Swerea Group; develops, improves solutions for materials research; areas of research incl.: application of instrumental methods for chemical analysis, welding, brazing and soldering; hot working, cold forming and microscopy; the relationship between microstructure and properties; solidification processes and their industrial applications; continuous casting; powder metallurgy; corrosion problems in connection with microstructure with a special interest in stainless steels; library of 2,000 books, 50 periodicals; Chair. TOMAS THORVALDSSON; Man. Dir STAFFAN SÖDERBERG; Deputy Man. Dir ARNE MELANDER; Librarian ANDERS MÅRTENSON.

Swerea MEFOS: POB 812, SE-971 25 Luleå; tel. (920) 20-19-00; fax (920) 25-58-32; e-mail mefos@swerea.se; internet www.swereamefos.se; research in process metallurgy, heating, metalworking and energy technology; Man. Dir GÖRAN CARLSSON.

Swerea SICOMP: POB 271, SE-941 26 Piteå; tel. (911) 744-01; fax (911) 744-99; e-mail hans.hansson@swerea.se; internet www.swerea.se/sicomp; research in polymer fibre composites; Man. Dir HANS HANSSON.

Swerea SWECAST: POB 2033, SE-553 22 Jönköping; tel. (36) 30-12-00; fax (36) 16-68-66; e-mail swecast@swerea.se; internet www.swerea.se/swecast; research in cast metals; CEO MATS HOLMGREN.

Ytkemiska Institutet (Institute for Surface Chemistry): Drottning Kristinas Väg 45, POB 5607, SE-114 86 Stockholm; tel. (10) 516-60-00; fax (8) 20-89-98; e-mail info@yki.se; internet www.yki.se; research in applied surface and colloid chemistry; located on campus of Royal Institute of Technology; library of 5,100 vols; Chair. PER LINDBERG; Sec. PETER ALBERIUS.

Libraries and Archives

Alvesta

Alvesta Bibliotek (Alvesta Library): Allbogatan 17, SE-342 80 Alvesta; tel. (472) 152-69; fax (472) 152-70; e-mail biblioteket@alvesta.se; internet www.alvesta.se; 4 br. libraries, 1 mobile library; Chief Librarian ANN-KATRIN URSBERG.

Borås

Bibliotek & läranderesurser, Högskolan i Borås (University of Borås Library & Learning Resources): SE-501 90 Borås; Järnvägsgatan 1, Borås; tel. (33) 435-40-50; fax (33) 435-40-04; e-mail biblioteket@hb.se; f. 1972; 158,000 vols, 38,000 e-books, 9,000 e-journals; Dir CATTA TORHELL.

Borås stadsbibliotek (Borås City Library): POB 856, SE-501 15 Borås; Västerbrogatan 8, Borås; tel. (33) 35-76-20; fax (33) 35-76-75; e-mail boras.stadsbibliotek@boras.se; internet www.boras.se/kultur/stadsbiblioteket; f. 1931, present location 1974; 300,000 vols; Chief Librarian BRITT-INGER LINDQVIST.

Eskilstuna

Eskilstuna stads- och länsbibliotek (Eskilstuna Municipal and County Library): Kriebsensgatan 4, SE-632 20 Eskilstuna; tel. (16) 710-51-10; fax (16) 13-29-49; internet eskilstuna.se/default2____152775.aspx; f. 1925; 550,000 vols; 3 brs in Lagersberg, Torshälla and Årby; Head BARBARA ÅHLIN; Head KARIN ZETTERBERG.

Gävle

Gävle stadsbibliotek (Gävle City Library): POB 801, SE-801 30 Gävle; Slottstorget 1, Gävle; tel. (26) 17-96-00; fax (26) 61-06-78; e-mail info@gavlebibliotek.nu; f. 1907; 700,000 vols; Dir of Libraries LISBETH FORSLUND.

Gothenburg

Chalmers Bibliotek (Chalmers Library): Chalmers Tvärgata 1, SE-412 96 Gothenburg; tel. (31) 772-37-37; fax (31) 18-35-44; e-mail request.lib@chalmers.se; internet www.lib.chalmers.se; f. 1829; attached to Chalmers Univ. of Technology; 530,000 vols, 620 journals, 7,200 electronic journals; Chair. STEFAN BENGTSSON; Dir ANNIKA SVERRUNG; Asst Dir ANNELIE JANRED.

Attached Libraries:

Arkitekturbiblioteket: Sven Hultins gata 6, SE-412 96 Gothenburg; tel. (31) 772-24-13; fax (31) 772-24-19; e-mail arch.lib@chalmers.se; Head Librarian ELISABETH KIHLÉN.

Lindholmenbiblioteket: Forskningsgången 6, SE-412 96 Gothenburg; tel. (31) 772-57-84; fax (31) 772-57-82.

Göteborgs stadsbibliotek (Gothenburg City Library): Götaplatsen, POB 5404, SE-402 29 Gothenburg; tel. (31) 368-33-00; fax (31) 368-35-98; e-mail info.stadsbiblioteket@kultur.goteborg.se; f. 1861; 405,807 vols, incl. 2,90,000 books; Chief Librarian CHRISTINA PERSSON.

Göteborgs universitetsbibliotek (Gothenburg University Library): POB 222, SE-405 30 Gothenburg; Renströmsgatan 4, Gothenburg; tel. (31) 786-17-49; fax (31) 786-44-11; e-mail universitetsbiblioteket@ub.gu.se; internet www.ub.gu.se; f. 1861; 2.7m. vols, 5,070 journals, 15,960 e-journals; legal deposit library for Swedish publs; spec. collns incl. MSS colln, women's history colln, Snoilsky colln (early Swedish literature), sound and video archives; Dir AGNETA OLSSON; publ. *Acta*.

Halmstad

Halmstads Stadsbibliotek (Halmstad City Library): POB 4083, SE-300 04 Halmstad; Axel Olsons Gata 1, SE-302 27 Halmstad; tel. (35) 13-71-81; fax (35) 13-71-82; e-mail stadsbiblioteket@halmstad.se; f. 2006; public library; 209,000 vols; Chief Librarian ANETTE HAGBERG; Librarian BENEDICTE SÖDERGREN.

Jönköping

Högskolebiblioteket i Jönköping: Högskoleområdet, House C, Gjuterigatan 5, SE-553 16 Jönköping; tel. (36) 10-10-10; fax (36) 10-03-59; internet hj.se/bibl; f. 1914; attached to Jönköping University; 200,000 books, 60,000 e-books, 15,000 journals; Library Dir ANNIKA SWEDÉN.

Stadsbibliotek Jönköpings (Jönköping city library): POB 1029, SE-551 11 Jönköping; Dag Hammarskjölds plats 1, Jönköping; tel. (36) 10-55-75; fax (36) 10-70-44; e-mail stadsbibl@jonkoping.se; internet lingonline.jonkoping.se; f. 1916; 600,000 vols (incl. 700 newspapers and magazines, CDs, DVDs, audio books); Head ULF MOBERG.

Kalmar

Kalmar Stadsbibliotek (Kalmar City Library): Huvudbiblioteket, POB 610, SE-391 26 Kalmar; Tullslätten 4, Kalmar; tel. (480) 45-06-30; fax (480) 45-06-32; e-mail stadsbiblioteket@kalmar.se; f. 1922; 510,000 vols, 300 Swedish periodicals, 25 journals; Chief Librarian SUZANNE HAMMARGREN.

Linnéuniversitetets Biblioteket (Linnaeus University Library): SE-391 82 Kalmar; Nygatan 18A Kalmar; tel. (480) 44-61-00; fax (480) 44-61-15; e-mail kalmar.ub@lnu.se SE-351 95 Växjö; Universitetsplatsen 2, Växjö; tel. (470) 70-84-00; fax (470) 845-23; e-mail vaxjo.ub@lnu.se; internet lnu.se/ub; 360,000 vols; Library Dir (vacant); Deputy Library Dir ANDERS RYDQVIST.

Karlskrona

Blekinge Tekniska Högskola Library (Blekinge Institute of Technology Library): Library Gräsvik, SE-371 79 Karlskrona; Library Gräsvik, Vallhallavägen 1, Karlskrona; tel. (455) 38-51-01; fax (455) 38-51-07; e-mail biblioteket@bth.se Library Piren, SE-374 24 Karlshamn; Biblioteksgatan 4, Karlshamn; tel. (455) 38-51-28; fax (454) 191-04; e-mail piren@bth.se; internet www.bth.se/bib; 2 units: Library Gräsvik, Karlskrona; Library Piren, Karlshamn; incls. learning lab and educational devt; Dir ANNIKA ANNEMARK.

Köpings

Köpings Stadsbibliotek (Köpings City Library): Folkets Hus, SE-731 41 Köpings; tel. (221) 251-82; fax (221) 251-98; e-mail stadsbiblioteket@koping.se; internet www.koping.se; Chief Librarian INGER FELLDIN.

Kristianstad

Högskolan Kristianstad Biblioteket (Kristianstad University College Library): SE-291 39 Kristianstad; Elmetorpsvägen 15, House 7, Kristianstad; tel. (44) 20-30-59; fax (44) 20-30-53; e-mail biblioteket@hkr.se; internet www.hkr.se; Head CHRISTINA JÖNSSON ADRIAL.

Linköping

Linköpings Stadsbibliotek (Linköping City Library): POB 1984, SE-581 19 Linköping; Östgötagatan 5, Linköping; tel. (13) 20-66-00; fax (13) 20-66-50; e-mail stadsbiblioteket@linkoping.se; f. 1926; 666,000 vols; Chief Librarian LINDA FAGERLUND.

Linköpings Universitetsbibliotek (Linköping University Library): SE-581 83 Linköping; tel. (13) 28-19-10; fax (13) 28-44-24; e-mail hb@bibl.liu.se; internet www.bibl.liu.se; f. 1969; 5 campus libraries; 400,000 books, 2,000 journals, 10,000 e-journals; Dir MARIANNE HÄLLGREN; Asst Dir HELENA WEDBORN; publ. *Publikation*.

Luleå

Luleå Stadsbiblioteket (Luleå City Library): Skeppsbrogatan 17, SE-971 79 Luleå; tel. (920) 45-59-51; e-mail biblioteket@kulturen.lulea.se; Chief Librarian LENA LUNDBERG VESTERLUND.

Luleå Universitetsbibliotek (Luleå University library): SE-971 87 Luleå; Betahouse, Univ. campus, Porsön, Luleå; tel. (920) 49-15-20; fax (920) 49-20-40; e-mail lulelibrary@ltu.se; internet www.ltu.se/lib; campus libraries at Luleå, Piteå, Skellefteå; research library for Norrbotten County Council; 240,932 vols, 15,663 journals, 66,884 e-books; Chair. ERIK HÖGLUND; Chief Librarian TERJE HÖISETH.

Lund

Landsarkivet i Lund (Lund Regional Archives): POB 2016, SE-220 02 Lund; Dalbyvägen 4, Lund; tel. (10) 476-82-00; fax (10) 476-82-20; e-mail landsarkivet@landsarkivet-lund.ra.se; f. 1903; holds records of govt bodies in S Sweden (counties of Halland, Skåne, Blekinge); spec. collns: estate archives; library: 42,000 shelf m of records, 900 shelf m, mainly genealogy and topography; Chief Archivist JAN DAHLIN.

Universitetsbiblioteket, Lunds Universitet (Lund University Library): POB 3, Helgonabacken, SE-221 00 Lund; tel. (46) 222-00-00; fax (46) 222-42-43; internet www.ub.lu.se; f. 1671; 5,000,000 vols, 129,000 MSS, 120,000 items of microforms; legal deposit library and nat. lending library; MSS incl *Necrologium Lundense*, the oldest Scandinavian MS; spec. collns: *Bibliotheca Gripenhielmiana* (6,000 vols 16th- and 17th-century prints), Taussig colln of Schubert MSS, Broman colln of Elsevier prints, De La Gardie colln of prints and MSS; Dir CHRISTINA FRISTRÖM.

Malmö

Malmö Stadsbibliotek (Malmö City Library): SE-205 81 Malmö; Kung Oscars väg 11, SE-211 33 Malmö; tel. (40) 660-85-00; fax (40) 660-86-81; e-mail info.stadsbiblioteket@malmo.se; internet malmo.stadsbibliotek.org; f. 1905; 1,003,469 vols; Librarian ELSEBETH TANK.

Norrköping

Archives for UFO Research: POB 11027, SE-600 11 Norrköping; tel. (703) 68-32-21; e-mail afu@ufo.se; internet www.afu.info; f. 1973; repositories for UFO data and UFO-related folklore; colln of 600 m; Chair. and Man. ANDERS LILJEGREN.

Norrköpings Stadsbibliotek (Norrköping City Library): POB 2113, SE-600 02 Norrköping; Södra Promenaden 105, Norrköping; tel. (11) 15-26-65; fax (11) 10-38-45; e-mail stadsbiblioteket@norrkoping.se; internet www.nsb.norrkoping.se; f. 1913; 7 br. libraries, 3 bookmobiles; 472,785 vols; Chief Librarian BIRGITTA HJERPE.

Örebro

Örebro stadsbibliotek (City Library and County Library of Örebro län): POB 325 10, SE-701 35 Örebro; Näbbtorgsgatan 12, Örebro; tel. (19) 21-10-00; fax (19) 21-61-62; e-mail biblinfo@orebro.se; f. 1862; 780,000 vols; Chief Librarian CHRISTER KLINGBERG; publ. *Samfundet Örebro Stads- och Länsbiblioteks vänner. Meddelande 1929–*.

Östersund

Jämtlands Läns Bibliotek (Jämtland's County Library): SE-831 80 Östersund; Rådhusgatan 25–27, SE-831 80 Östersund; tel. (63) 14-30-50; e-mail lansbiblioteket@ostersund.se; internet www.jlb.ostersund.se; f. 1816, present location 1958; 1 main library, 3 area libraries, 1 mobile library, 2 hospital libraries; 550,000 vols; Chief Librarian BODIL KOPSEN.

Skara

Stifts- och Landsbiblioteket i Skara (State County and City Library of Skaraborgs Län): POB 194, SE-532 23 Skara; Prubbatorget 1, Skara; tel. (511) 32-060; fax (511) 32-069; e-mail skarabibliotek@skara.se; f. 1938; 400,000 vols, 200 running m MSS; Chief Librarian PEMA MALMGREN; publ. *Acta*.

Skövde

Högskolebiblioteket i Skövde (University of Skövde Library): POB 408, SE-541 28 Skövde; tel. (500) 44-80-60; fax (500) 44-80-59; e-mail biblioteket@his.se; internet www.his.se/biblioteket; 100,000 vols, 8,000 journals, 7,000 e-journals; Library Dir TOMAS LUNDÉN.

Stockholm

Antikvarisk-topografiska arkivet (Antiquarian Topographical Archives): POB 5405, SE-114 84 Stockholm; Östra stallet, Informationstorget, Storgatan 41, Stockholm; tel. (8) 519-180-50; fax (8) 519-180-88; e-mail ata@raa.se; f. 1786; archives of the Collegium Antiquitatum and the Royal Archives of Antiquities (1666–1786), archives and collns of the Royal Academy of Letters, History and Antiquities (1786–1975) and of the Central Board of Antiquities and Nat. Historical Museums, archives of the office of monuments (1918–67) of the Nat. Board of Public Bldgs; 300 private archives; 120,000 maps and drawings; 1,100,000 negatives and photographs; open to the public; Dir Dr ANN HÖRSELL.

Handelshögskolans i Stockholm—Bibliotek (Stockholm School of Economics Library): POB 6501, SE-113 83 Stockholm; tel. (8) 736-97-02; e-mail library@hhs.se; internet www.hhs.se/library; f. 1909; 157,000 vols, 15,000 e-journals, 60 databases, 4,500 m of printed materials; provides access to information within the fields of business, economics and the social sciences that is relevant to the teaching and research carried out at Stockholm School of Economics; Dir MARIE-LOUISE FENDIN.

Karolinska Institutet, Universitetsbiblioteket (Karolinska Institute University Library): POB 200, SE-171 77 Stockholm; Solna Br.: Solna, Berzelius väg 7B, Stockholm; Huddinge Br.: Huddinge, Alfred Nobels allé 8, SE-141 83 Stockholm; tel. (8) 524-840-00; fax (8) 524-843-10; e-mail ub@ki.se; internet kib.ki.se; f. 1810; Chief Librarian CHRISTER BJÖRKLUND.

Konstbiblioteket, Nationalmuseum och Moderna Museet (Joint Art Library of the Nationalmuseum and the Museum of Modern Art): POB 16 176, SE-103 24 Stockholm; Holmamiralens väg 2, Skeppsholmen, Stockholm; tel. (8) 519-543-52; fax (8) 519-543-76; e-mail konstbiblioteket@nationalmuseum.se; internet www.nationalmuseum.se; f. late 19th century; 330,000 vols, 247 serials, 2,390,000 cuttings, 900 journal titles; literature on Western art since the Renaissance; jt library of the Nat. Museum and Moderna Museet; Librarian MARIA SYLVÉN.

Kungliga biblioteket—Sveriges nationalbibliotek (National Library of Sweden): POB 5039, SE-102 41 Stockholm; Humlegården, Stockholm; tel. (10) 709-30-00; fax (10) 709-39-25; e-mail kungl.biblioteket@kb.se; internet www.kb.se; f. early 16th century; Nat. Library of Sweden with most complete colln of Swedish printed books and audiovisual material in the world; foreign holdings in humanities; important collns of Old Swedish and Icelandic MSS; spec. collns incl. incunabula, Elzevirs, maps, portraits, heraldry; responsible for the union catalogue *LIBRIS* and for cooperation among scientific libraries (Nat. Cooperation Dept); 4,000,000 vols; Nat. Librarian Dr GUNNAR SAHLIN; Deputy Nat. Librarian MAGDALENA GRAM; publ. *Acta Bibliothecæ regiæ Stockholmiensis*.

Kungl. Skogs- och Lantbruksakademiens Bibliotek (Royal Swedish Academy of Agriculture and Forestry Library): POB 6806, SE-113 86 Stockholm; Drottninggatan 95B, Stockholm; tel. (8) 545-477-20; fax (8) 545-477-30; e-mail kslab@ksla.se; internet www.kslab.ksla.se; f. 1813; 85,000 vols, 400 periodicals; colln of books on rural and agricultural history, horticulture, forestry and related fields; Chief Librarian LARS LJUNGGREN; publs *Miscellanea*, *Skogs- och Lantbrukshistoriska Meddelanden* (irregular).

Kungliga Tekniska Högskolans Bibliotek (Royal Institute of Technology Library): Osquars Backe 25, SE-100 44 Stockholm; Osquars Backe 31, Stockholm; tel. (8) 790-70-88; fax (8) 790-71-22; e-mail sekr@lib.kth.se; internet www.lib.kth.se; f. 1827; centre for computerized information and documentation services in science and technology; 877,000 vols, 27,000 e-books, 9,000 e-journals (incl. br. libraries); Chief Librarian GUNNAR LAGER; publ. *Stockholm Papers in History and Philosophy of Science and Technology*.

Kurdiska Biblioteket (Kurdish Library): POB 13029, SE-103 01 Stockholm; Vattugatan 16, SE-172 73 Stockholm; tel. (8) 679-88-03; fax (8) 679-88-04; e-mail info@kurdlib.org; internet www.kurdlib.org; f. 1997; collects, preserves and makes available all printed works written by Kurds or has relationship with the Kurds and Kurdistan; 10,000 titles, 600 serials; Chair. ANNE MURRAY; Vice-Chair. AYCAN BOZARSLAN; Library Dir and Sec. of Board NEWZAD HIRORI; Librarian MEHMET TAYFUN.

Östasiatiska Biblioteket (Far Eastern Library — Library of the Museum of Far Eastern Antiquities): POB 16381, SE-103 27 Stockholm; Tyghusplan, Skeppsholmen, Stockholm; tel. (8) 519-557-76; fax (8) 519-557-55; e-mail helena.rundkrantz@ostasiatiska.se; internet www.ostasiatiska.se; f. 1986; 3,500 linear m; colln of Chinese periodicals, Japanese colln of A.E. Nordenskiöld, colln of Chinese congshu, colln of Western-language books on Asia; library is administered within the MFEA Unit for Research and Devt (Head: Dr EVA MYRDAL); Librarian HELENA RUNDKRANTZ.

Regeringskansliet Utrikesdepartementets Bibliotek (Library of the Swedish Ministry for Foreign Affairs): SE-103 33 Stockholm; tel. (8) 405-10-00; internet www.regeringen.se; not open to the public; Librarian ELISABETH LARSON OLIN.

Riksarkivet (National Archives of Sweden): POB 12541, SE-102 29 Stockholm; Fyrverkarbacken 13, Stockholm; tel. (10) 476-70-00; fax (10) 476-71-20; e-mail riksarkivet@riksarkivet.ra.se; internet www.riksarkivet.se; f. 1618, present status 2010; 670,000 m of archival holdings; regional archives at Gothenburg, Härnösand, Lund, Östersund, Uppsala, Vadstena, Visby; Military archives and Research Center SVAR are also attached; Dir-Gen. BJÖRN JORDEL; publs *Årsbok för Riksarkivet och landsarkiven* (1 a year), *Glossarium till medeltidslatinet i Sverige*, *Skrifter utgivna av Riksarkivet*, *Svenskt diplomatarium*.

Riksdagsbiblioteket (Library of the Swedish Parliament): SE-100 12 Stockholm; Storkyrkobrinken 7A; tel. (8) 786-40-00; fax (8) 786-58-70; e-mail biblioteket@riksdagen.se; internet www.riksdagen.se; f. 1851; serves the Riksdag, the admin. services and research; chiefly devoted to political science, administration, social science and law; open to the public; 700,000 vols; Chief Librarian GUNILLA LILIE BAUER; publ. *Fakta om folkvalda: Riksdagen 1985–* (biographical handbook, every 4 years).

Stockholms Stadsarkiv (Stockholm City Archives): POB 22063, SE-104 22 Stockholm; Kungsklippan 6, Stockholm; tel. (8) 508-283-00; fax (8) 508-283-01; e-mail stadsarkivet@stockholm.se; internet www.ssa.stockholm.se; f. 1930; provincial archives for Stockholm; documents from regional authorities and the municipal govt of Stockholm; archives on urban history of Stockholm; 130,000 vols, archives: 68,000 shelf m; City Archivist LENNART PLOOM; publs *Stadsarkivets småtryck* (irregular), *Stockholms stadsarkiv. Årsberättelse* (1 a year), *Stockholms tänkeböcker från år 1592* (irregular).

Musik- och teaterbiblioteket vid Statens musiksamlingar (Music and Theatre Library of Sweden): POB 16326, SE-103 26 Stockholm; Torsgatan 19, SE-113 21 Stockholm; tel. (8) 519-554-12; fax (8) 519-554-05; e-mail exp@muslib.se; internet www.muslib.se; f. 1771, present name and status 2010, merger of Theatre Library of Sweden (f. 1935); attached to Statens musiksamlingar; large colln of 18th century music and 19th century theatre material; about 300 archives and collns; incl. a documentation centre for Swedish music; 137,000 books on music and theatre, 400,000 scores of music, 50,000 plays, 28,000 MSS and about 15,000 letters, 500,000 photographs (theatre colln); Chief Librarian VESLEMØY HEINTZ; publ. *Dokumenterat: bulletin från Musik- och teaterbiblioteket* (online, www.muslib.se/publ/bulletin.html).

Statistiska Centralbyråns Information och Bibliotek (Statistics Sweden Information Centre and Library): POB 24300, SE-104 51 Stockholm; tel. (8) 506-950-66; fax (8) 661-52-61; e-mail library@scb.se; internet www.scb.se; f. 1858; research library for official Swedish statistics; all statistics published by Statistics Sweden; literature on statistical theories and methodology; colln of statistical results from most of the countries of the world and from 50 int. orgs and the EU's statistical office Eurostat till 2008; 230,000 vols, 1,400 periodicals; Chief Librarian LIGIA GODYMIRSKA; publ. *Statistics from International Organizations and other Issuing Bodies* (1 a year).

Stockholms stadsbibliotek (Stockholm Public Library): SE-113 80 Stockholm; Odengatan 63, Spelbomskan, Stockholm; tel. (8) 508-311-00; fax (8) 508-312-10; e-mail stadsbiblioteket@stockholm.se; internet www.biblioteket.stockholm.se; f. 1927; 40 libraries; 2,225,000 vols; Chief Librarian INGA LUNDÉN.

Stockholms universitetsbibliotek (Stockholm University Library): SE-106 91 Stockholm; Universitetsvägen 14D, Stockholm; tel. (8) 16-28-00; fax (8) 15-77-76; internet www.sub.su.se; f. 1877; 2,500,000 vols; 12 brs; Librarian Dr CATARINA ERICSON-ROOS.

Svenskt Visarkiv (Centre for Swedish Folk Music and Jazz Research): POB 16326, SE-103 26 Stockholm; Torsgatan 19, Stockholm; tel. (8) 519-554-88; fax (8) 519-554-49; e-mail info@visarkiv.se; internet www.visarkiv.se; f. 1951; attached to Swedish Nat. Collns of Music; collects, preserves, publishes material concerning instrumental folk music, folk songs, jazz and traditional music from the end of the 16th century till present; Dir DAN LUNDBERG.

Svenska Akademiens Nobelbibliotek (Nobel Library of the Swedish Academy): POB 2118, SE-103 13 Stockholm; Källargränd 4, Gamla Stan, Stockholm; tel. (8) 555-125-52; fax (8) 555-125-99; e-mail info@nobelbiblioteket.se; internet www.nobelbiblioteket.se; f. 1901; recent works of literature, literary criticism and linguistics; assists the Swedish Acad. in evaluations required for the Nobel Prize in Literature; 200,000 vols, 150 journals; Chief Librarian LARS RYDQUIST.

Sveriges Radio Förvaltings AB (Resources of the Swedish Broadcasting Corporation): Oxenstiernsgatan 20, SE-105 10 Stockholm; tel. (8) 784-54-00; fax (8) 660-72-57; internet www.srf.se; f. 1925; documents relating to Swedish public service broadcasting and television; Archivist BJÖRN BLOMBERG.

Vitterhetsakademiens Bibliotek (Library of the Royal Swedish Academy of Letters, History and Antiquities): POB 5405, SE-114 84 Stockholm; Östra stallet, Storgatan 41, Stockholm; tel. (8) 519-183-26; fax (8) 663-35-28; e-mail bibl@raa.se; internet www.raa.se/bibliotek; f. 1753, present name 1786; attached to Swedish Nat. Heritage Board; spec. collns on archaeology, medieval art and architecture, numismatics, preservation of cultural heritage; open to the public; affiliated library: Colln of Numismatic Books; 430,000 vols; Head of the Unit of Library Services LIGIA GODYMIRSKA; publ. *Fornvännen*.

Sundsvall

Universitetsbiblioteket, Mittuniversitetet (Mid Sweden University Library): SE-851 70 Sundsvall; Holmgatan 10, Sundsvall; tel. (60) 14-87-50; fax (60) 14-89-66; e-mail bibsvl@miun.se; internet www.bib.miun.se; campus libraries in Härnösand, Östersund; 220,000 vols, 20,000 e-journals, 60 electronic databases; Dir MORGAN PALMQVIST; Library Man. CATHRINE BERGGREN.

Umeå

Umeå stadsbibliotek (Umeå City Library): Rådhusesplanaden 6A, SE-901 78 Umeå; tel. (90) 16-33-00; fax (90) 16-33-04; e-mail stadsbiblioteket@umea.se; internet www.minabibliotek.se; f. 1903; 770,000 vols; Chief Librarian INGER EDEBRO SIKSTRÖM.

Umeå Universitetsbibliotek (Umeå University Library): SE-901 74 Umeå; Social Sciences Bldg, Umeå Univ., Umeå; tel. (90) 786-56-93; fax (90) 786-74-74; e-mail umub@ub.umu.se; internet www.ub.umu.se; f. 1950, as Scientific Library in Umeå, present name and status 1964; academic research; open to public; 1,500,000 vols, 18,000 journals, 12,000 e-journals; Chief Librarian GUNNI ÖBERG.

Uppsala

Sveriges lantbruksuniversitets bibliotek (Library of the Swedish University of Agricultural Sciences): POB 7071, SE-750 07 Uppsala; Undervisningsplan 10, Uppsala; tel. (18) 67-11-05; fax (18) 67-28-53; e-mail bib-esupport@slu.se; internet www.slu.se/sv/bibliotek; f. 1977; consists of Ultunabiblioteket (main library, in Uppsala) and 8 brs; Dir SNORRE RUFELT; Asst Dir CATHARINA ISBERG; Sr Librarian ULLA ANDERSSON; Librarian CHRISTINA TÖRNQVIST WESTIN.

Uppsala stadsbibliotek (Uppsala City Library): POB 643, SE-751 27 Uppsala; Svartbäcksgatan 17, SE-753 75 Uppsala; tel. (18) 727-17-00; fax (18) 727-06-40; e-mail stadsbibli.inf@uppsala.se; f. 1906; 800,000 vols; Chief Librarian MARIE-LOUISE RITON.

Uppsala universitetsbibliotek (Uppsala University Library): POB 510, SE-751 20 Uppsala; Carolina Rediviva, Dag Hammarskjölds väg 1, Uppsala; tel. (18) 471-39-00; fax (18) 471-39-13; e-mail info@ub.uu.se; internet www.ub.uu.se; f. 1620; consists of 14 library units and extensive cultural heritage collns; 5,500,000 vols, 17,500 electronic periodicals, 400,000 eBooks, 200 databases, 30 encyclopaedias and 62,000 MSS, incl. the famous *Codex argenteus*, the 'Silver Bible' from the 6th century, a translation of the Gospels into the Gothic language, Swedish and Icelandic medieval MSS, the Bibliotheca Walleriana (medical books), a colln of old music books and MSS, a colln of old maps, engravings and drawings, incl. the *Carta Marina* of 1539 by Olaus Magnus (earliest accurate map of Scandinavia); Dir Prof. ULF GÖRANSON; publs *Acta Bibliothecae R. Universitatis Upsaliensis*, *Acta Universitatis Upsaliensis*, *Scripta Minora Bibliothecae R. Universitatis Upsaliensis*, *Uppsala universitetsbiblioteks utställnings-kataloger* (exhibition catalogues), etc.

Varberg

Campusbiblioteket i Varberg (Campus Library in Varberg): Otto Torells gata 18, SE-432 44 Varberg; tel. (340) 69-74-46; fax (340) 69-74-45; e-mail varberg@bib.hh.se; internet www.campusbiblioteket.se; f. 2003; operated jtly by Varberg Kommun and Halmstad Univ.'s Varberg Campus; Librarian CHRISTINA GABRIELSSON; Librarian LENNART ERLING; Librarian VERONICA AASHEIM KVIST.

Varberg Bibliotek: Engelbrektsgatan 7, SE-432 80 Varberg; tel. (340) 886-00; fax (340) 69-70-50; e-mail biblioteket@kommunen.varberg.se; internet www2.varberg.se; 6 br. libraries, 1 mobile library; 250,000 titles; Chief Librarian PER FALK.

Värmland

Värmlandsarkiv (Värmland Archives): POB 475, SE-651 11 Karlstad; Hööksgatan 2, SE-651 11 Karlstad; tel. (54) 61-77-30; e-mail varmlandsarkiv@regionvarmland.se; internet varmlandsarkiv.regionvarmland.se; f. 1970, present status 2001; attached to Nat. Archives of Sweden; colln of 23,000 shelf m from middle ages to present; 25,000 vols.

Västerås

Mälardalens Högskolebiblioteket (Mälardalens University Library): POB 832, SE-721 22 Västerås; Högskoleplan 1, Västerås; tel. (21) 10-13-44; fax (21) 10-13-40 POB 329, SE-631 05 Eskilstuna; Drottninggatan 16, Eskilstuna; tel. (16) 15-37-00; fax (16) 15-36-75; e-mail biblioteket@mdh.se; internet www.mdh.se/library; 114,364 vols, 46,200 e-books, 318 journals, 10,421 e-journals; Chair. ROLAND SVENSSON; Library Dir ANNSOFIE OSCARSSON.

Västerås stadsbibliotek (Västerås City Library): Biskopsgatan 2, SE-721 87 Västerås; tel. (21) 39-46-01; fax (21) 39-46-80; e-mail stadsbibliotek@vasteras.se; internet www.bibliotek.vasteras.se; f. 1952; 571,000 vols; 6 associated libraries and a mobile library; Chief Librarian EVA MATSSON.

Växjö

Smålands Musikarkiv (Småland's Music Archive): Västergatan 13, SE-352 31 Växjö; tel. (470) 70-03-00; internet www.smalandsmusikarkiv.nu; f. 1992; attached to Musik i Syd; colln incl. music from Småland and adjacent landscape; 2,000 vols; Head MAGNUS GUSTAFSSON.

Växjö Bibliotek (City and County Library, Kronobergs län): POB 1202, SE-351 12 Växjö; Västra Esplanaden 7, SE-351 12 Växjö; tel. (470) 4-14-44; fax (470) 79-69-92; e-mail stadsbiblioteket@vaxjo.se; internet www.vaxjo.se/bibliotek; f. 1954, present bldg 2003; 460,000 vols; 15 brs; Chief Librarian ANNA-KARIN AXELSSON.

Visby

Almedalsbiblioteket (Almedals Library): POB 1121, SE-621 22 Visby; Cramérgatan 3–5, SE-621 22 Visby; tel. (498) 29-90-00; fax (498) 29-90-11; e-mail almedalsbiblioteket@hgo.se; internet www.almedalsbiblioteket.se; f. 1865; 502,000 vols; Chief Librarian KERSTIN SIMBERG.

Museums and Art Galleries

Falun

Dalarnas Museum: POB 22, SE-791 21 Falun; tel. (23) 76-55-00; fax (23) 283-58; e-mail info@dalarnasmuseum.se; internet www.dalarnasmuseum.se; f. 1962; shows cultural heritage from the Stone Age to present time; exhibits Archaeological Society colln activities from 1862; colln of costume and textiles, folk art, folk music, graphics, Selma Lagerlof's library; Dir. JAN RAIHLE; Deputy Dir ANNA BJÖRKMAN-HOLMGREN.

Gävle

Länsmuseet Gävleborgs (Gävleborg County Museum): POB 746, SE-801 28 Gävle; Södrastrandgatan 20, Gävle; tel. (26) 65-56-00; e-mail lansmuseetgavleborg@xlm.se; internet www.lansmuseetgavleborg.se; f. 1978 as Gävle Museum; exhibits art, silver and gold metal work, representations of circus life, archeology of Gävle, selection from Hedvig Ulfsparre's private colln of textiles, devt of modern mass production; Pres. LENNART GARD; Vice-Pres. NILS MALMLÖF.

Sveriges Järnvägsmuseum (Swedish Railway Museum): POB 407, SE-801 05 Gävle; Rälsgatan 1, Gävle; tel. (26) 14-46-15; fax (26) 14-45-98; e-mail jarnvagsmuseum@banverket.se; internet www.banverket.se/en/swedish-railway-museum; f. 1915; colln of locomotives, carriages, wagons, other railway items; photographs, pictures, historic film material, railway literature, and archival material; br. in Ängelholm; Dir ROBERT SJÖÖ; Admin. GÖRAN JÄDERHOLM.

Gothenburg

Aeroseum: Holmvägen 100, SE-417 46 Gothenburg; Säve Depå, Holmvägen, Gothenburg; tel. (31) 55-83-00; fax (31) 55-13-09; e-mail info@aeroseum.se; internet www.aeroseum.se; f. 1999, present status 2008; history and devt of aviation; preserves ex-military subterranean aircraft hangars; Chair. ROGER ELIASSON.

Goteborgs Konsthall: Gotaplatsen, SE-412 56 Gothenborg; tel. (31) 368 34 50; fax (31) 368 34 59; e-mail goteborgs.konsthall@kultur.goteborg.se; internet www.konsthallen.goteborg.se; f. 1923; exhibits contemporary art; organizes artist talks, tours, seminars and classes; presents group and solo exhibitions of nat. and int. artists; Dir. MIKAEL NANFELDT; Curators STINA EDBLOM, LAURA MOTT.

Göteborgs Naturhistoriska Museet (Gothenburg Museum of Natural History): POB 7283, SE-402 35 Gothenburg; Slottsskogen vid Linnéplatsen, Gothenburg; tel. (31) 775-24-00; fax (31) 12-98-07; e-mail info.naturhistoriska@vgregion.se; internet www.gnm.se; f. 1833, present location 1923; exhibits Swedish animal world and animals from around the world; themes incl. Earth's structure and life history, marine life, environmental problems, humans as biological beings and ecology concepts; specimens date from 18th century; zoological colln: 10m. animals, vertebrate colln: of 100,000 specimens; library of 80,000 vols; Dir Dr ANN STRÖMBERG; publ. *Årstryck*.

Göteborgs Stads Kulturförvaltning (Gothenburg Arts and Culture): Norra Hamngatan 8, SE-411 14 Gothenburg; tel. (31) 368-32-00; fax (31) 368-32-14; e-mail info@kultur.goteborg.se; internet www.goteborg.se/kultur; f. 1993; responsible for cultural activities in Gothenburg; Chair. of Trustees HELENA NYHUS; Vice-Chair. of Trustees LENNART S. WIDING.

Attached Museums:

Göteborgs Konstmuseum (Gothenburg Museum of Art): Götaplatsen, SE-412 56 Gothenburg; tel. (31) 368-35-00; fax (31) 368-35-26; e-mail info.konstmuseum@kultur.goteborg.se; internet www.konstmuseum.goteborg.se; f. 1925; European paintings, sculpture, prints and drawings from 1400, spec. collns of French art since 1820 and Scandinavian art incl. works by Monet, Picasso, Rembrandt, Van Gogh; art library; Dir ISABELLA NILSSON.

Göteborgs Stadsmuseum (Gothenburg City Museum): Norra Hamngatan 12, SE-411 14 Gothenburg; tel. (31) 368-36-00; fax (31) 774-03-58; e-mail stadsmuseum@kultur.goteborg.se; internet www.stadsmuseum.goteborg.se; f. 1861, present status 1993; archaeology since prehistoric times, industrial heritage; Dir KARL-GUNNAR NORDANSTAD.

Röhsska Museet (Röhss Museum of Applied Art and Design): Vasagatan 37–39, SE-400 15 Gothenburg; POB 53178, SE-400 15 Gothenburg; tel. (31) 368-31-50; fax (31) 368-31-78; e-mail info.designmuseum@kultur.goteborg.se; internet www.designmuseum.se; f. 1916, present status 1961; colln incl. 50,000 objects of crafts, applied arts and industrial design; Swedish and European decorative art, Greek and Roman antiquities, material from Japan and China; library of 30,000 vols; Dir TED HESSELBOM; publ. *Röhsska Konstslöjdmuseets årsbok* (Röhsska Museum Yearbook).

Sjöfartsmuseet Akvariet (Maritime Museum and Aquarium): Karl Johansgatan 1–3, SE-414 59 Gothenburg; tel. (31) 368-35-50; fax (31) 368-35-59; e-mail info.sjofartsmuseum@kultur.goteborg.se; internet www.sjofartsmuseum.goteborg.se; f. 1913; permanent exhibitions on world shipping significant for Gothenburg and W Sweden; themes incl. pirates, life at sea; temporary exhibitions and programme activities; library of 20,000 vols; Dir ANNA ROSENGREN; publ. *Unda Maris*.

Kvibergs Museum: Lilla Regementsvägen 33, SE-415 28 Gothenburg; tel. (31) 48-06-02; e-mail kvibergsmuseum@telia.com; internet www.kvibergsmuseum.se; f. 1895; highlights military action in Kviberg area; Dir TORGNY ALLVIN.

Världskulturmuseet (Museum of World Culture): POB 5303, SE-402 27 Gothenburg; Södra vägen 54, Gothenburg; tel. (31) 63-27-00; e-mail info@varldskulturmuseet.se; internet www.varldskulturmuseet.se; f. 2004; exhibitions and programs on contemporary issues about the world; library of 30,000 titles, 900 journals and yearbooks; Dir MARGARETA ALIN.

Hässleholms

Bjärnum Museum och Hembygdssamlingar (Bjärnum Museum and Local Historical Collections): Parkgatan, SE-280 20 Hässleholms; tel. (451) 200-91; e-mail info@bjarnumsmuseum.se; internet www.bjarnumsmuseum.se; 100,000 articles describing the lifestyle of ancestors; objects covering a period of approx. 11,000 years; Chair. ARNE WIGHAGEN; Sec. ANDERS SVENSSON.

Helsingborg

Dunkers Kulturhus (Arts Centre): Kungsgatan 11, SE-252 21 Helsingborg; tel. (0) 42-10-74-00; fax (0) 42-10-74-10; internet www.dunkerskulturhus.se; f. 2002; exhibitions with town history, cultural history; contemporary art exhibitions; theatre, ballet, modern dance, jazz, chamber music and world music concerts; Dir ELISABETH ALSHEIMER; Curator BENGT ADLERS.

Grafiska Museet (Printing Museum): c/o Fredriksdal Museums and Gardens, Gisela Trapps väg 5, SE-254 37 Helsingborg; tel. and fax (42) 10-45-24; e-mail info@grafiskamuseet.se; internet www.grafiskamuseet.se; f. 1990; working printing museum; Chair. BERTIL HAGBERG; Deputy Chair. GIDEON BEIL.

Höganäs

Höganäs Museum och Konsthall: Polhemsgatan 1, SE-263 37 Höganäs; tel. (42) 34-13 35; e-mail hoganas.museum@telia.com; internet www.hoganasmuseum.se; f. 1924, present status 1997; exhibits historical industrial period; art gallery; Chair. SIMON ARNE.

Karlskoga

Nobelmuseet i Karlskoga: Björkbornsvägen 10, SE-691 33 Karlskoga; tel. (46) 586-834-94; fax (46) 586-352-20; e-mail info@nobelmuseetikarlskoga.se; internet nobelmuseetikarlskoga.se; exhibits on Alfred Nobel and his home, laboratory on Björkborn Manor.

Karlskrona

Blekinge Museum: Borgmästaregatan 21, SE-371 35 Karlskrona; tel. (455) 30-49-65; fax (455) 30-49-73; e-mail blekingemuseum@karlskrona.se; internet www.blekingemuseum.se; f. 1899 as preservation society, present status 1983; exhibits history of Blekinge; Dir TULLAN GUNÉR; Librarian CHRISTIN NILSSON.

Museum The Kulenovic Collection: Stortorget 5, Karlskrona; tel. (455) 25573; e-mail rizah.kulenovic@telia.com; internet www.kulenoviccollection.se; f. 1997, as Museum Lionardo da Vinci Ideale; exhibition of paintings, drawings, etchings and prints, sculptures, artifacts, ceramics; Raphael, Leonardo da Vinci, Rembrandt, Caravaggio, van Gogh and Picasso and others; art objects in the form of figurines, vases and figurines dating from around 3000BC onwards; Dir RIZAH KULENOVIC.

Köpings

Köpings Museum: Östra Långgatan 37, SE-731 30 Köpings; tel. (221) 253-51; fax (221) 179-45; e-mail museum@koping.se; internet www.koping.se; f. 1887; shows Köpings history over 10,000 years; 4,000 glass plates, approx. 8,000 photographs from the 1860s until today; 25,000 magazines; Dir ROY CASSÉ.

Kristianstad

Regionmuseet Kristianstad (Regional Museum in Kristianstad): POB 134, SE-291 22 Kristianstad; Stora Torg, Kristianstad; tel. (44) 13-58-00; fax (44) 21-49-02; e-mail info@regionmuseet.se; internet www.regionmuseet.m.se; has 3 br. museums: Film Museum, Railway Museum and Åhus Museum; archive and photographic archive; colln incl. archaeological material, natural history: rocks, fossils, animals, military equipment, railway historical stock, movie historical stock, school and teaching materials; agricultural lot, textiles and clothing, business interiors, crafts, furniture, utensils, glass, porcelain, ceramic arts, crafts, toys, musical instruments; art colln by Scanian artists, oils, watercolours, prints and sculptures; Dir BARBRO MELLANDER; Asst Dir OLOF HERMELIN.

Kristinehamn

Kristinehamns Konstmuseum: Dr Enwalls väg 13B, SE-681 84 Kristinehamn; tel. (550) 88 200; fax (550) 180 99; e-mail info.konstmuseum@kristinehamn.se; internet www.kristinehamnskonstmuseum.com; f. 1997; modern and contemporary art; colln of works created by artists connected to Värmland; works of artists Bengt Olson and Stig Olson; Dir ANNA SVENSSON; Curator JOHAN MAGNUSSON.

Jokkmokk

Ájtte Svenskt Fjäll- och Samemuseum (Ajtte Swedish Mountain and Sami Museum): POB 116, SE-962 23 Jokkmokk; Kyrkogatan 3, SE-962 31 Jokkmokk; tel. (971) 170-70; fax (971) 120-57; e-mail info@ajtte.com; internet www.ajtte.com; exhibits Sami culture; spec. museum of mountain chain's, natural and cultural resources, information centre for mountain tourists; Dir KJELL-ÅKE ARONSSON.

Jönköping

Radiomuseet (Radio Museum): Tändsticksgränd 16, SE-553 15 Jönköping; tel. (36) 71-39-59; e-mail radiomuseet@telia.com; internet www.radiomuseet.com; f. 1988; exhibits loudspeaker equipment and microphones, historical radio broadcasting equipment, sound recording devices from Edison's wax cylinders to modern CD.

Landskrona

Tycho Brahe museet (Tycho Brahe Museum): Landsvägen 182, SE-260 13 St Ibb; tel. (418) 72530; e-mail goran.nystrom@landskrona.se; internet www.tychobrahe.com; f. 2005; colln of films, archaeological finds from field, reconstructed instruments, models, pictures and multimedia; incl. Tycho Brahe's underground observatory Stjärneborg, a reconstructed Renaissance Garden, Tycho Brahe museum, and science centre; Dir GÖRAN NYSTRÖM.

Lidingö

Millesgården: Carl Milles väg 2, SE-181 34 Lidingö; Herserudsvägen 32, Lidingö; tel. (8) 446-75-90; fax (8) 767-09-02; e-mail info@

millesgarden.se; internet www.millesgarden.se; f. 1936; four rooms for exhibition: art gallery, artist home and small studio; colln of sculptures made by artists; Dir ONITA WASS; Curator EVELINA JANSSON.

Linköping

Linköpings Slotts- och Domkyrkomuseum: Borggården, SE-582 28 Linköping; tel. (13) 12-23-80; fax (13) 14-23-80; e-mail info@lsdm.se; internet lsdm.se; displays aspects of medieval times, such as episode of bubonic plague, medical practices, status and regalia, pests, family banners.

Lund

Botaniska Museet (Botanical Museum): Östra Vallgatan 18, SE-223 61 Lund; tel. (46) 222-95-59; fax (46) 222-42-34; e-mail museichef@botmus.lu.se; internet www.biomus.lu.se/botaniska-museet; attached to Lund Univ.; colln includes about 2.5m. specimens of plants; fungi, lichens, mosses, vascular plants etc.; Dir Prof. INGVAR KÄRNEFELT.

Historiska museet (Historical museum): Lund University, Krafts torg 1, SE-223 50 Lund; tel. (46) 222-79-44; e-mail info@luhm.lu.se; internet www.luhm.lu.se; f. 1805; exhibits Kilian Stobaeus Cabinet of Curiosities from the 18th century, finds from excavations of the Iron Age city of Uppåkra and artefacts from the Scanian Stone, Bronze and Iron Ages; coin colln; dept of Medieval church art and Antique artefacts; Dir PER KARSTEN.

Kulturen in Lund (Cultural History Museum): POB 1095, Tegnérsplatsen, SE-221 04 Lund; Tegnérsplatsen, Lund; tel. (46) 35-04-00; fax (46) 30-42-60; e-mail info@kulturen.com; internet www.kulturen.com; f. 1882; ethnography, cultural history, medieval archaeology; open-air museum, town and country houses; applied arts (ceramics, textiles, silver, glass); weapons and uniforms; musical instruments; furniture and fittings; trades; commerce and crafts; fishery; farming; folk art; archaeological finds from medieval Lund; holds more than 30 historical bldgs, around 125,000 items and 1m. archaeological finds from 3000BC to present; Östarp, old farm with inn, 30 km from Lund; library of 35,000 vols; Dir ANKI DAHLIN; publ. *Kulturen* (yearbook).

Lund konsthall: Mårtenstorget 3, SE-223 51 Lund; tel. (46) 35-52-95; fax (46) 18-45-21; e-mail lundskonsthall@lund.se; internet www.lundskonsthall.se; f. 1957; nat. and int. art exhibition; visual and spatial articulation of exhibitions, catalogues, public talks, lectures and discussion events; in charge of producing public art projects for new buildings financed by the City of Lund; Dir ÅSA NACKING; Curator ANDERS KREUGER.

Skissernas Museum (Museum of Sketches): Finngatan 2, SE-223 62 Lund; tel. (46) 222-72-83; e-mail reception@skissernasmuseum.se; internet www.adk.lu.se; f. 1934; Swedish, Nordic and Int. collns; colln of sketches and models; sculpture colln; Dir ELISABET HAGLUND; Curator ANN LANDGREN.

Zoologiska Museet (Zoological Museum): Helgonavägen 3A, SE-223 62 Lund; tel. (46) 222-93-30; fax (46) 222-45-41; e-mail museichef@zool.lu.se; internet www.biomus.lu.se/zoologiska-museet; attached to Lund Univ.; scientific colln; contains approx. 10m objects, mostly insects and other invertebrates; Dir Prof. SVEN-AXEL BENGTSON; publ. *Entomologica scandinavica* (Scandinavian Entomology).

Lycksele

Skogsmuseet (Forestry Museum): POB 176, SE-921 23 Lycksele; Lapland, SE-921 23 Lycksele; tel. (950) 379-45; fax (950) 132-60; internet www.skogsmuseet.se; f. 1983; exhibitions on the manual logging era and the mechanized logging era showing woodland population; Birger Nordin Sami colln of art objects and books; Dir MAARIT KALELA-BRUNDIN.

Malmö

Idrottsmuseet (Sports Museum): Fritidsförvaltningen, POB 8111, SE-200 41 Malmö; Eric Perssons väg, Malmö; tel. (40) 34-26-88; e-mail idrottsmuseet@malmo.se; internet www.malmo.se/idrottsmuseet; material on people who have devoted their lives to sport, active athletes, managers or spectators; publ. *Skånsk Idrotts Historia*.

Malmö Konsthall: S:t Johannesgatan 7, POB 17 127, SE-200 10 Malmö; tel. (40) 34-60-00; fax (40) 30-15-07; e-mail info.konsthall@malmo.se; internet www.konsthall.malmo.se; f. 1975; exhibits int. and nat. art ranging from the classics of modernism to current experiments; the Schyl Collection; organizes theatre, film, poetry, video installations, multimedia, music, lectures and debates; Dir JACOB FABRICIUS; Chief Curator ANNA HOLMBOM.

Malmö Konstmuseum (Malmö Art Museum): POB 406, SE-201 24 Malmö; Malmöhusvägen 6, Malmö; tel. (705) 77-44-69; fax (708) 87-44-33; e-mail malmokonstmuseum@malmo.se; internet www.malmo.se; f. 1841 as Malmö Museum, reorganised 1932; collns incl. primarily Nordic art, European art, decorative art and design objects from the 1500s to the present; 40,000 works of art; Dir GÖRAN CHRISTENSON.

Malmö Museer (Malmö Museums): POB 406, SE-201 24 Malmö; Malmöhusvägen 6, Malmö; tel. (40) 34-44-00; fax (40) 12-40-97; e-mail malmomuseer@malmo.se; internet www.malmo.se; f. 1841; incl. commander's house, Ebba's house on Snapperupsgatan, Slottsmöllan at Mölleplatsen, Slottsholmen (with hus Castle), Technology & Maritime House, Wowragården in Southern Sallerup; Dir GÖRAN LARSSON.

Teatermuseet (Theatre Museum): Kalendegatan 5C, SE-211 35 Malmö; tel. (40) 12-48-83; e-mail info@teatermuseet.com; internet www.teatermuseet.com; preserves, documents history and traditions of theatre and the performing world; colln incl. Artillery Photographs from Hippodromteatern in Malmö dating from 1924 until closure in 1949, personal letters and photographs of Swedish actors, large colln of press clippings from Swedish newspapers on theatre activities from 1930s onwards, manuscripts from Skåne theatre history.

Mariefred

Swedish National Portrait Gallery: c/o Swedish National Portrait Gallery and Castles Collns, Nationalmuseum, POB 16176, SE-103 24 Stockholm; Gripsholm Castle, Mariefred; tel. (8) 519-543-00; fax (8) 519-544-56; e-mail elk@nationalmuseum.se; internet www.nationalmuseum.se; f. 1822; colln of Swedish portraits from 16th century till present day; Dir MAGNUS OLAUSSON.

Mora

Zornmuseet (Zorn Museum): Vasagatan 36, POB 32, SE-792 21 Mora; tel. (250) 59-23-10; fax (250) 184-60; e-mail info@zorn.se; internet www.zorn.se; f. 1939; divided into four parts: Zorn Museum, Zorn House, open-air museum Zorn's Gammelgård and Gopsmor; also consists of The Textile Museum; permanent exhibition: 'Midnight' (1891), 'Dairy Maid' (1908), 'Dance in the Gopsmor Cottage' (1913) as well as the two self portraits in red and in a wolfskin (both 1915); 'Mormor' (1883) and 'The Misses Salomon' (1888) and water studies; Zorn's etchings and silver collection; Chair. BIRGIT FRIGGEBO; Dir JOHAN CEDERLUND; Sec. KARIN HÖGBERG.

Norrköping

Norrköpings Konstmuseum (Norrköping Art Museum): Kristinaplatsen, SE-602 34 Norrköping; tel. (11) 15-26-00; fax (11) 13-58-97; e-mail konstmuseet@norrkoping.se; internet www.norrkoping.se/kultur-fritid/museer/konstmuseum; Swedish art from 1600s to present day; int. and nat. graphic colln; print colln consists of works from artists incl. Dürer, Rembrandt and Goya; sculpture park incl. works of Carl Milles, Bror Hjorth and Arne Jones; creative workshops, music, lectures, further training for teachers, corporate events.

Nyköping

Sörmlands museum: POB 314, SE-611 26 Nyköping; tel. (155) 24-57-00; e-mail info.museet@dll.se; internet www.sormlandsmuseum.se; archive of letters, diaries, records, maps, drawings, reports, stories; collns of wedding dresses from the 1700s, home furnishing, textiles; archipelago colln and archaeological colln; organizes courses, lectures, walks, field trips, travelling exhibitions; publishes books; Dir KARIN LINDVALL; Deputy Dir. CARINA WENDEL; Sec. INGER BERG.

Örebro

Örebro Läns Museum: POB 314, SE-701 46 Örebro; tel. (19) 602-87-00; e-mail info@olm.se; internet www.orebrolansmuseum.se; art colln ranges in time from late 1700s to present; painting; archeological colln; preserves local history, handicraft, artwork, and cultural heritage sites; organizes lectures, workshops, tours and children's activities; colln of antiques, fine jewellery and clothing, replica of a medieval church interior with altar paintings and shrines; Dir MIKAEL EIVERGÅRD; Admin. Man. LARS NORLING; Asst Dir MARIA UDDÉN.

Rattvik

Folkmusikens hus (Folk Music House): Dalagatan 7, SE-795 31 Rattvik; tel. (48) 79-70-50; fax (48) 129-15; e-mail kontakt@folkmusikenshus.se; internet www.folkmusikenshus.se; f. 1994; folk music centre; colln of CDs, sheet music and literature; serves as information hub for folk music and dance; organizes exhibitions, concerts, dances, education, archival services; Pres. LARS-ERIK KALLES; Vice-Pres. MATS HULANDER; Man. PER GUDMUNDSON.

Simrishamn

Österlens museum: Storgatan 24, SE-272 31 Simrishamn; tel. (414) 81-96-70; e-mail osterlens.museum@simrishamn.se; internet www.simrishamn.se/sv/kultur_fritid/osterlens_museum; f. 1917; colln relating to life on Swedish countryside; exhibits native plants, local agriculture, handicraft e.g. lace-making and metal work, fossils and archeological objects, tools, furniture, clothing and nautical equipment from Eastern Skåne; colln of coins and historical jewellery; Gislövs Forging Museum; Dir LENA ALEBO.

Skara

Västergötlands Museum: POB 253, SE-532 23 Skara; Stadsträdgården, SE-532 31 Skara; tel. (511) 260-00; fax (511) 260 1999; e-mail kansliet.skaramus@vgregion.se;

internet www.vastergotlandsmuseum.se; f. 1863; 3 permanent exhibitions: prehistoric colln of 17 bronze shields buried under water 3,000 years ago, Skara in the Middle Ages, and exposé on 19th-century artist Agnes de Frumerie; exhibits local handicraft and design, traditional games, energy conservation, school projects; Dir GRAZIELLA BELLONI; Curator JOHANNA AUSTRIN.

Skurup

Johanna Museet: POB 85, SE-274 22 Skurup; Sandåkra 6, Skurup; tel. (411) 427-80; fax (411) 425-30; e-mail info@johannamuseet.se; internet www.johannamuseet.se; f. 1983; objects exhibiting technological devts during the 1900s.

Svaneholms Slottsmuseum (Svaneholm Castle Museum): Svaneholms Slott, SE-274 91 Skurup; tel. and fax (411) 400-12; e-mail svaneholm.museum@telia.com; internet www.svaneholms-slott.se; f. 1935; textile collns of both upper-class and peasant class; colln incl. archaeological finds from the area, works of art, old toys, furniture, photographs and archives; Pres. BRITT-MARIE HANSSON; Vice-Pres. HELGE OLSSON; Treas. LENNART MÖRKING.

Stockholm

Aquaria Vattenmuseum (Aquaria Water Museum): Djurgården, Falkenbergsgatan 2, SE-115 21 Stockholm; tel. (8) 660-90-89; fax (8) 660-70-03; e-mail info@aquaria.se; internet www.aquaria.se; presents physical view of different climates and environments around the world with aquariums and indoor vegetation; centred on 3 themes: the Amazon rain forest, tropical seas, and Nordic waters.

Arkitekturmuseet (Swedish Museum of Architecture): Skeppsholmen, SE-111 49 Stockholm; tel. (8) 58-72-70-00; fax (8) 58-72-70-70; e-mail info@arkitekturmuseet.se; internet www.arkitekturmuseet.se; f. 1962; permanent architecture exhibition, drawings, models and photographs; organizes guided tours, debates, lectures, information, and activities on contemporary issues in architecture, design and planning; acts as platform for architecture, design and sustainable urban devt; library of 25,000 vols; Dir LENA RAHOULT; Asst Dir ULRIKA BEHM.

Biologiska Museet (Biological Museum): POB 27807, SE-115 93 Stockholm; Hazeliusporten, Djurgården, Stockholm; tel. (8) 442-82-15; fax (8) 442-82-98; e-mail bokning@skansen.se; internet www.biologiskamuseet.com; f. 1893; colln of Scandinavian mammals and birds in their natural, ecological habitat; use of dioramas to present natural habitat.

Dansmuseet (Dance Museum): Gustav Adolfs torg 22–24, SE-111 52 Stockholm; tel. (8) 441-76-50; fax (8) 20-06-02; e-mail info@dansmuseet.se; internet www.dansmuseet.se; f. 1933 in Paris as Archives Internationales de la Danse, 1953 in Sweden, present location 1999; performing arts museum; exhibitions of dance, theatre, visual art and photography; material from all over the world, notably Ballets Suédois; videotheque, folk dance dept, Rolf de Maré archive; Dir Dr ERIK NÄSLUND.

Etnografiska Museet (Museum of Ethnography): POB 27140, SE-102 52 Stockholm; Djurgårdsbrunnsvägen 34, SE-102 52 Stockholm; tel. (8) 519-550-00; fax (8) 519-550-70; e-mail info@etnografiska.se; internet www.etnografiska.se; f. 1880; colln of 150,000 artefacts from Africa, America, Asia, Australia and the Pacific; also houses the Sven Hedin Foundation; library of 45,000 books and journals; Dir ANDERS BJÖRKLUND; Librarian ZSUZSANNA MÜLLER; publs *Ethnos* (4 a year), Monograph Series.

Färgfabriken Contemporary Art Gallery: Lövholmsbrinken 1, SE-117 43 Stockholm; tel. (8) 645-07-07; internet www.fargfabriken.se; f. 1889; ind. foundation; works of art, architecture and community development; Dir RICHARD LESSE.

Fotografiska: Stadsgårdshamnen 22, SE-116 45 Stockholm; tel. (8) 50-90-05-00; e-mail info@fotografiska.eu; internet en.fotografiska.eu; f. 1940; exhibits contemporary photography; organizes seminars and courses; Dir JAN BROMAN; Vice-Pres. CHARLOTTE WIKING; Chief Curator MICHELLE ROY.

Galleri Kontrast: Hornsgatan 8, SE-118 20 Stockholm; tel. (8) 641-49-99; e-mail gkv@gallerikontrast.se; internet www.gallerikontrast.se; f. 1996; documentary photography; exhibits Swedish picture of the year, World Press Photo and work from Nordens Fotoskola; Chair. ROLF ADLERCREUTZ; Curator MIA KLINTEWALL.

Gustav III's Antikmuseum (Gustav III's Museum of Antiquities): Kungliga Slottet, SE-111 30 Stockholm; tel. (8) 402-61-30; fax (8) 402-61-67; internet www.royalcourt.se/royalcourt/royalpalaces/theroyalpalace/gustaviiismuseumofantiquities; f. 1794; art colln; private sculpture colln of Gustav III; sculptures and artifacts from late 18th century and belonging to Scandinavian region.

Historiska Museet (National Historical Museum): POB 5428, SE-114 84 Stockholm; Narvavägen 13–17, Stockholm; tel. (8) 519-556-00; fax (8) 519-556-40; e-mail info@historiska.se; internet www.historiska.se; comprises Museum of Nat. Antiquities and Royal Cabinet of Coins and Medals; collns comprise archaeological artefacts from Sweden and Swedish ecclesiastical art; Dir.-Gen. LARS AMRÉUS.

Judiska Museet (Jewish Museum): POB 6299, SE-102 34 Stockholm; Hälsingegatan 2, Stockholm; tel. (8) 31-01-43; fax (8) 31-84-04; e-mail info@judiska-museet.se; internet www.judiska-museet.a.se; f. 1987; adaptation of Jews to Swedish society and their contribution to culture, art, literature, trade, industry etc.; culture and religion of Jews, their manners and customs, in the synagogue and in their homes; history of the Swedish Jews; Dir YVONNE JACOBSSON.

Konstnärshuset: Smålandsgatan 7, SE-111 46 Stockholm; tel. (8) 611-10-09; e-mail storagalleriet.konstnarshuset@telia.com; internet www.konstnarshuset.com; f. 1899; exhibits architectural works and contemporary art; Sec. BO L. JOHANSSON.

Kulturhuset: POB 16414, SE-103 27 Stockholm; 7, Sergels torg, SE-103 72 Stockholm; tel. (50) 83-15-08; fax (50) 83-14-09; e-mail info.kulturhuset@stockholm.se; internet www.kulturhuset.stockholm.se; f. 1974; organizes photographic exhibitions, stories for children, concerts, literary discussions, films, debates, theatre; two libraries; Dir ERIC SJÖSTRÖM; Curators PIA KRISTOFFERSSON ESTELLE AF MALMBORG MARIA PATOMELLA.

Kungl. Myntkabinettet—Sveriges Ekonomiska Museum (Royal Coin Cabinet—National Museum of Economy): Slottsbacken 6, POB 5428, SE-114 84 Stockholm; tel. (8) 519-553-04; e-mail info@myntkabinettet.se; internet www.myntkabinettet.se; f. 1630; coin colln representing all ages; exhibition displays coins, banknotes, tokens, stock certificates, bank materials, wallets, piggy banks and related to economic history; exhibits medal's history and devt; Dir IAN WISÉHN.

Lars Bohman Gallery: Karlavägen 16, SE-114 31 Stockholm; tel. (8) 20-78-07; fax (8) 21-23-66; e-mail info@larsbohmangallery.com; internet www.larsbohmangallery.com; f. 1982; exhibits works of int. contemporary artists that incl. painting, drawing, sculpture, video and photography; Owner JAN HANSEN; Mans. MALIN LEVÉN, PELLE HÖGLUND.

Liljevalchs Konsthall: Djurgårdsvägen 60, SE-115 21 Stockholm; tel. (8) 50-83-13-30; e-mail info.liljevalchs@stockholm.se; internet www.liljevalchs.se; f. 1916; ind. and public art gallery for contemporary art; Head MARTEN CASTENFORS.

Livrustkammaren (Royal Armoury): Royal Palace, Slottsbacken 3, SE-111 30 Stockholm; tel. (8) 402-30-10; fax (8) 20-73-05; e-mail livrustkammaren@lsh.se; internet www.livrustkammaren.se; f. 1628; houses items once in the possession of Swedish monarchs and their families; most artefacts in the colln reflect official occasions such as state ceremonies, weddings, coronations and funerals; historical collns dating from mid-16th century; Swedish royal arms, costumes, jewels, coaches, etc.; library of 43,000 vols; Dir MAGNUS HAGBERG; Curator ELISABETH WESTIN BERG; Curator LENA RANGSTRÖM; Curator ANN GRÖNHAMMAR; publ. *Livrustkammaren* (Journal of Royal Armour, 1 a year).

Component Sites:

Hallwylska Museet: Hamngatan 4, SE-111 47 Stockholm; tel. (8) 402-30-99; e-mail hallwyl@lsh.se; internet www.hallwylskamuseet.se; f. c. 1900; private residence of Hallwyl family; colln of furniture, paintings, applied art, etc.; Dir HELI HAAPASALO; publ. *Hallwyliana*.

Skoklosters Slott: SE-746 95 Skokloster; tel. (8) 402-30-77; fax (18) 38-64-46; e-mail skokloster@lsh.se; internet sko.lsh.se; baroque castle built in 1654 by Count C. G. Wrangel; contains mainly 17th-century furniture, paintings, applied art and armour; library; library of 20,000 vols; Dir ANN KRISTIN CARLSTRÖM; Curator ELISABETH WESTIN BERG; publ. *Skokloster Studies*.

Magasin 3 Konsthall: Frihamnen, SE-115 56 Stockholm; tel. (8) 54-56-80-40; fax (8) 54-56-80-41; e-mail art@magasin3.com; internet www.magasin3.com; f. 1987; colln of contemporary art; three-dimensional works, drawings, photographic works and videos; 'Dawning' by James Turrell; Dir DAVID NEUMAN; Chief Curator RICHARD JULIN.

Medelhavsmuseet (Museum of Mediterranean and Near Eastern Antiquities): POB 16008, SE-103 21 Stockholm; Fredsgatan 2, Stockholm; tel. (8) 519-550-50; fax (8) 519-553-70; e-mail info@medelhavsmuseet.se; internet www.medelhavsmuseet.se; f. 1954 by merger of Egyptian Museum and Cyprus colln, present location 1982; archaeological collns of ancient and historical relics from Mediterranean countries; Dir SANNE HOUBY-NIELSEN; Deputy Dir SUZANNE UNGE-SÖRLING; Sec. CLAUDIE WIRÉN.

Moderna Museet (Museum of Modern Art): POB 16382, SE-103 27 Stockholm; Skeppsholmen, Stockholm; tel. (8) 519-552-00; fax (8) 519-552-10; e-mail info@modernamuseet.se; internet www.modernamuseet.se; f. 1958; contemporary paintings and sculptures by Swedish and foreign artists, also photographs and drawings; colln from 1900 to present day; br at Malmö; Dir DANIEL BIRNBAUM; Co-Dir ANN-SOFI NORING.

Museum Tre Kronor: Kungliga Slottet, SE-111 30 Stockholm; tel. (8) 402-61-00; fax (8) 402-61-67; internet www.royalcourt.se/kungligaslotten/kungligaslottet/museum-trekronor; f. 1999; colln of objects that rescued from fire of 1697 and newly created models; depicts the Tre Kronor Palace's devt from defence fort to the Renaissance palace of today.

Musik- & Teatermuseet (Stockholm Music and Theatre Museum): POB 16326, SE-103 26 Stockholm; Sibyllegatan 2, Stockholm; tel. (8) 519-554-90; fax (8) 663-91-81; e-mail museum@musikmuseet.se; internet www.musikmuseet.se; f. 1899 as Musikhistoriska Museet, present location 1979; attached to Swedish Nat. Collns of Music; more than 11,500 art and folk music instruments; exhibitions, archives and library; Dir HANS RIBEN.

Nationalmuseum: POB 16176, SE-103 24 Stockholm; Södra Blasieholmshamnen, Stockholm; tel. (8) 519-543-00; fax (8) 519-544-50; e-mail info@nationalmuseum.se; internet www.nationalmuseum.se; f. 1792; 16,000 paintings, sculptures and other objects, 500,000 drawings and prints, 30,000 items of applied art; also administers collns of several royal castles with 23,000 works of art; library: see Libraries and Archives; Dir Prof. SOLFRID SÖDERLIND; publs *Art Bulletin of Nationalmuseum Stockholm* (1 a year), *Nationalmuseums skriftserie. N. S.*.

Naturhistoriska Riksmuseet (Swedish Museum of Natural History): POB 50007, SE-104 05 Stockholm; Frescativägen 40, SE-114 18 Stockholm; tel. (8) 519-540-40; fax (8) 519-540-85; e-mail info@nrm.se; internet www.nrm.se; f. 1739; attached to Min. of Culture; collns and research units: vertebrates, entomology, invertebrates, palaeozoology, phanerogamic botany, cryptogamic botany, palaeobotany, mineralogy, isotope geology, DNA laboratory, contaminants; Dir JAN OLOV WESTERBERG; Dir for Admin. LENNART SANDBERG; Dir for Communication CHRISTINA KÅREMO SKÖLDKVIST; Dir for Public Engagement EWA BERGDAHL; Dir for Science PER ERICSON.

Nobelmuseet (Nobel Museum): POB 2245, SE-103 16 Stockholm; Börshuset, Stortorget, Gamla Stan, Stockholm; tel. (8) 53-48-18-00; fax (8) 23-25-07; e-mail bokning@nobel.se; internet www.nobelmuseum.se; honours Nobel Prize winners by highlighting their achievements and displaying some of their work; organizes lectures, group discussions , games, and interactive exhibitions; permanent colln: children's room educating about the Nobel Prizes in physics, chemistry, medicine, literature, peace, and economics; library of 5,000 vols; Dir OLOV AMELIN; Curator ARON AMBROSIANI.

Nordiska museet (Nordic Museum): POB 27820, SE-115 93 Stockholm; Djurgårdsvägen 6–16, Stockholm; tel. (8) 519-546-00; fax (8) 519-545-80; e-mail nordiska@nordiskamuseet.se; internet www.nordiskamuseet.se; f. 1873, present name and status 1907; nat. museum of cultural history since 16th century ethnological and industrial art collns; 10m. archive and photographic items; library of 250,000 vols; Pres. LARS O. GRÖNSTEDT; Dir CHRISTINA MATTSSON.

Observatoriemuseet (Observatory museum): Drottninggatan 120, SE-113 60 Stockholm; tel. (8) 545-483-90; fax (8) 545-483-95; e-mail observatoriet@kva.se; internet www.observatoriet.kva.se; f. 1991; organizes seminars, visits and excursions; exhibition on building's history; exhibits photographic work; Superintendent INGA EMQVIST SÖDERLUND.

Östasiatiska Museet (Museum of Far Eastern Antiquities): POB 16381, 103 27 Stockholm; Tyghusplan, Skeppsholmen, Stockholm; tel. (8) 519-557-50; fax (8) 519-557-55; e-mail info@ostasiatiska.se; internet www.ostasiatiska.se; f. 1926, present status 1999; Chinese paintings, sculptures and ceramics; Chinese pottery and bronze objects; Japanese, Korean, Southeast Asian and Indian collns; Far Eastern Library; Dir ANDERS BJÖRKLUND (acting); Deputy Dir and Curator EVA MYRDAL; Sec. KERSTIN BERGSTRÖM; publ. *Bulletin* (1 a year).

Postmuseum: POB 2002, SE-103 11 Stockholm; Lilla Nygatan 6T, Gamla Stan, Stockholm; tel. (8) 781-17-55; fax (8) 20-90-21; e-mail postmuseum@posten.se; internet www.postmuseum.posten.se; f. 1906; exhibits items connected with the Swedish Post Office and its history; colln of stamps, letter boxes and signs, postal art, furniture, cars, bicycles, stamp cancelling machines, uniforms, postal horns, emblems, mailmen's bags; collns of pictures and documents; philatelic collns; library of 60,000 vols, 180 journals; Dir OLLE SYNNERHOLM.

Prins Eugens Waldemarsudde: POB 16176, SE-103 24 Stockholm; Prins Eugens väg 6, Djurgården, Stockholm; tel. (8) 54-58-37-00; fax (8) 667-74-59; e-mail bokningen@waldemarsudde.se; internet www.waldemarsudde.se; f. 1995; colln of artwork by Carl Larsson, Anders Zorn, and Karl Nordström, Prince Eugen; sculptures by Carl Eldh, Per Hasselberg, Auguste Rodin, Carl Milles; exhibits sculpture, hand drawing, graphics and art medals; Admin. Man. HELEN WALDENSTRÖM; Chief Sec. CATRIN LUNDEBERG; Curator GÖRAN SÖDERLUND.

Skansen: POB 27807, SE-115 93 Stockholm; Djurgårdsslätten 49–51, SE-115 93 Stockholm; tel. (8) 442-80-00; fax (8) 442-82-82; e-mail info@skansen.se; internet www.skansen.se; f. 1891, present status 1963; open-air museum and zoological garden; Dir JOHN BRATTMYHR; Keeper of Bldgs CORTINA LANGE; Keeper of Zoo TOMAS FRISK.

Statens försvarshistoriska museer (National Swedish Museums of Military History): POB 14095, SE-104 41 Stockholm; Riddargatan 13, Stockholm; tel. (8) 519-563-10; e-mail info@sfhm.se; internet www.sfhm.se; f. 1976, merger of Army Museum in Stockholm, Navy Museum in Karlskrona, Air Force Museum in Linköping and Board of Military Traditions; attached to Min. of Culture; promotes knowledge about Swedish armed forces through the ages and their role in devt of society; responsible for a network of approximately 20 museums relating to particular units and for certain defence facilities of a culture historical value that previously had been under the auspices of the Swedish armed forces; supports other activities related to the cultural heritage of the armed forces at approximately 30 locations throughout Sweden; Dir-Gen. STAFFAN BENGTSSON; Deputy Dir-Gen. JOHAN ENGSTRÖM.

Statens maritima museer (National Maritime Museums): POB 27131, SE-102 52 Stockholm; Linnégatan 64, SE-114 54 Stockholm; tel. (8) 519-549-00; fax (8) 519-548-94; e-mail registrator@maritima.se; internet www.maritima.se; responsible for museums in Swedish state care that have maritime profile; Dir ROBERT OLSEN.

Component Museums:

Marinmuseum (Naval Museum): POB 48, SE-371 32 Karlskrona; Stumholmen, Karlskrona; tel. (455) 35-93-00; fax (455) 35-93-49; e-mail registrator@maritima.se; internet www.marinmuseum.se; f. 1752; 55,000 exhibits since 17th century; library of 22,000 vols, 4,000 maps and blueprints, 200,000 negatives and photographs; Dir RICKARD BAUER; publ. *Aktuellt-Marinmuseum* (yearbook).

Sjöhistoriska museet (Maritime Museum): POB 27131, SE-102 52 Stockholm; Djurgårdsbrunnsvägen 24, SE-115 27; tel. (8) 519-549-00; fax (8) 519-549-49; e-mail sjohistoriska@maritima.se; internet www.sjohistoriska.se; f. 1938; collns give a view of Swedish naval and merchant history, vessels of the past and of today as well as the history of Swedish shipbuilding; archive of drawings and photographs; colln comprises 100,000 objects, incl. over 1,500 models of ships and boats; library of 60,000 vols; Dir HANS-LENNART OHLSSON; publ. *Sjöhistorisk årsbok* (every 2 years).

Vasamuseet (Vasa Museum): POB 27131, SE-102 52 Stockholm; Galärvarvsvägen 14, Stockholm; tel. (8) 519-548-00; fax (8) 519-548-88; e-mail vasamuseet@maritima.se; internet www.vasamuseet.se; f. 1987; the Swedish warship *Vasa*, lost in 1628 and raised in 1961, and associated exhibits; also steam icebreaker *Sankt Erik* and lightship *Finngrundet*; Dir MARIKA HEDIN.

Stiftelsen Musikkulturens Främjande (Nydahl Collection): Riddargatan 35–37, SE-114 57 Stockholm; tel. and fax (8) 661-71-71; e-mail smf@nydahlcoll.se; internet www.nydahlcoll.se; f. 1920; colln of old music instruments; arranges concerts and lectures; music manuscript colln incl. works of composers Beethoven, Chopin, Donizetti, Mozart, Rossini, Schubert and Schumann, and Swedish and Scandinavian composers; colln of iconographic material, drawings, paintings and photos; a library of scores; colln of music literature belonging to Prof. Ingmar Bengtsson; Curators GÖRAN GRAHN, ROBERT HOLMIN, EDWARD KLINGSPOR.

Stockholms läns museum (Stockholm County Museum): Sickla Industriväg 5B, SE-131 54 Nacka; tel. (8) 586-194-00; e-mail museet@stockholmslansmuseum.se; internet www.stockholmslansmuseum.se; f. 1982; prehistoric finds; architectural and cultural history; library of 10,000 vols; Dir PETER BRATT.

Stockholms Stadsmuseum (Stockholm City Museum): POB 15025, SE-104 65 Stockholm; Ryssgården, Slussen; tel. (8) 508-316-00; fax (8) 508-316-99; e-mail info@stadsmuseum.stockholm.se; internet www.stadsmuseum.stockholm.se; f. 1937; history and devt of Stockholm; archaeology and cultural heritage; colln of photographs, maps, art and artefacts; incl. a library and archives; preserves 300,000 items of historical interest; 20,000 works of art, 3,000 oil paintings, 3m. photographs; library of 40,000 vols; Dir ANN-CHARLOTTE BACKLUND; publs *Blick* (articles covering the activity of the admin.), *Sankt Eriks årsbok* (yearbook).

Affiliated Museum:

Stockholms Medeltidsmuseum (Museum of Medieval Stockholm): SE-100 12 Stockholm; Strömparterren, Norrbro, Stockholm; tel. (8) 508-317-90; fax (8) 508-317-99; e-mail info.medeltidsmuseet@stockholm.se; internet www.medeltidsmuseet.stockholm.se; f. 1986; archaeological remains of Stockholm, reflecting its foundation and history from c. 1250–1550; Dir SOLBRITT BENNETH; Curator LIN ANNERBÄCK.

Strindbergsmuseet (Strindberg Museum): Drottninggatan 85, SE-111 60 Stockholm; tel. (8) 411-53-54; fax (8) 411-01-41; e-mail fornamn@strindbergsmuseet.se; internet www.strindbergsmuseet.se; colln of objects related to Strindberg; collns divided into 7 categories: cultural history, art, theatre, photographs, press clippings, library, audiovisual media; photographic archive with 2,500 photographs; library of 5,000 vols; Dir STEFAN BOHMAN; Curators ERIK HÖÖK, CAMILLA LARSSON.

Tekniska Museet (National Museum of Science and Technology): POB 27842, SE-115 93 Stockholm; Museivägen 7, SE-115 93 Stockholm; tel. (8) 450-56-00; fax (8) 450-56-01; e-mail info@tekniskamuseet.se; internet www.tekniskamuseet.se; f. 1924; history of science and technology; devt of Swedish industry and engineering; mining, iron and steel, steam power and machines, cars and aircraft, history of electricity, chemistry, computers, Polhem's colln of engineering models, mechanical workshop and model railway; Teknorama science centre; Cino4 special effects 3D films, archives of drawings and photographs; library of 50,000 vols; Dir ANN FOLLIN; publ. *Daedalus* (1 a year).

Thielska Gallery: Sjötullsbacken 8, SE-115 25 Stockholm; tel. (8) 662-58-84; fax (8) 544-85-112; e-mail info@thielska-galleriet.se; internet www.thielska-galleriet.se; f. 1926; colln of Nordic Heirloom Art; works of artists Edvard Munch, Carl Larsson, Bruno Liljefors and Eugène Jansson; Curator NINA ÖHMAN.

Vin & Sprithistoriska Museet (Historical Museum of Wines & Spirits): Dalagatan 100, SE-113 43 Stockholm; tel. (8) 51-91-86-50; fax (8) 31-39-28; e-mail ingrid.leffler@vinosprithistoriska.se; internet www.vinosprithistoriska.se; f. 1967, present status 1992; collns of objects, images, tags from period between late 1800s and present day; alcohol historical archives; colln of wine and liquor bottles; library of 4,500 vols, 150 journal titles; Dir INGRID LEFFLER; Curator EVA LENNEMAN.

Svalöv

Galleri Tapper-Popermajer (Tapper-Popermajer Art Gallery): Bantorget 2, SE-260 20 Teckomatorp; e-mail info@tapper-popermajer.com; internet www.tapper-popermajer.com; f. 2007; exhibits nat. and int. artists' work; organizes lecturers and musical events; Owner ILONA POPERMAJER.

Svedala

Statarmuseet i Skåne: Torupsvägen 606-59, SE-230 40 Bara; tel. (40) 44-70-90; fax (40) 41-49-67; e-mail brevladan@statarmuseet.com; internet www.statarmuseet.com; f. 1995; organizes training courses, seminars, theme days and events with the starting point of the seasons; has archive; exhibits kitchen commons, sleeping accommodation, and tiny garden plot of bonded labours of the time.; Dir BARBRO FRANCKIE.

Tjörn

Nordiska Akvarellmuseet (Nordic Watercolour Museum): Södra hamnen 6, SE-471 32 Skärhamn; tel. (304) 60-00-80; e-mail info@akvarellmuseet.org; internet www.akvarellmuseet.org; f. 1989; Nordic centre for contemporary art, research and training; exhibits works of contemporary int. watercolourists; organizes lectures, theatrical performance, dance, music and discussions; Dir BERA NORDAL.

Umea

Bild Museet (Image Museum): c/o Umeå Univ., SE-901 87 Umeå; tel. (90) 786-52-27; fax (90) 786-77-33; e-mail info@bildmuseet.umu.se; internet www.bildmuseet.umu.se; f. 1981; exhibits int. contemporary art, classical art; photographs, design, architecture and scientific images combines contemporary perspective with historical flashbacks; Dir KATARINA PIERRE (acting).

Pengsjö nybyggarmuseum (Pengsjö settler's museum): c/o Sven-Eric Nyman, Rönnbärsstigen 17, SE-903 46 Umea; tel. (90) 13-05-33; e-mail sven-eric.nyman@pengsjomuseum.se; internet www.pengsjomuseum.se; exhibits buildings from 17th, 18th and 19th centuries; colln from peasant and Sami culture; Head SVEN-ERIC NYMAN.

Västerbottens museum: POB 3183, SE-903 40 Umea; tel. (90) 17-18-00; fax (90) 77-90-00; e-mail info@vbm.se; internet www.vbm.se; f. 1886; collns of Sami culture with its gear and clothing; has photo archive; Chair. EVERTH GUSTAVSSON; Dir ULRICA GRUBBSTRÖM; publ. *Västerbotten* (4 a year).

Attached Museums:

Svenska Skidmuseet (Swedish Ski Museum):; f. 1928; colln of hand-made ski, snowshoe for both man and horse, prehistoric skis, ski equipment, world's oldest surviving pods, Kalvträsk scabbard.

Fiske- och sjöfartsmuseet (Fishing and Maritime Museum):; f. 1975; colln of pictures, models and objects related to boats, ships and sea industries.

Uppsala

Evolutionsmuseet (Museum of Evolution): Norbyvägen 16, SE-752 36 Uppsala; tel. (18) 471-27-39; fax (18) 471-27-94; e-mail info@em.uu.se; internet www.evolutionsmuseet.uu.se; f. 1999; 5m. fossils of animals, plants, fungi, lichens, minerals, dinosaurs; Dir MATS ERIKSSON.

Museum Gustavianum: Akademigatan 3, SE-753 10 Uppsala; tel. (18) 471-75-71; fax (18) 471-75-72; e-mail museum@gustavianum.uu.se; internet www.gustavianum.uu.se; f. 1997; exhibits Anatomical Theatre, the Augsburg Art Cabinet and objects from Valsgärde; the Antique colln; the Egyptian colln; the Nordic archaeology colln; the physical cabinet; art collns; coin cabinet; Head Curator MARGARETA NISSER-DALMAN; Curator ANNA SJÖGREN (acting); Asst Curator JOHAN LUNDBERG.

Upplandsmuseet (Upplands Museum): St Eriksgränd 6, SE-753 10 Uppsala; tel. (18) 16-91-00; fax (18) 69-25-09; e-mail info@upplandsmuseet.se; internet www.upplandsmuseet.se; f. 1959; provincial cultural history; collns of 750,000 objects and nearly 1.5m. glass negatives, film negatives and prints, extensive archive of topographic data, measurements, records and maps; Chair. ULF SCHMIDT; Vice-Chair. GUNILLA OLTNER; Dir BENT SYSE; Dir HÅKAN LIBY; publ. *Uppland*.

Varberg

Länsmuseet Varberg: Varbergs Fästning, SE-432 44 Varberg; tel. (340) 828-30; e-mail kansli@lansmuseet.varberg.se; internet www.lansmuseet.varberg.se; 50,000 historical items; 20,000 archaeological finds; 200,000 photographs; library of 20,000 vols; Dir AGNES BOQVIST.

Växjö

Smålands Museum, Sveriges Glasmuseum (Smålands Museum, Sweden's Museum of Glass): POB 102, SE-351 04 Växjö; Södra Järnvägsgatan 2, SE-351 04 Växjö; tel. (470) 70-42-00; fax (470) 397-44; e-mail reception@smalandsmuseum.se; internet www.smalandsmuseum.se; Swedish glass colln; collns incl. objects of cultural historical significance, visual art, textiles, church furnishings, archaeological finds and agricultural history; permanent exhibits on 2 themes: Småland's rural industrial landscape and five centuries of Swedish glass; castle ruins of Kronoberg; Kronoberg agricultural museum; numismatic colln; Dir ERICA MÅNSSON.

Viken

Beredskapsmuseet: Djuramossavägen 160, SE-260 40 Viken; tel. (42) 22-40-39; fax (42) 22-40-89; e-mail info@beredskapsmuseet.com; internet www.beredskapsmuseet.com; f. 1997; located in a Second World War underground military facility; exhibits Sweden's defences during the Second World War through equipment, photography etc.; Dir JOHAN ANDRÉE.

Universities

GÖTEBORGS UNIVERSITET (Gothenburg University)

POB 100, 405 30 Gothenburg
Telephone: (31) 786-00-00
Fax: (31) 786-44-73
E-mail: registrator@gu.se
Internet: www.gu.se

Founded 1891, became state univ. 1954
Academic year: September to June

Vice-Chancellor: PAM FREDMAN
Pro-Vice-Chancellor: LENNART WEIBULL
Pro-Vice-Chancellor: MARGARETA WALLIN PETERSON
Head of Admin.: PER-OLOF REHNQUIST
Librarian: AGNETA OLSSON

Library: see Libraries and Archives
Number of teachers: 2,500
Number of students: 37,000

Publication: *Acta Universitatis Gothoburgensis*

DEANS

Faculty of Arts: Prof. MARGARETA HALLBEERG
Faculty of Education: Prof. MIKAEL ALEXANDERSSON
Faculty of Fine, Applied and Performing Arts: Prof. ANNA LINDAL
Faculty of Science: Prof. DAVID TURNER
Faculty of Social Sciences: Prof. HELENA LINDHOLM-SCHULZ
IT Faculty: Prof. JAN SMITH
Sahlgrenska Academy: Prof. OLLE LARKÖ
School of Business, Economics and Law: Prof. ROLF WOLFF
Teacher Training: Prof. ELISABETH HESSLEFORS-ARKTOFT

PROFESSORS

Faculty of Arts (POB 200, SE-405 30 Gothenburg; tel. (31) 786-00-00; fax (31) 786-11-44; internet www.hum.gu.se):

AGRELL, B., Comparative Literature
AHLBERGER, C., History
AHLSÉN, E., Neurolinguistics
AIJMER, K., English
ALLWOOD, J., General Linguistics
ANDERSSON, L.-G., Modern Swedish
ANDERSSON, S.-G., German
BÄRMARK, J., Theory of Science
BENSON, K., Spanish
BERGH, G., English
BJÖRNBERG, A., Musicology
BORIN, L., Natural Language Processing
BOYD, S., General Linguistics
BYRSKOG, S., New Testament Exegesis
COOPER, R., Computational Linguistics
DAHL, E.-L., History of Science and Ideas
EDSTRÖM, K.-O., Musicology
ENGDAHL, E., Swedish
EKLUND, B.-L., Modern Greek
ERIKSSON, A., Phonetics
FLORBY, G., English Literature
FORSER, T., Comparative Literature
HAGLUND, D., Religious Studies
HALLBERG, M., Theory of Science
HANSSON, S., Comparative Literature
HELDNER, C., French
HOLMQUIST, I., Women Studies

JOHANNESSON, L., History of Art
KRISTIANSEN, K., Archaeology
LAGER, T., Computational Linguistics
LARSSON, L., Comparative Literature
LEGÈRE, K., African Languages
LIEDMAN, S.-E., History of Science and Ideas
LILJA, E., Comparative Literature
LILLIESTAM, L., Musicology
LINDBERG, B., History of Science and Ideas
LINDBERG, I., Swedish as a Second Language
LINDKVIST, T., Medieval History
LJUNGGREN, M., Russian Literature
MALM, M., Comparative Literature
MALMGREN, H., Theoretical Philosophy
MALMGREN, S.-G., Swedish
MALMSTEDT, G., History
MUNTHE, C., Practical Philosophy
NÄSSTRÖM, B.-M., History of Religion
NILSSON, B., History of Christianity
NILSSON, I., History of Science and Ideas
NORDBLADH, J., Archaeology
OHLANDER, S., English
OLAUSSON, L., Conditions in Science and Humanities
OLOFSSON, A., English
OLOFSSON, S., Old Testament Exegesis
PANKOW, C., German
PERSSON, I., Practical Philosophy
PERSSON, L., History
PLATEN, E., German Literature
RALPH, B., Northern Languages
RETSÖ, J., Arabic
SANDBERG, B., German
SJÖGREN, O., Film Studies
SKARIN-FRYKMAN, B., Ethnology
STÅLHAMMAR, M., English Terminology
STRANDBERG-OLOFSSON, M., Classical Archaeology and Ancient History
THUNMAN, N., Japanese
WESTERSTÅHL, D., Theoretical Philosophy
WINBERG, C., History
WISTRAND, M., Latin

Faculty of Education (POB 300, SE-405 30 Gothenburg; tel. (31) 786-00-00; fax (31) 786-22-42; e-mail kansli.ufn@ped.gu.se; internet www.ped.gu.se):

AHLBERG, A., Special Education and Educational Research
ALEXANDERSSON, M., Education and Educational Research—Didactics
ANDERSSON, B., Education and Educational Research—Didactics
BENGTSSON, J., Philosophy of Education
GUNNARSSON, L., Education and Educational Research
GUSTAFSSON, J.-E., Education and Educational Research
HOLMER, J., Work Science
LANDER, R., Education and Educational Research
LASSBO, G., Education and Educational Research
LINDBLAD, S., Education and Educational Research
LINDSTRÖM, B., Education and Educational Research
MARTON, F., Education and Educational Research
MUNCK, J., Education and Educational Research
NILSSON, L., Education and Educational Research
OHLANDER, S., English
OSCARSON, M., Education and Educational Research
OTT, A., Science Education
PATRIKSSON, G., Education and Educational Research
PRAMLING-SAMUELSSON, I., Education and Educational Research
SÄLJÖ, R., Education and Educational Science
SHANAHAN, H., Home Economics
SIMONSON, B., History
THÅNG, P.-O., Education and Educational Research
WENESTAM, C.-G., Education and Educational Research
WERNERSSON, I., Education and Educational Research

Faculty of Fine, Applied and Performing Arts (POB 141, SE-405 30 Gothenburg; tel. (31) 786-00-00; fax (31) 786-13-18; e-mail anna.lindal@konst.gu.se; internet www.konst.gu.se):

DAVIDSSON, H., Organ
DU RÉES, G., Film Directing
EKLUND, B., Trumpet
ELDENIUS, M., Music Theory
FOLKESTAD, G., Research in Music Education
GÅRDFELDT, G., Communication and Performance Skills, Drama
HYBBINETTE, P., Fine Arts in Design
JORMIN, A., Contrabass and Improvisation
LÜTZOW-HOLM, O., Composition
NÄSSEN, E., Voice
NIELSEN, E., Percussion and Contemporary Music
OLSSON, B., Research in Music Education
THORSÉN, S.-M., Music and Society
WASKO, R., Fine Arts
WIKLUND, A., Music Drama

Faculty of Science (POB 460, SE-405 30 Gothenburg; tel. (31) 786-00-00; fax (31) 773-48-39; e-mail info@science.gu.se; internet www.science.gu.se):

ÅBERG, P., Marine Ecology
ABRAMOWICZ, M., Astrophysics
ADLER, L., Marine Microbiology
AHLBERG, E., Inorganic Chemistry
AHLBERG, P., Organic Chemistry
ANDERSSON, L., Hydrosphere Science
ANDERSSON, M., Zooecology
ANDERSSON, S., Animal Ecology
ANDERSSON, S., Physics
ANDREASSON, L.-E., Molecular Biophysics
ARKERYD, L., Applied Mathematics
AXELSSON, M., Comparative Integrative Zoology
BADEN, S. P., Marine Ecology
BILLETER, M., Molecular Biophysics
BJÖRK, G., Polar Oceanography
BJÖRNSSON, B. T., Zoophysiology
BJURSELL, G., Molecular Biology
BLANCK, H., Plant Physiology
BLOMBERG, A., Functional Genomics
BOHLIN, T., Animal Ecology
BRZEZINSKI, J., Mathematics
CAMPBELL, E., Atomic and Molecular Physics
CARLSSON, P., Genetics
CEDERWALL, M., Theoretical Physics
CHEN, D., Physical Meteorology
CLARKE, A., Plant Molecular Biology
CORNELL, D., Geochemistry
DAVE, G., Environmental Protection
ELWING, H., Surface Biophysics
ERSÉUS, C., Evolutionary Morphology and Systematics
FÖRLIN, L., Zoophysiology
FRANZÉN, L., Physical Geography
GÖTMARK, F., Zooecology
HÅKANSSON, M., Organometallic Chemistry
HALL, P., Marine Sediment Diagenesis
HALLENBERG, N., Systematic Biology
HANSTORP, D., Experimental Physics
HELLSING, B., Physics
HERMANSSON, M., Marine Microbiology
HOHMANN, S., Molecular Microbial Physiology
HOLMGREN, S., Zoophysiology
HOLMLID, L., Physical Chemistry, especially Energy-related Basic Research
JAGNER, D., Analytical Chemistry
JOHANNESSON, H., Theoretical Physics
JOHANNESSON, K., Biology, Marine Ecology
JONSON, M., Condensed Matter Physics
JONSSON, P., Marine Ecology
KARLBERG, A.-T., Dermatochemistry and Skin Allergy
KJELLANDER, R., Physical Chemistry
KOMITOV, L., Physics
LARSON, S. A., Geology
LARSSON, Å., Environmental Protection
LEVAN, G., Genetics
LINDHE, U., Zoology (Structural and Animal)
LINDQVIST, O., Inorganic Chemistry
LINDQVIST, S., Physical Geography
LINDVALL, T., Mathematical Statistics
LJUNGSTRÖM, E., Atmospheric Science
LUTHMAN, K., Medicinal Chemistry
MALMGREN, B., Marine Geology
MEHLIG, B., Physics
MOLAU, U., Plant Ecology
NILSSON, S., Zoophysiology
NORDBERG, K., Paleoceanography
NORDHOLM, S., Physical Chemistry
NYMAN, G., Physical Chemistry
NYSTRÖM, T., Scientific Microbiology
OLSSON, O., Developmental Biology of Plants
OMSTEDT, A., Geosphere Dynamics
ÖSTLAND, S., Solid State Physics
PEDERSEN, K., Biology, Microbiology
PENDRILL, A.-M., Physics
PETTERSSON, J., Environmental Atmospheric Sciences
PIHL, L., Marine Fish Ecology
PLEIJEL, H., Environmental Protection
RODHE, J., Oceanography
ROSEN, A., Molecular Physics
ROSENBERG, R., Marine Ecology
RYDBERG, L., Oceanography
RYDSTRÖM, J., Biochemistry
SANDELIUS, A.-S., Plant Physiology
SELLDÉN, G., Tree Physiology, Influence of Air Pollution
SHCHERBINA, N., Mathematics
SHEKTER, R., Theoretical Physics
SILVERIN, B., Zoology (Structural and Animal)
SJÖGREN, P., Mathematics
SJÖLIN, L., Inorganic Chemistry
STENSON, J., Biology, Aquatic Ecology
STEVENS, R., Environmental and Quaternary Geology
STIGEBRANDT, A., Oceanography
STIGH, J., Bedrock Geology
STOLIN, A., Mathematics
SUNDBÄCK, K., Biology, Marine Botany
SUNDBERG, P., Zoomorphology
SUNDELL, K., Animal Zoophysiology
SUNDQVIST, CH., Plant Physiology
SUNNERHAGEN, P., Eucaryotic Molecular Biology
SVANSTEDT, N., Mathematics
TISELIUS, P., Marine Ecology
TURNER, D. R., Marine Chemistry
WALLENTINUS, I., Marine Botany
WALLIN PETERSSON, M., Zoophysiology
WEDBORG, M., Marine Analytical Chemistry
WERMUTH, N. E., Biostatistics
WETTERBERG, O., Conservation, specializing in integrated conservation of the built environment
WILLANDER, M., Experimental Physics
ZHUKOV, M., Theoretical Physics

Faculty of Social Sciences (POB 720, SE-405 30 Gothenburg; tel. (31) 786-10-00; fax (31) 786-19-40; e-mail lars-olof.karlsson@gu.se; internet www.samfak.gu.se):

ARCHER, T., Psychology
ASP, K., Journalism
BJERELD, U., Political Science
BJÖRNBERG, U., Sociology
BOHOLM, Å., Social Anthropology
BROBERG, A., Psychology
BRORSTRÖM, B., Management Economics
BÄCK, H., Public Administration
BÄCK-WIKLUND, M., Social Work

Demker, M., Political Science
Esaiasson, P., Political Science
Furåker, B., Sociology
Gilljam, M., Political Science
Glimell, H., Science and Technology Studies
Gustafsson, B., Social Work
Gärling, T., Psychology
Hansen, S., Psychology
Hettne, B., Peace and Conflict Research
Hjelmquist, E., Behavioural Studies of Disabilities and Handicap
Holmberg, S., Political Science
Hwang, P., Psychology
Höglund, L., Library and Information Science
Johansson, B., Psychology
Jonsson, D., Sociology
Lindahl, R., Political Science
Lundqvist, L. J., Political Science
Olsson, S., Social Work
Peterson, A., Sociology
Pierre, J., Political Science
Rombach, B., Management Economics
Rothstein, B., Political Science
Svensson, L. G., Sociology
Weibull, L., Mass Communication
Århem, K., Social Anthropology

IT-Faculty (Forskningsgången 6, SE-412 96 Gothenburg; tel. (31) 786-00-00; fax (31) 772-48-99; e-mail jan.smith@chalmers.se; internet www.itufak.gu.se):

Brenner, P., Mathematics
Coquand, T., Computer Science
Dahlbom, B., Informatics

Sahlgrenska Academy (POB 400, SE-405 30 Gothenburg; fax (31) 786-33-99; e-mail registrator@sahlgrenska.gu.se; internet www.sahlgrenska.gu.se):

Ahlman, H., Endocrine Surgery
Albertsson-Wikland, K., Paediatric Growth Research
Albrektsson, T., Handicap Research
Allebeck, P., Social and Preventive Medicine
Åman, P., Tumour Biology
Andersson, O., Medicine
Ashton, M., Biopharmacy
Axelsson, G., Hygiene
Axelsson, R., Psychiatry
Bagge, U., Anatomy
Barregård, L., Clinical Environmental Medicine
Bengtsson, B.-Å, Clinical Endocrinology
Bergbom, I., Nursing
Bergfeldt, L., Cardiology
Berggren, U., Odontological Psychology
Berglundh, T., Parodontology
Bergström, T., Clinical Microbiology
Betsholtz, Ch., Medical Biochemistry
Biber, B., Anaesthesiology and Intensive Care
Billig, B., Cellular Aging and Apoptosis
Birkhed, D., Cariology
Björkelund, C., General Medicine
Blennow, K., Clinical Neurochemistry
Blomstrand, C., Neurology
Bondjers, G., Cardiological Research
Borén, J., Cardiovascular Research
Braide, M., Anatomy
Breimer, M., Clinical Molecular Genetics
Bry, K., Paediatrics, especially Neonatology
Brännström, M., Obstetrics and Gynaecology
Carlsson, J., Physiotherapy
Carlsson, L., Clinical Metabolic Research
Carlsten, H., Rheumatology
Dahlén, G., Oral Microbiology
Dahlgren, C., Medical Microbiology
Dahlgren, U., Oral Immunology
Dahlström, A., Histology
Damber, J.-E., Urology
Dickson, S., Psychology, especially Neuro Endocrinology
Edén, S., Physiology, especially Endocrinology
Edenbrandt, L., Clinical Physiology, especially Nuclear Medicine
Ekroth, R., Thoracic Surgery
Ekström, J., Pharmacology
Elam, M., Clinical Neurophysiology
Elias, P., Medicinal Biochemistry
Emilson, C.-G., Cardiology
Enerbäck, S., Medical Genetics
Engel, J., Pharmacology
Ericson, L., Anatomy
Eriksson, E., Pharmacology
Eriksson, P., Neurobiology, especially Stem Cell Research
Fändriks, L., Integrative Physiology and Pharmacology
Fasth, A., Paediatric Immunology and Rheumatology
Fossell-Aronsson, E., Radiophysics
Fredman, P., Neurochemistry
Friberg, P., Clinical Physiology
Funa, K., Medical Cell Biology
Gaston-Johansson, F., Nursing Sciences
Gillberg, C., Child and Youth Psychiatry and Handicap Research
Granström, G., Otorhinolaryngology
Gröndahl, H.-G., Oral Diagnostic Radiology
Gröndahl, K., Oral Diagnostic Radiology
Gustafsson, B., Neurophysiology
Hagberg, H., Obstetrics and Gynaecology, especially Peridontology
Hagberg, M., Occupational Medicine
Haglid, K., Histology
Hamberger, L., Obstetrics and Gynaecology
Hansson, G., Biochemistry, especially Gastrointestinal Glycobiology
Hansson, H.-A., Histology
Hansson, T., Occupational Orthopaedics
Hansson Rönnbäck, E., Glia Cell Research
Härd, T., Structural Biology, especially Protein Chemistry
Haraldsson, B., Kidney Medicine with Experimental Alignment
Hedner, T., Clinical Pharmacology
Hellstrand, K., Immune Therapy
Hellström, A., Paediatric Ophtalmology, especially Growth Factors
Hellström, M., Diagnostic Radiology
Hjalmarsson, O., Paediatrics
Holm, S., Experimental Surgery
Holmgren, J., Medical Microbiology
Holmström, H., Plastic Surgery
Holmäng, A., Laboratory Medicine
Hultborn, R., Oncology
Hulthén, L., Clinical Nutrition, especially Human Trace Element Research
Isaksson, O., Endocrinology
Isgaard, J., Hormonal Regulation of the Heart, especially Growth and Repair Processes
Iwarson, S., Infectious Diseases
Jacobsson, L., Medical Radiophysics
Janson, P.-O., Obstetrics and Gynaecology
Jansson, J.-O., Tissue Regeneration
Jansson, T., Physiology, especially Perinatal Physiology
Jern, C., Neurology, especially Vascular Diseases and Vascular Genetics
Jern, S., Cardiovascular Physiology
Johansson, B. R., Anatomy
Jonason, J., Pharmacology
Jontell, M., Endocrinology with Oral Diagnostics
Kahnberg, K.-E., Dental Surgery
Karlsson, A., Experimental Rheumatology
Karlsson, J.-O., Histology
Karlsson, S., Prosthetic Dentistry
Kindblom, L.-G., Pathology
Kärrholm, J., Orthopaedic Surgery
Lagergård, T., Vaccine Research
Larkö, O., Dermatology and Venereal Disease
Larson, G., Laboratory Medicine, especially Glycobiology
Larsson, S., Pneumology
Lekholm, U., Oral Implant Surgery
Lindahl, A., Cartilage Tissue Regeneration
Lindblom, B., Eye Diseases
Linde, A., Oral Biochemistry
Lissner, L., Epidemiology
Lundholm, K., Surgery
Lycke, N., Clinical Immunology
Lötvall, J., Clinical Allergology
Magnusson, B., Oral Pathology
Mattsson, B., General Medicine
Meis-Kindblom, J., Pathology
Mellander, L., International Medicine
Milsom, I., Gynaecology and Obstetrics
Möller, C., Audiology
Mohlin, B., Orthodontics
Nilsson, O., Pathology
Nilsson, T., Functional Morphology
Nissbrandt, H., Pharmacology
Nordgren, S., Surgery
Norén, J., Paedodontics
Nygren, H., Histology
Nyström, E., Medicine
Ohlsson, C., Hormonal Regulation of Bone Metabolism and Growth
Olausson, M., Clinical Transplantation Surgery
Oldfors, A., Pathology
Olmarker, K., Experimental Spinal Pain Research, especially Neuropathic Pain Mechanism
Olofsson, S.-O., Medical Biochemistry
Olsson, J., Odontological Technology
Östman-Smith, I., Paediatric Cardiology
Pilhammar-Andersson, E., Nursing Pedagogics
Reit, C., Endodontology
Ridell, M., Medical Microbiology
Risberg, B., Surgery
Rosengren, A., Epidemiology
Roupe, G., Dermatology and Venereal Diseases
Rydevik, B., Orthopaedic Surgery
Rymo, L., Clinical Chemistry
Rönnbäck, L., Neurology
Samuelsson, B., Transfusion Medicine
Sandberg, M., Biochemistry
Semb, H., Evolutionary Biology
Sennerby, L., Handicap Research, especially Experimental and Clinical
Sillén, U., Paediatric Surgery
Sjöberg, B., Medical Biochemistry
Sjöström, L., Clinical Research
Sjövall, H., Physiology and Pathophysiology of the Digestive and Intestinal Channel
Skoog, I., Psychiatry, especially Social Psychiatry and Epidemiology
Smith, U., Medicine
Soussi, B., Experimental Medicine, especially NMR Spectroscopy
Steineck, G., Cancer Epidemiology
Stenevi, U., Ophthalmology
Stenman, G., Pathology
Strandvik, B., Paediatrics
Sullivan, M., Psychology
Svennerholm, A.-M., Infectious Diseases and Immunology
Swedberg, K., Medicine
Tarkowski, A., Rheumatology
Thelle, D., Cardiovascular Epidemiology and Prevention
Thomsen, P., Medical Biomaterials Research
Tylén, U., X-Ray Diagnostics
Wahlström, J., Clinical Genetics
Wallerstedt, S., Medicine
Wallgren, A., Radio Therapeutics
Wallin, A., Geriatric Neuropsychiatry
Wennerberg, A., Oral Prosthetics
Wennergren, G., Paediatrics
Wennström, J., Parodontology

WICK, M. J., Clinical and Experimental Immunology
WIGSTRÖM, H., Medical Physics
WIKKELSÖ, C., Neurology
WIKLUND, O., Medicine
WIKSTRÖM, M., Oral Microbiology

School of Business, Economics and Law (POB 600, SE-405 30 Gothenburg; tel. (31) 786-49-48; fax (31) 773-55-20; e-mail info@handels.gu.se; internet www.handels.gu.se):

ALVSTAM, C.-G., International Economic Geography
ANDERSSON, D. T., Marketing
BERGENDAHL, G., Managerial Economics
BIGSTEN, A., Economics
CRAMÉR, P., International Law, European Integration Law
CZARNIAWSKA, B., Business Administration
DOTEVALL, R., Commercial Law
FLOOD, L., Econometrics
FRISÉN, M., Statistics
GADD, C.-J., Economic History
HIBBS, D., Economics
HJALMARSSON, L., Economics
JENSEN, A., Transport Management
JOHANSSON STENMAN, O., Economics
JONSSON, S., Economic History
JÖNSSON, S., Business Administration
LINDBLOM, T., Business Administration
MÅRTENSSON, R., Business Administration
NORBÄCK, L.-E., Business Administration
NORDSTRÖM, L., Human Geography
OLSON, O., Accounting and Finance
OLSSON, U., Economic History
PÅHLSSON, R., Tax Law
POLESIE, T., Accounting and Finance
RAMBERG, C., Commercial Law
SANDELIN, B., Economics
SOLLI, R., Business Administration
STERNER, T., Environmental Economics
STJERNBERG, T., Management and Organization
TÖLLBORG, D., Legal Science
TÖRNQVIST, U., Business Administration
VILHELMSON, B., Human Geography
WESTERHÄLL, V. L., Public Law

KARLSTADS UNIVERSITET
(Karlstad University)

SE-651 88 Karlstad
Universitetsgatan 2, Karlstad
Telephone: (54) 700-10-00
Fax: (54) 700-14-60
E-mail: information@kau.se
Internet: www.kau.se

Founded 1967 as Universitetsfilialen; became Högskolan i Karlstad 1977, present name 1999
State control
Languages of instruction: English, Swedish
Academic year: August to June

Rector: KERSTIN NORÉN
Pro-Rector: THOMAS BLOM
Pro-Rector: GERD LINDGREN
Univ. Dir: ANNE-CHRISTINE LARSEN
Library Dir: EVA ARNDT KLING

Library of 180,000 vols
Number of teachers: 700
Number of students: 12,000

Publications: *Anslaget* (26 a year), *Utbilder* (6 a year)

DEANS

Faculty of Arts and Education: KENNETH NORDGREN
Faculty of Economic Sciences, Communication and IT: JOHN SÖREN PETTERSSON
Faculty of Social and Life Sciences: Prof. CURT RÄFTEGÅRD
Faculty of Technology and Science: JAN VAN STAM

LINKÖPINGS UNIVERSITET
(Linköping University)

SE-581 83 Linköping
Telephone: (13) 28-10-00
Fax: (13) 14-94-03
E-mail: liu@liu.se
Internet: www.liu.se

Founded 1970
Academic year: September to June

Rector: MILLE MILLNERT
Pro-Rector: KARIN FÄLTH-MAGNUSSON
Univ. Dir: CURT KARLSSON

Library: see Libraries and Archives
Number of teachers: 1,800
Number of students: 25,000

DEANS

Faculty of Arts and Sciences: BO HELLGREN
Faculty of Educational Sciences: KARIN MÅRDSJÖ BLUME
Faculty of Health Sciences: Prof. Dr MATS HAMMAR
Institute of Technology: HELEN DANNETUN

PROFESSORS

Faculty of Arts and Sciences:

ÅDELSWÄRD, V., Communication Studies
ÅHLUND, A, Ethnicity Studies
ALLARD, B., Water and Environmental Studies
ANSELM, J., Technology and Social Change
ANWARD, J., Language and Culture Studies
ARNESDOTTER, I., Business Law
ARONSSON OTTOSSON, K., Child Studies
BECKMAN, S., Technology and Social Change
BERNER, B., Technology and Social Change
BORGQUIST, L., Health and Society
CARLGREN, I., Education
CARSTENSEN, J., Health and Society
COLLSTE, G., Applied Ethics
DAHLGREN, L.-O., Education
EDQUIST, C., Technology and Social Change
ELLEGÅRD, K., Technology and Social Change
ELLSTÖM, P.-E., Education
ERIKSSON, B. E., Health and Society
FRODI, A., Psychology
GOLDKUHL, G., Information Systems
GRANSTÖM, K., Education
GRIMWALL, A., Statistics
HALLDÉN, G., Child Studies
HELLGREN, B., Management
HJORT AF ORNÄS, A., Water and Environmental Studies
HULTMAN, G., Education
HYDÉN, L.-C., Communication Studies
INGELSTAM, L., Technology and Social Change
JANSSON, J., Transport Economics
JOHANSSON, R., Ethnicity Studies
KYLHAMMER, J., Communication Studies
LINDKVIST, L., Management
LINELL, P., Communication Studies
LOHM, U., Water and Environmental Studies
LUNDQVIST, J., Water and Environmental Studies
LYKKE, N., Gender Studies
LYXELL, B., Psychology
MYRBERG, M., Education
NÄSMAN, E., Society and Cultural Studies
NELSON, M. C., History
NILSSON, G. B., Technology and Social Change
NORDENFELT, L., Health and Society
NORDIN, I., Health and Society
PETERSON, B., Philosophy
ÖBERG, G., Water and Environmental Studies
QVARSELL, R., Health and Society
RAHM, L., Water and Environmental Studies
RÖNNBERG, J., Psychology
SANDELL, R., Clinical Psychology
SANDIN, B., Child Studies
SJÖGREN, H., Technology and Social Change
SKOGH, G., Economics
SUNDIN, E., Technology and Social Change
SUNDIN, J., Health and Society
SVENSSON, B., Water and Environmental Studies

Faculty of Health Sciences:

ALM-CARLSSON, G., Medical Radiation Physics
ANDERSSON, R., Pharmacology
ARNQVIST, H., Medical Cell Biology
ASPENBERG, P., Orthopaedic Surgery
AXELSON, O., Occupational and Environmental Medicine
BERGDAHL, B., Medicine
BLOMQUIST, A., Pain Research
BORCH, K., Surgery
BRUNK, U., Pathology
CARLSSON, P., Health Technology Assessment
EK, A.-C., Caring Science
EKBERG, K., Work and Rehabilitation
FAGERHOLM, P., Ophthalmology
FORSBERG, P., Infectious Diseases
FORSUM, U., Clinical Microbiology
GERDLE, B., Rehabilitation Medicine
GRANERUS, A.-K., Geriatric Medicine
HAMMAR, M., Obstetrics and Gynaecology
HAMMARSTRÖM, S., Medical Cell Biology
HILDEBRAND, C., Medical Cell Biology
HULTMAN, P., Pathology
KÅGEDAL, B., Clinical Chemistry
KARLBERG, B., Medicine
KINLSTRÖM, E., Clinical Microbiology
LARSSON, S.-E., Orthopaedic Surgery
LENNQUIST, S., Disaster Medicine and Traumatology
LINDSTRÖM, S., Medical Cell Biology
LISANDER, B., Anaesthesiology
LUDVIGSSON, J., Paediatrics
LUNDBLAD, A., Clinical Chemistry
LUNDQUIST, P.-G., Otorhinolaryngology
MAGNUSSON, K.-E., Medical Microbiology
MARAISSON, J., Geriatrics
MESSNER, K., Skeletal Biology
MÅRDH, S., Cell Biology
NILSSON, L., Microbiology
NORDENSKJÖLD, B., Oncology
NORDIN, C., Psychiatry
ÖBERG, Å., Medical Engineering (Instrumentation)
ÕBERG, B., Physiotherapy
OLIN, C., Cardiothoracic Surgery
OLSSON, A. G., Internal Medicine
OLSSON, J.-E., Neurology
ÖSTRUP, L., Plastic Surgery
PAULETTE-HULTCRANTZ, E., Otorhinolaryngology
PETERSSON, C., Clinical Pharmacology
RAMMER, L., Forensic Science and Medicine
ROSDAHL, I., Dermatology and Venereology
ROSÉN, A., Inflammation and Tumour Biology
SERUP, J., Dermatology and Venereology
SJÖBERG, F., Critical Care, especially Burn Intensive Care
SMEDBY, Ö., Diagnostic Radiology
SMEDS, S., Surgery
STENDAHL, O., Medical Microbiology
STENMAN, G., Medical Genetics
STRANG, P., Palliative Medicine
STRÅLFORS, P., Medical Cell Biology
SUNDQUIST, T., Medical Microbiology, especially Inflammation
SVANBORG, E., Clinical Neuropsychology
SVANVIK, J., Surgery
SÖDERFELT, B., Neurology
SÖDERKVIST, P., Cell Biology, especially Medical Genetics
TAGESSON, C., Experimental Medicine
THEODORSSON, E., Neurochemistry

TIMPKA, T., Social Medicine and Public Health Sciences
TRELL, E., Primary Health Care and General Practice
WASTESON, Å., Medical Cell Biology
WIGERTZ, O., Medical Engineering (Medical Information Processing)
WIJMA, B., Women's Health
WRANNE, B., Clinical Physiology
WÅLINDER, J., Psychiatry

Institute of Technology:
ABRAHAMSSON, M., Logistics Management
AHRENBERG, L., Computational Linguistics
ANDERSSON, L.-E., Applied Mathematics
ARONSSON, G., Applied Mathematics
ARWIN, H., Applied Optics
ASK, P., Biomedical Engineering
BALTZER, L., Organic Chemistry
BERGGREN, C., Production Management
BERGGREN, K.-F., Theoretical Physics
BORÉN, H., Organic Chemistry
BRANDES, O., Industrial Marketing
BREGE, S., Industrial Marketing
CARLSSON, U., Biochemistry
CHEN, W., Materials Science
DADFAR, H., International Marketing
DAHLBERG, T., Solid Mechanics and Strength of Materials
DAHLGAARD, J. J., Quality Technology and Management
DOHERTY, P., Computer Science
EDGAR, B., Applied Mathematics
EKEDAHL, L.-G., Applied Physics, Catalytic Reactions
EKLUND, J., Industrial Ergonomics
ELDÉN, L., Numerical Analysis
ERICSON, T., Data Transmission
ERICSSON, T., Engineering Materials
FAHLMAN, A., Physics
FRITZSON, P., Computer Science
GLAD, T., Automatic Control
GRANLUND, G., Computer Vision
GRUBBSTRÖM, R. W., Production Economics
GUSTAFSSON, F., Communication Systems
HANSSON, G., Experimental Semiconductor Physics
HELMERSSON, U., Thin Film Physics
HOLLNAGEL, E., Industrial Ergonomics
HOLMBERG, K., Optimization
HOLTZ, P.-O., Materials Science
HULTMAN, L., Thin Film Physics
HÄGGLUND, S., Computer Science
INGANÄS, O., Biomolecular and Organic Electronics
INGEMARSSON, I., Information Theory
JANZÉN, E., Semiconductor Physics
JOHANSSON, L., Materials Science
JONSSON, B. H., Biochemistry
KAMKAR, M., Software Engineering
KARLSSON, B., Energy Systems
KARLSSON, J. M., Telecommunications
KLARBRING, A., Optimization Models in Structural Mechanics
KNUTSSON, H., Medical Informatics
KOSKI, T., Mathematical Statistics
KRUS, P., Fluid Power Technology
KRUSE, B., Digital Images and Media Technology
KVARNSTRÖM, I., Organic Chemistry
LIEDBERG, B., Sensor Science
LINDBERG, P.-O., Optimization
LINUSSON, S., Applied Mathematics
LIU, D., Computer Engineering
LJUNG, L., Automatic Control
LOYD, D., Applied Thermodynamics and Fluid Mechanics
LUND, A., Chemical Physics
LUNDGREN, J., Traffic Systems
LUNDSTRÖM, I., Applied Physics
MALUSZYNSKI, J., Programming Theory
MANDENIUS, C.-F., Biotechnology
MAZ'YA, V., Applied Mathematics
MILLNERT, M., Automatic Control
MONEMAR, B., Condensed Matter Physics
MOSFEGH, B., Energy Systems
MUKHERJEE, S. D., Electronic Production
NIELSEN, L., Vehicle Systems
NILSSON, G., Biomedical Instrumentation
NILSSON, L., Solid Mechanics
NOVAK, A., Production Engineering
ÖBERG, Å., Biomedical Engineering
OHLSSON, K., Industrial Ergonomics
PALMBERG, J.-O., Fluid Power Technology
PENG, Z., Computer Systems
PERSSON, J., Medical Technology Assessment
RAPP, B., Economic Information Systems
RAUCH, S., Applied Mathematics
RIKLUND, R., Theoretical Physics
RYDBERG, K.-E., Fluid Power Technology
RÖNNQVIST, M., Optimization
SALANECK, W., Surface Physics and Chemistry
SANDAHL, K., Software Engineering
SANDEWALL, E., Computer Science
SANDKULL, B., Industrial Organization
SERNELIUS, B., Theoretical Physics
SHAHMEHRI, N., Computer Science
SJÖLANDER, S., Zoology
STAFSTRÖM, S., Computational Physics
STRANDBERG, L., Traffic Safety and Environment
SVENSSON, C., Electronic Devices
TENGVALL, P., Applied Physics
UHRBERG, R., Surface and Semiconductor Physics
VÄRBRAND, P., Optimization
WANHAMMAR, L., Electronic Systems
WIGERTZ, O., Medical Informatics

LINNÉUNIVERSITETET
(Linnaeus University)

SE-391 82 Kalmar
Fax: (480) 44-60-32SE-351 95 Växjö
Telephone: (772) 28-80-00
Fax: (470) 832-17
E-mail: registrator@lnu.se

Founded 2010, following merger of Växjo Universitet (f. 1967 as a br. of Lunds Univ.) and Högskolan i Kalmar (f. 1977)
State control
Languages of instruction: Swedish, English
Academic year: September to June

Rector: STEPHEN HWANG
Pro-Rector: BO BERGBÄCK
Pro-Rector: LENA FRITZÉN
Library Dir: ANDERS RYDQVIST

Library: see Libraries and Archives
Number of teachers: 2,000
Number of students: 34,000 (15,000 full-time, 19,000 part-time)

HEADS OF FACULTY

Faculty of Economics and Design: Prof. HENRIETTE KOBLANCK
Faculty of Education Sciences: Prof. PER GERREVALL
Faculty of Health, Social Work and Behavioural Sciences: HÅKAN JENNER
Faculty of Humanities and Social Sciences: MATS SJÖLIN
Faculty of Science and Technology: Prof. BENGT PERSSON

LULEÅ TEKNISKA UNIVERSITET
(Luleå University of Technology)

SE-971 87 Luleå
Telephone: (920) 49-10-00
Fax: (920) 49-13-99
E-mail: registrator@ltu.se
Internet: www.ltu.se

Founded 1971
State control
Language of instruction: Swedish

Vice-Chancellor: JOHAN STERTE
Deputy Vice-Chancellor: ERIK HÖGLUND
Chief Admin. Officer: STAFFAN SARBÄCK
Univ. Librarian: TERJE HÖISETH

Library of 240,932 vols, 15,663 periodicals
Number of teachers: 650 (incl. researchers)
Number of students: 12,000

PROFESSORS

Department of Applied Physics and Mechanical Engineering:
FREDRIKSSON, S., Physics
GUSTAVSSON, H., Fluid Mechanics
HÖGLUND, E., Machine Elements
JINYUE, Y., Energy Engineering
KAPLAN, A., Systems Engineering
KARLSSON, L., Computer Aided Design
MOLIN, N. E., Experimental Mechanics
ODÉN, M., Engineering Materials
OLDENBURG, M., Solid Mechanics
VARNA, J., Polymer Engineering

Department of Business Administration and Social Sciences:
BERGSTRÖM, I., Management Control
DE RAADT, D., Informatics and Systems Sciences
HÄGERFORS, A., Computer and Systems Sciences
HANSSON, S., Political Science, History and Geography
HÖRTE, S.-A., Industrial Organization
KLEFSJÖ, B.
LUNDGREN, N.-G., Political Science, History and Geography
MICHANEK, G., Jurisprudence
RADETZKI, M., Economics
SALEHI-SANGARI, E., Industrial Marketing
WIKLUND, H., Quality and Environmental Management

Department of Communication and Languages:
MAGNUSSON, U., English
PERSSON, G., English

Department of Chemical and Metallurgical Engineering:
BERGLUND, K. A., Biochemical and Chemical Process Engineering
BJÖRKMAN, B., Process Metallurgy
FORSLING, W., Chemistry
FORSSBERG, E., Mineral Processing
STERTE, J., Chemical Technology

Department of Civil and Mining Engineering:
BORGBRANT, J., Construction Management
ELFGREN, L., Structural Engineering
JOHANSSON, B., Steel Structures
KLISINSKI, M., Structural Mechanics
KNUTSSON, S., Soil Mechanics and Foundation Engineering
KUMAR, U., Operation and Maintenance Engineering
LAGERQVIST, O., Steel Structures
LINDQVIST, P.-A., Rock Engineering
NORDLUND, E., Rock Mechanics
OLOFSSON, T., Structural Engineering

Department of Computer Science and Electrical Engineering:
DELSING, J., Embedded Internet Systems Laboratory (EISLAB)
MEDVEDEV, A., Automatic Control
WERNERSSON, Å., Embedded Internet Systems Laboratory (EISLAB)

Department of Environmental Engineering:
ELMING, S.-Å., Applied Geophysics
HANAEUS, J., Sanitary Engineering
LAGERKVIST, A., Water Science and Technology
NORDELL, B., Renewable Energy
ÖHLANDER, B., Applied Geology
ÖSTMAN, A., Geographical Information Technology
SELLGREN, A., Water Resources Engineering

Department of Human Work Sciences:
ÅGREN, A., Sound and Vibration

ALM, H., Engineering Psychology
JOHANSSON, J., Industrial Work Environment
PETTERSSON, D., Industrial Design

Department of Mathematics:
EULER, M., Applied Mathematics
HEABERG, T., Applied Mathematics
PERSSON, L.-E., Applied Mathematics
STRAESSER, R., Applied Mathematics

Department of Wood Technology:
GRÖNLUND, A., Wood Technology
MORÉN, T., Wood Physics
WESTERMARK, U., Wood Material Science

School of Education:
ALEXANDERSSON, M., Pedagogics

School of Music:
BRÄNDSTRÖM, S., Education and Teaching Methods in Music
ERICSSON, H.-O., Organ
SANDSTRÖM, J., Composition
WESTBERG, E., Choir Singing and Choir Conducting

LUND UNIVERSITY

POB 117, SE-221 00 Lund
Telephone: (46) 222-00-00
Fax: (46) 222-47-20
E-mail: info@rektor.lu.se
Internet: www.lu.se

Founded 1666
State control
Languages of instruction: Swedish, English
Academic year: September to June (two semesters)

Vice-Chancellor: PER ERIKSSON
Pro-Vice-Chancellor: EVA ÅKESSON
Head of Admin.: MARIANNE GRANFELT
Library: see Libraries and Archives
Number of teachers: 646
Number of students: 47,000
Publication: *LUM* (9 a year)

DEANS

Faculty of Engineering: Prof. ANDERS AXELSSON
Faculty of Fine and Performing Arts: HÅKAN LUNDSTRÖM
Faculty of Humanities and Theology: Prof. LYNN ÅKESSON
Faculty of Law: Prof. CHRISTINA MOËLL
Faculty of Medicine: Prof. BO AHRÉN
Faculty of Social Sciences: ANN-KATRIN BÄCKLUND
Faculty of Science: Prof. TORBJÖRN VON SCHANTZ
School of Economics and Mananagement: ALLAN T. MALM

PROFESSORS

Faculty of Humanities:
ANDERSSON, G., Musicology
ANDRÉN, A., Medieval Archaeology
BJÖRLING, F., Slavic Languages
BLOMQVIST, J., Greek Language and Literature
BROBERG, G., History of Ideas and Sciences
BRUCE, G., Phonetics
EDLUND, B., Musicology
EINARSSON, J., Scandinavian Languages
ENÉVIST, I., Spanish
FLORBY, G., English Literature
FRYKMAN, J., European Ethnology
GREATREX, R., Chinese
GÄRDENFORS, P., Cognitive Science
GUSTAFSSON, H., History
HAETTNER-AURELIUS, E., Literature
HÅKANSSON, G., General Linguistics
HANSSON, B., Theoretical Philosophy
HÅRDH, B., Archaeology
HEDLING, E., Film
HOADLEY, M., Southeast Asian History and Bahasa Indonesia
HOLMBERG, B., Semitic Languages
HORNBORG, A., Human Ecology
IREGREN, E., Historical Osteology
KARLSSON, K.-G., History
LARSSON, B., French
LARSSON, L., Archaeology
LARSSON, L., Literature
LÖFGREN, O., European Ethnology
LÖVKRONA, I., European Ethnology
MOLNÁR, V., German
NORDIN, S., History of Ideas and Science
OLAUSSON, D., Archaeology
OREDSSON, S., History
ÖSTERBERG, E., History
PALM, A., Literature
PERSSON, I., Practical Philosophy
PILTZ, A., Latin
PLATZACK, C., Scandinavian Languages
RABINOWICZ, W., Practical Philosophy
RAGVALD, L., Chinese
RIDDERSTAD, P. S., Book and Library History
RYDÉN, P., Literature
RYSTEDT, E., Classical Archaeology and Ancient History
SAHLIN, N.-E., Theoretical Philosophy
SALOMON, K., International History
SALOMOUSSON, A., European Ethnology
SANDQVIST, S., French
SCHLYTER, S., Romance Languages
SJÖBLAD, C., Literature
SJÖLIN, J.-G., History of Contemporary Art
SONESSON, G., Cultural Semiotics
STEENSLAND, L., Slavic Languages
STRÖMQVIST, S., Language Acquisition
SVANTESSON, J.-O., General Linguistics
SVENSSON, J., Swedish
SVENSSON, L.-H., English Literature
THORMÄHLEN, M., English Literature
VIBERG, Å., General Linguistics
WARREN, B., English
WEIMARCK, T., History of Contemporary Art
WIÉANDER, Ö., Classical Archaeology
WIENBERG, J., Medieval Archaeology

Faculty of Law:
BERGHOLTZ, G., Legal Procedure
BERGSTRÖM, S., Tax Law
BOGDAN, M., Comparative and Private International Law
FAHLBECK, R., Labour Law
GORTON, L., Banking Law
MELANDER, G., Public International Law
MODÉER, K. Å., Legal History
NUMHAUSER-HENNING, A., Private Law
NYSTRÖM, B., Private Law
PECZENIK, A., Jurisprudence
TRÄSKMAN, P. O., Criminal Law
VOGEL, H.-H., Public Law
WESTBERG, P., Legal Procedure

Faculty of Medicine:
ABRAHAMSSON, P.-A., Oncological Urology
AHRÉN, B., Clinical Metabolic Research
ÅKERLUND, M., Obstetrics and Gynaecology
ÅKERSTROM, B., Medical Chemistry
ALLING, CH., Medical Neurochemistry
ALM, P., Pathology
ANDERSSON, K.-E., Clinical Pharmacology
ANDERSSON, R., Surgery
ANDERSSON, T., Experimental Pathology
ARNER, A., Physiology
BÄCK, O., Dermatology
BELFRAGE, P., Medical Biochemistry
BERGLUND, G., Internal Medicine
BERGLUND, M., Clinical Alcohol Research
BJURSTEN, L.-M., Bio-implant Research
BJÖRCK, L., Medical Biochemistry
BJÖRKLUND, A., Histology
BORGSTRÖM, A., Surgery
BRUNDIN, P., Neuroscience
CARLSTEDT, I., Mucosal Biology
DAHLBÄCK, B., Coagulation Research
DEGERMAN, E., Experimental Diabetes Research
DEHLIN, O., Geriatric Medicine
DILLNER, J., Virology
EHINGER, B., Ophthalmology
EKBLOM, P., Molecular Cell Biology
EKDAHL, C., Physiotherapy
EKHBERG, O., Diagnostic Radiology
ELMESTÅHL, S., Geriatrics
ERLANSON-ALBERTSSON, C.
FENYÖ, E.-M., Virology
FORSGREN, A., Clinical Bacteriology
FRANSSON, L.-Å., Cell Biology
FÄSSLER, R., Experimental Pathology
GERDTHAM, U., Public Health Science
GROOP, L., Endocrinology
GRUBB, A., Clinical Biochemistry
GRÄNDE, P.-O., Anaesthesia and Intensive Care
GULLBERG, U., Haematology
GUSTAFSON, L., Geriatric Psychiatry
HAGANDER, B., Medicine
HAGMAR, L., Environmental Medicine
HEIJL, A., Ophthalmology
HEINEGÅRD, D., Medical Biochemistry
HELLSTRAND, P., Muscle Research
HERMERÉN, G., Medical Ethics
HESSLOW, G., Neuroscience
HOLMBERG, L., Paediatrics
HOLMDAHL, R., Medical Inflammation Research
HOLMER, N.-G., Biomedical Engineering
HOLM WALLENBERG, C., Molecular Cell Biology
HOLTÅS, S., Neuroradiology
HOVELIUS, B., General Practice
HÅKANSSON, R., Experimental Endocrinology
HÖGESTÄTT, E., Clinical Pharmacology
IHSE, I., Surgery
JACOBSEN, S. E., Stem Cell Biology
JANZON, L., Epidemiology
JEPPSSON, B., Surgery
JOHNELL, O., Orthopaedic Surgery
JONSON, B., Clinical Physiology
KARLSSON, S., Gene Therapy in Molecular Medicine
KILLANDER, D., Oncology
LANDBERG, G., Pathology
LEANDERSON, T., Immunology
LEED-LUNDBERG, F., Cellular and Molecular Physiology
LERNMARK, A., Experimental Diabetes Research
LEVANDER, S., Psychiatry
LIDGREN, L., Orthopaedics
LINDAHL, G., Medical Microbiology and Immunology
LINDGREN, B., Health Economics
LINDGREN, S., Medicine
LINDVALL, O., Restorative Neurology
LJUNGGREN, B., Dermatology and Venereology
LOHMANDER, S., Orthopaedics
LUNDBERG, D., Anaesthesiology
LUNDBORG, G., Hand Surgery
LUNDQUIST, I., Pharmacology
LUTHMAN, H., Genetic Epidemology
LÖFDAHL, C.-G., Lung Disease
LÖFQVIST, A., Logopaedic Phonetics
LÖWENHIELM, P., Forensic Medicine
MCNEIL, T., Medical Behavioural Research
MAGNUSSON, M., Otorhinolaryngology
MALMSTRÖM, A., Medical and Physiological Chemistry
MARSAL, K., Obstetrics and Gynaecology
MATTIASSON, A., Urology
MATTSON, R., Reproduction Immunology
MATTSSON, S., Medical Radiation Physics
MITELMAN, F., Clinical Genetics
NETTELBLADT, U., Logopaedics
NILSSON, Å., Internal Medicine
NILSSON, J., Experimental Cardiovascular Research
NILSSON-EHLE, P., Clinical Chemistry
NORRBY, R., Infectious Diseases

NORRVING, B., Neurology
ÖHMAN, R. L., Psychiatry
OLBRANT, K., Cell Biology
OLOFSSON, T., Haematology
OLSSON, B., Cardiology
OLSSON, H., Oncology
OLSSON, I., Haematology
OWMAN, CH., Histology
PERSSON, B., Medical Radiation Physics
PERSSON, C. G. A., Experimental Clinical Pharmacology
PESONEN, E., Child Cardiology
PETTERSSON, H., Diagnostic Radiology
PRELLNER, K., Otorhinolaryngology
PÅHLMAN, S., Molecular Medicine
RAHM-HALLBERG, I., Caring Sciences
RENCK, H., Anaesthesiology
RIPPE, B., Nephrology
RISBERG, J., Neuropsychology
RORSMAN, P., Membrane Physiology
ROSÉN, I., Clinical Neurophysiology
RÅSTAM, L., Applied Public Health
SALFORD, L., Neurosurgery
SCHOUENBORG, J., Physiology
SJÖBERG, N.-O., Obstetrics and Gynaecology
SKERFVING, S., Occupational Medicine
STEEN, S., Thoracic Surgery
STENFLO, J., Clinical Chemistry
SUNDLER, F., Histology
SUNDLER, R., Cell Biology
SVANBORG, C., Clinical Immunology
THORNGREN, K.-G., Orthopaedics
TRÄSKMAN BENDZ, L., Psychiatry
WADSTRÖM, T., Bacteriology
WIELOCH, T., Neurobiology
WINGSTRAND, H., Orthopaedics
WOLLMER, P., Clinical Physiology

Faculty of Political and Social Sciences:

AGNÉR SIGBO, G., Informatics
ÅKERSTRÖM, M., Sociology
ALLWOOD, C.-M., Psychology
ALVESSON, M., Business Administration
ANDERSSON, G., Social Work
ANDERSSON, S. I., Psychology
ARWIDI, O., Business Administration
ASHEIM, B. T., Economic Geography
ÅSTRÖM, K., Sociology of Law
BENGTSSON, T., Economic History
BERONIUS, M., Sociology
BORGLIN, A., Public Sector Economics
BRANTE, T., Sociology
CARLSSON, S., Informatics
CARLSSON WETTERBERG, C., Gender Studies
CLARK, E., Social Geography
DAHL, G., Sociology
DAHLGREN, P., Sociology of Communication
DJURFELDT, G., Sociology
EDEBALK, P.-G., Social Work
EDGERTON, D., Econometrics
EHN, P., Information and Computer Sciences
EKHOLM FRIEDMAN, K., Social Anthropology
ELGSTRÖM, O., Political Science
ELIASSON, R.-M., Social Work
ESSEVELD, J., Sociology
FLODGREN, B., Business Law
FRIEDMAN, J., Social Anthropology
GUNNARSSON, CHR., Economic History
HANSSON, B., Economics
HANSSON, G., International Economics
HETZLER, A., Social Policy
HOLMQUIST, B., Statistics
HYDÉN, H., Sociology of Law
JACOBSSON, B., Business Administration
JERNECK, M., Political Science
JOHANSSON, C. R., Industrial and Organizational Psychology
JÖNSSON, CHR., Political Science
LAGNEVIK, M., Business Administration
LANDSTRÖM, H., Entrepreneurship and Small Business
LARSSON, R., Business Administration
LINDBERG, S., Sociology
LINDÉN, A.-L., Sociology
LUNDQUIST, L., Political Science, especially Public Administration
LYTTKENS, C. H., Economics
MALM, A., Business Administration
NORBERG, C., Corporate Law and Tax Law
OHLSSON, R., Modern Economic and Social History
OLANDER, L.-O., Social and Economic Geography
OLERUP, A., Informatics
OLSSON, C.-A., Economic History
OXELHEIM, L., International Business
PERSSON, I., Economics, especially Women's Studies
ROSENBECK, B., Gender Studies
RUNDQUIST, F.-M., Social and Economic Geography
RYDÉN, O., Personality Psychology
SALONEN, T., Social Work
SAMUELSSON, P., Corporate Law and Capital Market Law
SCHÖN, L., Economic History
SELLERBERG, A.-M., Sociology
STENELO, L.-G., Political Science
STÅHL, I., Economics
SÖDERSTRÖM, L., Economics, especially Social Policy
STANKIEWICZ, R., Science and Technology Policy
SUNESSON, S., Social Work
SVENSSON, C., Business Administration
SVENSSON, L., Pedagogy
SVENSSON, L.-G., Economics
SWÄRD, H., Social Work

Faculty of Science:

ADLER, J.-O., Nuclear Physics
AHLBERG, P., Historical Geology and Palaeontology
ÅKESSON, T., Elementary Particle Physics
ALERSTAM, T., Animal Ecology
ALLEN, J. F., Plant Cell Biology
ALMBLADH, C.-O., Physics
ANDERSEN, T., Astronomy
ANDERSSON, B., Theoretical Physics
ANDERSSON, C., Inorganic Chemistry
ANDRÉASSON, P.-G., Mineralogy and Petrology
ARDEBERG, A., Astronomy
ARNASON, U., Evolutionary Genetics
ASMUSSEN, S., Mathematical Statistics
BENGTSSON, B. O., Genetics
BENGTSSON, G., Chemical Ecology and Ecotoxicology
BENGTSSON, S.-A., Systematic Zoology
BERG, U., Organic Chemistry
BJÖRCK, S., Quaternary Geology
BJÖRN, L. O., Plant Physiology
BRÖNMARK, C., Limnology
BÅÅTH, E., Microbial Ecology
CHAO, K., Theoretical Physics
CONSTANTIN, A., Mathematics
DRAVINS, D., Astronomy
EDSTRÖM, A., Zoophysiology
EEROLA, P., Experimental Particle Physics
ELDING, L. I., Inorganic Chemistry
ERIKSSON, M., Physics
EVERITT, E., Microbiology
FAGERSTRÖM, T., Theoretical Ecology
FAHLANDER, C., Physics
FALKENGRENGRERUP, U., Plant Ecology
FREJD, T., Organic Chemistry
GORTON, L., Analytical Chemistry
GRANELI, W., Limnology
GUSTAFSON, G., Theoretical Physics
GUSTAFSSON, H.-Å., High Energy Heavy Ion Physics
HANSSON, B., Chemical Ecology and Ecotoxicology
HANSSON, L.-A., Limnology
HEBERT, H., Molecular Biophysics
HEDENMALM, H., Mathematics
HELLBORG, R., Nuclear Physics
HELLDÉN, U., Physical Geography
HOLM, E., Radiation Physics
HOLMBERG, B., Inorganic Chemistry
HÖSSJER, O., Mathematical Studies
JAKOBSSON, B., Subatomic Physics
JANSSON, H.-B., Microbial Ecology
JARLSKOG, G., Physics
JEPPSSON, L., Historical Geology and Palaeontology
JERGIL, B., Biochemistry
JOHANSSON, S., Atomic Spectroscopy
JÖNSSON, B., Physical Chemistry
JÖNSSON, L., Elementary Particle Physics
JÖNSSON, J.-Å., Analytical Chemistry
KANJE, M., Zoological Cell Biology
KANTOR, I., Mathematics
KARLSTRÖM, G., Theoretical Physics
KJELLBOM, P., Plant Biochemistry
KÄRNEFELT, I., Systematic Botany
LARSSON, C., Plant Biochemistry
LARSSON, K., Historical Geology and Palaeontology
LARSSON, P., Chemical Ecology and Ecotoxicology
LARSSON, R., Zoology
LILJAS, A., Molecular Biophysics
LINDAU, I., Synchrotron Light Research
LINDH, A., Mineralogy and Petrology
LINDEGREN, L., Astronomy
LINDMAN, B., Physical Chemistry
LINDROTH, A., Physical Geography
LINGAS, A., Computer Sciences
LINSE, P., Macromolecular Chemistry
LITZÉN, U., Atomic Spectroscopy
LOFSTEDT, C., Ecology, Chemical Communication
LUNDBERG, P., Theoretical Ecology
LÖRSTAD, B., Elementary Particle Physics
MARTINSON, I., Atomic Physics
MATHIASSON, L., Analytical Chemistry
MAX MØLLER, I., Plant Physiology
MELIN, A., Mathematics
MEURMAN, A., Mathematics
NIHLGÅRD, B., Plant Ecology
NILSSON, D. E., Zoology
NILSSON, J.-A., Animal Ecology
NILSSON, N., Mathematics
NILSSON, S. G., Animal Ecology
NYHOLM, R., Synchrotron Radiation Instrumentation
OLSSON, U., Physical Chemistry
OREDSSON, S., Animal Physiology
OSCARSSON, Å., Inorganic Chemistry
PEETRE, J., Mathematics
PETERSON, C., Theoretical Physics
PETTERSON, G., Biochemistry
PICULELL, L., Physical Chemistry
PRENTICE, H., Systematic Botany
ROOS, B., Theoretical Chemistry
RUTBERG, B., Microbiology
RUTBERG, L., Microbiology
SANDGREN, P., Quaternary Geology
SCHRÖDER, B., Nuclear Physics
SJÖSTRAND, T., Theoretical Physics
SMITH, H., Animal Ecology
SOMMARIN, M., Plant Biochemistry
STENLUND, E., Cosmic and Subatomic Physics
STÅHLBERG, F., Magnetic Resonance
STRAND, S.-E., Radiation Physics
STYRING, S., Biochemistry
SUNDSTRÖM, V., Chemical Dynamics
SVENSSON, B. E. Y., Theoretical Physics
SYKES, M., Plant Ecology
SÖDERGREN, A., Chemical Ecology and Ecotoxicology
SÖDERLIND, G., Numerical Mathematics
SÖDERMAN, O., Physical Chemistry
SÖDERSTRÖM, B., Microbial Ecology
TJERNELD, F., Biochemistry
TUNLID, A., Microbial Ecology
TYLER, G., Plant Ecology
VON BARTH, U., Physics
VON SCHANTZ, T., Animal Ecology
WENNERSTRÖM, H., Physical Chemistry
WESTRÖM, B., Animal Physiology
WIDELL, S., Plant Physiology

Faculty of Technology:
- ÅBERG, S., Mathematical Physics
- ADLERCREUTZ, P., Biotechnology
- AKSELSSON, R., Ergonomics
- ÅKESSON, B., Applied Nutrition
- ALAKÜLA, M., Industrial Electrical Engineering
- ALDÉN, M., Laser-based Combustion Diagnostics
- ALY, G., Chemical Engineering
- ANDERSON, J. B., Digital Communications
- ANDERSSON, A., Chemical Engineering, especially Heterogenous Catalysis
- ANDERSSON-ENGELS, S., Experimental Physics
- ÅRZÉN, K.-E., Automatic Control
- ASP, N.-G., Applied Nutrition
- ÅSTRÖM, K. J., Mathematics
- AXELSSON, A., Chemical Engineering
- AXSÄTER, S., Production Management
- BARUP, K., Architectural Conservation and Restoration
- BENGTSSON, L., Water Resources Engineering
- BENGTSSON, P.-E., Laser-Based Combustion Diagnostics
- BENGTSSON, R., Mathematical Physics
- BERGENSTÅHL, B., Food Technology
- BERNDTSSON, R., Water Resources Engineering
- BERNHARDSSON, B., Automatic Control
- BJELM, L., Engineering Geology
- BJÖRK, I., Applied Nutrition and Food Chemistry
- BOHGARD, M., Ergonomics and Aerosol Technology
- BOLMSJÖ, G., Robotics
- BORREBAECK, C., Immunotechnology
- BOVIN, J.-O., Materials Chemistry and High-Resolution Electron Microscopy
- BÜLOW, L., Biochemistry
- BÖRJESSON, P.-O., Signal Processing
- DAHLBLOM, O., Structural Mechanics
- DAMS, M., Computer Science
- DEJMEK, P., Food Engineering
- ECKHARDT, C.-C., Industrial Design
- EDFORS, O., Radio Communications
- EDSTRÖM, M., Architectural Conservation and Restoration
- EKHOLM, A., Computer Aided Architectural Design
- ELIASSON, A.-C., Cereal Technology
- ELMROTH, A., Building Physics
- ENGSTRÖM, L., Experimental Physics, especially Atomic Physics and Optics
- FAGERLUND, G., Building Materials
- FREDLUND, B., Building Science
- FUCHS, L., Fluid Mechanics
- GONZALEZ, A., Theoretical and Applied Aesthetics
- GUSTAFSSON, P. J., Structural Mechanics
- HAGANDER, P., Automatic Control
- HAHN-HÄGERDAL, B., Applied Microbiology
- HALLE, B., Physical Chemistry
- HANSON, H., Water Resources Engineering
- HANSSON, B., Construction Management
- HELSING, J., Scientific Computing
- HEYDEN, A., Mathematics
- HOLMBERG, B., Traffic Planning
- HOLMSTEDT, G., Fire Safety Engineering
- HOLST, J., Mathematical Statistics
- HOLST, O., Biotechnology
- HOLST, U., Mathematical Statistics
- HYDÉN, C., Traffic Engineering
- HÄGGLUND, T., Automatic Control
- JACOBSON, B., Machine Elements
- JAMES, P., Proteomics
- JARLSKOG, C., Theoretical Particle Physics
- JENSEN, L. H., Building Services
- JENSEN, U., Real Estate Management
- JOHANNESSON, R., Information Theory
- JOHANNESSON, T., Materials Engineering
- JOHANSSON, B., Combustion Engines
- JOHANSSON, G., Ergonomics and Aerosol Technology
- JOHANSSON, R., Automatic Control
- JOHANSSON, T., Information Theory
- JOHANSSON, T.-B., Energy Systems Analysis
- JÖNSON, G., Packaging Logistics
- JÖNSSON, A. S., Chemical Engineering
- JÖNSSON, B., Physical Chemistry
- JÖNSSON, B., Rehabilitation Engineering
- KARLSSON, A., Electromagnetic Theory
- KARLSSON, H., Chemical Engineering, Process Chemistry and Catalysis
- KARLSSON, J. M., Communication Systems
- KRISTENSSON, G., Electromagnetic Theory
- KRÖLL, S., Atomic Physics
- KUCHINSKI, K., Computer Science
- KÜLLER, R., Environmental Psychology
- KÖRNER, U., Communication Systems
- L'HUILLIER, A., Atomic Physics
- LA COUR JANSEN, J., Water and Waste Water Engineering
- LARSON, M., Water Resources Engineering
- LARSSON, P.-O., Applied Biochemistry
- LAURELL, T., Electrical Measurements
- LIDÉN, G., Chemical Reaction Engineering
- LIDGREN, K., Environmental Economics
- LINDGREN, G., Mathematical Statistics
- LINDSTRÖM, K., Electrical Measurements
- LUNDHOLM, G., Combustion Engines
- MAGNUSSON, B., Software Technology
- MAGNUSSON, S.-E., Fire Safety Engineering
- MALMQVIST, K., Nuclear Physics
- MARTINSSON, B., Aerosol Physics
- MATTIASSON, B., Biotechnology
- MAURER, F., Polymer Technology
- MOLIN, G., Food Hygiene
- MOLISCH, A., Radio Communications
- MONTELIUS, L., Solid State Physics
- NILSSON, S., Technical Analysis Chemistry, especially Microanalytical Chemistry
- NYMAN, M., Food Chemistry
- ODENBRAND, I., Chemical Engineering, especially Environmental Catalysis
- OLSSON, G., Industrial Automation
- OMLING, P., Solid State Physics
- PAULSSON, M., Dairy Technology
- PERSSON, H. W., Electrical Measurements
- PETERSON, H., Structural Mechanics
- PHILIPSON, L., Computer Systems
- PIÓRO, M., Communication Systems
- PISTOL, M.-E., Solid State Physics
- RAGNARSSON, I., Mathematical Physics
- RANTZER, A., Automatic Control
- REUTERSWÄRD, L., Architecture and Development Studies
- RISTINMAA, M., Solid Mechanics
- RYCHLIK, I., Mathematical Statistics
- RYDÉN, T., Mathematical Statistics
- RÅDBERG, J., Urban Planning
- RÅDSTRÖM, P., Applied Microbiology, especially Genetic Applications
- SAABYE OTTOSEN, N., Solid Mechanics
- SAMUELSSON, L., Solid State Physics
- SANDBERG, G., Structural Mechanics
- SCHMELING, J., Mathematics
- SEIFERT, W., Solid State Physics
- SENTLER, L., Structural Engineering
- SMEETS, B., Information Theory
- SPARR, G., Mathematics
- STENSTRÖM, S., Chemical Engineering
- STERNER, O., Bio-organic Chemistry
- STÅHL, A., Traffic Planning
- STÅHL, J.-E., Production and Materials Engineering
- SUNDÉN, B., Heat Transfer
- SVANBERG, S., Atomic Physics
- SVERDRUP, H., Biogeochemistry
- SÄRNER, E., Water and Environmental Engineering
- SÖDERBERG, J., Construction Management
- SÖRNMO, L., Biomedical Signals Processing
- THAM, K., Architecture
- THELANDERSSON, S., Structural Engineering
- THÖRNQVIST, L., Energy Economics and Planning
- TORISSON, T., Thermal Power Engineering
- TORNBERG, E., Food Engineering
- TRÄGÅRDH, C., Food Engineering
- TRÄGÅRDH, G., Food Engineering, especially Membrane Technology
- WAHSTRÖM, C.-G., Experimental Physics
- WAHLUND, K.-G., Technical Analytical Chemistry
- WALLENBERG, R., Solid State Chemistry
- WANDEL, S., Engineering Logistics
- WARFVINGE, P., Biogeochemistry
- WERNE, F., Building Functions Analysis
- WHITLOW, H. J., Nuclear Physics, especially Ion Physics
- WIMMERSTEDT, R., Chemical Engineering
- WITTENMARK, B., Automatic Control
- WOHLIN, C., Software Systems Engineering
- YUAN, J., Circuit Design
- ZACCHI, G., Chemical Engineering
- ZIGANGIROW, K. S., Telecommunications Theory

Faculty of Theology:
- BEXELL, G., Ethics
- DAHLGREN, C., Sociology of Religion
- GEELS, A., Psychology of Religion
- GUSTAFSSON, G., Sociology of Religion
- HALLONSTEN, G., Systematic Theology
- HAMBERG, E., Immigration Studies
- HIDAL, S., Old Testament Exegesis
- HJÄRPE, J., Islamic Studies
- HOFMANN, M., Systematic Theology
- HOLMBERG, B., New Testament Exegesis
- JARLERT, A., Church History
- JEANROND, W., Systematic Theology
- LANDE, A., Missiology with Ecumenical Theology
- LINDSTRÖM, F., Old Testament Exegesis
- OLSSON, B., New Testament Exegesis
- OLSSON, T., History and Phenomenology of Religions
- METTINGER, T., Old Testament Exegesis
- RUBENSON, S., Church History
- STENQVIST, C., Philosophy of Religion
- TRAUTNER-KROMANN, H., Jewish Studies

MITTUNIVERSITETET
(Mid Sweden University)

SE-851 70 Sundsvall

Telephone: (771) 97-50-00
Fax: (771) 97-50-01
E-mail: info@miun.se
Internet: www.miun.se

Founded 1993, following merger of Univ. Colleges of Sundsvall/Härnösand and Östersund, merger of Sundsvall/Örnsköldsvik and Sundsvall Colleges of Health Sciences 1995, present status 2005

State control

Languages of instruction: English, Swedish

3 Campuses

Vice-Chancelllor: ANDERS SÖDERHOLM
Pro-Vice-Chancelllor: HÅKAN WIKLUND
Univ. Dir: YASMINE LINDSTRÖM
Library Dir: MORGAN PALMQVIST

Library: see Libraries and Archives
Number of teachers: 417
Number of students: 21,476

DEANS

Faculty of Human Sciences: PER SÖRLIN
Faculty of Science, Technology and Media: STURE PETERSSON

ÖREBRO UNIVERSITET
(University of Örebro)

SE-701 82 Örebro

Telephone: (19) 30-30-00
Fax: (19) 33-02-38
E-mail: registrator@oru.se
Internet: www.oru.se

Founded 1967 as Högskolan i Örebro, present name and status 1999

State control

Academic year: September to June
Vice-Chancellor: JENS SCHOLLINS
Pro-Vice-Chancellor: GUNILLA LINDSTRÖM
Sec.: MARIANNE ALVELÖV
Univ. Dir: JOHAN LUNDBORG
Head Librarian: PER AHLIN

Library of 325,000 vols, 10,000 periodicals
Number of teachers: 764
Number of students: 16,820

DEANS

Faculty of Economics, Natural and Engineering Sciences: Prof. SUNE KARLSSON
Faculty of Educational Science: Prof. OWE LINDBERG
Faculty of Humanities and Social Sciences: Prof. ÅSA KROON LUNDELL
Faculty of Medicine and Health: Prof. ROBERT BRUMMER

STOCKHOLMS UNIVERSITET (Stockholm University)

SE-106 91 Stockholm
Bloms hus, Universitetsvägen 16, Stockholm
Telephone: (8) 16-20-00
Fax: (8) 15-95-22
E-mail: press@su.se
Internet: www.su.se

Founded 1878, became State Univ. 1960
State control
Language of instruction: Swedish
Academic year: August to June

Rector: Prof. KÅRE BREMER
Pro-Rector: Prof. LENA GERHOLM
Vice-Rector: ANDERS GUSTAVSSON
Univ. Dir: JENNY GARDBRANT

Library: see Libraries and Archives
Number of teachers: 4,350
Number of students: 28,632

Publication: *Acta Universitatis Stockholmiensis*

DEANS

Faculty of Humanities: Prof. GUNNAR SVENSSON
Faculty of Law: Prof. SAID MAHMOUDI
Faculty of Science: Prof. STEFAN NORDLUND
Faculty of Social Sciences: Prof. GUDRUN DAHL

PROFESSORS

Faculty of Humanities

History-Philosophy Section:

AILI, H., Latin
ALBERG-JENSEN, P., Slavic Languages
ANDRÉN, A., Archaeology
BARTNING, I., French
BECKER, K., Journalism
BERGLIE, Q., Religion
BERGMAN, B., Sign Language
BILY, M., Slavic Languages
BODIN, P.-A., Slavic Languages
BOLTON, K., English
CARLSHAMRE, S., Theoretical Philosophy
CULLHED, A., Literary History
DAHL, Ö., General Linguistics
DAHLBÄCK, G., History of the Middle Ages
EKECRANTZ, J., Media and Communication
ENGSTRAND, O., Phonetics
FALK, C., Swedish Language
FALK, J., Spanish
FANT, L., Ibero-Romance Languages
FAWKNER, H., English
FERM, O., History
FORSGREN, M., French
GERHOLM, L., Ethnology
GERÖ, E.-C., Greek
GLETE, J., History
HALL, T., Scandinavian and Comparative Art History
HEED, S.-Å., Theatre Studies
HELANDER, K., Theatre Studies
HELLBERG, S., Scandinavian Languages
HVITFELT, H., Journalism
HYLTENSTAM, K., Bilingualism
INGDAHL KAZMIERA, A., Slavic Languages
IVERSEN, H., Latin
JARRICK, A., History
JOHANNESSON, N.-L., English
KANGERE, B., Baltic Languages
KOPTJEVSKAJA TAMM, M., General Linguistics
KÖLL, A. M., Baltic Studies
KOSKINEN, M., Film Studies
LACERDA, F., Phonetics
LANGE, S., Scandinavian Languages
LARSEN, H., Musicology
LEANDER-TOUATI, A.-M., Ancient Culture
LIDÉN, K., Archaeology
LILJA, S., History
LINDBERG-WADA, G., Japanology
LINDROTH, J., History of Athletics
LJUNGGREN, A., Russian
LODÉN, T., Language and Culture of China
LYSELL, R., History of Literature
MALMNÄS, P.-E., Theoretical Philosophy
MOLIN, K., History
MURDOCH, D., Theoretical Philosophy
NEEDHAM, P., Theoretical Philosophy
NEUGER, L., Polish
NIKOLAJEVA, M., History of Literature
NILSSON, L., History of Municipality
NYSTEDT, J., Italian
OETKE, C., Language and Culture of India
OHLSSON, R., Practical Philosophy
OLSSON, J., Film Studies
PAGIN, P., Theoretical Philosophy
RIAD, T., Scandinavian Languages
ROSÉN, S., Language and Culture of Korea
ROSENBERG, T., Gender Studies
ROSENDAHL, M., Latin American Studies
ROSSHOLM, G., History of Literature
ROSSHOLM LAGERLÖF, M., Art History
RÖHL, M., History of Literature
SAUTER, W., Theatre Studies
SCHEFFER, C., Ancient Culture
SJØVOLD, T., Historical Osteology
SMITH, W., Indology
STRAND, H., Swedish
STROUD, C., Bilingualism
SVARTHOLM, K., Swedish as a Second Language for the Deaf
SVENSSON, G., Theoretical Philosophy
SÖDERBERGH WIDDING, A., Film Studies
TEODOROWICZ-HELLMAN, E., Polish
TERSMAN, F., Practical Philosophy
TRAUNMÜLLER, H., Auditative Phonetics
TÄNNSJÖ, T., Practical Philosophy
VOLK, M., Computer Linguistics
WANDE, E., Finnish
WARDINI, E., Arabic
WESTIN, B., History of Literature
WÅGHALL NIVRE, E., German
ÅMARK, K., History

Faculty of Law:

BJARUP, J., Jurisprudence
BOHLIN, A., Public Law
BRING, O., International Law
DIESEN, C., Procedure
EBBESSON, J., Environmental Law
EDELSTAM, H., Procedure
EKLUND, R., Private Law, Labour Law
HEUMAN, L., Procedure
KLEINEMAN, J., Civil Law
KÄLLSTRÖM, K., Private Law
LEIJONHUFVUD, M., Penal Law
LEVIN, M., Private Law
MAGNUSSON SJÖBERG, C., Law and Informatics
MAHMOUDI, S., International Law
MELZ, P., Financial Law
PEHRSON, L., Economics and Economic Law
PETERSON, C., Legal History
ROSÉN, J., Civil Law
SANDGREN, C., Civil Law
SANDSTRÖM, M., History of Law
SCHIRATSKY, D., Theoretical Philosophy
SEIPEL, P., Law and Informatics
SILFVERBERG, C., Financial Law
VOGEL, H.-H., Public Law
WAHL, N., European Law
WAHLGREN, P., Law and Informatics
WARNLING-NEREP, W., Public Law
WENNBERG, S., Penal Law

Faculty of Science

Biology Section:

BERGMAN, B., Physiological Botany
BORG, H., Aquatic Environmental Chemistry
BROMAN, D., Aquatic Ecotoxicology
CANNON, B., Animal Physiology
ELMGREN, R., Marine Ecology
ERIKSSON, O., Plant Ecology
FOLKE, C., Management of Natural Resources
GRÄSLUND, A., Biophysics
HAGGÅRD, E., Genetics
ISAKSSON, L., Microbiology
KAUTSKY, N., Marine Ecotoxicology
LINDBERG, U., Zoological Cell Biology
MÖLLER, G., Immunology
NÄSSEL, D., Functional Zoomorphology
RADESÄTER, T., Ethology
RANNUG, U., Toxicological Genetics
SJÖBERG, B.-M., Molecular Biology
WALLES, B., Morphological Botany
WIESLANDER, L., Molecular Genome Research
WIKLUND, C., Ecological Zoology
WULFF, F., Marine Systems Ecology

Chemistry Section:

ANDERSSON, B., Biochemistry
BARTFAI, T., Neurochemistry
BERGMAN, Å., Environmental Chemistry
BRZEZINSKI, P., Biochemistry, esp. Molecular Energy Research
BÄCKVALL, J.-E., Organic Chemistry
DEPIERRE, J., Biochemistry, especially Enzymological Toxicology
HULTH, P.-O., Experimental Physics
JANSSON, B., Chemical Environmental Analysis
JOSEFSSON, B., Analytical Chemistry
KOWALEWSKI, J., Physical Chemistry
LEVITT, M., Chemical Spectroscopy
LIDIN, S., Inorganic Chemistry
NELSON, D., Biochemistry
NORDLUND, P., Structural Biochemistry
NORRESTAM, R., Structural Chemistry
NYGREN, M., Material Chemistry, Electroceramics
ODHAM, G., Analytical Environmental Chemistry
SONNHAMMER, E., Bioinformatics
VON HEIJNE, G., Theoretical Chemistry

Earth and Environmental Studies Section:

BACKMAN, J., General and Historical Geology
HALLBERG, R., Microbial Chemistry
HOLMGREN, K., Physical Geography
IHSE, M., Ecological Geography
INGRI, J., Geochemistry and Petrology
KARLÉN, W., Physical Geography
LUNDÉN, B., Remote Sensing
RINGBERG, B., Quaternary Geology
ROSSWALL, T., Water and Environmental Studies
WASTENSON, L., Remote Sensing

Mathematics-Physics Section:

BARGHOLTZ, C., Nuclear Physics
BJÖRK, J.-E., Mathematics
BOHM, C., Technology of Physical Systems
EKEDAHL, T., Mathematics
FRANSSON, C., Astrophysics
HANSSON, H., Theoretical Physics
HANSSON, H.-C., Air Pollution
HOLMGREN, S.-O., High-Energy Physics
KÄLLEN, E., Dynamic Meteorology
LARSSON, M., Experimental Molecular Physics

MARTIN-LÖF, A., Actuarial Mathematics and Mathematical Statistics
OLOFSSON, H., Astronomy
PALMGREN, J., Biostatistics
PASSARE, M., Mathematics
RODHE, H., Chemical Meteorology
ROOS, J. E., Mathematics
SCHUCH, R., Atomic Physics
SIEGBAHN, P., Theoretical Physics
SUNDQVIST, H., Meteorology
SVENSSON, R., Astrophysics with Cosmology

Faculty of Social Sciences:

AGELL, J., Economics
AHRNE, G., Sociology
ALMKVIST, O., Psychology
ARAI, M., Economics
BACKENROTH-OHSAKO, G., Psychology
BERG, P.-O., Business Administration
BERGLUND, B., Perception and Psychophysics
BERGMARK, A., Social Work
BERNHARDT, E., Demography
BJÖRKUND, A., Economics
CALMFORS, L., International Economics
CHINAPAH, V., International Education
CHRISTIANSSON, S.-Å., Psychology
DAHL, G., Social Anthropology, Development Research
DAHLERUP, O., Political Science
DAUN, H., International Education
EDWARDS, M., Political Science
EKBERG, J., Economics
EKENBERG, L., Computer and Systems Science
ERIKSON, R., Sociology
FÄGERLIND, I., International and Comparative Education
FLAM, H., International Economics
FLYGHED, J., Criminology
FORSBERG, G., Human Geography
FRANK, O., Statistics
GOLDMANN, K., Political Science
GUILLET DE MONTHOUX, P., Business Administration
GUMMESSON, E., Business Administration
HANNERZ, U., Social Anthropology
HART, T., Pacific Asia Studies
HEDBERG, B., Business Administration
HEDSTRÖM, P., Sociology, Population Processes
HESSLE, S., Social Work
HOEM, J., Demography
HORN AF RANTZIEN, H., International Economics
JOHANSSON, G., Working Life Psychology
JONSSON, E., Business Administration, Administrative Economics
KORPI, W., Social Politics
KÜHLHORN, E., Sociological Alcoholic Research
LENNTORP, B., Human and Economic Geography
LUNDBERG, B., Information Administration
LUNDBERG, U., Human Biological Psychology
MONTGOMERY, H., Cognitive Psychology
NILSSON, L.-G., Psychology
NORSTRÖM, T., Sociology, Social Politics
NYSTEDT, L., Psychology, Social Perception
ÖST, L.-G., Clinical Psychology
OVARSELL, B., Education
PALME, J., Computer and Systems Sciences
PALME, M., Social Security
PERSSON, M., International Economics
PERSSON, T., International Economics
PREMFORS, R., Political Science
SAHLIN-ANDERSON, K., Public Organization
SARNECKI, J., Criminology
SIVEN, C.-H., Economics, especially Economic Politics
SKÖLDBERG, K., Business Administration
SPORRONG, U., Geography, especially Human Geography
SVEDBERG, P., Development Economics
SVENSON, O., Nuclear Power Safety (Psychology)
SVENSSON, L., International Economics
SWEDBERG, R., Economic Sociology
SÖDERBERG, J., Economic History
TÅHLIN, M., Sociology
TARSCHYS, D., Political Science, especially Planning and Administration
THAM, H., Criminology
THORBURN, D., Statistics
THORSLUND, M., Social Work
VÅGERÖ, D., Medical Sociology
WADENSJÖ, E., Employment Policy
WESTIN, C., Immigration Research
WIJKANDER, H., International Economics
WIKANDER, U., Economic History
WITTROCK, B., Political Science

SVERIGES LANTBRUKSUNIVERSITET (Swedish University of Agricultural Sciences)

POB 7070, SE-750 07 Uppsala
Telephone: (18) 67-10-00
Fax: (18) 67-20-00
E-mail: registrator@slu.se
Internet: www.slu.se

Founded 1977 by merger of fmr Lantbrukshögskolan, Skogshögskolan and Veterinärhögskolan

Academic year: September to May

Vice-Chancellor: LISA SENNERBY FORSSE
Pro-Vice-Chancellor: LENA ANDERSSON-EKLUND
Pro-Vice-Chancellor: JOHN SCHNUR
Pro-Vice-Chancellor: GÖRAN STÅHL
Chair.: Prof. LARS-ERIK EDQVIST
Univ. Dir: ULF HEYMAN
Chief Librarian: SNORRE RUFELT

Library: see Libraries and Archives
Number of teachers: 500
Number of students: 3,793 full-time, 712 postgraduate

DEANS

Faculty of Forestry: TOMAS LUNDMARK
Faculty of Natural Resources and Agricultural Science: KRISTINA GLIMELIUS
Faculty of Veterinary Medicine and Animal Science: KERSTIN SVENNERSTEN SJAUNJA

PROFESSORS

(Some professors serve in more than one faculty)

Faculty of Forestry:

ÅGREN, G., Systems Ecology
ANDRÉN, H., Conservation Biology
ARNOLD, S. VON, Forest Cell Biology
BERGSTEN, U., Reforestation
BISHOP, K., Environmental Assessment
BORGEFORS, G., Remote Sensing and Image Analysis
CLARHOLM, M., Soil Ecology
DANELL, K., Wildlife Ecology
DANIEL, G., Wood Products
ELFVING, B., Forest Yield Research
ELOWSON, T., Wood Technology
ERICSSON, A., Forest Plant Physiology
ERIKSSON, L.-O., Aquaculture
ERIKSSON, L. O., Forest Planning
FINLAY, R., Forest Microbiology
GEMMEL, P., Forestry
GOBRAN, G., Ecology, Soil Science
GUSTAVSSON, L., Conservation Biology
HANSSON, L., Population Ecology
HÅNELL, B., Silviculture
HÄLLGREN, J.-E., Forest Plant Physiology
HÖGBERG, P., Soil Science
JEGLUM, J., Forest Peatland Science
JOHANSSON, M.-B., Forest Soil Science
JOHANSSON, T., Forest Management
JOHNSSON, R., Aquatic Ecology
KRISTRÖM, B., Natural Resources Economics
LARSSON, S., Forest Entomology
LINDER, S., Forest Ecology
LINDGREN, D., Forest Genetics
LOHMANDER, P., Forest Management
LUNDKVIST, H., Soil Ecology
LUNDQVIST, H., Fish Biology
LÅNGSTROM, B., Forest Protection from Insects
LÖNNSTEDT, L., Business Economics
MAGNHAGEN, C., Aquaculture
MORITZ, T., Forest Plant Physiology
NILSSON, M.-C., Forest Vegetation Ecology
NILSSON, P.-O., Energy System in Forestry
NILSSON, T., Ultrastructure and Disintegration of Wood
NILSSON, U., Reforestation
NYLINDER, M., Wood Measurement and Cross-Cutting
NYLUND, J.-E., Forest Microbiology
NÄSHOLM, T., Forest Plant Physiology
ODÉN, P. C., Forestry Seed Research
OLSSON, H., Remote Sensing applied to Forestry
OLSSON, M., Forest Soil Chemistry
PERSSON, H., Root Ecology
PERSSON, T., Biology of Forest Soils
RANNEBY, B., Forest Survey
ROSEN, K., Forest Soils
SALLNÄS, O., Forest Operations
SANDBERG, G., Morphogenesis of Trees
STENLID, J., Pathology of Forest Trees
STÅHL, G., Forest Survey
SUNDBERG, B., Forest Plant Physiology
VERWIJST, T., Forestry
WIBE, S., Forest Economics
WINGSLE, G., Forest Plant Physiology
WÄSTERLUND, I., Forestry Technology
ZACKRISSON, O., Forest Vegetation Ecology

Faculty of Natural Resources and Agriculture Science:

ÅMAN, P., Plant Products
ANDERSSON, G., Molecular Genetics
ANDERSSON, H., Agricultural Economics
ANDERSSON, I., Plant Biochemistry
ANDRÉN, O., Soil Biology and Agriculture
BENGTSSON, B., International Crop Production Science
BENGTSSON, J., Environmental Science and Conservation
BERGSTRÖM, L., Water Quality Management
BJÖRCK, L., Dairy Products Science
BJÖRNHAG, G., Animal Physiology
BOLIN, O., Economics of Agriculture, International Trade
BOTHMER, R. VON, Genetics and Breeding of Cultivated Plants
BRYNGELSSON, T., Molecular Plant Biology
BUCHT, E., Landscape Planning
BYLUND, A.-C., Meat Science
DANELL, B., Animal Breeding
DANELL, Ö., Reindeer Husbandry
EBBERSTEN, S., Organic Farming/Ecological Farming
EKBOM, B., Entomology
EKLUND, H., Structural Molecular Biology
EMMELIN, L., Environmental Impact Assessment
FLORGÅRD, C., Landscape Architecture
GEBRESENBET, G., Agricultural Engineering
GERHARDSON, B., Plant Pathology
GLIMELIUS, K., Genetics and Plant Breeding
GREN, J.-M., Natural Resource and Environmental Economics
GULLBERG, U., Plant Breeding
GUSTAFSON, A., Water Quality Management
GUSTAFSSON, L., Systems Analysis
GUSTAFSSON, M., Plant Disease Resistance
GUSTAFSSON, P., Landscape Architecture
GUSTAVSSON, R., Planting Design and Management
HANSSON, B. S., Plant Protection Sciences

HAVNEVIK, K., Rural Development
HUSS-DANELL, K., Crop Science
JANSSON, C., Molecular Cell Biology
JARVIS, N., Biogeophysics
JENSÉN, P., Horticultural Science
JILAR, T., Horticultural Building and Climate Technology
JÄGERSTAD, M., Food Chemistry
KENNE, L., Organic Chemistry
KIRCHMANN, H., Soil Fertility
KNIGHT, S., Biochemistry
LARSEN, R., Greenhouse Production, Horticultural Crops
LARSSON, L.-G., Molecular Genetics
LILJENSTRÖM, H., Biometry
LINDBERG, J.-E., Animal Nutrition and Management
LUNDQVIST, P., Work Science
LUNDSTRÖM, K., Meat Science
MEIJER, J., Molecular Cell Biology
MERKER, A., Plant Breeding
MOWBRAY, S., Biochemistry
MYRDAL, J., History of Agriculture
MÅRTENSSON, A., Soil Fertility
NILSSON, C., Building Science
NILSSON, I., Soil Chemistry and Pedology
NILSSON, J., Cooperation
NITSCH, U., Agricultural Communication
NORBERG, T., Inorganic Chemistry
NYBOM, H., Horticultural Genetics and Plant Breeding
NYBRANT, T., Agricultural Control Engineering
ÖBERG, K., Ergonomics
ÖHLMER, B., Agricultural Business Administration
OLOFSSON, C., Entrepreneurial Studies
OLSSON, K., Animal Physiology
OLWIG, K. R., Landscape Planning
PERSSON, I., Inorganic and Physical Chemistry
PETTERSSON, J., Applied Entomology
RABINOWICZ, E., Economic Analysis of Food and Agricultural Systems
RIDDERSTRÅLE, Y., Animal Physiology
RONNE, H., Molecular Genetics
ROSSWALL, T., Water and Environmental Studies
SCHNÜRER, J., Food Microbiology
SKÄRBÄCK, E., Comprehensive Landscape Planning
SORTE, G., Landscape Architecture
STYMNE, S., Plant Breeding, Biochemistry
SÄLLVIK, K., Agricultural Building Functions Analysis
TORSTENSSON, L., Soil Microbiology
UVNÄS-MOBERG, K., Animal Physiology
VALKONEN, J., Virology comprising Plant Viruses
VON ROSEN, D., Statistics
WELANDER, M., Horticultural Science
WIKTORSSON, H., Animal Nutrition and Management
YUEN, J., Plant Pathology

Faculty of Veterinary Medicine and Animal Science (tel. (18) 67-35-70):
ALENIUS, S., Medicine for Ruminants
ALGERS, B., Animal Hygiene
ALM, G., Immunology
ANDERSSON, L., Genetics
BELAK, S., Virology
BJÖRK, I., Medical and Physiological Chemistry
DANIELSSON-THAM, M.-L., Food Hygiene
DREVEMO, S., Anatomy and Histology
EINARSSON, S., Obstetrics and Gynaecology
ENGSTRÖM, W., Pathology
ERIKSSON, S., Medical and Physiological Chemistry
FELLSTRÖM, C., Swine Diseases
FORSBERG, M., Veterinary Diagnostic Endocrinology
GUSTAVSSON, I., Genetics
HEDHAMMER, H., Small Animal Medicine
JENSEN, P., Ethology
JENSEN-WAERN, M., Comparative Medicine
JONES, B., Clinical Chemistry
JÖNSSON, L., Pathology
KINDAHL, H., Obstetrics and Gynaecology
KVART, C., Clinical Physiology
LINDE-FORSBERG, C., Small Animal Reproduction
LINNÉ, T., Virology
LORD, P., Clinical Radiology
LUTHMAN, J., Medicine for Ruminants
MORENO-LOPEZ, J., Virology
NORRGREN, L., Aquatic Ecotoxicology
OSKARSSON, A., Food Hygiene
PLÖEN, L., Anatomy and Histology
PRINGLE, J., Equine Medicine
RODRÍGUEZ-MARTÍNEZ, H., Reproduction Biotechnology
SVENSSON, C., Production Diseases of Farm Animals
SVENSSON, S., Bacteriology
TJÄLVE, H., Toxicology
UGGLA, A., Parasitology

UMEÅ UNIVERSITET
(Umeå University)

SE-901 87 Umeå
Telephone: (90) 786-50-00
Fax: (90) 786-99-95
E-mail: umea.universitet@umu.se
Internet: www.umu.se

Founded 1965
State control
Languages of instruction: English, Swedish
Academic year: September to June
Vice-Chancellor: LENA GUSTAFSON
Pro-Vice-Chancellor: KJELL JONSSON
Deputy Vice-Chancellor for Education: Prof. ANDERS FÄLLSTRÖM
Deputy Vice-Chancellor for Research: MARIANNE SOMMARIN
Vice-Rector for Collaboration and Innovation: Prof. AGNETA MARELL
Univ. Dir: LARS LUSTIG
Head of Admin.: SIV OLOFSSON

Library: see under Libraries and Archives
Number of teachers: 1,928
Number of students: 33,474

DEANS

Faculty of Arts: Prof. BRITTA LUNDGREN
Faculty of Medicine: Prof. BENGT JÄRVHOLM
Faculty of Science and Technology: Prof. ÅSA RASMUSON-LESTANDER
Faculty of Social Sciences: (vacant)

PROFESSORS

Faculty of Humanities (internet www.humfak.umu.se):
ANDERSSON, G., Science of Science
BANNERT, R., Phonetics
BRÄNDSTRÖM, A., Historical Demography
EDLUND, L.-E., Scandinavian Languages
EDMAN, M., Philosophy and Science of Humanities
EHN, B., Ethnology
ERICSSON, T., History
FORSGREN, K.-Å., German Language
GENRUP, K., Ethnology
GRANQVIST, R., English Language
GROUNDSTROEM, A., Finnish Language
HATJE, A.-K., History
HENE, B., Swedish Language
JOHANSSON, I., Theoretical Philosophy
JONSSON, K., History of Science and Ideas
LARSSON, T., Archaeology
LILIEQUIST, M., Ethnology
LINDBLAD, I.-B., Media and Communications
LINDSTRÖM, S., Theoretical Philosophy
LUNDGREN, B., Ethnology
PETTERSSON, A., Comparative Literature
POUSSA, P., English Language
RAMQVIST, P., Archaeology
RINGBY, P., Comparative Literature
SJÖBERG TAUSSI, M., History in a Social Historic Perspective
SKÖLD, P., History, Lapp Culture
SMEDS, K., Museology
SÖRLIN, S., Environmental History
SPOLANDER, R., History of Art
STRAARUP, J., Religious Studies
STRANGERT, E., Phonetics
SUNDIN, B., History of Science and Ideas
SVONNI, M., Lapp Language and Culture
WERBART, B., Archaeology
WIKSTRÖM, E., Fine Arts

Faculty of Medicine (tel. (90) 786-64-65; internet www.medfak.umu.se):
ADOLFSSON, R., Psychiatry
ÅHLSTRÖM, K., X-Ray and Diagnostics
ALFREDSSON, H., Sports Medicine
ALSTERMARK, B., Physiology, especially Neurology
ASIKAINEN, S., Oral Microbiology
BERGENHEIM, T., Neurosurgery
BERGH, A., Pathology
BERGSTRÖM, S., Microbiology
BERNSPÅNG, B., Occupational Therapy
BJÖRNSTIG, U., Surgery, especially Trauma and Civil Defence Medicine
BOMAN, K., Medicine
BORÉN, T., Medical Chemistry
BROSTRÖM, L.-Å., Orthopaedics
BUCHT, G., Geriatrics
BÄCKSTRÖM, T., Obstetrics and Gynaecology
DAHLQUIST, G., Paediatrics, especially Diabetes
DAHLQVIST, S., Rheumatology
DANIELSSON, Å., Gastroenterology
DIJKEN, J. VAN, Cariology
DOORN, J. VAN, Logopedics
EDLUND, H., Molecular Development Biology
EDLUND, T., Molecular Genetics
EGELRUD, T., Dermatology and Venereology
EMDIN, S., Surgery
ERIKSSON, A., Forensic Medicine
ERIKSSON, J., Medicine
ERIKSSON, P.-O., Clinical Oral Physiology
FÄLLMAN, M., Medical Microbiology
FISHER, A., Occupational Therapy
FORSGREN, L., Neurology
FOWLER, C., Pharmacology
GOTHEFORS, L., Paediatrics
GRANKVIST, K., Clinical Chemistry, especially Experimental Toxicology
GRÖNBERG, H., Oncology
GROTH, S., Clinical Physiology
GRUNDSTRÖM, T., Tumour Biology
GUNNE, J., Prosthetic Dentistry
GUSTAFSON, Y., Geriatric Medicine
HALLMANS, G., Nutrition Research
HAMMARSTRÖM, A., Public Health (Gender Perspective)
HAMMARSTRÖM, M.-L., Immunology
HAMMARSTRÖM, S., Immunology
HENRIKSSON, R., Experimental Oncology
HERNELL, O., Paediatrics, especially Nutrition Research
HOLMBERG, D., Molecular Genetics
HULTMARK, D., Medical Molecular Biology
HÄGGLÖF, B., Child and Youth Psychiatry
HÖGBERG, U., Obstetrics and Gynaecology
JACOBSSON, L., Psychiatry
JANLERT, U., Public Health
JOHANSSON, I., Cariology
JOHANSSON, R., Physiology
JOHANSSON, S., Physiology
JÄRVHOLM, B., Occupational and Environmental Medicine
KARLSSON, M., Medical Radiation Physics
KELLERTH, J.-O., Anatomy
KULLGREN, G., Psychiatric Epidemiology
LALOS, A., Public Health (Gender Perspective)
LARSÉN, K., Sports Medicine

LERNER, U., Oral Cell Biology
LIBELIUS, R., Clinical Neurophysiology
LINDHOLM, L., Family Medicine
LINDSTRÖM, P., Histology and Cell Biology
LJUNGBERG, B., Urology
LORENTZON, R., Sports Medicine
LUNDGREN, E., Applied Cell Biology
LUNDGREN, S., Oral and Maxillofacial Surgery
LUNDMAN, B., Nursing
MARKLUND, S., Clinical Chemistry
MOLIN, M., Prosthetic Dentistry
NAREDI, P., Surgery
NILSSON, E., Surgery
NORBERG, A., Advanced Nursing
NORDBERG, G., Health and Hygiene
NORGREN, M., Biomedical Laboratory Sciences
NY, T., Medical and Physiological Chemistry
OLIVECRONA, G., Medical Chemistry
OLOFSSON, B.-O., Medicine
OLSSON, K., Physiology
OLSSON, T., Medicine
ROOS, G., Pathology
SANDMAN, P.-O., Advanced Nursing
SANDSTRÖM, T., Pulmonary Medicine
SCHLEUCHER, J., Medical Biophysics
SEHLIN, J., Histology and Cell Biology
SELSTAM, G., Physiology
SJÖLUND, B. H., Rehabilitation Medicine
SJÖSTEDT, A., Clinical Bacteriology
STENLING, R., Pathology
STIGBRAND, T., Immunochemistry
STRÖMBERG, I., Histology and Cell Biology
STRÖMBERG, N., Cardiology
SUNDELIN, G., Advanced Nursing
SUNDVIST, K. G., Clinical Immunology
SVENSSON, O., Orthopaedics
THELANDER, L., Medical and Physiological Chemistry
THORNELL, L.-E., Anatomy
TWETMAN, S., Paedodontics
TÄLJEDAL, I.-B., Histology
TÄRNVIK, A., Infectious Diseases
UHLIN, B. E., Medical Microbiology
WACHTMEISTER, L., Ophthalmology
WADELL, G., Virology
WALDENSTRÖM, A., Cardiology
WALL, S., Epidemiology and Public Health
WESTER, P., Medicine
WESTMAN, G., Family Medicine
WIBERG, M., Anatomy
WIDMARK, A., Oncology
WINKVIST, A., Epidemiology

Faculty of Science and Technology (fax (90) 786-97-96; e-mail teknat@adm.umu.se; internet www.teknat.umu.se):

ANDERSSON, B., Environmental Chemistry
AVONDOGLIO, P., Industrial Design
AXNER, O., Physics
BJÖRK, G., Microbiology
BONDESSON, L., Mathematical Statistics
BYSTRÖM, A., Microbiology
BÅMSTEDT, U., Marine Sciences
BRODIN, G., Physics
CEDERGREN, A., Analytical Chemistry
CEGRELL, U., Mathematics (Complete Analysis)
EDLUND, U., Organic Chemistry
EKLUND, P., Computer Science
ERICSON, L., Plant Ecology
ERIKSSON, E. S., Structural Biology
FRECH, W., Analytical Chemistry
GARDESTRÖM, P., Plant Physiology
GILLBRO, T., Biophysical Chemistry
GUSTAFSSON, P., Plant Molecular Biology
HEBY, O., Cellular and Developmental Biology
HÄGGKVIST, R., Discrete Mathematics
IRGUM, K., Analytical Chemistry
JANLERT, L.-E., Computing Science
JANSSON, M., Physical Geography
JANSSON, S., Plant Biology
JOHANSSON, L., Physical Chemistry
JOHNELS, D., Organic Chemistry
KASTBERG, A., Experimental Optical Physics
KIHLBERG, J., Organic Chemistry
KIRKWOOD, S., Atmospheric Physics
KLECZKOWSKI, L., Plant Physiology
KULLMAN, L., Physical Geography
KÅGSTRÖM, B., Numerical Analysis and Parallel Computing
LARSON, M., Applied Mathematics
LARSSON, J., Plasma Physics
LESTANDER, Å., Genetics
LI, H., Signal Processing
LINDAHL, O., Medical Technology
LINDBLOM, G., Physical Chemistry
LUNDIN, R., Space Physics
MALMQVIST, B., Ecology
MARKLUND, S., Environmental Chemistry
MINNHAGEN, P., Theoretical Physics
NILSSON, C., Landscape Ecology, especially Running Waters
NORDIN, A., Energy Technology
ÖHMAN, L.-O., Inorganic Chemistry
OKSANEN, L., Ecology
OLIVEBERG, M., Biochemistry
OTTO, CH., Animal Ecology
ÖQUIST, G., Plant Physiology
PALMGREN, B., Design
PERSSON, L., Aquatic Ecology
PERSSON, P., Chemistry, Molecular Chemistry
PETTERSSON, L., Inorganic Chemistry
RAMMER, J., Condensed Matter Theory
RENBERG, I., Ecological and Environmental Impact Assessment
RÖNNMARK, K., Theoretical Space Physics
SAMUELSSON, G., Plant Physiology
SANDAHL, I., Space Physics
SAURA, A., Genetics
SCHRÖDER, W., Biochemistry
SELLSTEDT, A., Plant Physiology
SHELANKOV, A., Condensed Matter Physics
SHINGLER, V., Microbiology
SHIRIAEV, A., Automatic Control Engineering
SJÖBERG, S., Inorganic Chemistry
SJÖSTRÖM, M., Inorganic Chemistry
STENFLO, L., Theoretical Plasma Physics
STOTT, M., Interaction Design
SUNDQVIST, B., Condensed Matter Physics
TYSKLIND, M., Environmental Chemistry
WEDIN, P.-Å., Numerical Analysis
WESTLUND, P.-O., Theoretical Chemistry
WOLD, S., Chemometrics
WOLF-WATZ, H., Applied Molecular Biology

Faculty of Social Sciences (fax (90) 786-66-75; internet www.umu.se/samfak):

ÅBERG, R., Sociology
ARMELIUS, B.-Å., Clinical Psychology
ARMELIUS, K., Clinical Psychology
ARONSSON, T., Environmental and Natural Resources Economics
BACKMAN, J., Pedagogics and Educational Psychology
BENGTSSON, M., Business Administration and Economics
BOTER, H., Business Administration and Economics
BROSTRÖM, G., Statistics
BRÄNNLUND, R., Economics
BRÄNNÄS, K., Econometrics
DAHLGREN, L., Medical Sociology
ECKERBERG, K., Political Science
EDSTRÖM, Ö., Legal Science
FRANKE, S., Pedagogics
GUNNARSSON, Å, Legal Science
GUSTAFSSON, G., Political Science
HALLERÖD, B., Sociology
HALLSTRÖM, P., Legal Science
HAMILTON, D., Pedagogics
HENRIKSSON, W., Pedagogics
HOLM, E., Social and Economic Geography, especially Social Community Planning and Financial Control
JOHANSSON, G., Nutritional Studies
JOHANSSON, M., Pedagogics (Sports)
JOHANSSON, O., Political Science
JOHANSSON, S., Social Work
JOHANSSON, U., Pedagogics
KAPTELININ, V., Informatics
LINDQVIST, R., Social Work
LÖFGREN, K.-G., Economics, especially Evaluating Labour Market Research
MALMBERG, G., Social and Economic Geography
MOLANDER, B., Psychology
MÄNTYLÄ, T., Psychology (Cognitive Science)
NIEMI-KIESILÄINEN, J., Legal Science
NILSSON, I., Pedagogics
NYBERG, L., Psychology
NYGREN, L., Social Work
PERSSON, O., Library and Information Science
RÄTHZEL, N., Sociology
SÖDERHOLM, A., Informatics
SKÖG, L. A., Business Administration
STAGE, C., Pedagogics
STOLTERMAN, E., Informatics
SUNDBOM, E., Clinical Psychology
SVALLFORS, S., Sociology
TESAR, G., Business Administration and Economics (Marketing and International Business Administration)
WATERWORTH, J., Informatics
WIBERG, U., Economic Geography, especially the Structural Issues of Sparsely Populated Areas

UPPSALA UNIVERSITET
(Uppsala University)

POB 256, SE-751 05 Uppsala
Telephone: (18) 471-00-00
Fax: (18) 471-20-00
E-mail: info@uadm.uu.se
Internet: www.uu.se

Founded 1477
Academic year: September to June

Vice-Chancellor: Prof. ANDERS HALLBERG
Deputy Vice-Chancellor: KERSTIN SAHLIN
Vice-Rector for Humanities and Social Sciences: MARGARETHA FAHLGREN
Vice-Rector for Medicine and Pharmacy: BRITT SKOGSEID
Vice-Rector for Science and Technology: JOSEPH NORDGREN
Univ. Dir: ANN FUST
Chief Librarian: ULF GÖRANSON

Library: see Libraries and Archives
Number of teachers: 3,600
Number of students: 20,000

Publications: *Acta Universitatis Upsaliensis*, *Multiethnica*, *Universen* (12 a year), *Uppsala Accelerator News*

DEANS

Faculty of Education: Prof. CAROLINE LIBERG
Faculty of History and Philosophy: Prof. JAN LINDEGREN
Faculty of Languages: Prof. BJÖRN MELANDER
Faculty of Law: Prof. TORBJÖRN ANDERSSON
Faculty of Medicine: Prof. GÖRAN MAGNUSSON
Faculty of Pharmacy: Prof. FRED NYBERG
Faculty of Science and Technology: Prof. JOSEPH NORDGREN
Faculty of Social Sciences: Prof. ANDERS MALMBERG
Faculty of Theology: Prof. MIKAEL STENMARK

PROFESSORS

Faculty of History and Philosophy

I. Historical-Philosophical Division:

ÅHLBERG, L.-O., Aesthetics and Cultural Studies
ALANEN, L., History of Philosophy
ARVASTSON, G., Ethnology
BEACH, H., Cultural Anthropology
BURMAN, L., Rhetoric

DANIELSSON, S. O., Practical Philosophy
FAHLGREN, M., Literature
FRÄNGSMYR, T., History of Science
HERSCHEND, F., Archaeology
IVARSDOTTER, A., Musicology
JANSSON, T., History
JOHANNISSON, K. M., History of Science and Ideas
KJELLBERG, E., Musicology
KYHLBERG, O., Archaeology
LANDGREN, B., Literature
LINDEGREN, J., History
PARKMAN, S., Musicology
PETTERSSON, T., Literature
RUNBLOM, H., History
SANTILLO FRIZELL, B., Archaeology
SINCLAIR, P., African Archaeology
SKUNCKE, M.-C., Literature
SVEDJEDAL, J. O., Literature
SÖDERLIND, S., Art History
TROY, L., Archaeology

II. Linguistic Division:

EKLUND, S. I., Latin
FRYCKSTEDT, M., English Literature
GREN-EKLUND, G., Indology
GUSTAVSSON, S. R., Slavic Languages
HELANDER, H. O., Latin
ISAKSSON, B., Semitic Languages
JONASSON, K., French Language
KINDSTRAND, J. F., Greek Language and Literature
KROHN, D., German Language
KRONNING, H., French Language
KYTÖ, M., English Language
LARSSON, L.-G., Finno-Ugrian Languages
LUNDÉN, R., American Literature
MAIER, I., Russian Language
MELANDER, B., Swedish Language
MULLER, G., German Language and Literature
NORDBERG, B., Sociolinguistics
PACKALEN, A. M., Polish Language
PALM MEISTER, C., German Language
PEDERSEN, O., Assyriology
PETERSON, L., Scandinavian Languages
RAAG, R., Finno-Ugric Languages
ROSENQVIST, J.-O., Byzantine Studies
STRANDBERG, S., Scandinavian Onomastics
SUNDELL, L.-G., French Language
SVANE, B., French Literature
SÅGVALL-HEIN, A., Computational Linguistics
THELANDER, M., Swedish Language
UTAS, B., Iranian Studies
VIBERG, Å, Linguistics
WILLIAMS, H., Swedish Language
WOLLIN, L., Scandinavian Languages

Faculty of Law:

ANDERSSON, H., Private Law
ANDERSSON, T., Private Law
CAMERON, I., International Law
ERIKSSON, M., International Law
FRÄNDBERG, Å., History of Law
JÄNTERÄ-JAREBORG, M., International Law
JAREBORG, N., Penal Law
LEHRBERG, B., Penal Law
LINDBLOM, P. H., Judicial Procedure
LINDELL, B., Judicial Procedure
LYSEN, G., International Law
MARCUSSON, L. M., Administrative Law
MATTSSON, N. G., Taxation
MÖLLER, M., Private Law
NYGREN, R. O., History of Law
ÖSTERDAHL, I., International Law
SALDEEN, Å., Private Law
THORELL, P. H., Business Law
WESTERLUND, S., Environmental Law

Faculty of Medicine:

ÅKERMAN, K., Cell Physiology
ÅKERSTRÖM, G., Endocrinological Surgery
AKUSJÄRVI, G., Microbiology
ALDSKOGIUS, H., Medical Structural Biology
ALM, A., Ophthalmology
ANDERSSON, A. E. V., Diabetes Research
ANDERSSON, J. H., Immunology
ANNIKO, M., Otorhinolaryngology
AQUILONIUS, S.-M., Neurology
ARNETZ, B., Social Medicine
AXELSSON, O. L., Women's and Children's Health
BERGQVIST, D., Vascular Surgery
BERNE, CH., Medicine
BLOMBERG, J., Clinical Virology
BOBERG, M., Social Medicine
BOMAN, G., Pulmonary Medicine
CARLSSON, J., Biomedical Radiation Science
CLAESSON-WELSH, L., Genetics and Pathology
DAHL, M.-L., Medicine
DAHL, N., Clinical Genetics
DUMANSKI, J., Genetics and Pathology
EBENDAL, T., Developmental Biology
EDLING, C., Occupational Medicine
ERIKSSON, U., Histology
FLEMSTRÖM, G. F., Physiology
FRIES, E., Cell Biology
FRIMAN, G., Infectious Diseases
GEBRE-MEDHIN, M., International Child Care
GERDIN, B., Intensive and Burns Care
GLIMELIUS, B., Oncology
GUSTAFSSON, J., Women's and Children's Health
GYLFE, E., Secretion Research
GYLLENSTEN, U., Medical Molecular Genetics
HAGLUND, U., Surgery
HÄLLGREN, R., Medicine
HAU, J., Comparative Medicine
HEDENSTIERNA, G., Medicine
HEYMAN, B., Genetics and Pathology
HILLERED, L., Clinical Neurochemistry
HOLMBERG, L., Surgery
JOHANSSON, S., Cell Biology
KARLSSON, A., Experimental Endocrinology
KJELLEN, L., Medical Biochemistry and Microbiology
KÄMPE, O., Molecular Medicine
LANDEGREN, U., Molecular Medicine
LARHAMMAR, D. S., Molecular Cell Biology
LARSSON, R., Medicine
LINDAHL, U., Medical Chemistry
LINDGREN, P. G., X-ray Diagnosis
LINDHOLM, D., Neurobiology
LINDMARK, G., International Mother and Child Health
LITHELL, H., Geriatrics
LJUNGHALL, S., Medicine
LUNDQVIST, H., Oncology
LÖNNERHOLM, G., Women's and Children's Health
MAGNUSSON, A., Oncology
MAGNUSSON, G., Molecular Virology
MÅRDH, P.-A., Medicine
NILSSON, K., Cell Pathology
NILSSON, O., Orthopaedics
NISTÉR, M., Experimental Pathology
NORLÉN, B. J., Urology
ÖBERG, K., Oncological Endocrinology
ORELAND, L. Å. M., Pharmacology
PERSSON, E., Physiology
PERSSON, L., Physiology
PETTERSSON, U. G., Medical Genetics
PÅHLMAN, L., Surgery
RAININKO, R., Neuroradiology
RASK, L., Medical Biochemistry
RASK-ANDERSEN, H., Surgery
RASTAD, J., Surgery
RAUSCHNING, W., Surgery
ROOMANS, G. M., Medical Ultrastructure
ROSENQVIST, U., Health Services Research
RUBIN, K., Connective Tissue Biochemistry
SALDEEN, T., Forensic Medicine
SANDLER, S., Medical Cell Biology
SCHWARTZ, S., Medical Biochemistry and Microbiology
SEDIN, G., Perinatal Medicine
SIEGBAHN, A., Medicine
SJÖDÉN, P.-O., Nursing and Health Care
SJÖQVIST, M. I. J., Physiology
STJERNSCHANTZ, J., Pharmacology
SVÄRDSUDD, K., Family Medicine
SYVÄNEN, A.-C., Medicine
TOREBJÖRK, E., Pain Research
TÖTTERMAN, T., Clinical Immunology
TURESSON, I., Oncology
TUVEMO, T., Paediatrics
ULMSTEN, U., Obstetrics and Gynaecology
VAHLQUIST, A., Dermatology and Venereology
VENGE, P., Clinical Chemistry
VON KNORRING, A.-L., Child Psychiatry
VON KNORRING, L., Psychiatry
WADELIUS, C., Genetics and Pathology
WALLENTIN, L., Cardiology
WESTERMARK, B. A., Tumour Biology
WESTERMARK, P., Pathology
WESTMAN, J. O., Anatomy
WIESEL, F.-A., Psychiatry
WIKLUND, L., Anaesthesiology

Faculty of Pharmacy:

ALDERBORN, G., Pharmacy
ARTURSSON, P., Pharmacy
BOHLIN, L., Pharmacognosy
BRITTEBO, E. B., Toxicology
DENCKER, L., Toxicology
ENGSTRÖM, S. O. A., Pharmacy
HALLBERG, A., Organic Pharmaceutical Chemistry
HAMMARLUND-UDENAES, M., Pharmacokinetics
ISACSON, D., Pharmacy
KARLSSON, M., Pharmacokinetics
LANG, M., Biochemistry
LENNERNÄS, H., Pharmacy
NYBERG, F., Pharmacological and Biological Research on Drug Dependence
NYSTRÖM, L.-CHR., Pharmacy
OLIW, E., Pharmacological and Biological Research on Drug Dependence
PETTERSSON, C., Analytical Pharmaceutical Chemistry
WESTERLUND, D., Analytical Pharmaceutical Chemistry
WIKBERG, J., Pharmacological and Biological Research on Drug Dependence
WIKVALL, K., Biochemistry

Faculty of Science and Technology:

ÅGREN, J., Ecological Botany
AHLÉN, A., Signal Processing
ALEKLETT, K., Nuclear Physics
ALEXEEV, A., Theoretical Physics
ALMGREN, M., Biochemistry
ANDERSSON, A., Computer Science
ANDERSSON, P., Organic Chemistry
ANDERSSON, S., Evolutionary Biology
ANNERSTEN, H. S., Mineral Chemistry and Petrology
ARNESEN, A., Physics
ÅQVIST, J., Evolutionary Biology
BADELEK, B., Experimental Physics
BENGTSSON, E., Computerized Image Analysis
BENNETT, K. D., Quaternary Geology
BERG, O., Molecular Evolution
BERG, S., Solid State Electronics
BERGER, R., Inorganic Chemistry
BERGLUND, A., Animal Ecology
BERGSTRÖM, Y., Materials Science
BJÖRKLUND, M., Animal Ecology
BOHMAN, O., Organic Chemistry
BOTNER, O., High Energy Physics
BRANDT, I., Ecotoxicology
BRANDT ANDERSSON, Y., Inorganic Chemistry
BREMER, B., Systematic Botany
BREMER, K., Systematic Botany
BRUNSTRÖM, B. O., Ecotoxicology
BRÄNDAS, E., Quantum Chemistry
CARLSSON, B., Systems and Control
CARLSSON, J.-O., Inorganic Chemistry
CHATTOPADHYAYA, J., Bio-organic Chemistry

COORAY, V., Electricity and Lightning
DAHLGREN CALDWELL, K., Surface Biotechnology
DANIELSSON, U., Theoretical Physics
EDWARDS, K., Physical Chemistry
EHRENBERG, M., Molecular Biology with Kinetics
EKELÖF, T., Experimental Elementary Particle Physics
EKMAN, J., Population Biology
ELLEGREN, H., Evolutionary Biology
ENGMAN, L., Organic Chemistry
ENGSTRÖM, P., Physiological Botany
ERICSSON, T., Materials Physics
ERIKSSON, O., Condensed Matter Physics
FROELICH, P., Quantum Chemistry
FÄLDT, G. L., Theoretical Physics
GEE, D. G., Orogenic Dynamics
GELIUS, U., Physics
GESTBLOM, B., Physics
GOSCINSKI, O., Quantum Chemistry
GRANQVIST, C.-G., Solid State Physics
GUNNINGBERG, P., Computer Communication
GUSTAFSSON, B., Numerical Analysis
GUSTAFSSON, B., Theoretical Astrophysics
GUSTAFSSON, L., Animal Ecology
GUT, A., Mathematical Statistics
HAGERSTEN, E., Computer Architecture
HAJDU, J., Biochemistry
HALLDIN, S., Hydrology
HALLGREN, A., Experimental Physics
HEJHAL, D. A., Mathematics
HELLMAN, L., Molecular and Comparative Immunology
HERMANSSON, K. G., Inorganic Chemistry
HILBORN, J., Polymer Chemistry
HOGMARK, S., Materials Science
HOLMER, L., Historical Geology and Palaeontology
HUGHES, D., Evolutionary Biology
HÅKANSSON, L., Sedimentology
HÅKANSSON, P., Ion Physics
HÖGLUND, J., Population Biology
HÖISTAD, B., Nuclear Physics
INGELMANN, G., High Energy Physics
ISRAELSSON, S. O., Meteorology
JACOBSON, S., Materials Science
JANSON, S., Mathematics
JANSSON, U., Inorganic Chemistry
JOHANSSON, B., Condensed Matter Theory
JOHANSSON, S., Materials Science
JOHANSSON, T., Nuclear Physics
JONES, A., Structural Molecular Biology
JONSSON, B., Computer Systems
JUHL-JÖRICKE, B., Mathematics
KAISER, S. G., Mathematics
KARLSSON, L., Experimental Physics
KIRSEBOM, L., Evolutionary Biology
KISELMAN, C. O., Mathematics
KOLSTRUP, E., Physical Geography
KÄLLNE, J., Neutron Physics
LANSHAMMER, H., Systems and Control
LEIJON, M., Electricity
LIBERMAN, M., Theoretical Statistical Physics
LILJAS, L., Evolutionary Biology
LINDBLAD, P., Evolutionary Biology
LINDER, C., Physical Didactics
LINDGREN, J. B. R., Inorganic Chemistry
LUNDAHL, P., Biochemistry
LUNDBERG, A., Evolutionary Biology
LUNDBERG, B., Solid Mechanics
LUNELL, S. G., Applied Quantum Chemistry
LÅNGSTROM, B., Radiopharmaceutical Organic Chemistry
LÖTSTEDT, P., Numerical Analysis
MANNERVIK, B., Biochemistry
MARKIDES, K., Analytical Chemistry
MATTSSON, O. L., Organic Chemistry
MCGREEVY, R. L., Neutron Research
MILBRINK, G., Animal Ecology
MOLLER, F., Computing Science
MÅRTENSSON, N., Physics of Metals and Metal Surfaces
NIEMI, A., Theoretical Physics
NIKLASSON, G., Materials Science and Solar Energy
NILSSON, A., Chemical Physics
NILSSON, A., Systematic Botany
NORDBLAD, P., Solid State Physics
NORDGREN, J., Soft X-ray Physics
NYHOLM, L., Analytical Chemistry
OHLSSON, R., Developmental Zoology
OLSSON, E., Experimental Physics
PAMILO, P., Conservation Biology
PAROSH, A., Computer Systems
PAVLENKO, V. P., Astronomy
PEDERSEN, L. B., Solid Earth Physics
PEEL, J. S., Historical Geology and Palaeontology
PETTERSSON, K. I., Evolutionary Biology
PILSTRÖM, L. H., Immunology
PISKOUNOV, N., Astronomy
POSSNERT, G., Accelerator Mass Spectrometry
RIBBING, C.-G., Solid State Physics
RICKMAN, H., Astronomy
ROBERTS, R., Solid Earth Physics
RODHE, A., Hydrology
RONQUIST, F., Systematic Zoology
ROOS, A., Solid State Physics
RYDIN, H., Plant Ecology
SAXENA, S., Theoretical Geochemistry
SCHWEITZ, J.-Å., Materials Science
SIEGBAHN, H., Atomic and Molecular Physics
SJÖBERG, S., Organic Chemistry
SKÖLD, K., Neutron Research
SMEDMAN, A.-S., Meteorology
STERNAD, M., Signals and Systems
STOICA, P., Systems Modelling
STOLTENBERG-HANSEN, V., Logic of Mathematics
STRÖMQUIST, L., Applied Environmental Impact Analysis
SUNDQVIST, B. U. R., Ion Physics
SVEDLINDH, P., Solid State Physics
SVENSSON, B. W., Animal Ecology
SVENSSON, S., Physics
SÖDERHÄLL, K. T., Physiological Mycology
SÖDERSTRÖM, T., Automatic Control
TALBOT, C. J., Geodynamics and Tectonics
TAPIA-OLIVARES, O., Physical Chemistry
TEGELSTRÖM, H., Conservation Biology and Genetics
TEGENFELT, J. S., Inorganic Chemistry
THOMAS, J. O., Solid State Electro-chemistry
THOTTAPPILLIL, R., Electricity
THULIN, M., Systematic Botany
THUNE, M., Scientific Computing
TIBELL, L. B., Systematic Botany
TINTAREV, K., Mathematics
TOTTMAR, O., Comparative Physiology
TRANVIK, L., Limnology
TÄRNLUND, S. A., Computer Science
VIRO, O., Mathematics
VIRTANEN, A., Molecular Cell Biology
WAGNER, G., Microbiology
WAHLBERG, C., Astronomy
WANG, Y., Computer Systems
WÄPPLING, R., Physics
ZILITINKEVICH, S., Meteorology

Faculty of Social Sciences:

AGELL, J., Economics
ANDERSSON, R. K. G., Housing and Urban Research
BLOMQUIST, S., Local Public Economics
BOHLIN, G., Developmental Psychology
BORGEGÅRD, L.-E., Urban Geography
BROADY, D., Education
BURNS, T., Sociology
BÄCK, L., Urban Geography
BÄCKMAN, L., Cognitive Psychology
BÖRJESSON, E. Å., Psychology
CARLSNAES, W., Political Science
CHRISTOFFERSSON, A. L., Statistics
DIMBERG, U., Psychology
EDIN, P.-A., Labour Market Relations
EKEHAMMAR, B., Psychology
ENGWALL, L., Business Studies
EYERMAN, R., Sociology
FOGELKLOU, A., East European Studies
FORSGREN, M. O., International Business Studies
FREDRIKSON, M., Clinical Psychology
GERNER, K., East European Studies
GOTTFRIES, N., Economics
GUSTAFSSON, C., Education
HADENIUS, A., Political Science
HAGEKULL, B., Developmental Psychology
HALLEN, L., Business Studies
HAMFELT, A., Computer Science
HAMMARSTRÖM, G., Sociology
HANSSON, Å., Computer Science
HEDLUND, S., East European Studies
HEDMAN, L., Media and Communication
HERMANSSON, B. J., Political Science
HOLMLUND, B., Economics
HOPPE, G., Economic Geography
HÅKANSSON, K. G., Sociology
ISACSON, M., Economic History
KEMENY, P. J., Urban Sociology
KLEVMARKEN, A., Econometrics
LEWIN, L., Political Science
LINDBLAD, S., Education
LINDH, T., Economics
LUNDGREN, E., Sociology
LUNDGREN, U. P., Education
MAGNUSSON, L., Economic History
MALMBERG, A., Economic Geography
MELIN, L. G., Clinical Psychology
ÖBERG, S., Social and Economic Geography
OHLSSON, H., Economics
PETERSSOHN, E., Business Administration
RIIS, U., Education
RISCH, T., Computer Science
SAHLIN-ANDERSSON, K., Business Studies
SOMMESTAD, L., Economic History
SÖDER, M., Sociology
SÖDERSTEN, J., Economics
TORNSTAM, L., Sociology
TURNER, B., Housing Economics
VEDUNG, E., Housing Policy
VON HOFSTEN, C., Perceptional Psychology
WALLENSTEEN, P. N., Peace and Conflict
WIGREN, R., Economics
WITTROCK, B., Advanced Study in the Social Sciences

Faculty of Theology:

BÄCKSTRÖM, A., Sociology of Religion
BEXELL, O., Ecclesiology
BRÅKENHIELM, C.-R., Studies of Faiths and Ideologies
BRODD, S.-E., Studies of Churches and Religious Denominations
DE MARINIES, VALERIE, Psychology of Religion
FRANZÉN, R., Church History
GRENHOLM, C.-H., Ethics
HERRMANN, E., Philosophy of Religions
HULTGÅRD, A., History of Religions
NORIN, S., Old Testament Exegesis
PETTERSSON, T., Sociology of Religion
SCHALK, P., History of Religions
SYREENI, K., New Testament Exegesis
WIKSTRÖM, O., Psychology of Religion

University Colleges

Ersta Sköndal Högskola (First Sköndal University College): POB 11, SE-100 61 Stockholm; tel. (8) 55-50-50; e-mail info@esh.se; internet www.esh.se; f. 1998; health sciences, psychotherapy, social work and theology; 1,100 students; Rector JAN-HÅKAN HANSSON.

Högskola Malmö (Malmo University College): SE-205 06 Malmö; tel. (40) 665-70-00; fax (40) 665-73-05; e-mail intsek@mah.se; internet www.mah.se; f. 1998; faculties of health and society and odontology; schools of arts and communication, international migration and ethnic relations, technology, and culture and society; 1,439 teachers; 25,000 students (full-time and part-time); Vice-Chancellor LENNART OLAUSSON.

Högskolan Dalarna (Dalarna University College): SE-791 88 Falun; tel. (23) 77-80-00; fax (23) 77-80-80; e-mail ioffice@du.se; internet www.du.se; f. 1977; schools of health and social sciences, humanities and media studies, technology and business studies; 666 teachers; 7,380 students; Chair. LARS-OVE STAFF; Vice-Chancellor MARITA HILLIGES; Library Dir MARGARETA MALMGREN.

Högskolan Halmstad (Halmstad University College): POB 823, SE-301 18 Halmstad; tel. (35) 16-71-00; fax (35) 14-85-33; e-mail registrator@hh.se; internet www.hh.se; f. 1983; academic year September to June; library: 125,000 vols, 10,500 e-journals, 500 periodicals; 253 teachers; 14,500 students(5,088 full-time, 9,412 part-time); Rector ROMULO ENMARK.

Högskolan i Borås (University College of Borås): Allégatan 1, SE-501 90 Borås; tel. (33) 435-40-00; fax (33) 435-40-03; e-mail registrator@hb.se; internet www.hb.se; f. 1977; offers courses in behavioural and education sciences, business and informatics, engineering, fashion and textile studies, library and information studies and health sciences; mem. of the European Univ. Asscn; library: see Libraries and Archives; 650 teachers; 15,000 students; Chair. ROLAND ANDERSSON; Rector Prof. LENA NORDHOLM; Head of Central Admin. KARIN CARDELL; Librarian INGER EIDE-JENSEN.

Högskolan i Gävle (Gävle University College): SE-801 76 Gävle; Kungsbackavägen 47, Gävle; tel. (26) 64-85-00; fax (26) 64-86-86; e-mail registrator@hig.se; internet www.hig.se; f. 1977; mathematics, natural sciences, and computer science, technology, humanities and social sciences, teacher training and health care; library: 90,000 vols, 550 periodicals; 500 teachers (incl. 40 profs, 150 senior lecturers); 12,000 students; Rector MAJ-BRITT JOHANSSON.

Högskolan i Jönköping (Jönköping University College): POB 1026, SE-551 11 Jönköping; Gjuterigatan 5, SE-553 18 Jönköping; tel. (36) 10-10-00; fax (36) 15-08-12; e-mail info@hj.se; internet www.hj.se; f. 1977; library: see Libraries and Archives; 500 teachers; 8,595 students; Rector ANITA HANSBO.

Högskolan på Gotland (Gotland University): Cramérgatan 3, SE-621 67 Visby; tel. (498) 29-99-00; fax (498) 29-99-62; e-mail info@hgo.se; internet www.hgo.se; f. 1998; primarily business administration and international management and coastal zone management, secondary subjects incl. archaeology, osteology, information technology and business administration, international business relations, technology, art and new media, building restoration, Russian, history, human geography, ethnology, ecology, art history and cross-cultural communication; 150 teachers; 2,396 students; Rector JORGEN THOLIN.

Högskolan i Skövde (Skövde University College): POB 408, SE-541 28 Skövde; tel. (500) 44-80-00; fax (500) 44-81-39; e-mail registrator@his.se; internet www.his.se; f. 1977, present status 1983; business administration, economics, engineering science, biosciences, computer science, languages, art, social science, nursing; library: see Libraries and Archives; 312 teachers; 10,904 students (4,381 full-time, 6,523 part-time); Rector SIGBRITT KARLSSON.

Högskolan Kristianstad (Kristianstad University College): Elmetorpsvägen 15, SE-291 88 Kristianstad; tel. (44) 20-30-00; fax (44) 12-96-51; e-mail info@hkr.se; internet www.hkr.se; f. 1977; languages of instruction: Swedish, English; depts of behavioural sciences, business studies, humanities and social sciences, health sciences and mathematics and science; school of engineering; library: see Libraries and Archives; 500 teachers; 12,000 students; Rector LARS CARLSSON.

Högskolan Väst (University West): SE-461 86 Trollhättan; tel. (520) 22-30-00; fax (520) 22-30-99; e-mail registrator@hv.se; internet www.hv.se; f. 1990 as Högskolan Trollhättan/Uddevalla, present name 2006; depts of economics and IT, engineering science, nursing, health and culture, social and behavioural studies; 500 teachers; 11,000 students; Vice-Chancellor Prof. LARS EKEDAHL.

Mälardalens Högskola (Mälardalen University College): POB 883, SE-721 23 Västerås; tel. (21) 10-13-00; fax (21) 10-15-44; e-mail info@mdh.se; internet www.mdh.se; f. 1977; library: see Libraries and Archives; 50 teachers; 13,000 students; Chair. MADELEINE CAESAR; Pres. Dr INGEGERD PALMÉR; Vice-Pres. KARIN AXELSSON.

Södertörns Högskola (Sodertorn University College): SE-141 89 Huddinge; Alfred Nobels allé 7, Flemingsberg, Huddinge; tel. (8) 608-40-00; fax (8) 608-40-10; e-mail international@sh.se; internet www.sh.se; f. 1996; faculties of humanities, social sciences and technology, science and teacher training and education studies; library: 119,313 vols; 450 teachers; 12,000 students; Vice-Chancellor Prof. MOIRA VON WRIGHT.

Sophiahemmet Högskola (Sophiahemmet University College): POB 5605, SE-114 86 Stockholm; Lindstedtsvägen 8, Solhemmet, Stockholm; tel. (8) 406-20-00; fax (8) 10-29-09; e-mail info@sophiahemmethogskola.se; internet www.sophiahemmethogskola.se; f. 1884 as Drottningens Sjuksköterskeskola (Queen's School of Nursing); Bachelors and Masters degree courses in nursing science; library: 20,000 vols, 100 periodicals; 1,300 students; Rector JAN ÅKE LINDGREN.

Other Institutes of University Standing

Blekinge Tekniska Högskola (Blekinge Institute of Technology): SE-371 79 Karlskrona; Campus Gräsvik, Karlskrona; tel. (455) 38-50-00; fax (455) 38-50-57; e-mail registrator@bth.se; internet www.bth.se; f. 1989; applied information technology and sustainable devt of industry and soc.; 140 teachers; 7,000 students; Rector URSULA HASS; Deputy Head ANDERS HEDERSTIERNA; Sec. ING-MARIE BILLGREN.

Chalmers Tekniska Högskola (Chalmers University of Technology): SE-412 96 Gothenburg; tel. (31) 772-10-00; fax (31) 772-38-72; e-mail info@adm.chalmers.se; internet www.chalmers.se; f. 1829; depts of applied information technology, applied mechanics, applied physics, architecture, chemical and biological engineering, civil and environmental engineering, computer science and engineering, earth and space sciences, energy and environment, fundamental physics, materials and manufacturing technology, mathematical sciences, microtechnology and nanoscience, product and production devt, shipping and marine technology, signals and systems, technology management and economics; maintains 44 attached centres; language of instruction: Swedish; academic year September to June; library: see Libraries and Archives; 1,590 teachers; 11,000 students; Pres. and CEO Prof. KARIN MARKIDES; First Vice-Pres. Prof. STEFAN BENGTSSON; Libraries Dir L. NELLDE.

Dramatiska Institutet (University College of Film, Radio, Television and Theatre): POB 27090, SE-102 51 Stockholm; Valhallavägen 189, SE-115 53 Stockholm; tel. (8) 55-57-20-00; fax (8) 55-57-20-05; e-mail kansli@draminst.se; internet www.dramatiskainstitutet.se; f. 1970; provides education for professional practice in film, radio, television and theatre; offers univ. diploma in performing arts and media, postgraduate courses and short courses within the field of theatre and media; Rector PER LYSANDER; Pro-Rector BOEL HÖJEBERG; Pro-Rector MARIA HEDMAN HVITFELDT.

Ersta Sköndal Högskola (Ersta Sköndal University College): Stigbergsgatan 30, POB 11189, SE-100 61 Stockholm; tel. (8) 555-050-00; fax (8) 550-050-60; e-mail info@esh.se; internet www.esh.se; f. 1998; studies and research in social work, nursing and health care, psychotherapy, theology and church music; Rector JAN-HÅKAN HANSSON; Sec. ANN-MARGRET BERGMAN.

Gymnastik- och Idrottshögskolan (Swedish School of Sport and Health Sciences): POB 5626, SE-114 86 Stockholm; Lidingövägen 1, SE-114 33 Stockholm; tel. (8) 402-22-00; fax (8) 402-22-80; e-mail registrator@gih.se; internet www.gih.se; f. 1813, fmrly Stockholm Univ. College of Physical Education and Sports, present name 2005; didactics, human biology, pedagogics, physical education, preventive health, sports coaching; library: 60,000 vols, 6000 periodicals; 60 teachers; 650 students; Rector Prof. KARIN HENRIKSSON-LARSEN; Vice-Rector KARIN REDELIUS.

Handelshögskolan i Stockholm (Stockholm School of Economics): POB 6501, SE-113 83 Stockholm; Sveavägen 65, Stockholm; tel. (8) 736-90-00; fax (8) 31-81-86; e-mail info@hhs.se; internet www.hhs.se; f. 1909; economics, financial economics, management, marketing, statistics and accounting; library: see Libraries; 166 teachers; 2,000 students; Chair. ERIK ÅSBRINK; Pres. Prof. LARS BERGMAN; Vice-Pres. ÖRJAN SÖLVELL.

Högskolan för Design och Konsthantverk (School of Design and Crafts): POB 131, SE-405 30 Gothenburg; Kristinelundsgatan 6–8, SE-405 30 Gothenburg; tel. (31) 786-00-00; fax (31) 786-48-88; e-mail info@hdk.gu.se; internet www.hdk.gu.se; f. 1848; attached to Gothenburg Univ.; product design, interior and graphic design, ceramic art, textile art, jewellery design, film scenography; library: 20,000 vols; 40 teachers; 250 students; Head EVA ENGSTRAND; Librarian KARIN SUNDÉN.

Högskolan för Scen och Musik (Academy of Music and Drama): POB 210, SE-405 30 Gothenburg; Fågelsången 1, Gothenburg; tel. (31) 786-40-20; fax (31) 786-40-30; e-mail kerstin.nilsson@hsm.gu.se; internet www.hsm.gu.se; f. 1916, present status 2005; attached to Göteborgs Univ.; music education, performing, church music, composition, world music, jazz, electro-acoustic composition, music technology; 150 teachers; 600 students; Prin. STAFFAN RYDÉN; Chief Librarian PIA SHEKHTER.

Internationella Handelshögskolan (Jönköping International Business School): POB 1026, SE-551 11 Jönköping; Gjuterigatan 5, Jönköping; tel. (36) 10-10-00; fax (36) 16-50-69; e-mail info@jibs.hj.se; internet hj.se/jibs.html; f. 1994; business administration, economics, political science, business informatics and commercial law; 220 staff (incl. 34 full professors, 10 assoc. professors); 2,100 students (incl. 750 int. students); Man. Dir and Dean Prof. NICLAS ADLER; Exec. Sec. KARIN STENBERG.

Karolinska Institutet: SE-171 77 Stockholm; Solna Br.: Nobels väg 5, Solna, Stockholm; Huddinge Br.: Alfred Nobels Allé 8, Huddinge, Stockholm; tel. (8) 524-800-00; fax (8) 31-11-01; internet www.ki.se; f. 1810; medical univ.; library: see Libraries and Archives; 476 teachers; 6,000 students; Pres. Prof. Dr HARRIET WALLBERG-HENRIKSSON; Vice-Pres. Prof. JAN ANDERSSON; Univ. Dir KARIN RÖDING; Chief Librarian CHRISTER BJÖRKLUND; publs *Computerized Publication Register* (information on all publs issued by the Institute), *Curriculum*, *Students' Handbook*.

Konstfack (University College of Arts, Crafts and Design): POB 3601, SE-126 27 Stockholm; LM Ericssons väg 14, SE-126 27 Stockholm; tel. (8) 450-41-00; fax (8) 450-41-29; e-mail registrator@konstfack.se; internet www.konstfack.se; f. 1844, present bldg 2004; graphic design and illustration, industrial design, interior architecture, furniture design, textile design, ceramics and glass, metalwork design, fine art, art education; library: 110,000 vols; 135 teachers; 900 students; Pres. Dr IVAR BJÖRKMAN.

Konsthögskolan Valand (Valand School of Fine Art): POB 132, SE-405 30 Gothenburg; Vasagatan 50, Gothenburg; tel. (31) 786-51-00; fax (31) 786-51-19; e-mail info@valand.gu.se; internet www.valand.gu.se; f. 1865 as Göteborgs Musei Ritskola, present name 1977, present status 1995; attached to Gothenburg Univ.; fine, applied and performing arts; 14 teachers; 100 students; Dir LESLIE JOHNSON.

Kungl. Konsthögskolan (Royal Institute of Art): POB 163 15, SE-103 26 Stockholm; Flaggmansv. 1, SE-111 49 Stockholm; tel. (8) 614-40-00; fax (8) 679-86-26; e-mail info@kkh.se; internet www.kkh.se; f. 1735, present location 1995, present name 2010; attached to Min. of Education; offers Bachelors and Masters courses in fine arts; library: 60,000 vols; 38 teachers; 230 students; Rector MÅNS WRANGE; Pro-Rector MARIA LANTZ; Librarian ANNAKARIN LINDBERG; Librarian ULF NORDQVIST; publs *Konsthögskolans Broschyr*, *Konsthögskolan Elevkatalog*.

Kungl. Musikhögskolan (Royal College of Music in Stockholm): POB 27711, SE-115 91 Stockholm; Valhallavägen 105, Stockholm; tel. (8) 16-18-00; fax (8) 664-14-24; e-mail info@kmh.se; internet www.kmh.se; f. 1771; classical music, Nordic folk music, music from other cultures, jazz, improvisation, composition, conducting, music and media technology, various forms of music education; 314 teachers; 1,000 students; Prin. JOHANNES JOHANSSON; Vice-Prin. CECILIA RYDINGER ALIN; Vice-Prin. STAFFAN SCHEJA.

Kungliga Tekniska Högskolan (Royal Institute of Technology): SE-100 44 Stockholm; Valhallavägen 79, Stockholm; tel. (8) 790-60-00; fax (8) 790-65-00; e-mail info@kth.se; internet www.kth.se; f. 1827, present location 1917; academic year September to June; offers Bachelors and Masters degrees in architecture, engineering, science; also offers licentiate or doctoral degrees; library: see Libraries and Archives; 479 professors; 14,877 students; Pres. PETER GUDMUNDSON; Deputy Pres. EVA MALMSTRÖM JONSSON; Vice-Pres. for Faculty Devt and Gender Equality GUSTAV AMBERG; Vice-Pres. for Int. Commitments RAMON WYSS; Vice-Pres. for Research Interactions with Society GUNNAR LANDGREN; Vice-Pres. for Research Structure and Content BJÖRN BIRGISSON; Univ. Dir ANDERS LUNDGREN; Chief Librarian G. LAGER; publs *Catalogue*, *Study Handbook* (1 a year).

Umeå Institute of Design: SE-901 87 Umeå; Östra Strandgatan 30, Umeå; tel. (90) 786-69-96; fax (90) 786-66-97; e-mail info@dh.umu.se; internet www.dh.umu.se; f. 1989; attached to Umeå Univ.; Bachelors, Masters and Doctoral programmes in industrial design and related specializations; 16 teachers, 76 visiting staff; Rector ANNA VALTONEN.

SWITZERLAND

The Higher Education System

Higher education institutions predate the proclamation of the Helvetic Republic in 1798, with the oldest being the Universität Basel, which was founded in 1460. Other long-standing institutions include the Université de Lausanne (founded in 1537), the Université de Genève (founded in 1559) and the Universität Luzern (founded in 1574; current status since 2000). There is no Federal agency for higher education, which is instead governed by the individual Cantons. There are 10 Cantonal universities, and the main languages of instruction are French, German or Italian, depending on the Canton. However, in 2007 the Swiss Conference of Cantonal Ministers of Education designed an inter-cantonal reform system (HarmoS) that endeavoured to unify the different education systems in the different Cantons. Once 10 Cantons have ratified the agreement individually, it will be legally binding on those that have signed it. Currently, four cCantons have ratified the agreement (Glarus, Jura, Schaffhausen, Vaud) and it is pending in most other cantons. Higher education is the joint responsibility of the Confederation and the Cantons. Other institutions of higher education include two Federal Institutes of Technology and universities of applied sciences (known as Fachhochoshulen, Hautes Ecoles Spécialisées or Scuole Universitarie Professionale). Switzerland participates in the Bologna Process to establish a European Higher Education Area, the first phase of which is to adopt a credit-based system of comparable degrees with two main cycles (undergraduate and graduate). In 2007 there were 225,862 students enrolled in higher education.

Either the Federal Maturity Certificate (Maturitätszeugnis, Certificat de Maturité, Baccalauréat or Attestato di Maturità) or the Federally recognized Cantonal Maturity Certificate (Eidgenössisch anerkanntes kantonales Maturitätszeugnis, Certificat de Maturité cantonal reconnu par la Confédération or Attestato di Maturità cantonale riconosciuto dalla Confederazione) is the main requirement for admission to university. The Cantonal Maturity Certificate (Kantonale Maturität, Maturité Cantonale or Maturità Cantonale) gives limited access to higher education, while the Certificate of Professional Maturity (Berufsmaturität, Maturité Professionelle or Maturità Professionale) is required for admission to the Fachhochoshulen, Hautes Ecoles Spécialisées or Scuole Universitarie Professionale. The two-tier Masters and Bachelors degree system is due to be fully implemented by 2010; meanwhile, old-style university degrees are still available from many institutions. The Bachelors is a three-year degree, equivalent to the old four-year Diplom, Diplôme, Licence or Lizentiat. The first postgraduate degree is the Masters, a one- to two-year programme following the Bachelors. Finally, the highest university degree is the Doctorate (Doktorat, Doctorat), which is awarded after between two and five years of research, culminating with defence of a thesis.

Technical and vocational education is regulated by Federal law and implemented by Cantonal authorities. Students split their time between the workplace and the classroom, and the primary qualification is the Federal Apprenticeship Certificate or Certificate of Proficiency (Fähigkeitszeugnis, Certificate de Capacité or Attestato di Capacità). There are also Advanced Vocational Schools (Ecoles Professionnelles Supérieures or Scuole Medie Professionale) offering advanced programmes in technical and vocational education.

The Centre of Accreditation and Quality Assurance of the Swiss Universities (OAQ) is an independent body which defines quality assurance requirements and regularly checks compliance with these and prepares guidelines for the national accreditation procedures. In addition it conducts accreditation procedures as well as other quality assessments such as evaluations and audits on behalf of the Swiss University Conference and the Federal Government. The political authorities have mandated the OAQ to undertake quality audits of the universities and federal institutes of technology every four years to determine whether their quality assurance systems are compatible with internationally accepted standards. A system of accreditation has been in place since 2002. It is a voluntary procedure open to academic institutions and their study programmes, both from the public and private sectors. It consists of a three-step procedure which comprises self-evaluation, external evaluation and finally decision on accreditation. The accreditation is based on an assessment of compliance with predefined, internationally accepted quality standards as mentioned above. The accreditation decision is made by the Swiss University Conference. An unconditional positive decision is granted for seven years.

Regulatory and Representative Bodies

GOVERNMENT

Staatssekretariat für Bildung und Forschung/Secrétariat d'Etat à l'éducation et à la recherche (State Secretariat for Education and Research): Hallwylstr. 4, 3003 Bern; tel. 313229691; fax 313227854; e-mail info@sbf.admin.ch; internet www.sbf.admin.ch; State Sec. MAURO DELL'AMBROGIO; Deputy Dir JÜRG BURRI.

ACCREDITATION

Organ für Akkreditierung und Qualitätssicherung der Schweizerischen Hochschulen/Organe d'accréditation et d'assurance de qualité des hautes écoles suisses (Swiss Center of Accreditation and Quality Assurance in Higher Education): Falkenplatz 9, POB, 3001 Bern; tel. 313801150; fax 313801155; e-mail info@oaq.ch; internet www.oaq.ch; f. 2001; promotes quality of teaching and research at univs; develops guidelines and quality standards for academic accreditation and carries out accreditation procedures on basis of guidelines introduced by SUK/CUS; Dir Dr CHRISTOPH GROLIMUND.

Schweizerische Universitätskonferenz/Conférence universitaire suisse (Swiss University Conference): Sennweg 2, POB 576, 3012 Bern 9; tel. 313066060; fax 313066070; e-mail cus@cus.ch; internet www.cus.ch; f. 1969, present status 2001; coordination of Swiss univs and institutes of higher education; empowered to accredit public or private academic instns and programmes; awards project-specific grants; issues directives on evaluation of teaching and research; 18 mems, representing cantons, univs, Nat. Union of Students, etc.; Pres. Dr BERNHARD PULVER; Sec.-Gen. Dr MARTINA WEISS; Deputy Sec.-Gen. VALÉRIE CLERC BOREL; publ. *SUK Info* (4 a year).

Swiss ENIC: Rectors' Conf. of the Swiss Univs., POB 607, 3000 Bern 9; tel. 313066041; fax 313066020; e-mail christine.gehrig@crus.ch; internet www.enic.ch; provides information on Swiss and foreign higher education systems and on recognition of qualifications; Head CHRISTINE GEHRIG.

FUNDING

Rat der Eidgenössischen Technischen Hochschulen/Conseil des Ecoles polytechniques fédérales (Board of the Swiss Federal Institutes of Technology): Häldeliweg 15, 8092 Zürich; tel. 446322367; fax 446321190; internet www.ethrat.ch; appointed by Swiss Fed. Council; allocates funds to Swiss Fed. Institutes of Technology in Zurich and Lausanne, the Paul Scherrer Institut, the Swiss Fed. Institute for Forest, Snow and Landscape Research, Materials Science and Technology Research Instn and Swiss Fed. Institute of Aquatic Science and Technology; centre in Bern; Pres. Dr FRITZ SCHIESSER; Vice-Pres. Prof. Dr PAUL L. HERRLING; Exec. Dir Dr MICHAEL KÄPPELI.

Schweizerischer Nationalfonds zur Förderung der wissenschaftlichen Forschung/Fonds national suisse de la Recherche scientifique (Swiss National Science Foundation): Wildhainweg 3, POB

8232, 3001 Bern; tel. 313082222; fax 313013009; e-mail pri@snf.ch; internet www.snf.ch; f. 1952; promotes ind. scientific research; supports basic research in all disciplines; supports applied research through Nat. Research Programmes; facilitates and promotes int. engagement for Swiss research community and provides funding opportunities; Pres., Foundation Council HANS ULRICH STÖCKLING; Dir DANIEL HÖCHLI; publs *Horizons* (4 a year), *SNSFinfo print* (3 a year).

NATIONAL BODIES

EDK/IDES (IDES Information and Documentation Centre): Speichergasse 6, POB 660, 3000 Bern 7; tel. 313095100; fax 313095110; e-mail idcs@ides.ch; internet www.edk.ch; f. 1962, (with partial integration of CESDOC 1994); collects information and documents about Swiss education system and makes them accessible; serves cantonal education and training depts; library of 8,000 vols, 400 periodicals, 6,000 documents; Pres. ISABELLE CHASSOT; Dir ANNEMARIE STREIT.

Rektorenkonferenz der Schweizer Universitäten (CRUS)/Conférence des Recteurs des Universités Suisses (CRUS) (Rectors' Conference of the Swiss Universities): Sennweg 2, 3012 Bern; tel. 313066036; fax 313066050; e-mail crus@crus.ch; internet www.crus.ch; f. 1904, present status 2001; 12 mem univs; responsible for exchange of information, harmonization of academic procedures and definitions and proper distribution of tasks among univs and polytechnics; library of 4,000 vols; Pres. Prof. Dr ANTONIO LOPRIENO; Sec.-Gen. Dr MATHIAS STAUFFACHER; publs *proff.ch* (online), *Studying in Switzerland: Universities*.

Schweizerische Konferenz der kantonalen Erziehungsdirektoren (EDK)/Conférence suisse des directeurs cantonaux de l'instruction publique (Swiss Conference of Cantonal Ministers of Education): Speichergasse 6, POB 660, 3000 Bern 7; tel. 313095111; fax 313095150; e-mail edk@edk.ch; internet www.edk.ch; assembly of the 26 cantonal govt ministers responsible for education, training, culture and sport; negotiating partner of federal govt for jt responsibility of education (high school, vocational education, univs) and represents cantons in foreign countries in educational and cultural affairs; centre in Bern; Pres. ISABELLE CHASSOT; Gen. Sec. HANS AMBÜHL.

Schweizerischer Wissenschafts- und Technologierat/Conseil Suisse de la Science et de la Technologie (Swiss Science and Technology Council): Inselgasse 1, 3003 Bern; tel. 313230048; fax 313239547; e-mail swtr@swtr.admin.ch; internet www.swtr.ch; advisory body to govt on all matters relating to science policy; provides and evaluates fundamentals of nat. policy on education, research and technology; Pres. Prof. Dr SUSANNE SUTER; Sec. DENISE WAGNER.

Vereinigung der Schweizerischen Hochschuldozierenden/Association Suisse des Enseignantes d'Université (Swiss University Teachers' Association): Buchhalden 5, 8127 Forch; tel. 446333399; fax 446331105; e-mail vsh-sekretariat@ethz.ch; internet www.hsl.ethz.ch; f. 1971; promotes public understanding of univ. matters and univ. professions; represents interests of univ. lecturers; maintains int. ties among univ. teachers; Pres. Prof. Dr CHRISTIAN BOCHET; Vice-Pres. (vacant); Gen. Sec. Prof. Dr GERNOT KOSTORZ.

Learned Societies

GENERAL

Akademie der Naturwissenschaften Schweiz/Académie des sciences naturelles (Swiss Academy of Sciences): Schwarztorstrasse 9, 3007 Bern; tel. 313104020; fax 313104029; e-mail info@scnat.ch; internet www.scnat.ch; f. 1815, present name 2004; promotes scientific integrity and ethically considered treatment of scientific knowledge and its application; promotes active exchange of opinion between science and society through information and promotional events on new areas of research, support of regional projects and awarding of prizes for outstanding communication of scientific content; 54 mems incl. expert asscns and Cantonal and Regional asscns; library: see Universitätsbibliothek Bern (Stadtbibliotheken); Pres. Prof. DENIS MONARD; Sec.-Gen. Dr JÜRG PFISTER; Treas. Prof. THIERRY J. L. COURVOISIER; publ. *SCNATinfo*.

Institut National Genevois: Promenade du Pin 1, 1204 Geneva; tel. 223104188; fax 223103453; internet www.inge.ch; f. 1853; divided into four sections: economics, moral and political sciences, fine arts, music and letters and science; encourages advancement and dissemination of science, literature, fine arts, industry, commerce and agriculture; 750 mems; Pres. PIERRE KUNZ; Sec.-Gen. MICHELLE SAUDIN; Treas. JEAN-CLAUDE MEYER; publ. *Mémoires*.

Schweizerische Akademie der Geistes- und Sozialwissenschaften/Académie Suisse des Sciences Humaines et Sociales (Swiss Academy of Humanities and Social Sciences): Hirschengraben 11, POB 8160, 3011 Bern; tel. 313131440; fax 313131450; e-mail sagw@sagw.ch; internet www.sagw.ch; f. 1946; represents concerns of humanities and social sciences to decision makers and authorities and to media and public; provides infrastructure for humanities and social science research; organizes confs and metings of nat. and int. mem. orgs; 60 mem. socs; Pres. Prof. Dr HEINZ GUTSCHER; Vice-Pres. Prof. Dr BEATRICE SCHMID; Sec.-Gen. Dr MARKUS ZÜRCHER.

Schweizerische Akademie der Technischen Wissenschaften/Académie Suisse des Sciences Techniques (Swiss Academy of Engineering Sciences): Seidengasse 16, 8001 Zürich; tel. 442265011; fax 442265019; e-mail info@satw.ch; internet www.satw.ch; f. 1981; co-operation with similar socs and acts in advisory capacity to govt; promotes utilization and devt of technology for benefit of soc.; 240 individual mems, 60 mem. orgs; Pres. Prof. Dr RENÉ DÄNDLIKER; Designated Pres. Prof. Dr ULRICH W. SUTER; Vice-Pres. Dr IRENE AEGERTER; Man. Dir Dr ROLF HÜGLI; publ. *Technoscope* (3 a year).

AGRICULTURE, FISHERIES AND VETERINARY SCIENCE

Association des Groupements et Organisations Romands de l'Agriculture—AGORA: Ave des Jordils 5, POB 128, 1000 Lausanne 6; tel. 216140477; fax 216140478; e-mail info@agora-romandie.ch; internet www.agora-romandie.ch; f. 1881, as Fédération des Sociétés d'Agriculture de Suisse Romande (FSASR), present name and status 1996; defends professional interests of Romande agriculture; promotes vocational training and devt of service activities; 21 corporate mems; library of 200 vols; Pres. FRANÇOIS HALDEMANN; Dir WALTER WILLENER; publs *d'arboriculture et d'horticulture* (6 a year), *Revue suisse d'agriculture* (6 a year), *Revue suisse de viticulture*.

Gesellschaft Schweizer Tierärztinnen und Tierärzte/Société des Vétérinaires Suisses: Brunnmattstr. 13, POB 45, 3174 Thörishaus; tel. 313073535; fax 313073539; e-mail info@gstsvs.ch; internet www.gstsvs.ch; f. 1813; represents professional interests of ind. and employed veterinarians; 2,700 mems; Pres. CHARLES TROLLIET; Man. Dir RUEDI HELFER-DÖLKER; publ. *Schweizer Archiv für Tierheilkunde* (12 a year).

ARCHITECTURE AND TOWN PLANNING

Bund Schweizer Architekten/Fédération des Architectes Suisses: Pfluggässlein 3, POB 907, 4001 Basel; tel. 612621010; fax 612621009; e-mail mail@bsa-fas.ch; internet www.architects-fsa.ch; f. 1908; represents professional interests of architects; provides information on architecture profession and its role in soc.; supports education, training and research of architecture; 858 mems; Pres. PAUL KNILL; Vice-Pres. ALDO NOLLI; Vice-Pres. ELISABETH BOESCH; Vice-Pres. ROLF SEILER; Treas. YVO THALMANN; publ. *Werk, Bauen und Wohnen* (12 a year).

Schweizer Heimatschutz (Swiss Heritage Society): Seefeldstr. 5A, POB 1122, 8032 Zürich; tel. 442545700; fax 442522870; e-mail info@heimatschutz.ch; internet www.heimatschutz.ch; f. 1905; promotes advancement of Switzerland's architectural heritage; preserves important landmarks, develops structural environment, and promotes good architectural design; 27,000 mems; Pres. PHILIPPE BIÉLER; Vice-Pres. RUTH GISI-WILLISEGGER; Vice-Pres. SEVERIN LENEL; Sec.-Gen. ADRIAN SCHMID; publ. *Heimatschutz / Patrimoine* (French and German, 4 a year).

Société Suisse des Ingénieurs et des Architectes/Schweizerischer Ingenieur- und Architektenverein: POB, 8027 Zürich; Selnaustr. 16, 8001 Zürich; tel. 442831515; fax 442831516; e-mail contact@sia.ch; internet www.sia.ch; f. 1837; promotes sustainable devt and quality of natural and built environment; guards professional interests of its mems; 14,683 mems; Pres. DANIEL KÜNDIG; Vice-Pres. ANDREAS BERNASCONI; Vice-Pres. LAURENT VULLIET; Sec. Gen. HANS-GEORG BÄCHTOLD; publs *TEC21*, *TRACÉS* (24 a year).

BIBLIOGRAPHY, LIBRARY SCIENCE AND MUSEOLOGY

Bibliothek Information Schweiz/Bibliothèque Information Suisse/Biblioteca Informazione Svizzera/Biblioteca Infurmaziun Svizra (Swiss National Association of Libraries and Librarians): Hallerstr. 58, 3012 Bern; tel. 313824240; fax 313824648; e-mail info@bis.info; internet www.bis.info; f. 1987, merger of Bibliotheken und der Bibliothekarinnen/Bibliothekare der Schweiz (BBS) and Schweizerische Vereinigung für Dokumentation (SVD) 2008; rep. of mems in politics and public; lobbying of decision makers from education, science and culture in fields of library policy and devt, intellectual, cultural promotion, professional training; organizes training programmes for mems; 1,950 mems incl. instns and professionals; Pres. YOLANDE ESTERMANN WISKOTT; Gen. .Sec. CHRISTINE SCHAAD HÜGLI; publ. *ARBIDO* (4 a year).

Genossenschaft der Urheber und Verleger von Musik/Coopérative des auteurs et éditeurs de musique (Cooperative Society of Music Authors and Publishers): Bellariastr. 82, POB 782, 8038 Zürich; tel. 444856666; fax 444824333; e-mail suisa@suisa.ch; internet www.suisa.ch; f. 1923; issues licences authorising its clients to perform, broadcast, disseminate and reproduce music; collects royalties of its members for public use of their works in Switzerland and Liechtenstein; centres in Lausanne and Lugano; 29,000 mems; Pres. HANS ULRICH LEHMANN; Vice-Pres. MARCO ZANOTTA; CEO ANDREAS WEGELIN; Gen. Dir ANDREAS WEGELIN.

Schweizer Diplombibliothekare, -innen/ Bibliothécaires diplômé(e)s suisses (Association of Swiss Graduate Librarians): POB 607, 3000 Bern 7; Sekretariat, c/o Martin Rohde, Sportweg 15, 3097 Liebefeld; tel. 4024854-2; e-mail info@sdb-bds.ch; internet www.sdb-bds.ch; f. 1988; promotes professional interests of qualified librarians; regional groups in Aarau, Basel, Bern, Lausanne, Zentralschweiz and Zürich; 500 mems; publ. *SDB/BDS News* (3 a year).

Schweizerische Bibliophilen Gesellschaft/Société Suisse des Bibliophiles: Alte Landstrasse 95, POB 151, 8804 Au; e-mail erfueter@gmx.ch; f. 1921; 600 mems; Pres. Dr AGLAJA HUBER; Hon. Treas. EDUARD R. FUETER; publs *Librarium 58* (3 a year), *Stultifera Navis 44–57*.

Verband der Museen der Schweiz/Association des Musées Suisses: c/o Landesmuseum Zürich, POB, 8021 Zürich; tel. 442186588; fax 442186589; e-mail info@museums.ch; internet www.museums.ch; f. 1966; asscn of Swiss museums and zoological and botanical gardens, to represent their interests; forms a link between Swiss museums and Int. Council of Museums (see International Organizations chapter); organizes annual conf. and work sessions on museology, conservation, restoration and other related topics; jt projects with univs, training; basic program for new museum professionals, spec. courses for guides, security and technical staff, academic museology courses in cooperation with univs; Int. Museum Day; 670 institutional mems; Pres. GIANNA A. MINA; Gen. Sec. DAVID VUILLAUME; publs *Revue museums.ch* (1 a year), *Schweizer Museumsführer/Guide des musées suisses* (irregular).

Verein Schweizerischer Archivarinnen und Archivare/Association des archivistes suisses (Association of Swiss Archivists): c/o Büro Pontri GmbH, Solothurnstr. 13, POB, 3322 Urtenen-Schönbühl; tel. 313122666; fax 313122668; e-mail info@vsa-aas.org; internet www.vsa-aas.org; f. 1922; ensures professionalization of archives; encourages establishment of coordinated archival heritage; represents interests of mems; advanced professional training, confs, lobbying, collaboration and coordination within and for Swiss archival community; 713 mems; Pres. Dr ANNA PIA MAISSEN; Vice-Pres. GREGOR EGLOFF; Sec. DANIEL KRESS; Treas. PHILIPPE KÜNZLER; publ. *ARBIDO* (4 a year).

ECONOMICS, LAW AND POLITICS

Bundesamt für Statistik/Office Fédéral de la Statistique (Federal Statistical Office): Espace de l'Europe 10, 2010 Neuchâtel; tel. 327136011; fax 327136012; e-mail info@bfs.admin.ch; internet www.statistik.admin.ch; f. 1860; nat. centre for public statistics; production and publication of statistics; Dir-Gen. Dr JÜRG MARTI; publ. *Statistical Yearbook* (1 a year).

Gottlieb Duttweiler Institute: Langhaldenstr. 21, POB 531, 8803 Rüschlikon/Zürich; tel. 447246111; fax 447246262; e-mail info@gdi.ch; internet www.gdi.ch; f. 1963; conducts scientific research in social and economic fields; monitoring of societal change; organizes confs, seminars and workshops; 35 mems; CEO Dr DAVID BOSSHART; Asst CEO INGRID SCHMID; publ. *GDI Impuls*.

Schweizerische Gesellschaft für Aussenpolitik/L'Association Suisse de Politique Extérieure: c/o Karin Büchli, Netzwerk Müllerhaus, Bleicherain 7, 5600 Lenzburg 1; tel. 628880120; fax 628880101; e-mail info@sga-aspe.ch; internet www.sga-aspe.ch; f. 1968; deals with matters of foreign, int. trade, integration and security policy; organizes lectures, confs and seminars on current foreign policy issues; 800 mems; Pres. HADORN ADRIAN; Sec.- Gen. Dr ULRICH E. GUT.

Schweizerische Gesellschaft für Volkswirtschaft und Statistik/Société Suisse d'Economie et de Statistique (Swiss Society of Economics and Statistics): c/o SNB/BNS, Börsenstrasse 15, 8022 Zürich; tel. 446313234; fax 446313901; e-mail mail@sgvs.ch; internet www.sgvs.ch; f. 1864; promotes and advances economic research and improves collaboration between domestic and int. research community, promotes young economists by providing appropriate platform to present their scientific work; awards SSES Young Economist Awards; 750 mems; library: see entry for Schweiz. Wirtschaftsarchiv; Pres. GEBHARD KIRCHGÄSSNER; Sec. and Treas. HEDY DORNAUER; publ. *Swiss Journal of Economics and Statistics/Schweizerische Zeitschrift für Volkswirtschaft und Statistik/Revue suisse d'économie et de statistique* (4 a year).

Schweizerische Vereinigung für Internationales Recht/Société Suisse de Droit International: c/o Dr Stefan Breitenstein, Lenz & Staehelin, Bleicherweg 58, 8027 Zürich; tel. 442041212; e-mail stefan.breitenstein@lenzstaehelin.com; internet www.svir-ssdi.ch; f. 1914; promotes qualitative implementation of int. law; promotes lawyers working in field of int. and European law; organizes Swiss conf. of int. law; 300 mems; Pres. Prof. CHRISTINE KADDOUS; Vice-Pres. Prof. DANIEL GIRSBERGER; Sec. Dr STEFAN BREITENSTEIN; Treas. Dr MONIQUE JAMETTI GREINER; publs *Schweizerische Zeitschrift für internationales und europäisches Recht* (5 a year), *Swiss Studies in International Law*.

Schweizerischer Anwaltsverband/Fédération Suisse des Avocats/Federazione Svizzera degli Avvocati (Swiss Bar Association): Marktgasse 4, POB 8321, 3011 Bern; tel. 313130606; fax 313130616; e-mail info@swisslawyers.com; internet www.swisslawyers.com; f. 1898; preserves and defends independent legal profession in Switzerland and abroad; represent Swiss law as against federal authorities and int. orgs; fosters relations among cantonal bar asscns; 8,620 mems; Pres. Avv. BRENNO BRUNONI; Vice-Pres. Dr BEAT VON RECHENBERG; Vice-Pres. PIERRE-DOMINIQUE SCHUPP; Gen. Sec. Lic. RENÉ RALL; publs *Anwaltsrevue/Revue de l'Avocat* (12 a year), *Schriftenreihe*.

Schweizerischer Notarenverband/Fédération Suisse des Notaires/Federazione Svizzera dei Notai: Tavelweg 2, 3074 Muri; tel. 313105840; fax 313105841; e-mail info@schweizernotare.ch; internet www.schweizernotare.ch; f. 1920; safeguards interests of freelance notary; rep. of professional notary to authorities and opinion on federal issues associated with exercise of notary in context; maintains relationships follow notary feds of other countries and int. orgs notary; 1,500 mems; Pres. Me PHILIPPE BOSSET; Sec. Me ANDREAS B. NOTTER.

FINE AND PERFORMING ARTS

Berufsverband Visuelle Kunst/Société Des Artistes Visuels (Visual Arts Asscociation): Räffelstrasse 32, 8045 Zürich; tel. 444621030; fax 444621610; e-mail office@visarte.ch; internet www.visarte.ch; f. 1865, present name and status 2001; defends visual artists' interests on political and social levels; seeks to ensure favourable conditions for artistic production and provides counsel to artists; 3,300 mems incl. 2,600 active mems; Pres. HEINRICH GARTENTOR; Vice-Pres. NATALIA SCHMUKI; Man. REGINE HELBLING; publs *Arte Svizzera*, *Art Suisse*, *Schweizer Kunst* (2 a year).

Hindemith Stiftung (Hindemith Foundation): Champ Belluet 41, 1807 Blonay; tel. 219430528; fax 219430529; e-mail administration@hindemith.org; internet www.hindemith.org; f. 1968; promotes and cultivates music, in particular contemporary music; maintains musical and literary heritage of Paul Hindemith, and encourages research in field of music and diffusion of research results; awards prizes; Pres. Prof. Dr ANDREAS ECKHARDT; Man. and Vice-Pres. FRANÇOIS MARGOT; publs *Frankfurter Studien*, *Hindemith-Forum* (1 or 2 a year), *Hindemith General Original Edition*, *Les Annales Hindemith* (1 a year).

Attached Institutions:

Hindemith-Institut Frankfurt: Eschersheimer Landstrasse 29–39, 60322 Frankfurt-am-Main, Germany; tel. (69) 5970362; fax (69) 5963104; internet www.paul-hindemith.org; archives of Hindemith's autograph scores and sketches, manuscript versions of musico-theoretical writings, autobiographical catalogues of works and extensive correspondence; Dir Dr SUSANNE SCHAAL-GOTTHARDT.

Centre de Musique Hindemith (Hindemith Centre for Music): Chemin Lacuez 3, 1807 Blonay; tel. 219430520; fax 219430521; internet www.hindemith.org; f. 1978; chamber music master classes; Dir MARCEL LACHAT.

Gesellschaft für Schweizerische Kunstgeschichte/Société d'histoire de l'art en Suisse: Pavillonweg 2, 3012 Bern; tel. 313083838; fax 313016991; e-mail gsk@gsk.ch; internet www.gsk.ch; f. 1880; studies and publicizes cultural heritage and diversity of Switzerland dating back to antiquity; 9,500 mems; Pres. Dr BENNO SCHUBIGER; Vice-Pres. Dr JACQUES BUJARD; Sec. Dr MATTHIAS EPPENBERGER; Treas. ERICH WEBER; publs *Beiträge zur Kunstgeschichte der Schweiz*, *Die Kunstdenkmäler der Schweiz*, *Inventar der neueren Schweizer Architektur*, *k+a* (4 a year), *Kunst Architektur in der Schweiz* (4 a year), *Kunstführer durch die Schweiz*, *Schweiz. Kunstführer* (20 a year).

Kunstverein St Gallen: Museumstr. 32, 9000 St Gallen; tel. 712420674; fax 712420672; e-mail kunstverein@kunstmuseumsg.ch; internet www.kunstmuseumsg.ch; f. 1827; organizes exhibitions; promotes int. contemporary art exhibitions; 2,000 mems; Pres. Dr BENNO GROSSMANN; Man. Dir ELVIRA HUBER.

Pro Helvetia (Swiss Arts Council): Hirschengraben 22, 8024 Zürich; tel. 442677171; fax 442677106; e-mail info@prohelvetia.ch; internet www.prohelvetia.ch; f. 1939; promotes artistic creation, fosters cultural outreach and facilitates cultural exchange with int. artists; offices in Warsaw, Cairo, Cape Town, New Delhi, Shanghai and Paris; Pres. MARIO ANNONI; Dir PIUS KNÜSEL; publ. *Passagen/Passages* (3 a year).

Schweizer Blasmusikverband/Association Suisse des Musiques (Swiss Wind-band Association): Gönhardweg 32, POB, 5001 Aarau; tel. 628228111; fax 628228110; e-mail info@windband.ch; internet www.windband.ch; f. 1862; 76,000 mems, 32 associated mem. orgs; Chair. VALENTIN BISCHOF; publ. *Unisono* (26 a year).

Schweizer Musikrat/Conseil Suisse de la Musique (Swiss Music Council): Haus der Musik, Gönhardweg 32, POB 3839, 5001 Aarau; tel. 628229423; fax 628229407; e-mail info@musikrat.ch; internet www.musikrat.ch; f. 1964; mem. of CIM (UNESCO); mem. of various musical orgs; rep. of interests of music creators to public and political bodies at fed. level and in educational and cultural issues; 61 mem. orgs; Pres. Dr ISABELLE MILI; Vice-Pres. MARKUS FLURY; Gen. Sec. HERR KURT HESS; publs *Guide for Musical Studies in Switzerland*, *Schweizer Muzikzeitung* (irregular).

Schweizerische Musikforschende Gesellschaft/Société Suisse de Musicologie: Universität Bern, Hallerstrasse 5, 3012 Bern; tel. 316315034; e-mail info@smg-ssm.ch; internet www.smg-ssm.ch; f. 1916, present name 1934; supports music research; organizes lectures, confs and congresses; country rep. of RILM (Répertoire Int. de Littérature Musicale); 7 sections in Basel, Bern, Luzern, St. Gallen-Zürich, Suisse Romande, Svizzera Italiana, Zürich; awards Glarean Prize and Jacques-Handschin Prize; 700 mems; Pres. Dr THERESE BRUGGISSER-LANKER; Vice-Pres. Prof. Dr LAURENZ LÜTTEKEN; Sec. Dr URS FISCHER; Treas. Lic. CHRISTOPH BALLMER; publs *Schweizer Jahrbuch für Musikwissenschaft* (1 a year), *Schweiz. Musikdenkmäler, Publikationen der SMG: Serie II.*

Schweizerischer Kunstverein/Société Suisse des Beaux-Arts/Società Svizzera di Belle Arti: Zeughausstrasse 55, 8026 Zürich; tel. 442983035; fax 44 2983038; e-mail info@kunstverein.ch; internet www.kunstverein.ch; f. 1806, present name 1839; promotes and protects interests of art assocs and art lovers on fed. level; lobbies and advocacies of mem. sections on nat. level; 44,000 individual mems of 34 local and regional art asscns; Pres. PETER STUDER (acting); publ. *Kunstbulletin* (10 a year).

Schweizerischer Tonkünstlerverein/Association Suisse des Musiciens: Ave du Grammont 11 bis, 1007 Lausanne 13; tel. 216143290; fax 216143299; e-mail info@asm-stv.ch; internet www.asm-stv.ch; f. 1900; advocates and promotes innovative music; protects interests of composers, soloists, improvisers, conductors and chorus, musicologists and music dirs; 950 mems; Pres. MATTHIAS ARTER; Vice-Pres. WILLIAM BLANK; Treas. SIMONA RYSER; Dir CSABA KÉZÉR; publ. *dissonanz/dissonance* (4 a year).

Schweizerischer Werkbund/Werkbund Suisse: Limmatstr. 118, POB, 8031 Zürich; tel. 442727176; fax 442727506; e-mail swb@werkbund.ch; internet www.werkbund.ch; f. 1913; organized into regional groups: Argovie, Bâle, Berne, Grisons, Suisse centrale, Suisse orientale, Romandie and Zurich; supports professionals from fields of creation, art and culture; organizes nationwide debates regarding design creation; 900 mems; Pres. IWAN RASCHLE; Treas. ALEXANDER ZOANNI; Sec.-Gen. BERND ZOCHER; publs *SWB-Dokumente*, *SWB-Information* (4 a year).

Schweizerisches Institut für Kunstwissenschaft/Institut Suisse pour l'Etude de l'Art (Swiss Institute for Art Research): Zollikerstr. 32, POB 1124, 8032 Zürich; tel. 443885151; fax 443815250; e-mail sik@sik-isea.ch; internet www.sik-isea.ch; f. 1951; registration of Swiss works of art and Swiss artists; studies in art and technology; research, documentation, dissemination of knowledge and information in fields of fine art, art business and art technology; 1,700 mems; library of 114,000 vols; Pres. ANNE KELLER-DUBACH; Vice-Pres. and CEO Dr TONI SCHÖNENBERGER; Treas. Dr ERICH HUNZIKER; Dir Dr ROGER FAYET; publs *Œuvrekataloge Schweizer Künstler*, *Kataloge Schweizer Museen und Sammlungen*, *KUNSTmaterial*, *Museen der Schweiz*, *outlines*.

SGD Swiss Graphic Designers: Bahnhofstrasse 11, POB 157, 9230 Flawil; tel. 713934535; fax 713934548; internet www.sgd.ch; f. 1972, by merger of VSG (Verband Schweizer Grafiker) and BGG (Bund Gestalter Grafische/Graphic Designers Asscn of AGC), present name 1993; protects and advances economic and professional interests of its members and offers advice and assistance; cooperates with nat. and int. orgs and with partners from economic and scientific worlds; 600 mems; Pres. DANILO SILVESTRI; Vice-Pres. MICHAELA VARIN; Sec.-Gen. ERIKA REMUND; publ. *SGD Information* (4 a year).

Société Suisse de Pédagogie Musicale/Società Svizzera di Pedagogia Musicale/Schweizerische Musikpädagogische Verband: Bollstrasse 43, 3076 Worb, Bern; tel. 313522266; fax 313522267; e-mail zentralsekretariat@smpv.ch; internet www.smpv.ch; f. 1893; 15 regional asscns; promotes musical education and research; 5,000 mems; Pres. BRIGITTE SCHOLL; Sec. LISA BUCHI; publ. *Agenda du musicien*.

HISTORY, GEOGRAPHY AND ARCHAEOLOGY

Antiquarische Gesellschaft in Zürich: c/o Staatsarchiv des Kantons Zürich, POB, 8057 Zürich; tel. 16356911; fax 446356905; e-mail sekretariat@antiquarische.ch; internet www.antiquarische.ch; f. 1832; concerned with history of Zürich and Swiss history in gen.; organizes lectures, meetings, field trips and guided tours; 550 mems; Pres. Dr ROLAND BÖHMER; publs *Mitteilungen der Antiquarischen Gesellschaft in Zürich* (1 a year), *Neujahrsblatt* (1 a year).

Archäologie Schweiz/Archéologie Suisse/Archeologia Svizzera: Petersgraben 51, POB 116, 4003 Basel; tel. 612613078; fax 612613076; e-mail info@archaeologie-schweiz.ch; internet www.archaeologie-schweiz.ch; f. 1907, present name 2005; supports research on archaeological heritage and disseminates knowledge; library of 30,000 vols; 2,200 mems; Pres. CARMEN BUCHILLER; Treas. WERNER H. GRAF; Sec. URS NIFFELER; publ. *Archäologie Schweiz/Archéologie Suisse* (4 a year).

Geographisch-Ethnographische Gesellschaft Zürich: Geographisches Institut der Universität Zürich, Winterthurerstr. 190, 8057 Zürich; tel. 16355111; fax 16356848; e-mail gegz@geo.unizh.ch; internet www.geo.unizh.ch/gegz; f. 1889, by merger of Ethnographic Society (f. 1888) and Geographical Society (f. 1897); promotes geographical and ethnographic knowledge and sustainable use of resources; understanding of foreign cultures and global connections; 450 individual and corporate mems; Pres. Prof. Dr MAX MAISCH; Vice-Pres. Prof. Dr ULRIKE MÜLLER-BÖKER; Sec. and Treas. Dr REGULA VOLKART; publ. *Geographica Helvetica* (4 a year).

Geographisch-Ethnologische Gesellschaft Basel/Société de Geographie et d'Ethnologie de Bâle: c/o Geographisches Institut, Klingelbergstr. 27, 4056 Basel; tel. 612673660; fax 612673651; e-mail info@gegbasel.ch; internet www.gegbasel.ch; f. 1923; provides knowledge on topics in geography and anthropology; maintains contact with univs and cultural instns for research and training; 428 mems; Pres. Prof. Dr HARTMUT LESER; Hon. Pres. Dr GEORG BIENZ; Treas. HANSPETER MEIER; publs *Basler Beiträge zur Geographie* (irregular), *Basler Beiträge zur Physiogeographie* (irregular), *Regio Basiliensis* (3 a year).

Geographische Gesellschaft Bern: Hallerstr. 12, 3012 Bern; tel. 316318869; fax 316318544; e-mail gb@giub.unibe.ch; internet www.swissgeography.ch/de/members/ggb.php; f. 1873; attached to Verband Geographie Schweiz; organizes lectures; 650 mems; Pres. LEKTORIN ELISABETH BÄSCHLIN; Sec. MONIKA WÄLTI; publs *Berner Geographische Mitteilungen* (1 a year), *Jahrbuch* (irregular).

Historische und Antiquarische Gesellschaft zu Basel: St. Alban-Vorstadt 5, 4002 Basel; tel. 612058605; fax 612058601; e-mail a.salvisberg@merianstiftung.ch; internet pages.unibas.ch/hag; f. 1836; aims to revive intellectual life in Basel; promotes historical studies and knowledge; organizes lectures, seminars and excursions for mems; 450 mems; library of 30,000 vols; Pres. Lic. ANDRÉ SALVISBERG; publ. *Basler Zeitschrift für Geschichte und Altertumskunde* (1 a year).

Historischer Verein des Kantons Bern: c/o Universitätsbibliothek Bern, Münstergasse 63, 3000 Bern 8; tel. 316319203; e-mail christian.luethi@ub.unibe.ch; internet www.hvbe.ch; f. 1846; promotes studies, dissemination of information and discussions on history of Bern among its mems; organizes lectures, publs and excursions for mems; 1,000 mems; Pres. Lic. CHRISTIAN LÜTHI; Vice-Pres. Lic. HEINRICH CHRISTOPH AFFOLTER; Vice-Pres. Dr CHARLOTTE GUTSCHER; Treas. SASCHA M. BURKHALTER; publs *Archiv des Historischen Vereins* (1 a year), *Berner Zeitschrift für Geschichte* (4 a year).

Historischer Verein des Kantons St Gallen: c/o Kantonsbibliothek Vadiana, Notkerstrasse 22, 9000 St Gallen; e-mail info@hvsg.ch; internet www.hvsg.ch; f. 1859; supports projects on preservation and study of heritage; promotes dialogues on topical issues related to history; demonstrates diversity of cultural history to life through meetings, study tours and film clips; 550 mems; Pres. Dr CORNEL DORA; publs *Neujahrsblatt (NJBL)* (1 a year), *St Galler Kultur und Geschichte* (together with the State Archives St Gallen).

Historischer Verein Obwalden: POB 1314, 6061 Sarnen; tel. 416606522; e-mail info@hvow.ch; internet www.hvow.ch; f. 1877, as Historisch-antiquarischer Verein von Obwalden; promotes understanding and interest in historical issues; preserves historic and ethnographic heritage in Canton; organizes publs, excursions and lectures; Pres. VICTOR BIERI; Vice-Pres. NOTKER DILLIER; Treas. ANNELIS ROHRER; publ. *Obwaldner Geschichtsblätter*.

Schweizerische Gesellschaft für Geschichte/Société Suisse d'Histoire/Società Svizzera di Storia: Villettemattstr. 9, 3007 Bern; tel. 313813821; e-mail generalsekretariat@sgg-ssh.ch; internet www.sgg-ssh.ch; f. 1841; promotes studies and training related to history; divided in four depts; defends professional interests of historians; rep. of historical branch to int. orgs; 1,400 mems; Pres. Prof. Dr REGINA WECKER; Vice-Pres. SACHA ZALA; Vice-Pres. MAURO CERUTTI; Gen-Sec Dr ERIKA FLÜCKIGER STREBEL; Treas. MAX HAUCK; publs *ITINERA* (irregular), *Quellen zur Schweizergeschichte*, *Schweizerische Zeitschrift für Geschichte* (1 a year).

Schweizerische Gesellschaft für Kartographie/Société Suisse de Cartographie

(Swiss Society of Cartography): Wolfgang-Pauli-Str. 15, 8093 Zürich; tel. 446333031; fax 446331153; e-mail sgk@kartografie.ch; internet www.kartographie.ch; f. 1969; promotes training of theoretical and practical cartography; acts as platform for int. relations with cartographic instns; represents interests of mems; organizes workshops, professional internal training courses, exhibitions and confs; 310 mems; Pres. STEFAN ARN; Sec. STEFAN RÄBER; Treas. MARTIN PROBST; publs *Cartographica Helvetica* (2 a year), *Topographic Maps: Map Graphics ad Generalisation*.

Schweizerische Numismatische Gesellschaft/Société Suisse de Numismatique (Swiss Numismatic Society): c/o J.-P. Righetti, Route de Fribourg 54, 1724 Ferpicloz; tel. 264130216; fax 264130215; e-mail pmzanchi@bluewin.ch; internet www.numisuisse.ch; f. 1879; promotes all branches of numismatic science through its publs dealing with classical, medieval and modern coins, paper money and medals; organizes annual numismatic days Switzerland; 650 mems; Pres. Lic. HORTENSIA VON ROTEN; Vice-Pres. Dr MARKUS PETER; Sec. PIERRE-ANDRÉ ZANCHI; Treas. JEAN-PIERRE RIGHETTI; publs *Schweizer Studien zur Numismatik*, *Schweizerische Numismatische Rundschau* (1 a year), *Schweizer Münzblätter* (4 a year), *Schweizer Münzkatalog*, *Typos*.

Schweizerische Vereinigung für Altertumswissenschaft/Association Suisse pour l'Étude de l'Antiquité: Universität Bern, Historisches Institut, Länggassstr. 49, 3000 Bern 9; tel. 31638341; e-mail thomas.spaeth@hist.unibe.ch; internet www.sagw.ch/svaw.html; f. 1943; promotes research and teaching in all areas of classical studies; fosters int. relations with corresponding asscns; 190 mems; Pres. Prof. Dr THOMAS SPÄTH; Treas. Prof. Dr PIERRE SANCHEZ; publs *Museum Helveticum* (4 a year), *Schweizerische Beiträge zur Altertumswissenschaft*.

Società Storica Locarnese: POB 1119, 6601 Locarno; e-mail info@societastoricalocarnese.ch; internet www.societastoricalocarnese.ch; f. 1954; colln and conservation of documents relating to history of Locarno area, promotes study of history and art of ancient church in the region of Locarno (Locarno and Maggia); organizes exhibitions, confs, and lectures; 150 mems; Pres. RODOLFO HUBER; Vice-Pres. DAMIJANA GRAMIGNA; Sec. ERICA BARLOCCHI; Treas. EMMY FERRARI.

Société d'Egyptologie, Genève: POB 26, 1218 Grand-Saconnex; tel. 227910974; e-mail info@segweb.ch; internet www.segweb.ch; f. 1978; promotes study of Egyptology and related disciplines (coptology, Islamic studies, etc.); organizes confs, seminars and courses; supports research; 400 mems; library of 2,000 vols; Pres. Dr PHILIPPE GERMOND; Vice-Pres. Dr RODOLPHE KASSER; Vice-Pres. JEAN-LUC CHAPPAZ; Sec. SANDRA GUARNORI NICOLLIN; Treas. DANIEL NICOLLIN; publ. *Cahiers* (irregular).

Société d'Histoire de la Suisse Romande: Chemin du Cerisier 1, 1004 Lausanne; e-mail mail@shsr.ch; internet www.shsr.ch; f. 1837; supports historical and archaeological research; organizes seminars and visits; tries to foster interest in history of western Switzerland in public; 530 mems; library: see Bibliothèque Cantonale et Universitaire de Lausanne; Pres. ALAIN CLAVIEN; Vice-Pres. FRANÇOISE DUBOSSON.

Société d'Histoire et d'Archéologie de Genève: c/o Bibliothèque de Genève, 1211 Geneva 4; internet www.shag-geneve.ch; f. 1838; preserves historical and archaeological past of Geneva; promotes research and disseminates results through publs; 440 mems; library of 10,000 vols, 1,000 MSS (contact: c/o Archives de la Ville de Genève, Palais Eynard, 4 rue de la Croix-Rouge, 1211 Geneva 3); Pres. Dr. MATTHIEU DE LA CORBIÈRE; Pres. FRANÇOIS JACOB; Sec. MARTINE PIGUET; Treas. ANDRÉ WAGNIÈRE; publs *Bibliographie genevoise* (1 a year), *Cahiers, Mémoires et Documents*.

Société de Géographie de Genève: Route de Malagnou 1, CP 6434, 1211 Geneva 6; tel. 223798347; fax 223798353; e-mail ruggero.crivelli@unige.ch; internet www.geographie-geneve.ch; f. 1858; promotes study advancement and dissemination of geographical science in all its brs; 250 mems; Pres. RUGGERO CRIVELLI; Vice-Pres. RENÉ ZWAHLEN; Sec. CHRISTIAN MOSER; Treas. CHRISTIANE OLSZEWSKI; publ. *Le Globe* (1 a year).

Société Vaudoise d'Histoire et d'Archéologie: 32 rue de la Mouline, 1022 Chavannes-près-Renens; tel. 213163711; fax 213163755; e-mail info@svha-vd.ch; internet www.svha-vd.ch; f. 1902; preserves historic monuments in Canton of Vaud; encourages genealogical research; organizes confs, visits to monuments and exhibitions excursions and study circles; 850 mems; Pres. DANIÈLE TOSATO-RIGO; Treas. and Sec. RUTH LINIGER; publ. *Revue historique vaudoise* (1 a year).

Verband Geographie Schweiz/Association Suisse de Géographie (Association of Swiss Geographers): Geographisches Institut der Universität Bern, Hallerstrasse 12, 3012 Bern; tel. 316318567; fax 316318511; e-mail pbachmann@giub.unibe.ch; internet www.swissgeography.ch; f. 1990; acts as umbrella asscn of Swiss Geographers; supports research in field of geosciences; rep. of Swiss geography in int. asscns and congresses; coordinates 6 regional and 4 thematic socs, and 8 univ. institutes; Central Cttee acts as nat. cttee of IGU; Pres. Prof. HANS-RUDOLF EGLI; Vice-Pres. Prof. CONRADIN A. BURGA; Sec. Dr PHILIPP BACHMANN; Treas. Prof. THOMAS HAMMER; publ. *GeoAgenda (Mitteilungsblatt der ASG)* (6 a year).

Vereinigung der Freunde Antiker Kunst/Association des Amis de l'Art Antique (Association of Friends of Classical Art): c/o Archäologisches Seminar der Universität, Schönbeinstr. 20, 4056 Basel; fax 612673063; tel. 612673068; e-mail editor@antikekunst.ch; internet www.antikekunst.ch; f. 1956; promotes interest in classical archaeology; offers lectures, guided visits to exhibitions, trips to Classical sites; six regional groups in Basel, Berne-Bienne-Solothurn, Fribourg, Geneva, Lausanne and Zurich; 1,050 mems; Pres. Prof. Dr MARTIN GUGGISBERG; publ. *Antike Kunst* (1 a year).

LANGUAGE AND LITERATURE

Alliance Française de Zurich: Merkurstr. 34, 8032 Zürich; tel. 442619306; fax 442619330; e-mail info@afz.ch; internet www.afz.ch; f. 1883; offers courses and exams in French language and culture and promotes cultural exchange with France; organizes confs, guided tours, lectures, cultural meetings; attached offices in Basel, Berne, Fribourg, Hermance, Locarno, Lucerne, Lugano, Lugnasco and St Gallen.

Autorinnen und Autoren der Schweiz AdS (Swiss Society of Writers): Konradstr. 61, 8031 Zürich; tel. 443500460; fax 443500461; e-mail sekretariat@a-d-s.ch; internet www.a-d-s.ch; f. 2003; supports professional interests of writers in field of political literary, linguistic and cultural asscn, in respect of copyright; creates relationships between AUTRIC, authors, translators, translators, language regions and countries; 940 mems; Pres. RETO FINGER; Dir-Gen. NICOLE PFISTER FETZ.

British Council: Sennweg 2, POB 532, 3000 Bern 9; tel. 315603794; fax 313011459; e-mail britishcouncil@britishcouncil.ch; internet www.britishcouncil.org/switzerland; offers courses and examinations in English language and British culture; promotes cultural exchange with the UK; Dir CAROLINE MORRISSEY; Deputy Dir SIMON BRIMBLECOMBE.

Collegium Romanicum: c/o Michele Loporcaro, Romanisches Seminar der, Universität Zürich, Zürichbergstrasse 8, 8032 Zürich; e-mail loporcar@rom.uzh.ch; internet www.sagw.ch/collegium-romanicum; f. 1947; study of Romance languages and literature; 200 mems; Pres. Prof. Dr MICHELE LOPORCARO; Vice-Pres. Prof. Dr YASMINA FOEHR-JANSSENS; Sec. Prof. Dr URSULA BÄHLER; publs *Romanica Helvetica*, *Versants* (2 a year), *Vox Romanica* (1 a year).

Deutschschweizer PEN-Zentrum: c/o Kristin T. Schnider, Russenhaus, 6484 Wassen; tel. 443507070; e-mail office@pen-dschweiz.ch; internet www.pen-dschweiz.ch; f. 1979; promotes literature and freedom of expression; works by int. PEN charter; 80 mems; Pres. DOMINIK RIEDO; Sec. KRISTIN T. SCHNIDER; publ. *Briefzeitung* (2 a year).

Gesellschaft für deutsche Sprache und Literatur in Zürich: c/o Deutsches Seminar, Schönberggasse 9, 8001 Zürich; e-mail gfdsl@ds.uzh.ch; internet www.ds.uzh.ch/gfdsl; f. 1894; promotes research of linguistics and literary studies; offers courses and lectures for mems; 170 mems; Pres. Dr PETER BICHSEL.

Institut dal Dicziunari Rumantsch Grischun: Ringstr. 34, 7000 Chur; tel. 812846642; fax 812840204; e-mail info@drg.ch; internet www.drg.ch; f. 1885; conservation and research into Romansch language; publ. of documented vocabulary of Romansh-speaking people of Switzerland; 1,000 mems; library of 18,000 vols; Pres. Dr CHRISTIAN COLLENBERG; Vice-Pres. CHASPER PULT; publs *Annalas* (1 a year), *Dicziunari Rumantsch Grischun* (2 a year).

Institut et Musée Voltaire: 25 rue des Délices, 1203 Geneva; tel. 224189560; fax 224189561; e-mail institut.voltaire@ville-ge.ch; internet www.ville-ge.ch/imv; f. 1954; research centre, exhibitions, confs; library of 22,000 vols and MSS, 2,500 printed editions of Voltaire's writings; Curator FRANÇOIS JACOB; publs *La Gazette des Délices* (4 a year), *La Ligne d'ombre* (irregular).

PEN Club de Suisse Romande (PEN Club of French-speaking Cantons of Switzerland): 23 Crêts de Pregny, 1218 Grand Saconnex; tel. 227882231; e-mail ergas@webcreatif.ch; internet www.penromand.ch; f. 1949; defends freedom of expression and promotes int. cultural exchanges; promotes peace according to the PEN Charter; 70 mems; Pres. CLAUDE KRUL; Sec. Gen. ZEKI ERGAS; Treas. ALFRED DE ZAYAS; publ. *Pages littéraires*.

Schweizerische Sprachwissenschaftliche Gesellschaft/Société Suisse de Linguistique/Società Svizzera di Linguistica: c/o Dr. Johanna Miecznikowski, Istituto di studi italiani, Università della Svizzera italiana, Via Giuseppe Buffi 13, 6904 Lugano; e-mail johanna.miecznikowskifuenfschilling@usi.ch; f. 1947; 207 mems; Pres. Prof. JACQUES MOESCHLER; Sec. Dr JOHANNA MIECZNIKOWSKI; publs *Bulletin Vals-Asla* (2 a year), *Cahiers Ferdinand de Saussure*.

MEDICINE

Académie Suisse des Sciences Médicales/Schweizerische Akademie der Medizinischen Wissenschaften (Swiss Academy of Medical Sciences): Peterspl. 13, 4051 Basel; tel. 612699030; fax 612699039; e-mail mail@samw.ch; internet www.samw.ch; f. 1943; promotes professional training of scientists, esp. in clinical research; supports research in biomedical and clinical research; clarifies ethical questions in connection with medical devts and their effects on society; 160 mems; Pres. Prof. PETER SUTER; Vice-Pres. Prof. PETER MEIER-ABT; Vice-Pres. Prof. WALTER REINHARD; Gen. Sec. Dr HERMAN AMSTAD; Treas. Dr DIETER SCHOLER.

Schweizerische Gesellschaft für Chirurgie/Société Suisse de Chirurgie: Bahnhofstr. 55, 5001 Aarau; tel. 628362098; fax 628362097; e-mail info@sgc-ssc.ch; internet www.sgc-ssc.ch; f. 1913; promotes scientific activity and generation of academics in field of surgery; rep. of professional interests of mems; 1,202 mems; Pres. Prof. Dr PHILIPPE MOREL; Vice-Pres. Prof. Dr RALPH A. SCHMID; Gen. Sec. Dr FRÉDÉRIC DUBAS; publ. *Swiss Surgery*.

Schweizerische Gesellschaft für Geschichte der Medizin und der Naturwissenschaften/Société Suisse d'Histoire de la Médecine et des Sciences Naturelles (Swiss Society for the History of Medicine and Sciences): c/o Prof. Hans Konrad Schmutz, Naturmuseum Winterthur, Museumstr. 52, 8400 Winterthur; tel. 522675166; fax 522675319; e-mail hubert.steinke@mhi.unibe.ch; internet www.sggmn.ch; f. 1921; promotes history of medicine and sciences; supports young scientists and confers Henry E. Sigerist Prize for promotion of young scholars; 300 mems; Pres. Prof. Dr. phil. HANS KONRAD SCHMUTZ; Vice-Pres. Dr Lic. IRIS RITZMANN; Sec. Dr HUBERT STEINKE; publ. *Gesnerus* (4 a year).

Schweizerische Gesellschaft für Innere Medizin/Société Suisse de Médecine Interne (Swiss Society of General Internal Medicine): POB 422, 4008 Bâle; Solothurnerstr. 68, 4053 Bâle; tel. 612259330; fax 612259331; e-mail info@sgim.ch; internet www.sgim.ch; f. 1932; supports professional and economic interests of Swiss postgraduate internees of management, economics, communication and medical humanities; promotes internal medical research; encourages networking partnership of hospital and ambulatory medicine; 2,100 mems; Pres. Prof. VERENA BRINER; Sec.-Gen. Dr REGULA SIEVERS-FREY.

Schweizerische Gesellschaft für Orthopädie und Traumatologie/Société Suisse d'Orthopédie et de Traumatologie: 15 Ave des Planches, 1820 Montreux; tel. 219632139; fax 219632149; e-mail office@cpconsulting.ch; internet www.sgosso.ch; f. 1942, present name 2006; promotes professional and economic interests of orthopaedic surgeons; promotes specialization in orthopaedics within field of research and teaching; 11 regional groups; 839 mems; Pres. Prof. Dr CHRISTIAN GERBER; Vice-Pres. Prof. Dr BERNHARD CHRISTEN; Sec. Dr THOMAS KEHL; Treas. Dr ANDREAS EGLI.

Schweizerischer Apothekerverband/Société Suisse des Pharmaciens: Stationsstr. 12, POB, 3097 Bern-Liebefeld; tel. 319785858; fax 319785859; e-mail info@pharmasuisse.org; internet www.pharmasuisse.org; f. 1843; promotes interests of pharmacy in areas of teaching, research, policy and practice; 5,528 mems; Pres. DOMINIQUE JORDAN; Vice-Pres. PETER BURKARD; Vice-Pres. CHRISTIAN ROUVINEZ; publs *Apotheken-Handbuch* (1 a year), *Index Nominum, Pharmactuel* (6 a year), *Schweizer Apothekerzeitung* (24 a year).

NATURAL SCIENCES

General

Naturforschende Gesellschaft in Basel: c/o Nunzio Putrino, Gartenst. 2, 6300 Zug; tel. 797223913; e-mail sekretariat@ngib.ch; internet www.ngib.ch; f. 1817; promotes natural history; organizes lectures for semester program; 600 mems; library of 74,000 vols; Pres. Prof. Dr ORESTE GHISALBA; Vice-Pres. Prof. Dr RETO BRUN; Sec. PUTRINO NUNZIO; Treas. Dr HANS-PETER SCHÄR; publ. *Mitteilungen der Naturforschenden Gesellschaften beider Basel*.

Naturforschende Gesellschaft in Bern: Universitätsbibliothek, Münstergasse 61, Postfach, 3000 Bern 8; tel. 313203231; fax 313203299; e-mail info@ngbe.ch; internet www.ngbe.ch; f. 1786; attached to Universität Bern; spreads scientific thought and new knowledge from various fields of natural sciences; organizes lecture cycles, field trips; 300 mems; Pres. Dr MARCO HERWEGH; Vice-Pres. Prof. Dr GÜNTER BAARS; Sec. Dr KURT GROSSENBACHER; Treas. MATTHIAS HAUPT; publ. *Mitteilungen* (1 a year).

Naturwissenschaftliche Gesellschaft Winterthur: Stadtbibliothek Winterthur, Museumstr. 52, 8401 Winterthur; internet www.ngw.ch; f. 1884; lectures, field trips, publs of scientific articles to foster understanding of natural sciences; 340 mems; Pres. PETER LIPPUNER; Vice-Pres. Dr HANS KONRAD SCHMUTZ; Sec. Dr SABINE OERTLI; Treas. Dr URS BLUMER; publ. *Mitteilungen* (every 3 years).

Schweizerische Energie-Stiftung/Fondation Suisse pour l'Energie (Swiss Energy Foundation): Sihlquai 67, 8005 Zürich; tel. 442715464; fax 442730369; e-mail info@energiestiftung.ch; internet www.energiestiftung.ch; f. 1976; promotes energy policy suitable for human beings and environment; and control of energy consumption; promotes alternative sources of energy and practice of conservation; 3,000 mems; Pres. GERI MÜLLER; Vice-Pres. DIETER KUHN; publs *Energie Umwelt* (4 a year), *SES-Reports* (irregular).

Schweizerische Stiftung für Alpine Forschungen/Fondation Suisse pour Recherches Alpines (Swiss Foundation for Alpine Research): Stadelhoferstr. 42, 8001 Zürich; tel. 442531200; fax 442531201; e-mail mail@alpinfo.ch; internet www.alpinfo.ch; f. 1939; supports scientific studies in field of mountains, mountain people and mountain sports; 11 mems; Pres. ETIENNE GROSS; Man. Dir THOMAS WEBER.

Società Ticinese di Scienze Naturali: c/o Museo cantonale di Storia naturale, viale Cattaneo 4, 6900 Lugano; tel. (91) 8154761; fax (91) 8154769; e-mail stsn-info@scnatweb.ch; internet stsn.ch; f. 1903; promotion and advancement of natural sciences; organizes confs, assembly, courses, exhibitions, excursions; promotes and supports: activities of Cantonal Museum of Natural History and Biology Centre Alpine Piora; 400 mems; Pres. Dr M. TONOLLA; Sec. SIMONA CASATI; publ. *Memorie*.

Société de Physique et d'Histoire Naturelle de Genève: POB 6434, Route de Malagnou, 1211 Geneva 6; tel. 224186300; fax 224186301; internet www.unige.ch/sphn; f. 1790; natural and exact sciences; organizes confs and excursions for mems; 195 mems; Pres. Dr MICHEL GRENON; Vice-Pres. PIERRE KUNZ; Sec. ETIENNE CHAROLLAIS; publ. *Archives des sciences* (2 a year).

Société Vaudoise des Sciences Naturelles: Palais de Rumine, 1005 Lausanne; tel. and fax 213124334; e-mail svsn@unil.ch; internet www.unil.ch/svsn; f. 1819; study, advancement and dissemination of natural sciences and related sciences; publication of research in biology, geology, chemistry, physics, mathematics, and history and methodology of science; 600 mems; library: 1,000 periodicals in library reading-room: see also Bibliothèque Cantonale et Universitaire de Lausanne; Pres. ALAIN MORARD; Vice-Pres. ANNE FREITAG; Treas. JEAN-LUC EPARD; publ. *Mémoires* (irregular).

Biological Sciences

Bernische Botanische Gesellschaft: Altenbergrain 21, 3013 Bern; tel. 313329233; fax 313322059; internet homepage.hispeed.ch/bebege; f. 1918; promotes private or business interest for vegetation science, plant ecology and floristics; organizes lectures floristic, geobotanical and ecophysiological issues; 380 mems; Pres. BRIGITTA AMMANN; Vice-Pres. STEFAN EGGENBERG; Vice-Pres. MARC HÄMMERLI; Treas. REGINE BLÄNKNER; Sec. RITA GERBER; publ. *Sitzungsberichte* (1 a year).

Schweizerische Botanische Gesellschaft/Société Botanique Suisse: Institute of Plant Sciences, University of Bern, Altenbergrain 21, 3013 Bern; tel. 316314928; fax 316314942; internet www.botanica-helvetica.ch; f. 1889; encourages plant sciences and initiatives aimed at protecting flora and conservation of its living environment; cultivates exchange of ideas and experiences and friendly relations between Swiss botanists; 700 mems; Pres. Prof. Dr MARKUS FISCHER; Vice-Pres. Prof. Dr PETER LINDER; Sec. CHRISTOPHE BORNAND; Treas. Dr STEFAN EGGENBERG; publ. *Alpine Botany* (2 a year).

Schweizerische Entomologische Gesellschaft/Société Entomologique Suisse: c/o Hannes Baur, Naturhistorisches Museum, Bernastr. 15, 3005 Bern; tel. 313507264; fax 313507499; e-mail hannes.baur@nmbe.ch; internet seg.scnatweb.ch; f. 1858; studies Swiss entomological fauna; develops entomological knowledge; mems are professional or amateur entomologists; 10 local sections Alpstein, Basel, Bern, Freiburg, Geneva, Lucerne, Neuenburg, Waadt, Wallis and Zürich; 293 mems; library of 18,000 vols; Pres. Dr DENISE WYNIGER; Vice-Pres. Dr DANIEL BURCKHARDT; Sec. HANNES BAUR; publ. *Insecta Helvetica / Fauna Helvetica*.

Mathematical Sciences

Schweizerische Mathematische Gesellschaft/Société Mathématique Suisse (Swiss Mathematical Society): Mathematisches Institut, Universität Bern, Sidlerstr. 5, 3012 Bern; tel. 316318834; fax 316318510; e-mail nicolas.monod@epfl.ch; internet www.math.ch; f. 1910; organizes confs and courses of mathematics at schools; 480 mems; Pres. BRUNO COLBOIS; Vice-Pres. CHRISTINE RIEDTMANN; Sec. and Treas. NICOLAS MONOD; publs *Commentarii Mathematici Helvetici* (4 a year), *Elemente der Mathematik* (4 a year).

Physical Sciences

Bundesamt für Meteorologie und Klimatologie (MeteoSchweiz) (Federal Office of Meteorology and Climatology (MeteoSwiss)): Krähbühlstr. 58, 8044 Zürich; tel. 442569111; fax 442569278; internet www.meteoschweiz.ch; f. 1880, present name 1996; meteorological and climatological services; rep. of Switzerland in World Meteorological Org.; three regional centres in Zurich,

Geneva and Locarno; 296 mems; library of 40,000 vols; Dir DANIEL K. KEUERLEBER; Librarian GREGOR STORK; publs *Annalen*, *Arbeitsberichte der MeteoSchweiz*, *Veröffentlichung der MeteoSchweiz*.

Schweizerische Astronomische Gesellschaft/Société Astronomique Suisse (Swiss Astronomical Society): c/o Geri Hildebrandt, Mittlere Gstücktstr. 14D, 8180 Bülach; tel. 319311446; e-mail ghildebrandt@hispeed.ch; internet sas .astronomie.ch; f. 1938; promote exchanges of information related to astronomy between mems and general public; 2,000 mems; Pres. Dr MAX HUBMANN; Vice-Pres. BRICE-OLIVIER DEMORY; Vice-Pres. HANS ROTH; Sec. GERI HILDEBRANDT; publ. *Orion* (6 a year).

Schweizerische Chemische Gesellschaft/Societe Suisse de Chimie (Swiss Chemical Society): Schwarztorstr. 9, 3007 Bern; tel. 313104090; fax 313104029; e-mail info@scg.ch; internet www.scg.ch; f. 1992 as Neue Schweizerische Chemische Gesellschaft, present name 2001; 2,500 mems; Pres. Prof E. PETER WUNDIG; Exec. Dir LUKAS WEBER; publ. *Chimia* (online, at www.chimia.ch).

Schweizerische Geologische Gesellschaft/Société Géologique Suisse (Swiss Geological Society): c/o Dr Gilles Borel, Musée cantonal de géologie, UNIL-L'Anthropole, 1015 Lausanne; tel. 216924474; fax 216924475; e-mail gilles .borel@unil.ch; internet www.geolsoc.ch; f. 1882; promotes advancement of earth sciences by organizing meetings supported by SCNAT, and by annual reunions of spec. interest groups; 1,000 mems; Pres. Dr GILLES BOREL; Vice-Pres. Dr NEIL MANKTELOW; Treas. Dr ROGERR RÜTTI; Sec. Dr STEPHAN DELL'AGNOLO; publ. *Eclogae geologicae Helvetiae* (Swiss Journal of Geosciences, 3 a year).

Schweizerische Paläontologische Gesellschaft/Société Paléontologique Suisse (Swiss Palaeontological Society): Naturmuseum Solothurn Klosterpl. 2, 4500 Solothurn; tel. (32) 6227021; fax (32) 6227052; e-mail sps@scnatweb.ch; internet spg.scnatweb.ch; f. 1921; attached to Swiss Academy of Sciences (SCNAT); organizes scientific symposia (Swiss Geoscience Meeting), short courses and guided excursions, annual assembly, awards Amanz Gressly-Award for outstanding contributions to Swiss palaeontology; addresses palaeontological questions from geological and biological points of view; 170 mems; Pres. Dr DAMIEN BECKER; Vice-Pres. Dr LIONEL CAVIN; Sec SILVAN THÜRING; publ. *Swiss Journal of Geosciences* (jtly with Swiss Geological and Mineralogical Socs).

Schweizerische Physikalische Gesellschaft/Société Suisse de Physique (Swiss Physical Society): Dept. Physik, Klingelbergstr. 82, 4056 Basel; fax 612673784; e-mail sps@unibas.ch; internet www.sps.ch; f. 1908; supports exchange of ideas within research community by offering workshops; SPS awards for outstanding achievements of young scientists; offers forum at interface of basic research and applied physics; 1,200 mems; Pres. Dr CHRISTOPHE ROSSEL; Vice-Pres. Prof. ULRICH STRAUMANN; Sec. Dr ANTOINE POCHELON; Treas. Dr PIERANGELO GRÖNING.

PHILOSOPHY AND PSYCHOLOGY

Schweizerische Gesellschaft für Psychologie/Société Suisse de Psychologie: Univ. of Neuchatel Dept of Work and Organisational Psychology, Rue Emile-Argand 11, 2009 Neuchâtel; tel. 789022695; fax 327181391; e-mail sekretariat@ssp-sgp.ch; internet www.ssp-sgp.ch; f. 1943; promotes scientific psychology in education, research and practice; protects professional interests of its mems; 560 mems; Pres. Prof. MARIANNE SCHMID MAST (acting); publ. *Swiss Journal of Psychology* (4 a year).

Schweizerische Philosophische Gesellschaft/Société Suisse de Philosophie: c/o Christophe Calame, 53 ave de Rumine, 1005 Lausanne; e-mail christophe .calame@bluewin.ch; internet www.sagw.ch/ philosophie; f. 1940; study and discussion of philosophical problems; organizes meetings; 800 mems; Pres. CHRISTOPHE CALAME; Vice-Pres. LEA BÄHLER; Sec. JULIA SCHEIDEGGER; Treas. Lic. HUBERT SCHNÜRIGER; publs *Studia philosophica* (1 a year), *Supplementa* (irregular).

Schweizerischer Berufsverband für Angewandte Psychologie/Association Professionnelle Suisse de Psychologie Appliquée/Associazone Professionale Svizzera della Psicologia Applicata: Vogelsangstr. 15, 8006 Zürich; tel. 432680405; fax 432680406; e-mail info@sbap .ch; internet www.sbap.ch; f. 1952; rep. of professional interests of its members and interests of applied psychology; 1,000 mems; Pres. HEIDI AESCHLIMANN; Sec. MANUELA LISIBACH.

RELIGION, SOCIOLOGY AND ANTHROPOLOGY

Schweizerische Gesellschaft für Afrikastudien/Société Suisse d'Etudes Africaines: Postfach 8212 3001 Bern; tel. 612672742; internet www.sagw.ch/africa; f. 1974; links and coordinates multidisciplinary research on Africa conducted at Swiss univs and research instns; organizes thematic confs and scientific meetings; 200 mems; Co-Pres. ANNE MAYOR; Co-Pres. Dr DIDIER PÉCLARD; Sec. Dr VEIT ARLT.

Schweizerische Gesellschaft für Soziologie/Société Suisse de Sociologie (Swiss Sociological Association): c/o Marie-Eve Zufferey, Département de Sociologie, Université de Genève, Blvd du Pont d'Arve 40, 1211 Geneva; tel. 223798309; fax 716785657; e-mail sss@unige.ch; internet www.sagw.ch/ soziologie; f. 1955; represents interests of Swiss sociology in relation to scientific and political instns; 600 mems; Pres. Prof. ERIC D. WIDMER; Vice-Pres. Prof. Dr KURT IMHOF; Gen. Sec. Prof. Dr CHRISTOPH MAEDER; publ. *Schweizerische Zeitschrift für Soziologie / Revue suisse de sociologie / Swiss Journal of Sociology* (3 a year).

Schweizerische Gesellschaft für Volkskunde/Société Suisse des Traditions Populaires: Spalenvorstadt 2, 4001 Basel; tel. 612671163; fax 612671163; e-mail sgv-sstp@volkskunde.ch; internet www .volkskunde.ch; f. 1896; documents Swiss popular culture in its historical and current forms; supports and promotes ethnographic research; 832 mems; Pres. Prof. Dr WALTER LEIMGRUBER; Sec. ERNST J. HUBER; Treas. HANS-ULRICH VOLLENWEIDER; publs *Schweizer Volkskunde* (4 a year), *Schweizerisches Archiv für Volkskunde* (2 a year).

Schweizerische Theologische Gesellschaft/Société Suisse de Théologie: c/o Prof. Dr Wolfgang Müller, Theologische Fakultät der Universiät Luzern, Gibraltarstrasse 3, POB 7763, 6000 Luzern 7; tel. 412286635; e-mail wolfgang.mueller@ unilu.ch; internet www.sagw.ch/sthg; f. 1965; promotes technical and theological debate and scientific research; organizes theological seminars and confs; 272 mems; Pres. Prof. Dr WOLFGANG W. MÜLLER; Vice-Pres. Prof. Dr DENIS MÜLLER; Treas. Prof. Dr PIERRE BÜHLER; Sec. KATHERINE SIEGENTHALER.

Schweizerische Trachtenvereinigung/Fédération Nationale des Costumes Suisses (Swiss National Costume Association): Rosswiesstr. 29, POB 8608 Bubikon; tel. 552631563; fax 552631561; e-mail info@ trachtenvereinigung.ch; internet www .trachtenvereinigung.ch; f. 1926; maintains and renews different Swiss costumes, folk dance records and descriptions, folk songs, folk music and folk theatre and dialects; organizes projects and courses; 23,400 mems; Pres. ROLAND MEYER-IMBODEN; Vice-Pres. FRITZ BRAND; Vice-Pres. GÉRARD QUELOZ; publ. *Tracht und Brauch / Costumes et Coutumes* (4 a year).

TECHNOLOGY

Fachleute Geomatik Schweiz/Professionnels Geomatique Suisse (Swiss Association of Surveyors): c/o André Franziska, Flühlistr. 30B, 3612 Steffisburg; tel. 334381462; fax 334381464; e-mail admin@ pro-geo.ch; internet www.pro-geo.ch; f. 1929 as Verband Schweizerische Vermessungsfachleute, present name 2005; supports interests of mems professionally and socially; provides apprenticeship training; 11 regional sections in Aargau, Basel, Bern, Fribourg, eastern Switzerland, Rätia, Ticino, Valais, W Switzerland, Central Switzerland, Zürich; 1,450 mems; Pres. BERSET LAURENT; Vice-Pres. BASCIO ALESSANDRA; Sec. and Treas. ANDRÉ FRANZISKA; publs *Geomatik Schweiz* (12 a year), *NotaBene* (2 a year).

Schweizerische Gesellschaft für Automatik/Association Suisse pour l'Automatique (Swiss Federation of Automatic Control): SGA Sekretariat, Christl Vogel, Eggwilstr. 16A, 9552 Bronschhofen; tel. 719118416; fax 719118449; e-mail sekretariat@sga-asspa.ch; internet www .sga-asspa.ch; f. 1956; promotes and develops knowledge of techniques of measurement, control and calculation, and their application in field of automation; 200 individual mems, 17 corporate mems; Pres. Dr JÜRG KELLER; Sec. CHRISTL VOGEL; publ. *Lernmodule* (4 a year).

Schweizerische Gesellschaft für Mikrotechnik/Association Suisse de Microtechnique: c/o FRSM, Ruelle DuPeyrou 4, CP 2353, 2001 Neuchâtel; tel. 327200900; fax 327200990; e-mail asmt@fsrm.ch; internet www.sgmt-asmt.ch; f. 1962; promotes working in Swiss microtechnology enterprises and instns; offers engineering education in univs, engineering schools; organizes confs, lectures, courses and study tours; 73 mems; Pres. PHILIPP FISCHER; Sec. SUZANNE SCHWENDENER.

Schweizerischer Verband der Ingenieur-Agronomen und der Lebensmittel-Ingenieure/Association suisse des ingénieurs agronomes et des ingénieurs en technologie alimentaire: Länggasse 79, 3052 Zollikofen; tel. 319105075; fax 319105070; e-mail svial@svial.ch; internet www.svial.ch; f. 1901; active in five areas: agricultural production and environment, food and nutrition, management of agricultural and food industry, training and consulting, govt and politics; promotes professional interests of its mems; 2,000 mems; Pres. NICOLAS FELLAY; Sec. ERNST BAUMANN; publ. *Journal* (4 a year).

Swiss Engineering–STV (Association of Engineers and Architects): Weinbergstr. 41, 8006 Zürich; tel. 442683711; fax 442683700; e-mail info@swissengineering.ch; internet www.swissengineering.ch; f. 1905; supports professional interests of mems; encourages engineering education and training and protection of traditional titles; 15,000 mems; Pres. MAURO PELLEGRINI; Sec.-Gen. STEFAN

ARQUINT; publs *Revue Technique Suisse, Schweizerische Technische Zeitschrift, Swiss Engineering STZ / Swiss Engineering rts* (10 a year).

Verband Schweizer Abwasser- und Gewässerschutzfachleute/Association suisse des professionnels de la protection des eaux (Swiss Water Association): Europastr. 3, Glattbrugg; tel. 433437070; fax 433437071; e-mail sekretariat@vsa.ch; internet www.vsa.ch; f. 1944; promotes waste-water technology and water pollution control through advanced technical training for its mems through confs, courses and on-the-job exchanges; publication of standards and guidelines; 1,350 mems, 2,400 reps; Pres. WÜRSTEN MARTIN; Vice-Pres. CHAIX OLIVIER.

Research Institutes

GENERAL

European Journalism Observatory: Via G. Buffi 13, 6904 Lugano; tel. 586664126; fax 586664647; e-mail ejo@lu.unisi.ch; internet it .ejo.ch; f. 2004; attached to Univ. della Svizzera Italiana; promotes links between newsrooms and communications research by aiding media managers, analysts, editors and journalists; analyzes research and trends in media industry; Dir Dr STEPHAN RUSS-MOHL; Co-Dir MARCELLO FOA.

Institute of Management: Via G. Buffi 13, 6900 Lugano; fax 586664647; internet www .ima.eco.unisi.ch; attached to Univ. della Svizzera Italiana; research in different fields of management studies: strategic management, clusters and regional competitiveness, entrepreneurship and family business, public administration and health care management; programmes at undergraduate and postgraduate levels.

Istituto di Marketing e Comunicazione Aziendale (Institute of Marketing and Communication Management): Via G. Buffi 13, 6900 Lugano; tel. 586664756; fax 58 6664647; e-mail ivan.snehota@usi.ch; internet www .imca.com.usi.ch; attached to Univ. della Svizzera Italiana; scientific and applied research on issues of teaching and communication in field of economic org.; Dir IVAN SNEHOTA.

Istituto Media e Giornalismo (Institute for Media and Journalism): Via G. Buffi 13, 6900 Lugano; tel. 586664738; fax 586664647; e-mail imeg.com@usi.ch; internet www.imeg .com.usi.ch; attached to Univ. della Svizzera italiana; research and teaching activities on two constituent parts of communication: content (text) and their containers (media); main characteristics of media in historical, economic and social context; forms of access and use of media and methods of use content from a variety of audiences; strategies of instns and companies dealing with nat. and int. media; Dir GIUSEPPE RICHERI; Co-Dir STEPHAN RUSS-MOHL.

Laboratorio di Storia delle Alpi: Largo Bernasconi 2, 6850 Mendrisio; tel. 586665819; fax 586665868; e-mail labisalp .arc@usi.ch; internet www.arc.usi.ch/ labisalp; f. 2000; attached to Univ. della Svizzera Italiana; research on alpine space, in its economic, social, cultural, demographic, and political aspects; Head LUIGI LORENZETTI; Sec. MONICA BANCALÀ; publ. *Histoire des Alpes / Storia delle Alpi / Geschichte der Alpen* (1 a year).

AGRICULTURE, FISHERIES AND VETERINARY SCIENCE

Office Fédéral de l'Agriculture/Bundesamt für Landwirtschaft (Federal Office for Agriculture): Ministry of Public Economy, Mattenhofstr. 5, 3003 Bern; tel. 313222511; fax 313222634; e-mail info@blw.admin.ch; internet www.blw.admin.ch; centre for federal agricultural research; promotes multi-functional agriculture; implements decisions taken by electorate, Swiss parliament and govt and plays active role in formulating agricultural policy; Dir-Gen. Dr MANFRED BÖTSCH; Deputy Dir Dr JACQUES CHAVAZ; publs *Agrarforschung* (12 a year), *Revue suisse d'agriculture* (12 a year).

Federal Agricultural Research Stations:

Agroscope: Route de Duillier, POB 1012, 1260 Nyon 1; tel. 223634444; fax 223621325; e-mail info@faw.admin.ch; internet www.agroscope.admin.ch; agricultural research for sustained economic activity in agricultural, nutritional and environmental sectors; develops scientific knowledge and technical principles for agricultural and environmental policy decisions and their legal implementation; Dir of Agroscope Changins-Wädenswil Dr JEAN-PHILIPPE MAYOR; Dir of Agroscope Liebefeld-Posieux-Haras Dr MICHAEL GYSI; Dir of Agroscope Reckenholz-Tänikon Dr PAUL STEFFEN; publs *Agrarforschung Schweiz / Recherche Agronomique Suisse, ALP aktuell, Revue suisse de viticulture arboriculture horticulture, Schweizer Zeitschrift für Obst- und Weinbau*.

ARCHITECTURE AND TOWN PLANNING

Fondazione Archivio del Moderno (Archive of the Modern): Largo Bernasconi 2, 6850 Medrisio; tel. 586665500; fax 586665555; e-mail archivio.arc@usi.ch; internet www .arc.usi.ch/archivio.htm; f. 1996; ind. research institute supporting Acad. of Architecture of Mendrisio, reinforcing its teaching and scholarly activities; acquisition, protection, preservation and exploitation of archives of architecture, urban planning, engineering, design, art and photography; promotes scientific research in fields of history of modern and contemporary architecture, art, design, territory and civil engineering, recognizing their leading role in current state of society; Dir LETIZIA TEDESCHI; Deputy Dir NICOLA NAVONE.

Istituto di Ricerca per il Progetto Urbano Contemporaneo (Institute for the Contemporary Urban Project): Largo Bernasconi 2, 6850 Medrisio; e-mail i.cup@arch .unisi.ch; internet www.arch.unisi.ch/ ris_ist_icup; f. 2004; attached to Univ. della Svizzera italiana; research studies on grounds of quantitative parameters: mobility, transport, energetic consumption, sustainability, re-use of existing architectures, effect of new infrastructures, economic capacity of territory; Dir Prof. JOSEP ACEBILLO.

ECONOMICS, LAW AND POLITICS

Center for Comparative and International Studies (CIS) Zürich: Haldeneggsteig 4, 8092 Zürich; tel. 446326385; fax 446321289; e-mail cispostmaster@gess .ethz.ch; internet www.cis.ethz.ch; f. 1997; research centre for comparative politics and int. relations; fosters cooperation in research and education; organizes research seminars, workshops and public events with leading academics and political practitioners; topics of research: democracy, political violence, markets and politics, and sustainable devt; Dir Prof. Dr KATHARINA MICHAELOWA; Vice-Dir Prof. LARS-ERIK CEDERMAN.

Institut Suisse de Droit Comparé/ Schweizerisches Institut für Rechtsvergleichung/Istituto Svizzero di Diritto Comparato (Swiss Institute of Comparative Law): 1015 Lausanne; tel. 216924911; fax 216924949; e-mail info@isdc.ch; internet www.isdc.ch; f. 1978; provides Fed. Govt with documents and studies necessary for legislation and for conclusion of int. conventions; participates in int. efforts towards approx. and unification of law; gives information and consultations to courts, admins, attorneys and interested persons; conducts its own scientific research, promotes and co-ordinates studies in Swiss univs and provides researchers in Switzerland with appropriate centre for study; library: see Libraries and Archives; Dir Prof. Dr CHRISTINA SCHMID; Vice-Dir Dr LUKAS HECKENDORN URSCHELER.

Institute for Microeconomics and Public Economics: Via Giuseppe Buffi 13, 6904 Lugano; tel. 586664783; fax 586664733; e-mail marisa.clemenz@usi.ch; internet www.mecop.eco.unisi.ch; f. 1998; attached to Univ. della Svizzera italiana; research in fields of public economics and public management; offers graduate and postgraduate courses; Dir MASSIMO FILIPPINI.

Institute of Finance: Via G. Buffi 13, 6900 Lugano; tel. 586664752; fax 586664734; e-mail abf.istfin.eco@usi.ch; internet www .istfin.eco.usi.ch; f. 1999; attached to Univ. della Svizzera Italiana; research about quantitative and institutional themes of financial markets; offers postgraduate studies; Dir GIOVANNI BARONE-ADESI.

Istituto di Diritto (Institute of Law): Via G. Buffi 13, 6900 Lugano; tel. 586664627; fax 586664647; e-mail marco.borghi@usi.ch; internet www.idusi.eco.usi.ch; attached to Univ. della Svizzera Italiana; offers post-graduate training and interdisciplinary activities; research in field law in Ticino; organizes exhibitions; Dir MARCO BORGHI.

Istituto di Ricerche Economiche (Institute for Economic Research): Via Maderno 24, CP 4361, 6904 Lugano; tel. 586664661; fax 586664662; e-mail ire.eco@usi.ch; internet www.ire.eco.usi.ch; attached to Univ. della Svizzera italiana; research on various aspects of regional and urban economics, ranging from regional growth and devt to competitiveness and innovation and from labour market issues to transportation and mobility; Dir RICO MAGGI; Vice-Dir SIEGFRIED ALBERTON.

Schweizerisches Institut für Auslandforschung/Institut Suisse de Recherches Internationales (Swiss Institute of International Studies): Frau Anja Spring Augustinerhof 1, 8001 Zürich; tel. 442121313; fax 442127854; e-mail info@siaf.ch; internet www.siaf.ch; f. 1943; attached to Univ. Zürich; deals with current issues in the fields of politics, economy, society, science and culture and selected for qualified and internationally renowned speakers; gives SIAF Award for outstanding theses, Licentiate and Masters theses at Univ. and ETH Zurich; Pres. KASPAR VILLIGER; Vice-Pres. Dr MARTIN MEYER; Treas. JOSEF MEIER; publ. *Sozialwissenschaftliche Studien* (1 a year).

EDUCATION

Institut de Recherche et de Documentation Pédagogique: Faubourg de l'Hôpital 43–45, CP 556, 2002 Neuchâtel; tel. 328898600; fax 328896971; e-mail secretariat@irdp.ch; internet www.irdp.ch; f. 1970; research in French-speaking Switzerland, into educational methods, organization and administration; creation and analysis of teaching aids; documentation; library of 10,000 vols; Dir MATTHIS BEHRENS; publ. *Le point sur la recherche* (irregular).

Institut Européen de l'Université de Genève: rue Jean-Daniel Colladon 2, 1204 Genève; tel. 223797850; fax 223797852;

internet www.unige.ch/ieug; f. 1963; directs, coordinates and promotes educational programs in European studies and research on Europe in interdisciplinary perspective; organizes symposia, seminars, workshops and confs; library of 18,000 vols, 25,000 monographs, 92 periodicals; Dir Prof. NICOLAS LEVRAT; Librarian JEAN-MARC MEMBREZ; publ. *Euryopa*.

Istituto di Studi Italiani: Via Lambertenghi 10A, 6904 Lugano; tel. 586664700; fax 586664259; e-mail ism.com@usi.ch; internet www.isi.com.usi.ch; f. 2007; attached to Univ. della Svizzera italiana; offers postgraduate studies in language, Italian literature and culture; scientific research projects in tradition of Italian studies; Dir CARLO OSSOLA.

HISTORY, GEOGRAPHY AND ARCHAEOLOGY

Institut d'Histoire de la Réformation: rue de-Candolle 5, 1211 Geneva 4; tel. 223797128; fax 223797133; e-mail marlene .jaouich@unige.ch; internet www.unige.ch/ ihr; f. 1969; attached to Univ. de Genève; promotes research and postgraduate studies in history of ideas, instns and practices of reformation; Dir MARIA-CRISTINA PITASSI; Sec. MARLÈNE JAOUICH.

LANGUAGE AND LITERATURE

Institut de langue et civilisation françaises (Institute of French Language and Civilisation): Faubourg de l'Hôpital 61–63, 2000 Neuchâtel; tel. 327181800; fax 327181801; e-mail ilcf.ce@unine.ch; internet www2.unine.ch/ilcf; f. 1892; attached to Univ. of Neuchâtel; research centre specialized in teaching French; Dir PHILIPPE TERRIER; Sec. BRIGITTE STEINER.

Istituto Linguistico-Semiotico (Institute for Linguistics and Semiotics): via Giuseppe Buffi 13, 6900 Lugano; tel. 586664791; fax 586664647; e-mail ils.com@usi.ch; internet www.ils.com.usi.ch; attached to Univ. della Svizzera italiana; research related to discourse, dialogue, argument, intercultural communication, linguistic structures and processes of interpretation of texts hypermedia; Dir EDDO RIGOTTI; Vice-Dir ANDREA ROCCI.

MEDICINE

Arbeitsstelle für Ethik in den Biowissenschaften (Unit for Ethics in the Biosciences): Univ. of Basel, Schönbeinstr. 20, 4056 Basel; Universität, Missionstr. 24, 4055 Basel; tel. 612601132; fax 612601133; e-mail christoph.rehmann-sutter@unibas.ch; internet www.aeb.unibas.ch; f. 1996; attached to Univ. of Basel; research on bioethics, philosophy of biology and ELSA research in genetics and genomics, esp. the patients' perspectives on gene therapy, genetic tests and societal perceptions of devts in genetics; library of 10,000 vols; Dir Prof. Dr CHRISTOPH REHMANN-SUTTER.

Centre Interfacultaire de Gérontologie (Interfaculty Centre for Gerontology): route de Drize 7, 1227 Carouge; tel. 223793790; fax 223793787; e-mail cig@unige.ch; internet cig .unige.ch; f. 1992; attached to Univ. de Genève; research on various aspects of aging, vulnerability and life course; Dir Prof. MICHEL ORIS.

Institut für Sucht- und Gesundheitsforschung Zürich: Konradstr. 32, POB, 8031 Zürich; tel. 444481160; fax 444481170; e-mail isgf@isgf.uzh.ch; internet www.isgf .uzh.ch; f. 1993; attached to Univ. of Zurich; research and service sectors, covering legal and illegal drugs, non substance-related addictive behaviour, health planning and economics, consulting and assessments and transfer of knowledge through training; Pres. Prof. Dr AMBROS UCHTENHAGEN; Vice-Pres. Prof. Dr RAINER HORNUNG.

Institute of Communication and Health: Via Lambertenghi 10, 6904 Lugano; tel. 586664487; e-mail nadia.galli@usi.ch; internet www.ich.com.usi.ch; attached to Univ. della Svizzera italiana; theoretical and applied researches for preservation and improvement of individual health; organizes social and organizational programs for promotion of health, wellness and health policy; offers postgraduate educational programs; Dir PETER J. SCHULZ.

Schweizerisches Institut für Allergie- und Asthmaforschung (Swiss Institute of Allergy and Asthma Research): Obere Str. 22, 7270 Davos; tel. 814100848; fax 814100840; e-mail siaf@siaf.uzh.ch; internet www.siaf.uzh.ch; f. 1988; attached to Univ. of Zurich; applied and basic research in field of allergies and asthma; Dir Prof. Dr CEZMI A. AKDIS.

Schweizerisches Tropen- und Public Health-institut (Swiss TPH)/Institut Tropical et de Santé Publique Suisse (Swiss Tropical and Public Health Institute): Socinstr. 57, 4051 Basel; Socinstr. 55A, Eulerstr. 54, 68, 77 4051 Basel; tel. 612848111; fax 612848101; e-mail library-sti@unibas.ch; internet www .swisstph.ch; f. 1943, present name 2010; provides teaching, research and services in field of int. health devt; library of 7,000 vols, 80 journals, 9000 monographs, annual reports, reprints, course programs and theses; Pres. Prof. Dr FELIX GUTZWILLER; Vice-Dir JÖRG H. SCHWARZENBACH; Dir Prof. Dr MARCEL TANNER; Deputy Dir NICOLAUS LORENZ; Deputy Dir NINO KÜNZLI.

NATURAL SCIENCES

General

Collegium Basilea (Institute of Advanced Study): Hochstr. 51, 4053 Basel; tel. 613619523; fax 613619524; e-mail cb@ unibas.ch; internet pages.unibas.ch/colbas; f. 1999; supports interdisciplinary postdoctoral research, mainly in biological, physical and chemical sciences, with emphasis on physicochemical foundations of living systems and in applications of complexity theory; library of 7,000 vols; Pres. Prof. Dr JEREMY J. RAMSDEN; publs *Journal of Biological Physics and Chemistry* (4 a year), *Nanotechnology Perceptions* (review of ultraprecision engineering and nanotechnology, 3 a year).

High Altitude Research Stations Jungfraujoch & Gornergrat Int: Sidlerstr. 5, 3012 Bern; tel. 316314052; fax 316314405; e-mail louise.wilson@space.unibe.ch; internet www.ifjungo.ch; f. 1930; high-altitude research in solar astronomy, astrophysics, environmental sciences, atmospheric physics, atmospheric chemistry, glaciology, meteorology, physics and biology; international foundation run by scientific organizations of Austria, Belgium, Germany, Italy, Switzerland and the UK; Hon. Pres. Prof. Dr HANS BALSIGER; Pres. Prof. Dr ERWIN O. FLÜCKIGER; Treas. KARL MARTIN WYSS; Dir Prof. Dr MARKUS LEUENBERGER; publ. *Review on Activity*.

Space Center: Station 11, 1015 Lausanne; tel. 216936948; fax 216936940; e-mail space .center@epfl.ch; internet space.epfl.ch; attached to Ecole Polytechnique Fédérale de Lausanne; promotes space technology across science, education and industry; Dir Prof. HERBERT SHEA.

Staatssekretariat für Bildung und Forschung SBF/Secretariat d'Etat a l'education et a la recherche SER (State Secretariat for Education and Research SER): Hallwylstr. 4, 3003 Bern; tel. 313229691; fax 313227854; e-mail info@sbf .admin.ch; internet www.sbf.admin.ch; f. 1969; prepares policy decisions for education and science and executes scientific policy; coordinates activities of Fed. bodies concerned with research and education; supports univs and other institutes of higher education and contributes to grants; is responsible for encouragement and general coordination of research and higher education; with other depts deals with int. scientific affairs; Dir MAURO DELL'AMBROGIO; Deputy Dir JÜRG BURRI.

Stiftung für Humanwissenschaftliche Grundlagenforschung/Fondation pour la Recherche de Base dans les Sciences de l'Homme: Kirchgasse 42, 8001 Zürich; tel. 443830922; f. 1970; basic research in human sciences; Pres. Prof. JULES ANGST; Dir Dr WALTER BODMER.

Biological Sciences

Centre d'Imagerie BioMedicale (Centre for Biomedical Imaging): Station 6, 1015 Lausanne; tel. 216934467; fax 216937960; e-mail info@cibm.ch; internet www.cibm.ch; attached to Ecole Polytechnique Fédérale de Lausanne; research on understanding of biomedical processes in health and disease, focusing on mechanisms of normal functioning, pathogenic mechanisms, characterization of disease onset prior to structural damage, metabolic and functional consequences of gene expression, and non-invasive insights into disease processes under treatment; Dir Prof. ROLF GRUETTER.

Conservatoire et Jardin botaniques de la Ville de Genève: POB 60, 1292 Chambésy; tel. 224185133; fax 224185101; e-mail periodiques.cjb@ville-ge.ch; internet www .ville-ge.ch/cjb; f. 1817; systematic botany, taxonomy, floristics, ecology, phytogeography; research in plant systematics, floristics, and population genetics; library of 100,000 vols, 1,1447 periodicals; Dir Prof. PIERRE-ANDRÉ LOIZEAU; publs *Boissiera*, *Candollea*.

Institut für Pflanzenwissenschaften (Institute of Plant Sciences): Altenbergrain 21, 3013 Bern; tel. 316314911; fax 316314942; e-mail ipsinfo@ips.unibe.ch; internet www.botany.unibe.ch; f. 1862; attached to Univ. Bern; consists of six ind. research sections; research covers vegetation ecology, plant ecology, paleoecology, molecular ecology and plant devt, plant breeding, plant nutrition, molecular physiology; teaching at all academic levels; receives c. one-third of budget from the Swiss National Science Foundation, EU and other orgs; Dir Prof. Dr DORIS RENTSCH; Sec. HELGA RODRIGUEZ.

Botanic Garden:

Botanischer Garten Bern: Altenbergrain 21, 3013 Bern; tel. 316314945; fax 316314993; e-mail info@botanischergarten .ch; internet boga.unibe.ch; f. 1859; Dir Prof. Dr MARKUS FISCHER.

Mathematical Sciences

Centre Interfacultaire Bernoulli (Bernoulli Interfaculty Centre of Mathematics): Station 15, 1015 Lausanne; tel. 216932583; internet cib.epfl.ch; attached to Ecole Polytechnique Fédérale de Lausanne; organizes programmes and symposiums related to research in field of mathematics; Dir TUDOR RATIU.

Physical Sciences

Centre Universitaire d'Ecologie Humaine et des Sciences de l'Environnement: route de Drize 7, 1227 Carouge; tel. 223790875; fax 223790860; internet www.unige.ch/ecohum; f. 1976, present status 2008; attached to Univ. de Genève; research and teaching in natural and social sciences; Dir B. BÜRGENMEIER; publ. *journées du cuepe*.

Eidgenössische Forschungsanstalt für Wald, Schnee und Landschaft (Swiss Federal Institute for Forest, Snow and Landscape Research): Zürcherstr. 111, 8903 Birmensdorf; tel. 447392111; fax 447392215; e-mail wslinfo@wsl.ch; internet www.wsl.ch; attached to ETH Zurich; concerned with use, devt and protection of natural and urban spaces; maintains experimental and research plots for studying rock fall or debris flow, study areas for monitoring effects of climate change on forests and sites damaged by storms or fires for investigating impact of natural hazards; library of 16,000 vols, 4,000 maps of Switzerland, 1,500 journals, 3,000 electronic journals; Dir Prof. Dr JAMES KIRCHNER; Deputy Dir Dr CHRISTOPH HEGG.

Institut für Astronomie: ETH Zürich, Wolfgang-Pauli-Str. 27, 8093 Zürich; tel. 446337608; fax 446331238; e-mail marcella@phys.ethz.ch; internet www.astro.phys.ethz.ch; f. 1864; attached to ETH Zürich; research on astronomy and astrophysics; Chair. Prof. Dr MARCELLA CAROLLO; Vice-Chair. Prof. MICHAEL MEYER.

Observatoire Astronomique de l'Université de Genève: 51 Ch. des Maillettes, 1290 Sauverny–Geneva; tel. 223792200; fax 223792205; e-mail gilbert.burki@obs.unige.ch; internet www.unige.ch/sciences/astro; f. 1772; attached to Univ. de Genève; astronomy, astrophysics research; 115 mems; library of 6,000 vols, 500 periodicals; Dir Prof. STÉPHANE UDRY; Librarian CLAUDE GUIDI.

Schweizerische Gesellschaft für Astrophysik und Astronomie/Société Suisse d'Astrophysique et d'Astronomie (Swiss Society for Astrophysics and Astronomy): Astronomisches Institut der Universität Bern, Sidlerstr. 5, 3012 Bern; e-mail thomas.schildknecht@aiub.unibe.ch; internet obswww.unige.ch/ssaa; f. 1968; research in astrophysics and astronomy; training of researchers through courses; Pres. Prof. DANIEL SCHAERER; Vice-Pres. MICHAEL MEYER; Treas. WERNER SCHMUTZ; Sec. Prof. THOMAS SCHILDKNECHT.

Specola Solare Ticinese, Locarno: Via ai Monti 146, 6600 Locarno; tel. 917562376; fax 917562375; e-mail scortesi@specola.ch; internet www.specola.ch; f. 1957; solar observation; determination of Wolf number; data collected sent regularly to SIDC; library of 600 vols; Pres. Prof. Dr PHILIPPE JETZER; Vice-Pres. Dr MARIO CAMANI; Treas. ALBERTO TABORELLI; Sec. Ing. FLAVIO DONATI.

WSL-Institut für Schnee- und Lawinenforschung (SLF) (WSL Institute for Snow and Avalanche Research): Flüelastr. 11, 7260 Davos Dorf; tel. 814170111; fax 814170110; e-mail contact@slf.ch; internet www.slf.ch; f. 1936; attached to Swiss Federal Institute for Forest, Snow and Landscape Research; research on physics and mechanics of snow and snow pack, avalanche formation and mechanics, protective structure, snow and avalanche interaction with forests, and an avalanche warning service; library of 20,000 vols; Dir Prof. Dr JAMES KIRCHNER; Deputy Dir Dr CHRISTOPH HEGG; publs *Mitteilungen*, *Unfallberichte*, *Winterbericht* (1 a year).

Libraries and Archives

Aarau

Aargauer Kantonsbibliothek: Aargauerpl., 5000 Aarau; tel. 628352362; fax 628352369; e-mail kantonsbibliothek@ag.ch; internet www.ag.ch/kantonsbibliothek; f. 1803; oldest document is written parchment from early 9th century; specialized in designed humanities; special collns: Zurlaubiana (history of Switzerland and Europe), Frank Wedekind archive; 700,000 vols, 2,000 periodicals, 850 incunabula, 1,500 MSS; Dir Dr RUTH WÜST; Deputy Dir Lic. ANITA GRESELE.

Staatsarchiv Aargau: Entfelderstr. 22, 5001 Aarau; tel. 628351290; fax 628351299; e-mail staatsarchiv@ag.ch; internet www.ag.ch/staatsarchiv; f. 1803; records of 1027 to 1803 and from district of establishing systematic documentation together until beginning of Canton; divided into dept; 130,000 entries; 70,000 records in Govt Council resolutions from 1971 to 1996, consisting of title and description; State Archivist Lic. ANDREA VOELLMIN; Sec. ANITA MÜLLER.

Basel

Allgemeine Bibliotheken der Gesellschaft für das Gute und Gemeinnützige: Im Schmiedenhof 10, 4051 Basel; tel. 612641111; fax 612641190; e-mail info@stadtbibliothekbasel.ch; internet www.stadtbibliothekbasel.ch; f. 1807; eight brs; 290,000 vols; central library and 8 br. libraries; Dir KLAUS EGLI; Vice-Dir MARIE-THÉRÈSE BANDERA.

Archiv für Schweizerische Kunstgeschichte: Im Laurenz-Bau, St. Alban-Graben 8, POB, 4010 Basel; tel. 612066292; fax 612066297; e-mail info-kunsthist@unibas.ch; internet kunsthist.unibas.ch/seminar/archiv-fuer-schweizerische-kunstgeschichte; attached to Universitätsgut; illustrations by monuments, works of painting, sculpture and ancient and modern decorative arts, literature on Swiss art history as reference library, projection images; 6,000 vols; Dir NIKLAUS MEIER.

Bibliothek des Museums der Kulturen Basel: Münsterpl. 20, 4051 Basel; tel. 612665630; fax 612665605; e-mail mkb.biblio@bs.ch; internet www.mkb.ch; f. 1901; specialized literature on ethnology on areas dealt with by museum's collns and scientific history of ethnology; 80,000 vols, 200 journals; Librarian ELISABETH IDRIS-HÖHENER.

Schweizerisches Wirtschaftsarchiv/Archives Economiques Suisses (Swiss Economic Archives): Peter Merian-Weg 6, 4002 Basel; tel. 612673219; fax 612673208; e-mail info@wwzb.unibas.ch; internet www.ub.unibas.ch/wwz-bibliothek-swa; f. 1910; nat. centre for economic information and economic history; open to gen. public; 650,000 vols, incl. business reports, periodicals, statistical publs, reports on social instns and professional socs; 2,500,000 newspaper cuttings; Dir IRENE AMSTUTZ; Sec. BARBARA DÜRR.

Staatsarchiv Basel-Stadt: Martinsgasse 2, 4001 Basel; tel. 612678601; fax 612676571; e-mail stabs@bs.ch; internet www.staatsarchiv.bs.ch; history of canton of Basel and its communities; Dir Lic. ESTHER BAUR; publ. *Quellen und Forschungen zur Basler Geschichte*.

Universitätsbibliothek Basel (University Library of Basel): Schönbeinstr. 18–20, 4056 Basel; tel. 612673100; fax 612673103; e-mail info-ub@unibas.ch; internet www.ub.unibas.ch; f. 1460; 3,300,000 vols, scientific works, 10,000 musical MSS, 3,000 incunabula, 35,000 topographic maps, 100,000 reproductions of portraits; Dir HANNES HUG; Vice-Dir FELIX WINTER; publs *Die Amerbachkorrespondenz*, *Die Matrikel der Universität Basel*, *Die mittelalterlichen Handschriften der Universitätsbibliothek Basel*.

Bern

Bibliothek des Musikschule Konservatorium Bern: Kramgasse 36, 3011 Bern; e-mail office@konsibern.ch; internet www.konsibern.ch; f. 1917; 50,000 vols; Pres. ANNAMARIE ZINSLI.

Burgerbibliothek Bern/Bibliothèque de la Bourgeoisie de Berne: Münstergasse 63, POB, 3000 Bern 8; tel. 313203333; fax 313203370; e-mail bbb@burgerbib.ch; internet www.burgerbib.ch; f. 1951; medieval MSS, Bongarsiana-Codices, documents concerning Swiss and Bernese history and bequests of important people such as Albrecht von Haller or Jeremias Gotthelf; acts as archival capacity for Burgergemeinde (civic community), guilds and Burgers' socs; 15,000 vols, 50 periodicals, 2,700 m of historical MSS, of which 50 m medieval MSS; Dir Dr CLAUDIA ENGLER; Sec. ANNELIES HÜSSY; publs *Bibliografie der Berner Geschichte*, *Kataloge der Burgerbibliothek Bern*, *Passepartout*, *Schriften der Burgerbibliothek Bern*.

Schweizerische Nationalbibliothek/Bibliothèque nationale suisse (Swiss National Library): Hallwylstr. 15, 3003 Bern; tel. 313228935; fax 313228408; e-mail info@nb.admin.ch; internet www.nb.admin.ch; f. 1895; contains all publs issued in Switzerland and foreign publs by Swiss authors or concerning Switzerland; Swiss union catalogue, SwissInfoDesk, Swiss Literary Archives, Prints and Drawings Dept, Swiss ISSN Centre, Centre Dürrenmatt Neuchâtel; 4,033,569 vols, 749,175 bound vols of periodicals, 384,056 engravings, photos and maps, 67,212 musical publs, 14,560 microforms and CD-ROMs, 18,397 audio-visual items, 277 collns in the Swiss Literary Archives, 68 collns in the Prints and Drawings Dept; Dir MARIE-CHRISTINE DOFFEY; Vice-Dir ELENA BALZARDI; publs *Bibliographie der Schweizergeschichte / Bibliographie de l'histoire suisse / Bibliografia della storia svizzera*, *Bulletin du Cercle d'études internationales Jean Starobinski*, *Passim* (Bulletin des Schweizerischen Literaturarchivs/Bulletin des Archives littéraires suisses/Bollettino dell'Archivio svizzero di letteratura/Bulletin da l'Archiv svizzer da litteratura), *The Swiss Book / Le Livre suisse / Das Schweizer Buch / Il libro svizzero* (24 a year), *Quarto* (Zeitschrift des Schweizerischen Literaturarchivs / Revue des Archives littéraires suisses / Rivista dell'Archivio svizzero di letteratura/Revista da l'Archiv svizzer da litteratura).

Schweizerisches Bundesarchiv (Swiss Federal Archives): Archivstr. 24, 3003 Bern; tel. 313228989; fax 313227823; e-mail bundesarchiv@bar.admin.ch; internet www.bar.admin.ch; f. 1798; appraises, secures, describes and provides access to archive-worthy records of Swiss Confederation; Dir ANDREAS KELLERHALS; Deputy Dir P. KUNZLER.

Staatsarchiv des Kantons Bern: Falkenpl. 4, POB 8424, 3001 Bern; tel. 316335101; fax 316335102; e-mail info.stab@sta.be.ch; internet www.sta.be.ch/staatsarchiv; collects, registers and preserves canton's archival heritage; microfilms of parish registers; State Archivist Dr PETER MARTIG; Sec. MADLEN TANNER; publ. *Das Staatsarchiv des Kantons Bern*.

Universitätsbibliothek Bern: Münstergasse 61, 3000 Bern 8; tel. 316319211; fax

316319299; e-mail info@ub.unibe.ch; internet www.ub.unibe.ch; f. 1528; 50 br. libraries; 4,600,000 vols, 17,000 online journals; Chief Librarian MARIANNE RUBLI SUPERSAXO.

Bubendorf

Fondation Bibliotheca Afghanica (Afghanistan Institute in Switzerland): Bruehlstr. 2, 4416 Bubendorf; tel. 619339877; fax 619339878; e-mail info@afghanistan-institut.ch; internet www.afghanistan-institut.ch; f. 1975; research institute and archive; Afghani nature, culture and contemporary history; material on Afghan history, geography, ethnography, religion and politics; German newspaper clippings; Mujahideen and Communist govt publs; 17,000 vols, 40,000 photographs; Dir PAUL BUCHERER-DIETSCHI.

Chur

Staatsarchiv Graubünden: Karlihofpl., 7001 Chur; tel. 812572803; fax 812572001; e-mail info@sag.gr.ch; internet www.sag.gr.ch; f. 1803; written works on history of Graubünden; admin. acts to preserve rights and interests of Graubünden; Dir Dr SILVIO MARGADANT.

Cologny

Bibliotheca Bodmeriana (Fondation Martin Bodmer): 19–21 route du Guignard, 1223 Cologny; tel. 227074433; fax 227074430; e-mail info@fondationbodmer.ch; internet www.fondationbodmer.org; f. 1972; 160,000 vols; spec. collns of papyrus, MSS, autographs, incunabula, music MSS, drawings; Dir Prof. CHARLES MÉLA.

Fribourg

Bibliothèque Cantonale et Universitaire/Kantons- und Universitätsbibliothek: rue Joseph-Piller 2, 1701 Fribourg; tel. 263051333; fax 263051377; e-mail bcu@fr.ch; internet www.fr.ch/bcuf; f. 1848; special colln of MSS and incunabula of middle ages to present; Heritage Fribourg colln; organizes cultural activities; 2,500,000 vols; Dir Dr MARTIN GOOD.

Geneva

Archives d'etat de Genève: 1 rue de l'Hôtel de Ville, 1211 Geneva 3; tel. 223279320; fax 223279321; e-mail archives@etat.ge.ch; internet www.ge.ch/archives; material on history of Geneva; Archivist PIERRE FLÜCKIGER; Librarian ISABELLE COLINI.

Bibliothèque d'Art et d'Archéologie des Musées d'art et d'histoire: 5 Promenade du Pin, 1204 Geneva; tel. 224182700; fax 224182701; e-mail info.baa@ville-ge.ch; internet www.ville-ge.ch/baa; f. 1911; library of Musées d'Art et d'Histoire and public art library; 400,000 vols, 6,200 periodicals, 140,000 exhibition and auction catalogues, CD-ROMs, databases, microforms, video cassettes, iconography; Conservator VÉRONIQUE GONCERUT ESTÈBE; publ. *Geneva* (annual review of Musées d'art et d'histoire).

Bibliothèque de l'ONUG (United Nations Office at Geneva Library): Palais des Nations, 1211 Geneva 10; tel. 229174181; fax 229170418; e-mail library@unog.ch; internet www.unog.ch/library; f. 1919; manages cultural activities at Palais des Nations, organizes c. 40 annual events (concerts, exhibitions, film festivals) in cooperation with Permanent Mission of the UN Member State; manages visits to its premises and research training for UNOG staff members; 1,100,000 vols, 4m. documents and publs of UN and its specialized agencies, 500,000 govt documents, 9,000 periodicals; archives of the League of Nations; Chief Librarian PIERRE LE LOARER; publs *Bibliographie Mensuelle* (12 a year), *Catalogue des Publications en Série* (serials catalogue).

Bibliothèque de Genève: Promenade des Bastions, 1211 Geneva 4; tel. 224182800; fax 224182801; e-mail info.bge@ville-ge.ch; internet www.ville-ge.ch/bge; f. 1562; 2,191,000 vols and pamphlets, 70,000 posters, 23,000 maps, 45,000 engravings, 400 painted portraits, 15,000 MSS; Dir JEAN-CHARLES GIROUD.

Bibliothèques Municipales: 10 rue de la Tour-de-Boël, CP 3930 1211 Geneva 3; tel. 224183250; fax 224183251; e-mail webbmu@ville-ge.ch; internet www.ville-ge.ch/bmu; f. 1931; 7 br. libraries, sports library, bookmobile service and prison library in Champ-Dollon; 700,000 vols; Dir HÉLENE RIVIER.

International Labour Office Library: 4 route des Morillons, 1211 Geneva 22; tel. 227998675; fax 227996516; e-mail inform@ilo.org; internet www.ilo.org/inform; f. 1919; core repository of ILO publs produced in Geneva and in ILO's offices around world; open to public on request; 2,000,000 vols and pamphlets, 3,000 current periodicals (incl. annuals and official gazettes); computerized data base (LABORDOC), containing 210,000 abstracts, available for online searching worldwide through facilities of ESA-IRS and Questel-ORBIT and on CD-ROM; Dir L. DRYDEN; publ. *ILO Thesaurus: labour*.

World Health Organization Library and Information Networks for Knowledge: 20 Ave Appia, 1211 Geneva 27; tel. 227912062; fax 227914150; e-mail library@who.int; internet www.who.int/library; f. 1948; WHO permanent colln, int. public health literature, journals and databases, historical colln, govt statistical reports, WHOLIS database; Librarian TOMAS ALLEN.

Grand Saint-Bernard

Bibliothèque de l'Hospice du Grand Saint-Bernard: 1946 Bourg-Saint-Pierre; tel. 277871236; fax 277871107; e-mail hospicestbernard@gsbernard.ch; internet www.gsbernard.ch; library of Austin Canons monastery; works on history, theology, Catholic literature, natural sciences (botany, entomology, zoology, ornithology, mineralogy), applied sciences (physics, arithmetic, chemistry, astronomy), geography and travel, philosophy, law (civil and canon) liturgy and numismatics, ancient MSS and maps; 32,500 vols, 8,000 periodicals.

Lausanne

Bibliothèque cantonale et Universitaire de Lausanne, Riponne-Palais de Rumine: 6, Place de la Riponne, 1014 Lausanne; tel. 213167880; fax 213167870; e-mail info-riponne@bcu.unil.ch; internet www.unil.ch/bcu; f. 1537; br. in Dorigny; legal deposit library of Vaud Canton; regional documentation; 2,000,000 vols, 170 incunabula; 29,500 CDs, 32,000 musical scores, 10,000 audiovisual materials and 2,500 LP records; Dir JEANNETTE FREY; publs *Catalogues des fonds de manuscrits*, *Catalogues des manuscrits musicaux*.

Bibliothèque de l'EPFL—Rolex Learning Centre: Rolex Learning Centre, Station 20, 1015 Lausanne; tel. 216932156; fax 216935100; e-mail questions.bib@epfl.ch; internet library.epfl.ch; f. 1945; open to public; specializes in fields of study and research at EPFL; organizes confs and publs; science and technology; 550,000 vols, 11,000 electronic journals, 100 databases; Dir DAVID AYMONIN.

Bibliothèque de l'Institut Suisse de Droit Comparé: Dorigny, 1015 Lausanne; tel. 216924911; fax 216924949; internet www.isdc.ch; f. 1982; collects legal material from all countries in all fields of law, incl. int. law; European Documentation Centre; 360,000 vols, 2,000 periodicals, 900 electronic resources; Head SADRI SAIEB.

Bibliothèque Municipale de la Ville de Lausanne: 11 pl. Chauderon, 1003 Lausanne; tel. 213156915; fax 213156007; e-mail bml@lausanne.ch; internet www.lausanne.ch/bibliotheque; f. 1934; 4 brs in Chailly, Entre-Bois, Montriond, Grand-Vennes; 445,000 vols; Dir PIERRE-YVES LADOR.

Bibliothèque Universitaire de Médecine: Centre Hospitalier Universitaire Vaudois, 1011 Lausanne; tel. 213145082; fax 213145070; e-mail bdfm@chuv.ch; internet www.chuv.ch/bdfm; f. 1968; colln on different areas of health and medicine; 60,000 vols, 2,000 periodicals, 12,000 electronic journals, microcomputer facilities, audio-visual library; Head Librarian ISABELLE DE KAENEL.

Lucerne

Staatsarchiv des Kantons Luzern: Schützenstr. 9, POB 7853, 6000 Lucerne 7; tel. 412285365; fax 412286663; e-mail staatsarchiv@lu.ch; internet www.staatsarchiv.lu.ch; f. 1803; Siegel colln, seal stamp colln, Clichésammlung, Autograph colln, copy colln, Photo and copy colln, photo negative and microfilm colln, newspapers; 25,000 vols; Archivist Dr JÜRG SCHMUTZ; publ. *Luzerner Historische Veröffentlichungen* (irregular).

Zentral- und Hochschulbibliothek Luzern: Sempacherstr. 10, 6002 Lucerne; tel. 412285312; fax 412108255; e-mail info@zhbluzern.ch; internet www.zhbluzern.ch; f. 1951; incl. Burghers' library, canton library and library of Univ. of Lucerne; Lucerne Documentary Heritage Colln; differentiated spectrum of technical, factual and entertainment media; 960,893 vols, 2,736 MSS, 134,638 engravings, photos and maps, 36,868 microforms; colln of Swiss publs up to 1848; Dir Dr ULRICH NIEDERER; Deputy Dir Dr WILFRIED LOCHBÜHLER.

Lugano

Biblioteca Cantonale: Lugano, Ticino: Viale C. Cattaneo 6, 6901 Lugano; tel. 918154611; fax 918154619; e-mail bclu-segr.sbt@ti.ch; internet www.sbt.ti.ch/bclugano; f. 1852; colln on religion, theology, art, language, philology, linguistics, literature, with particular reference to Italian culture; inc. *Libreria Patria*, special colln of 'Ticinensia', 40,000 vols; Archivio Prezzolini and collns on contemporary culture; 300,000 vols, 1,300 periodicals, 198 incunabula; Dir Prof. GERARDO RIGOZZI.

Neuchâtel

Archives de l'Etat de Neuchâtel: Le Château, 12 rue de la Collégiale, 2000 Neuchâtel; tel. 328896040; fax 328896088; e-mail service.archivesetat@ne.ch; internet www.ne.ch/archives; f. 1898; stores and manages documents of State and private documents relating to history of canton of Neuchâtel; maintains historical library and administrative library; State Archivist LIONEL BARTOLINI; Librarian GÉRALDINE GALFETTI.

Bibliothèque des Pasteurs: Fbg de l'Hôpital 41, 2000 Neuchâtel; tel. 327254666; e-mail carmen.burkhalter@unine.ch; f. 1538; theological library of 90,000 vols, 80,000 monographs; Librarian CECILIA GRIENER HURLEY.

Bibliothèque Publique et Universitaire: 3 pl. Numa-Droz, CP 1916, 2000 Neuchâtel; tel. 327177302; fax 327177309; e-mail secretariat.bpu@unine.ch; internet bpun

.unine.ch; f. 1788; 600,000 vols, 1,900 periodicals, 8,000 posters, 40,000 books of information and general knowledge and multimedia documents (DVD, CD-ROMs and audio books); Dir THIERRY CHÂTELAIN; publs *Bibliothèques et musées*, *Revue historique neuchâteloise*, and bulletins of chronometry, geography, and natural sciences.

St Gallen

Kantonsbibliothek Vadiana St Gallen: Notkerstr. 22, 9000 St Gallen; tel. 582292321; fax 582292329; e-mail kb .vadiana@sg.ch; internet www.kb.sg.ch; f. 1551; colln point for St Gallische literature; three specialty divs: Vadian colln, collns of county Library and St Gallen centre for book (Zebu); open to public; 800,000 vols; Dir Dr CORNEL DORA; publ. *Veröffentlichungen der Gesellschaft Pro Vadiana*.

Stiftsbibliothek St Gallen: Klosterhof 6D, POB, 9004 St Gallen; tel. 712273416; fax 712273418; e-mail stibi@stibi.ch; internet www.stiftsbibliothek.ch; f. 719; library of fmr Benedictine Abbey of St Gall; important colln of MSS from Carolingian and Ottonian periods (8th–11th centuries); colln shows devt of European culture and documents cultural achievements of Abbey of St Gall from 8th century to dissolution of monastery in 1805; 170,000 vols; Dir Prof. Dr ERNST TREMP.

Sion

Médiathèque Valais (Bibliothèque Cantonale)/Mediathek Wallis (Kantonsbibliothek): 18 Ave de Pratifori, CP 182, 1951 Sion; tel. 276064550; fax 276064554; e-mail mv.sion@mediatheque.ch; internet www.mediatheque.ch; f. 1853; four brs: Brig, Sion, Martigny, Saint-Maurice; spec. collns on Alps; 840,000 vols; Dir DAMIAN ELSIG.

Solothurn

Bibliomedia Schweiz Suisse Svizzera: Rosenweg 2, 4500 Solothurn; tel. 326249020; fax 326249028; e-mail solothurn@bibliomedia.ch; internet www .buchstart.ch; f. 1920; promotes devt of libraries and promotion of reading; brs at Solothurn, Lausanne and Biasca; 500,000 vols; Dir Dr PETER WILLE; Sec. BÉATRICE AEGERTER; publ. *Le Cri du Hibou* (irregular).

Zentralbibliothek: Bielstr. 39, 4502 Solothurn; tel. 326276262; fax 326276200; e-mail info@zbsolothurn.ch; internet www .zbsolothurn.ch; f. 1930; 800,000 vols, 900 incunabula, 13,200 MSS, 7,000 illustrations and graphics, 18,000 music scores, 42,000 records and cassettes, 550 current periodicals and series, 30,000 children's books; Dir for Collns Lic. VERENA BIDER; Dir PETER PROBST; publs *Kleine Reihe*, *Musik aus der Sammlung der Zentralbibliothek Solothurn* (edns of regional compositions), *Veröffentlichungen der Zentralbibliothek Solothurn*.

Winterthur

Stadtbibliothek: Obere Kirchgasse 6, POB 132, 8402 Winterthur; tel. 522675148; fax 522675140; e-mail stadtbibliothek@win.ch; internet www.winbib.ch; f. 1660; spec. collns of local history, numismatics, music, African languages, MSS, letters and literature; nonlending library book collns, incl. books, music notes and cards from 1465 to 1900; open to public; six brs; 900,000 vols; Dir Dr HERMANN ROMER; publ. *Neujahrsblatt* (1 a year).

Zürich

ETH-Bibliothek (Library of the Swiss Federal Institute of Technology (ETH Zurich)): Rämistr. 101, 8092 Zürich; tel. 446322135; fax 446321087; e-mail info@library.ethz.ch; internet www.library.ethz.ch; f. 1855; specializes in science and technology; colln of architecture, civil engineering, engineering sciences, natural sciences and mathematics, system-oriented natural sciences, management and social sciences; 7.6m. vols and documents, 2.8m. monographs and bound journals, 2.2m. microforms, 1.8m. images, 400,000 maps, 260,000 MSS, 277,000 electronic documents, 13,000 e-journals, 5,300 current journals (printed), 145 databases, 63,000 e-books, 129,000 abstracts and indices (NEBIS catalogue); Dir Dr WOLFRAM NEUBAUER; Deputy Dir ANDREAS KIRSTEIN; publs *Schriftenreihe A: History of Science* (irregular), *Schriftenreihe B: Library Science* (irregular).

Schweizerisches Sozialarchiv/Archives sociales suisses: Stadelhoferstr. 12, 8001 Zürich; tel. 432688740; fax 432688759; e-mail kontakt@sozialarchiv.ch; internet www .sozialarchiv.ch; f. 1906; centre of social documentation; open to public; collects corporate archives of traditional and new social movements and private documents of activists during such movements; 210,000 vols, 1,476 current periodicals, 186,000 brochures and pamphlets, 1,700,000 newspaper cuttings, 29,000 archival documents, 100,000 iconic documents, 130 electronic journals; Head Librarian Dr ANITA ULRICH; Deputy Dir Dr URS KÄLIN.

Staatsarchiv des Kantons Zürich: Winterthurerstr. 170, 8057 Zürich; tel. and fax 446356911; e-mail staatsarchivzh@ji.zh.ch; internet www.staatsarchiv.zh.ch; f. 1837; archives of canton of Zürich and specialized library (local publns and collns of statutes and numerous pamphlets); archives: 30,000 m; 92,000 vols; Dir Dr BEAT GNÄDINGER.

Zentralbibliothek Zürich: Zähringerpl. 6, 8001 Zürich; tel. 442683100; fax 442683290; e-mail zb@zb.uzh.ch; internet www.zb.uzh .ch; f. 1914; city, cantonal and univ. library, inc. libraries of Naturforschende Gesellschaft in Zürich, Antiquarische Gesellschaft in Zürich, Geographisch-Ethnographische Gesellschaft Zürich, Schweizerischer Alpenclub, Allgemeine MusikGesellschaft Zürich, Bibliotheca Fennica; 5,250,000 vols, 106,000 MSS and autographs, 11,260 incunabula, 249,000 maps, and spec. colln of graphic arts (222,000 items), 35,000 records and cassettes; 8,700 current print periodicals, 45,000 electronic periodicals, 190 newspapers; Dir Prof. SUSANNA BLIGGENSTORFER.

Zentrale für Betriebswirtschaft & Zentrale für Wirtschaftsdokumentation, Universität Zürich: Plattenstr. 14, 8032 Zürich; tel. 446343911; fax 446344995; e-mail bfb@business.uzh.ch; internet www.business .uzh.ch/libraries/libraryba.html; f. 1910, present status 1990; attached to Univ. of Zurich; large worldwide colln of annual reports of major companies; periodicals, OECD colln, online library catalogues in fields of business studies and economics, daily newspapers, magazines and statistical material available; 36,000 vols, 122 periodicals; Dir KATHARINA HERTZBERG-SCHILLING.

Museums and Art Galleries

Aarau

Aargauer Kunsthaus: Aargauerpl., 5001 Aarau; tel. 628352330; fax 628352329; e-mail kunsthaus@ag.ch; internet www .aargauerkunsthaus.ch; f. 1959; Swiss painting and sculpture since 1750; colln of paintings by Caspar Wolf (1735–83), Adolf Staebli, and Auberjonois, Brühlmann, Amiet, G. Giacometti, Hodler, Meyer-Amden, Louis Soutter, Vallotton; temporary exhibitions; Dir MADELEINE SCHUPPLI; Deputy Dir and Curator STEPHAN KUNZ.

Avenches

Musée Romain Avenches: 1580 Avenches; tel. 265573300; fax 265573313; e-mail musee .romain@vd.ch; internet www.aventicum .org; f. 1824; situated at 2nd century AD Roman amphitheatre; mosaics, funerary stelae and sculptures; excavations of Aventicum; temporary exhibitions; library of 18,000 vols; Pres. Prof. P. DUCREY; Dir Dr MARIE-FRANCE MEYLAN KRAUSE; publ. *Aventicum* (2 a year).

Basel

Antikenmuseum Basel und Sammlung Ludwig: St Alban Graben 5, 4010 Basel; tel. 612011212; fax 612011210; e-mail info@ antikenmuseumbasel.ch; internet www .antikenmuseumbasel.ch; f. 1961; exhibition of art and culture of the Mediterranean area; collns of Greek art (2500–100 BC), Roman art (100 BC–AD 300), Etruscan art and Egyptian art, spec. exhibitions; Dir Prof. Dr PETER BLOME; Vice-Dir Dr ANDREA BIGNASCA; Curator Lic. VERA SLEHOFER; Curator Dr ANDRÉ WIESE; Curator Dr ELLA VAN DER MEIJDEN.

Historisches Museum Basel: Verwaltung, Steinenberg 4, 4051 Basel; tel. 612058600; fax 612058601; e-mail historisches.museum@ bs.ch; internet www.hmb.ch; f. 1894; 4 brs containing colln of objects from Middle Ages to 20th century, civic culture of Basel in 18th and 19th centuries and colln of old musical instruments, numismatics, coaches and sleighs; library of 21,000 vols, 38 journals, 183 periodicals; Dir Dr BURKARD VON RODA; Librarian DANIEL SUTER; publ. *Basler Kostbarkeiten* (1 a year).

Kunstmuseum Basel: St Albangraben 16, 4010 Basel; tel. 612066262; fax 612066252; internet www.kunstmuseumbasel.ch; f. 1662; pictures from 15th century to present day, notably by Witz, Holbein and contemporary painters; colln incl. Grünewald, Rembrandt, 16th- and 17th-century Dutch painting, Cézanne, Gauguin and Van Gogh; colln of cubist art; sculptures by Rodin and 20th-century artists; American art since 1950; dept of prints and drawings with old Upper Rhine, German and Swiss masters and 20th-century works; library of 150,000 vols, 200 periodicals; Dir Dr BERNHARD MENDES BÜRGI; Man. Dir FAUSTO DE LORENZO; Head of Library RAINER BAUM.

Attached Museum:

Museum für Gegenwartskunst (Museum of Contemporary Art): St Alban-Rheinweg 60, 4010 Basel; tel. 612066262; fax 612066253; internet www .kunstmuseumbasel.ch/en/museum-fuer--gegenwartskunst; f. 1980; contemporary art from collns of Emanuel Hoffmann Foundation and Kunstmuseum; Dir Dr BERNHARD MENDES BÜRGI; Curator NIKOLA DIETRICH.

Museum der Kulturen Basel: Muensterpl. 20, 4051 Basel; tel. 612665600; fax 612665605; e-mail info@mkb.ch; internet www.mkb.ch; f. 1849; ethnographical collections from all parts of the world, esp. from Oceania, Indonesia, South America and Europe; textiles; historic photographs, incl. stocks of fmr Swiss Museum of Ethnology; 300,000 objects; temporary exhibitions; library: see under Libraries and Archives; Dir Dr ANNA SCHMID; Vice-Dir Lic. DOMINIK WUNDERLIN; publs *Basler Beiträge zur Ethnologie*, guides.

Bern

Historisches Museum Bern: Helvetiapl. 5, 3005 Bern; tel. 313507711; fax 313507799;

e-mail info@bhm.ch; internet www.bhm.ch; f. 1894; Burgundian tapestries, Königsfeld Diptych, Bern's silver treasure, Stone Age, Celts and Romans, art from Asia and Oceania, bronze hydria from Grächwil and series of ethnographic and numismatic collns; colln from early Middle Ages to Ancien Régime; Einstein museum; temporary exhibitions; Dir Dr JAKOB MESSERLI; Vice-Dir Prof. Dr FELIX MÜLLER.

Kunstmuseum (Museum of Fine Arts Bern): Hodlerstr. 8–12, 3000 Bern 7; tel. 313280944; fax 313280955; e-mail info@kunstmuseumbern.ch; internet www.kunstmuseumbern.ch; f. 1879; colln of 3,000 paintings and sculptures incl. Italian paintings from 14th to 16th centuries; works by Swiss masters from 15th to 19th centuries; works illustrating devt of art since 19th century by Manet, Cézanne, Monet, Pissaro, Renoir, Van Gogh, members of 'Blaue Ritter', 'Brücke', and Bauhaus movements, Rothko and Pollock, and other modern works by Hodler and other Swiss, French and German artists; Hermann and Margrit Rupf Foundation, incl. paintings by Picasso, Braque, Léger, Gris and Kandinsky; Adolf Wölfli Foundation; graphic art colln of more than 48,000 drawings, engravings, photographs, video cassettes and films; library of 110,000 vols; Dir Dr MATTHIAS FREHNER; Curator Dr THERESE BHATTACHARYA-STETTLER; Curator Dr KATHLEEN BÜHLER; publ. *Berner Kunstmitteilungen* (4 a year).

Naturhistorisches Museum: Bernastr. 15, 3005 Bern; tel. 313507111; fax 313507499; e-mail contact@nmbe.ch; internet www.nmbe.ch; f. 1832; colln incl. 220 dioramas of Swiss mammals and birds, big game (esp. African), Swiss fish, amphibians and reptiles, minerals of Swiss Alps, invertebrates, hall of skeletons; Earth science exhibition; three depts: Earth sciences, mineralogy and paleontology, invertebrates and vertebrates; promotes research in Univ. of Bern; Dir Prof. Dr MARCEL GÜNTERT; publ. *Contributions to Natural History* (2 a year).

Zentrum Paul Klee Bern: Monument im Fruchtland 3, 3000 Bern 31; tel. 313590101; fax 313590102; e-mail kontakt@zpk.org; internet www.zpk.org; f. 2005, 4,000 works of art by Paul Klee (1879–1940) and colln of biographical material; exhibition space for contemporary artists; children's museum 'Creaviva'; organizes concerts and theatre; CEO URSINA BARANDUN.

Biel

Museum Schwab: Seevorstadt 50, 2502 Biel; tel. 323227603; fax 323233768; e-mail info@muschwab.ch; internet www.bielbienne.ch/ww/de/pub/aktiv/kultur/museen/schwab.cfm; f. 1873; contains prehistoric exhibits, esp. of lake-dwelling culture, New Stone Age, Bronze Age, and 2nd Iron Age; colln of items from Roman period (Petinesca); temporary exhibitions; Dir MADELEINE BETSCHAVT.

Chur

Bündner Kunstmuseum: POB 7000 Chur; tel. 812572868; fax 812572172; e-mail info@bkm.gr.ch; internet www.buendner-kunstmuseum.ch; f. 1900; contains works by Swiss artists, Segantini, Hodler, Alberto, Augusto and G. Giacometti, E. L. Kirchner and Angelica Kauffmann; exhibitions of Swiss and foreign art; Dir Dr BEAT STUTZER; Curator Dr KATHARINA AMMANN.

Fribourg

Musée d'Art et d'Histoire: 12 rue de Morat, 1700 Fribourg; tel. 263055140; fax 263055141; e-mail mahf@fr.ch; internet www.fr.ch/mahf; f. 1823; housed in Hotel Ratzé (16th century); collns of prehistoric, Roman and medieval exhibits; important collns of Swiss sculpture and painting since 11th century; works from Marcello Foundation; monumental pieces by Jean Tinguely; stained glass gallery; works of art in Freiburg in 19th and 20th centuries; Dir VERENA VILLIGER STEINAUER; Curator STEPHAN GASSER.

Geneva

Fondation Baur, Musée des Arts d'Extrême-Orient (Baur Foundation-Museum of Far Eastern Art): 8 rue Munier Romilly, 1206 Geneva; tel. 227043282; fax 227891845; e-mail musee@fondationbaur.ch; internet fondation-baur.ch; f. 1964; 9,000 Chinese and Japanese art objects; Chinese imperial ceramic ware, jades and snuff bottles from 10th to 19th centuries and Japanese prints, lacquer, netsuke, and sword fittings, Chinese lacquer ware and export ceramics; temporary exhibitions related to Chinese and Japanese artwork; library of 5,500 vols; Dir MONIQUE CRICK; Curator HELEN LOVEDAY.

Musée d'art et d'histoire: 2 rue Charles Galland, 1206 Geneva 3; tel. 224182600; fax 224182601; e-mail mah@ville-ge.ch; internet ville-ge.ch/mah; f. 1910; contains local prehistory section; Mediterranean, Egyptian, Near Eastern, Byzantine and Coptic archaeology; Italian, Dutch, Flemish, German, French, English and Swiss (esp. Genevese) paintings, paintings since beginning of 20th century, European sculpture, applied art and numismatic colln; collns of timepieces, enamels, jewellery and miniatures; library of 300,000 vols, 5,900 periodicals, 70,000 auction catalogs from 1857 to today; Dir JEAN-YVES MARIN; publs *Genava* (1 a year), *Journal des Musées d'art et d'histoire* (4 a year).

Attached Museums:

Cabinet d'Arts Graphiques: 5 promenade du Pin, 1204 Geneva; tel. 224182770; fax 224182771; e-mail cde@ville-ge.ch; f. 1886, as separate institution, part of Musées d'art et d'histoire 1910; 350,000 items covering five centuries of printmaking; multiples and 20th- and 21st-century artist's books; Keeper Dr CHRISTIAN RÜMELIN.

Maison Tavel: 6 rue du Puits Saint-Pierre, 1204 Geneva; tel. 224183700; fax 224183701; e-mail mah@ville-ge.ch; f. 1986; history of city; exhibits of artifacts and images from 14th to 19th century; Curator CHAIX NATHALIE.

Musée Ariana: 10 ave de la Paix, 1202 Geneva; tel. 224185450; fax 224185451; f. 1884; European and Eastern ceramics and glass; Curator ROLAND BLAETTLER.

Musée d'Histoire des Sciences: 128 rue de Lausanne, 1202 Geneva; tel. 224815060; fax 224815061; f. 1964; scientific instruments; library of 10,000 vols; Curator NINIAN HUBERT VAN BLYENBURGH.

Musée Rath: Pl. Neuve, 1204 Geneva; tel. 224183340; fax 224183351; e-mail mah@ville-ge.ch; f. 1828; temporary exhibitions; Dir JEAN-YVES MARIN.

Musée d'Art Moderne et Contemporain (Museum of Modern and Contemporary Art): 10 rue des Vieux-Grenadiers, 1205 Geneva; tel. 223206122; fax 227815681; internet www.mamco.ch; f. 1994; specialises in works since 1960; temporary exhibitions; archives of works of art; Dir CHRISTIAN BERNARD; Deputy Dir and Chief Curator FRANÇOISE NINGHETTO; Sec.-Gen. VALÉRIE MALLET.

Musée d'ethnographie de Genève: CP 191, 1211 Geneva 8; tel. 224184550; fax 224184551; e-mail musee.ethno@ville-ge.ch; internet www.ville-ge.ch/meg; f. 1901; African colln; American colln; Asian colln; European colln; Oceanic colln; musical instruments; 400 film colln; colln of 130,000 historical photographs; also houses Société Suisse des Américanistes and Archives Internationales de Musique Populaire; library of 45,000 vols, 1,500 periodicals; Dir Dr BORIS WASTIAU; publ. *Totem* (3 a year).

Muséum d'Histoire Naturelle: Route de Malagnou 1, 1208 Geneva; tel. 224186300; fax 224186301; e-mail info.mhn@ville-ge.ch; internet www.ville-ge.ch/mhng; f. 1820; depts of mammalogy and ornithology, herpetology and ichthyology, invertebrates, arthropods and insects, entomology, archaeozoology, geology and palaeontology, mineralogy; library of 200,000 vols, 40,000 monographs, 4,000 geological and topographical maps, 2,000 periodicals (800 current), also manages Bibliothèque de l'Association Nos Oiseaux and Bibliothèque du Centre de Coordination Ouest pour l'Étude et la Protection des Chauves-souris; Dir Dr DANIELLE DECROUEZ; Librarian CHRISTELLE MOUGIN; publs *Catalogue des Invertébrés de la Suisse*, *Le Rhinolophe* (1 a year), *Revue suisse de Zoologie* (4 a year), *Revue de Paléobiologie* (2 a year).

Glarus

Kunsthaus Glarus: Im Volksgarten, POB 665, 8750 Glarus; tel. 556402535; fax 556402519; e-mail office@kunsthausglarus.ch; internet www.kunsthausglarus.ch; f. 1870; 19th and 20th century Swiss art, Swiss and foreign contemporary art; temporary exhibitions; Pres. KASPAR MARTI; Vice-Pres. THOMAS ASCHMANN; Dir SABINE RUSTERHOLZ.

La Chaux-de-Fonds

Musée des Beaux-Arts: 33 rue des Musées, 2300 La Chaux-de-Fonds; tel. 329676077; fax 327220763; e-mail mba.vch@ne.ch; internet cdf-mba.ne.ch; f. 1864; colln of paintings, sculptures, videos and prints from 19th century (Matisse, Renoir, Van Gogh, Constable, Rouault) to now; works of Swiss artists (Anker, Vallotton, Bailly, Hodler), particularly of Neuchâtel district (Robert, Kaiser, l'Eplattenier, Perrin, Humbert, Le Corbusier, etc.); colln of European and American artists; temporary exhibitions; Dir LADA UMSTÄTTER.

Musée International d'Horlogerie: 29 rue des Musées, 2301 La Chaux-de-Fonds; tel. 329676861; fax 327220761; e-mail mih.vch@ne.ch; internet www.mih.ch; f. 1902; artistic and technical collns of watches, clocks, instruments and objects connected with measurement of time; time research dept; modern carillon; library of 3,000 vols; Curator M. LUDWIG OECHSLIN.

Lausanne

Musée Cantonal des Beaux-Arts: Palais de Rumine, Pl. Riponne 6, 1014 Lausanne; tel. 213163445; fax 213163446; e-mail info.beaux-arts@vd.ch; internet www.musees.vd.ch/fr/musee-des-beaux-arts; f. 1841; colln of works since 18th century mainly by Swiss artists; int. exhibitions of classical, modern and contemporary art; has library; Dir BERNARD FIBICHER; Curator CATHERINE LEPDOR; Curator NICOLE SCHWEIZER.

Musée Historique de Lausanne: 4 Pl. de la Cathédrale, 1005 Lausanne; tel. 213154101; fax 213154102; e-mail musee.historique@lausanne.ch; internet www.lausanne.ch/mhl; f. 1918; permanent and temporary exhibitions; model of 17th-century Lausanne, collns relating to local and regional history: silver, furniture, paintings and drawings, plans of the town, musical instruments; library; history of city from medieval times to 19th century; colln in three depts: paintings and graphic arts, objects, photographic collns; organizes interactive workshops, meetings, performances and concerts; Dir LAURENT GOLAY; publ. *Mémoire vive* (1 a year).

The Olympic Museum/Le Musée Olympique: 1 Quai d'Ouchy , 1006, Lausanne; tel. 216216511; fax 216216512; internet www.olympic.org/museum; f. 1993; attached to Int. Olympic Cttee; themed exhibitions; philatelic and numismatic exhibition; works of Arnoldi, Berrocal, Botero, Calder, Chillida, Folon, Graham, Niki de Saint Phalle, Tàpies, Mitoraj in bronze, marble and steel to offer their interpretation of sport, athlete and Olympic ideals; library of 23,000 monograph vols, 420 journals, 20,000 historical archival files, 9,500 films, 35,000 hours of film footage, 6,500 hours of sound files, 610,000 photographic documents (120,000 digitized); Dir of the IOC Information Management Dept PHILIPPE BLANCHARD; publ. *Symposium on Olympism – Proceedings* (1 a year).

Ligornetto

Museo Vincenzo Vela: 6853 Ligornetto; tel. 916407044; fax 916473241; e-mail museo.vela@bak.admin.ch; internet www.bundesmuseen.ch/museo_vela; f. 1898; bequests of sculptor Lorenzo Vela and painter Spartaco Vela; colln of 19th-century Lombard and Piedmontese paintings, autograph drawings and private collns of photographs; portraits of leading figures of the Risorgimento; landscaped garden; temporary exhibitions; Dir Dr GIANNA A. MINA; Sec. MARIANGELA ROSIELLO-AGNOLA.

Locarno

Museo Civico e Archeologico, Servizi Culturali: Via B. Rusca 5, 6600 Locarno; tel. 917563180; fax 917563268; e-mail servizi.culturali@locarno.ch; f. 1970; 14th-century fortress housing archaeological colln and historical museum; Dir Prof. RICCARDO CARAZZETTI.

Pinacoteca Casa Rusca: Servizi Culturali, Via B. Rusca 5, 6600 Locarno; tel. 917563185; fax 917519871; e-mail servizi.culturali@locarno.ch; f. 1987; restored 17th-century building housing municipal art gallery; incl. Jean Arp colln, and works by Calder, Hans Richter, Van Doesburg, etc.; Dir Prof RICCARDO CARAZZETTI.

Lucerne

Historisches Museum (Museum of History): Altes Zeughaus, Pfistergasse 24, POB 7437, 6000 Lucerne 7; tel. 412285424; fax 412285418; e-mail historischesmuseum@lu.ch; internet www.historischesmuseum.lu.ch; f. 1986; colln of coat of mail worn by Leopold III at battle of Sempach 1386, Milanese round shields from battle of Giornico 1478, column on Weinmarkt fountain by Conrad Lux 1481, gothic altarpieces, baroque sleigh owned by Amrhyn-Göldlin family 1673, Pewter vessels, Swiss costumes, coats of arms in stained glass, industrial products; organizes theatre tours and temporary exhibitions; Dir Dr HEINZ HORAT; Asst Dir and Curator Lic. ALEXANDRA STROBEL; Curator KURT LUSSI; publs *Jahrbuch der Historischen Gesellschaft Luzern*, *Jahresbericht des Historischen Museums*.

Kunstmuseum Luzern (Museum of Art Lucerne): Europapl. 1, 6002 Lucerne; tel. 412267800; fax 412267801; e-mail info@kunstmuseumluzern.ch; internet www.kunstmuseumluzern.ch; f. 1925; 18th- to 20th-century Swiss landscape painting and portraiture, Swiss art after 1945, foreign contemporary art; temporary exhibitions of contemporary works of art; Dir PETER FISCHER; Curator CHRISTOPH LICHTIN.

Richard Wagner-Museum: Richard Wagner-Weg 27, 6005 Lucerne; tel. 413602370; fax 413602379; e-mail info@richard-wagner-museum.ch; internet www.richard-wagner-museum.ch; f. 1933; home of Richard Wagner from 1866 to 1872; contains original scores of *Siegfried-Idyll, Schusterlied (Meistersinger)*, etchings, paintings, busts and Erard grand piano which accompanied Wagner throughout Europe; maintains image archive; Dir KATJA FLEISCHER.

Verkehrshaus der Schweiz (Swiss Transport Museum): Lidostr. 5, 6006 Lucerne; tel. 413704444; fax 413706168; e-mail mail@verkehrshaus.org; internet www.verkehrshaus.org; f. 1959; transport by land, water and air, communication and tourism; transportation archives; IMAX Theatre; planetarium; Dir DANIEL SUTER.

Lugano

Museo Civico di Belle Arti: Villa Ciani, Parco Civico, 6900 Lugano; tel. 588667201; fax 588667497; e-mail museodibellearti@lugano.ch; f. 1903; works by artists of Ticino since 17th century, and by French and Italian artists.

Neuchâtel

Musée d'Art et d'Histoire: Esplanade Léopold Robert 1, 2000 Neuchâtel; tel. 327177920; fax 327177929; e-mail mahn@ne.ch; internet www.mahn.ch; f. 1885; pictures, drawings, prints and sculptures by local and other Swiss artists; French 18th-and 19th-century works (Courbet, Corot, and others); French Impressionists; furniture, coins and medals; colln of 18th-century automata by Jaquet-Droz; has art library; Curator of Dept of Applied Arts CAROLINE JUNIER; Curator of Numismatic Cabinet GILLES PERRET; Curator of Visual Arts WALTER TSCHOPP.

Attached Gallery:

Galeries de l'Histoire: Ave Du Peyrou 7, 2000 Neuchâtel; tel. 327177920; fax 327177959; e-mail mahn@ne.ch; internet www.mahn.ch; f. 2003; Curator CHANTAL LAFONTANT VALLOTTON.

Musée d'Ethnographie: 4 rue Saint-Nicolas, 2000 Neuchâtel; tel. 327181960; fax 327181969; e-mail secretariat.men@ne.ch; internet www.men.ch; f. 1795; collns incl. Africa, America, Asia, Ancient Egypt, Europe, South Sea Islands, Arctic; musical instruments; library of 25,000 vols, 300 periodicals; music archives of original recordings; Curator MARC-OLIVIER GONSETH.

Muséum d'Histoire Naturelle: Rue des Terreaux 14, 2000 Neuchâtel; tel. 327177960; fax 327177969; e-mail info.museum@unine.ch; internet www.museum-neuchatel.ch; f. 1835; zoological, entomological, geological and botanical collns; Curator CHRISTOPHE DUFOUR; publ. *Ville de Neuchâtel, Bibliothèques et Musées* (1 a year).

Olten

Kunstmuseum Olten: Kirchgasse 8, 4603 Olten; tel. 622128676; fax 622123466; e-mail info@kunstmuseumolten.ch; internet www.kunstmuseumolten.ch; f. 1845; drawings and paintings by Martin Disteli (1802–1844); paintings, drawings and sculptures by Swiss artists; organizes school workshops and temporary exhibitions; library of 500 vols; Curator PATRICIA NUSSBAUM.

St Gallen

Historisches und Völkerkundemuseum: Museumstr. 50, 9000 St Gallen; tel. 712420642; fax 712420644; e-mail info@hmsg.ch; internet www.hmsg.ch; f. 1877, as Historisches Museum; present name 2004 following merger with Völkerkundemuseum; historical-archeological section: prehistoric and early history, history of St-Gall; period rooms from 16th to 19th century, glass paintings, furniture, pewter art, Swiss folk art, porcelain, costumes, fire and light, kitchen, pharmacy, religious art, flags, weapons and uniforms; ethnological section: culture of ancient Egypt, masks and sculptures of Africa, cult objects from Oceania, Inuit cultures of North America, native Indian tribes of north, central and South-America; Islamic cultural area from North Africa to Central Asia; cultural areas of India incl. Sri Lanka, Indochina, Indonesia, China and Japan; children's museum; Dir Dr DANIEL STUDER.

Kunstmuseum: Museumstr. 32, 9000 St Gallen; tel. 712420671; fax 712420672; e-mail info@kunstmuseumsg.ch; internet www.kunstmuseumsg.ch; f. 1877; works by 19th-and 20th-century masters, post-war sculpture, contemporary art; Dir Lic. ROLAND WÄSPE; Deputy Dir and Curator Lic. KONRAD BITTERLI; Curator Lic. MATTHIAS WOHLGEMUTH.

Museum Kirchhoferhaus: Museumstr. 27, 9000 St Gallen; tel. 712447521; fax 712420644; e-mail info@hmsg.ch; prehistoric and historic exhibits; 17th–19th century paintings by Graff, Diogg, Stäbli, Hodler, Corot, Renoir and others; peasant art of eastern Switzerland; furniture, silverware; closed to public; Dir Dr DANIEL STUDER.

Naturmuseum St Gallen: Museumstr. 32, 9000 St Gallen; tel. 712420670; fax 712420672; e-mail info@naturmuseumsg.ch; internet www.naturmuseumsg.ch; f. 1846; 19th-century exhibits incl. birds, plants and insects; Nile crocodile from 1623 and skeleton of Anatosaurus; colln available for scientific research; library of 2,000 vols; Curator Dr TONI BÜRGIN; publ. *Museumsbriefe*.

Textilmuseum mit Textilbibliothek: Vadianstr. 2, 9000 St Gallen; tel. 712221744; fax 712234239; e-mail info@textilmuseum.ch; internet www.textilmuseum.ch; f. 1886; colln of tissues of Egyptian graves, historical embroideries from 14th century, handmade lace from major European centres of excellence, ethnographic textiles, historic fabrics and costumes, handmade utensils and objects of contemporary textile art; library of 20,000 vols; special colln of 2m. textile samples; Dir HANSPETER SCHMID; Curator URSULA KARBACHER; Librarian REGULA LÜSCHER.

Schaffhausen

Museum zu Allerheiligen: Baumgartenstr. 6, 8200 Schaffhausen; tel. 526330777; fax 526330788; e-mail admin.allerheiligen@stsh.ch; internet www.allerheiligen.ch; f. 1938; archaeology, history, natural history, numismatic and graphics colln; art of City and Canton of Schaffhausen and of Switzerland; Dir Dr PETER JEZLER.

Solothurn

Kunstmuseum Solothurn: Werkhofstr. 30, 4500 Solothurn; tel. 326244000; fax 326225001; e-mail kunstmuseum@solothurn.ch; internet www.kunstmuseum-so.ch; f. 1902; colln of works by Hans Holbein the younger; int. colln, incl. works by Van Gogh, Klimt, Matisse, Picasso and Braque; Swiss art colln from 1850 to 1990, incl. works by Hodler; paintings, drawings, water-colours; primitive art section; Curator Dr CHRISTOPH VÖGELE; Sec. CHRISTINE KOBEL.

Vevey

Musée Jenisch Vevey: 2 ave de la Gare, 1800 Vevey; tel. 219253520; fax 219253525;

e-mail info@museejenisch.ch; internet www.museejenisch.ch; f. 1898; comprises Fine Arts Museum (19th-and 20th-century Swiss and foreign artists, old master drawings, Oskar Kokoschka Foundation, Balthus Foundation) and Cantonal Museum of Prints (16th–20th century prints); Dir DOMINIQUE RODRIZZANI.

Winterthur

Kunstmuseum Winterthur: Museumstr. 52, POB 235, 8402 Winterthur; Museumstr. 52, 8402 Winterthur; tel. 522675162; fax 522675317; e-mail info@kmw.ch; internet www.kmw.ch; f. 1848; painting and sculpture from late 19th century to present, incl. works by Monet, Degas, Picasso, Gris, Léger, Klee, Schlemmer, Magritte, Arp, Kandinsky, Bonnard, Maillol, Van Gogh, Rodin, M. Rosso, Lehmbruck, Brancusi, Morandi, Giacometti, de Staël, Guston, Bishop, Marden, D. Rabinowitch, Richter, Fontana, Manzoni, Merz, Kounellis, Fabro, Paolini; drawings and prints; administered by Kunstverein Winterthur; Pres. Dr JÜRG SPILLER; Dir Dr DIETER SCHWARZ; publs *Jahresbericht des Kunstvereins Winterthur*, colln and exhibition catalogues.

Museum Oskar Reinhart am Stadtgarten: Stadthausstr. 6, 8400 Winterthur; tel. 522675172; fax 522676228; e-mail museum.oskarreinhart@win.ch; internet www.museumoskarreinhart.ch; f. 1951; public art gallery; exhibits paintings and drawings; Pres. ERNST WOHLWEND; Curator PETER WEGMANN.

Zürich

Botanischer Garten und Museum der Universität Zürich: Zollikerstr. 107, 8008 Zürich; tel. 446348461; fax 446348404; e-mail botanischer.garten@systbot.uzh.ch; internet www.bguz.uzh.ch; f. 1837; worldwide herbarium, esp. of African and New Caledonian flora; exhibitions on plants; organizes guided tours for public and schools, courses, exhibitions; library of 100,000 vols; Dir Prof. Dr HANS PETER LINDER; Head Curator PETER ENZ.

Graphische Sammlung der ETH Zürich (Collection of Prints and Drawings of ETH Zurich): Rämistr. 101, 8092 Zürich; tel. 446324046; fax 446321168; e-mail info@gs.ethz.ch; internet www.gs.ethz.ch; f. 1867; 150,000 prints and drawings from 15th century to present, with special reference to devt of graphic art in Switzerland; Chief Curator PAUL TANNER; Curator Dr MICHAEL MATILE; Curator and Registrar ALEXANDRA BARCAL.

Kunsthaus Zürich: POB, 8024 Zürich; Heimpl. 1, 8001 Zürich; tel. 442538484; fax 442538433; e-mail info@kunsthaus.ch; internet www.kunsthaus.ch; f. 1910; chiefly paintings and sculptures since 19th century by Swiss and foreign artists; selection of old masters; extensive colln covering all branches of graphic art since 16th century; unique Giacometti colln; Monet, Cézanne, van Gogh, Picasso and Chagall; contemporary artists incl. Baselitz, Beuys and Twombly; video colln; library of 244,000 vols, 320 journals; Dir Dr CHRISTOPH BECKER; Deputy Dir CHRISTIAN KLEMM; Curator TOBIA BEZZOLA; Curator BICE CURIGER; publ. *Kunsthaus-Magazin* (4 a year).

Musée Suisse/Schweizerisches Landesmuseum (Swiss National Museum): Museumstr. 2, 8021 Zürich; tel. 442186511; fax 442112949; e-mail kanzlei@snm.admin.ch; internet www.landesmuseen.ch; f. 1898; incl. Castle of Prangins, Forum of Swiss History Schwyz and collns centre in Affoltern and Albis; Switzerland's largest colln of objects regarding cultural history of Switzerland; permanent and spec. exhibitions cover all periods from prehistory to the 21st century; library of 90,000 vols, 2,000 periodicals; Pres. MARKUS NOTTER; Dir Dr ANDREAS SPILLMAN; Deputy Dir MARKUS LEUTHARD; publs *Kulturmagazin* (in German and French, 4 a year), *Zeitschrift für Schweizerische Archäologie und Kunstgeschichte* (4 a year).

Museum für Gestaltung Zürich (Museum of Design Zürich): POB, 8031 Zürich; Ausstellungsstr. 60, 8005 Zürich; tel. and fax 434466767; e-mail welcome@museum-gestaltung.ch; internet www.museum-gestaltung.ch; f. 1875; attached to Zurich Univ. of the Arts; design colln, graphic art colln, poster colln; temporary exhibitions, research, education and publishing; library: public library of 90,000 vols; Dir CHRISTIAN BRÄNDLE.

Affiliated Museum:

Museum Bellerive: Höschgasse 3, 8008 Zürich; tel. 434464469; fax 434464503; e-mail welcome@museum-gestaltung.ch; internet www.museum-bellerive.ch; f. 1968; colln of applied and fine arts in glass, ceramics, textiles, marionettes, musical instruments; two or three exhibitions annually exploring art and design, modern classics and recent trends; Man. JACQUELINE GREENSPAN; Asst Curator TANJA TRAMPE.

Museum Rietberg Zürich: Gablerstr. 15, 8002 Zürich; tel. 442063131; fax 442063132; e-mail museum.rietberg@zuerich.ch; internet www.stadt-zuerich.ch/kultur/de/index/institutionen/museum_rietberg.html; f. 1952; works of art from Asia, Africa, Oceania and Americas; E. von der Heydt colln; organizes tours and educational programmes; Dir Dr ALBERT LUTZ; Deputy Dir KATHARINA EPPRECHT; Chief Curator JOHANNES BELTZ.

Paläontologisches Institut und Museum der Universität: Karl Schmid-Str. 4, 8006 Zürich; tel. 446342339; fax 446344923; internet www.pim.uzh.ch; f. 1991; attached to Univ. Zürich; Triassic reptiles and fishes, Triassic and Jurassic invertebrates, Tertiary mammals; library of 5,500 vols, 30,000 publs; Curator Dr HEINZ FURRER.

Zoologisches Museum der Universität (Zoological Museum of the University of Zurich): Karl Schmid-Str. 4, 8006 Zürich; tel. 446343838; fax 446343839; e-mail zminfo@zm.uzh.ch; internet www.zm.uzh.ch; f. 1837; research in systematics, taxonomy, and population biology; exhibitions of birds, molluscs and mammals of world and Swiss fauna; public slide shows and films; library of 7,000 vols; Dir LUKAS F. KELLER.

Universities

ÉCOLE POLYTECHNIQUE FÉDÉRALE DE LAUSANNE

1015 Lausanne
Telephone: 216931111
Fax: 216934380
E-mail: webmaster@epfl.ch
Internet: www.epfl.ch

Founded 1853, present status 1969
Language of instruction: French
Federal state control
Academic year: October to July

Pres.: Prof. PATRICK AEBISCHER
Vice-Pres. for Academic Affairs: Prof. PHILIPPE GILLET
Vice-Pres. for Innovation and Technology Transfer: Prof. ADRIENNE CORBOUD FUMAGALLI
Vice-Pres. for Institutional Affairs: Prof. MARIN VETTERLI
Vice-Pres. for Planning and Logistics: Prof. FRANCIS-LUC PERRET
Gen. Sec.: JEAN-FRANÇOIS RICCI (acting)
Library Dir: DAVID AYMONIN

Library: see Libraries and Archives
Number of teachers: 275
Number of students: 6,000

DEANS

College of Human Sciences: Prof. FRANCESCO PANESE (acting)
College of Management of Technology: Dr MARTIN VETTERLI (acting)
School of Architecture, Civil and Environmental Engineering: Prof. MARC PARLANGE
School of Basic Sciences: Prof. THOMAS RIZZO
School of Computer and Communication Sciences: Dr MARTIN VETTERLI
School of Engineering: Prof. DEMETRI PSALTIS
School of Life Sciences: DIDIER TRONO

PROFESSORS

Department of Architecture:

ABOU-JAOUDÉ, G., Computer-Aided Design
BERGER, P., Architecture
CANTAFORA, A., Architecture
CHUARD, P., Building Techniques
DUTRY, G.
LAMUNIÈRE, I., History and Theory of Architecture
LUCAN, J., Architectural Theory
MANGEAT, V., Architecture
MARCHAND, B., History and Theory of Architecture
MESTELAN, P., Architecture
MOREL, C., Building Techniques
ORTELLI, L., Architectural Theory
SCARTEZZINI, J.-L., Solar Energy Research Building
STEINMANN, M., Architecture
THALMANN, P., Economics

Department of Biomedical Engineering:

EBRAHIMI, T., Visual Information Processing
LASSER, T., Biomedical Optics
SALATHE, R., Applied Optics
STERGIOPULOS, N., Cardiovascular Technology
UNSER, M., Biomedical Imaging
ZUPPIROLI, L., Optoelectronics

Department of Chemistry and Chemical Engineering:

BODENHAUSEN, G.
BÜNZLI, J.-C.
DYSON, P.
FREITAG, R., Laboratory of Cellular Biotechnology
GIRAULT, H., Institute of Physical Chemistry
GRAETZEL, M., Institute of Physical Chemistry
JOHNSSON, K.
KROSSING, I.
MERBACH, A.
MUTTER, M.
PITSCH, S.
RENKEN, A., Institute of Chemical Engineering III
RIZZO, T., Institute of Physical Chemistry
RÖTHLISBERGER, U.
ROULET, R.
SEVERIN, K.
VOGEL, H., Laboratory of Polymer Chemistry
VOGEL, P.
VON STOCKAR, U.

Department of Civil Engineering:

BADOUX, M., Institute of Reinforced and Prestressed Concrete
BOVY, P., Institute of Transportation and Planning
BRUEHWILER, E., Maintenance, Construction and Safety of Structures
DESCOEUDRES, F., Road Mechanics

DUMONT, A.-G., Institute of Soils, Rocks and Foundations
FAVRE, R., Institute of Structural Engineering
FREY, FR., Laboratory of Structural and Continuum Mechanics
GRAF, W.-H., Hydraulic Research
HIRT, M., Institute of Steel Structures
JACQUOT, P., Stress Analysis and Measurement
LAFITTE, R., Institute of Hydraulics and Energy
MARCHAND, J.-D., Economics of Infrastructure
NATTERER, J., Timber Construction
PARRIAUX, A., Geology
PERRET, F.-L., Construction Management
PFLUG, L., Optical Stress Analysis Laboratory
RIVIER, R., Institute of Transportation and Planning
SANDOZ, J.-L., Timber Construction
SARLOS, G., Institute of Hydraulics and Energy
SCHLEISS, A., Institute of Hydraulics and Energy
SMITH, I., Institute of Reinforced and Prestressed Concrete
VULLIET, L., Soil Mechanics

Department of Communications Systems:
HUBAUX, J.-P.
KUNT, M.
LE BOUDEC, J.-Y.
NUSSBAUMER, H.
PETITPIERRE, C.
VETTERLI, M.

Department of Computer Science:
BOURLARD, H., Artificial Intelligence Laboratory
CORAY, G., Dir, Theoretical Computer Science Laboratory
COULON, F. DE, Dir, Computer-Aided-Learning Laboratory
FALTINGS, B., Dir, Artificial Intelligence Laboratory
GERSTNER, W., Mini- and Micro-Computer Laboratory
HERSCH, R.-D., Dir, Peripheral Systems Laboratory
LE BOUDEC, J.-Y., Dir, Communication Network Laboratory
MANGE, D., Dir, Logic Systems Laboratory
NICOUD, J.-D., Dir, Mini- and Micro-Computer Laboratory
PETITPIERRE, C., Dir, Data Communication Laboratory
SANCHEZ, E., Logic Systems Laboratory
SCHIPER, A., Dir, Operating Systems Laboratory
SPACCAPIETRA, S., Dir, Databases Laboratory
STROHMEIER, A., Dir, Software Engineering Laboratory
THALMANN, D., Dir, Computer Graphics Laboratory
THIRAN, P., Institute of Data Communication
WEGMANN, A., Industrial Computer Engineering Laboratory
ZAHND, J., Dir, Logic Systems Laboratory

Department of Electrical Engineering:
DECLERCQ, M., Electronics Laboratory
ENZ, C., General Electronics
FAZAN, P., Electronics Laboratory
GERMOND, A., Electrical Installations Laboratory
IONESCU, M.-A., General Engineering
JUFER, M., Electromechanics Laboratory
KAYAL, M., General Electronics
KUNT, M., Signal Processing Laboratory
MLYNEK, D., Electronics Laboratory
MOSIG, J., Electromagnetism and Acoustics
ROBERT, PH., Metrology Laboratory
ROSSI, M., Electromagnetism and Microwaves Laboratory
RUFER, A.-C., Electronics Laboratory
SIMOND, J.-J., Electromechanics and Electrical Machines Laboratory
SKRIVERVIK, A., Electromagnetism and Acoustics
WAVRE, N., Electromechanics and Electrical Machines Laboratory

Department of Environmental Engineering:
BEY, I., Atmospheric Chemistry Modelling
HARMS, H., Pedology
HOLLIGER, C., Environmental Biotechnology
JOLLIET, O., Ecosystem Management
MERMOUD, A., Institute of Development of Earth and Water
MUSY, A., Institute of Agricultural Engineering
PÉRINGER, P., Institute of Environmental Engineering
SCHLAEPFER, R., Soils and Water
TARRADELLAS, J., Institute of Environmental Engineering
VAN DEN BERGH, H., Institute of Environmental Engineering
VÉDY, J.-C., Institute of Agricultural Engineering

Department of Materials Science and Engineering:
HOFMANN, H., Powder Technology Laboratory
JACQUOT, P., Meteorology and Photonics
KURZ, W., Metallurgy
LANDOLT, D., Chemical Metallurgy
MÅNSON, J.-A., Polymer Composite Technology
MATHIEU, H. J., Chemical Metallurgy Laboratory
MORTENSEN, A., Mechanical Metallurgy Laboratory
RAPPAZ, M., Physical Metallurgy Laboratory
SCRIVENER, K., Construction Materials
SETTER, N., Ceramics Laboratory

Department of Mathematics:
BARTHOLDI, L.
BAYER-FLUCKIGER, E.
BEN AROUS, G., Probability Theory
BUSER, P., Geometry
DACAROGNA, B., Analysis
DALANG, R., Probability Theory
DAVISON, A.
DERIGHETTI, A.
JORIS, H.
LIEBLING, T., Operational Research
MADDOCKS, J., Analysis
MORGENTHALER, S., Statistics
MOUNTFORD, T.
OJANGUREN, M., Mathematical Methodology
QUARTERONI, A.
RAPPAZ, J.
RATIU, T. S.
SHOKROLLAHI, A.
STUART, C., Numerical Analysis and Simulation
THÉVENAZ, J.
WERRA, D. DE, Operational Research

Department of Mechanical Engineering:
AVELLAN, F., Institute of Hydraulic Machinery and Fluid Mechanics
BÖLCS, A., Institute of Thermal Engineering
BONVIN, D., Institute of Automatic Control
BOTSIS, J., Applied Mechanics
CURNIER, A., Laboratory of Applied Mechanics
DEVILLE, M., Institute of Hydraulic Machinery and Fluid Mechanics
FAVRAT, D., Laboratory of Industrial Energy Systems
GIOVANOLA, J., Laboratory of Mechanical Systems Design
GLARDON, R., Applied Mechanics and Institute of Machine Design
LONGCHAMP, R., Institute of Automatics
MONKEWITZ, P., Institute of Hydraulic Machinery and Fluid Mechanics
OWEN, R., Fluid Mechanics
THOME, J., Laboratory of Applied Thermodynamics
XIROUCHAKIS, P., Applied Mechanics and Institute of Machine Design
ZYSSET, P., Laboratory of Applied Mechanics

Department of Microengineering:
BLEULER, H., Institute of Microtechnology
CLAVEL, R., Institute of Microtechnology
GIJS, M., Microsystems
HONGLER, M.-O., Microtechnology
JACOT-DESCOMBES, J., Institute of Microtechnology
LEBLEBICI, Y., Microelectronics
NICOLLIER, C., Institute of Microtechnology
PFLUGER, P., Institute of Microtechnology
POPOVIC, R., Institute of Microtechnology
RENAUD, P., Institute of Microtechnology
RYSER, P., Microtechnology
SIEGWART, R., Institute of Microtechnology

Department of Physics:
ANSERMET, J.-P., Experimental Physics Institute
BALDERESCHI, A., Applied Physics Institute
BARÈS, P.-A., Theoretical Physics
BENOIT, W., Nuclear Engineering Institute
BRÜESCH, P., General Physics of Solids
BUTTET, J., Experimental Physics Institute
CHÂTELAIN, A., Experimental Physics Institute
CHAWLA, R., Nuclear Engineering Institute
DEVEAUD-PLEDRAN, B., Micro- and Optoelectronics Institute
FIVAZ, R., Dir, Applied Physics Institute
GRUBER, C., Theoretical Physics Institute
ILEGEMS, M., Dir, Micro- and Opto-electronics Institute
KAPON, E., Micro- and Opto-electronics Institute
KERN, K., Experimental Physics Institute
KUNZ, H., Theoretical Physics Institute
LÉVY, F., Applied Physics Institute
MARGARITONDO, G., Applied Physics Institute
MARTIN, J.-L., Dir, Nuclear Engineering Institute
MARTIN, PH., Theoretical Physics Institute
MEISTER, J.-J., Applied Physics Institute
MONOT, R., Experimental Physics Institute
QUATTROPANI, A., Theoretical Physics Institute
REINHART, F. K., Micro- and Opto-electronics Institute
STERGIOPOULOS, N., Medical Engineering
ZUPPIROLI, L., Nuclear Engineering Institute

EIDGENÖSSISCHE TECHNISCHE HOCHSCHULE ZÜRICH (ETH)
(Swiss Federal Institute of Technology)

8092 Zürich
HG, Rämistr. 101, 8092 Zürich
Telephone: 446321111
Fax: 446321010
E-mail: praesidium@sl.ethz.ch
Internet: www.ethz.ch

Founded 1855
Languages of instruction: French, German
Federal State control
Academic year: October to July (two semesters)

Pres.: Prof. Dr RALPH EICHLER
Rector: Prof. HEIDI WUNDERLI-ALLENSPACH
Vice-Pres. for Research and Corporate Relations: Prof. Dr ROLAND Y. SIEGWART
Vice-Pres. for Finance and Control: Dr ROBERT PERICH

Vice-Pres. for Human Resources and Infrastructure: Prof. Dr ROMAN BOUTELLIER
Sec.-Gen.: HUGO BRETSCHER

Library: see Libraries and Archives
Number of teachers: 400
Number of students: 16,000

Publications: *ETH Globe* (4 a year), *ETH Life* (online magazine), *ETH Life Print* (9 a year)

PROFESSORS

Agriculture and Food Science (D-Agrl, ETH Zentrum, 8092 Zürich; tel. 446323887; fax 446321161; e-mail rutz@agrl.ethz.ch; internet www.agrl.ethz.ch/):

ABDULAI, A., Economics of Nutrition
AMADÒ, R., Food Chemistry
AMRHEIN, N., Plant Science
APEL, K., Plant Science
DORN, S., Applied Entomology
ESCHER, F., Food Technology
FROSSARD, E., Plant Nutrition
GRUISSEM, W., Plant Biotechnology
HURRELL, R. F., Human Nutrition
KREUZER, M., Animal Nutrition
KÜNZI, N., Animal Breeding
LANGHANS, W., Physiology and Animal Husbandry
LEHMANN, B., Farm and Agrobusiness Management
MCDONALD, B., Phytopathology
PUHAN, Z., Dairy Science
RIEDER, P., Agricultural Market and Policy
STAMP, P., Agronomy and Plant Breeding
STRANZINGER, G., Breeding Biology
TEUBER, M., Food Microbiology
WENK, C., Biology of Nutrition
WINDHAB, E., Food Engineering

Applied Biosciences (D-Anbi, Uni Irchel, Winterthurerstr. 110, 8057 Zürich; tel. 446356042; fax 446356883; e-mail wyrsck@anbi.ethz.ch; internet www.pharma.ethz.ch):

BOUTELLIER, U., Exercise Physiology
FOLKERS, G., Pharmaceutical Chemistry
MERKLE, H. P., Galenic Pharmacy
MÖHLER, H., Pharmacology
MÜNTENER, M., Anatomy
MURER, K.
NERI, D., Protein Engineering
SCHUBIGER, P. A., Radiopharmacy
STICHER, O., Pharmacognosy and Phytochemistry
WUNDERLI-ALLENSPACH, H., Biopharmacy

Architecture (D-Arch, ETH Honggerberg, 8093 Zürich; tel. 446332885; fax 446331053; e-mail michel@arch.ethz.ch; internet www.arch.ethz.ch):

ANGÉLIL, M., Architecture and Design
CAMINADA, G. A., Architecture and Design
CAMPI, M., Architecture and Design
DANIELS, K., Building Systems
DE MEURON, P., Architecture and Design
DEPLAZES, A., Architecture and Technology
DIENER, R., Architecture and Design
EBERLE, D., Architecture and Design
ENGELI, M., Architecture and Computer-Aided Architectural Design
FLÜCKIGER, H., Spatial Development
HERZOG, J., Architecture and Design
HOVESTADT, L., Computer-Aided Architectural Design
JENNY, P., Visual Design
KELLER, B., Building Physics
KÖHLER, B., History and Theory of Architecture
KOLLHOFF, H., Architecture and Technology
KRAMEL, H. E., Architecture and Technology
KRUCKER, B., Architecture and Design
KÜNZLE, O., Building Structures
LYNN, G., Spatial Conception and Exploration
MAGNAGO LAMPUGNANI, V., History of Urbanism
MEILI, M., Architecture and Design
MEYER, A., Architecture and Design
MEYER, P., Architecture and Building Realization
MÖRSCH, G., Preservation of Historical Monuments and Sites
OECHSLIN, W., History of Art and Architecture
OSWALD, F., Architecture and Urbanism
RUCHAT-RONCATI, F., Architecture and Design
RÜEGG, A., Architecture and Design
SCHETT, W., Architecture and Design
SCHMID, W. A., Regional Planning and Methodology
SCHMITT, G., Computer-Aided Architectural Design
SIK, M., Architecture and Design
THIERSTEIN, A., Spatial Development

Biology (D-Biol, ETH Zentrum, 8092 Zürich; tel. 446325942; fax 446321151; e-mail ulrich@biol.ethz.ch; internet www.biol.ethz.ch):

AEBI, M., Microbiology
BAILEY, J. E., Biotechnology
BARRAL, Y., Biochemistry
DIMROTH, P., Microbiology
EPPENBERGER, H. M., Cell Biology
FELDON, J., Behavioural Neurobiology
GLOCKSHUBER, R., Molecular Biology and Biophysics
HELENIUS, A., Biochemistry
HENGARTNER, H., Experimental Immunology
HENNECKE, H., Microbiology
KUTAY, U., Biochemistry
LEISINGER, TH., Microbiology
MANSUY, I., Neurobiology
MARTIN, K. A. C., Systematic Neurophysiology
RICHMOND, T. J., Molecular Biology and Biophysics
SCHWAB, M. E., Neuroscience
SUTER, U., Cell Biology
THÖNY-MEYER, L., Molecular Microbiology
WERNER, S., Cell Biology
WINKLER, F. K., Structural Biology
WITHOLT, B., Biotechnology
WÜRGLER, F. E., Genetics
WÜTHRICH, K., Molecular Biology and Biophysics

Chemistry (D-Chem, ETH Zentrum, 8093 Zürich; tel. 446323055; fax 446321058; e-mail hauser@chem.ethz.ch; internet www.chem.ethz.ch):

BAIKER, A., Chemical Engineering and Catalysis
CARREIRA, E. M., Organic Chemistry
CHEN, P., Physical-organic Chemistry
DIEDERICH, F., Organic Chemistry
GRÜTZMACHER, H., Inorganic Chemistry
GÜNTHER, D., Analytical Chemistry
HILVERT, D., Organic Chemistry
HÜNENBERGER, PH. H., Physical Chemistry
HUNGERBÜHLER, K., Safety and Environmental Protection
KOPPENOL, W. H., Bioinorganic Chemistry
MEIER, B. H., Physical Chemistry
MERKT, F., Physical Chemistry
MORBIDELLI, M., Chemical Reaction Engineering
NESPER, R., Inorganic Chemistry
PRINS, R., Industrial Chemistry
QUACK, M., Physical Chemistry
RÖTHLISBERGER, U., Computer-Aided Inorganic Chemistry
RYS, P., Technical Chemistry
SCHWEIGER, A., Physical Chemistry
SEEBACH, D., Organic Chemistry
TOGNI, A., Organometallic Chemistry
VAN GUNSTEREN, W. F., Computer-Aided Chemistry
VASELLA, A. T., Organic Chemistry
WILD, U. P., Physical Chemistry
WOKAUN, A., Chemistry
ZENOBI, R., Analytical Chemistry

Civil, Environmental and Geomatics Engineering (D-Baug, ETH Honggerberg, 8093 Zürich; tel. 446332691; fax 446331088; e-mail altenburger@baug.ethz.ch; internet www.baum.ethz.ch):

AMANN, P., Soil Engineering and Soil Mechanics
ANDERHEGGEN, E., Applied Computer Science
AXHAUSEN, K. W., Traffic Engineering
BACCINI, P., Material Flux and Waste Management
BÖHNI, H., Materials Science
BRÄNDLI, H., Traffic Engineering
BURLANDO, P., Hydrology and Water Resource Management
CAROSIO, A., Geodesy
FABER, M., Structural Engineering
FONTANA, M., Structural Engineering
GIGER, CH., Geographic Information Systems
GIRMSCHEID, G., Construction Management and Process Technology
GRÜN, A., Photogrammetry
GUJER, W., Sanitary Engineering
HERMANNS STENGELE, R., Geotechnics
HURNI, L., Cartography
INGENSAND, H., Geodesy
KAHLE, H.-G., Geodesy
KINZELBACH, W., Hydromechanics
KOVARI, K., Tunnelling
MARTI, P., Structural Engineering
MINOR, H.-E., Hydraulic Structures
SCHALCHER, H.-R., Planning and Construction Management
SCHMID, W. A., Rural Engineering and Planning
SPRINGMAN, S., Geotechnical Engineering
VIRTANEN, S., Metallic High-Performance Materials
VOGEL, TH., Structural Engineering
WITTMANN, F. H., Materials Science

Computer Science (D-Infk, ETH Zentrum, 8092 Zürich; tel. 446327220; fax 446321620; e-mail haeni@inf.ethz.ch; internet www.inf.ethz.ch):

ALONSO, G., Information Systems
BIERE, A., Computer Systems
GANDER, W., Scientific Computing
GONNET, G. H., Scientific Computing
GROSS, M., Computer Graphics
GROSS, TH., Computer Systems
GUTKNECHT, J., Computer Systems
MATTERN, F., Information Systems
MAURER, U., Theoretical Computer Science
NAGEL, K., Scientific Computing
NIEVERGELT, J., Theoretical Computer Science
NORRIE, M., Information Systems
RICHTER-GEBERT, J., Theoretical Computer Science
SCHEK, H.-J., Information Systems
SCHIELE, B., Scientific Computing
STÄRK, R., Theoretical Computer Science
STRICKER, TH. M., Computer Systems
WELZL, E., Theoretical Computer Science
WIDMAYER, P., Theoretical Computer Science
ZEHNDER, C. A., Information Systems

Earth Sciences (D-Erdw, ETH Zentrum, 8092 Zürich; tel. 446325647; fax 446321112; e-mail bonadurer@erdw.ethz.ch; internet www.erdw.ethz.ch):

BURG, J.-P., Structural Geology
GIARDINI, D., Seismology and Geodynamics
GREEN, A. G., Applied Geophysics
HALLIDAY, A. N., Isotope Geochemistry
HEINRICH, CH. A., Mineral Resources and Processes of the Earth's Interior
KUNZ, M., Crystallography
LÖW, S., Engineering Geology

LOWRIE, W., Geophysics
MCKENZIE, J., Earth System Sciences
SEWARD, T. M., Geochemistry
STEURER, W., Crystallography
THIERSTEIN, H. R., Micropalaeontology
THOMPSON, A. B., Petrology
TROMMSDORFF, V., Petrography

Electrical Engineering (D-Elek, ETH Zentrum, 8092 Zürich; tel. 446325002; fax 446321492; e-mail marcel.kreuzer@ee.ethz.ch; internet www.itet.ethz.ch):

ANDERSSON, G., Electrical Energy Systems and Processes
BÄCHTOLD, W., Electromagnetic Fields and Microwaves
DAHLHAUS, D., Mobile Radio Communication
EGGIMANN, F., Signal and Information Processing
ERLEBACH, TH., Theory of Communication Networks
FICHTNER, W., Integrated Systems
FRÖHLICH, K., Electric Power Transmission and High Voltage Technology
GUT, J., Military Security Technology
HUANG, Q., Integrated Systems
HUBBELL, J. A., Biomedical Engineering and Medical Informatics
HUGEL, J., Electrical Engineering Design
JÄCKEL, H., Electronics
KÜNDIG, A., Computer Engineering and Communication Networks
LAPIDOTH, A., Information Theory
LEUTHOLD, P., Communication Technology
LOELIGER, H.-A., Signals Processing
MORARI, M., Automatic Control
NIEDERER, P., Biomedical Engineering and Medical Informatics
PLATTNER, B., Computer Engineering and Communications Networks
SCHAUFELBERGER, W., Automatic Control
STILLER, B., Communication Systems
THIELE, L., Computer Engineering
TRÖSTER, G., Electronics
VAHLDIECK, R., Field Theory
VAN GOOL, L., Computer Vision

Environmental Sciences (D-Umnw, ETH Zentrum, 8092 Zürich; tel. 446322523; fax 446321309; e-mail secretariat@umnw.ethz.ch; internet www.env.ethz.ch/):

DAVIES, H. C., Atmospheric Physics, Dynamic Meteorology
EDWARDS, P., Plant Ecology
EWALD, K., Nature and Landscape Protection
FLÜHLER, H., Soil Physics
IMBODEN, D., Environmental Physics
KAISER, F. G., Human–Environmental Relations
KRETZSCHMAR, R., Soil Chemistry
MIEG, H. A., Human–Environmental Relations
OHMURA, A., Climatology
PETER, TH., Atmospheric Chemistry
ROY, B. A., Plant Biodiversity
SCHÄR, C., Hydrology and Climatology
SCHMID-HEMPEL, P., Experimental Ecology
SCHOLZ, R. W., Environmental Sciences
SCHULIN, R., Soil Protection
SCHWARZENBACH, R., Organic Environmental Chemistry
WALDVOGEL, A., Atmospheric Physics
WARD, J. V., Aquatic Ecology
WEHRLI, B., Aquatic Chemistry
ZEHNDER, A. J. B, Environmental Biotechnology
ZEYER, J., Soil Biology

Forest Sciences (D-Fowi, ETH Zentrum, 8092 Zürich; tel. 446326194; fax 446321575; e-mail benz@fowi.ethz.ch; internet www.fowi.ethz.ch):

BACHMANN, P., Forest Inventory and Planning
BUGMANN, H., Mountain Forest Ecology
HEINIMANN, H. R., Forestry Engineering
HOLDENRIEDER, O., Forest Pathology and Dendrology
KISSLING-NÄF, I., Forest Resource Economics
SCHMITHÜSEN, F., Forestry Policy and Economics
SCHÜTZ, J.-PH., Silviculture

Humanities, Social and Political Sciences (D-Gess, ETH Zentrum, 8092 Zürich; tel. 446322308; fax 446321027; e-mail margelisch@gess.ethz.ch; internet www.gess.ethz.ch):

BERNAUER, T., International Relations
BESOMI, O., Italian Language and Literature
BUCHMANN, M., Sociology
DÄLLENBACH, L., French Language and Literature
EISNER, M., Sociology
FREY, K., Education
GABRIEL, J. M., International Relations
GUGERLI, D., History of Technology
HERTIG, G., Law
HOLENSTEIN, E., Philosophy
KAPPEL, R., Problems of Developing Countries
NEF, U. CH., Law
NOWOTNY, H., Philosophy and Social Studies
RIS, R., German Language and Literature
RUCH, A., Law
SCHIPS, B., Economics
SCHUBERT, R., Economics
SPILLMAN, K. R., Security Studies and Conflict Research
SUTER, CH., Sociology
TOBLER, H. W., General History
VICKERS, B., English Language and Literature
WENGER, A., Swiss and International Security Policy

Industrial Management and Manufacturing Engineering (D-Bepr, ETH Zentrum, 8092 Zürich; tel. 446325718; fax 446321047; e-mail wismer@bepr.ethz.ch; internet www.bepr.ethz.ch/main.htm):

ABELL, D. F., Technology and Management
FAHRNI, F., Technology Management
GROTE, G., Work Psychology
HUBER, F., Industrial Engineering and Management
KOLLER, TH., Hygiene and Applied Physiology
KRUEGER, H., Ergonomics
MEYER, U., Textile Machinery
REISSNER, J., Forming Technology
SCHÖNSLEBEN, P., Industrial Engineering and Management
TSCHIRKY, H., Industrial Engineering and Management
WEHNER, T., Work and Organizational Psychology

Materials Sciences (D-Werk, ETH Zentrum, 8092 Zürich; tel. 446322520; fax 446321028; e-mail krombach@ifp.mat.ethz.ch; internet www.mat.ethz.ch):

GAUCKLER, L. J., Non-metallic Materials
LUISI, P. L., Macromolecular Chemistry
ÖTTINGER, H. CH., Polymer Physics
SMITH, P., Polymer Technology
SPEIDEL, M. O., Metals and Metallurgy
SPENCER, N. D., Surface Technology
STÜSSI, E., Biomechanics
SUTER, U. W., Macromolecular Chemistry
WINTERMANTEL, E., Biocompatible Materials

Mathematics (D-Math, ETH Zentrum, 8092 Zürich; tel. 446325615; fax 446321085; e-mail mathdept@math.ethz.ch; internet www.math.ethz.ch):

BÜHLMANN, P. L., Mathematics
BURGER, M., Mathematics
DELBAEN, F., Financial Mathematics
EMBRECHTS, P., Mathematics
FEICHTNER, E. M., Mathematics
FELDER, G., Mathematics
GROTE, M. J., Mathematics
HAMPEL, F., Statistics
ILMANEN, T., Mathematics
JELTSCH, R., Applied Mathematics
KIRCHGRABER, U., Mathematics
KNÖRRER, H., Mathematics
KNUS, M. A., Mathematics
KÜNSCH, H. R., Mathematics
LANFORD, O. E., III, Mathematics
LANG, U., Mathematics
LÜTHI, H.-J., Operations Research
MISLIN, G., Mathematics
NUCINKIS, B. E. A., Mathematics
OSTERWALDER, K., Mathematics
PINK, R., Mathematics
SALAMON, D. A., Mathematics
SALMHOFER, M., Mathematics
SCHWAB, CH., Applied Mathematics
STAMMBACH, U., Mathematics
STRUWE, M., Mathematics
SZNITMAN, A.-S., Mathematics
TRUBOWITZ, E., Mathematics
WÜSTHOLZ, G., Mathematics
ZEHNDER, E., Mathematics

Mechanical and Process Engineering (D-Mavt, ETH Zentrum, 8092 Zürich; tel. 446322596; fax 446321483; e-mail vonrohr@mavt.ethz.ch; internet www.mavt.ethz.ch):

ABHARI, R., Turbomachinery
DUAL, J., Mechanics
EBERLE, M., Internal Combustion Engines and Combustion Technology
ERMANNI, P., Composites and Structures
FILIPPINI, M., Economics and Energy Policy
GEERING, H. P., Measurement and Control
GUZZELLA, L., Internal Combustion Engines
JOCHEM, E., Economics and Energy Policy
KLEISER, L., Fluid Dynamics
KOUMOUTSAKOS, P., Fluid Dynamics
KRÖGER, W., Safety Technology
MAZZOTTI, M., Process Engineering
MEIER, M., Product Development
MEYER-PIENING, H.-R., Lightweight Structures and Ropeways
POULIKAKOS, D., Thermodynamics in Emerging Technology
PRATSINIS, S. E., Process Engineering
RÖSGEN, TH., Fluid Dynamics
RUDOLF VON ROHR, PH., Process Engineering
SAYIR, M., Mechanics
SCHWEITZER, G., Robotics
SEILER, A., Engineering and Management
STEINER, M., Control Systems
STEINFELD, Renewable Energy Carriers
STEMMER, A., Nanotechnology
YADIGAROGLU, G., Nuclear Engineering

Physics (D-Phys, ETH Hönggerberg, 8093 Zürich; tel. 446332585; fax 446331106; e-mail rafailidis@phys.ethz.ch; internet www.phys.ethz.ch):

BALTES, H., Quantum Electronics
BATLOGG, B., Solid State Physics
BLATTER, J. W., Theoretical Physics
DEGIORGI, L., Solid State Physics
DOUGLAS, R. J., Theoretical Neuroinformatics
EICHLER, R., Experimental Particle Physics
ENSSLIN, K., Solid State Physics
FRÖHLICH, J., Theoretical and Mathematical Physics
GRAF, G. M., Theoretical Physics
GÜNTER, P., Quantum Electronics
HEPP, K., Theoretical Physics
HOFER, H., Experimental Particle Physics
HUNZIKER, W., Theoretical Physics
KELLER, U., Quantum Electronics
KOSTORZ, G., Applied Physics
LANDOLT, M., Solid State Physics
LANG, J., Experimental Particle Physics

MARTIN, K. A. C., Systematic Neurophysiology
OTT, H. R., Solid State Physics
PAUSS, F., Experimental Particle Physics
PESCIA, D., Solid State Physics
RICE, TH. M., Theoretical Physics
RUBBIA, A., Experimental Particle Physics
SCHMID, CH., Theoretical Physics
STENFLO, J. O., Astrophysics
VAN ER VEEN, J. F., Experimental Particle Physics

UNIVERSITÀ DELLA SVIZZERA ITALIANA (University of Lugano)

Via Lambertenghi 10, 6904 Lugano
Telephone: (58) 6664000
Fax: (58) 6664647
E-mail: info@usi.ch
Internet: www.usi.ch

Founded 1996
State control
Language of instruction: Italian
Academic year: September to June

2 Campuses at Lugano and Mendrisio

Pres.: PIERO MARTINOLI
Gen. Sec.: Lic. phil. ALBINO ZGRAGGEN
Head Librarians: Dr GIUSEPPE ORIGGI (Lugano): SERGIO STEFFEN (Mendrisio)

Library of 70,000 vols
Number of teachers: 743
Number of students: 2,852

DEANS

Academy of Architecture: Prof. VALENTIN BEARTH
Faculty of Communication Sciences: Prof. Dr LORENZO CANTONI
Faculty of Economics: Prof. RICO MAGGI
Faculty of Informatics: MAURO PEZZÈ

UNIVERSITÄT BASEL

Peterspl. 1, POB, 4003 Basel
Telephone: 612671298
Fax: 612673013
E-mail: studienberatung@unibas.ch
Internet: www.unibas.ch

Founded 1460
Languages of instruction: German, English
Academic year: August to July

Rector: Prof. Dr ANTONIO LOPRIENO
Vice-Rector for Research and Professional Devt: Prof. Dr PETER MEIER-ABT
Vice-Rector for Devt: Prof. Dr ALEX N. EBERLE
Vice-Rector for Teaching: Prof. Dr HEDWIG J. KAISER
Exec. Dir: CHRISTOPH TSCHUMI
Librarian: H. HUG

Library: see under Libraries and Archives
Number of teachers: 1,300
Number of students: 11,360

DEANS

Faculty of Business and Economics: Prof. Dr. MANFRED BRUHN
Faculty of Humanities: Prof. Dr. C. OPITZ-BELAKHAL
Faculty of Law: Prof. Dr PETER JUNG
Faculty of Medicine: Prof. Dr ALBERT URWYLER
Faculty of Psychology: Prof. Dr MICHAELA WÄNKE
Faculty of Science: Prof. Dr MARTIN SPIESS
Faculty of Theology: Prof. Dr ALFRED BODENHEIMER

PROFESSORS

Faculty of Humanities:

HOLL, U., Media Sciences
MAASEN, SABINE, Social Studies of Science

Faculty of Economics (Wirtschaftswissenschaftliches Zentrum (WWZ), Petersgraben 51, 4003 Basel):

BORNER, S., Political Economics
BRUHN, M., Marketing and Management
KUGLER, P., Monetary Macroeconomics
MÜLLER, W. R., Business Administration
SCHIERENBECK, H., Business Administration
WEDER, R., Economics
ZIMMERMANN, H., Finance Theory

Faculty of Law (Peter Merian-Weg 8, 4056 Basel; tel. 612672531; fax 612672508; e-mail dekanat-ius@unibas.ch; internet www.ius.unibas.ch):

BEHNISCH, U., Public Law
GLESS, S., Criminal Law
HANDSCHIN, L., Private Law
KRAMER, E. A., Civil Law
NADAKAVUKAREN SCHEFER, K., Public Law
PETERS, A., Public Law, Swiss National Law
PIETH, M., Penal Law
RIVA, E., Public Law
SCHEFER, M., Swiss National Law
SCHWENZER, I., Civil Law
SEELMANN, K., Penal Law, Philosophy of Law
STÖCKLI, F., Private Law
SUTTER-SOMM, T., Civil Law and Civil Procedural Law
THURNHERR, D., Public Law
TOBLER, C., Public Law

Faculty of Medicine (Klingelbergstrasse 61, 4056 Basel; tel. 612652050; fax 612652230; internet www.medizin.unibas.ch):

ACKERMANN-LIEBRICH, U., Social and Prophylactic Medicine
BETTLER, B., Physiology
BÜHLER, F. R., Pharmaceutical Medicine
CHRISTOFORI, G., Biochemistry and Genetics
DE GEEST, S., Nursing
DICK, W., Orthopaedics
DITTMANN, V., Legal Medicine
ECKSTEIN, F., Cardiology
FLAMMER, J., Ophthalmology
GASSER, TH., Urology
GRATWOHL, A., Internal Medicine
HESS, C., Ambulant Internal Medicine
HOLLÄNDER, G., Paediatric Molecular Medicine
ITIN, P., Dermatology and Venereology
KAPPOS, L., Neurology
KRAPF, R., Internal Medicine
KÜNZLE, N., Social and Preventive Medicine
LAMBRECHT, J. TH., Dentistry
LUIGI, M., Neurosurgery
MARINELLO, C. P., Dentistry
MIHATSCH, M. J., General and Special Pathology
MORONI, CHR., Medical Microbiology
MÜLLER, V., Internal Medicine
MÜLLER-SPAHN, F. S., Adult Psychiatry
OERTLI, D., General Surgery
OSSWALD, S., Cardiology
PALMER, E., Experimental Transplantation Immunology and Nephrology
PFISTERER, M., Cardiology
PÜHSE, U., Science of Sports Medicine
QUERVAIN, D., Cognitive Neurosciences
RIECHER-RÖSSLER, Adult Psychiatry
ROLINK, A., Immunology
SCHAAD, U. B., Paediatrics
SCHEIDEGGER, D. H., Anaesthetics
SCHIFFERLI, J., Internal Medicine
SCHMIDT-TRUCKSÄSS, A., Sports Medicine
SKODA, R., Molecular Medicine
STEIGER, J., Internal Medicine
STEINBRICH, W., Medical Radiology
TOLNAY, M., Pathology
TYNDALL, L. A., Rheumatology
WEIGER, R., Dentistry
ZEILHOFER, H.-F., Reconstructive Surgery
ZELLER, R., Anatomy and Embryology
ZIMMERLI, W., Internal Medicine

Faculty of Philosophy and History (Bernoullistr. 28, 4056 Basel):

ANGEHRN, E., Philosophy
ARLT, W., Musicology
BERGMAN, M., Sociology
BEYER, A., Modern History of Art
BIERL, A., General Philology
BOEHM, G., History of Art
BURGHARTZ, S., History of the 14th–16th centuries
ENGLER, B., English Philology
FÖRSTER, T., Ethnology
GLAUSER, J., Nordic Philology
GUSKI, A., Slavonic Philology
HÄCKI BUHOFER, A., German Philology
HARICH-SCHWARZBAUER, H., Latin Philology
HAUMANN, H., History of Eastern Europe
HONOLD, A., Modern German Literature
KOPP, R., Romance Philology
KREBS, A., Philosophy
KREIS, G., Modern General History and Swiss History
LEIMGRUBER, W., Folklore, European Ethnology
LOPRIENO, A., Egyptology
LÜDI, G., Romance Philology
MÄDER, U., Sociology
MILLET, O., French Philology
MOOSER, J., History of the 20th Century
OPITZ-BELAKHAL, C., History of the 17th and 18th Centuries
PILLER, I., Sociolinguistics and Sociology of English as a Global Language
SCHAFFNER, M., Swiss History and Recent General History
SCHELLEWALD, B., History of Art
SCHMID, B., Ibero-Romance Philology
SCHNELL, R., German Philology
SCHOELER, G., Islamic Studies
SIEGMUND, F., Prehistory and Early History
SIMON, R., German Literary Studies
STÄHELI, U., Sociology
STUCKY, R., Classical Archaeology
TERZOLI, M. A., Romance Philology
THOLEN, G. C., Media Science
VON GREYERZ, K., Recent General History and Swiss History
VON MÜLLER, A, Medieval History
VON UNGERN-STERNBERG, J, Ancient History

Faculty of Psychology (Missionsstr. 60–62, 4055 Basel; tel. 612673528; fax 612673526; e-mail info-psycho@unibas.ch; internet www.unibas.ch/psycho):

GROB, A., Developmental Psychology
MARGRAF, J., Clinical Psychology
OPWIS, K., General Psychology and Methodology
WÄNKE, M., Social and Business Psychology

Faculty of Science (Pharmazentrum, Klingelbergstr. 50, 4056 Basel; tel. 612673053; fax 612671434; internet www.unibas.ch/philnat):

A'CAMPO, N., Mathematics
AEBI, U., Structural Biology
AFFOLTER, M., Neurobiology and Developmental Biology
ALEWELL, CH., Environmental Earth Sciences
BARDE, Y. A., Neurobiology
BICKLE, T. A., Microbiology
BOLLER, TH., Botany
BRUDER, C., Theoretical Physics
CONSTABLE, E., Inorganic Chemistry
CORNELIS, G., Microbiology
EBERT, D., Zoology
ENGEL, A., Structural Biology
ERNST, B., Molecular Pharmaceutics
FOLKERS, G., Pharmaceutical Chemistry

GASSER, S., Molecular Biology
GEHRING, W. J., Physiology of Development and Genetics
GIESE, B., Organic Chemistry
GROTE, M. S., Mathematics
GRZESIEK, S., Structural Biology
GÜNTHERODT, H.-J., Experimental Physics
HALL, M., Biochemistry
HAMBURGER, M. O., Pharmacy
HAURI, H., Cell Biology
IM HOF, H.-CHR., Mathematics
KELLER, W., Cell Biology
KÖRNER, CHR., Botany
KRAFT, H., Mathematics
LE TENSORER, J.-M., Pre- and Early History
LESER, H., Physical Geography
LEUENBERGER, H., Pharmaceutical Technology
LOSS, D., Theoretical Physics
MAIER, J. P., Physical Chemistry
MASSER, D., Mathematics
MEIER, W., Chemistry
PARLOW, E., Meteorology and Climatology
PFALTZ, A., Organic Chemistry
PHILIPPSEN, P., Applied Microbiology
REICHERT, H., Zoology
RÜEGG, M., Neurobiology
SCHMID, S. M., Geology and Palaeontology
SCHNEIDER-SLIWA, R., Human Geography
SCHÖNENBERGER, CH., Experimental Physics
SEELIG, J., Structural Biology
SPIESS, M., Biochemistry
TANNES, M., Epidemiology and Medical Parasitology
THIELEMANN, F. K., Theoretical Physics
TSCHUDIN, CH., Applied Information Technology
VETTER, T., Applied Information Technology
WIEMKEN, A. M., Botany
ZUBERBÜHLER, A., Inorganic Chemistry

Faculty of Theology (Nadelberg 10, 4051 Basel; tel. 612672901; fax 612672902; internet theolrel.unibas.ch):

BERNHARDT, R., Systematic Theology, Dogmatics
BRÄNDLE, R., New Testament, History of the Early Church
GÄBLER, U., Ecclesiastical and Dogmatic History
GRÖZINGER, A., Practical Theology
LIENEMANN, CH., Ecumenical Movement and Mission
MATHYS, H.-P., Old Testament and Semitic Languages
MOHN, J., Science of Religion
PFLEIDERER, G., Systematic Theology, Ethics
STEGEMANN, E., New Testament
WALRAFF, M., History of the Church and of Theology

Institute for Jewish Studies (Leimenstr. 48, 4051 Basel; tel. 612051636; fax 612051640; e-mail institut-judaistik@unibas.ch; internet www.jewishstudies.unibas.ch):

BODENHEIMER, A., Jewish Literature and History
PICARD, J., Modern Jewish History and Culture

UNIVERSITÄT BERN

Hochschulstr. 4, 3012 Bern
Telephone: 316318111
Fax: 316318008
E-mail: info@imd.unibe.ch
Internet: www.unibe.ch

Founded 1834, (inc. Theological School, f. 1528)
State control
Language of instruction: German
Academic year: September to August

Rector: Prof. Dr URS WÜRGLER
Vice-Rector for Research: Prof. Dr MARTIN TÄUBER
Vice-Rector for Univ. Education: Prof. Dr GUNTER STEPHAN
Admin. Dir: Dr DANIEL ODERMATT
Chief Librarian: Prof. Dr ROBERT BARTH

Number of teachers: 3,552
Number of students: 14,300

Publications: *uniaktuell* (online magazine), *UniPress–Forschung und Wissenschaft*

DEANS

Faculty of Economics and Social Science: Prof. Dr HARLEY KROHMER
Faculty of Humanities: Prof. Dr HEINZPETER ZNOJ
Faculty of Human Sciences: Prof. Dr ROLAND SEILER
Faculty of Law: Prof. Dr STEPHAN WOLF
Faculty of Medicine: Prof. Dr PETER EGGLI
Faculty of Science: Prof. Dr SILVIO DECURTINS
Faculty of Theology: Prof. Dr SILVIA SCHROER
Vetsuisse Faculty: Prof. Dr ANDREAS ZURBRIGGEN

UNIVERSITÄT LUZERN
(University of Lucerne)

Pfistergasse 20, 6003 Luzern
Pfistergasse 20, POB 7979, 6000 Lucerne 7
Telephone: 412285510
Fax: 412285505
E-mail: international@unilu.ch
Internet: www.unilu.ch

Founded 1574, univ. status 2000
Languages of instruction: German, English, French
Academic year: August to July

Rector: Prof. Dr PAUL RICHLI
Vice-Rector: Prof. Dr ANDREAS FURRER
Vice-Rector for Education and Int. Relations: Prof. Dr MARKUS RIES
Admin. Sec.: JUSTINA SCHMIDLIN
Librarian: Dr WOLFRAM LUTTERER

Number of teachers: 137
Number of students: 2,500

DEANS

Faculty of Culture and Social Sciences: Prof. Dr CHRISTIANE SCHILDKNECHT
Faculty of Law: Prof. Dr REGINA AEBI-MUELLER
Faculty of Theology: Prof. Dr MONIKA JAKOBS

UNIVERSITÄT ST GALLEN
(University of St Gallen)

Dufourstr. 50, 9000 St Gallen
Telephone: 712242111
Fax: 712242816
E-mail: info@unisg.ch
Internet: www.unisg.ch

Founded 1898, present name 2011
State control
Languages of instruction: German, English
Academic year: April to March

Pres.: Prof. Dr THOMAS BIEGER
Vice-Pres.: Lic. WERNER GÄCHTER
Exec. Dir: Lic. MARKUS BRÖNNIMANN
Library Dir: Dr XAVER BAUMGARTNER

Number of teachers: 2,223
Number of students: 6,726

Publications: *Aussenwirtschaft* (6 a year), *Electronic Markets* (4 a year), *Thexis* (6 a year)

DEANS

School of Economics and Political Science: Prof. MONIKA BÜTLER
School of Finance: Prof. Dr KARL FRAUENDORFER
School of Humanities and Social Sciences: Prof. ULRICH SCHMID
School of Management: Prof. WALTER BRENNER
Law School: Prof. LUKAS GSCHWEND

PROFESSORS

ANDEREGG, J., German Language and Literature
BACK, A., Information Processing
BAUDENBACHER, C., Private, Commercial and Economic Law
BAUMER, J.-M., Development Policy
BEHR, G., Business Administration
BELZ, C., Marketing
BERNET, B., Business Administration, Banking
BIEGER, T., Business Administration, Tourism
BOURQUI, C., Business Administration
BURMEISTER, K. H., History of Law
CHONG, L., Business Administration
DACHLER, P., Psychology
DOPFER, K., Foreign Trade and Development Theory
DRUEY, J. N., Civil and Commercial Law
DUBS, R., Business Pedagogy
DYLLICK, T., Business Administration
EHRENZELLER, B., Public Law
FICKERT, R., Business Administration
FISCHER, G., Economics
FRAUENDORFER, K., Operations Research
GÄRTNER, M., Economics
GEISER, T., Civil and Commercial Law
GOMEZ, P., Business Administration
GROSS, P., Sociology
GRÜNBICHLER, A., Finance
HALLER, M., Insurance and Business Administration, Risk Management
HAUSER, H., Foreign Trade Theory and Policy
HILB, M., Business Administration
INGOLD, F. P., Russian Language and Literature
JAEGER, F., Economic Policy
KAUFMANN, V., French Language and Literature
KEEL, A., Statistics
KIRCHGÄSSNER, G., Economics
KLEY, R., Political Science
KOLLER, A., Civil and Commercial Law
LECHNER, M., Empirical Economic Research and Econometrics
LEUENBERGER, T., Modern History
MANELLA, J., Business Administration
MARTINONI, R., Italian Language and Literature
MASTRONARDI, P., Public Law
MEIER, A., Economics
MEIER-SCHATZ, C., Civil and Commercial Law
METZGER, CH., Business Administration
MOHR, E., Economics
MÜLLER, H., Mathematics
MÜLLER-STEWENS, G., Business Administration
NOBEL, P., Private, Commercial and Economic Law
OESTERLE, H., Information Processing
PLEITNER, H. J., Business Administration
REETZ, N., Economics
RIKLIN, A., Political Science
ROBERTO, V., Private, Commercial and Economic Law
ROBINSON, A. D., English Language and Literature
RUIGROK, W., International Management
RUUD, F., Accounting
SCHEDLER, K., Public Management
SCHMID, B., Information Processing
SCHMID, H., Economics
SCHUH, G., Technology
SCHWANDER, I., Civil Law
SCHWEIZER, R., Public Law
SILES, J. R., Spanish Language and Literature
SPREMANN, K., Business Administration
STÄHLY, P., Operations Research
STIER, W., Empirical Social Research and Applied Statistics

TOMCZAK, T., Business Administration
TRECHSEL, ST., Criminal Law and Criminal Case Law
ULRICH, P., Economic Ethics
VALLENDER, C., Public Law and Law of Taxation
VON KROGH, F., Business Administration
WALDBURGER, R., Taxation Law
WINTER, R., Information Processing
WUNDERER, R., Business Administration
ZIMMERMANN, H., Financial Market Analysis

UNIVERSITÄT ZÜRICH

Rämistr. 71, 8006 Zürich
Telephone: 446341111
Fax: 446344901
Internet: www.uzh.ch

Founded 1833, as Universitas Turicensis, univ. status 1912
State control
Language of instruction: German
Academic year: October to July (2 semesters)

Pres.: Prof. Dr ANDREAS FISCHER
Vice-Pres. for Arts and Social Sciences: Prof. Dr OTTFRIED JARREN
Vice-Pres. for Medicine and Natural Sciences: Prof. Dr DANIEL WYLER
Vice-Pres. for Law and Economics: Prof. Dr EGON FRANCK
Admin. Dir. and Dir of Finance: Dipl.-Ing. STEFAN SCHNYDER
Sec.-Gen.: Dr KURT REIMANN
Librarian: Dr HEINZ DICKENMANN

Number of teachers: 512
Number of students: 25,854

Publications: *unijournal* (6 a year), *unimagazin* (4 a year), *unireport* (1 a year)

DEANS

Faculty of Arts: Prof. Dr BERND ROECK
Faculty of Economics: Prof. Dr JOSEF FALKINGER
Faculty of Law: Prof. Dr WOLFGANG WOHLERS
Faculty of Medicine: Prof. Dr KLAUS GRÄTZ
Faculty of Science: Prof. Dr MICHAEL HENGARTNER
Faculty of Theology: Prof. Dr CHRISTOPH UEHLINGER
Vetsuisse Faculty: Prof. Dr FELIX R. ALTHAUS

PROFESSORS

Centre for Dentistry, Oral and Maxillary Medicine (Plattenstr. 11, 8028 Zürich; tel. 446343203):

GRÄTZ, K., Oral Surgery
HÄMMERLE, C., Crowns and Bridges
IMFELD, T., Preventive Dentistry, Periodontology, Cardiology
PALLA, S., Dental Prosthesis
PELTOMÄKI, T., Children's Dentistry

Faculty of Economics (tel. 446342314; e-mail dekanatww@zuv.uzh.ch; internet www.oec.uzh.ch):

BACKES-GELLNER, U., Business Admin.
BERNSTEIN, A., Dynamic and Distributed Application Systems
CHESNEY, M., Quantitative Finance
DIETL, H., Service and Operation Management
DITTRICH, K. R., Computer Science
EWERHART, C., Information Economy
FALKINGER, J., Finance and Macroeconomics
FEHR, E., Economics
FRANCK, E., Business Admin.
GALL, H. C., Software Engineering
GEIGER, H., Banking and Finance
GIBSON-ASNER, R., Financial Economics
GLINZ, M., Informatics
HABIB, M., Corporate Finance Theory
HENS, T., Financial Economics
HOFFMANN, M., Int. Trade and Finance
HOTZ-HART, B., Economics
JANSSEN, M., Financial Economics
KLATTE, D., Mathematics and Economics
MEYER, C., Accountancy and Financial Control
OSTERLOH, M., Business Admin.
PAJAROLA, R., Multimedia
PAOLELLA, M., Empirical Finance
PFAFF, D., Accountancy and Financial Control
PFEIFER, R., Computer Science
RUUD, F., Accountancy and Financial Control
SAEZ-MARTI, F., Microeconomics
SCHAUER, H., Computer Science
SCHENKER-WICKI, A., Business Management
SCHERER, A. G., Business Admin.
SCHMUTZLER, A., Economics
SCHWABE, G., Information Management
STAFFELBACH, B., Business Admin.
STILLER, B., System and Communication
VOLKART, R., Banking and Finance
WEHRLI, H. P., Business Admin.
WINKELMANN, R., Empirical Economics
WOITEK, U., History of Economics and National Economy
ZILIBOTTI, F., National Economics
ZWEIFEL, P., Political Economy
ZWEIMÜLLER, J., Macroeconomics

Faculty of Law (tel. 446342233; e-mail dekrwf@ius.uzh.ch; internet www.jur.uzh.ch):

BIAGGINI, G., State, Administrative and European Law
BREITSCHMID, P., Private Law
BÜCHLER, A., Private Law
DONATSCH, A., Criminal Law
ERNST, W., Roman Law
FÖGEN, M. T., Roman Law and Comparative Law
FORSTMOSER, P., Trade Law
GÄCHTER, TH., State, Administrative and Securities Law
GRIFFEL, A., State and Administrative Law
HEINEMANN, A., Economic Law
HILTY, R., Private Law
HONSELL, H., Swiss and European Civil Law, Roman Law
HUGUENIN, C., Private Economic Law and European Law
JAAG, T., State and Administrative Law
JOSITSCH, D., Criminal Law
KAUFMANN, C., State and Administrative Law, Law of Nations
KELLER, H., State Law
KILLIAS, M., Criminal Law
KLEY, A., State Law
MEIER, I., Civil Case Law, Bankruptcy Law
NOBEL, P. J., Swiss and European Trading and Economic Law
OBERHAMMER, P., Civil Case Law
OTT, W., Philosophical and Swiss Civil Law
PORTMANN, W., Private and Industrial Law
RAUSCH, H., Environmental and Administrative Law
REICH, M., Tax, Fiscal and Administrative Law
REY, H., Swiss Civil Law
SCHNYDER, A., Private Economic Law
SENN, M., Philosophical Law
TAG, B., Criminal Law
THIER, A., History of Law
THÜRER, D., Law of Nations, State and Administrative Law
UHLMANN, F., State and Administrative Law
VON DER CRONE, H. C., Private and Business Law
WEBER, R., European Law
WEBER-DÜRLER, B., State and Administrative Law
WOHLERS, P., Private, Economic and European Law
ZOBL, D., Civil Law, Banking and Securities Law

Faculty of Medicine (Zürichbergstr. 14, 8091 Zürich; tel. 446341071; e-mail renate.gay@usz.ch; internet www.med.uzh.ch):

AGUZZI, A., Neuropathology
AKDIS, C., Immunology
ARAND, M., Pharmacology
ATTIN, TH., Preventive Dentistry
BÄR, W., Forensic Medicine
BASSETTI, C., Neurology
BERGER, E. G., Physiology
BERGER, W., Medical Molecular Genetics
BILLER-ANDORNO, N., Biomedical Ethics
BOLTSHAUSER, E., Paediatrics
BORGEAT, A., Anaesthesiology
BÖSIGER, P., Biomedical Technology
BÖTTGER, E. C., Medical Microbiology
BOUTELLIER, U., Physiology
BUCHER, H. U., Neonatology
BUCK, A., Nuclear Medicine
BUDDEBERG, C., Social Psychology
CLAVIEN, P. A., Abdominal Surgery
DIETZ, V., Paraplegology
FEHR, J., Haematology
FINK, D. A., Gynaecology
FONTANA, A., Clinical Immunology
FRENCH, L., Dermatology
FRIED, M., Gastroenterology
FRITSCHY, J. M., Neuropharmacology
GAY, S., Experimental Rheumatology
GENONI, M., Heart Surgery
GERBER, C., Orthopaedics
GIOVANOLI, P., Surgery
GRÄTZ, K., Pathology
GROSCURTH, P., Anatomy
GRÜTTER, M. G., Biochemistry, Macromolecular Crystallography
GUTZWILLER, F., Social and Preventive Medicine
HÄMMERLE, CH., Dentistry
HELD, L., Biostatics
HELL, D., Clinical Psychiatry
HELMCHEN, F., Neurology
HENGARTNER, H., Experimental Pathology
HENNET, TH., Human Biology
HOCK, C., Biological Pharmacology
HODLER, J., Radiology
HUG, E., Radiology
IMFELD, TH., Preventive Dentistry
IMTHURN, B., Gynaecological Endocrinology
JENNI, R., Cardiology
JIRICNY, J., Molecular Radiology
KAISSLING, B., Anatomy
KNUTH, A., Oncology
KOLLIAS, S., Radiology
KULLAK-UBLICK, G. A., Clinical Pharmacology
LANDAU, K., Ophthalmology
LIPP, H. P., Anatomy
LOFFING, J., Anatomy
LÜSCHER, T. F., Cardiology
LÜTOLF, U. M., Radiotherapy
MANSUY, I., Neurology
MARINCEK, B., Diagnostic Radiology
MEULI, M., Surgery
MICHEL, B., Rheumatology
MITSIADIS, TH., Oral Biology
MOCH, H., Pathology
MODESTIN, J., Clinical Psychiatry
MÖLLING, K., Virology
MURER, H., Physiology
NADAL, D., Paediatrics
NEUHASS, S., Neurobiology
NITSCH, R. M., Psychiatry
NOLL, G., Molecular Biology
PALLA, S., Prosthetics
PELTOMÄKI, T., Maxillary Orthopaedics
PLÜCKTHUN, A., Biochemistry
PRÊTRE, R., Children's Cardiac Surgery
PROBST, R. R., Otorhinolaryngology
PRUSCHY, M., Molecular Biology
REINECKE, M., Anatomy
ROGLER, G., Internal Medicine
RÖSSLER, W., Clinical Psychiatry
ROTH, J., Cell Molecular Pathology
RUDIN, M., Pharmacology

RUSSI, E., Internal Medicine
RÜTTIMANN, B., History of Medicine
SALLER, R., Naturopathy
SCHINZEL, A., Medical Genetics
SCHMID, E., Anaesthesia
SCHMID, S., Otorhinolaryngology
SCHNYDER, U., Psychiatry
SCHÖNLE, E., Paediatrics
SCHWAB, M. E., Neurology and Anatomy
SEGER, R., Children's Medicine, Immunology and Haematology
SENNHAUSER, F. H., Paediatrics
SONDEREGGER, P., Biochemistry
SPAHN, D. R., Anaesthesiology
SPINAS, G. A., Endocrinology, Diabetology and Pathophysiology
STEINHAUSEN, H.-C., Child and Youth Psychiatry
STEINMANN, B. U., Paediatrics
STEURER, J., Internal Medicine
SULSER, T., Urology
TRENTZ, O., Accident Surgery
VALAVANIS, A., Neuroradiology
VERREY, F., Physiology
VETTER, W., Internal Medicine
VON ECKARDSTEIN, A., Clinical Chemistry
VON SCHULTHESS, G. K., Nuclear Medicine
WAGNER, A., Bioinformatics
WEBER, R., Clinical Infectology
WEDER, W., Thorax Surgery
WENGER, R. H., Physiology
WIESER, H.-G., Neurology, Special Epileptology
WOGGON, B., Pharmacotherapy
WOLFER, D., Anatomy
WÜTHRICH, B., Dermatology and Venereology
ZEILHOFER, H. U., Pharmacology
ZIMMERMANN, R., Obstetrics and Gynaecology
ZINKERNAGEL, R. M., Experimental Pathology
ZÜND, G., Surgery

Faculty of Philosophy (tel. 446342234; fax 446344966; e-mail heidi.moor@access.unizh.ch; internet www.uzh.ch/fakultaet/phil):

BONFADELLI, H., Journalism
BOOTHE, B., Clinical Psychology
BORNSCHIER, V., Economic Sociology
BOSKOVSKA, N., History of Eastern Europe
BOSSONG, G., Romance Philology
BRANDSTÄTTER, V., General Psychology
BRONFEN, E., English and American Literature
BUCHMANN, M., Sociology
CLAUSSEN, P. C., Art History of the Middle Ages
CRIVELLI, T., Special Romance Literature
DELLA CASA, PH., History of Medieval Art
DESCOEDRES, G., History of Medieval Art
DUNKEL, G. E., Comparative Indo-German Linguistics
DURSCHEID, CH., German Language
EBERLE, F., Pedagogy
EBERT, K. H., General German Philology
EHLERT, U., Psychology
EIGLER, U., Classical Philology
ESSER, F., Journalism
ESTERHAMMER, A., English Literature
FATKE, R., Pedagogy, Special Social Pedagogics
FINKE, P., Ethnology
FISCH, J., General Modern History
FISCHER, A., English Philology
FREUD, A., Applied Psychology
FRIES, U., English Philology
FRÖHLICHER, P., History of French Literature
GASSMANN, R. H., Sinology
GESER, H., Sociology
GILOMEN, H. J., General Economic and Social History, Swiss History
GLASER, E., German Philology
GLAUSER, J., Nordic Philology
GLESSGEN, M.-D., Romance Philology
GLOCK, H.-J., Philosophy
GONON, P., Pedagogy
GRODDECK, W., New German Literature
GÜNTHER, H., History of Modern Art
GUTSCHER, H., Social Psychology
GYR, U., Folklore
HAUG, H.-J., Psychiatry
HAUSENDORF, H., German Language
HELBLING, J., Ethnology
HESS, M., Computer Linguistics
HEUSSER, M., English Literature
HINRICHSEN, H.-J., Musicology
HIRSIG, R., Psychological Methods
HORNUNG, R., Social Psychology
HUG, S., Political Science
IMHOF, K., Journalism
JÄNCKE, L., Neuropsychology
JARREN, O., Publicity Science
JONAS, K., Social Psychology
JUCKER, A., English Philology
KELLNER, B., Old German Literature
KIENING, C., German Literature
KLEINMANN, M., Psychology
KOHLER, G., Philosophy, Political Philosophy
KOLB, G., Ancient History
KRIESI, H., Political Science
KRÜGER, G., Modern History
KYBURZ-GRABER, R., Pedagogy
LA FAUCI, N., Romance Philology, Italian Linguistics
LABARTHE, P., Romance Literature
LEIST, A., Ethics
LIENHARD, M., Spanish
LINKE, W. A., German Literature
LOETZ, F., History
LOPEZ GUIL, I., Iberoromanic Literature
LOPORCARO, M., Romance Philology, History of Italian
LÜTTEKEN, L., Musicology
MAERCKER, A., Psychopathology
MAREK, CH., Ancient History
MARTIN, M., Gerontology
MARX, W., General Psychology
MICHAELOWA, K., Politology
MICHEL, P., Ancient German Literature
MOOS, C., General and Swiss Modern History
MÜLLER NIELABA, D., German Literature
NÄF, B., Ancient History
NAUMANN, B., German Literature
OELKERS, J., Pedagogy
OPPITZ, M., Ethnology
PETERS, J.-U., Slavic Philology
PICONE, M., Italian Literature
RANDERIA, S., Ethnology
REDDICK, A., English Literature
REUSSER, K., Pedagogy
RIATSCH, C., Romance Literature
RIEDWEG, C., Classical Philology, Ancient Greek Studies
RIEMENSCHNITTER, A., Chinese Philology
ROECK, B., General and Swiss History
ROSSI, L., Romance Literature
RUCH, W., Psychology
RUDOLPH, U., Islamic Sciences
RUF, U., Pedagogy
RULOFF, D., Political Science
SAPORITI, K., Philosophy
SARASIN, P., General and Swiss Modern History
SCHABER, P., Philosophy
SCHNEIDER, S., German Literature
SCHREIER, D., English Language
SCHREINER, P., Indology
SCHULTHESS, P., Philosophical Theory
SIEGERT, G., Journalism
STOTZ, P., Middle Latin Philology
SZYDLIK, M., Sociology
TANNER, J., General and Swiss Modern History
TEUSCHER, S., Medieval Studies
TRÖHLER, M., Cinema Studies
URSPRUNG, PH., Modern Art
WAGNER, K., German Literature
WEISS, D., Slavonic Languages
WILKENING, F., General Psychology
WIRTH, W., Publicity Science
ZEY, C., History

Faculty of Science (Winterthurerstr. 190, 8057 Zürich; tel. 446344002; fax 446346806; e-mail dekanat@mnf.uzh.ch; internet www.mnf.uzh.ch):

ACBERSOLD, R., Functional Genomics
ALBERTO, R., Inorganic Chemistry
AMSLER, C., Experimental Physics
BALDRIDGE, K., Computer-supported Chemistry
BARBOUR, A. D., Biomathematics
BASLER, K., Zoology, Molecular Development Genetics
BERKE, H. G. H., Inorganic Chemistry
BOLTHAUSEN, E., Mathematics, esp. Applied Mathematics
BRODMANN, M., Mathematics
BUCHER, H. F. R., Palaeontology
BURG, J.-P., Geology
CAFLISCH, A., Computer-supported Structural Biology
CATTANEO, A. S., Mathematics
CHIPOT, M. M., Mathematics
CONTI, E., Systematic Biology
DE LELLIS, C., Pure Mathematics
DOUGLAS, R., Neuroinformatics
EBERL, L., Microbiology
ENDRESS, P. K., Systematic Botany
FABRIKANT, S. I., Geography, esp. Geographical Information Science
FINK, H.-W., Experimental Physics
GEHRMANN, T., Theoretical Physics
GREBER, U., Zoology
GROSSNIKLAUS, U., Biology
HAEBERLI, W., Geography
HAHNLOSER, R., Neuroinformatics
HAMM, P., Physical Chemistry
HEINRICH, C. A., Crystallography and Petrography
HENGARTNER, M. O., Molecular Biology
HUTTER, J., Physical Chemistry
ITTEN, K. I., Geography
KAPPELER, T., Mathematics
KELLER, B., Plant Molecular Biology
KELLER, H., Physics of Condensed Matter
KÖNIG, B., Zoology, Behavioural Biology
KRESCH, A., Pure Mathematics
LAKE, G., Theoretical Physics
LEHNER, C. F., Developmental Biology
LINDER, H. P., Systematic Biology
MARTIN, K. A., Neurophysiology Systems
MARTINOIA, E., Plant Biology
MOORE, B., Theoretical Physics
MÜLLER-BÖKER, U., Anthropogeography
NOLL, M., Molecular Biology
OKONEK, CH., Mathematics
OSTERWALDER, J., Experimental Physics
REYER, H.-U., Zoology
ROBINSON, J. A., Organic Chemistry
ROSENTHAL, J. J., Mathematics
SAUTER, S. A., Mathematics
SCHAFFNER, W., Molecular Biology
SCHILLING, A., Experimental Physics
SCHMID, B., Environmental Science
SCHMIDT, M., Physical Geography
SCHMIDT, M. W., Crystalline Geology
SCHROEDER, V., Mathematics
SEEGER, S., Physical Chemistry
SELJAK, U., Theoretical Physics
SIEGEL, J. S., Organic Chemistry
STEINMANN-ZWICKY, M., Zoology
STENFLO, J. O., Astronomy
STEURER, W., Crystallography
STOECKLI, E., Neurobiology
STRAUMANN, U., Physics
THIERSTEIN, H. R., Micro-Palaeontology
THOMPSON, A. B., Petrology
VAN SCHAIK, C. P., Anthropology
VON MERING, CH., Bioinformatics
WARD, P., Zoology, Ecology
WEIBEL, R., Geography
WYLER, D., Theoretical Physics
ZOLLIKOFER, CH., Zoology

Faculty of Theology (Kirchgasse 9, 8001 Zürich; tel. 446344721; e-mail dekanat@theol.uzh.ch):

BERGIAN, S., History of Church and Dogma
BÜHLER, P., Systematic Theology
CAMPI, E., History of Church and Dogma
DALFERTH, I. U., Systematic Theology
FISCHER, J., Theological Ethics
KRÜGER, T., Old Testament
KUNZ, R., Practical Theology
SCHMID, K., Old Testament
UEHLINGER, C., History and Science of Religions
VOLLENWEIDER, S., New Testament
ZUMSTEIN, J., New Testament

Faculty of Veterinary Medicine (Winterthurerstr. 252, 8057 Zürich; tel. 446358121; fax 446358902; e-mail dekanat@vetadm.uzh.ch; internet www.vet.uzh.ch):

ACKERMANN, M., Virology
ALTHAUS, F., Pharmacology and Toxicology
AUER, J. A., Veterinary Surgery
BRAUN, U., Internal Medicine of Ruminants
BÜRKI, K., Laboratory Animal Science
DEPLAZES, P., Parasitology
EHRENSPERGER, F., Immunopathology
GASSMAN, M., Veterinary Physiology
HATT, J. M., Small Animals
HOTTIGER, M., Molecular Biology
HÜBSCHER, U., Biochemistry
KÄHN, W., Reproductive Medicine
LUTZ, H., Internal Medicine
LUTZ, TH., Physiology
MONTAVON, P. M., Surgery of Small Domestic Animals
NAEGELI, H. P., Toxicology
POSPISCHIL, A., Pathology
REUSCH, C., Internal Medicine (Small Animals)
SPIESS, B., Veterinary Ophthalmology
STEPHAN, R., Foodstuff Security
WANNER, M., Animal Nutrition
WITTENBRINK, M. M., Veterinary Bacteriology

UNIVERSITÉ DE FRIBOURG/ UNIVERSITÄT FREIBURG

1700 Fribourg
Telephone: 263007111
Fax: 263009700
E-mail: rectorat@unifr.ch
Internet: www.unifr.ch

Founded 1889
State control
Languages of instruction: French, German, English
Academic year: July to August
Rector: Prof. G. VERGAUWEN
Vice-Rector: Prof. A. EPINEY
Vice-Rector: Prof. J.-L. GURTNER
Vice-Rector: Prof. F. MÜLLER
Vice-Rector: Prof. J. PASQUIER
Librarian: M. GOOD
Library of 2,400,000 vols
Number of teachers: 200
Number of students: 10,000
Publications: *Uni Reflets* (6 a year), *Universitas Friburgensis* (4 a year)

DEANS

Faculty of Arts: Prof. THOMAS AUSTENFELD
Faculty of Economics and Social Sciences: Prof. M. WIDMER
Faculty of Law: Prof. MARCEL ALEXANDER NIGGLI
Faculty of Science: Prof. ROLF INGOLD
Faculty of Theology: Prof. MARIANO DELGADO

PROFESSORS

Faculty of Arts (Ave Europe 20, 1700 Fribourg; tel. 263007500; fax 263009709; e-mail lettres@unifr.ch; internet www.unifr.ch/lettres):

AUSTENFELD, T., American Literature
BERRENDONNER, A., French Linguistics
BERTHELE, R., Multilingualism
BILLERBECK, M., Classical Philology
BLESS, G., Therapeutic Pedagogy
BUDOWSKI, M., Social Policy
CASASUS, G., Contemporary History
CHRISTEN, H., Germanic Linguistics
CLAVIEN, A., General and Swiss Contemporary History
DARMS, G., Rhaeto-Romance Language and Culture
FRICKE, H., Modern German Literature
GHOSE, I., English Literature
GIORDANO, C., Ethnology
GURTNER, J.-L., General Pedagogy
HAUSER, C., General and Swiss Contemporary History
HERLTH, J., Slavistic Studies
HUBER, O., General Psychology
HUNKELER, T., French Literature
KARFIK, P., Philosophy of Antiquity
KRONIG, W., Special Education
KURMANN, P., History of Art
LAMBERT, J., Therapeutic Pedagogy
LUTZ, E., German Philology
MARTINI, A., Italian Literature
NIDA RUEMELIN, M., Philosophy
PEÑATE RIVERO, J., Spanish Literature
PERREZ, M., Clinical Psychology
PIÉRART, M., Ancient History
PYTHON, F., General and Swiss Contemporary History
REICHERTS, M., Clinical Psychology
REINHARDT, V., Early Modern History of Europe and Switzerland
SCHMIDT, H.-J., Medieval History of Europe and Switzerland
SCHMIDT, T., Classical Philology
SOLDATI, G., Modern and Contemporary Philosophy
SOULET, M., Social Work
SPIESER, J.-M., Early Christian Archaeology
STAMM, M., Education Science
STOICHITA, V., History of Art
SUAREZ NANI, T., Medieval Philosophy, Ontology
TURCHETTI, M., Early Modern History of Europe and Switzerland
VIEGNES, M., French Literature
WOLF, J.-C., Ethical and Political Philosophy
ZOPPELLI, L., History of Music

Faculty of Economics and Social Sciences (Blvd de Pérolles 90, 1700 Fribourg; tel. 263008200; fax 263009725; e-mail decanat-ses@unifr.ch; internet www.unifr.ch/economics):

BORTIS, H., History of Economic Theory
BOSSHART, L., Media and Communication
BOURGEOIS, D., Media and Communication
BRACHINGER, H.-W., Statistics
DAFFLON, B., Public Finance
DAVOINE, E., Administration of Human Resources
DESCHAMPS, P., Econometrics
EICHENBERGER, R., Public Finance
FRIBOULET, J.-J., Economic History
GMÜR, M., Management, NPO–Management
GÖX, R., Finance and Controlling
GRÖFLIN, H., Information Systems
GROSSMANN, V., Macro Economy
GRÜNIG, R., Management
GUGLER, P., Social and Political Economy
ISAKOV, D., Financial Management
MEIER, A., Informatics
MORSCHETT, D., International Management
PASQUIER-ROCHA, J., Informatics
ROSSI, S., Macro Economy
SCHÖNHAGEN, P., Media and Communication
TEUFEL, S., International Telecommunications Management
VANETTI, M., Marketing
WALLMEIER, M., Financial Management
WIDMER, M., Decision Support Systems
WOLFF, R., Economic Theory and Empirical Research

Faculty of Law (Ave Europe 20, 1700 Fribourg; tel. 263008000; fax 263009719; e-mail droit-decanat@unifr.ch; internet www.unifr.ch/droit):

AMSTUTZ, M., Private Law
BELSER, M., Private Law
BESSON, S., International Public Law, European Law
BORGHI, M., Swiss Public Law
BORS, M., Roman Law
EPINEY, A., Constitutional Law, International Public Law, European Law
HÄNNI, P., Constitutional and Administrative Law
HINNY, P., Tax Law
HÜRLIMANN-KAUP, B., Private Law
HURTADO POZO, J., Criminal Law
LE ROY, Y., History of Law, Canon Law
MURER, E., Labour and Social Insurance Law
NIGGLI, M., Criminal Law
PAHUD DE MORTANGES, R., History of Law
PICHONNAZ, P., Private Law
QUELOZ, N., Criminal Law
RUMO-JUNGO, A., Private Law
STEINAUER, P.-H., Civil Law
STÖCKLI, H., Civil Law, Trade Law
STOFFEL, W., International Private Law, Trade Law
TORRIONE, H., Tax Law and Philosophy of Law
VOLKEN, P., International and Commercial Law
WALDMANN, B., Public Law
WERRO, F., Private Law
ZUFFEREY, J. B., Public Law

Faculty of Science (Ch. du Musée 9, Pérolles, 1700 Fribourg; tel. 263008111; fax 263009729; e-mail science@unifr.ch; internet www.unifr.ch/sciences):

AEBI, P., Physics
BAERISWYL, D., Theoretical Physics
BERNHARD, C., Experimental Physics
BERRUT, J.-P., Mathematics
BERSIER, L.-F., Ecology and Evolution
BOCHET, C., Organic Chemistry
CELIO, M., Histology
CONZELMANN, A., Biochemistry
DESSAI, A., Mathematics
DE VIRGILIO, C., Biochemistry
FROMM, K., Inorganic Chemistry
HAUCK, C., Physical Geography
HIRSBRUNNER, B., Computer Science
HÖLZLE, M., Physical Geography
HUGHES, K., Microbiology
INGOLD, R., Computer Science
KELLERHALS, R., Mathematics
MAZZA, C., Statistics and Theory of Probability
MÉTRAUX, J.-P., Plant Biology
MONTANI, J.-P., Physiology
MÜLLER, F., Zoology
ROUILLER, E., Physiology
RÜEGG, C., Pathology
SCHEFFOLD, F., Experimental Physics
WEDER, C., Polymer Chemistry
WEIS, A., Experimental Physics
ZHANG, Y.-C., Theoretical Physics

Faculty of Theology (Ave Europe 20, 1700 Fribourg; tel. 263007370; fax 263009708; e-mail decanat-theol@unifr.ch; internet www.unifr.ch/theo):

DELGADO, M., History of Church
EMERY, G., Dogmatic Theology
HALLENSLEBEN, B., Dogmatic Theology

HOLDEREGGER, A., Moral Theology
KLÖCKENER, M., Moral Theology
KÜCHLER, M., New Testament Exegesis

UNIVERSITÉ DE GENÈVE

rue du Général-Dufour 24, 1211 Geneva 4
Telephone: 223797111
Fax: 223791134
E-mail: secretariat-rectorat@unige.ch
Internet: www.unige.ch

Founded 1559, univ. status 1873
Language of instruction: French
Academic year: October to July

Rector: Prof. JEAN-DOMINIQUE VASSALLI
Vice-Rector: Prof. ANIK DE RIBAUPIERRE
Vice-Rector: Prof. YVES FLÜCKIGER
Vice-Rector: Prof. PIERRE SPIERER
Sec.-Gen.: Dr STÉPHANE BERTHET
Library: see under Libraries and Archives
Number of teachers: 3,569
Number of students: 14,500
Publication: *Campus*

DEANS

Faculty of Arts: Prof. ERIC WEHRLI
Faculty of Economics and Social Science: Prof. BERNARD MORARD
Faculty of Law: Prof. CHRISTIAN BOVET
Faculty of Medicine: Prof. JEAN-LOUIS CARPENTIER
Faculty of Psychology and Educational Sciences: Prof. JEAN-PAUL BRONCKART
Faculty of Science: Prof. JEAN-MARC TRISCONE
Faculty of Theology: ANDREAS DETTWILER
School of Translation and Interpretation: LANCE HEWSON

PROFESSORS

Faculty of Arts (3 rue de Candolle, 1211 Geneva 4; tel. 223797111; fax 223791029; internet www.unige.ch/lettres):

ADAMZIK-BEVAND, K., German Literature and Civilization
ALVAR, C., Spanish Language and Literature
BARDAZZI, G., Romance Literature
BERELOWITCH, W., History
BOCCADORO, B., Musicology
BOLENS-JEANNERET, G., English Language and Literature
BORGEAUD, P., History of Ancient Religions
CAVIGNEAUX, A., Oriental Languages
CERUTTI, M., General History
CONRAD, C., History
DARBELLAY, E., Musicology
DE LIBERA, A., Philosophy
DESCOEUDRES, J.-P., Archaeology
FOEHR-JANSSENS, Y., Medieval French Literature
GAJO, G., Romance Literature
GAMBONI, L., Linguistics
GENEQUAND, C., Muslim and Arab Civilization
GROSRICHARD, A., French Literature
HAEBERLI, E., English Literature
HELG, A., General History
HURST, A., Classical Greek
JACCARD, J.-P., Russian Language
JENNY, L., French Literature
KOT, S., General History
LASSITHIOTAKIS, M., Modern Greek
LOMBARDO, P., French Literature
MADSEN, D., English Language and Literature
MANZOTTI, E., Italian Linguistics
MÉLA, CH., Medieval Romance Languages and Literature
MOESCHLER, J., General Linguistics
MORENZONI, F., History
MULLIGAN, K., Philosophy
NAEF, S., Arabic Language
NATALE, M., History of Art
NELIS, D., Latin Literature
PERUGI, M., Medieval Latin Language and Literature
PONT, J.-C., History of Sciences
PORRET, M., Modern History
POT, O., French Literature
RIGOLI, J., French Literature
SCHRADER, H. J., German Literature and Civilization
SCHUBERT, P., Modern Greek
SHLONSKY, UR., Linguistics
SOUYRI, P.-F., Japanese
SPURR, D. A., Modern English Literature
TALENS, C. J., Spanish Language and Literature
TILLIETTE, J.-Y., Medieval Latin Language and Literature
VALLOGGIA, M., Egyptology
WALTER, F., General History
WEHRLI, E., French Linguistics and Computer Science
WETZEL, R., German Literature and Civilization
WINKLER, M., German Literature and Civilization
WIRTH, J., History of Art in the Middle Ages
ZUFFEREY, Chinese Studies

Faculty of Economics and Social Science (40 blvd du Pont-d'Arve, 1211 Geneva 4; tel. 223797111; fax 223799919; internet www.unige.ch/ses):

ALLAN, P., Political Science
ANTILLE GAILLARD, G., Economics and Social Science
BALLMER-CAO, T.-H., Political Science
BENDER, A., Industrial Organization
BERGADAA DELMAS, M., Marketing
BRAILLARD, P., European Globalization
BURGENMEIER, B., Political Economy
CARLEVARO, F., Econometrics
CASSIS, Y., Economic History
CATTACIN, S., Sociology
CURZON-PRICE, V., Economics
DE BLASIS, J. P., Industrial Organization
DE LA GRANDVILLE, O., Political Economy
DE MELO, J., Political Economy
DEBARBIEUX, B., Geography
DENIS, J. E., Industrial Organization
DUMONT, P.-A., Industrial Organization
DUMONTIER, P., Accountancy
FLUECKIGER, Y., Political Economy
GILLI, M., Computer Science, Econometrics
HOESLI, M. E. R., Real Estate Financing
HORBER, E., Sociology
HUSSY, C., Geography
JARILLO, J.-C., Economic Strategy
KELLERHALS, J., Sociology
KONSTANTAS, D., Information Systems
KRISHNAKUMAR, J., Econometrics
LANE, J. E., Political Science
LAWRENCE, R. J., Human Ecology
LEFOLL, J., Industrial Organization
LEONARD, M., Computer Science applied to Business
LOUBERGÉ, H., Political Economy
MAGNENAT THALMANN, N., Information Systems
MIRONESCO, C., Political Science
MORARD, B., Accountancy
MÜLLER, T., Econometrics
ORIS, M., Economic History
OSSIPOW, W., Political Science
PROBST, G., Industrial Organization
RAFFOURNIER, B., Accountancy
RECORDON, P. A., Contracts
RITSCHARD, G., Econometrics
RONCHETTI, E., Industrial Organization
ROYER, D., Statistics
SAUVAIN, C., Demography
SCAILLET, O., Statistics and Probability
SCHMITT, N., Political Economy
SCIARINI, P., Political Science
SCHNEIDER, S. C., Industrial Organization
SCHULTHEISS, F., Sociology
THOENIG, M., Political Economy
VERLEY, P., Economic History
VERNEX, J. C., Geography
VIAL, J.-PH., Industrial Organization
VIALLON, P., Sociology
VICTORIA FESER, M.-P., Statistics and Probability
WEBER, L., Political Economy
WINDISCH, U., Sociology

Faculty of Law (40 blvd du Pont-d'Arve, 1211 Geneva 4; tel. 223797111; fax 223799916; internet www.unige.ch/droit):

AUBERT, G., Administrative Law
AUER, A., Constitutional Law
BADDELEY, M., Civil Law
BELLANGER, F., Fiscal Law
BOISSON DE CHAZOURNES, L., Public International Law
BOVET, C., Fiscal Law
BUCHER, A., Civil Law
CASSANI, U., Penal Law
CHAPPUIS, C., Business Law
DELLEY, J.-D., Constitutional Law
FLUECKIGER, A., Constitutional Law
FOEX, B., Civil Law
GREBER, P. Y., Administrative Law
HOTTELIER, M., Constitutional Law
JEANDIN, N., Civil Law
KADDOUS, C., Public International Law
KADNER, T., Civil Law
KAUFMANN-KOHLER, G., Private International Law
KELLER, A., History of Institutions and Law
LEVRAT, N., Public International Law
MALINVERNI, G., Constitutional Law, Introduction to the Science of Law
MANAÏ-WEHRLI, D., Civil Law
MONNIER, V., History of Institutions and Law
OBERSON, X. B., Fiscal Law
PETER, H., Civil Law
PETITPIERRE-SAUVAIN, A., Commercial Law
ROBERT, C. N., Penal Law, Criminology
ROTH, R., Penal Law
SASSOLI, M., Public International Law
STAUDER, B., German Commercial Law
STETTLER, M., Civil Law
TANQUEREL, T., Constitutional Law
THÉVENOZ, L., Civil Law
TRIGO TRINDADE, R. M., Business and Commercial Law
WINIGER, B., European and Civil Law

Faculty of Medicine (C.M.U., 1 rue Michel-Servet, 1211 Geneva 4; tel. 223795111; fax 223473334; internet www.unige.ch/medecine):

ANTONORAKIS, S., Genetics and Microbiology
ASSIMACOPOULOS, F., Medical Biochemistry
BADER, C., Oto-neuro-ophthalmology
BAEHNI, P., Dentistry
BAERTSCHI, A. J., Physiology
BAIROCH, A., Medical Biochemistry
BARRAZZONE, C., Paediatrics
BECKER, C., Radiology
BEGHETTI, M., Paediatrics
BELIN, D., Pathology
BELLI, D. C., Paediatrics
BELSER, U., Dentistry
BERNER, M., Paediatrics
BERNHEIM, L., Physiology
BERTRAND, D., Physiology
BERTSCHY, G., Psychiatry
BISCHOF, P. A., Gynaecology and Obstetrics
BORISCH, B., Pathology
BOUNAMEAUX, H., Medicine
CAPPONI, A., Endocrinology
CARPENTIER, J.-L., Morphology
CAVERZASIO, J., Medicine
CHARDOT, C., Paediatrics
CHEVROLET, J.-C., Medicine
CLERGUE, F., Cardiology
COLLART BUCKHARD, M., Medical Biochemistry

COSSON, P., Morphology
DAYER, J.-M., Medicine
DAYER, P., Pharmacology
DE TRIBOLET, N., Oto-neuro-ophthalmology
DEMAUREX, N., Physiology
DUBUISSON, J.-S., Gynaecology and Obstetrics
FANTINI, B., Medicine
FASEL, J., Morphology
FERRERO, F., Pharmacology
FRENCH, L., Oto-neuro-ophthalmology
GABAY, C., Medicine
GEISSBUHLER, A., Radiology
GENTA, R., Pathology
GEORGOPOULOS, C. P., Medical Biochemistry
GIANNAKOPOULOS, P., Psychiatry
GIRARDIN, E., Paediatrics
GOLAY, A., Medicine
GUYOT, J., Oto-neuro-ophthalmology
HADENGUE, A., Medicine
HALBAN, PH., Medicine
HARDING, T., Legal Medicine
HOCHSTRASSER, D., Medical Biochemistry
HOESSLI, D., Pathology
HOFFMEYER, P., Surgery
HUEPPI, P., Paediatrics
IMHOF, B., Pathology
ISELIN, C., Surgery
IZUI, S., Pathology
KATO, A. C., Oto-neuro-ophthalmology
KAYSER BENGT, E. J., Sports Medicine
KILIARIDIS, S., Orthodontics
KISS, J. Z., Morphology
KOLAKOFSKY, D., Microbiology
KRAUSE, K. H., Medicine
KREJCI, I., Dentistry
LANDIS, T., Oto-neuro-ophthalmology
LE COULTRE, C., Surgery
LERCH, R., Medicine
LEW, D. P., Microbiology
LINDER, P., Medical Biochemistry
LÜSCHER, C., Oto-neuro-ophthalmology
MAGISTRETTI, P., Psychiatry
MALAFOSSE, A., Psychiatry
MARTIN, P.-Y., Nephrology
MAURON, A., Clinical Ethics
MEDA, P., Morphology
MENTHA, G., Surgery
MICHEL, C., Oto-neuro-ophthalmology
MICHEL, J.-P., Geriatrics
MOMBELLI, A., Orthodontics
MONTESANO, R., Morphology
MORABIA, A., Social Medicine
MOREL, D., Cardiology
MOREL, PH., Surgery
MUHLETHALER, M., Neurophysiology
MÜLLER, D., Pharmacology
MÜLLER, F., Dental Prosthesis
PALACIO-ESPASA, F., Psychiatry
PANIZZON, R., Oto-neuro-ophthalmology
PELIZZONE, M., Oto-neuro-ophthalmology
PERNEGER, T., Social Medicine
PERRIER, A., Medicine
PETER, R., Surgery
PHILIPPE, J., Medicine
PITTET, D., Medicine
PITTET-CUENOD, B., Surgery
PRALONG, F., Medicine
RAPIN, CH.-H., Gerontology
RATIB, O., Radiology
REITH, W., Genetics, Microbiology
RICHTER, M. W., Surgery
ROCHAT, T., Medicine
ROSE, K., Medical Biochemistry
ROUGEMONT, A., Social Medicine
ROUX, L., Genetics, Microbiology
RUEFENACHT, D., Radiology
RUIZ-ALTABA, A., Stem Cells
SAFRAN, A.-B., Oto-neuro-ophthalmology
SAMSON, J., Dentistry
SAPPINO, P., Oncology
SAURAT, J.-H., Dermatology
SCHLEGEL, W., Medicine
SCHNIDER, A., Oto-neuro-ophthalmology
SIEGRIST, C.-A., Paediatrics
SIGWART, U., Medicine
SOLDATI-FAVRE, D., Genetics, Microbiology
STALDER, J., Medicine
STRUBIN, M., Genetics, Microbiology
SUTER, P., Surgery
SUTER, S., Paediatrics
VAN DER GOOT GRUNBERG, F., Genetics, Microbiology
VASSALLI, J.-D., Morphology
VILLEMURE, J.-G., Oto-neuro-ophthalmology
VU, NU. V., Medicine
WOLLHEIM, C., Medicine
ZUBLER, R., Medicine

Faculty of Protestant Theology (3 rue de Candolle, 1211 Geneva 4; tel. 223797111; fax 223797430; e-mail info@theologie.unige.ch; internet www.unige.ch/theologie):

BACKUS, I., History of the Reformation
BENEDICT, J., History of the Reformation
DERMANGE, F., Ethics
DETTWILER, A., New Testament Exegesis
GRANDJEAN, M., History of Christianity
NORELLI, E., New Testament Exegesis
PITASSI, M. C., History of the Reformation

Faculty of Psychology and Educational Sciences (40 blvd du Pont-d'Arve, 1211 Geneva 4; tel. 223797111; fax 223799020; internet www.unige.ch/fapse):

Section of Psychology:

BARISUKOV, K., Psychology of Mental Deficiency
BETRANCOURT, M., Training Technologies
CASPAR, F., Psychology
DE RIBAUPIERRE, A., Differential Psychology
EID, M., Data Analysis
FRAUENFELDER, U. H., Psycholinguistics
GENDOLLA, G., Psychology
GILLIÈRON-PALÉOLOGUE, C., Psychology, Epistemology
HAUERT, C.-A., Psychology of Development
KAISER, S., Verbal and Non-Verbal Communication
KERZEL, D., Cognitive Psychology
LORENZI-CIOLDI, F., Social Psychology
MOUNOUD, P., Psychology of Personality Development
MUGNY, G., Social Psychology
ROBERT-TISSOT, C., Child Psychotherapy
SCHERER, K., Social Psychology
VAN DER LINDEN, M., Psychopathology
VANHULLE, S., Psychology
VIVIANI, P., Statistics and Modelling in Psychology
ZESIGER, P. E., Language Disorders

Section of Educational Sciences:

ALLAL, L., Pedagogical Evaluation
AUDIGIER, F., Teaching of Social Science and Humanities
BAYER, E., Research Techniques in Education
BELLIER, S., Educational Sciences
BRONCKART, J.-P., Introduction to Language Theories
BUCHEL, F., Cognitive Education
CHATELANAT, G., Educational Sciences
CIFALI, M., Psycho-pedagogy
CRAHAY, M., Educational Sciences
DASEN, P., Introduction to Educational Sciences
DOLZ-MESTRE, J., Educational Sciences
DURAND, M., Adult Education
GIORDAN, A., Psycho-pedagogy in Sciences
HANHART, S., Education
HOFSTETTER-ROSET, R., Educational Sciences
JOBERT, G., Adult Education
MAGNIN, C. F., History of Education
PAYET, J. P., Sociology of Education
PERAYA, D., Educational Sciences
PERREGAUX, C., Cultural and Linguistic Diversity at School
PERRENOUD, P., General Pedagogy
SAADA-ROBERT, M., Learning Process
SCHNEUWLY, B., Introduction to Language Theories
SCHUBAUER, M.-L., Social Psychology
SCHURMANS BRONCKART, M. N., Social Construction of Knowledge

Faculty of Science (30 quai Ernest-Ansermet, 1211 Geneva 4; tel. 223796111; fax 223796698; internet www.unige.ch/sciences):

ALEXAKIS, A, Organic Chemistry
ALEXEEV, A., Mathematics
AUGUSTYNSKI, J., Applied Mineral Chemistry
BALLIVET, M., Biochemistry
BENY, J.-L., Animal Biology
BESSE, M., Anthropology, Ecology
BLECHA, A., Astronomy
BLONDEL, A., Nuclear Physics
BORKOVEC, M., Applied Mineral Chemistry
BOURQUIN, M., Nuclear Physics
BROUGHTON, W. J., Botany
BUCHS, D., Electronic Computing
BUETTIKER, M., Theoretical Physics
BUFFLE, J., Mineral Chemistry
BURKI, G., Astronomy
CARRUPT, P. A., Pharmacy
CHOPARD, B., Electronic Computing
CLARK, A. G., Nuclear Physics
CORAY, D., Mathematics
COURVOISIER, TH., Astronomy
DAVAUD, E. J., Geology
DE LA HARPE, P., Mathematics
DOELKER, E., Pharmacy
DOMINIK, J., History and Philosophy of Science
DROZ, M., Theoretical Physics
DUBOULE, D., Animal Biology
DUNGAN, M., Mineralogy
DURRER, R., Theoretical Physics
ECKMANN, J. P., Theoretical Physics and Mathematics
EDELSTEIN, S., Biochemistry
FISCHER, Ø., Physics
FONTBOTÉ, L., Mineralogy
GANDER, M.-J., Mathematics
GEOFFROY, M., Physical Chemistry
GIAMARCHI, T., Solid State Physics
GISIN, N., Theoretical Physics
GORIN, G. E., Geology
GRENON, M., Astronomy
GRUENBERG, J., Biochemistry
GULAÇAR, F., Physical Chemistry
GURNY, R., Pharmacy
HAIRER, E., Mathematics
HAUSER, A., Physical Chemistry
HOCHSTRASSER, D., Pharmacy
HOPFGARTNER, G., Pharmacy
HOSTETTMANN, K., Pharmacy
IZZAURRALDE, E., Molecular Biology
JEAN-PETIT-MATILE, S., Organic Chemistry
KIENZLE, M.-N., Solid State Physics
KINDLER, P., Geology and Palaeontology
KRAEMER BILBE, A., Cell Biology
KUNDIG, E. P., Organic Chemistry
LACHAL, B. M., Problems of Energy
LACHAVANNE, J.-B., Anthropology
LACOUR, J., Organic Chemistry
LANGANEY, A., Anthropology
LELUC, C., Nuclear Physics
MAEDER, A., Astronomy
MAGGIORE, M., Theoretical Physics
MARTINOU, J.-C., Cell Biology
MAYOR, M., Astronomy
MONOD, N., Mathematics
PALAZZO ROLIM, J., Electronic Computing
PASZKOWSKI, J., Vegetal Biology
PELLEGRINI, CH., Computer Science
PENEL, C., Botany
PFENNIGER, D., Astronomy
PICARD, D., Biology
PIGUET, C., Mineral Chemistry
POHL, M., Nuclear Physics
PONT, J.-C., History and Philosophy of Science
PUN, T., Computer Science

Rapin, D., Nuclear Physics
Riezman, H., Biochemistry
Rochaix, J.-D., Biology
Rodriguez, I., Animal Biology
Ronga, F., Mathematics
Ruegg, U.-T., Pharmacy
Sanchez-Mazas de Abreu, A., Anthropology
Scappozza, L., Pharmacy
Schaltegger, U., Mineralogy
Schibler, U., Molecular Biology
Shore, D., Molecular Biology
Smirnov, S., Mathematics
Spierer, P., Animal Biology
Strasser, R., Botany
Streit, F., Mathematics
Triscone, J.-M., Solid State Physics
van der Marel, D., Solid State Physics
Vauthey, E., Physical Chemistry
Veuthey, J.-L., Pharmaceutical Chemistry
Wanner, G., Mathematics
Wernli, R., Micropalaeontology
Wildi, W., Geology
Williams, A. F., Applied Mineral Chemistry
Wittwer, P., Theoretical Physics
Wolf, J.-P., Physics
Wolfender, J. L., Pharmacy
Yvon, K., Structural Crystallography
Zaninetti, L., Zoology and Palaeontology

Institute of Architecture (7 route de Drize, 1227 Carouge; tel. 223790799; fax 223799789; e-mail info@archi.unige.ch; internet www.unige.ch/ia):

Cêtre, J.-P., Materials and Structures
Mariani, R., Urban History
Reichlin, B., Theory of Architecture
Scheiwiller, A., Architectural Design and Arts and Crafts
Simonnet, C., Culture and History of Architecture and Arts and Crafts
Weber, W., Architecture

School of Translation and Interpretation (40 blvd du Pont-d'Arve, 1211 Geneva 4; tel. 223797111; fax 223798750; internet www.unige.ch/eti):

Abdel Hadi, M., Arabic
Armstrong, S., Use of Computers
Bocquet, C.-Y., French
Daniel, M., Translation with Computer Assistance
de Bessé, B., Terminology
Fantuzzi, M., Italian
Gemar, J.-C., French
Grin, F., French
Hewson Lance, S. F., English
Lee-Jahnke, H., German
Marchesini, G., Italian
Moser-Mercer, B., German
Setton, R. A. M., Interpretation
Weibel, L., French

ATTACHED SCHOOLS

École d'Education Physique et de Sport (School of Physical Education and Sport): tel. 223797722; attached to Faculty of Medicine; Dir P. Holenstein.

École de Langue et de Civilisation Françaises (School of French Language and Culture): tel. 223797111; fax 223797681; internet www.unige.ch/lettres/elcf; attached to Faculty of Arts; teaching activities, research and services in areas of French language (FLE), applied linguistics and multilingualism; Dir Prof. Laurent Gajo.

ASSOCIATED INSTITUTES

Institut Oecuménique de Bossey (Ecumenical Institute): Château de Bossey, POB 1000, 1299 Crans-près-Céligny;Château de Bossey, Chemin Chenevière 2, Bogis-Bossey; tel. 229607300; fax 229607367; e-mail bossey@wcc-coe.org; internet www.wcc-coe.org/bossey; f. 1946; Dir Ioan Sauca.

UNIVERSITÉ DE LAUSANNE

1015 Lausanne
Telephone: 216921111
Fax: 216922615
E-mail: uniscope@unil.ch
Internet: www.unil.ch
Founded 1537, present name and status 1890
Language of instruction: French
Academic year: September to July
Rector: Prof. Dominique Arlettaz
Vice-Rector for Human Resources and Infrastructure: Jean-Paul Dépraz
Vice-Rector for Research and Academic Affairs: Prof. Philippe Moreillon
Vice-Rector for Education: Prof. Danielle Chaperon
Vice-Rector for Valorization and Quality: Jacques Lanarès
Gen. Sec.: Marc de Perrot
Librarian: Jeannette Frey
Library: see Libraries and Archives
Number of teachers: 720
Number of students: 12,091
Publications: *Allez Savoir!*, *L'Enseignement*, *La Recherche*, *Uniscope*

DEANS

Faculty of Arts: Prof. François Rosset
Faculty of Biology and Medicine: Prof. Patrick Francioli
Faculty of Business and Economics: Prof. Daniel Oyon
Faculty of Geosciences and Environment: Prof. Jean Ruegg
Faculty of Law and Criminal Justice: Prof. Laurent Moreillon
Faculty of Social and Political Science: Prof. René Knüsel
Faculty of Theology and Religious Studies: Prof. Pierre Gisel

PROFESSORS

Faculty of Biology and Medicine (Rue du Bugnon 21, 1005 Lausanne; tel. 216925000; fax 216925005; e-mail info.fbm@unil.ch; internet www.unil.ch/fbm):

Acha-Orbea, H., Biochemistry
Aguet, M., ISREC
Ansermet, F., Child and Adolescent Psychiatry
Barrandon, Y., Experimental Surgery
Barras, V., History of Medicine and Public Health
Beckmann, J., Medical Genetics
Besson, J., Community Psychiatry
Bille, J., Medical Bacteriology
Biollaz, J., Clinical Pharmacology
Bischof-Delaloye, A., Nuclear Medicine
Bosman, F. T., Pathology
Bula, C., Geriatrics
Burnier, M., Nephrology
Calandra, T., Infectious Diseases
Chiolero, R. L., Intensive Surgical Care
Clarke, S., Neuropsychology and Neurorehabilitation
Danuser, B., Work Health
Demartines, N., Visceral Surgery
Desvergne, B., Genomics
Dotto, G.-P., Biochemistry
Egloff, D. V., Surgery
Fanconi, S., Paediatrics
Farmer, E. E., Molecular Biology
Farron, A., Orthopedics
Frackowiak, R., Neurology
Francioli, P., Preventive Hospital Medicine
Gaillard, R. C., Endocrinology and Metabolism
Gruetter, R., Biomedical Imagery
Guex, P., Psychiatry of Liaison
Guillou, L., Pathology
Haalfon, O., Infant and Adolescent Psychiatry
Haas, D., Basic Microbiology
Hernansez, N., Genomics
Herr, W., Genomics
Hohlfeld, P., Obstetrics
Hornung, J.-P., Cell Biology and Morphology
Jichlinski, P., Urology
Keller, L., Ecology and Evolution
Kern, C. G., Anesthesiology
Launois, P., Biochemistry
Lehr, H.-A., Pathology
Levi, F. G., Social and Preventive Medicine
Levivier, M., Neuro-Surgery
Leyvraz, P.-F., Locomotive Device
Magistretti, P., Psychiatric Neurosciences
Mangin, P., Forensic Medicine
Mayer, A., Biochemistry
Mermod, N., Biotechnology
Meuli, R., Radiodiagnostic and Radiology Intervention
Michaud, P.-A., Adolescent Health
Michetti, P., Gastroenterology and Hepatalogy
Mirimanoff, R.-O., Radiotherapy
Moessinger, A. C., Neonatology and Paediatrics
Monnier, P., Otorhinolaryngology
Moradpour, D., Gastroenterology and Hepatalogy
Moreillon, P., Basic Microbiology
Nicod, L., Pneumology
Nicod, P., Internal Medicine
Paccaud, F. M., Social and Preventive Medicine
Panizzon, R., Dermatology
Pantaleo, G., Allergology and Immunology
Pascual, M., Transplantation
Pécoud, A., General Medicine
Perrin, N., Ecology and Evolution
Ris, H.-B. F., Thoracic and Vascular Surgery
Saurat, J. H., Dermatology
Schenk, F., Physiology
Schild, L., Pharmacology and Toxiology
Schnyder, P.-A., Radiodiagnostics and Radiology Intervention
So, A., Rheumatology, Physical Medicine and Rehabilitation
Stamenkovic, I., Pathology
Stiefel, F., Psychiatry of Liasion
Tappy, L., Physiology
Telenti, A., Microbiology
Thorens, B., Genomics
Tissot, J.-D., Haematology
Tschopp, J., Biochemistry
Volterra, A., Cellular Biology, Morphology
von Segesser, L.-K., Cardiovascular Surgery
Waeber, B., Clinical Physiopathology
Waeber, G., Internal Medicine
Wahli, W., Genomics
Zografos, L., Ophthalmology

Faculty of Geosciences and Environment (tel. 216923500; fax 216923505; internet www.unil.ch/gse):

Baumgartner, P. O., Institute of Geology and Palaentology
Erkman, S., Institute of Territorial Politics and Human Ecology
Holliger, K., Institute of Geophysics
Jaboyedoff, M., Institute of Geomatics and Risk Analysis
Muntener, O., Institute of Mineralogy and Geochemistry
Reynard, E., Institute of Geography

Faculty of Law and Criminal Justice (tel. 216922740; fax 21692745; internet www.unil.ch/droit):

Bieri, L., Law of Obligation
Bonomi, A., Comparative Civil Law and International Private Law

BRIDEL, P., Political Economics, Centre Walras-Pareto
DONGOIS, N., Penal Law
FAVRE, A.-CH., Environment Law
HAHN, M., European Law
KAHIL-WOLFF, B., Social Security
KUHN, A., Criminology
MARGOT, P., Criminal Investigation
MARTENET, V., Constitutional Law
MEIER, PH., Civil Law
MOREILLON, L., Penal Law
MORIN, A., Law of Obligation
NOEL, Y., Tax Law
PETER, H., Roman Law, Bankruptcy Law
PIOTET, D., Civil Law
POLTIER, E., Administrative Law
RAPP, J.-M., Commercial Law
SCHULZE, G., German Law
TAPPY, D., Private Law, History of Public Institutions and Sources, Civil Procedure
ZIEGLER, A., Foreign Trade Law and International Public Law

Faculty of Letters (BFSH2, 1015 Lausanne; tel. 216922978; fax 216922905; internet www.unil.ch/lettres):

ADAM, J.-M., French Linguistics
ALBERA, F., History of Cinema
BÉRARD, C., Classical Archaeology
BERTHOUD, A.-C., Applied Linguistics
BOUVIER, D., Greek Language and Literature
BRONKHORST, J., Sanskrit, Indian Studies
CÉLIS, R., Philosophy
DUCREY, P., Ancient History
EBERENZ, R., Spanish Linguistics and Philology
ESFELD, M. A., Philosophy
FORSYTH, N., English Literature
HALTER, P., American Literature
HART-NIBBRIG, C., German Language and Literature
HELLER, L., Modern Russian Literature
HOFMANN, E., History
JEQUIER, F., Modern History
JOLIVET, R., Theoretical Linguistics, Sociolinguistics
JOST, H.-U., Modern Swiss History
KAEMPFER, J., French Literature
KELLER, E., Computing for the Humanities
LARA POZUELO, A., Spanish Language and Literature
MAGGETTI, D., French Literature
MARCHAND, J.-J., Italian Language and Literature
MICHEL, C., History of Art
MÜHLETHALER, J.-C., Medieval French
NESCHKE HENTSCHKE, A., Philosophy
PARAVICINI, A., Medieval History
PRALORAN, M., Italian Linguistics
REICHLER, C., French Language and Literature
ROMANO G. DI STURMECK, S., History of Art
SCHWARZ, A., German Linguistics
SCHWYTER, J., English Linguistics
SERIOT, P., Russian Linguistics and Philology
TILLEMANS, T., Oriental Languages and Civilizations
TOSCATO-RIGO, D., Modern History
UTZ, P., German Language and Literature
VAN MAL-MAEDER, D., German Language and Literature
WYSS, A., Modern French Language and Literature

Faculty of Social and Political Science (BFSH2, 1015 Lausanne; tel. 216923100; fax 216923115; internet www.unil.ch/ssp):

BATOU, J., European Political and Social History
BRAUN, D., Political Sciences
BUTERA, F., Social Psychology
DAUWALDER, J.-P., Psychology
FILLIEULE, O., Study of Social and Political Movements
FONTANA, B., History of Political Theory
GRAZ, J.-C., International Relations
GROSSEN, M., Clinical Psychosociology
HOFMANN, E., History and Social Sciences
KAUFMANN, L., Sociology of Communication and Culture
KILANI, M., Cultural and Social Anthropology
KNUSEL, R., Social Policy
LE FEUVRE, N., Sociology of Work and Employment
MERRIEN, F. X., Sociology, Social Policy
MORO, C., Developmental and Educational Psychology
MUNSCH, S., Child and Adolescent Clinical Psychology
OHL, F., Sociology of Sport
PAPADOPOULOS, I., Public Policy
PETITAT, A., Sociology, Education
ROMAN, P., Clinical Psychology
ROSSIER, J., Career Counselling and Vocational Psychology
SANTIAGO, M., Health Psychology
SCHENK, F., Neurosciences, Psychophysiology
VOLKEN, H., Applied Mathematics

Faculty of Theology and Religious Studies (BFSH2, 1015 Lausanne; tel. 216922700; fax 216922700; e-mail secretariattheologie@unil.ch; internet www.unil.ch/theol):

AMSLER, F., History of Christianity
BURGER, M., Science of Religions
EHRENFREUND, J., History of Jews and Judaism
GISEL, P., Dogmatics and Fundamental Theology
MULLER, D., Ethics
ROMER, TH., Old Testament
STOLZ, J., Religious Sociology

Business School (BFSH1, 1015 Lausanne; tel. 216923300; fax 216933005; internet www.hec.unil.ch):

ANTONAKIS, J., Organizational Behaviour
AUTIO, E., Strategic Technology Management
BERGMANN, A., Organizational Behaviour
BRÜLHART, M., International Economics, Applied Econometrics
BÜTLER, M., Economics, Public Finance
CADOT, O., International Economy
CATRY, B., Business Policy
CESTRE, G., Marketing
DANTHINE, J.-P., Monetary Theory and Policy, Macroeconomics, Quantitative Methods
DE TREVILLE, S., Productivity in Operations Management
DUBEY, A., Actuarial Mathematics
DUFRESNE, F., Economic and Actuarial Mathematics
DUPARC, J., Theoretical Computer Science
GARBINATO, B., Programming
GERBER, H.-U., Economic and Actuarial Mathematics
GHERNAOUTI HÉLIE, S., Information Systems
HAMERI, A., Operations Management
HOFFRAGE, U., Risk Theory
HOLLY, A., Econometrics
IMBS, J., Macroeconomics
JONDEAU, E., Finance
LIMAYEM, M., Information Technology
MATTEI, A., Microeconomics and Statistics
MORELLEC, E., Finance
MUNARI, S., System Management
OYON, D., Accounting
PIGNEUR, Y., Information Systems
RACINE, J.-B., Geographical Structures
ROCKINGER, M., Finance
ST-AMOUR, P., Macroeconomics
STETTLER, A., Financial Accounting
USUNIER, J.-C., International Marketing
VAN ACKERE, A., Decision Science
VON UNGERN, T., Analysis of Industrial Structures, Macroeconomics
WEISS, L., Financial Accounting
WENTLAND FORTE, M., Knowledge Management

School of Criminal Sciences (tel. 216924600; fax 216924605; e-mail info.esc@unil.ch; internet www.unil.ch/esc):

AEBI, M.F., Criminology and Penal Law
CHAMPOD, C., Scientific Police
MARGOT, P., Criminal Science

School of French as a Foreign Language (tel. 216923080; fax 216923085; e-mail efle@unil.ch):

ANDISON, L.
BLANC, G.
BREYMANN, T.
BUCHS, A.
CAPRÉ, R.
CERNUSCHI, A.
CORDONIER, D.
DE VRIES DE HECKELINGEN, B.
DELACRÉTAZ MAGGETTI, A. L.
FLÜTSCH, C.
GENOUD, I.
GIROUD, A.
GONZALEZ, A.
JAQUEROD, P.
KILANI SCHOCH, M.
MARCELLI, A.
NICOLLERAT GILLARD, M.
PANDAZIS-RUDER, A. C.
PFERSICH, H.
REYMOND, C.

UNIVERSITÉ DE NEUCHÂTEL

ave du 1er Mars 26, 2000 Neuchâtel
Telephone: 327181000
Fax: 327181001
E-mail: contact@unine.ch
Internet: www2.unine.ch

Founded 1838
Languages of instruction: French, English
Academic year: September to June

Rector: Dr MARTINE RAHIER
Vice-Rector for Education: Prof. PHILIPPE TERRIER
Vice-Rector for Quality: Prof. CLAIRE JAQUIER
Vice-Rector for Research Devt: Prof. NATHALIE TISSOT
Sec.-Gen.: PHILIPPE JEANNERET
Librarian: L. REGAMEY

Number of teachers: 120
Number of students: 4,056

Publications: *Recueils*, *UniNews* (5 a year)

DEANS

Faculty of Economics: JEAN-MARIE GRETHER
Faculty of Humanities: LAURENT TISSOT
Faculty of Law: JEAN-PHILIPPE DUNAND
Faculty of Science: Prof. PETER KROPF
Faculty of Theology: Prof. FÉLIX MOSER

PROFESSORS

Faculty of Economics (7 Pierre-à-Mazel, 2000 Neuchâtel; tel. 327181500; fax 327181501; e-mail secretariat.seco@unine.ch; internet www.unine.ch/seco):

BANGERTER, A.
BARANZINI, R.
BELKONIENE, A.
BERTHO-LAVENIR, C.
BLILI, S.
CHAPPUIS, F.
CHARDONNENS, J.
CIORASCU, I.
COTTIER, B.
DAL ZOTTO, C.
DE BONDT, W.
DE COULON, A.
DE SCHEPPER, W.
DEBRAINE, L.
DUBOIS, M.
DUMONTIER, P.
GRESSE, C.

GRETHER, J.
GRIZE, Y.
GUNTHERT, A.
HARAYAMA, Y.
HAZAN, P.
JEANRENAUD, C.
KASSANOS, E.
KLAPPROTH, S.
KORKMAZ, A.
KOSTECKI, M.
LACK, J.
LAVENIR-LECLERC, C.
MASSIANI, A.
MATEI, A.
MATHYS, N.
MELFI, G.
MINELLI, M.
NEDYALKOVA, D.
NIVAT, A.
NUSSBAUM, P.
PILET, J.
PLENEL, E.
RAFFOURNIER, B.
RAMACIOTTI, D.
REINER, G.
RIME, B.
ROGER, P.
ROTHENBUEHLER, P.
SALVA LOPEZ, C.
SBERGAMI, F.
SCHMID MAST, M.
SCHOENENBERGER, A.
SIMON, E.
SONNEY, F.
STANOEVSKA-SLABEVA, K.
STARICA, C.
STOFFEL, K.
TILLE, Y.
TSCHAN SEMMER, F.
ZARIN-NEJADAN, M.
ZUBER, J.

Faculty of Law (26 ave du 1er Mars, 2000 Neuchâtel; tel. 327181200; fax 327181201; e-mail secretariat.droit@unine.ch; internet www.unine.ch/droit):

AMARELLE, C.
BOHNET, F.
BRUCHEZ, C.
CERUTTI, D.
CHENAUX, J.
CLERC, E.
DANON, R.
DELIMATSIS, P.
DESPLAND, B.
DIACONU, M.
DISTEFANO, G.
DUNAND, J.
ENGEL, S.
GARIBIAN, S.
GUILLAUME, F.
GUILLOD, O.
GUY-ECABERT, C.
JEANNERET, Y.
JONGEN, F.
KRAUS, D.
KUHN, A.
LEMPEN, K.
MAHON, P.
MARCHAND, S.
MAVROIDIS, P.
MIZEL, C.
MUELLER, C.
NGUYEN, M.
OSWALD, D.
RIGOZZI, A.
SPRUMONT, D.
TISSOT, N.
WESSNER, P.
ZEN-RUFFINEN, P.

Faculty of Letters and Human Sciences (1 Espace Louis-Agassiz, 2000 Neuchâtel; tel. 327181700; fax 327181701; e-mail secretariat.lettres@unine.ch; internet www.unine.ch/lettres):

ACHERMANN, C.
ANDRES-SUAREZ, I.
ARSEVER, S.
AUBERT, J.
AUBERT SCHEURER, N.
BAGOU, O.
BARBIERI, L.
BARTOLINI, L.
BEGUELIN, M.
BENOVSKY, J.
BERLINCOURT, V.
BESSEYRE, M.
BETRIX KOEHLER, D.
BILLOD, C.
BOCHET, B.
BONNEFOIT, R.
BOREL, F.
BRANDT, C.
CHAPPUIS SANDOZ, L.
CHRISTIN, O.
CORBELLARI, A.
COTELLI FIOR, S.
COULIBALY, M.
CREVOISIER, O.
DAHINDEN, J.
D'AMATO, G.
DE BUZON, F.
DE MARCHI, P.
DE SAUSSURE, L.
DE WECK, G.
DEBARY, O.
DELACHAUX DJAPO YOGWA, S.
DELBARRE, S.
DIEMOZ, F.
DOERING, C.
DRIDI, H.
DUBOIS, M.
DUCRET, J.
EIGELDINGER, F.
ELMIGER, D.
FRESIA, M.
FUHRER, B.
GASSER, P.
GESLIN, P.
GESSLER, N.
GHASARIAN, C.
GILOMEN, H.
GINDROZ, J.
GLAUSER, R.
GODAT, C.
GRECO MORASSO, S.
GREMAUD, G.
GRIENER, P.
GRIENER HURLEY, C.
GROSSEN, M.
GYGER GASPOZ, D.
HAINARD, F.
HERTZ WERRO, E.
HONEGGER, M.
HUBERT VAN BLYENBURGH, N.
JAQUIER KAEMPFER, C.
KAESER, M.
KAMBER, A.
KAPOSSY, B.
KISSINE, M.
KLAPPROTH MUAZZIN, D.
KOHLER, A.
KRISTOL, A.
KUKORELLY LEVERINGTON, E.
LAGANARO, M.
LAMBOLEZ, S.
LAVILLE, Y.
LECHOT, P.
LUESCHER, J.
LUTZELSCHWAB, C.
MADRID, C.
MALFROY, S.
MANNO, G.
MARIAUX, P.
MARRO, P.
MARTY CRETTENAND, S.
MATTHEY, C.
MAYOR, G.
MAZZONI, E.
MCINTYRE, A.
MIEVILLE, D.
MOCCOZET, L.
MOINE, A.
MOREROD, C.
MOREROD, J.
MORIN, J.
MUELLER, W.
MULLER, B.
NÄF, A.
NEDELCU, M.
PADIGLIA, S.
PANG, B.
PEKAREK DOEHLER, S.
PERRET, J.
PERRET-CLERMONT, A.
PETER, P.
PETRIS, L.
PIGUET, E.
POCHON, L.
PROBST MARMIER, I.
RAMSEYER, D.
RATHGEB, J.
REBETEZ, M.
RERAT, P.
RIVAS, A.
RODRIGUEZ, A.
RUPP, K.
SALOMON CAVIN, J.
SÁNCHEZ MÉNDEZ, J.
SANGSUE, D.
SCHMID, G.
SCHMUTZ, T.
SCHNEIDER, J.
SCHNYDER, P.
SCHULTHESS, D.
SCHWAB, E.
SCHWEIZER, V.
SELMECI CASTIONI, B.
SESSA, M.
SGIER, L.
SKUPIEN DEKENS, C.
SÖDERSTRÖM, O.
SOUGY, N.
STEINBACH KOHLER, F.
STEINER, P.
SUTER, C.
TERRIER, P.
TISSOT, L.
TOLHURST, F.
TUDEAU-CLAYTON, M.
VAN ELSLANDE, J.
VERDON, V.
VERLEY, P.
VIBERT, D.
VINCENT, P.
VOLL, P.
VUILLEMIN, N.
WANNER, P.
WEBER, F.
WENDLING, T.
WERLY, S.
WERQUIN, P.
WILSON, D.
ZITTOUN, T.

Faculty of Science (11 rue Emile-Argand, 2000 Neuchâtel; tel. 327182100; fax 327182103; e-mail secretariat.sciences@unine.ch; internet www.unine.ch/sciences):

AEBI, P.
ANDRES, C.
ARAGNO, M.
BALLIF, C.
BEHREND, R.
BENAIM, M.
BENREY, B.
BERNASCONI FUSI, G.
BESSON, O.
BETSCHART, B.
BLAU, M.
BORER, M.
BSHARY, R.
CALLMANDER, M.
COLBOIS, B.
DE ROOIJ, N.
DERENDINGER, J.
DESCHENAUX, R.
DIEHL, P.

FARINE, P.
FELBER, F.
FELBER, P.
FOELLMI, K.
FREI HALLER, B.
GERMOND, J.
GOBAT, J.
GRAF, J.
GRANT, J.
GROEBLI, Y.
HAVLICEK, E.
HERZIG, H.
HUNKELER, D.
JOLISSAINT, P.
JUNIER, P.
KALT, A.
KESSLER, F.
KROPF, P.
LE BAYON, R.
LEHMANN, L.
MARIN, C.
MITCHELL, E.
MONTANDON, P.
MONTANI, J.
NEIER, R.
NEUHAUS, J.
PERROCHET, P.
PFISTER, K.
RAEBER, P.
ROUILLER, E.
SANDOZ, A.
SANGLARD, H.
SAVOY, J.
SCHILL, E.
SCHIRMER, M.
SCHLENK, F.
SEITZ, P.
SIEGRIST, H.
SUESS-FINK, G.
TACHER, L.
THERRIEN, B.
THOMANN, P.
TURLINGS, T.
TWERENBOLD, D.
VALETTE, A.
VERRECCHIA, E.
VUATAZ, F.
VUILLEUMIER, J.
WALTER-BARAKAT, I.
WILLI, Y.
ZUBER, M.
ZWAHLEN, F.

Faculty of Theology (41 Faubourg de l'Hôpital, 2000 Neuchâtel; tel. 327181900; fax 327181901; e-mail secretariat.factheol@unine.ch; internet www.unine.ch/theol):

BASSET, L.
DUBIED, P.
MOSER, F.
ROSE, M.

Other Institutes of Higher Education

INSTITUT DE HAUTES ÉTUDES EN ADMINISTRATION PUBLIQUE (IDHEAP)
(Swiss Graduate School of Public Administration)

Quartier UNIL Mouline, 1015 Lausanne
rue de la Mouline 28, 1022 Chavannes-près-Renens
Telephone: 215574000
Fax: 215574009
E-mail: idheap@idheap.unil.ch
Internet: www.idheap.ch
Founded 1981
Pres.: Dr BARBARA HAERING
Dir: Prof. JEAN-LOUP CHAPPELET
Gen. Sec.: JACQUES-ANDRÉ VULLIET
Library of 10,000 vols and 100 periodicals
Number of teachers: 12
Number of students: 384

INSTITUT DE HAUTES ÉTUDES INTERNATIONALES ET DU DÉVELOPPEMENT
(Graduate Institute of International and Development Studies)

rue de Lausanne 132, CP 136, 1211 Geneva 21
Telephone: 229085700
Fax: 229085710
E-mail: info@graduateinstitute.ch
Internet: graduateinstitute.ch
Founded 2008, by merger of Institut universitaire de hautes études internationales (f. 1927) and Institut universitaire d'études du développement (f. 1961)
Private control
Languages of instruction: English, French
Dir: PHILIPPE BURRIN
Deputy Dir: ELISABETH PRÜGL
Library of 300,000 vols, 850 journals, 5,500 DVDs and videotapes
Number of teachers: 43
Number of students: 810
Publications: *Journal International Relations* (in French), *International Development Policy* (in English and French).

INSTITUT UNIVERSITAIRE KURT BÖSCH
(Kurt Bösch University Institute)

CP 4176, 1950 Sion 4
Chemin de l'Institut 18, 1967 Bramois
Telephone: 272057300
Fax: 272057301
E-mail: institut@iukb.ch
Internet: www.iukb.ch
Founded 1989, present status 1992
Language of instruction: French
Academic year: September to June
Dir: Prof. PHILIP D. JAFFÉ
Vice-Dir: Prof. STÉPHANE NAHRATH.

UNIVERSITÄRE FERNSTUDIEN SCHWEIZ/FORMATION UNIVERSITAIRE À DISTANCE
(Distance Learning University)

Überlandstr. 12, POB 265, 3900 Brig
Telephone: 279223180
Fax: 279223185
E-mail: admin@fernuni.ch
Internet: www.fernuni.ch
Founded 2005, by merger of three regional study centres: Brig Study Centre of the Distance Learning University Switzerland, Brig VS, Pfäffikon Study Centre of the Distance Learning University Switzerland, Pfäffikon SZ and French-Swiss Distance Learning Centre CRED, Sierre VS
Public control
Languages of instruction: French, German
Rector: Prof. Dr PAUL VOLKEN
Dir for Service Centre and Coordination: STÉPHANE PANNATIER
Dir for Planning, Cooperation and e-Learning: Dr KURT GRÜNWALD
Number of students: 2,190

Universities of Applied Sciences

BERNER FACHHOCHSCHULE/HAUTE ÉCOLE SPÉCIALISÉE BERNOISE
(Bern University of Applied Sciences)

Hallerstr. 10, 3012 Berne
Telephone: 318483300
Fax: 318483303
E-mail: office@bfh.ch
Internet: www.bfh.ch
Founded 1997
Languages of instruction: English, French, German
Pres.: Dr RUDOLF GERBER
Number of teachers: 1,945 f.t.e.
Number of students: 5,673

FACHHOCHSCHULE NORDWESTSCHWEIZ
(University of Applied Sciences of Northwestern Switzerland)

Schulthess-Allee 1, POB 235, 5200 Brugg
Telephone: 564624911
Fax: 564624401
Internet: www.fhnw.ch
Founded 2006, by merger of three Univs of applied sciences (Aargau, Basel-Stadt and Basel-Landschaft, and Solothurn), School of Education of Solothurn and School of Education and Social Sciences of Basel-Stadt and Basel-Landschaft and Acad. of Music Basel
State control
Languages of instruction: English, German
Pres.: PETER SCHMID-SCHEIBLER
Vice-Pres.: PETER KOFMEL
Number of teachers: 1,265
Number of students: 9,231

FACHHOCHSCHULE OSTSCHWEIZ/ HAUTE ECOLE SPÉCIALISÉE DE LA SUISSE ORIENTALE
(University of Applied Sciences of Eastern Switzerland)

Bogenstr. 7, 9000 St. Gallen
Telephone: 712808383
Fax: 712808389
E-mail: info@fho.ch
Internet: www.fho.ch
Founded 1999
State control
Languages of instruction: English, German
Pres.: STEFAN KÖLLIKER
Vice-Pres.: MARTIN JÄGER
Head of Library: CRISTINA CARLINO
Number of students: 3,300
Publication: *Zeitschrift der Fachhochschule Ostschweiz* (2 a year).

HAUTE ÉCOLE SPÉCIALISÉE DE SUISSE OCCIDENTALE/ FACHHOCHSCHULE WESTSCHWEIZ
(University of Applied Sciences Western Switzerland)

Rue de la Jeunesse 1, CP 452, 2800 Delémont 1
Telephone: 324244900
Fax: 324244901
E-mail: info@hes-so.ch
Internet: www.hes-so.ch
Founded 1997
State control
Languages of instruction: English, French
Pres.: MARC-ANDRÉ BERCLAZ
Vice-Pres.: MARTIN KASSER
Number of students: 15,500

HOCHSCHULE LUZERN
(Lucerne University of Applied Sciences and Arts)

Frankenstr. 9, POB 2969, 6002 Lucerne
Telephone: 412284242
Fax: 412284243
E-mail: info@hslu.ch
Internet: www.hslu.ch

Founded 1997
State control

Rector: Prof. SABINE JAGGY
Exec. Dir: ANDREAS KALLMANN

Number of teachers: 661
Number of students: 8,438

Publication: *Hochschule Luzern – Das Magazin* (3 a year).

KALAIDOS FACHHOCHSCHULE

Wirtschaft AG, Hohlstr. 535, 8048 Zürich
Telephone: 442001919
Fax: 442001915
E-mail: info@kalaidos-fh.ch
Internet: www.kalaidos-fh.ch

Founded 1995
Private control

Rector: Lic. JÜRG EGGENBERGER

Number of teachers: 75
Number of students: 1,729

Publication: *Kalaidoskop*.

LES ROCHES-GRUYÈRE UNIVERSITY OF APPLIED SCIENCES

rue du Lac 118, 1815 Clarens
Telephone: 219892600
Fax: 219892645
E-mail: info@lrguas.ch
Internet: www.lrguas.ch/les_roches_gruyere

Founded 2008, by merger of Les Roches Int. School of Hotel Management and Glion Institute of Higher Education
Private control

Dir-Gen.: Dr DEBORAH PRINCE.

SCUOLA UNIVERSITARIA PROFESSIONALE DELLA SVIZZERA ITALIANA
(University of Applied Sciences and Arts of Southern Switzerland)

Le Gerre, 6928 Manno
Telephone: 586666000
Fax: 586666001
E-mail: info@supsi.ch
Internet: www.supsi.ch

Founded 1997
Public control

Pres.: ALBERTO COTTI
Dir: FRANCO GERVASON

Number of teachers: 652
Number of students: 5,000

ZÜRCHER FACHHOCHSCHULE

Walchepl. 2, POB, 8090 Zürich
Telephone: 432592348
Fax: 432595161
E-mail: info@zfh.ch
Internet: www.zfh.ch
State control
Languages of instruction: English, German

Gen. Sec.: Dr RETO THALER

Number of teachers: 1,322
Number of students: 14,000

Colleges

C. G. Jung Institute Zürich: Hornweg 28, 8700 Küsnacht; tel. 449141040; fax 449141050; e-mail cg@junginstitut.ch; internet wwww.junginstitut.ch; f. 1948; private teaching and research institute for analytical psychology as conceived by psychoanalyst, Carl Gustav Jung (1875–1961); clinical and professional training programme leading to Diploma; courses and seminars in German and English for qualified auditors; special training in child-psychotherapy (for German-speaking students); several further education programmes; counselling centre; int. picture archive and library; library: 15,000 vols; 100 teachers; 150 students; Pres. Dipl. DANIEL BAUMANN; Dir of Studies Lic. URSULA WEISS.

Eidgenössische Hochschulinstitut für Berufsbildung/Institut Fédéral des Hautes Études en Formation Professionnelle/Istituto Universitario Federale per la Formazione Professionale (Swiss Federal Institute for Vocational Education and Training): Kirchlindachstr. 79, 3052 Zollikofen; tel. 319103700; fax 319103701; internet www.ehb-schweiz.ch; f. 1972, present name 2007; regional campuses in Lugano, Lausanne and Zurich; teaching and research in areas of vocational pedagogy, vocational and professional education and training and career devt; Chair. Prof. Dr STEFAN C. WOLTER; Dir Dr DALIA SCHIPPER; Deputy Dir Dr ALEXANDER ETIENNE.

Facoltà Di Teologia Di Lugano: Via Giuseppe Buffi 13, CP 4663, 6904 Lugano; tel. 586664555; fax 586664556; e-mail info@teologialugano.ch; internet www.teologialugano.ch; f. 1993; research and teaching in liberal arts, particularly in fields of theology, canon law and philosophy; Rector AZZOLINO CHIAPPINI; Sec. Gen. and Treas. LUCA MATTIOLO; publ. *Rivista Teologica di Lugano (RTLu)* (in French, German and Italian).

Franklin College Switzerland: Via Ponte Tresa 29, 6924 Sorengo (Lugano); tel. 919852260; fax 919944117; e-mail info@fc.edu; internet www.fc.edu; f. 1969; language of instruction: English; academic year September to May; mem. of Asscn of American Int. Colleges and Univs, Ccl of Ind. Colleges; accredited by Middle States Asscn; 11 accredited undergraduate degree courses; library: 36,000 vols, 150 periodicals; 50 teachers; 450 students; Pres. ERIK O. NIELSEN.

Haute Ecole Pédagogique des Cantons de Berne, du Jura et de Neuchâtel—BEJUNE: Rue du Banné 23, 2900 Porrentruy; tel. 844886996; e-mail info@hep-bejune.ch; internet www.hep-bejune.ch; f. 2001; campuses at Bienne and La Chaux-de-Fonds; courses in teaching at pre-school, primary, secondary and further education level; Rector JEAN-PIERRE FAIVRE; publ. *Revue Académique Electronique* (1 a year).

Pädagogische Hochschule: Baslerstr. 43, 5201 Brugg; tel. 848012210; fax 564600609; e-mail info.ph@fhnw.ch; internet www.fhnw.ch/ph; courses in pre-school, primary and secondary teaching, special psychology and pedagogy and research and development in applied pedagogy; 2,000 students; Dir Prof. Dr HERMANN FORNECK; Exec. Sec. KATJA MINI.

Pädagogische Hochschule Bern: Weltistr. 40, 3006 Bern; tel. 313092711; fax 313092199; e-mail iinfo-iwb@phbern.ch; internet www.phbern.ch; f. 2005; institutes of pre-school and primary-level teaching, secondary-level teaching I and II, remedial pedagogy, further training and of educational media; 2,000 students; Rector Prof. Dr MARTIN SCHÄFER; Sec. ERICH SCHMID; Gen. Sec. Dr MONIKA PÄTZMANN.

Pädagogische Hochschule des Cantons St Gallen: Notkerstr. 27, 9000 St Gallen; tel. 712439400; fax 712439496; e-mail phs_sekretariat@unisg.ch; internet www.phsg.ch; f. 1983; campus at Gossau; courses in secondary-level teaching; 210 teachers; 810 students; Rector Prof. Dr ERWIN BECK; Exec. Dir MARKUS SEITZ.

Schiller International University—Switzerland: (For general information, see entry for Schiller International University in Germany chapter).

Campuses:

Schiller International University – American College of Switzerland: 1854 Leysin; tel. 244930309; fax 244930300; e-mail siuacsadmissions@bluewin.ch; internet www.american-college.com; f. 1963; degree courses in liberal arts and business administration; French and English Language Institute for EFL/ESL students (programme certificate); library of 48,000 vols; Pres. WALTER LEIBRECHT.

Schiller International University – Engelberg: Dorfstrasse 40, 6390 Engelberg; tel. 416397474; fax 416397475; e-mail info@schiller-university.ch; internet www.schiller-university.ch; f. 1978; Dir ROBERTA LO.

Staatsunabhängige Theologische Hochschule Basel (Basel Theological Seminary (State Independent)): Mühlestiegrain 50, 4125 Riehen BS; tel. 616468080; fax 616468090; e-mail info@sthbasel.ch; internet www.sthbasel.ch; f. 1970; masters and doctoral degree programmes in theology; distance-learning courses in Hebrew and Greek; excavation project in Israel; Rector Prof. Dr JACOB THIESSEN.

Theologische Hochschule Chur: Alte Schanfiggerstr. 7, 7000 Chur; tel. 812549999; fax 812549998; e-mail sekretariat@priesterseminar-thc.ch; internet www.thchur.ch; f. 1807, present status 2006; courses in philosophy and theology; library: 50,000 vols; Rector Prof. Dr EVA-MARIA FABER; Head of Library Prof. Dr MICHAEL DURST.

Schools of Art and Music

ART

Centre de Formation Professionnelle Arts Appliqués: 2 Rue Necker, 1201 Geneva; tel. 223885000; fax 223885059; internet edu.ge.ch/cfpaa; f. 1876, as École des Arts Industriels; jewellery, ceramics, stylism, interior architecture, dressmaking, graphic art, art expression; 7 buildings; library: 11,000 vols, 70 periodicals; 125 teachers; 600 students; Dir GUY MÉRAT.

École Çantonale d'Art de Lausanne/Haute École d'Art et de Design (University of Art and Design Lausanne): ave du Temple 5, CP 555, 1001 Lausanne; ave du Temple 5, 1020 Lausanne; tel. 213169933; fax 213169266; e-mail ecal@ecal.ch; internet www.ecal.ch; f. 1821; depts of fine arts, audiovisual studies, graphic design, multimedia and industrial design, film studies; 227 teachers; 574 students incl. exchange students; Dir PIERRE KELLER.

École Cantonale d'Art du Valais: rue Bonne-Eau 16, 3960 Sierre; tel. 274565511; fax 274565530; e-mail ecav@ecav.ch; internet www.ecav.ch; f. 1948, present name 1997;

courses in graphic design and visual arts; organizes summer acad. and workshops; library: 12,000 vols, 40 periodicals, 900 DVDs, VHS, CD-ROM and music CDs; 200 students; Dir SIBYLLE OMLIN.

Haute École d'Art et de Design-Genève (Geneva University of Art and Design): 15 blvd James-Fazy, 1201 Geneva; tel. 223885100; fax 223885159; e-mail info .head@hesge.ch; internet head.hesge.ch; f. 2006, by merger of École Supérieure des Beaux-arts (f. 1748) and Haute École d'Arts Appliqués (HEAA); courses in fine arts, cinema specialization and design; library: 7,000 vols, 2,500 CDs and DVDs, 50 periodicals, 4,500 exhibition catalogues; 97 teachers; 670 students; Dir JEAN-PIERRE GREFF; Deputy Dir MARC PICCAND; Exec. Sec. DIANE CHRISTINAZ.

MUSIC

Conservatoire de Fribourg: 8 route Louis Braille, CP 88, 1763 Granges-Paccot; tel. 263059940; fax 263059941; e-mail conservatoire@fr.ch; internet www.fr.ch/cof; f. 1904; attached to Dept of Culture, Directorate of Education, Culture and Sport (SCID); vocal and instrumental music, dance and drama; library: 12,000 vols, 20,000 printed music; 207 teachers; 5,000 students; Dir GIANCARLO GEROSA; Librarian CHRISTIANE ANTONIAZZA-TORCHE.

Conservatoire de Musique: 12 Rue de l'Arquebuse, CP 5155, 1211 Geneva; tel. 223196060; fax 223196062; e-mail cmg@ cmusge.ch; internet www.cmusge.ch; f. 1835; seven educational centres; all brs of music, dramatic art and classical ballet; library: 70,000 vols, music scores and 10,000 vols; 144 teachers; 2,400 full-time students; Dir EVA AROUTUNIAN; Librarian JACQUES TCHAMKERTEN.

Conservatoire de Musique de Neuchâtel: 21 Espace de l'Europe, 2000 Neuchâtel; tel. 328896912; fax 328891510; e-mail conservatoire.ne@cmne.ch; internet www .cmne.ch; f. 1918; pre-vocational courses, courses in all fields of music; library: 2,000 vols, 800 CDs, 20,000 scores; 2,100 students; Dir FRANÇOIS HOTZ; Librarian JOËLLE EICHENBERGER; publ. *Le Journal* (2 a year).

HEMU Lausanne (High School of Music in Lausanne): 2 rue de la Grotte, CP 5700, 1002 Lausanne; tel. 213213535; fax 213213536; e-mail info@hemu-cl.ch; internet www.hemu .ch; f. 1861; research and courses in classical and jazz; library: 20,000 scores and 4,000 reference books; 120 teachers; 1,400 students; Dir-Gen. HERVÉ KLOPFENSTEIN.

Konservatorium Winterthur: Tössertobelstr. 1, 8400 Winterthur; tel. 522681580; fax 522681501; e-mail info@konservatorium .ch; internet www.konservatorium.ch; f. 1873; courses and workshops related to music and musical instruments; lessons for children, adolescents and adults with disabilities; 105 teachers; 224 students; Dir HANS-ULRICH MUNZINGER.

Musik Akademie Basel: 6 Leonhardsstr., 4003 Basel; tel. 612645757; fax 612645713; e-mail info@mab-bs.ch; internet www .musik-akademie.ch; f. 1867; comprises 3 institutes: music school providing non-professional musical education, conservatory providing professional musical education, Schola Cantorum Basiliensis providing specialized education in early music; library: 100,000 vols; 430 staff; 9,000 students; Rector Dr ANDRÉ BALTENSPERGER; Exec. Dir MARC DE HALLER.

Musikschule Konservatorium Bern: Kramgasse 36, 3000 Bern 8; tel. 313265353; fax 313122053; e-mail office@konsibern.ch; internet www.konsibern.ch; f. 1858; library: 50,000 vols; 140 teachers; Dir GERHARD MÜLLER; Deputy Dir MARKUS PLATTNER.

Zürich Konservatorium Klassik und Jazz: Hirschengraben 1, 8001 Zürich; tel. 442504600; fax 442504601; e-mail info@konsi .ch; internet www.konsi.ch; f. 1875; 125 teachers; 2,700 students; Man. DANIEL KNECHT; Admin. Dir CHRISTINE GISLER.

SYRIA

The Higher Education System

Higher education institutions predate Syria's independence from France in 1946, with the oldest being the University of Damascus, which was founded in 1903 (when Syria was part of the Ottoman Turkish Empire).

The Ministry of Higher Education is responsible for the universities, Intermediate Institutes (also attached to other Ministries) and higher institutes, and the Council of Higher Education is the coordinating body. Higher education policy is planned centrally but implementation is decentralized. There is a Supreme Council of Intermediate Institutes which supervises the Intermediate Institutes. In 2001 Legislative Decree No. 36 authorised the establishment of private institutions of higher education. There were 279,614 students enrolled at state universities with another 6,000 at private universities in 2006/07. A further 2,500 were enrolled at the Syrian Virtual University (established in 2002, offering degree courses via the internet).

Applicants are legally required to possess the General Secondary Certificate to be admitted to university. The specific grade requirements for admission to programmes are determined by the Council of Higher Education. The Bachelors (*Licence*—French, or *Ijâza fi*—Arabic) is often a four-year degree, although some disciplines require longer, such as engineering, pharmacy, architecture (five years) and medicine (six years). The first postgraduate degree is the Diploma of Higher Studies or Postgraduate Diploma, a full-time course lasting one or two years. Additionally, there is a Diploma of Qualification and Specialization, which is a professional qualification in commerce, medicine and teacher training. Following the award of the Diploma of Higher Studies, the Masters degree is a one- to three-year course consisting of both taught and research elements. Finally, the highest university degree is the Doctor of Philosophy (PhD), which comprises both taught and research elements and culminates in submission and defence of a thesis.

The Intermediate Institutes are the main institutions for the provision of post-secondary technical and vocational education. Courses last two years and are administered either by the Ministry of Higher Education or one of the relevant Ministries. Upon completion of the course, students are awarded the Certificate of Assistant Bachelor.

Regulatory and Representative Bodies

GOVERNMENT

Ministry of Culture: rue George Haddad, ar-Rawda, Damascus; tel. (11) 3331556; fax (11) 3320804; Minister Riyad Na'asan Agha.

Ministry of Education: rue Shahbander, al-Masraa, Damascus; tel. (11) 4444703; fax (11) 4420435; e-mail mudhar@syrianeducation.org.sy; internet www.syrianeducation.org.sy; Minister Ali Sa'd.

Ministry of Higher Education: BP 9251, place Mezzeh Gamarik, Damascus; tel. (11) 2119865; fax (11) 2128919; e-mail mhe@shem.net; internet www.mhe.gov.sy; Minister Ghiath Barakat.

NATIONAL BODY

Council of Higher Education: BP 9355, Damascus; tel. (11) 2126336; fax (11) 2129298; regulates and oversees the higher education system; Minister Ghiath Barakat; Sec-Gen. Riad al-Ajlani.

Learned Societies

GENERAL

Arabic Language Academy of Damascus: BP 327, Damascus; tel. (11) 3713103; fax (11) 3733363; f. 1919; Arabic Islamic legacy and linguistic studies and terminology; 20 mems; Chair. Dr Marwan al-Mahasini; Sec.-Gen. Dr A. Wassek Chahid; publ. *Majallat Majmaa al-Lughah al-Arabiyyah bi-Dimashq* (review, 4 a year).

LANGUAGE AND LITERATURE

British Council: Maysaloun St, Shalaan, BP 33105, Damascus; tel. (11) 3310631; fax (11) 3321467; e-mail info@sy.britishcouncil.org; internet www.britishcouncil.org/syria; f. 1974; information services; Education UK teaching centre; offers courses and exams in English language and British culture and promotes cultural exchange with the UK; library of 7,000 vols; additional electronic resources and audiovisual materials; Dir Paul Doubleday; Teaching Centre Man. Amir Ramzan.

Goethe-Institut: Adnan Malki St 8, BP 6100, Damascus; tel. (11) 3719435; fax (11) 3719437; e-mail info@damascus.goethe.org; internet www.goethe.de/damaskus; offers courses and exams in German language and culture and promotes cultural exchange with Germany; library of 5,200 vols; Dir Manfred Ewel; Librarian Regina Abboud.

Instituto Cervantes: 10 Malek Abdel Aziz al Saud St, Sebki, Damascus; tel. (11) 3737061; fax (11) 3737062; e-mail cendam@cervantes.es; internet damasco.cervantes.es; offers courses and exams in Spanish language and culture and promotes cultural exchange with Spain and Spanish-speaking Latin and Central America; library of 10,000 vols; Dir Pablo Martin Asuero.

Research Institutes

GENERAL

Institut Français du Proche-Orient: BP 344, Damascus; tel. (11) 3330214; fax (11) 3327887; e-mail f.burgat@ifporient.org; internet www.ifporient.org; f. 1922 as Institut Français d'études Arabes de Damas (Ifead); 2003 merged with Centre d'études et de recherches sur le Moyen-Orient contemporain (Cermoc) and L'Institut français d'archéologie de Beyrouth; archaeological research, study of the classical Arab world, Islamic civilization, and history and studies of modern Syria; library of 100,000 vols, 1,500 periodicals; Dir François Burgat; Gen. Sec. Emmanuel Rattin; Librarian Martine Gillet; publ. *Bulletin d'Etudes Orientales* (1 a year).

AGRICULTURE, FISHERIES AND VETERINARY SCIENCE

Arab Centre for the Study of Arid Zones and Dry Lands: BP 2440, Damascus; tel. (11) 5743087; fax (11) 5743063; e-mail email@acsad.org; internet www.acsad.org; f. 1968 by the Arab League; studies problems of management conservation and devt of agricultural resources, incl. water, soil, plant and animal resources; emphasis on resources survey and assessment, causes of degradation and desertification, processes of conservation and devt, economic evaluation and social implications, proper management through appropriate technologies, technical training, processing and dissemination of pertinent scientific and technical knowledge and information; mems: 16 Arab states; library of 1,500 vols, 152 periodicals, 65,000 references; Dir-Gen. Dr Hassan Seoud; publs *Agriculture and Water in Arid Regions of the Arab World* (2 a year), *The Camel Newsletter* (2 a year).

EDUCATION

Arab Centre for Arabization, Translation, Authorship and Publication: Al-Afif St, 2 Senbul Jadet, BP 3752, Damascus; tel. (11) 3334876; fax (11) 3330998; e-mail acatap@net.sy; internet www.acatap.htmlplanet.com; f. 1989; attached to the Arab League Educational, Cultural and Scientific Organization (ALECSO); translates and prints recent educational, medical and scientific titles in Arabic; organizes seminars and workshops; library of 3,500 items; Dir Prof. Dr Zaid Ibraheem al Assaf; publ. *Arabization* (2 a year).

Libraries and Archives

Aleppo

Al Maktabah Al Wataniah: Bab El-Faradj, Aleppo; tel. (21) 236130; fax (21) 229184; f. 1924; Librarian Younis Roshdi.

Damascus

Al Zahiriah (Public Library): Bab el Barid, Damascus; f. 1919; main subjects are miscellaneous sciences, literature and language, history, biography, religion; 100,000 vols, 50,000 periodicals; spec. colln: rare pre-1900 Arabic books; Librarian SAMA EL MAHASSINI; publ. brochure of new additions (4 a year).

Assad National Library: Malki St, BP 3639, Damascus; tel. (11) 3320803; internet www.alassad-library.gov.sy; f. 1984, in process of formation; nat. deposit library; publishes National Bibliography, trains librarians; 280 staff; 147,124 vols, 19,000 Arabic MSS; Gen. Dir GHASSAN LAHHAM; publs *Analytical Index of Syrian Periodicals*, *Index of Syrian University Theses*, *National Bibliography* (1 a year).

University of Damascus Library: BP 3003, Damascus; tel. and fax (11) 2119840; e-mail damasuniv@syriatel.net; f. 1919; 150,000 vols, 2,700 periodicals; Librarian Dr NIZAR OYOUN EL SOUD; publs *Conférences Générales* (1 a year), *Statistic Collection* (1 a year).

Homs

Dar al-Kutub al-Wataniah (Public Library): Homs.

Latakia

Public Library of Latakia: Latakia; f. 1944; 12,000 vols; Dir MOHAMAD ALI NTAYFI.

Museums and Art Galleries

Aleppo

Aleppo National Museum: BP 6581, Aleppo; tel. (21) 212400; f. 1931; archaeology and modern art; spec. colln of Iron Age artefacts; library of 4,000 vols; Head Curator Dr SHAWQI SHAATH.

Busra

Busra Museum: Busra; tel. (15) 790105; traditional arts and crafts; Dir of Archaeological Research Dr SULEIMAN MOGHDAD.

Damascus

Adnan Malki Museum: Adnan Malki Sq., Damascus; dedicated to Lt Col. Malki, assassinated in 1955 failed Syrian Socialist Nationalist Party coup.

Agricultural Museum: Halbouni, Damascus; colln of agricultural tools; paintings of rural life.

Military Museum: Takeih Suleimanieh, Damascus; depictions of famous battles; colln of weapons.

Museum of Arabic Epigraphy: Jakmakieh Madressa, Damascus; tel. (11) 2219746; f. 1974; examples of calligraphy from different periods and colln of tools used in writing Arabic script; Dir FAYEZ HOMSI.

National Museum: Syrian University St, Damascus 4; tel. (11) 2219148; fax (11) 2247983; f. 1919; Sections: Prehistory; Ancient Oriental; Greek, Roman and Byzantine; Arab and Islamic; Modern Art; of special interest is the reconstruction of the Palmyrene Hypogeum of Yarhai (2nd century AD), of the Dura Synagogue (3rd century AD), of the Umayyad Qasr El-Hair El-Gharbi (8th century AD) and of the Damascus Hall (18th century AD); houses the Directorate-General of Antiquities and Museums, established by decree in 1947 to conserve Syrian antiquities and to supervise the archaeological museums and the excavations; Dir-Gen. of Antiquities and Museums ALI AL-KAYYEM; publs *Les Annales Archéologiques Arabes Syriennes*, *Les Chroniques Archéologiques en Syrie*.

Popular Traditions Museum Qasrelazem: Bzourieh St, Damascus; tel. (11) 2225418; f. 1954; traditions and crafts; library of 3,000 vols; Curator HASSAN KAMAL.

Deir ez-Zor

Deir ez-Zor Museum: Pl. du Président, Deir ez-Zor; tel. (51) 222530; f. 1974; archaeology; library of 1,000 vols; Dir ASSAD MAHMOUD; publ. *Les Annales Archéologiques de Syrie*.

Hama

Hama Museum: rue Abou al-Fida'a Hama; tel. (33) 224550; f. 1956; history and folklore; Dir ABDEL RAZZAQ ZAGZOUQ.

Homs

Homs Museum: rue al-Koutli, Homs dar Al-Thakafa; tel. (31) 220002; f. 1974; archaeology, folk and modern art; Curator MAJED EL MOUSSLI.

Palmyra

Palmyra National Museum: Palmyra; tel. (31) 910573; f. 1961; archaeological finds from prehistory to 16th century; attached is the museum of Syrian desert folklore, traditional handicraft industry and agriculture; Dir KHALED AL AS'AD.

Sweida

Sweida Museum: rue de Qanawat, Sweida; tel. (16) 232035; artefacts from Roman, Nabatean and Islamic periods; Curator M. HOUSSEIN ZEIN EL-DIN.

Tartos

Tartos Museum: Tartos; tel. (43) 220541; Islamic history; Curator RAMIZ HOUCHE.

Universities

AL-BAATH UNIVERSITY

BP 77, Homs
Telephone: (31) 431847
Fax: (31) 426716
E-mail: baath-univ@net.sy
Internet: www.albaath-univ.edu.sy

Founded 1979
State control
Language of instruction: Arabic
Academic year: September to June

Pres.: Prof. Dr YASSER HOURI
Vice-Pres. for Admin. and Student Affairs: Prof. Dr HOUSAM BARAKAT
Vice-Pres. for Scientific Affairs: Prof. Dr AUODI SALHA
Admin. Officer: KASSEM HAMMOUD
Dir of Int. Relations: ABDUL ILAH AL-ABDOU
Librarian: LINA MAASRANI

Library of 63,000 vols
Number of teachers: 802
Number of students: 26,730

DEANS

Faculty of Agriculture: Dr ABDULA AL-ISA
Faculty of Chemical and Petroleum Engineering: Dr SHARIF SADIQ
Faculty of Civil Engineering and Architecture: Dr MOHAMED HAKEMI (Architecture)
Faculty of Civil Engineering and Architecture: Dr BASSAM IBRAHIM (Civil Engineering)
Faculty of Dentistry: Dr MOUHAMED SABEH ARAB
Faculty of Education: Dr IBRAHIM KHADOUR
Faculty of Informatics: Dr MUHAMAD AL-RAJAB
Faculty of Literature: Dr AHMAD DAHMAN
Faculty of Mechanical and Electrical Engineering: Dr RADWAN AL-MASRI
Faculty of Medicine: Dr ISA TUMI
Faculty of Pharmacy: Dr IMAD HADAD
Faculty of Sciences: Dr MALEK ALI
Faculty of Veterinary Science (in Hama): Dr MOHAMED ALI AL-IMADI
Intermediate Institute of Computer Engineering: Dr MOHAMED AL-HAG YOUNES
Intermediate Institute of Engineering: Dr MOUFAK FAKHOURI
Intermediate Institute of Industry: Dr HASSAN FARAH
Intermediate Institute of Veterinary Medicine: Dr ASAD AL-ABID

UNIVERSITY OF ALEPPO

Aleppo
Telephone: (21) 2675900
Fax: (21) 229184
E-mail: alepuniv@alepuniv.shern.net
Internet: www.alepuniv.shern.net

Founded 1960
State control
Languages of instruction: Arabic, French, English
Academic year: September to June

Pres.: Dr MOHAMMAD NIZAR AKIL
Vice-Pres. for Scientific Affairs: Dr AHMAD KILLY
Vice-Pres. for Admin. and Student Affairs: Dr MAHMOUD KASSEM
Vice-Pres. for Research: Dr ABED YKAN
Vice-Pres. for Open Learning: Dr SAMIR SAAD
Chief Administrator and Secretary: MOHAMMAD WATTAR
Registrar: MAHMUD ELWANI
Librarian: MUSTAFA JASSOUMEH

Number of teachers: 3,377
Number of students: 53,465

Publications: *Journal for the History of Arabic Science*, *Newsletter of the Institute for the History of Arabic Science*, *Research Journal of Aleppo University* (comprises the following series: Arts and Humanities; Medical Sciences; Agricultural Sciences; Basic Sciences; Engineering Sciences; *Adiyat Halab*)

DEANS

Faculty of Agriculture: Dr JEMMA IBRAHIM
Second Faculty of Agriculture: Dr MUHIEDDEEN QARAWANI
Faculty of Architectural Engineering: Dr ABDUL GHANI AL SHEHABI
Faculty of Arts and Humanities: Dr MOUSTAFA JATAL
Faculty of Civil Engineering: Dr SAMEH JAZMATI
Faculty of Dentistry: Dr MOHAMMAD IKBAL MUSHREF
Faculty of Economics: Dr AHMAD ASHKAR
Faculty of Electrical and Electronic Engineering: Dr MISHEL HALLAK
Faculty of Law: Dr KHALED AL HAMOUD
Faculty of Mechanical Engineering: Dr SALMAN SAGHBINI
Faculty of Medicine: Dr MOUNZER BARAKAT
Faculty of Pharmacy: Dr SAMEER SA'AD
Faculty of Sciences: Dr NASSUH ALAYA

UNIVERSITY OF DAMASCUS

Damascus
Telephone: (11) 2232152
Fax: (11) 2236010
E-mail: w-mualla@scs-net.org
Internet: www.damascusuniversity.edu.sy

Founded 1903
State control
Language of instruction: Arabic
Academic year: September to June

Pres.: Dr WAEL MUALLA

Vice-Pres. for Academic Affairs: Dr MOHAMMAD SALEM AL-RIKAB
Vice-Pres. for Admin. and Student Affairs: Prof. Dr TAREK AL-KHAIR
Vice-Pres. for Postgraduate Studies and Scientific Research: Dr RAKAN RAZOUK
Registrar: YOUSEF KAHELEH
Librarian: KAIS SHAHEEN

Library of 51,500 vols, 70,000 vols in libraries of faculties
Number of teachers: 2,688
Number of students: 120,000 , 60,000 distant learning students

Publications: *Dirasat Tarikhiyyah* (historical review, 4 a year), *Journal for Agricultural Studies* (4 a year), *Journal for Basic and Applied Sciences* (4 a year), *Journal for the Arts, Humanities and Sciences* (4 a year), *Journal for the Economic and Legal Sciences* (4 a year), *Journal for the Medical Sciences* (4 a year), *Statistical Collections* (1 a year), *University Journal* (4 a year)

DEANS

Faculty of Agriculture: Prof. Dr HAMZEH BLAL
Faculty of Architecture: Dr PIERRE NANO
Faculty of Arts and Humanities: Prof. Dr WAHAB ROUMIEH
Faculty of Civil Engineering: Prof. Dr AMJAD ZENO
Faculty of Computer Science: Dr AMMAR KHEIR-BEK
Faculty of Dentistry: Prof. Dr M. HASAN YOUSEF
Faculty of Economics: Prof. Dr MUSTAFA AL-KAFRI
Faculty of Fine Arts: Prof. Dr MAHMOUD SHAHEEN
Faculty of Law: Prof. Dr MOHAMED AL-HUSEIN
Faculty of Mechanical and Electrical Engineering: (vacant)
Faculty of Medicine: Prof. Dr NEZAR ASSAD
Faculty of Pharmacy: Prof. Dr ANTOIN LAHHAM
Faculty of Political Science: Prof. Dr OMAR ABDULLAH
Faculty of Science: Prof. Dr ESSAM KASSEM
Faculty of Sharia: Prof. MOHAMED AL-HASAN AL-BOGHAA
Faculty of Tourism: Dr REEM RAMADAN

TISHREEN UNIVERSITY (University of October)

POB 2230, Latakia
Telephone and fax (41) 445290
E-mail: inter-rel@tishreen.shern.net
Internet: www.tishreen.shern.net

Founded 1971 as Univ. of Latakia
State control
Language of instruction: Arabic
Academic year: September to June

Rector: Prof. Dr MOHAMMAD YAHIA MOUALLA
Vice-Pres. for Academic Affairs: Dr MOHAMED YACINE KASSAB
Vice-Rector for Admin. and Students Affairs: Prof. Dr HASSAN BADDOUR
Vice-Rector for Open Learning: Prof. Dr TALAL AMEEN
Vice-Rector for Scientific Affairs: Prof. Dr MAHMOUD SAID
Vice-Rector for Scientific Affairs and Scientific Research: MUSTAFA FAWAL
Vice-Rector for Scientific Research and Postgraduate Studies: Prof. Dr NAZIEH ISSA
Registrar: SALAH SHAABAN
Librarian: MOUHAMMAD NAJIB SAKER

Library of 60,214 vols, 468 periodicals
Number of teachers: 892
Number of students: 25,621

Publications: *Journal of Agriculture*, *Journal of Arts and Humanities*, *Journal of Basic Science*, *Journal of Economics*, *Journal of Medical Science*, *Journal of Studies and Scientific Research*

DEANS

Faculty of Agriculture: Dr AHMAD JALLOUL
Faculty of Architecture: Dr NUHAD ABDALLA
Faculty of Arts: Dr MOHAMMAD JALAL OSMAN
Faculty of Civil Engineering: Dr ALI TURIKIEH
Faculty of Dentistry: Dr NAZIH ISSA
Faculty of Economics: Dr ALI HISMEH
Faculty of Education: Dr GHASSAN SALEH
Faculty of Electrical and Mechanical Engineering: Dr JARKAS TAJE DINE
Faculty of Medicine: Dr IBRAHIM SULAIMAN
Faculty of Nursing: NAJWA KERDOGHLI
Faculty of Pharmacology: Dr MARROUF AL KHAYER
Faculty of Physical Education: NOURI BARAKAT
Faculty of Science: Dr DAIFALLAH NASSOUR

Colleges

Arab Conservatory of Music: Sabil near Kalimeh Hospital, Aleppo; tel. (21) 2672600; fax (21) 2672600; f. 1963; depts of classical (Western) and Oriental (Middle Eastern) music; children's choir, chamber orchestra; 28 teachers; 600 students; Dir NABIL GHREWATI.

Higher Institute of Applied Sciences and Technology: BP 31983, Barzeh, Damascus; tel. (11) 5140520; fax (11) 2237710; e-mail info@hiast.edu.sy; internet www.hiast.edu.sy; f. 1983; awards BSc, MSc, PhD; depts of informatics, systems engineering, mathematics, physics, electronics, management, mechanics; language of instruction: Arabic; 120 teachers; 400 students; Dir Prof. Dr OMRAN KOUBA.

Higher Institute of Political Science: Al-Tall, Damascus; tel. (11) 5911704; fax (11) 5911526; f. 1976; depts of administration and public relations, international relations and political studies; library: 15,000 vols; 25 teachers; 434 students; Dean HUSEIN AL-SAYED HUSEIN.

TAIWAN

The Higher Education System

Until 1947 Taiwan was governed from the mainland of China; however, in 1947 the Chinese communists came to power in Beijing, and the National Government was forced to remove itself to Taipei, the capital of Taiwan, where it established the 'Republic of China', which later came to be known as Taiwan. The population is mainly Chinese in origin, and the official language is Mandarin (Guoyu); Taiwanese, Hakka and English are also spoken. Most universities have been founded since the establishment of the Republic of China, but some were formerly mainland institutions that either relocated during the Communist takeover or were refounded; these include Fu-Jen Catholic University (founded in 1925 in Beijing), National Central University (originally based in Nanking), National Chiao Tung University (founded in 1896 in Shanghai), National Tsing Hua University (founded in 1911 in Beijing), and Soochow University (founded in 1900 in the mainland province of Jiangsu). In 2008/09 there were 162 universities, junior colleges and independent colleges, most of which offer postgraduate facilities; total enrolment in higher education in that year was 1,337,455 students. In 1987 the nine teachers' junior colleges were upgraded to teachers' colleges. These admit senior secondary graduates for a four-year course. High-school teachers are trained at normal universities. Higher education is highly centralized and the Constitution places great emphasis on the importance of education. The higher education system is based on the US model.

The Ministry of Education supervises the Universities and Colleges Joint Entrance Examination, which is required for admission to higher education. Students, however, may also gain admission through two other methods, either by applying directly to the institution in question and meeting that institution's entry requirements, or through recommendation on grounds of academic excellence.

Junior colleges, which provide two- or five-year Junior College Diploma programmes, are the first level of higher education. Two-year junior colleges admit graduates from Senior and Senior Vocational High Schools, while five-year junior colleges accept students from Junior High Schools. The majority of junior colleges are privately-run. Institutes of technology operate on a similar basis: two-year institutes admit junior college graduates and four-year institutes admit senior vocational school graduates. There are also 'Open' universities which specialize in adult education.

The Bachelors degree is the main university undergraduate qualification, and usually lasts four years, although specialist programmes such as dentistry and medicine may take six or seven years. At postgraduate level, the Masters degree requires one to four years' study, while the final qualification, the Doctorate, requires two to seven years' study following the Masters. Technical and vocational education and training is provided by senior vocational schools and junior colleges. Periods of study vary between two to five years.

Regulatory Bodies

GOVERNMENT

Bureau of International Cultural and Educational Relations: Min. of Education, 13F, 5 Syujhou Rd, Jhongjheng Dist., Taipei 100; tel. (2) 23565608; fax (2) 23976978; e-mail cschang@mail.moe.gov.tw; internet english.moe.gov.tw; f. 1947; assists colleges and univs to enter into academic co-operation with foreign instns of higher learning; sponsors int. scholar exchange programmes; organizes bilateral confs on higher education; encourages Taiwan specialists, academics and doctoral students to participate in int. academic confs abroad; provides Taiwan Scholarships to encourage exceptional foreign students to pursue degrees in Taiwan; works with govts, cultural and educational instns and commercial enterprises to obtain scholarships for Taiwan students; Dir-Gen. Dr CHIN-SHENG CHANG.

Ministry of Education: 5 Chung Shan South Rd, Taipei 10051; tel. (2) 23566051; fax (2) 23976978; internet www.moe.gov.tw; Min. TU CHENG-SHENG.

Research, Development and Evaluation Commission: 6/F, 2-2 Chi Nan Rd, Sec. 1, Taipei 10051; tel. (2) 23419066; fax (2) 23969990; e-mail service@rdec.gov.tw; internet rdec.gov.tw; Minister SHIH NING-JYE.

Learned Societies

GENERAL

Academia Sinica: 128 Academia Rd, Section 2, Nankang, Taipei 11529; tel. (2) 27822120; fax (2) 27853847; internet www.sinica.edu.tw; f. 1928; 220 mems; attached research institutes: see Research Institutes; library of 2,236,000 vols; Pres. Dr YUAN-TSEH LEE; Dir-Gen. Dr YIH-HSIUNG YEH; Chief of Secretariat Dr CHI-CHIUNG LO; publs *Academia Economic* (papers), *Academia Sinica* (2 a year), *Asia-Major* (2 a year), *Asia-Pacific Forum* (4 a year), *Botanical Bulletin* (4 a year), *Bulletin of the Institute of Ethnology*, *Bulletin of the Institute of History and Philosophy*, *Bulletin of the Institute of Mathematics*, *Bulletin of the Institute of Modern History* (4 a year), *Disquisitions of the Past and Present* (2 a year), *EurAmerica Quarterly*, *Journal of Social Sciences and Philosophy*, *Language and Linguistics* (4 a year), *Mathmedia* (4 a year), *Research on Women in Chinese History* (1 a year), *Statistica Sinica* (4 a year), *Taiwan Economic Forecasts and Policies Academia Economic Papers*, *Taiwan Historical Research* (2 a year), *Taiwan Journal of Anthropology* (2 a year), *Taiwanese Sociological Review* (2 a year), *Zoological Studies* (4 a year).

China Academy: Hwa Kang, Yang Ming Shan; f. 1966; private instn for sinological studies, consisting of 20 academic asscns and research institutions and Chinese and foreign mems; 591 acads, 312 hon. acads, 1,815 fellows; library of 450,000 vols; Pres. CHANG CHI-YUN; Sec.-Gen. PAN WEI-HO; publs *Beautiful China Pictorial Monthly* (bilingual Chinese and English), *Chinese Culture* (in English, 4 a year), *Renaissance Monthly* (in Chinese), *Sino-American Relations* (in English, 4 a year), *Sinological Monthly* (in Chinese), *Sinological Quarterly* (in Chinese).

China National Association of Literature and the Arts: 4 Lane 22, Nuigpo St W, Taipei.

China Society: 7 Lane 52, Wenchow St, Taipei; f. 1960; centre for Chinese studies; 100 mems; Pres. Dr CHEN CHI-LU; publ. *Journal* (1 a year).

AGRICULTURE, FISHERIES AND VETERINARY SCIENCE

Agricultural Association of China: 14 Wenchow St, Taipei; tel. (2) 23636681; f. 1917; mems: 159 instns, 2,554 individuals; Pres. TSONG-SHIEN WU; publ. *Journal* (4 a year).

Chinese Forestry Association: 2 Sec. 1, Hang-chow South Rd, Taipei 100; tel. (2) 33221299; fax (2) 33221099; e-mail cfa@forest.gov.tw; internet www.forestry.org.tw; f. 1967; 1,219 mems; Chair. JEN-TEH YEN; publ. *Quarterly Journal of Chinese Forestry*.

BIBLIOGRAPHY, LIBRARY SCIENCE AND MUSEOLOGY

Library Association of the Republic of China (Taiwan): 20 Chungshan S. Rd, Taipei 10001; tel. (2) 23312475; fax (2) 23700899; e-mail lac@ncl.edu.tw; internet www.lac.org.tw; f. 1953; 2,060 mems; Pres. HSUEH-HUA CHEN; Sec.-Gen. WEI PENG; publs *Journal of Library and Information Science Research* (2 a year), *Library Association of the Republic of China (Taiwan) e-NEWs* (12 a year).

ECONOMICS, LAW AND POLITICS

Chinese National Foreign Relations Association: Third Fl., 94 Nanchang St, Sec. 1, Taipei; Pres. HUANG KUO-SHU.

National Bar Association: 124 Chungking South Rd, Sec. 1, Taipei.

HISTORY, GEOGRAPHY AND ARCHAEOLOGY

Academia Historica (Academy of History): 406 Sec. 2, Pei Yi Rd, Hsintien, Taipei; tel. (2) 22175500; fax (2) 22170317; internet www.drnh.gov.tw; f. 1947; responsible for researching and compiling material on Taiwanese national history; 175 mems; library of 10,000,000 items (nat. archives, books, documents); Pres. CHANG YEN HSIEN; Sec.-Gen. Prof. LI CHUNG KUANG; publs *Bulletin* (2 a year), *Journal* (2 a year).

LANGUAGE AND LITERATURE

British Council: 2F-1, 106 XinYi Rd, Sec. 5, Taipei 110; tel. (2) 87221000; fax (2) 87860985; e-mail enquiries@britishcouncil.org.tw; internet www.britishcouncil.org/taiwan; teaching centre; offers courses and exams in English language and British culture and promotes cultural exchange with the UK; attached office in Kaohsiung; Dir GORDON SLAVEN.

Chinese Language Society: c/o Taiwan Normal Univ., Hoping E Rd, Taipei; f. 1953; Dir MAO TZU-SHUI; publ. *Chinese Language Monthly*.

MEDICINE

Chinese Medical Association: 201 Shih-Pai Rd, Sec. II, Taipei; f. 1915; 1,672 mems; Pres. Dr KWANG-JUEI LO; Sec.-Gen. Dr YANG-TE TSAI; publ. *Chinese Medical Journal* (12 a year).

NATURAL SCIENCES

Mathematical Sciences

Chinese Statistical Association: 1 Nan Chung Rd, Sec. 1, Taipei; f. 1941; 1,082 mems; Pres. C. C. LEE; publ. *Chinese Statistical Journal*.

Mathematical Society of the Republic of China: Dept of Mathematics, Nat. Cheng Kung Univ., Tainan 70101; fax (6) 2743191; Pres. LEE YUH-JIA; Sec. HUANG YOUNG-YE.

Physical Sciences

Chemical Society: POB 1-18, Nankang, Taipei 115; tel. (2) 27898574; fax (2) 26530440; e-mail ccswww@gate.sinica.edu.tw; internet www.ccs.sinica.edu.tw; f. 1932; 3,000 mems; Sec.-Gen. LING-KANG LIU; publs *Hua Hsueh* (in Chinese, 4 a year), *Journal* (in English, 6 a year).

Committee on the Promotion of the Peaceful Uses of Atomic Energy: 110 Yenping South Rd, Taipei; Pres. MILTON J. T. SHIEH.

Physical Society of China: POB 23-30, Taipei.

PHILOSOPHY AND PSYCHOLOGY

Confucius-Mencius Society of the Republic of China: 45 Nanhai Rd, Taipei; f. 1960; spreads knowledge about Confucius and Mencius, seeks the improvement of public morals and the creation of a better society; 3,900 mems; Chair. Dr CHEN LI-FU; Sec. HUA CHUNG-LIN; publ. *Confucius-Mencius Monthly*, *Journal of Confucius-Mencius Society*.

RELIGION, SOCIOLOGY AND ANTHROPOLOGY

Chinese Association for Folklore: 422 Fulin Rd, POB 68-1292, Shihlin, Taipei; f. 1932; Chinese and Asian folklore; 47 mems; library of 1,000 vols and MSS; Chair. Prof. LOU TSU-KUANG; Sec. AMY LOU.

TECHNOLOGY

Chinese Institute of Civil and Hydraulic Engineering: 4th Fl., 1 Jen Ai Rd, 2 Taipei; tel. (2) 23926325; fax (2) 23964260; e-mail ciche@ciche.org.tw; internet www.ciche.org.tw; f. 1973; 7,500 mems; Pres. YU CHENG; publs *Journal of Civil and Hydraulic Engineering* (4 a year), *Journal of the Chinese Institute of Civil and Hydraulic Engineering* (4 a year).

Chinese Institute of Engineers: Fl. 3, No. 1 Ren-ai Rd, Sec. 2, Taipei 10055; tel. (2) 23925128; fax (2) 23973003; e-mail secretariat@cie.org.tw; internet www.cie.org.tw; f. 1912; 18,125 individual mems and 78 group mems; library of 7,500 vols, 60 periodicals; Sec. FENZA CHIANG; publs *Journal of the Chinese Institute of Engineers* (8 a year), *Newsletter* (4 a year), *Transactions* (6 a year).

Research Institutes

GENERAL

National Institute for Compilation and Translation: 179 Heping E Rd, Sector 1, Da-An District, Taipei City 10644; tel. (2) 33225558; fax (2) 33225559; e-mail trcnews@mail.nict.gov.tw; internet www.nict.gov.tw; f. 1932; translates foreign books, examines and approves textbooks, standardizes scientific and technical terms; 75 mems; library of 100,000 vols; Dir-Gen; PAN WEN-CHUNG; publs *Compilation and Translation Review* (print and online), *Journal of Textbook Research* (print and online).

AGRICULTURE, FISHERIES AND VETERINARY SCIENCE

Council of Agriculture: 37 Nanhai Rd, Taipei; tel. (2) 23812991; fax (2) 23310341; e-mail coa@mail.coa.gov.tw; internet www.coa.gov.tw; f. 1984; govt agency under the Exec. Yuan, with ministerial status; administers nat. agriculture, forestry, fisheries, livestock farming and food; library of 18,000 vols; Min. Dr WU-HSIUNG CHEN.

Taiwan Agricultural Research Institute: 189 Chung-Cheng Rd, Wan-Feng, Wu-Feng, Taichung; tel. (4) 3302301; fax (4) 3338162; e-mail mwf-doc@wufeng.tari.gov.tw; internet www.tari.gov.tw; f. 1895; insect colln; Dir LIN CHIEN-YIH; publ. *Journal of Agricultural Research of China* (4 a year).

Taiwan Fisheries Research Institute: 199 Hou-Ih Rd, Keelung 220; tel. (2) 24622101; fax (2) 24629388; f. 1933; library of 16,000 vols; Dir-Gen. I-CHIU LIAO; publs *Journal*, research reports.

Taiwan Forestry Research Institute: 53 Nan-Hai Rd, Taipei, 10066; tel. (2) 23039978; fax (2) 23142234; e-mail service@serv.tfri.gov.tw; internet www.tfri.gov.tw; f. 1985; library of 33,000 vols; Dir HEN-BIAU KING; Sec.-Gen. KUO-CHUAN LIN; publ. *Journal of Forest Science* (4 a year).

Taiwan Sugar Research Institute: 54 Sheng Chan Rd, Tainan; tel. (6) 2671911; fax (6) 2685425; e-mail tsc02@taisugar.com.tw; f. 1902; supported by Taiwan Sugar Corpn; library of 46,800 vols; Dir LONG-HUEI WANG; publs *Extension Bulletin*, *Report* (in Chinese, 4 a year, English summary), *Technical Bulletin*.

ECONOMICS, LAW AND POLITICS

Co-operative League of the Republic of China: 11-2 Fu Chow St, Taipei; tel. (2) 23219343; fax (2) 23517918; f. 1940; cooperative business research and education; Chair. YANG CHIA-LIN; Exec. Dir and Sec.-Gen. HSU WEN-FU; publs *CLC Co-operative News* (1 a year), *Co-operative Economics* (4 a year).

Institute of Economics: c/o Academia Sinica, Nankang, Taipei 11529; tel. (2) 27822791; fax (2) 27853946; internet www.sinica.edu.tw/~econ; f. 1962; attached to Academia Sinica; Dir Dr CHUNG-MING KUAN; publs *Academia Economic Papers* (4 a year), *Taiwan Economic Forecast and Policy* (2 a year).

FINE AND PERFORMING ARTS

National Taiwan Arts Education Centre: 47 Nan Hai Rd, Taipei; tel. (2) 23110574; fax (2) 23122555; internet www.arte.gov.tw; f. 1957; in charge of the research, extension and guidance of art education in Taiwan; Dir JOSEPH TSU-SHENG WU; publs *Journal of Aesthetic Education* (6 a year), *Newsletter of Arts Education* (12 a year), *The International Journal of Arts Education* (2 a year).

HISTORY, GEOGRAPHY AND ARCHAEOLOGY

Institute of History and Philology: c/o Academia Sinica, Nankang, Taipei 11529; tel. (2) 27829555; fax (2) 27868834; internet www.ihp.sinica.edu.tw/english; attached to Academia Sinica; Dir Prof. TUNG-KUEI KUAN.

Institute of Modern History: c/o Academia Sinica, Nankang, Taipei 11529; tel. (2) 27824166; attached to Academia Sinica; Dir Prof. KO-WU HUANG; Sec. SHU-LING CHIANG.

MEDICINE

Institute of Biomedical Sciences, Preparatory Office: c/o Academia Sinica, Nankang, Taipei 11529; attached to Academia Sinica; Dir Dr CHENG-WEN WU.

NATURAL SCIENCES

General

National Science Council: 106 Ho-ping E Rd, Section 2, Taipei 106; tel. (2) 27377981; fax (2) 27377672; e-mail klchou@nsc.gov.tw; internet www.nsc.gov.tw; f. 1959; br. of central govt; promotes nat. science and technology devt, supports academic research and establishes industrial parks; Sr Systems Coordinator K.L. CHOU; publs *East Asian Science, Technology and Society* (in English, 4 a year), *Indicators of Science and Technology* (in Chinese and English, 1 a year), *International Journal of Science and Mathematics Education* (in English, 4 a year), *Journal of Biomedical Science* (in English, 6 a year , open access journal since January 2009), *National Science Council Review* (in English and Chinese, 1 a year), *Science Development* (in Chinese, 12 a year).

Biological Sciences

Central Laboratory of Molecular Biology, Preparatory Office: c/o Academia Sinica, Nankang, Taipei 11529; attached to Academia Sinica; Dir Dr CHIEN HO.

Institute of Biological Chemistry: c/o Academia Sinica, Nankang, Taipei 11529; attached to Academia Sinica; Dir Dr WEN-CHANG CHANG (acting).

Institute of Botany: c/o Academia Sinica, Nankang, Taipei 11529; tel. (2) 27899590; fax (2) 27827954; e-mail boplshaw@ccvax.sinica.edu.tw; internet www.botany.sinica.edu.tw; f. 1929; attached to Academia Sinica; Dir Dr JEI-FU SHAW; publ. *Botanical Bulletin of Academia Sinica* (4 a year).

Institute of Zoology: c/o Academia Sinica, Nankang, Taipei 11529; attached to Academia Sinica; Dir Dr JEN-LEIH WU.

Mathematical Sciences

Institute of Mathematics: c/o Academia Sinica, Nankang, Taipei 11529; attached to Academia Sinica; Dir Dr KO-WEI LIH.

Institute of Statistical Science: c/o Academia Sinica, 128 Academia Rd Sec. 2, Taipei 11529; tel. (2) 27835611; fax (2) 27831523; internet www.stat.sinica.edu.tw; f. 1982; attached to Academia Sinica; Dir Dr KER-CHAU LI; publ. *Statistica Sinica* (4 a year).

Physical Sciences

Atomic Energy Council: 67 Lane 144, Keelung Rd, Sec. 4, Taipei 106; tel. (2) 23634180; fax (2) 23635377; f. 1955; govt agency for the peaceful application of atomic energy; library of 11,000 vols, deposit library at the Nat. Tsing Hua Univ. of 36,000 vols and 424,000 microcards; Chair. Dr YIH-YUN HSU; Sec.-Gen. KUANG-CHI LIU; publs *Nuclear Climate* (12 a year), *Nuclear Science Journal* (6 a year).

Central Geological Survey: POB 968, Taipei 100; tel. (2) 29462793; fax (2) 29429291; e-mail cgs@linx.moeacgs.gov.tw; internet www.moeacgs.gov.tw; f. 1946; maps; library of 50,000 vols and periodicals; Dir CHAO-CHUNG LIN; publs *Bulletin*, *Ti-Chih* (geology, 2 a year).

Institute of Atomic and Molecular Sciences, Preparatory Office: c/o Academia Sinica, Nankang, Taipei 11529; attached to Academia Sinica; Dir Dr CHAO-TIN CHANG.

Institute of Chemistry: c/o Academia Sinica, Nankang, Taipei 11529; attached to Academia Sinica; Dir Dr SUNNEY I. CHAN.

Institute of Earth Sciences: Academia Sinica, Nankang, Taipei 11529; tel. (2) 27839910; fax (2) 27839871; attached to Academia Sinica; Dir Dr BOR-MING JAHN.

Institute of Information Science: c/o Academia Sinica, Nankang, Taipei 11529; attached to Academia Sinica; Dir Dr YUE-SUN KUO (acting).

Institute of Nuclear Energy Research: POB 3, Lung-Tan 32500; tel. (2) 3651717; fax (3) 4711064; f. 1968; research in peaceful uses of atomic energy; Dir Dr HSIA DER-YU (acting); publ. *INER report series*.

Institute of Physics: c/o Academia Sinica, Nankang, Taipei 11529; attached to Academia Sinica; Dir Dr TUNG-MIN HO (acting).

PHILOSOPHY AND PSYCHOLOGY

Sun Yat-sen Institute for Social Sciences and Philosophy: c/o Academia Sinica, Nankang, Taipei 11529; tel. (2) 27821693; fax (2) 27854160; e-mail issp@www.issp.sinica.edu.tw; internet www.issp.sinica.edu.tw; f. 1981; attached to Academia Sinica; Dir Dr ANGELA KI CHE LEUNG; publ. *Journal of Social Sciences and Philosophy* (4 a year).

RELIGION, SOCIOLOGY AND ANTHROPOLOGY

Institute of Ethnology: c/o Academia Sinica, Nankang, Taipei 11529; tel. (2) 26523300; fax (2) 26523436; e-mail tja@gate.sinica.edu.tw; internet www.sinica.edu.tw/ioe; f. 1955; attached to Academia Sinica; main field of research: social and cultural anthropology; Dir Prof. HUANG SHU-MIN; publs *Field Materials*, *Taiwan Journal of Anthropology* (2 a year).

Institute of European and American Studies: Academia Sinica, Nankang, Taipei 11529; attached to Academia Sinica; Dir Dr WEN-CHING HO; publ. *EurAmerica* (4 a year).

TECHNOLOGY

Industrial Technology Research Institute: 195 Chung Hsing Rd, Sec. 4, Chu-Tung, Hsinchu; tel. (35) 820100; fax (35) 820045; f. 1973; library of 130,000 vols; Pres. Dr OTTO C. C. LIN; publs *Chemical Industry Notes*, *Electro-optics Development Journal*, *Energy-Resources and Environment* (in Chinese, 4 a year), *Materials and Society*, *Mechatronics Journal*, *Metrology Information* (in Chinese, 6 a year), *Mining Technology*, *MRL Bulletin of Research and Development* (in English, 2 a year), *Opto-Electronics and Systems*, *Reports of Center for Measurement Standards* (in Chinese, 12 a year), *Superconductor Applications News*, *UCL Chemical Information Digest*.

Research Laboratories:

Centre for Aviation and Aerospace: Hsinchu; Dir Dr RICHARD Y. H. LIN.

Centre for Industrial Safety and Health Technology: Hsinchu; Dir Dr ADA W. S. MA.

Centre for Measurement Standards: Hsinchu; Dir Dr CHANG HSU.

Centre for Pollution Control Technology: Hsinchu; Dir Dr LING-YUAN CHEN.

Computer and Communication Research Laboratories: Hsinchu; Dir Dr STEVEN CHENG.

Electronics Research and Service Organization: Hsinchu; Dir Dr DAVID C. T. HSING.

Energy and Resources Laboratories: Hsinchu; Dir Dr ROBERT J. YANG.

Materials Research Laboratories: Hsinchu and Kaohsiung; Dir Dr LI-CHUNG LEE.

Mechanical Industry Research Laboratories: Hsinchu; Dir Dr C. RICHARD LIU.

Opto-Electronics and Systems Laboratories: Hsinchu; Dir Dr MIN-SHYONG LIN.

Union Chemical Laboratories: Hsinchu; Dir Dr JOHN-SEE LEE.

National Bureau of Standards: Min. of Economic Affairs, 3rd Floor, 185 Hsinhai Rd, Sec. 2, Taipei 106; tel. (2) 27380007; fax (2) 27352656; f. 1947; nat. standards, weights and measures, patents, trademarks; library of 20,000 vols, 500 periodicals; Dir-Gen. MING-BANG CHEN; publs *Catalogue of Chinese National Standards* (1 a year), *Chinese National Standards* (irregular), *Official Gazette for Patents* (36 a year), *Official Gazette for Standards* (12 a year), *Official Gazette for Trademarks* (24 a year).

Libraries and Archives

Tainan

National Cheng Kung University Library: 1 Ta Hsueh Rd, Tainan 70101; tel. (6) 2757575; fax (6) 2378232; internet www.lib.ncku.edu.tw; f. 1927; 1,685,049 vols, 12,676 periodicals; Dir MING-TZONG YANG; publ. *Bulletin* (4 a year).

Taipei

Agricultural Science Information Centre: POB 7-636, Taipei 106; tel. (2) 23626222; internet www.asic.org.tw; f. 1977; 11,000 vols, 638 periodicals, databases; Dir WAN-JIUN WU.

Dr Sun Yat-sen Library: 2F, 505 Jen Ai Rd, Sec. 4, Taipei; tel. (2) 27297030; fax (2) 27582460; f. 1929; 299,345 vols on Dr Sun Yat-sen's writings and studies on San Min Chu Yih and modern Chinese history; Curator SHAW MING-HUANG; publ. *Modern China* (6 a year).

Fu Ssu-nien Library, Institute of History and Philology: 130 Yen Chiu Yuan Rd, Sec. 2, Nankang, Taipei 11521; tel. (2) 27829555; fax (2) 27868834; f. 1928; 420,000 vols, 3,000 periodicals; spec. collns incl. 33,889 stone and bronze rubbings, 13,100 folk plays, 310,000 cabinet records of Ming and Ch'ing dynasties; Dir JUEI-HSIU WU.

National Central Library: 20 Chung Shan South Rd, Taipei 100; tel. (2) 23619132; fax (2) 23110155; e-mail iechief@ncl.edu.tw; internet www.ncl.edu.tw; f. 1933; 4,198,475 vols, incl. 190,000 rare books, stone rubbings and historical material; Dir-Gen. Dr TSENG SHU-HSIEN; publs *Chinese National Bibliography* (12 a year), *Index to Chinese Periodicals* (4 a year), *NCL Bulletin* (2 a year), *NCL News Bulletin* (4 a year).

Branch Library:

Taiwan Branch Library, National Central Library: 1 Hsinshen South Rd, Sec. 1, Taipei; tel. (2) 27724724; internet www.ncltb.edu.tw; f. 1915; 592,023 vols; spec. collns incl. Taiwan and Southern Asia; Dir LIN WEI-JEI; publs *Catalogue of Materials for the Blind*, *Catalogue of NCL Taiwan Branch Collection on Southeast Asia*, *Catalogue on China in Japanese Languages*, *Catalogue on China in Western Languages*, *Index to Taiwan-Related Periodical Literature Collected in NCL Taiwan Branch*, *List of Non-Chinese Serials in NCL Taiwan Branch*, *The Annotative Catalogue of Taiwan Documents*, *Union Catalogue of Taiwan-Related Bibliographies*.

National War College Library: Yangmingshan, Taipei; 156,639 vols on political subjects; Librarian LO MOU-PIN.

Parliamentary Library, Legislative Yuan: 1 Chung Shan S Rd, Taipei 10051; tel. (2) 23585278; fax (2) 23585290; internet npl.ly.gov.tw; f. 1947; gen. reference, govt publs, legal documents; 248,235 vols; Dir Dr SHOW-RONG WANG; publs *Chinese legislative news review index* (12 a year), *Chinese legislative news reviews series* (irregular), *Code Amendment Cyclopedia* (irregular), *Code and reference book catalogue* (irregular), *Code resource pathfinder* (6 a year), *Collection of Interpellation Records* (irregular), *Gazette*, *Index to Chinese Legislative Literature* (6 a year), *Index to Legal Periodicals* (irregular), *Index of Legislative Records* (every 3 years), *LEGISIS thesaurus* (irregular), *Legislative Decision Support Service* (12 a year), *Legislative Microform Catalogue* (irregular), *Library Communications Quarterly*, *Newsletter of books and documentation* (4 a year), *Proceedings and Serials Catalogue* (irregular), *Selective Abstracts of US Congressional Records* (irregular), *Selected Dissemination of Information Series* (6 a year), *Subject Guide to Chinese Code* (irregular), *The Legislative Yuan Library Catalogue* (irregular).

Taipei City Library: 46 Chinan Rd, Sec. 2, Taipei; f. 1952; 125,000 vols; 4 brs; Dir CHIH-SHIH YANG; publ. *Taipei Municipal Library Annals*.

Museums and Art Galleries

Kaohsiung

Kaohsiung Museum of Fine Arts: 80 Meishukuan Rd, Kaohsiung; tel. (7) 5550331; fax (7) 5550307; e-mail service@kmfa.gov.tw; internet www.kmfa.gov.tw; f. 1994; Dir PEI-NI BEATRICE HSIEH.

Taichung

National Taiwan Museum of Fine Arts: 2, Sec. 1, Wu Chuan West Rd, Taichung 403;

tel. (4) 23723552; fax (4) 23721195; e-mail artnet@art.ntmofa.gov.tw; internet www.ntmofa.gov.tw; f. 1986; mostly works of Taiwan artists; library of 70,000 vols; Dir TSAI-LANG HUANG; publ. *Journal of National Taiwan Museum of Fine Arts* (4 a year).

Taipei

Chinese Postal Museum: 45 Chungking South Rd, Sec. 2, Taipei 100; tel. (2) 23945185; fax (2) 23518773; e-mail musol@mail.post.gov.tw; internet www.post.gov.tw/museum.htm; f. 1966; library of 27,000 vols; Dir SUSAN TENG-KUEI YU.

Hwa Kang Museum: 55 Hwa Kang Rd, Chinese Culture Univ., Yang Ming Shan, Taipei 111; tel. (2) 28610511; fax (2) 28621918; e-mail cuch@staff.pccu.edu.tw; internet www2.pccu.edu.tw/cuch; f. 1971; Chinese folk arts, pottery, porcelain, calligraphy and paintings; Dir MARGARET CHEN LEE.

National Museum of History: 49 Nan Hai Rd, Taipei 10066; tel. (2) 23610270; fax (2) 23610171; internet www.nmh.gov.tw; f. 1955; Chinese and Taiwanese historical and archaeological artefacts; library of 30,000 vols; Dir YUNG-CHUAN HUANG; publs *Bulletin of the National Museum of History* (in Chinese, 12 a year), *Journal of the National Museum of History* (in Chinese, 2 a year).

National Palace Museum: Wai-shuang-hsi, Shih-lin, Taipei; tel. (2) 28812021; fax (2) 28821440; internet www.npm.gov.tw; f. 1925; colln consists chiefly of historic and archaeological treasures brought from mainland China; library of 155,136 vols, 624 periodical titles, 200,907 rare books, 395,335 Ch'ing documents; Dir SHIH SHOU-CHIEN; publs *National Palace Museum Monthly of Chinese Art* (12 a year), *Research Quarterly* (4 a year).

National Taiwan Museum: 2 Siang-yang Rd, Taipei 100; tel. (2) 23822699; fax (2) 23822684; e-mail ntmmail@ntm.gov.uk; internet www.ntm.gov.uk; f. 1908; anthropology, earth sciences, zoology and botany; Dir HSIAO TSUNG-HUANG; publs *Journal of Taiwan Museum* (in English), *Taiwan Natural Science*.

National Taiwan Science Education Centre: 41 Nan Hai Rd, Taipei; tel. (2) 23116734; f. 1958; planetarium, science exhibitions, lectures and films; Dir SHIH-BEY CHEN; publ. *Science Study Monthly*.

Shung Ye Museum of Formosan Aborigines: 282 Chishan Rd Section 2, Shi-Lin Dist, Taipei 11143; tel. (2) 28412611; fax (2) 28412615; e-mail shungye@gate.sinica.edu.tw; internet www.museum.org.tw; f. 1994; holds a colln of artefacts of Taiwan's indigenous peoples; promotes understanding between ethnic groups and undertakes research and preservation of Aboriginal cultural works; Museum Curator and Dir ERIC H. Y. YU.

Taipei Astronomical Museum: 363 Kee-Ho Rd, Taipei 111; tel. (2) 28314551; fax (2) 28314405; e-mail tam001@tam.gov.tw; internet www.tam.gov.tw; f. 1996; exhibits hall, cosmic adventure, IMAX and 3D theatre, observation area; organizes lectures, astronomer workshops and programmes, teacher training; Pres. GUO-GUANG CIOU; Gen. Sec. CHING-HSIUNG WANG; publs *Astronomical Almanac* (1 a year), *Journal Taipei Astronomical Museum*, *Report on Sunspot Observations* (1 a year), *Taipei Skylight* (4 a year).

Taipei Fine Arts Museum: 181, Sec. 3, Zhong Shan N. Rd, Taipei 10461; tel. (2) 25957656; fax (2) 25944104; e-mail info@tfam.gov.tw; internet www.tfam.gov.tw; f. 1983; modern art; Dir TSAI-LANG HSIAO (acting); publs *Journal* (2 a year), *Modern Art* (6 a year).

Universities

CHINESE CULTURE UNIVERSITY

55 Hwa Kang Rd, Yang Ming Shan, Taipei
Telephone: (2) 28610511
Fax: (2) 28615031
Internet: www.pccu.edu.tw

Founded 1962
Private control

Colleges of agriculture, arts, business, engineering, foreign languages and literature, journalism and mass communication, law, liberal arts, science; graduate and evening schools

Pres.: LIN TSAI-MEI

Library of 630,000 vols, 3,500 periodicals
Number of teachers: 531
Number of students: 20,013

CHUNG YUAN CHRISTIAN UNIVERSITY

Chung Li
Telephone: (3) 4563171
Fax: (3) 4563160
Internet: www.cycu.edu.tw

Founded 1955
Private control
Academic year: August to July

Colleges of business, design, engineering, science; evening dept

Pres.: Dr SAMUEL K. C. CHANG

Library of 250,000 vols
Number of teachers: 12,491
Number of students: 11,798

Publications: *Chung Yuan Journal*, *CYCU News*.

FENG CHIA UNIVERSITY

100 Wenhwa Rd, Seatwen, Taichung 40724
Telephone: (4) 24517250
Fax: (4) 24514907
E-mail: linkages@fcu.edu.tw
Internet: www.fcu.edu.tw

Founded 1961
Private control
Languages of instruction: Chinese, English
Academic year: September to June

Pres.: AN-CHI LIU
Vice-Pres.: YUAN-TONG LEE
Sec.-Gen.: HAI-PING HSIEH
Chief Librarian: HSIANG-HOO CHING

Library of 590,000 vols
Number of teachers: 1,107
Number of students: 19,124 (17,517 undergraduate, 1,607 postgraduate)

Publications: *Accounting Journal*, *Architecture Quarterly*, *Banking and Insurance*, *Civil Engineering Journal*, *Computer Science*, *Co-operative Research*, *FCU Weekly*, *Finance Research*, *Industrial Engineering*, *International Trade*, *Mechanical Engineering*, *Statistics Journal*, *Textile Science*

DEANS

College of Business: PAO-LONG CHANG
College of Construction and Devt: BING-JEAN LEE
College of Continuing Education: YOU-REN SHIAU
College of Engineering: TONG-MIIN LIOU
College of Humanities and Social Studies: YEN CHU
College of Information and Electrical Engineering: CHUANG-CHIEN CHIU
College of Sciences: TAI-LEE HU

DIRECTORS OF GRADUATE INSTITUTES

Accounting and Taxation: YU-CHI LIN
Aeronautical Engineering: WEN-SHYONG KOU
Applied Mathematics: JIANN-CHERNG YANG
Architecture and Urban Planning: MEI-JUNG LAI
Automatic Control Engineering: CHERN-SHENG LIN
Business Administration: MEI-YANE CHUNG
Chemical Engineering: CHYI-TSONG CHEN
Chinese Literature: JIANN-HWA SONG
Civil and Hydraulic Engineering: YU-MIN KANG
Communications Engineering: CHENG-HO HSIN
Economics: CHI-CHU CHOU
Electrical and Communications Engineering: CHUANG-CHIEN CHIU
Electrical Engineering: CHANG-CHOU HWANG
Electronic Engineering: WEN-LUH YANG
Environmental Science and Engineering: JYA-JYUN YU
Finance: CHE-PENG LIN
History and Cultural Heritage Management: CHIH-CHIA HU
Industrial Engineering: ANGUS JEANG
Information Engineering: DON-LIN YANG
Insurance: GOW-NING YUAN
International Trade: TING-JI LIN
Land Management: JING-CHZI HSIEH
Materials Science: HSIN-CHIH LIN
Mechanical Engineering: JIN-HUANG HUANG
Optical Physics: YING-TE LEE
Statistics and Actuarial Science: WOAN-SHU CHEN
Textiles Engineering: TIEN-WEI SHYR
Traffic and Transportation Engineering and Management: TA-YIN HU

FU-JEN CATHOLIC UNIVERSITY

510 Chungcheng Rd, Hsin-Chuang, Taipei
Telephone: (2) 29031111
Fax: (2) 29017391
E-mail: fjuweb@mails.fju.edu.tw
Internet: www.fju.edu.tw

Founded 1925 in Beijing; re-opened in Taiwan 1961
Academic year: August to July

Pres.: Dr JOHN NING-YUEAN LEE
Vice-Pres: Dr PERRY C. CHIU, Dr PETER SHANG-SHING CHOU, Rev. LOUIS GENDRON
Sec.-Gen.: JOHN SHIANG-YANG HWANG
Dean of Academic Affairs: Dr YIU-LUNG CHEN
Dean of Gen. Affairs: Prof. ZERMAN HU
Dean of Research and Devt: Dr SHIH-MING KO
Dean of Student Affairs: Dr HUNG YAN CHEN
Registrar: TZU-CHI LI
Librarian: Dr H. H. CHENG

Library of 828,000 vols
Number of teachers: 1,591
Number of students: 23,658

Publications: *Catholic Observer*, *Fu Jen Philosophical Studies*, *Fu Jen Studies* (4 a year)

DEANS

College of Fine Arts: Dr MING-JIAN FANG
College of Foreign Languages: Dr NICHOLAS KOSS
College of Human Ecology: Dr SHAU-YEN HUANG
College of Law: Dr AH-YEE LEE
College of Liberal Arts: Dr THOMAS FU-BEING CHEN
College of Management: Dr DENG-YUAN HUANG
College of Medicine: Dr VINCENT HAN-SUN CHIANG
College of Science and Engineering: Dr JOSEPH L. G. HWA

Holistic Education Centre: Dr DAMIANUS JEN-LUNGKAO
School of Continuing Education: Dr CAJUS CHI-CHI LIN

NATIONAL CENTRAL UNIVERSITY

Chung-Li 320
Telephone: (3) 4227151
Fax: (3) 4226062
Internet: www.ncu.edu.tw

Founded 1968 as re-establishment of Nat. Central Univ. (Nanking)
Academic year: February to January

Pres.: Prof. CHAO-HAN LIU
Vice-Pres.: KUANG-FU CHENG
Dean of Academic Affairs: KUAN-CHING LEE
Dean of Gen. Affairs: EDMOND LIU-WU HOURNG
Dean of Research and Devt: WEI-LING CHIANG
Dean of Student Affairs: DYI-HWA TSENG
Dir of Secretariat: JIEN-MING JUE
Librarian: CHIEU-YIUG WANG

Number of teachers: 450
Number of students: 7,813

Publications: *Bulletin of Geophysics* (2 a year), *Journal of Humanities East/West* (2 a year)

DEANS

College of Earth Sciences: YI-BEN TSAI
College of Engineering: KUO-SHONG WANG
College of Information Technology and Electrical Engineering: SHING-TSAAN HUANG
College of Liberal Arts: JEH-HANG LAI
College of Management: JING-TWEN CHEN
College of Science: WING-HUEN IP

NATIONAL CHENG KUNG UNIVERSITY

1 Ta-Hsueh Rd, Tainan 70101
Telephone: (6) 2757575
Fax: (6) 2368660
E-mail: em50000@mail.ncku.edu.tw
Internet: www.ncku.edu.tw

Founded 1931 as Tainan Technical College, renamed Taiwan Provincial College of Engineering 1946, present name 1971
State control
Language of instruction: Chinese, some English
Academic year: September to June

Pres.: Dr CHIANG KAO
Dean of Academic Affairs: Dr YAN-KUIN SU
Registrar: SHIN-FU HUANG
Librarian: Dr JEN-FA MIN

Number of teachers: 1,200
Number of students: 19,000

Publications: *Bulletin of National Cheng Kung University* (1 a year), *Journal of National Cheng Kung University* (1 a year)

DEANS

College of Design: Dr MING-FU HSU
College of Electrical Engineering and Computer Science: Dr CHING-TING LI
College of Engineering: Dr WEN-TENG WU
College of Liberal Arts: Dr KAO-PING CHANG
College of Management Science: Dr WANN-YIH WU
College of Medicine: Dr RUEY-JEN SUNG
College of Sciences: Dr SHU-CHENG YU
College of Social Sciences: Dr JENN-YEU CHEN

Graduate institutes are attached to the College of Engineering, the College of Liberal Arts, the College of Management Science, the College of Medicine, the College of Sciences and the College of Social Sciences

NATIONAL CHENGCHI UNIVERSITY

64 Zhinan Rd Sec. 2, Wenshan 116, Taipei
Telephone: (2) 29393091
Fax: (2) 29379611
E-mail: oic@nccu.edu.tw
Internet: www.nccu.edu.tw

Founded 1927, univ. status 1946; state-funded
Public control
Languages of instruction: Chinese, English
Academic year: September to June (2 semesters)

Pres.: SE-HWA WU
Vice-Pres. and Dean of Academic Affairs: LIEN-KONG TSAI
Dean of General Affairs: TAI-MING BEN
Dean of Student Affairs: MEI-LIE CHU
Dir of Library: JYI-SHANE LIU

Library of 2,106,128 vols
Number of teachers: 684 (full- and part-time)
Number of students: 16,038

DEANS

College of Commerce: CHUEN-LUNG CHEN
College of Communication: CHIH-YU CHAN
College of Education: WEI-WEN CHUNG
College of Foreign Languages: NAI-MING YU
College of Int. Affairs: CHUNG-CHIAN TENG
College of Law: KAI-LIN FAUNG
College of Liberal Arts: WHEI-MING CHOU
College of Science: ARBEE CHEN
College of Social Sciences: SONG-LING YANG

NATIONAL CHIAO TUNG UNIVERSITY

1001 Ta Hsueh Rd, Hsinchu
Telephone: (35) 712121
Fax: (35) 721500
Internet: www.nctu.edu.tw

Founded 1896, re-established in Hsinchu 1958
Languages of instruction: Chinese, English
Academic year: August to July (2 semesters)

Pres.: Dr CHI-FU DEN
Dean of Academic Affairs: Dr LONG-ING CHEN
Dean of Gen. Affairs: Dr CHUNG-BIAU TSAY
Dean of the Research and Devt Ccl: Dr CHUNG-YU WU
Dean of Student Affairs: Dr FU-WHA HAN
Chief Sec.: Prof. HSIN-SEN CHU
Registrar: Assoc. Prof. CHIN-SHYONG CHEN
Chief Librarian: Dr RUEI-CHUAN CHANG

Library of 170,329 vols, 2,373 periodicals
Number of teachers: 415 (full-time)
Number of students: 4,896

Publications: *Chiao Ta Management Review*, *List of Publications of Faculty Members*, abstracts of papers and research reports

DEANS

College of Electrical Engineering and Computer Science: Dr CHE-HO WEI
College of Engineering: Dr TAI-YAN KAM
College of Management: Dr PAO-LONG CHANG
College of Science: Dr DER-SAN CHUU

DIRECTORS OF GRADUATE INSTITUTES

Applied Arts (Design and Music): Dr MING-CHUEN CHUANG
Applied Chemistry: Dr CHAIN-SHU HSU
Applied Mathematics: Dr GERARD J. CHANG
Biological Science and Technology: Dr CHENG ALLEN CHANG
Civil Engineering: Dr YUNG-SHOW FANG
Communication Engineering: Dr CHUNG-JU CHANG
Communication Studies: Dr SHIN-MIN CHEN
Computer and Information Science: Dr RONG-HONG JAN
Computer Science and Information Engineering: Dr SHU-YUEN HWANG
Control Engineering: Dr DER-CHERNG LIAW
Electronics: Dr TAN-FU LEI
Electro-Optical Engineering: Dr CI-LING PAN
Electrophysics: Dr MING-CHIH LEE
Environmental Engineering: Dr JEHNG-JUNG KAO
Industrial Engineering: Dr CHAO-TON SU
Information Management: Dr CHI-CHUN LO
Management Science: Dr SOUSHAN WU
Management Technology: Dr SHANG-JYH LIU
Materials Science and Engineering: Dr TZENG-FENG LIU
Mechanical Engineering: Dr HSIN-SEN CHU
Physics: Dr JSIN-FU JIANG
Statistics: Dr CHAO-SHENG LEE
Traffic and Transportation: Dr YUAN-CHING HSU

DIRECTORS OF RESEARCH CENTRES

Centre for Telecommunications Research: Dr SIN-HORNG CHEN
Computer Centre: Dr RUEI-CHUAN CHANG
Microelectronics and Information Science and Technology Research Centre: Dr MING SZE
National Nano Device Centre: Dr CHUN-YEN CHANG
Semiconductor Research Centre: (vacant)

NATIONAL CHUNG HSING UNIVERSITY

250 Kuokuang Rd, Taichung
Telephone: (4) 2872991
Fax: (4) 2853813
Internet: www.nchu.edu.tw

Founded 1961

Pres.: Dr CHENG-CHANG LI
Sec.-Gen.: MU-CHIOU HUANG
Librarian: WOEI LIN

Number of teachers: 980
Number of students: 17,625

DEANS

College of Agriculture: MING-TSAO CHEN
College of Engineering: SHIH-SHYN WU
College of Law and Commerce: SEN-TIAN WU
College of Liberal Arts: CHUNG-HSUAN TUNG
College of Life Science: SCHENG-MING TSCHEN
College of Science: TENG-KUEI YANG

HEADS OF INSTITUTES

Institute of Agricultural Biotechnology: FENG-NAN HOU
Institute of Agricultural Extension and Education: CHING-YING HUANG
Institute of Biochemistry: JUNGYIE KAO
Institute of Computer Science: SYING-JYAN WANG
Institute of Library and Information Science: WOEI LIN
Institute of Materials Engineering: FUN-SHENG SHEIU
Institute of Molecular Biology: LIANG-JWU CHEN
Institute of Natural Resource Management: DAIGEE SHAW
Institute of Urban Planning: HSUEH-TAO CHIEN
Institute of Veterinary Microbiology: LONG-HUW LEE
Institute of Veterinary Pathology: CHENG-I LIU

NATIONAL OPEN UNIVERSITY

172 Chung Cheng Rd, Lu Chow, Taipei 24702
Telephone: (2) 22829355
Fax: (2) 22831721
E-mail: elec007@mail.nou.edu.tw
Internet: www.nou.edu.tw

Founded 1986
Language of instruction: Chinese

Academic year: September to June
Pres.: Dr SHENG-SHIUNG HUANG
Registrar: LI-CHI HSIEH
Dean of Academic Affairs: Dr CHIA-SHING YANG
Number of teachers: 2,037 (88 full-time, 1,949 part-time)
Number of students: 40,000
Publication: *National Open University Learning Journal* (24 a year)

CHAIRMEN OF DEPARTMENTS

Arts in Commerce: JIN-HO YUAN
General Affairs: TSAI HSIANG-HUEI
General Studies: SZE-LU NA
Instructional Media: DWO-YAN CHANG
Liberal Arts: YUAN-JEN FANG
Living Sciences: WEN-CHIN CHOU
Management and Information: SUNG-BO CHEN
Public Administration: SHIH-PEI LAI
Research and Development: JUDY HUANG
Social Sciences: JEHNG OUYANG
Student Affairs: JESSE C. CHOU

NATIONAL PINGTUNG UNIVERSITY OF SCIENCE AND TECHNOLOGY

1 Hseuh-Fu Rd, Nei Pu Hsiang, Pingtung Hsien 912
Telephone: (8) 7703660
Fax: (8) 7702226
E-mail: choumasa@mail.npust.edu.tw
Internet: www.npust.edu.tw
Founded 1954 as Taiwan Provincial Institute of Agriculture; became National Pingtung Institute of Agriculture 1981 and National Pingtung Polytechnic Institute 1991; present name and status 1997
Pres.: CHANG-HUNG CHOU
Library of 227,198 vols
Number of teachers: 324
Number of students: 9,000
Publication: *Bulletin* (1 a year)
Colleges of agriculture, engineering, management and humanities, social sciences.

NATIONAL TAIWAN NORMAL UNIVERSITY

162 East Ho Ping Rd, Sec. 1, Taipei 10610
Telephone: (2) 23625101
Fax: (2) 23922673
Internet: www.ntnu.edu.tw
Founded 1946
Language of instruction: Chinese
State control
Academic year: August to July (2 semesters)
Pres.: MAW-FA CHIEN
Vice-Pres.: CHUNG-YANG TSAI
Sec.-Gen.: HSI-PING WANG
Dean of General Affairs: DAR-CHIN RAU
Dean of Internship Supervision and Placement: (vacant)
Dean of Research and Devt: LILLIAN MEEI-JIN HUANG
Dean of Students: HU-HSIUNG LI
Dean of Studies: C. H. GEORGE KAO
Registrar: AN-PAN LIN
Library Dir: HARRY LIANG
Number of teachers: 1,131
Number of students: 9,716
Publications: *A-V Education* (6 a year), *Bulletin*, *NTNU Alumni* (12 a year), *Secondary Education* (6 a year), graduate institutional and departmental journals

DEANS

College of Education: WU-TIEN WU
College of Fine and Applied Arts: CHING-LANG CHANG
College of Liberal Arts: WEN-HSING WU
College of Sciences: CHU-NAN CHANG
College of Sports and Recreation: YAO-HUI CHIEN
College of Technology: LUNG-SHERN LEE
Extension Division: SUZ-WEI YANG

NATIONAL TAIWAN OCEAN UNIVERSITY

2 Pei-Ning Rd, Keelung
Telephone: (2) 24622192
Fax: (2) 24623563
Internet: www.ntou.edu.tw
Founded 1953 (fmrly Nat. Taiwan College of Marine Science and Technology)
Language of instruction: Mandarin
Academic year: August to July
Pres.: KUO-TIEN LEE
Vice-Pres.: SAN-SHYAN LIN
Vice-Pres.: CHING-FONG CHANG
Dean of Academic Affairs: KUO-KAO LEE
Dean of General Affairs: KUO-CHENG YANG
Dean of Research and Devt: HSUAN-HSIH LEE
Dean of Student Affairs: TAN-KIN WANG
Librarian: YIN-HWANG LIN
Library of 423,000 vols, 3,000 periodicals
Number of teachers: 325
Number of students: 7,731
Publication: *Journal of Marine Science and Technology* (4 a year)

DEANS

Electrical Engineering and Computer Science: CHUNG-CHENG CHANG
Engineering: JIAHN-HORNG CHEN
Life and Resource Science: DENG-FWU HWANG
Maritime Science and Management: CHIH-CHING CHANG
Ocean Science and Resource: MING-AN LEE

NATIONAL TAIWAN UNIVERSITY

1 Roosevelt Rd, Section 4, Taipei 10617
Telephone: (2) 3366-3366
Fax: (2) 2362-7651
E-mail: secretor@ntu.edu.tw
Internet: www.ntu.edu.tw
Founded 1928 during the Japanese occupation as the Taihoku Imperial Univ.; taken over and renamed by Chinese Govt in 1945
Language of instruction: Chinese
Academic year: August to July (2 semesters)
Pres.: Dr SI-CHEN LEE
Vice-Pres. for Academic Affairs: Dr TAI-JEN GEORGE CHEN
Vice-Pres. for Admin. Affairs: TZONG-HO BAU
Vice-Pres. for Financial Affairs: MING-JE TANG
Dean of Academic Affairs: BEEN-HUANG CHIANG
Dean of Gen. Affairs: Dr HONG-KI HONG
Dean of Int. Affairs: TUNG SHEN
Dean of Research and Devt: JI-WANG CHERN
Dean of Student Affairs: JOYCE YEN FENG
Library Dir: SHIUE-HUA CHEN
Library of 3,000,000 vols
Number of teachers: 3,509
Number of students: 33,416
Publications: *Acta Botanica Taiwania*, *Acta Geologica Taiwanica*, *Acta Oceanographica Taiwanica*

DEANS

College of Bio-Resources and Agriculture: BAO-JI CHEN
College of Electrical Engineering and Computer Science: SOO-CHANG PEI
College of Engineering: HUAN-JANG KEH
College of Law: MING-CHEN TSAI
College of Liberal Arts: KUO-LIANG YEH
College of Life Science: GRACE CHU-FANG LO
College of Management: MAO-WEI HUNG
College of Medicine: PAN-CHYR YANG
College of Public Health: DUNG-LIANG JIANG
College of Science: CHING-HUA LO
College of Social Sciences: YUNG-MAU CHAO
School of Dentistry: CHUN-PIN LIN
School of Professional and Continuing Studies: RUEI-SHIANG GUO
School of Veterinary Medicine: CHEN-HSUAN LIU (Chair.)

DIRECTORS OF GRADUATE INSTITUTES

Accounting: SHU-HSING LI
Agricultural Chemistry: DAR-YUAN LEE
Agricultural Economics: SHIH-HSUN HSU
Agronomy: YUN-MING PONG
Anatomy and Cell Biology: KUO-SHYAN LU
Animal Science and Technology: LEANG-SHIN WU
Anthropology: YUAN-CHAO TUNG
Applied Mechanics: MAO-KUEN KUO
Applied Physics: YEE-BOB HSIUNG
Art History: MING-LIANG HSIEH
Astrophysics: YEE-BOB HSIUNG
Atmospheric Sciences: CHUN-CHIEH WU
Biochemical Sciences: GEEN-DONG CHANG
Biochemistry and Molecular Biology: LU-PING CHOW
Bioenvironmental Systems Engineering: HUNG-PIN HUANG
Bio-Industrial Mechatronics Engineering: TA-TE LIN
Bio-Industry Communication and Development: ER-ROU LAI
Biomedical Electronics and Bioinformatics: PAI-CHI LI
Biomedical Engineering: TAI-HORNG YOUNG
Biotechnology: HUU-SHENG LUR
Building and Planning: CHU-JOE HSIA
Business Administration: SHU-CHENG STEVE CHI
Chemical Engineering: LI-JEN CHEN
Chemistry: PI-TAI CHOU
Chinese Literature: YU-YU JENG
Civil Engineering: KUO-CHUN CHANG
Clinical Dentistry: CHUN-PIN LIN
Clinical Laboratory Sciences and Medical Biotechnology: CHUN-NAN LEE
Clinical Medicine: PEI-JER CHEN
Clinical Pharmacy: FE-LIN LIN
Communications Engineering: HUEI WANG
Computer Science and Information Engineering: YUH-DAUH LYUU
Drama and Theatre: WEI-JAN CHI
Economics: CHIEN-FU CHOU
Electrical Engineering: JENN-GWO HWU
Electronics Engineering: SHEY-SHI LU
Engineering Science and Ocean Engineering: JING-FA TSAI
Entomology: CHENG-JEN SHIH
Environmental Engineering: SHIAN-CHEE WU
Environmental Health: GEN-SHUH WANG
Epidemiology: WEN-CHUNG LEE
Finance: MING-SHEN CHEN
Fisheries Science: WANN-NIAN TZENG
Food Science and Technology: AN-I YEH
Foreign Languages and Literature: YAN-WING LEUNG
Forensic Medicine: YAO-CHANG CHEN
Forestry and Resource Conservation: HANN-CHUNG LO
Geography: SUE-CHING JOU
Geosciences: HONGEY CHEN
Health Care Organization Administration: MING-CHIN YANG
Health Policy and Management: LAN LEE
History: HUAI-CHEN KAN
Horticulture: YANN-JOU LIN
Immunology: PING-NING HSU
Industrial Engineering: ARGON CHEN
Information Management: CHING-CHIN CHERN
Interdisciplinary Legal Studies: TAY-SHENG WANG
International Business: HSIOU-WEI LIN
Japanese Language and Literature: SHING-CHING SHYU
Journalism: DENNIS WENG-JENG PENG

Law: MING-CHENG TSAI
Library and Information Science: CLARENCE TSA-KANG CHU
Linguistics: HINTAT CHEUNG
Materials Science and Engineering: JER-REN YANG
Mathematics: GERARD-JENNHWA CHANG
Mechanical Engineering: SHUO-HUNG CHANG
Microbiology: SHOW-LIN CHEN
Microbiology and Biochemistry: TZU-MING PAN
Molecular and Cellular Biology: HUAI-JEN TSAI
Molecular Medicine: FANG-JEN LEE
Musicology: YING-FEN WANG
National Development: RONG-JEO CHIU
Networking and Multimedia: YI-PING HUNG
Nursing: LIAN-HUA HUANG
Occupational Medicine and Industrial Hygiene: TSUN-JEN CHENG
Occupational Therapy: KEH-CHUNG LIN
Oceanography: LING-YUN CHIAO
Oral Biology: YEN-PING KUO
Pathology: CHUNG-WU LIN
Pharmacology: CHING-CHOW CHEN
Pharmacy: SHOEI-SHENG LEE
Philosophy: HSIAO-CHIH SUN
Photonics and Optoelectronics: SHENG-LUNG HUANG
Physical Therapy: SUH-FANG JENG
Physics: YEE-BOB HSIUNG
Plant Biology: KAI-WUN YEH
Plant Pathology and Microbiology: CHAO-YING CHEN
Political Science: TSAI-TSU SU
Political Science and Engineering: WEN-CHANG CHEN
Preventive Medicine: WEI-CHU CHIE
Psychology: LI-JEN WENG
Physiology: KUO-CHU CHANG
Public Health: WEI-JIAN CHEN
Social Work: YEUN-WEN KU
Sociology: HOLIN LIN
Taiwan Literature: CHIA-LING MEI
Toxicology: SHING-HWA LIU
Veterinary Clinical Science: LI-SEN YEH
Veterinary Medicine: ZHEN-XUAN LIU
Zoology: JIUN-HONG CHEN

NATIONAL TAIWAN UNIVERSITY OF SCIENCE AND TECHNOLOGY

43 Keelung Rd, Sec. 4, Taipei
Telephone: (2) 27376101
Fax: (2) 27376107
E-mail: president@mail.ntust.edu.tw
Internet: www.ntust.edu.tw

Founded 1974
Academic year: August to July (2 semesters)

Pres.: SHUN-TYAN CHEN
Dean of Studies: CHENG-SEEN HO

Library of 279,326 vols
Number of teachers: 315
Number of students: 8,106

NATIONAL TSING HUA UNIVERSITY

101, Sec. 2, Kuang Fu Rd, Hsinchu 30013
Telephone: (3) 5715131
Fax: (3) 5710582
E-mail: presid@my.nthu.edu.tw
Internet: www.nthu.edu.tw

Founded 1911, re-founded 1956
Language of instruction: Chinese
Academic year: August to July

Pres.: WEN-TSUEN CHEN
Librarian: HSIAO-CHIN HSIEH

Number of teachers: 604
Number of students: 11,381

Publication: *Tsing Hua Journal of Chinese Studies* (Chinese literature and community science, 4 a year)

DEANS

College of Electrical Engineering and Computer Science: JYUO-MIN SHYU
College of Engineering: HONG HOCHENG
College of Humanities and Social Sciences: WEI-AN CHANG
College of Life Science: RONG-LONG PAN
College of Nuclear Science: CHIN PAN
College of Science: HUAN-CHIU KU
College of Technology Management: CHIN-TAY SHIH
Commission of General Education: HWAI-PWU CHOU

SOOCHOW UNIVERSITY

70 Linhsi Rd, Shihlin, Taipei 111
Telephone: (2) 28819471
Fax: (2) 28829310
E-mail: secretary@scu.edu.tw
Internet: www.scu.edu.tw

Founded 1900
Private control
Languages of instruction: Chinese, English
Academic year: September to June (2 semesters)

Pres.: CHAO-SHUIAN LIU
Vice-Pres.: CHUN-MEI MA
Vice-Pres. for Academic Affairs: MAO-TING CHIEN
Registrar: CHENG-TSUN LIN
Librarian: YUAN-JEE DING

Library of 692,767 vols
Number of teachers: 1,149 (including part-time teachers)
Number of students: 15,085

Publications: *Journal of Chinese Studies* (1 a year), *Journal of Economics and Business* (4 a year), *Journal of Foreign Languages and Cultures* (1 a year), *Journal of History* (1 a year), *Journal of Japanese Language Teaching* (1 a year), *Journal of Mathematics* (1 a year), *Journal of Philosophical Studies* (2 a year), *Journal of Political Science* (2 a year), *Journal of Sociology* (2 a year), *Law Review* (2 a year)

DIRECTORS

School of Arts and Social Sciences: SIU KEUNG WONG
School of Business: YUNG-HO CHIU
School of Foreign Languages and Cultures: TSONG-MINN LIN
School of Law: WEI-DA PAN
School of Science: HIN-CHUNG WONG
Extension School: PING-WEN LIN

TAIPEI NATIONAL UNIVERSITY OF THE ARTS

1 Hsueh Yuan Rd, Kuan-Tu, Taipei 112
Telephone: (2) 28961000
Fax: (2) 28945124
E-mail: www@www.tnua.edu.tw
Internet: www.tnua.edu.tw

Founded 1982 as National Institute of the Arts; university status 2004

Library of 300,000 vols
Number of teachers: 127
Number of students: 1,726

Pres.: Dr KUN-LIANG CHIU

Publications: *Arts Review* (1 a year), *Guandu Music Journal* (2 a year), *Journal of Cultural Resources* (1 a year), *Taipei Theatre Journal* (2 a year)

DEANS

Faculty of Culture Resources: HUI-CHENG LIN
Faculty of Dance: CHUNG-SHIUAN CHANG
Faculty of Fine Art: CHANG-HU LIN
Faculty of Music: HWANG-LONG PAN
Faculty of Theatre: MING-TE CHUNG

TAMKANG UNIVERSITY

151 Ying-Chuan Rd, Tamsui, Taipei 25137
Telephone: (2) 26215656
Fax: (2) 26237384
Internet: www.tku.edu.tw

Founded 1950 (formerly Tamkang College of Arts and Sciences)
Private control
Languages of instruction: Chinese, English
Academic year: August to July

Pres.: Dr HORNG-JINH CHANG
Vice-Pres. for Academic Affairs: Dr CHAO-KANG FENG
Vice-Pres. for Admin.: Dr FLORA CHIA-I CHANG
Sec.-Gen.: Dr TUN-LI CHEN
Dean of Academic Affairs: Dr HIS-JEN FU
Dean of General Affairs: Prof. CHING-JEN HUNG
Dean of Student Affairs: Dr HUAN-CHAO KEH
Librarian: Prof. HONG-CHU HUANG

Library of 753,911 vols, 6,901 periodicals
Number of teachers: 2,033
Number of students: 26,600

Publications: *Educational Media and Library Science*, *International Journal of Information and Management Science*, *Journal of Future Studies*, *Tamkang Journal*, *Tamkang Journal of International Affairs*, *Tamkang Mathematics*, *Tamkang Review*

DEANS OF COLLEGES

Business: Dr JONG-RONG CHIOU
Engineering: Dr SHI-CHIH CHU
Foreign Languages and Literature: Dr YAOFU LIN
International Studies: Dr WOU WEI
Liberal Arts: Dr SHIH-HSION HUANG
Management: Dr LIANG-YU OUYANG
Science: Dr KAN-NAN CHEN
Technocracy: Prof. HSIN-FU TSAI
Extension Education Centre: Prof. YAO-LUNG HAN

DIRECTORS OF GRADUATE INSTITUTES

Accounting: Dr CHEN-LI HUANG
Aerospace Engineering: Dr TZENG-YUAN CHEN
American Studies: Dr I-HSIN CHEN
Applied Statistics: Dr JONG-WUU WU
Architecture: Prof. HOANG-ELL JENG
Chemical Engineering: Dr KUO-JEN HWANG
Chemistry: Dr HUEY-CHUEN KAO
Chinese Literature: Dr PO-YUAN KAO
China Studies: Dr ANDY W. Y. CHANG
Civil Engineering: Dr CHO-SEN WO
Educational Media Library Science: Dr JEONG-YEOU CHIU
Educational Technology: Dr CHIEN-HUA WANG
Electrical Engineering: Dr JEN-CHIUN CHIANG
European Studies: Dr TZUNG-JEN TSAI
History: Dr TZENG-CHYUAN LIOU
Industrial Economics: Dr JIUNN-RONG CHIOU
Information Engineering: Dr KUO-CHEN SHIH
Information Management: Dr CHEN-CHUNG HUANG
International Affairs and Strategic Studies: Dr MING-HSIEN WONG
International Business: Dr JYH-HORNG LIN
Japanese Studies: Dr CHANG-HUEI LIU
Latin-American Studies: Dr KWO-WEI KUNG
Management Science: Dr PEI-CHI LEE
Mass Communication: Dr SHU-HUA CHANG
Mathematics: Dr CHIN-MEI KAU
Mechanical Engineering: Dr FENG-HUI YEH
Money, Banking and Finance: Dr GIN-CHUNG LIN
Physics: Dr WAY-FAUNG PONG
Public Administration: Dr MING-SIANG CHEN
Slavic Studies: Dr ALEXANDER PISAREV
South-East Asian Studies: Dr JUO-YU LIN
Transportation Management: Dr HSIAO-HSIEN LUO

Water Resources and Environmental Engineering: Dr PO-CHIEN LU
Western Languages and Literature: Dr CHUN-CHUNG LIN

TUNGHAI UNIVERSITY

181 Taichung Harbour Rd, Sec. 3, Taichung 40704
Telephone: (4) 23590200
Fax: (4) 23590361
E-mail: kpwang@mail.thu.edu.tw
Internet: www.thu.edu.tw
Founded 1955 under the auspices of the United Board for Christian Higher Education in Asia
Languages of instruction: Chinese, English
Academic year: September to July (2 semesters)
Pres.: KANG-PEI WANG
Dean of Academic Affairs: CHENG-TUNG LIN
Dean of General Affairs: I-CHAO HSIAO
Dean of Student Affairs: HUNG-DER FU
Librarian: CHUNG-LIN LU
Number of teachers: 826
Number of students: 14,500
Publications: *The Vineyard*, *Tunghai Bulletin*, *Tunghai Journal*, *Tunghai News*

DEANS

College of Agriculture: TSUN-CHUNG TSAI
College of Arts: HAI-YUN HUANG
College of Engineering: JEN-TENG TSAI
College of Management: TSAI-DING LIN
College of Science: CHING-SHENG CHEN
College of Social Sciences: JENN-HWAN WANG

Colleges and Institutes

China Medical College: 91 Hseuh Shih Rd, Taichung 404; tel. (4) 2057153; f. 1958; Private control; 2 campuses (in Taichung and Peikang), 6 graduate institutes, 12 undergraduate schools, Chiang Kai-shek Medical Center, 2 teaching hospitals; 4,666 students; Pres. MASON CHEN.

Kaohsiung Medical University: 100 Shih Chuan 1st Rd, Kaohsiung 807; tel. (7) 3117820; fax (7) 3212062; internet www.kmu.edu.tw; f. 1954; Private control; colleges of medicine, dental medicine, pharmacy, nursing, health sciences, life sciences; undergraduate division of 19 schools; 12 postgraduate institutes; 7 research centres: health and social services, industrial hygiene, gender studies, tropical medicine, orthopaedics, genomics, protcomics; 428 teachers; 6,106 students; library: 175,802 vols, 2,970 periodicals; Pres. Dr GWO-JAW WANG; publ. *Kaohsiung Journal of Medical Sciences* (12 a year).

National Kaohsiung University of Applied Sciences: 415 Chien-Kung Rd, Kaohsiung 807; tel. (7) 3814526; fax (7) 3838435; f. 1963; depts of accounting, applied foreign languages, business administration, chemical, civil, cultural industries development, electrical, electronic, finance, human resource development, industrial management, information management, international trade, mechanical, mould- and die-making engineering, taxation and finance, tourism; graduate institutes of civil engineering and disaster prevention, commerce, electrical energy and control, electronic and information engineering, finance and information, mechanical and precision engineering, tourism management; library: 171,674 vols; 415 teachers; 10,727 students; Pres. Dr REN-YIH LIN; publ. *Journal* (1 a year).

Taipei Institute of Technology: 3, Sec. 1, Shin-sheng South Rd, Taipei; f. 1912; 8,973 students; library: 112,000 vols; Pres. Dr CHIH TANG.

Taipei Medical University: 250 Wu Hsing St, Taipei, 110; tel. (2) 27361661; fax (2) 27387795; f. 1960; Private control; undergraduate and graduate programmes; 1,000 teachers incl. full-time and part-time; 6,000 students; library: 132,015 vols, 650 periodicals; Pres. Prof. WEN-TA CHIU; Vice-Pres. Prof. TA-LIANG CHEN; publ. *Journal* (2 a year).

Tatung University: 40 Chungshan N Rd, Sec. 3, Taipei; tel. (2) 25925252; fax (2) 25941371; e-mail registrar@ttu.edu.tw; internet www.ttu.edu.tw; f. 1956; private control; depts of applied mathematics, bioengineering, business management, chemical engineering, computer science and engineering, electrical engineering, industrial design, information management, materials engineering, mechanical engineering; graduate institutes in electro-optical engineering and communications engineering; 200 teachers; 2,500 students; library: 159,683 vols; Pres. T. S. LIN; Dean of Studies JAN-CHEN HONG.

School of Art and Music

National Taiwan College of Arts: Panchiao, Taipei; tel. (2) 22722181; fax (2) 29687563; internet www.ntca.edu.tw; f. 1955; Chinese music, cinema, dance, drama, fine arts, graphic arts, industrial arts, music, painting, radio and television, sculpture; 364 teachers; 2,300 students; library: 104,000 vols; Pres. MING-SHEAN WANG.

TAJIKISTAN

The Higher Education System

Higher education institutions predate the independence of Tajikistan (formerly Tajik SSR) from the USSR in 1991, with the oldest being Tajik State Pedagogical University S. Aini and Tajik Agricultural University, both of which were founded in 1931. In 2000 the Presidents of Kazakhstan, Kyrgyzstan and Tajikistan co-signed a charter of foundation for a new University of Central Asia, which was to be established in Khorog (in Kuhistoni Badakhshon Autonomous Viloyat) and administered by the Aga Khan Development Network, based in Geneva, Switzerland. This began admitting students in 2006. In 2003 constitutional amendments abolished free higher education. In 2007/08 some 154,200 students were enrolled at 33 institutes of higher education.

The Diploma of Completed Secondary Education or the Diploma of Completed Vocational Education are the main requirements for admission to higher education. The Specialist Diploma is the Soviet-style undergraduate degree which lasts five or six years and grants students the right to enter directly into doctoral-level studies upon successful completion. Alternatively, the Bachelors (Bakalavr) degree is a four-year programme of study, after which a graduate may study for the Masters (Magister), the first postgraduate degree. The Masters is a two-year course culminating in the submission of a thesis; students who have successfully completed the Masters may undertake doctoral-level studies. Both the Soviet-style Candidate of Science (Kandidat Nauk) and European-style Doctorate are available and are awarded after two to three years of independent research. The highest university degree is the Doctor of Sciences, which is purely an academic degree, aimed at students who wish to pursue a career in academia or research.

Technical and vocational education at the post-secondary level consists of two-year programmes of study leading to the title of Junior Specialist.

Regulatory and Representative Bodies

GOVERNMENT

Ministry of Culture: 734025 Dushanbe, Xiyoboni Rudaki 34; tel. (372) 21-03-05; fax (372) 21-47-01; Minister MIRZOSHOHRUKH ASROROV.

Ministry of Education: 734025 Dushanbe, Kuchai Chexov 13A; tel. (372) 21-46-05; fax (372) 21-70-41; Minister ABDUJABBOR RAHMONOV.

Learned Societies

GENERAL

Academy of Sciences of the Republic of Tajikistan: 734025 Dushanbe, Pr. Rudaki 33; tel. (372) 21-50-83; fax (372) 21-49-11; e-mail ilolovm@gmail.com; internet www.ant.tj; f. 1951; divs of Physical-Mathematical, Chemical and Geological Sciences (Chair. S. ODINAEV, Scientific Sec. R. I. KOSTOVA), Biological and Medical Sciences (Chair. M. YAKUBOVA, Scientific Sec. M. QURBANOVA), Social Sciences (Chair. K.OLIMOV, Scientific Sec. SH. UMAROVA); attached research institutes: see Research Institutes; 79 mems (36 full, 43 corresp.); library: see Libraries and Archives; Pres. Prof. MAMADSHO ILOLOV; Vice-Pres. Prof. KAROMATULLO OLIMOV; Vice-Pres. Prof. SAIDMUHAMMAD ODINAEV; Vice-Pres. Prof. MUHIBA YAKUBOVA; Gen. Sec. Dr KHAKIM AHMEDOV; publs *Proceedings* (each div. publishes its own edn, 4 a year), *Doklady* (Reports), *Problemy gastroenterologii*, *Izvestiya* (bulletins: Physical-Engineering and Geological Sciences, Biological Sciences, History and Philology, Philosophy, Economics and Law).

LANGUAGE AND LITERATURE

British Council:see chapter on Uzbekistan.

Research Institutes

GENERAL

Khatlon Scientific Centre: Kulob; tel. (332) 22-36-36; f. 1985; attached to Tajik Acad. of Sciences; Dir TILLO BOBOEV.

Khudzhand Scientific Centre: 735714 Khudzhand, Ul. Syrdarinskaya 26; tel. (379) 25-17-74; attached to Tajik Acad. of Sciences; Chair. M. R. DZHALILOV; Scientific Sec. M. SUBKHONOV.

ARCHITECTURE AND TOWN PLANNING

Institute of Earthquake Engineering and Seismology: 734029 Dushanbe, Ul. Aini 121; tel. (372) 25-06-69; fax (372) 24-43-83; e-mail tisss@iscuk.td.silk.org; f. 1951; attached to Tajik Acad. of Sciences; library of 6,000 vols, 40 periodicals; Dir SOBIT KH. NEGMATULLAEV; Sec. PULAT A. YASUNOV; publs *Prognoz zemletryasenii* (in Russian, 1 a year), *Zemletryaseniya Sredney Azii i Kazakhstana* (in Russian, 1 a year).

BIBLIOGRAPHY, LIBRARY SCIENCE AND MUSEOLOGY

Institute of Oriental Studies and Written Heritage: 734025 Dushanbe, Kirov 35; tel. (372) 27-34-04; attached to Tajik Acad. of Sciences; Dir D. NAZRIYEV.

ECONOMICS, LAW AND POLITICS

Institute of Economics: 734000 Dushanbe, Ul. Aini 44; tel. (372) 21-67-50; fax (372) 21-57-65; f. 1951; attached to Tajik Acad. of Sciences; Dir R. K. RAKHIMOV.

Institute of State and Law: 734025 Dushanbe, Pr. Rudaki 19; tel. (372) 21-65-72; fax (372) 21-65-72; e-mail isalanrt@rambler.ru; f. 2005; attached to Tajik Acad. of Sciences; library of 5,000 vols; 40 mems; Dir SAITUMBAR ADINAEVICH RAJABOV; publ. *Izvestiya Akademii Nauk RT, seriya Philosophiya i Pravo.*

HISTORY, GEOGRAPHY AND ARCHAEOLOGY

Donish Institute of History, Archaeology and Ethnography: 734025 Dushanbe, Pr. Rudaki 33; tel. (372) 22-37-42; f. 1932; attached to Tajik Acad. of Sciences; Dir R. M. MASOV.

LANGUAGE AND LITERATURE

Rudaki Institute of Language and Literature: 734025 Dushanbe, Pr. Rudaki 21; tel. (372) 21-60-11; f. 1932; attached to Tajik Acad. of Sciences; Dir A. M. MANIYAZOV.

MEDICINE

Institute of Gastroenterology: 734002 Dushanbe, Parvin 12; tel. (372) 21-77-82; fax (372) 23-49-17; e-mail mansurov@academy.td.silk.org; f. 1959; attached to Tajik Acad. of Sciences; library of 5,000 vols; Dir Prof. G. MIRODJEV; publ. *Problems of Gastroenterology* (4 a year).

NATURAL SCIENCES

Biological Sciences

Institute of Botany: 734017 Dushanbe, Ul. Karamova 27; tel. (372) 24-71-88; f. 1941; attached to Tajik Acad. of Sciences; Dir U. I. ISMOILOV.

Institute of Plant Physiology and Genetics: 734063 Dushanbe, Ul. Aini 299/2; tel. (372) 25-26-44; e-mail akotibbm@ac.tajik.net; f. 1964; attached to Tajik Acad. of Sciences; Dir Prof. KHURSHED KARIMOV.

Pamir Biological Institute: 736000 Khorog, Gorno-Badakhshan Autonomous Region; f. 1969; attached to Tajik Acad. of Sciences; Chair. U. KH. KHOLDOROV.

Pavlovskii, E. N., Institute of Zoology and Parasitology: 734025 Dushanbe, Post Office 70; tel. (372) 25-58-71; f. 1941; attached to Tajik Acad. of Sciences; Dir A. K. GAFUROV.

Mathematical Sciences

Institute of Mathematics: 734063 Dushanbe, Ul. Aini 299; tel. (372) 25-77-76; e-mail usmanov@ac.tajik.net; f. 1973; attached to Tajik Acad. of Sciences; Dir Z. D. USMANOV.

Physical Sciences

Institute of Astrophysics: 734042 Dushanbe, Ul. Bukhoro 22; tel. (372) 27-46-14; e-mail astro@ac.tajik.net; f. 1958; attached to

Tajik Acad. of Sciences; Dir KHURSAND I. IBADINOV; publ. *Bulletin* (2 a year).

Institute of Geology: 734063 Dushanbe, Ul. Aini 267; tel. (372) 25-32-67; f. 1941; attached to Tajik Acad. of Sciences; Dir M. R. DHALILOV.

Institute of Water Problems, Hydropower and Ecology: 734002 Dushanbe, Parvin 12; tel. and fax (372) 24-52-31; e-mail kobuliev@mail.ru; f. 2002; attached to Acad. of Sciences of the Republic of Tajikistan; Dir Prof. ZAINALOBUDIN KOBULIEV.

Nikitin, V. I., Institute of Chemistry: 734063 Dushanbe, Ul. Aini 299/2; tel. (372) 25-26-04; e-mail sarvar@ac.tajik.net; f. 1946; attached to Tajik Acad. of Sciences; Dir U. M. MIRSAYIDOV.

PHILOSOPHY AND PSYCHOLOGY

Institute of Philosophy: 734025 Dushanbe, Pr. Rudaki 33; tel. (372) 23-77-96; e-mail noibprez@ac.tajik.net; attached to Tajik Acad. of Sciences; f. 1991; Dir M. DINORSHOYEV.

RELIGION, SOCIOLOGY AND ANTHROPOLOGY

Institute of Demography: 734025 Dushanbe, Rudaki Ave 33; tel. (372) 21-89-39; e-mail inst.demography.tj@gmail.com; internet www.demography.tj; f. 2003; attached to Tajik Acad. of Sciences; population, fertility, mortality, family issues, internal and external migration processes, policy making; library of 100 vols; Dir Prof. SADULLO IBODOVICH ISLOMOV.

Institute of Humanities: 736000 Khorog, Lenin 35; tel. (352) 22-67-55; f. 1991; attached to Tajik Acad. of Sciences; Dir SHODIKHON YUSUFBEKOV.

Institute of Oriental Studies and Written Heritage: 734025 Dushanbe, Kiroka 35; tel. (372) 27-23-36; e-mail ogonazar@ac.tajik.net; f. 1958; attached to Tajik Acad. of Sciences.

TECHNOLOGY

Nuclear and Radiation Safety Agency: 734025 Dushanbe, Pr. Rudaki 33; tel. (372) 23-36-09; fax (372) 21-55-48; f. 2003; attached to Tajik Acad. of Sciences; Dir ULMAS MIRSAIDOVICH MIRSAIDOV.

Umarov, S. U., Physical-Technical Institute: 734063 Dushanbe, Ul. Aini 299/1; tel. (37) 225-80-92; fax (37) 225-79-14; e-mail phti@tascampus.eastera.net; internet www.phti.tj; f. 1964; attached to Tajik Acad. of Sciences; theoretical and mathematical physics (classical and quantum statistics, field theory, non-linear science); materials science (crystal physics, polymer science); nanoscience and nanotechnology; lasers and infrared spectroscopy; cryophysics; mathematical modelling of climate and climate change; application of nuclear physics methods; instrumentation and detectors; radiation safety and ecology; renewable energy sources; Dir Dr KHIKMAT KH. MUMINOV.

Libraries and Archives

Dushanbe

Central Scientific Library of the Tajik Academy of Sciences: 734025 Dushanbe, Pr. Rudaki 33; tel. (372) 22-42-24; f. 1933; 1,500,000 vols; Dir Dr A. A. ASLITDINOVA.

Firdavsi Tajik National Library: 734025 Dushanbe, Pr. Rudaki 36; tel. (372) 27-47-26; 3,059,281 vols; Dir SH. TOSHEW.

State Patent and Technical Library of Republic of Tajikistan: 734042 Dushanbe, Ul. Aini 14A; tel. (372) 27-58-77; fax (372) 21-71-54; f. 1965; 148m. vols (incl. 14m. patents); Dir BOBOJON BOYZODA.

Tajik State University Library: 734016 Dushanbe, Pr. Rudaki 17; tel. (372) 23-39-81; f. 1948; 1,039,000 vols; Dir R. YARBABAYEV; publ. *Vestnik* (1 a year).

Museum

Dushanbe

Tajik State Historical Museum: 734012 Dushanbe, Ul. Aini 31; tel. (372) 23-15-44; history, culture, art; library of 14,000 vols; Dir M. MAKHMUDOV.

Universities

AVICENNA TAJIK STATE MEDICAL UNIVERSITY

734003 Dushanbe, Pr. Rudaki 139

Telephone: (372) 24-12-53
Fax: (372) 24-36-87
E-mail: tajmedun@rambler.ru
Internet: www.tajmedun.tj

Founded 1939 as Tajik Medical Institute, fmrly Tajik Abu-Ali Ibn-Cina State Medical Institute, present name 2009
State control
Languages of instruction: Tajik, Russian, English
Academic year: September to July

Rector: Prof. UBAIDULLO KURBANOV

Library of 515,035 vols
Number of teachers: 855
Number of students: 6,222

DEANS

Dentistry Faculty: SAID SHARIPOV
Medical Faculty: MUHIDDIN TABAROV
Pharmaceutical Faculty: ERMAHMAD KHOLOV
Public Health Faculty: GULNORA USMONOVA

CENTRAL INSTITUTE OF ADVANCED QUALIFICATION OF TEACHERS

734013 Dushanbe, Chechova 13

Telephone: (372) 21-54-57
Fax: (372) 27-16-27
E-mail: ciftmail@tajnet.com

Founded 1935
State control

Rector: ABUNAZAR A. SOIBOV
Vice-Rector: ABDUHALIM GAFFAROV

Number of students: 2,000

Faculties of economics, educational administration, foreign languages education, pedagogy, psychology, science education and teacher training.

FISCAL–LEGAL INSTITUTE

734013 Dushanbe, Drujby Narodov 96

Telephone: (3772) 21-59-48
Fax: (3772) 21-74-59
State control

Rector: D. G. GULMIRZOYEV

Faculties of economics and law.

HIGHER SCHOOL OF THE MINISTRY OF THE INTERIOR

734025 Dushanbe, Vose 123

Telephone: (372) 27-06-07
Fax: (372) 21-72-21
State Control

Faculties of history, law.

INSTITUTE OF ENTREPRENEURSHIP AND SERVICE

734055 Dushanbe, Borbad Ave 48/5

Telephone: (372) 34-88-00
Fax: (372) 34-88-02
E-mail: dsx_ips@mail.ru
Internet: www.dsx.tj

Founded 1991
State control
Languages of instruction: Russian, Tajik
Academic year: September to June

Rector: Prof. Dr FAIZALI S. KOMILOV
Deputy Rector for Education: Assoc. Prof. BAHRIDDIN B. JABBOROV (acting)
Deputy Rector for Science and International Relations: Dr Prof. SAID AHMADOV
Deputy Rector for Teaching: Assoc. Prof. SHERMAHMAD B. JONMAMMADOV
Librarian: JAMILA KHOLOVA

Library of 42,839 vols
Number of teachers: 171
Number of students: 3,302

Publications: *Payom 9* (1 a year), *Sohibkor* (12 a year)

DEANS

Entrepreneurship and Management: AKRAMJON NAJMIDDINOV
Financial Services: SABZALI AMIROV
Tourism and Hospitality: FAIZIDDIN QODIROV

KHOROG INSTITUTE OF SOCIAL SCIENCES

Khorog

Telephone and fax (352) 22-58-86
E-mail: jangibekov@land.ru
Public control
Languages of instruction: English, Russian
Academic year: September to June

Rector: SH. YUSUFBEKOV

Number of teachers: 280
Number of students: 5,005

KHOROG STATE UNIVERSITY

736000 Khorog

Telephone: (342) 20-22-18
Fax: (342) 20-43-99

Founded 1992
State control

Rector: M. SHABOZOV

Faculties of economics, history, mathematics, natural sciences and philology.

KHUJAND B. GAFUROV STATE UNIVERSITY

735700 Khujand, B. Mavlonbekova 1

Telephone: (342) 26-52-73
Fax: (342) 26-51-37
E-mail: hgu-rector@sugdien.com

Founded 1991
State control
Languages of instruction: English, Russian, Tajik, Uzbek

Rector: SALIMOV NOSIRJON

Library of 500,000 vols
Number of teachers: 754
Number of students: 10,599

DEANS

Art: G. JURAYEV
Cybernetics and World Economics: A., ABDULLOYEV
Drawing and Graphics: S. OLOV
Eastern Languages (Arabic and Persian): U. GAFFOROVA
Economics: A., ABDULLOYEV

Finance and Marketing: A. MAJIDOV
Foreign Languages: M. AZIMOVA
History: U. GAFFOROV
Law: IKROM KASIMOV
Mathematics: A. KASHIDOV
Natural Sciences: S. KARIMOV
Pedagogy: S. SHAROPOV
Physics and Technology: S. YAKUBOV
Russian and Literature: A. AZIZOV
Tajik Philology: N. F. FAIZULLAYEV
Uzbek Language: I. MAVLONBERDIYEV

KULYAB STATE UNIVERSITY

735360 Kulyab, Safarov 26
Telephone: (332) 22-35-06
State control
Faculties of economics, history, mathematics, pedagogy, philology and physics.

MODERN HUMANITARIAN UNIVERSITY

735700 Khujand, Microraion 17
Telephone: (342) 22-19-58
Fax: (342) 26-19-91
Founded 1998
State control
Language of instruction: Russian
Rector: M. I. BAKIYEV
Number of teachers: 36
Number of students: 380

DEANS

Faculty of Computer Science: U. V. SIT
Faculty of Languages: SH. D. KHODJAYEV
Faculty of Law: N. T. RAKHIMOV
Faculty of Management: G. A. USUPOVA

REPUBLICAN INSTITUTE OF ADVANCED TEACHERS' STUDIES

734013 Dushanbe, Chehova 13
Telephone: (372) 21-64-67
State control.

'SHIRINSHO SHOTEMUR' TAJIK AGRARIAN UNIVERSITY

734003 Dushanbe, Pr. Rudaki 146
Telephone and fax (372) 24-72-07
E-mail: rectortau31@mail.ru
Internet: www.tajagroun.tj
Founded 1931
State control
Languages of instruction: Tajik, Russian
Academic year: September to June
Rector: Dr SATTORI IZZATULLO
Vice-Rector for Cultural Upbringing: Doc. HASANOV NAHTULLO RAHMATOVICH
Vice-Rector for Economy: Doc. MAHMUDOV KAMOLJON BURHONOVICH
Vice-Rector for Education: Prof. SALIMOV AMONULLO FAIZULLOEVICH
Vice-Rector for Int. Relations: Doc. KODIROV TURA ABDULLOEVICH
Vice-Rector for Science: Prof. Dr SARDOROV MAHMADIYOR NAIMOVICH
Head of Educational Dept: Doc. MIRZOEV BOBO
Dir of Library: DAVLATOV ODINA YOROVICH
Library of 366,567 vols, 61 periodicals
Number of teachers: 496
Number of students: 8,323
Publication: *Kishovarz* (Peasant)

DEANS

Faculty of Accounting and Finance: Prof. Dr SAMANDAROV ISKANDAR HUSEINOVICH
Faculty of Agrobusiness: Prof. Dr NOROV MASTIBEK SAMADOVICH
Faculty of Agronomy: Doc. HAYDAROV ZIKRIYOKHON YOKUBOVICH
Faculty of Animal Science: Doc. KOSIMOV RAJABEK BOBORAJABOVICH
Faculty of Economy: Doc. BAEVA NODIRA KHOLMURADOVNA
Faculty of Horticulture and Agricultural Biotechnology: Prof. Dr KARIMOV MUZAFFAR KARIMOVICH
Faculty of Hydromeliorative: Doc. AKRAMOV ABDUGAFFOR
Faculty of Mechanization of Agriculture: Doc. AHMADOV BAHROM RAJABOVICH
Faculty of Veterinary Medicine: Prof. Dr HABIBOV ABDUJALIL KHALILOVICH

TAJIK INSTITUTE OF MANAGEMENT

Kairakkum
Telephone: (344) 32-24-85
State control
Rector: YU. MADJIDOV
Faculties of management and marketing.

TAJIK ISLAMIC UNIVERSITY

734001 Dushanbe, Shodmoni 58
Telephone: (372) 24-92-61
State control
Rector: ABDUJALOL ALIZODA
Faculties of general studies, Islamic law and religious studies.

TAJIK M. OSIMI TECHNICAL UNIVERSITY

734042 Dushanbe, Pr. Acad Rajabovs 10
Telephone: (372) 21-35-11
Fax: (372) 21-71-35
E-mail: techuni@tajnet.com
Founded 1956
State control
Languages of instruction: Tajik, Russian
Number of teachers: 530
Number of students: 6,000
Rector: SAIDMUHAMAD ODINAYEV

DEANS

Business Engineering: S. KAMOLIDDINOV
Chemical Technology and Metallurgy: A. SHARIFOV
Construction and Architecture: A. FAZILOV
Energy Engineering: R. JALILOV
Mechanical Technology: S. ZULFANOV
Transport and Road Engineering: A. TURSUNOV

TAJIK OPEN UNIVERSITY

735500 Penjikent, Rudaki 108
Telephone: (347) 55-53-09
Fax: (347) 55-40-50
E-mail: tou@pnjk.tajik.net
Founded 1991
State control
Languages of instruction: Tajik, Russian
Prin.: AHMADJON HOTAMOV
Number of teachers: 138 (full-time)
Number of students: 413
Divs of computing and programming, law and management.

TAJIK–RUSSIAN SLAVONIC UNIVERSITY

734032 Dushanbe, M. Tursunzade 30
Telephone: (372) 22-35-50
Fax: (372) 21-05-79
State control
Prin.: A. S. SATTAROV
Faculties of economics, history, international relations, law and philology.

TAJIK STATE INSTITUTE OF FINE ARTS

734032 Dushanbe, Ul. Borbada 73A
Telephone: (372) 31-45-45
E-mail: tgii@tajnet.com
Founded 1967
Rector: Prof. TALABKHUJA SATTOROV
Library of 70,000 vols
Number of students: 1,500
Faculties of cultural science, performing arts, library science and information, musical-pedagogical studies and theatre.

TAJIK STATE INSTITUTE OF LANGUAGES

734064 Dushanbe, F. Muhammadiyeva 13
Telephone: (372) 32-95-29
Fax: (372) 32-95-15
E-mail: mabdullaeva@yandex.ru
Founded 1980
State control
Languages of instruction: Tajik, Russian
Rector: MAVLUDA ABDULLAYEVA
Vice-Rector: KHURSHED ZIYOYEV
Library of 113,000 vols
Number of teachers: 65
Number of students: 763

DEANS

Faculty of Foreign Languages: KHALIDA ASTANOVA
Faculty of Philology: KAHHOR AVAZOV

TAJIK STATE NATIONAL UNIVERSITY

734025 Dushanbe, Pr. Rudaki 17
Telephone: (372) 21-77-11
Fax: (372) 21-48-84
E-mail: tgnu@mail.ru
Internet: www.tgnu.tarena.tj
Founded 1948 (present status 1997)
State control
Languages of instruction: Tajik, Russian
Academic year: September to July
Rector: Prof. KH. S. SAFIEV
Vice-Rector for Educational Affairs: Prof. D. KH. SAFAROV
Vice-Rector for Int. Relations: N. N. JUMAEV
Vice-Rector for Scientific Affairs: A. A. AMINJANOV
Librarian: R. I. YARBABAEV
Number of teachers: 1,228
Number of students: 13,060
Publications: *Guli murod* (Government and Law, 4 a year), *Science* (1 a year), *Vestnik* (4 a year)

DEANS

Faculty of Accounting: D. U. UROKOV
Faculty of Biology: Dr M. GIYOSOV
Faculty of Chemistry: L. KUDRATOVA
Faculty of Economics and Management: Prof. T. B. GANIEV
Faculty of Finance and Credit: SH. D. DUSTBOEV
Faculty of History: Prof. N. M. MIRZOEV
Faculty of Journalism and Translation Studies: Prof. A. SAIDULLOEV (acting)
Faculty of Law: M. A. MAKHMUDOV
Faculty of Mechanics and Mathematics: Dr R. M. MUSTAFOKULOV
Faculty of Mountain Geology: M. M. PHOZILOV
Faculty of Oriental Languages: S. SH. SHUKROEVA
Faculty of Philosophy: Prof. A. MUKHABATOV (acting)
Faculty of Physics: K. K. KOMILOV
Faculty of Tajik Philology: M. S. IMOMOV

TAJIK STATE PEDAGOGICAL UNIVERSITY S. AINI

734001 Dushanbe, Pr. Rudaki 121
Telephone: (37) 224-13-83
Fax: (37) 224-13-83
E-mail: info@tgpu.tj
Internet: www.tgpu.tj

Founded 1931
State control

Rector: NUR SAID

Faculties of economics and management, finance and accountancy, history, law, mechanics and mathematics, pedagogics and philology.

TAJIK STATE UNIVERSITY OF COMMERCE

734055 Dushanbe, Dehoti 1/2
Telephone: (372) 34-86-22
Fax: (372) 34-83-94
E-mail: kaa77@tajik.net

Founded 1991
State control
Languages of instruction: Russian, Tajik
Academic year: September to June

Rector: KHAMIDULLOKHON FAKIROV
Vice-Rector: N. SANGINOV

Number of teachers: 168
Number of students: 2,380

DEANS

Faculty of Customs: KHAMID MADJIDOV
Faculty of Distance Education: MUKHIDDIN KHOMIDOV
Faculty of Economics and Management: SAFIULLO HABIBOV
Faculty of World Economics and Financing: ZUYORATSHO AKOBIROV

TAJIK UNIVERSITY OF LAW, POLICY AND BUSINESS

Soghd Oblast, 735700 Khujand
Telephone: (342) 22-38-11
State control

Rector: H. R. PULATOV.

TECHNOLOGICAL UNIVERSITY OF TAJIKISTAN

734061 Dushanbe, N. Narabayev 63/3
Telephone: (372) 34-79-87
Fax: (372) 34-79-88
E-mail: rektorat@tat.tajik.net

Founded 1992
State control
Languages of instruction: Tajik, Russian, English
Academic year: September to June

Rector: AMIR H. KATAYEV
Vice-Rector: NURALI N. SHOYEV

Library of 70,000 vols
Number of teachers: 158
Number of students: 1,050

Publications: *Collection of Scientific Works* (2 a year), *Herald of Ecology* (12 a year)

DEANS

Faculty of Industrial Informatics: MIRZO YUSUPOV
Faculty of International Studies: NASRULLO HOJAYOROV
Faculty of Textile Technology and Mechanical Engineering: VALIJON M. MIRAKILOV

TANZANIA

The Higher Education System

Higher education institutions predate the formation of the United Republic of Tanzania (by a merger of the independent states of Tanganyika and Zanzibar) in 1964, with the oldest being St Augustine University of Tanzania (formerly Nyegezi Social Training Centre), which was founded in 1960. In 2006 there were 55,293 students enrolled in 103 public and private institutions of higher education, which included universities, technical colleges, teacher training colleges and other higher education institutions. Higher education is administered by the Ministry of Education and Vocational Training.

Students are required to gain three passes in the Advanced Certificate of Secondary Education and five passes at CSE level in order to gain admission to higher education. Examinations are administered by the National Examinations Council of Tanzania. Undergraduate Bachelors degrees usually last three years, although programmes of study in mainly professional fields of study last longer, such as engineering, nursing, pharmacy (four years) and medicine (five years). Following the award of the Bachelors, graduates may take the one-year Postgraduate Diploma or the Masters degree, which lasts one to three years. The highest university degree is the Doctor of Philosophy (PhD), a two-year period of research culminating with the submission of a thesis.

Post-secondary technical and vocational education is offered by Technical Colleges, National Vocational Training Centres, Folk Development Colleges, Technical Secondary Schools, Private Vocational Schools and Training Schools. Qualifications include the Diploma and Advanced Diploma.

Regulatory Bodies

GOVERNMENT

Ministry of Education and Vocational Training: POB 9121, Dar es Salaam; tel. (22) 2120403; fax (22) 2113271; e-mail psmoevt@moe.go.tz; internet www.moe.go.tz; Minister Prof. JUMANNE ABDALLAH MAGHEMBE; Permanent Sec. HAMISI O. DIHENGA.

Ministry of Information, Culture and Sports: Dar es Salaam; internet www.hum.go.tz; Minister GEORGE MKUCHIKA.

Learned Societies

GENERAL

Tanzania Society: POB 511, Dar es Salaam; f. 1936; a non-profit society catering for the geographical, ethnological, historical, and general scientific interests of Tanzania; 1,200 mems; publ. *Tanzania Notes and Records* (1 a year).

UNESCO Dar es Salaam Cluster Office: POB 31473, Dar es Salaam; Plot 127C, Mafinga St (off Kinondoni Rd), Dar es Salaam; tel. (22) 2666623; fax (22) 2666927; e-mail dar-es-salaam@unesco.org; designated Cluster Office for Comoros, Madagascar, Mauritius, Seychelles and Tanzania; library of 2,500 vols; Dir and Rep. VIBEKE JENSEN.

AGRICULTURE, FISHERIES AND VETERINARY SCIENCE

Tanzania Veterinary Association: POB 3174, Chuo Kikuu Morogoro; tel. (23) 2604979; fax (23) 2604647; e-mail deanfvm@suanet.ac.tz; f. 1968; 350 mems; Chair. Prof. D. M. KAMBARAGE; publs *Annual Proceedings of the Tanzania Veterinary Association Scientific Conferences*, *Tanzania Veterinary Journal*.

BIBLIOGRAPHY, LIBRARY SCIENCE AND MUSEOLOGY

Tanzania Library Association: POB 33433, Dar es Salaam; tel. and fax (22) 2775411; e-mail tla_tanzania@yahoo.com; internet www.tlatz.org; f. 1965 as a br. of the East African Library Association, reorganized 1973 as an independent body; 200 mems; Chair. Dr ALLI MCHARAZO; Sec. P. MUNUDHI; publ. *Matukio* (Newsletter, irregular).

ECONOMICS, LAW AND POLITICS

East Africa Law Society: POB 6240, Arusha; 64 Haile Selassie Rd, Arusha; tel. (27) 2503135; fax (27) 2508707; e-mail eals@habari.co.tz; f. 1996; 5,000 mems; CEO DONALD DEYA; publs *The East African Human Rights Report* (1 a year), *The East African Lawyer* (4 a year).

HISTORY, GEOGRAPHY AND ARCHAEOLOGY

Historical Association of Tanzania: c/o Department of History, University of Dar es Salaam, POB 35050, Dar es Salaam; tel. (22) 2410397; f. 1966; 2,000 mems; Chair. Prof. K. I. TAMBILA; Sec. Dr E. P. A. N. MIHANJO; publ. *Tanzania Zamani*.

LANGUAGE AND LITERATURE

Alliance Française: Ali Hassan Mwinyi Rd (behind Las Vegas Casino), Upanga, POB 2566, Dar es Salaam; tel. (22) 2111331; fax (22) 2666576; offers courses and exams in French language and culture and promotes cultural exchange with France; attached teaching centre in Arusha.

British Council: Samora Ave/Ohio St, POB 9100, Dar es Salaam; tel. (22) 2116574; fax (22) 2112699; e-mail info@britishcouncil.or.tz; internet www.britishcouncil.org/tanzania; teaching centre; offers courses and exams in English language and British culture and promotes cultural exchange with the UK; Dir TOM COWIN.

Research Institutes

GENERAL

Tanzania Commission for Science and Technology: POB 4302, Dar es Salaam; tel. (22) 2700745; fax (22) 2775313; e-mail costech@costech.or.tz; internet www.costech.or.tz; f. 1986; 73 mems; library of 8,000 vols; Dir.-Gen. Dr HASSAN MSHINDA; publ. *Tanzania Science and Technology Newsletter* (4 a year).

AGRICULTURE, FISHERIES AND VETERINARY SCIENCE

Agricultural Research Institute (Mlingano): ARI Mlingano, POB 5088, Tanga; tel. (27) 2647647; fax (27) 2642577; e-mail mlingano@iwayafrica.com; internet www.kilimo.go.tz/research-training/mlingano.htm; f. 1934; research on cultivation of sisal and other crops, soils, resourcing of efficient farming methods, horticulture; germplasm collection of tropical and subtropical fruits, spices and essential oils; Dir Dr A. NYAKI.

Forestry and Beekeeping Division: c/o Ministry of Natural Resources and Tourism, POB 426, Dar es Salaam; tel. (22) 2864249; e-mail dfob@mnrt.go.tz; internet www.nfp.co.tz; forest surveying, mapping, industrial development, economics, management and education as part of the National Forest Policy and National Beekeeping Policy (both adopted 1998); library of 2,500 vols; Dir Dr FELICIAN KILAHAMA.

Mikocheni Agricultural Research Institute: POB 6226, Kinondoni District, Dar es Salaam; tel. (22) 2700552; fax (22) 2775549; e-mail mari@mari.or.tz; integrated pest management, with emphasis on biological control of coconut pests; Dir Dr ALOIS KULLAYA.

National Livestock Research Institute: POB 202, Mpwapwa, Dodoma; tel. and fax (26) 2320853; f. 1905; research in dairy science, breeding and nutrition of livestock, Mpwapwa cattle and Malya goats, pastural agronomy and multidisciplinary research; Nat. Livestock Research Institute; research information documentation and dissemination; library of 4,000 vols, 40 periodicals; Dir Dr REGINALD P. MBWILE; publ. *Progressive Stockman* (4 a year).

Tanzania Forestry Research Institute: Silviculture Research Centre, POB 95, Lushoto; f. 1951; library of 3,000 vols; Officer-in-Charge T. H. MSANGI; publs *TAFORI Newsletter*, *Tanzania Silviculture Research Notes* (4 a year), *Technical Notes*.

Tanzania Wildlife Research Institute: POB 661, Arusha; tel. (27) 2509871; fax (27) 2548240; e-mail info@tawiri.org; internet www.tawiri.org; research into wildlife, with the objective of providing scientific information and advice to the Govt of Tanzania and local wildlife management authorities on the sustainable conservation of wildlife; Chair Prof. PETER MSOLLA.

Tropical Pesticides Research Institute: POB 3024, Arusha; tel. (27) 2548813; fax (27) 2548217; e-mail tpri@habari.co.tz; internet www.habari.co.tz/tpri; f. 1962; research into all aspects of pesticide application and behaviour; library of 5,000 vols; Dir Dr GRATIAN BAMWENDA.

HISTORY, GEOGRAPHY AND ARCHAEOLOGY

Geological Survey of Tanzania: c/o Min. of Energy and Minerals, POB 903, Dodoma; tel. (26) 2324943; e-mail madini-do@gst.go.tz; internet www.gst.go.tz; f. 1925; attached to Min. of Energy and Minerals; regional mapping, mineral exploration and assessment; supporting laboratory facilities; reprints, bulletins, memoirs, books and maps; library of 4,000 books; Chief Exec., Geological Survey of Tanzania Prof. A. H. MRUMA (acting); Librarian/Information Officer E. LUHOKO; publs *Bulletins*, *Records of the Geological Survey of Tanzania*.

LANGUAGE AND LITERATURE

Eastern African Centre for Research on Oral Traditions and African National Languages (EACROTANAL): POB 600, Zanzibar; f. 1979 as a regional and intergovernmental organization to encourage research and develop means of collection, analysis, conservation and diffusion of oral traditions and promotion of national languages; provides short-term training courses on these subjects; library of 3,000 vols (incl. 148 old Arabic MSS from Zanzibar); one of 3 African regional centres, set up by Burundi, Comoros, Ethiopia, Madagascar, Mauritius, Mozambique, Somalia, Sudan, Tanzania; Exec. Dir KHATIB MAKAME OMAR (acting); publs annotated bibliography of the Arabic MSS (every 2 years), *Paukwa Pakawa* (traditional tales, 1 a year).

Institute of Kiswahili Research: POB 35110, Dar es Salaam; tel. (22) 2410757; e-mail tuki@ikr.udsm.ac.tz; internet www.udsm.ac.tz/ikr/; f. 1970; initiates and conducts fundamental research in all aspects of Kiswahili language; cooperates with local public authorities and int. organizations; promotes the standardization of orthography and the development of language generally; preparing new standard dictionary, technical dictionaries, grammars, monographs on oral literature; library of 3,000 vols; Dir Prof. M. M. MULOKOZI; publs *Kiswahili* (1 a year), *Mulika* (1 a year).

MEDICINE

National Institute for Medical Research (NIMR): Headquarters, Ocean Rd, POB 9653, Dar es Salaam; tel. (22) 2121400; fax (22) 2121360; e-mail headquarters@nimr.or.tz; internet www.nimr.or.tz; f. 1949 at Muheza as the Malaria Unit; investigation into human vector-borne diseases, especially malaria, bancroftian filariasis, and onchocerciasis; Dir Dr ANDREW KITUA.

National Institute for Medical Research, Mwanza Centre: POB 1462, Mwanza; tel. (28) 250189; f. 1949; investigations into various tropical diseases with emphasis on bilharziasis, and other soil-transmitted helminths, bacterial diseases, sanitation and water, diarrhoeal diseases, sexually transmitted diseases, HIV/AIDS; library of 2,300 vols; Dir Dr R. M. GABONE; publs *NIMR Bulletin*, *Proceedings of the Annual NIMR Joint Scientific Conference*.

Libraries and Archives

Dar es Salaam

Tanzania Information Services Department: POB 9142, Dar es Salaam; tel. (22) 2122771; fax (22) 2113814; e-mail maelezo@pmo.go.tz; reference books on Tanzania, journalism, photography, social sciences, geography and history; newspapers and periodicals.

Tanzania Library Services Board: Bibi Titi Mohamed Rd, POB 9283, Dar es Salaam; tel. (22) 2150048; fax (22) 2151100; e-mail tlsb@africaonline.co.tz; internet www.tlsb.or.tz; f. 1964; 16 brs; Dir-Gen. ELIEZER A. MWINYIMVUA.

Tanzania National Archives: Vijibweni St, POB 2006, Dar es Salaam; tel. (22) 2151279; fax (22) 2150634; e-mail dram@intafrica.com; internet www.tanzania.go.tz/psrp/record1.html; f. 1963; German and British colonial archives, post-independence archives; Dir J. M. KARUGILA; publ. *Guide to Archives*.

University of Dar es Salaam Library: POB 35092, Dar es Salaam; tel. and fax (22) 2410241; e-mail director@libis.udsm.ac.tz; internet www.udsm.ac.tz/library; f. 1961; legal deposit library; 600,000 vols, 280 journals, spec. collns: E Africana Colln, UN Colln, Law Colln; 8,000 periodicals; Dir JANGAWE MSUYA.

Morogoro

Sokoine National Agricultural Library: POB 3022, Morogoro; tel. (23) 2604639; fax (23) 2604388; e-mail library@suanet.ac.tz; internet www.suanet.ac.tz; f. 1964 as library for the College of Agriculture, library for Faculty of Agriculture, Forestry and Veterinary Medicine of the Univ. of Dar es Salaam 1972, Sokoine Univ. of Agriculture Library 1984, present name and status 1991; attached to Sokoine Univ. of Agriculture; learning, teaching, research, consultancy and outreach services; 75,000 vols, 100 periodicals; Library Dir Dr DORIS. S. MATOVELO.

Mwanza

Ladha Meghji Indian Public Library: POB 70, Mwanza; tel. (28) 2500482; fax (28) 2500222; e-mail desaitz@yahoo.com; f. 1935; 11,130 vols; runs English, French, oriental language and computer classes; Librarian RAMAN DESAI.

Zanzibar

Agricultural Department Library: POB 159, Zanzibar; 1,100 vols, 50 periodicals.

Museum Research Library: c/o Dept of Antiquities, Archives and Museum, Zanzibar National Archives, POB 116, Zanzibar; tel. (22) 30342; e-mail dama@zitec.org; f. 1930; reference library; 15,000 vols and 1,000 periodicals; Head of the Library SULEIMAN SEIF.

Zanzibar National Archives: POB 116, Zanzibar; tel. and fax (22) 35241; f. 1956; history and administration; 3,500 vols; Archivist HAMAD OMAR.

Museums and Art Galleries

Dar es Salaam

National Museums of Tanzania: POB 511, Dar es Salaam; tel. (22) 2122030; internet www.museum.or.tz; f. 1937 as King George V Memorial Museum, name changed 1963; ethnography, palaeoanthropology, history and marine biology; houses the *Zinjanthropus* skull and other material from Olduvai Gorge and other Palaeolithic sites; also houses reference library; Dir-Gen. Dr N. A. KAYOMBO.

Branch Museums:

- **Arusha Declaration Museum:** POB 7423, Arusha; tel. (27) 2507800; e-mail adm-arusha@habari.co.tz; internet www.arushamuseum.ac.tz; f. 1977; preservation and exhibition of political, social and economic history; Curators CONSTANTINUS MISAGO NYAMABONDO, FABIAN LYIMO.
- **Arusha Natural History Museum:** POB 2160, Arusha; tel. (27) 2507540; e-mail nnhm@habari.co.tz; internet www.museum.or.tz; Curator FELISTA MANGALU.
- **Village Museum:** POB 511, Dar es Salaam; tel. (22) 2700437; e-mail villagemuseum@raha.com; f. 1967; traditional house styles and crafts; Curator JACKSON M. KIHIYO.

Zanzibar

Zanzibar Government Museum: POB 116, Zanzibar; tel. (24) 2230342; fax (24) 2235241; e-mail dama@zitec.org; internet www.museum.com/jb/museum?id=24191; f. 1925; operates Peace Memorial Museum at Mnazi Minoja (history, ethnography, natural history and archaeology of Zanzibar, f. 1925), Palace Museum at Mizingani (history of the Zanzibar sultans, f. 1994), Pemba Museum at Chake (history of Pemba Island, f. 2000), House of Wonders Museum at Forodhani (history and culture of Zanzibar and Swahili Coast civilization, f. 2001); Dir H. H. OMAR.

Universities

UNIVERSITY OF DAR ES SALAAM

POB 35091, Dar es Salaam
Telephone: (22) 2410500
Fax: (22) 2410078
E-mail: vc@admin.udsm.ac.tz
Internet: www.udsm.ac.tz

Founded 1961; univ. status 1970
Language of instruction: English
Academic year: October to June (two semesters)

Chancellor: Ambassador F. KAZAURA
Vice-Chancellor: Prof. RWEKAZA MUKANDALA
Deputy Vice-Chancellor for Academic Affairs: Prof. M. A. H. MABOKO
Deputy Vice-Chancellor for Admin.: Prof. Y. D. MGAYA
Dir for Postgraduate Studies: Prof. B. M. MWINYIWIWA
Dir for Research: Prof. J. V. TESHA
Library: see Libraries and Archives
Number of teachers: 1,172
Number of students: 19,650

Publication: *Research Bulletin* (2 a year)

DEANS

College of Arts and Social Sciences: B. B. MAPUNDA
College of Engineering Technology: J. H. Y. KATIMA
College of Natural and Applied Sciences: Prof. F. S. S. MAGINGO
Dar es Salaam University College of Education: Prof. S. B. MISANA
Mkwawa University College of Education: Prof. P. A. K. MUSHI
School of Education: Prof. E. P. BHALALUSESA
School of Informatics and Communication Technologies: Prof. J. R. IKINGURA
School of Journalism and Mass Communication: Dr B. KILLIAN
School of Law: P. J. KABUDI

PROFESSORS

CHAMBEGA, D., Electrical Power Engineering
CHAMI, F., History and Archaeology
FIMBO, G., Economic Law
GALABAWA, J., Educational Planning and Administration
ISHUMI, A., Educational, Management, Foundations and Lifelong Studies
JOHN, G., Energy Engineering
KIMAMBO, I., History and Archaeology
LUHANGA, M., Electrical and Computer Systems Engineering
MAGHIMBI, S., Sociology and Anthropology
MASANJA, V., Mathematics
MASSAMBA, D., Institute of Kiswahili Research
MBAGO, M., Statistics
MBUNDA, F., Educational Psychology and Curriculum Studies
MLAWA, H., Institute of Development Studies
MOSHA, H., Educational Management, Foundations and Learning
MPANGALA, G., Institute of Development Studies
MSAKI, P., Physics
MSAMBICHAKA, L., Economics
MTALO, F., Water Resources Engineering
MUHONGO, S., Geology
MUNISHI, G., Political Science and Public Administration
MUSHI, P., Adult Education and Extension
MUSHI, S., Political Science and Public Administration
MUTAHABA, G., Political Science and Public Administration
MUTAKYAHWA, M., Geology
NGANA, J., Institute of Resource Assessment
NGWARE, S., Institute of Development Studies
NJAU, E., Physics
NYICHOMBA, B., Design and Production Engineering
OMARI, I., Curriculum and Teaching
OSORO, E., Economic Development
PETER, C., Private Law
RUGUMAMU, S., Institute of Development Studies
RUGUMAMU, W., Geography
RUTASHOBYA, L., Marketing
SHISHIRA, E., Institute of Resource Assessment
SHIVJI, I., Chairs

HUBERT KARIUKI MEMORIAL UNIVERSITY

POB 65300, 322 Regent Estate, Dar es Salaam
Telephone: (22) 2700021
Fax: (22) 2775591
E-mail: secvc@hkmu.ac.tz
Internet: www.hkmu.ac.tz

Founded 1997; univ. status 2000
Language of instruction: English
Academic year: September to August

Vice-Chancellor: Prof. KETO E. MSHIGENI
Deputy Vice-Chancellor for Finance, Planning and Admin.: Prof. PASCHALIS RUGARABAMU
Dir of Postgraduate Studies and Research Institute: Prof. SYLVESTER L. B. KAJUNA
Dean of Students: Dr ALPHAGE LIWA
Sr Librarian: STANSLAUS NGADAYA

DEANS

Faculty of Medicine: Dr FELICIAN RUTACHUNZIBWA
Faculty of Nursing: Prof. PAULINE P. MELLA

PROFESSORS

LUTAHOIRE, S., Medicine
MELLA, P., Nursing
MSAMATI, B. C., Medicine
MWAIKAMBO, E., Medicine

INTERNATIONAL MEDICAL AND TECHNOLOGICAL UNIVERSITY

Mbeze Beach area, New Bagamoyo Rd, POB 77594, Dar es Salaam
Telephone: (22) 2647036
Fax: (22) 2647038
E-mail: imtu@costech.or.tz
Internet: www.imtu.edu

Founded 1995 by Vignan Educational Foundation (India) and Tanzanian Govt

Number of teachers: 23

Vice-Chancellor: Dr V. P. KIMATI
Deputy Vice-Chancellor for Academic Affairs: V. S. RAKESH
Dir of Finance: P. B. KUMAR
Dean of Students: Dr RENJU THOMAS.

MZUMBE UNIVERSITY (Chuo Kikuu Mzumbe)

POB 1, Mzumbe, Morogoro
Telephone: (23) 2604380
Fax: (23) 2604382
E-mail: mu@mzumbe.ac.tz
Internet: www.mzumbe.ac.tz

Founded 1972 as Institute of Devt Management; present name and univ. status 2001
State control
Language of instruction: English
Academic year: October to June

Chancellor: Hon. Judge (retd) BARNABAS SAMATTA
Vice-Chancellor: Prof. JOSEPH ANDREW KUZILWA
Deputy Vice-Chancellor for Academic Affairs: Prof. MAGISHI NKWABI MGASA
Deputy Vice-Chancellor for Admin. and Finance: Prof. FAUSTIN KAMUZORA
Registrar: Prof. HAMISI I. MAHIGI
Dir of Research and Postgraduate Studies: Dr AGGREY KIHOMBO
Dir of Library and Technical Services: MATILDA KUZILWA
Dir of Information and Communications Technology: ALMAS MAGUYE
Dir of MU Mbeya campus: ROSS KINEMO

Library of 50,000 books, 900 current periodicals
Number of teachers: 270
Number of students: 3,551

Publications: *Economics and Development Papers*, *Journal of Public Policy and Administration*, *Uongozi Journal of Management and Development Dynamics* (4 a year)

DEANS

Dar es Salaam Business School: Dr ANDREW MBWAMBO
Faculty of Commerce: Dr JOSEPH A. KIMEME
Faculty of Law: ELEUTER G. MUSHI
Faculty of Public Administration and Management: Prof. JOSEPHAT ITIKA
Faculty of Science and Technology: Prof. Dr PHILBERT NDUNGURU
Faculty of Social Science: Prof. Dr EULALIA I. TEMBA

ATTACHED RESEARCH INSTITUTES

Institute of Continuing Studies: POB, Mzumbe; tel. (23) 2604380; fax (23) 2604382; e-mail ics@mzumbe.ac.tz; Dir ALOYCE MAZIKU.

Institute of Development Studies: POB 83, Mzumbe; tel. (23) 2604380; fax (23) 2604382; e-mail ids@mzumbe.ac.tz; Dir Dr IDDI MAKOMBE.

Institute of Public Administration: POB 2, Mzumbe; tel. (23) 2604380; fax (23) 2604382; e-mail ipa@mzumbe.ac.tz; Dir Dr EMMANUEL MATIKU.

OPEN UNIVERSITY OF TANZANIA

Kawawa Rd, Kinondoni Municipality, POB 23409, Dar es Salaam
Telephone: (22) 2668992
Fax: (22) 2668759
E-mail: vc@out.ac.tz
Internet: www.out.ac.tz

Founded 1992
State control
Languages of instruction: English, Kiswahili
Academic year: January to December

Chancellor: Dr JOHN SAMWEL MALECELA
Vice-Chancellor: Prof. TOLLY S. A. MBWETTE
Deputy Vice-Chancellor for Academic Affairs: Prof. DONATUS A. KOMBA
Registrar: Prof. USWEGE M. MINGA
Librarian: A. S. SAMZUGI

Library of 5,000 vols
Number of teachers: 113 (33 full-time, 80 part-time)
Number of students: 12,945

Publication: *HURIA Journal*

PROFESSORS

AMAA, K. O., Business Management
KIWANGA, C. A., Science, Technology and Environmental Studies
KOMBA, D. A., Education
MASENGE, R. W. P., Science, Technology and Environmental Studies
MUKOYOGO, M. C., Law
TEMU, A. J., Arts and Social Sciences

23 regional centres and 69 study centres

ST AUGUSTINE UNIVERSITY OF TANZANIA

POB 307, Mwanza
Telephone: (28) 2552725
Fax: (28) 2550167
E-mail: saut@saut.ac.tz
Internet: www.saut.ac.tz

Founded 1960 as Nyegezi Social Training Centre; present status and name 1998
Private control (Catholic Church)
Language of instruction: English
Academic year: October to June

Vice-Chancellor: Prof. CHARLES KITIMA

Library of 15,000 vols, 30 periodicals
Number of teachers: 44
Number of students: 404

DEANS

Faculty of Business Administration: ILDEFONS CHONYA (acting)
Faculty of Humanities and Mass Communication: JOSEPH MLACHA (acting)

SOKOINE UNIVERSITY OF AGRICULTURE

POB 3000, Chuo Kikuu, Morogoro
Telephone: (23) 2603511
Fax: (23) 2604651
E-mail: sua@suanet.ac.tz
Internet: www.suanet.ac.tz

Founded 1984, previously a faculty of Univ. of Dar es Salaam
State control
Language of instruction: English
Academic year: September to June

Chancellor: AL NOOR KASSUM
Vice-Chancellor: Prof. G. C. MONELA
Deputy Vice-Chancellor for Academic Affairs: Prof. D. M. KAMBARAGE
Deputy Vice-Chancellor for Admin. and Finance: Prof. A. E. PEREKA
Dir, Solomon Mahlangu Campus: Assoc. Prof. N. D. URIO
Registrar: Assoc. Prof. H. O. DIHENGA
Librarian: D. S. MATOVELO

Library: see Libraries and Archives

Number of teachers: 452
Number of students: 3,619 (2,925 undergraduate, 694 postgraduate)

DEANS

Faculty of Agriculture: Prof. B. P. TIISEKWA
Faculty of Forestry and Nature Conservation: Prof. P. R. GILLAH
Faculty of Science: Dr Y. C. MUZANILA
Faculty of Veterinary Medicine: Assoc. Prof. P. N. WAMBURA

PROFESSORS

ABELI, W., Forest Engineering
ASSEY, R., Veterinary Anatomy
BALTHAZARY, S., Physiology, Biochemistry, Pharmacology and Toxicology
BATAMUZI, E., Surgery and Theriogenology
BITEGEKO, S., Surgery and Theriogenology
CHAMSHAMA, S., Forest Biology
GWAKISA, P., Microbiology and Parasitology
HAMZA, K., Wood Utilization
ISHENGOMA, R., Wood Utilization
KAJEMBE, G., Forest Mensuration and Management
KAMBARAGE, D., Veterinary Medicine and Public Health
KASSUKU, A., Veterinary Microbiology and Parasitology
KAZWALA, R., Veterinary Medicine and Public Health
KESSY, B., Veterinary Surgery and Theriogenology
KIFARO, G., Animal Science
KILONZO, B., Veterinary Microbiology and Parasitology
KIMAMBO, A., Animal Science
KINABO, L., Veterinary Physiology, Biochemistry, Pharmacology and Toxicology
KURWIJILA, R., Animal Science
LASWAI, G., Animal Science
LASWAI, H., Food Science and Production
LEKULE, F., Animal Science
LULANDALA, L., Forest Biology
LWOGA, A., Crop Science and Production
MABAGALA, R., Crop Science and Production
MACHANG'U, R., Veterinary Microbiology and Parasitology
MADOFE, S., Forest Biology
MALIMBWI, R., Forest Mensuration
MALIONDO, S., Forest Biology
MASELLE, R., Veterinary Pathology
MATOVELO, J., Veterinary Pathology
MBASSA, G., Veterinary Anatomy
MDOE, N., Agricultural Economics and Agribusiness
MGASA, M., Veterinary Surgery and Theriogenology
MGONGO, F., Veterinary Surgery and Theriogenology
MISANGU, R., Crop Science and Production
MLAMBITI, M., Agricultural Economics and Agribusiness
MLANGWA, J., Veterinary Medicine and Public Health
MLOZI, M., Agricultural Education and Extension
MONELA, G., Forest Economics
MOSHA, R., Veterinary Physiology, Biochemistry, Pharmacology and Toxicology
MSANYA, B., Soil Science
MTAMBO, M., Veterinary Medicine and Public Health
MTENGA, L., Animal Science
MUHIKAMBELE, V., Animal Science
MUNISHI, P., Forest Biology
MUTAYOBA, B., Veterinary Physiology, Biochemistry, Pharmacology and Toxicology
NGOMUO, A., Veterinary Physiology, Biochemistry, Pharmacology and Toxicology
NYARUHUCHA, C., Food Science
PEREKA, A., Veterinary Physiology, Biochemistry, Pharmacology and Toxicology
REUBEN, S., Crop Science and Production
RUTATORA, D., Agricultural Education and Extension
SEMOKA, J., Soil Science
SEMUGURUKA, W., Veterinary Pathology
SENKONDO, E., Agricultural Economics and Agribusiness
SHAYO, N., Food Science and Production
SHEM, M., Animal Science
SIBUGA, K., Crop Science and Production
SILAYO, R., Veterinary Microbiology and Parasitology
TARIMO, A., Agricultural Engineering and Land Planning
TIISEKWA, B., Food Science and Production

ATTACHED CENTRES

Computer Centre: POB 3218, Chuo Kikuu, Morogoro; e-mail ccentre@suanet.ac.tz; Dir Prof. S. D TUMBO.

Development Studies Institute: POB 3024, Chuo Kikuu, Morogoro; e-mail dsi@suanet.ac.tz; Dir Prof. A. Z. MATTEE.

Directorate of Research and Postgraduate Studies: POB 3151, Morogoro; tel. and fax (23) 2604388; e-mail drpgs@suanet.ac.tz; Dir Prof. J. A. MATOVELO.

Institute of Continuing Education: POB 3044, Morogoro; tel. (23) 2604549; fax (23) 2603718; e-mail ice@suanet.ac.tz; Dir Assoc. Prof. G. G. KIMBI.

SUA Centre for Sustainable Rural Development: POB 3035, Morogoro; tel. (23) 2604360; fax (23) 2604758; e-mail suajica@suanet.ac.tz; Dir Prof. D. F. RUTATORA.

SUA Pest Management Centre: POB 3110, Morogoro; tel. (23) 2604621; e-mail pestman@suanet.ac.tz; Dir Prof. R. H. MAKUNDI.

TUMAINI UNIVERSITY

POB 55, Usa River, Arusha
Telephone: (27) 2541144
Fax: (27) 2541146
E-mail: tu@kilinet.co.tz
Internet: www.tumainiuniversity.ac.tz
Founded 1996, present status 2001
Private control (Evangelical Lutheran Church in Tanzania)
Language of instruction: English
Vice-Chancellor: Prof. JOHN F. SHAO
Number of teachers: 400
Number of students: 9,000
Publication: *Tumaini Hill* (Newsletter, 4 a year).

CONSTITUENT COLLEGES

Iringa University College

POB 200, Iringa
Telephone: (26) 2720900
Fax: (26) 2720904
Founded 1993
Provost: NICOLAS BANGU
Deputy Provost for Academic Affairs: Rev. Dr RICHARD LUBAWA

DEANS

Faculty of Arts and Social Sciences: EGIDIO Y. CHAULA
Faculty of Business and Economics: EMMANUEL LUVANDA
Faculty of Law: THOMAS MWAHOMBELA
Faculty of Theology: PETER FUE

Kilimanjaro Christian Medical College

POB 2240, Moshi
Telephone: (27) 2754377
Fax: (27) 2754381
E-mail: kcmcadmin@kcmc.ac.tz
Internet: www.kcmc.ac.tz
Founded 1997
Provost: EGBERT M. KESSI
Deputy Provost for Academic Affairs: Prof. AUGUSTINE MALLYA

DEANS

Faculty of Medicine: KIEN MTETA
Faculty of Nursing: MARCELINA H. MSUYA
Faculty of Rehabilitative Science: HAROLD G. SHANGALI

Makumira University College

POB 55, Usa River, Arusha
Telephone: (27) 2541034
Fax: (27) 2541030
E-mail: provost@makumira.ac.tz
Internet: www.makumira.ac.tz
Founded 1954
Provost: Rev. Prof. JOSEPH W. PARSALAW
Deputy Provost for Academic Affairs: Prof. ISMAEL R. MBISE
Dean of Students: ZAKARIA MATINDA
Dean of Students: Rev. Dr E.A. MUNGURE

DEANS

Faculty of Humanity and Social Sciences: APOLO A. MUGYENYI
Faculty of Law: DANIEL PALLANGYO
Faculty of Theology: Rev. HABAKUKI LWENDO

Sebastian Kolowa University College

POB 370, Lushoto
Telephone: (27) 2640114
Fax: (27) 2640107
E-mail: admin@sekuco.org
Internet: www.sekuco.org
Provost: Rev. Dr ANNETH MUNGA

DEANS

Faculty of Education: PAUL O. NWAOGU
Faculty of Law: MUTABAZI LUGAZIYA (acting)
Faculty of Science: NATHAN MUNYIAMBA (acting)

Stefano Moshi Memorial University College

POB 881, Moshi
Telephone: (27) 2757070
Fax: (27) 2757880
E-mail: masoka@kilinet.co.tz
Provost: ARNOLD TEMU (acting)
Deputy Provost for Academic Affairs: Prof. PETER CHONJO (acting)

DEANS

Faculty of Business and Management: ERNEST KASHESHI (acting)
Faculty of Education: ISMAIL NKYA (acting)
Faculty of Science and Technology: (vacant)

Tumaini University Dar es Salaam College

POB 77588, Lushoto
Telephone: (22) 2760335
Fax: (22) 2760432
E-mail: provost@tumainidsm.ac.tz
Internet: www.tumainidsm.ac.tz

DEANS

Faculty of Arts and Social Sciences: ROBERT MFUGALE
Faculty of Business Administration: GILLIARD LOTH
Faculty of Law: MASUMBUKO LAMWAI

UNIVERSITY OF BUKOBA

POB 1725, Bukoba
Telephone: (28) 2220691
Fax: (28) 2222341
E-mail: uobtz@yahoo.com
Internet: uobtz.tripod.com
Founded 1999

State control
Language of instruction: English
Academic year: October to June

Chancellor: C. G. KAHAMA
Vice-Chancellor: Prof. M. HODD
Deputy Vice-Chancellor: Prof. ISRAEL KATOKE
Registrar: SAMUEL MUTASA

Library of 1,000 vols
Number of teachers: 20
Number of students: 50

DEANS

Faculty of Commerce and Management: JOSEPH MWABUKI
Faculty of Social and Natural Science: CHRISTOPHER RWIZA (acting)

ZANZIBAR UNIVERSITY

POB 2440, Zanzibar
Telephone: (24) 2232642
Fax: (24) 2236388
E-mail: info@zanvarsity.ac.tz
Internet: www.zanvarsity.ac.tz

Founded 1998
State control
Language of instruction: English

Faculties of arts and social science, business administration, and law and Shariah

Vice-Chancellor: MUSTAFA A. A. ROSHASH (acting)

Library of 3,000 vols
Number of teachers: 24
Number of students: 393

Colleges

College of African Wildlife Management, Mweka: POB 3031, Moshi; tel. (27) 2756451; fax (27) 2756414; e-mail mweka@mwekawildlife.org; internet www.mwekawildlife.org; f. 1963; professional and technical training, research and consultancy services in African wildlife management; qualifications awarded include certificate, diploma, advanced diploma and postgraduate diploma in wildlife management; library: 10,000 vols; 16 teachers; 150 students; Prin. DEO-GRATIAS M. GAMASSA.

College of Business Education: POB 1968, Dar es Salaam; tel. (22) 2150177; e-mail principalcbe@yahoo.com; f. 1965; 55 teachers; 1,300 students; two- and three-year diploma courses in business administration and metrology; certificate course in business administration; postgraduate course in business administration; Prin. S. M. HYERA.

Dar es Salaam Institute of Technology: Private Bag 2958, Dar es Salaam; tel. (22) 2150174; fax (22) 2152504; e-mail principaldit@intafrica.com; internet www.dit.ac.tz; f. 1957; civil, mechanical, electrical, electronics and telecommunications engineering courses; science and laboratory technology and computing studies courses; library: 27,000 vols; 180 teachers; 3,600 students (1,200 full-time, 2,400 part-time); Prin. Prof. J. W. A. KONDORO.

Eastern and Southern African Management Institute: POB 3030, Arusha; tel. (27) 2508384; fax (27) 2508285; e-mail esamihq@esamihq.ac.tz; internet www.esami-africa.org; f. 1974, reconstituted 1980; country offices in Kenya, Malawi, Mozambique, Namibia, Swaziland, Tanzania, Uganda, Zambia, Zimbabwe; conducts management development programmes; programmes in corporate entrepreneurship, energy and environment management, finance and banking, gender development and management, governance and public sector management, human resource management, information technology, transport and infrastructure development, health services management and administration; also Executive MBA and MBA in Transport Economics and Logistics Management; 44 teachers (24 full-time, 20 associate); library: 12,000 vols, 15,000 pamphlets; Dir-Gen. Dr BONARD MWAPE; publs *African Management Development Forum* (2 a year), *ESAMI Newsletter* (4 a year).

Institute of Finance Management: Shaaban Robert St, POB 3918, Dar es Salaam; tel. (22) 2112931; fax (22) 2112935; e-mail principal@africaonline.co.tz; internet www.ifm.ac.tz; f. 1972; courses incl. certificates in insurance, social security administration, information technology and computer science; library: 32,000 vols, 100 periodicals; 80 teachers; 1,710 students; Chief Exec. Prof. JOSHUA DORIYE (acting); Dir of Studies Dr ISAYA JAIRO (acting); publ. *African Journal of Finance and Management* (2 a year).

Kivukoni Academy of Social Sciences: POB 9193, Dar es Salaam; tel. (22) 2820041; fax (22) 2820816; e-mail kass@kasstz.org; internet www.kasstz.org; f. 1961; two-year diploma courses in social sciences, economic development and gender issues in development; one-year certificate in youth work; library: 27,000 vols; 30 teachers; 250 students; Prin. Dr JOHN M. J. MAGOTTI.

Moshi University College of Cooperative and Business Studies: POB 474, Sokoine Rd, Moshi; tel. (27) 2751183; fax (27) 2750806; e-mail moshiuniversity@yahoo.com; internet www.muccobs.ac.tz; f. 1963; library: 37,000 vols; Gender Documentation Centre on cooperatives and development; Health Information Centre; 90 teachers; 900 students; Prin. Prof. S. A. CHAMBO; publs *Journal of Cooperative and Business Studies* (2 a year), *Research Abstracts* (every 3 years), *Research Report Series*.

National Social Welfare Training Institute: POB 3375, Dar es Salaam; tel. (22) 2700918; f. 1974; 20 teachers; 180 students; library: 7,172 vols; Prin. T. F. NGALULA; publ. *Jamii Journal*.

University College of Lands and Architectural Studies: POB 35176, Dar es Salaam; tel. (22) 2775004; fax (22) 27755391; e-mail uclas@uclas.ac.tz; internet www.uclas.ac.tz; f. 1996; architecture, building economics, land management and valuation, land surveying, geomatics, environmental engineering, urban and rural planning; Institute of Human Settlements Studies (applied research and documentation services in housing, building, planning and environmental management), Centre for Information Communication Technology (geographic information systems, remote sensing and ICT Studies); library: 20,000 vols; spec. colls of UN publications, theses and masterplans; 111 teachers; 1,060 students; Prin. Prof. IDRIS KIKULA; publ. *Journal of Building and Land Development* (3 a year).

THAILAND

The Higher Education System

The oldest institution of higher education is Chulalongkorn University, which was founded in 1917. Following the National Education Act (1999; amended 2002) and the Act for Streamlining of Ministries and Government Agencies (2003), the Ministry of Education, Ministry of University Affairs and Office of the National Education Commission were incorporated into a supra-Ministry of Education. Higher education is the responsibility of the Ministry of Education's Higher Education Commission. The Education Act also specified that a quality assurance system should be in place by 2003. After initial assessment, individual institutions would be revisited every five years. In 2004 there were 1,891,693 students enrolled in 166 institutions under the authority of the Higher Education Commission.

The main requirements for admission to higher education are 12 years of secondary school education and the MAW 6 (M6) certificate. Applicants to state institutions must sit the Written Entrance Examination, and private institutions may also require applicants to fulfil additional criteria for admission. The principal undergraduate degree is the Bachelors, which is a four-year programme of study, although degrees in mainly professional fields of study may last longer, such as dentistry, architecture, pharmacy (five years) and medicine (six years). The first postgraduate degree is the Masters, which usually lasts two years and may be either a taught or a research degree. The highest university degree is the Doctor of Philosophy (PhD), which requires a minimum of three years and a maximum of eight years of classwork and research.

Post-secondary vocational and technical education is overseen by the Ministry of Education Vocational Education Commission. Qualifications offered include Diploma in Vocational Education, Higher Certificate (Technician Level) and Higher Diploma of Technical Education (all two years).

Regulatory and Representative Bodies

GOVERNMENT

Ministry of Culture: Thanalongkorn Bldg, Thanon Boromrachanonnee, Bangplud, Bangkok 10700; tel. (2) 522-8888; e-mail webmaster@m-culture.go.th; internet www.m-culture.go.th; Minister ANUSORN WONGWAN.

Ministry of Education: Wang Chankasem, Thanon Ratchadamnoen Nok, Bangkok 10300; tel. (2) 281-9809; fax (2) 281-9241; e-mail website@emisc.moe.go.th; internet www.moe.go.th; Min. CHINNAWORN BOONYAKIAT.

NATIONAL BODIES

Association of Private Higher Education Institutions of Thailand: Siam Univ., 235 Petchkasem Rd, Phasi-charoen, Bangkok 10160; tel. (2) 354-5689; fax (2) 457-3982; e-mail webmaster@siam.edu; internet www.apheit.com; f. 1976; Pres. Assoc. Prof. Dr CHIRADET OUSAWAT.

Commission on Higher Education: 328 Si Ayutthay Rd, Ratchathewi, Bangkok 10400; tel. (2) 610-5200; fax (2) 354-5524; e-mail pr_mua@mua.go.th; internet www.mua.go.th/default1.html; part of Min. of Education; makes policy recommendations, sets standards and plans devt in higher education; devises criteria and guidelines for the allocation of resources; tests and assesses academic and professional standards for purposes of quality assurance; coordinates and promotes research activities; Chair. THE MIN. OF EDUCATION ; Sec.-Gen. Dr SUMATE YAMNOON; publ. *Thai Higher Education Review* (4 a year).

Council of University Presidents of Thailand (CUPT): 333 Moo 1, Muang Dist., Chiangrai 57100; tel. (53) 706-175; fax (53) 706-174; e-mail postmaster@mua.go.th; internet www.mfu.ac.th; f. 1972; 24 mem. univs and institutes of higher learning; Pres. Assoc. Prof. Dr WANCHAI SIRICHANA.

Rectors' Conference of Thailand: Planning Division, Ministry of University Affairs, Si-Ayuthya Rd, Bangkok 10400; f. 1971; to exchange ideas and discuss problems of common concern to univs; 14 mems; Chair. Prof. Dr NATTH BHAMARAPRAVATI; Sec. Asst Prof. Dr UTHAI BOONPRASERT.

Learned Societies

GENERAL

Office of the National Culture Commission: Ratchadapisek Rd, Huay Khwang, Bangkok 10320; tel. 247-0013; fax 248-5841; internet www.culture.go.th; f. 1979; advises the Ministerial Council on cultural policy, and promotes coordination and cooperation in cultural activities (e.g. ASEAN projects, UNESCO programmes, intraregional music workshop, cultural exchanges, varied research); 300 mems; library of 30,000 vols; Sec.-Gen. ARTORN CHANDAVIMOL; publ. *Thai Culture Magazine* (52 a year).

Royal Institute: The Royal Grand Palace Grounds, Thanon, Na Phra Lan Rd, Bangkok 10200; tel. 221-4822; fax 224-9910; e-mail royal_institute@mozart.inet.co.th; f. 1933; promotes investigation and encouragement of all branches of knowledge, the exchange of knowledge and advises the Government; 151 mems; library of 25,000 vols; Pres. Prof. Dr PRAYOON KANCHANADUL; Sec.-Gen. CHAMNONG TONGPRASERT.

Siam Society under Royal Patronage: 131 Soi 21 (Asoke), Asokemontri Rd, Wattana, Bangkok 10110; tel. (2) 661-6470; fax (2) 258-3491; e-mail info@siam-society.org; internet www.siam-society.org; f. 1904; promotes the preservation of Thai heritage, culture, art, flora and fauna; 2,000 mems; library of 35,000 vols; Pres. M. R. CHAKRAROT CHITRABONGS; Hon. Sec. MONITA SINGHAKOWIN; publs *Journal*, *Natural History Bulletin* (2 a year).

BIBLIOGRAPHY, LIBRARY SCIENCE AND MUSEOLOGY

Thai Library Association: 273 Vibhavadee Rangsit Rd, Phyathai, Bangkok 10400; tel. 271-2084; f. 1954; 1,524 mems; Pres. M. CHAVALIT; Sec. K. SUCKCHAROEN; publs *TLA Bulletin*, *The World of Books*.

EDUCATION

UNESCO Office Bangkok and Asia and Pacific Regional Bureau for Education: Prakanong Post Office, POB 10110, Bangkok; located at: 920 Sukhumvit Rd, Bangkok 10110; tel. (2) 391-0577; fax (2) 391-0866; e-mail bangkok@unesco.org; internet www.unesco.org/bangkok; f. 1961; designated Cluster Office for Cambodia, Laos, Myanmar, Thailand and Viet Nam; Dir SHELDON SHAEFFER.

LANGUAGE AND LITERATURE

Alliance Française: 29 Thanon Sathorn Tai, Bangkok 10120; tel. (2) 670-4200; fax (2) 670-4200; e-mail bangkok@alliance-francaise.or.th; internet www.alliance-francaise.or.th; offers courses and exams in French language and culture and promotes cultural exchange with France; attached teaching centres in Chiang Mai, Chiang Rai and Phuket; Dir of Operations, Thailand ANDRÉ SCHMITT.

British Council: 254 Chulalongkorn Soi 64, Siam Sq., Phayathai Rd, Pathumwan, Bangkok 10330; tel. (2) 652-5480; fax (2) 253-5312; e-mail info@britishcouncil.or.th; internet www.britishcouncil.or.th; teaching centre; offers courses and exams in English language and British culture and promotes cultural exchange with the UK; attached teaching centres in Chiang Mai, Ladprao, Pinklao and Srinakarin; Dir PETER UPTON.

Goethe-Institut: 18/1 Soi Goethe, Sathorn 1 Rd, Bangkok 10120; tel. (2) 287-0942; fax (2) 287-1829; e-mail info@bangkok.goethe.org; internet www.goethe.de/bangkok; f. 1960; offers courses and exams in German language and culture and promotes cultural exchange with Germany; library of 8,000 vols; Dir Dr NORBERT SPITZ.

MEDICINE

Medical Association of Thailand: 3 Silom St, Bangkok; f. 1921; 3,057 mems; Pres. Prof. Dr SONGKRANT NIYOMSEN; Hon. Sec. Prof. Dr SANONG UNAKOL; publ. *Journal*.

NATURAL SCIENCES

General

Science Society of Thailand: Faculty of Science, Chulalongkorn University, Phyathai Rd, Bangkok 10330; tel. (2) 2527987; fax (2) 2527987; f. 1948; aims to promote education and research in all branches of natural science; 2,500 mems; Pres. Prof. Dr MONTRI CHULAVATNATOL; Sec.-Gen. Dr PIAMSOOK PONGSAWASDI; publs *Journal* (in English, 4 a year), *Science* (26 a year).

Research Institutes

AGRICULTURE, FISHERIES AND VETERINARY SCIENCE

Fishery Technological Development Division: Dept of Fisheries, Ministry of Agriculture and Co-operatives, Charoen Krung Rd, Yannawa, Bangkok 10120; tel. (2) 2111261; f. 1954; fish handling, processing and utilization; analytical and sanitary certificate for export; Dir UDOM SUNDRARAVIPAT.

Forest Products Research and Development Division: Royal Forest Dept, Ministry of Agriculture and Co-operatives, 61 Paholyothin Rd, Jatujak, Bangkok 10900; f. 1935; wood and non-wood products research and utilization; library of 20,000 vols; Dir of Division WANIDA SUBANSENEE.

Rubber Research Centre: Hat Yai, Songkhla, Dept of Agriculture, Ministry of Agriculture and Co-operatives, Bangkok.

NATURAL SCIENCES

Biological Sciences

Marine Biology Centre: Marine Fisheries Division, 89/1 Sapanpla, Yanawa, Bangkok 12; f. 1968; research and training of marine biologists; Dir DEB MENASWETA.

RELIGION, SOCIOLOGY AND ANTHROPOLOGY

Buddhist Research Centre: Wat Benchamabopitr, Bangkok; f. 1961; sponsored by Department of Religious Affairs, Ministry of Education; publs *Pali-Thai-English Dictionary, vol. 1*.

TECHNOLOGY

Department of Alternative Energy Development and Efficiency: Kasatsuk Bridge, Rama I Rd, Bangkok 10330; tel. (2) 2230021; fax (2) 2261416; e-mail dede@dede.go.th; internet www.dede.go.th; f. 1953; conducts research and inspection, surveys and gathers data on energy resources; lays down safety regulations, sets up standards for the sale of energy, promotes the use of energy to improve the economy; library of 13,000 vols; Dir-Gen. SIRIPORN SAILASUTA; publs *Electric Power in Thailand* (1 a year), *Oil and Thailand* (1 a year), *Thailand Alternative Energy Situation* (1 a year), *Thailand Energy Situation* (1 a year).

Department of Mineral Resources: Ministry of Industry, Rama VI Rd, Bangkok 10400; geological mapping, mineral prospecting, mining, mineral dressing and metallurgical research; Dir-Gen. Dr PRABHAS CHAKKAPHAK.

Department of Science Service: Rama VI Rd, Bangkok 10400; tel. 2461387-95; f. 1891; testing, calibration and analysis services; research in food technology, industrial fermentation, pulp and paper raw materials, chemical engineering processes, air and water pollution control; research in ceramics; scientific and technological information service; library: see Libraries; Dir-Gen. CHODCHOI EIUMPONG; publ. *Journal* (3 a year).

Office of Atomic Energy for Peace: Vibhavadi Rangsit, Chatuchuk, Bangkok 10900; tel. 579-5230; fax 561-3013; f. 1961; 401 staff; library of 11,000 vols, 265 periodicals; Sec.-Gen. KRIENGSAK BHADRAKOM; publ. *OAEP Newsletter* (4 a year).

Thailand Institute of Scientific and Technological Research: Technopolis Klong 5, Klong Luang, Pathumthani, Bangkok 10120; tel. (2) 577-4157; fax (2) 577-4160; e-mail tistr@tistr.or.th; internet www.tistr.or.th; f. 1963; principal govt research agency; research depts: pharmaceuticals and natural products, food industry, chemical industry, biotechnology, building technology, electronics industry, engineering industry, materials technology, agricultural technology, energy technology, environmental and resources management, ecological research, Thai packaging centre; 690 staff; Governor Dr SURAPOL VATANAWONG (acting).

Libraries and Archives

Bangkok

Asian Institute of Technology Library: POB 4, Klong-Luang, Pathumthani 12120; tel. (2) 5245853; fax (2) 5245870; e-mail ref@ait.ac.th; internet www.library.ait.ac.th; f. 1959; provides services and training in library and information services; 250,000 vols, 900 periodicals; Head of Library BOONTHAREE PHOONCHAI.

Chulalongkorn University, Center of Academic Resources: Phyathai Rd, Bangkok 10330; tel. 218-2905; fax 215 3617; internet www.car.chula.ac.th; f. 1910; Central Library (995,264 vols), Thailand Information Center (73,400 vols), Audio Visual Center (14,269 vols), International Information Center (20,147 vols), Academic Development and Service Center; Dir Dr KAMALES SANTIVEJKUL (acting).

Kasetsart University, Main Library: Bangkok 10900; tel. (2) 9405834; fax (2) 5611369; e-mail lib@ku.ac.th; internet www.lib.ku.ac.th; f. 1943; 279,465 vols, 647 periodicals, 48,218 theses, 107,631 jackets of microjacket, 9,408 titles of audiovisual materials; Dir Mrs AREE THUNKIJJANUKIJ; publ. *Buffalo Bulletin* (4 a year).

Knowledge Centre: 196 Phahonyothin Rd, Chatuchak, Bangkok 10900; tel. (2) 579-1121; fax (2) 579-8594; e-mail klc@tistr.or.th; internet klc.tistr.or.th; f. 1961; documentation services to science and technology; 53,861 vols, monographs in Thai 18,864 vols, monographs in English 36,894 vols, periodicals (110 in English, 175 in Thai); Dir Dr NARUMOL RUENWAI.

Library of the Scientific and Technological Information Division, Department of Science Service: Ministry of Science, Technology and Environment, Rama VI Rd, Ratchathewi District, Bangkok 10400; tel. (2) 245-5271; fax (2) 247-9468; internet www.dss.moeste.go.th; f. 1918; 450,000 vols; spec. library and technical information services incl. patents, standards and trade literature; Dir MAYUREE PONGPUDPUNTH.

National Archives of Thailand: Fine Arts Dept, Samsen Rd, Bangkok 10300; tel. (2) 281-1599; fax (2) 281-5341; e-mail taweta2001@yahoo.com; f. 1952; historical and research resources services for official agencies, scholars and public; 5 major classes of documentary material: textual (10,274 ft), audiovisual (24,508 glass plates, 442,149 photographs, 808,693 film negatives and slides, 19,840 maps, drawings and blueprints, 2,496 posters, 4,427 calendars, 4,467 audio tapes, 3,941 video cassettes, 962 microfilm rolls, 734 CDs, 34 digital tapes), bound vols, govt publs and rare books (42,418 titles), documents, memory records and contemporary records (1,867 titles), clippings and news items (677,112 titles); Dir SUREERAT WONGSANGIM.

National Library of Thailand: Samsen Rd, Bangkok 10300; tel. 2817927; fax 2817543; e-mail nlt@nlt.go.th; internet www.nlt.go.th; f. 1905; nat. research library; depository for UN publs and UNESCO documents and collns; controls Int. Standard Serial Number (ISSN–Thailand), ISSN Regional Centre for Southeast Asia (ISSN-SEA); 2,496,505 vols, unique and rare collns: 163,607 rare books, 355,172 MSS, 132,239 indexes, 336,000 bibliographies, digitized materials: 53,655 rare books, 26,420 MSS, 221,839 microfilms, depository colln: 263,878 books, 325,246 periodicals, 738,449 newspapers, 11 nat. and spec. databases; Dir WILAWAN SAPPHANSAEN; publs *Thai National Bibliography*, *ISSN-SEA Bulletin*, *NLT Newsletter*.

Neilson Hays Library: 195 Suriwongse Rd, Bangkok; tel. (2) 2331731; fax (2) 2334999; e-mail neilson@loxinfo.co.th; internet www.neilsonhays.com; f. 1869; Librarian PRAPHEN CHITRAKDI.

Siriraj Medical Library, Mahidol University: Siriraj Hospital, Bangkok 10700; tel. 411-3112; fax 412-8418; f. 1897; 159,600 vols, 3,918 periodicals; Librarian K. CHOLLAMPE; publs *Siriraj Hospital Gazette*, *Journal of the Medical Association of Thailand*, *Newsletter* (12 a year).

Srinakharinwirot University, Central Library: Sukhumvit 23, Wattana, Bangkok 10110; tel. 258-4002; fax 260-4514; e-mail library@swu.ac.th; internet lib.swu.ac.th; f. 1954; audiovisual centre; campus in Ongkarak, Nakornnayok; 492,123 vols, 78,600 theses and dissertations, 14,910 periodicals; Dir Asst Prof. NONGNATH CHAIRAT; publ. *New Books of the Month—A Bibliography*.

Thammasat University Libraries: 2 Prachand Rd, Bangkok 10200; tel. (2) 6235171; fax (2) 6235173; e-mail tulib@tu.ac.th; internet www.library.tu.ac.th; f. 1934; 2,099,267 vols (social sciences and humanities, medical science, science and technology), 4,782 periodicals, 63 databases, 75,538 audiovisual items; 11 br. libraries; Dir SRICHAN CHANCHEEWA; publ. *Dom That* (2 a year).

United Nations Economic and Social Commission for Asia and the Pacific Library: United Nations Bldg, Rajdamnern Ave, Bangkok 10200; tel. (2) 288-1360; fax (2) 288-1000; e-mail escap_libref.unescap@un.org; internet www.unescap.org/unis/library/weblib.htm; economic and social development; 150,000 vols; Chief Librarian EVELYN DOMINGO-BARKER; publs *Asian and Pacific Bibliography* (1 a year), *ESCAP Documents and Publications* (1 a year).

Museum

Bangkok

National Museum Bangkok: Na Phra That Rd, Phra Borom Maha Ratchawang, Phra Nakhon, Bangkok 10200; tel. and fax 2241396; internet www.bangkok-museum.go.th; f. 1874; permanent exhibitions on Thai history, archaeology and art history of Thailand from the prehistoric period to the Bangkok period, decorative arts and ethnology; prehistoric artefacts, bronze and stone sculptures, costumes, textiles, ancient weapons, coins, wood-carvings, ceramics, royal regalia, theatrical masks and dresses, marionettes, shadow-play figures, funeral chariots, illustrated books, musical instruments, monuments, historic bldgs; lectures on Thai art and culture; library; Dir SOMCHAI NA NAKHONPANOM; publs *Guide to Old Sukhothai*, *Guide to the National Museum*, *Official Guide to Ayutthaya and Bang Pa-in*, *Thai Cultural Series*.

Universities and Technical Institutes

ASIAN INSTITUTE OF TECHNOLOGY

POB 4, Klong Luang, Pathumthani 12120
Telephone: (2) 5160110
Fax: (2) 5162126
E-mail: provost@ait.ac.th
Internet: www.ait.ac.th

Founded 1959

Ind. graduate institute, open to graduates from all countries; 2 semesters per year leading to Diploma; 4 semesters (2 years) course leading to a Masters degree; further 3 years leading to Doctoral degree
Language of instruction: English
Academic year: January to December

Pres.: Prof. MARIO T. TABUCANON (acting)
Provost: Prof. MARIO T. TABUCANON
Dir of Promotion Activities: SANJEEV JAYASINGHE
Sec.: KARMA RANA
Library: see Libraries and Archives
Number of teachers: 110
Number of students: 2,000

DEANS

School of Advanced Technologies: Prof. M. T. TABUCANON (acting)
School of Civil Engineering: Prof. CHONGRAK POLPRASERT (acting)
School of Environment, Resources and Development: Prof. CHONGRAK POLPRASERT
School of Management: Dr NAZRUL ISLAM (acting)

ASIAN UNIVERSITY

POB 15, Baan Amphur Post Office, Baan Amphur, Chonburi 20250
89 Moo 1, Highway 331 Rd, Huayyai, Banglamung, Chonburi 20260
Telephone: (38) 253700
Fax: (38) 253747
E-mail: admissions@asianust.ac.th
Internet: www.asianust.ac.th

Founded 1993
Private control
Language of instruction: English
Academic year: August to July (2 semesters)

Pres.: Dr VIPHANDH ROENGPITHYA
Vice-Pres. for Admin.: PANIT NILUBOL
Registrar: LADDA THIRAPORN
Librarian: PREEYAGARN JAISA-ARD

Number of teachers: 43
Number of students: 200

DEANS

Faculty of Business: Dr VIPHANDH ROENGPITHYA
Faculty of Engineering: Asst. Prof. Dr APICHAT TUNGTHANGTHUM
Faculty of Liberal Arts: CHARURAT TANTRAPORN

ASSUMPTION UNIVERSITY

Hua Mak Campus, 682 Ramkhamhaeng 24 Rd, Hua Mak, Bangkapi, Bangkok 10240
Bang Na Campus, 88 Moo 8, K. M. 26 Bang Na-Trad Rd, Samutprakarn 10540
Telephone: (2) 300-4543
Fax: (2) 300-4563
E-mail: abac@au.edu
Internet: www.au.edu

Founded 1969, became university in 1990, formerly Assumption Business Administration College
Private control (Catholic: Brothers of St Gabriel)
Language of instruction: English
Academic year: June to March

Pres.: Rev. Bro. BANCHA SAENGHIRAN
Vice-Pres. for Academic Affairs: Rev. Bro. VISITH SRIVICHAIRATANA
Vice-Pres. for Admin. Affairs: Dr CHAVALIT MEENNUCH
Vice-Pres. for Financial Affairs: Rev. Bro. ANUPATT P. YUTTACHAI
Vice-Pres. for Information Technology: Prof. Dr SRISAKDI CHARMONMAN
Vice-Pres. for Research Affairs: Asst Prof. Dr JIRAWAT WONGSWADIWAT
Vice-Pres. for Student Affairs: Rev. Bro. LOECHAI LAVASUT
Registrar: KAMOL KITSAWAD
Dir of Central Library: SUPRATA SINCHAISUK
Library of 500,000 vols
Number of teachers: 1,233
Number of students: 20,000
Publications: *ABAC Journal*, *ABAC Today*, *AU Journal of Technology*, *English Teacher*, *Galaxy*, *International Journal of Computer and Engineering Management (IJCEM)*, *Journal of Risk Management and Insurance*, *Prajna-Vihara (The Journal of Philosophy and Religion)*

DEANS

Graduate School of Business: Rev. Bro. VINAI VIRIYADIDHAYAVONGS
Graduate School of Computer Engineering Management (MS Programme): Dr CHAMNONG JUNGTHIRAPANICH
Graduate School of Computer Information Systems (MS Programme): Air Marshal Dr CHULIT MEESAJJEE
Graduate School of Computer Information Systems (PhD Programme): Asst Prof. Dr VICHIT AVATCHANAKORN
Graduate School of Counselling Psychology: Dr DOLORES DE LEON
Graduate School of Education: Assoc. Prof. Dr METHI PILANTHANANOND
Graduate School of Internet and E-Commerce Technology: Rear Admiral PRASART SRIBHADUNG
Graduate School of Philosophy and Religion: Asst Prof. Dr WARAYUTH SRIWARAKUEL
School of Architecture: PISIT VIRIYAVADHANA
School of Arts: Dr PIMPORN CHANDEE
School of Biotechnology: Dr CHURDCHAI CHEOWTIRAKUL
School of Business: Dr CHERDPONG SIBANRUANG
School of Communication Arts: CHALIT LIMPANAVECH
School of Engineering: Dr SUDHIPORN PATUMTAEWAPIBAL
School of Law: Assoc. Prof. PORNCHAI SOONTHORNPAN
School of Nursing Science: Dr NANTHAPHAN CHINLUMPRASERT
School of Risk Management and Industrial Services: BANCHA THEERASATIANKUL (acting)
School of Science and Technology: Asst Prof. SUPAVADEE NONTAKAO

BANGKOK UNIVERSITY

Rama 4 Rd, Klong-Toey, Bangkok 10110
Telephone: (2) 350-3500
Fax: (2) 249-6274
E-mail: buiao@bu.ac.th
Internet: www.bu.ac.th

Founded 1962 as Thai Polytechnic Institute; became Bangkok College 1965; present status 1984
Private control
Languages of instruction: Thai, English
Academic year: August to May
Academic year: June to March

Pres.: Asst Prof. Dr MATHANA SANTIWAT
Advisor to the Pres.: Prof. Dr POTE SAPIANCHAI
Vice-Pres. for Academic Affairs: Asst Prof. Dr TIPARATANA WONGCHAROEN
Vice-Pres. for Admin. Affairs: Assoc. Prof. LAKSANA SATAWEDIN
Vice-Pres. for External Affairs: Dr SUPONG LIMTHANAKOOL
Vice-Pres. for Financial Affairs: NARUMON OSATHANUGRAH
Vice-Pres. for Int. College: JARED DORN
Vice-Pres. for Planning and Devt: Dr QUANCHAI AUNGTRAKUL
Vice-Pres. for Student Affairs: SOMMAI DOKMAI
Dir of Library: Dr SHANANA RODSOODTHI
Library of 400,000 vols
Number of teachers: 1,104
Number of students: 26,884
Publications: *BU Academic Journal* (2 a year), *Executive Journal* (4 a year)

DEANS

Graduate School: Asst Prof. Dr SIVAPORN WANGPIPATWONG
International College: Assoc. Prof. Dr SUTHINAN POMSUWAN
School of Accounting: Dr SUTHA JIARANAIKULVANICH
School of Business Administration: Asst Prof. Dr VEERAPONG MALAI
School of Communication Arts: Asst Prof. Dr TERAPON POORAT
School of Economics: Dr UKRIST TUCHINDA
School of Engineering: Dr NATTHAPHOB NIMPITIWAN
School of Fine and Applied Arts: Asst Prof. SANSERN MILINDASUTA
School of Humanities: Asst. Prof. Dr SOMYOT WATTANAKAMOLCHAI
School of Law: Asst Prof. Dr AUNYA SINGSANGOB
School of Science and Technology: Dr WUTNIPONG WARAKRAISAWAT

BURAPHA UNIVERSITY

169 Saen Sook, Muang Chonburi 20131
Telephone: (38) 745-900
Fax: (38) 390-049
Internet: www.adm.buu.ac.th

Founded 1955
State control
Language of instruction: Thai
Academic year: June to March

Pres.: Prof. Dr SUCHART UPATHAM
Vice-Pres. for Academic Affairs: Assoc. Prof. Dr RENA PONRUENGPHANT
Vice-Pres. for Admin.: Assoc. Prof. BOONSERM POOHSANGUAN
Vice-Pres. for Finance and Property Affairs: Assoc. Prof. SUDA SUWANNAPIROM
Vice-Pres. for Int. Relations: Asst Prof. PICHAN SAWANGWONG
Vice-Pres. for Planning and Devt: VIRAT KARAVAPITTAYAKULA
Vice-Pres. for Research Affairs: Prof. Dr SOMSAK PHANTUWATTANA

Vice-Pres. for Student Affairs: Asst Prof. BOOMKA THAIKRA
Librarian: Dr KWANCHADIL PHISALPHONG
Library of 231,635 vols
Number of teachers: 657
Number of students: 10,000 (8,000 undergraduate, 2,000 postgraduate)
Publication: *Journal of Science, Technology and Humanity*

DEANS

Faculty of Education: Assoc. Prof. Dr CHALONG TUBSEE
Faculty of Engineering: Asst Prof. Dr WIRONGA RUENGPHRATHUENGSUKA
Faculty of Fine and Applied Arts: Prof. THESAKAI THONANOPKONG
Faculty of Humanities and Social Sciences: Assoc. Prof. Dr CHARAN CHAKANDANG
Faculty of Marine Technology: Dr PINCHAI SONCHAENG
Faculty of Nursing: Asst Prof. Dr SUNTHARAWADEE THEMPICHET
Faculty of Public Health: Assoc. Prof. Dr SASTRI SAOWAKONTHA
Faculty of Science: Assoc. Prof. Dr KASHANE CHALERMWAT
Faculty of Science and Art: Asst. Prof. RANOP PRAVATNGAM
Graduate School: Assoc. Prof. Dr PRATOOM MUONGMEE

CHIANG MAI UNIVERSITY

239 Huay Keaw Rd, Muang Dist., Chiang Mai 50200
Telephone: (53) 943665
Fax: (53) 942670
E-mail: irdcmu@chiangmai.ac.th
Internet: www.cmu.ac.th

Founded 1964
Autonomous Univ.
Languages of instruction: Thai, English
Academic year: June to May (3 semesters)

Pres.: Prof. Dr PONGSAK ANGKASITH
Vice-Pres. for Academic and Educational Quality Affairs: Asst Prof. Dr PONG-IN RAKARIYATHAM
Vice-Pres. for Gen. Admin. and Human Resource Management: Asst Prof. SUPHACHAI CHUARATANAPHONG
Vice-Pres. for Int. Relations and Alumni Affairs: Assoc. Prof. Dr JAKKAPAN SIRITHUNYALUG
Vice-Pres. for Planning, Financial and Property Management: Assoc. Prof. Dr PAIROTE WIRIYACHAREE
Vice-Pres. for Research and Academic Services: Asst Prof. Dr NAT VARAYOS
Vice-Pres. for Student Devt and Spec. Affairs: Assoc. Prof. AMNAT YOUSUKH
Vice-Pres. for Univ. Ccl Affairs and Information Technology: Asst Prof. SUPHACHAI CHUARATANAPHONG
Vice-Pres. for Physical and Campus Management: Asst Prof. Dr PRAYOTE OUNCHANUM
Registrar: Asst Prof. TODSAPORN PICHAIYA
Librarian: PENSUWAN NAKHAPREECHA

Number of teachers: 2,108
Number of students: 34,603 (623 int. students)
Publications: *Arts Journal* (2 a year), *Bulletin of Chiang Mai Associated Medical Sciences* (4 a year), *Chiang Mai Journal of Science* (4 a year), *Chiang Mai Medical Journal* (4 a year), *Chiang Mai University Journal of Natural Sciences* (2 a year), *Chiang Mai University Journal of Social Sciences and Humanities* (1 a year), *Chiang Mai Veterinary Journal* (2 a year), *CM Dental Journal* (2 a year), *Determination* (1 a year), *Educational Research Journal* (1 a year), *Engineering Journal Chiang Mai University* (3 a year), *Graduate Research Conference Proceeding*, *Journal of Agriculture* (3 a year), *Journal of East Review* (1 a year), *Journal of Economics* (3 a year), *Journal of Education* (2 a year), *Journal of Human Sciences* (1 a year), *Journal of Social Sciences* (1 a year), *Nursing Journal* (4 a year), *The Thai Feminist Review* (1 a year)

DEANS

Chiang Mai Univ. Int. College: Assoc. Prof. ANNOP PONGWAT
College of Arts, Media and Technology: Dr NOPASIT CHAKPITAK (Dir)
Faculty of Agriculture: Assoc. Prof. THEERA VISITPANICH
Faculty of Agro-Industry: Asst Prof. Dr CHARIN TECHAPUN
Faculty of Architecture: Dr EKKACHAI MAHAEK
Faculty of Associated Medical Sciences: Asst Prof. Dr WASNA SIRIRUNGSI
Faculty of Business Administration: BOONSAWART PRUGSIGANONT
Faculty of Dentistry: Assoc. Prof. THONGNARD KUMCHAI
Faculty of Economics: Dr PISIT LEEAHTAM
Faculty of Education: Assoc. Prof. Dr NIMANONG NGAMPRAPASOM
Faculty of Engineering: Assoc. Prof. Dr SERMKIAT JOMJUNYONG
Faculty of Fine Arts: Assoc. Prof. PONGDEJ CHAIYAKUT
Faculty of Humanities: Assoc. Prof. ROME CHIRANUKROM
Faculty of Law: Assoc. Prof. CHATREE RUENGDETNARONG
Faculty of Mass Communications: Assoc. Prof. KULISARA KRIWARAKARN
Faculty of Medicine: Assoc. Prof. NIWES NANTACHIT
Faculty of Nursing: Assoc. Prof. Dr THANARUK SUWANPRAPISA
Faculty of Pharmacy: Assoc. Prof. WANDEE TAESOTIKUL
Faculty of Political Science and Public Admin.: Assoc. Prof. PAIRAT TRAKARNSIRINONT
Faculty of Social Sciences: Dr SIDTHINAT PRABUDHANITISARN
Faculty of Veterinary Medicine: Assoc. Prof. Dr LERTRAK SRIKITJAKARN
Graduate School: Assoc. Prof. Dr SURASAK WATANESK

CHULALONGKORN UNIVERSITY

254 Phayathai Rd, Pathumwan, Bangkok 10330
Telephone: (662) 215-0871
Fax: (662) 215-4804
E-mail: info@chula.ac.th
Internet: www.chula.ac.th

Founded 1917
State control
Language of instruction: Thai
Academic year: June to March

Pres.: Prof. PIROM KAMOLRATANAKUL
Vice-Pres. for Academic Affairs: Asst Prof. M. R. KALAYA TINGSABADH
Vice-Pres. for Admin.: Assoc. Prof. CHESADA SANGSUBHAN
Vice-Pres. for Finance: Assoc. Prof. DUNUJA KUNPANITCHAKIT
Vice-Pres. for Information Technology: Asst Prof. BOONCHAI SOWANWANICHCHAKUL
Vice-Pres. for Int. Relations: Prof. KUA WONGBOONSIN
Vice-Pres. for Physical Resources Management: Assoc. Prof. LERSOM STHAPITANONDA
Vice-Pres. for Property Management: Assoc. Prof. Gr. Capt. PERMYOT KESOLBHAND
Vice-Pres. for Research and Innovations: Prof. KUA WONGBOONSIN
Vice-Pres. for Strategy and Planning: Assoc. Prof. Dr SITTICHAI TUDSRI
Vice-Pres. for Student Affairs: Assoc. Prof. TANIT TONGTHONG
Registrar: Assoc. Prof. PRADISTHA INTARAKOSIT

Library: see Libraries and Archives
Number of teachers: 2,427
Number of students: 20,419 undergraduate, 11,477 postgraduate
Publications: *Chula Samphan* (26 a year), *Data on Freshmen Entering Chulalongkorn University*, *Fact Book* (1 a year), *'Pra Keaw' Students' Handbook* (1 a year), *Research Journal* (1 a year), *University Newsletter* (4 a year)

DEANS

Faculty of Allied Health Sciences: Asst Prof. Dr VANIDA NOPPONPUNTH
Faculty of Architecture: Prof. Dr BUNDIT CHULASAI
Faculty of Arts: Asst Prof. Dr PRAPOD ASSAVAVIRULHAKARN
Faculty of Commerce and Accountancy: Assoc. Prof. Dr ANNOP TANLAMAI
Faculty of Communication Arts: Assoc. Prof. Dr YUBOL BENJARONGKIJ
Faculty of Dentistry: Assoc. Prof. WACHARAPORN TASACHAN
Faculty of Economics: Prof. Dr TEERANA PONGMAKAPAT
Faculty of Education: Prof. Dr SIRICHAI KANJANAWASEE
Faculty of Engineering: Assoc. Prof. Dr BOONSOM LERDHIRUNWONG
Faculty of Fine and Applied Arts: Assoc. Prof. Dr SUPPAKORN DISATAPUNDHU
Faculty of Law: Assoc. Prof. SAKDA THANITCUL
Faculty of Medicine: Prof. Dr ADISORN PATRADUL
Faculty of Nursing: Asst Prof. Capt. YUPIN AUNGSUROCH
Faculty of Pharmaceutical Sciences: Assoc. Prof. PINTIP PONGPECH
Faculty of Political Science: Prof. Dr CHARAS SUWANMALA
Faculty of Psychology: Asst Prof. Dr KAKANANG MANEESRI
Faculty of Science: Prof. Dr SUPOT HANNONGBUA
Faculty of Veterinary Science: Prof. Dr MONGKOL TECHAKUMPHU
Graduate School: Assoc. Prof. Dr PORNPOTE PIUMSOMBOON
School of Sport Science: Assoc. Prof. Dr VIJIT KANUNGSUKKASEM
Petroleum and Petrochemical College: Asst Prof. POMTHONG MALAKUL
College of Population Studies: Assoc. Prof. VIPAN PRACHUABMOH
College of Public Health Science: Prof. Dr SURASAK TANEEPANICHSKUL

DHURAKIJPUNDIT UNIVERSITY

110/1-4 Prachacheun Rd, Laksi, Bangkok 10210
Telephone: (2) 9547300
Fax: (2) 9547904
E-mail: dpuic@dpu.ac.th
Internet: www.dpu.ac.th

Founded 1968
Private control
Languages of instruction: Chinese, Thai, English
Academic year: June to February (2 semesters)

Pres.: Assoc. Prof. Dr VARAKORN SAMAKOSES
Registrar: Aj. BUPHA ANUNTARASIRICHAI
Librarian: Aj. SUWAKHON SIRIWONGWORAWAT

Library of 213,396 vols
Number of teachers: 555

Number of students: 31,444
Publication: *Sudhiparidhasna* (Univ. journal)

DEANS

Faculty of Accounting: Asst Prof. UMPORN TEINGTRAKUL
Faculty of Arts and Sciences: Assoc. Prof. PREEYA UNARATANA
Faculty of Business Administration: Assoc. Prof. Dr UPATHAM SAISANGJAN
Faculty of Communication Arts: Aj. PRADIT RATANAWIJARN
Faculty of Economics: DUANGCHAN WORAKAMIN
Faculty of Engineering: Asst Prof. Dr NIT PETCHARAK
Faculty of Fine and Applied Arts: Assoc. Prof. Dr SULUCK SRIBURI
Faculty of Information Technology: Assoc. Prof. Dr NUEHAREE PREMEHAISWADI
Faculty of Law: Prof. Dr KANIT NAVAKORN
Faculty of Public Admin.: POONSAK PRANOOTNARAPARN
Graduate School: Assoc. Prof. Dr THANIDA CHITANOMRAT
Int. College: Prof. Dr CHARLES S. NEWTON
Language Institute: Dr HARALD KRAUS

HUACHIEW CHALERMPRAKIET UNIVERSITY

18/18 Bangna-Trad Rd, Bangplee Dist., Samutprakarn 10540
Telephone: (2) 312-6300
Fax: (2) 312-6237
E-mail: regist@hcu.ac.th
Internet: www.hcu.ac.th

Founded 1942 as Midwifery School; became a college 1981; present name and status 1992
Private control
Language of instruction: Thai
Academic year: June to May

Pres.: Assoc. Prof. Dr PRACHAK POOMVISES
Vice-Pres.: PISANU RIENMAHASARN
Vice-Pres. for Academic Affairs: Asst. Prof. Dr URAIPAN JANVANICHYANONT
Vice-Pres.: SANGUANSRI KENGKIJKOSOL
Vice Pres.: Assoc. Prof. Dr CHANTRA SHAIPANICH (acting)
Vice-Pres. for Planning and Devt: Assoc. Prof. Dr CHIRADET OUSAWAT
Vice-Pres. for Student Affairs: KANOGWAN CHANTHANAMONGKOL
Dir of Library and Information Centre: SUCHANYA CHIRABANDHU

Library of 209,803 books, 1,157 periodicals
Number of teachers: 476
Number of students: 8,934 (8,620 undergraduate, 226 postgraduate, 88 certificate)

DEANS

Faculty of Business Administration: Prof. Lt-Gen. PISANU RIENMAHASARN
Faculty of Communication Arts: Asst. Prof. Dr URAIPAN JANVANICHYANONT
Faculty of Law: Lt. Gen. SUPHOT NA BANGCHANG
Faculty of Liberal Arts: Assoc. Prof. Dr SUREERAT MARAPO
Faculty of Medical Technology: Asst Prof. ISAYA JANWITHYANUCHIT
Faculty of Nursing: Assoc. Prof. Dr JARIYAWAT KOMPAYAK
Faculty of Pharmaceutical Science: Assoc. Prof. Dr CHANTRA SHAIPANICH
Faculty of Physical Therapy: BOONRAT NGOWTRAKUL
Faculty of Public and Environmental Health: Asst. Prof. Dr SAOVALUG LUKSAMIJARULKUL
Faculty of Science and Technology: Assoc. Prof. RACHNEE RUKVEERADHUM

Faculty of Social Work and Social Welfare: NUANYAI WATTANAKOON
Faculty of Traditional Chinese Medicine: UDOM CHANTHARAKSRI
Graduate School: Asst Prof. PANNARAI SANGVICHIEN

KASETSART UNIVERSITY

Bangkhen Campus: 50 Phahonyothin Rd, Chatuchak, Bangkok 10900
Kamphaeng Saen Campus: 1 Moo 6, Tambon Kamphaeng Saen, Amphur Kamphaeng Saen, Nakhon Pathom 73140
Si Racha Campus: 199 Moo 6, Sukhumvit Rd, Tambon Tungsukla, Amphur Si Racha, Changwat Chon Buri 20230
Chalermprakiat Sakon Nakhon Province Campus: 59 Moo 1, Chiangkrua, Muang, Sakonnakhon 47000
Telephone: (2) 942-8171
Fax: (2) 942-8170
E-mail: fro@ku.ac.th
Internet: www.ku.ac.th

Founded 1943
State control
Languages of instruction: Thai, English
Academic year: June to March (two semesters)

Pres.: Assoc Prof. VUDTECHAI KAPILAKANCHANA
Vice-Pres. for Academic Affairs: Assoc. Prof. Dr PANIT KHEMTHONG
Vice-Pres. for Central Management: Asst Prof. MAYUREE THESPOL
Vice-Pres. for Chalermprakiat Sakon Nakorn Campus: Assoc. Prof. Dr PONGSAK SURIYAVANAGUL
Vice-Pres. for Information Technology: Assoc Prof. YUEN POOVARAWAN
Vice-Pres. for Int. Affairs: Assoc. Prof. Dr SORNPRACH THANISAWANYANGKURA
Vice-Pres. for Kamphaeng Saen Campus: Assoc. Prof. Dr CHAWALIT HONGPRAYOON
Vice-Pres. for Financial and Property Management: PREUNGBOON CHAKKAPHAK
Vice-Pres. for Quality Assurance: Assoc. Prof. KAMOLPUN NAMWONGPROM
Vice-Pres. for Research: Assoc. Prof. Dr SAMAKKEE BOONYAWAT
Vice-Pres. for Si Racha Campus: Assoc. Prof. Dr CHAIWAT CHAIKUL
Vice-Pres. for Spec. Projects: Asst Prof. THANWA JITSANGUAN
Vice-Pres. for Student Affairs and Physical Devt: NIPHON LIMLEAMTHONG
Registrar: Assoc. Prof. SAKDA INTRRAVICHAI
Librarian: AREE THUNKIJJANUKIJ

Library: see Libraries and Archives
Number of teachers: 3,166
Number of students: 57,116 (45,810 undergraduate, 11,306 postgraduate)
Publications: *Kasetsart Journal* (natural sciences edn, 4 a year; social sciences edn, 3 a year), *Knowledge of the Land* (university's academic affairs, in English, 1 a year)

DEANS

College of Environment: KASEM CHUNKAO
College of Graduate Studies (Si Racha): SRION SOMBOONSUP
Faculty of Agriculture: VICHAN VICHUKIT
Faculty of Agriculture (Kamphaeng Saen): VORAVIT SIRIPHOLVAT
Faculty of Agro-Industry: SIREE CHAISERI
Faculty of Architecture: RATCHOT CHOMPUNICH
Faculty of Business Administration: SAMPAN HANPAYON
Faculty of Economics: SAROJ AUNGSUMALIN
Faculty of Education: PORNTIP CHAISO
Faculty of Education and Development Sciences: BUNJOB PIROMKAM

Faculty of Engineering: NONTAWAT JUNJAREON
Faculty of Engineering (Kamphaeng Saen): BANCHA KWANYUEN
Faculty of Engineering (Si Racha): KIATYUTH KVEEYARN
Faculty of Fisheries: SURIYAN TUNKIJJANUKIJ
Faculty of Forestry: WANCHAI ARUNPRAPARUT
Faculty of Humanities: WILAISAK KINGKHAM
Faculty of Liberal Arts and Management Science: ORASA ARAMRATTANA
Faculty of Liberal Arts and Science: CHANAN SUDSUKH
Faculty of Management Sciences: AMNART THEERAVANICH
Faculty of Natural Resources and Agro-Industry: NITSRI SANGDUEN
Faculty of Resources and Environment: RUJA ARUNBANJERDKUL
Faculty of Science: SURAPOL PATHARAKORN
Faculty of Science and Engineering: SUPAKIT NONTANANANDH
Faculty of Social Science: MANITPOL URABUNNUALCHAT
Faculty of Sport Sciences: SIRIPORN SASIMONTONKUL
Faculty of Veterinary Medicine: THAVAJCHAI SAKPUARAM
Faculty of Veterinary Technology: WORAWUT RERKAMNUAYCHOKE
Graduate School: GUNJANA THEERAGOOL
International Maritime College: SUPIT UMNUAY

PROFESSORS

ATTATHOM, T., Entomology
CHANDRAPATYA, A., Entomology
CHAREONVIRIYAPHAP, T., Entomology
HORMCHAN, P., Entomology
KAMDEE, D., Philosophy and Religion
KANCHANALAI, T., Civil Engineering
KETSA, S., Horticulture
LAOHAKOSOL, V., Mathematics
LIMTONG, S., Microbiology
LIMTRAKUL, J., Chemistry
MAKARABHIROM, K., English Literature
NAIVIKUL, O., Food Science and Technology
NA-NAKORN, U., Aquaculture
PANICHSAKPATANA, S., Soil Science
PONGTONGKAM, P., Genetics
ROADRANGKA, V., Education
ROJANARIDPICHED, C., Agronomy
RUJOPAKARN, W., Transportation Engineering
SIRIPHANICH, J., Horticulture
SRINIVES, P., Agronomy
SUPRASERT, A., Anatomy
TASANACHAIKUL, N., Political Science and Public Administration
TUDSRI, S., Agronomy
YINGJAJAVAL, S., Soil Physics
YONGSMITH, B., Microbiology

KHON KAEN UNIVERSITY

123 Mitraparb Rd, Amphur Muang, Khon Kaen 40002
Telephone: (4320) 222241
Fax: (4324) 1216
Internet: www.kku.ac.th

Founded 1964
State control
Language of instruction: Thai
Academic year: June to March (two semesters)

Pres.: Assoc. Prof. Dr SUMON SAKOLCHAI
Vice-Pres. for Academic and Int. Affairs: Assoc. Prof. Dr KUTHILDA TUAMSUK
Vice-Pres. for Admin. Affairs: Assoc. Prof. DUMRONG HORMDEE
Vice-Pres. for Planning and Information Technology: Asst Prof. AROM TATAWASART
Vice-Pres. for Research: Asst Prof. PUSAN SIRITHORN

Vice-Pres. for Spec. Affairs: Asst Prof. WICHAI NEERATANAPHAN
Vice-Pres. for Student Affairs: Asst Prof. Dr ANAN HIRANSALEE
Vice-Pres. for Student Devt: Assoc. Prof. LIKHIT AMARTTAYAKONG
Vice-Pres. for Univ. Facilities: SURACHET MANGMEESRI

Library of 339,614 vols
Number of teachers: 1,810
Number of students: 18,457

Publications: *Academic Services Newsletter* (12 a year), *Architecture Journal* (4 a year), *Bulletin of Medical Technology and Physical Therapy* (4 a year), *Humanities and Social Sciences Journal* (4 a year), *Information* (2 a year), *I-San Journal of International Medicine* (4 a year), *Journal of Library and Information Science* (4 a year), *Journal of Learning and Teaching Competency* (4 a year), *Journal of Learning and Teaching Innovation* (4 a year), *Journal of Medical Technology and Physical Therapy* (4 a year), *Journal of Mekong Societies* (4 a year), *Journal of Nursing* (4 a year), *Kaen Kaset* (4 a year), *Khon Kaen Agriculture Journal* (6 a year), *KKU Daily News*, *KKU Dental Journal* (2 a year), *KKU Engineering Journal* (4 a year), *KKU Engineering Quarterly*, *KKU Health Sciences Center Bulletin* (6 a year), *KKU Health Sciences Center Newsletter* (52 a year), *KKU Journal of Education* (4 a year), *KKU Journal of Management Science* (1 a year), *KKU Newsletter* (26 a year), *KKU Quality Assurance Journal* (2 a year), *KKU VET Journal* (2 a year), *Science Journal* (4 a year), *Srinagarind Medical Journal* (4 a year)

DEANS

Faculty of Agriculture: Asst Prof. ASSANEE PRACHINBURAVAN
Faculty of Architecture: Asst. Prof. TANOO POLWAT
Faculty of Associated Medical Sciences: Assoc. Prof. YUPA UAVIJTIAROON
Faculty of Dentistry: Asst Prof. Dr NIWUT JUNTAVEE
Faculty of Education: Assoc. Prof. Dr SAMPAN PANPURK
Faculty of Engineering: Assoc. Prof. Dr WINIT CHINSUWAN
Faculty of Fine and Applied Arts: Assoc. Prof. Dr CHALERMSAK PIKULSRI
Faculty of Humanities and Social Sciences: Assoc. Prof. SRIPANYA CHAIYAI
Faculty of Management Sciences: Assoc. Prof. SUMETH KAENMANEE
Faculty of Medicine: Asst Prof. SUCHART AREEMITR
Faculty of Nursing: Asst Prof. Dr WANAPA SRITANYARAT
Faculty of Pharmaceutical Sciences: Assoc. Prof. SUMON SAKOLCHAI
Faculty of Public Health: Assoc. Prof. AROON JIRAWATKUL
Faculty of Sciences: Asst Prof. Dr WANCHAI SOOMLEG
Faculty of Technology: Asst Prof. Dr KRIENGSAK SRISUK
Faculty of Veterinary Medicine: Assoc. Prof. PRACKAK PUAPERMPOONSRI
Graduate School: Assoc. Prof. Dr SOMMAI PRIPREM

KING MONGKUT'S INSTITUTE OF TECHNOLOGY LADKRABANG

Chalongkrung Rd, Ladkrabang District, Bangkok 10520
Telephone: (2) 326-9157
Fax: (2) 326-7333
E-mail: inter@kmitl.ac.th
Internet: www.kmitl.ac.th

Founded 1960
State control
Academic year: June to March

Pres.: Assoc. Prof. PRAKIT TANGTISANON
Vice-Pres. for Academic Affairs: SUCHEEP SUKSUPATH
Vice-Pres. for Admin.: KITTI TIRASESTH
Vice-Pres. for Chumporn Campus: SURAPOL SETHABUTR
Vice-Pres. for Devt: AMNOUY PANITKULPONG
Vice-Pres. for Finance and Property: WILAIWAN WONYODPUN
Vice-Pres. for Int. Affairs: DUSANEE THANABORIPAT
Vice-Pres. for Planning: KULTHORN LUERNSHAVEE
Vice-Pres. for Student Affairs: PACHERNCHAI CHAIYASITH
Admin. Officer: RUAMPORN INTARAPRASONG
Dir of Central Library: OUEN PIN-NGERN

Library of 67,000 vols
Number of teachers: 808
Number of students: 15,052

Publications: *IT Journal* (2 a year), *Journal* (2 a year), *Journal of Science—Ladkrabang* (2 a year), *Ladkrabang Engin* (4 a year), *Research Abstracts* (irregular)

DEANS

Faculty of Agricultural Technology: JUTARAT SETHAKUL
Faculty of Architecture: EKAPHONG CHULASANIE
Faculty of Engineering: TAWIL PAUNGMA
Faculty of Industrial Education: PREEYAPORN WONGANUTROHD
Faculty of Information Technology: SURASIT VANNAKRAIROJN
Faculty of Science: THEERAWAT MONGKOLAUSSAWARATNA
Graduate School: MANAS SANGWORASIL

KING MONGKUT'S INSTITUTE OF TECHNOLOGY NORTH BANGKOK

1518 Pibulsongkram Rd, Bangsue, Bangkok 10800
Telephone: (2) 913-2500
Fax: (2) 587-4350
E-mail: iro@kmitnb.ac.th
Internet: www.kmitnb.ac.th
Founded 1959
State control
Languages of instruction: Thai, English
Academic year: June to March

Pres.: Prof. Dr TERAVUTI BOONYASOPON
Vice-Pres. for Academic Affairs: Assoc. Prof. Dr CHANASAK BAITIANG
Vice-Pres. for Admin. and Int. Affairs: Asst Prof. WATANA PINSEM
Vice-Pres. for Finance: Asst Prof. ACHARA SUNGSUWAN
Vice-Pres. for Prachinburi Campus: Asst Prof. WORAWIT CHATURAPANICH
Vice-Pres. for Research and Quality Assurance: Assoc. Prof. CHARN THANADNGARN
Vice-Pres. for Student Affairs: Asst Prof. WITTAYA WIPAWIWAT
Vice-Pres. for Univ. Devt and Promotion: ARUN PUTHAYANGKURA
Registrar: SANGOB KONGKA
Dir of Central Library: MONTREE KHEMRACH

Number of teachers: 626
Number of students: 16,445

Publications: *Journal of King Mongkut's Institute of Technology North Bangkok* (in Thai, 6 a year), *Technical Education Development* (in Thai, 4 a year)

DEANS

College of Industrial Technology: Asst Prof. PREECHA ONG-AREE
Faculty of Agro-Industry: Asst Prof. MALEE SIMSRISAKUL (acting)
Faculty of Applied Arts: Assoc. Prof. SURAPHI TONSIENGSOM (acting)
Faculty of Applied Science: Asst Prof. WICHAI SURACHERDKIATI
Faculty of Engineering: Asst Prof. Dr SIRISAK HARNCHOOWONG
Faculty of Information Technology: Assoc. Prof. Dr MONCHAI TIANTONG (acting)
Faculty of Technical Education: Asst Prof. Dr PISIT METHAPATARA
Faculty of Technology and Industrial Management: PEERASAK SAREKUL
Graduate College: Asst Prof. Dr VIBOON CHUNKAG

KING MONGKUT'S UNIVERSITY OF TECHNOLOGY THONBURI

126 Pracha-utit Rd, Bangmod, Thungkruh, Bangkok 10140
Telephone: (2) 470-8000
Fax: (2) 427-9860
E-mail: int.off@kmutt.ac.th
Internet: www.kmutt.ac.th

Founded 1960 as Thonburi Technical Institute, combined with two other Institutes to form King Mongkut's Institute of Technology 1971, but regained autonomy as King Mongkut's Institute of Technology Thonburi 1986, present name and status 1998
State control
Languages of instruction: Thai, English
Academic year: June to March

Pres.: Assoc. Prof. Dr SAKARINDR BHUMIRATANA
Senior Vice-Pres. for Academic Affairs: Assoc. Prof. Dr SUVIT TIA
Senior Vice-Pres. for Admin. Affairs: Assoc. Prof. PRASERT KANTHAMANON
Vice-Pres. for Human Resources: Asst Prof. SUPANEE LERTTRILUCK
Vice-Pres. for Planning and Information: THANITSORN CHIRAPORNCHAI
Vice-Pres. for Property and Finance: Asst Prof. Dr TIPPAWAN PINANICHKUL
Vice-Pres. for Research: Asst Prof. Dr BUNDIT FUNGTAMMASAN
Vice-Pres. for Student Devt: Assoc. Prof. Dr CHAOWALIT LIMMANEEVICHITR
Registrar: APAKORN PADUNGSATAYAWONG

Library of 120,000 books, 2,200 periodicals, 2,000 CD-ROMs, 14 online databases
Number of teachers: 576
Number of students: 12,453

Publication: *Research and Development Journal* (4 a year)

DEANS

Faculty of Engineering: Assoc. Prof. Dr BUNCHAREON SIRINAOWAKUL
Faculty of Science: Assoc. Prof. Dr WORANUJ KIRDSINCHAI
Graduate School of Management and Innovation: Asst. Prof. Dr PASIT LORTERAPONG
Joint Graduate School of Energy and Environment: Assoc. Prof. Dr BUNDIT FUNGTHAMMASAN
School of Architecture and Design: MICHAEL PAIRPOL
School of Bioresources and Technology: Assoc. Prof. NARUMON JEYASHOKE
School of Energy, Environment and Materials: Dr PATTANA RAKKAWAMSUK
School of Industrial Education and Technology: Assoc. Prof. Dr SITTICHAI KAEWKUEKOOL
School of Information Technology: Asst Prof. Dr BORWORN PAPASRATORN
School of Liberal Arts: Asst Prof. Dr PORNAPIT DARASAWANG

PROFESSORS

CHUCHEEPSAKUL, S., Civil Engineering
CHULLABODHI, C., Energy Management Technology

JIRARATANANON, R., Chemical Engineering
SOPONRONNARIT, S., Energy Technology
WONGWISES, S., Mechanical Engineering

KRIRK UNIVERSITY

43/1111 Ram-Indra Rd, Bangkhem, Bangkok 10220
Telephone: (2) 552-3500
Fax: (2) 552-3511
E-mail: phakaphan@krirk.ac.th
Internet: www.krirk.ac.th
Founded 1952
Private control
Academic year: June to May
President: DHATTONG VIRIYAVEJAKUL
Vice-Presidents: BENJA MANGALAPRUEK, Assoc. Prof. Dr MANOON PAHIRAH
Library of 68,000 books, 419 periodicals
Number of teachers: 130
Number of students: 3,445 (2,955 undergraduate, 490 postgraduate)

DEANS

Faculty of Business Administration: SANONG DEPRADIT
Faculty of Communication Arts and Liberal Arts: Prof. Maj.-Gen. SANITPONG KHEMTONG
Faculty of Economics: Asst Prof. Dr BUNSERM BUNCHAROENPOL
Faculty of Law: Pol. Maj.-Gen. Dr SAWADI SORALUM
Graduate School: Assoc. Prof. Dr MANOON PAHIRAH (acting)

MAE FAH LUANG UNIVERSITY

333 Moo 1, Muang Dist., Chiangrai 57100
Telephone: (53) 916-000
Fax: (53) 916-031
E-mail: pr@mfu.ac.th
Internet: www.mfu.ac.th
Founded 1998
Public Autonomous University
Academic year: June to March (2 semesters)
Schools of agricultural technology, biotechnology, information technology, liberal arts, management science and science.
Pres.: Assoc. Prof. Dr VANCHAI SIRICHANA (acting)
Vice-Pres.: Assoc. Prof. Dr TED TESPRATEEP, Asst Prof. PRITANA PRADIPASEAN, PORNTHIP PHUTIYOTHIN, Assoc. Prof. NAREEWAN CHINTAKANOND, Assoc. Prof. GANNAGA SATITTADA, Assoc. Prof. Group Capt. YUTANA TRA-NGARN
Library Dir: Dr PATHA SUWANNARAT
Library of 200,000 vols
Number of teachers: 350
Number of students: 9,186 (59 diploma, 8,183 undergraduate, 944 postgraduate)

DEANS

School of Agro-Industry: Assoc. Prof. Dr ORAPIN BHUMIBHAMON
School of Anti-Ageing and Regenerative Medicine: Prof. Dr THAMTHIWAT NARARATWANCHAI
School of Cosmetic Science: Assoc. Prof. Dr PANVIPA KRISDAPHONG
School of Health Science: Dr SAMRUENG KANJANAMETHAKUL
School of Information Technology: Group Capt. Dr THONGCHAI YOOYATIVONG
School of Law: Assoc. Prof. Dr CHALOR WONGWATTANAPHIKULA
School of Liberal Arts: Assoc. Prof. CHAKRAPAND WONGBURANAVART
School of Management: Assoc. Prof. Dr CHUTA MANUSPHAIBOON
School of Nursing: Assoc. Prof. SUPRANEE ATHASERI
School of Science: Prof. Dr SIRIWAT WONGSIRI

MAEJO UNIVERSITY

Sansai, Chiang Mai 50290
Telephone: (53) 873-000
Fax: (53) 498-861
Internet: www.mju.ac.th
Founded 1934; present name 1992 (fmrly Maejo Institute of Agricultural Technology)
State control
Language of instruction: Thai
Academic year: June to March
Pres.: Prof. Dr THEP PHONGPARNICH
Vice-Pres. for Admin.: Prof. ARKORN KANJANAPHACHOT, Asst. Prof. Dr CHAMNIAN YOSRAJ
Vice-Pres. for Assets and Spec. Affairs: PRAMOTE KLIBNGERN
Vice-Pres. for Education Quality Standards: Asst. Prof. PRASAN WONGMANEERUNG
Vice-Pres. for Information Technology and Communications: Asst. Prof. Dr. SIRICHAI UNSRISONG
Vice-Pres. for Planning and Int. Affairs: Prof. Dr NUMCHAI THANUPON
Vice-Pres. for Research and Academic Affairs: Assoc. Prof. Dr CHALERMCHAI PUNYADEE
Vice-Pres. for Student Devt and Alumni Relations: Prof. MANAS GUMPUKUL, Assoc. Prof. ARKOM KANJANAPHACHOTE (acting)
Registrar: KRISSADA BHACKDEE
Librarian: WASSANA PHONGPAL
Library of 1,357 vols, 1,032 periodicals
Number of teachers: 1,190
Number of students: 12,925
Publications: *Journal of Agricultural Research and Extension* (6 a year, in Thai, with English summaries), *Maejo International Journal of Science and Technology*, *Maejo Journal* (6 a year, in Thai)

DEANS

Faculty of Agricultural Business: Asst. Prof. Dr PRAPHANT OSATHAPHANT
Faculty of Architecture and Environmental Design: SIRICHAI HONGVITYAKORN
Faculty of Business Admin.: BOONSOM SUKHAJIT
Faculty of Economics: Asst Prof. THANARUG MECKHAYAI
Faculty of Engineering and Agro-Industry: RACHATA CHEUVIROJ
Faculty of Fisheries Technology and Aquatic Resources: Assoc. Prof. Dr KRIANGSAK MENG-AMPAN
Faculty of Information and Communication: Assoc. Prof. Dr WITTAYA DAMRONGKIATTISAK
Faculty of Liberal Arts: Asst Prof. Dr SAOWALUCK CHAYTAWEEP
Faculty of Science: Asst Prof. PHUENGPORN NIUMSUP
School of Admin. Science: PRADTANA YOSSUCK
School of Tourism Devt: Assoc. Prof. Dr WEERAPON THONGMA

MAHANAKORN UNIVERSITY OF TECHNOLOGY

51 Cheum Sampan Rd, Nong Chok, Bangkok 10530
E-mail: www@mut.ac.th
Internet: www.mut.ac.th
Founded 1990 as Mahanakorn College
Chancellor: Prof. Dr YONGYUT SATJAVANIT
Vice-Chancellor: YOUNGSAK KANATANAVANIT
Depts of accountancy, anatomy, business communication arts, business computer, chemical engineering, chemistry, civil engineering, computer engineering, control and instrument engineering, electrical engineering, electrical power engineering, finance and banking, industrial management, management, marketing, mathematics, mechanical engineering, microbiology, parasitology, pathology, pharmacology, physics, physiology, telecommunication engineering.

MAHASARAKHAM UNIVERSITY

Tambon Kamriang, Kantarawichai Dist., Maha Sarakham 44150
Telephone and fax (43) 75-4241
E-mail: iroffice@msu.ac.th
Internet: www.inter.msu.ac.th
Founded 1968 as Mahasarakham College of Education, became Mahasarakham campus of Srinakharinwirot Univ. in 1974, present name and status 1994
State control
Academic year: June to March
Languages of instruction: Thai, English
Pres.: Asst Prof. Dr SUPACHAI SAMAPPITO
Vice-Pres. for Academic Affairs and Research: Assoc. Prof. Dr PREECHA PRATHEPHA
Vice-Pres. for Admin.: Asst Prof. THIENSAK MAKKAPAN-OPAS
Vice-Pres. for Gen. Management: Asst Prof. PIYAPUN SANTAVEESUK
Vice-Pres. for Personnel Devt and Univ. Ccl Affairs: Assoc. Prof. THIENSAK MEKKAPAN-OPAS
Vice-Pres. for Spec. Affairs: Assoc. Prof. SURACHA AMORNPAN
Vice-Pres. for Student Affairs: Asst Prof. Dr SUJIN BUTDISUWAN
Dir of Academic Resource Centre: Dr SURITHONG SRISA-ARD
Library of 424,705 books, 2,171 periodicals
Number of teachers: 991
Number of students: 39,117

DEANS

College of Graduate Studies: Assoc. Prof. Dr PAITOOL SUKSRINGARM
College of Music: Assoc. Prof. Dr SUPANNEE LEAUBOONSHOO
College of Politics and Governance: Assoc. Prof. SIDA SORNSRI
Faculty of Accounting and Management: Assoc. Prof. PHAPRUKE USSAHAWANITCHAKIT
Faculty of Architecture, Urban Design and Creative Arts: PUANGPEN WIBOONSAWAT
Faculty of Education: Assoc. Prof. PRAWIT ERAWAN
Faculty of Engineering: Prof. Dr PRADIT TERDTOON
Faculty of Environment and Resource Studies: Assoc. Prof. Dr CHALEE NAWANUKHROH
Faculty of Fine and Applied Arts: NONTHIVATHN CHANDHANAPHALIN
Faculty of Hotel and Tourism Management: YUWADEE TAPANEEYAKORN
Faculty of Humanities and Social Sciences: Asst Prof. Dr SOMKIET POOPATWIBOON
Faculty of Informatics: Assoc. Prof. WIRAT PONGSIRI
Faculty of Medicine: Prof. Dr SOMPORN PHOTHINAM
Faculty of Nursing: Assoc. Prof. WALAIPORN NUNSUPHAWAT
Faculty of Pharmacy: Asst Prof. Dr CHANTIP KANCHANASIN
Faculty of Public Health: Prof. Dr SOMJIT SUPANNATAS
Faculty of Science: Assoc. Prof. JEERAPAN SUKSRINGARM
Faculty of Technology: Asst Prof. Dr RAMPAI KENSAKOO
Faculty of Tourism and Hotel Management: Asst Prof. SURACHET CHETTAMART
Faculty of Veterinary Medicine and Animal Science: Assoc. Prof. SAELI DONKAEWBUA

MAHIDOL UNIVERSITY

999 Phuttamonthon 4 Rd, Salaya, Phuttamonthon, Nakorn Pathom 73170
Telephone: (2) 2849-6230-3
Fax: (2) 2849-6237

E-mail: opinter@mahidol.ac.th
Internet: www.mahidol.ac.th

Founded 1888, as Siriraj Medical School; present name 1969

State control

Pres.: Prof. PIYASAKOL SAKOLSATAYADORN
Vice-Pres.: Prof. NAPATAWN BANCHUIN
Vice-Pres. for Academic Infrastructures Devt: Assoc. Prof. SUPACHAI TANGWONGSAN
Vice-Pres. for Admin. and Univ. Ccl Sec.: Prof. PASSIRI NISALAK
Vice-Pres. for Amnaj Charoen Campus: BOONSANONG BOONMEE
Vice-Pres. for Campus Devt: Asst Prof. NAKORN HAMAH
Vice-Pres. for Collaboration and Networking: Assoc. Prof. CHURNRURTAI KANCHANACHITRA
Vice-Pres. for Education: Assoc. Prof. SUNANTA VIBULJAN
Vice-Pres. for Finance and Assets: Assoc. Prof. SATIT HOTRAKITYA
Vice Pres. for Human Resources and Quality Devt: Prof. PRASIT WATANAPA
Vice Pres. for Int. Relations: Assoc. Prof. EMORN WASANTWISUT
Vice-Pres. for Law and Regulation Devt: Asst Prof. SINGHAPAN TONGSAWAS
Vice-Pres. for Nakhon Sawan Campus: Dr SOMPONG YOONGTONG
Vice-Pres. for Policy and Informatics Technology: Assoc. Prof. SORANIT SILTHARM
Vice-Pres. for Research and Academic Affairs: Prof. SANSANEE CHAIYAROJ
Vice-Pres. for Student and Univ. Affairs: Assoc. Prof. PREECHA SOONTRANAN

Library of 540,118 vols, 186,663 bound periodicals, 4,247 current periodicals, 15,961 audiovisual units, 97,786 theses, 79 online databases; 38,193 e-journals and 65,976 e-books, 21 libraries

Number of teachers: 3,598 (168 full profs, 791 assoc. profs, 822 asst profs and 1,817 Lecturers)

Number of students: 25,129

Publications: *Environment and Natural Resources Journal* (2 a year), *Journal of Applied Animal Science* (3 a year), *Journal of Health Education* (3 a year), *Journal of Language and Culture* (2 a year), *Journal of Nursing Science* (3 a year), *Journal of Population and Social Studies* (2 a year), *Journal of Public Health* (3 a year), *Journal of Public Health Admin.* (2 a year), *Journal of Public Health and Devt* (3 a year), *Journal of Public Health Nursing* (3 a year), *Journal of Ratchasuda College for Research and Development of Persons with Disabilities* (2 a year), *Journal of Religion and Culture* (2 a year), *Journal of Sahasat* (2 a year), *Journal of Tropical Medicine and Parasitology* (2 a year), *Mahidol Journal* (2 a year), *Mahidol Dental Journal* (3 a year), *Mahidol University Journal of Pharmaceutical Sciences* (4 a year), *MUMJ-Mahidol University Music Journal* (2 a year), *Music Journal* (12 a year), *Quality of Life and Law Journal* (2 a year), *Pacific Journal of Allergy and Immunology* (4 a year), *Ramathibodi Medical Journal* (4 a year), *Ramathibodi Nursing Journal* (4 a year), *ScienceAsia—Journal of the Science Society of Thailand* (4 a year), *Siriraj Medical Journal* (12 a year), *South-east Asian Journal of Tropical Medicine and Public Health* (4 a year), *The Journal: Journal of the Faculty of Arts* (2 a year), *Thai Journal of Phytopharmacy* (2 a year)

DEANS

Faculty of Dentistry: Assoc. Prof. THEERALAKSNA SUDDHASTHIRA
Faculty of Engineering: Asst Prof. RAWIN RAVIWONGSE
Faculty of Environmental and Resource Studies: Asst Prof. SITTIPONG DILOKWANICH
Faculty of Graduate Studies: Prof. BANCHONG MAHAISAVARIYA
Faculty of Information and Communication Technology: Assoc. Prof. JARERNSRI MITRPANONT
Faculty of Liberal Arts: Prof. PRASIT WATANAPA (acting)
Faculty of Medical Technology: Prof. VIRAPONG PRACHAYASITTIKUL
Faculty of Medicine, Ramathibodi Hospital: Prof. RAJATA RAJATANAVIN
Faculty of Medicine, Siriraj Hospital: Clinical Prof. TEERAWAT KULTHANAN
Faculty of Nursing: Assoc. Prof. FONGCUM TILOKSKULCHAI
Faculty of Pharmacy: Assoc. Prof. CHUTHAMANEE SUTHISISANG (acting)
Faculty of Physical Therapy: Assoc. Prof. ROONGTIWA VACHALATHITI
Faculty of Public Health: Assoc. Prof. PHITAYA CHARUPOONPHOL
Faculty of Science: Prof. SKORN MONGKOLSUK
Faculty of Social Sciences and Humanities: Assoc. Prof. WARIYA CHINWANNO
Faculty of Tropical Medicine: Assoc. Prof. PRATAP SINGHASIVANON
Faculty of Veterinary Science: Assoc. Prof. PARNTEP RATANAKORN

NARESUAN UNIVERSITY

Phitsanulok 65000
Telephone: (55) 261000
E-mail: international@nu.ac.th
Internet: www.nu.ac.th

Founded 1990
State control
Academic year: June to March

Library of 120,000 vols
Number of teachers: 867
Number of students: 21,435

Publications: *Naresuan University Journal*, *Naresuan University Newsletter* (12 a year).

NATIONAL INSTITUTE OF DEVELOPMENT ADMINISTRATION

118 Seri Thai Rd, Klongchan, Bangkapi, Bangkok 10240
Telephone: (2) 377-7400
Fax: (2) 375-8798
E-mail: nisnida@nida.nida.ac.th
Internet: www.nida.ac.th

Founded 1966
State control
Languages of instruction: Thai, English
Academic year: June to May (3 semesters)

Pres.: Assoc. Prof. Dr PREECHA JARUNGIDANAN
Vice-Pres. for Academic Affairs: Assoc. Prof. Dr SAGOL JARIYAVIDYANONT
Vice-Pres. for Admin.: Assoc. Prof. CHAMAIPORN KUNAKEMAKORN
Vice-Pres. for Planning: Prof. Dr CHARTCHAI NA CHIANGMAI

Library of 233,000 vols
Number of teachers: 155
Number of students: 10,391

Publications: *NIDA Bulletin* (6 a year), *Thai Journal of Development Administration* (4 a year)

DEANS

School of Applied Statistics: Assoc. Prof. Dr JIRAWAN JITHAVECH
School of Business Administration: Dr THAKOL NUNTHIRAPAKORN
School of Development Economics: Asst Prof. Dr WISARN PUPPHAVESA
School of Language and Communication: Assoc. Prof. Dr PATCHAREE POKASAMRIT
School of Public Administration: Prof. Dr SOMBAT THAMRONGTHANYAWONG
School of Social Development: Asst Prof. Dr TONG-ON MUNJAITON

DIRECTORS

Graduate Development Centre: Assoc. Prof. Dr SAGOL JARIYAVIDYANONT (acting)
Graduate Programme in Human Resource Development: Asst Prof. Dr MANEEWAN CHAT-UTHAI (acting)
Library and Information Centre: SIRIPORN SUWANNA
Research Centre: Assoc. Prof. Dr SAGOL JARIYAVIDYANONT (acting)
Training Centre: Dr BOORAPA CHODCHOEY (acting)

PROFESSORS

School of Applied Statistics (tel. (2) 375-8944; fax (2) 374-4061; e-mail jirawan@nida.nida.ac.th):

SUWATTEE, P., Statistics

School of Business Administration (tel. (622) 375-8874; fax (662) 374-3282; e-mail thakol@nida.nida.ac.th):

CHAMNONG, V., Organizational Behaviour

School of Public Administration (tel. (662) 375-1296; fax (662) 375-1297; e-mail sombat@nida.nida.ac.th):

CHANGRIEN, P., Political Science
PERMANJIT, G., City and Regional Planning
THAMRONGTANYAWONG, S., Public Policy and Planning

School of Social Development (tel. (662) 375-9111; fax (662) 375-0941; e-mail tangon@nida.nida.ac.th):

BHANTHUMNAVIN, D., Social Psychology
NORANITPADUNGKARN, C., Social Sciences
SMUCKARN, S., Social Psychology

PAYAP UNIVERSITY

Amphur Muang, Chiang Mai 50000
Telephone: (53) 851-478
Fax: (53) 241-983
E-mail: intexch@payap.ac.th
Internet: www.payap.ac.th

Founded 1974
Private control
Languages of instruction: Thai, English
Academic year: June to March (Thai Programme); September to April (English Programme)

Pres.: Dr BOONTHONG POOCHAROEN
Vice-Pres. for Academic Affairs: Dr YUWALAK CHIVAKIDAKARN
Vice-Pres. for Finance: Dr RUX PROHMPALIT
Vice-Pres. for Int. Affairs: MARTHA G. BUTT
Vice-Pres. for Planning and Devt: Dr TAWEESAK SUPASA
Vice-Pres. for Religious Affairs: Dr ESTHER WAKEMAN
Librarian: SUNTREE RATAYA-ANANT

Library of 125,100 vols
Number of teachers: 390
Number of students: 9,000

Publication: *Payap Journal* (1 a year)

DEANS

Faculty of Accountancy, Finance and Banking: MANIT PABUT
Faculty of Business Administration: YUVALUCK CHIVAKIDAKARN
Faculty of Humanities: Dr NARONG PRACHAKHESUWAT
Faculty of Law: Dr KHETTAI LANGKARPINT
Faculty of Nursing: KAMOLWAN DISABUT
Faculty of Science: DUANGDUEN POOCHAROEN
Faculty of Social Science: MONTHATHIP RUNGRUANGSRI
Faculty of Theology: Rev. WILLIAM J. YODER
Graduate School: Dr RATANAPORN SETHAKUL
International College: Dr TAWAT BUNREUANG

PRINCE OF SONGKLA UNIVERSITY

71/1 Moo 5 Thanon Karnjanavanich Tambon Kor-Hong, POB Hat-Yai, Hat-Yai Dist., Songkla 90110
Fax: (74) 211030 (Hat-Yai Campus); (74) 212828
E-mail: hatyai-pr@psu.ac.th
Internet: www.psu.ac.th
Founded 1967
State control
Languages of instruction: Thai, English
Academic year: June to March (two semesters)

Pres.: Assoc. Prof. Dr SUNTHORN SOTTHIBANDHU
Vice-Pres. for Academic Affairs (Hat-Yai Campus): Dr PAIRAT SA-NGUANSAI
Vice-Pres. for Academic Affairs (Pattani Campus): Asst Prof. Dr SUWIMON KIEWKAEW
Vice-Pres. for Devt: Asst Prof. Dr SUJITRA JARAJIT
Vice-Pres. for Devt Affairs (Pattani Campus): PRAMOTE KRAMUT
Vice-Pres., Hat-Yai Campus: Asst Prof. Dr METHI SUNBHANICH
Vice-Pres., Pattani Campus: Asst Prof. PRAPAN WISETRATTAKAM
Vice-Pres. for Planning and Devt: Assoc. Prof. UDOM CHOMCHAN
Vice-Pres. for Research and Int. Relations: Assoc. Prof. Dr PRASERT CHITAPONG
Vice-Pres. for Spec. Affairs (Pattani Campus): PANN YAUNLAIE
Asst Pres. (Hat-Yai Campus): Asst Prof. Dr SUJITRA JORAJIT (Academic Affairs), PARIPON PATTANASATTAYAVONG (Physical Facilities), Asst Prof. SUPOTE KOVITAVA (Student Activities), JEDSADA MOKHAGUL (Student Devt), Asst Prof. Dr WINIT JUNGCHAROENTHAM (System Devt)
Asst Pres. (Pattani Campus): Asst Prof. SUTHEP SANTIVARANON (Academic Affairs), SOMKIAT SUKNUNPONG (Admin.), PHAYAM PHETKLA (Int. Relations), Asst Prof. WERA MANUSAVANICH (Student Affairs)
Number of teachers: 1,428
Number of students: 13,048
Publication: *PSU Arts and Culture*

DEANS

College of Islamic Studies: Dr ISMA-AE ALEE (Dir)
Faculty of Agro-Industry (Hat-Yai Campus): Assoc. Prof. PAIBOON THAMMARATWASIK
Faculty of Dentistry (Hat-Yai Campus): KRASSANAI WONGRANGSIMAKUL
Faculty of Education (Pattani Campus): Asst Prof. Dr WIRAT THUMMARPORN
Faculty of Engineering (Hat-Yai Campus): PICHIT RERNGSANGVATANA
Faculty of Environmental Management Establishment Project (Hat-Yai Campus): Asst Prof. Dr CHADCHAI RATANACHAI
Faculty of Hospitality and Tourism: Assoc. Prof. MANAT CHAISAWAT (Dir)
Faculty of Humanities and Social Sciences (Pattani Campus): Asst Prof. PRAPAN WISETRATAKAN
Faculty of Management Science (Hat-Yai Campus): Asst Prof. Dr SOMPORN FUANGCHAN
Faculty of Medicine (Hat-Yai Campus): Assoc. Prof. PUNTIPYA SANGUANCHUA
Faculty of Natural Resources (Hat-Yai Campus): Assoc. Prof. Dr SOMKIAT SAITANOO
Faculty of Nursing (Hat-Yai Campus): Asst Prof. Dr SUNUTTRA TABOONPONG
Faculty of Pharmaceutical Science (Hat-Yai Campus): Asst Prof. Dr PITI TRISDIKOON
Faculty of Science (Hat-Yai Campus): Prof. PUANGPEN SIRIRUGSA
Faculty of Science and Technology (Pattani Campus): Asst Prof. PREECHA PONGBHAI
Phuket Community College: Asst Prof. PUVADON BUTTRAT (Dir)
Surat Thani Community College: SORAT MAGBOON (Dir)
Trang Province Educational Extension Project: Assoc. Prof. SOMKAEW RUNGIERDKRIENGKRAI (Dir)

RAMKHAMHAENG UNIVERSITY

Ramkhamhaeng Rd, Huamark, Bangkok 10240
Telephone: (2) 310-8118
Fax: (2) 310-8022
E-mail: admin@ram1.ru.ac.th
Internet: www.ru.ac.th
Founded 1971
State control
Languages of instruction: Thai, English
Academic year: June to March (two semesters)

Rector: Prof. RANGSAN SAENGSOOK
Vice-Rector for Academic Affairs and Research: Prof. Dr CHUTA THIANTHAI
Vice-Rector for Admin.: Assoc. Prof. PRASAT SANGASILP
Vice-Rector for Amnartcharoen Province Regional Campus: Asst Prof. CHALERMCHAI PIWRUANGNONT
Vice-Rector for Campus Affairs: Assoc. Prof. KIM CHAISANSOOK
Vice-Rector for Cultural Affairs: Dr WICHAI SUNGPRAPAI
Vice-Rector for Devt: Assoc. Prof. WIRAT SANGUANWONWAN
Vice-Rector for Educational Technology: Asst Prof. Dr PANYA SIRIROJ
Vice-Rector for Finance: Assoc. Prof. SOMCHINTANA SIVALI
Vice-Rector for Gen. Affairs: Assoc. Prof. ARUNTAVADEE PHATNIBUL
Vice-Rector for Int. Affairs: Assoc. Prof. RAMPAI SIRIMANAKUL
Vice-Rector for Khon Kaen Province Regional Campus: Assoc. Prof. VICHAI THARANONT
Vice-Rector for Legal Affairs and Property: Prof. SURACHAI SUWANPREECHA
Vice-Rector for Nakhornpanom Province Regional Campus: Asst Prof. VIBOON TOVANABOOT
Vice-Rector for Nakhornratsrima Province Regional Campus: Assoc. Prof. VISIT TAWEESET
Vice-Rector for Nakhornsrithammarat Province Regional Campus: Assoc. Prof. Dr AROM CHANUANCHIT
Vice-Rector for Policy and Planning: Assoc. Prof. MANOP PRAMANACHOTE
Vice-Rector for Prachinburi Province Regional Campus: Asst Prof. CHAMNAN TEMMUANGPUK
Vice-Rector for Prae Province Regional Campus: Assoc. Prof. KULYANEE TARASUEB
Vice-Rector for Public Relations: Assoc. Prof. Dr WISANU SUWANA-PERM
Vice-Rector of the Rector's Office: Assoc. Prof. Dr KHOSIT INTAWONGSE
Vice-Rector for Sri Sa Ket Province Regional Campus: WICHIAN CHUENCHOB
Vice-Rector for Student Affairs: Assoc. Prof. SUMETH KAEWPRAG
Vice-Rector for Sukhothai Province Regional Campus: Asst Prof. SAMRAN SOMBOONPHOL
Vice-Rector for Trang Regional Campus: Assoc. Prof. PETJARAPORN JANTARASUT
Vice-Rector for Univ. Affairs: Assoc. Prof SITTIPAN BUDDHAHUN
Vice-Rector for Uthaithani Province Regional Campus: Asst Prof. ROENGRAK JAMPANGOEN
Vice-Rector for Welfare: Assoc. Prof. NOPPAKUN KUNACHEVA
Number of teachers: 852
Number of students: 340,231 (329,599 undergraduate, 10,632 graduate)
Publication: *Ramkhamhaeng University Newsletter* (52 a year)

DEANS

Faculty of Business Administration: Prof. RANGSAN SAENGSOOK (acting)
Faculty of Economics: Assoc. Prof. VANCHAI RIMVITAGAYORN
Faculty of Education: Assoc. Prof. RAVIWAN SRIKRAMKRAN
Faculty of Engineering: Asst Prof. SUVAT SRIVITHAYARAKS
Faculty of Humanities: Assoc. Prof. Dr PIT SOMPONG
Faculty of Law: Assoc. Prof. JARAL LENGVITTAYA
Faculty of Political Science: Assoc. Prof. PRONCHAI DHEBPANYA
Faculty of Science: Assoc. Prof. SUPOTE CHAITIUMVONG

RANGSIT UNIVERSITY

52/347, Muang Ake, Phaholyothin Rd, Tambon-Lakhok, 12000 Pathum Thani
Telephone: (2) 997-2200
Fax: (2) 997-2200
E-mail: info@rangsit.rsu.ac.th
Internet: www.rsu.ac.th
Founded 1985
Private control
Languages of instruction: Thai, English
Academic year: May to April

Pres.: Dr ARTHIT OURAIRAT
Vice-Pres. for Academic Affairs: Asst Prof. Dr NARES PANTARATORN
Vice-Pres. for Admin.: DUMRONG INDHRAMEESUP
Vice-Pres. for Planning and Quality Devt: Asst Prof. Dr SUEBSANG PROMBOON
Vice-Pres. for Student Affairs: AKECHART SOMPONGSE
Library Dir: Dr MALIRAN PRADITTEERA
Library of 106,895 vols
Number of teachers: 703
Number of students: 13,713 (662 undergraduate, 13,051 postgraduate)
Publication: *Bulletin of Health, Science and Technology*

HEADS OF COLLEGES

Division of Art and Design:
- College of Architecture: Asst Prof. Dr NARUPOL CHAIYOT
- College of Art and Design: AUMNOUVUT SARASALIN
- Conservatory of Music: Dr DENNY EUPRASERT

Division of Engineering and Technology:
- College of Biotechnology: Asst Prof. Dr VARAPORN LAKSANALAMAI
- College of Engineering: Dr ARTAWIT OURAIRAT

Division of Humanities and Social Sciences:
- College of Accounting: Dr NIMNUAN KHAEWRAT
- College of Business Administration: Dr PHONGPHAT RAKAROM
- College of Communication Arts: ANUSORN SRIKAEW
- College of Economics: Dr ANUSORN TAMAJAI
- College of Education: Assoc. Prof. Dr RUJA PHOLSWARD (acting)
- College of Law: Dr SOMPHONG SUCHARITKUL
- College of Liberal Arts: Dr PIYASUDA MAWAI
- College of Social Innovation: WITAYAKORN CHIENGKUL
- College of Tourism and the Hospitality Industry: SEREE WANGPAICHITR
- Graduate College: Asst Prof. Plt. off. Dr WANNEE SOOKSATRA
- Institute of Public Administration: Assoc. Prof. Dr PATOM MANIROJANA

International College: Dr NUANANONG PANWANEE

Division of Medicine and Health Sciences:

College of Dentistry: Group Captain Dr SUCHADA WUTTAKANOK
College of Medical Technology: PISIT NAMJNTRA
College of Medicine: SURAWICH TATUWANAN
College of Nursing Science: Asst Prof. Dr AMPAPORN PUAVILAI
College of Optology: Dr WIT PREEDACHOTSUTTHI
College of Oriental Medicine: LVECHA WANARAT
College of Pharmacy: Assoc. Prof. Dr ORAPHAN MATANGKASOMBUT
College of Physical Therapy: Asst Prof. PORNPIMON CHANTARAWIROJ
College of Science: Assoc. Prof. Dr CHATCHAI TRAKULRUNGSI

SIAM UNIVERSITY

235 Petchkasem Rd, Phasi-Charoen, Bangkok 10160
Telephone: (2) 867-8088
Fax: (2) 457-6657
E-mail: siam@siam.edu
Internet: www.siam.edu

Founded 1973
Private control
Academic year: June to March

Pres.: Dr PORNCHAI MONGKHONVANIT
Vice-Pres. for Academic Affairs: Prof. Dr NIMNUAN SRICHAD
Vice-Pres. for Planning and Devt: Dr PAYUNGSAK JANTRASURIN
Vice-Pres. for Public Affairs and Cooperative Education: THANAVADEE BOONLUE
Vice-Pres. for Research: Prof. Dr NIPONE SOOKPREEDEE
Registrar: SURADEJ PRUGSAMATZ
Librarian: JIRAPAT HARNNUSSORN

Library of 161,561 vols
Number of teachers: 530
Number of students: 14,299

Publications: *Cultural Approach* (2 a year), *Engineering Journal of Siam University* (2 a year), *Journal of Nursing, Siam University* (2 a year), *Siam Business Review* (3 a year), *Siam University Law Journal* (1 a year), *Siam University Review* (6 a year)

DEANS

Graduate School of Business: Dr VICHIT SUPINIT
Graduate School of Communication Arts: Assoc. Prof. Dr THANAVADEE BOONLUE
Graduate School of Education: Assoc. Prof. Dr AMORNCHAI TANTIMEDH
Graduate School of Engineering: Dr VANCHAI RIJIRAVANICH
Graduate School of Information Technology: Assoc. Prof. Dr WICHIAN PREMCHAISWADI
Graduate School of Public Administration: Assoc. Prof. Dr SURAPOL KANCHANACHITRA
School of Business Administration: Dr SUMRIT TIANDUM
School of Communication Arts: Assoc. Prof. Dr SIRICHAI SIRIKAYA
School of Engineering: Assoc. Prof. SARAVUTH VORASUMANTA
School of Law: Dr SOMMAI CHANRUANG
School of Liberal Arts: Dr SUBORDAS WARMSINGH
School of Nursing Science: Assoc. Prof. ORNTIPA SONGSIRI
School of Science: Dr KANJANA MAHATTANATAWEE

SILPAKORN UNIVERSITY

22 Boromrachachonnani Rd, Taling-Chan, Bangkok 10170
Telephone: (2) 880-7374
Fax: (2) 880-7372
E-mail: webmaster@su.ac.th
Internet: www.su.ac.th

Founded 1943
State control
Language of instruction: Thai
Academic year: June to March (2 semesters)

Pres.: Dr UTHAI DULYAKASEM
Vice-Pres. for Academic and Research Affairs: Assoc. Prof. Dr MANEE LUANGTANA-ANAN
Vice-Pres. for Admin. Affairs: Asst Prof. RAPEEPUN CHALONGSUK
Vice-Pres. for Art and Culture: Asst Prof. YANAWIT KUNCHAETHONG
Vice-Pres. for Planning and Devt: Assoc. Prof. CHARUNPAT PUVANANT
Vice-Pres. for Student Affairs: PORNSAWAN AMARANONTA
Vice-Pres. for Quality Assurance in Education: Asst Prof. Dr RENU VEJARATPIMOL
Registrar: SAICHON SAJJANIT
Librarian: KANCHANA SUKONTHAMANEE

Library of 552,330 vols
Number of teachers: 1,016
Number of students: 22,340

Publication: *Viridian* (newsletter)

DEANS

Faculty of Music: THANATORN JIARAKUN
Graduate School: Assoc. Prof. Dr SIRICHAI CHINATANKUL
Silpakorn University International College (SUIC): Assoc. Prof. Dr SOMPID KATTIYAPIKUL (Dir)

CONSTITUENT CAMPUSES

Phetchaburi Information Technology Campus: 1 Moo 3, Cha-am, Pranburi Rd, Samphraya, Amphoe Cha Am, Phetchaburi 76120; tel. (3) 259-4043; fax (3) 259-4026

DEANS

Faculty of Animal Sciences and Agricultural Technology: Assoc. Prof. Dr KRIENGSAK POONSUK
Faculty of Information and Communication Technology: Asst Prof. CHAICHARN THAVARAVEJ
Faculty of Management Sciences: Asst Prof. Dr WANCHAO SUTANANTA

Sanamchand Palace Campus: 6 Rajamaka Nai Rd, Mueang Dist., Nakhon Pathom 73000; tel. (34) 253910; fax (34) 255099; Vice-Pres. Dr CHACORN VIPUSANAVANISH; Asst Pres. for Student Affairs Asst Prof. Dr BUSARAKORN MAHAYOTHEE; Librarian KANCHANA SUKONTHAMANEE

DEANS

Faculty of Arts: Asst Prof. Dr MANEEPIN PHROMSUTHIRAK
Faculty of Education: Assoc. Prof. Dr KANIT KHEOVICHAI
Faculty of Engineering and Industrial Technology: Asst Prof. Dr JESDAWAN WICHITWECHKARN
Faculty of Pharmacy: Assoc. Prof. Dr JURAIRAT NANTANIT
Faculty of Science: Asst Prof. Dr JARUNGSAENG LAKSANABOONSONG

Wang Thapra Palace Campus: 31 Na-Phra Lan Rd, Phra Nakhorn Dist., Bangkok 10200; tel. (2) 623-6115; fax (2) 225-7258; Vice-Pres. Asst Prof. SOMCHAI EKPANYAKUL; Asst Pres. for Student Affairs Assoc. Prof. TINNAKORN KASORNSUWAN

DEANS

Faculty of Archaeology: Assoc. Prof. SAYAN PRAICHARNJIT (acting)
Faculty of Architecture: Assoc. Prof. CHINASAK TANDIKUL
Faculty of Decorative Arts: Assoc. Prof. EAKACHART JONEURAIRATANA
Faculty of Painting, Sculpture and Graphic Arts: Assoc. Prof. PARINYA TANTISUK

SOUTH-EAST ASIA UNIVERSITY

19/1 Phetkasem Rd, Nona Khaem, Bangkok 10160
Telephone: (2) 807-4500
Fax: (2) 807-4528
E-mail: webmaster@sau.ac.th
Internet: www.sau.ac.th

Pres.: Assoc. Prof. Dr NARONG SINSAWASDI

Founded 1973 as South-East Asia College, univ. status 1992

Faculties of arts and sciences, business administration, engineering, law; graduate school; language institute

Library of 68,000 vols, 650 journals
Number of students: 5,191

SRINAKHARINWIROT UNIVERSITY

114 Sukhumvit 23, Bangkok 10110
Telephone: (2) 664-1000
Fax: (2) 258-4006
E-mail: ird@swu.ac.th
Internet: www.swu.ac.th

Founded 1954; univ. status 1974
State control
Language of instruction: Thai
Academic year: June to May

Pres.: Assoc. Prof. Dr SUMONTHA PROMBOON
Vice-Pres. for Academic Affairs: Assoc. Prof. Dr SAKCHAI NIRUNTHAWEE
Vice-Pres. for Admin. Affairs: Assoc. Prof. Dr PAISAL WANGPHANICH
Vice-Pres. for Arts and Culture: VINAI BHURAHONGSE
Vice-Pres. for Finance and Personnel: Assoc. Prof. Dr PINITI RATANANUKUL
Vice-Pres. for Int. Relations: Dr SUTASSI SMUTHKOCHORN
Vice-Pres. for Planning and Devt: Asst Prof. Dr CHAVANEE TONGROACH
Vice-Pres. for Research: Prof. Dr SERMSAK WISALAPORN
Vice-Pres. for Student Affairs: Asst Prof. MANEE THONGGOOM
Registrar: ORAPIN KAEWLAI
Dir of Central Library: Asst Prof. NONGNATH CHAIRAT

Library: see Libraries and Archives
Number of teachers: 1,523
Number of students: 16,877

Publication: journals in humanities, nursing, pharmaceutical science, physical education and science, each 2 a year

DEANS

Faculty of Dentistry: Assoc. Prof. Dr TIPAPORN VONGSURASIT
Faculty of Education: Assoc. Prof. Dr KHOMPET CHATSUPAKUL
Faculty of Engineering: AREE HANSUEBSAI
Faculty of Fine Arts: Prof. Dr WIROON TUNGCHAROEN
Faculty of Health Science: Assoc. Prof. Dr WITTAYA TONSUWONNONT
Faculty of Humanities: Asst Prof. SUPA PANCHAROEN
Faculty of Medicine: Assoc. Prof. ARUNWONG THEPCHATRI
Faculty of Nursing: Assoc. Prof. Dr TASSANA BOONTHONG
Faculty of Pharmaceutical Sciences: Lt-Col Dr NOPDOL THONGNOPNUA

Faculty of Physical Education: Asst Prof. PHAN JIARANAI
Faculty of Science: Dr YUVADEE NAKAPADUNGRUT
Faculty of Social Sciences: Asst Prof. KAWEE WORRAKAWIN
Graduate School: Assoc. Prof. Dr NAPAPORN HAWANONDHA

DIRECTORS OF RESEARCH INSTITUTES

Arts and Culture Research Institute: Asst Prof. AMNARD YENSABYE
Behavioural Science Research Institute: Assoc. Prof. Dr DUSADEE YOELAO
Institute of Asia Pacific Studies: Asst Prof. PLUPLUNG KONGCHANA
Institute of Eco-Tourism: Assoc. Prof. Dr PHYOM THAMABUTHRA
Institute of Environment and Resources: Assoc. Prof. Dr VINAI VEERAVATNANOND
Institute for Research for the Gifted and Talented: Asst Prof. PRIT SUPASETSIRI

SRIPATUM UNIVERSITY

Bangkhen Campus, 61 Phaholyotin Rd, Jatujak, Bangkok 10900
Telephone: (2) 579-1111
Fax: (2) 561-1721
E-mail: webspu@spu.ac.th
Internet: www.spu.ac.th

Founded 1970
Languages of instruction: Thai, English
Academic year: August to April

Pres.: RUTCHANEEPORN POOKAYAPORN PHUKKAMARN
Vice-Pres. for Academic Affairs: Asst Prof. Dr NIMNUAN SRICHAD
Vice-Pres. for Admin.: CHUA MAICHAROEN
Vice-Pres. for Student Affairs: SOPIT PANOMAI
Vice-Pres. for Technology: Assoc. Prof. Dr SUCHAI THANAWASTIEN
Library Dir: Asst Prof. Dr NAMTIP VIPAWIN

Library of 104,000 vols
Number of teachers: 493
Number of students: 16,442 (16,000 undergraduate, 442 postgraduate)

DEANS

Faculty of Accounting: KALAYAPORN BANMARUNG BURKE
Faculty of Architecture: Asst Prof. SUTHON VIRIYASOMBOON
Faculty of Business Administration: Dr KAMOL CHAIYAWAT
Faculty of Communication Arts: Assoc. Prof. ARUNEEPRAPA HOMSETHI
Faculty of Economics: SOMNUEK TANGEHAROEN
Faculty of Engineering: Assoc. Prof. NARONG U-THANOM
Faculty of Informatics: AMNUAY MUTHITAJAROEN
Faculty of Law: PARINYA PATHUMPONG
Faculty of Liberal Arts: Asst Prof. Dr GLORIA VIDHEECHAROEN
Graduate School: Dr NITINAI BUNNAG

SUKHOTHAI THAMMATHIRAT OPEN UNIVERSITY

Bangpood, Pakkred, Nonthaburi 11120
Telephone: (2) 503-2121
Fax: (2) 503-3607
E-mail: stou@samsorn.stou.ac.th
Internet: www.stou.ac.th

Founded 1978
State control
Language of instruction: Thai
Academic year: July to April (2 semesters)

Pres.: Prof. Dr IAM CHAYA-NGAM
Vice-Pres. for Academic Affairs: Assoc. Prof. Dr JUMPOL NIMPANICH
Vice-Pres. for Admin.: Assoc. Prof. NATEE KHLIBTONG
Vice-Pres. for Devt: Assoc. Prof. Dr CHOW ROJANASANG (acting)
Vice-Pres. for Operations: Assoc. Prof. CHUTIMA SACCHANAND
Vice-Pres. for Planning: Assoc. Prof. Dr CHOW ROJANASANG (acting)
Vice-Pres. for Services: Assoc. Prof. NATEE KHLIBTONG (acting)
Vice-Pres. for Spec. Affairs: Assoc. Prof. CHUTIMA SACCHANAND (acting)
Registrar: Assoc. Prof. Dr SOMSAK MEESAPLAK

Library of 651,000 vols, 1,930 periodicals
Number of teachers: 393
Number of students: 221,269

DEANS

School of Agricultural Extension and Cooperatives: Asst Prof. Dr PONGPHAN THIENHIRUN
School of Communication Arts: Assoc. Prof. SUMON YUESIN
School of Economics: Asst Prof. Dr SOMCHIN SUNTAVARUK
School of Educational Studies: Assoc. Prof. Dr SOMPRASONG WITTAYAGIAT
School of Health Science: Asst Prof. Dr ADISAK SATTAM
School of Home Economics: Assoc. Prof. Dr JUMPOL NIMPANICH (acting)
School of Law: THIENCHAI NA NAKORN
School of Liberal Arts: Assoc. Prof. Dr PAITOON MIKUSOL
School of Management Science: Assoc. Prof. SUNA SITHILERTPRASIT
School of Political Science: Assoc. Prof. ROSALIN SIRIYAPHAN
School of Science and Technology (pending official approval): Assoc. Prof. Dr JUMPOL NIMPANICH

SURANAREE UNIVERSITY OF TECHNOLOGY

111 University Ave, Muang Dist., Nakhon Ratchasima 30000
Telephone: (44) 224-141
Fax: (44) 224-4140
E-mail: cenintaf@ccs.sut.ac.th
Internet: www.sut.ac.th

Founded 1990
State control
Languages of instruction: Thai, English
Academic year: May to April

Rector: Prof. Dr WICHIT SRISA-AN
Vice-Rector for Academic Affairs: Assoc. Prof. Dr KASEM PRABRIPUTALOONG
Vice-Rector for Admin. Affairs: Assoc. Prof. Dr THAI TIPSUWANNAKUL
Vice-Rector for Devt: Assoc. Prof. Dr KANOK PHALARAKSH
Vice-Rector for Planning: Dr WISITPORN WATANAWATIN
Vice-Rector for Student Affairs: Asst Prof. Captain Dr KONTORN CHAMNIPRASART
Registrar: Asst Prof. Dr AIM-ORN TASSANASORN
Librarian: Assoc. Prof. Dr PRAPAVADEE SUEBSONTHI

Library of 55,000 books, 600 periodicals
Number of teachers: 205
Number of students: 4,623 (4,419 undergraduate, 204 postgraduate)

DEANS

Institute of Agricultural Technology: Assoc. Prof. Dr TERD CHAROENWATANA
Institute of Engineering: Asst Prof. Dr TAVEE LERTPANYAVIT
Institute of Medicine: Prof. VITOON OSATHANONDH
Institute of Science: Assoc. Prof. Dr TASSANEE SUKOSOL
Institute of Social Technology: Assoc. Prof. Dr KRICH SUEBSONTHI

THAKSIN UNIVERSITY

140 Moo 4 Tambon Khao Roop Chang, Muang Dist., Song Khla 90000
Telephone: (74) 311-885
Fax: (74) 324-440
E-mail: tsuinter@tsu.ac.th
Internet: www.tsu.ac.th

Founded 1996

Pres.: SOMBOON CHITPONG

Faculties of education, humanities and social sciences, science; institute of Southern Thai studies.

THAMMASAT UNIVERSITY

2 Prachand Rd, Bangkok 10200
Telephone: (2) 221-6111
Fax: (2) 224-8105
E-mail: inter@tu.ac.th
Internet: www.tu.ac.th

Founded 1934
State control
Languages of instruction: Thai, English
Academic year: June to February (2 semesters), summer session March to May

Rector: Prof. Dr SURAPON NITIKRAIPOT
Vice-Rector for Academic Affairs: Prof. Dr SIRILUCK ROTCHANAKITUMNUAI
Vice-Rector for Devt Planning and Technology: Asst Prof. Dr PRODPRAN SIRITHEERASAS
Vice-Rector for Financial Admin.: Asst Prof. SURASAK LIKASITWATANAKUL
Vice-Rector for Gen. Admin. (Lampang Center): Asst Prof. KAMONTHIP CHAMKRAJANG
Vice-Rector for Gen. Admin. (Rangsit Center): Assoc. Prof. GASINEE WITOONCHART
Vice-Rector for Gen. Admin. (Tha Prachan Center): Assoc. Prof. Dr UDOM RATHAMARIT
Vice-Rector for Int. Affairs: Assoc. Prof. Dr CHULACHEEP CHINWANNO
Vice-Rector for Personnel: Assoc. Prof. HARIRAK SUTABUTRA
Vice-Rector for Research Devt: Assoc. Prof. Dr PREECHA WANICHSETAKUL
Vice-Rector for Student Affairs: Asst Prof. Dr PARINYA THEWANARUEMITKUL
Registration Office Dir: Asst Prof. Dr VIRAVAT CHANTACHOTE
Librarian: SRICHAN CHANCHEEWA

Library: see Libraries
Number of teachers: 1,623
Number of students: 32,507

Publications: *Faculty Bulletin*, *Journal of Business Administration*, *Journal of Political Science*, *Social Work Journal*, *Thammasat Law Journal*, *Thammasat University Journal*

DEANS

College of Innovative Education: Assoc. Prof. M. R. PONGSVAS SVASTI
College of Interdisciplinary Studies: Assoc. Prof. Dr NANTANA RONAKIAT
Faculty of Allied Health Science: Prof. Dr VITHOON VIYANANT
Faculty of Architecture and Planning: Prof. Dr SANTIRAK PRASERTSUK
Faculty of Commerce and Accountancy: Assoc. Prof. Dr KULPATRA SIRODOM
Faculty of Dentistry: YUVABOON CHANCHAMCHAROON
Faculty of Economics: Assoc. Prof. Dr PATAMAWADEE SUZUKI
Faculty of Engineering: Assoc. Prof. Dr URUYA WEESAKUL
Faculty of Fine and Applied Arts: SUTHIDA KALAYANAROOJ

Faculty of Journalism and Mass Communication: Asst Prof. Dr PORNCHIT SOMBUTPHANICH
Faculty of Law: Prof. Dr SOMKIT LERTPAITHOON
Faculty of Liberal Arts: Assoc. Prof. Dr CHATCHAWADEE SARALAMBA
Faculty of Medicine: Assoc. Prof. CHITTINAD HAVANOND
Faculty of Nursing: Asst Prof. Dr SIRIPORN KHAMPALIKIT
Faculty of Political Science: Assoc. Prof. Dr SIRIPORN WAJJWALKU
Faculty of Public Health: Assoc. Prof. Dr NUNTAVARN VICHIT-VADAKAN
Faculty of Science and Technology: Assoc. Prof. SAITONG AMORNWICHET
Faculty of Social Administration: Asst Prof. Dr DECHA SUNGKAWAN
Faculty of Sociology and Anthropology: Asst Prof. PORNCHAI TRAKULWARANONT
Graduate School: Assoc. Prof. MANOON PAHIRAH
Pridi Banomyong International College: Assoc. Prof. Dr PIMPAN VESSAKOSOL
Sirindhon International Institute of Technology: Prof. Dr CHONGRAK POLPRASERT

UBON RATCHATHANI UNIVERSITY

University Administrative Building Warinchamrap, Ubon Ratchathani 34190
Telephone: (45) 288-398
Fax: (45) 288-398
E-mail: ira@ubu.ac.th
Internet: www.ubu.ac.th

Founded 1990
State control
Academic year: May to March

Pres.: Prof. Dr PRAKOB WIROJANAGUD
Vice-Pres. for Academic Affairs: Asst. Prof. Dr UTITH INPRASIT
Vice-Pres. for Admin.: SUPACHAI HATHONGKUM
Vice-Pres. for Facilities: NITISAK KAEWSENA
Vice-Pres. for Int. Relations: Prof. Dr PATAREEYA WISAIJORN
Vice-Pres. for Planning and Information: Asst. Prof. Dr MANOON SRIVIRAT
Vice-Pres. for Research and Academic Services: Asst. Prof. Dr KUNGWAN THUMMASAENG
Vice-Pres. for Student Affairs: THAI SANGTHEAN
Librarian: SUOACHAI HATHONGKHAM

Library of 170,734 books, 30,028 periodicals, 15,836 audio visuals
Number of teachers: 610
Number of students: 11,567 (11,052 undergraduate, 33 certificate, 366 masters and 116 doctoral)

DEANS

Faculty of Agriculture: Asst Prof. WATCHARAPONG WATTANAKUL
Faculty of Applied Arts and Design: Prof. Dr PRAKOB WIROJANAKUD (acting)
Faculty of Engineering: Prof. Dr SATHAPORN PHOKA
Faculty of Law: BUNLEU KONGCHAN
Faculty of Liberal Arts: Assoc. Prof. INTHIRA SAHEE (acting)
Faculty of Management Science: APICHAI PUNTASEN (acting Dir)
Faculty of Pharmaceutical Science: Assoc. Prof. NONGNIT TEERAWATANASUK
Faculty of Political Science: Prof. Dr YUWAT WUTTIMATEE
Faculty of Science: Asst Prof. JANPEN INTARAPRASERT

UNIVERSITY OF THE THAI CHAMBER OF COMMERCE

126/1 Vibhavadi Rangsit Rd, Bangkok 10320
Telephone: (2) 276-1040
Fax: (2) 276-2126
E-mail: nitima@morakot.nectec.or.th
Internet: www.utcc.ac.th

Founded 1940 as College of Commerce; present name and status 1984

Pres.: CHIRADET OUSAWAT

Library of 100,000 vols, 6,000 periodicals.

WALAILAK UNIVERSITY

222 Thaiburi, Thasala Dist., Nakhon Si Thammarat 80160
Telephone: (75) 384-000
Fax: (75) 384-258
E-mail: wu@praduu.wu.ac.th
Internet: www.wu.ac.th

Pres.: Dr SUPAT POOPAKA

Founded 1992
State control

Institutes of agricultural technology, allied health sciences and public health, engineering and resources management, information science, liberal arts, management, nursing and science.

Colleges and Institutes

AGRICULTURE

Ayuthaya Agricultural College: Ayuthaya.

Bang Phra Agricultural College: Bang Phra, Cholburi; tel. (38) 777503 ext. 118; fax (38) 341808; e-mail bp_library@hotmail.com; internet www.bparg.rit.ac.th; f. 1957; teacher training, training in farming; library: 10,000 vols; 130 teachers; 1,600 students; Dir Dr SURAPHOL SANGUANSRI.

Rajamangola Institute of Technology, Surin Campus: Surin; tel. (44) 511022; fax (44) 519034; e-mail webmaster@surin.rit.ac.th; internet www.surin.rit.ac.th; f. 2001 (fmrly Surin Agricultural College); 143 teachers; 2,289 students; Dir Asst Prof. Dr WIEHIEN OUNRUEN.

TECHNOLOGY

Northern Technical Institute: Huay Kaew Rd, Chiang Mai; f. 1957; library: 50,777 vols; 2–3-year diploma courses; Dir C. SUWATHEE.

Rajamangala Institute of Technology, Bangkok Technical Campus: 2 Nang Linchee Rd, Bangkok 10120; tel. 2863991; f. 1952; degree courses, 2- to 5-year certificate and diploma courses; library: 61,048 vols; 431 teachers; 6,111 students; Dir SKUL VEJAKORN.

Rajamangala Institute of Technology, Khon Kaen Campus: 150 Srichan Rd, Khon Kaen; tel. (43) 236-451; f. 1963 (fmrly Thai-German Technical Institute); specializes in industrial technology; 3-year vocational certificate course, 2-year higher vocational diploma, 2-year BS; library: 11,186 vols (mainly industrial education); Dir SUBHAN TUENGSOOK.

Southern Technical Institute: Songkla.

TIMOR-LESTE

The Higher Education System

Universidade Nasionál Timór Lorosa'e (formerly Universitas Timor Timur), which was founded in 2000, predates Timor-Leste (formerly East Timor)'s independence from Indonesia in 2002. It is Timor-Leste's principal institution of higher education. It was largely destroyed during civil unrest in 1999, but reopened in 2001. In that year there were an estimated 6,349 students enrolled in tertiary education. The Ministry of Education, Culture, Youth and Sport is responsible for the provision of higher education.

Since 2000 there has been significant growth in the higher education sector with the number of institutions growing from six in 1999 to over 20 in 2007 with a total enrolment of over 17,000. The National Commission for Academic Assessment and Accreditation was established in 2006 to take full responsibility for defining standards and criteria for academic accreditation and assessment and for accrediting higher education institutions and their programmes.

Regulatory Body

GOVERNMENT

Ministry of Education, Culture, Youth and Sport: Díli; e-mail education@gov.east-timor.org; Minister JOÃO CÂNCIO.

Research Institutes

LANGUAGE AND LITERATURE

Instituto Nacional de Linguística (National Institute of Linguistics): Liceu 'Dr Francisco Macado', Avda Cidade de Lisboa, Díli; tel. 3313-142; fax 3321-211; e-mail indldili@yahoo.com; internet www.shlrc.mq.edu.au/~leccles; f. 2001 to study, protect and foster the official languages of Timor-Leste, Tetum and Portuguese; official govt body with the charter of coordinating and overseeing all indigenous language research and development projects; attached to National University of East Timor; Dir-Gen. Prof. Dr BENJAMIM DE ARAÚJO E CORTE-REAL; Dir of Research and Publications Prof. Dr GEOFFREY HULL; publ. *Research Bulletin* (electronic, 2 a year).

NATURAL SCIENCES

Centro Nacional de Investigação Científica (National Centre of Scientific Research): Liceu Dr Francisco Machado, Avda Cidade de Lisboa, Díli; tel. 3332-705; e-mail cnic_timor@yahoo.com; internet www.cnictimor.org; f. 2001 to develop the economic, social and political welfare of Timor-Leste by means of scientific research; areas of research: agriculture, business and economics, education, political and social sciences, technology; Dir Prof. HELDER DA COSTA.

Libraries and Archives

Díli

National University of Timor Lorosa'e Library: Avda Cidade de Lisboa, Díli; fmrly library of Universitas Timor Timur; large part of its collection removed or destroyed during civil unrest in 1999; University Librarian VENCESLAO DO REGO.

Xanana Gusmão Reading Room: Rua Belarmina Lobo Lecidere, POB 3, Díli; tel. 3322-831; e-mail xgrroom@mail.timortelecom.tp; internet www.xgrroom.org; f. 2000; Dir KIRSTY SWORD GUSMÃO.

University

UNIVERSIDADE NASIONÁL TIMÓR LOROSA'E
(National University of East Timor)

Avda Cidade de Lisboa, Díli

Telephone: 3321-210
Fax: 3322-535
E-mail: bcorte_real@hotmail.com

Founded 2000; succeeded Universitas Timor Timur, (f. 1986, under Indonesian control) which was largely destroyed during civil unrest in 1999
State control

Rector: Prof. Dr BENJAMIM DE ARAÚJO E CORTE-REAL
Univ. Librarian: VENCESLAU DO REGO
Number of students: 7,000.

ATTACHED INSTITUTE

Instituto Nacional de Linguística (National Institute of Linguistics): see Research Institutes.

TOGO

The Higher Education System

The principal institution of higher education is the Université de Lomé (formerly University of Benin), which was founded in 1965 as the Institut Supérieur de Bénin (Advanced Institute of Benin) in conjunction with the neighbouring state of Benin. Higher education is the responsibility of the Ministry of Education and the Ministry of Technical Education and Professional Training. The funding of higher education is administered by the General Higher Education Council (Grand Conseil des Universités), which determines institutional budgets following consultation with the institutions.Students' tuition fees account for approximately 5% of income. In 2000/01 18,455 students were enrolled in tertiary education. The Université du Lomé had about 14,000 students in the early 2000s, and scholarships to French universities are also available. A second university opened in Kara, in the north of Togo, in early 2004.

The secondary school Baccalauréat is the main requirement for admission to higher education. Applicants without the Baccalauréat are required to sit an entrance examination. The university degree system is based on the French system of three cycles. The first cycle lasts two years and leads to the award of the undergraduate Diplôme d'Études Universitaires Générales. The second cycle consists of one year of study leading to the award of the Licence, followed by a further year leading to the award of the Maîtrise. Finally, the third cycle comprises firstly a one- to two-year period of study leading to the award of the Diplôme d'Études Supérieures, Diplôme d'Études Supérieures Specialisées or Diplôme d'Études Approfondies, and secondly a two-year period of study culminating with the award of the Doctorat. Professional degrees lasting longer than four years are offered by faculties of the university and specialist schools, such as Diplôme d'Ingénieur Agronome (five years), Diplôme d'Ingénieur de Conception (five years) and Doctorat de Médecine (seven years).

Regulatory Bodies

GOVERNMENT

Ministry of Communication, Culture and Civic Training: BP 40, Lomé; tel. 221-29-30; fax 221-43-80; e-mail info@republicoftogo.com; Minister CORNÉLIUS AÏDAM.

Ministry of Higher Education and Research: rue Colonel de Roux, BP 12175, Lomé; tel. 222-09-83; fax 222-07-83; Minister MESSAN ADIMADO ADUAYOM.

Learned Societies

BIBLIOGRAPHY, LIBRARY SCIENCE AND MUSEOLOGY

Association Togolaise pour le Développement de la Documentation, des Bibliothèques, Archives et Musées: c/o Bibliothèque de l'Université de Bénin, BP 1515, Lomé; f. 1959; promotes research in the field of documentation and library science; participates in the education of adults and young people; holds conferences, etc.; 60 mems; Pres. KOFFI ATTIGNON; Sec.-Gen. EKOUE AMAH.

LANGUAGE AND LITERATURE

Goethe-Institut: 25, Rue Kokéti, angle Rue de l'Eglise, BP 914, Lomé; tel. 2210894; fax 2220777; e-mail info@lome.goethe.org; internet www.goethe.de/lome; offers courses and exams in German language and culture and promotes cultural exchange with Germany; Dir TORSTEN OERTEL.

Research Institutes

GENERAL

Institut de Recherche pour le Développement (IRD): BP 375, Lomé; tel. 221-43-44; fax 221-03-43; e-mail ird_lome@netcom.tg; f. 1949; agronomy, geology, pedology, geography, sociology, hydrology, geophysics, library; Admin. Agent BERNADETTE NAKU; (see main entry under France).

AGRICULTURE, FISHERIES AND VETERINARY SCIENCE

Institut de Recherches Agronomiques Tropicales et des Cultures Vivrières (IRAT): BP 1163, Lomé; tel. 221-21-48; Dir M. SARAGONI; (see main entry under France).

Institut de Recherches du Café, du Cacao et Autres Plantes Stimulantes (IRCC): BP 90, Kpalimé; tel. 441-00-34; fax 441-00-60; f. 1967; research to improve quality and production of coffee, cocoa and other stimulants; experimental unit at Tové; Dir K. EDEM DJIEKPOR.

Institut Togolais de Recherche Agronomique/Centre de Recherche Agronomique de la Savane Humide: BP 01, Kolokopé Anié; tel. 444-30-00; fax 444-30-02; e-mail crash@laposte.tg; f. 1948; (see main entry under France); Dir M. BONFOH BEDIBETE; publ. *Coton et Fibres Tropicales*.

NATURAL SCIENCES

General

Institut National de la Recherche Scientifique: BP 2240, Lomé; tel. 221-01-39; f. 1965; initiation of national scientific research; rural development research; 12 permanent staff; library of 5,000 vols; publ. *Etudes Togolaises* (2 a year).

TECHNOLOGY

Service des Mines du Togo: c/o Ministère des Mines, Ave de la Marina, Lomé; Dir-Gen. ANKOUM P. AREGBA.

Libraries and Archives

Lomé

Archives Nationales du Togo: POB 1002, Lomé; tel. 221-04-10; f. 1976; administered by the Nat. Ministry for Education and Scientific Research; 2,500 vols, specializing in colonial history, tropical agronomy, stock breeding, health; Curator SENGHOR MOUSSA.

Bibliothèque du Ministère de l'Intérieur: Rue Albert Sarraut, Lomé; Librarian KWAOVI GABRIEL JOHNSON.

Bibliothèque Nationale: BP 1002, Lomé; tel. 221-04-10; fax 222-19-67; e-mail dban@tg.refer.org; German and French archives; 18,050 vols, 400 periodicals (incl. 74 current); Dir WENMI-AGORE M. COULIBALEY.

Museum

Lomé

Direction du Musée National, des Sites et Monuments: BP 12156, Lomé; tel. 221-68-07; fax 221-43-80, f. 1974; Curator of the National Museum NAYONDJOUA DJANGUENANE.

Universities

UNIVERSITÉ DE KARA

BP 43, Kara

Telephone: 661-02-56
Fax: 660-12-74

Founded 2004
State Control

Pres.: AÏSSAH AGBÉTRA

Number of teachers: 30
Number of students: 1,477

Faculties of arts and humanities, economics and management, law and politics.

UNIVERSITÉ DE LOMÉ

BP 1515, Lomé

Telephone: 221-35-00
Fax: 221-85-95
E-mail: ngayiber@tg.refer.org
Internet: www.ub.tg

Founded 1965 as a Higher Institute; univ. status 1970; incl. all the instns of higher education in the country
State control
Language of instruction: French
Academic year: October to June (three terms)

Pres.: Prof. NICOUÉ L. GAYIBOR
Vice-Pres.: THIOU T. K. TCHAMIE
Sec.-Gen.: ABALO KODJO TABO
Librarian: A. B. F. GBIKPI-BENISSAN

Library of 70,000 vols
Number of teachers: 650
Number of students: 14,168

Publications: *Livret de l'Etudiant*, *Annales (Lettres, Sciences, Médecine, Droit-Economie)*, *Actes des Journées Scientifiques*, *Annuaire statistique*, *Journal de la Recherche Scientifique*, *Campus Actualités*

DEANS AND DIRECTORS

Faculty of Economics and Business Management: K. AYASSOU
Faculty of Law: Prof. PEDRO AKUETE SANTOS
Faculty of Letters and Humanities: Prof. KOMLA M. F. NUBUKPO
Faculty of Medicine: Prof. KOFFI N'DAKENA
Faculty of Sciences: Prof. M. GBEASSOR
CIC-CAFMICRO (Computer Centre): TSATSOU FIADJOE
Distance Learning Centre: MARYSE A. QUASHIE
Higher School of Agriculture: K. AGBEKO
Higher Secretarial School: A. MAGNAN
Medical Training School: Prof. BATOMA SOSSOU
National Higher School of Engineering: E. K.-S. BEDJA
National Institute of Education: A. KOMLAN
University Technical Institute of Food and Biological Sciences: Prof. COMLAN A. DE SOUZA
University Technical Institute of Management: N. BIGOU-LARE

Colleges

Centre de Formation Professionnelle Agricole de Tove: BP 401, Kpalimé; f. 1901; 21 teachers; 230 students; library: 3,500 vols; Dir S. N. KANKARTI; Sec.-Gen. I. KUEVI.

Ecole Africaine des Métiers d'Architecture et d'Urbanisme: BP 2067, Lomé; tel. 221-62-53; fax 222-06-52; f. 1975; specialist courses in architecture and town planning; in-service courses for trained architects; library: 1,957 vols; 23 staff; 102 students; Dir AHMED ASKIA SIDI.

Ecole Nationale d'Administration: Ave de la Libération, Lomé; tel. 221-21-30; fax 221-35-29; f. 1958; provides training for Togolese civil servants; 100 teachers; 500 students; library: 1,000 vols; Dir DAGO YABRE; Sec.-Gen. KOMIKUMA DOGBEVI.

TONGA

The Higher Education System

Institutions of higher education pre-date the independence of Tonga from the United Kingdom in 1970, with the oldest being the 'Atenisi Institute, which was founded in 1966. There were four technical and vocational colleges in 1999, with a total of 467 students, and one teacher-training college, with 288 students. In 1990 there were 230 Tongans studying overseas. Some degree courses are offered at the university division of the 'Atenisi Institute. The University of the South Pacific has a centre in Tonga. A new establishment offering higher education, the 'Unuaki-'o-Tonga Royal University, opened in 2004.

Higher Education is overseen by the Tonga National Qualifications and Accreditation Board (TNQAB). The Board was created by legislation drafted in 1999 and by the TNQAB Bill in 2004 which was enacted in 2007.

Among the qualifications required for admission to higher education are the Higher Leaving Certificate, New Zealand University Entrance Certificate and Pacific Secondary Certificate. There is also a one-year Preliminary or Foundation Programme for applicants to the University of the South Pacific. The Bachelors is the undergraduate degree and lasts three years, although the Bachelors in medicine at the Fiji School of Medicine is a four-year degree. Following completion of the Bachelors, graduates may study for the Masters, which is a one- or two-year course of study. The highest university degree is the Doctorate, requiring a further two years of study following award of the Masters.

The Government provides over half of all facilities and training for post-secondary vocational and technical education. Institutions providing such education include the Community Development Training Centre, the Tonga Institute of Science and Technology, the Civil Service Training Centre and the Royal School of Science and Technology.

Regulatory Body

GOVERNMENT

Ministry of Education, Women's Affairs and Culture: POB 61, Vuna Rd, Kolofo'ou, Nuku'alofa; tel. 23-511; fax 23-596; e-mail moe@kalianet.to; Minister Dr TEVITA HALA PALEFAU.

ACCREDITATION

Tonga National Qualifications and Accreditation Board: New City Bldg, Nuku'alofa; tel. 28-124; f. 2007; attached to Min. of Education, Women's Affairs and Culture; has oversight to qualifications for both public and private post-secondary education in Tonga; reviews and approves qualifications and positions them on a graded framework used to inform learners, education providers, employers and others regarding the status and standard of awards provided; CEO Dr 'UHILA-MOE-LANGI FASI.

Learned Society

BIBLIOGRAPHY, LIBRARY SCIENCE AND MUSEOLOGY

Tonga Library Association: c/o USP Tonga Centre, POB 278, Nuku'alofa; tel. 29-055; fax 29-249; e-mail taufui_l@usp.ac.fj; f. 1981; training courses and library-related activities; 40 mems; Pres. LOSALINE TAUFU'I.

Libraries and Archives

Nuku'alofa

Ministry of Education Library: POB 123, Nuku'alofa; tel. 21-588; fax 24-105; f. 1976; provides supplementary reading and text books for students and public library service; 12,432 vols; special collection: Pacific (1,515 vols); Librarian TU'ILOKAMANA TUITA.

University of the South Pacific, Tonga Campus Library: POB 278, Nuku'alofa; tel. 29-240; fax 29-249; e-mail taufui_l@usp.ac.fj; 10,000 vols; Library Officer LOSALINE TAUFU'I.

Museum

Nuku'alofa

Tupou College Museum: POB 25, Nuku'alofa; tel. 32-240; f. 1866; museum within Tupou College; artefacts from Tonga's history; Principal Rev. SIOSAIA PELE.

Universities

'ATENISI UNIVERSITY

POB 90, Nuku'alofa
Telephone: 24-819
Fax: 24-868
E-mail: office@atenisi.edu.to
Internet: www.atenisi.edu.to

Founded 1975

Private control; attached to 'Atenisi Institute

Schools of arts, humanities, natural sciences, social sciences

Dean: Dr MICHAEL G. HOROWITZ
Assoc. Dean: FIRITIA VELT
Library Coordinator: ROBERT H. BECK.

'UNUAKI'-O-TONGA ROYAL UNIVERSITY

Taufa'ahau Rd, Haveluloto Nuku'alofa, POB 2936, Tongatapu
Telephone: 25-663
Fax: 25-664
E-mail: admission@tongaroyaluniversity.com
Internet: www.tongaroyaluniversity.com

Founded 2004

Chair.: HRH Princess SALOTE MAFILE'O PILOLEVU TUITA
Pres. and Vice-Chair.: Prof. 'ETUATE LAVULAVU
Vice-Pres. for Academic Affairs and Chief Exec. Dir: Prof. Dr MICHAEL FAIA
Exec. Vice-Pres.: SIONE TUALAU VIMAHI
Vice-Pres.: Prof. VINOD TRIVEDI
Dir for Admin. and Int. Relations: MELE LUPEHA'AMOA 'ILAIU
Dir for Technical and Vocational Training: PITA LIKILIKI PUA
Dir for Finance: MEHTA BHAVIK
Dir for Student Services: TELESIA LAVULAVU
Dir for Admissions: KALOLAINE KOLUSE
Dir for Research and Deputy Dir of Admissions: SIONA TALANOA FIFITA.

ATTACHED RESEARCH INSTITUTES

Asian Region Extension: 17, L/L, Harekrishna Complex opp. Kothawala Flats, Paldi Ahmedabad 380007, India; tel. 79-66613205; fax 79-26579891; e-mail ravishshah@tongaroyaluniversity.com; Exec. Dir Prof. VINOD TRIVEDI.

'Eua Community Education and Health Institute: Dir 'ANA FILI.

Ha'apai Community Education and Health Institute: Dir MO'ALE FINAU.

Tongatapu Community Education and Health Institute: Dir SIONE TUALAU VIMAHI.

Vava'u Community Education and Health Institute: Dir 'ETA HARRIS TAUMALOLO.

Colleges

'Atenisi Institute: POB 90, Nuku'alofa; tel. 24-819; fax 24-868; e-mail office@atenisi.edu.to; internet www.atenisi.edu.to; private control; f. 1966; anthropology, astronomy, chemistry, economics, global history, languages, life science, literature, mathematics, music and art, philosophy, physics, politics, psychology, sociology; comprises univ. (*q.v.*) and performing arts centre; library: 5,000 vols; Institute Dir SISI'UNO HELU; Library Coordinator ROBERT H. BECK.

Hango Agricultural College: POB 16, Ohonua, Eua; tel. 50-044; fax 50-128; f. 1968; part of Free Wesleyan Church Education System; 1-year diploma course in paraveterinary studies, 1-year diploma course in horticulture/cropping, 2-year certificate course; library: 1,200 vols; 7 teachers; 55 students.

Tonga Institute of Science and Technology: POB 485, Nuku'alofa; tel. 22-667; fax 24-334; e-mail tist1uf@kalianet.to; f. 1985; offers training in maritime studies and technical trades; library: 300 vols; 20 teachers; 160 students; Prin. Dr 'UHILA-MOE-LANGI FASI.

University of the South Pacific, Tonga Centre: POB 278, Nuku'alofa; tel. 29-240; fax 29-249; e-mail fukofuka_s@usp.ac.fj; extension centre with responsibilities for distance education, adult non-formal education; interests in village and community development and appropriate technology; library: see Libraries and Archives; Dir SALOTE FUKOFUKA.

TRINIDAD AND TOBAGO

The Higher Education System

The Trinidad campus of the University of the West Indies (UWI) at St Augustine offers undergraduate and postgraduate programmes. The UWI Institute of Business offers postgraduate courses, and develops programmes for local companies. Other institutions of higher education are the Eric Williams Medical Sciences complex, the Polytechnic Institute and the East Caribbean Farm Institute. The country has one teacher-training college and three government-controlled technical institutes and vocational centres, including the Trinidad and Tobago Hotel School. In the late 1990s the Government established the Trinidad and Tobago Institute of Technology and the College of Science, Technology and Applied Arts of Trinidad and Tobago. In March 2004 a steering committee was appointed to conduct a strategic review of tertiary education and distance and lifelong learning in an attempt to improve consistency within the tertiary sector, and in relation to the education system as a whole. In 2004/05 there were 16,920 students in three institutions of higher education.

Applicants are required to have a minimum of two GCE A-Levels for admission to undergraduate courses, and either the Caribbean Examinations Council Secondary Education Certificate or GCE O-Levels for admission to preliminary science, evening or part-time courses. Two-year Associate degrees are awarded by institutions such as the College of Nursing and the National Institute of Higher Education, and the undergraduate Bachelors degree is a three-year programme of study at the University of the West Indies. The postgraduate degrees are the two-year Masters and Doctorate programmes.

Post-secondary technical and vocational education is administered according to a framework of national vocational qualifications (TTNVQs). There are five levels: Pre-Craft, Craft, Technician, Professional, and Chartered or Advanced Professional. TTNVQs are offered by a range of professional institutes and centres.

The Accreditation Council of Trinidad and Tobago is the governing body for the assurance of quality in post-secondary and tertiary education in Trinidad and Tobago.

Regulatory and Representative Bodies

GOVERNMENT

Ministry of Education: 18 Alexandra St, St Clair; tel. 622-2181; fax 622-4892; e-mail mined@tstt.net.tt; internet www.moe.gov.tt; Min. Dr TIM GOPEESINGH; Permanent Sec. ANGELA JACK.

Ministry of Science, Technology and Tertiary Education: The International Waterfront Centre, Levels 16–18, Tower C, 1A Wrightson Rd, Port-of-Spain; tel. 623-9922; fax 625-5428; e-mail stte@stte.gov.tt; internet www.stte.gov.tt; Min. FAZAL KARIM KANGALOO.

Ministry of the Arts and Multiculturalism: JOBCO Bldg, 51–55 Frederick St, Port-of-Spain; tel. 625-8519; fax 627-4991; e-mail culturedivision.tt@gmail.com; internet www.culture.gov.tt; Min. WINSTON PETERS.

ACCREDITATION

Accreditation Council of Trinidad and Tobago (ACTT): Level 3, Bldg B, ALGICO Plaza, 91–93 St Vincent St, Port-of-Spain; tel. 623-2500; fax 624-5711; e-mail info@actt.org.tt; internet www.actt.org.tt; f. 2004; assures the quality and integrity of higher education through the recognition, registration and accreditation of instns and programmes; br. in Tobago; board of 10 mems; Chair. Dr MICHAEL DOWLATH; Exec. Dir MICHAEL BRADSHAW (acting).

Learned Societies

AGRICULTURE, FISHERIES AND VETERINARY SCIENCE

Agricultural Society of Trinidad and Tobago: POB 256, 13A Pembroke St, Port-of-Spain; tel. 627-3087; fax 623-7797; e-mail agrisoc@tstt.net.tt; internet www.agriculture.gov.tt; f. 1894; 528 mems; Pres. WENDY LEE YUEN; publ. *Journal* (1 a year).

Sugar Manufacture Association of Trinidad and Tobago: 80 Abercromby St, POB 230, Port-of-Spain; tel. 623-6106; f. 1967; to promote information of interest to the sugar industry; 272 mems; Pres. T. N. SKINNER; Sec. M. Y. KHAN; publ. *Proceedings*.

Tobago District Agricultural Society: Main St, Scarborough; Pres. Capt. R. H. HARROWER; Sec. S. A. DAVIES.

ARCHITECTURE AND TOWN PLANNING

Trinidad and Tobago Institute of Architects: POB 585, Port-of-Spain; tel. 624-8842; fax 624-5217; e-mail info@ttiarch.com; internet www.ttiarch.com; f. 1954, present name 1982; 90 mems (incl. overseas); Pres. MARK RAYMOND; Sec. STEVE JAMESON; publ. *Journal* (1 a year).

BIBLIOGRAPHY, LIBRARY SCIENCE AND MUSEOLOGY

Library Association of Trinidad and Tobago: POB 1275, Port-of-Spain; e-mail secretary@latt.org.tt; internet www.latt.org.tt; f. 1960; Pres. Dr LILLIBETH ACKBARALI; Exec. Sec. SALLY ANNE MONTSERIN; publ. *Bulletin*.

ECONOMICS, LAW AND POLITICS

Law Association of Trinidad and Tobago: POB 534, Port-of-Spain; tel. 625-9350; fax 625-2478; e-mail lawassociationtt@gmail.com; internet www.lawassociationtt.com; f. 1986; 750 mems; Pres. MARTIN G. DALY; Sec. PATRICIA DINDYAL; publ. *The Lawyer* (2 a year).

FINE AND PERFORMING ARTS

Trinidad Music Association: Bishop Anstey High School, Abercromby St, Port-of-Spain; f. 1941; 102 mems; Pres. ROBERT JOHNSTONE; Hon. Sec. VELMA JARDINE.

HISTORY, GEOGRAPHY AND ARCHAEOLOGY

Historical Society of Trinidad and Tobago: c/o POB 780, Port-of-Spain; f. 1932; 45 mems; Pres. MAX B. IFILL; Hon. Sec. and Treas. KENT VILLAFANA.

LANGUAGE AND LITERATURE

Alliance Française: 17 Alcazar St, Clair, POB 1288, Port-of-Spain; tel. 622-6726; fax 628-8226; e-mail info@alliancetnt.com; internet www.alliancetnt.com; offers courses and exams in French language and culture, and promotes cultural exchange with France.

British Council: c/o British High Commission, 19 St Clair Ave, St Clair, POB 778, Port-of-Spain; tel. 628-0565; fax 622-2853; e-mail information@britishcouncil.org.tt; internet www.britishcouncil.org/tt; offers courses and exams in English language and British culture, and promotes cultural exchange with the UK; Man. HARRIET MASSINGBERD.

MEDICINE

Pharmacy Board of Trinidad and Tobago: Professional Centre Building, Wrightson Rd Extension, Port-of-Spain; tel. 627-6731; fax 627-6731; e-mail pboftt@tstt.net.tt; f. 1899; 300 mems; Pres. ANDREW RAHAMAN; Hon. Sec. NORMA INNISS.

NATURAL SCIENCES

Physical Sciences

Geological Society of Trinidad and Tobago: POB 3524, La Romaine, Trinidad; tel. 679-6064; fax 679-6064; e-mail gstt@tstt.net.tt; internet www.gstt.org; f. 1976; 250 mems; library of 2,000 vols; Pres. Dr FAZAL HOSEIN; Pres. Elect CURTIS ARCHIE.

Research Institute

AGRICULTURE, FISHERIES AND VETERINARY SCIENCE

Caribbean Agricultural Research and Development Institute (CARDI): University Campus, St Augustine, Trinidad; tel. 645-1205; fax 645-1208; e-mail infocentre@cardi.org; internet www.cardi.org; f. 1975; sites in 13 Caribbean countries; Exec. Dir FRANK B. LAUCKNER.

Libraries and Archives

Port-of-Spain

Central Library of Trinidad and Tobago: POB 547, corner Duke and Pembroke Sts, Port-of-Spain; tel. 624-3120; fax 625-5369; f. 1941; a division of the Office of the Prime Minister; 442,000 vols; public library; Heritage Library held jointly with Trinidad Public Library; 13 brs; Dir PAMELLA BENSON; publ. *Trinidad and Tobago National Bibliography*.

National Archives: The Government Archivist, POB 763, 105 St Vincent St, Port-of-Spain; tel. 626-2874; fax 625-2689; e-mail nattenquires@moi.gov.tt; internet www.natt.gov.tt; f. 1960; records from 1797; govt and private archives; microfilm copies of Trinidad and Tobago records in other countries; Govt Archivist SHERYL LEE KIM; publ. *Select Documents*.

National Library and Information System Authority: National Library of Trinidad and Tobago, corner Hart and Abercromby Sts, Port-of-Spain; tel. 624-4496; fax 625-6096; e-mail nalis@nalis.gov.tt; internet www2.nalis.gov.tt; f. 1998; 23 public libraries; heritage library; 124 school libraries; 29 spec. libraries; 24 br libraries; colln of 729,715 items; Exec. Dir ANNETTE WALLACE.

St Augustine

University of the West Indies, Main Library: St Augustine; tel. 662-2002 ext. 2132; fax 662-9238; e-mail mainlib@sta.uwi.tt; internet www.mainlib.uwi.tt; f. 1960; 403,503 vols, 49,455 bound serials, 22,783 microfilms, 27,000 other non-book items, 1,418 maps, 4,054 multimedia items, 5,804 photographs, 10,721 vertical files, 816 video cassettes, 1,323 audio cassettes, 1,610 vinyl records; spec. collns: W Indiana, Oral and Pictorial Records Collns Index, journal articles on the W Indies or by W Indians; Campus Librarian JENNIFER JOSEPH.

San Fernando

San Fernando Carnegie Free Library: Harris Promenade, San Fernando; tel. 652-2921; fax 653-9645; internet www.nalis.gov.tt; f. 1919; lending and reference service for children and adults; 36,109 vols; special collection: West Indies, Carnival; Librarian REYNOLD BASSANT.

Museum and Art Gallery

Port-of-Spain

National Museum and Art Gallery of Trinidad & Tobago: 117 Frederick St, Port-of-Spain; tel. 623-5941; fax 624-7116; e-mail nationalmuseum117@gmail.com; internet www.nmag.gov.tt; f. 1892; art, archaeology, history, Carnival, petroleum technology, natural history; Curator VEL A. LEWIS.

University

UNIVERSITY OF THE WEST INDIES, ST AUGUSTINE CAMPUS

St Augustine, Trinidad
Telephone: 662-2002
Fax: 663-9684
Internet: www.sta.uwi.edu

Founded 1948 by the Govts of the Caribbean Commonwealth Territories with the cooperation of the British Govt
Autonomous
Language of instruction: English
Academic year: August to July

Serves Jamaica, Trinidad and Tobago, Barbados and the Commonwealth Territories in the Caribbean

Chancellor: Sir GEORGE ALLEYNE
Vice-Chancellor: Prof. E. NIGEL HARRIS
Pro-Vice-Chancellor and Campus Prin.: Prof. CLEMENT SANKAT
Deputy Prin.: Prof. RHODA REDDOCK
Registrar: JEREMY CALLAGHAN
Librarian: JENNIFER JOSEPH

Library of 403,503 vols, 49,455 bound serials, 10,047 periodicals, 22,783 microforms, 5,804 photographs, 1,418 maps, 1,323 CDs, 816 video cassettes, 811 audio cassettes
Number of teachers: 726
Number of students: 16,408

Publications: *Caribbean Agro Economic Society* (conf. proceedings), *Caribbean Dialogue* (policy bulletin of Caribbean affairs), *Caribbean Review of Gender Studies* (online), *Creating Language Links*, *History in Action* (online), *Journal of Business, Finance and Economics in Emerging Economies*, *Journal of Caribbean Curriculum*, *Journal of Caribbean History*, *Journal of Tropical Agriculture*, *Journal of West Indian Literature*, *St Augustine News*, *UWI Today Newspaper*, *West Indian Journal of Engineering*

DEANS

Faculty of Engineering: Prof. BRIAN COPELAND
Faculty of Humanities and Education: Dr FUNSO AIYEJINA
Faculty of Medical Sciences: Prof. SAMUEL RAMSEWAK
Faculty of Science and Agriculture: Prof. DYER NARINESINGH
Faculty of Social Sciences: Dr H. GHANY

PROFESSORS

ADESIYUN, A., Public Health
ADDAE, J., Physiology
ADOGWA, A., Anatomy
AGARD, J., Life Sciences
AGOZINO, O., Criminology
AIYEJINA, F., Literature
AKINGBALA, J., Chemical Engineering
ALI, Z., School of Medicine
BERTRAND, W., Chemical Engineering
BHATT, B., Math and Computer Science
BISSESSAR, A., Public Management
BRATHWAITE, R., Food Production
CHADWICK, A., Civil Engineering
COOPER, J., Pathology
COPELAND, B., Electrical and Computer Engineering
DAISLEY, H., Anatomical Pathology
DAWE, R., Chemical Engineering
EKWUE, E., Mechanical Engineering
EZENWAKA, C., Para-Clinical Sciences
EZEOKOLI, C., Veterinary Surgery
GIFT, S., Electrical Engineering
GIRVAN, N., International Relations
HUTCHINSON, G., Clinical Medical Sciences
IMBERT, C., Mechanical Engineering
KOCHHAR, G., Mechanical Engineering
LALLA, B., Linguistics
LAWRENCE, A., Environmental Biology
LEWIS, T., Civil Engineering
LEWIS, W., Mechanical Engineering
MAHARAJH, H., Clinical Medical Science
MCRAE, A., Human Anatomy
MOHAMMED, P., Center for Gender and Development Studies
MONTEIL, M., Para Clinical Science
MURTI, P., Histopathology
NARAYNSINGH, V., Surgery
NARINESINGH, D., Chemistry
OPADEYI, J., Land and Surveying
PANTIN, D., Economics
PINTO PEREIRA, L., Basic Health Science
PITT-MILLER, P., Anesthetics
POSTHOFF, C., Maths and Computer Science
PUN, K., Mechanical Engineering
RAMDATH, D., Basic Health Science
RAMNARINE, I., Life Sciences
RAMSARAN, R., International Relations
RAMSEWAK, S., Obstetrics and Gynaecology
REDDOCK, R., Gender, Social Change and Development
ROBERTSON, I., Linguistics
SAHAI, A., Math and Computer Science
SAUNDERS, R., Physics
SEEMUNGAL, T., School of Medicine
SHARMA, C., Electrical and Computer Engineering
SHAW, P., Food Production
SINGH, G., Chemistry
STEVENSON, A., Centre for Medical Science Education
SURYA RAO, D., Civil Engineering
SYAN, C., Mechanical Engineering
TEELUCKSINGH, S., School of Medicine
THEODORE, K., Economics
TYLER, B., Chemical Engineering
UMAHARAN, P., Life Sciences
YOUSSEF, V., Linguistics

UNIVERSITY OF TRINIDAD AND TOBAGO (UTT)

74–98 O'Meara Industrial Park, Arima
Telephone: 642-8888
Fax: 643-1617
E-mail: utt.marketing@utt.edu.tt
Internet: utt.edu.tt

Founded 2004
State control
Language of instruction: English
Academic year: September to July
Accredited by Accreditation Ccl of Trinidad and Tobago

Pres.: Prof. KENNETH RAMCHAND
Provost: Prof. DAVID MCGAW
Vice-Provost for Postgraduate Studies: Prof. ADEL SHARAF
Assoc. Provost, Humanities, Soc. Sciences and the Academies: JEANETTE MORRIS
Assoc. Provost, Science, Engineering and Technology: Prof. PRAKASH PERSAD
Vice-Pres. for Finance, Admin. and Procurement: FEONA LUE PING WA
Vice-Pres. for Quality Assurance and Institutional Advancement: Dr RUBY S. ALLEYNE
Asst Vice-Pres. for Human Resources: CEDRIC CONNOR
Asst Vice-Pres. for Student Support Services: STEPHEN SHEPPARD
Registrar and Corporate Sec.: DEBBIE SIRJUSINGH
Chief Univ. Librarian: Dr MARTHA PREDDIE

Library of 59,488 vols, 684 print journals, 1146 multimedia items
Number of teachers: 540
Number of students: 7,275

Publications: *Caribbean Journal of Criminology and Public Safety*, *Caribbean Journal of Teacher Education and Pedagogy*, *Talkaree*

PROFESSORS

AL-TAWEEL, A., Process Engineering
ATHRE, K., Mechanical Engineering
BLAIR, P., Sports and Leisure Studies
DEOSARAN, R., Criminology and Public Safety Programmes
EL-SAYED, M., Utilities Engineering
GAINHAM, K., Performing Arts
JOSEPH, A., Environmental Science and Management
KHAN, J., Biosciences, Agriculture and Food Technologies
LIVERPOOL, H., Carnival Studies Programmes
MORRIS, J., Cognition, Learning and Education
PERSAD, P., Undergraduate Studies, Design and Manufacturing
SHARAF, A., Research and Postgraduate Studies, Energy Systems
SMITH, M., Information, Computing and Telecommunications and Digital Media Studies
STEVENSON, C., Maritime Programmes
SUITE, W., Civil Engineering Programmes

TUNISIA

The Higher Education System

The University of Tunisia was founded in 1960, and divided in 1986 into three universities: Tunis, Centre and Sfax-South. In 1987 the university at Tunis was divided into four subject-based institutions, which in turn were later reorganized into multidisciplinary institutions. Several private universities have received accreditation since 2000. In 2007/08 there were 335,649 full-time students at 190 institutions of higher education. Higher education is funded from the national budget. Institutions of higher education are accredited by the Ministry of Higher Education and Scientific Research. Private higher education institutions operate on the basis of a licence granted by the Ministry. This licence enables them to offer specific courses in specific fields. Licences are reviewed periodically in order to maintain standards of quality.

The secondary school Baccalauréat is the main requirement for admission to higher education. Tunisia has traditionally followed the French system of higher education but is currently undergoing reform. It aims to introduce a three-tier system of Licence–Masters–Doctorate (LMD) and bring Tunisian education into line with the European Bologna Process. The implementation of the LMD started in 2006 with the aim of enrolling all students onto these new programmes by 2009. The LMD is expected to be fully implemented by 2012. The traditional university degrees are divided into three cycles: the first cycle ends with the award of the Diplôme Universitaire d'Études Scientifiques or Diplôme Universitaire d'Études Littéraires; the second cycle comprises the Licence or a Maîtrise; and the third cycle the doctoral-level degrees, specifically Diplôme d'Études Approfondies and Doctorat d'État. The professional title Diplôme d'Ingénieur is a second-cycle degree awarded after three years and the Docteur en Médecine is awarded after seven years. The new LMD system comprises three awards. The Licence is an undergraduate degree awarded three years after the Baccalauréat de l'Enseignement Secondaire. There are two types of Licence available, namely the Licence Fondamentale and the Licence Appliquée. The Masters is a postgraduate degree awarded two years after the Licence. There are two types of Masters available, namely the Master Recherché and the Master Professionnel. The first year is classroom based, the second year contains independent research or professional training, including project work. The Doctorat is a postgraduate research degree awarded three years after the Masters degree. Studies are organized in credit points (60 credit points correspond to one year of study) similar to the European Credit Transfer System within the Bologna System. All programmes are organized into units.

Technical and vocational programmes are administered by the Ministry of Education. The leading qualification of post-secondary technical and vocational education is the Brevet de Technicien Supérieur, which requires the Baccalauréat or Brevet de Technicien Professionnel.

Regulatory Bodies

GOVERNMENT

Ministry of Culture: 8 rue 2 mars 1934, la Kasbah, 1006 Tunis; tel. (71) 56-26-61; fax (71) 57-45-80; e-mail mcu@ministeres.tn; internet www.culture.tn; Min. EZZEDINE BESCHAOUCH.

Ministry of Education: ave Bab Benat, 1030 Tunis; tel. (71) 56-87-68; e-mail med@ministeres.tn; internet www.education.tn; Min. TAÏB BACCOUCHE.

Ministry of Higher Education and Scientific Research: ave Ouled Haffouz, 1030 Tunis; tel. (71) 78-63-00; fax (71) 78-67-01; e-mail mes@mes.rnu.tn; internet www.mes.tn; Min. RIFAAT CHAABOUNI.

Learned Societies

GENERAL

Comité Culturel National: 105 ave de la Liberté, 1002 Tunis; tel. (71) 28-81-54; fax (71) 79-26-39; f. 1968; central body co-ordinating national and international cultural activities, sponsored by the Min. of Culture and by foreign embassies; regional and local cultural committees throughout the country; 16 mems; Pres. MOHAMED TALBI; Sec.-Gen. SAMIR BELHAJ YAHIA.

BIBLIOGRAPHY, LIBRARY SCIENCE AND MUSEOLOGY

Association Tunisienne des Bibliothécaires, Documentalistes et Archivistes: BP 380, 1015 Tunis; f. 1965; information sciences; 250 mems; Pres. ABDELBAKI DALY; publ. *Rassid* (multilingual, 4 a year).

Comité National des Musées: Musée National du Bardo, Tunis; f. 1961; Pres. HABIB BEN YOUNES; publ. *Les musées de Tunisie*.

EDUCATION

Arab League Educational, Cultural and Scientific Organization (ALECSO) (Organisation Arabe pour l'Education, la Culture et la Science): POB 1120, ave Mohamed V, Tunis; tel. (71) 78-44-66; fax (71) 78-44-96; e-mail alecso@email.ati.tn; internet www.alecso.org.tn; f. 1970; regional units: Arab Centre for Arabization, Translation, Authorship and Publication (Damascus, Syria), Institute of Arab Manuscripts (Cairo, Egypt), Institute of Arab Research and Studies (Cairo, Egypt), Khartoum International Institute for Arabic Language (Khartoum, Sudan), Arabization Coordination Bureau (Rabat, Morocco); promotes devt of education, culture and sciences in Arab countries; 21 Arab countries; library of 7,000 vols, 110 periodicals; Dir-Gen. MONGI BOUSNINA; publs *Arab Journal of Culture* (2 a year), *Arab Journal of Education* (2 a year), *Arab Journal of Sciences and Information* (2 a year), *Journal of Mass Education* (1 a year).

FINE AND PERFORMING ARTS

Union Nationale des Arts Plastiques: Musée du Belvédère, Tunis.

LANGUAGE AND LITERATURE

British Council: c/o British Embassy, 5 place de la Victoire, BP 229, 1015 Tunis; tel. (71) 25-90-53; fax (71) 35-34-11; e-mail info@tn.britishcouncil.org; internet www.britishcouncil.org.tn; offers courses and exams in English language and British culture, and promotes cultural exchange with the UK; library of 8,000 vols; Dir WILL TODD (acting).

Teaching Centre:

Teaching Centre: 2nd/3rd Fl., 47 ave Habib Bourguiba, Tunis 1001; tel. (71) 35-35-68; fax (71) 35-39-85; Man. TANIA PUGLIESE (acting).

Goethe-Institut: 6 place d'Afrique, rue du Sénégal, 1002 Tunis-Belvédère; tel. (71) 84-82-66; fax (71) 84-17-51; internet www.goethe.de/wm/tun/deindex.htm; offers courses and examinations in German language and culture, and promotes cultural exchange with Germany; Dir ECKEHART VOGT.

Institut des Belles Lettres Arabes: 12 rue Jamâa al Haoua, 1008 Tunis Bab Menara; tel. (71) 56-01-33; fax (71) 57-26-83; e-mail ibla@gnet.tn; internet www.iblatunis.org; f. 1930; cultural centre; language of instruction: Arabic, French; library of 32,000 vols on Tunisian studies and Arabic literature; Dir Dr JEAN FONTAINE; publ. *IBLA* (2 a year).

Instituto Cervantes: 120 ave de la Liberté, 1002 Tunis Belvédère; tel. (71) 78-88-47; fax (71) 79-38-25; e-mail centun@cervantes.es; internet tunez.cervantes.es; offers courses and examinations in Spanish language and culture, and promotes cultural exchange with Spain and Spanish-speaking Latin and Central America; library of 16,000 vols; Dir FRANCISCO CORRAL SÁNCHEZ-CABEZUDO.

Union des Écrivains Tunisiens: 20 ave de Paris, 1000 Tunis; tel. (71) 25-78-07; fax (71) 34-42-65; e-mail uniondesecrivains@yahoo.fr; internet www.uet.c.la; f. 1970; 560 mems; Pres. D. SHAHEDDINNE BOUJAH; Sec.-Gen. SLAHEDDINNE LAHMADI; publ. *El Massar*.

Research Institutes

GENERAL

Centre d'Études Maghrébines à Tunis: 19 bis rue d'Angleterre, Impasse Menabrea, BP 404, 1049 Tunis-Hached; tel. (71) 32-62-19; fax (71) 32-83-78; e-mail cemat@planet.tn; internet www.la.utexas.edu/research/mena/cemat; f. 1985; operated by American Institute for Maghreb Studies, Univ. of Arizona, Tucson; sponsors research by scholars of all nationalities and in all disciplines; gives research grants to Americans and Maghribis; facilitates liaison with North African scholars; holds annual research conf. and frequent lectures; library of 2,300 vols, 1,000 dissertations; Dir Dr LAURENCE MICHALAK.

Institut de Recherche pour le Développement (IRD): see main entry under France: 5 impasse Chahrazed, BP 434, 1004 Tunis El Menzah; tel. (71) 75-00-09; fax (71) 75-02-54; f. 1958; pedology, hydrology, microbiology, medical entomology, agricultural economics, archaeology, desertification, remote detection; library; Dir J. CLAUDE.

Institut National de Recherche Scientifique et Technique (INRST): BP 95, Hammam-Lif 2050; premises at: route Touristique, Borj-Cedria, Soliman; tel. (72) 43-02-15; fax (72) 43-09-34; f. 1969; applied physics, biology, chemistry, biotechnology, earth sciences, development of the use of domestic and industrial waste; library of 1,500 vols, 100 in spec. colln; Dir MOHAMED ENNABLT; Sec.-Gen. MESSAOUD CHAHTOUR.

AGRICULTURE, FISHERIES AND VETERINARY SCIENCE

Centre de Recherche du Génie Rural: BP 10, Ariana 2080; tel. (71) 71-80-55; f. 1959; agronomy, irrigation, etc.; Dir MOHAMED NEJIB REJEB; publ. *Cahier du CRGR*.

Institut de la Recherche Vétérinaire de Tunisie: rue Djebel Lakhdhar La Rabta, 1006 Tunis; tel. (71) 56-26-02; fax (71) 56-96-92; e-mail hammami.salah@iresa.agrinet.tn; f. 1887; veterinary research, laboratory disease diagnosis, food hygiene; library of 3,000 vols; Dir-Gen. Prof. Dr HAMMAMI SALAH; publ. *Bulletin of Epidemiology*.

Institut National de la Recherche Agronomique de Tunisie (INRAT): rue Hédi Karray 2049, Ariana; tel. (71) 23-00-24; fax (71) 75-28-97; e-mail netij.benmechlia@iresa.agrinet.tn; f. 1914; improvement of vegetable and livestock production through the use of appropriate agroecological and socioeconomic methods; 7 research laboratories, 2 research units, 13 regional experimental stations; library of 8,000 vols, 1,500 periodicals; Dir Dr N. BEN MECHLIA; publ. *Annales* (1 a year).

Institut National de Recherches Forestières de Tunisie: BP 2-2080, Ariana; f. 1967 under present title; research in all aspects of forestry; library: Documentation Centre comprises 2,981 vols and 3,144 documents; Dir M. DAHMAN; publs *Bulletin d'Information* (2 or 3 a year), *Annales*, *Notes de Recherches*.

Institut National des Sciences et Technologies de la Mer: 28 rue 2 mars 1934, 2025 Salammbô; tel. (71) 73-04-20; fax (71) 73-26-22; e-mail messaoudi.saida@instm.rnrt.tn; internet www.instm.rnrt.tn; f. 1924; fisheries research, aquaculture, fishing technology, marine environment, toxicology, algology; marine museum; library of 40,000 vols; Dir-Gen. Prof. RIDHA MRABET; Librarian SAIDA MESSAOUDI; publs *Bulletin*, *INSTM* (1 a year), *Notes* (3 a year).

BIBLIOGRAPHY, LIBRARY SCIENCE AND MUSEOLOGY

Institut National du Patrimoine: 4 place du Château, 1008 Tunis; tel. (71) 26-16-22; f. 1957; archaeology, museography, ethnography, research, protection and evaluation of the national heritage; library of 25,000 vols; Dir ABDELAZIZ DAOULATLI; publ. *Africa*.

EDUCATION

Institut National des Sciences de l'Éducation: 17 rue d'Irak, 1002 Tunis-Belvédère; tel. (71) 28-77-22; fax (71) 79-54-23; f. 1969; conducts research, undertakes assessment of curricula, books, students and teaching techniques, develops the use of audiovisual aids in education, organizes seminars and conferences; library of 30,000 vols; Dir NEJIB AYED; publs *Bulletin pédagogique*, *Cahiers de l'INSE*, *Revue Tunisienne des Sciences de l'Education*.

MEDICINE

Institut Pasteur: BP 74, 13 place Pasteur, 1002 Tunis Belvédère; tel. (71) 78-96-08; fax (71) 79-18-33; f. 1893; research in health sciences; library of 4,500 vols, 200 periodicals; Dir Prof. K. DELLAGI; publ. *Archives* (4 a year).

TECHNOLOGY

Centre National de l'Informatique: 17 rue Belhassen Ben Chaâbane, El-Omrane, 1005 Tunis; tel. (71) 78-30-55; fax (71) 78-18-62; f. 1976; assistance, training, development of computer applications and software, management of processing centres; library of 4,000 vols; Dir MONGI MILED.

Office National des Mines: BP 215, 1080 Tunis Cedex; premises at: 24 rue 8601, La Charguia, 2035 Tunis; tel. (71) 78-88-42; fax (71) 79-40-16; f. 1962; geological research and map-making; bibliographic database on geology of Tunisia; library of 15,000 vols, 450 periodicals; Pres. and Dir-Gen. MOHAMED FADHEL ZERELLI; publs *Annales des Mines et de la Géologie*, *Notes du service géologique*.

Libraries and Archives

Tunis

Archives Nationales: Le Premier Ministère, La Casbah, 1020 Tunis; tel. (71) 56-05-56; fax (71) 56-91-75; f. 1874; 5,000 vols, MSS in Arabic, Turkish, French, Italian and English; Dir MONCEF FAKHFAKH; publ. *Inventaires des documents d'archives conservés*.

Bibliothèque Nationale: BP 42, 1000 Tunis; tel. (71) 57-27-06; fax (71) 57-28-87; e-mail bibliothequenationale@email.at.tn; internet www.bnt.nat.tn; f. 1885; depository of books published in Tunisia (mostly in Arabic); documentation and information dept; 1.5m. vols in 12 languages; 15,000 periodicals; 40,000 Arabic and Oriental MSS; Curator SAMIA KAMARTI; publs *Catalogue général des manuscrits* (1 a year), *Le Livre Tunisien* (1 a year).

Bibliothèques Publiques: Head Office: 39 rue Asdrubal, Lafayette, 1002 Tunis; tel. (71) 78-25-52; fax (71) 79-77-52; f. 1965; 2,746,678 vols in 293 public libraries throughout the country, notably at Tunis, Béjà, Bizerte, Gabès, Gafsa, Jendouba, Kairouan, Kasserine, El Kef, Medenine, Monastir, Nabeul, Sfax, Sousse, Siliana, Mahdia, Ariana, Ben Arous, Zagnouan, Sidi Bouzid, Tozeur, Kébili and Tetaouine; 233 children's libraries, 266 local and community libraries and 27 mobile libraries; Chief Curator ALI MARZOUKI; publs *Bulletin* (1 a year), *Répertoire*, *Statistics of public libraries*.

Centre de Documentation Nationale: blvd 7 Novembre, 1004 Tunis-El Menzah; tel. (71) 70-49-60; fax (71) 79-22-41; e-mail csi.cdn@email.ati.tn; f. 1966; 13,500 monographs, 2,400 periodicals, 210,000 press articles, 30,000 photographs; Dir-Gen. SAHRAOURI GAMAOUN.

Museums and Art Galleries

Carthage

Musée National de Carthage: BP 3, 2016 Carthage; tel. (71) 73-00-36; fax (71) 73-00-99; f. 1964; library of 5,000 vols on archaeology (special collection: antiquity); Dir ABDELMAJID ENNABLI.

El Jem

Musée Archéologique d'El Jem: El Jem; tel. (73) 630093; fax (73) 630969; e-mail ibenjerbania@yahoo.fr; Archaeologist in Charge of Research BEN JERBANIA IMED.

Kairouan

Musée d'Art Islamique: Kairouan.

Makthar

Musée Archéologique de Makthar: Makthar; Punic and Roman.

Monastir

Musée d'Art Islamique du Ribat: Monastir.

Sbeïtla

Musée de Sbeïtla: Sbeïtla; Roman antiquities.

Sfax

Musée Archéologique de Sfax: Sfax.

Sousse

Musée Archéologique de Sousse (Kasbah): Sousse.

Tunis

Maison des Arts: Parc du Belvédère, 1002 Tunis; tel. (71) 28-37-49; fax (71) 79-58-60; f. 1992; art exhibition, musical and cultural activities; library of 6,000 vols; Dir ALI LOUATI.

Musée National du Bardo: 2000 Le Bardo, Tunis; tel. (71) 51-36-50; fax (71) 51-40-50; f. 1888; contains prehistoric collections, relics of Punic, Greek and Roman art, and ancient and modern Islamic arts, largest collection in the world of Roman mosaics; library of 4,700 vols; Dir HABIB BEN YOUNES; publ. *Les Nécropoles Puniques de Tunisie*.

Universities

UNIVERSITÉ DU 7 NOVEMBRE À CARTHAGE

29 rue Asdrubal, 1002 Tunis
Telephone: (71) 78-75-02
Fax: (71) 78-87-68
E-mail: pu7nc@univ7nc.rnu.tn
Internet: www.univ7nc.rnu.tn/fr/indexfr.htm

Founded 1988 as Université de Droit, d'Économie et de Gestion; present name 2000

Pres.: Prof. TAÏEB HADHRI
Sec.-Gen.: MOHAMED AMEUR ISMAÏL

Number of teachers: 2,003
Number of students: 30,590

DEANS

Faculty of Economics and Management (Nabeul): EZZEDDINE ZOUARI
Faculty of Law, Political and Social Sciences (Tunis): (vacant)
Faculty of Sciences (Bizerte): CHAABANE CHEFI

UNIVERSITÉ DU CENTRE, SOUSSE

rue Khalifa El Karoui Sahloul, BP 526, 4002 Sousse
Telephone: (73) 36-81-25
Fax: (73) 36-81-26
E-mail: universite.centre@uc.rnu.tn
Internet: www.uc.rnu.tn

Founded 1986 as Université de Monastir pour le Centre; present name 1991
State control

Pres.: MOHAMED ALI HAMZA

Number of teachers: 2,585
Number of students: 51,490

DEANS

Faculty of Arts and Humanities, Khairouan: SAHBI ALLANI
Faculty of Arts and Humanities, Sousse: HÉDI JATLAOUI
Faculty of Dental Medicine, Monastir: KHALED BOURAOUI
Faculty of Economics and Management, Mahdia: ALI FRAJ
Faculty of Law, Economics and Political Science, Sousse: MONGI TARCHOUNA
Faculty of Medicine, Monastir: HABIB SABBAH
Faculty of Medicine, Sousse: BECHIR BEL HADJ ALI
Faculty of Pharmacy, Monastir: MOHAMED KALLEL
Faculty of Science, Monastir: MONGI BEN AMARA

UNIVERSITÉ EZZITOUNA

21 rue Sidi Jelizi, place Maakel Ezzaïm, 1008 Tunis
Telephone: (71) 57-55-14
Fax: (71) 57-61-51
Internet: www.uz.rnu.tn

Founded 1988 from existing faculties
State control

Pres.: SALEM BOUYAHIA

Faculties of theology and religious studies

Publications: *Al-Miskat* (1 a year), *Ettanwir* (1 a year).

UNIVERSITÉ DE LA MANOUBA

Campus Universitaire de la Manouba, la Manouba 2010
Telephone: (71) 60-14-99
Fax: (71) 60-22-11
E-mail: mail@uma.rnu.tn
Internet: www.uma.rnu.tn

Founded 2001
State control

Pres.: SLAHEDDINE GHERISSI
Vice-Pres.: MOHAMED EL KADHI
Sec.-Gen.: SAID GHRAB
Number of students: 30,557.

ATTACHED RESEARCH INSTITUTES

Faculty of Letters: tel. (71) 60-10-45; fax (71) 60-09-10; Dean CHOKRI MABKHOUT; Sec.-Gen. AHMED EL BOUKHARI CHETOUI.

Higher Institute for the Promotion of the Handicapped: IPH, 2 rue Jabrane Khalil Jabrane, la Manouba 2010; tel. (70) 60-40-91; fax (71) 60-40-71; e-mail directeur .iph@iph.org.tn; internet www.iph.nat.tn; Dir LOFTI BELLALEHOM; Sec.-Gen. MOUNIRA CHAABOUNI.

Higher Institute of Accounting and Business Administration: tel. (71) 60-18-90; fax (71) 60-24-04; Dir SAMIR EL GHAZOUANI; Sec.-Gen. LOTFI CHABBI.

Higher Institute of Documentation: tel. (71) 60-16-50; fax (71) 60-02-00; Dir KHALED MILED; Sec.-Gen. ABDERRAOUF BOUBAKAR.

Higher Institute of Multimedia Arts: ISAMM, Charguia 1; tel. (70) 83-72-06; fax (70) 83-76-03; Dir CHIRAZ LAATIRI.

Higher Institute of Sport and Physical Education: ISSEP, Kssar Essaid, la Manouba 2010; tel. (71) 54-84-32; fax (71) 65-42-82; e-mail crd@issep-ks.rnu.tn; internet www .issep-ks.rnu.tn; Dir MOURAD JALEL MAAOUI; Sec.-Gen. ALI NCIRI.

Higher Institute of the History of the National Movement: Dir MOHAMED LOFTI CHAIBI.

Higher School of Commerce: tel. (71) 60-27-60; fax (71) 60-13-11; internet www.esct .rnu.tn; Dir HAFEDH BEN ABDENNEBI; Sec.-Gen. HAMDA YAAKOUBI.

Higher School of Sciences and Design Technology: ESSTD, ave de l'Indépendance, Denden 2011; tel. (71) 61-07-00; fax (71) 61-07-50; Dir RAIF MALEK; Sec.-Gen. ADEL HENID.

Institute of Press and Communications Science (IPSI): tel. (71) 60-03-55; fax (71) 60-05-70; e-mail ipsi@ipsi.rnu.tn; internet www.ipsi.rnu.tn; Dir MOHAMED HAMDANE; Sec.-Gen. AHMED HADJI.

National School of Computer Sciences: tel. (71) 60-04-44; fax (71) 60-04-49; internet www.ensi.rnu.tn; Dir KHALID GHEDIRA.

School of e-Commerce: tel. (71) 60-29-19; fax (71) 60-26-62; Dir MALEK GHANIMA.

School of Veterinary Medicine: Dir MOHAMED HABIB JEMLI.

Sidi Thabet Higher Institute of Biotechnology: ISB, Sidi Thabet 2020; tel. (71) 52-05-88; fax (71) 52-12-67; Dir RAFIKA CHEKIR; Sec.-Gen. HAYET MANSOURI.

UNIVERSITÉ DE SFAX POUR LE SUD

route de l'Áeroport, 3029 Sfax
Telephone: (74) 24-44-23
Fax: (74) 24-09-13
E-mail: uss@uss.rnu.tn
Internet: www.mes.tn/uss

Founded 1986 from existing faculties; campus at Gafsa
State control
Languages of instruction: Arabic, French

Pres.: MOHAMED HEDI KTARI
Sec.-Gen.: MOHSEN BEN MANSOUR

Number of teachers: 2,495
Number of students: 48,514

DEANS

Faculty of Arts and Humanities: MOHSEN DHIEB
Faculty of Economics and Administration: ALI CHKIR
Faculty of Law: AHMED OMRANE
Faculty of Medicine: ADNANE HAMMAMI
Faculty of Science, Gafsa: (vacant)
Faculty of Science, Sfax: ABDELHAMID BEN SALAH

CONSTITUENT INSTITUTES

Higher Institute of Applied Humanities Studies, Gafsa: Dir IBRAHIM JADLA.

Higher Institute of Business Administration: Dir ABDELWAHEB REBAI.

Higher Institute of Business Administration, Gafsa: Dir MALEK OURIMI.

Higher Institute of Crafts and Technical Training: Dir NOURREDINE ELHENI.

Higher Institute of Electronics and Telecommunications Technology: Dir LOFTI KAMOUN.

Higher Institute of Industrial Management: Dir HABIB CHABCHOUB.

Higher Institute of Information Technology and Media Studies: Dir ABDELMAJID BEN HAMADOU.

Higher Institute of Management Training, Gafsa: Dir AMMAR AKRIMI.

Higher Institute of Music: Dir MOURAD SIALA.

Higher Institute of Sport and Physical Education: Dir JALEL MILADI.

Higher Institute of Technology, Gafsa: Dir JALEL KHDIRI.

Higher Institute of Technology, Sfax: Dir SLIMÈNE GABSI.

Institute of Advanced Business Studies: Dir FAIKA SCANDER CHARFI.

National School of Commerce: Dir ABDELKADER CHAABANE.

National School of Engineering: Dir BOUBAKER EL EUCH.

National School of Health Science and Technology: Dir MONGIA HACHICHA.

Olivier Institute: Dir TAÎ MILADI.

Preparatory Institute for Engineers: Dir FATHI LAADHAR.

RESEARCH CENTRE

Biotechnology Centre: Dir HAMADI AYADI.

UNIVERSITÉ DE SOUSSE

ave Khelifa Karoui, Sahloul IV, Sousse
Telephone: (73) 36-81-29
Fax: (73) 36-81-26
E-mail: universite.centre@uc.rnu.tn
Internet: www.uc.rnu.tn

Founded 1986
State control
Languages of instruction: Arabic, French
Academic year: September to July

Pres.: AHMED NOUREDDINE HELAL
Vice-Pres.: NEJIB BELAID

Library of 277,010 vols
Number of teachers: 2,100
Number of students: 33,500

DEANS

Faculty of Arts and Humanities: ADBELLATIF MRABET
Faculty of Law and Economic And Political Sciences: JAMEL DIMASSI
Faculty of Medicine: NAJIB MRIZAK
Institute of Agronomy of Chott Meriem: TIJANI MEHOUACHI
Institute of Applied Sciences and Technology: SALEM OURAJINI
Institute of Computer Sciences and Communication Techniques of Hammam Sousse: HABIB YOUSSEF
Institute of Finance and Fiscality: EZZEDDINE ZOUARI
Institute of Fine-Arts: MONGI SOYAD
Institute of Higher Commercial Studies: MOUNIR BELLOUMI
Institute of Management: KHAIREDDINE JEBSI
Institute of Music: MONCEF CHAARANA
Institute of Nursing Sciences: MOUNIR GRIRA
Institute of Science and Health Technics: SIHEM HMISSA
Institute of Sciences and Technology of Hammam Sousse: MONGI BEN AMARA
Institute of Transport and Logistics: ADEL KALBOUSSI
National School of Engineers: NAJOUWA SOUKRI BEN AMARA

UNIVERSITÉ DE TUNIS

92 blvd du 9 avril 1938, 1007 Tunis
Telephone: (71) 56-73-22
Fax: (71) 56-06-33

Founded 1988 as Université des Lettres, des Arts et des Sciences Humaines (Tunis I) from existing faculties, present name 2001

Pres.: ABDERRAOUF MAHBOULI
Sec.-Gen.: LAMJED MESSOUSSI

Library of 186,000 vols
Number of teachers: 1,280
Number of students: 32,000

Publications: *Les Annales de l'Université* (in Arabic), *Les Cahiers de Tunisie* (multilingual), *La Revue des Langues* (multilingual), *La Revue Tunisienne des Sciences de la Communication*, *Revue Géographique* (multilingual)

DEANS AND DIRECTORS

Centre for Economic and Social Studies and Research: HACHMI LABAÏED
Faculty of Humanities and Social Sciences: HABIB DLALA
Faculty of Law, Economics and Management: CHOKRI MAMOGHLI
Faculty of Letters: (vacant)
Higher Documentation Institute: HENDA HAJAMI BEN GHZALA
Higher Institute of Applied Studies in Humanities: JAMEL BEN TAHAR
Higher Institute of Cultural Studies and Heritage Professions of Tunis: HABIB BAKLOUTI
Higher Institute of Drama: MOHAMED MESSAOUD DRISS
Higher Institute of Education and Training: MALIKA TRABELSI
Higher Institute of Management: ABDELWAHED TRABELSI
Higher Institute of Music: MUSTAPHA ALOULOU
Higher Institute for Youth and Cultural Activity: MONCEF JAZZAR
Higher Teacher Training School: MABROUK EL MANNAÏ
National Institute of Heritage: BÉJI BEN MAMI
Preparatory Institute for Engineering Studies: MOHAMED ABEDELMANAF BEN ABDRABOU
Tunis College of Science and Technology: JILANI LAMLOUMI
Tunis Higher Institute of Fine Arts: MOHAMED BEN TAHER GUIGA

UNIVERSITÉ DE TUNIS EL MANAR

Campus Universitaire, Manar II, 2092 Tunis
Telephone: (71) 87-33-66
Fax: (71) 87-20-55
E-mail: unitumanar@tun2.rnu.tn

Founded 1988 as Université des Sciences, des Techniques et de Médecine de Tunis (Tunis II) from existing faculties; present name 2001

Pres.: Prof. YOUSSEF ALOUANE
Sec.-Gen.: ISMAIL KHALIL

Number of teachers: 2,733
Number of students: 23,488

Publication: *Revue de l'Université* (6 a year)

DEANS AND DIRECTORS

Bourguiba Institute of Modern Languages: ABED EL MAJID EL BEDOUI
El Khawarizmi Computer Centre: HENDA HADJAMI BEN GHEZELA
El Manar Preparatory School of Engineering: MOHAMED EL ABAAD
Faculties of Economics and Management: MOHAMED HADDAR
Faculty of Mathematics, Physics and Natural Sciences: CHEDLI TOUBLI
Faculty of Medicine: RACHID MECHMECH
Faculty of Law and Political Science: CHAFIK SAÏED
Higher Institute of Computer Science: SAMIR BEN AHMED
Higher Institute of Humanities: MOHAMED MAHJOUB
Higher Institute of Medical Technology: FATMA SLIM EL HILA
Higher Institute for Sport and Physical Education: ABDELAZIZ SFAR
Higher School of Food Technology: ABDELKADER CHERIF
Higher School of Health Sciences and Technology: MOHAMED HABIB JAAFOURA
Higher School of Posts and Telecommunications: NACEUR AMMAR
Higher School of Science and Technology: SLAHEDDINE EL-GHRISSI
Institute for the Advancement of Disabled People: RAOUF BEN AMMAR
Kef Higher School of Agriculture: BOUZID NASRAOUI
Kef Institute for Sport and Physical Education: YOUSSEF FEKIH
Mateur Higher School of Agriculture: HEDI ABDOULI
Mateur Preparatory School of Engineering: MOHAMED BEJAOUI
Medjez el Bab Higher School of Rural Engineering: ABDERRAZEK SUISSI
Mograne Higher School of Agriculture: TIJANI MAHOUACHI
Nabeul Preparatory Institute of Engineering: MONCEF HADDED
National Agricultural Research Institute: SALAH MEKNI
National Institute of Agronomy: MONCEF EL-HARRABI
National Research Institute of Rural Engineering for Water and Forests: NEJI RAJEB
National Research Institute of Sciences and Technology: MOHAMED NOBIL
National School of Computer Science: FAROUK KAMMOUN
National School of Engineering: KHALIFA MAÂLEL
National University Centre for Scientific and Technical Documentation: FATMA CHAMMAM BEN ABDALLAH
Pasteur Institute: KOUSSAI EDALAJI
Polytechnic Institute: TAIEB HADHRI
Preparatory Institute of Scientific Studies and Technology: FAOUZIA CHARFI
School of Civil Aviation and Meterorlogy: MOHAMED TOUIL
Sidi Thabet National School of Veterinary Medicine: ATEF MALEK
Tabarka Forestry School: HAMDA SAOUDI
Veterinary Research Institute: MALEK ZRELLI

Other Institutions of Higher Education

Centre Culturel International d'Hammamet: ave des Nations Unies, 8050 Hammamet; tel. (72) 28-04-10; fax (72) 28-07-22; f. 1962; theatrical techniques, history and sociology of the theatre and video; Dir TAOUFIK BESBÈS.

Conservatoire National de Musique, de Danse et d'Arts Populaires: 20 ave de Paris, Tunis.

École Nationale d'Administration: 24 ave du Docteur Calmette, Mutuelleville, Tunis; tel. (71) 28-83-00; f. 1964; library: 53,000 vols; 1,050 students; Dir MAHER KAMOUN; publ. *Revue Tunisienne d'Administration Publique* (3 a year).

École Nationale de la Statistique: BP 65, Tunis; f. 1969; 1- and 2-year diploma courses.

Institut d'Économie Quantitative: 27 rue de Liban, 1002 Tunis; tel. (71) 28-36-33; fax (71) 78-70-34; f. 1964; methodological research in planning and documentation in social and economic fields; library: 7,500 vols, 300 periodicals; Dir-Gen. GHORBEL HÉDI.

Institut National du Travail et des Études Sociales: Z. I. Charguia II, BP 692, 1080 Tunis; tel. (71) 70-62-07; fax (71) 70-34-64; e-mail intes@intes.rnu.tn; internet www.intes.rnu.tn; language of instruction: Arabic; library: 5,000 vols; 110 teachers (34 full-time, 76 part-time); 2,200 students; Dir Prof. MUSTAPHA NASRAOUI; publ. *Travail et Développement* (2 a year).

TURKEY

The Higher Education System

Universities are administered by the YöK (Council of Higher Education), which sets institutional budgets and defines criteria for the award of degrees. Institutions of higher education include universities, faculties, institutes, colleges, conservatories, vocational colleges and research centres. In 2005/06 2,181,217 students attended 1,306 higher education institutes. Turkey joined the Bologna Process in 2001. Reforms to the degree structure were not required since the Turkish higher education system was already based on three cycles. Quality assurance remains based on internal institutional evaluation, with some degree programmes assessed by specialized agencies, but full implementation of a national quality assurance system is planned. The Lisbon Convention was signed in 2004 and came into force in 2007. The National Qualifications Framework is currently under development and pilot implementation is planned for 2010, with full implementation by the end of 2012.

The main criteria for admission to higher education is the State University Entrance Examination (Ögrenci Secme Sinavi—ÖSS), administered by the Student Selection and Placement Centre (ÖSYM). Universities set their own entrance requirements based on scores in the ÖSS. Since 2002 the two-year Associate Degree (Ön Lisans Diplomasi) has been broadened to encompass technical and vocational education. The Bachelors (Lisans Diplomasi) is mostly a four-year programme of study, although some disciplines require longer periods of study, such as dentistry, architecture, veterinary medicine (five years) and medicine (six years). The first postgraduate degree is the Masters (Yüsek Lisans Diplomasi), which is a two-year programme and admission to which is on the basis of a competitive examination administered by the ÖSYM. The final university degree is the Doctor of Philosophy (Doktora); again, admission is on the basis of a competitive examination administered by the ÖSYM, and students are required to complete a four-year period of study and research for the award of the final degree.

Technical and vocational education is legally defined as one of three categories: formal vocational education, apprenticeship training or vocational courses. Since 2002 students have been allowed to enter vocational higher education without taking an entrance examination. In terms of formal vocational training, the main institutions are specialist vocational schools attached to universities, in addition to two-year colleges of technology and commercial colleges. Students who successfully complete the course of study are awarded the ön lisans (followed by subject name) and title of tekniker (Technician). Apprenticeship training is offered largely at the secondary level, and vocational courses are aimed at adults who have left formal education.

Regulatory and Representative Bodies

GOVERNMENT

Ministry of Culture and Tourism: Kültür ve Turizm Bakanlığı, Atatürk Bul. 29, 06050 Opera, Ankara; tel. (312) 309-08-50; fax (312) 312-43-59; e-mail info@kulturturizm.gov.tr; internet www.kultur.gov.tr; Minister ERTUĞRUL GÜNAY.

Ministry of National Education: Milli Eğitim Bakanlığı, Atatürk Bul., Bakanlıklar, Ankara; tel. (312) 419-14-10; fax (312) 417-70-27; e-mail meb@meb.gov.tr; internet www.meb.gov.tr; Minister Dr HÜSEYIN ÇELIK.

ACCREDITATION

ENIC/NARIC Turkey: European Union and Int. Relations Office, Yüksekögretim Kurulu Baskanligi (YÖK), 06539 Bilkent, Ankara; tel. (312) 298-72-43; fax (312) 266-47-44; e-mail naric@yok.gov.tr; Head DENIZ ATES.

NATIONAL BODIES

Türk Üniversite Rektörleri Komitesi (Turkish University Rectors' Committee): Yükseköğretim Kurulu, Bilkent, Ankara; tel. (312) 266-47-25; fax (312) 266-51-53; f. 1967; rectors of all Turkish univs, with 5 former rectors; advises the Higher Education Ccl and the Interuniversity Board on university affairs, promotes cooperation between univs; Pres. Prof. Dr KEMAL GÜRÜZ; Sec. Prof. Dr UĞUR BÜGET.

Yükseköğretim Kurulu (Council of Higher Education): 06539 Bilkent, Ankara; tel. (312) 298-70-00; fax (312) 266-47-59; e-mail webadmin@yok.gov.tr; internet www.yok.gov.tr; f. 1981; NGO responsible for the organization and governance of the higher education instns, and for the teaching and research carried out; 22 mems; Pres. Prof. Dr YUSUF ZIYA ÖZCAN; Gen. Sec. TURGUT KILIÇ.

Learned Societies

AGRICULTURE, FISHERIES AND VETERINARY SCIENCE

Türk Veteriner Hekimleri Birliği (Turkish Veterinary Medical Association): 73/8, Kocatepe, Cankaya, Ankara; tel. and fax (312) 435-54-15; e-mail merkezkonseyi@tvhb.org.tr; internet www.tvhb.org.tr; f. 1954; 20,000 mems; Pres. MEHMET ALKAN; Vice-Pres. Prof. Dr ARIF ALTINTAS; Gen-Sec. ALI KOC; publ. *Turkish Veterinary Medical Association / Turk Veteriner Hekimleri Birligi Dergisi* (3 or 4 a year).

BIBLIOGRAPHY, LIBRARY SCIENCE AND MUSEOLOGY

Türk Kütüphaneciler Derneği (Turkish Librarians' Association): Necatibey Cad. Elgün Sok. 8/8, 06440 Kızılay, Ankara; tel. (312) 230-13-25; fax (312) 232-04-53; e-mail tkd.dernek@gmail.com; internet www.kutuphaneci.org.tr; f. 1949; 2,000 mems; Pres. ALI FUAT KARTAL; Sec.-Gen. EMRE HASAN AKBAYRAK; publ. *Türk Kütüphaneciliği* (4 a year).

ECONOMICS, LAW AND POLITICS

Türk Hukuk Kurumu (Turkish Law Association): 2 Cad. 55/6 Bahçelievler, Ankara; f. 1934; publs *La Turquie* (Vie Juridique des Peuples, Paris), *Türk Hukuk Lûgati* (Turkish Law Dictionary).

HISTORY, GEOGRAPHY AND ARCHAEOLOGY

Türk Tarih Kurumu (Turkish Historical Society): Kızılay Sok. 1, 06100 Sıhhıye Ankara; tel. (312) 310-23-68; fax (312) 310-16-98; e-mail ttkinfo@ttk.org.tr; internet www.ttk.org.tr; f. 1931; 40 mems; library of 228,577 vols; Pres. Prof. Dr YUSUF HALAÇOĞLU; publs *Belgeler* (1 a year), *Belleten* (3 a year).

LANGUAGE AND LITERATURE

British Council: Posta Kutusu 34, Çankaya, Ankara; tel. (312) 455-36-00; fax (312) 455-36-36; internet www.britishcouncil.org/turkey; f. 1940; offers courses and exams in English language and British culture and promotes cultural exchange with the UK; attached offices in Istanbul (teaching centre) and Izmir; Dir of Operations, Turkey JEFF STREETER.

Goethe-Institut: Atatürk Bulvarı 131, Bakanlıklar, 06640 Ankara; tel. (312) 419-52-83; fax (312) 418-08-47; e-mail il@ankara.goethe.org; internet www.goethe.de/om/ank; offers courses and exams in German language and culture and promotes cultural exchange with Germany; attached centres in Istanbul and Izmir; library of 15,000 vols; Dir Dr THOMAS LIER.

Instituto Cervantes: Tarlabasi Bulvarı, Zambak Sokak 33, 80080 Istanbul; tel. (212) 292-65-36; fax (212) 292-65-37; e-mail cenest@cervantes.es; internet estambul.cervantes.es; offers courses and exams in Spanish language and culture and promotes cultural exchange with Spain and Spanish-speaking Latin and Central America; library of 7,500 vols; Dir PABLO MARTÍN ASUERO.

PEN Yazarlar Derneği (Turkish PEN Centre): Istiklal Cad., 225, Beyoglu is Merkezi, B Blok, Kat 2, 143, Beyoglu, Istanbul; e-mail pprtr@superonline.com; f. 1989; 200

mems; Pres. VECDI SAYAR; publ. *Turkish PEN Reader* (in English, 2 a year).

Türk Dil Kurumu (Turkish Language Institute): Atatürk Bulvarı 217, Kavaklıdere, 06680 Ankara; tel. (312) 428-61-00; fax (312) 468-07-83; e-mail bim@tdk.org.tr; internet www.tdk.org.tr; f. 1932; 40 mems; library of 35,000 vols on Turkish studies; Pres. Prof. Dr ŞÜKRÜ HALUK AKALIN; Sec.-Gen. ALI KARAÇALI; publs *Tercüme Yıllığı* (Yearbook of Translation), *Türk Dili Araştırmaları Yıllığı* (Yearbook of Turkic Studies), *Türk Dili Dergisi* (Journal of Turkish Language, 12 a year), *Türk Dünyası Dergisi* (Journal of Turkish World, 2 a year).

MEDICINE

Türk Cerrahi Derneği (Turkish Surgical Society): Koru Mah. Ihlamur Cad. 26, 06810 Çayyolu, Ankara; tel. (312) 241-99-90; fax (312) 241-99-91; e-mail turkcer@turkcer.org.tr; internet www.turkcer.org.tr; f. 1929.

Türk Mikrobiyoloji Cemiyeti (Turkish Microbiological Society): PK 57, 34492 Beyazit, Istanbul; tel. and fax (212) 531-70-89; e-mail tmc@tmc-online.org; internet www.tmc-online.org; f. 1931; 350 mems; Pres. Prof. Dr NEHAZAT GÜRLER; Sec.-Gen. Doc. Dr ORHAN CERN AKTEPE; publ. *Türk Mikrobiyoloji Cemiyeti Dergisi* (Journal, 4 a year).

Türk Nöropsikiyatri Derneği (Turkish Neuropsychiatric Society): Op. Dr. Raif Bey Sok. 31/2, 34360 Sisli, Istanbul; tel. (212) 219-97-77; fax (212) 343-00-95; f. 1914; 1,200 mems; meetings to discuss aspects of psychiatry and neurology; Pres. Prof. PEYKAN GÖKOLP; publ. *Nöropsikiyatri Arşivi* (Archives of Neuropsychiatry, 4 a year).

Türk Ortopedi ve Travmatoloji Birliği Derneği (Turkish Association of Orthopaedics and Traumatology): Bayraktar Mahallesi Ikizdere Sok. 21/12, Kat 2 GOP, Ankara; tel. (312) 436-11-40; fax (312) 436-27-16; internet www.totbid.org.tr; Pres. Prof. Dr BÜLEIT ALPARSLAN.

Türk Oto-Rino-Larengoloji Cemiyeti (Turkish Otorhinolaryngological and Head and Neck Surgery Society): Buyudere Cad. Tankaya 18/1 Kat 1, Şişli, 80260 Istanbul; tel. (212) 233-11-26; fax (212) 233-11-27; e-mail kbb@kbb.org.tr; internet www.kbb.org.tr; f. 1930; 2,500 mems; Pres. Prof. Dr ASIM KAYTAZ; Gen. Sec. Prof. Dr FERHAN ÖZ; publ. *Turkish Archives of Otolaryngology* (3 a year).

Türk Tabipleri Birliği (Turkish Medical Association): GMK Bul. Şehit Daniş Tunalıgil Sok. 2 Kat 4, Maltepe, 06570 Ankara; tel. (312) 231-31-79; fax (312) 231-19-52; e-mail ttb@ttb.org.tr; internet www.ttb.org.tr; f. 1953; 98,500 mems; Pres. Dr ERIŞ BILALOĞLU; Gen. Sec. Dr FERIDE AKSU TANIK.

Türk Tibbi Elektro Radyografi Cemiyeti (Turkish Electro-Radiographical Society): Valikonagi Cad. 10, Harbiye, Istanbul; f. 1924.

Türk Tıp Tarihi Kurumu (Turkish Medical History Society): c/o Uludağ Üniversitesi, Tıp Fakültesi, Deontoloji ve Tıp Tarihi Anabilim Dalı, Bursa; tel. (532) 452-94-37; e-mail ademirer@yahoo.com; f. 1938; 120 mems; library of 70,000 vols; Pres. Prof. Dr AYŞEGÜL ERDEMIR DEMIRHAN.

Türk Tüberküloz ve Toraks Derneği (Turkish Association of Tuberculosis and Thorax): Ankara Üniversitesi, Tıp Fakültesi, Göğüs Hastalıkları Anabilim Dalı, 06100 Cebeci- Ankara; tel. (312) 319-00-27; fax (312) 319-00-46; e-mail akaya@medicine.ankara.edu.tr; internet www.tubtoraks.org; Dir Dr ÖZLEM ÖZDEMIR KUMBASAR; publ. *Journal* (4 a year).

Türk Üroloji Derneği (Turkish Urological Society): c/o Prof. Nurettin Öktem Sokak, Lale Palas Apt. 18/2, 34382 Şişli, Istanbul; tel. and fax (212) 232-46-89; e-mail uroturk@uroturk.org.tr; internet www.uroturk.org.tr; f. 1933; 1,093 mems; Pres. Prof. VURAL SOLOK; publ. *Türk Uroloji Dergisi* (Turkish Journal of Urology, 4 a year).

NATURAL SCIENCES

Mathematical Sciences

Türkiye Matematik Derneği (Mathematical Society of Turkey): Sabancı Üniversitesi, Karaköy İletişim Merkezi, Bankalar Cad. 2, 80020 Karaköy, Istanbul; tel. (212) 292-49-39; e-mail emrah@su.sabanciuniv.edu; internet www.tmd.org.tr; f. 1948; development of mathematics among young people; 509 mems; Pres. Prof. Dr TOSUN TERZIOĞLU; Gen. Sec. Prof. Dr HÜLYA ŞENKON; publ. *Matematik Dünyası* (2 a year).

Physical Sciences

Türkiye Kimya Derneği (Chemical Society of Turkey): Halaskârgazi Cad. 53, D. 8 Uzay Apt, Harbiye, Istanbul; tel. (212) 240-73-31; e-mail tkd@turchemsoc.org; internet www.turchemsoc.org; f. 1919; 1,500 mems; Pres. Prof. Dr OSMAN YAVUZ ATAMAN'IN; publ. *Kimya ve Sanayi* (Chemistry and Industry).

PHILOSOPHY AND PSYCHOLOGY

Türkiye Felsefe Kurumu (Philosophical Society of Turkey): Ahmet Rasim Sok. 8/2, Çankaya, 06550 Ankara; tel. (312) 440-74-08; fax (312) 441-02-97; e-mail toc@tfk.org.tr; internet www.tfk.org.tr; f. 1974.; promotes philosophy and philosophical education in Turkey; encourages philosophical thinking in public life and secures int. cooperation through seminars, symposia and courses; 175 individual mems; Pres. IOANNA KUÇURADI; Sec.-Gen. GULRIZ UYGUR; publ. *Bülten* (3 a year).

Yeni Felsefe Cemiyeti (New Philosophical Society): Işık Lisesi, Nişantaşı, Istanbul; f. 1943.

TECHNOLOGY

TMMOB Jeoloji Mühendisleri Odası (Chamber of Geological Engineers of Turkey): PK 464, Yenişehir, 06444 Ankara; tel. (312) 434-36-01; fax (312) 434-23-88; e-mail jmo@jmo.org.tr; internet www.jmo.org.tr; f. 1974; 9,780 mems; library of 17,000 vols; Pres. AYDÝN CELEBI; Sec.-Gen. BAHATTIN MURAT DEMIR; publs *Abstracts of the Geological Congress of Turkey* (1 a year), *Abstracts of Geological Research in Turkey* (1 a year), *Blue Planet* (2 a year), *Bulletin News* (4 a year), *Geological Bulletin of Turkey* (2 a year), *Journal of Geological Engineering* (2 a year).

Research Institutes

GENERAL

Research Centre for Islamic History, Art and Culture (IRCICA): POB 24, Beşiktaş, 80692 Istanbul; Yildiz Sarayi, Seyir Kosku Barbaros Bulvarı, Besiktas, 34349 Istanbul; tel. (212) 259-17-42; fax (212) 258-43-65; e-mail ircica@ircica.org; internet www.ircica.org; f. 1979; a subsidiary of the Organization of the Islamic Conference; activities relating to research, publishing, documentation and information on subjects concerning the Islamic civilisation and Muslim cultures incl. history of Muslim nations, history of science, archaeology, architecture and urbanism, fine arts and handicrafts, preservation of cultural heritage, and cultural devt issues; organization of conferences, symposia, exhibitions, workshops, training courses and competitions; publishes books in various languages, newsletter appears quarterly in English, French and Arabic; library of 70,000 vols, 1,592 periodicals, 70,000 photographs, 1,500 maps, 1,150 microfilms, 200 CDs and DVDs, 1,860 audio cassettes, 5,210 archive documents, 4,000 calligraphy plates; Dir-Gen. Dr HALIT EREN.

Türk Kültürünü Araştırma Enstitüsü (Turkish Cultural Research Institute): 17° Sok. 38, Bahçelievler, Ankara; tel. (312) 213-31-00; fax (312) 213-41-35; f. 1961; scholarly research into all aspects of Turkish culture; Dir Dr ŞÜKRÜ ELÇIN; publs *Cultura Turcica* (1 a year), *Türk Kültürü* (12 a year), *Türk Kültürü Araştırmaları* (1 a year).

Türkiye Bilimsel ve Teknik Araştırma Kurumu (Scientific and Technical Research Council of Turkey): Tunus Cad. 80, 06100 Kavaklıdere, Ankara; tel. (312) 468-53-00; fax (312) 427-74-89; e-mail www-adm@tubitak.gov.tr; internet www.tubitak.gov.tr; f. 1963; library of 19,000 vols, 426 periodicals; govt body which carries out, sponsors, promotes and coordinates research activities in pure and applied sciences; Pres. Prof. Dr NÜKET YETIS; Sec.-Gen. IBRAHIM BERBEROGLU (acting); publs *Bilim ve Teknik* (Science and Technology, 12 a year), *Turkish Journal of Agriculture and Forestry Sciences* (6 a year), *Turkish Journal of Biology* (6 a year), *Turkish Journal of Botany* (6 a year), *Turkish Journal of Chemistry* (6 a year), *Turkish Journal of Earth Sciences* (6 a year), *Turkish Journal of Electrical Engineering and Computer Sciences* (3 a year), *Turkish Journal of Engineering and Environmental Sciences* (6 a year), *Turkish Journal of Mathematics* (6 a year), *Turkish Journal of Medical Sciences* (6 a year), *Turkish Journal of Physics* (6 a year), *Turkish Journal of Veterinary and Animal Sciences* (6 a year), *Turkish Journal of Zoology* (6 a year).

Attached Institutes:

Basic Science Research Institute:.

Cukurova Advanced Agricultural Research and Development Institute:.

Defence Research and Development Institute: PK 16 Mamak, 06261 Ankara; tel. (312) 399-03-38; fax (312) 212-37-49; Dir Prof. Dr ERES SÖYLEMEZ.

Marmara Araştırma Merkezi (Marmara Research Centre): PK 21, 41470 Gebze, Kocaeli; tel. (262) 677-20-00; fax (262) 641-23-09; e-mail info@mam.gov.tr; internet www.mam.gov.tr; f. 1972; materials science, optoelectronics, earth sciences, food science, nutrition, information technology, chemistry, chemical technology, environmental technology and energy; library of 30,000 vols, 90,000 bound periodicals; Dir (vacant).

TÜBİTAK Marmara Araştırma Merkezi Gen Mühendisliği ve Biyoteknoloji Araştırma Enstitüsü (TÜBİTAK Marmara Research Centre Genetic Engineering and Biotechnology Institute): Anibal Cad. Barış Mah., PK 21, 41470 Gebze, Kocaeli; tel. (262) 677-20-00; fax (262) 641-23-09; e-mail gmbe.web@mam.gov.tr; internet www.rigeb.gov.tr; f. 1983; Dir Asst Prof. AYNUR BASALP.

TÜBİTAK Uzay Teknolojileri Araştırma Enstitüsü (TUBITAK Space Technologies Research Institute): Middle E Technical Univ. (ODTÜ) Campus, 06531 Ankara; tel. (312) 210-13-10; fax (312) 210-13-15; e-mail info@uzay.tubitak.gov.tr; internet www.uzay.tubitak.gov.tr; f. 1985; research and devt in space technologies, electronics, software, power electronics, power distribution systems; Dir Dr UGUR MURAT LELOGLU.

Ulusal Elektronik ve Kriptoloji Araştırma Enstitüsü (National Electronics and Cryptology Research Institute): PK 74, 41470 Gebze, Kocaeli; tel. (262) 648-10-00; fax (262) 648-11-00; e-mail uekae@uekae.tubitak.gov.tr; internet www.uekae.tubitak.gov.tr; library of 2,700 vols, 70 periodicals; Dir Prof. Dr AYHAN TÜRELI.

AGRICULTURE, FISHERIES AND VETERINARY SCIENCE

Kavak ve Hızlı Gelişen Tür Orman Ağaçları Araştırma Müdürlüğü (Poplar and Fast-Growing Forest Trees Research Institute): PK 93, 41001 Izmit, Kocaeli; tel. (262) 311-69-64; fax (262) 311-69-72; e-mail kavak@kavak.gov.tr; internet www.kavak.gov.tr; f. 1962; attached to the Ministry of Forests; development of forest nursery and reafforestation techniques, introduction of new forest tree species, increase of wood production, research in poplar cultivation and management techniques; library of 3,700 vols; Dir Dr FARUK Ş. ÖZAY; publs *Annual Bulletin*, *Magazine*, *Technical Bulletin*.

Tarım ve Köyişleri Bakanliği, Zirai Mücadele Araştırma Enstitüsü (Ministry of Agricultural and Rural Affairs, Plant Protection Research Institute): Yenimahalle, Gayret Mahallesi Fatih Sultan Mehmet Bulv. 66, 06172 Ankara; tel. (312) 344-74-30; fax (312) 315-15-31; internet www.zmmae.gov.tr; f. 1934; depts dealing with research into combating plant diseases, pests and weeds; engaged in phytopathology, entomology, insect taxonomy and toxicology, nematology; analyzes pesticides and crop pesticide residues; library of 5,000 vols; Dir Dr ALI TAMER; publ. *Bitki Koruma Bülteni* (Plant Protection Bulletin, English, French or German summary, irregular).

HISTORY, GEOGRAPHY AND ARCHAEOLOGY

British Institute at Ankara: Tahran Cad. 24, 06700 Kavaklıdere, Ankara; tel. (312) 427-54-87; fax (312) 428-01-59; e-mail library@biaatr.org; internet www.biaa.ac.uk

London Office: c/o Claire McCafferty, British Institute at Ankara, British Academy, 10 Carlton House Terrace, London, SW1Y 5AH, UK; f. 1947; supports, promotes and publishes British research focused on Turkey and the Black Sea littoral, in all academic disciplines within the arts, humanities and social sciences; maintains a centre of excellence in Ankara, focused on the archaeology and related subjects of Turkey; library of 50,000 vols; Dir Dr LUTGARDE VANDEPUT; Admin. CLAIRE MCCAFFERTY; publs *Anatolian Archaeology* (1 a year), *Anatolian Studies* (1 a year), *BIAA Monographs*.

Deutsches Archäologisches Institut İstanbul Şubesi (Deutsches Archäologisches Institut Istanbul Branch): 34437 Gümüşsuyu/Inönü Caddesi 10, Istanbul; tel. (212) 393-76-00; fax (212) 393-76-14; e-mail sekretariat@istanbul.dainst.org; internet www.dainst.de; f. 1929; research into archaeology and cultural history in Turkey from prehistory to the Ottoman period; library of 60,000 vols; Dir Prof. Dr F. PIRSON; publs *Byzas*, *Istanbuler Beihefte*, *Istanbuler Forschungen*, *Istanbuler Mitteilungen des DAI* (1 a year).

Hollanda Araştırma Enstitüsü (Netherlands Institute in Turkey): Istiklâl Caddesi 181, Beyoğlu, Istanbul; tel. (212) 293-92-83; fax (212) 251-38-46; e-mail nit@nit-istanbul.org; internet www.nit-istanbul.org; f. 1958; library of 15,000 vols; Dir Dr FOKKE GERRITSEN; Librarian GÜLTEN YILDIZ; publ. *Anatolica* (1 a year).

Institut Français d'Etudes Anatoliennes d'Istanbul (Fransız Anadolu Araştırmaları Enstitüsü/French Institute of Anatolian Studies, Istanbul): PK 54, Palais de France, Nuru Ziya Sok, 80072 Beyoğlu-Istanbul; tel. (212) 244-17-17; fax (212) 252-80-91; e-mail ifea@ifea-istanbul.net; internet www.ifea-istanbul.net; f. 1930; Anatolian studies from prehistory to contemporary period; 15 mems; library of 24,000 vols; Dir PIERRE CHUVIN; publs *Anatolia antiqua* (1 a year), *Anatolia moderna* (1 a year).

Orient-Institut Istanbul/Alman Şarkiyat Cemiyeti'nin Orient Enstitüsü, İstanbul (Orient Institute of the German Oriental Society, Istanbul): Susam Sokak 16-18, D.8, 34433 Cihangir, Istanbul; tel. (212) 293-60-67; fax (212) 249-63-59; e-mail oiist@oidmg.org; internet www.oidmg.org; f. 1987; Turkish, Ottoman and Central Asian Studies; library of 37,000 vols, 1,320 periodicals; Turkish, Ottoman and central Asian studies; Dir Prof. Dr RAOUL MOTIKA; Asst Dir Dr RICHARD WITTMANN.

MEDICINE

Çocuk Sağlişi Enstitüsü, Hacettepe Üniversitesi Ihsan Doğramacı Çocuk Hastanesi (Institute of Child Health at Hacettepe University Children's Hospital): İhsan Doğramacı Çocuk Hastanesi 2, Blok 3, 06100 Yenisehir-Ankara; tel. (312) 324-42-91; fax (312) 324-32-84; e-mail tkutluk@hacettepe.edu.tr; internet www.cocuk.hacettepe.edu.tr; f. 1958; Masters and PhD training in paediatric sub-specialties; Dir Prof. Dr TEZER KUTLUK; publs *Çocuk Sağlıgı ve Hastalıkları Dergisi* (abstracts in English, 4 a year), *Turkish Journal of Paediatrics* (4 a year).

NATURAL SCIENCES

General

İstanbul Universitesi Deniz Bilimleri ve Işletmeciliği Enstitüsü (University of Istanbul Institute of Marine Sciences and Management): Müskule Sok 1 Vefa, 34410 Istanbul; tel. (212) 528-25-39; fax (212) 526-84-33; e-mail kcguven@yahoo.com.tr; internet www.istanbul.edu.tr/enstituler/denizbilimleri/denizbilimleri.htm; f. 1993; marine sciences; library of 11,243 vols; Dir Prof. Dr KASIM CEMAL GUVEN; publ. *Turkish Journal of Marine Science* (3 a year).

Türk Bilim Tarihi Kurumu (Turkish Society for History of Science): POB 24, 34349 Beşiktaş, Istanbul; tel. (212) 259-17-42; fax (212) 258-43-65; e-mail ircica@superonline.com; f. 1989; research and publication on history of science with emphasis on Ottoman history of science; organization of symposia; Pres. Prof. Dr EKMELEDDIN İHSANOĞLU.

Physical Sciences

Maden Tetkik ve Arama Genel Müdürlüğü (MTA) (General Directorate of Mineral Research and Exploration): İsmet İnönü Bulvarı, Ankara; tel. (312) 287-34-30; fax (312) 287-91-88; e-mail mta@mta.gov.tr; internet www.mta.gov.tr; f. 1935; conducts the Geological Survey of Turkey and evaluates mineral resources; library: see Libraries and Archives; Dir-Gen. A. KEMAL ISIKER; publs *Bulletin of Mineral Research and Exploration* (2 a year, in English), annual reports and maps.

RELIGION, SOCIOLOGY AND ANTHROPOLOGY

Islâm Araştırmaları Merkezi (Centre for Islamic Studies): Altunizade, İcadiye Bağlarbaşı Cad. 40, Bağlarbaşı, 81200 Üsküdar, Istanbul; tel. (216) 474-08-50; fax (216) 474-08-74; e-mail isam@isam.org.tr; internet www.isam.org.tr; f. 1988; library of 160,000 vols, 2,400 periodicals; Chair. Prof. Dr M. ÂKIF AYDIN; publ. *Turkish Journal of Islamic Studies*.

TECHNOLOGY

Afet İşleri Genel Müdürlüğü Deprem Araştırma Dairesi (General Directorate of Disaster Affairs Earthquake Research Department): Yüksel Cad. 7/B, Yenişehir, Ankara; tel. (312) 287-36-45; e-mail zemin@deprem.gov.tr; internet www.deprem.gov.tr; f. 1969; 78 staff; attached to the Ministry of Public Works and Resettlement; establishment, operation and maintenance of nationwide strong ground motion recorder network; earthquake prediction; preparation of codes and regulations for earthquake-resistant design and construction; research on earthquake hazard minimization; education and information for the public; comprises Earthquake Engineering, Seismology and Laboratory Divisions; Dir MUSTAFA TAYMAZ; publ. *Bulletin* (4 a year).

Araştırma Dairesi Başkanlığı (Demiryollar, Limanlar ve Hava Meydanları Inşaatı Genel Müdürlüğünün) (Department of Research and Materials (General Directorate of Railways, Harbour and Airport Construction)): Macun mah. Serpme Sok 3, 06338 Yenimahalle, Ankara; tel. (312) 397-33-50; fax (312) 397-38-11; e-mail dlharastirma1@ttnet.net.tr; internet www.dlh.gov.tr/arastirma; f. 1948; road materials testing, pavement design, soil and rock mechanics and geotechnical investigations; 60 staff; library of 2,467 vols; Dir YUSUF ZIYA BOYACI; publ. *Research Bulletin*.

Devlet Su Işleri, Teknik Araştırma ve Kalite Kontrol Dairesi (State Hydraulic Works, Technical Research and Quality Control Department): Ismet Inonu Bul., 06100 Yücetepe, Ankara; tel. (312) 417-83-00; fax (312) 418-24-98; e-mail takk@dsi.gov.tr; internet www.dsi.gov.tr; f. 1958; research and laboratory work on hydraulic engineering, soil mechanics, construction materials and concrete, chemistry, isotopes for hydrology; *in situ* research on water works; library; Dir HAYDAR KOÇAKER; publ. *DSI Teknik Bülteni* (original papers, some in foreign languages).

Marmara Research Centre: POB 21, 41470 Gebze, Kocaeli; tel. (262) 641-23-00; fax (262) 641-23-09; e-mail bilgi@mam.gov.tr; internet www.mam.gov.tr; f. 1972; research on basic and applied sciences, and industrial research; library of 90,000 vols, 746 periodicals; Dir Prof. ÖMER KAYMAKÇALAN.

Sarayköy Nükleer Araştırma ve Eğitim Merkezi (Sarayköy Nuclear Research and Training Centre): Saray Mahallesi, Atom Caddesi, 27 Kazan, 06983 Ankara; tel. (312) 815-43-00; fax (312) 815-43-07; internet www.anaem.gov.tr; f. 1967; attached to the Turkish Atomic Energy Authority; applied research in radiation chemistry and physics, electronics, nuclear agriculture, materials sciences and plasma physics; library of periodicals and technical reports; Dir I. TUKENMEZ; publ. *Turkish Journal of Nuclear Sciences* (2 a year).

Libraries and Archives

Afyon

Gedik Ahmed Paşa Library: Dumlupınar Mah. Şeyh Mehmet, Cad. 1, Afyon; tel. and fax (272) 213-54-33; f. 1785; 30,000 vols.

Ankara

Ankara Üniversitesi, Kütüphane ve Dokümantasyon Daire Başkanlığı (Ankara University Libraries and Documentation Centre): Sevket Aziz Kansu Bldg, İncitaşı Sok, Beşevler, Ankara; tel. (312) 223-57-61; fax (312) 213-95-32; e-mail atilgan@ankara.edu.tr; internet www.ankara.edu.tr; f. 1946; 722,309 vols, 33,000 e-books, 621 printed periodicals, 11,000 e-journals, 4,308 audiovisual materials, 17,872 MSS and 29,029 dissertations and theses; Library Dir Dr DOGAN ATILGAN; publs *Ankara Avrupa Çalışmaları Dergisi*, *Ankara Üniversitesi Dil ve Tarih-Coğrafya Fakültesi Dergisi*, *Ankara Üniversitesi Hukuk Fakültesi Dergisi*, *Ankara Üniversitesi Siyasal Bilgiler Fakültesi Dergisi*, *Ankara Üniversitesi Tıp Fakültesi Mecmuası*, *Ankara Üniversitesi Veteriner Fakültesi Dergisi*, *Ankara Üniversitesi Ziraat Fakültesi Tarım Bilimleri Dergisi*.

Library of National Defence: Ankara; f. 1877; 8,678 vols in Turkish, 5,820 vols in other languages; state-governed.

Maden Tetkik ve Arama Genel Müdürlüğü Kütüphanesi (General Directorate of Mineral Research and Exploration Library): İsmet İnönü Bulvarı, Ankara; f. 1935; 180,000 vols in various languages, 2,118 periodicals; Librarian ÜMİT ERKMEN; publ. *Bulletin* (in Turkish and English).

Middle East Technical University Library: Universiteler Mahallesi, Dumlupina Bulvarı, 06800 Ankara; tel. (312) 210-27-80; fax (312) 210-27-78; e-mail lib-hot-line@metu.edu.tr; internet www.lib.metu.edu.tr; f. 1956; maintains custody of the univ.'s recording, microfilm and projection equipment; 430,247 vols, 177,144 bound periodicals, 1,263 journal subscriptions; 54,681 electronic journals, 91,596 electronic books in 152 databases, 17,260 master and doctoral theses; Dir CEVAT GÜVEN.

Milli Kütüphane (National Library of Turkey): Bahçelievler, Ankara 06940; tel. (312) 222-38-12; fax (312) 223-04-51; e-mail info@mkutup.gov.tr; internet www.mkutup.gov.tr; f. 1946; 1,136,997 vols, 911,675 vols of periodicals, 35,024 MSS, 197,577 non-book items; Pres. TUNCEL ACAR; publs *Türkiye Bibliyografyası* (Turkish National Bibliography, 12 a year), *Türkiye Makaleler Bibliyografyası* (Bibliography of articles in Turkish periodicals, 12 a year).

Public Library: Ankara; f. 1922; 21,000 vols in Turkish, 10,200 vols in European languages, over 1,200 MSS in Arabic and Persian.

Türkiye Büyük Millet Meclisi Kütüphane ve Dokümantasyon Merkezi (Grand National Assembly Library and Documentation Centre): TBMM Kutuphanesi, 06543 Bakanlıklar, Ankara; tel. (312) 420-68-35; fax (312) 420-75-48; e-mail kutuphane@tbmm.gov.tr; internet www.tbmm.gov.tr/kutuphane; f. 1920; 271,298 vols in social sciences incl. 107,196 in Turkish, 24,788 in English, 10,847 in French, 1,000 in Arabic and Persian, 60 MSS, 59,134 vols of periodicals; Dir ISMET BAYDUR; publ. *Bilgi* (4 a year).

Antalya

Antalya Tekelioğlu İl Halk Kütüphanesi (Tekelioğlu Library): Ucgen Mah. 96. Sok. 54, Antalya; tel. (242) 344-51-37; f. 1924; 5,000 vols, nearly 2,000 MSS in Persian, Arabic and Turkish; Dir AYŞE D. SAVGUN.

Balıkeşir

Il Halk Kütüphanesi, Balıkeşir (Provincial Public Library, Balıkeşir): Bahçelievler Mah Kıralı Sok., Balıkeşir; tel. (266) 241-32-33; fax (266) 243-04-12; f. 1901; 1,286 MSS in Turkish, Arabic and Persian, 49,000 vols in Turkish, Arabic and English, 766 in other languages, 5,088 periodicals; Dir A. ERCAN TIĞ.

Darende

Mehmet Paşa Library: Darende; f. 1776; 4,000 vols, 800 MSS.

Edirne

Selimiye Library: Edirne; f. 1575; 36,113 vols (incl. 3,172 MSS and 3,894 vols in Arabic); Librarian Mrs OZLEM AĞIRGAN.

Isparta

Halil Hamit Paşa Library: Isparta; f. 1783; 20,200 vols, over 850 MSS; Dir MAHMUT KAYICI.

Istanbul

Atatürk Kitaplığı (Ataturk Library): Mete Caddesi 45, Taksim, Istanbul; tel. (212) 249-56-83; fax (212) 251-79-72; f. 1929; public library; 184,000 vols.

Beyazıt Devlet Kütüphanesi (Beyazit State Library): Turan Emeksiz Sok 6, 344450 Beyazıt, Istanbul; tel. (212) 522-31-67; f. 1882; legal deposit library; 500,000 vols in various languages, 11,120 MSS, 32,992 photographs, 21,616 periodicals; Dir YUSUF TAVACI.

Boğaziçi University Library: Bebek, 80815 Istanbul; tel. and fax (212) 257-50-16; e-mail bulib@boun.edu.tr; internet www.library.boun.edu.tr; f. 1863; 375,000 vols in English and other languages, incl. a special colln of over 30,332 vols on the Near East, 10,000 rare books and MSS; 220 periodicals, 2,500 records and 200 CDs; Librarian HATICE ÜN.

Ecumenical Patriarchate Library: İstanbul Rum Patrikliği, Sadrazam Ali Paşa Caddesi 35, 34220 Fener, Istanbul; internet www.patriarchate.org; foundation dates from beginning of Patriarchate, reorganization 1890; 25,000 vols in main library, and 1,500 MSS; 45,000 vols in branch library at Orthodox Seminary of Heybeliada; Dir Rev. PANAĞHIOTIS THEODORIDIS (under the jurisdiction of the Holy Synod).

Institute of Turkology Library: Istanbul University, 34452 Beyazıt, Istanbul; f. 1924; 50,000 vols relating to Turkish language, literature, history and culture.

Istanbul Teknik Üniversitesi Kütüphane ve Dokümantasyon Daire (Istanbul Technical University Library and Documentation Division): Ayazağa Kampüsü, Maslak 34469, Istanbul; tel. (212) 285-35-96; fax (212) 285-33-02; e-mail kutuphane@itu.edu.tr; internet www.library.itu.edu.tr; f. 1795; six separate libraries on five university campuses; 372,000 vols; Dir of Libraries AYHAN KAYGUSUZ.

Istanbul University Library and Documentation Centre: University PTT 34452, Beyazıt, Istanbul; tel. (212) 455-57-83; fax (212) 455-57-84; e-mail uko@istanbul.edu.tr; internet www.kutuphane.istanbul.edu.tr; f. 1925; comprises the central university library and 17 faculty libraries; 500,000 vols, 18,606 MSS, 18,000 periodicals (3,100 current), 35,000 theses; Dir Doç. Dr ÜMIT KONYA.

Köprülü Yazma Eser Kütüphanesi (Köprülü Library): Divan Yolu Cad. 29, Cemberlitas-Eminonu, Istanbul; tel. (212) 516-83-13; f. 1677; 3,000 vols, 2,755 MSS, of which 193 are from early Ottoman presses, and 42 handwritten works from before the 10th century.

Millet Kütüphanesi (Public Library): Macar Kardeşler Cad. 85, 34260 Fatih, Istanbul; tel. (212) 631-36-07; f. 1916; 33,980 vols, 8,844 MSS.

Nuruosmaniye Library: Camii Avlusu, Cagaloglu, Istanbul; tel. (212) 527-20-04; f. 1755; 6,000 vols, 5,000 MSS.

Süleymaniye Kütüphanesi (Süleymaniye Library): Aysekadin Hamami Sok. 35, Beyazıt, Istanbul; tel. (212) 520-64-60; fax (212) 520-64-62; f. 1557; 113,068 vols and 66,117 MSS in Turkish, Uyghur, Arabic and Persian; 109 different collections incl. those from Ayasofya, Fatih and Husrev Pasha; MS restoration service; brs at Atif Efendi, Hacı Selim Ağa, Köprülü, Nuru-Osmaniye, Ragıppaşa; Dir Dr NEVZAT KAYA.

Women's Library and Information Center Foundation: Fener Mahallesi, Fener Vapur Iskelesi Karşısı, Fener Haliç, 34220 Istanbul; tel. (212) 534-95-50; fax (212) 523-74-08; 6,500 vols; Dir BEKIR KEMAL ATAMAN.

Izmir

National Library of Izmir: Milli Kütüphane Cad. 39, Konak- Izmir; f. 1912; 299,000 vols in Turkish, 40,000 vols in European languages, 19,000 vols in Oriental scripts, 4,000 MSS, 4,843 periodicals; Dir ALİ RIZA ATAY.

Konya

Public Library: Purcuklu Mah., Turbe Cad. 23, Karatoy, Konya; f. 1947; 20,000 vols, 6,000 MSS.

Nevşehir

Damat Ibrahim Paşa Library: Nevşehir; f. 1727; 5,500 vols, 600 MSS.

Museums and Art Galleries

Adana

Adana Bölge Müzesi (Adana Regional Museum): Adana; f. 1926; depts of archaeology and ethnography; conference hall, laboratories, library and administrative sections; more than 107,000 items from the Neolithic to Roman and Byzantine periods; unique statue of a god made from natural crystal dating from Hittite Empire.

Amasya

Amasya Müzesi: Atatürk Cad. 91 Amasya; tel. (358) 218-45-13; fax (358) 218-69-57; f. 1926, moved 1961 to the Gök Medrese Mosque; archaeological finds from the early Bronze Age to Ottoman period; includes mummies dating from the Imperial period.

Ankara

Anadolu Medeniyetleri Müzesi (Museum of Anatolian Civilizations): Samanpazarı, Ankara; tel. (312) 324-31-60; fax (312) 311-28-39; f. 1921; exhibits cover the Palaeolithic, Neolithic, Chalcolithic, Early Bronze Age, Hittite, Phrygian, Urartian and Classical periods; Hittite reliefs from Alaca, Carchemish, Sakcagözü and Aslantepe and Ankara regions; collections represent excavations at Karain, Çatal Hüyük, Hacılar, Can Hasan, Alacahöyük, Ahlatlıbel, Karaz, Alişar, Karaoğlan, Karayavşan, Oymaağaç, Merzifon, Beycesultan, Kültepe, Acemhöyük, İnandık, Boğazköy, Eskiyapar, Patnos, Adilcevaz, Uşak-İkiztepe, Pazarlı, Gordion (now Yassihoyuk), Altıntepe, with special sections for cuneiform tablets and coins; library of 6,567 vols; Dir İLHAN TEMİZSOY; publs *The Anatolian Civilizations Museum Periodical*, *Museum Annual*, *Museum Conference Annual*, *Museum Lectures* (1 a year), *Museum News* (2 a year).

Anıtkabir Atatürk Müzesi (Atatürk's Mausoleum and Museum): Anıt Caddesi, Tandoğan, Ankara; tel. (312) 231-79-75; fax (312) 231-53-80; internet www.tsk.mil.tr./anitkabir; f. 1953; official and civil possessions of Mustafa Kemal Atatürk (1881–1938), founder of the Turkish Republic and its first Pres.; colln incl. documents, medals, plaques and albums; panoramas and paintings of the most important battles of the founding of the Turkish republic; library of 3,123 vols from the private library of Atatürk; Museum Commander Lt-Col HALIM KURT.

Ethnographical Museum: Talatpasa Bulvarı, Ankara; tel. (312) 311-95-56; f. 1930; specimens of Turkish and Islamic art, archives and Islamic seals; library of 6,245 vols; Dir Mrs SEMA KOÇ.

Kurtuluş Savaşl ve Cumhuriyet Müzeleri (Museums of the Turkish Independence War and Turkish Republic): Cumhuriyet Bulvarı No. 14–22, Ulus, Ankara; f. 1961; located in former Grand National Assembly buildings; library of 60,000 vols and 20,000 documents; Dir MUSTAFA SÜEL.

Natural History Museum: MTA, Genel Müdürlüğü, Eskişehir Yolu Balgat, 06520 Ankara; tel. (312) 286-32-89; fax (312) 284-14-77; e-mail muze1@mta.gov.tr; internet www.mta.gov.tr; f. 1968; attached to General Directorate of Mineral Research and Exploration; Dir Dr ALAADIN VURAL.

Antakya

Hatay Museum: Gündüz Cad. 1, Antakya, Hatay; tel. (326) 214-61-68; fax (326) 213-33-86; f. 1934; collection of mosaics from Roman Antioch, also finds from Al-Mina, Atchana, Çatal Hüyük, Judeidah and Tainat excavations; Dir MEHMET ERDEM.

Antalya

Antalya Müzesi (Antalya Museum): Konyaaltı Caddesi, Antalya; tel. (242) 238-56-88; fax (242) 238-56-87; f. 1922; prehistory, archaeology, numismatics, ethnography, children's section and garden exhibition; library of 7,500 vols; Dir SELAHATTIN EYÜP AKSU.

Aydın

Aydın Müzesi: Hasan Efendi Mahallesi, Kapalı Spor Salonu yanı Aydın; tel. (256) 225-22-59; fax (256) 213-35-91; f. 1959; archaeology, ethnography, historical coins.

Bergama

Pergamon Museum: Cumhurıyet Cadd. 10, 35700 Bergama-Izmir; tel. (232) 631-28-83; fax (232) 631-07-77; f. 1936; houses the historical relics discovered as the result of excavations conducted at Pergamon; Dir ADNAN SARIOĞLU.

Bodrum

Bodrum Sualtı Arkeoloji Müzesi (Bodrum Museum of Underwater Archaeology): 48000 Bodrum; tel. (252) 316-25-16; fax (252) 313-76-46; e-mail bodrum-museum@yahoo.com; internet www.bodrum-museum.com; f. 1964 in the castle of Bodrum (built 15th century, by the Knights of St John from Rhodes); finds from land and underwater, incl. ceramics, metal, stone, gold and glass, from the Mycenaean, Attic, Hellenic, Roman, Byzantine and Ottoman eras; remains of late Bronze age ship; Dir (vacant).

Bursa

Bursa Arkeoloji Müzesi: Kültürpark, Bursa; tel. (224) 234-49-18; fax (224) 234-49-19; f. 1902; archaeological finds from Bursa, Balıkesir and Bilecik; prehistoric, Roman and Byzantine finds, stone, ceramic, glass and metal objects, coins; library of 3,824 vols; Chief Officer SALIH KÜTÜK.

Bursa Türk ve Islâm Eserleri Müzesi (Bursa Turkish and Islamic Art Museum): Yeşil, Bursa; tel. (224) 327-75-39; f. 1975 in the Yeşil Medrese, built by the Ottoman Sultan Mehmet I Çelebi; items from 12th century to late Ottoman period; illuminated MSS, samples of calligraphy, woodwork, metalwork, embroidery, costumes, ceramics; open-air museum of gravestones.

Çanakkale

Truva Müzesi (Troy Museum): Çanakkale; at the entrance to the ruins of Troy in Çanakkale; small exhibitions of pottery, figurines, statues and glass objects.

Eskişehir

Eskişehir Arkeoloji Müzesi: Akarbaşı Mahallesi, Hasan Polatkan Bul. 64, Eskişehir; tel. (222) 230-13-71; fax (222) 230-17-49; e-mail muze2603@kultur.gov.tr; f. 1935; plant and animal fossils; prehistory (ceramics, idols, stone and bone objects); the walls are decorated with late Roman mosaics found in excavations at Doryleum; Museum Head M. DURSUN ÇAĞLAR.

Istanbul

Âsiyan Museum: Aşiyan Yokuşu, 80810 Bebek, Istanbul; tel. (212) 263-69-86; home of Turkish poet and artist T. Fikret (1867–1915).

Askeri Müze ve Kültür Sitesi Komutanlığı (Military Museum and Cultural Centre): Harbiye, Istanbul; tel. (212) 233-27-20; fax (212) 296-86-18; f. 1846; military uniforms, weapons, tents, trophies, flags and standards from ancient times; library of 20,000 vols; Dir Col AHMET TEKIN.

Ayasofya (Saint Sophia) Museum: Sultanahmet, Eminonu, 34400 Istanbul; tel. (212) 522-09-89; fax (212) 512-54-74; e-mail ayasofyamuzesi@hotmail.com; internet www.kultur.gov.tr; f. 1935; the Museum is housed in the Byzantine Basilica; built by Justinian and dedicated in AD 537, it was a church until 1453, after which it became a mosque; in 1935 it was made a state museum; contains Byzantine and Turkish antiquities; Pres. Assoc. Prof. A. HALUK DURSUN; publ. *The Annual of St Sophia*.

Istanbul Arkeoloji Müzeleri (Archaeological Museums of Istanbul): Gülhane, 34400 Istanbul; tel. (212) 520-77-40; fax (212) 527-43-00; f. 1891; includes Archaeological, Turkish Tiles and Ancient Orient museums, with Sumerian, Akkadian, Hittite, Assyrian, Egyptian, Urartu, Phrygian, Greek, Roman and Byzantine works of art; more than 1m. exhibits; library of 80,000 vols; Dir HALIL ÖZEKNLI.

Istanbul Deniz Müzesi (Istanbul Naval Museum): Deniz Müzesi K.ligi, Beşiktaş, Istanbul; tel. (212) 327-43-45; fax (212) 236-68-93; f. 1897; cannons, important collection of historical caiques, models, torpedoes and mines, Turkish standards, medals, costumes, paintings; library of 20,000 vols, 22,436 archive files (Ottoman Empire period); Dir Capt. ALI RIZA ISIPEK.

Istanbul Resim ve Heykel Müzesi (Museum of Painting and Sculpture): Beşiktaş, Istanbul; tel. (212) 261-42-98; fax (212) 244-03-98; f. 1937; Turkish paintings and sculptures since 19th century; international art exhibitions; Dir Prof. KEMAL İSKENDER.

Sabancı Üniversitesi Sakıp Sabancı Müzesi (Sabancı University Sakıp Sabancı Museum): Sakıp Sabancı Cad. 42, Emirgan 34467, Istanbul; tel. (212) 277-22-00; fax (212) 229-49-14; e-mail muze@sabanciuniv.edu; internet muze.sabanciuniv.edu; f. 2002, in the former private residence of the Sabancı family; permanent colln of calligraphic items since 15th century, paintings since 19th century; temporary exhibitions; Dir Dr NAZAN ÖLÇER.

Tanzimat Müzesi (Tanzimat Museum): Gülhane Parkı, 94400 Sirkeci, Istanbul; tel. (212) 512-63-04; f. 1952 in Ihlamur Pavilion, current site since 1983; operated by Istanbul Metropolitan Municipality; documents, paintings and objects pertaining to the Tanzimat period of reform 1839–76; Curator FADIME GELEŞ.

Topkapı Palace Museum: Sultanahmet 34400, Istanbul; tel. (212) 522-44-22; fax (212) 528-59-91; internet www.kultur.gov.tr; palace built by Mehmed II; collections of Turkish armour, cloth, embroidery, glass and porcelain, copper- and silver-ware, treasure, paintings, miniatures, illuminated manuscripts, royal coaches, collections of Sèvres and Bohemian crystal and porcelain, clocks, important collection of Chinese and Japanese porcelain amassed by the Sultans, collection of manuscripts, Ottoman tent; Audience Hall, Council Hall of Viziers, Baghdad and Revan Köşks, Harem; library of 18,000 MSS and 200,000 archive documents; Dir FILIZ ÇAĞMAN.

Türk ve Islam Eserleri Müzesi (Museum of Turkish and Islamic Art): Ibrahim Paşa Sarayı, At Meydani 46, Sultanahmet, Istanbul 34400; tel. (212) 518-18-05; fax (212) 518-18-07; internet www.tiem.org; f. 1914; Turkish and Islamic rugs, illuminated MSS, sculpture in stone and stucco, woodcarvings, metalwork and ceramics, traditional crafts and ethnographical material, all gathered from Turkish mosques and tombs; library: 4,142 MSS and 3,279 vols; Dir NAZAN ÖLCER.

Izmir

Izmir Arkeoloji Müzesi: Halit Rıfat Paşa Cad. 4, Konak, Izmir; tel. (232) 489-07-96; fax (232) 483-28-37; e-mail izmirmuze@ttnet.net.tr; f. 1927; works from the Archaic, Classical and Hellenistic periods of the Ionian civilization; Dir MEHMET TUNA.

Konya

Konya Museums: Il Kültür Müdürlüğü, Müze Müdürlüğü, Konya Valiliği; Dir of Museums Dr ERDOĞAN EROL.

Attached Museums:

Atatürk Museum:colln of documents and objects connected with Atatürk, also Konya clothing and other ethnographic exhibits.

Classical Museum:collns of Neolithic, early Bronze Age, Hittite, Phrygian, Greek, Roman and Byzantine monuments.

Mevlâna Museum:; f. in Mevlâna Turbe; Seljuk, Ottoman and Turkish collections, clothing, carpets, coins, library.

Seljuk Museum:; f. in Ince Minare; contains stone and wooden works of the Seljuk period.

Sirçali Medresseh:sarcophagus and inscription, collections of Seljuk and Ottoman period.

Turkish Ceramics Museum:; f. in Karatay Medresseh; contains ceramics from 13th–18th centuries.

Polatlı

Gordion Museum: Polatlı, Ankara; tel. (312) 638-21-88; fax (312) 311-28-39; e-mail anmedmuz@marketweb.net.tr; f. 1965; built near the Great Tumulus believed to be that of the Phrygian king Midas; archaeological items found during excavations at Gordion (now Yassıhöyük); Dir ILHAN TEMIZSOY.

Selçuk

Efes Müzesi Müdürlügü (Ephesus Museum): Kusadasi Cad., 35920 Selçuk-Izmir; tel. (232) 892-60-10; fax (232) 892-70-02; f. 1929; art (mostly statues and reliefs) excavated from Ephesus; library of 3,200 vols; Dir SELAHATTIN ERDEMGIL; publ. *Efes Müzesi Yıllıgı* (1 a year).

Selimiye

Side Müzesi: Manavgat-Antalya, Side (Selimiye); tel. (242) 753-10-06; fax (242) 753-27-49; f. 1962; museum is located in a Late Roman bath; statues and busts of Roman gods, goddesses and emperors; library of 985 vols; Dir ORHAN ATVUR.

Van

Van Müzesi: Şerefiye Mahallesi, Hacıosman Sokak 9 Van; tel. (432) 216-11-39; fax (432) 214-25-10; f. 1947; archaeological finds from the Urartu Civilization.

Universities

ABANT IZZET BAYSAL ÜNİVERSİTESİ

Gölköy Kampüsü, 14280 Gölköy- Bolu
Telephone: (374) 254-10-00
Fax: (374) 253-45-06
Internet: www.ibu.edu.tr
Founded 1992
State control
Languages of instruction: Turkish, English
Academic year: September to June
Pres.: Prof. Dr HAYRI COSKUN
Vice-Pres.: Prof. Dr AKCAHAN GEPDIREMEN
Vice-Pres.: Prof. Dr MEHMET BAHAR
Vice-Pres.: Prof. Dr RESUL ERYIGIT
Number of teachers: 927
Number of students: 17,449

DEANS

Faculty of Arts and Sciences: Prof. Dr AHMET VARILCI
Faculty of Dentistry: Prof. Dr ISMET DURAN
Faculty of Economics and Admin. Sciences: Prof. Dr RAMAZAN GOZEN
Faculty of Education: Prof. Dr CANAN CETINKANAT
Faculty of Engineering: Prof. Dr MAHMUT ACIMIS
Faculty of Fine Arts: Prof. Dr HAYRI COSKUN (acting)
Faculty of Medicine: Prof. Dr HASAN KOCOGLU

ADNAN MENDERES ÜNİVERSİTESİ

Aytepe Mevkii, Merkez Kampus, 09010 Aydin
Telephone: (256) 212-76-79
Fax: (256) 225-32-40
Internet: www.adu.edu.tr
Founded 1992
State control
Academic year: September to June
Rector: Prof. Dr MUSTAFA GUREL
Vice-Rectors: Dr OSMAN KAYA, Prof. Dr ERGUN ONUR, Prof. Dr ISMAIL TURGUT
Sec.-Gen.: ZIYAETTIN TEKMEN
Number of teachers: 960
Number of students: 10,000
Publications: *Bulletin* (4 a year), *Journal of Medical Faculty*

DEANS

Faculty of Agriculture: MUSTAFA ALI KAYNAK
Faculty of Economics and Administration: ERDOGAN GURSOY
Faculty of Medicine: TURGAY AKTUNE
Faculty of Science and Letters: ALI ERSIN KARAGOZLER
Faculty of Veterinary Science: HASAN ELEN

AFYON KOCATEPE ÜNIVERSITESI

Ahmet Necdet Sezer Kampusü, Gazligol Yolu, 03200 Afyonkarahisar
Telephone: (272) 444-03-03
Fax: (272) 228-14-08
E-mail: rektor@aku.edu.tr
Internet: www.aku.edu.tr
Founded 1992
State control
Rector: Prof. Dr ALI ALTUNTAŞ
Vice-Rectors: Prof. Dr BELKIS ÖZKARA, Prof. Dr KEMALETTIN ÇONKAR, Prof. Dr NECAT İMIRZALIOĞLU
Gen. Sec.: İSMET DOĞAN
Librarian: ABDULLAH KÜNDEYİ
Library of 127,592 print vols and e-books, 840 periodicals
Number of teachers: 1,032
Number of students: 28,849 (27,339 undergraduate, 1,510 graduate)

DEANS

Faculty of Arts and Sciences: Prof. Dr BELKIS ÖZKARA
Faculty of Arts and Sciences (Uşak): Prof. Dr LÜTFI ÖZAV
Faculty of Economics and Administrative Sciences (Uşak): Prof. Dr H. HÜSEYIN BAYRAKLI
Faculty of Economics and Management Science: Prof. Dr KEMALETTIN ÇONKAR
Faculty of Education: Prof. Dr MUSTAFA ERGÜN
Faculty of Education (Uşak): Prof. Dr ADNAN ŞIŞMAN
Faculty of Engineering: Prof. Dr RAMAZAN ŞEVİK
Faculty of Engineering (Uşak): Prof. Dr FIKRI ŞENOL
Faculty of Fine Arts: Prof. Dr RIZA AŞIKOĞLU
Faculty of Medicine: Prof. Dr NECAT İMIRZALIĞOLU
Faculty of Technical Education: Prof. Dr GALIP SAİD
Faculty of Veterinary Medicine: Prof. Dr HIFZI OĞUZ SARIMEHMETOĞLU

Research Centres incl. Animal Breeding Research Centre, Atatürk and History of Revolution Research and Application Centre, Experimental Animal Research and Application Centre, Food Control Research and Application Centre, Kocatepe Great Attack Research Centre, Technology Application and Research Centre, Turkish Handicrafts Research and Application Centre, Turkish World Research Centre

AKDENİZ ÜNİVERSİTESİ

Dumlupınar Bulvarı Kampus, 07058 Antalya
Telephone: (242) 227-59-83
Fax: (242) 227-55-40
E-mail: international@akdeniz.edu.tr
Internet: www.akdeniz.edu.tr
Founded 1982; previously affiliated to Ankara Univ.
State control
Language of instruction: Turkish
Academic year: October to June
Rector: Prof. Dr MUSTAFA AKAYDIN
Vice-Rectors: Prof. Dr MEHMET RIFKI AKTEKİN, Prof. Dr SADIK ÇAKMAKÇI, Prof. Dr MUSTAFA PEKMEZCI
Gen. Sec.: NUSRET ÇELIK
Librarian: NEVZAT SABAN
Number of teachers: 1,646
Number of students: 19,090
Publications: *Journal of the Faculty of Agriculture*, *Journal of the Faculty of Medicine* (4 a year), *University Bulletin*

DEANS

Faculty of Agribusiness: Prof. Dr AHMET AKTAŞ
Faculty of Agriculture: Prof. Dr HALIL İBRAHIM UZUN
Faculty of Arts and Sciences: Prof. Dr MUSTAFA GÖKÇEOĞLU
Faculty of Communications: Prof. Dr ÜMIT ATABEK
Faculty of Economics and Administrative Sciences: Prof. Dr FULYA SARVAN
Faculty of Education: Prof. Dr MEHMET YALÇIN
Faculty of Engineering: Prof. Dr HIKMET RENDE
Faculty of Fine Arts: Prof. Dr ABDULLAH UZ
Faculty of Fisheries: Prof. Dr RAMAZAN İKIZ
Faculty of Law: Prof. Dr MERAL SAĞIR ÖZTOPRAK
Faculty of Medicine: Prof. Dr MUSTAFA MELİKOĞLU
Faculty of Veterinary Science: Prof. Dr BAYRAM ALI YUKARI

There are 4 Vocational Schools within Akdeniz University, 8 Vocational Schools in Antalya and 4 Graduate Schools.

ANADOLU ÜNIVERSITESI
(Anatolian University)

Yunus Emre Kampüsü, 26470 Eskişehir
Telephone: (222) 335-05-80
Fax: (222) 335-36-16
E-mail: webadmin@anadolu.edu.tr
Internet: www.anadolu.edu.tr
Founded 1958
State control
Languages of instruction: Turkish, English
Academic year: October to June
Rector: Prof. Dr DAVUT AYDIN
Vice-Rector: Prof. Dr AYDIN ZIYA OZGUR
Vice-Rector: Prof. Dr MERYEM AKOGLAN KOZAK
Vice-Rector: Prof. Dr MUSTAFA CAVCAR
Vice-Rector: Prof. Dr ENDER SUVACI
Vice Rector: Prof. Dr NACI GUNDOGAN
Registrar and Sec.-Gen.: CETIN KAYA
Librarian: ADNAN YILMAZ
Number of teachers: 1,885
Number of students: 1,761,631 (incl. open-education students)
Publications: *Journal of Sciences and Technology* (2 a year), *Journal of Social Sciences* (2 a year), *Online International Journal of Communication Studies* (2 a year), *Turkish Online Journal of Distance Education* (2 a year)

DEANS

Faculty of Business Administration: Prof. Dr M. NECDET TIMUR
Faculty of Communication Sciences: Prof. Dr NEJDET ATABEK
Faculty of Economics: Prof. Dr RIDVAN KARLUK
Faculty of Economics and Administrative Sciences: Prof. Dr RECAI DONMEZ
Faculty of Education: Prof. Dr YUKSEL KOCADORU
Faculty of Engineering and Architecture: Prof. Dr TUNCAY DOGEROGLU
Faculty of Fine Arts: Prof. ZEHRA COBANLI
Faculty of Law: Prof. Dr NÜVIT GEREK
Faculty of Letters: Prof. Dr NADIR SUGUR
Faculty of Open Education: Prof. Dr AYDIN ZIYA OZGUR
Faculty of Pharmacy: Prof. Dr YASEMIN YAZAN
Faculty of Sciences: Prof. Dr MUSTAFA SENYEL

ATTACHED SCHOOLS

School of Civil Aviation: Dir Prof. Dr MUSTAFA KARA.

School of Drama and Music: Dir NAZLI GÜLMEZ.

School of Foreign Languages: Dir Assoc. Prof. HANDAN YAVUZ.

School of Industrial Arts: Dir Prof. Dr YAŞAR HOŞCAN.

School of Physical Education and Sports: Dir Prof. Dr COŞKUN BAYRAK.

School of Tourism and Hotel Management: Dir Prof. Dr DENIZ BÜLER.

College for the Handicapped: Dir Prof. Dr AHMET KONROT.

GRADUATE SCHOOLS

Graduate School of Health Sciences: Dir Prof. Dr YUSUF ÖZTÜRK.

Graduate School of Science: Dir Prof. Dr ORHAN ÖZER.

Graduate School of Social Sciences: Dir Prof. Dr ALTUĞ İFTAR.

Handicapped Research Institute: Dir Prof. Dr GÖNÜL SELVER KIRCAALÜ.

Institute of Communication Sciences: Dir (vacant).

Institute of Educational Sciences: Dir Prof. Dr İLKNUR KEÇIK.

Institute of Fine Arts: Dir Prof. Dr ATILLA ATAR.

Institute of Satellite and Space Sciences: Dir Assoc. Prof. Dr CAN AYDAY.

Institute of Transport Economics: Dir Prof. Dr NEZIH VARCAN.

ANKARA ÜNİVERSİTESİ

06100 Tandoğan, Ankara
Telephone: (312) 212-60-40
Fax: (312) 212-60-49
Internet: www.ankara.edu.tr

Founded 1946
State control
Language of instruction: Turkish
Academic year: October to June

Rector: Prof. Dr CEMAL TALUĞ
Vice-Rector: Prof. Dr NILGÜN HALLORAN
Vice-Rector: Prof. Dr N. YASEMIN YALIM
Vice-Rector: Prof. Dr ARGUN KARACABEY
Gen.–Sec.: SERPIL GÜNER
Registrar: Prof. Dr S. TUNA KARAHAN
Registrar: SINEM ÖZKARA
Librarian: Prof. Dr DOĞAN ATILGAN

Library of 800,000 vols and 7,984 periodicals
Number of teachers: 3,553
Number of students: 44,514

Publications: *Ankara Üniversitesi Yıllığı* (Annals of the University), *Turkish Journal of Geographical Sciences*, and faculty and research institute publications

DEANS

Çankırı Faculty of Forestry: Prof. Dr İLHAMİ KÖKSAL
Faculty of Agriculture: Prof. Dr AHMET ÇOLAK
Faculty of Communication: Prof. Dr ESER KÖKER
Faculty of Dentistry: Prof. Dr ADNAN ÖZTÜRK
Faculty of Divinity: Prof. Dr NESIMI YAZICI
Faculty of Education: Prof. Dr GÖNÜL AKÇAMETE
Faculty of Engineering: Prof. Dr ALI ULVİ YILMAZER
Faculty of Health Education: Prof. Dr ŞENGÜL HABLEMITOĞLU
Faculty of Law: Prof. Dr MUSTAFA AKKAYA
Faculty of Humanities: Prof. Dr RAHMI ER
Faculty of Medicine: Prof. Dr İLKER ÖKTEN
Faculty of Natural and Applied Science: Prof. Dr MUAMMER CANEL
Faculty of Pharmacy: Prof. Dr MAKSUT COŞKUN
Faculty of Political Science: Prof. Dr CELAL GÖLE
Faculty of Veterinary Medicine: Prof. Dr İBRAHİM BURGU

DIRECTORS OF APPLIED RESEARCH CENTRES

Astronomy and Aerospace Sciences: Prof. Dr BERAHITDIN ALBAYRAK
Atatürk's Principles: Prof. Dr ÜNSAL YAVUZ
Autistic Children: Prof. Dr EFSER KERIMOĞLU
Biotechnology: Prof. Dr TUNCER ÖZDAMAR
Cardiology: Prof. Dr DERVİŞ ORAL
Children's Studies: Prof. Dr BEKIR ONUR
Communications: Prof. Dr ASKER KARTARI
Continuous Training: Prof. Dr NEJLA TURAL
Cyprus: Prof. Dr FÜSUN ARSAVA
Distance Learning: Doç. Dr NURETTIN ŞIMŞEK
Earthquake Science: Prof. Dr AHMET TUĞRUL BAŞOKUR
Education-Rehabilitation: Prof. Dr EFSER KERİMOĞLU
Environmental Problems: Prof. Dr NEVIN AKPINAR
European Communities: Prof. Dr M. NAIL ALKAN
Fishery Products: Prof. Dr GÜLTEN KÖKSAL
Foreign Language Teaching: Prof. Dr ERSİN ONULDURAN
Gastroenterology: Prof. Dr ALI ÖZDEN
Human Resource Management: Doç. Dr RECEP VARÇIN
Intellectual and Industrial Property: ARZU OĞUZ
International Agriculture: Prof. Dr NEŞET KILINÇER
Medical and Scented Plants: Prof. Dr SEMRA KURUNCU
Oncology: Prof. Dr FİKRİ İÇLİ
Ottoman History: Prof. Dr ESIN KAHYA
Pediatric Haemotology and Oncology: Prof. Dr ŞÜKRÜ CIN
Psychiatric Crisis: Prof. Dr IŞIK SAYIL
Public Finance and Politics: Prof. Dr AHMET KIRMAN
River, Lake and Sea Geology: Prof. Dr MUSTAFA ERGIN
Science and Technology: Prof. Dr TAMER BAYKARA
Strategic Research: Prof. Dr YAVUZ ERCAN
Turkish Geography: Doç. Dr ALİ ÖZÇAĞLAR
Turkish Language Teaching Centre: Doç. Dr ENGIN UZUN
Women's Studies: SERPIL ÜŞÜR

ATTACHED INSTITUTES

Graduate Institute of Biotechnology: Dir Prof. Dr NEJAT AKAR.

Graduate Institute of Education: Dir Prof. Dr MERAL UYSAL.

Graduate Institute of Hepatology: Dir Prof. Dr S. CIHAN YURDAYDIN.

Graduate Institute of the History of the Turkish Revolution: Dir Prof. Dr YAVUZ ERCAN.

Graduate Institute of Medical Jurisprudence: Dir Prof. Dr HALIL GÜMÜŞ.

Graduate Institute of Medical Sciences: Dir Prof. Dr RIFAT VURAL.

Graduate Institute of Science: Dir Prof. Dr METIN OLGUN.

Graduate Institute of Social Sciences: Dir Prof. Dr CAN HAMAMCI.

ATTACHED SCHOOLS AND COLLEGES

Çankırı School of Health: Dir Prof. Dr MEHMET KIYAN.

School of Başkent: Dir Prof. Dr HANDE K. ERSOY.

School of Beypazarı: Dir Prof. Dr İLHAN KARAÇAL.

School of Çankırı: Dir Prof. Dr SABAHATTİN BALCI.

School of Cebeci Health Services: Dir Doç. Dr TÜLIN BEDÜK.

School of Dikimevi Health Services: Dir Prof. Dr AHMET DERYA AYSEV.

School of Foreign Languages: Dir Prof. Dr ERSIN ONULDURAN.

School of Home Economics (Faculty of Agriculture): Dir Prof. Dr EMINE GÖNEN.

School of Justice (Faculty of Law): Dir Doç. Dr HALUK KONURALP.

School of Kalecik: Dir Prof. Dr DOĞAN ERDOĞAN.

School of Kastamonu: Dir Prof. Dr BAHRİ GÖKÇEBAY.

School of Physical Education and Sports: Dir Prof. Dr EMIN ERGEN.

State Conservatory: Dir Prof. Dr NURHAN KARADAĞ.

ATATÜRK ÜNİVERSİTESİ

Rektörlüğü, 25240 Erzurum
Telephone: (442) 231-10-30
Fax: (442) 236-10-14
E-mail: ata@atauni.edu.tr
Internet: www.atauni.edu.tr

Founded 1957, reorganized 1982 following the Higher Education Reform
State control
Language of instruction: Turkish
Academic year: October to June

Pres.: HIKMET KOÇAK
Sec.-Gen.: USTUN OZEN
Head of Int. Affairs Office: FAHRI YAVUZ

Library of 300,000 vols
Number of teachers: 2,527 (incl. teaching assts)
Number of students: 40,191

Publications: *Atatürk Dergisi* (2 a year), *Atatürk Üniversitesi Diş Hekimliği Fakültesi Dergisi* (4 a year), *Atatürk Üniversitesi Erzincan Hukuk Fakültesi Dergisi* (2 a year), *Atatürk Üniversitesi İlahiyat Fakültesi Dergisi* (2 a year), *Atatürk Üniversitesi Tıp Dergisi* (4 a year), *Erzincan Eğitim Fakültesi Dergisi* (2 a year), *Güzel Sanatlar Enstitüsü Dergisi* (2 a year), *Güzel Sanatlar Fakültesi Sanat Dergisi* (2 a year), *İktisadi ve İdari Bilimler Dergisi* (2 a year), *Kazım Karabekir Eğitim Fakültesi Dergisi* (2 a year), *Sosyal Bilimler Dergisi* (2 a year), *Sosyal Bilimler Enstitüsü Dergisi* (2 a year), *Türkiyat Araştırmalari Enstitüsü Dergisi* (2 a year), *Ziraat Fakültesi Dergisi* (4 a year)

DEANS

Faculty of Agriculture: MUSTAFA YILDIRIM CANBOLAT
Faculty of Arts: Prof. Dr YILMAZ ÖZBEK
Faculty of Arts and Sciences (Erzincan): Prof. Dr MUHARREM GÜLERYÜZ
Faculty of Communication and Journalism: Prof. Dr ÖNDER BARLI
Faculty of Dentistry: Prof. Dr ABUBEKIR HARORLI
Faculty of Economics and Administrative Sciences: Prof. Dr SUPHI ORHAN
Faculty of Education: Prof. Dr SAMIH BAYRAKÇEKEN
Faculty of Education (Ağrı): Prof. Dr BILGE SEYİDOĞLU
Faculty of Education (Bayburt): Prof. Dr AHMET GÜRSES
Faculty of Education (Erzincan): Prof. Dr ERDOĞAN BÜYÜKKASAP
Faculty of Engineering: Prof. Dr CAFER ÇELİK

Faculty of Fine Arts: Prof. Dr KEMALETTIN YİĞİTER
Faculty of Law School (Erzincan): Prof. Dr AHMET NEZIH KÖK
Faculty of Medicine: Prof. Dr M. SELÇUK ATAMANALP
Faculty of Pharmacy: Prof. Dr FATIH AKÇAY
Faculty of Science: Ö. IRFAN KÜFREVIOĞLU
Faculty of Theology: Prof. Dr BAHATTIN KÖK
Faculty of Veterinary Sciences: Prof. Dr MUSTAFA ATASEVER

ATILIM ÜNIVERSITESI

Kızılcaşar Mah. Köyü, 06836 İncek Gölbası, Ankara
Telephone: (312) 586-80-00
Fax: (312) 586-80-91
E-mail: iro@atilim.edu.tr
Internet: www.atilim.edu.tr
Private control
President: Prof. Dr ABDURRAHIM ÖZGENOĞLU
Gen. Sec.: Prof. Dr ABDÜLAZIZ ŞEREN
Vice-Presidents: Prof. Dr İSMAIL BIRCAN, Prof. Dr İHSAN TARAKÇIOĞLU

DEANS

Faculty of Arts and Sciences: Prof. Dr OYA BATUM MENTEŞE
Faculty of Engineering: Prof. Dr KAMIL İBRAHIM AKMAN
Faculty of Law: Prof. Dr NAMI ÇAĞAN
Faculty of Management: Prof. Dr HALIL İBRAHIM ÜLKER

DIRECTORS

Graduate School of Natural and Applied Sciences: Prof. Dr SELÇUK SOYUPAK
Graduate School of Social Sciences: Prof. Dr ERTUĞRUL ÇETINER
Preparatory School: AYTUNA KOCABIYIKOĞLU

BAHÇEŞEHİR ÜNİVERSİTESİ

34538 Bahçeşehir, Istanbul
Telephone: (212) 669-65-23
Fax: (212) 669-43-98
E-mail: info@bahcesehir.edu.tr
Internet: www.bahcesehir.edu.tr
Founded 1998
Rector: Prof. Dr SÜHEYL BATUM
Vice-Presidents: Prof. Dr NURBAY GÜLTEKIN, Prof. Dr ESER KARAKAŞ
Library of 43,095 vols, 22,000 e-books, 472 periodicals and 3,106 e-journals
Number of teachers: 150
Number of students: 1,207

DEANS

Faculty of Architecture: Prof. Dr ERHAN A. BALKAN
Faculty of Arts and Science: Prof. Dr ÖMER ASIM SAÇLI
Faculty of Engineering: Prof. Dr ŞENAY YALÇIN
Faculty of Law: Prof. Dr CUMHUR ÖZAKMAN
Faculty of Management: Prof. Dr İLKAY SUNAR

BALİKESİR ÜNİVERSİTESİ

Soma Cad., 10100 Balikesir
Telephone: (266) 245-96-50
Fax: (266) 245-96-63
E-mail: hacioglu@balikesir.edu.tr
Internet: www.balikesir.edu.tr
State control
Academic year: September to July
Rector: Prof. Dr NECDET HACIOĞLU
Gen. Sec.: Prof. Dr FAIZ TÜRKAN
Library of 14,520 vols, 294 periodical subscriptions, 17 databases
Number of teachers: 607
Number of students: 22,141 full-time, 9,108 evening

DEANS

Faculty of Arts and Sciences: OKTAY ARSLAN
Faculty of Economics and Administration: ADEM ÇABUK
Faculty of Education: BEDRIYE TUNÇSIPER
Faculty of Engineering and Architecture: ŞERIF SAYLAN

DIRECTORS

Geothermal Research Institute: OSMAN ÇENET
Olive Trade and Agribusiness Institute: SAKIN VURAL VARLI

BAŞKENT ÜNİVERSİTESİ

Baglica Kampusu Eskisehir Yolu 20 km, Baglica, 06530 Etimesgut, Ankara
Telephone: (312) 234-10-10
Fax: (312) 234-12-16
E-mail: webmaster@baskent.edu.tr
Internet: www.baskent.edu.tr
Founded 1993
Private control
Rector: Prof. Dr MEHMET HABERAL
Library of 117,044 vols, 1,041 periodicals
Number of teachers: 947
Number of students: 8,489 undergraduate, 858 postgraduate

DEANS

Faculty of Commercial Sciences: Prof. Dr DOĞAN YAŞAR AYHAN
Faculty of Communications: Prof. Dr AHMET NEDIM TULUNGÜÇ
Faculty of Dentistry: Prof. Dr KENAN ARAZ
Faculty of Economic and Administrative Sciences: Prof. Dr ABDULKADIR VAROĞLU
Faculty of Education: Prof. Dr ŞEREF MIRASYEDIOĞLU
Faculty of Engineering: Prof. Dr BERNA DENGIZ
Faculty of Fine Arts, Design and Architecture: Prof. Dr ADNAN TEPECIK
Faculty of Health Sciences: Prof. Dr KORKUT ERSOY
Faculty of Law: Prof. Dr KUDRET GÜVEN
Faculty of Medicine: Prof. Dr HALDUN MÜDERRISOĞLU
Faculty of Science and Letters: Prof. Dr RAHMI YAĞBASAN

BEYKENT ÜNİVERSİTESİ

34900 Beykent, Istanbul
Telephone: (212) 872-64-32
Fax: (212) 872-24-89
E-mail: info@beykent.edu.tr
Internet: www.beykent.edu.tr
Founded 1997
Language of instruction: English
Academic year: October to June
Rector: Prof. Dr MEHMET FIKRET GEZGIN
Vice-Rector: Prof. Dr MUSTAFA DELICAN, Prof. Dr ÜNSAL OSKAY
Gen. Sec.: Prof. Dr NURETTIN ERDEM
Library and Learning Centre Man.: UĞUR BULGAN
Library of 27,500 vols, 165 periodicals, 2,000 CDs, 850 audio tapes
Number of teachers: 200
Number of students: 2,500

DEANS

Faculty of Arts and Science: ZAFER ASLAN
Faculty of Economics and Administrative Sciences: Prof. Dr MEHMET ZELKA
Faculty of Engineering and Architecture: Prof. Dr ERTAN ÖZKAN
Faculty of Fine Arts: Prof. Dr ÜNSAL OSKAY
Preparatory School: MUSTAFA MELEK (Dir)

BİLKENT ÜNİVERSİTESİ
(Bilkent University)

Bilkent, 06800 Ankara
Telephone: (312) 266-41-25
Fax: (312) 266-41-27
E-mail: contact@bilkent.edu.tr
Internet: www.bilkent.edu.tr
Founded 1984
Private control (educational foundation)
Language of instruction: English
Academic year: September to June
Pres., Bd of Trustees: Prof. ALI DOĞRAMACI
Rector: Prof. ABDULLAH ATALAR
Vice-Rector for Academic Affairs and Provost: Prof. METIN HEPER
Vice-Rector for Admin. and Financial Affairs and Gen. Sec.: Prof. KÜRŞAT AYDOĞAN
Vice-Rector for Student Affairs: Prof. ORHAN AYTÜR
Vice-Rector and Librarian: Dr PHYLLIS L. ERDOĞAN
Number of teachers: 1,100
Number of students: 12,000

DEANS

Faculty of Art, Design and Architecture: Prof. BÜLENT ÖZGÜÇ
Faculty of Business Administration: Prof. ERDAL EREL
Faculty of Economic, Administrative and Social Sciences: Prof. DILEK ÖNKAL
Faculty of Education: Prof. MEHMET BARAY
Faculty of Engineering: Prof. LEVENT ONURAL
Faculty of Humanities and Letters: Prof. TALAT HALMAN
Faculty of Law: Prof. OSMAN BERAT GÜRZUMAR
Faculty of Music and Performing Arts: Assoc. Prof. IŞIN METIN
Faculty of Science: Prof. HASAN ERTEN
School of Applied Languages: TANJU İNAL
School of English Language: JOHN O'DWYER
Vocational School of Computer Technology and Office Management: KAMER RODOPLU
Vocational School of Tourism and Hotel Services: KAMER RODOPLU

BOĞAZIÇI ÜNİVERSİTESİ
(Boğaziçi University)

34342 Bebek, Istanbul
Telephone: (212) 358-15-00
Fax: (212) 265-63-57
E-mail: halkilis@boun.edu.tr
Internet: www.boun.edu.tr
Founded 1863; fmrly Robert College
State control
Languages of instruction: Turkish, English
Academic year: September to July
Rector: Dr AYSE SOYSAL
Vice-Rectors: Prof. Dr CEM BEHAR, Prof. Dr GULEN AKTAS GREENWOOD, Prof. Dr TURAN ÖZTURAN
Dean of Students: Prof. Dr ALI IZZET TEKCAN
Sec.-Gen.: MINE KALENDEROĞLU
Registrar: ZELIHA BALKAN
Librarian: HATICE ÜN
Number of teachers: 984
Number of students: 9,973
Publications: *Boğaziçi University Journal* (1 a year), *Biomedical Engineering Bulletin* (4 a year), *Education Bulletin* (2 a year)

DEANS

Faculty of Arts and Sciences: Prof. Dr OMER OGUZ
Faculty of Economics and Administrative Sciences: Prof. Dr ESER BORAK
Faculty of Education: Prof. Dr CEM ALPTEKİN
Faculty of Engineering: Prof. Dr ALI RIZA KAYLAN

ATTACHED SCHOOLS AND COLLEGES

School of Applied Disciplines: Dir Prof. Dr MELTEM ÖZTURAN.

School of Foreign Languages: Dir Prof. Dr ESER TAYLAN.

School of Vocational Education: Dir Prof. Dr MELTEM ÖZTURAN.

ÇAĞ ÜNIVERSITESI

Adana-Mersin, Karayolu üzeri, 33800 Yenice/Mersin
Telephone: (324) 651-48-00
Fax: (324) 651-48-11
E-mail: cag@cag.edu.tr
Internet: www.cag.edu.tr

Founded 1997
Private control
Languages of instruction: Turkish, English
Academic year: September to June

Rector: Prof. Dr H. ÇETIN BEDESTENCİ
Vice-Rector: Prof. Dr MUSTAFA BAŞARAN
Librarian: ESRA İŞCAN

Library of 100,000 vols
Number of teachers: 160
Number of students: 3,000

Publication: *Journal of Social Sciences* (2 a year)

DEANS

Faculty of Arts and Sciences Faculty: Prof. Dr M. EMIN ÖZEL
Faculty of Economics and Admin. Science: Prof. Dr SÜLEYMAN TÜRKEL
Faculty of Law: Prof. Dr YÜCEL ERTEKİN
Higher Vocational School: Prof. Dr MUSTAFA BAŞARAN
Institute of Social Sciences: Assoc. Prof. Dr HALUK KORKMAZYÜREK

ÇANAKKALE ONSEKİZ MART ÜNİVERSİTESİ

Terziodlu Kampüsü, 17020 Çanakkale
Telephone: (286) 218-00-18
Fax: (286) 218-06-08
E-mail: comurek@comu.edu.tr
Internet: www.comu.edu.tr

Founded 1992
State control
Academic year: October to June

Rector: Prof. Dr RAMAZAN AYDİN
Asst Rectors: Prof. Dr SUZAN ERBAŠ, Prof. Dr ALI ÖZPİNAR, Prof. Dr ALI OSMAN ÖZTÜRK

Number of teachers: 695
Number of students: 15,000

DEANS

Faculty of Agriculture: Prof. Dr KENAN KAYNAŠ
Faculty of Economics and Administrative Studies: Prof. Dr ALI AKDEMIR
Faculty of Education: Prof. Dr REMZI Y. KİNCAL
Faculty of Engineering and Architecture: Prof. Dr SALIH ZEKI TUTKUN
Faculty of Fine Arts: Prof. Dr MUSTAFA APAYDİN
Faculty of Fisheries: Prof. Dr ŠÜKRAN CIRIK
Faculty of Sciences and Arts: Prof. Dr KAZIM KAYA
Faculty of Theology: Prof. Dr NASUHI ÜNAL KARAARSLAN

PROFESSORS

Faculty of Agriculture (Terziodlu Kampüsü, 17020 Çanakkale):

ALTAY, H.
BAYTEKIN, H.
GÖKKUŠ, A.
KAPTAN, H.
KAYNAŠ, K.
KUMUK, T.
ÖZPİNAR, A.
ŠENER, S.
SEREZ, M.

Faculty of Economics and Administrative Studies (Biga) (Biga, Çanakkale):

AKDEMIR, A.
ERDOĐAN, E.

Faculty of Education (Terziodlu Kampüsü, 17020 Çanakkale):

ERBAŠ, S.
METE TUNÇOKU, A.
OSMAN ÖZTÜRK, A.
YİLDİRİM, H.
Y KİNCAL, R.
YÜCE, K.

Faculty of Engineering and Architecture (Terziodlu Kampüsü, 17020 Çanakkale):

BILIŠLI, A.
GÜVEN, S.
YIĐITBAŠ, E.
ZEKI TUTKUN, S.

Faculty of Fine Arts (Terziodlu Kampüsü, 17020 Çanakkale):

APAYDİN, M.
UYANİK, M.

Faculty of Fisheries (Terziodlu Kampüsü, 17020 Çanakkale):

ALPASLAN, M.
CIRIK, Š.
KARAFISTAN, A. İ.
TUNCER, S.

Faculty of Sciences and Arts (Terziodlu Kampüsü, 17020 Çanakkale):

AYDİN, N.
AYDİN, R.
AYSEL, V.
BARAN, Y.
DEMIRCAN, O.
İBRAHIMOV, A.
KAYA, K.
ÖDEN, Z. G.
ÖZDEMIR, E.
ÖZEL, M. E.
TOK, V.
UĐUZMAN, T.
UYSAL, A. O.

Faculty of Theology (Terziodlu Kampüsü, 17020 Çanakkale):

KARAARSLAN, N. Ü.

ATTACHED SCHOOLS AND INSTITUTES

Natural and Applied Sciences Institute: Terziodlu Kampüsü, 17020 Çanakkale; Dir Prof. Dr MEHMET EMIN ÖZEL.

School of Health Services: Saglik Yuksekokulu, Onsekiz Mart Univs, 17100 Canakkale; tel. (286) 217-10-01; fax (286) 217-10-01; internet www.syo.comu.edu.tr; Dir Prof. GUNHAM ERDEM.

School of Tourism and Health Management: Terziodlu Kampüsü, 17020 Çanakkale.

Social Studies Institute: Terziodlu Kampüsü, 17020 Çanakkale; Dir Assoc. Prof. R. CENGIZ AKÇAY.

ÇANKAYA ÜNİVERSİTESİ

Öğretmenler Cad. 14, Yüzüncü Yil, 06530 Balgat, Ankara
Telephone: (312) 284-45-00
Fax: (312) 285-96-31
E-mail: webadmin@cankaya.edu.tr
Internet: www.cankaya.edu.tr

Founded 1997
Private control
Languages of instruction: Turkish, English
Academic year: September to June

President: SITKI ALP
Vice-Presidents: İSMAIL AKINALTUĞ, YUSUF GUNGOR
Rector: Prof. Dr ZIYA AKTAŞ
Vice-Rector: Prof. Dr KENAN TAS
Secretary-General: LÜTFI ÖNSOY
Director of Library: FATIH KUMSEL

Library of 9,278 vols, 140 periodicals
Number of teachers: 207
Number of students: 3,182 (2,977 undergraduate, 205 postgraduate)

DEANS

Faculty of Arts and Sciences: Prof. Dr EMEL DOGRAMACI
Faculty of Economics and Administrative Sciences: Prof. Dr AHMED YALNIZ
Faculty of Engineering and Architecture: Prof. Dr ZIYA AKTAŞ
Faculty of Law: Prof. Dr TURGUT ÖNEN

DIRECTORS

Graduate School of Natural and Applied Sciences: Prof. Dr YURDAHAN GÜLER
Graduate School of Social Sciences: Prof. Dr ÖZHAN ULUATAM
Preparatory School: Prof. Dr CENGIZ TOSUN
Vocational School: Asst Prof. Dr NÜZHET AKİN

CELAL BAYAR ÜNİVERSİTESİ

45000 Manisa
Telephone: (236) 237-28-86
Fax: (236) 237-24-42
E-mail: kutuphane@bayar.edu.tr
Internet: www.bayar.edu.tr

Founded 1992
State control

Rector: Prof. Dr CEMIL ÖZCAN
Vice-Rectors: Prof. Dr ÜLGEN OK, Prof. Dr CENGIZ YILMAZ

Number of teachers: 1,094
Number of students: 21,435

Publications: *Journal of Management and Economics* (2 a year), *Journal of Social Sciences* (2 a year)

DEANS

Faculty of Arts and Sciences: Prof. ŞULE AYCAN
Faculty of Economic and Administrative Sciences: Prof. SEMRA ÖNCÜ
Faculty of Education: Prof. NAZMI TOPÇU
Faculty of Engineering: Prof. ERGUN KÖSE
Faculty of Medicine: Prof. EROL ÖZMEN

ÇUKUROVA ÜNIVERSITESI

Balcalı Kampüsü, 01330 Balcalı, Adana
Telephone: (322) 338-60-84
Fax: (322) 338-64-11
E-mail: international@cu.edu.tr
Internet: www.cu.edu.tr

Founded 1973
State control
Language of instruction: Turkish
Academic year: September to July

Rector: Prof. Dr ALPER AKINOĞLU
Vice-Rector: Prof. Dr BANU İNANÇ
Vice-Rector: Prof. Dr M. RIFAT ULUSOY
Vice-Rector: Prof. Dr SÜLEYMAN GÜNGÖR
Sec.-Gen.: NAZAN KARATAŞ
Librarian: TURHAN YILMAZ

Library of 140,000 vols
Number of teachers: 1,899
Number of students: 36,050

Publications: *University Bulletin* (2 a year), faculty journals (all 3 a year)

DEANS

Faculty of Agriculture: Prof. Dr AYZIN B. KÜDEN
Faculty of Arts and Sciences: Prof. Dr SADULLAH SAKALLIOĞLU

Faculty of Communication: Prof. Dr VEDAT PEŞTEMALCI
Faculty of Dentistry: Prof. Dr İLTER UZEL
Faculty of Divinity: Prof. Dr ALI OSMAN ATEŞ
Faculty of Economics and Admin. Sciences: Prof. Dr MUAMMER TEKEOĞLU
Faculty of Education: Prof. Dr A. NECMI YAŞAR
Faculty of Engineering and Architecture: Prof. Dr BEŞIR ŞAHIN
Faculty of Fine Arts: Prof. Dr YUSUF GÜRÇINAR
Faculty of Fisheries: Prof. Dr OYA IŞIK
Faculty of Law: Prof. Dr ALPER AKINOĞLU
Faculty of Medicine: Prof. Dr BEHNAN ALPER

CUMHURIYET ÜNİVERSİTESİ
(Republic University)

58140 Campus-Sivas
Telephone: (346) 219-11-58
Fax: (346) 219-11-03
E-mail: rektor@cumhuriyet.edu.tr
Internet: www.cumhuriyet.edu.tr

Founded 1974, reorganized 1982
State control
Language of instruction: Turkish
Academic year: October to June

Rector: Prof. Dr FERİT KOÇOĞLU
Vice-Rectors: Prof. Dr ZAFER KARS, Prof. Dr HALDUN SÜMER, Prof. Dr ORHAN TATAR
Sec.-Gen.: Dr EROL ŞANLI
Librarian: AYGÜL ÜNAL

Number of teachers: 1,322
Number of students: 20,000

DEANS

Faculty of Arts and Sciences: Prof. Dr RAIF GÜLER
Faculty of Dentistry: Prof. Dr TIMUR ESENER
Faculty of Economic and Administrative Sciences: Prof. Dr M. ALI AKPINAR
Faculty of Education: Prof. Dr NEVZAT BATTAL
Faculty of Engineering: Prof. Dr ALI ÖZTÜRK
Faculty of Fine Arts: Prof. Dr KADIR KARKİN
Faculty of Medicine: Prof. Dr REYHAN EĞILMEZ
Faculty of Theological Studies: Prof. Dr N. YAŞAR AŞIKOĞLU YILMAZ

DIRECTORS OF INSTITUTES

Basic Sciences: Prof. Dr RAUF EMIROV
Medical Sciences: Prof. Dr ÖGE ÇETINKAYA
Social Sciences: Prof. Dr BAYRAM KAGMAZOĞLU

DICLE ÜNİVERSİTESİ
(Tigris University)

21280 Diyarbakır
Telephone: (412) 248-80-30
Fax: (412) 248-80-47
E-mail: fcan@dicle.edu.tr
Internet: www.dicle.edu.tr

Founded 1966 as branch of Ankara Univ., ind. 1973
State control
Academic year: October to June

Rector: Prof. Dr FIKRI CANORUÇ
Vice-Rectors: Prof. Dr ERALP ARIKAN, Prof. Dr ZÜLKÜF GÜLSÜN
Gen. Sec.: MEHMET TEKDÖŞ
Librarian: SEVGI EKMEKÇILER
Academic year: October to May

Library of 72,000 books, 6,000 periodicals, 1,350 theses and 3 CD databases
Number of teachers: 700
Number of students: 9,000

Publications: *Medical Faculty Journal*, *University Annual*

DEANS

Faculty of Agriculture: Prof. Dr DOĞAN ŞAKAR
Faculty of Dentistry: Prof. Dr FATMA ATAKUL
Faculty of Education: Prof. Dr ÖMER SAYA
Faculty of Education (Siirt): Assoc. Prof. YÜKSEL COŞKUN
Faculty of Engineering and Architecture: Assoc. Prof. FIKRI KAHRAMAN
Faculty of Law: Assoc. Prof. Dr FAZIL HÜSNÜ ERDEM
Faculty of Medicine: Assoc. Prof. Dr RECEP IŞIK
Faculty of Science and Letters: Prof. Dr HALIL HOŞGÖREN
Faculty of Technical Education (Batman): Prof. Dr O. ZEKI HEKİMOĞLU
Faculty of Theology: Assoc. Prof. ABDULKERIM ÜNALAN
Faculty of Veterinary Medicine: Prof. Dr SAVAŞ HATİPOĞLU

PROFESSORS

Faculty of Arts and Sciences:

BAŞARAN, D., Botany
BİLGİN, F. H., Zoology
GÜLSÜN, Z., Atomic and Molecular Physics
GÜMGÜM, B., Inorganic Chemistry
GÜNİGÜNİ, B., Inorganic Chemistry
TEZ, Z., Physical Chemistry
YILMAZ, A., General Physics

Faculty of Education:

ASLAN, E., Turkish Language and Literature
SÖNMEZ, A., Physics

Faculty of Medicine:

ARIKAN, E., Microbiology
AYDINOL, B., Biochemistry
BAHÇECİ, M., Internal Diseases
BAYHAN, N., Anaesthesiology
BUDAK, T., Medical Biology
CANORUÇ, F., Internal Diseases
ÇELİK, S., Biophysics
DEĞERTEKİN, H., Internal Diseases
DERİCİ, M., Dermatology
ERDOĞAN, F., Physical Rehabilitation
GÜL, T., Gynaecology and Obstetrics
GÜRGEN, F., Psychiatry
İLÇİN, E., Public Health
IŞIKOĞLU, B., Internal Diseases
KELLE, A., Medical Biology
METE, Ö., Microbiology
MÜFTÜOĞLU, E., Internal Diseases
NERGİS, Y., Histology
ÖZAYDIN, M., Pathology
ÖZGEN, G., Cardiovascular and Thoracic Surgery
TAŞ, M. A., Public Health
TOPCU, I., Otorhinolaryngology
TOPRAK, N., Internal Diseases
YILMAZ, N., Gynaecology and Obstetrics

DOGUS UNIVERSITY

Acıbadem, Zeamet Sok 21, 34722 Kadıköy, Istanbul
Telephone: (216) 544-55-55
Fax: (216) 544-55-32
E-mail: info@dogus.edu.tr
Internet: www.dogus.edu.tr

Founded 1997
Private control
Languages of instruction: Turkish, English
Academic year: September to June

Rector: Prof. Dr MITAT UYSAL
Gen. Sec.: MINE KALENDEROGLU
Library and Documentation Centre: SÖNMEZ ÇELIK

Library of 107,200 vols, 300 print journals, 23,700 electronic journals
Number of teachers: 464
Number of students: 4,187 (3,940 undergraduate, 247 postgraduate)

Publication: *Dogus University Journal*

DEANS

Faculty of Arts and Sciences: Prof. Dr DILEK DOLTAŞ
Faculty of Economic and Administrative Sciences: Prof. Dr ERTAN OKTAY
Faculty of Engineering: Prof. Dr FÜSUN ÜLENGIN
Faculty of Fine Arts and Design: Prof. Dr RIFAT ÇELEBI
Faculty of Law: Prof. Dr HASAN FEHIM ÜÇIŞIK
Institute of Science and Technology: Prof. Dr AHMET NURI CERANOGLU
Institute of Social Sciences: Prof. Dr ELIF ÇEPNI
Vocational School: MEHMET EEMEK

DOKUZ EYLÜL ÜNİVERSİTESİ
(Ninth September University)

Cumhuriyet Bul. 144, 35210 Alsancak, Izmir
Telephone: (232) 464-8068
Fax: (232) 464-8135
E-mail: webadmin@deu.edu.tr
Internet: www.deu.edu.tr

Founded 1982 from existing faculties and schools
State control
Academic year: October to July

President: Prof. Dr EMİN ALICI
Vice-Presidents: Prof. Dr ADIL ESEN, Prof. Dr IREM ÖZKARAHAN, Prof. Dr ÖMÜR ÖZMEN
Sec.-Gen.: Assoc. Prof. Dr SELMA BAKTİR
Librarian: HALE BALTEPE

Library of 262,000 vols
Number of teachers: 2,938
Number of students: 41,000

Publications: *IIBF Dergisi* (Faculty of Economics and Administrative Sciences, 2 a year), *İlahiyat Fakültesi Dergisi* (Faculty of Theology Review), *Sosyal Bilimler Enstitüsü Dergisi* (Social Sciences Institute Review, 2 a year), *Tip Fakültesi Dergisi* (Faculty of Medicine Review)

DEANS

Faculty of Architecture: Prof. Dr ORCAN GÜNDÜZ
Faculty of Arts and Sciences: Prof. Dr NILGÜN MORALİ
Faculty of Business Administration: Prof. Dr ORHAN İAÖZ
Faculty of Economics and Administrative Sciences: Prof. Dr ŞENAY ÜÇDOĞRUK
Faculty of Education: Prof. Dr FERDA AYSAN
Faculty of Engineering: Prof. Dr CÜNEYT GÜZELIŞ
Faculty of Fine Arts: Prof. Dr ÇETIN TÜRKAÜ
Faculty of Law: Prof. Dr ŞEREF ERTAŞ
Faculty of Medicine: Prof. Dr ŞEBNEM ÖZKAN
Faculty of Theology: Prof. Dr SELÂHATTIN PARLADIR

DIRECTORS

Conservatory: Prof. GÜLSER ERYÜMLÜ
Graduate School of Atatürk Principles and Turkish Revolution: Prof. Dr ERGÜN AYBARS
Graduate School of Education: Prof. Dr SEDEF GIDENER
Graduate School of Health Sciences: Prof. Dr GÜL GÜNER
Graduate School of Science and Engineering: Prof. Dr CAHİT HELVACI
Graduate School of Social Sciences: Prof. Dr ALİ NAZIM SÖZER
Institute of Marine Sciences and Technology: Prof. Dr MUSTAFA ERGÜN
Institute of Oncology: Prof. Dr NUR OLGUN
İzmir Vocational School: Prof. Dr RECEP YAPAREL
School of Maritime Business and Management: Prof. Dr GÜLDEM CERİT
School of Nursing: Prof. Dr GÜLSEREN KOCAMAN

School of Physical Therapy and Rehabilitation: Prof. Dr SERAP ALPER
Torbalı Vocational School: Prof. Dr BURHAN ERDOĞAN
Vocational School of Health Services: Prof. Dr NEDİM GAKIR
Vocational School of Juridical Practice: Prof. Dr HAKAN PEKCANİTEZ
Vocational School of Religion: Prof. Dr DURMUŞ TEZCAN

DUMLUPINAR ÜNİVERSİTESİ

M. Kampüs Rektörlük Binası Tavşanlı, Yolu 10 km 43100 Kütahya
Telephone: (274) 265-20-31
Fax: (274) 265-20-14
E-mail: ssevim@dumlupinar.edu.tr
Internet: www.dumlupinar.edu.tr
Founded 1992
State control
Academic year: November to July
Rector: Prof. Dr GÜNER ÖNCE
Vice-Rectors: Prof. Dr BAHRI ÖTEYAKA, Prof. Dr ALI SARIKOYUNCU
Sec.-Gen.: YALÇIN KALAY
Registrar: MIKTAT BEKTAŞ
Head of Library: İSMAIL BAYRAM
Library of 28,000 books, 168 periodicals
Number of teachers: 515
Number of students: 19,000

DEANS

Faculty of Arts and Sciences: Prof. ALI SARIKOYUNCU
Faculty of Economic and Administrative Sciences (Bilecik): Prof. BAHRI ÖTEYAKA
Faculty of Education: Prof. Dr AHMET YAMIK
Faculty of Engineering: Prof. CEM ŞENSÖĞÜT
Faculty of Fine Arts: Prof. Dr ADNAN TEPECİK
Faculty of Technical Education (Simav): Prof. GÜNER ÖNCE
Graduate School of Science and Engineering: Assoc. Prof. İSKENDER IŞIK
Graduate School of Social Sciences: Prof. AHMET KARAASLAN

EGE ÜNİVERSİTESİ
(Aegean University)

Bornova, Izmir
Telephone: (232) 388-01-10
Fax: (232) 339-90-90
E-mail: ulkubay@med.ege.edu.tr
Internet: www.ege.edu.tr
Founded 1955
State control
Languages of instruction: Turkish and, in some departments, English
Academic year: October to June
Rector: Prof. Dr ÜLKÜ BAYINDIR
Vice-Rectors: Prof. Dr HALUK BAYLAS, Prof. Dr FIKRET İKIZ, Prof. Dr MUSTAFA METIN
Gen. Sec.: CIHANGIR SOYGÜL
Librarian: NURCAN ESLİK BAYKAL
Number of teachers and assistants: 992
Number of students: 30,887
Publications: *Aegean Medical Journal*, *Fen Dergisi*, *Tıp Fakültesi Mecmuası*, *Ziraat Fakültesi Dergisi*, and faculty publications

DEANS

Faculty of Agriculture: Prof. Dr SEMIH ERKAN
Faculty of Communications: Prof. Dr AHMET BÜLENT GÖKSEL
Faculty of Dentistry: Prof. Dr SELDA ERTÜRK
Faculty of Economics and Administrative Sciences: Prof. Dr REZAN TATLIDİL
Faculty of Education: Prof. Dr KADIR ASLAN
Faculty of Engineering: Prof. Dr MUSTAFA TÜRKSEVER
Faculty of Fisheries: Prof. Dr AHMET KOCATAŞ
Faculty of Medicine: Prof. Dr ATA ERDENER
Faculty of Pharmacy: Prof. Dr ERÇIN ERCİYAS
Faculty of Science: Prof. Dr BEKIR ÇETİNKAYA
Faculty of Science and Letters: Prof. Dr KASIM EĞİT

DIRECTORS

Conservatory of Turkish Music: Prof. Dr REFET SAYGILI
Institute for Medical Sciences: Prof. Dr NECMETTİN ZEYBEK
Institute for Nuclear Sciences: Prof. Dr SELMAN KINACI
Institute for Science: Prof. Dr FERİDUN TOPALOĞLU
Institute for Solar Energy: Prof. Dr MEHMET AYDIN
Professional School: Prof. Dr MEHMET DOKUZOĞUZ
School of Nursing: Prof. Dr İNCİ EREFE
School of Press and Publications: Prof. Dr ÖZCAN ÖZAL
School of Water Products: Prof. Dr ATİLLA ALPBAZ

RESEARCH CENTRES

Agricultural Research Center: Dir Prof. Dr TAYFUN ÖZKAYA.
Botanical Garden and Herbarium Research Center: Dir Prof. Dr ÖZCAN SEÇMEN.
Cancer Surveillance and Research Center: Dir Prof. Dr AYFER HAYDAROĞLU.
Centre for Strategic Studies.
Environmental Studies Research Center: Dir Prof. Dr ÜMIT ERDEM.
European Languages and Cultures Research Center (ADİKAM): Dir Prof. Dr GERTRUDE DURUSOY.
Family Planning and Infertility Research Center.
Genetic Disease Research Center: Dir Prof. Dr CIHANGIR ÖZKINAY.
Health Research Center (University Hospital).
Information and Communication Technologies Research Center: Dir Prof. Dr FAZIL APAYDIN.
Izmir Research Center: Dir Prof. Dr IŞIK TARAKÇIOĞLU.
Natural History Research Center (The Museum of Natural History): Dir Prof. Dr NIMET ÖKTEM.
Organ Transplantation Research Centre: Dir Prof. Dr ÖZDEMİR YARARBAŞ.
Poison Research Center.
Principles of Atatürk and Recent Turkish History Research Center: Dir Prof. Dr FAZILET VARDAR-SUKAN.
Science and Technology Research Center: Dir Prof. Dr S. ŞUHA SUKAN.
Seed Technology Research Center: Dir Prof. Dr BENIAN ESER.
Submarine Research Center.
Textile and Apparel Manufacturing Research Center: Dir Prof. Dr IŞIK TARAKÇIOGLU.
Women's Studies Research Center.

ERCİYES ÜNİVERSİTESİ

38039 Kayseri
Telephone: (352) 437-49-22
Fax: (352) 437-49-31
E-mail: info@erciyes.edu.tr
Internet: www.erciyes.edu.tr
Founded 1978
State control
Language of instruction: Turkish
Academic year: October to June
Rector: Prof. Dr FAHRETTIN KELEŞTEMUR
Vice-Rectors: Prof. Dr METIN HÜLAGÜ, MUSTAFA ÇETIN, Prof. Dr IBRAHIM UZMAY
Registrar: Dr SEMA ASLAN
Librarian: GÜLNUR YAKAN
Library of 240,000 vols, 67,400 electronic books, 40,550 electronic journals, 71,000 journals
Number of teachers: 1,171
Number of students: 35,533
Publications: *Journal of the Faculty of Economics and Administrative Sciences*, *Journal of the Medical School*, *Journals of the Graduate School of Health Sciences*, *Journals of the Graduate School of Sciences*, *Journals of the Graduate School of Social Sciences*, *Journals of the Theology Faculty*, *Journals of the Veterinary Medicine Faculty*

DEANS

Faculty of Agriculture: Prof. Dr ALI İRFAN İLBAŞ SEVİĞ
Faculty of Architecture: Prof. Dr İBRAHIM UZMAY
Faculty of Arts: Prof. Dr ÜMIT TOKATLI
Faculty of Business Administration (Yozgat): Prof. Dr OSMAN UNUTULMAZ
Faculty of Business Administration and Management (Nevşehir): Prof. Dr MAHIR NAKİP
Faculty of Communication: Prof. Dr HAMZA ÇAKIR
Faculty of Dentistry: Prof. Dr ALPER ALKANİM
Faculty of Economics and Administrative Sciences: Prof. Dr EKREM ERDEM
Faculty of Education: Prof. Dr ABDULLAH SAYDAMİRCİ
Faculty of Engineering: Prof. Dr MUSTAFA ALÇI
Faculty of Engineering and Architecture (Yozgat): Prof. Dr RECEP KILIK
Faculty of Fine Arts: Prof. Dr FAHRETTIN KELEŞTEMUR
Faculty of Health Science: Prof. Dr ÜMIT SEVİĞ
Faculty of Law: Doç. Dr İSMAIL KAYAR
Faculty of Medicine: Prof. Dr MUHAMMET GÜVEN
Faculty of Pharmacy: Prof. Dr MÜBERRI KOŞARİN
Faculty of Science: Prof. Dr HÜSEYIN ALTINDIŞ
Faculty of Theology: Prof. Dr M. ZEKI DUMAN
Faculty of Veterinary Medicine: Prof. Dr HALIT CANATAN

PROFESSORS

Faculty of Architecture (Erciyes University, 38039 Kayseri; tel. (352) 437-52-82; fax (352) 437-65-54; internet www.erciyes.edu.tr/mimart.htm):

LÖKÇE, S.
ÖZCAN, Z.
YURTSEVER, H.

Faculty of Arts and Science (Erciyes University, 38039 Kayseri; tel. (352) 437-52-62; fax (352) 437-49-33; internet www.matrix.erciyes.edu.tr):

AKÇAMUR, Y.
AKKURT, M.
AKTAN, A.
ALTİNDİŞ, H.
ALTURAL, B.
ARGUNŞAH, H.
ARGUNŞAH, M.
AYYİLDIZ, E.
AYYİLDIZ, N.
BARAN, M.
BAYRAKTAR, B.
BOR, H.
ÇOBAN, A.
GÖRKEM, İ.
GÜLENSOY, T.
GÜNDÜZ, M.

GÜZEL, Y.
HÜLAGÜ, M. M.
KARAÖRS, M. M.
KARTAL, Ş.
KESKİN, M.
KESKİN, M.
KÖK, T. R.
MANAŞLI, N.
MUCUK, O.
ÖNEM, Ş C.
ÖZDEMIR, M.
ÖZKAN, N.
ÖZSOY, S.
PATAT, Ş.
SARIPINAR, E.
SOYLAK, M.
TAŞDEMİRCİ, E.
TOKATLI, U.
TUNÇBILEK, A. Ş.
TÜRKMEN, K.
ÜLGEN, A.
YILDIRIM, İ.
YUVALI, A.

Faculty of Arts and Science (Yozgat) (Erciyes University, Yozgat; tel. (354) 263-82-70; fax (354) 263-82-71; internet www.yozgatfef.erciyes.edu.tr):

AKÇAMUR, Y.

Faculty of Communication (Erciyes University, 38039 Kayseri; tel. and fax (352) 437-52-61; internet iletsim.erciyes.edu.tr):

AKDOĞAN, Ş.
YERLIKAYA, İ.

Faculty of Dentistry (Erciyes University, 38039 Kayseri; tel. and fax (352) 437-49-01; internet dent.erciyes.edu.tr):

KESIM, B.

Faculty of Economics and Administrative Sciences (Erciyes University, 38039 Kayseri; tel. (352) 437-49-13; fax (352) 437-52-39; e-mail iibf@erciyes.edu.tr; internet www.iibf.erciyes.edu.tr):

AKDOĞAN, A. A.
AKDOĞAN, M. Ş.
ANDAÇ, F.
ATALAY, M.
BİLGİNOĞLU, M. A.
ÇALIŞKAN, F.
DURA, C.
DURSUN, Y.
ERDEM, E.
NAKİP, M.
ÖZGÜVEN, C.
SAATÇİ, M.
SÖNMEZ, İ. H.
UNUTULMAZ, O.
YILDIZ, R.

Faculty of Economics and Administrative Sciences (Nevşehir) (Erciyes University, Nevşehir; tel. (384) 215-20-07; fax (384) 215-20-10; internet www.iibf.eunev.edu.tr):

YILDIZ, R.

Faculty of Economics and Administrative Sciences (Yozgat) (Erciyes University, Yozgat; tel. (354) 263-82-48; fax (354) 263-82-81; internet yiibf.erciyes.edu.tr):

UNUTULMAZ, O.

Faculty of Education (Erciyes University, 38039 Kayseri; tel. and fax (352) 437-32-06; internet egitim.erciyes.edu.tr):

TAŞDEMIRCI, E.

Faculty of Engineering (Erciyes University, 38039 Kayseri; tel. (352) 437-57-55; fax (352) 437-57-84; internet mf.erciyes.edu.tr):

ALÇİ, M.
APALAK, M. K.
BILIŞIK, A.
DANIŞMAN, K.
GÜNEY, K.
HAKTANIR, T.
KARABOĞA, D.
KARAMIŞ, M. B.
KILIK, R.
TAŞPİNAR, H.
UZMAY, İ.
YAPİCİ, H.
YETIM, H.

Faculty of Engineering and Architecture (Yozgat) (Erciyes University, Yozgat; tel. (354) 263-82-72; fax (354) 263-82-76; internet ymmf.erciyes.edu.tr):

KILIK, R.

Faculty of Fine Arts (Erciyes University, 38039 Kayseri; tel. (352) 437-52-81; fax (352) 437-36-52; internet guzelsanat.erciyes.edu.tr):

YENER, S.

Faculty of Law (Erciyes University, 38039 Kayseri; tel. (352) 437-49-01; fax (352) 437-49-31; internet hukuk.erciyes.edu.tr):

KAYAR, İ.

Faculty of Medicine (Erciyes University, 38039 Kayseri; tel. (352) 437-49-10; fax (352) 437-52-85; internet tip.erciyes.edu.tr):

AKÇALI, Y. F.
AKDEMİR, H.
AKTAS, E.
ALTUNBAŞ, M.
ALTUNTAŞ, H.
ARGUN, M.
ARITAŞ, Y.
ARMAN, F.
AŞÇIOĞLU, M.
AŞÇIOĞLU, Ö.
AYCAN, K.
AYDOĞAN, S.
AYGEN, B.
AYGEN, E. M.
AYKUT, M.
BAKTIR, A.
BALKANLI, S.
BAŞAK, E.
BAŞBUĞ, M.
BAŞTÜRK, M.
BAYRAM, F.
BOYACİ, A.
CANER, Y.
ÇETİN, N.
ÇETİN, S.
ÇETİNKAYA, F.
CEYHAN, O.
ÇOKSEVIM, B.
DEMİR, R.
DEMIRTAŞ, H.
DOĞAN, H.
DOĞANAY, M.
DÜNDAR, M.
DÜNDAR, M.
DURAK, A. C.
DURSUN, N.
DÜŞÜNSEL, R.
EMİROĞULLARİ, O. N.
ERENMEMİŞOĞLU, A.
ERGIN, A.
ERKAN, M.
ERKILIÇ, K.
ERSOY, A. Ö.
ESMAOĞLU, A.
GÖLGELİ, A.
GÜLEÇ, M.
GÜLMEZ, İ.
GÜLMEZ, İ.
GÜNAY, G. K.
GÜNAY, O.
GÜNDÜZ, Z.
GÜNEY, E.
GÜVEN, K.
KAHRAMAN, H. C.
KARACAGİL, M.
KARAKÜÇÜK, M. S.
KELEŞTİMUR, H. F.
KENDİRCİ, M.
KİLİÇ, H.
KIRNAP, M.
KOÇ, A. N.
KOÇ, R. K.
KONTAŞ, O.
KÖSE, S. K.
KÜÇÜKAYDIN, M.
KÜLAHLİ, İ.
KUMANDAŞ, S.
KURTOĞLU, S.
MADENOĞLU, H.
MİRZA, G. E.
MİRZA, M.
MÜDERRIS, İ. İ.
MUHTAROĞLU, S.
NARIN, N.
OKTEN, T.
OKUR, H.
OYMAK, O.
ÖZBAKİR, Ö.
ÖZBAL, Y.
ÖZCAN, N.
ÖZDAMAR, M. A.
ÖZDEMİR, M. A.
ÖZESMİ, Ç.
ÖZESMİ, M.
ÖZKUL, Y.
ÖZTÜRK, F.
ÖZTÜRK, M. A.
ÖZTÜRK, M. K.
ÖZTÜRK, Y.
PATIROĞLU, T.
PATIROĞLU, T. E.
ŞAHİN, İ.
ŞAHİN, Y.
SELÇUKLU, A.
SOFUOĞLU, S.
SOYUER, A.
SÖZÜER, E. M.
SÜER, C.
SÜMERKAN, A. B.
TALASLIOĞLU, A.
TATLIŞEN, A.
TAYYAR, M.
TEKOL, Y.
TERCAN, E.
TURAN, C.
TÜRK, C. Y.
TUTUŞ, A.
UKŞAL, Ü.
ÜNAL, A.
ÜNLÜ, Y.
ÜSTDAL, K. M.
UTAŞ, C.
UTAŞ, S.
ÜZUM, K.
YAKAN, B.
YIĞITBAŞI, , O. G.
YILMAZ, Z.
YÜCESOY, M.

Faculty of Pharmacy (Erciyes University, 38039 Kayseri; tel. (352) 437-49-01; fax (352) 437-49-31; internet pharmacy.erciyes.edu.tr):

BERÇIN, E.

Faculty of Theology (Erciyes University, 38039 Kayseri; tel. (352) 437-60-64; fax (352) 437-42-00; internet ilahiyat.erciyes.edu.tr):

APAYDIN, H. Y.
ATİK, M. K.
AYDİN, M. Ş.
BAĞÇECİ, M.
COŞKUN, A.
DEMİRCİ, A.
DUMAN, M. Z.
GÜNAY, Ü.
GÜNGÖR, H.
KIRCA, C.
KOÇ, T.
PAZARBAŞI, E.
POLAT, S.
ŞAHİN, H.
ŞAMUR, S.
SEVERCAN, Ş.
TAŞTAN, A.
TOKSARI, A.
TUNÇ, C.
UĞUR, A.

Faculty of Veterinary Science (Erciyes University, 38039 Kayseri; tel. (352) 339-94-84; fax (352) 337-27-40; internet www.erciyes.edu.tr/veterinert.htm):

ATASEVER, A.
AYDIN, F.
BEKYÜREK, T.
İNCI, A.
İŞCAN, K. M.
LIMAN, B. C.
LIMAN, N.
NUR, İ. H.

FATİH ÜNİVERSİTESİ

34500 Büyükçekmece, Istanbul
Telephone: (212) 866-33-00
Fax: (212) 866-33-37
E-mail: info@fatih.edu.tr
Internet: www.fatih.edu.tr
Founded 1996
Private control
Language of instruction: English(in faculties)
Language of instruction: Turkish (in Vocational Schools)
Academic year: September to June
Rector: Prof. Dr SERIF ALI TEKALAN
Vice-Rectors: Prof. Dr FAHRETTIN GUCIN, Prof. Dr AYHAN BOZKURT, Prof. Dr MUHAMMET RAMAZAN YIGITOGLU (acting)
Sec.-Gen.: ERTUGRUL MESCIOGLU
Dir of Financial Affairs: MUTTALIP YILMAZ
Dir of Int. Programs Office: FERHAT ARSLAN
Dir of Int. Students Office: ERDOGAN TUZEN
Dir of Library and Documentation: ERCUMENT DEMIRBOZAN
Dir of Student Affairs Office: CUNEYT UMUTLU
Librarian: ERCÜMENT DEMIRBOZAN
Library of 69,760 vols, 47,092 e-books, 7,651 journals, 979 theses, 70,000 e-theses, 40 periodicals, 882 CDs
Number of teachers: 344
Number of students: 11,808
Publications: *Civilacademy: Journal of Social Sciences* (3 a year), *EJEPS, European Journal of Economic and Political Studies*, *Fatih Bulletin*, *Genc Kariyer*, *Journal of Economic and Social Research* (2 a year), *Kariyer Penceresi*, *Peers (Student Journal)* (2 a year), *Politics, Reflections (Student Journal)* (2 a year), *Text (Student Journal)* (3 a year)

DEANS

Ankara Vocational School: YUKSEL NIZAMOGLU
Ankara Vocational School of Medical Sciences: YUKSEL NIZAMOGLU
Faculty of Arts and Sciences: Prof. Dr CEVDET NERGIZ
Faculty of Economics and Admin. Sciences: Prof. Dr MURAT KARAGOZ
Faculty of Education: Prof. Dr FAHRETTIN GUCIN
Faculty of Engineering: Prof. Dr CEVDE MERIC
Faculty of Law: Prof. OSMAN KASIKCI
Faculty of Medicine: Prof. Dr MUHAMMET RAMAZAN YIGITOGLU (acting)
Faculty of Theology: Prof. Dr MUHIT MERT
Graduate School of Biomedical Engineering: Prof. SADIK KARA
Graduate School of Sciences and Engineering: Assoc. Prof. NURULLAH ARSLAN
Graduate School of Social Sciences: Assoc. Prof. MEHMET KARAKUYU
Istanbul Vocational School: Assoc. Prof. OSMAN NURI ARAS
School of Nursing: Prof. SENOL DANE
Vocational School of Justice: Prof. OSMAN KASIKCI

FİRAT ÜNİVERSİTESİ
(Euphrates University)

23119 Elaziğ
Telephone: (424) 212-85-10
Fax: (424) 212-27-10
E-mail: okalem@firat.edu.tr
Internet: www.firat.edu.tr
Founded 1975
Language of instruction: Turkish
Academic year: October to June
Rector: Prof. Dr MEHMET HAMDI MUZ
Vice-Rectors: Prof. Dr A. Y. ERKIN OĞUR, Prof. Dr HARUN ÖZER
Gen. Sec.: GAZI ÖZCAN
Librarian: Prof. Dr FAHRETTIN GÖKTAŞ
Number of teachers: 1,558
Number of students: 15,906
Publications: *Journal of Health Sciences* (2 a year), *Journal of Science and Engineering* (2 a year), *Journal of Social Sciences* (2 a year)

DEANS

Faculty of Agriculture (Bingöl): (vacant)
Faculty of Aquatic Sciences: Prof. Dr BÜLENT ŞEN
Faculty of Arts and Sciences: Prof. Dr İBRAHIM YILMAZÇELIK
Faculty of Communication: Prof. Dr ASAF VAROL
Faculty of Economic and Management Sciences (Tunceli): (vacant)
Faculty of Education: Prof. Dr MEHMET AYDOĞDU
Faculty of Education (Muş): (vacant)
Faculty of Engineering: Prof. Dr DURSUN PEHLİVAN
Faculty of Medicine: Prof. Dr ÖZGE ARDIÇOĞLU
Faculty of Technical Education: Prof. Dr ALI İNAN
Faculty of Theology: Doç. Dr MUSTAFA ÖZTÜRK
Faculty of Veterinary Medicine: Prof. Dr H. BASRI GÜLCÜ

ATTACHED SCHOOLS AND COLLEGES

College of Health Sciences: Dir Prof. Dr EMINE ÜNSALDI.

College of Health Sciences (Elazig): Dir Prof. Dr ZÜLAL AŞCI TORAMAN.

College of Physical and Sports Education (Elazig): Dir Prof. Dr MEHMET ÜLKER.

College of Social Sciences (Elazig): Dir Doç. Dr ORHAN KILIÇ.

College of Technical Sciences (Elazig): Dir Doç. Dr NECATI KULOĞLU.

College of Vocational Education (Bingöl): Dir Prof. Dr MÜKREMIN APAYDIN.

College of Vocational Education (Maden): Dir Doç. Dr ALI İNAN.

College of Vocational Education (Malazgirt): Dir Prof. Dr KADIR SERVI.

College of Vocational Education (Muş): Dir Doç. Dr KADIR SERVİ.

College of Vocational Education (Sivrice): Dir Prof. Dr HARUN ÖZER.

College of Vocational Education (Tunceli): Dir Prof. Dr SALIH ÖZÇELİK.

Fine Arts–Music: Dir Assoc. Prof. Dr GÜLDENIZ EKMEN AGİŞ.

Keban Sleyman Demırel College of Vocational Education: Dir Assoc. Prof. Dr HÜSAMETTIN KAYA.

Kemaliye Hacı Ali Akin College of Vocational Education: Dir Prof. Dr MEHMET CEBECİ.

GALATASARAY ÜNİVERSİTESİ

Ciragan Cad. 36, 34357 Ortaköy, Istanbul
Telephone: (212) 227-44-80
E-mail: dyarsuvat@gsu.edu.tr
Internet: www.gsu.edu.tr
Founded 1992
Academic year: October to June
State control
Rector: Prof. Dr DUYGUN YARSUVAT
Vice-Rectors: Prof. Dr SEYFETTIN GÜRSEL, Prof. Dr PIERRE LE MIRE, Prof. Dr ETHEM TOLGA, Prof. Dr NECMI YÜZBAŞIOĞLU
Gen. Sec.: Prof. Dr İSMAIL ÖZTÜRK
Library of 42,000 vols
Number of teachers: 140
Number of students: 1,674

DEANS

Faculty of Communications: Prof. Dr E. ÖZDEN CANKAYA
Faculty of Engineering and Technology: Prof. Dr ETHEM TOLGA
Faculty of Law: Prof. Dr HAMDI YASAMAN
Faculty of Science and Letters: Prof. Dr KENAN GÜRSOY

GAZİ ÜNİVERSİTESİ

06500 Teknikokullar, Ankara
Telephone: (312) 202-22-22
Fax: (312) 221-32-02
E-mail: rektor@gazi.edu.tr
Internet: www.gazi.edu.tr
Founded 1982
State control
Language of instruction: Turkish
Academic year: September to June
Rector: Prof. Dr RIZA AYHAN
Vice-Rectors: Prof. Dr METIN AKTAS, Prof. Dr CUMHUR SAHIN, Prof. Dr DURAN ALTIPARMARK
Sec.-Gen.: Prof. Dr BAHTIYAR AKYILMAZ
Librarian: TÜNSEL CANATALI
Library of 308,723 vols
Number of teachers: 3,756
Number of students: 64,663 (55,068 undergraduate, 9,595 postgraduate)
Publication: *Gazi Üniversitesi Bülteni* (6 a year)

DEANS

Faculty of Architecture: Prof. Dr HÜSNU CAN
Faculty of Arts and Design: Prof. Dr FATMA ALI SINANOGLU
Faculty of Commerce and Tourism: Prof. Dr NEVZAT AYPEK
Faculty of Communication: Prof. Dr NACI BOSTANCI
Faculty of Dentistry: Prof. Dr DERVIS YILMAZ
Faculty of Economic and Administrative Sciences: Prof. Dr KADIR ARIKI
Faculty of Economics and Administrative Sciences (Çorum): Prof. Dr HASAN KAVAL
Faculty of Education (Gazi): Prof. Dr MUSTAFA SAFRAN
Faculty of Education (Kastamonu): Prof. Dr ALEMI YETIM
Faculty of Education (Kırşehir): Prof. Dr SELAHATTİN SALMAN
Faculty of Engineering (Çorum): Prof. Dr NAIL UNSAL
Faculty of Forestry (Kastamonu): Prof. Dr HASAN VURDU
Faculty of Fine Arts: Prof. Dr ALEV CAKMAOGLU KURU
Faculty of Health Sciences: Prof. Dr A. GULSAN TURKOZSUCAK
Faculty of Industrial Arts Education: Prof. Dr İRFAN SÜER
Faculty of Law: Prof. Dr IHSAN ERDOGAN
Faculty of Medicine: Prof. Dr PEYAM CINAZ
Faculty of Pharmacy: Prof. Dr TURHAN BAYKAL

Faculty of Sciences (Kırşehir): Prof. Dr İRFAN AKGÜN
Faculty of Technical Education: Prof. Dr CEMIL CETINKAYA
Faculty of Theology (Çorum): Prof. Dr HASAN ONAT
Faculty of Vocational Education: Prof. Dr FATMA ALI SINANOGLU

GRADUATE SCHOOLS

Graduate School of Accident Research and Prevention: Dir Prof. Dr ALİ BUMİN.
Graduate School of Educational Sciences: Dir Prof. Dr SEMIH YALÇIN.
Graduate School of Health Sciences: Dir OKTAY ÜNER.
Graduate School of Natural Sciences: Maltepe, Ankara; Dir Prof. Dr AHMET BIGER.
Graduate School of Social Sciences: Kavaklıdere, Ankara; Dir Prof. Dr İHSON ERDOĞAN.

GAZİANTEP ÜNİVERSİTESİ

POB 300, 27310 Gaziantep
Telephone: (342) 360-10-10
Fax: (342) 360-10-13
E-mail: gensek@gantep.edu.tr
Internet: www.gantep.edu.tr
Founded 1987
Academic year: October to June
Rector: Prof. Dr ERHAN EKİNCİ
Number of teachers: 2,821
Number of students: 49,250
Publications: *Sosyal Bilimler Dergisi* (social sciences, 1 a year), *Tıp Fakültesi Dergisi* (medicine, 2 a year)

DEANS

Faculty of Arts and Science: IHSAN UNVER
Faculty of Arts and Science (Kilis): ÖMER BAKKALOGLU
Faculty of Economics and Business Administration: ISMAIL H. ÖZSABUNCUOĞLU
Faculty of Education: MUHSIN MACIT
Faculty of Education (Adiyaman): HACI DURAN
Faculty of Education (Kilis): ALI RIZA TEKIN
Faculty of Engineering: MUSTAFA ÖZAKÇA
Faculty of Medicine: ABDURAHMAN KADAYIFÇI

GAZİOSMANPAŞA ÜNIVERSITESI

60150 Tokat
Telephone: (356) 252-14-52
Fax: (356) 252-14-52
E-mail: tokat@gop.edu.tr
Internet: www.gop.edu.tr
Founded 1992
State control
Academic year: October to June
Rector: Prof. Dr ZEHRA SEYFIKLI
Vice-Rector: Prof. Dr MEHMET ARSLAN
Vice-Rector: Prof. Dr MEHMET TEKIN
Librarian: ERDAL ŞAHİNİ
Library of 60,063 vols, 1,425 theses, 375 periodicals, 48 musical notes, 40 diskettes, 295 CD-ROMs, 19 electronic databases
Number of teachers: 842
Number of students: 13,328 (12,520 undergraduate, 808 postgraduate)

DEANS

Faculty of Agriculture: Prof. Dr GÜNGÖR YILMAZ
Faculty of Arts and Sciences: Prof. Dr HANEFI VURAL
Faculty of Economic and Administrative Sciences: Prof. Dr OSMAN KARAKACIER
Faculty of Education: Prof. Dr MUSTAFA BALOĞLU
Faculty of Medicine: Prof. Dr MURAT FIRAT
Faculty of Natural Sciences and Engineering: (vacant)

GEBZE YÜKSEK TEKNOLOJİ ENSTİTÜSÜ

PK 101, 41400, Gebze Kocaeli
Telephone: (262) 60515-01
Fax: (262) 653-84-90
E-mail: okalem@gyte.edu.tr
Internet: www.gyte.edu.tr
Founded 1992
Languages of instruction: Turkish, English
State control
Rector: Prof. Dr ALINUR BÜYÜKAKSOY
Vice-Rectors: Prof. Dr VASFI ELDEM, Prof. Dr ORHAN ŞAHIN
Library of 10,000 vols, 8 electronic databases, 9,705 online periodicals, 33 printed periodicals
Number of students: 1,063 undergraduate; 1,560 graduate
Faculties of architecture, business and administration, economics, engineering, science.

HACETTEPE ÜNİVERSİTESİ

Hacettepe Üniversitesi, 06100 Ankara
Telephone: (312) 305-5000
Fax: (312) 310-5552
E-mail: information@hacettepe.edu.tr
Internet: www.hacettepe.edu.tr
Founded 1967
State control
Languages of instruction: French, German, Turkish, English
Academic year: September to August
Rector: Prof. Dr UĞUR ERDENER
Vice-Rectors: Prof. Dr HASAN KAZDAĞLI, Prof. Dr HÜSEYIN SELÇUK GEÇIM, Prof. Dr SEVIL GÜRGAN
Sec.-Gen.: TURHAN MENTEŞ
Registrar: A. RIFKI GÖKMEN (Deputy Registrar)
Dir of Libraries: AYŞEN KÜYÜK (Deputy Director)
Library: Beytepe campus library of 185,554 vols, 34,940 journals, 1,216,181 theses, 1,996 CDs, 1,071 record albums
Number of teachers: 3,645
Number of students: 30,000
Publications: *Hacettepe Tıp/Cerrahi Bülteni* (4 a year), and several faculty bulletins

DEANS

Beytepe Campus:

Faculty of Economics and Adminstrative Sciences: Prof. Dr AHMET BURÇIN YERELI
Faculty of Communication: Prof. Dr SUAVI AYDIN
Faculty of Education: Prof. Dr BUKET AKKOYUNLU
Faculty of Engineering: Prof. Dr HAYRI YILMAZ KAPTAN
Faculty of Fine Arts: Prof. Dr UĞURCAN AKYÜZ
Faculty of Law: Prof. Dr SELMA ÇETINER
Faculty of Letters: Prof. Dr MUSA YAŞAR SAĞLAM
Faculty of Science: Prof. Dr MEHMET AŞKIN TÜMER

Hacettepe Campus:

Faculty of Dentistry: Prof. Dr CELAL TÜMER
Faculty of Health Sciences: Prof. Dr HALIT TANJU BESLER
Faculty of Medicine: Prof. Dr SARP SARAÇ
Faculty of Pharmacy: Prof. Dr A. AHMET BAŞARAN

Sihhiye Campus:

Faculty of Pharmacy: Prof. Dr LÜTFIYE ÖMÜR DEMIREZER
Kastamonu Faculty of Medicine: Prof. Dr SÜLEYMAN SIRRI KES

DIRECTORS

Ankara State Conservatoire: Prof. EROL BELGIN
Hacettepe Vocational School: Prof. Dr NEJDET BAŞTÜRK
Kaman Vocational School: Doç. Dr M. ALİ HİNDİSTAN
Polatlı Vocational School: Prof. Dr AHMET KART
Polatlı Vocational School of Health Services: Prof. Dr FATIH ERBAHÇECI
Polatlı Vocational School of Technical Sciences: Prof. Dr AHMET KART
School of Foreign Languages: Prof. Dr NALAN BÜYÜKKANTARCIOĞLU AKKOYUNLU
School of Health Administration: Prof. Dr HİKMET PEKCAN
School of Health Technology: Prof. Dr TÜRKAN MERDOL
School of Home Economics: Prof. Dr MÜBERRA BABAOĞLU
School of Nursing: Prof. Dr GÜLÜMSER KUBILAY
School of Physical Therapy and Rehabilitation: Prof. Dr HÜLYA KAYIHAN
School of Social Work: Prof. Dr AYŞE BERİL TUFAN
School of Sport Sciences and Technology: Prof. Dr CANER AÇIKADA
Vocational School (Ankara): Prof. Dr İLHAN TOMANBAY
Vocational School of Health Services: Prof. Dr GÜLŞEN HASÇELIK
Vocational School of Social Sciences: Prof. Dr CELAL REHA ALPAR
Vocational School of Sports Sciences and Technology: Dr CANER AÇIKADA
Vocational School of Woodwork Technology: Prof. Dr MEHMET DOĞAN

PROFESSORS

Faculty of Dentistry:

ALPARSLAN, M. G., Oral and Dental Therapeutics
ALTAY, A., Paediatric Dentistry
ANİL (GAZI), N., Prosthesis
ASLAN, Y., Prosthesis
AVCI, M., Prosthesis
BAŞEREN, N. M., Oral and Dental Therapeutics
BERKER, A. E., Periodontics
BOLAY (SARİOĞLU), Ş., Oral and Dental Therapeutics
CANAY (OLGUN), R. Ş., Prosthesis
ÇAĞLAYAN, F., Periodontics
ÇAĞLAYAN, G., Periodontics
ÇALT, T., Endodontics
ÇIĞER, S., Orthodontics
DAYANGAÇ, B., Oral and Dental Therapeutics
DAYANGAÇ, B., Prosthesis
DEMIREL (USLU), F., Prosthesis
DURMAZ, V., Oral and Dental Therapeutics
ERATALAY, Y. K., Periodontics
GÖKALP, S., Oral and Dental Therapeutics
GÖRDUYSUS, M., Endodontics
GÖRÜCÜ, J., Oral and Dental Therapeutics
GÜRGAN, S., Oral and Dental Therapeutics
HERSEK, N. E., Prosthesis
KANSU, A. Ö., Oral and Dental Therapeutics
KANSU, H., Oral and Dental Therapeutics
KEYF (HAMARAT), F., Prosthesis
KOCADERELI, İ., Orthodontics
KÖPRÜLÜ, H., Oral and Dental Therapeutics
KÖSEOĞLU, O. T., Dental Surgery
KURANER, T., Oral and Dental Therapeutics
NAZLIEL, H., Periodontics
NOHUTÇU, R. M., Periodontics
ÖKTEMER, M., Prosthesis

ÖLMEZ, M. S., Paediatric Dentistry
ÖNEN, A., Oral and Dental Therapeutics
ÖZÇELİK, B., Oral and Dental Therapeutics
ÖZGÜNALTAY, H. G., Oral and Dental Therapeutics
ŞAHİN, E., Prosthesis
ŞAHİN (SÖKMEN), S., Prosthesis
ŞAHMALİ, S., Prosthesis
ŞAYGİLİ, G., Prosthesis
ŞENGÜN, F. D., Periodontics
SERPER, A., Endodontics
TAŞAR, F., Dental Surgery
TAŞMAN, F., Endodontics
TUNCER, M., Periodontics
URAN, N., Oral Surgery
YAMALIK, N., Periodontology
YENİGÜL, M., Prosthesis

Faculty of Economics and Administrative Sciences:

AKALIN, G., Public Finance
AKTAN, O. H., Economics
BİLİCİ, N., Public Finance
ÇAĞLAR, A., Public Administration
CAN, H., Economics
ERDOĞAN, M., Public Administration
İPÇİ, M. Ö., Accounting and Finance
KARAN, M., Business Administration
KAZDAĞLI, H., Economics
MORGİL, O., Economics
ŞAHİNÖZ, A., Economics
ŞIŞIK, Ü., Economics
TANYERİ, İ, Economics
TELATAR, M. E., Economics
TİMUR, H., Economics
TOKAT, M., Economics
UYGUN, H., Economics

Faculty of Education:

ABAK, M., Physics
ACAR, N., Counselling and Guidance
AKKOYUNLU, B., Computer Education and Instructional Technologies
AKMAN, B., Pre-School Teaching
AŞKAR, P., Computer Education and Instructional Technologies
BAŞAR, H., Education
BAŞKAN, A. G., Educational Administration, Supervision, Planning and Economics
BÜLBÜL, A., Mathematics Teaching
DEMİREL, Ö., Education
DEMİREZEN, M., Language Studies
ERATALAY, N., French
ERÇETIN, Ş. Ş., Educational Administration, Supervision, Planning and Economics
EREN, A., Physics
ERSEVER, O. G., Counselling and Guidance
ERTEM, C., Language and Literature
GENÇ, A., German Language Teaching
HAMAN, S., Physics Teaching
KAVAK, Y., Education
KESKIL, G., English Language Teaching
KIRAN, A., Language Studies
KİZİROĞLU, İ, Biology
MORGİL, I., Analytical Chemistry
ÖNALP, B., Biology
ÖNSOY, R., Education
ÖZ, H., English Language Teaching
PATİR, S., Chemistry
SAĞLAM, N., Biology
SALİHOĞLU, H., Language Studies
SENEMOĞLU, N., Education
SİPAHILER, F., Biology
SÖNMEZ, V., Education
SORAN, H., Biology
TUĞRUL, B., Pre-School Teaching

Faculty of Engineering:

ACAR, J., Food
AKSU, Z., Process and Reactor Design
ALPER, E., Chemistry
APAYDIN, F., Physics
ARIKAN, A., Hydrogeology
AYDAR, E., Mineralogy, Petrography
AYTAÇ, S., Food Sciences
BAYARİ, S. C., Hydrogeology
BAYHAN, H., Geology
BEŞKARDEŞ, O., Chemistry
BİRGÜL, Ö., Nuclear Physics
BOZDEMİR, M. T., Unit Operations and Thermodynamics
ÇADIRCI, I., Electrical Engineering
ÇAĞLAR, A., Chemistry
ÇANKURTARAN, M., Physics
ÇELEBİ, S. S., Chemistry
ÇELİK, H., Physics
ÇELİK, S., Food Sciences
ÇELİK, T., Physics
ÇİNER, T. A., Geology
ÇOLAK, Ü., Nuclear Physics
DEMIRCIOĞLU, H., Electrical Engineering
DEMİREL, H., Mining Engineering
DURUBOY, H. Z., Physics
DURUSOY (DÖRTER), B. T., Mining Engineering
ERAY, A., Solid State Physics
ERCAN, B., Electrical Engineering
ERKAN, Y., Geology
FIRAT, T., Physics
GEÇİM, S., Electrical Engineering
GİRGİN, İ, Mining Engineering
GÜMÜŞDERELİOĞLU, M., Chemistry
GÜNDÜC, Y., Electrical Engineering
HÖKELEK, T., Physics
İDE, S., General Physics
İNAN, İ. D., Physics
KAPTAN, Y., Physics
KARAKAŞ, M. Ü., Computer Science Engineering
KARAYIĞIT, A., Mineral Deposits, Geochemistry
KASAPOĞLU, K. E., Geology
KAYHAN, S., Telecommunications
KENDİ, E., General Physics
KÖKSAL, A., Electromagnetic Waves and Microwaves
KÖKSEL, H., Food
KORKMAZ, M., Physics
KULAKSIZ, S., Mining and Mineral Processing
KUTSAL, T., Chemistry
MUTLU, M., Food
ÖKTÜ, Ö., General Physics
ÖNDER, M., Physics
ÖNER, M., Mining Engineering
ÖNER, M., Mining and Mineral Processing
ORAL, B., Physics
ÖZBAŞ, Y., Food Technology
ÖZBAY (DANACİ), S., General Physics
ÖZBEY, T., Physics
ÖZDURAL, A. R., Chemistry
ÖZTECİN, E., Physics
PİŞKİN, E., Chemistry
SAATÇI, A., Computer Science Engineering
ŞAFAK, M., Electrical Engineering
SAĞ, Y., Process and Reactor Design
SALDAMLI, İ., Food
SARAÇ, C., Mineral Deposits, Geochemistry
SAYDAM, A., Environmental Engineering
ŞENYUR, M. G., Mining and Mineral Processing
ŞIMŞEK, S., Hydrogeology
SUNGAR, R., General Physics
SÜNNETÇIOĞLU, M., Physics
TABAK, F., Physics
TANYOLAÇ, A., Chemistry
TEMEL, A., Mineral Deposits, Geochemistry
TEMİZ, A., Food
TERCAN, A., Mining and Mineral Processing
TOLUNAY, H., Solid State Physics
TOPAÇLI, C., Physics
TOPAÇLİ(SUNGUR), A., Atomic and Molecular Physics
TÖRECİ, E., Computer Science Engineering
TUNCEL, S. A., Process and Reactor Design
TUNOĞLU, C., General Geology
ÜLKÜ, D., Physics
ULUSAY, R., Applied Geology
ÜNVER, B., Mining and Mineral Processing
US, F., Food
VURAL, H., Food Sciences
YARIMAĞAN, Ü., Computer Science Engineering
YAZGAN, E., Electrical Engineering

Faculty of Fine Arts:

AKYÜZ, U., Graphic Art
AYDINÖZ, A. A., Art
DAKAK, H., Painting
GENCAYDIN, Z., Fine Arts
KAYA, İ., Graphic Art
MISMAN, H. A., Painting
PEKMEZCI, H., Painting
PEKTAŞ, H., Graphic Art
SAVAŞ, R., Sculpture

Faculty of Letters:

AKAN, A. V., Sociology
AKKOYUNLU, Z., Folklore Studies
AKSOY, B. M., English Translation and Interpretation
AKSOY, E., Western Language and Literature
ALTAY (AKANSEL), A., English Translation and Interpretation
ARİKAN (GÜRER), G., Sociology
AYDIN, O., Experimental Psychology
BAĞCİ, S., History of Art
BAYDUR, K. G., Librarianship
BAYKAN, F., Philosophy
BOZBEYOĞLU, S., French Language and Literature
BOZER, A. D., English Language and Literature
ÇAKIN, İ., Librarianship
ÇELIK, A., Librarianship
ÇELIK-ŞAVK, Ü., Turkish Language and Literature
DİKEÇLİĞİL, F. B., Sociometry
DOĞAN, Ş., German Language and Literature
ERCİLASUN, B., Literature
ERGAN, N., Sociology
ERKENAL, A., History of Art
ERLAT, J., French Studies
EROL, B., English Language and Literature
HORATA, O., Turkish Language and Literature
İÇLİ, T., Sociology
İNAL, T., French Studies
İZGI, Ö., General Turkish History
KARAKAŞ, S., Experimental Psychology
KIRAN, Z., French Studies
KÖNİG, G., Linguistics
KULA, O., German Language and Literature
KURBANOĞLU, S. S., Librarianship
OCAK, A. Y., History
OCAK, F. T., History
OPPERMANN (TUNÇ), S., English Language and Literature
ÖTÜKEN, S. Y., Archaeology
ÖZ, M., History
ÖZBEK, M., Social Anthropology
ÖZGEN, E., Archaeology
ÖZMEN, K., French Studies
ÖZÖNDER, M. C., Sociology
ÖZYER, N., German Language and Literature
SAĞLAM, M. Y., German Language and Literature
TEPE, H., Philosophy
TONTA, Y., Librarianship
UMUNÇ, H., English Language and Literature
UNAN, F., History
YILDIRIM, D., Literature
YILDIZ, S., German Studies
YİMAZ, E., Turkish Language and Literature

Faculty of Medicine:

ABBASOĞLU, O., Internal Medicine
AÇAN, L., Biochemistry
ACAROĞLU, R.E., Orthopaedics
ADALAR, N., Internal Medicine
ADALIOĞLU, G., Paediatrics

AKALAN, N., Neurosurgery
AKALIN, N., Neurosurgery
AKAN, H. T., Dermatology
AKATA, D., Radiology
AKHAN, H. M. O., Radiology
AKIN, A., Community Health
AKİNCİ, F.A., Physical Therapy and Rehabilitation
AKOVA, M., Internal Medicine
AKŞİT, D., Anatomy
AKSÖYEK, S., Cardiology
AKSU, A. T., Obstetrics and Gynaecology
AKYOL, F. H., Oncology
AKYOL, Ö., Biochemistry
AKYOL, U. M., Otorhinolaryngology
AKYÜZ (CELEPOĞLU), C., Oncology
ALAÇAM, R., Microbiology
ALEHAN, D., Paediatrics
ALPAR, C., Biostatistics
ALPARSLAN, M., Orthopaedics
ANLAR, B. F., Paediatrics
ARAN, Ö., Surgery
ARAS (SULHUN), T., Nuclear Medicine
ARIKAN, S., Microbiology
ARIOĞLU, S., Internal Medicine
ARİYÜREK, O. M., Radiology
ARSLAN, S., Internal Medicine
AŞAN, E., Morphology
ATAHAN, İ. L., Oncology
ATAKAN, Z. N., Dermatology
AYAS, K., Ear, Nose and Throat Surgery
AYDIN, E., Medical Ethics and History
AYDİNGÖZ, Ü., Radiology
AYHAN, A., Obstetrics and Gynaecology
AYPAR, Ü., Anaesthesiology
AYSUN, S., Paediatrics
AYTAR, Ş., Medical Biology
BAKKALOĞLU, A., Paediatrics
BAKKALOĞLU, A. M., Urology
BALCI, S., Paediatrics
BALKANCI, F., Radiology
BARIŞTA, İ., Internal Medicine
BAŞAR, R., Anatomy
BAŞGÖZE, O., Physical Therapy and Rehabilitation
BATMAN, F., Internal Medicine
BAYRAKTAR, M., Internal Medicine
BAYRAKTAR, Y., Internal Medicine
BEKSAÇ, S., Obstetrics and Gynaecology
BELGİN, E., Ear, Nose and Throat Surgery
BENLİ, K., Neurosurgery
BEŞBAŞ, N., Paediatrics
BESİM, A., Radiology
BİLGİÇ, S., Ophthalmology
BİLİR, N., Community Health
BÖKE, E., Cardiovascular and Thoracic Surgery
BOZKURT, A., Pharmacology
BÜLBÜL, F. F., Plastic and Reconstructive Surgery
BÜYÜKPAMUKÇU, M., Oncology
BÜYÜKPAMUKÇU, N., Paediatric Surgery
ÇAĞLAR, M., Nuclear Medicine
ÇAĞLAR, M., Paediatrics
ÇAKAR, A. N., Morphology
ÇAKMAK, F., Urology
ÇALGÜNERİ, M., Internal Medicine
CANER, B. E., Nuclear Medicine
ÇEKIRGE, H., Radiology
ÇEKIRGE, I. S., Radiology
ÇELEBİOĞLU, B., Anaesthesiology
ÇELIK, H. H., Anatomy
ÇELİKER, A., Paediatrics
ÇELİKER, A. R., Physical Therapy and Rehabilitation
ÇELİKER, V., Anaesthesiology and Reanimation
ÇETIN, M., Paediatrics
CEYHAN, M., Paediatrics
ÇIFTÇI, A., Paediatrics
CIĞER, A., Institute of Neurological Sciences
CILA, A., Radiodiagnostics
ÇOKUĞRAŞ, N. A., Biochemistry
ÇÖPLÜ, L., Thoracic Diseases
COSKUN, T., Paediatrics

ÇUHADAROĞLU, F., Psychiatry
CUMHUR, M., Morphology
DAĞDEVİREN, A., Histology and Embryology
DALKARA, N. E. T., Institute of Neurological Sciences
DEMİRCİN, M., Cardiovascular and Thoracic Surgery
DEMIRKAZIK, F., Radiology
DEMIRPENÇE (TANSEL), E., Biochemistry
DİNÇER, F., Physical Therapy and Rehabilitation
DİNÇER, P. R., Medical Biology
DOĞAN, P., Biochemistry
DOĞAN, R., Cardiovascular and Thoracic Surgery
DORAL, M. N., Orthopaedics
DUMAN, O., Physiology
DÜNDAR, S., Internal Medicine
DURUKAN, T., Obstetrics and Gynaecology
ELDEM, M. B., Ophthalmology
ELİBOL, B., Neurology
EMRE (DÖKMECI), S., Internal Medicine
ERBAŞ, A. T., Internal Medicine
ERBAŞ, B. H., Nuclear Medicine
ERDEM, Y., Internal Medicine
ERDENER, U., Ophthalmology
ERGEN, A., Urology
ERGÜVEN (DİKEL), S., Microbiology
ERK, Y., Plastic Surgery
ERKAN, İ., Urology
ERSOY, F. N., Paediatrics
ERSOY, Ü., Cardiovascular and Thoracic Surgery
ERTENLİ, A. İ., Internal Medicine
GEDİK, O., Internal Medicine
GEDIKOĞLU, G., Pathology
GÖKLER, B., Psychiatry
GÖKÖZ, A., Pathology
GÜÇ, D., Oncology
GÜÇ, M. O., Pharmacology
GÜLER, Ç., Community Health
GÜLER, E. N., Internal Medicine
GÜLLÜ, İ., Oncology
GÜMRÜK, F., Paediatrics
GÜNALP, G. S., Obstetrics and Gynaecology
GÜNGEN, Y. Y., Pathology
GÜR (AKMAN), D., Paediatrics
GÜRAKAN, H., Paediatrics
GÜRGAN, T., Obstetrics and Gynaecology
GÜRGERY, A., Paediatrics
GÜRKANYNAK, H. M., Oncology
GÜRLEK, Ö. A., Internal Medicine
GÜRSEL, B., Ear, Nose and Throat Surgery
HALILOĞLU, M., Radiology
HAMALOĞLU, E., General Surgery
HASÇELİK, A. G., Microbiology
HASÇELİK, H. Z., Physical Therapy and Rehabilitation
HAZNEDAROĞLU, C., Internal Medicine
HOŞAL, A., Otorhinology
İLGİ, N. S., Morphology
İLHAN, M., Pharmacology
İRKEÇ, M., Ophthalmology
KABAKÇİ, M.G., Cardiology
KALAYCİ, C., Paediatrics
KALE, G., Paediatrics
KALYONCU, A. F., Thoracic Diseases
KANBAK (SOYLU), M., Anaesthesiology and Reanimation
KANDEMIR, N., Paediatrics
KANSU, E., Oncology
KANSU, T., Institute of Neurological Sciences
KARAAĞAOĞLU, A. E., Medical Biology
KARABUDAK, R., Neurology
KARADUMAN, A., Dermatology
KARS, S. A., Internal Medicine
KART, A., Medical Biology
KAYA, S., Ear, Nose and Throat Surgery
KAYNAROLĞU, Z. V., Surgery
KEÇİK, A., Plastic Surgery
KENDİ, S., Urology
KES, S., Internal Medicine
KILINÇ, K., Biochemistry
KİPER, E. N., Childhood Health and Diseases

KIRATLI, H., Ophthalmology
KÖLEMEN, F., Dermatology
KÜÇÜKALİ, T., Pathology
KUŞ, M. S., Biochemistry
KUTLUK, M. T., Paediatrics
KUTSAL, F. Y., Physical Therapy and Rehabilitation
MAVİLİ, M. E., Plastic and Reconstructive Surgery
MOCAN, G., Pathology
MÜFTÜOĞLU, S., Histology and Embryology
MUŞDAL, Y., Orthopaedics and Traumatology
NAZLI, N., Internal Medicine, Cardiology
NURLU (ÖZGÜR), G., Neurology
OCAL, M. T., Anaesthesiology
ÖĞRETMENOĞLU, O., Otorhinology
ÖĞÜŞ, İ. H., Biochemistry
ÖKTEM (BONCUK), F., Psychiatry
ONAT, D., Surgery
ÖNDEROĞLU, L. S., Obstetrics and Gynaecology
ÖNDEROĞLU, S., Anatomy
ÖNER, Z. N., Surgery
ÖNERCİ, T. M., Ear, Nose and Throat Surgery
ONUR, E. R., Pharmacology
ORAN, M. B., Radiology
ORER, H., Pharmacology
ORHAN, M., Ophthalmology
OTO, M. A., Internal Medicine
ÖVÜNÇ, K., Cardiology
ÖZCAN, E. O., Neurosurgery
ÖZCEBE, L. H., Community Health
ÖZCEBE, O. İ., Internal Medicine
ÖZÇELIK, H., Paediatrics
ÖZDEMİR, A., Surgery
ÖZDEN, A. K., Medical Biology
ÖZEN, H., Paediatrics
ÖZEN, H. A., Urology
ÖZEN, S., Paediatrics
ÖZENÇ, A. M., Surgery
ÖZER, E. S., Paediatrics
ÖZER, N., Biochemistry
ÖZGEN, T., Institute of Neurological Sciences
ÖZGEN (ULUPİNAR), S., Anaesthesiology
ÖZGÜÇ, M., Medical Biology
ÖZGÜNEŞ, N., Biochemistry
ÖZİŞIK, Y. Y., Oncology
ÖZKAN, S., Ear, Nose and Throat Surgery
ÖZKARA (ŞAHİN), A., Biochemistry
ÖZKUTLU, H., Internal Medicine
ÖZKUTLU, S., Paediatrics
ÖZKUYUMCU, C., Microbiology
ÖZMEN, F., Internal Medicine
ÖZMEN, M. N., Radiology
ÖZMERT, E., Paediatrics
ÖZTEK, A. Z., Community Medicine
ÖZTÜRK, N., Biophysics
ÖZYAR, E., Radiation Oncology
ÖZYAZICI, A., Morphology
PALAOĞLU, Ö. S., Institute of Neurological Sciences
PEKCAN, H., Community Health
PURALİ, N., Biophysics
ŞAFAK, T., Plastic and Reconstructive Surgery
ŞAHIN, A., Urology
ŞAHİN, A. A., Internal Medicine
ŞAHİN, S., Dermatology
SANAÇ, A. Ş., Ophthalmology
SANAL, S. Ö., Paediatrics
SARGON, M. F., Anatomy
SAYEK, İ., Surgery
SAYGI (SÜTÇÜ), S., Neurology
SEÇMEER, G., Paediatrics
ŞEFTALİOĞLU, A., Histology
ŞEKEREL, B., Paediatrics
SELÇUK, Z., Chest Diseases
SELEKLER, K., Neurology
ŞENER, B., Microbiology
ŞENER, E. C., Ophthalmology
SENNAROĞLU, L., Ear Nose and Throat Surgery
ŞENOCAK, M. E., Paediatric Surgery

ŞIMŞEK, H., Internal Medicine
SIVRİ, B., Internal Medicine
SÖYLEMEZOĞLU, F., Pathology
SÖZEN, T., Internal Medicine
SÖZER, A. B., Ear, Nose and Throat Surgery
SUNGUR, A. A., Oncology
SURAT, A., Orthopaedics
TAN, M. E., Neurology
TANYEL, F. C., Paediatric Surgery
TASAR, C., Oncology
TATAR, G., Internal Medicine
TEKGÜL, S., Urology
TEKİNALP, G., Paediatrics
TEKUZMAN, G., Oncology
TEZCAN, F., Biochemistry
TEZCAN, F. İ., Paediatrics
TEZCAN, S., Community Medicine
TOKATLI, A., Paediatrics
TOKGÖZOĞLU, M., Orthopaedics and Traumatology
TOKGÖZOĞLU, S. L., Internal Medicine
TOPALOĞLU, H., Paediatrics
TOPALOĞLU, R., Paediatrics
TOPÇU, M., Institute of Neurological Sciences
TUNCEL, H. M., Anatomy
TUNÇBİLEK, E., Paediatrics
TUNCER, A., Paediatrics
TUNCER, A. M., Paediatrics
TUNCER, M., Pharmacology
TUNCER, Z. S., Obstetrics and Gynaecology
TUNÇKANAT, F. F., Microbiology
TURAN, E., Ear, Nose and Throat Surgery
TURGAN, Ç., Internal Medicine
UĞUR, Ö., Nuclear Medicine
ULUĞ, B., Psychiatry
ULUŞAHIN, N. A., Psychiatry
ÜNAL, M. F., Child Psychiatry
ÜNAL, S., Internal Medicine
UNGAN, P., Biophysics
ÜNSAL, M., Radiology
US (ERSÖZ), A. D., Microbiology
USMAN, A., Internal Medicine
USTAÇELEBİ, S., Microbiology
UZUN (ÖZMEN), Ö., Internal Medicine
VARLI, K., Neurology
YALÇIN, Ş., Internal Medicine
YALÇINRIDVANAĞAOĞLU, A., Physiology
YARALİ, H., Obstetrics and Gynaecology
YASAVUL, Ü., Internal Medicine
YAZICI, M., Orthopaedics
YAZICI, M. K., Psychiatry
YETKİN, S., Paediatrics
YİĞİT, Ş., Paediatrics
YILMAZ, E., Medical Biology
YORDAM, N., Paediatrics
YÖRÜKAN, S., Physiology
YÜCE, A., Childhood Health and Diseases
YÜCE, K., Obstetrics and Gynaecology
YURDAKÖK, K., Paediatrics
YURDAKÖK, M., Paediatrics
YURTER (ERDEM), H., Medical Biology
ZORLU, A. F., Radiation Oncology

Faculty of Pharmacy:

ALTİNÖZ SARİSOY, S., Analytical Chemistry
BALKAN (TAYHAN), A., Pharmaceutical Chemistry
BAŞARAN, A. A., Pharmacognosy
BAŞARAN (GÜNDÜZ), N., Pharmaceutical Toxicology
BAŞÇİ, N., Analytical Chemistry
BİLGİN, A., Pharmaceutical Chemistry
ÇALIŞ, İ., Pharmacognosy
ÇALİŞ, Ü., Pharmaceutical Chemistry
ÇALİŞ, Y. S., Pharmaceutical Technology
ÇAPAN, Y., Pharmaceutical Technology
DALKARA, S., Pharmaceutical Chemistry
DEMİRDAMAR, S. R., Pharmacy
DEMIREZEN, L.Ö., Pharmacognosy
DEMİREZER, L. Ö., Pharmacognosy
ELDEM (ER), T., Pharmaceutical Biotechnology
ERDEMLİ(ŞAHİN), İ., Pharmaceutical Toxicology
ERDOĞAN, H., Pharmaceutical Chemistry
ERSÖZ, T., Pharmacognosy
ERTAN, M., Pharmaceutical Chemistry
EZER, N., Pharmaceutical Botanics
HEKİMOĞLU (KONUR), S., Pharmaceutical Chemistry
HINCAL, A., Galenic Pharmacy
HINCAL, F., Pharmaceutical Toxicology
KIR (KOT), S., Analytical Chemistry
ÖNER, A. F., Pharmaceutical Chemistry
ÖNER, L., Pharmaceutical Chemistry
ÖZALTIN (LEBLEBİC), N., Analytical Chemistry
ÖZER, A. Y., Pharmaceutical Chemistry
ÖZER, İ., Biochemistry
ÖZGÜNES, H., Pharmaceutical Toxicology
PALASKA, E., Pharmaceutical Chemistry
PEKINER, C., Pharmacology
ŞAFAK, C., Pharmaceutical Toxicology
ŞAHIN, G., Pharmaceutical Toxicology
SAKAR, M. K., Pharmaceutical Chemistry
SARAÇ, S., Pharmaceutical Chemistry
SARAÇOĞLU, İ., Pharmacognosy
ŞENEL, S., Pharmaceutical Technology
SÜMER (İLKİZ), N. A., Biochemistry
ŞUMLU, M., Pharmaceutical Technology
TEMİZER, A., Analytical Chemistry
UMA, S., Pharmaceutical Toxicology
ÜNLÜ (KARABABA), N., Pharmaceutical Technology
YEŞİADA, A., Pharmacy

Faculty of Science:

AKAY, M. T., Zoology
AKGÜN, A., Molecular Biology
AKSÖZ, E., Molecular Biology
AKSÖZ, N., General Biology
BALCIOĞLU, N., Organic Chemistry
BARLAS (EMIR), N., Zoology
BEKTAŞ, F. S., Analytical Chemistry
BOŞGELMEZ, A., Zoology
BOZCUK, A. N., Biology
BOZCUK, S., Biology
BROWN, L. M., Mathematics
ÇAĞATAY, N., Zoology
ÇAĞLAR, P., Analytical Chemistry
CANSUNAR, E., General Biology
CIHANGIR, N., Biotechnology
ÇİNGİ, H., Statistics
ÇIRAKOĞLU, Ç., Molecular Biology
DEMIREZEN, Ş., General Biology
DEMİRSOY, A., Zoology
DENİZLİ, A., Biochemistry
DİRİL, N., Molecular Biology
DOĞAN, M., Analytical Chemistry
DURUSOY, M., Molecular Biology
DÜZ, S. F., Chemistry
EKMEKÇİ, F. G., Hydrobiology
ERIK, S., Botany
ERK, A. F., Hydrobiology
EŞ, A. H., Mathematics
ESENSOY, Ö., Statistics
GÖKOĞLU, E., Analytical Chemistry
GÜNAY, S., Statistics
GÜNDÜZ, E., Hydrobiology
GÜNER, A., Polymer and Theoretical Chemistry
GÜVEN, O., Physical Chemistry
HARMANCI, A., Mathematics
İMAMOĞLU, Y., Analytical Chemistry
İNAL, C., Statistics
KALAYCIOĞLU, A., Molecular Biology
KARAN (ZÜMREOĞLU), B., Inorganic Chemistry
KAZANCI, N., Hydrobiology
KESKIN (ELDEM), N., Applied Biology
KILBARER, A. G., Physical Chemistry
KIŞ, M., Physical Chemistry
KOLANKAYA, D., Zoology
KOLANKAYA, N., General Biology
OKAY, G., Organic Chemistry
ORAL (HOCAOĞLU), G., Statistics
ÖNER, Ç., Molecular Biology
ÖNER (ÖZDÖNMEZ), R., Biotechnology
ÖZÇAĞ, E., Mathematics
PEKMEZ, K., Analytical Chemistry
PEKMEZ (ÖZÇIÇEK), N., Analytical Chemistry
RZAYEV, Z. M. O., Chemistry
SALİH, B., Physical Chemistry
ŞENEL (UYANİK), S., Physical Chemistry
SOLTANOV, K. N., Mathematics
SORKUN, K., Applied Biology
SÖZER, T., Statistics
TATLIDİL, H., Statistics
TERCAN, A., Algebra and Theory of Numbers
TERZİOĞLU, S., Botany
TIRAŞ, Y., Algebra and Theory of Numbers
TOKTAMIŞ, Ö., Statistics
TÜMER, M. A., General Biology
TÜNOĞLU, N., Organic Chemistry
ÜNALEROĞLU, C., Organic Chemistry
ÜNLÜ, H., General Biology
YALVAÇ, T., Mathematics, Geometry and Topology
YERLİ, S. V., Hydrobiology
YILDIRIMLI, Ş., Botany
YILDIZ, A., Analytical Chemistry

HALİÇ ÜNİVERSİTESİ
(Haliç University)

Büyükdere Cad. 101, 34394 Mecidiyeköy, Istanbul
Telephone: (212) 275-20-20
Fax: (212) 274-81-22
E-mail: info@halic.edu.tr
Internet: www.halic.edu.tr

Founded 1998

Pres.: Prof. Dr GÜNDÜZ GEDIKOĞLU

Library of 11,000 vols
Number of teachers: 200
Number of students: 1,200

Faculties of arts and science, business administration, engineering and medicine.

HARRAN ÜNİVERSİTESİ

Sanlıurfa
Telephone: (414) 312-84-56
Fax: (414) 312-81-44
E-mail: rektor@harran.edu.tr
Internet: www.harran.edu.tr

Founded 1992
State control

President: Prof. Dr UGUR BUYUKBURC
Vice-Presidents: Prof. Dr URAL DINÇ, Prof. Dr I. HALIL MUTLU, Prof. Dr SELCUK YUCESAN

Number of teachers: 794
Number of students: 5,900

DEANS

Faculty of Agriculture: Prof. Dr MEHMET AKTAS
Faculty of Arts and Sciences: Prof. Dr GÖKSENIN ESELLER
Faculty of Economics: Prof. Dr MUSTAFA PIRILI
Faculty of Engineering: Prof. Dr BILGE ERDILLER
Faculty of Medicine: Prof. Dr SELCUK YUCESAN
Faculty of Theology: Prof. Dr IBRAHIM DUZEN
Faculty of Veterinary Sciences: Prof. Dr NAFIZ YURDAYDIN

DIRECTORS

Institute of Health Sciences: Prof. Dr A. ZIYA KARAKILCIK
Institute of Natural Sciences: Prof. Dr IBRAHIM BOLAT
Institute of Social Sciences: Prof. Dr ZUHAL KARAHAN KARA

İNÖNÜ ÜNİVERSİTESİ

Elazığ Yolu 15. km, 44280 Malatya
Telephone: (422) 341-00-28

Fax: (422) 341-00-34
E-mail: rektor@inonu.edu.tr
Internet: www.inonu.edu.tr
Founded 1975
State control
Language of instruction: Turkish (English in Faculty of Medicine)
Academic year: October to July
Rector: Prof. Dr FATIH HILMIOĞLU
Vice-Rectors: Prof. Dr SADIK KELEŞ, Prof. Dr MUSTAFA KILIÇ, Prof. Dr HASAN KÜÇÜKBAY
Sec.-Gen.: REŞAT ÖZKAN
Librarian: NEZIHA ÜSTÜNER
Number of teachers: 2,112
Number of students: 19,137

DEANS
Adıyaman Faculty of Science and Literature: Prof. Dr ENGIN ŞENER
Faculty of Economics and Administrative Sciences: Prof. Dr MUSTAFA KILIÇ
Faculty of Education: Prof. Dr K. BÜLENT BİROL
Faculty of Engineering: Prof. Dr MUSA SARIKAYA
Faculty of Fine Arts: (vacant)
Faculty of Medicine: Prof. Dr ÖZCAN ERSOY
Faculty of Pharmacy: Prof. Dr ENGIN ŞARER
Faculty of Religious Studies: Prof. Dr ASLAN AKSOY
Faculty of Science and Literature: Prof. Dr ÖZFER YEŞILADA

DIRECTORS
Institute of Health Sciences: Asst Prof. Dr TAYFUN GÜLDÜR
Institute of Science: Asst Prof. Dr ALI ŞAHİN
Institute of Social Sciences: Prof. Dr KEMAL KARTAL

IŞIK ÜNİVERSİTESİ

Kumbaba Mevkii, 34980 Sile, Istanbul
Telephone: (216) 528-70-45
Fax: (216) 712-14-68
E-mail: isikun@isikun.edu.tr
Internet: www.isikun.edu.tr
Founded 1885; univ. status 1996
Private control
Academic year: October to June
Pres.: Prof. Dr ERSIN KALAYCIOĞLU

DEANS
Faculty of Arts and Sciences: Prof. ÖNDER PEKCAN
Faculty of Economics and Administrative Sciences: Prof. Dr MEHMET KAYTAZ
Faculty of Engineering: Prof. YORGO İSTEFANOPULOS
Institute of Science and Engineering: Prof. Dr HÜSNÜ A. ERBAY
Institute of Social Sciences: Prof. Dr TOKER DERELI

İSTANBUL ÜNİVERSİTESİ

Beyazıt, 34052 Istanbul
Telephone: (212) 440-00-00
Fax: (212) 440-00-10
E-mail: postmaster@istanbul.edu.tr
Internet: www.istanbul.edu.tr
Founded 1453, reorganized 1933
State control
Languages of instruction: Turkish, English
Academic year: October to February, March to July
Rector: Prof. Dr MESUT PARLAK
Vice-Rectors: Prof. Dr TAYLAN AKKAYAN, Prof. Dr OSMAN ÖZDEMIR, Prof. Dr NUR SERTER
Admin. Officer: NURETTİN ERDEM
Number of teachers and assistants: 5,000
Number of students: 49,000

DEANS
Faculty of Communication: Prof. Dr SUAT GEZGIN
Faculty of Dentistry: Prof. Dr BETÜL TUNCELLI
Faculty of Economics: Prof. Dr MITHAT ZEKI DINÇER
Faculty of Engineering: Prof. Dr CUMA BAYAT
Faculty of Fisheries and Aquatic Science: Prof. Dr MEHMET SALIH ÇELIKKALE
Faculty of Forestry: Prof. Dr BÜLENT SEÇKIN
Faculty of Law: Prof. Dr TANKUT CENTEL
Faculty of Letters: Prof. Dr TANER TARHAN
Faculty of Management: Prof. Dr HAYRİ ÜLGEN
Faculty of Medicine: Prof. Dr FARUK ERZENGIN
Faculty of Medicine (Cerrahpaşa): Prof. Dr FIKRET SIPAHIOĐLU
Faculty of Pharmacy: Prof. Dr AYSEL GÜRSOY
Faculty of Political Science: Prof. Dr FERYAL ORHON BASİK
Faculty of Science: Prof. Dr NURETTİN MERIÇ
Faculty of Theology: Prof. Dr EMRULLAH YÜKSEL
Faculty of Veterinary Science: Prof. Dr AHMET ALTINEL

İSTANBUL BİLGİ ÜNİVERSİTESİ (Istanbul Bilgi University)

İnönü Cad. 28, Kuştepe, 34387 Şişli, Istanbul
Telephone: (212) 311-50-00
Fax: (212) 216-24-00
E-mail: bilgi@bilgi.edu.tr
Internet: www.bilgi.edu.tr
Founded 1994, as Istanbul School of International Studies; present name and status 1996
Private control
Language of instruction: English
Academic year: October to July
Rector: Prof. Dr HALIL GÜVEN
Vice-Rector: Prof. Dr REMZI SANVER
Sec.-Gen.: ÇAĞRI BAĞCIOĞLU
Registrar: MICHEL PAUS
Library of 68,000 vols
Number of teachers: 574
Number of students: 8,640
Publications: *Bilgi Bellek*, *Foreign Policy* (6 a year)

DEANS
European Institute: Prof. Dr AYHAN KAYA
Faculty of Architecture: Prof. Dr İHSAN BILGIN
Faculty of Arts and Sciences: Prof. Dr DIANE SUNAR
Faculty of Communication: Prof. Dr HALIL NALÇAOĞLU
Faculty of Economics and Administrative Sciences: Dr EGE YAZGAN
Faculty of Engineering: Prof. Dr LALE DURUIZ
Faculty of Law: Prof. Dr TURGUT TARHANLI
Institute of Natural and Applied Sciences (Graduate School): Prof. Dr DOĞAN GÜNEŞ
Social Science Institute (Graduate School): Dr GÖKSEL AŞAN

İSTANBUL KÜLTÜR ÜNİVERSİTESİ

E5 Karayolu Üzeri, 22 Ataköy Metro Istasyonu Karsısı, Sirinevler, 34510 Istanbul
Telephone: (212) 639-30-24
Fax: (212) 551-11-89
E-mail: kultur@iku.edu.tr
Internet: www.iku.edu.tr
Founded 1997
Private control
Languages of instruction: Turkish, English
Academic year: October to May
Rector: Prof. Dr DURSUN KOÇER
Vice-Rectors: Prof. Dr GETIN BOLCAL, Prof. Dr TAMER KOÇEL
Registrar: Asst Prof. Dr METIN BOLCAL
Library of 6,800 books
Number of teachers: 114
Number of students: 2,109 (2,064 undergraduate, 45 postgraduate)
Publication: *Journal* (4 a year)

DEANS
Faculty of Arts: Prof. Dr NÜKET GÜZ
Faculty of Business Administration: Prof. Dr TAMER KOÇEL
Faculty of Engineering and Architecture: Prof. Dr OKAY EROSKAY
Faculty of Law: Prof. Dr TAYFUN AKGÜNER
Faculty of Science and Letters: Prof. Dr LATIF TOPAKTAŞ
Vocational School: Prof. Dr TANER BULAT

İSTANBUL TEKNİK ÜNİVERSİTESİ

Ayazağa Kampüsü, 34469 Istanbul
Telephone: (212) 285-30-30
Fax: (212) 285-29-10
E-mail: karadogan@itu.edu.tr
Internet: www.itu.edu.tr
Founded 1773
State control
Languages of instruction: Turkish, English
Academic year: October to July (two semesters)
Rector: Prof. FARUK KARUDOGAN
Vice-Rectors: Prof. A. FUAT ANDAY, Prof. HALUK KARADOĞAN, Prof. S. ERKIN NASUF
Provost: NEVZAT ÖZKÖK
Librarian: AYHAN KAYGUSUZ
Library: see Libraries and Archives
Number of teachers: 1,861
Number of students: 17,500
Publications: *ARI* (physical and engineering sciences, 4 a year), *Catalog* (every 2 years), *ITU'den Haberler* (4 a year)

DEANS
Faculty of Aeronautics and Astronautics: Prof. FEVZI ÜNAL
Faculty of Architecture: Prof. CENGIZ GIRITLIOĞLU
Faculty of Chemical and Metallurgical Engineering: Prof. HASAN CAN OKUTAN
Faculty of Civil Engineering: Prof. DERIN ORHON
Faculty of Electrical and Electronic Engineering: Prof. HAKAN KUNTMAN
Faculty of Management: Prof. AHMET FAHRI ÖZOK
Faculty of Mechanical Engineering: Prof. TANER DERBENTLI
Faculty of Mines: Prof. MAHIR VARDAR
Faculty of Naval Architecture and Ocean Engineering: Prof. ÖMER GÖREN
Faculty of Science and Letters: Prof. FIGEN KADIRGAN (Deputy)
Faculty of Textile Technologies and Design: Prof. BÜLENT ÖZIPEK
Maritime Faculty: Prof. SAMI AYDIN ŞALCI
Turkish Music Conservatory: Prof. CAN ETILI ÖKTEM

ATTACHED CONSERVATORY AND DEPARTMENTS

Department of Fine Arts: Dir AYLA ÖDEKAN.

Department of Languages and History: Dir ÖNER GÜNÇAVDI.

Department of Physical Education and Sports: Dir EMİN TACER.

Turkish Music Conservatory: Dir CAN ETİLİ ÖKTEM.

ATTACHED GRADUATE INSTITUTES

Institute of Energy: Dir HASAN SAYGIN.

Institute of Eurasia Earth Sciences: Dir OKAN TÜYSÜZ.

Institute of Informatics: Dir NÜZHET DALFES.

Institute of Science and Technology: Dir MEHMET KARACA.

Institute of Social Sciences: Dir NURAN ZEREN GÜLERSOY.

İSTANBUL TİCARET ÜNİVERSİTESİ
(Istanbul Commerce University)

Ragıp Gümüşpala Cad. 84, 34378 Eminönü, Istanbul
Telephone: (212) 511-41-50
Fax: (212) 553-94-22
E-mail: rektorluk@iticu.edu.tr
Internet: www.iticu.edu.tr

Pres.: Prof. Dr A. HAYRI DURMUŞ

Library of 17,400 vols

DEANS

Faculty of Arts: Prof. Dr NECDET TEKİN
Faculty of Commercial Science: Prof. Dr MÜNEVVER TURANLI
Faculty of Communications: Prof. Dr JALE SARMAŞIK
Faculty of Engineering: Prof. Dr NECDET TEKİN
Faculty of Science: Prof. Dr AYSEL ÇELİKEL

İZMIR EKONOMI ÜNIİVERSITESİI
(Izmir University of Economics)

Sakarya Caddesi 156, 35330 Balçova, İzmir
Telephone: (232) 279-25-25
Fax: (232) 279-26-26
E-mail: oia@ieu.edu.tr
Internet: www.ieu.edu.tr

Founded 2001
Private control
Language of instruction: English
Academic year: September to June

Rector: Prof. Dr ATTILA SEZGİN
Vice-Rector: Prof. Dr M. CEMALI DİNÇER
Vice-Rector: Prof. Dr OĞUZ ESEN
Vice-Rector: Prof. Dr TUNÇDAN BALTACIOĞLU
Provost: Prof. Dr M. CEMALI DİNÇER
Sec.-Gen: LEVENT GÖKÇEER
Dean of Students: MINE KAYICAN
Librarian: ALI TUTAL

Number of teachers: 440
Number of students: 6,206

DEANS

Faculty of Arts and Sciences: Prof. Dr İSMIHAN BAYRAMOĞLU
Faculty of Communication: Prof. Dr SEVDA ALANKUŞ
Faculty of Economics and Administrative Sciences: Prof. Dr ALEV KATRINLI
Faculty of Engineering and Computer Science: Prof. Dr TURHAN TUNALI
Faculty of Fine Arts and Design: Prof. Dr TEVFIK BALCIOĞLU

İZMİR YÜKSEK TEKNOLOJİ ENSTİTÜSÜ
(İzmir Institute of Technology)

Gülbahçe Köyü, 35430 Urla, İzmir
Telephone: (232) 750-60-01
Fax: (232) 750-60-15
E-mail: semraulku@iyte.edu.tr
Internet: www.iyte.edu.tr

Founded 1992
State control
Languages of instruction: Turkish, English
Academic year: October to June

Rector: Prof. Dr SEMRA ÜLKÜ
Vice-Rectors: Prof. Dr CEMAL ARKON, Prof. Dr RECAI ERDEM
Librarian: GULIZAR USLU

Library of 21,492 books, 96 periodicals, 6,443 online scientific periodicals
Number of teachers: 423
Number of students: 1,733 (1,203 undergraduate, 530 postgraduate)

DEANS

Faculty of Architecture: Prof. Dr CEMAL ARKON
Faculty of Engineering: Prof. Dr MUHSIN ÇIFTIÇOGLU
Faculty of Science: Prof. Dr SEMRA ÜLKÜ
Graduate School of Engineering and Sciences: Assoc. Prof. SEMAHAT ÖZDEMIR

KADİR HAS ÜNİVERSİTESİ

Cibali Merkez Kampüsü, Hisarattı Cad., 34230-01 Cibali-Fatih, Istanbul
Telephone: (212) 533-65-32
Fax: (212) 533-65-15
E-mail: info@khas.edu.tr
Internet: www.khas.edu.tr

Founded 1997
Private control (Foundation)
Languages of instruction: Turkish, English
Academic year: October to June

Pres.: Prof. Dr YÜCEL YILMAZ
Vice-Pres.: Prof. Dr NÜKHET TAN
Gen.–Sec.: Dr AHMET B. SÖĞÜTLÜOĞLU
Registrar: SELMA DÖNMEZ
Head Librarian: ERTUĞRUL ÇIMEN

Library of 13,857 vols
Number of teachers: 142
Number of students: 1,500

DEANS

Faculty of Arts and Sciences: Prof. Dr KEMAL YELEKÇI
Faculty of Communications: Prof. Dr DENIZ BAYRAKDAR SEVGEN
Faculty of Economics and Business Administration: Prof. Dr EROL ÜÇDAL
Faculty of Engineering: Prof. Dr TUNCAY SAYDAM
Faculty of Fine Arts: Prof. Dr FATMA OYA BOYLA (acting)
Faculty of Law: Prof. Dr SELÇUK ÖZTEK

KAFKAS ÜNİVERSİTESİ

Rektörlüğü, Pasacayiri Mh., 36040 Kars
Telephone: (474) 242-68-00
Fax: (474) 242-68-47
E-mail: bidab@kafkas.edu.tr
Internet: www.kafkas.edu.tr

Founded 1992
State control

Rector: Prof. Dr NECATI KAYA

Number of teachers: 481
Number of students: 10,000

Publications: *University Bulletin* (1 a year), *University Gazette* (4 a year).

KAHRAMANMARAŞ SÜTÇÜ IMAM ÜNİVERSİTESİ

KSÜ Rektörlüğü, Avşar Kampüsü, 46100 Kahramanmaraş
Telephone: (344) 219-10-00
Fax: (344) 219-10-12
E-mail: baytorun@ksu.edu.tr
Internet: www.ksu.edu.tr

Founded 1992
State control
Academic year: October to June

Rector: Prof. Dr A. NAFI BAYTORUN
Vice-Rectors: Prof. Dr ORHAN DOĞAN, Prof. Dr CAFER MART, Prof. Dr CEMAL TUNCER
Sec.-Gen.: RÜŞTÜ ERTUĞRUL
Librarian: ŞEREF AKBEN

Library of 25,000 books and periodicals
Number of teachers: 700
Number of students: 11,000

DEANS

Faculty of Agriculture: Prof. Dr ERFAN EFE
Faculty of Economics and Administrative Sciences: Prof. Dr AHMET HAMDI AYDIN
Faculty of Education: Prof. Dr ADNAN KÜÇÜKÖNDER
Faculty of Engineering and Architecture: Prof. Dr MEHMET NURI BODUR
Faculty of Forestry: Prof. Dr ORHAN ERDAŞ
Faculty of Medicine: Prof. Dr İLHAMI TANER KALE
Faculty of Sciences and Literature: Prof. Dr ALI DOĞAN
Faculty of Theology: Prof. Dr M. KAMAL ATIK

KARADENİZ TEKNİK ÜNİVERSİTESİ
(Karadeniz Technical University)

61080 Trabzon
Telephone: (462) 377-30-00
Fax: (462) 325-32-05
E-mail: head@ktu.edu.tr
Internet: www.ktu.edu.tr

Founded 1955
State control
Languages of instruction: Turkish, English
Academic year: October to August

Rector: Prof. Dr İBRAHIM ÖZEN
Vice-Rectors: Prof. Dr SELAHATTIN KÖSE, Prof. Dr NECATI TÜYSÜZ, Prof. Dr ORHAN AYDIN
Gen. Sec.: Assoc. Prof. CÜNEYT ŞEN
Librarian: Prof. Dr MEHMET ARSLAN

Library of 220,000 vols
Number of teachers: 1,568
Number of students: 38,000

Publications: *KTÜ Bu Hafta* (univ. news bulletin, 48 a year), *KTÜ Bülteni* (bulletin, 2 a year), *KTÜ Education Activities* (1 a year)

DEANS

Faculty of Agriculture (Ordu): Prof. Dr Y. NURETTIN İSMAILÇELEBIOĞLU
Faculty of Architecture: Prof. Dr AYŞE SAĞSÖZ
Faculty of Arts and Sciences (Rize): Prof. Dr NAZMI TURAN OKUMUŞOĞLU
Faculty of Communication: Prof. Dr MUSTAFA EMİR
Faculty of Dentistry: Prof. Dr MEHMET TOSUN
Faculty of Economics and Administrative Sciences: Prof. Dr KAMIL YAZICI
Faculty of Economics and Administrative Sciences (Giresun): Prof. Dr METIN BERBER
Faculty of Education (Artvin): Prof. Dr OKTAY TORUL
Faculty of Education (Fatih): Prof. Dr ALIPAŞA AYAS
Faculty of Education (Giresun): Prof. Dr MEHMET TÜFEKÇI
Faculty of Education (Rize): Prof. Dr MEHMET AKBAŞ
Faculty of Engineering: Prof. Dr MUSTAFA AYTEKIN
Faculty of Engineering (Gümüşhane): Prof. Dr FIKRI BULUT
Faculty of Fine Arts: Prof. Dr MUSTAFA KANDİL
Faculty of Forestry: Prof. Dr ZAFER CEMAL ÖZKAN
Faculty of Law: Prof. Dr OSMAN PEHLİVAN
Faculty of Marine Sciences: Prof. Dr İBRAHIM OKUMUŞ
Faculty of Marine Sciences (Sürmene): Prof. Dr ERTUĞ DÜZGÜNEŞ
Faculty of Medicine: Prof. Dr SÜLEYMAN BAYKAL
Faculty of Pharmaceutical Sciences: Prof. Dr RASIN ÖZYAVUZ
Faculty of Science and Literature: Prof. Dr KENAN İNAN
Faculty of Science and Literature (Giresun): Prof. Dr ZIYA YAPAR

Faculty of Technology: Prof. Dr KENAN GELİŞİ
Faculty of Theology: Prof. Dr S. KEMAL SANDIKÇI

PROFESSORS

Faculty of Agriculture (Ordu) (Ordu; tel. (452) 225-05-77; fax (452) 225-12-61; e-mail ziraat@ktu.edu.tr):

İSMAİLÇELEBİOĞLU, Y. N., Soil Science
ŞILBIR, Y., Field Crops

Faculty of Architecture (Kanuni Kampüsü, 61080 Trabzon; tel. (462) 377-26-70; fax (462) 325-55-88):

ÇEVIK, S., Architecture
GÜR, Ş., Architecture
KANDIL, M., Architecture
PEHLEVAN, A., Architecture
SAĞSÖZ, A., Architecture
USTA, G., Architecture
YAŞAR, Y., Architecture

Faculty of Arts and Sciences (Giresun) (Gazi Cad. Kışla Hamam Sok., Giresun; tel. (454) 216-25-20; fax (454) 216-45-18):

YANMAZ, E., Physics

Faculty of Arts and Sciences (Rize) (Engindere Mah., Köy Hizmetleri Yanı, 53100 Rize; tel. (464) 223-53-75; fax (464) 223-53-76):

OKUMUŞOĞLU, N. T., Physics

Faculty of Economics and Administrative Sciences (Kanuni Kampüsü, 61080 Trabzon; tel. (462) 325-32-12; fax (462) 325-72-81; e-mail iibf@ktu.edu.tr):

ACUNER, T., Business Administration
AKSAR, Y., International Relations
AKTAŞ, H., International Relations
AKYAZI, H., Economics
ARAFAT, M., International Relations
BOCUTOĞLU, E., Economics
ÇELIK, K., Economics
ÇİFTÇİ, O., Labour Economics and Industrial Relations
ÇIKRIKÇI, M., Management
DAĞLI, H., Business Administration
EMIR, M., Business Administration
KARAMUSTAFA, O., Business Administration
KESİM, A., Economics
KOÇER, G., International Relations
KÜÇÜKKALE, Y., Economics
ÖZYURT, H., Economics
SÜRMEN, Y., Business Administration
TANDOĞAN, A., Economics
TERZI, H., Economics
TÜREDİ, H., Management
YAMAK, N., Economics
YAZICI, K., Business Administration
YAZICI, K., Management
ZENGIN, H., Econometrics

Faculty of Economics and Administrative Sciences (Giresun) (Giresun):

BERBER, M., Economics

Faculty of Education (Artvin) (Artvin):

TORUL, O., Chemistry

Faculty of Education (Fatih) (Söğütlü, Trabzon; tel. (462) 248-23-05; fax (462) 248-73-44):

AKDENIZ, A., Secondary Science and Mathematics Education
AYAS, A., Secondary Science and Mathematics Education
BAĞIROV, N., Fine Arts Education
BAKI, A., Secondary Science and Mathematics Education
ÇAPA, M., Secondary Social Science Education
ÇEPNI, S., Primary Education
KARANIS, N., Turkish Education
ŞAHIN, B., Secondary Science and Mathematics Education
SESLI, E., Secondary Science and Mathematics Education

Faculty of Education (Giresun) (Giresun; tel. (454) 215-53-72; fax (464) 215-53-75; e-mail gef@ktu.edu.tr):

TÜFEKÇİ, M., Chemistry

Faculty of Education (Rize) (Rize; tel. (464) 532-67-92; fax (464) 532-86-12; e-mail ktu.cayeli@superonline.com):

TORUL, O., Chemistry

Faculty of Engineering (Gümüşhane) (Gümüşhane; tel. (456) 233-74-27; fax (456) 233-74-27):

BULUT, F., Geology
DURMUŞ, A., Civil Engineering
UZMAN, Ü., Civil Engineering

Faculty of Engineering (Kanuni Kampüsü, 61080 Trabzon; tel. (462) 325-31-72; fax (462) 325-74-05):

AKÇAY, M., Geological Engineering
AKPINAR, A., Electrical and Electronics Engineering
AKYOL, N., Geomatics Engineering
ALTAŞ, İ., Electrical and Electronics Engineering
ARICI, M., Mechanical Engineering
ARSLAN, F., Metallurgical and Materials Engineering
ARSLAN, M., Geological Engineering
AYDIN, O., Mechanical Engineering
AYTEKIN, M., Civil Engineering
AYVAZ, Y., Civil Engineering
BAYDAR, E., Mechanical Engineering
BAYRAKTAR, A., Civil Engineering
BEKTAŞ, O., Geological Engineering
BERKÜN, M., Civil Engineering
BILGIN, A., Mechanical Engineering
BIYIK, C., Geomatics Engineering
BIYIKLIOĞLU, A., Mechanical Engineering
BULUT, F., Geological Engineering
ÇAKIROĞLU, A.O., Civil Engineering
ÇAPKINOĞLU, Ş., Geological Engineering
ÇELIK, F., Civil Engineering
ÇUHADAROĞLU, B., Mechanical Engineering
DALOĞLU, A., Civil Engineering
DALOĞLU, A., Mechanical Engineering
DILAVER, A., Geomatics Engineering
DOĞAN, M., Mechanical Engineering
DUMANOĞLU, A., Civil Engineering
DURGUN, O., Mechanical Engineering
DURMUŞ, A., Civil Engineering
ERDOĞDU, Ş., Civil Engineering
ERDÖL, R., Civil Engineering
ERTAŞ, B., Civil Engineering
GELIŞLI, K., Geophysical Engineering
GENÇ, S., Geological Engineering
GÖKALP, E., Geomatics Engineering
GÜRÜNLÜ, C., Electrical and Electronics Engineering
HÜSEM, M., Civil Engineering
KARADENIZ, S., Mechanical Engineering
KARALI, C., Geomatics Engineering
KAYA, A., Geomatics Engineering
KESIMAL, A., Mining Engineering
KORKMAZ, S., Geological Engineering
NABIYEV, V., Computer Engineering
ÖNSOY, H., Civil Engineering
SADIKLAR, M., Geological Engineering
SAVAŞKAN, T., Mechanical Engineering
ŞEN, K., Geomatics Engineering
SOFUOĞLU, H., Mechanical Engineering
TÜYSÜZ, N., Geological Engineering
ÜNAL, A., Mechanical Engineering
UZMAN, Ü., Civil Engineering
UZUNER, B., Civil Engineering
YALÇINKAYA, M.
YAZICI, R., Computer Engineering
YILMAZ, Ç., Geological Engineering
YÜKSEK, Ö., Civil Engineering

Faculty of Fine Arts (İnönü Cad. 53, 61300 Akçaabat, Trabzon; tel. (462) 228-12-02; fax (462) 228-12-83):

ALESKEROV, A., Painting

Faculty of Forestry (Kanuni Kampüsü, 61080 Trabzon; tel. (462) 377-28-28; fax (462) 325-74-99):

ACAR, C., Landspace Architecture
ACAR, H., Foresty Engineering
ALTUN, L., Foresty Engineering
AY, N., Forest Industrial Engineering
BAŞKENT, E., Foresty Engineering
BILGILI, E., Foresty Engineering
ÇOLAKOĞLU, G., Forest Industrial Engineering
DEMIRCI, A., Foresty Engineering
DEMIREL, Ö., Landspace Architecture
DENIZ, İ., Forest Industrial Engineering
EROĞLU, M., Foresty Engineering
GERÇEK, Z., Foresty Engineering
GÜMÜŞ, C., Foresty Engineering
KALAYCIOĞLU, H., Forest Industrial Engineering
KIRCI, H., Forest Industrial Engineering
KÖSE, S., Foresty Engineering
NEMLI, G., Forest Industrial Engineering
ÖZBILEN, A., Landspace Architecture
ÖZKAN, Z., Foresty Engineering
TERZIOĞLU, S., Foresty Engineering
TÜRKER, M., Foresty Engineering
TURNA, İ., Foresty Engineering
ÜÇLER, A., Foresty Engineering
USTA, M., Forest Industrial Engineering
YAHYAOĞLU, Z., Foresty Engineering
YAVUZ, H., Foresty Engineering
YILDIZ, Ü., Forest Industrial Engineering

Faculty of Marine Sciences (Sürmene) (Çamburnu, Trabzon; tel. (462) 752-28-05; fax (462) 752-21-58):

BORAN, H., Fisheries Technology Engineering
DINÇER, H., Fisheries Technology Engineering
KÖSE, H., Naval Architecture & Marine Engineering
DÜZGÜNEŞ, E., Fisheries Technology Engineering
KARAÇAM, H., Fisheries Technology Engineering
SEYHAN, H., Fisheries Technology Engineering

Faculty of Medicine (Kanuni Kampüsü, 61080 Trabzon; tel. (462) 377-54-05; fax (462) 325-22-70):

AĞAOĞLU, N., General Surgery
AK, İ., Psychiatry
AKGÜN, A., Physiology
AKYOL, N., Ophtalmology
ALHAN, E., General Surgery
ALIOĞLU, Z., Neurology
ARSLAN, M., General Surgery
ARSLAN, M., Internal Medicine
ASLAN, Y., Paediatrics
AYAR, A., Physiology
AYDIN, F., Internal Medicine
AYNACI, O., Orthopedics and Traumatology
BAHADIR, S., Dermatology
BAKI, A., Paediatrics
BAKI, C., Orthopedics and Traumatology
BAYKAL, S., Neurosurgery
BOZKAYA, H., Obstetrics and Gynaecology
ÇAN, G., Public Health
ÇALIK, A., General Surgery
ÇIMŞIT, G., Dermatology
ÇINEL, A., General Surgery
CIVELEK, A., Cardiovascular Surgery
DEĞER, O., Biochemistry
DILBER, E., Paediatrics
DINÇ, H., Radiodiagnostic
ERCEYES, H., Anaesthesiology and Reanimation
ERDURAN, E., Paediatrics
EREM, C., Internal Medicine
ERSÖZ, H., Internal Medicine
ERTÜRK, M., Microbiology
GEDIK, Y., Paediatrics
GÖKÇE, M., Cardiology
GÖR, A., Urology
GÜLER, M., Physical Medicine and Rehabilitation
GÜMELE, H., Radiodiagnostic
İMAMOĞLU, H., Ophtalmology
İMAMOĞLU, M., Otorhinolaryngology
IŞIK, A., Otorhinolaryngology

KALAYCIOĞLU, A., Anatomy
KALKAN, A., Infectious Diseases
KALYONCU, N., Pharmacology
KANDIL, S., Paediatric Psychiatry
KARAGÜZEL, A., Medical Biology
KARAHAN, S., Biochemistry
KEHA, E., Biochemistry
KÖKSAL, İ., Infectious Diseases
KUTLU, M., Cardiology
KUZEYLI, K., Neurosurgery
ODACI, E., Histology and Embriology
ÖKTEN, A., Paediatrics
OMAY, S., Internal Medicine
ÖNCÜ, M., General Surgery
ÖNDER, Ç., Orthopedics and Traumatology
ÖNDER, E., Biochemistry
ÖREM, A., Biochemistry
ORHAN, F., Paediatrics
OVALI, E., Internal Medicine
ÖZCAN, F., Cardiovascular Surgery
ÖZEN, İ., Anaesthesiology and Reanimation
ÖZGÜR, G., Urology
ÖZGÜR, O., Internal Medicine
ÖZLÜ, T., Chest Disease
ÖZMENOĞLU, M., Neurology
ÖZORAN, Y., Pathology
ÖZTÜRK, M., Radiodiagnostic
ÖZYAVUZ, R., Urology
REIS, A., Pathology
SARI, A., Radiodiagnostic
SARI, R., Internal Medicine
SARIHAN, H., Paediatric Surgery
SÖNMEZ, F., Paediatrics
TESTERECI, H., Biochemistry
TOSUN, M., Physical Medicine and Rehabilitation
TURGUTALP, H., Pathology
TURHAN, A., Orthopedics and Traumatology
ULUSOY, Ş., Internal Medicine
UZUN, D., Internal Medicine
VELIOĞLU, S., Neurology
YANDI, M., General Surgery
YARIŞ, E., Pharmacology
YENILMEZ, E., Histology and Embryology
YILDIZ, K., Pathology
YILDIZ, M., Orthopedics and Traumatology

Faculty of Science and Literature (Kanuni Kampüsü, 61080 Trabzon; tel. (462) 325-31-41; fax (462) 325-31-95):

ABBASOV, R., Chemistry
AHMET AYAZ, F., Biology
AKBAŞ, M.
AKBAŞ, M., Mathematics
ALAADDIN YALÇINKAYA, M., History
ALTUNBAŞ, M., Physics
AYAZ, S., Biology
BEYAZOĞLU, O., Biology
ÇAVUŞ, A., Mathematics
ÇELEBI, S., Physics
ÇELIK, A., Turkish Language and Literature
ÇEVIK, U., Physics
ÇIÇEK, K., History
COŞKUN, E.
COŞKUN, E., Mathematics
DEMIRBAĞLU, Z., Biology
DOĞAN, A., Turkish Language and Literature
HINTISTAN, S., Nursing
İHSAN KOBYA, A., Physics
İNAN, K., History
İSMAYILOV, Z.
İSMAYILOV, Z., Mathematics
KADIOĞLU, A., Biology
KANTEKIN, H., Chemistry
KARABÖCEK, S., Chemistry
KARAL, H., Physics
KARSLIOĞLU, S., Chemistry
KAYGUSUZ, K., Chemistry
KEMAL KAYRA, O., Turkish Language and Literature
KHADJIEV, D., Mathematics
KÜÇÜKÖMEROĞLU, B., Physics
ÖKSÜZ, H., History
OSMAN BELDÜZ, A., Biology
ŞENTÜRK, H., Chemistry
SÖKMEN, A., Chemistry
SÖKMEN, M., Biology
TIRAŞOĞLU, E., Physics
TÜFEKÇI, M., Chemistry
ÜNVER, İ., Mathematics
YALÇINKAYA, M., History
YANMAZ, E., Physics
YAPAR, Z., Mathematics
YAYLI, N., Chemistry
YEREBAKAN, İ., English Language and Literature
YEŞILÇIÇEK ÇALIK, K., Midwifery
YILMAZ, S., Chemistry

Faculty of Theology (Rize) (Atatürk Cad., Piri Çelebi Mah., Rize; tel. (464) 214-11-20; fax (464) 214-11-24; e-mail ilahiyat@ktu.edu.tr):

SANDIKÇI, S. K., Islamic Education

Faculty of Water Resource Sciences (Rize) (İyidere, Rize; tel. (464) 223-52-39; fax (464) 223-41-18):

KADIOĞLU, A., Biology

GRADUATE SCHOOLS

Graduate School of Health Sciences: Dir Prof. Dr ORHAN DEĞER.

Graduate School of Natural and Applied Sciences: Dir Prof. Dr SALIH TERZIOĞLU.

Graduate School of Social Sciences: Dir Prof. Dr HAYDAR AKYAZI.

KIRIKKALE ÜNİVERSİTESİ

Ankara Karayolu 7 km, 71450 Kırıkkale
Telephone: (318) 357-36-44
Fax: (318) 357-36-94
E-mail: rektorluk@kku.edu.tr
Internet: www.kku.edu.tr

Founded 1992
State control
Academic year: October to July (two semesters)

Rector: Prof. Dr EKREM YILDIZ
Vice-Rector: Prof. Dr ADNAN KARAISMAILOGLU
Vice-Rector: Prof. Dr OSMAN CAGLAYAN
Librarian: AHMET ÖZKAN

Library of 63,000 vols, 87 periodicals
Number of teachers: 849
Number of students: 15,542

DEANS

Faculty of Dentistry: Prof. Dr ABDÜRRAHIM ŞENGÜN
Faculty of Economics and Administrative Sciences: Prof. Dr MUSTAFA ACAR
Faculty of Education: Prof. Dr MEHMET KUTLU
Faculty of Engineering: Prof. Dr VELI ÇELIK
Faculty of Fine Arts: Prof. Dr SALIH AKKAŞ
Faculty of Law: Prof. Dr ENVER BOZKURT
Faculty of Medicine: Prof. Dr MURAT KAÇMAZ
Faculty of Science and Letters: Prof. Dr MUSTAFA YIĞITOĞLU
Faculty of Veterinary Medicine: Prof. Dr ERTUĞUL ELMA
School of Physical Education and Sports: Asst Prof. Dr MEHMET ÖÇALAN

KOÇ UNIVERSITY

Rumelifeneri Yolu, 34450 Sarıyer, Istanbul
Telephone: (212) 338-10-00
E-mail: information@ku.edu.tr
Internet: www.ku.edu.tr

Founded 1993
Private control
Languages of instruction: Turkish, English
Academic year: October to June

Pres.: Prof. Dr ATTILA AŞKAR
Provost and Vice-Pres. for Academic Affairs: Prof. Dr YAMAN ARKUN
Vice-Pres. for Admin.: Prof. Dr ÖMER YEDEKÇIOĞLU
Gen. Sec.: MEHMET CELAYIR
Librarian: DIDAR BAYIR

Library of 82,000 vols
Number of teachers: 126
Number of students: 1,054

DEANS

College of Administrative Sciences and Economics: Prof. Dr H. METE SONER
College of Arts and Sciences: Prof. Dr ERSIN YURTSEVER
College of Engineering: Prof. Dr IRSADI AKSUN
Graduate School of Business: Prof. BARIŞ TAN
School of Health Sciences: Prof. Dr ELIZABETH ANNE HERDMAN
School of Law: Prof. Dr TUĞRUL ANSAY

KOCAELI ÜNİVERSİTESİ

Eski Istanbul Yolu 10 km., 413080 Limuteppe, Izmit/Kocaeli
Telephone: (262) 303-10-00
Fax: (262) 303-10-03
E-mail: intoffice@kou.edu.tr
Internet: www.kou.edu.tr

Founded 1992
State control
Academic year: October to June

Rector: Prof. Dr BAKI KOMSUOGLU
Vice-Rector for Academic Services: Prof. Dr YUNUS KISHALI
Vice-Rector for Admin. Services: Prof. Dr OZER KENAR
Vice-Rector for Financial Services: Prof. Dr YUSUF CAGLAR
Chief Librarian: MAHMUT SEMERCI

Library of 45,000 vols, 10,000 periodicals
Number of teachers: 1,752
Number of students: 10,521

Publications: *Journal of Social Sciences Institute* (2 a year), *Kocaeli University Communication Faculty Research Journal* (2 a year), *Kocaeli University Law Faculty Journal* (2 a year)

DEANS

Faculty of Arts: Prof. Dr NURI TEMIZSOYLU
Faculty of Communication: Prof. Dr HASRET COMAK
Faculty of Economics: Prof. Dr AHMET İSLAMOĞLU
Faculty of Education: Prof. Dr SERVETTIN BILIR
Faculty of Engineering: Prof. SAVAS AYBERK
Faculty of Law: Prof. Dr HAMDI YILMAZ
Faculty of Medicine: Prof. Dr ALI GÖKALP
Faculty of Science: Prof. Dr YÜKSEL GÜNEY
Faculty of Technical Education: Prof. Dr SATILMIŞ TEKINDAL

MALTEPE ÜNİVERSİTESİ

Marmara Eğitim Köyü, 34857 Maltepe, Istanbul
Telephone: (216) 626-10-50
Fax: (216) 626-10-70
E-mail: maltepe@maltepe.edu.tr
Internet: www.maltepe.edu.tr

Founded 1997
State control
Languages of instruction: Turkish, English
Academic year: October to June

Rector: Prof. Dr MESUT RAZBONYAH
Librarians: NAZAN KARAKAŞ, BURCU ESENER, ARZU ACAR

Library of 17,230 vols, 531 periodicals
Number of teachers: 240
Number of students: 2,220

Publications: *Fen-Edebiyat Fakültesi Dergisi* (Science and Letters Faculty Journal, 2 a year), *Hukuk Fakültesi Dergisi* (Law Faculty Journal, 2 a year), *İktisadi ve İdari Bilimler Fakültesi Dergisi* (Economics and Business Administration Faculty Journal, 2 a year), *İletişim Fakültesi Dergisi* (Communication Faculty Journal, 2 a year)

DEANS

Faculty of Architecture: Prof. Dr ERKUT ÖZEL
Faculty of Communication: Prof. Dr SABRI ÖZAYDIN
Faculty of Economics and Business Administration: Prof. Dr ERTAN OKTAY
Faculty of Education: Prof. Dr İSA EŞME
Faculty of Engineering: Prof. Dr MESUT RAZBONYALI
Faculty of Law: Prof. Dr AYDIN AYBAY
Faculty of Medicine: Prof. Dr ŞEFIK GÜNEY
Faculty of Science and Letters: Prof. Dr MÜCELLA ULUĞ

MARMARA ÜNİVERSİTESİ

Sultanahmet, 34413 Istanbul
Telephone: (212) 518-16-00
Fax: (212) 518-16-15
Internet: www.marun.edu.tr
Founded 1883, reorganized 1982
State control
Languages of instruction: Turkish, English, French, German
Academic year: September to July
Rector: Prof. Dr TUNÇ EREM
Vice-Rector: Prof. Dr AHMET HAYRİ PURMUŞ
Gen. Sec.: Dr ALTAN KİTAPÇI
Librarian: SEVINC KAZAZ
Number of teachers: 2,500
Number of students: 45,000
Publication: various faculty journals

DEANS

Atatürk Faculty of Education: Prof. Dr AYLA OKTAY
Faculty of Communication: Prof. Dr MELDA CİNMAN ŞİMŞEK
Faculty of Dentistry: Prof. Dr SELÇUK BASA
Faculty of Economics and Business Administration: Prof. Dr AHMET HAYRİ DURMUŞ
Faculty of Engineering: Prof. Dr A. ALP SAYAR
Faculty of Fine Arts: Prof. Dr HÜSAMETTIN KOÇAN
Faculty of Health Education: Prof. Dr NILGÜN SARP
Faculty of Law: Prof. Dr MERIH KEMAL OMAĞ
Faculty of Medicine: Prof. Dr TOLGA DAĞLI
Faculty of Pharmacy: Prof. Dr MÜRŞIT PEKİN
Faculty of Science and Letters: Prof. Dr EMINE GÜRSOY NASKALI
Faculty of Technical Education: Prof. Dr SEMRA ÜNAL
Faculty of Theology: Prof. Dr MUSTAFA FAYDA

MERSİN ÜNİVERSİTESİ

Çiftlik Köyü Kampüsü, 33343 Mersin
Telephone: (324) 361-00-22
Fax: (324) 361-00-15
E-mail: webadmin@mersin.edu.tr
Internet: www.mersin.edu.tr
Founded 1992
State control
Rector: Prof. Dr UĞUR ORAL
Librarian: HÜSEYIN GÖLALMIŞ
Number of teachers: 100
Number of students: 18,000

DEANS

Faculty of Architecture: Prof. Dr TAMER GÖK
Faculty of Communication: Prof. Dr SELIM AKSÖYEK
Faculty of Economics and Administrative Sciences: Prof. Dr TAYFUR ÖZŞEN
Faculty of Education: Prof. Dr ZAFER GÖKÇAKAN
Faculty of Engineering: Prof. Dr CEMIL CENGIZ ARCASOY
Faculty of Fine Arts: Prof. Dr E. BERIKA İPEKBAYRAK
Faculty of Fisheries: Prof. Dr GÜRKAN EKİNGEN
Faculty of Medicine: Prof. Dr ESAT YILGÖR
Faculty of Pharmacy: Prof. Dr ATILLA YALÇIN
Faculty of Science and Letters: Prof. Dr AYHAN SEZER
Faculty of Technical Education (Tarsus): Prof. Dr ÖZDEN BAŞTÜRK

MIMAR SINAN GÜZEL SANATLAR ÜNIVERSITESI
(Mimar Sinan Fine Arts University)

Fındıklı, 80040 Istanbul
Telephone: (212) 145-00-00
E-mail: ulik@msu.edu.tr
Internet: www.msu.edu.tr
Founded 1883, univ. status 1982
State control
Language of instruction: Turkish
Rector: Prof. Dr ÝSMET VILDAN ALPTEKIN
Chief Admin. Officer: ERDAL KÜPELI
Librarian: ASİYE ALAGÖZOĞLU
Library of 51,200 vols
Number of teachers: 420
Number of students: 3,509

DEANS

Faculty of Architecture: Prof. ÝLGI YÜCE AŞKÝN
Faculty of Fine Arts: Prof. RAHMI AKSUNGUR
Faculty of Sciences and Literature: Prof. Dr GÜLAY BAŞARÝR KÝROĞLU

MUĞLA ÜNİVERSİTESİ

48000 Kötekli, Muğla
Telephone: (252) 211-10-00
Fax: (252) 211-15-00
E-mail: intoffice@mu.edu.tr
Internet: www.mu.edu.tr
Founded 1992; present status 2002
State control
Academic year: September to June
Rector: Prof. Dr ŞENER OKTIK
Vice-Rectors: Prof. Dr İBRAHIM YOKAŞ, Prof. Dr ATILA YÜCEL
Library of 76,000 vols, 750 periodicals, 60,000 electronic journals
Number of teachers: 660
Number of students: 17,140

DEANS

Faculty of Aquaculture and Fisheries Biology: Prof. Dr AHMET NURI TARKAN
Faculty of Arts and Sciences: Prof. Dr MURAT BARLAS
Faculty of Economics and Administrative Sciences: Prof. Dr CEMIL ERTUĞRUL
Faculty of Education: Prof. Dr ŞULE AYCAN
Faculty of Engineering: Prof. Dr ERDAL OZHAN
Faculty of Fine Arts: Prof. Dr ATILA YÜCEL (Deputy)
Faculty of Technical Education: Prof. Dr MUHAMMED ELTEZ

DIRECTORS

Institute of Natural Sciences (Graduate School): Prof. Dr MUSTAFA DİLEK
Institute of Social Sciences (Graduate School): Prof. Dr OMER GÜRKAN
School of Foreign Languages: Prof. Dr MUSTAFA KINSIZ
School of Health (Fethiye): Prof. Dr NESRIN AŞTI
School of Health (Muğla): Prof. Dr LALE AFRASYAP
School of Physical Education and Sports: Prof. Dr ERDAL ZORBA
School of Tourism and Hotel Management: Prof. Dr ASLAN EREN (Deputy)

There are 8 Vocational Schools.

MUSTAFA KEMAL ÜNİVERSİTESİ

31000 Antakya, Hatay
Telephone: (326) 221-33-17
Fax: (326) 221-33-00
Internet: www.mku.edu.tr
Founded 1992
State control
Rector: Prof. Dr METIN GÜRKANLAR
Vice-Rectors: Prof. Dr KAMURAN GÜÇLÜ, Prof. Dr SERMIN ÖRNEKTEKIN, Prof. Dr CEMAL YÜKSELEN
Number of teachers: 650
Number of students: 13,000 undergraduate, 350 postgraduate

Faculties of agriculture, aquaculture, economics and business administration, education, engineering and architecture, fine arts, medicine, public administration, science and humanities and veterinary science.

NİĞDE ÜNİVERSİTESİ

Niğde Üniversitesi Rektörlüğü, 51100 Niğde
Telephone: (388) 225-26-04
Fax: (388) 225-26-00
E-mail: ozelkalem@nigde.edu.tr
Internet: www.nigde.edu.tr
Founded 1992
State control
Academic year: September to June
Rector: Prof. Dr ADNAN GÖRÜR
Vice-Rectors: Prof. Dr MEHMET ŞENER
Vice-Rector: Prof. Dr MURAT ALP
Sec.-Gen.: Assoc. Prof. Dr MUSTAFA BAYRAK
Dir of the Library and Documentation Dept: MAZLUME VURAN
Library of 13,000 books, 100 periodicals
Number of teachers: 654
Number of students: 13,913 (13,136 undergraduate, 777 postgraduate)
Publications: *Natural Sciences*, *Social Sciences*

DEANS

Faculty of Arts and Science: MUSA ŞAŞMAZ
Faculty of Economics and Business Administration: ZEKI DOĞAN
Faculty of Education: MURAT ALP
Faculty of Engineering: SAIR KAHRAMAN
Faculty of Architecture: MEHMET ŞENER

OKAN ÜNİVERSİTESİ

Hasanpaşa Uzunçayır Cad. 6, Kadıköy, Istanbul
Telephone: (216) 325-48-18
Fax: (216) 339-61-36
E-mail: okan@okan.edu.tr
Internet: www.okan.edu.tr
Founded 2003
Rector: Prof. Dr SADIK KIRBAŞ
Vice-Rector: Prof. Dr CEVDET OĞÜT
Librarian: KENAN ÖZTOP
Number of students: 450

DEANS

Faculty of Arts and Sciences: Prof. Dr HASAN ÖZEKES
Faculty of Economics and Administrative Sciences: Prof. Dr SADIK KIRBAŞ
Faculty of Engineering: Asst Prof. Dr CEVDET ÖĞÜT

DIRECTORS

School of Computer Sciences and Tourism and Hotel Management: Prof. Dr ALI RIZA BÜYÜKUSLU
Social Institute: Asst Prof. Dr GONCA TELLI YAMAMOTO

ONDOKUZ MAYIS ÜNİVERSİTESİ (Ondokuz Mayis University)

Kurupelit, 55139 Samsun
Telephone: (362) 312-19-19
Fax: (362) 457-60-91
E-mail: inter@omu.edu.tr
Internet: www.omu.edu.tr

Founded 1975
State control
Language of instruction: Turkish
Academic year: September to June

Rector: Prof. Dr HÜSEYIN AKAN
Vice-Rector: Prof. AHMET BULUT
Vice-Rector: FERŞAT KOLBAKIR
Vice-Rector: Prof. Dr SAIT BILGIÇ
Sec.-Gen.: Asst Prof. SELAHATTIN ÖZYURT
Registrar: NURİYE GÜRKANLI
Librarian: ÖMER BOZKURT

Number of teachers: 1,944
Number of students: 36,076

Publications: *Faculty Journals* (12 a year), *Ondokuz Mayıs University News Bulletin* (4 a year)

DEANS

Faculty of Aeronautics and Space Sciences: Prof. Dr. ERDEM KOÇ
Faculty of Agriculture: Prof. Dr MEHMET KURAN
Faculty of Arts and Sciences: Prof. Dr ŞENOL EREN
Faculty of Communication: Prof. Dr. ZEKERIYA ULUDAĞ
Faculty of Dentistry: Prof. Dr SELIM ARICI
Faculty of Economics and Administrative Sciences: Prof. Dr FATIH YÜKSEL
Faculty of Education: Prof. Dr CEVDET YILMAZ
Faculty of Engineering: Prof. Dr FEHMI YAZICI
Faculty of Law: Prof. Dr. HAKAN HAKERI
Faculty of Medicine: Prof. Dr HAYDAR ŞAHINOĞLU
Faculty of Theology: Prof. Dr YAVUZ ÜNAL
Faculty of Veterinary Medicine: Prof. Dr MUSTAFA ALISARI

PROFESSORS

Faculty of Agriculture (Kurupelit 55139 Samsun; tel. (362) 457-60-86; fax (362) 457-60-34; e-mail iac-agric@omu.edu.tr; internet www.omu.edu.tr/a/en/academics/faculties/agriculture):

ACAR, Z., Agronomy
APAN, M., Agricultural Structures and Irrigation
BİLGENER, Ş., Horticulture
CİNEMRE, H. A., Agricultural Economics
DEMİR, Y., Agricultural Structures and Irrigation
ECEVİT, O., Plant Protection
ERENER, G., Feeds and Animal Nutrition
GÜLÜMSER, A., Agronomy
KEVSEROĞLU, K., Agronomy
KORKMAZ, A., Soil Science
KURAN, M., Agricultural Biotechnology
MEYDAN, M. A., Agricultural Machinery
MENNAN, H., Plant Protection
ODABAŞ, F., Horticulture
OKUMUS, A., Biometry-Genetics
ÖZCAN, M., Horticulture
ÖZDEMİR, N., Soil Science
ÖZTÜRK, T., Agricultural Structures and Irrigation
PINAR, Y., Agricultural Machinery
SARICA, M., Animal Science
SARIÇIÇEK, B. Z., Animal Science
TUNCER, C., Entomology
TUNALI, B., Phytopathology

Faculty of Arts and Sciences (Ordu) (Ordu Fen-Edebiyat Fakültesi, Perşembe, 52750 Ordu; tel. (452) 517-43-70; fax (452) 517-43-68; internet www.ome.edu.tr/akad/fklt/ordufen/index.html):

AKÇİN, Ö. E., Biology
EKİNCİ, İ., History
MAĞDEN, S., Mathematics
YAPAR, C., Mathematics

Faculty of Arts and Sciences (Samsun) (Kurupelit 55139 Samsun; tel. (362) 457-60-80; fax (362) 457-60-81; internet www.omu.edu.tr/a/en/academics/faculties/science-art):

AFŞİN, B., Chemistry
ALPASLAN, F., Statistics
BATI, B., Chemistry
BİÇER, ENDER, Physical Chemistry
BİLGENER, M., Biology
BÜYÜKGÜNGÖR, O., Physics
ÇALIŞKAN, M., Mathematics
ÇALIŞKAN, N., Physics
ÇELİK, F., Physics
DİNÇER, M., Physics
DEMİR, H., Applied Mathematics
EDİNSEL, K., Psychology
ERDÖNMEZ, A., Physics
EREN, Z., Biology
ERLER, M. Y., History
GÖNÜLOL, A., Biology
GÜLEL, A., Biology
GÜMRÜKÇÜOĞLU, İ. E., Chemistry
GÜMÜŞ, H., Physics
GÜRKANLI, A. T., Mathematics
İPEK, N., Born Modern
IŞILDAK, İ., Chemistry
KARACAN, T., Turkish
KARTAL, I., General Physics
KARTAL, V., Biology
KEFELİOĞLU, H., Biology
KILINÇ, M., Biology
KÖKSAL, F., Physics
KORKMAZ, H., Chemistry
KUTBAY, H. G., Biology
MENEK, N., Chemistry
NİŞANCI, A., Geography
OKUMUŞOĞLU, N. T., Physics
ÖLMEZ, H., Chemistry
ONAR, A. N., Chemistry
ÖZBALCI, M., Turkish
ÖZKANCA, R., Biology
ÖZKAPLAN, H., Physics
ÖZKOÇ, İ., Biology
PANCAR, A., Mathematics
POLAT, N., Biology
SAĞLIK, S., New Turkish Language
ŞENEL, G., Biology
ŞENEL, İ., Physics
TAPRAMAZ, R., Physics
TARAKÇI, C., Turkish
USTA, N., Sociology
UZUN, A., Physical Geography
YAVUZ, M., Physics
YILMAZ, M., Mathematics
YILMAZ, V. T., Chemistry
ZEYBEKOĞLU, Ü., Biology

Faculty of Arts and Sciences (Sinop) (Sinop Fen-Edebiyat Fakültesi, Sinop; tel. (368) 271-55-20; fax (368) 271-55-24; e-mail sinopfenedebiyat@yahoo.com; internet www.omu.edu.tr/akad/sinopfen):

ÇANKAYA, E., Statistics
DEMİRCİ, K., Mathematics
SIVACI, R., Biology

Faculty of Dentistry (Dişhekimliği Fakültesi, Kurupelit, 55139 Samsun; tel. (362) 457-60-30; fax (362) 457-60-32; e-mail dentistry@omu.edu.tr; internet www.omu.edu.tr/a/en/academics/faculties/dentistry/index.php):

AYDEMİR, H., Endodontics
AÇIKGÖZ, G., Periodontology
ALKAN, A., Oral and Maxillofacial Surgery
ÇELENK, P., Oral Diagnosis and Radiology
CEYLAN, G., Prosthodontics
KÖPRÜLÜ, H., Dental Diseases and Treatment
KOYUTÜRK, A. E., Pedodontics
TOLLER, M. Ö., Oral and Maxillofacial Surgery
TÜRK, T., Orthodontics

Faculty of Economics and Administrative Sciences (Samsun) (İktisadi ve İdari Bilimler Fakültesi, Kurupelit Kampüsü, 55139 Samsun; tel. (362) 312-19-19; fax (362) 457-60-17):

KÖKTAŞ, M. E., Political Science and Social Science
GÜZEL, H. A., Economics

Faculty of Economics and Administrative Sciences (Ünye) (Ünye İktisadi ve İdari Bilimler Fakültesi, Ünye; tel. (452) 323-86-96; fax (452) 323-82-56; e-mail gurolo@omu.edu.tr):

ÖZCÜRE, G., Economics

Faculty of Education (Amasya) (Amasya Eğitim Fakültesi, Amasya; tel. (358) 252-62-30; fax (358) 252-62-22; e-mail amasyaeg@omu.edu.tr; internet www.omu.edu.tr/akad/fklt/aegt/amsegtgiris.htm):

KARAMUSTAFAOĞLU, O., Computers and Teaching Technology
ORBAY, M., Primary Education
ÜSTÜN, A., Education
YİĞİT, M., Turkish
ZİYAGİL, M. A., Physical Education and Sport

Faculty of Education (Samsun) (Eğitim Fakültesi, Kurupelit, 55139 Samsun; tel. (362) 312 19 19; fax (362) 457 60 78; internet www.omu.edu.tr/a/en/academics/faculties/education):

AKBULUT, D. A., History
AYDIN, M., Turkish Language
BARUT, Y., Special Education
BAŞAR, E., Primary Education
BAYRAKTARKATAL, E., Music
BOLAT, H., Foreign Languages
ÇOLAK, M., Foreign Languages
ÇORUH, U., Computer Education and Educational Technology
DİNDAR, B., Education
ENGİN, A., Natural Sciences and Mathematics
ERSANLI, K., Education
KIRCI, M., Turkish
KOYUNCU, S., Fine Arts

Faculty of Education (Sinop) (Sinop Eğitim Fakültesi, Sinop; tel. (368) 271-55-35; fax (368) 271-55-30; e-mail sinopegit@omu.edu.tr; internet www.ome.edu.tr/akad/sinop-egt):

AYDIN, H., Computers and Teaching Technology
BAŞAR, E., Primary Education
BOSTANCI, B. A., Foreign Languages
MENTEŞE, S., Education
ÖZDEMIR, O., Primary Education

Faculty of Engineering (Kurupelit , 55139 Samsun; tel. (362) 457-60-36; fax (362) 457-60-35; e-mail onergun@omu.edu.tr; internet www.omu.edu.tr/a/en/academics/faculties/engineering):

BAYRAKLI, F., Environmental Engineering
BEKTAŞ, S., Geodesy and Photogrammetric Engineering
BÜYÜKGÜNGÖR, H., Environmental Engineering
ÇAKIRCIOĞLU, M., Civil Engineering
EFENDİYEV, Ç., Telecommunications
ELEVLİ, B., Industrial Engineering
ERGUN, O. N., Environmental Engineering
HURŞİT, A., Food Engineering
KASIMZADE, A., Civil Engineering
KOCA, F., Food Engineering

Önbilgin, G., Electrical and Electronic Engineering
Topaloğlu, B., Machine Engineering
Ulutaş, M., Computer Engineering

Faculty of Fisheries (Sinop) (Su Ürünleri Fakültesi, Akliman Kampüsü, 57000 Sinop; tel. (368) 287-62-62; fax (368) 287-62-55; internet www.omu.edu.tr/akad/fklt/ssu/anamenu.html):

Bat, L., Basic Fisheries Sciences
Bircan, R., Fish Breeding
Büyükhatipoğlu, Ş., Fish Breeding
Erdem, M., Fish Breeding
Erkoyuncu, İ., Fishing and Fish Processing Technology
Kalma, M., Fish Breeding
Samsun, O., Fishing and Fish Processing Technology

Faculty of Medicine (Kurupelit 55139 Samsun; tel. (362) 457-60-70; fax (362) 457-60-41; internet www.omu.edu.tr/akad/fklt/tip/anamenu.htm):

Acar, S., Paediatric Oncology
Ağar, E., Physiology
Akan, H., Radiodiagnostics
Akbaş, S., Child Psychiatry
Akpolat, İ., Pathology
Akpolat, M. T., Nephrology
Albayrak, D., Paediatric Haematology
Alper, T., Obstetrics and Gynaecology
Alvur, M., Biochemistry
Anlar, F. Y., Paediatrics
Arik, A. C., Psychiatry
Arik, N., Nephrology
Aritürk, E., Paediatric Surgery
Aşçi, R., Urology
Aydin, M., Paediatric Endocrinology
Bağci, H., Medical Biology
Bakir, T., Gastroenterology
Bariş, S., Pathology
Başoğlu, A., Thoracic Surgery
Başoğlu, T., Nuclear Medicine
Baysal, M. K., Paediatrics
Bedir, A., Biochemistry
Bek, Y., Bio-statistics
Bernay, R. F., Paediatric Surgery
Bilgiç, S., Anatomy
Birinci, , Ophthalmology
Büyükalpelli, R., Urology
Cantürk, F., Physical Medicine and Rehabilitation
Cantürk, T., Dermatology
Çelik, F., Neurosurgery
Çelik, S., Pharmacology
Cengiz, K., Nephrology
Çiftçi, N., Histology and Embryology
Dabak, N., Orthopaedics and Traumatology
Dikici, M. F., Family Practice
Diren, H. B., Radiodiagnostics
Duru, F., Paediatrics
Durupinar, B., Microbiology
Elbistan, M., Medical Biology
Erkan, D., Ophthalmology
Erkan, L., Thoracic Diseases
Erzurumlu, K., General Surgery
Geptiremen, A., Pharmacology
Gökçe, Ş. Ç., Radiation Oncology
Güldoğuş, F., Anaesthesiology
Gülman, B., Orthopaedics and Traumatology
Günal, N., Paediatrics
Günaydin, M., Microbiology
Gürmen, N., Radiodiagnostics
Güven, H., First Aid and Emergency Aid
İçten, N., Anatomy
Incesu, L., Radiodiagnostics
Işlek, İ., Paediatrics
İyigün, Ö., Neurosurgery
Kahraman, H., Endocrinology
Kalayci, A. G., Paediatrics
Kandemir, B., Pathology
Kaplan, S., Histology and Embryology
Karacalar, A., Plastic and Reconstructive Surgery
Karagöz, F., Pathology
Karaismailoğlu, N., Orthopaedics and Traumatology
Keçeligil, H. T., Cardiovascular Surgery
Kesim, M., General Surgery
Kesim, Y., Pharmacology
Kocakavak, C., Cardiology
Kökçü, A., Obstetrics and Gynaecology
Kolbakir, F., Cardiovascular Surgery
Kopuz, C., Anatomy
Korkmaz, A., Histology and Embryology
Koyuncu, M., Otorhinolaryngology
Küçüködük, Ş., Paediatrics
Kuru, O., Physical Medicine and Rehabilitation
Leblebicioğlu, H., Clinical Bacteriology and Infectious Diseases
Malatyalioğlu, E., Obstetrics and Gynaecology
Malazgirt, Z., General Surgery
Marangoz, C., Physiology
Öge, İ., Ophthalmology
Oğur, M. G., Paediatrics
Ökten, G., Medical Biology
Onar, M. K., Neurology
Özbenli, T., Neurology
Özen, N., General Surgery
Özkan, K., General Surgery
Öztürk, F., Paediatrics
Pekşen, Y., Public Health
Rakunt, C., Neurosurgery
Rizalar, R., Paediatric Surgery
Şahin, A. R., Psychiatry
Şahin, M., Cardiology
Şahin, M., Nuclear Medicine
Şahinoğlu, H., Anaesthesiology
Saniç, A., Microbiology
Sarihasan, B., Anaesthesiology and Reanimation
Sarikaya, Ş., Urology
Selçuk, M. B., Radiodiagnostics
Şeşen, T., Otolaryngology
Tanyeri, F., Internal Medicine (Endocrinology)
Tanyeri, Y., Otorhinolaryngology
Taşçi, N., Physiology
Taşdemir, H. A., Paediatrics
Tekat, A., Otorhinolaryngology
Tülek, N., Clinical Bacteriology and Infectious Diseases
Tunali, G., Neurology
Tür, A., Anaesthesiology
Turanli, A. Y., Dermatology
Türe, U., Neurosurgery
Turla, A., Forensic Medicine
Ulusoy, A. N., General Surgery
Ünal, R., Otorhinolaryngology
Üstün, C., Obstetrics and Gynaecology
Üstün, F. E., Anaesthesiology
Yeşildağ, O., Cardiology
Yilmaz, A. F., Urology
Yilmaz, Ö, Cardiology
Yücel, İ., Internal Medicine (Oncology)

Faculty of Theology (Kurupelit 55139 Samsun; tel. (362) 457-60-84; fax (362) 457-60-83; e-mail ilhdek@omu.edu.tr; internet www.omu.edu.tr/a/en/academics/faculties/divinity):

Can, Y., Islamic History and Arts
Doğan, İ., Basic Islamic Sciences
Güner, O., Basic Islamic Sciences
Kaya, M., Teaching Ethics and Religious Culture in Primary Education
Koçak, M., Basic Islamic Sciences
Köylü, M., Philosophy and Religious Sciences
Peker, H., Philosophy and Religion
Terzi, M. Z., Islamic History and Art
Turan, A., Basic Islamic Sciences
Yazici, İ., Basic Islamic Sciences
Yetik, E., Basic Islamic Sciences
Zümrüt, O., Islamic History and Art

Faculty of Veterinary Medicine (Kurupelit, 55139 Samsun; tel. (362) (362) 312-19-19 ext. 2800; fax (362) (362) 4576922):

Aksoy, A., Pharmacology And Toxicology
Alisarli, M., Food Hygiene and Technology
Celebi, M., Reproduction And Artificial Insemination
Findik, M., Obstetrics And Gynecology
Gulbahar, M. Y., Pathology
Muğlali, H., Animal Science and Animal Nutrition
Umur, Ş., Parasitology
Yurdusev, N., Microbiology

ORTA DOĞU TEKNİK ÜNİVERSİTESİ (Middle East Technical University)

İsmet İnönü Bulvarı, Ankara 06531
Telephone: (312) 210-20-00
Fax: (312) 210-11-05
E-mail: rektor@metu.edu.tr
Internet: www.metu.edu.tr

Founded 1956
State control
Languages of instruction: Turkish, English
Academic year: October to June (two semesters)

Pres.: Prof. Dr Ahmet Acar
Gen. Sec.: Prof. Dr Tanju Mehmetoğlu (acting)
Registrar: Nesrin Ünsal
Librarian: Cevat Güven (acting)

Library: see Libraries and Archives
Number of teachers: 2,529
Number of students: 23,624

Publications: *METU Journal of Faculty of Architecture* (2 a year), *METU Journal of Human Sciences* (2 a year), *METU Studies in Development* (4 a year)

DEANS

Faculty of Architecture: Prof. Dr Haluk Pamir
Faculty of Arts and Sciences: Prof. Dr Cüneyt Can
Faculty of Economic and Administrative Sciences: Prof. Dr Yaşar Eyüp Özveren
Faculty of Education: Prof. Dr M. Yaşar Özden
Faculty of Engineering: Prof. Dr Zafer Dursunkaya

PROFESSORS

Faculty of Architecture (tel. (312) 210-22-01; fax (312) 210-11-08; e-mail facultyweb@arc.metu.edu.tr; internet www.arch.metu.edu.tr):

Aktüre, S., City and Regional Planning
Bakirer, Ö., Architecture
Balamir, M., City and Regional Planning
Eraydin, A., City and Regional Planning
Ersoy, M., City and Regional Planning
Erzen, J. A., Architecture
Evyapan, G., Architecture
Gedik, A., City and Regional Planning
Güven, S., Architecture
İmamoğlu, V., Architecture
Pamir, H., Architecture
Saltik, E., Architecture
Tuna, N., City and Regional Planning
Türel, A., City and Regional Planning
Yavuz, A., Architecture
Yavuz, Y., Architecture

Faculty of Arts and Sciences (tel. (312) 210-31-01; fax (312) 210-12-79; e-mail wwwfef@metu.edu.tr; internet www.fef.metu.edu.tr):

Adali, O., Biology
Akbulut, U., Chemistry
Akgün, S., History
Akinoğlu, G. B., Physics
Akkaya, E. U., Chemistry
Akkaya, M., Chemistry
Akşit, B., Sociology
Akyildiz, E., Mathematics
Alpay, Ş., Mathematics
Alyürük, K., Chemistry

ARAS, L., Chemistry
ARINÇ, E., Biology
ATAMAN, O. Y., Chemistry
AYATA, S., Sociology
AYDIN, R., Physics
AYGÜN, R. S., Chemistry
AYHAN, H. Ö., Statistics
AYTUNA, A., Mathematics
BALCI, M., Chemistry
BAYIN, S. Ş., Physics
BAYKAL, A., Physics
BAYRAMLI, E., Chemistry
BİLHAN, M., Mathematics
BİLİKMEN, K. S., Physics
CAN, C., Physics
ÇELEBİ, O., Mathematics
CEYLAN, Y., Philosophy
CIVELEK, F. R., Physics
DEMİR, A. S., Chemistry
DEMİRCİ, Ş., Chemistry
DOĞAN, M., Biology
ECEVİT, A., Physics
ECEVİT, M. C., Sociology
ECEVİT, Y., Sociology
ELLİALTIOĞLU, Ş., Physics
ERÇELEBİ, A. Ç., Physics
ERGÜDEN, A., Philosophy
ERKOÇ, Ş., Physics
ERTÜRK, Y., Sociology
GÖKALP, A., Physics
GÖKMEN, A., Chemistry
GÖKMEN, İ. G., Chemistry
GÖKTÜRK, E. H., Chemistry
GÜLEN, D., Physics
GÜNAL, İ., Physics
GÜNDÜZ, U., Biology
GÜRAY, T., Biology
HACALOĞLU, J., Chemistry
HASIRCI, N., Chemistry
HASIRCI, V. N., Biology
İLTAN, E. O., Physics
İMAMOĞLU, O., Psychology
İNAM, A., Philosophy
İŞCAN, M., Biology
IŞÇİ, H., Chemistry
KARANCI, N. A., Psychology
KARASÖZEN, B., Mathematics
KARASU, A., Physics
KATIRCIOĞLU, B., Physics
KATIRCIOĞLU, Ş., Physics
KAYA, A., Mathematics
KAYA, Z., Biology
KAYRAN, H. C., Biology
KENCE, A., Biology
KILDIR, M., Chemistry
KIRBIYIK, H., Physics
KISAKÜREK, D., Chemistry
KIZILOĞLU, N., Physics
KIZILOĞLU, Ü., Physics
KOCABIYIK, S., Biology
KÜÇÜKYAVUZ, S., Chemistry
KÜÇÜKYAVUZ, Z., Chemistry
KUZUCUOĞLU, M., Mathematics
MUTLU, M. K., Sociology
MUTMAN, M., Sociology
NALBANTOĞLU, H. Ü., Sociology
NURLU, Z., Mathematics
ÖKTEM, H. A., Biology
ÖNAL, A. M., Chemistry
ÖNDER, T., Mathematics
ÖNSİPER, H., Mathematics
ÖZCENGİZ, G., Biology
ÖZDEMİR, S., Physics
ÖZKAN, H., Physics
ÖZKAN, İ., Chemistry
ÖZKAR, S., Chemistry
ÖZSAN, F. S., Physics
PAK, N. K., Physics
PEYNİRCİOĞLU, N. B., Chemistry
SAVCİ, M., Physics
SEVER, R., Physics
SEVERCAN, F., Biology
TALASLI, U., Psychology
TANYELİ, C., Chemistry
TARHAN, O., Chemistry
TAŞELİ, H., Mathematics
TATLI, A., Physics
TEZER, C., Mathematics
TEZER, M., Mathematics
TİNÇER, T., Chemistry
TOGAN, İ, Biology
TOGAN, İ, History
TOMAK, M., Physics
TOPPARE, L. K., Chemistry
TUNCEL, S., Chemistry
TURAN, G., Physics
TURAN, R., Physics
TÜRKER, L., Chemistry
ULA, A. T., Statistics
USANMAZ, A., Chemistry
UZUN, A., Statistics
VOLKAN, M., Chemistry
YİLMAZ, O., Physics
YÜCEL, M., Biology
YURTSEVEN, H., Physics
ZAFER, A., Mathematics
ZEYREK, T. M., Physics

Faculty of Economic and Administrative Sciences (tel. (312) 210-11-07; fax (312) 210-11-07; e-mail feas@feas.metu.edu.tr; internet www.feas.metu.edu.tr):

ACAR, A., Management
ACAR, A. F., Political Sciences and Public Administration
AKDER, H., Economics
AKSOY, Ş., Political Sciences and Public Administration
AYATA, A., Political Sciences and Public Administration
BAĞCI, H., International Relations
BÖLÜKBAŞIOĞLU, S., International Relations
ÇAKMAK, E. H., Economics
DAĞI, D. İ., International Relations
ERALP, Y. A., International Relations
ERLAT, G., Economics
ERLAT, H., Economics
EROL, C., Management
GITMEZ, A. S., Management
GÖKTAN, E., Management
KAYA, A. R., Political Sciences and Public Administration
MUĞAN, F. N. C., Management
ÖZUEREN, E., Economics
ŞENSES, F., Economics
TANSEL, A., Economics
TAYMAZ, E., Economics
TİLEYLİOĞLU, A., Management
TONAK, E., Economics

Faculty of Education (tel. (312) 210-40-01; fax (312) 210-11-12; e-mail top@metu.edu.tr; internet www.fedu.metu.edu.tr):

AKSU, M., Educational Sciences
ALPSAN, D., Science Education
AYDIN, A. G., Educational Sciences
BERBEROĞLU, G. H., Science Education
ÇILELI, M., Foreign Language Education
DEMIR, A. G., Educational Sciences
ENGİNARLAR, H., Foreign Language Education
ERTEPINAR, H., Science Education
GEBAN, Ö., Science Education
İÇÖZ, N., Foreign Language Education
KAŞ, A. D., Foreign Language Education
KÖNIG, W., Foreign Language Education
KORKUSUZ, F., Physical Education and Sports
ÖZDEN, Y., Computer Education and Instructional Technology
ŞİMŞEK, H., Educational Sciences
TEZER, E., Educational Sciences
YILDRIM, A., Educational Sciences
ZEYREK, D., Foreign Language Education

Faculty of Engineering (tel. (312) 210-25-01; fax (312) 210-11-10; e-mail engfac@eng.metu.edu.tr; internet www.eng.metu.edu.tr):

AKDENİZ, V., Metallurgical Engineering
AKGÖZ, Y. C., Engineering Sciences
AKGÜN, A. M., Aeronautical Engineering
AKIN, T., Electrical and Electronic Engineering
AKKÖK, M., Mechanical Engineering
AKMANDOR, İ. S., Aeronautical Engineering
AKSEL, H. M., Mechanical Engineering
AKYILMAZ, M. Ö., Civil Engineering
ALBAYRAK, K., Mechanical Engineering
ALEMDAROĞLU, N., Aeronautical Engineering
ALTINBİLEK, D. H., Civil Engineering
ALTINER, D., Geological Engineering
ANKARA, A., Metallurgical Engineering
ARIKAN, M. A. S., Mechanical Engineering
ARINÇ, F., Mechanical Engineering
AROL, A. İ., Mining Engineering
AŞKAR, M., Electrical and Electronic Engineering
ATALA, H., Metallurgical Engineering
ATALAY, Ü. M., Mining Engineering
ATIMTAY, A., Environmental Engineering
ATIMTAY, E., Civil Engineering
BAÇ, N., Chemical Engineering
BAĞCI, A. S., Petroleum and Natural Gas Engineering
BAKIR, U. B., Chemical Engineering
BALKAN, T., Mechanical Engineering
BAYINDIRLI, A., Food Engineering
BAYINDIRLI, L. A., Food Engineering
BAYKA, A. D., Mechanical Engineering
BAYKAL, A. D., Electrical and Electronic Engineering
BEŞIKÇI, C., Electrical and Electronic Engineering
BİLGEN, S., Electrical and Electronic Engineering
BİRAND, M. T., Electrical and Electronic Engineering
BİRLİK, G. A., Engineering Sciences
BOR, Ş., Metallurgical Engineering
BOZKURT, E., Geological Engineering
BOZOĞLU, F. T., Food Engineering
BOZŞAHIN, E. N. Ö., Industrial Engineering
BOZYİĞIT, M., Computer Engineering
BÖLÜKBAŞI, N., Mining Engineering
BÜYÜKDURA, O. M., Electrical and Electronic Engineering
ÇALIŞKAN, M., Mechanical Engineering
CANATAN, F., Electrical and Electronic Engineering
ÇELENLİGİL, M. C., Aeronautical Engineering
ÇİLİNGİR, F. C., Industrial Engineering
ÇOKÇA, E., Civil Engineering
ÇULFAZ, A., Chemical Engineering
DARENDELILER, H., Mechanical Engineering
DEMİRAL, B., Petroleum and Natural Gas Engineering
DEMİRBAŞ, K., Electrical and Electronic Engineering
DEMİREKLER, M., Electrical and Electronic Engineering
DİLEK, F. B., Environmental Engineering
DOĞAÇ, A., Computer Engineering
DOĞU, T., Chemical Engineering
DOYUM, A. B., Mechanical Engineering
DOYURAN, V., Geological Engineering
DURSUNKAYA, Z., Mechanical Engineering
ERALP, O. C., Mechanical Engineering
ERGİN, A., Civil Engineering
ERGÜL, R., Electrical and Electronic Engineering
ERGÜN, M. U., Civil Engineering
ERKİP, N., Industrial Engineering
ERKMEN, A., Electrical and Electronic Engineering
ERKMEN, İ., Electrical and Electronic Engineering
ERMIŞ, M., Electrical and Electronic Engineering
EROĞLU, İ., Chemical Engineering
EROL, A. O., Civil Engineering
ERSAK, A., Electrical and Electronic Engineering
ERTAN, B. H., Electrical and Electronic Engineering

ERTAŞ, A., Electrical and Electronic Engineering
ESİN, A., Food Engineering
EYÜBOĞLU, B. M., Electrical and Electronic Engineering
GEÇİT, M. R., Engineering Sciences
GENÇ, F. P., Computer Engineering
GENÇER, G. N., Electrical and Electronic Engineering
GEVECİ, A., Metallurgical Engineering
GÖĞÜŞ, M., Civil Engineering
GÖKÇAY, C. F., Environmental Engineering
GÖKLER, M. İ., Mechanical Engineering
GÖNCÜOĞLU, C., Geological Engineering
GÜLEÇ, N., Geological Engineering
GÜLKAN, P., Civil Engineering
GÜMRAH, F., Petroleum and Natural Gas Engineering
GÜNALP, T. N., Electrical and Electronic Engineering
GÜNDÜZ, G., Chemical Engineering
GÜRAN, H., Electrical and Electronic Engineering
GÜRBUZ, R., Metallurgical Engineering
GÜRKAN, T., Chemical Engineering
GÜRÜZ, G., Chemical Engineering
GÜVEN, A. N., Electrical and Electronic Engineering
GÜVEN, Ç., Industrial Engineering
GÜYAGÜLER, T., Mining Engineering
HALICI, U., Electrical and Electronic Engineering
HAMAMCI, H., Food Engineering
HIÇYILMAZ, C., Mining Engineering
HIZAL, A., Electrical and Electronic Engineering
HIZAL, M., Electrical and Electronic Engineering
HOŞTEN, Ç., Mining Engineering
İDER, S. K., Mechanical Engineering
İNAL, A., Civil Engineering
KAFTANOĞLU, B., Mechanical Engineering
KALKANLI, A., Metallurgical Engineering
KARAHANOĞLU, N., Geological Engineering
KARAKAYA, İ., Metallurgical Engineering
KARPUZ, C., Mining Engineering
KAYALIGIL, S., Industrial Engineering
KILIÇ, E. S., Mechanical Engineering
KINCAL, N. S., Chemical Engineering
KİPER, A., Computer Engineering
KIRCA, Ö., Industrial Engineering
KISAKÜREK, B., Chemical Engineering
KOCAOĞLAN, E., Electrical and Electronic Engineering
KOÇYİĞİT, A., Geological Engineering
KÖK, M. V., Petroleum and Natural Gas Engineering
KÖKSALAN, M., Industrial Engineering
KUZUOĞLU, M., Electrical and Electronic Engineering
LEBLEBİCİOĞLU, K., Electrical and Electronic Engineering
MEHMETOĞLU, T., Petroleum and Natural Gas Engineering
ÖGEL, B., Metallurgical Engineering
ÖGEL, Z. B. S., Food Engineering
OKANDAN, E., Petroleum and Natural Gas Engineering
ÖNAL, I., Chemical Engineering
ÖNDER, H., Civil Engineering
ORAL, S., Mechanical Engineering
ORÇAN, Y., Engineering Sciences
ÖSKAY, R., Mechanical Engineering
ÖZAY, N., Electrical and Electronic Engineering
ÖZBAYOĞLU, G., Mining Engineering
ÖZBELGE, Ö., Chemical Engineering
ÖZBELGE, T., Chemical Engineering
ÖZCEBE, G., Civil Engineering
ÖZENBAŞ, M., Metallurgical Engineering
ÖZGEN, C., Chemical Engineering
ÖZGÖREN, K., Mechanical Engineering
ÖZGÜVEN, N., Mechanical Engineering
ÖZHAN, E., Civil Engineering
ÖZKAN, M. Y., Civil Engineering
ÖZTÜRK, A., Metallurgical Engineering
ÖZTÜRK, T., Metallurgical Engineering
PARLAKTUNA, M., Petroleum and Natural Gas Engineering
PARNAS, L., Mechanical Engineering
PAYKOÇ, E., Mechanical Engineering
PLATİN, B. E., Mechanical Engineering
POLAT, F., Computer Engineering
SAATÇİOĞLU, Ö., Industrial Engineering
SAKA, M. P., Engineering Sciences
SARIOĞLU, F., Metallurgical Engineering
SAYAN, G. T., Electrical and Electronic Engineering
SELÇUK, E., Metallurgical Engineering
SELÇUK, N., Chemical Engineering
ŞENDİL, U., Civil Engineering
SEVAIOĞLU, O., Electrical and Electronic Engineering
SEVERCAN, M., Electrical and Electronic Engineering
SEVİNÇ, N., Metallurgical Engineering
SEVÜK, A. S., Civil Engineering
ŞORMAN, A. Ü., Civil Engineering
SÖYLEMEZ, E., Mechanical Engineering
SOYLU, R., Mechanical Engineering
SUCUOĞLU, H., Civil Engineering
SÜRÜCÜ, G., Environmental Engineering
TANIK, Y., Electrical and Electronic Engineering
TANKUT, A. T., Civil Engineering
TEKİN, E., Metallurgical Engineering
TİMUÇİN, M., Metallurgical Engineering
TOKDEMİR, T., Engineering Sciences
TOKER, C., Electrical and Electronic Engineering
TOKYAY, M., Civil Engineering
TOPKAYA, Y., Metallurgical Engineering
TOPRAK, G. M. V., Geological Engineering
TOSUN, İ., Chemical Engineering
TULUNAY, E., Electrical and Electronic Engineering
TULUNAY, Y., Aeronautical Engineering
TÜMER, T. S., Mechanical Engineering
TUNCEL, G., Environmental Engineering
TUNCER, İ. H., Aeronautical Engineering
TURHAN, D., Engineering Science
TÜRKMENOĞLU, A. G., Geological Engineering
ÜÇTUĞ, Y., Electrical and Electronic Engineering
ÜNAL, E., Mining Engineering
ÜNER, D., Chemical Engineering
UNGAN, S., Food Engineering
ÜNLÜ, K., Environmental Engineering
ÜNLUSOY, Y. S., Mechanical Engineering
ÜNVER, Z., Electrical and Electronic Engineering
UTKU, M., Civil Engineering
VURAL, F. T., Computer Engineering
VURAL, H., Mechanical Engineering
YALABIK, N., Computer Engineering
YAMAN, Y., Aeronautical Engineering
YANMAZ, M. A., Civil Engineering
YAZICI, A., Computer Engineering
YAZICIGİL, H., Geological Engineering
YEŞİN, A. O., Mechanical Engineering
YEŞİN, T., Mechanical Engineering
YETİŞ, U., Environmental Engineering
YILDIRIM, N., Electrical and Electronic Engineering
YILDIRIM, R. O., Mechanical Engineering
YILDIZ, F., Food Engineering
YILMAZ, Ç., Civil Engineering
YILMAZ, L., Chemical Engineering
YILMAZER, Ü., Chemical Engineering
YÜCEL, H., Chemical Engineering
YÜCEMEN, M. S., Civil Engineering
YÜKSEL, Y. Ö., Electrical and Electronic Engineering
YÜNCÜ, H., Mechanical Engineering

Graduate School of Marine Sciences (33731 Erdemli; tel. (324) 521-21-50; fax (324) 521-23-27; e-mail ilkay@imf.metu.edu.tr; internet www.ims.metu.edu.tr):

BİNGEL, F., Marine Sciences
KIDEYŞ, E. A., Marine Sciences
LATIF, M. A., Marine Sciences
OĞUZ, I. T., Marine Sciences
ÖZSOY, E., Marine Sciences
TUĞRUL, S., Marine Sciences
YILMAZ, A., Marine Sciences

OSMANGAZİ ÜNİVERSİTESİ

Meşelik Kampüsü, 26480 Eskişehir
Telephone: (222) 239-49-37
Fax: (222) 229-14-18
E-mail: ogubim@ogu.edu.tr
Internet: www.ogu.edu.tr

Founded 1970
State control
Languages of instruction: Turkish, English
Academic year: October to September

Chancellor: (vacant)
Vice-Chancellor: (vacant)
Rector: Prof. Dr NECAT A. AKGUN
Vice-Rectors: Prof. Dr MACIT YAMAN, Prof. Dr ATİLLA YILDIRIM
Registrar: ESAT ÇELİK

Library of 33,883 books, 7,521 periodicals
Number of teachers: 866
Number of students: 8,790 (7,930 undergraduate, 860 postgraduate)

Publications: *Journal of the Faculty of Engineering and Architecture* (2 a year), *Journal of the Faculty of Medicine* (2 a year)

DEANS

Faculty of Agriculture: Prof. Dr YAŞAR PANCAR
Faculty of Arts and Sciences: Prof. Dr YALÇIN ŞAHİN
Faculty of Economic and Administrative Sciences: Prof. Dr FAZIL TEKİN
Faculty of Education: Prof. Dr NACI EKEM
Faculty of Engineering and Architecture: Prof. Dr ERCENGİZ YILDIRIM
Faculty of Medicine: Prof. Dr EROL GÖKTÜRK
Faculty of Theology: Prof. Dr MEHMET MAKSUDOĞLU

PAMUKKALE ÜNİVERSİTESİ

Kinikli Campus, 20070 Denizli
Telephone: (258) 296-23-56
Fax: (258) 296-23-30
E-mail: internationaloffice@pau.edu.tr
Internet: pau.edu.tr/pau

State control
Languages of instruction: English, Turkish

Rector: Prof. Dr HUSEYIN BAGCI
Vice-Rector: Prof. Dr ALI KESKIN
Vice-Rector: Prof. Dr SEBAHATTIN NAS

Number of teachers: 698
Number of students: 31,581

DEANS

Faculty of Arts and Sciences: Prof. Dr HALIL CETISLI
Faculty of Economic and Administrative Sciences: Prof. Dr ALI İHSAN KARAALP
Faculty of Education: Prof. Dr SELAHITTIN OZCELIK
Faculty of Engineering: Prof. Dr MUZAFFER TOPCU
Faculty of Medicine: Prof. Dr MUSTAFA KILIC
Faculty of Technical Education: Prof. Dr RASIM KARABACAK

SABANCI ÜNİVERSİTESİ

Orhanli, 34956 Tuzla, Istanbul
Telephone: (216) 483-90-00
Fax: (216) 483-90-05
E-mail: db@sabanciuniv.edu
Internet: www.sabanciuniv.edu

Founded 1994
Private control

Languages of instruction: English, Turkish
Academic year: October to July

Rector: Prof. TOSUN TERZIOĞLU
Gen. Sec.: HALUK BAL
Librarian: HILMI ÇELIK

Library of 60,000 vols, 56 databases
Number of teachers: 410
Number of students: 2,010

DEANS

Faculty of Arts and Social Sciences: Prof. AHMET ALKAN
Faculty of Engineering and Natural Sciences: Prof. KEMAL İNAN
Graduate School of Management: Prof. NAKIYE AVDAN BOYACIGILLER

SAKARYA ÜNIVERSITESI

Esentepe Kampüsü, 54187 Sakarya
Telephone: (264) 295-54-54
Fax: (264) 295-50-36
E-mail: basin@sakarya.edu.tr
Internet: www.sakarya.edu.tr

Founded 1992
State control
Languages of instruction: Turkish, English
Academic year: September to June

Rector: Prof. Dr MEHMET DURMAN
Vice-Rectors: Prof. Dr MUZAFFER ELMAS, Prof. Dr H. RIZA GÜVEN, Prof. Dr H. BINNAZ BAYTEKIN
Sec.-Gen.: Dr ZAFER DEMIR
Dir of Library: MUSTAFA ESMELI

Library of 100,008 vols
Number of teachers: 1,241
Number of students: 45,576

Publications: *Adapazarı Meslek Yüksekokulu Dergisi Akademik İncelemeler, Saü Bulletin, TOJET: The Turkish Online Journal of Educational Technology*

DEANS

Faculty of Arts and Humanities: Prof. Dr MURAT TUTUNCU
Faculty of Economic and Administrative Sciences: Prof. Dr ENGIN YILDIRIM
Faculty of Education: Prof. VAHDETTIN SEVINÇ
Faculty of Engineering: Prof. Dr MEHMET ALI YALÇIN
Faculty of Fine Arts: Prof. Dr NILGÜN BILGE
Faculty of Technical Education: Prof. Dr HÜSEYIN EKIZ
Faculty of Theology: Prof. Dr ALI ERBAŞI
School of Health Sciences: Prof. Dr SEVIN ALTINKAYNAK
School of Physical Education and Sports: Asst. Prof. Dr ERTUĞRUL GELEN

SELÇUK ÜNIVERSITESI

Vali Izzet Bey Cad., Karatay Müzesi Karşisi, 42151 Konya
Telephone: (332) 350-70-05
Fax: (332) 352-09-98
E-mail: mesaj@selcuk.edu.tr
Internet: www.selcuk.edu.tr

Founded 1975
State control
Language of instruction: Turkish
Academic year: October to May

Rector: Prof. Dr SÜLEYMAN OKUDAN
Vice-Rectors: Prof. Dr DINÇER BEDÜK, Prof. Dr ŞEFIK BILIR, Prof. Dr KÜRŞAT TURGUT
Librarian: Dr CENGIZI KORKMAZ

Number of teachers: 3,264
Number of students: 75,000

Publications: *Journal of Faculty of Engineering and Architecture* (2 a year), *Journal of the Faculty of Medicine* (4 a year), *Journal of Veterinary Science* (4 a year)

DEANS

Faculty of Agriculture: Prof. Dr MUSTAFA ONDER
Faculty of Communication: Prof. Dr HALUK HADI SUMER
Faculty of Dentistry: Prof. Dr TAMER ATAOGLU
Faculty of Economics and Administrative Sciences: Prof. Dr SERIF SIMSEK
Faculty of Economics and Administrative Sciences (Konya): Prof. Dr ORHAN GÖKÇE
Faculty of Education: Prof. Dr MUSA GURSEL
Faculty of Engineering and Architecture: Prof. Dr CEVAT INAL
Faculty of Fine Arts: Prof. Dr FEVZI GUNUC
Faculty of Law: Prof. Dr MEHMET AYAN
Faculty of Literature: Prof. Dr AHMET TIRPAN
Faculty of Medicine (Meram): Prof. Dr AHMET OZKAGNICI
Faculty of Medicine (Selcuklu): Prof. Dr KAGAN KARABULUT
Faculty of Science: Prof. Dr İSMET UCAN
Faculty of Technical Education: Prof. Dr ALI UNUVAR
Faculty of Theology: Prof. Dr AHMET ONKAL
Faculty of Veterinary Sciences: Prof. Dr ZAFER DURGUN
Faculty of Vocational Education: Prof. Dr KADIRCAN OZKAN

SÜLEYMAN DEMIREL ÜNIVERSITESI

Merkez Kampüs, Çünür, 32260 Isparta
Telephone: (246) 211-10-00
Fax: (246) 237-04-31
E-mail: ozelkalem@sdu.edu.tr
Internet: www.sdu.edu.tr

Founded 1992
State control
Academic year: September to July

Rector: Prof. Dr METIN LÜTFI BAYDAR
Vice-Rector: Prof. Dr VECIHI KIRDEMIR
Vice-Rector: Prof. Dr MEHMET KITIŞ
Vice-Rector: Prof. Dr M. ALI DULUPÇU
Gen. Sec.: AZIZ BAYRAK
Librarian: UĞUR BULGAN

Library of 178,000 vols, 40,000 periodicals
Number of teachers: 3,000
Number of students: 50,000

Publications: *Cell Membranes and Free Radical Research* (in English, 1 a year), *European Journal of Mineral Processing and Environmental Protection* (3 a year), *International Journal of Technological Sciences* (in Turkish, 2 a year), *Journal of Engineering Science of Design* (in Turkish, 2 a year), *Journal of Natural and Applied Sciences* (in Turkish, 1 a year), *Journal of SDU Faculty of Dentistry* (in Turkish, 2 a year), *Journal of Sleep Health* (in Turkish, 2 a year), *Journal of the Faculty of Administrative Sciences and Education* (in Turkish, 2 a year), *Journal of the Faculty of Agriculture* (in Turkish, 2 a year), *Journal of the Faculty of Forestry* (in Turkish, 2 a year), *Medical Journal* (in Turkish, 4 a year), *Medical Journal of Suleyman Demirel University* (in Turkish, 4 a year), *SDÜ Art-e* (in Turkish, 2 a year), *SDÜ Eğirdir Su Ürünleri Fakültesi Dergisi* (in Turkish, 1 a year), *SDÜ Egzersiz Dergisi* (in Turkish, 1 a year), *SDÜ Fen Bilimleri Enstitüsü Dergisi* (in Turkish, 3 a year), *SDU Journal of Science* (in Turkish, 2 a year), *SDÜ Sağlık Bilimleri Enstitüsü Dergisi* (in Turkish, 2 a year), *SDÜ Teknik Bilimler Dergisi* (in Turkish, 2 a year), *SDÜ Türk Sanatları Araştırmaları Dergisi* (in Turkish, 2 a year), *SDÜ Vizyoner Dergisi* (in Turkish, 2 a year), *SDÜ Yaşam Dergisi* (in Turkish, 2 a year), *SDÜ Yekarum Dergisi* (in Turkish, 2 a year), *Suleyman Demirel University Journal of Faculty of Economics & Administrative Sciences* (in Turkish, 3 a year)

DEANS

Faculty of Agriculture: Prof. Dr İBRAHIM ERDAL
Faculty of Arts and Sciences: Prof. Dr YUSUF AYVAZ
Faculty of Dentistry: Prof. Dr FATMA YEŞIM KIRZIOĞLU
Faculty of Economic and Admin. Sciences: Prof. Dr HASAN İBICIOĞLU
Faculty of Education: Prof. Dr SONGÜL SALLAN GÜL
Faculty of Engineering and Architecture: Prof. Dr SIDDIKA NILAY KESKIN
Faculty of Fine Arts: Prof. Dr KUBILAY AKTULUM
Faculty of Fisheries: Prof. Dr ÖZNUR DİLER
Faculty of Forestry: Prof. Dr MUSA GENÇ
Faculty of Health: Prof. Dr SÜLEYMAN KUTLUHAN
Faculty of Law: Prof. Dr FARUK TURHAN
Faculty of Medicine: Prof. Dr HÜSEYIN YORGANCIGIL
Faculty of Technical Education: Prof. Dr MÜMIN FILIZ
Faculty of Technology: Prof. Dr OSMAN İPEK
Faculty of Theology: Prof. Dr KEMAL SÖZEN
Graduate School of Fine Arts: Doç. Dr ALI MUHAMMET BAYRAKTAROĞLU
Graduate School of Health Sciences: Prof. Dr SERPIL DEMIRCI
Graduate School of Natural and Applied Sciences: Prof. Dr MUSTAFA KUŞÇU
Graduate School of Social Sciences: Prof. Dr İLKER HÜSEYIN ÇARIKÇI
Graduate School of Water: Prof. Dr ATA UTKU AKÇIL

TRAKYA ÜNİVERSİTESİ

22050 Karaağaç, Edirne
Telephone: (284) 223-40-04
Fax: (284) 223-42-03
E-mail: rectorsoffice@trakya.edu.tr
Internet: www.trakya.edu.tr

Founded 1982 from existing faculties in Edirne
Academic year: October to June

Rector: Prof. Dr ENVER DURAN
Vice-Rectors: Prof. Dr BEYHAN KARAMANLIOGLU, Prof. Dr TIMUR KIRGIZ, Prof. Dr ALI KEMAL KUTLU
Librarian: ENDER BİLAR

Number of teachers: 1,238
Number of students: 20,265

Publications: *Journal of the Faculty of Agriculture* (2 a year), *Journal of the Faculty of Medicine* (4 a year), *Medical Journal Of Trakya University* (3 a year), *Trakya University Journal of Scientific Research* (2 a year)

DEANS

Faculty of Arts and Sciences: Prof. Dr BÜNYAMIN ÖZGÜLTEKİN
Faculty of Economics and Administrative Sciences: Prof. Dr DERMAN KÜÇÜKALTAN
Faculty of Education: Prof. Dr HILMI IBAR
Faculty of Engineering and Architecture: Prof. Dr AHMET CAN
Faculty of Health Sciences: Prof. Dr FERDA ÖZDEMİR
Faculty of Medicine: Prof. Dr MURAT DİKMENGİL
Faculty of Science and Letters: Prof. Dr ŞEVKET EROL OKAN

UFUK ÜNİVERSİTESİ

Mevlana Bulvarı (Konya Yolu) 86-88, 06520 Balgat, Ankara
Telephone: (312) 284-77-77

Fax: (312) 287-23-90
E-mail: ufukuni@ufuk.edu.tr
Internet: www.ufuk.edu.tr

Founded 1972; present name and status 1999

Rector: Prof. Dr A. ERGÜN ERTUĞ
Gen. Sec.: İSMET ATIK

Number of teachers: 23
Number of students: 66

Faculties of arts and science, economics and administration, education, law and medicine.

ULUDAĞ ÜNİVERSİTESİ

Görükle Kampüsü, Rektörlük Uluslararası İlişkiler Ofisi, 16059 Bursa
Telephone: (224) 442-80-06
Fax: (224) 442-90-44
E-mail: intoffice@uludag.edu.tr
Internet: www.uludag.edu.tr

Founded 1975 as Bursa Üniversitesi; present name and structure 1982
State control
Language of instruction: Turkish
Academic year: September to June

Rector: Prof. Dr MUSTAFA YURTKURAN
Vice-Rectors: Prof. Dr ERDAL EMEL, Prof. Dr MEHMET GENÇ, Prof. Dr ALI KARABULUT
Sec.-Gen.: İSMET TOPUZ
Head of Libraries and Documentation Centre: NEŞE ARAT

Library of 67,493 vols
Number of teachers: 2,102
Number of students: 41,057

Publications: *Agriculture* (1 a year), *Education* (1 a year), *Engineering* (1 a year), *Medicine* (1 a year), *Science and Literature* (1 a year), *Theology* (1 a year), *Veterinary Science* (1 a year)

DEANS

Faculty of Agriculture: Prof. Dr VAHAP KATKAT
Faculty of Economics and Administrative Sciences: Prof. Dr HALIS ERTÜRK
Faculty of Education: Prof. Dr MUSTAFA CEMILOĞLU
Faculty of Engineering and Architecture: Prof. Dr SEDAT ÜLKÜ
Faculty of Medicine: Prof. Dr MÜFIT PARLAK
Faculty of Science and Letters: Prof. Dr MUSTAFA BAYRAKTAR
Faculty of Theology: Prof. Dr HÜSEYIN ALGÜL
Faculty of Veterinary Medicine: Prof. Dr HASAN BATMAZ

YAŞAR ÜNİVERSİTESİ

Şehitler Cad. 1522, Sok 6, 35230 Alsancak, Izmir
Telephone: (232) 463-33-44
Fax: (232) 463-07-80
E-mail: info@yasar.edu.tr
Internet: www.yasar.edu.tr

Founded 1998; present status 2001

Rector: Prof. Dr NECATI SEN
Gen. Sec.: DIDEM ÖKTEM

DEANS

Faculty of Business Economics and Administration: Prof. Dr CENGIZ PINAR
Faculty of Communications: Prof. Dr CENGIZ PINAR (Deputy)
Faculty of Engineering and Architecture: Prof. Dr DEMIR ASLAN
Faculty of Law: Prof. Dr DEMIR ASLAN (Deputy)
Faculty of Science and Letters: Prof. Dr COŞKUN IŞÇI

DIRECTORS

School of Foreign Languages: Asst Prof. Dr SENA TULPAR
Vocational School: Prof. Dr HASAN HÜSNÜ ÇATALCA

YEDİTEPE ÜNİVERSİTESİ

26 Agustos Yerlesimi, Kayışdağı Caddesi, 34755 Ataşehir, Istanbul
Telephone: (216) 578-00-00
Fax: (216) 578-02-44
E-mail: halklailiskiler@yeditepe.edu.tr
Internet: www.yeditepe.edu.tr

Founded 1996
Private control

Rector: Prof. Dr NURCAN BAÇ
Vice-Rector: Prof. Dr MELIH BORAL
Vice-Rector: Prof. Dr NEDRET KURAN BURÇOĞLU
Sec.-Gen.: LEYLA YEŞİLADA (acting)
Number of students: 17,380

DEANS

Faculty of Architecture and Engineering: Prof. Dr İBRAHIM FAHIR BORAK
Faculty of Arts and Sciences: Prof. Dr AHMET İNCE
Faculty of Commercial Sciences: Prof. Dr ÖMER GÖKAY
Faculty of Communication: Prof. Dr SUAT ANAR
Faculty of Dentistry: Prof. Dr TURKER SANDALLI
Faculty of Economics and Administrative Sciences: Prof. Dr KADIR AYKUT TOP
Faculty of Education: AYŞE SEMRA AKYEL
Faculty of Fine Arts: Prof. Dr BIKE KOCAOĞLU
Faculty of Law: Prof. Dr HALUK KABAALIOĞLU
Faculty of Medicine: Prof. Dr AYÇA VİTRİNEL
Faculty of Pharmacy: Prof. Dr DILEK EROL

YILDIZ TEKNİK ÜNİVERSİTESİ

80750 Beşiktaş, Istanbul
Telephone: (212) 259-70-70
Fax: (212) 261-42-84
E-mail: uerden@yildiz.edu.tr
Internet: www.yildiz.edu.tr

Founded 1911; reorganized 1982 (fmrly State Acad. of Engineering and Architecture)
Academic year: October to July

Rector: Prof. Dr DURUL ÖREN
Vice-Rector for Admin.: Prof. Dr SALIH DURER
Vice-Rector for Education: Prof. Dr ZEKERIYA POLAT
Vice-Rector for Research and Planning: Prof. Dr GÖRÜN ARUN
Sec.-Gen.: ÜMIT ERDEN

Number of teachers: 1,111
Number of students: 17,000

Publication: *Periodical* (4 a year)

DEANS

Faculty of Architecture: Prof. Dr EMRE AYSU
Faculty of Art and Design: Prof. Dr TOMUR ATAGÖK
Faculty of Arts and Sciences: Prof. Dr DURUL OREN
Faculty of Chemical and Metallurgical Engineering: Prof. Dr SABRIYE PIŞKIN
Faculty of Civil Engineering: Prof. Dr YALÇIN YÜKSEL
Faculty of Economic and Administrative Sciences: Prof. Dr AYKUT POLATOĞLU
Faculty of Electrical and Electronic Engineering: Prof. Dr GALIP CANSEVER
Faculty of Mechanical Engineering: Prof. Dr HASAN HEPERKAN

ATTACHED COLLEGES

School of Foreign Languages: Dir Prof. Dr NÜKET ÖCAL.

School of Vocational Studies: Dir Assoc. Prof. Dr MUSTAFA SUNU.

YÜZÜNCÜ YIL ÜNİVERSİTESİ
(Centennial University)

65080 Van
Telephone: (432) 225-10-10
Fax: (432) 225-10-09
Internet: www.yyu.edu.tr

Founded 1982
State control
Language of instruction: Turkish
Academic year: October to July

Rector: Prof. Dr YÜCEL AŞKIN
Vice-Rectors: Prof. Dr HASAN CEYLAN, Prof. Dr ALI FUAT DOĞU, Prof. Dr AYŞE YÜKSEL
Gen. Sec.: Dr IŞIK TEPE
Librarian: (vacant)

Library of 31,000 vols
Number of teachers: 300
Number of students: 6,100

Publications: *Artos* (Universities and Colleges in Literature, 1 a year), *Eastern Journal of Physical Medicine and Rehabilitation* (12 a year), *Journal of Agricultural Sciences* (1 a year), *Journal of the Faculty of Arts and Sciences (Sciences)* (irregular), *Journal of the Faculty of Education (Sciences)* (12 a year), *Journal of the Faculty of Education (Social Sciences)* (12 a year), *Journal of the Faculty of Theology* (12 a year), *Journal of the Faculty of Veterinary Science* (12 a year), *Journal of the Graduate School of Sciences* (irregular), *Journal of Health Sciences* (12 a year), *Journal of the Institute of Social Sciences* (irregular), *Rahva* (education, 12 a year), *University Bulletin* (12 a year), *Van Medical Journal* (12 a year), *Yeldegirmeni* (Arts, 12 a year)

DEANS

Faculty of Agriculture: Prof. Dr FIRAT CENGİZ
Faculty of Arts and Sciences: Prof. Dr ERKSIN GÜLEÇ
Faculty of Economic and Administrative Sciences: Prof. Dr BÜLENT KARAKAŞ
Faculty of Education: Prof. Dr RAUF YILDIZ
Faculty of Education (Hakkari): Prof. Dr RECAI KARAHAN
Faculty of Engineering: Prof. Dr A. ÜMIT TOLLUOĞLU
Faculty of Fine Arts: Prof. Dr ZUHRE ŞENTÜRK
Faculty of Medicine: Prof. Dr MANSUR KAMACI
Faculty of Theology: Prof. Dr SELAHATTIN KIYICI
Faculty of Veterinary Science: Prof. Dr NIHAT MERT

PROFESSORS

Faculty of Agriculture:
AKYUZ, N.
ASKİN, Y.
COKSOYLER, N.
ŞEN, S. M.
YASAR, B.

Faculty of Arts and Science:
AMİRALİ, G.
CEYLAN, H.
KARAKAS, B.
ONLER, Z.
OZTURK, A.
RASİMGIL, R.
TİLEKLİOĞLU, B.
ULUCAM, A.
YİLMAZ, A.

Faculty of Education:
SAVAS, E.
TOZLU, N.

Faculty of Engineering:
ORCEN, S.
TOLLUOĞLU, A. U.

Faculty of Medicine:
AKSOY, H.

Atay, G.
Burdurlu, Y.
Ceylan, A.
Dalkilic, A. E.
Demirors, A. P.
Goksoy, T.
Kamaci, M.
Odabas, D.
Turan, F.
Yakut, C.
Yetkin, Y.
Yuksel, A.

Faculty of Veterinary Science:

Agaoğlu, Z. T.
Bolat, D.
Boynukara, B.
Karadag, H.
Mert, N.

ZONGULDAK KARAELMAS ÜNİVERSİTESİ

67100 Zonguldak
Telephone: (372) 257-41-30
Fax: (372) 257-21-40
Internet: www.karaelmas.edu.tr
Founded 1992
State control
Academic year: September to July
Rector: Prof. Dr Bektaş Açikgöz
Vice-Rectors: Prof. Dr Turgay Atalay, Prof. Dr H. Yilmaz Kaptan, Prof. Dr Yadigar Müftüoğlu
Chief Librarian: Fatma Ceylan
Library of 35,000 vols, 12,000 periodicals
Number of teachers: 1,194
Number of students: 10,194 full-time, 2,143 evening
Publications: *Journal of the Faculty of Engineering* (4 a year), *Journal of the Faculty of Forestry* (2 a year)

DEANS

Faculty of Arts and Science (Devrek): Prof. Dr Türkan Kopaç
Faculty of Economics and Administration (Çaycuma): Prof. Dr Güven Murat
Faculty of Education (Ereğli): Prof. Dr Baki Hazer
Faculty of Engineering: Prof. Dr H. Yilmaz Kaptan
Faculty of Forestry (Bartın): Prof. Dr Hüdaverdi Eroğlu
Faculty of Medicine: Prof. Dr Gamze Moçan Kuzey
Faculty of Technical Education (Karabük): Prof. Dr Etem Sait Öz

DIRECTORS

Graduate School of Health Sciences: Prof. Dr Z. Nur Banoğlu
Graduate School of Natural and Applied Sciences: Prof. Dr Etem Kişioğlu
Graduate School of Social Sciences: Prof. Dr Turhan Korkmaz

TURKMENISTAN

The Higher Education System

Institutions of higher education pre-date the independence of Turkmenistan (formerly Turkmen SSR) from the USSR in 1991, with the oldest being the Turkmen State Medical Institute, which was founded in 1931. Following independence, a policy of bilim (education) was initiated, aimed at distancing Turkmenistan from its Soviet (and hence, Russian) past; a key element in this policy was the reformation of the Turkmen language, primarily through the substitution of the Latin for the Cyrillic alphabet. Free education at Turkmenistan's universities was reported to have been abolished in 2003, while it was reported that the number of places for students in educational establishments had been sharply reduced since the mid-1990s. In 2004 a presidential decree invalidating all higher-education degrees received abroad came into effect; all teachers with such degrees were to be dismissed. Some 13,800 students were enrolled at the country's 18 institutions of higher education in 2007/08. In 2007 the new President extended the period of higher education from two to five years (effective from the beginning of the 2007/08 school year) and announced that the Turkmenistan Academy of Sciences, which had been closed in 1993, was to reopen.

The main requirements for admission to higher education are the Secondary School Leaving Certificate and results in competitive entrance examinations. The main undergraduate qualifications are the Soviet-style Specialist Diploma, which lasts five years, and the Bachelors (Bakalavr), which lasts four years. There is no postgraduate education in Turkmenistan.

Post-secondary technical and vocational education consists of short-term courses of up to one-and-a-half years open to students who have completed nine years of secondary education. Qualifications studied for include Certificates and Diplomas.

Regulatory Bodies

GOVERNMENT

Ministry of Culture, Television and Radio Broadcasting: 744000 Ashgabat, ul. Pushkin 14; tel. (12) 35-41-05; fax (12) 35-35-60; Minister GULMURAT MURADOV.

Ministry of Education: 744000 Ashgabat, ul. Gurungan 2; tel. (12) 35-58-03; fax (12) 39-88-11; Minister GULSAT MAMMEDOWA.

Learned Societies

GENERAL

Academy of Sciences of Turkmenistan: 744000 Ashgabat, ul. Gogolia 15; tel. (12) 25-44-74; fax (12) 25-53-67; internet science.gov.tm; f. 1951; Pres. GURBANMYRAT MEZILOV; Deputy Pres. P. KOUWANDYK.

Research Institutes

GENERAL

National Institute of Deserts, Flora and Fauna: 744000 Ashgabat, Bitarap Turkmenistan 15; tel. (12) 39-54-27; fax (12) 35-37-16; e-mail desert@online.tm; internet science.gov.tm/en/organisations/desert_institute; f. 1962; attached to Min. of Nature Protection; fundamental and applied research on problems of biology, ecology, human environment; rational use of nature with regard to functional peculiarities of arid ecosystem; Dir Prof. AGADJAN G. BABAEV (acting); publ. *Problems of Desert Development* (4 a year).

AGRICULTURE, FISHERIES AND VETERINARY SCIENCE

Gara-Kala Experimental Station for Plant Genetic Resources: Balkan Province, Gara-Kala; tel. (48) 3-17-99; f. 1900; Dir ASHIRMUKHAMET SAPARMURADOV.

Research Institute of Cotton Growing of the MAWR: 746423 Maryiskiy velayat, Eloten Region, Institutskiy v.; tel. (560) 2-26-02; Dir Prof. SEITBARDY KURBANGELDIEV; Deputy Dir Dr AKMUKHAMMET CHAPAU.

Research Institute of Livestock and Veterinary Science: 744012 Ashgabat, ul. Gerogly 70; tel. (12) 34-82-97; fax (12) 34-97-98; Chair. NURMURAT ATAEV.

Scientific Research Institute of Farming: 744000 Ashgabat, ul. Ostrovskiy 30; tel. (12) 34-74-35; fax (12) 35-74-12; f. 1900; attached to Ministry of Agriculture; Dir ORAZ SOUNOV.

Scientific Research Institute of Grain Crops: 744205 Akhal, Esnev Village, ul. O. Jumaev 1; tel. (13) 73-64-76; f. 1900; Head KHUDAYBERDI KADJIEV.

Turkmen Research Institute of Grain: 744012 Ashgabat, ul. Ostrovskiy 1; tel. (12) 34-74-35; fax (12) 34-74-72; Dir Dr AKMUKHAMMED DURDIEV.

ECONOMICS, LAW AND POLITICS

Institute of Economics: 744032 Ashgabat, Bikrova Sad Keshi 28; tel. (12) 24-02-52; Dir G. M. MURADOV.

Institute of Philosophy and Law: 744000 Ashgabat, ul. Gogolia 15; tel. (12) 25-41-69; Dir O. MUSAYEV.

HISTORY, GEOGRAPHY AND ARCHAEOLOGY

Institute of History: 744000 Ashgabat, ul. Azady 2011; tel. (12) 35-31-38; fax (12) 39-86-87; e-mail history@online.tm; f. 2009; attached to Acad. of Sciences of Turkmenistan; research on the history of Turkmenistan and the Turkmen people from prehistory to present; Dir GULSHAT ORAZMUHAMMEDOWA.

Southern Turkmen Multidisciplinary Archaeological Expedition: 744000 Ashgabat, ul. Gogolia 15; tel. (12) 25-15-25; Man. KAKAMURAD KURBANSAKHATOV.

LANGUAGE AND LITERATURE

Bailyev Institute of Linguistics: 744000 Ashgabat, ul. Gogolia 15; tel. (12) 25-27-73; Dir M. SOYEGOV.

Magtymguly Institute of Literature: 744000 Ashgabat, ul. Bitarap 15; tel. (12) 35-35-09; e-mail diledeninstitut@rambler.ru; Dir GYZYLGUL HAKBERDYEVNA KYYASOVA.

MEDICINE

Scientific Clinical Centre of Cardiology: 744006 Ashgabat, ul. Gerogly 31; tel. (12) 39-04-90; fax (12) 33-01-07; e-mail kykmh@mail.ru; attached to Ministry of Health and Medical Industry.

Scientific Clinical Center of Eye Diseases: 744000 Ashgabat, ul. 1973 32; tel. and fax (12) 35-48-70; f. 1932; Dir A. SHAMURAT.

Turkmen Research Institute of Preventive and Clinical Medicine: 744006 Ashgabat, ul. 2009 31; tel. (12) 29-01-88; fax (12) 24-11-93; f. 1989; Dir Dr NINA KERIMI.

Turkmenistan Scientific-Clinical Centre of Oncology: 744020 Ashgabat, ul. Gorogly 53; tel. (12) 34-48-03; fax (12) 34-50-19; improves the methods of medical treatment of cancer in Turkmenistan.

NATURAL SCIENCES

Biological Sciences

Institute of Botany: 744000 Ashgabat, ul. 2033 79; tel. (12) 25-37-58; Dir NURJAMAL ORAZOVNA ORAZMUHAMMEDOVA.

Institute of Physiology: 744011 Ashgabat, ul. 2053 30; tel. (12) 24-74-18; f. 1959; Dir K. AMMANEPESOV.

Institute of Zoology: 744000 Ashgabat, ul. Engelsa 6; tel. (12) 25-37-91; Dir T. TOGKAYEV.

Physical Sciences

Institute of Chemistry: 744012 Ashgabat, ul. Esgerler 92; tel. (12) 34-05-08; fax (12) 34-41-71; e-mail chem@online.tm; f. 1957; Dir GELDYEV OTUZBAY ANNABAEVICH.

Institute of Oil and Gas: Ashgabat, ul. Tehran 6; tel. and fax (12) 39-18-46; f. 1970 as Institute 'Turkmen Gas Technology', present name 1993; Dir Dr KHOSHGELDY BABAEV.

Research Institute of Geology: 744000 Ashgabat, Magtymguly Ave 81; tel. (12) 39-17-65; fax (12) 35-52-33; f. 1998; Dir ODEK A. ODEKOV.

Research Institute of Seismology: 744000 Ashgabat, ul. Acad T. Berdyev 20; tel. (12) 39-06-92; fax (12) 39-06-13; e-mail gaip@icctm.org; f. 1998; attached to Min. of Construction; Dir MYRAT MERETLIEVICH CHARYEV; publ. *Seismological Report* (2 a year).

Turkmensuvylymtaslama Institute: 744000 Ashgabat, ul. Beki Seytakov 1; tel. and fax (12) 35-18-35; e-mail tgvh@online.tm; water economy of Turkmenistan; Dir Dr MOSES SARKISOV; Deputy Dir USMAN SAPAROV.

TECHNOLOGY

Biotechnology Scientific Technological Centre: 744000, Ashgabat, ul. Bitarap 15; tel. and fax (3632) 35-14-39; attached to Acad. of Sciences; Head Dr TACHDURDY GEDEMOV.

Institute of Mathematics and Mechanics: 744000 Ashgabat, ul. Gogolia 15; tel. (12) 29-87-13; Dir M. B. ORAZOV.

Physical Engineering Institute: 744000 Ashgabat, ul. Gogolia 15; tel. (12) 25-42-85; Dir A. BERKELIYEV.

Libraries and Archives

Ashgabat

Central Scientific Library: 744007 Ashgabat, ul. 2002 15A; tel. (12) 35-65-71; internet library.science.gov.tm; f. 1941, present status 1957; attached to High Ccl for Science and Technology; colln of rare and valuable edns of valuable stock CSL Turkmen books with various graphics (Arabic, Latin, Cyrillic) for the period up to 1917 and subsequent years; publishes scientific support bibliographical aids; received books on all brs of science from the Central Reservoir libraries of Russia (Moscow); 2,130,000 vols; Dir A. B. YAZBERDIYEV.

Magtymguly Turkmen State University Library: 744005 Ashgabat, Sapamurat Turkmenbashi shayely 31; tel. (12) 5-39-22; f. 1950 within the Institute of Pedagogy; provides scientific information; participates in educational process; promotes culture; 542,000 vols; Dir. A. T. VOROBEVA.

National Library of Turkmenistan: 744000 Ashgabat, pl. 2001, Berzengi, National Cultural Centre; tel. (12) 35-74-89; fax (12) 25-38-43; f. 1895; 5,500,000 vols; Dir OGULGOZEL MUHAMMETGULYEVA.

Museums and Art Galleries

Ashgabat

Carpet Museum: 744000 Ashgabat, ul. Gorogly 5; f. 1994; colln of more than 8,000 Turkmen carpets from 17th to 20th century; museum workshop shows the weaving of carpets; Dir TUVAKBIBI K. DURDYEVA.

Central Botanical Garden: 744012 Ashgabat, ul. Timiryazeva 17; tel. (12) 24-18-57; f. 1929; spec. collns of native flora, tropical and subtropical plants, Crataegus, Astragalus, Lonicera, Cotoneaster, Quercus, Juniperus, Pinus, Rosa, Allium; Dir Dr B. B. KERBABAEV.

National Museum of Turkmenistan: 744000 Ashgabat, ul. Novofiruzinskoye 30; tel. (12) 51-90-20; fax (12) 51-90-22; e-mail vip@online.tm; f. 1998 by merger of Nat. Museum of History and Ethnography of Turkmenistan, State Museum of History of Turkmenistan and Turkmen State Museum of Fine Art; over 166,000 unique exhibits depicting history, ethnography, fine art; library of 8,830 vols; Dir OVEZMUHAMED MAMETNUROV.

Universities

INTERNATIONAL TURKMEN-TURKISH UNIVERSITY

744012 Ashgabat, ul. Gyorogly 84
Telephone: (12) 34-85-38
Fax: (12) 51-08-09
E-mail: ikez@mail.ru
Internet: www.ittu.edu.tm

Founded 1994

Rector: YUSUF ERDOGAN
Vice-Chancellor: ZEKI PEKTAŞ

Faculties of economics, education, engineering.

MAGTYMGULY TURKMEN STATE UNIVERSITY

744014 Ashgabat, Saparmurat Turkembashi shayely 31
Telephone: (12) 39-89-97
Fax: (12) 35-11-59
E-mail: math3@online.tm

Founded 1931 as Ashgabat Pedagogical Institute, present status and name 1950
State control

Rector: Prof. KALAYEV REDJEPMURAD CHARYEVICH
Pro-Rector: Prof. ATDAYEV SAPARGELDY ATDAYEVICH

Number of teachers: 544
Number of students: 11,000

Faculties of biology, chemistry, foreign languages, geography, history, humanities and social sciences, law and int. relations, management and int. trade, mathematics and applied maths, physics, Russian philology, theology, Turkmen philology.

TURKMEN AGRICULTURAL UNIVERSITY

744012 Ashgabat, ul. 2009 62
Telephone: (12) 34-26-52
Fax: (12) 34-68-80

Founded 1930
State control

Rector: A. MAMEDOV

Library of 136,000 vols
Number of teachers: 216
Number of students: 2,000

Depts of accounting, agrochemistry, animal husbandry, fruit and vegetable growing, mechanization, veterinary science, viticulture.

Other Higher Educational Institutes

D. Azadi Turkmen National Institute of World Languages: 744011 Ashgabat, ul. Ostrovskogo 47; tel. (12) 34-54-24; fax (12) 34-39-88; European languages: English, French, German, Russian language and literature; Eastern languages: Arabic, Persian, Turkish, Turkmen language and literature; Rector NEPESOVA ROZA; Vice-Rector TAGANDURDYEV TAGANDURDY.

State Academy of Arts: 744012 Ashgabat, ul. Salavat Yulaeva 1; tel. (12) 34-61-07; fax (12) 34-66-65; painting (graphic solution of cinema, machine drawing, theatrical-decorative); graphics; sculpture; architecture; design; national art (carpets, ceramics, jewellery); art criticism; Rector BEGMYRADOV GULNAZAR; Vice-Rector TADJYMOVA JEREN.

Turkmen Institute of National Economy: 744027 Ashgabat, Atamurad Nyyazov shayely 46; tel. (12) 41-90-36; fax (12) 46-98-05; faculties of accounting, economic planning, trade economics; Rector MAKHAMMETGELDI ANNAAMANOV.

Turkmen National Conservatory: 744000 Ashgabat, ul. Pushkina 22; tel. (12) 35-32-55; musicology; composition; orchestral string instruments; history, theory of Turkmen music; chorus conducting; solo singing; national instruments; wind and percussion instruments; Turkmen music; piano; musical teaching; Rector BOZAGAN H. AMANOV; Vice Rector KHUDAYGULYEV BAYRAMDURDY.

Turkmen National Institute of Sport and Tourism: 744001 Ashgabat, Atamyrad Nyyazov Shayely15A; tel. (12) 36-25-40; fax (12) 36-24-56; Rector B. ANNAORAZOV.

Turkmen Polytechnic Institute: 744025 Ashgabat, ul. 1916 62; tel. (12) 47-67-01; fax (12) 47-67-02; faculties of construction, oil and gas, chemical technology, energy, economics, computer technology and sanitation technology; managing of production; Rector YAZ MOVLAMOV.

Turkmen S. Seydi State Pedagogical Institute: 746100 Türkmenabat, ul. Shabende 7; tel. (42) 26-21-30; fax (42) 26-20-31; languages, teacher training; Chancellor G. MEZILOV.

Turkmen State Institute of Culture: 744000 Ashgabat, Magtymguly Shayely 4; tel. (12) 47-39-44; fax (12) 47-43-11; e-mail miras@cpart.org; theatrical art, production; archives; Rector CHOPANOV YAZMURAT; Vice-Rector GOSHAYEV DADEBAY.

Turkmen State Institute of Energy: 745400 Mary, ul. Bayramali 62; tel. and fax (52) 26-04-12; electrical systems and networks; manual and automatic management of technical systems; production of electronics; work up and technology of metals and machines; apparatus of chemical industry; chemical technology of inorganic matters; Rector JUMAGYLYJOV ANNAGULY; Vice-Rector KAKABAYEV SAPAR.

Turkmen State Institute of Transport and Communications: 744028 Ashgabat, ul. Oguzhana 13; tel. (12) 41-06-42; fax (12) 42-55-83; e-mail durdyev@online.tm; Rector M. ASHIRBAYEV.

Turkmen State Medical Institute: 744001 Ashgabat, ul. 2028 58; tel. (12) 25-40-96; fax (12) 35-19-53; e-mail medins@online.tm; f. 1931; library: 191,000 vols; Rector GURBANGULY M. BERDYMUKHAMMEDOV (acting).

TUVALU

The Higher Education System

There was no higher education in Tuvalu before 1979. In that year the University of the South Pacific (Fiji) established an extension centre at Funafuti. The only other tertiary institution is the Maritime Training School at Amatuku on Funafuti. About 60 people graduate from the school annually. The Ministry of Education, Sports and Culture in Funafuti is responsible for higher education.

Regulatory Body

GOVERNMENT

Ministry of Education, Sports and Culture: Vaiaku, Funafuti; tel. 20405; fax 20832; Minister Dr Falesa Pitoi.

Libraries and Archives

Funafuti

National Library and Archives: POB 36, Funafuti; tel. 20711; fax 20832; depositary library for all govt documents; 19,500 vols, 150 periodicals; Librarian Mila Tafao.

Parliamentary Library: Tuvalu Parliament, Vaiaku, Funafuti; tel. 20739; fax 20800; f. 1984; Librarian Paulson Panapa.

University

UNIVERSITY OF THE SOUTH PACIFIC, TUVALU CENTRE

POB 21, Funafuti
Telephone: 20811
Fax: 20704
E-mail: manuella_d@usp.ac.fj
Internet: www.usp.ac.fj/index.php?id=4502#tuvalu
Founded 1979
Dir: David Manuella
Library of 3,000 vols.

UGANDA

The Higher Education System

Institutions of higher education predate Uganda's independence from the United Kingdom in 1962, the oldest being Makerere University in Kampala, which was founded in 1922 as a technical college for students from British East Africa. After 1949 it was affiliated to the University of London (United Kingdom), and in 1970 it was declared an independent university. There is also a university of science and technology at Mbarara, and a small Islamic university located in Mbale. Public institutions of higher education receive funding from the Ministry of Education and Sports and the Public Sector Commission. In 2004 there were 58,823 students enrolled at 18 universities. According to the Ministry of Education, the number of students enrolled at university had increased to roughly 97,000 in 2008.

Six passes in the Uganda Advanced Certificate of Education and two passes in the Uganda Certificate of Education are the main requirements for admission to undergraduate degrees. Sub-degree Certificate and Diploma courses lasting one or two years are offered in a range of subjects, often relating to professional fields of study. The principal undergraduate degree is the Bachelors, which is usually a three-year programme of study, although degrees in agriculture, engineering and veterinary science last four years, and degrees in medicine and pharmacy five years. The Bachelors is required for admission to a Masters degree programme. Masters degrees last between 18 months and three years, although gradually two years is becoming the norm. Following the Masters is the Doctorate, the highest university degree, which is awarded after a minimum of three years' study.

Post-secondary technical and vocational education is offered by a range of institutions, among them technical colleges, colleges of commerce, vocational training institutes and cooperative colleges. There is no national framework of qualifications, but awards are broadly classified as Craft, Technician or Higher Technician. The National Council for Higher Education is responsible for accreditation and quality assurance, and institutions seeking to award degrees or other programmes of higher education must fulfil a number of requirements. Once an institution has been awarded a provisional licence by the Council it then has three years to apply for chartered status.

Regulatory and Representative Bodies

GOVERNMENT

Ministry of Education and Sports: Embassy House and Devt Bldg, Plot 9/11, Parliament Ave, POB 7063, Kampala; tel. (41) 4234451; fax (41) 42230437; e-mail akibenge@education.go.ug; internet www.education.go.ug; Min. NAMIREMBE BITAMAZIRE; Permanent Sec. F. X. K. LUBANGA.

ACCREDITATION

National Council for Higher Education: POB 7634, Cavers Crescent, Kyambogo, Kampala; tel. (31) 2262140; fax (31) 2262145; e-mail nche@infocom.co.ug; internet www.unche.or.ug; f. 2001; statutory agency regulating the management of higher education instns and the quality of higher education; accredits public and private tertiary instns and licenses private tertiary instns; Exec. Dir Prof. A. B. K. KASOZI.

NATIONAL BODIES

Association for Teacher Education in Africa: c/o Assoc. Prof. J. C. B. Bigala, Makerere University, POB 7062, Kampala; f. 1970; to develop and co-ordinate syllabuses and materials to be used in teacher education instns; 50 mem. instns in anglophone Africa; Pres. Prof. M. MOHAPELOA; Sec. Assoc. Prof. J. C. B. BIGALA; publs *Journal of West African Education*, *Education in Eastern Africa*.

Inter-University Council for East Africa: POB 7110, Kampala; tel. (41) 4256251; fax (41) 4342007; e-mail info@iucea.org; internet www.iucea.org; f. 1980 as a corporate body to succeed the Inter-University Committee for East Africa; aims to facilitate contact and cooperation between the universities of Kenya, Tanzania and Uganda, to provide a forum for discussion on academic matters, and to maintain comparable academic standards; also provides secretariat for the Asscn of Eastern and Southern African Universities (see under International); 36 mem. univs and colleges; Chair. Prof. F. I. B. KAYANJA (Vice-Chancellor, Mbarara University of Science and Technology); Exec. Sec. Prof. CHACHA NYAIGOTTI-CHACHA.

Learned Societies

GENERAL

Uganda Society: POB 4980, Kampala; e-mail ncid@infocom.co.ug; internet www.africa.upenn.edu/ugandasoc/ugandasociety.htm; f. 1923; present name 1933; premises in the Uganda Museum, Kira Rd, Kampala; membership open to persons of all nationalities and institutions, to promote interest in literary, historic, scientific and general cultural matters, discovering and recording facts about the country, arranging lectures and establishing contacts; library of 1,600 vols and periodicals; Pres. Prof. E. H. K. NSUBUGA; Sec. NANNY CARDER; publ. *The Uganda Journal* (2 a year).

BIBLIOGRAPHY, LIBRARY SCIENCE AND MUSEOLOGY

Uganda Library and Information Association: POB 40227, Kampala; tel. (41) 2495592; fax (41) 2540817; internet www.ou.edu/cas/slis/ula/ula_index.htm; f. 1972; 356 mems; Chair. MAGARA ELISAM; Sec. C. BATAMBUZE; publ. *Uganda Library and Information Science Journal* (2 a year).

LANGUAGE AND LITERATURE

Alliance Française: National Theatre, 1st Fl., POB 4314, Kampala; tel. (41) 2344490; fax (41) 2349812; e-mail afka@bushnet.net; offers courses and exams in French language and culture and promotes cultural exchange with France.

British Council: Rwenzori Courts, Plot 2 and 4A, Nakasero Rd, POB 7070, Kampala; tel. (41) 2234725; fax (41) 2254853; internet www.britishcouncil.org/uganda; offers courses and examinations in English language and British culture and promotes cultural exchange with the UK; library of 5,000 vols, 40 periodicals; Dir KATE EWART-BIGGS.

MEDICINE

Uganda Medical Association: Plot 8, 41–43 Circular Rd, POB 2243, Kampala; tel. (41) 2321795; fax (41) 2345597; e-mail myers28@hotmail.com; f. 1961; 1,500 mems; library of 700 vols; Pres. Dr MARGARET MUNGHERERA; Sec. Dr MYERS LUGEMWA; publ. *Uganda Medical Journal*.

Research Institutes

AGRICULTURE, FISHERIES AND VETERINARY SCIENCE

Animal Health Research Centre: POB 24, Entebbe; f. 1926; research and field work in animal diseases, husbandry and nutrition; herbarium; library of 13,950 vols; Dir Veterinary Research Services Prof. O. BWANGAMOI; Librarian H. R. KIBOOLE; publs *Research Index* (irregular), *Research Bulletin* (irregular).

Kawanda Agricultural Research Institute: POB 7065, Kampala; tel. and fax (41) 2567649; e-mail karidir@imul.com; f. 1937; research on bananas and coffee, horticulture, post-harvest soil and soil fertility management, integrated pest management, biometrics, plant breeding, plant pathology; 9 research staff; library of 2,600 vols; plant herbarium; insect museum; Dir of Research Dr MATTHIAS MAGUNDA.

Nakawa Forestry Research Centre: POB 8668, Kampala; tel. (41) 2256261; fax (41) 2241682; f. 1952; logging, milling and building research; preservation and seasoning tests; small specialized library.

Namulonge Agricultural and Animal Production Research Institute: POB 7084, Kampala; tel. (41) 2573016; fax (41) 2726554; e-mail fopio@naro-ug.org; internet www.naro.go.ug/institute/namulonge; f. 1949; aims to increase efficiency and yield of crop and livestock production; specific objectives are genetic improvement of crops and livestock, pest and disease control, management of mandate crops, feed resource development and management for livestock; 127 scientific staff; library of 1,700 vols, 155 periodicals; Dir of Research Dr FINA OPIO.

ECONOMICS, LAW AND POLITICS

Centre for Basic Research: 15 Baskerville Ave, Kololo, POB 9863, Kampala; tel. (41) 2342987; fax (41) 2235413; internet www.cbr-ug.org; f. 1988; non-governmental organization active in social research; library of 14,000 vols; Exec. Dir Dr SIMON RUTABAJUUKA.

Makerere University Institute of Social Research: POB 16022, Kampala; tel. (41) 2554582; fax (41) 2532821; internet misr.mak.ac.ug; f. 1948; conducts independent research into social, political and economic problems of East Africa; 6 Research Fellows, University staff in depts of economics, political science, rural economy and extension, environmental studies, women's studies, sociology, social work and social administration; library of 10,000 vols, 70 current periodicals; Dir Dr NAKANYIKE B. MUSISI; Research Sec. PATRICK MULINDWA; publs working papers, USSC Conference papers (1 a year), *East African Studies* (irregular), *East Africa Linguistic Studies* (irregular), *Mawazo Journal* (2 a year), *Policy Abstracts and Research Newsletter*.

MEDICINE

Uganda Virus Research Institute: Entebbe; tel. (41) 4321094; fax (41) 4321124; e-mail information@iavi.or.ug; f. 1936 as Yellow Fever Research Institute; East African Virus Research institute 1950; present name 1977; attached to Uganda National Health Research Organization, under Ministry of Health control; carries out scientific research concerning communicable diseases, especially viral diseases threatening to public health, and advises the govt on strategies for disease control and prevention; Communications Officer DAVID WALUGEMBE.

NATURAL SCIENCES

Physical Sciences

Geological Survey and Mines Department: POB 9, Entebbe; tel. (41) 2320559; fax (41) 2320364; e-mail muinda@energy.go.ug; internet www.energyandminerals.go.ug; f. 1919; library of 22,900 vols; Commissioner J. T. TUHUMWIRE.

Government Chemist Department: POB 2174, Kampala; tel. (41) 2250470; forensic chemical examination, bacteriological examination of foods and water, chemical analysis of water, food and drugs, pollution control, identification and assay of drugs, general chemical analysis of soils and ores, isolation and identification of active principles of medicinal plants; Dir GEOFFREY ONEN.

Libraries and Archives

Kampala

Cabinet Office Library: POB 7168, Kampala; tel. (41) 2254881; fax (41) 2235459; f. 1920; for government officials and for research workers; 10,000 vols; Librarian HERBERT R. KIBOOLE; publ. *Catalogue*.

Forestry Department Library: POB 7124, Kampala; tel. (41) 2347085; fax (41) 2347086; f. 1904; specialized library (open to students by special arrangement with the Commissioner for Forestry): literature on forestry and related sciences; 20,000 vols; Librarian W. M. BWIRUKA.

Makerere University, Albert Cook Library: Makerere Univ., College of Health Sciences, POB 7072, Kampala; tel. (41) 4534149; fax (41) 4530024; e-mail cooklib@chs.mak.ac.ug; internet mulib.mak.ac.ug/acooklib; f. 1946; 60,000 vols, 500 periodicals, covering all medical subjects, especially East African and tropical medicine, spec. collns: history of medicine, Mengo Notes, WHO publs, database of Ugandan health literature; Head and Sr Librarian RACHEL NAKALEMBE (acting); publ. *Uganda Health Information Digest* (3 a year).

Makerere University Library Service: POB 16002, Kampala; tel. (41) 2531041; fax (41) 2540374; e-mail info@mulib.mak.ac.ug; internet www.makerere.ac.ug/mulib; f. 1940; consists of a Main Library, functioning as National Reference Library, with seven sub-libraries: five located on the main campus: East African School of Library and Information Science Library, Education Library, Institute of Adult and Continuing Education Library, Makerere Institute of Social Research Library and the Veterinary Library; and two off-campus: Albert Cook Library at the Medical School, Mulago; and Makerere University Agricultural Research Institute Library at the Agricultural Institute, Kabayoro; 384,000 vols, 330 current periodicals, spec. colln on East Africa, Uganda legal deposit, and private archives; book-bank system of basic textbooks kept in departmental libraries, comprising 182,000 vols; Librarian Dr MARIA G. N. MUSOKE; publ. publs incl. *East African Studies*, *Makerere Law Journal*, *Makerere Political Review*, *Mawazo*.

National Library of Uganda: Buganda Rd, POB 4262, Kampala; tel. (41) 233633; fax (41) 348625; e-mail library@infocom.co.ug; internet www.nlu.go.ug; f. 1964 as Public Libraries Board; present name 2003; organizes the collection and management of the nation's documented heritage, for current and future use; assists local govts in the management of public libraries; provides bibliographic control and aims to promote a reading culture among Ugandans, through reading tents and book donations to schools; provides an information referral service on Uganda; 157,000 vols, 200 serial titles; Dir GERTRUDE KAYAGA MULINDWA; publ. *National Bibliography of Uganda*.

Museums and Art Galleries

Entebbe

Entebbe Botanical Gardens: Lugard Rd, POB 295, Entebbe; tel. (41) 2320638; fax (41) 2321070; e-mail curator@infocom.co.ug; f. 1898; conservation and devt of native and exotic plants, colln and planting of local medicinal plants; Curator JOHN MULUMBA-WASSWA; publ. *Index Seminum* (1 a year).

Game and Fisheries Museum, Aquarium and Library: Johnstone Rd, POB 4, Entebbe; collections of heads of game animals, reptiles, fish and butterflies, hunting and fishing implements and weapons; library of 1,100 vols; Commissioner for Fisheries CHRISTOPHER DHATEMWA; Commissioner for Wildlife MOSES OKUA.

Geological Survey Museum and Documentation Centre: POB 9, Entebbe; tel. (41) 2320559; fax (41) 2320364; e-mail minerals@infocom.co.ug; f. 1919; attached to Geological Survey and Mines Department; about 37,500 specimens of rocks and minerals; library of over 9,850 vols and 3,850 periodicals.; Commissioner of the Geological Survey and Mines Department JOSHUA T. TUHUMWIRE.

Uganda Wildlife Education Centre: 56–57 Johnston St, POB 369, Entebbe; tel. (41) 4322169; fax (41) 4320073; e-mail info@uwec.ug; internet www.uweczoo.org; f. 1952, present name and status 1994; conservation, education, rescue and rehabilitation of orphaned, injured and/or confiscated wildlife; captive breeding of endangered wildlife species; Exec. Dir Dr JAMES MUSINGUZI.

Kampala

Uganda Museum: 5–7 Kira Rd, POB 365, Kampala; tel. (41) 2244060; fax (41) 2245580; f. 1908; natural history, geology, ethnology, archaeology, palaeontology; science and industry pavilion; special collection of African musical instruments; centre for archaeological research in Uganda; library of 4,000 vols; Curator Dr E. KAMUHANGIRE.

Universities

GULU UNIVERSITY

POB 166, Gulu
Telephone: (47) 1432095
Fax: (47) 1432094
Internet: www.gu.ac.ug

Founded 2002
State control
Language of instruction: English
Academic year: August to May

Rector: JACK H. PEN-MOGI NYOKI
Univ. Sec.: VINCENT M. OKOTH-OGOLA
Academic Registrar: GEOFFREY LAMTOO
Librarian: AREGU RAPHAEL

Library of 23,000 vols, 33 periodicals
Number of teachers: 188
Number of students: 3,831

DEANS

Faculty of Agriculture and Environment: Prof. CALLISTUS W. BALIDDAWA
Faculty of Business and Development Studies: UWONDA GILBERT
Faculty of Education and Humanities: OKUMU CHARLES
Faculty of Medicine: Prof. EMILIO OVUGA
Faculty of Science: Dr ANDOGAH GEOFFREY

ISLAMIC UNIVERSITY IN UGANDA

POB 2555, Mbale
Telephone: (35) 2512100
Fax: (45) 4433502
E-mail: iuiumbalecampus@yahoo.com
Internet: www.iuiu.ac.ug

Founded 1988
Private control
Languages of instruction: English, Arabic
Academic year: August to July

Rector: Dr AHMAD KAWESA SENGENDO
Vice-Rector for Academic Affairs: Dr MPEZAMIHIGO MOUHAMAD
Vice-Rector for Finance and Administration: Dr KAZIBA MPAATA ABDUL
Univ. Sec.: MASOKOYI WASSWA (acting)
Academic Registrar: SULAIT D. KABALI
Librarian: Dr SESSANGA IDRIS

Library of 19,315 books, 100 periodicals

Number of teachers: 263
Number of students: 6,622
Publications: *Islamic University Journal* (2 a year), *IUIU Law Journal* (1 a year)

DEANS

Faculty of Arts and Social Sciences: MWANGA MOSES
Faculty of Education: NIMULORA MAIMUNA
Faculty of Islamic Studies and Arabic Language: BOWA MUHAMMAD
Faculty of Law: SAIDAT NAKITTO
Faculty of Management Studies: KITAKULE MUBI HUSSEIN
Faculty of Science: SARAH NACHUHA

KAMPALA UNIVERSITY

POB 25454, Kampala
Telephone: (41) 2258219
E-mail: kuniv@afsat.com
Private control
Vice-Chancellor: Prof. BADRU KATEREGA.

KYAMBOGO UNIVERSITY

POB 1, Kyambogo
Telephone: (41) 4285001
Fax: (41) 4220464
Internet: www.kyu.ac.ug
Founded 1954 as Uganda Polytechnic Kyambogo; univ. status 2001 following merger with Institute of Teacher Education Kyambogo and Uganda Nat. Institute for Special Education
State control
Chancellor: Dr ERIC TIYO SSEKEBUGA ADRIKO
Ccl Chair.: JAMES KALEBO
Vice-Chancellor: Prof. ISAIAH OMOLO NDIEGE
Univ. Sec.: PATRICK MADAYA (acting)
Dean of Students: CYRIACO KABAGAMBE
Registrar: ANDREW CULA (acting)
Librarian: JUSTINE KIYIMBA
Library of 150,000 vols, 12,000 periodicals
Number of students: 25,000

DEANS

Faculty of Arts and Social Sciences: Dr CYPRIAN ADUPA
Faculty of Education: Dr JOHN KAHEERU-KATIGO
Faculty of Engineering: DAUDI MUGISA
Faculty of Science: AARON WANYAMA
Faculty of Special Needs Education and Rehabilitation: Dr J. B. OKECH
Faculty of Vocational Studies: Dr WILLIAM EPEJU
School of Management and Entreneurship: JOCOB OYUGI

MAKERERE UNIVERSITY

POB 7062, Kampala
Telephone: (41) 2542803
Fax: (41) 2541068
E-mail: helpme@dicts.mak.ac.ug
Internet: mak.ac.ug
Founded 1922 as technical school; became Univ. College 1949, attained Univ. status 1970
State control
Language of instruction: English
Academic year: October to June
Chancellor: H. E. THE PRES. OF UGANDA
Vice-Chancellor: Prof. J. P. SEBUWUFU
Deputy Vice-Chancellor: Prof. J. EPELU-OPIO
Sec.: S. R. BYANAGWA
Academic Registrar: AMOS OLAL-ODUR
Librarian: J. MUGASHA
Number of teachers: 1,089
Number of students: 27,976
Publication: *Mawazo*

DEANS

Faculty of Agriculture: Assoc. Prof. E. N. SABIITI
Faculty of Arts: Dr O. NDOLERIIRE
Faculty of Commerce: WASWA-BALUNYWA
Faculty of Forestry and Nature Conservation: Dr J. KABOGGOZA
Faculty of Law: Assoc. Prof. J. OLOKA-ONYANGO
Faculty of Medicine: Assoc. Prof. N. SEWANKEMBO
Faculty of Science: Dr H. ORYEM-ORIGA
Faculty of Social Sciences: Dr JOY KWESIGA
Faculty of Technology: Dr B. M. KIGGUNDU
Faculty of Veterinary Medicine: Assoc. Prof. E. KATUNGA-RWAKISHAYA
School of Education: Dr C. MASEMBE-SSEBUNGA
Margaret Trowell School of Industrial and Fine Arts: J. MUKASA

PROFESSORS

Faculty of Agriculture (tel. (41) 2542277; fax (41) 2531641; e-mail dean@foamak.ug.com; internet www.makerere.ac.ug):

EKWAMU, A., Crop Science
BAREEBA, F. B., Animal Science
KITUNGULU-ZAKE, Y. J., Soil Science
KIWUWA, G. H., Animal Science
OSIRU, D. O., Crop Science
RUBAIHAYO, P. R.
RUYOOKA, D., Forestry

Faculty of Arts (tel. (41) 2542241; fax (41) 2542265; e-mail faculty@arts.mak.ac.ug):

BYARUHANGA-AKIIKI, A. B. T., Religious Studies and Philosophy
DALFOVO, A. T., Philosophy
MUKAMA, R.
TIBENDERANA, P. K., History

Faculty of Law (tel. (41) 2542284; fax (41) 2543110; e-mail lawdean@muklaw.ac.ug):

BAKIBINGA, D. J., Commercial Law
KAKOOZA, J. M. N., Law and Jurisprudence

Faculty of Medicine (tel. (41) 2530020; fax (41) 2531091; e-mail sewankam@infocom.co.ug):

ANOKBONGGO, W. W., Pharmacology and Therapeutics
BULWA, F. M., Obstetrics and Gynaecology
MMIRO, F. A., Obstetrics and Gynaecology
MUGERWA, J. W., Pathology
MUNUBE, J., Microbiology
NDUGWA, C. M., Paediatrics and Child Health
ODOI-ADOME, R., Pharmacy
OTIM, M. A., Medicine
OWOR, R., Pathology
SWEANKAMBO, N. K., Medicine

Faculty of Science (tel. (41) 2541258; fax (41) 2531061; e-mail deansci@mak.ac.ug):

BANAGE, W. B., Zoology
BANDA, E. K. J., Physics
ILUKOR, J. O., Physics
KAHWA, Y., Physics
KAKONGE, E., Biochemistry
LUBOOBI, L. S., Mathematics
MUGAMBE, P. E., Physics
MUGAMBI, P. E., Mathematics
OKWAKOL, M. N., Zoology
OLWA-ODYEK, Chemistry
POMEROY, D. E., Zoology
SEKAALO, H., Chemistry
TALIGOOLA, H. K., Botany
TUKAHIRWA, E., Environmental Science

Faculty of Social Sciences (tel. (41) 2545040; fax (41) 2530815; e-mail deanfss@mak.ac.ug):

AKIIKI-MUJAJU, A. B., Political Science
GINGYERA-PINYCWA, A. C. G., Political Science
MWAKA, V. M.

School of Education (tel. (41) 2540733; e-mail deaneduc@mak.ac.ug):

MUSAAZI, J. S., Higher Education
OCITTI, J., Geography
ODAET, C. F., Educational Foundations and Management
OPOLOT, J. A., Psychology

Institute of Statistics and Applied Economics (tel. (41) 2534224):

NTOZI, S. P. N.
TULYA-MUHIKA

ATTACHED INSTITUTES

East African School of Librarianship: Kampala; f. 1963 to train librarians for all parts of East Africa; 3-year course leads to degree in Library and Information Science; Dir S. A. H. ABIDI.

Institute of Adult and Continuing Education: Kampala; f. 1953; three divisions: Adult Education and Communication Studies, Community Education and Extra-Mural Studies, Distance Education; one-year post-secondary school courses; shorter courses are also arranged both at the centre and in surrounding rural areas; Dir NUWA SENTONGO.

Institute of Statistics and Applied Economics: a joint enterprise of the Government of Uganda and the United Nations Development Programme; depts of Planning and Applied Statistics, Population Studies, and Statistical Methods; 3-year degree courses; Dir Dr X. R. MUGISHA.

Makerere Institute of Social Research: see under Research Institutes.

MBARARA UNIVERSITY OF SCIENCE AND TECHNOLOGY

POB 1410, Mbarara
Telephone: (48) 5221623
Fax: (48) 5220782
E-mail: vc@must.ac.ug
Internet: www.must.ac.ug
Founded 1989
State control
Language of instruction: English
Academic year: October to August
Chancellor: Prof. RAPHAEL OWOR
Vice-Chancellor: Prof. F. I. B. KAYANJA
Registrar: S. B. BAZIRAKE
Librarian: ANNE GAKIBAYO
Library of 22,100 vols
Number of teachers: 144
Number of students: 1,104
Publications: *Medical Journal* (1 a year), *Science Journal* (1 a year)

DEANS

Faculty of Development Studies: Prof. PAMELA MBABAZI
Faculty of Medicine: Prof. J. KABAKYENGA
Faculty of Science Education: Prof. J. BARANGA

PROFESSORS

BARANGA, J., Biology
BEGUMYA, Y. R., Physiology
JAEGER, B., Dermatology
KAYANJA, F. I. B., Histology
PEPPER, L., Medicine

ATTACHED INSTITUTE

Institute of Tropical Forest Conservation: POB 7487, Kampala; fax 245597; Dir Dr A. MCNEILAGE.

NAMASAGALI UNIVERSITY

POB 241, Kamuli
Telephone: (77) 2861961
Founded 1975; present status 1998

Private control
Vice-Chancellor: SAMWIRI KIGWANA
Library of 5,000 vols
Number of teachers: 58
Number of students: 531

DEANS
Faculty of Education: PETER MUBIRU
Faculty of Management and Development Studies: WILLIAM SAAZI

NDEJJE UNIVERSITY

POB 7088, Kampala
Telephone: (77) 2630319
Fax: (77) 2610132
Founded 1992
Private control
Academic year: October to June
Library of 40,000 vols
Number of teachers: 60
Number of students: 1,515
Vice-Chancellor: Bishop Dr MICHAEL SENYIMBA
Schools of business administration and computer science, education.

UGANDA CHRISTIAN UNIVERSITY

POB 4, Mukono
Telephone: (41) 4565800
Fax: (41) 2290800
E-mail: ucu@ucu.ac.ug
Internet: www.ucu.ac.ug
Founded 1913 as Bishop Tucker Theological College, present name and status 1997
Private control
Language of instruction: English
Academic year: September to August
Chancellor: HENRY LUKE OROMBI
Vice-Chancellor: Dr JOHN MUSISI SENYONYI
Deputy Vice-Chancellor for Development and External Relations: DOUG FOUNTAIN
Deputy Vice-Chancellor for Finance and Administration: Dr FLORENCE BAKIBINGA SAJJABI
Deputy Vice-Chancellor for Academic Affairs: Dr ALEX KAGUME
Dir of Student Affairs: MILTON TWEHEYO
Univ. Librarian: FREDRICK NATHANIEL MUKUNGU
Library of 120,000 vols, 70 periodicals
Number of teachers: 175
Number of students: 7,395

DEANS
Bishop Tucker School of Divinity and Theology: Dr OLIVIA NASSAKA BANJA
Faculty of Business and Administration: VINCENT KISENYI
Faculty of Education and Arts: Dr MEDARD RUGYENDO
Faculty of Law: Dr LILLIAN TIBATEMWA-ERIKIKUBINZA KALYEGIRA
Faculty of Science and Technology: FABIAN NABUGOOMU
Faculty of Social Sciences: Dr ELIZABETH BACWAYO KUKUNDA
School of Research and Post Graduate Studies: Dr FABIAN NABUGOOMU

UGANDA MARTYRS UNIVERSITY

POB 5498, Kampala
Telephone: (38) 2410611
Fax: (38) 2410100
E-mail: umu@umu.ac.ug
Internet: www.fiuc.org/umu
Founded 1993
Private control
Academic year: August to September
Chancellor: Rt Rev. Bishop MATTHIAS SSEKAMANYA
Vice-Chancellor: Prof. Dr CHARLES OLWENY
Deputy Vice-Chancellor for Academic Affairs: Asst. Prof. Dr JOSEPH KISEKKA
Deputy Vice-Chancellor Finance and Admin.: Asst. Prof. Dr SIMEON WANYAMA
Registrar: INNOCENT BYUMA
Librarian: JUDITH NANNOZI
Library of 31,735 vols
Number of teachers: 242
Number of students: 4,697
Publications: *Health Policy Journal*, *Journal of Science*, *Mtafiti Mwafrika* (African Researcher, 3 a year)

DEANS
Centre for Extra-Mural Studies: Dr MARTIN O'REILLY (Head)
Department of Good Governance and Peace Studies: Dr MAXIMIANO NGABIRANO (Head)
Department of Information and Communications Technology: CYPRIAN LWANGA (Head)
Department of Information Systems: Prof. Dr PETER KALEMA (Head)
East African School of Diplomacy, Governance and Int. Studies: SAMUEL BALIGIDDE (Dir)
Faculty of Agriculture: Dr CHARLES KUDAMBA
Faculty of Built Environment: CONNIE NSHEMEREIRWE
Faculty of Business Administration and Management: Dr ALEX IJO
Centre for Distance Learning: Dr GUDULA NAIGA BASAZA
Faculty of Education: Prof. BARNABAS OTAALA
Faculty of Health Sciences: Dr VINCENT BWETE
Faculty of Sciences: HENRY KIWANUKA
Institute of Ethics and Development Studies: Dr JUDE SSEBUWUFU (Dir)
School of Postgraduate Studies: Prof. Dr PETER KANYANDAGO (Dir)

UKRAINE

The Higher Education System

Institutions of higher education predate Ukraine (formerly Ukrainian SSR)'s independence from the USSR in 1991, the oldest being National University of Kyiv-Mohyla Academy, which was founded in 1615. The next oldest institution is National University of Lviv 'Ivan Franko', which was founded in 1661. During the period of Soviet rule (1920–91) over 60 universities, academies and institutions of higher education were founded.

Since independence the Law on Education (1991) is the defining legislation for all levels of the education system, and an accreditation system of licensing, assessment and certification of educational establishments has been in place since 1992. Ukraine has also become a member of the European Quality Assurance Register. Other than the Ministry of Education and Science, institutions of higher education may also be attached to the relevant ministry. Ukraine signed up for the Bologna Process in 2005, the first phase of which is to adopt a credit-based system of comparable degrees with two main cycles (undergraduate and graduate). Since 2006/07 European Credit Transfer and Accumulation System (ECTS) has been introduced for all programmes of the first and second cycles, directly corresponding with the national system of credits. Specialists in the fields of medicine and veterinary medicine, however, still follow a long integrated cycle. A national qualification framework is currently under development, and planned for completion by 2010. Higher education is classified into four levels, in ascending order: technical colleges (Level I), colleges (Level II), institutes (Level III) and universities, academies and institutes (Level IV). In 2008/09 there were 2,763,800 students enrolled in higher education.

The main requirements for admission to higher education are award of the general secondary education certificate (Atestat pro Povnu Zagal'nu Sersdniu Osvitu) and satisfactory performance in entrance examinations or interviews. Ukraine has introduced a two-tier Bachelors and Masters degree system in accordance with the principles of the Bologna Process; however, the old-style degrees are still available. The Bachelors (Dyplom Bakalavra) is an undergraduate degree of four years, and is offered parallel to the Specialist Diploma (Dyplom Spetsialista), an integrated five-year programme of study mostly offered by institutes. The first postgraduate degree under the new system is the Masters (Dyplom Magistra), and it lasts for one or two years after the award of the Bachelors or Specialist Diploma. Finally, doctoral-level studies consist of two awards, both lasting three years, Diploma of Candidate of Sciences (Dyplom pro Prysudzhenia Naukovogo Stupenia Kandydata Nauk) and Diploma of Doctor of Sciences (Dyplom pro Prysudzhenia Naukovogo Stupenia Doktora Nauk).

Regulatory and Representative Bodies

GOVERNMENT

Ministry of Culture and Tourism: 01601 Kyiv, vul. Ivana Franka 19; tel. (44) 226-26-45; fax (44) 235-32-57; e-mail ministr@mincult.gov.ua; internet www.mincult.gov.ua; Min. VASYL V. VOVKUN.

Ministry of Education and Science: 01601 Kyiv, blv T. Shevchenka 16; tel. (44) 226-26-61; fax (44) 274-10-49; e-mail press@mon.gov.ua; internet www.mon.gov.ua; Min. IVAN O. VAKARCHUK.

ACCREDITATION

ENIC/NARIC Ukraine: Dept for Licensing and Accreditation, Min. of Education and Science, Youth and Sports, 10 Ave Pobedy, 01135 Kyiv; tel. and fax (44) 486-74-09; e-mail dlan@mon.gov.ua; internet www.mon.gov.ua; attached to Dept for Scientific Researches and Licensing, Min. of Education and Science, Youth and Sports of Ukraine; recognizes academic foreign qualifications; verifies educational documents issued in Ukraine (apostille); int. academic mobility; Dir MICHAEL GONCHARENKO.

NATIONAL BODIES

Academy of Pedagogical Sciences of Ukraine: 04053 Kyiv, Artema vul. 52A; tel. (44) 211-94-01; fax (44) 226-31-80; e-mail info@apsu.org.ua; internet www.apsu.org.ua; f. 1992; Pres. Prof. VASYL H. KREMEN; publs *Biolohiya i Khimiya v Shkoli* (Biology and Chemistry at School, 4 a year), *Compyuter v Shkoli i Simyi* (Computer at School and at Home, 4 a year), *Defektolohiya* (Defectology, 4 a year), *Fizyka i Astronomiya v Shkoli* (Physics and Astronomy at School, 4 a year), *Heohrafiya i Osnovy Ekonomiky v Shkoli* (Geography and Fundamentals of Economics at School, 4 a year), *Istoriya v Shkolakh Ukrainy* (History in Ukrainian Schools, 4 a year), *Matemmatyka v Shkoli* (Mathematics at School, 4 a year), *Mystetstvo i Osvita* (Arts and Education, 4 a year), *Nauka i Osvita* (Science and Education, 2 a year), *Obdarovana Dytyna* (Gifted Child, 6 a year), *Pedahohichna Hazeta* (Pedagogical Newspaper, 12 a year), *Pedahohika i Psykholohiya* (Pedagogy and Psychology, 4 a year), *Praktychna Psykholohiya i Sotsialna Robota* (Applied Psychology and Social Work, 12 a year), *Profesiyno-Tekhnichna Osvita* (Vocational and Technical Education, 4 a year), *Shlyakh Osvity* (A Way of Education, 4 a year), *Ukrainska Literatura v Zahalnoosvitniy Shkoli* (Ukrainian Literature at Secondary School, 6 a year), *Ukrainska Mova i Literatura v Shkoli* (Ukrainian Language and Literature at School, 4 a year), *Vyshcha Osvita Ukrainy* (Higher Education in Ukraine, 4 a year), *Zarubizhna Literatura v Navchalnykh Zakladakh* (Foreign Literature at Educational Institutions, 12 a year).

Association of Non-State-owned Educational Institutions of Ukraine: 252115 Kyiv, 16-v Vernadsky Ave; tel. (44) 452-76-55; fax (44) 444-05-44; e-mail assoc@ufimb.kiev.ua; internet www.ambernet.kiev.ua/~tlc/aeiunfp/index_e.htm; f. 1993; aims to improve the educational system in the Ukraine; 68 mem. instns; Head Prof. IVAN TIMOSCHENKO.

Council of Rectors of Ukrainian Institutions of Higher Education: 01017 Kyiv, Taras Shevchenko Kyiv Nat. Univ., vul. Volodymyrska 60; internet www.univ.kiev.ua; Pres. Prof. Dr VIKTOR V. SKOPENKO.

Learned Societies

GENERAL

National Academy of Sciences of Ukraine: 01601 Kyiv, Volodymyrska 54; tel. (44) 225-22-39; fax (44) 224-32-43; e-mail prez@nas.gov.ua; internet www.nas.gov.ua; f. 1918; sections of physical-technical and mathematical sciences (Chair. A. K. SHIDLOVSKIY), chemical and biological sciences (Chair. V. D. POKHODENKO), social sciences and humanities (Chair. I. F. KURAS); depts of chemistry (V. V. GONCHARUK), earth sciences (Academician-Sec. V. I. STAROSTENKO), economics (Academician-Sec. V. M. GEYETS), general biology (Academician-Sec. D. M. GRODZINSKIY), history, philosophy and law (Academician-Sec. O. S. ONYSHCHENKO), informatics (Academician-Sec. I. V. SERGIENKO), literature, language and art criticism (Academician-Sec. I. M. DZYUBA), mathematics (Academician-Sec. I. V. SKRYPNIK), mechanics (Academician-Sec. V. V. PYLYPENKO), molecular biology, biochemistry and experimental and clinical physiology (Academician-Sec. G. KH. MATSUKA), physical and technical problems of materials science (Academician-Sec. I. K. POKHODNYA), physical and technical problems of power engineering (Academician-Sec. B. S. STOGNIY), physics and astronomy (Academician-Sec. A. G. NAUMOVETS); attached research institutes: see Research Institutes; 708 mems (207 full, 378 corresp., 123 foreign); library: see Libraries and Archives; Pres. Acad. BORIS PATON; Vice-Pres. Acad. ANATOLIY SHPAK; Chief Scientific Sec. ANATOLIY ZAGORODNY; publs in Ukrainian and English: *Dopovidi NAN Ukrainy*, *Ekonomika Ukrainy* (Economy of Ukraine, 12 a year), *Kosmichna Nauka i Tekhnologiya* (Space Science and Engineering, 6 a year), *Kyivska Starovyna* (Kiev Antiquities, 6 a year), *Visnyk NAN Ukrainy* (Journal of the National Academy of Sciences of Ukraine, in Ukrainian and English, 12 a year).

Shevchenko Scientific Society: 290013 Lviv, vul. Gen. Chuprynka 21; tel. (322) 34-51-63; fax (322) 76-04-97; e-mail ntsh@ipm.lviv.ua; f. 1873; broad range of arts and sciences; library of 30,000 vols; Pres. Prof. O. M. ROMANIV; Sec. O. A. KUPCHYNSKY; publ. *Memoires* (2 a year).

AGRICULTURE, FISHERIES AND VETERINARY SCIENCE

Ukrainian Academy of Agricultural Sciences: 01010 Kyiv, vul. Suvorova 9; tel. (44) 290-10-85; fax (44) 290-94-73; internet www.aginukraine.com/uaas; f. 1990; 4,900 mems; attached research institutes: see Research Institutes; publ. *Visnyk Agrarnoi Nauky* (Bulletin of Agricultural Science, 12 a year).

ARCHITECTURE AND TOWN PLANNING

National Union of Architects of Ukraine: 01001 Kyiv, vul. Hrychenka 7; tel. (44) 279-98-09; fax (44) 228-13-11; Pres. IHOR SHPARA.

BIBLIOGRAPHY, LIBRARY SCIENCE AND MUSEOLOGY

Association of Libraries of Ukraine: 03039 Kyiv, pr. Richchya Zhovtnya 3; tel. (44) 265-81-04; fax (44) 264-33-98; e-mail nlu@csl.freenet.kiev.ua; internet www.nbuv.gov.ua; Pres. OLEKSIY S. ONYSCHENKO.

ECONOMICS, LAW AND POLITICS

Academy of Legal Sciences of Ukraine: 61024 Kharkiv, vul. Pushkinska 70; tel. (57) 704-19-01; fax (57) 704-19-10; e-mail aprnu@online.kharkiv.com; internet www.aprnu.kharkiv.org; f. 1993; Pres. Acad. VASIL YA. TATSIY.

FINE AND PERFORMING ARTS

National Artists' Union of Ukraine: 04053 Kyiv, vul. Sichovykh Striltsiv 1–5; tel. (44) 212-01-33; fax (44) 212-14-54; e-mail spilka@nbi.com.ua; internet www.nshu.org.ua; f. 1938; 33 regional constituent orgs; 4,330 mems; Head VOLODYMYR A. CHEPELNIK.

National Union of Cinematographers of Ukraine: 01033 Kyiv, vul. Saksahanskoho 6; tel. and fax (44) 287-75-57; e-mail ukrkino@ln.ua; internet www.ukrkino.com.ua; f. 1958; 1,251 mems; Head BORIS I. SAVCHENKO.

National Writers' Union of Ukraine: 01024 Kyiv, vul. Bankova 2; tel. (44) 293-45-86; e-mail nspu@i.kiev.ua; internet www.nspu.kiev.ua; f. 1934 as part of the Writers' Union of the former USSR; 1,600 mems; Head VOLODYMYR O. YAVORIVSKY.

HISTORY, GEOGRAPHY AND ARCHAEOLOGY

Ukrainian Geographical Society: 03022 Kyiv, vul. Vasilkivska 90; fax (44) 266-54-17; e-mail vpsh@icchq.univ.kiev.ua; Head PETRO H. SHISHCHENKO.

LANGUAGE AND LITERATURE

Alliance Française: 03150 Kyiv, c/o CCCL, 104 vul. Gorki; tel. (44) 269-41-57; fax (44) 269-85-28; e-mail alliance.francaise@ifu.kiev.ua; offers courses and exams in French language and culture and promotes cultural exchange with France; attached offices in Dneprodzerzhinsk, Donetsk, Enerdogar, Feodossia, Gorlivka, Izmail, Kharkiv, Khmelnystkyi, Kramatorsk, Lougansk, Mykolaiv, Odessa, Oujgorod, Poltava, Rivne, Sebastopol, Simferopol, Slaviansk, Tchernivtsy, Ternopil, Vinnitsia and Zaporijjia.

British Council: 04070 Kyiv, 4/12 vul. Hryhoriya Skovorody; tel. (44) 490-56-00; fax (44) 490-56-05; e-mail enquiry@britishcouncil.org.ua; internet www.britishcouncil.org/ukraine; teaching centre; offers courses and exams in English language and British culture and promotes cultural exchange with the UK; attached offices in Donetsk, Kharkiv, Lviv and Odessa; training and professional development centre; Dir TERRY SANDELL; Teaching Centre Man. TONY HUBBARD.

Goethe-Institut: 04070 Kyiv, vul. Voloska, 12/4; tel. (44) 496-97-85; fax (44) 496-97-89; e-mail info@kiew.goethe.org; internet www.goethe.de/ins/ua/kie/; f. 1994; offers courses and exams in German language and culture and promotes cultural exchange with Germany; Dir MARION HAASE.

MEDICINE

Academy of Medical Sciences of Ukraine: 04050 Kyiv, vul. Gertsena 12; tel. (44) 213-34-11; fax (44) 219-39-81; e-mail beb@rcrm.kiev.ua; internet www.amnu.kiev.ua; f. 1993; 31 mems; 44 corresp. mems; 5 foreign mems; attached research institutes: see Research Institutes; Pres. Prof. OLEKSANDR F. VOZIANOV; Chief Scientific Sec. Prof. VOLODYMYR A. MIKHNOV; publ. *Journal* (4 a year).

Gerontology and Geriatrics Society: Institute of Gerontology, 252655 Kyiv 114, Vyshgorodska vul. 67; tel. (44) 430-40-68; fax (44) 432-99-56; e-mail admin@geront.kiev.ua; f. 1963; 250 mems; library of 72,000 vols; Chair. V. V. BEZRUKOV; Chief Learned Sec. O.K. KULTCHITSKY; publ. *Problems of Ageing and Longevity* (4 a year).

Ukrainian Association of Radiologists: 03022 Kyiv, vul. Lomonsova 33/43; tel. and fax (44) 258-97-86; e-mail aru-kiev@ukr.net; internet www.aruk.org; f. 1992; 6,000 mems; Chair. Prof. VLADIMIR E. MEDVEDEV; publ. *Radiodiagnostics and Radiotherapy* (4 a year).

Ukrainian Physiological Society: 01024 Kyiv, vul. Bohomoltsya 4; tel. (44) 253-29-09; fax (44) 256-20-00; e-mail pkostyuk@biph.kiev.ua; internet uaphsoc.biph.kiev.ua; Head Acad. PLATON H. KOSTYUK; publ. *Fiziologichnyi Zhurnal* (Physiological Journal, 6 a year).

Ukrainian Scientific Society of Cardiologists: c/o Institute of Cardiology 'M. D. Strazhevska', 03151 Kyiv, vul. Narodnogo Opolcheniya 5; tel. (44) 449-70-03; internet www.ukrcardio.org; Pres. VOLODYMYR KOVALENKO.

Ukrainian Scientific Society of Hygienists: 02660 Kyiv, vul. Popudrenka 50; tel. and fax (44) 559-90-90; e-mail regina@usch.kiev.ua; f. 1953; Head ANDRIY M. SERDYUK.

Ukrainian Society of Allergology and Clinical Immunology: c/o Dept of Immunology and Allergy, National Medical University 'O. Bohomolets', 04053 Kyiv, vul. Kotsyubinskoho 9a; tel. (44) 216-54-03; fax (44) 216-24-02; Chair. Prof. H. DRANNIK.

Ukrainian Society of Ophthalmologists: c/o Institute of Eye Diseases and Tissue Therapy, 'V. P. Filatov', 65061 Odessa, bul. Frantsuzsky 49/51; tel. (048) 60-34-46; fax (048) 68-48-51; e-mail iryna.ods@gmail.com; f. 1936; 1,102 mems.

NATURAL SCIENCES

General

Scientific and Technical Societies—National Headquarters: 252053 Kyiv, vul. Artema 21; tel. (44) 212-42-34.

Biological Sciences

Ukrainian Biochemical Society: c/o Palladin Institute of Biochemistry, 01601 Kyiv, vul. Leontovicha 9; tel. (44) 234-59-74; fax (44) 279-63-65; e-mail secretar@biochem.kiev.ua; internet www.biochemistry.org.ua; f. 1928; organizes congresses, seminars and confs; 680 mems; library of 86,000 vols; Chair. Prof. SERHIY V. KOMISARENKO; publs *Biotechnologia* (Biotechnology, 6 a year, in Ukrainian, English and Russian), *Ukrainskyi Biokhimichnyi Zhurnal* (Ukrainian Biochemical Journal, 6 a year, in Ukrainian, English and Russian).

Physical Sciences

Ukrainian Physical Society: 03680 Kyiv, pr. Glushkova 4; tel. and fax (44) 526-40-36; e-mail krav@univ.kiev.ua; internet www.ups.kiev.ua; f. 1990; 425 mems; Pres. Prof. VOLODYMYR G. LITOVCHENKO.

Ukrainian Society of Geodesy, Aerospace Surveying and Cartography: c/o Ministry of Environment and Natural Resources of Ukraine, 02094 Kyiv, vul. Popudrenka 54; tel. (44) 268-21-09; fax (44) 559-73-89; e-mail ssavchuk@polynet.lviv.ua; Pres. IHOR TREVOHO.

PHILOSOPHY AND PSYCHOLOGY

Ukranian Psychological Society: 01032 Kyiv, bul. T. Shevchenka 27A, Office 305; tel. and fax (44) 246-54-59; e-mail ucap@ukr.net; internet www.ucap.kiev.ua; Dir Dr VITALIY PANOK.

RELIGION, SOCIOLOGY AND ANTHROPOLOGY

Sociological Association of Ukraine: 01021 Kyiv, vul. Shovkovychna 12; tel. and fax (44) 291-52-46; e-mail sau@mail.kar.net; Dir Dr N. SHULGA.

TECHNOLOGY

Chornobyl Center for Nuclear Safety, Radioactive Waste and Radioecology: 07100 Kyiv, Slavutych, vul. Hvardeyskoi Divizii 77, 7/1; tel. (44) 792-30-16; fax (44) 792-81-44; e-mail center@chornobyl.net; internet www.chornobyl.net; f. 1996; Coordinating Dir Prof. YEVGEN V. GARIN.

Ukrainian Society of Mechanical Engineers: c/o Br. of Mechanics of the Nat. Acad. of Sciences of Ukraine, 49600 Dnipropetrovsk, vul. Leshko-Popelya 15; tel. (56) 745-12-38; fax (56) 247-34-13; e-mail itm@pvv.dp.ua; internet www.itm.dp.ua; Pres. Acad. VIKTOR PYLYPENKO.

Ukrainian Society for Non-Destructive Testing: 03680 Kyiv, vul. Bozhenko 11; tel. (44) 287-26-66; fax (44) 289-21-66; e-mail usndt@ukr.net; internet www.usndt.com.ua; f. 1990; 200 mems; Pres. Prof. VOLODYMYR TROITSKIY.

Ukrainian Society for Soil Mechanics, Geotechnics and Foundation Engineering: 03680 Kyiv, Ivana Klimenka 5/2; tel. and fax (44) 248-89-42; e-mail adm-inst@ndibk.kiev.ua; f. 2001; promotes theory and practice of stabilization of weak soils in bases; interaction of upper structure and soil; devt of new technologies for bases preparation; other practical issues in the field of building; 138 mems; Pres. Prof. PETRO KRYVOSHEIEV; publ. *Geotechnic World*.

Research Institutes

AGRICULTURE, FISHERIES AND VETERINARY SCIENCE

Dairy and Meat Technology Institute: 02660 Kyiv, M. Raskovoi 4A; tel. (44) 517-17-37; fax (44) 517-02-28; e-mail verb@timm.kiev.ua; internet www.timm.kiev.ua; f. 1959; attached to Ukrainian Acad. of Agricultural Sciences; library of 27,000 vols; Dir G. A. ERESKO; publ. *Meat and Milk* (6 a year).

Institute of Agricultural Economics: 03680 Kyiv, vul. Geroev Oborony 10; tel. (44) 261-43-21; fax (44) 266-05-65; e-mail info@iae.com.ua; f. 1956; attached to Ukrainian Acad. of Agricultural Sciences; Dir PETRO SABLUK; publ. *Economics of AIC* (12 a year).

Institute of Agriculture: 08162 Kievska oblast, Kyevo-Svyatoshinsky raion, Chabani; tel. (44) 526-23-27; fax (44) 526-11-07; e-mail selectio@ukrpack.net; f. 1900; attached to Ukrainian Acad. of Agrarian Sciences; agriculture, crop-growing technologies, agricultural crops selection; library of 35,900 vols in scientific library; 100,000 in total; publs *Agriculture* (1 a year), *Proceedings of the International and All-Ukrainian Congresses*.

Institute of Beekeeping, P. I. Prokopovych: 03143 Kyiv, vul. Zabolotnogo 19; tel. (44) 266-67-98; fax (44) 266-31-89; e-mail prokopovych@ukr.net; f. 1989; attached to Ukrainian Acad. of Agrarian Sciences; library of 4,000 vols; Dir LEONID BODNARCHUK; publs *Apiary* (12 a year), *Beekeeping* (1 a year), *Ukrainian Beekeeper*.

Institute of Cereals: 49600 Dnipropetrovsk, vul. Dzerzhinskogo 14; tel. (56) 244-45-49; fax (56) 236-26-18; f. 1930; attached to Ukrainian Acad. of Agrarian Sciences; maize, winter wheat, other cereals and leguminous plants; library of 110,000 vols; Dir Dr YEVGEN LEBID; publ. *Bulletin* (2 a year).

Institute for Fisheries: 03164 Kyiv, vul. Obukhivska 165; tel. (44) 423-74-61; fax (44) 423-74-58; e-mail vitbekh@online.com.ua; attached to Ukrainian Acad. of Agrarian Sciences; research and devt into the exploitation of aquatic living resources in inland waters; fish genetics and selection; environmental safety; stock conservation and rehabilitation of rare and endangered species; and economic efficiency of Ukrainian fisheries; library of 50,000 vols; Dir OLEKSANDR TRETYAK; publ. *Rybne Gospodarstvo* (1 a year).

Institute for Mechanization of Animal Husbandry: 69097 Zaporizhzya, Island Khortitca; tel. and fax (612) 289-81-44; e-mail imtuaan@ukr.net; internet www.imt.zp.ua; f. 1930; attached to Nat. Acad. of Agrarian Sciences of Ukraine; research centre for electrification of agriculture; library of 45,000 vols; Dir Dr hab. IGOR ARKADIEVICH SHEVCHENKO; publ. *Mechanization, Ecology, Conversion of Bioresources in Animal Husbandry* (4 a year).

Institute of Plant Protection: 03022 Kyiv, 33 Vasilkovskaya; tel. (44) 257-11-24; fax (44) 257-21-85; e-mail plant_prot@ukr.net; internet ippuaan.by.ru; f. 1946; attached to Ukrainian Acad. of Agrarian Sciences; Dir Acad. Prof. Dr VITALIY FEDORENKO; publs *Karantyn i Zahyst Roslyn* (Plant Quarantine and Protection, 12 a year), *Ukrainian Entomological Journal* (2 a year), *Zahayst i Karantyn Roslyn* (Plant Protection and Quarantine, 2 a year).

Institute of Veterinary Research of the Ukrainian Academy of Agricultural Sciences: 03151 Kyiv, vul. Donetska 30; tel. and fax (44) 245-78-05; e-mail vet@ivm.kiev.ua; internet www.ivm.kiev.ua; attached to Ukrainian Acad. of Agricultural Sciences; Dir ANATOLIY OBRAZHEV; publ. *Veterinary Biotechnology* (2 a year).

Land Use Research Institute: 03151 Kyiv, Narodnogo Opolcheniya 3; tel. (44) 275-73-88; f. 1961; attached to Ukrainian Acad. of Agrarian Sciences; Dir DMITRO S. DOBRYAK; publ. *Land-Use Systems* (4 a year).

Magarach Institute of the Vine and Wine: 334200 the Autonomous Republic of Crimea, Yalta, ul. Kirova 31; tel. (65) 432-55-91; fax (65) 423-06-08; e-mail magarach@yalita.yalta.iuf.net; f. 1828; Dir A. M. AVIDZBA; publs *Magarach–Vinogradarstvo i Vinodelie* (in Russian, also English summaries, 4 a year), *Proceedings of the Magarach Institute for Vine and Wine* (in Russian, 2 a year), *Proceedings of the Scientific Centre of Viticulture and Oenology* (in Russian, 2 a year).

Pig Breeding Institute 'O. V. Kvasnitsky': 36006 Poltava, Shvedska Mogila 1; tel. (53) 252-74-19; fax (53) 222-27-53; e-mail slsvin@e-mail.pl.ua; internet web.poltava.ua/firms/slsvin; f. 1930; library of 60,000 vols; Dir Prof. VALENTIN P. RYBALKO; publ. *Pig Breeding* (1 a year).

Plant Breeding and Genetics Institute: 65036 Odessa, Ovidiopolskaya doroga 3; tel. (482) 39-54-01; fax (482) 39-52-89; e-mail sgi-uaan@ukr.net; f. 1912; attached to National Acad. of Agricultural Sciences of Ukraine; devt of breeding and seed production theory, as well as new varieties and hybrids of winter wheat, spring and winter barley, triticale, maize, sunflower, soybean, alfalfa, Sudan grass, sorghum; operates 7 experimental farms for seed production; conferences and workshops on the problems of plant breeding; courses for agronomists and seed-growers; 3-year post-doctoral courses; assistance to agricultural research stations and institutes; organizes research, confs and workshops; library of 115,863 vols; Dir Dr VYACHESLAV SOKOLOV; publ. *Collected Scientific Papers* (2 a year).

'V. M. Remeslo' Mironovka Institute of Wheat: 08853 Kievska oblast, P/o Tsentralne Mironovka; tel. (45) 747-41-35; fax (45) 747-44-46; e-mail mwheats@ukr.net; f. 1911; attached to Nat. Acad. of Agrarian Sciences of Ukraine; wheat and barley breeding, seed production and plant growing; library of 40,000 vols; Dir V. S. KOCHMARSKYI; publ. *Annual Collected Papers*.

Sugar Beet Research Institute: 03141 Kyiv, Klinichna vul. 25; tel. (44) 275-50-00; e-mail isb@isb.kiev.ua; internet www.sugarbeet.com.ua; f. 1922; attached to Ukrainian Acad. of Agrarian Sciences; library of 28,000 vols, 30,000 periodicals; Dir M. V. ROIK; publ. *Tsukrovi buryaky* (Sugar Beet, 6 a year).

Ukrainian Research Institute of Water Management and Ecological Problems: 252010 Kyiv, Inzhenerny prov. 4B; tel. and fax (44) 280-03-02; e-mail undiwep@ukrwecol.kiev.ua; internet www.nbuv.gov.ua/undiwep; f. 1974; library of 10,000 vols; Dir Prof. A. V. YATSYK.

Ukrainian Scientific Research Institute of Ecological Problems: 61166 Kharkiv, vul. Bakulina 6; tel. and fax (57) 702-15-92; e-mail director@niiep.kharkov.ua; internet www.niiep.kharkov.ua; f. 1971 as the All-Union Scientific Research Institute for Protection of Water; Dir Dr GRIGORY D. KOVALENKO (acting).

Zakarpatsky Institute of Agroindustrial Production: 90252 Zakarpatska oblast, Beregovo raion, Selo V. Bakhta; tel. and fax (3141) 2-34-04; e-mail insbakta@bereg.net.ua; f. 1989; 114 mems; library of 40,000 vols; Dir A. V. BAYLAN; publ. *Problems of Agroindustrial Complex of Karpaty* (every 2 years).

ARCHITECTURE AND TOWN PLANNING

Research Institute of Automated Systems in Construction: 03037 Kyiv, vul. M. Krivonosa 2A; tel. and fax (44) 249-72-30; e-mail office@ndiasb.kiev.ua; internet www.ndiasb.kiev.ua; Dir BORIS A. VOLOBOEV.

State Research Institute of Building Constructions: 03680 Kyiv, Ivan Klimenko 5/2; tel. (44) 249-72-34; fax (44) 248-89-09; e-mail adm-inst@ndibk.kiev.ua; internet www.niisk.com; f. 1943; bldg structures: modelling, designing, testing; 500 mems; library of 49,000 vols, 72,000 patents; Dir Dr VASILYY TARASYUK (acting); publs *Building Construction* (2 a year), *World of Geotechnics* (3 a year).

Ukrainian Zonal Scientific and Research Design Institute of Civil Engineering: 01133 Kyiv, bul. L. Ukrainki 26; tel. (44) 286-36-72; fax (44) 285-74-81; e-mail zniiep@adam.kiev.ua; internet www.zniiep.com.ua; f. 1963; library of 125,000 vols; Dir VLADIMIR B. SHEVELEV.

ECONOMICS, LAW AND POLITICS

Council for the Study of Productive Forces of Ukraine: 01032 Kyiv 32, bul. T. Shevchenka 60; tel. (44) 216-90-70; fax (44) 244-66-70; attached to Nat. Acad. of Sciences of Ukraine; 6 attached scientific schools; Dir A. N. ALYMOV.

Institute of Economics: 01011 Kyiv, vul. Panasa Mirnogo 26; tel. (44) 290-84-44; fax (44) 290-86-63; e-mail instecon@ln.ua; f. 1936; attached to Nat. Acad. of Sciences of Ukraine; Dir I. I. LUKINOV.

Institute for Economic Research and Policy Consulting: 01034 Kyiv, Reytarska 8/5-A; tel. (44) 278-63-42; fax (44) 278-63-36; e-mail institute@ier.kiev.ua; internet www.ier.kiev.ua; Dir IGOR BURAKOVSKY.

Institute of Industrial Economics: 83048 Donetsk, Universitetska vul. 77; tel. (62) 55-78-44; fax (62) 345-06-71; e-mail admin@iep.donetsk.ua; f. 1969; attached to Nat. Acad. of Sciences of Ukraine; Dir A. I. AMOSHA; publ. *Ekonomika Promyslovosti* (4 a year, Economics of Industry, in Ukrainian and Russian).

Institute of State and Law 'V. M. Koretsky': 01601 Kyiv, vul. Tryokhsviatitelskai 4; tel. (44) 278-51-55; fax (44) 278-54-74; e-mail jus@ukrpack.net; f. 1948; attached to Nat. Acad. of Sciences of Ukraine; research into the theory and practice of law and state-bldg; Dir YU. S. SHEMSHUCHENKO; publs *Lawful State* (1 a year), *Pravo Ukrainy* (Law of Ukraine, in Ukrainian and English, 12 a year).

Institute of World Economy and International Relations: 01030 Kyiv, vul. Leontovicha 5; tel. (44) 235-70-22; fax (44) 235-51-27; e-mail iweir_nas@iweir.org.ua; internet www.iweir.org.ua; f. 1992; attached to Nat. Acad. of Sciences of Ukraine; Dir Y. M. PAKHOMOV.

HISTORY, GEOGRAPHY AND ARCHAEOLOGY

Institute of Archaeology: 04210 Kyiv, Heroyiv Stalingrada 12; tel. (44) 418-27-75; fax (44) 418-33-06; e-mail sekretar@iananu.kiev.ua; internet www.iananu.kiev.ua; attached to Nat. Acad. of Sciences of Ukraine; Dir P. P. TOLOCHKO; publ. *Arkheologia* (Archaeology, 4 a year, in Ukrainian and English).

Krypiakevych, I., Institute of Ukrainian Studies: 79026 Lviv, Kozelnytska vul. 4; tel.

(32) 270-70-22; fax (32) 270-70-21; e-mail inukr@inst-ukr.lviv.ua; internet www.inst-ukr.lviv.ua; f. 1951; attached to Nat. Acad. of Sciences of Ukraine; archaeology, history, philology, political science; library of 10,000 vols; Dir YAROSLAV D. ISAIEVYCH; publs *Istorychni ta kulturolohichni studii* (4 a year), *Shashkevychiana* (1 a year), *Ukraina: kulturna spadshchyna, natsionalna svidomist, derzhavnist* (2 a year), *Ukrainska dialektna ta istorychna leksyka* (1 a year).

Ukrainian Institute of History: 01001 Kyiv, vul. Hrushevsky 4; tel. and fax (44) 229-63-62; e-mail institute@history.org.ua; internet www.history.org.ua; attached to Nat. Acad. of Sciences of Ukraine; Dir V. A. SMOLIY; publ. *Ukrainsky Istorychny Zhurnal* (Ukrainian Historical Journal, 6 a year, in Ukrainian and English).

LANGUAGE AND LITERATURE

Institute of Linguistics 'O. O. Potebni': 01001 Kyiv, vul. Hrushevsky 4; tel. (44) 229-02-92; fax (44) 228-43-83; attached to Nat. Acad. of Sciences of Ukraine; Dir V. H. SKLIARENKO; publ. *Movoznavstvo* (Linguistics, 6 a year, in Ukrainian and English).

Institute of Literature 'Shevchenko, T. G.': 01001 Kyiv 1, Hrushevskoho 4; tel. (44) 279-10-84; fax (44) 278-52-81; e-mail admin@ilnan.gov.ua; internet www.ilnan.gov.ua; f. 1926; attached to Nat. Acad. of Sciences of Ukraine; history of Ukrainian literature; source and textual researches of Ukrainian literature; Shevchenko studies; history of foreign literatures; theory of literature and methodology of literary researches; comparative literature; literature bibliography; library of 150,000 vols; Dir MYKOLA ZHULYNSKY; publ. *Slovo i Chas* (Word and Time, 12 a year, in Ukrainian).

MEDICINE

Donetsk Scientific Research Institute of Traumatology and Orthopaedics: 83048 Donetsk, vul. Artema 106; tel. (62) 311-05-08; fax (62) 335-14-61; e-mail info@dniito.org.ua; internet www.dniito.org.ua; f. 1953; Dir Prof. Dr VOLODYMYR KLYMOVYTSKYY; publ. *Trauma* (4 a year).

Filatov Institute for Eye Diseases and Tissue Therapy: 65061 Odessa, vul. Frantsi 49–51; tel. (48) 268-62-18; fax (48) 268-48-51; e-mail filatovorg@ukr.net; internet www.filatovinstitut.com.ua; f. 1936; library of 81,000 vols; Dir Prof. IVAN M. LOGAI; publ. *Ophthalmological Journal* (8 a year).

Institute of Cardiovascular Surgery, M. Amosov: 03110 Kiev, M. Amosova vul. 6; tel. and fax (44) 275-43-22; e-mail gvknyshov@ukr.net; f. 1983; 980 mems; Dir Prof. GENNADY V. KNYSHOV; Deputy Dir Prof. VITALY B. MAKSYMENKO; publ. *Annual of Cardiovascular Surgery* (1 a year).

Institute of Clinical Radiology: 04075 Kyiv, Pushcha-Voditsa, vul. Gamarnikova 42; attached to Ukrainian Acad. of Medical Sciences; Dir VOLODYMYR BEBESHKO.

Institute of Dermatology and Venereology: 61057 Kharkiv, Chernyshevskogo vul. 7/9; tel. (57) 706-32-00; fax (57) 706-32-03; e-mail idvamnu@mail.ru; internet www.idvamnu.com.ua; f. 1924; attached to Acad. of Medical Sciences of Ukraine; library of 40,000 vols; Dir Prof. IVAN I. MAVROV; publ. *Journal of Dermatology and Venereology* (4 a year).

Institute of Epidemiology and Infectious Diseases 'L. V. Gromashevsky': 01601 Kyiv, vul. S. Razina 4; tel. (44) 277-37-11; Dir A. F. FROLOV.

Institute of Gerontology: 04114 Kyiv, Vyshgorodska vul. 67; tel. (44) 430-40-68; fax (44) 432-99-56; e-mail ig@geront.kiev.ua; internet www.geront.kiev.ua; f. 1958; attached to Ukrainian Acad. of Medical Sciences; Dir VLADISLAV V. BEZRUKOV; publ. *Problemy stareniya i dolgoletiya* (Problems of Ageing and Longevity, 4 a year).

Institute of Medical Radiology 'S. P. Hrihoryev': 61024 Kharkiv, vul. Pushkinska 82; tel. (57) 704-10-65; fax (57) 700-05-00; e-mail imr@ukr.net; internet www.imr.kharkov.ua; f. 1920; library of 70,000 vols; Dir Prof. Dr MYKOLA I. PILIPENKO; publ. *Ukrainian Journal of Radiology* (4 a year).

Institute for Occupational Health: 01033 Kyiv, vul. Saksakanskogo 75; tel. (44) 284-34-27; fax (44) 289-66-77; e-mail yik@nanu.kiev.ua; f. 1928; attached to Ukraine Acad. of Medical Sciences; library of 50,000 vols; Dir Prof. Y. I. KUNDIEV; publ. *Ukrainian Journal of Occupational Health* (4 a year).

Institute of Pediatrics, Obstetrics and Gynaecology: 04050 Kyiv, Platona Maybborody 8; tel. (44) 483-80-67; fax (44) 483-80-26; e-mail ipag@ukr.net.

Institute for Problems of Cryobiology and Cryomedicine: 61015 Kharkiv, Pereyaslavskaya St 23; tel. (57) 373-41-43; fax (57) 373-30-84; e-mail cryo@online.kharkov.ua; internet www.cryo.org.ua; f. 1972; attached to Nat. Acad. of Sciences of Ukraine; library of 54,011 vols; Dir Acad. Prof. Dr ANATOLIY N. GOLTSEV (acting); publ. *Problemy Kriobiologii* (Problems of Cryobiology, 4 a year, in Ukrainian, Russian and English).

Institute of Surgery and Transplantology: 03680 Kyiv, vul. Geroev Sevastopolya 30; tel. (44) 488-13-74; fax (44) 488-19-09; e-mail surgery@i.com.ua; internet www.surgery.org.ua; f. 1972; library of 25,000 vols; Dir Prof. VALERY SAYENKO; publ. *Clinical Surgery* (12 a year).

R. E. Kavetsky Institute of Experimental Pathology, Oncology and Radiobiology: 03022 Kyiv, Vasylkivska str. 45; tel. (44) 259-01-83; fax (44) 258-16-56; e-mail iepor@onconet.kiev.ua; internet www.onconet.kiev.ua; f. 1960; attached to Nat. Acad. of Sciences of Ukraine; investigation of tumor cell biology and its microenvironment in devt of molecular and cellular mechanisms of oncogenesis; evaluation of molecular and cellular markers of initiation, promotion, progression and devt of methods for diagnostics of malignant tumours; determination of molecular aspects of pharmacological correction of carcinogenesis and drug resistance formation of malignant cell and epigenetic approaches; investigation of nanoparticles and nanocomposite's influence on normal and tumour cells metabolism; devt of approaches to target therapy and sorption detoxification of organism; library of 59,952 vols, 19,650 books, 273 periodicals; Dir Prof. Acad. VASYL F. CHEKHUN; publs *Eksperimentalnaya Onkologia* (Experimental Oncology, 4 a year, in Ukrainian and English), *Oncologia* (4 a year, in Ukrainian and Russian).

Kyiv 'N. D. Strazhesko' Research Institute of Cardiology: 03151 Kyiv, vul. Narodnogo Opolchenia 5; tel. (44) 277-66-22; fax (44) 228-72-72; f. 1936; 650 mems; library of 65,000 vols; Dir Prof. V. A. BOBROV.

Kyiv Research Institute of Oncology: Kyiv, vul. Lomonosova 33/43; tel. (44) 266-75-67; f. 1920; library of 27,000 vols; Dir V. L. GANUL.

Kyiv Research Institute of Otolaryngology: 03057 Kyiv, Zoologichna 3; tel. (44) 483-22-02; fax (44) 483-73-68; e-mail amtc@kndio.kiev.ua; f. 1960; diagnostics, conservative and surgical treatment of patients with ENT-diseases; library of 33,000 vols; Dir Prof. DMYTRO ZABOLOTNYI; publs *Journal of Ear, Nose and Throat Diseases* (6 a year), *Rhinology* (4 a year).

Lviv Scientific Research Institute of Hereditary Pathology: 79000 Lviv, vul. Lysenko 31A; tel. (32) 276-54-99; fax (32) 275-38-44; f. 1940; library of 28,000 vols; Dir O. Z. HNATEIKO; publ. *Medychna Genetyka* (every 2 years, in Ukrainian with Russian and English abstracts).

L. I. Medved's Institute of Ecohygiene and Toxicology: 03680 Kyiv, Heroiv Oborony St 6; tel. (44) 526-97-00; fax (44) 526-96-43; e-mail office@medved.kiev.ua; internet www.medved.kiev.ua; f. 1964; library of 42,000 vols; Dir Prof. Dr MYKOLA PRODANCHUK; publs *Modern Problems of Toxicology* (4 a year), *Preventive Medicine* (4 a year), *Problems of Nutrition* (4 a year).

Phthisiology and Pulmonology Research Institute: vul. M. Amosova 10, 03680 Kyiv; tel. (44) 275-04-02; fax (44) 275-21-18; e-mail admin@ifp.kiev.ua; internet www.ifp.kiev.ua; f. 1922; Dir YURI I. FESCHENKO; publs *Asthma and Allergy* (4 a year), *Ukrainian Chemotherapeutic Journal* (4 a year), *Ukrainian Journal of Pulmonology* (4 a year).

Research Centre for Radiation Medicine: 04050 Kyiv, vul. Melnikova 53; tel. (44) 213-06-37; fax (44) 213-72-02; e-mail baz@rcrm.kiev.ua; f. 1986; attached to Ukrainian Acad. of Medical Sciences; library of 30,000 vols; Dir Prof. V. G. BEBESHKO; publs *International Journal of Radiation Medicine* (6 a year), *Problems of Radiation Medicine* (4 a year).

Research Institute of Physical Methods of Treatment and Medical Climatology 'I. M. Sechenov': 98603 Yalta, Polikurovska vul. 25; tel. (65) 432-75-91; f. 1914; non-medical treatment and prophylaxis of lung diseases and diseases of the cardiovascular and nervous systems; Dir Prof. SERGEI SOLDATCHENKO.

Research Institute of Psychology 'G. S. Kostyuk': 03037 Kyiv, vul. Pankivska 2; tel. (44) 224-19-63; attached to Nat. Acad. of Pedagogical Sciences of Ukraine.

Romodanov, A., Institute of Neurosurgery: 04050 Kyiv, vul. Manuilskogo 32; tel. and fax (44) 483-95-73; e-mail neuro.kiev@gmail.com; internet www.neuro.kiev.ua; f. 1950; diagnosis, surgical and combined treatment of cerebral and spinal tumors, pathogenesis, diagnosis and treatment of CNS damage and its after-effects, surgical treatment of the most complex cerebrovascular pathologies, study of immune responses in patients with neurological CNS pathology; library of 77,000 vols; Dir Acad. Prof. YURIY ZOZULIA; publ. *Ukrainian Neurosurgical Journal* (4 a year).

State Scientific Centre of Drugs: Kharkiv 310085, Astronomicheska vul. 33; tel. (57) 744-10-33; fax (57) 744-11-18; e-mail samatov@phukr.kharkov.ua; internet farmacomua.narod.ru; f. 1920; production and devt of finished drugs and technologies for preparation of phytochemicals; library of 28,000 vols; Dir Prof. V. P. GEORGIEVSKY; publ. *Pharmacom* (4 a year, in Ukrainian and Russian,).

Sytenko Institute of Spine and Joint Pathology: 61024 Kharkiv, Pushkinska vul. 80; tel. (57) 715-75-06; e-mail post@sytenko.org.ua; internet www.sytenko.org.ua; f. 1907; attached to Acad. of Medical Sciences of Ukraine; library of 40,500 vols; Dir Prof. MYKOLA O. KORZH; publ. *Orthopaedics, Traumatology and Prosthetics* (4 a year).

Ukrainian Institute of Public Health: 01601 Kyiv, vul. Dymytrova 5, korp. 10-A, 7th Fl.; tel. (44) 284-39-38; fax (44) 284-39-37; e-mail health@uiph.kiev.ua; internet www .uiph.kiev.ua; f. 1997; attached to Ukrainian Min. of Health; Dir Prof. V. M. PONOMARENKO; publ. *Bulletin of the Social Hygiene and Health Protection Organization of Ukraine* (4 a year).

Ukrainian Research Institute of Traumatology and Orthopaedics: 01601 Kyiv, vul. Vorovskogo 27; tel. (44) 216-42-49; fax (44) 216-44-62; e-mail travma@rql.net.ua; f. 1919; library of 57,000 vols; Dir G. V. GAIKO; publs *Statistical Data Report on Traumatological and Orthopaedic Aid to Ukrainians* (1 a year), *Vestnik Ortopedii, Travmatologii i Protezirovaniia* (Orthopaedics, Traumatology and Prosthesis, 4 a year).

Ukrainian Scientific Centre of Hygiene: 02094 Kyiv, vul. Popudrenko 50; tel. (44) 559-73-73; fax (44) 559-90-90; e-mail usch@ usch.kiev.ua; f. 1931; incl. Institute of General and Communal Hygiene, and Institute of Medical Genetics; library of 102,213 vols; Dir Dr ANDRIY SERDIUK; publ. *Environment and Health* (4 a year).

NATURAL SCIENCES

Biological Sciences

Institute of Biology of Southern Seas: Pr. Nakhimov 2, 99011 Sevastopol; tel. (69) 254-41-10; fax (69) 255-78-13; e-mail ibss@ ibss.iuf.net; internet www.ibss.iuf.net; f. 1871; attached to Nat. Acad. of Sciences of Ukraine; library of 150,000 vols; 350 mems; Dir Dr V. N. EREMEEV; publs *Ekologiya Morya* (Ecology of the Sea, 4 a year), *Morskoj Ekologicheskij Zhurnal* (Marine Ecological Journal, 3 a year).

Institute of Botany 'M. G. Kholodny': 01601 Kyiv, Tereshchenkivska vul. 2; tel. (44) 224-40-41; fax (44) 224-10-64; e-mail inst@botan.kiev.ua; f. 1921; attached to Nat. Acad. of Sciences of Ukraine; library of 106,000 vols; Dir K. M. SYTNIK; publs *Algologiya* (Algology, 4 a year, in Ukrainian and English), *Ukrainsky Botanichny Zhurnal* (Ukrainian Botanical Journal, 6 a year, in Ukrainian and English).

Institute of Cellular Biology and Genetic Engineering: 03143 Kyiv, Vul. Zabolotnogo 148; tel. (44) 526-71-09; fax (44) 526-71-04; e-mail cytogen@iicb.kiev.ua; internet www.cytgen.com; f. 1967; attached to Nat. Acad. of Sciences of Ukraine; Dir YA. B. BLUME; Exec. Sec. FEDYUK ; publ. *Tsitologia i Genetika* (Cytology and Genetics, 6 a year, in Ukrainian and English).

Institute of Hydrobiology: 04210 Kyiv-210, pr. Geroyiv Stalingrada 12; tel. (44) 419-39-81; fax (44) 418-22-32; e-mail hydrobiol@ igb.ibc.com.ua; attached to Nat. Acad. of Sciences of Ukraine; Dir VIKTOR D. ROMANENKO; publ. *Gidrobiologichesky Zhurnal* (Hydrobiological Journal, 6 a year, in Ukrainian and English).

Institute of Molecular Biology and Genetics: 03680 Kyiv vul. Acad. Zabolotnoho 150; tel. (44) 526-11-69; fax (44) 526-07-59; e-mail inform@imbg.org.ua; internet www .imbg.org.ua; f. 1973; attached to Nat. Acad. of Sciences of Ukraine; central trends of molecular biology, genetics and biotechnology: structural and functional genomics; proteomics and protein engineering; regulatory systems and signal transduction mechanisms; bioinformatics and computational modelling; gene and cell biotechnologies, gene therapy and diagnostics; library of 90,000 vols; Dir Prof. Dr ANNA V. EL'SKAYA; Scientific Sec. Dr YANINA R. MISHCHUK; publ. *Biopolymers and Cell* (Biopolymers and Cell, 6 a year, in Ukrainian and English).

Institute of Plant Physiology and Genetics: 03022 Kyiv, Vasylkivska vul. 31/17; tel. (44) 257-01-14; fax (44) 257-51-50; e-mail editor@ifrg.freenet.kiev.ua; f. 1946; attached to Nat. Acad. of Sciences of Ukraine; Dir VLADIMIR V. MORGUN; publ. *Fiziologia i Biokhimia Kulturnykh Rastenii* (Physiology and Biochemistry of Cultivated Plants, in Ukrainian, Russian and English, 6 a year).

Institute for Sorption and Endoecology Problems: 03164 Kyiv, pr. Naumova 13; tel. (44) 452-93-28; fax (44) 452-93-27; e-mail ispe@ispe.kiev.ua; f. 1991; attached to Nat. Acad. of Sciences of Ukraine; Dir V. V. STRELKO.

Schmalhausen Institute of Zoology: 01601 Kyiv, vul. B. Khmelnytskoho 15; tel. (44) 235-10-70; fax (44) 234-15-69; e-mail iz@ izan.kiev.ua; internet www.izan.kiev.ua; f. 1930; attached to Nat. Acad. of Sciences of Ukraine; zoological museum; zoological scientific research; library of 161,947 vols; Dir Prof. IGOR A. AKIMOV; Scientific Dir Dr VITALIY KHARCHENKO; Scientific Dir Prof. IGOR DOVGAL; publ. *Vestnik Zoologii* (Zoological Journal, online, 6 a year, in Ukrainian and English).

'O. O. Bohomolets' Institute of Physiology: 01601 Kyiv, vul. Bohomoltsa 4; tel. (44) 293-20-13; fax (44) 253-64-58; e-mail pkostyuk@serv.biph.kiev.ua; attached to Nat. Acad. of Sciences of Ukraine; Dir P. H. KOSTYUK; publs *Fiziologichny Zhurnal* (Physiological Journal, 6 a year, in Ukrainian and English), *Neirofiziologia* (Neurophysiology, 6 a year, in Ukrainian and English).

Palladin Institute of Biochemistry: 01601 Kyiv 30 vul. Leontovicha 9; tel. (44) 234-59-74; fax (44) 279-63-65; e-mail secretar@biochem.kiev.ua; internet www .biochem.kiev.ua; f. 1925; attached to Nat. Acad. of Sciences of Ukraine; 360 mems; Dir Prof. SERGIY KOMISARENKO; publs *Biotechnologia* (Biotechnology, 6 a year, in Ukrainian, Russian and English), *Ukrainsky Biokhimichny Zhurnal* (Ukrainian Biochemical Journal, 6 a year, in Ukrainian, Russian and English).

Zabolotny Institute of Microbiology and Virology: 03143 Kyiv, vul. Akademika Zabolotnogo 154; tel. (44) 266-11-79; fax (44) 266-23-79; e-mail smirnov@imv.kiev.ua; internet www.imv.kiev.ua; f. 1928; attached to Nat. Acad. of Sciences of Ukraine; library of 121,000 vols; Dir V. V. SMIRNOV; publ. *Mikrobiolohichny Zhurnal* (Microbiology Journal, 6 a year, in Ukrainian, Russian and English).

Mathematical Sciences

Institute of Mathematics: 01601 Kyiv, vul. Repina 3; tel. (44) 234-53-16; fax (44) 235-20-10; e-mail institute@imath.kiev.ua; internet www.imath.kiev.ua; attached to Nat. Acad. of Sciences of Ukraine; Dir A. M. SAMOILENKO; publ. *Ukrainsky Matematychny Zhurnal* (Ukrainian Mathematical Journal, 12 a year, in Ukrainian and English).

Physical Sciences

A. V. Bogatsky Physico-Chemical Institute of the National Academy of Sciences of Ukraine: 65080 Odessa, Lustdorfskaya doroga 86; tel. (48) 766-20-44; fax (48) 765-96-02; e-mail medchem_department@ukr.net; internet physchemin-nas.od.ua/index.php; f. 1977; attached to Nat. Acad. of Sciences of Ukraine; 198 mems; Dir SERGEI ANDRONATI.

Bogolyubov Institute for Theoretical Physics: 03680 Kyiv, vul. Metrologichna 14B; tel. (44) 526-53-62; fax (44) 526-59-98; e-mail itp@bitp.kiev.ua; internet www.bitp .kiev.ua; f. 1966; attached to Nat. Acad. of Sciences of Ukraine; Dir Prof. A. G. ZAGORODNY; publ. *Ukrainian Journal of Physics* (12 a year).

Gas Institute: 03113 Kyiv, Degtiarivksa vul. 39; tel. (44) 456-44-71; fax (44) 456-88-30; e-mail ig-secr@i.com.ua; internet ingas .org.ua; f. 1949; attached to Nat. Acad. of Sciences of Ukraine; library of 110,000 vols; Dir Prof. B. I. BONDARENKO; publ. *Ekotekhnologia i Resursosberezheniye* (Energy Technologies and Resource Saving, 6 a year, in Russian with summary in Ukrainian and English).

Institute of Bio-organic Chemistry and Petrochemistry: 02660 Kyiv, vul. Murmanska 1; tel. (44) 558-53-88; fax (44) 573-25-52; e-mail users@bpci.kiev.ua; f. 1987; attached to Nat. Acad. of Sciences of Ukraine; Dir Prof. V. P. KUKHAR; publ. *Katalys i Neftekhimiya* (Catalysis and Petrochemistry, 4 a year).

Institute of Colloid Chemistry and Water Chemistry 'A. V. Dumansky': 03680 Kyiv 142, Vernadsky pr. 42; tel. (44) 424-01-96; fax (44) 423-82-24; f. 1968; attached to Nat. Acad. of Sciences of Ukraine; Dir V. V. GONCHARUK; publ. *Khimiya i Tekhnologiya Vody* (Water Chemistry and Engineering, 6 a year, in Russian and English).

Institute of General and Inorganic Chemistry 'V. I. Vernadsky': 03680 Kyiv, pr. Akademika Palladina 32/34; tel. (44) 444-34-61; fax (44) 444-30-70; e-mail office@ionc .kiev.ua; internet www.ionc.kar.net; f. 1918; attached to Nat. Acad. of Sciences of Ukraine; fundamental and applied research in inorganic chemistry, coordination chemistry, chemistry of solids, nanochemistry, electrochemistry and physical chemistry of melts, aqueous and non-aqueous solutions, processing of original and recycled metal-containing materials; study of structure and properties of ionic melts, solid electrolytes, inorganic sorbents, coordination compounds of rare, rare-earth and other metals, liquid ionic crystals, membrane materials; research in priority directions of inorganic and physico- inorganic chemistry in the branches of high-temperature coordination chemistry in the melts, gas phases and plasma; synthesis and characterization of novel dielectric, semiconductive, optical, ultrapure oxide materials, superconductors and high-temperature ceramics; Dir Prof. Dr SERGIY V. VOLKOV; Dir Prof. Dr VASILY PEKHNYO; publ. *Ukrainsky Khimichesky Zhurnal* (Ukrainian Chemistry Journal, 12 a year, in Russian, Ukrainian and English).

Institute of Geochemistry, Mineralogy and Ore Formation: 03680 Kyiv-142, pr. Palladina 34; tel. (44) 424-01-05; fax (44) 424-12-70; e-mail pavlenko@igmr.relc.com; f. 1969; attached to Nat. Acad. of Sciences of Ukraine; library of 30,000 vols, 35 periodicals; Dir MYKOLA P. SHCHERBAK; publ. *Mineralogichesky Zhurnal* (Mineralogical Journal, 6 a year, in Ukrainian and English).

Institute of Geological Sciences: 01054 Kyiv, vul. Honchar 55B; tel. (44) 216-94-46; fax (44) 216-98-34; f. 1926; attached to Nat. Acad. of Sciences of Ukraine; Dir Prof. PETRO F. HOZHYK; publ. *Geolohichny Zhurnal* (Geological Journal, 4 a year, in Ukrainian and English).

Institute of Geology and Geochemistry of Combustible Minerals: 79060 Lviv, Naukova vul. 3A; tel. (32) 263-25-41; fax (32) 263-22-09; e-mail igggk@mail.lviv.ua; f. 1951; attached to Nat. Acad. of Sciences of Ukraine; Dir V. E. ZABIGAILO; publ. *Geologia i*

Geokhimia Horiuchykh Kopalyn (Geology and Geochemistry of Mineral Fuels, 4 a year, in Ukrainian and English).

Institute of Geophysics: 03680 Kyiv, pr. Akademika Palladina 32; tel. (44) 424-01-12; fax (44) 450-25-20; e-mail earth@igph.kiev.ua; internet www.igph.kiev.ua; f. 1960; attached to Nat. Acad. of Sciences of Ukraine; Dir V. I. STAROSTENKO; publ. *Geofizichesky Zhurnal* (Geophysical Journal, 6 a year, in Russian, Ukrainian and English).

Institute of Ionosphere: 61002 Kharkiv, Krasnoznamennaya str. 16; tel. and fax (57) 706-22-87; e-mail iion@kpi.kharkov.ua; internet www.iion.org.ua; f. 1991; attached to Nat. Acad. of Sciences of Ukraine and Min. of Education and Science of Ukraine; incoherent scatter method, geophysics, geospace plasma, ionosphere, radio physics; Dir Prof. VITALY TARAN.

G. V. Kurdyumov Institute for Metal Physics: 03680 Kyiv, Acad. Vernadsky blvd 36; tel. (44) 424-10-05; fax (44) 424-25-61; e-mail metall@imp.kiev.ua; internet www.imp.kiev.ua; f. 1946; attached to Nat. Acad. of Sciences of Ukraine; Dir Acad. A. P. SHPAK; Academic Sec. S. A. BESPALOV; publs *Metallofizika i Noveishie Tekhnologii* (Metal Physics and Advanced Technology, 12 a year, in Ukrainian and English), *Uspehi Fiziki Metallov* (Developments in the Physics of Metals).

Institute of Nuclear Research: 03680 Kyiv, pr. Nauky 47; tel. (44) 265-23-49; fax (44) 265-44-63; e-mail interdep@kinr.kiev.ua; internet www.kinr.kiev.ua; f. 1970; attached to Nat. Acad. of Sciences of Ukraine; nuclear physics, atomic energy, radiation physics and radiation material science, physics of plasma, radiation ecology and biology; Dir IVAN M. VYSHNYEVSKIY; Deputy Dir VOLODYMYR OSTASHKO; publ. *Scientific Papers* (irregular).

Institute of Organic Chemistry: 02660 Kyiv, Murmanska vul. 5; tel. (44) 552-71-50; fax (44) 573-26-43; f. 1939; Dir MYRON O. LOZYNSKIY.

Institute of Physical-Organic Chemistry and Coal Chemistry 'L. M. Litvinenko': 83114 Donetsk, vul. R. Lyuksemburg 70; tel. and fax (62) 311-68-30; e-mail postmaster@infou.donetsk.ua; f. 1975; attached to Nat. Acad. of Sciences of Ukraine; coal and products of its processing; synthesis and investigation of the structure and properties of heterocyclic compounds, incl. biologically active ones; library of 110,000 vols, 13 periodicals; Dir Acad. ANATOLY F. POPOV.

Institute of Physics: 03028 Kyiv, pr. Nauky 46; tel. (44) 525-12-20; fax (44) 525-15-89; e-mail fizyka@iop.kiev.ua; internet www.iop.kiev.ua; f. 1929; attached to Nat. Acad. of Sciences of Ukraine; Dir M. S. BRODYN; publ. *Ukrainsky Fizychny Zhurnal* (Ukrainian Physics Journal, 12 a year, in Ukrainian and English).

Institute of Radio Astronomy: 61002 Kharkiv, Chervonopraporna vul. 4; tel. (57) 706-14-10; fax (57) 706-14-15; e-mail rai@ri.kharkov.ua; internet www.ri.kharkov.ua; f. 1985; attached to Nat. Acad. of Sciences of Ukraine; Dir LEONID M. LYTVYNENKO; publ. *Radiofizyka i Radioastronomiya* (Radio Physics and Radio Astronomy, 4 a year, in Ukrainian, Russian and English).

Institute of Single Crystals: 61001 Kharkiv, pr. Lenina 60; tel. (57) 341-01-66; fax (57) 340-93-43; e-mail info@isc.kharkov.com; internet www.isc.kharkov.com; f. 1961; attached to Nat. Acad. of Sciences of Ukraine; Dir Dr VYACHESLAV M. PUZIKOV; publ. *Functional Materials* (4 a year, in English).

Chuiko Institute of Surface Chemistry: 03164 Kyiv, vul. Naumova, 17; tel. (44) 422-96-04; fax (44) 424-35-67; e-mail info@isc.gov.ua; internet www.isc.gov.ua; f. 1986; attached to Nat. Acad. of Sciences of Ukraine; library of 20,000 vols; Dir Prof. M. T. KARTEL; publs *Chemistry, Physics and Technology of Surface* (4 a year), *Surface*.

V. Lashkaryov Institute of Semiconductor Physics: 03028 Kyiv, pr. Nauky 41; tel. (44) 525 40-20; fax (44) 525-83-42; e-mail info@isp.kiev.ua; internet www.isp.kiev.ua; f. 1960; attached to Nat. Acad. of Sciences of Ukraine; library of 171,628 vols; 23,707 books; Dir Acad. V. F. MACHULIN; Exec. Dir VASYL TOMASHYK; publs *Optoelektronika i Poluprovodnikovaya Tekhnika* (Optoelectronics and Semiconductor Technology, 1 a year), *Semiconductor Physics, Quantum Electronics and Optoelectronics* (4 a year, in English).

Main Astronomical Observatory: 03680 Kyiv, vul. Akademika Zabolotnogo 27; tel. (44) 526-31-10; fax (44) 526-21-47; e-mail director@mao.kiev.ua; internet www.mao.kiev.ua; f. 1944; attached to Nat. Acad. of Sciences of Ukraine; Dir YA. S. YATSKIV; publs *Kinematika i Fizika Nebesnykh Tel* (Kinematics and Physics of Celestial Bodies, 6 a year, in Ukrainian and English), *Space Science and Technology* (4 a year).

Marine Hydrophysical Institute: 99011 Sevastopol, vul. Kapitanska 2; tel. (69) 254-04-52; fax (69) 255-43-53; e-mail vaivanov@alpha.mhi.iuf.net; internet www.mhi.iuf.net; attached to Nat. Acad. of Sciences of Ukraine; Dir Prof. VITALY A. IVANOV; publs *Morskoy Gidrofizichesky Zhurnal* (Marine Hydrophysical Journal, in Ukrainian, Russian and English), *Physical Oceanography* (6 a year).

Pisarzhevsky, L. V., Institute of Physical Chemistry: 03028 Kyiv, Pr. Nauki 31; tel. (44) 265-11-90; fax (44) 265-62-16; e-mail ipcukr@sovam.com; internet www.inphyschem_nas.kiev.ua; f. 1927; attached to Nat. Acad. of Sciences of Ukraine; Dir Prof. V. D. POKHODENKO; publ. *Teoreticheskaya i Eksperimentalnaya Khimiya* (Theoretical and Experimental Chemistry, 6 a year, in Russian and English).

Research and Design Institute of Basic Chemistry: 61002 Kharkiv, Mironositska vul. 25; tel. (57) 700-01-23; fax (57) 700-48-25; e-mail office@niochim.kharkov.ua; internet www.niochim.kharkov.ua/niochim1.htm; f. 1923; library of 185,000 vols; Dir E. I. VELIEV.

Ukrainian State Geological Research Institute: 04114 Kyiv, vul. Avtozavodska 78; tel. (44) 430-70-24; fax (44) 430-41-76; e-mail ukrdgri@ukrdgri.gov.ua; internet www.ukrdgri.gov.ua; f. 1953; brs in Chirnigiv, Dnipropetrovsk, Lviv, Poltava and Simferopol; Dir MYKHAYLO D. KRASNOZHON.

PHILOSOPHY AND PSYCHOLOGY

'H. S. Skovoroda' Institute of Philosophy: 01001 Kyiv, vul. Tryokhsviatytelska 4; tel. (44) 278-06-05; fax (44) 278-63-66; e-mail if-ukr@i.kiev.ua; internet www.filosof.com.ua; f. 1946; attached to Nat. Acad. of Sciences of Ukraine; researching in different areas of philosophy; library of 65,000 vols; Dir Prof MYROSLAV POPOVYCH; publs *Filosofska Dumka* (Philosophical Thought, 6 a year, in Ukrainian), *Filosofski Obryi* (Philosophical Horizons, 2 a year, in Ukrainian), *Praktychna Filosofia* (Practical Philosophy, 4 as year), *Religiyna Panorama* (Religious Panorama, 12 a year).

RELIGION, SOCIOLOGY AND ANTHROPOLOGY

Institute of Art, Folklore Studies and Ethnography 'M. T. Rylsky': 01001 Kyiv, vul. Kirova 4; tel. (44) 266-20-08; e-mail etnolog@etnolog.kiev.ua; internet www.etnolog.kiev.ua; f. 1936; attached to Nat. Acad. of Sciences of Ukraine; Dir Prof. Dr H. A. SKRYPNYK; publ. *Folklore Studies*.

Institute of Sociology: 01021 Kyiv, Shovkovychna 12; tel. (44) 255-74-09; fax (44) 291-56-96; e-mail i-soc@i-soc.org.ua; internet www.i-soc.com.ua; f. 1990; attached to Nat. Acad. of Sciences of Ukraine; Dir Prof. VALERIY M. VORONA; publ. *Sotsiolohiya: Teoriya, Metody, Marketing* (Sociology: Theory, Methods, Marketing, 6 a year, in Ukrainian and English).

TECHNOLOGY

Donetsk Institute for Physics and Engineering 'O. O. Galkin': 83114 Donetsk, vul. R. Lyuksemburg 72; tel. (62) 311-52-27; fax (62) 342-90-18; e-mail scsecr@scsecr.fti.ac.donetsk.ua; internet www.fti.ac.donetsk.ua/zhurnal.htm; f. 1965; attached to Nat. Acad. of Sciences of Ukraine; 12 scientific depts, 2 scientific-auxiliary depts, 12 auxiliary subdiv., 1 spec. scientific and technical br., centre for collective use; electronic and kinetic properties of solids, physics of magnetic phenomena, phase transitions, spectroscopy of solids, physics of strength and plasticity, physical material science, pressure treatment of materials, physical process of mining, high-pressure equipment, experimental technique, production equipment; library of 160,000 vols; Dir Prof. Dr VIKTOR N. VARYUKHIN; Vice-Dir VIKTOR A. BELOSHENKO; Scientific Sec. ELENA G. PASHINSKA; publ. *Fizika i Tekhnika Vysokikh Davleniy* (High-pressure Physics and Technology, 4 a year, in Ukrainian and English).

E. O. Paton Electric Welding Institute: 03680 Kyiv, vul. Bozhenko 11; tel. (44) 200-60-16; fax (44) 206-17-87; e-mail office@paton.kiev.ua; internet www.paton.kiev.ua; f. 1934; attached to Nat. Acad. of Sciences of Ukraine; Dir Prof. B. E. PATON; publs *Avtomaticheskaya Svarka* (Automatic Welding, 12 a year, in Russian and English), *Sovremennaya Elektrometallurgiya* (Electrometallurgy Today, 4 a year, in Russian), *Tekhnicheskaya Diagnostika i Nerazrushayushchiy Control* (Technical Diagnostics and Non-destructive Testing, 4 a year, in Russian and English).

Frantsevich, I. N., Institute of Problems of Materials Science: 03142 Kyiv, vul. Krzhizhanovskoho 3; tel. (44) 424-01-02; fax (44) 424-21-31; e-mail dir@materials.kiev.ua; f. 1952; attached to Nat. Acad. of Sciences of Ukraine; Dir V. V. SKOROHOD; publ. *Poroshkovaya Metallurgia* (Powder Metallurgy, 12 a year, in Ukrainian and English).

Institute of Applied Mathematics and Mechanics: 83114 Donetsk, vul. R. Lyuksemburg 74; tel. (622) 55-23-94; fax (622) 55-22-65; e-mail math@iamm.ac.donetsk.ua; internet www.iamm.ac.donetsk.ua; f. 1965; attached to Nat. Acad. of Sciences of Ukraine; library of 89,415 vols; Dir ALEKSANDR M. KOVALEV; publs *Mekhanika Tverdogo Tela* (1 a year), *Nelineinye Granichnye Zadachi* (1 a year), *Trudy Instituta Prikladnoi Matematiki i Mehaniki NAN Ukrainy* (1 a year), *Ukrains'kyi Matematychnyi Visnyk* (Ukrainian Mathematical Bulletin, 4 issues in 1 vol, 1 a year).

Institute of Cybernetics 'V. M. Hlushkov': 03680 Kyiv MSP, Glushkova 20; tel. (44) 266-20-08; fax (44) 266-74-18; e-mail aik@public.icyb.kiev.ua; internet www.icyb.kiev.ua; attached to Nat. Acad. of Sciences of

Ukraine; Dir I. K. SERHIENKO; publs *Kibernetika i Sistemny Analiz* (Cybernetics and Systems Analysis, 6 a year, in Ukrainian and English), *Problemy Upravlenia i Informatiki* (Problems of Control and Informatics, 6 a year, in Ukrainian and English), *Upravlyauschie Sistemy i Mashiny* (Control Systems and Computers, 6 a year, in Ukrainian and English).

Institute of Electrodynamics: 03680 Kyiv, Peremohy 56; tel. (44) 456-01-51; fax (44) 456-94-94; internet www.ied.org.ua; f. 1947; attached to Nat. Acad. of Sciences of Ukraine; Dir O. V. KYRYLENKO; publs *Tekhnichna Elektrodynamika* (Technical Electrodynamics, 6 a year, in Ukrainian, Russian and English), *Works of Institute of Electrodynamics* (3 a year, in Ukrainian and Russian).

Institute of Engineering Mechanics 'A. M. Pidhorny': 61046 Kharkiv, vul. Pozharskoho 2/10; tel. (57) 294-55-14; fax (57) 294-46-35; e-mail root@ipmach.kharkov.ua; internet www.ipmach.kharkov.ua; attached to Nat. Acad. of Sciences of Ukraine; Dir YURI M. MATSEVITIY; publ. *Problemy Mashinostroenia* (Problems of Mechanical Engineering, 4 a year, in Ukrainian and English).

Institute of Engineering Thermophysics: 03057 Kyiv, vul. Zhelyabova 2A, k. 102; tel. (44) 456-62-82; fax (44) 456-60-91; e-mail admin@ittf.kiev.ua; internet www.ittf.kiev.ua; attached to Nat. Acad. of Sciences of Ukraine; Dir ANATOLIY A. DOLINSKIY; publ. *Promyshlennaya Teplotekhnika* (Industrial Thermal Engineering, in Ukrainian and English, 6 a year).

Institute of Geotechnical Mechanics: 320095 Dnipropetrovsk, Simferopolska vul. 2A; tel. (56) 246-01-51; fax (56) 246-24-26; e-mail nanu@igtm.dp.ua; internet www.igtm.narod.ru; f. 1962; attached to Nat. Acad. of Sciences of Ukraine; library of 109,000 vols; Dir A. F. BULAT; publ. *Geotechnical Mechanics* (4 a year).

Institute of Hydromechanics: 03057 Kyiv, vul. Zhelyabova 8/4; tel. (44) 456-43-13; fax (44) 455-64-32; e-mail office@hydromech.com.ua; internet www.hydromech.kiev.ua; f. 1926; attached to Nat. Acad. of Sciences of Ukraine; library of 84,727 vols; Dir VIKTOR T. GRINCHENKO; publs *Acoustics Bulletin* (4 a year), *Applied Hydromechanics* (4 a year).

Institute for Information Recording: 03113 Kyiv, vul. Shpaka 2; tel. (44) 446-83-89; fax (44) 241-72-33; e-mail petrov@ipri.kiev.ua; internet www.ipri.kiev.ua; f. 1987; attached to Nat. Acad. of Sciences of Ukraine; optical storage, information-analytical systems, information security, digital transfer of Edison cylinders with audio-cultural heritage, expert decision-making support systems; 210 mems; Dir V. V. PETROV; publs *Reestracia Zberezenna i Obrobka Danih* (Data Recording, Storage and Processing, 4 a year, in Ukrainian, Russian and English), *Ukrainsky Referatyvny Zhurnal 'Dzherelo'* (Ukrainian Journal of Abstracts 'Dzherelo', 6 a year, in Ukrainian and English).

Institute of Low-Temperature Physics and Engineering 'B. I. Verkin': 61103 Kharkiv, pr. Lenina 47; tel. (57) 340-22-23; fax (57) 340-33-70; e-mail ilt@ilt.kharkov.ua; internet www.ilt.kharkov.ua; f. 1960; attached to Nat. Acad. of Sciences of Ukraine; library of 40,000 vols; Dir Prof. SERGEI LEONIDOVICH GNATCHENKO; publs *Fizika Nizkikh Temperatur* (Low-temperature Physics, 12 a year, in Ukrainian, Russian and English), *Matematicheskaya Fizika, Analiz, Geometria* (Mathematical Physics, Analysis, Geometry, 4 a year, in Ukrainian, Russian and English).

Institute of Mining and the Chemical Industry: 79026 Lviv, Striiska vul. 98; tel. (32) 297-13-77; fax (32) 234-40-61; e-mail ghp@ghp.lviv.ua; internet www.glrhimprom.narod.ru; f. 1956; Chair. I. I. ZOZULIA.

Institute of Pulse Research and Engineering: 54018 Mykolayiv, Zhovtnevy pr. 43A; tel. (51) 222-41-13; fax (51) 222-61-40; e-mail iipt@iipt.com.ua; internet www.iipt.com.ua; f. 1962; attached to Nat. Acad. of Sciences of Ukraine; library of 126,000 vols; Dir O. I. VOVCHENKO.

Institute of Radiophysics and Electronics 'O. Ya. Usikov': 61085 Kharkiv, vul. Akademika Proskury 12; tel. (57) 244-83-19; fax (57) 244-11-05; e-mail ire@ire.kharkov.ua; internet www.ire.kharkov.ua; f. 1955; attached to Nat. Acad. of Sciences of Ukraine; Dir VLADIMIR M. YAKOVENKO.

Institute for Superhard Materials: 04074 Kyiv, Avtozavodska vul. 2; tel. (44) 468-86-32; fax (44) 468-86-25; internet www.ism.ua; f. 1961; attached to Nat. Acad. of Sciences of Ukraine; Dir Prof. N. V. NOVIKOV; publs *Instumentalnyi Swit* (World of Tools, 6 a year), *Sverkhtviordye Materialy* (Superhard Materials, 6 a year, in Russian and English).

Iron and Steel Institute 'Z. I. Nekrasov': 49050 Dnipropetrovsk, pl. Akademika Starodubova 1; tel. (56) 776-53-15; fax (56) 776-59-24; e-mail isi-nasu@a-teleport.com; internet www.isi.dnepr.net; f. 1939; attached to Nat. Acad. of Sciences of Ukraine; Dir Prof. Dr VADIM I. BOLSHAKOV; publ. *Fundamental and Applied Problems of the Steel Industry* (proceedings, 1 a year).

Physical Mechanical Institute 'Karpenko': 79060 Lviv, vul. Naukova 5; tel. (32) 263-30-88; fax (32) 264-94-27; e-mail pminasu@ipm.lviv.ua; internet www.ipm.lviv.ua; f. 1951; attached to Nat. Acad. of Sciences of Ukraine; library of 100,000 vols; problems of modern materials science, physicochemical fracture mechanics of materials and strength of structures; Dir Acad. V. V. PANASYUK; publs *Fizyko-Khimichna Mekhanika Materialiv* (Physical and Chemical Mechanics of Materials, 6 a year, in Ukrainian and English), *Vidbir i Obrobka Informatsii* (Information Extraction and Processing, 2 a year, in Ukrainian).

Pidstryhach Institute of Applied Problems of Mechanics and Mathematics: 79060 Lviv, Naukova str. 3B; tel. (32) 263-83-77; fax (32) 263-62-70; e-mail adm@iapmm.lviv.ua; internet www.iapmm.lviv.ua; f. 1973; attached to Nat. Acad. of Sciences of Ukraine; Dir Prof. ROMAN M. KUSHNIR; Deputy Dir VOLODYMYR PELYKH; publs *Applied Problems of Mechanics and Mathematics* (1 a year), *Mathematical Methods and Physicomechanical Fields* (4 a year).

G. S. Pisarenko Institute for Problems of Strength: 01014 Kyiv, Timiryazevska vul. 2; tel. (44) 285-16-87; fax (44) 286-16-84; e-mail ips@ipp.kiev.ua; internet www.ipp.kiev.ua; f. 1966; attached to Nat. Acad. of Sciences of Ukraine; Dir V. T. TROSHCHENKO; publ. *Problemy Prochnosti* (Strength of Materials, 6 a year, in Russian and English).

Research and Development Institute of the Merchant Marine of Ukraine: 65026 Odessa, Lanzheronovska vul. 15A; tel. (48) 741-17-04; fax (48) 741-11-77; e-mail unii@paco.net; internet www.unii.odessa.ua; f. 1947; Dir ALEXANDER LESNIK.

Research Institute of the Sewn Goods Industry: 03680 Kyiv, vul. P. Lyubchenko 15; tel. (44) 528-55-41; fax (44) 528-64-57; e-mail legprom@i.kiev.ua; internet www.iptelecom.net.ua/~legprom; f. 1961; library of 22,500 vols; Dir V. P. KRYSKO.

State Research and Design Institute of Chemical Engineering 'Khimtekhnologiya': 93400 Luhansk oblast, Severodonetsk, vul. Vilesova 1; tel. (64) 523-42-20; fax (64) 522-50-42; internet www.ixt.lg.ua; f. 1950; library of 130,000 vols; Dir PETR P. BORISOV; publ. *Collected Research Papers* (12 a year).

State Titanium Research and Design Institute: 69035 Zaporizhia, Lenina 180; tel. (61) 233-23-23; fax (61) 224-67-01; e-mail common@timag.org; internet www.timag.org; f. 1956; design and devt of non-ferrous metallurgical processes, production of semiconductors and carbon-graphite materials; Dir-Gen. Dr IGOR V. ZABELIN.

Timoshenko, S. P., Institute of Mechanics: 03057 Kyiv, vul. Nesterova 3; tel. (44) 456-93-51; fax (44) 456-03-19; e-mail ang@imech.freenet.kiev.ua; internet www.inmech.kiev.ua; library of 20,000 vols; f. 1918; mechanics of composite and inhomogenous materials; structural mechanics; mechanics of coupled fields in materials and structures; mechanics of fracture and fatigue; dynamics and stability of mechanical system motion; attached to Nat. Acad. of Sciences of Ukraine; Dir Prof. Dr ALEXANDER N. GUZ; publs *International Applied Mechanics* (12 a year, in English), *Prikladnaya Mekhanika* (12 a year, in Russian).

Ukrainian State Research and Design Institute of Mining Geology, Rock Mechanics and Mine Surveying (UkrNIMI): 83121 Donetsk, vul. Chelyuskintsev 291; tel. (62) 348-16-48; fax (62) 348-16-47; e-mail ukrnimi@ukrnimi.donetsk.ua; internet www.ukrnimi.donetsk.ua; f. 1929; attached to Nat. Acad. of Science of Ukraine; Dir Dr A. V. ANTSIFEROV.

Vniichimprojekt Institute: 02002 Kyiv-2, vul. M. Raskovoi 11; tel. (44) 517-05-81; fax (44) 517-15-18; e-mail vniichim@nbi.com.ua; internet www.himpro.com.ua; f. 1970; develops synthetic detergents, personal care products and packaging materials; library of 38,800 vols; Pres. VALERY N. KRIVOSHEI; publs *Khimichna Promyslovist Ukrainy* (6 a year), *Upakovka* (6 a year).

Yuzhniigiprogaz Institute OJSC: 83121 Donetsk, vul. Artema 169G; tel. (62) 305-76-61; fax (62) 305-71-76; e-mail ex@yuzh-gaz.donetsk.ua; internet www.ungg.org; f. 1933; library of 38,000 vols; Dir V. D. BONDARTSOV.

Libraries and Archives

Chernivtsi

Scientific Library Yuriy Fedkovych Chernivtsi National University: 58000 Chernivtsi, vul. Lesi Ukrainki 23; tel. (37) 258-47-60; e-mail biblio@chnu.cv.ua; internet www.library.chnu.edu.ua; f. 1852; 2.6m. vols; Dir MYKHAILO B. ZUSHMAN.

Dnipropetrovsk

Dnipropetrovsk National University Library 'O. Gonchar': 49050 Dnipropetrovsk, vul. Kozakova 8; tel. (56) 246-61-95; internet www.dsu.dp.ua/lib.html; 1,417,000 vols; Dir S. V. KUBYSHKINA.

Donetsk

Scientific Library of Donetsk National University: 83055 Donetsk, Universitetska vul. 24; tel. (62) 299-23-78; fax (62) 292-71-12; e-mail bdongu@dongu.donetsk.ua; internet library.dongu.donetsk.ua; f. 1937; 1,052,763 vols; Dir N. A. KARYAGINA.

Kharkiv

Kharkiv V. N. Karazin National University Central Scientific Library: 61077 Kharkiv, pl. Svobody 4; tel. (57) 707-52-86; fax (57) 707-12-55; e-mail cnb@univer.kharkov.ua; internet www.library.univer.kharkov.ua; f. 1804; 3.4m. vols, incl. 50,000 rare editions, 19 incunabula, more than 1,000 manuscripts, books by classical writers and scholars published in their lifetimes; Dir IRINA K. ZHURAVLYOVA (acting).

Kyiv

Archives of Ukraine:

Attached Archives:

Central State Archive and Museum of Literature and Art of Ukraine: 01601 Kyiv, Volodymyrska vul. 22A; tel. and fax (44) 278-44-81; f. 1966; Dir LEONID SKRYPKA.

Central State Archive of Public Organizations of Ukraine: 01011 Kyiv, Kutuzova vul. 24; tel. (44) 295-55-32; e-mail cdago@online.com.ua.

Central State Archive of Supreme Bodies of Power and Government of Ukraine:tel. (44) 275-36-66; e-mail tsdavo@archives.gov.ua.

Central State CinePhotoFono Archive of Ukraine 'H. S. Pshenychniy': 03110 Kyiv, Solomyanska vul. 24; tel. (44) 275-37-77; e-mail tsdkffa@archives.gov.ua; internet www.tsdkffa.archives.gov.ua; Dir NINA TOPISHKO.

Central State Historical Archive of Ukraine in Kyiv: 03110 Kyiv, Solomyanska vul. 24; tel. and fax (44) 275-30-02; e-mail mail@cdiak.archives.gov.ua; internet www.archives.gov.ua; f. 1852; Dir IVAN KISIL.

State Archive of Kyiv Oblast: 04119 Kyiv, Melnykova vul. 38; tel. (44) 213-75-72.

State Archive of the City of Kyiv: 04060 Kyiv, Oleny Telihy vul. 23; tel. (44) 440-54-16; e-mail archiv@archiv.kyiv-city.gov.ua.

State Committee on Archives of Ukraine: 03110 Kyiv, Solomyanska vul. 24; tel. (44) 275-27-77; fax (44) 275-36-55; e-mail mail@archives.gov.ua; internet www.archives.gov.ua; f. 1919; Dir-Gen. OLHA HINZBURH.

Kyiv National University 'Taras Shevchenko' Library: 01601 Kyiv, vul. Volodymyrska 58; tel. (44) 235-70-98; fax (44) 235-70-98; e-mail info@libcc.univ.kiev.ua; internet www.library.univ.kiev.ua; f. 1834; 3,559,000 vols; Dir VALENTINA G. NESTERENKO.

National Parliamentary Library of Ukraine: 01001 Kyiv, vul. M. Hrushevskoho 1; tel. (44) 228-85-12; fax (44) 228-85-12; internet www.nplu.kiev.ua; f. 1866; 4,000,000 vols; Dir A. P. KORNIENKO; publ. *Kalendar znamennikh i pamyatnikh dat* (4 a year).

National Scientific Medical Library: 01033 Kyiv, vul. L. Tolstogo 7; tel. (44) 234-51-97; fax (44) 235-11-35; e-mail medlib@library.gov.ua; internet www.library.gov.ua; f. 1930; 1.5m. vols; Gen. Dir RAISA I. PAVLENKO.

State Archival Service of Ukraine: 03110 Kyiv, Solamianska St 24; tel. (44) 275-27-77; fax (44) 275-36-55; internet www.archives.gov.ua; f. 1919; Head OLHA HINZBURH.

State History Library: 01015 Kyiv vul. Sichnevoho Povstannya 21; tel. (44) 290-46-17; e-mail shlu@shlu.freenet.kiev.ua; f. 1939; Dir OLENA VINOHRADOVA.

State Scientific Agricultural Library of Ukrainian Academy of Agricultural Sciences: 03680 Kyiv, vul. Heroyiv Oborony 10; tel. (44) 527-80-75; fax (44) 526-05-09; e-mail cnsgb@faust.kiev.ua; internet dnsgb.kiev.ua; f. 1921; 1,017,323 vols; Dir Dr VIKTOR A. VERGUNOV; publs *Agropromysloviy Complex Ukrainy* (abstract journal, 4 a year), *Akademiky Ukrainskoi Akademii Agrarnykh Nauk* (bibliographic series, 6–7 a year), *Silskohospodarki Knyhy* (4 a year).

State Scientific and Technical Library of Ukraine: 03650 Kyiv, vul. Antonovicha 180; tel. (44) 528-21-85; fax (44) 529-34-91; e-mail alex@gntb.gov.ua; internet gntb.gov.ua; f. 1935; 20m. vols, incl. books, documents and patents related to science and technology; Dir V. H. DRYGAYLO.

Ukrainian Institute of Scientific-Technical and Economic Information: 03680 Kyiv, vul. Horkogo 180; tel. (44) 268-25-79; fax (44) 268-25-41; Dir N. N. ERMOSHENKO.

Vernadsky National Library of Ukraine: 03039 Kyiv, pr. 40 Richja Zhovtnja 3; tel. (44) 265-81-04; fax (44) 264-33-98; e-mail nlu@csl.freenet.kiev.ua; internet www.nbuv.go.ua; f. 1919; over 14m. vols; colln incl. books, newspapers, magazines, serials, maps, music scores, fine arts materials, manuscripts, old and rare books, incunabula, documents; colln of Slavic writings; archives of outstanding Ukrainian and foreign scientists; archives of the National Academy of Sciences of Ukraine; 40 departments and centres of preservation and restoration, culture and education, computer technologies, and publishing; Dir-Gen. O. S. ONYSHCHENKO; publs *Bibliotechnyi Visnyk* (Library Journal, 6 a year, in Ukrainian and English), *Naukovi Pratsi* (Scientific Works, 2 or 3 a year).

Lviv

Lviv Ivan Franko State University Library: 290602 Lviv, vul. Dragomanova 5; tel. (32) 273-04-94; 2.5m. vols; Dir V. K. POTAICHUK.

Lviv National Stefanyk Scientific Library of Ukraine: 79000 Lviv, vul. Stefanyka 2; tel. (32) 274-43-72; fax (32) 2272-91-47; e-mail library@lsl.lviv.ua; internet www.lsl.lviv.ua; f. 1940; 6m. vols; Dir MIROSLAV. M. ROMANYUK.

Odesa

Scientific Library of the Odessa National I. I. Mechnikov University: 65082 Odessa, st. Preobrazhenska 24; tel. and fax (48) 726-04-01; e-mail library@onu.edu.ua; internet www.library.onu.edu.ua; f. 1817; 3,700,000 vols; Dir MARINA A. PODREZOVA; Deputy Dir and IT-Man. ZAYCHENKO ALLA; publ. *Odessa National University Herald. Series: Library studies, Bibliography studies, Bibliology.*

Simferopol

Taurida National University 'V. I. Vernadsky', Library: 95007 Simferopol, pr. Vernaskogo 4; tel. (65) 251-69-98; fax (65) 251-71-35; e-mail library@crimea.edu; 776,000 vols; Librarian V. I. SPIROVA.

Uzhhorod

Uzhorod National University Library: Uzhgorod, Kapytulna vul. 9; tel. (31) 223-72-29; internet www.univ.uzhgorod.ua/~library; 1.5m. vols; Dir OLENA I. POCHEKUTOVA.

Museums and Art Galleries

Alupka

Alupka State Palace and Park Preserve: Alupka, Dvortsove shosse 10; tel. and fax (65) 472-29-51; f. 1921; Russian noble culture and way of life in 19th century; spec. colln of 17th century maps of Europe and America; library of 10,000 vols; Dir K. K. KASPEROVICH.

Alushta

Alushta Literary Memorial Museum of S. M. Sergeev-Tsensky: Alushta, vul. Sergeeva-Tsenskogo 15; tel. (65) 603-06-64; house where the author lived; Dir T. A. FEFYUZA.

Bakhchisarai

Bakhchisarai Historical and Cultural State Preserve: 98405 Crimea, Bakhchisarai, ul. Richna 133; tel. and fax (65) 544-28-81; e-mail hansaray@crimeastar.net; internet www.hansaray.org.ua; f. 1917; works of art, architectural monuments, the Khan Palace of Bakhchisarai (built 1532), cave towns; archeological sites; archeology and ethnographic collns; library of 12,000 vols; Dir-Gen. EUGENY PETROV; Deputy Dir OLEKSA HAIWORONSKI.

Chernihiv

Chernihiv Literary Museum 'Mikhailo Kotsyubinsky': 14000 Chernihiv, vul. Kotsyubinskogo 3; tel. (46) 224-04-59; f. 1934; life and work of Kotsyubinsky; library of 11,000 books; Dir IGOR KOTSYUBINSKY; publ. *Collections* (every 5 years).

Chernivtsi

Chernivtsi Memorial Museum 'Yu. A. Fedkovych': Chernivtsi, vul. Pushkina 17; tel. (37) 22-56-78; f. 1945; life and work of the writer A. Fedkovich; Dir D. FYLYPCHUK.

Dniprodzerzhynsk

Dniprodzerzhynsk Museum of Town History: 51931 Dniprodzerzhynsk; tel. (56) 923-11-10; f. 1931; library of 10,000 vols; Dir NATALIA BULANOVA.

Dnipropetrovsk

Dnipropetrovsk Historical Museum 'D. I. Yavornystkiy': Dnipropetrovsk, vul. K. Marksa 16; tel. (56) 246-24-28; fax (56) 246-05-12; e-mail muzeum@a-teleport.com; internet www.museum.dp.ua; Dir NADEZHDA KAPUSTINA.

Dnipropetrovsk State Art Museum: 49044 Dnipropetrovsk, vul. Shevchenko 21; tel. (56) 247-32-65; e-mail info@globe.dp.ua; internet www.artmuseum.dp.ua; Dir VLADIMIR KULICHIKHIN.

Donetsk

Donetsk Art Museum: 83055 Donetsk, Pushkina 35; tel. (62) 304-83-03.

Donetsk Botanical Gardens: 83059 Donetsk, pr. Ilicha 110; tel. (62) 294-12-80; fax (62) 294-61-57; e-mail herb@herb.dn.ua; f. 1964; attached to Nat. Acad. of Sciences of Ukraine; Dir A. Z. GLUKHOV.

Kamyanets-Podilsky

Kamyanets-Podilsky State Historical Museum-Preserve: 32300 Khmelnitska oblast, Kamyanets-Podilsky, vul. Ioanno-Predtechenska 2; tel. (38) 492-37-84; f. 1890; Dir L. P. STANISLAVSKA.

Kerch

Kerch State Archaeological Museum: 98300 Crimea, Kerch, Sverdlova 7; tel. and fax (65) 2-04-75; e-mail museum@kerch.com

.ua; f. 1826; library of 20,000 vols; Dir P. I. IVANENKO; publ. *Arkheologiya i istoriya Bospora* (irregular).

Kharkiv

Kharkiv State Art Museum: 61002 Kharkiv, Sovnarkomivska vul. 11; tel. and fax (57) 706-33-95; e-mail artmuseum_kharkiv@i.ua; internet artmuseum.kharkov.ua; f. 1920; Ukrainian, Russian and foreign art from 15th–21st centuries; 24,000 exhibits; library of 19,000 vols; Dir V. V. MYZGINA.

Kharkiv State Historical Museum: 61003 Kharkiv, Universitetska vul. 10; tel. and fax (57) 223-20-94; Dir N. A. VOEVODIN.

Khomutovo

Ukrainian Steppe Nature Reserve: 87620 Donetsk oblast, Novoazov raion, Khomutov; tel. (62) 792-73-25; f. 1961; attached to Nat. Acad. of Sciences of Ukraine; Dir Dr ANATOLIY P. GENOV.

Kolomiya

Kolomiya State Museum of Folk Art: Ivano-Frankivska oblast, Kolomiya, Teatralna vul. 25; tel. and fax (34) 332-39-12; e-mail jatkachuk@hutsul.museum; internet hutsul.museum; f. 1926; exhibitions, confs, festivals, scientific work; 87 mems; library of 6,000 vols; Dir Y. TKACHUK; publ. *People's House* (6 a year).

Kyiv

Bohdan and Varvara Khanenko Museum of Arts: 01004 Kyiv, Tereshchenkivska 15–17; tel. (44) 235-02-25; fax (44) 235-02-06; e-mail khanenkomuseum@ukr.net; f. 1919; holds more than 20,000 items of western European, Oriental and ancient art; Dir VIRA VYNOHRADOVA; publ. *Khanenko Readings* (1 a year).

Kyiv Museum of Russian Art: 01004 Kyiv, Tereshchenkivska vul. 9; tel. (44) 451-40-27; fax (44) 234-61-07; e-mail museumru@ukr.net; f. 1922; library of 17,000 vols; Dir IURII VAKULENKO.

Kyiv State Literary Museum 'Lessya Ukrainka': 01032 Kyiv, vul. Saksaganskogo 97; tel. (44) 220-57-52; f. 1962; life and work of the Ukrainian poets and artists of the 19th and early 20th centuries; library of 5,000 vols; Dir IRINA L. VEREMEYEVA.

Museum of Theatrical, Musical and Cinematographic Art of Ukraine: 01015 Kyiv, vul. I. Mazepy 21/24; tel. and fax (44) 280-16-22; e-mail tmf-museum@ukr.net; internet www.tmf-museum.kiev.ua; f. 1923; library of 30,000 vols; Dir IRYNA DROBOT.

National Art Museum of Ukraine: 01001 Kyiv, vul. M. Hrushevskoho 6; tel. (44) 228-13-57; fax (44) 228-74-54; e-mail namu@i.com.ua; f. 1899; painting and wood-carving since the Middle Ages; Dir A. I. MELNIK.

National Botanical Gardens 'M. M. Gryshko': 01014 Kyiv, Timiryazevska vul. 1; tel. (44) 285-41-05; fax (44) 285-26-49; e-mail nbg@nbg.kiev.ua; f. 1935; attached to Nat. Acad. of Sciences of Ukraine; library of 39,041 vols; Dir Prof. Dr N. V. ZAIMENKO.

National Kyiv-Pechersk Lavra Museum: 01015 Kyiv, vul. Sichnevogo Povstannya 25; tel. (44) 254-22-57; e-mail lavra@lavra.kiev.ua; internet www.lavra.kiev.ua; ancient monastery, icons.

National Museum of the History of Ukraine: 01034 Kyiv, vul. Volodymyrska 2; tel. (44) 228-65-45; fax (44) 228-43-23; e-mail mhistory@i.com.ua; f. 1899; history, archaeology, religion, ethnography, 600,000 exhibits; Dir SERHIY CHAIKOVSKYI.

National Taras Shevchenko Museum: 12 Taras Shevchenko bulv., 01004 Kyiv; tel. (44) 234-25-23; e-mail m-shevchenka@ukr.net; life and work of the poet T. G. Shevchenko; f. 1940; Dir S. A. HALCHENKO.

St Sophia of Kiev National Conservation Area: 01034 Kyiv, Volodymyrska vul. 24; tel. (44) 278-26-20; fax (44) 278-67-06; e-mail stsophia@i.kiev.ua; internet www.sophia.org.ua; f. 1934; comprises 11th-century St Sofia cathedral (with early frescoes and mosaics) and other, 18th-century bldgs; attached museums incl. St Cyril Church Museum, St Andrew Church Museum, Golden Gates Museum (11th-century town gatehouse) and, in the Crimea, 6th–15th-century Sudak fortress; Dir-Gen. NELYA M. KUKOVALSKA.

Ukrainian Museum of Folk and Decorative Art: 01015 Kyiv, vul. Sichnevoho Povstannya 21; tel. (44) 290-13-43; f. 1954; library of 3,180 vols; Dir V. G. NAGAI; publ. *Folk Creative Work and Ethnography*.

Lviv

Lviv Historical Museum: 79008 Lviv, pl. Rynok 4/6/24; tel. (322) 74-33-04; f. 1893; Dir BOGDAN CHAYKOVSKIY.

Lviv State Picture Gallery: 79000 Lviv, vul. Stefanika 3; tel. (32) 272-39-48; fax (32) 272-30-09; f. 1907; West European and Ukrainian contemporary art; library of 34,276 vols; Dir BORIS VOZNITSKY.

The Andrey Sheptytsky National Museum in Lviv: 79008 Lviv, Svobody 20; tel. (32) 2235-88-46; fax (32) 2235-88-49; e-mail nml_shept@ukr.net; f. 1905; colln of over 160,000 artworks; preservation, devt, study and promotion of 11th–21st century Ukrainian art; library of 30,000 scientific vols; Dir IHOR KOZHAN; Academic Sec. ANGELINA ZABYTIVSKA; publ. *Litopys* (Chronicle of the Andrey Sheptytsky National Museum in Lviv, 1 a year).

State Museum of Ethnography, Arts and Crafts: Lviv, pr. Svoboda 15; tel. (32) 2727012; f. 1873; attached to Nat. Acad. of Sciences of Ukraine.

State Natural History Museum: 79008 Lviv, Teatralna vul. 18; tel. and fax (32) 274-23-07; e-mail museum@museum.lviv.net; internet museum.lviv.net; f. 1870; attached to Nat. Acad. of Sciences of Ukraine; library of 69,000 vols; Dir Prof. YURIY M. CHORNOBAY; publ. *Proceedings* (1 a year).

Odesa

Odessa Archaeological Museum: 65026 Odessa, vul. Lanzheronovska 4; tel. 722-01-71; e-mail archaeology@farlep.net; internet www.archaeology.farlep.odessa.ua; f. 1825; history of the Northern Black Sea Coast area; library of 28,000 vols; Dir V. P. VANCHUGOV; Librarian H. P. UKRAINSKA.

Odessa Fine Arts Museum: 65082 Odesa, Sofievska vul. 5A; tel. (48) 223-82-72; fax (48) 223-83-93; e-mail ofam@tm.odessa.ua; internet www.museum-finearts.odessa.ua; f. 1899; Ukrainian and Russian art since 15th century; library of 15,000 vols; Dir NATALYA S. POLISHCHUK.

Odessa Museum of Western and Eastern Art: 270026 Odesa, Pushkinsha vul. 9; tel. and fax (482) 22-48-15; e-mail oweamuseum@hotbox.ru; internet www.oweamuseum.odessa.ua; f. 1920; library of 14,000 vols; Dir VICTOR S. NIKIFOROV.

Poltava

Poltava Art Museum: 314020 Poltava, Spaska 11; tel. (53) 227-27-11; f. 1919; library of 4,000 vols; Curator KIM SKALATSKY.

Poltava State Museum: Poltava, Lenina 2; life and work of the writers P. Mirnyi, J. Kotlyarevsky, V. G. Korolenko, N. V. Gogol; library of 80,000 vols; Dir GALINA P. BELOUS.

Sevastopol

National Preserve of Tauric Chersonesos: 99045 Crimea, Sevastopol, vul. Drevnyaya 1; tel. and fax (69) 255-02-78; e-mail info@chersonesos.org; internet www.chersonesos.org; f. 1892; archaeological park incorporating museum and ruins of Greek colony and Byzantine city of Tauric Chersonesos; library of 30,000 vols; Dir Dr LEONID V. MARCHENKO; publ. *Khersonesskyi Sbornik* (Chersonesos Collected Articles, 1 a year).

Shevchenkovo

Shevchenko, T. G., State Memorial Museum: Cherkasska oblast, Zvenigorodsky raion, Shevchenkovo; f. 1939; life and work of T. G. Shevchenko; library of 3,000 vols; Dir T. V. GULAK.

Sumy

Sumy Art Museum 'Nukanor Onatsky': 40030 Sumy, Krasnaya pl. 1; tel. (54) 222-04-81; internet www.city.sumy.ua/artgallery; f. 1920; Dir GALINA V. AREFEVA.

Yalta

Nikita Botanical Gardens: 98648 Crimea, Yalta, Nikita; tel. (65) 433-55-30; fax (65) 433-53-86; e-mail nbs1812@gmail.com; internet www.nbg.crimea.ua; f. 1812; attached to Ukrainian Acad. of Agrarian Sciences; library of 213,000 vols; 50,000 species and hybrids of flowers, fruits, and woody, subtropical, industrial, oil-bearing and medical plants; Dir Prof. Dr V. N. EZHOV; publs *Bulletin* (3 a year), *Collected Scientific Works* (3 a year).

Universities

AGRARIAN UNIVERSITIES

BILA TSERKVA STATE AGRARIAN UNIVERSITY

09117 Kyivska obl., Bila Tserkva, bul. 50-Richchya Perermoti 96

Telephone: (44) 633-11-01
E-mail: rector@btsau.kiev.ua
Internet: www.btsau.kiev.ua

Founded 1750, present name and status 1995

Faculties of agronomy, biotechnology, culture and art, economics, external studies, languages, law, physical education, qualification improvement, veterinary medicine

Rector: Dr MYKHAILO M. BARANOVSKIY
First Pro-Rector: Prof. Dr VITALIY P. NOVAK
Pro-Rector for Distance Studies: Prof. Dr SVETLANA I. TSEKHMISTRENKO
Pro-Rector for Finance: Dr TATYANA V. ARBUZOVA
Pro-Rector for Research: Prof. Dr IHOR L. YAKIMENKO
Pro-Rector for Studies: Prof. Dr LYLIYA V. BARANOVSKAYA

Publication: *Vestnik BSGAU* (Bila Tserkva State Agrarian University Bulletin).

CRIMEAN AGROTECHNOLOGICAL UNIVERSITY

95492 Simferopol, Agrarnoye

Telephone: (65) 226-33-52
Fax: (65) 222-39-66
E-mail: rectorat@csau.crimea-ua.com
Internet: www.csau.crimea-ua.com

Founded 1922
Public control
Languages of instruction: Russian, Ukrainian

Academic year: September to July
Dir: Prof. MYKHAYLO M. MELNIKOV
Library of 542,425 vols
Number of teachers: 380
Number of students: 4,047

DEANS

Faculty of Agronomy: Dr VALERIY F. VIL'CHINSKIY
Faculty of Economics and Management: Dr VITALIY M. DYATEL
Faculty of Land Planning and Geodesy: Dr VOLODYMYR M. GORBATYUK
Faculty of Mechanization of Producing and Technology of Processing of Agricultural Production: Dr YURI B. GERBER
Faculty of Veterinary Medicine: Dr VIKTOR I. SKRIPNIK

DNIPROPETROVS'K STATE AGRARIAN UNIVERSITY

49600 Dnipropetrovsk, vul. Voroshilova 25
Telephone: (56) 744-81-32
E-mail: interdsau@gmail.com
Internet: www.dsau.dp.ua
Founded 1922
Academic year: September to June
Rector: Prof. ANATOLIY S. I. KOBETS'
First Pro-Rector for Education: Prof. Dr DMYTRO M. ONOPRIYENKO
Pro-Rector for Research: Prof. Dr YURI I. GRYTSAN
Librarian: A. H. BRATCHYK
Library of 372,000 vols
Number of teachers: 488
Number of students: 6,314 (3,653 full-time, 2,661 external)
Publications: *Bulletin* (2 a year), *Transactions* (2 a year)

DEANS

Faculty of Accounting and Finance: Dr L. A. ZAPARA
Faculty of Agricultural Mechanization: Dr P. M. KUKHARENKO
Faculty of Agronomy: Dr O. O. MYTSYK
Faculty of Biotechnology: Dr S. G. PISHCHAN
Faculty of Ecology and Irrigation: Dr A. V. TKACHUK
Faculty of Marketing and Management: T. M. SAMILYK
Faculty of Veterinary Medicine: Dr I. A. BIBEN

KHARKIV STATE AGRARIAN UNIVERSITY 'V. V. DOKUCHAYEV'

62483 Kharkiv, P/O 'Komunist-1', vul. Mazepy 10
Telephone: (57) 293-71-46
Fax: (57) 293-60-67
Internet: www.hgau.narod.ru
Founded 1816
Rector: Prof. MYKOLA D. YEVTUSHENKO
Library of 600,000 vols
Number of teachers: 258
Number of students: 5,195
Publications: *Agrochemistry*, *Common Agriculture, Forestry, Plant Growing and Vegetable Production*, *Series on Crop Production*, *Series on Economics and Natural Sciences*, *Series on Soil Science*

DEANS

Faculty of Agrochemistry and Soil Science: VASYL DEKHTYARYOV
Faculty of Agronomy: YEVGEN OGURTSOV
Faculty of Continuing Education: VOLODYMYR PUZIK
Faculty of Correspondence Studies: VOLODYMYR BILIUSKO
Faculty of Economics: OLEKSANDR ULYANCHENKO
Faculty of Forestry: ANATOLIY POLYVYANIY
Faculty of Land Management: VASYL BALAKYRSKY
Faculty of Plant Protection: VOLODYMYR TURENKO

LVIV STATE AGRARIAN UNIVERSITY

80381 Lviv oblast, Zhovkva raion, Dublyany
Telephone: (32) 279-33-45
E-mail: lday@mail.lviv.ua
Internet: www.lday.lviv.ua
Founded 1856
Departments of agricultural accounting, agronomy, architecture, economics, farm building, mechanization
Library of 521,000 vols
Number of teachers: 390
Number of students: 9,000
Rector: Prof. Dr VOLODYMYR V. SNITYNSKYY
Publication: *Transactions.*

NATIONAL AGRICULTURAL UNIVERSITY OF UKRAINE

03041 Kyiv, vul. Heroyiv Oborony 15
Telephone: (44) 267-81-19
Fax: (44) 261-42-34
E-mail: inter@nauu.kiev.ua
Internet: www.nauu.kiev.ua
Founded 1898
Rector: DYMTRO O. MELNYCHUK
Library: 1m. vols
Number of teachers: 2,827
Number of students: 22,034
Brs in Berezhany, Boyarka, Irpin, Nemishayiv, Nizhyn, Zalishchiky
Publication: *For Agricultural Specialists* (6 a year)

DEANS

Faculty of Agricultural Biology: ANATOLIY V. BYKIN
Faculty of Agricultural Management: KOVTUN O. ANATOLIVNA
Faculty of Agricultural Mechanical Engineering: YAROSLAV M. MYKHAYLOVYCH
Faculty of Animal Health: VITALIY Y. LUBETSKIY
Faculty of Animal Husbandry, Output Production and Processing Technology: YURIY V. ZASUKHA
Faculty of Construction and Design: KONSTYANTYN H. LOPATKO
Faculty of Ecology and Biotechnology: NATALYA M. RIDEY
Faculty of Economics: SERHIY M. KVASHA
Faculty of Electrification and Automation of Agriculture: IVAN P. RADKO
Faculty of Forestry: SERHIY B. KOVALEVSKY
Faculty of Land Management: BOHDAN I. NOVAK
Faculty of Landscape Engineering: ANATOLIY I. KUSHNIR
Faculty of Law: VOLODYMYR I. KURILO
Faculty of Quality and Safety of Agricultural Production: OLGA M. YAKUBCHAK
Faculty of Small Animal Health: OLEG F. PETRENKO
Faculty of Social Pedagogy: PETRO H. LUZAN
Faculty of Water Resources and Aquaculture: PETRO H. SHEVCHENKO

STATE AGROECOLOGICAL UNIVERSITY

10008 Zhytomyr, Stary bul. 7
Telephone: (41) 237-49-31
Fax: (41) 222-14-02
Internet: www.academy.zt.ua
Founded 1922
Depts of agricultural ecology, agricultural engineering, animal husbandry, economics and agribusiness, veterinary medicine
Rector: V. P. SLAVOV
Library of 370,000 vols
Number of teachers: 276
Number of students: 2,859

UKRAINIAN NATIONAL FORESTRY UNIVERSITY

79057 Lviv, vul. Gen. Chuprynka 103
Telephone: (32) 237-80-94
Fax: (32) 237-89-05
E-mail: nltu@ukr.net
Rector: YURIY YU. TUNYTSYA
Vice-Rector: HRYHORIY T. KRYNYTSKYY
Library of 450,000 vols
Number of teachers: 310
Number of students: 3,600
Publications: *Naukovyy visnyk* (Scientific bulletin), *Ukrainski lis* (Ukrainian Forest)

DEANS

Extra Mural Faculty: Dr YAROSLAV LYKO
Faculty of Economy: Dr YAROSLAV KULCHYTSKYY
Faculty of Forest Mechanics: Prof. Dr MYKOLA KIRYK
Faculty of Forestry: Prof. Dr STEPAN MYKLUSH
Faculty of Technology: Prof. Dr VOLODYMYR MAKSYMIV
Institute of Ecological Economics: Dir: Dr LYUDMYLA MAKSYMIV

HUMANITIES AND SCIENCES UNIVERSITIES

CHERNIVTSI NATIONAL UNIVERSITY 'YURIY FEDKOVYCH'

58012 Chernivtsi, vul. Kotsyubinskoho 2
Telephone: (37) 222-62-35
Fax: (37) 255-29-14
E-mail: rector@chnu.cv.ua
Internet: www.chnu.cv.ua
Founded 1875
State control
Language of instruction: Ukrainian
Academic year: September to June
Rector: STEPAN V. MELNYCHUK
First Pro-Rector, Pro-Rector for Research: S. V. MELNYCHUK
Pro-Rector for Academic Affairs: ROMAN I. PETRYSHYN
Pro-Rector for Academic Devt: TAMARA V. MARUSYK
Librarian: OLEG I. SHLYUK
Library: see Libraries and Archives
Number of teachers: 786
Number of students: 14,103 (7,421 full-time, 6,682 part-time)
Publications: *Scientific University Annual*, *Universitetsky Visnyk* (12 a year)

DEANS

Faculty of Applied Mathematics: R. I. PETRYSHYN
Faculty of Biology: M. M. MARCHENKO
Faculty of Chemistry: O. S. LYAVYNETS
Faculty of Computer Science: (vacant)
Faculty of Economics: L. S. BILYK
Faculty of Engineering and Technology: Prof. O. V. ANGELSKIY
Faculty of Foreign Languages: R. V. VATSEBA
Faculty of Geography: V. P. RUDENKO
Faculty of History, Politology and International Relations: O. V. DOBRZHANSKIY
Faculty of Law: P. S. PATSURKIVSKIY
Faculty of Pedagogy: I. M. ZVARYCH
Faculty of Philology: B. I. BUNCHUK

Faculty of Philosophy and Theology: V. O. BALUKH
Faculty of Physics: I. V. GUTSUL

DNIPROPETROVSK NATIONAL UNIVERSITY

49050 Dnipropetrovsk, vul. Naukova 13
Telephone: (56) 246-00-95
Fax: (56) 776-58-33
E-mail: admin@dsu.dp.ua
Internet: www.dsu.dp.ua
Founded 1918
Languages of instruction: Ukrainian, Russian
Academic year: September to July
Pres.: MYKOLA POLYAKOV
Vice-Pres. and President's Deputy: O. O. KOCHUBEY
Vice-Pres. for Academic Affairs: V. G. MUSIYAKA
Vice-Pres. for Foreign Affairs: V. V. KOSTYRKO
Vice-Pres. for Research: M. M. DRON
Librarian: L. S. KUBISHKINA
Library: see Libraries and Archives
Number of teachers: 1,233
Number of students: 13,260
Publication: *Dnipropetrovsk University Newspaper* (12 a year)

DEANS

Faculty of Applied Mathematics: S. V. CHERNYSHENKO
Faculty of Biology and Ecology: O. Y. PAKHOMOV
Faculty of Chemistry: V. F. VARGALYUK
Faculty of Geology and Geography: V. V. BOGDANOVICH
Faculty of History: S. I. SVITLENKO
Faculty of International Economics: N. Y. BOYTSUN
Faculty of Law: P. I. GNATENKO
Faculty of Mass Media: V. D. DEMCHENKO
Faculty of Mechanics and Mathematics: V. O. SYASEV
Faculty of Medicine: J. S. SAPA
Faculty of Philology: O. V. RODNY
Faculty of Physics: R. S. TUTIK
Faculty of Psychology and Pedagogics: I. V. RASPOPOV
Faculty of Radio Physics: V. M. DOLGOV
Faculty of Ukrainian Philology and Art History: I. S. POPOVA
Institute of Economics: S. O. SMIRNOV
Institute of Physics and Technology: Y. A. DZUR

DONETSK NATIONAL UNIVERSITY

83001 Donetsk, vul. Universytetska St 24
Telephone: (62) 337-19-45
Fax: (62) 335-22-56
E-mail: postmaster@univ.donetsk.ua
Internet: www.donnu.edu.ua
Founded 1965, Donetsk State Univ. until 2000
State control
Languages of instruction: Ukrainian, Russian
Academic year: September to July
Rector: Prof. V. P. SHEVCHENKO
Deputy Rector: Prof. P.V. YEGOROV
Vice-Rector: Prof. N.P. IVANITSYN
Librarian: N. O. KORYAGINA
Library: see Libraries and Archives
Number of teachers: 900 .
Number of students: 17,500
Publications: *Bulletin* (1 a year), *Donetsk Archaeological Bulletin* (1 a year), *Eastern Ukraine Linguistic Collected Articles* (2 a year), *Economical Cybernetics* (4 a year), *Finance, Accounting, Banks* (2 a year), *Historical and Political Studies* (4 a year), *Juridical Studies* (4 a year), *Management Models in Market Economy* (2 a year), *New Pages in the History of Donbass* (2 a year), *Philological Studies* (2 a year), *Theoretical and Applied Mechanics* (1 a year).

DONETSK NATIONAL UNIVERSITY OF ECONOMICS AND TRADE 'M. TUHAN-BARANOVSKIY'

83050 Donetsk, vul. Shchorsa 31
Telephone: (62) 335-10-29
Fax: (62) 304-83-16
E-mail: info@donduet.edu.ua
Internet: www.donduet.edu.ua
Founded 1920
State control
Academic year: September to June
Languages of instruction: Ukrainian, Russian, English
Rector: O. O. SHUBIN
First Vice-Rector: L. O. OMELYANOVYCH
Vice-Rector for Social and Educational Affairs: S. V. DROZHZHINA
Vice-Rector for Scientific Affairs: A. A. SADEKOV
Vice-Rector for Scientific-Pedagogical Activity and Int. Relations: V. G. POGREBNYAK
Vice-Rector Economic and Technical Provisions: A. B. ROMANOV
Librarian: T. P. TKACHENKO
Library of 67,000 vols, 75,000 periodicals
Number of teachers: 450
Number of students: 14,876

DEANS

Institute of Accounting and Finance: V. A. ORLOVA
Institute of Economics and Management: L. V. FROLOVA
Institute of Foodstuff Industries: V. A. SUKMANOV
Faculty of Marketing, Trade and Customs Activity: Prof. I. KH. BASHYROV
Faculty of Restaurant and Hotel Business: Prof. T. V. NUZHNA
International Faculty of Foreign Specialist Training: V. E. VOYLOSHNIKOVA

VOLODYMYR DAHL EAST UKRAINIAN NATIONAL UNIVERSITY

91034 Luhansk, Kvartal Molodezhnyi 20A
Telephone: (64) 241-70-22
Fax: (64) 241-31-60
E-mail: uni@snu.edu.ua
Internet: www.snu.edu.ua
Founded 1920
Public control
Languages of instruction: English, Russian, Ukrainian
Academic year: September to June
Rector: Prof. Dr OLEKSANDR L. GOLUBENKO (acting)
First Vice-Rector: Prof. Dr MYKHAILO F. SMYRNY (acting)
Vice-Rector for International Affairs: Prof. Dr VALERIY DYADYCHEV (acting)
Library: 1m. vols
Number of teachers: 2,750
Number of students: 36,000
Publications: *Actual Issues of Law: Theory and Practice*, *Applied Ecology*, *Economics. Management. Enterpreneurship*, *Historical Notes: Collection of Scientific Papers*, *Information Security*, *Marketing: Theory and Practice*, *Materials and Investigation on Archeology of East of Ukraine*, *Philosophical Investigations*, *Political Science Notes*, *Project Management and Development of Production*, *Scientific Conducts of Dahl University* (online), *Scientific Media Notes*, *Scientific Works of Lugansk Branch of International Academy of Informatization*, *Spiritual Identity: Methodology, Theory and Practice*, *Theoretical and Practical Problems of Psychology*, *Visnyk of Volodymyr Dahl East Ukrainian National University on-Technic-Economics-History-Chemical-Physics and Mathematics*

DEANS

Economics Management Department: Prof. MARYNA A. MELNYK
Educational and Scientific Institute of Housing and Communal Services and Building: Prof. MYKOLA D. ANDIYCHUK
Faculty of Applied Mechanics and Material Science: Prof. VLADYMYR I. SOKOLOV
Faculty of Computer Sciences and Technologies: Prof. LARYSA O. GUBACHEVA
Faculty of Electrotechnical Systems: Prof. OLEKSANDR S. ZAKHARCHUK
Faculty of Financial Management: Asst Prof. OLEKSANDR M. ROZMYSLOV
Faculty of Foreign Citizens Training: Asst Prof. EVGEN I. KHARCHENKO
Faculty of Innovation Economics and Cybernetics: Prof. SULTAN K. RAMAZANOV
Faculty of Law: Prof. LIDIA I. LAZOR
Faculty of Management: Prof. VITALIY M. DANICH
Faculty of Mass Communications: Asst Prof. TETYANA A. MIRONOVA
Faculty of Mathematics And Informatics: Asst Prof. YURIY I. STATYVKO
Faculty of Nanoelectronics and Nanotechnologies: Prof. OLEKSANDR P. KRAVCHENKO
Faculty of Natural Sciences: Prof. SERGIY D. KRYVONOSOV
Faculty of Philology: Asst Prof. OLGA E. KRSEK
Faculty of Philosophy: Prof. VIKTORIA K. SUKHANTSEVA
Faculty of Rail Communications Systems: Prof. VALENTYN I. MOGYLA
Faculty of Transport Systems and Logistics: Prof. GRYGORIY I. NECHAEV

V. N. KARAZIN KHARKIV NATIONAL UNIVERSITY

61077 Kharkiv, pl. Svobody 4
Telephone: (57) 705-12-47
Fax: (57) 705-12-36
E-mail: postmaster@univer.kharkov.ua
Internet: www.univer.kharkov.ua
Founded 1804
Public control
Languages of instruction: Russian, Ukrainian
Academic year: September to June
Library: 3.5m. vols
Rector: Prof. V. S. BAKIROV
Vice-Rector: Prof. V. V. ALEKSANDROV
Vice-Rector: Prof. YU. V. KHOLIN
Vice-Rector: Prof. M. O. AZARENKOV
Vice-Rector: Prof. I. I. ZALYUBOVSKIY
Vice-Rector: Asst Prof. Z. F. NAZYROV
Vice-Rector: Asst Prof. A. M. UDOD
Vice-Rector: V. M. RYSHKOV
Librarian: I. K. ZHURAVLYOVA
Number of teachers: 1,500
Number of students: 12,000
Publication: *Visnyk*

DEANS

International Students Education Centre: (vacant)
School of Biology: Asst Prof. L. I. VOROBYOVA
School of Chemistry: Asst Prof. O. M. KALUGIN
School of Computer Science: Asst Prof. L. V. VASILIEVA (acting)
School of Ecology: Asst Prof. N. L. RICHAK (acting)

School of Economics: Prof. L. I. BULAYENKO
School of Foreign Languages: Prof. V. G. PASYNOK
School of Further Education: Asst Prof. L. P. KRUPSKA
School of Geology and Geography: Prof. V. A. PERESADKO
School of History: Prof. S. I. POSOKHOV
School of International Economic Relations and Tourist Industry: Prof. V. I. SIDOROV
School of Law: Asst Prof. T. YE. KAGANOVSKA
School of Mathematics and Mechanical Engineering: Prof. G. M. ZHOLTKEVYCH
School of Medicine: Prof. V. M. SAVCHENKO
School of Philology: Prof. YU. M. BEZKHUTRIY
School of Philosophy: Prof. I. V. KARPENKO
School of Physics: Asst Prof. A. A. ZAVGORODNIY
School of Physics and Energy: Prof. K. E. NYEMCHENKO
School of Physics and Technology: Prof. I. O. GIRKA
School of Psychology: Prof. N. P. KREYDYN
School of Radiophysics: Prof. S. M. SHULGA
School of Sociology: Prof. V. M. NIKOLAYEVSKIY

KHARKIV NATIONAL UNIVERSITY OF ECONOMICS

61001 Kharkiv, 9a pr. Lenina
Telephone: (57) 702-03-04
Fax: (57) 702-07-17
E-mail: mail@hneu.edu.ua
Internet: www.hdeu.edu.ua

Founded 1930
State control
Languages of instruction: English, Russian, Ukrainian
Academic year: September to June

Rector: Prof. Dr VOLODYMYR PONOMARENKO
Vice-Rector for Int. Relations: Prof. VOLODYMYR YERMACHENKO
Librarian: NATALYA BOZHKO

Library of 864,329 vols, 13,679 periodicals, 2,070 copies of theses and thesis abstracts
Number of teachers: 712
Number of students: 14,000 (incl. 205 postgraduate and doctoral)
Publications: *Business Inform*, *Development Management*, *Economy of Development*

DEANS

Correspondence Faculty: Prof. Dr SERGIJ LUKASHOV
Faculty of Accounting and Audit: Prof. Dr GRIGORY AZARENKOV
Faculty of Economic Informatics: Prof. Dr VOLODYMYR GRACHOV
Faculty of Economy and Law: Prof. Dr TETYANA SERIKOVA
Finance Faculty: Prof. Dr PAVLO PRONOZA
Faculty of Int. Economic Relations: Prof. Dr IVAN PIDDUBNY
Faculty of Management and Marketing: Prof. Dr OLEKSANDR TIMONIN

KHMELNYTSKY STATE UNIVERSITY

29016 Khmelnytsky, vul. Instytutska 11
Telephone: (38) 272-80-76
Fax: (38) 222-32-65
E-mail: centr@mailhub.tub.km.ua
Internet: www.tup.km.ua

Founded 1962

Rector: MYKOLA SKYBA
Deputy Rectors: SERGIY KOSTOGRYZ (Academic Work), MYKHAYLO VOYNARENKO (Academic Work), ANATOLIY FOMOV (Admin. Work), VIKTOR NYZHNYK (Finance and Economic Activity), MYKOLA YOKHNA (Int. Relations), VITALIY KAPLUN (Scientific Work)

Number of teachers: 637
Number of students: 12,976
Publications: *Measuring and Computing Devices in Technological Processes* (2 a year), *Problems of Trybology International Scientific Journal* (2 a year), *University Herald* (6 a year)

DEANS

Faculty of Applied Mathematics and Computer Technologies: SERGIY KOVALCHUK
Faculty of Business: LIDIYA TORGOVA
Faculty of Correspondence Studies 1: VITALIY KARAZEY
Faculty of Correspondence Studies 2: VIRA BEGNYAK
Faculty of Distance Studies: MYKOLA MAZUR
Faculty of Economics: MYKOLA BONDARENKO
Faculty of Engineering Mechanics: GEORGIY DRAPAK
Faculty of Humanities and Pedagogics: LYUDMYLA STANISLAVOVA
Faculty of International Relations: VITALIY TRETKO
Faculty of Management: LYUDMYLA LYUBOKHYNETS
Faculty of Pre-University and Post-University Training: MYKOLA BABYCH
Faculty of Radio Electronics and Computer Engineering: VOLODYMYR KOSENKOV
Faculty of Technology and Design: DOMBROVSKIY

DIRECTORS

Institute of Correspondence and Distance Studies: YAROSLAV GLADKIY
Institute of Economy and Management: MYKOLA BONDARENKO
Institute of Humanities: VITALIY TRETKO
Institute of Mechanics and Computer Studies: GEORGIY DRAPAK
Institute of Technology, Design and Service: GEORGIY PARASKA
Institute of Telecommunication and Computer Systems: VOLODYMYR KOSENKOV

KYIV NATIONAL LINGUISTIC UNIVERSITY

03680 Kyiv GSP 150, vul. Chervonoarmiyska 73
Telephone: (44) 227-33-72
Fax: (44) 227-67-88
E-mail: knlu@knlu.kiev.ua
Internet: www.knlu.kiev.ua

Founded 1948
Public control
Academic year: September to June

Rector: Dr ROMAN V. VASKO

Library: 1m. vols
Number of teachers: 605
Number of students: 6,230
Publications: *Methods in Foreign Language Teaching* (4 a year, in Ukrainian and other languages), *Philology of Foreign Languages* (4 a year, in Ukrainian and other languages)

DEANS

Faculty of Economics and Law: MYKOLA HAMZYUK
Faculty of German Philology: IRYNA MOYSEYENKO
Faculty of Oriental Studies: SERGUY SOROKIN
Faculty of Romance Philology: ANATOLIY CHERNUKHA
Faculty of Slavic Philology: ALLA KENDYUSHENKO
Faculty of Translation: OKSANA FRANKO

KYIV NATIONAL UNIVERSITY OF TRADE AND ECONOMICS

02156 Kyiv, vul. Kioto 19
Telephone: (44) 531-47-73
Fax: (44) 513-85-36
E-mail: rio@knteu.kiev.ua
Internet: www.knteu.kiev.ua

Rector: Prof. Dr ANATOLIY A. MAZARAKI
First Pro-Rector: Prof. Dr OLEAKSANDR P. KOROLCHUCK
Pro-Rector for Admin. and Economic Affairs: Prof. Dr LEONID SHAPOVAL
Pro-Rector for Education: Prof. Dr NATALIYA PRYTULSKA
Pro-Rector for International Relations: Prof. Dr VALERII M. SAI
Pro-Rector for Capital Construction: Prof. Dr GALYNA VOVK

Library of 800,000 vols
Number of students: 39,000

DEANS

Faculty of Accounting and Economics: Prof. Dr ANATOLIY D. BUTKO
Faculty of Economics, Management and Law: Dr NATALIYA M. HULYAYEVA
Faculty of Finance and Banking: Dr IGOR V. SMOLIN
Faculty of the Restaurant, Hotel and Tourist Industry: Prof. Dr MYKHAILO I. PERESICHNYY
Commodity Science Faculty: Prof. VICTOR OSYKA

NATIONAL UNIVERSITY OF KYIV-MOHYLA ACADEMY

04070 Kyiv, vul. Skovorody 2
Telephone: (44) 416-45-15
Fax: (44) 463-67-83
E-mail: rec@ukma.kiev.ua
Internet: www.ukma.kiev.ua

Founded 1615, closed 1817, re-established 1991, nat. univ. 1994
State control
Languages of instruction: Ukrainian, English
Academic year: September to June

Pres.: VYACHESLAV BRYUKHOVETSKY
First Vice-Pres. and Vice-Pres. for Research and Devt: MYKHAILO BRYK
Vice-Pres. for Academic Affairs: VADYM ZUBKO
Vice-Pres. for Devt: NATALYA SHUMKOVA
Vice-Pres. for Finance and Admin.: LYUDMYLA DYACHENKO
Vice-Pres. for Foreign Cooperation: VOLODYMYR PANCHENKO
Vice-Pres. for Graduate and Postgraduate Studies: LYUDMYLA DYACHENKO
Dean of Students: OLENA TRETYAKOVA
Registrar: NATALIA HRYBCHUK
Librarian: TETYANA YAROSHENKO

Library of 300,000 vols
Number of teachers: 157
Number of students: 2,300
Publications: *Magisterium* (4 a year), *Mandrivets* (Traveller, 6 a year), *Naukovi Zapysky* (Scientific Notes, 13 a year)

DEANS

Faculty of Computer Science: MYKOLA HLYBOVETS
Faculty of Economics: Prof. YURIY BAZHAL
Faculty of Humanities: Prof. VITALIY SCHERBAK
Faculty of Legal Sciences: Dr ANDRIY A. MELESHEVICH
Faculty of Natural Sciences: Dr IRYNA VYSHENSKA
Faculty of Social Sciences and Technology: Prof. SERHIY M. KVIT
Kyiv-Mohyla Business School: PAVLO M. SHEREMETA

'TARAS SHEVCHENKO' NATIONAL UNIVERSITY OF KYIV

01033 Kyiv, vul. Volodymyrska 64
Telephone: (44) 225-20-82
Fax: (44) 224-61-66
E-mail: stationery@univ.kiev.ua
Internet: www.univ.kiev.ua
Languages of instruction: Ukrainian, English

Founded 1834
State Control

Rector: Prof. Dr LEONID V. HUBERSKY
First Pro-Rector: Prof. Dr OLEG K. ZAKUSYLO
Pro-Rector for Int. Relations: Prof. Dr PETRO O. BEKH
Pro-Rector for Perspective Devt: Prof. Dr EUGENIY F. TOMIN
Pro-Rector for Research and Education: Prof. Dr OLEKSANDR A. NIKITUK
Pro-Rector for Science and Educational Work: Assoc. Prof. Dr VOLODYMYR P. BUGROV
Pro-Rector for Scientific Work: Prof. Dr VALERIY I. HRYHORUK
Librarian: VALENTYNA G. NESTERENKO

Library: see Libraries and Archives
Number of teachers: 2,175 ; 1,251 scientists
Number of students: 22,500

Publication: *Vestnik Kievskogo Universiteta*

DEANS

Faculty of Biology: Prof. Dr LYUDMYLA I. OSTAPCHENKO
Faculty of Chemistry: Prof. YULIAN M. VOLOVENKO
Faculty of Cybernetics: Prof. ANATOLIY V. ANISIMOV
Faculty of Economics: Prof. VIKTOR D. BAZYLEVICH
Faculty of Geography: Prof. YAROSLAV B. OLIYNYK
Faculty of Geology: Prof. SERHIY A. VYZHVA
Faculty of History: Prof. VIKTOR F. KOLESNYK
Faculty of Law: Prof. IVAN S. HRYTSENKO
Faculty of Mechanics and Mathematics: Prof. MYKHAILO F. HORODNIY
Faculty of Philosophy: Prof. ANATOLIY YE. KONVERSKYI
Faculty of Physics: Prof. MYKOLA V. MAKARETS
Faculty of Psychology: Prof. IRYNA P. MANOKHA
Faculty of Radiophysics: Prof. IHOR O. ANISIMOV
Faculty of Sociology: ANDRIY P. HORBACHYK
Preparatory Faculty: Prof. TETIANA V. TABENSKA

ATTACHED INSTITUTES

Astronomical Observatory: 01033 Kyiv, Observatorna St 3; tel. (44) 486-26-91; fax (44) 486-26-30; e-mail director@observ.univ.kiev.ua; internet www.observ.univ.kiev.ua/mainu.htm; Dir B. I. HNATYK.

Centre for Ukrainian Studies: 01033 Kyiv, Volodymyrska St 60, Rm 105; tel. (44) 239-31-84; e-mail uaznavstvo@mail.univ.kiev.ua; internet uaznavstvo.univ.kiev.ua; Dir Prof. MYKOLA I. OBUSHNYI.

Information and Computer Centre: 01033 Kyiv, Academician Glushkov Ave 2, Bldg 6; tel. and fax (44) 521-35-14; e-mail admin@univ.kiev.ua; internet www.icc.univ.kiev.ua; Dir Dr YURIY V. BOYKO.

Institute of International Relations: 01033 Kyiv, Melnykova St 36/1; tel. (44) 481-44-37; fax (44) 483-10-43; e-mail decanat_relat@univ.kiev.ua; internet www.iir.kiev.ua; Dir Prof. VALERIY V. KOPIYKA.

Institute of Journalism: 01033 Kyiv, Melnykova St 36/1; tel. (44) 481-44-01; fax (44) 483-09-81; e-mail inst@journ.univ.kiev.ua; internet www.journ.univ.kiev.ua; Dir Prof. VOLODYMYR V. RIZUN.

Institute of Management and Finance: 01033 Kyiv, Vasylkivska St 90A; tel. (44) 521-33-37; e-mail kiembi@econom.univ.kiev.ua; internet www.imf.kiev.ua; Dir DMYTRO M. CHERVANOV.

Institute of Philology: tel. (44) 239-33-02; fax (44) 239-31-13; e-mail philolog@univ.kiev.ua; internet www.philology.kiev.ua; Dir HRIHORIY F. SEMENIUK.

Institute of Postgraduate Education: 01033 Kyiv, Vasylkivska St 36; tel. (44) 521-35-60; fax (44) 257-71-32; e-mail ipe@ipe.univ.kiev.ua; internet www.ipe.univ.kiev.ua; Dir Prof. VALERIY M. PERESEKIN.

Military Institute: 01033 Kyiv, Academician Glushkov Ave 2, Bldg 8; tel. and fax (44) 521-32-92; e-mail balabin@mil.univ.kiev.ua; internet www.mil.univ.kiev.ua; Dir Col VIKTOR V. BALABIN.

Scientific and Research Department: 01033 Kyiv, Lev Tolstoj St 14A, Rm 17; tel. (44) 289-85-80; fax (44) 239-32-40; internet science.univ.kiev.ua; Vice-Rector Prof. Dr VALERIY I. HRYHORUK.

Ukrainian Humanitarian Lyceum: 01033 Kyiv, Kozlovskyi Lane 3; tel. (44) 253-07-89; e-mail upgl@upgl.edu.ukrsat.com; internet www.uhl-edu.kiev.ua; Dir Prof. HALYNA S. SAZONENKO.

Ukrainian Physico–Mathematical Lyceum: 01033 Kyiv, Academician Glushkov Ave 6; tel. (44) 259-03-94; e-mail fizmat_dir@ukr.net; internet www.upml.univ.kiev.ua; Dir OLEH M. KHOMIAKOV.

NATIONAL UNIVERSITY OF LVIV 'IVAN FRANKO'

79000 Lviv, Universytetska vul. 1
Telephone: (32) 274-12-62
Fax: (32) 2297-16-68
E-mail: kyrylych@franko.lviv.ua
Internet: www.franko.lviv.ua

Founded 1661
Language of instruction: Ukrainian
Academic year: September to June

Rector: Prof. V. VYSOCHANSKY
Vice-Rector for Admin. Affairs: V. VLASEVYCH
Vice-Rector for Economic and Financial Affairs: M. LOZYNSKY
Vice-Rector for Int. Affairs: V. KYRYLYCH
Vice-Rector for Research: B. KOTUR
Vice-Rector for Student Affairs: ZVENISLAVA MAMCHUR
Vice-Rector for Teaching and Educational Affairs: M. ZUBRYTSKA
Provost: V. VYSOCHANSKY
Librarian: VASYL KMET

Library: see Libraries and Archives
Number of teachers: 1,709
Number of students: 31,000

Publications: *Filolohiya* (Philology), *Inozemna Filologiya* (Foreign Philology), *Matematychni Studii* (Mathematical Studies), *Mineralogichniy Zbirnyk* (Proceedings on Mineralogy), *Paleontologichniy Zbirnyk* (Proceedings on Palaeontology), *Teoretychna Elektrotekhnika* (Theoretical Electrical Engineering), *Ukrainske Literaturoznavstvo* (Ukrainian Literature Studies), *Ukraina Moderna* (Modern Ukraine), *Zhurnal Fizychnykh Doslidzhen* (Journal of Physical Research)

DEANS

Dept of Life Safety: Prof. ZYNOVIY YAREMKO
Dept of Pedagogy: Prof. DMYTRO HERTSYUK
Dept of Physical Culture and Sport: Dr ROMANNA SIRENKO
Faculty of Applied Mathematics and Informatics: Prof. YAREMA G. SAVULA
Faculty of Biology: Assoc. Prof. SVITLANA HNATUSH
Faculty of Chemistry: Prof. MYKHAYLO KALYCHAK
Faculty of Economics: Prof. STEPAN PANCHYSHYN
Faculty of Electronics: Prof. IHOR POLOVINKO
Faculty of Foreign Languages: Assoc. Prof. VOLODYMYR SULYM
Faculty of Geography: Assoc. Prof. YAROSLAV KHOMYN
Faculty of Geology: Prof. MYKOLA PAVLUN
Faculty of History: Assoc. Prof. POMAN SHUST
Faculty of International Relations: MARKIAN MALSKY
Faculty of Journalism: Assoc. Prof. MYKHAYLO PRYSIAZHNY
Faculty of Law: Prof. ANDRIY BOYKO
Faculty of Mechanics and Mathematics: MYKAILO ZARICHNY
Faculty of Philosophy: VOLODYMYR MELNYK
Faculty of Physics: PETRO YAKYBCHUK
Faculty of Pre-University Training: Assoc. Prof. ROMAN O. KROKHMALNY

ODESSA NATIONAL UNIVERSITY 'I. I. MECHNIKOV'

65082 Odessa, vul. Dvoryanska 2
Telephone: (48) 723-52-54
Fax: (48) 723-35-15
E-mail: rector@onu.edu.ua
Internet: www.onu.edu.ua

Founded 1865
State control
Languages of instruction: Ukrainian, Russian
Academic year: September to July

Rector: Prof. Dr IGOR KOVAL
Pro-Rector for Academic Affairs: Assoc. Prof. ALEXANDR ZAPOROZHCENKO
Pro-Rector for Academic and Methodological Work: Prof. EVGENIY STRELTSOV
Pro-Rector for Administrative Work: VYACHESLAV IGNATENKO
Pro-Rector for Int. Relations: Assoc. Prof. SERGEY SKOROKHOD
Pro-Rector for Scientific Research: Prof. VLADIMIR IVANITSA
Librarian: MARINA PODREZOVA

Library: see under Libraries and Archives
Number of teachers: 1,700
Number of students: 13,000

Publications: *Fisika aerodispersnikh sistem* (1 a year), *Fotoelektronika* (1 a year), *Odessa State University Herald* (1 a year), *Studies in Literature* (1 a year)

DEANS

Faculty of Biology: Assoc. Prof. VENIAMIN ZAMOROV
Faculty of Chemistry: Assoc. Prof. VASILIY MENCHUK
Faculty of Economics and Law: Assoc. Prof. VYACHESLAV TRUBA
Faculty of Geology and Geography: Prof. EVGENIY CHERKEZ
Faculty of History: Assoc. Prof. VYACHESLAV KUSHNIR
Faculty of Philology: Prof. EVGENIY CHERNOIVANENKO
Faculty of Philosophy: Assoc. Prof. ALEXANDR CHAYKOVSKY
Faculty of Physics: Prof. YURY VAKSMAN
Faculty of Romance and Germanic Philology: Assoc. Prof. LIDIYA GOLUBENKO
Institute of Innovation and Postgraduate Education: Prof. L. DUNAEVA
Institute of Mathematics, Economics and Mechanics: Prof. VIKTOR KRUGLOV
Institute of Social Studies: Prof. VIKTOR GLEBOV
Illiychevsk Institute of ONU: Prof. GRIGORIY DRAGAN

Pervomaysk Educational Centre Of Science: Assoc. Prof. NATALIA MIKHAL'CHENKO
Preparatory Faculty for Foreign Citizens: Assoc. Prof. SERGEY FEDORKO
Preparatory Faculty: Assoc. Prof. NIKOLAY PASCHENKO

ODESSA STATE ECONOMIC UNIVERSITY

65082 Odessa, Preobrazhenska vul. 8
Telephone: (48) 723-61-58
Fax: (48) 232-04-46
E-mail: rector@oseu.edu.ua
Internet: www.oseu.edu.ua

Founded 1921
State control

Rector: M. I. ZVERYAKOV
Vice-Rector: GEORGE SHUBARTOVSKIY

Library of 423,000 vols
Number of teachers: 455
Number of students: 6,355

POLTAVA UNIVERSITY OF ECONOMICS AND TRADE

36014 Poltava, vul. Kovalya 3
Telephone: (53) 222-18-36
Fax: (53) 250-97-95
E-mail: rector@uccu.org.ua
Internet: www.pusku.edu.ua

Founded 1974, fmrly known as Poltava Univ. of Consumer Cooperatives in Ukraine, present name 2010
State control
Languages of instruction: Ukrainian, Russian, English
Academic year: September to June

Rector: Prof. OLEKSIY O. NESTULYA
Vice-Rector: Prof. MYKOLA G. ROGOZA
Vice-Rector for Research and International Relations: Prof. OLGA V. KARPENKO
Dir of Library: S. SADOVA

Library of 365,645 vols, 9,464 periodical titles
Number of teachers: 485
Number of students: 11,000

Publications: *PUET Scientific Bulletin*, *University Newsletter*

DEANS

Department of Economics and Management: S. VAHTIN
Department of Finance and Accounting: O. KOROSTASHOV
Department of Food Technology: V. SHKARUPA
Department of Merchandise and Commerce: N. TYAGUNOVA
Extramural Department: U. STROCHIHIN

ATTACHED INSTITUTE

Institute of Continuing and Transition Education: courses in accounting and auditing, business, corporate economics, finance, marketing and international management.

PRECARPATHIAN NATIONAL UNIVERSITY 'VASYL STEFANYK'

76025 Ivano-Frankivsk, vul. Shevchenka 57
E-mail: inst@pu.if.ua
Internet: www.pu.if.ua

Founded 1940

Rector: Prof. Dr BOHDAN. K. OSTAFIYCHUK
First Pro-Rector: Prof. Dr BOHDAN. V. VASYLYSHYN.

TAURIDA NATIONAL 'V. I. VERNADSKY UNIVERSITY'

95007 Simferopol, pr. Vernadskoho 4
Telephone: (65) 251-64-98
Fax: (65) 251-71-35
E-mail: rector@tnu.crimea.ua
Internet: www.tnu.crimea.ua

Founded 1918, present name 1999
State control
Language of instruction: Russian
Academic year: September to July

Rector: NIKOLAY V. BAGROV
Vice-Rectors: ELENA N. CHUJAN, VIKTOR F. SHULGIN, ALEXANDER M. TIMOHIN
Registrar: NIKOLAY V. PRAVDIN
Librarian: VIKTORIA I. SPIROVA

Library: see Libraries and Archives
Number of teachers: 800
Number of students: 15,000

Publications: *Dynamic Systems* (1 a year), *Ecological Aspects of Nature Protection in the Crimea* (1 a year), *Ecological Study of the Mountainous Crimea* (1 a year), *Ecosystems of the Mountainous Crimea in Studies of Nature Protection* (1 a year), *Notes of Geologists*, *Pontida: Journal of The Association for the Support of Biological and Landscape Diversity* (1 a year), *Scientific Notes* (1 a year), *The Black Sea Peoples' Culture* (1 a year)

DEANS

Faculty of Biology: SERGEY F. KOTOV
Faculty of Chemistry: VLADIMIR O. KURJANOV
Faculty of Crimean Tatar and Oriental Philology: AIDER M. MEMETOV
Faculty of Economics: SVETLANA V. KLIMCHUK
Faculty of Foreign Languages: ALEXANDER D. PETRENKO
Faculty of Geography: BORIS A. VAKHRUSHEV
Faculty of History: ALEXANDER G. GERTSEN
Faculty of Jurisprudence: LUDMILA D. DONSKAYA
Faculty of Management: VLADIMIR A. PODSOLONKO
Faculty of Mathematics: ALEXANDER I. RUDSKOY
Faculty of Philosophy: YURI A. KATUNIN
Faculty of Physical Training: VLADIMIR F. KROVYAKOV
Faculty of Physics: MARINA V. GLUMOVA
Faculty of Psychology: EVGENIY V. CHERNY
Faculty of Slavic Philology and Journalism: GALINA YU BOGDANOVICH
Faculty of Ukrainian Philology and Ukranian Studies: YRIY F. PRADID

PROFESSORS

AKULOV, M. R., History of Ukraine
APATOVA, N. V., Information Systems in Economics
ARIFOV, L. YA, Theoretical Physics
BERESTOVSKAYA, D. S., History of World Culture
BERZHANSKY, V. N., Experimental Physics
BOKOV, V. A., Geography
BUROV, G. M., Ancient and Medieval History
CHEKHOV, V. N., Theoretical and Applied Mechanics
CHIRVA, V. YA, Organic and Analytical Chemistry
DEMENTIEV, N. E., History of Russia
DONSKOY, V. I., Informatics
EMIROVA, A. M., Russian Language
FEDORENKO, A. M., Chemistry
FILIMONOV, S. B., History of Ukraine
GABRIELYAN, O. A., Political Science and Sociology
GUBANOV, I. G., Geography
GUBAR, A. I., Ukrainian Language
KALIN, V. K., General Psychology, History of Psychology
KALNOY, I. I., Social Philosophy
KASHENKO, S. G., History of Russian Law
KAZARIN, V. P., Russian and General Literature
KIRICHENKO, A. A., Law
KOPACHEVSKY, N. D., Mathematical Analysis
KORENYUK, I. I., Human and Animal Physiology
KOZLOV, A. S., Greek Language
KRAMARENKO, V. I., Management
KRICHEK, P. M., Ukrainian Literature
KRYUCHKOV, I. V., Economics
KUDRYASHOV, A. P., Political Economy
KUZHEL, A. V., Theory of Functions and Functional Analysis
LAZAREV, F. V., Philosophy
LYSENKO, N. I., General Land Science
MANAKOV, M. K., Physiology of Plants
MARTYNYUK, YU. N., Philosophy
MEMETOV, A. A., Philosophy
MISHNEV, V. G., Botany
NAGORSKAYA, M. N., Management
NIKOLKO, V. N., Philosophy
NOVIKOVA, M. A., Russian and General Literature
OLIFEROV, A. N., Oceanology
OREKHOVA, L. A., Russian Literature
PERSIDSKY, S. K., Differential and Integral Equations
PETRENKO, A. D., German Language
PODSOLONKO, V. A., Economics
POMERANETS, V. N., Economics
POPOV, V. K., Law
REGUSHEVSKY, E. S., Linguistics
RUDYAKOV, A. N., Linguistics
SHARAPA, V. F., History
SHEVLYAKOV, YU. M., Applied Mathematics
SHULGIN, V. F., Chemistry
SIDYAKIN, V. G., Human and Animal Physiology
SOKOLOVSKAYA, ZH. P., Philology
STADNIK, I. P., Theoretical Physics
STASHKOV, A. M., Animal Biophysics
TEMURYANTS, N. A., Human and Animal Physiology
TEREZ, E. K., Astronomy and Teaching Methods of Physics
UNKOVSKAYA, T. E., Management
URSU, D. P., Modern and Contemporary History
VOLYAR, A. V., Physics
YENA, V. G., Geography
YEFIMENKO, A. M., Theoretical Foundations of Physical Culture
YURAKHNO, M. V., Zoology

TERNOPIL NATIONAL ECONOMIC UNIVERSITY

46020 Ternopil, vul. Lvivska 11
Telephone: (35) 247-50-51
Fax: (35) 247-61-33
E-mail: rector@tneu.edu.ua
Internet: www.tneu.edu.ua

Founded 1966
State control
Languages of instruction: Ukrainian, English, German, Polish
Academic year: September to July

Rector: Prof. Dr SERHIY I. YURIY
Vice-Rector for Educational Research (Int. Relations): Dr BOHDAN LUTSIV
Vice-Rector for Educational Research (Organizational Work): Prof. ANDRII KRYSOVATYI
Vice-Rector for Educational Research (Teaching): Dr MYKOLA SHYNKARYK
Vice-Rector for Educational Research (Territory, Distant Structural Subdivisons, Accreditation, Licensing): Prof. HRYHORII ZHURAVEL
Vice-Rector for Humanities and Extra-Curricular Activities: Dr BOHDAN ADAMYK
Vice-Rector for Research: Prof. ALLA MELNYK
Vice-Rector for Social and Economic Devt: VASYL BULAVYNETS
Librarian: KAZYMYR VOZNIY

Library of 448,327 vols
Number of teachers: 1,005
Number of students: 88,508

Publications: *Computing*, *Economic Analysis*, *Journal of European Economy* (in English, Russian, Ukrainian), *Psychologiya I Suspilstvo* (Psychology and Society), *Regional Aspects of The Development and Placement of Productive Forces in Ukraine*, *Svit Finaciv* (World of Finances), *TNEU Herald*, *Ukrainian Science: Past, Nowadays and Future* (colns of research papers), *Young Science*

DEANS

Faculty of Accounting and Audit: Prof. YAROSLAV D. KRUPKA
Faculty of Agrarian Economics and Management: Prof. ROMAN HEVKO
Faculty of the Banking Business: Dr VASYL TKACHUK
Faculty of Computer and Information Technologies: Prof. MYKOLA P. DYVAK
Faculty of Economics and Investment Management: Prof. BOGDAN LITVIN
Faculty of Economics and Management: Prof. YEVHEN KACHAN
Faculty of Finances: Prof. IHOR HUTSAL
Faculty of International Business and Management: Prof. ANATOLIY M. TYBIN
Faculty of Law: Dr VOLODYMYR VOZNIY
Faculty of Pre-University, Postgraduate Education and Master Training: Prof. OLEH IVASHCHUK

UZHHOROD NATIONAL UNIVERSITY

88000 Uzhhorod, vul. Pidhirna 46
Telephone and fax (31) 223-33-41
E-mail: admin@univ.uzhgorod.ua
Internet: www.univ.uzhgorod.ua

Founded 1945
State control
Language of instruction: Ukrainian
Academic year: September to July

Rector: Prof. Dr MYKOLA M. VEHESH
Pro-Rector for Academic Affairs: OLEXANDR H. SLYVKA
Pro-Rector for Admin. and Economic Affairs: VOLODYMYR V. SHETELYA
Pro-Rector for Research: IHOR P. STUDENJAK
Pro-Rector for Social Devt and Capital Construction: YAROSLAV S. HUK
Registrar: ROSTISLAV. V. ROMANYUK
Librarian: OLENA I. POCHEKUTOVA

Library: see Libraries and Archives
Number of teachers: 600
Number of students: 8,000

Publication: *Bulletin* (series: Biology, Chemistry, Mathematics, Medicine, Philology, Physics, Romance and Germanic Philology, annual)

DEANS

Faculty of Biology: Asst Prof. V. I. NIKOLAYCHUK
Faculty of Chemistry: Asst Prof. VASYL LENDYEL
Faculty of Economics: Prof. VASIL MIKLOVDA
Faculty of Engineering: Asst Prof. IVAN TURYANYTSYA
Faculty of History: Asst Prof. VOLODYMYR FENYCH
Faculty of International Relations: Prof. M. A. LENDYEL
Faculty of Law: Prof. VASIL YAREMA
Faculty of Mathematics: Asst Prof. MYKHAYLO PAHYRYA
Faculty of Medicine: Asst Prof. BOLDIZHAR BOLDIZHAR
Faculty of Philology: Asst Prof. IVAN SABADOSH
Faculty of Physical Education and Sport: Asst Prof. STEPAN LASUR
Faculty of Physics: Prof. Dr VOLODYMYR LASUR
Faculty of Postgraduate Studies: Prof. IVAN MIKHAYLOVYCH
Faculty of Romance and Germanic Philology: Asst Prof. STEPAN BOBYNETS

VADYM HETMAN KYIV NATIONAL UNIVERSITY OF ECONOMICS

03057 Kyiv, pr. Peremohi 54/1
Telephone: (44) 371-61-12
Fax: (44) 226-25-73
E-mail: rector@kneu.kiev.ua
Internet: www.kneu.kiev.ua

Founded 1906
State control
Language of instruction: Ukrainian
Academic year: September to June

Rector: Prof. Dr ANATOLII PAVLENKO
Librarian: TETYANA KYRYLENKO

Library of 1,301,706 vols, 156 journals
Number of teachers: 1,512 (incl. full-time and part-time)
Number of students: 37,174

Publications: *International Economic Policy*, *Marketing in Ukraine*

DEANS

Faculty of Accounting: Prof. Dr VASYL IEFIMENKO
Faculty of Agroindustrial Complex: Prof. Dr MYKHAILO M. KOTSUPATRYY
Faculty of Crediting: Prof. Dr MYKHAILO I. DYBA
Faculty of Economics and Management: Prof. Dr ANATOLII P. NALIVAIKO
Faculty of Finance: Dr VOLODYMYR K. KHLIVNYY
Faculty of Information Systems and Technologies: Prof. Dr OLEKSANDR D. SHARAPOV
Faculty of International Economics and Management: Prof. Dr DMYTRO H. LUKYANENKO
Faculty of Law: Prof. Dr VITALII F. OPRYSHKO
Faculty of Personnel Management and Marketing: Prof. Dr OLEKSANDR SHAFALIUK

ZAPORIZHZHYA NATIONAL UNIVERSITY

69063 Zaporizhia, vul. Zhukovskoho 66
Telephone: (61) 264-45-46
Fax: (61) 262-71-61
E-mail: rektor@zsu.zp.ua
Internet: www.zsu.edu.ua

Founded 1985
State control
Languages of instruction: Russian, Ukrainian
Academic year: September to July

Rector: Prof. V. A. TOLOK
Pro-Rector for Admin.: I. G. YAKUSHEV
Pro-Rector for Curriculum: V. V. HIRZHON
Pro-Rector for Research and Int. Cooperation: V. Z. HRYSTCHAK
Pro-Rector for Social Devt: V. G. TKACHENKO
Registrar: S. A. EVSTAFENKO
Librarian: V. A. HERASYMOVA

Number of teachers: 541
Number of students: 8,200

Publications: *Antiquities of the Steppe, Black Sea Region and Crimea*, *Bulletin*, *Cultural Bulletin* (scientific-theoretical annual of the Lower Dnieper region), *New Paradigm*, *New Philology*, *Notes of the Scientific Research Laboratory of the Southern Ukraine*, *Problems of Bioindication*, *Renaissance Studies*, *Zaporizhzhya Legacy* (history of the Southern Ukraine in the 18th century)

DEANS

Faculty of Biology: Dr V. I. DOMNICH
Faculty of Economics: Prof. V. V. KIRICHEVSKIY
Faculty of Foreign Philology: Prof. V. I. SKIBINA
Faculty of History: Prof. F. G. TURCHENKO
Faculty of Law: Dr T. A. DENISOVA
Faculty of Management: Dr I. G. SHAVKUN
Faculty of Mathematics: Prof. N. G. TAMUROV
Faculty of Philology: Prof. O. D. TURGAN
Faculty of Physical Training: Dr V. N. ZAYTSEVA
Faculty of Physics: Dr A. Y. OSIPOV
Faculty of Postgraduate Education: Dr L. D. KRIVEGA
Faculty of Social Pedagogics: Prof. L. I. MISCHIK
Faculty of Sociology and Administration: Prof. V. P. BEKH

PROFESSORS

BAYKINA, N. G., Sports
BEKH, V. P., Politics and Theory of Administration
BESSONOVA, V. P., Biology
BOVT, V. D., Biology
BYLOUSENKO, P. I., Ukrainian Language
CHABANENKO, V. A., General Linguistics
FROLOV, A. K., Human Physiology
GRISTCHAK, V. Z., Applied Mathematics
IVANENKO, V. K., Methods of Teaching Philological Disciplines
KARAGODIN, A. I., History
KIRICHEVSKIY, V. V., Applied Mathematics
LYAKH, S. R., History of Ukraine
MISCHIK, L. I., Pedagogics and Psychology
MOROZOV, L. V., Finance and Credit
NAUMENKO, A. M., German Philology
NOVIKOV, Y. F., Theory and Practice of Management
PAKHOMOVA, T. A., Methods of Teaching Philological Disciplines
PROZOROVA, N. S., History and Theory of State and Law
PRYKHODKO, N. I., Problems of Administration and Social Pedagogics
PRYVARNIKOV, A. K., Algebra and Geometry
PSARYOV, V. I., Physics
SERGEYEV, A. V., Physics
TAMUROV, N. G., Applied Mathematics
TOLOK, V. A., Applied Mathematics
TURCHENKO, F. G., History of the Ukraine
TURGAN, O. D., Theory of Literature and Journalism
TYKHOMIROV, V. N., Foreign Literature
TYMCHENKO, S. M., History of the Ukraine
YESHENKO, V. A., Physiology and Civil Defence
ZATSNIY, Y. A., Theory and Practice of Translation

MEDICAL UNIVERSITIES

BUKOVINIAN STATE MEDICAL UNIVERSITY

58000 Chernivtsi, Teatralna pl. 2
Telephone: (372) 55-37-54
Fax: (372) 55-37-54
E-mail: bma@bsmu.edu.ua
Internet: www.bsmu.edu.ua

Founded 1944 as Chernivtsi State Medical Institute; as Bukovinian State Medical Acad. 1997; present name and Univ. status 2005
State control
Academic year: September to June

Rector: VASIL P. PISHAK
First Vice-Rector: MIHAILO Y. KOLOMOETS
Vice-Rector for Int. Relations: YURIY M. NECHYTAYLO

Library of 350,000 vols
Number of teachers: 435
Number of students: 3,100

Publications: *Bukovinian Medical Herald* (4 a year), *Clinical Anatomy and Operative Surgery* (4 a year), *Clinical and Experimental Pathology* (4 a year)

DEANS

VOLODYMYR HLUBOCHENKO
OLEKSANDR POLISCHUK
VIKTOR POLYOVIY
TAMILA SOROKMAN

CRIMEAN STATE MEDICAL UNIVERSITY 'S. I. GEORGIEVSKY'

95006 Simferopol, bul. Lenina 5/7
Telephone: (65) 227-44-62
Fax: (65) 227-20-92
E-mail: office@crsmu.com
Internet: www.crsmu.com

Founded 1931

Rector: Prof. A. A. BABANIN

Library of 634,371 vols
Number of teachers: 629
Number of students: 4,556

Publications: *Bulletin of Physiotherapy and Balneology* (4 a year), *Problems, Achievements and Perspectives of the Development of Biomedical Sciences and Practical Public Health of Ukraine* (colln of scientific works, 4 a year), *Tavrian Biomedical Bulletin* (4 a year), *Tavrian Journal of Psychiatry* (4 a year)

DEANS

First Medical Faculty: Prof. A. I. KRADINOV
Second Medical Faculty: Prof. S. N. KRUTIKOV
Faculty of Stomatology: Prof. L. I. AVDONINA
International Faculty: Prof. M. N. GRISHIN
Postgraduate Faculty: Prof. N. P. BUGLAK

I. HORBACHEVSKY TERNOPIL STATE MEDICAL UNIVERSITY

46001 Ternopil, Maydan Voli 1
Telephone: (35) 252-44-92
Fax: (35) 252-41-83
E-mail: university@tdmu.edu.te.ua
Internet: www.tdmu.edu.te.ua

Founded 1957
Public control
Languages of instruction: English, Russian, Ukrainian
Academic year: September to July

Rector: Prof. LEONID Y. KOVALCHUK

Library of 500,000 vols
Number of teachers: 560
Number of students: 4,000

Publications: *Achievements of Clinical and Experimental Medicine* (2 a year), *Hospital Surgery* (4 a year), *Infectious Diseases* (4 a year), *Medical Chemistry* (4 a year), *Medical Education* (4 a year), *Scientific Research Newsletter* (4 a year)

DEANS

Faculty of Dentistry: Prof. YAROSLAV NAGIRNY
Faculty of Foreign Students: Prof. MYKHAYLO KORDA
Faculty of Medicine: Prof. ARKADIY SHULGAY
Faculty of Pharmacy: Prof. LIUDMYLA SOKOLOVA
Faculty of Postgraduate Education: Prof. MARYAN GREBENYK

KHARKIV NATIONAL MEDICAL UNIVERSITY

61022 Kharkiv, pr. Lenina 4
Telephone: (57) 705-07-11
Fax: (57) 700-41-32
E-mail: meduniver@knmu.kharkov.ua
Internet: www.knmu.kharkov.ua

Founded 1805, present name and status 2007
State control
Languages of instruction: Ukrainian, English, Russian
Academic year: September to June

Rector: Prof. Dr VLADIMIR N. LESOVOY
First Vice-Rector for Research and Education: Prof. VALERY A. KAPUSTNYK
Vice-Rector for Research and Education: Prof. VALERIY V. MYASOEDOV
Librarian: ISABELLA SH. IVANOVA

Library of 986,384 vols, 237 periodicals
Number of teachers: 701
Number of students: 5,438

Publications: *Experimental Clinical Medicine* (4 a year), *Medical Practice* (6 a year), *Medicine Today and Tomorrow* (2 a year), *Ultrasonic Perinatal Diagnosis* (2 a year)

DEANS

Faculty for Postgraduate Education: Asst Prof. VALERIY V. VYUN
Medical Faculty I: Prof. ANATOLIY O. TERESCHENKO
Medical Faculty II: Prof. VASYL O. OLKHOVSKIY
Medical Faculty III: Prof. MYKOLA V. PANCHENKO
Medical Faculty IV: Prof. VALERIY V. MINUKHIN
Medical Faculty V for Training Foreign Students: Asst Prof. DMYTRO I. MARAKUSHYN
Medical Faculty VI for Training Foreign Students: Asst Prof. DMYTRO V. KATSAPOV
Stomatological Faculty: Asst Prof. VIKTOR V. NIKONOV

LUHANSK STATE MEDICAL UNIVERSITY

91045 Luhansk, Kvartal 50-richchya Oborony Luhanska 1
Telephone: (64) 254-84-03
Fax: (64) 253-20-36
E-mail: kanc@lsmu.edu.ua
Internet: www.lsmu.edu.ua

Founded 1956, present name and status 1994

Faculties of dentistry, health care, nursing, paediatrics and pharmacy

Rector: Prof. VALERIY K. IVCHENKO

Library of 420,000 vols
Number of teachers: 394
Number of students: 2,815

LVIV NATIONAL MEDICAL UNIVERSITY 'DANYLO HALYTSKIY'

79010 Lviv, Pekarska Str. 69
Telephone: (32) 272-26-60
Fax: (32) 276-79-73
E-mail: zimenkovsky@meduniv.lviv.ua
Internet: www.meduniv.lviv.ua

Founded 1784

Rector: Prof. Dr BORYS ZIMENKOVSKY

Library of 520,000 vols
Number of teachers: 1,200
Number of students: 4,977

DEANS

Faculty of Dentistry: ROSTYSLAV M. STUPNYTSKYI
First Medical Faculty: BOGDAN V. DYBAS
Second Medical Faculty: YURI YA. KRYVKO
Faculty of Nursing: VIRA I. PIROGOVA
Faculty of Pharmacy: ROMAN B. LESYK
Faculty of Stomatology: IVAN M. HOT
Faculty of Postgraduate Education: OREST YE. SICHKORIZ
International Faculty: EUGENE VARYVODA
External Faculty: ROMAN EU. DARMOGRAIY

NATIONAL O. BOHOMOLETS MEDICAL UNIVERSITY

01601 Kyiv, bul. T. Shevchenka 13
Telephone: (44) 234-40-62
Fax: (44) 234-92-76
E-mail: interdeptnmu@gmail.com
Internet: www.nmu.edu.ua

Founded 1841
Public control
Languages of instruction: English, Russian, Ukrainian
Academic year: September to June

Rector: Prof. Dr VITALIY MOSKALENKO
Vice-Rector for International Affairs Research and Education: Prof. Dr OLESYA HULCHIY

Library of 750,000 vols
Number of teachers: 1,200
Number of students: 10,000

Publications: *East European Journal Of Public Health, Health Care in Ukraine, Scientific Journal of National O. Bohomolets Medical University*

DEANS

Faculty for International Students: Prof. ALEXANDER SAVYCHUK
Medical Faculty I (General Medicine): Prof. VICTOR CHERKASOV
Medical Faculty II (General Medicine): Prof. VASYL NETYAZHENKO
Medical Faculty III (Paediatrics): Prof. VASYL PETRENKO
Medical Faculty IV (Preventive Care): Prof. SERHIY OMELCHUK
School for Continuing Education for Trainers: Prof. YURIY MARUSHKO
School of Dentistry: Prof. VALERIY NESPRYADKO
School of Medical Engineering: Prof. VALENTYN YATSENKO
School of Medical Psychology: Prof. SERHIY MAKSYMENKO
School of Pharmacy: Prof. IRYNA NIZHENKIVSKA
School of Military Medicine: Col OLEG VLASENKO

NATIONAL UNIVERSITY OF PHARMACY

61002 Kharkiv, vul. Pushkinskaya 53
Telephone: (57) 706-35-81
Fax: (57) 714-25-40
E-mail: mail@ukrfa.kharkov.ua
Internet: www.pharm.kharkiv.edu

Founded 1805
Public control
Languages of instruction: English, Russian, Ukrainian
Academic year: September to June (10 semesters)

Rector: Prof. Dr VALENTIN P. CHERNYKH
Vice-Rector For Scientific, Educational Work And International Affairs: Prof. Dr SERGEY B. POPOV
Librarian: NATALIYA B. LISOVOL

Library: 1m. vols
Number of teachers: 830
Number of students: 17,000

Publications: *Clinical Pharmacy* (4 a year), *Fisiologichno-Aktivni Rechovini* (Physiologically Active Substances, 2 a year), *Klinichna Farmatsiya* (Clinical Pharmacy, 4 a year), *Organic and Pharmaceutical Chemistry* (4 a year), *Visnik Farmatsii* (Pharmacy Bulletin, 4 a year), *Zdorovya Cheloveky* (Health to Mankind, 4 a year)

DEANS

Faculty of Correspondence and Distance Learning: Assoc. Prof. SVETLANA G. KALAYCHEVA
Faculty of Economics and Management: Assoc. Prof. VOLODYMYR V. MALY
Faculty of Foreign Students' Training: Assoc. Prof. VLADIMIR D. GORYACHIY

Faculty of Industrial Pharmacy: Assoc. Prof. Dr TATYANA KRUTSKIKH
Faculty of Medical Pharmacy: Assoc. Prof. Dr OLGA I. NABOKA
Faculty of Pharmacy: Assoc. Prof. Dr LILIYA I. VISHNEVSKAYA
Preparatory Faculty for Foreign Citizens: ZOYA I. KOVALENKO

NATIONAL UNIVERSITY OF PHYSICAL EDUCATION AND SPORTS OF UKRAINE

03680 Kyiv, vul. Fizkultury 1
Telephone: (44) 227-54-52
Fax: (44) 287-61-91
E-mail: rectorat@uni-sport.edu.ua
Internet: www.uni-sport.edu.ua

Founded 1930

Faculties of Olympic and professional sport, physical rehabilitation and sports medicine, physical education, recreation and health-related physical culture; faculty of external studies

Rector: Prof. Dr VOLODYMYR M. PLATONOV
First Pro-Rector for Education: Prof. Dr YURIY M. SHKREBTIY
Pro-Rector for Research: Dr TETYANA YU. KRUTSEVICH.

VINNITSA NATIONAL MEDICAL UNIVERSITY 'M. I. PYROHOV'

21018 Vinnytsya, pr. Lenina 9
Telephone: (432) 32-06-85
Fax: (432) 32-16-13
E-mail: admission@vsmu.vinnica.ua
Internet: www.vnmu.vn.ua

Founded 1921

Rector: Prof. Dr VASYL M. MOROZ

Library of 500,000 vols
Number of teachers: 554
Number of students: 3,600

PEDAGOGICAL UNIVERSITIES

KHARKIV NATIONAL PEDAGOGICAL UNIVERSITY 'H. S. SKOVORODA'

61168 Kharkiv, vul. Blyukhera 2
Telephone: (57) 700-69-09
E-mail: rector@pu.ac.kharkov.ua
Internet: pu.ac.kharkov.ua

Founded 1804

Rector: Prof. Dr IVAN F. PROKOPENKO

Library of 714,689 vols

DEANS

Faculty of Art and Design: Prof. Dr NADEZDA V. SHYLOVTSEVA
Faculty of Economics: Prof. Dr HANNA M. GUZENKO
Faculty of Elementary Education: Prof. Dr NATALIYA M. YAKUSHKO
Faculty of Foreign Languages: Dr NATALIYA V. TUCHYNA
Faculty of History: Assoc. Prof. SVETLANA V. BEREZNAYA
Faculty of Law: Prof. Dr VIKTOR O. PROTSEVSKYY
Faculty of Music Education: Assoc. Prof. TETYANA A. SMIRNOVA
Faculty of Natural Sciences: Prof. Dr IGOR IONOV
Faculty of Physical Education: Prof. Dr MYKOLA I. GORODYSKYY
Faculty of Physics and Mathematics: Prof. Dr OLEKSANDR I. GONCHAROV
Faculty of Pre-School Education: Prof. Dr TETYANA P. TANKO
Faculty of Psychology and Sociology: Prof. Dr OKSANA G. VOLKOVA
Faculty of Russian Language and World Literature: Prof. Dr TAMARA P. STAKANKOVA
Faculty of Ukrainian Language and Literature: Prof. Dr IRYNA V. TYMCHENKO
External Faculty: Assoc. Prof. VIKTORIYA M. TYKHONOVICH

DIRECTORS

Institute of Post-Diploma Education: Prof. Dr MYKOLA V. GADETSKYY
Institute of World Languages: Prof. Dr TAMARA P. STAKANKOVA

NATIONAL PEDAGOGICAL DRAGOMANOV UNIVERSITY

01601 Kyiv, vul. Pyrohova 9
Telephone: (44) 234-11-08
Fax: (44) 234-11-08
E-mail: shcf-npu@ukr.net
Internet: www.npu.kiev.ua

Founded 1834 as Gorky Kievan Pedagogical Institute, became Kievan State Pedagogical Univ. 1991, present name and status 1997

Rector: Acad. Prof. Dr VIKTOR P. ANDRUSHCHENKO
First Vice-Rector: Dr VOLODYMYR P. BEKH
Vice-Rector for Academic Affairs: Prof. PETRO V. DMYTRENKO
Vice-Rector for Academic and Methodical Affairs: Prof. ROMAN M. VERNYDUB
Vice-Rector for Distance Learning and Innovational Technologies of Learning: Prof. ANATOLYI P. KUDIN
Vice-Rector for Finance and Organizational Effectiveness: Dr OLEG S. PADALKA
Vice-Rector for Int. Relations: Dr VOLODYMYR G. LAVRYNENKO
Vice-Rector for Research Work: Prof. HRIHORIY I. VOLYNKA
Vice-Rector: Prof. Dr ANATOLYI T. AVDIEVSKIY
Dir of Library: LYUDMYLA V. SAVENKOVA

Library of 1,233,252 vols, 863,673 books, 150,351 periodicals, 7,149 foreign edns, 125 magnetic tapes and discs, 2,563 theses and dissertations defended within the Univ.

TECHNICAL UNIVERSITIES

DNIPRODZERZHYNSK STATE TECHNICAL UNIVERSITY

51948 Dnipropetrovska oblast, Dniprodzerzhynsk, vul. Dniprobudivska
Telephone: (56) 955-13-89
Fax: (56) 955-13-07
E-mail: science@dstu.dp.ua
Internet: www.dstu.dp.ua

Founded 1920, present name and status 1994

Rector: Prof. IHOR O. PAVLYUCHENKOV
First Pro-Rector: Dr VITALIY M. HULYAYEV

DEANS

Faculty of Chemical Technology: Dr OLEH I. POLYANCHYKOV
Faculty of Economics and Management: Dr SERHIY H. DRONOV
Faculty of Electronics and Computer Technology: Prof. OLEKSANDR M. SYANOV
Faculty of Mechanical Engineering: Dr VOLODYMYR SOLOD
Faculty of Metallurgy: Dr OLEKSANDR V. HRESS
Faculty of Post-Diploma Education: Prof. I. V. HUBARYEV
Faculty of Power Engineering: Prof. ANATOLIY M. PAVLENKO
Faculty of Sociology and Philology: Prof. MYKOLA S. KONOKH
External Faculty: Prof. YEVHEN B. LEYKO

DNIPROPETROVSK NATIONAL TECHNICAL UNIVERSITY OF RAILWAY TRANSPORT 'V. LAZARYAN'

49700 Dnipropetrovsk-10, vul. Lazaryana 2
Telephone: (56) 776-59-47
Fax: (56) 247-18-66
E-mail: dnuzt@diit.edu.ua
Internet: www.diit.edu.ua

Founded 1930

Specialist faculties incl. bridges and tunnels, economics and management in transport, industrial and civil engineering, management of transport processes in railway transport, mechanics, organization of railway construction and track maintenance, technical cybernetics and military training

Rector: Prof. Dr ALEXANDER N. PSHINKO
First Pro-Rector for Education: Prof. Dr BORIS E. BODNAR
Pro-Rector for Research: Dr SERHEY MYAMLYN

Library of 800,000 vols
Number of students: 4,200

DONBASS STATE TECHNICAL UNIVERSITY

94204 Alchevsk, pr. Lenina 16
Telephone: (64) 422-31-23
Fax: (64) 422-68-87
E-mail: info@dmmi.edu.ua
Internet: www.dmmi.edu.ua
Public control
Languages of instruction: English, Russian, Ukrainian
Academic year: September to July
Rector: Prof. Dr ANATOLIY I. AKMAYEV
First Vice-Rector for Academic Affairs: Dr VASILIY N. OKALELOV
Vice-Rector for Research: Dr NIKOLAY N. ZABLODSKIY
Library of 700,000 vols
Number of teachers: 470
Number of students: 14,000

Publication: *Impulse* (52 a year).

DONETSK NATIONAL TECHNICAL UNIVERSITY

83000 Donetsk, Artema 58
Telephone: (62) 337-17-33
Fax: (62) 304-12-78
E-mail: info@dgtu.donetsk.ua
Internet: www.donntu.edu.ua

Founded 1921

Rector: Prof. Dr ALEKSANDR A. MINAEV
First Pro-Rector: Prof. Dr ALEKSANDR A. TROYANSKIY
Pro-Rector for Academic Affairs: Dr ALEKSANDR V. LEVSHOV
Pro-Rector for Admin.: HEORHIY A. ROMANKO
Pro-Rector for Internal Communications and Economic Affairs: ILYA P. NAVKA
Pro-Rector for Research: Prof. Dr EVGENIY A. BASHKOV
Librarian: ANNA A. PETROVA

Library: 1.5m. vols
Number of teachers: 1,500
Number of students: 23,000

Publications: *Development of Mining Minerals* (2 a year), *Problems of Ecology* (1 a year)

Campuses in Gorlovka and Krasnoarmeysk

DEANS

Faculty of Computing Technology and Information Science: Dr ALEKSANDR ANOPRIENKO
Faculty of Ecology and Chemical Technology: Dr ALEKSANDR S. PARFENYUK
Faculty of Economics and Management: Prof. VYACHESLAV V. DEMENTYEV

Faculty of Electrotechnical Engineering: Prof. Nilolay Grebchenko
Faculty of Geotechnology and Management in Manufacturing: Prof. Yuri F. Bulgakov
Faculty of Information Technologies and Automation: Dr Aleksandr V. Khorkhordin
Faculty of Mechanical Engineering: Dr Sergey A. Selivra
Faculty of Mining and Geology: Prof. Oleg I. Kalinichenko
Faculty of Physics and Metallurgy: Prof. Sergey Safyants
Faculty of Power Mechanics and Automation: Dr Sergey A. Selivra
Faculty of Radiotechnology: Prof. Pavel V. Stefanenko
English-Language Technical Faculty: Dr Sergey A. Kovalev
French-Language Faculty of Engineering: Prof. Gennadiy S. Klyagin
German-Language Technical Faculty: Dr Viktor I. Kalashnikov
Polish-Language Technical Faculty: Dr Aleksandr Yu. Makeyev
Foreign Students: Dr Sergey F. Sukov

IVANO-FRANKIVSK NATIONAL TECHNICAL UNIVERSITY OF OIL AND GAS

76019 Ivano-Frankivsk, vul. Karpatska 15
Telephone: (34) 224-22-64
Fax: (34) 224-21-39
E-mail: admin@nung.edu.ua
Internet: www.ifdtung.if.ua

Founded 1967

Faculties of automation and electrification, economics and management, engineering ecology, gas and oil industry, gas and oil pipelines, geological prospecting, mechanical, mechanics and technology

Rector: Y. I. Kryzhanivsky

Library of 790,000 vols
Number of teachers: 413
Number of students: 4,453

KHARKIV NATIONAL AUTOMOBILE AND HIGHWAYS UNIVERSITY

61002 Kharkiv, vul. Petrovskoho 25
Telephone: (57) 700-38-65
Fax: (57) 700-38-66
E-mail: admin@khadi.kharkov.ua
Internet: www.khadi.kharkov.ua

Founded 1930

Rector: Prof. Dr Anatoliy N. Turenko
First Pro-Rector: Prof. Dr Ivan P. Gladkiy
Pro-Rector for Research: Prof. Dr Viktor A. Bogomolov

Library of 450,000 vols
Number of teachers: 458
Number of students: 10,956 full-time, 7,042 external

DEANS

Faculty of Automotive Technology: Volodymyr Volkov
Faculty of Business and Management: Ilya Dmitriev
Faculty of Distance Education: Nikolay Aleksa
Faculty of Postgraduate Studies: Nikolay Kaslin
Faculty of Road Construction: Igor Kiyashko
Faculty of Transport Systems: Yuri Beketov

KHARKIV NATIONAL UNIVERSITY OF RADIOELECTRONICS

61166 Kharkiv, pr. Lenina 14
Telephone: (57) 702-18-07
Fax: (57) 702-10-13
E-mail: info@kture.kharkov.ua
Internet: www.kture.kharkov.ua

Founded 1930

Rector: Prof. Dr Mykhaylo F. Bondarenko

Library of 750,000 vols
Number of students: 8,500

DEANS

Faculty of Applied Mathematics and Management: Leonid I. Shklyarov
Faculty of Computer Engineering and Management: Gennadiy F. Krivulya
Faculty of Computer Sciences: Vladimir P. Mashtalir
Faculty of Electronic Devices: Vladimir A. Storozhenko
Faculty of Electronic Technology: Yuri N. Aleksandrov
Faculty of Radiotechnology: Sergey N. Sakalo
Faculty of Telecommunications and Electronics: Igor N. Presnyakov
Foreign Students' Preparatory Faculty: Vladimir P. Nemchenko
Postgraduate Faculty: Zoya V. Dudar

DIRECTORS OF INSTITUTES

Institute of Computing and Information Technologies: Viktor M. Levykin
Institute of Radioengineering and Electronics: Vladimir M. Shokalo
Institute of Telecommunications: Viktor M. Levykin

KHARKIV POLYTECHNICAL INSTITUTE (NATIONAL TECHNICAL UNIVERSITY)

61002 Kharkiv, vul. Frunze 21
Telephone: (57) 243-26-81
Fax: (57) 240-06-01
E-mail: omsroot@kpi.kharkov.ua
Internet: www.kpi.kharkov.ua

Founded 1885

Rector: Leonid L. Tovazhnyansky
Pro-Rector for Education and Int. Relations: Valeriy O. Kravets
Pro-Rector for Research: Yevgen I. Sokol

Number of teachers: 1,235
Number of students: 20,000

DEANS

Faculty of Automation and Instrument Making: Prof. Anatoliy I. Hapon
Faculty of Business Administration: Prof. Viktor Ya. Zaruba
Faculty of Business and Finance: Prof. Oleksandr M. Havris
Faculty of Chemical Engineering: Dr Oleksiy M. Passokha
Faculty of Computing and Information Technologies: Prof. Mykola I. Zapolovskiy
Faculty of Distance and Pre-University Training: Dr Mykola M. Sirenko
Faculty of Economics: Prof. Petro H. Perverva
Faculty of Economics and Law: Prof. Leonid M. Ivin
Faculty of Electrical Engineering: Prof. Volodymyr V. Voinov
Faculty of Engineering: Dr Mikhailo S. Stepanov
Faculty of Engineering Physics: Dr Dmitro V. Breskslavskiy
Faculty of Information Science and Management: Prof. Vyacheslav H. Bazhenov
Faculty of Inorganic Substances Technology: Prof. Mikhailo I. Rischenko
Faculty of Mechanics and Technology: Dr Mykola Pohribniy
Faculty of Organic Substances Technology: Prof. Oleksandr P. Nekrasov
Faculty of Physics and Technology: Prof. Serhiy M. Kosmachov
Faculty of Power Engineering: Prof. Mykola O. Tarasenko
Faculty of Transport Engineering: Dr Vitaliy V. Yepifanov
German Technical Faculty: Dr Vira M. Shamardina

KHARKIV STATE TECHNICAL UNIVERSITY OF CIVIL ENGINEERING AND ARCHITECTURE

61002 Kharkiv, Sumska ul. 40
Telephone: (57) 700-10-66
Fax: (57) 700-02-50
E-mail: office@kstuca.kharkov.ua
Internet: www.kstuca.kharkov.ua

Founded 1930

Rector: Prof. Dr Yuriy Shkodovskiy

Library of 683,000 vols
Number of teachers: 590
Number of students: 6,500

DEANS

Faculty of Architecture: Prof. Oleksandr Vasilenko
Faculty of Construction: Dr Yevgen Yakovlev
Faculty of Economics and Management: Dr Oleksandr Syrovatskiy
Faculty of External Education: Dr Oleksandr F. Pugachov
Faculty of Mechanical-Technical Engineering: Dr Yuriy Zhuravlev
Faculty of Postgraduate Education: Dr Gennadiy Sukhorukov
Faculty of Pre-University Preparation: Dr Igor Emets
Faculty of Sanitary Engineering: Dr Viktor Shylin

KHERSON NATIONAL TECHNICAL UNIVERSITY

73008 Kherson, Beryslavske shose 24
Telephone and fax (55) 255-40-11
E-mail: kstu@tlc.kherson.ua
Internet: www.kstu.edu.ua

Founded 1957

Rector: Frants B. Rohalskiy

Library of 400,000 vols
Publication: *Proceedings* (2 a year)

DEANS

Faculty of Cybernetics: Prof. Nadiya A. Sokolova
Faculty of Distance Education: Prof. N. A. Pustovaya
Faculty of Economics: Prof. Volodymyr. E. Tursh
Faculty of International Economics: Prof. V. V. Kryuchovskiy
Faculty of Machine Building: Prof. Hrihoriy Dynevich
Faculty of Technology and Design: Prof. N. I. Valko
Preparatory Faculty: Prof. N. S. Mykolaychuk

KIROVOHRAD NATIONAL TECHNICAL UNIVERSITY

25006 Kirovohrad, Universitetska 8
Telephone: (52) 255-93-59
Fax: (52) 255-92-53
E-mail: relintern@kdtu.kr.ua
Internet: www.kdtu.kr.ua

Founded 1929

Rector: Prof. Dr Mykhailo I. Chernovol
Pro-Rector for Education: Prof. Mykola M. Petrenko
Pro-Rector for Science and Research: Dr Volodymyr M. Kropivniy

Library of 406,000 vols

Number of teachers: 400
Number of students: 7,000

DEANS

Faculty of Agricultural Mechanics: Prof. VASYL M. SALO
Faculty of Automation, Power Engineering and Programming: Prof. LARISA H. VIKHROVA
Faculty of Economics: Prof. HRIHORIY M. DAVIDOV
Faculty of Machine Design and Development: Dr VOLODYMYR V. YATSUN
Faculty of Mechanics and Technology: Prof. BORIS YE. NADVORNIY
Preparatory and Specialists' Retraining Faculty: Prof. YEVGEN K. SOLOVYKH
Preparatory Faculty for Foreign Specialists: Prof. OLEKSANDR Y. MAZHEYKA

KYIV NATIONAL UNIVERSITY OF CONSTRUCTION AND ARCHITECTURE

03037 Kyiv, Vozdukhoflotskii pr. 31
Telephone: (44) 248-49-05
Fax: (44) 248-49-01
E-mail: knuba@knuba.edu.ua
Internet: www.knuba.edu.ua

Founded 1930
Academic year: September to July
Rector: A. M. TUGAY
Library of 1,213,000 vols
Number of teachers: 850
Number of students: 6,800

'KYIV POLYTECHNIC INSTITUTE' NATIONAL TECHNICAL UNIVERSITY OF UKRAINE

03056 Kyiv, pr. Peremohy 37
Telephone and fax (44) 236-69-13
E-mail: zgur@zgurov.kiev.ua
Internet: www.ntu-kpi.kiev.ua

Founded 1898
Languages of instruction: Ukrainian, Russian, English
Academic year: September to June

19 Educational depts, 10 educational research institutes, 13 research institutes and 17 other scientific subdivisions (incl. design bureaux, engineering centres)

Rector: Acad. MYKHAYLO Z. ZGUROVSKIY
Library: 3m. vols
Number of students: 40,000
Publications: *Kyivsky Politekhnik* (newspaper, 48 a year), *Vesti* (2 a year)

DEANS

Faculty of Aircraft and Space Systems: Prof. OLEKSANDR V. ZBRUTSKIY
Faculty of Applied Mathematics: Prof. OLEKSANDR A. MOLCHANOV
Faculty of Biotechnology and Bioengineering: Prof. OLEKSIY M. DUGAN
Faculty of Chemical Engineering: Prof. YEVGEN M. PANOV
Faculty of Chemical Technology: Prof. IHOR M. ASTRELIN
Faculty of Electric Power Engineering and Automation: Prof. OLEKSANDR S. YANDULSKIY
Faculty of Electronics: Prof. VALERIY YA. ZHUYKOV
Faculty of Heat Power Engineering: Prof. YEVGEN M. PISMENNIY
Faculty of Informatics and Computer Science: Prof. OLEKSANDR A. PAVLOV
Faculty of Instrument Design and Engineering: Prof. HRIHORIY S. TYMCHYK
Faculty of Law and Sociology: Prof. ANATOLIY P. TUZOV
Faculty of Linguistics: Prof. NATALYA S. SAYENKO
Faculty of Management and Marketing: Prof. VASYL H. HERASIMCHUK
Faculty of Physics and Engineering: Prof. PETRO I. LOBODA
Faculty of Physics and Mathematics: Acad. Prof. VIKTOR H. BARYAKHTER
Faculty of Radio Engineering: Prof. OLEKSANDR I. RYBIN
Faculty of Welding: SERHIY K. FOMICHOV
Intercollegiate Faculty of Medical Engineering: Prof. V. P. YATSENKO

'LVIV POLYTECHNIC' NATIONAL UNIVERSITY

79013 Lviv, vul. St Bandery 12
Telephone: (32) 272-47-33
E-mail: rudavsky@polynet.lviv.ua
Internet: www.lp.edu.ua

Founded 1844
Rector: Prof. Dr YURIY K. RUDAVSKIY
First Pro-Rector: Prof. Dr PETRO P. KOSTROBIY
Pro-Rector for Education and Foreign Affairs: Prof. Dr YURIY M. RASHKEVYCH
Pro-Rector for Research: Prof. Dr YURIY YA. BOBALO
Library: 3m. vols
Number of teachers: 2,000
Number of students: 17,000
Publication: *Journal* (15 series annual)

DIRECTORS

Institute of Applied Mathematics and Fundamental Sciences: Prof. PETRO I. KALENYUK
Institute of Architecture: Prof. BOGDAN S. CHERKES
Institute of Chemistry and Chemical Technologies: Prof. YOSYP Y. YATCHYSHYN
Institute of Civil and Environmental Engineering: Prof. MYROSLAV A. SANYTSKY
Institute of Computer Sciences and Information Technologies: Prof. VOLODYMYR V. HRYTSYK
Institute of Computer Technologies, Automation and Metrology: Prof. BOHDAN I. STADNYK
Institute of Economics and Management: Prof. OLEH Y. KUZMIN
Institute of Engineering Mechanics and Transport: Prof. ZINOVIY A. STOTSKO
Institute of Geodesy: Prof. PETRO M. ZAZULYAK
Institute of Liberal Arts: Prof. LEONTIY E. DESCHYNSKIY
Institute of Power Engineering and Control Systems: Prof. PETRO M. ZAZULYAK
Institute of Telecommunications, Radioelectronics and Electronic Engineering: Prof. BOHDAN A. MANDZIY
Institute of Distance Education: Prof. BORYS M. ROMANYSHYN

NATIONAL AEROSPACE UNIVERSITY KHARKIV AVIATION INSTITUTE

61070 Kharkiv, Chkalova vul. 17
Telephone: (57) 315-10-56
Fax: (57) 315-11-31
E-mail: khai@khai.edu
Internet: www.khai.edu

Founded 1930
Rector: Prof. VLADIMIR S. KRIVTSOV
Library: 1m. vols
Number of teachers: 850
Number of students: 9,500

DEANS

Faculty of Aircraft Control Systems: ANATOLIY S. KULIK
Faculty of Aircraft Design: VITALIY N. KOBRIN
Faculty of Aircraft Radio-Electronic Systems: VIKTOR I. ILYUSHKO
Faculty of Aviation Engine-Building and Power Systems: ANATOLIY I. DOLMATOV
Faculty of Distance Education: YAKOV V. SAFRONOV
Faculty of Economics and Management: IGOR V. CHUMACHENKO
Faculty of Humanities: VOLODYMYR A. KOPILOV
Faculty of Pre-University Training and Professional Skills Improvement: VLADYSLAV F. DEMENKO
Faculty of Rocket Engineering: OLEKSIY G. NIKOLAEV

NATIONAL AVIATION UNIVERSITY

03680 Kyiv, pr. Kosmonavta Komarova 1
Telephone: (44) 406-72-08
Fax: (44) 497-33-85
E-mail: interdep@nau.edu.ua
Internet: www.nau.edu.ua

Founded 1933
Languages of instruction: Ukrainian, Russian, English
Library: 3m. vols
Academic year: September to June
Publications: *Aviator*, *Biplan*, *Bulletin of Engineering Academy of Ukraine*, *Business and Management*, *Development Strategy of Ukraine: Sociology, Economics, Law, Science and Youth*, *Information Security Scientific and Technical Magazine*, *Economics, Electronics and Control Systems*, *Higher Institution Establishments*, *Humanities Education in Engineering*, *Information Bulletin of Ministries of Industrial Policy of Ukraine in Standardation*, *Juridical Bulletin: Air and Space Law*, *Metrology and Guality management*, *National Aviation University Bulletin*, *Problems of Improving of Effectiveness and Infrastructure*, *Problems of Informatization and Management*, *Problems of Systems Approach in Economics*, *Scientific Bulletin of International Relation Institute*, *Security of Information*

Rector: Prof. Dr MYKOLA KULYK
First Vice-Rector: Prof. Dr MAKSYM LUTSKVI
Vice-Rector for Administrative-Economic Work: MYKOLA MYKHALKO
Vice-Rector for Corporate Management: Prof. Dr RYNAT SALIMOV
Vice-Rector for Educational Issues: Prof. Dr ANATOLIY POLUKHIN
Vice-Rector for Educational-Methodological Cooperation: Prof. Dr SERGIV IVANOV
Vice-Rector for Scientific-Research Work: Prof. Dr VOLODYMYR KHARCHENKO

DIRECTORS

Aeronavigation Institute: Prof. Dr VOLODYMYR VASYLIEV
Aerospace Institute: Prof. Dr VALERIY SHMAROV
Department of International Relations: OLGA SHEVCHENKO
Electronics and Control Systems Institute: Prof. Dr VIKTOR M. SYNEGLAZOV
Humanities Institute: Prof. Dr ARTHUR HUDMANYAN
Information-Diagnostic Systems Institute: Prof. Dr SERGIY F. FILONENKO
Institute of Computer Technologies: Prof. Dr IGOR A. ZHUKOV
Institute of Continuing Education: OLEKSANDR SAVINOV
Institute of Extramural and Distance Education: Dr PAVLO BORSUK
Institute of Innovative Technologies: Dr OLEKSANDR YUDIN
Institute of International Relations: OLEH DYOMIN

Institute of Municipal Activity: Prof. Dr OLEKSANDR ZAPOROZHETS
Land Use and Information Technologies Institute: Dr DMYTRO BAISSA
Management and Economics Institute: VYACHESLAV MATVEEV
International Civil Aviation Organization (ICAO) Institute: Prof. GALYNA SUSLOVA
Preparatory Institute: Dr NATALIYA P. MURANOVA
Zhytomyr S.P. Korolyov Military Institute: Prof. MYKHAILO PICHUGIN

NATIONAL MINING UNIVERSITY OF UKRAINE

49027 Dnipropetrovsk, pr. K. Marksa 19
Telephone: (56) 247-07-66
Fax: (56) 247-07-66
E-mail: dfr@nmuu.dp.ua
Internet: www.nmuu.dp.ua

Founded 1899

Faculties of construction electrical engineering, construction of mines, economics, engineering, geotechnology, law, mining and prospecting

Rector: Prof. GENNADIY PIVNYAK

Library: 1.3m. vols
Number of teachers: 708
Number of students: 10,897

Publications: *University Monthly*, *University Newspaper* (52 a year).

NATIONAL SHIPBUILDING UNIVERSITY 'ADMIRAL MAKAROV'

54025 Kyiv, Mikolaiv, pr. Heroiv Stalinhrada
Telephone: (51) 235-91-48
Fax: (51) 242-46-52
E-mail: vc@usmtu.edu.ua
Internet: www.usmtu.edu.ua

Founded 1929

Rector: Prof. Dr HEORHIY F. ROMANOVSKIY
First Pro-Rector: Prof. Dr OLEKSANDR M. DUBOVIY
Pro-Rector for Research: Prof. Dr VYACHESLAV F. KVASNITSKIY

DIRECTORS

Institute of Automation and Electrical Technology: Prof. VOLODYMYR S. BLINTSOV
Institute of External and Distance Education: Acad. Prof. OLEKSANDR O. MOCHALOV
Institute of Humanities: Prof. OLEKSANDR M. DUBOVIY
Institute of Machine Building: Prof. VIKTOR M. HORBOV
Institute of Shipbuilding: Prof. KOSTYANTIN KOSHKIN
Institute of Postgraduate Studies: Prof. MYKOLA V. FATEEV
1st of May Polytechnic Institute: Prof. TETYANA I. KOSTYUKOVA
Feodosia Polytechnic Institute: (vacant)

DEANS

Faculty of Engineering Economics: Prof. OLEKSANDR YU. YEGANOV
Preparatory Faculty: Prof. V. I. KONDRATENKO

NATIONAL TRANSPORT UNIVERSITY

01010 Kyiv, vul. Suvorova 1
Telephone: (44) 280-82-03
Fax: (44) 290-82-03
E-mail: general@ntu.edu.ua
Internet: www.ntu.edu.ua

Founded 1944

Rector: Prof. Dr MYKOLA F. DMYTRYCHENKO
First Pro-Rector: Prof. Dr MYKOLA O. BILYAKOVYCH
Pro-Rector for Research: Prof. Dr MYKOLA M. DYMYTRIEV

Library of 440,000 vols
Number of teachers: 909
Number of students: 15,000

DEANS

Faculty of Economics, Management and Law: LYUDMILA KOZAK
Faculty of Motor Mechanics: YURIY HUTAREVICH
Faculty of Road Building: VYACHESLAV SAVENKO
Faculty of Transport and Information Technologies: Prof. VICTOR DANCHUK

NATIONAL UNIVERSITY OF FOOD TECHNOLOGIES

01601 Kyiv, Volodymyrska vul. 68
Telephone: (44) 220-95-55
Fax: (44) 220-01-02
E-mail: indepart@nuft.edu.ua
Internet: www.nuft.edu.ua

Founded 1930 as Kyiv Institute of Sugar Refinery Production, present name and status 2002
State control
Languages of instruction: Ukrainian, Russian
Academic year: September to June

Rector: Prof. SERGII IVANOV

Library of 1,163,050 vols, 120 periodicals
Number of teachers: 742
Number of students: 13,019

Publications: *Food Industry* (4 a year), *Latest Achievements in the Food Industry and Scientific Research*, *Research Papers of the National University of Food Technologies* (4 a year), *Scientific Works*

DEANS

Faculty of Accounting, Finance and Business: OLEG SHEREMET
Faculty of Automation and Computer Systems: LIUDMILA MANOHA
Faculty of Biotechnology and Food Products Examination: ANDRIY CHAGAIDA
Faculty of Economics and Management: TATIANA MOSTENSKA
Faculty of Fermentation and Baking Industry: PETRO SHIYAN
Faculty of Hotel-Restaurant Business and Tourism: GALINA SEMAKHINA
Faculty of Mechanical Engineering and Packing Technologies: SERGIY BLAZHENKO
Faculty of Power Engineering: MYKHAILO MASLIKOV
Faculty of Sugar, Meat and Dairy Products: OKSANA KOCHUBEY-LITVINENKO
Preparatory Dept: VALENTINA KUDINA

NATIONAL UNIVERSITY OF WATER MANAGEMENT AND NATURE RESOURCES USE

33028 Rivne, vul. Soborna 11
Telephone: (36) 222-10-86
Fax: (36) 222-21-97
Internet: www.nuwm.rv.ua

Founded 1922
State control

Rector: VASYL A. HURYN
Vice-Rector of Science and Academic Affairs: OLEKSANDR TKACHUK (acting)
Vice-Rector of Research: MYKOLA HIROL
Vice-Rector of Admin. and Social Affairs: VOLODYMYR M. YAKYMCHUK (acting)
Vice-Rector of Science and Int. Relations: HRYHORIY SAPSAY
Vice-Rector of Science and Teaching Methods: ANATOLIY BILESTSKIY

Library of 900,000 vols
Number of teachers: 715
Number of students: 14,000

Publications: *Bulletin* (4 a year), *Hydroamelioration and Hydrotechnical Engineering* (1 a year), *Resource Saving Materials, Construction, Buildings and Structures* (4 a year)

DEANS

Faculty of Applied Mathematics and Computer-Integrated Systems (tel. (362) 23-14-60):
ANATOLIY P. VLASIUK
Faculty of Building and Architecture (tel. (36) 222-20-07):
HRYHORIY H. MASIUK
Faculty of Ecology and Natural Resource Application (tel. (36) 223-14-17):
MYKOLA O. KLYMENKO
Faculty of Economy and Business (tel. (36) 222-23-30):
SVITLANA O. LEVYTSKA
Faculty of Hydrotechnical Engineering and Hydroenergetics (tel. (36) 223-52-63):
ANATOLIY M. MAKOVSKIY
Faculty of Land Management and Geoinformation (tel. (36) 223-72-82):
PETRO H. CHERNIAGA
Faculty of Management (tel. (36) 223-00-95):
VITALIY P. OKORSKIY
Faculty of Mechanical and Power Engineering (tel. (36) 222-35-11):
MYKOLA M. MARCHUK
Faculty of Water Management (tel. (36) 226-64-55):
VASYL TURCHENIUK

ODESSA NATIONAL POLYTECHNIC UNIVERSITY

65044 Odessa, pr. Shevchenko 1
Telephone: (48) 222-34-74
E-mail: ospu@ospu.odessa.ua
Internet: www.ospu.odessa.ua

Founded 1918

Faculties of automation and computer technology, automation and electrification of industry, chemical technology, engineering economics, mechanical technology, nuclear power, radio engineering, robot systems, thermal power

Rector: Prof. Dr VALERIY P. MALAKHOV
Pro-Rector for Studies and Education: Prof. Dr YURIY S. YAMOLSKY
Pro-Rector for Studies and Research: Prof. Dr VALERIY P. MALAKHOV

Library of 1,500,000 vols
Number of teachers: 4,000
Number of students: 20,000

DIRECTORS

Institute of Basic Automation and Electrical Power Supply: Dr O. A. ANDRYUSCHENKO
Institute of Business, Economics and Informational Technologies: Dr HEORHIY N. VOSTROV
Institute of Computer Systems: Prof. SERHIY A. NESTERENKO
Institute of Industrial Technologies, Design and Management: Dr GENNADIY A. OBORSKIY
Institute of Machine Engineering: Prof. ALEKSANDR F. DASCHENKO
Institute of Power Engineering: Prof. ANTON S. MAZURENKO
Institute of Radioelectronics and Telecommunications: Dr PORFIRIY YU. BARANOV
Institute of Pre-University Preparation: (vacant)

ODESA STATE ENVIRONMENTAL UNIVERSITY

65016 Odesa, vul. Lvivska 15
Telephone: (48) 263-62-09
Fax: (48) 242-77-67
E-mail: synop@ogmi.farlep.odessa.ua
Internet: www.odeku.edu.ua

Founded 1932
Academic year: September to June

Rector: Prof. SERHIY M. STEPANENKO
Vice-Rector: Dr MYKOLA H. SERBOV
Chief of Int. Dept: V. M. SYTOV
Dean of Continuing Education and Training: L. M. POLETAEVA

Library of 273,000 vols
Number of teachers: 245
Number of students: 3,790

Publication: *Meteorology, Climatology and Hydrology* (4 a year)

DEANS

Faculty of Computer Science and Management: V. V. AUROV
Faculty of Environmental Studies: O. H. VOLODYMYROVA
Faculty of Hydrology, Hydrometeorological Institute: M. P. EKHNICH (Dir)
Faculty of Metrology: G. P. IVUS

PROFESSORS

Faculty of Computer Science:
KORBAN, V. KH.
KRUGLYAK, Y. M.
PREPELIZHA, G. P.

Faculty of Environmental Studies:
GERASIMOV, O. I.
LOEVA, I. D.
MINICHEVA, G. G.
SAFRANOV, T. A.
SOKOLOV, Y. M.
ZHYKALO, A. N.

Hydrometeorological Institute:
EFIMOV, V. A.
GOPCHENKO, E. D.
LOBODA, N. S.
MICHAYLOV, V. I.
MISCHENKO, Z. A.
POLEVOY, A. M.
SHKOLNY, E. P.
STEPANENKO, S. N.
TUCHKOVENKO, Y. S.

POLTAVA NATIONAL TECHNICAL UNIVERSITY 'YU. KONDRATYUKA'

36601 Poltava, Pershotravnevyy pr. 24
Telephone: (53) 222-28-50
Fax: (53) 227-38-02
E-mail: v57@pntu.edu.ua
Internet: www.pntu.edu.ua

Founded 1930, present name and status 2002
State control

Rector: Prof. Dr VOLODYMYR O. ONYSHCHENKO
First Vice-Rector: Dr BOGDAN O. KOROBKO
Vice-Rector for Academic Work: Dr BOGDAN KOROBKO
Vice-Rector for Science and Innovations: Prof. Dr hab. VICTOR PASHYNSKY
Vice-Rector for Corporative Management: ANATOLIY MARTYNENKO
Vice-Rector for Social and Int. Affairs: YURI BEREZA
Chief Librarian: VELENTINA SIDORENKO

Library of 500,000 vols, 116 periodicals
Number of teachers: 540
Number of students: 10,000

DEANS

Faculty of Architecture: Prof. Dr hab. VASYL SHULYK
Faculty of Civil Engineering: Dr LEONID SHCHERBININ
Faculty of Management and Business: Dr VOLODYMYR PENTS
Faculty of Electro-Mechanical Engineering: Dr MYKOLA SHPYLKA
Faculty of Finance and Economics: Dr RAYISA V. SHYNKARENKO
Faculty of Information, Telecommunication Technologies and Systems: Dr OLEG ODARUSHCHENKO
Faculty of Sanitary Engineering: Dr STANISLAV POPOV
External Faculty: Dr I. O. IVANYTSKA
Postgraduate Study Centre: GENNADIY GOLOVKO

SEVASTOPOL NATIONAL TECHNICAL UNIVERSITY

99053 Sevastopol, Streletsky Bay, Studgorodok, ul. Mazepy 10
Telephone: (69) 223-50-08

Founded 1963

Rector: M. Z. LAVRINENKO

Library of 1,200,000 vols, spec. collns on machine-building and environmental monitoring
Number of teachers: 550
Number of students: 7,000

UKRAINIAN STATE UNIVERSITY OF CHEMICAL TECHNOLOGY

49005 Dnipropetrovsk, Gagarin Ave. 8
Telephone: (56) 247-08-13
Fax: (56) 247-33-16
E-mail: ughtu@dicht.dp.ua
Internet: www.udhtu.com.ua

Founded 1930
Public control
Academic year: July to September
Languages of instruction: Russian, Ukrainian

Rector: Prof. Dr MYKHAYLO V. BURMISTR
Vice Rector of Science and Education: Prof. Dr VIKTOR GOLEUS
Vice Rector of Science: Prof. Dr OLEG GIRIN
First Vice Rector: Prof. Dr MYKOLA NIKOLENKO

Library of 800,000 vols
Number of teachers: 484
Number of students: 7,813

Publications: *Chemistry and Chemical Technology Questions* (4 a year), *Scientific-Technological Digest* (4 a year), *Voprosy himii i himicheskoi tehnologii* (6 a year)

DEANS

Advanced Technologies: ANGELA VACULICH
Faculty of Economics: NATALIA CHUPRINA
Faculty of High-Molecular Compounds Technology: SVETLANA VOLKOVA
Faculty of Inorganic Technology: OLEXANDER PIVOVAROV
Faculty of Mechanical: ILLYA NACHOVNYY
Faculty of Organic Technology: NATALYA EVDOKIMENKO
Faculty of Silicate Technology: OLGA RYZHOVA

VINNYTSIA NATIONAL TECHNICAL UNIVERSITY

21036 Vinnytsia, Khmelnitske shose 95
Telephone: (43) 232-57-18
Fax: (43) 246-57-72
E-mail: vstu@vstu.vinnica.ua
Internet: www.vstu.edu.ua

Founded 1960

Rector: Prof. BORIS I. MOKIN
First Pro-Rector for Research, Int. Relations and Economic and Political Affairs: VOLODYMYR V. HRABKO

Library of 820,000 vols
Number of teachers: 542
Number of students: 7,492

Publications: *Proceedings* (6 a year), *University News* (12 a year)

DIRECTORS

Institute of Civil Engineering and Gas Supply: HEORHIY S. RATUSHNYAK
Institute of Electronics and Computer Systems' Management: ANATOLIY S. VASYURA
Institute of Information Technologies and Computer Engineering: OLEKSIY D. AZAROV
Institute of Machine Building and Transport: YURIY A. BURYENNIKOV
Institute of Management: MYKOLA I. NEBAVA
Institute of Power Engineering, Ecology and Electrical Mechanics: MYKOLA P. SVRYDOV
Institute of Radio engineering, Telecommunications and Electronic Instrument Engineering: VASYL M. KYCHAK

ZAPORIZHZHIA NATIONAL TECHNICAL UNIVERSITY

69063 Zaporizhzhya, vul. Zhukovskoho 64
Telephone: (61) 764-25-06
Fax: (61) 764-21-41
E-mail: rector@zntu.edu.ua
Internet: www.zntu.edu.ua

Founded 1900
Public control
Languages of instruction: Russian, Ukrainian
Academic year: September to June

Rector: SERHIY B. BYELIKOV
First Pro-Rector for Education: VOLODYMYR G. PRUSHKIVSKY
Pro-Rector for Education: SERHIY T. YARYMBASH
Librarian: RAISA I. KUCHERUK

Library: 1m. vols
Number of teachers: 770
Number of students: 13,000

Publications: *Bulletin of Propulsion Engineering, Computer Science and Control* (2 a year), *Electrotechnics and Electroenergetics, Journal* (12 a year), *New Materials and Technology in Metallurgy and Machine Construction, Radio Electronics*

DIRECTORS

Institute of Continuous Training: Dr SERGIY T. YARYMBASH
Institute of Economics and Humanities: Dr VOLODYMYR G. PRUSHKIVSKIY
Institute of Information Science and Radio-electronics: Prof. DMYTRO M. PIZA
Institute of Machine Building: Acad. Prof. LEONID Y. IVSCHENKO
Institute of Management and Law: VALENTYNA M. ZAYTSEVA
Institute of Physics and Technology: Acad. Prof. VALENTYN V. LUNOV

Academies

Dnipropetrovsk State Medical Academy: 49044 Dnipropetrovsk, vul. Dzerzhinskoho 9; tel. (56) 245-15-65; fax (56) 370-96-38; e-mail dsma@dsma.dp.ua; internet www.dsma.dp.ua; f. 1916; main specialities: clinical pharmacology, dentistry, general practice, paediatrics, sanitary hygiene; library: 656,600 vols; 598 teachers; 4,045 students; Rector Dr GEORGY V. DZYAK; publs *Dermatology, Cosmetics and Sexual Pathology* (4 a year), *Medical Perspectives* (4 a year), *Urology* (4 a year).

Donbass State Academy of Civil Engineering and Architecture: 86123 Donetsk obl., Makeyevka vul. Derzhavina 2; tel. (62) 290-29-38; fax (62) 222-06-16; e-mail mailbox@dgasa.dn.ua; internet www.dgasa.dn.ua; f. 1972; faculties: architecture, basic and general engineering training, civil engineering, economics, environmental engineering, mechanical engineering, marketing and management; extra-mural preparatory dept for foreign students, humanities; library: 400,000 vols; 399 teachers; 5,769 students; Rector YEVHEN V. HOROKHOV; publs *Academy News* (12 a year), *Bulletin* (6 a year), *Metal Construction* (4 a year).

Donbass State Engineering Academy: 84313 Kramatorsk, vul. Shkadinova 72; tel. (62) 641-67-94; fax (62) 641-63-15; e-mail postmaster@dgma.edu.donetsk.ua; faculties: automation, automation of metal-shaping processes, economics, engineering and economics, humanities, machine-building.

Ivano-Frankivsk State Medical Academy: 76000 Ivano-Frankivsk, Halytska 2; tel. and fax (34) 222-42-95; e-mail ma@ifdma.if.ua; internet www.ifdma.if.ua; f. 1945; library: 319,000 vols; 389 teachers; 4,994 students; Rector Dr YE. NEIKO.

Kharkiv State Academy of Railway Transport: 61003 Kharkiv, pl. Feierbakha 7; tel. (57) 732-20-67; fax (57) 220-60-19; e-mail info@kart.kharkov.com; internet www.kart.edu.ua; f. 1930; faculties: automation, mechanics, construction, economics, telemechanics and communication, traffic management; brs in Donetsk, Kyiv; library: 700,000 vols; Rector NIKOLAY I. DANKO.

Kharkiv State Academy of Zooveterinary Science: 62341 Kharkiv obl., Dergachevskiy raion, P/O Malaya Danilovka; tel. (57) 635-74-65; fax (57) 635-70-76; e-mail zoovet@zoovet.kharkov.ua; f. 1851; library: 250,000 vols; 190 teachers; 2,500 students; Rector VALERY GOLOVKO.

Kharkiv State Municipal Academy: 61002 Kharkiv, vul. Revolyutsii 12; tel. (57) 243-21-62; fax (57) 247-65-00; e-mail root@ksma.kharkov.ua; f. 1930; faculties: accounting and auditing, architecture, economics of civil engineering enterprises, economics of municipal economy enterprises, electric and underground transport, engineering ecology, landscape architecture, management in hotel business and tourism, management of public services and municipal finances, retraining, technical maintenance of buildings, urban electric power supply and lighting, urban planning and development; Electromechanical College, Municipal Economy College; library: 890,000 vols; 1,000 teachers; 12,000 students; Rector Prof. L. N. SHUTENKO.

Lviv Academy of Veterinary Medicine: 79301 Lviv, vul. Pekarska 50; tel. (32) 275-67-84; fax (32) 279-32-31; e-mail vetacademy@hotmail.com; internet www.vetacad.lviv.ua; f. 1784; faculties: biology and technology, economics and management, extra-mural studies, food technology, veterinary medicine; 292 teachers; 4,500 students; library: 333,000 vols; Rector Prof. Dr R. J. KRAVTSIV.

Lviv Commercial Academy: 79005 Lviv, vul. Tuhan-Baranovskoho 10; tel. (32) 275-65-50; e-mail academy@lac.lviv.ua; internet www.lac.lviv.ua; f. 1899; faculties: commodity science, commerce, economics, international economic relations, law, management; 300 teachers; 5,740 students; library: 600,000 vols; Rector YA. A. HONCHARUK.

National Metallurgical Academy of Ukraine: 49600 Dnipropetrovsk, pr. Gagarina 4; tel. (56) 245-31-56; fax (56) 247-44-61; e-mail dmeti@dmeti.dp.ua; internet dmeti.dp.ua; f. 1899; faculties: computing systems and automation, ecology and chemical technologies, economic cybernetics, economics, electrometallurgy, energy and electromechanics, humanities, management, materials sciences and metal forming, mechanics and machine building, metallurgy; library: 524,327 vols; 732 teachers; 12,199 students; Rector OLEKSANDR H. VELYCHKO; publ. *Theory and Practice of Metallurgy* (4 a year).

Odessa National Academy of Food Technologies: 65039 Odessa, vul. Kanatna 112; tel. (482) 29-11-40; fax (482) 25-32-84; e-mail fedosov@optima.com.ua; internet www.osaft.odessa.ua; f. 1902; State control; academic year September to June; faculties: automation of technological processes; economics, management and business; food preserving technology and winemaking; grain and grain products technology; meat and dairy products technology and ecology; mechanical engineering; technology of bread, confectionery and nutrition; 566 teachers (incl. 53 full professors); 10,400 students; library: 600,000 vols; Rector Prof. BOGDAN YEGOROV; publs *Collection of Scientific Works* (2 a year), *Grain Products and Mixed Fodders* (4 a year).

Odessa National Maritime Academy: 65029 Odessa, Didrikhson 8; tel. (48) 777-57-74; fax (48) 234-52-67; e-mail info@ma.odessa.ua; internet www.ma.odessa.ua; f. 1944; faculties: automation, electrical engineering, marine engineering, maritime law, navigation, radio electronics; brs in Mariupol, Izmail, correspondence depts and the maritime college of the technical fleet; library: 578,000 vols; 401 teachers; 7,134 students; Rector Prof. MYKHAYLO V. MIYUSOV; publs *Automization of Ship's Technical Devices* (2 a year), *Marine Transportation and Transport Complexes* (1 a year), *Navigation* (2 a year), *Sea Review* (4 a year), *Ship's Power Plants* (2 a year).

Odessa State Academy of Civil Engineering and Architecture: 65029 Odessa, Didrikhson 4; tel. (482) 20-41-82; fax (482) 23-35-10; e-mail rektorat@gs.org.ua; internet www.ogasa.odessa.ua; f. 1930; faculties: architecture, construction engineering, power engineering, industrial and civil construction, technical engineering, sanitary engineering; library: 600,000 vols; Rector Prof. VITALIY S. DOROFEEV.

Odessa State Academy of Refrigeration: 65026 Odessa, vul. Dvoryanska 1/3; tel. (48) 223-22-20; fax (48) 223-89-31; e-mail admin@osar.odessa.ua; internet www.osar.odessa.ua; f. 1922; faculties: automation and robot engineering, cryogenic engineering, environmental protection and rational use of natural resources, heat technology, mechanical engineering, refrigeration engineering, systems of automatized projection, thermophysics; library: 487,173 vols; 288 teachers; 3,500 students; Rector V. V. PRITULA; publ. *Refrigeration Engineering and Technology* (2 a year).

Poltava State Agrarian Academy: 314003 Poltava, vul. Skovorody 1/3; tel. (5322) 2-26-10; fax (5322) 2-29-57; e-mail antonov@agroak.poltava.ua; internet agroak.poltava.ua; f. 1920; depts: accounting and auditing, agronomy, economy of enterprises, farm mechanization, finance, management of organizations, veterinary medicine, zoological engineering; library: 315,000 vols; 247 teachers; 7,000 students; Rector Dr V. N. PISARENKO; publ. *Poltava Agrarian News* (4 a year).

Prydniprovska State Academy of Civil Engineering and Architecture: 49600 Dnipropetrovsk, Chernyshevskeho 24A; tel. and fax (562) 47-16-88; e-mail dik@pgasa.dp.ua; internet www.pgasa.dp.ua; f. 1930; faculties: architecture, building technology, civil engineering, construction, correspondence, economics, mechanics; library: 662,000 vols; 467 teachers; 6,392 students; Rector Prof. V. I. BOLSHAKOV.

State Academy of Food Technology and Management: 61051 Kharkiv, Klochkivska 333; tel. (57) 236-89-79; fax (57) 237-85-35; e-mail hdatoh@kharkov.com; internet www.hdatoh.kharkov.com; f. 1967; faculties: accountancy and auditing, economics, food industry machines and equipment, food science and food trade, food technology, industrial management, marketing, services management; 350 teachers; 5,000 students; library: 380,000 vols; Rector A. I. CHEREVKO; publ. *Zbirnyk naukovykh prats* (1 a year).

Ukrainian Engineering Pedagogics Academy: 61003 Kharkiv, Department of Foreign Relations, vul. Universytetska 16; tel. (572) 731-28-62; fax (572) 731-32-36; e-mail docents@vl.kharkov.ua; f. 1958; faculties: electrical and technological, electromechanics and computer systems, machine-building, mechanical and technological, mining engineering, power engineering, radio-electronics, social-economical; training centres for foreign citizens and engineering educators; library: 1m. vols; 350 teachers; 11,000 students; Rector ELENA KOVALENKO.

Yaroslav Mudry National Law Academy of Ukraine: 61024 Kharkiv, Pushkinskaya ul. 77; tel. (57) 704-11-20; fax (57) 704-11-71; e-mail uracad@bestnet.kharkov.ua; internet www.uracad.kharkiv.edu; f. 1804; library: 1m. vols, 1,000 dissertations, 29,000 rare books and MSS; 600 teachers; 15,000 students; Rector VASYL YA. TATSIY.

Zaporizhzhya State Engineering Academy: 69006 Zaporizhia, pr. Lenina 226; tel. (612) 15-90-34; fax (612) 12-38-87; e-mail admin@zgia.zp.ua; internet www.zgia.zp.ua; f. 1959; faculties: building and water resources, economics of enterprises, electronics and electronic technologies, information technologies, management and finance, mechanics and technology, metallurgy, post-graduate studies, power engineering and energy-saving; library: 501,777 vols; 350 teachers; 10,000 students; Rector Dr V. I. POZHUEV.

Institutes of Higher Education

Donetsk Musical-Pedagogical Institute: 340086 Donetsk, vul. Artema 44; tel. (622) 93-81-22; depts: choral conducting, composition, folk instruments, musicology, orchestral instruments, piano, singing.

Institute of National Economy: 03057 Kyiv, pr. Pobedy 54/1; tel. (44) 446-50-55; fax (44) 226-25-73; f. 1912; depts: accounting and audit, agricultural management, economics and management, engineering economics, finance, international relations, marketing; br. in Krivoi Rog; 600 teachers; 11,000 students; library: 800,000 vols; Rector ANATOLY PAVLENKO.

Kamyanets-Podilsk Institute of Agriculture: 32300 Khmelnytska r-n, Kamyanets-Podilsk, ul. Shevchenko 13; tel. (3849) 2-52-18; fax (3849) 3-92-20; f. 1920; depts: agronomy, animal husbandry, economics, mechanization of agriculture, veterinary medicine; library: 600,000 vols; Rector M. I. SAMOKISH.

Kharkiv Institute of Agricultural Mechanization and Electrification: 61078 Kharkiv, vul. Artema 44; tel. (57) 222-37-86; f. 1929; library: 150,000 vols; Rector M. K. EVSEEV.

Kherson A. D. Tsuryupa Agricultural Institute: 325006 Kherson, vul. Rozy Lyuksemburga 23; tel. (55) 2-64-71; f. 1874; faculties of agricultural construction and hydromelioration, agronomy, animal husbandry, economics and agrobusiness jurisdiction; library: 300,000 vols; Rector V. A. USHKARENKO.

Kirovograd Higher Flying School of Civil Aviation: 316005 Kirovograd oblastnoi, vul. Dobrovolskogo 1; tel. (5222) 2-38-64; faculties: air navigation, air traffic control, flying.

Krivoi Rog Ore Mining Institute: 324027 Krivoi Rog, vul. 22 Partsezda 11; tel. (564) 23-22-30; fax (564) 74-84-12; f. 1922; faculties: construction, electrical engineering, engineering, geology and dressing, mine surveying and geodesy, open-cast mining, underground mining; geological museum; 4,500 students; library of 1.2m. vols; Rector V. F. BIZOV; publ. *Collection of Works* (2 a year).

Lugansk Agricultural Institute: 348008 Lugansk 8; tel. (642) 95-20-40; depts: accounting, agronomy, economics, mechanization.

Mariupol Metallurgical Institute: 87500 Mariupol, Republiki 7; tel. (62) 934-30-97; f. 1929; faculties: industrial energy, mechanical engineering, metallurgy, technology, welding; library: 580,000 vols; 444 teachers; 5,600 students; Rector I. V. ZHEZHELENKO.

Melitopol Institute of Agricultural Mechanization: 72300 Zaporizhia oblast, Melitopol, pr. B. Khmelnitskoho 18; tel. (61) 22-21-32; f. 1932; 315 teachers; 4,045 students; library: 330,000 vols; Rector N. L. KRIZHACHKOVSKII; publ. publs collns of scientific articles (4 a year).

Odessa Agricultural Institute: 270039 Odessa, Ul. Sverdlova 99; tel. (48) 222-37-23; fax (48) 224-01-84; f. 1918; depts: accounting, agronomy, animal husbandry, economics and management, fruit and vegetable growing, land management, mechanization, veterinary medicine, viticulture; br. in Nikolaev; 1,000 teachers; 5,200 students; library: 280,000 vols; Rector YU. S. TSUKANOV.

Odessa N. I. Pirohov Medical Institute: 270100 Odessa, per. Nariman Narimanova 2; tel. (48) 223-35-67; library: 433,000 vols.

Poltava Medical Stomatological Institute: 314024 Poltava, vul. Shevchenko 23; tel. (53) 22-88-25; Rector N. S. SKRIPNIKOV.

Ukrainian Institute of Printing: 290020 Lviv, vul. Podholosko 19; tel. (32) 259-94-01; faculties: book illustration, economics, editorial, mechanics, technology,; library: 384,000 vols; Rector Dr STEPAN HUNKO; publ. *Journal of Printing and Publishing*.

Zaporizhzhia Medical Institute: 330074 Zaporizhzhia, vul. Mayakovskoho 26; tel. (61) 233-01-49; f. 1965; Rector I. I. TOKARENKO.

Schools of Art and Music

Kharkiv State Academy of Culture: 61003 Kharkiv, Bursatski Uzviz 4; tel. (57) 712-81-05; fax (57) 712-81-05; e-mail shciko@ic.ac.kharkov.ua; internet www.ic.ac.kharkov.ua; f. 1929; departments: Library and Information Science, Cultural Studies, Documentation and Information Work, Art, Music, Theatre, Cinema and Television; library: 400,000 vols; 257 teachers; 3,393 students; Rector Prof. VASYL M. SHEYKO; publs *Journal* (1 a year), *Kultura Ukrainy* (12 a year).

Kyiv State Institute of Culture: 01133 Kyiv, vul. Shchorsa 36; tel. (44) 269-98-44; fax (44) 212-10-48; departments: folk culture, library science.

Kharkiv Institute of Industrial and Applied Arts: 61002 Kharkiv, vul. Krasnoznamennaya 8; tel. (57) 243-28-73; fax (57) 243-28-73; e-mail root@design.kharkov.ua; f. 1927 and renamed 1963; faculties: industrial design, interior design; library: 88,000 vols; 154 teachers; 577 students; Rector V. DANYLENKO.

Kharkiv State Institute of Arts: 310003 Kharkiv, pl. Sovetskoi Ukrainy 11/13; tel. (572) 22-56-28; acting (puppets), choral conducting, composition, directing (puppets), musicology, orchestral instruments, piano, singing, theatre studies; library: 100,000 vols.

Kyiv State Academy of Fine Arts and Architecture: 04053 Kyiv, vul. Smirnova-Lastochkina 20; tel. (44) 212-15-40; fax (44) 212-10-48; f. 1917; faculties: architecture, art history, arts management, graphic art, restoration, sculpture, painting, theatrical decorative art; 130 teachers; 800 students; library: 130,000 vols; Rector Prof. ANDREI V. CHEBYKIN.

Lviv Academy of Arts: 79011 Lviv, vul. Kubiyovycha 38; tel. (32) 276-14-82; fax (32) 276-14-77; e-mail artacademy@mail.lviv.ua; internet www.artacademy.lviv.ua; f. 1946; faculties: decorative and applied arts, design, fine art and restoration, history and theory of art; library: 90,000 vols; 250 teachers; 1,000 students; Rector Prof. ANDRIY BOKOTEY; Vice-Rectors Prof. IGOR GOLOD, Prof. OREST HOLUBETZ; publ. *Scientific Messenger* (1 a year).

Odessa State Conservatoire 'A. V. Nezhdanova': 65021 Odessa, vul. Ostrovidova 63; tel. (48) 226-78-76; fax (48) 223-75-37; f. 1913; choral conducting, composition, musicology, orchestral and folk instruments, piano, singing; 140 teachers; 680 students; library: 100,000 vols; Rector OLEKSANDR V. SOKOL.

State Academy of Music 'Mykola Lysenko': 79005 Lviv, vul. Nyzhankivsky 5; tel. (32) 274-31-06; fax (32) 272-36-13; e-mail musinst@lviv.gu.net; internet musicacademy.lviv.ua; f. 1852; faculties: choral conducting, composition, folk instruments, musicology, operatic and symphonic conducting, orchestral instruments, piano, singing; library: 200,000 vols; 175 teachers; 550 students; Rector IHOR PYLATIUK.

Ukrainian National Academy of Music 'P. Tchaikovsky': 01001 Kyiv, Gorodetska vul. 1–3/11; tel. (44) 229-07-92; fax (44) 229-35-30; e-mail nmau@iptelecom.net.ua; f. 1913; faculties: choral conducting, composition, folk instruments, music production, music education, opera and symphony orchestra conducting, orchestral instruments, piano, singing, theory and history of music; 304 teachers; 1,156 students; library: 355,000 vols; Rector OLEG TIMOSHENKO; publ. *Ukrainian Musicology* (1 a year).

UNITED ARAB EMIRATES

The Higher Education System

The United Arab Emirates has five universities: the United Arab Emirates University (founded 1976), Zayed University (founded 1998 with two campuses in Abu Dhabi, two in Dubai), Abu Dhabi University (founded 2003), Ajman University of Science and Technology (founded 1988) and University of Sharjah (founded 1997). A branch of the Sorbonne University, based in Paris, France, opened in Abu Dhabi in 2006 and two American universities are in operation in Sharjah and Dubai. In September 1988 four higher colleges of technology (two for male and two for female students) opened, admitting a total of 1,150 students in 1992/93, all of whom were citizens of the United Arab Emirates; in 2007/08 a total of 77,428 students were enrolled in university and other higher education institutions. Many other students currently receive higher education abroad. The Ministry of Higher Education and Scientific Research, founded in 1992, is responsible for all post-secondary education. It is also responsible for the regulation of private institutions in higher education. The Commission for Academic Accreditation, a department in the Ministry, licenses institutions and accredits degree programmes.

Admission to higher education is on the basis of an average score of at least 80% in the Tawjihiyya examinations. Students are awarded degrees on a credit basis. The undergraduate Bachelors degree is a four-year programme of study (medicine lasts seven years). The Masters degree is a one-year course following the Bachelors degree.

Post-secondary technical and vocational education is offered by higher colleges of technology and other colleges. Higher colleges of technology are funded by the Ministry of Finance and provide training for professional and technology careers in the public and private sectors. Admission is on the basis of a score of at least 60% in the Tawjihiyya and the Common English Proficiency Examination. Among the qualifications offered by the higher colleges of technology are Certificates (two years), Diplomas (one to three years) and Higher Diplomas (three years).

There are a number of foreign institutions, such as the Birla Institute of Technology and Science Pilani (India), that operate programmes not accredited by the UAE Commission for Academic Accreditation, but accredited by foreign governments and accreditation bodies.

Regulatory Bodies

GOVERNMENT

Ministry of Culture, Youth and Community Development: POB 17, Abu Dhabi; tel. (2) 4453000; fax (2) 4452504; Minister ABD AR-RAHMAN MUHAMMAD AL-OWAIS.

Ministry of Education: POB 295, Abu Dhabi; tel. (2) 6213800; fax (2) 6351164; e-mail moe@uae.gov.ae; internet www.moe.gov.ae; Minister Dr HANIF HASSAN ALI.

Ministry of Higher Education and Scientific Research: POB 45253, Abu Dhabi; tel. (2) 6428000; fax (2) 6427262; e-mail mohe@uae.gov.ae; internet www.uae.gov.ae/mohe; Minister Sheikh NAHYAN BIN MUBARAK AN-NAHYAN.

ACCREDITATION

Commission for Academic Accreditation: Ministry of Higher Education, Al Najdah St, POB 41533, Abu Dhabi; tel. (2) 6427772; fax (2) 6428488; e-mail badr.aboulela@mohesr.ae; internet www.caa.ae; f. 2000; 4 mems; Dir MOHAMED BADR ELDIN ABOUL-ELA.

Learned Societies

LANGUAGE AND LITERATURE

Alliance Française: POB 2646, Abu Dhabi; tel. (2) 6666232; fax (2) 6669044; e-mail alliancefrancaise@af-aboudabi.net; internet www.af-aboudabi.net; offers courses and exams in French language and culture and promotes cultural exchange with France; attached teaching centre in Dubai.

British Council: Villa no. 7, Al Nasr St, Khalidya, Abu Dhabi, POB 46523; tel. (2) 6659300; fax (2) 6664340; e-mail information@ae.britishcouncil.org; internet www.britishcouncil.org/uae; teaching centre; offers courses and exams in English language and British culture and promotes cultural exchange with the UK; attached teaching centres in Dubai and Sharjah; Dir, United Arab Emirates JO MAHER; Deputy Dir PAUL MASON.

Research Institutes

GENERAL

Centre for Documentation and Research: POB 5884, Abu Dhabi; tel. (2) 4183333; fax (2) 4445811; e-mail dg@cdr.gov.ae; internet www.cdr.gov.ae; f. 1968; attached to Ministry of Presidential Court; documents, books, maps and articles relating to the Arabian Gulf and the Arabian Peninsula; publishes specialized research studies; convenes nat., regional and int. seminars and conferences; organizes exhibitions relating to the UAE; library of 32,000 vols in many languages, 6,481 microfiches, 7m. documents; Pres. Sheik MANSOUR BIN ZAYED AL-NAHYAN.

AGRICULTURE, FISHERIES AND VETERINARY SCIENCE

Agricultural Information Centre: POB 176, Ras al-Khaimah; tel. (2) 4495100; fax (2) 4495150; e-mail info@moew.gov.ae; f. 1975 as a UNDP-FAO assisted project, present name 1984; run by Ministry of Environment and Water; conducts research into irrigation, plant protection, vegetable varieties, vegetables under plastic houses, soil fertility; c. 48 staff; library of 500 vols; Research Dir MOHAMMED HASSAN AL-SHAMSI.

Libraries and Archives

Abu Dhabi

National Archives: POB 2380, Abu Dhabi; tel. (2) 4447797; fax (2) 4445639; internet www.cultural.org.ae; f. 1985; attached to the Cultural Foundation, an independent government body; cares for current and historical public records; Dir Dr NASSIR ALI AL-HIMIRI.

National Library: POB 2380, Abu Dhabi; tel. (2) 6336483; fax (2) 6217472; internet www.cultural.org.ae; f. 1981; 900,000 vols, 1,500 periodical titles, 8,000 audiovisual items; UN Deposit Centre; Dir JUMAA ALQUBAISI; publs *National Bibliography* (in Arabic and English), *Union Catalogue of Periodicals in the UAE* (in Arabic and English).

Dubai

Dubai Municipality Public Libraries: POB 67, Dubai; tel. (4) 2262788; fax (4) 2266226; e-mail libraries@dm.gov.ae; internet login.dm.gov.ae; f. 1963; 205,970 vols, 1,707 periodicals; spec. colln of Arab Islamic art books; Head MOHAMMAD JASSIM AL-ERIADI.

Museums and Art Galleries

Al-Ain

Al-Ain Museum: POB 15715, Al-Ain; tel. (3) 764559; fax (3) 764559; e-mail antigan@emirates.net.ae; internet www.aam.gov.ae; f. 1971; archaeology and ethnography; library of 200 vols; archaeological sites at al-Ain and Umm al-Nar island; Dirs SAIF BIN ALI AL-DARMAKI, Dr WALID YASIN.

Sharjah

Sharjah Museums: POB 39939, Sharjah; tel. (6) 5566002; fax (6) 5566003; e-mail info@sharjahmuseums.ae; internet www.sharjahmuseums.ae; f. 1995; Dir SHIEKHA HOOR AL-QASIMI.

Universities

ABU DHABI UNIVERSITY

POB 59911, Abu Dhabi
Internet: www.adu.ac.ae

Founded 2003
Private control

Accredited by Ministry of Education and Scientific Research

Chancellor: Prof. Dr NABIL IBRAHIM
Librarian: OMAR ABBAS
Number of students: 4,000

DEANS

College of Arts and Sciences: (vacant)
College of Business Administration: Dr MOHAMED KHALIFA
College of Engineering and Computer Science: Dr ALY S. NAZMY
University College: Dr JEHAN ZITAWI

AL-AIN UNIVERSITY OF SCIENCE AND TECHNOLOGY

POB 64141, Al-Ain
Telephone: (3) 7611185
Fax: (3) 7611198
Internet: alain-university.com

Founded 2005
Private control

Accredited by Ministry of Education and Scientific Research

Pres.: Prof. FUAD SHEIKH SALEM

Colleges of business administration, education, engineering and IT, law, pharmacy.

AL-GHURAIR UNIVERSITY

POB 37374, Dubai
Telephone: (4) 4200223
Fax: (4) 4200224
E-mail: admissions@agu.ac.ae
Internet: www.agu.ae

Founded 1999
Private control

Accredited by Ministry of Education and Scientific Research

Pres.: Dr ABDURAHEM MOHAMMED AL-AMEEN

Colleges of business studies, computing, engineering and applied sciences; school of design.

AL-HOSN UNIVERSITY

POB 38772, Abu Dhabi
Telephone: (2) 4070700
Fax: (2) 4070799
Internet: www.alhosnu.ae

Founded 2003
Private control

Accredited by Ministry of Education and Scientific Research

Vice-Chancellor: Prof. ABDUL RAHIM SABOUNI
Provost: Dr HAMDI SHEIBANI
Library Dir: Dr ALHAJ SALIM MUSTAFA

Publication: *Journal of Engineering and Applied Sciences* (every 2 years)

DEANS

Faculty of Arts and Social Sciences: Prof. HASSAN MUSTAPHA
Faculty of Business: Prof. AHMAD ZOHDI
Faculty of Engineering and Applied Sciences: Dr HAMDI SHEIBANI

AJMAN UNIVERSITY OF SCIENCE AND TECHNOLOGY (AUST)

POB 346, Ajman
Telephone: (6) 7482222
Fax: (6) 7438888
E-mail: info@ajman.ac.ae
Internet: www.ajman.ac.ae

Founded 1988
Private control

Pres.: Dr SAEED ABDULLAH SALMAN
Vice-Pres. for Admin. and Financial Affairs: THAMER SAEED ABDULLA ALI SALMAN
Vice-Pres. for External Relations and Cultural Affairs: AHMED ANKIT

DEANS

Faculty of Business Administration: Dr YAHYA HADDAD
Faculty of Computer Science: Dr MAHMOUD ABO-NAAJ
Faculty of Dentistry: (vacant)
Faculty of Education and Basic Science: Dr SALEH AWADH OMAR ARAM
Faculty of Engineering: Prof. FAHAR HAYATI
Faculty of Foreign Languages: Dr THARWAT SAKRAN
Faculty of Information, Mass Communication and Public Relations: (vacant)
Faculty of Pharmacy and Health Sciences: Dr SAMIR ISSA BLOUKH

AMERICAN UNIVERSITY IN DUBAI

POB 28282, Dubai
Telephone: (4) 3999000
Fax: (4) 3998899
Internet: www.aud.edu

Founded 1995
Private control

Accredited by Ministry of Education and Scientific Research

Pres.: Dr LANCE DE MASI
Exec. Vice-Pres.: ELIAS BOU SAAB
Provost: Dr JIHAD S. NADER
Library Dir: LIZ OESLEBY

Library of 77,334 vols, 345 periodicals

DEANS

School of Business and Administration: Dr DWAYNE A. BANKS
School of Communication and Information Studies: (vacant)
School of Engineering: Dr ALAA K. ASHMAWY

AMERICAN UNIVERSITY IN THE EMIRATES

Block 6, Dubai International Academic City, Dubai
Telephone: (4) 4291200
Fax: (4) 4291205
E-mail: info@aue.ae
Internet: www.aue.ae
Private control

Colleges of business admin., computer information technology, fine arts and design, media and mass communication.

AMERICAN UNIVERSITY OF SHARJAH

POB 26666, Sharjah
Telephone: (6) 5155555
Internet: www.aus.edu

Founded 1997
Private control

Accredited by Ministry of Education and Scientific Research

Chancellor: Dr PETER HEATH

DEANS

College of Arts and Sciences: WILLIAM HEIDCAMP
College of Engineering: YOUSEF AL-ASSAF
School of Architecture and Design: FATIH RIFKI
School of Business and Management: R. MALCOLM RICAHRDS

BRITISH UNIVERSITY IN DUBAI

POB 502216, Dubai
Telephone: (4) 3913626
Fax: (4) 3664698
E-mail: info@buid.ac.ae
Internet: www.buid.ac.ae

Founded 1997
Private control

Accredited by Ministry of Education and Scientific Research

Vice-Chancellor: Dr ABDULLAH M. ALSHAMSI

Faculties of business, education, engineering, informatics.

CANADIAN UNIVERSITY OF DUBAI

POB 117781, Dubai
Telephone: (4) 3218866
Fax: (4) 3211991
E-mail: info@cud.ac.ae
Internet: www.cud.ac.ae

Founded 2006
Private control

Accredited by Ministry of Education and Scientific Research

Pres.: ANN BULLER

Schools of architectural studies and interior design, business, engineering, applied science and technology, environment and health.

GULF MEDICAL UNIVERSITY

POB 4184, Ajman
Telephone: (4) 7431333
Fax: (4) 7431222
E-mail: gmcajman@emirates.net.ae
Internet: www.gmcajman.com

Founded 1998 as Gulf Medical College; univ. status 2008
Private control; Thumbay Group

Accredited by Ministry of Higher Education and Scientific Research

Dir: MOIDEEN THUMBAY

Bachelors and Masters degree programmes.

HAMDAN BIN MOHAMMED E-UNIVERSITY

POB 71400, Dubai
Telephone: (4) 4241111
Fax: (4) 4393939
E-mail: hbmeu@hbmeu.ac.ae
Internet: www.hbmeu.ac.ae

Fmrly Electronic Total Quality Management (E-TQM College)
Private control

Accredited by Ministry of Higher Education and Scientific Research

Chancellor: Dr MANSOOR MOHAMED AQIL AL-AWAR
Vice-Chancellor: Dr IBRAHIM MAHMOOD BIN ABDULRAHMAN

DEANS

e-School of Business and Quality Management: Dr KHALID HAFEEZ
e-School of Health and Environmental Studies: Prof. RACHID HADJ-HAMOU
School of e-Education: Prof. ALAIN R. SENTENI

ITTIHAD UNIVERSITY

POB 2286, Ras al-Khaimah
Telephone: (7) 2059999
Fax: (7) 2059982
E-mail: ittihadu@emirates.net.ae
Internet: www.ittihad.ac.ae

Founded 1999
Private control

Chancellor: Dr ADNAN AL-BAZI.

KHALIFA UNIVERSITY OF SCIENCE, TECHNOLOGY AND RESEARCH

POB 573, Sharjah
Telephone: (6) 5611333
E-mail: info@kustar.ac.ae
Internet: www.ku.ac.ae

Founded 2007 incorporating the former Etisalat Univ. College as the Sharjah branch campus

Abu Dhabi Campus is under devt
Private control

Accredited by Ministry of Higher Education and Scientific Research

Pres.: Dr ARIF SULTAN AL-HAMMADI

Undergraduate and postgraduate degrees in Engineering.

MIDDLESEX UNIVERSITY DUBAI

POB 500697, Dubai
Telephone: (4) 3678100
Fax: (4) 3672956
E-mail: info@mdx.ac
Internet: www.mdx.ac

Founded 2005
Private control; Middlesex University, London (UK)

Dir: Prof. RAED AWAMLEH

Schools of Arts and Education, Business, Engineering and Information Sciences, Health and Social Science
Number of students: 1,200

NYU ABU DHABI

POB 113100, Abu Dhabi
Telephone: (2) 4069677
E-mail: nyuad@nyu.edu
Internet: nyuad.nyu.edu

Founded 2009
Private control; New York Univ. (USA)

Provost: MARIËT WESTERMANN.

PARIS-SORBONNE UNIVERSITY ABU DHABI

POB 38044, Abu Dhabi
Telephone: (2) 5090555
Fax: (2) 5090656
E-mail: admissions@psuad.ac.ae
Internet: www.paris-sorbonne-abudhabi.ae

Founded 2006
Private control.

RAS AL-KHAIMAH MEDICAL AND HEALTH SCIENCES UNIVERSITY

POB 11172, Ras al-Khaimah
Telephone: (7) 2269999
Fax: (7) 2269998
E-mail: admissions@rakmhsu.ae
Internet: www.rakmhsu.com

Founded 1993
Jointly controlled by Ras Al Khaimah Govt, Al Ghurair Investments and ETA Ascon Group, Dubai

Accredited by Ministry of Higher Education and Scientific Research

Vice-Chancellor: Dr S. GURUMADHVA RAO

Colleges of dental sciences, medical sciences, nursing, pharmaceutical sciences.

UNITED ARAB EMIRATES UNIVERSITY

POB 15551, Al-Ain
Telephone: (3) 7555557
Fax: (3) 7545277
E-mail: vice_chancellor@uaeu.ac.ae
Internet: www.uaeu.ac.ae

Founded 1976
State control
Languages of instruction: Arabic, English
Academic year: September to June

Chancellor: HH Sheikh NAHAYAN MABARAK AL-NAHAYAN
Vice-Chancellor: Dr ABDULLA AL-KHANBASHI
Provost, Chief Academic Officer and CEO: Dr WYATT R. HUME
Sec.-Gen.: Dr FATIMA AL-SHAMSI
Assoc. Provost for Academic Affairs: Prof. DONALD E. BOWEN
Asst Provost and Dean of Students: Dr COURTNEY STRYKER
Asst Provost for IT and Chief Information Officer: NICK MITCHELL CHOBAN
Asst Provost for Research: Dr MAITHA S. AL-SHAMSI

Library of 439,651 vols, 929 periodicals
Number of teachers: 667
Number of students: 17,000

Publication: individual faculty journals published annually

DEANS

College of Education: Dr GARY M. INGERSOLL
College of Engineering: Prof. REYADH ALMEHAIDEB
College of Food and Agriculture: Prof. GHALEB ALHADRAMI
College of Humanities and Social Sciences: Prof. DONALD BAKER
College of Information Technology: Dr BOUMEDIENE BELKHOUCHE
College of Law: Prof. JASSIM ALI SALEM ALSHAMSI
College of Science: Prof. M. NAIM ANWAR
Faculty of Business and Economics: Prof. DAVID GRAF
Faculty of Medicine and Health Sciences: Prof. GEORGE CARRUTHERS

UNIVERSITY OF ATLANTA—GULF REGION

41st Fl., Jumeirah Emirates Tower, Dubai
E-mail: dubai@uofa.edu
Internet: www.uofa.edu
Private control

Dir: Dr STEVE HERMES.

UNIVERSITY OF DUBAI

POB 14143, Dubai
Telephone: (4) 2072600
Fax: (4) 2242151
E-mail: info@ud.ac.ae
Internet: www.ud.ac.ae

Founded 1997 as Dubai Univ. College; present status 2006

Accredited by UAE Ministry of Higher Education and Scientific Research; member of the Association to Advance Collegiate Schools of Business (AACSB), the Accrediting Board for Engineering and Technology (ABET) and the European Foundation for Management Development (EFMD)
Under the control of the state-funded Dubai Chamber of Commerce and Industry
Languages of instruction: Arabic, English

Pres.: M. OMAR HEFNI

Number of teachers: 48
Number of students: 630

DEANS

College of Business Administration: Assoc. Prof. ANANTH RAO
College of Information Technology: Dr FAOUZI KAMOUN

UNIVERSITY OF SHARJAH

POB 27272, Sharjah
Telephone: (6) 5585000
Fax: (6) 5585099
E-mail: info@sharjah.ac.ae
Internet: www.sharjah.ac.ae

Founded 1997
Private control

Chancellor: Prof. SAMY A. MAHMOUD
Vice-Chancellor for Academic Affairs: Prof. SALIM SABRI
Vice-Chancellor for Admin. and Financial Affairs: Dr MOHAMMED ISMAIL
Vice-Chancellor for Medical Colleges: Prof. MOHAMMED HUSAM AL-DIN HAMDI
Dir of Libraries: QASIM MUHAMMAD AL-KHALIDI

DEANS

College of Arts, Humanities and Social Sciences: Prof. HAMID M. AL-NAIMIY
College of Business Admin.: Prof. MAHENDRA RAJ
College of Communication: Prof. MUHAMMED KIRAT
College of Dentistry: Prof. RANI SHAMSUDIN
College of Engineering: Prof. BOUALEM BOASHASH
College of Fine Arts and Design: Dr HASSAN ABDALLA
College of Health Sciences: Prof. BASSAMAT OMAR
College of Law: Prof. ADNAN SIRHAN
College of Medicine: Prof. MOHAMMED HUSAM AL-DIN HAMDI
College of Pharmacy: Prof. MAZEN KHALIL AL-QATO
College of Shari'a and Islamic Studies: Prof. EL-GURASHI EL-BASHIR (acting)
College of Sciences: Prof. HAMID M. AL-NAIMIY

UNIVERSITY OF WOLLONGONG IN DUBAI

POB 20183, Dubai
Telephone: (4) 3672400
Fax: (4) 3672760
E-mail: info@uowdubai.ac.ae
Internet: www.uowdubai.ac.ae

Founded 1993
Private control

Accredited by Ministry of Higher Education and Scientific Research

Pres.: Prof. ROB WHELAN
Number of students: 3,500

Faculties of business and management, computer science and engineering, finance and accounting.

ZAYED UNIVERSITY

POB 19282, Dubai
Telephone: (4) 4021111
Fax: (4) 4021008
E-mail: info@zu.ac.ae
Internet: www.zu.ac.ae

Founded 1998
State control

Pres.: Sheikh NAHAYAN MABARAK AL-NAHAYAN
Vice-Pres.: Dr SULAIMAN AL-JASSIM
Provost: DAN JOHNSON
Assoc. Provost for Academic and Int. Affairs: BOB CRYAN
Chief Admin. and Finance Officer: ANDRÉ RACETTE
Dean of Libraries: PATRICIA WAND

DEANS

College of Arts and Sciences: MICHAEL ALLEN
College of Business Sciences: MICHAEL OWEN

College of Communication and Media Sciences: MARILYN ROBERTS
College of Education: PEGGY BLACKWELL
College of Information Technology: LEON JOLOLIAN

Colleges

Al-Khawarizmi International College: POB 25669, Abu Dhabi; tel. (2) 6789700; fax (2) 6789300; e-mail ceo@khawarizmi.com; internet www.khawarizmi.com; f. 1985; private control; accredited by Ministry of Higher Education and Scientific Research; affiliated to Liverpool John Moores Univ., UK; campus in Al-Ain; BSc in Computer Technology; Pres. NAEEM RADI.

American College of Dubai: POB 12867, Dubai; tel. (4) 2829992; fax (4) 2828060; e-mail info@acd.ae; internet www.centamed.com; private control; accredited by Ministry of Higher Education and Scientific Research; business, IT, liberal arts; library: 30,000 vols; Pres. WILLIAM J. O'BRIEN; Provost Dr NIGEL THORPE; Dean of Academic and Faculty Affairs Dr POONAN SINGH; Dean of Business Dr ZAFAR QUERESHI; Dean of Student Affairs S. SHARMA; Registrar CHRISTINE MASCARENHAS; Librarian RANI MANI.

Birla Institute of Technology and Science, Pilani—Dubai: POB 345055, Dubai; tel. (4) 4200700; fax (4) 4200555; internet www.bitsdubai.com; private control.

Boston University Institute for Dental Research and Education: POB 505097, Dubai; tel. (4) 4248787; fax (4) 4248687; e-mail info@bududubai.ae; internet www.bududubai.ae; private control; CEO Dr STEVEN MORGANO.

Computer College: Dubai; tel. (4) 2826880; fax (4) 2826902; e-mail sales@computer-centre.ae; internet www.cc-uae.com; f. 1993; private control; accredited by Ministry of Higher Education and Scientific Research; business admin. and IT.

Dubai Aerospace Enterprise Flight Academy: POB 10227, Ras al-Khaimah; tel. (7) 2043524; fax (7) 2043600; e-mail admissions@daeflightacademy.com; internet www.daeflightacademy.com; f. 2006; private control; Man. Dir Capt RICHARD MORRIS.

Dubai Medical College for Girls: POB 20170, Dubai; tel. (4) 2646465; fax (4) 2646130; internet www.dmcg.edu; private control; accredited by Ministry of Higher Education and Scientific Research; BSc in medicine and surgery; Dean Prof. MOHAMMED GALAL EL-DIN.

Dubai Pharmacy College: POB 19099, Dubai; tel. (4) 2646968; fax (4) 2646740; internet www.dpc.edu; f. 1999; private control; accredited by Ministry of Higher Education and Scientific Research; Dean Dr SAEED AHMED KHAN.

Dubai Police Academy: POB 53900 Dubai; tel. (4) 3482255; fax (4) 3481144; e-mail college@dubaipolice.gov.ae; internet www.dubaipolice.gov.ae; f. 1989; accredited by Ministry of Higher Education and Scientific Research; Dean Dr MOHAMMED AHMED BIN FAHAD.

Dubai School of Government: POB 72229, Dubai; tel. (4) 3293290; fax (4) 3293291; e-mail info@dsg.ae; internet www.dsg.ae; f. 2005; private control; masters degrees in public admin., public policy; Dean TARIK YOUSEF.

Emirates Academy of Hospitality Management: POB 29662, Dubai; tel. (4) 3155555; fax (4) 3155556; e-mail info@emiratesacademy.edu; internet www.jumeirah.com/en/jumeirah-group/the-emirates-academy; f. 2001; private control; Jumeirah Group; accredited by Ministry of Higher Education and Scientific Research; 400 students; Man. Dir RON HILVERT.

Emirates Aviation College – Aerospace and Academic Studies: POB 53044, Dubai; tel. (4) 2824000; fax (4) 2824222; internet www.emiratesaviationcollege.com; f. 1991 by Dept of Civil Aviation; private control; Emirate Group; accredited by Ministry of Higher Education, bachelors degrees in aeronautical engineering, business admin. (air transport management); Vice-Pres. Dr AHMED AL-ALI.

Emirates College for Management and Information Technology: POB 39292, Dubai; tel. (4) 2675016; fax (4) 2675048; e-mail admissions@ecmit.ac.ae; internet www.ecmit.ac.ae; f. 1998; private control; Emirate Group; accredited by Ministry of Higher Education and Scientific Research; British Accreditation Council for Independent Further and Higher Education; Assoc. Science degrees in Business and Information Technology; Pres. and CEO SUDHIR KARTHA; Librarian SEENA SHAHAN.

Emirates College of Advanced Education: POB 126662, Abu Dhabi; tel. (2) 6964300; fax (2) 6421641; e-mail info@ecae.ac.ae; internet www.ecae.ac.ae; private control; Vice-Chancellor IAN HASLAM.

Emirates College of Technology: POB 41009, Abu Dhabi; tel. (2) 6266010; fax (2) 6276664; e-mail ectuae@emirates.net.ae; internet www.ectuae.com; f. 1993 as Emirates Institute of Technology; private control; accredited by Ministry of Higher Education and Scientific Research; diplomas in accounting, banking and finance, business admin. and computer information systems, computer graphic design and animation, e-commerce and marketing, human resource management; Pres. MOHAMED AL-MAZROUI.

Emirates Institute for Banking and Financial Studies: POB 4166, Sharjah; tel. (6) 5728880; fax (6) 5728080; e-mail info@eibfs.com; internet www.eibfs.com; f. 1983; private control; Diploma and short courses; br. in Abu Dhabi; Chair. AHMAD HUMAID AL-TAYER; Gen. Man. JAMAL AL-JASSMI.

European University College Brussels: POB 500691, Dubai; tel. (4) 3672323; fax (4) 3672777; e-mail admissions@ehsal-dubai.net; internet www.ehsal-dubai.net; private control; f. 2003; Dir-Gen. Dr KIRK DE CEULAER.

Falcon College of Hotel Management and Tourism: POB 43319, Abu Dhabi; tel. (2) 4491450; fax (2) 4494594; e-mail fchmuae@emirates.net.ae; f. 2007; private control; accredited by Ministry of Higher Education and Scientific Research; affiliated to Cesar Ritz Colleges, Switzerland; Chair. ABDULLA ABDULJALIL AL-FAHIM; Dean Dr OSKAR R. SYKORA.

Fujairah College: POB 1207, Fujairah; tel. (2) 2244499; fax (2) 2244488; e-mail info@fc.ac.ae; internet www.fc.ac.ae; f. 2006; state control; accredited by Ministry of Higher Education and Scientific Research; Assoc. degrees in Business Admin. and Information Technology; Exec. Dir Prof. GHASSAN AL-QAIMIRI.

Heriot Watt University – Dubai: Dubai International Academic City, Dubai; tel. (4) 3616999; e-mail dubaienquiries@hw.ac.uk; internet www.hw.ac.uk/dubai; private control; undergraduate degrees in management, construction, quantity surveying, engineering, textiles and fashion design; masters programmes in petroleum engineering, construction, management, energy, information technology.

Higher Colleges of Technology: POB 32092, Abu Dhabi; tel. (2) 6815654; fax (2) 6812637; e-mail enquiries@hct.ac.ae; internet www.hct.ac.ae; f. 1988; divs of applied communications, business, education, engineering technology, general education, graduate studies, health sciences, information technology; campuses at Al-Ain, Dubai, Fujairah, Ras al-Khaimah, Sharjah; library: 160,000 vols; 950 teachers; 16,000 students; Chancellor H. E. Sheikh NAHAYAN MABARAK AL-NAHAYAN; Vice-Chancellor Dr TAYEB KAMALI.

Institute of Management Technology: POB 345006, Dubai; tel. (2) 3604844; fax (2) 3604838; e-mail info@imtdubai.ac.ae; internet imtdubai.ac.ae; f. 2006; private control; accredited by Ministry of Higher Education and Scientific Research; MBA programmes; Dir Dr FARHAD RAD-SERECHT.

Islamic and Arabic Studies College: Dubai; tel. (2) 3604844; fax (2) 3604838; e-mail iasc@emirates.net.ae; internet www.islamic-college.co.ae; f. 1986; Private Control; accredited by Ministry of Higher Education and Scientific Research; bachelors, masters and PhDs in Arabic language, Arabic literature, Islamic Fiqh, Islamic studies, Shariah; 3,489 students.

Mahatma Gandhi University Off Campus Centre: Block 3, Dubai Knowledge Village, Dubai; tel. (4) 3902981; fax (4) 3664661; e-mail contact@mgudxboc.com; internet www.mgudxboc.com; f. 2003; private control; BSc in computer science, bachelor in fashion technology, BTS in tourism studies; 700 students.

Manipal University, Dubai Campus: Block 7, Academic City, Dubai; tel. (4) 4291214; fax (4) 3694541; e-mail admissions@mahedubai.com; internet www.mahedubai.com; private control; programmes in civil engineering, electronics and communication engineering, instrumentation and control engineering, mechanical engineering, mechatronics engineering.

Masdar Institute of Science and Technology: POB 54115, Abu Dhabi; tel. (2) 6988133; fax (2) 6988123; e-mail rorfali@masdar.ae; internet www.mist.ac.ae; f. 2006; private control; masters and PhD programmes in science and engineering disciplines.

Michigan State University – Dubai: POB 345001, Dubai; tel. (4) 5015314; e-mail dubai@msu.edu; internet www.dubai.msu.edu; private control; bachelors and masters degrees.

Murdoch University International Study Center: POB 345005, Dubai; tel. (4) 4355700; fax (4) 4355704; e-mail info@murdochdubai.ac.ae; internet www.murdochdubai.com; private control; Dir Prof. JOHN GRAINGER.

Naval College: POB 800, Abu Dhabi; tel. (2) 6157600; fax (2) 6157692; f. 1997; state control; accredited by Ministry of Higher Education and Scientific Research; bachelors degree in naval studies.

New York Institute of Technology: POB 5464, Abu Dhabi; tel. (2) 4048611; fax (2) 4450830; internet www.nyit.edu/nyit_worldwide/united_arab_emirates; f. 2005; private control; New York Institute of Technology (USA); initial accreditation by the Ministry of Higher Education and Scientific Research for Bachelor of Fine Arts in Interior Design programme.

Petroleum Institute: POB 2533, Abu Dhabi; tel. (2) 6075100; fax (2) 6075200; e-mail enquiries@pi.ac.ae; internet www.pi

.ac.ae; f. 2001; private control; accredited by Ministry of Higher Education and Scientific Research; BSc degrees in electrical engineering, chemical engineering, mechanical engineering, petroleum engineering, petroleum geosciences; Masters of engineering in electrical engineering, chemical engineering, mechanical engineering, petroleum engineering; Provost and Pres. Dr MICHAEL OHADI (acting).

Police College: POB 163, Abu Dhabi; tel. (2) 4447700; fax (2) 4449720; e-mail general-manager@policecollege.ac.ae; internet www.policecollege.ac.ae; f. 1985; state control, Ministry of the Interior; accredited by Ministry of Higher Education and Scientific Research; Bachelors degree in law and policing sciences; Dir-Gen. MUSTAFA SHIHAB AL-HASHMI.

Police Sciences Academy Sharjah: POB 1510, Sharjah; tel. (6) 5585888; fax (6) 5585588; e-mail info@psa.ac.ae; internet www.psa.ac.ae; f. 1995; state control; accredited by Ministry of Higher Education and Scientific Research; bachelor of police sciences.

Rochester Institute of Technology—Dubai: POB 341055, Dubai; tel. (4) 5015314; e-mail dubai@rit.edu; internet www.rit.edu/dubai; private control; graduate degrees in business admin., finance, electrical engineering, mechanical engineering, networking and systems admin., service leadership and innovation; Pres. Dr MUSTAFA ABUSHAGUR.

Royal College of Applied Science and Technology: POB 10141, Ras al-Khaima; tel. (7) 2359080; fax (7) 2359081; e-mail bitic-uae@rcast.org; internet www.rcast.org; f. 2004; private control; Sudhir Gopi Holdings (India); 2-year MBA programmes in finance, human resource management, marketing and IT; Pres. Prof. Dr PRAVEEN DHYANI.

SAE Institute Dubai: POB 500648, Dubai; tel. (4) 3616173; fax (4) 3686800; e-mail infodubai@sae.edu; internet www.sae-dubai.com; private control.

Shaheed Zulfikar Ali Bhutto Institute of Science and Technology: POB 345004, Dubai; tel. (4) 3664601; fax (4) 3664607; e-mail info@szabist.ac.ae; internet www.szabist.ac.ae; private control.

Skyline University College: POB 1797, Sharjah; tel. (6) 5441155; fax (6) 5441166; e-mail admissions@skylineuniversity.com; internet www.skylinecollege.info; f. 1990; private control; accredited by Ministry of Higher Education and Scientific Research; bachelor and masters in business admin.; Pres. KAMAL PURI.

Syscoms College: POB 72574, Abu Dhabi; tel. (2) 6760800; fax (2) 6760890; e-mail info@syscomscollege.com; internet www.syscomscollege.com; f. 1990; private control, EMKE Group; accredited by Ministry of Higher Education and Scientific Research; assoc. of science degree in information technology.

Troy University ITS Sharjah Campus: POB 5398, Sharjah; tel. (6) 5313111; fax (6) 5314545; e-mail info@shjcollege.ac.ae; internet www.shjcollege.ac.ae; f. 1990; private control; Troy Univ. (USA); assoc. and bachelor degrees in business admin., computer science; Pres. Dr E. M. S. EDIRISINGHE.

Universal Empire Institute of Medical Sciences: POB 500332, Dubai; tel. (4) 4332773; fax (4) 4370305; e-mail administration@ueims.com; internet www.ueims.com; private control; Universal Empire Int.; Chair. and Man. Dir SUDHIR GOPI.

UNITED KINGDOM

The Higher Education System

Institutions of higher education date from the 13th century, with the oldest being the University of Oxford, the oldest college of which was founded in 1249; the next oldest university is the University of Cambridge, the oldest college of which was founded in 1284. The oldest Scottish universities are the University of St Andrews and the University of Aberdeen, which were both founded in the 15th century. The 19th century saw a great expansion of the higher education system, with the foundation of over 90 universities, colleges and institutes in the United Kingdom. In 2006/07 there were 124 universities (including the Open University) and 45 other higher education institutions, together with the privately funded University of Buckingham, offering courses of higher education. In 2005/06 there were 1,055,000 full-time and 3,395,400 part-time students (including from overseas) taking higher education courses. Notable legislation pertaining to higher education includes the Further and Higher Education Act 1992, which brought to an end the binary system by which universities and polytechnics were treated separately and enabled former polytechnics to achieve university status, and the Higher Education Act 2004, which brought in changes to the funding of higher education by introducing a scheme whereby students contributed towards their tuition. Institutions of higher education include universities, university colleges, colleges of higher education and some further education colleges. Institutions of higher education are established by a Royal Charter and most receive some funding from the Government. However, they are autonomous bodies in which admissions, staffing and teaching are administered independently of the Government.

Until 2007 the Secretary of State for Education and Skills was responsible, in principle, for all sectors of education in England. In that year some of these responsibilities, as well as some of those from the Department of Trade and Industry, were transferred to a newly created Department for Innovation, Universities and Skills. In practice the individual Local Education Authorities (LEAs) have substantial autonomy over the education system in their area. The Secretary of State for Wales is responsible for all non-university education in Wales and, since April 1993, for the University of Wales College, Newport. Government finance for publicly funded higher education institutions is distributed by the Higher Education Funding Council (HEFC) in England, the Scottish Funding Council in Scotland, the Department for Education, Culture and Welsh Language in Wales, and the Department for Employment and Learning in Northern Ireland. Student loans are the main form of support for assistance with living costs for higher education students. The amount of loan depends on where a student lives or studies, the length of the academic year, the course of study, the year of the course and the student's and their family's income. Since 2006/07 universities have been entitled to set variable fees. Since the academic year 2000/01, eligible full-time Scottish-domiciled or EU students who are studying in Scotland no longer pay tuition fees. Other additional forms of student support include dependant's allowances, young and mature student bursaries, hardship funds, disabled students' allowance and care leavers' grant, and the Higher Education (HE) Grant, introduced in September 2004.

Students in England, Wales and Northern Ireland enter university upon completion of 13 years of education. Universities set their own standards for admission, which are usually based on a student's performance in their A-Level examinations. However, other awards at level 3 on the National Qualifications Framework (NQF) may also be accepted, for example the BTEC National Diploma. All undergraduate admissions in the UK (including Scotland) are dealt with by the University and College Admissions Service (UCAS). This organization does not set admission standards, which are established by each individual institution, but it oversees the process of university admission and provides information to students on entry requirements for specific courses. The UK joined the Bologna Process in 1999. Since the UK already had a three-cycle degree structure based on Bachelors, Masters and doctorate-level qualifications, no changes were necessary. Higher education institutions are autonomous bodies and so implementation of Bologna reforms such as the use of ECTS and the issuing of the Diploma Supplement remains at institutional discretion. The Quality Assurance Agency for Higher Education is responsible for the accreditation and quality assurance of higher education in the UK. The review process in Wales is slightly different from that of England and Northern Ireland, reflecting the new framework for quality assurance which is being developed by the Higher Education Funding Council for Wales. The principal undergraduate degrees are the Bachelor of Arts (BA Hons) and Bachelor of Science (BSc Hons). These are usually full-time, three-year courses but can also be taken as longer part-time courses and may be available through distance learning. In Scotland, where students usually start a year earlier, a full-time first degree generally takes four years for Honours and three years for the broad-based Ordinary degree. The Foundation degree is a new higher education qualification (since 2001) of one year, with a vocational focus. It aims to increase the number of people qualified at higher technician and associate professional level (e.g. legal executives, engineering technicians, personnel officers, laboratory technicians, teaching assistants). Both full- and part-time courses are offered in a variety of work-related subjects and offer progression to a full Honours degree. The Higher National Diploma (HND) or Diploma of Higher Education (Dip HE) are two-year, full-time programmes, and there is the option of turning them into an Honours degree by studying for a further year. Some students go on to do postgraduate studies, usually leading to a Masters degree, such as a Master of Arts (MA), or Master of Science (MSc), or to a Doctorate (PhD). A Masters degree usually lasts one year full-time or two years part-time. A PhD usually lasts three years full-time or six years part-time. Since 2003 a four-year PhD has been introduced.

The Learning and Skills Act 2000 integrated all planning and funding for post-compulsory learning below higher education, including that provided in schools, into one overarching sector under the auspices of the Learning and Skills Council (LSC), which consists of a network of 10 regional directors and local branches. From 1986 onwards the National Council for Vocational Qualifications (NCVQ) established a framework on National Vocational Qualifications (NVQs) in England, Wales and Northern Ireland. In 1997 the Council's work was taken over by the Qualifications and Curriculum Authority. The framework is based on five defined levels of achievement, ranging from Level 1, broadly equating to foundation skills in semi-skilled occupations, to Level 5, equating to professional/senior management occupations. The competence-based system has also been extended in Scotland through a system of Scottish Vocational Qualifications (SVQs) along similar lines to the NVQs. General National Vocational Qualifications (GNVQs), along with General Scottish Vocational Qualifications (GSVQs) have also been introduced. The work of the Qualifications, Curriculum and Assessment Authority for Wales has been taken over by the Welsh Assembly Government.

The principal vocational qualifications now awarded in England, Wales and Northern Ireland are Vocational A-levels, introduced in September 2000, and the new A-Levels in applied subjects. These were designed to replace the Advanced GNVQ, with the aim of improving the standing of vocational qualifications and increasing flexibility within the system. Since September 2002, the Vocational GCSE has also replaced the Foundation, Intermediate and Part One GNVQs. From September 2008 the new 14–19 Diploma has been offered to students aged 14–19 who wish to combine their studies within the national curriculum with applied learning and relevant work experience. The LSC is responsible for funding the further education sector in England. It is also responsible for funding provision for non-prescribed higher education in further education sector colleges and further education provided by LEA-maintained and other institutions, referred to as 'external institutions'. In Wales, the Department for Education, Culture and Welsh Language funds further education provision made by further education institutions via a third party or sponsored arrangements. The Scottish Funding Council funds further education colleges in Scotland, while the Department for Employment and Learning funds further education colleges in Northern Ireland. Further and higher education may be pursued through vocational or academic courses, on a full-time, part-time or 'sandwich' basis.

Regulatory and Representative Bodies

In the following section entries whose activities cover the whole of the United Kingdom are listed under the General subheading. Those active in specific nations, for example devolved government departments, are then listed separately under the relevant subheadings which appear in alphabetical order.

GOVERNMENT

England

Department for Business, Innovation and Skills: 1 Victoria St, London, SW1H 0ET; Kingsgate House, 66–74 Victoria St, London, SW1E 6SW; tel. (20) 7215-5000; e-mail info@dius.gsi.gov.uk; internet www.bis.gov.uk; Sec. of State Dr VINCE CABLE; Min. of State for Univs and Science DAVID WILLETTS; Min. of State for Further Education, Skills and Lifelong Learning JOHN HAYES; Min. of State for Business and Enterprise MARK PRISK; Permanent Sec. MARTIN DONNELLY (acting); Parliamentary Sec. for Business, Innovation and Skills Baroness WILCOX.

Department for Culture, Media and Sport: 2–4 Cockspur St, London, SW1Y 5DH; tel. (20) 7211-6000; fax (20) 7211-6032; e-mail enquiries@culture.gov.uk; internet www.culture.gov.uk; Sec. of State for Culture, Olympics, Media and Sport JEREMY HUNT; Min. for Tourism and Heritage JOHN PENROSE; Min. for Sport and the Olympics HUGH ROBERTSON; Min. for Culture, Communications and Creative Industries ED VAIZEY; Permanent Sec. JONATHAN STEPHENS.

Department for Education: Castle View House, E Lane, Cheshire, WA7 2GJ; fax (1928) 738248; internet www.education.gov.uk; Sec. of State MICHAEL GOVE; Min. of State for Schools NICK GIBB; Min. of State for Children and Families SARAH TEATHER; Min. of State for Further Education, Skills and Lifelong Learning JOHN HAYES; Parliamentary Under-Sec. of State for Children and Families TIM LOUGHTON; Parliamentary Under-Sec. of State for Schools LORD HILL; Permanent Sec. DAVID BELL.

Northern Ireland

Department of Culture, Arts and Leisure: Causeway Exchange, 1–7 Bedford St, Belfast, BT2 7EG; tel. (28) 9025-8825; fax (28) 9025-3450; e-mail dcal@dcalni.gov.uk; internet www.dcalni.gov.uk; Min. NELSON MCCAUSLAND; Permanent Sec. ROSALIE FLANAGAN.

Department of Education: Rathgael House, Balloo Rd, Bangor, BT19 7PR; tel. (28) 9127-9279; fax (28) 9127-9100; e-mail mail@deni.gov.uk; internet www.deni.gov.uk; Min. CAITRÍONA RUANE; Permanent Sec. PAUL SWEENEY; Deputy Sec. JOHN MCGRATH; Chief Inspector of Education and Training Inspectorate STANLEY GOUDIE.

Department for Employment and Learning: Adelaide House, 39–49 Adelaide St, Belfast, BT2 8FD; tel. (28) 9025-7777; fax (28) 9025-7778; e-mail del@nics.gov.uk; internet www.delni.gov.uk; Min. DANNY KENNEDY; Permanent Sec. ALAN SHANNON.

Wales

Department for Children, Education, Lifelong Learning and Skills: Welsh Assembly Govt, Cathays Park, Cardiff, CF10 3NQ; e-mail dcells.enquiries@wales.gsi.gov.uk; internet new.wales.gov.uk; Dir-Gen. EMYR ROBERTS; Min. LEIGHTON ANDREWS; Permanent Sec. Dr DAME GILLIAN MORGAN.

ACCREDITATION

General

Accreditation Service for International Colleges (ASIC): 13 Yarm Rd, Stockton-on-Tees, TS18 3NJ; tel. (1740) 617-920; fax (1740) 617-929; e-mail info@asic.org.uk; internet www.asic.org.uk; CEO MAURICE DIMMOCK.

British Accreditation Council (BAC): 44 Bedford Row, London, WC1R 4LL; tel. (20) 7447-2584; fax (20) 7447-2585; e-mail info@the-bac.org; internet www.the-bac.org; f. 1984; acts as nat. accrediting body for private post-16 education in the UK; independent, registered charity comprising Council and Accreditation Cttee; accreditation by BAC is recognized by the Home Office as a qualifying requirement for institutions wishing to enrol visa students; works closely with and is itself monitored by Ofsted on behalf of the Home Office; BAC accreditation enables institutions to apply to UKBA (UK Border Agency) for entry on to the Sponsors Register in order to recruit non-EU students and staff; maintains close relationship with the British Council's Accreditation Unit UK and the Open and Distance–Learning Quality Council; Hon. Pres. LORD WATSON OF RICHMOND UPON THAMES; Chair. of Council TIM COX; CEO Dr GINA HOBSON; Head of Inspection Services Prof. STEVE BRISTOW; Chief Inspector SHIELA NEEDHAM; Accreditation Man. FRANCINE KOUBEL; Chair. of Accreditation Cttee DIANE BILLAM.

British Council Accreditation Unit: Bridgewater House, 58 Whitworth St, Manchester, M1 6BB; tel. (161) 957-7692; fax (161) 957-7074; e-mail accreditation.unit@britishcouncil.org; internet www.britishcouncil.org/accreditation.htm; develops, establishes and maintains quality standards for English language provision for int. students delivered by UK providers; accredits English language providers in the UK; provides an assurance of quality of English language provision accredited under the Scheme to int. students and their advisors; Man. ELIZABETH MCLAREN.

ENIC/NARIC United Kingdom: UK NARIC, Oriel House, Oriel Rd, Cheltenham, GL50 1XP; tel. (1242) 258-621; fax (1242) 258-611; e-mail info@naric.org.uk; internet www.naric.org.uk; provides information and advice on int. education and training systems and overseas skills and qualifications; incl. vocational, academic and professional qualifications; Head Dr CLOUD BAI-YUN.

Open and Distance Learning Quality Council: 79 Barnfield Wood Rd, Beckenham, BR3 6ST; tel. (20) 8658-8337; e-mail info@odlqc.org.uk; internet www.odlqc.org.uk; f. 1969 as Council for the Accreditation of Correspondence Colleges, present name and status 1995; enhances quality in education and training; Chair. JOHN AINSWORTH; Chief Exec. and Sec. to Council Dr DAVID MORLEY; Admin. Man. JULIE FOX.

Qualifications and Curriculum Development Agency (QCDA): 53–55 Butts Rd, Earlsdon Park, Coventry, CV1 3BH; tel. (300) 303-3010; fax (300) 303-3014; e-mail info@qcda.gov.uk; internet www.qcda.gov.uk; f. 1997 by merger of the Nat. Council for Vocational Qualifications (f. 1986) and the School Curriculum and Assessment Authority (f. 1993); a public body, sponsored by the Dept for Children, Schools and Families; maintains and develops the nat. curriculum and associated assessments, tests and examinations; accredits and monitors qualifications in schools, colleges and the workplace; offices in London and Northern Ireland; Chair. CHRISTOPHER TRINICK; CEO LIN HINNIGAN (acting); Exec. Dir of Education MICK WALKER; Exec. Dir for Policy Implementation SYLVIA MCNAMARA.

Scotland

Scottish Qualifications Authority (SQA): The Optima Bldg, 58 Robertson St, Glasgow, G2 8DQ; tel. (303) 333-0330; e-mail customer@sqa.org.uk; internet www.sqa.org.uk; sponsored by the Scottish Exec. Education Dept; nat. body in Scotland responsible for the devt, accreditation, assessment and certification of qualifications other than degrees; SQA qualifications incl. Higher Nat. Certificates and Diplomas, and Scottish Vocational Qualifications; has offices in Glasgow and Dalkeith; Chair. GRAHAM HOUSTON; Chief Exec. Dr JANET BROWN.

FUNDING

General

Arts and Humanities Research Council (AHRC): Polaris House, North Star Ave, Swindon, SN2 1FL; tel. (1793) 416-000; fax (1793) 416-001; e-mail enquiries@ahrc.ac.uk; internet www.ahrc.ac.uk; f. 2005 as successor to the Arts and Humanities Research Board (f. 1998); operates programmes throughout the UK to support the highest quality research and postgraduate training in the arts and humanities; divided into 8 subject panels (Panel 1: Classics, Ancient History and Archaeology; Panel 2: Visual Arts and Media: practice, history and theory; Panel 3: English Language and Literature; Panel 4: Medieval and Modern History; Panel 5: Modern Languages and Linguistics; Panel 6: Librarianship, Information and

Museum Studies; Panel 7: Music and Performing Arts; Panel 8: Philosophy, Law and Religious Studies); has an annual budget of more than £75m.; makes c. 550–600 awards in 7 research schemes and c. 1,500 awards in 3 postgraduate schemes; manages c. £10m. on an agency basis for the HEFCE to fund museums, galleries and other collns in English higher education instns; Chair. Prof. Sir ALAN WILSON; CEO Prof. RICK RYLANCE.

Skills Funding Agency: Cheylesmore House, Quinton Rd, Coventry, CV1 2WT; e-mail info@skillsfundingagency.bis.gov.uk; internet skillsfundingagency.bis.gov.uk; funds and regulates adult further education and skills training in England; Chief Exec. GEOFF RUSSELL.

UK Commission for Employment and Skills: 3 Callflex Business Park, Golden Smithies Lane, Wath-upon-Dearne, S63 7ER; tel. (1709) 774-800; fax (1709) 774-801; e-mail info@ukces.org.uk; internet www.ukces.org.uk; f. 2008; non-departmental public body providing strategic leadership on skills and employment issues in the four nations of the UK; 22 commissioners; Chair. CHARLIE MAYFIELD; Chief Exec. MICHAEL DAVIS.

England

Higher Education Funding Council for England (HEFCE): Northavon House, Coldharbour Lane, Bristol, BS16 1QD; tel. (117) 931-7317; fax (117) 931-7203; e-mail hefce@hefce.ac.uk; internet www.hefce.ac.uk; f. 1992; promotes and funds teaching and research; meets the needs of students, economy and the soc.; Chair. TIM MELVILLE-ROSS; Chief Exec. Sir ALAN LANGLANDS.

Scotland

Scottish Funding Council: Donaldson House, 97 Haymarket Terrace, Edinburgh, EH12 5HD; tel. (131) 313-6500; fax (131) 313-6501; e-mail info@sfc.ac.uk; internet www.sfc.ac.uk; f. 2005; replaced the Scottish Further Education Funding Council and the Scottish Higher Education Funding Council; a Non-Departmental Public Body of the Scottish Exec.; allocates resources for teaching and learning, research and other activities in Scotland's colleges and univs; Chair. JOHN MCCLELLAND; Chief Exec. MARK BATHO.

Wales

Higher Education Funding Council for Wales (HEFCW): Linden Court, Ilex Close, Llanishen, Cardiff, CF14 5DZ; tel. (29) 2076-1861; fax (29) 2076-3163; e-mail info@hefcw.ac.uk; internet www.hefcw.ac.uk; f. 1992; distribution of funds for education, research and related activities at higher education instns and courses at further education colleges in Wales; Chair. ROGER THOMAS; Chief Exec. Prof. PHILIP GUMMETT.

NATIONAL BODIES

General

Alliance of Sector Skills Councils (SSCs): Unit 50D, St Olav's Court, London, SE16 2XB; e-mail info@sscalliance.org; internet www.sscalliance.org; f. 2008; 25 mems; collective campaigning org. representing all of the licensed Sector Skills Councils in the UK; speaks for 90% of the UK's employers on skills issues in 1.7m. UK businesses; the 25 SSCs represent the skills and training interests of small to large business; has offices in London, Edinburgh, Cardiff and Belfast; CEO JOHN MCNAMARA.

City & Guilds: 1 Giltspur St, London, EC1A 9DD; tel. (20) 7294-2800; fax (20) 7294-2400; e-mail enquiry@cityandguilds.com; internet www.cityandguilds.com; f. 1878; awards vocational qualifications at all levels in 500 subjects at 8,500 training centres globally; Chair. MICHAEL HOWELL; Dir-Gen. CHRIS JONES.

College of Teachers: Institute of Education, 20 Bedford Way, London, WC1H 0AL; tel. (20) 7911-5536; fax (20) 7631-4865; e-mail enquiries@cot.ac.uk; internet www.collegeofteachers.ac.uk; f. 1846, incorporated by Royal Charter 1849; offers membership to educationists, awards qualifications by examination to experienced teachers of Associate, Licentiate (equivalent to university first degree), Diploma in the Advanced Study of Education, and Fellow; 1,630 mems; Patron HRH THE DUKE OF EDINBURGH; Pres. Dr RAPHAEL WILKINS; CEO and Registrar MATTHEW MARTIN; publ. *Education Today* (4 a year).

Council for the Curriculum, Examinations and Assessment: 29 Clarendon Rd, Clarendon Dock, Belfast, BT1 3BG; tel. (28) 9026-1200; fax (28) 9026-1234; e-mail info@ccea.org.uk; internet www.ccea.org.uk; f. 1994; reports to the Dept of Education of the Northern Ireland Exec.; advises Govt on what should be taught in Northern Ireland's schools and colleges, ensures that the qualifications and examinations offered by awarding bodies in Northern Ireland are of an appropriate quality and standard, and awards qualifications incl. GCSEs and GCE A and AS levels; Chief Exec. GAVIN BOYD.

GuildHE: Woburn House, 20 Tavistock Sq., London, WC1H 9HB; tel. (20) 7387-7711; fax (20) 7387-7712; e-mail info@guildhe.ac.uk; internet www.guildhe.ac.uk; f. 1978 as SCOP (the Standing Conference of Principals Ltd); present name 2006; acts as the rep. org. for higher education colleges, specialist instns and some univs; promotes institutional diversity and distinctiveness within the UK higher education sector; Chair. Prof. RUTH FARWELL; Chief Exec. ANDY WESTWOOD.

Learning and Skills Improvement Service (LSIS): Friars House, Manor House Dr., Coventry, CV1 2TE; tel. and fax (24) 7662-7900; e-mail enquiries@lsis.org.uk; internet www.lsis.org.uk; f. 2008 by merger of the Quality Improvement Agency (QIA) and the Centre for Excellence (CEL); accelerates improvement in the performance of learning and skills sector; builds the sector's capacity for self-improvement; helps the sector respond to strategic reforms; leads the sector quality improvement strategy; Chair. DAME SILVER; Chief Exec. ROB WYE; Deputy Chief Exec. MARGARET BENNETT.

National Conference of University Professors: c/o School of Construction Management and Engineering, Univ. of Reading, POB 219, Whiteknights, Reading, RG6 6AW; tel. (118) 3786753; fax (118) 9313856; e-mail ncup@reading.ac.uk; internet www.reading.ac.uk/ncup; f. 1989; supports univ. profs in carrying out their responsibilities for the maintenance of academic standards; provides a forum for discussion and a corporate voice on matters of concern to the nation's univ. system; improves public understanding of the work of univs; acts as a means of collecting and disseminating information relevant to univs; 640 univ. profs; Pres. Prof. UGUR TUZUN; Vice-Pres. Prof. JAWED SIDDIQI; Sec. HELEN SPENCE.

National Institute of Adult Continuing Education (England and Wales): Renaissance House, 20 Princess Rd W, Leicester, LE1 6TP; tel. (116) 204-4200; fax (116) 285-4514; e-mail enquiries@niace.org.uk; internet www.niace.org.uk; f. 1921 by incorporation of the British Institute of Adult Education and Nat. Foundation for Adult Education; promotes adult learning; 151 individual mems, 426 corporate mems; 45 hon. life mems; library of 20,000 vols; Pres. DAVID SHERLOCK; CEO ALAN TUCKETT; publs *Adults Learning* (12 a year), *CONCEPT—Journal of Contemporary Community Education Practice Theory* (3 a year), *Convergence* (4 a year), *Journal of Access Policy and Practice* (2 a year), *Journal of Adult and Continuing Education* (2 a year), *Studies in the Education of Adults* (2 a year).

National Society for Education in Art and Design: 3 Mason's Wharf, Corsham, SN13 9FY; tel. (1225) 810134; fax (1225) 812730; e-mail info@nsead.org; internet www.nsead.org; f. 1888; recognized professional body and trade union for principals, lecturers and teachers employed in colleges and schools of art and all specialist teachers of art, craft and design; promotes interests of art, craft and design education in the UK; 2,500 mems; Pres. ANDREW MUTTER; Gen. Sec. Dr JOHN STEERS; publ. *International Journal of Art and Design Education* (3 a year).

Nord Anglia Education: Nord House, Third Ave, Centrum 100, Burton-upon-Trent, DE14 2WD; tel. (1283) 496-500; e-mail enquiries@nordanglia.com; internet www.nordanglia.com; f. 1972; provider of education, training and childcare within the UK and overseas; aims to deliver quality learning experiences to people at every stage of their lives; comprises Int. Schools Div., Learning Services Div. and Leapfrog Day Nurseries; has offices in Burton-upon-Trent, Cheadle and London; CEO ANDREW FITZ-MAURICE.

Office for Fair Access: Northavon House Coldharbour Lane, Bristol, BS16 1QD; tel. (117) 931-7171; fax (117) 931-7083; e-mail enquiries@offa.org.uk; internet www.offa.org.uk; f. 2004; safeguards and promotes fair access to higher education; Dir Sir MARTIN HARRIS.

Office for Standards in Education, Children's Services and Skills (Ofsted): Royal Exchange Bldgs, St Ann's Sq., Manchester, M2 7LA; tel. (300) 123-4666; e-mail enquiries@ofsted.gov.uk; internet www.ofsted.gov.uk; f. 2007 by merger of the Office for Standards in Education (Ofsted) and the Adult Learning Inspectorate; inspects and regulates care for children and young people; inspects education and training for learners of all ages; reports directly to Parliament (and to the Lord Chancellor about children and family courts administration); has offices in Bristol, London, Manchester, and Nottingham; Chair. Baroness SALLY MORGAN; Chief Inspector CHRISTINE GILBERT; publ. *Ofsted News* (online).

Quality Assurance Agency for Higher Education: Southgate House, Southgate St, Gloucester, GL1 1UB; tel. (1452) 557-000; fax (1452) 557-070; e-mail comms@qaa.ac.uk; internet www.qaa.ac.uk; f. 1997; ind. body funded by subscriptions from univs and colleges of higher education, and through contracts with the main higher education funding bodies; safeguards public interest in sound standards of higher education qualifications, and encourages continuous improvement in the management of the quality of higher education; has offices in Gloucester and Glasgow; Chair. Sir RODNEY BROOKE; Chief Exec. ANTHONY MCCLARAN; publ. *QAA News* (online, 24 a year).

UK Council for Graduate Education: Lichfield Centre, The Friary, Lichfield, WS13 6QG; tel. (1543) 308-602; fax (1543) 308-604; e-mail ukcge@ukcge.ac.uk; internet www.ukcge.ac.uk; f. 1994; promotes distinct identity for graduate education and research in higher education; 125 full institutional mems, 8 assoc. institutional mems, 9 individual mems; Chair Prof. MALCOLM MCCRAE; Principal Officer CAROLYN RAVEN.

Universities and Colleges Admissions Service (UCAS): POB 28, Cheltenham, GL52 3LZ; Rosehill, New Barn Lane, Cheltenham, GL52 3LZ; tel. (1242) 222444; e-mail enquiries@ucas.ac.uk; internet www.ucas.com; manages applications to higher education courses in the UK; Chair. Prof. Sir ROBERT BURGESS; Chief Exec. MARY CURNOCK COOK.

Universities UK: Woburn House, 20 Tavistock Sq., London, WC1H 9HQ; tel. (20) 7419-4111; fax (20) 7388-8649; e-mail info@universitiesuk.ac.uk; internet www.universitiesuk.ac.uk; f. 2000. fmrly Cttee of Vice-Chancellors and Principals of the Univs of the UK (CVCP, f. 1918); promotes, encourages and develops British univs, and promotes understanding of the role, achievements and objectives of univs; 133 exec. heads of British univs; Pres. Prof. STEVE SMITH; Chief Exec. NICOLA DANDRIDGE.

University and College Union: Carlow St, London, NW1 7LH; tel. (20) 7756-2500; fax (20) 7756-2501; e-mail hq@ucu.org.uk; internet www.ucu.org.uk; f. 2006, merger of Asscn of Univ. Teachers (f. 1919) and Nat. Asscn for Teachers in Further and Higher Education (f. 1976); Pres. ALAN WHITAKER; Gen. Sec. SALLY HUNT; publs *Environmental news* (online, irregular), *Equality News* (6 a year), *FE news* (online), *HE news* (online), *Health and safety news* (online, 12 a year), *UC* (4 a year).

England

General Teaching Council for England: Victoria Sq. House, Victoria Sq., Birmingham, B2 4AJ; tel. (370) 001-0308; fax (121) 345-0100; e-mail info@gtce.org.uk; internet www.gtce.org.uk; f. 2000; ind. body that aims to help improve standards of teaching and the quality of learning; maintains a register of more than 500,000 qualified teachers in England and regulates the teaching profession in the public interest; the GTC is the awarding body for qualified teacher status (QTS) in England; has offices in Birmingham and London; Chief Exec. ALAN MEYRICK; publ. *Teaching* (3 a year).

Independent Schools Inspectorate: CAP House, 9–12 Long Lane, London, EC1A 9HA; tel. (20) 7600-0100; fax (20) 7776-8849; e-mail info@isi.net; internet www.isi.net; responsible under Statute for inspecting 1,200 ind. schools in England that are mems of the Ind. Schools Ccl; promotes and safeguards the welfare and education of children in these schools through inspections; inspects British curriculum schools worldwide; Chair. JUNE TAYLOR; Chief Inspector CHRISTINE RYAN.

Northern Ireland

Colleges Northern Ireland: Millennium Community Outreach Centre, Springfield Educational Village, 400 Springfield Rd, Belfast, BT12 7DU; tel. (28) 9090-0060; e-mail info@anic.ac.uk; internet www.anic.ac.uk; f. 1998 as Association of Northern Ireland's Colleges; liaison with Northern Ireland Assembly, govt depts.

Education and Training Inspectorate: Inspection Services Br., Dept of Education, Rathgael House, 43 Balloo Rd, Bangor, Co Down, BT19 7PR; tel. (28) 9127-9726; fax (28) 9127-9721; e-mail inspectionservices@deni.gov.uk; internet www.etini.gov.uk; provides inspection services for, and information about the quality of education in N Ireland to, the Dept of Education, Dept of Culture, Arts and Leisure, and Dept for Employment and Learning; promotes highest possible standards of learning, teaching and achievement throughout education, training and youth sectors; Chief Inspector STANLEY GOUDIE.

Scotland

Educational Institute of Scotland: 46 Moray Pl., Edinburgh, EH3 6BH; tel. (131) 225-6244; fax (131) 220-3151; e-mail enquiries@eis.org.uk; internet www.eis.org.uk; f. 1847; 60,110 mems; Pres. ALAN MUNRO; Gen. Sec. RONALD A. SMITH; publ. *Scottish Educational Journal*.

Her Majesty's Inspectorate of Education: Denholm House, Almondvale Business Park, Almondvale Way, Livingston EH54 6GA; tel. (1506) 600-200; e-mail enquiries@hmie.gov.uk; internet www.hmie.gov.uk; ind. agency accountable to the Scottish mins; promotes and contributes to sustainable improvements in standards, quality and achievements for all learners in a Scottish education system that is inclusive; Sr Chief Inspector BILL MAXWELL.

Scotland's Colleges: Argyll Court, Castle Business Park, Stirling, FK9 4TY; tel. (1786) 892-000; fax (1786) 892-001; e-mail info@scotcol.ac.uk; internet www.scotlandscolleges.ac.uk; f. 2009, merger of sector support functions; supports, represents and promotes the Scottish college sector; Chair. BRIAN KEEGAN; Chief Exec. JOHN HENDERSON.

Universities Scotland: 53 Hanover St, Edinburgh, EH2 2PJ; tel. (131) 226-1111; fax (131) 226-1100; e-mail info@universities-scotland.ac.uk; internet www.universities-scotland.ac.uk; 20 mem. univs and other instns; Convener Prof. Sir TIMOTHY O'SHEA (acting); Dir ALASTAIR SIM.

Wales

Estyn: Anchor Court, Keen Rd, Cardiff, CF24 5JW; tel. (29) 2044-6446; fax (29) 2044-6448; e-mail enquiries@estyn.gov.uk; internet www.estyn.gov.uk; office of Her Majesty's Inspectorate for Education and Training in Wales; Chief Inspector ANN KEANE.

Higher Education Wales: 2 Caspian Point, Caspian Way, Cardiff Bay, CF10 4DQ; tel. (29) 2044-8020; fax (29) 2048-9531; e-mail hew@hew.ac.uk; f. 1996; provides an expert resource on all aspects of higher education in Wales; Chair. Prof. NOEL LLOYD; Dir AMANDA WILKINSON; Deputy Dir GREG WALKER.

Learned Societies

GENERAL

Academy of Social Sciences: 30 Tabernacle St, London, EC2A 4UE; tel. (20) 7330-0898; e-mail administrator@acss.org.uk; internet www.acss.org.uk; f. 1999; composed of individual academicians and learned socs; responds to govt and other consultations on behalf of the social science community; organizes meetings and seminars; sponsors schemes to promote social sciences; 400 academicians, 40 mem. learned socs; Exec. Dir CAROLINE BUCKLOW; publs *21st Century Society* (3 a year), *eBulletin* (10 a year).

British Academy: 10 Carlton House Terrace, London, SW1Y 5AH; tel. (20) 7969-5200; fax (20) 7969-5300; e-mail secretary@britac.ac.uk; internet www.britac.ac.uk; f. 1950; sections of Classical Antiquity, of African and Oriental Studies, of Theology and Religious Studies, of Linguistics and Philology, of Early Modern Languages and Literature, of Modern Languages, Literature and Other Media, of Archaeology, of Medieval Studies: History and Literature, of Early Modern History to 1800, of Modern History from 1800, of History of Art and Music, of Philosophy, of Law, of Economics and Economic History, of Social Anthropology and Geography, of Sociology, Demography and Social Statistics, of Political Studies: Political Theory, Government and International Relations, of Psychology; 700 mems; Pres. Viscount RUNCIMAN; Sec. P. W. H. BROWN; Foreign Sec. Prof. C. N. J. MANN; publ. *Proceedings*.

British Council: 10 Spring Gardens, London, SW1A 2BN; tel. (20) 7930-8466; fax (20) 7389-6347; e-mail general.enquiries@britishcouncil.org; internet www.britishcouncil.org; f. 1934; promotes a wider knowledge of the United Kingdom and the English language abroad and develops closer cultural relations with other countries; operates in 109 countries; maintains English Teaching Centres in 53 countries, and 209 overseas libraries and information centres; arranges for the invigilation overseas of British examinations and, in collaboration with the University of Cambridge Local Examinations Syndicate, offers service to test English-language proficiency of foreign students seeking admission to British instns; grants scholarships and other awards to overseas scholars and research workers to enable them to pursue their studies in the United Kingdom, and is responsible for administering in the United Kingdom a number of Fellowships schemes on behalf of other bodies including the UN and the Foreign and Commonwealth Office; promotes liaison between scientists in the United Kingdom and abroad and provides information on British science, medicine and technology; promotes British writers, actors and other artists abroad; organizes overseas exhibitions of British books and periodicals; Chair. NEIL KINNOCK; Chief Exec. MARTIN DAVIDSON.

Commonwealth Institute: New Zealand House, 80 Haymarket, London, SW1Y 4TE; tel. (20) 7024-9822; fax (20) 7024-9833; e-mail information@commonwealth-institute.org; internet www.commonwealth.org.uk; aims to advance primary and secondary education across the Commonwealth; Company Sec. JUDY CURRY.

Attached Centre:

Centre for Commonwealth Education: jt venture between the Commonwealth Institute and the Faculty of Education at the University of Cambridge; Dir Prof. CHRISTOPHER COLCLOUGH.

English-Speaking Union (of the Commonwealth): Dartmouth House, 37 Charles St, Berkeley Sq., London, W1J 5ED; tel. (20) 7529-1550; fax (20) 7495-6108; e-mail esu@esu.org; internet www.esu.org; f. 1918; int. voluntary org., which through its educational programmes is devoted to the promotion of understanding and friendship; 35,000 mems worldwide; library of 3,000 vols; Pres. HRH PRINCE PHILIP, DUKE OF EDINBURGH; Chair. Lord HUNT OF WIRRAL; Dir-Gen. MICHAEL LAKE; publ. *Dialogue* (4 a year).

Northern Ireland Foundation: Carnegie Bldg, 121 Donegall Rd, Belfast, BT12 5JL; tel. (28) 9089-1799; e-mail info@nifoundation.net; internet nifoundation.net; f. 2008; private, charitable and ind. org.; addresses the legacy of conflict in Northern Ireland by developing leadership programmes and promoting relevant int. research; Chair. JAMES HOLMES; Dir ALLAN LEONARD; Sec. QUINTIN OLIVER.

Royal Society: 6–9 Carlton House Terrace, London, SW1Y 5AG; tel. (20) 7451-2500; fax

(20) 7930-2170; e-mail info@royalsoc.ac.uk; internet www.royalsoc.ac.uk; f. 1660; science, technology and engineering; 1,410 mems (1,280 fellows, 130 foreign mems); library: see Libraries and Archives; Pres. Prof. MARTIN REES, LORD REES OF LUDLOW; Vice-Pres. Prof. MARTIN TAYLOR; Biological Sec. Prof. DAVID READ; Foreign Sec. Prof. Dame JULIA HIGGINS; Physical Sec. Prof. MARTIN TAYLOR; Exec. Sec. STEPHEN COX; publs *Biology Letters* (4 a year), *Journal of the Royal Society Interface* (4 a year), *Notes and Records*, *Philosophical Transactions*, *Proceedings*.

Royal Society for the Encouragement of Arts, Manufactures and Commerce (RSA): 8 John Adam St, London, WC2N 6EZ; tel. (20) 7930-5115; e-mail general@rsa.org.uk; internet www.thersa.org; f. 1754; promotes arts, manufactures and commerce; 27,000 fellows; library of 8,000 vols, 11,000 MSS; Pres. HRH Prince PHILIP, DUKE OF EDINBURGH; Chair. LUKE JOHNSON; Chief Exec. MATTHEW TAYLOR; publ. *Journal* (4 a year).

Royal Society of Edinburgh: 22–26 George St, Edinburgh, EH2 2PQ; tel. (131) 240-5000; fax (131) 240-5024; e-mail rse@royalsoced.org.uk; internet www.royalsoced.org.uk; f. 1783; arts and sciences, business and enterprise research; enterprise fellowships; policy advice to govts, young people's programme, learned journals; 1,494 fellows (1,376 ordinary, 66 hon., 52 corresp.); Pres. Lord DAVID WILSON OF TILLYORN; Gen. Sec. Prof. GEOFFREY BOULTON; Chief Exec. Dr WILLIAM DUNCAN; publs *Proceedings A* (mathematics, 6 a year), *Transactions* (earth and environmental sciences, 4 a year).

Saltire Society: 9 Fountain Close, 22 High St, Edinburgh, EH1 1TF; tel. (131) 556-1836; e-mail saltire@saltiresociety.org.uk; internet www.saltiresociety.org.uk; f. 1936; conserves and fosters Scottish way of life through arts and crafts, architecture, education, literature; brs throughout Scotland; 1,000 mems; Pres. Lord CULLEN OF WHITEKIRK; Admin. (vacant).

AGRICULTURE, FISHERIES AND VETERINARY SCIENCE

Agricultural Economics Society: AES Secretariat, Tangley Mount, Tangley, Andover, SP11 0SH; tel. (1264) 730872; fax (1264) 730869; e-mail aesoc@btopenworld.com; internet www.aes.ac.uk; f. 1926 to promote the study and teaching of all disciplines relevant to agricultural economics as they apply to the agricultural, food and related industries; 500 mems; Pres. ALLAN BUCKWELL; publs *EuroChoices* (3 a year), *Journal of Agricultural Economics* (3 a year).

British Agricultural History Society: Dept of History, University of Exeter, Amory Building, Rennes Drive, Exeter, EX4 4RJ; tel. (1392) 263284; fax (1392) 263305; e-mail bahs@exeter.ac.uk; internet www.bahs.org.uk; f. 1952; 800 mems; Treasurer Prof. M. OVERTON; publ. *Agricultural History Review* (2 a year).

British Society of Animal Science: POB 3, Penicuik, EH26 0RZ; tel. (131) 445-4508; fax (131) 535-3103; e-mail bsas@sac.ac.uk; internet www.bsas.org.uk; f. 1944; UK mem. org. of the European Assen for Animal Production; 1,000 mems; Pres. Prof. NIGEL SCOLLAN; Chief Exec. MIKE STEELE; publ. *ANIMAL* (animal bioscience, 12 a year).

British Society of Soil Science: BSSS Administrative Centre, Bldg 53, Cranfield University, Cranfield MK43 0AL; tel. (1224) 752983; fax (1224) 752970; e-mail admin@soils.org.uk; internet www.soils.org.uk; f. 1947; advances the study of the soil itself and its management in agriculture, forestry, environmental matters and other fields; promotes public engagement with soil science; disseminates information and encourages discussion of soil science in a variety of fora; provides support for potential soil scientists and those on the boundary of soil science at all stages of their career; promotes soil science as a professional discipline; promotes the adoption of appropriate professional standards in all work involving soil science through the publication of professional competency statements for use by government and industry when conducting or contracting out soil science work; provides certification and accreditation of members and offers soil scientists a route to qualification as chartered scientists; 950 mems; Exec. Officer Dr KATHRYN ALLTON; publs *European Journal of Soil Science* (4 a year), *Soil Use and Management* (4 a year).

British Veterinary Association: 7 Mansfield St, London, W1G 9NQ; tel. (20) 7636-6541; fax (20) 7436-2970; e-mail bvahq@bva.co.uk; internet www.bva.co.uk; f. 1881; promotes and supports the interests of mems, and the animals under their care, and develops and maintains channels of communication not least with govt, parliamentarians and the media; 11,000 mems; Pres. Dr DAVID CATLOW; publs *In Practice* (10 a year), *Off The Record* (10 a year), *The Veterinary Record* (52 a year).

Institute of Chartered Foresters: 59 George St, Edinburgh, EH2 2JG; tel. (131) 240-1425; fax (131) 240-1424; e-mail icf@charteredforesters.org; internet www.charteredforesters.org; f. 1925, Royal Charter 1982; maintains and improves the standards of practice and understanding of forestry, and strives to be the professional body of the forestry profession and the only UK org. to award chartered forester status (MICFor and FICFor); 1,100 mems; Exec. Dir SHIREEN CHAMBERS; publs *Forestry* (5 a year), *The Chartered Forester* (members' magazine, 4 a year).

Institution of Agricultural Engineers (IAgrE): Bullock Bldg (Bldg 53), Univ. Way, Cranfield, Bedford, MK43 0GH; tel. (1234) 750876; fax (1234) 751319; e-mail secretary@iagre.org; internet www.iagre.org; f. 1938; professional body for all involved in land-based sectors incl. agriculture, horticulture, forestry, amenities and the environment; awards professional qualifications; administers the Land Based Technician Accreditation Scheme (LTA); 2,100 mems; Chief Exec. CHRISTOPHER R. WHETNALL; publs *Biosystems Engineering* (12 a year), *Landwards* (4 a year).

Royal Agricultural Society of England: Stoneleigh Park, CV8 2LZ; tel. (24) 7669-6969; fax (24) 7669-6900; e-mail info@rase.org.uk; internet www.rase.org.uk; f. 1838 (Royal Charter 1840); 11,000 mems; established National Agricultural Centre at Stoneleigh in 1963 to promote advancements in British Agriculture and disseminate information; organizes the Royal Show; arranges regular courses, conferences, etc.; agricultural history library; Chief Exec. BRIAN WARREN; publ. *RASE Journal* (1 a year).

Royal College of Veterinary Surgeons: Belgravia House, 62–64 Horseferry Rd, London, SW1P 2AF; tel. (20) 7222-2001; fax (20) 7222-2004; e-mail admin@rcvs.org.uk; internet www.rcvs.org.uk; f. 1844; governing body of the veterinary profession in the United Kingdom; maintains the Statutory Registers and the discipline of the profession and has supervisory functions in relation to veterinary education in British univs; possesses the foremost veterinary library in the United Kingdom, open to veterinary surgeons and *bona fide* scientific workers; 22,000 mems; Pres. Prof. SANDY TREES; Registrar JANE C. HERN; publ. *Directory of Veterinary Practices* (1 a year).

Royal Forestry Society: 102 High St, Tring, Herts, HP23 4AF; tel. (1442) 822028; fax (1442) 890395; e-mail rfshq@rfs.org.uk; internet www.rfs.org.uk; f. 1882 as the English Arboricultural Soc. to advance the knowledge and practice of forestry and arboriculture, and to disseminate knowledge of the sciences on which they are based; 4,000 mems; library of 1,500 vols; Chief Exec. Dr J. E. JACKSON; publs *E-news* (electronic, fortnightly), *Quarterly Journal of Forestry*.

Royal Highland and Agricultural Society of Scotland: Royal Highland Centre, Ingliston, Edinburgh, EH28 8NF; tel. (131) 335-6200; fax (131) 333-5236; e-mail info@rhass.org.uk; internet www.rhass.org.uk; f. 1784, inc. by Royal Charter 1787, for the promotion of agriculture and related industries and education; 14,000 mems; library of 6,000 vols; Chief Exec. STEPHEN HUTT; Sec. ADELE THOMSON.

Royal Horticultural Society: Exhibition Halls, Library and Offices, 80 Vincent Square, London, SW1P 2PE; tel. (20) 7834-4333; e-mail info@rhs.org.uk; internet www.rhs.org.uk; Gardens and School, Wisley, Woking, Surrey; Gardens at Rosemoor, Great Torrington, Devon, Hyde Hall, Chelmsford, Essex and Harlow Carr, Harrogate, North Yorkshire; f. 1804; 230,000 mems; library of 50,000 vols (Lindley Library); Pres. Sir RICHARD CARE POLE; Dir-Gen. Dr ANDREW COLQUHOUN; Sec. ANDREW SMITH; publs *The Garden* (12 a year), *The New Plantsman*, *Proceedings*, *Wisley Handbooks*, etc.

Royal Scottish Forestry Society: Potholm, Langholm, DG13 0NE; tel. and fax (1387) 383845; e-mail administrator@rsfs.org.uk; internet www.rsfs.org; f. 1854, fmrly known as The Royal Scottish Arboricultural Soc., present name 1930; meetings; seminars; forest visits; discussion groups; 1,400 mems; Pres. CHRISTOPHER BADENOCH; Dir RICHARD KAY; publ. *Scottish Forestry* (4 a year).

Royal Welsh Agricultural Society: Llanelwedd, Builth-Wells, Powys, LD2 3SY; tel. (1982) 553683; fax (1982) 553563; e-mail requests@rwas.co.uk; internet www.rwas.co.uk; f. 1904; organizes Royal Welsh Show, Royal Welsh Agricultural Winter Fair and Royal Welsh Smallholder and Garden Festival; promotes agriculture, horticulture, forestry and conservation, particularly in Wales; 16,500 mems; Chief Exec. D. WALTERS; publ. *Royal Welsh Journal* (1 a year).

Society of Dairy Technology: POB 12, Appleby in Westmorland, CA16 6YJ; tel. (1768) 354034; fax (1768) 352546; e-mail execdirector@sdt.org; internet www.sdt.org; f. 1943; supports advancement of dairy technology and encourages technical education and scientific enquiry in the dairy industry; organizes confs. and seminars; publishes multi-author technical series; 400 mems; Pres. Dr LIZ WHITLEY; Exec. Dir MAURICE WALTON; publ. *International Journal of Dairy Technology* (4 a year).

ARCHITECTURE AND TOWN PLANNING

Architectural Association (Inc.): 34–36 Bedford Sq., London, WC1B 3ES; tel. (20) 7887-4000; fax (20) 7414-0782; internet www.aaschool.ac.uk; f. 1847; serves the AA School of Architecture, offers facilities for architectural studies to undergraduates and graduates; professional courses; research programmes; 3,200 mems worldwide; library of 45,500 vols, 49,000 classified periodical articles, 150,000 slides; Pres. ERIC PARRY;

Company Sec. KATHLEEN FORMOSA; publs *AA Files* (3 a year), *Projects Review* (1 a year).

Association of Building Engineers: Lutyens House, Billing Brook Rd, Northampton, NN3 8NW; tel. (1604) 404121; fax (1604) 784220; e-mail building.engineers@abe.org.uk; internet www.abe.org.uk; f. 1925; trains, examines and qualifies professional body for those specializing in the technology of building; 7,000 mems; Chief Exec. Dr JOHN HOOPES; Deputy Chief Exec. KATE ILOTT; Hon. Sec. DAVID B. SMITH; publ. *Building Engineer* (12 a year).

Campaign to Protect Rural England (CPRE): 128 Southwark St, London, SE1 0SW; tel. (20) 7981-2800; fax (20) 7981-2899; e-mail info@cpre.org.uk; internet www.cpre.org.uk; f. 1926; nat. charity that helps people to protect and enhance their local countryside; 60,000 mems; Pres. Sir MAX HASTINGS; Dir KATE PARMINTER; publ. *Countryside Voice* (3 a year).

Church Buildings Council: Church House, Great Smith St, London, SW1P 3AZ; tel. (20) 7898-1863; fax (20) 7898-1881; e-mail enquiries@churchofengland.org; internet www.churchcare.co.uk; f. 1921; maintains highest standards in preservation, restoration and alteration of Anglican churches and their contents by making available sound artistic and technical advice; library of 12,000 vols; Chair. Very Rev. ANNE SLOMAN; Sec. JANET GOUGH.

Civic Society Initiative: Unit 101, 82 Wood St, The Tea Factory, Liverpool, L1 4DQ; tel. (151) 708-9920; e-mail admin@civicsocietyinitiative.org.uk; internet www.civicsocietyinitiative.org.uk; f. 2009, following closure of the Civic Trust; ensures the civic society movement has a strong national voice and an effective support structure; registered charity; supports over 1,000 local amenity societies; Dir TONY BURTON; Coordinator IAN HARVEY; publ. *Own the Future*.

Landscape Institute: 33 Great Portland St, London, W1W 8QG; tel. (20) 7299-4500; fax (20) 7299-4501; e-mail mail@landscapeinstitute.org; internet www.landscapeinstitute.org; f. 1929; objects: advancement of the art of landscape architecture, theory and practice of landscape design, promotion of research and education therein, maintenance of a high standard of professional qualification, promotion of the highest standard of professional service; the Institute is the chartered institute in the UK for landscape architects, incorporating designers, scientists and managers; 5,194 mems (comprising students, assocs, mems and fellows); library of 15,313 vols, journal articles and landscape drawings; visits to library and archive by non-members by appointment; Chief Exec. ALASTAIR MCCAPRA; publs *Landscape* (4 a year), *Landscape Journal Online* (24 a year).

London Society: Mortimer Wheeler House, 46 Eagle Wharf Rd, London, N1 7ED; tel. (20) 7253-9400; e-mail info@londonsociety.org.uk; internet www.londonsociety.org.uk; f. 1912; encourages a wider concern for the beauty of the capital city and the preservation of its charms; library: colln of books and MSS incl. journals since 1912, now housed at Mortimer Wheeler House; 848 mems; Pres. HRH THE DUKE OF GLOUCESTER; Chair. Exec. Cttee FRANK KELSALL; Hon. Sec. PATRICK GASKELL-TAYLOR; Admin. JANE JEPHCOTE; publ. *Journal* (2 a year).

National Trust for Places of Historic Interest or Natural Beauty: 36 Queen Anne's Gate, London SW1H 9AS; tel. (20) 7222-9251; fax (20) 7222-5097; e-mail enquiries@thenationaltrust.org.uk; internet www.nationaltrust.org.uk; f. 1895 for the purpose of promoting the permanent preservation of, and public access to, land of natural beauty and buildings of historic interest; 2.3m. mems; Chair. Sir SIMON JENKINS; Dir-Gen. FIONA REYNOLDS; publ. *Members' and Visitors' Handbook*.

National Trust for Scotland: Wemyss House, 28 Charlotte Sq., Edinburgh, EH2 4ET; tel. (131) 243-9300; fax (131) 243-9301; e-mail information@nts.org.uk; internet www.nts.org.uk; f. 1931; promotes the preservation of places of historical or architectural interest or natural beauty in Scotland; 250,000 mems.

Open Spaces Society: 25A Bell St, Henley-on-Thames, RG9 2BA; tel. (1491) 573535; fax (1491) 573051; e-mail hq@oss.org.uk; internet www.oss.org.uk; f. 1865; campaigns to protect common land, village greens, open spaces and public paths, and people's right to enjoy them; 2,300 mems; Chair. TIM CROWTHER (acting); Gen. Sec. KATE ASHBROOK; publ. *Open Space* (3 a year).

Oxford Preservation Trust: 10 Turn Again Lane, St Ebbes, Oxford, OX1 1QL; tel. (1865) 242918; fax (1865) 246706; e-mail info@oxfordpreservation.org.uk; internet www.oxfordpreservation.org.uk; f. 1927; preserves and enhances benefit of public amenities of Oxford and its surroundings; takes an active role in local planning; runs an annual Award Scheme to acknowledge projects that contribute to the conservation or enhancement of the built or natural environment; land ownership; membership and education programmes; restoration projects; small grant making programmes; 1,000 mems; Chair. Prof. ROGER AINSWORTH; Dir DEBORAH DANCE.

ROOM—the National Council for Housing and Planning: 41 Botolph Lane, London, EC3R 8DL; tel. (20) 7929-9494; fax (20) 7929-9490; e-mail room@rtpi.org.uk; internet www.room.org.uk; f. 1900 as the National Housing Reform Council to secure the abolition of unhealthy and socially undesirable houses; a campaigning organization with mems in both public and private sectors, seeking to promote the best standards of housing and planning; and to disseminate information on housing, planning and regeneration; 600 mems; Chair. CATHERINE CHATER; publ. *Axis* (6 a year).

Royal Incorporation of Architects in Scotland: 15 Rutland Sq., Edinburgh, EH1 2BE; tel. (131) 229-7545; fax (131) 228-2188; e-mail info@rias.org.uk; internet www.rias.org.uk; f. 1916 as a professional org.; 4,000 mems; Pres. DAVID DUNBAR; Sec. and Treas. NEIL BAXTER; publ. *Practice Information* (4 a year).

Royal Institute of British Architects: 66 Portland Pl., London, W1B 1AD; tel. (20) 7580-5533; fax (20) 7255-1541; e-mail info@inst.riba.org; internet www.architecture.com; f. 1834; 28,000 corporate mems; library: see entry for British Architectural Library; Pres. JACK PRINGLE; CEO RICHARD HASTILOW; publs *Directory of Practices* (1 a year), *RIBA Journal* (12 a year).

Royal Institution of Chartered Surveyors: 12 Great George St, Parliament Sq., London, SW1P 3AD; tel. (20) 7033-1600; fax (20) 7334-3811; e-mail contactrics@rics.org; internet www.rics.org; f. 1868; 140,000 mems; library of 35,000 vols; Chief Exec. LOUIS ARMSTRONG; Chief Operating Officer SEAN TOMPKINS; publ. *RICS Business* (12 a year).

Royal Town Planning Institute: 41 Botolph Lane, London EC3R 8DL; tel. (20) 7929-9494; fax (20) 7929-9490; e-mail online@rtpi.org.uk; internet www.rtpi.org.uk; f. 1914 to further the science and art of town planning for the benefit of the public; 20,000 mems; library of 10,000 vols; Pres. JIM CLAYDON; Sec.-Gen. ROBERT UPTON; publs *Planning Theory and Practice* (4 a year), *RTPI News* (52 a year).

Society for the Protection of Ancient Buildings: 37 Spital Sq., London, E1 6DY; tel. (20) 7377-1644; fax (20) 7247-5296; e-mail info@spab.org.uk; internet www.spab.org.uk; f. 1877 by William Morris; prevents the destruction of old bldgs and advises on their conservative repair through courses, campaigns, etc.; c. 8,500 mems; Pres. THE DUKE OF GRAFTON; Sec. PHILIP VENNING.

Town and Country Planning Association: 17 Carlton House Terrace, London, SW1Y 5AS; tel. (20) 7930-8903; fax (20) 7930-3280; e-mail tcpa@tcpa.org.uk; internet www.tcpa.org.uk; f. 1899 to campaign for garden cities; now concerns itself with all aspects of planning and the environment; campaigns for improvement to the environment by effective planning, community participation and sustainable development; holds conferences and study tours; 1,000 mems; Chair. LEE SHOSTAK; Chief Exec. GIDEON AMOS; publ. *Town and Country Planning* (11 a year).

Victorian Society: 1 Priory Gardens, Bedford Park, London, W4 1TT; tel. (20) 8994-1019; fax (20) 8747-5899; e-mail admin@victoriansociety.org.uk; internet www.victoriansociety.org.uk; f. 1958; promotes Victorian and Edwardian architecture; studies the art and built environment of the period; makes suggestions to the English heritage for bldgs to be added to the statutory list; judges applications for listed bldgs to be demolished or altered; represents at public inquiries on preservation of bldgs; 3,500 mems; Chair. Prof. HILARY GRAINGER; Dir Dr IAN DUNGAVELL; publs *Journal* (irregular), *The Victorian Magazine* (3 a year).

BIBLIOGRAPHY, LIBRARY SCIENCE AND MUSEOLOGY

Arlis UK and Ireland/Art Libraries Society of United Kingdom and Ireland: 18 College Rd, Bromsgrove, B60 2NE; tel. (1527) 579298; fax (1527) 579298; internet www.arlis.org.uk; f. 1969; aims to promote art librarianship particularly by acting as a forum for the interchange of information and materials; 710 mems (360 UK and Ireland, 350 overseas); Chair. MARGARET YOUNG; Admin. SONIA FRENCH; publs *Art Libraries Journal* (4 a year), *Directory* (1 a year), *News-sheet* (6 a year).

Aslib (The Association for Information Management): Howard House, Wagon Lane, Bingley, BD16 1WA; tel. (12) 7477-7700; fax (12) 7478-5201; internet www.aslib.com; f. 1924; asscn of industrial and commercial firms, govt depts, research asscns and instns, univs and learned socs in the UK and 40 other countries; provides consultancy; in-house training, short courses on all aspects of information work; organizes nat. and int. confs and meetings; 600 corporate mems and subscriber orgs; library: see Libraries and Archives; Man. Dir Dir JOHN PETERS; Dir REBECCA MARSH; publs *Aslib Book Guide* (12 a year), *Aslib Proceedings* (10 a year), *Current Awareness Abstracts* (10 a year), *Library Hi Tech News incorporating Online and CD Notes* (10 a year), *Managing Information* (10 a year, print and online), *Performance, Measurement and Metrics* (3 a year), *Program* (4 a year), *Records Management Journal* (12 a year), *The Journal of Documentation* (5 a year).

Association of Independent Libraries: c/o The Leeds Library, 18 Commercial St,

Leeds, LS1 6AL; tel. (113) 245-3071; e-mail enquiries@theleedslibrary.org.uk; internet www.independentlibraries.co.uk; f. 1989; 30 mems; Pres. ROBERT ANDERSON.

Bibliographical Society: c/o Inst. of English Studies, Univ. of London, Senate House, Malet St, London, WC1E 7HU; tel. (20) 7862-8679; fax (20) 7862-8720; e-mail secretary@bibsoc.org.uk; internet www.bibsoc.org; f. 1892; 1,000 mems; promotes study and research in the fields of historical, analytical, descriptive and textual bibliography and the history of printing, publishing, bookselling, bookbinding and collecting; holds meetings, at which papers are read and discussed; prints and publishes a journal and books concerned with bibliography; maintains bibliographical library; awards medals for services to bibliography, and grants and bursaries to support bibliographical research; Pres. Dr DAVID PEARSON; Hon. Sec. MARGARET L. FORD; publ. *The Library* (4 a year).

Booktrust: Book House, 45 East Hill, London, SW18 2QZ; tel. (20) 8516-2977; internet www.booktrust.org.uk; ind. educational charity; f. 1925 as The Nat. Book Council to extend the use and enjoyment of books of all kinds; provides book lists and a book information service; administers literary prizes, the Children's Laureate, Children's Book Week and Bookstart (books for babies); 1,000 mems; Pres. DORIS LESSING; Chief Exec. CHRIS MEADE.

Cambridge Bibliographical Society: Univ. Library, Cambridge, CB3 9DR; tel. (1223) 333123; fax (1223) 333160; f. 1949; historical bibliography and history of the book trade; lectures and visits; 450 mems; Hon. Sec. NICHOLAS SMITH; publs *Monographs* (irregular), *Transactions* (1 a year).

Chartered Institute of Library and Information Professionals (CILIP): 7 Ridgmount St, London, WC1E 7AE; tel. (20) 7255-0500; fax (20) 7255-0501; e-mail info@cilip.org.uk; internet www.cilip.org.uk; f. 2002, merger of Library Asscn and Institute of Information Scientists; professional body for librarians, information specialists and knowledge managers; provides practical career support for mems; 18,000 mems; Pres. BRIAN HALL; publ. *CILIP Update with Gazette* (12 a year).

Chartered Institute of Library and Information Professionals Scotland (CILIPS): 1st Floor, Block C, Brandon Gate, Leechlee Rd, Hamilton, ML3 6AU; tel. (1698) 458888; fax (1698) 283170; e-mail cilips@slainte.org.uk; internet www.slainte.org.uk; f. 1908, frmrly Scottish Library Association; attached to CILIP; 2,200 mems; Pres. ALAN HASSON; Dir ELAINE FULTON; publs *Information Scotland* (6 a year), *Scottish Library and Information Resources*.

Chartered Institute of Library and Information Professionals Wales (CILIP Wales): c/o The Executive Officer, Dept of Information Studies, Llanbadarn Fawr, Aberystwyth SY23 3AS; tel. (1970) 622174; fax (1970) 622190; e-mail cilip-wales@aber.ac.uk; internet www.cilip.org.uk/wales; f. 1931; a branch of the Chartered Institute of Library and Information Professionals; a professional body of librarians and information professionals in Wales concerned with all aspects of librarianship and related matters; 850 mems; Exec. Officer SUE MACE; publs *Wales Current Awareness* (e-mail bulletin every 2 weeks), *Y Ddolen* (3 a year).

Edinburgh Bibliographical Society: c/o National Library of Scotland, George IV Bridge, Edinburgh, EH1 1EW; tel. (131) 623-3894; fax (131) 623-3888; e-mail joseph.marshall@ed.ac.uk; internet mcs.qmuc.ac.uk/ebs; f. 1890; discusses and elucidates questions connected with books, printed or MSS, especially Scottish; promotes and encourages bibliographical studies, and printing of bibliographical works; 150 mems; Pres. IAN MCGOWAN; Hon. Sec. HELEN VINCENT; publ. *Journal* (1 a year).

Friends of the National Libraries: c/o Dept of Manuscripts, The British Library, 96 Euston Rd, London, NW1 2DB; tel. (20) 7412-7559; e-mail secretary@fnlmail.org.uk; internet www.friendsofnationallibraries.org.uk; f. 1931; promotes the acquisition of printed books, MSS and archives of historical, literary or artistic significance for libraries and record offices; 800 mems; Chair. Lord EGREMONT; Hon. Sec. MICHAEL BORRIE; publ. *Friends of the National Libraries*.

Museums Association: 24 Calvin St, London, E1 6NW; tel. (20) 7426-6910; fax (20) 7426-6961; e-mail info@museumsassociation.org; internet www.museumsassociation.org; f. 1889 to promote and improve museums and galleries and the training of museum staff; 6,011 mems; Exec. Dir MARK TAYLOR; publs *Museum Journal* (12 a year), *Museums and Galleries Yearbook*, *Museums Practice* (4 a year).

Museums, Libraries and Archives Council (MLA): Grosvenor House 14 Bennetts Hill, Birmingham, B2 5RS; tel. (121) 345-7300; fax (121) 345-7303; e-mail info@mla.gov.uk; internet www.mla.gov.uk. Wellcome Wolfson Building, 165 Queen's Gate, London, SW7 5HD; tel. (20) 7273-1444; fax (20) 7273-1404; f. 2000; advises the Govt on museum, library and archive affairs; exec. functions: allocates grants to Regional Agencies and coordinates funding and monitoring of other sectoral agencies; 15 mems; Chair. Prof. ANDREW MOTION; Chief Exec. ROY CLARE.

Society of College, National and University Libraries (SCONUL): 94 Euston St, London, NW1 2HA; tel. (20) 7387-0317; fax (20) 7383-3197; e-mail info@sconul.ac.uk; internet www.sconul.ac.uk; f. 1950; promotes the work of the nat. and univ. libraries of the UK and Ireland; 178 mem. institutions; Exec. Dir A. H. ROSSITER; Sec. A. J. C. BAINTON; publs *SCONUL Annual Library Statistics*, *SCONUL Focus*.

ECONOMICS, LAW AND POLITICS

Association of Chartered Certified Accountants: 29 Lincoln's Inn Fields, London, WC2A 3EE; tel. (20) 7059-7000; fax (20) 7059-7070; e-mail info@accaglobal.com; internet www.accaglobal.com; f. 1904; inc. by Royal Charter; 105,000 mems; Pres. CHRISTOPHER FORSTER; Chief Exec. ALLEN BLEWITT; publs *Accounting and Business* (12 a year), *Accountants' Guide*, *Student Accountant* (12 a year), *Teach Accounting* (4 a year).

British Academy of Forensic Sciences: Haematology, ICMS, Barts and the London, 4 Newark St, London, E1 2AT; tel. (20) 7882-2276; fax (20) 7882-2182; e-mail y.d.syndercombe-court@qmul.ac.uk; internet www.bafs.org.uk; f. 1959 to advance forensic science in all its aspects to the benefit of justice and the law; scientific and medico-legal meetings; publication of articles of interest to lawyers, doctors, scientists and law-enforcement officers; over 400 mems; Sec.-Gen. Dr DENISE SYNDERCOMBE-COURT; publ. *Medicine, Science and the Law* (4 a year).

British Institute of International and Comparative Law: Charles Clore House, 17 Russell Sq., London, WC1B 5JP; tel. (20) 7862-5151; fax (20) 7862-5152; e-mail info@biicl.org; internet www.biicl.org; f. 1958 by the amalgamation of the Grotius Society and the Society of Comparative Legislation and Int. Law; organizes the Commonwealth Legal Advisory Service and research in comparative law, int. law, and law of the European Communities; holds conferences, meetings and lectures in int. and comparative law; 800 mems; Chair. Lord BINGHAM OF CORNHILL; Dir Prof. ROBERT MCCORQUODALE; publs *Bulletin of International Legal Developments* (26 a year), *International and Comparative Law Quarterly* (4 a year), and other monographs on int. and comparative law.

Chartered Banker Institute: Drumsheugh House, 38B Drumsheugh Gardens, Edinburgh, EH3 7SW; tel. (131) 473-7777; fax (131) 473-7788; e-mail info@charteredbanker.com; internet www.charteredbanker.com; f. 1875; develops and promotes professional standards for bankers and provides professional qualifications for the financial services sector both in the UK and overseas; improves the qualifications of those engaged in banking, and raises their status and influence; 10,000 mems; Chief Exec. Prof. SIMON THOMPSON; publ. *Chartered Banker* (6 a year).

Chartered Institute of Management Accountants (CIMA): 26 Chapter St, London, SW1P 4NP; tel. (20) 7663-5441; fax (20) 7663-5442; internet www.cimaglobal.com; f. 1919, Royal Charter granted 1975; professional examining and membership body for chartered management accountants throughout the world; membership is gained through examination and practical experience; 62,000 mems in 155 countries; Pres. C. O. IGHODARO; Sec. C. TILLEY; publs *CIMA Insider* (12 a year), *Financial Management* (12 a year).

Chartered Institute of Public Finance and Accountancy: 3 Robert St, London, WC2N 6RL; tel. (20) 7543-5600; fax (20) 7543-5700; e-mail corporate@cipfa.org; internet www.cipfa.org.uk; f. 1885; professional accountancy body for public services; provides education and training in accountancy and financial management, and monitors professional standards; 13,500 mems; 3,000 students; CEO STEVE FREER; publs *PMPA* (4 a year), *Public Finance* (52 a year).

Chartered Insurance Institute: 42–48 High Rd, South Woodford, London, E18 2JP; tel. (20) 8989-8464; fax (20) 8530-3052; e-mail customer.serv@cii.co.uk; internet www.cii.co.uk; f. 1897; inc. by Royal Charter 1912 with the object of providing and maintaining a central organization for the promotion of professionalism and progress among insurance and financial services employees; primarily an educational and examining body; 70,000 mems; library of 15,000 vols; Dir-Gen. D. E. BLAND; Librarian R. L. CUNNEW; publ. *Journal* (6 a year).

Confederation of British Industry (CBI): Centre Point, 103 New Oxford St, London, WC1A 1DU; tel. (20) 7379-7400; fax (20) 7240-1578; internet www.cbi.org.uk; f. 1965; represents the interests of private enterprise and industry and seeks to influence govt policymaking; Pres. HELEN ALEXANDER; Dir-Gen. RICHARD LAMBERT; publs *Business Voice* (12 a year), *CBI Distributive Trades Survey*

(12 a year), *Economic Situation Report* (12 a year), *Industrial Trends Survey* (4 a year).

David Davies Memorial Institute of International Studies: c/o Dept of International Politics, Aberystwyth Univ., Aberystwyth, SY23 3FE; e-mail ddmstaff@aber.ac.uk; tel. (1970) 621770; fax (1970) 622709; internet www.aber.ac.uk/ddmi; f. 1951 to commemorate and continue the work of Lord Davies (1880–1944), on the means of establishing a viable world order; aims to advance and promote the devt of int. relations in the political, economic, legal, social, educational, ecological and other fields, and to carry out and instigate research; works through ad hoc groups, seminars, confs, bringing together experts in the relevant fields and publishing its findings; 2,500 mems; Dir Prof. KEN BOOTH; Deputy Dir Dr GRANT DAWSON.

Economics, Business and Enterprise Association: The Forum, 277 London Rd, Burgess Hill, RH15 9QU; tel. (1444) 240150; fax (1444) 240101; e-mail office@ebea.org.uk; internet www.ebea.org.uk; f. 1948; promotes and extends the study of economics, business studies, enterprise and related subjects in schools and colleges; acts as a rep. body for economics and business studies teachers in educational matters; promotes knowledge of and interest in economics and related subjects among the gen. public; annual conf.; 1,600 mems; Chief Exec. DUNCAN CULLIMORE; Office Admin. CLAIRE JOHNSON; publ. *Teaching Business and Economics* (3 a year).

Electoral Reform Society: 6 Chancel St, Blackfriars, London, SE1 0UU; tel. (20) 7928-1622; fax (20) 7401-7789; e-mail ers@electoral-reform.org.uk; internet www.electoral-reform.org.uk; f. 1884 as Proportional Representation Society, to secure an effective vote for every parliamentary and local government elector, by the adoption of the single transferable vote form of proportional representation, at all elections of representative bodies, and similarly for elections in all voluntary organizations; comprehensive reference library and archive; Electoral Reform (Ballot Services) Ltd (tel. (20) 8365-8909, fax (20) 8365-8587) provides advice and electoral administration service for UK organizations; Electoral Reform (International Services) (tel. (20) 7620-3794, fax (20) 7401-7789) provides advice for overseas organizations; the McDougall Trust is a charitable organization whose principal objective is to advance the knowledge of elections, voting systems and representative democracy; 2,000 mems; Pres. Rt Rev. COLIN BUCHANAN; Chair. ANDREW D. BURNS; Chief Exec. KATIE GHOSE.

European Movement: Southbank House, Black Prince Rd, London, SE1 7SJ; tel. (20) 3176-0543; e-mail emoffice@euromove.org.uk; internet www.euromove.org.uk; f. 1948; promotes European integration and unity at nat. and int. level; Pres. CHARLES KENNEDY; Chair. PETER LUFF.

Fabian Society: 11 Dartmouth St, London, SW1H 9BN; tel. (20) 7227-4900; fax (20) 7976-7153; e-mail info@fabian-society.org.uk; internet www.fabians.org.uk; f. 1884; public policy think-tank and socialist soc.; conducts research, organizes confs and seminars; 7,000 mems; Gen. Sec. SUNDER KATWALA; publs *Fabian Pamphlets* (6 a year), *Fabian Review* (4 a year).

Faculty of Actuaries: MacLaurin House, 18 Dublin St, Edinburgh, EH1 3PP; tel. (131) 240-1300; fax (131) 240-1313; e-mail faculty@actuaries.org.uk; internet www.actuaries.org.uk; f. 1856; 1,220 (1,174 fellows, 11 hon. fellows, 35 affiliates); library of 9,000 vols; 784 students; Sec. RICHARD MACONACHIE; publs *Annals of Actuarial Science*, *British Actuarial Journal* (4–5 a year).

Faculty of Advocates: Advocates Library, Parliament House, Edinburgh, EH1 1RF; tel. (131) 226-5071; fax (131) 225-3642; internet www.advocates.org.uk; f. 1532; the sole professional body for Advocates (Barristers) in Scotland; it maintains professional standards, examines Intrants and represents its mems; 739 mems; library: copyright library in respect of legal works of 100,000 law books associated with Nat. Library of Scotland; Dean RICHARD KEEN; Clerk CALUM S. WILSON; Keeper of the Library MUNGO BOVEY.

Federal Trust for Education and Research: 31 Jewry St, London, EC3N 2EY; tel. (20) 7320-3045; e-mail info@fedtrust.co.uk; internet www.fedtrust.co.uk; f. 1945; confs, study groups, publications; promotes and carries out research and education into federal solutions to nat., European and global problems, in particular the European Union; 500 mems; Dir BRENDAN DONNELLY.

General Council of the Bar: 289–293 High Holborn, London, WC1V 7HZ; tel. (20) 7242-0082; fax (20) 7831-9217; internet www.barcouncil.org.uk; f. 1894, present constitution 1987; governing body for the barristers' profession in England and Wales; Chief Exec. DAVID HOBART; publs *Code of Conduct*, *Counsel (*incorporating *Bar News)* (12 a year).

Hansard Society: 40–43 Chancery Lane, London, WC2A 1JA; tel. (20) 7438-1222; fax (20) 7438-1229; internet www.hansardsociety.org.uk; f. 1944; promotes parliamentary democracy, political education, political research and informed discussion of all aspects of modern parliamentary government; 400 mems; Pres. SPEAKER OF THE HOUSE OF COMMONS; Dir CLARE ETTINGHAUSEN; publ. *Parliamentary Affairs* (4 a year).

IFS School of Finance: IFS House, 4–9 Burgate Lane, Canterbury, CT1 2XJ; tel. (1227) 818609; fax (1227) 763788; e-mail customerservices@ifslearning.ac.uk; internet www.ifslearning.com; f. 1879; provides the educational foundation and qualifications for a career in banking, building societies or other financial services; publishes textbooks for the financial sector; 41,000 mems; library of 30,000 vols; Chair DONALD BRYDON; Prin. GAVIN SHREEVE; publs *Eclectic* (4 a year), *Financial World* (12 a year), *IFS News* (12 a year).

Institute for Fiscal Studies: 7 Ridgmount St, London, WC1E 7AE; tel. (20) 7291-4800; fax (20) 7323-4780; e-mail mailbox@ifs.org.uk; internet www.ifs.org.uk; f. 1969 to provide high-quality economic analysis of public policy; produces briefing notes and working papers and organizes conferences, seminars and briefings; c. 650 individual mems; 100 corporate and institutional mems; Dir PAUL JOHNSON; Research Dir RICHARD BLUNDELL; publ. *Fiscal Studies* (4 a year).

Institute of Actuaries: Staple Inn Hall, High Holborn, London, WC1V 7QJ; tel. (20) 7632-2100; fax (20) 7632-2111 Education Service and Library, Napier House, 4 Worcester St, Oxford, OX1 2AW; tel. (1865) 268200; fax (1865) 268211; e-mail institute@actuaries.org.uk; internet www.actuaries.org.uk; f. 1848, Royal Charter 1884; develops the role and standing of the actuarial profession; enhances its reputation in serving the public interest; sets examinations, courses in continuing professional devt; professional codes and disciplinary standards, awards research grants; 18,142 mems; 8,492 fellows; library of 15,000 vols, colln of rare books and archives incl. Archive of Equitable Life Assurance Society (London); Pres. NIGEL B. MASTERS; Chief Exec., Actuarial Profession CAROLINE M. INSTANCE; Head of Learning Dr TREVOR WATKINS; publs *Annals of Actuarial Science* (with Faculty of Actuaries, 2 a year), *British Actuarial Journal* (with Faculty of Actuaries, 3 a year).

Institute of Chartered Accountants in England and Wales: Chartered Accountants' Hall, Moorgate Pl., London, EC2P 2BJ; tel. (20) 7920-8100; fax (20) 7920-0547; internet www.icaew.co.uk; f. 1880 by Royal Charter; special collection of early European books on book-keeping; internationally important research library on the British accounting and tax systems; 128,000 mems; library of 40,000 vols, 40,000 journal records; Chief Exec. MICHAEL IZZA; Head of Library and Information Services SUSAN MOORE; publ. *Accountancy* (12 a year).

Institute of Chartered Accountants of Scotland: CA House, 21 Haymarket Yards, Edinburgh, EH12 5BH; tel. (131) 347-0100; fax (131) 347-0105; e-mail enquiries@icas.org.uk; internet www.icas.org.uk; f. 1854; deals with professional matters concerning its mems and the public in matters of chartered accountancy; runs information service; library of 3,000 books, 140 periodicals, online databases; 18,500 mems; Pres. IAIN MCLAREN; Chief Exec. ANTON COLELLA; publ. *CA Magazine* (12 a year).

Institute of Chartered Secretaries and Administrators: 16 Park Crescent, London, W1B 1AH; tel. (20) 7580-4741; fax (20) 7323-1132; e-mail info@icsa.co.uk; internet www.icsa.org.uk; f. 1891; 47,000 mems and students; qualifying body for company secretaries; authority on corporate governance; Information Manager SHEILA DOYLE; publs *Best Practice Guides* (irregular), *Chartered Secretary* (12 a year), *Company Secretarial Practice* (4 a year), *The Company Secretary* (12 a year).

Institute of Economic Affairs: 2 Lord North St, Westminster, London, SW1P 3LB; tel. (20) 7799-3745; fax (20) 7799-2137; e-mail iea@iea.org.uk; internet www.iea.org.uk; f. 1955; to improve understanding of economics and its application to business and public policy; Dir-Gen. JOHN BLUNDELL; publs *Hobart Papers*, *Research Monographs*, *IEA Readings*, *Occasional Papers*, *Current Controversies*, *Choice in Welfare*, *Economic Affairs*, *Journal* (4 a year).

Law Society: 113 Chancery Lane, London, WC2A 1PL; tel. (20) 7242-1222; fax (20) 7831-0344; e-mail info.services@lawsociety.org.uk; internet www.lawsociety.org.uk; f. 1825; regulator and representative body for solicitors in England and Wales; 93,000 mems; library: see Libraries and Archives; Chief Exec. JULIA PARASKEVA; publ. *Gazette* (weekly).

Political Studies Association of the United Kingdom: Dept of Politics, Newcastle Univ., Newcastle upon Tyne, NE1 7RU; tel. (191) 222-8021; fax (191) 222-3499; internet www.psa.ac.uk; f. 1950; promotes the devt of political studies; 1,600 mems; Chair. Prof. VICKEY RANDALL; Hon. Sec. Prof. PAUL CARMICHAEL; publs *British Journal of Politics and International Relations* (4 a year), *Political Studies* (4 a year), *Political Studies Review* (3 a year), *Politics* (3 a year).

Royal Economic Society: School of Economics and Finance, Univ. of St Andrews, St Andrews, KY16 9AL; tel. (13) 3446-2479; fax (13) 446-2444; e-mail royaleconsoc@st-andrews.ac.uk; internet www.res.org.uk; f. 1890; advances and disseminates economic knowledge; exchanges ideas; trains and supports younger mems; cooperates with int. assns of economists; promotes study of economic science in academics, govt service, banking, industry and public affairs; 3,000 mems; Pres. Prof. Sir JOHN VICKERS; Pres. Elect Prof. RICHARD BLUNDELL; Sec.-Gen. Prof. JOHN BEATH; publs *The Econometrics Journal* (online), *The Economic Journal* (8 a year).

Royal Faculty of Procurators in Glasgow: 12 Nelson Mandela Pl., Glasgow, G2 1BT; internet www.rfpg.org; f. inc. long prior to 1668, and by Royal Charter 1796; a legal soc.; 1,500 mems; library of 25,000 vols; Dean PAUL CARNAN; Chief Exec. and Faculty Librarian JOHN M. MCKENZIE.

Royal Institute of International Affairs: Chatham House, 10 St James's Sq., London, SW1Y 4LE; tel. (20) 7957-5700; fax (20) 7957-5710; e-mail contact@chathamhouse.org.uk; internet www.chathamhouse.org.uk; f. 1920; facilitates the scientific study of int. affairs; studies economic, political and security trends in int. relations; researches into Middle East, Asia-Pacific, Africa, Europe, Russia and Central Asia, and into energy and the environment, int. economics, law and security; 5,000 mems (all categories); library: see Libraries and Archives; Pres Sir JOHN MAJOR, Lord ROBERTSON OF PORT ELLEN, Lord ASHDOWN OF NORTON-SUB-HAMDON; Dir of Research Dr ROBIN NIBLETT; publs *International Affairs* (6 a year), *The World Today* (12 a year).

Royal Statistical Society: 12 Errol St, London, EC1Y 8LX; tel. (20) 7638-8998; fax (20) 7614-3905; e-mail rss@rss.org.uk; internet www.rss.org.uk; f. 1834; nurtures the discipline of statistics by publishing a journal, organising meetings, setting and maintaining professional standards, accrediting univ. courses and operating examinations; promotes the discipline of statistics by disseminating and encouraging statistical knowledge and good practice with both producers and consumers of statistics; provides effective and efficient services to members which supports their professional and academic interests and their endeavours; 7,000 mems; Pres. Prof. VALERIE ISHAM; Exec. Dir Dr MARTIN DOUGHERTY; publs *Applied Statistics* (journal, 4 a year), *Statistical Methodology* (journal, 4 a year), *Statistics in Society* (journal, 3 a year), *The Statistician* (journal, 4 a year).

Selden Society: c/o School of Law, Queen Mary–University of London, Mile End Rd, London, E1 4NS; tel. (20) 7882-3968; fax (20) 7882-7042; e-mail selden-society@qmul.ac.uk; internet www.selden-society.qmul.ac.uk; f. 1887; encourages the study and advances the knowledge of the history of English law mainly by the publication of the original records of the law and legal instns; publishes more than 150 vols on sources and other aspects of English legal history; 1,700 mems; Pres. Rt Hon. Lord IGOR JUDGE; Hon. Treas. CHRISTOPHER WRIGHT; Literary Dir Prof. Sir JOHN BAKER; Sec. VICTOR TUNKEL; publs *Selden Society Main Series* (1 a year), *Selden Society Supplementary Series* (irregular).

Stair Society: c/o Thomas H Drysdale, 6 The Glebe, Manse Rd, Dirleton East Lothian, EH39 5FB; fax (1620) 850264; e-mail stairsecretary@btinternet.com; internet www.stairsociety.org; f. 1934; encourages study and advances knowledge of history of Scots Law; 450 mems; Pres. Lord HOPE OF CRAIGHEAD; Chair. of Council Dr JOHN CAIRNS; Sec. THOMAS H. DRYSDALE.

EDUCATION

Advisory Centre for Education (ACE) Ltd: 1C Aberdeen Studios, 22–24 Highbury Grove, London, N5 2DQ; tel. (20) 7354-8318; fax (20) 7354-9069; e-mail enquiries@ace.dialnet.com; internet www.ace-ed.org.uk; f. 1960; aims to provide information on education for parents and others, to encourage close home-school relationships, and to arouse discussion on education issues; publs *ACE Bulletin* (6 a year), *Stop Press* (12 a year).

British Educational Leadership Management and Administration Society: Rm 50, Victoria Hall, Norfolk St, Sheffield, S1 2JB; tel. (114) 279-9926; fax (114) 279-6868; e-mail info@belmas.org.uk; internet www.belmas.org.uk; f. 1971; advances the practice of and research into educational admin.; maintains close contact with nat. and int. orgs and encourages the foundation of local groups; 600 mems; Chair. Dr MEGAN CRAWFORD; Sec. Prof. TIM SIMKIINS; Treas. Dr ALISON TAYSUM; publs *Educational Management Administration and Leadership* (6 a year), *Management in Education* (4 a year), *Networks*.

Council for Education in World Citizenship: 63 Gee St, London, EC1V 3RS; tel. (20) 7566-4141; fax (20) 7566-4131; e-mail info@citizenshipfoundation.org.uk; internet www.citizenshipfoundation.org.uk; f. 1939; an independent, non-political organization to assist schools and colleges in the teaching of international affairs and promote a more global perspective in curricula; 1,000 mem. schools; library: resources and reference material; Dir LES STRATTON; publs *Activities Sheet* (5 a year), *Broadsheet* (5 a year), *Broadsheet Digest* (5 a year).

University Association for Contemporary European Studies: School of Public Policy, Univ. College London, 29–30 Tavistock Sq., London, WC1H 9QU; tel. (20) 7679-4975; fax (20) 7679-4973; e-mail admin@uaces.org; internet www.uaces.org; f. 1968; brings together academics with a common interest in European studies (and specifically in European integration) with practitioners active in European affairs; circulates information to mems about devts in European studies; holds confs and seminars; provides documentation on European studies; 1,050 individual, 85 group mems; Exec. Dir. SUE DAVIS; publs *JCMS: Journal of Common Market Studies* (5 a year), *JCMS European Union Annual Review*, *UACES-Routledge Contemporary European Studies Book Series*, *JCER: Journal of Contemporary European Research* (online, www.jcer.net).

Workers' Educational Association (WEA): 4 Luke St, London, EC2A 4XW; tel. (20) 7426-3450; fax (20) 7426-3451; e-mail national@wea.org.uk; internet www.wea.org.uk; f. 1903; voluntary provider of adult education; co-operates with univs. and other voluntary asscns through all English regions and in Scotland for the provision of classes; these classes, although provided independently, are grant-aided by the Learning and Skills Ccl in England, the Scottish Office Education Dept, local education authorities and other funding bodies; 44,000 mems; 80,000 students; Gen. Sec. RICHARD BOLSIN.

FINE AND PERFORMING ARTS

Arts Council of England: 14 Great Peter St, London, SW1P 3NQ; tel. (20) 7333-0100; fax (20) 7973-6590; e-mail enquiries@artscouncil.org.uk; internet www.artscouncil.org.uk; f. 1940 as the Council for the Encouragement of Music and the Arts (CEMA), in 1945 became the Arts Council of Great Britain, present name 1994; nat. ind. and non-political body working to develop, sustain and promote the arts; distributes public money from govt and the National Lottery to artists and arts orgs, both directly and through the regional arts boards; Chair. Sir CHRISTOPHER FRAYLING; Chief Exec. PETER HEWITT; publ. *Development Funds*.

Arts Council of Northern Ireland: 77 Malone Rd, Belfast, BT9 6AQ; tel. (28) 9038-5200; fax (28) 9066-1715; e-mail info@artscouncil-ni.org; internet www.artscouncil-ni.org; f. 1943; devt agency for arts; offers support and funding to artists and arts orgs; Chair. ROSEMARY KELLY; Chief Exec. ROISIN MCDONOUGH; Dir NICK LIVINGSTON; publ. *Article* (2 a year).

Arts Council of Wales: Bute Pl., Cardiff, CF10 5AL; tel. (845) 8734-900; fax (845) 2044-1400; e-mail info@artswales.org.uk; internet www.artswales.org.uk; funded by the Welsh Assembly Government and distributor of National Lottery funding; 18 mems; Chair. Prof. DAI SMITH; Chief Exec. NICK CAPALDI.

BFI Southbank: Belvedere Rd, South Bank, Waterloo, London, SE1 8XT; tel. (20) 7928 3535; internet www.bfi.org.uk; f. 1933; nat. agency with responsibility for encouraging the arts of film and television and conserving them in the nat. interest; among its divisions and activities are the BFI Nat. Archive (*q.v.*), the Nat. Film Theatre, the London Film Festival, the London Lesbian and Gay Film Festival, education and library services, DVD and book publishing; 24,000 mems; in receipt of annual govt grant; Dir AMANDA NEVILL; publ. *Sight and Sound* (monthly, illustrated).

British Academy of Composers and Songwriters: British Music House, 26 Berners St, London, W1T 3LR; tel. (20) 7636-2929; fax (20) 7636-2212; e-mail info@britishacademy.com; internet www.britishacademy.com; f. 1999, following merger of Association of Professional Composers, British Academy of Songwriters, Composers and Authors, and Composers' Guild of Great Britain; represents the interests of composers and songwriters, providing initial career support and services and benefits for members, protects copyright, and promotes British songwriting and composition; 3,000 mems; Chief Exec. CHRIS GREEN.

British and International Federation of Festivals: Festivals House, 198 Park Lane, Macclesfield, SK11 6UD; tel. (1625) 428297; fax (1625) 503229; e-mail info@federationoffestivals.org.uk; internet www.federationoffestivals.org.uk; f. 1921; HQ of the Amateur Festival Movement; 800 mems; Patron HM THE QUEEN; Chief Exec. E. WHITEHEAD.

British Institute of Professional Photography: 1 Prebendal Court, Oxford Rd, Aylesbury, Bucks, HP19 8EY; tel. (1296) 718530; fax (1296) 336367; e-mail info@bipp.com; internet www.bipp.com; f. 1901; professional qualifying body; awards the designatory letters FBIPP, ABIPP and LBIPP; represents professional photographers and photographic technicians; aims to improve the quality of photography, to establish recognized examinations and standards of conduct and to safeguard the interests of the public and the profession; 3,500 mems; publ. *The Photographer* (12 a year).

British Society of Painters: 13 Manor Orchards, Knaresborough, North Yorkshire, HG5 0BW; tel. (1423) 540603; e-mail info@britpaint.co.uk; internet www.britpaint.co.uk; f. 1986; holds 2 exhibitions annually; awards prizes; 62 mems (12 fellows, 50 mems); Pres. DAVID SHEPHERD; Dir LESLIE SIMPSON.

Attached Societies:

British Watercolour Society: 13 Manor Orchards, Knaresborough, North Yorkshire, HG5 0BW; tel. (1423) 540603; f. 1911; holds 2 exhibitions annually; awards prizes; 150 mems; Pres. KENNETH ELMSLEY; Dir MARGARET SIMPSON.

Society of Miniaturists: 13 Manor Orchards, Knaresborough, North Yorkshire, HG5 0BW; tel. (1423) 540603; e-mail info@britpaint.co.uk; internet www.britpaint.co.uk; f. 1895; 35 mems; holds 2 exhibitions annually; awards prizes.

Commission for Architecture and the Built Environment (CABE): 1 Kemble St, London, WC2B 4AN; tel. (20) 7070-6700; fax (20) 7070-6777; e-mail enquiries@cabe.org.uk; internet www.cabe.org.uk; f. 1999; 11 mems; Chair. Sir STUART LIPTON; CEO JON ROUSE.

Contemporary Art Society: 11–15 Emerald St, London, WC1N 3QL; tel. (20) 7831-1243; fax (20) 7831-1214; e-mail info@contemporaryartsociety.org; internet www.contemporaryartsociety.org; f. 1910; nat. non-profit agency; supports contemporary artists through the promotion of collecting and commissioning by individuals, public and private instns across the UK; 1,500 mems; Chair. MARK STEPHENS; Dir PAUL HOBSON; Deputy Dir SOPHIA BARDSLEY.

English Folk Dance and Song Society: Cecil Sharp House, 2 Regent's Park Rd, London, NW1 7AY; tel. (20) 7485-2206; fax (20) 7284-0534; e-mail info@efdss.org; internet www.efdss.org; f. 1932, Folk Song Society 1898, English Folk Dance Society 1911; collects, studies and preserves English folk dances and songs and other folk music; encourages their performance; 5,000 mems; library: see Vaughan Williams Memorial Library; publs *English Dance and Song* (4 a year), *Folk Music Journal* (1 a year).

Federation of British Artists: 17 Carlton House Terrace, London, SW1Y 5BD; tel. (20) 7930-6844; fax (20) 7839-7830; e-mail info@mallgalleries.com; internet www.mallgalleries.org.uk; f. 1961; 650 mems; administers The Mall Galleries, The Mall, London, SW1, and holds annual exhibitions, open to all artists, for mem. socs.; Dir LEWIS MCNAUGHT.

Member Societies:

Hesketh Hubbard Art Society: 17 Carlton House Terrace, London, SW1Y 5BD; tel. (20) 7930-6844; fax (20) 7839-7830; e-mail info@mallgalleries.com; internet www.mallgalleries.org.uk; f. 1930 by the Royal Soc. of British Artists; weekly drawing sessions in Mall Galleries from life models; 200 mems; Pres. SIMON WHITTLE.

New English Art Club: 17 Carlton House Terrace, London, SW1Y 5BD; tel. (20) 7930-6844; fax (20) 7839-7830; e-mail info@mallgalleries.com; internet www.newenglishartclub.co.uk; f. 1886; exhibition held in autumn, open to all artists to submit work for selection; 87 mems; Pres. JASON BOWYER.

Pastel Society: 17 Carlton House Terrace, London, SW1Y 5BD; tel. (20) 7930-6844; fax (20) 7839-7830; e-mail info@mallgalleries.com; internet www.thepastelsociety.org.uk; f. 1898; annual open exhibition; 65 mems; Pres. JOHN IVOR STEWART.

Royal Institute of Oil Painters: 17 Carlton House Terrace, London, SW1Y 5BD; tel. (20) 7930-6844; fax (20) 7839-7830; e-mail info@mallgalleries.com; internet www.theroi.org.uk; f. 1882; annual exhibition; 69 mems; Pres. PETER WILEMAN.

Royal Institute of Painters in Water Colours: 17 Carlton House Terrace, London, SW1Y 5BD; tel. (20) 7930-6844; fax (20) 7839-7830; e-mail info@mallgalleries.com; internet www.mallgalleries.org.uk; f. 1831; annual exhibition (March/April) open to all artists to submit work for selection; 70 mems; Pres. RONALD MADDOX.

Royal Society of British Artists: 17 Carlton House Terrace, London, SW1Y 5BD; tel. (20) 7930-6844; fax (20) 7839-7830; e-mail info@mallgalleries.com; internet www.royalsocietyofbritishartists.org.uk; f. 1823; annual open exhibition; 110 mems (incl. 11 hon.); Pres. JAMES HORTON.

Royal Society of Marine Artists: 17 Carlton House Terrace, London, SW1Y 5BD; tel. (20) 7930-6844; fax (20) 7839-7830; e-mail info@mallgalleries.com; internet www.rsma-web.co.uk; f. 1939; annual open exhibition; 51 mems; Pres. DAVID HOWELL.

Royal Society of Portrait Painters: 17 Carlton House Terrace, London, SW1Y 5BD; tel. (20) 7930-6844; fax (20) 7839-7830; e-mail info@mallgalleries.com; internet www.therp.co.uk; f. 1891; annual exhibition (May); 54 mems; Pres. ALASTAIR ADAMS.

Society of Wildlife Artists: 17 Carlton House Terrace, London, SW1Y 5BD; tel. (20) 7930-6844; fax (20) 7839-7830; e-mail info@mallgalleries.com; internet www.swla.co.uk; f. 1963; annual open exhibition (September); 77 mems; Pres. HARRIET MEAD.

Guild of Church Musicians: c/o John Ewington, 'Hillbrow', Godstone Rd, Bletchingley, RH1 4PJ; tel. (1883) 743168; e-mail johnmusicsure@orbix.co.uk; internet www.churchmusicians.org; f. 1888; runs courses and seminars, conducts examinations for the Archbishops' Certificate in Church Music and the Archbishops' Certificate in Public Worship, and runs a Fellowship Programme (FGCM) at postgraduate diploma level; 800 mems; Pres. Dr MARY ARCHER; Warden Very Rev. Dr RICHARD FENWICK; Gen. Sec. JOHN EWINGTON; publs *Laudate* (2 or 3 a year), *Year Book*.

Incorporated Association of Organists: 17 Woodland Rd, Northfield, Birmingham, B31 2HU; tel. (121) 475-4408; fax (121) 475-4408; e-mail w.j.stormont@btinternet.com; internet iao.org.uk; f. 1913; 100 affiliated associations with 6,500 mems worldwide; aims to improve and advance the knowledge of organs, organ music and teaching methods by organizing an Annual Congress, residential and day courses, master-classes, recitals and lectures; administers a Benevolent Fund for organists; Pres. Dr SIMON LINDLEY; Hon. Sec. JOHN STORMONT; publ. *Organists' Review* (4 a year).

Incorporated Society of Musicians: 10 Stratford Pl., London, W1C 1AA; tel. (20) 7629-4413; fax (20) 7408-1538; e-mail membership@ism.org; internet www.ism.org; f. 1882; professional association for all musicians (performers, teachers and composers); 5,000 mems; Pres. GAVIN HENDERSON; Chief Exec. DEBORAH ANNETTS; publs *Yearbook and Register of Members*, *Register of Professional Private Music Teachers* (1 a year), *Music Journal* (12 a year), *Register of Performers and Composers* (1 a year), *Register of Musicians in Education* (1 a year).

Institute of Contemporary Arts: Nash House, The Mall, London, SW1Y 5AH; tel. (20) 7930-0493; fax (20) 7873-0051; internet www.ica.org.uk; f. 1947; contemporary cultural centre; organizes exhibitions, lecture series, films, performances and musical events, etc.; c. 6,000 mems; Dir EKOW ESHUN; Chair. ALAN YENTOB; publs *ICA Documents*, *Monthly Bulletin of Events*.

Oriental Ceramic Society: POB 517, Cambridge, CB21 5BE; tel. (1223) 881328; e-mail ocslondon@btinternet.com; internet www.ocs-london.com; f. 1921 to increase knowledge and appreciation of Asian art, in particular ceramics; 750 mems. worldwide; monthly lectures, discussions and handling sessions; visits to important collns in the UK and abroad; Pres. ROSEMARY SCOTT; Admin. MARY PAINTER; publ. *Transactions of the Oriental Ceramic Society* (1 a year).

Plainsong and Mediaeval Music Society: c/o RSCM, 19 The Close, Salisbury, SP1 2EB; tel. (1306) 872800; fax (1306) 887260; e-mail admin@plainsong.org.uk; internet www.plainsong.org.uk; f. 1888; promotes the study and appreciation of plainsong and medieval music, especially by publs and performances; organizes annual conf.; 90 mems; Chair. Dr LISA COLTON; Sec. Prof. THOMAS SCHMIDT-BESTE; publ. *Plainsong and Medieval Music* (2 a year).

Professional Photographers Association of Northern Ireland: 142 Bridge St, Portadown, BT63 5AP; tel. (28) 3835-1055; e-mail honsec@ppani.co.uk; internet www.ppani.co.uk; f. 1966; helps improve the standard of photography in the community; Pres. CIARAN O'NEILL; Vice-Pres. SIMON O'NEILL; Hon. Sec. MARIE ALLEN; Hon. Treas. DAVID COOTE.

Royal Academy of Arts in London: Burlington House, Piccadilly, London, W1J 0BD; tel. (20) 7300-8000; fax (20) 7300-8001; internet www.royalacademy.org.uk; f. 1768; fine arts; runs art school; 80 Acads; Pres. Sir NICHOLAS GRIMSHAW; Sec. and Chief Exec. CHARLES SAUMAREZ SMITH; Keeper MAURICE COCKRILL; publs *RA Illustrated* (summer exhibition souvenir, 1 a year), *RA Magazine* (4 a year).

Royal British Society of Sculptors: 108 Old Brompton Rd, London, SW7 3RA; tel. (20) 7373-8615; fax (20) 7370-3721; e-mail info@rbs.org.uk; internet www.rbs.org.uk; f. 1904 for the promotion and advancement of the art of sculpture; Pres. Prof. BRIAN FALCONBRIDGE; Administrator FLORENCIA GUILLEN; publ. *Sculpture97*.

Royal Cambrian Academy of Art: Crown Lane, Conwy, LL32 8AN; tel. and fax (1492) 593413; e-mail rca@rcaconwy.org; internet www.rcaconwy.org; f. 1882; promotes the arts of painting, engraving, sculpture, and other forms of art in Wales; 125 mems; Pres. MAURICE COCKRILL; Hon. Sec. TIM PUGH; Curator GILL BIRD.

Royal Fine Art Commission for Scotland: Bakehouse Close, 146 Canongate, Edinburgh, EH8 8DD; tel. (131) 556-6699; fax (131) 556-6633; e-mail plan@royfinartcomforsco.gov.uk; internet www.royfinartcomforsco.gov.uk; f. 1927; independent body advising ministers and local authorities on the visual impact and quality of design of construction projects; during the Edinburgh International Festival an annual exhibition is held on a topic related to the Commission's work; 12 mems; Sec. CHARLES PROSSER.

Royal Musical Association:; tel. (161) 861-7542; fax (161) 861-7543; e-mail jeffrey.dean@stingrayoffice.com; internet www.rma.ac.uk; f. 1874, inc. 1904, for the investigation and discussion of subjects connected with the art, science and history of music; annual conf., research students' conf., 4–6 annual regional study days; 1,000 mems; Pres. Prof. PHILIP OLLESON; Exec. Officer Dr JEFFREY DEAN; Hon. Treas. LAWRENCE WRAGG; publs *Journal of the Royal Musical Association* (2 a year), *Royal Musical Association Monographs* (1 a year), *Royal Musical Association Research Chronicle* (1 a year).

Royal Photographic Society of Great Britain: Fenton House, 122 Wells Rd, Bath, BA2 3AH; tel. (1225) 325733; fax (1225) 448688; e-mail reception@rps.org; internet www.rps.org; f. 1853 for the advancement of the science and art of photography; 9,500 mems; library of 20,000 vols and periodicals; permanent colln of 200,000 photographs and 8,000 items of photographic equipment; Pres. Dr BARRY SENIOR; Dir Gen. STUART BLAKE; publs *Imaging Abstracts* (6 a year), *RPS Journal* (10 a year), *The Imaging Science Journal* (4 a year).

Royal Scottish Academy of Art and Architecture: The Mound, Edinburgh, EH2 2EL; tel. (131) 225-6671; fax (131) 220-6016; e-mail info@royalscottishacademy.org; internet www.royalscottishacademy.org; f. 1826; ind., privately funded instn led by eminent artists and architects whose sole purpose is to promote and support the creation, understanding and enjoyment of the visual arts through exhibitions and related educational events; 129 mems (98 Acads, 31 hon. Acads); Programme Dir COLIN R. GREENSLADE; Collns Curator Dr JOANNA SODEN; Marketing Man. ALISA LINDSAY.

Royal Watercolour Society: Bankside Gallery, 48 Hopton St, Blackfriars, London, SE1 9JH; tel. (20) 7928-7521; fax (20) 7928-2820; e-mail info@banksidegallery.com; internet www.banksidegallery.com; f. 1804; small archive and diploma collection; 83 mems; Pres. FRANCIS BOWYER; Sec. JUDY DIXEY; publ. *Bankside Bulletin* (4 a year).

Royal West of England Academy: Queen's Rd, Clifton, Bristol, BS8 1PX; tel. (117) 973-5129; fax (117) 923-7874; e-mail info@rwa.org.uk; internet www.rwa.org.uk; f. 1844; encourages, advances and promotes the appreciation of the fine arts by exhibitions and occasional lectures and meetings; 160 academicians; library: small library, mainly exhibition catalogues; Chair. of Trustees NORMAN BIDDLE.

Society for Theatre Research: POB 53971, London, SW15 6UL; e-mail contact@str.org.uk; internet www.str.org.uk; f. 1948; encourages research into the history and technique of the British theatre; holds monthly lectures in the winter season; distributes research grants annually and offers an annual theatre book prize; 750 individual and corporate mems; Pres. TIMOTHY WEST; publ. *Theatre Notebook* (3 a year).

Society of Architectural Illustration: Rosemary Cottage, Bletchinglye Lane, Rotherfield, TN6 3NN; tel. (1892) 852578; fax (1892) 853578; e-mail info@sai.org.uk; internet www.sai.org.uk; f. 1975; has established a professional body and a recognized qualification for mems of the design professions who specialize in architectural illustration; confers SAI (Member), FSAI (Fellow), Hon. FSAI (Hon. Fellow); 359 mems; Pres. PHILIP CROWE; Admin. ERIC MONK.

Society of Scribes & Illuminators: c/o 6 Queen Sq., London, WC1N 3AT; tel. and fax (1524) 251534; e-mail scribe@calligraphyonline.org; internet www.calligraphyonline.org; f. 1921; re-establishes and perpetuates the tradition of craftsmanship, calligraphy and fine lettering; advanced training scheme; reference library; 500 mems; Hon. Sec. GILLIAN HAZELDINE; publ. *The Scribe* (2 a year).

SPNM–Promoting New Music: St Margaret's House, 4th Floor, 18–20 Southwark St, London, SE1 1TJ; tel. (20) 7407-1640; fax (20) 7403-7652; e-mail spnm@spnm.org.uk; internet www.spnm.org.uk; f. 1943; 1,700 mems; concerts and workshop performances of new music; educational projects and collaborations with venues and ensembles in United Kingdom; professional development and training for emerging composers; Pres. Sir PETER MAXWELL DAVIES; Exec. Dir ABIGAIL POGSON; publ. *New Notes* (12 a year).

HISTORY, GEOGRAPHY AND ARCHAEOLOGY

Ancient Monuments Society: St Ann's Vestry Hall, 2 Church Entry, London, EC4V 5HB; tel. (20) 7236-3934; e-mail office@ancientmonumentssociety.org.uk; internet www.ancientmonumentssociety.org.uk; f. 1924; studies and conserves ancient monuments, historic bldgs of all ages and types, fine old craftsmanship, in partnership with the Friends of Friendless Churches; 2,200 mems; Pres. Earl of Leicester EDWARD COKE; Chair. GILES QUARME; Sec. M. J. SAUNDERS; publ. *Transactions* (1 a year).

Archives and Records Association UK and Ireland: Prioryfield House, 20 Canon St, Taunton, TA1 1SW; tel. (1823) 327030; fax (1823) 271719; e-mail ara@archives.org.uk; internet www.archives.org.uk; f. 1947; 2,000 mems; Chair. KATY GOODRUM; Chief Exec. JOHN CHAMBERS; publs *ARC Magazine* (12 a year), *Journal* (2 a year).

Baptist Historical Society: Baptist House, POB 44, 129 Broadway, Didcot, OX11 8RT; internet www.baptisthistory.org.uk; f. 1908; promotes the study of and records the history of the Baptists; assists researchers, and gives advice to Churches on care and preservation of records; library administered jtly with Angus Library, Regent's Park College, Oxford; 550 mems; Pres. Prof. J. H. Y. BRIGGS; Sec. Rev. S. L. COPSON; publ. *The Baptist Quarterly*.

British Archaeological Association: c/o John McNeill, 18 Stanley Rd., Oxford, OX4 1QZ; internet www.britarch.ac.uk/baa; f. 1843; 700 mems; Hon. Pres. Prof. LINDY GRANT; Hon. Sec. JOHN MCNEILL; publs *Conference Transactions* (1 a year), *Journal* (1 a year).

British Cartographic Society: c/o Royal Geographic Soc., 1 Kensington Gore, London, SW7 2AR; tel. (1823) 665775; fax (1823) 665775; e-mail admin@cartography.org.uk; internet www.cartography.org.uk; f. 1963; 700 mems; promotes the art and science of map-making through cartography, history of cartography, map library curatorship, GIS, technical devts and automation in cartography, design and technology and education and careers in cartography; Pres. MARY SPENCE; Admin. KEN ATHERTON; Hon. Sec. Dr TIM RIDEOUT; publs *Cartographic Journal* (4 a year), *Cartographiti* (newsletter of the map curators' group, 3 a year), *Maplines* (newsletter, 3 a year), *Maps & Surveys* (irregular newsletter of the Historical Military Mapping Group).

British Numismatic Society: c/o Warburg Institute, Woburn Sq., London, WC1H 0AB; tel. (20) 7323-8255; e-mail secretary@britnumsoc.org; internet www.britnumsoc.org; f. 1903; 636 mems; Pres. Dr M. A. S. BLACKBURN; Sec. R. M. KELLEHER; publ. *British Numismatic Journal* (1 a year).

British Records Association: c/o Finsbury Library, 245 St John St, London, EC1V 4NB; tel. (20) 7833-0428; fax (20) 7833-0416; e-mail britrecassoc@hotmail.com; internet www.britishrecordsassociation.org.uk; f. 1932 for the preservation and use of records (archives), and for the coordination of the work of institutions and individuals interested in the subject; 1,000 mems; annual conference, training day; Pres. RT HON. THE MASTER OF THE ROLLS; Hon. Sec. KATHERINE TAYLOR; publ. *Archives* (2 a year).

Cambrian Archaeological Association: c/o Heather James, Braemar, Llangunnor Rd, Carmarthen, SA31 2PB; tel. (1267) 231793; internet www.orchardweb.co.uk/cambrians; f. 1846; 544 mems incl. 132 corporate, 47 corresp. socs; Pres. Rev. J. WYN EVANS; Gen. Sec. HEATHER JAMES; publ. *Archaeologia Cambrensis* (1 a year).

Canterbury and York Society: c/o Borthwick Institute, Univ. of York, York, YO10 5DD; internet www.canterburyandyork.org; f. 1904; 249 mems; Pres. Dr P. ZUTSHI; Sec. Dr C. FONGE; publ. *Medieval Bishops' Registers and other Ecclesiastical Records*.

Catholic Record Society: c/o Hon. Sec., 12 Melbourne Pl., Wolsingham, DL13 3EH; tel. (1388) 527747; internet www.catholic-history.org.uk/crs; f. 1904; publishes documentary material on Catholic history in England and Wales since the Reformation; int. membership; Hon. Sec. Dr LEO GOOCH; publ. *Monographs* (irregular).

Council for British Archaeology: St Mary's House, 66 Bootham, York, YO30 7BZ; tel. (1904) 671417; fax (1904) 671384; e-mail info@britarch.ac.uk; internet www.britarch.ac.uk; f. 1944; promotes the study and safeguarding of Britain's historic environment; provides a forum for archaeological opinion; improves public knowledge of Britain's past; 600 institutional mems, 5,600 individual mems; Pres. K. PRETTY; Dir M. HEYWORTH; publ. *British Archaeology* (6 a year).

Council of British Geography: c/o Royal Geographical Society (with the Institute of British Geographers), 1 Kensington Gore, London, SW7 2AR; tel. (20) 7591-3000; fax (20) 7591-3001; f. 1988; provides a formal org. linking all British geographical socs for the advancement of British geography; coordinates policies of mem. socs, and takes initiatives in educational, academic, research or policy matters; Chair. Prof. M. ROBERTS; Hon. Sec. Prof. P. WOOD.

Ecclesiastical History Society: Dr Sheridan Gilley, Dept of Theology and Religion, Univ. of Durham, Abbey House, Palace Green, Durham, DH1 3RS; e-mail sheridan.gilley@talktalk.net; internet www.history.ac.uk/ehsoc; f. 1961; furthers the study of ecclesiastical history and maintains relations between British ecclesiastical historians and scholars abroad; 960 mems; Pres. Dr SHERIDAN GILLEY; Sec. STELLA FLETCHER; publs *Studies in Church History* (1 a year), *Subsidia* (irregular).

Economic History Society: Dept of Economic and Social History, Univ. of Glasgow, Lilybank House, Bute Gardens, Glasgow, G12 8RT; tel. (141) 330-4662; fax (141) 330-4889; e-mail ehsocsec@arts.gla.ac.uk; internet www.ehs.org.uk; f. 1927; promotes the study of economic and social history; establishes closer relations between students and teachers of economic and social history; holds annual conf.; cooperates with other orgs having kindred purposes; provides fellowships; training course for postgraduate students; 1,300 mems; Pres. Prof. K. J. HUMPHRIES; Hon. Sec. Dr W. P. HOWLETT; publ. *Economic History Review* (4 a year).

Egypt Exploration Society: 3 Doughty Mews, London, WC1N 2PG; tel. (20) 7242-1880; fax (20) 7404-6118; e-mail contact@ees.ac.uk; internet www.ees.ac.uk; f. 1882; excavation in Egypt and publication of work, lectures and study days; 3,000 mems;

library of 20,000 vols, journals and pamphlets; Dir Dr PATRICIA SPENCER; Deputy Dir CHRIS NAUNTON; Librarian and Archivist Dr ALICE STEVENSON; publs *Archaeological Survey* (irregular), *Egyptian Archaeology* (2 a year), *Excavation Memoirs* (irregular), *Graeco-Roman Memoirs* (1 a year), *Journal of Egyptian Archaeology* (1 a year).

English Place-Name Society: School of English Studies, University of Nottingham, Nottingham, NG7 2RD; tel. (115) 951-5919; fax (115) 951-5924; e-mail janet.rudkin@nottingham.ac.uk; internet www.nottingham.ac.uk/english/ins; f. 1923 for the publication of a yearly volume on the place-names of a county, or part of a county; 650 mems; Hon. Dir RICHARD COATES; publ. *Journal* (1 a year).

Friends Historical Society: c/o Friends House, Euston Rd, London, NW1 2BJ; f. 1903; 400 mems; Clerk of Exec. GIL SKIDMORE; publ. *Journal* (1 a year).

Geographical Association: 160 Solly St, Sheffield, S1 4BF; tel. (114) 296-0088; fax (114) 296-7176; e-mail info@geography.org.uk; internet www.geography.org.uk; f. 1893 to further the interests of teachers of geography and the study and teaching of geography generally; 6,000 mems; CEO Prof. DAVID LAMBERT; publs *Geography* (3 a year), *Teaching Geography* (3 a year), *Primary Geographer* (3 a year).

Hakluyt Society: c/o Map Library, British Library, 96 Euston Rd, London, NW1 2DB; tel. (1428) 641850; fax (1428) 641933; e-mail office@hakluyt.com; internet www.hakluyt.com; f. 1846; publishes primary source material of early exploratory voyages, travel and other geographical records; 1,600 mems; Pres. Prof. W. F. RYAN.

Harleian Society: c/o College of Arms, Queen Victoria St, London, EC4V 4BT; tel. (20) 7236-7728; fax (20) 7248-6448; e-mail info@harleian.org.uk; internet harleian.org.uk; f. 1869, inc. 1902, for the transcribing, printing and publishing of the Heraldic Visitations of Counties, Parish Registers or any MSS relating to genealogy, family history and heraldry; 300 subscribers; Chair. T. WOODCOCK; Hon. Sec. and Treas. T. H. S. DUKE (Chester Herald of Arms).

Heraldry Society: POB 772, Guildford, Surrey, GU3 3ZX; tel. (1483) 237373; internet www.theheraldrysociety.com; f. 1947 to further the study of heraldry, armory, chivalry, genealogy and kindred subjects; 1,000 mems; Patron THE DUKE OF NORFOLK; publs *The Coat of Arms* (4 a year), *The Heraldry Gazette* (4 a year).

Historic Buildings and Monuments Commission for England (English Heritage): POB 569, Swindon, SN2 2YP; tel. (870) 333-1181; fax (1793) 414-926; e-mail customers@english-heritage.org.uk; internet www.english-heritage.org.uk; f. 1983; executive non-departmental public body sponsored by the Department for Culture, Media and Sport; responsible for all aspects of protecting and promoting historic buildings and landscapes throughout England; funded by the UK Govt and from revenue earned from its historic properties; Chair. Sir NEIL COSSONS; publs *Buildings at Risk Register* (1 a year), *Conservation Bulletin* (4 a year), *Register of Parks and Gardens*.

Attached Organizations:

Centre for Archaeology: Fort Cumberland, Fort Cumberland Rd, Eastney, Portsmouth, PO4 9LD; tel. (23) 9285-6700; e-mail cfa@english-heritage.org.uk.

National Monuments Record: Kemble Dr., Swindon, SN2 2GZ; tel. (1793) 414600; fax (1793) 414606; e-mail nmrinfo@english-heritage.org.uk; internet www.english-heritage.org.uk/nmr; over 1m. photographs, plans, drawings, reports, records and publs covering England's archaeology, architecture, social and local history; library of 60,000 vols, 400 current journals.

Historical Association: 59A Kennington Park Rd, London, SE11 4JH; tel. (20) 7735-3901; fax (20) 7582-4989; e-mail enquiry@history.org.uk; internet www.history.org.uk; f. 1906; aims to advance the study and teaching of history at all levels, to increase public interest in all aspects of the subject and to develop it as an essential element in the education of all; colln of history textbooks; 60 brs nationally; 6,500 mems; Pres. ANNE CURRY; Chief Exec. REBECCA SULLIVAN; publs *The Historian* (4 a year), *History* (4 a year), *Primary History* (3 a year), *Teaching History* (4 a year).

Honourable Society of Cymmrodorion: 30 Eastcastle St, London, W1W 8DJ; tel. (20) 7631-0502; e-mail aelodau1751we@yahoo.co.uk; internet www.cymmrodorion1751.org.uk; f. 1751; promotes the practice and devt of literature, the arts and sciences insofar as they are of spec. interest to Wales, the Welsh people and those interested in Wales; Royal Charter 1951; 900 mems; Patron HRH THE PRINCE OF WALES; Pres. Prof. PRYS MORGAN; Hon. Sec. JON PERRY; publs *Dictionary of Welsh Biography*, *Transactions* (1 a year).

Huguenot Society of Great Britain and Ireland: The Huguenot Library, UCL, Gower St, London, WC1E 6BT; tel. (20) 6795-199; e-mail library@huguenotsociety.org.uk; internet www.huguenotsociety.org.uk; f. 1885; 1,385 mems (9 hon. fellows, 1,376 ordinary fellows); promotes the publication and exchange of knowledge about the Huguenots in the UK and Ireland; aims to form a bond of fellowship among those who, whether or not of Huguenot descent, respect and admire the Huguenots and seek to perpetuate their memory; library of 5,500 vols, colln of MSS and rare books, genealogical material; Pres. MICHAEL COURAGE; Hon. Sec. ANNE NUGENT; Librarian LUCY GWYNN; publs *New Series* (irregular), *Proceedings* (1 a year), *Quarto Series* (irregular).

Institute of Heraldic and Genealogical Studies: 79–82 Northgate, Canterbury, Kent, CT1 1BA; tel. (1227) 768664; fax (1227) 765617; e-mail admin@ihgs.ac.uk; internet www.ihgs.ac.uk; f. 1961; provides courses in family history and related subjects using traditional classroom methods and a correspondence course available online or by post, leading to accredited qualifications; spec. collns; 250 mems; library of 35,000 vols, 20,000 case studies; Pres. Rt Hon. THE EARL OF LYTTON; Prin. C. R. HUMPHERY-SMITH; Reg. MICHELLE WEBBER; publs *Atlas and Index of Parishes*, *Family History* (4 a year), *Syllabus of Study*, *Teacher's Aids*.

Jewish Historical Society of England: 33 Seymour Place, London, W1H 5AP; tel. (20) 7723-5852; fax (20) 7723-5852; e-mail info@jhse.org; internet www.jhse.org; f. 1893; Jewish Studies Library, University College, London; 800 mems; Administrator DAVID FREEMAN; Hon. Sec. Dr GERRY BLACK; publ. *Transactions* (1 a year).

London and Middlesex Archaeological Society: c/o Museum of London, London Wall, London, EC2Y 5HN; tel. (20) 7814-5734; internet www.lamas.org.uk; f. 1855; promotes and publishes archaeological and historical research on the London area; 644 mems; Pres. Prof. MARTIN BIDDLE; Hon. Sec. JACKIE KEILY; publ. *Transactions* (1 a year).

London Record Society: POB 691, Exeter, EX1 9PH; e-mail londonrecordsoc@btinternet.com; internet www.londonrecordsociety.org.uk; f. 1964; publishes original sources for the history of London and encourages public interest in archives relating to London; 292 mems; Chair. Prof. CAROLINE BARRON; Hon. Membership Sec. Dr STEPHANIE HOVLAND; Hon. Sec. Dr HELEN BRADLEY; Hon. Treas. Dr DAVID LEWIS.

London Topographical Society: 10 Tremaine Rd, London, SE20 7TZ; tel. (20) 8659-2405; e-mail m.galinou@virgin.net; internet www.topsoc.org; f. 1880; 1,100 mems; publishes material to assist in the study and appreciation of London's history, growth and topography, incl. reproductions of historic maps and views of London; Patron HRH THE DUKE OF EDINBURGH; Hon. Sec. MIREILLE GALINOU; publs *London Topographical Record* (every 5 years), maps, views and books.

Manchester Geographical Society: Meadowbank, Ringley Rd, Radcliffe, Manchester, M26 1FW; tel. (161) 834-2965; e-mail secretary@mangeogsoc.org.uk; internet www.mangeogsoc.org.uk; f. 1884; promotes the study of all brs of geographical science; lecture programme, funding research, publishing; 100 mems; library of 4,500 vols (now on permanent loan to the Univ. of Manchester); Hon. Sec. Dr PAUL HINDLE; publ. *North West Geography* (electronic journal, 2 a year).

Monumental Brass Society: c/o H. M. Stuchfield, Lowe Hill House, Stratford St Mary, CO7 6JX; e-mail martin.stuchfield@intercitygroup.co.uk; internet www.mbs-brasses.co.uk; f. 1887 to promote the study of and interest in, better preservation of monumental brasses, and to compile and publish a full and accurate list of all extant and lost brasses, English and foreign; Pres. Rev. Canon D. G. MEARA; Hon. Sec. H. M. STUCHFIELD; publs *Bulletin* (3 a year), *Portfolio* (irregular), *Transactions* (1 a year).

Palestine Exploration Fund: 2 Hinde Mews, Marylebone Lane, London, W1U 2AA; tel. (20) 7935-5379; fax (20) 7486-7438; e-mail execsec@pef.org.uk; internet www.pef.org.uk; f. 1865; 900 subscribers; promotes research into the archaeology and history, manners, customs and culture, topography, geology and natural sciences of biblical Palestine and the Levant (modern-day Syria, Lebanon, Jordan and Israel); specialist library and archaeological collns (restricted to mems); library of 5,000 vols; Exec. and Curator FELICITY COBBING; Consultant Financial Administrator IVONA LLOYD-JONES; Librarian ANDREA ZERBINI; publ. *Palestine Exploration Quarterly* (3 a year).

Prehistoric Society: c/o Institute of Archaeology, University College London, 31–34 Gordon Sq., London, WC1H 0PY; internet www.ucl.ac.uk/prehistoric; f. 1908; furthers prehistoric archaeology; 2,000 mems; Pres. Prof. GRAEME BARKER; Hon. Sec. Dr ALEX GIBSON; publs *Past* (3 a year), *Proceedings* (1 a year).

Regional Studies Association: POB 2058, Seaford, BN25 4QU; tel. (1323) 899698; fax (1323) 899798; e-mail info@rsa-ls.ac.uk; internet www.regional-studies-assoc.ac.uk; f. 1965; an interdisciplinary group exclusively concerned with regional issues at sub-nat. level; provides a forum for the exchange of ideas and information on regional problems, publishes the results of regional research, and stimulates studies and research in regional planning and related fields; holds meetings, confs and seminars; organizes study groups; 6 branches; 7 int. sections and present in more than 40 countries; 850 individual, 200 corporate mems, including government depts, ministries, local authorities, educational institutions, etc.; Chair. DAVID BAILEY;

Chief Exec. SALLY HARDY; Hon. Sec. GILLIAN BRISTOW; publs *Regional Insights* (1 a year), *Regional Studies* (10 a year), *Regions* (4 a year), *Special Economic Analysis* (4 a year).

Royal Geographical Society (with the Institute of British Geographers): 1 Kensington Gore, London, SW7 2AR; tel. (20) 7591-3000; fax (20) 7591-3001; e-mail info@rgs.org; internet www.rgs.org; f. 1830; furtherance of geographical research, teaching and expeditions; 14,000 mems; library of 150,000 books, 1m. maps and charts, 4,500 atlases, 500,000 mid-19th-century to contemporary pictures and photographs; Pres. MICHAEL PALIN; Dir and Sec. Dr RITA GARDNER; publs *Area* (4 a year), *Geographical* (12 a year), *Geographical Journal* (4 a year), *Transactions* (4 a year).

Royal Historical Society: Univ. College London, Gower St, London, WC1E 6BT; tel. (20) 7387-7532; fax (20) 7387-7532; e-mail royalhistsoc@ucl.ac.uk; internet www.royalhistoricalsociety.org; f. 1868; 3,000 mems; library of 3,000 vols; Pres. Prof. COLIN D. H. JONES; Exec. Sec. SUSAN CARR; publs *Transactions* (1 a year), *Camden* (5th series, 2 vols a year).

Royal Numismatic Society: c/o Dept of Coins and Medals, British Museum, London, WC1B 3DG; tel. (20) 7323-8272; fax (20) 7323-8171; e-mail info@numismatics.org.uk; internet www.numismatics.org.uk; f. 1836; 1,000 mems; Pres. J. CRIBB; Secs V. S. CURTIS, S. MOORHEAD; publ. *Numismatic Chronicle* (1 a year).

Royal Philatelic Society London: 41 Devonshire Pl., London, W1G 6JY; tel. (20) 7486-1044; fax (20) 7486-0803; e-mail secretary@rpsl.org.uk; internet www.rpsl.org.uk; f. 1869; 1,600 mems; Pres. ALAN N. MOORCROFT; Sec. CHRISTINE A. EARLE; publ. *The London Philatelist* (10 a year).

Royal Scottish Geographical Society: Lord John Murray House, 15–19 North Port, Blackfriars, Perth, PH1 5LU; tel. (1738) 455-050; e-mail enquiries@rsgs.org; internet www.rsgs.org; f. 1884 to further the science of geography in all its branches; symposia, illustrated talks and schools conferences; provides research grants and support to scientific expeditions; library of 20,000 vols, 30,000 maps, 200 current periodicals, special collection of early maps of Scotland; 2,200 mems; Pres. THE EARL OF LINDSAY; Chief Exec. MIKE ROBINSON; publ. *The Scottish Geographical Journal* (4 a year).

Scottish History Society: Dept of Scottish History, Univ. of St Andrews, St Katharine's Lodge, The Scores, St Andrews, KY16 9AL; e-mail katie.stevenson@st-andrews.ac.uk; internet www.scottishhistorysociety.org; f. 1886 for the printing of unpublished documents illustrating the history of Scotland; 800 mems; Pres. Dr IAIN HUTCHISON; Hon. Sec. Dr KATIE STEVENSON.

Society for Army Historical Research: c/o National Army Museum, Royal Hospital Rd, London, SW3 4HT; internet www.sahr.co.uk; f. 1921; army and regimental history; military antiquities and pictures, uniforms, badges and medals, arms and equipment, customs and traditions and the history of land warfare in general; 1,000 mems; Pres. Field Marshal Sir JOHN CHAPPLE; Hon. Sec. GEORGE EVELYN; publ. *Journal* (4 a year).

Society for Medieval Archaeology: c/o Dept of Archaeology, Univ. of Sheffield, Northgate House, W St, Sheffield, S1 4ET; tel. (114) 222-2920; fax (114) 272-2563; e-mail d.m.hadley@sheffield.ac.uk; internet www.medievalarchaeology.org; f. 1957; studies archaeology of the post-Roman period; organizes regular confs; offers funds for research; 1,500 mems; library of 54 vols; Pres. LESLIE WEBSTER; Hon. Sec. DAWN HADLEY; Hon. Treas. Prof. STEPHEN RIPPON; Hon. Editor Dr SALLY FOSTER; publs *Medieval Archaeology* (1 a year), *Monograph Series* (irregular).

Society for Nautical Research: c/o 6 Ashmeadow Rd, Arnside, via Carnforth, LA5 0AE; tel. (1524) 761616; e-mail honsecretary.snr@btinternet.com; internet www.snr.org.uk; f. 1910; annual public lecture; 1,500 mems; Pres. HRH THE DUKE OF YORK; Chair. Prof. R. HARDING; Sec. P. D. WINTERBOTTOM; publ. *The Mariners' Mirror* (4 a year).

Society for Post-Medieval Archaeology Ltd: c/o David Cranstone, 267 Kells Lane, Low Fell, Gateshead NE9 5HU; tel. (191) 482-1037; fax (191) 482-2343; e-mail cranconsult@btinternet.com; internet www.spma.org.uk; f. 1967; 400 mems; Pres. Dr DAVID GAIMSTER; Sec. DAVID CRANSTONE; publ. *Post-Medieval Archaeology* (2 a year).

Society for Renaissance Studies: c/o Michelle O'Malley, Centre for Research in the History of Art, University of Sussex, Falmer, Brighton, BN1 9RQ; e-mail m.o-malley@sussex.ac.uk; internet www.sas.ac.uk/srs/default.htm; f. 1967 to advance scholarship on the Renaissance, including literature, philosophy, science, art and music; 550 mems; Hon. Chair. Dr DAVID CHAMBERS; Hon. Sec. Dr MICHELLE O'MALLEY; publs *Bulletin* (2 a year), *Renaissance Studies* (4 a year).

Society of Antiquaries of London: Burlington House, Piccadilly, London, W1J 0BE; tel. (20) 7479-7080; fax (20) 7287-6967; e-mail admin@sal.org.uk; internet www.sal.org.uk; f. 1707; 2,800 Fellows; library: see Libraries and Archives; Pres. Prof. MAURICE HOWARD; Gen. Sec. and CEO Dr DAVID GAIMSTER; publs *Archaeologia* (1 a year), *The Antiquaries Journal* (1 a year).

Society of Antiquaries of Scotland: c/o National Museums Scotland, Chambers St, Edinburgh, EH1 1JF; tel. (131) 247-4133; fax (131) 247-4163; e-mail info@socantscot.org; internet www.socantscot.org; f. 1780; study of Scottish antiquities and history, particularly by archaeological research; grants and awards available for research relating to Scotland; 3,000 mems; Pres. Dr BARBARA CRAWFORD; Dir Dr SIMON GILMOUR; publs *Proceedings of the Society of Antiquaries of Scotland* (1 a year), *Scottish Archaeological Internet Reports* (online).

Society of Genealogists: 14 Charterhouse Bldgs, Goswell Rd, London, EC1M 7BA; tel. (20) 7251-8799; fax (20) 7250-1800; e-mail library@sog.org.uk; internet www.sog.org.uk; f. 1911; 12,000 mems; promotes the study, science and knowledge of genealogy and family history, through education and library programmes; library of 127,000 vols and other items, incl. video cassettes, microfiches and CDs; Pres. PATRIC DICKINSON; Chief Exec. JUNE PERRIN; publ. *Genealogists' Magazine* (4 a year).

Ulster Archaeological Society: c/o School of Geography and Palaeoecology, Queens Univ., 42 Fitzwilliam St, Belfast, BT9 6AX; e-mail arcpal@qub.ac.uk; internet www.uas.society.qub.ac.uk; f. 1853; promotes education in archaeology and history of Ulster; organizes public lectures and field trips; has survey group; 300 mems; Pres. BARRIE HARTWELL; Vice-Pres. TOM HAYES; Vice-Pres. Dr HARRY WELSH; Vice-Pres. Dr CHRIS LYNN; Hon. Sec. KEN PULLIN; Hon. Treas. JOHN MOORE; publ. *Ulster Journal of Archaeology* (1 a year).

United Reformed Church History Society: Westminster College, Madingley Rd, Cambridge, CB3 0AA; tel. (1223) 741300; e-mail hw374@cam.ac.uk; f. 1972 to incorporate the Congregational Historical Soc. (f. 1899), the Presbyterian Historical Soc. of England (f. 1913) and the Churches of Christ Historical Soc. (f. 1981); 250 mems; library of 5,000 vols; Hon. Sec. Rev. ELIZABETH J. BROWN; publ. *Journal* (2 a year).

Wesley Historical Society: c/o Dr John A. Hargreaves, 7 Haugh Shaw Rd, Halifax, HX1 3AH; tel. (1422) 250780; e-mail johnahargreaves@blueyonder.co.uk; internet www.wesleyhistoricalsociety.org.uk; f. 1893 to promote the study of the history and literature of all brs. of Methodism; annual lecture, supporting programme; residential conf. every 3 years; access to network of regional historical socs; 600 mems; library: library at Westminster Institute of Education, Oxford Brookes Univ., Harcourt Hill Campus, Oxford, OX2 9AT; Pres. Rev. Dr JOHN A. NEWTON; Gen. Sec. Dr JOHN A. HARGREAVES; publ. *Proceedings* (3 a year).

LANGUAGE AND LITERATURE

Academi Gymreig, Yr/Welsh Academy, The: Mount Stuart House, 3rd Floor, Mount Stuart Sq., Cardiff, CF10 5FQ; tel. (29) 2047-2266; fax (29) 2049-2930; e-mail post@literaturewales.org; internet www.literaturewales.org; f. 1959; promotes interests of writers and literatures of Wales; 730 mems (250 in Welsh-language section, 480 in English-language section); Pres. (English language) DANNIE ABSE; Pres. (Welsh language) BOBI JONES; Co-Chairs Dr HARRI PRITCHARD-JONES, Dr JOHN PIKOULIS; Chief Exec. PETER FINCH; publs *Listings Magazine* (4 a year), *Taliesin* (3 a year).

Alliance Française: 1 Dorset Sq., London, NW1 6PU; tel. (20) 7723-6439; fax (20) 7224-9512; e-mail info@alliancefrancaise.org.uk; internet www.alliancefrancaise.org.uk; offers courses and exams in French language and culture and promotes cultural exchange with France; attached offices in Bath, Belfast, Bristol, Cambridge, Exeter, Glasgow, Jersey, Loughborough, Manchester, Milton Keynes, Oxford, Totnes, York; Dir CHRYSTEL HUG.

Alliance of Literary Societies: 59 Bryony Rd, Birmingham, B29 4BY; tel. (121) 475-1805; e-mail l.j.curry@bham.ac.uk; internet www.allianceofliterarysocieties.org.uk; f. 1973; provides a voice for literary and authors' societies in defence of sites and legacies of literary importance; annual general meeting; information resource for literary socs in the UK; 125 mem. socs; Chair. LINDA CURRY; Hon. Sec. ANITA FERNANDEZ-YOUNG; Hon. Treas. and Membership Sec. JULIE SHORLAND; publ. *ALSo* (1 a year).

Association for Language Learning: 150 Railway Terrace, Rugby, CV21 3HN; tel. (1788) 546443; fax (1788) 544149; e-mail langlearn@all-languages.org.uk; internet www.all-languages.org.uk; f. 1990; offers help, in-service training and support to language teachers; promotes the learning and use of foreign languages; 3,500 mems; Dir LINDA PARKER; publs *Language Learning Journal*, *Rusistika* (1 a year), *Tuttitalia*, *Vida Hispánica*, *Deutsch: Lehren und Lernen*, *Francophonie* (all 2 a year), *Language World* (4 a year).

Association of British Science Writers: Wellcome Wolfson Bldg, 165 Queen's Gate, London, SW7 5HD; e-mail absw@absw.org.uk; internet www.absw.org.uk; f. 1947; study trips, briefings, workshops, lunches and social events; 600 mems; Chair. Dr NATASHA LODER; Admin. ANGELA NICOLAIDES; publ. *The Science Reporter* (4 a year and online).

British Association for Applied Linguistics: c/o Dovetail Management Consultancy,

POB 6688, London, SE15 3WB; tel. (20) 7639-0090; fax (20) 7635-6014; e-mail admin@baal.org.uk; internet www.baal.org.uk; f. 1967; promotes study of language in use; fosters interdisciplinary collaboration, provides common forum for those engaged in theoretical study of language and those interested in its practical use; 750 individual mems, 30 mem. publishers and univ. depts; Chair. GUY COOK; Sec. CAROLINE COFFIN; publs *Applied Linguistics* (4 a year, in asscn with American Asscn for Applied Linguistics), *British Studies in Applied Linguistics* (Edited Proceedings of Annual Meetings).

British Association of Academic Phoneticians: Phonetics Laboratory, Dept of English Language, Univ. of Glasgow, G12 8QQ; tel. (141) 330-6340; fax (141) 330-3531; e-mail m.macmahon@englang.arts.gla.ac.uk; internet www.phon.ucl.ac.uk/home/baap; f. 1984; 150 mems; Sec. and Archivist Prof. M. K. C. MACMAHON.

Brontë Society: The Brontë Parsonage Museum, Haworth, Keighley, W Yorks., BD22 8DR; tel. (1535) 642323; fax (1535) 647131; e-mail bronte@bronte.org.uk; internet www.bronte.org.uk; f. 1893, inc. 1902, to collect and act as guardian of Brontë letters, MSS, and personal belongings that are housed in the Brontë Parsonage Museum, fmr home of the Brontës and now in the care of the Soc.; 3,000 mems; Library and Information Officer Dr SARAH LAYCOCK; publ. *Brontë Studies* (3 a year).

Canadian Linguistic Association/Association Canadienne de Linguistique: Département d'Études Françaises, University of Western Ontario, London, N6A 3K7; fax (519) 661-2111; internet www.chass.utoronto.ca/~cla-acl; f. 1954; advances study of linguistics and languages in Canada; 220 mems; Pres. FRANCE MARTINEAU; Sec. ILLEANA PAUL; Treas. CARRIE DYCK; publ. *The Canadian Journal of Linguistics/La Revue Canadienne de Linguistique* (4 a year).

Charles Lamb Society: BM Elia, London, WC1N 3XX; f. 1935; to promote the study of the lives and works of Charles Lamb and his circle and to form a collection of Eliana; 300 mems; library: library housed in the Guildhall Library, Corporation of London; Pres. Prof. J. R. WATSON; Chair. NICHOLAS POWELL; publ. *The Charles Lamb Bulletin* (4 a year).

Chartered Institute of Linguists: Saxon House, 48 Southwark St, London, SE1 1UN; tel. (20) 7940-3100; fax (20) 7940-3101; e-mail info@iol.org.uk; internet www.iol.org.uk; f. 1910; promotes proficiency in modern languages worldwide amongst professional linguists, including translators, interpreters and educationalists, as well as those in the public and private sectors for whom languages are an important skill; helps to ensure equal access for all to the public services (law, health, local govt) by providing interpreting qualifications in most of the languages spoken in the United Kingdom and running the Nat. Register of Public Service Interpreters (NRPSI Ltd); a wholly owned subsidiary, IoL Language Services Ltd, offers translation, production and recruitment services, validation of language qualifications and assessments as well as training courses; IoL Educational Trust, an associated charity, is an accredited awarding body offering high-level examinations; 6,500 mems; library of 6,000 vols; Chief Exec. JOHN HAMMOND; publ. *The Linguist* (6 a year).

Classical Association: c/o Claire Daveport, Senate House, Malet St, London, WC1E 7HU; tel. (20) 7862-8706; fax (20) 7255-2297; e-mail office@classicalassociation.org; internet www.classicalassociation.org; f. 1903; 3,500 mems; Jt Secs Prof. DOUGLAS CAIRNS, BARBARA FINNEY; publs *CA News* (2 a year), *Classical Quarterly* (2 a year), *Classical Review* (2 a year), *Greece and Rome* (2 a year).

Dickens Fellowship: Dickens House, 48 Doughty St, London, WC1N 2LF; tel. (20) 7405-2127; fax (20) 7831-5175; internet www.dickens.fellowship.btinternet.co.uk; f. 1902 to knit together in a common bond of friendship lovers of Charles Dickens, and to assist in the preservation and purchase of buildings and objects associated with Dickens or mentioned in his works; 7,000 mems; Pres. HENRY DICKENS HAWKSLEY; Hon. Gen. Secs THELMA GROVE, Dr TONY WILLIAMS; publs *The Dickensian* (3 a year), *Mr Dick's Kite* (3 a year).

Early English Text Society: Lady Margaret Hall, Oxford, OX2 6QA; internet www.eets.org.uk; f. 1864; texts published annually; 900 mems; Hon. Dir Prof. ANNE HUDSON; Exec. Sec. Prof. VINCENT A. GILLESPIE.

English Association: Univ. of Leicester, Leicester, LE1 7RH; tel. (116) 229-7622; fax (116) 229-7623; e-mail engassoc@le.ac.uk; internet www.le.ac.uk/engassoc; f. 1906; promotes knowledge and appreciation of the English language and its literature, through confs, lectures and publs; 1,500 mems; Pres. Prof. PETER KITSON; Chair. Prof. MAUREEN MORAN; Chief Exec. HELEN LUCAS; publs *English* (4 a year), *English 4–11* (3 a year), *Essays and Studies*, *The Use of English* (3 a year), *The Year's Work in Critical and Cultural Theory*, *The Year's Work in English Studies*.

English Centre of International PEN: 6–8 Amwell St, London, EC1R 1UQ; tel. (20) 7713-0023; fax (20) 7837-7838; e-mail enquiries@englishpen.org; internet www.englishpen.org; f. 1921; 990 mems; Pres. Dr ALISTAIR NIVEN; Dir SUSANNA NICKLIN.

English Speaking Board: 26A Princes St, Southport, Merseyside, PR8 1EQ; tel. (1704) 501730; fax (1704) 539637; e-mail admin@esbuk.org; internet www.esbuk.org; f. 1953; promotes and encourages all aspects of oral communication in English; brings together people from educational, professional and industrial spheres who are concerned with oral education as a means of communication; individual and corporate mems in 34 countries; arranges courses and examinations in spoken English at all levels, from primary to higher education; certificates and diplomas awarded to teachers, professional speakers; assessments for individuals studying English as an acquired language; 450 mems; Hon. Pres. JOCELYN BELL; Chair. RICHARD ELLIS (acting); publ. *Speaking English* (2 a year).

Francis Bacon Society Inc.: c/o G. N. Salway, Flat 1, Lee House, 75A Effra Rd, London, SW19 8PS; tel. (20) 8542-4689; internet www.baconsocietyinc.org; f. 1886; registered charity; studies the works and life of Francis Bacon, and investigates evidence suggesting Bacon's authorship of plays attributed to Shakespeare; library; Pres. PETER A. WELSFORD; Sec. GERALD N. SALWAY; publ. *Baconiana*.

Goethe-Institut: 50 Princes Gate, Exhibition Rd, London, SW7 2PH; tel. (20) 7596-4000; fax (20) 7594-0240; e-mail mail@london.goethe.org; internet www.goethe.de/london; offers courses and exams in German language and culture and promotes cultural exchange with Germany; attached centres in Glasgow and Manchester; library of 17,000 vols; Dir Dr ROLAND GOLL.

Institute of Translation and Interpreting: Fortuna House, South Fifth St, Milton Keynes, MK9 2PQ; tel. (1908) 325250; fax (1908) 325259; e-mail info@iti.org.uk; internet www.iti.org.uk; f. 1986; promotes high standards in translation and interpreting; provides information on these services to govt, industry, the media and the gen. public; offers guidance to those entering the profession and advice to those who offer language services and their customers; 3,000 mems; Gen. Sec. ALAN WHEATLEY; publ. *ITI Bulletin* (6 a year).

Instituto Cervantes: 102 Eaton Sq., London, SW1W 9AN; tel. (20) 7235-0353; fax (20) 7235-0329; e-mail cenlon@cervantes.es; internet londres.cervantes.es; f. 1991; offers courses and exams in Spanish language and culture and promotes cultural exchange with Spain and Spanish-speaking Latin and Central America; attached centre in Manchester; library of 20,000 vols; Dir JUAN PEDRO APARICIO.

Joseph Conrad Society: c/o POSK, 238–246 King St, London, W6 0RF; e-mail theconradian@aol.com; internet www.josephconradsociety.org; f. 1973; provides a forum and resource for scholars of Conrad's work; 200 mems; library of 800 vols; Hon. Sec. HUGH EPSTEIN; publ. *The Conradian* (2 a year).

Kipling Society: 6 Clifton Rd, London, W9 1SS; tel. (20) 7286-0194; fax (20) 7286-0194; e-mail jmkeskar@btinternet.com; internet www.kipling.org.uk; f. 1927; honours and extends the influence of Rudyard Kipling; 5 meetings a year with guest speaker in London; Annual Luncheon in May also with guest speaker; 500 mems; Pres. Sir JOHN CHAPPLE; Hon. Sec. JANE KESKAR; publ. *The Kipling Journal* (4 a year).

Linguistics Association of Great Britain: c/o Dr Andrew Hippisley, School of Electronics and Physical Sciences, University of Surrey, Guildford, Surrey, GU2 7XH; e-mail a.hippisley@surrey.ac.uk; internet www.lagb.org; f. 1959 to promote the study of linguistics and provide a forum for discussion and co-operation in the field; annual general meeting; 600 mems; Pres. Prof. APRIL MCMAHON; Hon. Sec. Dr AD NEELEMAN; publ. *Journal of Linguistics* (2 a year).

Malone Society:; tel. (20) 7862-8679; e-mail canor.wyer@sas.ac.uk; internet ies.sas.ac.uk/malone; f. 1906; makes accessible materials for the study of English Renaissance drama up to 1642; publishes edns of 16th- and 17th-century plays from MSS, photographic facsimile edns of printed plays of the period, and edns of original documents relating to Renaissance theatre and drama; 170 vols published; back issues available; 670 mems; Chair. LEAH SCRAGG; Exec. Sec. Prof. KATHARINE CRAIK.

Philological Society: School of Oriental and African Studies, Univ. of London, Thornhaugh St, Russell Sq., London, WC1H 0XG; fax (20) 7898-4399; e-mail secretary@philsoc.org.uk; internet www.philsoc.org.uk; f. 1842, inc. 1879; investigates and promotes the study and knowledge of the structure, affinities, and history of languages; 832 mems; Pres. Prof. SYLVIA ADAMSON; Sec Dr MARTIN ORWIN; publ. *Transactions* (3 a year).

Poetry Society: 22 Betterton St, London, WC2H 9BX; tel. (20) 7240-9880; fax (20) 7240-4818; e-mail info@poetrysociety.org.uk; internet www.poetrysociety.org.uk; f. 1909; promotes study, appreciation and enjoyment of poetry; organises poetry reading, educational activities and the Nat. Poetry Competition; awards the Foyle Young Poets of Year prize; 4,000 mems; Dir JUDITH PALMER; publs *Poetry News* (4 a year), *Poetry Review* (4 a year).

Royal Society of Literature of the United Kingdom: Somerset House, Strand, London, WC2R 1LA; tel. (20) 7845-4676; fax (20) 7845-4679; e-mail info@rslit.org; internet www.rslit.org; f. 1820; lectures and literary discussions; awards 3 prizes annually; 1,350 mems; Pres. COLIN THUBRON; Chair. ANNE CHISHOLM; Sec. MAGGIE FERGUSSON.

Society for the Promotion of Hellenic Studies: Senate House, Malet St, London, WC1E 7HU; tel. (20) 7862-8730; fax (20) 7862-8731; e-mail hellenic@sas.ac.uk; f. 1879; 3,000 mems; library: see entry for Joint Library of the Hellenic and Roman Societies; Pres. Prof. MALCOLM SCHOFIELD; Hon. Sec. Dr PANTELIS MICHELAKIS; Exec. Sec. RICHELLA DOYLE; publs *Journal of Hellenic Studies* (1 a year), *Archaeological Reports* (in conjunction with the British School at Athens, 1 a year).

Society for the Promotion of Roman Studies: Senate House, Malet St, London, WC1E 7HU; tel. (20) 7862-8727; fax (20) 7862-8728; e-mail office@romansociety.org; internet www.romansociety.org; f. 1910; 3,000 mems; library: see entry for Library of the Hellenic and Roman Societies; Pres. Dr ANDREW BURNETT; Hon. Sec. SAM MOORHEAD; Sec. Dr FIONA HAARER; Hon. Treas. Dr PHILIP KAY; publs *Britannia* (1 a year), *Journal of Roman Studies* (1 a year).

Society for the Study of Medieval Languages and Literature: c/o Dr Corinne Saunders, Department of English Studies, University of Durham, Hallgarth House, 77 Hallgarth St, Durham, DH1 3AY; internet www.mod-langs.ox.ac.uk/ssmll; f. 1932; Editors Dr E. KENNEDY, Prof. N. PALMER, Dr C. SAUNDERS; publ. *Medium Ævum* (2 a year).

Society of Authors: 84 Drayton Gardens, London, SW10 9SB; tel. (20) 7373-6642; fax (20) 7373-5768; e-mail info@societyofauthors.org; internet www.societyofauthors.org; f. 1884; promotes and protects the rights of authors; 9,000 mems; Gen. Sec. NICOLA SOLOMON; publ. *The Author* (4 a year).

Wells, H. G., Society: c/o Paul Allen, 1 Nackington Rd, Canterbury, Kent, CT1 3NU; internet hgwellsusa.50megs.com; f. 1960; promotes an interest in and appreciation of the life, work and thought of H. G. Wells; organizes annual conf. (September); 200 mems; library of 300 vols (H. G. Wells Colln, Library, London Metropolitan Univ.–North London campus); Treas. PAUL ALLEN; publ. *The Wellsian* (1 a year).

MEDICINE

Academy of Medical Sciences: 10 Carlton House Terrace, London, SW1Y 5AH; tel. (20) 7969-5288; fax (20) 7969-5298; e-mail info@acmedsci.ac.uk; internet www.acmedsci.ac.uk; f. 1998; 943 fellows; Pres. Sir JOHN BELL; Exec. Dir HELEN MUNN.

Anatomical Society of Great Britain and Ireland: Dept of Anatomy and Human Sciences, King's College (Guy's Campus), Room HB4.1N, Hodgkin Bldg, London, SE1 1UL; tel. (20) 7848-8234; fax (20) 7848-8234; internet www.anatsoc.org.uk; f. 1887; promotes, develops and advances anatomical and related sciences; research into the anatomical and related sciences; publishes research relevant to anatomical sciences; promotes and advances education in the anatomical sciences; 700 mems; Exec. Admin. MARY-ANNE PIGGOTT; Hon. Sec. Prof. D. CERI DAVIES; publs *Ageing Cell* (12 a year), *Journal of Anatomy* (12 a year).

Apothecaries of London, Worshipful Society of: Apothecaries' Hall, Black Friars Lane, London, EC4V 6EJ; tel. (20) 7236-1180; fax (20) 7329-3177; e-mail examoffice@apothecaries.org; internet www.apothecaries.org; f. 1617 by King James I; grants a registrable medical qualification (LMSSA Lond.), also the postgraduate diplomas in Medical Jurisprudence (DMJ), in Genitourinary Medicine (DipGUM), HIV Medicine (DipHIV), the History of Medicine (DHMSA), Philosophy of Medicine (DPMSA), Musculo Skeletal Medicine (DMSM), Medical Care of Catastrophes (DMCC), Clinical Pharmacology (DCPSA), Forensic Medical Sciences (DFMS), Forensic Human Identification (DFHID), Mastership in Medical Jurisprudence (MMJ); 1,600 mems; Master Sir WILLIAM SHAND; Clerk ANDREW WALLINGTON-SMITH; Registrar KIM EDMUNDS.

Association for the Study of Medical Education: 12 Queen St, Edinburgh, EH2 1JE; tel. (131) 225-9111; fax (131) 225-9444; e-mail info@asme.org.uk; internet www.asme.org.uk; f. 1957 to exchange information and promote research into medical education; 1,200 individual mems, 85 corporate mems; Pres. Prof. Sir KENNETH CALMAN; Chair Prof. GRAHAM BUCKLEY; Chief Exec. Prof. FRANK SMITH; publs *Bulletin* (6 a year), *Medical Education* (12 a year), *The Clinical Teacher* (2 a year).

Association of Anaesthetists of Great Britain and Ireland: 21 Portland Pl., London, W1B 1PY; tel. (20) 7631-8801; e-mail info@aagbi.org; internet www.aagbi.org; f. 1932; promotes devt and study of anaesthetics and their administration and maintains the high standard of this branch of medicine; 10,000 mems; Pres. Dr BIRKS GEMMELL; Hon. Sec. Dr ROBERT BUCKLAND; publs *Anaesthesia* (12 a year), *Anaesthesia News* (12 a year).

Association of British Neurologists: Ormand House (4th Floor), 27 Boswell St, London, WC1N 3JZ; tel. (20) 7405-4060; fax (20) 7405-4070; e-mail info@theabn.org; internet www.theabn.org; f. 1933 to support neurologists and neurological trainees in their clinical practice and research, and advance the understanding of the nervous system and its disorders; 1,139 mems; Pres. Prof. DAVID CHADWICK; Hon. Sec. Dr DAVID BATEMAN.

Association of Surgeons of Great Britain and Ireland: c/o The Royal College of Surgeons, 35–43 Lincoln's Inn Fields, London, WC2A 3PN; tel. (20) 7973-0300; fax (20) 7430-9235; e-mail admin@asgbi.org.uk; internet www.asgbi.org.uk; f. 1920 for the advancement of the science and art of surgery; Pres. DENIS C. WILKINS; Hon. Sec. JONATHAN K. PYE.

British Association for Sexual Health and HIV: c/o Simon Croker, RSM, 1 Wimpole St, London, W1G 0AE; tel. (20) 7290-2968; fax (20) 7290-2989; f. 1922 as Medical Society for the Study of Venereal Diseases, to study sexually transmitted and allied diseases, incl., more recently, HIV/AIDS; 900 mems; Pres. Dr SIMON BARTON; Hon. Sec. Dr KEITH RADCLIFFE; publ. *Sexually Transmitted Infections* (6 a year).

British Association of Plastic, Reconstructive & Aesthetic Surgeons: c/o The Royal College of Surgeons, 35–43 Lincoln's Inn Fields, London, WC2A 3PE; tel. (20) 7831-5161; fax (20) 7831-4041; e-mail secretariat@baprass.co.uk; internet www.bapras.org.uk; f. 1946; protects and preserves public health by the promotion and development of plastic surgery; Pres. E. FREEDLANDER; Hon. Sec. D. J. COLEMAN; publs *British Journal of Plastic Surgery* (8 a year), *Journal of Plastic, Reconstructive and Aesthetic Surgery (JPRAS)*, *The Voice of Plastic Surgery*.

British Dental Association: 64 Wimpole St, London, W1G 8YS; tel. (20) 7935-0875; fax (20) 7487-5232; e-mail enquiries@bda.org; internet www.bda.org; f. 1880 as a professional asscn and subsequently became the trade union for the dental profession; 20,000 mems, 3,500 student mems; library of 10,000 vols; Chief Exec. Dr P. WARD; publ. *British Dental Journal* (24 a year).

British Dietetic Association: 5th Fl., Charles House, 148–149 Great Charles St Queensway, Birmingham, B3 3HT; tel. (121) 200-8080; e-mail info@bda.uk.com; internet www.bda.uk.com; f. 1936; 5,000 mems; Chair. SUSAN JONES; Sec. LORETTA COX; publ. *Journal of Human Nutrition and Dietetics* (6 a year).

British Geriatrics Society: 31 St John's Square, London, EC1M 4DN; tel. (20) 7608-1369; fax (20) 7608-1041; e-mail info@bgs.org.uk; internet www.bgs.org.uk; f. 1947 to improve standards of medical care for elderly patients and to encourage research into the problems of old age; 2,000 mems; Chief Exec. ALEX MAIR; publ. *Age and Ageing*.

British Institute of Radiology: 36 Portland Place, London, W1B 1AT; tel. (20) 7307-1400; fax (20) 7307-1414; e-mail admin@bir.org.uk; internet www.bir.org.uk; f. 1897; a centre for consultation on the medical, physical and biological applications of radiology; current and historic radiological library; 1,700 mems; Pres. PETER SHARPE; Gen. Sec. TONY HUDSON; publs *The British Journal of Radiology* (12 a year), *Imaging* (4 a year).

British Medical Association: BMA House, Tavistock Square, London, WC1H 9JP; tel. (20) 7387-4499; fax (20) 7383-6400; e-mail info.web@bma.org.uk; internet www.bma.org.uk; f. 1832; voluntary professional association for doctors; scientific and educational body, publisher of the British Medical Journal and provides services for members; 137,000 mems; library: see Libraries and Archives; Pres. Prof. ANTHONY KUMAR; Chair. JAMES JOHNSON; publs *BMA News* (weekly), *British Medical Journal* (weekly), and numerous journals on specialized medical subjects.

British Nutrition Foundation: High Holborn House, 52–54 High Holborn, London, WC1V 6RQ; tel. (20) 7404-6504; fax (20) 7404-6747; e-mail postbox@nutrition.org.uk; internet www.nutrition.org.uk; f. 1967; Hon. Pres. Prof. DEREK BURKE; Dir-Gen. Prof. JUDITH L. BUTTRISS; Sec. THOMAS BARCLAY; publ. *Bulletin* (4 a year).

British Orthodontic Society: c/o David Barnett, BOS Office, Eastman Dental Hospital, Grays Inn Rd, London, WC1X 8LD; tel. and fax (20) 7837-2193; internet www.bos.org.uk; f. 1994; Chair. W. G. WEBB; Sec. D. C. TIDY; publ. *British Journal of Orthodontics* (4 a year).

British Orthopaedic Association: 35–43 Lincoln's Inn Fields, London, WC2A 3PE; tel. (20) 7405-6507; fax (20) 7831-2676; e-mail secretary@boa.ac.uk; internet www.boa.ac.uk; f. 1918; the advancement of the science and art of orthopaedic surgery; 3,486 mems; Pres. CLARE MARX; Hon. Sec. J. DIAS; Chief Exec. D. C. ADAMS; publ. *Journal of Bone and Joint Surgery*.

British Pharmacological Society: 16 Angel Gate, City Rd, London, EC1V 2PT; tel. (20) 7239-0171; fax (20) 7417-0114; e-mail info@bps.ac.uk; internet www.bps.ac.uk; f. 1931; 2,700 mems; Chief Exec. K. BAILLIE; publs *British Journal of Clinical Pharmacology* (12 a year), *British Journal of Pharmacology* (24 a year).

British Psychoanalytical Society: Byron House, 112A Shirland Rd, Maida Vale, London, W9 2EQ; tel. (20) 7563-5000; fax (20) 7563-5001; e-mail ginette@goulston-lincoln.com; internet www.psychoanalysis.org.uk; f. 1913 as The London Psychoanalytical Society, present name

1919; training of psychoanalysts, devt of the theory and practice of psychoanalysis, advancement of psychoanalysis as a science; 400 mems; library of 22,000 vols, incl. 1,600 monographs, 300 journals; Pres. MICHAEL BREARLEY; Hon. Sec. C. POLMEAR; publ. *The International Journal of Psycho-Analysis* (6 a year).

British Society for Research on Ageing: c/o Dr Matthew Hardman, Faculty of Life Sciences, AV Hill Bldg, Univ. of Manchester, Manchester, M13 9PT; e-mail web@bsra.org.uk; internet www.bsra.org.uk; f. 1945; encourages gerontological research in Great Britain by acting as a forum for the report and discussion of new advances in ageing research; open to all who are engaged in experimental gerontology; Chair. Prof. ANNE MCARDLE; Sec. Dr MATTHEW HARDMAN; publs *e-Lifespan* (12 a year, online), *Lifespan* (2 a year), *Mechanisms of Ageing and Development*.

British Society for Rheumatology: Bride House, 18–20 Bride Lane, London, EC4Y 8EE; tel. (20) 7842-0900; fax (20) 7842-0901; e-mail bsr@rheumatology.org.uk; internet www.rheumatology.org.uk; f. 1984; promotes excellence in the treatment of people with arthritis and musculo-skeletal conditions and supports those delivering it; 1,500 mems; Pres. DEBORAH BAX; Exec. Sec. SAMANTHA PETERS; publs *Musculoskeletal Care*, *Rheumatology*.

British Society of Gastroenterology: 3 St Andrews Pl., Regent's Park, London, NW1 4LB; tel. (20) 7935-3150; fax (20) 7487-3734; e-mail enquiries@bsg.org.uk; internet www.bsg.org.uk; f. 1937; training programmes and research workshops; 3,400 mems; Pres. Prof. JONATHAN RHODES; Sec. Dr C. D. R. MURRAY; Sec. Dr CATHRYN EDWARDS; Chief Exec. Dr TOM SMITH; Treas. Dr M DAKKAK; publs *Frontline Gastroenterology* (6 a year), *Gut* (12 a year).

Central Council of Physical Recreation: CCPR, Burwood House, 14–16 Caxton St, London, SW1H 0QT; tel. (20) 7976-3900; fax (20) 7976-3901; e-mail info@ccpr.org.uk; internet www.ccpr.org.uk; f. 1935 as the Central Council of Recreative Physical Training to formulate and promote measures to improve and develop sport and physical recreation; promotes, protects and provides for sport and recreation; Pres. HRH PRINCE EDWARD, EARL OF WESSEX; Chair., Bd of Dirs BRIGID SIMMONDS; Chief Exec. TIM LAMB; Treas. JOHN CROWTHER.

Chartered Society of Physiotherapy: 14 Bedford Row, London, WC1R 4ED; tel. (20) 7306-6666; fax (20) 7306-6611; e-mail enquiries@csp.org.uk; internet www.csp.org.uk; f. 1894 as Society of Trained Masseuses, became Incorporated Society of Trained Masseuses 1900, granted a Royal Charter 1920, amalgamated with Institute of Massage and Remedial Gymnastics, present name 1944; professional, educational and trade union body for chartered physiotherapists, support workers and physiotherapy students in the UK; 50,000 mems; Chair. of Council ANN GREEN; Treas. SUE ENGLAND; Pres. Baroness ILORA FINLAY OF LLANDAFF; Chief Exec. PHIL GRAY; publs *Physiotherapy Frontline* (24 a year), *Physiotherapy Journal* (4 a year).

College of Optometrists: 42 Craven St, London, WC2N 5NG; tel. (20) 7839-6000; fax (20) 7839-6800; e-mail optometry@college-optometrists.org; internet www.college-optometrists.org; f. 1980 by The British Optical Asscn, The Scottish Asscn of Opticians and The Worshipful Co of Spectacle Makers; improves and conserves human vision; incl. a library and museum; 13,357 mems incl. over 9,000 practising UK Members and Fellows; library of 7,000 vols, incl. optical books, pamphlets and audiovisual titles, journals, British Standards, govt publs, college publs, gen. reference materials, historical collns; Pres. ROB HOGAN; Chair. and Vice-Pres. CINDY TROMANS; CEO BRYONY PAWINSKA; publs *Ophthalmic and Physiological Optics* (online, 6 a year), *Optometry in Practice* (print, 4 a year).

Diabetes UK: 10 Parkway, London, NW1 7AA; tel. (20) 7424-1000; fax (20) 7424-1001; e-mail info@diabetes.org.uk; internet www.diabetes.org.uk; f. 1934 to help all people with diabetes and those interested in diabetes, to promote greater public understanding of the condition and to support research into diabetes; 190,000 mems; Chair. of Board of Trustees Sir MICHAEL HIRST; Chief Exec. PAUL STREETS; publs *Balance for Beginners* (updated annually), *Balance Magazine* (6 a year), *Diabetic Medicine* (10 a year), *Diabetes Update* (4 a year).

Harveian Society of London: 11 Chandos St, London, W1G 9EB; tel. (20) 7580-1043; e-mail harveiansoclondon@btconnect.com; f. 1831; promotes the advancement of medical science; 250 mems; Pres. Prof. ROBERT DOUGLAS; Hon. Sec. Prof. JOHN WALKER-SMITH; Exec. Sec. Cmdr ROGER IRELAND; Exec. Sec. BETTY SMALLWOOD.

Institute of Biomedical Science: 12 Coldbath Sq., London, EC1R 5HL; tel. (20) 7713-0214; fax (20) 7837-9658; e-mail mail@ibms.org; internet www.ibms.org; f. 1912; promotes and develops biomedical science and its practitioners, and establishes and maintains professional standards; 18,000 mems; Chief Exec. ALAN R. POTTER; publs *British Journal of Biomedical Science* (4 a year), *The Biomedical Scientist* (12 a year).

Medical Society of London: Lettsom House, 11 Chandos St, London, W1G 9EB; tel. (20) 7580-1043; fax (20) 7631-4817; e-mail medicalsoclondon@btconnect.com; internet www.medsoclondon.org; f. 1773; 440 mems; library of 4,500 vols; Registrar ROGER IRELAND; publ. *Transactions* (1 a year).

MIND: Granta House, 15–19 Broadway, London, E15 4BQ; tel. (20) 8519-2122; fax (20) 8522-1725; e-mail info@mind.org.uk; internet www.mind.org.uk; f. 1946; works to create a better life for people with experience of mental distress; produces information and publs; offers services incl. advocacy, counselling, crisis helplines, drop-in centres, employment and training schemes, supported housing; 1,600 mems, 200 local asscns, 7 regional offices; Chief Exec. PAUL FARMER.

Northern Ireland Association for Mental Health: Central Office, 80 University St, Belfast, BT7 1HE; tel. (28) 9032-8474; e-mail alisondeane@niamh.co.uk; internet www.niamh.co.uk; f. 1959 as Beacon House; counselling, training and consultancy for employers on mental health in the workplace; Chief Exec. Prof ALAN FERGUSON; Chair. Dr GRAEME MCDONALD.

Nutrition Society: 10 Cambridge Court, 210 Shepherds Bush Rd, London, W6 7NJ; tel. (20) 7602-0228; fax (20) 7602-1756; e-mail office@nutsoc.org.uk; internet www.nutritionsociety.org.uk; f. 1941 to advance the scientific study of nutrition and its application to the maintenance of human and animal health; over 2,200 mems; Pres. Prof. J. J. STRAIN; publs *British Journal of Nutrition* (12 a year), *Nutrition Research Reviews* (2 a year), *Proceedings* (6 a year), *Public Health Nutrition* (8 a year).

Pathological Society: 2 Carlton House Terrace, London, SW1Y 5AF; tel. (20) 7976-1260; fax (20) 7930-2981; e-mail admin@pathsoc.org; internet www.pathsoc.org; f. 1906; 1,500 mems; Pres. Prof. A. H. WYLLIE; Meetings Sec. Prof. I. O. ELLIS; Gen.-Sec. Prof. C. SIMON HERRINGTON; Treas. Prof. ALASTAIR D. BURT; publ. *Journal of Pathology*.

Royal Association for Disability and Rehabilitation: 12 City Forum, 250 City Rd, London, EC1V 8AF; tel. (20) 7250-3222; fax (20) 7250-0212; e-mail radar@radar.org.uk; internet www.radar.org.uk; f. 1977; covers the whole field of disability; a co-ordinating organization concerned with the needs and rights of disabled people; Dir KATE NASH.

Royal College of Anaesthetists: Churchill House, 35 Red Lion Sq., London, WC1R 4SG; tel. (20) 7092-1500; fax (20) 7092-1730; e-mail info@rcoa.ac.uk; internet www.rcoa.ac.uk; f. 1948; responsible for the science of anaesthesia throughout the United Kingdom and for ensuring the quality of patient care through the maintenance of standards in anaesthesia, critical care and pain management; 14,000 fellows, mems and trainees; Pres. Dr JUDITH HULF; publs *British Journal of Anaesthesia* (12 a year), *Bulletin* (6 a year).

Royal College of General Practitioners: 14 Princes Gate, London, SW7 1PU; tel. (20) 7581-3232; fax (20) 7225-3047; internet www.rcgp.org.uk; f. 1952 to ensure the highest possible standards in general medical practice; 21,000 mems; Chair. Dr MAYUR LAKHANI; Hon. Sec. Dr MAUREEN BAKER; publ. *British Journal of General Practice* (12 a year).

Royal College of Nursing of the United Kingdom: 20 Cavendish Sq., London, W1M 0AB; tel. (20) 7409-3333; fax (20) 7355-1379; internet www.rcn.org.uk; f. 1916 to represent the interests of nurses and advance the provision of healthcare generally; library of 60,000 vols; Pres. SYLVIA DENTON; publ. *Nursing Standard* (weekly).

Royal College of Obstetricians and Gynaecologists: 27 Sussex Pl., Regent's Park, London, NW1 4RG; tel. (20) 7772-6200; fax (20) 7723-0575; e-mail coll.sec@rcog.org.uk; internet www.rcog.org.uk; f. 1929; 10,705 mems; library of 11,000 vols; Pres. Dr TONY FALCONER; College Administrator IAN WYLIE; publs *British Journal of Obstetrics and Gynaecology* (12 a year), *The Obstetrician and Gynaecologist* (4 a year).

Royal College of Ophthalmologists: 17 Cornwall Terrace, London, NW1 4QW; tel. (20) 7935-0702; fax (20) 7935-9838; internet www.rcophth.ac.uk; f. 1988 for the cultivation and promotion of ophthalmology; 3,200 mems; Pres. ALLAN TEMPLETON; Hon. Sec. BRENDA BILLINGTON; publ. *Eye* (6 a year).

Royal College of Paediatrics and Child Health: 5–11 Theobalds Rd, London, WC1X 8SH; tel. (20) 7092-6000; fax (20) 7092-6001; e-mail enquiries@rcpch.ac.uk; internet www.rcpch.ac.uk; f. 1928 to advance, for the benefit of the public, education in paediatrics and to relieve sickness by promoting the improvement of paediatric practice; 7,800 mems; Pres. Prof. ALAN CRAFT; Registrar Dr SHEILA SHRIBMAN; publ. *Archives of Disease in Childhood* (12 a year, with British Medical Association).

Royal College of Pathologists: 2 Carlton House Terrace, London, SW1Y 5AF; tel. (20) 7451-6700; fax (20) 7451-6701; e-mail info@rcpath.org; internet www.rcpath.org; f. 1962; 8,474 fellows and mems; library of 2,100 vols (spec. colln); Pres. Prof. ADRIAN NEWLAND; Chief Exec. DANIEL ROSS; publ. *Bulletin* (4 a year).

Royal College of Physicians: 11 St Andrews Pl., London, NW1 4LE; tel. (20) 7224-1539; fax (20) 7487-5218; e-mail infocentre@rcplondon.ac.uk; internet www.rcplondon.ac.uk; f. 1518; aims to promote the values of the medical profession, improve standards of clinical practice, support physicians in their practice of medicine through education and training, communicate with govt, the public and the profession and provide leadership on health and healthcare issues; 22,000 mems (13,000 fellows, 9,000 collegiate mems); library: see Libraries and Archives; Pres. Prof. I. GILMORE; Registrar Prof. R. BURNHAM; Chief Exec. M. ELSE; publ. *Clinical Medicine* (6 a year).

Royal College of Physicians and Surgeons of Glasgow: 232–242 St Vincent St, Glasgow, G2 5RJ; tel. (141) 221-6072; fax (141) 221-1804; internet www.rcpsg.ac.uk; f. 1599; a medical licensing corporation; 9,039 fellows and mems in medicine, surgery, dentistry and travel medicine; library: see Libraries and Archives; Pres. I. ANDERSON; Hon. Sec. Dr J. TAYLOR.

Royal College of Physicians of Edinburgh: 9 Queen St, Edinburgh, EH2 1JQ; tel. (131) 225-7324; fax (131) 220-3939; internet www.rcpe.ac.uk; f. 1681; 7,000 mems; library: see Libraries and Archives; Pres. Prof. N. J. DOUGLAS; Sec. Dr J. COLLINS; publ. *Journal* (4 a year).

Royal College of Psychiatrists: 17 Belgrave Sq., London, SW1X 8PG; tel. (20) 7235-2351; fax (20) 7245-1231; e-mail rcpsych@rcpsych.ac.uk; internet www.rcpsych.ac.uk; f. 1971 by Charter, previously Royal Medico-Psychological Association; 12,000 Fellows and mems; Pres. Prof. D. BHUGRA; Registrar Dr L. MYNORS-WALLIS; Chief Exec. V. CAMERON; publs *Advances in Psychiatric Treatment* (6 a year), *British Journal of Psychiatry* (12 a year), *The Psychiatrist* (12 a year).

Royal College of Radiologists: 38 Portland Pl., London, W1B 1JQ; tel. (20) 7636-4432; fax (20) 7323-3100; e-mail enquiries@rcr.ac.uk; internet www.rcr.ac.uk; f. 1939; practice of radiology and oncology; 6,600 mems; Chief Exec. ANDREW HALL; publs *Clinical Oncology* (8 a year), *Clinical Radiology* (12 a year).

Royal College of Surgeons of Edinburgh: Nicolson St, Edinburgh, EH8 9DW; tel. (131) 527-1600; fax (131) 557-6406; e-mail information@rcsed.ac.uk; internet www.rcsed.ac.uk; f. 1505; postgraduate education and assessment in surgery; 17,000 Fellows; Pres. D. A. TOLLEY; Chief Exec. A. ROONEY; publs *Surgeon News* (4 a year), *The Surgeon* (6 a year).

Royal College of Surgeons of England: 35–43 Lincoln's Inn Fields, London, WC2A 3PE; tel. (20) 7405-3474; fax (20) 7831-9438; e-mail education@rcseng.ac.uk; internet www.rcseng.ac.uk; f. 1800; supervises training of surgeons in approved posts; provides educational and practical workshops for surgeons and other medical professionals; promotes surgical research; acts as an advisory body to the Dept of Health and other health authorities, trusts, hospitals; attached information centre for surgeons in the library and museums; 14,300 fellows and mems; library of 100,000 vols; Pres. JOHN BLACK; publs *Annals of the Royal College of Surgeons of England* (8 a year), *Bulletin* (10 year).

Royal Institute of Public Health: 28 Portland Pl., London, W1B 1DE; tel. (20) 7580-2731; fax (20) 7580-6157; e-mail info@riphh.org.uk; internet www.riphh.org.uk; f. 1898; 3,000 mems; Chief Exec. NICHOLA WILKINS; publs *Health and Hygiene* (4 a year), *Public Health* (6 a year).

Royal Medical Society: Students' Centre, Bristo Sq., Edinburgh, EH8 9AL; tel. (131) 650-2672; e-mail enquiries@royalmedical.co.uk; internet www.royalmedicalsociety.co.uk; f. 1737; 2,000 mems; library of 2,000 vols; Pres. KRISTINA LEE; Sec. ANDREW BROOKES; Permanent Sec. ELIZABETH SINGH; publ. *Res Medica* (2 a year).

Royal Pharmaceutical Society of Great Britain: 1 Lambeth High St, London, SE1 7JN; tel. (20) 7572-2300; e-mail library@rpharms.com; internet www.rpharms.com; f. 1841; professional and regulatory body for pharmacists in England, Scotland and Wales; 47,621 mems (620 fellows, 47,001 mems); library of 80,000 vols, pamphlets and MSS, 300 journals, colln of pharmacopoeias and formularies; Pres. MARTIN ASTBURY; CEO HELEN GORDON; publs *Annual Register of Pharmaceutical Chemists*, *British National Formulary* (jtly with the British Medical Asscn), *The Hospital Pharmacist* (11 a year), *The International Journal of Pharmacy Practice* (4 a year), *Journal of Pharmacy and Pharmacology* (12 a year), *Martindale: The Extra Pharmacopoeia*, *Medicines and Ethics*, *The Pharmaceutical Journal* (weekly), *Pharmaceutical Sciences* (12 a year).

Royal Society for Public Health: 3rd Fl., Market Towers, 1 Nine Elms Lane, London, SW8 5NQ; tel. (20) 3177-1600; fax (20) 3177-1601; e-mail info@rsph.org.uk; internet www.rsph.org.uk; f. 2008 by merger of Royal Soc. for the Promotion of Health and the Royal Institute of Public Health; ind., multi-disciplinary org. dedicated to the promotion, protection and preservation of human health and wellbeing; examining body for food hygiene; holds confs. and lectures; 5,700 mems; Patron HM THE QUEEN; Pres. LORD HUNT OF KING'S HEATH; Chair of Ccl Dr SELWYN HODGE; publs *Perspectives in Public Health* (6 a year), *Public Health* (12 a year).

Royal Society of Medicine: 1 Wimpole St, London, W1G 0AE; tel. (20) 7290-2900; fax (20) 7290-2992; e-mail membership@rsm.ac.uk; internet www.rsm.ac.uk; f. 1805, first Royal Charter 1834; undertakes over 400 meetings a year covering 58 Sections of medicine and surgery; has own publishing house and publishes journals for other orgs and proceedings of sponsored meetings; runs hotel, bar, restaurant and lounges that mems can use when visiting London; 23,000 mems; library: see Libraries and Archives; Pres. Prof. ROBIN WILLIAMSON; publs *Aids and Hepatitis Digest* (6 a year), *Annals of Clinical Biochemistry* (online, 6 a year), *Clinical Governance Bulletin* (6 a year, also online), *Clinical Risk* (online, 6 a year), *Effective Health Care* (6 a year, also online), *Handbook of Practice Management* (online, quarterly), *Health Information on the Internet* (online, 6 a year), *Health Services Management Research* (4 a year, also online), *International Journal of STD and AIDS* (12 a year, also online), *Journal of Health Services Research and Policy* (online, 4 a year), *Journal of Integrated Care Pathways* (3 a year), *Journal of Laryngology and Otology* (12 a year, also online), *Journal of Medical Biography* (4 a year), *Journal of Medical Screening* (4 a year, also online), *Journal of Telemedicine and Telecare* (online, 6 a year), *Journal of the British Menopause Society* (4 a year, also online), *Journal of the Royal Society of Medicine* (12 a year, also online), *Laboratory Animals* (online, 4 a year), *Phlebology* (4 a year, also online), *Tropical Doctor* (4 a year).

Royal Society of Tropical Medicine and Hygiene: 50 Bedford Sq., London, WC1B 3DP; tel. (20) 7580-2127; fax (20) 7436-1389; e-mail info@rstmh.org; internet www.rstmh.org; f. 1907 to promote and advance the study, control and prevention of disease in humankind and other animals in the tropics and warm climates, and to facilitate the discussion and exchange of information among those interested in tropical medicine and international health; 2,000 mems; Pres. Prof. HAZEL DOCKRELL; Hon. Secs Prof. M. J. NEWPORT, Dr J. R. STOTHARD; Chief Exec. GERRI MCHUGH; publs *International Health* (4 a year), *Transactions* (12 a year).

Society for Endocrinology: 22 Apex Court, Woodlands, Bradley Stoke, Bristol, BS32 4JT; tel. (1454) 642200; fax (1454) 642222; e-mail info@endocrinology.org; internet www.endrocrinology.org; f. 1939; promotes the advancement of endocrinology; 1,900 mems; Chair. J. BUCKINGHAM; publs *Endocrine-Related Cancer* (4 a year, online), *Journal of Endocrinology* (12 a year), *Journal of Molecular Endocrinology* (6 a year, print; 12 a year, online), *The Endocrinologist* (4 a year).

Society of British Neurological Surgeons: c/o Suzanne Murray, 35–43 Lincoln's Inn Fields, London, WC2A 3PE; tel. (20) 7869-6892; fax (20) 7869-6890; e-mail admin@sbns.org.uk; internet www.sbns.org.uk; f. 1926; promotes high standards of professional practice through the Soc.'s involvement in the education and the examination of neurosurgeons and through its meetings and associated activities in the continual professional devt of neurosurgeons; 384 mems; Pres. Prof. JOHN PICKARD; Pres. Elect PHILIP VAN HILLE; publ. *Proceedings* (in *British Journal of Neurosurgery*).

Society of Occupational Medicine: 6 St Andrew's Pl., London, NW1 4LB; tel. (20) 7486-2641; fax (20) 7486-0028; e-mail admin@som.org.uk; internet www.som.org.uk; f. 1935; concerned with the protection of the health of people at work and the prevention of occupational diseases and injuries; stimulates research and education in occupational medicine; 1,800 mems; Pres. Dr O. H. CARLTON; Hon. Sec. Dr E. S. WILKINSON; publ. *Occupational Medicine* (8 a year).

St John's Dermatological Society: St John's Institute of Dermatology, St Thomas' Hospital, Lambeth Palace Rd, London, SE1 7EH; tel. (20) 7188-9352; e-mail nuala.odonoghue@imperial.nhs.uk; internet www.st-johns-society.co.uk; meeting at St John's Hospital for Diseases of the Skin; f. 1911 to promote the knowledge and study of dermatology by presentation and discussion of rare and interesting cases; 250 Fellows; Pres. Dr ANDREW PEMBROKE; Hon. Sec. Dr NUALA O'DONOGHUE; publ. *Clinical and Experimental Dermatology* (1 a year).

Stroke Association: 240 City Rd, London, EC1V 2PR; tel. (845) 303-3100; e-mail info@stroke.org.uk; internet www.stroke.org.uk; f. 1899, fmrly The Chest, Heart and Stroke Asscn; provides practical support to people who have had strokes and to their families, through community services and welfare grants; prevents strokes through health education; Chair. of Council Sir CHARLES GEORGE; Chief Exec. JON BARRICK; publ. *Stroke News* (4 a year).

Tavistock Institute of Medical Psychology: The Tavistock Centre, 120 Belsize Lane, London, NW3 5BA; tel. (20) 7435-7111; fax (20) 7435-1080; e-mail timp@tccr.org.uk; internet www.tccr.org.uk; f. 1929; promotes the study and practice of psychotherapy and provides grants for related small research projects; administers the Tavistock Centre for Couple Relationships, which offers a professional service to couples experiencing difficulty in relationships and trains counsellors; and Relationship Counselling for London, which provides a counselling consultation service and trains counsellors;

Chair. Dr A. OBHOLZER; Company Sec. D. OBADINA; publ. *In Brief* (1 a year).

NATURAL SCIENCES

General

Association for Science Education: College Lane, Hatfield AL10 9AA; tel. (1707) 283000; fax (1707) 266532; e-mail membership@ase.org.uk; internet www.ase.org.uk; f. 1901; organizes meetings and workshops locally and nationally; aims to improve science teaching and to provide a medium of expression for science teachers; 21,000 mems; Chief Exec. Dr D. S. MOORE; publs *Education in Science* (5 a year), *Primary Science Review* (5 a year), *School Science Review* (4 a year), *Science Teacher Education* (3 a year).

British Science Association: Wellcome Wolfson Bldg, 165 Queen's Gate, London, SW7 5HD; tel. (870) 770-7101; fax (20) 7581-6587; e-mail info@britishscienceassociation.org; internet www.britishscienceassociation.org; f. 1831; promotes and advances public understanding and awareness of science and technology and their effect on soc.; 5,670 mems; Chief Exec. ROLAND JACKSON; publ. *People & Science* (4 a year).

British Society for the History of Science: POB 3401, Norwich, NR7 7JF; tel. (1603) 516236; fax (1252) 641135; e-mail execsec@bshs.org.uk; internet www.bshs.org.uk; f. 1947; promotes and furthers the study of the history and philosophy of science, technology and medicine; organizes meetings and confs; 750 mems; Exec. Sec. L TETLOW; publs *British Journal for the History of Science* (4 a year), *Viewpoint* (newsletter, 3 a year).

Cambridge Philosophical Society: Central Science Library, Arts School, Bene't St, Cambridge, CB2 3PY; tel. (1223) 334743; e-mail philosoc@hermes.cam.ac.uk; internet www.cambridgephilosophicalsociety.org; f. 1819; promotes scientific enquiry and facilitates the communication of facts connected with the advancement of science; 1,900 mems; Exec. Sec. B. LARNER; publs *Biological Reviews* (4 a year), *Mathematical Proceedings* (6 a year).

Council for Environmental Education: 94 London St, Reading, RG1 4SJ; tel. (118) 950-2550; fax (118) 959-1955; e-mail enquiries@cee.org.uk; internet www.cee.org.uk; f. 1968 to increase the effectiveness of the environmental education movement by developing and influencing policy and supporting and encouraging good practice; umbrella org. for national and associated orgs working in environmental and sustainable development education; library: reference library and resource centre; 84 mems; Dir LIBBY GRUNDY; publs *CEEmail* (3 a year), *CEEview* (4 a year), *Earthlines* (3 a year).

Environment Council: 212 High Holborn, London, WC1V 7BF; tel. (20) 7836-2626; fax (20) 7242-1180; e-mail info@envcouncil.org.uk; internet www.the-environment-council.org.uk; f. 1969, fmrly Ccl for Environmental Conservation; works with business, industry, government, non-governmental organizations and the community to find sustainable solutions to environmental problems; 2,000 mems; Chief Exec. WINSOME MACLAURIN; publ. *elements* (6 a year).

Field Studies Council: Preston Montford, Montford Bridge, Shrewsbury, SY4 1HW; tel. (1743) 852100; fax (1743) 852101; e-mail fsc.headoffice@field-studies-council.org; internet www.field-studies-council.org; f. 1943; ind. educational charity; operates 17 residential and day centres throughout the UK, offering a range of courses for schools and colleges; leisure learning and professional devt courses are offered in the UK and overseas; provides outreach education, training and consultancy; publishes a number of titles to support its work, incl. identification guides; 4,000 mems; Pres. Prof. I. D. MERCER; Chair. Prof. T. P. BURT; Dir A. D. THOMAS.

Foundation for Science and Technology: 10 Carlton House Terrace, London, SW1Y 5AH; tel. (20) 7321-2220; fax (20) 7321-2221; e-mail office@foundation.org.uk; internet www.foundation.org.uk; f. 1977; debates science, engineering, technology and medical science policy; Chief Exec. Dr DOUGAL GOODMAN; publ. *FST Journal* (4 a year).

Institution of Environmental Sciences: 38 Ebury St, London, SW1W 0LU; tel. (20) 7730-5516; fax (20) 7730-5519; internet www.ies-uk.org.uk; f. 1971 for consultation in matters of an environmental nature; aims to promote interdisciplinary studies of the environment, to diffuse information relating to environmental sciences at nat. and int. levels, and to bring together into a corporate professional body all persons throughout the world possessing responsibilities for environmental affairs; 1,003 individual mems; Chair. CAROLYN ROBERTS; Hon. Sec. J. R. BLUMHOF; publ. *The Environmental Scientist* (3 a year).

London Natural History Society: c/o The Secretary, 381B Whitton Ave, Greenford UB6 0JU; tel. (20) 8426-6621; e-mail davidhowdon@yahoo.co.uk; internet www.lnhs.org.uk; f. 1858 for people interested in the study of natural history, archaeology and related subjects, esp. within a radius of 20 miles from St Paul's Cathedral; 1,000 individual mems, 25 corporate mems; field meetings, talks, training days, recording of species and habitats; reading circles distribute a wide range of journals; sections cater for spec. interests: botany, entomology and general ecology, ornithology; library of 3,500 books and 5,000 periodicals; Library at the Angela Marmont Centre for UK Biodiversity at the Natural History Museum, London, is open to public; Pres. Prof. JOHN EDGINGTON; Treas. MICHAEL WEST; Sec. DAVID HOWDON; publs *London Bird Report* (1 a year), *The London Naturalist* (1 a year).

Royal Institution of Great Britain: 21 Albemarle St, London, W1S 4BS; tel. (20) 7409-2992; fax (20) 7629-3569; e-mail ri@ri.ac.uk; internet www.rigb.org; f. 1799; promotes science to the public through lectures, demonstrations and discussions; Davy Faraday Research Laboratory conducts research into the chemistry and physics of materials; active heritage dept; 3,200 mems; library: library: see Libraries and Archives; museum: see Museums and Art Galleries; Pres. HRH THE DUKE OF KENT; Sec. Prof. ALAN MARIES; Chief Exec. CHRIS ROFE; Dir of the Davy Faraday Research Laboratory Prof. QUENTIN PANKHURST.

Scottish Field Studies Association: Kindrogan Field Centre, Enochdhu, Blairgowrie PH10 7PG; tel. (1250) 881286; fax (1250) 881433; e-mail kindrogan@btinternet.com; internet www.kindrogan.com; f. 1945; provides residential courses and a venue for fieldwork in biology and geography; 400 mems; Chair. ROBIN NOBLE.

United Kingdom Science Park Association: Chesterford Research Park, Little Chesterford, Cambridge, CB10 1XL; tel. (1799) 532050; fax (1799) 532049; e-mail admin@ukspa.prestel.co.uk; internet www.ukspa.org.uk; f. 1984 to act as a forum for those concerned with the planning and management of science parks, and to promote awareness of science parks and provide information on their objectives and achievements; mems: 65 science parks; Chair. JANE DAVIES; Sec. PAUL CARVER; publs *Directory*, *Innovation Into Success*, *The Development and Operation of Science Parks*.

Wildlife Trusts: The Kiln, Waterside, Mather Rd, Newark, NG24 1WT; tel. (1636) 677711; fax (1636) 670001; e-mail enquiry@wildlifetrusts.org; internet www.wildlifetrusts.org; f. 1912 as Royal Society for Nature Conservation; inc. by Royal Charter 1916 and 1976, to promote the conservation of nature for study and research and to educate the public in the understanding and appreciation of nature, the awareness of its value and the need for its conservation; acts as the nat. office for the 46 Wildlife Trusts, Urban Wildlife Groups and Wildlife Watch (junior br.); 800,000 mems; Pres. Prof. DAVID BELLAMY; publ. *Natural World* (3 a year).

Biological Sciences

Association for the Study of Animal Behaviour: c/o Prof. F. Huntingford, Graham Kerr Building, University of Glasgow, Glasgow, G12 8QQ; tel. (141) 330-6643; fax (141) 330-5971; e-mail gbza10@udcf.gla.ac.uk; internet www.societies.ncl.ac.uk/asab; f. 1936; 2,000 mems; Pres. Prof. F. HUNTINGFORD; Sec. Dr C. MAGNHAGEN; publ. *Animal Behaviour* (12 a year).

Association of Applied Biologists: Warwick Enterprise Park, Wellesbourne, Warwick, CV35 9EF; tel. (1789) 472020; fax (1789) 470234; internet www.aab.org.uk; f. 1904; promotes study and advancement of all brs of biology, with spec. reference to their applied aspects; 800 mems; Pres. Prof. TREVOR HOCKING; Gen. Sec. Dr ELIZABETH STOCKDALE; publ. *Annals of Applied Biology* (6 a year).

Biochemical Society: Charles Darwin House, 12 Roger St, London, WC1N 2JU; tel. (20) 7685-2400; e-mail genadmin@biochemistry.org; internet www.biochemistry.org; f. 1911; advancement of the science of biochemistry; 5,000 mems; Chair. Prof. COLIN KLEANTHOUS; Chief Exec. Dr C. J. KIRK; publs *Biochemical Journal* (24 a year), *Biochemical Society Transactions* (6 a year), *Clinical Science* (12 a year), *Essays in Biochemistry* (2 a year), *Symposia* (1 a year), *The Biochemist* (6 a year), *Biology of the Cell* (on behalf of the Société de Biologie Cellulaire de France and the Société Française des Microscopies, 12 a year), *Biotechnology and Applied Biochemistry* (on behalf of the International Union of Biochemistry and Molecular Biology, 6 a year).

Biosciences Federation: Peer House, 8–14 Verulam St, London, WC1X 8LZ; tel. (1223) 400181; e-mail info@bsf.ac.uk; internet www.bsf.ac.uk; f. 2002; 50 mem. socs; Pres. Prof. Dame NANCY ROTHWELL; CEO Dr RICHARD DYER.

Botanical Society of Scotland: c/o Royal Botanic Garden Edinburgh, 20A Inverleith Row, Edinburgh, EH3 5LR; tel. (131) 552-7171; internet www.botsocscot.org.uk; f. 1836 (fmrly Botanical Soc. of Edinburgh); incorporates the Cryptogamic Soc. of Scotland; 300 mems and fellows; Pres. Prof. C. E. JEFFREE; Hon. Gen. Sec. Dr B. A. HARVIE; publ. *Plant Ecology and Diversity* (2 a year).

Botanical Society of the British Isles: c/o Dept of Botany, Natural History Museum, Cromwell Rd, London, SW7 5BD; tel. (20) 7942-5002; internet www.bsbi.org.uk; f. 1836; studies British native flowering plants and ferns; exhibitions, confs, field meetings; 2,800 mems; Hon. Gen. Sec. LYNNE FARRELL; publs *BSBI News* (3 a year), *Watsonia* (2 a year).

British Biophysical Society: c/o Prof. John Seddon, Dept of Chemistry, Imperial College, London SW7 2AZ; tel. (20) 7594-5797; e-mail j.seddon@imperial.ac.uk; internet www.britishbiophysics.org.uk; f. 1960; 450 mems; Sec. Prof. JOHN M. SEDDON.

British Ecological Society: Charles Darwin House, 12 Roger St, London, WC1N 2JU; tel. (20) 7685-2500; fax (20) 7685-2501; e-mail info@britishecologicalsociety.org; internet www.britishecologicalsociety.org; f. 1913; publ. of scientific literature, incl. five internationally renowned journals; funding of numerous grant schemes, education work and policy work; 4,000 mems; Exec. Dir Dr HAZEL J. NORMAN; publs *Symposium* (1 a year), *Journal of Ecology* (6 a year), *Journal of Animal Ecology* (6 a year), *Journal of Applied Ecology* (6 a year), *Functional Ecology* (6 a year).

British Mycological Society: The Wolfson Wing, Jodrell Laboratory, Royal Botanic Gardens, Kew, Richmond, Surrey, TW9 3AB; tel. (23) 9284-2024; fax (23) 9252-5902; e-mail admin@britmycolsoc.info; internet www.britmycolsoc.org.uk; f. 1896; promotes mycology through scientific meetings, publs and education; 1,206 mems and 644 assocs; Pres. Prof. LYNNE BODDY; Gen. Sec. Dr GEOFFREY D. ROBSON; publs *Field Mycology* (4 a year), *Mycological Research* (12 a year), *Mycologist* (4 a year).

British Ornithologists' Union: Dept of Zoology, University of Oxford, South Parks Rd, Oxford, OX1 3PS; tel. and fax (1865) 8281842; e-mail bou@bou.org.uk; internet www.bou.org.uk; f. 1858 for the advancement of the science of ornithology; 1,800 ordinary mems, plus hon. mems and corresp. mems; Pres. Prof. C. M. PERRINS; Hon. Sec. N. J. BUCKNELL; publ. *Ibis* (4 a year).

British Society for Plant Pathology: Marlborough House, Basingstoke Rd, Spencers Wood, Reading, RG7 1AG; e-mail secretary@bspp.org.uk; internet www.bspp.org.uk; f. 1981; 650 mems; Pres. Prof. SARAH GURR; Sec. ROGER WILLIAMS; publs *BSPP News* (4 a year), *Molecular Plant Pathology* (6 a year), *New Disease Reports* (4 a year), *Plant Pathology* (6 a year).

British Trust for Ornithology: The Nunnery, Thetford, IP24 2PU; tel. (1842) 750050; fax (1842) 750030; e-mail info@bto.org; internet www.bto.org; f. 1933; promotes and encourages wider understanding, appreciation and conservation of birds through scientific studies using the combined skills and enthusiasm of its mems, other bird watchers and staff; projects incl. Nat. Bird Ringing Scheme, Nest Records Scheme, Wetland Bird Survey, Breeding Bird Survey, Garden Bird Watch, Bird Atlas; offers advisory services to ecologists, land use planners, conservationists, developers; 13,000 mems; Pres. Baroness YOUNG OF OLD SCONE; Dir Dr F. A. CLEMENTS; publs *Bird Study* (4 a year), *Bird Table* (4 a year), *BTO News* (6 a year), *Ringing and Migration* (2 a year).

Fauna & Flora International: 4th Fl, Jupiter House, Station Rd, Cambridge, CB1 2JD; tel. (1223) 571000; fax (1223) 461481; e-mail info@fauna-flora.org; internet www.fauna-flora.org; f. 1903; world's oldest international wildlife conservation society working to save endangered species from extinction; especially concerned with the prevention of illegal trade; publishes information and news about wildlife conservation throughout the world; 2,000 mems; Pres. LINDSAY BURY; Chair. MARTIN FISHER; publ. *Oryx* (4 a year).

Freshwater Biological Association: The Ferry Landing, Ambleside, LA22 0LP; tel. (15394) 42468; fax (15394) 46914; e-mail info@fba.org.uk; internet www.fba.org.uk; f. 1929; promotes study and application of freshwater biology, and encourages adoption of freshwater science as best way to understand, protect and manage water resources; ferry landing on shores of Windermere, Cumbria; River Laboratory, East Stoke, Wareham, Dorset sited on River Frome; 1,650 mems; library of 150,000 vols, 10,000 vols. of scientific periodicals; Pres. Prof. ALAN HILDREW; Chair. of Ccl Prof. CHRIS SPRAY; Sec. and Dir Dr MICHAEL DOBSON; publs *FBA News* (4 a year), *FBA Scientific Publications* (irregular), *Freshwater Forum* (2 a year), *Freshwater Reviews* (online, 2 a year).

Genetics Society: c/o Jayne Richards, Roslin Institute, Roslin, Midlothian, EH25 9PS; tel. (131) 200-6391; fax (131) 200-6401; e-mail mail@genetics.org.uk; internet www.genetics.org.uk; f. 1919; all aspects of genetics, pure and applied; 2,000 mems; Pres. Prof. JONATHAN HODGKIN; Hon. Sec. Dr JOHN ARMOUR; publs *Genes and Development* (every 2 weeks), *Genetics Society News* (12 a year), *Heredity* (12 a year).

Linnean Society of London: Burlington House, Piccadilly, London, W1J 0BF; tel. (20) 7434-4479; fax (20) 7287-9364; e-mail info@linnean.org; internet www.linnean.org; f. 1788; possesses the unique colln of Linnaeus's plants and animals and other collns; library and archive; holds scientific meetings; 2,100 Fellows, incl. 50 Foreign Mems and 20 Hon. Fellows; library: see Libraries and Archives; Exec. Sec. Dr RUTH TEMPLE; Pres. Dr VAUGHN SOUTHGATE; Sec. for Botany Dr SANDRA KNAPP; Sec. for Collections SUSAN GOVE; Sec. for Editorial Dr JOHN EDMONDON; Sec. for Zoology Dr MALCOLM SCOBLE; publs *Biological Journal* (12 a year), *Botanical Journal* (12 a year), *Pulse* (4 a year), *Symposium* (vols), *Synopses of the British Fauna* (irregular), *The Linnean Newsletter and Proceedings* (4 a year), *Zoological Journal* (12 a year).

Malacological Society of London: c/o Dr V. Flari, Central Science Laboratory, Sand Hutton, York, YO4 1LZ; tel. (1904) 462349; e-mail vasiliki@flari.fsnet.co.uk; internet www.malacsoc.org.uk; f. 1893 to promote all aspects of the study of Mollusca; library: Radley Library deposited at University College London; 300 mems; Hon. Sec. Dr VASILIKI FLARI; publs *Journal of Molluscan Studies* (4 a year), *The Malacologist* (bulletin of the Society, 3 a year).

Marine Biological Association of the United Kingdom: The Laboratory, Citadel Hill, Plymouth, PL1 2PB; tel. (1752) 633207; fax (1752) 633102; e-mail sec@mba.ac.uk; internet www.mba.ac.uk; f. 1884 to promote scientific research into all aspects of life in the sea and to make public the results; the Assn receives grants from univs, research charities and other public bodies and is active in the Oceans 2025 UK strategic science programme; 1,250 mems; library: National Marine Biological Library; 60,000 vols; Pres. Sir GEOFFREY HOLLAND; Sec. and Dir Prof. COLIN BROWNLEE; publs *JMBA Global* (2 a year), *Journal* (8 a year).

Physiological Society: Peer House, Verulam St, London, WC1X 8LZ; tel. (20) 7269-5710; fax (20) 7269-5720; e-mail admin@physoc.org; internet www.physoc.org; f. 1876; promotes the advancement of physiology and facilitates communication between physiologists at home and abroad; 2,900 mems; Chief Exec. MIKE COLLIS; publs *Experimental Physiology* (12 a year online, 6 a year in print), *The Journal of Physiology* (26 a year), *The Physiological Society Magazine* (4 a year).

Ray Society: c/o Natural History Museum, Cromwell Rd, London, SW7 5BD; tel. (20) 7942-5560; e-mail t.ferrero@nhm.ac.uk; f. 1844; publishes works primarily concerned with the natural history of the British Isles and north-west Europe; 270 mems; Pres. E. PLATTS; Hon. Sec. Dr T. J. FERRERO.

Royal Entomological Society: The Mansion House, Chiswell Green Lane, St Albans, AL2 3NS; tel. (1727) 899387; fax (1727) 894797; e-mail info@royensoc.co.uk; internet www.royensoc.co.uk; f. 1833; 2,025 Fellows; library of 11,000 vols, 750 periodicals, 30,000 reprints; Pres. Prof. LIN FIELD; Registrar W. H. F. BLAKEMORE; publs *Agricultural and Forest Entomology* (4 a year), *Antenna* (4 a year), *Ecological Entomology* (4 a year), *Insect Molecular Biology* (4 a year), *Medical and Veterinary Entomology* (4 a year), *Physiological Entomology* (4 a year), *Systematic Entomology* (4 a year).

Royal Society for the Protection of Birds: The Lodge, Sandy, SG19 2DL; tel. (1767) 680551; fax (1767) 692365; internet www.rspb.org.uk; f. 1889, inc. 1904; protects wild birds and their natural habitat; 1m. mems; library of 9,000 vols; Chair. IAN DARLING; Chief Exec. Dr MIKE CLARKE; publs *Bird Life* (6 a year), *Birds* (4 a year), and occasional titles.

Royal Zoological Society of Scotland: Scottish National Zoological Park, Edinburgh, EH12 6TS; tel. (131) 334-9171; fax (131) 314-0382; e-mail info@rzss.org.uk; internet www.edinburghzoo.org.uk; f. 1909, inc. by Royal Charter 1913, to promote, through the presentation of the Soc.'s living collns, the conservation of animal species and wild places by captive breeding, environmental education and scientific research; 23,000 mems; Chief Exec. HUGH ROBERTS; publ. *Lifelinks* (4 a year).

Scottish Association for Marine Science: Dunstaffnage Marine Laboratory, Dunbeg, Oban, PA37 1QA; tel. (1631) 559000; fax (1631) 559001; internet www.sams.ac.uk; f. 1884 for research and education in marine science; 470 mems, 150 staff; Pres. Prof. Sir JOHN ARBUTHNOTT; Dir Prof. LAWERCE MEE.

Selborne Society Ltd: 89 Daryngton Dr., Greenford, UB6 8BH; tel. (78) 7859-4290; e-mail contact@selbornesociety.org.uk; internet www.selbornesociety.org.uk; f. 1885; perpetuates the memory of Gilbert White of Selborne and promotes the study of natural history, esp. among schoolchildren; library: large colln of documents incl. originals of 'The Natural History of Selborne', back copies in-house magazine and MSS by Gilbert White; 1,024 mems; Hon. Sec. ANDREW PEDLEY.

Society for General Microbiology: Marlborough House, Basingstoke Rd, Spencers Wood, Reading, RG7 1AG; tel. (118) 988-1800; fax (118) 988-5656; e-mail admin@sgm.ac.uk; internet www.sgm.ac.uk; f. 1945; promotes the advancement of microbiology; provides a common meeting ground for those working in specialized fields incl. medical, veterinary, agricultural and economic microbiology; 5,300 individual mems, 550 schools; Pres. Prof. HILARY LAPPIN-SCOTT; Chief Exec. Dr R. S. S. FRASER; publs *International Journal of Systematic and Evolutionary Microbiology* (12 a year), *Journal of General Virology* (12 a year), *Journal of Medical Microbiology* (12 a year), *Microbiology* (12 a year), *Microbiology Today* (4 a year).

Society of Biology: Charles Darwin House, 12 Roger St, London, WC1N 2JU; tel. (20) 7685-2550; e-mail info@societyofbiology.org; internet www.societyofbiology.org; f. 2009 by merger of the Biosciences Federation and the Institute of Biology; to create a single unified voice for UK biology, representing the discipline and its practitioners; 80,000 mems; Pres. Prof. Dame NANCY ROTHWELL; Chief Exec. Dr MARK DOWNS; publ. *Journal of Biological Education*.

Systematics Association: c/o Botany Dept, Natural History Museum, Cromwell Rd, London, SW7 5BD; tel. (20) 7942-5910; fax (20) 7942-5529; e-mail j.brodie@nhm.ac.uk; internet www.systass.org; f. 1937; studies systematics in relation to biology and evolution; 400 mems; Pres. Prof. JULIET BRODIE; Sec. for Programmes Dr J. COTTON; Sec. Dr P. WILKIE; Sec. for Grants and Awards Dr T. RICHARDS.

Zoological Society of London: Regent's Park, London, NW1 4RY; tel. (20) 7722-3333; fax (20) 7449-6411; internet www.zsl.org; f. 1826; consists of: ZSL London Zoo and ZSL Whipsnade Zoo; conservation programmes, Institute of Zoology, library and fellowship services; 40,000 mems; library of 180,000 vols, 1,300 periodicals; Pres. Prof. Sir PATRICK BATESON; Dir-Gen. RALPH ARMOND; publs *Animal Conservation* (6 a year), *Conservation Science and Practice Book Series* (2 a year), *International Zoo Yearbook* (1 a year), *Journal of Zoology* (12 a year), *Nomenclator Zoologicus* (9 vols).

Mathematical Sciences

British Society for the History of Mathematics: 20 Dunvegan Close, Exeter, Devon, EX4 4AF; internet www.bshm.org; f. 1971; provides a forum for all interested in the history and development of mathematics and related disciplines; organizes conferences, workshops, visits; 500 mems; Hon. Sec. TONY MANN; publ. *Bulletin* (3 a year).

Institute of Mathematics and its Applications: Catherine Richards House, 16 Nelson St, Southend-on-Sea, SS1 1EF; tel. (1702) 354020; fax (1702) 354111; e-mail post@ima.org.uk; internet www.ima.org.uk; f. 1964, inc. by Royal Charter 1990; extends and diffuses knowledge of mathematics and of the applications of mathematics in science, engineering, economics; promotes education in mathematics; 5,000 mems; Pres. Prof. MICHAEL WALKER; Exec. Dir DAVID YOUDAN; publs *IMA Journal of Applied Mathematics* (6 a year), *IMA Journal of Management Mathematics* (4 a year), *IMA Journal of Mathematical Control and Information* (4 a year), *IMA Journal of Numerical Analysis* (4 a year), *IMA Teaching Mathematics and its Applications* (int. journal, 4 a year), *Mathematical Medicine and Biology* (4 a year).

London Mathematical Society: De Morgan House, 57–58 Russell Sq., London, WC1B 4HS; tel. (20) 7637-3686; fax (20) 7323-3655; e-mail lms@lms.ac.uk; internet www.lms.ac.uk; f. 1865 for the promotion and extension of mathematical knowledge; 2,450 mems; Pres. Prof. E. B. DAVIES; Hon. Sec. Prof. C. M. GOLDIE; Exec. Sec. P. R. COOPER; publs *Bulletin* (6 a year), *Journal* (6 a year), *Nonlinearity* (6 a year), *Proceedings* (6 a year).

Physical Sciences

Association of Public Analysts: Burlington House, Piccadilly, London W1V 0BN; tel. (1224) 491648; fax (1224) 276873; e-mail nmichie@aberdeencity.gov.uk; internet www.the-apa.co.uk; f. 1953 as a body to support analysts engaged in the public protection enforcement service, where chemical analysis and related testing are undertaken, especially in relation to the composition of foodstuffs, fertilizers, animal feed and other areas of consumer protection; 120 mems and Associate mems; Pres. NORMAN MICHIE; Hon. Sec. RON ENNION; publ. *Journal of the Association of Public Analysts* (online).

British Astronomical Association: Burlington House, Piccadilly, London, W1J 0DU; tel. (20) 7734-4145; fax (20) 7439-4629; e-mail office@britastro.org; internet www.britastro.org; f. 1890; asscn of amateur astronomical observers; 3,000 mems; publs *Handbook* (1 a year), *Journal* (6 a year).

British Cryogenics Council: POB 227, Wantage, OX12 2DP; tel. (1372) 376544; fax (1372) 376544; e-mail admin@bcryo.org.uk; internet www.bcryo.org.uk; f. 1967 to foster and encourage the development and application of cryogenics in Britain by means of contacts, education and research; 10 mem. instns; Chair. Prof. HARRY JONES; Hon. Sec. CHARLES MONROE; publ. *Low Temperature News* (4 a year).

British Horological Institute: Upton Hall, Upton, Newark, NG23 5TE; tel. (1636) 813795; fax (1636) 812258; internet www.bhi.co.uk; f. 1858; promotes the science and practice of horology; 3,000 mems; Pres. Dr J. K. LLOYD JONES; Sec. M. TAYLOR; publ. *The Horological Journal* (12 a year).

British Interplanetary Society: 27/29 South Lambeth Rd, London, SW8 1SZ; tel. (20) 7735-3160; fax (20) 7587-5118; e-mail mail@bis-spaceflight.com; internet www.bis-spaceflight.com; f. 1933; promotes study and research in science, engineering and technology of astronautics; organizes evening lectures; symposia; confs; visits; 3,300 mems (1,800 fellows, 1,500 mems); Pres. ROBERT PARKINSON; Exec. Sec. SUSZANN PARRY; publs *Journal* (12 a year), *Space Chronicle* (2 a year), *Spaceflight* (12 a year).

British Nuclear Energy Society: 1–7 Great George St, London, SW1P 3AA; tel. (20) 7665-2241; fax (20) 7799-1325; internet www.bnes.com; f. 1962 in succession to British Nuclear Energy Conference to provide a forum for discussion, and directed to the broader aspects of nuclear energy, covering engineering and scientific disciplines; 12 constituent institutions; 1,200 mems; Sec. ANDREW TILLBROOK; publs *Nuclear Energy* (6 a year), *Conference Proceedings* (irregular).

Challenger Society for Marine Science: c/o National Oceanography Centre Empress Dock, European Way, Southampton, SO14 3ZH; tel. (23) 8059-5106; fax (23) 8059-5107; e-mail jennifer.jones@noc.ac.uk; internet www.challenger-society.org.uk; f. 1903; promotes study of oceanography, marine sciences; 500 mems; Pres. Prof. HARRY BRYDEN; publ. *Ocean Challenge* (2 a year).

Geological Society of London: Burlington House, Piccadilly, London, W1J 0BG; tel. (20) 7434-9944; fax (20) 7439-8975; e-mail enquiries@geolsoc.org.uk; internet www.geolsoc.org.uk; f. 1807; investigates the mineral structure of the Earth; 10,000 mems; library: see Libraries and Archives; Pres. Dr BRYAN LOVELL; Exec. Sec. EDMUND NICKLESS; publs *Geochemistry, Exploration, Environment, Analysis* (4 a year), *Journal* (6 a year), *Petroleum Geoscience* (4 a year), *Quarterly Journal of Engineering Geology and Hydrogeology* (4 a year).

Geologists' Association: Burlington House, Piccadilly, London, W1J 0DU; tel. (20) 7434-9298; fax (20) 7287-0280; e-mail geol.assoc@btinternet.com; internet www.geologist.demon.co.uk; f. 1858 to foster the progress and diffusion of the science of geology and to encourage research and the development of new methods; 2,000 mems; Pres. Dr ROBIN COCKS; Exec. Sec. SARAH STAFFORD; publs *GA Magazine* (4 a year), *Proceedings* (4 a year).

Institute of Acoustics: 77A St Peter's St, St Albans, AL1 3BN; tel. (1727) 848195; fax (1727) 850553; e-mail ioa@ioa.org.uk; internet www.ioa.org.uk; f. 1974; 3,000 mems; Pres. TREVER COX; Chief Exec. KEVIN MACAN-LIND; publ. *Acoustics Bulletin* (6 a year).

Institute of Physics: 76 Portland Place, London, W1B 1NT; tel. (20) 7470-4800; fax (20) 7470-4848; e-mail physics@iop.org; internet www.iop.org; f. 1918, chartered 1970; professional body for physicists in the UK and Ireland; 34,500 mems; Pres. Sir JOHN ENDERBY; Hon. Sec. Prof. JOHN BEEBY; Chief Exec. Dr ROBERT KIRBY-HARRIS; publs *Chinese Physics* (12 a year), *Chinese Physics Letters* (12 a year), *Combustion Theory and Modelling* (4 a year), *European Journal of Physics* (6 a year), *Inverse Problems* (6 a year), *Journal of Cosmology and Astroparticle Physics* (online only), *Journal of High Energy Physics* (online only), *Journal of Micromechanics and Microengineering* (12 a year), *Journal of Physics* (series A 50 a year, B 24 a year, CM 50 a year, D 24 a year and G 12 a year), *Journal of Radiological Protection* (4 a year), *Journal of Turbulence* (online only), *Measurement Science and Technology* (12 a year), *Metrologia* (6 a year), *Modelling and Simulation in Materials Science and Engineering* (8 a year), *Nanotechnology* (12 a year), *New Journal of Physics* (online only, at www.njp.org), *Nonlinearity* (6 a year), *Nuclear Fusion* (12 a year), *Physics Education* (6 a year), *Physics in Medicine and Biology* (24 a year), *Physiological Measurement* (6 a year), *Plasma Physics and Controlled Fusion* (12 a year), *Plasma Sources Science and Technology* (4 a year), *Reports on Progress in Physics* (12 a year), *Semiconductor Science and Technology* (12 a year), *Smart Materials and Structures* (6 a year), *Superconductor Science and Technology* (12 a year).

Mineralogical Society of Great Britain and Ireland: 12 Baylis Mews, Amyand Park Rd, Twickenham, Middx, TW1 3HQ; tel. (20) 8891-6600; fax (20) 8891-6599; e-mail info@minersoc.org; internet www.minersoc.org; f. 1876 by Joseph Henry Collins; scientific publishing and promotion of the mineral sciences through scientific meetings and special interest groups; 1,000 mems; Pres. Prof. BEN HARTE; Gen. Sec. Dr MARK HODSON; Exec. Sec. Dr ADRIAN LLOYD-LAWRENCE; publs *Clay Minerals* (4 a year), *Mineralogical Magazine* (6 a year).

Palaeontographical Society: c/o Dept of Palaeontology, Natural History Museum, Cromwell Rd, London, SW7 5BD; tel. (20) 7942-5195; fax (20) 7942-5546; e-mail s.long@nhm.ac.uk; internet www.nhm.ac.uk/hostedsites/palsoc; f. 1847; illustration and description of British fossils; 181 individual mems, 174 mem. orgs; Pres. Dr A. B. SMITH; Sec. Dr S. L. LONG; Sec. Dr P. M. BARRETT; publ. *Monograph of the Palaeontographical Society* (1 a year).

Quekett Microscopical Club: c/o Natural History Museum, Cromwell Rd, London, SW7 5BD; tel. (20) 7942-5213; internet www.quekett.org; f. 1865 to encourage the study of every branch of microscopical science; 500 mems; library of 1,000 vols; publ. *Quekett Journal of Microscopy* (2 a year).

Royal Astronomical Society: Burlington House, Piccadilly, London, W1J 0BQ; tel. (20) 7734-4582; fax (20) 7494-0166; e-mail info@ras.org.uk; internet www.ras.org.uk; f. 1820, granted Royal Charter in 1831; 3,200 mems; library: see Libraries and Archives; Pres. Prof. K. WHALER; Exec. Sec. D. ELLIOTT; publs *Astronomy and Geophysics* (6 a year), *Geophysical Journal International* (12 a year), *Monthly Notices of the Royal Astronomical Society* (every 10 days).

Royal Meteorological Society: 104 Oxford Rd, Reading, Berks, RG1 7LS; tel. (1734)

568500; fax (1734) 568571; e-mail execdir@rmets.org; internet www.rmets.org; f. 1850; 3,000 mems; Pres. Prof. C. G. COLLIER; Gen. Sec. Dr P. RYDER; publs *Quarterly Journal*, *International Journal of Climatology* (15 a year), *Weather* (12 a year), *Meteorological Applications* (4 a year), *Atmospheric Science Letters* (online), *Weather Front* (12 a year).

Royal Microscopical Society: 37–38 St Clements, Oxford, OX4 1AJ; tel. (1865) 248768; fax (1865) 791237; e-mail info@rms.org.uk; internet www.rms.org.uk; f. 1839, granted Royal Charter in 1866; for the promotion of microscopical science and its applications in the academic and industrial fields; 1,400 mems; Pres. Prof. CHRIS HAWKS; Exec. Dir ROBERT FLAVIN; publs *Journal of Microscopy* (12 a year), *Proceedings* (4 a year).

Royal Society of Chemistry: Thomas Graham House, Science Park, Milton Rd, Cambridge, CB4 0WF; tel. (1223) 420066; fax (1223) 426017; e-mail sales@rsc.org; internet www.rsc.org; f. 1980 from unification of the Chemical Soc. (f. 1841) and the Royal Inst. of Chemistry (f. 1877); 46,000 fellows and mems (designated Chartered Chemists), assoc. mems and affiliates, incl. 4,000 students; library: see Libraries and Archives; Pres. Prof. JIM FEAST; Chief Exec. Dr RICHARD PIKE; publs *The Analyst* (12 a year), *Analytical Abstracts* (12 a year), *Catalysts and Catalysed Reactions* (12 a year), *Chemical Biology* (12 a year), *Chemical Communications* (52 a year), *Chemical Science* (12 a year), *Chemical Society Reviews* (12 a year), *Chemical Technology* (12 a year), *Chemistry World* (12 a year), *Chromatography Abstracts* (published in collaboration with the Chromatographic Soc., 12 a year), *CrystEngComm* (electronic only, 12 a year), *Dalton Transactions* (52 a year), *Education in Chemistry* (6 a year), *Faraday Discussions* (3 a year), *Green Chemistry* (12 a year), *Journal of Analytical Atomic Spectroscopy* (12 a year), *Journal of Environmental Monitoring* (12 a year), *Journal of Materials Chemistry* (52 a year), *Lab on a Chip* (12 a year), *Laboratory Hazards Bulletin* (12 a year), *Mass Spectrometry Bulletin* (12 a year), *Methods in Organic Synthesis* (12 a year), *Molecular BioSystems* (12 a year), *Natural Product Reports* (6 a year), *Natural Product Updates* (12 a year), *New Journal of Chemistry* (published on behalf of the CNRS, 12 a year), *Organic and Biomolecular Chemistry* (26 a year), *PCCP–Physical Chemistry Chemical Physics* (jtly owned by Royal Soc. of Chemistry, Deutsche Bunsen-Gesellschaft für Physikalische Chemie and the chemical societies of Denmark, Finland, Ireland, Israel, Italy, the Netherlands, Norway, Spain, Sweden, Switzerland and Turkey, weekly), *Photochemical and Photobiological Sciences* (published on behalf of European Soc. for Photobiology (ESP), European Photochemistry Asscn (EPA), the Asia and Oceania Soc. for Photobiology (AOSP) and the Korean Soc. of Photoscience (KSP), 12 a year), *Soft Matter* (12 a year).

SCI (Society of Chemical Industry): International Headquarters, 14/15 Belgrave Square, London, SW1X 8PS; tel. (20) 7598-1500; fax (20) 7598-1545; internet www.soci.org; f. 1881; interdisciplinary network connecting industry, research and consumer affairs at all levels throughout the world; provides opportunities for people working in the areas of process and materials technologies, energy, water, agriculture, food, pharmaceuticals, construction and environmental protection to exchange ideas and gain new perspectives on markets, technologies and strategies; 6,000 mems; Pres. THOMAS M. SWAN; Gen. Sec. RICHARD DENYER; publs *Chemistry & Industry* (2 a month), *Journal of Chemical Technology and Biotechnology* (12 a year), *Journal of the Science of Food and Agriculture* (15 a year), *Pest Management Science* (12 a year), *Polymer International* (12 a year), *SCI Bulletin* (12 a year).

Yorkshire Geological Society: c/o Prof. Patrick Boylan, 2A Compass Rd, Leicester, LE5 2HF; tel. (116) 220-5496; e-mail p.boylan@city.ac.uk; internet www.yorksgeolsoc.org.uk; f. 1837; 600 mems; library of 5,000 vols; Pres. Dr NOEL WORLEY; Gen. Sec. (vacant); Hon. Treas. Prof. PATRICK BOYLAN; publs *Circular* (7 a year), *Proceedings* (2 a year).

PHILOSOPHY AND PSYCHOLOGY

Aristotelian Society: Room 281, Stewart House, Russell Sq., London, WC1B 5DN; tel. (20) 7862-8685; e-mail mail@aristoteliansociety.org.uk; internet www.aristoteliansociety.org.uk; f. 1880 for the systematic study of philosophy, its historic devt and its methods and problems; meets fortnightly in London, throughout the academic year, to hear and discuss philosophical papers; papers are drawn from an int. base of contributors and discuss issues across a broad range of philosophical traditions, incl. those that are of greatest current interest; meetings are open to the public and the papers are subsequently published in the Soc.'s Journal; also an annual conference held in conjunction with the Mind Asscn; papers given at the conference are published in a Supplementary Vol; 700 individual mems, 1,357 mem. libraries; Exec. Sec. R. E. CARTER; publs *Proceedings* (annual; online journal, 3 a year), *Supplementary Volume* (1 a year).

British Psychological Society: St Andrews House, 48 Princess Rd East, Leicester, LE1 7DR; tel. (116) 254-9568; fax (116) 247-0787; e-mail mail@bps.org.uk; internet www.bps.org.uk; f. 1901; 40,000 mems; Pres. Dr GERRY MULHERN; Hon. Gen. Sec. Prof. PAM MARAS; publs *British Journal of Clinical Psychology* (4 a year), *British Journal of Developmental Psychology* (4 a year), *British Journal of Educational Psychology* (4 a year), *British Journal of Health Psychology* (4 a year), *British Journal of Mathematical & Statistical Psychology* (4 a year), *British Journal of Psychology* (4 a year), *British Journal of Social Psychology* (4 a year), *Journal of Occupational & Organisational Psychology* (4 a year), *Legal and Criminological Psychology* (4 a year), *Psychology and Psychotherapy: Theory, Research and Practice* (4 a year), *Selection & Development Review* (4 a year), *The Psychologist* (12 a year).

British Society of Aesthetics: c/o Prof. Graham McFee, The Chelsea School, Univ. of Brighton, 1 Denton Rd, Eastbourne, BN20 7SP; e-mail kathleen@british-aesthetics.org; internet www.british-aesthetics.org; f. 1960 to promote study, research and discussion in aesthetics and the growth of artistic taste among the public, and to facilitate communications between scholars at an international and European level; Pres. RICHARD WOLLHEIM; Sec. KATHLEEN STOCK; publ. *British Journal of Aesthetics* (4 a year).

Experimental Psychology Society: Dept of Experimental Psychology, Univ. of Bristol, 12A Priory Rd, Bristol, BS8 1TU; internet www.eps.ac.uk; f. 1946; furthers scientific enquiry in the field of psychology; 756 mems; Pres. Prof. V. BRUCE; Hon. Sec. Prof. C. JARROLD; publ. *Quarterly Journal of Experimental Psychology*.

Leeds Philosophical and Literary Society Ltd: c/o Armley Mills Museum, Canal Rd, Leeds, LS12 2QF; internet www.leedsphilandlit.org.uk; f. 1820 to promote the advancement of science, literature and the arts in the city of Leeds and elsewhere; organizes public lectures and visits; provides assistance for scholarly research and publication; 135 mems; Sec. Dr J. LYDON.

Manchester Literary and Philosophical Society: MMU Business School, Aytoun St, Manchester, M1 3GH; tel. (161) 247-6774; fax (161) 247-6773; e-mail admin@manlitphil.co.uk; internet www.manlitphil.co.uk; f. 1781; promotes advancement of education and encourages public interest in, and appreciation of, any form of literature, science, the arts and public affairs; varied lectures throughout the academic year; 500 mems; library of 4,000 vols; Administrator ALLAN JEFFERIS; Administrator MARGARET GALLAGHER; Hon. Sec. PETER BARNES; Hon. Sec. DEREK CALDWELL; publ. *Manchester Memoirs* (1 a year).

Mind Association: c/o Dr Miranda Fricker, Dept of Philosophy, Birkbeck College, Malet St, London, WC1E 7HX; tel. (20) 7631-6383; e-mail m.fricker@bbk.ac.uk; internet www.mindassociation.org; f. 1900; organizes annual confs jtly with the Aristotelian Soc.; 300 mems; Hon. Sec. Dr MIRANDA FRICKER; publ. *MIND* (4 a year).

Philosophical Society of England: 6 Craghall Dean Ave, Newcastle upon Tyne, NE3 1QR; tel. (191) 284-1223; fax (191) 284-1223; e-mail m.c.bavidge@ncl.ac.uk; internet www.philsoc.co.uk; f. 1913; spreads knowledge of philosophy among public; organizes lectures, confs and workshops; sponsors local philosophical groups; 150 mems; Pres. Prof. BRENDA ALMOND; Chair. MICHAEL BAVIDGE; publ. *The Philosopher* (2 a year).

Royal Institute of Philosophy: 14 Gordon Square, London, WC1H 0AR; tel. (20) 7387-4130; fax (20) 7387-4061; e-mail j.garvey@royalinstitutephilosophy.org; internet www.royalinstitutephilosophy.org; f. 1925; 700 mems; Pres. Lord QUINTON; Chair. Lord SUTHERLAND OF HOUNDWOOD; Dir Prof. A. O'HEAR; Sec. Dr JAMES GARVEY; publs *Conference Proceedings* (1 a year), *Philosophy* (4 a year), *Think* (4 a year).

Royal Philosophical Society of Glasgow: D12, 160 Bothwell St, Glasgow, G2 7EL; tel. (141) 564-3841; e-mail info@royalphil.org; internet www.royalphil.org; f. 1802; organizes lectures and promotes philosophical debate; 916 mems; Pres. Prof. Sir RODDY MACSWEEN; Hon. Sec. MAIRI MITCHELL; Hon. Treas. MERVYN LOVAT.

Victoria Institute, or Philosophical Society of Great Britain (operates as Faith and Thought): 96 Hadleigh Rd, Leigh on Sea, SS9 2LZ; tel. and fax (1702) 472-710; e-mail apkerry@aol.com; internet www.faithandthought.org.uk; f. 1865; Pres. Sir JOHN HOUGHTON; publs *Faith&Thought* (2 a year), *Science and Christian Belief* (jtly with Christians in Science, 2 a year).

William Morris Society: Kelmscott House, 26 Upper Mall, London, W6 9TA; tel. (20) 8741-3735; fax (20) 8748-5207; e-mail william.morris@care4free.net; internet www.morrissociety.org; f. 1955 to encourage wider appreciation and understanding of the life, work and influence of William Morris and his circle; 1,400 mems; library of 2,000 vols; Hon. Sec. PETER FAULKNER; publ. *Journal* (2 a year).

RELIGION, SOCIOLOGY AND ANTHROPOLOGY

African Studies Association of the United Kingdom: 36 Gordon Sq., London, WC1H 0PD; tel. (20) 3073-8335; fax (20)

3073-8340; e-mail asa@soas.ac.uk; f. 1963; advances academic studies relating to Africa by providing facilities for the interchange of information and ideas; holds inter-disciplinary confs, symposia; 1,000 mems; Hon. Pres. Prof. WILLIAM BEINART; Hon. Sec. Dr JUNE BAM-HUTCHISON.

British Association for South Asian Studies: c/o Royal Asiatic Society, 14 Stephenson Way (Second Fl.), London, NW1 2HD; tel. (20) 7388-5490; e-mail basas@basas.org.uk; internet www.basas.org.uk; f. 1972 as the Soc. for S Asian Studies; merged with British Asscn for S Asian Studies 2007; supports research and training in the arts, humanities and social sciences of S Asia; 600 mems; Chair. Prof. KUNAL SEN; Sec. Dr LAWRENCE SAEZ; publs *Contemporary South Asia* (1 a year), *South Asian Studies* (1 a year).

British Association for the Study of Religions: c/o Dr James Cox, Univ. of Edinburgh, New College, Mound Place, Edinburgh, EH1 2LX; tel. (131) 650-8942; fax (131) 650-7952; e-mail j.cox@ed.ac.uk; internet basr.open.ac.uk; f. 1954; affiliated to Int. Association for the History of Religions; organizes an annual conference; 250 mems; Pres. and Chair Dr JAMES COX; Hon. Sec. Dr GRAHAM HARVEY; publ. *Bulletin* (3 a year).

British Society for Middle Eastern Studies: Institute for Middle Eastern and Islamic Studies, Univ. of Durham, Al-Qasimi Bldg, Elvet Hill Rd, Durham, DH1 3TU; tel. (191) 334-5179; fax (191) 334-5661; e-mail a.l.haysey@durham.ac.uk; internet www.brismes.ac.uk; f. 1973; promotes the study of the Middle Eastern region from the end of classical antiquity and the rise of Islam, encouraging discussion and debate and fostering cooperation among teachers, researchers and students of the Middle East, both within the UK and int.; co-operation with similar societies is being consolidated and expanded; 550 mems; Pres. Sir HAROLD WALKER; Exec. Dir Dr ZAHIA SALHI; publ. *British Journal of Middle Eastern Studies* (3 a year).

British Sociological Association: Bailey Suite, Palatine House, Belmont Business Park, Belmont, Durham, DH1 1TW; tel. (191) 383-0839; fax (191) 383 0782; e-mail enquiries@britsoc.org.uk; internet www.britsoc.co.uk; f. 1951; promotes interest in sociology; advances its study and application in the United Kingdom; encourages contacts between workers in all relevant fields of enquiry; holds confs, seminars and workshops; 2,500 mems; Pres. Prof. JOHN BREWER; Exec. Team Chair Prof. ROBERT MEARS; Chief Exec. JUDITH MUDD; publs *Cultural Sociology* (3 a year), *Network* (3 a year), *Sociology* (6 a year), *Work Employment and Society* (4 a year).

Ecclesiological Society: EcclSoc, 38 Rosebery Ave, New Malden, Surrey, KT3 4JS; tel. (20) 8942-2111; e-mail info@ecclsoc.org; internet www.ecclsoc.org; f. 1879 as St Paul's Ecclesiological Soc.; lectures, confs, visits, publs; 950 mems; Pres. Rt Rev. DAVID STANCLIFFE; Chair. TREVOR COOPER; publ. *Ecclesiology Today* (2 a year).

Folklore Society: c/o Warburg Inst., Woburn Sq., London, WC1H 0AB; tel. (20) 7862-8564; e-mail enquiries@folklore-society.com; internet www.folklore-society.com; f. 1878; c. 1,000 mems and subscribers; library of 11,000 vols; Pres. ROBERT MCDOWALL; Hon. Sec. Prof. JAMES H. GRAYSON; publ. *Folklore* (3 a year).

Galton Institute: 19 Northfields Prospect, London, SW18 1PE; tel. (20) 8874-7257; e-mail betty.nixon@talk21.com; internet www.galtoninstitute.org.uk; f. 1907; advances public knowledge and understanding of human genetics and population problems; 400 mems; Pres. Prof. Sir WALTER BODMER; Gen. Sec. BETTY NIXON.

Henry Bradshaw Society: Music Collections, The British Library, 96 Euston Rd, London, NW1 2DB; e-mail nicolas.bell@bl.uk; internet www.henrybradshawsociety.org; f. 1890; publishes facsimiles and editions of rare texts relating to the liturgy of the medieval Christian church; 134 institutional mems, 152 individual mems; Chair. Prof. MICHAEL LAPIDGE; Sec. NICOLAS BELL.

Institute of Race Relations: 2–6 Leeke St, King's Cross Rd, London, WC1X 9HS; tel. (20) 7837-0041; fax (20) 7278-0623; e-mail info@irr.org.uk; internet www.irr.org.uk; f. 1958 to promote scientific study and publication on race and racism, and to make information and proposals available on race relations; Dir A. SIVANANDAN; publ. *Race & Class* (4 a year).

Maghreb Studies Association: c/o The Maghreb Bookshop, 45 Burton St, London, WC1H 9AL; tel. and fax (20) 7388-1840; e-mail maghreb@maghrebreview.com; internet www.maghrebreview.com; f. 1981; promotes the study of the history, politics and environment of North Africa and the broader Middle East and Islamic world; 155 mems; Chair. Prof. HÉDI BOURAOUI; Exec. Sec. M. BEN-MADANI; publ. *Maghreb Review* (4 a year).

Modern Church: c/o Rev. Jonathan Clatworthy, 9 Westward View, Liverpool, L17 7EE; tel. (845) 345-1909; e-mail office@modchurchunion.org; internet www.modchurchunion.org; f. 1898; for the advancement of liberal religious thought; 650 mems; Pres. Rt Rev. JOHN SAXBEE; Chair. Rev. JOHN PLANT; Gen. Sec. Rev. JONATHAN CLATWORTHY; Administrator CHRISTINE ALKER; publ. *Modern Believing* (4 a year).

National Society (Church of England) for Promoting Religious Education: Church House, Great Smith St, Westminster, SW1P 3AZ; tel. (20) 7898-1518; fax (20) 7898-1493; e-mail info.natsoc@churchofengland.org; internet www.churchofengland.org/national-society; f. 1811; promotes religious education in accordance with the principles of the Church of England; Chair. The BISHOP OF OXFORD; Gen. Sec. Rev. JANINA AINSWORTH.

Royal African Society: 36 Gordon Sq., London, WC1H 0PD; tel. (20) 3075-8335; fax (20) 3075-8340; e-mail ras@soas.ac.uk; internet www.royalafricansociety.org; f. 1901; hosts regular programme of lectures in London, Bristol and Edinburgh; 1,000 mems; Chair. Lord MALLOCH-BROWN; Sec. GEMMA HAXBY; publ. *African Affairs* (4 a year).

Royal Anthropological Institute of Great Britain and Ireland: 50 Fitzroy St, London, W1T 5BT; tel. (20) 7387-0455; fax (20) 7388-8817; e-mail admin@therai.org.uk; internet www.therai.org.uk; f. 1843; lectures and film festivals; manages various trust and scholarship funds; awards medals and prizes; raises funds for research; 1,600 mems; library: borrowing rights to 120,000 vols; film-hire library; photographic archive; Pres. Prof. ROY ELLEN; Dir Dr DAVID SHANKLAND; Hon. Sec. Dr ERIC HIRSCH; publs *Anthropology Today* (6 a year), *Journal of the Royal Anthropological Institute* (incorporating *Man*, 5 a year).

Royal Asiatic Society of Great Britain and Ireland: 14 Stephenson Way, London, NW1 2HD; tel. (20) 7388-4539; fax (20) 7391-9429; e-mail info@royalasiaticsociety.org; internet www.royalasiaticsociety.org; f. 1823; studies the history, religions, instns, customs, languages, literature and art of Asia; 600 subscribing libraries; brs in various Asian cities; 800 mems; library: see Libraries and Archives; Dir ALISON OHTA; Exec. Officer CAMILLA LARSEN; publ. *Journal* (4 a year).

Royal Commonwealth Society: 18 Northumberland Ave, London, WC2N 5BJ; tel. (20) 7930-6733; fax (20) 7930-9705; e-mail info@rcsint.org; internet www.rcsint.org; f. 1868; 10,000 mems worldwide.

Royal Society for Asian Affairs: 2 Belgrave Sq., London, SW1X 8PJ; tel. (20) 7235-5122; fax (20) 7259-6771; e-mail info@rsaa.org.uk; internet www.rsaa.org.uk; f. 1901; promotes greater knowledge and understanding of Asia and countries from the Middle East to Japan; hosts lectures and encourages debate on topics, from literature and the arts, exploration and the environment, to cultural, military and political history and current affairs; organises mem. tour to a country in part of Asia or the Middle East; 1,080 mems with knowledge of, and interest in, Asia; library of 5,000 vols; Pres. Lord DENMAN; Chair. Sir DAVID JOHN; Sec. Col NEIL S. PORTER; publ. *Asian Affairs* (3 a year).

Swedenborg Society: 20–21 Bloomsbury Way, London, WC1A 2TH; tel. (20) 7405-7986; fax (20) 7831-5848; e-mail richard@swedenborg.org.uk; internet www.swedenborg.org.uk; f. 1810; translates and publishes writings of Emanuel Swedenborg, Swedish scientist, philosopher and theologian; organizes lectures and meetings to further knowledge of Swedenborg's life, works and influence; also incl. publishing; maintains a library; library of 15,000 vols; works of Swedenborg in Latin and translated in modern languages; colln of collateral literature (mainly 19th century); periodicals dating back to 1790; approx. 850 mems; Pres. Dr LARS BERGQUIST; Sec. RICHARD LINES; Librarian JAMES WILSON; publ. *Journal of the Swedenborg Society* (1 a year).

Young Foundation: 18 Victoria Park Sq., London, E2 9PF; tel. (20) 8980-6263; fax (20) 8981-6719; e-mail reception@youngfoundation.org; internet www.youngfoundation.org; f. 1954, fmrly Institute of Community Studies; social research on poverty, deprivation and comparative social policy; housing, urban planning and community; education; Dir Dr GEOFF MULGAN.

TECHNOLOGY

British Computer Society: 1 Sanford St, Swindon, Wilts., SN1 1HJ; tel. (1793) 417417; fax (1793) 480270; e-mail bcshq@bcs.org.uk; internet www.bcs.org.uk; f. 1957; industry body for Information Technology professionals; sets standards for education and training through the BCS Professional Examination and through the inspection and accreditation of university courses and company training schemes; awards the Chartered IT Professional (CITP) qualification; licensed by the Engineering Council and the Science Council to appoint chartered and incorporated engineers and chartered scientists; 45,000 mems; library: joint library with Instn of Electrical Engineers; Pres. DAVID MORRISS; Registrar MANDY BRYAR; publs *The Computer Journal* (6 a year), *IT Now* (6 a year), *IEE Proceedings —Software* (6 a year, in conjunction with IEE), *Interacting with Computers Journal* (4 a year), *Formal Aspects of Computing Journal* (6 a year).

British Society of Rheology: c/o Prof. Simon Cox, Institute of Mathematics and Physics, Aberystwyth Univ., Aberystwyth SY23 2AX; tel. (1970) 622764; fax (1970) 622826; e-mail secretary@bsr.org.uk;

internet www.bsr.org.uk; f. 1940; promotes rheology, the science of the deformation and flow of matter; library at Univ. of Wales, Aberystwyth; 400 mems; Pres. BILL FRITH; Sec. Prof. SIMON COX; publs *Bulletin* (4 a year), *Rheology Abstracts*.

BSI Group (British Standards Institution): 389 Chiswick High Rd, London, W4 4AL; tel. (20) 8996-9000; fax (20) 8996-7400; e-mail cservices@bsi-global.com; f. 1901 as Engineering Standards Committee; inc. 1918 as British Engineering Standards Association, f. 1929 under Royal Charter and Supplemental Charter in 1931, when scope was extended; independent certification of management systems and products; product-testing services; operates BSI British Standards, the national standards body of the UK, which develops standards for industry and the population in general; 15,000 subscribing mems; CEO STEVAN BREEZE; Dir of Legal Affairs and Company Sec. RICHARD CATT; publs *British Standards*, *BSI Catalogue* (1 a year), *Business Standards* (4 a year), *Standards Update* (12 a year).

Chartered Institute of Building: Englemere, Kings Ride, Ascot, SL5 7TB; tel. (1344) 630700; fax (1344) 630777; e-mail reception@ciob.org.uk; internet www.ciob.org.uk; f. 1834, inc. by Royal Charter 1980; professional body for managers in the construction industry; 39,000 mems; Pres. STUART HENDERSON; Chief Exec. CHRIS BLYTHE; publs *Construction Information Quarterly* (4 a year), *Construction Manager/Construction Computing* (10 a year), *New Constructor* (3 a year).

Chartered Institute of Logistics and Transport: Earlstrees Court, Earlstrees Rd, Corby, NN17 4AX; tel. (20) 1536 740100; fax (20) 1536 740101; e-mail enquiry@ciltuk.org.uk; internet www.cilt-international.com; f. 1919, inc. by Royal Charter 1926 to promote, encourage, and coordinate the study and advancement of the science and art of transport in all its branches, and to provide a source of authoritative views on transport; brs in Argentina, Australia, Bangladesh, Canada, Cyprus, Ghana, Greece, Hong Kong, India, Ireland, Kenya, Malawi, Malaysia, Malta, Mauritius, Nepal, New Zealand, Nigeria, Pakistan, Singapore, South Africa, Spain, Sri Lanka, Thailand, Uganda, United Arab Emirates, USA, West Indies, Zambia, Zimbabwe and elsewhere; 32,000 mems; Pres. RICHARD HUNT; Dir-Gen. CYRIL BLEASDALE; publ. *CILT World* (newsletter, 3 a year).

Chartered Institute of Patent Attorneys: 95 Chancery Lane, London, WC2A 1DT; tel. (20) 7405-9450; fax (20) 7430-0471; e-mail mail@cipa.org.uk; internet www.cipa.org.uk; f. 1882, chartered 1891, present name 2006; professional and examining body; 3,250 mems; Sec. MICHAEL RALPH; publs *CIPA* (12 a year), *Register of Patent Attorneys* (1 a year).

Chartered Institution of Building Services Engineers: 222 Balham High Rd, London, SW12 9BS; tel. (20) 8675-5211; fax (20) 8675-5449; e-mail enquiries@cibse.org; internet www.cibse.org; promotes the science and practice of such engineering services as are associated with the built environment and industrial processes and the advancement of education and research in building services engineering; 15,000 mems; Chief Exec. and Sec. JULIAN AMEY; publs *Building Services Engineering Research and Technology* (4 a year), *Building Services Journal* (12 a year), *Lighting Research and Technology* (4 a year).

Chartered Institution of Water and Environmental Management: 15 John St, London, WC1N 2EB; tel. (20) 7831-3110; fax (20) 7405-4967; e-mail admin@ciwem.org.uk; internet www.ciwem.org.uk; f. 1895; to advance the science and practice of water and environmental management for the public benefit and to promote education, training, study and research in those areas; 12,000 mems; Pres. PETER TREADGOLD; Exec. Dir NICK REEVES; publs *Journal* (4 a year), *Water and Environment Magazine* (12 a year).

Chartered Management Institute: 2 Savoy Court, Strand, London, WC2R 0EZ; and Management House, Cottingham Rd, Corby, Northants., NN17 1TT; tel. (1536) 204222; fax (1536) 201651; e-mail enquiries@managers.org.uk; internet www.managers.org.uk; f. 1947 as British Institute of Management, name changed 1992; granted Royal Charter 2002; encourages and supports the lifelong development of managers; influences policy-makers and opinion-formers on management issues; 84,000 individual mems, 600 company mems; library: 80,000 items, 200 periodicals; Dir-Gen. MARY M. CHAPMAN; Sec. VALERIE HAMILL; publ. *Professional Manager* (6 a year).

Chartered Society of Designers: 1 Cedar Court, Royal Oak Yard, Bermondsey St, London, SE1 3GA; tel. (20) 7357-8088; fax (20) 7407-9878; e-mail info@csd.org.uk; internet www.csd.org.uk; f. 1930, incorporated by Royal Charter 1976; professional body for designers practising in product design, fashion and textiles design, interiors and graphics, design management, education and professional development; 4,000 mems; Pres. ADRIANNE LEMAN; publ. *CSD Magazine* (4 a year).

Crafts Council: 44A Pentonville Rd, London, N1 9BY; tel. (20) 7278-7700; fax (20) 7837-6891; e-mail reference@craftscouncil.org.uk; internet www.craftscouncil.org.uk; f. 1971 as the Crafts Advisory Cttee, present name 1979; directly funded by Arts Council England; nat. org. for contemporary crafts in Great Britain, offering exhibition and education programmes; Nat. Register of Makers; research library; library of 7,200 vols, 190 periodicals; Chair. JOANNA FOSTER; Dir ROSY GREENLEES; publ. *Crafts* (6 a year).

Design Council: 34 Bow St, London, WC2E 7DL; tel. (20) 7420-5200; fax (20) 7420-5300; e-mail info@designcouncil.org.uk; internet www.designcouncil.org.uk; f. 1944 to inspire, in the world context, the best use of design by the UK to improve prosperity and well-being; Chair. of Council Sir MICHAEL BICHARD; Chief Exec. DAVID KESTER.

Energy Institute: 61 New Cavendish St, London, W1G 7AR; tel. (20) 7467-7100; fax (20) 7255-1472; e-mail info@energyinst.org; internet www.energyinst.org; f. 2003 following the merger of the Institute of Petroleum (f. 1913) and the Institute of Energy (f. 1927), to promote the safe, environmentally responsible and efficient supply and use of energy; research into oil, gas and other primary fuels and renewable sources of energy; power generation, transmission and distribution, sustainable devt, demand-side management and energy efficiency; publishes codes of safe practice, measurement manuals, test methods, journals; organizes conferences, training courses; participates in careers and education work and offers an extensive library and information service; 12,000 individual mems and 400 group mems; library of 17,000 vols, 200 periodicals; Pres. Dr JAMES SMITH; Chief Exec. LOUISE KINGHAM; Hon. Sec. JOANNE WADE; publs *Energy World* (11 a year), *Journal of the Energy Institute*, *Petroleum Review* (12 a year).

Engineering Council UK: 246 High Holborn, London, WC1V 7EX; tel. (20) 3206-0500; fax (20) 3206-0501; e-mail info@engc.org.uk; internet www.engc.org.uk; f. 1981 by Royal Charter; advances the education and training of engineers and technologists; improves the supply of qualified engineers and technologists; sets up and maintains relevant professional, educational and training standards; Chair. Prof. KEL FIDLER; CEO ANDREW RAMSAY.

Ergonomics Society: The Elms, Elmsgrove, Loughborough, LE11 1RG; tel. (1509) 234904; fax (1509) 235666; e-mail ergsoc@ergonomics.org.uk; internet www.ergonomics.org.uk; f. 1949; promotes ergonomics and the work of ergonomists in solving problems that arise between people, their working environment and things that they use; organizes confs and one-day events about ergonomics applications, incl. patient safety, human and organizational factors in the oil, gas and chemical industries, and access and integration into schools; 1,400 mems; Pres. JOHN WILSON; Chief Exec. DAVID O'NEILL; publs *Applied Ergonomics*, *Behaviour and Information Technology*, *Ergonomics*, *Injury Control & Safety Promotion*, *Theoretical Issues in Ergonomic Science*, *Work and Stress*.

Faculty of Royal Designers for Industry: RSA, 8 John Adam St, London, WC2N 6EZ; tel. (20) 7930-5115; fax (20) 7839-5805; e-mail rdi@rsa.org.uk; internet www.thersa.org.uk; f. 1936; furthers the devt of design and in particular its application to industrial purposes; number of holders of RDI limited to 200 (132 at present plus 56 Hon.); Chair. LUKE JOHNSON; Master ROBIN LEVIEN; Sec. EMILY CAMPBELL.

Gemmological Association Great Britain: 27 Greville St, London, EC1N 8TN; tel. (20) 7404-3334; fax (20) 7404-8843; e-mail information@gem-a.com; internet www.gem-a.com; f. 1908; promotes study of gemmology and the scientific and industrial study of all materials and articles used or dealt in by persons interested in the science of gems; 3,000 mems; CEO Dr JACK OGDEN; publs *Gem and Jewellery* (1 a year), *Journal of Gemmology* (4 a year), *MailTalk*.

Heritage Crafts Association: 132 The Glade, Old Coulsdon CR5 1SP; e-mail info@heritagecrafts.org.uk; internet www.heritagecrafts.org.uk; f. 2009; advocacy body for traditional heritage crafts; supports and promotes heritage crafts as a fundamental part of the UK's living heritage; researches the status of heritage crafts, identifying those crafts in decline or in imminent danger of being lost, and addressing the issues to ensure their survival; communicates the vital importance of the heritage crafts to Government, key agencies and organizations; raises awareness and the status of heritage craft skills with the wider public through a programme of public relations, communications and showcase events; works in partnership with key agencies in the education and learning sectors to identify and support new ways to ensure that the highest standard of heritage skills are passed from one generation to the next and where necessary recorded for posterity; supports heritage crafts through a range of means, including advice, networking, training and access to public and private funding; 200 mems; Chair. ROBIN WOOD; Vice-Chair. PATRICIA LOVETT; Treas. IAN LOVETT (acting); Sec. BRIAN CROSSLEY.

Institute of Corrosion: Corrosion House, Vimy Court, Vimy Rd, Leighton Buzzard, Beds., LU7 1FG; tel. (1525) 851771; fax (1525) 376690; e-mail admin@icorr.demon.co

.uk; internet www.icorr.org; f. 1975; 1,600 mems; Pres. DAVID DEACON; Hon. Sec. JIM BURNELL-GRAY; publs *Corrosion Management* (6 a year), *Corrosion Science* (12 a year).

Institute of Food Science and Technology: 5 Cambridge Court, 210 Shepherd's Bush Rd, London, W6 7NJ; tel. (20) 7603-6316; fax (20) 7602-9936; e-mail info@ifst.org; internet www.ifst.org; f. 1964 to promote the knowledge, devt and application of science and technology of food, and the provision of a professional body for food scientists and technologists; 2,000 mems; Pres. Prof. CAROL PHILLIPS; Hon. Sec. S. TOMLINSON; Chief Exec. H. G. WILD; publs *Food Science and Technology* (4 a year), *International Journal of Food Science and Technology* (12 a year).

Institute of Management Services: Brooke House, 24 Dam St, Lichfield, Staffs., WS13 6AA; tel. (1543) 266909; fax (1543) 257848; e-mail admin@ims-stowe.fsnet.co.uk; internet www.ims-productivity.com; f. 1941; promotion, practice and devt of methodologies and techniques for the improvement of productivity and quality; 1,800 mems; Chair. D. BLANCHFLOWER; publ. *Management Services Journal* (4 a year).

Institute of Marine Engineering, Science and Technology (IMarEST): 80 Coleman St, London, EC2R 5BJ; tel. (20) 7382-2600; fax (20) 7382-2670; e-mail info@imarest.org; internet www.imarest.org; f. 1889 as Institute of Marine Engineers, present name 2002; professional society representing those involved in marine engineering, science and technology; 15,000 mems; library: library and Marine Information Centre; Sec. K. F. READ; publs *Marine Engineers' Review* (10 a year), *Journal of Offshore Technology* (6 a year), *The Marine Scientist* (4 a year), *Proceedings* (Parts A and B), *Maritime Electronics* (6 a year).

Institute of Materials, Minerals and Mining: 1 Carlton House Terrace, London, SW1Y 5DB; tel. (20) 7451-7300; fax (20) 7839-1702; e-mail admin@iom3.org; internet www.iom3.org; f. 2002, merger of Institute of Materials and Institution of Mining and Metallurgy; advances the science and practice of engineering; facilitates the acquisition and preservation of knowledge pertaining to the associated professions; establishes, upholds and advances the industry standards of education, training and competence; organizes meetings and confs worldwide; administers scholarships and fellowships; 22,000 mems; library of 65,000 vols, 1,000 periodicals; Pres. Dr BARRY LYE; Chief Exec. Dr B. A. RICKINSON; publs *Advances in Applied Ceramics* (4 a year), *British Corrosion Engineering, Science and Technology* (4 a year), *Clay Technology* (6 a year), *Energy Materials* (4 a year), *Historical Metallurgy* (2 a year), *Interdisciplinary Science Reviews* (4 a year), *International Heat Treatment and Surface Engineering* (6 a year), *International Materials Reviews* (6 a year), *International Wood Products Journal* (2 a year), *Ironmaking and Steelmaking* (8 a year), *Materials Science and Technology* (12 a year), *Materials World* (12 a year), *Plastics, Rubber and Composites* (10 a year), *Powder Metallurgy* (4 a year), *Science and Technology of Welding and Joining* (8 a year), *Steel World* (2 a year), *Surface Engineering* (4 a year), *The Packaging Professional* (6 a year), *Transactions* of the fmr Institute of Mining and Metallurgy (12 a year), *Tribology* (4 a year), *Wood Focus* (3 a year).

Institute of Measurement and Control: 87 Gower St, London, WC1E 6AF; tel. (20) 7387-4949; fax (20) 7388-8431; e-mail ceo@instmc.org.uk; internet www.instmc.org.uk; f. 1944, inc. by Royal Charter 1975; to promote the advancement and application of the science and practice of measurement and control; to co-ordinate and disseminate information and to conduct examinations; 4,100 mems; Chief Exec. PETER MARTINDALE; publs *Measurement and Control* (10 a year, incl. *Inst MC Interface*, of which 2 a year), *Transactions* (5 a year), *Instrument Engineer's Yearbook*.

Institute of Physics and Engineering in Medicine: Fairmount House, 230 Tadcaster Rd, York, YO24 1ES; tel. (1904) 610821; fax (1904) 612279; e-mail office@ipem.ac.uk; internet www.ipem.ac.uk; f. 1995; promotes advancement of physics and engineering applied to medicine and biology and advances public education in the field; 3,700 mems; Pres. Dr C. J. GIBSON; Gen. Sec. ROBERT W. NEILSON; publs *Medical Engineering and Physics* (10 a year), *Physics in Medicine and Biology* (26 a year), *Physiological Measurement* (12 a year).

Institute of Quarrying: 7 Regent St, Nottingham, NG1 5BS; tel. (115) 941-1315; fax (115) 948-4035; e-mail mail@quarrying.org; internet www.quarrying.org; f. 1917; professional body to provide a professional qualification, to improve science and practice of quarrying and to provide a forum for technical discussion; over 5,000 home and overseas mems; Exec. Dir J. W. BERRIDGE; Sec. L. BRYDEN; publ. *Quarry Management* (12 a year).

Institute of Refrigeration: Kelvin House, 76 Mill Lane, Carshalton, Surrey, SM5 2JR; tel. (20) 8647-7033; fax (20) 8773-0165; e-mail ior@ior.org.uk; internet www.ior.org.uk; f. 1899 (as the Cold Storage and Ice Association) for the general advancement of refrigeration in all its applications; 2,600 mems; Pres. J. ELLIS; Sec. M. J. HORLICK; publ. *Proceedings*.

Institute of Science and Technology: Kingfisher House, 90 Rockingham St, Sheffield, S1 4EB; tel. (114) 2763197; fax (114) 2726354; e-mail office@istonline.org.uk; internet www.istonline.org.uk; f. 1954 from the Science Technologists' Assoc. (f. 1948); present name 2008; professional and qualifying body for specialist, technical and managerial staff; provides training for vocational qualifications and continuing professional devt; provides awards and prizes; 1,000 mems; Pres. ROBERT HARDWICK; Chair. JOHN ROBINSON; Hon Sec. AMANDA TAYLOR; publ. *Science Technology Journal* (2 a year).

Institute of Scientific and Technical Communicators: Airport House, Purley Way, Croydon, CR0 0XZ; tel. (20) 8253-4506; fax (20) 8253-4510; e-mail istc@istc.org.uk; internet www.istc.org.uk; f. 1972; establishes and maintains professional codes of practice for people engaged in all brs of scientific and technical communication; 1,500 mems; Pres. PAUL BALLARD; Exec. Administrator ELAINE COLE; publ. *Communicator* (4 a year).

Institution of Chemical Engineers: 165–189 Railway Terrace, Rugby, CV21 3HQ; tel. (1788) 578214; fax (1788) 560833; e-mail tjevans@icheme.org.uk; internet www.icheme.org; f. 1922, incorporated by Royal Charter to promote the science and practice of chemical engineering, to improve the standards and methods of education therein, and to act as a qualifying body for chemical engineers, etc.; 25,000 mems; Chief Exec. Dr T. J. EVANS; publs *Chemical Engineering Research and Design* (12 a year), *Food and Bioproducts Processing* (4 a year), *Process Safety and Environmental Protection* (6 a year), *The Chemical Engineer* (12 a year).

Institution of Civil Engineers: 1 Great George St, Westminster, London, SW1P 3AA; tel. (20) 7222-7722; fax (20) 7222-7500; e-mail secretariat@ice.org.uk; internet www.ice.org.uk; f. 1818; inc. by Royal Charter in 1828 for the general advancement of mechanical science and more particularly for promoting the acquisition of knowledge which constitutes the profession of a Civil Engineer, namely the art of directing natural sources of power for the use and convenience of man; two principal roles: (i) qualifying body for all three levels of registration: Chartered Engineers, Incorporated Engineers and Engineering Technicians; (ii) learned society; as a qualifying body the Institution is concerned with academic and professional achievements and with continuing education, and as a learned society it is concerned with the acquisition and dissemination of knowledge; 80,000 corporate and non-corporate mems; library of 100,000 vols; Pres. Prof. PAUL JOWITT; Dir-Gen. and Sec. TOM FOULKES; publs *Advances in Cement Research*, *Geotechnique* (4 a year), *Ground Improvement*, *Magazine of Concrete Research*, *Nuclear Energy*, *Proceedings* (in 16 parts: *Civil Engineering, Geotechnical Engineering, Structures & Building, Municipal Engineer, Transport, Water, Maritime Engineering, Bridge Engineering, Construction Materials, Energy, Engineering History and Heritage, Engineering Sustainability, Engineering and Computational Mechanics, Management, Procurement and Law, Urban Design and Planning, Waste and Resource Management, Water Management*, all 4 a year except the last which is 6 a year).

Institution of Electronics: 12 Bentfield Close, Higher Bebington, Wirral, CH63 8NB; tel. (151) 608-4236; e-mail info@institutionofelectronics.ac.uk; internet www.institutionofelectronics.ac.uk; f. 1930, inc. 1935; furtherance of the science of electronics and other scientific subjects; over 2,500 mems; Chair. ALAN HOLLINSHEAD-JONES; Membership Officer TIM HATCH; publs *Electron* (online, 4 a year), *Proceedings* (online, 4 a year).

Institution of Engineering and Technology: Savoy Place, London, WC2R 0BL; tel. (20) 7240-1871; fax (20) 7240-7735; internet www.theiet.org; f. 1871 (and inc. by Royal Charter in 1921, inc. the Institution of Radio and Electronic Engineers 1988 and Institution of Manufacturing Engineers 1991, Society of Engineers inc. into the Institution of Incorporated Engineers in 2005 and both merged with IET in 2006); to promote the general advancement of science, engineering and technology, and to facilitate the exchange of information and ideas on those subjects; fmrly Institution of Electrical Engineers; 150,000 mems; library: see Libraries and Archives; Pres. Sir ROBIN SAXBY; CEO Dr A. ROBERTS; publs *Communications Engineer* (6 a year), *Computing and Control Engineering* (6 a year), *Electronics Education* (3 a year), *Electronics Letters* (every 2 weeks), *Electronics Systems and Software* (6 a year), *Engineering Management* (6 a year), *Engineering & Technology* (12 a year), *Flipside* (6 a year), *Information Professional* (6 a year), *Manufacturing Engineer* (6 a year), *Power Engineer* (6 a year), *Proceedings* (6 a year), *Systems Biology* (4 a year).

Institution of Engineering Designers: Courtleigh, Westbury Leigh, Westbury, Wilts., BA13 3TA; tel. (1373) 822801; fax (1373) 858085; e-mail staff@ied.org.uk; internet www.ied.org.uk; f. 1945 to advance education in engineering, particularly in engineering and product design and to constitute a body of members qualified to a recognized high standard; a nominated body of the Engineering Council; 5,300 mems; Sec. ELIZABETH BRODHURST; publ. *Engineering Designer* (6 a year).

Institution of Engineers and Shipbuilders in Scotland: Clydeport, 16 Robertson St, Glasgow, G2 8DS; tel. (141) 248-3721; fax (141) 221-2698; e-mail secretary@iesis.org; internet www.iesis.org; f. 1857 to facilitate the exchange of information and ideas amongst its mems, and to promote the advancement of the science and practice of engineering and shipbuilding; 800 mems; Chair. E. CHAMBERS; publs *Transactions* (1 a year), *Year Book and List of Members* (every 2 years).

Institution of Fire Engineers: London Rd, Moreton-in-Marsh, GL56 0RH; tel. (1608) 812580; fax (1608) 812581; e-mail info@ife.org.uk; internet www.ife.org.uk; f. 1918, and inc. 1924, to promote, encourage, and improve the science of fire engineering and technology; 11,000 home and overseas mems; CEO ELLEN JESSETT; publ. *Fire Prevention and Fire Engineers Journal* (monthly, online).

Institution of Gas Engineers and Managers: IGEM House, 28 High St, Kegworth, DE74 2DA; tel. (844) 375-4436; fax (1509) 283110; e-mail general@igem.org.uk; internet www.igem.org.uk; f. 1863; Royal Charter 1929, to promote by research, discussion and education the sciences necessary for the better production, distribution or utilization of gas and of the by-products of its production; 5,000 mems; library of 10,000 vols; Chief Exec. JOHN WILLIAMS; publ. *Journal*.

Institution of Highways and Transportation: 119 Britannia Walk, London, N1 7JE; tel. (20) 7336-1555; fax (20) 7336-1556; e-mail info@iht.org; internet www.iht.org; f. 1930 as the Institution of Highway Engineers; present name 1987; concerned with the design, construction, maintenance and operation of sustainable transport systems and infrastructure; serves as a representative body for the profession, to implement best practice and technical excellence, to bring fellow professionals and ideas together and to provide training and professional competence; 11,000 UK-based mems, several hundred overseas mems; 18 UK-based brs, several overseas brs incl. Republic of Ireland, Hong Kong and Malaysia; Chief Exec. MARY LEWIS; publ. *Transportation Professional* (10 a year).

Institution of Lighting Engineers: Regent House, Regent Place, Rugby, Warwicks., CV21 2PN; tel. (1788) 576492; fax (1788) 540145; e-mail info@ile.org.uk; internet www.ile.org.uk; f. 1924 to promote, encourage and improve the science and art of efficient lighting in all fields, and to facilitate the exchange of information and ideas on this subject; 1,900 mems; Pres. DEREK ROGERS; Chief Exec. RICHARD FROST; publ. *Lighting Journal* (6 a year).

Institution of Mechanical Engineers: 1 Birdcage Walk, London, SW1H 9JJ; tel. (20) 7222-7899; fax (20) 7222-4557; internet www.imeche.org.uk; f. 1847, inc. by Royal Charter 1930; principal organization for professional mechanical engineers in the UK, and qualifying body for chartered and incorporated mechanical engineers; 75,000 mems worldwide; library of 60,000 books and various other documents; Pres. WILLIAM EDGAR; Chief Exec. ANDREW IVES; publs *Automotive Engineer* (10 a year), *Environmental Engineering* (4 a year), *Institution of Diesel and Gas Turbine Engineers* (6 a year), *Journal of Strain Analysis*, *Professional Engineering* (22 a year).

Institution of Nuclear Engineers: Allan House, 1 Penerley Rd, London, SE6 2LQ; tel. (20) 8698-1500; fax (20) 8695-6409; e-mail inucewh@aol.com; internet www.inuce.org.uk; f. 1959 for the advancement of nuclear engineering technology and its related fields; 1,700 mems; Pres. Dr P. A. BEELEY; publ. *The Nuclear Engineer* (6 a year).

Institution of Structural Engineers: 11 Upper Belgrave St, London, SW1X 8BH; tel. (20) 7235-4535; fax (20) 7235-4294; e-mail mail@istructe.org; internet www.istructe.org; f. 1908 as the Concrete Inst., present name 1922; inc. by Royal Charter 1934, to promote the general advancement of the science and art of structural eng.; library of 15,000 vols; 21,000 mems; Pres. DAVID HARVEY; Chief Exec. Dr KEITH J. EATON; publ. *The Structural Engineer* (2 a month).

National Society for Clean Air and Environmental Protection: 44 Grand Parade, Brighton, East Sussex, BN2 9QA; tel. (1273) 878770; fax (1273) 606626; e-mail admin@nsca.org.uk; internet www.nsca.org.uk; f. 1899 as Coal Smoke Abatement Soc. and merged with the Smoke Abatement League of Great Britain in 1929; air pollution, contaminated land and noise control, environmental protection; 1,500 mems, incl. learned socs, local authorities, industrial concerns, etc.; Pres. Lord JULIAN HUNT; Chief Exec. PHILIP MULLIGAN (acting); publs *NSCA Briefing* (12 a year), *NSCA Pollution Handbook* (overview of pollution control legislation, annual).

Newcomen Society for the Study of the History of Engineering and Technology: Science Museum, Exhibition Rd, S Kensington, London, SW7 2DD; tel. and fax (20) 7371-4445; e-mail office@newcomen.com; internet www.newcomen.com; f. 1920; encourages the study of the history of engineering and technology worldwide; regular evening meetings in London and other regional centres; visits to sites of engineering interest; annual summer meeting and other visits at home and abroad; 1,000 mems and subscribers; Exec. Sec. TIM CRICHTON; publs *Links* (Bulletin of the Newcomen Society, 4 a year), *Transactions of the Newcomen Society / The International Journal for the History of Engineering and Technology* (2 a year).

Oil and Colour Chemists' Association: Priory House, 967 Harrow Rd, Wembley, Middlesex, HA0 2SF; tel. (20) 8908-1086; fax (20) 8908-1219; e-mail enquiries@occa.org.uk; internet www.occa.org.uk; f. 1918 to promote by discussion and scientific investigation the technology of the paint, oil, printing ink, and allied industries; 2,400 mems; Pres. D. FOULGER; Gen. Sec. C. PACEY-DAY; publs *Surface Coatings International Part A* (10 a year), *Surface Coatings International Part B* (4 a year), *Surface Coating Reviews*, *Surface Coating Monographs*.

Radio Society of Great Britain: 3 Abbey Court, Fraser Rd, Priory Business Park, Bedford, MK44 3WH; tel. (1234) 832700; fax (1234) 831496; e-mail ar.dept@rsgb.org.uk; internet www.rsgb.org; f. 1913 to promote interest in the science of radio-communication by amateurs, and to safeguard the interests of those of its members who operate or aspire to operate amateur transmitting stations; 30,000 mems; Gen. Man. PETER A. KIRBY; publ. *Radio Communication* (12 a year).

Remote Sensing and Photogrammetry Society: c/o School of Geography, Univ. of Nottingham, Nottingham, NG7 2RD; tel. (115) 951-5435; fax (115) 951-5249; e-mail rspsoc@nottingham.ac.uk; internet www.rspsoc.org; f. 2001; theory, techniques, instrumentation, applications in surveying, engineering, mapping, geographic information; annual conference; 1,000 mems; library of 2,000 vols; Hon. Gen. Sec. Dr PHILIPPA MASON; Exec. Sec. KAREN LAUGHTON; publs *International Journal of Remote Sensing* (24 a year), *The Photogrammetric Record* (4 a year).

Royal Academy of Engineering: 3 Carlton House Terrace, London, SW1Y 5DG; tel. (20) 7766-0600; fax (20) 7930-1549; internet www.raeng.org.uk; f. 1976; conducts engineering and educational studies, sponsors links between industry and higher education, co-sponsors with industry academic posts at higher education instns; 1,390 mems (1,266 fellows, 90 foreign mems, 34 hon. fellows); Pres. Lord JOHN BROWNE OF MADINGLEY; Chief Exec. PHILIP GREENISH; publ. *Ingenia* (4 a year).

Royal Aeronautical Society: 4 Hamilton Place, London, W1J 7BQ; tel. (20) 7499-3515; fax (20) 7499-6230; internet www.aerosociety.com; f. 1866; 18,500 mems; library of 27,000 books, 1,300 periodicals (of which 300 current), 20,000 technical reports, 100,000 photographs; Dir KEITH MANS; publs *Aerospace International* (12 a year), *Aerospace Professional* (12 a year), *The Aeronautical Journal* (12 a year).

Royal Institution of Naval Architects: 10 Upper Belgrave St, London, SW1X 8BQ; tel. (20) 7235-4622; fax (20) 7259-5912; e-mail hq@rina.org.uk; internet www.rina.org.uk; f. 1860, to advance naval architecture and marine technology; 8,500 mems; Pres. STEPHEN PAYNE; Chief Exec. TREVOR BLAKELEY; publs *Transactions Part A: International Journal of Maritime Engineering* (4 a year), *Transactions Part B: International Journal of Small Craft Technology* (2 a year), *The Naval Architect* (10 a year), *Ship and Boat International* (6 a year), *Ship Repair and Conversion Technology* (4 a year), *Significant Ships* (1 a year), *Significant Small Ships* (1 a year), *Warship Technology* (5 a year), *Offshore Marine Technology* (4 a year).

Royal Television Society: Kildare House, 3 Dorset Rise, London, EC4Y 8EN; tel. (20) 7822-2810; fax (20) 7822-2811; e-mail info@rts.org.uk; internet www.rts.org.uk; f. 1927; advances the art of television; forum for discussion and debate on all aspects of the profession; annual awards; 14 regional centres; over 3,000 mems; Pres. Sir ROBERT PHILLIS; Chief Exec. SIMON ALBURY; publ. *Television* (10 a year).

SCI (Steel Construction Institute): Silwood Park, Ascot, SL5 7QN; tel. (1344) 636525; fax (1344) 636570; e-mail reception@steel-sci.com; internet www.steel-sci.org; f. 1986; develops and promotes the proper and effective use of steel as a construction material; 850 mems; library of 11,000 vols; Dir Dr G.H. COUCHMAN; publ. *New Steel Construction* (6 a year).

Society for Underwater Technology: 80 Coleman St, London, EC2R 5BJ; tel. (20) 7382-2601; fax (20) 7382-2684; e-mail info@sut.org; internet www.sut.org.uk; f. 1966; to promote the further understanding of the underwater environment, and to advance the development of the techniques and tools needed to explore, study and exploit the oceans; provides sponsorship for undergraduate and 1-year postgraduate students studying in an appropriate subject area; 1,000 individual and 110 corporate mems; Exec. Sec. I. N. L. GALLETT; publ. *Underwater Technology* (4 a year).

Society of Consulting Marine Engineers and Ship Surveyors: 202 Lambeth Rd, London, SE1 7JW; tel. (20) 7261-0869; fax (20) 7261-0871; e-mail sec@scmshq.org; internet www.scmshq.org; f. 1920 to provide a central org. for consulting marine engineers, naval architects and ship surveyors, and generally to elevate the status and procure the advancement of the interests of the profession; Sec. P. R. OWEN.

Society of Designer Craftsmen: 24 Rivington St, London, EC2A 3DU; tel. (20) 7739-3663; fax (20) 7739-3663; e-mail info@societyofdesignercraftsmen.org.uk; internet www.societyofdesignercraftsmen.org.uk; f. 1887, as Arts and Crafts Exhibition Society; annual exhibitions for mems and invited guests; occasional regional exhibitions; active licentiate scheme to assist recently graduated designer-makers; 650 mems; Pres. Prof. CHRISTOPHER FRAYLING; Chair. FIONA ZOBOLE; Mem and Finance Sec. JEANNE DANIEL.

Society of Dyers and Colourists: Perkin House, POB 244, 82 Grattan Rd, Bradford, BD1 2JB; tel. (1274) 725138; fax (1274) 392888; e-mail info@sdc.org.uk; internet www.sdc.org.uk; f. 1884; promotes the advancement of the science and technology of colour and coloration; awards chartered qualifications; colour experience; 2,500 mems; Pres. JOHN MORRIS; Chief Exec. SUSIE HARGREAVES; publs *Colour Index*, *Coloration Technology* (6 a year), *The Colourist* (4 a year).

Society of Glass Technology: 9 Churchill Way, Chapeltown, Sheffield, S35 2PY; tel. (114) 263-4455; fax (114) 263-4411; e-mail info@sgt.org; internet www.sgt.org; f. 1916; promotes the assocn of persons interested in glass technology; publishes books, journals and conf. proceedings; hosts and organizes int. and local confs on glass; provides information and holds a library and archive on glass; supports students with travel bursaries and final year project prizes; British rep. on int. bodies such as the Int. Commission on Glass and European Soc. of Glass Science and Technology; 600 mems; library of 10,000 vols; located at Univ. of Sheffield Applied Science Library; Hon. Sec. JOHN HENDERSON; publs *Glass Technology: European Journal of Glass Science and Technology Part A* (6 a year), *Physics and Chemistry of Glasses: European Journal of Glass Science and Technology Part B* (6 a year).

Society of Operations Engineers: 22 Greencoat Pl., London, SWIP 1PR; tel. (20) 7630-1111; fax (20) 7630 6677; e-mail soe@soe.org.uk; internet www.soe.org.uk; f. 2000 by merger of Institute of Road Transport Engineers (IRTE) and Instn of Plant Engineers (IPlantE), to represent mems of the road transport, plant engineering and engineer surveying industries; 15,000 mems; Pres. CHRIS GRIME; Chief Exec. NICK JONES; publs *Operations Engineer* (10 a year), *Plant Engineer* (6 a year), *Transport Engineer* (12 a year).

South Wales Institute of Engineers Educational Trust: Empire House, Mount Stuart Sq., Cardiff, CF10 5FN; tel. (29) 2063-0561; fax (29) 2063-0666; e-mail info@swieet.org.uk; internet www.swieet.org.uk; f. 1857 for the encouragement and advancement of eng. science and practice; Sec. D. M. MORGAN; publ. *Proceedings* (every 2 years).

Textile Institute: see under International Organizations (Engineering and Technology).

TWI: Granta Park, Great Abington, Cambridge, CB21 6AL; tel. (1223) 899000; fax (1223) 892588; e-mail twi@twi.co.uk; internet www.twi.co.uk; f. 1946 to undertake gen. and contract research, to advance welding technology in all aspects, to provide consultancy and laboratory services, to provide education and training and to improve the professional status and qualification of mems; specialized information services on materials-joining technology; training courses in welding engineering, welding inspection, practical welding, non-destructive testing, structural integrity, microjoining; 10,500 mems (3,500 research, 7,000 professional); library of 10,000 vols; Chief Exec. R. JOHN; publs *Connect* (6 a year), *Contact* (news video, annual).

Research Institutes

GENERAL

Asia Research Centre: Houghton St, London, WC2A 2AE; f. 1997; attached to London School of Economics and Political Science, Univ. of London; conducts social science research on Asia; Dir Dr C. HUGHES.

Bill Douglas Centre for History of Cinema and Popular Culture: Academic Services, Univ. of Exeter, The Old Library, Prince of Wales Rd, Exeter, EX4 4SB; tel. (1392) 724321; e-mail soe.pgoffice@exeter.ac.uk; internet www.billdouglas.org; f. 1994; attached to Univ. of Exeter; study of twentieth century's art form and its precursors; Academic Dir Prof. STEVE NEALE.

Cambridge Programme for Sustainability Leadership: 1 Trumpington St, Cambridge CB2 1QA; tel. (1223) 768850; fax (1223) 768831; e-mail info@cpsl.cam.ac.uk; internet www.cpsl.cam.ac.uk; attached to Univ. of Cambridge; Dir POLLY COURTICE.

Centre for Alcohol and Drug Studies: Paisley Campus, Paisley, PA1 2BE; tel. (141) 848-3788; fax (141) 848-3891; attached to Univ. of the West of Scotland; Dir K. BARRIE.

Centre for Business Research: The Judge Business School Bldg, Trumpington St, Cambridge, CB2 1AG; tel. (1223) 765320; fax (1223) 765338; e-mail enquiries@cbr.cam.ac.uk; internet www.cbr.cam.ac.uk; attached to Univ. of Cambridge; Dir Prof. ALAN HUGHES (Sidney Sussex College).

Centre for Civil Society: Houghton St, London, WC2A 2AE; f. 1999; attached to London School of Economics and Political Science, Univ. of London; conducts research on problems and issues in management of voluntary agencies and NGOs; Dir Prof. J. HOWELL.

Centre for Early Modern Studies: The Centre for the Early Modern History, History Dept, School of Humanities and Social Sciences, Armory Bldg, Rennes Dr., Exeter, EX4 4RJ; tel. (1392) 264297; fax (1392) 263305; e-mail histoff@ex.ac.uk; internet centres.exeter.ac.uk/cems; f. 2007; attached to Univ. of Exeter; rareas of research incl. religious culture, social and economic relations, political and intellectual thought, gender and sexuality, space, landscape and national identities, history of the book, theatre and performance for the period between 1500 and 1800; Dir Prof. ALEX WALSHAM; Asst Dir Prof. ANDREW MCRAE.

Centre for Enterprise and Regional Development: College Rd, Bangor, Gwynned, LL57 2DG; attached to Bangor Univ.; Dir S. JONES.

Centre for Gymnastics Research: Loughborough, LE11 3TU; e-mail m.r.yeadon@lboro.ac.uk; f. 2004; attached to Loughborough Univ.; Dir Prof. FRED YEADON.

Centre for International Studies: Houghton St, London, WC2A 2AE; f. 1967; attached to London School of Economics and Political Science, Univ. of London; promotes research in all aspects of int. studies; Chair. of Steering Cttee Dr JOHN KENT.

Centre for Leadership Studies: XFI Bldg, Rennes Dr., Exeter, EX4 4ST; tel. (1392) 262555; fax (1392) 262559; e-mail leadership@exeter.ac.uk; internet centres.exeter.ac.uk/cls; f. 1997; attached to Univ. of Exeter; research area ranges from applied evaluation of leadership devt processes to the philosophical underpinnings of modern leadership; Dir Prof. JONATHAN GOSLING.

Centre for Olympic Studies & Research: School of Sport, Exercise and Health Sciences, Loughborough Univ., Loughborough, LE11 3TU; e-mail cosar@lboro.ac.uk; f. 2004; attached to Loughborough Univ.; promotes, facilitates and conducts academic research into Olympism and Olympic movement; Dir Prof. IAN HENRY.

Centre for Research in Human Rights: tel. (20) 8392-3661; fax (20) 8392-3231; e-mail l.gearon@roehampton.ac.uk; attached to Roehampton Univ.; Dir Dr LIAM GEARON.

Centre For Service Research: Univ. of Exeter Business School, Streatham Court, Rennes Dr., Exeter, EX4 4PU; tel. (1392) 263458; fax (1392) 263242; e-mail cserv@exeter.ac.uk; internet centres.exeter.ac.uk/cserv; attached to Univ. of Exeter; research focuses on customer, process, people, environment working together towards the service experience; Dir of Service Pricing, Revenue Management, Customer Commitment and Relationships Prof. IRENE NG; Dir of Service Quality Management, Service Processes Prof. ROGER MAULL.

Centre for the Study of Human Rights: Houghton St, London, WC2A 2AE; tel. (20) 7955-6428; fax (20) 7955-6934; e-mail z.gillard@lse.ac.uk; internet www2.lse.ac.uk/humanrights; f. 1998; attached to London School of Economics and Political Science, Univ. of London; promotes study of human rights; Dir Prof. CHETAN BHATT; Man. ZOE GILLARD.

Centre for the Study of War, State and Society: History Dept, School of Humanities and Social Sciences, Armory Bldg, Rennes Dr., Exeter, EX4 4RJ; tel. (1392) 264297; fax (1392) 263305; e-mail histoff@ex.ac.uk; internet centres.ex.ac.uk/wss; f. 2005; attached to Univ. of Exeter; researches on effects of armed conflict on states, societies, cultures; explores themes of warfare and societal transformation; Dir Prof. RICHARD OVERY.

Centre of Commonwealth Studies: Stirling, FK9 4LA; tel. (1786) 467495; fax (1786) 466210; e-mail english@stir.ac.uk; internet www.english.stir.ac.uk/research/profile/ccws.php; f. 1985; attached to Univ. of Stirling; postgraduate and undergraduate work relating to Commonwealth countries, particularly in fields of African history, African and Caribbean culture and writing, African and Caribbean religion, Australian writing and painting, literature of India and of New Zealand, and post-colonial critical theory; Dir Prof. DAVID RICHARDS.

Communications Research Centre: Dept of Social Sciences, Loughborough Univ., Loughborough, LE11 3TU; tel. (1509) 223365; e-mail e.a.van-zoonen@lboro.ac.uk; internet www.lboro.ac.uk/departments/ss/research/crc; attached to Loughborough Univ.; communication studies, culture and media, discourse and social interaction; Dir LIESBAT VAN ZOONEN; Dir CHARLES ANTAKI.

David Livingstone Institute of Overseas Development Studies: McCance Bldg, 16 Richmond St, Glasgow, G1 1XQ; attached to Univ. of Strathclyde; Dir Prof. J. PICKETT.

Early Childhood Research Centre: Dept of Education, Roehampton Univ., Froebel College, London, SW15 5PJ; tel. (20) 8392-3689; fax (20) 8392-3322; e-mail k.brehony@roehampton.ac.uk; attached to Roehampton

Univ.; interdisciplinary research in children's thinking, early childhood history and policy, measures of quality in early years provision, professional devt; Dir Prof. KEVIN J. BREHONY.

European Construction Institute: Loughborough, LE11 3TU; tel. (1509) 222620; fax (1509) 260118; e-mail eci@lboro.ac.uk; internet www.eci-online.org; f. 1990; attached to Loughborough Univ.; Pres. MICHEL VIRLOGEUX; Chair. JOHN OLIVER.

European Institute: Houghton St, London, WC2A 2AE; f. 1991; attached to London School of Economics and Political Science, Univ. of London; coordinates and develops research and research training on European issues; Dir Prof. PAUL TAYLOR.

European Research Institute: Edgbaston, Birmingham, B15 2TT; tel. (121) 414-6346; e-mail p.a.carr@bham.ac.uk; internet www.eri.bham.ac.uk; f. 2001; attached to Univ. of Birmingham; research in the fields of culture and society, economics, European politics, history, law; Chair. Dr TIM HAUGHTON.

Exeter Centre for Strategic Processes and Operations (XSPO): Univ. of Exeter Business School, Streatham Court, Rennes Dr, Exeter, EX4 4PU; tel. (1392) 262557; fax (1392) 263242; e-mail xspo@exeter.ac.uk; internet centres.exeter.ac.uk/xspo; attached to Univ. of Exeter; research focuses on business process management; Dir for Service Quality Management Prof. ROGER MAULL; Dir for Service Process Management Prof. ANDI SMART.

Exeter Interdisciplinary Institute (EII): Univ. of Exeter, Queen's Dr., Exeter, Devon, EX4 4QJ; tel. (1392) 269302; e-mail r.gagnier@exeter.ac.uk; internet centres.exeter.ac.uk/interdisciplinaryinstitute; attached to Univ. of Exeter; researches across Exeter's strengths in cultural, natural, built environments with needs and opportunities in public sphere; Dir Prof. REGENIA GAGNIER.

Institute for Retail Studies: Stirling, FK9 4LA; tel. (1786) 467386; fax (1786) 466290; e-mail irst1@stir.ac.uk; internet www.management.stir.ac.uk; attached to Univ. of Stirling; Dir Prof. PAUL FREATHY; Deputy Dir Prof. LEIGH SPARKS.

Institute of Creative Enterprises: Coventry Univ. Enterprises, Puma Way, Coventry, CV1 2TT; tel. (24) 7615-8300; e-mail c.hamilton@coventry.ac.uk; internet wwwm.coventry.ac.uk/researchnet/ice; attached to Coventry Univ.; applied research activities for arts practice, communication and cultural studies, media, performing arts; postgraduate courses in performance, media, digital art; Dir CHRISTINE HAMILTON.

Institute of Rehabilitation: 215 Anlaby Rd, Kingston upon Hull HU3 2PG; tel. (1482) 675602; fax (1482) 675636; e-mail d.m.sharp@hull.ac.uk; internet www2.hull.ac.uk/pgmi/cmr/rehabilitation.aspx; f. 1997; attached to Univ. of Hull; Dir Dr DONALD SHARP (acting).

Institute of Sport and Leisure Policy: Loughborough, LE11 3TU; tel. (1509) 226365; fax (1509) 226301; e-mail p.downward@lboro.ac.uk; f. 1990, present name 1997; attached to Loughborough Univ.; theoretical analysis of sport and leisure policy; Dir PAUL DOWNWARD.

Institute of Youth Sport: Loughborough, LE11 3TU; e-mail c.e.taylor@lboro.ac.uk; f. 1998; attached to Loughborough Univ.; Dir MARY NEVILL.

Interdisciplinary Institute of Management: Houghton St, London, WC2A 2AE; f. 1990; attached to London School of Economics and Political Science, Univ. of London; promotes interdisciplinary research into management; research is closely linked with Centre for Economic Performance; Dir Prof. DIANE REYNIERS.

Loughborough Design School: Loughborough, LE11 3TU; tel. (1509) 226900; e-mail dsoffice@lboro.ac.uk; internet www.lboro.ac.uk/departments/lds; f. 2010 by merger of Dept of Design and Technology, Dept of Human Sciences (Ergonomics) and the Ergonomics and Safety Research Institute (ESRI); attached to Loughborough Univ.; Dir TONY HODGSON (acting).

LSE Gender Institute: Houghton St, London, WC2A 2AE; f. 1993; attached to London School of Economics and Political Science, Univ. of London; multi-disciplinary centre; addresses major intellectual challenges posed by contemporary changes in gender relations; Dir Prof. ANNE PHILLIPS.

Paisley Enterprise Research Centre: Paisley, Renfrewshire, PA1 2BE; f. 1995; attached to Univ. of the West of Scotland; Dir Prof. DAVID DEAKINS.

Peter Harrison Centre for Disability Sport: School of Sport Exercise and Health Sciences, Loughborough Univ., Loughborough, LE11 3TU; tel. (1509) 226387; e-mail phc@lboro.ac.uk; internet www.peterharrisoncentre.org.uk; f. 2005; attached to Loughborough Univ.; promotes knowledge in disability sport through applied research; Dir Dr VICKY TOLFREY; publs *Health and Well-being, Sport Culture and Science, Sport Science*.

Professional and Management Development Centre: Sir Richard Morris Bldg, Loughborough Univ., Loughborough, LE11 3TU; tel. (1509) 223140; fax (1509) 223963; e-mail pmdc@lboro.ac.uk; internet www.lboro.ac.uk/departments/sbe/pmdc; attached to Loughborough Univ.; Dir J. WHITTAKER.

Research Centre Wales: Bangor, Gwynned, LL57 2DG; tel. (1248) 382220; fax (1248) 388081; e-mail cyc@bangor.ac.uk; f. 1985; attached to Bangor Univ.; Dir Prof. C. R. BAKER.

Social Science Research Unit, Institute of Education: 18 Woburn Sq., London, WC1H 0NR; tel. (20) 7612-6391; fax (20) 7612-6400; e-mail ssru@ioe.ac.uk; internet www.ioe.ac.uk/ssru; f. 1990; attached to Institute of Education, Univ. of London; Dir Prof. DAVID GOUGH; Deputy Dir SANDY OLIVER.

Stirling Centre for Scottish Studies: Stirling, FK9 4LA; tel. (1786) 467495; fax (1786) 466210; e-mail english@stir.ac.uk; internet www.english.stir.ac.uk/research/profile/centerofscottishstudies.php; f. 1996; attached to Univ. of Stirling; promotes research, publ. and postgraduate recruitment in Scottish Studies, literature, art, music, history, media, philosophy, politics, social issues and cultural theory; Dir MICHAEL PENMAN.

Stirling Media Research Institute: Stirling, FK9 4LA; tel. (1786) 467520; fax (1786) 466855; e-mail stirling.media@stir.ac.uk; attached to Univ. of Stirling; Dir Dr RICHARD HAYNES; publ. *International Journal of Media and Cultural Politics*.

AGRICULTURE, FISHERIES AND VETERINARY SCIENCE

Agri-Food and Biosciences Institute: AFBI HQ, Newforge Lane, Belfast, BT9 5PX; tel. (28) 9025-5689; fax (28) 9025-5035; e-mail info@afbini.gov.uk; internet www.afbini.gov.uk; f. 2006, by merger of Dept of Agriculture and Rural Development (DARD) Science Service and the Agricultural Research Institute of Northern Ireland (ARINI); non-dept public body (NDPB); conducts high technology research and devt, statutory, analytical and diagnostic testing functions; offers scientific capabilities in areas of agriculture, animal health, food, environment and biosciences; Chair. SEÁN HOGAN; CEO Dr S. KENNEDY.

Animal Health and Welfare: Dept of Agriculture and Rural Development, Dundonald House, Upper Newtownards Rd, Belfast, BT4 3SB; tel. (28) 9052-4999; fax (28) 9052-4420; e-mail dardhelpline@dardni.gov.uk; internet www.dardni.gov.uk; attached to Dept of Agriculture and Rural Devt; animal and animal product imports and by-products, diseases, control and prevention, animal welfare, artificial reproduction, export certification; library of 11,000 vols.

Animal Health Trust: Lanwades Park, Kentford, Newmarket, Suffolk, CB8 7UU; tel. (8700) 502424; fax (8700) 502425; e-mail info@aht.org.uk; internet www.aht.org.uk; f. 1942; aims to advance veterinary science and provide specialist clinical services for all companion animals; Pres. HRH The PRINCESS ROYAL; CEO Dr PETER WEBBON.

Biotechnology and Biological Sciences Research Council: Polaris House, North Star Ave, Swindon, SN2 1UH; tel. (1793) 413200; fax (1793) 413201; internet www.bbsrc.ac.uk; f. 1994; responsible to the Office of Science and Technology; supports fundamental and strategic multidisciplinary research, with emphasis on the biological sciences, biotechnology and engineering, in its institutes and univs; Chair. Dr TOM BLUDELL; Chief Exec. Prof. DOUGLAS KELL.

Institutes and Units:

Babraham Institute: Babraham Hall, Babraham, Cambridge, CB2 4AT; tel. (1223) 496000; fax (1223) 496021; internet www.babraham.ac.uk; f. 1948; research to advance understanding of function in animal cells and systems, with emphasis on cell signalling, recognition mechanisms and mammalism devt; Dir Dr R. J. BICKNELL (acting).

Institute for Animal Health: Ash Rd, Pirbright, GU24 0NF; tel. (1635) 578411; fax (1635) 577237; e-mail iahweb@bbsrc.ac.uk; internet www.iah.ac.uk; f. 1986; undertakes basic, strategic and applied research required for the understanding of the aetiology, pathogenesis, epidemiology and diagnosis of diseases of farm animals, incl. those exotic diseases that could spread to the United Kingdom, the study of newly recognized diseases and the influence of disease control measures on food safety and quality; Institute Dir Prof. JOHN FAZAKERLEY; Dir of Research Prof. DAVID PATON.

Sites:

Institute for Animal Health—Compton Laboratory: Compton, Nr Newbury, RG20 7NN; tel. (1635) 578411; fax (1635) 577237.

Institute for Animal Health—Pirbright Laboratory: Ash Rd, Pirbright, Woking, GU24 0NF; tel. (1483) 232441; fax (1483) 232448; Head Dr A. I. DONALDSON.

Neuropathogenesis Unit: Ogston Bldg, West Mains Rd, Edinburgh, EH9 3JF; tel. (131) 667-5204; fax (131) 668-3872.

Institute of Food Research: Norwich Research Park, Colney Lane, Norwich, NR4 7UA; tel. (1603) 255-000; fax (1603) 507-723; internet www.ifr.ac.uk; research into harnessing food for health and preventing food-related diseases; centred around the characterisation of the gut as an integrated biological system; helping to ensure competitiveness of agri-food and allied industries; Dir Prof. DAVID BOXER.

Institute of Biological, Environmental and Rural Sciences - IBERS, Aberystwyth University: Edward Llwyd Building, Pengalis Campus, Aberystwyth, SY23 3DA; tel. (1970) 622-316; fax (1970) 622-350; e-mail ibers@aber.ac.uk; internet www.aber.ac.uk/en/ibers; f. 2008; basic and strategic research into grassland and environmental research related to non-arable agriculture; increases understanding of genetic and competitive processes in pastures and natural plant populations in response to grazing and climatic variables, to elucidate processes controlling intake, growth, body composition and lactation in ruminants; investigates consequences of climatic and management changes on grassland agriculture and the opportunities for alternative animals and crops and studies the fluxes of nutrients and utilization efficiencies of inputs with reference to losses and environmental pollution; Dir Prof. W. POWELL; publ. *IBERS Knowledge-Based Innovations* (1 a year).

Sites:

Institute of Biological, Environmental and Rural Sciences (IBERS) - Gogerddan Research Centre: Plas Gogerddan, Aberystwyth, SY23 3EB; tel. (1970) 823-000; fax (1970) 828-357; e-mail ibers@aber.ac.uk; internet www.aber.ac.uk/en/ibers; f. 2008; library of 300 vols, 250 journals; Dir Prof. WAYNE POWELL; publ. *IBERS Knowledge-Based Innovations* (1 a year).

Institute of Grassland and Environmental Research—Bronydd Mawr Research Centre: Trecastle, Brecon, Powys, LD3 8RD; tel. (1874) 636-480; fax (1874) 636-542; Officer in charge J. M. M. MUNRO.

John Innes Centre: Colney Lane, Norwich, NR4 7UH; tel. (1603) 450-000; fax (1603) 450-045; internet www.jic.ac.uk; carries out fundamental research on plants and bacteria; describes the basis of the control of plant and bacterial form, behaviour and metabolism so that genetically modified plants and bacteria may be improved or changed to offer new industrial potentialities; Dir Prof. MIKE BEVAN (acting).

Rothamsted Research, North Wyke: Okehampton, EX20 2SB; tel. (1837) 883-500; e-mail nwlibrary@bbsrc.ac.uk; Assoc. Head of Dept Dr PHIL MURRAY.

Roslin Institute (Edinburgh): Roslin, Midlothian, EH25 9PS; tel. (131) 527-4200; fax (131) 440-0434; internet www.roslin.ac.uk; f. 1945; basic and strategic research on farm animals; Dir Prof. DAVID HUME.

Rothamsted Research: Rothamsted, Harpenden, AL5 2JQ; tel. (1582) 763-133; fax (1582) 760-981; internet www.rothamsted.ac.uk; f. 1843; basic, strategic and applied research on soils and crop plants; Dir Prof. IAN R. CRUTE.

Attached Site:

Broom's Barn Research Centre: Higham, Bury St Edmunds, IP28 6NP; tel. (1284) 812-200; fax (1284) 811-191; e-mail brooms.barn@bbsrc.ac.uk; internet www.broomsbarn.ac.uk; research into sugar beet and other crops; Dir BILL CLARK.

Sustainable Bioenergy Centre: e-mail info.bsbec@bbsrc.ac.uk; internet bsbec.bbsrc.ac.uk; six dedicated programmes in bioenergy research; centres have offices at universities incl. Cambridge, Dundee, Nottingham and York.

Centre for Applied Marine Sciences: Menai Bridge Anglesey, Bangor, LL59 5AB; tel. (1248) 713808; e-mail enquiries@cams.bangor.ac.uk; f. 1977; attached to Bangor Univ.; Dir Prof. A. J. ELLIOTT.

Centre for Rural Policy Research: Dept of Politics, College of Social Sciences & Int. Studies, Armory Bldg, Rennes Dr., Exeter, Devon, EX4 4RJ; tel. (1392) 722438; e-mail crprmail@exeter.ac.uk; internet centres.exeter.ac.uk/crpr; f. 1960 as Agricultural Economics Unit, renamed as Centre for Rural Research, present name and location 2007; attached to Univ. of Exeter; researches into aspects of rural economy and society with focus on agricultural, environmental and bioenergy policy; sustainable land management; agro-food regulation; sustainable communities; social and economic devt of agriculture; impacts of climate change on farming and land use; Dir Prof. MICHAEL WINTER; Asst Dir Dr MATT LOBLEY; publ. *Farm Management Handbook*.

Centre for the Environment, Fisheries and Aquaculture Science (CEFAS): Pakefield Rd, Lowestoft, NR33 0HT; tel. (1502) 562244; fax (1502) 513865; e-mail lowlibrary@cefas.co.uk; internet www.cefas.co.uk; exec. agency of the Dept for the Environment, Food and Rural Affairs; provides contract research, consultancy and training services in environmental impact assessment, environmental research and monitoring, aquaculture health and hygiene, and fisheries science and management; extensive research library; br at Weymouth; Chief Exec. R. JUDGE; Library Man. S. CARTER.

Food and Environment Research Agency (FERA): Sand Hutton, York, YO41 1LZ; tel. (1904) 462000; fax (1904) 462111; e-mail info@fera.gsi.gov.uk; internet www.defra.gov.uk/fera; f. 2009; exec. agency of the Dept for Environment, Food and Rural Affairs; research and advice in the fields of: plant health; the authenticity, chemical and microbiological safety and nutritional value of the food supply; pesticide safety (incl. the monitoring of residues in food); veterinary drug residues; proficiency testing schemes; the control of pests and diseases of growing and stored crops; the impact of food production on the environment and the consumer; alternative crops and biotechnology; animal health and welfare; and conservation and wildlife management; response and recovery from unforeseen and emergency situations; Chief Exec. ADRIAN BELTON.

Forest Research: Alice Holt Lodge, Wrecclesham, Farnham, GU10 4LH; tel. (1420) 22255; fax (1420) 23653; e-mail research.info@forestry.gsi.gov.uk; internet www.forestresearch.gov.uk; f. 1997; attached to Forestry Commission, f. 1919; advances research and technology related to forestry; informs and supports forestry's contribution to UK governmental policies; provides the evidence base for UK forestry practices and supports innovation; provides a range of products and services to support the land management and environmental technologies sectors; comprises 2 research stations with biological sections for biometrics, surveys and statistics, ecology, environmental and human sciences, forest management, tree health, supporting services incl. photographic library; 250 mems; library of 20,000 vols, 200 current journals; Chief Exec. Dr JAMES PENDLEBURY; Research Dir Prof. PETER FREER-SMITH; publs *Forest Research Corporate Publications*, *Scientific and technical publications*.

Research Stations:

Northern Research Station: Roslin, EH25 9SY; tel. (131) 445-2176; fax (131) 445-5124; e-mail nrs@forestry.gsi.gov.uk.

Henry Doubleday Research Association: Ryton Organic Gardens, Coventry, CV8 3LG; tel. (24) 7630-3517; fax (24) 7663-9229; e-mail enquiry@hdra.org.uk; internet www.hdra.org.uk; f. 1954; conducts research in organic agriculture, with focus on commercial organic horticulture in temperate regions and subsistence agriculture in developing countries; maintains vegetable seed colln; sets standards for organic amenity horticulture; services to the public incl. membership of the Asscn and access to organic display gardens; Dir of Research Dr MARGI LENNARTSSON.

National Institute of Agricultural Botany: Huntingdon Rd, Cambridge, CB3 0LE; tel. (1223) 342200; fax (1223) 277602; e-mail info@niab.com; internet www.niab.com; f. 1919; applied, basic and translational research in crops and agronomy, genetics and breeding, varieties and seeds; Chair. TONY PEXTON; CEO Dr TINA BARSBY.

NIAB: Huntingdon Rd, Cambridge, CB3 0LE; tel. (1223) 276381; fax (1223) 277602; e-mail info@niab.com; internet www.niab.com; f. 1919 to promote the improvement of existing varieties of seeds, plants and crops in the UK; incl. Official Seed Testing Station for England and Wales, and other depts that are particularly concerned with crop variety testing and description, seed certification and seed production techniques; library of 10,000 vols; Dir Prof. BRIAN J. LEGG; Sec. J. W. HALL; publs *Plant Genetic Resources Characterization and Utilization* (print and online), *Varieties of Cereals, Oilseeds, Pulses* (2 a year), *Grass and Herbage Legumes Variety Book* (1 a year), *Potato Variety Handbook*.

Oxford Forestry Institute: University of Oxford, Department of Plant Sciences, South Parks Rd, Oxford, OX1 3RB; tel. (1865) 275000; fax (1865) 275074; e-mail ofi@plants.ox.ac.uk; internet www.plants.ox.ac.uk/ofi; f. 1924 (as Imperial, later Commonwealth Forestry Inst.), now fully inc. into the Dept. of Plant Sciences; library of 200,000 vols, in conjunction with CAB International; research and higher studies in forestry; Dir Prof. J. BURLEY.

Science and Advice for Scottish Agriculture: Roddinglaw Rd, Edinburgh, EH12 9FJ; tel. (131) 244-8890; fax (131) 244-8940; e-mail info@sasa.gsi.gov.uk; internet www.sasa.gov.uk; f. 2008, fmrly the Scottish Agricultural Science Agency; attached to Scottish Govt Rural Payments and Inspections Directorate; carries out scientific exec. work, associated research and consultation on: seed testing, testing of candidate cultivars of crop plants for Nat. Listing and Plant Breeders' Rights, certification of seed and planting stock, production of disease-tested clonal stocks of potatoes, statutory aspects of pest and disease control, pesticide usage assessment, pesticide residues, ecology of mammals and birds of actual or potential pest status; Head of SASA Prof. GORDON C. MACHRAY.

Research Institutes:

Hannah Research Institute: Ayr, KA6 5HL; tel. (1292) 674000; fax (1292) 674003; internet www.hri.sari.ac.uk; f. 1928; researches into human health and nutrition; programme areas: metabolism; life and death of the cell; CHARIS (food science and technology research); Dir Prof. C. KNIGHT (acting).

Macaulay Land Use Research Institute: Craigiebuckler, Aberdeen, AB15 8QH; tel. (1224) 395000; fax (1224) 311556; e-mail enquries@macaulay.ac.uk; internet www.macaulay.ac.uk; f. 1930; interdisciplinary research across the environmental and social sciences; supports the protection of natural resources, creation of integrated land-use systems and the devt of sustainable rural communities; Chief Exec. Prof. RICHARD ASPINALL.

Moredun Research Institute: Pentlands Science Park, Bush Loan, Penicuik, EH26 0PZ; tel. (131) 445-5111; fax (131) 445-6111; e-mail info@moredun.ac.uk; internet www.moredun.ac.uk; f. 1920; researches on livestock diseases that undermine biological efficiency, impair welfare or threaten public health; Dir Prof. JULIE FITZPATRICK.

Rowett Research Institute: Greenbank Rd, Bucksburn, Aberdeen, AB21 9SB; tel. (1224) 712751; fax (1224) 715349; internet www.rowett.ac.uk; f. 1913; researches into how nutrition can prevent disease, into improving health and into enhancing the quality of food production in agriculture; Dir Prof. PETER MORGAN.

James Hutton Institute: Invergowrie, Dundee, DD2 5DA; tel. (8449) 285428; fax (8449) 285429; e-mail info@hutton.ac.uk; internet www.hutton.ac.uk; f. 2011 by merger of Macaulay Land Use Research Institute and SCRI; researches on plants and their interactions with the environment, particularly in managed ecosystems; addresses the public goods of sustainability and high quality and healthy food; crops of potatoes, barley and soft fruit are of particular interest; Chief Exec. Prof. IAIN GORDON; Chief Operating Officer Dr KAREN SHAW.

University of Hull International Fisheries Institute: Cottingham Rd, Hull, HU6 7RX; f. 1989; attached to Univ. of Hull; Dir Prof. Dr IAN G. COWX.

Veterinary Laboratories Agency: Woodham Lane, Addlestone, Surrey, KT15 3NB; tel. (1932) 341111; fax (1932) 347046; internet www.vla.gov.uk; exec. agency of the Dept for Environment, Food and Rural Affairs; f. 1917; Dir Prof. PETER BORRIELLO.

Woburn Experimental Station (Lawes Agricultural Trust): Husborne Crawley, Bedford; f. 1876 for the investigation of manurial and other problems of British crops; run as outstation of Rothamsted Experimental Station; Dir L. FOWDEN.

ARCHITECTURE AND TOWN PLANNING

Built Environment Research Institute: Room 04F14, School of The Built Environment, Univ. of Ulster, Jordanstown campus, Shore Rd, Newtownabbey, BT37 0QB; tel. (28) 9036-6566; e-mail adbe@ulster.ac.uk; internet www.beri.ulster.ac.uk; attached research centres: Centre for Sustainable Technologies (CST), Centre for Research on Property and Planning (RPP), Fire Safety Engineering Research and Technology Centre (FireSERT), Hydrogen Safety Engineering and Research (HySAFER); conducts research that enhances the quality of the built environment and addresses the changing needs of society in a more sustainable manner; Dir STANLEY MCGREAL; Sec. SADIE MAGEE.

Cities Programme: Houghton St, London, WC2A 2AE; f. 1996; attached to London School of Economics and Political Science, Univ. of London; undertakes design-based teaching and research on social, technical and economic aspects of cities and urban systems; Dir R. BURDETT.

Housing Policy and Practice Unit: School of Applied Social Science, Colin Bell Bldg, Univ. of Stirling, Stirling, FK9 4LA; tel. (1786) 467719; fax (1786) 466323; e-mail hppu1@stir.ac.uk; internet www.dass.stir.ac.uk; attached to Univ. of Stirling; teaching and research in sociology, social policy, social work, housing, services to people with dementia and addictions; Dir Prof. ISOBEL ANDERSON.

Innovative Manufacturing and Construction Research Centre: Wolfson School of Mechanical and Manufacturing Engineering, Loughborough Univ., Loughborough, LE11 3TU; tel. (1509) 227598; fax (1509) 227501; e-mail a.n.baldwin@lboro.ac.uk; internet www.lboro.ac.uk/eng/research/imcrc; f. 2001; attached to Loughborough Univ.; research in business and management, computer science, construction, design, manufacturing, processes and materials, systems engineering; Dir Prof. ANDREW BALDWIN.

Land Value Information Unit: Paisley, Renfrewshire, PA1 2BE; attached to Univ. of the West of Scotland; statistical research on behaviour of Scottish property market; Dir D. MARTIN.

LSE Housing: Houghton St, London, WC2A 2AE; f. 1989; attached to London School of Economics and Political Science, Univ. of London; centre for research, devt and consultancy work in areas of housing policy and management; residents' consultation and involvement, tenant involvement, inner-city problems, difficult estates; European housing issues; Coordinator Dr ANNE POWER.

Parallelism, Algorithms and Architectures Research Centre: Dept of Computer Science, Loughborough Univ., Loughborough, LE11 3TU; tel. (1509) 222692; fax (1509) 211586; e-mail h.e.bez@lboro.ac.uk; internet parc.lboro.ac.uk; attached to Loughborough Univ.; research areas incl. coding and signal processing, concurrency, fundamental theoretical research, future architectures of parallel computers, parallel algorithms, vision and visualisation; Co-Dir Dr HELMUT BEZ; Co-Dir Dr ONDREJ SYKORA.

The Prince's Foundation for the Built Environment: 19–22 Charlotte Rd, London, EC2A 3SG; tel. (20) 7613-8507; fax (20) 7613-8599; e-mail enquiry@princes-foundation.org; internet www.princes-foundation.org; f. 1992; research into all areas of sustainable traditional architecture, urbanism, regeneration and building crafts; public lectures, seminars and exhibitions; educational courses and consultancy; library of 9,500 vols; Librarian CARLA MARCHESAN.

ECONOMICS, LAW AND POLITICS

Bedford Group for Lifecourse and Statistical Studies: 20 Bedford Way, London, WC1H 0AL; f. 2002; combines Centre for Longitudinal Studies, Centre for Multilevel Modelling, DfES Centre for the Economics of Education, DfES Centre for Research on the Wider Benefits of Learning, DfES Nat. Centre for Research and Devt in Adult Literacy and Numeracy and Int. Centre for Research on Assessment; attached to Institute of Education, Univ. of London; Dir Prof. JOHN BYNNER.

Centre for Comparative Criminology and Criminal Justice: College Rd, Bangor, Gwynned, LL57 2DG; f. 1992; attached to Bangor Univ.; Dir Dr J. WARDHAUGH.

Centre for Economic Performance: Houghton St, London, WC2A 2AE; f. 1990; attached to London School of Economics and Political Science, Univ. of London; conducts interdisciplinary research on economic performance, focusing particularly on performance of firms; Dir Prof. J. VAN REENEN; Dir Prof. RICHARD FREEMAN.

Centre for Elections, Media and Parties (CEMaP): c/o Univ. of Exeter, Queen's Dr., Exeter, Devon, EX4 4QJ; tel. (1392) 723183; e-mail j.karp@exeter.ac.uk; internet centres.exeter.ac.uk/cemap; f. 2008; attached to Univ. of Exeter; research on campaigns, elections, political parties from both a British and comparative perspective; Dir Prof. JEFFREY KARP.

Centre for European Governance: Dept of Politics, Univ. of Exeter, Armory Bldg, Rennes Dr., Exeter, Devon, EX4 4RJ; tel. (1392) 264490; e-mail s.j.heeks@exeter.ac.uk; internet centres.exeter.ac.uk/ceg; f. 1979 as Centre for European Studies; merged with the Centre for Regulatory Governance; attached to Univ. of Exeter; provides training and conducts research in EU politics, regulatory governance, public opinion, constitutional politics, political economy of European integration; Dir Prof. CLAUDIO RADAELLI.

Centre for European Legal Studies: School of Law, Univ. of Exeter, Armory Bldg, Rennes Dr., Exeter, EX4 4RJ; tel. (1392) 263365; fax (1392) 263196; e-mail lawlib@exeter.ac.uk; internet socialsciences.exeter.ac.uk; f. 1972; attached to Univ. of Exeter; conducts research on European Union and comparative law; evaluates its effects in the United Kingdom and other mem. states; Dir Prof. LEONE NIGLIA.

Centre for Legal History Research: c/o Univ. of Exeter, Armory Bldg, Rennes Dr., Exeter, EX4 4RJ; f. 2009; attached to Univ. of Exeter; Dir Prof. CHANTAL STEBBINGS; Dir Prof. ANTHONY MUSSON.

Centre for Professional Legal Studies: Graham Hills Bldg, 50 George St, Glasgow, G1 1BA; tel. (141) 548-3738; internet www.strath.ac.uk/humanities/lawschool; attached to Univ. of Strathclyde; Dir Prof. ALAN PATERSON.

Centre for Research into Economics and Finance in Southern Africa: Houghton St, London, WC2A 2AE; f. 1990; attached to London School of Economics and Political Science, Univ. of London; undertakes research into management of int. finance, foreign-exchange policy and domestic financial policy in South Africa, and macroeconomic and financial issues in S African region; Dir Dr J. LEAPE.

Centre for Studies in Security and Diplomacy: Muirhead Tower, Univ. of Birmingham, Edgbaston, Birmingham, B15 2TT; tel. (121) 414-3344; fax (121) 414-2693; e-mail cssd-bham@bham.ac.uk; internet www.cssd.bham.ac.uk; attached to Univ. of Birmingham; Dir Sir FRANCIS RICHARDS; Deputy Dir JUDY BATT; Assoc. Dir DANIELLE BESWICK.

Centre for the Study of Public Policy: McCance Bldg, 16 Richmond St, Glasgow, G1 1XQ; attached to Univ. of Strathclyde; Dir Prof. R. ROSE.

Development Studies Institute: Houghton St, London, WC2A 2AE; f. 1990; attached to London School of Economics and Political Science, Univ. of London; a multidisciplinary centre for teaching economic research and devt studies, covering problems from around globe, of third-world and Europe; Head Prof. JOHN HARRISS.

Economic Research Council: 55 Tufton St, London, SW1P 3QL; tel. (20) 7340-6016; e-mail info@ercouncil.org; internet www

.ercouncil.org; f. 1943; non-profit-making research and educational org. in the field of economics and monetary practice; Pres. Lord LAMONT; Chair. DAMON DE LASZLO; Hon. Sec. JIM BOURLET; publ. *Britain and Overseas* (4 a year).

Economic Research Institute of Northern Ireland: Floral Bldgs, 2–14 East Bridge St, Belfast, BT1 3NQ; tel. (28) 9072-7350; fax (28) 9031-9003; e-mail contact@erini.ac.uk; internet www.erini.ac.uk; f. 2003, merger of Northern Ireland Economic Research Centre (NIERC) and the Northern Ireland Economic Council (NIEC) 2004; ind. economic research and analyses; public policy making; research consultancy; Dir VICTOR HEWITT; Head of Research Dr MICHAEL ANYADIKE-DANES; publs *ERINI Research Reports*, *ERINI Working Papers* (print and online, irregular), *NIEC Publications* (print and online, irregular), *NIERC Northern Ireland Studies* (print and online, irregular), *NIERC Reports* (print and online, irregular).

European Policies Research Centre: EAC Bldg, 141 St James' Rd, Glasgow, G4 0LT; attached to Univ. of Strathclyde; Dir Prof. D. M. YUILL; Dir Prof. K. J. ALLEN.

Exeter Centre for Ethno-Political Studies (EXCEPS): Institute of Arab and Islamic Studies, Stocker Rd, Univ. of Exeter, Exeter, EX4 4ND; tel. (1392) 269250; fax (1392) 264035; e-mail l.newberry@exeter.ac.uk; internet centres.exeter.ac.uk/exceps; f. 2007; attached to Univ. of Exeter; conducts interdisciplinary research covering culture, memory and conflict, dynamics and management of ethnic conflict, unrecognised states, migrations and diasporas, language, literature and culture, security and terrorism; Dir Prof. GARETH STANSFIELD; Deputy Dir Prof ILAN PAPPE; Deputy Dir Dr JONATHAN GITHENS-MAZER.

Financial Markets Group: Houghton St, London, WC2A 2AE; f. 1987; attached to London School of Economics and Political Science, Univ. of London; undertakes first-rate basic research into the nature and operation of financial markets; Dir Prof. D. WEBB.

Fraser of Allander Institute for Research on the Scottish Economy: Curran Bldg, 131 St James' Rd, Glasgow, G4 0LS; attached to Univ. of Strathclyde; Dir B. K. ASHCROFT.

Greater London Group: Houghton St, London, WC2A 2AE; f. 1958; attached to London School of Economics and Political Science, Univ. of London; undertakes research and issues publs on govt and economy of Greater London and SE region; Chair. Prof. G. W. JONES; Dir TONY TRAVERS.

Institute for Democracy and Conflict Resolution: Univ. of Essex, Wivenhoe Park, Colchester, CO4 3SQ; tel. (1206) 872129; fax (1206) 872129; e-mail info@idcr.org.uk; internet www.idcr.org.uk; attached to Univ. of Essex; research in areas of democracy, conflict, human rights, justice and governance; dissemination of knowledge to policy makers, think tanks, non-governmental orgs, and private companies; Dir Prof. TODD LANDMAN.

Institute for Social and Economic Research: Wivenhoe Park, Colchester, CO4 3SQ; annual panel survey of 5,000 British households, examines income distribution, etc., labour market behaviour, household formation and dissolution; attached to Univ. of Essex; Dir Prof. J. I. GERSHUNY.

Institute of Development Studies: Univ. of Sussex, Falmer, Brighton, BN1 9RE; tel. (1273) 606261; f. 1966; attached to Univ. of Sussex; nat. centre concerned with Third World devt and relationships between rich and poor countries; offers teaching and supervision for univ. graduate degrees; official depository for UN publs; library of 200,000 vols; Dir KEITH BEZANSON; publ. *IDS Bulletin* (4 a year).

Institute of Economic Research: Bangor, Gwynned, LL57 2DG; f. 1969; attached to Bangor Univ.; research in regional economics, economics of developing countries, tourism and economics of ports, policy-making and planning; data analysis; Dir Prof. R. R. MACKAY.

Institute of European Finance: Bangor, Gwynned, LL57 2DG; tel. (1248) 382277; fax (1248) 364760; e-mail ief@bangor.ac.uk; f. 1973; attached to Bangor Univ.; Dir Prof. E. P. M. GARDENER.

Institute of European Law: Birmingham Law School, Univ. of Birmingham, Edgbaston, Birmingham, B15 2TT; tel. (121) 414-6312; fax (121) 414-3585; e-mail iel@contacts.bham.ac.uk; internet www.iel.bham.ac.uk; f. 1989; attached to Univ. of Birmingham; provides interdisciplinary centre for research on European law; Dir Prof. MARTIN TRYBUS; Deputy Dir Dr LUCA RUBINI.

Institute of European Public Law: Cottingham Rd, Hull, HU6 7RX; tel. (1482) 465-742; f. 1992; attached to Univ. of Hull; Dir Prof. P. BIRKINSHAW.

Institute of Judicial Administration: Birmingham Law School, Univ. of Birmingham, Edgbaston, Birmingham, B15 2TT; tel. (121) 414-3637; fax (121) 414-3585; e-mail law@bham.ac.uk; internet www.law.bham.ac.uk/research/ija.shtml; f. 1968; attached to Univ. of Birmingham; initiates, coordinates and develops teaching and research in all aspects of the admin. of justice in England and Wales; Dir Dr MARIANNE WADE.

International Institute for Strategic Studies: Arundel House, 13–15 Arundel St, London, WC2R 3DX; tel. (20) 73797676; fax (20) 78363108; e-mail iiss@iiss.org; internet www.iiss.org; f. 1958; aims to promote discussion and research on the problems of international security arising from all causes; international membership, Council, and staff; 2,141 mems (1,623 ordinary, 391 assoc., 127 student), 165 corporate mems; Chair. of the Council FRANÇOIS HEISBOURG; Dir Dr JOHN CHIPMAN; publs *Strategic Comments* (electronic publ., 10 a year), *Survival* (4 a year), *The Military Balance* (1 a year), *Strategic Survey* (1 a year), *Adelphi Papers* (8–10 a year).

Jill Dando Institute for Crime Science: Third Fl., 1 Old St, London, EC1V 9HL; tel. (20) 7324-3000; fax (20) 7324-3003; e-mail jdi@ucl.ac.uk; internet www.jdi.ucl.ac.uk; f. 2001; attached to Univ. College London; Dir Prof. RICHARD WORTLEY.

LSE London: Houghton St, London, WC2A 2AE; f. 1998; attached to London School of Economics and Political Science, Univ. of London; studies economic and social issues of London region, as well as problems and potential of other urban and metropolitan regions; Dir Prof. I. GORDON.

Mannheim Centre of Criminology and Criminal Justice: Houghton St, London, WC2A 2AE; f. 1990; attached to London School of Economics and Political Science, Univ. of London; coordinates research in field of criminology and criminal justice; Dir Prof. DAVID DOWNES.

Midlands Centre for Criminology and Criminal Justice: Brockington Bldg, Loughborough Univ., Loughborough, LE11 3TU; tel. (1509) 228369; e-mail g.farrell@lboro.ac.uk; attached to Loughborough Univ.; research areas incl. crime prevention, criminal justice system, drug policy, policing; Dir Prof. GRAHAM FARRELL.

National Institute of Economic and Social Research: 2 Dean Trench St, Smith Sq., London, SW1P 3HE; tel. (20) 7222-7665; fax (20) 7654-1900; e-mail enquiries@niesr.ac.uk; internet www.niesr.ac.uk; f. 1938; library of 10,000 vols, 300 periodicals; Pres. Lord BURNS; Dir JONATHAN PORTES; publ. *National Institute Economic Review* (4 a year).

Overseas Development Institute: 111 Westminster Bridge Rd, London, SE1 7JD; tel. (20) 7922-0300; fax (20) 7922-0399; e-mail odi@odi.org.uk; internet www.odi.org.uk; f. 1960 to act as an independent think-tank on international development and humanitarian issues; works to inspire and inform policy and practice that lead to the reduction of poverty, the alleviation of suffering and the achievement of sustainable livelihoods in developing countries; has 14 research and policy groups and programmes; works with partners in the public and private sectors, in both developing and developed countries; library of 20,000 vols; Chair. Baroness MARGARET JAY OF PADDINGTON; Dir SIMON MAXWELL; publs *Development Policy Review* (4 a year), *Disasters: The Journal of Disaster Studies and Management* (4 a year), research work in the form of books, opinions, briefing papers and working papers.

Policy Studies Institute: 50 Hanson St, London, W1W 6UP; tel. (20) 7911-7500; fax (20) 7911-7501; e-mail website@psi.org.uk; internet www.psi.org.uk; f. 1978; attached to Univ. of Westminster; undertakes and publishes research studies relevant to social, economic, industrial and environmental policy; Dir MALCOLM RIGG.

Royal United Services Institute for Defence and Security Studies: Whitehall, London, SW1A 2ET; tel. (20) 7930-5854; fax (20) 7321-0943; e-mail information@rusi.org; internet www.rusi.org; f. 1831; professional forum in the UK for those concerned with nat. and int. defence and security; research programmes, lectures, confs and seminars; individual, corporate and diplomatic mems; library: see Libraries and Archives; Dir Rear Admiral RICHARD COBBOLD; publs *Chinese Military Update* (12 a year), *Documents of British Foreign and Security Policy* (irregular, jointly with the Stationery Office), *Homeland Security and Resilience Monitor* (10 a year), *Journal* (6 a year), *Newsbrief* (12 a year), *World Defence Systems* (3 a year).

Scottish Economic Policy Network: Stirling, FK9 4LA; tel. (1786) 473171; fax (1786) 463000; attached to Univ. of Stirling; Dir Prof. D. BELL.

Suntory and Toyota International Centres for Economics and Related Disciplines: Houghton St, London, WC2A 2AE; f. 1978; attached to London School of Economics and Political Science, Univ. of London; promotes research into applied economics and related fields; incl. Centre for Analysis of Social Exclusion; Dir Prof. TIMOTHY BESLEY.

Tayside Economic Research Centre: Bell St, Dundee, DD1 1HG; attached to Univ. of Abertay Dundee; Dir NEIL C. MCGREGOR.

Transitional Justice Institute: Jordanstown Campus, Shore Rd, Newtownabbey, BT37 0QB; tel. (28) 9036-6202; fax (28) 9036-8962 Magee Campus, Northland Rd, Londonderry, BT48 7JL; tel. (28) 7137-5146; fax (28) 7137-5184; e-mail transitionaljustice@ulster.ac.uk; internet transitionaljustice.ulster.ac.uk; attached to Univ. of Ulster; promotes theoretical and practical understanding of 'transitional justice'; raises awareness of gender and other issues in the realization of peace and justice; Assoc. Dir Prof CHRISTINE BELL; Co-Dir Prof. COLM CAMPBELL; Co-Dir Prof. FIONNUALA NÍ AOLÁIN.

EDUCATION

Academic Innovation and Continuing Education: Stirling, FK9 4LA; tel. (1786) 473171; fax (1786) 463000; attached to Univ. of Stirling; Dir Prof. J. FIELD.

Centre for Applied Research in Educational Technologies (CARET): First Fl., 16 Mill Lane, Cambridge CB2 1SB; tel. (1223) 765357; fax (1223) 765505; e-mail stephanie@caret.cam.ac.uk; internet www.caret.cam.ac.uk; attached to Univ. of Cambridge; Administrator STEPHANIE SAUNDERS.

Centre for Educational Research: Houghton St, London, WC2A 2AE; f. 1990; attached to London School of Economics and Political Science, Univ. of London; carries out research into current educational topics incl. choice of schools, schools' admissions, nat. curriculum, funding of education, and European and int. issues; Dir Dr A. WEST.

Centre for Educational Research and Development: Brayford Pool, Univ. of Lincoln, Lincoln, LN6 7TS; tel. (1522) 837017; fax (1522) 886023; e-mail email:jhubbard@lincoln.ac.uk; internet www.lincoln.ac.uk/cerd; attached to Univ. of Lincoln; Dir Prof. MIKE NEARY.

Centre for Educational Studies: Wilberforce Bldg, Univ. of Hull, Cottingham Rd, Hull, HU6 7RX; tel. (1482) 466216; fax (1482) 466137; e-mail admissions-ces@hull.ac.uk; internet www2.hull.ac.uk/ifl/ces; attached to Univ. of Hull; undergraduate, postgraduate and professional training programmes; Head ANGELA SHAW.

Centre for International Education and Research: School of Education, Univ. of Birmingham, Edgbaston, Birmingham, B15 2TT; tel. (121) 414-4809; fax (121) 414-4865; e-mail m.schweisfurth@bham.ac.uk; internet www.education.bham.ac.uk/research/cier; attached to Univ. of Birmingham; promotes role of education in economic, social, political devt; Dir Dr MICHELE SCHWEISFURTH.

Centre for Learning Development: Cottingham Rd, Hull, HU6 7RX; e-mail cld@hull.ac.uk; attached to Univ. of Hull; Head Prof. G. CHAMBERS (acting).

Centre for Mediterranean Studies: Dept of Classics and Ancient history, Univ. of Exeter, Queen's Dr., Exeter, Devon, EX4 4QJ; tel. (1392) 264203; e-mail l.g.mitchell@ex.ac.uk; internet centres.exeter.ac.uk/cms; f. 1992; attached to Univ. of Exeter; promotes interdisciplinary teaching and research into history, culture and people of Mediterranean; Dir Dr LYNETTE MITCHELL.

Centre for Research in the Arts, Social Sciences and Humanities: 17 Mill Lane, Cambridge, CB2 1RX; tel. (1223) 766886; fax (1223) 315794; e-mail crassh-admin@lists.cam.ac.uk; internet www.crassh.cam.ac.uk; attached to Univ. of Cambridge; Dir Dr ANDREW WEBBER (acting) (Churchill College).

Centre for Russian and East European Studies: Muirhead Tower, 6th Fl., Univ. of Birmingham, Edgbaston, Birmingham, B15 2TT; tel. (121) 414-6346; fax (121) 414-3423; e-mail d.l.averre@bham.ac.uk; internet www.crees.bham.ac.uk; f. 1963; attached to Univ. of Birmingham; research programmes incl. studies of Russian, Ukrainian and Central European politics, society and culture, post-socialist economic transformation, history of Russia and the Soviet Union, security studies; library of 90,000 vols; Dir Dr DEREK AVERRE; Deputy Dir KATARYNA WOLCZUK.

Centre for the Economics of Education: Houghton St, London, WC2A 2AE; f. 2000; attached to London School of Economics and Political Science, Univ. of London; Dir Prof. S. MACHIN.

Centre of Advanced International Studies: c/o Politics Dept, Univ. of Exeter, Armory Bldg, Rennes Dr., Exeter, EX4 4RJ; tel. (1392) 263164; fax (1392) 263305; e-mail politics@exeter.ac.uk; internet centres.exeter.ac.uk/cais; f. 2000; attached to Univ. of Exeter; researches into aspects of global social relations across political, economic, cultural realms; Dir Prof. MICK DUMPER; Assoc. Dir Dr BICE MAIGUASHCA; Assoc. Dir Dr NICK VAUGHAN-WILLIAMS; publ. *European Journal of International Relations*.

Centre of African Studies: Mond Bldg, Free School Lane, Cambridge, CB2 3RF; tel. (1223) 334396; fax (1223) 769329; e-mail afrenq@hermes.cam.ac.uk; internet www.african.cam.ac.uk; attached to Univ. of Cambridge; Dir Prof. MEGAN VAUGHAN (King's College).

Centre of Latin American Studies: Second Fl., 17 Mill Lane, Cambridge, CB2 1RX; tel. (1223) 335390; fax (1223) 335397; e-mail general@latin-american.cam.ac.uk; internet www.latin-american.cam.ac.uk; attached to Univ. of Cambridge; Dir Dr GEOFFREY KANTARIS.

Centre of South Asian Studies: Laundress Lane, Cambridge, CB2 1SD; tel. (1223) 338094; fax (1223) 767094; e-mail webmaster@s-asian.cam.ac.uk; internet www.s-asian.cam.ac.uk; attached to Univ. of Cambridge; Dir Prof. C. A. BAYLY.

Institute for Advanced Studies: Hope Park Sq., Edinburgh, EH8 9NW; tel. (131) 650-4671; fax (131) 668-2252; e-mail iash@ed.ac.uk; internet www.iash.ed.ac.uk; f. 1969; attached to Univ. of Edinburgh; Dir SUSAN MANNING.

Institute for Cultural Research: POB 2227, London, NW2 3BW; tel. (20) 8452-0960; fax (20) 8438-0311; e-mail admin@i-c-r.org.uk; internet i-c-r.org.uk; f. 1966; promotes and conducts research, advances public education in man's heritage of knowledge; 200 mems; library of 56 monographs; Chair. of Council CLARE MAXWELL-HUDSON; Hon. Sec. PATTI SCHNEIDER; Hon. Treas. T. R. WILLS.

Institute of Continuing Education: Madingley Hall, Madingley, Cambridge, CB23 8AQ; tel. (1223) 746222; e-mail enquiry@madingleyhall.co.uk; internet www.cont-ed.cam.ac.uk; attached to Univ. of Cambridge; Dir Dr REBECCA LINGWOOD.

Library and Information Statistics Unit: Holywell Park, Loughborough Univ., Loughborough, LE11 3TU; tel. (1509) 635680; fax (1509) 635699; e-mail lisu@lboro.ac.uk; internet www.lboro.ac.uk/departments/ls/lisu; f. 1987; attached to Loughborough Univ.; research and information centre for library and information services; collects, analyses, interprets, publishes statistical information for and about the library domain in the UK; Dir CLAIRE CREASER.

National Foundation for Educational Research: The Mere, Upton Park, Slough, SL1 2DQ; tel. (1753) 574123; fax (1753) 691632; e-mail enquiries@nfer.ac.uk; internet www.nfer.ac.uk; f. 1946; provides independent research, assessment and information services for education, training and children's services; improves the practice and understanding of those who work with and for learners; library of 20,000 vols, 300 journals; Pres. Sir JAMES ROSE; Chair. RICHARD BUNKER; Chief Exec. SUE ROSSITER; publs *Educational Research* (2 a year), *Impact: NFER's Research News for Schools* (2 a year), *Practical Research for Education* (2 a year).

SCRE Centre: St Andrew's Bldg, 11 Eldon St, Glasgow, G3 6NH; tel. (141) 330-3490; fax (141) 330-3491; e-mail scre.info@scre.ac.uk; internet www.scre.ac.uk; f. 1928 as Scottish Council for Research in Education; conducts educational research of the highest quality and supports the use of research outcomes through the dissemination of findings; Dir Prof. PAUL BRNA.

Society for Research into Higher Education Ltd: 76 Portland Pl., London, W1B 1NT; tel. (20) 7637-2766; fax (20) 7637-2781; e-mail srheoffice@srhe.ac.uk; internet www.srhe.ac.uk; f. 1964 to encourage research and development in higher education and collect and disseminate the results; 237 corporate mems; Pres. Prof. Sir DAVID WATSON; Dir HELEN PERKINS; publs *Research into Higher Education Abstracts* (3 a year), *Studies in Higher Education* (4 a year), *Higher Education Quarterly*, *Newsletter* (3 a year), *International Newsletter* (3 a year).

FINE AND PERFORMING ARTS

Art and Design Research Institute: Room 82E02, School of Art and Design, Univ. of Ulster, Belfast campus, Belfast, BT15 1ED; tel. (28) 9026-7267; e-mail adbe@ulster.ac.uk; internet www.adbe.ulster.ac.uk/research/artdes_ri; attached to Univ. of Ulster; research, knowledge and technology exchange, teaching; research in fine and applied arts, fashion and textile design, 2-d and 3-d design, visual communication, history and theory of art and design; Dir Prof KAREN FLEMING.

Centre for Advanced Welsh Music Study: College Rd, Bangor, LL57 2DG; tel. (1248) 382181; fax (1248) 383895; attached to Bangor Univ.; Dir Dr SALLY HARPER.

Centre for Dance Research: Roehampton Univ., Roehampton Lane, London SW15 5PH; tel. (20) 8392-3379; e-mail a.grau@roehampton.ac.uk; attached to Roehampton Univ.; research projects in historical, analytical, anthropological, cultural studies and professional choreography; Dir Prof. ANDRÉE GRAU.

Centre for Research in Film and Audiovisual Cultures: Queen's Bldg, Roehampton Univ., Roehampton Lane, London, SW15 5PH; tel. (20) 8392-3513; e-mail p.mcdonald@roehampton.ac.uk; attached to Roehampton Univ.; critical, historical, analytic and practical research relating to film and other audiovisual media; supports research on cinema, television, video/DVD, interactive platforms and online media; Dir Prof. MICHAEL CHANAN; Dir Dr HEATHER NUNN.

Sainsbury Institute for the Study of Japanese Arts and Culture: 8A The Close, Norwich, NR1 4DH; tel. (1603) 624349; fax (1603) 625011; e-mail sisjac@sainsbury-institute.org; internet www.sainsbury-institute.org; f. 1999; attached to Univ. of East Anglia; Dir NICOLE COOLIDGE ROUSMANIERE.

HISTORY, GEOGRAPHY AND ARCHAEOLOGY

Business History Unit: Houghton St, London, WC2A 2AE; f. 1978, jtly with Imperial College London; attached to London School of Economics and Political Science, Univ. of London; promotes research into business history, incl. technological aspects; Dir Dr T. GOURVISH.

Centre for City and Regional Studies: Cottingham Rd, Hull, HU6 7RX; tel. (1482)

465330; fax (1482) 465006; attached to University of Hull; Dir Prof. DAVID GIBBS; Dir Prof. G. HAUGHTON.

Centre for Contemporary British History: Institute of Historical Research, Senate House, Malet St, London, WC1E 7HU; tel. (20) 7862-8740; fax (20) 7862-8812; e-mail ccbhinfo@sas.ac.uk; internet www.ccbh.ac.uk; f. 1986, fmrly Institute of Contemporary British History; manages research projects, incl. colln of oral testimony for present and future historians; Dir Dr RICHARD ROBERTS (acting); publs *Contemporary British History* (4 a year), *Modern History Review* (4 a year), *Twentieth Century British History* (4 a year).

Centre for Medieval Studies: Univ. of Exeter, The Queen's Dr., Exeter, Devon, EX4 4QJ; tel. (1392) 264364; e-mail y.m.plumley@exeter.ac.uk; internet centres.exeter.ac.uk/medievalstudies; attached to Univ. of Exeter; Dir Dr YOLANDA PLUMLEY.

Centre for Research in History and Theory: Roehampton Lane, London, SW15 5PH; tel. (20) 8392-5793; e-mail w.gallois@roehampton.ac.uk; internet www.roehampton.ac.uk/researchcentres/chat/index.html; f. 2006; attached to Roehampton Univ.; research in art history, classical civilisation, dance, and drama, history, philosophy, theology and religious studies; Dir Prof. WILLIAM GALLOIS.

Centre for Research in Polish History: Stirling, FK9 4LA; tel. (1786) 467580; fax (1786) 467581; e-mail historyandpolitics@stir.ac.uk; internet ww.historyandpolitics.stir.ac.uk; f. 2000; attached to Univ. of Stirling; Dir Dr PETER D. STACHURA.

Centre for Research in Renaissance Studies:tel. (20) 8392-3334; e-mail s.greenhalgh@roehampton.ac.uk; internet www.roehampton.ac.uk/researchcentres/renaissance/index.html; attached to Roehampton Univ.; research in classics, drama, English, history and art history, particularly in the fields of Italian Renaissance history; 17th-century politics; Shakespearean after lives in literature, theatre, and the media; gender and performance; early modern court and domestic cultures; textual editing; and Renaissance visual cultures and mythographies; Dir SUSANNE GREENHALGH.

Centre for South-Western Historical Studies: c/o Devon and Exeter Institution, 7 The Close Exeter, EX1 1EZ; tel. (1392) 263292; fax (1392) 263305; e-mail r.burt@exeter.ac.uk; internet people.exeter.ac.uk/rburt/swhs; f. 1985; attached to Univ. of Exeter; promotes historical research into all aspects of counties of Cornwall, Devon, Dorset, Somerset; Dir Prof. ROGER BURT.

German Historical Institute: 17 Bloomsbury Sq., London, WC1A 2NJ; tel. (20) 7309-2050; e-mail ghil@ghil.ac.uk; internet www.ghil.ac.uk; f. 1976; research in medieval, modern and comparative British and German history; study of int., esp. Anglo-German, relations; European history; 9 research fellows; library of 75,000 vols, 200 periodicals; Dir Prof. Dr ANDREAS GESTRICH; Admin. Officer WOLFGANG HAACK; publ. *Bulletin* (2 a year).

Royal Archaeological Institute: c/o Society of Antiquaries of London, Burlington House, Piccadilly, London, W1J 0BE; tel. (7826) 755779; e-mail admin@royalarchaeolinst.org; internet www.royalarchaeolinst.org; f. 1844; has a lecture programme; holds meetings for mems; awards grants for archaeological research and excavations; undergraduate and masters dissertations; library of 166 vols; 1,500 mems; Pres. Prof. DAVID BREEZE; Hon. Sec. Dr GILL HEY; Admin. SHARON GERBER-PARFITT; publ. *Archaeological Journal* (1 a year).

Scott Polar Research Institute: Univ. of Cambridge, Lensfield Rd, Cambridge, CB2 1ER; tel. (1223) 336540; fax (1223) 336549; e-mail enquiries@spri.cam.ac.uk; internet www.spri.cam.ac.uk; f. 1920; research and information centre on the Polar regions (glaciology, geophysics, oceanography, remote sensing, history, anthropology, socio-economics); exhibits; also offers Bachelors, Masters, MPhil and PhD courses; library of 100,000 vols, 700 periodicals; archives; photographic library; Dir Prof. JULIAN A. DOWDESWELL; Librarian and Keeper of Collections HEATHER LANE; publs *Polar and Glaciological Abstracts* (3 a year), *Polar Record* (4 a year).

Wetland Archaeology and Environments Research Centre: Cottingham Rd, Hull, HU6 7RX; attached to Univ. of Hull; Dir Dr M. LILLIE.

LANGUAGE AND LITERATURE

Arts and Humanities Research Council: Whitefriars, Lewins Mead, Bristol, BS1 2AE; tel. (117) 987-6500; fax (117) 987-6600; e-mail enquiries@ahrc.ac.uk; internet www.ahrc.ac.uk; f. 2005 to provide financial and practical support for research and postgraduate training in the arts and humanities, as well as funding for museums and art galleries; Chief Exec. Prof. PHILIP ESLER; Chair. Prof. Sir ALAN WILSON; publ. *Arcady Newsletter* (irregular).

Centre for Advanced Research in English: Edgbaston, Birmingham, B15 2TT; e-mail m.c.m.devereux@bham.ac.uk; internet www.care.bham.ac.uk; attached to Univ. of Birmingham; Dir Dr M. KNOWLES; Admin. MICHELLE DEVEREUX.

Centre for English Language Studies: Westmere House, Univ. of Birmingham, Edgbaston, Birmingham, B15 2TT; tel. (121) 414-5695; fax (121) 414-3298; e-mail cels@bham.ac.uk; internet www.cels.bham.ac.uk; attached to Univ. of Birmingham; Dir CHRIS J. KENNEDY.

Centre for Scottish Cultural Studies: Level 6, Livingstone Tower, 26 Richmond St, Glasgow, G1 1XH; attached to Univ. of Strathclyde; Dir Dr K. G. SIMPSON.

Centre for South West Writing: Univ. of Exeter, Queen's Dr., Exeter, Devon, EX4 4QJ; tel. (1392) 264343; e-mail t.kendall@exeter.ac.uk; internet centres.exeter.ac.uk/southwestwriting; attached to Univ. of Exeter; promotes the appreciation of the region's many important creative writers; Dir ANDY BROWN.

Centre for the Standardisation of Terminology: Bangor, Gwynned, LL57 2DG; f. 1996; attached to Bangor Univ.; develops standardized dictionaries and glossaries of contemporary technical terms in Welsh; Dir Dr LLION JONES.

CILT, the National Centre for Languages: 3rd Fl., 111 Westminster Bridge Rd, London, SE1 7HR; tel. (20) 7633-3300; fax (20) 7379-5082; e-mail info@cilt.org.uk; internet www.cilt.org.uk; f. 1966; independent, registered charity, supported by govt grants; nat. centre for information on learning and teaching languages and on languages for employment; has an enquiry service, specialized library and multimedia colln, training and conference programme; library of 14,000 titles; Chief Exec. ISABELLA MOORE.

Dictionary Research Centre: Edgbaston, Birmingham, B15 2TT; tel. (121) 414-3364; fax (121) 414-5668; e-mail english@bham.ac.uk; internet www.english.bham.ac.uk/drc.shtml; f. 2001; attached to Univ. of Birmingham; research activities incl. work on Johnson's A Dictionary of the English Language, sourcing of Johnson's citations; corpus-based lexicography; bilingual and multilingual lexicography; lexicographical description of collocation; language of definitions; perceptions of dictionaries; metaphor and dictionaries; Dir Dr ROSAMUND MOON.

Foreign Language Centre: Univ. of Exeter, 2nd Fl., Queen's Bldg, Queen's Dr., Exeter, Devon, EX4 4QH; tel. (1392) 724306; e-mail languages@exeter.ac.uk; internet www.sall.ex.ac.uk/flc; attached to Univ. of Exeter; Dir JONATHAN LIPPMAN.

Hispanic Research Centre:tel. (20) 8392-3572; e-mail i.santaolalla@roehampton.ac.uk; attached to Roehampton Univ.; Dir Dr ISABEL SANTAOLALLA.

Institute for Advanced Research in Arts and Social Sciences: 91 Oakfield Rd, Selly Park, Birmingham, B29 7HL; attached to Univ. of Birmingham; Hon. Dir Prof. E. W. IVES.

Institute of Cornish Studies: Tremough Campus, Treliever Rd, Penryn, Cornwall, TR1 9EZ; Univ. of Exeter, Cornwall Campus, Penryn, Cornwall, TR104 9EZ; tel. (1326) 371811; internet www.exeter.ac.uk/cornwall/academic_departments/huss/ics/icsresearch.shtml; f. 1970, present bldg 2004; attached to Univ. of Exeter; Dir Prof. PHILIP J. PAYTON; Asst Dir Dr GARRY TREGIDGA; publ. *Cornish Studies* (1 a year).

Leopardi Centre: Edgbaston, Birmingham, B15 2TT; tel. (121) 414-5996; e-mail f.dintino@bham.ac.uk; internet www.leopardi.bham.ac.uk; f. 1998; attached to Univ. of Birmingham; promotes study and knowledge of Leopardi and his European context at postdoctoral, postgraduate, undergraduate level; facilitates research on Leopardi and on related topics, incl. the European reception of Leopardi's work; acts as a UK focus for research into the cultures of 18th and 19th century Italy; organizes research seminars and colloquia with specialists in 18th and 19th century studies and related fields from Italy, the UK and other countries; maintains and enhances colln of publs relating to Leopardi in the European languages; collects relevant bibliographical material; Dir Dr FRANCO D'INTINO.

Modern Humanities Research Association: 1 Carlton House Terrace, London, SW1Y 5AF; e-mail mail@mhra.org.uk; internet www.mhra.org.uk; f. at Cambridge Univ. in 1918; encourages advanced studies in modern and medieval languages and literatures; publishes journals and monographs; provides funding assistance for academic publishing, research and conferences; 400 mems; Hon. Sec. Dr BARBARA BURNS; publs *Annual Bibliography of English Language and Literature*, *Austrian Studies*, *Modern Language Review* (4 a year), *Portuguese Studies* (2 a year), *The Slavonic and East European Review* (4 a year), *Yearbook of English Studies* (2 a year), *The Year's Work in Modern Language Studies*.

National Centre for Research in Children's Literature:tel. (20) 8392-3346; e-mail k.reynolds@roehampton.ac.uk; internet www.ncrcl.ac.uk; attached to Roehampton Univ.; Dir Prof. KIM REYNOLDS.

R. S. Thomas Study Centre: Bangor, Gwynned, LL57 2DG; tel. (1248) 382113; internet rsthomas.bangor.ac.uk; f. 2000; attached to Bangor Univ.; Dir Dr JASON WALFORD DAVIES; Dir Prof. TONY BROWN.

Shakespeare Institute: Mason Croft, Stratford upon Avon, CV37 6HP; tel. (1789) 293138; e-mail shakespeare@bham.ac.uk; Dir Prof. KATE MCLUSKIE.

MEDICINE

Arthritis Research UK: Copeman House, St Mary's Court, St Mary's Gate, Chesterfield, Derbyshire, S41 7TD; tel. (1246) 558033; fax (1246) 558007; e-mail enquiries@arthritisresearchuk.org; internet www.arthritisresearchuk.org; f. 1936 as the Arthritis and Rheumatism Council; raises funds to promote medical research into causes, treatment and cure of arthritis and related musculoskeletal conditions; educates medical students, doctors and allied healthcare professionals about arthritis; provides information to people affected by arthritis and to the general public; basic science and clinical research is carried out in medical schools and univs across the UK; Chief Exec. Dr LIAM O'TOOLE; publ. *Reports on Rheumatic Diseases* (3 a year).

Asthma UK: Summit House, 70 Wilson St, London, EC2A 2DB; tel. (20) 7786-4900; fax (20) 7256-6075; e-mail info@asthma.org.uk; internet www.asthma.org.uk; f. 1927; ind. UK charity; funds research into asthma and provides advice and information; works with asthma patients, health professionals and researchers; influences healthcare policies; 7,000 mems; Chair. Dr ROB WILSON; Chief Exec. NEIL CHURCHILL; publ. *Asthma Magazine* (4 a year).

Bone and Joint Research Unit: John Vane Bldg, Charterhouse Sq., London, EC1M 6BQ; e-mail y.chernajovsky@qmul.ac.uk; internet www.whri.qmul.ac.uk/research/boneandjoint.html; f. 1978; attached to Queen Mary's School, Univ. of London; Dir Prof. YUTI CHERNAJOVSKY.

British Heart Foundation National Centre for Physical Activity and Health: School of Sport, Exercise and Health Sciences, Loughborough Univ., Epinal Way, Loughborough, LE11 3TU; tel. (1509) 226421; fax (1509) 226420; e-mail bhfnc@lboro.ac.uk; internet www.bhfactive.org.uk; f. 2000; attached to Loughborough Univ.; promotes physical activity and health; Admin. ANJNA NAGAR.

Burden Neurological Institute: Frenchay Park Rd, Bristol, BS16 1JB; tel. (117) 918-6720; e-mail burdeninstitute@hotmail.com; internet www.bristol.ac.uk/neuroscience/clinical/bni; f. 1939 to conduct research in neurology, neurophysiology, neuropsychology and psychiatry; stem cell research into multiple sclerosis; library of 4,000 vols; Dir Prof. NEIL J. SCOLDING; Sec. RODNEY C. NORTH.

Cancer Research UK: 61 Lincoln's Inn Fields, London, WC2A 3PX; tel. (20) 7242-0200; fax (20) 7269-3101; internet www.cancerresearchuk.org; f. 2002, by merger of Imperial Cancer Research Fund (f. 1902) and Cancer Research Campaign (f. 1923); library of 4,000 vols, 300 periodicals; Chair. DAVID NEWBIGGING; Chief. Exec. Prof. ALEX MARKHAM; publ. *Scientific Report* (1 a year).

Cancer Research UK Beatson Institute for Cancer Research: Garscube Estate, Switchback Rd, Bearsden, Glasgow, G61 1BD; tel. (141) 330-3953; fax (141) 942-6521; e-mail beatson@gla.ac.uk; internet www.beatson.gla.ac.uk; f. 1990; incorporates Beatson Institute for Cancer Research and the Univ. of Glasgow depts of Medical Oncology and Radiation Oncology; research in molecular and cell biology of cancer and related diseases; library of 1,000 textbooks, 83 journals; Dir of the Beatson Institute for Cancer Research K. H. VOUSDEN; publ. *Scientific Report* (1 a year).

Centre for Child and Family Research: Dept of Social Sciences, Schofield Bldg, Loughborough Univ., Loughborough, LE11 3TU; tel. (1509) 228355; fax (1509) 223943; e-mail ccfr@lboro.ac.uk; internet www.lboro.ac.uk/research/ccfr; f. 2002; attached to Loughborough Univ.; Dir Prof. HARRIET WARD.

Centre for Mechanisms of Human Toxicity: Hodgkin Bldg, Univ. of Leicester, POB 138, Lancaster Rd, Leicester, LE1 9HN; tel. (116) 252-5544; fax (116) 252-5616; internet www.le.ac.uk/cmht; f. 1993; Dir Prof. ANNE WILLIS.

Centre for Medical History: Armory Bldg, Rennes Dr., Exeter, EX4 4RJ; tel. (1392) 263289; fax (1392) 263305; e-mail cfmhmail@exeter.ac.uk; internet centres.exeter.ac.uk/medhist; f. 1997; attached to Univ. of Exeter; researches within the field of medical history, social study of contemporary medical and health-related activities; Dir Dr KATE FISHER; Asst Dir Prof. JO MELLING.

Children's Health and Exercise Research Centre: Univ. of Exeter, St Luke's Campus, Exeter, EX1 2LU; tel. (1392) 262884; e-mail sshs-school-office@exeter.ac.uk; internet centres.exeter.ac.uk/cherc; f. 1987; attached to Univ. of Exeter; research in paediatric exercise science; Dir Prof. NEIL ARMSTRONG; Co-Dir Assoc. Prof. CRAIG WILLIAMS; Assoc. Dir Dr RICHARD WINSLEY.

Dementia Services Development Centre: Stirling, FK9 4LA; tel. (1786) 473171; fax (1786) 463000; attached to Univ. of Stirling; Dir Prof. JUNE ANDREWS.

Essex Biomedical Sciences Institute: University of Essex, Wivenhoe Park, Colchester, CO4 3SQ; tel. (1206) 872918; e-mail klenovae@essex.ac.uk; internet www.essex.ac.uk/bs/ebsi; attached to Univ. of Essex; promotes clinically-relevant, biomedical and health-related translational research; Dir Prof. ELENA KLENOVA; Assoc. Dir Dr TONY ELSTON.

Health and Rehabilitation Sciences Research Institute: Room 01B102, School of Health Sciences, Jordanstown Campus, Univ. of Ulster, Shore Rd, Newtownabbey, BT37 0QB; tel. (28) 9036-6851; internet www.science.ulster.ac.uk/hrsri; attached to Univ. of Ulster; research in physiotherapy, speech and language therapy, occupational therapy, radiography, podiatry and clinical physiology; Dir Prof STEPHANIE MCKEOWN; Sec. ANNA MOONEY.

Health and Social Services Institute: Wivenhoe Park, Colchester, CO4 3SQ; applied teaching, training and research in health and social services; attached to Univ. of Essex; Dir Prof. N. SOUTH.

Health Protection Agency: Porton Down, Salisbury, SP4 0JG; tel. (1980) 612100; fax (1980) 611096; e-mail business@hpa.org.uk; internet www.hpa.org.uk; f. 2003; attached to Dept of Health; protects the UK population against biological, chemical and radiological health threats.

History of Medicine Unit: 90 Vincent Dr., Edgbaston, Birmingham, B15 2SP; tel. (121) 415-8174; fax (121) 414-4036; e-mail k.k.hallan@bham.ac.uk; internet www.medicine.bham.ac.uk/histmed; f. 2000; attached to Univ. of Birmingham; supports and promotes teaching and research in the history of medicine; Dir Dr JONATHAN REINARZ; Sec. KIRAN HALLAN.

Institute for Ageing and Health: c/o Lynn Patterson, Wolfson Research Centre, Newcastle General Hospital, Newcastle upon Tyne, NE4 6BE; tel. (191) 256-3014; fax (191) 256-3011; internet www.ncl.ac.uk/iah; f. 1994 to undertake clinical research into gerontology and the health-related issues of the ageing process; 200 mems; small specialist library; Dir Prof. TOM KIRKWOOD.

Institute of Cancer Research: see under University of London.

Institute of Medical and Social Care Research: Bangor, Gwynned, LL57 2DG; tel. (1248) 388771; e-mail imscar@bangor.ac.uk; f. 1998; attached to Bangor Univ.; Dir Prof. I. T. RUSSELL.

Institute of Neurology: The Nat. Hospital, Queen Sq., London, WC1N 3BG; tel. (20) 7837-3611; fax (20) 7278-5069; internet www.ucl.ac.uk/ion; postgraduate institute of UCL; eight research depts doing clinical and basic research in themes: neurodegenerative disease; molecular neuroscience, clinical and experimental epilepsy; motor neuroscience and movement disorders; imaging neuroscience; brain repair and rehabilitation, neuroinflammation and clinical neurosciences; library of 16,000 vols; Dir Prof. A. THOMPSON; Sec. ROBERT WALKER.

Institute of Nursing Research: Room G 242, School of Nursing, Univ. of Ulster, Coleraine Campus Cromore Rd, Coleraine, BT52 1SA; tel. (28) 7012-4094; fax (28) 7012-4951; internet www.science.ulster.ac.uk/inr; attached to Univ. of Ulster; activities related to developmental disabilities and child health, managing chronic illness, maternal fetal and infant research, intellectual and developmental disabilities; Dir Prof BRENDAN MCCORMACK; Sec. JULIE CUMMINS.

Liverpool School of Tropical Medicine: Pembroke Pl., Liverpool, L3 5QA; tel. (151) 705-3100; fax (151) 705-3370; e-mail ruth.pollard@liv.ac.uk; internet www.liv.ac.uk/lstm; f. 1898 and received its Charter of Incorporation 1905; affiliated to the Univ. of Liverpool; its objects are to train medical and paramedical personnel in all aspects of individual or community medicine in the tropics, to conduct original research into tropical diseases and their control, and to organize and conduct clinical and prophylactic measures against tropical diseases; also undertakes research and technical assistance work in other health sector areas; library of 50,000 vols and periodicals, incl. Ronald Ross collection; Dir Prof. JANET HEMINGWAY; publs *Annals of Tropical Medicine and Parasitology*, *Annals of Tropical Paediatrics*.

LSE Health and Social Care: Houghton St, London, WC2A 2AE; f. 2000; attached to London School of Economics and Political Science, Univ. of London; undertakes research, consultancy and training in int. comparative health policy; coordinates European Health Policy Research Network; Dir Dr E. MOSSIALOS; Dir Prof. MARTIN KNAPP.

Medical Research Council (MRC): 20 Park Crescent, London, W1B 1AL; tel. (20) 7636-5422; fax (20) 7436-6179; e-mail corporate@headoffice.mrc.ac.uk; internet www.mrc.ac.uk; f. 1913; promotes research for improvement of human health; undertakes research in molecular science and public health in a network of 64 research establishments complementing the research resources of univs and hospitals; supports research training by means of fellowships, studentships and grants to scientists; Chair. Sir JOHN CHISHOLM; Chief Exec. Prof. LESZEK BORYSIEWICZ; publs *Annual Review*, *Research Strategy* (1 a year).

Attached Research Establishments:

Centre for Brain Ageing and Vitality: Univ. of Newcastle Upon Tyne, Campus for Ageing & Vitality, Newcastle Upon Tyne, NE4 5PL; tel. (191) 248-1200; fax (191) 248-1101; e-mail hazel.glass@ncl.ac.uk; internet www.ncl.ac.uk/biomedicine/

research/centres/cbav.htm; Dir Prof. DOUG TURNBULL.

Centre for Cognitive Ageing and Cognitive Epidemiology: Dept of Psychology, Univ. of Edinburgh, 7 George Sq., Edinburgh, EH8 9JZ; tel. (131) 650-8275; fax (131) 651-1771; e-mail ccace@ed.ac.uk; internet www.ccace.ed.ac.uk; Dir Prof. IAN J. DEARY.

Crucible Centre: Univ. College London, Gower St, London, WC1E 6BT; tel. (20) 7679-1597; e-mail r.thoreau@ucl.ac.uk; internet www.ucl.ac.uk/crucible; research on all aspects of ageing process from philosophy, biology, economics, clinical practice to design of the built environment; Dir Prof. NICK TYLER.

MRC Anatomical Neuropharmacology Unit: Mansfield Rd, Oxford, OX1 3TH; tel. (1865) 271865; fax (1865) 271647; e-mail mary.gilgunn-jones@pharm.ox.ac.uk; internet mrcanu.pharm.ox.ac.uk; f. 1984; Dir Prof. PETER SOMOGYI.

MRC Asthma UK Centre in Allergic Mechanisms of Asthma: King's College London, School of Medicine, 5th Floor, Thomas Guy House, Guy's Hospital, London, SE1 9RT; tel. (20) 7188-1943; fax (20) 7403-8640 Imperial College London, S Kensington Campus, Sir Alexander Fleming Bldg, London, SW7 2AZ; tel. (20) 7594-3159; internet www.asthma-allergy.ac.uk; Dir at KCL Prof. TAK LEE; Dir at ICL Prof. TIM WILLIAMS.

MRC Biomedical Nuclear Magnetic Resonance Centre: Nat. Institute for Medical Research, The Ridgeway, Mill Hill, London, NW7 1AA; tel. (20) 8816-2026; fax (20) 8906-4477; e-mail tom.frenkiel@nimr.mrc.ac.uk; internet www.nmrcentre.mrc.ac.uk; f. 1980; Head Dr TOM FRENKIEL.

MRC Biostatistics Unit: Institute of Public Health, Univ. Forvie Site, Robinson Way, Cambridge, CB2 0SR; tel. (1223) 330366; fax (1223) 330365; internet www.mrc-bsu.cam.ac.uk; f. 1970; Hon. Dir Prof. SIMON THOMPSON.

MRC Cambridge Centre for Brain Repair: E. D. Adrian Bldg, Forvie Site, Robinson Way, Cambridge, CB2 0PY; tel. (1223) 331160; fax (1223) 331174; e-mail pj214@cam.ac.uk; internet www.brc.cam.ac.uk; Chair. Prof. J. W. FAWCETT.

MRC Cancer Cell Unit: Hutchison/MRC Research Centre, Hills Rd, Cambridge, CB2 0XZ; tel. (1223) 763240; fax (1223) 763241; e-mail reception@hutchison-mrc.cam.ac.uk; internet www.hutchison-mrc.cam.ac.uk; f. 2002; Dir Prof. ASHOK VENKITARAMAN; Dir Prof. BRUCE PONDER; Dir Prof. RON LASKEY.

MRC/Cancer Research UK/BHF Clinical Trial Service Unit & Epidemiological Studies Unit (CTSU): Richard Doll Bldg, Old Rd Campus, Roosevelt Dr., Oxford, OX3 7LF; tel. (1865) 743743; fax (1865) 743985; e-mail secretary@ctsu.ox.ac.uk; internet www.ctsu.ox.ac.uk; Co-Dir Prof. RORY COLLINS; Co-Dir Prof. RICHARD PETO.

MRC Cell Biology Unit: MRC Laboratory for Molecular Cell Biology, Univ. College London, Gower St, London, WC1E 6BT; tel. (20) 7679-7806; fax (20) 7679-7805; internet www.ucl.ac.uk/lmcb; Dir Prof. MARK MARSH.

MRC Centre for Behavioural and Clinical Neuroscience Institute (BCNI): Dept of Experimental Psychology, Univ. of Cambridge, Downing Site, Cambridge, CB2 3EB; tel. (1223) 333558; fax (1223) 314547; internet www.psychol.cam.ac.uk; Dir Prof. TREVOR ROBBINS.

MRC Centre for Causal Analyses in Translational Epidemiology: Oakfield House, 15–23 Oakfield Grove, Clifton, BS8 2BN; tel. (117) 331-0098; fax (117) 331-0123; e-mail info-caite@bristol.ac.uk; internet www.bristol.ac.uk/caite; f. 2007; develops and applies novel methods that can be used to determine causes of health and disease in population; covers range of disease and health-related outcomes, incl cardiovascular disease, obesity, diabetes, cancer, mental ill-health, smoking, alcohol and physical activity; Dir Prof. GEORGE DAVEY SMITH; Deputy Dir Prof. DEBBIE LAWLOR; Deputy Dir Prof. IAN DAY.

MRC Centre for Developmental and Biomedical Genetics: Dept of Biomedical Science, Firth Court, Univ. of Sheffield, Western Bank, Sheffield, S10 2TN; tel. (114) 222-2710; fax (114) 276-5413; e-mail cdbg@sheffield.ac.uk; internet cdbg.shef.ac.uk; f. 1997 as Centre for Developmental Genetics, present status 2004; Dir Prof. MARYSIA PLACZEK.

MRC Centre for Developmental Neurobiology: King's College London, New Hunt's House, 4th Fl., Guy's Hospital Campus, London, SE1 1UL; tel. (20) 7848-8148; fax (20) 7848-6550; e-mail lauren.ryan@kcl.ac.uk; internet www.kcl.ac.uk; Dir Prof. ANDREW LUMSDEN.

MRC Centre for Drug Safety Science: School of Biomedical Sciences, Univ. of Liverpool, Liverpool, L69 3BX; tel. (151) 794-5852; fax (151) 794-5540; e-mail neil.french@liverpool.ac.uk; internet www.liv.ac.uk/drug-safety; Dir Prof. KEVIN PARK.

MRC Centre for Genomics and Global Health: Roosevelt Dr., Oxford, OX3 7BN; tel. (1865) 287500; fax (1865) 287501; e-mail victoria.cornelius@well.ox.ac.uk; internet www.cggh.ox.ac.uk; Dir Prof. DOMINIC KWIATKOWSKI.

MRC Centre, London: Stephenson House, 158–160 N Gower St, London, NW1 2ND; tel. (20) 7670-4600; fax (20) 7670-4690; e-mail enquiries@centre-london.mrc.ac.uk; internet www.centre-london.mrc.ac.uk; Head of Centre Dr IAN VINEY.

MRC Centre for Neurodegeneration Research: King's College London, Institute of Psychiatry, POB 55, De Crespigny Park, Denmark Hill, London, SE5 8AF; tel. (20) 7848-0611; fax (20) 7708-0017; internet cnr.iop.kcl.ac.uk; Dir Prof. CHRISTOPHER SHAW.

MRC Centre for Neuromuscular Diseases: POB 102, Nat. Hospital for Neurology and Neurosurgery, Queen Sq., London, WC1 3BG; tel. (845) 155-5000; fax (20) 7692-1208; e-mail admin-cnmd@ion.ucl.ac.uk; internet www.cnmd.ac.uk; Dir Prof. MIKE HANNA.

MRC Centre for Neuropsychiatric Genetics and Genomics: Dept of Psychological Medicine and Neurology, Cardiff Univ., Henry Wellcome Bldg, Heath Park, Cardiff, CF14 4XN; tel. (29) 2068-7065; Dir Prof. MICHAEL OWEN.

MRC Centre for Nutritional Epidemiology in Cancer Prevention and Survival (CNC): Dept of Public Health and Primary Care, Univ. of Cambridge, Cambridge, CB1 8RN; tel. (1223) 740151; fax (1223) 740147; internet www.srl.cam.ac.uk/cnc; Dir Prof. KAY TEE KHAW.

MRC Centre, Oxford: Old Rd Campus, Oxford Univ., Oxford, OX3 9DU; tel. (1865) 222580; fax (1865) 222549; Head Dr ANNE-MARIE CORIAT.

MRC Centre for Obesity and Related Metabolic Diseases: Univ. of Cambridge Metabolic Research Laboratories, Level 4, Institute of Metabolic Science, POB 289, Addenbrooke's Hospital, Cambridge, CB2 0QQ; tel. (1223) 336792; internet www.mrc-cord.org; f. 2007; Dir Prof. STEVE O'RAHILLY.

MRC Centre for Outbreak Analysis and Modelling: Imperial College Faculty of Medicine, St Mary's Campus, Norfolk Pl., London, W2 1PG; tel. (20) 7594-3296; internet www1.imperial.ac.uk; Dir Prof. NEIL FERGUSON.

MRC Centre for Protein Engineering: Hills Rd, Cambridge, CB2 0QH; tel. (1223) 402136; fax (1223) 402140; e-mail murphyp@mrc-lmb.cam.ac.uk; internet www.mrc-cpe.cam.ac.uk; f. 1989; Dir Prof. Sir ALAN FERSHT.

MRC Centre for Regenerative Medicine: Chancellor's Bldg, 49 Little France Crescent, Edinburgh, EH16 4SB; tel. (131) 242-6630; fax (131) 242-6629; internet www.scrm.ed.ac.uk; Dir Prof. IAN WILMUT.

MRC Centre for Stem Cell Biology and Regenerative Medicine: Cambridge Stem Cell Initiative, Univ. of Cambridge, Cambridge, CB2 2XY; tel. (1223) 763366; e-mail contact@stemcells.cam.ac.uk; internet www.stemcells.cam.ac.uk; Dir Prof. ROGER PEDERSON.

MRC Centre for Synaptic Plasticity: Dept of Anatomy, School of Medical Sciences, Univ. Walk, Bristol, BS8 1TD; tel. (117) 331-1905; internet www.bris.ac.uk/synaptic; Dir Prof. G. L. COLLINGRIDGE.

MRC Centre for Transplantation: King's College London, 5th Fl. Tower Wing, Guy's Hospital, Great Maze Pond, London, SE1 9RT; tel. (20) 7188-8711; fax (20) 7188-5660; e-mail mrccentre@kcl.ac.uk; internet transplantation.kcl.ac.uk; Dir Prof. STEVE SACKS.

MRC Centre of Epidemiology for Child Health: Institute of Child Health, 30 Guilford St, London, WC1N 1EH; tel. (20) 7905-2602; fax (20) 7905-2381; internet www.ich.ucl.ac.uk; Dir Prof. CAROL DEZATEUX.

MRC Clinical Sciences Centre: Faculty of Medicine, Imperial College London, Hammersmith Hospital Campus, Du Cane Rd, London, W12 0NN; tel. (20) 8383-8249; fax (20) 8383-8337; e-mail wmaster@csc.mrc.ac.uk; internet www.csc.mrc.ac.uk; f. 1994; Dir Prof. AMANDA FISHER.

MRC Clinical Trials Units: 222 Euston Rd, London, NW1 2DA; tel. (20) 7670-4700; fax (20) 7670-4818; e-mail contact@ctu.mrc.ac.uk; internet www.ctu.mrc.ac.uk; f. 1998; Dir Prof. MAX PARMAR.

MRC Cognition and Brain Sciences Unit: 15 Chaucer Rd, Cambridge, CB2 7EF; tel. (1223) 355294; fax (1223) 359062; e-mail info@mrc-cbu.cam.ac.uk; internet www.mrc-cbu.cam.ac.uk; f. 1944; investigates fundamental human mental processes such as attention, emotion, memory and knowledge, speech and language; conducts behavioural experiments to probe the functional properties of psychological systems and build computer models of their operation; carries out neuropsychological and neuroimaging (PET, MRI, MEG, EEG) studies of the underlying neural mechanisms in the brain and explores the clinical implications of the research for patient therapy and rehabilitation; Dir Prof. SUSAN GATHERCOLE.

MRC Collaborative Centre for Human Nutrition Research: Elsie Widdowson Laboratory, Fulbourn Rd, Cambridge, CB1 9NL; tel. (1223) 426356; fax (1223) 437515; internet www.mrc-hnr.cam.ac.uk; f. 1998; Dir Dr ANN PRENTICE.

MRC Epidemiology Resource Centre: Southampton Gen. Hospital, Southampton, SO16 6YD; tel. (23) 8077-7624; fax (23) 8070-4021; e-mail postmaster@mrc.soton.ac.uk; internet www.mrc.soton.ac.uk; f. 1979 as Environmental Epidemiology Unit; present status 2003; Dir Dr CYRUS COOPER.

MRC Epidemiology Unit: Institute of Metabolic Science, POB 285, Addenbrooke's Hospital, Hills Rd, Cambridge, CB2 0QQ; tel. (1223) 330315; fax (1223) 330316; internet www.mrc-epid.cam.ac.uk; Dir Prof. NICK WAREHAM.

MRC Functional Genomics Unit: Univ. of Oxford, Dept of Physiology, Anatomy and Genetics, Le Gros Clark bldg, South Parks Rd, Oxford, OX1 3QX; tel. (1865) 285867; fax (1865) 282862; e-mail mrc.fgu@dpag.ox.ac.uk; internet www.mrcfgu.ox.ac.uk; Hon. Dir Prof. KAY DAVIES.

MRC General Practice Research Framework (GPRF): Stephenson House, 158–160 N Gower St, London, NW1 2ND; tel. (20) 7670-4850; fax (20) 7670-4890; e-mail contact@gprf.mrc.ac.uk; internet www.gprf.mrc.ac.uk; Dir Prof. IRWIN NAZARETH.

MRC Harwell: Harwell Science and Innovation Campus, Harwell, OX11 0RD; tel. (1235) 841000; fax (1235) 841172; internet www.mgu.har.mrc.ac.uk; Dir Prof. S. BROWN.

MRC Human Genetics Unit: Western Gen. Hospital, Crewe Rd, Edinburgh, EH4 2XU; tel. (131) 332-2471; fax (131) 467-8456; e-mail enquiries@hgu.mrc.ac.uk; internet www.hgu.mrc.ac.uk; f. 1967; Dir Prof. NICK D. HASTIE.

MRC Human Immunology Unit: Weatherall Institute of Molecular Medicine, Univ. of Oxford, John Radcliffe Hospital, Headington, Oxford, OX3 9DS; tel. (1865) 222443; fax (1865) 222737; internet www.imm.ox.ac.uk; Dir Prof. Sir ANDREW MCMICHAEL.

MRC Human Reproductive Sciences Unit: Centre for Reproductive Biology, Queen's Medical Research Institute, 47 Little France Crescent, Edinburgh, EH16 4TJ; tel. (131) 242-9100; fax (131) 242-6197; e-mail enquiries@hrsu.mrc.ac.uk; internet www.hrsu.mrc.ac.uk; Dir Prof. R. P. MILLAR.

MRC Immunochemistry Unit: Dept of Biochemistry, South Parks Rd, Oxford, OX1 3QU; tel. (1865) 275354; fax (1865) 275729; internet www.bioch.ox.ac.uk/immunoch; Dir Prof. K. B. M. REID.

MRC Institute of Hearing Research: Univ. of Nottingham, Nottingham, NG7 2RD; tel. (115) 922-3431; fax (115) 951-8503; e-mail enquiries@ihr.mrc.ac.uk; internet www.ihr.mrc.ac.uk; f. 1977; Dir Prof. DAVE MOORE.

MRC International Nutrition Group: Nutrition & Public Health Intervention Research Unit, London School of Hygiene & Tropical Medicine, Keppel St, London, WC1E 7HT; tel. (20) 7958-8140; Dir Prof. ANDREW PRENTICE.

MRC Laboratories, The Gambia: POB 273, Banjul, Gambia; tel. 4495442; fax 4495919; e-mail communications@mrc.gm; internet www.mrc.gm; f. 1947; researches into improvement of health care for developing countries; areas of speciality include virology, malaria, bacterial diseases and genetics; Dir and Chair. Prof. CORRAH TUMANI.

MRC Laboratory for Molecular Cell Biology: Univ. College London, Gower St, London, WC1E 6BT; tel. (20) 7679-7806; fax (20) 7679-7805; internet www.ucl.ac.uk/lmcb; Dir Prof. C. R. HOPKINS.

MRC Laboratory of Molecular Biology (LMB): Hills Rd, Cambridge, CB2 0QH; tel. (1223) 248011; fax (1223) 213556; e-mail webmaster@mrc-lmb.cam.ac.uk; internet www2.mrc-lmb.cam.ac.uk; f. 1947, moved to present site in 1962; Dir HUGH PELHAM.

MRC Mitochondrial Biology Unit: Wellcome Trust/MRC Bldg, Hills Rd, Cambridge, CB2 0XY; tel. (1223) 252700; fax (1223) 252715; internet www.mrc-mbu.cam.ac.uk; Dir Prof. Sir JOHN WALKER.

MRC Molecular Haematology Unit: Weatherall Institute of Molecular Medicine, John Radcliffe Hospital, Headington, Oxford, OX3 9DS; tel. (1865) 222359; fax (1865) 222500; Hon. Dir Prof. DOUG HIGGS.

MRC Muscle and Cell Motility Unit: New Hunts House, GKT School of Biomedical Sciences, London Bridge, London, SE1 1UL; tel. (20) 7848-6434; fax (20) 7848-6435; Hon. Dir Prof. R. M. SIMMONS.

MRC Prion Unit: Institute of Neurology, Queen Sq., London, WC1N 3BG; tel. (20) 7837-4888; fax (20) 7676-8047; e-mail pacollinge@prion.ucl.ac.uk; internet www.prion.ucl.ac.uk; f. 1998; Dir Prof. JOHN COLLINGE.

MRC Protein Phosphorylation Unit: Sir James Black Centre, College of Life Sciences, Univ. of Dundee, Dundee, DD1 5EH; tel. (1382) 384238; fax (1382) 223778; internet www.ppu.mrc.ac.uk; f. 1990; Hon. Dir Prof. Sir PHILIP COHEN.

MRC Social and Public Health Sciences Unit: 4 Lilybank Gardens, Glasgow, G12 8RZ; tel. (141) 357-3949; fax (141) 357-2389; e-mail enquiries@sphsu.mrc.ac.uk; internet www.sphsu.mrc.ac.uk; f. 1998; Dir Prof. SALLY MACINTYRE.

MRC Social, Genetic and Developmental Psychiatry Centre: Institute of Psychiatry, De Crespigny Park, Denmark Hill, London, SE5 8AF; tel. (20) 7848-0873; fax (20) 7848-0866; internet www.iop.kcl.ac.uk; Dir Prof. ROBERT PLOMIN.

MRC Technology: 20 Park Crescent, London, W1B 1AL; tel. (20) 7291-5300; fax (20) 7291-5325; e-mail info@tech.mrc.ac.uk; internet www.mrctechnology.org; CEO Dr DAVID TAPOLCZAY.

MRC Toxicology Unit: Hodgkin Bldg, Univ. of Leicester, POB 138, Lancaster Rd, Leicester, LE1 9HN; tel. (116) 252-5544; fax (116) 252-5616; internet www.le.ac.uk/mrctox; f. 1947; Dir Prof. G. COHEN (acting).

MRC Unit for Lifelong Health and Ageing: 33 Bedford Pl., London, WC1B 5JU; tel. (20) 7670-5700; fax (20) 7580-1501; internet www.nshd.mrc.ac.uk; includes MRC Nat. Survey of Health and Devt; Dir Prof. DI KUH.

MRC/University College London Centre for Medical Molecular Virology: Univ. College London, Windeyer Bldg, 46 Cleveland St, London, W1T 4JF; tel. (20) 7679-9119; Dir Prof. MARY COLLINS.

MRC/University of Birmingham Centre for Immune Regulation: Dept of Immunology, Univ. of Birmingham, Edgbaston, Birmingham, B15 2TT; tel. (121) 414-4068; fax (121) 414-3599; e-mail a.s.shakespeare@bham.ac.uk; internet www.mrcbcir.bham.ac.uk; Dir Prof. ERIC J. JENKINSON.

MRC/University of Edinburgh Centre for Inflammation Research: Queen's Medical Research Institute, 47 Little France Crescent, Edinburgh, EH16 4TJ; tel. (131) 242-9195; fax (131)242-6578; e-mail paula.saikko@ed.ac.uk; internet www.cir.med.ed.ac.uk; Dir Prof. JOHN IREDALE.

MRC/University of Sussex Centre in Genome Damage and Stability: Science Park Rd, Univ. of Sussex, Falmer, Brighton, BN1 9RQ; tel. (1273) 678123; fax (1273) 678121; e-mail gdsc@sussex.ac.uk; internet www.sussex.ac.uk/gdsc; Dir Prof. ANTHONY CARR.

MRC/UVRI Uganda Research Unit on AIDS, Uganda: Uganda Virus Research Institute, POB 49, Entebbe, Uganda; tel. (417) 704000; fax (414) 321137; e-mail mrc@mrcuganda.org; internet www.mrcuganda.org; f. 1989; Dir Dr HEINER GROSSKURTH.

MRC Virology Unit: Institute of Virology, Church St, Glasgow, G11 5JR; tel. (141) 330-4017; fax (141) 337-2236; e-mail enquiries@mrcvu.gla.ac.uk; internet www.mrcvu.gla.ac.uk; Dir Prof. CHRIS M. PRESTON (acting).

National Institute for Medical Research: The Ridgeway, Mill Hill, London, NW7 1AA; tel. (20) 8959-3666; fax (20) 8906-4477; e-mail enquiries@nimr.mrc.ac.uk; internet www.nimr.mrc.ac.uk; f. 1913; Dir Prof. JIM SMITH; publs *Influenza Bibliography* (irregular), *Mill Hill Essays* (1 a year).

Oxford Centre for Molecular Sciences: New Chemistry Laboratory, Univ. of Oxford, South Parks Rd, Oxford, OX1 3QT; tel. (1865) 275627; fax (1865) 275905; internet www.ocms.ox.ac.uk; Dir Prof. C. M. DOBSON.

Radiation Oncology and Biology Initiative: Radiobiology Research Institute, Churchill Hospital, Headington, Oxford, OX3 7LJ; tel. (1865) 857532; fax (1865) 857533; internet www.rob.ox.ac.uk; Dir Prof. GILLIES MCKENNA.

Scottish Collaboration for Public Health Research and Policy: MRC Human Genetics Unit, W. Gen. Hospital, Crewe Rd, Edinburgh, EH4 2XU; tel. (131) 332-2471; Dir Prof. JOHN FRANK.

UK Human Genome Mapping Project Resource Centre: Hinxton Hall, Cambridge, CB10 1SB; tel. (1223) 496750; fax (1223) 496751; e-mail support@hgmp.mrc.ac.uk; internet www.hgmp.mrc.ac.uk; Dir Dr D. CAMPBELL.

Miles Dyslexia Centre: Bangor, Gwyne, LL57 2DG; tel. (1248) 382203; fax (1248) 383614; internet www.dyslexia.bangor.ac.uk; attached to Bangor Univ.; Dir MARKETA CARAVOLAS.

National Centre for Training and Education in Prosthetics and Orthotics: Curran Bldg, 131 St James' Rd, Glasgow G4 0LS; attached to University of Strathclyde; Dir Prof. J. HUGHES.

Paterson Institute for Cancer Research: Christie Hospital (NHS) Trust, Wilmslow Rd, Withington, Manchester, M20 9BX; tel. (161) 446-3000; fax (161) 446-3109; e-mail inquiries@picr.man.ac.uk; internet www.paterson.man.ac.uk; f. 1932; conducts basic and clinical cancer research; Dir NIC JONES.

Peninsula Magnetic Resonance Research Centre: Peninsula Medical School, Univ. of Exeter, St Lukes Campus,

Magdalen Rd Exeter, EX1 2LU; tel. (1392) 262982; fax (1392) 262926; e-mail a.benattayallah@exeter.ac.uk; internet centres.exeter.ac.uk/pmrrc; collaboration of the Univ. of Exeter, the Peninsula Medical School and the Univ. of Plymouth; jtly run by the Schools of Physics, Sports Science and Psychology at Exeter, the Institute of Neuroscience at Plymouth and the Peninsula Medical School; Dir IAN R. SUMMERS.

Public Health Laboratory Service: 61 Colindale Ave, London, NW9 5HT; tel. (20) 8200-4400; fax (20) 8200-7874; internet www.phls.co.uk; f. 1946; library of 35,000 vols; Dir (vacant); publs *Communicable Disease and Public Health* (4 a year), *Communicable Disease Report* (52 a year), *PHLS Food and Environment Bulletin* (12 a year), *PHLS HIV Bulletin*, *PHLS Library Bulletin* (weekly).

Scottish Network for Chronic Pain Research: Stirling, FK9 4LA; tel. (1786) 473171; fax (1786) 463000; attached to Univ. of Stirling; Dir Dr E. BRODIE.

Strangeways Research Laboratory: Worts' Causeway, Cambridge, CB1 8RN; tel. (1223) 740145; fax (1223) 740147; internet www.srl.cam.ac.uk; f. 1912; research into cell biology, developmental biology, cancer; primary research into cancer genetics, epidemiology, cardiovascular disease and diabetes; Dirs Prof. J. DANESH, Prof. B. PONDER.

Strathclyde Institute for Drug Research: Royal College Bldg, 204 George St, Glasgow G1 1XW; attached to Univ. of Strathclyde; Dir Prof. A. L. HARVEY.

Thomas Coram Research Unit: 27–28 Woburn Sq., London, WC1H 0AA; f. 1973; multi-disciplinary designated research unit of the Dept of Health; research in health, education and devt of children; attached to Institute of Education, Univ. of London; Dir Prof. PETER AGGLETON.

Trafford Centre for Medical Research: University of Sussex, Falmer, Brighton, BN1 9RH; attached to Univ. of Sussex; Dir Prof. A. L. MOORE (acting).

Wellcome Trust/Cancer Research UK Gurdon Institute: Tennis Court Rd, Cambridge, CB2 1QN; tel. (1223) 334088; fax (1223) 334089; e-mail info@gurdon.cam.ac.uk; internet www.gurdon.cam.ac.uk; attached to Univ. of Cambridge; Chair. Prof. J. C. SMITH (Christ's College).

NATURAL SCIENCES

General

Engineering and Physical Sciences Research Council: Polaris House, North Star Ave, Swindon, SN2 1ET; tel. (1793) 444100; fax (1793) 444005; e-mail infoline@epsrc.ac.uk; internet www.epsrc.ac.uk; f. 1994; supports basic, strategic and applied research and related postgraduate training in engineering and the physical sciences; funds engineers and physical scientists to conduct research; Chair. JOHN ARMITT; CEO Prof. DAVID DELPY; publs *Connect*, *Impact* (www.impactworld.org.uk), *Newsline*, *Pioneer*, *Spotlight*.

Natural Environment Research Council (NERC): Polaris House, North Star Ave, Swindon, SN2 1EU; tel. (1793) 411500; fax (1793) 411501; e-mail requests@nerc.ac.uk; internet www.nerc.ac.uk; f. 1965; funds and conducts research to help find sustainable solutions to problems concerning biodiversity, environmental risks and hazards, global change, natural resource management, and pollution and waste; trains ind. environmental scientists; Chair. ROB MARGETTS; Chief Exec. Prof. JOHN LAWTON.

Component Institutes of the Council:

British Antarctic Survey: High Cross, Madingley Rd, Cambridge, CB3 0ET; tel. (1223) 221400; fax (1223) 362616; e-mail information@bas.ac.uk; internet www.antarctica.ac.uk; f. 1945 as Falkland Islands Dependencies Survey; present name 1962; operates 5 research stations, 2 Royal Research Ships and 5 aircraft in and around Antarctica; undertakes a programme of science in the Antarctic and related regions and aims to address key global and regional issues; undertakes jt research projects and over 120 nat. and int. collaborations; library of 8,500 vols, 350 periodicals; Dir Prof. C. RAPLEY, Prof. NICHOLAS OWENS.

British Geological Survey: Kingsley Dunham Centre, Nicker Hill, Keyworth, Nottingham, NG12 5GG; tel. (115) 936-3100; fax (115) 936-3200; e-mail enquiries@bgs.ac.uk; internet www.bgs.ac.uk; f. 1835; library: earth science reference library; Nat. Geoscience Data Centre; Exec. Dir Prof. JOHN LUDDEN; publ. *Earthwise* (2 a year).

Centre for Ecology & Hydrology: Maclean Bldg, Benson Lane, Crowmarsh Gifford, Wallingford, OX10 8BB; tel. (1491) 838800; fax (1491) 692424; e-mail enquiries@ceh.ac.uk; internet www.ceh.ac.uk; Dir Prof. PATRICIA NUTTALL.

Constituent Institutes:

CEH Bangor: Environment Centre Wales, Deinol Rd, Bangor, LL57 2UW; tel. (1248) 374500; fax (1248) 355363; internet www.ceh.ac.uk/sites/bangor.html; Head Prof. BRIDGET EMMETT.

CEH Edinburgh: Bush Estate, Penicuik, EH26 0QB; tel. (131) 445-4343; fax (131) 445-3943; internet www.ceh.ac.uk; Dir Prof. J. NEIL CAPE.

CEH Lancaster: Lancaster Environment Centre, Library Ave, Bailrigg, Lancaster, LA1 4AP; tel. (1524) 595800; fax (1524) 61536; e-mail lancaster@ceh.ac.uk; internet www.ceh.ac.uk/sites/lancaster.html; Head of Site Dr BRENDA HOWARD.

CEH Wallingford: Maclean Bldg, Benson Lane, Crowmarsh Gifford, Wallingford, OX10 8BB; tel. (1491) 838800; fax (1491) 629424; e-mail jsw@ceh.ac.uk; internet www.nwl.ac.uk; Dir Prof. JIM WALLACE.

Proudman Oceanographic Laboratory: 6 Brownlow St, Liverpool, L3 5DA; tel. (151) 795-4800; fax (151) 795-4801; e-mail polenquiries@pol.ac.uk; internet www.pol.ac.uk; Dir Dr ANDREW WILLMOTT.

Centre for Atmospheric Science: Dept of Chemistry, Univ. of Cambridge, Lensfield Rd, Cambridge, CB2 1EP; tel. (1223) 336473; fax (1223) 336473; internet www.atm.ch.cam.ac.uk/acmsu; Dir Dr J. A. PYLE.

Centre for Population Biology: Imperial College London, Silwood Park Campus, Ascot, SL5 7PY; tel. (20) 7594-2475; fax (1344) 873173; internet www.imperial.ac.uk/cpb; Dir Prof. GEORGIA MACE.

Environmental Systems Science Centre: Univ. of Reading, Harry Pitt Bldg, 3 Earley Gate, POB 238, Reading, RG6 6AL; tel. (118) 931-8741; fax (118) 931-6413; e-mail admin@mail.nerc-essc.ac.uk; internet www.nerc-essc.ac.uk; Head Prof. R. J. GURNEY.

National Centre for Atmospheric Science (NCAS): Dept of Meteorology, Univ. of Reading, POB 243, Earley Gate, Reading, RG6 6BB; tel. (118) 378-8315; fax (118) 378-8316; e-mail n.d.bray@reading.ac.uk; internet www.cgam.nerc.ac.uk; Dir for Climate Prof. JULIA SLINGO.

National Oceanography Centre: Univ. of Southampton Waterfront Campus, European Way, Southampton, SO14 3ZH; tel. (23) 8059-6666; fax (23) 8059-6032; internet www.noc.soton.ac.uk; Dir Prof. ED HILL.

Plymouth Marine Laboratory: Prospect Pl., Plymouth, PL1 3DH; tel. (1752) 633100; fax (1752) 633101; e-mail forinf@pml.ac.uk; internet www.pml.ac.uk; f. 2002; CEO Prof. STEPHEN DE MORA.

Sea Mammal Research Unit: Gatty Marine Laboratory, Univ. of St Andrews, St Andrews, KY16 8LB; tel. (1334) 462630; fax (1334) 462632; e-mail smru.office@smru.st-and.ac.uk; internet smub.st-and.ac.uk; Dir Prof. P. HAMMOND.

Tyndall Centre for Climate Change Research: School of Environmental Sciences, Univ. of East Anglia, Norwich, NR4 7TJ; tel. (1603) 593900; fax (1603) 593901; internet www.tyndall.ac.uk; Dir Prof. KEVIN ANDERSON.

Biological Sciences

Biocomposites Centre: Deiniol Rd, Bangor, LL57 2UW; tel. (1248) 370588; fax (1248) 370594; e-mail bc@bangor.ac.uk; internet www.bc.bangor.ac.uk; f. 1991; attached to Bangor Univ.; conducts contract research on processing of wood and plant materials; Dir Dr PAUL FOWLER.

Biomedical Sciences Research Institute:tel. (28) 7032-3091; fax (28) 7032-4965; e-mail km.coyles@ulster.ac.uk; internet biomed.science.ulster.ac.uk/bmsri; f. 2004; attached to Univ. of Ulster; studies of biological mechanisms associated with degenerative diseases like cancer, diabetes, heart disease, osteoporosis and visual deterioration.

BIOS: Houghton St, London, WC2A 2AE; f. 2003; attached to London School of Economics and Political Science, Univ. of London; int. centre for research and policy on social aspects of life sciences and biomedicine; Dir Prof. NIKOLAS ROSE.

Biosciences Graduate Research School: Edgbaston, Birmingham, B15 2TT; tel. (121) 414-5560; fax (121) 414-5925; e-mail biosciences-phd@bham.ac.uk; internet www.biosciences.bham.ac.uk/study/graduate/research/phd.shtml; attached to Univ. of Birmingham; Dir Prof. C. M. THOMAS.

Bristol University Botanic Garden: Waltham Cottage Yard, Hollybush Lane, Stoke Bishop, Bristol, BS9 1JB; tel. (117) 331-4912; fax (117) 331-4909; internet www.bris.ac.uk/depts/botanicgardens; f. 1882 to advance public education and promote teaching and research into botany and its related subjects; adult education programme, courses and tours; school groups welcome; Curator NICHOLAS WRAY; publ. *Annual Seed List*.

Cambridge University Botanic Garden: Cory Lodge, Bateman St, Cambridge, CB2 1JF; tel. (1223) 336265; fax (1223) 336278; e-mail enquiries@botanic.cam.ac.uk; internet www.botanic.cam.ac.uk; f. 1762 (1846 on present site); teaching and research in botany and horticulture; library of 11,000 (incl. early vols of *Gardeners Chronicle* annotated by Charles Darwin); Dir Prof. J. S. PARKER; publ. *Seed List* (1 a year).

Chelsea Physic Garden: 66 Royal Hospital Rd, London, SW3 4HS; tel. (20) 7352-5646; fax (20) 7376-3910; e-mail enquiries@chelseaphysicgarden.co.uk; internet www.chelseaphysicgarden.co.uk; f. 1673; botanic garden and centre for research and education on plants, conservation of rare plants, and a public amenity; specializes in medicinal plants, tropical corridor glasshouse, cool fernery, listed pond rockery, beehives; adult learning programme of lectures and short courses; library: restricted-access library of 300 vols, incl. Society of Apothecaries Dale bequest; Curator R. ATKINS; publ. *Index Seminum* (1 a year).

Economic and Social Research Council Centre for Genomics in Society (Egenis Centre): Univ. of Exeter, Byrne House, St German's Rd, Exeter, Devon, EX4 4PJ; tel. (1392) 269140; fax (1392) 264676; e-mail egenis@ex.ac.uk; internet www.genomicsnetwork.ac.uk/egenis; f. 2002 as part of the ESRC Genomics Network; attached to Univ. of Exeter; conducts research on social impact of devts in genomic science; Dir Prof. JOHN DUPRÉ; Co-Dir Prof. S. BARRY BARNES; Deputy Dir Dr CHRISTINE HAUSKELLER.

Institute of Zoology: Zoological Society of London, Regent's Park, London, NW1 4RY; tel. (20) 7449-6610; fax (20) 7586-2870; e-mail enquiries@ioz.ac.uk; internet www.zoo.cam.ac.uk/ioz; f. 1977; studies aimed at the scientific advancement of conservation, breeding and management of animals in the wild and in captivity; research groups in reproductive biology (gamete biology, endocrinology, physiological ecology), genetics (population genetics, molecular genetics), veterinary science (incl. wildlife disease and comparative medicine), ecology (behavioural ecology and population dynamics); incorporates Nuffield Laboratories of Comparative Medicine and Wellcome Laboratories of Comparative Physiology; library and publs: see Zoological Society of London; Dir Prof. TIM BLACKBURN (acting); publ. *Science for Conservation* (1 a year).

Interdisciplinary Research Centre in Biomedical Materials: Mile End Rd, London, E1 4NS; f. 1991; attached to Queen Mary, University of London; funded by EPSRC as nat. centre; innovation of analogue biomaterials for tissue and joint replacement; second generation implants and prostheses for medical and dental applications; offers PhD, MD and MS degrees.

International Bee Research Association (IBRA): 16 North Rd, Cardiff, CF10 3DY; tel. (29) 2037-2409; fax (56) 0113-5640; e-mail mail@ibra.org.uk; internet www.ibra.org.uk; f. 1949; charity working to increase awareness of the vital role of bees in the environment and to encourage the use of bees as wealth creators; has a UK Council (8 mems) and an Int. Council (9 mems); library: transferred to the Nat. Library of Wales; Pres. Prof. OCTAAF VAN LAERE (Belgium); Chair. HANS KJAERSGAARD; Exec. Dir SARAH JONES; publs *Bee World* (4 a year), *Journal of Apicultural Research* (e-journal, 4 a year), *Journal of ApiProduct and ApiMedical Science* (e-journal, 4 a year).

National Institute for Biological Standards and Control: Blanche Lane, South Mimms, Potters Bar, Herts, EN6 3QG; tel. (1707) 641000; fax (1707) 641050; e-mail enquiries@nibsc.ac.uk; internet www.nibsc.ac.uk; f. 1976; the National Biological Standards Board is responsible for control and standardization of biological substances used in human medicine, and its functions are executed through the Institute; biological substances include all vaccines such as poliomyelitis, measles, rubella and whooping cough, also blood products, certain hormones and a number of antibiotics; research and development work is an important part of the Institute's activities; designated a WHO Int. Laboratory for Biological Standards; library of 4,000 vols, 200 periodicals; Dir Dr G. C. SCHILD; publ. *Biological Reference Materials*.

Royal Botanic Garden, Edinburgh: 20A Inverleith Row, Edinburgh, EH3 5LR; tel. (131) 552-7171; fax (131) 248-2901; e-mail d&m@rbge.org.uk; internet www.rbge.org.uk; f. 1670; int. centre for the study of plant biodiversity and conservation; courses leading to HND in horticulture with plantsmanship; MSc course in biodiversity and plant taxonomy; Inverleith House Gallery with art exhibitions inspired by nature; regional gardens—Benmore Botanic Garden, near Dunoon, Argyll; Logan Botanic Garden, Stranraer, Wigtownshire; Dawyck Botanic Garden, Stobo, Peeblesshire; Herbarium of 2,000,000 specimens; library: see Libraries and Archives; Regius Keeper Prof. STEPHEN BLACKMORE; publ. *Edinburgh Journal of Botany* (3 a year).

Royal Botanic Gardens, Kew: Richmond upon Thames, TW9 3AB; tel. (20) 8332-5000; fax (20) 8332-5197; e-mail info@kew.org; internet www.kew.org; f. 1759, became a public institution in 1841; taxonomic botany, horticulture, conservation, economic botany, biochemistry, genetics, mycology, propagation and seed storage; also gardens and facilities at Wakehust Place, W Sussex; library: see Libraries and Archives; Dir and CEO Prof. STEPHEN HOPPER; publs *Curtis's Botanical Magazine* (4 a year), *Kew Bulletin* (4 a year), *Kew Record of Taxonomic Literature* (4 a year).

Attached Institute:

Millennium Seed Bank Project: Wakehurst Pl., Ardingly, Haywards Heath, RH17 6TN; tel. (1444) 894100; fax (1444) 894110; e-mail msbsci@kew.org; internet www.kew.org/science-conservation/conservation-climate-change/millennium-seed--bank; aims to save 25% of the world's plant species from extinction by 2020 through collection and conservation of seeds, incl. all UK native seed-bearing flora; undertakes British and int. programmes of seed collection; Convention to Combat Desertification est. to protect drylands flora species; Head of Seed Conservation PAUL SMITH.

University of Oxford Botanic Garden: Rose Lane, Oxford, OX1 4AZ; tel. (1865) 286690; fax (1865) 286693; e-mail postmaster@obg.ox.ac.uk; internet www.botanic-garden.ox.ac.uk; f. 1621; 6,000 different plant species in glasshouses, walled garden, water garden, rock garden and seasonal borders; educational lectures and tours; Harcourt Arboretum south of Oxford; library of 1,000 vols on horticulture; Dir TIMOTHY WALKER; publ. *Guide*.

Wildfowl & Wetlands Trust: Slimbridge, Glos., GL2 7BT; tel. (1453) 891900; fax (1453) 890827; e-mail enquiries@wwt.org.uk; internet www.wwt.org.uk; f. 1946; concerned with all aspects of biology/ecology of wetlands and wildfowl, particularly those related to conservation, research, education and recreation; the world's largest comparative collection of living wildfowl is maintained at Slimbridge; other centres open to the public all year round at Arundel, Sussex; Castle Espie, Co. Down; Martin Mere, Lancs.; Washington, Tyne and Wear; Welney, Norfolk; Llanelli, Dyfed; Caerlaverock, Dumfriesshire; Barnes, London; education staff and facilities at all centres; 100,000 mems; library: research library at Slimbridge; Man. Dir MARTIN SPRAY; publ. *Wildfowl* (1 a year).

Mathematical Sciences

Centre for Applicable Mathematics: College Rd, Bangor, LL57 2DG; f. 1988; attached to Bangor Univ.; Dir Dr G. W. ROBERTS.

Hull Institute for Mathematical Science and Applications: Cottingham Rd, Hull, HU6 7RX; attached to Univ. of Hull; Dir Prof. V. VLADIMIROV.

Isaac Newton Institute for Mathematical Sciences: 20 Clarkson Rd, Cambridge, CB3 0EH; tel. (1223) 335999; fax (1223) 330508; e-mail info@newton.ac.uk; internet www.newton.ac.uk; attached to Univ. of Cambridge; Dir Sir DAVID WALLACE (Churchill College).

Mathematics Education Centre: Schofield Bldg, Loughborough Univ., Loughborough, LE11 3TU; tel. (1509) 228250; fax (1509) 228211; internet mec.lboro.ac.uk; f. 2002; attached to Loughborough Univ.; research in different fields of mathematics; curriculum devt projects; organizes courses and seminars; Dir Dr CAROL ROBINSON.

National Computing Centre: Oxford Rd, Manchester, M1 7ED; tel. (161) 242-2121; fax (161) 242-2499; e-mail info@ncc.co.uk; internet www.ncc.co.uk; f. 1966; a membership organization run on a commercial basis to promote the effective use of information technology; acts as a focus for its mems and represents their views at nat. and int. level; provides consultancy and training services, software packages and other products; cooperates with other bodies to foster standards and best practices; Exec. Chair. MICHAEL GOUGH; Man. Dir STEFAN FOSTER.

Scottish Informatics, Mathematics, Biology and Statistics: Bell St, Dundee, DD1 1HG; attached to Univ. of Abertay Dundee; Dir Prof. JOHN W. PALFREYMAN.

XFi Centre for Finance and Investment: Univ. of Exeter Business School, Streatham Court, Rennes Dr., Exeter, EX4 4ST; tel. (1392) 263463; fax (1392) 262475; e-mail m.l.bishop@exeter.ac.uk; internet xfi.exeter.ac.uk; f. 2001; attached to Univ. of Exeter; financial market research; Dir Prof. ALAN GREGORY.

Physical Sciences

Astronomy Unit: School of Mathematical Sciences, Queen Mary, Univ. of London, London, E1 4NS; tel. (20) 7882-5514; fax (20) 7882-7684; e-mail w.white@qmul.ac.uk; internet www.maths.qmul.ac.uk/research/astronomy; attached to Queen Mary, Univ. of London; nat. centre conducting research in areas of astronomy; UK Cluster Science Centre is located in Unit.

Armagh Observatory: College Hill, Armagh, BT61 9DG; tel. (28) 3752-2928; fax (28) 3752-7174; e-mail info@arm.ac.uk; internet www.arm.ac.uk; f. 1790 by Archbishop Richard Robinson; study of astronomy, climate, stellar astrophysics and the solar system; library of 15,000 vols; Dir Prof. MARK E. BAILEY; Admin. LAWRENCE F. YOUNG.

Astrophysics Group, Cavendish Laboratory: JJ Thomson Ave, Cambridge, CB3 0HE; tel. (1223) 337294; fax (1223) 354599; e-mail k.scrivener@mrao.cam.ac.uk; internet www.mrao.cam.ac.uk; f. 1945; Head Dr PAUL ALEXANDER; publ. scientific papers.

Cambridge University Institute of Astronomy: Madingley Rd, Cambridge, CB3 0HA; tel. (1223) 337548; fax (1223) 337523; e-mail ioa@ast.cam.ac.uk; internet www.ast.cam.ac.uk; f. inc. fmr Observatory (f. 1824), Solar Physics Observatory (f. 1913) and Institute of Theoretical Astronomy (f. 1967); works on observational and theoretical astrophysics; library of 35,800 vols; Dir Prof. R. C. KENNICUTT.

Centre for Applicable Mathematics: College Rd, Bangor, LL57 2DG; f. 1988; attached to Bangor Univ.; Dir Dr G. W. ROBERTS.

Centre for Arid Zone Studies: College Rd, Bangor, LL57 2DG; f. 1984; attached to Bangor Univ.; specializes in natural resource management and rural devt in drought-prone areas; Dir Dr W. I. ROBINSON.

Centre for Electromagnetic Materials Research (CEMR): Harrison Bldg, N Park Rd, Exeter, EX4 4QF; tel. (1392) 263628; fax (1392) 217965 Physics Bldg, Stocker Rd, Exeter, EX4 4QL; tel. (1392) 264151; fax (1392) 264111; e-mail cemr@exeter.ac.uk; internet centres.exeter.ac.uk/cemr; attached to Univ. of Exeter; research areas include diffractive optics, photonic control of light-matter interactions, thin-film magnetics, magnetic, optical, probe data storage, microwave photonics and plasmonics, phase-change materials, photonics in biology, Terahertz photonics and plasmonics, liquid crystals; Dir Prof. KEN EVANS.

Centre for Energy and Environment: Room 303, Physics Bldg, Univ. of Exeter, Stocker Rd, Exeter, Devon, EX4 4QL; tel. (1392) 724144; fax (1392) 724111; e-mail g.s.j.hitchcock@exeter.ac.uk; internet emps.exeter.ac.uk/research/cee; f. 1975; attached to Univ. of Exeter; researches on issues surrounding sustainable bldgs, energy, transport; Dir Dr GUY HITCHCOCK.

Centre for Environmental Studies: Loughborough, LE11 3TU; tel. (1509) 222558; fax (1509) 223925; e-mail l.e.child@lboro.ac.uk; internet www.lboro.ac.uk/research/cens; attached to Loughborough Univ.; teaching and research in environmental topics; vocational training and education in environmental studies at undergraduate and postgraduate level; Dir Prof. P. WARWICK.

Centre for Hazard & Risk Management: Loughborough, LE11 3TU; tel. (1509) 222155; fax (1509) 223991; e-mail m.jost@lboro.ac.uk; attached to Loughborough Univ.; applied research in environmental pollution control, human factors and safety culture, organisational health and safety management, risk and continuing professional devt; Dir CHARLES HANCOCK.

Centre for Maritime Historical Studies: College of Humanities, Armory Bldg, Rennes Dr., Exeter, EX4 4RJ; e-mail history@exeter.ac.uk; internet centres.exeter.ac.uk/cmhs; f. 1991; attached to Univ. of Exeter; promotes research into economic, social, political, naval, environmental aspects of British maritime with help from European and int. experience; Dir Dr MARIA FUSARO.

Centre for Philosophy of Natural and Social Science: Houghton St, London, WC2A 2AE; f. 1990; attached to London School of Economics and Political Science, Univ. of London; promotes study of philosophical and methodological issues; Dir Dr CARL HOEFER.

Centre for Renewable Energy Systems Technology: Dept of Electronic and Electrical Engineering, Loughborough Univ., Loughborough, LE11 3TU; internet www.lboro.ac.uk/departments/el/research/centres/crest; f. 1993; attached to Loughborough Univ.; research and education in renewable energy technology; Dir Prof. PHIL EAMES.

Centre for Research in Ecology: Dept of Life Sciences, Whitelands College, Roehampton Univ., Holybourne Ave, London, SW15 4JD; tel. (20) 8392-3457; fax (20) 8392-3527; e-mail a.robertson@roehampton.ac.uk; internet www.roehampton.ac.uk/researchcentres/cre; attached to Roehampton Univ.; research on ecology and behavioural-physiology of animals, both vertebrates and invertebrates; Dir Dr ANNE ROBERTSON.

Centre for Research in Environmental History: Stirling, FK9 4LA; tel. (1786) 467-580; fax (1786) 467-581; f. 2002; attached to Univ. of Stirling; research on disciplinary backgrounds, incl. history, environmental science, philosophy and economics; Dir Dr RICHARD ORAM.

Centre for Sustainable Design: Falkner Rd, Farnham, Surrey, GU9 7DS; tel. (1252) 892772; fax (1252) 892747; e-mail cfsd@ucreative.ac.uk; internet www.cfsd.org.uk; f. 1995; attached to Univ. for the Creative Arts; Dir MARTIN CHARTER; publ. *The Journal of Sustainable Product Design* (4 a year).

Centre for Water Systems (CWS): School of Engineering, Computing and Mathematics, Univ. of Exeter, N Park Rd, Exeter, EX4 4QF; tel. (1392) 263637; fax (1392) 217965; e-mail d.savic@exeter.ac.uk; internet centres.exeter.ac.uk/cws; f. 1994; attached to Univ. of Exeter; researches into water systems engineering focusing mainly on water supply and distribution systems, waste water and urban drainage systems, integrated modelling, risk and uncertainty, whole-life costing, water efficiency, catchment-based management, spatial water management; Head Prof. DAVID BUTLER; Head Prof. DRAGAN SAVIC.

Centre of Environmental and Waste Management: Paisley, PA1 2BE; tel. (141) 848-3146; e-mail cewm@uws.ac.uk; f. 1991; attached to Univ. of the West of Scotland; Dir Dr JENNIFER MCQUAID-COOK.

Environmental Sciences Research Institute: Room G157, School of Environmental Sciences, Univ. of Ulster, Coleraine, BT52 1SA; tel. (28) 7032-4242; e-mail science@ulster.ac.uk; internet www.science.ulster.ac.uk/esri; attached to Univ. of Ulster; promotes understanding of the Earth systems for effective management of environment; Dir SANDY STEACY (acting).

Exeter Biocatalysis Centre: Henry Wellcome Bldg for Biocatalysis, Stocker Rd, Exeter, Devon, EX4 4QD; tel. (1392) 263489; e-mail j.a.littlechild@exeter.ac.uk; internet centres.exeter.ac.uk/biocatalysis; f. 2003; attached to Univ. of Exeter; researches into aspects of biocatalysis incl. relationships between protein structure and function, protein engineering, molecular graphics, protein crystallography; Dir Prof. JENNIFER LITTLECHILD.

Graduate School of Environmental Studies: Level 7, Graham Hills Bldg, 50 Richmond St, Glasgow, G1; attached to Univ. of Strathclyde; Dir J. FORBES.

Hull Environment Research Institute (HERI): Cottingham Rd, Hull, HU6 7RX; internet www2.hull.ac.uk/science/heri.aspx; f. 2004; attached to Univ. of Hull; research across interdisciplinary span of environmental science; Dir Prof. L. FROSTICK.

Institute of Estuarine and Coastal Studies: Cottingham Rd, Hull, HU6 7RX; tel. (1482) 464120; fax (1482) 464130; e-mail iecs@hull.ac.uk; research on coastal environment ranging from biological and physical environments (topography, vegetation, ornithology, benthic and pelagic fauna) to coastal planning, environmental quality, marine law and environmental impact assessment; attached to Univ. of Hull; Dir Dr M. ELLIOTT.

Jodrell Bank Observatory/University of Manchester: Macclesfield, Cheshire, SK11 9DL; tel. (1477) 571321; fax (1477) 571618; e-mail lisa.mcdermott@manchester.ac.uk; internet www.jb.man.ac.uk; f. 1945; the observatory uses 7 large steerable radio telescopes, including the Lovell (fmrly Mark 1A) 250-ft diameter radio telescope; these can be connected into MERLIN array which extends to Cambridge (base-line: 230 km) to study radio objects in any part of the sky; research on galactic and extra-galactic astrophysical continuum and spectral line radio emissions and cosmic microwave background; observations of radio emission from quasars, pulsars and stars; multi-telescope interferometry and very long base-line interferometry; Dir Prof. PHILIP DIAMOND.

Met Office: Fitzroy Rd, Exeter, EX1 3PB; tel. (1392) 885680; fax (1392) 885681; e-mail enquiries@metoffice.gov.uk; internet www.metoffice.gov.uk; f. 1854; provides a nat. meteorological service and is responsible for implementing the objectives of the World Meteorological Org. (see Int. Org.); provides comprehensive forecasting and consultative services; involved with major research into all aspects of meteorology, climatology and atmospheric science, partly in cooperation with univs and other nat. and int. agencies; work on the physics and dynamics of the atmosphere ranges in scale from global numerical analyses and forecasts to the microphysics of clouds; library: see Libraries and Archives; Chief Exec. J. HIRST; publ. *Scientific and Technical Review*.

Attached Research Centre:

Met Office Hadley Centre: Fitzroy Rd, Exeter, EX1 3PB; tel. (870) 9000100; fax (870) 9005050; e-mail enquiries@metoffice.gov.uk; internet www.metoffice.gov.uk/climate-change; f. 1990; monitors, understands and predicts global and regional climate variability and change; provides advocacy services to govt on climate change issues; Head Dr CHRIS GORDON; publ. *COP Climate Change* (1 a year).

Oxford Institute for Energy Studies: 57 Woodstock Rd, Oxford, OX2 6FA; tel. (1865) 311377; fax (1865) 310527; e-mail information@oxfordenergy.org; internet www.oxfordenergy.org; f. 1982; attached to Univ. of Oxford; library of 12,500 vols; Dir CHRISTOPHER ALLSOP.

Science and Technology Facilities Council: Polaris House, N Star Ave, Swindon, SN2 1SZ; tel. (1793) 442000; fax (1793) 442002; internet www.stfc.ac.uk; granted Royal Charter in 2007; operates large-scale research facilities and provides strategic advice to British govt on their devt; manages int. research projects in support of a broad cross-section of the UK research community; directs, coordinates and funds research, education and training; Chair. Prof. MICHAEL STIRLING; Chief Exec. Prof. KEITH MASON; publ. *Fascination*.

Attached Centre:

UK Astronomy Technology Centre: Royal Observatory, Blackford Hill, Edinburgh, EH9 3HJ; tel. (131) 668-8313; fax (131) 668-8314; e-mail library@roe.ac.uk; internet www.roe.ac.uk; f. 1998; manages the 3.8-m infra-red telescope and the James Clerk Maxwell mm-wave telescope in Hawaii, USA; responsible for the optical telescope at La Palma Observatory, Canary Islands, Spain; houses the Dept of Astronomy of Edinburgh Univ.; has a Starlink data processing centre and a Super-COSMOS high-speed plate scanning machine; library of 75,000 vols; Dir Dr IAN ROBSON.

Scottish Institute for Wood Technology: Bell St, Dundee, DD1 1HG; attached to Univ. of Abertay Dundee; Sr Research Dir Prof. JOHN W. PALFREYMAN.

Strathclyde Fermentation Centre: Royal College Bldg, 204 George St, Glasgow, G1 1XW; attached to Univ. of Strathclyde; Dir Prof. B. KRISTIANSEN.

Tyndall Centre for Climate Change Research: School of Environmental Sciences, Norwich, NR4 7TJ; tel. (1603) 593900; fax (1603) 593901; e-mail tyndall@uea.ac.uk; internet www.tyndall.ac.uk;

attached to Univ. of East Anglia; Dir Prof. MIKE HULME.

Science and Technology Facilities Council: Chilton, Didcot, OX11 0QX; tel. (1235) 821900; fax (1235) 445808; e-mail enquiries@stcc.ac.uk; internet www.scitech .ac.uk; f. 1995; provides advanced and large-scale laboratory facilities, and expertise, to support univ. and industrial research; Chief Exec. Prof. KEITH MASON; publ. *Science and Technology* (3 a year).

Laboratories:

Daresbury Laboratory: Keckwick Lane, Daresbury Science and Innovation Campus, Warrington, WA4 4AD; tel. (1925) 603000; fax (1925) 603100; e-mail enquiries@stfc.ac.uk; internet www.scitech .ac.uk; f. 1958; operates synchrotron X-ray source; provides advanced surface science and other materials facilities, and computational support in a broad range of disciplines; Chief Exec. Prof. KEITH MASON.

Rutherford Appleton Laboratory: Harwell Science and Innovation Campus, Didcot, OX11 0QX; tel. (1235) 445000; fax (1235) 445808; e-mail enquiries@stfc.ac.uk; internet www.stfc.ac.uk; f. 1957; operates pulsed source of neutrons and muons (ISIS), high-power lasers, microelectronic design and microengineering facilities, and space engineering and data centres; provides supercomputing, detector technology and particle physics support; Chief Exec. Prof. KEITH MASON.

United Kingdom Atomic Energy Authority: Manor Court, Chilton, Didcot, Oxon., OX11 0RN; tel. (1235) 431810; fax (1235) 436899; internet www.ukaea.org.uk; f. 1954; has responsibility for the safe management and decommissioning of the nuclear reactors and other research and development facilities used to develop the UK's nuclear power programme, together with the safe disposal of the radioactive waste; implements the UK's contribution to the European fusion programme; sites at Dounreay (Caithness), Windscale (Cumbria), Risley (Cheshire), Culham (Oxfordshire), Harwell (Oxfordshire), Winfrith (Dorset); Chair. Sir KENNETH EATON; Chief Exec. Dr JOHN MCKEOWN.

University of London Observatory: 553 Watford Way, Mill Hill Park, London, NW7 2QS; tel. (20) 8959-0421; fax (20) 8238-8872; e-mail vmp@star.ucl.ac.uk; internet www.ulo .ucl.ac.uk; f. 1929; part of Dept of Physics and Astronomy, University College, London; teaching and research in astronomy; specialized astronomical library; Dir Prof. I. D. HOWARTH; publ. *Communications* (irregular, online only).

PHILOSOPHY AND PSYCHOLOGY

Anna Freud Centre: 21 Maresfield Gdns, London, NW3 5SD; tel. (20) 7794-2313; fax (20) 7794-6506; e-mail info@annafreud.org; internet www.annafreudcentre.org; f. 1947 by Anna Freud, daughter of Sigmund Freud, 1952–1982 as the Hampstead Child Therapy Course and Clinic, present name 1982; psychoanalytical treatment of troubled children and young people; offers academic training in child psychotherapy and conducts research into psychotherapeutic techniques and the emotional devt of children; library open only to those working at the Centre; library of 2,500 vols; Chair. of Directorial Team LINDA MAYES; Chief Exec. PETER FONAGY; Professional Dir MARY TARGET.

Centre for Attention Perception and Motor Control: College Rd, Bangor, LL57 2DG; studies interaction between vision and movement and role of selective attention and memory in control of goal-directed behaviour; attached to Bangor Univ.; Dir Prof. S. TIPPER.

Centre for Experimental Consumer Psychology: College Rd, Bangor, LL57 2DG; tel. (1248) 382211; e-mail psychology@ bangor.ac.uk; attached to Bangor Univ.; Dir Prof. JANE RAYMOND.

Clinical and Health Psychology Research Centre: Department of Psychology, Whitelands College, Roehampton University, Holybourne Ave, London, SW15 4JD; tel. (20) 8392-3744; e-mail l.gibson@ roehampton.ac.uk; internet www .roehampton.ac.uk/researchcentres/chp; attached to Roehampton Univ.; investigates interaction of behavioural, biological environmental and sociocultural factors in the aetiology, maintenance and prevention of health problems, and in health promotion; developmental, food, neuropsychological and psychophysiological laboratories; Dir Dr LEIGH GIBSON.

Psychology Research Institute: Room G213, School of Psychology, Coleraine Campus, Cromore Rd, Coleraine, BT52 1SA; tel. (28) 7032-4656; internet www.science.ulster .ac.uk/psyri; attached to Univ. of Ulster; research groups: Behavioural Neuroscience, Peace and Conflict, Health Psychology, and Measurement and Statistical Modelling; Dir Prof. MAURICE STRINGER; Sec. FIONA HARKIN.

RELIGION, SOCIOLOGY AND ANTHROPOLOGY

Centre for Analysis of Social Exclusion: Houghton St, London, WC2A 2AE; 5th Fl., Lionel Robbins Bldg, Portugal St 10, London, WC2A 2HD; tel. (20) 7955-6679; fax (20) 7955-6951; e-mail j.dickson@lse.ac.uk; internet sticerd.lse.ac.uk/case; f. 1997; attached to London School of Economics and Political Science, Univ. of London; research and consultancy on different dimensions of social disadvantage, particularly from longitudinal and neighbourhood perspectives, and examination of impact of public policy; organizes seminars and co-organizes monthly welfare policy and analysis seminar; Dir Prof. JOHN HILLS.

Centre for Biblical Studies: c/o Univ. of Exeter, Queen's Dr., Devon, Devon, EX4 4QJ; tel. (1392) 724288; e-mail d.g.horrell@ exeter.ac.uk; internet centres.exeter.ac.uk/ cbs; f. 2008; attached to Univ. of Exeter; Dir Prof. DAVID HORRELL.

Centre for Research in Evolutionary Anthropology: Department of Life Sciences, Whitelands College, Roehampton University, Holybourne Ave, London, SW15 4JD; tel. (20) 8392-3645; fax (20) 8392-3527; e-mail a.maclarnon@roehampton.ac.uk; internet www.roehampton.ac.uk/ researchcentres/crea; f. 2002; attached to Roehampton Univ.; research on fields in primatology, incl. socioecology, life history strategies, communication, welfare, reproductive endocrinology, comparative morphology and crop-raiding behaviour; Dir Prof. ANN MACLARNON.

Centre for Research in Social Policy: Loughborough, LE11 3TU; e-mail a.p .france@lboro.ac.uk; internet www.lboro.ac .uk/study/postgraduate/courses/departments/socialsci/research/centreforresearchinsocialpolicy; attached to Loughborough Univ.; research in field of social policy; provides information on which policy decisions are made; Dir Prof. ALAN FRANCE.

Centre for the Advanced Study of Religion in Wales: Bangor, LL57 2DG; tel. (1248) 382079; e-mail theology@bangor.ac .uk; f. 1998; attached to Bangor Univ.; Dir Prof. D. DENSIL MORGAN; Dir Dr ROBERT POPE.

Centre for the Study of Migration: Mile End Rd, London, E1 4NS; f. 1994; attached to Queen Mary, Univ. of London; acts as focal point for those engaged in study of migration locally, nationally and internationally.

Centre for the Study of the Christian Church: Dept of Theology, Univ. of Exeter, Exeter, Devon, EX4 4QH; tel. (1392) 264242; e-mail theology@exeter.ac.uk; internet centres.exeter.ac.uk/cscc; attached to Univ. of Exeter; promotes scholarly study of the Christian Church; Dir Rev. Dr PAUL AVIS; publ. *International Journal for the Study of the Christian Church* (2 a year).

Economic and Social Research Council: Polaris House, North Star Ave, Swindon, SN2 1UJ; tel. (1793) 413000; fax (1793) 413001; internet www.esrcsocietytoday.ac .uk; f. 1965; ind. org. funded mainly by Govt; research and training agency; aims to provide research on issues of importance to business, public sector and govt; Chair. FRANCES CAIRNCROSS; Chief Exec. Prof. IAN DIAMOND; publs *The Edge* (3 a year), *Social Sciences* (3 a year).

European Muslim Research Centre: Armory Bldg, Rennes Dr., Exeter, EX4 4RJ; tel. (1392) 723367; e-mail emrc@exeter.ac.uk; internet centres.exeter.ac.uk/emrc; attached to Univ. of Exeter; researches on roles that Muslim communities play in European soc.; Co-Dir Dr JONATHAN GITHENS-MAZER; Co-Dir Dr ROBERT LAMBERT.

Exeter Centre for the Study of Esotericism (EXESESO): c/o Univ. of Exeter, Queen's Dr., Exeter, Devon, EX4 4QJ; tel. (1392) 661000; e-mail n.goodrick-clarke@ exeter.ac.uk; internet centres.exeter.ac.uk/ exeseso; attached to Univ. of Exeter; researches into historical and comparative aspects of esoteric traditions from Hellenistic period in late antiquity through Renaissance and early modern period to present; Dir Prof. NICHOLAS GOODRICK-CLARKE.

Exeter Turkish Studies: Armory Bldg, Rennes Dr., Exeter, EX4 4RJ; tel. (1392) 264195; fax (1392) 263305; e-mail exts@ exeter.ac.uk; internet centres.exeter.ac.uk/ exts; attached to Univ. of Exeter; researches on Turkish history and culture; Dir STEPHEN MITCHELL; Co-Dir GERALD MACLEAN.

Family Assessment and Support Unit: Cottingham Rd, Hull, HU6 7RX; attached to Univ. of Hull; Dir T. ALLCOTT.

Institute of Applied Social Studies: Muirhead Tower, Birmingham, B15 2TT; tel. (121) 414-2676; fax (121) 414-5726; internet www .iass.bham.ac.uk; attached to Univ. of Birmingham; research in social policy and social work; Dir DAVE MARSH.

Institute of Arab and Islamic Studies: Stocker Rd, Univ. of Exeter, Exeter, EX4 4ND; tel. (1392) 725250; fax (1392) 264035; e-mail iais-info@ex.ac.uk; internet huss .exeter.ac.uk/iais; f. 1999, present bldg 2001; attached to Univ. of Exeter; researches in areas within field of Arab, Middle Eastern, Islamic studies; Dir Prof. GARETH STANSFIELD; Deputy Dir Prof. IAN NETTON; Librarian PAUL AUCHTERLONIE.

Institute of Ismaili Studies: 210 Euston Rd, London, NW1 2DA; tel. (20) 7756-2700; fax (20) 7756-2740; e-mail info@iis.ac.uk; internet www.iis.ac.uk; f. 1977 by the Aga Khan; research into Islam, with emphasis on Shi'ism and Ismaili tariqah; library of 25,000 vols, MSS and audiovisual items; Dir Prof. AZIM NANJI.

ISTD: Centre for Crime and Justice Studies: King's College London, Strand, London, WC2R 2LS; tel. (20) 7848-1688; fax

(20) 7848-1689; e-mail info@crimeandjustice.org.uk; internet www.crimeandjustice.org.uk; f. 1931; ind. objective forum for all criminal justice professionals and those with a lay interest in crime; arranges confs, courses and visits; Chair. of Council ELIZABETH HILL; Dir RICHARD GARSIDE; publs *British Journal of Criminology* (4 a year), *Criminal Justice Matters* (4 a year).

London Middle East Institute: SOAS, Russell Sq., London, WC1H 0XG; tel. (20) 7898-4330; fax (20) 7898-4329; e-mail lmei@soas.ac.uk; internet www.lmei.soas.ac.uk; attached to the School of Oriental and African Studies (SOAS), Univ. of London; Dir Dr HASSAN HAKIMIAN; publ. *The Middle East in London* (12 a year).

Methodology Institute: Houghton St, London, WC2A 2AE; f. 1991, jtly with external research bodies; attached to London School of Economics and Political Science, Univ. of London; researches methodological aspects of social surveys; Dir Prof. G. GASKELL.

Muslim Institute: 109 Fulham Palace Rd, London, W6 8JA; tel. (20) 8563-1995; fax (20) 8563-1993; e-mail info@musliminstitute.com; internet www.musliminstitute.com; f. 1972; research in early history of Islam, Islamic economics, philosophy of science, international relations, global Islamic movement; teaching (short courses) in political thought, philosophy of science, Arabic language, journalism; monthly meetings of academics, writers and activists dealing with issues such as reform within Islam, Islamic identity and citizenship and the future of Islam in Europe; library of 600 vols; Dir Dr FARIDA OWAISI.

Network for Religion in Public Life: Armory Bldg, Rennes Dr., Devon, EX4 4RJ; Univ. of Exeter, Dept of Theology, Exeter, Devon, EX4 4RJ; tel. (1392) 264241; fax (1392) 264195; e-mail e.d.reed@exeter.ac.uk; internet centres.exeter.ac.uk/nrpl; f. 2007; attached to Univ. of Exeter; promotes understanding and cooperation between academics and religious communities; Dir Dr ESTHER D. REED.

Oxford Centre for Buddhist Studies: Linton Rd, Oxford, OX2 6UD; tel. (1865) 274098; e-mail info@ocbs.org; internet www.ocbs.org; attached to Univ. of Oxford; Exec. Dir GEOFFREY BAMFORD; Academic Dir Prof. RICHARD GOMBRICH.

Oxford Centre for Hebrew and Jewish Studies: Yarnton Manor, Yarnton, Kidlington, OX5 1PY; tel. (1865) 377946; fax (1865) 375079; e-mail enquiries@ochjs.ac.uk; internet www.ochjs.ac.uk; f. 1972; attached to Univ. of Oxford; Master of Studies (MSt) degree; library: Leopold Muller Memorial Library: Kressel colln of 30,000 vols and pamphlets and 400,000 newspaper cuttings, Elkoshi colln of 17,000 vols, Yizkor colln of 450 Holocaust memorial books; Pres. Dr DAVID ARIEL; publ. *the Journal of Jewish Studies*.

Oxford Centre for Hindu Studies: 13–15 Magdalen St, Oxford, OX1 3AE; tel. (1865) 304300; fax (1865) 304301; e-mail info@ochs.org.uk; internet www.ochs.org.uk; attached to Univ. of Oxford; Dir SHAUNAKA RISHI DAS; Academic Dir Prof. GAVIN FLOOD.

Oxford Centre for Islamic Studies: George St, Oxford, OX1 2AR; tel. (1865) 278730; fax (1865) 248942; e-mail islamic.studies@oxcis.ac.uk; internet www.oxcis.ac.uk; attached to Univ. of Oxford; f. 1985; Dir FARHAN AHMAD NIZAMI (Magdalen College); publ. *The Journal of Islamic Studies* (3 a year).

Population Investigation Committee: Houghton St, London, WC2A 2AE; f. 1936; attached to London School of Economics and Political Science, Univ. of London; promotes and undertakes research into population questions and promotes study of demography in both its quantitative and qualitative aspects; Chair. Prof. J. HOBCRAFT.

School of Theology and Ministry Studies: Brayford Pool, Lincoln, LN6 7TS; attached to Univ. of Lincoln; Head Rev. Dr MARK HOCKNULL.

Social Work Research Centre: Stirling, FK9 4LA; tel. (1786) 473171; fax (1786) 463000; attached to Univ. of Stirling; Dir Prof. G. MCIVOR.

Tavistock Institute: 30 Tabernacle St, London, EC2A 4UE; tel. (20) 7417-0407; fax (20) 7417-0566; e-mail central.admin@tavinstitute.org; internet www.tavistockinstitute.org; f. 1947; study of human relations in conditions of well-being, conflict or breakdown in the family, the work group, the community and the larger organization; disciplines range from social science to organizational development; Sec. DEBBIE SORKIN; publs *Evaluation* (4 a year), *Human Relations* (12 a year).

Welsh National Centre for Religious Education: Bangor, LL57 2DG; tel. (1248) 383594; e-mail ems023@bangor.ac.uk; internet wncre.bangor.ac.uk; f. 1979; attached to Bangor Univ.; promotes the devt of religious education in schools, colleges and churches of all types throughout Wales; Head VAUGHAN SALISBURY; Dir Prof. L. FRANCIS.

TECHNOLOGY

Advanced Virtual Reality Research Centre: Loughborough, LE11 3TU; tel. (1509) 635678; fax (1509) 211586; e-mail r.s.kalawsky@lboro.ac.uk; internet www.lboro.ac.uk/departments/el/research/centres/avrrc; attached to Loughborough Univ.; research and devt in advanced modelling, simulation and visualization techniques; Dir Prof. ROY KALAWSKY.

Animation Research Centre: Falkner Rd, Farnham, Surrey, GU9 7DS; f. 2000; attached to Univ. for the Creative Arts; Dir Dr SUZANNE BUCHAN.

BHR Group Ltd: Fluid Eng. Centre, Cranfield, Beds., MK43 0AJ; tel. (1234) 750422; fax (1234) 750074; e-mail solutions@bhrgroup.com; internet www.bhrgroup.com; f. 1947; provides research, devt and consultancy on all aspects of fluid eng. and process technology, for a wide range of industries; specializes in abrasive water-jet cutting, fluid power, hydraulics, mixing, pumping, process intensification, chemical reaction eng., micromaterials and nanomaterials technology, multiphase flow, pipe networks, sealing and containment, slurry transport; biodiesel; field studies; conferences and specialist training courses; technical information services; Chief Exec. J. A. R. MUIR.

BMT Group Ltd: Goodrich House, 1 Waldegrave Rd, Teddington, TW11 8LZ; tel. (20) 8943-5544; fax (20) 8943-5347; internet www.bmt.org; f. 1985; provides industry with high-level research and technical assistance; solutions to the problems of designers and operators of structures and vehicles on land, coastal terrain and at sea; 22 subsidiary and assoc. operating companies; Chair. Dr NEIL CROSS; Chief. Exec. PETER FRENCH; publs *BMT Abstracts* (12 a year), *Focus*.

British Textile Technology Group (BTTG): Wira House, West Park Ring Rd, Leeds, LS16 6QL; tel. (113) 259-1999; fax (161) 278-0306; e-mail info@bttg.co.uk; internet www.bttg.co.uk; f. 1918; engaged in research, devt, testing and evaluation for textile and related industries; undertakes product devt and testing, int. consulting work; Man. Dir STEPHEN DONNELLY.

Building Research Establishment: Bucknalls Lane, Garston, Watford, WD25 9XX; tel. (1923) 664000; fax (1923) 664010; e-mail enquiries@bre.co.uk; internet www.bre.co.uk; f. 1921; research and consultancy covering building, construction, energy efficiency and the prevention and control of fire; certification of building products, accreditation of product installers and energy assessors; Chair. Dr MARTIN WYATT; Chief Exec. Dr PETER BONFIELD; Chief Exec. CAROL ATKINSON; publs *BRE: Constructing the Future* (4 a year), *BRE Digest series* (4 a year), *BRE Report Series*.

Centre for Automotive Management: Loughborough, LE11 3TU; tel. (1509) 223294; e-mail s.e.hollick@lboro.ac.uk; internet www.lboro.ac.uk/departments/sbe/pmdc/areas/automotive/index.html; f. 1997; attached to Loughborough Univ.; research within the automotive industry; specialist training and devt for practising dealer principals, managers, supervisors and team leaders; Dir Prof. JIM SACKER.

Centre for Computational Chemistry: College Rd, Bangor, LL57 2DG; develops industrial applications of modelling in materials science for natural and advanced materials; attached to Bangor Univ.; Dir Dr J. N. MACDONALD.

Centre for Electrical Power Engineering: Royal College Bldg, 204 George St, Glasgow, G1 1XW; attached to Univ. of Strathclyde; Dir Prof. O. FARISH.

Centre for Innovative and Collaborative Construction Engineering: Loughborough, LE11 3TU; tel. (1509) 228549; fax (1509) 223982; e-mail cice@lboro.ac.uk; internet www.lboro.ac.uk/cice; f. 1999; attached to Loughborough Univ.; training and research in engineering and management of the construction field; Dir Prof. DINO BOUCHLAGHEM.

Centre for Internet Computing: Cottingham Rd, Hull, HU6 7RX; attached to Univ. of Hull; Head Dr C. GASKELL.

Centre for Magnetic Resonance Investigations: Anlaby Rd, Hull, HU3 2JZ; tel. (1482) 674078; fax (1482) 320137; f. 1992; attached to Univ. of Hull; Dir Prof. L. W. TURNBULL.

Centre for Mobile Communications Research: Loughborough, LE11 3TU; tel. (1509) 227006; fax (1509) 227008; internet www.lboro.ac.uk/departments/el/research/centres/cmcr; f. 1998; attached to Loughborough Univ.; research in the design of antennas and associated components for mobility applications;encourages cross fertilization between physical, firm and soft aspects of communications technology; Dir YIANNIS VARDAXOGLOU.

Centre for Particle Characterization and Analysis: Paisley, PA1 2BE; tel. (141) 848-3241; e-mail cpca@uws.ac.uk; attached to Univ. of the West of Scotland; Man. Dr A. HURSTHOUSE.

CERAM Research Ltd: Queens Rd, Penkhull, Stoke-on-Trent, ST4 7LQ; tel. (1782) 764444; fax (1782) 412331; e-mail enquiries@ceram.com; internet www.ceram.com; f. 1948; researches into ceramics and materials processing, manufacture of ceramic components and the use of ceramic products for clients involved in metals, composites, construction and the environment; services incl. contract research and devt, manufacturing consultancy, testing and analysis; library of 13,000 vols and 60,000 pamphlets; Chair.

DAVID DRY; Chief Exec. Dr NEIL SANDERSON; publ. *World Ceramics Abstracts* (online).

CIRIA: Classic House, 174–180 Old St, London, EC1V 9BP; tel. (20) 7549-3300; fax (20) 7253-0523; e-mail enquiries@ciria.org; internet www.ciria.org; f. 1960; improves the quality, efficiency, cost-effectiveness and safety in both the provision and operation of the modern built environment; 500 mem. orgs; Chief Exec. BILL HEALY; publ. *Evolution* (2 a year).

Computer Science Research Institute: Room D092, School of Computing and Information Engineering, Univ. of Ulster, Coleraine campus, Cromore Rd, Coleraine, BT52 1SA; tel. (28) 7032-4648; internet www.compeng.ulster.ac.uk/csri.php; f. 2004; attached to Univ. of Ulster; research in artificial intelligence and applications, information and communication engineering, intelligent systems and smart environments; attached research centres: Electronics Production and Innovation (EPI) Centre, Intelligent Systems Research Centre, Wireless Technology Research Centre; Dir Prof B. W. SCOTNEY.

Computer Security Research Centre: Houghton St, London, WC2A 2AE; f. 1991; attached to London School of Economics and Political Science, Univ. of London; studies computer security issues from organizational, management, social and technical perspectives; Dir Dr J. BACKHOUSE.

Defence Science and Technology Laboratory (DSTL): Porton Down, Salisbury, Wilts, SP4 0JQ; tel. (1980) 613121; fax (1980) 613085; e-mail central-enquiries@dstl.gov.uk; internet www.dstl.gov.uk; f. 2001 following re-organization of the former Defence Evaluation and Research Agency (DERA); part of the Ministry of Defence; locations: Alverstoke, Fort Halstead, Harwell, Porton Down, Portsdown West; library: MOD Scientific Reports Collection of 750,000 items from WWII to the present; publs *Defence Reports Abstracts* (monthly; available only to the MOD, its agencies and contractors), *Defence Technology Alerts* (monthly, information about technological developments in the defence community; available only to the MOD, its agencies and contractors).

Engineering Centre for Excellence in Teaching and Learning: Keith Green Bldg, Faculty of Engineering, Loughborough University, Loughborough, LE11 3TU; tel. (1509) 227191; fax (1509) 227181; e-mail engcetl@lboro.ac.uk; internet engcetl.lboro.ac.uk; f. 2005; attached to Loughborough Univ.; pedagogic research and evaluation to underpin teaching and learning; Man. Dr ADAM CRAWFORD; Assoc. Dir FIONA LAMB.

Engineering Innovation Institute: Cottingham Rd, Hull, HU6 7RX; tel. (1482) 466470; attached to Univ. of Hull; Dir GAVIN CUTLER.

Hasselblad Centre for High Resolution Digital Imaging: Fort Pitt, Rochester, Kent, ME1 1DZ; attached to Univ. for the Creative Arts; Contact Prof. ORI GERSHT.

Health Design and Technology Institute: Coventry Univ. Technology Park, Puma Way, Coventry, CV1 2TT; tel. (24) 76158000; e-mail hdti.info@coventry.ac.uk; internet www.coventry.ac.uk/hdti; attached to Coventry Univ.; research in areas such as bldg and vehicle adaptations, walking aids and wheelchairs, consumer health products and healthcare technology for the elderly and people with disabilities; Dir SIMON FIELDEN.

Industrial Control Centre: Marland House, 40 George St, Glasgow, G1 1BA; attached to Univ. of Strathclyde; Dir Prof. M. GRIMBLE.

Infoterra Ltd: Delta House, Southwood Crescent, Southwood, Farnborough, Hants., GU14 0NL; tel. (1252) 362000; fax (1252) 375016; e-mail info@infoterra-global.com; internet www.infoterra-global.com; f. 1989 to commercialize the National Remote Sensing Centre and Earth Observation Centre; supplier of products and services based on information extracted from data acquired by Earth observation satellites and aerial photography; consultancy services; Marketing Dir ANTHONY DENNISS.

Institute of Bioelectronic and Molecular Microsystems: Dean St, Bangor, LL57 1UT; tel. (1248) 382010; fax (1248) 361429; e-mail info@ibmm-microtech.co.uk; internet www.eng.bangor.ac.uk; f. 1983; attached to Bangor Univ.; Dir Prof. D. M. TAYLOR.

Institute of Development Engineering: Loughborough, LE11 3TU; incl. Water, Engineering and Devt Centre (WEDC); research on infrastructure needs of underdeveloped countries for the British Govt's Dept for Int. Devt, int. orgns, foreign govts and agencies; attached to Loughborough Univ.; Dir I. SMOUT.

Interdisciplinary Research Centre in Materials Processing: Edgbaston, Birmingham, B15 2TT; tel. (121) 414-3446; fax (121) 414-3441; internet www.irc.bham.ac.uk; f. 1989, present name 2001; attached to Univ. of Birmingham; research on metals and ceramics, covering processing, property and microstructural studies; Head Dr S. BLACKBURN.

International Centre for Computer Games and Virtual Entertainment: Bell St, Dundee, DD1 1HG; f. 2001; attached to Univ. of Abertay Dundee; academic research and devt centre for computer games and digital entertainment industry; Head Prof. LACHLAN MACKINNON.

John Logie Baird Centre for Research in Television and Film: Livingstone Tower, 26 Richmond St, Glasgow G1 1XH; attached to University of Strathclyde; Dir Prof. S. W. FRITH.

National Physical Laboratory: Hampton Rd, Teddington, Middx, TW11 0LW; tel. (20) 8977-3222; fax (20) 8943-6458; e-mail enquiry@npl.co.uk; internet www.npl.co.uk; f. 1900; nat. standards laboratory; establishes measurement standards, and undertakes research into improved techniques, engineering materials and information technology; Dir Dr BRIAN BOWSHER.

Natural Resources Institute: Univ. of Greenwich, Central Ave, Chatham Maritime, Kent, ME4 4TB; tel. (1634) 880088; fax (1634) 880066; e-mail nri@greenwich.ac.uk; internet www.nri.org; f. 1987; became an institute of the Univ. of Greenwich 1996; supplier of research, consultancy and training services in the environment and natural resources sector to support devt assistance programmes, sustainable management of natural resources, environmental sciences, cost-effective and environmentally safe pest management, devt and transfer of technologies to improve food security, social, economic and institutional analysis to enhance the impact of devt projects and policies; training (some courses accredited for postgraduate qualifications); library of 300,000 vols and information service; Dir Dr ANDREW WESTBY; publ. *NRI Annual Review*.

Pera International: Nottingham Rd, Melton Mowbray, LE13 0PB; tel. (1664) 501501; fax (1664) 501554; e-mail innovation@pera.com; internet www.pera.com; f. 1946; a multi-disciplinary technology centre specializing in all aspects of manufacture, incl. materials, quality training, methods, computer applications, human resources and manufacturing integration; Non-Exec. Chair. ROGER WHYSALL; Chief Exec. JOHN HILL.

QinetiQ: Cody Technology Park, Ively Rd, Farnborough, GU14 0LX; tel. (8700) 100942; internet www.qinetiq.com; f. 2001 as government-owned UK PLC following reorganization of the former Defence Evaluation and Research Agency (DERA); researches and develops services and technologies in various fields: defence, maritime, aviation, security, energy and power, automative, finance, health, highways and traffic, public sector, rail, space, telecoms, media and electronics; locations: Aberporth, Bedford, Bincleaves, Bishopton, Boscombe Down, Bridgwater, Bristol, Buckingham Gate (London), Burntisland, BUTEC (Rosshire), Chertsey, Cobbett Hill, Defford, Eskmeals, Farnborough, Fort Halstead, Foulness, Fraser (Portsmouth), Funtington (Chichester), Haslar, Hebrides, Kirkcudbright, Larkhill, Llanbedr, Loch Goil, Malvern, Pendine, Pershore, Plymouth, Portland Bill, Portsdown, Portsdown West, Rona, Rosneath, Rosyth, Shoeburyness, Skipness, Sundridge, West Freugh, Weston-Super-Mare, Winfrith; CEO LEO QUINN.

Scottish Microelectronics Centre: The Kings Bldgs, W Mains Rd, Edinburgh, EH9 3JF; tel. (131) 650-7474; fax (131) 650-7475; internet www.scotmicrocentre.co.uk; attached to Univ. of the West of Scotland; research and devt in semiconductor sector; delivers services in four areas: incubation, analytical, processing and assembly; Chief Exec. IAIN HYSLOP; Dir Prof. ANTHONY J. WALTON.

Scottish Transputer Centre & DTI Centre for Parallel Signal Processing: Royal College Bldg, 204 George St, Glasgow, G1 1XW; attached to Univ. of Strathclyde; Dir Prof. T. DURRANI.

Scottish Universities Environmental Research Centre: Rankine Ave, Scottish Enterprise Technology Park, E Kilbride, Glasgow, G75 0QF; tel. (1355) 223332; fax (1355) 229898; e-mail maleana.provan@glasgow.ac.uk; internet www.glasgow.ac.uk/suerc; f. 1963; provides research and teaching facilities in radioactive and stable isotopes in the environment, ultratrace analysis, radiation mapping, nuclear waste disposal, thermoluminescence dating and dosimetry, food irradiation, radiochemistry, environmental studies, geochronology, isotope geology, stable isotope geochemistry, carbon dating and cosmogenic isotope analysis, including accelerator mass spectrometry; Dir Prof. ANGUS B. MACKENZIE; Dir of Research Prof. ROBERT M. ELLAM.

Smart Structures Research Institute: Royal College Bldg, 204 George St, Glasgow, G1 1XW; attached to Univ. of Strathclyde; Dir P. GARDINER.

Smith Institute: Surrey Technology Centre, Surrey Research Park, Guildford, GU2 7GG; tel. (1483) 579108; fax (1483) 568710; e-mail gillian@smithinst.co.uk; internet www.smithinst.co.uk; f. 1993; non-profit organization; mathematics and computing depts of univs throughout the UK; joint industry/academic institute for research in industrial mathematics and system engineering; training in energy, telecommunications and insurance sectors; Dir Dr ROBERT LEESE; Business Devt Dir Dr HEATHER TEWKESBURY.

Sports Technology Institute: Loughborough Park, Loughborough Univ., Loughborough, LE11 3TU; tel. (1509) 564819; fax (1509) 564820; e-mail k.e.brand@lboro.ac.uk; internet sti.lboro.ac.uk; attached to Loughborough Univ.; Dir Prof. MIKE CAINE.

Science and Technology Policy Research Unit: Freeman Centre, Univ. of Sussex, Falmer, Brighton, BN1 9QE; tel. (1273) 686758; fax (1273) 685865; e-mail spru@sussex.ac.uk; internet www.sussex.ac.uk/spru; attached to Univ. of Sussex; analysis of science, technology and innovation; research in the field of social sciences; Dir Prof. GORDON MACKERRON.

Systems Engineering Innovation Centre: Sir Denis Rooke Bldg, Holywell Park, Loughborough University, Loughborough, LE11 3TU; tel. (1509) 635200; fax (1509) 635231; e-mail seic@lboro.ac.uk; internet www.seic-loughborough.com; f. 2003; attached to Loughborough Univ.; promotes systems engineering as a strategic discipline; Technical Head Dr PHIL GREENWAY.

Thin Film Centre: High St, Paisley, PA1 2BE; tel. (141) 848-3610; fax (141) 848-3627; e-mail thinfilmcentre@uws.ac.uk; internet www.thinfilmcentre.co.uk; f. 2000; devt of deposition processes for thin films; design and fabrication of thin film products; characterisation of thin films and dissemination of information about applications of thin films; Dir Prof. FRANK PLACIDO.

TRL Ltd: Crowthorne House, Nine Mile Ride, Wokingham, RG40 3GA; tel. (1344) 773131; fax (1344) 770356; e-mail info@trl.co.uk; internet www.trl.co.uk; f. 1933; ind. research and devt and consultancy org. specializing in road materials and construction, structures, road safety and traffic, vehicle safety, environment, security, travel behaviours and attitudes, software; library of 200,000 vols, 250 current journals, int. roads and transport database; Chief Exec. Dr SUSAN SHARLAND; publ. *TRL Journal of Research* (3 or 4 a year).

Tun Abdul Razak Research Centre: Brickendonbury, Hertford, SG13 8NL; tel. (1992) 584966; fax (1992) 554837; f. 1938; research and devt on natural rubber; library of 3,000 books and 200 periodicals, information retrieval system containing 100,000 items; Dir of Research Dr A. J. TINKER.

TUV NEL Ltd: East Kilbride, Glasgow, G75 0QF; tel. (1355) 220222; fax (1355) 272999; internet www.tuvnel.com; f. 1947; applied engineering research, development; calibration, consultancy and prototype manufacture for private and public sectors; Gen. Man. Dr F. KINGHORN; publs *Conference Proceedings*, technical papers, reports.

Urban Water Technology Centre: Level 5, Kydd Bldg, Bell St, Dundee, DD1 1HG; tel. (1382) 308170; fax (1382) 308117; e-mail uwtc@abertay.ac.uk; internet www.uwtc.tay.ac.uk; f. 1993; attached to Univ. of Abertay Dundee; provides research, academic and consultancy services to the water industry (in the UK and overseas); Head Dr CHRIS JEFFERIES.

WRc PLC: Frankland Rd, Blagrove, Swindon, SN5 8YF; tel. (1793) 865000; fax (1793) 865001; e-mail solutions@wrcplc.co.uk; internet www.wrcplc.co.uk; f. 1927; ind. research and devt and consultancy org. specializing in water and environmental management; Chief Exec. RON CHAPMAN.

Libraries and Archives

Aberdeen

Aberdeen City Council Library and Information Services: Central Library, Rosemount Viaduct, Aberdeen, AB25 1GW; tel. (1224) 652500; fax (1224) 641985; internet www.aberdeencity.gov.uk/libraries; f. 1884; 17 brs; Central Library—Adult Lending Library, Children's Library, Media Centre, Internet access, Aberdeen College Learning Centre, information service, Local Studies, Community Contacts Directory; Careers Information Point, Scottish Parliament Partner Library, Nat. Library of Scotland Partner, Europe Direct Centre Enquiry and Research service, Migrant Communities Information Point, Enquire on-line nat. reference service; 500,000 vols; spec. collns incl. Scottish genealogy, local photographs, North Sea oil, British patent abstracts, 10,000 standard specifications, trade marks, business information; Library and Information Services Manager FIONA CLARK.

Robert Gordon University Library: Garthdee Rd, Aberdeen, AB10 7QE; tel. (1224) 263450; fax (1224) 263460; e-mail library@rgu.ac.uk; internet www.rgu.ac.uk/library; f. 1992; 205,470 vols; Dir of Library Services MICHELLE ANDERSON.

University of Aberdeen: Library and Historic Collections: Univ. Library, Meston Walk, Aberdeen, AB24 3UE; tel. (1224) 273600; fax (1224) 273596; e-mail library@abdn.ac.uk; internet www.abdn.ac.uk/library; f. 1495; 1,200,000 vols; McBean Jacobite colln, O'Dell railway colln, Biesenthal Hebrew colln, Taylor psalmody colln, G. W. Wilson photographic colln, Gregory, Melvin and other spec. collns; consists of Queen Mother Library, Taylor Library and European Documentation Centre, Medical Library; Special Libraries and Archives on King's College Campus; Librarian and Dir CHRIS BANKS.

Aberystwyth

Ceredigion County Library: Public Library, Corporation St, Aberystwyth, SY23 2BU; tel. (1970) 633703; fax (1970) 625059; e-mail llyfrgell.library@ceredigion.gov.uk; f. 1996; 290,000 vols; 7 brs, 6 mobile libraries; County Libraries Officer WILLIAM H. HOWELLS.

National Library of Wales: Aberystwyth, Ceredigion, SY23 3BU; tel. (1970) 632800; fax (1970) 615709; internet www.llgc.org.uk; f. 1907; legal deposit library; 5,000,000 printed books, 30,000 MSS, over 3,500,000 deeds and docs and 200,000 maps, prints and drawings, incl. the finest existing Welsh colln; diaries and correspondence of David Lloyd George; Librarian ANDREW M. W. GREEN; publ. *The National Library of Wales Journal* (2 a year).

University of Wales Aberystwyth, Hugh Owen Library: Penglais Campus, Aberystwyth, Ceredigion, SY23 3DZ; tel. (1970) 622391; fax (1970) 622404; e-mail libinfo@aber.ac.uk; internet www.aber.ac.uk; f. 1872; 730,000 vols, 3,647 periodicals; spec. collns in Hugh Owen Library incl. Celtic Colln (13,000 vols), Gregynog Press books and private press books since beginning of 20th century, George Powell Colln (19th-century English and French literature, fine art and music), James Camden Hotten Collection, Rudler Collection of geological pamphlets, Duff Colln of pamphlets (Classics), League of Nations and UN Documents, microforms incl. Early American Imprints 1639–1800, David De Lloyd Papers (Welsh folksongs), Lily Newton Papers (water pollution), Thomas Webster letters (19th-century geologist), British Soc. of Rheology Library; spec. collns in Thomas Parry Library (incl. Welsh Institute of Rural Studies Library) incl. Horton Colln (early children's books), Appleton Colln (Victorian colour printing and binding); Dir of Information Services REBECCA DAVIES.

Aldershot

Prince Consort's Library: Knollys Rd, Aldershot, Hants., GU11 1PS; tel. (1252) 349381; fax (1252) 349382; e-mail pcl@dstl.gov.uk; f. 1860; public access by written appointment only; military history library; 60,000 vols; Head of Library Services TIM WARD.

Amagh

Southern Education and Library Board: 3 Charlemont Pl., The Mall, Armagh, BT61 9AX; tel. (28) 3751-2200; e-mail selb.hq@selb.org; internet www.selb.org; f. 1973; 23 brs, 6 mobile libraries;serves the district council areas of Armagh, Banbridge, Cookstown, Craigavon, Dungannon and South Tyrone, Newry and Mourne; 1,450,000 vols; Chief Exec. TONY MURPHY.

Armagh Public Library: 43 Abbey St, Armagh, BT61 7DY; tel. (28) 3752-3142; fax (28) 3752-4177; e-mail admin@armaghpubliclibrary.co.uk; internet armaghpubliclibrary.arm.ac.uk; f. 1771, by Archbishop Richard Robinson, museum status 2001; 17th- and 18th-century books on theology, philosophy, classic and modern literature, voyages and travels, history, medicine and law; library colln incl. subjects on art, history, religion, Ireland, Armagh City and County, Jonathan Swift, St. Patrick, Church of Ireland, Rokeby Colln (prints), Beresford Colln (Irish artefacts); library incl. Ref. Dept with 39,000 vols; Keeper Very Rev. PATRICK ROOKE.

Ashton under Lyne

Tameside Metropolitan Borough Council Libraries and Customer Services Department: Council Offices, Wellington Rd, Ashton under Lyne, OL6 6DL; tel. (161) 342-8355; fax (161) 342-3744; e-mail information.direct@tameside.gov.uk; internet www.tameside.gov.uk/libraries; f. 1974; 288,078 vols, 150 periodicals; spec. collns: local studies and archives, sound recordings, video cassettes, computer software; Head of Library Services MANDY KINDER.

Aylesbury

Buckinghamshire County Library: County Offices, Walton St, Aylesbury, HP20 1UU; tel. (845) 230-3232; e-mail library@buckscc.gov.uk; internet www.buckscc.gov.uk/libraries; f. 1918; 927,000 vols; 34 brs; Library Systems Man. HAZEL EDWARDS.

Ballymena

North Eastern Education and Library Board: County Hall, 182 Galgorm Rd, Ballymena, BT42 1HN; tel. (28) 2566-3333; fax (28) 2563-2038; e-mail foi@neelb.org.uk; internet www.neelb.org.uk; f. 1973; 28 brs, 8 mobile libraries; 2m. vols; Chief Exec. SHANE MCCURDY.

Bangor

University of Wales, Bangor, Information Services: Bangor, LL57 2DG; tel. (1248) 382961; fax (1248) 382979; e-mail library@bangor.ac.uk; internet www.bangor.ac.uk/is/library; f. 1884; 500,000 vols; Bangor Cathedral Library; local Estate archives; 6 brs; Dir EINION WYN THOMAS.

Barry

Vale of Glamorgan Library and Information Service: Provincial House, Kendrick Rd, Barry, CF62 8UF; tel. (1446) 709381; fax (1446) 709448; internet www.valeofglamorgan.gov.uk/libraries; 10 brs; Chief Librarian SIAN E. JONES.

Bath

University of Bath Library: Bath, BA2 7AY; tel. (1225) 385000; fax (1225) 386229; e-mail library@bath.ac.uk; internet www.bath.ac.uk/library; 440,000 vols; contains Sir

Isaac Pitman's Library; Univ. Librarian H. D. NICHOLSON.

Bedford

Bedford Borough Libraries: Bedford Borough Council, Borough Hall, Cauldwell St, Bedford MK42 9AP; tel. (1234) 267422; e-mail bedfordshirelibraries@bedford.gov.uk; internet www.bedford.gov.uk/leisure_and_culture/libraries.aspx; 5 brs and 1 mobile library; Man. ANDY BAKER.

Central Bedfordshire Libraries: Central Bedfordshire Council, Priory House, Monks Walk, Chicksands, Shefford SG17 5TQ; tel. (300) 300-8000; 12 brs.

Belfast

Belfast Education & Library Board: 40 Academy St, Belfast, BT1 2NQ; tel. (28) 9056-4000; e-mail info@belb.co.uk; internet www.belb.org.uk; f. 1973; Central Library, 20 community libraries and 2 mobile libraries; Central Lending Library 57,000 vols; Central Reserve colln 100,000 vols; Humanities and Gen. Reference Library 120,000 vols; Irish Library 40,000 books, pamphlets and MSS on all aspects of Ireland, Ulster and Belfast; Fine Arts and Literature 74,000 vols; Music Library 12,000 vols, 24,000 scores, 24,000 records and cassettes; Business, Science and Technology Library 68,000 vols; other spec. collns: bibliographies, govt and agency publs, patents, rare books, microfilms; Chief Librarian KATHERINE MCCLOSKEY.

Linen Hall Library: 17 Donegall Sq., North, Belfast, BT1 5GB; tel. (28) 9032-1707; fax (28) 9043-8586; e-mail info@linenhall.com; internet www.linenhall.com; f. 1788 as Belfast Reading Society, still known as Belfast Library and Society for Promoting Knowledge for legal purposes; noted for its Irish colln of 70,000 vols, incl. early Ulster printing and major colln of political ephemera relating to civil conflict since 1968; 5,000 17th-century pamphlets, 18th- and 19th-century travel, biography; 250,000 vols; Dir BRIAN ADGEY; Deputy Dir PATRICIA SAUNDERS; Pres. G. PRIESTLEY; Vice-Pres. A. DAVIES; Hon. Sec. S. BURNSIDE; Hon. Treas. C. HUNTER; Librarian JOHN KILLEN; Deputy Librarian MONICA MCERLANE.

Public Record Office of Northern Ireland: 2 Titanic Blvd, Belfast, BT3 9HQ; tel. (28) 9025-5905; fax (28) 9025-5999; e-mail proni@dcalni.gov.uk; internet www.proni.gov.uk; f. 1923; attached to Dept of Culture, Arts and Leisure for Northern Ireland; an exec. agency within the Dept of Culture, Arts and Leisure for Northern Ireland; retains official and private records relating mainly to the history of Northern Ireland (dating from c. 1600 to the present day); Chair. and Chief Exec. Dr GERRY SLATER; Dir and Deputy Keeper of the Records AILEEN MCCLINTOCK.

Queen's University Library: Information Services, Queen's Univ., Belfast, BT7 1NN; tel. (28) 9097-6322; fax (28) 9032-3340; e-mail library@qub.ac.uk; internet www.qub.ac.uk/lib; f. 1849; 1.2m. vols, periodicals, pamphlets, MSS, theses and microforms; spec. collns: Hibernica Colln (incl. R. M. Henry Colln, O'Rahilly Colln), Antrim Presbytery Library, MacDouall Colln (Philology), Hamilton Harty Music Colln, Thomas Percy Library; Asst Dir for Library Services and Research Support ELIZABETH TRAYNOR; Asst Dir for Resources Management TREVOR LYTTLE; Sr Subject Librarian for Arts and Humanities DEIRDRE WILDY; Sr Subject Librarian for Medicine and Health Sciences ANGELA THOMPSON; Sr Subject Librarian for Science and Engineering DAN HOLDEN; Sr Subject Librarian for Social Sciences, Education and Law JOHN KNOWLES.

South Eastern Education and Library Board: Grahambridge Rd, Dundonald, Belfast, BT16 2HS; tel. (28) 9056-6200; fax (28) 9056-6366; e-mail info@seelb.org.uk; internet www.seelb.org.uk; f. 1973; 24 brs, 5 mobile libraries; 652,000 vols, 6,000 maps, 18,000 microforms, 22,000 CDs, 3,000 video recordings, 2,000 DVDs; Chief Exec. and Accounting Officer STANTON G. SLOAN.

Birmingham

Aston University Library and Information Services: Aston Triangle, Birmingham, B4 7ET; tel. (121) 204-4525; fax (121) 204-4530; e-mail library@aston.ac.uk; internet www.aston.ac.uk/lis; f. 1895; 237,000 vols, 88 print journal titles, 14,620 e-journal titles; Dir Dr N. R. SMITH.

Birmingham Library Services: Central Library, Chamberlain Sq., Birmingham, B3 3HQ; tel. (121) 303-4511; fax (121) 303-2861; e-mail libraries@birmingham.gov.uk; internet www.birmingham.gov.uk/libraries; f. 1861; 1,362,708 vols incl. 134 incunabula; 39 community libraries; reference library (f. 1866); depts: archives (incl. Diocesan Record Office and Boulton and Watt colln); arts, business information, language and literature (including John Ash Oberammergau Passion Play colln, King's Norton Parish Library, Sheldon Rector's Library, Parker colln of early children's books and games, Samuel Johnson, Milton, Cervantes, Baskerville and war poetry collns, early printed books, fine bindings and private press books, and Shakespeare Library—f. 1864, 45,000 vols in 90 languages), local studies and history (incl. Priestley colln, Sir Benjamin Stone colln of photographs, Marston Rudland colln of engraved portraits, Francis Frith negative archive, Bedford Photographic colln, and Warwickshire Photographic Survey), Music Library, Science and Technology , Social Sciences , Learning Centre; Head of Library and Archives Services LINDA BUTLER.

Orchard Learning Resources Centre (University of Birmingham): Hamilton Drive, Weoley Park Rd, Selly Oak, Birmingham, B29 6QW; tel. (121) 415-8454; fax (121) 415-8476; e-mail olrc@bham.ac.uk; internet www.olrc.bham.ac.uk; f. 1997; anthropology and world area studies, communications, development economics, Islamics, Christian theology and missiology, social studies, world religions, education, child and youth studies; 225,000 vols; Greek papyri; spec. collns incl. Harold W. Turner Colln on New Religious Movements; Mingana Collection of Arabic and Syriac MSS, archives relating to Christian mission and Christian education; Resource Centre Man. DOROTHY VUONG.

University of Birmingham Library: Edgbaston, Birmingham, B15 2TT; tel. (121) 414-5816; fax (121) 471-4691; internet www.is.bham.ac.uk; f. 1880 (as Mason Science College Library); 2,655,251 vols, 7,500 current periodicals, 3,000,000 MSS; special collections include: archives of Joseph, Austen and Neville Chamberlain, Anthony Eden, W. H. Dawson, Francis Brett Young, Harriet Martineau, Bishop E. W. Barnes, Sir Oliver Lodge, Church Missionary Society Archives (pre-1950), YMCA archives; St Mary's, Warwick and Bengeworth parish libraries, Wigan Library from Bewdley, Worcs, Baskerville collection; Birmingham and Midland Institute pamphlet collection; Librarian M. I. SHOEBRIDGE.

Blackburn

Blackburn with Darwen Library and Information Services: Central Library, Town Hall St, Blackburn, BB2 1AG; tel. (1254) 661221; fax (1254) 678898; e-mail library@blackburn.gov.uk; internet www.blackburn.gov.uk/libraries; f. 1998; unitary authority with 5 public libraries and mobile services; Head of Library and Information Services KATH SUTTON; Senior Librarian CATHERINE SNELLING.

Blackpool

Blackpool Library Service: Leisure, Culture and Community Learning, Progress House, Clifton Road, Blackpool, FY4 4US; tel. (1253) 478111; fax (1253) 478072; e-mail library.info@blackpool.gov.uk; 152,284 vols, 43 periodicals; Head of Libraries ANNE ELLIS.

Bournemouth

Bournemouth Libraries: 22 The Triangle, Bournemouth, BH2 5RQ; tel. (1202) 454848; fax (1202) 454840; e-mail bournemouth@bournemouthlibraries.org.uk; 277,404 vols, 41,237 audiovisual items, 13,276 sheet music, 16,720 microforms, 2,339 maps, 532 newspapers and periodicals; Area Services and Arts Manager CAROLYN DATE.

Bracknell

Bracknell Forest Borough Library and Information Service: Bracknell Library, Town Sq., Bracknell, RG12 1BH; tel. (1344) 352400; fax (1344) 411392; e-mail bracknell.library@bracknell-forest.gov.uk; internet www.bracknell-forest.gov.uk/libraries; f. 1998; 9 brs; Head of Libraries, Arts and Heritage RUTH BURGESS.

Bradford

Bradford Libraries: Prince's Way, Bradford, BD1 1NN; tel. (1274) 753600; fax (1274) 395108; internet www.bradford.gov.uk; f. 1887; 1,000,000 vols; 32 libraries and 3 mobile libraries, provide general collections; Central Library specializes in: local history, business information, Asian languages, and audio and video services; Head of Service JOHN TRIFFITT.

University of Bradford Library: Bradford, BD7 1DP; tel. (1274) 233301; fax (1274) 233398; e-mail library@bradford.ac.uk; internet www.bradford.ac.uk/library; f. 1966; 580,000 vols; J. B. Priestley Library; Management Library; Commonweal Colln; spec. collns incl. J. B. Priestley Colln; Head of Library Services GRACE HUDSON; publ. occasional bibliographies and guides.

Bridgend

Bridgend County Borough Library and Information Service: Ravens' Court, Brewery Lane Bridgend, CF31 4AP; tel. (1656) 754800; fax (1656) 642431; e-mail blis@bridgend.gov.uk; internet www.bridgend.gov.uk/libraries; 13 brs; Prin. Officer Libraries MARGARET GRIFFITHS.

Bridgwater

Somerset County Council, Library Service: Mount St, Bridgwater, TA6 3ES; tel. (1823) 336370; fax (1823) 272178; e-mail enquiry@somerset.gov.uk; internet www.somerset.gov.uk/libraries; f. 1919; 933,217 vols and sound recordings; 34 brs, 6 mobile libraries; a remote information service based in Taunton dealing with all information enquiries incl. business information; Group Man., Heritage and Libraries Group TOM MAYBERRY.

Brighton

Brighton and Hove City Libraries: Jubilee Library, Jubilee St, Brighton, BN1 1GE; tel. (1273) 290800; fax (1273) 296951; e-mail libraries@brighton-hove.gov.uk; internet www.citylibraries.info; Head of Libraries and Information Services SALLY MCMAHON.

Constituent Library:

Jubilee Library: Jubilee St, Brighton, BN1 1GE; tel. (1273) 290800; e-mail brightonlibrary@brighton-hove.gov.uk; internet www.citylibraries.info/jubilee/default.asp; f. 2005; holdings include 45,000 rare and historical books.

University of Sussex Library: Falmer, Brighton, BN1 9QL; tel. (1273) 606755; fax (1273) 678441; e-mail library@sussex.ac.uk; internet www.sussex.ac.uk/library; f. 1961; 750,000 vols; Librarian KITTY INGLIS.

Bristol

Bristol City Council—Culture and Leisure: Central Library, College Green, Bristol, BS1 5TL; tel. (117) 903-7200; fax (117) 922-1081; e-mail refandinfo@bristol.gov.uk; f. 1613; 27 brs, 1 mobile library; reference library; learning centre; 876,332 vols; Dir S. WRAY.

University of Bristol Library: Tyndall Ave, Bristol, BS8 1TJ; tel. (117) 928-9000; fax (117) 925-5334; e-mail library-enquiries@bris.ac.uk; internet www.bris.ac.uk/is/library; f. 1909; 1,500,000 vols and pamphlets; spec. collns incl. the English novel to 1850, the Sir Allen Lane Penguin colln, business histories, early geology, medicine, mathematics, chemistry and physics, Pinney Papers (17th–19th century), Brunel workbooks and papers, British philosophers, landscape gardening, courtesy books, Gen. Election addresses (part of the Nat. Liberal Club Library), Wiglesworth Ornithological Library, EDC, Addington Symonds Papers, Papers of the Somerset Miners' Assoc.; Dir of Library Services CATHRYN GALLACHER.

Caernarfon

Gwynedd Library and Information Service: Gwynedd Council, Council Offices, Caernarfon, LL55 1SH; tel. (1286) 679504; fax (1286) 677347; e-mail library@gwynedd.gov.uk; internet www.gwynedd.gov.uk; f. 1996; 383,989 vols; 17 brs; Principal Librarian HYWEL JAMES.

Cambridge

British and Foreign Bible Society's Library: Cambridge Univ. Library, West Rd, Cambridge, CB3 9DR; tel. (1223) 333000 ext. 33075; fax (1223) 333160; e-mail bslib@lib.cam.ac.uk; internet www.lib.cam.ac.uk; f. 1804; large colln of printed Bibles, over 40,000 vols of Scripture in more than 2,500 languages; archives of the Bible Society from 1804; Librarian P. M. MEADOWS.

Cambridge University Library: West Rd, Cambridge, CB3 9DR; tel. (1223) 333000; fax (1223) 333160; e-mail library@lib.cam.ac.uk; internet www.lib.cam.ac.uk; f. 1400; legal deposit library; 7,115,065 printed books and serial vols, numerous spec. collns, 157,186 MSS, large collns of papers and correspondence, 1,151,087 maps, 1,800,324 microforms; the collns have been accumulating since the beginning of the 15th century; Librarian ANNE JARVIS.

College Libraries:

Christ's College Library: Cambridge, CB2 3BU; tel. (1223) 334950; fax (1223) 334973; e-mail library@christs.cam.ac.uk; internet www.christs.cam.ac.uk; f. 1448, refounded 1505; 100,000 vols, incunabula, periodicals; spec. collns: works of John Milton, incl. items published before 1700, Charles Lesingham Smith colln of early mathematical and scientific books, William Robertson Smith Oriental Library, Sir Stephen Gaselee colln of Coptic studies, A. H. Wratislaw colln of Slavonic language and literature, W. H. D. Rouse colln of Indian studies and 16th-century English books, D. Dickson colln of C.P. Snow, David Stanbury Darwin colln; Librarian NAZLIN BHIMANI; Librarian Dr GAVIN ALEXANDER.

Churchill College Library: Cambridge, CB3 0DS; tel. (1223) 336138; e-mail librarian@chu.cam.ac.uk; internet www.chu.cam.ac.uk; f. 1960; 53,000 vols; spec. collns incl. political, military and scientific archives mainly since late 19th century, Powys colln, Winston Churchill's books on Napoleon; Librarian MARY KENDALL.

Clare College Library: Memorial Court, Clare College, Cambridge, CB3 9AJ; tel. (1223) 333202; fax (1223) 765560; e-mail library@clare.cam.ac.uk; internet www.clare.cam.ac.uk/academic/libraries; f. 1326; 36,000 vols; comprises Fellows' Library (8,000 vols); Forbes Mellon Library (28,000 vols); spec. collns: Cecil Sharp MSS, Geoffrey Elton papers; Fellows' Librarian Dr HUBERTUS JAHN; Forbes Mellon Librarian ANNE C. HUGHES.

Corpus Christi College: Parker Library: Trumpington St, Cambridge, CB2 1RH; tel. (1223) 338025; fax (1223) 338041; e-mail parker-library@corpus.cam.ac.uk; internet www.corpus.cam.ac.uk; f. 1352; spec. collns: Parker bequest of MSS and early printed books, Lewis colln of coins, gems and other antiquities (at present on loan to the Fitzwilliam Museum); Stokes colln on Jewish history; readers by appointment; 20,000 books, 600 MSS; Fellow Librarian Dr C. DE HAMEL.

Downing College: The Maitland Robinson Library: Regent St, Cambridge, CB2 1DQ; tel. (1223) 334829; internet www.dow.cam.ac.uk; f. 1800, Maitland Robinson Library opened 1993; 50,000 vols; spec. collns of Bowtell MSS relating to the city and univ. of Cambridge; library of 500 vols of Naval history and navigation and large colln of law, Civil War and Interregnum newspapers; College Librarian KAREN LUBARR.

Emmanuel College Library: St Andrew's St, Cambridge, CB2 3AP; tel. (1223) 334233; e-mail library@emma.cam.ac.uk; internet www.emma.cam.ac.uk/teaching/library; f. 1584; 72,000 vols, rare book collns, incl. the Graham Watson Colln and library of William Sancroft, Archbishop of Canterbury; 400 MSS (readers by appointment only); Librarian Dr H. C. CARRON.

Fitzwilliam College Library: Cambridge, CB3 0DG; tel. (1223) 332042; fax (1223) 477976; e-mail library@fitz.cam.ac.uk; internet www.fitz.cam.ac.uk/library; f. 1963; 39,000 vols; Librarian CHRISTINE ROBERTS LEWIS.

Girton College Library: Cambridge, CB3 0JG; tel. (1223) 338970; fax (1223) 339890; e-mail library@girton.cam.ac.uk; internet www-lib.girton.cam.ac.uk; f. 1869; spec. collns: Blackburn Colln of women's rights materials, Newall Colln of Scandinavian material, Frere Colln of Hebrew MSS, Crews Colln of Judeo-Spanish material, Somerville Colln of science and mathematics, Bibas Colln of 18th-century French works; College Archive covers the history of higher education for women via the College's institutional records and numerous collns of personal papers; 95,000 vols, 100 periodicals; Librarian and Curator FRANCES GANDY.

Gonville and Caius College Library: Cambridge, CB2 1TA; tel. (1223) 332419; e-mail library@cai.cam.ac.uk; internet www.cai.cam.ac.uk; f. 1348; 85,000 vols, 900 incunabula, 1,000 MSS related to medieval law and science; Librarian MARK STATHAM; Fellow Librarian Prof. D. S. H. ABULAFIA.

Jesus College Old Library: Jesus College, Cambridge, CB5 8BL; tel. (1223) 339405; fax (1223) 324910; f. 1500; spec. collns: Civil War tracts, military science, library of the Malthus family, large theological colln; 8,600 vols, 39 incunabula, 80 medieval MSS from north-country monasteries, 17 Oriental MSS; Keeper of the Old Library Prof. S. C. HEATH.

King's College Library: Cambridge, CB2 1ST; tel. (1223) 331232; fax (1223) 331891; e-mail library@kings.cam.ac.uk; internet www.kings.cam.ac.uk/library; f. 1441; spec. collns: MSS of Sir Isaac Newton (available on microfilm in the Univ. Library), 20th-century MSS, notably major collns of Rupert Brooke, E. M. Forster, T. S. Eliot, J. M. Keynes, Joan Robinson; incl. the Rowe Music Library; f. 1928; 25,000 vols; 125,000 vols; Librarian P. M. JONES.

Magdalene College Old Library: Cambridge, CB3 0AG; tel. (1223) 332125; e-mail library@magd.cam.ac.uk; MSS of works by Thomas Hardy, Rudyard Kipling, T. S. Eliot, I. A. Richards and 38 medieval MSS, incl. a 13th-century Apocalypse; papers of Ferrar family of Little Gidding; incunabula, foreign-printed books of 16th, 17th and 18th centuries, early theological works; Diaries of A. C. Benson, W. R. Inge and letters of George Mallory; access by appointment only (made in writing); 17,000 vols; Keeper Dr RICHARD LUCKETT.

Newnham College Library: Cambridge, CB3 9DF; tel. (1223) 335740; e-mail librarian@newn.cam.ac.uk; internet www.library.newn.cam.ac.uk; f. 1871; 9 medieval MSS, incunabula, early editions of poets, dramatists and chroniclers of 16th and 17th centuries; Skilliter Centre for Ottoman Studies holds 4,500 vols relating to Ottoman history; 90,000 vols; Librarian DEBORAH HODDER.

Pembroke College Library: Cambridge, CB2 1RF; tel. (1223) 338121; fax (1223) 338163; e-mail library@pem.cam.ac.uk; f. 1347; spec. collns; papers of Gray, William Mason, R. Storrs; 65,000 vols, 317 medieval MSS; Librarian PATRICIA ASKE.

Pepys Library (Magdalene College): Cambridge, CB3 0AG; tel. (1223) 332125; e-mail pepyslibrary@magd.cam.ac.uk; f. 1724 in its present location; Pepys's own colln (MSS, books, music, maps, prints and drawings), not added to since his death in 1703; Pepys's own catalogue; spec. collns: Pepys MSS (incl. Diary), medieval MSS, naval and historical MSS (mostly English, 16th- and 17th-century), colln of calligraphy, prints of London and Westminster, incunabula, broadside ballads, plays; 3,000 vols in original bookcases; Pepys Librarian Dr RICHARD LUCKETT.

Peterhouse (Perne) Library: Cambridge, CB2 1RD; tel. (1223) 338251; fax (1223) 337578; e-mail perne@pet.cam.ac.uk; internet www.pet.cam.ac.uk; f. 1594; 5,000 vols, 80 incunabula, 280 medieval MSS, 16th- and 17th-century musical MSS (on permanent deposit in Univ. Library); spec. collns incl. first editions of classics in science, 16th-century theological books; Librarian S. H. MANDELBROTE.

Queens' College Old Library: Cambridge, CB3 9ET; tel. (1223) 335549; fax (1223) 335522; e-mail librarian@queens.cam.ac.uk; internet www.queens.cam.ac.uk; f. 1448; colln incl. medieval MSS and incunabula, library of over 28,000 vols; catalogue by Thomas Hartwell Horne (1827); Milner colln of works on history of Reformation and 18th-century science and mathematics; Thomas Smith colln of Renaissance humanist writings; Keeper of the Old Library Dr I. PATTERSON.

St Catharine's College Library: Cambridge, CB2 1RL; tel. (1223) 338343; fax (1223) 338340; e-mail librarian@caths.cam.ac.uk; internet www.caths.cam.ac.uk/library; f. 1473; 69,000 vols (44,000 vols in undergraduate library; 25,000 vols in spec. collns: 17th-century political and religious tracts, 184 vols of 18th-century medical works (Addenbrooke colln), medieval Romance literature, Spanish books and MSS of 16th and 17th centuries (Chaytor colln); MSS, 30 incunabula); Librarian Dr COLIN HIGGINS.

St John's College Library: Cambridge, CB2 1TP; tel. (1223) 338662; fax (1223) 337035; e-mail library@joh.cam.ac.uk; internet www.joh.cam.ac.uk/library; f. 1511; MSS; spec. collns: 15th-century books, Matthew Prior bequest, Sir Soulden Lawrence law colln, Thomas Baker's colln of printed books and MSS, Samuel Butler colln, Smith colln of Rabelais literature, Wordsworthiana, papers of Sir Cecil Beaton, mathematical works of historical interest from libraries of Adams, Todhunter and Pendlebury, Udny Yule colln of Thomas à Kempis edns, Hugh Gatty colln, Sparrow bequest of Samuel Parr books, papers of Sir Fred Hoyle; Librarian Dr MARK NICHOLLS.

Selwyn College Library: Grange Rd, Cambridge, CB3 9DQ; tel. (1223) 335880; e-mail lib@sel.cam.ac.uk; internet www.sel.cam.ac.uk/library; f. 1896; 40,000 vols, MSS, incunabula; spec. collns incl. diaries and papers of George Augustus Selwyn (1809–78) Primate of New Zealand and later Bishop of Lichfield, large colln of theological works including 19th-century sermons, 19th-century missionary colln with particular emphasis on Melanesia and New Zealand, and 3,000 19th-century English ecclesiastical pamphlets; Librarian SARAH STAMFORD.

Sidney Sussex College Library: Cambridge, CB2 3HU; tel. (1223) 338852; fax (1223) 338884; e-mail librarian@sid.cam.ac.uk; internet www.sid.cam.ac.uk/life/lib; f. 16th century; 38,000 vols, 70 periodicals; Muniment Room: 7,300 vols, 119 MSS, incunabula; spec. collns incl. 18th- and 19th-century mathematical books; Taylor Mathematical Library (separately administered); Librarian ALAN STEVENS.

Trinity College Library: Cambridge, CB2 1TQ; tel. (1223) 338488; fax (1223) 338532; e-mail trin-lib@lists.cam.ac.uk; internet www.trin.cam.ac.uk; f. 1546; 300,000 vols; spec. collns incl. medieval western and oriental MSS; literary MSS of Milton, Tennyson, Housman, Capell colln of Shakespeareana; Rothschild library of 18th-century English literature; Isaac Newton's library; papers of economists, philosophers, politicians since 19th century; Librarian Prof. D. MCKITTERICK.

Trinity Hall Library: Cambridge, CB2 1TJ; tel. (1223) 332546; fax (1223) 332537; e-mail library@trinhall.cam.ac.uk; f. 1350; 25,000 vols, 31 MSS; spec. collns incl. early canon law, Larman Bequest of books and MSS relating to Reformation and Tudor periods, particularly heraldry, ecclesiastical history and theology; Dir of Library Services DOMINIQUE RUHLMANN.

Special Libraries:

Balfour and Newton Libraries: Univ. of Cambridge, Dept of Zoology, Downing St, Cambridge, CB2 3EJ; tel. (1223) 336648; fax (1223) 336676; e-mail library@zoo.cam.ac.uk; internet www.zoo.cam.ac.uk/library; Balfour Library f. 1883, Newton Library f. 1907; 155,000 vols, incl. 19,600 books, 22,600 periodicals and over 110,000 reprints; Librarian CLAIR M. CASTLE.

Churchill Archives Centre: Churchill College, Cambridge, CB3 0DS; tel. (1223) 336087; fax (1223) 336135; e-mail archives@chu.cam.ac.uk; internet www.chu.cam.ac.uk/archives; f. 1973; houses papers of Sir Winston Churchill, Lady Thatcher and many other senior political figures; Dir of the Archives ALLEN PACKWOOD.

Marshall Library of Economics: Sidgwick Ave, Cambridge, CB3 9DB; tel. (1223) 335217; fax (1223) 335475; e-mail marshlib@econ.cam.ac.uk; f. 1925; 97,000 vols; Librarian ROWLAND THOMAS.

Squire Law Library: 10 West Rd, Cambridge, CB3 9DZ; tel. (1223) 330077; fax (1223) 330048; f. 1904; 130,000 vols; spec. collns incl. Roman law, legal history, comparative law, conflict of laws, int. law, environmental law, intellectual property, political biographies; research library; Librarian D. F. WILLS.

Cambridgeshire Libraries, Archives and Information: 7 Lion Yard, Cambridge, CB2 3QD; tel. (345) 045-5225; fax (1223) 712011; e-mail your.library@cambridgeshire.gov.uk; internet www.cambridgeshire.gov.uk/library; f. 1974; 1,155,000 vols; 32 brs, 4 mobile libraries; Central Library Supervisor MARGOT EAGLE; Head of Libraries, Archives and Information CHRISTINE MAY (acting).

Needham Research Institute: E Asian History of Science Library, 8 Sylvester Rd, Cambridge, CB3 9AF; tel. (1223) 311545; fax (1223) 362703; e-mail admin@nri.org.uk; internet www.nri.org.uk; f. 1976; from collns assembled since 1942 by Dr Joseph Needham and Dr Lu Gwei-Djen, from sources in China and the West, primarily intended for the research on which is based the series 'Science and Civilization in China' (24 vols of which have so far been published); governed by the Needham Research Institute Trust (fmrly E Asian History of Science Trust, f. 1968), an educational charity; a unique colln specialized in works in the history of science, technology and medicine in E Asia and consisting of books, periodicals, off-prints, MSS in Asian and European languages, also archival and iconographic material (notes, photographs, maps, microfilms, etc.); open to research scholars by appointment, 30,000 monographs; Dir Dr CHRISTOPHER CULLEN; Librarian JOHN P. C. MOFFETT.

Tyndale House Library: 36 Selwyn Gardens, Cambridge, CB3 9BA; tel. (1223) 566604; fax (1223) 566608; e-mail librarian@tyndale.cam.ac.uk; internet www.tyndale.cam.ac.uk; f. 1944; a residential centre for biblical research; intended for postgraduate and post-doctoral study in biblically related fields, with a view to promoting evangelical scholarship; 46,000 vols; Librarian Dr ELIZABETH MAGBA; publ. *Tyndale Bulletin* (2 a year).

Canterbury

Canterbury Cathedral Archives and Library: The Precincts, Canterbury, CT1 2EH; tel. (1227) 865330 (Archives); tel. (1227) 865287 (Library); fax (1227) 865222; e-mail archives@canterbury-cathedral.org; internet www.canterbury-cathedral.org; f. c. 597; books and archives have been used and maintained here throughout the cathedral's existence; documents since 8th century; MSS of Christ Church Cathedral Priory and the Dean and Chapter of Canterbury; archives of the Diocese of Canterbury; archives of Canterbury City and District Parish; records for parishes in the Archdeaconry of Canterbury (eastern Kent); 52,000 printed books: early printed books, Bibles, prayer books, Catholic and anti-Catholic writings, natural science, travel, theology, history, 17th–19th century pamphlets, material on the slave trade, music; 2 parish libraries (Elham and Preston-next-Wingham); Cannon Librarian CHRISTOPHER IRVINE; Sr Library Asst KAREN BRAYSHAW; Archivist CRESSIDA WILLIAMS.

University of Kent, The Templeman Library: Canterbury, CT2 7NU; tel. (1227) 764000; fax (1227) 823984; e-mail library-enquiry@kent.ac.uk; internet www.kent.ac.uk; f. 1964; 800,000 vols; special collections include Cartoon Centre (80,000 original political cartoons), Victorian and Edwardian Popular Theatre (Pettingell, Melville and Reading-Rayner MSS and printed plays, mainly 19th century), Maddison collection (history of science), C. P. Davies Wind and Watermill collection, the papers of Lord Weatherill; Dir of Information Services and Librarian MARGARET M. COUTTS.

Cardiff

Amgueddfa Cymru – National Museum Wales Library: Cathays Park, Cardiff, CF10 3NP; tel. (29) 2057-3202; fax (29) 2057-3321; e-mail library@museumwales.ac.uk; internet www.museumwales.ac.uk; 210,000 vols, books and periodicals relevant to the museum collns; spec. collns: Tomlin (conchology), Willoughby Gardner (early natural history), Vaynor (James) Colln (early works on astronomy); also houses libraries of Cardiff Naturalists' Soc. and Cambrian Archaeological Asscn; Librarian J. R. KENYON.

Cardiff Central Library: Central Library, The Hayes, Cardiff, CF10 1FL; tel. (29) 2038-2116; fax (29) 2078-0989; e-mail centrallibrary@cardiff.gov.uk; internet www.cardiff.gov.uk/libraries; f. 1862, present bldg 2009; main library incl. lending and reference books; music and sound recordings library; DVD colln; children's library; local studies library incl. maps, prints and MSS, large colln of Welsh history; facilities for disabled; 547,269 vols incl. 10,000 Welsh language and 10,000 community language items; Central Library Man. NIC RICHARDS; Operational Man., Libraries ELSPETH MORRIS.

Cardiff University Library Service: Information Services Directorate, 40–41 Park Pl., Cardiff, CF10 3BB; tel. (29) 2087-4818; fax (29) 2087-4285; e-mail library@cardiff.ac.uk; internet www.cardiff.ac.uk/1495; f. 1883; consists of 17 libraries: Aberconway (Business, Economics and Transport), Archie Cochrane (Medicine), Architecture, Arts and Social Studies, Biomedical Sciences, Brian Cooke Dental, Bute, Cancer Research Wales, Law, Legal Practice, Music, Nursing and Healthcare Studies, School of Nursing and Midwifery Studies, Science, Senghennydd (Mathematics and Lifelong Learning), Sir Herbert Duthie (Medicine), Trevithick (Engineering and Science); research collns: Ann Griffiths colln, Architecture Rare Books colln, Arts and Social Studies Special colln, Cochrane archive, Cudlipp colln, David Bainton archive, European Documentation Centre, First Edition archive, Historical Book colln (Healthcare), Osman archive (Photojournalism), Salisbury colln (Welsh History), UCAC (Undeb Cenedlaethanol Athrawon Cymru) archive; Dir of Libraries and Univ. Librarian JANET PETERS.

Carlisle

Cumbria Libraries: Arroyo Block, The Castle, Carlisle, CA3 8UR; tel. (1228) 227295; fax (1228) 607299; e-mail libraries@

cumbriacc.gov.uk; internet www.cumbria.gov.uk/libraries.

Carmarthen

Carmarthenshire County Library: Public Library, St Peter's St, Carmarthen, SA31 1LN; tel. (1267) 224824; fax (1267) 221839; e-mail library@carmarthenshire.gov.uk; 660,000 vols; 17 brs, 5 mobile libraries; spec. collns: coal mine plans, Theodore Nichol Collection, the library of the Carmarthenshire Antiquarian Society; Library Services Man. MARK JEWELL; Library Services Man. MYRDDIN MORGAN; Library Services Man. WIL PHILLIPS.

Chelmsford

Anglia Ruskin University Library: Rivermead Campus, Bishop Hall Lane, Chelmsford, CM1 1SQ; tel. (1245) 493131; fax (1245) 490835; 250,000 vols; Librarian NICOLA KERSHAW.

Essex County Council Libraries: County Hall, Market Rd, Chelmsford, CM1 1LH; tel. (845) 603-7628; e-mail answers.direct@essex.gov.uk; internet www.essex.gov.uk/libraries; 73 brs, 12 mobile libraries; Dir of Libraries and Culture SUSAN CARRAGHER.

Chester

Cheshire Libraries: Cheshire County Council, Libraries and Culture, Room 286, County Hall, Chester, CH1 1SF; tel. (1244) 606034; fax (1244) 602767; e-mail webmaster@cheshire.gov.uk; internet www.cheshire.gov.uk/library/home.htm; f. 1922; 1,500,000 vols; 35 full-time, 6 part-time, 3 dual use brs, 6 mobile libraries and 1 research library; HQ special collections; Education Library Service; County Libraries Officer I. DUNN.

Chichester

West Sussex County Council Library and Information Service: Greyfriars, 61 N St, Chichester, West Sussex, PO19 1NB; tel. (1243) 382541; fax (1243) 382554; e-mail county.libraries@westsussex.gov.uk; internet www.westsussex.gov.uk/libraries; f. 1925; 1,117,000 vols; 36 brs, 3 mobile libraries; Service Man. Libraries LESLEY SIM.

Colchester

University of Essex, The Albert Sloman Library: Wivenhoe Park, Colchester, CO4 3SQ; tel. (1206) 873333; fax (1206) 872289; internet www.essex.ac.uk; f. 1964; 1m. vols and microforms, 9,690 current periodicals; spec. collns: Latin America, fmr USSR, Social Democratic Party (SDP) archives, SDP papers of Lord Rodgers of Quarrybank, Tawney Soc. archives, Nat. Viewers' and Listeners' Assen archives, Boundary Comm. for England archives (1992–93 public enquiries), papers and publs of the Cttee on Standards in Public Life (Nolan Cttee), Sigmund Freud and related collns (papers and publs), papers of Lord Alport, Sir Vincent Evans colln, Paul Sieghart memorial archive, SCOPE-ENUWAR archive, papers of Lord Brimelow, Gaudier-Brzeska colln, Royal Statistical Soc. (historical) colln, Essex Soc. for Archaeology and History Library, John Hassall colln, Lord Hill of Wivenhoe papers, T. E. Lawrence letters, Samuel Harsnett Library (Archbishop of York, 1629–31), Ellis East European Elections colln, Windscale Inquiry (1977) papers, archives of the Talking Newspaper Assen of the UK, Margery Allingham/Philip Youngman Carter colln, Bernie Hamilton (Human Rights) archive, Georg Groddeck archive, papers of Sir Frederick Warner, Papers of Enid Balint (Psychoanalyst), Papers of Lord Brimelow (under-sec. of State, Foreign Office, 1969–73), Charter 88 Archives (1990–97); Librarian R. BUTLER.

Conwy

Conwy County Borough Council Library, Information and Culture Service: Bodlondeb, Conwy, LL32 8DU; tel. (1492) 576140; fax (1492) 592061; e-mail llyfr.lib.pencadlys.hq@conwy.gov.uk; f. 1996; 200,000 vols; 13 brs, 1 mobile library; special collections: local history, Welsh language and literature; Head of Service: Library, Information and Culture RONA ALDRICH.

Coventry

Coventry Libraries and Information Services: Central Library, Smithford Way, Coventry, CV1 1FY; tel. (24) 7683-2314; fax (24) 7683-2440; e-mail central.library@coventry.gov.uk; internet www.coventry.gov.uk/libraries; f. 1868; 480,000 vols; spec. collns on trade unions and industrial relations; 16 community libraries and 1 mobile library; Head of Libraries and Information Services CARMEL REED; Central Library Man. CAROL ROBINSON (acting).

University of Warwick Library: Gibbet Hill Rd, Coventry, CV4 7AL; tel. (24) 7652-3523; fax (24) 7652-4211; e-mail library@warwick.ac.uk; internet library.warwick.ac.uk; f. 1963; 1,000,000 vols; spec. collns: British and foreign statistical serials (trade, finance, production), current and retrospective, pre-1948 collections of Howard League for Penal Reform, Modern Records Centre (labour history, employers' records, industrial relations), Modern German Literature; Librarian ANNE BELL.

Cwmbran

Monmouthshire Libraries and Information Service: Chepstow Library, Manor Way, Chepstow, NP16 5HZ; tel. (1291) 635730; fax (1291) 635736; e-mail infocentre@monmouthshire.gov.uk; internet libraries.monmouthshire.gov.uk; 6 brs, 1 mobile library; 150,000 vols; Prin. Librarian ANN JONES.

Darlington

Darlington Libraries: Central Library, Crown St, Darlington, DL1 1ND; tel. (1325) 462034; fax (1325) 381556; e-mail crown.street.library@darlington.gov.uk; internet www.darlington.gov.uk/library; f. 1885; Head of Libraries and Community Learning RUTH BERNSTEIN; Information Services Man. LYNNE LITCHFIELD; Business Support Man. CHRISTINE MCCALLUM.

Derby

Derby City Libraries: Roman House, Heritage Gate, Friary St, Derby, DE1 1XB; tel. (1332) 641723; fax (1332) 715549; e-mail libraries@derby.gov.uk; internet www.derby.gov.uk/libraries; f. 1997; Head of Library Services DAVID POTTON.

Dorchester

Dorset County Library: Colliton Park, Dorchester, DT1 1XJ; tel. (1305) 225000; fax (1305) 224344; e-mail dorsetlibraries@dorsetcc.gov.uk; internet www.dorsetcc.gov.uk; f. 1920, reorganized 1997; 34 brs; 5 mobile libraries; special collns: Dorset colln, Thomas Hardy colln, Powys colln; 625,000 vols; Head of Community Services P. LEIVERS.

Dundee

Dundee City Council Central Library: The Wellgate, Dundee, DD1 1DB; tel. (1382) 431500; fax (1382) 431558; e-mail central.library@dundeecity.gov.uk; internet www.dundeecity.gov.uk/library/central; f. 1869; 13 brs, mobile library; spec. collns: local history and genealogy, commerce, music, Wighton Collection of National Music (620 vols), British Standards, Audio Library, video library; Dir. for Leisure and Communities STEWART MURDOCH.

University of Dundee Library and Learning Centre: Dundee, DD1 4HN; tel. (1382) 384087; fax (1382) 386228; e-mail library@dundee.ac.uk; internet www.dundee.ac.uk/library; f. 1881; 684,352 vols, 4,804 periodicals; Dir RICHARD PARSONS.

Durham

Durham Arts, Libraries and Museums Department: POB, County Hall, Durham, DH1 5TY; tel. (191) 383-3595; fax (191) 384-1336; e-mail enquiries@durhamcityarts.org.uk; f. 1923; 876,000 vols; 38 full-time brs, 2 trailers, 4 mobile and 3 travelling libraries, 1 bookbus for the elderly; Dir PATRICK CONWAY.

University of Durham Library: Main Univ. Library, Stockton Rd, Durham, DH1 3LY; tel. (191) 334-2968; fax (191) 334-2971; e-mail main.library@durham.ac.uk; internet www.dur.ac.uk/library; f. 1833; 1,500,000 printed items on 4 sites, incl. Middle East Documentation Unit; dept of Archives and Spec. Collns houses extensive spec. collns of early printed books, MSS, maps, prints, photographs; printed book spec. collns incl. those formed by Bishop Cosin, M. J. Routh, Bishop Maltby, Dr Winterbottom, and the Sharp Library from Bamburgh Castle; 200 incunabula, 2,200 STC, 10,000 Wing; collns of MSS and archives incl. medieval MSS, modern literary MSS (C. C. Abbott, Basil Bunting, William Plomer Collns), Earl Grey Papers, Malcolm MacDonald Papers, Durham Cathedral Archives, Durham diocesan and probate records, Howard of Naworth Papers and other collns of local family and estate records, Sudan Archive; Librarian JON PURCELL; publ. *Durham University Library Publications* (irregular).

Ebbw Vale

Blaenau Gwent Libraries: Facilities Section, Municipal Offices, Civic Centre, Ebbw Vale, NP23 6XB; tel. (1495) 355311; fax (1495) 355468; 120,000 vols; 7 brs, 2 mobile libraries; County Borough Librarian MARY JONES.

Edinburgh

Edinburgh City Libraries and Information Services: Central Library, George IV Bridge, Edinburgh, EH1 1EG; tel. (131) 242-8000; fax (131) 242-8009; e-mail eclis@edinburgh.gov.uk; internet www.edinburgh.gov.uk/libraries; f. 1890; 1,365,000 items; 25 community libraries, 4 mobile libraries; Central Reference (incl. business information, British Standards, electronic information; 346,229 items); spec. colln: Edinburgh Room (contains information on life in Edinburgh and on Scott, Stevenson, Ballantyne; press cuttings; illustrations; playbills; 120,000 items), Scottish (especially genealogy, history and Scottish Parliament information; 97,000 items), Music and Audio (CDs, scores, Scottish music; 148,000 items), Fine Art (includes costume, fashion and photography; slides, Japanese prints, video cassettes, artists' books, press cuttings on Scottish art, architecture, design and photography; 90,000 items); City Librarian BILL WALLACE.

Edinburgh University Library, Museums and Galleries: George Square, Edinburgh, EH8 9LJ; tel. (131) 650-3384; fax (131) 650-3380; e-mail library@ed.ac.uk; internet www.lib.ed.ac.uk; f. 1580; 3,462,947 printed items, 279,814 microforms, 111,832 maps in sheets, 7,700 metres of MSS and archives, 33,808 theses, 6,826 audiovisual items, 4,417 electronic and 4,430 print current periodicals; Drummond (of Hawthornden) Collection; Laing Charters and MSS; Halliwell-Phillipps Collection; MSS on Scottish history and the Scottish literary renaissance; Arthur Koestler MSS and part library; Corson Sir Walter Scott Collection; New Zealand Studies Collection; MSS and printed books on early 20th-century English literature; Scottish Enlightenment; history of science and medicine; African, East Asian, Islamic and Middle Eastern studies; includes the Main Library, Law and Europa Library, Moray House Library (Education), New College Library (Divinity), Science Libraries and Royal (Dick) School of Veterinary Studies Libraries, Royal Infirmary Library, Reid Concert Hall Museum of Instruments (John Donaldson Collection), St Cecilia's Hall Museum of instruments (Raymond Russell Collection of Early Keyboard Instruments) and the Talbot Rice Gallery; Dir of Library Services SHEILA E. CANNELL.

Heriot-Watt University Library: Riccarton, Edinburgh, EH14 4AS; tel. (131) 451-3570; fax (131) 451-3164; e-mail library@hw.ac.uk; internet www.hw.ac.uk; f. 1821; 145,000 vols, 1,500 periodicals; Librarian (vacant).

National Archives of Scotland: HM General Register House, Edinburgh, EH1 3YY; tel. (131) 535-1314; fax (131) 535-1360; e-mail enquiries@nas.gov.uk; internet www.nas.gov.uk; f. 1993 as an Executive Agency; national archives of Scotland; local and church records, and records of Scottish government and law since 12th century; also contains many private and business collns; Keeper of the Records of Scotland GEORGE P. MACKENZIE.

National Library of Scotland: George IV Bridge, Edinburgh, EH1 1EW; tel. (131) 623-3700; fax (131) 623-3701; e-mail enquiries@nls.uk; internet www.nls.uk; f. 1680 as the Advocates' Library; legal deposit library; contains 13,000,000 vols and pamphlets and a large colln of MSS; Library's Inter-Library Services (33 Salisbury Pl., Edinburgh, EH9 1SL) maintain a stock (120,000 vols) of scarce books to supplement the reserves of Scottish public libraries, act as the headquarters for Scottish inter-library co-operation, and house Scottish Union Catalogue; Chair. of the Trustees Prof. MICHAEL ANDERSON; Nat. Librarian MARTYN WADE; publ. *Discover NLS* (4 a year).

Attached Library:

National Library of Scotland Map Library: 159 Causewayside, Edinburgh, EH9 1PH; tel. (131) 623-3970; fax (131) 623-3971; e-mail maps@nls.uk; internet maps.nls.uk; f. 1958; modern topographic and thematic map coverage of most parts of the world; particular interest in early/modern maps with Scottish association; Sr Map Curator CHRIS FLEET.

National Museums Scotland Library: Chambers St, Edinburgh, EH1 1JF; tel. (131) 247-4137; fax (131) 247-4311; e-mail library@nms.ac.uk; internet www.nms.ac.uk; f. 1854; 320,000 vols, esp. European decorative arts, N European archaeology and Scottish history; MS collns incl. Society of Antiquaries of Scotland, Harvie Brown (natural sciences), William Spiers Bruce (Antarctic exploration), Sir William Jardine (natural sciences); Head of Information Services EVELYN SIMPSON.

Royal Botanic Garden Library: Edinburgh, EH3 5LR; 20A Inverleith Row, Edinburgh, EH3 5LR; tel. (131) 522-7171; fax (131) 248-2901; e-mail library@rbge.org.uk; internet www.rbge.ac.uk; f. 1670; incorporates the botanical libraries of the Plinian (1841), Wernerian (1858) and Botanical (1872) societies of Edinburgh, Dr John Hope (1899), Cleghorn Memorial Library (1941) and Mr Robert Scarlett (1975); compiles indexes to Monographs, Floras, Gardens, botanists, botanical expeditions, etc.; 100,000 vols, including pre-Linnean literature on botany, horticulture, agriculture and medicine; 100,000 pamphlets and separates; 4,000 (1,500 current) periodicals; extensive colln of botanical drawings and prints, photographs, cuttings, etc., correspondence, diaries, maps, plans, MSS, etc., relating to the early Regius Keepers and Curators and botanists and horticulturists in the UK and abroad; Head of Library Services JANE HUTCHEON; publs *British Fungus Flora* (irregular), *Catalogue of Plants* (irregular), *Edinburgh Journal of Botany* (3 a year), *Sibbaldia: an occasional series of horticultural notes* (irregular).

Royal College of Physicians of Edinburgh Library: 9 Queen St, Edinburgh, EH2 1JQ; tel. (131) 225-7324; fax (131) 220-3939; e-mail library@rcpe.ac.uk; internet www.rcpe.ac.uk; f. 1681; 50,000 books, 1,000 vols of MSS; open to all *bona fide* enquirers; particularly rich in the early sources of medical knowledge; colln of periodicals; Librarian I. A. MILNE.

Royal College of Surgeons of Edinburgh Library and Archive: Nicolson St, Edinburgh, EH8 9DW; tel. (131) 527-1630; fax (131) 557-6406; e-mail library@rcsed.ac.uk; internet www.library.rcsed.ac.uk; f. 1505; 50,000 vols, 170 periodicals; historical and contemporary medical and surgical stock; images library; college archive since 1505; private library for Fellows and members (access to researchers by appointment); CEO ALISON ROONEY; publs *Surgeons' News*, *The Surgeon*.

Signet Library: Parliament Sq., Edinburgh, EH1 1RF; tel. (131) 225-4923; fax (131) 220-4016; e-mail library@wssociety.co.uk; internet www.signetlibrary.co.uk; f. date of foundation 1594, but there were Writers to Her Majesty's Signet as early as 1460; 90,000 vols; the Library of the Society of Writers to Her Majesty's Signet is devoted chiefly to Scots law and Scottish history and genealogy, and is the library of a private society; Librarian FELICITY CROSS.

Eton

Eton College Library: Eton College, Windsor, SL4 6DB; tel. (1753) 671221; fax (1753) 801507; e-mail collections@etoncollege.org.uk; f. 1440; 85,000 items, incl. 200 medieval MSS, 200 incunabula; important collns of edns of classical writers and related material (16th–18th centuries), early science, Elizabethan, Jacobean and Restoration drama, large colln of Civil War and early 18th-century English pamphlets, 16th-century Italian books; bindings, English and Continental, since 12th century; Topham colln of drawings and engravings (c. 2,500 items); Etoniana colln (c. 5,000 printed books, drawings, prints, scrap-books, MSS); School Books colln; Parikian colln of Armenian printed books 1500–1900; Kessler colln of books on China and Russia; English literature since 19th century, incl. Elizabeth Barrett Browning, Anne Thackeray Ritchie, Thomas Hardy, Edward Gordon Craig, Moelwyn Merchant collections; mezzotint colln (1,000 items); Librarian M. C. MEREDITH; Archivist P. C. HATFIELD.

Exeter

Devon Libraries: Great Moor House, Bittern Rd, Sowton, Exeter, EX2 7NL; tel. (1392) 384315; fax (1392) 384316; e-mail devlibs@devon.gov.uk; internet www.devon.gov.uk/libraries; f. 1924; 50 brs, 8 mobile libraries; 1,169,987 vols; Head of Libraries CIARA EASTELL.

Exeter Cathedral Library: West Wing, The Palace, Palace Gate, Exeter, EX1 1HX; tel. (1392) 495954; fax (1392) 285986; e-mail library@exeter-cathedral.org.uk; internet www.exeter-cathedral.org.uk/admin/library.html; f. 11th century when Bishop Leofric gave 66 MS vols to the Cathedral Church; 20,000 items; MS vols incl. Exeter Book of Old English Poetry and Exon Domesday Book; spec. collns incl. Cathedral MSS and archives, early printed books in medicine and science, Cook Colln (16th–19th century works, early linguistics), printed tracts (mainly English Civil War period), Harington Collection (16th–19th century theology, ecclesiastical history, history); archive of 50,000 items; Cathedral Librarian PETER W. THOMAS; Cathedral Archivist ANGELA DOUGHTY.

National Meteorological Library and Archive: Met Office, Fitzroy Rd, Exeter, EX1 3PB; tel. (1392) 884841; fax (1392) 885681; e-mail metlib@metoffice.gov.uk; internet www.metoffice.gov.uk/learning/library; f. 1870; nat. library and archive for meteorology, climatology; incl. comprehensive records of data published by British and foreign instns; early weather diaries; official weather records and charts; ships' weather log books; open to the public; separate record stores for Scotland (Edinburgh) and N Ireland (Belfast); 300,000 vols and 5,000 images.

University of Exeter Library: Stocker Rd, Exeter, EX4 4PT; tel. (1392) 263869; fax (1392) 263871; e-mail library@exeter.ac.uk; internet www.library.ex.ac.uk; f. 1937; 1,200,000 vols; administers Library of Devon and Exeter Institution (36,000 vols); Dir of Academic Services MICHELE SHOEBRIDGE.

Falkirk

Falkirk Council Library Services: Public and Schools Library Service, Victoria Bldgs, Queen St, Falkirk, FK2 7AF; tel. (1324) 506800; fax (1324) 506801; e-mail library.support@falkirk.gov.uk; internet www.falkirk.gov.uk; local history colln; Prin. Librarian SHONA HILL (acting); publ. *Current Awareness Bulletin* (48 a year).

Glasgow

Glasgow Caledonian University Library: The Saltire Centre, Glasgow Caledonian University, Cowcaddens Rd, Glasgow, G4 0BA; tel. (141) 273-1000; fax (141) 331-3005; e-mail librarye@gcal.ac.uk; internet www.gcal.ac.uk/library; f. 1993; 350,000 vols and access to 12,000 journals online; Chief Information Officer JEFF MURRAY (acting).

Glasgow Libraries: 20 Trongate, Glasgow, G1 5ES; tel. (141) 287-4350; fax (141) 287-5151; e-mail info@glasgowlife.org.uk; internet www.glasgowlife.org.uk; 32 district libraries; spec. collns of foreign literature and local history; 2,145,000 vols; Head of Libraries and Community Facilities KAREN CUNNINGHAM.

Attached Library:

Mitchell Library: North St, Glasgow, G3 7DN; tel. (141) 287-2999; fax (141) 287-2815; e-mail archives@csglasgow.org; internet www.mitchelllibrary.org; f. 1874; 1,235,000 vols; special collns: on Glasgow (20,000 vols), music (43,000 vols), Robert Burns (5,000 vols), Scottish poetry (12,000 vols) and Patent Depositary Library; business users' service; receives a copy of every publication issued by HMSO, and is also a

Depository Library for the unrestricted publications of the UN, UNESCO and FAO; Librarian F. MACPHERSON.

Royal College of Physicians and Surgeons of Glasgow Library: 234 St Vincent St, Glasgow, G2 5RJ; tel. (141) 227-3234; fax (141) 221-1804; e-mail library@rcpsg.ac.uk; internet www.rcpsg.ac.uk; f. 1698; 35,000 vols; houses works on all aspects of medicine and surgery incl. very fine and early examples of medical texts from the 16th and 17th centuries; Glasgow Colln, books relating to the history of Glasgow and the West of Scotland; archives from 1602 until the present day.; Librarian JAMES BEATON; Library and Heritage Man. CAROL PARRY.

University of Glasgow Library: Hillhead St, Glasgow, G12 8QE; tel. (141) 330-6704; fax (141) 330-4952; e-mail library@lib.gla.ac.uk; internet www.lib.gla.ac.uk; f. 15th century; 1.3m. books, 7,308 m of MSS, archives; 15,000 serial titles; incorporates Trinity College Glasgow Library (Church of Scotland); Hunterian Books and MSS, Euing Collns of the Bible and music, Farmer Music Colln, Laver, MacColl and Wright Papers on fine art, Hamilton Colln of philosophy, Ferguson Colln of the history of chemistry, Stirling Maxwell Colln of Emblem books, J. M. Whistler archive, David Murray regional history colln, Scottish Theatre Archive, Edwin Morgan Papers, Trotsky Colln; Univ. Librarian HELEN DURNDELL.

University of Strathclyde Library: 101 St James' Rd, Glasgow, G4 0NS; tel. (141) 548-4620; fax (141) 552-3304; e-mail library@strath.ac.uk; internet www.lib.strath.ac.uk; f. 1796; 986,330 vols; spec. collns incl. Anderson colln (founder's library), Young colln (alchemy and early chemistry), Laing colln (mathematics vols from the 18th and 19th centuries), Robertson colln (Scottish history and topography), annual company reports; 938,000 vols, 6,290 periodicals; Asst Dir STUART BROUGH.

Gloucester

Gloucestershire Libraries and Information HQ: Quayside House, Shire Hall, Gloucester, GL1 2HY; tel. (845) 230-5420; fax (1452) 425042; e-mail libraryhelp@gloucestershire.gov.uk; internet www.libraries.gloucestershire.gov.uk; spec. collns incl. Gloucestershire Colln; Library Services Man. for Strategy SUE LAURENCE; Library Services Man. for Operations JO HAND.

Grays

Thurrock Libraries: Grays Library, Orsett Rd, Grays, RM17 5DX; tel. (1375) 413973; e-mail grays.library@thurrock.gov.uk; internet www.thurrock.gov.uk/libraries; 10 brs, 1 mobile library; Head of Libraries ANN HALLIDAY.

Guildford

Surrey Libraries: Enquiries Direct, Guildford Library, 77 North St, Guildford, GU1 4AL; tel. (1483) 543599; fax (1483) 543597; e-mail libraries@surreycc.gov.uk; internet www.surreycc.gov.uk; offers a public library service to Surrey; 52 brs and an enquiries dept; 1,913,000 vols, 78,400 audiovisual items; Head of Libraries and Culture PETER MILTON.

University of Surrey Library: Guildford, GU2 7XH; tel. (1483) 683325; fax (1483) 689500; e-mail library-enquiries@surrey.ac.uk; internet www.surrey.ac.uk/library; f. 1894; 625,000 vols, 7,900 periodicals; spec. collns incl. National Resource Centre for Dance, E. H. Shepard archive; Dir of Library and Learning Support Services J. SAVIDGE.

Hatfield

Hertfordshire Libraries Culture and Learning: New Barnfield, Travellers Lane, Hatfield, Herts., AL10 8XG; tel. (1438) 737333; fax (1438) 737334; e-mail hertsdirect@hertscc.gov.uk; internet www.hertsdirect.org; f. 1925; 1,373,048 vols, other media 119,852 items; 49 brs, 13 mobile libraries, 1 prison library; spec. collns: performing arts, local history, business information, official publs; Head of Libraries GLENDA WOOD.

Haverfordwest

Pembrokeshire County Library: Dew St, Haverfordwest, SA61 1SU; tel. (1437) 775244; fax (1437) 769218; e-mail gill.gilliland@pembrokeshire.gov.uk; internet www.pembrokeshire.gov.uk; reference library, incl. the Pembrokeshire Colln; local studies colln; 12 br. lending libraries; Information and Cultural Services Man. NEIL BENNETT.

Hawarden

Gladstone's Library: Hawarden, Deeside, Flintshire, CH5 3DF; tel. (1244) 532350; fax (1244) 520643; e-mail enquiries@gladlib.org; internet www.gladstoneslibrary.org; f. 1894 by William Ewart Gladstone (1809–98); 200,000 vols, 50,000 pamphlets, and MSS material; theology, philosophy, history (esp. 19th century), classics, English literature, Gladstonian studies; accommodation for 40 residents; Warden Rev. PETER FRANCIS; Librarian PATRICIA WILLIAMS.

Hereford

Herefordshire Council Libraries: Shire Hall, Hereford, HR1 2HX; tel. (1432) 261644; fax (1432) 260127; e-mail libraries@herefordshire.gov.uk; internet www.herefordshire.gov.uk/leisure/libraries/1566.asp; f. 1998; 10 libraries, 2 mobile libraries and 1 volunteer-run service; Libraries Man. JON CHEDGZOY.

Huddersfield

Kirklees Culture and Leisure Services: Headquarters, Red Doles Lane, Huddersfield, W Yorks., HD2 1YF; tel. (1484) 226300; fax (1484) 226342; e-mail cultural.services@kirklees.gov.uk; f. 1974; 1,250,000 vols; Head of Culture and Leisure Services KIMIYO RICKETT.

University of Huddersfield Learning Centre: Queensgate, Huddersfield, Lw Yorks., HD1 3DH; tel. (1484) 473888; fax (1484) 517987; internet www.hud.ac.uk; f. 1841; 450,000 vols; Dir of Library Services PHIL SYKES.

Ipswich

Suffolk County Council—Libraries, Archives and Information: Endeavour House, Russell Rd, Ipswich, IP1 2BX; tel. (1473) 584263; fax (1473) 216847; e-mail help@suffolklibraries.co.uk; internet www.suffolklibraries.co.uk; f. 1974 by merger with fmr Suffolk library authorities; 1.2m. vols; Head of Service Delivery, Libraries, Archives and Information ROGER MCMASTER.

Keele

University of Keele Library: Keele, ST5 5BG; tel. (1782) 733535; fax (1782) 734502; e-mail libhelp@lib.keele.ac.uk; internet www.keele.ac.uk/depts/li; f. 1949; 620,000 vols; Librarian P. R. REYNOLDS.

Keyworth

British Geological Survey Library: British Geological Survey, Keyworth, Nottingham, NG12 5GG; tel. (115) 936-3205; fax (115) 936-3200; e-mail libuser@bgs.ac.uk; internet www.bgs.ac.uk; f. 1837; 500,000 vols, 400 current periodicals, 200,000 maps, 20,000 archives, nat. collns of 100,000 photographs largely illustrating British scenery and geology; regional office library at Edinburgh; information office in London; open access repository; Head of Research Knowledge Services KEN HOLLYWOOD.

Kingston upon Hull

Kingston upon Hull Libraries: Central Library, Albion St, Hull, HU1 3TF; tel. (1482) 616904; fax (1482) 616827; e-mail rosemary.reed@hullcc.gov.uk; internet www.hullcc.gov.uk; public library reference and information service; Asst Head of Service (Libraries and Information) MICHELLE ALFORD.

University of Hull, Library and Learning Innovation: Cottingham Rd, Hull, HU6 7RX; tel. (1482) 466581; fax (1482) 466205; e-mail libhelp@hull.ac.uk; internet www.hull.ac.uk/lib; f. 1929; 1,000,000 vols; spec. collns: SE Asia, India, British Labour history; Dir of Library and Learning Innovation and Univ. Librarian R. G. HESELTINE.

Kirkcaldy

Fife Council Libraries and Museums: East Fergus Pl., Kirkcaldy, Fife, KY1 1XT; tel. (1592) 583204; e-mail fife.libraries@fife.gov.uk; internet www.fifedirect.org.uk/libraries; 628,000 vols; Service Man. DOROTHY BROWSE.

Lampeter

University of Wales, Lampeter Library: Lampeter, Ceredigion, SA48 7ED; tel. (1570) 422351; fax (1570) 423875; e-mail library@lamp.ac.uk; internet www.lamp.ac.uk; 200,000 vols, incl. Tract colln of 11,000 items; Librarian A. PRESCOTT (acting); publ. *Trivium.*

Lancaster

University of Lancaster Library: Bailrigg, Lancaster, LA1 4YH; tel. (1524) 592515; fax (1524) 63806; f. 1963; 936,000 vols, pamphlets and other items, 3,000 current serials; spec. collns: business history, Quaker, Redlich (music), Socialist, European Documentation Centre; Librarian JACQUELINE WHITESIDE; publ. *Report of the Librarian.*

Branch Library:

Ruskin Library and Research Centre: Univ. of Lancaster, Bailrigg, Lancaster, LA1 4YH; tel. (1524) 593587; fax (1524) 593580; e-mail ruskin.library@lancaster.ac.uk; internet www.lancs.ac.uk/depts/ruskinlib; Whitehouse colln of documents relating to the writer and thinker, John Ruskin (1819–1900), (incl. 1,700 works of art by Ruskin and his circle, Ruskin's exhaustive diaries, 8,000 of his letters, 200 MSS, 3,500 books and 1,000 original photographs); Dir and Curator Prof. STEPHEN WILDMAN; Sec. JEN SHEPHERD.

Leeds

Leeds Library and Information Services: Central Library, Calverley St, Leeds, LS1 3AB; tel. (113) 2478282; fax (113) 3951833; e-mail businessandresearch@leedslearning.net; internet www.leeds.gov.uk/libraries; f. 1884; Central Library, 52 br. libraries, 5 mobile libraries; specialist Central Depts: Business and Patents, Local and Family History, Art and Music and The Information Centre housing special collections such as the Porton Collection of Judaica, Gott Bequest of early gardening books and the Gascoigne Collection of militaria; Chief Officer, Libraries, Arts and Heritage CATHERINE BLANSHARD.

Leeds University Library: Leeds, LS2 9JT; tel. (113) 233-6388; fax (113) 233-5561; f. 1874; 2,500,000 vols, pamphlets and microforms including the Brotherton Collection which contains over 50,000 vols and pamphlets and a large number of MSS, deeds and letters; includes fmr Ripon Cathedral Library containing early MSS, Service Books, Books of Hours, MSS since the 13th century, important printed books from 15th–18th century; Liddle Collection of First World War archive materials; Librarian M. COUTTS; publs *Al-Masaq*, *Journal of Educational Administration and History*, *Leeds Studies in English*, *Leeds Texts and Monographs*, *Northern History*, *Proceedings of the Leeds Philosophical and Literary Society: literary and historical section*, *Proceedings of the Leeds Philosophical and Literary Society: scientific section*, *Proceedings of the Yorkshire Geological Society*, *Publications of the Thoresby Society*, *University of Leeds Review*.

Leicester

De Montfort University Library: Kimberlin Library, The Gateway, Leicester, LE1 9BH; tel. (116) 257-7042; fax (116) 257-7046; e-mail justask@dmu.ac.uk; internet www.library.dmu.ac.uk; Head of Library Services KATHRYN ARNOLD.

Leicester City Libraries: New Walk Centre, Welford Place, Leicester, LE1 6ZG; tel. (116) 252-6762; fax (116) 255-9257; e-mail libraries@leicester.gov.uk; internet www.leicester.gov.uk/libraries; Head of Library and Information Services ADRIAN WILLS.

Leicestershire Library Services: County Hall, Glenfield, Leicester, LE3 8SS; tel. (116) 305-6988; fax (116) 265-7370; e-mail libraries@leics.gov.uk; internet www.leics.gov.uk/libraries; f. 1974.

University of Leicester Library: POB 248, University Rd, Leicester, LE1 9QD; tel. (116) 252-2042; fax (116) 252-2066; e-mail library@le.ac.uk; internet www.le.ac.uk/library; f. 1921; 1,000,000 items; spec. collns of local history of England and Wales, papers of Joe Orton and of Sue Townsend; Dir of Library Services L. JONES.

Lewes

East Sussex Library and Information Service: C15G, County Hall, St Anne's Crescent, Lewes, BN7 1UE; tel. (1273) 481870; fax (1273) 481716; 750,000 vols; 24 full-time and part-time brs; Asst Dir: Libraries and Culture Dr IRENE CAMPBELL.

Lichfield

Dean Savage Reference Library: 19A The Close, Lichfield, Staffs., WS13 7LD; tel. (1543) 306100; f. 1924; 6,000 vols, mostly theology and ecclesiastical history; for use, apply to above address.

Lincoln

Lincolnshire County Council Communities Directorate—Libraries: County Offices, Newland, Lincoln, LN1 1YL; tel. (1522) 552222; fax (1522) 552811; e-mail library.support@lincolnshire.gov.uk; internet www.lincolnshire.gov.uk; f. 1974 from 7 fmr Lincolnshire library authorities; 1,528,773 vols; 46 brs, 11 mobile libraries; spec. collns: Music, Drama, Lincolnshire material, Alfred Lord Tennyson; Head of Libraries JONATHAN PLATT.

Liverpool

Liverpool Libraries and Information Services: Central Library, William Brown St, Liverpool, L3 8EW; tel. (151) 233-5835; fax (151) 233-5886; e-mail refbt.central.library@liverpool.gov.uk; f. 1852; 1,500,000 vols, pamphlets, MSS, etc.; reference services (incl. Hornby Library: rare books, fine bindings, MSS, prints, etc. and patents library), services to business, record office, family history service; EU depository library; Head of Service JOYCE LITTLE.

University of Liverpool Library: POB 123, Liverpool, L69 3DA; tel. (151) 794-2674; fax (151) 794-2681; e-mail libcontactelec@liverpool.ac.uk; internet www.liv.ac.uk/library; f. 1881; over 1,900,000 vols, 4,900 current periodicals; spec. collns incl. 254 incunabula, the T. G. Rylands collection (early cartography, Lancashire and Cheshire history), the William Blake colln, the Scott Macfie colln (gypsy studies), the William Noble colln (Kelmscott and other private presses), the Knowsley colln (17th- to 19th-century English pamphlets), the Peers colln (Spanish Civil War), the Fraser colln (c. 900 books and pamphlets on tobacco; also much material on positivism and secularism), the Robert Graves Colln, Merseyside poets; modern MS holdings incl. the Rathbone, Blanco White, Brunner and Glasier papers, Science Fiction Foundation Colln, Olaf Stapledon colln; the Education Library contains an important colln of children's books; Librarian P. SYKES; publ. *Guide to Special Collections*.

Llandrindod Wells

Powys Library and Archive Service: Cefnllys Lane, Llandrindod Wells, Powys, LD1 5LD; tel. (1597) 826860; fax (1597) 826872; f. 1974; 300,000 vols; 18 brs; special local history collections; County Librarian T. L. ADAMS.

Llangefni

Isle of Anglesey County Library: Llangefni Library, Lon-y-Felin, Llangefni, Anglesey, LL77 7RT; tel. (1248) 752092; fax (1248) 750197; e-mail jrtlh@ynysmon.gov.uk; internet www.ynysmon.gov.uk; Head of Services JOHN REES THOMAS.

London

Aslib-IMI Information and Library Service: Temple Chambers, 3–7 Temple Ave, London, EC4Y 0HP; tel. (20) 7583-8900; fax (20) 7583-8401; e-mail aslib@aslib.co.uk; internet www.aslib.com/info; 16,000 vols on information management, incl. documentation, information science, special libraries and related subjects, 370 current periodicals of the world and about 25,000 references to articles, reports, etc., on library and information science; publs *Aslib Book Guide* (12 a year), *Aslib Guide to Copyright* (3 a year), *Aslib Proceedings* (10 a year), *Current Awareness Abstracts* (10 a year), *Forthcoming International Scientific and Technical Conferences* (4 a year), *Journal of Documentation* (5 a year), *Managing Information* (10 a year), *Online and CD Notes* (10 a year), *Program: Electronic Library and Information Systems* (4 a year), *Records Management Journal* (3 a year).

Barking and Dagenham Libraries: Barking Library, 2 Town Sq., Barking, IG11 8DQ; tel. (20) 8724-8725; fax (20) 8724-8733; e-mail 3000direct@lbbd.gov.uk; internet www.lbbd.gov.uk/leisureartsandlibraries/libraries/pages; f. 1888; 600,000 vols; public library service in the London Borough of Barking and Dagenham; 10 brs throughout the borough, mem. of the LLC (London Libraries Consortium); Group Man. Libraries ZOINUL ABIDIN.

Barnet Education—Libraries: Bldg 4, North London Business Park, Oakleigh Rd South, London, N11 1NP; internet www.barnet.gov.uk; f. 1965; 66,000 vols; special collection of Sociology; Head of Libraries, Museums and Local Studies P. A. LITTLE.

Bexley Library Service: Ground Floor, Footscray Offices, Maidstone Rd, Sidcup, DA14 5HS; tel. (20) 8303-7777; fax (20) 8309-4142; e-mail libraries@bexley.gov.uk; internet www.bexley.gov.uk; 600,000 vols; 12 brs; 3 mobile libraries, reference library; Local Studies and Archive Centre; Library Services Man. JUDITH MITLIN.

Brent Library Service: Brent Council, Town Hall, Forty Lane, Wembley, Middlesex, HA9 9HD; tel. (20) 8937-3144; fax (20) 8937-3023; e-mail libraryservice@brent.gov.uk; internet ww.brent.gov.uk/library.nsf; f. 1965; 580,000 vols; 12 brs, mobile library, housebound service, Grange Museum of Local History; Head of Library Service KAREN TYERMAN.

British Architectural Library: RIBA, 66 Portland Pl., London, W1B 1AD; tel. (20) 7580-5533; fax (20) 7631-1802; e-mail info@inst.riba.org; internet www.architecture.com; f. 1834; 150,000 vols, 700 current serials, 1,400 dead runs, 1.5m. photographs, 300,000 negatives, 700 m of MSS, and a colln of 600,000 drawings (housed at the Henry Cole Wing, Victoria and Albert Museum, London); one of the most comprehensive architectural libraries in the world; Dir Dr IRENA MURRAY; publs *APId: Architectural Publications Index* (on disc, 4 a year), *Architectural Periodicals Index and Books catalogued by the British Architectural Library* (4 a year), *RIBA List of Recommended Books* (1 a year).

BFI National Archive: 21 Stephen St, London, W1T 1LN; tel. (20) 7255-1444; fax (20) 7436-0165; internet www.bfi.org.uk/nftva; f. 1935 as a division of the British Film Institute; 50,000 fiction films, over 100,000 non-fiction titles and around 625,000 television programmes; preserves for posterity, and makes available for study, cinematograph films and television programmes, stills, posters and set designs of artistic and historical value; incl. J. Paul Getty Jr Conservation Centre (in Berkhamsted), Nat. Film and Television Archive and Ind. Television Comm. Library; 63,000 books, 4,000 audiotapes, 500 spec. collns, 5,000 serials, 2m. newspaper cuttings; Head Librarian DAVID SHARP; Head of Collns and Information DARREN LONG.

British Geological Survey London Information Office: Natural History Museum, Cromwell Rd, London, SW7 5BD; tel. (20) 7589-4090; fax (20) 7584-8270; e-mail bgslondon@bgs.ac.uk; internet www.bgs.ac.uk; f. 1986; information and advisory service; public reference colln of British Geological Survey; publs incl. geological maps, memoirs, reports, research reports and information illustrating the geology of the British Isles; online access to British Geological Survey databases; some overseas maps and textbooks; Man. CLARE M. TOMBLESON.

British Library: St Pancras, 96 Euston Rd, London, NW1 2DB; tel. (843) 208-1144; e-mail press-and-pr@bl.uk; internet www.bl.uk; f. 1973; legal deposit library; 150m. items in most known languages, incorporating books, newspapers, periodicals, manuscripts, maps, prints and drawings, music scores, patents and the National Sound Archive; document supply service at Boston Spa, Wetherby, West Yorks., LS23 7BQ; Chair. Sir COLIN LUCAS; Chief Exec. LYNNE BRINDLEY; publ. *British Library Journal* (online only).

British Library of Political and Economic Science: London School of Economics, 10 Portugal St, London, WC2A 2HD; tel. (20) 7955-7229; fax (20) 7955-7454; e-mail e.chapman@lse.ac.uk; internet www.lse.ac.uk/library; f. 1896 as The British Library of

Political Science, present name 1925; 4m. bibliographic items comprising journals, govt publs from all over the world, other serial publs and 1.2m. monographs; colln mainly covers economics, political science, law (esp. int), sociology, history and geography; Dir of Library Services ELIZABETH CHAPMAN; Head of Library Services MAUREEN WADE; publ. *The International Bibliography of the Social Sciences* (1 a year, also online).

British Medical Association Library: BMA House, Tavistock Sq., London, WC1H 9JP; tel. (20) 7383-6625; fax (20) 7388-2544; e-mail bma-library@bma.org.uk; internet www.bma.org.uk; f. 1887; provides expert medical information services to members and staff; specialises in current clinical practice, medical ethics and education; 30,000 vols, 2,000 periodicals, 3,500 films and video cassettes; Librarian JACKY BERRY; Sub-Librarian FIONA ROBERTSON; Sub-Librarian LINA COELHO; publ. *BMA Library Bulletin* (online only).

Bromley Public Libraries: Central Library, High St, Bromley, BR1 1EX; tel. (20) 8460-9955; fax (20) 8466-7860; e-mail informationservices@bromley.gov.uk; f. 1894; 44,581 audiovisual items, 1,399 multimedia items, 98,878 microtext items, spec. collns: Crystal Palace, Walter de la Mare, H. G. Wells; Prin. Library Services Man. DAVID BROCKHURST.

Camden Leisure and Community Services (Libraries, Arts and Tourism): The Crowndale Centre, 218–220 Eversholt St, London, NW1 1BD; tel. (20) 7974-1647; fax (20) 7974-1615; 759,537 vols; Head of Libraries DAVID JONES.

Canning House Library: Canning House, 2 Belgrave Sq., London, SW1X 8PJ; tel. (20) 7235-2303 ext. 208; fax (20) 7838-9258; e-mail library@canninghouse.org; internet www.canninghouse.org; f. 1947; attached to Hispanic and Luso-Brazilian Council; collns on the Spanish- and Portuguese-speaking countries covering disciplines such as Social Sciences and Humanities; 70,000 vols on Latin America, Caribbean, Spain and Portugal; Library and Information Services Man. ALAN BIGGINS; publ. *British Bulletin of Publications on Latin America, the Caribbean, Portugal and Spain* (2 a year).

City of Westminster Libraries and Archives: Dept of Environment and Leisure, Westminster City Hall, Victoria St, London, SW1E 6QP; tel. (20) 7641-1300; fax (20) 7641-6594; internet www.westminster.gov.uk/services/libraries; 11 community libraries, total stock: 1,196,903 books and other materials; Dir DAVID RUSE; Head of Library Operations IONA CAIRNS.

Notable Constituent Libraries:

City of Westminster Archives Centre: 10 St Ann's St, London, SW1P 2DE; tel. (20) 7641-5180; e-mail archives@westminster.gov.uk; internet www.westminster.gov.uk/archives; collns document the socio-economic, cultural, admin. and community history; houses the archives of Jaeger, Liberty and Gillows; 200,000 books, pamphlets, directories, newspapers, journals, maps and plans, prints, drawings and photographs, local government records, electoral registers, census returns, parish registers and business archives; Archives Man. ADRIAN AUTTON; Local Studies Librarian JUDITH BOTTOMLEY.

Westminster Music Library: 160 Buckingham Palace Rd, London, SW1W 9UD; tel. (20) 7641-1300; fax (020) 7641-4281; e-mail musiclibrary@westminster.gov.uk; internet www.westminster.gov.uk/services/libraries/special/music; f. 1946; 62,400 items on music (not recordings).

Westminster Reference Library: 35 St Martin's St, London, WC2H 7HP; tel. (20) 7641-1300; fax (20) 7641-5232; e-mail referencelibrarywc2@westminster.gov.uk; internet www.westminster.gov.uk/libraries/findalibrary/westref.cfm; 432,000 vols; key collns incl. law and British official publs (Hansard, LexisNexis); performing arts (theatre, film, television, radio, dance); art and design (MLA designated colln of nat. importance); business information (market research reports, directories and on-line services); Gen. Reference Librarian EVELEEN ROONEY.

College of Arms: Queen Victoria St, London, EC4V 4BT; tel. (20) 7248-2762; fax (20) 7248-6448; e-mail enquiries@college-of-arms.gov.uk; internet www.college-of-arms.gov.uk; f. 1484; 30,000 vols; genealogica, lheraldic, antiquarian collns; Arundel MSS, deeds and charters; Archivist MATTHEW JONES; Librarian PETER O'DONOGHUE.

Croydon Public Libraries: Katharine St, Croydon, CR9 1ET; tel. (20) 8726-6900; fax (20) 8253-1004; internet www.croydon.gov.uk; f. 1888; 695,017 vols, 23,592 audio items; Libraries Officer A. BATT.

Department for Children, Schools and Family Library: Sanctuary Bldgs, Great Smith St, London, SW1P 3BT; tel. (20) 7925-5040; fax (20) 7925-5085; e-mail enquiries.library@dcfs.gsi.gov.uk; internet www.dcfs.gov.uk; f. 1854; 210,000 vols; Chief Librarian GILL BAKER.

Department of Health Library: Skipton House, 80 London Rd, London, SE1 6LH; tel. (20) 7972-6541; fax (20) 7972-5976; e-mail library.skh@dh.gsi.gov.uk; internet www.dh.gov.uk; f. 1834; 200,000 vols and pamphlets, 650 print periodicals and various databases and electronic journals on public health, health services policy and management, medicine, hospitals, and social care; Head of Library and Information Services PEK LAN BOWER; Senior Librarian JAMES DENMEAD; publs *DH-Data* (online), *DH-Data Thesaurus* (print), *HMIC* (online and CD-ROM).

Associated Library:

Department of Health Library (Leeds): Room 1W28, Quarry House, Quarry Hill, Leeds, LS2 7UE; tel. (113) 254-5080; fax (113) 254-5084; e-mail library.enquiries@dh.gsi.gov.uk; Sr Librarian NATALIE GUDGEON.

Dr Williams's Library: 14 Gordon Sq., London, WC1H 0AR; tel. (20) 7387-3727; e-mail enquiries@dwlib.co.uk; internet www.dwlib.co.uk; f. 1729; lending and reference library of theological, philosophical and historical works, relating in particular to religious Non-conformity and especially to Congregational, English Presbyterian and Unitarian traditions; 300,000 vols; Dir Dr DAVID L. WYKES; Prin. Librarian ALICE FORD-SMITH; publs *Bulletin* (1 a year), *Lectures of Friends of Dr Williams's Library* (1 a year).

Attached Library:

Congregational Library: 14 Gordon Sq., London, WC1H 0AR; tel. (20) 7387-3727; e-mail enquiries@dwlib.co.uk; internet www.dwlib.co.uk; f. 1831; 70,000 vols, mainly relating to Church history, the history and activities of the Nonconformists, theology, religious liberty and hymnology.

Ealing Libraries: Perceval House, ISW, 14/16 Uxbridge Rd, London, W5 2HL; tel. (20) 8825-9297; f. 1965; 650,000 vols; Prin. Library Man. HEATHER FARRAR.

Enfield Libraries: Enfield Town Library, 66 Church St, Enfield, EN2 6AX; tel. (20) 8379-8393; fax (20) 8379-8331; e-mail enfield.town.library@enfield.gov.uk; internet www.enfield.gov.uk/library; f. 1965; 620,000 vols; 16 brs, 3 reference libraries, mobile library; spec. collns: linguistics, local history; mobile library; Head of Library Services JULIE GIBSON.

Geological Society of London, Library: Burlington House, Piccadilly, London, W1J 0BG; tel. (20) 7432-0999; fax (20) 7439-3470; e-mail library@geolsoc.org.uk; internet www.geolsoc.org.uk; f. 1807; 300,000 vols, 40,000 maps; lending restricted to the UK, via British Library Document Supply Centre; reference access by appointment; Chief Librarian SHEILA MEREDITH.

Gray's Inn Library: South Sq., Gray's Inn, London, WC1R 5ET; e-mail library.information@graysinn.org.uk; internet www.graysinn.org.uk; f. c. 1522; 40,000 vols; Legal Reference Library, for mems of Gray's Inn, others admitted on application; spec. collns: 12th–14th century MSS, Baconiana; Librarian T. L. THOM.

Greenwich Libraries: Library Support Services, Plumstead Library, 232 Plumstead High St, London, SE18 1JL; tel. (20) 8317-4466; internet www.greenwich.gov.uk/council/publicservices/libraries.htm; f. 1905; 750,833 vols, 85,213 sound recordings; Borough Librarian and Head of Community Services JULIA NEWTON.

Guardian News and Media Archive: Kings Pl., 90 York Way, London, N1 9GU; tel. (20) 3353-3304; fax (20) 7837-2114; e-mail archives@guardian.co.uk; internet www.guardian.co.uk/gnm-archive; f. 2002 as the Newsroom; archives of orgs and people associated with the Guardian and Observer newspapers; photographic libraries; microfilm, bound hard-copy and digital back-issues; permanent display details history of the two newspapers; Archivist MARIAM YAMIN.

Guildhall Library, City of London: Aldermanbury, London, EC2V 7HH; tel. (20) 7332-1868; fax (20) 7600-1098; e-mail guildhall.library@cityoflondon.gov.uk; internet www.cityoflondon.gov.uk/guildhalllibrary; f. c. 1425; MSS records of the city livery cos, stock exchange, St Paul's cathedral, Lloyd's of London and Christ's hospital; public reference library, particularly rich in books on all aspects of London history business history, maritime history, food and wine, clock making; Dir of Libraries and Guildhall Art Gallery DAVID PEARSON.

Branch Library:

City Business Library, City of London: Guildhall, Aldermanbury, London, EC2V 7HH; tel. (20) 7332-1812; fax (20) 7332-1847; e-mail cbl@cityoflondon.gov.uk; internet www.cityoflondon.gov.uk/cbl; f. 1970; finance, investment and banking; contains co-financial data, country information (incl. global markets) and market research information; Business Librarian G. CONSIDINE.

Hackney Library Services: Hackney Central Library, 1 Reading Lane, London, E8 1GQ; e-mail reference.library@hackney.gov.uk; internet www.hackney.gov.uk/cl-libraries; f. 1965; 900,000 vols; 7 brs, ref. library; spec. collns: mechanic trades, woodwork and furniture, local history, John Dawson Colln; Head of Library Services, Archives and Information Services EDWARD ROGERS.

Hammersmith and Fulham Public Libraries: Hammersmith Library, Shepherds Bush Rd, London, W6 7AT; tel. (20) 8753-3813; fax (20) 8753-3815; internet www.lbhf.gov.uk; f. 1888; 550,000 vols, 48,000 audio items; special collections: law, politics, Christianity, HMSO publs since 1970, video and audio cassettes, DVDs, CDs; Head of Libraries DAVID HERBERT.

Haringey Libraries: Central Library, High Rd, Wood Green, London, N22 6XD; tel. (20) 8489-2781; e-mail library.service@haringey.gov.uk; internet www.haringey.gov.uk/data/libraries; Head of Libraries DIANA EDMONDS.

Harrow Public Library Service: POB 4, Civic Centre, Station Rd, Harrow, HA1 2UU; tel. (20) 8424-1055; fax (20) 8424-1971; e-mail civiccentre.library@harrow.gov.uk; internet www.harrow.gov.uk; f. 1965; 412,000 vols; 38,000 audiovisual items; spec. collns: architecture and building; 11 brs; Head of Service, Libraries and Culture JOHN E. PENNELLS.

Havering Library Service: Central Library, St Edward's Way, Romford, RM1 3AR; tel. (1708) 432389; fax (1708) 432391; e-mail central.library@havering.gov.uk; internet www.havering.gov.uk/libraries; f. 1964; 500,000 vols; 9 brs; Library Services Man. ANN RENNIE.

Hillingdon Libraries, London Borough of Hillingdon: Central Library, 14 High St, Uxbridge, Middx., UB8 1HD; tel. (1895) 250600; fax (1895) 239794; e-mail librarycontact@hillingdon.gov.uk; internet www.hillingdon.gov.uk/libraries; f. 1965; 843,105 vols; Dir (vacant).

Home Office Information Services Centre: Lower Ground, Seacole Bldg, 2 Marsham St, London, SW1P 4DF; tel. (20) 7035-6699; fax (20) 7035-4022; e-mail informationservicescentre@homeoffice.gsi.gov.uk; internet www.homeoffice.gov.uk; 42,000 vols, 100,000 microforms, 2,000 periodicals; social sciences, esp. official publs, criminal law and admin. of justice, criminology, police, immigration, nationality, probation and community relations; regular access for Home Office staff only; access for staff from other govt depts by appointment; Library and Information Services JACKIE KING; Customer Liaison Man. JANET COCKAYNE.

Hounslow Library Network: Hounslow Community Services, CentreSpace, Treaty Centre, High St, Hounslow, Middx, TW3 1ES; tel. and fax (845) 456-2800; e-mail hounslow-info@laing.com; internet www.hounslow.info; Dir of Culture and Heritage (vacant).

House of Commons Library: London, SW1A 0AA; tel. (20) 7219-4272; e-mail hoclibserials@parliament.uk; f. 1818; over 150,000 vols, plus Parliamentary Papers; reference library files contain more than 1,500 periodicals and newspapers; research div. issues internal reference sheets and background papers on subjects of current interest to mems; library private to MPs; Information Office handles enquiries on Parliament from the gen. public; Dir-Gen. of Information Services and Librarian JOHN PULLINGER; Head of Library Resources KATHARINE MARKE; publs *Research Papers*, *Sessional Digest*, *Weekly Information Bulletin*.

House of Lords Library: London, SW1A 0PW; tel. (20) 7219-5242; fax (20) 7219-6396; e-mail hllibrary@parliament.uk; f. 1826; 120,000 vols, legal and Parliamentary history, gen. literature and reference; Dir of Information Services and Librarian Dr ELIZABETH HALLAM SMITH.

Imperial College of London Libraries: South Kensington, London, SW7 2AZ; tel. (20) 7594-8820; fax (20) 7594-8876; e-mail library@imperial.ac.uk; internet www.imperial.ac.uk/library; central library and 5 departmental libraries on South Kensington campus; 5 Faculty of Medicine libraries at Charing Cross, Chelsea and Westminster, Royal Brompton, St Mary's and Wellcome Library, Hammersmith campuses; also Michael Way Library at Silwood Park and The Kempe Centre at Wye campus; 580,000 vols, 25,000 e-journal titles, 1,000 print titles; Dir of Library Services DEBORAH SHORELY.

Inner Temple Library: Inner Temple, London, EC4Y 7DA; tel. (20) 7797-8217; fax (20) 7583-6030; e-mail library@innertemple.org.uk; internet www.innertemplelibrary.org.uk; f. 1500; 80,000 vols, mostly legal and historical; contains, in addition to British law and legal history, an extensive colln of law relating to the Commonwealth; spec. colln of 10,000 MSS, including Petyt MSS, available to the public (by written application, access granted at Librarian's discretion) for historical research; Librarian MARGARET CLAY.

Institute of Advanced Legal Studies Library: Univ. of London, 17 Russell Sq., London, WC1B 5DR; tel. (20) 7862-5790; fax (20) 7862-5850; e-mail ials@sas.ac.uk; internet www.ials.sas.ac.uk; f. 1947; serves academic researchers nationally and internationally; a premium information service is available for clients outside the higher education sector; 300,000 vols, 3,073 current serials; comprehensive colln of legal literature (except for Oriental laws and literature of East European law in East European languages), with spec. emphasis on the legal systems of the UK, the Commonwealth, the USA, Western Europe and Latin America; comparative law; int. law; incl. the Foreign and Commonwealth Office Commonwealth Law Library; the Records of Legal Education Archives; Dir of Institute Prof. AVROM SHERR; Librarian and Assoc. Dir of Institute JULES WINTERTON.

Institute of Historical Research Library: Univ. of London, Senate House, London, WC1E 7HU; tel. (20) 7862-8760; e-mail ihr.library@sas.ac.uk; internet www.history.ac.uk; f. 1921; 170,000 vols; Librarian JENNIFER HIGHAM.

Institution of Engineering and Technology Library and Archives: Savoy Place, London, WC2R 0BL; tel. (20) 7344-5461; fax (20) 7344-8467; e-mail libdesk@theiet.org; internet www.theiet.org/library; f. 1871; 75,000 books, 200,000 bound vols of periodicals, 850 current periodicals, 20,000 reports and pamphlets; spec. collns of historical electrical works; Sir Francis Ronalds Colln (6,000 vols and pamphlets), Sylvanus P. Thompson Library (4,500 vols and 8,000 pamphlets), Faraday MSS, and library, notebooks and MSS of Oliver Heaviside; holds library of British Computer Society; produces INSPEC database and provides specialized information services; Man. of Library and Archives Services JOHN W. COUPLAND; publs *Electronics Letters* (24 a year), *Engineering and Technology* (12 a year), *IET Proceedings* (6 a year), *IET Research Journals*.

Islington Library and Heritage Services: Central Library, 2 Fieldway Crescent, London, N5 1PF; tel. (20) 7527-6900; fax (20) 7527-6939; e-mail library.informationunit@islington.gov.uk; internet www.islington.gov.uk/libraries; 10 libraries incl. the Central Reference Library, Lewis Carroll Children's Library, Islington Local History Centre, Islington museum, and two adult learning centres: First Steps Learning Centre and Islington Computer Skills Centre; f. 1905; 544,357 vols; Head of Library and Heritage Service ROSEMARY DOYLE.

Joint Library of the Hellenic and Roman Societies: Senate House, Malet St, London, WC1E 7HU; tel. (20) 7862-8709; fax (20) 7862-8735; e-mail colin.annis@sas.ac.uk; internet icls.sas.ac.uk/library/home.htm; f. 1879, since 1953 run in assen with Univ. of London's Institute of Classical Studies Library; classical archaeology, art, history, religion, philosophy, language and literature; 130,000 books, 19,500 periodicals, 650 current periodicals; classified colln of 6,800 coloured slides, 200 CD-ROMs; Librarian COLIN ANNIS.

Kensington and Chelsea Library Service: Central Library, Phillimore Walk, London, W8 7RX; tel. (20) 7361-3010; e-mail libraries@rbkc.gov.uk; internet www.rbkc.gov.uk/leisureandlibraries; f. 1888; 620,000 vols; system incl.: Central Library, Phillimore Walk; Chelsea Library, Chelsea Old Town Hall, Kings Rd, London, SW3 5EZ; 4 brs; spec. collns: genealogy and heraldry, biography, languages, folklore, costume and local history; Head of Libraries JANE BATTYE.

King's College London Library: Chancery Lane, London, WC2A 1LR; tel. (20) 7848-2424; fax (20) 7848-1777; e-mail libraryenquiry@kcl.ac.uk; internet www.kcl.ac.uk/library; f. 1829; sites incl. Chancery Lane (humanities, law, science), Denmark Hill Campus (medicine, dentistry), Guy's Campus (medicine, dentistry, biomedical sciences), St Thomas's Campus (medicine) and Waterloo Campus (life sciences, nursing and midwifery, education, management); 1,200,000 vols; Dir of Library Services ROBERT HALL.

Kingston upon Thames Public Libraries: Fairfield Rd, Kingston upon Thames, KT1 2PS; tel. (20) 8547-6413; fax (20) 8547-6426; internet www.kingston.gov.uk/browse/leisure/libraries.htm; f. 1882; 230,000 vols; Strategic Manager Library and Heritage Service GRACE MCELWEE.

Lambeth Libraries and Archives: 1st Fl., Blue Star House, 234–244 Stockwell Rd, Brixton, London, SW9 9QS; tel. (20) 7926-0750; fax (20) 7926-0751; e-mail libraries@lambeth.gov.uk; internet www.lambeth.gov.uk; f. 1888; 9 brs; mobile library and home visit library service; archives and local history service; over 600,000 vols; Head of Service SANDRA GOODWIN.

Lambeth Palace Library: Lambeth Palace Rd, London, SE1 7JU; tel. (20) 7898-1400; fax (20) 7928-7932; e-mail archives@churchofengland.org; internet www.lambethpalacelibrary.org; f. 1610; 200,000 printed items (esp. Church history) and 4,500 vols of 9th–20th century MSS; Sion College Library MSS and early printed books; archives; Librarian and Archivist GILES MANDELBROTE.

Law Society Library: 113 Chancery Lane, London, WC2A 1PL; tel. (20) 7320-5946; fax (20) 7831-1687; e-mail library@lawsociety.org.uk; internet www.lawsociety.org.uk/library; f. 1828; private library for solicitors who are mems of the Law Society of England and Wales; 45,000 vols; Librarian CHRIS HOLLAND.

Lewisham Library Service: Town Hall, Catford, London, SE6 4RU; tel. (20) 8314-6399; e-mail libraries@lewisham.gov.uk; internet www.lewisham.gov.uk/leisureandculture/libraries; f. 1890; 700,000 vols; 12 brs, Central Reference Library, Local History Centre, Open Learning Centre; Head of Library and Information Services JOHN HUGHES; publs *Looking Back at Lewisham*, local history publs.

Library of Anti-Slavery International: Thomas Clarkson House, The Stableyard, Broomgrove Rd, London, SW9 9TL; tel. (20) 7501-8939; fax (20) 7738-4110; e-mail library@antislavery.org; internet www.antislavery.org; f. 1839; literature, photographs and video cassettes on historical and contemporary slavery and human rights issues (modern issues incl. bonded labour, child labour, descent-based slavery, forced labour, indigenous peoples and trafficking; historical issues incl. the Transatlantic Slave Trade and colonialism); Librarian JEFF HOWARTH.

Library of the Religious Society of Friends in Britain: Friends House, Euston Rd, London, NW1 2BJ; tel. (20) 7663-1135; fax (20) 7663-1001; e-mail library@quaker.org.uk; internet www.quaker.org.uk/library; f. 1673; collects and preserves Quakers' historic and continuing recorded heritage; increases access to information about the Society of Friends; encourages study in Quaker and related activities; 80,000 vols of books and pamphlets; 3,000 vols of periodicals, 4,000 MSS, 40,000 prints and photographs; Head of Library and Archives BEVERLEY KEMP.

Lilian Storey Memorial Library Foundation for Theosophical Studies: 50 Gloucester Pl., London, W1U 8EA; tel. (20) 7563-9816; fax (20) 7935-9543; e-mail books@theosoc.org.uk; internet www.theosoc.org.uk; f. 1875; 14,000 vols, visitors by appointment; Librarian; publ. *Esoterica*.

Lincoln's Inn Library: Holborn, London, WC2A 3TN; tel. (20) 7242-4371; fax (20) 7404-1864; e-mail library@lincolnsinn.org.uk; internet www.lincolnsinn.org.uk; f. by 1475; 170,000 vols on law and 2,000 vols of MSS, incl. the Hale Colln; Librarian G. F. HOLBORN.

Linnean Society Library: Burlington House, Piccadilly, London, W1J 0BF; tel. (20) 7434-4479; fax (20) 7287-9364; e-mail library@linnean.org; internet www.linnean.org; f. 1788; 95,000 vols on natural history, incl. Linnaeus's own library and a colln of MSS, engravings and portraits; Librarian LYNDA BROOKS; publs *Pulse*, *Synopses of the British Fauna (New Series)*, *The Linnean*.

London Borough of Redbridge Libraries Service: Central Library, Clements Rd, Ilford, Essex, IG1 1EA; tel. (20) 8708-2420; fax (20) 8708-2431; e-mail central.library@redbridge.gov.uk; internet www.redbridge.gov.uk; f. 1965; adult, children's, reference and reserve: 633,104 vols; Central Library Man. (vacant).

London Library: 14 St James's Sq., London, SW1Y 4LG; tel. (20) 7930-7705; fax (20) 7766-4766; e-mail membership@londonlibrary.co.uk; internet www.londonlibrary.co.uk; f. 1841; open to subscribing mems; an educational charity; 1,000,000 vols mainly in the humanities and social sciences; Librarian INEZ T. P. A. LYNN.

London Oratory Library: The Oratory, Brompton Rd, South Kensington, London, SW7 2RP; tel. (20) 7808-0900; fax (20) 7584-1095; e-mail bromptonoratory@aol.com; internet www.bromptonoratory.com; f. 1854; contains 40,000 vols and 3,000 pamphlets on theology and Church history; separate library (4,000 vols) of David Lewis, Tractarian convert; Librarian and Archivist Father LIBRARIAN.

London School of Hygiene and Tropical Medicine Library: Keppel St, London, WC1E 7HT; tel. (20) 7927-2283; fax (20) 7927-2273; e-mail library@lshtm.ac.uk; internet www.lshtm.ac.uk/library; f. 1924; public health and tropical medicine in all aspects; many series of medical reports; archives incl. the papers of Sir Ronald Ross and many other eminent public health and tropical medicine professionals; Head of Library and Archives Service CAROLINE LLOYD.

Marx Memorial Library: Marx House, 37A Clerkenwell Green, London, EC1R 0DU; tel. (20) 7253-1485; fax (20) 7251-6039; e-mail info@marx-memorial-library.org; internet www.marx-memorial-library.org; f. 1933; 150,000 vols; pamphlets, files of Labour, Socialist and Communist periodicals; spec. collns: Peace Movement, Spanish Civil War, USA, and the Hunger Marches; James Klugmann colln of Chartist and early British working-class history; research, reading and lending; lectures and discussion conferences; Dir of Archives and Librarian Dr JOHN CALLOW (acting); publ. *Bulletin* (2 a year).

Merton Libraries and Heritage Service: Merton Civic Centre, London Rd, Morden, SM4 5DX; tel. (20) 8545-3783; fax (20) 8545-3237; e-mail library.admin@merton.gov.uk; internet www.merton.gov.uk; f. 1887; 500,000 vols; spec. collns: William Morris, Nelson; Head of Library and Heritage Services INGRID LACKAJIS.

Middle Temple Library (The Hon. Society of the Middle Temple): Middle Temple Lane, London, EC4Y 9BT; tel. (20) 7427-4830; fax (20) 7427-4831; e-mail library@middletemple.org.uk; internet www.middletemplelibrary.org.uk; f. 1641; private library for members of The Hon. Soc. of the Middle Temple; non-mems admitted at the discretion of the Keeper of the Library; a charge may be made for services to non-mems; contains 125,000 vols of works on British, American, Public Int. and European Communities law; spec. collns: 80 incunabula, misc. tracts, mainly 17th-century, 83 vols from John Donne's library; Librarian V. HAYWARD.

Ministry of Defence, Information Services: Ministry of Defence Main Bldg, Whitehall, London, SW1A 2HB; tel. (20) 7218-4445; fax (20) 7218-5413; e-mail cio-svcslibrary-office@mod.uk; covers defence policy, defence forces, military, naval and aviation strategy and technology, int. relations, politics, management and computer science; 50,000 vols, 300 periodicals; Chief Librarian PATRICK RYAN.

National Archives: Ruskin Ave, Kew, Richmond upon Thames, TW9 4DU; tel. (20) 8876-3444; fax (20) 8878-8905; e-mail enquiry@nationalarchives.gov.uk; internet www.nationalarchives.gov.uk; f. 2003 following merger of the Public Record Office (f. 1838) and the Historical Manuscripts Commission (f. 1869); national archives for England and Wales and for the United Kingdom; holds the records of central government and the central courts of law since 11th century; central UK advisory body on archives and manuscripts relating to British history; Keeper of Public Records and Historical Manuscripts Commissioner SARAH TYACKE; publ. *National Register of Archives* (previously published by the Historical Manuscripts Commission and containing 43,000 indexed unpublished lists of MSS).

National Art Library: Victoria and Albert Museum, Cromwell Rd, London, SW7 2RL; tel. (20) 7942-2400; fax (20) 7942-2401; e-mail nal.enquiries@vam.ac.uk; internet www.vam.ac.uk/nal; f. 1837; attached to Victoria and Albert (V&A) Museums; reference library for the int. documentation of art and design; 1,000,000 vols on art and allied subjects; spec. collns: Dyce (1869) and Forster (1876) literary libraries, Clements Colln of armorial book-bindings, Piot Colln of festival literature, and many others; Keeper of the Word and Image Dept JULIUS BRYANT.

Attached Archive:

Archive of Art and Design: 23 Blythe Rd, Olympia, London, W14 0QX; tel. (20) 7603-1514, ext. 209; fax (20) 7602-0980; e-mail archive@vam.ac.uk; internet www.vam.ac.uk/resources/archives/aad; f. 1978; colln of principally 20th-century archives of designers, design asscns and cos involved in the design process; Keeper of the Word and Image Dept JULIUS BRYANT.

Natural History Museum, Library and Information Services: Cromwell Rd, London, SW7 5BD; tel. (20) 7942-5460; fax (20) 7942-5559; e-mail library@nhm.ac.uk; internet www.nhm.ac.uk; f. 1881; 1,000,000 vols covering botany, entomology, museum techniques, palaeontology, mineralogy, parasitology, physical anthropology, zoology, ornithology; spec. collns: Carl Linnaeus, Sir Joseph Banks, Alfred Russel Wallace; 1,800 MSS, 400,000 original works of art; Head, Library and Information Services GRAHAM HIGLEY; publs *Journal of Systematic Palaeontology* (4 a year), *Systematics and Biodiversity* (4 a year).

Newham Public Libraries: East Ham Library, High St South, London, E6 6EL; tel. (20) 8430-2000; fax (20) 8430-2412; e-mail customer.services@newham.gov.uk; internet www.newham.gov.uk/services/libraryservices; f. 1965; 500,530 vols, 57,243 reference stock, 14,031 audio items; Chief Librarian (vacant).

Queen Mary, University of London, Library: Mile End Rd, London, E1 4NS; tel. (20) 7882-7379; e-mail library-acquisitions@qmul.ac.uk; internet www.library.qmul.ac.uk; f. 1887; 600,000 vols on the arts, sciences, engineering, medicine, social studies and law; European Documentation Centre; Dir of Library Services EMMA BULL.

Medical Libraries:

St Bartholomew's and the Royal London, Queen Mary's School of Medicine and Dentistry, Libraries: Turner St, London, E1 2AD; tel. (20) 7882-7112; fax (20) 7882-7113; internet www.library.qmul.ac.uk; incl. Whitechapel, W Smithfield, London Chest Hospital, Wolfson Institute of Preventive Medicine.

Richmond upon Thames Public Libraries: Central Lending Library, Little Green, Richmond upon Thames, TW9 1QL; Central Reference Library, Old Town Hall, Whittaker Ave, Richmond upon Thames, Surrey, TW9 1TP; tel. (20) 8734-3303 (CLL); tel. (20) 8734-3308 (CRL); fax (20) 8734-3330 (CLL); fax (20) 8940-6899 (CRL); f. 1880; incl. Borough Local Studies Colln; Head of Libraries and Culture IAN DODDS.

Royal Academy of Arts Library: Burlington House, London, W1J 0BD; tel. (20) 7300-5737; fax (20) 7300-5765; e-mail library@royalacademy.org.uk; internet www.royalacademy.org.uk; f. 1768; 60,000 vols on the fine arts and standard reference books; also original drawings, MSS, prints and photographs; Librarian ADAM WATERTON.

Royal Academy of Music Library: Marylebone Rd, London, NW1 5HT; tel. (20) 7873-7323; fax (20) 7873-7322; e-mail library@ram.ac.uk; internet www.ram.ac.uk; f. 1822; 150,000 vols, 5,500 sets of orchestral parts, sound recordings; special collns include MSS and early editions, Sir Henry Wood Library, Angelina Goetz Library, David Munrow Library, Sullivan Archive, Robert Spencer Colln, Foyle Menuhin Archive; Librarian KATHRYN ADAMSON.

Royal Asiatic Society Library: 14 Stephenson Way, London, NW1 2HD; tel. (20) 7388-4539; fax (20) 7391-9429; e-mail library@royalasiaticsociety.org; internet www.royalasiaticsociety.org; f. 1823; holds monthly lectures, organizes study days; 60,000 vols; colln incl. 1,500 Asian MSS,

2,000 paintings and drawings, 5,000 photographs; Librarian KATHY LAZENBATT; publ. *Journal* (4 a year).

Royal Astronomical Society Library and Archives: Burlington House, Piccadilly, London, W1J 0BQ; tel. (20) 7734-4582; fax (20) 7494-0166; e-mail info@ras.org.uk; internet www.ras.org.uk; f. 1820; 31,000 vols, plus archives, dealing with astronomy, history of astronomy and geophysics; Librarian P. D. HINGLEY.

Royal Botanic Gardens, Kew, Library, Art & Archives: Kew, Richmond upon Thames, TW9 3AE; tel. (20) 8332-5414; fax (20) 8332-5430; e-mail library@kew.org; internet www.kew.org; f. 1852; botany (esp. taxonomic, floristic and economic aspects), history of gardening, botanical art, conservation, biochemistry, anatomy, genetics, molecular systematics, propagation and seed science and storage; 300,000 vols, 160,000 monographs, 3,800 periodicals, 150,000 pamphlets, 200,000 botanical illustrations, 4,600 collns within archives consisting of 250,000 letters and MSS and registered files; Head of Library, Art and Archives CHRISTOPHER MILLS.

Royal College of Art Library: Kensington Gore, London, SW7 2EU; tel. (20) 7590-4224; fax (20) 7590-4217; e-mail library@rca.ac.uk; internet www.rca.ac.uk; f. 1953; 70,000 vols on the visual arts, history and philosophy of design, history and criticism of the arts; Colour Reference Library: comprehensive colln of books and articles on all aspects of colour; admittance by appointment only; Head of Information and Learning Services PETER HASSELL; Library Man. DARLENE MAXWELL.

Royal College of Music Library: Prince Consort Rd, South Kensington, London, SW7 2BS; tel. (20) 7591-4325; fax (20) 7591-4326; e-mail library@rcm.ac.uk; internet www.rcm.ac.uk/library; f. 1883; more than 400,000 vols, incl. MSS and early printed music; admission for reference only; Chief Librarian PAMELA THOMPSON.

Royal College of Physicians' Library Archive and Museum Services Department: 11 St Andrews Pl., Regent's Park, London, NW1 4LE; tel. (20) 3075-1539; fax (20) 7486-3729; e-mail infocentre@rcplondon.ac.uk; internet www.rcplondon.ac.uk; f. 1518; services incl. enquiry service, exhibitions, research facilities, tours, weekly health digest; services for fellows and mems incl. loans, expert search and information retrieval; medical education resource centre; 60,000 vols (mostly related to history of medicine, but some on current medical issues), 100 incunabula, 200 linear m of MSS, 30,000 portrait photographs and other pictorial items; Man. JULIE BECKWITH; publs *Evan Bedford Library of Cardiology: catalogue*, *Munk's Roll* (Lives of Fellows of the College, 11 Vols 1878–2004), *The Royal College of Physicians and its Collections* (illustrated history).

Royal College of Surgeons of England Library and Lumley Study Centre: 35–43 Lincoln's Inn Fields, London, WC2A 3PE; tel. (20) 7869-6555; fax (20) 7405-4438; e-mail library@rcseng.ac.uk; internet www.rcseng.ac.uk; f. 1800; 150,000 vols on surgery and dentistry, 400 current periodicals; Librarian THALIA KNIGHT; publ. *Annals*.

Royal College of Veterinary Surgeons Trust Library: Belgravia House, 62–64 Horseferry Rd, London, SW1P 2AF; tel. (20) 7202-0752; fax (20) 7202-0751; e-mail library@rcvstrust.org.uk; internet www.rcvslibrary.org.uk; f. 1844; open to qualified veterinary surgeons and veterinary nurses; open to mems of the public by appointment; 30,000 vols; Librarian CLARE BOULTON.

Royal Geographical Society (with the Institute of British Geographers) Library: Kensington Gore, London, SW7 2AR; tel. (20) 7591-3044; fax (20) 7591-3001; e-mail enquiries@rgs.org; internet www.rgs.org; f. 1830; 250,000 books and bound periodicals; 500 current periodicals; map room contains 1m. maps and charts, 3,000 atlases, large selection of gazetteers and expedition reports; picture library of 500,000 images; archives; Prin. Librarian E. M. RAE; Map Curator D. MCNEILL; publs *Area*, *Geographical Journal*, *Transactions*.

Royal Institute of International Affairs Library: Chatham House, 10 St James's Sq., London, SW1Y 4LE; tel. (20) 7957-5723; fax (20) 7957-5710; e-mail libenquire@chathamhouse.org.uk; internet www.chathamhouse.org.uk/library; f. 1920; 75,000 vols, vols; 200 current periodicals; Chatham House archives; private research library; visiting scholars welcome by prior arrangement; Library and Information Services Man. DAVID BATES.

Royal Institution of Great Britain Archives: 21 Albemarle St, London, W1S 4BS; tel. (20) 7409-2992; fax (20) 7629-3569; e-mail archivist@ri.ac.uk; internet www.rigb.org; f. 1799; 25,000 vols on all brs of science, spec. collns: early scientific books and journals especially of 18th and 19th centuries, accessible through archive; Head of Collns and Heritage Prof. FRANK JAMES.

Royal National Institute for Deaf People (RNID) Library: 330–332 Gray's Inn Rd, London, WC1X 8EE; tel. (20) 7915-1553; f. 1911; 18,000 books and 200 current journals on all aspects of deafness and other communication disorders; Librarian MARY PLACKETT.

Royal Society Centre for History of Science: 6–9 Carlton House Terrace, London, SW1Y 5AG; tel. (20) 7451-2606; fax (20) 7930-2170; e-mail library@royalsociety.org; internet royalsociety.org; f. 1660; history of science and scientists, science policy, science education, science and the public; 150,000 vols; Library Man. RUPERT BAKER; Head of Library and Information Services KEITH MOORE; publ. *Notes and Records of The Royal Society* (scholarly journal covering history of science activities, 4 a year).

Royal Society of Chemistry Library and Information Centre: Burlington House, Piccadilly, London, W1J 0BA; tel. (20) 7440-3373; fax (20) 7287-9798; e-mail library@rsc.org; internet www.rsc.org; f. 1841; 100,000 vols; Librarian NIGEL LEES.

Royal Society of Medicine Library: 1 Wimpole St, London, W1G 0AE; tel. (20) 7290-2940; fax (20) 7290-2939; e-mail library@rsm.ac.uk; internet www.rsm.ac.uk/library; f. 1805; 500,000 vols, 1,200 current periodicals, 10,000 back titles; lending restricted to mems; back-up library to British Library; worldwide mail order photocopy service; historical colln from 1474; medical portrait colln; Dir of Library Services WAYNE SIME; Librarian NICOLA WOOD.

Royal United Services Institute Library of Military History: 61 Whitehall, London, SW1A 2ET; tel. (20) 7930-5854; fax (20) 7747-2636; e-mail library@rusi.org; internet www.rusi.org/about/library; f. 1831; maintains 3 in-house research depts covering int. security studies, military science and nat. security and resilience; organizes lectures, seminars and conferences; 16,000 vols on military history incl. British regimental and unit histories; c. 4,000 biographies, memoirs and personal experiences (published works, the library does not keep MSS or similar documents); books lent to RUSI mems and to other libraries, mems of the public should apply to the librarian for reference access; Librarian JOHN MONTGOMERY; publs *Homeland Security and Resilience Monitor* (10 a year), *RUSI Defence Systems* (3 a year), *RUSI Journal* (6 a year), *Whitehall Papers* (2 a year), *Whitehall Reports* (irregular).

St Bride Library: Bride Lane, Fleet St, London, EC4Y 8EE; tel. (20) 7353-4660; e-mail nigelroche@stbridefoundation.org; internet www.stbride.org; f. 1891, opened 1895; printing, papermaking, bookbinding, illustration, graphic design; 50,000 books and pamphlets, 3,500 periodical titles; early technical literature, drawings, MSS, prospectuses, patents, materials for printing and type founding; programme of exhibitions and lectures; 3 annual confs; printing workshop educational programme; Librarian NIGEL ROCHE; publs *Printing History News* (4 a year), *Ultrabold* (2 a year).

St Paul's Cathedral Library: London, EC4M 8AE; tel. (20) 7246-8342; fax (20) 7248-3104; e-mail library@stpaulscathedral.org.uk; internet www.stpauls.co.uk; f. 1707; 13,500 vols and 11,500 pamphlets; early printed books of theology and Greek and Latin classics, 20 medieval MSS; Librarian JO WISDOM.

School of Oriental and African Studies Library: Univ. of London, Thornhaugh St, Russell Square, London, WC1H 0XG; tel. (20) 7898-4160; fax (20) 7898-4159; internet www.soas.ac.uk; f. 1916; 859,000 vols and pamphlets, 4,500 periodicals, 2,700 MSS and archive collections dealing with Asian and African languages, literature, philosophy, religions, history, law, cultural anthropology, art and archaeology, social sciences; back-up library to the British Library for loans; Librarian ANNE POULSON.

Science Museum Library: Imperial College Rd, South Kensington, London, SW7 5NH; tel. (20) 7942-4242; fax (20) 7942-4243; e-mail smlinfo@sciencemuseum.org.uk; internet www.sciencemuseum.org.uk/library; f. 1883; 500,000 vols; collns housed in London incl. history, biography and social context of all brs of science, technology and medicine, also 400 current journal titles; collns housed in Swindon incl. contemporary science technology and medicine books and journals, published in 15th–20th centuries, reports, directories, trade literature; also at Swindon the Archives colln containing original MSS, letters, company records, drawings, etc. on scientific, technical and medical subjects; access to Swindon collns by appointment; printed and archive collns; provides access to academics, students, authors, general public, and schools; Head of Library and Archives RUPERT WILLIAMS.

Senate House Library, University of London: Senate House, Malet St, London, WC1E 7HU; tel. (20) 7862-8500; fax (20) 7862-8480; e-mail shl.enquiries@london.ac.uk; internet www.shl.lon.ac.uk; f. 1838; 2,000,000 titles; research library principally in the arts, humanities and social sciences, for reference and loan, including spec. colln, e.g., Goldsmiths' Library of Economic Literature, Harry Price Collection, Sterling Library, Durning-Lawrence Library, Eliot-Phelips Collection, Bromhead Library, Carlton Shorthand Collection, Porteus Library, Malcolm Morley Theatre Collection and the Libraries of the Canadian and Australian High Commissions; Dirs PAUL MCLAUGHLIN (Technical Services), CHRISTINE MULLER (User Services).

Sir John Soane's House and Museum Library: 13 Lincoln's Inn Fields, London, WC2A 3BP; tel. (20) 7440-4251; fax (20)

7831-3957; e-mail library@soane.org.uk; internet www.soane.org; f. 1837; contains Sir John Soane's colln of 8,000 vols on art, antiquities, architecture, classical and gen. literature, architectural drawings, personal and business archive; Librarian Dr STEPHANIE COANE.

Society of Antiquaries Library & Collections: Burlington House, Piccadilly, London, W1J 0BE; tel. (20) 7479-7084; fax (20) 7287-6967; e-mail library@sal.org.uk; internet www.sal.org.uk; f. 1707; 100,000 vols, 650 current periodicals on British and foreign archaeology and history, heraldry, genealogy, etc.; MSS, prints, drawings, early printed books, brass rubbings, paintings, museum objects, seal casts; Head of Library and Collns HEATHER ROWLAND; publ. *Antiquaries Journal* (1 a year).

Southwark Culture, Libraries, Learning and Leisure: 160 Tooley St, London, SE1 2QH; tel. (20) 7525-2000; fax (20) 7525-1586; e-mail southwark.libraries@southwark.gov.uk; internet www.southwark.gov.uk/libraries; 600,000 vols; 12 brs; 1 museum; Head of Culture, Libraries, Learning and Leisure ADRIAN WHITTLE.

Supreme Court Library: Royal Courts of Justice, Ministry of Justice, Strand, London, WC2A 2LL; tel. (20) 7947-6587; fax (20) 7947-6661; internet www.justice.gov.uk; f. 1970; 300,000 vols; spec. collns: Court of Appeal (Civil Div.) Transcripts 1950–; old edns of legal textbooks (in Supreme Court Library—Bar—f. 1883); Librarian J. ROBERTSON.

Sutton Library Service: Central Library, St Nicholas Way, Sutton, Surrey, SM1 1EA; tel. (20) 8770-4700; fax (20) 8770-4777; f. 1936; 9 libraries; 316,100 vols; 26,759 audio items, 9,067 visual items; spec. colln: genealogy and heraldry; Heads of Libraries and Heritage C. MCDONOUGH, A. FLETCHER.

Thames Valley University Learning Resource Centre: Walpole House, 18–22 Bond St, Ealing, London, W5 5AA; tel. (20) 8231-2246; fax (20) 8231-2631; internet lrs.tvu.ac.uk; f. 1992; 259,000 vols in 5 sites; Head of Learning Resources J. I. WOLSTENHOLME.

Tower Hamlets Idea Stores and Libraries: c/o Head of Idea Stores, Shadwell Centre, 455 The Highway, London, E1 3HP; tel. (20) 7364-4332; e-mail ideastore@towerhamlets.gov.uk; internet www.ideastore.co.uk; f. 1965; 627,564 vols; Local History library; collection of books in Urdu, Bengali, Punjabi, Hindi, Gujarati, Chinese and Vietnamese; gramophone records and tape cassettes; video cassettes, compact discs; Head of Idea Stores JUDITH ST JOHN.

Treasury and Cabinet Office Library: Parliament St, London, SW1P 3AG; tel. (20) 7270-5290; fax (20) 7270-5681; 120,000 vols; 1,500 periodicals; covers economics, finance and public administration; Librarian JEAN CLAYTON.

UCL Library Services: Gower St, London, WC1E 6BT; tel. (20) 7679-7700; fax (20) 7679-7373; e-mail library@ucl.ac.uk; internet www.ucl.ac.uk/library; f. 1828; comprises Main (Arts and Humanities) and Science sites at Gower St; Cruciform and Royal Free medical libraries; libraries of Bartlett (Faculty of the Built Environment), Human Communication Science, Institute of Archaeology, Institute of Laryngology and Otology (incorporating RNID), Institute of Orthopaedics, UCL School of Slavonic and East European Studies; libraries of Eastman Dental Institute; Institute of Child Health, Institute of Neurology, Institute of Ophthalmology, Language & Speech Science Library, School of Slavonic & East European Studies, Library and Information Services, Spec. Collns; 2,000,000 books, c. 30,000 journals printed and electronic format; Dir PAUL AYRIS.

University of Greenwich Information and Library Services: Old Royal Naval College, Greenwich, London, SE10 9LS; tel. (20) 8331-8196; fax (20) 8331-9084; internet www.gre.ac.uk/lib; Head of Learning Services ANN MURPHY.

Upper Norwood Joint Library: Westow Hill, London, SE19 1TJ; tel. (20) 8670-2551; fax (20) 8670-5468; e-mail info@uppernorwoodlibrary.org; internet www.uppernorwoodlibrary.org; f. 1900; 60,000 vols; collns on the Crystal Palace and its historical background, the Gerald Massey colln, the J. B. Wilson colln; Chief Librarian BRADLEY MILLINGTON.

Vaughan Williams Memorial Library: English Folk Dance and Song Soc., Cecil Sharp House, 2 Regents Park Rd, London, NW1 7AY; tel. (20) 7485-2206; fax (20) 7284-0523; e-mail library@efdss.org; internet www.efdss.org/library.htm; f. 1930; maintained by English Folk Dance and Song Soc. (*q.v.*); England's main source of information on traditional song, dance, customs and folk culture; 20,000 vols, MS collns, microfilms, press cuttings, broadsides, 10,000 audiovisual items, 15,000 photographic images; open to public for reference; Library Dir MALCOLM TAYLOR; publs *English Dance and Song (EDS)* (4 a year), *Folk Music Journal* (1 a year).

Victoria and Albert Museum, Library of the: see National Art Library.

Waltham Forest Public Libraries: Walthamstow Library, High St, Walthamstow, London, E17 7JN; tel. (20) 8496-5134; fax (20) 8509-9539; e-mail wf.libs@walthamforest.gov.uk; internet www.walthamforest.gov.uk; f. 1893; 448,427 vols; spec. collns: Cookery, Domestic Economy, Fiction Authors U, V; Librarian CAROLINE RAE.

Wandsworth Public Libraries: Town Hall, Wandsworth High St, London, SW18 2PU; tel. (20) 8871-8536; fax (20) 8871-7630; e-mail libraries@wandsworth.gov.uk; internet www.wandsworth.gov.uk/libraries; f. 1883; 721,101 vols; 12 brs; reference library, 2 music libraries, local history library, home delivery library service; special collns: architecture, town planning, European history, geography and travel, occult sciences, local history, early children's books, G. A. Henty; Head of Library and Heritage Service ANDREW GREEN.

Warburg Institute Library: Woburn Sq., London, WC1H 0AB; tel. (20) 7862-8949; fax (20) 7862-8939; e-mail warburg.library@sas.ac.uk; internet warburg.sas.ac.uk/mnemosyne/entrance.htm; f. 1922; cultural and intellectual history of Europe from Classical Antiquity to modern times, incl. history of art, literature, science, religion, humanism; houses libraries of the Royal and British Numismatic Socs; 350,000 vols, 1,300 current serials, 450,000 photographs; Librarian Prof. JILL KRAYE; publ. *Journal of the Warburg and Courtauld Institutes* (1 a year).

Wellcome Library: 183 Euston Rd, London, NW1 2BE; tel. (20) 7611-8722; fax (20) 7611-8369; e-mail library@wellcome.ac.uk; internet library.wellcome.ac.uk; f. 1890, opened to the public in 1949; records medicine and its role in society, past and present; includes popular science, biomedical ethics and the public understanding of science; 700 incunabula; 700,000 books; ephemera; 55,000 pamphlets, 2,700 periodical titles; 9,000 Western MSS; 12,000 Oriental MSS in 43 languages; 200,000 prints, drawings, photographs, paintings; 700 collns of medical archives; 2,500 films; Head Librarian Dr SIMON CHAPLIN.

Westminster Abbey Library and Muniment Room: E Cloister, London, SW1P 3PA; tel. (20) 7654-4830; fax (20) 7654-4827; e-mail library@westminster-abbey.org; internet www.westminster-abbey.org; f. 1623; 20,000 vols since the 16th century, predominantly theological but also general literature and music; Abbey records and other documents since the 11th century; Librarian and Head of Abbey Collns Dr TONY TROWLES; Keeper of Muniments Dr R. MORTIMER.

The Wiener Library Institute of Contemporary History: 4 Devonshire St, London, W1W 5BH; tel. (20) 7636-7247; fax (20) 7436-6428; e-mail info@wienerlibrary.co.uk; internet www.wienerlibrary.co.uk; f. in Amsterdam in 1933 by Dr Alfred Wiener, moved to London 1939; 65,000 vols incl. books and pamphlets; 3,000 periodicals; 900 catalogued documents on the Holocaust, anti-Semitism, the Third Reich, Fascism, Neo-Fascism, contemporary German-Jewish history and exile studies; Dir BEN BARKOW; Sr Librarian KATHARINA HÜBSCHMANN; publ. *Wiener Library News*.

Women's Library, London Metropolitan University: 25 Old Castle St, London, E1 7NT; tel. (20) 7320-2222; fax (20) 7320-2333; e-mail moreinfo@thewomenslibrary.ac.uk; internet www.londonmet.ac.uk/thewomenslibrary; f. 1926; documents changing role of women in soc.; attached to London Metropolitan Univ.; 43,000 books, 2,500 periodicals, 17,000 pamphlets; Collns Man. TERESA DOHERTY.

Zoological Society of London Library: Regent's Park, London, NW1 4RY; tel. (20) 7449-6293; fax (20) 7586-5743; e-mail library@zsl.org; internet www.zsl.org; f. 1826; contains 180,000 vols, 1,300 current periodicals connected with zoology and animal conservation; photograph library; archives of Zoological Soc. of London; information about zoos; Librarian ANN SYLPH; Archivist MICHAEL PALMER; publs *Animal Conservation*, *International Zoo Yearbook*, *Journal of Zoology*.

Loughborough

Loughborough University-Pilkington Library: Loughborough, LE11 3TU; tel. (1509) 222360; fax (1509) 223993; e-mail library@lboro.ac.uk; internet www.lboro.ac.uk; f. 1909; incl. the Univ. Archives; 550,000 vols, 4,000 periodicals; Univ. Librarian RUTH JENKINS.

Luton

Luton Cultural Services Trust: Luton Libraries, St George's Sq., Luton, LU1 2NG; tel. (1582) 547440; fax (1582) 547461; e-mail libraryinfo@lutonculture.com; internet www.lutonlibraries.co.uk; Luton Libraries is now part of Luton Cultural Services Trust, a charity delivering cultural services on behalf of Luton Borough Ccl; Dir of Libraries JEAN GEORGE.

Maidenhead

Royal Borough of Windsor and Maidenhead Libraries: Maidenhead Library, St Ives Rd, Maidenhead, SL6 1QU; tel. (1628) 796969; fax (1628) 766971; Head of Library, Information, Heritage and Art MARK TAYLOR.

Maidstone

Kent Libraries and Archives: Springfield, Maidstone, ME14 2LH; tel. (1622) 696438; fax (1622) 696445; e-mail libraries.informationservices@kent.gov.uk; internet www.kent.gov.uk/libraries; f. 1921; 70,000 vols; Head of Libraries and Archives CATH ANLEY.

Manchester

Chetham's Library: Long Millgate, Manchester, M3 1SB; tel. (161) 834-7961; fax (161) 839-5797; e-mail librarian@chethams.org.uk; internet www.chethams.org.uk; f. 1653 as a free public reference library; 100,000 vols, incl. many works from the 17th and 18th centuries; local history records; Librarian Dr MICHAEL POWELL.

John Rylands University Library, University of Manchester: Oxford Rd, Manchester, M13 9PP; tel. (161) 275-3751; fax (161) 273-7488; internet www.library.manchester.ac.uk; f. 2004 by merger of the John Rylands University Library of Manchester (f. 1972 by merger of John Rylands Library—f. 1900 with Manchester University Library—f. 1851) and the Library of UMIST (f. 1824); 4,500,000 printed books, 1,000,000 MSS or archival items, 800,000 titles on microform, 9,000 serials currently received; numerous spec. colln, several of international renown such as Althorp Library of 2nd Earl Spencer and manuscript portion of Bibliotheca Lindesiana, containing, *inter alia*, 220,000 books printed before 1801, among them 4,500 incunabula and 1,500 Aldines; Librarian and Dir WILLIAM G. SIMPSON; publ. *Bulletin* (3 a year).

Manchester Libraries and Theatres: Central Library, St Peter's Sq., Manchester, M2 5PD; tel. (161) 234-1900; fax (161) 234-1963; internet www.manchester.gov.uk/libraries; f. 1852; 2,430,000 vols, 141,000 audiovisual items; includes social sciences, commercial, arts, music, Chinese, languages and literature, technical, local studies and archives, European information and general libraries, and a unit for visually impaired people: 2 library theatres with resident company; 23 brs, offering Afro-Caribbean, Asian, Vietnamese and community resource services, with 3 mobile libraries and a housebound readers' service; libraries in old people's homes, hospitals and prisons; special collections incl. the Newman Flower, Henry Watson, and Gaskell; Library Theatre Company; Dir LIS PHELAN.

Manchester Metropolitan University Library: Sir Kenneth Green Library, All Saints, Manchester Metropolitan University, Manchester, M15 6BH; tel. (161) 247-6104; fax (161) 247-6349; internet www.mmu.ac.uk/library; f. 1970; 867,000 vols; Librarian GILL BARRY.

Matlock

Derbyshire County Council, Cultural and Community Services, Libraries and Heritage Division:; e-mail roger.jones@derbyshire.gov.uk County Hall, Matlock, DE4 3AG; tel. (845) 605-8058; fax (1629) 585995; e-mail derbyshire.libraries@derbyshire.gov.uk; internet www.derbyshire.gov.uk/leisure/libraries; f. 1923; 1,000,000 vols; 46 brs; 190,000 mems; Strategic Dir of Cultural and Community Services MARTIN MOLLOY.

Merthyr Tydfil

Merthyr Tydfil County Borough Library: Central Library, High St, Merthyr Tydfil, CF47 8AF; tel. (1685) 723057; fax (1685) 370690; e-mail library.services@merthyr.gov.uk; internet www.libraries.merthyr.gov.uk; f. 1935; Public Library Service with active collection and promotion of local history; 163,210 vols; 2 brs; Head of Libraries GERAINT H. JAMES.

Middlesbrough

Middlesbrough Libraries and Information: Central Library, Victoria Sq., Middlesbrough, TS1 2AY; tel. (1642) 729001; fax (1642) 729953; 400,000 vols; central library, 12 brs; Chief Librarian JEN BRITTAIN (acting).

University of Teesside Library: Library and Information Services, Borough Rd, Middlesbrough, Tees Valley, TS1 3BA; tel. (1642) 342100; fax (1642) 342190; internet lis.tees.ac.uk; 290,000 vols; Dir LIZ JOLLY.

Milton Keynes

Milton Keynes Council Library Service: Milton Keynes Central Library, 555 Silbury Blvd, Central Milton Keynes, MK9 3HL; tel. (1908) 254050; fax (1908) 254088; e-mail central.library@milton-keynes.gov.uk; internet www.mkweb.co.uk/library-services; f. 1981; Reference and Information Librarian AGGIE O'HARA.

Library Services The Open University: Walton Hall, Milton Keynes, MK7 6AA; tel. (1908) 659001; fax (1908) 653571; e-mail lib-help@open.ac.uk; internet www.open.ac.uk/library; f. 1969; 206,000 books, 450 current periodicals, 50,000 online journal titles; Dir of Library Services NICKY WHITSED.

Mold

Flintshire Library and Information Service: County Hall, Mold, CH7 6NW; tel. (1352) 704400; fax (1352) 753662; 16 libraries, 2 mobile libraries, 1 library for the housebound; spec. collns: Arthurian literature, local studies; Wales Euro Information Centre; Head of Libraries and Archives LAWRENCE RAWSTHORNE.

Morpeth

Northumberland County Library: Beachfield, Gas House Lane, Morpeth, NE61 1TA; tel. (1670) 500397; fax (1670) 534513; e-mail shirley.cross@northumberland.gov.uk; internet www.northumberland.gov.uk; f. 1924; 635,000 vols; 35 brs, 5 mobile libraries; spec. colln: local history, vocal scores, cinema, drama, Northern Poetry Library; Divisional Dir (Libraries, Arts and Heritage) D. E. BONSOR.

Newbury

West Berkshire Libraries: W Berkshire District Ccl, Market St, Newbury, RG14 5LD; tel. (1635) 519900; fax (1635) 519906; e-mail newburylibrary@westberks.gov.uk; internet www.westberks.gov.uk; f. 1998; public library; Library Services Man. CHRISTINE OWEN; Librarian FIONA DAVIES.

Newcastle upon Tyne

Newcastle Libraries and Information Service: Charles Avison Bldg, 33 New Bridge St W, Newcastle upon Tyne, NE1 8AX; tel. (191) 277-4100; fax (191) 277-4137; e-mail information@newcastle.gov.uk; internet www.newcastle.gov.uk/libraries; f. 1880; 600,000 vols, 50,000 audiovisual items; extensive local and family history resources; Thomas Bewick Colln (first edns, engravings, original woodblocks, Bewick's worktable and toolbox), Thomlinson Library (4,351 vols from the 16th, 17th and 18th centuries, mainly theological); City Library and 17 brs; Library and Information Officer NICK STOPFORTH.

Newcastle University The Robinson Library: Newcastle upon Tyne, NE1 7RU; tel. (191) 222-7662; fax (191) 222-6235; e-mail lib-readerservices@ncl.ac.uk; internet www.ncl.ac.uk/library; f. 1871 as Library of Durham College of Physical Science; spec. collns incl. Pybus (medical history), Robert White, Gertrude Bell, Runciman Papers, Trevelyan Papers, Catherine Cookson, Wallis, Butler, Booktrust (children's literature); 1.2m. vols, 10,000 periodicals (electronic and print); Librarian WAYNE CONNOLLY.

Newport (Gwent)

Newport Community Learning and Libraries: Central Library, John Frost Sq., Newport, NP20 1PA; tel. (1633) 656656; fax (1633) 222615; e-mail central.library@newport.gov.uk; internet www.newport.gov.uk/libraries; 12 brs; Community Learning and Libraries Man. GILL JOHN.

Newport (Isle of Wight)

Isle of Wight Council Library Services: 5 Mariners Way, Somerton Industrial Estate, Cowes, Isle of Wight, PO31 8PD; tel. (1983) 203880; fax (1983) 203899; e-mail libraries@iow.gov.uk; internet www.iwight.com/thelibrary; f. 1904; 11 brs; Head of Libraries and Information Services (vacant).

Newtownabbey

University of Ulster Learning Resource Centre: Shore Rd, Newtownabbey, BT37 0QB; tel. (28) 9036-6399; fax (28) 9036-6849; internet library.ulster.ac.uk; f. 1985; campus learning resource centres at Belfast, Coleraine, Jordanstown and Londonderry; 640,994 vols (all campuses); Asst Dir for Library COLETTE MCKENNA (acting).

Campus Libraries:

Belfast Campus Library: York St, Belfast, BT15 1ED; tel. (28) 9026-7268; fax (28) 9026-7278; e-mail illbfast@ulster.ac.uk; 68,226 vols, mostly arts-related: painting, history of art and architecture, sculpture, design, fashion, film and photography, museum studies, Irish language; Man. MARION KHORSHIDIAN.

Coleraine Campus Library: Cromore Rd, Coleraine, BT52 1SA; tel. (28) 7032-4345; fax (28) 7032-4928; e-mail illcol@ulster.ac.uk; 297,689 vols; European Documentation Centre; spec. collns: First and Second World Wars, Henry Davis Gift of incunabula, Henry Morris Colln of Irish material, Stelfox natural history colln; Man. STEPHANIE MCLAUGHLIN.

Jordanstown Campus Library: Shore Rd, Newtownabbey, BT37 0QB; tel. (28) 9036-6399; fax (28) 9036-6849; e-mail illjord@ulster.ac.uk; 273,004 vols; American and women's studies; UK, US and Irish radical newspapers and periodicals on microfilm; Man. LAURA MILLS.

Magee Campus Library: Northland Rd, Londonderry, BT48 7JL; tel. (28) 7137-5264; fax (28) 7137-5626; e-mail illmagee@ulster.ac.uk; internet library.ulster.ac.uk/lib/maglib.htm; 82,000 vols; history, modern languages, music, drama, dance, American studies, informatics, law and social work; Irish Colln of 5,400 books and 800 pamphlets, rare books Colln. Derry & Raphoe Diocesan Library; Man. CIARAN CREGAN.

Northallerton

North Yorkshire County Library: County Library Headquarters, Grammar School Lane, Northallerton, North Yorks., DL6 1DF; tel. (1609) 767800; fax (1609) 780793; e-mail julie.blaisdale@northyorks.gov.uk; 1,059,000 vols; 45 brs; Head of Libraries, Archives and Arts JULIE BLAISDALE.

Northampton

Northamptonshire Libraries and Information Service: POB 216, John Dryden House, 8–10 The Lakes, Northampton, NN4 7DD; tel. (1604) 237955; fax (1604) 237937; e-mail nlis@northamptonshire.gov.uk;

internet www3.northamptonshire.gov.uk/leisure/libraries; f. 1927; 1,224,000 vols; 107,000 sound recordings and video cassettes; 35 brs, 6 mobile libraries; Supervisor (Libraries) WENDY SMITH.

Norwich

Norfolk Library and Information Service: County Hall, Martineau Lane, Norwich, NR1 2UA; tel. (844) 800-8006; fax (1603) 222422; e-mail libraries@norfolk.gov.uk; internet www.norfolk.gov.uk; public; f. 1925, reorganized 1974; 1,153,295 vols; 47 libraries incl. Norfolk and Norwich Millennium Library, 14 mobiles, services to hospitals, prisons, residential settings, School Library Service, Home Library service; Dir of Cultural Services PAUL ADAMS.

Norwich Cathedral Library: 12 The Close, Norwich, NR1 4DH; tel. (1603) 218443; fax (1603) 766032; e-mail library@cathedral.org.uk; internet www.cathedral.org.uk/learning; a medieval monastic (Benedictine) foundation; privately managed by Norwich Cathedral, for public use; 20,000 vols modern theology loan colln; 8,000 vols historic colln, some incunabula and MSS; houses 450 vols of the Swaffham Parochial Church Library and other parish books; Canon Librarian Dr P. DOLL; Librarian GUDRUN WARREN.

University of East Anglia Library: Norwich, NR4 7TJ; tel. (1603) 592425; fax (1603) 259490; internet www.lib.uea.ac.uk; f. 1962; 725,000 vols; Dir of Library and Learning Resources JEAN STEWARD.

Nottingham

Nottingham City Libraries and Information Service: Central Library, Angel Row, Nottingham, NG1 6HP; tel. (115) 915-2828; fax (115) 915-2840; e-mail enquiryline@nottinghamcity.gov.uk; internet www.nottinghamcity.gov.uk/libraries; f. 1868; 480,000 vols, 33,000 sound recordings; spec. collns incl. local history, D. H. Lawrence, Byron and Robin Hood; Head of Service CHRISTINA DYER.

University of Nottingham Information Services: University Park, Nottingham, NG7 2RD; tel. (115) 951-4555; fax (115) 951-4558; internet www.nottingham.ac.uk/is; f. (University College) 1881; 1,000,000 vols and pamphlets, 5,450 current periodicals, 7,600 electronic journals; MSS and archives (Portland, Newcastle, Middleton, Manvers, etc.) 3m. items; spec. collns incl. D. H. Lawrence, early children's books, French Revolution, meteorology, ornithology; incl. Hallward Library (arts, social sciences and law), George Green Library of Science and Engineering, James Cameron Gifford Library of Agricultural and Food Sciences (Sutton Bonington), Greenfield Medical Library and Djanogly Learning Resources Centre (education, business and computer science); Chief Information Officer STEPHEN PINFIELD.

Oakham

Rutland Library Service: Oakham Library, Catmos St, Oakham, LE15 6HW; tel. (1572) 722918; fax (1572) 724906; e-mail libraries@rutland.gov.uk; internet www.rutland.gov.uk/libraries; f. 1997; 54,943 vols; Head of Culture and Leisure ROBERT CLAYTON; Prin. Librarian EMILY BARWELL.

Omagh

Western Education & Library Board: 1 Hospital Rd, Omagh, BT79 0AW; tel. (28) 8241-1411; fax (28) 8241-1400; e-mail info@welbni.org; internet www.welbni.org; provides library services in the council areas of Omagh, Fermanagh, Londonderry, Strabane and Limavady; Chair. Rev. R. HERRON; Vice-Chair. P. DUFFY; Chief Exec. B. MULHOLLAND.

Oxford

Bodleian Library: Oxford, OX1 3BG; tel. (1865) 277000; fax (1865) 277182; e-mail reader.services@bodleian.ox.ac.uk; internet www.bodleian.ox.ac.uk; f. 1602; legal deposit library; the principal library of Oxford University; includes the Old Library, the Radcliffe Camera, New Library and the following dependent libraries: Radcliffe Science Library, Hooke Library, Bodleian Law Library, Indian Institute Library, Bodleian Library for Commonwealth and African Studies (at Rhodes House), Vere Harmsworth Library (for the history of the United States), Bodleian Japanese Library, Philosophy Library, Oriental Institute Library and Institute for Chinese Studies Library; 9,000,000 vols; Librarian SARAH E. THOMAS; publ. *The Bodleian Library Record* (2 a year).

Oxfordshire Libraries Headquarters: Customer Services Unit, Library Support Services, Holton, Oxford, OX33 1QQ; tel. (1865) 810240; e-mail librarycustomerservicesunit@oxfordshire.gov.uk; internet www.oxfordshire.gov.uk/libraries; 930,000 vols, 11,000 maps, 272,000 photographs and slides, 40,000 scores, 18,000 sound recordings, 38,000 video cassettes and DVDs; 43 static libraries, 5 mobile libraries; County Librarian KAREN WARREN.

Sackler Library: St John St, Oxford, OX1 2LG; tel. (1865) 288190; fax (1865) 278098; e-mail enquiries@saclib.ox.ac.uk; internet www.saclib.ox.ac.uk; f. 2001, fmrly Ashmolean Library (since 1683); 270,000 vols; archaeology, ancient history and ancient Near Eastern studies, and Byzantine studies, numismatics, classical languages and literature, Western art and architecture. Special collections include Grenfell and Hunt Papyrological Library, Griffith Egyptological Library, Haverfield and Richmond Archives and original documentation of principal archaeological expeditions and explorations and classification of artefacts; Librarian-in-Charge Dr G. PIDDOCK.

Taylor Institution Library: Oxford Univ. Library Services, St Giles', Oxford, OX1 3NA; tel. (1865) 278158; fax (1865) 278165; e-mail enquiries@taylib.ox.ac.uk; internet www.taylib.ox.ac.uk; f. 1847; 600,000 vols; medieval and modern continental European (and related) languages and literature (esp. French, German, Italian, Spanish, Portuguese, incl. the languages and literature of Latin America, the literature of Canada, and North and sub-Saharan Africa); Dutch, Yiddish, Celtic, Afrikaans, Romanian; linguistics and philology; spec. collns incl.: Voltaire and the French Enlightenment; Dante and Futurist holdings; the G. B. Guarini colln; Golden Age literature; literature of the former German Democratic Republic; Luther *Flugschriften* and the Fiedler colln; letters and papers of Modern European writers; and the Strachan colln of *livres d'artistes*; Slavonic, East European and Modern Greek languages and literature housed separately at 47 Wellington Sq., Oxford, OX1 2JF; the Taylor Instn houses the Taylor Instn Modern Languages Faculty Library, as well as the Main Library; Librarian in Charge A. J. PETERS.

University of Oxford Libraries:.

Constituent Libraries:

Balliol College Library: Oxford, OX1 3BJ; tel. (1865) 277709; fax (1865) 277803; e-mail library@balliol.ox.ac.uk; internet www.balliol.ox.ac.uk; f. 1263; 120,000 vols; Librarian Dr P. A. BULLOCH.

Brasenose College Library: Oxford, OX1 4AJ; tel. (1865) 277827; e-mail library@bnc.ox.ac.uk; internet www.bnc.ox.ac.uk; f. 1509; 60,000 vols; Fellow Librarian Dr E. H. BISPHAM; College Librarian LIZ KAY.

Christ Church Library: Oxford, OX1 1DP; tel. (1865) 276169; e-mail library@chch.ox.ac.uk; internet www.chch.ox.ac.uk; f. 1546; 130,000 vols.

Codrington Library (All Souls College): Oxford, OX1 4AL; tel. (1865) 279318; fax (1865) 279299; e-mail codrington.library@all-souls.ox.ac.uk; internet www.all-souls.ox.ac.uk; f. 1710; 178,000 vols; spec. collns: medieval and modern history, military history, strategic studies and law; Librarian Prof. I. MACLEAN.

Corpus Christi College Library: Oxford, OX1 4JF; tel. (1865) 276744; fax (1865) 276767; e-mail library.staff@ccc.ox.ac.uk; internet www.ccc.ox.ac.uk/library-and-archives; f. 1517; 80,000 vols, MSS; spec. collns: incunabula, early English printed books, 17th- and 18th-century Italian books, English, French and German books on 19th-century philosophy; Fellow Librarian Dr. H. MOORE; Librarian J. SNELLING.

Exeter College Library: Oxford, OX1 3DP; tel. (1865) 279600; fax (1865) 279630; e-mail library@exeter.ox.ac.uk; f. 1314; 41,000 vols on open shelves, 35,000 vols in spec. collns; Librarian J. CHADWICK.

Green Templeton College Library: Oxford, OX2 6HG; tel. (1865) 274770; fax (1865) 274796; e-mail gill.edwards@gtc.ox.ac.uk; internet library.green.ox.ac.uk; f. 1979; 12,000 vols; Medicine and Social Science Librarian GILL EDWARDS; Business Studies Librarian DEBORAH FARRELL.

Hertford College Library: Oxford, OX1 3BW; tel. (1865) 279409, e-mail susan.griffin@hertford.ox.ac.uk; internet www.hertford.ox.ac.uk; 50,000 vols; 17th-century colln from Magdalen Hall (forerunner of Hertford College); Fellow Librarian Dr T. C. BARNARD; Librarian S. M. GRIFFIN.

Jesus College Library: Oxford, OX1 3DW; tel. (1865) 279700; e-mail librarian@jesus.ox.ac.uk; internet www.jesus.ox.ac.uk; f. 1571; 65,000 vols, incl. periodicals; Celtic colln; Fellows' Library (f. 1571): 12,000 early printed books, 150 MSS; spec. collns: library of Lord Herbert of Cherbury, material relating to T. E. Lawrence (of Arabia); Meyricke Library (f. 1865): undergraduate library; college's archives are separately maintained; Fellow Librarian Prof. T. CHARLES-EDWARDS; College Librarian OWEN MCKNIGHT; Archivist C. JEENS.

Keble College Library: Oxford, OX1 3PG; tel. (1865) 272797; e-mail library@keb.ox.ac.uk; f. 1876; 40,000 vols in working library; spec. collns: medieval MSS, incunabula and early printed books, Brooke colln, Millard colln, Hatchett-Jackson colln, Port-Royal, John Keble's own library, part of Henry Liddon's library, 19th-century archive material; Librarian M. M. SZURKO.

Lincoln College Library: Oxford, OX1 3DR; tel. (1865) 279831; e-mail library@lincoln.ox.ac.uk; f. 1427; 40,000 vols; Librarian F. M. PIDDOCK.

Magdalen College Library: Oxford, OX1 4AU; tel. (1865) 276045; fax (1865) 276057; e-mail library@magd.ox.ac.uk; internet www.magd.ox.ac.uk/college_life/libraries_and_archives.shtml; f. 1458; 120,000 vols; spec. collns: 16th- to 18th-century books, late medieval English history, late medieval MS books, early printed botanical books, early printed medical books; Fellow Librarian Dr C. Y. FERDINAND; Deputy Librarian HILARY PATTISON; Asst Librarian TABITHA TUCKETT.

Merton College Library: Oxford, OX1 4JD; tel. (1865) 276380; fax (1865) 276361; e-mail library@merton.ox.ac.uk; internet www.merton.ox.ac.uk; f. 1264; 70,000 vols; Librarian Dr JULIA WALWORTH.

New College Library: Holywell St, Oxford, OX1 3BN; tel. (1865) 279580; fax (1865) 279590; e-mail naomi.vanloo@new.ox.ac.uk; internet www.new.ox.ac.uk/the_library; f. 1379; 100,000 vols; spec. collns: medieval MSS, incunabula, early archives, modern papers of Milner Colln (deposited in Bodleian Library); Librarian NAOMI VAN LOO.

Nuffield College Library: Oxford, OX1 1NF; tel. (1865) 278550; fax (1865) 278621; e-mail librarian@nuffield.ox.ac.uk; internet www.nuffield.ox.ac.uk/library; f. 1937; 200,000 vols; postgraduate research library in the social sciences covering politics, int. relations, sociology and economics; spec. collns: modern political MSS, labour history, trade unions, political parties, William Cobbett, Daniel Defoe, William Morris, Lord Nuffield; Librarian ELIZABETH MARTIN.

Oriel College Library: Oxford, OX1 4EW; tel. (1865) 276558; e-mail library@oriel.ox.ac.uk; f. 1326; 100,000 vols; spec. colln of personages who attended Oriel College; Librarian MARJORY SZURKO.

Pembroke College, McGowin Library: Oxford, OX1 1DW; tel. (1865) 276409; fax (1865) 276418; e-mail library@pmb.ox.ac.uk; internet www.pmb.ox.ac.uk; f. 1624; 40,000 vols; Chandler colln of Aristotelia; Librarian LUCIE WALKER.

Queen's College Library: High St, Oxford, OX1 4AW; tel. (1865) 279130; fax (1865) 790819; e-mail library@queens.ox.ac.uk; internet www.queens.ox.ac.uk/library; f. 1341; 150,000 vols; Librarian A. J. SAVILLE.

St Edmund Hall Library: Queen's Lane, Oxford, OX1 4AR; tel. (1865) 279000; internet www.seh.ox.ac.uk/index.cfm?do=library; f. 17th century; 54,000 vols; spec. collns: Emden (naval and military history), Aularian (Hall members' publs), John Oldham, Thomas Hearne; Librarian DEBORAH EATON.

St John's College Library: Oxford, OX1 3JP; tel. (1865) 277300; fax (1865) 277435; e-mail library@sjc.ox.ac.uk; internet www.sjc.ox.ac.uk/385/library-and-archives; f. c. 1598; 80,000 vols, spec. collns incl. 400 MSS (200 Medieval); 20,000 early printed books; archives of papers of Robert Graves, A.E. Housman & Spike Milligan; Librarian STEWART TILEY.

Trinity College Library: Oxford, OX1 3BH; tel. (1865) 279863; fax (1865) 279902; e-mail alison.felstead@trinity.ox.ac.uk; internet www.trinity.ox.ac.uk/college/library; Librarian ALISON FELSTEAD.

University College Library: Oxford, OX1 4BH; tel. (1865) 276621; fax (1865) 276987; e-mail library@university-college.ox.ac.uk; internet www.lib.ox.ac.uk/libraries/guides/uni.html; f. 1249; 50,000 vols; spec. collns, incl. the Attlee Papers, are deposited in the Bodleian Library (see above); Librarian C. M. RITCHIE.

Wadham College Library: Oxford, OX1 3PN; tel. (1865) 277914; e-mail library@wadh.ox.ac.uk; f. 1610; 55,000 vols; spec. collns: 16th-century theology, 17th-century science; Persian history and literature; Fellow Librarian Prof. R. W. FIDDIAN.

Worcester College Library: Oxford, OX1 2HB; tel. (1865) 278354; fax (1865) 278387; internet www.worc.ox.ac.uk/library; f. 1714; 75,000 vols; spec. collns: Clarke Papers (Civil War and Commonwealth documents), architectural books and drawings (Inigo Jones, Hawksmoor), English poetry and drama from 1550–1750, Pottinger colln of 19th-century pamphlets, 17th- and 18th-century print colln; Librarian Dr JOANNA PARKER.

Paisley

Paisley Campus Library: High St, Paisley, PA1 2BE; tel. (141) 848-3758; fax (141) 848-3761; e-mail library@uws.ac.uk; internet library.paisley.ac.uk; attached to Univ. of West of Scotland Library; vols, 12,114 online journals; Univ. Librarian GORDON HUNT (acting).

Renfrewshire Libraries: Abbey House, Paisley, Renfrewshire, PA1 1AJ; tel. (141) 840-3003; fax (141) 840-3004; e-mail libraries.els@renfrewshire.gov.uk; internet www.renfrewshire.gov.uk/libraries; 13 libraries, incl. Paisley Central Reference Library; toy library; 2 mobile libraries; 321,500 vols; 29,000 audiovisual items; Libraries Man. JENIFER MCFARLANE (acting).

Peterborough

Peterborough Cathedral Library: c/o Chapter Office, Minster Precincts, Peterborough, PE1 1XS; tel. (1733) 562125; fax (1733) 552465; e-mail fiona.west@peterborough-cathedral.org.uk; f. c. 1670 by Dean Duport; 8,000 vols, some important medieval MSS and some early printed books (books and MSS printed before 1800 are now deposited in the Cambridge University Library, save those of local concern); Librarian Canon J. HIGHAM.

Peterborough City Libraries: Peterborough Central Library, Broadway, Peterborough, PE1 1RX; tel. (1733) 742700; fax (1733) 555277; e-mail libraryenquiries@peterborough.gov.uk; internet www.peterborough.gov.uk/page-37; f. 1892; 8 brs, 2 mobile libraries; Library Service Man. HEATHER WALTON.

Plymouth

City of Plymouth Libraries and Information Services: Central Library, Drake Circus, Plymouth, PL4 8AL; tel. (1752) 305923; fax (1752) 305929; e-mail library@plymouth.gov.uk; internet www.plymouth.gov.uk/libraries; 16 brs; City Librarian ALASDAIR MACNAUGHTAN.

Pontllanfraith

Caerphilly Library Service: Penallta House, Tredomen Park, Ystrad Mynach, Hengoed, CF82 7PG; tel. (1443) 864068; e-mail libraries@caerphilly.gov.uk; internet www.caerphilly.gov.uk; 19 brs, 1 mobile library; Sr Man. GARETH EVANS.

Pontypool

Torfaen Libraries: Torfaen County Borough Council, County Hall, Croesyceiliog, Cwmbran, Torfaen, NP44 2WN; tel. (1633) 628943; fax (1633) 648088; e-mail christine.george@torfaen.gov.uk; internet www.torfaen.gov.uk/leisureandculture/libraries/home; 110,000 vols; 3 brs; Strategic Library and Information Man. CHRISTINE GEORGE.

Poole

Borough of Poole Libraries: Poole Central Library, Dolphin Centre, Poole, Dorset, BH15 1QE; tel. (1202) 262421; fax (1202) 262442; e-mail centrallibrary@poole.gov.uk; internet www.boroughofpoole.com; Head of Service KEVIN MCERLANE.

Port Talbot

Neath Port Talbot Library and Information Service: Reginald St, Velindre, Port Talbot, SA13 1YY; tel. (1639) 899829; fax (1639) 899152; e-mail npt.libhq@neath-porttalbot.gov.uk; internet www.neath-porttalbot.gov.uk; f. 1996; 391,000 vols; 18 brs, 2 mobile libraries; Coordinator (Cultural Services) J. L. ELLIS.

Porth

Rhondda Cynon Taff County Borough Library Services: Ty Trevithick, Abercynon, Mountain Ash, CF45 4UQ; tel. (1443) 744029; fax (1443) 744023; internet www.rhondda-cynon-taff.gov.uk/libraries; 550,000 vols; 28 brs, 4 mobile libraries; Head of Libraries ROS WILLIAMS (acting).

Portsmouth

Portsmouth City Libraries: Central Library, Guildhall Square, Portsmouth, PO1 2DX; tel. (23) 9281-9311; fax (23) 9283-9855; e-mail library.admin@portsmouthcc.gov.uk; internet www.portsmouth.gov.uk/leisure/libraries; f. 1976; Library Services Man. COLIN BROWN (acting).

University of Portsmouth Library: Univ. of Portsmouth, Cambridge Rd, Portsmouth, PO1 2ST; tel. (23) 9284-3222; fax (23) 9284-3233; e-mail library@port.ac.uk; internet www.port.ac.uk/departments/studentsupport/library; 600,000 vols; Librarian ROISIN GWYER.

Preston

Lancashire County Library: Bowran St, Preston, PR1 2UX; tel. (1772) 534003; fax (1772) 534200; f. 1924; 3,018,000 vols; 84 brs, 12 mobile libraries, 2 trailer libraries; Admin. Officer LINDA WHITFIELD.

Reading

Reading Borough Libraries: Central Library, Abbey Sq., Reading, RG1 3BQ; tel. (118) 901-5950; e-mail info@readinglibraries.org.uk; internet www.readinglibraries.org.uk; f. 1883; 280,000 vols; 7 brs, 2 mobile libraries; Local Studies Library; Head of Cultural Services AMAR DAVE.

University of Reading Library: Whiteknights, POB 233, Reading, RG6 6AE; tel. (118) 378-8770; fax (118) 378-6636; e-mail library@reading.ac.uk; internet www.reading.ac.uk/library; f. 1892; 1.2m. catalogued items, 12,860 current periodical subscriptions, 12,000 electronic periodicals; University Museums and Special Collections Service, Redlands Rd, gives access to MLA Designated Collections of British Publishers' Archives and material by and about Samuel Beckett; also Overstone Library, Stenton Library on English history, Cole Library on early zoology, Finzi collns of music and English poetry, Turner Collection of French Revolution pamphlets, Stendhal Collection, agricultural history, children's books, papers of Lord and Lady Astor; Librarian JULIA MUNRO.

Rochester

Medway Council: Chatham Library, Gun Wharf, Dock Rd, Chatham, ME4 4TX; tel. (1634) 337799; fax (1634) 337800; e-mail chatham.library@medway.gov.uk; internet www.medway.gov.uk/libraries; f. 1998; 16 brs, 2 mobile library, Medway Archives and Local Studies Centre; Head of Libraries MARTIN GARLICK.

Runcorn

Halton Borough Libraries: Halton Borough Council, Municipal Building, Kingsway, Widnes, Cheshire, WA8 7QF; tel. (303) 333-4300; fax (1928) 790221; internet www2 .halton.gov.uk; f. 1998; 4 brs, 1 mobile library; Head of Libraries PAULA RILEY-COOPER.

Ruthin

Denbighshire Library Service: Yr Hen Garchar, 46 Clwyd St, Ruthin, Denbighshire, LL15 1HP; tel. (1824) 708204; fax (1824) 708202; e-mail library.services@ denbighshire.gov.uk; internet www .denbighshire.gov.uk; 8 libraries, 1 mobile library, 1 home library service; special collections: Welsh music, local history; 219,260 vols; Head of Libraries R. ARWYN JONES.

St Andrews

University of St Andrews Library and Information Services: North St, St Andrews, KY16 9TR; tel. (1334) 462281; fax (1334) 462282; e-mail library@st-andrews.ac .uk; internet www.st-andrews.ac.uk/library; f. 1612; 1m. MSS, maps and numerous special collns, incl. Donaldson (Classics and Education), J. D. Forbes (Science), and Von Hügel (Theology and Philosophy), 150,000 early and rare printed vols, MSS holdings and photographic colln; 12,000 e-journals; Dir of Library Services J. UPTON (acting).

Salford

HM Revenue and Customs Library: Ralli Quays, 3 Stanley St, Salford, M60 9LA; tel. (161) 827-0465; fax (161) 827-0491; f. 1991; also at Revenue and Customs Library, 100 Parliament St, London, SW1A 2BQ; tel. (20) 7147-2195; fax (20) 7147-0232; 5,000 vols; Chief Librarian LORNA BANKES.

University of Salford Information Services Division: Clifford Whitworth Bldg, Peel Park Campus, The Crescent, Salford, M5 4WT; tel. (161) 295-2444; fax (161) 295-5888; e-mail isd-servicedesk@salford.ac.uk; internet www.isd.salford.ac.uk; f. 1896; 675,000 items, 5,000 periodicals; Dir of Information Services TONY LEWIS.

Salisbury

Salisbury Cathedral Library: The Cathedral, Salisbury, SP1 2EN; f. 11th century; contains printed books and medieval MSS; open only to *bona fide* research students by appointment; an exhibition of books and documents incl. an original Magna Carta is on show in the Chapter House from March to December; Librarian SUZANNE EWARD.

Sheffield

Sheffield Hallam University Learning and Information Services: Adsetts Centre, City Campus, Howard St, Sheffield, S1 1WB; tel. (114) 225-3333; fax (114) 225-3859; e-mail learning.centre@shu.ac.uk; internet www.shu.ac.uk/services/sls/ learning; 550,000 vols, 16,000 subscribed journal titles, 38,000 e-journals; Dir EDWARD OYSTON.

Sheffield Libraries and Information Services: Central Library, Surrey St, Sheffield, S1 1XZ; tel. (114) 273-4712; fax (114) 273-5009; e-mail libraries@sheffield.gov.uk; internet www.sheffield.gov.uk; f. 1856; 915,000 vols (excluding MSS); 28 community libraries, 5 mobile libraries; services such as housebound, hospital and schools' library service, Reference and Information services incl. material on arts, humanities, social sciences, business, science and technology, local spec. collns incl. 19th-century periodicals, botanical illustrations, sports and climbing library, patents, standards and the World Metal Index; central library (incl. private press books, books printed in England 1765–79); business, science and technology standards, local studies, circulation services (incl. Whitworth Colln of organ books, Sports Library and Information Service), Sheffield Archives (incl. Strafford papers, Edmund Burke papers, Edward Carpenter papers, Fairbank map colln); Head of Libraries, Archives and Information Services MARTIN DUTCH.

University of Sheffield Library: Western Bank, Sheffield, S10 2TN; tel. (114) 222-7200; fax (114) 222-7290; e-mail library@ sheffield.ac.uk; internet www.shef.ac.uk/ library; f. 1905; 1,400,000 vols; spec. collns: Sir Charles Firth's collection of 17th-century tracts and 19th-century broadside ballads, the Samuel Hartlib Papers, the papers of Sir Hans Krebs (FRS and Nobel Laureate), National Fairground Archive, Sir Thomas Beecham Music Library; Dir of Library Services and Univ. Librarian M. J. LEWIS.

Shrewsbury

Shropshire Libraries: Shirehall, Abbey Foregate, Shrewsbury, SY2 6ND; tel. (1743) 255000; fax (1743) 255050; e-mail libraries@ shropshire.gov.uk; internet www.shropshire .gov.uk/library.nsf; f. 1925; 510,000 vols, audiovisual collns; 22 brs, 8 mobile libraries; Head of Libraries and Information JAMES ANTHONY-EDWARDS.

Slough

Slough Borough Council Libraries and Information Service: Slough Library, High St, Slough, SL1 1EA; tel. (1753) 535166; fax (1753) 825050; internet www.sloughlibrary .org.uk; 3 brs, 1 mobile library; Head of Libraries and Information YVONNE COPE.

Southampton

Southampton City Libraries: Central Library, Civic Centre, Southampton, SO14 7LW; tel. (23) 8091-7582; fax (23) 8033-6305; internet www.southampton.gov.uk/libraries; Libraries Man. DAVID BALDWIN; Central Librarian MARTIN PAVEY.

University of Southampton Library: Southampton, SO17 1BJ; tel. (23) 8059-2180; fax (23) 8059-3007; e-mail libenqs@ soton.ac.uk; internet www.library.soton.ac .uk; f. 1862 as Hartley Institution; main and branch libraries; 1,300,000 vols, 8,000 current periodicals, Wessex Medical Library, Ford Collection of Parliamentary Papers (since 1801), Wellington Papers, Broadlands Archives (Palmerston, Shaftesbury, Mountbatten), Cope collection of Hampshire material, Perkins Agricultural Library, Parkes Library (relationship between Jewish and non-Jewish worlds), archive collections relating to Anglo-Jewry, Hampshire Field Club Library; Librarian Dr MARK BROWN.

Southend on Sea

Southend on Sea Borough Libraries Department: Southend Library, Victoria Ave, Southend on Sea, Essex, SS2 6EX; tel. (1702) 215011; fax (1702) 469241; e-mail library@southend.gov.uk; internet www .southend.gov.uk/libraries; 7 brs; Head of Service SIMON MAY.

Stafford

Staffordshire Library and Information Services: Tipping St, Stafford, ST16 2DH; tel. (1785) 278311; fax (1785) 278319; internet www.staffordshire.gov.uk; f. 1916; 1,067,000 vols, 38,000 CDs, 17,000 DVDs, 43 static libraries, 8 mobile libraries; Commissioner for Culture and Leisure JANENE COX; Libraries Man. CATHERINE MANN.

Stirling

Stirling Council Library Services: Borrowmeadow Rd, Stirling, FK7 7TN; tel. (1786) 432383; fax (1786) 432395; e-mail libraryheadquarters@stirling.gov.uk; internet www.stirling.gov.uk; 330,000 vols; Libraries and Archives Man. R. RUTHVEN.

University of Stirling Library: Stirling, FK9 4LA; tel. (1786) 467235; fax (1786) 466866; e-mail library@stir.ac.uk; internet www.is.stir.ac.uk; f. 1966; 450,000 vols, 4,000 periodicals; colln of works by Sir Walter Scott and contemporaries, John Grierson archive, Lindsay Anderson archive, Howietoun Fish Farm archive, labour history collection; facilities for online information retrieval; some spec. collns will be inaccessible due to redevelopment work between May 2009 and August 2010; Dir of Information Services MARK TOOLE.

Stockport

RNIB National Library Service: Far Cromwell Rd, Bredbury, Stockport, SK6 2SG; tel. (303) 123-9999; fax (161) 355-2098; e-mail library@rnib.org.uk; internet www .rnib.org.uk; f. 1882, present status 2008 by merger of the Nat. Library for the Blind and the Royal Nat. Institute of Blind People; contains 400,000 vols, incl. music, in Braille and Moon types; giant print and audio incl. talking books; Head of Nat. Library Service HELEN BRAZIER; publs *New Books* (4 a year), *Read On* (4 a year).

Stoke on Trent

Staffordshire University Library: POB 664, College Rd, Stoke on Trent, ST4 2XS; tel. (1782) 294443; fax (1782) 295799; 300,000 vols; Librarian LIZ HART.

Stoke on Trent City Council Libraries and Archives: City Central Library, Bethesda St, Hanley, Stoke on Trent, ST1 3RS; tel. (1782) 238455; fax (1782) 238499; e-mail libraries@stoke.gov.uk; internet www .stoke.gov.uk/libraries; 352,000 vols; Solon ceramics colln; Strategic Man. JANET THURSFIELD; Head of Community Services IAN VAN ARKADIE; City Archivist CHRIS LATIMER.

Stratford upon Avon

Shakespeare Centre Library and Archive, Shakespeare Birthplace Trust: Henley St, Stratford upon Avon, CV37 6QW; tel. (1789) 204016; fax (1789) 296083; e-mail scla@shakespeare.org.uk; internet www .shakespeare.org.uk; f. 1864; 55,000 vols, comprising the combined collns of the Shakespeare Birthplace Trust (the Shakespeare collns—all aspects of Shakespeare's life, work and times; the local collns—history of Stratford-upon-Avon and surrounding area) and the Royal Shakespeare Company Archive (incl. its administrative and production archives, prompt books, photographs, programmes, press clippings, playbills and ephemera); Head of Collections Devt DELIA GARRATT; Head of Local Collns MAIRI MACDONALD.

Swansea

City and County of Swansea Library and Information Service: Central Library, Civic Centre, Oystermouth Rd, Swansea, SA1 3SN; tel. (1792) 636430; fax (1792) 636235; e-mail libraryline@swansea.gov.uk; internet www.swansea.gov.uk/libraries; 986,546 vols; spec. collns: Dylan Thomas, Welsh and Local History; Head of Libraries STEVE HARDMAN.

Swansea University Library: Singleton Park, Swansea, SA2 8PP; tel. (1792) 295697; fax (1792) 295851; e-mail library@ swansea.ac.uk; internet www.swan.ac.uk/lis/ index.asp; f. 1920; 800,000 items; Dir of

Library and Information Services CHRISTOPHER WEST.

Swindon

Swindon Borough Libraries: Central Library, Regent Circus, Swindon, SN1 1QG; tel. (1793) 463238; e-mail central.library@swindon.gov.uk; internet www.swindon.gov.uk/libraries; f. 1943; Librarian ROGER TRAYHURN; Libraries Services Manager ALLYSON JORDAN; publs *Swindon Evening Advertiser*, *The Times (London) and Times Digitial*.

Telford

Telford and Wrekin Libraries: Telford Town Centre Library, St Quentin Gate, Telford, TF3 4JG; tel. (1952) 292151; fax (1952) 292078; e-mail telfordlibrary@hotmail.com; internet twlibraries.enta.net; 9 brs, 1 mobile library; Libraries and Heritage Services Man. PAT DAVIS.

Torquay

Torbay Library Services: Torquay Library, Lymington Rd, Torquay, TQ1 3DT; tel. (1803) 208310; fax (1803) 208311; e-mail tqadminlib@torbay.gov.uk; internet www.torbay.gov.uk/libraries; f. 1907; 190,955 vols; 4 brs, 1 mobile library; local studies colln; Group Man., Cultural and Community Services KATIE LUSTY.

Trowbridge

Wiltshire Libraries and Heritage and Arts: Bythesea Rd, Trowbridge, BA14 8BS; tel. (300) 456-0100; fax (1225) 713993; internet www.wiltshire.gov.uk; f. 1919; 869,000 vols, cassettes, compact discs, video cassettes, etc.; 31 brs, 4 mobile libraries; special collections: Wiltshire, agriculture, life of Christ, anthropology and sociology of the family; public and private archives for Wiltshire and the Diocese of Salisbury; Assistant Dir, Libraries and Heritage PAULINE PALMER.

Truro

Cornwall Library Service: Unit 17, Threemilestone, Truro, Cornwall, TR4 9LD; tel. (1872) 324676; fax (1872) 223509; e-mail library@cornwall.gov.uk; internet www.cornwall.gov.uk/library; f. 1925; 835,000 vols; 29 brs; Asst Dir, Education, Arts and Libraries CHRIS RAMSEY.

Warrington

Warrington Borough Libraries: Warrington Library, Museum St, Warrington, WA1 1JB; tel. (1925) 442890; fax (1925) 411395; e-mail library@warrington.gov.uk; internet www.warrington.gov.uk/libraries; f. 1848; 11 brs; Head of Culture, Libraries and Heritage MARTIN GAW.

Warwick

Warwickshire Library and Information Service: Barrack St, Warwick, CV34 4TH; tel. (1926) 412657; fax (1926) 412471; e-mail librarieslearningandculture@warwickshire.gov.uk; internet www.warwickshire.gov.uk/libraries; f. 1920; 1,105,000 vols; 34 libraries; 5 mobile and community libraries; spec. collns: Warwickshire Colln, George Eliot Colln; Head of Libraries and Culture SIMON ROBSON; Head of Communities and Wellbeing RON WILLIAMSON.

West Bretton

National Arts Education Archive, Lawrence Batley Centre for: University of Leeds, Special Collections, Bretton Hall Campus, West Bretton, WF4 4LG; tel. (1924) 832020; fax (1924) 832077; e-mail s.kielty@leeds.ac.uk; internet naea.leeds.ac.uk; f. 1985; to establish an illustrated 'trace' of work in art and design education 1880 to date, to make this available to scholars and the general public, and to promote academic research and more informed teaching through its use; colln of works of art illustrating the development of the Child Art and Basic Design movements in art education; includes many thousands of original papers, letters, slides, films, video cassettes, tapes and books; Senior Library Asst SONJA KIELTY.

Winchester

Hampshire Library and Information Service: 5/6 Moorside Place, Moorside Rd, Winchester, SO23 7FZ; tel. (1962) 826600; fax (1962) 856615; e-mail library@hants.gov.uk; internet www3.hants.gov.uk/library/library-finder.htm; f. 1974; 2,840,000 vols; 53 brs; 9 mobile libraries; Head of Operations ALEC KENNEDY.

Worcester

Worcestershire Libraries and Learning Service: Culture and Community Services, Worcestershire County Council, County Hall, Spetchley Rd, Worcester, WR5 2NP; tel. (1905) 822819; fax (1905) 766930; e-mail librarieshq@worcestershire.gov.uk; internet www.worcestershire.gov.uk/libraries; f. 1998; 21 library brs, 5 mobile libraries; Strategic Libraries and Learning Man. KATHY KIRK.

Wrexham

Wrexham County Borough Council, Library and Information Service: Lambpit St Wrexham, LL11 1AR; tel. (1978) 297430; fax (1978) 297448; e-mail library@wrexham.gov.uk; internet www.wrexham.gov.uk/libraries; 214,746 vols; 12 libraries, 1 mobile library, 1 library for the housebound; special collections: open learning, Japanese life and culture; business information centre; Chief Officer ALAN WATKIN.

York

City of York Libraries: York Central Library, Museum St, York, YO1 7DS; tel. (1904) 655631; fax (1904) 552835; internet www.york.gov.uk/libraries; f. 1893; Head of Library Service FIONA WILLIAMS.

University of York Library and Archives: Heslington, York, YO10 5DD; tel. (1904) 433873; fax (1904) 433866; e-mail lib-enquiry@york.ac.uk; internet www.york.ac.uk/library; f. 1963; 1,000,000 vols; Dir STEPHEN TOWN.

York Minster Library: Dean's Park, York, YO1 7JQ; tel. (0844) 9390021; fax (1904) 611119; e-mail library@yorkminster.org; internet www.yorkminster.org/learning/the-old-palace-archives-conservation-and-library; f. 7th–8th century; 125,000 vols, 115 incunabula, 101 medieval MSS, 200 music MSS; spec. collns incl. Civil War Tracts and Yorkshire local history (120,000 vols); Librarian SARAH GRIFFIN; Archivist PETER YOUNG.

Museums and Art Galleries

Aberdeen

Aberdeen Art Gallery and Museums: Schoolhill, Aberdeen, AB10 1FQ; tel. (1224) 523700; fax (1224) 632133; e-mail info@aagm.co.uk; internet www.aberdeencity.gov.uk; Art Gallery and Museums Man. CHRISTINE REW.

Selected Museums and Galleries:

Aberdeen Art Gallery: Schoolhill, Aberdeen, AB10 1FQ; tel. (1224) 523700; fax (1224) 632133; e-mail info@aagm.co.uk; internet www.aberdeencity.gov.uk; f. 1885; fine and decorative arts; major collns of British art since the 18th century; Art Gallery and Museums Man. CHRISTINE REW.

Aberdeen Maritime Museum: Shiprow, Aberdeen, AB11 5BY; tel. (1224) 337700; fax (1224) 213066; e-mail info@aagm.co.uk; internet www.aagm.co.uk; f. 1984; displays covering all aspects of Aberdeen and the North East of Scotland's maritime heritage; Head of Collns JOHN EDWARDS.

Alloway

Burns Cottage and Museum: Murdoch's Lone, Alloway, Ayr, Ayrshire, KA7 4PQ; tel. (1292) 443700; fax (1292) 441750; internet www.burnsheritagepark.com; f. 1881; birthplace of the poet Robert Burns; MSS and correspondence; Visitor Services Supervisor JOHN MANSON.

Anstruther

Scottish Fisheries Museum: St Ayles, Harbourhead, Anstruther, KY10 3AB; tel. (1333) 310628; e-mail enquiries@scotfishmuseum.org; internet www.scotfishmuseum.org; f. 1969; visual historical record of every aspect of the Scottish fishing industry from prehistoric times to the present; touring boat; library: reference library and archive of 1,000 vols (open by appointment); photographic archive; Dir TOM SUNTER.

Bangor

Gwynedd Museum and Art Gallery, Bangor: Ffordd Gwynedd, Bangor, Gwynedd, LL57 1DT; tel. (1248) 353368; fax (1248) 370149; e-mail gwyneddmuseum@gwynedd.gov.uk; internet www.gwynedd.gov.uk/museums; f. 1884; artefacts relating to North Wales, incl. archaeology, furniture, costume and Welsh textiles; Curator ESTHER ROBERTS.

Barnard Castle

The Bowes Museum: Barnard Castle, DL12 8NP; tel. (1833) 690606; fax (1833) 637163; e-mail info@thebowesmuseum.org.uk; internet www.thebowesmuseum.org.uk; f. 1892; collns formed 1862–75 by John and Joséphine Bowes, mainly of all forms of European fine and decorative art, incl. works by Goya, El Greco and Canaletto; ceramics, furniture and textiles; ongoing programme of exhibitions; education work; Dir ADRIAN JENKINS.

Bath

American Museum in Britain: Claverton Manor, Bath, BA2 7BD; tel. (1225) 460503; fax (1225) 469160; e-mail info@americanmuseum.org; internet www.americanmuseum.org; f. 1961; illustrates the devt of American decorative arts from the 17th to the 19th century; textile colln; printed maps from the 15th and 16th centuries; Native American colln; library: reference library of 10,500 vols; Curator LAURA BERESFORD; Dir Dr RICHARD WENDORF; publ. *America in Britain* (1 a year).

Holburne Museum of Art: Great Pulteney St, Bath, BA2 4DB; tel. (1225) 466669; e-mail holburne@bath.ac.uk; internet www.bath.ac.uk/holburne; f. 1893; paintings, silver, sculpture, porcelain and furniture in an 18th-century building; Dir ALEXANDER STURGIS.

Beamish

Beamish Museum: Beamish, Co. Durham, DH9 0RG; tel. (191) 370-4000; fax (191) 370-4001; e-mail museum@beamish.org.uk; internet www.beamish.org.uk; f. 1970 to study, collect, preserve and exhibit buildings, machinery, objects and information illustrating the devt of industry, social history, agriculture and way of life in the N of England; the museum covers more than 300 acres and includes a colliery village, railway station, a working farm and The Town of around 1913; Pockerley Manor and horse yard illustrate yeoman farming lifestyle in early 19th century; working replica of George Stephenson's *Locomotion No. 1* railway engine, and *Steam Elephant* of 1815; library of 20,000 vols, 10,000 trade catalogues; photographic archive containing 250,000 photographs; oral history colln with 800 tape recordings; Dir (vacant).

Beaulieu

National Motor Museum: Beaulieu, Brockenhurst, Hants., SO42 7ZN; tel. (1590) 614600; fax (1590) 612655; e-mail nmmt@beaulieu.co.uk; internet www.beaulieu.co.uk; f. 1968; houses designated collns of 270 vehicles, 38,000 motor objects, motoring reference, film and video library; Caravan Club Collection; Shell Art Collection; library: reference library, film library, photograph library; Man. Dir RUSSELL BOWMAN.

Belfast

National Museums Northern Ireland: Cultra, Holywood, BT18 0EU; tel. (845) 608-0000; fax (28) 9042-8728; e-mail info@nmni.com; internet www.nmni.com; Chair. DAN HARVEY; Vice-Chair. TOM SHAW; Chief Exec. TIM COOKE.

Constituent Museums:

Armagh County Museum: The Mall East, Armagh, BT61 9BE; tel. (28) 3752-3070; e-mail acm.info@nmni.com; internet www.nmni.com; f. 1935; collns in archaeology, art, domestic life, history, natural world, transport, textiles and costumes, social life and traditions; library: extensive reference library; Curator Dr GREER RAMSEY; Learning and Outreach Officer RACHEL MCCANCE.

Ulster American Folk Museum: 2 Mellon Rd, Castletown, Omagh, BT78 5QU; tel. (28) 8224-3292; internet www.folkpark.com; f. 1976; open-air museum illustrating history of emigration from Ulster to the USA during the 18th and 19th centuries; reconstructions of bldgs and activities; full-size reconstruction of 19th-century sailing ship; Curator Dr PHILIP MOUNT.

Ulster Folk and Transport Museum: Cultra, Holywood, BT18 0EU; tel. (28) 9042-8428; internet www.uftm.org.uk; f. 1964; nat. museum comprising open-air museum with authentic bldgs illustrating Ulster folk life, both rural and urban; separate transport museum; library of 18,000 vols; Chair. of Bd of Trustees M. ELLIOTT; Divisional Head JONATHAN BELL; publ. *Ulster Folklife* (1 a year).

Ulster Museum: Botanic Gardens, Belfast, BT9 5AB; tel. (845) 608-0000; internet www.ulstermuseum.org.uk; f. 1833; fine and applied arts, archaeology, ethnography, history, botany, geology, zoology; Chief Exec. TIM COOKE.

Birmingham

Birmingham Museums and Art Gallery: Chamberlain Sq., Birmingham, B3 3DH; tel. (121) 303-2834; fax (121) 303-1394; e-mail bmag_enquiries@birmingham.gov.uk; internet www.bmag.org.uk; f. 1867; Departments of Fine and Applied Art (foreign schools from Renaissance, English from the 17th century, early English watercolours and Pre-Raphaelite paintings and drawings, modern art, sculpture, silver, metalwork, costume, glass, stained glass, ceramics and textile collections); Staffordshire Hoard, Archaeology, Ethnography and Local History (collections from Ancient Egypt, Ur, Nineveh, Jericho, Nimrud, Vinca, Jerusalem, Petra, Vounos (Cyprus), Mexico and Peru, Prehistoric, Roman and British Medieval antiquities, British 20th century); Pacific ethnography collection; British coin collection; restricted access to comprehensive collections of minerals, gemstones and molluscs, British birds, lepidoptera and coleoptera; Midlands flora; prints (access by appointment only); br. museums incl. Aston Hall, Blakesley Hall, Weoley Castle, Sarehole Mill, Soho House, Museum of the Jewellery Quarter; picture library; Head RITA MCLEAN; Head, Museum Operations SIMON CANE.

Thinktank, Birmingham Museum: Millennium Point, Curzon St, Birmingham, B4 7XG; tel. (121) 202-2222; e-mail findout@thinktank.ac; internet www.thinktank.ac; consists of 10 galleries of interactive exhibits on science, technology, medicine, natural and local history; also planetarium; Chief Exec. NICK WINTERBOTHAM.

Bishop's Stortford

Bishop's Stortford Museum: South Rd, Bishop's Stortford, CM23 3JG; tel. (1279) 651746; fax (1279) 467171; e-mail museum@rhodesbishopsstortford.org.uk; internet www.rhodesbishopsstortford.org.uk; f. 1938 as the Rhodes Memorial Museum; present name 2005; exhibits relating to the life and times of colonialist Cecil Rhodes (1853–1902); African art and culture; also incorporates local history museum; Curator SARAH TURNER.

Blackburn

Blackburn Museum and Art Gallery: Museum St, Blackburn, Lancs., BB1 7AJ; tel. (1254) 667130; fax (1254) 685541; f. 1874; local history, Indian and Pakistani textiles and jewellery, military history, icons, coins, books, MSS, early printed books, fine and decorative arts, Japanese prints.

Bradford

National Media Museum: Bradford, West Yorks., BD1 1NQ; tel. (870) 701-0200; fax (1274) 723155; e-mail talk@nationalmediamuseum.org.uk; internet www.nationalmediamuseum.org.uk; f. 1983 as part of the National Museum of Science and Industry; explores the history, art and science of photography, film and television, with interactive exhibits; photographic colln incorporates the Kodak Museum colln and colln of the Royal Photographic Society; cinematography colln focuses on film-making; also exhibits of books, posters, designs and ephemera; the Museum houses an IMAX projection system, with cinema screen and a Cinerama cinema; library: access to the Kraszna-Krausz personal library and to other relevant books, MSS and periodicals; Head COLIN PHILPOTT.

Brighton

Booth Museum of Natural History: 194 Dyke Rd, Brighton, BN1 5AA; tel. (1273) 292777; fax (1273) 292778; e-mail boothmuseum@brighton-hove.gov.uk; internet www.brighton-hove-rpml.org.uk/museums/boothmuseum/pages; f. 1874; displays of British birds in recreated natural settings, and galleries of butterflies from all over the world and geology and vertebrate evolution; reference collections of eggs, insects, minerals, palaeontology, osteology, skins and herbaria; library of 15,000 vols; Keeper of Natural Sciences Dr GERALD LEGG; Curator of Natural Sciences LEE ISMAIL.

Brighton Museum and Art Gallery: Royal Pavilion Gardens, Brighton, East Sussex, BN1 1EE; tel. (1273) 290900; fax (1273) 292871; e-mail museums@brighton-hove.gov.uk; internet www.brighton.virtualmuseum.info; f. 1873; collection of paintings since the 15th century, drawings and prints; English pottery and porcelain, including the Willett Collection; decorative art and furniture of Art Nouveau and Art Deco periods; fashion gallery; ethnography; local history; Assistant Dir of Heritage PAULINE SCOTT-GARRETT.

Royal Pavilion: Brighton, E Sussex, BN1 1EE; tel. (3000) 290900; fax (1273) 292871; e-mail visitor.services@brighton-hove.gov.uk; internet www.royalpavilion.org.uk; f. 1851; Regency seaside palace of King George IV with Mughal-style exterior and Chinese-style interiors; audioguides in English, French, German, Spanish, Italian, Cantonese, Mandarin; Head of Museums and Royal Pavilion JANITA BAGSHAWE.

Bristol

Bristol City Museums and Art Gallery: Queen's Rd, Bristol, BS8 1RL; tel. (117) 922-3571; fax (117) 922-2047; e-mail general_museum@bristol-city.gov.uk; internet www.bristol-city.gov.uk/museums; galleries incl. Old Masters, French School, British collection, Modern Art and Bristol School; decorative arts collection incl. Eastern Art, ceramics, silverware and glassware; minerals, fossils and natural history collections; archaeological collection; also 16th-century Red Lodge (Park Row), Georgian House (Gt George St), Blaise Castle House Museum (Henbury), Bristol Industrial Museum (Princes Wharf); Kingsweston Roman Villa; Dir KATE BRINDLEY; publ. *Events* (3 a year).

British Empire and Commonwealth Museum: Clock Tower Yard, Temple Meads, Bristol, BS1 6QH; tel. (117) 925-4980; fax (117) 954-4849; e-mail admin@empiremuseum.co.uk; internet www.empiremuseum.co.uk; f. 2002; charts the history of the British empire and examines its legacy in contemporary Britain; holds over 1m. items incl. documents, photographs, film, paintings, prints, costumes, textiles, domestic and personal artefacts, books, music and an extensive oral history archive; Bristol site closed in 2008 to relocate to new premises in London in 2012; Dir Dr GARETH GRIFFITHS.

Burnley

Towneley Hall Art Gallery and Museums: Towneley Hall, Towneley Park, Burnley, BB11 3RQ; tel. (1282) 424213; fax (1282) 436138; e-mail towneleyhall@burnley.gov.uk; internet www.towneleyhall.org.uk; f. 1902; collections incl. natural history, Egyptology, local history, textiles, decorative art and furniture; art collection focuses on 19th-century British artists; Curator MIKE TAREND.

Caernarfon

Segontium Roman Fort Museum: Beddgelert Rd, Caernarfon, Gwynedd, LL55 2LN; tel. (1286) 676767; fax (1286) 676767; internet www.segontium.org.uk; f. 1924; exhibits relating to the Roman occupation of Wales, relics from Segontium Roman fort.

Cambridge

Fitzwilliam Museum: Trumpington St, Cambridge, CB2 1RB; tel. (1223) 332900; fax (1223) 332923; e-mail fitzmuseum-enquiries@lists.cam.ac.uk; internet www.fitzmuseum.cam.ac.uk; f. 1816; art collns of the Univ. of Cambridge; paintings, drawings, prints, sculpture; coins and medals; ceramics, glass, textiles, arms and armour, and other applied arts; Greek,

Roman, Cypriot, western Asiatic and Egyptian antiquities; library of 250,000 vols and medieval, literary and music MSS, autograph letters, early printed books, printed music, books on history of art; Assis. Dir KATE CARRENO; publ. *Biennial Review*.

University Museum of Archaeology and Anthropology: Downing St, Cambridge, CB2 3DZ; tel. (1223) 333516; fax (1233) 333517; e-mail admin@maa.cam.ac.uk; internet maa.cam.ac.uk; f. 1884; anthropology and prehistoric archaeology of all parts of the world; also local archaeology of all periods; Dir and Curator Prof. N. J. THOMAS.

University Museum of Zoology: Downing St, Cambridge, CB2 3EJ; tel. (1223) 336650; fax (1223) 336679; e-mail umzc@zoo.cam.ac.uk; internet www.museum.zoo.cam.ac.uk; f. 1815; collns of recent and fossil zoological species; Collns Man. MATHEW LOWE.

Cardiff

Amgueddfa Cymru/National Museum Wales: Cathays Park, Cardiff, CF10 3NP; tel. (29) 2057-3951; fax (29) 2057-3321; internet www.museumwales.ac.uk; f. 1907; Pres. PAUL LOVELUCK; Dir-Gen. DAVID ANDERSON.

Associated Museums:

Big Pit: National Coal Museum: Blaenafon, Torfaen, NP4 9XP; tel. (1495) 790311; internet www.museumwales.ac.uk/en/bigpit; f. 1980; working coal mine and exhibits relating to Welsh mining history; Man. PETER WALKER.

National Museum Cardiff: Cathays Park, Cardiff, CF10 3NP; tel. (29) 2039-7951; internet www.museumwales.ac.uk/en/cardiff; f. 1907; houses the Welsh nat. colln of fine and applied art; also archaeological, numismatic, natural history and geological collns; library of 2,000,000 vols; also print and drawings study room open by appointment; Dir MICHAEL TOOBY.

National Roman Legion Museum: High St, Caerleon, NP18 1AE; tel. (1633) 423134; internet www.museumwales.ac.uk/en/roman; f. 1850; fmr Roman fortress, comprising ruins and relevant exhibits; open by appointment; Man. DAI PRICE.

National Slate Museum: Llanberis, Gwynedd, LL55 4TY; tel. (1286) 870630; fax (1286) 871906; internet www.museumwales.ac.uk/en/slate; f. 1972; machinery, relics and bldgs relating to the Wales slate industry; library: open by appointment; Keeper DAFYDD ROBERTS.

National Waterfront Museum: Oystermouth Rd, Maritime Quarter, Swansea, SA1 3RD; tel. (1792) 638950; internet www.museumwales.ac.uk/en/swansea; 15 themed display areas on the effect of the Industrial Revolution on Welsh life.

National Wool Museum: Dre-fach Felindre, near Newcastle Emlyn, Llandysul, Sir Gaerfyrddin, Carmarthenshire, SA44 5UP; tel. (1559) 370929; fax (1559) 370929; e-mail gwlan@amgueddfacymru.ac.uk; internet www.amgueddfacymru.ac.uk; f. 1976; displays of bldgs and artefacts relating to the Welsh woollen industry, incl. working historic textile machinery and textile gallery; Man. ANN WHITTALL.

St Fagans: National History Museum: St Fagans, Cardiff, CF5 6XB; tel. (29) 2057-3500; internet www.museumwales.ac.uk/en/stfagans; f. 1948; museum of Welsh social history, with over 40 original bldgs re-erected on site; library: library open by appointment; Dir BETHAN LEWIS.

Turner House Gallery: Plymouth Rd, Penarth, CF64 3DM; tel. (29) 2070-8870; e-mail post@nmgw.ac.uk; internet www.nmgw.ac.uk; f. 1921; art gallery; Dir MICHAEL TOOBY.

Carmarthen

Carmarthenshire County Museum: Abergwili, Carmarthen, SA31 2JG; tel. (1267) 228696; fax (1267) 223830; e-mail museums@carmarthenshire.gov.uk; internet www.carmarthenshire.gov.uk; f. 1978; local authority museum; geology, archaeology, social history, folk life, furniture, ceramics, art, costume; County Museums Man. A. DORSETT.

Chawton

Jane Austen's House: Chawton, Alton, Hampshire; tel. (1420) 83262; e-mail enquiries@jane-austens-house-museum.org.uk; internet www.jane-austens-house-museum.org.uk; f. 1949; portraits, documents, furniture and objects relating to Jane Austen and her family; Dir T. F. CARPENTER.

Cirencester

Corinium Museum: Park St, Cirencester, GL7 2BX; tel. (1285) 655611; e-mail coriniummuseum@cotswold.gov.uk; internet www.cotswold.gov.uk/go/museum; important colln of Roman material; mosaic pavements, sculpture, military and civil tombstones, household domestic utensils, personal ornaments, and Samian and coarse pottery, all giving ample evidence of the importance and wealth of Corinium, which was the second largest town in Roman Britain; regional museum for the Cotswolds; Museums Service Man. Dr JOHN PADDOCK.

Colchester

Colchester Museums: Museum Resource Centre, 14 Ryegate Rd, Colchester, Essex, CO1 1YG; tel. (1206) 282931; fax (1206) 282925; internet www.colchestermuseums.org.uk; f. 1860 from the collections of Essex Archaeological Society; local human and natural history; large collns in the Norman Castle, with extensive Roman section; 3 br. museums (covering Natural History, social history, Colchester Clocks); Head of Museums PETER BERRIDGE.

Devizes

Wiltshire Heritage Museum, Gallery and Library: The Museum, 41 Long St, Devizes, Wilts., SN10 1NS; tel. (1380) 727369; fax (1380) 722150; e-mail wanhs@wiltshireheritage.org.uk; internet wiltshireheritage.org.uk; f. 1853; archaeological and historical collns from Wiltshire, incl. Stonehenge, with emphasis on Bronze Age period; Wiltshire art colln; archives relating to Wiltshire; library of 8,000 vols; Chair. W. A. PERRY; Curator P. H. ROBINSON; Librarian Dr L. HAYCOCK; publ. *Wiltshire Archaeological and Natural History Magazine* (1 a year).

Doncaster

Doncaster Museum and Art Gallery: Chequer Rd, Doncaster, DN1 2AE; tel. (1302) 734293; fax (1302) 735409; e-mail museum@doncaster.gov.uk; internet www.doncaster.gov.uk/museums; f. 1909; regional natural history, geology, archaeology and local history collns; permanent art colln, paintings, ceramics and glass; Regimental colln of the King's Own Yorkshire Light Infantry; Man. C. DALTON; Assist Man. J. ADAMS.

Dorchester

Dorset County Museum and Dorset Natural History and Archaeological Society: High West St, Dorchester, Dorset, DT1 1XA; tel. (1305) 262735; fax (1305) 257180; e-mail dorsetcountymuseum@dor-mus.demon.co.uk; internet www.dorsetcountymuseum.org; f. 1846 (Museum), merged with Society (f. 1875) in 1928; natural history, palaeontology, archaeology, fine arts, geology, literature (incl. Thomas Hardy), and the local history of Dorset; lectures, conferences and seminars are held in the Museum during the first half of the calendar year; Pres. CAROLINE MONTAGU, COUNTESS OF SANDWICH; Dir of the Museum and Sec. to the Society JUDY LINDSAY; publ. *The Proceedings of the Dorset Natural History and Archaeological Society* (1 a year).

Dumfries

Dumfries Museums: The Observatory, Rotchell Rd, Dumfries, DG2 7SW; tel. (1387) 253374; fax (1387) 265081; e-mail dumfriesmuseum@dumgal.gov.uk; internet www.dumgal.gov.uk/museums; f. 1836 as an observatory and Camera Obscura; building erected as a windmill c. 1790; exhibits Roman relics, Stone and Bronze Age artefacts, natural and local history from Dumfries and Galloway; incorporates Dumfries Museum, Thornhill Museum, Langholm Museum and Myrseth Museum collns; MSS concerning Carlyle and Barrie; Camera Obscura; period rooms at Old Bridge House (1660) nearby; Robert Burns Centre in Dumfries Town Mill (1781): exhibitions on Burns and his life in South West Scotland; Burns House: period house occupied by Burns 1793–96 and where he died: exhibits incl. MSS, first editions, personal belongings; Sanquhar Museum in Adam-designed Town House (1735) covers local history and geology; Museum Officer SIOBHAN RATCHFORD.

Dundee

Dundee City Council: Leisure and Communities Department: McManus: Dundee's Art Gallery & Museum, Albert Sq., Meadowside, Dundee, DD1 1DA; tel. (1382) 307200; fax (1382) 307207; e-mail themcmanus@dundeecity.gov.uk; internet www.themcmanus-dundee.gov.uk; f. 1873; operates 4 heritage sites open to the public: McManus: Dundee's Art Gallery & Museum (Victorian Scottish paintings, contemporary art and photography, decorative arts, local history displays from time of earliest settlers to modern era, costume gallery, natural history); Broughty Castle Museum (history of Broughty Ferry, natural history of the seashore, a selection of paintings from the Orchar Colln), Mills Observatory (10-inch Victorian telescope, modern 12-inch reflecting telescope with 'go to' technology, displays on the solar system and space exploration, displays of historic equipment and information of local importance; planetarium), McManus Collns Unit (new permanent home for the city's History, Archaeology and Natural History Collns); Cultural Services Man. BILLY GARTLEY.

Durham

Durham University, Oriental Museum: Elvet Hill, off South Rd, Durham, DH1 3TH; tel. (191) 334-5694; fax (191) 334-5694; e-mail oriental.museum@durham.ac.uk; internet www.dur.ac.uk/oriental.museum; f. 1960; Duke of Northumberland's colln of Egyptian antiquities; MacDonald colln of Chinese ceramics; Charles Hardinge colln of Chinese jades; Henry de Laszlo colln of Chinese art and other examples of oriental art and archaeology covering Ancient Egypt and the Near East, the Indian subcontinent, Japan and SE Asia; Curator CRAIG P. BARCLAY.

Killhope, the North of England Lead Mining Museum: nr Cowshill, Upper Weardale, Co. Durham, DL13 1AR; tel. (1388) 537505; fax (1388) 537617; e-mail info@killhope.org.uk; internet www.killhope.org.uk; f. 1984 as Killhope Lead Mining Centre; present name 2000; fully restored 19th-century lead mine; Man. IAN FORBES.

Edinburgh

Edinburgh City Museums and Art Galleries: City Art Centre, 2 Market St, Edinburgh, EH1 1DE; tel. (131) 529-2427; fax (131) 529-3977; e-mail museumsandgalleries@edinburgh.gov.uk; comprise Museum of Edinburgh, 142 Canongate (local history), People's Story, Canongate Tolbooth, 163 Canongate (life and work of Edinburgh's people), Museum of Childhood, 42 High St, Writers' Museum, Lawnmarket (collection of Scott, Burns and Stevenson), City Art Centre (museum headquarters), Market St (temporary exhibitions and artists since the 19th century), Lauriston Castle, Cramond Rd South (furniture collection in Edwardian interior), Queensferry Museum, South Queensferry (local history); Newhaven (local history); Brass Rubbing Centre, Chalmers Close, Royal Mile; Head of Museums and Arts LYNNE HALFPENNY.

National Galleries of Scotland: The Mound, Edinburgh, EH2 2EL; tel. (131) 624-6200; e-mail enquiries@nationalgalleries.org; internet www.nationalgalleries.org; f. 1859; collns of Western art ranging from the Middle Ages to the present day; Dir-Gen. JOHN LEIGHTON; publ. *eBulletin* (describing new acquisitions, exhibitions, events, public programme highlights of the 4 nat. galleries,12 a year).

Constituent Galleries:

Dean Gallery: 73 Belford Rd, Edinburgh, EH4 3DS; tel. (131) 624-6200; e-mail gmainfo@nationalgalleries.org; internet www.nationalgalleries.org; f. 1999; Paolozzi gift of sculpture and graphic art, Dada and Surrealist colln; library and archive; Dir Dr SIMON GROOM.

National Gallery of Scotland: The Mound, Edinburgh, EH2 2EL; tel. (131) 624-6200; fax (131) 220-0917; e-mail nginfo@nationalgalleries.org; internet www.nationalgalleries.org; f. 1859; European and Scottish paintings up to 1900; also drawings, prints and sculpture; Dir MICHAEL CLARKE.

Royal Scottish Academy: The Mound, Edinburgh, EH2 2EL; tel. (131) 225-6671; fax (131) 220-6016; internet www.royalscottishacademy.org; f. 1826; collns of painting, sculpture and architecture from academicians since 1831; contemporary art; colln of William Gillies; library: library of material on fine arts and architecture; open by appointment; Pres. IAN MCKENZIE-SMITH.

Scottish National Gallery of Modern Art: 75 Belford Rd, Edinburgh, EH4 3DR; tel. (131) 624-6200; fax (131) 343-2802; e-mail gmainfo@nationalgalleries.org; internet www.nationalgalleries.org; f. 1960; displays Scottish and European paintings, drawings, prints and sculptures since beginning of 20th century; int. post-war works; library of 50,000 vols; Dir Dr SIMON GROOM.

Scottish National Portrait Gallery: 1 Queen St, Edinburgh, EH2 1JD; tel. (131) 624-6200; fax (131) 558-3691; e-mail pginfo@nationalgalleries.org; internet www.nationalgalleries.org; f. 1889; portraits of Scottish historical interest; an extensive reference section of engravings and photographs of portraits; the nat. photography colln (closed for refurbishment until 2011); Dir JAMES HOLLOWAY.

National Museums Scotland: Chambers St, Edinburgh, EH1 1JF; tel. (131) 225-7534; fax (131) 220-4819; e-mail info@nms.ac.uk; internet www.nms.ac.uk; f. 1985; Dir Dr GORDON RINTOUL.

Constituent Museums:

Museum of Flight: East Fortune Airfield, East Lothian, EH39 5LF; tel. (131) 247-4238; fax (131) 247-4442; e-mail info@nms.ac.uk; internet www.nms.ac.uk/flight; colln of aircraft, rockets and aeroengines displayed in the hangars of a former RAF wartime station; houses a decommissioned Concorde aircraft; archives, propellers, incl. reference library; Curator ALISTAIR DODDS.

Museum of Rural Life: Philipshill Rd, Wester Kittochside, East Kilbride, G76 9HR; tel. (131) 247-4369; fax (1355) 571290; e-mail info@nms.ac.uk; internet www.nms.ac.uk/our_museums/museum_of_rural_life.aspx; f. 2001, fmrly Museum of Scottish Country Life; includes Georgian farmhouse and a 1950s working farm; Gen. Man. DUNCAN DORNAN.

Museum of Scotland: Chambers St, Edinburgh, EH1 1JF; tel. (131) 225-7534; fax (131) 220-4819; e-mail info@nms.ac.uk; internet www.nms.ac.uk/scotland; f. 1998; history and geology of Scotland; Dir Dr GORDON RINTOUL.

National Museum of Costume: New Abbey, DG2 8HQ; tel. (131) 247-4030; fax (1387) 850461; e-mail info@nms.ac.uk; internet www.nms.ac.uk/costume; f. 1977; 19th-century country house; changing exhibitions of costume from the 1870s to the 1950s; Man. MARGARET ROBERTS.

National War Museum of Scotland: Edinburgh Castle, Edinburgh, EH1 2NG; tel. (131) 247-4413; fax (131) 225-3848; e-mail info@nms.ac.uk; internet www.nms.ac.uk/war; f. 1930; collns of the Scottish experience of war and military service since 1700; Curator ALLAN CARSWELL.

Royal Museum: Chambers St, Edinburgh, EH1 1JF; tel. (131) 247-4422; fax (131) 220-4819; e-mail info@nms.ac.uk; internet www.nms.ac.uk/royal; f. 1854; int. collns of decorative arts, archaeology, ethnography, natural history, geology, science and technology; Dir Dr GORDON RINTOUL.

Gateshead

BALTIC Centre for Contemporary Art: Gateshead Quays, South Shore Rd, Gateshead, NE8 3BA; tel. (191) 478-1810; fax (191) 478-1922; e-mail info@balticmill.com; internet www.balticmill.com; f. 2002; Dir GODFREY WORSDALE; Head of Learning and Engagement EMMA THOMAS.

Glasgow

Glasgow Museums: 200 Woodhead Rd, Nitshill Glasgow, G53 7NN; tel. (141) 276-9300; fax (141) 276-9305; e-mail museums@csglasgow.org; internet www.glasgowmuseums.com; colln displayed in 10 venues across the city of Glasgow;incl. Glasgow Museums Resource Centre; Museum Man. CAROLINE BARR; publ. *Preview Magazine* (4 a year).

Constituent Museums:

Burrell Collection: Pollok Country Park, 2060 Pollokshaws Rd, Glasgow G43 1AT; tel. (141) 287-2550; fax (141) 287-2597; e-mail museums@glasgowlife.org.uk; internet www.glasgowlife.org.uk; f. 1983; colln of c. 8,000 objects bequeathed to City of Glasgow by Sir William Burrell 1944; antiquities from Iraq, Egypt, Greece and Italy; Oriental art, incl. Chinese ceramics, bronzes and jades, Japanese prints, Near Eastern carpets, rugs, ceramics and metal work; European decorative arts of 14th–18th centuries including tapestries, stained glass, sculpture, furniture, glass, silver and ceramics; fine art, especially French 19th-century works by Degas, Boudin, Monet and Daumier; Sr Curator, Ancient Civilizations SIMON ECCLES.

Gallery of Modern Art (GOMA): Royal Exchange Sq., Glasgow G1 3AH; tel. (141) 229-1996; fax (141) 204-5316; e-mail museums@csglasgow.org; internet www.glasgowmuseums.com; f. 1996; exhibits work by local, nat. and int. artists; aims to address contemporary social issues through major biennial projects; museum bldg combines old and new architecture and incorporates a number of artists' commissions; Man. VICTORIA HOLLOWS.

Glasgow Museums Resource Centre (GMRC): 200 Woodhead Rd, Nitshill, Glasgow, G53 7NN; tel. (141) 276-9300; fax (141) 276-9305; e-mail museums@csglasgow.org; internet www.glasgowmuseums.com; f. 2003; publicly accessible store of 200,000 items held by Glasgow's museum service; home of the Open Museum; daily public tours and formal and informal learning programmes; research facilities; Man. CAROLINE BARR.

Kelvingrove Art Gallery and Museum: Argyle St, Glasgow, G3 8AG; tel. (141) 287-2699; fax (141) 287-2690; e-mail museums@csglasgow.org; internet www.glasgowmuseums.com; f. 1901; collns incl. Dutch and French Impressionist paintings, Scottish colourists, arms and armour, Charles Rennie Mackintosh and the Glasgow Style, natural history, technology, costume; discovery and study centres.

Museum of Transport: Kelvin Hall, 1 Bunhouse Rd, Glasgow, G3 8DP; tel. (141) 287-2720; fax (141) 287-2692; e-mail museums@csglasgow.org; internet www.glasgowmuseums.com; f. 1964; history of transport and technology; displays incl. Glasgow trams and buses, Scottish-built cars, commercial vehicles, cycles and motor cycles, railway locomotives, fire engines, horse-drawn vehicles, ship models; toy cars, prams, the oldest surviving pedal cycle in the world and a reproduction of a typical Glasgow street of 1938; Manager LAWRENCE FITZGERALD.

People's Palace and Winter Gardens: Glasgow Green, Glasgow, G40 1AT; tel. (141) 271-2962; fax (141) 271-2960; e-mail museums@csglasgow.org; internet www.glasgowmuseums.com; f. 1898; local and social history museum; story of the city of Glasgow and its inhabitants since 1750; the Winter Gardens houses exotic palms and plants; Curator FIONA HAYES.

Pollok House: Pollok Country Park, 2060 Pollokshaws Rd, Glasgow, G43 1AT; tel. (844) 493-2202; fax (844) 493-2203; e-mail pollokhouse@nts.org.uk; internet www.nts.org.uk; 18th-century Palladian house with Edwardian additions, furnished c. 1750–1820 and with Stirling Maxwell colln of Spanish and European paintings; managed by the Nat. Trust of Scotland on behalf of Glasgow Museums; Property Man. IAN MCGREEVY (acting); Admin. Asst ALISON SIMMS.

Provand's Lordship: 3 Castle St, Glasgow, G4 0RB; tel. (141) 276-1625; fax (141) 276-1626; e-mail museums@glasgowlife.org.uk; internet www.glasgowlife.org.uk/museums; built 1471, the oldest house in Glasgow, with period room displays; home to the St Nicholas Garden, a herb garden containing 15th-century medicinal plants, the Tontine Faces (colln of carved stone faces originally carved for the new Town Hall 1740); Man. SANDRA EWIRI.

St Mungo Museum of Religious Life and Art: 2 Castle St, Glasgow, G4 0RH; tel. (141) 276-1625; fax (141) 276-1626; e-mail museums@glasgowlife.org.uk; internet www.glasgowlife.org.uk/museums; f. 1993; art objects associated with religious faiths; displays on religion in art, world faiths, religion in Scottish history; permanent Zen garden; Man. SANDRA EWIRI.

Scotland Street School Museum: 225 Scotland St, Glasgow, G5 8QB; tel. (141) 287-0500; fax (141) 287-0515; e-mail museums@csglasgow.org; internet www.glasgowmuseums.com; f. 1906; designed by Charles Rennie Mackintosh between 1903 and 1906; history of Scotland Street Public School, and developments in education in Scotland; reconstructed classrooms from the Victorian period, World War II, the 1950s and 1960s; colln of old school photographs; Curator, Decorative Arts ALISON BROWN; Curator, Costumes and Textiles REBECCA QUINTON.

Hunterian Museum and Art Gallery: University of Glasgow Main/Gilbert-Scott Bldg, University Ave, Glasgow, G12 8QQ; tel. (141) 330-4221; fax (141) 330-3617; e-mail hunter@museum.gla.ac.uk; internet www.hunterian.gla.ac.uk; f. 1807; based around the collns of the Surgeon Extraordinary to Queen Charlotte, William Hunter (1718–83); geological, prehistoric, Roman, ethnographical and coin collns, scientific instruments; zoological, anatomical and pathological collns in univ. depts of Zoology, Anatomy and Pathology; books and MSS in univ. library; Dir EWEN SMITH.

Attached Gallery:

Hunterian Art Gallery: University of Glasgow, 82 Hillhead St, Glasgow, G12 8QQ; tel. (141) 330-5431; fax (141) 330-3618; e-mail hunter@museum.gla.ac.uk; internet www.gla.ac.uk/museum; f. 1980; collns of C. R. Mackintosh and J. M. Whistler; works by Chardin, Stubbs and Reynolds; Scottish painting since the 18th century; Old Master and modern prints; Dir EWEN SMITH.

Gloucester

City Museum and Art Gallery: Brunswick Rd, Gloucester, GL1 1HP; tel. (1452) 396131; fax (1452) 410898; e-mail city.museum@gloucester.gov.uk; internet www.gloucester.gov.uk; f. 1859; natural history, archaeology (before AD 1500), fine and applied art; temporary art, science, archaeology, natural sciences and textile exhibitions; collns online at livinggloucester.co.uk.

Gloucester Folk Museum: 99–103 Westgate St, Gloucester, GL1 2PG; tel. (1452) 396868; fax (1452) 330495; e-mail folk.museum@gloucester.gov.uk; internet www.gloucester.gov.uk/folkmuseum; f. 1935; local history, crafts, trades and industries of City and County of Gloucester since 1500; housed in Tudor and Jacobean timber-framed buildings with new extensions; regular special exhibitions, activities and events; social history reference colln (access by appointment); Man. CHRIS MORRIS.

Grasmere

Dove Cottage and the Wordsworth Museum: Dove Cottage, Grasmere, Ambleside, LA22 9SH; tel. (1539) 435544; fax (1539) 435748; e-mail enquiries@wordsworth.org.uk; internet www.wordsworth.org.uk; f. 1890; fmr home of William and Dorothy Wordsworth and, later, of Thomas de Quincey; contains original furniture and personal effects, and a museum containing MSS, books, paintings, diaries, letters, poetry books, manuscripts as well as personal items, clothing, pictures, sculptures, objects relating to the poet, and to Grasmere life of the period; library: major research library for the Romantic period, The Jerwood Centre; access by appointment; Dir MICHAEL MCGREGOR.

Grays

Thurrock Museum: Thameside Complex, Orsett Rd, Grays, RM17 5DX; tel. (1375) 413965; fax (1375) 392666; e-mail thurrock.museum@thurrock.gov.uk; internet www.thurrock.gov.uk/museum; f. 1956; archaeology and history of Thurrock with accent on the growth of technology in a Thameside landscape; Museum and Heritage Officer JONATHAN CATTON.

Haverfordwest

Pembrokeshire Museum Service: The County Library, Dew St, Haverfordwest, Pembs., SA61 1SU; tel. (1437) 779500; fax (1437) 779500; internet www.pembrokeshire.gov.uk; f. 1967; Museums Officer NICK SUFFOLK.

Attached Museums:

Penrhos Cottage: Pembrokeshire Museum Service, The County Library, Dew St, Haverfordwest, Pembs., SA61 1SU; Llanycefn, Clunderwen; tel. (1437) 779500; fax (1437) 779500; f. 1971; traditional thatched Welsh cottage with original furniture; open by appointment only; Museums Officer NICK SUFFOLK.

Scolton Manor Museum: Spittal, Haverfordwest; tel. (1437) 731328; fax (1437) 779500; f. 1972; regional history of Pembrokeshire; includes period rooms in early Victorian manor, World War II exhibition, railway exhibits, geology, river fishing, coal mining, servant life, costume; history of the domestic iron; Museums Officer NICK SUFFOLK.

High Wycombe

National Trust, Hughenden Manor: Hughenden Manor, High Wycombe, Bucks., HP14 4LA; tel. (1494) 755573; fax (1494) 474284; e-mail hughenden@nationaltrust.org.uk; internet www.nationaltrust.org.uk/hughendenmanor; f. 1947; Disraeli's country estate; contains Disraeli's books, furniture, paintings and personal effects; property of the National Trust (*q.v.*); library of 4,000 vols; Gen Man. JIM FOY; Regional Curator LUCY PORTEN.

Huddersfield

Tolson Memorial Museum: Ravensknowle Park, Wakefield Rd, Huddersfield, HD5 8DJ; tel. (1484) 223830; fax (1484) 223843; e-mail tolson.museum@kirklees.gov.uk; f. 1922; illustrates natural and human history of the district; prehistory, folk-life, development of woollen industry; colln of costume and textiles, decorative and applied art, music, weapons and war, coins and medals, personalities, science and technology, vehicles.

Ironbridge

Ironbridge Gorge Museums: Coach Rd, Coalbrookdale, Shropshire, TF8 7DQ; tel. (1952) 884391; fax (1952) 435999; e-mail information@ironbridge.org.uk; internet www.ironbridge.org.uk; f. 1968; explains and interprets the industrial and social history of the East Shropshire Coalfield, regarded as the 'Birthplace of the Industrial Revolution'; 6-mile site on the River Severn comprising: Coalbrookdale Museum of Iron and Darby Furnace, Ironbridge with the Museum of the Gorge, the world's first Iron Bridge (built 1779), Blists Hill Victorian Town, Coalport China Museum, Jackfield Tile Museum, Ironbridge Institute at Coalbrookdale, Rosehill and Dale House (restored home of the Darby family), Tar Tunnel (200-year-old source of natural bitumen), Broseley Pipeworks, 'Enginuity' (engineering and technological exhibits); designated a World Heritage Site by UNESCO; library of 50,000 vols; Chief Exec. STEVE MILLER.

Kendal

Abbot Hall Art Gallery and Museum of Lakeland Life & Industry: Kendal, LA9 5AL; tel. (1539) 722464; e-mail info@abbothall.org.uk; internet www.abbothall.org.uk; f. 1962 (gallery), 1971 (museum); gallery provides changing exhibitions of local and int. interest; houses permanent collns of 18th-century furniture, paintings and *objets d'art*, modern paintings, sculpture and drawings; museum features the working and social life of the area; Chief Exec. GORDON WATSON; Dir EDWARD KING.

Attached Museum:

Blackwell, The Arts & Crafts House: Bowness-on-Windermere, Cumbria, LA23 3JT; tel. (1539) 446139; fax (1539) 488486; e-mail info@blackwell.org.uk; internet www.blackwell.org.uk; f. 2001; bldg designed by Baillie Scott and built 1898–1900; period house with Arts and Crafts interiors and exhibitions of historic and contemporary crafts; Dir EDWARD KING.

Kendal Museum of Natural History and Archaeology: Station Rd, Kendal, Cumbria, LA9 6BT; tel. (1539) 721374; fax (1539) 737976; e-mail info@kendalmuseum.org.uk; internet www.kendalmuseum.org.uk; f. 1796; Westmorland Gallery of local history and archaeology, World Wildlife gallery, Natural History gallery of geology, flora and fauna of the district; Curator MORAG CLEMENT.

Kirkcaldy

Kirkcaldy Museum and Art Gallery: War Memorial Gardens, Kirkcaldy, Fife, KY1 1YG; tel. (1592) 583213; e-mail kirkcaldy.museum@fife.gov.uk; internet www.fifedirect.org.uk/museums; f. 1925; local history, archaeology, earth and natural sciences, industrial history, decorative arts, costume, ceramics; Scottish paintings since 19th century; Service Devt Man., Heritage and Art DALLAS MECHAN.

Leeds

Leeds Museums and Galleries: Carlisle Road, Hunslet, Leeds, LS10 1LB; tel. (113) 224-4370; e-mail museumsandgalleries@leeds.gov.uk; internet www.leeds.gov.uk/museumsandgalleries; f. 1820; Dir TIM CORUM; publ. *Museums and Galleries Review* (1 a year).

Selected Museums and Galleries:

Abbey House Museum: Abbey Walk, Kirkstall, Leeds, LS5 3EH; tel. (113) 230-5492; fax (113) 230-5499; e-mail abbey.house@leeds.gov.uk; internet www.leeds.gov.uk/abbeyhouse; f. 1927; gatehouse of Kirkstall Abbey (www.leeds.gov.uk/kirkstallabbey), recreation of Victorian Leeds; Curator SAMANTHA FLAVIN.

Armley Mills (Leeds Industrial Museum): Canal Rd, Armley, Leeds, LS12 2QF; tel. (113) 263-7861; fax (113) 263-7861; e-mail armley.mills@leeds.gov.uk; internet www.leeds.gov.uk/armleymills; f. 1969; textiles, printing, cinematography, history of engine and locomotive manufacturing in Leeds; manager's and mill-workers' houses; Keeper NINA BAPTISTE.

Leeds Art Gallery: The Headrow, Leeds, LS1 3AA; tel. (113) 247-8256; e-mail city.art.gallery@leeds.gov.uk; internet www.leeds.gov.uk/artgallery; f. 1888; 19th-century English and European paintings; early English watercolours, incl. Kitson and Lupton collns; modern paintings and sculpture; library: Print Room and Art Library; linked with Henry Moore Institute Archive and Library supporting the study of sculpture; Curator, Contemporary Art NIGEL WALSH.

Lotherton Hall: Lotherton Lane, Aberford, Leeds, LS25 3EB; tel. (113) 281-3259; fax (113) 281-2100; internet www.leeds.gov.uk/lothertonhall; f. 1969; country house dating from the 19th and 20th centuries; Gascoigne Colln of furniture, silver, ceramics, costume and paintings from the 17th to 19th centuries; modern crafts; oriental gallery; Curator ADAM WHITE.

Temple Newsam House: Temple Newsam Rd, off Selby Rd, Leeds, LS15 0AE; tel. (113) 264-5535; fax (113) 260-2285; e-mail temple.newsam@leeds.gov.uk; internet www.leeds.gov.uk/templenewsam; f. 1923; Tudor-Stuart house, birthplace of Lord Darnley; contains extensive collns of old master and Ingram family paintings and the decorative arts; Curators ANTHONY WELLS-COLE, JAMES LOMAX.

Royal Armouries Museum: Armouries Dr., Leeds, LS10 1LT; tel. (113) 220-1999; fax (113) 220-1955; e-mail enquiries@armouries.org.uk; internet www.royalarmouries.org; f. 1996; nat. colln of arms and armour and artillery; Dir Gen. Dr JONATHON RILEY; Chief Exec. JANICE MURRAY; publ. *Arms and Armour: Journal of the Royal Armouries*.

Leicester

Leicestershire Museums: Leicestershire County Council, Leicester Rd, Glenfield, Leicester, LE3 8TB; tel. (116) 305-6642; fax (116) 265-6844; e-mail museums@leics.gov.uk; internet www.leics.gov.uk/museums; f. 1849; local museums incl. Charnwood Museum, Donington-le-Heath Manor House, Harborough Museum, Melton Carnegie Museum, Snibston Discovery Park and the Record Office at Wigston Magna; Leicester 'Open Museum' comprises exhibits for hire within the county; museums concentrate on archaeology, natural life, cultural life, working life, Leicestershire history and education; Head Y. C. COURTNEY.

National Space Centre: Exploration Dr., Leicester, LE4 5NS; fax (116) 261-0261; e-mail info@spacecentre.co.uk; internet www.spacecentre.co.uk; f. 2001; displays about space and space exploration; incl. space science research unit; Chief Exec. CHAS BISHOP.

Lincoln

Lincolnshire Heritage Services: Cultural Services Branch, Lincolnshire County Council Offices, Newland, Lincoln, LN1 1YQ; tel. (1522) 552222; e-mail education@lincolnshire.gov.uk; internet www.lincolnshire.gov.uk; f. 1974; operates 7 museums (see below) and several other sites, incl. Lincoln Castle, Judge's Lodgings, Battle of Britain Memorial Flight Visitor Centre, Lincolnshire Archives, and windmills in Alford, Burgh le Marsh, Heckington and Lincoln; Head of Heritage and Regeneration HEATHER CUMMINS.

Attached Museums:

Church Farm Museum: Church Rd South, Skegness, PE25 2HF; tel. (1754) 766658; fax (1754) 898243; e-mail info@churchfarmvillage.org.uk; f. 1976; a complex of 18th- and 19th-century farmhouse and agricultural bldgs with displays of agricultural equipment typical of the area; farmhouse furnished to period c. 1900; Chair. STEVE KIRK.

The Collection: Art and Archaeology in Lincolnshire: Danes Terrace, Lincoln, LN2 1LP; tel. (1522) 550990; fax (1522) 550991; e-mail thecollection@lincolnshire.gov.uk; internet www.thecollection.lincoln.museum; f. 1906 as City and County Museum, present status 2005; comprises exhibits from the former City and County Museum (artefacts since medieval era, incl. collns of coins, medals, arms and natural science) and the Usher Gallery (fine, decorative and contemporary arts); Collns Officer DAWN HEYWOOD; Collns Officer ANTONY LEE.

Gainsborough Old Hall: Parnell St, Gainsborough, DN21 2NB; tel. (1427) 612669; fax (1427) 612779; e-mail gainsborougholdhall@lincolnshire.gov.uk; internet www.lincolnshire.gov.uk/gainsborougholdhall; f. 1974; 15th-century timber framed manor house with great hall, medieval kitchen; guided tours; events and exhibits; heritage education programme; Site Coordinator VICTORIA MASON.

Grantham Museum: St Peter's Hill, Grantham, NG31 6PY; tel. (1476) 568783; fax (1476) 592457; e-mail grantham.museum@lincolnshire.gov.uk; f. 1923; local prehistoric artefacts, Roman and Saxon archaeology, Grantham local history, trades and industries, display of Victorian dolls, and a colln devoted to notable figures born locally, incl. Sir Isaac Newton and Margaret Thatcher; District Man. NICOLA ROGERS.

Museum of Lincolnshire Life: Burton Rd, Lincoln, LN1 3LY; tel. (1522) 528448; fax (1522) 521264; e-mail lincolnshire_museum@lincolnshire.gov.uk; f. 1969; displays illustrating the social, agricultural and industrial history of Lincolnshire over the 17th–20th centuries; also contains Lincolnshire Regiment Museum; manages the Ellis Windmill; Dist. Man. N. ROGERS.

Stamford Museum: Broad St, Stamford, PE9 1PJ; tel. (1780) 766317; fax (1780) 480363; e-mail stamford_museum@lincolnshire.gov.uk; internet www.lincolnshire.gov.uk/stamfordmuseum; f. 1980; local archaeology and history incl. Stamford Ware pottery, the visit of Daniel Lambert and the Stamford Tapestry; Site Coordinator LEA RICKARD.

Usher Gallery: Lindum Rd, Lincoln, LN2 1NN; tel. (1522) 527980; fax (1522) 550991; e-mail usher.gallery@lincolnshire.gov.uk; internet www.thecollection.lincoln.museum; houses the Usher colln of watches, miniatures and decorative art, and a colln of fine art, sculpture and coins, incl. works by De Wint, Lowry, Turner and contemporary artists Grayson Perry and Terry Frost; attached to The Collection (county archaeological collns; see above); Area Service Man. JEREMY WEBSTER.

Liverpool

National Museums Liverpool: 127 Dale St, Liverpool,; tel. and fax (151) 207-0001; internet www.liverpoolmuseums.org.uk; f. 1986 as Nat. Museums and Galleries on Merseyside, present name 2003; groups the 7 museums of Liverpool, incl. the Museum of Liverpool; Dir DAVID FLEMING.

Constituent Museums and Galleries:

Lady Lever Art Gallery: Port Sunlight Village, Wirral, CH62 5EQ; tel. (151) 478-4136; internet www.liverpoolmuseums.org.uk/ladylever; f. 1922; colln of British 18th- and 19th-century paintings, 18th-century furniture; colln of Wedgewood and Chinese porcelain.

Merseyside Maritime Museum: Albert Dock, Liverpool, L3 4AQ; tel. (151) 478-4499; fax (151) 478-4590; internet www.liverpoolmuseums.org.uk/maritime; f. 1980; set in Liverpool's docklands; displays and exhibits on the region's maritime past; gallery of maritime paintings; library: reference library of maritime material, incl. archives and records.

National Conservation Centre: Whitechapel, Liverpool, L1 6HZ; tel. (151) 478-4999; internet www.liverpoolmuseums.org.uk; f. 1996; illustrates the arts and science of the conservation of museum exhibits; depts of ceramics, conservation science, frames, metals, organics, paintings, paper, sculpture, shipkeeping, taxidermy and textiles; Head of Conservation SALLY ANN YATES.

Seized! Border and Customs Uncovered: Merseyside Maritime Museum, Albert Dock, Liverpool, L3 4AQ; tel. (151) 478-4499; internet www.liverpoolmuseums.org.uk/maritime; f. 1994 fmrly HM Customs and Excise National Museum; exhibits relating to smuggling and revenue colln since 1700; holds nat. colln of Dept of Customs and Excise and UK Border Agency; displays of equipment, prints, paintings and photographs; Press Assist. ALISON CORNMELL.

Sudley House: Mossley Hill Rd, Liverpool; tel. (151) 724-3245; internet www.liverpoolmuseums.org.uk; f. 1986; fmr home of 19th-century shipowner; 18th- and 19th-century art incl. works by Gainsborough, Landseer and artists of the Pre-Raphaelite movement; Dir of Art Galleries REYAHN KING.

Walker Art Gallery: William Brown St, Liverpool L3 8EL; tel. (151) 478-4199; fax (151) 478-4190; internet www.liverpoolmuseums.org.uk/walker; collns of European art since 1300; sculpture gallery; Keeper JULIAN TREUHERZ.

World Museum Liverpool: William Brown St, Liverpool, L3 8EN; tel. (151) 478-4399; fax (151) 478-4390; internet www.liverpoolmuseums.org.uk/wml; f. 1851, rebuilt 1964–69, present name 2005; spec. collns incl. the Mayer-Fejérváry Gothic ivories, the Bryan Fausset group of Anglo-Saxon antiquities, the Lord Derby and Tristram ornithological collns; bug house, aquarium, ethnology, time and space gallery, planetarium, Clore natural history centre, Weston discovery centre; Dir Dr STEVE JUDD.

London

Bank of England Museum: Threadneedle St, London, EC2R 8AH; tel. (20) 7601-5545; fax (20) 7601-5808; e-mail museum@bankofengland.co.uk; internet www.bankofengland.co.uk/education/museum; f. 1694; illustrates the history of the Bank and its current work; collns incl. banknotes and coins, furniture, pictures and photographs, silver; Curator JOHN KEYWORTH.

British Museum: Great Russell St, London, WC1B 3DG; tel. (20) 7323-8000; e-mail information@thebritishmuseum.ac.uk; internet www.thebritishmuseum.ac.uk; f. 1753 in pursuance of the will of Sir Hans Sloane, and with the addition of the Cottonian and Harleian Libraries; opened 1759, present bldgs begun 1823, completed 1852; collns and exhibitions of prehistoric, Egyptian, Assyrian, medieval, oriental and other archaeological collns, ethnography, prints, drawings, ceramics, coins, medals and banknotes;

many catalogues and reproductions are published; Chair. of Board of Trustees NIALL FITZGERALD; Dir NEIL MACGREGOR; Keepers of Depts JONATHAN KING (Africa, Oceania and the Americas), VIVIAN DAVIES (Ancient Egypt and Sudan), Dr JOHN CURTIS (Ancient Near East), JAN STUART (Asia), JOE CRIBB (Coins and Medals), DAVID SAUNDERS (Conservation, Documentation and Scientific Research), Dr DYFRI WILLIAMS (Greek and Roman Antiquities), JONATHAN WILLIAMS (Prehistory and Europe), ANTHONY GRIFFITHS (Prints and Drawings).

British Postal Museum & Archive: Freeling House, Phoenix Place, London, WC1X 0DL; tel. (20) 7239-2570; fax (20) 7239-2576; e-mail info@postalheritage.org.uk; internet www.postalheritage.org.uk; f. 1966; colln of stamps, essays, drawings and official documents dating back to Rowland Hill's proposals for Uniform Penny Postage in 1837–39; also the Post Office collection of stamps of the world and of British stamps since the early 20th century, and the philatelic archives (1855–1965) of Thomas De La Rue and Co., security printers, on microfilm; postboxes and other postal exhibits; Dir ADRIAN STEEL.

Carlyle's House: 24 Cheyne Row, Chelsea, London, SW3 5HL; tel. (20) 7352-7087; e-mail carlyleshouse@nationaltrust.org.uk; built 1708; occupied by the Victorian writer, Thomas Carlyle (1834–81) and his wife Jane; National Trust property; contains books, paintings, furniture, and personal relics.

Courtauld Gallery: Somerset House, Strand, London, WC2R 0RN; tel. (20) 7848-2526; fax (20) 7848-2589; e-mail galleryinfo@courtauld.ac.uk; internet www.courtauld.ac.uk/gallery; f. 1932; Old Master, Impressionist and Post-Impressionist paintings, prints and drawings, (incl. works by Botticelli, Cézanne, Goya, Manet, Michelangelo, Rembrandt, Renoir, Rubens, Tiepolo, Turner and Van Gogh); sculpture and applied arts; Head Dr ERNST VEGELIN.

Cuming Museum (Borough of Southwark): 151 Walworth Rd, London, SE17 1RS; tel. (20) 7525-2332; fax (20) 7525-2345; e-mail cuming.museum@southwark.gov.uk; internet www.southwark.gov.uk; f. 1906; worldwide collns of the Cuming family joined with the local history of Southwark, from Roman times to the present; Collns Man. DEYAN SUDJIC.

Design Museum: Butler's Wharf, 28 Shad Thames, London, SE1 2YD; tel. (20) 7403-6933; fax (20) 7378-6540; internet www.designmuseum.org; f. 1981; ind. museum set up by the Conran Foundation, to promote awareness of the importance of design in education, industry, commerce and culture; colln of mass-produced design; Chair. LUQMAN ARNOLD; Dir DEYAN SUDJIC.

Dulwich Picture Gallery: Gallery Rd, London, SE21 7AD; tel. (20) 8693-5254; fax (20) 8299-8700; e-mail enquiries@dulwichpicturegallery.org.uk; internet www.dulwichpicturegallery.org.uk; f. 1811; houses colln of Old Masters incl. Rembrandt, Rubens, Cuyp, Van Dyck, Teniers, Poussin, Claude, Watteau, Raphael, Tiepolo, Gainsborough, Murillo, etc.; schedule of temporary exhibitions and educational activities; Curator Dr. XAVIER BRAY; Dir IAN DEJARDIN.

Estorick Collection of Modern Italian Art: 39A Canonbury Sq., London, N1 2AN; tel. (20) 7704-9522; fax (20) 7704-9531; e-mail curator@estorickcollection.com; internet www.estorickcollection.com; f. 1998; 20th-century Italian art, especially Futurist; also sculpture; library of 2,000 vols, periodicals and catalogues: library open by appointment; Dir ROBERTA CREMONCINI.

Fashion and Textile Museum: 83 Bermondsey St, London, SE1 3XF; tel. (20) 7407-8664; fax (20) 7089-9416; e-mail info@ftmlondon.org; internet www.ftmlondon.org; f. 2003; British and world fashion and textile design; Operations Man. CHRISTOPHER LEE.

Foundling Museum: 40 Brunswick Sq., London, WC1N 1AZ; tel. (20) 7841-3600; fax (20) 7841-3601; e-mail enquiries@foundlingmuseum.org.uk; internet www.foundlingmuseum.org.uk; f. 2004; documents history of the Foundling Hospital (f. 1739), London's first home for abandoned children, and of its founder, philanthropist Thomas Coram, artist William Hogarth and composer George Frideric Handel; collns of art, social history and music in a restored and refurbished bldg adjacent to the original site of the Hospital; Chair. Dr ALAN BORG; Dir LARS THARP.

Freud Museum: 20 Maresfield Gardens, London, NW3 5SX; tel. (20) 7435-2002; fax (20) 7431-5452; e-mail info@freud.org.uk; internet www.freud.org.uk; f. 1986; fmr London home of Sigmund Freud and his daughter Anna; incl. Sigmund Freud's colln of antiquities, including 1,500 Egyptian, Greek, Roman and Oriental antiquities; his psychoanalytical couch, library and furniture; also a psychoanalysis research centre; library of 1,600 vols from Sigmund Freud's colln; reference library relating to the history of psychoanalysis; archive containing Freud family documents and photographs; Dir CAROL SEIGEL; Librarian KEITH DAVIES.

Geffrye Museum: 136 Kingsland Rd, London, E2 8EA; tel. (20) 7739-9893; fax (20) 7729-5647; e-mail info@geffrye-museum.org.uk; internet www.geffrye-museum.org.uk; f. 1914; English furniture, textiles, domestic objects and paintings arranged in a series of period rooms from 1600–2000; herb and period gardens; library: reference library of books and periodicals on the arts and social history; Dir DAVID DEWING.

Hampton Court Palace: Surrey, KT8 9AU; tel. (844) 482-7777; e-mail hamptoncourt@hrp.org.uk; internet www.hrp.org.uk; home of Henry VIII, contains a collection of paintings and tapestries, including Andrea Mantegna's nine great tempera paintings of 'The Triumphs of Julius Caesar'; Palace Dir RODNEY GIDDINS; Superintendent of the Royal Collection C. STEVENS.

Hayward Gallery: South Bank Centre, Belvedere Rd, London, SE1 8XZ; tel. (20) 7921-08138; fax (20) 7401-2664; e-mail hginfo@hayward.org.uk; internet www.hayward.org.uk; f. 1968; contemporary perspectives on art past and present, focusing on individual artists, historical themes and artistic movements, other cultures, and contemporary art; administers national touring exhibitions and the Arts Council Collection (7,500 items); Dir CAROLINE FELTON (acting).

Horniman Museum and Gardens: 100 London Rd, Forest Hill, London, SE23 3PQ; tel. (20) 8699-1872; fax (20) 8291-5506; e-mail enquiry@horniman.ac.uk; internet www.horniman.ac.uk; f. 1901; three major collns: ethnography, natural history and musical instruments (incl. archive documents); Aquarium; 16 acres of gardens; education activities with schools, community groups and individual researchers; library of 35,000 vols, mainly on African history, entomology, botany, ethnography, natural history, incl. ecology, sustainabilty, and musical instruments; Dir JANET VITMAYER.

Hunterian Museum at the Royal College of Surgeons: 35–43 Lincoln's Inn Fields, London, WC2A 3PE; tel. (20) 7869-6560; fax (20) 7869-6564; e-mail museums@rcseng.ac.uk; internet www.rcseng.ac.uk/museums; f. 1800, built around the colln of anatomist and surgeon John Hunter (1728–93); collns of comparative anatomy and pathology specimens, skeletons, skulls and teeth, teaching models, historical surgical and dental instruments, paintings, drawings and sculpture; temporary exhibitions, lectures, family events and educational workshops; Dir of Museums and Archives Dr SAMUEL ALBERTI; Curator (vacant) SARAH PEARSON; Head of Conservation Unit MARTYN COOKE.

Imperial War Museum: Lambeth Rd, London, SE1 6HZ; tel. (20) 7416-5320; fax (20) 7416-5374; e-mail mail@iwm.org.uk; internet www.iwm.org.uk; f. 1917, to illustrate and record the operations in which the Armed Forces of the British Commonwealth have been engaged since 1914; nat. museum and picture gallery; contains many exhibits on all aspects of war, incl. 19,000 works of art, 6m. photographs, 120m. ft of film and 46,000 hours of sound and video recordings; library of 270,000 items, incl. pamphlets, periodicals, maps and drawings; Chair. of the Board of Trustees Sir PETER SQUIRE; Dir-Gen. DIANE LEES; publ. *Imperial War Museum Review* (1 a year).

Branches:

Churchill Museum and Cabinet War Rooms: Clive Steps, King Charles St, London, SW1A 2AQ; tel. (20) 7766-0120; fax (20) 7839-5897; e-mail cwr@iwm.org.uk; internet cwr.iwm.org.uk; Churchill's underground headquarters; incorporates the Churchill Museum (churchillmuseum.iwm.org.uk), exploring the life of Winston Churchill (1874–1965); Dir P. REED.

HMS Belfast: Morgans Lane, Tooley St, London, SE1 2JH; tel. (20) 7940-6300; fax (20) 7403-0719; internet hmsbelfast.iwm.org.uk; Second World War cruiser moored in the Pool of London; Dir E. J. WENZEL.

Imperial War Museum Duxford: Duxford, Cambridgeshire, CB22 4QR; tel. (1223) 835000; fax (1223) 837267; e-mail duxford@iwm.org.uk; internet www.iwm.org.uk/duxford; f. 1977; airfield that featured in the Battle of Britain (1940), housing historic colln of aircraft, military vehicles, tanks and artillery; incl. American Air Museum (aam.iwm.org.uk); interactive exhibitions; Dir RICHARD ASHTON.

Imperial War Museum North: The Quays, Trafford Wharf Rd, Manchester, M17 1TZ; tel. (161) 836-4000; fax (161) 836-4090; e-mail iwmnorth@iwm.org.uk; internet www.iwm.org.uk/north; f. 2002; war and its impact on the 20th and 21st centuries, through exhibits, audiovisual shows and interactive exhibits and a changing programme of events; Dir JIM FORRESTER.

Iveagh Bequest: Kenwood, Hampstead Lane, London, NW3 7JR; tel. (20) 8348-1286; left to the nation by Edward Cecil Guinness, first Earl of Iveagh, in 1927; includes paintings of British, Dutch, Flemish and French Schools, housed in an 18th-century mansion (Kenwood House) designed by Robert Adam, containing an ornate library; exhibitions on aspects of 18th-century art; Admin. Trustee English Heritage (HBMC); Dir of E. H. London Region RICHARD FREELAND; publs catalogues.

London Transport Museum: 39 Wellington St, Covent Garden, London, WC2E 7BB; tel. (20) 7379-6344; fax (20) 7565-7254; e-mail enquiry@ltmuseum.co.uk; internet www.ltmuseum.co.uk; f. 1978, opened on present site 1980; governing body: Transport for London; conserves and explains London's transport heritage; exhibits of vehicles, posters, equipment, uniforms, film, photographs, maps, signs and models; film and photo library; library of 12,000 books, journals and spec. collns on the history and devt of Londons's transport from 1800 to the present day, incl. art, design and architecture; 100 current journals; Dir SAM MULLINS.

Museum of London: London Wall, London, EC2Y 5HN; tel. (20) 7001-9844; fax (20) 7600-1058; e-mail info@museumoflondon.org.uk; internet www.museumoflondon.org.uk; formed from amalgamation of London Museum and Guildhall Museum; social history of London from prehistory to 20th century; exhibits include the Lord Mayor's coach, 18th-century prison cell, Victorian shop fronts; Chair. of Board of Govs MICHAEL CASSIDY; Dir Prof. JACK LOHMAN.

National Army Museum: Royal Hospital Rd, Chelsea, London, SW3 4HT; tel. (20) 7730-0717; fax (20) 7823-6573; internet www.nam.ac.uk; f. 1960; displays depicting the history of the British Army since 1066 until the present day, the Indian Army until Independence in 1947, and colonial land forces; reference collections of 43,000 books, 30,000 pamphlets, 1,000 ft of archives, 50,000 prints, drawings and watercolours, 5,000,000 photographs; 80,000 uniforms, 250,000 badges; 20,000 medals and weapons; personal equipment and a sound and film archive; Dir Dr ALAN J. GUY.

National Gallery: Trafalgar Sq., London, WC2N 5DN; tel. (20) 7747-2885; fax (20) 7747-2423; e-mail information@ng-london.org.uk; internet www.nationalgallery.org.uk; f. 1824; contains examples of all the principal schools of Western European painting from 1250 to 1900; a selection of British painters from Hogarth to Turner; guided tours and public lectures; picture library; Chair. MARK GETTY; Senior Curator DAVID JAFFÉ; Dir of Collections SUSAN FOISTER; Dir of Conservation LARRY KEITH; Dir of Scientific Research Dr ASHOK ROY.

National Maritime Museum: Park Row, Greenwich, London, SE10 9NF; tel. (20) 8858-6516; fax (20) 8312-6599; internet www.nmm.ac.uk; f. 1934; opened 1937; illustrates British maritime history; the collection includes portraits and sea pieces, models, ship's plans, instruments, maps and charts, weapons, medals, a library of books and MSS; photo library of 330,000 images and negatives; Queen's House: 17th-century royal apartments of Queen Henrietta Maria; also the Royal Observatory Greenwich, where the displays illustrate themes concerned with astronomy, time and navigation, the meridian line, and a planetarium; library of 20,000 vols on maritime history; Dir ROY CLARE; publ. *Journal for Maritime Research*.

National Portrait Gallery: St Martin's Pl., London, WC2H 0HE; tel. (20) 7306-0055; fax (20) 7306-0056; internet www.npg.org.uk; f. 1856; portraits of the most eminent people in British history; library of 40,000 vols; Dir SANDY NAIRNE; Chair. of Trustees Prof. DAVID CANNADINE.

Natural History Museum: Cromwell Rd, South Kensington, London, SW7 5BD; tel. (20) 7942-5000; internet www.nhm.ac.uk; originates from the Natural History Depts of the British Museum, and a br. comprising the Natural History Museum at Tring, Herts.; separate instn 1963; incorporates the Geological Museum; library: see Libraries and Archives; Chair. of the Board of Trustees OLIVER STOCKEN; Dir (vacant); Science Dir RICHARD PAUL LANE; Keeper of Botany Dr JOHANNES VOGEL; Keeper of Entomology Dr MALCOLM SCOBLE; Keeper of Mineralogy Dr ANDREW FLEET; Keeper of Palaeontology Prof. NORMAN MACLEOD; Keeper of Zoology Prof. PHIL RAINBOW.

Polish Institute and Sikorski Museum: 20 Princes Gate, London, SW7 1PT; tel. (20) 7589-9249; f. 1945; archives, museum, research centre and publishing house; includes the Sikorski Collection (personal belongings, memorabilia, wartime diary, etc. of Gen. Wladyslaw Sikorski, 1881–1943), militaria (over 10,000 items), maps, paintings and engravings, sculptures, porcelain, miniatures, coins and medals.

Royal Academy of Arts: Burlington House, Piccadilly, London, W1J 0BD; tel. (20) 7300-8000; internet www.royalacademy.org.uk; f. 1768 by Joshua Reynolds, first President of the Academy; permanent colln includes works by Turner, Gainsborough, Reynolds and Hockney; temporary exhibitions of works borrowed from major instns worldwide; Pres. Sir NICHOLAS GRIMSHAW.

Royal Air Force Museum London: Grahame Park Way, London, NW9 5LL; tel. (20) 8205-2266; fax (20) 8200-1751; e-mail london@rafmuseum.org; internet www.rafmuseum.org; f. 1963, opened 1972; grant-aided through the Ministry of Defence; exhibits 100 full-size British and foreign aircraft from 1909 to the present day, together with supporting material recording the history of the Royal Air Force and the development of aviation generally; activities cover many aspects of aviation, including military, civil, artistic, scientific, industrial and political; br. at Cosford (West Midlands); library of 100,000 vols, and archives and photographic collection; Dir-Gen. PETER DYE.

Royal Armouries: HM Tower of London, London, EC3N 4AB; tel. (20) 7480-6358; fax (20) 7481-2922; e-mail enquiries@armouries.org.uk; internet www.royalarmouries.org and Royal Armouries Museum, Armouries Drive, Leeds, W. Yorks., LS10 1LT; tel. (113) 220-1999; fax (113) 220-1995 and Artillery Collection, Fort Nelson, Down End Rd, Portsdown Hill, Fareham, PO17 6AN; tel. (1329) 233734; fax (1329) 822092; the nat. museum of arms and armour and museum of the Tower of London, originating from the working arsenal at the Tower and the collection of royal armours begun by Henry VIII; first open to the public c. 1660; the national and royal collections cover the development of arms and armour since c. AD 1000; Leeds-based picture library of 167,000 prints, transparencies and slides; archives relating to the history of the museum and the Royal Small Arms Factory; library: Leeds-based reference library of 40,000 vols; also libraries at the Tower of London and Fort Nelson; Chief Exec. PAUL EVANS; Chair. ANN GREEN; Museum Dir PETER ARMSTRONG; publ. *Arms and Armour* (2 a year).

Royal College of Music Museum of Instruments: Prince Consort Rd, South Kensington, London, SW7 2BS; tel. (20) 7591-4842; fax (20) 7589-7740; e-mail museum@rcm.ac.uk; internet www.cph.rcm.ac.uk; f. 1970; colln of instruments and accessories since 1480, incl. Donaldson, Tagore, Hipkins, Ridley, Hartley, Fleming, Walton and Steele-Perkins collns; Curator JENNY NEX.

Royal Institution of Great Britain Michael Faraday Museum: 21 Albemarle St, London, W1S 4BS; tel. (20) 7409-2992; fax (20) 7670-2920; e-mail archivist@ri.ac.uk; internet www.rigb.org; f. 1799; contains original apparatus made and used by Faraday and other key scientists such as Humprhy Davy, John Tyndall and William and Lawrence Bragg; also incl. Faraday's magnetic laboratory, restored to the form it was known to have in 1845 and containing much of his apparatus; library of 30,000 vols (works on physics and chemistry since the 1700s); Head of Collns and Heritage Prof FRANK JAMES.

Saatchi Gallery: Duke of York's HQ, King's Rd, Sloane Sq., Chelsea, London, SW3 4SQ; internet www.saatchi-gallery.co.uk; f. 1985; colln of mostly modern art from contemporary British artists (incl. Damien Hirst, Tracey Emin, Sarah Lucas, Jenny Saville, Chapman brothers), new art from China; also exhibits work of lesser-known int. artists; Dir PHILLY ADAMS.

Science Museum: South Kensington, London, SW7 2DD; tel. (870) 870-4771; fax (20) 7942-4302; internet www.sciencemuseum.org.uk; f. 1857; official title the National Museum of Science and Industry; collns: Science, Medicine, Information and Communications Technologies, Engineering Technologies; Science Library: see Libraries and Archives; Dir Prof. CHRIS RAPLEY.

Sir John Soane's House and Museum: 13 Lincoln's Inn Fields, London, WC2A 3BP; tel. (20) 7440-4251; fax (20) 7831-3957; e-mail library@soane.org.uk; internet www.soane.org; f. 1837 (built by Sir John Soane 1812, est. by Act of Parliament for the promotion of the study of architecture and allied arts 1833); colln incl. paintings by Hogarth, the Egyptian Sarcophagus of Seti I, Italian bronzes, paintings, antique sculpture, 18th-century English sculpture, models, 30,000 architectural drawings; library: library: see Libraries and Archives; Dir TIM KNOX.

South London Gallery: 65 Peckham Rd, London, SE5 8UH; tel. (20) 7703-6120; fax (20) 7252-4730; e-mail mail@southlondongallery.org; internet www.southlondongallery.org; f. 1891; regular exhibitions of innovative contemporary art supported by a full programme of education events and workshops; Dir MARGOT HELLER; Programme Man. SIMON PARRIS.

Tate: Millbank, London, SW1P 4RG; tel. (20) 7887-8888; fax (20) 7887-8007; e-mail information@tate.org.uk; internet www.tate.org.uk; f. 1897; Dir Sir NICHOLAS SEROTA.

Constituent Museums:

Tate Britain: Millbank, London, SW1P 4RG; tel. (20) 7887-8008; fax (20) 7887-8007; e-mail information@tate.org.uk; internet www.tate.org.uk; f. 1897 by Sir Henry Tate; nat. gallery of British art since 1500, incl. works by Hogarth, Blake, Constable and the Pre-Raphaelites, with the Turner Collection housed in the Clore Gallery; Dir STEPHEN DEUCHAR..

Research Centre:

Tate Library and Archive: Hyman Kreitman Reading Rooms, Tate Britain, Millbank, London, SW1P 4RG; tel. (20) 7887-8838; fax (20) 7887-3952; e-mail reading.rooms@tate.org.uk; internet www.tate.org.uk/research/researchservices/readingrooms; f. 2002; library: art library and archive; Library colln (250,000 vols), covers British art from 1500 and international art from 1900; Archive colln (700 individual archives) covers British art from 1900, incl. unpublished material on British artists, art world figures and orgs; Gallery Records colln; exhibition catalogues, monographs, artists' books, ephemera; Head of Library and Archive JANE BRAMWELL.

Tate Liverpool: Albert Dock, Liverpool, L3 4BB; tel. (151) 702-7400; e-mail visiting.liverpool@tate.org.uk; internet www.tate.org.uk/liverpool; f. 1988; home of the Nat. Colln of Modern Art in the North; 4 floors displaying work selected from the Tate Colln and spec. exhibitions of artwork loaned from around the world; modern and contemporary art since 1900, incl. painting and sculpture, photography, video installations; tours and lectures; Dir CHRISTOPH GRUNENBERG.

Tate Modern: Bankside, London, SE1 9TG; tel. (20) 7887-8008; fax (20) 7887-8007; e-mail information@tate.org.uk; internet www.tate.org.uk; f. 2000; int. modern art since 1900; Dir VICENTE TODOLÍ.

Tate St Ives: Porthmeor Beach, St Ives, TR26 1TG; tel. (1736) 796226; e-mail tatestives@tate.org.uk; internet www.tate.org.uk; f. 1993; modern painting, sculpture and ceramics by artists associated with St Ives, as well as int. figures; incl. Barbara Hepworth Museum and Sculpture Garden; Dir SUSAN DANIEL-MCELROY.

Victoria and Albert (V&A) Museums:.

Constituent Museums:

Victoria and Albert Museum (V&A): South Kensington, London, SW7 2RL; tel. (20) 7942-2000; e-mail vanda@vam.ac.uk; internet www.vam.ac.uk; f. 1852; all forms of art and design, with collns of ceramics, furniture, fashion, glass, jewellery, metalwork, sculpture, textiles and paintings; library: library: see entry for Nat. Art Library; Dir MARK JONES; Keepers BETH MCKILLOP (Asian Dept), C. WILK (Furniture, Textiles and Fashion Dept), JULIUS BRYANT (Prints, Drawings and Painting/ Nat. Art Library Dept), Dr P. WILLIAMSON (Sculpture, Metalwork, Ceramics and Glass Dept).

V&A Department of Theatre and Performance—National Museum for the Performing Arts: Reading Room, Blythe House, 23 Blythe Rd, London, W14 0QX; tel. (20) 7942 2697; fax (20) 7471 9864; e-mail tmenquiries@vam.ac.uk; internet www.vam.ac.uk/page/t/theatre-and-performance; f. 1974, opened to the public 1987; nat. record of stage performance; history, craft and practice of the performing arts in Britain; library of 100,000 vols (incorporating British Theatre Asscn colln and library of the Soc. for Theatre Research); spec. archive collns incl. D'Oyly Carte Co, English Stage Co, Engish Shakespeare Co, Arts Council of Great Britain, Diaghilev's Ballets Russes and Edward Gordon Craig; spec. photographic archives incl. Houston Rogers, Gordon Anthony and Anthony Crickmay; Nat. Video Archive of Performance; Dir GEOFFREY MARSH.

V&A Museum of Childhood: Cambridge Heath Rd, London, E2 9PA; tel. (20) 8983-5200; fax (20) 8983-5225; e-mail moc@vam.ac.uk; internet www.vam.ac.uk/moc; f. 1872; children's toys, games, costume, nursery furniture; Chair. SAMIR SHAH; Dir RHIAN HARRIS.

Wallace Collection: Hertford House, Manchester Square, London, W1U 3BN; tel. (20) 7563-9500; fax (20) 7224-2155; e-mail enquiries@wallacecollection.org; internet www.wallacecollection.org; f. 1900; library of 15,000 vols; collns of 18th-century French pictures, furniture, Sèvres porcelain and sculpture, 17th-century paintings, armoury and *objets d'art*, bequeathed to the nation in 1897 by Lady Wallace; Dir ROSALIND SAVILL.

White Cube: 48 Hoxton Sq., London, N1 6PB; tel. (20) 7930-5373; fax (20) 7749-7480; e-mail enquiries@whitecube.com; internet www.whitecube.com; f. 2000; modern British art; Man. Dir JAY JOPLING.

Whitechapel Gallery: 77–82 Whitechapel High St, London, E1 7QX; tel. (20) 7522-7888; fax (20) 7377-1685; e-mail info@whitechapelgallery.org; internet www.whitechapelgallery.org; f. 1901, reopened in 2009; temporary exhibitions, principally of modern or contemporary art; no permanent colln; charitable trust supported by the Arts Council, local authorities, charitable bodies and the business community; Chair. of Trustees ROBERT TAYLOR; Dir IWONA BLAZWICK.

Manchester

Manchester City Galleries: Mosley St, Manchester, M2 3JL; tel. (161) 235-8888; fax (161) 235-8899; internet www.manchestergalleries.org; f. 1823; dept of Manchester City Ccl, operates 4 galleries in and around Manchester.

Constituent Galleries:

Gallery of Costume: Platt Hall, Rusholme, Manchester, M14 5LL; tel. (161) 245-7245; e-mail m.lambert@manchester.gov.uk; internet www.manchestergalleries.org; f. 1947; 18th-century fmr textile merchant's house; 20,000 items of clothing and fashion accessories from 17th century to the present; library of 20,000 vols, 25000 portrait photographs, fashion journals, tailoring and etiquette books, shop catalogues, paper patterns; Senior Man. Dr MILES LAMBERT.

Heaton Hall: Heaton Park, Prestwich, Manchester, M25 5SW; tel. (161) 773-2581; fax (161) 235-8805; e-mail galleryeducation@notes.manchester.gov.uk; internet www.manchestergalleries.org; Grade I listed, 18th-century neo-classical country house; interiors restored to illustrate life as it was in the late 18th and 19th centuries.

Manchester Art Gallery: Mosley St, Manchester, M2 3JL; tel. (161) 235-8888; fax (161) 235-8899; e-mail galleryeducation@notes.manchester.gov.uk; internet www.manchestergalleries.org; f. 2002 following re-organization of the fmr Manchester City Art Gallery; 25,000 items; fine art colln includes 2,000 oil paintings, 3,000 watercolours and drawings, 250 sculptures, 90 miniatures, 1,000 prints, notable works by the Pre-Raphaelites: Rossetti, Millais, Hunt, Burne-Jones; colln of decorative arts ranges from ancient Greek pottery to contemporary furniture; contemporary local art and design, incl. works by Lowry; gallery of craft and design.

Wythenshawe Hall: Wythenshawe Park, Northenden, Manchester, M23 0AB; tel. (161) 990-5083; fax (161) 235-8805; e-mail galleryeducation@notes.manchester.gov.uk; internet www.manchestergalleries.org; f. 1926; Tudor house.

Manchester Museum: Univ. of Manchester, Oxford Rd, Manchester, M13 9PL; tel. (161) 275-2634; fax (161) 275-2676; e-mail museum@manchester.ac.uk; internet www.manchester.ac.uk/museum; f. 1821; archaeology, Egyptology, ethnology, geology, botany, zoology, entomology, archery, numismatics; education and exhibition services; 15 galleries; public events for families and adults; Dir Dr NICHOLAS MERRIMAN.

Museum of Science and Industry in Manchester: Liverpool Rd, Castlefield, Manchester, M3 4FP; tel. (161) 832-2244; e-mail collections@msim.org.uk; internet www.msim.org.uk; f. 1983; housed in the world's oldest passenger railway station; explores the history, science and industry of Manchester, with displays focusing on textiles, communications, utilities, steam power and the railways, cameras, aircraft; Xperiment! (interactive science centre); Dir IAN GRIFFIN (acting).

Urbis: Cathedral Gardens, Manchester, M4 3BG; tel. (161) 605-8200; e-mail info@urbis.org.uk; internet www.urbis.org.uk; f. 2002; exhibits on social, historical and cultural aspects of city life, with interactive galleries; Learning Admin. ALEXIA ANTHONY.

Newcastle upon Tyne

Tyne and Wear Museums: Discovery Museum, Blandford Sq., Newcastle upon Tyne, NE1 4JA; tel. (191) 232-6789; fax (191) 230-2614; internet www.twmuseums.org.uk; f. 1974; Dir ALEC COLES.

Selected Museums and Galleries:

Arbeia Roman Fort: Baring St, South Shields, NE33 2BB; tel. (191) 456-1369; fax (191) 427-6862; internet www.twmuseums.org.uk/arbeia; f. 1953; Roman coins, military equipment, pottery, jewellery; excavations and reconstructions; Curator ALEX CROOM.

Discovery Museum: Blandford Sq., Newcastle upon Tyne, NE1 4JA; tel. (191) 232-6789; fax (191) 230-2614; e-mail discovery@twmuseums.org.uk; internet www.twmuseums.org.uk/discovery; f. 1934; displays of fashion, military history, social history and maritime history, and ship *Turbinia*; Museum Man. HAZEL EDWARDS.

Great North Museum: Barras Bridge, Newcastle upon Tyne, NE2 4PT; tel. (191) 222-6765; fax (191) 261-7537; internet www.twmuseums.org.uk/greatnorthmuseum; f. 2009, incorporates collns from the Hancock Museum (f. 1829), Newcastle Univ.'s Museum of Antiquities (f. 1813), the Shefton Museum (f. 1956) and the Hatton Gallery; reserve natural science and archaeology collns comprising 500,000 items; large-scale, interactive model of Hadrian's Wall, displays of the animal and plant kingdoms, objects from ancient Greece, mummies from ancient Egypt, planetarium.

Laing Art Gallery: New Bridge St, Newcastle upon Tyne, NE1 8AG; tel. (191) 232-7734; e-mail laing@twmuseums.org.uk; internet www.twmuseums.org.uk/laing; f. 1904; British oil paintings and watercolours since 1700 (incl. works by Reynolds, Gainsborough, Turner, Landseer, Burne-Jones, Holman Hunt, Spencer, etc.); silver, ceramics and glass (incl. display of enamelled glass by William Beilby); Curator JULIE MILNE.

Monkwearmouth Station Museum: North Bridge St, Sunderland, SR5 1AP; tel. (191) 567-7075; fax (191) 510-9415; internet www.twmuseums.org.uk/monkwearmouth; f. 1973; collns relating to transport, incl. rolling stock, printed material, photographs and models; Curator JULIET HORSLEY.

Segedunum Roman Fort, Baths and Museum: Buddle St, Wallsend, NE28 6HR; tel. (191) 236-9347; fax (191) 295-5858; internet www.twmuseums.org.uk/segedunum; f. 2000; Roman collection incl. defensive missiles from the fort; Industry Gallery has artefacts associated with coal-mining and shipbuilding, incl. model of the ship *Carpathia*; Curator GEOFF WOODWARD.

Shipley Art Gallery: Prince Consort Rd, Gateshead, NE8 4JB; tel. (191) 477-1495; e-mail shipley@twmuseums.org.uk; internet www.twmuseums.org.uk/shipley; f. 1917; contemporary craft; design; decorative arts; British and European paintings; Curator AMY BARKER.

South Shields Museum and Art Gallery: Ocean Rd, South Shields, NE33 2JA; tel. (191) 456-8740; fax (191) 456-7850; internet www.twmuseums.org.uk/

southshields; local history in relation to South Tyneside; Catherine Cookson gallery; local art and crafts; Curator ALISDAIR WILSON.

Stephenson Railway Museum: Middle Engine Lane, North Shields, NE29 8DX; tel. and fax (191) 200-7146; internet www.twmuseums.org.uk/stephenson; colln of steam, diesel and electric locomotives, incl. the early locomotive *Billy*; social history relating to railways; Curator JOHN CLAYSON.

Sunderland Museum and Winter Gardens: Burdon Rd, Sunderlands SR1 1PP; tel. (191) 553-2323; fax (191) 553-7828; internet www.twmuseums.org.uk/sunderland; f. 1846; archaeology, local history, geology, glass, pottery, paintings (incl. by Lowry), natural history; ethnography; Curator JULIET HORSLEY.

Newport (Gwent)

Newport Museum and Art Gallery: John Frost Square, Newport, NP20 1PA; tel. (1633) 840064; e-mail museum@newport.gov.uk; internet www.newport.gov.uk; f. 1888; collns of Roman material from Caerleon and Caerwent; oils, early English watercolours and prints, and other paintings (incl. by Lowry); teapot displays; ceramics; natural and local history collections; Museums Officer (Collections) BRUCE CAMPBELL; Museums and Heritage Officer MIKE LEWIS.

Norwich

Norfolk Museums and Archaeology Service: The Shirehall, Market Ave, Norwich, NR1 3JQ; tel. (1603) 493625; fax (1603) 493623; e-mail museums@norfolk.gov.uk; internet www.museums.norfolk.gov.uk; Head of Museums VANESSA TREVELYAN.

Selected Museums:

Ancient House Museum: White Hart St, Thetford; tel. (1842) 752599; e-mail ancient.house.museum@norfolk.gov.uk; 15th-century timber-framed bldg; local history; Curator OLIVER BONE.

Bridewell Museum: Bridewell Alley, Norwich, NR2 1AQ; tel. (1603) 629127; fax (1603) 614018; e-mail hannah.maddox@norfolk.gov.uk; local industries and crafts in medieval house; Curator HANNAH MADDOX.

Cromer Museum: Cromer; tel. (1263) 513543; e-mail cromer.museum@norfolk.gov.uk; internet www.museums.norfolk.gov.uk; f. 1978; local history, archaeology, geology, natural history; Curator ALISTAIR MURPHY; Area Museum Officer JAMIE EVERITT.

Elizabethan House Museum: Great Yarmouth; tel. (1493) 745526; fax (1493) 745459; domestic life, toys, porcelain, glassware.

Gressenhall Farm and Workhouse: Gressenhall; tel. (1362) 860563; e-mail gressenhall.museum@norfolk.gov.uk; historic workhouse; social and rural history displays and collections; farm with rare breeds of animal.

Lynn Museum: Market St, King's Lynn, PE30 1NL; tel. (1553) 75001; e-mail lynn.museum@norfolk.gov.uk; social history, natural history, archaeology and geology of West Norfolk.

Norwich Castle Museum and Art Gallery: Castle Meadow, Norwich, NR1 3JN; tel. (1603) 493625; fax (1603) 4939623; e-mail museums@norfolk.gov.uk; f. 1894; Norman keep; fine art, ceramics, social history, natural history, archaeology.

Royal Norfolk Regimental Museum: Market Ave, Norwich, NR1 3JQ; tel. (1603) 493650; e-mail museums@norfolk.gov.uk; social history of the county regiment since 1685.

Time and Tide: Great Yarmouth; tel. (1493) 743930; various aspects of East Anglian maritime history.

Tolhouse Museum: Great Yarmouth; tel. (1493) 745526; fax (1493) 745459; e-mail yarmouth.museums@norfolk.gov.uk; internet www.museums.norfolk.gov.uk; history of crime and punishment in Great Yarmouth.

Town House: 46 Queen St, King's Lynn, PE30 5DQ; tel. (1553) 773450; social history of King's Lynn.

Sainsbury Centre for Visual Arts: Univ. of East Anglia, Norwich, Norfolk, NR4 7TJ; tel. (1603) 593199; e-mail scva@uea.ac.uk; internet www.scva.ac.uk; f. 1978; modern European art and art, sculpture and design of other cultures and periods; library of 13,000 vols (mainly non-Western art and anthropology); Dir Prof. PAUL GREENHALGH.

Nottingham

Nottingham Castle Museum: Friar Lane, off Maid Marian Way, Nottingham, NG1 6EL; tel. (115) 915-3700; fax (115) 915-3653; e-mail castle@ncmg.org.uk; internet www.nottinghamcity.gov.uk; f. 1878; archaeology and ethnography, fine and applied arts, military, social and local history; Dir MICHAEL WILLIAMS.

Nottingham Natural History Museum: Wollaton Hall, Nottingham, NG8 2AE; tel. (115) 915-3900; fax (115) 915-3940; internet www.nottinghamcity.gov.uk; f. 1867; collections of botanical, zoological, and geological material; extensive British and foreign herbaria, Crowfoot collection of exotic butterflies, Pearson collection of European butterflies, Fowler collection of British Coleoptera, Hollier collection of Wenlock Limestone fossils, Carrington series of Mountain Limestone fossils; library of 3,500 vols; Nottinghamshire environmental database; controlled by Nottingham City Council; Senior Keeper G. WALLEY.

Overton

National Coal Mining Museum for England: Caphouse Colliery, New Rd, Overton, Wakefield, WF4 4RH; tel. (1924) 848806; fax (1924) 840694; e-mail info@ncm.org.uk; internet www.ncm.org.uk; f. 1988; mine workings and mine exhibits; library of 15,000 vols, library of material on all aspects of coal-mining; Museum Dir Dr MARGARET FAULL; Librarians ANISHA CHRISTISON, JUDITH DENNIS.

Oxford

Ashmolean Museum, University of Oxford: Beaumont St, Oxford, OX1 2PH; tel. (1865) 278000; fax (1865) 278018; internet www.ashmolean.org; f. 1683; contains the art and archaeological collns of the Univ. of Oxford; British, European, Mediterranean, Egyptian and Near Eastern archaeology; Italian, Dutch, Flemish, French and English oil paintings; Old Master and modern drawings, watercolours and prints; miniatures; European ceramics; sculpture and bronzes; English silver; objects of applied art; Hope colln of engraved portraits; coins and medals of all countries and periods; Chinese and Japanese porcelain, paintings and lacquer; Chinese bronzes, Tibetan art; Indian sculpture and painting; Islamic pottery and metalwork; Dir Dr CHRISTOPHER BROWN.

Modern Art Oxford: 30 Pembroke St, Oxford, OX1 1BP; tel. (1865) 722733; fax (1865) 722573; e-mail info@modernartoxford.org; internet www.modernartoxford.org.uk; f. 1965; exhibits contemporary and 20th-century painting, sculpture, design, photography, architecture, film and video; Dir MICHAEL STANLEY.

Pitt Rivers Museum, University of Oxford: South Parks Rd, Oxford, OX1 3PP; tel. (1865) 270927; fax (1865) 270943; e-mail prm@prm.ox.ac.uk; internet www.prm.ox.ac.uk; f. 1884; attached to Univ.'s School of Anthropology and Museum of Ethnography; contains the ethnographic, archaeological and related photographic and manuscript collns of the Univ.; library of 30,000 vols, 250 periodicals; spec. collns of historic photographs and MSS; Dir Dr MICHAEL O'HANLON.

Plymouth

Plymouth City Museum and Art Gallery: Drake Circus, Plymouth, PL4 8AJ; tel. (1752) 304774; fax (1752) 304775; e-mail museum@plymouth.gov.uk; internet www.plymouth.gov.uk; f. 1897; illustrates the arts and sciences of the West Country; comprises the Cottonian Colln of early printed and illuminated books, Old Master engravings and drawings, portraits by Sir Joshua Reynolds; gen. collns of Fine Art (since 16th century) and of Decorative Arts incl. Plymouth silver and William Cookworthy's Plymouth and Bristol porcelain; natural history, ethnography, archaeology and local history; the Merchant's House (f. 1977), 33 St Andrew's St (16th–17th centuries); the Elizabethan House (f. 1929), 32 New St (16th century) and Smeaton's Tower lighthouse, The Hoe; Curator NICOLA MOYLE.

Portsmouth

Portsmouth City Museum and Records Office: Museum Rd, Portsmouth, PO1 2LJ; tel. (23) 9282-7261; fax (23) 9287-5276; e-mail mvs@portsmouthcc.gov.uk; internet www.portsmouthmuseums.co.uk; f. 1972; local history, fine and decorative art; re-creation of domestic interiors from various periods; Arthur Conan Doyle Colln; Fine and Decorative Art Gallery; Records Office contains official records of the City of Portsmouth since 14th century; Museums and Records Services Man. Dr JANE MEE.

Branch Museums:

Charles Dickens Birthplace: 393 Old Commercial Rd, Portsmouth, PO1 4QL; tel. (23) 9282-7261; fax (23) 9287-5276; e-mail mvs@portsmouthcc.gov.uk; internet www.portsmouthmuseums.co.uk; f. 1904; built 1805; birthplace of Charles Dickens in 1812; a small terraced house restored, decorated and furnished in the Regency style; Museums and Records Services Man. Dr JANE MEE.

D-Day Museum and Overlord Embroidery: Clarence Esplanade, Southsea, PO5 3NT; tel. (23) 9282-7261; fax (23) 9287-5276; e-mail mvs@portsmouthcc.gov.uk; internet www.ddaymuseum.co.uk; f. 1984; houses the 'Overlord Embroidery', commemorating the D-Day Landings; displays of original archive material, vehicles, uniforms and artefacts; Museums and Records Services Man. Dr JANE MEE.

Southsea Castle: Clarence Esplanade, Southsea, PO5 3PA; tel. (23) 9282-7261; fax (23) 9287-5276; e-mail mvs@portsmouthcc.gov.uk; internet www.portsmouthmuseums.co.uk; f. 1967; built 1544 by Henry VIII to protect Portsmouth harbour; 'Life in the Castle' experience; history of the defences of Portsmouth; displays on the Tudors, the English Civil War, 18th century and the Victorian period; audiovisual show and underground passages; Museums and Records Services Man. Dr JANE MEE.

Preston

Harris Museum and Art Gallery: Market Sq., Preston, Lancs., PR1 2PP; tel. (1772) 258248; fax (1772) 886764; e-mail harris .museum@preston.gov.uk; internet www .harrismuseum.org.uk; f. 1893; fine art, decorative art, costumes and textiles, archaeology, local history, photography; Head of Arts and Heritage Services ALEXANDRA WALKER.

Reading

Museum of English Rural Life: Univ. of Reading, Redlands Rd, Reading, RG1 5EX; tel. (118) 378-8660; fax (118) 378-5632; e-mail merl@reading.ac.uk; internet www .reading.ac.uk/merl; f. 1951; nat. colln of objects, photographs, archives, records and publs relating to English rural and agricultural history; 1m. photographic prints and negatives; library of 70,000 vols incl. large sections on agricultural sciences and technology and pre-1950 agricultural devt overseas; Head of Univ. Museums and Collns Services K. ARNOLD-FOSTER.

Museum of Reading: Blagrave St, Reading, Berks, RG1 1QH; tel. (118) 939-9800; fax (118) 939-9881; e-mail curator@ readingmuseum.org.uk; internet www .readingmuseum.org.uk; f. 1883; collns cover art, archaeology, local history, world history and natural history; over 400,000 objects of local, regional and nat. importance incl. archaeological finds from the Roman site at Silchester, British artworks from between the wars, Romanesque carvings from Reading Abbey and the Huntley and Palmers Colln relating to the famous Reading biscuit company; also offers Hands-on Learning programme for schools and community groups, incl. loan box service; Sr Curator MATTHEW WILLIAMS.

Salisbury

Salisbury and South Wiltshire Museum: The King's House, 65 The Close, Salisbury, Wilts., SP1 2EN; tel. (1722) 332151; fax (1722) 325611; e-mail museum@ salisburymuseum.org.uk; internet www .salisburymuseum.org.uk; f. 1860; archaeology, local history, ceramics, costume, Pitt Rivers colln, topographical pictures, numismatics; temporary exhibitions; Dir P. R. SAUNDERS.

Selborne

Gilbert White's House and Garden and the Oates Museum: The Wakes, High St, Selborne, Alton, Hants; tel. (1420) 511275; f. 1954; private collections funded by the Oates Memorial Trust; furnished period rooms, original MSS about the natural history of Selborne; 18th-century plants grown in the garden; exploration in Africa by Frank Oates and in Antarctica by Capt. Lawrence Oates; Oates Memorial Library.

Sheffield

Kelham Island Museum: Alma St, Sheffield, S3 8RY; tel. (114) 272-2106; fax (114) 275-7847; e-mail postmaster@simt.co.uk; internet www.simt.co.uk/kelham; f. 1982; objects, pictures and archives relating to Sheffield's industrial heritage; Exec. Dir JOHN HAMSHERE.

Weston Park Museum: Western Bank, Sheffield, S10 2TP; tel. (114) 278-2600; e-mail info@sheffieldgalleries.co.uk; internet www.sheffieldgalleries.org.uk; f. 1875 as Sheffield City Museum and Mappin Art Gallery; collns of Sheffield cutlery, Old Sheffield Plate, British and European cutlery, coins and medals, ceramics, local archaeology, natural sciences, local geology, etc.; Victorian paintings, Old Masters; Dir NICK DODD.

Singleton

Weald and Downland Open Air Museum: Singleton, Chichester, PO18 0EU; tel. (1243) 811363; fax (1243) 811475; e-mail courses@ wealddown.co.uk; internet www.wealddown .co.uk; f. 1967 to save interesting examples of vernacular architecture from South-east England that have been threatened with demolition; more than 45 bldgs ranging from early medieval times to the 19th century have been re-erected on the site; working exhibits incl. a watermill and treadwheel; working farm with animals; continuing education courses for adults in building conservation, traditional building methods and traditional rural trades and crafts; diverse curriculum of subjects offered to schools, Masters degree course in building conservation and timber building conservation; library: research library and archive; Dir RICHARD HARRIS; Head of Learning DIANA ROWSELL.

Southampton

Southampton City Art Gallery: Civic Centre, Commercial Rd, Southampton, SO14 7LP; tel. (23) 8083-2277; fax (23) 8083-2153; e-mail art.gallery@southampton .gov.uk; internet www.southampton.gov.uk/ leisure/arts; f. 1916 by a bequest fund for purchase and display of works of art; opened 1939; collns incl. Old Masters, French 19th- and 20th-century Schools, British painting since the 18th century, with emphasis on the Camden Town School; large colln of British contemporary painting and sculpture; library of 1,500 vols; Curator of Art TIM CRAVEN.

Southport

Atkinson Art Gallery: Lord St, Southport, PR8 1DH; tel. (151) 934-2110; fax (151) 934-2109; internet www.seftonarts.co.uk; f. 1878 for the exhibition of the town's permanent colln; British oils and watercolours since the 18th century; contemporary sculpture, paintings and prints; closed for refurbishment until 2013; Arts and Cultural Services Man. (Museums and Galleries) JOANNA JONES.

Stoke on Trent

Chatterley Whitfield Mining Museum: Tunstall, Stoke on Trent, ST6 8UN; tel. (1782) 813337; f. 1979 at a former colliery; aims to demonstrate the realities of mining development; recreation of surface and underground conditions; reference library; mining artefacts, photographs, films, documents, maps and plans, and oral history recordings; Dir JAMES HUTCHINSON; publs *Chatterley Whitfield News*, *Primary Teachers' Pack*, *Schools Roadshow Pack*.

Stoke on Trent Museums: Bethesda St, Hanley, Stoke on Trent, ST1 3DW; tel. (1782) 232323; fax (1782) 232500; e-mail museums@ stoke.gov.uk; internet www.stokemuseums .org.uk; Head of Museums IAN LAWLEY.

Constituent Museums:

Etruria Industrial Museum: Lower Bedford St, Etruria, Stoke on Trent, ST4 7AF; tel. (1782) 233144; fax (1782) 233141; e-mail museums@stoke.gov.uk; internet www.stokemuseums.org.uk; steam-powered potter's mill.

Ford Green Hall: Ford Green Rd, Smallthorne, Stoke on Trent, ST6 1NG; tel. (1782) 233195; fax (1782) 233194; e-mail ford.green.hall@stoke.gov.uk; internet www.stokemuseums.org.uk; 17th-century timber-framed bldg and period garden.

Gladstone Pottery Museum: Uttoxeter Rd, Longton, Stoke on Trent, ST3 1PQ; tel. (1782) 237777; fax (1782) 237076; e-mail gladstone@stoke.gov.uk; internet www .stokemuseums.org.uk; f. 1974; complete Victorian pottery factory; workshops demonstrating traditional skills; Visitor Services KERRY WALTERS, ALISON PORTER.

Potteries Museum and Art Gallery: Bethesda St, City Centre, Stoke on Trent, ST1 3DW; tel. (1782) 232323; fax (1782) 232500; e-mail museums@stoke.gov.uk; internet www.stokemuseums.org.uk; Staffordshire pottery and porcelain, art, natural history, archaeology, local history; Strategic Man. KEITH BLOOR.

Wakefield

Wakefield Metropolitan District Council Access and Culture—Libraries and Museums: Wakefield Art Gallery, Wentworth Terrace, Wakefield, WF1 3QW; tel. (1924) 305796; fax (1924) 305770; e-mail cmacdonald@wakefield.gov.uk; internet www.wakefield.gov.uk/culture; f. 1934; museums and sites incl. Wakefield Art Gallery, Wakefield Museum, Pontefract Museum, Castleford Museum Room, Pontefract Castle, Sandal Castle, Clarke Hall Educational Museum; Head of Libraries and Museums COLIN MACDONALD.

Weybridge

Brooklands Museum: Brooklands Rd, Weybridge, Surrey, KT13 0QN; tel. (1932) 857381; fax (1932) 855465; e-mail info@ brooklandsmuseum.com; internet www .brooklandsmuseum.com; f. 1991; cars, motorcycles, aircraft, historic Brooklands racetrack, interactive science gallery; Dir ALLAN WINN.

Widnes

Catalyst—Science Discovery Centre and Museum: Mersey Rd, Widnes, WA8 0DF; tel. (151) 420-1121; e-mail info@catalyst.org.uk; internet www.catalyst.org.uk; f. 1987; informs the public about the role of chemistry in society past and present, incl. its relationship to the environment; enthuses school pupils about science through workshops, science demonstrations and interactive galleries; colln of relevant artefacts; library: reference library on history of the chemical industry; archive of historical photographs, industry archives; Marketing Officer MERYL JAMESON.

Wolverhampton

Wolverhampton Art Gallery and Museums: Lichfield St, Wolverhampton, WV1 1DU; tel. (1902) 552055; fax (1902) 552053; internet www.wolverhamptonart .org.uk; f. 1884; collns of fine art since the 18th century and temporary exhibitions; br. museums: Bantock House (period house, enamels, japanned ware); Bilston Craft Gallery (contemporary craft and temporary exhibitions); Head of Arts and Museums CORINNE MILLER.

York

Jorvik Viking Centre: Coppergate, York, YO1 9WT; tel. (1904) 615505; fax (1904) 627097; e-mail jorvik@yorkat.co.uk; internet www.vikingjorvik.com; f. 1984; reconstruction of part of the Viking city of Jorvik, based on archaeological evidence; many artefacts from the York Archaeological Trust's excavation are on display in the Gallery; Dir of Attractions SARAH MALTBY.

National Railway Museum: Leeman Rd, York, YO26 4XJ; tel. (844) 815139; e-mail nrm@nrm.org.uk; internet www.nrm.org.uk; f. 1975; part of the Science Museum (*q.v.*);

houses a large part of the National Railway Colln reflecting over 150 years of British railway heritage; full-size rolling stock of diesel, electric and steam locomotives, carriages and wagons, models, signalling equipment, railway relics, posters, prints, films, technical drawings, photographs and paintings; Institute of Railway Studies, based at the Museum, provides university-level teaching on history and heritage of rail and urban transport; library of 15,000 vols; Head STEVE DAVIES.

York Castle Museum: Eye of York, York, YO1 9RY; tel. (1904) 687687; e-mail castle.museum@ymt.org.uk; internet www.yorkcastlemuseum.org.uk; f. 1938; England's first major folk museum; Kirk collection illustrates English life since the 17th century, including reconstructed shops and streets; also costumes, arms and armour, craft workshops, 1960s exhibition and the 18th-century Castle Prison; Museums Man. IAN CARLISLE.

York City Art Gallery: Exhibition Sq., York, YO1 7EW; tel. (1904) 687687; fax (1904) 697966; e-mail art.gallery@ymt.org.uk; internet www.yorkartgallery.org.uk; f. 1879; paintings of the Italian, Dutch, Flemish, German, French, Spanish and British Schools; William Etty colln; large colln of 20th-century studio ceramics; library of 7,000 vols; Gallery Man. LORNA SERGEANT; Curator LAURA TURNER.

Yorkshire Museum: Museum Gardens, York, YO1 7FR; tel. (1904) 687687; e-mail yorkshire.museum@ymt.org.uk; internet www.yorkshiremuseum.org.uk; f. 1822; archaeology (Roman, Anglo-Saxon, Viking and medieval life), natural history, geology, numismatics and ceramics; Museums Man. HELEN YOUNG.

Universities in England

ANGLIA RUSKIN UNIVERSITY

Chelmsford Campus: Bishop Hall Lane, Chelmsford, CM1 1SQ
Cambridge Campus: East Rd, Cambridge, CB1 1PT
Telephone: (1245) 493131
Fax: (1245) 490835
E-mail: answers@apu.ac.uk
Internet: www.anglia.ac.uk
Founded 1858, present status 1992; present name 2005
Academic year: September to July
Chancellor: Lord ASHCROFT
Vice-Chancellor: Prof. MICHAEL THORNE
Deputy Vice-Chancellor: Prof. ALAN SIBBALD
Deputy Vice-Chancellor: Prof. HELEN VALENTINE
Deputy Vice-Chancellor: Prof. LESLEY DOBREE
Librarian: NICKY KERSHAW
Number of teachers: 709
Number of students: 31,000

DEANS

Ashcroft International Business School: Dr TREVOR BOLTON (acting)
Faculty of Arts, Law and Social Science: DERRIK FERNEY
Faculty of Education: Prof. HELEN VALENTINE
Faculty of Health & Social Care: Prof. DAVID HUMBER
Faculty of Science and Technology: Prof. EAMON STRAIN

ASTON UNIVERSITY

Aston Triangle, Birmingham, B4 7ET
Telephone: (121) 204-3000
Fax: (121) 204-3696
E-mail: prospectus@aston.ac.uk
Internet: www.aston.ac.uk
Founded 1895, present status 1966
Academic year: October to June
Chancellor: Sir MICHAEL BETT
Pro-Chancellor: Dr PAUL GOLBY
Vice-Chancellor: Prof. JULIA KING
Sr Pro-Vice-Chancellor: Prof. HELEN HIGSON
Pro-Vice-Chancellor for Learning and Teaching Innovation: Prof. ALISON HALSTEAD
Pro-Vice-Chancellor for Business Partnerships and Knowledge Transfer: Dr PHIL EXTANCE
Pro-Vice-Chancellor for Research: Prof. MARTIN GRIFFIN
Univ. Sec.: ADELE MACKINLAY
Dir of Library and Information Services: Dr NICK SMITH
Library: see under Libraries and Archives
Number of teachers: 343
Number of students: 6,623 (5,700 full-time, 923 part-time)

DEANS

Aston Business School: Prof. MIKE WEST
School of Engineering and Applied Science: Prof. ROBERT BERRY
School of Languages and Social Science: Prof. PAM MOORES
School of Life and Health Sciences: Prof. HELEN GRIFFITHS

PROFESSORS

ANDERSON, S., Clinical Neuroscience
BAILEY, C., Pharmacology
BARKER, P., Chemical Engineering
BENNET, D., Technology Management and Head of International Liaison, Aston Business School
BENNION, I., Opto Electronics
BHATTACHARYYA, G., Sociology
BLOW, K., Photonic Systems
BOOTH, R., Occupational Health and Safety
BRETT, P., Medical Engineering
BRIDGWATER, T., Engineering and Applied Science
BRIGNALL, S., Finance Accounting and Law, Aston Business School
BROOKES, J., Life and Health Sciences
BROWN, M., Pharmacy
CHELLEY-STEELEY, P., Finance Accounting and Law, Aston Business School
COLEMAN, M., Toxicology, Medicinal Chemistry
COULTHARD, M., Forensic Linguistics
FLOOD, J., Electronic Engineering
FURLONG, P., Clinical Neuroimaging
GAFFNEY, J., Languages and Social Sciences
GEOFFREY, G., Chemical Engineering
GEORGESON, M., Vision Sciences
GIBSON, J., Ophthalmology
GILMARTIN, B., Optometry
GREEN, S., Languages and Social Sciences
GRIFFIN, M., Biochemistry
HARDING, G., Life and Health Sciences
HART, M., Small Business and Entrepreneurship
HOMER, J., Chemistry
HORNUNG, A., Chemical Engineering
JARZABKOWSKI, P., Strategic Management, Aston Business School
JOSEPH, N., Finance Accounting and Law, Aston Business School
LOWE, A., Finance Accounting and Law, Aston Business School
LOWE, D., Informatics
MARRIOTT, J., Pharmacy Practice
NABNEY, T., Computer Science
PEARCE, G., Finance Accounting and Law, Aston Business School
PENNY, J., Engineering Systems and Management
POOLE, J., Commercial Law
PORTER, K., Chemical Engineering
REERSHEMIUS, G., German Linguistics
ROBERTS, B., Auditory Perception
ROGERS, M., Economics and Strategy, Aston Business School
ROPER, S., Business Innovation, Aston Business School
SAAD, D., Information Maths
SAUNDERS, J., Marketing, Aston Business School
SCHWALBE, C., Medicinal Chemistry
SCOTT, G., Chemical Engineering
SERI, S., Clinical Neurophysiology
SHAW, D., Operations and Information Management, Aston Business School
SILLINCE, J., Operations and Information Management, Aston Business School
STEELEY, J., Finance Accounting and Law, Aston Business School
STEVENS, A., European Studies
SULLIVAN, J., Surface Science
TANSLEY, G., Mechanical Engineering
THANASSOULIS, E., Operations and Information Management, Aston Business School
TIGHE, J., Polymer Chemistry
TISDALE, M., Cancer Biochemistry
TURITSYN, S., Electronic Engineering
ZHANG, L., Electronic Engineering

BATH SPA UNIVERSITY

Newton Park Campus: Newton St Loe, Bath, BA2 9BN
Telephone: (1225) 875875
Fax: (1225) 875444
Sion Hill Campus: Lansdown, Bath, BA1 5SF
Telephone: (1225) 875875
Fax: (1225) 875666
E-mail: enquiries@bathspa.ac.uk
Internet: www.bathspa.ac.uk
Founded 1898, granted taught degree-awarding powers 1992; present name and status 2005
Academic year: September to June
Vice-Chancellor: Prof. FRANK MORGAN
Deputy Vice-Chancellor: Dr ALUN THOMAS
Deputy Vice-Chancellor: Prof. NEIL SAMMELLS
Deputy Vice-Chancellor: JON BRADY
Registrar: CHRISTOPHER ELLICOTT
Head of Library and Information Services: Prof. ALISON BAUD
Number of teachers: 600
Number of students: 5,500

BIRMINGHAM CITY UNIVERSITY

Perry Barr, Birmingham, B42 2SU
Telephone: (121) 331-5000
Fax: (121) 331-7994
E-mail: choices@bcu.ac.uk
Internet: www.bcu.ac.uk
Founded 1971, as Birmingham Polytechnic, gained university status in 1992 and was renamed Univ. of Central England in Birmingham, present name 2007
Academic year: October to July
Chancellor: The Lord Mayor of Birmingham, Cllr MICHAEL NANGLE
Vice-Chancellor: Prof. DAVID TIDMARSH
Pro-Vice-Chancellor: SALLY WESTNEY
Pro-Vice-Chancellor: Prof. MARY CARSWELL
Pro-Vice-Chancellor for Corporate Devt: Prof. DAVID MAGUIRE
Univ. Sec.: CHRISTINE ABBOTT

Library of 950,000 vols, 9,000 journals
Number of teachers: 700
Number of students: 25,000

DEANS

Birmingham City Business School: Prof. CHRISTOPHER PRINCE
Birmingham Institute of Art and Design: Prof. CHRIS O'NEIL
Faculty of Education, Law and Social Sciences: Prof. R. WOODS
Faculty of Health: Prof. IAN BLAIR
Faculty of Performance, Media and English: Prof. JOHN ROUSE
Faculty of Technology, Engineering and Environment: Prof. MELVYN LEES

BOURNEMOUTH UNIVERSITY

Fern Barrow, Poole, BH12 5BB
Telephone: (1202) 524111
Fax: (1202) 962736
E-mail: enquiries@bournemouth.ac.uk
Internet: www.bournemouth.ac.uk

Founded 1976, as Dorset Institute of Higher Education, became Bournemouth Polytechnic 1990, present name and status 1992
Academic year: September to July
Chancellor: Rt Hon. Lord NICHOLAS PHILLIPS
Vice-Chancellor: Prof. JOHN VINNEY
Deputy Vice-Chancellor: DAVID WILLEY
Pro-Vice-Chancellor for Academic Affairs: Prof. PAUL LUKER
Pro-Vice-Chancellor for Corporate Development and Finance: DAVID WILLEY
Registrar: NOEL RICHARDSON
Librarian: DAVID BALL
Library of 150,000 vols
Number of teachers: 391
Number of students: 17,502 incl. full-time and part-time

DEANS

Business School: Prof. ANDROS GREGORIOU
Media School: STEPHEN JUKES
School of Applied Sciences: Prof. MATTHEW BENNETT
School of Design, Engineering and Computing: Prof. JIM ROACH
School of Health and Social Care: Dr B. GAIL THOMAS
School of Tourism: Dr KEITH WILKES

BRUNEL UNIVERSITY

Kingston Lane, Uxbridge, UB8 3PH
Telephone: (1895) 274000
Fax: (1895) 232806
E-mail: admissions@brunel.ac.uk
Internet: www.brunel.ac.uk

Founded 1966 as Brunel College of Technology, College of Advanced Technology 1962, Univ. Charter 1966, inc. W London Institute into the Univ. in 1995
State control
Academic year: September to June
Chancellor: The Rt Hon. Lord WAKEHAM
Pro-Chancellor: Lord LINGFIELD
Vice-Chancellor and Prin.: Prof. CHRIS JENKS
Vice-Prin.: Prof. MANSOOR SARHADI
Pro-Vice-Chancellor for Strategy and Devt: Prof. STEVE DIXON
Pro-Vice-Chancellor for External Relations: Prof. IAN CAMPBELL
Pro-Vice-Chancellor for Research: Prof. GEOFF RODGERS
Pro-Vice-Chancellor for Student Experience and Staff Devt: Prof. KEN DARBY-DOWMAN
Academic Registrar: BOB WESTAWAY
Library of 458,000 vols, 17,000 journals
Number of teachers: 1,057
Number of students: 15,201

PROFESSORS

ABASS, A., Law
AKEMANN, G., Mathematical Sciences
AL-RAWESHIDY, H., Electronic and Computer Engineering
ANDERSON, N., Business and Management
ANDREWS, B., Brunel Institute of Bioengineering
ANGELIDES, M., Mechanical Engineering
BAHAI, H., Mechanical Engineering
BALACHANDRAN, W., Electronic and Computer Engineering
BALMER, J. M. T., Business and Management
BANTEKAS, I., Law
BEASLEY, J., Mathematical Sciences
BENNETT, J., Economics and Finance
BERESFORD, P., Social Care
BIRRINGER, J., Drama
BRACKENRIDGE, C., Sport
BRAGANZA, A., Business and Management
BROADHURST, S., Drama
BUCKINGHAM, S., Social Care
BUNCE, D., Psychology
BUXTON, M., Health Economics Research Group
CAMPOS, N., Economics and Finance
CAPEL, S., School of Sport and Education
CAPORALE, G., Economics and Finance
CHENG, K., Mechanical Engineering
CHIGARA, B., Law
COSMAS, J., Electronic and Computer Engineering
DESOUZA, L., School Health Sciences and Social Care
DICKSON, K., Business and Management
ESAT, I., Mechanical Engineering
EVANS, R., Biological Sciences
FISHER, D., Brunel Institute of Bioengineering
FISHER, J., Politics and History
FITZGERALD, G., Information Systems
FOX, C., Music
FOX-RUSHBY, J., Health Economics Research Group
GAN, T., Electronic and Computer Engineering
GIACOMIN, J., Design
GILBERT, D., Information Systems
GILHOOLY, M., Health Studies and Community Health
GOBET, F., Psychology
GONZALEZ-ALONSO, J., Sport
GOODWIN, R., Psychology
HACKNEY, R., Business and Management
HARRISON, D., Design
HARWIN, J., Social Care
HIERONS, R., Information Systems
HOBSON, P., Electronic and Computer Engineering
IOSSA, E., Economics and Finance
IRANI, Z., Brunel Business School
IRVING, M., Electronic and Computer Engineering
JAFFEY, P., Law
JARVIS, R., Business and Management
KAIKOBAD, K., Law
KAPLUNOV, J., Mathematical Sciences
KARANASOS, M., Economics and Finance
KARAYIANNIS, T., Mechanical Engineering
KATHIRGAMANATHAN, P., Wolfson Centre
KHAN, A., Electronic and Computer Engineering
KING, G., Film and Television
KLEINBERG, J., Politics and History
KOLOKOTRONI, M., Electronic and Computer Engineering
KOSHY, V., Education
KRZYWINSKA, T., Film and Television
KULJIS, J., Mathematical Sciences
KUMAR RAY, A., Wolfson Centre
LEASK, M., Education
LEROY, S., Environmental Studies
LIU, G., Business and Management
LIU, X., Information Systems
LOUVIERIS, P., Information Systems
LUNT, P., Sociology and Communication
MACREDIE, R., Information Systems
MCCONNELL, A., Sport
MIKHAILOV, S., Mathematical Sciences
MORGAN, K., Politics and History
MOUSSY, F., Brunel Institute of Bioengineering
MUSHKAT, R., Law
MYERS, L., Psychology
NEOCLEOUS, M., Politics and History
NEWBOLD, R., Cancer, Genetics and Pharmaceuticals
NOBUS, D., School of Social Sciences
OLOWOFOYEKU, A., Brunel Law School
PETLEY, J., Film and Television
PIPER, C., Law
POLDEN, P., Law
RAWLINS, A., Mathematical Sciences
REHMAN, J., Law
RITA VICTOR, C., Health Studies and Community Health
RIVERS, I., Sport
ROJEK, C., Sociology and Communication
SADKA, A., Electronic and Computer Engineering
SCAMANS, G., BCAST
SHARIF, A., Business and Management
SHEPPERD, M., Information Systems
SIMPSON, R., Business and Management
SONG, J., Mechanical Engineering
STELARC, X., Performance Arts
STOLARSKI, T., Mechanical Engineering
STONHAM, T., Electronic and Computer Engineering
SUMPTER, J., Institute for the Environment
TASSOU, S., School of Engineering and Design
TEW, P., English Studies
VASEGHI, S., Electronic and Computer Engineering
WANG, Z., Mathematical Sciences
WARLEIGH-LACK, A., Politics and History
WATKIN, W., English Studies
WATTS, M., Education
WELDON, F., English Studies
WHITEMAN, J., Mathematical Sciences
WIEGOLD, P., Music
WITHNALL, R., Wolfson Centre
WOODS, A., Business and Management
WOOLRICH, J., Music
WRIGHT, D., Design
WRIGHT, M., Psychology
WROBEL, L., Mechanical Engineering
WYDELL, T., Sociology and Communication
YOUNG, T., Information Systems
ZHAO, H., Mechanical Engineering

BUCKINGHAMSHIRE NEW UNIVERSITY

Queen Alexandra Rd, High Wycombe, HP11 2JZ
Telephone: (1494) 522141
Fax: (1494) 524392
E-mail: advice@bucks.ac.uk
Internet: bucks.ac.uk

Founded 1893; present name and status 2007
Vice-Chancellor and CEO: Prof. RUTH FARWELL
Deputy Vice-Chancellor: Prof. DEREK GODFREY
Pro-Vice-Chancellor: Prof. CHRIS KEMP
Pro-Vice-Chancellor: Prof. DAVID SINES
Pro-Vice-Chancellor: Prof. TREVOR NICHOLLS
Dir for Business Planning: STEPHEN DEWHURST
Number of students: 9,017

DEANS

Faculty of Design, Media and Management: Prof. CHRIS KEMP
Faculty of Society and Health: Prof. DAVID SINES

School of Advanced and Continuing Practice: LAUREN GRIFFITHS (Head)
School of Applied Management and Law: Dr LORRAINE WATKINS-MATHYS (Head)
School of Applied Production and New Media: FRAZER MACKENZIE (Head)

CANTERBURY CHRIST CHURCH UNIVERSITY

North Holmes Rd, Canterbury, CT1 1QU
Telephone: (1227) 767700
Fax: (1227) 470442
E-mail: admissions@canterbury.ac.uk
Internet: www.canterbury.ac.uk

Founded 1962 as a Church of England Teacher Training College; University College 1995; present name and status 2005

Chancellor: Dr ROWAN WILLIAMS
Vice-Chancellor: Prof. ROBIN BAKER
Pro-Chancellor: Prof. PETER HERMITAGE
Deputy Pro-Chancellor: STEPHEN CLARK
Sr Pro-Vice-Chancellor: Prof. JANET DRUKER
Pro-Vice-Chancellor: Dr PAUL DALTON
Pro-Vice-Chancellor: Prof. TONY LAVENDER
Pro-Vice-Chancellor for Academics: Prof. SUE PIOTROWSKI
Pro-Vice-Chancellor for Learning and Quality: Dr KEITH GWILYM
Pro-Vice-Chancellor for Students: Prof. MARGARET ANDREWS
Strategic Dir: ANDREW IRONSIDE

Number of teachers: 1,334 (f.t.e.)
Number of students: 16,755

Publication: *Inspire*

DEANS

Faculty of Arts and Humanities: Dr PAUL DALTON
Faculty of Business and Management: Prof. GIOIA PESCETTO
Faculty of Education: Dr JOHN MOSS
Faculty of Health and Social Care: HAZEL COLYER
Faculty of Social and Applied Sciences: Prof. TONY LAVENDER

CITY UNIVERSITY

Northampton Sq., London, EC1V 0HB
Telephone: (20) 7040-5060
Fax: (20) 7040-5070
E-mail: registry@city.ac.uk
Internet: www.city.ac.uk

Founded 1894 as Northampton Institute, Northampton College of Advanced Technology 1957, Univ. Charter 1966

Academic year: September to July

Chancellor: THE LORD MAYOR OF LONDON
Vice-Chancellor: Prof. PAUL CURRAN
Deputy Vice-Chancellor: Prof. JULIUS WEINBERG
Deputy Vice-Chancellor for Education: Prof. DAVID BOLTON
Deputy Vice-Chancellor for Research and Int.: Prof. DINOS ARCOUMANIS
Pro-Vice-Chancellor for External Affairs: Prof. COSTAS GRAMMENOS
Univ. Sec.: FRANK TOOP
Librarian: B. M. CASEY

Library of 350,000 vols
Number of teachers: 1,842
Number of students: 21,727

Publication: *City*

DEANS

Cass Business School: Prof. COSTAS GRAMMENOS
City Law School: SUSAN NASH (Dir)
School of Arts: CHRISTINA SLADE (acting)
School of Community and Health Sciences: MARTIN CARAHER (acting)
School of Engineering and Mathematical Sciences: KEN GRATTAN
School of Informatics: KEN GRATTAN
School of Social Sciences: CHRISTINA SLADE

PROFESSORS

ATKINSON, J. H., Soil Mechanics
BADEN-FULLER, C., Business Strategy
BARBUR, J. L., Optics and Visual Science
BARONE-ADESI, G., Financial Engineering
BATCHELOR, R., Banking and Finance
BOOTH, P., Real Estate Finance
BOSWELL, L. F., Civil Engineering
BOWERS, L., Psychiatric Nursing
BOYLAN, P. J., Arts Policy and Management
BRADLEY, K., Management
BRYER, R.
BUCKLEY, R. J., Ocular Medicine
BURN, E. H., Law
BURRIDGE, P., Economics
BYNG, S., Communication Disability
CAPIE, F. H., Economic History
CARSON, E. R., Systems Science
COHEN, B., Computing
COLLINS, M. A., Marketing Research
CONNELL, T. J., Languages for the Professions
COYLE, A., Sociology
CRESSY, R., Accounting and Finance
CROMPTON, R., Sociology
CUBBIN, J., Economics
D'ANDREA, V., Educational Development
DANIELS, P. G., Applied Mathematics
DICKINSON, G. M., International Insurance
DINENIS, E., Investment and Risk Management
DOCKRAY, M. S., Law
DONE, G. T. S., Aeronautics
DOUGLAS, R. H., Visual Science
FAHLE, M., Optometry
FINKELSTEIN, L., Measurement and Instrumentation
GARDINER, J. M., Psychology
GEMMILL, G. T., Finance
GLEN, S., Nursing
GLYCOPANTIS, D., Economics
GOLOMBOK, J. M., Psychology
GRAMMENOS, C. TH., Shipping, Trade and Finance
GRANT, R. M., Management
GRATTAN, K. T. V., Measurement and Instrumentation
GREENSLADE, R., Journalism
HABERMAN, S., Actuarial Science
HAINES, C. R., Mathematics Education
HAMPTON, J., Psychology
HEFFERNAN, S. A., Banking and Finance
HENDRY, C., Organizational Behaviour
HEYMAN, B., Nursing
HINES, M., Psychology
HOLTHAM, C. W., Information Management
KARCANIAS, N., Control Theory and Design
LASSFER, M., Finance
LEVIS, M., Finance
LITTLEWOOD, B., Software Engineering
LOVELAND, I., Law
MCGUIRE, A. J., Economics
MARKS, D., Psychology
MARTIN, P. P., Mathematical Physics
MATHON, J., Mathematical Physics
MENOU, M., Information Policy
MEYER, J., Adult Nursing
MINTZ, B., Engineering Materials
MOODY, E., Arts Policy and Management
NEWBY, J., Statistical Science
PALMER, A. W., Electrical Engineering
PARKIN, D., Health Economics
PEAKE, D. J., Aero and Fluid Dynamics
PHYLAKTIS, E., International Finance
PRICE, S., Economics
PURDUE, H. M., Law
RAHMAN, A., Photonic Devices
RAPER, J. F., Information Science
RATTANSI, A., Sociology
RYAN, C. L., Law
SALMON, M., Financial Markets
SAMUEL, R., Music
SANDALL, J., Midwifery
SELIM, G., Internal Auditing
SMALLEY, D., Music
SMITH, I. K., Applied Thermodynamics
STEPHENSON, H., Journalism
STOSIC, N., Positive Displacement Compressor Technology
STRIGINI, L., Systems Engineering
TAYLOR, R. N., Geotechnical Engineering
THOMAS, P.
THORLEY, A. R. D., Fluid Engineering
TUMBER, H., Sociology
TUNSTALL, C. J., Sociology
VERRALL, R., Actuarial Science and Statistics
VIRDI, K. S., Structural Engineering
WATTS, M., Psychology
WEINBERG, J.
WILLETTS, P., Global Politics
WILLIAMS, A. P. O., Organizational and Occupational Psychology
WOLL, B., Sign Language and Deaf Studies
WOOD, G., Economics
WOODIWISS, A., Sociology
WOODWARD, E. G., Optometry and Visual Science
WOOTTON, L. R., Engineering

COVENTRY UNIVERSITY

Priory St, Coventry, CV1 5FB
Telephone: (24) 7688-7688
Fax: (24) 7688-8638
E-mail: info.rao@coventry.ac.uk
Internet: www.coventry.ac.uk

Founded 1970, by merger of Coventry College of Art, Lanchester College of Technology and Rugby College of Engineering Technology, present name and status 1992

Academic year: September to June

Chancellor: Sir JOHN EGAN
Vice-Chancellor: Prof. MADELAINE ATKINS
Deputy Chancellor for Business Devt: JOHN LATHAM
Deputy Vice-Chancellor for Acad.: Prof. IAN MARSHALL
Deputy Vice-Chancellor for Planning and Resources: DAVID SOUTTER
Pro-Vice-Chancellor for Continuous Improvement: DONNA KENDALL
Pro-Vice-Chancellor for Int. Experience and Mobility Service: Dr DAVID PILSBURY
Pro-Vice-Chancellor for Student Empowerment: IAN DUNN
Registrar and Sec.: KATE QUANTRELL
Librarian: P. NOON

Library of 400,000 vols
Number of teachers: 600
Number of students: 18,000

Publications: *Biological Agriculture and Horticulture* (4 a year), *Coventry University Law Journal* (2 a year), *The Holocene*, *International Journal of Media and Cultural Politics*, *Ultrasonics – Sonochemistry*

DEANS

Faculty of Business, Environment and Society: Prof. DAVID NOON
Faculty of Engineering and Computing: Prof. PAUL IVEY
Faculty of Health and Life Sciences: Dr LINDA MERRIMAN
School of Art and Design: Prof. JILL JOURNEAUX
School of Lifelong Learning Staff: SUE RIVERS (acting)

PROFESSORS

Faculty of Business, Environment and Society:

BAKER, B., African Security
BARRETT, H., Development Geography
BEIDER, H., Community Cohesion
BRODERICK, A., Marketing/Advertising
CANTLE, E.
CHADWICK, S., Sport Management and Marketing
DONNELLY, T., Automotive Business
FARNELL, R., Neighbourhood Regeneration
FORBES, N., International History
HARRIS, P., Plant Design
HUNTER, A., Asian Studies
MCINTOSH, M., Human Security
MITCHELL, B., Criminal Law and Criminal Justice
NESI, H., English Language
NOON, D., Economic Regeneration
RENWICK, N., Global Security
RIGBY, A., Peace Studies
SKINNER, D., Human Resource Management
WORRALL, L., Strategic Analysis

Faculty of Engineering and Computing:

BENJAMIN, S., Fluid Dynamics
BLUNDELL, M., Vehicle Dynamics and Impact
BURNHAM, K., Industrial Control Systems
CHAO, K., Computing
CLAISSE, P., Construction Materials
HOLDO, A., Energy and Environment
IVEY, P.
JAMES, A., Data Systems Architecture
LAWSON, D., Mathematics and Education
LEHANEY, B., Statistics and Operational Research Subject Group
MOLOKOV, S., Applied Mathematics
NAGUIB, R., Biomedical Computing
POPPLEWELL, K., Engineering Manufacture and Management
WHITE, P., Thermofluid Dynamics

Faculty of Health and Life Sciences:

BARLOW, J., Health Psychology
HARRISON, K., Physiotherapy and Dietetics
MASON, T., Chemistry
SAVIN-BADEN, M., Higher Education Research
TOFT, B., Patient Safety
WALLACE, L., Psychology and Health
WOOLLARD, M., Pre-Hospital and Emergency Care

School of Art and Design:

DUTTON, S., Creative Practice
HALL, G., Media and Performing Arts
JOURNEAUX, J., Fine Art Education
RICHARDS, C., Information Design
WHATLEY, S., Dance
WOODCOCK, A., Educational Ergonomics and Design

CRANFIELD UNIVERSITY

Cranfield campus: Cranfield, MK43 0AL
Telephone: (1234) 750111
Fax: (1234) 750875
Shrivenham campus: CDT, Shrivenham, Swindon, SN6 8LA
Telephone: (1793) 785810
Fax: (1793) 783878
E-mail: info@cranfield.ac.uk
Internet: www.cranfield.ac.uk

Founded 1946 as College of Aeronautics; became Cranfield Institute of Technology 1969; took responsibility for academic work at Royal Military College of Science, Shrivenham, 1984; present name 1993

Academic year: October to September

Chancellor: Baroness BARBARA YOUNG OF OLD SCONE
Pro-Chancellor: GORDON PAGE
Vice-Chancellor: Prof. Sir JOHN O'REILLY
Deputy Vice-Chancellor: Prof. CLIFFORD FRIEND
Pro-Vice-Chancellor: Prof. DAVID J. STEPHENSON
Sec. and Registrar: Prof. WILLIAM STEPHENS
Univ. Librarian: Dr HAZEL WOODWARD

Library of 440,915 vols, 9,708 journals (electronic and print)

Number of students: 4,300 , 13,000 short-course delegates per annum

PROFESSORS

AKHAVAN, J., Explosive Chemistry
ALLEN, D., Microengineering
ASPINALL, R., Translational Medicine
BAINES, T., Strategic Manufacturing
BARR, H., Medicine and Biosciences
BELLAMY, C.
BOLTON, S., Creative Design
BONACHE, J., International HRM
BOURNE, M., Business Performance
BRAITHWAITE, G., Air Transport
BRENNAN, F., Offshore
BUCHANAN, D., Organizational Behaviour
BURKE, A., Entrepreneurship
CARR, K., Human Systems
CHIVERS, H., Information Systems
COLLINS, B.
CULLEN, D., Bioanalytical Technology
DRIKAKIS, D., Aerospace Sciences
EDWARDS, C., Management Information Systems
EVANS, S., Life Cycle Engineering
FIELDING, J., Aerospace Engineering
FRIEND, C.
GARRY, K., Aerodynamics Group
GELMAN, L., Vibro-Acoustic Monitoring
GOFFIN, K., Innovation and New Product Development
GRAYSON, D., Corporate Social Responsibility
GUENOV, M., Engineering Design
HARRIS, J., Environmental Technology
HARRISON, A., Operations and Logistics
HETHERINGTON, J.
HIGSON, S., Bio- and Electroanalysis
HORSFALL, I., Armour Systems
HORWITZ, F., Management
IRVING, P., CAA Damage Tolerance
JENKINS, M., Business Strategy
JOHN, P., Dept of Systems Engineering and Human Factors
JUDD, S., Membrane Technology
KAKABADSE, A., Management Development
KAYVANTASH, K., Automotive Technology
KIBBLEWHITE, M., Applied Soil Science
KIRK, G., Soil Systems
KNOWLES, K., Aeromechanical Systems
KNOX, S., Brand Marketing
LAWTON, T., Strategic Management
LUNEC, J., Health
MAGAN, N., Applied Mycology
MATTHEWS, R., Defence Economics
MORRELL, P., Air Transport Economics and Finance
MURRAY, S., Ordnance Science and Technology
NEAL, D., Defence Strategic Change
NEELY, A., Research
NELLIS, J., International Management Economics
NICHOLLS, J., Coatings Technology
OAKEY, J., Energy Technology
ORMONDROYD, R., Communication Networks
PARSONS, S., Water Sciences
PARTRIDGE, I., Polymer Composites
PATEL, M., Engineering
PEPPARD, J., Information Systems
PILETSKY, S., Bio-Organic Polymer Chemistry
PILIDIS, P., Power and Propulsion
POLL, D., Aerospace Engineering
POLLARD, S., Environmental Risk Management
POSHAKWALE, S., International Finance
RAMSDEN, J., Nanotechnology
REINMOELLER, P., Strategic Management
RICKSON, R., Soil Erosion and Conservation
RITZ, K., Soil Biology
ROGERS, K., Materials/Medical Science
ROY, R., Competitive Design
RYALS, L., Strategic Sales—Account Management
SAVILL, A., Computational Aerodynamics Design
SHORE, P., Ultra Precision Engineering
SMITH, H., Security and Resilience
STEPHENSON, D., Materials Processing
STEPHENSON, T., Applied Sciences
TATAM, R., Engineering Photonics Group
TAYLOR, J., Land Resources Monitoring
THOMPSON, C., Applied Mathematics and Computing
TSOURDOS, A., Control Engineering
TURNBULL JAMES, K., Executive Learning
TURNER, A., Biotechnology
VAUGHAN, N., Automotive Engineering Group
VIGNJEVIC, R., Applied Mechanics
VINNICOMBE, S., Organizational Behaviour
WALLACE, I.
WANG, F., e-Science and Grid Computing
WARD, J., Strategic Information Systems
WARNER, P., Molecular Diagnostics
WEBB, P., Engineering
WHITE, S., Integrated Catchment Management
WILDING, R., Supply Chain Risk Management
WILLIAMS, S., Welding Science and Technology
WILSON, H., Strategic Marketing
WITTY, R., Information Systems Engineering
ZBIKOWSKI, R., Control Engineering

DE MONTFORT UNIVERSITY

The Gateway, Leicester, LE1 9BH
Telephone: (116) 255-1551
Fax: (116) 250-6204
E-mail: enquiry@dmu.ac.uk
Internet: www.dmu.ac.uk

Founded 1969, as Leicester Polytechnic, later became Leicester Polytechnic; present name and status 1992

Chancellor: Lord WAHEED ALLI
Pro-Chancellor: DAVID STEVENS
Vice-Chancellor: Prof. DOMINIC SHELLARD
Pro-Vice-Chancellor for Research: (vacant)
Pro-Vice-Chancellor for Teaching, Learning and Student Experience: Prof. HEIDI MACPHERSON
Acad. Registrar: EUGENE CRITCHLOW
Univ. Librarian: K. ARNOLD

Library of 479,135 vols, 16,490 periodicals
Number of teachers: 3,240
Number of students: 20,500

DEANS

Faculty of Art and Design: Dr GERARD MORAN
Faculty of Business and Law: Prof. DAVID WILSON
Faculty of Health and Life Sciences: Prof. BARRY MITCHELL
Faculty of Humanities: Prof. TIM O'SULLIVAN
Faculty of Technology: Prof. ADRIAN HOPGOOD

EDGE HILL UNIVERSITY

St Helens Rd, Ormskirk, L39 4QP
Telephone: (1695) 575171
Fax: (1695) 579997
Internet: www.edgehill.ac.uk

Founded 1885, present status 2008

Chancellor: Prof. TANYA BYRON
Pro-Chancellor: CHRIS TRINICK

Vice-Chancellor: Dr John Cater
Pro-Vice-Chancellor for Academic Affairs: Prof. Bill Bruce
Pro-Vice-Chancellor for Students and External Relations: Dr David Law
Pro-Vice-Chancellor for Resources: Steve Igoe
Univ. Sec. and Clerk to Governors: Lesley Munro
Academic Registrar: Ian Jones
Dean of Learning Services: Alison Mackenzie

Number of teachers: 4,000
Number of students: 24,000

DEANS

Faculty of Arts and Sciences: George Talbot
Faculty of Education: Robert Smedley
Faculty of Health: Seth Crofts

KINGSTON UNIVERSITY

River House, 53–57 High St, Kingston upon Thames, KT1 1LQ
Telephone: (20) 8417-9000
Fax: (20) 8547-7980
E-mail: admissions-info@kingston.ac.uk
Internet: www.kingston.ac.uk

Founded 1899, as Kingston Technical Institute, present name and status 1992
Academic year: September to July

Chancellor: Sir Peter Hall
Vice-Chancellor: Dr. David Mackintosh (acting)
Deputy Vice-Chancellor: Dr. David Mackintosh
Pro-Vice Chancellor for Acad. Support and Student Services: Prof. Martyn Jones
Pro-Vice Chancellor for Corporate Affairs and Univ. Sec.: Neil Latham
Pro-Vice-Chancellor for Research and Enterprise: Prof. Penny Sparke
Acad. Registrar: Dr David Ashton
Head of Library Services: Graham Bulpitt

Library of 450,000 vols
Number of teachers: 661
Number of students: 22,782
Publication: *Kingston review*

DEANS

Faculty of Art, Design and Architecture: Dr Simon Ofield-Kerr
Faculty of Arts and Social Sciences: Prof. Martin Mc Quillon
Faculty of Business and Law: Prof. Jean-Noel Ezingrard
Faculty of Computing, Information Systems and Mathematics: Prof. Timothy Ellis
Faculty of Engineering: Prof. Peter Mason
Faculty of Health and Social Care Sciences: Prof. Fiona Ross
Faculty of Science: Prof. Andy Augousti

LEEDS METROPOLITAN UNIVERSITY

City Campus, Leeds, LS1 3HE
Telephone: (113) 812-0000
E-mail: helpzone@leedsmet.ac.uk
Internet: www.leedsmet.ac.uk

Founded 1970 as Leeds Polytechnic; present name and status 1992

Chancellor: Brendan Foster
Vice-Chancellor: Prof. Susan Price
Pro-Vice-Chancellor and Provost: Sally Brown
Deputy Vice-Chancellor for Research and Enterprise: Prof. Andrew Slade
Deputy Vice-Chancellor for Strategic Devt: Dr Paul Smith
Deputy Vice-Chancellor for Student Experience: Prof. Sally Glen
Sec. and Registrar: Steve Denton
Dir of Libraries and Learning Innovation: Jo Norry

Library of 330,000 vols, 22,000 periodicals
Number of teachers: 3,000
Number of students: 30,000

DEANS

Faculty of Arts, Environment & Technology: Prof. Christopher Bailey
Faculty of Business and Law: Barbara Colledge
Faculty of Health and Social Sciences: Prof. Ieuan Ellis
Carnegie Faculty of Sports and Education: Gareth Davies

LIVERPOOL HOPE UNIVERSITY

Hope Park, Liverpool, L16 9JD
Telephone: (151) 291-3000
Fax: (151) 291-3100
E-mail: admission@hope.ac.uk
Internet: www.hope.ac.uk

Founded 1844; present name 1995, present status 2005
Academic year: September to July

Chancellor: Baroness Caroline Cox
Vice-Chancellor and Rector: Prof. Gerald Pillay
Pro-Vice-Chancellor for External Relations and Widening Participation: Prof. Bill Chambers
Pro-Vice-Chancellor for Research and Acad. Devt: Prof. Kenneth Newport
Pro-Vice-Chancellor for Resource Management and Planning: Dr Ian Vandewalle
Pro-Vice-Chancellor for Student Support and Well-being: Bishop Ian Stuart
Univ. Sec.: Graham Donelan
Number of students: 7,000

DEANS

Arts and Humanities: Dr Terry Philips
Business and Computer Sciences: Dr John Brinkman
Education: Prof. Bart McGettrick
Sciences and Social Sciences: Dr Penny Haughan

LIVERPOOL JOHN MOORES UNIVERSITY

Roscoe Court, 4 Rodney St, Liverpool, L1 2TZ
Telephone: (151) 231-5090
Fax: (151) 231-3194
Internet: www.livjm.ac.uk

Founded 1825, as Liverpool Mechanics' School of Arts, present name and status 1992
Academic year: September to May

Chancellor: Dr Brian May
Vice-Chancellor and Chief Exec.: Prof. Michael Brown
Pro-Vice-Chancellor for Admin. and Univ. Sec.: Alison Wild
Pro-Vice-Chancellor for Acad. and Enhancement: Prof. Diana Burton
Pro-Vice-Chancellor for Student Experience: Steve Kenny
Pro-Vice-Chancellor for Infrastructure: Allan Bickerstaffe
Dir of Learning and Information Services: Maxine Melling

Number of teachers: 2,800
Number of students: 24,000

DEANS

Faculty of Business and Law: Prof. Roger Webster
Faculty of Education, Community and Leisure: Kate Johnston
Faculty of Health and Applied Social Sciences: Prof. Godfrey Mazhindu
Faculty of Media, Arts and Social Science: Prof. Roger Webster
Faculty of Science: Prof. Peter Wheeler
Faculty of Technology and Environment: Prof. Diane Meehan

LONDON METROPOLITAN UNIVERSITY

London City campus: 133 Whitechapel High St, London, E1 7QA
North London campus: 166–220 Holloway Rd, London, N7 8DB
Telephone: (20) 7423-0000
E-mail: admissions@londonmet.ac.uk
Internet: www.londonmet.ac.uk

Founded 2002, by merger of Univ. of North London and London Guildhall Univ.

Pres.: Sir Roderick Castle Floud
Vice-Chancellor and Chief Exec.: Prof. Malcolm Gillies
Deputy Vice-Chancellor for Acad. Affairs: Bob Aylett
Deputy Vice-Chancellor for Planning and Resources: Max Weaver
Deputy Vice-Chancellor for Research and Devt: Prof. Paul Lister
Acad. Registrar: Jill Grinstead
Number of students: 33,000
Publication: *The Metropolitan* (1 a year).

LONDON SOUTH BANK UNIVERSITY

103 Borough Rd, London, SE1 0AA
Telephone: (20) 7928-8989
Fax: (20) 7815-8155
E-mail: lsbuinfo@lsbu.ac.uk
Internet: www.lsbu.ac.uk

Founded 1970 as South Bank Polytechnic, present name and status 1992
State control
Academic year: September to July

Chancellor: Sir Trevor McDonald
Vice-Chancellor: Prof. Martin J Earwicker
Pro-Vice-Chancellor for Academic Affairs: Prof. Phil Cardew
Pro-Vice-Chancellor for External Affairs: Bev Jullien
Univ. Sec.: James Stevenson
Registrar: R. Phillips
Librarian: J. Akeroyd

Library of 280,000 vols
Number of teachers: 652
Number of students: 25,441

DEANS

Business School: Jane Houzer
Faculty of Arts and Human Sciences: Prof. Mike Molan
Faculty of Engineering, Science and Built Environment: Prof. Rao Bhamidimarri
Faculty of Health and Social Care: Prof. Judith Ellis

LOUGHBOROUGH UNIVERSITY

Loughborough, LE11 3TU
Telephone: (1509) 263171
Fax: (1509) 223901
Internet: www.lboro.ac.uk

Founded 1966, as univ.; fmrly Loughborough College of Advanced Technology, univ. charter 1966
Academic year: September to June

Chancellor: Sir Nigel Rudd
Vice-Chancellor and Pres.: Prof. Shirley Pearce
Deputy Vice-Chancellor and Provost: Prof. Neil Halliwell
Pro-Vice-Chancellor for Teaching: Prof. Morag Bell
Pro-Vice-Chancellor for Research: Prof. Ken Parsons
Pro-Vice-Chancellor for Enterprise: Prof. Phill Dickens
Registrar: John Town

Librarian: RUTH JENKINS
Library of 500,000 vols, 19,000 e-journals
Number of teachers: 764
Number of students: 16,629

DEANS

Faculty of Engineering: Prof. STEVE ROTHBERG
Faculty of Science: Prof. CHRIS LINTON
Faculty of Social Sciences and Humanities: Prof. TERRY KAVANAGH

PROFESSORS

ACKERS, P., Industrial Relations and Labour History
ALEXANDROV, A., Theoretical Physics
ALLEN, D., European and International Politics
ANDERSON, J., Physical Geography
ANDREWS, J., Risk and Reliability Analysis
ANTAKI, C., Language and Psychology
ANUMBA, C., Construction Engineering and Informatics
ARNOLD, J., Organizational Behaviour
AUSTIN, S., Structural Engineering
BABITSKY, V., Dynamics
BACKHOUSE, C., Product Innovation
BAGILHOLE, B., Social Policy and Equal Opportunities
BAIRNER, A., Sport and Social Theory
BELL, M., Cultural Geography
BIDDLE, S., Exercise and Sport Psychology
BILLIG, M., Social Sciences
BOUCHLAGHEM, D., Architectural Engineering
BOWMAN, R., Organic Chemistry
BRISTOW, A., Transport Studies
BUCK, T., International Business
BURNS, N., Manufacturing Systems
CADOGAN, J., Marketing
CAINE, M., Sports Technology and Innovation
CALLOW, G., Industrial Professor
CAMERON, N., Human Biology
CARRILLO, P., Strategic Management in Construction
CASE, K., Computer aided Engineering
CHAMBERS, J., Communications and Signal Processing
CHUNG, P., Computer Science
COHEN, L., Organization Studies
CONWAY, P., Manufacturing Processes
COUPLAND, J., Applied Optics
CRAMER, D., Psychological Health
CREASER, C., Analytical Chemistry
DAINTY, A. R. J., Construction Sociology
DAMODARAN, L., Participative Design and Change Management
DANIELS, K., Organizational Psychology
DAVIDSON, I., Accounting and Finance
DICKENS, J., Engineering Education
DICKENS, P., Manufacturing Technology
DIXON, N., Geotechnical Engineering
DOBSON, P., Competition Economics
DOHERTY, N., Information Management
EBBATSON, R., English Studies
EDWARDS, D., Psychology
EVANS, J., Sociology of Education and Physical Education
FARRELL, G., Criminology
FAULKNER, R., Physical Metallurgy
FEATHER, J., Library and Information Studies
FITZGERALD, L., Management Accounting
FLETCHER, S., Physical Chemistry
FORBES, W., Accounting and Finance
GANE, M., Sociology
GARNER, C., Applied Thermodynamics
GERSTNER, E., Marketing and Retail
GIBB, A., Construction Engineering Management
GILBERT, M., Polymer Technology
GLEESON, M., Exercise Biochemistry
GOLDING, P., Sociology
GOODALL, R., Control Systems Engineering
GREEN, C., Banking and Finance
GRIFFITHS, J., Applied Mathematics
GRIMSHAW, R. H. J., Mathematical Sciences
GROVES, M., Mathematics
HAGUE, R., Innovative Manufacturing
HALL, M., Banking and Financial Regulation
HALLIWELL, N., Optical Engineering
HANKINSON, G., Safety Engineering
HANTRAI, L., European Social Policy
HARGRAVE, G., Optical Diagnostics
HASLAM, R., Health and Safety Ergonomics
HAVENITH, G., Environmental Physiology and Ergonomics
HENRY, I., Leisure Policy and Management
HENSHAW, M., Systems Engineering
HEWITT, C., Pharmaceutical Engineering
HOBBY, E., 17th-century Studies
HOCKING, B., International Relations
HOGERVORST, E., Psychology
HOLDICH, R., Chemical Engineering
HORNE, J., Psychophysiology
HOULIHAN, B., Sport Policy
HOWCROFT, B., Retail Banking
HUBBARD, P., Urban Social Geography
HUNTLEY, J., Applied Mechanics
ISON, S., Transport Policy
JONES, R., Organic and Biological Chemistry
JONES, R., Sports Technology
KALAWSKY, R., Human-Computer Integration
KAVANAGH, T., Design
KHOMSKII, D., Novel Material
KING, M., Management Sciences
KONG, M., Bioelectrics Engineering
KORCZYNSKI, M., Sociology of Work
KRYLOV, V., Acoustics and Vibration
KUSMARTSEV, F., Condensed Matter Theory
LINTON, C., Applied Mathematics
LISTER, R., Social Policy
LIU, J., Operations Management
LLEWELLYN, D., Money and Banking
LOUCOPOULOS, P., Information Systems
LOUGHLAN, J., Aerospace Structures
LOVEDAY, D., Building Physics
MCCAFFER, R., Construction Management
MCGUIGAN, J., Cultural Analysis
MCGUIRK, J., Aerodynamics
MCIVER, P., Applied Mathematics
MCKEE, V., Inorganic Chemistry
MCKNIGHT, C., Information Studies
MAGUIRE, J., Sociology of Sport
MATTHEWS, G., Information Management
MAUGHAN, R., Sport and Exercise Nutrition
MILLS, T., Applied Statistics and Econometrics
MORGAN, K., Gerontology
MORRIS, A., Information Science
MORTIMER, R., Physical Chemistry
NEISHTADT, A., Applied Mathematics
NIMMO, M., Exercise Physiology
OPPENHEIM, C., Information Science
OVERTON, W., Literature
PAGE, P., Organic Chemistry
PARISH, D., Communication Networks
PARKIN, R., Mechatronics
PARRY-JONES, R., Industrial Professor
PARSONS, K., Environmental Ergonomics
PENTECOST, E., Economics
PORTER, M., Design Ergonomics
POTTER, J., Discourse Analysis
POYAGO-THEOTOKY, J., Microeconomics
PRICE, A., Project Management
RADLEY, A., Social Psychology
RAHNEJAT, H., Dynamics
RAMAN, K., Marketing
RAOOF, M., Structural Engineering
RASTOGI, S., Polymer Technology
REID, I., Physical Geography
RENDELL, H., Physical Geography
RIELLY, C., Chemical Engineering
ROTHBERG, S., Vibration Engineering
SEAL, W., Accounting
SHAW, M., English
SHIONO, K., Environmental Hydrodynamics
SILBERSCHMIDT, V., Mechanics of Materials
SINGH, S., Autonomous Systems
SKELTON, T., Critical Geographies
SLATER, D., Human Geography
SMITH, D., Sociology
SMITH, I., Electrical Power Engineering
SMITH, M., European Politics
SMITH, R., Analytical Chemistry
SMITH, R., Mathematical Engineering
STAROV, V., Chemical Engineering
STOBART, R. K., Automotive Engineering
STURGES, P., Library Studies
SUMMERS, R., Information Science
TAYLOR, P., Geography
THOMAS, P., Analytical Chemistry
THOMSON, R., Materials Engineering
THORPE, A., Construction Information Technology
THRING, R., Fuel Cell Engineering
TIPPETT, M., Accounting and Finance
TIWARI, A., Renewable Energy Systems
VARDAXOGLOU, Y., Wireless Communications
VESELOV, A., Mathematics
WAKEMAN, R., Chemical Engineering
WARD, H., Child and Family Research
WARWICK, P., Environmental Radiochemistry
WELLS, P., Animation
WESTON, R., Flexible Automation
WEYMAN-JONES, T., Industrial Economics
WHEATLEY, A., Water Technology
WILKINSON, S., Feminisim and Health Studies
WILLIAMS, C., Sports Science
WILLIAMS, D., Healthcare Engineering
WILSON, J., Operational Research
WOLFREYS, J., Modern Literature and Culture
WOOD, N., Literature
WOODHEAD, M., Systems Engineering
WOODWARD, B., Underwater Acoustics
WRIGHT, J., Building Optimization
YANG, S., Networks and Control
YEADON, F., Computer Simulation in Sport
ZHAO, H., Mathematics
ZIEBECK, K., Physics

MANCHESTER METROPOLITAN UNIVERSITY

All Saints Bldg, Manchester, M15 6BH
Telephone: (161) 247-2000
Fax: (161) 247-6390
E-mail: enquiries@mmu.ac.uk
Internet: www.mmu.ac.uk

Founded 1970, as Manchester Polytechnic, present name and status 1992
Academic year: September to July

Chancellor: Rt Hon. Dame JANET SMITH
Pro-Chancellor: ALAN BENZIE
Vice-Chancellor: Prof. JOHN BROOKS
Deputy Vice-Chancellor for Student Experience: Prof. KEVIN BONNETT
Deputy Vice-Chancellor for Strategic Planning: Prof. GERRY KELLEHER
Registrar: GWYN ARNOLD
Librarian: Prof. C. HARRIS

Library: see under Libraries and Archives
Number of teachers: 2,592
Number of students: 35,728

Publication: *Success*

DEANS

Business School: Prof. RUTH ASHFORD
Faculty Hollings: Prof. RICHARD MURRAY
Faculty of Art and Design: Prof. DAVID CROW
Faculty of Health, Psychology and Social Care: Prof. V. K. RAMPROGUS
Faculty of Humanities, Law and Social Science: Prof. J. BEER
Faculty of Science and Engineering: Prof. M. NEAL
Institute of Education: ANDY JONES
MMU Cheshire: DENNIS DUNN

MIDDLESEX UNIVERSITY

The Burroughs, London, NW4 4BT
Telephone: (20) 8411-5555
Fax: (20) 8411-5649
E-mail: intadmissions@mdx.ac.uk

Internet: www.mdx.ac.uk

Founded 1973, as Middlesex Polytechnic, present name and status 1992; comprises fmr Enfield and Hendon Colleges of Technology, Hornsey College of Art, New College of Speech and Drama, Trent Park College of Education, College of All Saints and North London College of Health Studies

Academic year: September to July

Chancellor: Rt Hon. Lord SHEPPARD OF DIDGEMERE

Vice-Chancellor: Prof. MICHAEL DRISCOLL

Deputy Vice-Chancellor: STEVE KNIGHT

Deputy Vice-Chancellor: KATIE BELL

Deputy Vice-Chancellor for International Affairs: Dr TERRY BUTLAND

Deputy Vice-Chancellor for Academic: Prof. MARGARET HOUSE

Deputy Vice-Chancellor for Finance and External Relations: MELVYN KEEN

Deputy Vice-Chancellor for Research and Enterprise: Prof. WAQAR AHMAD

Library of 540,000 vols, 130,000 vols of periodicals

Number of teachers: 853

Number of students: 35,000

DEANS

School of Arts and Education: Prof. EDWARD J. ESCHE

School of Engineering and Information Sciences: Prof. MARTIN LOOMES

School of Health and Social Sciences: Prof. JAN WILLIAMS

Middlesex University Business School: ANNA KYPRIANOU

NEWCASTLE UNIVERSITY

Registrar's Office, 6 Kensington Terrace, Newcastle upon Tyne NE1 7RU

Telephone: (191) 222-6000

Fax: (191) 222-8685

E-mail: postmaster@ncl.ac.uk

Internet: www.ncl.ac.uk

Founded 1851, incorporated as separate Univ. in 1963

Academic year: September to June

Chancellor: Sir LIAM DONALDSON

Chair. of Ccl and Pro-Chancellor: OLIVIA GRANT

Vice-Chancellor: Prof. CHRIS BRINK

Deputy Vice-Chancellor: Prof. ELLA RITCHIE

Dean for Int. Business Devt and Student Recruitment: Prof. GERARD CORSANE

Pro-Vice-Chancellor for Medical Sciences: Prof. CHRIS P. DAY

Pro-Vice-Chancellor for Planning and Resources: Prof. TONY STEVENSON

Pro-Vice-Chancellor for Research and Innovation: Prof. NICK WRIGHT

Pro-Vice-Chancellor for Science, Agriculture and Engineering: Prof. OLIVER R. HINTON

Pro-Vice-Chancellor for Teaching and Learning: Prof. Dr ELLA RITCHIE

Registrar: Dr JOHN HOGAN

Librarian: WAYNE CONNOLLY

Library of 1,000,000 electronic resources, 10,000 periodicals

Number of teachers: 2,171

Number of students: 20,456

DEANS

Faculty of Humanities and Social Sciences: Prof. GERARD DOCHERTY (Dean of Research: Prof. ERIC CROSS (Dean of Cultural Affairs: Prof. NEILL MARSHALL (Dean of Postgraduate Affairs: SIMON PALLETT (Dean of Undergraduate Affairs)

Faculty of Medical Sciences: Prof. TIM CAWSTON (Dean of Research: Prof. MICHAEL WHITAKER (Dean of Devt: Prof. ALASTAIR BURT (Dean of Clinical Medicine: Prof. BARRY HIRST (Dean of Postgraduate Studies: Prof. SUZANNE CHOLERTON (Dean of Undergraduate Studies)

Faculty of Science, Agriculture and Engineering: Prof. TONY ROSKILLY (Dean of Research: Prof. TOM ANDERSON (Dean of Business Devt: Dr BRYN JONES (Dean of Postgraduate Studies: Dr CHRIS PHILLIPS (Dean of Undergraduate Studies)

PROFESSORS

Faculty of Humanities and Social Sciences:

ALDER, J. E., Law
ANDERSON, L. R., Modern English and American Literature
APPLEYARD, A. R., Accounting and Finance
BABINGTON, B. F., Film Studies
BALLANTYNE, A. N., Architectural Science
BATCHELOR, J. B., English Literature
BONNETT, A., Social Geography
BURTON-ROBERTS, N. C., English Language and Linguistics
CAIN, T. G. S., Early Modern Literature
CARRINGTON, L. B., Education
CHARLES, D. R., Business Innovation
CHEDGZOY, K., Renaissance Literature
COLLIER, R. S., Law and Social Theory
COOK, V. J., Applied Linguistics
COOMBES, M. G., Geographic Information
DAVIS, P. S., Museology
DOLKON, P. J., Economics
FIRTH, J. E., Law
GILLESPIE, A. E., Communications Geography
GRAHAM, D. F., Poetry
GUY, S. C., Law
HAIMES, E. V., Sociology
HANSEN, R., Politics
HILLIER, J. S., Town and Country Planning
HOLMBERG, J. A., Theoretical Linguistics
HOWARD, D., Research Development
JONES, P. N., Political Philosophy
KARANASOS, M., Financial Economics
LAMONT, C., English Romantic Literature
LEOPOLD, J. W., Human Resources Management
LI, W., Applied Linguistics
MAC AN GHAILL, M., Education
MADANI POUR, A., Urban Design
MARSHALL, J. N., Economic Geography
MIDDLETON, R., Music
MINCA, C., Human Geography
MOLES, J. L., Latin
MOULAERT, F., European Planning and Development
MYLES, F., French Linguistics
NEWSON, M. D., Physical Geography
PERRIAM, C. G., Hispanic Studies
PINCOMBE, M. J., Tudor and Elizabethan Literature
POWRIE, P. P., French Cultural Studies
REYNOLDS, K. K., Children's Literature
RICHARDSON, L. D., Sociology and Social Policy
RIORDAN, C. B., German
RODGERS, C. P., Law
SAUNDERS, D. B., History of the Russian Empire
SHUCKSMITH, D. M., Town Planning
SPAWFORTH, A. J. S., Ancient History
STANLEY, L., Sociology
STIMPSON, B. E., French Studies
TOMANEY, J., Regional Governance
TOOLEY, J. N., Policy Studies in Education
VAN DER EIJK, P. J., Greek
WALKER, J. A., Family Policy
WARD, I., Law
WHALEY, D. C., Law
WHEELOCK, J., Socio-economics
WILLIS, K. G., Economics of the Environment
WRIGHT, T. R., English Literature
WYNARCZYK, P., Small Enterprise Research

Faculty of Medical Sciences:

AGIUS, L., Metabolic Biochemistry
ARGENT, B. E., Cellular Physiology
BARER, D. H., Clinical Geriatric Medicine
BARTON, J. R., Clinical Medicine
BASSENDINE, M. F., Hepatology
BATES, D., Clinical Neurology
BILOUS, R. W., Clinical Medicine
BLAIN, P. G., Environmental Medicine
BLAMIRE, A. M., Magnetic Resonance Physics
BOND, J., Social Gerontology and Health Services Research
BOND, S., Nursing Research
BURN, J., Clinical Genetics
BURT, A. D., Pathology
BUSHBY, K. M. D., Neuromuscular Genetics
CALVERT, A. H., Medical Oncology
CARDING, P., Voice Pathology
CAWSTON, T. E., Rheumatology
CHINNERY, P. F., Neurogenetics
CONNOLLY, B. A., Biochemistry
CORRIS, P. A., Thoracic Medicine
CRAFT, A. W., Child Health
DALY, A. K., Pharmacogenetics
DARK, J. H., Cardiothoracic Surgery
DARRINGTON, A. M., Psychology, Brain and Behaviour
DAY, C. P., Liver Medicine
DICKINSON, A. M., Marrow Transplant Biology
DONALDSON, C., Health Economics
DUNLOP, W., Obstetrics and Gynaecology
ECCLES, M. P., Primary Care Research
EDWARDSON, J. A. E., Neuroendocrinology
ELLISON, D. W., Neuropathology
EYRE, J. A., Paediatric Neuroscience
FERRIER, I. N., Psychiatry
FLECKNELL, P. A., Comparative Biology
FORD, G. A., Pharmacology of Old Age
FREESTON, M., Clinical Psychology
GATEHOUSE, A. M. R., Invertebrate Molecular Biology
GIBSON, G. J., Respiratory Medicine
GILBERT, H. J., Agricultural Biochemistry and Nutrition
GILLESPIE, J. I., Human Physiology
GOODSHIP, J. A., Medical Genetics
GOODSHIP, T. H. J., Renal Medicine
GOSLING, L. M., Animal Behaviour
GRAY, C. S., Clinical Geriatric Medicine
GRIFFITHS, T. D., Cognitive Neurology
GRUBIN, D., Forensic Psychiatry
HALL, A. G., Experimental Haematology
HARRIS, J. B., Experimental Neurology
HARWOOD, C. R., Molecular Microbiology
HAWKINS, A. R., Molecular Genetics
HEASMAN, P. A., Periodontology
HENDRICK, D. J., Occupational Respiratory Medicine
HESKETH, J. E., Mammalian Molecular Biology
HILL, P. M., Postgraduate Medical Education
HIRST, B. H., Cellular Physiology
HOME, P. D., Diabetes Medicine
HUGHES, M. A., Plant Molecular Genetics
INGRAM, C. D., Psychobiology
ISAACS, J., Clinical Rheumatology
JAMES, O. F. W., Geriatric Medicine
JONES, D. E. J., Liver Immunology
KEHOE, M. A., Microbiology
KENNY, R. A., Cardiovascular Research
KIRBY, J. A., Immunobiology
KIRKWOOD, T. B. L., Medicine
LAKEY, J. H., Structural Biochemistry
LE COUTEUR, A. S., Child and Adolescent Psychiatry
LENNARD, T. W. J., Breast and Endocrine Surgery
LEUNG, H. Y., Urological Oncology
LIGHTOWLERS, R. N., Molecular Neuroscience
LYDALL, D. A., Biology of Ageing
MCCABE, J. F., Dental Materials Science
MCCASKIE, A. W., Orthopaedic Surgery
MCGUCKIN, C., Regenerative Medicine
MCKEITH, I. G., Old Age Psychiatry

McNeil, C. J., Biological Sensor Systems
Marshall, S. M., Diabetes
Mathers, J. C., Human Nutrition
May, C., Medical Sociology
Mendelow, A. D., Neurosurgery
Morgan, B. A., Yeast Molecular Biology
Newell, D. R., Cancer Therapeutics
O'Brien, J. T., Old Age Psychiatry
Parker, L., Paediatric Epidemiology
Pearson, A. D. J., Paediatric Oncology
Perry, E. K., Neurochemical Pathology
Perry, R. H., Neuropathology
Petrie, M., Behavioural Ecology
Proctor, S. J., Haematological Oncology
Purves, I. N., Health Informatics
Rawlins, M., Clinical Pharmacology
Reynolds, N. J., Dermatology
Robinson, J. H., Immunology
Robinson, N. J., Molecular Genetics
Robson, S. C., Foetal Medicine
Russell, R. R. B., Oral Biology
Self, C. H., Clinical Biochemistry
Seymour, R. A., Restorative Dentistry
Simmons, N. L., Epithelial Physiology
Slater, C. R., Neuroscience
Soames, J. V., Oral Pathology
Spencer, J. A., Medical Education in Primary Health Care
Stansby, G., Vascular Surgery
Steele, J. G., Dental Sciences
Strachan, T., Human Molecular Genetics
Straub, V. W., Medicine
Taylor, R., Medicine and Metabolism
Thiele, A., Visual Neuroscience
Thomason, J. M., Prosthodontics and Oral Rehabilitation
Thomson, P. J., Oral and Maxillofacial Surgery
Thomson, R. G., Epidemiology and Public Health
Turnbull, D. M., Neurology
van Zwanenberg, T. D., Postgraduate General Practice
von Zglinicki, T., Cellular Gerontology
Walker, M., Molecular Diabetic Medicine
Walls, A. W. G., Restorative Dentistry
Westley, B. R., Molecular Pathology
Whitaker, M. J., Physiology
Williams, F. M., Toxicology
Wilson, J. A., Otolaryngology and Head and Neck Surgery
Young, A. H., General Psychiatry

Faculty of Science, Agriculture and Engineering:

Akay, G., Chemical Engineering
Anderson, G. K., Environmental Engineering
Anderson, T., Computing Science
Aplin, A. C., Petroleum Geosciences
Atlar, M., Ship Hydrodynamics
Barenghi, C. F., Fluid Dynamics
Birmingham, R. W., Small Craft Design
Blythe, P. T., Transport
Braiden, P. M., Manufacturing Engineering
Bruce, G. J., Ship Repair and Conversion
Bull, S. J., Surface Engineering
Burdess, J. S., Engineering Dynamics
Calder, I. R., Land Use and Water Resources Management
Carrasco, R. A., Mobile Communications
Clare, A. S., Marine Science
Clarke, B. G., Geotechnical Engineering
Clegg, W., Structural Crystallography
Cram, W. J., Plant Biology
Crowe, A., Physics
Cullinane, K., Marine Transport and Management
Dickinson, A. S., Theoretical Atomic Physics
Donnelly, T., Integrated Pollution Control
Edwards, S. A., Agriculture
Embley, T. M., Evolutionary Molecular Therapy
Finch, J. W., Electrical Control Engineering
Frid, C. L., Marine Systems Geology
Gibson, A. G., Composite Materials Engineering
Golding, B. T., Organic Chemistry
Goodfellow, M., Microbial Systematics
Gosling, L. M., Animal Behaviour
Griffin, R. J., Medicinal Chemistry
Hall, J. W., Animal Behaviour
Hall, J. W., Earth System Engineering
Harriman, A. M., Physical Chemistry
Harrison, M. D., Informatics
Harvey, D. R., Agricultural Economics
Henderson, O. R., Statistics
Henderson, R. A., Inorganic Chemistry
Hinton, O. R., Signal Processing
Hofmann, D. A., Gear Systems Design and Development
Incecik, A., Offshore Engineering
Jack, A. G., Electrical Engineering
Jaros, M., Philosophical Studies
Johnson, G. R., Rehabilitation Engineering
Jones, C. B., Computing Science
Jones-Lee, M. W., Economics
Kapoor, A., Mechanical Engineering Innovation
Koutny, M., Computing Science
Larter, S. R., Geology
Lee, P. A., Computing Science
Leifert, C., Ecological Agriculture
Li, F., e-Business Development
Lowe, P. D., Rural Economy
McLoughlin, I. P., Management
Manning, D. C., Soil Science
Martin, E. B., Industrial Statistics
Matthews, J. N. S., Medical Statistics
Mecrow, B. C., Electrical Power Engineering
Metcalfe, I. S., Chemical Engineering
Mitrani, I., Computing Science
Montague, G. A., Bioprocess Control
Moore, P., Geomatics
Morris, A. J., Process Control
Moss, I. G., Theoretical Cosmology
Nelson, J. D., Public Transport Systems
North, M., Organic Chemistry
O'Connell, P. E., Water Resources Engineering
O'Donnell, A. G., Soil Microbiology and Molecular Ecology
Olive, P. J. W., Reproductive Biology
O'Neill, A. G., Microelectronics
Page, T. F., Engineering Materials
Parker, D., Geomatics
Procter, S., Management
Reeks, M. W., Multiphase Flow
Ritson, C., Agricultural Marketing
Robertson, A. G., Pure Mathematics
Roskilly, A. P., Marine Engineering
Ryan, P. Y. A., Computing Science
Scott, K., Electrochemical Engineering
Sen, P., Marine Design and Construction
Sergeev, Y. A., Engineering Mathematics
Sharif, B. S., Digital Communications
Shrivastava, S. K., Computing Science
Shukurov, A., Astrophysics and Fluid Dynamics
Snowdon, K. J., Research Development
Thomas, K. M., Carbon Science
Thompson, D. P., Engineering Ceramics
Upstill-Goddard, R. C., Marine Biogeochemistry
Wagner, T., Earth Systems Science
Watson, P., Computer Science
White, J. R., Polymer Science and Engineering
Wright, A. R., Chemical Engineering
Wright, N. G., Electronic Materials
Yakovlev, A. V., Computing Systems Design
Young, N. J., Pure Mathematics
Younger, P. L., Hydrogeochemical Engineering

NORTHUMBRIA UNIVERSITY

Ellison Pl., Newcastle upon Tyne NE1 8ST
Telephone: (191) 232-6002
Fax: (191) 227-3903
E-mail: er.pressoffice@northumbria.ac.uk
Internet: www.northumbria.ac.uk

Founded 1969, as Newcastle upon Tyne Polytechnic, present name and status 1992

Academic year: September to July

Chancellor: Lord Stevens of Kirkwhelpington
Chair and Pro-Chancellor: Sir Leslie Elton
Vice-Chancellor and Chief Exec.: Prof. Andrew Wathey
Deputy Vice-Chancellor and Finance Dir: David Chesser
Deputy Vice-Chancellor for Learning and Teaching: Prof. Paul Croney
Deputy Vice-Chancellor for Region, Engagement and Partnerships: Lucy Winskell
Deputy Vice-Chancellor for Research and Innovation: Prof. Peter Golding
Deputy Vice-Chancellor for Strategic Planning: Prof. Ian Postlethwaite
Academic Registrar: Paul Kelly
Univ. Sec.: Philip Booth (acting)

Library of 550,000 vols with 2,500 titles available as e-books

Number of teachers: 924 (full-time)

Number of students: 34,018 (23,185 full-time and sandwich, 10,833 part-time)

DEANS

School of Arts and Social Sciences: Prof. Lynn Dobbs
School of Built and Natural Environment: Stephen Hodgson (acting)
School of Computing, Engineering and Information Science: Prof. Alistair Sambell
School of Design: Prof. Steven Kyffin
School of Health, Community and Education Studies: Prof. Kath McCourt (acting)
School of Life Sciences: Prof. Pam Briggs
Newcastle Business School: Prof. Sharon Mavin (acting)
Northumbria Law School: Prof. Philip Plowden

NOTTINGHAM TRENT UNIVERSITY

Burton St, Nottingham, NG1 4BU
Telephone: (115) 941-8418
Fax: (115) 848-4852
E-mail: cor.web@ntu.ac.uk
Internet: www.ntu.ac.uk

Founded 1843, as Nottingham Government School of Design, present name and status 1992

Academic year: September to July

Chancellor: Sir Michael Parkinson
Vice-Chancellor: Prof. Neil T. Gorman
Sr Pro-Vice-Chancellor: Prof. Peter Jones
Pro-Vice-Chancellor: Prof Yvonne Barnett
Pro-Vice-Chancellor: Prof. Nigel Hastings
Pro-Vice-Chancellor: Ann Priest
Registrar: D. W. Samson
Librarian: Sue McKnight

Library of 467,299 vols, 2,550 periodicals, 7,150 electronic journals, 261 databases

Number of teachers: 927 (767 full-time, 160 part-time)

Number of students: 24,000

Publications: *Collapsing Soil Communique* (2 a year), *Comparative American Studies* (4 a year), *Gearing and Transmissions Journal* (2 a year), *Interventions Journal* (3 a year), *John Clare Society Journal* (1 a year), *Journal of Construction Procurement* (2 a year), *Journal for Critical Realism* (3 a year), *Journal of Strategic Change* (8 a year), *Loess Letter* (2 a year), *Mercian Geologist* (1 a year), *Nottingham Law*

Journal (2 a year), *Studies in Travel Writing* (2 a year)

DEANS

School of Animal, Rural and Environmental Sciences: Dr EUNICE SIMMONS
School of Architecture, Design and Built Environment: PETER WESTLAND
School of Art and Design: Prof. JUDITH MOTTRAM
School of Arts and Humanities: Prof. MURRAY PRATT
School of Education: Dr GILL SCOTT
School of Science and Technology: Prof. ROGER ECCLESTON
School of Social Sciences: CHRIS POLE
Nottingham Business School: Prof. BABACK YAZDANI
Nottingham Law School: ANDREA NOLLENT

OPEN UNIVERSITY

Walton Hall, Milton Keynes, MK7 6AA
POB 197, Milton Keynes, MK7 6BJ
Telephone: (1908) 274066
Fax: (1908) 653744
E-mail: general-enquiries@open.ac.uk
Internet: www.open.ac.uk
Founded 1969
Academic year: variable; teaching takes place over up to 9 months, depending on courses
Chancellor: Lord PUTTNAM
Pro-Chancellor: Baron HASKINS OF SHIDBY
Treas.: RICHARD DEL BRIDGE
Vice-Chancellor: MARTIN BEAN
Pro-Vice-Chancellor for Curriculum and Qualifications: Prof ALAN TAIT
Pro-Vice-Chancellor for Learning, Teaching and Quality: Prof DENISE KIRKPATRICK
Pro-Vice-Chancellor for Research and Staff: Prof. BRIGID HEYWOOD
Pro-Vice-Chancellor for Strategy and External Affairs: Prof. DAVID VINCENT
Pro-Vice-Chancellor for Students, Quality and Standards: Prof. ALAN COCHRANE
Univ. Sec.: FRASER WOODBURN
Finance Dir: HILES HEDGET
Dir, Students: WILLIAM SWANN
Dir of Library Services: NICKY WHITSED
Number of teachers: 8,200 incl. 7,000 tutors and 1,200 full-time
Number of students: 250,000
Publications: *Open Business School Brochure*, *PGCE Brochure*, *Research Degree Prospectus*, *Studying with the Open University*, *Taught Master's Degree Prospectuses*

DEANS

Faculty of Arts: Prof DAVID ROWLAND
Faculty of Education and Language Studies: Dr SHARON DING
Faculty of Health and Social Care: JEREMY ROCHE
Faculty of Mathematics, Computing, and Technology: Prof. ANNE DE ROECK
Faculty of Science: Prof PHILIP POTTS
Faculty of Social Sciences: Prof SIMON BROMLEY
Open University Business School: Prof. JAMES FLECK

DIRECTORS OF UNITS

Institute of Educational Technology: Prof. JOSIE TAYLOR
Knowledge Media Institute: Dr PETER SCOTT

REGIONAL DIRECTORS

East Midlands Region: G. LAMMIE
East of England Region: HELEN WILDMAN
Ireland: Dr R. HAMILTON
London Region: ROSEMARY MAYES
North Region: DAVID KNIGHT
North West Region: LYNDA BRADY
Scotland: PETER SYME
South East Region: LIZ GRAY
South Region: CELIA COHEN
South West Region: LINDA BRIGHTMAN
Wales: ROB HUMPHREYS
West Midlands Region: Dr MICHAEL ROOKES
Yorkshire Region: NICK BERRY

PROFESSORS

ALDGATE, P. J., Social Care
ALLEN, J. R., Social Science
APPLEBY, C., Business Development
ATKINSON, D., Learning Disability
BASSINDALE, A., Organometallic Chemistry
BENNETT, T., Sociology
BENTON, T. J., Art History
BERRY, F., Inorganic Chemistry
BISSELL, C. C., Telematics
BLOWERS, A. T., Social Sciences
BORNAT, J., Oral History
BRAITHWAITE, N., Engineering Physics
BRANNAN, D. A., Pure Mathematics
BROWN, S., Philosophy
BURROWS, D. J., Music
BURTON, K. W., Isotope Geochemistry
BUSH, P.
CANDLIN, C. N., Applied Linguistics
CHAMBERS, E.
CHATAWAY, J. C., Development Manager
CLARKE, J., Social Policy
COCHRANE, A., Public Policy
COCKELL, C. S., Geomicrobiology
COLEMAN, J. A., Languages
COLLINS, R. E., Media Studies
COOK, G., Education
CRITCHLEY, F., Statistics
CROSS, N. G., Design Studies (Technology)
DANIEL, E. M., Information Management
DAVIES, C., Health Care
DE ROECK, A. N., Computing
DOBSON, A. N. H., Politics
DU GAY, P. L. J., Sociology
EARL, C., Engineering Product Design
EDWARDS, L., Structural Integrity
EISENSTADT, M., Artificial Intelligence
ELLIOTT, D., Technology Policy
EMSLEY, C., Arts
ENGLANDER, R., History
FORRESTER-PATON, R., Social Enterprise
GARTHWAITE, P. H., Statistics
GELLATLY, A. R. H., Cognitive Psychology
GLATTER, R. G., Education
GOODMAN, D. C., History of Science and Technology
GOWER, J. C., Statistics
GRANNELL, M. J., Pure Mathematics
GRANT, J., Education in Medicine
GRAY, J. J., History of Mathematics
GRIGGS, T. S., Pure Mathematics
HALL, P. A. V., Computing
HALLIDAY, T. R., Evolutionary Biology
HAMMERSLEY, M., Educational and Social Research
HARDWICK, L. P., Classical Studies
HARRIS, N. B. W., Tectonics
HARRISON, C. T., Art History
HERBERT, T., Music
HIMMELWEIT, S. F., Economics
HOLLWAY, W., Psychology
INCE, D. C., Computing
ISON, R. L., Systems
JOHNSON, J., Complexity, Science and Design
JONES, B. W., Astronomy
JONES, M. C., Statistics
KAYE, G. R., Information Management
KING, C., Art History
LAING, A. W., Marketing
LAURENCE, E. A., History
LENTIN, A., History
LEWIS, V., Education
MCCORMICK, R., Learning Schools Programme
MCDONNELL, J. A., Planetary Space Science
MACKINTOSH, M., Economics
MALE, D., Immunology
MASON, J. H., Mathematics Education
MASON, N., Physics
MASON, R., Educational Technology
MASSEY, D. B., Geography
MERCER, N., Education
MONK, J. S., Digital Systems
MOON, R. E., Education
MUNCIE, J. P., Criminology
NAUGHTON, J., Public Understanding of Technology
NEWMAN, J. E., Social Policy
NUSEIBEH, B., Computing
O'DAY, R., History
OWENS, W. R., Art
PETERS, G., Systems Strategy
PHOENIX, A. A., Psychology
PILLINGER, C. T., Planetary Sciences
PLUMBRIDGE, W. J., Materials
POND-JANZEN, C. M., Biological Sciences
QUINTAS, P. R., Knowledge Management
RICHARDS, D., Applied Mathematics
RICHARDSON, J. T. E., Student Learning and Assessment
ROSE, S. P. R., Biology
ROY, R., Design and Environment
RUTTERFORD, J., Financial Management
SALAMAN, G., Organization Studies
SAWARD, M., Politics
SCANLON, E., Educational Technology
SEGAL-HORN, S., International Strategy
SELF, S., Volcanology
SHUKER, D. E. G., Organic Chemistry
SILVERTOWN, J. W., Ecology
SLAPPER, G., Law
SLATER, J. B.
SPICER, R. A., Earth Sciences
STEWART, D.
STEWART, M. G., Neuroscience
STOREY, J., Human Resource Management
SWITHENBY, S. J., Physics
THOMPSON, G. F., Political Economy
THORPE, M. S., Educational Technology
WALDER, D. J., Literature
WATSON, S., Sociology
WETHERELL, M., Business
WHATMORE, S. J., Geography
WIELD, D. V., Innovation and Development
WILKINSON, M., Applied Mathematics
WILSON, R. C. L., Earth Sciences
WOLFFE, J. R., Religious History
ZARNECKI, J., Space Sciences

OXFORD BROOKES UNIVERSITY

Gipsy Lane, Headington, Oxford, OX3 0BP
Telephone: (1865) 484848
Fax: (1865) 483073
E-mail: query@brookes.ac.uk
Internet: www.brookes.ac.uk
Founded 1865, as Oxford School of Art, became Oxford Polytechnic 1970, university status 1992
State control
Academic year: September to July
Chancellor: SHAMI CHAKRABARTI
Pro-Chancellor: DANBY BLOCH
Vice-Chancellor: Prof. JANET BEER
Pro-Vice-Chancellor for Research: Prof DIANA WOODHOUSE
Pro-Vice-Chancellor for Student Experience: Prof. JOHN RAFTERY
Registrar: PAUL LARGE (acting)
Library of 500,000 vols
Number of teachers: 750
Number of students: 18,167
Publication: *Observe*

DEANS

Faculty of Business: Prof. CHRIS COOPER
Faculty of Health and Life Sciences: JUNE GIRVIN
Faculty of Humanities and Social Sciences: DEREK ELSOM

Faculty of Technology, Design and Environment: MARS STREET

ROEHAMPTON UNIVERSITY

Erasmus House, Roehampton Lane, London, SW15 5PU
Telephone: (20) 8392-3232
Fax: (20) 8392-3470
E-mail: enquiries@roehampton.ac.uk
Internet: www.roehampton.ac.uk

Founded 1841, present status 2004

Chancellor: JOHN SIMPSON
Pro-Chancellor: WILLIAM MACINTYRE
Pro-Vice-Chancellor: ANDREW MASHETER
Vice-Chancellor: Prof. PAUL O'PREY
Deputy Vice-Chancellor and Provost: Prof. JANE BROADBENT
Pro-Vice-Chancellor: CHRIS COBB
Pro-Vice-Chancellor: ANDY MASHETER
Dir for Finance: REGGIE BLENNERHASSETT
Univ. Sec. and Registrar: ROBIN GELLER
Prin. of Digby Stuart College: PAUL HODGES
Prin. of Froebel College: SIMON DORMAN
Prin. of Southlands College: YVONNE GUERRIER
Prin. of Whitelands College: Rev. Prof. GEOFFREY WALKER

DEANS

School of Arts: LYNDIE BRIMSTONE
School of Business and Social Sciences: Prof. YVONNE GUERRIER
School of Education: Dr JEANNE KEAY
School of Human and Life Sciences: MICHAEL BARHAM
Business School: Prof. ELAINE HARRIS (Dir)

PROFESSORS

School of Arts:
FISHER, A., Art History
JORDAN, S., Dance
READ, A., Drama and Theatre Studies

School of Business and Social Sciences:
BALES, K., Sociology
EADE, J., Sociology and Anthropology
FENNELL, G., Sociology and Social Policy
GLOVER, J., Employment Studies
GUERRIER, Y., Organizational Studies

School of Education:
BREHONY, K. J., Early Childhood Studies
HARGREAVES, D., Child Development
MAHONY, P., Education
MASON, R., Art Education
WATTS, M., Education

School of English and Modern Languages:
COATES, J., English Languages and Linguistics
DOBSON, M., English Literature
HARTLEY, J., English Literature
HEADLAM-WELLS, R., English Literature
LEADER, Z., English Literature
PRIESTMAN, M., English Literature

School of Humanities and Cultural Studies:
DEAN, T., Medieval History
EDWARDS, P., History
GIBSON, A., Philosophy
TOSH, J., History

School of Initial Teacher Education:
BEST, R., Education

School of Human and Life Sciences:
MACLARNON, A., Evolutionary Anthropology

School of Psychology and Therapeutic Studies:
BEAUMONT, G., Neuropsychology
ESSAU, C., Developmental Psychopathology
REID, M., Nutritional Psychology
VOGELE, C., Clinical and Health Psychology

SHEFFIELD HALLAM UNIVERSITY

City Campus, Howard St, Sheffield, S1 1WB
Telephone: (114) 225-5555
Fax: (114) 225-4449
E-mail: admissions@shu.ac.uk
Internet: www.shu.ac.uk

Founded 1969, as Sheffield Polytechnic, later Sheffield City Polytechnic; present name and status 1992

Academic year: September to June

Chancellor: Lord WINSTON
Vice-Chancellor: PHILIP JONES
Deputy Vice-Chancellor: CLIFF ALLAN
Pro-Vice-Chancellor for Research: MIKE SMITH
Dir of Human Resources: PHILL DIXON
Sec. and Registrar: LIZ WINDERS
Academic Registrar: GWYN ARNOLD

Library of 540,000 vols
Number of teachers: 955
Number of students: 28,279 (20,993 undergraduate, 7,286 postgraduate)

DEANS

Faculty of Arts, Computing Engineering and Sciences: Prof. ALISTAIR SAMBELL
Faculty of Devt and Society: SYLVIA JOHNSON
Faculty of Health and Wellbeing: Prof. RHIANNON BILLINGLSEY
Sheffield Business School: CHRISTINE BOOTH

SOUTHAMPTON SOLENT UNIVERSITY

East Park Terrace, Southampton, SO14 0YN
Telephone: (23) 8031-9000
Fax: (23) 8033-4161
E-mail: ask@solent.ac.uk
Internet: www.solent.ac.uk

Founded 1855, as a school of art; present name and status 2005

Chancellor: Admiral The Rt Hon. Lord WEST OF SPITHEAD
Vice-Chancellor: Prof. VAN GORE
Deputy Vice-Chancellor: Dr RICHARD BLACKWELL
Deputy Vice-Chancellor: Prof. JANE LONGMORE
Deputy Vice-Chancellor: Dr MIKE WILKINSON
Number of students: 16,000

Publications: *headway*, *Issue*

DEANS

Faculty of Business, Sport and Enterprise: Prof. JENNY ANDERSON
Faculty of Media, Arts and Society: Prof. ROD PILLING
Faculty of Technology: Prof. JOHN REES
Warsash Maritime Academy: JOHN MILLICAN

STAFFORDSHIRE UNIVERSITY

College Rd, Stoke on Trent, ST4 2DE
Telephone: (1782) 294000
Fax: (1782) 292796
E-mail: international@staffs.ac.uk
Internet: www.staffs.ac.uk

Founded 1970 as North Staffordshire Polytechnic, became Staffordshire Polytechnic 1988; present name and status 1992

Academic year: September to July

Chancellor: Sir Lord BILL MORRIS
Vice-Chancellor and Chief Exec.: Prof. MICHAEL GUNN
Deputy Vice-Chancellor and Deputy Chief Exec.: PAUL RICHARDS
Univ. Sec.: KEN SPROSTON
Academic Registrar: FRANCESCA FRANCIS
Librarian: LIZ HART

Library of 300,000 vols, 2,000 periodicals
Number of teachers: 589
Number of students: 16,575 (10,991 full-time undergraduate, 1,972 postgraduate, 3,612 part-time)

Publications: *Horizon* (journal for former students; 3 a year), *Research Report* (1 a year), *Shine On* (1 a year)

DEANS

Business School: Prof. SUSAN FOREMAN
Faculty of Arts, Media and Design: Dr ASTRID HERHOFFER
Faculty of Computing, Engineering and Technology: Prof. MIKE GOODWIN
Faculty of Health: HILARY JONES
Faculty of Sciences: Prof. DAVID WHITE (acting)
Law School: ROSEMARY EVANS

THAMES VALLEY UNIVERSITY

St Mary's Rd, Ealing, London, W5 5RF
Telephone: (20) 8579-5000
Fax: (20) 8566-1353
E-mail: learning.advice@tvu.ac.uk
Internet: www.tvu.ac.uk

Wellington St, Slough, Berks, SL1 1YG
Telephone: (1753) 534585

Founded 1860, as Lady Byron School, present name and status 1992

Academic year: September to July

Chancellor: Lord BILIMORIA
Vice-Chancellor: Prof. PETER JOHN
Pro-Vice-Chancellor for Academic Affairs and Student Services: Prof. KATH MITCHELL
Deputy Vice-Chancellor for Enterprise and External Services: Dr IAN TUNBRIDGE
Univ. Sec. and Clerk to the Board: MAUREEN SKINNER
Head of Registry Services: (vacant)

Library of 270,000 vols, 1,300 print journals
Number of teachers: 638 (388 full-time, 250 part-time)
Number of students: 25,741 (9,004 full-time and sandwich, 16,737 part-time and distance learning)

DEANS

Faculty of Arts: ROSY CREHAN
Faculty of Health and Human Sciences: ANDREW MACCALLUM
Faculty of Professional Studies: Prof. DAVID JONES

UNIVERSITY FOR THE CREATIVE ARTS

Canterbury campus: New Dover Rd, Canterbury, Kent, CT1 3AN
Telephone: (1227) 817302
Fax: (1227) 817500
E-mail: admissionscanterbury@ucreative.ac.uk

Epsom campus: Ashley Rd, Epsom, Surrey, KT18 5BE
Telephone: (1372) 728811
Fax: (1372) 747050
E-mail: admissionsepsom@ucreative.ac.uk

Farnham campus: Falkner Rd, Farnham, Surrey, GU9 7DS
Telephone: (1252) 722441
Fax: (1252) 892616
E-mail: admissionsfarnham@ucreative.ac.uk

Maidstone campus: Oakwood Park, Maidstone, Kent, ME16 8AG
Telephone: (1622) 620000
Fax: (1622) 621100
E-mail: admissionsmaidstone@ucreative.ac.uk

Rochester campus: Fort Pitt, Rochester, Kent, ME1 1DZ
Telephone: (1634) 888702

Fax: (1634) 820700
E-mail: admissionsrochester@ucreative.ac.uk
Internet: www.ucreative.ac.uk

Founded 2005, as Univ. College for Creative Arts by merger of Kent Inst. of Art and Design (f. 1987) and Surrey Inst. of Art and Design, University College (f. 1995); present name 2008
Academic year: September to May
Vice-Chancellor: Prof. ELAINE THOMAS
Deputy Vice-Chancellor: Prof. MARK HUNT
Pro-Vice-Chancellor for Corporate Resources: ALAN COOKE
Pro-Vice-Chancellor for Further Education and Widening Participation: Prof. DIANNE TAYLOR GEARING
Pro-Vice-Chancellor for Learning and Teaching: Prof. PAUL COYLE
Pro-Vice-Chancellor for Research and Devt: Dr SEYMOUR ROWORTH-STOKES
Sec.: MARION WILKS
Number of students: 6,500

UNIVERSITY OF BATH

Claverton Down, Bath, BA2 7AY
Telephone: (1225) 388388
Fax: (1225) 386559
E-mail: registry@bath.ac.uk
Internet: www.bath.ac.uk

Founded 1856, designated College of Advanced Technology 1960, independent instn with direct-grant status 1962, Univ. Charter 1966
Academic year: September to June
Chancellor: Lord TUGENDHAT OF WIDDINGTON
Vice-Chancellor: Prof. GLYNIS BREAKWELL
Deputy Vice-Chancellor: Prof. KEVIN EDGE
Pro-Vice-Chancellor for Learning and Teaching: Prof. BERNIE MORLEY
Pro-Vice-Chancellor for Research: Prof. JANE MILLAR
Sec.: MARK HUMPHRISS
Librarian: HOWARD NICHOLSON

Library: see Libraries and Archives
Number of teachers: 533
Number of students: 13,959

DEANS

Faculty of Engineering and Design: Prof. GARY HAWLEY
Faculty of Humanities and Social Sciences: Prof. ROGER EATWELL
Faculty of Science: Prof. DAVID BIRD
School of Management: Prof. RICHARD ELLIOTT

PROFESSORS

ACHARYA, K. R., Biology and Biochemistry
AGGARWAL, R. K., Electronic and Electrical Engineering
ALMOND, D. P., Materials Science
BENDING, S. J., Physics
BIRD, D. M., Physics
BLAKE, D. R., Medical Sciences
BRAMLEY, A. N., Engineering and Applied Sciences
BRITTON, N., Mathematical Sciences
BROOKS, S. W., European Studies and Modern Languages
BROWN, A. D., Management
BUDD, C. J., Applied Mathematics
BULL, A., European Studies and Modern Languages
BURSTALL, F. E., Mathematical Sciences
CARUSO, A., Architecture and Civil Engineering
CHARNLEY, A. K., Biology and Biochemistry
CHAUDHURI, J. B., Chemical Engineering
COLEMAN, P. G., Physics
CRITTENDEN, B. D., Chemical Engineering
CRONIN, N. J., Physics
DANIELS, H. R., Education
DANSON, M. J., Biochemistry
DAVENPORT, J. H., Information Technology
DAVIDSON, M. G., Chemistry
DAVIES, J. J., Physics
EATWELL, R., European Studies and Modern Languages
EDGE, K., Mechanical Engineering
EGGLESTONE, C., Psychology
EISENTHAL, R., Biology and Biochemistry
FFRENCH-CONSTANT, R., Biology and Biochemistry
FINEMAN, S., Management
FITCH, J. P., Software Engineering
FORD, I. D., Management
FRAENKEL, L. E., Mathematical Sciences
GALAKTIONOV, V. A., Mathematical Sciences
GARLAND, C. J., Pharmacy and Pharmacology
GILLESPIE, D., Russian
GOODING, D. C., Psychology
GOUGH, I. R., Social Sciences
GOULD, N., Social and Policy Sciences
GRAHAM, I. G., Mathematical Sciences
GREEN, R. H., Management
GURSUL, I., Mechanical Engineering
GUY, R., Pharmacy and Pharmacology
HAMMOND, G. P., Environmental Engineering
HARLAND, C. M., Management
HASTE, H. E., Psychology
HAWLEY, J. G., Mechanical Engineering
HOLMAN, G. D., Biochemistry
HOPE, V., Management
HORROCKS, M., School for Health
HUDSON, J. R., Economics and International Development
HUNT, G. W., Mechanical Engineering
HURST, L. D., Biology
IBELL, T. J., Architecture and Civil Engineering
IOANNIDIS, C., Management
JENNISON, C., Statistics
JOHNSON, P., Computer Science
JONES, P. R., Economics and International Development
KERWIN, D. G., Sport and Exercise Science
KNIGHT, J. C., Physics
KOLACZKOWSKI, S. T., Chemical Engineering
LAUDER, H., Education
LEWIS, A., Psychology
LEWIS, M. A., Management
LOGEMANN, H., Mathematical Sciences
MCKAY, A., Economics and International Development
MARKANDYA, A., Economics and International Development
MARSH, R. J., Modern Languages
MARSHALL, J., Management
MARTIN, B., Marketing
MAYER, M., Strategic Management
MEDLAND, A. J., Design Engineering
MILEHAM, A. R., Mechanical Engineering
MILES, A. W., Mechanical Engineering
MILLAR, J., Social Policy
MITCHELL, N., Electronic and Electrical Engineering
MOLLOY, K., Chemistry
MONRO, D. M., Electronics
MORTON, K. W., Mathematical Sciences
NANDEIBAM, S., Economics and International Development
NAUDE, P., Management
ORTON, P., School for Health
PACE, N. G., Physics
PARKER, S. C., Chemistry
PENROSE, M., Mathematical Sciences
PETER, L. M., Physical Chemistry
POTTER, B. V. L., Pharmacy
POWELL, P., Management
PURCELL, J., Management
PYM, D., Computer Science
RAITHBY, P. R., Chemistry
REASON, P., Management
REDFERN, P., School for Health
REYNOLDS, S. E., Biology
RICKELLS, P., Architecture
RODGER, D., Electronic and Electrical Engineering
ROOM, G. J., Social Sciences
RUSSELL, P. ST. J., Physics
RYAN, E. P., Mathematical Sciences
SCOTT, R. J., Biology and Biochemistry
SCOTT, W. A. H., Education
SKEVINGTON, S. M., Psychology
SLACK, J. M. W., Cell and Molecular Biology
SMITH, A. W., Pharmacy
SMYSHLYAEV, V., Mathematical Sciences
SPENCE, A., Numerical Analysis
STABLES, A. W., Education
STEVENS, R., Engineering and Applied Science
TATE, G. D., European Studies and Modern Languages
TAVERNOR, R. W., Architecture
TAYLOR, J. T., Electronic and Electrical Engineering
TOLAND, J. F., Mathematics
TURNBULL, D., Architecture and Civil Engineering
TYRELL, R. M., Pharmacy and Pharmacology
VASSILIEV, D. G., Mathematical Sciences
VIDGEN, R, Management
VINCENT, J. F. V., Mechanical Engineering
WALLACE, A. M., Education
WANG, W. N., Physics
WARD, S., Pharmacy and Pharmacology
WELHAM, M., Pharmacy and Pharmacology
WHITMAN, R., Politics
WILKINSON, B., Management
WILLIAMS, I., Chemistry
WILLIAMS, J. M. J., Chemistry
WILLIS, P. J., Mathematical Sciences
WONNACOTT, S. J., Biology and Biochemistry
WOOD, G. D., Economics and International Development

UNIVERSITY OF BEDFORDSHIRE

Park Sq., Luton, Bedfordshire, LU1 3JU
Telephone: (1582) 489286
Fax: (1582) 489323
E-mail: admission@beds.ac.uk
Internet: www.beds.ac.uk

Founded 2006, by merger of Univ. of Luton (f. 1993) and De Montfort Univ.'s Bedford campus
Academic year: September to September
Chancellor: ALISTAIR DARLING
Vice Chancellor and Chief Exec.: Prof. LES EBDON
Deputy Vice-Chancellor for Acad. Affairs: Prof. MARY MALCOLM
Deputy Vice-Chancellor for Resources: DONALD HARLEY
Registrar: ALICE HYNES
Librarian: TIM STONE

Library of 250,000 vols
Number of teachers: 1,200
Number of students: 21,000

DEANS

Bedfordshire Business School: Prof. PAUL BURNS
Faculty of Creative Arts, Technologies and Science: Prof. JAMES CRABBE
Faculty of Education, Sport and Tourism: Prof. MARILYN LEASK
Faculty of Health and Social Sciences: Prof. MICHAEL PRESTON-SHOOT

UNIVERSITY OF BIRMINGHAM

Edgbaston, Birmingham, B15 2TT
Telephone: (121) 414-3344
Fax: (121) 414-3971
Internet: www.bham.ac.uk

Founded 1900
Academic year: September to June
Chancellor: Sir DOMINIC CADBURY
Vice-Chancellor and Prin.: Prof. DAVID EASTWOOD

Provost and Vice-Prin.: Prof. MICHAEL SHEPPARD
Pro-Vice-Chancellor for Estates and Infrastructure: Prof. JOHN HEATH
Pro-Vice-Chancellor for Research and Knowledge Transfer: (vacant)
Pro-Vice-Chancellor for Teaching, Learning and Quality: Prof. ADRIAN RANDALL
Registrar and Sec.: LEE SANDERS
Librarian: M. SHOEBRIDGE (acting)

Library: see Libraries and Archives
Number of teachers: 2,291
Number of students: 26,073

Publications: *Court Reporter* (1 a year), *Medlines* (2 a year), *The Birmingham Magazine* (1 a year)

PROFESSORS

ABELL, S., Functional Materials
ADAMS, D. H., Hepatology
AHMED, A., Reproductive Physiology
AL-RUBEAI, M., Biotechnology
ALCOCK, P., Social Policy and Administration
ALEXANDER, D., Accounting
ALLEMANN, R., Chemical Biology
AMANN, R., Soviet Politics
ARNULL, A. M., European Law
BACKHOUSE, R. E., History and Philosophy of Economics
BACON, P. A., Rheumatology
BALDWIN, J., Judicial Administration
BALE, J. S., Environmental Biology
BANFIELD, S. D., Music
BARBER, K., African Popular Culture
BARKER, A., Classics
BARNDEN, J., Artificial Intelligence
BARNETT, A. H., Diabetic Medicine
BATLEY, R. A., Development Administration
BEEVERS, D. G., Medicine
BELL, T., Metallurgy
BESRA, G., Biosciences
BIDDLESTONE, A. J., Chemical Engineering
BIRKETT, J., French Studies
BLACKBURN, S., Solids Processing
BLAKE, J. R., Applied Mathematics
BOOTH, D. A., Psychology
BOOTH, I. W., Paediatric Gastroenterology and Nutrition
BOWEN, P., Mechanical Metallurgy
BOWERY, N. G., Pharmacology
BRADBURY, A., Vascular Surgery
BREUILLY, J. J., Modern History
BROOKS, N. P., Medieval History
BROWN, N. L., Molecular Genetics and Microbiology
BROWNE, K., Forensic and Family Psychology
BRYAN, S., Health Economics
BUCKLEY, C., Rheumatology
BURKE, F., Primary Dental Care
BUSBY, S. J. W., Biochemistry
BUTLER, M. G., Modern German Literature
BUTLER, P. J., Comparative Physiology
CAESAR, M. P., Italian
CALLOW, J. A., Botany
CAMPBELL, J., Casting Technology
CARROLL, D., Applied Psychology
CHAPPLE, I., Periodontology
CHENG, K. K., Public Health and Epidemiology
CHILD, J., Commerce (International Management and Organization)
CHIPMAN, J., Cell Toxicology
CLARK, L. A., Structural Engineering
CLARKE, M., Public Policy
CLIFFORD, C. M., Nursing
COCHRANE, R., Psychology
COLE, J. A., Microbial Physiology and Biochemistry
COOPER, J. M., Russian Economic Studies
COOTE, J. H., Physiology
COULTHARD, R. M., English Language and Linguistics
COX, A. W., Business Strategy and Procurement
CROFT, S. J., International Relations
CROSSLEY, E. C. D., 19th-century French Studies
CRUIKSHANK, G. S., Neurosurgery
CRUISE, A. M., Astrophysics and Space Research
CURTIS, R., Combinatorial Algebra
DADSON, T. J., Hispanic Studies
DANIELS, H. R. J., Special Education and Educational Psychology
DANIELS, P. W., Geography
DAVIES, G., Engineering
DAVIES, L., English
DAVIES, M. L., International Education
DAVIS, A., Social Work
DAWE, D. J., Structural Mechanics
DE CHERNATONY, L., Brand Marketing
DEAN, T. A., Manufacturing Engineering
DEB, S., Neuropsychiatry and Intellectual Disability
DELECLUSE, H.-J., Molecular Pathology
DENT, N. J. H., Philosophy
DICKENSON, D., Global Ethics
DOE, W., Medicine
DOLING, J. F., Housing Studies
DOWDEN, K., Classics
DUDA, J., Sports Psychology
DUTTA, J., Economics
EDWARDS, A., Education
EDWARDS, P. P., Inorganic Chemistry
ELLIS, E. D., Public Law
ELLIS, S., English Literature
ENONCHONG, N., Law
EVANS, H., Metallurgy and Materials
FADDY, M., Statistics
FELDMAN, D. J., Jurisprudence
FENDER, J., Macroeconomics
FORGAN, E. M., Condensed Matter Physics
FRAME, J. W., Oral Surgery
FRANKLIN, F., Plant Molecular Biology
FRANKLYN, J. A., Medicine
FREEMANTLE, N., Clinical Epidemiology and Biostatistics
FRYER, P. J., Chemical Engineering
GALLIMORE, P. H., Cancer Studies
GARVEY, J., Particle Physics
GORDON, J., Cellular Immunology
GRAY, R., Medical Statistics
GREAVES, C., Solid State Chemistry
GUNN, J. M. F., Theoretical Physics
HALDON, J. F., Byzantine Studies
HALL, P. S., Communications Engineering
HAM, C. J., Health Policy and Management
HARBER, C., International Education
HARRIS, I. R., Materials Science
HARRIS, J., Law
HARRIS, K. D. M., Structural Chemistry
HARRISON, R. M., Environmental Health
HAWKEY, P., Immunology
HAY, C., Political Analysis
HEATH, J. K., Biochemistry
HENDERSON, W., Continuing Education
HICKS, C., Health Care Psychology
HOBBS, F. D. R., Primary Care and General Practice
HUGHES, A., 20th-century French Literature
HUMPHREYS, G. W., Cognitive Psychology
HUNTER, J. R., Ancient History and Archaeology
HUTTON, P., Anaesthetics and Intensive Care
JACKSON, J. B., Bioenergetics
JEFFERIES, R., Molecular Immunology
JEFFERY, C., German Politics
JEFFERYS, J. G. R., Basic Neuroscience
JENKINSON, E. J., Experimental Immunology
JENNINGS, J., Political Theory
JOHNSON, P., Oncology and Translational Research
JONES, D. A., Sport and Exercise Sciences
JONES, E. L., Pathology
JONES, I. P., Physical Metallurgy
JONES, P. M., French History
JONES, R. H., Public Sector Accounting
JUNG, A., Computer Science
KAPLAN, J., Drama and Theatre Arts
KEARSEY, M., Biometrical Genetics
KEIGHLEY, M. R. B., Surgery
KELSEY, D., Economic Theory
KENDALL, K., Chemical Engineering
KENDALL, M., Clinical Pharmacology
KERALI, R., Highway Engineering and Management
KILBY, M., Maternal and Foetal Medicine
KINSON, J. B., High Energy Physics
KLAPPER, J., Foreign Language Pedagogy
KNIGHT, D., Water Engineering
KNOTT, J. F., Metallurgy and Materials
KNOWLES, P. J., Theoretical Chemistry
KWIATKOWSKA, M., Computer Science
LAIRD, W. R. E., Prosthetic Dentistry
LANCASTER, M., Communications Engineering
LAWRANCE, A. J., Statistics
LE SUEUR, A., Jurisprudence
LEATHER, P., Urban and Regional Studies
LERNER, I., Theoretical Physics
LEWIS, A., Special Education and Educational Psychology
LILFORD, R., Public Health and Epidemiology
LLOYD-BOSTOCK, S., Law and Psychology
LOGAN, A., Molecular Neuroscience
LOTE, C., Experimental Nephrology
LUCAS, W., American Studies
LUESLEY, D. M., Gynaecology
LYDDIATT, A., Process Biotechnology
MACARTHUR, C., Maternal and Child Epidemiology
MACASKIE, L., Applied Microbiology
MCCASKIE, T., Asante History
MACKAY, R., Hydrogeology
MACLENNAN, I. C. M., Immunology
MADELIN, K. B., Civil Engineering
MAHER, E., Medical Genetics
MALLIN, C., Business Finance
MARQUIS, P. M., Biomaterials
MARSH, D., Political Science and International Studies
MARSHALL, J. M., Cardiovascular Science
MARTIN, G. R., Avian Sensory Science
MCLEOD, D. H., Church History
MENON, A., European Studies
MICHELL, R. H., Biochemistry
MILLER, C. J., English Law
MINNIKIN, D., Microbial Chemistry
MOAYYEDI, P., Primary Care and General Practice
MORRISON, K., Neurology
MORTON, D. B., Biomedical Science and Biomedical Ethics
MOSS, P. A. H., Haematology
MULLINEUX, A. W., Global Finance
MURIE, A., Urban and Regional Studies
MURINDE, V., Developmental Finance
MURRAY, P. I., Ophthalmology
NASH, G., Cardiovascular Rheology
NEAL-STURGESS, C. E., Automotive Engineering
NELSON, J. M., Nuclear Physics
NIELSEN, J., Theology
NIENOW, A. W., Biochemical Engineering
NOONAN, H., Philosophy
NORTON, J. P., Control Engineering
OLIVER, C., Clinical Psychology
ORFORD, J. F., Clinical and Community Psychology
PALIWODA, S., Marketing
PALLEN, M., Infection
PALMER, R. E., Experimental Physics
PARKER, D., Textual Criticism and Palaeography
PARLE, J., Primary Care
PARRATT, J., Third-World Theologies
PATERSON, W. E., German Studies
PECK, E., Health Services Management
PENN, C., Molecular Microbiology
PERRIE, M., Russian History
PERRY, J. G., Civil Engineering
PETTS, G., Physical Geography
PETTS, J., Environmental Risk Management
PIDDOCK, L., Microbiology
PILKINGTON, H., Sociology and Russian Area Studies
PONMAN, T., Astrophysics

PRESTON, P., Political Sociology
PREWETT, P., Microsystems Manufacture
RAFTERY, J. P., Health Economics
RAINE, J., Management in Criminal Justice
RAKODI, C., Public Policy
RANDALL, A. J., English Social History
RANSON, P. R. S., Education
REDDY, U., Computer Science
REDMOND, J., European Studies
RICHARDS, S., Public Management
RICKINSON, A. B., Cancer Studies
RIDDOCH, M., Cognitive Neuropsychology
ROBINSON, G., Pure Mathematics
ROGERS, C., Geotechnical Engineering
RUSSELL, M., Electronic and Electrical Engineering
SALMON, M., Experimental Rheumatology
SAMUELS, J. M., Business Finance
SAVAGE, C., Nephrology
SCASE, W., Medieval English Literature
SCHOFIELD, A., Theoretical Physics
SCOTT, I. R., Law
SEN, S., Development Economics
SEVILLE, J. P. K., Chemical Engineering
SHARPLES, M., Educational Technology
SHEPPARD, M. C., Medicine
SHUTE, S., Criminal Law and Criminal Justice
SIEBERT, W. S., Labour Economics
SIMNETT, G. M., High-Energy Astrophysics
SINCLAIR, P. J. N., Economics
SKELCHER, C., Local Government Studies
SLOMAN, A., Artificial Intelligence and Cognitive Science
SMALL, I. C., English Literature
SMITH, A., Oral Biology
SMITH, M., Experimental Neurology
SORAHAN, T., Occupational Epidemiology
SOUTHWOOD, T., Paediatric Rheumatology
SPEIRS, R. C., German
SPENCER, K. M., Local Policy
SPURGEON, P. C., Health Services Management
STEVENS, A., Public Health
STEWART, P. M., Medicine
STRAIN, A., Biochemistry
SUGDEN, R., Commerce
SUGIRTHARAJAH, R., Biblical Hermeneutics
SWANSON, R., Medieval Ecclesiastical History
TANN, J., Commerce
TAYLOR, A., Economics
TAYLOR, A. M. R., Cancer Genetics
TAYLOR, E. W., Animal Physiology
TAYLOR, M., World Faiths Development Dialogue
TELLAM, J., Hydrogeology
TEMPLE, J. G., Surgery
TEUBERT, W., English
THEOBALD, M. F., Accounting
THOMAS, C. M., Molecular Genetics
THOMAS, C. R., Biochemical Engineering
THOMAS, H. R., Economics of Education
TIMMS, C. R., Music
TOOLAN, M., Applied English Linguistics
TRAYER, I. P., Biochemistry
TURNBULL, P., Marketing
TURNER, B. M., Experimental Genetics
TZIOVAS, D. P., Modern Greek Studies
USTORF, W., Mission
VERDI, R., Fine Art and Art History
VINZENT, M., Theology
WAKELAM, M. J. O., Molecular Pharmacology
WALMSLEY, A., Dentistry
WALSH, M., English Literature
WALTON, D., Mechanical Engineering
WEBBER, J., Theology
WEST, S., Art History
WESTBROOK, G. K., Geophysics
WESTBURY, D. R., Physiology
WHARTON, C., Biochemistry
WHEATLEY, K., Medical Statistics
WHENHAM, E., Music History
WHITEHAND, J. W. R., Urban Geography
WHITTLE, M. J., Foetal Medicine
WICKHAM, C. J., Early Medieval History
WILSON, J. S., Pure Mathematics
WILSON, R., Group Theory
WING, A. M., Human Movement
WINTERBOTTOM, J., Chemical Reaction Engineering
WOOD, D. M., French Literature
WOODMAN, G., Comparative Law
WRIGHTSON, P., Physiotherapy
YAO, X., Computer Science
YOUNG, F. M., Theology
YOUNG, L. S., Cancer Biology

UNIVERSITY OF BOLTON

Deane Rd, Bolton, BL3 5AB
Telephone: (1204) 900600
Fax: (1204) 399074
E-mail: enquiries@bolton.ac.uk
Internet: www.bolton.ac.uk

Founded 1824, present status 2005
State control
Language of instruction: English
Academic year: September to July

Chancellor: Baroness MORRIS OF BOLTON
Vice-Chancellor: Dr GEORGE HOLMES
Pro-Vice-Chancellor: Prof. ROB CAMPBELL
Dean of Students: SARAH RICHES
Library Manager: KAREN SENIOR

Library of 171,000 books, 2,587 periodicals
Number of teachers: 320
Number of students: 12,644 (9,455 undergraduate, 2,241 postgraduate, 948 further education)
Publication: *The Bolt* (4 a year)

DEANS

School of Arts, Media and Education: SAM JOHNSON
School of Built Environment and Engineering: ANDY GRAHAM
School of Business and Creative Technologies: Prof. STAN OLIVER
School of Health and Social Sciences: Dr MARGARET BONEHAM (Dir)

UNIVERSITY OF BRADFORD

Richmond Rd, Bradford, BD7 1DP
Telephone: (1274) 232323
Fax: (1274) 236260
E-mail: enquiries@bradford.ac.uk
Internet: www.bradford.ac.uk

Founded 1882, as Bradford Technical College, Royal Charter 1966
Academic year: September to May to May (2 semesters)

Chancellor: IMRAN KHAN
Vice-Chancellor and Prin.: Prof. MARK CLEAREY
Pro-Chancellor and Chair.: PAUL JAGGER
Treas. and Pro-Chancellor: ROLAND CLARK
Pro-Chancellor: DIANA CHAMBERS
Sec.: MARY-ROSE MILLIN
Deputy Vice-Chancellor: S. KERSHAW
Deputy Vice-Chancellor for Academic Affairs: Prof. GEOFF LAYER
Dir of Learning Resources Unit: Dr S. J. HOUGHTON
Librarian: J. J. HORTON

Library: see Libraries and Archives
Number of teachers: 536
Number of students: 8,435
Publications: *News and Views*, *Vice-Chancellor's Research Report* (1 a year)

DEANS

Engineering, Design and Technology: Prof. A. S. WOOD
Health Studies: Prof. G. BRADSHAW
School of Computing, Informatics and Media: Dr I. J. PALMER
School of Life Sciences: Prof. D. COATES
School of Lifelong Education and Devt: N. MIRZA
School of Management: Prof. A. FRANCIS
School of Social and Int. Studies: Prof. J. CUSWORTH

PROFESSORS

ALDERSON, G., Medical Microbiology
ANDERSON, D., Biomedical Sciences
ASHLEY, R. M., Urban Water
ASHMORE, M. R., Environmental Science
BAILES, P. J., Process Engineering
BALMER, J. M. T., Corporate Identity
BARRY, B. W., Pharmaceutical Technology
BENKREIRA, H., Coating and Polymer Processing
BIBBY, M. C., Cancer Research
CHALMERS, M. G., International Politics
CHOUDHRY, T., Finance
CHRYSTYN, H., Clinical Pharmacy
CLARK, B. J., Pharmaceutical Technology
COATES, P. D., Polymer Engineering
COSTALL, B., Neuropharmacology
COWLING, P. I., Computing
CUSWORTH, J. W., International Development Management
DANDO, M. R., International Security
DAY, A. J., Quality Engineering
DOUBLE, J. A., Experimental Cancer Chemotherapy
DOWNS, M. G., Dementia Studies
DUNCAN, S. S., Comparative Social Policy
EARNSHAW, R. A., Electronic Imaging
EDWARDS, H. G. M., Molecular Spectroscopy
EXCELL, P. S., Applied Electromagnetics
FELL, A. F., Pharmaceutical Chemistry
FILOTOTCHEV, I. R., Strategic Management
FRANCIS, F. A. S., Management
GALLAGHER, T. G. P., Ethnic Conflict and Peace
GARDINER, J. G., Electronic Engineering
GARDNER, M. L. G., Physiological Biochemistry
GRAVES-MORRIS, P. R., Numerical Analysis
GREEN, J. N., Romance Linguistics
HOGARTH-SCOTT, S., Marketing and Entrepreneurship
HOPE, C. A., Service Quality
HUSBAND, C. H., Social Analysis
JAMES, A. L., Social Sciences
JAMES, P. W., Environmental Sciences
JENKINS, T. C., Drugs Design
JIANG, J., Electronic Imaging and Media Communications
JOBBER, D., Marketing
KOUVATSOS, D. D., Computer Systems Modelling
LAYER, G. M., Lifelong Learning
LUCAS, J., Learning and Teaching
MCCOLM, I. J., Ceramic Materials
MELLORS, C., Political Science
MIRZA, H. R., International Business
MUHLEMANN, A. P., Operations Management
NAYLOR, R. J, Pharmacology
NEWELL, R. J., Nursing Research
O'HEAR, A., Philosophy
OSTELL, A. E., Organizational Health and Behaviour
PEARCE, J. V., Latin American Politics
PIKE, R. H., Finance and Accounting
POLLARD, A. M., Archaeological Sciences
PRICE, D. H. R., Operational Research
RADAELLI, C. M., Public Policy
RAMSBOTHAM, O. P., Peace Studies
RANDALL, V. A., Biomedical Sciences
ROGERS, P. F., Peace Studies
SCHALLREUTER, K. U., Clinical and Experimental Dermatology
SEAWARD, M. R. D., Environmental Biology
SHEPHERD, S. J., Cryptography and Computer Communications Security
SHERIFF, R. E., Mobile Communications
SMALL, N. A., Community and Primary Care
TAYLOR, W. A., Business Information Systems
TOROPOV, V. V., Computational Mechanics
VOURDAS, A., Computing
WALLS, J. R., Chemical Engineering

WEISS, J. A., Development Economics
WHALLEY, R., Mechanical Engineering
WHITAKER, D. J., Optometry
WILLIAMS, A. C., Contemporary German Studies
WINN, B., Optometry
WOOD, J. M., Medical Biochemistry
WOODHOUSE, T., Conflict Resolution
WOODWARD, M. E., Telecommunications
YORK, P., Physical Pharmaceutics
ZAIRI, M., Best Practice Management

UNIVERSITY OF BRIGHTON

Mithras House, Lewes Rd, Brighton, BN2 4AT
Telephone: (1273) 600900
Fax: (1273) 642607
E-mail: enquiries@brighton.ac.uk
Internet: www.brighton.ac.uk

Founded 1970 as Brighton Polytechnic, present name and status 1992
Academic year: September to June

Vice-Chancellor: Prof. JULIAN CRAMPTON
Deputy Vice-Chancellor: STUART LAING
Pro-Vice-Chancellor for Business and Marketing: COLIN MONK
Pro-Vice-Chancellor for Research: Prof. BRUCE BROWN
Registrar and Sec.: CAROL BURNS
Dir of Finance: SUE MCHUGH
Dir of Information Services: MARK TOOLE

Library of 550,000 vols
Number of teachers: 1,122 (f.t.e.)
Number of students: 23,000

DEANS

Brighton and Sussex Medical School: Prof. JON COHEN
Faculty of Arts: Prof. BRUCE BROWN
Faculty of Education and Sport: PAUL GRIFFITHS
Faculty of Health and Social Science: Prof. DAVID TAYLOR
Faculty of Management and Information Sciences: Prof. DAVID ARNOLD
Faculty of Science and Engineering: Prof. ANDREW LLOYD

UNIVERSITY OF BRISTOL

Senate House, Tyndall Ave, Bristol, BS8 1TH
Telephone: (117) 928-9000
Fax: (117) 925-1424
Internet: www.bristol.ac.uk

Founded 1909, previously established as Univ. College, Bristol, 1876
Academic year: October to July

Chancellor: Rt Hon. the Baroness HALE OF RICHMOND
Vice-Chancellor: Prof. ERIC THOMAS
Deputy Vice-Chancellor: Prof. DAVID CLARKE
Pro-Vice-Chancellor for Education and Students: Prof. AVRIL WATERMAN-PEARSON
Pro-Vice-Chancellor for Enterprise: Prof. GUY ORPEN
Registrar: DEREK PRETTY

Library: see under Libraries and Archives
Number of teachers: 2,129
Number of students: 18,615

Publications: *re:search*, *Subtext*

DEANS

Faculty of Arts: Prof. CHARLES MARTINDALE
Faculty of Engineering: Prof. NICK LIEVEN
Faculty of Medical and Veterinary Sciences: Prof. CLIVE ORCHARD
Faculty of Medicine and Dentistry: Prof. PETER MATHIESON
Faculty of Science: Prof. JON KEATING
Faculty of Social Sciences and Law: Prof. JUDITH SQUIRES

PROFESSORS

(Some professors serve in more than one faculty)

Faculty of Arts (Senate House, Tyndall Ave, Bristol, BS8 1TH; tel. (117) 928-8897; internet www.bris.ac.uk/depts/artspgc/facart.htm):

BANFIELD, S. D., Music
BANN, S., History of Art
BENNETT, A. J., English
BIRD, A. J., Philosophy
BROOKSHAW, D. R., Luso-Brazilian Studies
BRYCE, J. H., Italian
BUXTON, R. G. A., Greek Language and Literature
CLARK, E. G., Ancient History
CORNWELL, N. J., Russian and Comparative Literature
DOYLE, W., History
FOWLER, R. L. H., Greek
FREEMAN, M. J., French Language and Literature
HARRISON, R. J., European Prehistory
HOOK, D., Hispanic Studies
HOPKINS, D. W., English Literature
HUTTON, R. E., History
KENNEDY, D. F., Latin Literature and Theory of Criticism
KERSHAW, B. R., Drama
KOSENINA, A., German
LOWE, R., Contemporary History
MARTINDALE, C. A., Latin
OFFORD, D. C., Russian Intellectual History
PARKIN, J., French Literary Studies
PARRY, M. M., Italian Linguistics
POOLE, G. R., Composition
PUNTER, D. G., English
SAMPSON, R. B. K., Romance Philology
STREET, S. C. J., Film
UNWIN, T. A., French
VINCENT, J. R., History
WEBB, E. T., English
WHITE, M. E., Theatre
WILLIAMS, P. M., Indian and Tibetan Philosophy

Faculty of Engineering (Queen's Building, University Walk, Bristol, BS8 1TR; tel. (117) 928-9760; internet www.fen.bris.ac.uk):

ADAMS, R. D., Applied Mechanics
BEACH, M. A., Radio Systems Engineering
BLOCKLEY, D. I., Civil Engineering
BOWES, S. R., Electrical and Electronic Engineering
BULL, D. R., Digital Systems Processing
CANAGARAJAH, C. N., Multimedia Signal Processing
CHALMERS, A. G., Computer Graphics
CHAMPNEYS, A. R., Applied Non-linear Mathematics
CLUCKIE, I. D., Worldwide Water Management
DAGLESS, E. L., Microelectronics
FLACH, P. A., Artificial Intelligence
FRISWELL, M. I., Aerospace Engineering
HOGAN, S. J., Mathematics
JOSZA, R. O., Computer Science
KRAUSKOPF, B., Applied Non-linear Mathematics
LIEVEN, N. A. J., Aerospace Dynamics
MAY, M. D., Computer Science
MCGEEHAN, J. P., Communications Engineering
MELLOR, P. H., Electrical Engineering
MUIR WOOD, D., Civil Engineering
NIX, A. R., Wireless Communication Systems
PRADHAN, D. K., Computer Science
QUARINI, G. L., Process Engineering
RAILTON, C. J., Electrical and Electronic Engineering
RARITY, J. G., Optical Communications Systems
SMART, N. P., Cryptology
SMITH, D. J., Mechanical Engineering
STOTEN, D. P., Dynamics and Control
TAYLOR, C. A., Earthquake Engineering
WISNOM, M. R., Aerospace Structures

Faculty of Medical and Veterinary Sciences (University Walk, Bristol, BS8 1TD; tel. (117) 331-7484; internet www.bristol.ac.uk/fmvs/):

BANTING, G. S., Molecular Cell Biology
BASHIR, Z. I., Cellular Neuroscience
BENNETT, P. M., Bacterial Genetics
BRADY, R. L., Biochemistry
BROWN, M. W., Anatomy and Cognitive Neuroscience
CLARKE, A. R., Biochemistry
COLLINGRIDGE, G., Neuroscience in Anatomy
CULLEN, P. J., Biochemistry
DAY, M. J., Veterinary Pathology
DENTON, R. M., Biochemistry
DUFFUS, W. P. H., Veterinary Medicine
GRUFFYDD-JONES, T. J., Feline Medicine
HALESTRAP, A. P., Biochemistry
HALFORD, S. E., Biochemistry
HALL, E. J., Companion Animal Studies
HALL, L., Molecular Genetics
HASSAN, A. B., Adult Oncology
HEADLEY, P. M., Physiology
HENDERSON, G., Pharmacology
HENLEY, J. M., Molecular Neuroscience
HEYDERMAN, R. S., Infectious Diseases and International Health
HOLT, P. E., Veterinary Surgery
HUMPHREY, T. J., Veterinary Zoonotic Bacteriology
KUWABARA, P. E., Genomics
LAWSON, S. N., Physiology
LISNEY, S. J. W., Physiology
MACGOWAN, A. P., Clinical Microbiology and Antimicrobial Therapeutics
MARRION, N. V., Neuroscience
MARTIN, P. B., Cell Biology
MOLNAR, E., Anatomy
MULLER, R. L., Neuroscience
NICOL, C. J., Animal Welfare
ORCHARD, C. H., Physiology
PARASKEVA, M. M., Experimental Oncology
PATON, J. F. R., Physiology
PIGNATELLI, M., Histopathology
RIVETT, A. J., Biochemistry
ROBERTS, P. J., Neurochemical Pharmacology
RUTTER, G. A., Biochemistry and Cell Biology
SIDDELL, S. G., Virology
STOKES, C. R., Mucosal Immunology
TAVARE, J. M., Biochemistry
VAZQUEZ-BOLAND, J. A., Veterinary Molecular Biology
VIRJI, M., Molecular Microbiology
WATERMAN-PATERSON, A. E., Veterinary Anaesthesia
WILLIAMS, N. A., Immunology
WOOD, J. D., Food Animal Science
WRAITH, D. C., Pathological Sciences

Faculty of Medicine and Dentistry (Senate House, Tyndall Ave, Bristol, BS8 1TH; tel. (117) 928-9951; internet www.medici.bris.ac.uk/medf):

ADDY, M., Periodontology
ALDERSON, D., Gastrointestinal Surgery
ANGELINI, G., Cardiac Surgery
ARMITAGE, W. J., Opthalmology
BINGLEY, P. J., Diabetes
CAMPBELL, A. V., Ethics in Medicine
COLLINGRIDGE, G., Neuroscience in Anatomy
COWPE, J. G., Oral Surgery
DAVEY SMITH, G., Clinical Epidemiology
DICK, A. D., Ophthalmology
DONOVAN, J. L., Social Medicine
EBRAHIM, S. B. J., Epidemiology of Ageing
EMOND, A. M., Community Child Health
EVESON, J. W., Head and Neck Pathology
FINN, A. H. R., Paediatrics

FLEMING, P. J., Infant Health and Developmental Psychology
FRANKEL, S. J., Epidemiology and Public Health Medicine
GALE, E. A. M., Diabetic Medicine
GOLDING, M. J., Paediatric and Perinatal Epidemiology
GUNNELL, D. J., Epidemiology
HANKS, G. W. C., Palliative Medicine
HARRISON, G. L., Mental Health
HOLLANDER, A. P., Rheumatology and Tissue Engineering
HOLLY, J. M. P., Clinical Sciences
JAGGER, D. C., Restorative Dentistry
JENKINSON, H. F., Oral Microbiology
KARSCH, K. R., Cardiology
KIRWAN, J. R., Rheumatic Diseases
LEARMONTH, I. D., Orthopaedic Surgery
LEWIS, G. H., Psychiatric Epidemiology
LIGHTMAN, S. L., Medicine
LOPEZ BERNAL, A., Human Reproductive Biology
LOVE, S., Neuropathology
MATHIESON, P. W., Renal Medicine
MURPHY, D., Experimental Medicine
NEWBY, A. C., Vascular Cell Biology
NUTT, D. J., Psychopharmacology
PETERS, T. J., Primary Health Care Services Research
PIGNATELLI, M. M., Histopathology
PRIME, S. S., Experimental Pathology
REES, M. R., Clinical Radiology
SALISBURY, C. J., Primary Health Care
SANDY, J. R., Orthodontics
SCOLDING, N. J., Clinical Neurosciences
SHARP, D. J., Primary Health Care
SOOTHILL, P. W., Maternal and Foetal Medicine
STEVENS, M. C. G., Paediatric Oncology
THORESEN, M., Neo-natal Neuroscience
UNEY, J. B., Molecular Neuroscience
WHITELAW, A. G. L., Neonatal Medicine
WILCOCK, G. K., Care of the Elderly
WILLIAMS, G., Medicine and Dentistry
WOLF, A. R., Anaesthesia
WYNICK, D., Molecular Medicine

Faculty of Science (Senate House, Tyndall Ave, Bristol, BS8 1TH; tel. (117) 928-9957; internet www.bris.ac.uk/depts/science/sciweb.htm):

AGGARWAL, V. K., Synthetic Organic Chemistry
ALAM, M. A., Physics
ALLAN, N. L., Physical Chemistry
ALLEN, G. C., Materials Science
ANDERSON, M. G., Geography
ANNETT, J. F., Physics
ASHFOLD, M. N. R., Physical Chemistry
BALINT-KURTI, G. G., Theoretical Chemistry
BAMBER, J. L., Geography
BATES, P. D., Hydrology
BENTON, M. J., Vertebrate Palaeontology
Sir BERRY, MICHAEL, Physics
BIRKINSHAW, M., Cosmology and Astrophysics
BLUNDY, J. D., Petrology
BRERETON, R. G., Chemometrics
CHERNS, D., Physics
CLOKE, P. J., Geography
CONNELLY, N. G., Inorganic Chemistry
CONREY, J. B., Number Theory
COSGROVE, T., Physical Chemistry
CUTHILL, I. C., Behavioural Ecology
DAVIS, A. P., Supramolecular Chemistry
EASTOE, J. G., Chemistry
EDWARDS, K. J., Cereal Functional Genomics
EGGERS, J. G., Applied Mathematics
EVANS, D. V., Applied Mathematics
EVANS, R., Physics
EVERSHED, R. P., Chemistry
FOSTER, B., Physics
FRANKS, N. R., Animal Behaviour and Ecology
FREEMAN, N. H., Cognitive Development
GALLAGHER, T. C., Organic Chemistry
GIBSON, W. C., Protozoology
GOLDSTEIN, H., Statistics
GREEN, B. J., Pure Mathematics
GREEN, P. J., Statistics
HANNAY, J. H., Theoretical Physics
HARRIS, S., Environmental Sciences
HAWKESWORTH, C. J., Earth Sciences
HAYDEN, S. M., Physics
HAYES, P. K., Biology
HEATH, G. P., Physics
HELFRICH, G. R., Seismology
HENSHAW, D. L., Physics
HOOD, B. M., Development Psychology
HOUSTON, A. I., Theoretical Biology
JONES, G., Biological Sciences
JONES, K., Human Quantitative Geography
KEATING, J. P., Mathematical Physics
KEMPSON, H. E., Personal Finance and Social Policy Research
KENDALL, J.-M., Earth Sciences
LARNER, W. J., Human Geography and Sociology
LINDEN, N., Theoretical Physics
LISKEVICH, V., Mathematics
LLOYD-JONES, G. C., Chemistry
MANN, S., Chemistry
MCNAMARA, J. M., Mathematics and Biology
MANNERS, I., Inorganic Materials and Chemistry
MILES, M. J., Physics
NASON, G. P., Statistics
OBERAUER, K., Psychology
ORPEN, A. G., Structural Chemistry
ORR-EWING, A. J., Chemistry
PEREGRINE, D. H., Applied Mathematics
POPESCU, S., Physics
PRENTICE, I. C., Earth System Science
PRINGLE, P. G., Inorganic Chemistry
RAGNARSDOTTIR, K. V., Environmental Geochemistry
RICHARDSON, R. M., Physics
RICKARD, J. C., Mathematics
ROBERT, D., Bionanoscience
ROBERTS, A., Zoology
ROGERS, P. J., Biological Psychology
SCHOFIELD, A. H., Pure Mathematics
SHERMAN, D. M., Geochemistry
SIEGERT, M. J., Physical Geography
SIMPSON, T. J., Organic Chemistry
SMART, P. L., Geography
SPARKS, R. S. J., Geology
STEEDS, J. W., Physics
STOBART, A. K., Plant Biochemistry
TICKELL, A. T., Human Geography
TINSLEY, R. C., Zoology
TRANTER, M., Geography
TROSCIANKO, T. S., Psychology
VALDES, P. J., Physical Geography
VAN DEN BERG, M., Pure Mathematics
VINCENT, B., Physical Chemistry
VINEY, M. E., Biological Sciences
WALL, R. L., Zoology
WALSBY, A. E., Botany
WELCH, P. D., Mathematics
WIGGINS, S. R., Applied Mathematics
WILLIS, C. L., Organic Chemistry
WOOD, B. J., Earth Sciences
WORRALL, D. M., Physics

Faculty of Social Sciences and Law (Senate House, Tyndall Ave, Bristol, BS8 1TH; tel. (117) 928-7797; internet www.bris.ac.uk/depts/socsci):

ASHTON, D. J., Accountancy and Finance
ATTFIELD, C. L. F., Econometrics
BAILEY-HARRIS, R. J., Law
BRADLEY, H. K., Sociology
BREWER, A. A., History of Economics
BURGESS, S. M., Economics
CARVER, T. F., Political Theory
COWAN, D. S., Law and Policy
CROSSLEY, M. W., Comparative and International Education
DEEM, R., Education
DOYAL, L., Health and Social Care
DUGDALE, D., Management Accounting
FARMER, E. R. G., Child and Family Studies
FENTON, C. S., Sociology
FORREST, R. S., Urban Studies
FORSTER, A. W., Politics and International Relations
FOX, K. R., Exercise and Health Sciences
FRIEDMAN, A. L., Management and Economics
GORDON, D., Social Justice
GREGG, P. A., Economics
GROUT, P. A., Political Economy
HESTER, M., Gender, Violence and International Policy
HILL, J. D., Law
HUGHES, R. M., Education
JOHNSON, M. L., Health and Social Policy
KERRIDGE, J. R., Law
KYLE, J. G., Deaf Studies
LEVITAS, R., Sociology
LITTLE, R., International Politics
MCFARLANE, A. E., Education
MCLENNAN, G., Sociology
MCMEEL, G. P., Law
MODOOD, T., Sociology, Politics and Public Policy
MOK, K. J., East Asian Studies
OSBORN, M. J., Education
PARK, I.-U., Industrial Organization
PARTINGTON, T. M., Law
PRIDHAM, G. F. M., European Politics
PROPPER, C., Economics
PROSSER, J. A. W., Public Law
QUINTON, D. L., Psychosocial Development
REA-DICKINS, P. M., Applied Linguistics in Education
ROBERTSON, S. L., Education (Sociology)
ROSE, F. D., Commercial Law
SKULTANS SHELLEY, V., Social Anthropology
STANTON, K. M., Law
SUFRIN, B. E., Law
SUTHERLAND, R. J., Education
TEMPLE, J. R. W., Economics
WARD, L. M., Disability and Social Policy
WEBSTER, A., Educational Psychology

UNIVERSITY OF BUCKINGHAM

Hunter St, Buckingham, MK18 1EG
Telephone: (1280) 814080
Fax: (1280) 822245
E-mail: info@buckingham.ac.uk
Internet: www.buckingham.ac.uk

Founded 1976, Royal Charter 1983
Private control
Academic year: January to December (4 10-week terms)

Chancellor: Lord TANLAW
Chairman of Ccl: CHLOE WOODHEAD
Vice-Chancellor: Dr TERENCE KEALEY
Deputy Vice-Chancellor: Prof. ANDREW MILES
Registrar: Prof. LEN EVANS
Librarian: LOUISE HAMMOND

Number of teachers: 164 (93 full-time, 91 part-time)
Number of students: 1,000
Publication: *Denning Law Journal* (1 a year)

DEANS

School of Business: Dr JANE TAPSELL
School of Humanities: Prof. MARTIN RICKETTS
School of Law: Prof. SUSAN EDWARDS
School of Medicine: Prof. KAROL SIKORA (Dean-Elect)
School of Sciences: Prof. MIKE CAWTHORNE

PROFESSORS

ADAMS, C. J., Information Systems
ADAMSON, J., Modern History
ALCOCK, A., Corporate Law
ALDERMAN, G., Politics and Contemporary History

ARCH, J., Metabolic Research
CAWTHORNE, M. A., Metabolic Research
CLARKE, J. C., History
DURAND, A., European Law
EDWARDS, S., Law
FOSTER, N., European Law
GLEES, A., Security/Intelligence Studies
JASSIM, S., Mathematics
O'HEAR, A., Philosophy and Education
O'KEEFE, D., Education
RICKETTS, M., Economic Organisation
RIDLEY, J., History
SMITHERS, A., Education
WOOD, G., Economics
WOODHEAD, C., Education

UNIVERSITY OF CAMBRIDGE

Cambridge CB2 1TN
Telephone: (1223) 337733 (Central Switchboard); (1223) 332200 (Central Administration)
Fax: (1223) 339669
E-mail: communications@admin.cam.ac.uk
Internet: www.cam.ac.uk

Founded 13th century
Academic year: October to June

Chancellor: HRH PRINCE PHILIP, THE DUKE OF EDINBURGH
Vice-Chancellor: Prof. Sir LESZEK BORYSIEWICZ
Pro-Vice-Chancellor for Education: Prof. JOHN RALLISON
Pro-Vice-Chancellor for Int. Strategy: Dr JENNIFER BARNES
Pro-Vice-Chancellor for Institutional Affairs: Prof. IAN WHITE
Pro-Vice-Chancellor for Planning and Resources: Prof. STEVE YOUNG
Pro-Vice-Chancellor for Research: Prof. LYNN GLADDEN
High Steward: Dame BRIDGET OGILVIE
Registrary: Dr J. NICHOLLS
Librarian: P. K. FOX

Number of teachers: 1,500
Number of students: 15,821 (11,160 undergraduate, 4,661 postgraduate)

PROFESSORS

Faculty of Archaeology and Anthropology (Pembroke St, Cambridge, CB2 3QY; tel. (1223) 762846; fax (1223) 335460; e-mail archanth-enquiries@lists.cam.ac.uk; internet www.archanth.cam.ac.uk):

BARKER, G., Archaeology (St John's College)
CHAKRABARTI, D., McDonald Institute for Archaeological Research
FOLEY, R. A., Human Evolution (King's College)
HUMPHREY, C., Collaborative Anthropology (King's College)
JONES, M. K., Archaeological Science
KEMP, B., McDonald Institute for Archaeological Research
LEGGE, A. J., McDonald Institute for Archaeological Research
MASCIE-TAYLOR, C. G. N., Biological Anthropology (Churchill College)
MELLARS, P. A., Prehistory and Human Evolution (Corpus Christi College)
MILLETT, M. J., Classical Archaeology (Fitzwilliam College)
MOORE, H. L., Social Anthropology (Jesus College)
POSTGATE, N., Assyriology (Trinity College)
RAY, J., Egyptology (Selwyn College)
Lord RENFREW, Archaeology

Faculty of Architecture and History of Art (1–5 Scroope Terrace, Trumpington St, Cambridge, CB2 1PX; tel. (1223) 332950; fax (1223) 332960; e-mail enquiries@aha.cam.ac.uk; internet www.aha.cam.ac.uk):

BINSKI, P., History of Medieval Art (Gonville and Caius College)
ECHENIQUE, M. H., Land Use and Transport Studies (Churchill College)
HOWARD, D. J., Architectural History (St John's College)
JOANNIDES, P. E., Art History
MASSING, J. M., History of Art (King's College)
SHORT, A., Architecture (Clare Hall)
STEEMERS, K., Sustainable Design (Wolfson College)

Faculty of Asian and Middle Eastern Studies (Sidgwick Ave, Cambridge, CB3 9DA; tel. (1223) 335106; fax (1223) 335110; e-mail enquiries@ames.cam.ac.uk; internet www.ames.cam.ac.uk):

BOWRING, R., Japanese Studies (Downing College)
DE LANGE, N., Hebrew and Jewish Studies (Wolfson College)
GORDON, R., Hebrew (St Catharine's College)
KHAN, G., Semitic Philology
KORNICKI, P., East Asian Studies (Robinson College)
MELVILLE, C., Persian History (Pembroke College)
MONTGOMERY, J., Classical Arabic (Trinity Hall)
POSTGATE, N., Assyriology (Trinity College)
RAY, J., Egyptology (Selwyn College)
STERCKX, R., Chinese (Clare College)
SULEIMAN, Y., Modern Arabic Studies (King's College)
VAN DE VEN, H., Modern Chinese History

Faculty of Biology (School of the Biological Sciences, 17 Mill Lane, Cambridge, CB2 1RX; tel. (1223) 766894; fax (1223) 332355; e-mail mb422@admin.cam.ac.uk; internet www.bio.cam.ac.uk/index.html):

AFFARA, N. A., Pathology (Hughes Hall)
ASHBURNER, M., Genetics (Churchill College)
BARLOW, H. B., Physiology, Development and Neuroscience (Trinity College)
BATE, C. M., Developmental Biology (King's College)
BAULCOMBE, D. C., Plant Sciences
Sir BLUNDELL, TOM, Biochemistry (Sidney Sussex College)
BURROWS, M., Neurobiology (Wolfson College)
CLAYTON, N. S., Comparative Cognition (Clare College)
CLUTTON-BROCK, T. H., Animal Ecology (Magdalen College)
COLLINS, V. P., Histopathology
COOKE, A., Pathology (King's College)
CRAWFORD, A. C., Neurophysiology (Trinity College)
DAVIES, N. B., Behavioural Ecology (Pembroke College)
DICKINSON, A., Comparative Psychology (Hughes Hall)
ELLAR, D. J., Biochemistry (Gonville and Caius College)
ELLINGTON, C. P., Zoology (Downing College)
EVERITT, B. J., Behavioural Neuroscience (Downing College)
FIELD, M. C., Pathology
FITZSIMONS, J. T., Physiology, Development and Neuroscience (Gonville and Caius College)
FOWDEN, A. L., Biological Sciences (Girton College)
GILLIGAN, C. A., Mathematical Biology (King's College)
GLOVER, D. M., Genetics (Fitzwilliam College)
GRAY, J. C., Plant Molecular Biology (Robinson College)
GRIFFITHS, H., Plant Sciences (Clare College)
HARRIS, W. A., Physiology, Development and Neuroscience (Clare College)
HUANG, C. L.-H., Cell Physiology (Murray Edwards College)
HUGHES, C., Pathology (Trinity College)
IRVINE, R. F., Molecular Pharmacology (Corpus Christi College)
JACKSON, R. J., Biochemistry (Pembroke College)
JACKSON, S. P., Zoology (St John's College)
JOHNSON, M. H., Reproductive Sciences (Christ's College)
KEVERNE, E. B., Behavioural Neuroscience (King's College)
LASKEY, R. A., Animal Embryology (Darwin College)
LAUE, E. D., Biochemistry (St John's College)
LAUGHLIN, S. B., Zoology (Churchill College)
LEADLAY, P. F., Biochemistry (Clare College)
LOKE, Y. W., Reproductive Immunology (King's College)
MCNAUGHTON, P. A., Pharmacology (Christ's College)
METCALFE, J. C., Mammalian Cell Biochemistry (Darwin College)
MINSON, A. C., Virology (Wolfson College)
MOLLON, J. D., Visual Neuroscience (Gonville and Caius College)
MOORE, B. C. J., Auditory Perception (Wolfson College)
PARKER, J. S., Plant Cytogenetics (St Catharine's College)
PERHAM, R. N., Structural Biochemistry (St John's College)
ROBBINS, T. W., Cognitive Neuroscience (Downing College)
ROBERTS, A. C., Behavioural Neuroscience (Girton College)
RUDD, C E, Pathology
SALMOND, G. P. C., Biochemistry (Wolfson College)
SCHULTZ, W., Neuroscience (Churchill College)
SMITH, A., Wellcome Trust Centre for Stem Cell Research
SMITH, J. C., Zoology (Christ's College)
STANLEY, M. A., Pathology (Christ's College)
SURANI, M. A. H., Physiology of Reproduction (King's College)
SUTHERLAND, W. J., Conservation Biology (Clare College)
TAYLOR, C. W., Pharmacology (Downing College)
TYLER, L. K., Cognitive Neuroscience (Clare College)
WARING, M. J., Pharmacology (Jesus College)
WATT, F. M., Molecular Genetics
WYLLIE, A. H., Pathology (St John's College)

Faculty of Classics (Sidgwick Site, Sidgwick Ave, Cambridge, CB3 9DA; tel. (1223) 335151; fax (1223) 335409; internet www.classics.cam.ac.uk):

BEARD, M., Classics (Newnham College)
CARTLEDGE, P. A., Greek History and Greek Culture (Clare College)
DIGGLE, J., Greek and Latin (Queens' College)
GOLDHILL, S., Greek Literature and Culture (King's College)
HENDERSON, J., Classics (King's College)
HOLTON, D. W., Modern Greek
HORROCKS, G. C., Comparative Philology (St John's College)
HUNTER, R. L., Greek (Trinity College)
MILLETT, M. J., Classical Archaeology (Fitzwilliam College)
OAKLEY, S. P., Latin (Emmanuel College)
OSBORNE, R., Ancient History (King's College)

SCHOFIELD, M., Ancient Philosophy (St John's College)
SEDLEY, D. N., Ancient Philosophy (Christ's College)

Faculty of Divinity (West Rd, Cambridge, CB3 9BS; tel. (1223) 763002; fax (1223) 763003; e-mail faculty-office@divinity.cam.ac.uk; internet www.divinity.cam.ac.uk):

COAKLEY, S., Divinity (Murray Edwards College)
DAVIES, G. I., Old Testament Studies (Fitzwilliam College)
DE LANGE, N. R. M., Hebrew and Jewish Studies (Wolfson College)
DUFFY, E., History of Christianity (Magdalene College)
FORD, D. F., Divinity (Selwyn College)
LIEU, J., Divinity (Robinson College)
LIPNER, J., Hinduism and Comparative Study of Religion (Clare Hall)

Faculty of Earth Sciences and Geography (Downing Place, Cambridge, CB2 3EN; tel. (1223) 333393; e-mail secretary@esg.cam.ac.uk; internet www.esg.cam.ac.uk):

ADAMS, B., Conservation and Development (Downing College)
ARTACHO, E., Mineral Sciences
BENNETT, R. J., Geography (St Catharine's College)
BICKLE, M. J., Tectonics, Basin and Crustal Development and Sedimentology (Queens' College)
CARPENTER, M. A., Mineralogy and Mineral Physics (Magdalene College)
CLIFF, A. D., Theoretical Geography (Christ's College)
CONWAY MORRIS, S., Evolutionary Palaeoecology (St John's College)
DOVE, M., Mineralogy and Mineral Physics
DOWDESWELL, J. A., Physical Geography (Jesus College)
ELDERFIELD, H., Environmental Change and Marine Geochemistry (St Catharine's College)
HAINING, R. P., Human Geography (Fitzwilliam College)
HODELL, D. A., Climate Change and Earth-Ocean-Atmosphere Systems
HUPPERT, H., Geological Fluid Mechanics (King's College)
JACKSON, J., Geophysics, Geodynamics and Tectonics
LEADER-WILLIAMS, N., Conservation Leadership (Dir (Churchill College)
MCKENZIE, D. P., Geophysics, Geodynamics and Tectonics (King's College)
MARTIN, R. L., Economic Geography (St Catharine's College)
OWENS, S., Environment and Policy (Newnham College)
PRIESTLEY, K., Geophysics, Geodynamics and Tectonics
REDFERN, S., Mineral Sciences
RICHARDS, K. S., Geography (Emmanuel College)
SALJE, E. K. H., Mineralogy and Petrology (Darwin College)
SMITH, R., Historical Geography and Demography (Downing College)
WHITE, R. S., Geophysics, Geodynamics and Tectonics (St Edmund's College)
WOODS, A. W., Geophysics, Geodynamics and Tectonics (St John's College)

Faculty of Economics (Austin Robinson Bldg, Sidgwick Ave, Cambridge, CB3 9DD; tel. (1223) 335200; fax (1223) 335475; e-mail faculty@econ.cam.ac.uk; internet www.econ.cam.ac.uk):

BROWN, W. A., Industrial Relations (Darwin College)
Sir DASGUPTA, PARTHA, Economics (St John's College)
GOYAL, S., Economics (Christ's College)
HARRIS, C. J., Economics (King's College)
HARVEY, A. C., Econometrics (Corpus Christi College)
NEWBERY, D. M. G., Economics (Churchill College)
OGILVIE, S., Economic History
PESARAN, M. H., Economics (Trinity College)
RUSTICHINI, A., Political Economy
SABOURIAN, H., Economics and Game Theory (King's College)
SMITH, R. J., Economic Theory and Economic Statistics (Gonville and Caius College)

Faculty of Education (184 Hills Rd, Cambridge, CB2 8PQ; tel. (1223) 767600; fax (1223) 767602; e-mail reception@educ.cam.ac.uk; internet www.educ.cam.ac.uk):

ARNOT, M., Sociology of Education (Jesus College)
COLCLOUGH, C., Education and Development
GOSWAMI, U., Education (St John's College)
GRAY, J. M., Education
GRONN, P., Education (Hughes Hall)
HOWE, C., Education (Lucy Cavendish College)
MERCER, N., Education (Hughes Hall)
NIKOLAJEVA, M., Education
REAY, D., Education
RUTHVEN, K., Education (Hughes Hall)

Faculty of English (9 West Rd, Cambridge, CB3 9DP; tel. (1223) 335070; fax (1223) 335075; e-mail english-faculty@lists.cam.ac.uk; internet www.english.cam.ac.uk):

COLLINI, S. A., English
COOPER, H., English (Magdalene College)
DE BOLLA, P., English (King's College)
GLEN, H. J., English (Murray Edwards College)
HAWKINS, J., Research Centre for English and Applied Linguistics
HEATH, S., English (Jesus College)
JACOBUS, M. L., English (Churchill College)
JARVIS, S., English (Robinson College)
KERRIGAN, J. F., English (St John's College)
LEIGHTON, A., English (Trinity College)
POOLE, A., English (Trinity College)
TROTTER, D., English (Gonville and Caius College)
WINDEATT, B. A., English (Emmanuel College)

Faculty of History (West Rd, Cambridge, CB3 9EF; tel. (1223) 335340; fax (1223) 335968; e-mail gen.enq@hist.cam.ac.uk; internet www.hist.cam.ac.uk):

ABULAFIA, D. S. H., History of the Mediterranean Countries in the Middle Ages (Gonville and Caius College)
ANDREW, C. M., Modern and Contemporary History (Corpus Christi College)
BADGER, A. J., American History since 1930 (Clare College)
Sir BAYLY, CHRISTOPHER, Modern Indian History and the History of the Expansion of Europe (St Catharine's College)
CARPENTER, M. C., Medieval English History
CLARK, C., Modern Europe (St Catharine's College)
DAUNTON, M. J., Economic History (Trinity Hall)
DUFFY, E., Religious History (Magdalene College)
EVANS, R. J., Modern European History (Gonville and Caius College)
HASLAM, J., History of International Relations (Corpus Christi College)
HATCHER, M. J., Economic History (Corpus Christi College)
HILTON, B., British History (Trinity College)
MANDLER, P., British History since 1800 (Gonville and Caius College)
MCKITTERICK, R. D., Medieval History (Sidney Sussex College)
MORRILL, J. S., British and Irish History (Selwyn College)
O'BRIEN, M., Modern Intellectual Culture (Jesus College)
PARRY, J. P., British Political and Constitutional History (Pembroke College)
REYNOLDS, D., International History (Christ's College)
SMITH, R., Historical Demography (Downing College)
STEDMAN-JONES, G., Modern European Political Thought (King's College)
THOMPSON, D., Church History (Fitzwilliam College)
TOMBS, R., Modern French and European History (St John's College)
VAUGHAN, M., African History (King's College)

Faculty of Law (10 West Rd, Cambridge, CB3 9DZ; tel. (1223) 330033; fax (1223) 330055; e-mail enquiries@law.cam.ac.uk; internet www.law.cam.ac.uk):

ALLAN, T. R. S., Public Law and Jurisprudence (Pembroke College)
Sir BAKER, JOHN H., Laws of England (St Catharine's College)
BARNARD, C., European Union Law (Trinity College)
BELL, J. S., Law (Pembroke College)
BENTLY, L. A. F., Intellectual Property (Emmanuel College)
Sir BOTTOMS, ANTHONY E., Criminology (Fitzwilliam College)
CHEFFINS, B. R., Corporate Law (Trinity Hall)
CLARKE, M. A., Commercial Contract Law (St John's College)
CORNISH, W. R., Intellectual Property Law (Magdalene College)
CRAWFORD, J. R., International Law (Jesus College)
DASHWOOD, A. A., European Law (Sidney Sussex College)
FARRINGTON, D. P., Psychological Criminology (Darwin College)
FELDMAN, D., English Law (Downing College)
FERRAN, E. V., Company and Securities Law (St Catharine's College)
FORSYTH, C. F., Public Law and Private International Law (Robinson College)
GRAY, C. D., International Law (St John's College)
GRAY, K. J., Law (Trinity College)
HOOLEY, R. J. A., Law (Fitzwilliam College)
IBBETSON, D. J., Civil Law (Corpus Christi College)
KOSKENNIEMI, M. A., Legal Science (Jesus College)
KRAMER, M. H., Legal and Political Philosophy (Churchill College)
LIEBLING, A., Criminology
LÖSEL, F., Institute of Criminology (Dir)
SHERMAN, L. W., Criminology
SIMESTER, A. P., Law (Wolfson College)
SPENCER, J. R., Law (Selwyn College)
TILEY, J., Law of Taxation (Queens' College)
VIRGO, G. J., English Private Law (Downing College)
WIKSTROM, P. O., Ecological and Developmental Criminology
YATES, A. D., Law (Robinson College)

Faculty of Mathematics (Centre for Mathematical Sciences, Wilberforce Rd, Cambridge, CB3 0WA; tel. (1223) 765000; fax (1223) 765900; e-mail reception@maths.cam.ac.uk; internet www.maths.cam.ac.uk):

BAKER, A., Pure Mathematics (Trinity College)
BARROW, J. D., Applied Mathematics (Clare Hall)

COATES, J. H., Pure Mathematics (Emmanuel College)
DAVIS, A.-C., Theoretical Physics
DAWID, A. P., Statistics
DOREY, N., Theoretical Physics
FOKAS, T., Nonlinear Mathematical Science
GIBBONS, G. W., Theoretical Physics (Clare College)
GOLDSTEIN, R. E., Complex Physical Systems
GOWERS, W. T., Mathematics (Trinity College)
GREEN, B. J., Pure Mathematics (Trinity College)
GREEN, M. B., Theoretical Physics (Clare Hall)
GRIMMETT, G. R., Mathematical Statistics (Churchill College)
GROJNOWSKI, I., Mathematics
HAWKING, S. W., Gravitational Physics
HAYNES, P. H., Applied Mathematics
HINCH, E. J., Fluid Mechanics (Trinity College)
HORGAN, R. R., Theoretical and Mathematical Physics
HUPPERT, H. E., Theoretical Geophysics (King's College)
HYLAND, J. M. E., Mathematical Logic (King's College)
ISERLES, A., Numerical Analysis of Differential Equations (King's College)
JOHNSTONE, P. T., Foundations of Mathematics (St John's College)
JOZSA, R., Applied Mathematics and Theoretical Geophysics
KELLY, F. P., Mathematics of Systems (Christ's College)
KÖRNER, T. W., Fourier Analysis (Trinity Hall)
LEADER, I. B., Pure Mathematics (Trinity College)
LISTER, J. R., Fluid Dynamics (Trinity College)
MANTON, N. S., Mathematical Physics (St John's College)
MARKOWICH, P. A., Applied Mathematics
NORRIS, J. R., Stochastic Analysis (Churchill College)
OSBORN, H., Mathematics
PATERNAIN, G. P., Mathematics (Trinity College)
PEAKE, N., Applied Mathematics (Emmanuel College)
PROCTOR, M. R. E., Astrophysical Fluid Dynamics (Trinity College)
QUEVEDO, F.
RALLISON, J. M., Fluid Dynamics (Trinity College)
ROGERS, L. C. G., Statistical Science (St John's College)
SAXL, J., Algebra (Gonville and Caius College)
SCHOLL, A. J., Number Theory and Algebra
SHELLARD, E. P.
SHEPHERD-BARRON, N. I., Algebraic Geometry (Trinity College)
SPIEGELHALTER, D. J., Public Understanding of Risk
SUHOV, Y. M., Applied Probability (St John's College)
TAVARÉ, S., Applied Mathematics and Theoretical Geophysics
THOMASON, A. G., Combinatorial Mathematics (Clare College)
TOTARO, B. J., Astronomy and Geometry
TOWNSEND, P. K., Theoretical Physics (Queens' College)
WADHAMS, P., Ocean Physics
WEBER, R. R., Mathematics for Operational Research (Queens' College)
WILSON, P. M. H., Algebraic Geometry (Trinity College)
WORSTER, M. G., Mathematics for Natural Sciences (Trinity College)

Faculty of Modern and Medieval Languages (Sidgwick Ave, Cambridge, CB3 9DA; tel. (1223) 335000; fax (1223) 335062; e-mail mml-faculty-office@lists.cam.ac.uk; internet www.mml.cam.ac.uk):

BARANSKI, Z. G., Italian (Murray Edwards College)
BAYLEY, P., French (Gonville and Caius College)
BENNETT, W., French Philology and Linguistics (Murray Edwards College)
BOYLE, N., German (Magdalene College)
FINCH, A.
FORD, P. J., French and Neo-Latin Literature (Clare College)
FRANKLIN, S. C., Slavonic Studies (Clare College)
HAWKINS, S., Phonetic Sciences (Clare Hall)
HOLTON, D. W., Modern Greek (Selwyn College)
HUOT, S., Medieval French Literature (Pembroke College)
KIRKPATRICK, R., Italian and English (Robinson College)
LISBOA, M. M., Portuguese Literature and Culture (St John's College)
NOLAN, F. J., Phonetics (Fitzwilliam College)
ROBERTS, I. G., Linguistics (Downing College)
SINCLAIR, A., Modern Spanish Literature and Intellectual History (Clare College)
SMITH, P. J., Spanish (Trinity Hall)

Faculty of Music (11 West Rd, Cambridge, CB3 9DP; tel. (1223) 763481; fax (1223) 335067; e-mail tkw23@cam.ac.uk; internet www.mus.cam.ac.uk):

COOK, N. J., Music (Darwin College)
FENLON, I. A., Historical Musicology (King's College)
HOLLOWAY, R. G., Musical Composition (Gonville and Caius College)
RANKIN, S. K., Medieval Music (Emmanuel College)
RINK, J. S., Musical Performance Studies

Faculty of Philosophy (Sidgwick Ave, Cambridge, CB3 9DA; tel. (1223) 335090; fax (1223) 335091; e-mail phil-admin@lists.cam.ac.uk; internet www.phil.cam.ac.uk):

BLACKBURN, S. W., Philosophy (Trinity College)
CRANE, T., Philosophy (Peterhouse)
GEUSS, R., Philosophy
HEAL, B. J., Philosophy (St John's College)

Faculty of Physics and Chemistry (Institute of Astronomy, Madingley Rd, Cambridge, CB3 0HA; tel. (1223) 766644; fax (1223) 337523; e-mail smo@ast.cam.ac.uk; internet www.ast.cam.ac.uk/physchemfaculty):

ABELL, C., Biological Chemistry (Christ's College)
BALASUBRAMANIAN, S., Medicinal Chemistry (Trinity College)
BAUMBERG, J. J., Nanophotonics (Jesus College)
BEST, S. M., Materials Science
BHADESHIA, H. K. D. H., Metallurgy (Darwin College)
BLAMIRE, M. D., Device Materials
BURSTEIN, G. T., Materials Chemistry and Corrosion (Selwyn College)
CAMERON, R. E., Materials Science (Lucy Cavendish College)
CHEETHAM, A. K., Materials Science (Downing College)
CLARKE, C. J., Institute of Astronomy
CLYNE, T. W., Mechanics of Materials (Downing College)
COOPER, J. R. C., Quantum Matter (Darwin College)
COOPER, N. R., Theoretical Physics (Pembroke College)
DAVIES, P. B., Laser Spectroscopy (Corpus Christi College)
DOBSON, C. M., Chemistry (St John's College)
DONALD, A. M., Biological and Soft Systems (Robinson College)
DONALD, A. M., Experimental Physics (Robinson College)
DRISCOLL, J. L., Materials Science (Robinson College)
EFSTATHIOU, G. P., Astrophysics (King's College)
ELLIOTT, S. R., Chemistry (Trinity College)
EVANS, W., Institute of Astronomy
EVETTS, J. E., Device Materials (Pembroke College)
FABIAN, A. C., Institute of Astronomy
Sir FERSHT, ALAN, Organic Chemistry (Gonville and Caius College)
FRENKEL, D., Chemistry (Trinity College)
Sir FRIEND, RICHARD, Physics (St John's College)
GIBSON, V., High Energy Physics (Trinity College)
GILMORE, G. F., Institute of Astronomy (King's College)
GLEN, R. C., Chemistry (Clare College)
GREENHAM, N. C., Optoelectronics (Clare College)
GREER, A. L., Materials Science
GREY, C. P., Materials Chemistry
GULL, S., Physics (St John's College)
HANIFF, C. A., Astrophysics (Downing College)
HANSEN, J.-P., Chemistry (Corpus Christi College)
HEWETT, P. C., Institute of Astronomy
HILLS, R. E., Physics (St Edmund's College)
HUCK, W. T. S., Nanotechnology (Gonville and Caius College)
HUMPHREYS, C. J., Materials Science (Selwyn College)
JONES, R., Photochemistry (Queens' College)
JONES, W., Materials Chemistry (Sidney Sussex College)
KENNICUTT, R. C., Astronomy and Experimental Philosophy
KHMELNITSKII, D. E., Theory of Condensed Matter (Trinity College)
Sir KING, DAVID, Physical Chemistry (Downing College)
KLENERMAN, D., Chemistry (Christ's College)
KLINOWSKI, J., Chemistry (Peterhouse)
LAMBERT, R. M., Chemistry (King's College)
LASENBY, A. N., Astrophysics and Cosmology (Queens' College)
LEY, S. V., Organic Chemistry (Trinity College)
LITTLEWOOD, P. B., Theoretical Physics (Trinity College)
LONZARICH, G. G., Theoretical Physics (Trinity College)
MACKAY, C. D., Institute of Astronomy
MACKAY, D., Natural Philosophy
MIDGLEY, P. A., Materials Science
NEEDS, R., Theoretical Physics (Robinson College)
OSTRIKER, J., Astronomy (Clare College)
PARKER, A., High Energy Physics (Peterhouse)
PATERSON, I., Chemistry (Jesus College)
PAYNE, M. C., Theory of Condensed Matter (Pembroke College)
PETTINI, M., Institute of Astronomy
PHILLIPS, R. T., Physics (Clare College)
PRINGLE, J. E., Astronomy (Emmanuel College)
PYLE, J. A., Atmospheric Chemistry (St Catharine's College)
RITCHIE, D. A., Experimental Physics (Robinson College)
SANDERS, J. K. M., Inorganic Chemistry (Selwyn College)

SIMONS, B. D., Theoretical Physics (St John's College)
SIRRINGHAUS, H., Electron Device Physics (Churchill College)
SMITH, C. G., Semiconductor Physics (Clare Hall)
SPRIK, M., Chemistry (Clare College)
STEINER, U., Physics of Materials (St Edmund's College)
STIRLING, J., Natural Philosophy (Peterhouse)
TERENTJEV, E. M., Polymer Physics (Queen's College)
THOMSON, E., Experimental Particle Physics (Emmanuel College)
WALES, D., Chemistry (Emmanuel College)
WARD, D. R., Particle Physics (Queen's College)
WARNER, M., Theoretical Physics (Corpus Christi College)
WEBBER, B. R., Theoretical High Energy Physics (Emmanuel College)
WINDLE, A. H., Materials Science (Trinity College)
WITHINGTON, S., Analytical Physics (Downing College)

Faculty of Politics, Psychology, Sociology and International Studies (Free School Lane, Cambridge, CB2 3RQ; tel. (1223) 334520; fax (1223) 334550; e-mail enquiries@ppsis.cam.ac.uk; internet www.ppsis.cam.ac.uk; merger of Faculty of Social and Political Sciences and Centre of International Studies (CIS) 2009):

BORN, G. E. M., Sociology, Anthropology and Music
DUNN, J. M., Political Theory (King's College)
GAMBLE, A. M., British Political Economy
GOLOMBOK, S., Family Research (Newnham College)
HASLAM, J. G., History of International Relations (Corpus Christi College)
HILL, C. J., International Relations (Sidney Sussex College)
HINES, M., Psychology (Churchill College)
LAMB, M., Social and Development Psychology
MAYALL, J. B. L., International Relations (Sidney Sussex College)
RUST, J., Psychometrics Centre (Dir)
SCOTT, J. L., Empirical Sociology (Queens' College)
SIMMS, B. P., History of International Relations
THERBORN, G., Sociology
THOMPSON, J. B., Sociology (Jesus College)

School of Clinical Medicine (Addenbrooke's Hospital, Box 111, Hills Rd, Cambridge, CB2 0SP; tel. (1223) 336700; fax (1223) 336709; e-mail school-enquiries@medschl.cam.ac.uk; internet www.medschl.cam.ac.uk):

ALLAIN, J.-P., Transfusion Medicine (Corpus Christi College)
BARON, J.-C., Stroke Medicine
BENNETT, M. R., Cardiovascular Sciences
BLACKWELL, J. M., Molecular Parasitology (Newnham College)
BOBROW, M., Medical Genetics (Wolfson College)
BRADLEY, J. A., Surgery
BRAYNE, C. E. G., Public Health (Darwin College)
BROWN, M. J., Clinical Pharmacology (Gonville and Caius College)
BULLMORE, E. T., Psychiatry
CALDAS, C., Cancer Medicine
CARRELL, R. W., Haematology (Trinity College)
CHATTERJEE, V. K. K., Endocrinology (Churchill College)
CHILVERS, E. R., Respiratory Medicine (St Edmund's College)
CLAYTON, D., Biostatistics
COMPSTON, D. A. S., Neurology (Jesus College)
COMPSTON, J. E., Bone Medicine
COX, T. M., Medicine (Sidney Sussex College)
DANESH, J., Public Health and Primary Care
DAY, N. E., Public Health and Primary Care (Hughes Hall)
DUNGER, D. B., Paediatrics
EDWARDS, A. W. F., Public Health and Primary Care (Gonville and Caius College)
FAWCETT, J. W., Medicine (King's College)
FEARON, D. T., Immunology (Trinity College)
FFRENCH-CONSTANT, C. K., Neurological Genetics (Pembroke College)
FLETCHER, P., Psychiatry
GASTON, J. S. H., Rheumatology (St Edmund's College)
GOODYER, I. M., Child and Adolescent Psychiatry (Wolfson College)
GREEN, A. R., Haematology
GRIFFITHS, G., Medicine
GRIFFITHS, J., Molecular Imaging
HODGES, J. R., Medicine (King's College)
HOLLAND, A. J., Learning Disability
HUGHES, I. A., Paediatrics (Clare Hall)
HUPPERT, F., Psychology (Darwin College)
JODRELL, D., Cancer Therapeutics
JONES, P. B., Psychiatry
KARET, F. E., Nephrology
KHAW, K.-T., Clinical Gerontology (Gonville and Caius College)
KINMONTH, A. L., General Practice (St John's College)
LEHNER, P. J., Medicine
LEVER, A. M. L., Infectious Diseases (Peterhouse)
LOMAS, D. A., Respiratory Medicine (Trinity College)
LOMAS, D. J., Radiology
LUZIO, J. P., Clinical Biochemistry (St Edmund's College)
MANT, J., Primary Care Research
MENON, D. K., Anaesthesia (Queens' College)
MORRELL, N. W., Cardiopulmonary Medicine
MURPHY, G., Oncology
NEAL, D. E., Surgery
O'RAHILLY, S., Clinical Biochemistry and Medicine (Churchill College)
OWEN, D., Clinical Biochemistry
PEDERSEN, R., Regenerative Medicine
PETERS, A. M., Nuclear Medicine (New Hall)
Sir PETERS, KEITH, Physic (Christ's College)
PICKARD, J. D., Neurosurgery (St Catharine's College)
PONDER, B. A. J., Clinical Oncology (Jesus College)
READ, R. J., Haematology
ROBINSON, M., Clinical Biochemistry
ROLAND, M., Health Services Research
ROSENGARD, B. R., Surgery
RUBINSZTEIN, D., Molecular Neurogenetics
RUDD, C., Pathology
RUSHTON, N., Orthopaedic Research
SAHAKIAN, B. J., Clinical Neuropsychology
ST GEORGE-HYSLOP, P., Clinical Neurosciences
SIDDLE, K., Clinical Biochemistry (Churchill College)
SINCLAIR, J. H., Infectious Diseases
SISSONS, J. G. P., Infectious Diseases (Darwin College)
SMITH, G. C. S., Obstetrics and Gynaecology
SMITH, K. G. C., Experimental Medicine
SUTTON, S. R., Behavioural Science
TAVARÉ, S., Bioinformatics
TODD, J. A., Medical Genetics (Gonville and Caius College)
TROWSDALE, J., Pathology
VENTIKARAMAN, A. R., Cancer Research (New Hall)
WAREHAM, N., Epidemiology
WEISSBERG, P. L., Cardiovascular Medicine (Wolfson College)
WICKER, L., Medical Genetics

Department of Chemical Engineering and Biotechnology (New Museums Site, Pembroke St, Cambridge, CB2 3RA; tel. (1223) 334777; fax (1223) 334796; e-mail webmaster@ceb.cam.ac.uk; internet www.ceb.cam.ac.uk):

CHASE, H., Biochemical Engineering (Magdalene College)
GLADDEN, L. F., Chemical Engineering (Trinity College)
HALL, E. A. H., Analytical Biotechnology (Queens' College)
KRAFT, M., Chemical Engineering (Churchill College)
LOWE, C., Biotechnology (Trinity College)
MACKLEY, M. R., Chemical Engineering (Robinson College)
SLATER, N. K. H., Chemical Engineering (Fitzwilliam College)

Department of Engineering (Trumpington St, Cambridge, CB2 1PZ; tel. (1223) 332600; fax (1223) 332662; e-mail reception@eng.cam.ac.uk; internet www.eng.cam.ac.uk):

AINGER, C., Engineering
AMARATUNGA, G. A. J., Electrical Engineering (Churchill College)
BOLTON, M. D., Soil Mechanics (Churchill College)
BRITTER, R. E., Engineering (Pembroke College)
CALLADINE, C., Engineering
CAMPBELL, A. M., Engineering (Christ's College)
CANT, R. S., Engineering (Selwyn College)
CARDWELL, D. A., Superconducting Engineering
CEBON, D., Mechanical Engineering (Queens' College)
CIPOLLA, R., Information Engineering (Jesus College)
CLARKSON, P. J., Engineering Design
COLES, H. J., Electrical Engineering (St Catharine's College)
COLLINGS, N., Engineering (Robinson College)
COLOURIS, G., Engineering
CONTI, R., Engineering
DAVIDSON, P., Fluid Mechanics
DAWES, W. N., Aeronautical Engineering (Churchill College)
Dame DOWLING, ANN, Mechanical Engineering (Sidney Sussex College)
EARL, C. F., Engineering
FITZGERALD, W. J., Applied Statistics and Signal Processing
FLECK, N. A., Mechanics of Materials (Pembroke College)
GHAHRAMANI, Z., Information Engineering
GLOVER, K., Information Engineering (Sidney Sussex College)
GODSILL, S. J., Statistical Signal Processing (Corpus Christi College)
GREGORY, M. J., Manufacturing Engineering (Churchill College)
GUTHRIE, P. M., Engineering (St Edmund's College)
HOCHGREB, S., Engineering
HODSON, H. P., Aerothermal Engineering (Girton College)
HOPPER, A., Communications (Corpus Christi College)
HUTCHINGS, I. M., Manufacturing Engineering (St John's College)
IWAI, Y., Engineering
KELLY, M. J., Technology (Trinity Hall)
KINGSBURY, N. G., Signal Processing
KITTELSON, D., Engineering
LANGLEY, R. S., Mechanical Engineering (Fitzwilliam College)

LIDDELL, W. I., Engineering
McFARLANE, D., Service and Support Engineering
MACIEJOWSKI, J. M., Control Engineering
MAIR, R. J., Geotechnical Engineering (Jesus College)
MASTORAKOS, E., Energy Technologies (Fitzwilliam College)
MIGLIORATO, P., Electrical Engineering (Trinity College)
MILNE, W. I., Electrical Engineering (Churchill College)
NEELY, A., Institute for Manufacturing
NEWLAND, D. E., Engineering (Selwyn College)
PALMER, A. E., Engineering
PEAKE, N., Applied Mathematics
PELLEGRINO, S., Engineering (Corpus Christi College)
PENTY, R. V., Photonics
PRAGER, R. V., Medical Imaging (Queens' College)
ROBERTSON, J., Electrical Engineering (Churchill College)
SMITH, M. C., Control Engineering (Gonville and Caius College)
SOGA, K., Civil, Structural and Environmental Engineering
STRONGE, W. J., Applied Mechanics (Jesus College)
TUCKER, P. G., Engineering
UDREA, F., Electrical Engineering (Girton College)
WALLACE, K. M., Engineering (Selwyn College)
WELLAND, M. E., Nanotechnology (St John's College)
WHITE, I. H., Electrical Engineering (Jesus College)
WILLIAMS, J. A., Engineering Tribology
WOLPERT, D., Engineering (Trinity College)
WOODHOUSE, J., Engineering (Clare College)
WOODLAND, P., Information Engineering (Peterhouse)
XU, L., Turbomachinery (Downing College)
YOUNG, J. B., Applied Thermodynamics (King's College)
YOUNG, S. J., Information Engineering (Emmanuel College)

Department of History and Philosophy of Science (Free School Lane, Cambridge, CB2 3RH; tel. (1223) 334500; fax (1223) 334554; e-mail hps-admin@lists.cam.ac.uk; internet www.hps.cam.ac.uk):

FORRESTER, J. P., History and Philosophy of Psychoanalysis and Human Sciences (King's College)
JARDINE, N., History and Philosophy of the Sciences (Darwin College)
SCHAFFER, S., History of Physical Science
SECORD, J., Social History of Science

Department of Land Economy (19 Silver St, Cambridge, CB3 9EP; tel. (1223) 337147; fax (1223) 337130; e-mail landecon-ugadmissions@lists.cam.ac.uk; internet www.landecon.cam.ac.uk):

ALLMENDINGER, P., Land Economy

Department of Veterinary Medicine (Madingley Rd, Cambridge, CB3 0ES; tel. (1223) 337694; fax (1223) 337610; e-mail enquiries@vet.cam.ac.uk; internet www.vet.cam.ac.uk):

ALLEN, W. R., Equine Reproduction (Robinson College)
BLAKEMORE, W. F., Neuropathology (Wolfson College)
BROOM, D. M., Animal Welfare (St Catharine's College)
FRANKLIN, R., Neuroscience
HEENEY, J. L., Comparative Pathology
HERRTAGE, M. E., Animal Welfare
JEFFERY, N., Veterinary Clinical Studies
KAUFMAN, J., Pathology
McCONNELL, I., Veterinary Science (Clare Hall)
MASKELL, D. J., Farm Animal Health, Food Science and Food Safety (Wolfson College)
WOOD, J., Equine and Farm Animal Science

Judge Business School (Trumpington St, Cambridge, CB2 1AG; tel. (1223) 339700; fax (1223) 339701; e-mail enquiries@jbs.cam.ac.uk; internet www.jbs.cam.ac.uk; Judge Institute of Management Studies renamed to present 2005):

Dame DAWSON, SANDRA, Management (Sidney Sussex College)
Lord EATWELL, Financial Policy (Queens' College)
HUGHES, A., Enterprise Studies (Sidney Sussex College)
KILDUFF, M. J., Management Studies
MEEKS, G., Financial Accounting
NOLAN, P. H., Chinese Management (Jesus College)
PRABHU, J., Indian Business and Enterprise
RALPH, D., Operations Research
SCHOLTES, S., Health Management
WALSHAM, G., Management Studies

Computer Laboratory (William Gates Bldg, 15 J. J. Thomson Ave, Cambridge, CB3 0FD; tel. (1223) 763500; fax (1223) 334678; e-mail departmental-secretary@cl.cam.ac.uk; internet www.cl.cam.ac.uk):

ANDERSON, R. J., Security Engineering
BACON, J. M., Distributed Systems (Jesus College)
CROWCROFT, J. A., Communications Systems (Trinity College)
DAUGMAN, J. G., Computer Vision and Pattern Recognition
DAWAR, A., Logic and Algorithms (Robinson College)
GORDON, M. J. C., Computer Assisted Reasoning (King's College)
HOPPER, A., Computer Technology (Corpus Christi College)
LESLIE, I. M., Computer Science (Christ's College)
MYCROFT, A., Computing (Robinson College)
PAULSON, L., Computational Logic (Clare College)
PITTS, A. M., Theoretical Computer Science (Darwin College)
ROBINSON, P., Computer Technology (Gonville and Caius College)
WINSKEL, G., Computer Science (Emmanuel College)

WOMEN'S COLLEGES

Lucy Cavendish College: Lady Margaret Rd, Cambridge, CB3 0BU; tel. (1223) 332190; fax (1223) 332178; e-mail lcc-admin@lists.cam.ac.uk; internet www.lucy-cav.cam.ac.uk; f. 1965; library of 27,000 vols; Pres. Prof. JANET TODD.

Murray Edwards College: New Hall, University of Cambridge, Cambridge, CB3 0DF; tel. (1223) 762100; fax (1223) 763110; e-mail enquiries@murrayedwards.cam.ac.uk; internet www.newhall.cam.ac.uk; f. 1954; New Hall was re-named as present name 2008; Pres. Dr JENNIFER BARNES.

Newnham College: Sidgwick Ave, Cambridge, CB3 9DF; tel. (1223) 335700; fax (1223) 357898; internet www.newn.cam.ac.uk; f. 1871; library of 90,000 vols; Prin. Dame PATRICIA HODGSON.

MIXED COLLEGES

Christ's College: St Andrew's St, Cambridge, CB2 3BU; tel. (1223) 334900; fax (1223) 334973; e-mail library@christs.cam.ac.uk; internet www.christs.cam.ac.uk; f. 1505 for men; library of 80,000 vols; women admitted 1978; Master Prof. FRANK KELLY.

Churchill College: Storey's Way, Cambridge, CB3 0DS; tel. (1223) 336000; fax (1223) 336180; internet www.chu.cam.ac.uk; f. 1960 for men; women admitted 1972; Master Sir DAVID WALLACE.

Clare College: Trinity Lane, Cambridge, CB2 1TL; tel. (1223) 333200; fax (1223) 333219; internet www.clare.cam.ac.uk; f. 1326 for men; women admitted 1972; Master Prof. A. J. BADGER.

Corpus Christi College: Trumpington St, Cambridge, CB2 1RH; tel. (1223) 338000; fax (1223) 338061; internet www.corpus.cam.ac.uk; f. 1352 for men; women admitted 1983; Master STUART LAING.

Downing College: Regent St, Cambridge, CB2 1DQ; tel. (1223) 334800; fax (1223) 363852; e-mail college-office@dow.cam.ac.uk; internet www.dow.cam.ac.uk; f. 1800 for men; women admitted 1978; Master Prof. BARRY EVERITT.

Emmanuel College: St Andrew's St, Cambridge, CB2 3AP; tel. (1223) 334200; fax (1223) 334426; internet www.emma.cam.ac.uk; f. 1584 for men; women admitted 1978; Master Lord WILSON OF DINTON.

Fitzwilliam College: Storey's Way, Cambridge, CB3 0DG; tel. (1223) 332000; fax (1223) 464162; internet www.fitz.cam.ac.uk; f. 1966 for men; women admitted 1978; Master Prof. ROBERT LETHBRIDGE.

Girton College: Huntington Rd, Cambridge, CB3 0JG; tel. (1223) 338999; fax (1223) 338896; internet www.girton.cam.ac.uk; f. 1869 for women, men admitted 1977; Mistress Prof. SUSAN J. SMITH.

Gonville and Caius College: Trinity St, Cambridge, CB2 1TA; tel. (1223) 332400; fax (1223) 332456; internet www.cai.cam.ac.uk; f. 1348 for men; women admitted 1978; Master Sir CHRISTOPHER HUM.

Homerton College: Hills Rd, Cambridge, CB2 8PH; tel. (1223) 747111; fax (1223) 747120; e-mail porters@homerton.cam.ac.uk; internet www.homerton.cam.ac.uk; f. 1824 as a Training College (Approved Society 1976); men re-admitted 1978; Prin. Dr KATE PRETTY.

Hughes Hall: Mortimer Rd, Cambridge, CB1 2EW; tel. (1223) 334898; fax (1223) 311179; internet www.hughes.cam.ac.uk; f. 1885 as the Cambridge Training College for Women (Approved Foundation 1968); Pres. SARAH SQUIRE.

Jesus College: Jesus Lane, Cambridge, CB5 8BL; tel. (1223) 339339; fax (1223) 339313; internet www.jesus.cam.ac.uk; f. 1497 for men; women admitted 1978; Master Prof. ROBERT MAIR.

King's College: King's Parade, Cambridge, CB2 1ST; tel. (1223) 331100; fax (1223) 331315; e-mail info@kings.cam.ac.uk; internet www.kings.cam.ac.uk; f. 1441 for men; women admitted 1972; library of 130,000 vols; Provost Prof. ROSS HARRISON.

Magdalene College: Magdalene St, Cambridge, CB3 0AG; tel. (1223) 332100; fax (1223) 363637; internet www.magd.cam.ac.uk; f. 1428 for men; women admitted 1987; Master DUNCAN ROBINSON.

Pembroke College: Trumpington St, Cambridge, CB2 1RF; tel. (1223) 338100; fax (1223) 338163; e-mail enquiries@pem.cam.ac.uk; internet www.pem.cam.ac.uk; f. 1347 for men; women admitted 1983; Master Sir ROGER TOMKYS.

Peterhouse: Trumpington St, Cambridge, CB2 1RD; tel. (1223) 338200; fax (1223) 337578; e-mail info@pet.cam.ac.uk; internet www.pet.cam.ac.uk; f. 1284 for men; women admitted 1984; Master Prof. ADRIAN DIXON.

Queens' College: Silver St, Cambridge, CB3 9ET; tel. (1223) 335511; fax (1223) 335522; e-mail enquiries@quns.cam.ac.uk; internet www.quns.cam.ac.uk; f. 1448 for men; women admitted 1979; Pres. Prof. Lord EATWELL.

Robinson College: Grange Rd, Cambridge, CB3 9AN; tel. (1223) 339100; fax (1223) 351794; internet www.robinson.cam.ac.uk; f. 1979; Warden Prof. DAVID YATES; Dir of Studies MIA GRAY.

St Catharine's College: Trumpington St, Cambridge, CB2 1RL; tel. (1223) 338300; fax (1223) 338340; internet www.caths.cam.ac.uk; f. 1473 for men; women admitted 1978; Master Prof. Dame JEAN THOMAS.

St Edmund's College: Mount Pleasant, Cambridge, CB3 0BN; tel. (1223) 336250; fax (1223) 762822; e-mail college.office@st-edmunds.cam.ac.uk; internet www.st-edmunds.cam.ac.uk; f. 1896 for men; (Approved Foundation 1975); women admitted 1978; Master Prof. J. PAUL LUZIO.

St John's College: St John's St, Cambridge, CB2 1TP; tel. (1223) 338600; fax (1223) 337720; e-mail enquiries@joh.cam.ac.uk; internet www.joh.cam.ac.uk; f. 1511 for men; women admitted 1981; Master Prof. C. M. DOBSON.

Selwyn College: Grange Rd, Cambridge, CB3 9DQ; tel. (1223) 335846; fax (1223) 335837; internet www.sel.cam.ac.uk; f. 1882 for men; women admitted 1976; Master Prof. RICHARD BOWRING.

Sidney Sussex College: Sidney St, Cambridge, CB2 3HU; tel. (1223) 338800; fax (1223) 338884; e-mail enquiries@sid.cam.ac.uk; internet www.sid.cam.ac.uk; f. 1596 for men; women admitted 1976; Master Dr ANDREW WALLACE-HADRILL.

Trinity College: Trinity St, Cambridge, CB2 1TQ; tel. (1223) 338400; fax (1223) 338564; e-mail college.office@trin.cam.ac.uk; internet www.trin.cam.ac.uk; f. 1546 for men; women admitted 1977; library of 300,000 vols; Master Lord REES OF LUDLOW.

Trinity Hall: Trinity Lane, Cambridge, CB2 1TJ; tel. (1223) 332500; fax (1223) 332537; e-mail info@trinhall.cam.ac.uk; internet www.trinhall.cam.ac.uk; f. 1350 for men; women admitted 1977; Master Prof. MARTIN DAUNTON.

MIXED COLLEGES FOR GRADUATE STUDENTS

Clare Hall: Herschel Rd, Cambridge, CB3 9AL; tel. (1223) 332360; fax (1223) 332333; e-mail college.secretary@clarehall.cam.ac.uk; internet www.clarehall.cam.ac.uk; f. 1966 (Approved Foundation); Pres. Sir MARTIN HARRIS.

Darwin College: Silver St, Cambridge, CB3 9EU; tel. (1223) 335660; fax (1223) 335667; e-mail deanery@darwin.cam.ac.uk; internet www.dar.cam.ac.uk; f. 1964; Master Prof. WILLIAM A. BROWN; Dean Dr LEO HOWE.

Wolfson College: Barton Rd, Cambridge, CB3 9BB; tel. (1223) 335900; fax (1223) 335908; e-mail registrar@wolfson.cam.ac.uk; internet www.wolfson.cam.ac.uk; f. 1965; academic year October to September; Pres. Prof. RICHARD EVANS.

UNIVERSITY OF CENTRAL LANCASHIRE

Preston, PR1 2HE

Telephone: (1772) 201201
Fax: (1772) 892911
E-mail: cenquiries@uclan.ac.uk
Internet: www.uclan.ac.uk

Founded 1828, as Instn for the Diffusion of Knowledge, present name and status 1992

Academic year: September to July

Chancellor: Sir RICHARD EVANS
Vice-Chancellor: Dr MALCOLM MCVICAR
Deputy Vice-Chancellor for Academic Affairs: GRAHAM BALDWIN
Deputy Vice-Chancellor for Strategic Planning and Performance Management: DAVE PHOENIX
Pro-Vice-Chancellor for Student Experience: ROD DUBROW-MARSHALL
Pro-Vice-Chancellor for Research: (vacant)
Pro-Vice-Chancellor for International Affairs: ANGELA MURPHY
Librarian: KEVIN ELLARD

Number of teachers: 1,006
Number of students: 35,000

DEANS

Faculty of Arts, Humanities and Social Sciences: JOHN JOUGHIN
Faculty of Health: EILEEN MARTIN
Faculty of Management: DHARMA KOVVURI
Faculty of Science and Technology: DAVID PHOENIX
Lancashire Business School: DAVID HAMBLIN

UNIVERSITY OF CHESTER

Parkgate Rd, Chester, CH1 4BJ

Telephone: (1244) 511000
Fax: (1244) 511300
E-mail: enquiries@chester.ac.uk
Internet: www.chester.ac.uk

Founded 1839; present status 2005

Vice-Chancellor and Prin.: Prof. TIMOTHY WHEELER
Sr Pro-Vice-Chancellor for Resources and Quality: Dr MALCOLM RHODES
Pro-Vice-Chancellor: Prof. PETER HARROP
Pro-Vice-Chancellor for Student Experience and Corporate Performance: Dr CHRIS HASLAM
Pro-Vice-Chancellor for Acad. Sec.: ADRIAN LEE
Pro-Vice-Chancellor for Acad.: Prof. MIKE THOMAS
Univ. Sec.: DAVID STEVENS

Number of teachers: 413
Number of students: 14,000

DEANS

Applied Sciences: Prof. SARAH ANDREW
Arts and Media: BRENDAN O'SULLIVAN
Business, Enterprise and Lifelong Learning: Prof. PHIL HARRIS
Education and Children's Services: ANNA SUTTON
Health and Social Care: Prof. MICHAEL THOMAS
Humanities: Prof. ROB WARNER
Social Sciences: DAVID BALSAMO

UNIVERSITY OF CHICHESTER

Bishop Otter Campus, College Lane, Chichester, PO19 6PE

Telephone: (1243) 816000
E-mail: admissions@chi.ac.uk
Internet: www.chi.ac.uk

Founded 1839; became University College Chichester 1999, present name and status 2005

Vice-Chancellor: Prof. CLIVE BEHAGG

Publication: *Scene*

DEANS

Faculty of Business, Arts and Humanities: GILL BUTLER
Faculty of Sport, Education and Social Sciences: MARK MASON

UNIVERSITY OF DERBY

Kedleston Rd, Derby, DE22 1GB

Telephone: (1332) 590500
Fax: (1332) 294861
E-mail: askadmissions@derby.ac.uk
Internet: www.derby.ac.uk

Founded 1851, present name and status 1993, merged with High Peak College 1998

Academic year: September to June

Chancellor: Duke Of Devonshire PEREGRINE CAVENDISH
Vice-Chancellor and Chief Exec.: Prof. JOHN COYNE
Pro-Vice-Chancellor: Prof. LIZ BARNES
Pro-Vice-Chancellor: Prof. MICHAEL GUNN
Librarian: RICHARD FINCH

Library of 550,000 vols
Number of teachers: 595
Number of students: 23,000

DEANS

Faculty of Arts, Design and Technology: Prof. HUW DAVIES
Faculty of Business, Computing and Law: Dr KEITH HORTON
Faculty of Education, Health and Sciences: Prof. HELEN LANGTON
University of Derby College, Buxton: Prof. PETER DEWHURST

UNIVERSITY OF DURHAM

University Office, Old Elvet, Durham, DH1 3HP

Telephone: (191) 334-2000
Fax: (191) 334-6250
E-mail: pro.directory@durham.ac.uk
Internet: www.dur.ac.uk

Founded 1832

Academic year: October to June (3 terms)

Chancellor: BILL BRYSON
Vice-Chancellor and Warden: Prof. CHRISTOPHER HIGGINS
Deputy Warden: Prof. JOHN ASHWORTH
Pro-Vice-Chancellor for Education: Prof. ANTHONY FORSTER
Pro-Vice-Chancellor for Research: Prof. TOM MCLEISH
Pro-Vice-Chancellor for the Faculty of Arts and Humanities: Prof. SETH KUNIN
Pro-Vice-Chancellor for the Faculty of Science: Prof. ANDREW DEEKS
Pro-Vice-Chancellor for the Faculty of Social Sciences and Health: Prof. ROBIN CONINGHAM
Pro-Vice-Chancellor: Prof. RAY HUDSON
Registrar and Sec.: CAROLYN FOWLER
Treas.: PAULINA LUBACZ
Librarian: JON PURCELL

Library: see Libraries and Archives
Number of teachers: 1,449
Number of students: 15,768

PROFESSORS

Faculty of Arts and Humanities:
ARCHER, R. L. A., Spanish
BAGULEY, D., French
BARCLAY, J. M. G., Divinity
BARNES, G. L., Japanese
BROOKS, C. W., History
BROWN, D. W., Divinity
CLARK, T. J. A., English Studies
COOPER, D. E., Philosophy
COWLING, D. J., French
DAVIES, D. J., Study of Religion
DIBBLE, J. C., Music
HALL, E. M., Greek Cultural History
HARRIS, E., Classics and Ancient History
HARRIS, H. J., History
HAYWARD, C. T. R., Hebrew
LOUTH, A., Patristic and Byzantine Studies
LOWE, E. J., Philosophy
MANNING, P. D., Music

MICHIE, R. C., History
O'MEARA, P., Russian
O'NEILL, M. S. C., English Studies
PADDISON, M. H., Music
PRESTWICH, M. C., History
REGAN, S., English Studies
RHODES, P. J., Ancient History
ROLLASON, D. W., History
ROWE, C. J., Greek
SANDERS, A. L., English Studies
SAUL, N. D. B., German
STUCKENBRUCK, L. T., Biblical Studies
TAYLOR, J. H. M., French
WAUGH, P., English Studies
WILLIAMSON, P. A., History

Faculty of Science:

ABRAM, R. A., Physics
ABRASHKIN, V. A., Mathematics
ADAMS, C. S., Physics
APPLETON, E., Engineering
BADYAL, J. P., Chemistry
BENNETT, K. H., Engineering
BOWER, R. G., Physics
BROERSMA, H. J., Computer Science
BRYCE, M. R., Chemistry
CAMPBELL, A. C., Psychology
CHAMBERLAIN, J. M., Applied Physics
CROUCH, R., Engineering
DAVIDSON, J. P., Earth Sciences
DOREY, P. E., Mathematics
EDWARDS, R., Biological and Biomedical Sciences
FARBER, M. S., Pure Mathematics
FINDLAY, J. M., Psychology
FLOWER, D. R., Physics
FOULGER, G. R., Earth Sciences
FRENK, C. S., Fundamental Physics
GATHERCOLE, S. E., Psychology
GLOVER, E. W. N., Physics
GOLDSTEIN, M., Statistics
GOULTY, N. R., Earth Sciences
HATTON, P. D., Physics
HE, L., Engineering
HEYWOOD, C. A., Psychology
HOLDSWORTH, R. E., Earth Sciences
HOWARD, J. A. K., Chemistry
HUNTLEY, B., Biological and Biomedical Sciences
HUSSEY, P. J., Plant Molecular Cell Biology
HUTCHISON, C. J, Animal Cell Biology
HUTSON, J. M., Chemistry
LINDSAY, S. W., Biological and Biomedical Sciences
LINDSEY, K., Plant Molecular Biology
MANSFIELD, P., Mathematics
MARDER, T. B., Chemistry
MAROPOULOS, P., Engineering
MENSHIKOV, M. V., Statistics
MILNER, A. D., Cognitive Neuroscience
MONKMAN, A. P., Physics
MUNRO, M., Computer Science
NIU, Y., Earth Sciences
PARKER, D., Chemistry
PENNINGTON, M. R., Mathematical Sciences and Physics
PETTY, M. C., Engineering
PURVIS, A., Engineering
QUINLAN, R. A., Biomedical Sciences
SALOUS, S., Engineering
SEARLE, R. C., Geophysics
SHANKS, T., Physics
SHARPLES, R. M., Physics
SLABAS, A. R., Plant Sciences
STEWART, I. A., Computer Science
STIRLING, W. J., Mathematical Sciences and Physics
STRAUGHAN, B., Numerical Analysis
TANNER, B. K., Physics
TAVNER, P., Engineering
THOMPSON, R. N., Geology
TUCKER, M. E., Geological Sciences
UNSWORTH, A., Engineering
WALMSLEY, A. R., Infectious Diseases
WARD, M. J., Physics
WARD, R. S., Mathematics
ZAKRZEWSKI, W. J., Mathematics

Faculty of Social Sciences and Health:

ABHYANKAR, A., Finance
ALLEN, T., Law
ALLISON, R. J., Geography
AMIN, A., Geography
ANTONIOU, A., Business School
BAILEY, D., Applied Social Sciences
BAILIFF, I. K., Archaeology
BARR, D. G., Business School
BASU, P., Economics
BILSBOROUGH, A., Anthropology
BLACKMAN, T. J., Applied Social Sciences
BOHLANDER, M., Law
BOYNE, R. D., Sociology and Social Policy
BURT, T. P., Geography
BYRAM, M. S., Education
BYRNE, D. S., Applied Social Sciences
CAMPBELL, D., Cultural and Political Geography
CAMPBELL, I. D., Law
CARRITHERS, M. B., Anthropology
CLARK, T., Organizational Behaviour
COCKERILL, T. A. J., Business Management and Economics
COOPER, B., Education
DARNELL, A. C., Business School
DEGELING, P., Clinical Management Development
DIXON, R., Managerial Accounting
EHTESHAMI, A., Middle Eastern and Islamic Studies
ELLIOTT, J., Education
EVANS, H. M., Humanities in Medicine
FENWICK, H. M., Law
FERGUSON, R. I., Physical Geography
GLOVER, G. R., Public Mental Health
GOTT, R., Education
GRAHAM, S., Geography
GREAVES, R.-M., European Law
HAMILTON, J. D., Academic Director of Phase 1 Medicine
HOBBS, R. F., Law
HOLMES, P. R., Business School
HUDSON, R., Geography
HUNGIN, A. P. S., Health
HUNTER, D. J., Health Policy and Management
JOHNSON, P. S., Business School
KOUKRAKOS, P., Law
LAFFIN, M., Public Policy and Management
LANE, S., Geography
LAYTON, R. H., Anthropology
LEIGH, I. D., Law
LINSTEAD, S., Organizational Analysis
LONG, A. J., Geography
MASON, J., Health
MCGLYNN, C. M. S., Law
MCKENDRICK, D. G., Strategy
MEYER, J. H. F., Education
MOORE, G., Business School
NEWTON, L. D., Education
PAINTER, J. M., Geography
PALMER-COOPER, J. A., Education
PARKER, S. C., Entrepreneurship
PAUDYAL, K., Business School
POLOS, L., Business School
PRICE, A. J., Archaeology
READ, D., Business School
REDMAN, T., Business School
RIDGWAY, J. E., Education
RIGG, J. D., Geography
ROBERTS, C. A., Archaeology
SCOTT, S. J., Applied Social Sciences
SHENNAN, I., Geography
SHONE, R., Business School
SILLITOE, P., Anthropology
SMITH, R. D., Education
SMITH, S. J., Human Geography
SULLIVAN, G. R., Law
TOWNSEND, A. R., Regional Regeneration and Development Studies
TYMMS, P. B., Education
VAN WITTELOOSTUIJN, A., Strategy
WARBRICK, C. J., Law
WATSON, R., Financial Management
WILLIAMS, R. J., Politics
WILSON, R. J. A., Middle Eastern and Islamic Studies
WRIGHT, G., Management

COLLEGES

College of St Hild and St Bede: Durham, DH1 1SZ; tel. (191) 334-8300; fax (191) 334-8301; internet www.dur.ac.uk/hild-bede; f. 1975, by merger of College of the Venerable Bede (for men) and St Hild's College (for women); Prin. Prof. CHRIS HUTCHISON; Vice-Prin. LAURA WILSON.

Collingwood College: South Rd, Durham, DH1 3LT; tel. (191) 334-5000; fax (191) 334-5035; internet www.dur.ac.uk/collingwood; f. 1972; 1,100 students; Prin. Prof. EDWARD CORRIGAN.

Grey College: South Rd, Durham, DH1 3LG; tel. (191) 334-5900; fax (191) 334-5901; e-mail grey.college@durham.ac.uk; internet www.dur.ac.uk/grey.college; f. 1959; Master Prof. J. M. CHAMBERLAIN.

Hatfield College: North Bailey, Durham, DH1 3RQ; tel. (191) 334-2633; fax (191) 334-1541; e-mail hatfield.reception@durham.ac.uk; internet www.dur.ac.uk/hatfield.college; f. 1846; Master Prof. TIM BURT (acting).

John Snow College: Stockton-on-Tees, TS17 6BH; tel. (191) 334-0046; e-mail snow.college@durham.ac.uk; internet www.dur.ac.uk/johnsnow.college; f. 2001; Prin. Prof. CAROLYN SUMMERBELL.

Josephine Butler College: South Rd, Durham, DH1 3DF; tel. (191) 334-7260; fax (191) 334-7259; internet www.dur.ac.uk/butler.college; f. 2001; 800 students; Prin. ADRIAN SIMPSON.

Queen's Campus, Stockton: Thornaby, Stockton-on-Tees, TS17 6BH; tel. (191) 334-0022; fax (191) 334-0010; internet www.dur.ac.uk/queens-campus; f. 1992, as Univ. College Stockton, to award joint qualifications of Universities of Durham and Teesside; Dean Prof. TIM BLACKMAN.

St Aidan's College: Windmill Hill, Durham, DH1 3LJ; tel. (191) 334-5769; fax (191) 334-5770; internet www.dur.ac.uk/st-aidans.college; f. 1895, known as St Aidan's Society until 1961; Prin. J. S. ASHWORTH.

St Chad's College: 18 North Bailey, Durham, DH1 3RH; tel. (191) 334-3358; fax (191) 334-3371; e-mail chads@dur.ac.uk; internet www.dur.ac.uk/stchads; f. 1904; 500 students; Prin. Rev. Canon Dr J. P. M. CASSIDY.

St Cuthbert's Society: 12 South Bailey, Durham, DH1 3EE; tel. (191) 334-3400; fax (191) 334-3401; e-mail st-cuthberts.society@durham.ac.uk; internet www.dur.ac.uk/st-cuthberts.society; f. 1888, known as non-Collegiate until 1947; Prin. Prof. GRAHAM TOWL.

St John's College with Cranmer Hall: 3 South Bailey, Durham, DH1 3RJ; tel. (191) 334-3894; fax (191) 334-3501; e-mail enquiries@cranmerhall.co; internet www.dur.ac.uk/cranmerhall; f. 1909; Prin. Rev. Dr DAVID WILKINSON.

St Mary's College: Elvet Hill Road, Durham, DH1 3LR; tel. (191) 334-5719; fax (191) 334-5720; internet www.dur.ac.uk/st-marys.college; f. 1899; Prin. Prof. PHILIP GILMARTIN.

Stephenson College: Stockton-on-Tees, TS17 6JZ; tel. (191) 334-0560; fax (191) 334-0054; e-mail stephenson@durham.ac.uk; internet www.dur.ac.uk/stephenson; f. 2001; Prin. Prof. A. C. DARNELL.

Trevelyan College: Elvet Hill Rd, Durham, DH1 3LN; tel. (191) 334-7000; fax (191) 334-5371; e-mail admissions.trevelyan@durham.ac.uk; internet www.dur.ac.uk/trevelyan

.college; f. 1966; 600 students; Prin. Prof. H MARTYN EVANS.

University College: Durham Castle, Palace Green, Durham, DH1 3RW; tel. (191) 334-4099; fax (191) 334-3801; internet www.dur.ac.uk/university.college; f. 1832; Master Prof. M. E. TUCKER.

Ushaw College: Durham, DH7 9RH; tel. (191) 373-8517; e-mail courses@ushaw.ac.uk; internet www.ushaw.ac.uk; f. 1808; Rector Rev. T. P. DRAINEY.

Ustinov College: Howlands Farm, Durham, DH1 3DE; tel. (191) 334-7241; fax (191) 334-7231; e-mail ustinov.college@durham.ac.uk; internet www.dur.ac.uk/ustinov.college; f. 1965; Prin. Dr PENELOPE WILSON (acting).

Van Mildert College: Mill Hill Lane, Durham, DH1 3LH; tel. (191) 334-7100; e-mail vm.reception@durham.ac.uk; f. 1963; 1,000 students; Master Prof. PATRICK O'MEARA; publ. *VMA News*.

UNIVERSITY OF EAST ANGLIA

Norwich, NR4 7TJ
Telephone: (1603) 456161
Fax: (1603) 458553
Internet: www.uea.ac.uk
Founded 1963
Academic year: September to June
Chancellor: Sir BRANDON GOUGH
Vice-Chancellor: Prof. EDWARD ACTON
Pro-Vice-Chancellor for Academics: Prof. TOM WARD
Pro-Vice-Chancellor for Research, Enterprise and Engagement: Prof. TREVOR DAVIES
Registrar and Sec.y: BRIAN SUMMERS
Librarian: JEAN C. STEWARD
Library of 800,000 items (700,000 books, CDs and DVDs, 100,000 print periodicals)
Number of teachers: 1,000
Number of students: 14,313
Publications: *Pretext* (2 a year), *Reactions* (1 a year), *Scandinavica* (2 a year)

DEANS

Faculty of Arts and Humanities: Prof. DAVID PETERS CORBETT
Faculty of Health: Prof. IAN HARVEY
Faculty of Science: Prof. DAVID RICHARDSON
Faculty of Social Sciences: Prof. NEIL WARD

PROFESSORS

School of American Studies (tel. (1603) 592220; fax (1603) 507728; e-mail wwweas@uea.ac.uk; internet www.uea.ac.uk/eas):

BIGSBY, C. W. E.
CROCKATT, R.
HOMBERGER, E.

School of Biological Sciences (tel. (1603) 593503; fax (1603) 592250; e-mail diana.cook@uea.ac.uk; internet www.uea.ac.uk/bio):

DAWSON, A., Biology
DUNCAN, G., Biology
EDWARDS, D. R., Cancer Studies
HEWITT, G. M., Biology
JOHNSTON, A. W. B., Biology
REYNOLDS, J., Biology
RICHARDSON, D. J.
SUTHERLAND, W. J., Biology
WATKINSON, A. R., Ecology

School of Chemical Sciences and Pharmacy (tel. (1603) 593145; fax (1603) 592003; e-mail k.e.bezants@uea.ac.uk; internet www.uea.ac.uk/cap):

ANDREWS, D. L., Chemistry
BELTON, P., Chemistry
BOCHMANN, M., Chemistry
COOK, M. J., Chemistry
CRAIG, D., Pharmacy
FIELD, R., Chemistry
MOORE, G. R., Chemistry
ROBINSON, B. H., Chemistry
RUSSELL, D., Chemistry
THOMSON, A. J., Chemistry

School of Computing Sciences (tel. (1603) 592847; fax (1603) 593345; e-mail www-admin@uea.ac.uk; internet www.cmp.vea.uea.ac.uk):

BANGHAM, J. A., Electronic Systems Engineering
GLAUERT, J., Computing Science
FINLAYSON, G., Information Systems
FORREST, A. R., Computing Science
RAYWARD-SMITH, V. J., Computing Science
SLEEP, M. R., Computing Science

School of Developmental Studies (tel. (1603) 592807; fax (1603) 451999; e-mail dev.general@uea.ac.uk; internet www.uea.ac.uk/dev):

ELLIS, F. T., Development Studies
JENKINS, R., Development Studies
SEDDON, D., Development Studies
STOCKING, M. A., Development Studies

School of Economics (tel. (1603) 592070; fax (1603) 250434; e-mail m.watling@uea.ac.uk; internet www.uea.ac.uk/eco):

CUBITT, R., Economics
DAVIES, S. W., Economics
HARGREAVES HEAP, S. P., Economics
LAWSON, S., International Relations
LOOMES, G., Economics
LYONS, B. R., Economics
SUGDEN, R., Economics

School of Education and Lifelong Learning (tel. (1603) 591451; fax (1603) 593446; e-mail edv.reception@uea.ac.uk; internet www.uea.ac.uk/edu):

BRIDGES, D., Education
ELLIOTT, J., Education
NORRIS, N. F. J., Education
SCHOSTAK, J. F., Education
TICKLE, L., Education
WALKER, R., Education

School of Environmental Sciences (tel. (1603) 592542; fax (1603) 592327; e-mail env@uea.ac.uk; internet www.uea.ac.uk/env):

BATEMEN, I., Environmental Sciences
BENTHAM, C. G., Environmental Sciences
BRIMBLECOMBE, P., Environmental Sciences
HEY, R. D., Environmental Sciences
HULME, M., Environmental Sciences
JICKELLS, T. D., Environmental Sciences
LEEDER, M. R., Environmental Sciences
LISS, P. S., Environmental Sciences
O'RIORDAN, T., Environmental Sciences
PENKETT, S. A., Environmental Sciences
PIDGEON, N. F., Environmental Sciences
PLANE, J. M. C., Environmental Sciences
SCHELLNHUBER, J., Environmental Sciences
TURNER, R. K., Environmental Studies
VINCENT, C. E., Environmental Sciences
WATKINSON, A. R., Ecology
WIGLEY, T. M. C., Environmental Sciences

School of Film and Television Studies (tel. (1603) 593820; fax (1603) 507728; e-mail k.durnford@uea.ac.uk; internet www.uea.ac.uk/eas):

BARR, C. J. A., Film Studies
HIGSON, A., Film Studies
JANCOVICH, M., Film Studies
TASKER, Y., Contemporary Popular Culture

School of History (tel. (1603) 593521; fax (1603) 593519; e-mail h.ashdown@uea.ac.uk; internet www.uea.ac.uk/his):

CHARMLEY, J. D., Modern British History
DAVIS, J. C., English History
HARPER-BILL, C., English History
HOWE, A. C., Modern History
RAWCLIFFE, C., English History
SANDERSON, M., Modern Social History
VINCENT, N., English and European History

School of Language, Linguistics and Translation Studies (tel. (1603) 592750; fax (1603) 250599; e-mail pg.llt@uea.ac.uk; internet www.uea.ac.uk/llt):

CHILTON, P., Linguistics

School of Law (tel. (1603) 593042; fax (1603) 250245; e-mail pglaw@uea.ac.uk; internet www.uea.ac.uk/law):

HVIID, M., Competition and Contract Law
MULLIS, A., International Commercial Law
PATTENDEN, R. D., Law
PRIME, T., Law
SMITH, I. T., Employment Law
WINSHIP, P., Law

School of Literature and Creative Writing (tel. (1603) 593820; fax (1603) 507728; e-mail k.durnford@uea.ac.uk; internet www.uea.ac.uk/eas):

DUNCKER, P., Creative Writing
HOLMES, R., Literature
ROBERTS, M., Creative Writing
ROBINSON, M., Scandinavian Studies
SAGE, V., Literature
SALES, R., English Literature
SCOTT, C., European Literature (French)
YARROW, R., Drama

School of Management (tel. (1603) 593029; fax (1603) 593343; e-mail pg.mgt@uea.ac.uk; internet www.mgt.uea.ac.uk):

DREW, S., Management
FLETCHER, K. P., Management
TZOKAS, N., Customer Relationship Management
WADDAMS, C., Management

School of Mathematics (tel. (1603) 592597; fax (1603) 593868; e-mail ann.barnes@uea.ac.uk; internet www.mth.uea.ac.uk):

EVEREST, G. R., Mathematics
JOHNSON, J. A., Mathematics
VANDER-BROECK, J. M., Applied Mathematics
WARD, T., Pure Mathematics
ZALESSKII, A., Pure Mathematics

School of Medicine (tel. (1603) 593061; fax (1603) 593752; e-mail e.newport@uea.ac.uk; internet www.med.uea.ac.uk):

BACHMANN, M., Healthcare Interfaces
BARRETT, A., Clinical Oncology
HARVEY, I., Epidemiology and Public Health
HOWE, A. C., Clinical Professor
HUNTER, P. R., Clinical Professor
MACGREGOR, A., Public Health
MUGFORD, M., Health Economics
REYNOLDS, S., Medicine

School of Music (tel. (1603) 592452; fax (1603) 250454; e-mail n.swan@uea.ac.uk; internet www.uea.ac.uk/mus):

CHADD, D., Music

School of Nursing and Midwifery (tel. (1603) 421422; fax (1603) 421505; e-mail nam.admissions@uea.ac.uk; internet www.uea.ac.uk/nam):

SALTER, B., Health Services Research

School of Philosophy (tel. (1603) 593717; fax (1603) 250434; e-mail m.watling@uea.ac.uk; internet www.uea.ac.uk/phi):

O'HAGAN, T., Philosophy

School of Political, Social and International Studies (tel. (1603) 593717; fax (1603) 250434; e-mail m.watling@uea.ac.uk; internet www.uea.ac.uk/psi):

GOODWIN, B., Politics
LAWSON, S., International Relations
STREET, J. R., Politics

School of Social Work and Psychosocial Sciences (tel. (1603) 592068; fax (1603) 593552; e-mail pgswk@uea.ac.uk; internet www.uea.ac.uk/swk):

HOWE, D. K., Social Work
THOBURN, J., Social Work

School of World Art Studies and Museology (tel. (1603) 592817; fax (1603) 593642; e-mail pgwam1@uea.ac.uk; internet www.uea.ac.uk/art):

HODGES, R. A., Visual Arts
JORDANOVA, L., Visual Arts
ONIANS, J. B., Visual Arts

UNIVERSITY OF EAST LONDON

University Way, Docklands, London, E16 2RD
Telephone: (20) 8223-3000
Fax: (20) 8223-4072
E-mail: study@uel.ac.uk
Internet: www.uel.ac.uk

Founded 1970, as North East London Polytechnic, later became Polytechnic of East London, present name and status 1992
Academic year: September to July

Chancellor: Lord RIX
Vice-Chancellor: Prof. PATRICK MCGHEE
Deputy Vice-Chancellor: Prof. JOHN JOUGHIN
Pro-Vice-Chancellor: NIRMAL BORKHATARIA
Pro-Vice-Chancellor for Learning, Teaching and Student Experience: GRAHAM CURTIS
Pro-Vice-Chancellor for Int.: JOHN SHAW
Pro-Vice-Chancellor for Strategic Planning and External Devt: SELENA BOLINGBROKE
Univ. Sec. and Registrar: JILL GRINSTEAD
Librarian: ANDREW MCDONALD

Library of 248,000 vols, 1,400 current periodicals
Number of teachers: 530 (485 full-time, 45 part-time)
Number of students: 23,000

DEANS

Cass School of Education: ANN SLATER
Royal Docks Business School: Prof. LEN SHACKLETON
School of Architecture & the Visual Arts: PETE COBB (acting)
School of Computing, Information Technology and Engineering: Prof. MOHAMMAD DASTBAZ
School of Health and Bioscience: Prof. NEVILLE PUNCHARD
School of Humanities and Social Sciences: STEVEN P. TREVILLION
School of Law: FIONA FAIRWEATHER
School of Psychology: Prof. MARK DAVIES

UNIVERSITY OF ESSEX

Wivenhoe Park, Colchester, CO4 3SQ
Telephone: (1206) 873333
Fax: (1206) 873598

East 15 (Loughton) Campus, Hatfields, Rectory Lane, Loughton, IG10 3RY
Telephone: (20) 8508-5983
Fax: (20) 8508-7521

Southend Campus, Elmer Approach, Southend-on-Sea, SS1 1LW
Telephone: (1702) 328200
Fax: (1702) 328201
E-mail: admit@essex.ac.uk
Internet: www.essex.ac.uk

Founded 1964
Academic year: October to July

Chancellor: Lord PHILLIPS OF SUDBURY
Vice-Chancellor: Prof. COLIN RIORDAN
Pro-Vice-Chancellor for Research and Enterprise: Prof. DAVID SANDERS
Pro-Vice-Chancellor for Academic and Regional Devt: Prof. NIGEL SOUTH
Pro-Vice Chancellor for Academic Standards: Prof. JANE WRIGHT
Pro-Vice Chancellor for Learning and Teaching: Prof. ANDY DOWNTOWN
Deputy Vice-Chancellor and Pro-Vice-Chancellor for Sustainability and Resources: Prof. JULES PRETTY
Dean, Univ. of Essex Southend: Prof. STUART MANSON
Dean, Academic Partnerships: Dr AULAY MACKENZIE
Registrar and Sec.: Dr TONY RICH
Librarian: ROBERT BUTLER

Library: see under Libraries and Archives
Number of teachers: 610
Number of students: 10,280

DEANS

Faculty of Health: Prof. JOHN CLIBBENS
Faculty of Humanities and Comparative Studies: Dr LEON BURNETT
Faculty of Law and Management: PETER LUTHER
Faculty of Science and Engineering: Dr DAVID PEVALIN
School of Social Sciences: Dr MIKE JONES
Graduate School: Prof. PAM COX

PROFESSORS

ADAMS, M., Computer Science And Electronic Engineering
ADES, D., Art History And Theory
BAKER, N., Biological Sciences
BALKAN, A., Computer Science And Electronic Engineering
BARRY, C., Psychology
BENEKE, R., Biological Sciences
BENTON, E., Sociology
BLACKBURN, R., Sociology
BOOTH, A., Economics
BORSLEY, R., Language And Linguistics
BOYLE, C., Law
BUSFIELD, N., Sociology
CALLAGHAN, V., Computer Science And Electronic Engineering
CHAMBERS, M., Economics
CLAHSEN, H., Language And Linguistics
CLIBBENS, J., Faculty Of Science And Engineering
COAKLEY, J., Ebs-Essex Business School
COLBECK, I., Biological Sciences
COLES, M., Economics
COOPER, C., Biological Sciences
COX, N., Art History And Theory
DEWS, P., Philosophy
DORUSSEN, H., Government
DOWNTON, A., Computer Sci And Electronic Engineering
ELSON, D., Sociology
ERMISCH, J., Iser
FERNANDEZ, N., Biological Sciences
FIGLIO, K., Centre For Psychoanalytic Studies
FOX, E., Psychology
FRANCESCONI, M., Economics
FRASER, V., Art History And Theory
GALEOTTI, A., Economics
GEIDER, R., Biological Sciences
GHANBARI, M., Computer Science And Electronic Engineering
GHIGLINO, C., Economics
GILBERT, G., Law
GILLIES, J., Literature, Film, And Theatre Studies
GLEDITSCH, K., Government
GLUCKSMANN, M., Sociology
GOBERT, J., Law
GRAY, R., Literature, Film, And Theatre Studies
GREEN, G., Health And Human Sciences
HADFIELD, B., Law
HAGRAS, H., Computer Science And Electronic Engineering
HAMILTON, C., Law
HAMPSON, F., Law
HANLEY, J., Psychology
HAN-PILE, B., Philosophy
HARVEY, M., Sociology
HATTON, T., Economics
HAWKINS, R., Language And Linguistics
HAWKSFORD, M., Computer Science And Electronic Engineering
HENNING, I., Computer Science And Electronic Engineering
HENSON, M., Computer Science And Electronic Engineering
HIGGINS, P., Mathematical Sciences
HIGGS, E., History
HINSHELWOOD, R., Centre For Psychoanalytic Studies
HOPFL, H., Ebs-Essex Business School
HU, H., Computer Science And Electronic Engineering
HULME, P., Literature, Film, And Theatre Studies
HUNT, P., Law
IVERSEN, M., Art History And Theory
JENKINS, S., Iser
KING, A., Government
LANDMAN, T., Government
LANDMAN, T., Inst For Democracy & Conflict Resolution
LEADER, S., Law
LUBBOCK, J., Art History And Theory
LUCAS, S., Computer Science And Electronic Engineering
LYNN, P., Iser
MANSON, S., Ebs-Essex Business School
MARKOSE-CHERIAN, S., Economics
MARTIN, W., Philosophy
MCDONALD-MAIER, K., Computer Science And Electronic Engineering
MEDDIS, R., Psychology
MILLARD, F., Government
MIRSHEKAR-SYAHKAL, D., Computer Science And Electronic Engineering
MITRA, J., Ebs-Essex Business School (Southend)
MORAWSKA, E., Sociology
MORRIS, L., Sociology
MUGASHA, A., Law
MULLINEAUX, P., Biological Sciences
NANKERVIS, J., Ebs-Essex Business School
NEDWELL, D., Biological Sciences
NORTON, J., Biological Sciences
ORBELL, S., Psychology
PACKER, F., Human Rights Centre
PAPADOPOULOS, R., Centre For Psychoanalytic Studies
PATRICK, P., Language And Linguistics
PEERS, S., Law
PLUMPER, T., Government
POLI, R., Computer Science And Electronic Engineering
PRETTY, J., Biological Sciences
PUDNEY, S., Iser
RADFORD, A., Language And Linguistics
RAINES, C., Biological Sciences
RANDALL, M., Government
RAVEN, J., History
REYNOLDS, C., Biological Sciences
ROBERSON, D., Psychology
RODLEY, N., Law
ROPER, M., Sociology
RUBIN, L., East 15 Acting School, Loughton Campus
RUSSO, R., Psychology
SACKER, A., Iser
SADLER, L., Language And Linguistics
SAMUELS, A., Centre For Psychoanalytic Studies
SANDERS, D., Government
SANTOS SILVA, J., Economics
SCHURER, K., Uk Data Archive
SHERER, M., Ebs-Essex Business School
SIKKA, P., Ebs-Essex Business School
SIMEONIDOU, D., Computer Science And Electronic Engineering
SMITH, E., Economics
SMITH, S., History
SOUTH, N., Sociology

SPENCER, A., Language And Linguistics
SQUINTANI, F., Economics
STANWAY, G., Biological Sciences
STONE, P., Law
STONES, R., Sociology
SUNKIN, M., Law
SUTHERLAND, H., Iser
TEMPLE, C., Psychology
TSANG, E., Computer Science And Electronic Engineering
TURNER, R., Computer Science And Electronic Engineering
UNDERWOOD, G., Biological Sciences
UPTON, G., Mathematical Sciences
VEGA-REDONDO, F., Economics
VERGO, P., Art History And Theory
WALKER, S., Computer Science And Electronic Engineering
WALTER, J., History
WARD, H., Government
WARD, G., Psychology
WARNER, M., Literature, Film, And Theatre Studies
WHITELEY, P., Government
WILKINS, A., Psychology
WILSON, M., Biological Sciences
WRIGHT, J., Law
ZHANG, Q., Computer Science And Electronic Engineering

UNIVERSITY OF EXETER

Mail Room, The Old Library, Exeter, EX4 4SB
Telephone: (1392) 661000
Fax: (1392) 723060
E-mail: ug-ad@exeter.ac.uk
Internet: www.exeter.ac.uk

Founded 1922, as University College, present status 1955
Academic year: October to July

Chancellor: Baroness FLOELLA BENJAMIN
Vice-Chancellor and Chief Exec.: Prof. STEVE SMITH
Sr Deputy Vice-Chancellor for Education: Prof. JANICE KAY
Deputy Vice-Chancellor for Research and Knowledge Transfer: Prof. NICHOLAS J. TALBOT
Deputy Vice-Chancellor for Int. Affairs: Prof. NEIL ARMSTRONG
Deputy Vice-Chancellor for External affairs: Prof. MARK OVERTON
Registrar and Deputy Chief Exec.: DAVID ALLEN
Chief Library Officer: ALASDAIR PATERSON
Library: see under Libraries and Archives
Number of teachers: 3,025
Number of students: 17,210 (15,760 full-time, 1,450 part-time)
Publications: *Bracton Law Journal* (1 a year), *Cornish Studies* (1 a year), *FACT: focus on alternative and complementary therapies* (4 a year), *New Arabian Studies* (1 a year), *Studies in Theatre Production* (2 a year)

DEANS

Business School: Prof. RICHARD LAMMING
College of Engineering, Mathematics and Physical Sciences: Prof. KEN EVANS
College of Humanities: Prof. NICK KAYE
College of Life and Environmental Sciences: Prof. MARK GOODWIN
College of Social Sciences and International Studies: Prof. DEBRA MYHILL (acting)
Peninsula College of Medicine and Dentistry: Prof. STEVE THORNTON

UNIVERSITY OF GLOUCESTERSHIRE

The Park, Cheltenham, GL50 2RH
Telephone: (1242) 714666
Fax: (1242) 714827
E-mail: admissions@glos.ac.uk
Internet: www.glos.ac.uk

Founded 1990, as Cheltenham and Gloucester College of Further Education through merger of existing colleges, present name and status 2001
State control

Chancellor: Lord CAREY OF CLIFTON
Vice-Chancellor and Chief Exec.: Dr. PAUL HARTLEY
Deputy Vice-Chancellor: Dr PETER EASY
Academic Registrar and Clerk to the Council: JULIE THACKRAY
Head of Learning Centres: ANN MATHIE
Number of teachers: 293
Number of students: 9,092 (5,525 full-time and sandwich, 3,567 part-time)
Publications: *Business School Research Journal* (4 a year), *Contexts* (2 a year), *Journal of Learning and Teaching* (2 a year), *Landscape Issues* (2 a year)

HEADS OF SCHOOLS

School of Art, Media and Design: DAVE KESKEYS
School of Education: PETER MANSFIELD
School of Environment: CAROLYN ROBERTS
School of Health and Social Sciences: GUY DALY
School of Humanities: LINDEN PEACH
School of Sport and Leisure: MIKE COGGER
Gloucestershire Business School: JIM SIMPSON

UNIVERSITY OF GREENWICH

Telephone: (20) 8331-8590
Fax: (20) 8331-8145
E-mail: courseinfo@greenwich.ac.uk
Internet: www.greenwich.ac.uk

Founded 1890, later became Thames Polytechnic; present name and status 1992
Academic year: September to July

Chancellor: Lord HART OF CHILTON
Vice-Chancellor: Baroness TESSA BLACKSTONE
Deputy Vice-Chancellor for Academic Development: Prof. SIMON JARVIS
Deputy Vice-Chancellor for Resources: Prof. NEIL GARROD
Deputy Vice-Chancellor for Research and Enterprise: Prof. TOM BARNES
Registrar and Sec.: LINDA CORDING
Librarian: D. HEATHCOTE
Library of 610,000 vols
Number of teachers: 709
Number of students: 24,843
Publications: *Applied Mathematical Modelling* (12 a year), *Computational Fluid Dynamics News* (4 a year)

DEANS

Business School: Prof. BARRY CURNOW
Greenwich Maritime Institute: Prof. CHRIS BELLAMY (Dir)
Medway School of Pharmacy: Prof. IAIN CUMMING
Natural Resources Institute: Prof. ANDREW WESTBY (Dir)
School of Architecture and Construction: Prof. NEIL SPILLER
School of Computing and Mathematical Sciences: Dr LIZ BACON
School of Education: CHRIS PHILPOTT
School of Engineering: Prof. NDY EKERE
School of Health and Social Care: LIZ MEERABEAU
School of Humanities and Social Sciences: Prof. JOANNE FINKELSTEIN
School of Science: Prof. MARTIN SNOWDEN
Urban Renaissance Institute: LOUISE THOMAS (Dir)

UNIVERSITY OF HERTFORDSHIRE

College Lane, Hatfield, AL10 9AB
Telephone: (1707) 284800
Fax: (1707) 284870
E-mail: admissions@herts.ac.uk
Internet: www.herts.ac.uk

Founded 1952, as Hatfield Technical College, became Hatfield Polytechnic in 1969; present name and status 1992
Main campus in Hatfield and Law campus in St Albans
Academic year: October to June

Chancellor: Lord MACLAURIN OF KNEBWORTH
Vice-Chancellor: Prof. QUINTIN MCKELLAR
Deputy Vice-Chancellor: Prof. GRAHAM GALBRAITH
Pro-Vice-Chancellor for Int. Affairs: Prof. BARRY HUNT
Pro-Vice-Chancellor for Enterprise: JULIE NEWLAN
Pro-Vice-Chancellor for Research: Prof. JOHN SENIOR
Pro-Vice-Chancellor for Regional Affairs: Dr STEPHEN BOFFEY
Pro-Vice-Chancellor for Student Experience: Dr ANDREW CLUTTERBUCK
Sec. and Registrar: PHILIP E. WATERS
Librarian: D. MARTIN
Library of 600,000 vols
Number of teachers: 2,700
Number of students: 24,500

DEANS

Business School: JULIE NEWLAN
Faculty of Engineering and Information Sciences: Prof. JOHN SENIOR
Faculty of Health and Human Sciences: Prof. BARRY HUNT
Faculty of Humanities, Law and Education: Dr ANDREW CLUTTERBUCK
Faculty of Interdisciplinary Studies: Dr STEPHEN BOFFEY

UNIVERSITY OF HUDDERSFIELD

Queensgate, Huddersfield, HD1 3DH
Telephone: (1484) 422288
Fax: (1484) 516151
E-mail: admissions@hud.ac.uk
Internet: www.hud.ac.uk

Founded 1841, formerly Huddersfield College of Technology, became Polytechnic of Huddersfield in 1970; present name and status 1992
Academic year: September to June

Chancellor: Prof. Sir PATRICK STEWART
Vice-Chancellor: Prof. BOB CRYAN
Deputy Vice-Chancellor: Prof. PETER SLEE
Pro-Vice-Chancellor for Teaching and Learning: Prof. TIM THORNTON
Pro-Vice-Chancellor for Research and Enterprise: Prof. ANDREW BALL
Univ. Sec.: TONY MEARS
Acad. Registrar: Dr V. P. JEFFS
Library of 416,000 vols
Number of teachers: 1,900
Number of students: 23,000

DEANS

Business School: Prof. CHRIS COWTON
School of Applied Sciences: Prof. BOB CYWINSKI
School of Art, Design and Architecture: EMMA HUNT
School of Computing and Engineering: Prof. JIM YIP (acting)
School of Education and Professional Devt: Dr CHRISTINE JARVIS
School of Human and Health Sciences: SUE BERNHAUSER
School of Music and Humanities: Prof. TIM THORNTON

UNIVERSITY OF HULL

Cottingham Rd, Hull, HU6 7RX
Telephone: (1482) 346311
Fax: (1482) 465936
Internet: www.hull.ac.uk

Founded 1928, as University College of Hull, Univ. Charter 1954
Academic year: September to June

Chancellor: Rt Hon. Baroness BOTTOMLEY
Vice-Chancellor: Prof. CALIE PISTORIUS
Deputy Vice-Chancellor and Pro-Vice Chancellor for Acad. Affairs: Prof. J. W. BRUCE
Pro-Vice-Chancellor for Engagement: Prof. JOHN LEACH
Pro-Vice-Chancellor for Learning and Teaching: Prof. GLENN BURGESS
Pro-Vice-Chancellor for Research and Enterprise: Prof. BARRY WINN
Quality Dir, Univ. Registrar and Sec.: FRANCES OWEN
Librarian and Academic Services Dir: Dr R. G. HESELTINE

Library: see under Libraries and Archives
Number of teachers: 1,026
Number of students: 20,000

DEANS

Business School: Prof. M. JACKSON
Faculty of Arts and Social Sciences: Prof. VALERIE SANDERS (acting)
Faculty of Education: DINA LEWIS
Faculty of Health and Social Care: CHRISTINE ENGLISH
Faculty of Science: DEREK P. WILLS
Hull York Medical School: Prof. TONY KENDRICK
Postgraduate Medical Institute: Prof. NICHOLAS D. STAFFORD

PROFESSORS

ALEKSEEVSKY, D., Mathematics
ATTENBOROUGH, K., Engineering
BENNETT, J., Hull York Medical School
BINKS, B., Chemistry
BIRKINSHAW, P. J., Law
BOSCH, P., Mathematics
BOTTERY, M., Educational Studies
BROOKES, G. R., Computer Science
BURGESS, M., Politics
BURGESS, P., History
CAMPION, P. D., Public Health and Primary Care Medicine
CARVALHO, G., Biological Science
CHESTERS, G., IfL Office
CLELAND, J., Cardiology
COLQUHOUN, D., Educational Studies
CRAIG, G., Comparative and Applied Social Sciences
CROUCH, D., History
CUMMINGS, A., Engineering Design and Manufacture
CUTLAND, N. J., Pure Mathematics
DAVIES, K., International Leadership Centre
DYER, P. E., Physics
ELTIS, D., Economic Studies
FLETCHER, P. D., Chemistry
FROSTICK, L. E., Geography and Earth Resources
GIBBS, D. C., Geography and Earth Resources
GILBERT, P., Philosophy
GILLESPIE, W., Hull York Medical School
GOODBY, J. W., Chemistry
GRABBE, L. L., Theology
GREEN, R., Economics
GRIFFIN, G., Gender Studies
HARDISTY, J. H., Geography and Earth Resources
HARRIS, R. J., Politics
HASWELL, S., Chemistry
HAUGHTON, G., Geography
HAYWOOD, S., Engineering
HOPPEN, T., History
JACKSON, M., Business School
JESSHOPE, C., Computer Science
JOHNSTON, R., Psychology
KILLICK, S. R., Obstetrics and Gynaecology
KING, V. T., Politics
KITCHEN, P., Business School
LA TORRE, M., Law
LEIGHTON, A., English
LIND, M. J., Oncology
LLOYD, H. A., History
LOVEJOY, P., History
MCCOLLUM, P. T., Surgery
MCNAUGHTON, L., Sport Science
MAUNDERS, K. T., Accounting, Business and Finance
MONSON, J. R. T., Surgery
MORICE, A. H., Respiratory Medicine
MORTIMER, A., Psychiatry
Lord NORTON OF LOUTH, Politics
OKELY, J. M., Comparative and Applied Social Sciences
O'SULLIVAN, N. K., Politics
PATTON, R. J., Electronic Engineering
PHILLIPS, R., Computer Science
RATLEDGE, C., Biological Science
RICHARDSON, P. D., Economic Studies
RIGBY, B., English
SANDERS, V., English Literature
SCHLUDERMANN, B., Dutch Studies
SHNIRELMAN, A., Mathematics
SMITH, P. M., French
STAFFORD, N., Otolaryngology and Head and Neck Surgery
SWIFT, K. G., Engineering Design and Manufacture
TOWNSHEND, A., Chemistry
TURNBULL, L. W., Magnetic Resonance Investigation
TURNER, G., Biological Science
TURNER, M. E., Economic Studies
VLADIMIROV, V., Mathematics
WALKER, L., Rehabilitation
WATSON, R., Care of the Older Person
WILLIAMS, D., French

UNIVERSITY OF KEELE

Keele, ST5 5BG
Telephone: (1782) 732000
E-mail: undergraduate@acad.keele.ac.uk
Internet: www.keele.ac.uk

Founded 1949, as Univ. College of North Staffordshire, present name and status 1962
Academic year: September to August

Chancellor: Prof. Sir DAVID WEATHERALL
Vice-Chancellor: Prof. NICK FOSKETT
Deputy Vice-Chancellor: RAMA THIRUNAMACHANDRAN
Pro-Vice-Chancellor: Prof. MARILYN ANDREWS
Pro-Vice-Chancellor: KEVIN MATTINSON
Univ. Sec. and Registrar: SIMON MORRIS
Librarian: PAUL REYNOLDS

Library: see under Libraries and Archives
Number of teachers: 360
Number of students: 9,000

Publications: *British Journal for the History of Philosophy*, *Sociological Review*

DEANS

Faculty of Health: Prof. ANDY GARNER
Faculty of Humanities and Social Sciences: Prof. DAVID SHEPHERD
Faculty of Natural Sciences: Prof. PATRICK BAILEY

PROFESSORS

ALLAN, G., Sociology
ALLIN, S., Organic Chemistry
AMIGONI, D., Victorian Literature
ANDREW, J., Literature and Culture
ANDREWS, M., Professional Education in Health
BAILEY, P., Natural Sciences
BELL, I., American Literature
BERNARD, M., Social Gerontology
BLADEN-HOVELL, R., Economics
BLENKINSOPP, A., Practice of Pharmacy
BRADNEY, A., Law
BRUCE, S., English
CHAPMAN, C., Applied Mathematics
CHAPMAN, S., Prescribing Studies
COWNIE, F., Law
CROOK, M., French History
CROPPER, S., Management
DOBSON, A., Politics
DOBSON, J., Biophysics and Biomedical Engineering
DOYLE, T., Politics and International Relations
EGGLESTON, P., Molecular Entomology
EVANS, A., Astrophysics
FARRELL, W., Human Genomics
FISCHMAN STEREMBERG, R., Composition
FORSYTH, V., Biophysics
FOX, M., Law
FU, Y., Applied Mathematics
GARNER, A., Health Sciences
GIFFORD, L., Pharmacy Education
GODFREY, B., Criminology
GOKAY, B., International Relations
GREENHOUGH, T., Structural Biology
HALEY, M., Property Law
HARRIS, O., American Studies
HAYCOCK, P., Environmental Engineering
HELLIER, C., Astrophysics
HOLDSWORTH, C., Social Geography
HOOLE, D., Fish Diseases
HORTON, J., Political Philosophy
HOWELL, J., Organometallic Chemistry
HUGHES, A., Early Modern History
HUNT, K., British History
HURD, H., Parasitology
JACKSON, P., Medieval History
JESTER, R., Orthopaedic Nursing
JONES, P., Statistics
KELEMEN, M., Management Studies
KELLY, B., Musicology
KING, C., Earth Science Education
KITCHENHAM, B., Quantitative Software Engineering
KLAES, M., Commerce
LANOT, G., Economics
LAWRENCE, P., Development Economics
LIPPENS, R., Criminology
MAIN, C., Psychology (Pain Management)
MASLIN-PROTHERO, S., Nursing
MAXWELL, D., African History
MCCABE, D., Organisational Analysis
MCCRACKEN, M., English Literature
MILAS, C., Finance/Financial Relations
MURRAY, M., Psychology
NEWEY, G., Politics and International Relations
ONG, B., Health Services Research
ORMEROD, R., Inorganic Materials Chemistry
PATON, C., Public Policy
PHILLIPSON, C., Applied Social Studies and Social Gerontology
PUGH, R., Social Work
QUINNEY, D., Computer Assisted Learning in Mathematics
RAMSDEN, C., Organic Chemistry
RANGACHARI, P., Health Education
ROGERSON, G., Applied Mathematics
ROTENBERG, K., Psychology
SCHARF, T., Social Gerontology
SEMENOV, S., Imaging
SHARPE, A., Law
SHEPHERD, D., Humanities and Social Sciences
SHRIRA, V., Applied Mathematics
SIM, J., Health Care Research
SPANEL, P., Trace Gas Analysis
STENNING, P., Criminology
STRANGE, R., Clinical Biochemistry
STYLES, P., Applied and Environmental Geophysics
THOMSON, M., Law, Culture and Society
TOWNSHEND, C., International History

VAN DER WINDT, D., Primary Care Epidemiology
VAUGHAN, M., Humanities
WARD, R., Medical Entomology
WASIK, M., Criminal Justice
WASS, V., Medical Education
WEARDEN, J., Psychology
WENZELBURGER, J., Economics
WERBNER, P., Social Anthropology
WILKINSON, S., Bioethics
WILLIAMS, C., Social Justice
WILLIAMS, G., Structural Geology
WILLIAMS, G., Biochemistry
WILLIS, P., Cultural Theory and Qualitative Social Research

UNIVERSITY OF KENT

The Registry, Canterbury, CT2 7NZ
Telephone: (1227) 764000
E-mail: information@kent.ac.uk
Internet: www.kent.ac.uk

Founded 1965
State control
Academic year: September to June

Chancellor: Sir ROBERT WORCESTER
Vice-Chancellor: Prof. JULIA GOODFELLOW
Sr: DAVID NIGHTINGALE
Deputy Vice-Chancellor: Prof. KEITH MANDER
Deputy Vice-Chancellor: DENISE EVERITT
Pro Vice-Chancellor: Prof. JOHN BALDOCK
Pro Vice-Chancellor: Prof. ALEX HUGHES
Sec. of Council: KAREN GOFFIN
Head of Library Services: CAROLE PICKAVER

Library: 1.3m. vols
Number of teachers: 630
Number of students: 17,000

DEANS

Faculty of Humanities: Prof. KARL LEYDECKER
Faculty of Sciences: Prof. MARK BURCHELL
Faculty of Social Sciences: Prof. JOHN WIGHTMAN

PROFESSORS

Faculty of Humanities (Marlowe Bldg, Univ. of Kent, Canterbury, CT2 7NR; tel. (1227) 764000; fax (1227) 827127):

ANDERSON, G., Classics
ANDREWS, M. Y., Victorian and Visual Studies
BRADLEY, K., Social History and Policy
BOLT, C. A., American History
CARDINAL, R. T., Literary and Visual Studies
DAVIS, G. M., Drama
DURRANI, O., German
ELLIS, D., English
FLOWER, J., French
GILL, R., Theology
INNES, C. L., Post-colonial Literatures
IRWIN, M., English Literature
NORMAN, R. J., Moral Philosophy
READ, P. F., French
SMITH, C. W., History of Science
SMITH, M., Film Studies
WELCH, D. A., Modern European History

Faculty of Sciences (School of Mathematics, Statistics and Actuarial Science, Univ. of Kent Canterbury, CT2 7NR; tel. (1227) 764000; fax (1227) 827154):

BROWN, P. J., Medical Statistics
BULL, A., Microbial Technology
CHADWICK, A. V., Physical Chemistry
CLARKSON, P., Mathematics
COLCHESTER, A. C. F., Clinical Neuroscience and Medical Image Computing
DAVIES, P. A., Optical Communications
DORE, J., Condensed-Matter Physics
FAIRHURST, M. C., Computer Vision
FLEISCHMAN, P., Mathematics
GEEVES, M. A., Physical Biochemistry
GULLICK, W., Cancer Biology
JACKSON, D. A., Applied Optics
JEFFRIES, P., Mycology
LININGTON, P. F., Computer Communication
MANDER, K., Computer Science
MORGAN, B. J. T., Applied Statistics
NEWPORT, R., Materials Physics
PANNELL, C. N., Optical Physics
SOBHY, M. I., Electronic Engineering
STRANGE, J. H., Experimental Physics
THOMPSON, S., Logic and Computation
TUITE, M., Molecular Biology
WARREN, M. J., Biochemistry
WELCH, P. H., Parallel Computing

Faculty of Social Sciences (Marlowe Bldg, University of Kent, Canterbury, CT2 7NR; tel. (1227) 764000; fax (1227) 823959):

ABRAMS, W. D. J., Social Psychology
ALASZEWSKI, A., Sociology of Health Studies
BALDOCK, J., Social Policy
BRIDE, I., Biodiversity Management
CALNAN, M., Sociology of Health Studies
CARRUTH, A., Economics
CONAGHAN, J., Law
ELLEN, R. F., Anthropology and Human Ecology
EVANS, M. S., Women's Studies
FUNNELL, W., Accounting and Finance
FUREDI, F., Sociology
GREEN, F., Economics
HALE, C., Criminology
HARROP, S., Wildlife Management Law
HOWARTH, W., Environmental Law
JOHNSTON, R., Cognitive Psychology
LUI, S. W., Management Science and Computational Mathematics
MANSELL, J., Applied Psychology of Learning Disability
MIALL, A., International Relations
MURPHY, G., Applied Psychology of Learning Disability
PAHL, J., Social Policy
PICKVANCE, C. G., Urban Studies
RAY, L., Sociology
RUBIN, G., Law
RUTTER, D., Health Psychology
SAKWA, R., Russian and European Politics
SALHI, S., Management Science
STEPHENSON, G., Social Psychology
SAMUEL, G., Law
SAYERS, J., Psychoanalytic Psychology
STEPHENSON, G., Social Psychology
TAYLOR-GOOBY, P., Social Policy
THIRLWALL, A. P., Applied Economics
TWIGG, J., Social Policy and Sociology
UGLOW, S., Criminal Justice
VICKERMAN, R. W., Regional and Transport Economics

UNIVERSITY OF LANCASTER

Univ. House, Lancaster, LA1 4YW
Telephone: (1524) 65201
Fax: (1524) 843087
E-mail: ugadmissions@lancaster.ac.uk
Internet: www.lancs.ac.uk

Founded 1964
Academic year: October to July

Chancellor: Sir CHRISTIAN BONINGTON
Pro-Chancellor: BRYAN GRAY
Vice-Chancellor: Prof. PAUL WELLINGS
Deputy Vice-Chancellor: Prof. ROBERT MCKINLAY
Pro-Vice-Chancellor for Colleges and Student Experience: Prof. AMANDA CHETWYND
Pro-Vice-Chancellor for Research: Prof. TREVOR J. MCMILLAN
Univ. Sec.: FIONA AIKEN
Librarian: CLARE POWNE

Library: see under Libraries and Archives
Number of teachers: 800
Number of students: 16,500

DEANS

Faculty of Arts and Social Sciences: Prof. TONY MCENERY
Faculty of Science and Technology: Prof. MARY SMYTH
School of Health and Medicine: Prof. TONY GATRELL
Management School: Prof. SUE COX

PROFESSORS

ACKROYD, S. C., Organizational Behaviour
ALDERSON, J. C., Linguistics and English Language Education
ALLSOP, D., Neuroscience
ARAUJO, L., Industrial Marketing
ARCHARD, D., Philosophy
ASTON, E., Theatre Studies
BARDGETT, R. D., Ecology
BARTON, D., Language and Literacy
BELLANY, I., Politics
BEVEN, K. J., Environmental Science
BINLEY, A., Hydrogeophysics
BLACKLER, F. H. M., Behaviour in Organizations
BLAIR, G. S., Distributed Systems
BLINKHORN, R. M., History
BLOOMFIELD, B., Organizational Behaviour
BRADLEY, S., Economics
BRAY, R. W., Music
BREMNER, J. G., Developmental Psychology
BURGOYNE, J. G., Management Learning
BYGATE, M., Linguistics
CARTER, R. G., Electronic Engineering
CHADWICK, R., Philosophy
CHAPMAN, G. P., Geography
CHETWYND, A. G., Mathematics and Statistics
CLARK, D., Medical Sociology
CLARKE, I., Marketing
COLLINSON, D., Management Learning
COULSON, G., Distributed Systems
COX, S. J., Safety and Risk Management
CROUCHLEY, R., Applied Statistics
DAVIES, N.A. J., Computing
DAVIES, W. J., Environmental Physiology
DAVISON, W., Environmental Chemistry
DENVER, D. T., Politics
DIGGLE, P. J., Mathematics and Statistics
DILLON, G. M., Politics
DIX, A., Computing
DUFFIELD, M., Politics
EASTERBY-SMITH, M. P. V., Management Learning
EASTON, G., Marketing
EMERSON, E., Clinical Psychology
EVANS, E. J., Social History
FAIRCLOUGH, N. L., Linguistics
FALKO, V., Condensed Matter Theory
FIDDLER, A., German and Austrian Studies
FILDES, R. A., Management Science
FINDLAY, A., Renaissance Drama
FORDE, B., Plant Biotechnology
FOX, S., Social and Management Learning
FRANCIS, B. J., Social Statistics
FRANKLIN, S., Sociology
GATRELL, A. C., Health
GELLERSEN, H.-W., Computing
GRAHAM, H., Social Policy
HAMILTON, M. E., Adult Learning and Literacy
HANLEY, K. A., English Literature
HARMAN, P. M., History of Science
HATTON, C. R., Psychology, Health and Social Care
HEELAS, P. L. F., Religion and Modernity
HENDERSON, R., Biostatistics
HETHERINGTON, A. M., Plant Cell Physiology
HEWITT, C. N., Atmospheric Chemistry
HONARY, B., Communications Engineering
HONARY, F., Space Plasma and Radio Science
HOPKINS, J. B., Psychology
HUGHES, J. A., Sociological Analysis
HUTCHISON, D., Computing
INTRONA, L., Organization, Technology and Ethics
IVANIC, R., Linguistics and Education

JESSOP, R. D., Sociology
JOHNES, G., Economics
JOHNSON, K., Linguistics and Language Education
JONES, K. C., Environmental Chemistry and Ecotoxicology
KATAMBA, F. X., Linguistics
KIRBY, M. W., Economic History
KRIER, A., Semiconductor Physics
KUHN, A. F., Film Studies
LAMBERT, C. J., Theoretical Condensed Matter Physics
LAMBRECHT, B. M., Accounting and Finance
LAW, J., Sociology
LEA, P. J., Biological Sciences
LEWIS, C. N., Family and Developmental Psychology
LYTH, D., Astro-Particle Physics
MACDONALD, R., Environmental Science
MAHER, B., Geography
MAY-CHAHAL, C., Applied Social Science
MCCLINTOCK, P. V. E., Physics
MCENERY, A. M., English Language and Linguistics
MCMILLAN, T. J., Cancer Biology
MCNEILL, M., Women's Studies and Cultural Studies
MORRIS, P. E., Psychology
MULLETT, M. A. A., Cultural and Religious History
NIEDUSZYNSKI, I. A., Connective Tissue Biochemistry
O'HANLAN, J. F., Finance
O'NEILL, J. F., Philosophy
ORMEROD, T., Cognitive Psychology
OTLEY, D. T., Accounting and Finance
PAYNE, J. P., German Studies
PEARCE, L., Literary Theory and Women's Writing
PEASNELL, K. V., Accounting and Finance
PENN, R. D., Economic Sociology and Statistics
PERCY, K. A., Adult Continuing Education
PICCIOTTO, S., Law
PICKETT, G. R., Low Temperature Physics
PIDD, M., Management Science
PINKERTON, H., Physical Volcanology
POOLEY, C. G., Geography
POPAY, J., Social and Public Health
POPE, P. F., Accounting and Finance
POWER, S. C., Mathematics
RATOFF, P. N., Experimental Particle Physics
READER, I. J., Religious Studies
REYNOLDS, P. M., Management Learning
RICHARDS, J. M., Cultural History
RICHARDSON, A. M. D., Microsystems Engineering
ROBERTS, G., Mathematics
RODWELL, J. S., Plant Ecology
ROGERS, C. G., Educational Research
ROSE, M., Entrepreneurship
ROTHSCHILD, R., Economics
ROWE, P., Law
SAUNDERS, M. S., Evaluation in Education and Work
SAYER, R. A., Sociology
SEGAL, R., Theories of Religion
SEWARD, D. W., Engineering Design
SHAPIRO, D. Z., Sociology
SHORT, M. H., Linguistics
SIEWIERSKA, A. M., Linguistics
SMITH, D. B., Criminology
SMITH, L., Educational Research
SMYTH, M. M., Experimental Psychology
SOMMERVILLE, I. F., Computing
SOOTHILL, K. L., Social Research
STACEY, J., Women's Studies and Cultural Studies
STRINGER, K. J., Medieval British History
SUCHMAN, L., Sociology
SUGARMAN, D., Law
TAWN, J. A., Statistics
TAYLOR, J., Economics
TAYLOR, S. J., Finance
THORPE, D. H., Applied Social Science
TIHANOV, G., Comparative Literature
TROWLER, P., Higher Education
TUCKER, R. W., Mathematical Physics
TURVEY, G. J., Engineering Mechanics
URRY, J. R., Sociology
WEBER, C. L., Politics
WHITELEY, N. S., Visual Arts
WHITTAKER, J. B., Biological Sciences
WHITTON, D. W., French Theatre
WHYTE, I. D., Historical Geography
WIGMORE, J. K., Condensed Matter Physics
WILSON, L., Environmental Science
WILSON, R. F., Renaissance Studies
WISE, S., Social Justice
WYNNE, B. E., Science Studies
XYDEAS, C. S., Communications Engineering
YADAV, P. K., Accounting and Finance

UNIVERSITY OF LEEDS

Leeds, LS2 9JT
Telephone: (113) 243-1751
Fax: (113) 244-3923
E-mail: enquiry@leeds.ac.uk
Internet: www.leeds.ac.uk

Founded 1874 as Yorkshire College of Science, Univ. Charter 1904
Academic year: September to June
Chancellor: The Rt Hon. Lord BRAGG
Pro-Chancellor: LINDA POLLARD
Vice-Chancellor: Prof. MICHAEL ARTHUR
Deputy Vice-Chancellor: Prof. JOHN FISHER
Pro-Vice-Chancellor for Int. Partnerships: Prof. RICHARD WILLIAMS
Pro-Vice-Chancellor for Student Education: Prof. VIVIEN JONES
Pro-Vice-Chancellor for Research and Innovation: Prof. ANDREW THOMPSON
Pro-Vice-Chancellor for Staff: Prof. STEPHEN SCOTT
Sec: ROGER GAIR
Librarian and Keeper of Brotherton Colln: MARGARET COUTTS

Library: see under Libraries and Archives
Number of students: 32,500

DEANS

Faculty of Arts: Prof. FRANK FINLAY
Faculty of Biological Sciences: Prof. STEVE HOMANS
Faculty of Business: Prof. PETER MOIZER
Faculty of Education, Social Sciences and Law: Prof. JEREMY HIGHAM (acting)
Faculty of Engineering: Prof. PETER JIMACK
Faculty of Environment: Prof. JANE FRANCIS
Faculty of Mathematics and Physical Sciences: Prof. MICHAEL WILSON
Faculty of Medicine and Health: Prof. PETER MCWILLIAM
Faculty of Performance, Visual Arts and Communications: Prof. DAVID COOPER

PROFESSORS

Faculty of Arts:
AGIUS, D. A., Arabic and Islamic Material Culture
ATACK, M. K., French
BLACK, R. D., Renaissance History
BROCK, R. W., Renaissance History
BUTLER, M. H., Renaissance Drama
CANTOR, G. N., History of Science
CHARTRES, J. A., Social and Economic History
CHILDS, J. C. R., Military History
DIXON, S. M., Modern History
ELLIOTT, J. K., New Testament Textual Criticism
FAIRER, D., 18th-century English Literature
FINLAY, F. J., German
FRENCH, S. R. D., Philosophy of Science
GARNER, P., Spanish
GIDLEY, CM., American Literature
GOOCH, J., International History
HAMMOND, P., 17th-century English Literature
HARTLEY, T., Translation Studies
HEATH, M. F., Greek Language and Literature
HILL, J., Visiting Professor
HOLMES, D., French
HUGGAN, G., Commonwealth and Post-colonial Literatures
JOHNSON, S., Linguistics
JONES, V., 18th-century Gender and Culture
KILLICK, R., Quebec Studies and 19th-century French Studies
KING, V. T., South-East Asian Studies
KNIGHT, R. A., Language Centre
KNOTT, K., Religious Studies
KOCIENSKI, P., Chemistry
LARRISSY, E., English Literature
LEVENE, D. S., Latin Language and Literature
LINDLEY, D., Renaissance Literature
LOOSELY, D. L., Contemporary French Culture
LOUD, G. A., Medieval Italian History
MALTBY, R., Latin Philology
MCFADYEN, A. I., Theology and Religious Studies
MORRIS, R. H., Medieval Studies
NAGIB, L., Centenary Professor of World History
NELSON, M. T., Philosophy
NETTON, I. R., Arabic Studies
PLATTEN, D. P., French
POIDEVIN, R. LE, Metaphysics
RICHARDSON, B. F., Italian
SILVERMAN, M., Modern French Studies
SIMONS, P. M., Philosophy
SPIERS, E. M., Strategic Studies
SUTTON, J. F., Russian
TABERNER, S. J., German
TOLLIDAY, S. W., Economic History
WAWN, A., Anglo-Icelandic Studies
WILLIAMS, M. B., East Asian Studies
WILSON, K. M., International Politics
WOOD, I. N., Early Medieval History

Faculty of Biological Sciences:
ALEXANDER, R. M., Biology
ALTRINGHAM, J. D., Biomechanics
ATKINSON, H. J., Nematology
BALDWIN, S. A., Biochemistry
BAUMBERG, S., Bacterial Genetics
BEECH, D. J., Cellular and Molecular Physiology
BENTON, T. G., Population Ecology
BOOTH, A. G., Online Learning
BROWN, S. B., Biochemistry
BUCKLEY, N. J., Neuroscience
CARDING, S., Molecular Immunology
CHOPRA, I., Microbiology
FINDLAY, J. B. C., Biochemistry
FORBES, J. M., Agricultural Sciences
GILMARTIN, P. M., Plant Molecular Genetics
HANDYSIDE, A., Developmental Biology
HENDERSON, P. J. F., Biochemistry and Molecular Biology
HOLDEN, A. V., Computational Biology
HOLLAND, K. T., Microbiology
HOMANS, S. W., Structural Biology
HOOPER, N. M., Biochemistry
HUGHES, I. E., Pharmacology Education
INGHAM, E., Medical Immunology
ISAAC, R. E., Comparative Biochemistry
KILLINGTON, R. A., Virology Education
KRAUSE, J., Behavioural Ecology
MCPHERSON, M. J., Biochemistry and Molecular Biology
MEYER, P., Plant Genetics
ORCHARD, C. H., Physiology
PHILLIPS, S. E. V., Biophysics
RADFORD, S. E., Structural Molecular Biology
RAYNER, J. M. V., Zoology
ROBERTSON, B., Neurobiology

ROWLANDS, D. J., Molecular Virology
SHORROCKS, B., Population Biology
SMITH, J. E., Parasitology
STOCKLEY, P. G., Biological Chemistry
TRINICK, J. A., Animal Cell Biology
TURNER, A. J., Biochemistry
WARD, S. A., Sport and Exercises
WILCOX, M. H., Medical Microbiology
WITHINGTON, D. J., Auditory Neuroscience
WOOD, E. J., Biochemistry
WRAY, D. A., Pharmacology
YATES, M. S., Biomedical Sciences

Faculty of Earth and Environment:

ALEXANDER, R. M., Biology
BAILEY, A. J., Population Geography
BELL, M., Traffic and Environmental Pollution
BEST, J. L., Process Sedimentology
BONSALL, P. W., Transport Planning
CARSTEN, O., Transport Safety
CLARKE, G. P., Business Geography
CLARKE, M. C., Geographic Modelling
FAIRHEAD, J. D., Applied Geophysics
FORBES, R. D., Business Geography
FRANCIS, J. E., Paleoclimatology
GUBBINS, D., Geophysics
HAISEMAN, G. A., Geophysics
KNEALE, P. E., Applied Hydrology
KNIPE, R. J., Structural Geology
KROM, M. D., Marine and Environmental Geochemistry
LLOYD, J. J., Centenary Professor of Earth Science Systems
MCDONALD, A. T., Environmental Management
MACKIE, P. J., Transport Studies
MAY, A. D., Transport Engineering
MOBBS, S. D., Atmospheric Dynamics
NASH, C. A., Transport Economics
RAISWELL, R. W., Sedimentary Geochemistry
REES, P. H., Population Geography
SMITH, M. H., Atmospheric Physics
SMITH, N. J., Project and Transport Infrastructure Management (joint post with Faculty of Engineering)
STILLWELL, J. C. H., Migration and Regional Development
TZEDAKIS, P. C., Quarternary Earth System History
VALENTINE, G., Human Geography
WATLING, D., Centenary Professor of Transport Analysis
WILSON, B. M., Igneous Petrogenesis
YARDLEY, B. W. D., Metamorphic Geochemistry

Faculty of Education, Social Sciences and Law:

ACKERS, H. L., European Law
BAGGULEY, P., Sociology and Social Policy
BARNES, C., Disability Studies
BATES, I., Education and Work
BAYNHAM, M. J., TESOL
BELL, D. S., French Government and Politics
BLUTH, C., International Studies
CAMERON, L. J., Applied Linguistics
CHASE, M. S., Continuing Education
CRAWFORD, T. A., Criminology and Criminal Justice
DEACON, A. J., Social Policy
DONNELLY, J. F., Science Education
HALSON, D. R., Law
HODKINSON, P. M., Lifelong Learning
KEAY, A., Corporate and Commercial Law
KERR, A., Sociology
LEACH, J., Science Education
LODGE, J., European Studies
MCCARGO, D., Politics and International Studies
MCMULLEN, J., Labour Law
ORMEROD, D., Law
OSLER, A. H., Education
PEARSON, R., Development Studies
RADICE, H. K., International Political Economy
ROSENEIL, S., Sociology and Gender Studies
SCOTT, P., Science Education
SHORROCKS-TAYLOR, D., Assessment and Evaluation in Education
SUBEDI, S. P., International Law
SUGDEN, D. A., Special Needs in Education
THEAKSTON, K., British Government
VINCENT-JONES, P., Law
WALKER, C. P., Criminal Justice
WALL, D. S., Legal History
WILLIAMS, F., Social Policy
ZUKAS, M., Adult Education

Faculty of Engineering:

ANDREWS, G. E., Combustion Engineering
BARTON, D. C., Solid Mechanics
BELL, A. J., Electronic Materials
BERZINS, M., Scientific Computation
BIGGS, S. R., Particle Science and Technology
BONSALL, P. W., Transport Planning
BOYLE, R. D., Computing
BRADLEY, D., Mechanical Engineering
BRODLIE, K. W., Visualization
CHILDS, T. H. C., Manufacturing Engineering
COHN, A. G., Automated Reasoning
DAVIES, A. G., Electronic and Photonic Engineering
DE PENNINGTON, A., Computer-aided Engineering
DEW, P. M., Computer Science
DOWSON, D., Mechanical Engineering
DYER, M. E., Theoretical Computer Science
EDMONDS, D. V., Metallurgy
FAIRWEATHER, R. M., Thermofluids and Combustion
FISHER, J., Mechanical Engineering
GASKELL, P. H., Fluid Mechanics
GHADIRI, M., Chemical Engineering
HARRISON, P. H., Quantum Electronics
HOGG, D. C., Artificial Intelligence
HOWES, M. J., Electronic Engineering
HOYLE, B. S., Vision and Image Systems
HUNTER, I. C., Microwave Signal Processing
JHA, A., Applied Materials Science
JIMACK, P., Scientific Computing
JIN, Z. M., Computational Biomechanics/Bioengineering
LINFIELD, E., Terahertz Electronics
MARA, D. D., Civil Engineering
MARKARIAN, G., Communication Systems
MCINTOSH, A. C., Thermodynamics and Combustion Theory
MILES, R. E., Semiconductor Electronics
NEVILLE, A., Engineering Tribology
PAGE, C. L., Civil Engineering Materials
POLLARD, R. D., High-frequency Measurements
POURKASHANIAN, M., High Temperature Combustion Processes
PRIEST, M., Engineering Tribology
RAND, B., Ceramics
RHODES, J. D., Electronic and Electrical Engineering
ROBERTS, K. J., Chemical Engineering
ROBERTSON, I. D., Centenary Professor of Microwave and Millimetre Wave Circuits
SHEPPARD, C. G. W., Applied Thermodynamics and Combustion Science
SMITH, N. J., Project and Transport Infrastructure Management (joint position with Transport Studies)
VIRK, G. S., Robotics and Control
WILLIAMS, P. T., Environmental Engineering
WILLIAMS, R. A., Mineral and Process Engineering
XU, J., Computing

Faculty of Mathematics and Physical Sciences:

BATCHELDER, D. N., Physics
BEDDARD, G., Chemical Physics
BLOOR, M. I. G., Applied Mathematics
BODEN, N., Physical Chemistry
BRINDLEY, J., Applied Mathematics
COOPER, S. B., Pure Mathematics
CRAWLEY-BOEVEY, W. W., Pure Mathematics
CYWINSKI, R., Experimental Physics
DALES, H. G., Pure Mathematics
DICKINSON, E., Food Colloids
DYSON, J. E., Astronomy
EVANS, S. D., Molecular and Nanoscale Physics
FALLE, S. A. E. G., Astrophysical Fluid Dynamics
FORDY, A. P., Nonlinear Mathematics
GREIG, D., Physics
GRIFFITHS, J. F., Functional Dye Chemistry
GRIGG, R. E., Organic Chemistry
GUTHRIE, J. T., Polymer and Surface Coatings, Science and Technology
HAMLEY, I. W., Polymer Materials
HARTQUIST, T. W., Astrophysics
HEARD, D. E., Atmospheric Chemistry
HICKEY, B., Physics
HILLAS, A. M., Physics
HUGHES, D. W., Applied Mathematics
INGHAM, D. B., Applied Mathematics
JOHNSON, A. P., Computational Chemistry
KENNEDY, J. D., Inorganic Chemistry
KENT, J. T., Statistics
KOCIEŃSKI, P. J., Organic Chemistry
LANCE, E. C., Pure Mathematics
LAWRIE, I. D., Theoretical Physics
LEWIS, D. M., Colour Chemistry
LUO, M. R., Colour and Imaging Science
MACPHERSON, H. D., Pure Mathematics
MARDIA, K. V., Applied Statistics
MCLEISH, T. C. B., Polymer Physics
MERKIN, J. H., Applied Mathematics
MIKHAILOV, A. V., Mathematical Physics
MORGAN, G. J., Theoretical Physics
MORGAN, M. R., Food Biochemistry
NIJHOFF, F. W., Mathematical Physics
PARTINGTON, J. R., Pure Mathematics
PILLING, M. J., Physical Chemistry
POVEY, M. J. W., Food Physics
RATHJEN, M., Pure Mathematics
READ, C. J., Pure Mathematics
ROBINSON, D. S., Food Science
RODSON, J. C., Pure Mathematics
SAVAGE, M. D., Thin Liquid Films and Coatings
SCOTT, S. K., Mathematical Chemistry
SLEEMAN, B. D., Applied Mathematics
TAYLOR, C. C., Statistics
TRUSS, J. K., Pure Mathematics
VEDRAL, V., Centenary Professor of Quantum Information Science
VERETENNIKOV, A. Y., Statistics
WAINER, S. S., Pure Mathematics
WARD, I. M., Physics
WATSON, A. A., Physics
WEDZICHA, B. L., Food Science
WHITAKER, B. J., Chemical Physics
WILSON, M. J., Applied Mathematics
WOOD, J. C., Pure Mathematics

Faculty of Medicine and Health:

ADAMS, C., Adult Psychiatry and Mental Health Services Research
ALIMO-METCALFE, B. M., Leadership Studies
BALL, S. G., Cardiology
BARKHAM, M., Clinical and Counselling Psychology
BIRD, H. A., Pharmacological Rheumatology
BISHOP, T., Genetic Epidemiology
BLUNDELL, J. E., Psychobiology
BONIFER, C., Experimental Haematology
BONTHRON, D. T., Molecular Medicine
BOYLSTON, A. W., Pathology
BRUNTON, P. A., Restorative Dentistry
CADE, J., Nutritional Epidemiology and Public Health

CHEATER, F., Public Health Nursing
CLEREHUGH, M. A., Periodontology
CLOSS, J., Nursing Research
COTTRELL, D. J., Child and Adolescent Psychiatry
CUCKLE, H. S., Reproductive Epidemiology
DICKSON, R. A., Orthopaedic Surgery
DRIFE, J. O., Obstetrics and Gynaecology
DUGGAL, M. S., Child Dental Health
EMERY, P., Rheumatology
FORMAN, D., Cancer Epidemiology
GIANNOUDIS, P. P., Orthopaedic Surgery
GRANT, P. J., Molecular Vascular Medicine
GREEN, A., International Health Planning
GUILLOU, P. J., Surgery
HALE, C., Clinical Nursing
HALL, A. S., Clinical Cardiology
HANBY, A. M., Breast Pathology
HAWARD, R., Cancer Studies
HAY, A., Environmental Toxicology
HEWISON, J., Healthcare Psychology
HEYWOOD, P. L., Primary Care
HILLHOUSE, E., Dean of the School of Medicine and Health
HOPKINS, P. M., Anaesthesia
HOUSE, A. O., Liaison Psychiatry
HOWDLE, P. D., Clinical Education
HULL, M. A., Molecular Gastroenterology
HUME, W. J., Oral Pathology
INGLEHEARN, C., Molecular Ophthalmology
KAPLAN, R. S., Clinical Cancer Studies
KEEN, J., Health Politics and Information Management
KELLETT, M., Restorative Dentistry
KIRKHAM, J., Oral Biology
KNOWLES, M., Experimental Cancer Research
LEVENE, M. I., Paediatrics and Child Health
LONG, A., Health Systems Research
MACLENNAN, K., Tumour Pathology
MARKHAM, A. F., Medicine
MARSH, P. D., Oral Microbiology
MCDERMOTT, M., Experimental Rheumatology
MCGONAGLE, D., Investigative Rheumatology
MCMAHON, M. J., Surgery
MCWILLIAM, P. N., Cardiovascular Physiology
MORLEY, S. J., Clinical Psychology
MURDOCH-EATON, D., Medical Education
PEERS, C. S., Cellular Physiology
QUIRKE, P., Pathology
RAYNOR, D. K., Pharmacy Practice, Medicine and their Users
ROBERTS, T. E., Medical Education
ROBINSON, C., Oral Biology
RODGERS, R. J., Behavioural Pharmacology
SANDLE, G. I., Clinical Science
SELBY, P. J., Cancer Medicine
SEYMOUR, M., Gastro-intestinal Medicine
TENNANT, A., Rehabilitation Studies
TWELVES, C. J., Clinical Pharmacology and Oncology
WALKER, J. J., Obstetrics and Gynaecology
WILD, C., Molecular Epidemiology
WILLIAMS, S. A., Oral Health Services Research
WISTOW, G., Health and Social Care
WOOD, D. J, Dental Materials
WOOD, E. J., Biochemistry

Faculty of Performance, Visual Arts and Communications:

BARBER, G. D., Performance Studies (Music)
BOON, R., Performance Studies
BROWN, C., Applied Musicology
BROWN, R. C. M., International Communications
BURKINSHAW, S. M., Textile Chemistry
CASSIDY, T., Design
COOPER, D. G., Music
DANIELS, S. M., Performance and Cultural Industries
GREEN, V., Fine Art, Film and Media
HANN, M. A., Design Theory
HAY, K. G., Contemporary Art Practice
HILL, D., Fine Art
LAWRENCE, C. A., Textile Engineering
MCQUILLAN, M., Fine Art, History of Art and Cultural Studies
MORRISON, D. E., Communications Research
ORTON, L. F., Art History and Theory
PALMER, R., Fine Art
POLLOCK, G. F. S., Social and Critical Histories of Art
RASTALL, G. R., Historical Musicology
TAYLOR, P. M., International Communications
WALLIS, M., Performance and Culture
WESTLAND, S., Colour Science and Technology

Leeds University Business School:

BUCKLEY, P. J., International Business
CLEGG, L. J., European Integration and International Business Management
COLLINS, M., Financial History
GERRARD, W. J., Sport Management and Finance
HAYES, J., Management Studies
HILLIER, D., Financial Markets
HODGKINSON, G. P., Organizational Behaviour and Strategic Management
KATSIKEAS, C. S., Marketing and International Management
KEASEY, K., Financial Services
LOCK, A. R., Marketing and Business Administration
MACKIE, P. J., Transport Studies
MAULE, A. J., Human Decisions
MCNULTY, T. H., Management and Governance
MICHELL, P. C. N., Marketing and Communications
MOIZER, P., Accounting
NASH, C. A., Transport Economics
NOLAN, P. J., Industrial Relations
OAKLAND, J. S., Business Excellence and Quality Management
PEARMAN, A. D., Management Decision Analysis
PÉROTIN, V., Economics
SAWYER, M. C., Economics
SCHENK-HOPPÉ, K. R., Renaissance History
SHIN, Y., Applied Econometrics
STUART, M., Human Resources Management and Employment Relations
THORPE, R., Management Development
WILSON, N., Credit Management

UNIVERSITY OF LEICESTER

University Rd, Leicester, LE1 7RH
Telephone: (116) 252-2522
Fax: (116) 252-2200
Internet: www.le.ac.uk

Founded 1918 as Univ. College; Charter 1950; Univ. Charter 1957

Academic year: September to June

Visitor: HER MAJESTY THE QUEEN
Chancellor: (vacant)
Pro-Chancellor: R. H. BETTLES
Pro-Chancellor: P. BATEMAN
Vice-Chancellor: Prof. Sir R. G. BURGESS
Sr Pro-Vice-Chancellor: Prof. M. P. THOMPSON
Pro-Vice-Chancellor: C. FYFE
Pro Vice-Chancellor: Prof. K. SCHÜRER
Registrar and Sec.: D. E. HALL
Head of Library Services: L. JONES

Library: see under Libraries and Archives
Number of teachers: 751 full-time
Number of students: 23,000

Publications: *Graduates' Review* (1 a year), *Insider*, *LE1* (2 a year)

PRO-VICE-CHANCELLORS AND HEADS OF COLLEGE

College of Arts, Humanities and Law: Prof. D. TALLACK
College of Medicine, Biological Sciences and Psychology: Prof. D. WYNFORD-THOMAS
College of Science and Engineering: Prof. M. BARSTOW
College of Social Sciences: Prof. E. MURPHY

PROFESSORS

Faculty of Arts (tel. (116) 252-2679; fax (116) 252-5213; e-mail arts@le.ac.uk; internet www.le.ac.uk/arts):

BARKER, G. W., Archaeology
BONNEY, R. J., Modern History
CAMPBELL, G. R., Renaissance Literature
CULL, N. J., American Studies
EKSRDJIAN, D., History of Art and Film
FOXHALL, L., Ancient History
HOOPER-GREENHILL, E. R., Museum Studies
HOUSLEY, N. J., History
LITTLEJOHNS, R., Modern Languages
MATTINGLY, D. J., Roman Archaeology
NEWEY, V., English
PALMER, M., Industrial Archaeology
PEARCE, S. M., Museum Studies
RUGGLES, C. L. N., Archaeoastronomy
SHATTOCK, E. J., Victorian Literature
SHIPLEY, D. G. J., Ancient History
STANNARD, M. J., Modern English Literature
TREHAME, E. M., English
WALKER, G. M., Early Modern Literature and Culture
WOOD, S., Modern Languages
YARRINGTON, A., Art History

Faculty of Education and Continuing Studies (tel. (116) 252-3688; fax (116) 252-3653; e-mail soed@le.ac.uk; internet www.le.ac.uk/education):

BELL, L. A., Educational Management
COOPER, P. W., Education
DIMMOCK, C. A. J., Educational Management
FOGELMAN, K. R., Education

Faculty of Law (tel. (116) 252-2363; fax (116) 252-5023; e-mail law@le.ac.uk; internet www.le.ac.uk/law):

BRADNEY, A. G. D., Law
CLARKSON, C. M. V., Law
GRAHAM, C., Law
MCHALE, J. V., Law
SHAW, M. N., International Law
SZYSZCZAK, E. M., Competition and Labour Law
THOMPSON, M. P., Law
WHITE, R. C. A., Law

Faculty of Medicine and Biological Sciences (tel. (116) 252-2969; fax (116) 252-3013; e-mail med-admis@le.ac.uk; internet www.le.ac.uk/medicine):

ABRAMS, K. R., Epidemiology and Public Health
ANDREW, P. W., Microbial Pathogenesis
BAGSHAW, C. R., Biochemistry
BAKER, R. H., Quality in Health Care
BARER, M. R., Clinical Microbiology
BARNETT, D. B., Clinical Pharmacology
BELL, P. R. F., Surgery
BELL, S. C., Reproductive Sciences
BRAMMAR, W. J., Biochemistry
BRUGHA, T. S., Psychiatry
BURTON, P. R., Genetic Epidemiology
CAMP, R. D. R., Dermatology
CHERRYMAN, G. R., Radiology
COLLEY, A. M., Psychology
COLMAN, A. M., Psychology
CRITCHLEY, D. R., Biochemistry
CUNDLIFFE, E., Biochemistry
DAVIES, G. M., Psychology
DAVIES, M., Diabetes Medicine
DUGGAN, C. F., Forensic Mental Health
DYER, M. J. S., Pathology

EPERON, I. C., Biochemistry
EVANS, D. H., Medical Physics
FIELD, D. J., Neonatal Medicine
FORSYTHE, I. D., Neuroscience
FRASER, R. C., General Practice
FURNESS, P. N., Renal Pathology
GALINANES, M., Cardiac Surgery
GOTTLOB, I., Ophthalmology
GRANT, W. D., Environmental Microbiology
HALLIGAN, A. W. F., Foetal-Maternal Medicine
HARPER, W. M., Orthopaedic Surgery
HESLOP-HARRISON, J. S., Plant Cell Biology, Molecular Cytogenetics
HOLLIN, C. R., Criminological Psychology
JAGGER, C., Epidemiology
Sir JEFFREYS, A., Genetics
JONES, D. R., Medical Statistics
JOSEPH, M. H., Behavioural Neuroscience
KETLEY, J. M., Genetics
KYRIACOU, C. P., Behavioural Genetics
LAUDER, I., Pathology
LINDESAY, J. E. B., Psychiatry for the Elderly
LONDON, N. J. M., Surgery
LOUIS, E. J., Genetics
LUNEC, J., Chemical Pathology
MELLON, J. K., Urology
NAHORSKI, S. R., Pharmacology and Therapeutics
NG, L. L., Medicine and Therapeutics
NICHOLSON, K. G., Infectious Diseases
NICHOLSON, M. L., Transplant Surgery
O'CALLAGHAN, C. L. P., Paediatrics
PANERAI, R. B., Physiological Measurement
PARKER, G., Community Care
PASI, K. J., Haematology
PETERSEN, S. A., Medical Education
POTTER, J. F., Medicine for the Elderly
REVELEY, M. A., Psychiatry
ROBERTS, G. C. K., Biochemistry
ROWBOTHAM, D. J., Anaesthesia and Pain Management
RUTTY, G. N., Forensic Pathology
SAMANI, N. J., Cardiovascular Medicine
SCHWAEBLE, W. J., Microbiology and Immunology
SCRUTTON, N. S., Biochemistry
SILVERMAN, M., Child Health
SMITH, G., Anaesthesia
SMITH, R. H., Biology
STACE, C. A., Plant Taxonomy
STAMMERS, R. B., Occupational Psychology
STANDEN, N. B., Physiology
STEWARD, W. P., Oncology
TAYLOR, D. J., Obstetrics and Gynaecology
THOMPSON, J. R., Ophthalmology
THURSTON, H., Medicine
TREMBATH, R. C. P., Medical Genetics
TWELL, D., Plant Biology
VOSTANIS, P., Child and Adolescent Psychiatry
WALKER, R. A., Pathology
WARDLAW, A. J., Respiratory Medicine
WHITELAM, G. C., Plant Molecular Physics
WILLIAMS, B., Medicine
WILLIAMS, P. H., Microbiology
WOODS, K. L., Therapeutics
ZIEGLER-HEITBROCK, H.-W. L., Immunology

Faculty of Science (tel. (116) 252-5012; fax (116) 252-2770; e-mail science@le.ac.uk; internet www.le.ac.uk/science):

ALDRIDGE, R. J., Palaeontology
BENDELL, A., Quality and Reliability Management
BINNS, C., Physics and Astronomy
BOWLER, I. R., Human Geography
BRADSHAW, M. J., Human Geography
COCKS, A. C. F., Mechanical Engineering
COWLEY, S. W. H., Solar-Planetary Physics
CULLIS, P. M., Organic Chemistry
DISSADO, L. A., Engineering
FISHER, P. F., Geographical Information
FOTHERGILL, J. C., Engineering
FRASER, G. W., Detector Physics
GOSTELOW, J. P., Engineering
HARVEY, P. K. H., Geomathematics
HILLMAN, A. R., Physical Chemistry
HOLLOWAY, J. H., Inorganic Chemistry
HOPE, E. G., Inorganic Chemistry
KING, A. R., Astrophysics
KOENIG, S. C., Pure Mathematics
LEIMKUHLER, B. J., Applied Mathematics
LESTER, M., Physics and Astronomy
LEWIS, G. T., Human Geography
LIGHT, W. A., Mathematics
LOVELL, M. A., Petrophysics
MAGUIRE, P. K. H., Geophysics
MILLINGTON, A. C., Physical Geography
NORRIS, C., Surface Physics
PAN, J., Mechanics and Materials
PARRISH, R. R., Isotope Geology
PARSONS, A. J., Physical Geography
PERCY, J. M., Chemistry
POLLOCK, C., Electrical Engineering
PONTER, A. R. S., Engineering
POSTLETHWAITE, I., Engineering
RAMAN, R., Computer Science
ROBINSON, T. R., Space Plasma Physics
SAUNDERS, A. D., Geochemistry
SIVETER, D. J., Palaeontology
SPURGEON, S. K., Engineering
STEWART, A., Computer Science
THOMAS, R. M., Mathematics and Computer Science
WARD, M. J., X-Ray Astronomy
WARWICK, R. S., X-Ray Astronomy

Faculty of the Social Sciences (tel. (116) 252-2842; fax (116) 252-5073; e-mail socsci@le.ac.uk; internet www.le.ac.uk/socsci):

BARBALET, J. M., Sociology
BENDELL, A., Quality and Reliability Management
BENYON, J. T., Political Studies
BRESNEN, M., Organizational Behaviour
BURRELL, G., Organization Theory
CHAREMZA, W., Economics
COTTRELL, P. L., Economic and Social History
DEMETRIADES, P. O., Financial Economics
DYER, C. C., Regional and Local History
FEARON, P. S., Modern Economic and Social History
FIELDING, D. J., Economics
FRASER, C. D., Economics
GILL, M., Criminology
HANLON, G., Organizations and Society
HOFFMAN, J. A., Political Theory
HYDE-PRICE, A. G. V., Politics and International Relations
JACKSON, P. M., Economics; Public Sector Economics
KOOP, G., Economics
LAYDER, D. R., Social Theory
LEE, K. C., Economics
MUELLER, F., Management
OSWICK, C., Organization Theory and Development
PARKER, M., Organization Management
PUDNEY, S. E., Economics
RODGER, R. G., Urban History
SCHOTT, D. M. S., History of Urban Planning
SNELL, K. D. M., English Local History
SREBERNY, A., Mass Communications
THOMPSON, R. S., Economics
UNWIN, L. W., Vocational Education
WILLIAMS, C., Management

UNIVERSITY OF LINCOLN

Brayford Pool, Lincoln, LN6 7TS
Telephone: (1522) 882000
Fax: (1522) 886041
E-mail: enquiries@lincoln.ac.uk
Internet: www.lincoln.ac.uk

Founded 1861 as School of Art and Design; as Humberside College of Higher Education 1978; Humberside Polytechnic 1990; University of Humberside 1992; University of Lincolnshire and Humberside 1996; incorporated Lincoln School of Art and Lincolnshire School of Agriculture 2001; present name and status 2001

Vice-Chancellor: Prof. MARY STUART
Sr Deputy Vice-Chancellor for Research, Innovation and Enterprise: Prof. ANDREW ATHERTON
Deputy Vice-Chancellor for Devt: Dr FRANCES MANNSAKER
Deputy Vice-Chancellor for Teaching Quality and Student Experience: Prof. SCOTT DAVIDSON
Registrar: EDMUND FITZPATRICK
Dir of Learning Support: MICHELLE ANDERSON

Library of 240,000 vols, 1,000 periodicals
Number of teachers: 573
Number of students: 10,682
Publications: *Institute of Communication Ethics* (4 a year), *Lincoln Magazine*

DEANS

Faculty of Agriculture, Food and Animal Sciences: VAL BRAYBROOKS
Faculty of Art, Architecture and Design: Prof. NORMAN CHERRY
Faculty of Business and Law: Prof. DAVID HEAD
Faculty of Health, Life and Social Science: Prof. SARA OWEN
Faculty of Media, Humanities and Technology: Prof. DAVID SLEIGHT

UNIVERSITY OF LIVERPOOL

Liverpool, L69 3BX
Telephone: (151) 794-2000
Fax: (151) 708-6502
Internet: www.liv.ac.uk

Founded 1882, as Univ. College, Royal Charter 1903

Chancellor: Prof. Sir DAVID KING
Pro-Chancellor: Prof. JAMES KEATON
Vice-Chancellor: Prof. Sir HOWARD NEWBY
Deputy Vice-Chancellor: Prof. JON SAUNDERS
Exec. Pro-Vice-Chancellor: Prof. ANDREW DERRINGTON
Exec. Pro-Vice-Chancellor: Prof. STEPHEN HOLLOWAY
Exec. Pro-Vice-Chancellor: Prof. IAN GREER
Pro-Vice-Chancellor for Int. Affairs: Prof. MICHAEL HOEY
Pro-Vice-Chancellor for Student Experience: Prof. KELVIN EVEREST
Registrar: M. D. CARR
Librarian: PHILIP SYKES

Library: see under Libraries and Archives
Number of teachers: 1,400
Number of students: 18,000
Publications: *Bulletin of Hispanic Studies* (4 a year), *Third World Planning Review* (4 a year), *Town Planning Review* (4 a year)

PROFESSORS

Faculty of Arts:

BATE, A. J., English Literature
BELCHEM, J. C., History
CLARK, S. R. L., Philosophy
DAVIES, J. K., Ancient History and Classical Archaeology
ELLIOTT, M., Irish Studies
EVEREST, K. D., Modern English
FISHER, J. R., Latin-American History
FORSDICK, C., French
GASKIN, R. M., Philosophy
GOWLETT, J. A. J., Archaeology, Classics and Oriental Studies
HIGGINS, J., Latin American Literature
HOEY, M. P., English Language
LEE, W. R., Economic and Social History
MEE, C., Archaeology, Classics and Oriental Studies

MILLARD, A. R., Hebrew and Ancient Semitic Languages
MILLS, A. D., English Language and Literature
SAUL, N. D. B., German
SEED, D., English
SEVERIN, D. S., Spanish
SHAW, J., Archaeology, Classics and Oriental Studies
SLATER, E. A., Archaeology
STAFFORD, P. A., History
TALBOT, M. O., Music
WRIGHT, R. H. P., Hispanic Studies

Faculty of Engineering:

BACON, D. J., Materials Science and Engineering
BUNGEY, J. H., Civil Engineering
BURROWS, R., Environmental Hydraulics
CANTWELL, W. J., Engineering
CHALKER, P. R., Engineering
ECCLESTON, W., Electronic Engineering
ESCUDIER, M. P., Mechanical Engineering
FANG, M. T. C., Applied Electromagnetism
GOODHEW, P. J., Materials Engineering
HALL, S., Electrical Engineering and Electronics
HON, K. K. B., Manufacturing Systems
JONES, G. R., Electrical Engineering and Electronics
JONES, N., Mechanical Engineering
LUCAS, J., Electrical Engineering and Electronics
MOTTERSHEAD, J. E., Applied Mechanics
NANDI, A. K., Electrical Engineering and Electronics
OWEN, I., Mechanical Engineering
PADFIELD, G. D., Engineering
POND, R. C., Materials Science and Engineering
TATLOCK, G. J., Engineering
WATKINS, K. G., Engineering
WU, Q. H., Electrical Engineering

Faculty of Medicine:

ASHFORD, R. W., Parasite and Vector Biology
BACK, D. J., Pharmacology and Therapeutics
BURGOYNE, R. D., Physiology
CALVERLEY, P. M. A., Rehabilitation Medicine
CAPEWELL, S. J., Public Health
CARTY, H. M. L., Paediatric Radiology
CAWLEY, J. C., Haematology
CHADWICK, D. W., Neurology
COOKE, R. W. I., Paediatric Medicine
DIMALINE, R., Physiology
DOCKRAY, G. J., Physiology
DOWRICK, C. F., Primary Care
EMBERY, G., Clinical Dental Sciences
FIELD, J. K., Molecular Oncology
FOSTER, C. S., Pathology
FRASER, W. D., Clinical Chemistry
FROSTICK, S. P., Orthopaedics
GALLAGHER, J. A., Human Anatomy and Cell Biology
GARNER, P. A., Tropical Medicine
GOSDEN, C. M., Medical Genetics
GOWERS, S. G., Adolescent Psychiatry
GRIERSON, I., Experimental Ophthalmology
GRIFFITHS, R. D., Medicine
HART, C. A., Medical Microbiology
HART, G., Medicine
HILL, J., Child and Development Psychiatry
HOMMEL, M., Tropical Medicine
HUNTER, J. M., Anaesthesia
JACKSON, M. J., Cellular Pathophysiology
JOHNSON, P. M., Immunology
KROEGER, A., International Community Health
LEUWER, M., Anaesthesia
LLOYD, D. A., Paediatric Surgery
MOLYNEUX, M. E., Tropical Medicine
MORRISS, R. K., Psychiatry
NEILSON, J. P., Obstetrics and Gynaecology
NEOPTOLEMOS, J. P., Surgery
NURMIKKO, T. J., Neurology
PARK, B. K., Pharmacology and Therapeutics
PETERSEN, O. H., Physiology
PINE, C. M., Clinical Dental Sciences
PIRMOHAMED, M., Pharmacology and Therapeutics
QUINN, J. P., Human Anatomy and Cell Biology
RHODES, J. M., Medicine
ROBERTS, J. N., Magnetic Resonance
SALMON, P., Clinical Psychology
SCOTT, J., Oral Diseases
SHENKIN, A., Clinical Chemistry
SMYTH, R. L., Child Health
STEWART, J. P., Medical Microbiology
TEPIKIN, A. V., Physiology
THEAKSTON, R. D. G., Tropical Medicine
TOWNSON, H., Medical Entomology
TRAYHURN, P., Medicine
TREES, A. J., Tropical Medicine
VARRO, A., Physiology
WALLEY, T. J., Clinical Pharmacology
WARD, S., Tropical Medicine
WARENIUS, H. M., Research Oncology
WARNKE, P. C., Neurology
WATSON, A. J. M., Medicine
WATTS, A., Restorative Dentistry
WEINDLING, A. M., Child Health
WHITEHEAD, M. M., Public Health
WILKINSON, D. G., Liaison Psychiatry
WILLIAMS, D. F., Clinical Engineering
WILLIAMS, G., Medicine
WILSON, K. C. M., Psychiatry of Old Age
WINSTANLEY, P. A., Pharmacology and Therapeutics
WRAY, S. C., Physiology

Faculty of Science:

ALLPORT, P., Physics
APPLEBY, P. G., Mathematical Sciences
BEGON, M. E., Biological Sciences
BHANSALI, R. J., Mathematical Sciences
BOWCOCK, T. J. V., Physics
BRUCE, J. W., Pure Mathematics
CANTER, D. V., Psychology
COOPER, S. J., Psychology
COSSINS, A. R., Biological Sciences
CRAMPTON, J. M., Molecular Biology
DAINTON, J. B., Physics
DEROUANE, E. G. J., Chemistry, Innovative Catalysis
DONALD, I., Psychology
DUNBAR, R. I. M., Psychology
EDWARDS, C., Biological Sciences
EDWARDS, S. W., Biological Sciences
ELLIOTT, T. J., Geology
FISHER, M. D., Computer Science
FLINT, S. S., Earth Sciences
GIBLIN, P., Mathematical Sciences
GORYUNOV, W., Mathematical Sciences
HEATON, B. T., Inorganic Chemistry
HETHERINGTON, M. M., Psychology
HOLLOWAY, S., Chemical Physics
IRVING, A. C., Mathematical Sciences
JONES, A. C., Chemistry
KEMP, S. J., Biological Sciences
KUSZNIR, N. J., Geophysics
MARRS, R. H., Applied Plant Biology
MAYES, A. R., Psychology
MCCARTHY, A. J., Biological Sciences
MCLENNAN, A. G., Biological Sciences
MICHAEL, C., Theoretical Physics
MORTON, H. R., Mathematical Sciences
MOSS, B., Botany
MOVCHAN, A., Mathematical Sciences
MUELLER, M. M., Psychology
NIKULIN, W., Mathematical Sciences
NORTON, T. A., Marine Biology
PARKER, G. A., Zoology
RAVAL, R., Chemistry
REES, H. H., Biological Sciences
REES, S. M., Mathematical Sciences
RITCHIE, D. A., Genetics
ROBERTS, S. M., Organic Chemistry
ROSSEINSKY, M. J., Chemistry
RUDLAND, P. S., Biochemistry
SAUNDERS, J. R., Genetics and Microbiology
SCHIFFRIN, D. J., Physical Chemistry
SHAW, J., Earth Sciences
STIRLING, W. G., Experimental Physics
TOMSETT, A. B., Biological Sciences
VAN DEN BERG, C. M. G., Earth Sciences
VAN DER HOEK,, W., Computer Science
VEDRINE, J., Chemistry
WEIGHTMAN, P., Physics
WOOLDRIDGE, M. J., Computer Science

Faculty of Social and Environmental Studies:

ARORA, A., Law
BARON, J. S., Management
BATEY, P. W. J., Town and Regional Planning
CORNER, J., Politics and Communication Studies
DEARING, J. A., Geography
DELANTY, G., Sociology
DRUMMOND, H., Decision Sciences
DUNSTER, D., Architecture
ELLIOTT, D., Management
GIBBS, B. M., Acoustics
GILLESPIE, R., Politics
GOULD, W. T. S., Geography
HADRI, K., Economics and Accounting
HARVEY, A. M., Geography
HILL, J. J., Management
HOJMAN, D. E., Economics and Accounting
JONES, C., Social Policy and Social Work
JONES, M. A., Law
KAVANAGH, D. A., Politics and Communication Studies
KEHOE, D. F., Management
LYON, C. M., Common Law
MACLEOD, J. K., Law
MCCABE, B. P. M., Economics
MCGOLDRICK, D., Law
MUNCK, R. P., Sociology
NEUWAHL, N. A. E. M., European Law
OLDHAM, D. J., Building Engineering
PEPPER, S. M., Architecture and Building Engineering
ROBERTS, K., Sociology
RUSSELL, T., Centre for Research into Primary Science and Technology
SADLER, D., Geography
SAPSFORD, D. R., Economics and Accounting
SMITH, D., Management
SMITHERS, A. G., Education
TAYLOR, P. J., Economics and Accounting
WARBURTON, J., Law
WONG, Y. L. C., Civic Design
WOODS, R. I., Geography

Faculty of Veterinary Science:

BENNETT, M., Veterinary Pathology
BEYNON, R. J., Veterinary Pre-Clinical Science
CARTER, S. D., Veterinary Science
DOBSON, H., Veterinary Reproduction
EDWARDS, G. B., Equine Studies
GASKELL, C. J., Small Animal Studies
GASKELL, R. M., Veterinary Pathology
HURST, J. L., Animal Science
INNES, J. F., Veterinary Clinical Science and Animal Husbandry
MORGAN, K. L., Epidemiology
SHIRAZI-BEECHEY, S. P., Veterinary Pre-Clinical Science

UNIVERSITY OF LONDON

Senate House, Malet St, London, WC1E 7HU
Telephone: (20) 7862-8000
Fax: (20) 7862-8358
E-mail: enquiries@london.ac.uk
Internet: www.london.ac.uk

Founded 1836, as examining body, became also a teaching body in 1898

Chancellor: HRH THE PRINCESS ROYAL
Vice-Chancellor: Prof. GEOFFREY CROSSICK

Deputy Vice-Chancellor: Prof PAUL WEBLEY
Dir of Admin.: CATHERINE SWARBRICK
Academic Registrar: GILLIAN ROBERTS

Library: see under Libraries and Archives
Number of teachers: 7,881
Number of students: 170,000 incl. students of distance learning.

COLLEGES OF THE UNIVERSITY

Birkbeck, University of London

Malet St, London, WC1E 7HX
Telephone: (20) 7631-6000
Fax: (20) 7631-6270
Internet: www.bbk.ac.uk

Founded 1823, Charter of Incorporation 1926
State control
Academic year: September to July

Master: Prof. DAVID S. LATCHMAN
Vice-Master: Prof. PHILIP DEWE
Dean of College: Dr KATE MACKENZIE DAVEY
Sec.: KEITH HARRISON
Registrar: B. A. HARWOOD
Librarian: PHILIP PAYNE

Library of 364,102 vols
Number of teachers: 927 (incl. 575 part-time)
Number of students: 19,000

DEANS

School of Arts: Prof. HILARY FRASER
School of Business, Economics and Informatics: Prof. PHILIP POWELL
School of Law: Prof. PATRICIA TUITT
School of Science: Prof. NICHOLAS KEEP
School of Social Sciences, History and Philosophy: Prof. MIRIAM ZUKAS

PROFESSORS

ANNETTE, J., Citizenship and Lifelong Learning
ARCHIBUGI, D., Innovation, Governance and Public Policy
BARNES, J., Psychology
BARNES, P., Applied Crystallography
BELSKY, J., Psychology
BOURKE, J., History
BRAH, A., Sociology
BRAKE, L., Literature and Print Culture
BRINER, R., Organizational Psychology
BRUMMELHUIS, R., Mathematical Finance
CHRISTIE, I., Film and Media History
CLARK, S., Renaissance Literature
CONNOR, S., Modern Literature and Theory
COOLE, D., Political and Social Theory
COOMBES, A., Material and Visual Culture
DAVIES, D., Chemistry
DENCH, E., Ancient History
DEWE, P., Organizational Behaviour
DICKENSON, D., Medical Ethics and Humanities
DOUZINAS, C., Law
DOWNES, H., Geochemistry
DRIFFILL, J., Economics
EDWARDS, C., Ancient History and Culture
EIMER, M., Psychology
FIGES, O., History
FITZPATRICK, P., Law
FRASER, H., Nineteenth-century Studies
FROSH, S., Psychology
GOLDSWORTHY, G. J., Biology
GRAYLING, A., Applied Philosophy
HEALY, T., Renaissance Studies
HILEY, B., Physics
HORNSBY, J., Philosophy
HOUNSELL, E., Biological Chemistry
HOWELLS, R., French
HUNTER, M., History
JAMES, S., Philosophy
JENKINS, R., Political Science
JOHNSON, M. H., Psychology
JONES, R. C., Creative Writing
KELLY, J., Industrial Relations
LEVENE, M., Computer Science
LOVENDUSKI, J., Politics
MACMILLAN, F., Law
MAYBANK, S., Computer Science
MCAUSLAN, P., Law
MELHUISH, E., Psychology
MIRKIN, B., Computer Science
MORAN, L., Law
MOSS, D., Biomolecular Structure
MULCAHY, L., Law and Society
MÜLLER, H., Cognitive Psychology
MULVEY, L., Film Studies
NEAD, L., History of Art
OUGHTON, C., Management
POLLARD, P., French
POULOVASSILIS, A., Computer Science
PRICE, G. D., Mineral Physics
PSARADAKIS, Z., Econometrics
ROWE, W., Poetics
SAIBIL, H., Structural Biology
SEGAL, L., Psychology and Gender Studies
SHEPHERD, J., Geography
SIBERT, A., Economics
SINGH, R., Politics
SMITH, R., Applied Economics
SNOWER, D. J., Economics
SOLA, M., Economics
THOMPSON, W., Political Economy
USHER, M., Psychology
WAKSMAN, G., Structural Molecular Biology
WALLACE, B., Crystallography
WELLS, D. A., German

Courtauld Institute of Art

Somerset House, Strand, London, WC2R 0RN
Telephone: (20) 7848-2777
Fax: (20) 7848-2410
E-mail: ugadmissions@courtauld.ac.uk
Internet: www.courtauld.ac.uk

Founded 1932, became an ind. college of the Univ. of London 2002
Academic year: September to July

Dir: Dr DEBORAH SWALLOW
Dean and Deputy Dir: Prof. DAVID SOLKIN
Sec. and Registrar: MICHAEL ARTHUR
Academic Registrar: Dr GARETH MORGAN

Number of teachers: 29
Number of students: 381 (329 full-time, 52 part-time)

Publication: *Journal of the Warburg and Courtauld Institutes* (1 a year)

PROFESSORS

CORMACK, R., History of Art
CROSSLEY, P., History of Art
CUNO, J., History of Art
GREEN, C., History of Art
HOUSE, J., History of Art
LOWDEN, J., History of Art
RIBEIRO, A., History of Dress
RUBIN, P., History of Art
SOLKIN, D., History of Art

Goldsmiths, University of London

New Cross, London, SE14 6NW
Telephone: (20) 7919-7171
Fax: (20) 7919-7975
E-mail: ext-comms@gold.ac.uk
Internet: www.gold.ac.uk

Founded 1891
Academic year: September to June

Warden: Prof. PAT LOUGHREY (acting)
Pro-Warden for Academic Devt: Prof. SIMON MCVEIGH
Pro-Warden for Research and Enterprise: Prof. JANE POWELL
Pro-Warden of Students and Learning Devt: Dr PHILLIP BROADHEAD
Registrar and Sec.: HUGH JONES

Library of 221,000 vols
Number of teachers: 396 and 319 visiting tutors and 169 assoc. tutors
Number of students: 9,415 (7,497 full-time, 1,918 part-time)

Publications: *African Affairs* (historical and cultural studies), *African Identities, Death and Dying* (sociological), *Economy and Society* (4 a year), *Goldsmiths Journal of Education* (2 a year), *History Workshop Journal* (4 a year), *Journal of Buddhist Ethics* (historical and cultural studies), *Scriblerian* (English language and literature, 2 a year), *Social Identities, Street Signs* (urban and community research, 2 a year), *Third Text* (historical and cultural studies)

PROFESSORS

ADKINS, L., Sociology
AHMED, S., Media and Communications
ALEXANDER, S., History
ATKINSON, D., Educational Studies
BACK, L., Sociology
BALDICK, C., English and Comparative Literature
BELL, V., Sociology
BERRY, C., Media and Communications
BESSON, J., Anthropology
BLAMIRES, A., English and Comparative Literature
BOND, F., Psychology
BOWERS, J., Design
CAPLAN, P., Anthropology
CARR, H., English and Comparative Literature
CASSIDY, R., Anthropology
CAYGILL, H., History
CHITTY, C., Educational Studies
COHEN, J., English and Comparative Literature
COULDRY, N., Media and Communications
CURRAN, J. P. P., Media and Communications
DAVIDOFF, J., Psychology
DAY, S., Anthropology
DE VILLE, N., Visual Arts
D'INVERNO, M., Computing
DOWNIE, A., English and Comparative Literature
DRYDEN, W., Professional and Community Education
DUNWOODIE, P., English and Comparative Literature
DUTTMAN, A., Visual Cultures
DUTTON, M., Politics
FLETCHER, C., Psychology
FOL LEYMARIE, F., Computing
FRENCH, C., Psychology
GAVER, B., Design
GEORGE, R., Educational Studies
GORDON, R., Drama
GREGORY, E., Educational Studies
GRUZELIER, J., Psychology
HEMSWORTH, G., Art
HEWITT, R., Sociology
HUTNYK, J., Cultural Studies
IVASHKIN, A., Music
JEFFERIES, J., Computing
JONES, K., Educational Studies
KEOWN, D., History
KIMBELL, R. A., Design
KNOWLES, C., Sociology
LASH, S., Cultural Studies
LATHAM, W., Computing
LOMAX, Y., Art
LURY, C., Sociology
MARGOLIES, D., English and Comparative Studies
MAYO, M., Professional and Community Education
MCDONALD, R., English and Comparative Literature
MCROBBIE, A., Media and Communications
MCVEIGH, S., Music
MICHAEL, M., Sociology
MOORE-GILBERT, B., English and Comparative Literature
MORLEY, D., Media and Communications
MORRIS, B., Anthropology
MORRISON, B., English and Comparative Literature

NEGUS, K., Music
NEWMAN, M., Art
NUGENT, S., Anthropology
OHTANI, N., Design
PAECHTER, C., Educational Studies
PEARSON, G., Professional and Community Education
PICKERING, A., Psychology
PLATT, L., Professional and Community Education
POWELL, J., Psychology
PRING, L., Psychology
PROPHET, J. A., Computing
RIFKIN, A., Art
ROBINS, K., Media and Communications
ROGOFF, I., Visual Cultures
SEIDLER, V., Sociology
SETH, S., Politics
SHEVTSOVA, M., Drama
SHOBEN, A., Computing
SIMONE, A. M., Sociology
SKEGGS, B., Sociology
SMITH, P. K., Psychology
STABLES, K., Design
STIEGLER, B., Cultural Studies
VALENTINE, T., Psychology
VELMANS, M., Psychology
VERGES, F, Cultural Studies
WALLER, D., Professional and Community Education
WIGGINS, G., Computing
WOOD, J., Design
ZIMMER, R., Computing

Heythrop College

Univ. of London, Kensington Sq., London, W8 5HN
Telephone: (20) 7795-6600
Fax: (20) 7795-4200
E-mail: enquiries@heythrop.ac.uk
Internet: www.heythrop.ac.uk

Founded 1614, became part of Univ. of London 1970
Academic year: September to June
Specialist courses in theology and philosophy; receives HEFCE grant
Prin.: Rev. Dr JOHN MCDADE SJ
Academic Registrar: ANNABEL CLARKSON
Asst Registrar: ANTONY CHARLES
Library of 180,000 vols
Number of teachers: 42
Number of students: 920
Publications: *Heythrop Journal* (4 a year), *Heythrop Studies in Contemporary Philosophy, Religion and Theology* (2 a year).

Imperial College London

South Kensington Campus, London, SW7 2AZ
Telephone: (20) 7589-5111
Fax: (20) 7584-7596
E-mail: info@imperial.ac.uk
Internet: www.imperial.ac.uk

Founded 1907 by fed. of Royal College of Science, Royal School of Mines, and City and Guilds College, (1988) St Mary's Hospital Medical School, (1995) National Heart and Lung Institute, (1997) Charing Cross and Westminster Medical School and Royal Postgraduate Medical School, and (2000) Wye College
Academic year: October to June
Rector: Sir KEITH O'NIONS (acting)
Deputy Rector: Prof. JEFF MAGEE
Deputy Rector for Research: Prof. Sir PETER KNIGHT
Pro-Rector for Education and Academic Services: Prof. JULIA BUCKINGHAM
Pro-Rector for Enterprise: EDWARD ASTLE
Pro-Rector for Health: Prof. STEPHEN SMITH
Pro-Rector for Int. Affairs: Prof. MARY RITTER
College Sec.: Dr RODNEY EASTWOOD
Academic Registrar: NIGEL WHEATLEY
Dir of Library Services: DEBORAH SHORLEY
Number of teachers: 1,240
Number of students: 13,019

PRINCIPALS

Business School: Prof. DAVID BEGG
Faculty of Engineering: Prof. STEPHEN RICHARDSON
Faculty of Medicine: Prof. ANTHONY NEWMAN TAYLOR
Faculty of Natural Sciences: MAGGIE DALLMAN
Graduate School of Engineering and Physical Sciences: Prof. RICHARD KITNEY (Dir)
Graduate School of Life Sciences and Medicine: Prof. ANDREW GEORGE (Dir)

PROFESSORS

ADCOCK, I. M., Respiratory Cell and Molecular Biology
ALBANESE, C., Mathematical Finance
ALBERTI, J. G. M. M., Metabolic Medicine
ALIABADI, F. M. H., Aerostructures
ALLDAY, M. J., Virology
ALLEN-MERSH, T. G., Gastrointestinal Surgery
ALTON, E. W. F. W., Gene Therapy
AMIS, A. A., Orthopaedic Biomechanics
ANAND, P., Clinical Neurology
ANDERSON, R. M., Infectious Disease Epidemology
APSIMON, H. M., Air Pollution Studies
ARMSTRONG, A., Organic Chemistry
ARST, H. N., Microbial Genetics
ATKINSON, A., Materials Chemistry
ATKINSON, C., Applied Mathematics
BALDING, D. J., Statistical Genetics
BALOGH, A., Space Physics
BANGHAM, C., Immunology
BARBER, J., Biochemistry
BARLOW, J. G., Technology and Innovation Management
BARNES, P. J., Thoracic Medicine
BARNES, T. R. E., Clinical Psychiatry
BARNHAM, K. W. J., Physics
BARRETT, A. G. M., Organic Chemistry
BARRETT, J. W., Numerical Analysis
BEDDINGTON, J. R., Applied Population Biology
BEGG, D. K. H., Economics
BELL, A. R., Plasma Physics
BELL, J. N. B., Environmental Pollution
BELL, M. G. H., Transport Operations
BELVISI, M., Respiratory Pharmacology
BENNETT, P. R., Obstetrics and Gynaecology
BLACKMOND, D. G., Catalysis
BLANE, D., Medical Sociology
BLOMLEY, M. J., Radiology
BLOOM, S. R., Metabolic Medicine
BLUNT, M. J., Petroleum Engineering
BOOBIS, A. R., Biochemical Pharmacology
BOSANQUET, N. F. G., Health Policy
BOTTO, M., Rheumatology
BRADLEY, D. D. C., Experimental Solid State Physics
BRANDON, N. P., Sustainable Development in Energy
BRENNAN, F. M., Immunopathology
BRIDSON, M. R., Pure Mathematics
BRIGGS, D. J., Public Health
BRINSON, C. E. J., German Studies
BRISCOE, B. J., Interface Engineering
BRONSTEIN, A. M., Clinical Neurology
BROOKS, D. J., Neurology
BROSENS, J. J., Reproductive Sciences
BUCHANAN, D. L., Mining Geology
BUCK, K. W., Plant and Fungal Virology
BUCK, M., Molecular Microbiology
BUCKINGHAM, J. C., Pharmacology
BUENFELD, N. R., Concrete Structures
BULPITT, C. J., Geriatric Medicine
BUSH, A., Paediatric Respirology
BUTLER, D., Water Engineering
CALLAN, M. F. C., Immunology and Rheumatology
CARGILL, P. J., Physics
CASH, J. R., Numerical Analysis
CASS, A. E. G., Chemical Biology
CAWLEY, P., Mechanical Engineering
CHADWICK, D., Applied Catalysis
CHATURVEDI, N., General Practice
CHEN, Y., Mathematical Physics
CHEUNG, P., Digital Systems
CHRISTOFIDES, N., Operational Research
CHUNG, K. F., Respiratory Medicine
CLARK, K. L., Computational Logic
COLLINS, P., Clinical Cardiology
CONNERADE, J.-P., Atomic and Molecular Physics
CONSTANTINIDES, A. G., Signal Processing
CONWAY, G. R., Int. Devt
COOK, H. T., Renal Pathology
COOKSON, W. O. C., Respiratory Genetics
COOMBES, R. C. D. S., Medical Oncology
COUCHMAN, J. R., Cell Biology
COUTELLE, C. C., Gene Therapy
COWBURN, R. P., Nanotechnology
COWIE, M. R., Cardiology
COWLEY, S. R., Plasma Physics
CRAIG, D. D. C., Organic Synthesis
CRASTER, R. V., Applied Mathematics
CRAWLEY, M. J., Community Ecology
CRISANTI, A., Molecular Parasitology
CROWDER, M. J., Stochastic Modelling
CUMPSTY, N. A., Mechanical Engineering
CUTHBERTSON, K., Finance
DAINTY, J. C., Applied Optics
DALLMAN, M. J., Immunology
DAMZEN, M. J., Experimental Laser Physics
DARLINGTON, J., Programming Methodology
DARZI, A., Minimal Access Surgery
DAVIS, M. H. A., Mathematics
DE BELLEROCHE, J. S., Neurochemistry
DE MELLO, A. J., Chemical Nanosciences
DELL, A., Carbohydrate Biochemistry
DERWENT, R. G., Atmospheric Chemistry
DJAMGOZ, M. B. A., Neurobiology
DOKAL, I. S., Haematology
DONALDSON, S. K., Pure Mathematics
DONNELLY, C., Statistical Epidemiology
DORNAN, P. J., Experimental Particle Physics
DOUGHERTY, M. K., Space Physics
DREW, J. E., Astrophysics
DRIVER, C., Economics
DUGWELL, D. R., Chemical Engineering
DURHAM, S. R., Allergy and Clinical Immunology
DURUCAN, S., Mining and Environmental Engineering
EDALAT, A., Computer Science and Mathematics
EDGERTON, D. E. H., History of Science, Technology and Medicine
EDWARDS, A. D., Neonatology
ELGIN, J. N., Applied Mathematics
ELLAWAY, P. H., Physiology
ELLIOTT, P., Epidemiology and Public Health Medicine
EVANS, A. W., Risk Management
EVANS, J., Tropical Forestry
EWINS, D. J., Vibration Engineering
FARRELL, P. J., Tumour Virology
FELDMAN, M., Cellular Immunology
FENNER, R. T., Engineering Computation
FENWICK, A., Tropical Parasitology
FERENCZI, M. J., Physiological Sciences
FERGUSON, N. M., Mathematical Biology
FIRMIN, D., Biomedical Imaging
FIRTH, J. A., Anatomy
FISK, D. J., Engineering for Sustainable Development
FISK, N. M., Obstetrics and Gynaecology
FOSTER, R. G., Molecular Neurology
FOULKES, W. M. C., Physics
FOXWELL, B. M., Immune Cell Signalling
FRANKEL, G., Molecular Pathenogenesis
FRANKS, N. P., Biophysics
FRANKS, S., Reproductive Endocrinology
FRASER, R. W., Agricultural Economics
FREEMONT, P. S., Structural Biology
FRENCH, P. M. W., Physics

FRIEDLAND, J. S., Infectious Diseases and Microbiology
FROGUEL, P., Genomic Medicine
GABRA, H., Medical Oncology
GABRIEL, J., Organizational Theory
GANN, D. M., Technology and Innovation Management, Built Environment
GARNETT, G., Microparasite Epidemiology
GARRALDA HUALDE, M. E., Child and Adolescent Psychiatry
GAUNTLETT, J. P., Theoretical Physics
GELENBE, S. E., Computer and Communication Networks
GEORGE, A., Molecular Immunology
GHATEI, M., Peptide Endocrinology
GHOSH, S., Gastroenterology
GIBBON, J. D., Applied Mathematics
GIBSON, S. E., Chemistry
GIBSON, V. C., Organic Chemistry
GILKS, C. F., International Health
GILLON, R., Medical Ethics
GLAISTER, S., Transport and Infrastructure
GLOVER, V. A., Perinatal Psychobiology
GODFRAY, H. C. J., Evolutionary Biology
GOGOLIN, A. O., Mathematical Physics
GORDON, M. Y. A., Experimental Haematology
GOSMAN, A. D., Computational Fluid Dynamics
GOTCH, F. M., Immunology
GRAEBER, M., Neuroscience
GRAHAM, J. M. R., Unsteady Aerodynamics
GRAHAM, N. J. D., Environmental Engineering
GRASBY, P. M., Psychiatry
GREENHALGH, R. M., Surgery
GRIFFITHS, D. S., Human Resource Management
GRIGORYAN, A., Pure Mathematics
GRIMES, R. W., Materials Science
GRIMM, S. W., Toxicology
GRINGARTEN, A., Petroleum Engineering
GRUZELIER, J. G., Psychology
GUO, Y., Computing Science
HABIB, N. A., Hepto-biliary Surgery
HAIGH, J. D., Atmospheric Physics
HAJNAL, J. V., Imaging Science
HALL, G., Physics
HALL, P., Applied Mathematics
HALL, S. G. F., Economics
HALLIWELL, J. J., Theoretical Physics
HAND, D. J., Statistics
HANKINS, M. W., Visual Neuroscience
HARDIE, R. J., Insect Physiology
HARDING, S., Cardiac Pharmacology
HARRIES, J. E., Earth Observation
HARRISON, N., Chemistry
HARRISON, P. G., Computing Science
HASKARD, D. O., Cardiovascular Medicine
HASSELL, M. P., Insect Ecology
HENCH, L. L., Ceramic Materials
HENRY, J. A., Accident and Emergency Medicine
HIGGINS, C. F., Clinical Sciences
HIGGINS, J. S., Polymer Science
HILL, B., Policy Analysis
HILLIER, R., Compressible Flow
HINDS, E. A., Quantum Optics
HODKINSON, I., Logic and Computation
HODSON, M. E., Respiratory Medicine
HOLDEN, D. W., Molecular Microbiology
HOLM, D. D., Applied Mathematics
HOLMES, A. B., Organic and Polymer Chemistry
HOPKINS, C. R., Biochemistry
HUDSON, J. A., Rock Mechanics
HUGHES, A. D., Clinical Pharmacology
HUGHES, S. F. R., Orthopaedic Surgery
HUHTANIEMI, I. T., Reproductive Biology
HULL, C., Theoretical Physics
IMREGUN, M., Computational Engineering Dynamics
ISHAM, C. J., Theoretical Physics
IVANOV, A. A., Pure Mathematics
IWATA, C. J., Biochemistry
JACKSON, G., Chemical Physics
JAMES, G. D., Pure Mathematics
JARDINE, R. J., Geomechanics
JARVELIN, M., Lifecourse Epidemiology
JEGER, M., Agroecology
JENSEN, H. J., Mathematics
JOHNSON, H. D., Petroleum Geology
JOHNSTON, D. G., Clinical Endocrinology
JOHNSTON, S. L., Respiratory Medicine
JONES, T. S., Physical Chemistry
JONES, W. G., High Energy Physics
JONES, W. P., Combustion
KANDIYOTI, R., Chemical Engineering
KELSALL, G. H., Electrochemical Engineering
KENNARD, C., Clinical Neurology
KILNER, J. A., Materials Science
KING, P. R., Petroleum Engineering
KINLOCH, A. J., Adhesion
KITNEY, R. I., Biomedical Systems Engineering
KLUG, D., Chemical Biophysics
KLUMPES, P. J. M., Accounting
KNIGHT, P. L., Quantum Optics
KORNYSHEV, A. A., Chemical Physics
KRAMER, J., Distributed Computing
KRUSHELNICK, K. M., Plasma Physics
KYDD, J., Agricultural Economics and Business Management
LALANI, E. M. A., Molecular and Cell Pathology
LANE, D. A., Molecular Haematology
LAWRENCE, C., Fluid Mechanics
LAYCOCK, J. F., Endocrine Physiology
LEATHERBARROW, R., Chemical Biology
LESCHZINER, R., Computational Aerodynamics
LESTER, J. N., Water Technology
LEUNG, K. K., Internet Technology
LEVER, M. J., Physiological Mechanics
LEVIN, M., Paediatrics
LIEBECK, M. W., Pure Mathematics
LIMEBEER, D. J. N., Control Engineering
LINDSTEDT, R. P., Thermofluids
LIVINGSTON, A. G., Chemical Engineering
LLOYD SMITH, D., Structural Mechanics
LOMAX, M. A., Animal Sciences
LONG, K. R., Experimental Particle Physics
LUCKHAM, P. F., Particle Technology
LUK, W. W.-C., Computer Engineering
MACCHIETTO, S., Process Systems Engineering
MACCULLOCH, R. J., Economics
MACDERMOT, J., Clinical Pharmacology
MACKINNON, A., Theoretical Solid State Physics
MADEN, A., Psychiatry
MAGEE, A. I., Membrane Biology
MAGEE, J. N., Computing Science
Sir MAINI, R. N., Rheumatology
MAJEED, F. A., Primary Healthcare and General Practice
MAMDANI, E. H., Telecommunications Strategy and Services
MANSFIELD, J., Biology
MARANGOS, J. J., Laser Physics
MAROS, I., Computational Methods of Operations Research
MARSTON, S. B., Cardiovascular Biochemistry
MATHIAS, C. J., Neurovascular Medicine
MATTHEWS, S. J., Chemical and Structural Biology
MAXWELL, P. H., Nephrology
MAZE, M., Anaesthetics
MCCLURE, M. O., Retrovirology
MEADE, N., Quantitative Finance
MEIKLE, W. P. S., Astrophysics
MILLER, A., Organic Chemistry and Structural Biology
MITCHELL, J., Pharmacology in Critical Care
MOORE, G. E., Molecular Genetics
MUGGLETON, S. H., Bioinformatics
MUMFORD, J., Natural Resource Management
MUNTONI, F., Paediatric Neurology
NAGASE, H., Rheumatology
NETHERCOT, D. A., Civil Engineering
NEW, G. H. C., Non-linear Optics
NICHOLSON, J. K., Biological Chemistry
NORTHOVER, J. M. A., Intestinal Surgery
OPENSHAW, P. J. M., Experimental Medicine
OWENS, I., Evolutionary Ecology
PANTELIDES, C. C., Chemical Engineering
PARKER, K. H., Physiological Fluid
PARKER, M. G., Obstetrics and Gynaecology
PARRY, A. O., Statistical Physics
PARRY, G., Applied Physics
PARRY, S., Radiochemistry
PARTRIDGE, M. R., Respiratory Medicine
PASVOL, G., Infection and Tropical Medicine
PAVLOVIC, M., Structural Engineering and Mechanics
PENDRY, J. B., Theoretical Solid-state Physics
PENNELL, D. J., Cardiology
PEPPER, J., Cardiothoracic Surgery
PERRAUDIN, W. R. M., Finance
PETERS, N. S., Cardiac Electrophysiology
PHILLIPS, C. C., Experimental Solid-state Physics
PHILLIPS, D., Physical Chemistry
PISTIKOPOULOS, E. N., Chemical Engineering
PLANT, J. A., Applied Geochemistry
PLAYFORD, R., Gastroenterology
PLENIO, M. B., Quantum Physics
POLAK, J. M., Endocrine Pathology
POTTS, D. M., Analytical Soil Mechanics
POULTER, N. R., Preventative Cardiovascular Medicine
PRABHU, J. C., Marketing
PUSEY, C. D., Renal Medicine
QUIRKE, N., Physical Chemistry
RAWLINGS, R. D., Materials Science
REED, M. J., Steroid Biochemistry
REGAN, L., Obstetrics and Gynaecology
REYNOLDS, R., Cellular Neurobiology
RICHARDS, B., Computing Science
RICHARDSON, S., Public Health
RICHARDSON, S. M., Chemical Engineering
RITTER, M. A., Immunology
RIVERS, R. J., Theoretical Physics
ROBB, M. A., Chemistry
ROBERTS, I., Paediatrics Haematology
ROSE, M. L., Transport Immunology
ROWAN-ROBINSON, G. M., Astrophysics
RUDD, C. E., Haematology
RUSSELL, N. J., Biology
RUSTEM, B., Computational Methods in Operations
RZEPA, H. S., Computational Fluid Dynamics
SAKLATVALA, J., Experimental Pathology
SANDERSON, D. J., Geology
SCHROTER, R. C., Biological Mechanics
SCHWARTZ, S. J., Space Physics
SCOTT, J., Medicine
SCREATON, G. R., Medicine
SEABRA, M. C., Molecular Genetics
SECKL, M., Molecular Cancer Medicine
SEDDON, J. M., Physical Chemistry
SEFTON, J. A., Economics
SELKIRK, M. E., Biochemical Parasitology
SENSKY, J., Applied Mathematics
SERGOT, M. J., Computational Logic
SEVER, P. S., Clinical Pharmacology and Therapeutics
SEVERS, N. J., Cell Biology
SHAH, N., Process Systems Engineering
SHAUNAK, S., Infectious Diseases
SHAW, R. J., Thoracic Medicine
SHERIDAN, D. J., Clinical Cardiology
SINDEN, R. E., Parasite Cell Biology
SKOROBOGATOV, A. N., Pure Mathematics
SLOMAN, M. S., Distributed Systems Management
SMITH, G. L., Experimental Pathology
SMITH, R. A., Mechanical Engineering
SMITH, R. W., Physics
SOBEY, R. J., Fluid Mechanics
SOUTHWOOD, D. J., Physics
SPIKES, H. A., Lubrication
SPRATT, B. G., Molecular Microbiology
SQUIRE, J. M., Structural Biophysics
STAMP, G. W. M., Histopathology
STARK, J., Applied Mathematics
STEER, P. J., Obstetrics and Gynaecology
STELLE, K. S., Physics

STERNBERG, M. J. E., Structural Bioinformatics
STUCKEY, D. C., Biochemical Engineering
SUGDEN, P. H., Cellular Biochemistry
SUMMERFIELD, J. A., Experimental Medicine
SUMNER, T. J., Experimental Astrophysics
SUTTON, A. P., Nanotechnology
SWAN, C., Hydrodynamics
SYMS, R. R., Microsystems
SZYMANSKI, S. A., Economics
TAYLOR, A., Neurophysiology
TAYLOR, A. M. K. P., Thermofluids
TAYLOR, J. R., Ultrafast Physics and Technology
TAYLOR, K. M., Cardiac Surgery
TEMPLER, R., Biophysical Chemistry
THIRTLE, C. G., Agricultural Economics
THOMAS, H. C., Medicine
THOMPSON, R. C., Experimental Physics
TOUMAZOU, C., Analogue Circuit Design
TRUSLER, J. P. M., Thermophysics
TSEYTLIN, A., Theoretical Physics
TYRER, P. J., Community Psychiatry
UNDERWOOD, S. R., Cardiac Imaging
VAN HEEL, M., Structural Biology
VASSILICOS, C., Fluid Mechanics
VAZ DE MELO, J., Molecular Haematology
VENABLES, P. J., Viral Immunorheumatology
VINEIS, P., Environmental Epidemiology
VINTER, R. B., Control Theory
VIRDEE, T. S., Physics
VVEDENSKY, D., Theoretical Solid-State Physics
WAAGE, J. K., Applied Ecology
WALDEN, A. T., Statistics
WANG, Y., Reservoir Geophysics
WARK, D. L., High Energy Physics
WARNER, M. R., Geophysics
WARWICK, A. C., History of Science
WAXMAN, J., Medical Oncology
WEBER, J. N., Genito-urinary Medicine and Communicable Diseases
WEBSDALE, D. M., Physics
WEBSTER, J. P. G., Agricultural Business Management
WHEATER, H. S., Hydrology
WILKINS, M. R., Clinical Pharmacology
WILLIAMS, A. J., Membrane Biophysics
WILLIAMS, T. J., Applied Pharmacology
WINSTON, R. M., Fertility Studies
WISE, C. M., Civil Engineering Design
WISE, R. J. S., Neurology
WOOD, D. A., Clinical Epidemiology
WOODS, J. D., Oceanography
WRIGHT, D. J., Pest Management
YANG, G. Z., Medical Image Computing
YOUNG, D. B., Medical Microbiology
ZEGARLINSKI, B., Pure Mathematics

Institute of Education

20 Bedford Way, London, WC1H 0AL
Telephone: (20) 7612-6000
Fax: (20) 7612-6126
E-mail: info@ioe.ac.uk
Internet: www.ioe.ac.uk

Founded 1902 as London Day Training College, transferred to control of Univ. of London in 1932, became School of Univ. in 1987
Academic year: September to June

Dir: Prof. CHRIS HUSBANDS
Sec.: BRYN MORRIS
Academic Registrar: Dr LORETO LOUGHRAN
Librarian: ANNE PETERS

Library of 270,000 vols, 1,160 periodicals
Number of teachers: 176
Number of students: 4,424 (1,372 full-time, 3,052 part-time)
Publication: *London Review of Education* (3 a year)

PROFESSORS

AGGLETON, P., Education
ALDERSON, P., Childhood Studies
ALDRICH, R., History of Education
BALL, S., Sociology of Education
BARNETT, R., Higher Education
BARTON, L., Inclusive Education
BLATCHFORD, P., Education and Psychology
BRANNEN, J., Sociology of the Family
BRIGHOUSE, H., Philosophy of Education
BUCKINGHAM, D., Education
BYNNER, J., Education
CAMERON, D., Languages
DAVID, N., Educational Technology
DOCKRELL, J., Psychology and Special Needs
DOLTON, P., Education
ELBOURNE, D., Evidence-informed Policy and Practice
EVANS, K., Education (Lifelong Learning)
GILLBORN, D., Education
GOLDSTEIN, H., Statistical Methods
GORDON, P., History of Education
GREEN, A., Education
GUNDARA, J., Education
HALPIN, D., Education
HIRST, P., Education
HOYLES, C. M., Mathematics Education
JOSHI, H., Education
KENT, A., Geography Education
KRESS, G., English
LAWTON, D., Education
LEONARD, D., Sociology of Education and Gender
LEVACIC, R., Economics and Finance of Education
LITTLE, A., Education with spec. reference to Developing Countries
LUNT, I., Educational Psychology
MACGILCHRIST, B., Education
MAYALL, B., Childhood Studies
MOSS, P., Early Childhood Provision
NOSS, R., Mathematics Education
OAKLEY, A. R., Sociology and Social Policy
POWER, S., Education
REISS, M., Science Education
ST JAMES ROBERTS, I., Child Development
SAMMONS, P., Education
SHATTOCK, M., Higher Education Management
SIRAJ-BLATCHFORD, I., Early Childhood Education
WELCH, G., Music Education
WHITE, J., Philosophy of Education
WHITTY, G. J., Sociology of Education
WOLF, A., Education

King's College London

Strand, London, WC2R 2LS
Telephone: (20) 7836-5454
Denmark Hill campus: 10 Cutcombe Rd, London, SE5 9RJ
Guy's campus: New Hunts House, London, SE1 1UL
Telephone: (20) 7848-6004
St Thomas' campus: Westminster Bridge Rd, London, SE1 7EH
Telephone: (20) 7188-7188
Waterloo campus: James Clerk Maxwell Bldg, 57 Waterloo Rd, London, SE1 8WA
E-mail: ceu@kcl.ac.uk
Internet: www.kcl.ac.uk

Founded 1829 by merger of Queen Elizabeth College and Chelsea College 1985, the Institute of Psychiatry 1997, and United Medical and Dental Schools of Guy's and St Thomas' Hospitals 1998
Academic year: September to June

Prin. and Pres.: Prof. RICK TRAINOR (acting)
Vice-Prin. for Arts and Sciences: Prof. KEITH HOGGART
Vice-Prin. for Education: Prof. EEVA LEINONEN
Vice-Prin. for Health: Prof. ROBERT LECHLER
Vice-Prin. for Research and Innovation: CHRIS MOTTERSHEAD
Vice-Prin. for Strategy and Devt: Prof. Sir LAWRENCE FREEDMAN
Head of Admin. and College Sec.: IAN CREAGH
Chief Information Officer and College Librarian: KAREN STANTON

Library: see Libraries and Archives
Number of teachers: 1,535
Number of students: 23,000 (incl. School of Medicine and Dentistry)
Publications: *Dispatches* (3 a year), *King's College Law Journal* (2 a year)

PROFESSORS

Guy's, King's and St Thomas' School of Biomedical Sciences (1st Fl., Henrietta Raphael House, London, SE1 1UL; tel. (20) 7848-6400; fax (20) 7848-6399; e-mail biomed.admin@kcl.ac.uk):

BERRY, M., Anatomy
BRAIN, S. D., Pharmacology
BUCKLAND-WRIGHT, J. C., Radiological Anatomy
CICLITIRA, P. J., Gastroenterology
FILE, S. E., Psychopharmacology
FRASER, L. R., Reproductive Biology
GOULD, H. G., Biophysics
HALLIWELL, B., Biochemistry
HEARSE, D. J., Cardiovascular Biochemistry
HOLDER, N. H., Anatomy
HOWELL, S. L., Physiology
JENNER, P. G., Pharmacology
JONES, G. E., Cell Biology
LITTLETON, J. M., Pharmacology
LUMSDEN, A. G. S., Developmental Neurobiology
MADEN, M., Developmental Biology
MANN, G. E., Vascular Physiology
MARSHALL, J., Ophthalmology
MCMAHON, S. B., Physiology
MCNAUGHTON, P. A., Physiology
NAFTALIN, R. J., Physiology
NEAL, M. J., Pharmacology
PAGE, C. P., Pharmacology
PATIENT, R. K., Molecular Genetics
PEARSON, J. D., Physiology
PRICE, R. G., Biochemistry
QUINN, P. J., Biochemistry
RICE-EVANS, C., Biochemistry
RITTER, J. M., Clinical Pharmacology
RUTTER, M., Psychopathology
SIMMONS, R., Biophysics
STANDRING, S. M., Applied Neurobiology
THURSTON, C. F., Microbiology
TIMBRELL, J. A., Biochemical Toxicology
WEBSTER, K., Anatomy
WILLIAMS, W. P., Environmental Science

Guy's, King's and St Thomas' School of Dentistry (Guy's Tower, Guy's Hospital, London, SE1 9RT; tel. (20) 7188-7188; fax (20) 7188-1159):

BEIGHTON, D., Oral Microbiology
CHALLACOMBE, S. J., Oral Medicine
ELEY, B. M., Periodontology
GELBIER, S., Dental Public Health
GIBBONS, D. E., Oral Health Services Research
JOHNSON, N., Dental Sciences
KIDD, E. A., Cariology
LANGDON, J., Oral and Maxillofacial Surgery
LINDEN, R., Craniofacial Biology
MCGURK, M., Oral and Maxillofacial Surgery
MEIKLE, M. C., Orthodontics
MEREDITH SMITH, M., Evolutionary Dento-skeletal Biology
PALMER, R. M., Implant Dentistry and Periodontology
PITT-FORD, T. R., Endodontology
SHARPE, P. T., Craniofacial Biology
SMITH, B. G. N., Conservative Dental Surgery
SMITH, N. J. D., Dentistry

WADE, W. G., Oral Microbiology
WATSON, R., Prosthetic Dentistry

School of Education (Franklin-Wilkins Bldg (WBW), Waterloo Rd, London, SE1 9NN; tel. (20) 7848-3183; fax (20) 7848-3182):

BROWN, M. L., Education
COX, M. J., Information Technology in Education
DUSCHL, R., Science Education
JOHNSON, D. C., Education
STREET, B. U., Language in Education
WILLIAM, D. A. P. R., Educational Assessment

School of Health and Life Sciences (Franklin-Williams Bldg, 150 Stamford St, London, SE1 9NN; e-mail health-life@kcl.ac.uk):

CAMMACK, R., Health and Life Siences
COWAN, D. A., Pharmaceutical Toxicology
COWLEY, S. A., Community Practice Development
EBRINGER, A. M. A., Immunology
FRANK, L. S., Children's Nursing Research
GEISSLER, C. A., Nutrition
HALL, D. O., Health and Life Sciences
HIDER, R. C., Pharmacy
MARRIOTT, C., Pharmacy
REDFERN, S. J., Nursing Studies
ROSS MURPHY, S. B., Life Sciences
SANDERS, T. A., Nutrition
STAINES, N. A., Immunology
TINKER, A. M., Gerontology
WHILE, A. E., Nursing Studies
WILSON-BARNETT, J., Nursing Studies

School of Humanities (Strand, London, WC2R 2LS; tel. (20) 7848-2374; fax (20) 7848-2415; e-mail humanities@kcl.ac.uk):

ADLER, J. D., German
BANNER, M. C., Moral and Social Theology
BEATON, R. M., Modern Greek
BIRTWISTLE, H., Musical Composition
BOND, B. J., War Studies
BRIDGE, C., Australian Studies
BUSH, C., American Literature
BUTT, J. W., Modern Hispanic Studies
CHABAL, P. E., Lusophone-African Studies
CLARKE, M., Defence Studies
CLARKE, P. B., History and Sociology of Religion
DANDEKER, C., Military Sociology
DEATHRIDGE, J. W., King Edward Chair of Music
DOCKRILL, M. L., Diplomatic History
DREYFUS, L., Music
FREEDMAN, L. D., War Studies
GANZ, D., Palaeography
GARNETT, J., Defence Studies
GAUNT, S. B., French Language and Literature
GILLIES, D. A., Philosophy of Science and Mathematics
GRIFFITHS, R. M., French Studies
HAMNETT, C., Human Geography
HEATH, M. J., French Literature
HELM, P., Theology and Religious Studies
HERRIN, J. E., Late Antique and Byzantine Studies
HOGGART, K., Geography
HOOK, D., Spanish Medieval Studies
IFE, B. W., Spanish and Spanish-American Studies
JORDANOVA, L., Modern History
KARSH, E., Mediterranean Studies
KNIBB, M. A., Old Testament Studies
LAPPIN, S., Linguistics
LIEU, J., New Testament Studies
MCCABE, M. M. A., Ancient Philosophy
MACEDO, H. M., Portuguese and Brazilian Studies
MACHOVER, M., Philosophy
MAYER, R. G. M., Classics
NELSON, J. L., Medieval History
NEWITT, M. D. D., History
NEWSON, L. A., Geography
NOKES, D. L., English Literature
ORMOND, L., Victorian Studies
OVERY, R. J., Modern History
PAPINEAU, D. C., Philosophy
PORTER, A. N., History
PROUDFOOT, G. R., English
ROBERTS, J. A., English Language and Medieval Literature
ROSEVEARE, H. G., History
RUSSELL, C. S. R., History
SABIN, P. A. G., Strategic Studies
SAINSBURY, R. M., Philosophy
SAVILE, A. B., Philosophy
SCHIESARO, A., Latin Language and Literature
SILK, M. S., Latin Language and Literature
SORABJI, R. R. K., Philosophy
STOKES, J., English Literature
THORNES, J. B., Geography
WAYWELL, G. B., Classics
WHITE, J. J., German

School of Law (Strand, London, WC2R 2LS; tel. (20) 7836-5454; e-mail gen.genlaw@kcl.ac.uk):

BLACKBURN, R., Law
EECKHOUT, P. O. V., Law
EWING, K. D., Law
GEARTY, C. A., Human Rights Law
GLOVER, J. C. B., Ethics (Dir)
GUEST, A. G., Law
HAYTON, D. J., Law
LOMNICKA, E. Z., Law
MARTIN, J. E., Law
MORSE, C. G., Law
MULLERSON, R., International Law
NORRIE, A. W., Criminal Law and Criminal Justice
PHILLIPS, J. C., Law
WHISH, R., Law

Guy's, King's and St Thomas' School of Medicine (1st Fl., Hodgkin Bldg, London, SE1 9RT; tel. (20) 7848-6971; fax (20) 7848-6969):

ADAM, A., Interventional Radiology
ADAMS, A. P., Anaesthetics
AMIEL, S., Diabetic Medicine
BANATVALA, J. E., Clinical Virology
BATES, G. P., Neurogenetics
BENJAMIN, I., Surgery
BOURAS, N., Psychiatry of Learning Difficulties
BRAUDE, P. R., Obstetrics and Gynaecology
BURNAND, K. G., Vascular Surgery
BURNEY, P. G. J., Public Health Medicine
COLLINS, W. P., Obstetrics and Gynaecology
CRAIG, T. K., Community Psychiatry
DAVID, A., Cognitive Neuropsychiatry
DAVIS, H. M., Child Health Psychology
DOHERTY, P., Cell Biology
EADY, R. A., Experimental Dermatopathology
EASTERBROOK, P. J., Medicine
EYKYN, S. J., Clinical Microbiology
FABRE, J., Clinical Sciences
FARZANEH, F., Molecular Medicine
FENTIMAN, I. S., Surgical Oncology
FOGELMAN, I., Nuclear Medicine
FORSLING, M. L., Neuroendocrinology
FRENCH, G. L., Medical Microbiology
GARETY, P. A., Clinical Psychology
GIANNELLI, F. B., Molecular Genetics
GLEESON, M. J., Otolaryngology
GREAVES, M. W., Dermatology
GREENOUGH, A., Clinical Respiratory Physiology
HART, I. R., Cancer Research
HAWK, J. L. M., Dermatological Photobiology
HAWKES, D. J., Computational Imaging
HAY, R. J., Cutaneous Medicine
HAYCOCK, G. B., Paediatrics
HAYDAY, A. C., Immunobiology
HEATLEY, F. W., Orthopaedic Surgery
HENDRY, B., Renal Medicine
HIGGINSON, I., Palliative Care
HIGGS, R., General Practice
HUGHES, R. A. C., Neurology
JACKSON, S., Clinical Gerontology
JONES, R. H., General Practice
KALRA, L., Stroke Medicine
KEMENY, D. M., Immunology
KOPELMAN, M. D., Neuropsychiatry
LEE, T. H., Allergy and Respiratory Medicine
LEHNER, T., Basic and Applied Immunology
LOWY, C., Endocrinology
LUCAS, S. B., Clinical Histopathology
MACDONALD, A. J. D., Old-Age Psychiatry
MAISEY, M. N., Radiological Sciences
MARTEAU, T. M., Health Psychology
MATHEW, C. G. P., Molecular Genetics
MCGREGOR, A., Medicine
MILLS, K. R., Clinical Neurophysiology
MILNER, A. D., Neonatology
MUFTI, G., Haematological Oncology
NICOLAIDES, K., Obstetrics and Gynaecology
PANAYI, G. S., Rheumatology
PEARSON, T. C., Haematology
PETERS, T. J., Clinical Biochemistry
POLKEY, C., Neurosurgery of Epilepsy
POSTON, L., Foetal Health
RAMIREZ, A. J., Liaison Psychiatry
RICHARDS, M. A., Palliative Medicine
ROBERTS, V. C., Clinical Prof.
ROBINSON, R. O., Paediatric Neurology
ROSS, E., Community Paediatrics
RUBENS, R. D., Clinical Oncology
SACKS, S. H., Nephrology
SAVIDGE, G. F., Coagulation Medicine
SCOTT, D. L., Clinical Rheumatology
SELLER, M. J., Developmental Genetics
SHEPHERD, G. W., Mental Health Rehabilitation
SIMONOFF, E. A., Child and Adolescent Psychiatry
SOLOMON, E., Human Genetics
SONKSEN, P. H., Endocrinology
SWAMINATHAN, R., Clinical Biochemistry
SWIFT, C., Health Care of the Elderly
TYNAN, M. J., Paediatric Cardiology
VIBERTI, G., Diabetes and Metabolic Medicine
WATSON, J. P., Psychiatry
WEINMAN, J. A., Psychology Applied to Medicine
WESSELEY, S., Liaison Psychiatry
WILLIAMS, D. G., Medicine

Florence Nightingale School of Nursing and Midwifery (James Clerk Maxwell Bldg, 57 Waterloo Rd, London, SE1 8WA; tel. (20) 7848-4698; e-mail nightingale@kcl.ac.uk; internet www.kcl.ac.uk/nursing):

COWLEY, S.
FRANCK, L.
HUMPHREY, C.
NORMAN, I.
RICHARDSON, A.
SANDALL, J.
WHILE, A.

School of Physical Sciences and Engineering (Strand, London, WC2R 2LS; tel. (20) 7848-2267; fax (20) 7848-2766; e-mail pse.schooloffice@kcl.ac.uk):

AGHVAMI, A. H., Telecommunications Engineering
BUSHNELL, C. J., Mathematics
CLARKSON, T. G., Electrical Engineering
COLLINS, A. T., Physics
DAVIES, A. C., Electrical Engineering
DAVIES, E. B., Mathematics
DAVIES, G., Physics
GABBAY, D. M., Logic
GAUNT, D. S., Physics
GIBSON, S. E., Chemistry
GOSPEL, H. F., Management
HALL, T. J., Optoelectronics
HEATH, C. C., Work and Orgs
HIBBERT, F., Chemistry
HOLWILL, M. E. J., Biological Physics

HOWE, P. S., Applied Mathematics
HUGHES, M. N., Chemistry
LAUGHLIN, R., Physical and Engineering Sciences
PIKE, E. R., Physical and Engineering Sciences
PRESSLEY, A. N., Mathematics
ROBB, M. A., Chemistry
ROBINSON, D. C., Mathematics
ROGERS, A. J., Electrical Engineering
SAFAROV, Y., Mathematics
SANDLER, M. B., Signal Processing
SARKAR, S., Theoretical Physics
SAUNDERS, P. T., Mathematics
STREATER, R. F., Mathematics
SWANSON, J. G., Electrical Engineering
TURNER, C. W., Electrical Engineering
UFF, J., Engineering Law
WEST, P. C., Mathematics
WINDER, R., Computer Science
YIANNESKIS, M., Fluid Mechanics

Institute of Psychiatry (De Crespigny Park, London, SE5 8AF; tel. (20) 7836-5454; e-mail spjgams@iop.kcl.ac.uk; internet www.iop.kcl.ac.uk):

ANDERTON, B. H., Neuroscience
BANERJEE, S. S., Mental Health and Ageing
BARKER, G. J., Magnetic Resonance Physics
BOLTON, D., Philosophy and Psychopathology
CHALDER, T., Psychological Medicine
CRAIG, T. K. J., Psychological Medicine
GOODMAN, R., Child and Adolescent Psychiatry
HEMSLEY, D. R., Psychology
HOTOPF, M., General Hospital Psychiatry
HUXLEY, P. J., Social Work
JONES, E., History of Medicine and Psychiatry
KNAPP, M. R. J., Health Economics
MACDONALD, A. J. D., Psychological Medicine
MCGUFFIN, P., Social, Genetic and Developmental Psychiatry
MORRIS, R. G., Neuropsychology
SALKOVSKIS, P. M., Psychology
STOLERMAN, I., Behavioural Pharmacology
STRANG, J., Addiction Research
WESSELY, S., Epidemiological and Liaison Psychiatry

ATTACHED CENTRE

Centre for Defence Studies: King's College London, Strand, London, WC2R 2LS; tel. (20) 7848-2338; fax (20) 7848-2748; e-mail cds@kcl.ac.uk; internet www.kcl.ac.uk/depsta/rel/cds; f. 1990; Dir Prof. MICHAEL CLARKE; publ. *Conflict, Security and Development* (3 a year).

London Business School

Regent's Park, London, NW1 4SA
Telephone: (20) 7000-7000
Fax: (20) 7000-7001
E-mail: webenquiries@london.edu
Internet: www.london.edu
Founded 1965
Academic year: August to July
Dean: Sir ANDREW LIKIERMAN
Deputy Dean for Programmes: Prof. ANDREW SCOTT
Deputy Dean for Faculty: Prof. STEPHEN SCHAEFER
Number of teachers: 158
Number of students: 1,700 (postgraduate); over 8,000 exec. education participants

PROFESSORS

BIRKINSHAW, J., Strategic and International Management
BUNN, D. W., Decision Science
CORNELLI, F., Finance
DEGRAEVE, Z., Decision Sciences
DIMSON, E., Finance
FRANKS, J. R., Finance
GOFFEE, R. E., Organizational Behaviour
GRATTON, L., Organizational Behaviour
HENNESSY, C., Finance
LIKIERMAN, A., Accounting (Dean)
MARKIDES, C., Strategic and International Management
NAIK, N., Finance
NICHOLSON, N., Organizational Behaviour
PETERSON, R., Organizational Behaviour
PILLUTLA, M., Organizational Behaviour
PORTES, R., Economics
RAMDAS, K., Management Science and Operations
REY, H., Economics
SCOTT, A., Economics
SHIVAKUMAR, L., Accounting
TALMOR, E., Accounting
WARREN, K., Management Science and Operations
WEBER, B., Management Science and Operations

ATTACHED RESEARCH INSTITUTES

Aditya Birla India Centre: e-mail indiacentre@london.edu; Co-Dir NIRMALYA KUMAR; Co-Dir PHANISH PURANAM.

Centre for Corporate Governance: e-mail vfarnell@london.edu; Academic Dir JULIAN FRANKS.

Coller Institute of Private Equity: e-mail peinstitute@london.edu; Founder and Chair. Prof. ELI TALMOR.

Foundation and Endowment Asset Management: e-mail sacharya@london.edu; Academic Dir ELROY DIMSON.

Hedge Fund Centre: e-mail hedgefunds@london.edu; Dir NARAYAN NAIK.

Management Lab: e-mail jbirkinshaw@london.edu; Co-founder and Research Dir JULIAN BIRKINSHAW.

London School of Economics and Political Science

Houghton St, London, WC2A 2AE
Telephone: (20) 7405-7686
Fax: (20) 7955-6001
E-mail: stu.rec@lse.ac.uk
Internet: www.lse.ac.uk
Founded 1895
Academic year: October to July
Dir (vacant)
Pro-Dir for Planning and Resources: Prof. GEORGE GASKELL
Pro-Dir for Teaching and Learning: Prof. JANET HARTLEY
Pro-Dir: Prof. S CORBRIDGE
Sec. and Dir of Admin.: ADRIAN HALL
Library: see Libraries and Archives
Number of teachers: 579 (full-time)
Number of students: 9,500 (8,700 full-time, 800 part-time)
Publications: *BioSocieties* (4 a year), *British Journal of Industrial Relations* (4 a year), *Economica* (4 a year journal of economics, economic history and statistics), *Journal of Global History* (3 a year), *Journal of Transport Economics and Policy* (3 a year), *Population Studies* (3 a year), *The British Journal of Sociology* (4 a year), *The International Bibliography of the Social Sciences* (4 vols, 1 a year)

PROFESSORS

ALPERN, S. R., Mathematics
ANDERSON, R. W., Accounting and Finance
ANGELL, I. O., Information Systems
BALDWIN, R., Law
BALFOUR, S., Govt
BARKER, E. V., Sociology
BARKER, R. S., Govt
BARR, N. A., European Institute
BEAN, C. R., Economics/CEP
BESLEY, T. J., Economics
BHATTACHARYA, S., Accounting and Finance
BIGGS, N. L., Mathematics
BLOCH, M. E. F., Anthropology
BRIGHTWELL, G. R., Mathematics
BROMWICH, M., Accounting and Finance
BROWN, C. J., International Relations
BUZAN, B. G., International Relations
CARTWRIGHT, N. L. D., Philosophy
CHANT, S. H., Geography and Environment
CHARVET, J. C. R., Govt
CHESHIRE, P. C., Geography and Environment
CHINKIN, C. M., Law
CIBORRA, C., Information Systems
COHEN, S., Sociology
COLEMAN, J., Govt
COLLEY, L. J., European Institute
COLLINS, H. G., Law
CONNOR, G., Accounting and Finance
CORBRIDGE, S. E., Geography and Environment
COWELL, F. A., Economics
COX, M., International Relations
CRAFTS, N. F. R., Economic History/CEP
DAVIES, P. L., Law
DESAI, LORD, Economics
DOWDING, K. M., Govt
DOWNES, D. M., Social Policy
DUNLEAVY, P., Govt
DYSON, T. P., Population Studies
EPSTEIN, S. R., Economic History
FEATHERSTONE, K., European Institute
FELLI, L., Economics
FREEMAN, R. B., CEP
FULLER, C. J., Anthropology
GALLIERS, R., Information Systems
GASKELL, G. D., Social Psychology
GEARTY, C. A., Sociology
GORDON, I. R., Geography and Environment
GRAY, J. N., Govt
GREENWOOD, C. J., Law
HALLIDAY, F., International Relations
HARDMAN MOORE, J., Economics
HARRISS, J. C., Development Studies Institute
HARTLEY, T. C., Law
HELD, D., Govt
HEMMER, T., Accounting and Finance
HIDALGO, F. J., Economics
HILL, C. J., International Relations
HILLS, J. R., STICERD
HOBCRAFT, J. N., Population Studies, Social Policy
HOWSON, C., Philosophy
HUMPHREY, N. K., Centre for Philosophy of Natural and Social Science
HUMPHREY, P. C., Social Psychology
HUTTER, B. M., Centre for Analysis of Risk and Regulation
HYMAN, R., Industrial Relations
JACKMAN, R. A., Economics
JOHNSON, P. A., Economic History
JONES, D. K. C., Geography and Environment
JONES, G. W., Govt
KALDOR, M. H., Centre for the Study of Global Governance
KELLY, J. E., Industrial Relations
KIERNAN, K. E., Social Policy
KIYOTAKI, N., Economics
KNAPP, M. R. J., Social Policy
KNOX, M. B., International History
LACEY, N. M., Law
LAYARD, P. R. G., Economics/CEP
LE GRAND, J., Social Policy
LIEVEN, D. C. B., Govt
LIGHT, M. M., International Relations
LINTON, O., Economics
LIVINGSTONE, S. M., Social Psychology
LOUGHLIN, M., Law
MACVE, R. H., Accounting and Finance
MANNING, A. P., Economics
MANSELL, R. E., Sociology
MARSDEN, D. W., Industrial Relations
MCGUIRE, A. J., Social Policy
METCALF, D. H., Industrial Relations/CEP

MILLER, P. B., Accounting and Finance
MOORE, H. L., Anthropology
MORGAN, M. S., Economic History
MOUZELIS, N. P., Sociology
MURPHY, M. J., Population Studies
MURPHY, T., Law
NEWBURN, W. H. T., Social Policy
NICKELL, S. J., Economics
NORBERG, R., Statistics
O'LEARY, B., Govt
PAGE, E. C., Govt
PARRY, J. P., Anthropology
PHILIP, G. D. E., Govt
PHILLIPS, A. M., Gender Institute
PIACHAUD, D. F. J., Social Policy
PICCIONE, M., Economics
PISCHKE, J. S., Economics
PISSARIDES, C. A., Economics
POWER, A. E., Social Policy
POWER, M. K., Accounting and Finance
PRESTON, P., International History
QUAH, D., Economics
RAWLINGS, R., Law
REES, J. A., Geography and Environment
REINER, R., Law
REYNIERS, D. J., Interdisciplinary Institute of Management
ROBERTS, S. A., Law
ROBINSON, P. M., Economics
ROCK, P. E., Sociology
RODRIGUEZ-SALGADO, M., International History
ROSE, N. S., Sociology
ROSENHEAD, J. V., Operational Research
RYDIN, Y. J., Geography and Environment
SAITH, A., Development Studies Institute
SASSEN, S., Geography and Environment
SENNETT, R., Sociology
SHIN, H. S., Accounting and Finance
SMITH, A. D. S., Govt
STERN, N. H., Economics
STEVENSON, D., International History
SUTTON, J., Economics
TAYLOR, P. G., International Relations
TEUBNER, G., Law
TIMMERMANN, A. G., Accounting and Finance
TONG, H., Statistics
VENABLES, A. J., Economics
WADE, R., Development Studies Institute
WALLACE, W., International Relations
WEBB, D. C., Accounting and Finance
WHITEHEAD, C. M. E., Economics
WILLIAMS, H. P., Operational Research
WORRALL, J., Philosophy
YAHUDA, M. B., International Relations
YAO, Q., Statistics

London School of Hygiene and Tropical Medicine

Keppel St, London, WC1E 7HT
Telephone: (20) 7636-8636
Fax: (20) 7436-5389
E-mail: registry@lshtm.ac.uk
Internet: www.lshtm.ac.uk

Founded 1899
Academic year: September to September

Dir: PETER PIOT
Sec. and Registrar: WENDY SURRIDGE

Library: see Libraries and Archives
Number of teachers: 432 (incl. research staff)
Number of students: 1,800

Publications: *Health Policy and Planning*, *Journal of Tropical Medicine and Hygiene*

PROFESSORS

ACKERS, J., Postgraduate Education in Public Health
BERRIDGE, V., History
BLACK, N. A., Health Services Research
CAIRNCROSS, A. M., Environmental Health
CAIRNS, J., Health Economics
CLELAND, J., Medical Demography
COLEMAN, M. P., Epidemiology and Vital Statistics
COUSENS, S. N., Epidemiology and Medical Statistics
CROFT, S. L., Parasitology
CURTIS, C., Medical Entomology
DOCKRELL, H., Immunology
DOWIE, J., Health Impact Analysis
ELBOURNE, D., Health Care Evaluation
FINE, P. E. M., Communicable Disease Epidemiology
FLETCHER, A., Epidemiology and Ageing
FOSTER, A., International Eye Health
GREENWOOD, B. M., Communicable Diseases
GRUNDY, E., Demographic Gerontology
HALL, A. J., Infectious Disease Epidemiology
HAYES, R. J., Epidemiology and International Health
HILL, A. A., Community Nutrition
KAYE, P. M., Cellular Immunology
KELLY, J. M., Molecular Biology
KENWARD, M. G., Biostatistics
KIRKWOOD, B. R., Epidemiology and International Health
LEON, D., Epidemiology
MABEY, D., Communicable Diseases
MCADAM, K. P. W., Clinical Tropical Medicine
MCKEE, C. M., European Public Health
MILES, M. A., Medical Protozoology
MILLS, A. J., Health Economics and Policy
MULHOLLAND, K., Infectious Disease Epidemiology
NOAH, N. D., Public Health
PETO, J., Cancer Epidemiology
POCOCK, S. J., Medical Statistics
PRENTICE, A., International Nutrition
RILEY, E. M., Infectious Disease Immunology
ROBERTS, I., Epidemiology and Public Health
RODRIGUES, L., Infectious Disease Epidemiology
ROY, P., Virology
SMITH, P. G., Tropical Epidemiology
TAYLOR, M. G., Medical Helminthology
UAUY, R., Public Health Nutrition
WALT, G., International Health Policy
WELLINGS, K., Sexual and Reproductive Health
WHITWORTH, J. A., International Public Health
WREN, B. W., Microbial Pathogenesis

Queen Mary, University of London

Mile End Rd, London, E1 4NS
Telephone: (20) 7882-5315
Fax: (20) 7882-5556
E-mail: international-office@qmul.ac.uk
Internet: www.qmul.ac.uk

Founded 1989 as Queen Mary and Westfield College, following merger of Queen Mary College (f. 1934) and Westfield College (f. 1882); present name 2000
Academic year: September to June

Prin.: Prof. SIMON GASKELL
Sr Vice-Prin.: Prof. PHILIP OGDEN
Vice-Prin. for External Relations: Prof. RAY PLAYFORD
Vice-Prin. for Humanities and Social Sciences: Prof. MORAG SHIACH
Vice-Prin. for Science and Engineering: Prof. JEREMY KILBURN (acting)
Vice-Prin. for Research and Int. Affairs: Prof. EVELYN WELCH
Vice-Prin. for Teaching and Learning: Prof. SUSAN DILLY
Vice-Prin. and Warden, Barts and the London School of Medicine and Dentistry: Prof. RICHARD TREMBATH
Chief Admin. Officer: DEAN CURTIS
Sec. to Council and Academic Registrar: WENDY APPLEBY
Dir of Library Services: E. J. BULL

Library: see Libraries and Archives
Number of teachers: 1,000
Number of students: 16,500

PROFESSORS

Faculty of Arts:

ADAMOWICZ, E., French
ADGER, D. J., Linguistics
BOFFEY, J., English
CHESHIRE, J. L., Linguistics
DADSON, T. J., Hispanic Studies
DELGADO, M. M., Drama and Theatre Arts
DEYERMOND, A. D., Spanish
EDWARDS, M. J., Classics
ELLIS, M., English Literary History
EVANS, P. W., Film Studies
GOERNER, R., German
GUSSENHOVEN, C., Linguistics
HAMILTON, P. W. A., English
HENNESSY, P. J., Contemporary History
HOBSON JEANNERET, M. E., French Language and Literature
JACKSON, J., History
JANOWITZ, A., English
JARDINE, L. A., English and Drama
MILLER, J. L., History
MORIARTY, M. M., French Literature and Thought
OLSCHNER, L. M., German
PARSONS, D. W., Public Policy
PENNY, R. J., Romance Philology
RAMSDEN, J. A., Modern History
RANAWAKE, S. A., German
RAYFIELD, D., Russian
REES, G. C., English
ROSE, J., English
RUBIN, M., History
SASSOON, D., History
SHIACH, M., Cultural History

Faculty of Engineering and Mathematical Sciences:

ALIABADI, M. H., Engineering
ANDREWS, E. H., Materials
ARROWSMITH, D. K., Mathematics
ASHBY, D., Mathematics
BADER, D. L., Engineering
BAILEY, R. A., Statistics
BULLET, S. R., Mathematics
CAMERON, P. J., Mathematics
CARR, B. J., Mathematics and Astronomy
CLARRICOATS, P., Electrical Engineering
CROOKES, R., Combustion Engineering
CUTHBERT, L. G., Electronic Engineering
DAVIES, K. L., Materials
DONKIN, S., Pure Mathematics
DRIKAKIS, D., Engineering
EDIRISINGHE, M., Materials
EVANS, J., Materials
GASTER, M., Experimental Aerodynamics
GOLDSHEID, I., Probability Theory
GUO, Z. X., Materials
HODGES, W. A., Mathematics
HOGG, P., Materials
LAUGHTON, M. A., Electrical and Electronic Engineering
LAWN, C. J., Thermo-fluids Engineering
LEEDHAM-GREEN, C. R., Pure Mathematics
LESCHZINER, M. A., Engineering
LINDSAY, P., Electrical Engineering
MACCALLUM, M. A. H., Applied Mathematics
MURRAY, C. D., Mathematics and Astronomy
O'HEARN, P., Computer Science
OLVER, A. D., Electrical and Electronic Engineering
PAKER, Y., Parallel Computing
PAPALOIZOU, J. C. B., Mathematics and Astronomy
PARINI, C., Antenna Engineering
ROBINSON, E., Computer Science
ROSE, J. W., Mechanical Engineering
ROXBURGH, I. W., Mathematics and Astronomy
SCHWARTZ, S. J., Space Plasma Physics
STARK, J. P. W., Aeronautical Engineering
TANNER, K., Materials
WEHRFRITZ, B. A. F., Pure Mathematics

WILLIAMS, I. P., Mathematics and Astronomy

Faculty of Law and Social Sciences:

ADAMS, J., Property Law
ATKINSON, B. W., Geography
BAILLIE, R. T., Economics
BLAKENEY, M., Intellectual Property Law
COTTERRELL, R. B. M., Legal Theory
CURTIS, S., Geography
FITZPATRICK, P., Law
FLETCHER, I. F., Commercial Law
GHIGLINO, C., Economics
HASKEL, J., Economics
LAHORE, J. C., Intellectual Property Law
LEE, R., Geography
MALGOSIA, F.
MCCONVILLE, S. D. M., Criminal Justice
NORTON, J. J., Banking Law
O'DONOVAN, K., Law
OGDEN, P. E., Geography
REED, C., Electronic Commerce Law
RICHARDSON, G. M., Public Law
SMITH, D. M., Geography
SORGER, G., Economics
SPENCE, N. A., Human Geography
THOMAS, G., Equity and Property Law
TZAVALIS, E., Economics
VAN BUEREN, G., International Human Rights Law
YELLAND, J. L., Law

Faculty of Natural Sciences:

ADE, P. A. R., Experimental Astrophysics
AYLETT, B. J., Chemistry
BONNETT, R., Research Chemistry
BRADLEY, D. C., Chemistry
BUGG, D. V., Nuclear Physics
CARTER, A. A., Particle Physics
CHARAP, J. M., Theoretical Physics
CLEGG, P. E., Astrophysics
COVNEY, P. V., Physical Chemistry
DUCKETT, J. G., Botany
DUNSTAN, D. J., Experimental Physics
EDGINGTON, J. A., Physics
EMERSON, J., Physics
GRIFFITHS, D. V., Organic Chemistry
HILDREW, A. G., Ecology
KALMUS, P., Physics
LICHTENSTEIN, C. P., Molecular Biology
MARTIN, D., Physics
PERCIVAL, I. C., Physics
PYE, J. D., Biological Sciences
RANDALL, E. W., Research Chemistry
SEWELL, G., Physics
SULLIVAN, A., Inorganic Chemistry
THOMPSON, G., Physics
THORPE, A., Biology
UTLEY, J. H. P., Organic Chemistry
VLCEK, A., Inorganic Chemistry
WARREN, M. J., Biological Sciences
WHITE, G. J., Physics and Astronomy
WILSON, E. G., Physics

Barts and the London School of Medicine and Dentistry (Turner St, London, E1 2AD; tel. (20) 7377-7611; fax (20) 7377-7612; e-mail medicaladmissions@qmul.ac.uk; internet www.mds.qmul.ac.uk):

ANSEAU, M. R., Institute of Dentistry
ARMSTRONG, P., Haematology, Oncology and Imaging
ARMSTRONG-JAMES, M. A., Biomedical Sciences
ASHBY, D., Wolfson Institute of Preventive Medicine
BENJAMIN, N., Pharmacology
BERRY, C. L., Molecular Pathology, Infection and Immunity
BESSER, G. M., Metabolism
BRADLEY, P. F., Institute of Dentistry
BRITTON, K. E., Haematology, Oncology and Imaging
BROCKLEHURST, K., Biomedical Sciences
BURRIN, J., Metabolism
CARTER, Y. H., Community Sciences
CHARD, T., Haematology, Oncology and Imaging
CLARK, A. J. L., Metabolism
COHEN, R. D., Metabolism
COID, J. W., Community Sciences
COSTELOE, K., Metabolism
CURTIS, M., Oral Microbiology
DAVIES, R. J., Molecular Pathology, Infection and Immunity
DOYAL, L., Metabolism
ELLIOTT, J. C., Institute of Dentistry
FELDMAN, R. A., Surgery, Clinical Neuroscience and Intensive Care
FLOWER, R. J., Pharmacology
GALTON, D., Metabolism
GOODE, A. W., Surgery, Clinical Neuroscience and Intensive Care
GOWLAND, G., Pharmacology
GROSSMAN, A., Metabolism
GRUDZINSKAS, J. G., Community Sciences
HAJ, M., Metabolism
HAJEK, P., Clinical Psychology
HARDIE, J. M., Institute of Dentistry
HEATH, M., Institute of Dentistry
HILLIER, S. M., Community Sciences
HITMAN, G. A., Metabolism
HUGHES, F., Periodontology
ILES, R. A., Metabolism
JACOBS, I., Gynaecological Oncology
JEFFRIES, R. A., Molecular Pathology, Infection and Immunity
KOPELMAN, P. G., Metabolism
KUMAR, P., Clinical Medical Education
LEIGH, I. M., Haematology, Oncology and Imaging
LESLIE, R. D. G., Metabolism
LILLEYMAN, J. S., Metabolism
LISTER, T. A., Haematology, Oncology and Imaging
LOWE, D. G., Molecular Pathology, Infection and Immunity
LUMLEY, J. S., Surgery, Clinical Neurosurgery and Intensive Care
MACDONALD, T. T., Metabolism
MARTIN, J. E., Molecular Pathology, Infection and Immunity
MILLER, G., Epidemiology
MILLER, N. E., Metabolism
MONSON, J., Clinical Endocrinology
NEWLAND, A. C., Haematology, Oncology and Imaging
OLIVER, R. T. D., Haematology, Oncology and Imaging
OXFORD, J., Molecular Pathology, Infection and Immunity
PERRETT, D., Metabolism
PHILLIPS, I. R., Biomedical Sciences
PINCHING, A. J., Molecular Pathology, Infection and Immunity
PRICE, C. P., Metabolism
PRIEBE, S., Community Sciences
PRIESTLEY, J. V., Biomedical Sciences
REES, L. H., Metabolism
REZNEK, R., Haematology, Oncology and Imaging
SANDERSON, I. R., Metabolism
SAVAGE, M., Metabolism
STRUNIN, L., Surgery, Clinical Neuroscience and Intensive Care
SUGDEN, M. C., Biomedical Sciences
SWAIN, C., Gastrointestinal Endoscopy
SWASH, M., Surgery, Clinical Neuroscience and Intensive Care
TABAQCHALI, S., Molecular Pathology, Infection and Immunity
THIEMERMANN, C., Pharmacology
TOMLINSON, D. R., Biomedical Sciences
TROTT, K. R., Haematology, Oncology and Imaging
VINSON, G. P., Biomedical Sciences
WALD, N. J., Wolfson Institute of Preventive Medicine
WHITTLE, B. J., Pharmacology
WILLIAMS, D. M., Institute of Dentistry
WILLIAMS, N. S., Surgery, Clinical Neuroscience and Intensive Care
WILLOUGHBY, D. A., Pharmacology
WINGATE, D. L., Metabolism

Royal Academy of Music

Marylebone Rd, London, NW1 5HT
Telephone: (20) 7873-7373
Fax: (20) 7873-7374
E-mail: go@ram.ac.uk
Internet: www.ram.ac.uk

Founded 1822, inc. by Royal Charter 1830
State control

Pres.: HRH THE DUCHESS OF GLOUCESTER
Prin.: Prof. JONATHAN FREEMAN-ATTWOOD
Deputy Prin.: MARK RACZ
Deputy Prin. for Programmes and Research: TIMOTHY JONES
Academic Registrar: PHILIP WHITE

Library of 125,000 vols, incl. colln of early sheet music and MSS
Number of teachers: 155
Number of students: 700

Publication: *RAM Magazine* (2 a year).

Royal Holloway, University of London

Egham Hill, Egham, TW20 0EX
Telephone: (1784) 434455
Fax: (1784) 437520
E-mail: admissions@rhul.ac.uk
Internet: www.rhul.ac.uk

Founded 1886 as Royal Holloway College, present status 1985

Prin.: Prof. PAUL LAYZELL
Deputy Prin.: Prof. ROB KEMP
Dir of Library Services: JOHN TUCK

Library of 600,000 vols, 17,000 e-journals
Number of teachers: 1,525
Number of students: 8,500

DEANS

Faculty of Arts: Prof. KATIE NORMINGTON
Faculty of History and Social Sciences: Prof. ROSEMARY DEEM
Faculty of Science: Prof. PHILIP BEESLEY

PROFESSORS

Faculty of Arts:

ALSTON, R., Classics
ARMSTRONG, T. D., English Literature
BOEHMER, E. D., English
BOWIE, A., German
BRADBY, D. H., Drama and Theatre Studies
BRATTON, J. S., Theatre and Cultural History
BRUZZI, S., Film Studies
CARROLL, J. F. M., Philosophy and German
CAVE, R. A., Drama and Theatre Studies
CHARLTON, D. P., Music
COOK, N. J., Music
DZELAINIS, M. M., Early Modern Literature and Thought
ELLIS, J. C. P., Media Arts
EVERSON, J. E., Italian Literature
GARNETT, A., Media Arts
GIBSON, A. W., Modern Literature and Theory
GOULD, W. L., English Literature
GUNDLE, S., Italian
HAMPSON, R. G., Modern Literature
HILL, W. J., Media Arts
HUGHES, E. J., Modern French Literature
HUGHES, J., German and Comparative Literature
KAHANE, A., Classics
LEE SIX, A. E., Hispanic Studies
LONGERICH, P., German History
MERCK, A. J., Media Arts
MOTION, A., Creative Writing
O'BRIEN, J. P., French Renaissance Literature
PIKE, L., Music
POWELL, J. G. F., Classics
RINK, J., Music
ROBERTSON, E., French

RYAN, K. J. P., English Language and Literature
SAMSON, J., Music
SCHAFER, E. J., Drama
TOSI, A., Italian Studies
VILAIN, R. L., German and Comparative Literature
VILASECA, D., Spanish
WATHEY, A., Music History
WHITE, I. A., German
WILES, D., Theatre
WILLIAMS, J., French Literature and Film

Faculty of History and Social Sciences:

ANSARI, K. H., Islam and Culture
BARN, R., Health and Social Care
BARRON, C. M., History of London
BROADBENT, P. J., Management
CESARANI, D., History
CHAMPION, J. A. I., Early Modern Ideas
CLAEYS, G. R., History of Political Thought
CORFIELD, P. J., History
CROFT, J. P., Early Modern History
DENNEY, D., Applied Social Studies
DREWRY, G., Public Admin.
EDWARDS, J. R., Social Policy
FAULKNER, D. O., Management
FERLIE, E. B., Management
FRANK, J. L., Economics
GRAHAM, H. E., History
HACKLEY, C. E., Marketing
HEYES, A., Economics
LEE, R. M., Social Research Methods
MCSWEENEY, L. B., Management
MANDLER, M., Economics
MATTEN, D., Management
MCCONVILLE, S. D. M., Criminal Justice
NEWELL, S. M., Management
NORMAN, H., Economics
PILBEAM, P., Modern European History
ROBINSON, F. C. R., History of Southeast Asia
ROSENBERG, D., Information and Communication Management
SAUL, N. E., Medieval History
SELZER, A., Economics
SMITH, C. D., Organization Studies
SPAGAT, M., Economics
STONE, D., Modern History

Faculty of Science:

ANDREWS, B. D., Abnormal Psychology
BLACKBURN, S., Mathematics
BLAIR, G. A., Physics
BOLWELL, G. P., Plant Biochemistry
BOWYER, J. R., Plant Biochemistry
BRADLEY, C., Health Psychology
BRAMLEY, P. M., Biochemistry
BRYSBAERT, M. M. C., Psychology
CASTIELLO, U., Psychology
CATCHPOLE, C. K., Animal Behaviour
CHERVONENKIS, A. Y., Computer Science
COHEN, D. A., Computer Science
COLLINSON, M. E., Plant Palaeobiology
COWAN, B. P., Physics
CRANG, P. A., Geography
DAVIES, E. R., Machine Vision
DICKSON, J. G., Molecular Cell Biology
DRIVER, F. F., Human Geography
DUDEN, R., Biological Sciences
EBINGER, C. J., Tectonics
EYSENCK, M. W., Psychology
FOWLER, C. M. R., Geography
FUNNELL, E., Neuropsychology
GAMBLE, C. S., Geography
GAMMERMAN, A., Computer Science
GREEN, M. G., Particle Physics
GUTIN, Z., Computer Science
HALL, R., Geology
HARMAN, G., Mathematics
HARRIS, M., Psychology
IMRIE, R. F., Human Geography
JANSEN, V., Mathematical Biology
KEMP, R. A., Physical Geography
LEA, M. J., Physics
LOEWENTHAL, C., Psychology
LOWE, J. J., Geography
LUO, Z., Computer Science
MACLEOD, A. K., Psychology
MCCLAY, K. R., Structural Geology
MENZIES, M. A., Geochemistry
MITCHELL, C. J., Information Security
MOORE, A. M., Crystallography
MURPHY, S. P., Mathematics
MURTAGH, F., Computer Science
NISBET, E. G., Geology
O'MAHONY, P. F., Applied Mathematics
PATERSON, K. G., Mathematics
PETRASHOV, V. T., Physics
ROSE, J., Geography
SAUNDERS, J., Low Temperature Physics
SCHACK, R., Mathematics
SCOTT, A. C., Applied Palaeobotany
SIMON, D., Development Geography
SMITH, A. T., Psychology
SOLOVYEV, W., Computer Science
STRONG, J. A., Experimental Physics
THIRLWALL, M. F., Isotope Geochemistry
UNWIN, P. T., Geography
VAPNIK, V., Computer Science
VOVK, V. G., Computer Science
WILD, P. R., Mathematics
ZANKER, J. M., Neuroscience

Royal Veterinary College

Royal College St, London, NW1 0TU
Telephone: (20) 7468-5000
Fax: (20) 7388-2342
E-mail: registry@rvc.ac.uk
Internet: www.rvc.ac.uk

Founded 1791
Academic year: September to July

Prin.: Prof. STUART REID
Asst Prin. and Sec.: ELAINE ACASTER
Librarian: SIMON JACKSON

Number of teachers: 109
Number of students: 1,058

PROFESSORS

BROWNLIE, J., Veterinary Pathology
CHANTLER, P. D., Veterinary Molecular and Cellular Biology
CHURCH, D. B., Small Animal Studies
ELLIOTT, J., Pharmacology
GOODSHIP, A. E., Orthopaedic Sciences
GREGORY, N. G., Animal Welfare Physiology
HOWARD, C. R., Veterinary Microbiology and Parasitology
JACOBS, D. E., Veterinary Parasitology
JOHNSTON, A. M., Veterinary Public Health
LANYON, L., Veterinary Anatomy
LEES, P., Veterinary Pharmacology
LLOYD, D. H., Veterinary Dermatology
MAY, S. A., Equine Medicine and Surgery
MCGOWAN, M., Farm-Animal Medicine and Surgery
PFEIFFER, D. U., Veterinary Epidemiology
SCARAMUZZI, R. J., Veterinary Physiology
SKERRY, T. M., Developmental Biology
SMITH, R., Equine Orthopaedics
STICKLAND, N. C., Veterinary Anatomy
STOKER, N. G., Molecular Bacteriology
WATHES, D. C., Veterinary Reproduction
WATSON, P. F., Reproductive Biology
WILLIAMS, A. E., Veterinary Pathology

St George's Hospital Medical School

Cranmer Terrace, London, SW17 0RE
Telephone: (20) 8672-9944
Fax: (20) 8725-3426
E-mail: webmaster@stgeorges.nhs.uk
Internet: www.sghms.ac.uk

Founded 1751
Academic year: September to August

Prin.: Prof. PETER KOPELMAN
Deputy Prin.: Prof. SEAN HILTON
Academic Registrar and Sec.: SOPHIE BOWEN

Library of 150,000 vols
Number of teachers: 400
Number of students: 6,068

PROFESSORS

ANDERSON, H. R., Epidemiology and Public Health
AUSTEN, B. M., Protein Science
BELL, B. A., Neurosurgery
BENNETT, D. C., Anatomy
BENNETT, E. D., Anaesthesia
BLAND, J. M., Medical Statistics
BOLTON, T. B., Pharmacology
BROWN, N., Anatomy and Developmental Biology
BURNS, T. P., Community Psychiatry
CAMM, A. J., Clinical Cardiology
CAMPBELL, S., Obstetrics and Gynaecology
CAPPUCCIO, F., General Practice and Primary Care
CARTER, N. D., Developmental Biochemistry
CHALMERS, R. A., Paediatric Metabolism
CHAMBERS, T. J., Tissue Pathology
CLEMENS, M. J., Biochemistry
COATES, A. R. M., Medical Microbiology
COLLIER, J. G., Clinical Pharmacology
COOK, D., Epidemiology
DALGLEISH, A. G., Oncology
DUFF, M. J. B., Physiological Medicine
EASTMAN, N. L. G., Psychiatry
FISHER, L. M., Biochemistry
GHODSE, A. H., Psychiatry of Addictive Behaviour
GILLBERG, C., Psychiatry
GORDON-SMITH, E. C., Haematology
GRIFFIN, G. E., Infectious Diseases and Medicine
GRIFFITHS, J. R., Medical Biochemistry
HALL, G. M., Anaesthesia
HAY, F. C., Immunology
HERMON-TAYLOR, J., Surgery
HILTON, S. R., General Practice and Primary Care
HOLLINS, S. C., Psychiatry of Learning Disability
HORTON, R., Clinical Pharmacology
HOWLIN, P. A., Clinical Psychology
JOHNSTONE, A. P., Molecular Immunology
JONES, I., Sociology of Health and Illness
JONES, P. W., Medicine
KASKI, J. C., Cardiological Sciences
KRISHNA, S., Infectious Diseases
LACEY, J. H., Psychiatry
LARGE, W. A., Pharmacology
LEVICK, J. R., Physiology
MACGREGOR, G. A., Cardiovascular Medicine
MALIK, M., Cardiology
MARKUS, H., Clinical Neuroscience
MCKENNA, W. J., Cardiac Medicine
MCLAREN, S., Nursing
MORTIMER, P. S., Physiological Medicine
OLIVEIRA, D. B. G., Renal Medicine
PATTON, M., Medical Genetics
ROSS, F., Nursing Primary Care
SEYMOUR, C. A., Clinical Biochemistry and Metabolism
STRACHAN, D. P., Public Health
VICTOR, C. R., Public Health Sciences
WALLER, G., Psychiatry
WALTERS, D. V., Child Health
WEST, R. J., Psychology
WHINCUP, P. H., Public Health Sciences
WHIPP, B. J., Physiology
XU, Q., Cardiological Sciences

School of Oriental and African Studies

Thornhaugh St, Russell Sq., London, WC1H 0XG
Telephone: (20) 7637-2388
Fax: (20) 7436-3844
E-mail: study@soas.ac.uk
Internet: www.soas.ac.uk

Founded 1916
Academic year: September to June

Dir and Prin.: Prof. PAUL WEBLEY
Pro-Dir for Learning and Teaching: Prof. NIRMALA RAO

Pro-Dir for Research and Enterprise: Prof. GRAHAM FURNISS
Vice-Prin. for External Relations: Prof. ELISABETH CROLL
Registrar and Sec.: DONALD BEATON
Library: see Libraries and Archives
Number of teachers: 200
Number of students: 4,700
Publications: *Journal of African Law*, *The Bulletin*, *The China Quarterly*

DEANS

Faculty of Arts and Humanities: Prof. IAN BROWN
Faculty of Languages and Cultures: Prof. ANNE PAUWELS
Faculty of Law and Social Sciences: Prof. MATTHEW CRAVEN

PROFESSORS

ABDEL-HALEEM, M. A. S., Islamic Studies
ABU-DEEB, K. M., Arabic
ARNOLD, D., History of South Asia
ASH, R. F., Taiwan Studies
BARRETT, T. H., East Asian History
BEHRENS-ABOUSEIF, D., Islamic Art and Archaeology
BERNSTEIN, H., Development Studies
BOCKING, B., Study of Religions
BOOTH, A. E., Economics (Asia)
BRAGINSKY, V. I., South East Asian Languages and Literatures
BROWN, I., Economic History (South East Asia)
CLARENCE-SMITH, W. G., Economic History (Asia and Africa)
CROLL, E., Chinese Anthropology
CRUISE O'BRIEN, D. B., Politics of Africa
DIKOTTER, F., Modern Chinese History
FARDON, R., Anthropology (West Africa)
FINE, B., Economics
FURNISS, G., African Languages, Literature and Popular Culture
GEORGE, A., Babylonian
GERSTLE, C. A., Japanese Studies
HAFEZ, S., Modern Arabic
HALE, W., Turkish Politics
HARDING, A., Law
HARRIS, L., Economics
HAWKINS, J. D., Ancient Anatolian Languages
HAWTING, G., History (Near and Middle East)
HEWITT, B. G., Caucasian Languages
HOWE, C., Chinese Business and Management
INGHAM, B., Arabic Linguistic Studies
KRATZ, U., Indonesian and Malay
PALMER, M., Law
PEEL, J. D. Y., Anthropology and Sociology (Africa)
PICTON, J., African Art
POTTIER, J., Anthropology (Africa)
RATHBONE, R. J. A. R., Modern African History
ROBB, P. G., History of India
RUBEN, D.-H., Philosophy
SENDER, J., Economics (Africa)
SHACKLE, C., Modern Languages of South Asia
SIMS-WILLIAMS, N., Iranian and Central Asian Studies
TAPPER, R. L., Anthropology (Middle East)
WEEKS, J., Development Economics
WRIGHT, O., Musicology of the Middle East

School of Pharmacy

29–39 Brunswick Sq., London, WC1N 1AX
Telephone: (20) 7753-5800
Fax: (20) 7753-5829
E-mail: registry@pharmacy.ac.uk
Internet: www.pharmacy.ac.uk
Founded 1842, Royal Charter of Incorporation 1952
Academic year: October to June
Dean and Prin.: Prof. ANTHONY W. SMITH
Chief Operating Officer: MAUREEN BOYLAN
Head of Registry: JOHN PECK
Head of Library and Information Services: MICHELLE WAKE
Number of teachers: 53
Number of students: 1,200

PROFESSORS

ALPAR, O., Drug Delivery Research
BARBER, N., Practice and Policy
BATES, I., Pharmacy Education
BEEZER, A., Biophysical Chemistry
BROCCHINI, S., Chemical Pharmaceuticals
BUCKTON, G., Pharmaceutics
HADGRAFT, J., Biophysical Pharmaceutics
HEINRICH, M., Pharmacognosy and Phytotherapy
HORNE, R., Behavioural Medicine
MOFFAT, A. C., Pharmaceutical Analysis
NEIDLE, S., Chemical Biology
SMITH, F., Pharmacy Practice
STEPHENSON, F. A., Molecular Neuroscience
TAYLOR, D., Pharmaceutical and Public Health Policy
TAYLOR, K., Clinical Pharmaceutics
TAYLOR, P., Microbiology
THOMSON, A. M., Pharmacology
THURSTON, D., Pharmaceutical and Biological Chemistry
UCHEGBU, I., Pharmaceutical Nanoscience
WONG, I., Paediatric Pharmacy

University College London

Gower St, London, WC1E 6BT
Telephone: (20) 7679-2000
Fax: (20) 7387-8057
E-mail: international@ucl.ac.uk
Internet: www.ucl.ac.uk
Founded 1826, merged with Royal Free Hospital School of Medicine 1998
Pres. and Provost: Prof. MALCOLM GRANT
Vice-Provost for Academic and Int. Affairs: Prof. MICHAEL WORTON
Vice-Provost for Enterprise: Prof. STEPHEN CADDICK
Vice-Provost for Health: Prof. Sir JOHN TOOKE
Vice-Provost for Operations: REX KNIGHT
Vice-Provost for Research: Prof. G. DAVID PRICE
Registrar: CHRISTOPHER HALLAS
Library: see Libraries and Archives
Number of teachers: 4,078
Number of students: 21,126
Publications: *The World of UCL*, *UCL Universe*

DEANS

Faculty of Arts and Humanities: Prof. HENRY WOUDHUYSEN
Faculty of Biomedical Sciences: Prof. IAN JACOBS
Faculty of the Built Environment: Prof. ALAN PENN
Faculty of Engineering Sciences: Prof. ANTHONY C W FINKELSTEIN
Faculty of Laws: Prof. Dame HAZEL GENN
Faculty of Life Sciences: Prof. MARY K. L. COLLINS
Faculty of Mathematical and Physical Sciences: Prof. RICHARD CATLOW
Faculty of Social and Historical Sciences: Prof. STEPHEN R. SMITH

PROFESSORS

ADLER, M. W., Sexually Transmitted Diseases
AEPPLI, G., Physics
AGHION, P., Economics of Public Policy
AIELLO, L. C., Biological Anthropology
AIKEN, J., Fine Art
AKBAR, A. N., Immunology
ALLSOP, R. E., Transport Studies
ANDERSON, J. E., Organic Chemistry
ANDERSON, J. M., Mathematics
ANDERSON, P. N., Experimental Neuroscience
ANDERSON, R. H., Paediatric Cardiac Morphology
ANDREWS, D. J., Engineering Design
ARRIDGE, S. R., Image Processing
ASHMORE, J. F., Biophysics
ASHTON, R. D., English Language and Literature
ATKINSON, J., Psychology
ATTANASIO, O. P., Economics
ATTWELL, D. I., Physiology
AYAZI SHAMLOU, P., Biochemical Engineering
AYNSLEY-GREEN, A., Child Health
BABIKER, A. G., Medical Statistics and Epidemiology
BALL, K. M., Mathematics
BANISTER, D. J., Transport Planning
BARENDT, E. M., Law of Media of Communication and Expression
BARKER, J. A., Hydrogeology
BARLOW, M. J., Astrophysics
BARNES, M. P., Scandinavian Studies
BARTLETT, R. P., Russian History
BARTLEY, M., Medical Sociology
BATE, S. P., Health Services Management
BATTARBEE, R. W., Environmental Change
BATTY, J. M., Spatial Analysis and Planning
BAYVEL, P., Optical Communications and Networks
BEBBINGTON, P. E., Social and Community Psychiatry
BEGENT, R. H. J., Oncology
BERGER, M. A., Mathematics
BETTERIDGE, D. J., Endocrinology and Metabolism
BEVAN, S. J., Pharmacology
BEVERLEY, P. C. L., Tumour Immunology
BHATTACHARYA, S. S., Experimental Ophthalmology
BINDMAN, D., History of Art
BIRD, A. C., Clinical Ophthalmology
BISHOP, S. R., Non-linear Dynamics
BLUNDELL, R., Economics
BLUNN, G. W., Biomedical Engineering
BOGLE, I. D. L., Chemical Engineering
BOLSOVER, S. R., Cell Physiology
BORDEN, I. M., Architecture and Urban Culture
BORGERS, T., Economics
BOSHOFF, C. H., Cancer Medicine
BOSTOCK, H., Neurophysiology
BOULOS, P. B., Surgery
BOWLING, A., Health Services Research
BOWMAKER, J., Visual Research
BOWN, S. G., Laser Medicine and Surgery
BOYD, I. W., Electronic Materials
BRAMWELL, S. T., Physical Chemistry
BREWIN, C. R., Clinical Psychology
BRIDGE, M. G., Commercial Law
BROCKES, J. P., Cell Biology
BRODY, M. B., Linguistics
BROWN, D. A., Pharmacology
BROWN, M. M., Stroke Medicine
BROWN, R. A., Tissue Engineering
BROWN, S. N., Mathematics
BROWNE, E. J., History of Medicine
BRUCKDORFER, K. R., Biochemistry
BRYSON, W. N., History and Theory of Art
BURGESS, J. A., Geography
BURK, K. M., Modern and Contemporary History
BURNHAM, P. C., Social Anthropology
BURNSTOCK, G., Anatomy
BURROUGHS, A. K., Hepatology
BUTLER, W. E., Comparative Law
BUTTERWORTH, B. L., Cognitive Neuropsychology
BUXTON, B. F., Information Processing
BYNUM, W. F., History of Medicine
CALLARD, R., Immunology
CAMPBELL, J. A., Computer Science
CAMPBELL, R., Communication Disorders
CARLIN, W. J., Economics
CATLOW, C. R. A., Chemistry

CHAIN, B. M., Immunology
CHARLES, I. G., Molecular Biology
CHESHER, A. D., Economics
CLARK, J. B., Neurochemistry
CLARK, R. J. H., Chemistry
CLARKE, P. E. L., Physics
CLAYTON, P. T., Paediatric Metabolic Disease and Hepatology
CLOUT, H. D., Geography
COCKCROFT, S., Cell Physiology
COLHOUN, H. M., Clinical Epidemiology
COLLINGE, J., Neurodegenerative Disease
COLLINS, M. K. L., Immunology
COLQUHOUN, D., Pharmacology
CONWAY, S. R., History
COOK, P. F. C., Architecture
COOTER, R. J.
COPP, A. J., Developmental Neurobiology
COVENEY, P. V., Physical Chemistry
CRAGGS, M. D., Applied Neurophysiology
CRAIG, G., Paediatric Genetics
CRANE, T. M., Philosophy
CRAWFORD, M. H., Ancient History
CROLL, J. G. A., Civil and Environmental Engineering
CROSS, P. A., Geomatic Engineering
CULHANE, J. L., Physics
CULL-CANDY, S. G., Pharmacology
CURRAN, H. V., Psychopharmacology
CUZNER, M. L., Neurochemistry
D'AVRAY, D. L., History
DACRE, J. E., Medical Education
DANPURE, C. J., Molecular Cell Biology
DARBYSHIRE, J. H., Epidemiology
DAVIDSON, B. R., Surgery
DAVIES, S. W., Experimental Neuropathology
DAVIES, W. E., History
DAWID, A. P., Statistics
DAYAN, P., Computational Neuroscience
DEAN, M. C., Anatomy
DEEMING, A. J., Chemistry
DELETANT, D. J., Romanian Studies
DELHANTY, J. D. A., Human Genetics
DELPY, D. T., Medical Photonics
DENNIS, I. H., English Law
DEZATEUX, C. A., Paediatric Epidemiology
DHILLON, A. P., Histopathology
DICKENSON, A. H., Neuropharmacology
DIMITRIOU, H., Planning Studies
DOLAN, R., Neuropsychiatry
DOLPHIN, A., Pharmacology
DOWD, P. M., Dermatology
DOWMAN, I. J., Photogrammetry and Remote Sensing
DRIVER, J. S., Psychology
DUCHEN, M. R., Physiology
DUNCAN, J. S., Clinical Neurology
DUNNILL, P., Biochemical Engineering
DUSHEIKO, G. M., Medicine
DWORKIN, R. M., Jurisprudence
EDWARDS, J. C. W., Connective-tissue Medicine
EDWARDS, Y. H., Human Genetics
EKINS, R. P., Biophysics
ELL, P. J., Nuclear Medicine
ELTON, L., Higher Education
EMERY, V. C., Virology
EVANS, A. W., Transport Safety
EVANS, M. C. W., Plant Chemistry
FEARN, T., Applied Statistics
FERGUSSON-PELL, M., Neuromuscular Restoration and Rehabilitation
FINE, L. G., Medicine
FINKELSTEIN, A. C. W., Software Systems Engineering
FINNEY, J. L., Physics
FISH, D. R., Clinical Neurophysiology and Epilepsy
FISHER, A. J., Physics
FISHER, E. M. C., Neurogenetics
FITZGERALD, M., Developmental Neurobiology
FITZKE, F. W., Visual Optics
FLETCHER, I. F., International Commercial Law
FONAGY, P., Psychoanalysis
FOOT, M. M., Library and Archive Studies
FOREMAN, J. C., Immunopharmacology
FORGACS, D. A., Italian
FORGE, A., Auditory Cell Biology
FORTY, J. A., History of Architecture
FOURNIER, C. L., Architecture and Urban Planning
FOWLER, C. J., Uro-neurology
FRACKOWIAK, R. S. J., Cognitive Neurology
FRANCK, L. S., Children's Nursing Research Studies
FREEMAN, M. D. A., English Law
FRENCH, D. W., History
FRISTON, K. J., Imaging Neuroscience
FRITH, C. D., Neuropsychology
FRITH, U., Cognitive Development
FRY, C. H., Cellular Physiology
FULBROOK, M. J. A., German History
FULLER, J. H., Clinical Epidemiology
FURNHAM, A. F., Psychology
GABELLA, G., Histology and Cytology
GAGE, S. A., Innovative Technology in Architecture
GALLIVAN, S., Mathematics
GARB, T., History of Art
GARDINER, R. M., Paediatrics
GARDNER-MEDWIN, A. R., Physiology
GARTHWAITE, J., Experimental Neuroscience
GELLER, M. J., Jewish Studies
GENN, H. G., Socio-Legal Studies
GILBERT, A. G., Geography
GILLAN, M. J., Physics
GILLESPIE, S. H., Medical Microbiology
GOADSBY, P. J., Clinical Neurology
GODOVAC-ZIMMERMANN, J., Protein Biochemistry
GOLDSPINK, G., Anatomy
GOLDSTEIN, D. B., Evolutionary and Population Genetics
GOLDSTONE, A. H., Haematology
GOODSHIP, A. E., Orthopaedic Sciences
GOODWIN, P. B., Transport Policy
GOSWAMI, U., Cognitive Developmental Psychology
GRAFFY, J. J., Russian Literature and Cinema
GRANTHAM-MCGREGOR, S. M., Child Health and Nutrition
GRASS, A. J., Fluid Mechanics
GREEN, C. J., Surgery
GREENHALGH, P. M., Primary Care Development
GREENWOOD, J., Biomedical Research
GREGORY, J., Water Chemistry
GRIFFITHS, H. D., Electronics
GRIFFITHS, P. D., Virology
GUERRINI, R., Paediatric Neurology
GUEST, J. E., Planetary Science
GUEST, S. F. D., Legal Philosophy
GURLING, H. M., Molecular Psychiatry
HALE, K. J., Chemistry
HALL, A., Molecular Biology
HALL, C., Modern British Social and Cultural History
HALL, C. M., Paediatric Radiology
HALL, P. G., Planning Studies
HAMILTON-MILLER, J. M. T., Medical Microbiology
HAMMOND, P., Dental and Medical Informatics
HANN, I., Paediatric Haematology and Oncology
HANSON, J. M., House Form and Culture
HARRIS, J. M., Linguistics
HARRIS, R., Geography
HARRISON, C. M., Geography
HARRISON, M. J. G., Clinical Neurology
HART, S. M., Hispanic Studies
HARTLEY, J. A., Cancer Studies
HARVEY, N. J. W., Judgement and Decision Research
HASSAN, F. A., Archaeology
HATCH, D. J., Paediatric Anaesthesia
HAUSSER, M. A., Neuroscience
HAWKINS, P. N., Medicine
HAWLEY, C., Architectural Studies
HAWORTH, S. G., Developmental Cardiology
HAZELL, R. J. D., Govt and the Constitution
HEBDEN, J. C., Biomedical Optics
HERMANS, T. J., Dutch and Comparative Literature
HERTZMAN, C., Paediatric Radiology
HEYDECKER, B. G., Transport Studies
HEYES, C. M., Psychology
HILLIARD, J., Fine Art Media
HILLIER, W. R. G., Architectural and Urban Morphology
HILLSON, S. W., Bioarchaeology
HITCHINGS, R. A., Glaucoma and Allied Studies
HOARE, M., Biochemical Engineering
HOBKIRK, J. A., Dental Prosthetics
HOBSON, R. P., Developmental Psychopathology
HOCKEY, S. M., Library and Information Studies
HODGSON, H., Medicine
HOMEWOOD, K. M., Human Ecology
HOPPIT, J., British History
HORNBLOWER, N. S. R., Classics and Ancient History
HORNE, F. P., English Language and Literature
HORTON, M. A., Bone Biology and Mineral Metabolism
HOSKING, G. A., Russian History
HOWARTH, I. D., Astronomy
HOWELL, P., Experimental Psychology
HUDSON, R. A., Linguistics
HUGHES, L. A. J., Russian History
HUMBERSTON, J. W., Physics
HUMPHRIES, S. E., Cardiovascular Genetics
HUNT, D. M., Molecular Genetics
HUNT, J. C. R., Climate Modelling
HUNT, N. P., Orthodontics
HUNT, S. P., Molecular Neurobiology
HYAMS, J. S., Cell Biology
ICHIMURA, H., Economics
INGRAM, D., Health Informatics
ISENBERG, D. A., Rheumatology
ISHAM, V. S., Probability and Statistics
JANOSSY, G., Immunology
JARVIS, M. J., Health Psychology
JAUNIAUX, E. R. M., Obstetrics and Fetal Medicine
JAYNE, J. E., Mathematics
JEHIEL, P., Economics
JESSEN, K. R., Developmental Neurobiology
JOHNSON, A. M., Primary Care and Population Sciences
JOHNSON, E. R., Mathematics
JOHNSON, F. E. A., Mathematics
JOHNSTON, A., Psychology
JONES, A. G., Chemical Engineering
JONES, D. T., Bioinformatics
JONES, J. S., Human Genetics
JONES, T. W., Physics
JORDAN, D., Physiology
JOWELL, J. L., Public Law
KAPLAN, B. J., Dutch History
KARLIN, D. R., English
KATONA, C. L. E., Psychiatry of the Elderly
KATZ, D. R., Immunopathology
KEMP, D. T., Auditory Biophysics
KHAW, P. T., Glaucoma Studies and Wound Healing
KING, M., Primary Care Psychiatry
KINNON, C., Molecular Immunology
KIRBY, D. G., Modern History
KIRSTEIN, P. T., Computer Systems
KLIER, J. D., Modern Jewish History
KOERNER, J. L., History of Art
KOLANKIEWICZ, J. M., Sociology
KUHRT, A. T. L., Ancient Near Eastern History
KULLMANN, D. M., Neurology
LARMAN, D. G., Mathematics
LAST, D. M., Anthropology
LATCHMAN, D. S., Human Genetics
LAURENT, G. J., Pulmonary Biochemistry
LAWRENCE, C. J., History of Medicine
LAYCOCK, G. K., Crime Science
LEES, A. J., Clinical Neurology

LEES, W. R., Medical Imaging
LEMON, R. N., Neurophysiology
LEONARD, J. V., Paediatric Metabolic Disease
LEWIS, A. D. E., Comparative Legal History
LIEBERMAN, A. R., Anatomy
LIGHTMAN, S. L., Clinical Ophthalmology
LIM, L., Neurochemistry
LINCH, D. C., Clinical Haematology
LINDON, J. M. A., Italian Studies
LITTLEWOOD, R., Anthropological Psychiatry
LLOYD, M. H., General Practice
LONDEI, M., Autoimmunity
LONGLEY, P. A., Geographic Information
LUMLEY, R., Italian Cultural History
LUND, V. J., Rhinology
LUTHERT, P. J., Pathology
LUXON, L. M., Audiological Medicine
LYDYARD, P. M., Immunology
MACHIN, S. J., Economics
MACHIN, S. J., Haematology
MACKETT, R. L., Transport Studies
MACLEAN, A. B., Obstetrics and Gynaecology
MACRORY, R. B., Environmental Law
MAJEED, F. A., Primary Care and Public Health
MALLET, J., Biological Diversity
MALONE-LEE, J. G., Geriatric Medicine
MARGETTS, H. Z., Political Science
MARKESINIS, B., Common Law and Civil Law
MARMOT, M. G., Epidemiology and Public Health
MARTIN, B. R. C., Physics
MARTIN, J. F., Cardiovascular Medicine
MARTIN, M. G. F., Philosophy
MARTIN, P., Tissue Repair
MASON, K. O., Astronomy
MASTERS, J. R. W., Experimental Pathology
MATHEWS, T. P., French
MATHIAS, C. J., Neurovascular Medicine
MCARTHUR, J. M., Geochemistry
MCCARTHY, M., Public Health
MCDOWELL, L. M., Economic Geography
MCEWEN, K. A., Physics
MCGUIRE, W. J., Geological Hazards
MCLEAN, P., Fine Art
MCMANUS, I. C., Psychology and Medical Education
MCMILLAN, P. F., Solid State Chemistry
MCMILLIN, A. B., Russian Literature
MCMULLEN, P., Mathematics
MEGHIR, C. H. D., Economics
MEREDITH, P. G., Rock Physics
MIDWINTER, J. E., Electrical Engineering
MILLA, P. J., Paediatric Gastroenterology
MILLER, A. I., History and Philosophy of Science
MILLER, D. H., Clinical Neurology
MILLER, D. J., Physics
MILLER, D. M. S., Anthropology
MIRSKY, R., Developmental Neurobiology
MOBBS, P. G., Physiology
MONCADA, S., Experimental Biology and Therapeutics
MONK, M., Molecular Embryology
MOORE, A. T., Ophthalmology
MORRIS, P. W. G., Construction and Project Management
MOSS, S. E., Biomedical Research
MOSS, S. J., Molecular Pharmacology and Cell Biology
MOTHERWELL, W. B., Chemistry
MULLER, J.-P. A. L., Image Understanding and Remote Sensing
MUNDY, A. R., Urology
MUNTON, R. J. C., Geography
MYTHEN, M. G., Paediatric Anaesthesia
NAZARETH, I. D., Primary Care and Population Science
NEILD, G. H., Nephrology
NEVILLE, B., Paediatric Neurology
NEWELL, M. L., Paediatric Epidemiology
NEWELL, W. R., Physics
NEWMAN, A. F., Economics
NEWMAN, S. P., Health Psychology
NORTH, J. A., History
NUGENT, J. H. A., Plant Biochemistry
NUTT, B. B., Facility and Environment Management
NUTTON, V., History of Medicine
O'DALY, G. J. P., Latin
O'HARE, M. J., Cell Biology
O'HIGGINS, P., Anatomy
O'KEEFE, J., Cognitive Neuroscience
O'KEEFFE, D., European Law
O'NEILL, M. E., Mathematics
O'REILLY, J. J., Telecommunications
ODA, H., Japanese Law
OLIVER, A. D. H., Constitutional Law
OLSEN, I., Cell Biology and Tissue Engineering
ONO, S. J., Ocular Immunology
ORDIDGE, R. J., Medical Physics
ORENGO, C. A., Bioinformatics
ORESZCZYN, T., Energy and Environment
ORTON, C. R., Quantitative Archaeology
OWEN, J. S., Molecular Medicine
PALMER, N. E., Law of Art and Cultural Property
PARKIN, I. P., Chemistry
PARMAR, M. K. B., Medical Statistics and Epidemiology
PARNAVELAS, J. G., Neuroanatomy
PARTRIDGE, L., Biometry
PATTISON, J. R., Medical Microbiology
PEARCE, D. W., Economics
PEARCE, F. L., Biological Chemistry
PECKHAM, C., Paediatric Epidemiology
PEPYS, M., Medicine
PERKINS, R. M., Norse Studies
PERKINS, S. J., Structural Biochemistry
PETTET, B. G., Company and Capital Markets Law
PHILLIPS, A., Epidemiology and Biostatistics
PICKERING, K. T., Sedimentology and Stratigraphy
PIERRO, A., Paediatric Surgery
PIPER, P. W., Molecular Microbiology
PITT, C. W., Electrical Engineering
PLATT, J. P., Geology
PLOTKIN, H. C., Psychobiology
POLLOCK, A. M., Health Services Policy
POMIANKOWSKI, A., Genetics
PORTER, J. B., Haematology
PORTER, S. R., Oral Medicine
POULTER, L. W., Immunology
POUNDER, R. E., Medicine
POVEY, M. S., Human Somatic Cell Genetics
POWER, C., Epidemiology and Public Health
POWIS, S. H., Renal Medicine
PRASHER, D. K., Audiology
PREECE, M., Child Health and Growth
PREISS, D., Pure Mathematics
PRICE, C. A., Archaeological Conservation
PRICE, G. D., Mineral Physics
PRICE, S. D., Chemical Physics
PRICE, S. L., Chemistry
PROWSE, P., Theatre Design
PYNSENT, R. B., Czech and Slovak Literature
QUINN, N. P., Clinical Neurology
RADEMACHER, T. W., Molecular Medicine
RAWSON, P. F., Geology
REHREN, T. H. H., Archaeological Materials and Technologies
REVELL, P. A., Histopathology
RICH, P. R., Bioenergetics
RICHARDS, C. D., Experimental Physiology
RICHARDS, P., Anthropology
RICHARDSON, W. D., Biology
ROBERTS, B. P., Chemistry
ROBERTS, G. J., Children's Dentistry
ROBERTSON, M. M., Neuropsychiatry
RODECK, C. H., Obstetrics and Gynaecology
ROEMER, C. E., Papyrology
RON, M. A., Neuropsychiatry
ROOK, G. A. W., Medical Microbiology
ROSEN, F. R., History of Political Thought
ROSEN, S., Speech and Hearing Sciences
ROTHWELL, J. C., Human Neurophysiology
ROWLAND, S. C. W., Higher Education
ROWLANDS, M. J. J., Material Culture
RUBIN, G. S., Visual Function and Rehabilitation
RUSSELL, M. A., Addiction
RYAN, J. M., Post-Conflict Recovery
SAGGERSON, E. D., Biochemistry
SALT, J., Geography
SALT, T. E., Visual Science
SALVERDA, R., Dutch Language and Literature
SAMMONDS, P. R., Geophysics
SANDER, J. W. A., Epilepsy
SANDS, P. J., Law
SAUNDERS, M. I., Oncology
SCAMBLER, G. N., Medical Sociology
SCAMBLER, P. J., Molecular Medicine
SCARAVILLI, F., Neuropathology
SCHAPIRA, A. H. V., Neurology
SCHOFIELD, T. P., History of Legal and Political Thought
SCULLY, C. M., Special Needs Dentistry
SEEDS, A. J., Opto-electronics
SEGAL, A. W., Medicine
SENN, S. J., Pharmaceutical and Health Statistics
SEYMOUR, R. M., Mathematics
SHALLICE, T., Psychology
SHANKS, D. R., Experimental Psychology
SHARPLES, R. W., Classics
SHEIHAM, A., Dental Public Health
SHENNAN, S. J., Theoretical Archaeology
SHEPHARD, E. A., Molecular Biology
SHEPHERD, P. R., Cellular Signalling
SHERR, L., Clinical and Health Psychology
SHORVON, S. D., Clinical Neurology
SILLITO, A. M., Visual Science
SIMONS, S. J. R., Chemical Engineering
SINDET-PEDERSEN, S., Oral Implantology
SINGER, A., Gynaecological Research
SINGER, M., Intensive Care Medicine
SLATER, M., Virtual Environments
SMART, T. G., Pharmacology
SMITH, A., Detector Physics
SMITH, A. H., Political Economy
SMITH, F. T., Mathematics
SMITH, N. V., Linguistics
SMITH, S. R., Economics
SNOWDON, P. F.
SOMMER, V., Evolutionary Anthropology
SOUTHGATE, L. J., Primary Care and Education
SPEIGHT, P. M., Oral Pathology
SPELLER, R. D., Medical Physics
SPIRO, S. G., Respiratory Medicine
SPOOR, C. F., Evolutionary Anatomy
SPYER, K. M., Physiology
STANFORD, J. L., Medical Microbiology
STEADMAN, J. P., Urban and Built Form Studies
STEPHENS, J. A., Physiology
STEPTOE, A. P. A., Psychology
STOCKMAN, A., Investigative Eye Research
STOCKS, J., Respiratory Medicine
STONEHAM, A. M., Physics
STOREY, P. J., Physics
STROBEL, S., Paediatrics and Clinical Immunology
SURTEES, R. A. H., Paediatric Neurology
SUTHERLAND, J. A., Modern English Literature
SUTTON, S. R., Social and Health Psychology
SWALES, M. W., German
SWALLOW, D. M., Biology
SWANN, P. F., Molecular Oncology
SWANSON, T. M., Law and Economics
TAIT, W. J., Egyptology
TAYLOR, B., Community Child Health
TAYLOR, I., Surgery
TEDDER, R. S., Medical Virology
TENNYSON, J., Physics
THIMBLEBY, H. W., Human Interaction with Systems
THOMAS, D. G. T., Neurological Surgery
THOMAS, K. D., Human Palaeoecology
THOMPSON, A. J., Clinical Neurology and Neurorehabilitation
THOMPSON, E. J., Neurochemistry
THORNTON, J. M., Biomolecular Structure
THRASHER, A. J., Paediatric Immunology

TILLEY, C. Y., Anthropology and Archaeology
TITCHENER-HOOKER, N. J., Biochemical Engineering
TOBIAS, J. S., Cancer Medicine
TODD, C. J., Network Science
TODD-POKROPEK, A. E., Medical Physics
TOFTS, P. S., Medical Physics
TOMKINS, A. M., International Child Health
TONETTI, M., Periodontology
TOOK, J. F., Dante Studies
TRELEAVEN, P. C., Computer Science
TRIMBLE, M. R., Behavioural Neurology
TURNER, M. W., Molecular Immunology
TURNER, R., Anthropology
TWINING, W. L., Jurisprudence
TYLER, N. A., Communities and Transport
UCKO, P. J., Comparative Archaeology
UNWIN, R., Nephrology and Physiology
VALLANCE, P., Clinical Pharmacology
VAN DER LELY, H. K. J., Developmental Language Disorders and Cognitive Neuroscience
VAN GRIETHUYSEN, W. J., Naval Architecture
VAN REENEN, J. M., Economics
VARGHA-KHADEM, F., Developmental Cognitive Neuroscience
VERGANI, D., Immunopathology
WAKELY, P. I., Urban Development
WALTON, S. J., Norwegian
WARDLE, F. J., Clinical Psychology
WARNER, A. E., Developmental Biology
WASHBROOK, J., Computer Science
WATERFIELD, M. D., Biochemistry
WEIS, R. J., English
WEISS, R. A., Viral Oncology
WELLER, I. V. D., Sexually Transmitted Diseases
WELLS, J. C., Phonetics
WESTON, H. D., History of Art
WHITEHOUSE, R. D., Archaeology
WIGZELL, F. C. M., Russian Literature and Culture
WILBUR, S. R., Distributed Systems
WILKIN, C., Physics
WILLIAMS, G. H., Histopathology
WILLIAMS, R. S., Hepatology
WILLIS, A. J., Astronomy
WILSON, D. S. M., Linguistics
WILSON, E. J., Latin American Literature
WILSON, M., Microbiology
WILSON, S. W., Developmental Genetics
WINCHESTER, B. G., Biochemistry
WINGHAM, D. J., Climate Physics
WINSLET, M. C., Surgery
WINTER, R. M., Clinical Genetics
WOLEDGE, R. C., Experimental Physiology
WOLFF, J., Philosophy
WOLPERT, D. M., Motor Neuroscience
WOLPERT, L., Biology as applied to Medicine
WOO, P. M. M., Paediatric Rheumatology
WOOD, N. W., Clinical Neurogenetics
WOOD, P. A., Geography
WOOLF, A. S., Nephrology
WORTON, M. J., French Language and Literature
WOTTON, R. S., Biology
WOUDHUYSEN, H. R., English Language and Literature
WRIGHT, A., Otorhinolaryngology
WU, G., Computational Fluid Dynamics
WYATT, J. S., Neonatal Paediatrics
YANG, Z., Statistical Genetics
YATES, J. G., Chemical Engineering
YELLON, D. M., Cellular Cardiology
YIP, M. J., Linguistics
YOUSRY, T. A., Neuroradiology
YUDKIN, J. S., Medicine
ZEKI, S., Neurobiology
ZUMLA, A., Infectious Diseases and International Health

SCHOOL OF THE COLLEGE

UCL School of Slavonic and East European Studies: Univ. of London, London, WC1E 7HU; tel. (20) 7636-8000; f. 1915, merged with Univ. College London 1999; library of 400,000 vols; 60 teachers; 500 students (460 full-time, 40 part-time); Dir. Dr ROBIN P. AIZLEWOOD; Academic Registrar CAROL PEARCE; publ. *The Slavonic and East European Review* (4 a year).

UNIVERSITY INSTITUTES

University of London Institute in Paris

9–11 rue de Constantine, 75340 Paris Cedex 07, France
Telephone: (1) 44-11-73-73
Fax: (1) 45-50-31-55
E-mail: french@ulip.lon.ac.uk
Internet: www.ulip.lon.ac.uk

Founded 1894 as 'Guilde Franco-Anglaise', attached to Univ. of Paris 1927, now a central institute of Univ. of London, partner of Queen Mary and Royal Holloway, Univ. of London
Academic year: September to July
Languages of instruction: French, English

Dean: Prof. ANDREW HUSSEY
Project Man.: ANNA GRAY
Office Man.: COLLETTE BROWN
Librarian: ERICA BURNHAM

Library of 10,000 vols; 25 journals and electronic subscriptions
Number of teachers: 13
Number of students: 160 f.t.e.

PROFESSORS

HUSSEY, A., French Studies

University Marine Biological Station Millport

Millport, Isle of Cumbrae, Scotland, KA28 0EG
Telephone: (1475) 530581
Fax: (1475) 530601
E-mail: tracy.price@millport.gla.ac.uk
Internet: www.gla.ac.uk/marinestation

Founded 1970 in assen with Univ. of Glasgow

Teaches and researches in marine biology

Library of 5,000 vols

Dir: Prof. JIM ATKINSON (acting)
Deputy Dir: FIONA HANNAH
Sec.: TRACY E. PRICE

PROFESSORS

ATKINSON, R. J. A., Marine Biology
MOORE, P. G., Marine Biology.

CONSTITUENT INSTITUTES OF THE SCHOOL OF ADVANCED STUDY

Dean of the School of Advanced Study: Prof. C. N. J. MANN

School of Advanced Studies

17 Russell Sq., London, WC1B 5DR
Telephone: (20) 7862-5800
Fax: (20) 7862-5850
E-mail: ials@sas.ac.uk
Internet: www.ials.sas.ac.uk
Academic year: October to December

Founded 1947

Man.: MARGARET R. WILSON
Assoc. Dir and Librarian: JULES WINTERTON

Library: see Libraries and Archives

Publication: *Amicus Curiae*

PROFESSORS

DAINTITH, T. C., Constitutional and Admin. Law, Economic Law
RIDER, B. A. K., Company Law, Commercial Criminal Law
SHERR, A. H., Legal Education, the Legal Profession, Legal Services

Institute of Classical Studies

Senate House, Malet St, London, WC1E 7HU
Telephone: (20) 7862-8705
Fax: (20) 7862-8722
E-mail: icls.publications@sas.ac.uk
Internet: www.icls.sas.ac.uk/institute

Founded 1953

Library of basic research books complemented by library of Hellenic and Roman Societies (jt library of 100,000 vols); research courses and seminars held for postgraduate students

Dir: Prof. MIKE EDWARDS
Sec.: Dr OLGA KRZYSZKOWSKA

Publications: *Bulletin* (1 a year), *Bulletin Supplements*.

Institute of Commonwealth Studies

Second Fl., S Block, Senate House, Malet St, London, WC1E 7HU
Telephone: (20) 7262-8844
Fax: (20) 7262-8813
E-mail: ics@sas.ac.uk
Internet: commonwealth.sas.ac.uk

Founded 1949
Academic year: September to June

Dir: Prof. PHILIP MURPHY
Admin. Man.: ALISON STEWART
Information Resources Man.: DAVID CLOVER

Library of 190,000 vols, 9,000 periodical and serial publs, 230 archival collns
Number of teachers: 5 (full-time)
Number of students: 80

Publication: *Journal of Imperial and Commonwealth History* (4 a year)

PROFESSORS

HOLLAND, R., Imperial and Commonwealth History
MANOR, J., Emeka Anyaoku prof. of Commonwealth Studies
MURPHY, P., British and Commonwealth History

ATTACHED INSTITUTE

Commonwealth Policy Studies Unit (CPSU): internet www.cpsu.org.uk; Head Dr VICTORIA TE VELDE; Asst Dir Dr LEO ZEILIG.

Institute of English Studies

School of Advanced Study, Senate House, Malet St, London, WC1E 7HU
Telephone: (20) 7862-8675
Fax: (20) 7862-8720
E-mail: ies@sas.ac.uk
Internet: ies.sas.ac.uk

Founded 1991 as Centre for English Studies; present name 1999
State control
Academic year: September to June

Dir: Prof. WARWICK GOULD

Number of teachers: 35
Number of students: 28

Institute of Germanic and Romance Studies

Senate House, Malet St, London, WC1E 7HU
Telephone: (20) 7862-8677
Fax: (20) 7862-8672
E-mail: igrs@sas.ac.ukGermanic Studies Library: 29 Russell Sq., London, WC1B 5DP
Telephone: (20) 7862-8967
Fax: (20) 7862-8970
E-mail: igslib@sas.ac.uk
Internet: igrs.sas.ac.uk

Founded 2004, by merger of Institute of Germanic Studies (f. 1950) and Institute of Romance Studies (f. 1989)

Academic year: October to June
Dir: Prof. NAOMI SEGAL
Admin. Sec.: ROSEMARY LAMBETH
Librarian: WILLIAM ABBEY; 1,320 mems
Library of 100,000 vols
Number of teachers: 6
Number of students: 25
Publications: *Journal of Romance Studies* (3 a year), *London German Studies* (irregular).

Institute of Historical Research

Senate House, Malet St., London, WC1E 7HU
Telephone: (20) 7862-8740
Fax: (20) 7862-8745
E-mail: ihr@sas.ac.uk
Internet: www.history.ac.uk
Founded 1921
Academic year: October to August
Dir: Prof. MILES TAYLOR
Institute Administrator: ELAINE WALTERS
Librarian: ALISON GAGE
Library: see Libraries and Archives
Number of teachers: 8
Number of students: 57
Publications: *Historical Research* (4 a year), *Past and Future*, *Teachers of History* (1 a year), *Theses in Progress and Theses Completed* (1 a year)

PROFESSORS

ROBERTS, R., Contemporary British History
TAYLOR, M., Modern History
THANE, P., Contemporary British History

Institute of Musical Research

Senate House, Malet St, London, WC1E 7HU
Telephone: (20) 7664-4865
Fax: (20) 7664-4867
E-mail: music@sas.ac.uk
Internet: music.sas.ac.uk
Founded 2005, began operating 2006
Funded by HEFCE; fosters collaborative research; hosts visiting scholars; organizes confs and other events; provides research training support for postgraduate students
Dir: Prof. JOHN IRVING
Administrator: VALERIE JAMES.

Institute of Philosophy

Senate House, Malet St, London, WC1E 7HU
Telephone: (20) 7862-8683
Fax: (20) 7862-8639
E-mail: philosophy@sas.ac.uk
Internet: www.philosophy.sas.ac.uk
Founded 2005
Promotes and disseminates research in philosophy
Dir: Prof. BARRY C. SMITH
Administrator: Dr SHAHRAR ALI.

Institute for the Study of the Americas

Senate House, Malet St, London, WC1H 7HU
Telephone: (20) 7862-8870
Fax: (20) 7862-8886
E-mail: americas@sas.ac.uk
Internet: www.americas.sas.ac.uk
Founded 2004 by merger of Institute of Latin American Studies (f. 1964) and Institute of United States Studies (f. 1965)
Academic year: October to July
Dir: Prof. MAXINE MOLYNEUX
Admin. Man.: PAUL SULLIVAN
Librarian: CHRISTINE ANDERSON
Number of teachers: 9
Number of students: 80
Publication: *Journal of Latin American Studies* (4 a year)

PROFESSORS

MIDDLEBROOK, K., Politics
MOLYNEUX, M., Sociology
MORGAN, I., United States Studies

Warburg Institute

Woburn Sq., London, WC1H 0AB
Telephone: (20) 7862-8949
Fax: (20) 7862-8955
E-mail: warburg@sas.ac.uk
Internet: www.warburg.sas.ac.uk
Founded 1921
Academic year: October to September
Dir: Prof. P. W. MACK
Sec. and Registrar: ANITA C. POLLARD
Librarian: Prof. JILL KRAYE
Library: see Libraries and Archives
Number of teachers: 5
Number of students: 21
Publications: *Journal of the Warburg and Courtauld Institutes* (1 a year), *Warburg Institute Colloquia* (1 a year), *Warburg Studies and Texts* (irregular)

PROFESSORS

BURNETT, C. S. F., History of Islamic Influences in Europe
HOPE, C., History of the Classical Tradition
KRAYE, J. A., History of Renaissance Philosophy
MCGRATH, E., History of Art.

ASSOCIATE INSTITUTION

The following institution has recognized teachers of the University of London on its staff and offers courses leading to degrees of the University.

Institute of Cancer Research: 123 Old Brompton Rd, London, SW7 3RP; tel. (20) 7352-8133; fax (20) 7370-5261; internet www.icr.ac.uk; f. 1909; library of 25,000 vols; Chief Exec. Prof. ALAN ASHWORTH; Sec. CATHY SCIVIER; Academic Dean Prof. ALAN HORWICH.

UNIVERSITY OF MANCHESTER

Oxford Rd, Manchester, M13 9PL
Telephone: (161) 306-6000
E-mail: ug-admissions@manchester.ac.uk
Internet: www.manchester.ac.uk
Founded 2004 following merger of Univ. of Manchester (f. 1851) and UMIST (f. 1824)
Academic year: September to June
Chancellor: TOM BLOXHAM
Pres. and Vice-Chancellor: Prof. Dame NANCY J. ROTHWELL
Deputy Pres. and Deputy Vice-Chancellor: Prof. ROD COOMBS
Pro-Chancellor: NORMAN ASKEW (Chair. of the Board of Governors)
Pro-Chancellor: Sir JOHN KERR
Registrar and Sec.: ALBERT MCMENEMY
Vice-Pres.: Prof. COLIN BAILEY
Vice-Pres.: Prof. KEITH BROWN
Vice-Pres.: Prof. MARTIN HUMPHRIES
Vice-Pres.: Prof. ALAN NORTH
Vice-Pres. for Research and Innovation: Prof. LUKE GEORGHIOU
Vice-Pres. for Teaching and Learning: Prof. COLIN STIRLING
Univ. Librarian: JAN WILKINSON
Library: See John Rylands Univ. Library of Manchester
Number of teachers: 3,972
Number of students: 37,021

DEANS

Faculty of Engineering and Physical Sciences: Prof. COLIN BAILEY
Faculty of Humanities: Prof. KEITH BROWN
Faculty of Life Sciences: Prof. MARTIN HUMPHRIES
Faculty of Medical and Human Sciences: Prof. ALAN NORTH

PROFESSORS

Faculty of Engineering and Physical Sciences

School of Chemical Engineering and Analytical Science:

ALDER, J. F.
CILLIERS, J.
DAVEY, R.
DEWHURST, R.
DYAKOWSKI, T.
FIELDEN, P.
GODDARD, N.
GRIFFITHS, R.
HEGGS, P.
MANN, R.
MAVITUNA, F.
MCCARTHY, J.
PERSAUD, K.
ROBERTS, S.
SHARRATT, P.
SMITH, R.
SNOOK, R.
TIDDY, G.
VICKERMAN, J.
WEBB, C.

School of Chemistry:

ANDERSON, N. W.
BAILEY, P. D.
CLARKE, J. H. R.
CLAYDEN, J. P.
CONNOR, J. N. L.
GASKELL, S. J.
HELLIWELL, J. R.
HILLIER, I. H.
KELL, D. B.
LIVENS, F. R.
MORRIS, G. A.
MUNN, R. W.
O'BRIEN, P.
STOODLEY, R. J.
SUTHERLAND, J.
TAIT, P. J. T.
THOMAS, E. J.
TURNER, M.
VICKERMAN, J. C.
WAUGH, K. C.
WINPENNY, R.
WOODPENNY, L. V.

School of Computer Science:

ACZEL, P.
BARRINGER, H.
BARTON, S.
BREE, D.
FURBER, S.
GOBLE, C.
GURD, J.
HORROCKS, I.
HUBBOLD, R.
KAHN, H.
MIDDLETON, B.
PATON, N.
RECTOR, A.
TAYLOR, C.
VORONKOV, A.
WARBOYS, B.
WATSON, I.

School of Earth, Atmospheric and Environmental Sciences:

CHOULARTON, T. W., Atmospheric Physics
CURTIS, C., Geochemistry
GAWTHORPE, R., Sedimentation and Tectonics
HENDERSON, M., Petrology
JONAS, P. R., Atmospheric Physics
PATTRICK, R., Earth Sciences
RUTTER, E., Earth Sciences
SELDEN, P., Earth Sciences
TURNER, G., Earth Sciences
VAUGHAN, D., Mineralogy
VAUGHAN, G., Atmospheric Sciences
ZUSSMAN, Z., Earth Sciences

School of Electrical and Electronic Engineering:

ALLINSON, N. M.
BROWN, A. K.
DAVIS, L. E.
GOTT, G. F.
HICKS, P. J.
JENKINS, N.
KIRSCHEN, D.
MCCANN, H.
MISSOUS, M.
MUNRO, N.
PEAKER, A. R.
REZAZADEH, A.
STRBAC, G.
WANG, H.
WILLIAMSON, S.
YORK, T. A.

School of Materials:

DERBY, B., Materials Science
FREER, R., Materials Science
HUMPHREYS, F. J., Materials Science
LORIMER, G., Materials Science
LOVELL, P., Polymer Science
O'BRIEN, P., Inorganic Materials, Chemistry
ROBERTS, J., Textiles and Paper
SALE, F., Chemical Metallurgy and Materials Science
SHERRY, A., Corrosion and Protection
STANFORD, J., Polymer Materials Science
STOTT, H., Corrosion and Protection
THOMPSON, G., Corrosion and Protection
WITHERS, P., Materials Science
YOUNG, R., Polymer Science and Technology

School of Mathematics:

ABRAHAMS, I. D., Applied Mathematics
ACZEL, P. H., Mathematical Logic and Computing Science
BOROVIK, A., Pure Mathematics
BROOMHEAD, D., Applied Mathematics
BRYANT, R., Pure Mathematics
DODSON, K., Geometry
DOLD, J., Applied Mathematics
DONEY, R. A., Probability Theory
DUCK, P. W., Applied Mathematics
GLENDINNING, P., Applied Mathematics
HIGHAM, N. J., Applied Mathematics
PARIS, J. B., Pure Mathematics
PLYMEN, R. J., Pure Mathematics
PREMET, A. A., Algebra
PREST, M., Pure Mathematics
RAY, N., Pure Mathematics
ROWLEY, P., Mathematics
RUBAN, A., Computational Fluid Dynamics
SILVESTER, D., Applied Mathematics
SUBBA RAO, T., Statistics
TAYLOR, M. J., Pure Mathematics
WOOD, R. M. W., Algebra

School of Mechanical, Aerospace and Civil Engineering:

AL-HASSANI, S. T. S., Mechanical Engineering
BAILEY, C., Structural Engineering
BALL, A. D., Maintenance Engineering
COOPER, J. E., Engineering
DAVIES, M., Structural Engineering
HAYHURST, D. R., Design, Manufacture and Materials
HINDUJA, S., Mechanical Engineering
JACKSON, J. D., Mechanical and Nuclear Engineering
LAUNDER, B. E., Mechanical Engineering
LAURENCE, D., Computational Fluid Dynamics
LEUNG, A., Engineering
LEVERMORE, G., Built Environment
LI, L., Laser Engineering
MARSDEN, B., Nuclear Graphite Technology
REID, S. R., Mechanical Engineering
SANDOZ, D. J., Control Engineering
SMITH, I., Geotechnics
STANSBY, P., Hydrodynamics
THOMPSON, G., Mechanical Engineering
TURAN, A., Mechanical Engineering
VARLOW, B. R., Industrial Liaison
WINCH, G., Construction Project Management
WOOD, N., Aerospace Engineering
WRIGHT, J. R., Mechanical Engineering

School of Physics and Astronomy:

BARLOW, S. J., Particle Physics
BISHOP, R. F., Theoretical Physics
BRAY, A. J., Theoretical Physics
DIAMOND, P. D., Astronomy and Astrophysics
DURELL, J. L., Nuclear Physics
FLAVELL, W. R., Photon Physics
FORSHAW, J. R., Particle Physics
GEIM, A. K., Condensed Matter Physics
GLEESON, H. F., Nonlinear and Liquid Crystal Physics
KING, G. C., Photon Physics
KING, T. A., Photon Physics
LAFFERTY, G. D., Particle Physics
LU, J., Biological Physics
LYNE, A. G., Astronomy and Astrophysics
MARSHALL, R., Particle Physics
MILLAR, T. J., Astronomy and Astrophysics
MOORE, M. A., Theoretical Physics
MULLIN, T., Nonlinear and Liquid Crystal Physics
WALET, N. R., Theoretical Physics
WILKINSON, P. N., Astronomy and Astrophysics
WYATT, T. R., Particle Physics
ZIJLSTRA, A. A., Astronomy and Astrophysics

Faculty of Humanities

School of Arts, Histories and Culture:

ADAMSON, S., Linguistics and Literary History
ALEXANDER, P., Post-Biblical Jewish Studies
BERGIN, J., Modern History
BROOKE, G. J., Biblical Studies
CASKEN, J., Music
CAUSEY, A., Modern Art History
COOPER, B., Music
CORNELL, T., Ancient History
CROWLEY, T., Modern English Literature
DENISON, D., English Linguistics
EAGLETON, T., Cultural Theory
FALLOWS, D., Music
FANNING, D., Music
FOURACRE, P., History
GARDNER, V., Theatre Studies
GATRELL, P., Modern History
GRAHAM, E. L., Social and Pastoral Theology
GRANGE, P., Music
HAMMOND, G., English Literature
HOGG, R. M., English Language and Medieval English Literature
JACKSON, B. S., Modern Jewish Studies
JANTZEN, G. M., Philosophy of Religion
JONES, A., History of Art
JOYCE, P., Modern History
LANGSLOW, D., Classics
LING, R., Archaeology
MILLWARD, R., Economic History
PARKIN, T., Ancient History
PEARSON, J., English Literature
PITTOCK, M., Scottish and Romantic Literature
SCRAGG, D., Anglo-Saxon Studies
SHARROCK, A., Classics
SUMMERFIELD, P., Modern History
THOMAS, J., Archaeology
WARD, B., American Studies
WARD, G., Contextual Theology
WOOLFORD, J., 19th-century Literature and Culture

School of Education:

AINSCOW, M., Education
BAMFORD, J., Audiology and Deaf Education
CONTI-RAMSDEN, G., Specific Language Impairment
DAVIES, A., Education
DYSON, A., Education
FARRELL, P., Educational Psychology
THOMPSON, L., Language and Literacy Studies
WEST, M., Educational Leadership
WILLIAMS, J. S., Mathematics Education

School of Environment and Development:

AGNEW, C., Geography
ALLOTT, T., Geography
BEBBINGTON, A., Management in International Development
BRADFORD, M., Geography
CASTREE, N., Geography
COOK, P., Economics and Development Policy
DOUGLAS, I., Geography
HANDLEY, J., Land Restoration and Management
HEBBERT, M., Town Planning
HENDERSON, J., International Economic Sociology
HULME, D., Development Studies
KIRKPATRICK, C., Development Economics
MACDOUGALL, G., Architecture and Advanced Technology
ROBSON, B., Geography
STONEHOUSE, R., Architecture
THOMAS, R., Geography
WILLIAMS, G., Urban Planning and Development
WOOD, C., Environmental Planning

School of Informatics:

BLENKHORN, P., Interactive Systems Design
KEANE, J., Data and Decision Engineering
LOUCOPOULOS, P., Information Systems
MACAULAY, L., System Design
RAMSAY, A., Data and Decision Engineering
SUTCLIFFE, A., Interactive Systems Design
WASTELL, D., Information Systems
WOOD, J., Information Systems
WOOD-HARPER, A., Information Systems

School of Languages, Linguistics and Cultures:

ALEXANDER, P. S., Middle Eastern Studies
BERGER, S., Modern German and Comparative European History
DURRELL, M., German
GÜNSBERG, M., Italian
LAWRANCE, J., Spanish
PARKER, S., German
PERRIAM, C., Hispanic Studies
SMITH, G. R., Middle Eastern Studies
TOLZ, V., Russian

School of Law:

BRAZIER, M., Law
BRAZIER, R., Law
DOBASH, R., Law
DUXBURY, N., Law
GIBBONS, T., Law
HARRIS, J., Law
HARRIS, N., Law
HÄYRY, M., Law
JACONELLI, J., Law
MCCORMACK, G., Law
MCGEE, A., Law
MILLMAN, D., Law
OGUS, A., Law
QURESHI, A., Law
SANDERS, A., Law
SHAW, J., Law
TSUJII, J., Text Mining

Manchester Business School:

BARRAR, P., Operations Management
BOWE, M., International Finance
BRUCE, M., Design Management and Retailing

CHITTENDEN, F., Small Business Finance
CONYON, M., Corporate Governance
COOMBS, R., Technology Management
DAVIDSON, M., Managerial Psychology
DAVIES, G., Corporate Reputation
EASINGWOOD, C., Marketing
EDWARDS, P., Accountancy
FRENCH, S., Information and Decision Sciences
GARRETT, I., Accounting and Finance
GEORGHIOU, L., Technology and Entrepreneurship Management and Policy
GHAURI, P., International Business
GREEN, K., Technology and Entrepreneurship Management and Policy
HASSARD, J., Organizational Analysis
HIGGINS, J., Health Policy
HOWELLS, J., Innovation and Competition
HUMPHREY, C., Accounting
JACKSON, P., Corporate Communications
KANG, J., Marketing
LEWIS, B., Marketing
LITTLER, D., Strategic Management
MARCHINGTON, M., Human Resource Management
MCGOLDRICK, P., Retailing
MILES, I., Technology and Entrepreneurship Management and Policy
NAUDÉ, P., Marketing
NEWMAN, M., Management Accounting and Information Systems
OAKEY, R., Business Development
OGDEN, S., Accounting and Finance
O'LEARY, T., Accounting
PAXSON, D., Finance
POON, S.-H., Finance
RICKARDS, T., Creativity and Organizational Change
ROBSON, K., Accounting
RUBERY, J., Comparative Employment Systems
SANGHAVI, N., Retail Marketing and Strategy
SCAPENS, R., Management Accounting and Information Systems
SPARROW, P., International Human Resource Management
STAPLETON, R., Finance
STARK, A., Accounting
STEPHEN, F., Regulation
STRONG, N., Finance
TURLEY, S., Accounting
WADDINGTON, J., Human Resource Management
WALKER, M., Finance and Accounting
WALSH, V., Innovation Management
WALSHE, K., Health Policy and Management
WILLIAMS, K., Accounting and Political Economy
YANG, J.-B., Decision Sciences and Operations Management

School of Social Sciences:

AGÉNOR, P.-R., Economics
BLACKBURN, K., Economics
CALLAHAN, W., International Politics
COLMAN, D., Economics
EVSTIGNEEV, I., Economics
GLEDHILL, J., Social Anthropology
HARVEY, P., Social Anthropology
HENLEY, P., Social Anthropology
MADDEN, P., Economics
MASON, J., Sociology
METCALFE, S., Economics
NIXSON, F., Economics
OSBORN, D., Economics
SMART, C., Sociology
WADE, P., Social Anthropology
WERBNER, R., Social Anthropology
YOUNG, T., Economics

Faculty of Life Sciences:

ABADI, R.
ATTWOOD, T.
BALMENT, R.
BARNES, G.
BRASS, A.
BROWN, T. A.
BULLEID, N.
CASE, M.
CHARMAN, W.
CRONLY-DILLON, J.
CROSSMAN, A.
DAVID, R.
DIXON, M.
DUNNE, M.
EDDY, A.
EFRON, N.
FERGUSON, M.
FOSTER, D.
GARROD, D.
GRANT, M.
GRENCIS, R.
HARDINGHAM, T.
HIGH, S.
HUMPHRIES, M.
HUTCHINSON, I.
HYDE, J. E.
ITZHAKI, R.
KADLER, K.
KAUPPINEN, R.
KIELTY, C.
KULIKOWSKI, J.
LIAN, L. Y.
LOUDON, A.
MCCARTHY, J. E. G.
MOORE, A.
NORTH, R. A.
OLIVER, S.
PICKSTONE, J.
POLLER, L.
ROBERTS, I.
ROTHWELL, N.
SHARROCKS, A.
SIBLEY, C.
STERN, P.
STIRLING, C.
STREULI, C.
TERENGHI, G.
TOMLINSON, D.
TRINCI, A.
TURNER, S.
VERKHRATSKY, A.
WESTON, A.
WHETTON, A. D.
WHITE, A.
WORBOYS, M.

Faculty of Medical and Human Sciences

School of Dentistry:

BLINKHORN, A. S., Oral Health
DIXON, M. J., Dental Genetics
FERGUSON, M. W. J., Basic Dental Sciences
O'BRIEN, K. D., Orthodontics
SHAW, W. C., Orthodontics and Dentofacial Development
SLOAN, P., Experimental Oral Pathology
THORNHILL, M. H., Medicine in Dentistry
WILSON, N. H. F., Restorative Dentistry

School of Medicine:

ADAMS, J. E., Diagnostic Radiology
AGIUS, R., Occupational and Environmental Medicine
BIRCH, J. M., Cancer Research Campaign, Paediatric and Familial Cancer Research Group
BOULTON, A. J. M., Medicine
BURNIE, J. P., Medical Microbiology
CASE, R. M., Physiology
CHERRY, N. M., Occupational and Environmental Medicine
CROSSMAN, A. R., Anatomy
DAVID, T. J., Child Health and Paediatrics
DAVIS, J. R. E., Medicine
DUNN, G., Biomedical Statistics
DURRINGTON, P. N., Medicine
EDEN, O. B., Paediatric Oncology
EISNER, D., Cardiac Physiology
FREEMONT, A. J., Tissue Pathology
GALASKO, C. S. B., Orthopaedic Surgery
GALLAGHER, S. T., Oncology
GARROD, D. R., Developmental Biology
GORDON, D., Medicine
GRANT, M. E., Medical Biochemistry
GREEN, R., Physiology
GRENCIS, R. K., Immunology
GRIFFITHS, C. E. M., Dermatology
HAWKINS, R. E., Medical Oncology
HEAGERTY, A., Medicine
HELLER, R., Public Health
HERHOLZ, K., Clinical Neurosciences
HICKMAN, J., Molecular Pharmacology
HORAN, M. A., Geriatric Medicine (South)
HOWELL, A., Medical Oncology
HUTCHINSON, I. V., Immunology
IRVING, M. H., Surgery
JACKSON, A., Neuroradiology
KIERNAN, C. C., Behavioural Studies in Mental Handicap
KIRKWOOD, T. B. L., Biological Gerontology
KITCHENER, H. C., Gynaecological Oncology
LOWENSTEIN, P. R., Molecular Medicine and Gene Therapy
MALLICK, N. P., Renal Medicine
MAWER, E. B., Bone and Mineral Metabolism
MAYES, A., Cognitive Neuroscience
MCALLISTER, I., Medicine
MCCLURE, J., Pathology
MCCOLLUM, C. N., Surgery
MCCORD, J. F., Restorative Care of the Elderly
MCLEOD, D., Ophthalmology
MÜLLER, R., Pharmaceutics, Biopharmaceutics and Biotechnology
O'BRIEN, K. D., Orthodontics
OLLIER, W. E. R., Immunogenetics
POLLARD, B. J., Anaesthesia
PRICE, P., Radiation Oncology
READ, A. P., Human Genetics
RECTOR, A. L., Medical Informatics
ROLAND, M. O., General Practice
SCARFFE, J. H., Oncology
SEYMOUR, L., Gene Therapy
SIBBALD, B. S., Health Services Research
SIBLEY, C. P., Child Health and Physiology
SILMAN, A. J., Rheumatic Diseases Epidemiology
STANLEY, J. K., Hand Surgery
TALLIS, R. C., Geriatric Medicine (Salford)
TAYLOR, C. J., Medical Biophysics
THATCHER, N., Oncology
THOMPSON, D. G., Gastroenterology
VADGAMA, P., Clinical Biochemistry
WHITE, A., Endocrine Sciences
WHITEHOUSE, C. R., Teaching Medicine in the Community
WILKIN, D., Health Services Research
WOODMAN, C. B. J., Cancer Epidemiology and Public Health
YATES, D. W., Accident and Emergency Surgery

School of Nursing, Midwifery and Social Work:

CARLISLE, E., Education in Nursing and Midwifery
LUKER, K., Nursing and Midwifery
THOMSON, A., Midwifery
TODD, C., Primary Care and Community Health
WATERMAN, H., Nursing and Midwifery

School of Pharmacy and Pharmaceutical Sciences:

ATTWOOD, D.
CANTRILL, J.
CLARKE, D.
COLLETT, J.
DIVE, C.
DOUGLAS, K.
GIFFORD, L.
GILBERT, P.
HOUSTON, J. B.
NOYCE, P.
ROWLAND, M.
STRATFORD, I.

School of Psychological Sciences:
BAMFORD, J.
BARROWCLOUGH, C.
BEATTIE, G.
BENTALL, R.
CONTI-RAMSEN, G.
DAVIS, A.
LAMBON-RALPH, M.
LIEVEN, E.
MEUDELL, P.
PARKER, D.
TARRIER, N.
WEARDEN, J. H.

UNIVERSITY OF NORTHAMPTON

Park Campus, Boughton Green Rd, Northampton, NN2 7AL
Ave Campus, St George's Ave, Northampton, NN2 6JD
Telephone: (1604) 735500
Fax: (1604) 720636
E-mail: study@northampton.ac.uk
Internet: www.northampton.ac.uk

Founded 1975 by merger of College of Education, College of Technology and College of Art, present name and status 2005
Academic year: September to July

Chancellor: Baroness FALKNER OF MARGRAVINE
Vice-Chancellor: ANN TATE
Vice-Chancellor: Prof. NICK PETFORD
Pro-Vice-Chancellor for Acad.: Prof. PETER BUSH
Pro-Vice-Chancellor for Research and Devt: Dr FRANK BURDETT
Pro-Vice-Chancellor for Strategic Planning and Resources: JOHN HOSKINSON

Library of 375,000 vols, 15,000 journals
Number of teachers: 465
Number of students: 10,000

DEANS
School of Education: Prof. ANN SHELTON MAYES
School of Health: Dr SUE ALLEN
School of Science and Technology: Prof. KAMAL BECHKOUM
School of Social Sciences: CHRIS MOORE
School of the Arts: PAUL MIDDLETON
Northampton Business School: Dr IAN BROOKS

UNIVERSITY OF NOTTINGHAM

University Park, Nottingham, NG7 2RD
Telephone: (115) 951-5151
Fax: (115) 951-3666
Internet: www.nottingham.ac.uk

Founded 1881, Univ. Charter 1948
Academic year: September to August

Chancellor: Prof. YANG FUJIA
Vice-Chancellor: Prof. Sir DAVID GREENAWAY
Pro-Vice-Chancellor for Environment, Infrastructure and Information Services: Prof. ALAN DODSON
Pro-Vice-Chancellor for Human Resources, Access and Community Relations: Prof. KAREN COX
Pro-Vice-Chancellor for Internationalization: Prof. CHRISTINE ENNEW
Pro-Vice-Chancellor for Knowledge Transfer, Business Engagement, Devt and Alumni Relations Office: Prof. CHRIS RUDD
Pro-Vice-Chancellor for Research and Graduate School: Prof. BOB WEBB
Pro-Vice-Chancellor for Teaching and Learning: Prof. SAUL TENDLER
Registrar: Dr PAUL GREATRIX

Library: see Libraries and Archives
Number of teachers: 2,700
Number of students: 32,044

Publications: *Exchange Magazine*, *Gazette*, *Global Review*

DEANS
Faculty of Arts: Prof. ALAN FORD
Faculty of Engineering: Prof. HAI-SUI YU
Faculty of Medicine and Health Sciences: Prof. IAN HALL
Faculty of Science: Prof. EDMUND BURKE
Faculty of Social Sciences: Prof. SARAH O'HARA
Graduate School: Prof. CLAIRE O'MALLEY

PROFESSORS
AITKENHEAD, A., Anaesthesia and Intensive Care
ALDRICH, R. J., Politics
ARCHER, D. B., Microbiology
ARMOUR, E. A. G., Mathematical Physics
ARROWSMITH, S. L., Law
ASHER, G. M., Electrical and Electronic Engineering
ASHWORTH, J., American and Canadian Studies
AZZOPARDI, B. J., Chemical, Environmental and Mining Engineering
BACKHOUSE, R. C., Computer Science and Information Technology
BAILEY, S. H., Law
BALL, F. G., Statistics
BARNARD, C. J., Animal Behaviour and Ecology
BATES, C., Physics and Astronomy
BATH, P., Stroke Medicine
BECKER, A. A., Mechanical Engineering
BECKETT, J. V., History
BEHNKE, J. M., Infections and Immunity
BELAVKIN, V., Mathematical Physics
BENFORD, S. D., Computer Science and Information Technology
BENNETT, M. J., Plant Science
BENNETT, T., Biomedical Sciences
BENSON, T. M., Electrical and Electronic Engineering
BERRY, R. H., Accounting and Finance
BETON, P. H., Physics and Astronomy
BINKS, M. R., Institute for Enterprise and Innovation
BIRCH, D. J., Law
BLACK, C. R., Plant Science
BLEANEY, M. F., Economics
BOWLEY, R. M., Physics and Astronomy
BOWTELL, R. W., Physics and Astronomy
BRADLEY, J. E., Infections and Immunity
BRADSHAW, C. M., Psychiatry
BRAILSFORD, D. F., Computer Science and Information Technology
BRIGGS, D., Pharmaceutical Sciences
BRINCAT, M. P., Nurture Unit
BRITTON, J., Respiratory Medicine
BROOK, J. D., Genetics
BROUGHTON-PIPKIN, F., Obstetrics and Gynaecology
BROWN, A. D., Business School
BROWN, S. F., Civil Engineering
BRUCE, A. C., Economics and Insurance
BURKE, E. K., Computer Science and Information Technology
BURKHARDT, H., Education
BUTTERY, P. J., Nutritional Biochemistry
BYCROFT, B. W., Pharmaceutical Sciences
CALLEN, A. E., Art History
CAMPBELL, K. H., Animal Physiology
CARDWELL, R. A., Hispanic and Latin American Studies
CARTER, R. A., English Studies
CASEY, P. M., Theology
CHALLIS, R. E., Electrical and Electronic Engineering
CHESTERS, M. A., Physical Chemistry
CHOI, K.-S., Fluid Mechanics
CHOONARA, I., Human Devt
CHRISTOPOULOS, C., Electrical and Electronic Engineering
CLARK, J. S., Organic Chemistry
CLARKE, B., Genetics
CLARKE, D. D., Psychology
COLES, P., Physics and Astronomy
COLLIS, J., Atmospheric Environment
CONNERTON, I., Food Sciences
COOKE, M., Music
COX, K., Nursing
COX, T. R., Institute of Work, Health and Orgs
CREMONA, J. E., Mathematical Sciences
CURRIE, G., Business School
CURRIE, G., Philosophy
DANCHEV, A., Int. Relations
DANIELS, S., Geography
DAVIES, M. C., Pharmaceutical Sciences
DAVIS, S. S., Pharmaceutical Sciences
DAVIS, T., Orthopaedic and Accident Surgery
DAY, C., Education
DENBY, B., Chemical, Environmental and Mining Engineering
DERRINGTON, A. M., Psychology
DEVLIN, J., Marketing
DIACON, S. R., Business School
DINGWALL, R. W. J., Institute for the Study of Genetics, Biorisks and Society
DISNEY, R. F., Economics
DODSON, A. H., Civil Engineering
DONNELLY, R., Vascular Medicine
DOWD, K., Centre for Risk Insurance Studies
DRYDEN, I. L., Statistics
DUNCAN, A. S., Economics
EAVES, L., Physics and Astronomy
ELLIMAN, D. G., Computer Science and Information Technology
ENNEW, C. T., Business School
EVETTS, J. A., Sociology and Social Policy
FALVEY, R. E., Economics
FAWCETT, A. P., Architecture
FAWCETT, J. J., Law
FENN, P. T., Business School
FESENKO, I., Pure Mathematics
FINCH, R., Microbiology and Infectious Diseases
FLINT, A. P. F., Animal Physiology
FORBES, I., Politics
FORD, G. A., Theology
FORD, P. H., Computer Science and Information Technology
FOXON, C. T. B., Physics and Astronomy
FRANCIS, R. A., French
FRASER, D., Midwifery
GARDINER, S. M., Biomedical Sciences
GARNER, C. D., Inorganic Chemistry
GARVEY, S. D., Mechanical Engineering
GEARY, R. J., History
GILL, P. M. W., Physical Chemistry
GILLIES, P. A., Public Health Sciences
GINDY, N. N. Z., Manufacturing Engineering and Operations Management
GLASS, R. E., Genetics
GOW, I. T., Business School
GRAVELLS, N. P., Law
GREENAWAY, D., Economics
GREENHAFF, P. L., Biomedical Sciences
GRIERSON, D., Plant Science
GRIFFITHS, A., Institute of Work, Health and Orgs
HALL, I., Therapeutics
HAMMOND, B. S., English Studies
HARDING, S. E., Food Sciences
HARGREAVES, A., Education
HARRIS, D. J., Law
HARRISON, C., Education
HASLAM, C., Institute of Work, Health and Orgs
HEFFERNAN, M. J., Geography
HENDERSON, J., Archaeology
HEPTINSTALL, S., Cardiovascular Medicine
HERVEY, T. K., Law
HEWITT, N., French
HEYWOOD, P. M., Politics
HILL, S. J., Biomedical Sciences
HOLLIS, C., Psychiatry
HOPKINSON, B., Vascular Surgery
HOWDLE, S. M., Inorganic Chemistry
HYDE, T. H., Mechanical Engineering

IRVING, W., Microbiology and Infectious Diseases
JACKSON, S., Psychology
JAKEMAN, E., Electrical and Electronic Engineering
JAKEMAN, E., Theoretical Mechanics
JAMES, R., Microbiology and Infectious Diseases
JAMES, V. C., Nursing
JENSEN, O. E., Theoretical Mechanics
JESCH, J., English Studies
JOHNSON, C. M., French
JOHNSON, I. R., Human Devt
JONES, R. G., Physical Chemistry
JORDAN, T. R., Psychology
KENDALL, D. A., Biomedical Sciences
KENNER, J., European Law
KING, J. R., Theoretical Mechanics
KING, R. H., American and Canadian Studies
KNIGHT, D. M., French
LANGLEY-EVANS, S., Human Nutrition
LARKINS, E., Electrical and Electronic Engineering
LAYBOURN-PARRY, J., Life and Environmental Sciences
LEDGEWAY, T., Vision Research
LEICESTER, M., Continuing Education
LEYBOURNE, S. J., Economics
LEYSHON, A., Geography
LINCOLN, N. B., Psychology
LLOYD, R. G., Genetics
MCCARTNEY, D. G., Materials Engineering and Materials Design
MCCORQUODALE, R. G., Law
MCCOUSTRA, M., Chemical Physics
MACDONALD, I. A., Biomedical Sciences
MCGUIRK, B. J., Hispanic and Latin American Studies
MCRAE, J., English Studies
MADELEY, R., Community Health Sciences
MAHAJAN, R., Anaesthesia and Intensive Care
MANNING, N. P., Sociology and Social Policy
MARLOW, N., Human Devt
MARSDEN, C. A., Biomedical Sciences
MATHER, P. M., Geography
MAYER, R. J., Biomedical Sciences
MAYHEW, T. M., Biomedical Sciences
MELLER, H. E., History
MEPHAM, B., Biosciences
MERRIFIELD, M. R., Physics and Astronomy
MESSENT, P. B., American and Canadian Studies
MILES, N. J., Chemical, Environmental and Mining Engineering
MILLINGTON, M. I., Hispanic and Latin American Studies
MILNE, L. M., Russian and Slavonic Studies
MILNER, C. R., Economics
MITCHELL, J. R., Food Sciences
MITCHELL, P., Psychology
MITHEN, R. F., Agricultural Sciences
MONTEITH, S., American Studies
MOON, J., Int. Centre for Corporate Social Responsibility
MOORE, T., Engineering Surveying and Space Geodesy
MORGAN, W. J., Continuing Education
MORRIS, P. G., Physics and Astronomy
MORSE, G. K., Law
MURPHY, R. J. L., Education
MURPHY, S., Biomedical Sciences
NEWBOLD, P., Economics
NEWMAN, J. A., American and Canadian Studies
O'BRIEN, C., Manufacturing Engineering and Operations Management
O'CONNELL-DAVIDSON, J., Sociology and Social Policy
O'SHEA, P. S., Biomedical Sciences
OC, T., Built Environment
PARKER, S., Continuing Education
PASHBY, I. R., Manufacturing Engineering and Operations Management
PATIENT, R. K., Genetics
PATTENDEN, G., Chemistry
PEBERDY, J. F., Institute for Enterprise and Innovation
PERKINS, A., Human Devt
PIERSON, C., Politics
POLIAKOFF, M., Inorganic Chemistry
POWER, H., Mechanical Engineering
PRINGLE, M., General Practice
PRITCHARD, D. I., Pharmaceutical Sciences
RAY, D., Biomedical Sciences
REES, W., Int. Security
REEVE, D. E., Civil Engineering
RIFFAT, S. B., Built Environment
RILEY, D. S., Theoretical Mechanics
ROBERTS, J. A., Plant Science
RODDEN, T. A., Computer Science and Information Technology
ROSSLYN, W., Russian and Slavonic Studies
ROWLANDS, B. J., Gastrointestinal Surgery
RUDD, C. D., Mechanical Engineering
RUSSELL, N., Haematology
SABLITZKY, F., Genetics
SARRE, P. J., Physical Chemistry
SCHOLEFIELD, J., Surgery
SCHRODER, M., Inorganic Chemistry
SEABROOK, M. F., Agricultural Sciences
SEDDON, A. B., Materials Engineering and Materials Design
SHAKESHEFF, K., Pharmaceutical Sciences
SHARP, P. M., Genetics
SHAW, P. E., Biomedical Sciences
SHAW, R., Obstetrics and Gynaecology
SHAYLER, P. J., Mechanical Engineering
SIMESTER, A. P., Law
SIMPKINS, N. S., Organic Chemistry
SINCLAIR, M. T., Business School
SNAPE, C. E., Chemical, Environmental and Mining Engineering
SOCKET, E., Bacterial Genetics
SOMEKH, M. G., Electrical and Electronic Engineering
SOMMERSTEIN, A. H., Classics
SPIESS, M. K., Pure Mathematics
STARKEY, K. P., Business School
STARMER, C. V., Economics
STEPHENSON, T., Child Health
STEVENS, M. F. G., Pharmaceutical Sciences
STILL, J. M., French
TALLACK, D. G., American and Canadian Studies
TATTERSFIELD, A., Respiratory Medicine
TAYLOR, A. J., Food Sciences
TENDLER, S. J. B., Pharmaceutical Sciences
THORNE, C. R., Geography
THORNTON, J., Obstetrics and Gynaecology
TOMS, J. S., Business School
TUCK, B., Electrical and Electronic Engineering
TUCKER, G. A., Nutritional Biochemistry
TURVILLE-PETRE, T. F. S., English Studies
TYNAN, A. C., Business School
UNDERWOOD, G., Psychology
VAN ZYL SMIT, D., Law
WAITES, W. M., Food Sciences
WALKER, R. L., Sociology and Social Policy
WALLACE, W. A., Orthopaedic and Accident Surgery
WARD, C., Rehabilitation and Ageing
WEBB, R., Agricultural Sciences
WESTHEAD, P., Business School
WHITE, N. D., Law
WHYNES, D. K., Economics
WILCOX, R. G., Cardiovascular Medicine
WILKINSON, R., Epidemiology and Public Health Sciences
WILLIAMS, H., Medical and Surgical Sciences
WILLIAMS, P., Institute of Infections and Immunity
WILLIAMS, P., Pharmaceutical Sciences
WILSON, J., Business School
WILSON, J. R., Manufacturing Engineering and Operations Management
WILSON, R. J. A., Archaeology
WINGFIELD, J., Pharmaceutical Sciences
WOOD, A. T., Statistics
WOOD, D. J., Psychology
WOOD, J. V., Materials Engineering and Materials Design
WOODS, R. A. M., German
WORTHEN, J., English Studies
WRIGHT, D. M., Business School
WRIGHT, N., Environmental Fluid Mechanics
WRIGLEY, C. J., History
YOUNG, J. W., History
YOUNG, L., Molecular Embryology
YU, H., Civil Engineering

UNIVERSITY OF OXFORD

Univ. Offices, Wellington Sq., Oxford, OX1 2JD
Telephone: (1865) 270000
Fax: (1865) 270708
E-mail: information.officer@admin.ox.ac.uk
Internet: www.ox.ac.uk

Founded 12th century
Academic year: October to June

Chancellor: Rt Hon. the Lord PATTEN OF BARNES
High Steward: Rt Hon. the Lord RODGER OF EARLSFERRY
Vice-Chancellor: Dr ANDREW HAMILTON
Pro-Vice-Chancellor for Devt and External Relation: Prof. NICK RAWLINS (acting)
Pro-Vice-Chancellor for Education: Dr SALLY MAPSTONE
Pro-Vice-Chancellor for Personnel and Equality: Dr STEPHEN GOSS
Pro-Vice-Chancellor for Planning and Resources: Prof. WILLIAM JAMES
Pro-Vice-Chancellor for Research, Academic Services and Univ. Collns: Prof. IAN WALMSLEY
Registrar: Prof. EWAN MCKENDRICK
Academic Registrar and Sec. of Faculties: MICHAEL SIBLY
Bodley's Librarian and Dir, Library Services: Dr SARAH THOMAS
Library: the Bodleian Libraries comprise some 40 libraries, excl. college libraries, and holds over 9m. vols
Number of teachers: 1,600 f.t.e.
Number of students: 21,535 (incl. 19,803 full-time and 1,732 part-time)

PROFESSORS

Note: Faculties, Schools, Depts, etc. are grouped by Div. (each div. has a full-time head and an elected board who are responsible for day-to-day operations incl. finance and planning) as follows: *Humanities Div.*(-Rothermere American Institute, Faculty of Classics, Faculty of English Language and Literature, Faculty of Linguistics, Philology and Phonetics, Faculty of Medieval and Modern European Languages, Faculty of History, Faculty of Music, Faculty of Oriental Studies, Faculty of Philosophy, Ruskin School of Drawing and Fine Art, Faculty of Theology); *Mathematical, Physical and Physical Sciences Div.*(Dept of Chemistry, Dept of Computer Science, Dept of Earth Sciences, Dept of Engineering Science, Dept of Materials, Mathematical Institute, Dept of Physics, Dept of Plant Sciences, Dept of Statistics, Dept of Zoology, e-Research Centre); *Medical Sciences Div.*(Clinical Depts: Nuffield Dept of Anaesthetics, Dept of Cardiovascular Medicine, Nuffield Dept of Clinical Laboratory Sciences, Nuffield Dept of Clinical Medicine, Dept of Clinical Neurology, Dept of Clinical Pharmacology, Medical Oncology, Weatherall Institute of Molecular Medicine, Nuffield Dept of Obstetrics and Gynaecology, Nuffield Laboratory of Ophthalmology, Nuffield Dept of Orthopaedics, Rheumatology and Musculoskeletal Science, Dept of Paediatrics, Dept of Primary Health Care, Dept of Psychiatry, Dept of Public Health, Nuffield Dept of Surgical Sciences. Non-Clinical Depts: Dept of Biochemistry, Dept of Experimental

Psychology, Sir William Dunn School of Pathology, Dept of Pharmacology, Dept of Physiology, Anatomy and Genetics); *Social Sciences Div.*(School of Anthropology and Museum Ethnography, School of Archaeology, Interdisciplinary Area Studies, Dept of Economics, Dept of Education, School of Geography and the Environment, Oxford Internet Institute, Faculty of Law, Faculty of Management (Saïd Business School), Dept of Politics and International Relations, Dept of International Development, Dept of Social Policy and Intervention, Dept of Sociology). *Dept for Continuing Education* is not part of a Div.

Nuffield Department of Anaesthetics (John Radcliffe Hospital, Headley Way, Headington, Oxford, OX3 9DU; tel. (1865) 231515; fax (1865) 234844; e-mail anaesthetics@nda.ox.ac.uk; internet www.nda.ox.ac.uk):

TRACEY, I. M. C., Anaesthetic Science (Pembroke College)

Rothermere American Institute (1A South Parks Rd, Oxford, OX1 3UB; tel. (1865) 282710; fax (1865) 282720; e-mail enquiries@rai.ox.ac.uk; internet www.rai.ox.ac.uk):

WOLFE, A., American Government (Balliol College)

School of Anthropology and Museum Ethnography (51 Banbury Rd, Oxford, OX2 6PE; tel. (1865) 274624; fax (1865) 274630; e-mail info@anthro.ox.ac.uk; internet www.anthropology.ox.ac.uk):

BANKS, M. J., Visual Anthropology (Wolfson College)
BARNES, R. H., Social Anthropology (St Antony's College)
DUNBAR, R. I. M., Evolutionary Anthropology (Magdalen College)
GELLNER, D. N., Social Anthropology (All Souls College)
KEITH, M., Personal Professorship (Merton College)
ULIJASZEK, S. J., Human Ecology (St Cross College)
VERTOVEC, S., Transnational Anthropology (Linacre College)
WHITEHOUSE, H., Social Anthropology (Magdalen College)

School of Archaeology (34–36 Beaumont St, Oxford, OX1 2PG; tel. (1865) 278240; fax (1865) 278254; e-mail administrator@arch.ox.ac.uk; internet www.arch.ox.ac.uk):

BARTON, R. N. E., Palaeolithic Archaeology (Hertford College)
GOSDEN, C. H., European Archaeology (Keble College)
HAMEROW, H. F., Archaeology (St Cross College)
LEE-THORP, J., Scientific Archaeology (St Cross College)
MITCHELL, P. J., African Archaeology (St Hugh's College)
POLLARD, A. M., Archaeological Science (Linacre College)
RAMSEY, C. B., Archaeological Science
ROBINSON, M. A., Environmental Archaeology (St John's College)

Department of Biochemistry (South Parks Rd, Oxford, OX1 3QU; tel. (1865) 613200; fax (1865) 613201; e-mail admin@bioch.ox.ac.uk; internet www.bioch.ox.ac.uk):

ARMITAGE, J. P., Biochemistry (Merton College)
BROCKDORFF, N., Biochemistry
DAVIS, I., Cell Biology (Jesus College)
ENDICOTT, J. A., Structural Biology (St Cross College)
FERGUSON, S. J., Biochemistry (St Edmund Hall)
GARMAN, E. F., Molecular Biophysics (Brasenose College)
HANDFORD, P. A., Biochemistry (St Catherine's College)
HODGKIN, J. A., Genetics (Keble College)
MAHADEVAN, L. C., Biochemistry (Trinity College)
MELLOR, E. J. C., Biochemistry (The Queen's College)
NASMYTH, K., Biochemistry (Trinity College)
NOBLE, M. E. M., Structural Biology (Somerville College)
NOVÁK, B., Integrative Systems Biology (Merton College)
SANSOM, M. S. P., Molecular Biophysics (Corpus Christi College)
WATTS, A., Biochemistry (St Hugh's College)
WHITBY, M. C., Molecular Genetics

Department of Cardiovascular Medicine (Level 6, West Wing, John Radcliffe Hospital, Headington, Oxford, OX3 9DU; tel. (1865) 234657; fax (1865) 234658; e-mail enquiries@cardiov.ox.ac.uk; internet www.cardiov.ox.ac.uk):

BHATTACHARYA, S., Cardiovascular Medicine (Green Templeton College)
CASADEI, B., Cardiovascular Medicine
CHANNON, K. M., Cardiovascular Medicine (Lady Margaret Hall)
FARRALL, M., Cardiovascular Genetics (Keble College)
NEUBAUER, S., Cardiovascular Medicine (Christ Church)
WATKINS, H. C., Cardiovascular Medicine (Exeter College)

Department of Chemistry (Chemistry Research Laboratory, 12 Mansfield Rd, Oxford, OX1 3TA; tel. (1865) 285000; fax (1865) 275633; internet www.chem.ox.ac.uk):

ANDERSON, H. L., Chemistry (Keble College)
ARMSTRONG, F. A., Chemistry (St John's College)
BATTLE, P. D., Chemistry (St Catherine's College)
BAYLEY, J. H. P., Chemical Biology (Hertford College)
BEER, P. D., Chemistry (Wadham College)
BROUARD, M., Chemistry (Jesus College)
CLARY, D. C., Chemistry (Magdalen College)
COMPTON, R. G., Chemistry (St John's College)
DAVIES, S. G., Chemistry (Magdalen College)
DAVIS, B. G., Chemistry (Pembroke College)
DIXON, D. J., Chemistry (Wadham College)
DONOHOE, T. J., Chemistry (Magdalen College)
EDWARDS, P. P., Inorganic Chemistry (St Catherine's College)
EGDELL, R. G., Inorganic Chemistry (Trinity College)
FAULKNER, S., Chemistry (Keble College)
FLEET, G. W. J., Chemistry (St John's College)
FOORD, J. S., Chemistry (St Catherine's College)
GOUVERNEUR, V., Chemistry (Merton College)
HANCOCK, G., Chemistry (Trinity College)
HODGSON, D. M., Chemistry (Oriel College)
HORE, P. J., Physical Chemistry (Corpus Christi College)
HOWARD, B. J., Chemistry (Pembroke College)
LOGAN, D. E., Theoretical Chemistry (University College)
MANOLOPOULOS, D. E., Theoretical Chemistry (St Edmund Hall)
MCGRADY, J., Computational Inorganic Chemistry (New College)
MOUNTFORD, P., Chemistry (St Edmund Hall)
O'HARE, D. M., Chemistry (Balliol College)
ROBINSON, C. V., Chemistry (Exeter College)
SCHOFIELD, C. J., Chemistry (Hertford College)
SOFTLEY, T. P., Chemical Physics (Merton College)
TSANG, S. C. E., Chemistry (University College)
WELLER, A. S., Chemistry (Magdalen College)

Faculty of Classics (Ioannou Centre for Classical and Byzantine Studies, 66 St Giles, Oxford, OX1 3UL; tel. (1865) 288391; fax (1865) 288386; e-mail enquiries@classics.ox.ac.uk; internet www.classics.ox.ac.uk):

HARRISON, S. J., Classical Languages and Literature (Corpus Christi College)
HOWGEGO, C. J., Greek and Roman Numismatics (Wolfson College)
HUTCHINSON, G. O., Greek and Latin Languages and Literature (Exeter College)
JENKYNS, R. H. A., The Classical Tradition (Lady Margaret Hall)
KURTZ, D. C., Classical Art (Wolfson College)
LEIGH, M. G. L., Classical Languages and Literature (St Anne's College)
LEMOS, I. S., Classical Archaeology (Merton College)
PARKER, R. C. T., Ancient History (New College)
PELLING, C. B. R., Greek (Regius) (Christ Church)
PURCELL, N., Ancient History (Brasenose College)
REINHARDT, T., Latin Language and Literature (Corpus Christi College)
SMITH, R. R. R., Classical Archaeology and Art (Lincoln College)
WILLI, A., Comparative Philology (Worcester College)
WILSON, A. I., Archaeology of the Roman Empire (All Souls College)

Nuffield Department of Clinical Laboratory Sciences (Level 4, Academic Block, John Radcliffe Hospital, Headington, Oxford, OX3 9DU; tel. (1865) 221166; fax (1865) 220524; e-mail enquiries@ndcls.ox.ac.uk; internet www.ndcls.ox.ac.uk):

BELL, J. I., Medicine (Regius) (Christ Church)
BRUNNER, T., Translational Clinical Oncology
FERGUSON, D. J. P., Ultrastructural Morphology
GATTER, K. C., Pathology (St John's College)
HELLEDAY, T., Cancer Therapeutics
HIGGS, D. R., Haematology (Brasenose College)
JACOBSEN, S. E. W., Developmental and Stem Cell Biology (St Cross College)
MCKENNA, W. G., Radiation Oncology and Biology (Wolfson College)
MUSCHEL, R. J., Molecular Pathology (St Hilda's College)
PEZZELLA, F., Tumour Pathology
ROBERTS, D. J., Haematology (Trinity College)
VOJNOVIC, B., Biophysics
WAINSCOAT, J. S., Haematology
WATT, S. M., Haematology
WILKIE, A. O. M., Pathology (Merton College)

Nuffield Department of Clinical Medicine (John Radcliffe Hospital, Headington, Oxford, OX3 9DU; tel. (1865) 221325; fax (1865) 222901; e-mail enquiries@ndm.ox.ac.uk; internet www.ndm.ox.ac.uk):

ARMITAGE, J. M., Clinical Trials and Epidemiology
BAIGENT, C., Epidemiology

BERAL, V., Epidemiology (Green Templeton College)
BUCHAN, A. M., Clinical Geratology (Green Templeton College)
CERUNDOLO, V., Immunology (Merton College)
CHAPEL, H., Clinical Immunology
CHEN, Z., Epidemiology (Green Templeton College)
COLLINS, R. E., Medicine and Epidemiology
CORNALL, R. J., Immunology
CROOK, D. W. M., Microbiology
DARBY, S. C., Medical Statistics (Green Templeton College)
DAVIS, S. J., Molecular Immunology
DAY, N. P. J., Tropical Medicine
ENVER, T., Molecular Haematology
FARRAR, J., Tropical Medicine
FRAYN, K. N., Human Metabolism (Green Templeton College)
GAUGUIER, D., Mammalian Genetics
HARPER, S., Gerontology (Nuffield College)
HILL, A. V. S., Human Genetics (Magdalen College)
HOLMAN, R. R., Diabetic Medicine
JONES, E. Y., Protein Crystallography (Jesus College)
KLENERMAN, P., Immunology (Brasenose College)
KNAPP, S., Structural Biology
LU, X., Cancer Medicine
MARSH, K., Tropical Medicine
MCCARTHY, M., Diabetic Medicine (Green Templeton College)
MCMICHAEL, A. J., Molecular Medicine (Corpus Christi College)
MOTT, R., Bioinformatics and Statistical Genetics
NEWBOLD, C. I., Tropical Medicine (Green Templeton College)
NOSTEN, F., Tropical Medicine
Sir PETO, RICHARD, Medical Statistics and Epidemiology (Green Templeton College)
PETO, T. E. A., Medicine
PHILLIPS, R. E., Clinical Medicine
POWRIE, F. M., Gastroenterology (Green Templeton College)
PUGH, C. W., Renal Medicine (Kellogg College)
RATCLIFFE, P. J., Clinical Medicine (Magdalen College)
RORSMAN, P., Diabetic Medicine (Harris Manchester College)
ROWLAND-JONES, S. L., Immunology (Christ Church)
SNOW, R. W., Tropical Public Health
STRADLING, J. R., Respiratory Medicine
STUART, D. I., Biochemistry (Hertford College)
THAKKER, R. V., Medicine (Somerville College)
TOMLINSON, I., Molecular and Population Genetics (The Queen's College)
WASS, J. A. H., Endocrinology (Green Templeton College)
WHITE, N. J., Tropical Medicine (St John's College)

Department of Clinical Neurology (Level 6, West Wing, John Radcliffe Hospital, Headley Way, Headington, Oxford, OX3 9DU; tel. (1865) 231909; fax (1865) 231914; internet www.clneuro.ox.ac.uk):

BEESON, D. M. W., Neurosciences
EBERS, G. C., Clinical Neurology (St Edmund Hall)
FUGGER, L., Clinical Neuroimmunology (Oriel College)
JEZZARD, P., Neuroimaging
KENNARD, C., Clinical Neurology (Green Templeton College)
ROTHWELL, P. M., Clinical Neurology
SMITH, S. M., Biomedical Engineering

Department of Clinical Pharmacology (Old Rd Campus Research Bldg, Old Rd Campus, Roosevelt Dr., Oxford, OX3 7DQ; tel. (1865) 617024; fax (1865) 617100; e-mail admin@clinpharm.ox.ac.uk; internet www.clinpharm.ox.ac.uk):

LA THANGUE, N. B., Cancer Biology (Linacre College)
SEYMOUR, L. W., Genetic Therapy (Wolfson College)

Department of Computer Science (Wolfson Bldg, Parks Rd, Oxford, OX1 3QD; tel. (1865) 273838; fax (1865) 273839; e-mail enquiries@cs.ox.ac.uk; internet www.cs.ox.ac.uk):

ABRAMSKY, S., Computing (Wolfson College)
BENEDIKT, M., Computing Science (University College)
BURRAGE, K., Computational and Systems Biology (New College)
DAVIES, J. W. M., Software Engineering (Kellogg College)
DE MOOR, O., Computing Science (Magdalen College)
GAVAGHAN, D. J., Computational Biology (New College)
GILES, M., Scientific Computing (St Hugh's College)
GOTTLOB, G., Computing Science (St Anne's College)
HORROCKS, I. R., Computing Science (Oriel College)
JEAVONS, P. G., Computer Science (St Anne's College)
KWIATKOWSKA, M. Z., Computing Systems (Trinity College)
LOWE, G., Computer Science (St Catherine's College)
MELHAM, T. F., Computing Science (Balliol College)
ONG, C. H. L., Computing Science (Merton College)
PULMAN, S. G., Computational Linguistics (Somerville College)
ROSCOE, A. W., Computing Science (University College)
SMITH, N. P., Computational Biology (St John's College)

Continuing Education (1 Wellington Sq., Oxford, OX1 2JA; tel. (1865) 270360; fax (1865) 270309; e-mail enquiries@conted.ox.ac.uk; internet www.conted.ox.ac.uk):

DU SAUTOY, M. P. F., Public Understanding of Science (New College)
MICHIE, J., Innovation & Knowledge Exchange (Kellogg College)

Ruskin School of Drawing and Fine Art (74 High St, Oxford, OX1 4BG; tel. (1865) 276940; fax (1865) 276949; e-mail info@ruskin-sch.ox.ac.uk; internet www.ruskin-sch.ox.ac.uk):

CATLING, B. D., Fine Art (Linacre College)
CHEVSKA, M., Fine Art (Brasenose College)

Department of Earth Sciences (South Parks Rd, Oxford, OX1 3AN; tel. (1865) 272000; fax (1865) 272072; e-mail enquiries@earth.ox.ac.uk; internet www.earth.ox.ac.uk):

BRASIER, M. D., Palaeobiology (St Edmund Hall)
BURTON, K. W., Earth Sciences
ENGLAND, P. C., Geology (University College)
FRASER, D. G., Earth Sciences (Worcester College)
HALLIDAY, A. N., Geochemistry (St Hugh's College)
HENDERSON, G. M., Earth Sciences (University College)
HESSELBO, S. P., Stratigraphy (St Peter's College)
PARSONS, B. E., Geodesy and Geophysics (St Cross College)
PYLE, D. M., Earth Sciences (St Anne's College)
SEARLE, M. P., Earth Sciences (Worcester College)
SIVETER, D. J., Earth Sciences (St Cross College)
WATTS, A. B., Marine Geology and Geophysics (Wolfson College)
WOOD, B., Earth Sciences (Wolfson College)
WOODHOUSE, J. H., Geophysics (Worcester College)

Department of Economics (Manor Rd Bldg, Manor Rd, Oxford, OX1 3UQ; tel. (1865) 271089; fax (1865) 271094; e-mail reception@economics.ox.ac.uk; internet www.economics.ox.ac.uk):

ALLEN, R. C., Recent Social and Economic History (Nuffield College)
ANAND, S., Quantitative Economic Analysis (St Catherine's College)
BROWNING, M. J., Economics (Nuffield College)
COLLIER, P., Economics (St Antony's College)
CRAWFORD, V. P., Political Economy (All Souls College)
ELLISON, M., Economics (Exeter College)
FAFCHAMPS, M., Development Economics (Mansfield College)
HENDRY, D. F., Economics (Nuffield College)
KELLER, R. G., Microeconomic Theory
KLEMPERER, P. D., Economics (Nuffield College)
MALCOMSON, J. M., Economics (All Souls College)
MUELLBAUER, J. N. J., Economics (Nuffield College)
MUKERJI, S., Economics (University College)
NEARY, J. P., Economics (Merton College)
NOCKE, V., Industrial Economics (Jesus College)
OFFER, A., Economic History (All Souls College)
QUAH, J. K.-H., Economic Theory (St Hugh's College)
ROBERTS, K. S. W., Economics (Nuffield College)
SHEPHARD, N., Economics (Nuffield College)
STEVENS, M. J., Economics (Lincoln College)
VENABLES, A. J., Economics (New College)
VINES, D. A., Economics (Balliol College)
WALLACE, C. C., Economics (Economic Theory) (Trinity College)
WREN-LEWIS, S., Economics (Merton College)
YOUNG, H. P., Economics (Nuffield College)

Department of Education (15 Norham Gardens, Oxford, OX2 6PY; tel. (1865) 274024; fax (1865) 274027; e-mail general.enquiries@education.ox.ac.uk; internet www.education.ox.ac.uk):

BAIRD, J. A., Educational Assessment (St Anne's College)
FURLONG, J., Educational Studies (Green Templeton College)
MACARO, E., Applied Linguistics and Second Language Acquisition (Worcester College)
MARSH, H. W., Educational Studies (St Cross College)
NUNES, T., Educational Studies (Harris Manchester College)
OZGA, J., Sociology of Education (Green Templeton College)
PHILLIPS, D., Comparative Education (St Edmund Hall)
WATSON, A., Mathematics Education (Linacre College)

Department of Engineering Science (17 Parks Rd, Oxford, OX1 3PJ; tel. (1865) 273000; fax (1865) 273010; e-mail enquiries@eng.ox.ac.uk; internet www.eng.ox.ac.uk):

BHATTACHARYA, A., Engineering Science
BLAKEBOROUGH, A., Engineering Science (Worcester College)
BORTHWICK, A. G. L., Engineering Science (St Edmund Hall)
BUCKLEY, C. P., Engineering Science (Balliol College)
COCKS, A. C. F., Materials Engineering (St Anne's College)
COUSSIOS, C. C., Biomedical Engineering (Magdalen College)
CUI, Z. F., Chemical Engineering (Hertford College)
DANIEL, R. W., Engineering Science (Brasenose College)
DARTON, R. C., Engineering Science (Keble College)
DUNCAN, S. R., Engineering Science (St Hugh's College)
DUNNE, F. P. E., Engineering Science (Hertford College)
EDWARDS, D. J., Engineering Science (Wadham College)
ELSTON, S. J., Engineering Science (St John's College)
FOX, J. P., Engineering Science
HILLS, D. A., Engineering Science (Lincoln College)
HOULSBY, G. T., Civil Engineering (Brasenose College)
IRELAND, P. T., Turbomachinery (St Catherine's College)
KORSUNSKY, A. M., Engineering Science (Trinity College)
KOUVARITAKIS, B., Engineering Science (St Edmund Hall)
LIMEBEER, D. J. N., Control Engineering (New College)
MURRAY, D. W., Engineering Science (St Anne's College)
NOBLE, J. A., Biomedical Engineering (St Hilda's College)
NOWELL, D., Engineering Science (Christ Church)
ROBERTS, S. J., Engineering Science (Somerville College)
STONE, C. R., Engineering Science (Somerville College)
TARASSENKO, L., Electrical and Electronic Engineering (St John's College)
TAYLOR, P. H., Engineering Science (Keble College)
THOMPSON, I. P., Engineering Science
WILLIAMS, M. S., Engineering Science (New College)
WILSON, T., Engineering Science (Hertford College)
ZISSERMAN, A. P., Computer Vision Engineering

Faculty of English Language and Literature (St Cross Bldg, Manor Rd, Oxford, OX1 3UL; tel. (1865) 271055; fax (1865) 271054; e-mail english.office@ell.ox.ac.uk; internet www.english.ox.ac.uk):

BALLASTER, R. M., Eighteenth-century Studies (Mansfield College)
BOEHMER, E. D., World Literatures in English (Wolfson College)
BREWER, C. D., English Language and Literature (Hertford College)
BUSH, R. L., American Literature (St John's College)
CAMERON, D. J., Language and Communication (Worcester College)
CUNNINGHAM, V. D., English Language and Literature (Corpus Christi College)
GILLESPIE, V. A., English Language and Literature (Lady Margaret Hall)
GODDEN, M. R., Anglo-Saxon (Pembroke College)
HANNA, R., Palaeography (Keble College)
HILL, G. W., Poetry (Keble College)
MAGUIRE, L. E., English Literature (Magdalen College)
MARCUS, L., English Literature (New College)
MCCABE, R. A., English Language and Literature (Merton College)
MUGGLESTONE, L. C., History of English (Pembroke College)
NEWLYN, L. A., English Language and Literature (St Edmund Hall)
NORBROOK, D. G. E., English Literature (Merton College)
ROMAINE, S., English Language (Merton College)
STAFFORD, F. J., English Language and Literature (Somerville College)
SUTHERLAND, K., Bibliography and Textual Criticism (St Anne's College)
WOMERSELY, D. J., English Literature (St Catherine's College)
WU, S., English Language and Literature (St Catherine's College)

Oxford e-Research Centre (7 Keble Rd, Oxford, OX1 3QG; tel. (1865) 610600; fax (1865) 610624; e-mail info@oerc.ox.ac.uk; internet www.oerc.ox.ac.uk):

CHEN, M., Scientific Visualisation (Pembroke College)
TREFETHEN, A. E., Scientific Computing (Keble College)

Department of Experimental Psychology (9 South Parks Rd, Oxford, OX1 3UD; tel. (1865) 271444; fax (1865) 310447; e-mail general@psy.ox.ac.uk; internet www.psych.ox.ac.uk):

BISHOP, D. V. M., Developmental Neuropsychology (St John's College)
FLINT, J., Neuroscience (Merton College)
GAFFAN, D., Behavioural Neuroscience
HEYES, C. M., Psychology (All Souls College)
HEWSTONE, M. R. C., Social Psychology (New College)
MARTIN, R. M. A., Abnormal Psychology (St Edmund Hall)
NATION, K., Experimental Psychology (St John's College)
NOBRÉ, A. C. DE O., Cognitive Neuroscience (New College)
PLUNKETT, K. R., Cognitive Neuroscience (St Hugh's College)
RAWLINS, J. N. P., Psychology (Wolfson College)
ROGERS, B. J., Experimental Psychology (Pembroke College)
RUSHWORTH, M. F. S., Cognitive Neuroscience
SPENCE, C. J., Experimental Psychology (Somerville College)

School of Geography and the Environment (Dyson Perrins Bldg, South Parks Rd, Oxford, OX1 3QY; tel. (1865) 285070; fax (1865) 275885; e-mail enquiries@ouce.ox.ac.uk; internet www.ouce.ox.ac.uk):

ALLEN, M. R. (Linacre College)
BANISTER, D., Transport Studies (St Anne's College)
CLARK, G. L., Geography (St Peter's College)
LIVERMAN, D. M., Environmental Policy and Development (Linacre College)
MALHI, Y. S., Terrestrial Ecology (Oriel College)
MCDOWELL, L. M., Human Geography (St John's College)
PALLOT, J., Human Geography of Russia (Christ Church)
THOMAS, D. S. G., Geography (Hertford College)
VILES, H. A., Biogeomorphology and Heritage Conservation (Worcester College)
WHATMORE, S. J., Environment and Public Policy (Linacre College)
WHITTAKER, R. J., Biogeography (St Edmund Hall)

Faculty of History (Old Boys' School, George St, Oxford, OX1 2RL; tel. (1865) 615000; fax (1865) 250704; internet www.history.ox.ac.uk):

BLAIR, W. J., Medieval History and Archaeololgy (Queen's College)
BROCKLISS, L. W. B., Early Modern French History (Magdalen College)
BROWN, J. M., History of the British Commonwealth (Balliol College)
CAPLAN, J., Modern European History (St Antony's College)
CLUNAS, C., History of Art (Trinity College)
CORSI, P., History of Science (Linacre College)
FOSTER, R. F., Irish History (Hertford College)
GILDEA, R. N., Modern History (Worcester College)
HAMEROW, H. F., Archaeology (St Cross College)
HARRISON, M., History of Medicine (Green Templeton College)
HOTSON, H. B., Early Modern Intellectual History (St Anne's College)
HUMPHRIES, K. J., Economic History (All Souls College)
KNIGHT, A. S., History of Latin America (St Antony's College)
LANGFORD, P., Modern History (Lincoln College)
MACLEAN, I. W. F., Renaissance Studies (All Souls College)
MITTER, R. S. R., History and Politics of Modern China (St Cross College)
O'ROURKE, K. H., Economic History (All Souls College)
ROPER, L. A., Modern History (Regius) (Oriel College)
SERVICE, R. J., Russian History (St Antony's College)
SHARPE, R., Diplomatic (Wadham College)
STRACHAN, H. F. A., History of War (All Souls College)
TYRRELL, I., American History (Queen's College)
WICKHAM, C. J., Medieval History (All Souls College)

School of Interdisciplinary Area Studies (12 Bevington Rd, Oxford, OX2 6LH; tel. (1865) 284996; fax (1865) 284992; e-mail enquiries@area.ox.ac.uk; internet www.area-studies.ox.ac.uk):

ANDERSON, D. MCBEATH, African Politics (St Cross College)
BEINART, W., Race Relations (St Antony's College)
FOWERAKER, J. W., Latin American Politics (St Antony's College)
GOODMAN, R. J., Modern Japanese Studies (St Antony's College)
HARRISS-WHITE, B., Development Studies (Wolfson College)
KARIYA, T., Sociology of Japanese Society (St Antony's College)
NEARY, I. J., Politics of Japan (St Antony's College)
PAYNE, L. A, Sociology (Latin American Societies) (St Antony's College)
SHUE, V., Contemporary China (St Antony's College)

Department of International Development (3 Mansfield Rd, Oxford, OX1 3TB; tel. (1865) 281800; fax (1865) 281801; e-mail qeh@qeh.ox.ac.uk; internet www.qeh.ox.ac.uk):

ALEXANDER, J., Development Studies (Linacre College)
DERCON, S., Development Economics (Wolfson College)
FITZGERALD, E. V. K., International Development (St Antony's College)

HARRISS-WHITE, B., Development Studies (Wolfson College)
WOOD, A., International Development (Wolfson College)
ZETTER, R., Refugee Studies (Green Templeton College)

Oxford Internet Institute (1 St Giles, Oxford, OX1 3JS; tel. (1865) 287210; fax (1865) 287211; e-mail enquiries@oii.ox.ac.uk; internet www.oii.ox.ac.uk):

DUTTON, W. H., Internet Studies (Balliol College)
MARGETTS, H., Society and the Internet (Mansfield College)
MAYER-SCHÖNBERGER, V., Internet Governance and Regulation (Keble College)

Faculty of Law (St Cross Bldg, St Cross Rd, Oxford, OX1 3UL; tel. (1865) 271491; fax (1865) 271493; e-mail lawfac@law.ox.ac.uk; internet www.law.ox.ac.uk):

ARMOUR, J. H., Law and Finance (Oriel College)
ASHWORTH, A. J., English Law (All Souls College)
BRIGGS, A., Private International Law (St Edmund Hall)
BRIGHT, S. L., Land Law (New College)
CARTWRIGHT, J., Law of Contract (Christ Church)
CRAIG, P. P., English Law (St John's College)
DAVIES, P. L., Corporate Law (Jesus College)
DINWOODIE, G. B., Intellectual Property and Information Technology Law (St Peter's College)
DOUGLAS-SCOTT, S., European and Human Rights Law (Lady Margaret Hall)
EDELMAN, J. J., Law of Obligations (Keble College)
ENDICOTT, T. A. O., Legal Philosophy (Balliol College)
FREDMAN, S. D., Law (Exeter College)
FREEDLAND, M. R., Employment Law (St John's College)
FREEDMAN, J. A., Taxation Law (Worcester College)
GALLIGAN, D. J., Socio-legal Studies (Wolfson College)
GARDNER, J. B., Jurisprudence (University College)
GREEN, L., Philosophy of Law (Balliol College)
LOADER, I., Criminology (All Souls College)
LOWE, A. V., Public International Law (All Souls College)
MCCRUDDEN, J. C., Human Rights Law (Lincoln College)
MCKENDRICK, E. G., English Private Law (Lady Margaret Hall)
ROBERTS, J. V., Criminology (Worcester College)
SAROOSHI, D., Public International Law (Queen's College)
SIRKS, A. J. B., Civil Law (Regius) (All Souls College)
VOGENAUER, S., Comparative Law (Brasenose College)
WEATHERILL, S. R., European Community Law (Somerville College)
WHITTAKER, S. J., European Comparative Law (St John's College)
ZEDNER, L. H., Criminal Justice (Corpus Christi College)
ZUCKERMAN, A. A. S., Civil Procedure (University College)

Centre for Linguistics and Philology (Clarendon Institute, Walton St, Oxford, OX1 2HG; tel. (1865) 280400; fax (1865) 280412; e-mail enquiries@ling-phil.ox.ac.uk; internet www.ling-phil.ox.ac.uk):

COLEMAN, J. S., Phonetics (Wolfson College)
DALRYMPLE, M. E., Linguistics (Linacre College)
LAHIRI, A., Linguistics (Somerville College)
WILLI, A., Comparative Philology (Worcester College)

Faculty of Management (Saïd Business School, Park End St, Oxford, OX1 1HP; tel. (1865) 288800; fax (1865) 288805; e-mail reception@sbs.ox.ac.uk; internet www.sbs.ox.ac.uk):

BARNETT, M., Strategy (St Anne's College)
DENRELL, J., Strategy and Organisation (Keble College)
DEVEREUX, M., Business Taxation (Oriel College)
DOPSON, S., Organisational Behaviour (Green Templeton College)
FLYVBJERG, B., Major Programme Management (St Anne's College)
FUEST, C., Business Taxation
HOLT, D. B., Marketing (Worcester College)
JENKINSON, T. J., Finance (Keble College)
MAYER, C. P., Management Studies (St Edmund Hall)
MORRIS, T. J., Management Studies (Green Templeton College)
MORRISON, A. D., Finance (Merton College)
NOE, T. H., Management Studies (Balliol College)
PETTIGREW, A. M., Strategy and Organisation (Brasenose College)
POWELL, T. C., Strategy (St Hugh's College)
RAYNER, S., Science and Civilisation (Keble College)
SAKO, M., Management Studies (Green Templeton College)
SCOTT, L., Entrepreneurship and Innovation (Green Templeton College)
TAYLOR, J. W., Decision Science (St Cross College)
UPTON, D. M., Operations Management (Christ Church)
WESTBROOK, R. K., Operations Management (St Hugh's College)
WHITTINGTON, R. C., Strategic Management (New College)
WOOLGAR, S. W., Marketing (Green Templeton College)

Department of Materials (16 Parks Rd, Oxford, OX1 3PH; tel. (1865) 273700; fax (1865) 273789; e-mail enquiries@materials.ox.ac.uk; internet www.materials.ox.ac.uk):

BRIGGS, G. A. D., Nanomaterials (St Anne's College)
GRANT, P. S., Materials Science (St Catherine's College)
GROVENOR, C. R. M., Materials (St Anne's College)
KIRKLAND, A. J., Materials (Linacre College)
MARROW, T. J., Energy Materials (Mansfield College)
MARZARI, N., Materials Modelling (St Anne's College)
ROBERTS, S. G., Materials (St Edmund Hall)

Mathematical Institute (24–29 St Giles, Oxford, OX1 3LB; tel. (1865) 273525; fax (1865) 273583; e-mail enquiries@maths.ox.ac.uk; internet www.maths.ox.ac.uk):

Sir BALL, J. M., Natural Philosophy (The Queen's College)
BATTY, C. J. K., Analysis (St John's College)
BRESSLOFF, P., Applied Mathematics (Jesus College)
BRIDSON, M. R., Pure Mathematics (Magdalen College)
CANDELAS, P., Mathematics (Wadham College)
CHAPMAN, S. J., Mathematics and its Applications (Mansfield College)
COLLINS, M. J., Mathematics (University College)
DRUTU BADEA, C., Mathematics (Exeter College)
DU SAUTOY, M. P. F., Public Understanding of Science (New College)
EKERT, A., Quantum Information (Merton College)
ETHERIDGE, A. M., Probability (Magdalen College)
FLYNN, E. V., Mathematics (New College)
GILES, M. B., Scientific Computing (St Hugh's College)
GORIELY, A., Mathematical Modelling (St Catherine's College)
GOULD, N. M., Numerical Optimization (Exeter College)
GUI-QIANG, G. C., Analysis of Partial Differential Equations (Keble College)
HAYDON, R. G., Mathematics (Brasenose College)
HEATH-BROWN, D. R., Pure Mathematics (Worcester College)
HITCHIN, N. J., Geometry (New College)
HOWISON, S. D., Applied Mathematics (Christ Church)
JOYCE, D. D., Mathematics (Lincoln College)
KIRCHHEIM, B., Mathematics (Trinity College)
KIRWAN, F. C., Mathematics (Balliol College)
KRAMKOV, D., Mathematical Finance
LACKENBY, M., Mathematics (St Catherine's College)
LENNOX, J. C., Mathematics (Green Templeton College)
LYONS, T. J., Mathematics (St Anne's College)
MAINI, P. K., Mathematical Biology (Brasenose College)
MASON, L., Mathematics (St Peter's College)
NIETHAMMER, B., Applied Mathematics (St Edmund Hall)
PRIESTLEY, H. A., Mathematics (St Anne's College)
RIORDAN, O., Discrete Mathematics (St Edmund Hall)
ROUQUIER, R., Pure Mathematics (Magdalen College)
SCOTT, A. D., Mathematics (Merton College)
SEGAL, D., Mathematics (All Souls College)
SEREGIN, G. A., Pure Mathematics (St Hilda's College)
SÜLI, E., Numerical Analysis (Worcester College)
TILLMANN, U. L., Mathematics (Merton College)
TOD, K. P., Mathematical Physics (St John's College)
TREFETHEN, L. N., Numerical Analysis (Balliol College)
VASSEUR, A. F., Mathematics (Lincoln College)
WENDLAND, H., Numerical Analysis (Exeter College)
WOODHOUSE, N. M. J., Mathematics (Wadham College)
ZHOU, X., Mathematical Finance (St Hugh's College)
ZILBER, B., Mathematical Logic (Merton College)

Department of Medical Oncology (Churchill Hospital, Oxford, OX3 7LJ; tel. (1865) 235310; fax (1865) 235986):

ELLIOTT, T. J., Immunology (Balliol College)
GODING, C. R., Oncology
HARRIS, A. L., Medical Oncology (St Hugh's College)
MIDDLETON, M. R., Experimental Cancer Medicine

Faculty of Medieval and Modern European Languages (47 Wellington Sq., Oxford, OX1 2JF; tel. (1865) 270570; fax (1865) 270757; e-mail reception@mod-langs.ox.ac.uk; internet www.mod-langs.ox.ac.uk):

BETHEA, D. M., Russian Studies (Wadham College)
CHARLES-EDWARDS, T. M. O., Celtic (Jesus College)
COOPER, R. A., French (Brasenose College)
CRONK, N. E., French Literature (St Edmund Hall)
EARLE, T. F., Portuguese Studies (St Peter's College)
FIDDIAN, R. W., Spanish (Wadham College)
HOWELLS, C. M., French (Wadham College)
JEFFERSON, A. M., French Literature (New College)
KELLY, C. H. M., Russian (New College)
KOHL, K. M., German Literature (Jesus College)
LAUXTERMANN, M. D., Modern Greek Language and Literature (Exeter College)
LEEDER, K. J., Modern German Literature (New College)
MAIDEN, M. D., Romance Languages (Trinity College)
MCGUINNESS, P. R. A., French and Comparative Literature (St Anne's College)
MCLAUGHLIN, M. L., Italian Studies (Magdalen College)
PALMER, N. F., German Medieval and Linguistic Studies (St Edmund Hall)
PARISH, R. J., French (St Catherine's College)
PEARSON, R. A. G., French (Queen's College)
PHELAN, A., German Romantic Literature (Keble College)
ROBERTSON, R. N. N., German Language and Literature (The Queen's College)
SHERINGHAM, M. H. T., French Literature (All Souls College)
VIALA, A., French Literature (Lady Margaret Hall)
VOLFING, A. M., Medieval German Studies (Oriel College)
WATANABE-O'KELLY, H., German Literature (Exeter College)
WILLIAMSON, E. H., Spanish Studies (Exeter College)
ZORIN, A. L., Russian (New College)

Weatherall Institute of Molecular Medicine (John Radcliffe Hospital, Headington, Oxford, OX3 9DS; tel. (1865) 222443; fax (1865) 222737; internet www.imm.ox.ac.uk):

BEESON, D., Neuroscience
CERUNDOLO, V., Immunology (Merton College)
DAVIS, S.
ENVER, T., Stem Cell Biology
FUGGER, L., Clinical Neuroimmunology (Oriel College)
HARRIS, A. L., Clinical Oncology (Oriel College)
HASSAN, B., Medical Oncology (Lincoln College)
HICKSON, I., Molecular Oncology
HIGGS, D. R., Heamatology (Brasenose College)
JACKSON, D., Human Immunology
JACOBSEN, S. E. W., Developmental and Stem Cell Biology (St Cross College)
Sir MCMICHAEL, A. J., Molecular Medicine (Corpus Christi College)
NEWBOLD, C. I., Tropical Medicine (Green Templeton College)
PATIENT, R., Developmental Haemopoiesis
ROWLAND-JONES, S., Immunology (Christ Church)
TOWNSEND, A. R. M., Molecular Immunology (New College)
WILKIE, A. O. M., Pathology
WOOD, W. G., Haematology

Faculty of Music (St Aldate's, Oxford, OX1 1DB; tel. (1865) 276125; fax (1865) 276128; e-mail office@music.ox.ac.uk; internet www.music.ox.ac.uk):

CLARKE, E. F., Music (Wadham College)
CROSS, J. G. E., Musicology (Christ Church)
DREYFUS, L., Music (Magdalen College)
FRANKLIN, P. R., Music (St Catherine's College)
HIGGINBOTTOM, E., Choral Music (New College)
SAXTON, R. L. A., Composition (Worcester College)

Nuffield Department of Obstetrics and Gynaecology (John Radcliffe Hospital, Oxford, OX3 9DU; tel. (1865) 221004; fax (1865) 769141; e-mail enquiries@obs-gyn.ox.ac.uk; internet www.obs-gyn.ox.ac.uk):

MARDON, H. J., Reproductive Science (St Catherine's College)
POULTON, J., Mitochondrial Genetics (Lady Margaret Hall)
SARGENT, I. L., Reproductive Science (Mansfield College)

Nuffield Laboratory of Ophthalmology (Level 5, West Wing, John Radcliffe Hospital, Headington, Oxford, OX3 9DU; tel. (1865) 234782; fax (1865) 234795; e-mail enquiries@eye.ox.ac.uk; internet www.eye.ox.ac.uk):

FOSTER, R. G., Circadian Neuroscience (Brasenose College)
HANKINS, M. W., Visual Neuroscience
MACLAREN, R., Ophthalmology (Merton College)

Faculty of Oriental Studies (Oriental Institute, Pusey Lane, Oxford, OX1 2LE; tel. (1865) 278200; fax (1865) 278190; e-mail orient@orinst.ox.ac.uk; internet www.orinst.ox.ac.uk):

ALLAN, J. W., Eastern Art (St Cross College)
BAINES, J. R., Egyptology (The Queen's College)
FLOOD, G. D., Hindu Studies
FRELLESVIG, B., Japanese Linguistics (Hertford College)
GOODMAN, M. D., Jewish Studies (Wolfson College)
HERZIG, E., Persian Studies (Wadham College)
HOLES, C. D., Contemporary Arab World (Magdalen College)
JOHNS, J., Art and Archaeology of the Islamic Mediterranean (Wolfson College)
MINKOWSKI, C. Z., Sanskrit (Balliol College)
O'HANLON, R., Indian History and Culture (St Cross College)
RAMADAN, T., Contemporary Islamic Studies (St Antony's College)
SANDERSON, A. G. J. S., Eastern Religions and Ethics (All Souls College)
SMITH, M. J., Egyptology (University College)
VAN GELDER, G. J. H., Arabic (St John's College)
VAN LINT, T. M., Armenian Studies (Pembroke College)
WALLACE, V. A., Buddhist Studies (Balliol College)
WATSON, O. J., Islamic Art and Architecture (Wolfson College)
WILLIAMSON, H. G. M., Hebrew (Regius) (Christ Church)

Nuffield Department of Orthopaedics, Rheumatology and Musculoskeletal Sciences (Nuffield Orthopaedic Centre, Windmill Rd, Headington, Oxford, OX3 7LD; tel. (1865) 227374; fax (1865) 737640; internet www.ndos.ox.ac.uk):

ARDEN, N. K., Rheumatology and Musculoskeletal Sciences (Lady Margaret Hall)
ATHANASOU, N. A., Osteoarticular Pathology (Wadham College)
BULSTRODE, C. J. K., Orthopaedic Surgery (Green Templeton College)
CARR, A. J., Orthopaedic Surgery (Worcester College)
COOPER, C., Musculoskeletal Sciences (St Peter's College)
FAIRBANK, J. C. T., Spinal Surgery
LAMB, S. E., Trauma Rehabilitation (Wadham College)
MURRAY, D., Orthopaedic Surgery
OPPERMANN, U. C. T., Musculoskeletal Sciences (St Catherine's College)
WILLETT, K. M., Orthopaedic Trauma Surgery (Wolfson College)
WORDSWORTH, B. P., Rheumatology (Green Templeton College)

Department of Paediatrics (Level 2, Children's Hospital (John Radcliffe), Headington, Oxford, OX3 9DU; tel. (1865) 234239; fax (1865) 234242; e-mail enquiries@paediatrics.ox.ac.uk; internet www.paediatrics.ox.ac.uk):

GOULDER, P. J. R., Immunology (Brasenose College)
HOLLANDER, G. A. P., Paediatrics (Jesus College)
KWIATKOWSKI, D. P., Tropical Paediatrics (St John's College)
POLLARD, A. J., Paediatric Infection and Immunity (St Cross College)
WILKINSON, A. W., Paediatrics (All Souls College)

Sir William Dunn School of Pathology (South Parks Rd, Oxford, OX1 3RE; tel. (1865) 275500; fax (1865) 275515; e-mail enquiries@path.ox.ac.uk; internet www.path.ox.ac.uk):

ACUTO, O., Molecular Cell Signalling (Lincoln College)
BARCLAY, A. N., Chemical Pathology (Lincoln College)
BELL, S. D., Microbiology (Wadham College)
COOK, P. R., Cell Biology (Lincoln College)
HALE, G., Therapeutic Immunology
JAMES, W. S., Virology (Brasenose College)
LEA, S., Chemical Pathology (Brasenose College)
PROUDFOOT, N. J., Molecular Biology (Brasenose College)
SATTENTAU, Q. J., Immunology (Magdalen College)
VAN DER MERWE, P. A., Molecular Immunology (Brasenose College)
WALDMANN, H., Pathology (Lincoln College)

Department of Pharmacology (Mansfield Rd, Oxford, OX1 3QT; tel. (1865) 271850; fax (1865) 271853; e-mail info@pharm.ox.ac.uk; internet www.pharm.ox.ac.uk):

GALIONE, A. G., Pharmacology (Lady Margaret Hall)
GARLAND, C. J., Vascular Pharmacology (Magdalen College)
Baroness GREENFIELD, S., Pharmacology (Lincoln College)
PLATT, F. M., Biochemistry and Pharmacology (Merton College)
SIM, E., Pharmacology (St Peter's College)
TERRAR, D. A., Cardiac Electrophysiology (Worcester College)

Faculty of Philosophy (10 Merton St, Oxford, OX1 4JJ; tel. (1865) 276926; fax (1865) 276932; e-mail enquiries@philosophy.ox.ac.uk; internet www.philosophy.ox.ac.uk):

ARNTZENIUS, F., Philosophy (University College)
BOSTROM, N. R. L., Applied Ethics (St Cross College)
BROOME, J. R., Moral Philosophy (Corpus Christi College)
BROWN, H. R., Physics (Wolfson College)

CHARLES, D. O. M., Philosophy (Oriel College)
COOPE, U. C., Ancient Philosophy (Corpus Christi)
CRISP, R. S., Moral Philosophy (St Anne's College)
DAVIES, M. K., Mental Philosophy (Corpus Christi College)
HAWTHORNE, J., Metaphysical Philosophy (Magdalen College)
HYMAN, J., Aesthetics (The Queen's College)
IRWIN, T. H., Ancient Philosophy (Keble College)
MOORE, A. W., Philosophy (St Hugh's College)
MULHALL, S. J., Philosophy (New College)
RODRIGUEZ-PEREYRA, G., Metaphysics (Oriel College)
SAUNDERS, S. W., Philosophy of Physics (Linacre College)
SAVULESCU, J., Practical Ethics (St Cross College)
SHIELDS, C. J., Classical Philosophy (Lady Margaret Hall)
TRIFOGLI, C., Medieval Philosophy (All Souls College)
WEDGWOOD, R., Philosophy (Merton College)
WILLIAMSON, T., Logic (New College)

Department of Physics (Clarendon Laboratory, Parks Rd, Oxford, OX1 3PU; tel. (1865) 272200; fax (1865) 272400; e-mail enquiries@physics.ox.ac.uk; internet www.physics.ox.ac.uk):

ABRAHAM, D. B., Statistical Mechanics (Wolfson College)
ANDREWS, D. G., Physics (Lady Margaret Hall)
BILLER, S. D., Particle Physics (Mansfield College)
BINNEY, J. J., Physics (Merton College)
BLUNDELL, K. M., Astrophysics (St John's College)
BLUNDELL, S. J., Physics (Mansfield College)
BOOTHROYD, A. T., Physics (Oriel College)
BURROWS, P. N., Accelerator Physics (Jesus College)
CAVALLERI, A., Physics (Merton College)
CHALKER, J. T., Physics (St Hugh's College)
CLOSE, F., Theoretical Physics (Exeter College)
COOPER, S., Experimental Physics (St Catherine's College)
COOPER-SARKAR, A. M., Particle Physics (St Hilda's College)
DAVIES, R. L., Astrophysics (Christ Church)
DEVENISH, R. C. E., Physics (Hertford College)
DIMOPOULOS, S., Physics (New College)
ESSLER, F. H. L., Physics (Worcester College)
EWART, P., Physics (Worcester College)
FERREIRA, P. G., Astrophysics (Oriel College)
FOOT, C. J., Physics (St Peter's College)
FOSTER, B., Experimental Physics (Balliol College)
GLAZER, A. M., Physics (Jesus College)
GREGG, J. F., Physics (Magdalen College)
HARNEW, N., Physics (St Anne's College)
HOOK, I. M., Astrophysics (Christ Church)
HOOKER, S. M., Atomic and Laser Physics (Merton College)
JELLEY, N. A., Physics (Lincoln College)
JONES, H., Condensed Matter Physics
JONES, J. A., Physics (Brasenose College)
JONES, M. E., Experimental Cosmology
KRAUS, H. A. P., Physics (Corpus Christi College)
LUKAS, A., Theoretical Physics (Balliol College)
MARCH-RUSSELL, J., Physics (New College)
MARSHALL, D. P., Physical Oceanography (St Hugh's College)
NICHOLAS, R. J., Physics (University College)
PALMER, T. N., Physics (Jesus College)
PEACH, K., Physics (Wolfson College)
PODSIADLOWSKI, P., Physics (St Edmund Hall)
RADAELLI, P., Experimental Philosophy (Wadham College)
RAWLINGS, S. G., Physics (St Peter's College)
READ, P. L., Physics (Trinity College)
RENTON, P. B., Physics
ROCHE, P. F., Physics (Hertford College)
ROSS, G. G., Theoretical Physics (Wadham College)
RYAN, J. F., Physics (Christ Church)
SARKAR, S., Physics (Linacre College)
SERYI, A., Accelerator Physics
SILVER, J. D., Physics (New College)
STEANE, A. M., Physics (Exeter College)
TAYLOR, F. W., Physics (Jesus College)
TAYLOR, R., Condensed Matter Physics (The Queen's College)
THATTE, N., Astrophysics (Keble College)
TURBERFIELD, A. J., Physics (Magdalen College)
VEDRAL, V., Quantum Information Science (Wolfson College)
WALMSLEY, I. A., Experimental Physics (St Hugh's College)
WARK, J. S., Physics (Trinity College)
YASSIN, G., Astrophysics
YEOMANS, J. M., Physics (St Hilda's College)

Department of Physiology, Anatomy and Genetics (Le Gros Clark Bldg, South Parks Rd, Oxford, OX1 3QX; tel. (1865) 272169; fax (1865) 272420; e-mail enquiries@dpag.ox.ac.uk; internet www.dpag.ox.ac.uk):

ASHCROFT, F. M., Physiology (Trinity College)
BLAKEMORE, C. B., Physiology (Magdalen College)
CLARKE, K., Physiological Biochemistry (Merton College)
Dame DAVIES, K. E., Anatomy (Hertford College)
KING, A. J., Neurophysiology (Lincoln College)
MCVEAN, G. A. T., Statistical Genetics (Linacre College)
MIESENBÖCK, G., Physiology (Magdalen College)
PAREKH, A. K., Physiology (Keble College)
PARKER, A. J., Physiology (St John's College)
PATERSON, D. J., Cardiovascular Physiology (Merton College)
PONTING, C. P., Genomics
RILEY, P. R., Development and Reproduction (Jesus College)
ROBBINS, P. A., Physiology (Queen's College)
SATTELLE, D. B., Molecular Neurobiology
VAUGHAN-JONES, R. D., Cellular Physiology (Exeter College)

Department of Plant Sciences (South Parks Rd, Oxford, OX1 3RB; tel. (1865) 275000; fax (1865) 275074; e-mail reception@plants.ox.ac.uk; internet www.plants.ox.ac.uk):

DOLAN, L., Botany (Magdalen College)
GURR, S. J., Molecular Plant Pathology (Somerville College)
HARBERD, N. P., Plant Sciences (St John's College)
LANGDALE, J. A., Plant Development (Queen's College)
RATCLIFFE, R. G., Plant Sciences (New College)
SMITH, J. A. C., Plant Sciences (Magdalen College)
TSIANTIS, M. S., Plant Developmental Genetics (Wadham College)

Department of Politics and International Relations (Manor Rd, Oxford, OX1 3UQ; tel. (1865) 278700; fax (1865) 278725; e-mail enquiries@politics.ox.ac.uk; internet www.politics.ox.ac.uk):

BERMEO, N., Comparative Politics (Nuffield College)
CANEY, S., Political Theory (Magdalen College)
CAPLAN, R. D., International Relations (Linacre College)
CAPOCCIA, G., Comparative Government (Corpus Christi College)
CEADEL, M. E., Politics (New College)
DEIGHTON, A. F., European International Politics (Wolfson College)
DUCH, R., Quantitative Political Science (Nuffield College)
EVANS, G., Sociology of Politics (Nuffield College)
FOOT, R. J., International Relations (St Antony's College)
FOWERAKER, J. W., Latin American Politics (St Antony's College)
FREEDEN, M. S., Politics (Mansfield College)
HOOD, C. C., Government (All Souls College)
HURRELL, A. J., International Relations (Balliol College)
KHONG, Y. F., International Relations (Nuffield College)
KING, D. S., American Government (Nuffield College)
MACFARLANE, S. N., International Relations (St Anne's College)
MATTLI, W., International Political Economy (St John's College)
MCBEATH ANDERSON, D., African Politics (St Antony's College)
MCNAY, L., Theory of Politics (Somerville College)
NEARY, I. J., Politics of Japan (St Antony's College)
NICOLAÏDIS, K. A., International Relations (St Antony's College)
ROBERTSON, D. B., Politics (St Hugh's College)
RUEDA, D., Comparative Politics (Merton College)
SHLAIM, A., International Relations (St Antony's College)
SKACH, C., Comparative Government
SNIDAL, D. J., International Relations (Nuffield College)
SNIJDERS, T. A. B., Statistics in the Social Sciences (Nuffield College)
SOSKICE, D., Comparative Political Economy (Nuffield College)
WALDRON, J. J., Social and Political Theory (All Souls College)
WARE, A. J., Politics (Worcester College)
WELSH, J. M., International Relations (Somerville College)
WHITEFIELD, S. D., Comparative Russian and East European Politics and Society (Pembroke College)
WOODS, N. T., International Political Economy (University College)
ZIELONKA, J., European Politics (St Antony's College)

Department of Primary Health Care (23–38 Hythe Bridge St, Oxford, OX1 2ET; tel. (1865) 289288; fax (1865) 289287; internet www.primarycare.ox.ac.uk):

FARMER, A. J., General Practice (Exeter College)
GLASZIOU, P. P., Evidence-based Medicine (Kellogg College)
HOBBS, F. D. R., General Practice (Harris Manchester College)
NEIL, H. A. W., Clinical Epidemiology (Wolfson College)

Department of Psychiatry (Warneford Hospital, Oxford, OX3 7JX; tel. (1865) 223635;

fax (1865) 793101; e-mail information@psych.ox.ac.uk; internet www.psych.ox.ac.uk):

BURNS, T. P., Social Psychiatry (Kellogg College)
COWEN, P. J., Psychopharmacology
EBMEIER, K. P., Old Age Psychiatry (Linacre College)
FAIRBURN, C. J. A. G., Psychiatry (Merton College)
FLINT, J., Molecular Psychiatry (Merton College)
GEDDES, J., Epidemiological Psychiatry
GOODWIN, G. M., Psychiatry (Merton College)
HARRISON, P. J., Psychiatry (Wolfson College)
HAWTON, K. E., Psychiatry (Green Templeton College)
LLEWELYN, S. P., Clinical Psychology (Harris Manchester College)
ROGERS, R. D., Cognitive Neuroscience (Jesus College)
STEIN, A. J., Child and Adult Psychiatry (Linacre College)

Department of Public Health (Old Rd, Headington, Oxford, OX3 7LF; tel. (1865) 289200; fax (1865) 289260; internet www.dphpc.ox.ac.uk):

BROCKLEHURST, P., Perinatal Epidemiology
FITZPATRICK, R. M., Public Health and Primary Health Care (Nuffield College)
GOLDACRE, M. J., Public Health (Magdalen College)
GRAY, A. M., Health Economics
HOPE, R. A., Medical Ethics (St Cross College)
JAFFE, H. W., Public Health (St Cross College)
JENKINSON, C. P., Health Services Research (Harris Manchester College)
PARKER, M. J., Bioethics (St Cross College)

Department of Social Policy and Intervention (Barnett House, 32 Wellington Sq., Oxford, OX1 2ER; tel. (1865) 270325; fax (1865) 270324; internet www.spi.ox.ac.uk):

COLEMAN, D. A., Demography
GARDNER, F. E. M., Child and Family Psychology (Wolfson College)
KEMP, P. A., Social Policy (St Cross College)
NOBLE, M. W. J., Social Policy (Green Templeton College)
RINGEN, S., Sociology and Social Policy (Green Templeton College)
WALKER, R. L., Social Policy (Green Templeton College)

Department of Sociology (Manor Rd, Oxford, OX1 3UQ; tel. (1865) 281740; fax (1865) 286171; e-mail enquiries@sociology.oxford.ac.uk; internet www.sociology.ox.ac.uk):

DE GRAAF, N. D., Sociology (Nuffield College)
GAMBETTA, D., Sociology (Nuffield College)
GERSHUNY, J., Sociology (St Hugh's College)
HARPER, S., Gerontology (Nuffield College)
HESTROM, P., Sociology (Nuffield College)
KARIYA, T., Sociology of Japanese Society (St Antony's College)
PAYNE, L. A., Sociology (Latin American Societies) (St Antony's College)
VARESE, F., Criminology (Linacre College)

Department of Statistics (1 South Parks Rd, Oxford, OX1 3TG; tel. (1865) 272860; fax (1865) 272595; e-mail info@stats.ox.ac.uk; internet www.stats.ox.ac.uk):

DONNELLY, P. J., Statistical Science (St Anne's College)
ETHERIDGE, A. M., Mathematics (Magdalen College)
GRIFFITHS, R. C., Mathematical Genetics (Lady Margaret Hall)
HEIN, J. J., Bioinformatics (University College)
HOLMES, C., Biostatistics (Lincoln College)
LAURITZEN, S. L., Statistics (Jesus College)
MCDIARMID, C. J. H., Combinatronics (Corpus Christi College)
MCVEAN, G. A. T., Statistical Genetics (Linacre College)
REINERT, G., Statistics (Keble College)
RIPLEY, B. D., Applied Statistics (St Peter's College)
SILVERMAN, B. W., Statistics (Green Templeton College)
SNIJDERS, T. A. B., Statistics in the Social Sciences (Nuffield College)

Nuffield Department of Surgical Sciences (John Radcliffe Hospital, Headington, Oxford, OX3 9DU; tel. (1865) 220532; fax (1865) 768876; e-mail enquiries@nds.ox.ac.uk; internet www.nds.ox.ac.uk):

AUSTYN, J. M., Immunobiology (Wolfson College)
AZIZ, T. Z., Neurosurgery
BYRNE, J. V., Neuroradiology
FRIEND, P. J., Transplantation (Green Templeton College)
HAMDY, F. C., Surgery (Balliol College)
JOHNSON, P. R. V., Paediatric Surgery (St Edmund Hall)
TAGGART, D. P., Cardiothoracic Surgery
WOOD, K. J., Immunology (Green Templeton College)

Faculty of Theology (Theology Faculty Centre, 41 St Giles, Oxford, OX1 3LW; tel. (1865) 270790; fax (1865) 270795; internet www.theology.ox.ac.uk):

Rev. BARTON, J., Interpretation of Holy Scripture (Oriel College)
BIGGAR, N. J., Moral and Pastoral Theology (Regius) (Christ Church)
BOCKMUEHL, M., Biblical and Early Christian Studies (Keble College)
DAY, J., Old Testament Theology (Lady Margaret Hall)
FIDDES, P. S., Systematic Theology (Regent's Park College)
FOOT, S. R. I., Ecclesiastical History (Regius) (Christ Church)
HARRISON, P., Science and Religion (Harris Manchester College)
LEFTOW, B., Philosophy of the Christian Religion (Oriel College)
MACCULLOCH, D. N. J., History of the Church (St Cross College)
PATTISON, G. L., Divinity (Christ Church)
ROWLAND, C. C., Exegesis of Holy Scripture (Queen's College)
STROUMSA, G. G., Study of the Abrahamic Religions (Lady Margaret Hall)
TUCKETT, C. M., New Testament Studies (Wolfson College)

Department of Zoology (South Parks Rd, Oxford, OX1 3PS; tel. (1865) 271234; fax (1865) 310447; internet www.zoo.ox.ac.uk):

GODFRAY, H. C. J., Zoology (Entomology) (Jesus College)
GRAFEN, A., Theoretical Biology (St John's College)
GUILFORD, T. C., Animal Behaviour (Merton College)
GUPTA, S., Epidemiology of Infectious Diseases (Linacre College)
HARVEY, P., Zoology (Jesus College)
HOLLAND, P. W. H., Zoology (Merton College)
KACELNIK, A., Behavioural Ecology (Pembroke College)
Lord KREBS, Zoology (Jesus College)
MACDONALD, D. W., Wildlife Conservation (Lady Margaret Hall)
MAIDEN, M. C. J., Molecular Epidemiology (Hertford College)
Lord MAY, Zoology (Merton College)
MCLEAN, A. R., Mathematical Biology (St Catherine's College)
RANDOLPH, S. E., Parasite Ecology (Oriel College)
ROGERS, D. J., Ecology (Green Templeton College)
SHELDON, B. C., Field Ornithology (Wolfson College)
THOMAS, A. L. R., Biomechanics (Lady Margaret Hall)
THOMAS, J. A., Ecology (New College)
WEST, S. A., Evolutionary Biology
WILLIS, K. J., Biodiversity (Merton College)

DIRECTORS AND HEADS OF UNIVERSITY INSTITUTIONS AND DEPARTMENTS

Institute of Archaeology (34–36 Beaumont St, Oxford, OX1 2PG; tel. (1865) 278240; fax (1865) 278254; e-mail administrator@arch.ox.ac.uk; internet www.archinst.ox.ac.uk):

A. I. WILSON, Archaeology of the Roman Empire (All Souls College)

Institute for Chinese Studies (Clarendon Institute Bldg, Walton St, Oxford, OX1 2HG; tel. (1865) 280387; fax (1865) 280435; e-mail enquiries@chinese.ox.ac.uk; internet www.orinst.ox.ac.uk/ea/chinese):

Chinese Studies: (vacant)

Institute of European and Comparative Law (St Cross Bldg, St Cross Rd, Oxford, OX1 3UL; tel. (1865) 281610; fax (1865) 281611; e-mail enquiries@iecl.ox.ac.uk; internet www.iecl.ox.ac.uk):

S. VOGENAUER, Comparative Law (Brasenose College)

Institute of Social and Cultural Anthropology (51 Banbury Rd, Oxford, OX2 6PF; tel. (1865) 274624; fax (1865) 274630; e-mail info@anthro.ox.ac.uk; internet www.isca.ox.ac.uk):

M. J. BANKS, Visual Anthropology (Wolfson College)

Centre for Criminology (Manor Rd, Oxford, OX1 3UQ; tel. (1865) 274444; fax (1865) 281924; e-mail ccr@crim.ox.ac.uk; internet www.crim.ox.ac.uk):

Dir I. LOADER, Criminology (All Souls College)

Centre for Linguistics and Philology (Walton St, Oxford, OX1 2HG; tel. (1865) 280400; fax (1865) 280412; e-mail enquiries@ling-phil.ox.ac.uk; internet www.ling-phil.ox.ac.uk):

Curator A. LAHIRI, Linguistics (Somerville College)

Centre for Socio-Legal Studies (Manor Rd, Oxford, OX1 3UQ; tel. (1865) 284220; fax (1865) 284221; internet www.csls.ox.ac.uk):

Dir Dr F. PIRIE, Socio-Legal Studies (St Cross College)

Environmental Change Institute (Oxford University Centre for the Environment, South Parks Rd, Oxford, OX1 3QY; tel. (1865) 275848; fax (1865) 275850; e-mail enquiries@eci.ox.ac.uk; internet www.eci.ox.ac.uk):

Dir J. HALL, Climate and Environmental Risks (Linacre College)

Nissan Institute of Japanese Studies (27 Winchester Rd, Oxford, OX2 6NA; tel. (1865) 274570; fax (1865) 274574; e-mail secretary@nissan.ox.ac.uk; internet www.nissan.ox.ac.uk):

Dir I. J. NEARY, Politics of Japan (St Antony's College)

Oriental Institute (Pusey Lane, Oxford, OX1 2LE; tel. (1865) 278200; fax (1865) 278190; e-mail orient@orinst.ox.ac.uk; internet www.orinst.ox.ac.uk):

Chair. of the Faculty Prof. E. HERZIG, Persian Studies (Wadham College)

Oxford Learning Institute (Littlegate House, 16/17 St Ebbe's St, Oxford, OX1 1PT; tel. (1865) 286808; fax (1865) 286801; e-mail services@learning.ox.ac.uk; internet www.learning.ox.ac.uk):

S. GOSS, Teaching and Learning in Higher Education (Wadham College)

Language Centre (12 Woodstock Rd, Oxford, OX2 6HT; tel. (1865) 283360; fax (1865) 283366; e-mail admin@lang.ox.ac.uk; internet www.lang.ox.ac.uk):

Dir R. N. VANDERPLANK (Kellogg College)

Latin American Centre (St Antony's College, Oxford, OX2 6JF; tel. (1865) 274486; fax (1865) 274489; e-mail enquiries@lac.ox.ac.uk; internet www.lac.ox.ac.uk):

T. J. POWER, Latin American Politics (St Cross College)

Philosophy Centre (10 Merton St, Oxford, OX1 4JJ; tel. (1865) 276926; fax (1865) 276932; e-mail enquiries@philosophy.ox.ac.uk; internet www.philosophy.ox.ac.uk):

Chair. of the Faculty Dr M. K. DAVIES, Mental Philosophy (Corpus Christi College)

Department of the History of Art and Centre for Visual Studies (Littlegate House, St Ebbes, Oxford, OX1 1PT; tel. (1865) 286830; fax (1865) 286831; e-mail admin@hoa.ox.ac.uk; internet www.hoa.ox.ac.uk):

Head A. C. CLUNAS, History of Art (Trinity College)

Ruskin School of Drawing and Fine Art (74 High St, Oxford, OX1 4BG; tel. (1865) 276940; fax (1865) 276949; internet www.ruskin-sch.ox.ac.uk):

Head J. GAIGER, Fine Art

Inorganic Chemistry Laboratory (South Parks Rd, Oxford, OX1 3QR; tel. (1865) 272600; fax (1865) 272690; internet www.chem.ox.ac.uk/icl):

Head P. P. EDWARDS, Inorganic Chemistry (St Catherine's College)

Organic Chemistry Laboratory (Chemistry Research Laboratory, 12 Mansfield Rd, Oxford, OX1 3TA; tel. (1865) 285000; fax (1865) 275632; internet www.chem.ox.ac.uk/oc):

Head T. J. DONOHOE, Organic Chemistry (Magdalen College)

Phonetics Laboratory (41 Wellington Sq., Oxford, OX1 2JF; tel. (1865) 270444; fax (1865) 270445; e-mail enquiries@phon.ox.ac.uk; internet www.phon.ox.ac.uk):

Dir J. S. COLEMAN, Phonetics (Wolfson College)

Physical and Theoretical Chemistry Laboratory (South Parks Rd, Oxford, OX1 3QZ; tel. (1865) 275400; fax (1865) 275410; internet www.chem.ox.ac.uk/ptcl):

Head G. HANCOCK, Chemistry (Trinity College)

Research Laboratory for Archaeology and the History of Art (Dyson Perrins Bldg, South Parks Rd, Oxford, OX1 3QY; tel. (1865) 285222; fax (1865) 285220; internet www.rlaha.ox.ac.uk):

A. M. POLLARD, Archaeological Science (Linacre College)

University Archives (Bodleian Library, Broad St, Oxford, OX1 3BG; tel. (1865) 277145; fax (1865) 277187; e-mail enquiries@oua.ox.ac.uk; internet www.oua.ox.ac.uk):

Keeper S. BAILEY (Linacre College)

Ashmolean Museum of Art and Archaeology (Beaumont St, Oxford, OX1 2PH; tel. (1865) 278002; fax (1865) 278018; internet www.ashmolean.org):

C. P. H. BROWN (Worcester College)

Museum of the History of Science (Old Ashmolean Bldg, Broad St, Oxford, OX1 3AZ; tel. (1865) 277280; fax (1865) 277288; internet www.mhs.ox.ac.uk):

Dir J. A. BENNETT (Linacre College)

Pitt Rivers Museum (South Parks Rd, Oxford, OX1 3PP; tel. (1865) 270927; fax (1865) 270943; e-mail prm@prm.ox.ac.uk; internet www.prm.ox.ac.uk):

Dir M. O'HANLON (Linacre College)

University Museum of Natural History (Parks Rd, Oxford, OX1 3PW; tel. (1865) 272950; fax (1865) 272970; e-mail info@oum.ox.ac.uk; internet www.oum.ox.ac.uk):

Natural History: (vacant)

Bodleian Library (Broad St, Oxford, OX1 3BG; tel. (1865) 277000; fax (1865) 277182; e-mail enquiries@bodley.ox.ac.uk; internet www.ouls.ox.ac.uk/bodley):

Bodley's Librarian and Dir of Univ. Library Services S. E. THOMAS (Balliol College)

Botanic Garden (Rose Lane, Oxford, OX1 4AZ; tel. (1865) 286690; fax (1865) 286693; e-mail postmaster@obg.ox.ac.uk; internet www.botanic-garden.ox.ac.uk):

Dir T. WALKER (University College)

National Perinatal Epidemiology Unit (Old Rd Campus, Headington, Oxford, OX3 7LF; tel. (1865) 289700; fax (1865) 289701; e-mail general@npeu.ox.ac.uk; internet www.npeu.ox.ac.uk):

Dir P. BROCKLEHURST

Transport Studies Unit (Oxford University Centre for the Environment, South Parks Rd, Oxford, OX1 3QY; tel. (1865) 285070; fax (1865) 275885; internet www.tsu.ox.ac.uk):

Dir D. BANISTER, Transport Studies (St Anne's College)

Wellcome Unit for the History of Medicine (45–47 Banbury Rd, Oxford, OX2 6PE; tel. (1865) 274600; fax (1865) 274605; e-mail wuhmo@wuhmo.ox.ac.uk; internet www.wuhmo.ox.ac.uk):

Dir M. HARRISON, History of Medicine (Green Templeton College)

COLLEGES

All Souls College: High St, Oxford, OX1 4AL; tel. (1865) 279379; internet www.all-souls.ox.ac.uk; f. 1438; for Fellows only; Warden Prof. Sir JOHN VICKERS.

Balliol College: Broad St, Oxford, OX1 3BJ; tel. (1865) 277777; fax (1865) 277803; e-mail academic.registrar@balliol.ox.ac.uk; internet www.balliol.ox.ac.uk; f. 1263; Master ANDREW GRAHAM; publ. *Floreat Domus* (1 a year).

Brasenose College: Radcliffe Sq., Oxford, OX1 4AJ; tel. (1865) 277830; fax (1865) 277822; e-mail college.office@bnc.ox.ac.uk; internet www.bnc.ox.ac.uk; f. 1509; Prin. Prof. ROGER CASHMORE; Prin. Prof. ALAN K. BOWMAN (acting).

Christ Church: St Aldates, Oxford, OX1 1DP; tel. (1865) 276150; fax (1865) 286588; internet www.chch.ox.ac.uk; f. 1546; Dean The Very Rev. CHRISTOPHER LEWIS.

Corpus Christi College: Merton St, Oxford, OX1 4JF; tel. (1865) 276700; fax (1865) 276767; e-mail college.office@ccc.ox.ac.uk; internet www.ccc.ox.ac.uk; f. 1517; Pres. Prof. RICHARD CARWARDINE.

Exeter College: Turl St, Oxford, OX1 3DP; tel. (1865) 279600; fax (1865) 279645; e-mail academic.administrator@exeter.ox.ac.uk; internet www.exeter.ox.ac.uk; f. 1314; Rector FRANCES CAIRNCROSS.

Green Templeton College: Woodstock Rd, Oxford, OX2 6HG; tel. (1865) 274770; fax (1865) 274796; internet www.gtc.ox.ac.uk; f. 2008; Prin. Sir DAVID WATSON.

Harris Manchester College: Mansfield Rd, Oxford, OX1 3TD; tel. (1865) 271006; fax (1865) 271012; e-mail enquiries@hmc.ox.ac.uk; internet www.hmc.ox.ac.uk; f. 1786 for mature students; Prin. The Rev. Dr RALPH WALLER.

Hertford College: Catte St, Oxford, OX1 3BW; tel. (1865) 279400; fax (1865) 279437; internet www.hertford.ox.ac.uk; f. 1740; Prin. Dr JOHN LANDERS.

Jesus College: Turl St, Oxford, OX1 3DW; tel. (1865) 279700; fax (1865) 279687; e-mail lodge@jesus.ox.ac.uk; internet www.jesus.ox.ac.uk; f. 1571; Prin. Lord KREBS.

Keble College: Parks Rd, Oxford, OX1 3PG; tel. (1865) 272727; fax (1865) 272705; e-mail enquiries@keble.ox.ac.uk; internet www.keble.ox.ac.uk; f. 1870; Warden Sir JONATHAN PHILLIPS.

Kellogg College: Banbury Rd, Oxford, OX2 6PN; tel. (1865) 612000; fax (1865) 612001; e-mail college.office@kellogg.ox.ac.uk; internet www.kellogg.ox.ac.uk; f. 1990 for adult, part-time and professional devt students; Pres. Prof. Dr JONATHAN MICHIE.

Lady Margaret Hall: Norham Gardens, Oxford, OX2 6QA; tel. (1865) 274300; fax (1865) 274313; e-mail lodge@lmh.ox.ac.uk; internet www.lmh.ox.ac.uk; f. 1878; Prin. Dr FRANCES LANNON.

Linacre College: St Cross Rd, Oxford, OX1 3JA; tel. (1865) 271650; fax (1865) 271668; e-mail college.secretary@linacre.ox.ac.uk; internet www.linacre.ox.ac.uk; f. 1962, as Linacre House for graduates; Prin. Dr NICK BROWN.

Lincoln College: Turl St, Oxford, OX1 3DR; tel. (1865) 279800; fax (1865) 279802; e-mail info@lincoln.ac.uk; internet www.linc.ox.ac.uk; f. 1427; Rector Prof. PAUL LANGFORD.

Magdalen College: High St, Oxford, OX1 4AU; tel. (1865) 276000; fax (1865) 276030; internet www.magd.ox.ac.uk; f. 1458; Pres. Prof. DAVID CLARY.

Mansfield College: Mansfield Rd, Oxford, OX1 3TF; tel. (1865) 270999; fax (1865) 270970; e-mail admissions@ox.ac.uk; internet www.mansfield.ox.ac.uk; f. 1886; Prin. Dr DIANA WALFORD.

Merton College: Merton St, Oxford, OX1 4JD; tel. (1865) 276310; fax (1865) 276361; internet www.merton.ox.ac.uk; f. 1264; Warden Prof. Sir MARTIN TAYLOR.

New College: Holywell St, Oxford, OX1 3BN; tel. (1865) 279555; fax (1865) 289189; internet www.new.ox.ac.uk; f. 1379; Warden Sir CURTIS PRICE.

Nuffield College: New Rd, Oxford, OX1 1NF; tel. (1865) 278500; fax (1865) 278621; e-mail lodge@nuffield.ox.ac.uk; internet www.nuff.ox.ac.uk; f. 1958; Warden Prof. STEPHEN NICKELL.

Oriel College: Oriel Sq., Oxford, OX1 4EW; tel. (1865) 276555; fax (1865) 791823; e-mail lodge@oriel.ox.ac.uk; internet www.oriel.ox.ac.uk; f. 1326; Provost Sir DEREK MORRIS.

Pembroke College: St Aldate's, Oxford, OX1 1DW; tel. (1865) 276444; fax (1865) 276418; internet www.pmb.ox.ac.uk; f. 1624; Master GILES HENDERSON.

Queen's College, The: High St, Oxford, OX1 4AW; tel. (1865) 279120; fax (1865) 790819; internet www.queens.ox.ac.uk; f. 1341; Provost Prof. PAUL MADDEN.

St Anne's College: Woodstock Rd, Oxford, OX2 6HS; tel. (1865) 274800; fax (1865) 274899; e-mail enquiries@st-annes.ox.ac.uk;

internet www.st-annes.ox.ac.uk; f. 1878 as Society of Oxford Home Students; Prin. TIM GARDAM.

St Antony's College: Woodstock Rd, Oxford, OX2 6JF; tel. (1865) 284700; fax (1865) 274526; internet www.sant.ox.ac.uk; f. 1953; Warden Prof. MARGARET MACMILLAN.

St Catherine's College: Manor Rd, Oxford, OX1 3UJ; tel. (1865) 271700; fax (1865) 271685; e-mail college.office@stcatz.ox.ac.uk; internet www.stcatz.ox.ac.uk; f. 1868, reconstituted as a full College 1963; Master Prof. ROGER W. AINSWORTH.

St Cross College: St Giles, Oxford, OX1 3LZ; tel. (1865) 278490; fax (1865) 278484; internet www.stx.ox.ac.uk; f. 1965 for graduates; Master Prof. ANDREW GOUDIE.

St Edmund Hall: Queen's Lane, Oxford, OX1 4AR; tel. (1865) 279000; fax (1865) 279090; e-mail college.secretary@seh.ox.ac.uk; internet www.seh.ox.ac.uk; f. c. 1278; Prin. Prof. KEITH GULL.

St Hilda's College: Cowley Pl., Oxford, OX4 1DY; tel. (1865) 276884; fax (1865) 276816; e-mail outreach@st-hildas.ox.ac.uk; internet www.st-hildas.ox.ac.uk; f. 1893; Prin. SHEILA FORBES.

St Hugh's College: St Margaret's Rd, Oxford, OX2 6LE; tel. (1865) 274900; fax (1865) 274912; e-mail academic.administrator@st-hughs.ox.ac.uk; internet www.st-hughs.ox.ac.uk; f. 1886; Prin. ANDREW DILNOT.

St John's College: St Giles', Oxford, OX1 3JP; tel. (1865) 277300; fax (1865) 277435; e-mail college.office@sjc.ox.ac.uk; internet www.sjc.ox.ac.uk; f. 1555; Pres. Sir MICHAEL SCHOLAR.

St Peter's College: New Inn Hall St, Oxford, OX1 2DL; tel. (1865) 278900; fax (1865) 278855; internet www.spc.ox.ac.uk; f. 1929 as St Peter's Hall; Master MARK DAMAZER (acting); Dean Dr ROGER ALLEN.

Somerville College: Woodstock Rd, Oxford, OX2 6HD; tel. (1865) 270600; fax (1865) 270601; e-mail secretariat@some.ox.ac.uk; internet www.some.ox.ac.uk; f. 1879; Prin. Dr ALICE PROCHASKA.

Trinity College: Broad St, Oxford, OX1 3BH; tel. (1865) 279900; fax (1865) 279902; internet www.trinity.ox.ac.uk; f. 1555; Pres. Sir IVOR ROBERTS.

University College: High St, Oxford, OX1 4BH; tel. (1865) 276602; internet www.univ.ox.ac.uk; f. 1249; Master Sir IVOR CREWE.

Wadham College: Parks Rd, Oxford, OX1 3PN; tel. (1865) 277900; fax (1865) 277937; internet www.wadham.ox.ac.uk; f. 1610; Warden Sir NEIL CHALMERS.

Wolfson College: Linton Rd, Oxford, OX2 6UD; tel. (1865) 274100; fax (1865) 274125; internet www.wolfson.ox.ac.uk; f. 1965 for graduates; Pres. Prof. HERMIONE LEE (acting).

Worcester College: Walton St, Oxford, OX1 2HB; tel. (1865) 278300; fax (1865) 278369; internet www.wor.ox.ac.uk; f. 1714; Provost RICHARD G. SMETHURST.

PERMANENT PRIVATE HALLS

Blackfriars: 64 St Giles', Oxford, OX1 3LY; tel. (1865) 278400; e-mail secretary@bfriars.ox.ac.uk; internet www.bfriars.ox.ac.uk; f. 1221; Regent Very Revd Dr RICHARD FINN.

Campion Hall: Brewer St, Oxford, OX1 1QS; tel. (1865) 286100; fax (1865) 286148; e-mail enquiries@campion.ox.ac.uk; internet www.campion.ox.ac.uk; f. 1896; Master Rev. BRENDAN CALLAGHAN.

Regent's Park College: Pusey St, Oxford, OX1 2LB; tel. (1865) 288120; fax (1865) 288121; e-mail enquiries@regents.ox.ac.uk; internet www.rpc.ox.ac.uk; f. 1810; Prin. Rev. Dr ROBERT ELLIS.

St Benet's Hall: 38 St Giles, Oxford, OX1 3LN; tel. (1865) 280556; fax (1865) 280792; e-mail enquiries@stb.ox.ac.uk; internet www.st-benets.ox.ac.uk; f. 1897; Master Father FELIX STEPHENS.

St Stephen's House: 16 Marston St, Oxford, OX4 1JX; tel. (1865) 613500; fax (1865) 613513; e-mail enquiries@ssho.ox.ac.uk; internet www.ssho.ox.ac.uk; f. 1876; Prin. Rev. Canon Dr ROBIN WARD.

Wycliffe Hall: 52–54 Banbury Rd, Oxford, OX2 6PW; tel. (1865) 274200; fax (1865) 274215; e-mail enquiries@wycliffe.ox.ac.uk; internet www.wycliffe.ox.ac.uk; f. 1877; Prin. Rev. Dr RICHARD TURNBULL.

UNIVERSITY OF PLYMOUTH

Drake Circus, Plymouth, PL4 8AA
Telephone: (1752) 600600
Fax: (1752) 232293
E-mail: publicrelations@plymouth.ac.uk
Internet: www.plymouth.ac.uk

Founded 1970 as Plymouth Polytechnic, name changed to Polytechnic South West in 1989, present name and status 1992

Academic year: September to June

Vice-Chancellor and Chief Exec.: Prof. WENDY PURCELL
Deputy Vice-Chancellor: Prof. MARY WATKINS
Pro-Vice-Chancellor for Research: Prof. JOHN SCOTT
Pro-Vice-Chancellor: Prof. JULIAN BEER
Pro-Vice-Chancellor: Prof. RICHARD STEPHENSON
Pro-Vice-Chancellor: DAVID COSLETT
Pro-Vice-Chancellor: Prof. DAVID WHEELER
Dean of Students: Dr ANITA JELLINGS
Univ. Sec. and Acad. Registrar: JANE HOPKINSON
Dir for Information Learning Services: PENNY HOLLAND (acting)
Dir for Marketing and Communications: JANE CHAFER
Dir for Human Resources: ROLAND BUCKLEY
Dir for Research and Enterprise: Prof. JULIAN BEER

Library of 450,000 vols, 14,000 journal titles
Number of teachers: 2,942
Number of students: 32,933

Publication: *Research Report*

DEANS

Faculty of Arts: DAVID COSLETT
Faculty of Education: WILL MCBURNIE (acting)
Faculty of Health and Social Work: Prof. JOHN CLIBBENS (acting)
Faculty of Science and Technology: Prof. RICHARD GIBB
Faculty of Social Science and Business: Prof. Dr JOAN CHANDLER
Faculty of Technology: Prof. NEIL JAMES
Peninsula College of Medicine and Dentistry: Prof. STEVE THORNTON
Plymouth Business School: Prof. DAVID WHEELER
University of Plymouth Colleges: Dr COLIN WILLIAMS

UNIVERSITY OF PORTSMOUTH

University House, Winston Churchill Ave, Portsmouth, PO1 2UP
Telephone: (23) 9284-8484
Fax: (23) 9284-3082
E-mail: info.centre@port.ac.uk
Internet: www.port.ac.uk

Founded 1869, as Portsmouth School of Science and Art, became Portsmouth Polytechnic in 1969; present name and status 1992

Academic year: September to June

Chancellor: Lord PALUMBO
Vice-Chancellor: Prof. JOHN CRAVEN
Deputy Vice-Chancellor: REBECCA BUNTING
Pro-Vice-Chancellor: Dr DAVID ARRELL
Pro-Vice-Chancellor: Prof. JOHN TURNER
Acad. Registrar: A. REES
Univ. Librarian: ROISIN GWYER

Library of 600,000 vols
Number of teachers: 1,200
Number of students: 19,000

DEANS

Faculty of Creative and Cultural Industries: Dr SIMON CLARIDGE
Faculty of Humanities and Social Sciences: DAVE RUSSELL
Faculty of Science: Prof. PAUL HAYES
Faculty of Technology: Prof. DJAMEL AIT-BOUDAOUD
Portsmouth Business School: ANN RIDLEY

UNIVERSITY OF READING

Whiteknights, POB 217, Reading, RG6 6AH
Telephone: (118) 987-5123
Fax: (118) 931-4404
E-mail: communications@reading.ac.uk
Internet: www.reading.ac.uk

Founded 1892, as Univ. Extension College, univ. status 1926

Academic year: October to July

Chancellor: Sir JOHN MADEJSKI
Vice-Chancellor: Prof. GORDON MARSHALL
Deputy Vice-Chancellor: Prof. TONY DOWNES
Pro-Vice-Chancellor for Int. and External Engagement: Prof. STEVEN MITHEN
Pro-Vice-Chancellor for Research and Innovation: Prof. CHRISTINE WILLIAMS
Pro-Vice-Chancellor for Teaching and Learning: Prof. ROB ROBSON
Dir of Student Services: JENNIFER GHANDHI
Treas.: Dr PETER WARRY
Librarian: JULIA MUNRO

Library: see Libraries and Archives
Number of teachers: 2,005
Number of students: 17,500

Publication: *Research Review* (2 a year)

DEANS

Faculty of Arts and Humanities: Prof. SUE WALKER
Henley Business School: Prof. CHRIS BONES
Faculty of Life Sciences: Prof. RICHARD ELLIS
Faculty of Science: Prof. GAVIN BROOKS
Faculty of Social Sciences: Prof. DIANNE BERRY

PROFESSORS

(Some professors serve in more than one faculty)

Faculty of Arts and Humanities (Whiteknights, POB 218, Reading, RG6 6AA; tel. (118) 931-8063; fax (118) 931-0748):

ARNOLD, B. C. B., History
BARANSKI, Z., Italian Studies
BARBER, M. C., History
BIDDISS, M. D., History
BROWN, C. C., English and American Literary Studies
BUCKLEY, S., Arts and Communication Design
BULL, J., Arts and Communication Design
BULLEN, J. B., English and American Literary Studies
COOK, G.W. D., Linguistics and Applied Language Studies
COOPER, P. J., Psychology
COTTINGHAM, J. G., Humanities
CURRY, A. E., History
DANCY, J. P., Humanities

DUNSBY, J. M., Arts and Communication Design
ELIOT, S. J., Arts and Communication Design; English and American Literary Studies
EVANS, A. W., Environmental Economics
GARMAN, M. A. G., Linguistics and Applied Language Studies
GILCHRIST, R., Archaeology
HOOKER, B., Humanities
HOULBROOKE, R.A., History
HOWELLS, C. A., English and American Literary Studies
JAMES, E. F., History
LUNA, P., Arts and Communication Design
NOBLE, P. S., Modern Languages
PARRINDER, J. P., English and American Literary Studies
PILLING, J., English and American Literary Studies
POTTS, A., Humanities
ROACH, P. J., Lingustic and Applied Language Studies
ROBEY, D. J. B., Modern Languages
RUTHERFORD, I. C., Humanities
SANDFORD, J. E., Modern Languages
SEGAL, N., Modern Languages
STRAWSON, G. J., Humanities
TUCKER, G. H., Modern Languages
WALLACE-HADRILL, A. F., Humanities
WARBURTON, I. P., Linguistic Science
WILKINS, D. A., Linguistics and Applied Language Studies
WOODWARD, P. R., Politics

Faculty of Economic and Social Sciences (Whiteknights, POB 218, Reading, RG6 6AA; tel. (118) 931-8183; fax (118) 931-6658; e-mail fasug@reading.ac.uk):

BELLAMY, R., Politics and Sociology
BREHENY, M. J., Business
BUCKLEY, R. A., Law
BUSH, A. W., Education
CANTWELL, J. A., Business
CASSON, M. C., Business
CROLL, P., Education
CROSBY, F. N., Business
DAVIES, J. C. H., Politics and Sociology
DOWNES, T. A., Law
EDWARDS, V. K., Education
EVANS, A. W., Business
FIDLER, F. B., Education
FRANZONI, R., Politics and Sociology
GHANDI, P. R., Law
GILBERT, J. K., Education
GRAY, C. S., Politics and Sociology
JONES, G. G., Business
KEENE, J., Health and Social Care
LIZIERI, C. M., Business
MALVERN, D. D., Education
MURDOCH, J. R., Law
NOBES, C. W., Business
PATTERSON, K. D., Business
PEMBERTON, J., Business
POPE, M. L., Education
RICHARDS, B. J., Education
SCOTT-QUINN, B., Business
SOUTHWORTH, G. W., Education
STYCHIN, C., Law
UTTON, M. A., Business
WADDINGTON, P. A. J., Politics and Sociology
WARD, C. W., Business
WOODWARD, P. R., Politics and Sociology

Faculty of Life Sciences (Whiteknights, POB 200, Reading, RG6 6AF; tel. (118) 931-8342; fax (118) 931-5509; e-mail sciug@reading.ac.uk):

BARNETT, J. R., Plant Sciences
BEEVER, D. E., Agriculture, Policy and Development
BISBY, F. A., Plant Sciences
BROWN, V. K., Agriculture, Policy and Development
CALIGARI, P. D. S., Plant Sciences
COLLINS, M. D., Food Biosciences
CRABBE, M. J. C., Animal and Microbial Sciences
DUNWELL, J. M., Plant Sciences
ELLIS, R. H., Agriculture, Policy and Development
FRANCE, J., Agriculture, Policy and Development
GARFORTH, C. J., Agriculture, Policy and Development
GIBSON, G. R., Food Biosciences
HADLEY, P., Plant Sciences
HOLLAND, P. W. H., Animal and Microbial Sciences
JOHN, P., Plant Sciences
JONES, I. M., Animal and Microbial Sciences
KNIGHT, P. G., Animal and Microbial Sciences
LEDWARD, D. A., Food Biosciences
LOWRY, P. J., Animal and Microbial Sciences
MOTTRAM, D. V., Food Biosciences
OWEN, E., Agriculture, Policy and Development
PAGEL, M., Animal and Microbial Sciences
PAYNE, C. C., Plant Sciences
PYLE, D. L., Food Biosciences
ROBSON, R. L., Animal and Microbial Sciences
SCHOFIELD, J. D., Food Biosciences
SIBLY, R. M., Animal and Microbial Sciences
STRANGE, P., Animal and Microbial Sciences
SWINBANK, A., Agriculture, Policy and Development
TRAILL, B., Agriculture, Policy and Development
WHITEHEAD, J. R., Applied Statistics
WILLIAMS, C. M., Food Biosciences

Faculty of Science (Whiteknights, POB 200, Reading, RG6 6AF; tel. (118) 931-8342; fax (118) 975-5509; e-mail sciug@reading.ac.uk):

ALLOWAY, B. J., Human and Environmental Sciences
ANDREWS, B., Computer Science, Cybernetics and Electronic Engineering
ASTILL, G. G., Human and Environmental Sciences
ATKINS, A. G., Construction Management and Engineering
BAKER, K. D., Computer Science, Cybernetics and Electronic Engineering
BASSETT, D. C., Mathematics, Meteorology and Physics
BERRY, D. C., Psychology
BON, R., Construction Management and Engineering
BOWKER, M., Chemistry
BRADLEY, R. J., Human and Environmental Sciences
BROWNING, K. A., Mathematics, Meteorology and Physics
CARDIN, D. J., Chemistry
CHAPLIN, C. R., Construction Management and Engineering
CHAPMAN, R. W., Human and Environmental Sciences
CLEMENTS-CROOME, T. D. J., Construction Management and Engineering
CODLING, K., Mathematics, Meteorology and Physics
COLEMAN, M. L., Human and Environmental Sciences
COLQUHOUN, H. M., Chemistry
COOPER, P. J., Psychology
DREW, M. G. B., Chemistry
FISHER, G. N., Construction Management and Engineering
FLANAGAN, R., Construction Management and Engineering
FULFORD, M. G., Human and Environmental Sciences
GILBERT, A., Chemistry
GILCHRIST, R., Human and Environmental Sciences
GREGORY, P. J., Human and Environmental Sciences
GURNEY, R., Mathematics, Meteorology and Physics
HAINES, K., Mathematics, Meteorology and Physics
HARRISON, R., Computer Science, Cybernetics and Electronic Engineering
HARWOOD, L. M., Chemistry
HILTON, A. J. W., Mathematics, Meteorology and Physics
HOSKINS, B. J., Mathematics, Meteorology and Physics
JERONIMIDIS, G., Construction Management and Engineering
MCKENNA, F. P., Psychology
MEGSON, G. M., Computer Science, Cybernetics and Electronic Engineering
MITCHELL, G. R., Mathematics, Meteorology and Physics
MITHEN, S. J., Human and Environmental Sciences
MURRAY, L., Psychology
NEEDHAM, D. J., Mathematics, Meteorology and Physics
NICHOLS, N. K., Mathematics, Meteorology and Physics
O'NEILL, A., Mathematics, Meteorology and Physics
PORTER, D., Mathematics, Meteorology and Physics
RICE, D. A., Chemistry
SELLWOOD, B. W., Human Sciences
SHARKEY, P. M., Computer Science, Cybernetics and Electronic Engineering
SHINE, K. P., Mathematics, Meteorology and Physics
SLINGO, G. M., Mathematics, Meteorology and Physics
SMITH, P. T., Psychology
THORPE, A. J., Mathematics, Meteorology and Physics
VALDES, P. J., Mathematics, Meteorology and Physics
WADGE, G. M., Mathematics, Meteorology and Physics
WALSH, R., Chemistry
WANN, J. P., Psychology
WARBURTON, D. M., Psychology
WARWICK, K., Computer Science, Cybernetics and Electronic Engineering
WHITEHEAD, P. G., Human and Environmental Sciences
WRIGHT, A. C., Mathematics, Meteorology and Physics
WRIGHT, J. D. M., Mathematics, Meteorology and Physics

Rural History Centre (Whiteknights, POB 229, Reading, RG6 6AG; tel. (118) 931-8342; fax (118) 931-5509; e-mail rhc@reading.ac.uk):

HOYLE, R. W.

UNIVERSITY OF SALFORD

Salford, Greater Manchester, M5 4WT
Telephone: (161) 295-5000
Fax: (161) 295-5999
E-mail: office-exrel@salford.ac.uk
Internet: www.salford.ac.uk

Founded 1896, as the Royal Technical Institute, later Royal College of Advanced Technology, Univ. Charter granted 1967
Academic year: October to July

Chancellor: Dr IRENE KHAN
Vice-Chancellor: Prof. MARTIN HALL
Deputy Vice-Chancellor and Registrar and Sec.: Dr ADRIAN GRAVES
Pro-Vice-Chancellor for Academic: Prof. HUW MORRIS
Pro-Vice-Chancellor for International Affairs: Prof. CYNTHIA PINE

Pro-Vice-Chancellor for Research and Innovation: Prof. GHASSAN AOUAD
Pro-Vice-Chancellor for Strategic Partnerships: KEITH BARNES
Dir of Academic Information Services and Librarian: TONY LEWIS

Number of teachers: 800
Number of students: 18,000

DEANS

Arts and Social Sciences: Prof. HUW MORRIS
Health and Social Care: Prof. CYNTHIA PINE
Science and Technology: Prof. GHASSAN AOUAD

PROFESSORS

ALEXANDER, K., Construction and Property Management
ALSHAWI, M., Surveying
AOUAD, G., Surveying
ARMOUR, D. G., Physics
ARNELL, R. D., Aeronautical, Mechanical and Manufacturing Engineering
AVIS, N., Information Technology Institute
AYLETT, R., Information Systems Institute
BAKER, R. D., Accounting, Economics and Management Service
BARIC, L. F., Information Technology Institute
BARRETT, P. S., Surveying
BETTS, M. P., Surveying
BLAKEMORE, D. L., Modern Languages
BOARDMAN, A. D., Physics
BOOTH, J. G., Physics
BOTHAM, D., Management
BOWKER, P., Rehabilitation
BRANDON, P. S., Surveying
BROWN, G. R., Surveying
BRYANT, C. G. A., Sociology
BULL, M. J., Politics and Contemporary History
CALDWELL, D., Electronic and Electrical Engineering
CARTER, G., Physics
CHADWICK, D. W., Information System Institute
CHRISTER, A. H., Computer and Mathematics Science
COLLIER, C. G., Civil and Environmental Engineering
COLLIGON, J. S., Electronic and Electrical Engineering
COLLINS, D. N., Geography
COLQUHOUN, H. M., Chemistry and Applied Chemistry
COOK, R., Media and Performance
COOPER, G., Information Technology
COOPER, I., Centre for Regional Development and Sustainability
COOPER, R., Art and Design Technology
CRAIG, P. S., Biological Sciences
CROSSLEY, T. R., Aeronautical, Mechanical and Manufacturing Engineering
DANGERFIELD, B. C., Accounting, Economics and Management Science
DANSON, F. M., Environment and Life Sciences
DAVIES-COOPER, R., Art and Design Technology
DONNELLY, S. E., Physics
EASSON, A. W., English
EDGELL, S. R., Sociology
EDWARDS, J., Rehabilitation
EKERE, N. N., Aeronautical, Mechanical and Manufacturing Engineering
FERNANDO, T. P., Information Systems Institute
FLYNN, R., Sociology
GARSIDE, P. L., European Studies Research Institute
GERBER, R., Physics
GLEAVE, M. B., Geography
GOLDSMITH, M. J. F., Politics and Contemporary History
GRAY, J. O., Electronic and Electrical Engineering
GRUNDY, P. J., Physics
HARDING, A., Regional Development and Urban Politics
HARRIS, G. T., Modern Languages
HICKEY, L. D., Modern Languages
HILL, R., Computer and Mathematical Sciences
HORNER, A., English
HUGHES, R., Chemistry and Applied Chemistry
KAY, S., Health and Social Care
KEIGER, J. F. V., Modern Languages
KOBBACY, K. A. H., Accounting, Economics and Management Science
LAM, Y. W., Acoustics and Electronic Engineering
LARMOUTH, J., Information Technology Institute
LAWSON, R., Biological Sciences
LEONARD, J., Sciences
LINGE, N., Electronic and Electrical Engineering
LONG, A. F., Health Care Practice
LONGHURST, B. J., English, Sociology, Politics and Contemporary History
LORD, D., Physics
MARVIN, S., Centre for Regional Development and Sustainability
MASON, R. S., Business Studies
MAY, T., Sociology
MELBOURNE, C., Civil and Environmental Engineering
MORGAN, C. G., Biological Sciences
NAGY, F. L. N., Information Technology
NEAL, F., European Studies
PEMBLE, M. E., Chemistry and Applied Chemistry
POPAY, J., Public Health Research and Resource Centre
POWELL, J. A., Information Technology
PROCTER, G., Chemistry and Applied Chemistry
RAYNES, N., Health and Social Care
REZGUI, Y., Information Systems Institute
RICHARDS, J., Science
ROSS, D. K., Physics
SAMPSON, A. A., Economics
SANGER, D. J., Aeronautical, Mechanical and Manufacturing Engineering
SARSHAR, M., Construction and Property Management
SCOTT, D. B., Music
SHARDLOW, S. M., Social Work
SIMMONS, C., Accounting, Economics and Management Science
STEELE, A., Environment and Life Sciences
STOREY, D. M., Biological Sciences
TAYLOR, I. R., Sociology
TOLZ, V., English, Sociology, Politics and Contemporary History
TOMLINSON, P., Languages
TONGE, J., English, Sociology, Politics and Contemporary History
TOWELL, R. J., Modern Languages
VADERA, S., Sciences
WALKDEN, F., Computer and Mathematics Science
WEBSTER, P. J., Civil and Environmental Engineering
WHITEHEAD, C., Physics
WHITELEY, S., Media, Music and Performance
WHITELOCK, J., Management
WOOD, J. R. G., Computer and Mathematical Sciences, Information and Educational and Materials Development
WOOD, L., Business and Informatics
WOOD-HARPER, A. T., Computer and Mathematics Science
WRIGHT, F., Surveying
WYN JONES, E., Chemistry and Applied Chemistry

UNIVERSITY OF SHEFFIELD

Firth Court, Western Bank, Sheffield, S10 2TN
Telephone: (114) 222-2000
Fax: (114) 279-8603
E-mail: externalrelations@sheffield.ac.uk
Internet: www.sheffield.ac.uk

Founded 1879 as Univ. College, Royal Charter 1905
Academic year: September to June
Chancellor: Lord DAINTON
Pro-Chancellor: K. E. RIDDLE
Pro-Chancellor: P. FIRTH
Pro-Chancellor: ANTHONY PAUL PEDDER
Vice-Chancellor: Prof. KEITH BURNETT
Pro-Vice-Chancellor for Learning and Teaching: Prof. PAUL WHITE
Pro-Vice-Chancellor for Research and Innovation: Prof. RICHARD JONES
Pro-Vice-Chancellor for Internaional Affairs: Prof. REBECCA HUGHES
Pro-Vice-Chancellor for the Faculty of Arts and Humanities: Prof. MICHAEL BRADDICK (acting)
Pro-Vice-Chancellor for the Faculty of Engineering: Prof. MICHAEL HOUNSLOW
Pro-Vice-Chancellor for the Faculty of Medicine, Dentistry and Health: Prof. ANTHONY WEETMAN
Pro-Vice-Chancellor for the Faculty of Science: Prof. ANTHONY RYAN
Pro-Vice-Chancellor for the Faculty of Social Sciences: Prof. ANTHONY PAYNE
Registrar and Sec.: P. HARVEY
Librarian: MARTIN LEWIS

Library: see Libraries and Archives
Number of teachers: 1,500
Number of students: 24,916

PROFESSORS

(Some staff serve in more than one faculty)

Faculty of Architectural Studies:

BLUNDELL JONES, P. M., Architecture
CAMPBELL, H., Town and Regional Planning
CROOK, A. D. H., Town and Regional Planning
HENNEBERRY, J., Town and Regional Planning
KANG, J., Architecture
LAWSON, B. R., Architecture
PLANK, R. J., Architecture
SWANWICK, C. A., Landscape
TILL, J., Architecture
TREGENZA, P. R., Architecture

Faculty of Arts:

AINSWORTH, P. F., French
Canon ALEXANDER, L. C. A., Biblical Studies
BARRETT, J. C., Archaeology
BELL, D. A., Philosophy
BENNET, J., Archaeology
BRADDICK, M. J., History
BRANIGAN, K., Archaeology
BROOKSBANK JONES, A., Hispanic Studies
CLARKE, E. F., Music
CLINES, D. J. A., Biblical Studies
COLLIS, J. R., Archaeology and Prehistory
COOK, R. J., History
CROSS, M. F., French
DENNELL, R. W., Archaeology
DIVERS, J., Philosophy
DUFFIELD, N. G., English Language and Linguistics
ENGLAND, J. P., Hispanic Studies
EXUM, J. C., Biblical Studies
GREENGRASS, M., History
HAFFENDEN, J., English Literature
HATTAWAY, M., English Literature
HILL, P. H. A. W., Music
HOOKWAY, C. J., Philosophy
HOPKINS, R., Philosophy
JONES, G. E. M., Archaeology

Sir KERSHAW, I., Modern History
KING, E. J., History
LEATHERBARROW, W. J., Russian and Slavonic Studies
LINN, A. R., English Language and Linguistics
MCMAHON, A. M. S., English Language and Linguistics
OWENS, D. J., Philosophy
PERRAUDIN, M. F., Germanic Studies
PHIMISTER, I. P., International History
ROBERTS, N. J., English Literature
RUSSELL, R., Russian and Slavonic Studies
SAUL, J. M., Philosophy
SHELLARD, D. M., English Literature
SHEPHERD, D. G., Russian and Slavonic Studies
SHOEMAKER, R. B., History
SHUTTLEWORTH, S. A., English Literature
SIMEONE, N. A., Music
STAUB, M. H., History
STERN, R. A., Philosophy
STOCK, J. P. J., Music
SWANSON, P., Hispanic Studies
WALKER, D. H., French
WHITELAM, K. W., Biblical Studies
ZVELEBIL, M., Archaeology

Faculty of Engineering:
ALLEN, R. W. K., Chemical and Process Engineering
ALLERTON, D. J., Automatic Control and Systems Engineering
ALLINSON, N. M., Electronic and Electrical Engineering
ANDERSON, W. F., Civil and Structural Engineering
ASHLEY, R. M., Civil and Structural Engineering
ASKES, H., Civil and Structural Engineering
BANKS, S. P., Automatic Control and Systems Engineering
BANWART, S. A., Civil and Structural Engineering
BEYNON, J. H., Metallurgy
BILLINGS, S. A., Control Engineering
BOLLER, C., Mechanical Engineering
BROWN, M. W., Mechanical Engineering
BURGESS, I. W., Civil and Structural Engineering
CHAMBERS, B., Electronic and Electrical Engineering
CULLIS, A. G., Electronic and Electrical Engineering
DALEY, S., Automatic Control and Systems Engineering
DAVID, J. P. R., Electronic and Electrical Engineering
DAVIES, H. A., Engineering Materials
FLEMING, P. J., Automatic Control and Systems Engineering
GIBBS, M. R. J., Engineering Materials
HARDING, J., Engineering Materials
HOUNSLOW, M. J., Chemical and Process Engineering
HOUSTON, P. A., Electronic and Electrical Engineering
HOWARD, I. C., Mechanical Engineering
HOWE, D., Electrical Engineering
JAMES, P. F., Engineering Materials
JOHNSON, C. M., Electronic and Electrical Engineering
JONES, F. R., Engineering Materials
JONES, H., Engineering Materials
LEE, W. E., Engineering Materials
LERNER, D. N., Civil Engineering
MACNEIL, S., Tissue Engineering
MATTHEWS, A., Engineering Materials
OWENS, D. H., Automatic Control and Systems Engineering
PAVIC, A., Civil and Structural Engineering
PILAKOUTAS, K., Civil and Structural Engineering
QIN, N., Mechanical Engineering
RAINFORTH, W. M., Engineering Materials
REES, G. J., Electronic and Electrical Engineering
RIDGWAY, K., Mechanical Engineering
SAUL, A. J., Civil and Structural Engineering
SHARIFI, V. N., Chemical and Process Engineering
SHORT, R. D., Engineering Materials
SOUTIS, C., Aerospace Engineering
SWITHENBANK, J., Chemical and Process Engineering
TOMLINSON, G. R., Engineering Dynamics
UNGAR, G., Engineering Materials
WALDRON, P., Civil and Structural Engineering
WEST, A. R., Engineering Materials
WILSON, C. W., Mechanical Engineering
WORDEN, K., Mechanical Engineering
WRIGHT, P. C., Chemical and Process Engineering
WRIGHT, P. V., Engineering Materials
YATES, J. R., Mechanical Engineering
ZHU, Z. Q., Electronic and Electrical Engineering

Faculty of Law (fax (114) 222-6832):
ADAMS, J. N., Intellectual Property
BEYLEVELD, D., Law
BIRDS, J. R., Commercial Law
BRADGATE, J. R., Commercial Law
BRADNEY, T. A., Law
DIGNAN, J., Criminology and Restorative Justice
DITTON, J., Criminology
HARDEN, I., Law
HOLDAWAY, S. D., Sociology
KINDERLERER, J., Biotechnical Law
LEWIS, N. D., Constitutional Law, Sociology of Law
LUXTON, P., Property Law
MERRILLS, J. E. G., International Law
SHAPLAND, J. M., Criminal Justice

Faculty of Medicine (Beech Hill Rd, Sheffield, S10 2RX; fax (114) 271-3960):
AHMEDZAI, S., Palliative Medicine
AKEHURST, R. L., Health Economics
BARBER, D. C., Medical Imaging and Medical Physics
BAX, N. D. S., Medical Education
BISHOP, N. J., Paediatric Bone Disease
BOISSONADE, F. M., Oral and Maxillofacial Surgery
BRAZIER, J. E., Health Economics
BROOK, A. H., Oral Health and Development
BROOK, I. M., Oral and Maxillofacial Surgery
BROOKER, C. G. D., Mental Health
BROWN, B. H., Medical Physics
BROWN, B. L., Cell Signalling and Endocrinology
BROWN, N. J., Surgical Sciences
CAMPBELL, M. J., Medical Statistics
CANNINGS, C., Mathematics and Informatics
COLEMAN, R., Medical Oncology
CROSSMAN, D. C., Cardiology
CROUCHER, P. I., Bone Biology
DOLAN, P. H. R., Health Economics
DOWER, S. K., Molecular Immunology
DUFF, G. W., Molecular Medicine
EASTELL, R., Bone Metabolism
EL-NAHAS, A. M., Nephrology
ENDERBY, P. M., Community Rehabilitation
FORREST, A. R. W., Clinical Chemistry
GERRISH, K., Nursing Practice Development
GRANT, G. W. B., Cognitive Disability
GRIFFITHS, P. D., Academic Radiology
Sir HALL, D. M. B., Community Paediatrics
HAMDY, F., Urology
HANCOCK, B. W., Clinical Oncology
HATTON, P. V., Adult Dental Care
HELLEWELL, P. G., Vascular Biology
HENDERSON, I. W., Functional Genomics
HUTCHINSON, A., Public Health Medicine
INCE, P., Neuropathology
KERSHAW, B., Nursing and Midwifery
KIRKHAM, M. J., Midwifery
LEDGER, W. L., Obstetrics and Gynaecology
LENNON, M. A., Oral Health and Development
LEWIS, C. E., Molecular and Cellular Pathology
MACNEIL, S., Tissue Engineering
MATHERS, N., General Practice
MEUTH, M., Cellular Genetics
MILROY, C. M., Forensic Pathology
MOORE, H. D. M., Reproductive Biology
NICHOLL, J. P., Medical Care Research Centre
NICOLSON, P., Health Psychology
NOLAN, M. R., Gerontological Nursing
PALEY, M. N. J., Magnetic Resonance Physics
PARKER, S. G., Health Care for Elderly People
PARRY, G. D., Applied Psychological Therapies
PAYNE, S., Palliative Care Nursing
PEAKE, I. R., Molecular Medicine
PERKINS, M. R., Human Communications Science
PHILP, I., Health Care for Elderly People
POCKLEY, A. G., Immunobiology
POWERS, H. J., Nutritional Biochemistry
QWARNSTRÖM, E. E., Cell Biology
READ, R. C., Infectious Diseases
READ, S. M., Acute and Critical Care Nursing
REED, M. W. R., Surgical Oncology
REILLY, C. S., Anaesthesia
RENNIE, I. G., Ophthalmology
ROBINSON, P. G., Oral Health and Development
ROBINSON, P. P., Oral and Maxillofacial Surgery
ROLF, C. G., Sports Medicine
ROSS, R. J. M., Endocrinology
SAYERS, J. R., Functional Genomics
SHAW, P. J., Neurology
SPEIGHT, P. M., Oral Pathology
STACKHOUSE, R. J., Human Communication Science
TANNER, M. S., Paediatrics
TANTAM, D. J. H., Psychotherapy
TAYLOR, C. J., Paediatric Gastroenterology
THOMPSON, D. R., Acute and Critical Care
TUCKER, G. T., Molecular Pharmacology and Pharmacogenetics
UNDERWOOD, J. C. E., Pathology
VAN NOORT, R., Adult Dental Care
WALSH, T. F., Adult Dental Care
WARNES, A. M., Social Gerontology
WEETMAN, A. P., Medicine
WELLS, M., Gynaecological Pathology
WELLS, W. B., Human Communication Science
WHYTE, M. K. B., Respiratory Medicine
WOLL, P. J., Medical Oncology
WOODRUFF, P. W. R., Academic Clinical Psychiatry

Faculty of Pure Science:
ANDERSON, C. W., Mathematics and Statistics
ANDREWS, P. W., Biomedical Science
ARMS, S. P., Chemistry
ARMSTRONG, H. W., Geography
ARTYMIUK, P. J., Molecular Biology and Biotechnology
ATKIN, R. J., Applied Mathematics
BAILEY, G. J., Applied Mathematics
BEERLING, D. J., Palaeoclimatology
BIGG, G. R., Geography
BIGGINS, J. D., Probability and Statistics
BINGHAM, N. H., Probability and Statistics
BIRKHEAD, T. R., Zoology
BLACKSTOCK, W., Molecular Biology and Biotechnology

BULLOUGH, P. A., Molecular Biology and Biotechnology
BURKE, T. A., Molecular Ecology
BUTLIN, R. K., Evolutionary Biology
CALLAGHAN, T. V., Arctic Ecology
CALOW, P., Zoology
CARSWELL, D. A., Geology
CHATWIN, P. C., Applied and Computational Mathematics
CIRAVEGNA, F., Computer Science
COOKE, M. P., Computer Science
DEAN, P., Psychology
DERRICK, J., Computer Science
DORLING, D. F. L., Geography
EBDON, J. R., Chemistry
EISER, C., Psychology
EISER, J. R., Psychology
FLEMING, A. J., Plant Sciences
FOSTER, S. J., Molecular Biology and Biotechnology
FRISBY, J. P., Psychology
GAIZAUSKAS, R., Computer Science
GASTON, K. J., Biodiversity and Conservation
GEHRING, G. A., Solid State Physics
GREEN, J., Molecular Biology and Biotechnology
GREEN, P. D., Computer Science
GREENLEES, J. P. C., Probability and Statistics
GREGSON, N., Geography
GRUNDY, D., Biomedical Science
HARDY, G., Clinical Psychology
HEATHWAITE, A. L., Geography
HIGGINS, J. A., Molecular Biology and Biotechnology
HOCKEY, G. R. J., Psychology
HOLCOMBE, W. M. L., Computer Science
HOLLEY, M. J., Biomedical Science
HORTON, P., Molecular Biology and Biotechnology
HUGHES, D. W., Physics and Astronomy
HUNTER, C. A., Chemistry
HUNTER, C. N., Molecular Biology and Biotechnology
INGHAM, P. W., Biomedical Science
JACKSON, P. A., Human Geography
JACKSON, R. F. W., Synthetic Chemistry
JONES, R. A. L., Physics
JORDAN, D. A., Pure Mathematics
KELLY, D. J., Molecular Biology and Biotechnology
LEE, J. A., Environmental Biology
LEEGOOD, R. C., Plant Biochemistry
LEGGETT, G. J., Nanoscale Analytical Science
MALTBY, L., Environmental Biology
MANN, B. E., Chemistry
MAYHEW, J. E. W., Psychology
MCLEOD, C. W. M., Chemistry
MOERDIJK, I., Pure Mathematics
MOORE, H. D. M., Reproductive Biology
MOORE, R., Computer Science
NICOLSON, R. I., Psychology
NIRANJAN, M., Computer Science
O'HAGAN, A., Probability and Statistics
OUTHWAITE, C. W., Mathematics and Statistics
PARSONS, L. M., Psychology
PATTIE, C. J., Geography
PICKUP, B. T., Chemistry
PIPER, P., Molecular Biology and Biotechnology
PLACZEK, M., Biomedical Science
POOLE, R. K., Molecular Biology and Biotechnology
PRESS, M. C., Physiological Ecology
QUEGAN, S., Applied and Computational Mathematics
QUICK, W. P., Plant Physiology
RATNIEKS, F. L. W., Apiculture
READ, D. J., Plant Sciences
REDGRAVE, P., Psychology
REES, M., Plant Ecology
RICE, D. W., Molecular Biology and Biotechnology
ROSZKOWSKI, L., Physics and Astronomy
RUDERMAN, M. S., Applied Mathematics
RYAN, A. J., Chemistry
SCHOLES, J. D., Plant and Microbial Science
SHARKEY, N. E., Computer Science
SHARP, R. Y., Pure Mathematics
SHEERAN, P., Psychology
SIEGAL, M., Psychology
SKOLNICK, M. S., Experimental Condensed Matter
SLADE, P., Clinical Psychology
SMALLWOOD, R., Computer Science
SMYTHE, C., Biomedical Science
SMYTHE, E., Biomedical Science
SNAITH, V. P., Pure Mathematics
SPENCER, C. P., Psychology
SPOONER, N. J. C., Physics
STRICKLAND, N. P., Pure Mathematics
SURPRENANT, A., Biomedical Science
TADHUNTER, C. N., Physics and Astronomy
THOMPSON, M.J., Applied Mathematics
TURNER, G., Genetics
TURPIN, G., Clinical Psychology
VALENTINE, G., Geography
VON FÁY-SIEBENBÜRGEN, R., Applied Mathematics
WALL, T. D., Psychology
WALKER, M., Computer Science
WALTHO, J. P., Molecular Biology and Biotechnology
WARD, M. D., Chemistry
WHITE, P. E., Geography
WILKS, Y., Computer Science
WILLIAMSON, M. P., Molecular Biology and Biotechnology
WOODWARD, F. I., Plant Ecology
WYATT, L. R., Applied Mathematics
ZINOBER, A. S. I., Applied Mathematics

Faculty of Social Sciences:
ADCOCK, C. J., Financial Econometrics
ARMSTRONG, D., Education
BEAULIEU, M., Management
BOOTH, T. A., Social Policy
BROOKES, R. G., Education
CARR, W., Education
CASSELL, C. M., Management
CHAPPELL, D., Mathematical Economics
CLEGG, C. W., Work Psychology
COLE, P., Journalism
CORRALL, S., Librarianship and Information Management
FORD, N. J., Information Studies
FRANKLIN, R., Media Communications
GAMBLE, A. M., Politics
GEDDES, A. P., Politics
GRAYSON, J. H., East Asian Studies
GRUGEL, J. B., Politics
GUNTER, B., Journalism
HANNON, P. W., Education
HEALD, D. E. A, Management
HOCKEY, J. L., Sociological Studies
HOOK, G. D., Japanese Studies
HOOPER, B. J., East Asian Studies
JAMES, A., Sociological Studies
JENKINS, R., Sociology
KENNEDY-PIPE, C., International Relations, Politics
MACDONALD, S., Management
MALTBY, J. A., Management
MARSH, P., Child and Family Welfare
MCCONNELL, D., Education
MOSLEY, P., Economics
NIXON, J. D., Education
NORRIS, C. A., Sociology
PARRY, G., Education
PAYNE, A. J., Politics
REDMAN, T. A., Management
SMITH, M. J., Politics
STANDISH, P., Education
TAYLOR, A. J., Politics
TAYLOR, P. D., Leisure Management
TYLECOTE, A. B., Economics and Management of Technological Change
USHERWOOD, R. C., Information Studies
VINCENT, A. W., Politics
WALKER, A. C., Social Policy
WEBB, S. C., Institute of Lifelong Learning
WELLINGTON, J. J., Education
WHITTAKER, S. J., Information Studies
WILLETT, P., Information Studies
WOOD, S. J., Work Psychology
WRIGHT, T., East Asian Studies

ATTACHED SCHOOLS

School of Health and Related Research: Dean Prof. R. L. AKEHURST.

School of Management: Dir Prof. M. BEAULIEU.

UNIVERSITY OF SOUTHAMPTON

University Rd, Southampton, SO17 1BJ
Telephone: (23) 8059-5000
Fax: (23) 8059-3131
E-mail: admissns@soton.ac.uk
Internet: www.soton.ac.uk

Founded 1952; opened as the Hartley Institution 1862; incorporated as the Hartley University College 1902

Academic year: October to July

Vice-Chancellor: Prof. DON NUTBEAM
Provost and Deputy Vice-Chancellor: Prof. ADAM WHEELER
Pro-Vice-Chancellor: Prof. PHILIP NELSON
Pro-Vice-Chancellor: Prof. ALISTAIR FITT
Pro-Vice-Chancellor for Education: Prof. DEBRA HUMPHRIS
Registrar and Chief Operating Officer: SIMON HIGMAN
Director of Student Services: Dr JANICE RIPPON
Head of Student Systems and Operations: CHRISTINE SMITH
Librarian: Dr MARK BROWN

Library: see under Libraries and Archives
Number of teachers: 950
Number of students: 19,896 (15,446 full-time, 4,450 part-time)

DEANS

Faculty of Business and Law: Prof. NATALIE LEE (Chair., Transitional Leadership Team)
Faculty of Engineering and the Environment: Prof. WILLIAM POWRIE
Faculty of Health Sciences: Prof. JESSICA CORNER
Faculty of Humanities: Prof. ANNE CURRY
Faculty of Medicine: Prof. IAIN CAMERON
Faculty of Natural and Environmental Sciences: Prof. STEPHEN HAWKINS
Faculty of Physical and Applied Sciences: Prof. Dame WENDY HALL
Faculty of Social and Human Sciences: Prof. JUDITH PETTS

PROFESSORS

Faculty of Engineering, Science and Mathematics (tel. (23) 8059-4184):
ALLEN, R., Institute of Sound and Vibration Research
ARNELL, N. W., Geography
ASHBURN, P., Electronics and Computer Science
ATTARD, G. S., Chemistry
BAILEY, A. G., Electronics and Computer Science
BARBER, K. E., Geography
BARNES, K. J., Physics and Astronomy
BARTLETT, P. N., Chemistry
BAUMBERG, J. J., Physics and Astronomy
BEDUZ, C., Cryogenics
BOWDITCH, B. H., Mathematics
BRADLEY, M., Chemistry
BROWN, A. D., Electronics and Computer Science
BROWN, T., Chemistry
BRYDEN, H., Oceanography

BUTLER, M. J., Electronics and Computer Science
CARLING, P. A., Geography
CASTRO, I. P., Aeronautics and Astronautics
CHAPLIN, J. R., Civil and Environmental Education
CHARLES, P. A., Physics and Astronomy
CHENG, R. C. H., Mathematics
CLARK, M. J., Geography
CLAYTON, C. R. I., Civil and Environmental Education
COLES, H. J., Physics and Astronomy
COLLINS, M. B., Oceanography
CURRAN, P. J., Geography
D'INVERNO, R. A, Mathematics
DAVIES, A. E., Electrical Engineering
DEAN, A. J., Physics and Astronomy
DE GROOT, P. A. J., Physics and Astronomy
DE ROURE, D. C., Electronics and Computer Science
DUNMUR, D. A., Chemistry
DYKE, J. M., Chemistry
EASON, A. B., Optoelectronics Research Centre
EASON, R. W., Physics and Astronomy
ELLIOTT, S. J., Institute of Sound and Vibration Research
EVANS, A. G. R, Electronics and Computer Science
EVANS, J., Chemistry
FASHAM, M. J. R., Oceanography
FITT, A. D., Mathematics
FOODY, G. M., Geography
FRAMPTON, C. S., Chemistry
GREGSON, P. J., Engineering Materials
GRIFFIN, M. J., Institute of Sound and Vibration Research
GRIFFITHS, G., Oceanography
GRUDININ, A. B., Optoelectronics Research Centre
HALL, W., Electronics and Computer Science
HAMMOND, J. K., Institute of Sound and Vibration Research
HANNA, D. C., Physics and Astronomy
HANZO, L., Electronics and Computer Science
HARNAD, S. R., Electronics and Computer Science
HARRIS, C. J., Electronics and Computer Science
HAYDEN, B. E., Chemistry
HEARN, G. E., Ship Science
HENDERSON, P., Electronics and Computer Science
HEY, A. J. G., Electronics and Computer Science
HOLLIGAN, P. M., Oceanography
HUGHES, J. F., Electrical Engineering
HURSTHOUSE, M. B., Chemistry
JENKINS, W. J., Chemical Oceanography
JENNINGS, N. R., Electronics and Computer Science
JONES, G. A., Mathematics
KEANE, A. J., Mechanical Engineering
KEMP, A. E. S., Oceanography
KILBURN, J. D., Chemistry
KILLWORTH, P. D., Oceanography
KING, R. C., Mathematics
KING, S. F., Physics and Astronomy
LEE, M. M. K., Civic and Environmental Engineering
LEIGHTON, T. G., Institute of Sound and Vibration Research
LEVASON, W., Chemistry
LEVITT, M. H., Chemistry
LEWIS, S., Mathematics
LOCKWOOD, M., Physics and Astronomy
LUCKHURST, G. R., Chemistry
LUTMAN, M. E., Institute of Sound and Vibration Research
MAROTZKE, J., Oceanography
MARTIN, D. J., Geography
MASON, C., Geography
MCBRIDE, J. W., Mechanical Engineering
MCDONALD, M., Civil and Environmental Engineering
MCHARDY, I. M., Physics and Astronomy
MELLOR, J., Chemistry
MORFEY, C. L., Institute of Sound and Vibration Research
MURRAY, J. W., Geology
NELSON, P. A., Institute of Sound and Vibration Research
NESBITT, R. W., Oceanography
PALMER, M. R., Oceanography
PARKER, G. I., Electronics and Computer Science
PAYNE, D. N., Optoelectronics Research Centre
PLEASE, C. P., Mathematics
PLETCHER, D., Chemistry
POTTS, C. N., Mathematics
POWRIE, W., Civil and Environmental Engineering
PRESCOTT, P., Mathematics
PRICE, W. G., Ship Science
RAINFORD, B. D., Physics and Astronomy
REDMAN-WHITE, W., Electronics and Computer Science
RICHARDSON, D. J., Optoelectronics Research Centre
ROBINSON, I. S., Oceanography
ROE, H. S., Oceanography
ROGERS, E. T. A., Electronics and Computer Science
ROSS, D. A., Physics and Astronomy
RUTT, H. N., Electronics and Computer Science
SACHRAJDA, C. T. C., Physics and Astronomy
SANDHAM, N. D., Aeronautics and Astronautics
SASSONE, V., Electronics and Computer Science
SHADBOLT, N. R., Electronics and Computer Science
SHENOI, R. A., Ship Science
SHEPHERD, J., Oceanography
SINGERMAN, D., Mathematics
SINHA, M. C., Oceanography
SLUCKIN, T. J., Mathematics
SNAITH, V., Mathematics
STOW, D. A., Oceanography
SYKULSKI, J. K., Electrical Engineering
TANTON, T. W., Civil and Environmental Engineering
TEMAREL, P., Ship Science
THOMSON, J., Oceanography
TROPPER, A. C., Physics and Astronomy
TYLER, P. A., Oceanography
VICKERS, J. A., Mathematics
WEAVER, P. P. E., Oceanography
WELLER, M. T., Chemistry
WELSH, A. H., Mathematics
WHEELER, A. A., Mathematics
WHITBY, R. J., Chemistry
WILKINSON, J. S., Optoelectronics Research Centre
WILLOUGHBY, A. F. W., Engineering Materials
WILSON, P. A., Ship Science
WRIGLEY, N., Geography
ZERVAS, M. N., Optoelectronics Research Centre
ZHANG, X., Aeronautics and Astronautics
ZHELUDEV, N. I., Physics and Astronomy

Faculty of Law, Arts and Social Sciences (tel. (23) 8059-2206; fax (23) 8059-3987; e-mail artsrec@soton.ac.uk; internet www.soton.ac.uk/~arts):

ANDERLINI, L., Economics
ARNOLD, D. R., Archaeology
BANCE, A. F., German
BOURNE, G. M., Education
BRADLEY, B., Psychology
BRUMFIT, C. J., Education
CALVERT, P. A. R., Politics
CANOVA, F., Economics
CESARANI, D., History
CHAMBERS, R. L., Social Statistics
CHAMPION, T. C., Archaeology
CHAPMAN, C. B., Management
CHEYETTE, B. H., English
CLIFF, D., Electronics and Computer Science
COLEMAN, P. G., Social Work Studies
COLLIER, A. S., Philosophy
COOK, N. J., Music
COOK, P., Film and Media Studies
CREMER, J., Economics
CROUAN, K. M., Winchester School of Art
DALE, R. S., Management
DOMINELLI, L. R., Social Work Studies
DEBATTISTA, C., Law
EVERIST, M. E., Music
FINNISSY, M., Music
FOSKETT, N., Education
GAMBLE, C. S., Archaeology
GASKELL, N. J., Law
GIBBONS, J., Winchester School of Art
GODDARD, A. R., Management
GRIME, R. P., Law
HAMLIN, A., Economics
HANNIGAN, B. M., Law
HILLIER, G. H., Economics
HINTON, D. A., Archaeology
JOHNSON, J. E. V., Management
KAPLAN, C., English
KARP, L., Economics
KEAY, S. J., Archaeology
KELLY, M. H., French
KUSHNER, A. R., History
LABANYI, J., Spanish
LUSTGARTEN, L., Law
MAR-MOLINERO, C., Spanish
MARTIN, R., Management
MASON, A., Politics
MCCORMICK, B., Economics
MCGREW, A., Politics
MCKENZIE, G. W., Management
MCLUSKIE, K. E., English
MEINHOFF, U., German
MERKIN, R., Law
MITCHELL, R., Management
MIZON, G. E., Economics
MOGG, K., Psychology
MONK, R., Philosophy
MONTGOMERY, J. R., Law
NAPIER, C. J., Management
NEWTON, K., Politics
NICHOLLS, D., Music
PEACOCK, D. P. S., Archaeology
PILGRIM, P. J., Winchester School of Art
Lord PLANT OF HIGHFIELD, Politics
PRINGLE, R., Sociology
RAPAPORT, H., English
REMINGTON, R. E., Psychology
REUTER, T. A., History
ROSEMAN, M., History
RUTHERFORD, A. F., Law
SEDIKEDES, C., Psychology
SHARPE, K. M., History
SIMONS, H., Education
SIMPSON, J., Politics
SKINNER, C. J., Social Statistics
SONUGA-BURKE, E., Psychology
STEVENSON, J. E., Psychology
SUTCLIFFE, C. M. S., Management
TAYLOR, B., Winchester School of Art
TAYLOR, M., History
THOMAS, C. A., Politics
THOMAS, L., Management
THOMAS, S. H., Management
TRIDIMAS, T., European Community Law
ULPH, A. M., Economics
UNGERSON, C. E., Sociology and Social Policy
VALIMAKI, J., Economics
WIKELEY, N. J., Law
ZILLIBOTI, F., Economics

Faculty of Medicine, Health and Life Sciences
(Some professors also serve in the Faculty of Engineering, Science and Mathematics)

ANTHONY, C., Biochemistry
ARTHUR, M. J. P., Medicine
ASHBURN, A. M., Rehabilitation
BARKER, D. J. P., Clinical Epidemiology
BARNITT, R., Occupational Therapy
BRIGGS, R. S. J., Geriatric Medicine
BYRNE, C. D. T., Endocrinology
CAMERON, I. T., Obstetrics
CHURCH, M. K., Experimental Immunopharmacology
CLARKE, I. N., Virology
COGGON, D., Environmental Epidemiology
COLEMAN, P. G., Social Gerontology
COOPER, C., Rheumatology
CROSS, N. C., Human Genetics
DAY, I. N. M., Genetics
ELIA, M., Human Nutrition
ELLIOTT, T. J., Oncology
FLEMING, T. P., Biological Sciences
FOX, K. R., Biological Sciences
FREW, A. J., Molecular Biology
FRIEDMAN, P., Dermatology
GABBAY, J., Public Health Medicine
GETLIFFE, K., Nursing
GLASPER, E. A., Nursing Studies
GLENNIE, M., Immunochemistry
GRIMBLE, R. F., Nutrition
HALL, J. L., Biological Sciences
HAMBLIN, T. J., Immunohaematology
HANSON, M. A., Foetal Origins of Adult Disease
HAWKINS, S. J., Biology
HECKELS, J. E., Molecular Microbiology
HOLGATE, S. T., Immunopharmacology
JACKSON, A. A., Human Nutrition
JACOBS, P. A., Genetics
JOHNSON, P., Medical Oncology
KENDRICK, T., Primary Medical Care
KINGDON, D., Mental Health Care Delivery
LATHLEAN, J., Nursing
LEE, A. G., Biochemistry
MACDONALD, T. T., Tissue Repair
MACLEAN, N., Biological Sciences
Dame MACLEOD CLARK, J., Nursing
MCLELLAN, D. L., Rehabilitation
NICOLL, J. A., Clinical Neurosciences
O'CONNOR, D., Biological Sciences
PERRY, V. H., Biological Sciences
PEVELER, M., Psychiatry
PRIMROSE, J. N., Surgery
RENWICK, A., Clinical Pharmacology
ROCHE, W. R., Pathology
SEDGWICK, E. M., Neurophysiology
SHEARMAN, C. P., Human Nutrition
SHOOLINGIN-JORDAN, P. M., Biochemistry
STEVENSON, F. K., Cancer Sciences
THOMPSON, C., Psychiatry
THORNTON, R., Neurosurgery
WALKER, R. J., Physiology and Pharmacology
WARD, M. E., Medical Microbiology
WARNER, J. O., Child Health
WELLER, R. O., Neuropathology
WHEAL, H. V., Physiology and Pharmacology
WILSON, D. I., Human Genetics
WOOD, S. P., Biological Sciences

UNIVERSITY OF SUNDERLAND

Edinburgh Bldg, City Campus, Chester Rd Sunderland, SR1 3SD
Telephone: (191) 515-2000
Fax: (191) 515-2960
E-mail: student-helpline@sunderland.ac.uk
Internet: www.sunderland.ac.uk

Founded 1969 as Sunderland Polytechnic; present name and status 1992
Academic year: September to June
Chancellor: STEVE CRAM
Vice-Chancellor and Chief Exec.: Prof. PETER FIDLER
Deputy Vice-Chancellor for Resources: SHIRLEY ATKINSON
Deputy Vice-Chancellor for Academic: Prof. PETER STRIKE
Deputy Vice-Chancellor for Academic: Prof. JULIE MENNELL
Sec. and Clerk to the Board: J. D. PACEY
Dir of Information Services: Prof. ANDREW MACDONALD
Library of 280,000 vols
Number of teachers: 1,302
Number of students: 18,944

DEANS

Faculty of Applied Sciences: Prof. JOHN MACINTYRE
Faculty of Arts, Design and Media: GRAEME THOMPSON
Faculty of Business and Law: VIVIAN KINNAIRD
Faculty of Education and Society: Prof. G. SHIELD

PROFESSORS

ALABASTER, T., Environmental Informatics
ARTHUR, W. W., Population Biology
BAINBRIDGE, E., Fine Art
BRAYNE, H., Law
CHILTON, P., Politics and Peace Studies
COCKTON, G., Computer Software Engineering
COX, C. S., Control Engineering
CRISELL, A. P., Broadcasting Studies
CROZIER, G., Education
DARBY, J., Humanities
EDWARDS, H. M., Computer Software Engineering
ELLIOTT, J., Education
ELLIS, P., Performance Arts
FLETCHER, E. J., Applied Computing
GROUNDWATER, P. W., Organic Chemistry
HANMER, J., Humanities
HARVEY, B. P., Humanities
HEPBURN, A., Modern Irish History
HESTER, M., Social Studies
HARRISON, R., Renewable Energy
ITZIN, C., Health and Community Studies
LEES, G., Neurophysiology and Neuropharmacology
LILLEY, T. H., Physical Chemistry
MACINTYRE, J., Computer Software Engineering
MALIN, N. A., Health Services Research
MOSCARDINI, A. O., Mathematical Modelling
O'BRIEN, M., Librarian, Communication and Media Studies
OVER, D. E., Philosophical Logic
PALOVA, Z., Design and Creative Arts
PETROVA, S., Glass
PODCZECK, G. F., Pharmaceutics
PRENTICE, R. C., Tourism
PRINGLE, K., Comparative Social Policy
REED, M. A., Criminal and Private International Law
RICHARDS, D. S., International Business and Cross-Cultural Management
SIM, S. D., Critical Theory
SINGH, G., Pharmacy
STOREY, J. C., Librarian, Communication and Media Studies
TAIT, J. I., Computer Software Engineering
THOMPSON, B., Design and Creative Arts
THORNHAM, S., Librarian, Communication and Media Studies
TINDLE, J., Computer Software Engineering
VAN LEEUWEN, C. C., Psychology
VAN ZON, H., Social Studies
WALDRON, P., Modern European History
WERMTER, S., Information Systems
WILSON, P. H., Early Modern History

UNIVERSITY OF SURREY

Guildford, GU2 5XH
Telephone: (1483) 300800
Fax: (1483) 683948
Internet: www.surrey.ac.uk

Founded 1891 as Battersea Polytechnic Institute, designated a College of Advanced Technology 1956, University Charter 1966
Academic year: October to June
Chancellor: HRH THE DUKE OF KENT
Vice-Chancellor and Chief Exec.: Prof. CHRISTOPHER M. SNOWDEN
Sr Deputy Vice-Chancellor: Prof. NIGEL SEATON
Deputy Vice-Chancellor for Academic Devt: Prof. GILLIAN NICHOLLS
Deputy Vice-Chancellor for Research and Innovation: Prof. STEPHEN WILLIAMSON
Pro-Vice-Chancellor for Int. Relations: Prof. COLIN GRANT
Univ. Registrar: CAROLINE JOHNSON (acting)
Dir of Corporate Services: GREG MELLY
Dir of Finance: DAVID SHARKEY
Dir of Information Services and University Librarian: T. J. A. CRAWSHAW
Number of teachers: 997 (incl. 350 part-time associate lecturers)
Number of students: 15,187
Publication: *Surrey Matters*

DEANS

Faculty of Arts and Human Sciences: Prof. PHILLIP POWRIE
Faculty of Engineering and Physical Sciences: Prof. MICHAEL KEARNEY
Faculty of Health and Medical Sciences: Prof. JOHN HAY
Faculty of Management and Law: Prof. DAVID ALLEN

PROFESSORS

School of Arts:

ANDERMAN, G. M., Translation Studies
BARTA, P., Russian and Cultural Studies
CORBETT, G. G., Linguistics and Russian Language
EADE, J.
FLOCKTON, C. H., European Economic Studies
FLOOD, C. G., European Studies
FORBES, S.
GRANT, C. B., Communication Studies
HOLFORD, J. A. K.
HUTCHINGS, S. C., Russian
JARVIS, P., Continuing Education
JUDGE, A., French
LANSDALE, J. H., Dance Studies
LUTZEIER, P. R., German
MCNAIR, S., Education
MIDDLEHURST, R. M., Higher Education
MOORE, A., Music
UPEX, R. V., Law

School of Biomedical and Life Sciences:

ADAMS, M. R., Food Microbiology
BUSHELL, M. E., Microbial Physiology
CLIFFORD, M. N., Food Safety
DALE, J. W., Molecular Microbiology
DANIL DE NAMOR, A., Chemistry
FERNS, G. A. A., Metabolic and Molecular Medicine
GIBSON, G. G., Molecular Toxicology
GOLDFARB, P. S. G., Molecular Biology
HAY, J. N., Materials Chemistry
HEYES, D. M., Chemistry
HINDMARCH, I., Human Psychopharmacology
HOURANI, S. M. O., Pharmacology
HOWELL, N. K., Food Science
KITCHEN, I., Neuropharmacology
LYNCH, J. M., Life Sciences
MCFADDEN, J., Molecular Genetics
MILLWARD, D. J., Nutrition
ROBERTSON, W. R.
SERMON, P., Physical Chemistry
SKENE, D. J., Neuroendocrinology
SLADE, R. C. T., Inorganic Chemistry
SMITH, C., Functional Genomics

School of Electronics and Physical Sciences:
ADAMS, A. R.
AHMAD, KH., Artificial Intelligence
ALLAM, J., Ultra-fast Optoelectronics
BRIDGES, T. J., Mathematics
CLOUGH, A. S.
COWERN, N. E. B., Nanoscale Materials Processing
EVANS, B. G., Information Systems
GELLETLY, W.
HESS, O., Computational Quantum Electronics
HOMEWOOD, K. P., Semiconductor Optoelectronics
ILLINGWORTH, J., Machine Vision
KEARNEY, M. J., Electronic Device Engineering
KITTLER, J. V., Machine Intelligence
KONDOZ, A. M., Multimedia Communication Systems
KRAUSE, P. J., Software Engineering
MCDONALD, P. J.
MELBOURNE, I., Mathematics
PAVLOU, G., Communication and Information Systems
PETROU, M., Image Analysis
REED, G. T., Optoelectronics
ROBERTS, R. M., Mathematics
ROGERS, A. J.
SANDSTEDE, B., Mathematical Sciences
SCHNEIDER, S. A., Computing
SEALY, B. J., Solid State Devices and Ion Beam Technology
SILVA, S. R. P., Solid State Electronics
SPYROU, N. M.
Sir SWEETING, MARTIN, Satellite Engineering
TAFAZOLLI, R., Mobile Communications
THOMPSON, I. J.
TOSTEVIN, J. A.
WALKER, P. M.
WEBB, R. P., Ion Beam Physics
WEISS, B. L., Microelectronics

School of Engineering:
AZAPAGIC, A., Sustainable Engineering
CHEW, J. W., Mechanical Engineering
CHRYSSANTHOPOULOS, M. K., Structural Systems
CLIFT, R., Environmental Technology
CROCOMBE, A. D., Structural Mechanics
GILLAN, M. A., Aerospace Engineering
GORINGE, M. J., Materials
HOLLAWAY, L. C., Composite Structures
JACKSON, T., Sustainable Development
JEFFERIS, S., Civil Engineering
KOKOSSIS, A. C., Process Systems Engineering Optimization
LAWSON, M., Construction Systems
LLOYD, B. J., Environmental Health Engineering
NOOSHIN, H., Space Structures
PARKE, C. A. R., Structural Engineering
PARKER, G. A., Mechanical Engineering
ROBINS, A. G., Environmental Fluid Mechanics
SMITH, P. A., Composite Materials
THORPE, R., Multiphase Engineering
TOY, N., Fluid Mechanics
TSAKIROPOULOS, P., Metallurgy
TÜZÜN, U., Process Engineering
WATTS, J. F., Materials Science

School of Human Sciences:
ARBER, S. L., Sociology
BAG, P., Economics
BARRETT, M. D., Psychology
BIRD, G. R., Economics
BROWN, J. M., Forensic Psychology
BULMER, M. I. A., Sociology
CRAWFORD, I., Economics
DAVIES, I. R. L., Psychology
EMLER, N., Social Psychology
FIELDING, N. G., Sociology
GILBERT, G. N., Sociology
GROEGER, J. A., Cognitive Psychology
HAMPSON, S. E., Psychology and Health
HUNT, L. C., Economics
LEVINE, P., Economics
OGDEN, J., Health Psychology
RICKMAN, N. J., Economics
SHEPHERD, R., Psychology
STERR, A., Cognitive Neuroscience and Neuropsychology
TARLING, R., Sociology
UZZELL, D. L., Environmental Psychology
ZIJLSTRA, F., Occupational and Organizational Psychology

School of Management:
AIREY, D. W., Tourism Management
ARCHER, G. S. H., Financial Management
BUTLER, R. W., Tourism
DESOMBRE, T., Health Care Management
GILBERT, D., Marketing
HALES, C., Organizational Behaviour
JONES, P. L. M., Productions and Operations Management
KIRBY, D., Entrepreneurship
LIU, X., International Business
LOCKWOOD, A. J., Hospitality Management
LOWE, M., Retail Management
O'KEEFE, R. M., Information Management
PHILLIPS, P. A., Hotel Management
RILEY, M. J., Organizational Behaviour
SADLER-SMITH, E., Management Development and Organizational Behaviour

European Institute of Health and Medical Sciences:
BRYAN, K., Clinical Practice
BUCKLE, P., Health Ergonomics
HUNT, G.
POPE, R., Nurse Education
ROBBINS, I., Mental Health Practice
SMITH, P. A., Nurse Education
STUBBS, D. A., Ergonomics

Postgraduate Medical School:
FARMER, R. D. T., Epidemiology
THOMAS, H., Oncology

UNIVERSITY OF SUSSEX

Sussex House, Brighton, BN1 9RH
Telephone: (1273) 606755
Fax: (1273) 678335
E-mail: information@sussex.ac.uk
Internet: www.sussex.ac.uk

Founded 1961
Academic year: October to June

Chancellor: SANJEEV BHASKAR
Vice-Chancellor: Prof. MICHAEL FARTHING
Deputy Vice-Chancellor and Pro Vice-Chancellor for Research: Prof. BOB ALLISON
Pro Vice-Chancellor for Int. Affairs: Prof. CHRIS MARLIN
Pro Vice-Chancellor for Teaching and Learning: Prof. CLARE MACKIE
Registrar and Sec.: JOHN DUFFY
Librarian: KITTY INGLIS
Library: see Libraries and Archives
Number of teachers: 552
Number of students: 11,478

PROFESSORS
ABBS, P. F., Creative Writing
ABRAHAM, J. W., Sociology
ABRAHAM, S. C. S., Psychology
ARMES, S. P., Chemistry
BACON, J. P., Neuroscience
BAILIN, D., Theoretical Physics
BEEBEE, J. J. C., Molecular Ecology
BENJAMIN, P. R., Neuroscience
BILLINGHAM, N. C., Chemistry
BLISS, J. F., Education
BODEN, M. A., Philosophy and Psychology
BUXTON, H., Visual Intelligence
CAWSON, A., Digital Media
CHATWIN, C. R., Manufacturing Systems
CHERRY, D., History of Art
CLARK, A. J., Philosophy
CLARK, T. D., Physical Electronics
CLOKE, F. G. N., Chemistry
CLUNAS, A. C., History of Art
COATES, R. A., Linguistics
COLCLOUGH, C. L., Development Studies
COLLETT, T. S., Neurobiology
COPELAND, E. J., Theoretical Physics
DARWIN, C. J., Experimental Psychology
DAVEY, G. C. L., Psychology
DEARLOVE, J. N., Politics
DOMBEY, N. D., Theoretical Physics
DU BOULAY, J. B. H., Artificial Intelligence
DUNFORD, M. F., Economic Geography
DYHOUSE, C. A., History
ERAUT, M. R., Education
FAIRHEAD, J., Social Anthropology
FALLOWFIELD, L. J., Psycho-Oncology
FENDER, S. A., American Studies
FIELDING, A. J., Human Geography
FLOWERS, T. J., Plant Physiology
GANN, D. M., Science and Technology Policy Research
GARDINER, J. M., Psychology
GARNHAM, A., Experimental Psychology
GAZDAR, G. J. M., Computational Linguistics
GOLDIE, C. M., Statistics
GOUGH, M. P., Space Science
GRAY, F. G., Continuing Education
GRIFFITH-JONES, S., Development Studies
GRILLO, R. D., Social Anthropology
GRIMSDALE, R. L., Electronic Engineering
HANSON, J. R., Chemistry
HART, V. M., American Studies
HENNESSY, M., Computer Science
HINDS, E. A., Experimental Physics
HIRSCHFELD, J. W. P., Mathematics
HOBDAY, M. G., Science and Technology Policy Research
HOLMWOOD, J. M., Sociology
HOWKINS, A. J., Social History
HUMPHREY, C. J., Development Studies
HUTCHINGS, M. J., Ecology
JAYAWANT, B. V., Electrical and Systems Engineering
KAPLINSKY, R. M., Development Studies
KEDWARD, H. R., History
KING, R. L., Geography
Sir KROTO, H. W., Chemistry
LAND, M. F., Neurobiology
LEACH, M. A., Development Studies
LEHMANN, A. R., Molecular Genetics
LEWIN, K. M., Education
LIDDLE, A. R., Astrophysics
LISTER, P. F., Electronics
LLEWELLYN, N. G., History of Art
MANOR, J. G., Development Studies
MARTIN, B. R., Science and Technology Policy Research
MATHER, G. W., Experimental Psychology
MCCAFFERY, A. J., Chemistry
MELLOR, D. A., History of Art
MILNER-GULLAND, R. R., Russian
MITTER, P., History of Art
MOORE, A. L., Biochemistry
MOORE, M. P., Development Studies
MURPHY, R. J., German, Comparative Literature and Film
NICHOLLS, P. A., English and American Literature
NIXON, J. F., Chemistry
O'SHEA, M. R., Neuroscience
OAKHILL, J. V., Experimental Psychology
OSMOND-SMITH, D., Music
OUTHWAITE, R. W., Sociology
PAIN, V. M., Biochemistry
PARSONS, P. J., Organic Chemistry
PAVITT, K. L. R., Science and Technology Policy Studies
PENDLEBURY, J. M., Experimental Physics
PERRY-ROBINSON, J. P., Science and Technology Policy Research
PLATT, J. A., Sociology
POWNER, E. T., Electronic Engineering
PRASSIDES, K., Chemistry
RAJAK, H. H., Law
RICHARDS, R. L., Chemistry

RÖHL, J. C. G., History
ROLLO, J. M. C., European Economic Integration
ROPER, T. J., Biology
ROSS, M. G., European Law
ROYLE, N. W. O., English
RUSSELL, I. J., Neurobiology
RYAN, C. J., Italian
SAMPSON, G. R., Natural Language Computing
SCHMITZ, H., Development Studies
SHAW, M., International Relations and Politics
SHORT, B. M., Geography
SINFIELD, A. J., English
SKELDON, R., Geography
SMITH, L. J., English
SMITH, P. B., Social Psychology
SMITH, P. H., Media Studies
SOBOLEV, A. V., Mathematics
STACE, A. J., Chemistry
STEINMUELLER, W. E., Science and Technology Policy Research
STEPHENS, D. N., Experimental Psychology
STOBART, R. K., Automotive Engineering
SUMNER, M. T., Economics
TAPPER, E. R., Politics
TAYLOR, I. J., Social Care and Social Work
TEMKIN, J., Law
TIDD, J., Science and Technology Policy Research
TIMMS, E. F., German Studies
TORRANCE, H., Education
TOWNSEND, P. D., Experimental Physics
TROSCIANKO, T., Psychology
TURNER, A. B., Mechanical Engineering
VAN DER PIJL, K., International Relations
VAN GELDEREN, M. A. J., Intellectual History
VANCE, R. N. C., English
VINCENT, R., Medical Science
VON TUNZELMANN, G., Economics of Science and Technology
WAGSTAFF, R. A. S., Economics
WALLIS, M., Biochemistry
WARK, D. L., Physics
WATTS, C. T., English
WEBB, P. D., Politics
WILKINSON, R. G., Trafford Centre for Graduate Medical Education and Research
WINTERS, L. A., Economics
WORDEN, A. B., Early Modern History
YOUNG, D. W., Chemistry
ZHANG, K., Pure Mathematics

UNIVERSITY OF TEESSIDE

Borough Rd, Middlesbrough, TS1 3BA
Telephone: (1642) 218121
Fax: (1642) 342067
E-mail: enquiries@tees.ac.uk
Internet: www.tees.ac.uk

Founded 1929 as Constantine College of Technology, became Teesside Polytechnic 1970, present name and status 1992

Chancellor: Lord SAWYER OF DARLINGTON
Vice-Chancellor and Chief Exec.: Prof. GRAHAM HENDERSON
Sr Deputy Vice-Chancellor: Prof. KATHERINE LENI OGLESBY
Deputy Vice-Chancellor for Devt: Prof. EILEEN MARTIN
Deputy Vice-Chancellor for Learning and Student Experience: Prof. CAROLINE MACDONALD
Deputy Vice-Chancellor for Research and Enterprise: Prof. CLIFF HARDCASTLE
Univ. Sec. and Clerk to the Governors: J. MORGAN MCCLINTOCK
Academic Registrar: TIM COBBETT
Dir, Library and Information Services: LIZ JOLLY

Library of 369,641 vols
Number of teachers: 701 (574 full-time, 127 part-time)
Number of students: 29,285 incl. full-time and part-time

DEANS

School of Arts and Media: Prof. GERDA ROPER
School of Computing: Dr SIMON STOBART
School of Health and Social Care: Prof. PAUL KEANE
School of Science and Engineering: Prof. SIMON HODGSON
School of Social Sciences and Law: Dr MARK SIMPSON
Teesside Univ. Business School: ALASTAIR THOMSON

UNIVERSITY OF THE ARTS LONDON

272 High Holborn, London, WC1V 7EY
Telephone: (20) 7514-6000
Fax: (20) 7514-6131
E-mail: info@arts.ac.uk
Internet: www.arts.ac.uk

Founded 2004

Rector: Sir NIGEL CARRINGTON
Deputy Rector of Academic Devt and Quality: ELIZABETH ROUSE
Deputy Rector of Planning and Operations: WILLIAM BRIDGE
Dir of Information Services: PAT CHRISTIE

Library of 400,000 vols, 3,500 magazines and periodicals, 10,000 video cassettes and other media, 130 databases, 170 electronic resources and 12,000 e-journals
Number of teachers: 1,228
Number of students: 22,051.

COLLEGES OF THE UNIVERSITY

Camberwell College of Arts

Peckham Rd, London, SE5 8UF
Telephone: (20) 7514-6302
Fax: (20) 7514-6310
E-mail: info@camberwell.arts.ac.uk
Internet: www.camberwell.arts.ac.uk

Founded 1898

Main subject areas: ceramics, design products, conservation, drawing, graphic design, illustration, painting, photography, sculpture; another campus at Wilson Rd

Head: CHRIS WAINWRIGHT
Dean: NATALIE BRETT

Number of teachers: 150
Number of students: 1,746

Central Saint Martins College of Art and Design

Southampton Row, London, WC1B 4AP
Telephone: (20) 7514-7022
Fax: (20) 7514-7254
E-mail: info@csm.arts.ac.uk
Internet: www.csm.arts.ac.uk

Founded 1989 by merger of Central School of Arts and Crafts (f. 1896) and St Martin's School of Art (f. 1854), incorporated Drama Centre London (f. 1962) 1999 and London Studio Centre 2003

Incl. Drama Centre London and the Cochrane Theatre; three schools: school of art, school of graphic and industrial design, school of fashion and textiles

Head: JANE RAPLEY

Library of 80,000 vols
Number of students: 4,883 students

Chelsea College of Art and Design

Millbank, London, SW1P 4JU
Telephone: (20) 7541-7751
Fax: (20) 7514-7778
E-mail: enquiries@chelsea.arts.ac.uk
Internet: www.chelsea.arts.ac.uk

Founded 1895

Main subject areas: fine art, communication design, interior and spatial design, textile design, history and theory of visual and multimedia cultures

Dean: Prof. DAVID GRACIA
Head: Prof. CHRIS WAINWRIGHT

Number of teachers: 80
Number of students: 1,751

London College of Communication

Elephant and Castle, London, SE1 6SB
Telephone: (20) 7514-6500
Fax: (20) 7514-6476
E-mail: info@lcc.arts.ac.uk
Internet: www.lcc.arts.ac.uk

Founded 1894, fmrly London College of Printing, present name 2004

Main subject areas: animation, graphic design, graphic communication, journalism, media, photography

Head: Prof. SANDRA KEMP
Number of students: 5,432 .

London College of Fashion

20 John Princes St, London, W1G 0BJ
Telephone: (20) 7514-7400
Fax: (20) 7514-7484
E-mail: enquiries@fashion.arts.ac.uk
Internet: www.fashion.arts.ac.uk

Founded 1906, as Shoreditch Technical Institute Girls School

Head of College: FRANCES CORNER
Number of students: 5,113

Publication: *Pigeons and Peacocks*.

Wimbledon College of Art

Merton Hall Rd, London, SW19 3QA
Telephone: (20) 7514-9641
Fax: (20) 7514-9642
E-mail: info@wimbledon.ac.uk
Internet: www.wimbledon.arts.ac.uk

Founded 1890,as an Art Class in the Rutlish School for Boys, present name and status 2006

Schools of specialist art and design

Head: CHRIS WAINWRIGHT
Dean: Prof. GEORGE BLACKLOCK

Library of 28,000 vols
Number of teachers: 47
Number of students: 1,124

UNIVERSITY OF THE WEST OF ENGLAND (UWE)

Frenchay Campus, Coldharbour Lane, Bristol, BS16 1QY
Telephone: (117) 965-6261
Fax: (117) 328-2810
E-mail: admissions@uwe.ac.uk
Internet: www.uwe.ac.uk

Founded 1969 as Bristol Polytechnic, present name and status 1992
Language of instruction: English
Academic year: September to June

Chancellor: Rt Hon Baroness BUTLER-SLOSS
Vice-Chancellor: Prof. STEVEN WEST
Deputy Vice-Chancellor For Academic Affairs: Prof. PAUL GOUGH
Deputy Vice-Chancellor For Resources, Planning and Infrastructure: JOHN RUSHFORTH
Academic Registrar: TESSA HARRISON
Librarian: CATHY REX

Library of 581,523 vols, 8,538 periodicals, 22,027 electronic books
Number of teachers: 1,165
Number of students: 30,130 (21,025 full-time and 9,105 part-time)

DEANS

Faculty of Business and Law: Dr JANE HARRINGTON
Faculty of Arts, Creative Industries and Education: ALEX GILKISON (acting)
Faculty of Environment and Technology: Prof. PAUL OLOMOLA
Faculty of Health and Life Sciences: Prof. HELEN LANGTON

UNIVERSITY OF WARWICK

Coventry CV4 7AL
Telephone: (24) 7652-3523
Fax: (24) 7646-1606
Internet: www2.warwick.ac.uk
Founded 1965
Academic year: September to June
Chancellor: Sir RICHARD LAMBERT
Vice-Chancellor: Prof. NIGEL THRIFT
Deputy Vice-Chancellor: Prof. MARK SMITH
Pro-Vice-Chancellor for Research (Faculties of Arts and Social Studies): Prof. RICHARD HIGGOTT
Pro-Vice-Chancellor for Research (Faculties of Science and Medicine): Prof. KOEN LAMBERTS
Pro-Vice-Chancellor for Student Experience: Prof. ANN CAESAR
Registrar: JON BALDWIN
Librarian: ANNE BELL
Library: 1m. vols
Number of teachers: 1,046
Number of students: 21,598

CHAIRS OF FACULTY BOARDS

Faculty of Arts: Prof. STELLA BRUZZI
Faculty of Medicine: Prof. PETER WINSTANLEY (acting)
Faculty of Science: Prof. TIM JONES
Faculty of Social Sciences: Prof. CHRISTINA HUGHES
Graduate Studies: Prof. JACKIE LABBE

PROFESSORS

Faculty of Arts (internet www2.warwick.ac.uk/fac/arts):

BASSNETT, S. E., Centre for Translation and Comparative Cultural Studies
BATE, J., English and Comparative Literary Studies
BEACHAM, R. C., Theatre Studies
BELL, M., English
BENNETT, O., Theatre Studies
BERG, M. L., History
BRUNSDON, C. M., Film and Television Studies
BURNS, R. A., German Studies
CAESAR, A., Italian
CAPP, B. S., History
CLARK, C. F., History
DABYDEEN, D., Caribbean Studies
DAVIS, C. J., French Studies
DAVIS, J., Theatre Studies
DOCHERTY, T., English and Comparative Literary Studies
DYER, R. W., Film and Television Studies
GARDNER, J., History of Art
HEUMAN, G. J., Caribbean Studies, History
HILL, L. J., French Studies
HINDLE, S., History
HINTON, J. S., History
HUGHES, D. W., English
JONES, C. D. H., History
KING, J. P., History
LAZARUS, N., English
MACK, P. W. D., English
MCFARLANE, A. J., History
MULRYNE, J. R., English
NYE, D., History
O'BRIEN, K., English and Comparative Literary Studies
PATERSON, L. M., French Studies
READ, C. J., History
ROSENTHAL, M. J., History of Art
RUTTER, C. C., English and Comparative Literary Studies
SHARPE, K., English
STEEDMAN, C. K., Social History
SWAIN, S. C. R., Classics
TREGLOWN, J. D., English
VINCENDEAU, G. O. R., Film and Television Studies
WHITBY, L. M., Classics

Faculty of Medicine, Warwick Medical School (internet www2.warwick.ac.uk/fac/med):

CARTER, Y., Dean, Warwick Medical School
DALE, J., Division of Health in the Community
FULFORD, K. W. N., Philosophy and Mental Health
GRIFFIN, D., Orthopaedics and Trauma
HUNDT, G. A., School of Health and Social Studies
KUMAR, S., Medicine, Diabetes and Metabolism
LAMB, S., Physiotherapy and Rehabilitation
LEHNERT, H., Medicine
PEILE, E., Medical Education
SINGER, D., Clinical Pharmacology
SPANSWICK, D., Molecular Neurosciences
STANFIELD, P. R., Dept of Biological Sciences
STEWART-BROWN, S., Public Health
THORNTON, S., Biological Sciences
THOROGOOD, M., Epidemiology
WEICH, S., Psychiatry

Faculty of Science (internet www2.warwick.ac.uk/fac/sci; some members also serve in the Faculty of Medicine):

ANDERSON, D., Civil and Mechanical Engineering
BALL, R. C., Theoretical Physics
BARKLEY, D., Mathematics
BHATTACHARYYA, S. K., Manufacturing Systems
BRIGHT, S.
BROWN, G. D. A., Psychology
BRYANSTON-CROSS, P. J., Civil and Mechanical Engineering
BUGG, T. D. H., Biological Chemistry
BURNS, I.
CAMPBELL-KELLY, M., Computer Science
CARPENTER, P. W., Mechanical Engineering
CHAPMAN, S. C., Physics
CHATER, N., Psychology
CHETWYND, D. G., Civil and Mechanical Engineering
COOPER, M. J., Physics
COPAS, J. B., Statistics
CRITOPH, R. E., Civil and Mechanical Engineering
DALE, N., Biological Sciences
DALTON, H., Biological Sciences
DAVEY, J., Biological Sciences
DERRICK, P. J., Chemistry
DIMMOCK, N. J., Biological Sciences
DOWSETT, M. G., Physics
DOWSON, C. G., Biological Sciences
DUPREE, R., Physics
EASTON, A. J., Biological Sciences
ELWORTHY, K. D., Mathematics
FIRTH, D., Statistics
FLOWER, J. O., Engineering
FREEDMAN, R. B., Biological Sciences
FRIESECKE, G., Mathematics
FULFORD, K. W. M., Philosophy and Mental Health
FULOP, V., Biological Sciences
GARDNER, J. W., Electronic Engineering
GODFREY, K. R., Electrical and Electronic Engineering
GREEN, R. J., Electronic Communication Systems
HADDLETON, D. M., Chemistry
HARRISON, P. F., Physics
HOLT, D. F., Mathematics
HUANG, T., Civil and Mechanical Engineering
HUTCHINS, D. A., Electrical and Electronic Engineering
HUTTON, J. L., Statistics
JONES, G. V., Psychology
JONES, J. D. S., Mathematics
KEMP, T. J., Chemistry
KENDALL, W. S., Statistics
KERR, R., Mathematics
KERR, R. M., Civil and Mechanical Engineering
LAMBERTS, K., Psychology
LAWRENCE, A. J., Statistics
LEWIS, M. H., Physics
LORD, J. M., Biological Sciences
MACKAY, R., Mathematics
MANN, N. H., Biological Sciences
MARSH, T., Physics
MAYOR, E. A., Psychology
MCCONVILLE, C. F., Physics
MCCRAE, M. A., Biological Sciences
MEDLEY, G. F. H., Biological Sciences
MILLAR, A. J., Biological Sciences
MILLS, P.
MOND, D. M. Q., Mathematics
MOORE, P., Chemistry
MURRELL, J. C., Biological Sciences
NUDD, G. R., Computer Science
PARKER, E. H. C., Semiconductor Physics
PATERSON, M. S., Computer Science
PAUL, D. MCK., Physics
PELED, D., Computer Science
POLLICOTT, M., Mathematics
RAND, D. A., Mathematics
RAWNSLEY, J. H., Mathematics
REID, M. A., Mathematics
ROBERTS, L. M., Biological Sciences
ROBINSON, C., Biological Sciences
RODGER, P. M.
ROURKE, C. P., Mathematics
SCOTT, P., Chemistry
SERIES, C. M., Mathematics
SHIPMAN, M., Chemistry
SMITH, J. Q., Statistics
SMITH, M. E., Physics
STANFIELD, P. R., Biological Sciences
STAUNTON, J. B., Physics
STEEL, M. F., Statistics
STEWART, I. N., Mathematics
STRIEN, S. VAN, Mathematics
STUART, A., Mathematics
TAYLOR, P. R., Chemistry
THOMAS, B.
THORNTON, S., Obstetrics and Gynaecology
UNWIN, P. R., Chemistry
WALTERS, P., Mathematics
WELLINGTON, E. M. H., Biological Sciences
WHALL, T. E., Physics
WHIPPS, J.
WILLS, M., Chemistry
WILSON, A. J., Medical Physics
WILSON, R. G., Computer Science
WILSON, T. M. A., Biological Sciences
WOODLAND, H. R., Biological Sciences
WOODRUFF, D. P., Physics

Faculty of Social Studies (internet www2.warwick.ac.uk/fac/soc; some members also serve in the Faculty of Medicine):

ALI, S. S., Law
ANSELL-PEARSON, K., Philosophy
ANWAR, M., Ethnic Relations
ARCHER, M. S, Sociology
ARULAMPALAM, S. W., Economics
AUBREY, C., Institute of Education
BAXI, U., Law
BEALE, H. G., Law
BECKFORD, J. A., Sociology
BENINGTON, J., Business Studies
BLACKORBY, A. B., Economics
BRESLIN, S., Politics and International Studies
BREWER, B., Philosophy
BRIDGES, L. T., Law
BROADBERRY, S. N., Economics

BRYER, R. A., Accounting and Finance
BURNELL, P. J., Politics and International Studies
BURNHAM, P., Politics and International Studies
BURRIDGE, R. H. M., Law
CAMPBELL, R. J., Institute of Education
CARNALL, C., Business Studies
CAVE, M., Centre for Management under Regulation
CHARLES, N., Sociology
CLARKE, S. R. C., Sociology
CLUBB, C., Accounting and Finance
COHEN, R., Sociology
COWLING, K. G., Industrial Economics
CROUCH, C., Governance and Public Management
CURRIE, W., Information Systems
DALE, J., Primary Care
DAVIES, R., Business Studies
DEVEREUX, M. P., Economics and Business Studies
DICKENS, L. J., Business Studies
DUTTA, B., Economics
DYSON, R. G., Business Studies
EDWARDS, P. K., Business Studies
EILAN, N. H., Philosophy
ELIAS, D. P. B., Employment Research
ELLIOTT, R., Business Studies
FAUNDEZ, J., Law
FINE, R. D., Sociology
FULFORD, K. W. M., Philosophy and Mental Health
FULLER, S., Sociology
GEMMILL, G., Accounting and Finance
GHOSAL, S., Economics
GLEESON, D., Institute of Education
GRANT, W. P., Politics and International Studies
HARRIS, A., Institute of Education
HARRIS, J., Health and Social Studies
HARRISON, R. M., Economics
HARTLEY, J., Local Government Centre
HIGGOTT, R. A., Politics and International Studies
HODGES, S. D., Financial Management
HOSKIN, K. W., Business Studies
HOULGATE, S., Philosophy
HUDDLESTON, P. J., Institute of Education
HURLEY, S., Politics and International Studies
IRELAND, N. J., Economics
JACKSON, R. M. D., Institute of Education
JOHNSTON, R., Business Studies
JOLY, D., Centre for Research in Ethnic Relations
LAYTON-HENRY, Z. A., Politics and International Studies
LEGGE, K., Business Studies
LEWANDO-HUNDT, G., Social Sciences and Health
LINDLEY, R. M., Employment Research
LINDSAY, G. A., Special Educational Needs
LOCKWOOD, B., Economics
LOVELL, T. A., Women and Gender
LUNTLEY, M., Philosophy
MARGINSON, P., Industrial Relations
MASSON, J. M., Law
MAWSON, J., Local Government Centre
MCCONVILLE, M. J., Law
MCELDOWNEY, J. F., Law
MCGEE, J., Marketing and Strategic Management
MILLER, M. H., Economics
MITCHELL, C., Centre for Management under Regulation
MORGAN, G., Industrial Relations
MULLENDER, A., Social Work
NAYLOR, R. A., Economics
NEAL, A., Law
NEUBERGER, A., Accounting and Finance
OSWALD, A. J., Economics
PALIWALA, A., Law
PERRONI, C., Economics
PHIZACKLEA, A. M., Sociology
PIERCY, N., Marketing and Strategic Management
POGANY, S. I., Law
RAI, S. M., Politics and International Studies
RANKIN, N., Economics
RATCLIFFE, P. B., Sociology
REEVE, A. W., Politics and International Studies
SALMON, M., Accounting and Finance
SARNO, L., Business Studies
SCARBOROUGH, H., Business Studies
SCHOLTE, J. A., Politics and International Studies
SKIDELSKY, R., Political Economy
SLACK, N. D. C., Manufacturing and Strategy Policy
SLADE, M., Economics
SMITH, H., Politics and International Studies
SMITH, R. J., Economics
SPENCER, N. J., Community Paediatrics
STEWART, M. B., Economics
STONEMAN, P., Business Studies
STOREY, D. J., Business Studies
STURDY, A., Industrial Relations and Organizational Behaviour
SWAN, J. A., Organizational Behaviour
SZCZEPURA, A., Business Studies
TALL, D. O., Institute of Education
TAYLOR, M. P., Economics
TERRY, M. A., Business Studies
THOMAS, H., Business Studies
TRIGG, R. H., Philosophy
TSOUKOS, H., Industrial Relations and Organizational Behaviour
WAGNER, P., Sociology
WALKER, I., Economics
WARHURST, A., Corporate Citizenship Unit
WATERSON, M. J., Economics
WENSLEY, J. R. C., Marketing and Strategic Management
WHALLEY, J., Development Economics
WHITE, B., Politics and International Studies
WHITESIDE, N., Sociology
WILLCOCKS, L., Information Management and e-Business
WILSON, D. C., Strategic Management
WOODERS, M., Economics
WRAY, D., Institute of Education

UNIVERSITY OF WESTMINSTER

309 Regent St, London W1B 2UW
Telephone: (20) 7911-5000
Fax: (20) 7911-5858
E-mail: course-enquiries@westminster.ac.uk
Internet: www.westminster.ac.uk

Founded 1838 as Polytechnic Institution; became Royal Polytechnic Institution 1839 and Polytechnic of Central London 1970; present name and status 1992
Academic year: September to August

Vice-Chancellor and Rector: Prof. GEOFFREY PETTS
Deputy Vice-Chancellor and Pro-Vice-Chancellor: Prof. RIKKI MORGAN-TAMOSUNAS
Pro-Vice-Chancellor: Dr MYSZKA GUZKOWSKA
Registrar and Sec.: CAROLE MAINSTONE
Dir for Finance: MICHAEL WEBB

Library of 420,000 vols
Number of teachers: 1,204
Number of students: 23,000

DEANS

School of Architecture and Built Environment: Prof. JEREMY TILL
School of Life sciences: Prof. JANE LEWIS
School of Informatics: Prof. GRAHAM MEGSON
School of Law: Prof. ANDREW BOON
School of Media, Arts and Design: SALLY FELDMAN
School of Social Sciences, Humanities and Languages: Dr JEREMY COLWILL
Westminster Business School: Prof. JEAN WOODALL

UNIVERSITY OF WINCHESTER

Sparkford Rd, Winchester, SO22 4NR
Telephone: (1962) 841515
Fax: (1962) 842280
E-mail: course.enquiries@winchester.ac.uk
Internet: www.winchester.ac.uk

Founded 1840; present name and status 2005

Chancellor: MARY FAGAN
Vice-Chancellor: Prof. JOY CARTER
Univ. Librarian: DAVID FARLEY
Deputy Vice-Chancellor: TOMMY GEDDES
Pro-Vice-Chancellor: Prof. ELIZABETH STUART
Dir for Finance and Strategy: SIMON COWHIG

Library of 250,000 vols
Number of teachers: 650 (f.t.e.)
Number of students: 5,906

DEANS

Faculty of Arts: Prof. ANTHONY DEAN
Faculty of Business, Law and Sport: Prof. NEIL MARRIOTT
Faculty of Education, Health and Social Care: Prof. JOYCE GOODMAN
Faculty of Humanities and Social Sciences: Prof. KRISTYAN SPELMAN MILLER

UNIVERSITY OF WOLVERHAMPTON

Molineux St, Wolverhampton, WV1 1SB
Telephone: (1902) 321000
Fax: (1902) 322680
E-mail: enquiries@wlv.ac.uk
Internet: www.wlv.ac.uk

Founded 1969 as Wolverhampton Polytechnic; present name and status 1992

Constituent Colleges: City of Wolverhampton College, Dudley College, Rodbaston College, Sandwell College, South Birmingham College, Telford College of Arts and Technology, Walsall College of Arts and Technology

Chancellor: Rt Hon. Lord PAUL OF MARYLEBONE
Vice-Chancellor: Prof. CAROLINE GIPPS
Deputy Vice-Chancellor: Prof. GEOFF HAMPTON
Deputy Vice-Chancellor and Dir of Finance: GARRY SPROSTON
Pro-Vice-Chancellor for Academic Affairs: Prof. SALLY GLEN
Pro-Vice-Chancellor and Dir for Corporate Services: HELEN LLOYD WILDMAN
Pro-Vice-Chancellor for Student Affairs: JANE NELSON
Pro-Vice-Chancellor for Research and Enterprise: Prof. IAN OAKES
Registrar: PAUL TRAVILL
Dir for Learning and Information Services: FIONA PARSONS
Dean for Students: JON ELSMORE
Univ. Sec.: A. W. (TONY) LEE

Library of 363,471 vols
Number of teachers: 978
Number of students: 23,084

DEANS

Applied Sciences: Prof. JOHN DARLING
Art and Design: Dr BRYONY CONWAY
Education: Prof. KIT FIELD
Health and Wellbeing: Prof. LINDA LANG
Institute for Learning Enhancement: Dr GLYNIS COUSIN
Law, Social Sciences and Communications: Dr JUDITH BURNETT
Sport, Performing Arts and Leisure: JOHN PYMM
Technology: Prof. ROBERT MORETON
University of Wolverhampton Business School: Prof. KIT FIELD (acting)

UNIVERSITY OF WORCESTER

Henwick Grove, Worcester, WR2 6AJ
Telephone: (1905) 855000
E-mail: admissions@worc.ac.uk
Internet: www.worc.ac.uk

Founded 1946, as Emergency Teacher Training College, present name and status 2005
Academic year: September to May
Chancellor: HRH PRINCE RICHARD, THE DUKE OF GLOUCESTER
Vice-Chancellor and Chief Exec.: Prof. DAVID GREEN
Deputy Vice-Chancellor: Prof. ROSALIND FOSKETT
Pro-Vice-Chancellor for Resources: Dr MARTIN DOUGHTY
Registrar and Univ. Sec.: JOHN RYAN
Library of 130,000 vols, 800 periodicals
Number of teachers: 700
Number of students: 9,545

UNIVERSITY OF YORK

Heslington, York, YO10 5DD
Telephone: (1904) 320000
Fax: (1904) 323433
E-mail: admissions@york.ac.uk
Internet: www.york.ac.uk

Founded 1963
Academic year: October to June (three terms)
Chancellor: GREG DYKE
Pro-Chancellor: Sir CHRISTOPHER O'DONNELL
Pro-Chancellor: LESLEY WILD
Pro-Chancellor: Dr ROBERT BRECH
Vice-Chancellor: Prof. BRIAN CANTOR
Deputy Vice-Chancellor: Prof. TREVOR SHELDON
Pro-Vice-Chancellor: Prof. COLIN MELLORS
Pro-Vice-Chancellor: ELIZABETH HEAPS
Pro-Vice-Chancellor: Dr JANE GRENVILLE
Pro-Vice-Chancellor: Prof. JOHN LOCAL
Registrar and Sec.: Dr DAVID DUNCAN
Dir for Corporate Planning: DAVID MUCKERSIE
Dir for Estates and Campus Services: JON MEACOCK
Dir for External Relations: JOAN CONCANNON
Dir for Finance: GRAHAM GILBERT
Dir for Human Resources: PAT LOFTHOUSE
Dir for Information and Univ. Librarian: STEPHEN TOWN
Dir for Research and Enterprise: MARK MORTIMER
Library: see under Libraries and Archives
Number of teachers: 770
Number of students: 13,000
Publication: *University of York Magazine* (6 a year)

PROFESSORS

ABADIR, K., Economics, Mathematics
AFSHAR, H., Politics
ANDREWS, R., Educational Studies
ARTHURS, A. M., Mathematics
ATTRIDGE, D., English
BABIKER, M., Physics
BALDWIN, T. R., Philosophy
BARRELL, J. C., English
BEHRINGER, W., History
BERTHOUD, J. A., English
BESSEL, R., History
BILLER, P., History
BOWLBY, R., English
BOWLES, D. J., Biology
BRADSHAW, J. R., Social Policy
BRAUNSTEIN, S., Quantum Computing
BURNS, A., Computer Science
BURR, A., Electronics
CALLINICOS, A., Politics
CAMPBELL, C., Sociology
CARR-HILL, R., Health Economics
CARVER, M. O., Archaeology
CLARK, J. H., Chemistry
CORRIGAN, E., Mathematics
CRESSER, M., Environment
CULYER, A. J., Economics
DE FRAJA, G., Economics
DITCH, J. S., Social Policy and Social Work
DIVALL, C., Railway Studies
DIXON, H. D., Economics
DODSON, E., Chemistry
DODSON, G. G., Chemistry
DODSON, M., Mathematics
DOLLIMORE, J., English
DRUMMOND, M. F., Health Economics
EL-GOMATI, M. M., Electronics
ELLIS, A. W., Psychology
FITTER, A. H., Biology
FORD, J. R., Housing Policy
FORREST, A. I., History
FOUNTAIN, J., Mathematics
GILBERT, B. C., Chemistry
GODBY, R., Physics
GODFREY, C., Centre for Health Economics, Health Services
GODFREY, L. G., Social and Economic Statistics
GRAHAM, I., Biology
GRAVELLE, H. S. E., Economics
GUEST, H., English
HALL, G., Psychology
HARRISON, M. D., Computer Science
HARTLEY, K., Economics
HEY, J. D., Social and Economic Statistics
HITCH, G., Psychology
HOLMAN, J., Chemistry
HOWARD, D., Electronics
HOWELL, D., Politics
HUBBARD, R., Chemistry
HULME, C., Psychology
HUTTON, J. P., Economics and Econometrics
INESON, P., Biology
JACKSON, S. F., Women's Studies
JONES, A., Economics
KEMP, P., Social Policy Research Unit
KITZINGER, C., Sociology
KLEIJNEN, J. E., Centre for Reviews and Dissemination
LAMARQUE, P., Philosophy
LAMBERT, P., Economics
LE FANU, N., Music
LEESE, H. J., Biology
LEWIN, R. J., Health Studies
LINDSAY SMITH, J., Chemistry
LOCAL, J. K., Linguistics
MACPHAIL, E., Psychology
MAITLAND, N. J., Biology
MARKS, R., History of Art
MARSH, R., Music
MARVIN, A. C., Electronics
MATTHEW, J. A. D., Physics
MAYNARD, A. K., Health Studies
MAYNARD, M. A., Social Policy and Social Work
MAYSTON, D. J., Public Sector Economics
MCDERMID, J. A., Computer Science
MCDOUGALL, C., Criminal Justice
MCQUEEN-MASON, S., Biology
MENDUS, S., Politics
MILLAR, R., Educational Studies
MILNER, A. J., Biology
MINNIS, A. J., Medieval Literature
MONK, A., Psychology
MULKAY, M., Sociology
MULLER-DETHLEFS, K., Chemistry
O'CONNOR, T., Archaeology
O'GRADY, K., Physics
ORMROD, M., History
PARRY, G., English
PERRINGS, C., Environment
PERT, G. J., Computational Physics
PERUTZ, R. N., Chemistry
PHILLIPS, P., Economics
POSNETT, J., York Health Economics Consortium
PRUTTON, M., Physics
QURESHI, H., Social Policy and Social Work
RAFFAELLI, D., Environment
RAINEY, L. S., English
RIDDY, F J., English
ROBARDS, A. W., Biology
ROBINSON, J., Electronics
ROYLE, E., History
RUNCIMAN, C., Computer Science
RUSSELL, I. T., Health Sciences
SANDERS, D., Biology
SHARPE, J. A., History
SHAW, I., Social Work
SHELDON, T., Health Sciences
SIMMONS, P. J., Economics
SINCLAIR, I. A. C., Social Work
SLOPER, P., Social Policy Research Unit
SMITH, D. M., Borthwick Institute
SMITH, P. C., Economics
SNOWLING, M. S., Psychology
SOUTHGATE, J., Biology
SPARROW, J., Biology
STEIN, M., Social Work
SUDBERY, A., Mathematics
TAYLOR, R. J. K., Chemistry
THOMPSON, D. R., Health Studies
TYRRELL, A. M., Electronics
VULLIAMY, G., Educational Studies
WALTON, P., Chemistry
WALVIN, J., History
WAND, I. C., Computer Science
WARD, N. A.-M. F., English
WARNER, A. R., Language
WATT, I. S., Health Studies
WEBSTER, A., Sociology
WELLINGS, A. J., Computer Science
WICKENS, M. R., Economics
WILKINSON, A. J., Chemistry
WILLIAMS, A. H., Economics
WILSON, K., Chemistry
WILSON, R. A., Biology
WOOLHOUSE, R., Philosophy
YEARLEY, S., Sociology
YOUNG, A. W., Psychology
YOUNG, J. P. W., Biology

YORK ST JOHN UNIVERSITY

Lord Mayor's Walk, York, YO31 7EX
Telephone: (1904) 624624
Fax: (1904) 612512
Internet: w3.yorksj.ac.uk

Founded 1841, as York Diocesan Training School, present name and status 2006
Chancellor: Archbishop of York, Dr JOHN SENTAMU
Vice-Chancellor: Prof. DAVID FLEMING
Deputy Vice-Chancellor: Prof. DAVID MAUGHAN BROWN
Registrar: PAULINE ALDOUS
Number of teachers: 235
Number of students: 5,627
Publication: *The White Rose* (1 a year)

DEANS

Faculty of Arts: Prof. STEVE PURCELL
Faculty of Education and Theology: Prof. JULIAN STERN
Faculty of Health and Life Sciences: Prof. PAMELA DAWSON
York St John Business School: JACKIE MATHERS

University Colleges in England

University Colleges have taught degree awarding powers only and do not carry out research.

Arts University College at Bournemouth: Wallisdown, Poole, BH12 5HH; tel. (1202) 363-233; fax (1202) 363-378; e-mail general@aucb.ac.uk; internet www.aucb.ac.uk; f. 1885; specialist instn; diploma, undergraduate, postgraduate degree courses in art, design and creative media; library: 45,000 vols, 40,000 e-books, 300 specialist journals; 3,000 students.

Bishop Grosseteste University College: Lincoln, LN1 3DY; tel. (1522) 527347; fax (1522) 530243; e-mail info@bishopg.ac.uk; internet www.bishopg.ac.uk; f. 1862; undergraduate, postgraduate and work-based programmes in education, arts and humanities and cultural industries; Provost Dame JUDITH MAYHEW JONAS; Prin. Prof. MURIEL ROBINSON; Head of Library Services EMMA SANSBY.

BPP University College: Aldine House, Aldine Place, 142–144 Uxbridge Rd, London, W12 8AW; tel. (20) 7633-4410; fax (2074) 041389; e-mail admissions@bpp.com; internet www.bppuc.com; f. 1992; consists of business school and law school; undergraduate, postgraduate and professional programmes; campuses in Birmingham, Bristol, Leeds, Manchester and in 3 centres in London; acquired by Apollo Global, Inc.; library: 6,200 vols; 64 teachers; 600 full-time postgraduate students; Prin. CARL LYGO.

College of Law: Braboeuf Manor, Portsmouth Rd, St Catherines, Guildford, GU3 1HA; tel. (1483) 216-000; fax (1483) 460-305; internet www.college-of-law.co.uk; f. 1967, degree awarding powers 2006; postgraduate courses; brs in Birmingham, Bristol, Chester, London, Manchester and York; Chief Exec. Prof. NIGEL SAVAGE; Chair. DAVID YATES; Deputy Chair. JONATHAN HAW; Deputy Chair. GUY BERINGER.

Greenwich School of Management: Meridian House, Royal Hill, Greenwich, London SE10 8RD; tel. (20) 8516-7800; fax (20) 8516-7801; e-mail admissions@greenwich-college.ac.uk; internet www.greenwich-college.ac.uk; f. 1973 incorporates the Greenwich School of Law; provides univ. MBA, MSc, EMBA, BSc, LLB, BBA PhD, DBA, CIPS, undergraduate, postgraduate, doctoral programmes and professional courses; Prin. Dr WILLIAM HUNT.

Henley Business School: Whiteknights, Reading, RG6 6UD; tel. (118) 378-5044; fax (118) 378-4029; e-mail helpdesk@henley.com; internet www.henley.reading.ac.uk; f. 1945; attached to Univ. of Reading; has campus in Greenland; courses in accountancy, business, management, finance, real estate, planning, informatics, and coaching; 7,000 students; Dean Prof. JOHN BOARD; Deputy Dean Prof. GINNY GIBSON.

ifs School of Finance: 36 Monument St, London, EC3R 8LJ; tel. (20) 7444-7111; fax (20) 7444-7115; e-mail customerservices@ifslearning.ac.uk; internet www.ifslearning.ac.uk; f. 1879 as Institute of Bankers, present name 2006, acquisition of taught degree-awarding powers 2010; courses in banking and financial management; Chair. BRUCE CARNEGIE-BROWN; Prin. GAVIN SHREEVE; Treas. ROY RANSLEY.

Leeds Trinity University College: International Office, Brownberrie Lane, Horsforth, Leeds, LS18 5HD; tel. (1132) 837178; fax (1132) 837200; e-mail international@leedstrinity.ac.uk; internet www.leedstrinity.ac.uk; f. 1980 by merger of Leeds Trinity and All Saints College, power to award taught degrees and became univ. college 2009; undergraduate and postgraduate courses in media, business and marketing, arts and social sciences, forensic psychology, sports psychology; accredited by Leeds Univ.; 3,000 students; Prin. and Chief Exec. Dr FREDA BRIDGE; Deputy Prin. MARK SHIELDS; Vice-Prin. and Registrar JENNY SHARE.

Newman University College: Genners Lane, Bartley Green, Birmingham, B32 3NT; tel. (121) 476-1181; fax (121) 476-1196; e-mail admissions@newman.ac.uk; internet www.newman.ac.uk; f. 1968; offers foundation degrees, BA (Hons), professional graduate certificate of education, teacher training courses; postgraduate research students awarded by Univ. of Leicester; library: 90,000 books, 500 periodicals; Prin. and CEO Prof. PETER LUTZEIER; Vice-Prin. KATHRYN SOUTHWORTH; Registrar and Univ. College Sec. HEATHER SOMERFIELD.

Norwich University College of the Arts: 3–7 Redwell St, Norwich, NR2 4SN; tel. (1603) 610561; fax (1603) 615728; e-mail info@nuca.ac.uk; internet www.nuca.ac.uk; f. 1845, as Norwich School of Design, present name and status 2008; library: 30,000 vols, 2,500 DVDs, 100 journals; 1,500 students; Prin. Prof. JOHN LAST.

Royal Agricultural College: Stroud Rd, Cirencester, GL7 6JS; tel. (1285) 652-531; fax (1285) 650-219; e-mail admissions@rac.ac.uk; internet www.rac.ac.uk; f. 1842 royal charter in 1845; education, research and consultancy; undergraduate and postgraduate courses in agricultural, land, business management, food, equine, property industries; library: 40,000 vols, 1,000 journal subscriptions, 50,000 e-books; 49 full-time teachers; 25 visiting professors; 650 full-time students; Prin. Prof. CHRIS GASKELL.

St Mary's University College: Strawberry Hill, Twickenham, London TW1 4SX; tel. (20) 8240-4000; fax (20) 8240-4255; internet www.smuc.ac.uk; f. 1850, present status 2006; library: 11,500 vols, 13,500 journals; 100 teachers; Prin. Prof. PHILIP ESLER; Vice-Prin. Prof. MICHAEL HAYES; Vice-Prin. DAVID LEEN.

University College Birmingham: Summer Row, Birmingham, B3 1JB; tel. (121) 604-1000; internet www.ucb.ac.uk; f. 1918, present name and status 2007; library: 75,000 vols, 1,000 journals; 7,500 students; Prin. Prof. RAY LINFORTH.

University College Falmouth: Woodlane, Falmouth, TR11 4RH; tel. (1326) 211077; fax (1326) 213880; e-mail admissions@falmouth.ac.uk; internet www.falmouth.ac.uk; f. 1902, merged with Dartington college of arts in 2008, aims to become specialist arts univ. by 2012; college of arts;campuses at Woodlane in Falmouth and Tremough in Penryn; library: 100,000 vols; 80 teachers; 1,700 students; Rector and CEO Prof. ANNE CARLISLE.

University College Plymouth St Mark and St John: Derriford Rd, Plymouth, PL6 8BH; tel. (1752) 636700; fax (1752) 636819; e-mail info@ucpmarjon.ac.uk; internet www.marjon.ac.uk; f. 1926, by merger of St John's College and St Mark's College, present name and status 2007; library: 120,000 vols; 3,500 students; Prin. Prof. MARGARET NOBLE; Vice-Prin. for Academic Dr GEOFF STOAKES; Vice-Prin. for Resources KAREN COOK.

Colleges in England

These institutions are not able to award their own degrees, but offer courses leading to a degree from a recognized body.

GENERAL

Abingdon and Witney College: Wootton Rd, Abingdon, OX14 1GG; tel. (1235) 555585; fax (1235) 553168; e-mail enquiry@abingdon-witney.ac.uk; internet www.abingdon-witney.ac.uk; f. 2001 by merger of Abingdon College and West Oxfordshire College; five campuses; foundation courses, diploma, full-time, part-time academic and vocational degree courses; Prin. TERESA KELLY.

Accrington and Rossendale College: Broad Oak Rd, Accrington, BB5 2AW; tel. (1254) 389933; fax (1254) 354001; e-mail info@accross.ac.uk; internet www.accross.ac.uk; 3 campuses; degree courses in health, sports, technology; Prin. STEPHEN CARLISLE.

Alpha Meridian College: Meridian House, Greenwich High Rd, Greenwich, London, SE10 8TL; tel. (20) 8853-4111; fax (20) 8858-5553; e-mail info@alphameridian.co.uk; internet www.alphameridian.co.uk; f. 1994; private independent educational instn; graduate, postgraduate and diploma courses in computing, IT, accounting, business administration and management, travel, tourism, hospitality and English language.

Alton College: Old Odiham Rd, Alton, GU34 2LX; tel. (1420) 592200; fax (1420) 592253; e-mail admissions@altoncollege.ac.uk; internet www.altoncollege.ac.uk; Level 1–4 courses; subsidiary and extended diploma, Ofsted grade 1 ratings; library: 30,000 vols; Prin. JANE MACHELL; publ. *The Alternative* (student online magazine).

American InterContinental University London: 110 Marylebone High St, London, W1U 4RY; tel. (2074) 675640; e-mail aiuadministration@aiuniv.edu; internet www.aiuniv.edu/london; f. 1970; Bachelors and Masters in business, fashion, design, education and IT; 22 teachers; CEO and Pres. STEPHEN J. TOBER.

Ashton Sixth Form College: Darnton Rd, Ashton-under-Lyne, OL6 9RL; tel. (1613) 302330; fax (1613) 391772; e-mail contact@asfc.ac.uk; internet www.asfc.ac.uk; foundation degrees, BA (Hons) degrees; library: 10,000 printed resources and multimedia materials; Prin. Dr JANET NEVIN.

Aylesbury College: Oxford Rd, Aylesbury, HP21 8PD; tel. (1296) 588588; e-mail customerservices@aylesbury.ac.uk; internet www.aylesbury.ac.uk; f. 1962 as Aylesbury College of Further Education; vocational courses including hospitality and catering, construction, care, hair and beauty and sport; 5,500 (4500 part-time, 1000 full-time); Prin. and Chief Exec. PAULINE ODULINSKI.

Barking and Dagenham College: Rush Green Campus, Dagenham Rd, Romford, RM7 0XU; tel. (20) 8090-3020; fax (20) 8090-3021; internet www.barkingcollege.ac.uk; f. 1993; higher education courses incl. animation and creative video, business studies, computing, construction, fine art, graphic design, management, performing arts, photography, teacher training; Prin. and CEO CATHY WALSH.

Barnet College: Wood St., Barnet, EN5 4AZ; tel. (20) 8200-8300; fax (20) 8205-7177; e-mail info@barnet.ac.uk; internet www.barnet.ac.uk; campus at Grahame Park, two learning centres; offers 2,000 academic, professional, vocational and general interest courses; Prin. MARILYN HAWKINS.

Basingstoke College of Technology: Worting Rd, Basingstoke, RG21 8TN; tel. (1256) 354141; fax (1256) 306444; e-mail information@bcot.ac.uk; internet www.bcot.ac.uk; two sites and three outreach centres; higher education diploma in art and design, health, primary education; foundation degree in childhood studies, management; BA (Hons) in Textiles for Fashion, full time courses in business and sports; library: 24,000 vols, 100 journals; 7,000 (2000 full-time, 5,000 part-time); Prin. JUDITH ARMSTRONG.

Bedford College: Cauldwell St, Bedford, MK42 9AH; tel. (1234) 291000; fax (1234)

342674; e-mail info@bedford.ac.uk; internet www.bedford.ac.uk; higher education, professional and part-time courses; partnership with Univ. of Bedfordshire; library: 40,000 items, 8000 e-journals; Prin. and Chief Exec. IAN PRYCE.

Bishop Burton College: York Rd, Bishop Burton, Beverley, HU17 8QG; tel. (1964) 553000; fax (1964) 553101; e-mail enquiries@bishopburton.ac.uk; internet www.bishopburton.ac.uk; f. 1954; land-based college; degrees validated by Univ. of Hull, Leeds Metropolitan Univ.; library: 46,000 items; 370 journal and magazine subscriptions; Prin JEANETTE DAWSON.

Blackpool and The Fylde College: Ashfield Rd, Bispham, Blackpool, FY2 0HB; tel. (1253) 352-352; fax (1253) 356-127; e-mail visitors@blackpool.ac.uk; internet www.blackpool.ac.uk; attached to Lancaster Univ.; offers undergraduate, professional and vocational courses; 30,000 students; Prin. and Chief Exec. PAULINE WATERHOUSE.

Bradford College: Great Horton Rd, Bradford, BD7 1AY; tel. (1274) 433348; fax (1274) 741060; e-mail international@bradfordcollege.ac.uk; internet www.bradfordcollege.ac.uk; f. 1832; provides undergraduate, postgraduate and professional courses; consists of law school, business school and school of teaching, health and care; 23,000 students; Prin. MICHELE SUTTON.

Bromley College of Further and Higher Education: Rookery Lane, Bromley, BR2 8HE; tel. (20) 8295-7001; fax (20) 8295-7099; e-mail info@bromley.ac.uk; internet www.bromley.ac.uk; Bachelors degrees, foundation degrees and HNDs in vocational subjects; validated by Univ. of Greenwich; 600 teachers; 8,000 students; Prin. SAM PARRETT.

Burnley College: Princess Way, Burnley, BB12 0AN; tel. (1282) 733373; internet www.burnley.ac.uk; sixth form, university and adult education with a campus at the Univ. of Central Lancashire; Prin. HUGH BRAMWELL.

Castle College Nottingham: The People's Campus, Maid Marian Way, Nottingham, NG1 6AB; tel. (1158) 842218; e-mail international@castlecollege.ac.uk; internet www.castlecollege.ac.uk/castle; f. 2006 by merger of Broxtowe College and The People's College; 11 sites; associate college of De Montfort Univ., Nottingham Trent Univ., Univ. of Bedfordshire, Univ. of Northampton and Univ. of Derby; HNC, HND, foundation degrees and vocational courses; Interim Prin. MALCOLM COWGILL.

Cavendish College: 35–37 Alfred Place, London, WC1E 7DP; tel. (20) 7580-4074; fax (20) 7255-1591; e-mail learn@cavendish.ac.uk; internet www.cavendish.ac.uk; full-time and part-time, diploma, certificate; foundation, undergraduate and postgraduate degrees in management, hospitality, digital media, designing and English language.

Chesterfield College: Infirmary Rd, Chesterfield, S41 7NG; tel. (1246) 500500; fax (1246) 500587; e-mail advice@chesterfield.ac.uk; internet www.chesterfield.ac.uk; f. 1841; 3 campuses; provides foundation courses, A levels, vocational and professional qualifications, diplomas and degrees; library: 340,000 books, journals, magazines and DVDs; Prin. JUDITH MCARTHUR.

City College Brighton and Hove: Pelham St, Brighton, BN1 4FA; tel. (1273) 667788; fax (1273) 667703; e-mail info@ccb.ac.uk; internet www.ccb.ac.uk; has campuses at Preston Rd and Wilson Ave; vocational courses in digital design, business and finance, catering and hospitality, tourism, heritage engineering, instrumentation, automation and control engineering; library: 40,000 vols, 300 periodicals, 2,500 video cassettes and DVDs; 9,000 students; Prin. and Chief Exec. PHIL FRIER; Vice-Prin. for Curriculum and Planning STEVE LEWIS; Vice-Prin. for Learning and Quality JAMES METTYEAR; Vice-Prin. for Student and Learning Support REBECCA FOREMAN.

City College Norwich: Ipswich Rd, Norwich, NR2 2LJ; tel. (1603) 773-483; fax (1603) 773-301; e-mail cfitzger@ccn.ac.uk; internet www.ccn.ac.uk; in conjunction with Univ. of East Anglia; higher national certificates and diplomas, foundation degrees, undergraduate degrees, postgraduate degrees, English language qualification; library: 80,000 books, 700 periodicals; Prin. DICK PALMER.

City of Bath College: Avon St, Bath, BA1 1UP; tel. (1225) 312-191; fax (1225) 444-213; e-mail enquiries@citybathcoll.ac.uk; internet www.citybathcoll.ac.uk; 6 local centres; undergraduate, part-time, full-time courses in arts, crafts and design, business and management, computing and information technology, construction and engineering, early years, music and performing arts, sports and fitness, teacher training; library: 35,000 print resources; 100 journals; Prin. MATT ATKINSON.

City of London College: 80 Backchurch Lane, London, E1 1LX; tel. (20) 7553-0430; fax (20) 7553-0431; e-mail info@clc-london.ac.uk; internet www.clc-london.ac.uk; f. 1979; courses validated by Birmingham City Univ., Univ. of Greenwich, Unv. of London, Univ. of Wales, Trinity Univ. College; courses in accounting and finance, business and management, economics, social sciences, computing, hospitality management, travel and tourism management, health and social care, English language; library: 2,500 vols; 2,000 students; Man. Dir Dr S. YOUSUF; Prin. DAVID J. NIXON.

City of Sunderland College: Durham Rd, Sunderland, SR3 4AH; tel. (191) 511-6000; e-mail informationservices@citysun.ac.uk; internet www.citysun.ac.uk; HE degrees by Univ. of Sunderland; Prin. ANGELA O'DONOGHUE.

Colchester Institute: Colchester Campus, Sheepen Rd, Colchester Essex, CO3 3LL; tel. (1206) 712000; fax (1206) 712800; internet www.colchester.ac.uk; 6 campuses, vocational colleges, part-time, full-time courses, foundation, higher national certificate, diploma, undergraduate and postgraduate courses; validated by Univ. of Essex; Prin. DANNY CLOUGH.

College of West Anglia: King's Lynn campus, Tennyson Ave, King's Lynn, PE30 2QW; tel. (1553) 761144; fax (1553) 815555; e-mail enquiries@col-westanglia.ac.uk; internet www.cwa.ac.uk; f. 1894 as King's Lynn Technical School; four campuses; offers degrees, foundation degrees and higher national diplomas; partnership with Anglia Ruskin Univ.; Prin. DAVID POMFRET.

Cornwall College: Cornwall College Camborne, Trevenson Rd, Pool, Redruth, TR15 3RD; tel. (1209) 611-611; fax (1209) 611-612; e-mail enquiries@cornwall.ac.uk; internet www.cornwall.ac.uk; f. 1929; 7 campues; higher and further education college; 2,800 staff; 45,000 students (4,500 full-time, 40,500 part-time); Prin. and CEO DAVE LINNELL.

Craven College: High St, Skipton, BD23 1JY; tel. (1756) 708-008; fax (1756) 794-872; e-mail international@craven-college.ac.uk; internet www.craven-college.ac.uk; 2 campuses, 2 centres, 2 academies; foundation degrees, BA Hons, higher national diplomas and certificates; Prin. ALAN BLACKWELL.

Croydon College: College Rd, Croydon, CR9 1DX; tel. (20) 8760-5914; fax (20) 8760-5880; e-mail internationaloffice@croydon.ac.uk; internet www.croydon.ac.uk; 3 campuses; entry level courses, BTECs, A levels, Access courses and NVQs, univ. level courses; more than 350 qualifications; validation by Univ. of Sussex; library: 80,000 books, 400 newspaper and magazine titles; 13,000 students; Prin. and Chief Exec. FRANCES WADSWORTH.

Doncaster College: High Melton, DN5 7SZ; tel. (1302) 553-592; fax (1302) 553-591; e-mail international@don.ac.uk; internet www.don.ac.uk; 2 campuses, 539 courses at all levels; degrees validated by the Univ. of Hull; 1,072 teachers; 19,813 students; Prin. and Chief Exec. GEORGE TROW.

East Riding College: Beverley campus, Gallows Lane, Beverly, HU17 7DT; e-mail info@eastridingcollege.ac.uk; internet www.eastridingcollege.ac.uk; 3 campuses; part-time and full-time courses, A-level, nat. vocational qualifications, diploma courses, foundation degrees and Bachelors degree courses; Prin. and Chief Exec. DEREK BRANTON.

EThames Graduate School: 197 Marsh Wall, Docklands, London, E14 9SG; tel. (20) 7531-7320; fax (20) 7987-0762; internet etgs.org.uk; centre in Essex; 7 depts: business, finance, computing, health and social care, hospitality and tourism, English, corporate training; Prin. SUSAN J HINDLEY.

Exeter College: Hele Rd Centre, Hele Rd, Exeter, EX4 4JS; tel. (8451) 116-000; fax (1392) 205-842; e-mail info@exe-coll.ac.uk; internet www.exe-coll.ac.uk; f. 1970; 5 centres; higher national diploma/certificate, foundation degree Bachelors degree, postgraduate certificate in education, English language courses; 12,250 students (4,250 full-time, 8,000 part-time); Prin. RICHARD ATKINS.

Furness College: Channelside, Barrow-in-Furness, LA14 2PJ; tel. (1229) 825-017; e-mail info@furness.ac.uk; internet www.furness.ac.uk; full-time, part-time courses at school leaving, univ. education level; partnership with Univ. of Central Lancashire, Univ. of Cumbria and Lancaster Univ.; 5,000 students; Prin. ANNE ATTWOOD.

Gateshead College: Baltic Campus, Quarryfield Rd, Baltic Business Quarter, Gateshead, NE8 3BE; tel. (1914) 902-246; internet www.gateshead.ac.uk; 4 campuses; partnership with Northumbria Univ., Univ. of Sunderland, Univ. of Teesside; provides foundation degrees and Bachelors degree courses; 700 teachers; 13,000 students; Prin. and CEO RICHARD THOROLD.

Grimsby Institute of Further and Higher Education: Nuns Corner, Grimsby, DN34 5BQ; tel. and fax (1472) 311-238; e-mail international@grimsby.ac.uk; internet www.grimsby.ac.uk; 3 campuses; English teaching, International Foundation in Business, further education, higher national certificates/diplomas, foundation degrees, undergraduate, postgraduate degree programmes; 1,350 staff; Prin. and Chief Exec. SUE MIDDLEHURST.

Guildford College: Stoke Rd, Guildford, GU1 1EZ; tel. (1483) 448-688; fax (1483) 448-689; e-mail international@guildford.ac.uk; internet www.guildford.ac.uk; f. 1939; 3 campuses; English teaching, international A-level, univ. access, undergraduate and other college courses; library: 50,000 books, magazines, videos and DVDs; 10,000 students; Prin. and CEO CLIVE COOKE.

Harlow College: Velizy Ave, Harlow, CM20 3LH; tel. (1279) 868000; e-mail reception@

harlow-college.ac.uk; internet www.harlow-college.ac.uk; Anglia Ruskin Univ.'s Centre and courses; Chair. PAUL TAYLOR; Prin. COLIN HINDMARCH.

Havering College of Further and Higher Education: International Devt Unit, Ardleigh Green Rd Campus, Ardleigh Green Rd, Hornchurch, RM11 2LL; tel. (1708) 462-793; fax (1708) 462-736; e-mail international@havering-college.ac.uk; internet www.havering-college.ac.uk; 2 main campuses, 5 learning centres; 35 higher education programmes from higher national certificates/diplomas to foundation degrees, undergraduate degrees and postgraduate programmes in vocational and academic subjects; Prin. and Chief Exec. NOEL OTLEY.

Hertford Regional College: Broxbourne Campus, Turnford, Broxbourne, SG12 9JF; tel. (1992) 411-400; e-mail info@hrc.ac.uk; internet www.hrc.ac.uk; 2 campuses; partnership with Hertfordshire Univ. and Univ. of Greenwich; apprenticeship, vocational courses, adult and community learning courses, foundation degrees and degree level courses; 3,900 students; Prin. ANDY FORBES.

Holborn College: Woolwich Rd, London, SE7 8LN; tel. (20) 7403-8080; fax (20) 8317-6001; e-mail international@kaplan.co.uk; internet www.holborncollege.ac.uk; f. 1969; undergraduate, postgraduate law and business degrees validated by Univ. of Wales, Univ. of London, Liverpool John Moores Univ.; library: 10,000 vols; Dean TIM HARRIS.

Holy Cross College: Manchester Rd, Bury, BL9 9BB; tel. (1617) 624-500; fax (1617) 624-501; e-mail information@holycross.ac.uk; internet www.holycross.ac.uk; univ. centre and sixth form college; partnership with Liverpool Hope, Edge Hill, Surrey and Leeds Metropolitan Univ.; library: 20,000 vols; Prin. DAVID FROST.

Hull College: Queen's Gardens, Chesters Bldg, Hull, HU1 3DG; tel. (1482) 381-921; fax (1482) 598-733; e-mail info@hull-college.ac.uk; internet www.hull-college.ac.uk; English language courses; more than 1,000 courses from foundation level to BA (Hons) degrees; Prin. and Chief Exec. Dr ELAINE MCMAHON.

K College: Brook St, Tonbridge, TN9 2PW; tel. (845) 207-8220; e-mail info@kcollege.ac.uk; internet www.kcollege.ac.uk; f. 2010, by merger of South Kent College and West Kent College; 5 campuses in Ashford, Dover, Folkestone, Tonbridge and Tunbridge Wells; 20,000 students; Prin. and Chief Exec. BILL FEARON; Deputy Prin. ALISON MONK.

Kaplan International Colleges: Shepherds Bldg, Charecroft Way, London, W14 0EE; tel. (20) 8727-3515; fax (20) 8727-3566; e-mail ukireland@kaplaninternational.com; internet www.kaplaninternational.com; f. 1938, present name and status 2009; schools in UK, Ireland, USA, Canada, Australia and New Zealand; English language courses and degree programmes.

Manchester College: International Office, Nicholls House, Hyde Rd, Ardwick, Manchester, M12 6BA; tel. (1614) 552-434; fax (1619) 532-955; e-mail international@themanchestercollege.ac.uk; internet www.themanchestercollege.ac.uk; f. 2008 by merger of Manchester College of Arts and Technology and City College Manchester; partnership with Univ. of Salford; full-time and part-time higher national diplomas/certificates, foundation degrees and Bachelors degree courses; Prin. PETER TAVERNOR.

Middlesbrough College: Dock St, Middlesbrough, TS2 1AD; tel. (1642) 333-700; e-mail courseinfo@mbro.ac.uk; internet www.mbro.ac.uk; f. 2002 by merger of Middlesbrough College and Teesside Tertiary College; courses leading to foundation degrees, higher national diploma/certificates, BA (Hons), BSc (Hons), univ. certificates, professional qualifications; degrees awarded by Teesside Univ.; library: 45,000 vols, 6,000 on-line newspapers, journals; Prin. MIKE HOPKINS.

Ming-Ai (London) Institute: 1 Cline Rd, London, N11 2LX; tel. (20) 8361-7161; fax (20) 8361-4207; e-mail enquiry@ming-ai.org.uk; internet www.ming-ai.org.uk; f. 1993, assen with Middlesex Univ. 1995; attached to Middlesex Univ.; promotes social, cultural, educational and economic exchanges among people of Hong Kong, China and Britain; courses in languages, catering and hospitality, business and ICT skills, arts and leisure; Dir Dr W. H. SHAK.

New College Durham: Framwellgate Moor Campus, Durham, DH1 5ES; tel. (1913) 754-000; fax (1913) 754-222; e-mail help@newdur.ac.uk; internet www.newcollegedurham.ac.uk; f. 1977 by merger of Neville's Cross College and Durham Technical College; higher national diplomas/certificates, foundation degrees, degrees and professional qualifications in part time and full time courses in variety of subjects; library: 65,000 vols, 300 periodicals; Prin. and Chief Exec. JOHN WIDDOWSON.

New College Nottingham: International Office, The Adams Bldg, Stoney St Lace Market, Nottingham, NG1 1NG; tel. (1159) 104-615; e-mail internat5@ncn.ac.uk; internet www.ncn.ac.uk; 7 centres; English language, vocational, higher national certificate, foundation degree and undergraduate courses; 22,000 students; Prin. and Chief Exec. GEOFF HALL.

Newbold College of Higher Education: St Marks Rd, Binfield, Bracknell, RG42 4AN; tel. (1344) 407-407; fax (1344) 407-406; e-mail info@newbold.ac.uk; internet www.newbold.ac.uk; higher education courses in management, arts, theology, accredited by Open Univ. Validation Services, Univ. of Wales Lampeter; 36 teachers (28 full-time, 8 part-time); 300 students; Prin. Dr SVEIN MYKLEBUST.

Newham College: East Ham Campus, High St South, London, E6 6ER; tel. (20) 8257-4446; e-mail international@newham.ac.uk; internet www.newham.ac.uk; f. 1985 by merger of East Ham and West Ham technical colleges; 2 main campuses; courses offered in business, management, combined studies, counselling, professional devt; assoc. college of London Metropolitan Univ.; 20,000 students; Prin. and Chief Exec. DENISE BROWN-SACKEY.

North Hertfordshire College: Stevenage Centre, Monkswood Way, Stevenage, SG1 1LA; tel. (1462) 424-242; e-mail enquiries@nhc.ac.uk; internet www.nhc.ac.uk; 5 main centres, foundation degrees, BA Hons degree in computer science, business admin. and science; assoc. college of Univ. of Hertfordshire; library: 20,000 books, 100 journals; 15,000 students; Prin. FINTAN DONOHUE.

North Lindsey College: Kingsway, Scunthorpe, DN17 1AJ; tel. (1724) 281-111; fax (1724) 294-020; e-mail info@northlindsey.ac.uk; internet www.northlindsey.ac.uk; assoc. college of Univ. of Lincoln; wide range of foundation degrees, Bachelors degrees in education and training, business studies, English and history and social science; programmes validated by Univ. of Hull, Univ. of Huddersfield; Prin. Prof. ROGER BENNETT.

North West Kent College: Dartford Campus, Oakfield Lane, Dartford, DA1 2JT; tel. (1322) 629-400; fax (1322) 629-468; e-mail course.enquiries@nwkcollege.ac.uk; internet www.nwkcollege.ac.uk; 2 campuses; partnership with Univ. of Greenwich; BA (Hons), foundation degrees, higher national diplomas and certificates in art, design photography and multimedia, business studies, media studies, performing and technical arts, professional care, travel and tourism and management studies, construction and building services, engineering, hotel and catering, motor vehicle, professional care, refrigeration; Prin. DAVID GLEED.

Prince's School of Traditional Arts: 19–22 Charlotte Rd, London, EC2A 3SG; tel. (20) 7613-8532; fax (20) 7613-8599; e-mail enquiry@psta.org.uk; internet www.psta.org.uk; f. 2004; research and postgraduate degrees validated by Univ. of Wales; courses in arts and philosophy; Chair. Sir DAVID GREEN; Dir Dr KHALED AZZAM.

Redbridge College: Barley Lane, Romford, RM6 4XT; tel. (20) 8548-7400; e-mail info@redbridge-college.ac.uk; internet www.redbridge-college.ac.uk; Chair. LEE ROGERS; Prin. and Chief Exec. THERESA DROWLEY.

South Cheshire College: Dane Bank Ave, Cheshire, Crewe, CW2 8AB; tel. (1270) 654654; fax (1270) 651515; e-mail info@s-cheshire.ac.uk; internet www.s-cheshire.ac.uk; Chair. KEN LEA; Prin. and Chief Exec. PETER SWIFT.

South Essex College: Luker Rd, Southend-on-Sea, SS1 1ND; tel. (1702) 220-571; fax (1702) 432-320; e-mail learning@southessex.ac.uk; internet www.southessex.ac.uk; f. 2010, by merger of Thurrock and Basildon College and South East Essex College; degrees validated by Univ. of Essex, Univ. of East London, or Anglia Ruskin Univ.; campuses in Basildon and Thurrock; Prin. and Chief Exec. JAN HODGES.

South Nottingham College: 1 Station St, Nottingham, Bingham, NG13 8AP; tel. (1949) 838901; e-mail enquiries@snc.ac.uk; internet www.snc.ac.uk; centres in West Bridgford, Clifton; 7 schools: business, IT, and humanities, foundation learning, health and lifestyle, lifelong learning, sport, leisure, travel and tourism, visual arts and digital media, automotive training; Chair. KEITH BEAUMONT; Prin. MALCOM COWGILL; Deputy Prin. for Corporate Services JOHN SNOW.

South Thames College: Wandsworth High St, London, SW18 2PP; tel. (20) 8918-7777; internet www.south-thames.ac.uk; f. 1895, as Wandsworth Technical Institute; attached to Kingston Univ.; degrees validated by Kingston Univ., London South Bank Univ., Christ Church Canterbury Univ; 21,000 students; Prin. SUE RIMMER.

South Tyneside College: St. George's Ave, South Shields, NE34 6ET; tel. (191) 427-3500; e-mail info@stc.ac.uk; internet www.stc.ac.uk; degrees validated by Univ. of Sunderland, Northumbrian Univ., Univ. of Huddersfield; 17,000 students; Prin. and chief Exec. LINDSEY WHITEROD.

Spurgeon's College: South Norwood Hill, London, SE25 6DJ; tel. (20) 8653-0850; fax (20) 8771-0959; e-mail enquiries@spurgeons.ac.uk; internet www.spurgeons.ac.uk; degrees validated by Univ. of Wales; library: 60,000 vols; Chair. ROBERT AMESS; Prin. Dr NIGEL WRIGHT.

St-Patrick's International College: 24 Great Chapel St, London, W1F 8FS; tel. (20) 7287-6664; fax (20) 7287-6282; e-mail registrar@st-patricks.ac.uk; internet www

.st-patricks.ac.uk; f. 1803, as St. Patrick's School; courses in accounting, business management, technology, healthcare management, hospitality management, and law; Prin. and Chief Exec. GIRISH CHANDRA.

St Helens College: Water St, St Helens, WA10 1PP; tel. (1744) 733766; fax (1744) 623913; internet www.sthelens.ac.uk; degree courses validated by Univ. of Central Lancashire, Edge Hill Univ., Liverpool John Moores Univ., Univ. of Salford, Sheffield Hallam Univ.; library: 60,000 vols, 200 periodicals; Prin. PAT BACON.

St John's College: Chilwell Lane, Nottingham, NG9 3DS; tel. (115) 925-1114; fax (115) 943-6438; e-mail enquiries@stjohns-nottm.ac.uk; internet www.stjohns-nottm.ac.uk; undergraduate and postgraduate courses in theology for ministry and theology validated by Univ. of Chester; Prin. Dr CHRISTINA BAXTER.

St Mary's College: Shear Brow, Blackburn, BB1 8DX; tel. (1254) 580464; fax (1254) 665991; e-mail reception@stmarysblackburn.ac.uk; internet www.stmarysblackburn.ac.uk; honours degree validated by Liverpool Hope Univ.; courses in English, education and society, sport and health studies, management of information and enterprise; 1,500 students; Dir of Devt S. FLANAGAN; Librarian ZANIB MALIK.

Stanmore College: Elm Park, London; Stanmore, HA7 4BQ; tel. (20) 8420-7780; fax (20) 8385-7269; internet www.stanmore.ac.uk; library: 20,000 vols; Prin. JACQUI MACE.

Stroud College: Stratford Rd, Stroud, GL5 4AH; tel. (1453) 763424; e-mail enquire@stroudcol.ac.uk; internet www.stroud.ac.uk; courses in art, design, media and music, construction and engineering, computing and information technology; library: 14,000 vols; Prin. BERI HARE; Deputy Prin. and Dir of Finance ANDREW CLARE; Vice-Prin. for Quality, Planning and Innovation PETER CLEGG.

Swindon College: North Star Ave, Swindon, SN2 1DY; tel. (1793) 491591; internet www.swindon-college.ac.uk; degrees validated by Oxford Brookes Univ. and Univ. of Bath; library: 32,000 vols; 9,500 students; Prin. ANDREW MILLER; Deputy Prin. for Finance and Resources NICK LETCHET; Vice-Prin. for Curriculum and Quality JOHN EVANS.

Trafford College: Talbot Rd, Manchester, Stretford, M32 0XH; tel. (161) 886-7000; fax (161) 872-7921; e-mail enquiries@trafford.ac.uk; internet www.trafford.ac.uk; centres in Cheshire; 4 centres in Manchester; 11,000 students; Chair. GRAHAM LUCCOCK; Prin. Sir BILL MOORCROFT.

Tresham College of Further and Higher Education: George St, Corby, NN17 1QA; tel. (845) 658-8990; fax (1536) 413357; e-mail info@tresham.ac.uk; internet www.tresham.ac.uk; f. 1978 by merger of 2 technical colleges in Kettering and Corby, present name and status 1992 by merger of Wellingborough College and Tresham College; degree courses validated by Univ. of Northampton and Univ. of Bedfordshire; courses in engineering, business and management, sport, computing, art and design, accounting; 10,000 students; Chair. E. R. BAINES; Prin. and Chief Exec. MARK SILVERMAN.

Tyne Metropolitan College: Battle Hill Dr., Wallsend, NE28 9NL; tel. (191) 229-5000; e-mail enquiries@tynemet.ac.uk; internet www.tynemet.ac.uk; has campus in North Shields; courses in art and design, computing, health and social care, business, floristry and horticulture, first aid, sport, retail, engineering and technology, catering and hospitality, pharmacy and laboratory services; Prin. and CEO JON VINCENT; Deputy Prin. for Finance and Corporate Devt ANN-MARIE CROZIER; Deputy Prin. for Curriculum and Business Devt AUDREY KINGHAM.

University Campus Suffolk: Neptune Quay, Ipswich, IP4 1QJ; tel. (1473) 338000; e-mail info@ucs.ac.uk; internet www.ucs.ac.uk; f. 2007; centres in Bury St Edmunds, Great Yarmouth, Lowestoft and Otley; degrees jtly validated by Univ. of East Anglia and Univ. of Essex; Provost and CEO Prof. MIKE SAKS; Head of Learning Resources STEVE PHILIPS.

University Centre Yeovil: 91 Preston Rd, Yeovil, BA20 2DN; tel. (1935) 845454; fax (1935) 415483; e-mail ucy@yeovil.ac.uk; internet www.ucy.ac.uk; courses validated by Bournemouth Univ., Univ. of the West of England and Exeter Univ.; courses in heritage and horticulture, engineering, forensic science, health and care, education, design and media, business and computing.

Uxbridge College: Park Rd, Uxbridge, UB8 1NQ; tel. (1895) 853333; fax (1895) 853377; e-mail enquiries@uxbridgecollege.ac.uk; internet www.uxbridge.ac.uk; f. 1965; courses validated by Thames Valley Univ. and Univ. of Greenwich; Prin. LARAINE SMITH.

Wakefield College: Margaret St, Wakefield, WF1 2DH; tel. (1924) 789789; fax (1924) 789340; e-mail info@wakefield.ac.uk; internet www.wakefield.ac.uk; f. 1868; foundation and bachelors degrees validated by univs; 13,000 full-time and part-time students; Prin. SUE GRIFFITHS; Deputy Prin. JOHN FOSTER; Deputy Prin. KAYE FISHER.

Wesley College, Bristol: Henbury Rd, Bristol, BS10 7QD; tel. (117) 959-1200; e-mail admin@wesley-college-bristol.ac.uk; internet www.wesley-college-bristol.ac.uk; f. 1945, present name and status 1967; BA (Hons) and MA programmes validated by Univ. of Bristol; foundation degree validated by St Mary's Univ. College; Prin. Rev. Dr JONATHAN PYE; Librarian MIKE BREALEY.

West Cheshire College: Eaton Rd, Chester, CH4 7ER; tel. (1244) 677677; e-mail info@west-cheshire.ac.uk; internet www.west-cheshire.ac.uk; has campus at Ellesmere Port and technology campus at Chester; Prin. SARA MOGEL.

West London College: 35 North Row, Mayfair, London, W1K 6DB; tel. (20) 7491-1841; fax (20) 7499-5853; internet www.w-l-c.co.uk; courses in business admin., finance and accounting, information technology, tourism management, fashion design; 1,000 students; Prin. PAUL SMITH; Deputy Prin. NEIL TETHER; Librarian NICOLE JOURDAN.

West Thames College: London Rd, Isleworth, TW7 4HS; tel. (20) 8326-2000; e-mail info@west-thames.ac.uk; internet www.west-thames.ac.uk; foundation Degrees accredited by Kingston Univ., TVU and St Mary's Univ. College; 6,500 students; Chair. J. ROBERTS; Prin. M. SEMPLE.

Wiltshire College: Cocklebury Rd, Chippenham, SN15 3QD; tel. (1249) 464644; fax (1249) 465326; e-mail info@wiltshire.ac.uk; internet www.wiltshire.ac.uk; f. 2000, merger with Salisbury College 2008; courses in computing, social work, applied arts, engineering, animal science and management, degrees validated; campuses in Corsham, Devizes, Lackham, Salisbury, Warminster, Trowbridge; 9,300 students incl. part-time and full-time; Prin. DIANE DALE.

AGRICULTURE

Askham Bryan College: Askham Bryan, York, YO23 3FR; tel. (1904) 772277; fax (1904) 772288; e-mail enquiries@askham-bryan.ac.uk; internet www.askham-bryan.ac.uk; f. 1948, as Yorkshire Institute of Agriculture; degrees validated by Harper Adams Univ. College, Univ. of Leeds and York St John Univ.; courses in agriculture; animal management; arboriculture, business; 4,000 students; Prin. and Chief Exec. LIZ PHILIP.

Brooksby Melton College: Melton Campus, Asfordby Rd, Melton Mowbray, LE13 0HJ; tel. (1664) 855444; internet www.brooksbymelton.ac.uk; 4 campuses; independent college specializing in animal care and agriculture, also leading performing arts college; associate college for Univ. of Lincoln, Leicester De Montfort Univ.; Prin. CHRIS BALL.

Hadlow College: Hadlow Campus, Hadlow, Tonbridge, TN11 0AL; fax (1732) 853-207; e-mail enquiries@hadlow.ac.uk; internet www.hadlow.ac.uk; f. 1969 by merging Sittingbourne Farm Institute and Swanley Horticultural Institute; 3 campuses; higher national diploma and degree courses in agriculture and sustainability, animal management, conservation and wildlife, equestrian studies and outdoor activities, fisheries management, horticulture, landscape and design; library: 18,000 specialist resources; Prin. and Chief Exec. PAUL HANNAN.

Moulton College: West St, Moulton, NN3 7RR; tel. (1604) 491-131; fax (1604) 491-127; e-mail enquiries@moulton.ac.uk; internet www.moulton.ac.uk; foundation degrees, diplomas, undergraduate, postgraduate courses in land based, construction and furniture disciplines; 400 part time courses in 15 disciplines; links with Univ. of Northampton; Prin. CHRIS MOODY.

Reaseheath College: Nantwich, CW5 6DF; tel. (1270) 625131; e-mail enquiries@reaseheath.ac.uk; internet www.reaseheath.ac.uk; f. 1921, as Cheshire School of Agriculture; attached to Harper Adams Univ. College and Univ. of Chester; Bachelors degrees in veterinary, ecology, agricultural engineering, equine science, food industry, landscape design and management; 500 teachers; 6,250 students; Prin. MEREDYDD DAVID.

Writtle College: Chelmsford, CM1 3RR; tel. (1245) 424200; fax (1245) 420456; e-mail info@writtle.ac.uk; internet www.writtle.ac.uk; f. 1893; specialist college providing undergraduate and postgraduate courses focused on business and green industries; degrees validated by Univ. of Essex; library: 40,000 vols, 300 periodical titles; 2,600 students; Prin. DAVID BUTCHER.

ART AND DESIGN

Christie's Education London: 153 Great Titchfield St, London, W1W 5BD; tel. (20) 7665-4350; fax (20) 7665-4351; e-mail education@christies.com; internet www.christieseducation.com; degrees validated by Univ. of Glasgow; courses in art, style and design of Europe, modern and contemporary art; centre in New York; 160 students; Academic Dir Dr M. A. MICHAEL.

City and Guilds of London Art School: 124 Kennington Park Rd, London, SE11 4DJ; tel. (20) 7735-2306; fax (20) 7582-5361; e-mail info@cityandguildsartschool.ac.uk; internet www.cityandguildsartschool.ac.uk; f. 1879; BA (Hons) degree courses in painting, sculpture, fine arts; diploma courses in wood-carving and gilding, stone carving;

library: 5,500 vols, 750 films and cinema titles, 1400 slides, 30 journal subscriptions; 60 part-time teachers; 200 students; Prin. TONY CARTER.

Cleveland College of Art and Design: Green Lane, Linthorpe, Middlesbrough, TS5 7RJ; tel. (1642) 288-000; fax (1642) 288-828; internet www.ccad.ac.uk; 2 campuses; specialist art and design education; partnership with Univ. of Teeside; library: 25,000 books, 100 magazines and journals, 1,600 DVDs and videocassettes; Prin. MARTIN RABY.

Courtauld Institute of Art: part of University of London (see entry).

Hereford College of Arts: Folly Lane, Hereford, HR1 1LT; tel. (1432) 273-359; fax (1432) 341-099; e-mail enquiries@hca.ac.uk; internet www.hca.ac.uk; f. 1851; specialist art, design and performing arts college, courses from entry level through to foundation and undergraduate degrees; library: 24,000 books, 80 specialist journals; 37 teachers; 850 students; Prin. RICHARD HEATLY.

Inchbald School of Design: 7 Eaton Gate, London, SW1W 9BA; tel. (20) 7730-5508; e-mail interiors@inchbald.co.uk; internet www.inchbald.co.uk; f. 1960; 2 campuses; independent school of design offering Masters degree, diploma and certificate courses in architectural interior design, interior decoration and garden design, short courses in computer aided design; Prin. JACQUELINE DUNCAN.

Leeds College of Art: Blenheim Walk, Leeds, LS2 9AQ; tel. (113) 202-8000; fax (113) 202-8001; e-mail info@leeds-art.ac.uk; internet www.leeds-art.ac.uk; f. 1842, as Leeds School of Art; graduate degrees validated by Open Univ.; courses in creative arts and design; library: 30,000 vols, 140 nat. and int. magazines; Chair. PETER YENDELL; Prin. SIMONE WONNACOTT.

Norwich School of Art and Design: Francis House, 3–7 Redwell St, Norwich, NR2 4SN; tel. (1603) 610-561; fax (1603) 615-728; e-mail info@nuca.ac.uk; internet www.nuca.ac.uk; f. 1846 became Norwich University College of the Arts in 2008; undergraduate, postgraduate and doctoral courses in arts, design and media disciplines; library: 30,000 vols, 80,000 photographs, 2,500 DVDs, 100 journals; 1,500 students; Prin. JOHN LAST.

Plymouth College of Art: Tavistock Pl., Plymouth, PL4 8AT; tel. (1752) 203434; fax (1752) 203444; e-mail enquiries@plymouthart.ac.uk; internet www.plymouthart.ac.uk; f. 1856, as Plymouth School of Art; graduate and postgraduate degrees validated by Open Univ.; courses in design and fine arts; library: 20,000 vols, 130 journals, magazines and newspapers; Prin. Prof. ANDREW BREWERTON.

Ravensbourne College of Design and Communication: Ravensbourne, 6 Penrose Way, London, SE10 0EW; tel. (20) 3040-3500; fax (20) 8325-8320; e-mail info@rave.ac.uk; internet www.rave.ac.uk; f. 1962; degree courses in broadcast engineering and communication and technology, fashion design, furniture design, graphic design, interaction design, interior design, moving image design, product design, professional broadcasting; BTEC HNDs in broadcast operations, engineering and production; BTEC HNCs in broadcast post production, and digital technology for the creative industries; BTEC NC in broadcast engineering; foundation course in art design and media; MA in Interactive Digital Media; 137 teachers incl. 200 part-time; 1,500 students; Dir Prof. ROBIN BAKER.

Royal Academy Schools: Burlington House, Piccadilly, London, W1J 0BD; tel. (20) 7300-8000; fax (20) 7300-5856; internet www.royalacademy.org.uk; f. 1768; offers three-year, full-time postgraduate fine arts course; Pres. Sir NICHOLAS GRIMSHAW.

Royal College of Art: Kensington Gore, London, SW7 2EU; tel. (20) 7590-4444; fax (20) 7590-4500; e-mail admissions@rca.ac.uk; internet www.rca.ac.uk; f. 1837, awarded Charter 1967 empowering it to grant its own degrees; postgraduate instn receiving direct grant from HEFCE; library: 70,000 vols, 200 periodicals; 800 students; Visitor HRH The DUKE OF EDINBURGH; Provost Sir TERENCE CONRAN; Rector and Vice-Provost Prof. Sir CHRISTOPHER FRAYLING; Registrar ALAN SELBY.

School of Architecture, Architectural Association: 34–36 Bedford Square, London, WC1B 3ES; tel. (20) 7887-4000; fax (20) 7414-0782; e-mail info@aaschool.ac.uk; internet www.aaschool.ac.uk; f. 1847; 1-year foundation course; 5-year course leading to AA Dipl.; postgraduate courses and research in architecture, building conservation, conservation (landscape and gardens), emergent technologies and design, environment and energy, histories and theories of architecture, housing and urbanism, landscape urbanism; campus at Hooke Park; library: 46,000 vols, 2,000 architectural drawings, paintings, 150,000 slides; 120 teachers; 580 students; Dir BRETT STEELE; publ. *AA Files* (2 a year).

School of Design London: 1–15 Bradley Close, White Lion St, London, N1 9PN; tel. (20) 7713-1991; fax (20) 7713-1997; e-mail design.london@northumbria.ac.uk; internet www.northumbria.ac.uk/sd/academic/scd/london; attached to Northumbria Univ.; MA in fashion management and entrepreneurship; MA in design innovation management and entrepreneurship; MA in design craftsmanship and entrepreneurship; Dean STEVEN KYFFIN.

Slade School of Fine Art: University College London, Gower St, London, WC1E 6BT; tel. (20) 7679-2313; fax (20) 7679-7801; e-mail slade.enquiries@ucl.ac.uk; internet www.ucl.ac.uk/slade; f. 1871; attached to University College London; BA (Hons) degree course in Fine Art (painting, sculpture or fine art media); MA in Fine Art; MFA in Fine Art; MPhil/PhD in Fine Art; short, non-degree courses in drawing and painting; 38 teachers; 260 students; Dir and Slade Prof. Prof. JOHN AIKEN.

Somerset College: Wellington Rd, Somerset, TA1 5AX; tel. (1823) 366331; fax (1823) 366418; e-mail enquiries@somerset.ac.uk; internet www.somerset.ac.uk; f. 1856, as School of Art and Science; attached to Univ. of Plymouth; undergraduate courses in design, fine art and business admin.; Prin. and Chief Exec. RACHEL DAVIES.

Sotheby's Institute of Art: 30 Bedford Sq., London, WC1B 3EE; tel. (20) 7462-3232; fax (20) 7580-8160; e-mail info@sothebysinstitute.com; internet www.sothebysinstitute.com; campuses in New York and Singapore; postgraduate courses in art business, contemporary art, photography, fine and decorative art, east Asian art and contemporary design; library: 15,000 vols; Dir JOS HACKFORTH-JONES; Academic Dir MEGAN ALDRICH.

BUSINESS AND COMMERCE

Ashridge Business School: Berkhamsted, HP4 1NS; tel. (1442) 843-491; fax (1442) 841-209; e-mail contact@ashridge.org.uk; internet www.ashridge.org.uk; f. 1959; MBA, MSc, doctorate, diploma and executive devt programmes; 90 full-time teachers; 6,000 students; library: 8,000 vols, spec. colln incl. Ashridge learning guides; CEO KAI PETERS; publs *360°, the Ashridge Journal* (2 a year), *Converse* (1 a year), *Network, the Ashridge Magazine*.

Chartered Management Institute: 2 Savoy Court, Strand, London, WC2R 0EZ; tel. (20) 7497-0580; fax (20)74 97-0463; e-mail enquiries@managers.org.uk; internet www.managers.org.uk; awards Chartered Manager qualification; Chief Exec. RUTH SPELLMAN; publ. *Professional Manager*.

City Banking College: 7–13 Melior St, London, SE1 3QP; tel. (20) 7403-3770; fax (20) 7403-8355; e-mail admin@citybankingcollege.co.uk; internet www.citybankingcollege.co.uk; course provider in banking, finance and management; undergraduate and postgraduate courses in association with Roehampton University; 9 teachers; Prin. MOHAMED KHAN.

College of Estate Management: Whiteknights, Reading, RG6 6AW; tel. (1189) 214-696; fax (1189) 214-620; e-mail courses@cem.ac.uk; internet www.cem.ac.uk; f. 1919, Royal Charter 1922; undergraduate and professional distance learning courses in real estate; 270 teachers (245 external, 25 internal); 4,000 students.

European Business School London: Regent's College, Inner Circle, Regent's Park, London, NW1 4NS; tel. (20) 7487-7505; fax (20) 7487-7425; e-mail ebsl@regents.ac.uk; internet www.ebslondon.ac.uk; f. 1979 in UK, centres also in Germany, France, Italy, Japan, Russia, Spain and USA; BA (Hons) degree in European Business Administration, and other degrees with business and language mix; summer courses; library: 25,500 vols; 750 full-time students; Dir Prof. MICHAEL SCRIVEN.

European College of Business and Management: 69–71 Great Eastern St, London, EC2A 3HU; tel. (20) 7749-5930; fax (20) 7729-6264; e-mail info@eurocollege.org.uk; internet www.eurocollege.org.uk; f. 1988 as British–German School for Vocational Training, present name 2000; Bachelors and Masters courses in business and management; centre in Germany; Dir RICHARD BILLS; Treas. PHIL SAMPSON.

European School of Economics: 8–9 Grosvenor Pl., London, SW1X 7SH; tel. (20) 7245-6148; fax (20) 7245-6164; e-mail info@eselondon.ac.uk; internet www.eselondon.ac.uk; private college of higher education in international business; Bachelors, Masters, MBA, and certificate programmes; validated by Univ. of Buckingham; Pres. ELIO D'ANNA.

Henley Business School: Greenlands, Henley-on-Thames, RG9 3AU; tel. (1491) 571-454; fax (1491) 571-635; e-mail helpdesk@henley.com; internet www.henley.reading.ac.uk; f. 1945 as the Administrative Staff College; attached to Univ. of Reading; undergraduate and postgraduate degrees in accountancy, business, management, finance, real estate, planning, informatics, and coaching; campus at Whiteknights, Reading; 113 teachers (53 full-time, 60 associate); 7,000 students; library: 18,000 vols; Dean Prof. JOHN BOARD; publ. *Journal of General Management*.

Kensington College of Business: Wesley House, 4 Wild Court, London, WC2B 4AU; tel. (20) 7404-6330; fax (20) 7404-6330; e-mail kcb@kensingtoncoll.ac.uk; internet www.kensingtoncoll.ac.uk; f. 1982; courses at undergraduate and postgraduate levels; Prin. IAN PIRIE.

London College of Accountancy: 19 Charter House St, London, EC1N 6RA; tel. (20) 7400-6789; fax (20) 7400-6799; internet www.londoncollege.org; accountancy and management courses; undergraduate and postgraduate programmes from Anglia Ruskin Univ.; 5,000 students; Man. Dir RAVI GILL.

London College of Business: 129 Oxford St, London, W1D 2UH; tel. (20) 7287-3040; fax (20) 7284-1166; e-mail info@lcbuk.org; internet www.lcbuk.org; centre in Birmingham and Essex; courses in sectors of business and information technology validated by Univ. of Wales; Pres. ZENON ADAMEK.

London College of Management and IT (LCMIT): Winchester House Campus, 80 Backchurch Lane, London, E1 1LX; tel. (20) 7553-0434; fax (20) 7553-0435; e-mail info@lcmit.com; internet lcmit.com; undergraduate, postgraduate, professional courses in accounting, management, computing and English language; library: 2,500 vols; Prin. DAVID NIXON.

London School of Accountancy and Management: 12–20 Camomile St, London, EC3A 7PT; tel. (20) 7623-8777; fax (20) 7623-8778; e-mail training@londonsam.ac; internet www.londonsam.org.uk; degrees validated by Staffordshire Univ. and Univ. of Wales; centres in Asia; Prin. Dr DAK PATEL.

London School of Commerce: Chaucer House, White Hart Yard, London, SE1 1NX; tel. (20) 7357-0077; fax (20) 7403-1163; e-mail info@lsclondon.co.uk; internet www.lsclondon.co.uk; degree, postgraduate and MBA courses in finance, management and business; associate college of Univ. of Wales Institute, Cardiff.

Manchester Business School: Booth St West, Manchester, M15 6PB; tel. (161) 275-6333; internet www.mbs.ac.uk; f. 2004, by merger of Institute of Innovation Research (IoIR), Victoria Univ. of Manchester's School of Accounting and Finance, UMIST's Manchester School of Management and Manchester Business School; courses in accounting and finance, business systems, marketing, int. business and strategy and management; 200 teachers; 2,000 students; Dir Prof. MICHAEL LUGER.

Oxford Business College: 65 George St, Oxford, OX1 2BQ; tel. (1865) 791908; fax (1865) 245059; e-mail enquiries@oxfordbusinesscollege.co.uk; internet www.oxfordbusinesscollege.net; courses in business management and accounting and travel and tourism; Vice-Prin. PRISCILLA CLARK-CHRISTOPHER.

Oxford House College: 30 Oxford St, London, W1D 1AU; tel. (20) 7436-4872; fax (20) 7323-4582; internet www.oxfordhousecollege.co.uk; f. 1974; degrees validated by Univ. of Sunderland; courses in business admin, int. tourism and hospitality management; Prin. TIM MATTHEW.

Rayat London College: 32–42 New Heston Rd, Heston, TW5 0LJ; tel. (20) 8754-3330; fax (20) 8754-3331; e-mail info@rayatlondoncollege.co.uk; internet www.rayatlondoncollege.co.uk; f. 2004; centre in New Delhi, India; validated by Univ. of Wales; courses in business, professional accounting, admin. management; Chair. NIRMAL SINGH RAYAT; Prin. Prof. C. MICHAEL WILKINSON.

Regent's Business School London: Inner Circle, Regent's Park, London, NW1 4NS; tel. (20) 7487-7505; fax (20) 7487-7425; e-mail rbsl@regents.ac.uk; internet www.rbslondon.ac.uk; f. 1997; foundation courses, undergraduate and postgraduate degrees in business, finance and management; 60 teachers; 430 students; Academic Dir Dr RICHARD GREGSON.

Resource Development International: 1A Brandon Lane, Coventry, CV3 3RD; tel. (24) 7651-5700; fax (24) 7651-5701; e-mail info@rdi.co.uk; internet www.rdi.co.uk; f. 1990; distance learning, undergraduate, postgraduate and vocational course; provides on campus degrees through Institute of Business and Management; 3,000 students; CEO Dr PHILIP HALLAM.

School of Technology and Management: Hannibal House, London, SE1 6TE; tel. (20) 7378-9061; fax (20) 7403-1163; e-mail info@stmlondon.co.uk; internet www.stmlondon.co.uk; attached to Univ. of East London; postgraduate courses in business and information technology.

TASMAC London School of Business: 1–3 Valley Dr., Kingsbury, NW9 9NG; tel. (20) 8206-0066; fax (20) 8206-1999; e-mail info@tasmac.org.uk; internet www.tasmac.org.uk; has campuses at Wembley, London and Pune, India; undergraduate and postgraduate business degree programmes accredited by Univ. of Wales and open and distance learning BA and MBA programmes from IGNOU; Head Prof. MARSHALL G. HALL.

Williams College: 5 Holborn Circus, Holborn, London, EC1N 2HB; tel. (20) 7583-9222; fax (20) 7583-9095; internet www.williamscollege.co.uk; f. 2002; MBA and BA or BSc degrees in various business related subjects incl. accounting, banking, finance, int. business, management, management information systems and marketing; Prin. Dr JOHN POMEROY.

MEDICINE, THERAPY, COUNSELLING AND HEALTHCARE

Anglo-European College of Chiropractic: 13–15 Parkwood Rd, Bournemouth, BH5 2DF; tel. (1202) 436200; fax (1202) 436312; e-mail admissions@aecc.ac.uk; internet www.aecc.ac.uk; f. 1965; chiropractic education and research at undergraduate and postgraduate level; assoc. college of Bournemouth Univ.; library: 10,000 vols, 100 current periodicals; Prin. Dr KENNETH VALL.

College of Integrated Chinese Medicine: 19–21 Castle St, Reading, RG1 7SB; tel. (1189) 508-880; fax (1189) 508-890; e-mail admin@cicm.org.uk; internet www.acupuncturecollege.org.uk; f. 1993; BSc (Hons) Acupuncture, MSc Chinese Medicine, Licentiate in Acupuncture validated by Kingston Univ.; 40 teachers; Dean PETER MOLE.

College of Medical and Dental Sciences: Edgbaston, Birmingham, B15 2TT; tel. (121) 414-3858; e-mail mdsenquiries@contacts.bham.ac.uk; internet www.medicine.bham.ac.uk; f. 2008; attached to Univ. of Birmingham; courses in medicine, medical sciences, dentistry, nursing and physiotherapy; 1,000 teachers; 750 students; Head Prof. LAWRENCE YOUNG.

College of Osteopaths: 13 Furzehill Rd, Borehamwood, WD6 2DG; tel. (20) 8905-1937; fax (20) 8953-6140; e-mail admin@collegeofosteopaths.ac.uk; internet www.collegeofosteopaths.ac.uk; f. 1948; foundation to masters courses in osteopathy; in collaboration with Keele Univ. and Middlesex Univ.; Prin. PAT HAMILTON.

European School of Osteopathy: Boxley House, The Street, Boxley, Maidstone, ME14 3DZ; tel. (1622) 671-558; fax (1622) 662-165; e-mail info@eso.ac.uk; internet www.eso.ac.uk; f. 1965; undergraduate and postgraduate courses; validated by Univ. of Greenwich; Prin. ADRIAN BARNES.

Hull York Medical School: John Hughlings Jackson Bldg, University of York, Heslington York, YO10 5DD; Hertford Bldg, Univ. of Hull, Hull HU6 7RX; tel. (1482) 463-074; fax (1482) 464-705; internet www.hyms.ac.uk/home.aspx; f. 2003; partnership between Univ. of Hull and Univ. of York; medical school with undergraduate, postgraduate courses; library: 2m. books, 20,000 journal titles; Dean Prof. TONY KENDRICK.

International College of Oriental Medicine: Green Hedges House, Green Hedges Ave, East Grinstead, RH19 1DZ; tel. (1342) 313-106; fax (1342) 335-104; e-mail info@orientalmed.ac.uk; internet www.orientalmed.ac.uk; f. 1972; accredited by the British Acupuncture Accreditation Board; BSc (Hons) Acupuncture validated by Univ. of Greenwich; 17 teachers; Joint Prin. PENNY KHARROUBI; Joint Prin. CRAIG MINTO.

Matrix College of Counselling and Psychotherapy: 18–20 Queen's Rd, Hethersett, NR9 3DB; tel. (1603) 812479; e-mail sue@matrix-training.org; internet www.matrix-training.org; f. 2001 as Matrix Integrative Training; programmes in integrative counselling validated by Middlesex Univ.; Dir Dr SUSIE JONES.

McTimoney College of Chiropractic: Kimber House, 1 Kimber Rd, Abingdon, OX14 1BZ; tel. (1235) 523-336; fax (1235) 523-576; e-mail courseoffice@mctimoney-college.ac.uk; internet www.mctimoney-college.ac.uk; f. 1972 as Oxfordshire School of Chiropractic; undergraduate, postgraduate courses in chiropractic; validated by Univ. of Wales; Prin. CHRISTINA CUNLIFFE.

Metanoia Institute: 13 North Common Rd, Ealing, London, W5 2QB; tel. (20) 8579-2505; fax (20) 8832-3070; e-mail info@metanoia.ac.uk; internet www.metanoia.ac.uk; professional training of counsellors, psychotherapists, counselling psychologists, coaching, organisational devt; courses validated by Middlesex Univ.; CEO SHEILA OWEN-JONES.

National Institute of Conductive Education: Cannon Hill House, 14 Russell Rd, Moseley, Birmingham, B13 8RD; tel. (1214) 491-569; e-mail mmccann@conductive-education.org.uk; internet www.conductive-education.org.uk; f. 1986; degree-level conductor training for handling children and adults with cerebral palsy; BA (Hons) Conductive Education from Univ. of Wolverhampton.

National Institute of Medical Herbalists: 54 Mary Arches St, Exeter, EX4 3BA; tel. (1392) 426022; fax (1392) 498963; e-mail info@nimh.org.uk; internet www.nimh.org.uk; f. 1864, as Nat. Asscn of Medical Herbalists; sets profession's educational standards and runs accreditation system for training establishments, maintains mandatory programmes of professional devt; publ. *European Journal of Herbal Medicine*.

School of Psychotherapy and Counselling Psychology: Regent's Park, London, NW1 4NS; tel. (20) 7487-7505; fax (20) 7487-7446; e-mail spc@regents.ac.uk; internet www.spc.ac.uk; f. 1990; attached to Regent's College; validation by Univ. of Wales; Head Dr JOHN NUTTALL (acting).

Sherwood Psychotherapy Training Institute: Thiskney House, 2 St James Terrace, Nottingham, NG1 6FW; tel. (115) 844-7904; fax (115) 924-2738; e-mail enquiries@spti.net; internet www.spti.net; f. 1987; full time and part time courses in psychotherapy and counselling; 200 students; Dir ROSEMARY LANGFORD-BELLABY.

MUSIC, DANCE AND DRAMA

Academy of Contemporary Music: Rodboro Bldgs, Bridge St, Guildford, GU1 4SB; tel. (1483) 500800; e-mail enquiries@acm.ac.uk; internet www.acm.ac.uk; music industry education; degree courses in music; other courses in music production; Founding Dir PHIL BROOKES.

Academy of Live and Recorded Arts: John Archer Way, London, SW18 3SX; tel. (20) 8870-6475; fax (20) 8875-0789; e-mail info@alra.co.uk; internet www.alra.co.uk; f. 1979; courses accredited by Nat. Council for Drama Training; centre in Wigan; course in acting, stage management; Chair. HARRY COWD; Co-Dir CLIVE DUNCAN; Co-Dir ADRIAN HALL.

Arts Educational Schools London: Cone Ripman House, 14 Bath Rd, Chiswick, London, W4 1LY; tel. (20) 8987-6666; fax (20) 8987-6699; internet www.artsed.co.uk; f. 1939 as the Cone Ripman School; undergraduate, postgraduate courses in acting, theatre and screenwriting; Prin. JANE HARRISON.

Bird College—Dance, Music and Theatre Performance: The Centre, 27 Station Rd, Sidcup, DA15 7EB; tel. (20) 8300-6004; fax (20) 8308-1370; e-mail luis.deabreu@birdcollege.co.uk; internet www.birdcollege.co.uk; f. 1946; performing arts college; offers degrees, foundation courses and diplomas validated by Univ. of Greenwich, Trinity College London; Prin. and Chief Exec. SHIRLEY COEN.

Birmingham School of Acting: International Office, Birmingham City Univ., Perry Barr, Birmingham, B42 2SU; tel. (1213) 316714; e-mail bcuinternational@enquiries.uk.com; internet www.bcu.ac.uk/pme/school-of-acting; f. 1936; attached to Faculty of Performance, Media and English at Birmingham City Univ.; specialist institution offering full-time higher education courses at undergraduate and postgraduate level; owned and operated by the Birmingham School of Speech and Drama Training Trust; 30 teachers; Dir STEPHEN SIMMS.

Brighton Institute of Modern Music: BIMM West, 38–42 Brunswick St, Hove, BN3 1EL; tel. (1273) 626666; e-mail info@bimm.co.uk; internet www.bimm.co.uk; 4 centres in Brighton and Bristol, 10 core courses in various areas; degree, diploma and certificate; validated by Univ. of Sussex; Prin. VASEEMA HAMILTON.

Bristol Old Vic Theatre School: 1–2 Downside Rd, Bristol, BS8 2XF; tel. (1179) 733-535; fax (1179) 809-258; e-mail enquiries@oldvic.ac.uk; internet www.oldvic.ac.uk; f. 1946; undergraduate and postgraduate courses in acting, stage management, theatre design, wardrobe and technical aspects of the theatre; Prin. PAUL RUMMER.

Central School of Speech and Drama: Embassy Theatre, 64 Eton Ave, London, NW3 3HY; tel. (20) 7722-8183; fax (20) 7722-4132; e-mail enquiries@csdd.ac.uk; internet www.cssd.ac.uk; f. 1906; attached to Univ. of London; undergraduate, postgraduate, PhD and research courses in art, design and the performing arts, in education and in therapy; 90 staff; 750 students; Prin. GARY HENDERSON.

Guildford School of Acting: Stag Hill Campus, Guildford, GU2 7XH; tel. (1483) 560-701; fax (1483) 684-070; e-mail gsaenquiries@gsa.surrey.ac.uk; internet www.conservatoire.org; f. 1964; subsidiary company of Univ. of Surrey; vocational training in acting, musical theatre, stage management; courses ranging from national diplomas and foundation degrees to postgraduate qualifications; 29 teachers; Dir. PETER BARLOW.

Guildhall School of Music and Drama: Silk St, Barbican, London, EC2Y 8DT; tel. (20) 7628-2571; fax (20) 7256-9438; e-mail info@gsmd.ac.uk; internet www.gsmd.ac.uk; f. 1880 by the Corpn of London; offers teaching in music, acting, technical theatre, professional devt and music therapy; 300 teachers; 800 students; Prin. BARRY IFE.

Italia Conti Academy of Theatre Arts: Italia Conti House, 23 Goswell Rd, London, EC1M 7AJ; tel. (20) 7608-0047; fax (20) 7253-1430; e-mail admin@italiaconti.com; internet www.italiaconti.com; f. 1911; offer full-time courses in theatre arts at secondary, further and higher education levels; Prin. A. M. SHEWARD.

Leeds College of Music: 3 Quarry Hill, Leeds, LS2 7PD; tel. (1132) 223-416; fax (1132) 438-798; e-mail enquiries@lcm.ac.uk; internet www.lcm.ac.uk; f. 1965 as Leeds Music Centre; offers higher and further education courses in jazz, classical and popular music, music production; 2,500 students (1,000 full-time, 1,500 part-time); Prin. PHILIP MEADEN.

Liverpool Institute for the Performing Arts: Mount St, Liverpool, L1 9HF; tel. (151) 330-3000; fax (151) 330-3131; e-mail reception@lipa.ac.uk; internet www.lipa.ac.uk; f. 1996; performing arts higher education instn; degrees administered by Liverpool John Moores Univ.; 80 teachers; 650 students; Chief Exec. and Prin. MARK FEATHERSTONE-WITTY.

London Academy of Music and Dramatic Art: 155 Talgarth Rd, London, W14 9DA; tel. (20) 8834-0500; fax (20) 8834-0501; e-mail enquiries@lamda.org.uk; internet www.lamda.org.uk; f. 1861; professional theatrical training, acting and stage management; Prin. JOANNA READ.

London Contemporary Dance School: The Place, 17 Duke's Rd, London, WC1H 9PY; tel. (20) 7121-1020; fax (20) 7121-1144; e-mail info@theplace.org.uk; internet www.theplace.org.uk/lcds; f. 1966; dance conservatoire; BA (Hons), postgraduate diploma, MA in contemporary dance; undergraduate course validated by Univ. of Kent; 27 teachers; Dir. VERONICA LEWIS.

London Studio Centre: 42–50 York Way, London, N1 9AB; tel. (20) 7837-7741; fax (20) 7837-3248; internet www.london-studio-centre.co.uk; f. 1978; Bachelors courses in classical ballet, contemporary dance, jazz theatre dance, music theatre validated by Univ. of the Arts London; Dir NIC ESPINOSA; Librarian FIONA COMPTON.

Mountview Academy of Theatre Arts: Ralph Richardson Memorial Studios, Clarendon Rd, Wood Green, London, N22; tel. (20) 8881-2201; fax (20) 8829-0034; e-mail enquiries@mountview.org.uk; internet www.mountview.org.uk; undergraduate, postgraduate diploma, degree courses in acting, musical theatre and production arts; national qualifications in professional acting, musical theatre, and production skills validated by Trinity College London.

Northern School of Contemporary Dance: 98 Chapeltown Rd, Leeds, LS7 4BH; tel. (113) 219-3000; fax (113) 219-3030; e-mail info@nscd.ac.uk; internet www.nscd.ac.uk; f. 1985; training programme and bachelor in performing arts: contemporary dance and choreography; Prin. GURMIT HUKAM; Vice-Prin. RUSSELL TRIGG (acting); Vice-Prin. DEBORA JOHNSON (acting).

Rose Bruford College of Theatre and Performance: Lamorbey Park, Burnt Oak Lane, Sidcup, DA15 9DF; tel. (20) 8308-2600; e-mail enquiries@bruford.ac.uk; internet www.bruford.ac.uk; f. 1951, as Rose Bruford Training College for Speech and Drama; MPhil and PhD research degrees validated by Univ. of London; honours degree in professional acting and theatre practice validated by Univ. of Manchester; Prin. and CEO Prof. MICHAEL EARLEY.

Royal Academy of Dance: 36 Battersea Sq., London, SW11 3RA; tel. (20) 7326-8000; e-mail info@rad.org.uk; internet www.rad.org.uk; f. 1920; undergraduate and postgraduate courses in dance validated by Univ. of Surrey; centres in Wales and Scotland; Chief Exec. LUKE RITTNER; publs *Dance Gazette*, *UK & Ireland diary* (3 a year).

Royal Academy of Dramatic Art (RADA): 62–64 Gower St, London, WC1E 6ED; tel. (20) 7636-7076; fax (20) 7323-3865; e-mail enquiries@rada.ac.uk; internet www.rada.ac.uk; f. 1904; vocational training for actors, stage managers, directors, designers and technical stage craft specialists; library: 30,000 vols, 1,000 videocassettes, 500 DVDs; Dir. EDWARD KEMP.

Royal Academy of Music: see University of London.

Royal College of Music: Prince Consort Rd, South Kensington, London, SW7 2BS; tel. (20) 7589-3643; fax (20) 7589-7740; e-mail info@rcm.ac.uk; internet www.rcm.ac.uk; f. 1882; BMus (Hons) degree, BSc in Physics with musical performance; Masters and Doctorate in music; 610 students; library: see under Libraries and Archives; Dir Prof. COLIN LAWSON.

Royal Northern College of Music: 124 Oxford Rd, Manchester, M13 9RD; tel. (161) 907-5200; fax (161) 273-7611; e-mail info@rncm.ac.uk; internet www.rncm.ac.uk; f. 1973; four-year BMus Hons in association with Univ. of Manchester; two-year foundation degree in popular music practice course; the Graduate School in Music; library: library contains extensive collection of MSS, reference works, gramophone records, tape cassettes, CDs, video cassettes, periodicals, and important archive material incl. an historical instrument collection; 150 teachers; 600 students; Prin. Prof. JONTY STOCKDALE.

Trinity Laban Conservatoire of Music and Dance: Trinity, King Charles Court, Old Royal Naval College, Greenwich, London, SE10 9JF; tel. (20) 8305-4444; fax (20) 8305-9444; e-mail info@tcm.ac.uk; internet www.trinitylaban.ac.uk; f. 2005 by merger of Trinity College of Music and Laban; undergraduate, postgraduate and one-year course programmes; 323 teachers; 570 students (500 full-time, 70 part-time); Prin. ANTHONY BOWNE; publ. *Dance Theatre Journal* (4 a year).

SCIENCE AND TECHNOLOGY

British Institute of Technology and E-Commerce: Avicenna House, 258–262 Romford Rd, London, E7 9HZ; tel. (20) 8552-3071; fax (20) 8552-3546; e-mail admissions@bite.ac.uk; internet bite.ac.uk; f. 2000; MBA, MA, MSc qualifications, LLM, BSc (Technology), BA (e-commerce), professional qualification, NVQs; degrees conferred by Univ. of East London, Coventry Univ. and Univ. of Wales; Prin. and Chief Exec. Dr MUHAMMAD FARMER; publ. *e-Britain*.

Camborne School of Mines: Cornwall Campus, Penryn, TR10 9EZ; tel. (1326) 371-800; fax (1326) 370-450; e-mail cornwall@exeter.ac.uk; internet www.ex.ac.uk/csm; f. 1888; attached to College of Engineering, Mathematics and Physical Sciences, Univ. of Exeter; undergraduate, postgraduate and research degree programmes in geology, mining, minerals processing and renewable energy; library: 30,000 vols; 25 teachers; 300 students; Head Prof. FRANCES WALL.

CECOS London College: 59 Compton Rd, Islington, London, N1 2YT; tel. (20) 7359-3316; fax (20) 7288-1599; e-mail info@cecos.co.uk; internet www.cecos.co.uk; f. 1998; courses in information technology, business admin., computer sciences; Dir Dr KEITH SHARP.

College of Technology London: 153–159 Bow Rd, London, E3 2SE; tel. (20) 8980-7888; fax (20) 8983-4911; e-mail info@ctlondon.ac.uk; internet www.ctlondon.ac.uk; 3 academic depts: business, information technology and academic English; library: 5,000 vols.

Farnborough College of Technology: Farnborough Campus, Boundary Rd, Farnborough, GU14 6SB; tel. (1252) 407-028; fax (1252) 407-041; e-mail admissions@farn-ct.ac.uk; internet www.farn-ct.ac.uk; f. 1957; 2 campuses, degrees by Univ. of Surrey; full-time, part-time and short courses in health, education, construction, education, engineering, business and media; Prin. CHRISTINE SLAYMAKER.

Herefordshire College of Technology: Hereford Campus, Folly Lane, Hereford, HR1 1LS; tel. (1432) 352-235; fax (1432) 353-449; e-mail enquiries@hct.ac.uk; internet www.hct.ac.uk; f. 1949; 2 campuses; 90 full-time vocational courses, courses available from foundation studies to Bachelors degree level; apprenticeships; library: 20,000 vols; 600 teachers; 7,000 students; Prin. and Chief Exec. IAN PEAKE.

National Computing Centre Education: Wilmslow Rd, Manchester, M20 2EZ; tel. (161) 438-6200; fax (161) 438-6240; e-mail customer.service@nccedu.com; internet www.nccedu.com; f. 1966; courses in business studies, business admin., computing and information systems; degrees validated by Univ. of Wales, Univ. of Greenwich and Univ. of Hertfordshire; centres in Asia (incl. Hong Kong), Africa, Middle East; Man. Dir Prof. FELIX STRAVENS.

National Film and Television School: Beaconsfield Studios, Station Rd, Beaconsfield, HP9 1LG; tel. (1494) 731-425; fax (1494) 674-042; e-mail info@nfts.co.uk; internet www.nftsfilm-tv.ac.uk; f. 1970 as National Film School; postgraduate and professional training for film and television production; 30 teachers; other visiting lecturers and tutors; 220 full-time students; 1,024 part-time; library: research and information library; Dir NIK POWELL.

Regents Theological College: West Malvern Rd, West Malvern, WR14 4AY; tel. (845) 302-6750; fax (845) 302-6752; e-mail info@regents-tc.ac.uk; internet www.regentstheologicalcollege.org.uk; graduate and postgraduate degrees validated by Univ. of Wales and Univ. of Bangor; library: 36,000 vols; Gen. Man. ANDREW CAVE; Academic Registrar JOHN OWEN.

SAE London: 1412 High Rd, London, N20 9BH; tel. (20) 7923-9159; fax (20) 7691-7653; e-mail london@sae.edu; internet london.sae.edu; f. 1985; degrees validated by Middlesex Univ.; courses in audio production, digital film making, media practice; campuses in Oxford, Liverpool, Glasgow; Man. LUCA BARASSI.

Telford College of Arts and Technology: Haybridge Rd, Wellington, TF1 2NP; tel. (1952) 642-200; fax (1952) 642-293; internet www.tcat.ac.uk; 800 teachers; 17,000 students; Chair. MIKE LOWE; Prin. JANET ELLIS.

THEOLOGY AND RELIGIOUS STUDIES

All Nations Christian College: Easneye, Ware, SG12 8LX; tel. (1920) 443500; fax (1920) 462997; internet www.allnations.ac.uk; f. 1971 by merger of three missionary colleges; certificate, diploma and graduate degree course in biblical and inter-cultural studies; library: 50,000 books, papers, maps and audiovisual items; 12 full-time, 12 visiting; Exec. Dir MIKE WALL.

Cambridge Theological Federation: Jesus Lane, Cambridge, CB5 8BQ; tel. (1223) 741055; e-mail general-enquiries@theofed.cam.ac.uk; internet www.theofed.cam.ac.uk; f. 1972; courses validated by Anglia Ruskin Univ. and Cambridge Univ.; courses in Christian theology and pastoral theology; Prin. CHRISTINE AMJAD-ALI.

Centre for Youth Ministry: Trinity Business Centre, Stonehill Green, Swindon, SN5 7DG; tel. (1793) 418336; e-mail enquiries@centreforyouthministry.ac.uk; internet www.centreforyouthministry.ac.uk; courses validated by Staffordshire Univ., Univ. of Gloucestershire; centres in Wales and Ireland; courses in schools, youth and community work and practical theology, reflective practice and applied theology; Asst Centre Dir ROBIN BARDEN.

Cliff College: Calver, Hope Valley, S32 3XG; tel. (1246) 584-200; e-mail ilc@cliffcollege.ac.uk; internet www.cliffcollege.ac.uk; full-time, part-time courses in theology and mission at undergraduate and postgraduate level and research degrees; accredited by Univ. of Manchester; library: 30,000 items; 9 teachers; Prin. Rev. Dr CHRIS BLAKE; publ. *Cliff Today* (3 a year).

College of the Resurrection: Stocksbank Rd, Mirfield, WF14 0BW; tel. (1924) 490441; fax (1924) 492738; e-mail hscott@mirfield.org.uk; internet college.mirfield.org.uk; graduate, postgraduate and research degrees validated by Univ. of Sheffield; library: 2,600,000 vols, 9,000 periodicals; Prin. Rev. Dr JOE KENNEDY.

Islamic College for Advanced Studies: The Islamic College, 133 High Rd, Willesden, London, NW10 2SW; tel. (20) 8451-9993; fax (20) 8451-9994; e-mail info@islamic-college.ac.uk; internet www.islamic-college.ac.uk; f. 1998; partnership with Middlesex Univ.; A-level, certificate, diploma, undergraduate, postgraduate courses in Islamic studies, culture and theology; 24 teachers; Prin. M. S. BAHMANPOUR; publ. *Journal of Shi'a Islamic Studies*.

Leo Baeck College: The Sternberg Centre, 80 East End Rd, London, N3 2SY; tel. (20) 8349-5600; fax (20) 8349-5619; internet www.lbc.ac.uk; f. 1956 as Jewish Theological College; five year rabbinic programme, MA in Jewish education, advanced diploma in professional devt for Jewish education, foundation courses for religion school teachers; Prin. Rabbi Prof. MARC SAPERSTEIN; publ. *European Judaism*.

Markfield Institute of Higher Education: Ratby Lane, Markfield, LE67 9SY; tel. (1530) 244-922; fax (1530) 243-102; e-mail info@mihe.org.uk; internet mihe.org.uk; f. 2000; study of Islam in an Islamic instn; postgraduate courses validated by Loughborough Univ.; library: 30,000 vols, 420 serials with 85 current journals; Dir Dr ATAULLAH SIDDIQUI.

Maryvale Institute: Maryvale House, Old Oscott Hill, Birmingham, B44 9AG; tel. (1213) 608-118; fax (1213) 666-786; internet www.maryvale.ac.uk; f. 1980; int. catholic distance-learning college for theology and religious education at undergraduate and postgraduate levels; courses validated by Open University; library: 15,000 vols; 21 teachers.

Oxford Centre for Mission Studies: Woodstock Rd, Oxford, OX2 6HR; tel. (1865) 556-071; fax (1865) 517-722; e-mail ocms@ocms.ac.uk; internet www.ocms.ac.uk; research degrees validated by Univ. of Wales and; library: 13,000 vols; Exec. Dir Dr WONSUK MA; Librarian RALPH BATES; publ. *Transformation*.

Queen's Foundation: Somerset Rd, Birmingham, B15 2QH; tel. (121) 454-1527; fax (121) 454-8171; e-mail enquire@queens.ac.uk; internet www.queens.ac.uk; f. 1828; research degrees validate by Univ. of Birmingham; graduate and postgraduate courses; library: 50,000 vols, 80 journals; Prin. Rev. Dr DAVID HEWLETT.

Redcliffe College: Horton Rd, Gloucester, GL1 3PT; tel. (1452) 308097; internet www.redcliffe.org; f. 1892; degrees validated by Univ. of Gloucestershire; courses in Asian studies, Bible and mission, global issues in contemporary mission, global leadership; Prin. ROB HAY.

Wesley Study Centre: 3 South Bailey, Durham, DH1 3RJ; tel. (191) 334-3850; fax (191) 334-3501; e-mail p.a.bissell@durham.ac.uk; internet www.dur.ac.uk/wsc.online; attached to Univ. of Durham; graduate and postgraduate theology and ministry courses validated by Univ. of Durham; Dir Rev. Dr CALVIN SAMUEL.

YMCA George Williams College: 199 Freemasons Rd, London, E16 3PY; tel. (20) 7540-4900; fax (20) 7511-4900; e-mail registry@ymca.ac.uk; internet www.ymca.ac.uk; f. 1970; undergraduate courses in youth and community work validated by Canterbury Christ Church Univ.; library: 25,000 vols; 1,000 students; Prin. MARY WOLFE; Librarian SAMANTHA MAKWANA.

Universities in Northern Ireland

QUEEN'S UNIVERSITY BELFAST

University Rd, Belfast, BT7 1NN
Telephone: (28) 9024-5133
Fax: (28) 9024-7895
E-mail: vc.office@qub.ac.uk
Internet: www.qub.ac.uk

Founded 1845, as Queen's College, original Univ. Charter 1908, present Charter 1982
State control
Language of instruction: English
Academic year: September to September

Chancellor: KAMALESH SHARMA
Pro-Chancellor: Sir DAVID FELL
Pro-Chancellor: ROTHA JOHNSTON
Pres. and Vice-Chancellor: Prof. PETER GREGSON
Pro-Vice-Chancellor for Education and Students: Prof. ELLEN DOUGLAS-COWIE
Pro-Vice-Chancellor for Academic Planning and External Relations: Prof. TONY GALLAGHER
Pro-Vice-Chancellor for Research and Postgraduates: Prof. JAMES McELNAY
Registrar: JAMES O'KANE
Library Systems Man.: ELIZABETH TRAYNOR

Library: see under Libraries and Archives
Number of teachers: 1,600 full-time
Number of students: 17,500 (full-time and part-time); 10,000 part-time students enrolled at Institute of Lifelong Learning

DEANS

Faculty of Arts, Humanities and Social Sciences: Prof. SHANE O'NEILL

Faculty of Engineering and Physical Sciences: Prof. TOM MILLAR
Faculty of Medicine, Health and Life Sciences: Prof. SEAN GORMAN

PROFESSORS

Faculty of Arts, Humanities and Social Sciences (73 University Rd, Belfast, BT7 1NN; tel. (28) 9097-5347; fax (28) 9024-9864; e-mail deansofficeahss@qub.ac.uk; internet www.qub.ac.uk/fhum):

ALCORN, M., Music and Sonic Arts
ANDREW, M., English
BALES, R., Languages, Literatures and (Performing) Arts
BELL, D., Languages, Literatures and (Performing) Arts
BEW, P., Politics, International Studies and Philosophy
BOWLER, P., History and Anthropology
BURNETT, M., English
CAMPBELL, J., History and Anthropology
CARAHER, B., English
CAREY, M., Management and Economics
CARSON, C., English
CLOUGH, P., Education
CONNOLLY, P., Education
CONNOLLY, S., History and Anthropology
CULLEN, B., Politics, International Studies and Philosophy
DALY, M., Sociology, Social Policy and Social Work
DAVIES, S., Languages, Literatures and (Performing) Arts
DAWSON, N., Law
DEMIRAG, S., Management and Economics
DICKSON, B., Law
DONNAN, H., History and Anthropology
DOUGLAS COWIE, E., Arts, Humanities and Social Sciences
ELWOOD, J., Education
ENGLISH, R., Politics, International Studies and Philosophy
EVANS, J., Politics, International Studies and Philosophy
FORKER, J., Management and Economics
GALLAGHER, A., Education
GARDNER, J., Arts, Humanities and Social Sciences
GEOGHEGAN, V., Politics, International Studies and Philosophy
GORMAN, J., Politics, International Studies and Philosophy
GRAY, P., History and Anthropology
GREEN, I., History and Anthropology
GUELKE, A., Politics, International Studies and Philosophy
HARVEY, C., Law
HAYTON, D., History and Anthropology
HELLAWELL, P., Music and Sonic Arts
HILLYARD, P., Sociology, Social Policy and Social Work
HYNDMAN, N., Management and Economics
JACKSON, J., Law
JEFFCUTT, P., Management and Economics
JEFFERY, K., History and Anthropology
JOHNSTON, D., Languages, Literatures and (Performing) Arts
KENNEDY, L., History and Anthropology
LEITH, P., Law
MACDONALD, C., Politics, International Studies and Philosophy
MAGENNIS, H., English
MANN, M., Sociology, Social Policy and Social Work
MCEVOY, J., Politics, International Studies and Philosophy
MCEVOY, K., Law
MCKILLOP, D., Management and Economics
MCLAUGHLIN, E., Sociology, Social Policy and Social Work
MILTON, K., History and Anthropology
MOORE, M., Management and Economics
MORISON, J., Law
MULLETT, M., History and Anthropology
O'DOWD, L., Sociology, Social Policy and Social Work
O'DOWD, M., History and Anthropology
O'HEARN, D., Sociology, Social Policy and Social Work
O'NEILL, S., Politics, International Studies and Philosophy
PHILIP, G., Management and Economics
PINKERTON, J., Sociology, Social Policy and Social Work
PRIOR, L., Sociology, Social Policy and Social Work
SCRATON, P., Law
SHEEHAN, E., English
SIMPSON, P., English
SMACZNY, J., Music and Sonic Arts
TEAGUE, P., Management and Economics
THOMPSON, J., English
TURNER, J., Management and Economics
TURNER, S., Law
WALKER, B., Politics, International Studies and Philosophy
WALKER, G., Politics, International Studies and Philosophy
WHEELER, S., Law
WHITEHEAD, D., History and Anthropology
WHITEHOUSE, H., History and Anthropology
WIENER, A., Politics, International Studies and Philosophy
WILFORD, R., Politics, International Studies and Philosophy
WILLIAMS, F., Arts, Humanities and Social Sciences
WOODFIELD, I., Music and Sonic Arts

Faculty of Engineering and Physical Sciences (NI Technology Centre, Cloreen Park, Belfast, BT9 5HN; tel. (28) 9097-5443; fax (28) 9097-4536; e-mail deaneps@qub.ac.uk; internet www.qub.ac.uk/feng):

ALLEN, S. J., Chemical Engineering
ARMITAGE, D. H., Pure Mathematics
ARMSTRONG, C. G., Mechanical and Manufacturing Engineering
ARMSTRONG, G. A., Electrical and Electronic Engineering
ATKINSON, R., Physics and Astronomy
BASHEER, P. A. M., Civil Engineering
BELL, D. A., Computer Science
BELL, K. L., Applied Mathematics and Theoretical Physics
BLAIR, G. P., Mechanical and Aerospace Engineering
BOYD, D. R., Chemistry
BURCH, R., Chemistry
CAMPBELL, B., Geography
CLELAND, D. J., Civil Engineering
CLINT, M., Computer Science
COWAN, C. F. N., Electrical and Electronic Engineering
COWIE, R., Psychology
CRAWFORD, R., Mechanical and Aerospace Engineering
CROOKES, D., Computer Engineering
CROSSLEY, P., Electrical and Electronic Engineering
CROTHERS, D. S. F., Applied Mathematics and Theoretical Physics
DE SILVA, A. P., Chemistry
DOUGLAS, R., Mechanical and Manufacturing Engineering
DUFTON, P. L., Physics and Astronomy
FEE, A. J., Mechanical and Manufacturing Engineering
FINNIS, M. W., Physics and Astronomy
FLECK, R., Mechanical and Manufacturing Engineering
FUSCO, V. F., Electrical and Electronic Engineering
GAMBLE, H. S., Electrical and Electronic Engineering
GRAHAM, W. G., Physics and Astronomy
HALL, V., Archaeology and Palaeoecology
HARDACRE, C., Chemistry
HARKIN-JONES, E. M. A., Mechanical and Manufacturing Engineering
HEPPER, P., Psychology
HIBBERT, A., Applied Mathematics and Theoretical Physics
HOWE, J., Environmental Planning
HU, P., Chemistry
IRWIN, G. W., Electrical and Electronic Engineering
KALIN, R. M., Civil Engineering
KEENAN, F. P., Applied Mathematics and Theoretical Physics
LATIMER, C. J., Physics and Astronomy
LEWIS, C. L. S., Physics and Astronomy
LIVINGSTONE, D. N., Mechanical and Aerospace Engineering
MAGEE, T. R. A., Chemical Engineering
MALLORY, J., Archaeology and Palaeoecology
MANN, J., Chemistry
MARSHALL, A. J., Electrical and Electronic Engineering
MCCANNY, J. V., Electrical and Electronic Engineering
MCCORMAC, G., Archaeology and Palaeoecology
MCELDOWNEY, J. M., Environmental Planning
MCGARVEY, J. J., Chemistry
MCGUINNESS, C., Psychology
ORFORD, J. D., Geography
ORR, J. F., Mechanical and Manufacturing Engineering
PERROTT, R. H., Computer Science
RAGHUNATHAN, S. R., Aeronautical Engineering
SCOTT, N. S., Computer Science
SEDDON, K. R., Chemistry
SHEEHY, N., Psychology
SMITH, B., Geography
SMYTH, A., Environmental Planning
TAYLOR, K. T. A., Applied Mathematics and Theoretical Physics
WALMSLEY, D. G., Physics and Astronomy
WALTERS, H. R. J., Applied Mathematics and Theoretical Physics
WHALLEY, W. B., Geography
WHITAKER, M. A. B., Physics and Astronomy
WICKSTEAD, A. W., Pure Mathematics
WILLIAMS, I., Physics and Astronomy
WOODS, R., Electrical and Electronic Engineering
WOOLLEY, T. A., Architecture

Faculty of Medicine, Health and Life Sciences (Whitla Medical Bldg, 97 Lisburn Rd, Belfast, BT9 7BL; tel. (28) 9097-5177; e-mail dean-mhls@qub.ac.uk; internet www.qub.ac.uk/fmhs):

AMES, J., Biological and Food Sciences
CAMPBELL, F., Biomedical Sciences
CHAKRAVARTHY, U., Biomedical Sciences
COSBY, S., Biomedical Sciences
DAVIES, R., Biological and Food Sciences
DRING, M., Biological and Food Sciences
ELBORN, J., Medicine and Dentistry
ELWOOD, R., Biological and Food Sciences
ENNIS, M., Medicine and Dentistry
EVANS, A., Medicine and Dentistry
FEE, J., Medicine and Dentistry
FREEMAN, R., Medicine and Dentistry
GORMAN, S., Pharmacy
HALL, P., Medicine and Dentistry
HAMILTON, P., Biomedical Sciences
HARKIN, D., Biomedical Sciences
HAY, R., Medicine and Dentistry
HIRST, D., Pharmacy
HUGHES, A., Medicine and Dentistry
HUGHES, C., Pharmacy
HUTCHINSON, G., Biological and Food Sciences
JOHNSTON, G., Medicine and Dentistry
JOHNSTON, J., Biomedical Sciences
JOHNSTON, P., Biomedical Sciences
JONES, D., Pharmacy

KEE, F., Medicine and Dentistry
LAMEY, P., Medicine and Dentistry
LAPPIN, T., Biomedical Sciences
LARKIN, M., Biological and Food Sciences
LEWIS, S., Medicine and Dentistry
LINDEN, G., Medicine and Dentistry
LYNCH, E., Medicine and Dentistry
MAGGS, C., Biological and Food Sciences
MAULE, A., Biological and Food Sciences
MAXWELL, A., Medicine and Dentistry
MCCLURE, N., Medicine and Dentistry
MCDERMOTT, B., Medicine and Dentistry
MCELNAY, J., Medicine, Health and Life Sciences
MCVEIGH, G., Biomedical Sciences
MIRAKHUR, R., Medicine and Dentistry
MONTGOMERY, W., Biological and Food Sciences
ORR, J., Nursing and Midwifery
PORTER, S., Nursing and Midwifery
REILLY, P., Medicine and Dentistry
REYNOLDS, G., Medicine and Dentistry
RIMA, B., Biomedical Sciences
SAVAGE, J., Medicine and Dentistry
SHAW, C., Pharmacy
SHIELDS, M., Medicine and Dentistry
STITT, A., Biomedical Sciences
STOUT, R., Medicine and Dentistry
TRIMBLE, E., Medicine and Dentistry
VANDENBROECK, K., Pharmacy
WALKER, B., Pharmacy
WOOLFSON, D., Pharmacy
YOUNG, I., Medicine and Dentistry

UNIVERSITY OF ULSTER

Coleraine Campus, Cromore Rd, Coleraine, BT52 1SA
Jordanstown Campus, Shore Rd, Newtownabbey, BT37 0QB
Belfast Campus, York St, Belfast, BT15 1ED
Magee Campus, Northland Rd, Londonderry, BT48 7JL

Telephone: (28) 7012-3456
E-mail: online@ulster.ac.uk
Internet: www.ulster.ac.uk

Founded 1984 by Royal Charter following merger of New Univ. of Ulster and Ulster Polytechnic
State control
Academic year: September to May
Chancellor: Sir RICHARD NICHOLS
Pro-Chancellor: Prof. ROSEMARY PETER-GALLAGHER
Pro-Chancellor: Dr JEREMY HARBINSON
Pro-Chancellor: GERRY MALLON
Vice-Chancellor: Prof. RICHARD BARNETT (acting)
Pro-Vice-Chancellor for Communication and External Affairs: Prof. ALASTAIR ADAIR
Pro-Vice-Chancellor for Sport and Student Services: Prof. JIM ALLEN
Pro-Vice-Chancellor for Research and Innovation: Prof. NORMAN BLACK
Pro-Vice-Chancellor for Teaching and Learning: Prof. DENISE MCALISTER
Dean for Academic Planning and Magee: Prof. DEIRDRE HEENAN
Dean for Campus Devt, Coleraine Campus and Provost: Prof. ROBERT HUTCHINSON
Number of teachers: 1,092
Number of students: 25,339 (17,075 full time and 8,264 part time)

DEANS

Faculty of Arts: Prof. PÓL O'DOCHARTAIGH
Faculty of Art, Design and the Built Environment: Prof. IAN MONTGOMERY
Faculty of Computing and Engineering: Prof. RICHARD MILLAR (acting)
Faculty of Life and Health Sciences: Prof. HUGH MCKENNA
Faculty of Social Sciences: Prof. PAUL CARMICHAEL
Ulster Business School: Prof. MARIE MCHUGH

PROFESSORS

Faculty of Arts (Univ. of Ulster Coleraine Campus, Cromore Rd, Coleraine, BT52 1SA; tel. (28) 7032-4517; fax (28) 7032-4925; e-mail arts@ulster.ac.uk; internet www.arts.ulster.ac.uk):

BRADFORD, R. W., Literary History and Theory
GILLESPIE, J., French
JEDRZEJEWSKI, J., Comparative Literature
JONES, G. J., Social and Intellectual History
KENNEDY-ANDREWS, E., English
KOCKEL, U., Ethnology and Folk Life
LARRES, K., History and International Affairs
MACMATHÚNA, S., Irish Studies
MCLOONE, M., Film Studies
MCMINN, J. M., Anglo-Irish Literature
NIC CRAITH, M., Irish Culture and Language
O'CORRAIN, A. P., Modern Irish Studies
O'DOCHARTAIGH, P., German
TONER, G., Irish Languages and Literature
UPTON, C., Drama
MOORE, P., Creative Technologies
THATCHER, I., History

Faculty of Art, Design and the Built Environment (Univ. of Ulster, Belfast Campus, York St, Belfast, BT15 1ED; tel. (28) 9036-6310; fax (28) 9036-6816; e-mail jai.montgomery@ulster.ac.uk; internet www.adbe.ulster.ac.uk):

ALI, F., Building Services Engineering
BERRY, J. N., Urban Planning and Property Development
DELICHATSIOS, M., Fire Safety and Engineering
DOHERTY, W. J., Video Art
FLEMING, K., Textile Art
GRAY, P., Housing
HEANEY, G., Construction
HEWITT, N., Energy
HINE, J. P., Transport
KELLY, W., Irish Visual Culture
LLOYD, G. M., Urban Planning
MACLENNAN, M., Fine Art
MCCLELLAND, B., Design
MCGREAL, W. S., Property Research
MOLKOV, V., Hydrogen Fire Safety Science
MONTGOMERY, I., Design
NADJAI, A., Fire Structural Engineering
NOVOZHILOV, V., Fire Dynamics
PARSA, A. G., Urban Planning and Business Development
SEAWRIGHT, P., Photography
WOODSIDE, A. R., Highways Engineering
WRIGHT, T., Visual Arts
YOHANIS, Y., Building Services Engineering

Faculty of Computing and Engineering (Univ. of Ulster, Jordanstown Campus, Shore Rd, Newtownabbey, BT37 0QB; tel. (28) 9036-6855; fax (28) 9036-6803; e-mail engineering@ulster.ac.uk; internet www.compeng.ulster.ac.uk):

ANDERSON, J. M. C. C., Biomedical Engineering
ANDERSON, T. J., Interactive Computing
BROWN, N. M. D., Chemistry (Surface Science)
BUSTARD, D. W., Computing Science
CLARKE, R. B., Mechanical Engineering
DAVIS, J., Biomedical Sensors
ESCALONA, O. J., Cardiovascular Research
FARAHMAND, K., Mathematics
HULL, M. E. C., Computing Science
MAGUIRE, L. P., Computational Intelligence
MAGUIRE, P. D., Plasmas and Nanofabrication
MCCLEAN, S. I., Mathematics
MCGINNITY, T. M., Intelligent Systems Engineering
MCKEAG, D., Product Development
MCKEVITT, P., Digital Multimedia
MCLAUGHLIN, J. A., Advanced Functional Materials
MCTEAR, M., Knowledge Engineering
MEENAN, B. J., Biomedical Materials
MILLAR, R. J., Computer Science
MULVENNA, M. D., Computer Science
NUGENT, C. D., Biomedical Engineering
PAPKONSTANTINOU, P., Advanced Materials
PARR, G. P., Telecommunications
SCOTNEY, B. W., Informatics

Faculty of Life and Health Sciences (Univ. of Ulster, Coleraine Campus, Cromore Rd, Coleraine, BT52 1SA; tel. (28) 7032-4491; fax (28) 7032-4596; e-mail science@ulster.ac.uk; internet www.science.ulster.ac.uk):

ANDERSON, R. S., Vision Science
BANAT, I., Microbiology
BJOURSON, A. J., Genomics
BROWN, J., Primary Health Care—General Practice
BUNTING, B. P., Psychology
CAIRNS, S. E., Psychology
COATES, V., Nursing Research
COOK, T.,
COOPER, J. A. G., Coastal Studies
DAY, K. R., Environmental Sciences
DOBBS, F., Primary Care
DOLK, H. M., Epidemiology and Health Services Research
DOOLEY, J. S. G., Microbiology
DOWNES, C. S., Cancer Biology
DUBITZKY, W., Bioinformatics
EASTWOOD, D. A., Environmental Studies
FLATT, P. R., Biological and Biomedical Sciences
GILLAN, U., International Primary Health Care
HANNIGAN, B. M., Biomedical Sciences
HARRISON, S. J., Social Anthropology
HOWARD, V., Bioimaging
JACKSON, D., Coastal Geomorphology
KERNOHAN, W. G., Health Research
LESLIE, J., Psychology
LIDDELL, C., Psychology
LIVINGSTONE, M. B. E., Nutrition
MARCHANT, R., Microbial Biotechnology
MCCANCE, T., Nursing Research and Development
MCCARRON, P., Pharmaceutics
MCCLENAGHAN, N., Bio-Innovation and Enterprise
MCCLOSKEY, J., Geophysics
MCCONKEY, R. A., Developmental Disabilities
MCCORMACK, B., Nursing Research
MCDONOUGH, S. M., Health and Rehabilitation
MCDOWELL, D. A., Food Studies
MCHALE, A. P., Medical Biotechnology
MCKELVEY-MARTIN, V., Molecular Biosciences
MCKENNA, H. P., Nursing
MCKEOWN, S. R., Cancer Biology
MCMULLAN, G., Microbiology
MCNULTY, H. M., Nutritional Science
MURPHY, M., Sports and Exercise
O'HARTE, F. P. M, Endocrinology and Metabolism
PARAHOO, K. A., Nursing and Health Research
PIERSCIONEK, K., Vision Science
POULTON, B. C., Community Health Nursing
RAE, G., Psychology
RIPPEY, B., Environmental Science
RUSHTON, B. S., Botany
SAKMANN, B., Biomedical Sciences
SINCLAIR, M., Midwifery Research
SOTO, A., Cancer Development
SMYTH, W. F., Bio-analytical Chemistry
STEACEY, S., Earthquake Physics
STRAIN, J. J., Human Nutrition
STRINGER, M., Psychology
WALLACE, E., Sports Biomechanics

WALSH, D. M., Rehabilitation Research
WELSH, R., Food Science and Nutrition
WILSON, R., Psychology

Faculty of Social Sciences (Univ. of Ulster, Jordanstown Campus, Shore Rd, Newtownabbey, BT37 0QB; tel. (28) 9036-6157; fax (28) 9036-6806; e-mail socsci@ulster.ac.uk; internet www.socsci.ulster.ac.uk):

AUGHEY, A. H., Politics
BELL, C. M., Public International Law
BIRRELL, W. D., Social Administration and Policy
BOROOAH, V. K., Applied Economics
CAMPBELL, C., Law
CARMICHAEL, P., Public Policy/Government
ERRIDGE, A. F., Public Policy and Management
GEARY, F., Economic History
HAMBER, B., Incore
HARGIE, O. D. W., Communication
HEENAN, D. A., Social Policy
HENRY, A. M., Linguistics
HUME, J., Incore
KNOX, C. G., Comparative Public Policy
MCALEAVY, G. J., Further and Higher Education
MCALISTER, D. A., Health Policy
MCWILLIAMS, M. M., Women's Studies
MORAN, A., Education
NI AOLAIN, F., Law
O'CONNOR, J. S., Social Policy
OFFER, J. W., Social Theory and Policy
OSBORNE, R. D., Applied Policy Studies
OSMANI, S. R., Applied Economics
PATTERSON, H. H., Politics
ROBINSON, G., Social Research
ROLSTON, W. J., Sociology
SMITH, A., Education
THAIN, C., Politics
TRIDIMAS, G., Political Economy
WILSON, J., Communication

Ulster Business School (Univ. of Ulster, Coleraine Campus, Cromore Rd, Coleraine, BT52 1SA; tel. (28) 9036-6351; fax (28) 9036-6805; e-mail business@ulster.ac.uk; internet www.business.ulster.ac.uk):

BALLANTINE, J., Accounting
BOYD, S., Tourism
BROWN, S., Marketing Research
CARSON, D., Marketing
GILMORE, A. J., Services Marketing
GLASS, J. C., Applied Financial Economics
GREENAN, K., Management Education
HAMILL, P., Finance and Investment
HUMPHREYS, P. K., Operations Management
KIRK, R. J., Accounting and Finance
MCADAM, R., Innovation Management
MCCOY, J., Management Decvelopment
MCGOWAN, P., Entrepreneurship and Business Development
MCHUGH, M. L., Organizational Behaviour
MCIVOR, R., Operations Management
MURRAY, A. E., Hospitality Management
O'REILLY, M. D., International Business Strategy
QUINN, B., Retail Accounting
WARD, A. M., Accounting
WARD, J. D., Taxation

Colleges in Northern Ireland

These institutions are not able to award their own degrees, but offer courses leading to a degree from a recognized body.

Belfast Bible College: Glenburn Rd South, Belfast, Dunmurry, BT17 9JP; tel. (28) 9030-1551; e-mail info@belfastbiblecollege.com; internet www.belfastbiblecollege.com; f. 1943, as Belfast Bible School and Missionary Training Home; attached to Queen's Univ. Belfast; courses in youth and community work and practical theology; undergraduate and postgraduate programmes in conjunction with Queen's Univ. Belfast and Univ. of Cumbria; library: 16,000 vols, 87 journals; 200 students; Prin. IAN DICKSON (acting); Librarian DOROTHY ANDERSON.

Belfast Metropolitan College: The Directorate, Gerald Moag Campus, Bldg 1, Level 2, Room 9, 125–153 Millfield, Belfast, BT1 1HS; tel. (28) 9026-5459; fax (28) 9026-5401; e-mail central_admissions@belfastmet.ac.uk; internet www.belfastmet.ac.uk; f. 1991, from College of Technology (f. 1901), College of Business Studies and Rupert Stanley College; full-time courses conducted at Brunswick St, Castlereagh, College Sq., Millfield, Tower St, Whiterock Campus bldgs; acad. depts of business and management, community education and training, computing and admin. studies, continuing education, creative and health studies, general education, hospitality, leisure and tourism, technology; 1,000 teachers; 53,000 students; Chair. RICHARD O'RAWE; Dir and Chief Exec. MAIRE-THÉRÈSE MCGIVERN.

College of Agriculture, Food and Rural Enterprise: Greenmount Campus, 45 Tirgracy Rd, Antrim, BT41 4PS; tel. (28) 9052-4420; e-mail enquiries@cafre.ac.uk; internet www.cafre.ac.uk; higher national certificate, diploma and degree courses in agriculture and animal care; campuses in Antrim, Enniskillen, Loughry.

Irish Baptist College: 19 Hillsborough Rd, Moira, BT67 0HG; tel. (28) 9261-9267; internet www.irishbaptistcollege.co.uk; f. 1892; undergraduate and postgraduate courses, validated by the University of Chester, in theology, ministry and philosophy; 50 students; Prin. EDWIN EWART; Registrar VALERIE HAMILTON.

North West Regional College: Londonderry Campus, Strand Rd, Londonderry, BT48 7AL; tel. (28) 7127-6000; fax (28) 7126-0520; internet www.nwrc.ac.uk; f. 2007, by merger of Limavady College and North West Institute; campuses in Limavady, Londonderry and Strabane; smaller centres situated throughout North West; 24,000 students; Prin. and Chief Exec. S MURPHY; Library Man. JONATHAN MOOR.

Northern Regional College: Antrim Campus, Fountain St, Antrim, BT41 4AL; tel. (28) 9446-3916; fax (28) 9446-5132; internet www.nrc.ac.uk; campuses in Antrim, Ballymena, Ballymoney, Coleriane, Larne, Magherafelt and Newtownabbey; faculties of access, built environment and design, business, community, engineering, hair and beauty therapies, hospitality and catering, IT, media and performing arts, science, social care and early years, sport and essential skills, travel and tourism; library: 35,000 vols, 3,000 ebooks, 70 journal titles; Dir T. NEILANDS; Sec. JIM HUNTER.

Saint Mary's University College: 191 Falls Rd, Belfast, BT12 6FE; tel. (28) 9032-7678; fax (28) 9033-3719; internet www.stmarys-belfast.ac.uk; f. 1900, as St Mary's Training College, present name and status 1985; attached to Queen's Univ. Belfast; faculties of education, liberal arts; library: 90,000 vols, 100 periodicals and newspapers; Chair. Rev. NOEL TREANOR; Vice-Chair. Rev. DONAL MCKEOWN; Prin. Prof. PETER B. FINN; Librarian FELICITY JONES.

South Eastern Regional College: Lisburn Campus, 39 Castle St, Lisburn, BT27 4SU; tel. (28) 9267-7225; fax (28) 9267-7291; e-mail info@serc.ac.uk; internet www.serc.ac.uk; f. 1914; main campuses in Bangor, Downpatrick, Lisburn and Newtownards, Newcastle and Ballynahinch; Chair. BRIAN ACHESON; Prin. and Chief Exec. KEN WEBB.

South West College: Enniskillen Campus, Fairview, 1 Dublin Rd, Enniskillen, BT74 6AE; tel. (845) 603-1881; fax (28) 6632-6357; e-mail enquiries@swc.ac.uk; internet www.swc.ac.uk; campuses in Cookstown, Dungannon, Enniskillen and Omagh; 500 teachers; 18,500 students; Chair. JOSEPH MARTIN (acting).

Southern Regional College: The Directorate, SRC Newry Campus, Patrick St, Newry, BT35 8DN; tel. (28) 3026-1071; fax (28) 3025-9679; e-mail info@src.ac.uk; internet www.src.ac.uk; offers over 600 courses; campuses in Armagh, Banbridge, Newry, Portadown, Kikeel and Lurgan; 1,100 teachers; 45,000 students; Chief Exec. BRIAN DORAN; Chair. ANDREW SAUNDERS; Vice-Chair. ANGELA COFFEY.

Stranmillis University College: Stranmillis Rd, Belfast, BT9 5DY; tel. (28) 9038-1271; fax (28) 9066-4423; e-mail info@stran.ac.uk; internet www.stran.ac.uk; f. 1922; attached to Queen's Univ. Belfast; depts of initial teacher education, early childhood education, health and physical education; Chair. S. COSTELLO; Vice-Chair. S. E. D. BELL; Prin. and Chief Exec. Dr ANNE HEASLETT.

Union Theological College: 108 Botanic Ave, Belfast, BT7 1JT; tel. (28) 9020-5080; fax (28) 9020-5099; e-mail admin@union.ac.uk; internet www.union.ac.uk; f. 1978, by merger of Assembly's College (f. 1853) and Magee College (f. 1865); attached to Institute of Theology, Queen's University Belfast; 3 depts: biblical studies; systematic theology and church history; practical theology and min.; library: 60,000 vols, 20,000 pamphlets, 100 journals and periodicals; Registrar and Admin. SANDRA MCKINNEY; Librarian DAVID KERRY.

Universities in Scotland

EDINBURGH NAPIER UNIVERSITY

Merchiston Campus, 10 Colinton Rd, Edinburgh, EH14 1DJ
Telephone: (131) 455-3555
Fax: (131) 455-6464
E-mail: info@napier.ac.uk
Internet: www.napier.ac.uk
Founded 1964, as Napier Technical College, present name and status 2009
Academic year: August to May
Chancellor: TIM WATERSTONE
Prin. and Vice-Chancellor: Prof. Dame JOAN STRINGER
Vice-Prin.: Prof. JOHN DUFFIELD
Vice-Prin.: Dr JENNY REES
Univ. Sec.: Dr GERRY WEBBER
Dir of Learning Information Services: CHRIS PINDER
Library of 210,000 vols
Number of teachers: 879
Number of students: 17,605

DEANS

Business School: Prof. GEORGE STONEHOUSE
Faculty of Engineering, Computing and Creative Industries: Dr SANDRA CAIRNCROSS
Faculty of Health, Life and Social Sciences: Prof. MORAG PROWSE

GLASGOW CALEDONIAN UNIVERSITY

Cowcaddens Rd, Glasgow, G4 0BA
Telephone: (141) 331-3000
Fax: (141) 331-3005
E-mail: helpline@gcal.ac.uk

Internet: www.caledonian.ac.uk

Founded 1971 as Glasgow Polytechnic; merged with The Queen's College; present name and status 1993

State control

Academic year: September to June

Chancellor: Rt Hon Lord MACDONALD OF TRADESTON

Prin. and Vice-Chancellor: Prof. PAMELA GILLIES

Vice-Prin. and Pro-Vice-Chancellor for External Relations: Prof. KAREN STANTON

Vice-Prin. and Pro-Vice-Chancellor for Learning and Teaching: Prof. MIKE MANNION

Pro-Vice-Chancellor for Strategy: Prof. MIKE SMITH

Vice-Prin. and Exec. Dir of Finance: DAVID BEEBY

Vice-Prin. and Univ. Sec.: JAN HULME

Chief Information Officer: JEFF MURRAY (acting)

Number of students: 17,000

DEANS

Caledonian Business School: Prof. ŽELJKO SEVIĆ

School of Built and Natural Environment: Prof. PETER KENNEDY

School of Engineering and Computing: Prof. MALCOLM ALLAN (acting)

School of Health: Prof. FRANK CROSSAN

School of Law and Social Sciences: Prof. BILL HUGHES (acting)

School of Life Sciences: Prof. KEVAN M. A. GARTLAND

HERIOT-WATT UNIVERSITY

Edinburgh Campus: Edinburgh, EH14 4AS

Scottish Borders Campus: Netherdale, Galashiels, TD1 3HF

Telephone: (131) 449-5111 (Edinburgh); (1896) 753351 (Scottish Borders)

Fax: (131) 449-5153 (Edinburgh); (1896) 758965 (Scottish Borders)

E-mail: enquiries@hw.ac.uk

Internet: www.hw.ac.uk

Founded 1821 as Edinburgh School of Arts; became Heriot-Watt College 1885; present name and status 1966

Academic year: September to August

Chancellor: Baroness SUSAN GREENFIELD

Prin. and Vice-Chancellor: Prof. STEVE CHAPMAN

Vice-Prin.: Prof. JULIAN D. C. JONES

Sr. Deputy Prin.: Prof. ANDY C. WALKER

Deputy Prin. for Learning and Teaching: Prof, ROBERT J. M. CRAIK

Deputy Prin. for Research and Knowledge Transfer: Prof. ALAN MILLER

Sec.: ANN MARIE DALTON

Librarian: GILL A. MCDONALD (acting)

Number of teachers: 450

Number of students: 23,000

HEADS OF SCHOOLS

Edinburgh Business School: Prof. KEITH G. LUMSDEN (Dir)

Institute of Petroleum Engineering: Prof. S. STEWART

School of Built Environment: Prof. GARRY PENDER

School of Engineering and Physical Sciences: (vacant)

School of Life Sciences: Prof. D. HOPKINS

School of Management and Languages: Prof. G. HOGG

School of Mathematical and Computer Sciences: Prof. PHILIP DE WILDE

School of Textiles and Design: Prof. ALISON J. HARLEY (acting)

PROFESSORS

School of the Built Environment (tel. (131) 451-4644; fax (131) 451-4617; e-mail a.j.ormston@hw.ac.uk):

- ASPINALL, P., Building Engineering and Surveying
- BANFILL, P., Construction Materials
- BRAMLEY, G., Urban Studies
- CAO, Z., Civil Engineering
- CHRISP, T., Civil Engineering
- CRAIK, R., Acoustics, Deputy Principal (Teaching and Learning)
- DHILLON, B., Building Engineering and Surveying
- HULL, A., Spatial Planning
- JENKINS, P., Architecture & Human Settlements
- JONES, C., Estate Management
- JOWITT, P., Sustainable Technology
- KAKA, A., Construction Economics & Management and William Watson Chair, Dubai Campus
- MAY, I., Civil Engineering
- MCCARTER, W., Civil Engineering Materials
- OGUNLANA, S., Construction Project Management
- PAWSON, H., Housing Policy
- PENDER, G., Civil Engineering
- PRIOR, A., Planning and Housing
- ROAF, S., Architectural Engineering
- ROBERSTON, B., School of the Built Environment
- SWAFFIELD, J., Building Services Engineering
- WANG, Y., Urban Studies

School of Engineering and Physical Sciences (tel. (131) 451-3082; fax (131) 451-3136; e-mail l.bruce@hw.ac.uk):

- ADAMS, D., Chemistry
- BAKER, H., Physics
- BULLER, G., Physics
- CLOSE, A., Electrical Engineering
- DESMULLIEZ, M., Electrical Engineering
- GALBRAITH, I., Physics
- GREENAWAY, A., Physics
- GREENHALGH, D., Physics
- GUTOWSKI, M., Chemistry
- HALL, D., Physics
- HAND, D., Physics
- HARVEY, A., Electrical Engineering
- JOHN, P., Chemistry
- JONSON, M., Physics
- JONES, J., Physics
- KAR, A., Physics
- KEANE, M., Chemical Engineering
- LANE, D., Electrical Engineering
- MACGREGOR, S., Chemistry
- MARKX, G., Chemical Engineering
- MCCOUSTRA, M., Chemical Physics
- MCKENDRICK, K., Chemistry
- MOORE, A., Mechanical Engineering
- NI, X., Chemical Engineering
- OCONE, R., Chemical Engineering
- PETILLOT, Y., Electrical Engineering
- POWELL, A., Chemistry
- REAY, D., Electrical Engineering
- REID, D., Physics
- REUBEN, R., Mechanical Engineering
- RICHARDS, B., Mechanical Engineering
- RITCHIE, J., Mechanical Engineering
- TAGHIZADEH, M., Physics
- WALKER, A., Physics
- WALLACE, A., Electrical and Electronic Engineering
- WELCH, A., Chemistry
- WHERRETT, B., Theoretical Physics
- WILSON, J., Physics

School of Life Sciences (tel. (131) 451-3456; fax (131) 451-3009; e-mail j.e.j.lodder@hw.ac.uk):

- GREEN, P., Psychology
- HUGHES, P., Brewing and Distilling
- MAIR, J., Marine Biology
- NORTH, A., Psychology
- QUAIN, D., Brewing
- SCHWEIZER, H., Biological Sciences
- WILKINSON, M., Marine Biology

School of Management and Languages (tel. (131) 451-8143; fax (131) 451-3498; e-mail enquiries@sml.hw.ac.uk):

- BOSER, U., Languages and Intercultural Studies
- COBHAM, D., Economics
- CRAIG, V., Employment Law
- FERNIE, J., Retail Marketing
- HARE, P., Economics
- JAMASB, T., Economics
- MARSTON, C., Accountancy
- MASON, I., Languages
- MCKINNON, A., Logistics
- MELITZ, J., Economics
- PEREZ, I., Languages
- ROSLENDER, R., Accounting
- SAWKINS, J., Economics
- SCHAFFER, M., Economics
- SHARWOOD SMITH, M., Languages
- TOWERS, N., Business Management
- TURNER, G., Translation, Languages

School of Mathematical and Computer Sciences (tel. (131) 451-3420; fax (131) 451-3327; e-mail enquiries@macs.hw.ac.uk):

- AYLETT, R., Computer Science
- CAIRNS, A., Actuarial Mathematics and Statistics
- CARR, J., Mathematics
- CHANTLER, M., Computer Science
- CORNE, D., Computer Science
- DE WILDE, P., Computer Science
- DUNCAN, D., Mathematics
- EILBECK, J., Mathematics
- FOSS, S., Actuarial Mathematics and Statistics
- GIBSON, G., Statistics
- HOWIE, J., Mathematics
- JOHNSTON, D., Mathematics
- KAMAREDDINE, F., Computer Science
- KONSTANTOPOULOS, P., Actuarial Mathematics
- KUKSIN, S., Mathematics
- LACEY, A., Mathematics
- LORD, G., Mathematics
- MACDONALD, A., Actuarial Mathematics
- MCNEIL, A., Actuarial Mathematics
- MICHAELSON, G., Computer Science
- RYNNE, B., Mathematics
- SHERRATT, J., Mathematics
- SZABO, R., Mathematics
- TAYLOR, N., Computer Science
- TRINDER, P., Computer Science
- WATERS, H., Actuarial Mathematics and Statistics
- WILKIE, A., Actuarial Mathematics and Statistics
- WILLIAMS, M., Computer Science

Institute of Petroleum Engineering (tel. (131) 451-3567; fax (131) 451-3127; e-mail jane.wells@pet.hw.ac.uk):

- CHRISTIE, M., Reservoir Engineering
- CORBETT, P., Geoengineering
- COUPLES, G., Petroleum Engineering
- DAVIES, D., Petroleum Engineering
- FORD, J., Petroleum Engineering
- MACBETH, C., Reservoir Geophysics; Timelapse and Multi Components
- SIDE, J., Civil Engineering
- SMART, B., Petroleum Engineering
- SORBIE, K., Petroleum Engineering
- STEWART, S., Petroleum Engineering
- STOW, D., Petroleum Engineering
- TODD, A., Petroleum Engineering
- TOHIDI KALORAZI, B., Petroleum Engineering

School of Textiles and Design (tel. (1896) 753351; fax (1896) 758965; e-mail l.a.lindsay@hw.ac.uk):

- CHRISTIE, R., Colour Chemistry
- HARLEY, A., Textiles and Design

SHENK, P., Textile Design
STYLIOS, G., Textiles
WARDMAN, R., Textiles

Edinburgh Business School (tel. (131) 451-3090; fax (131) 451-3002; e-mail enquiries@ebs.hw.ac.uk):

KAY, N., Economics
LOTHIAN, N., Accounting
LUMSDEN, K., Economics
O'FARRELL, P., Consultant
POOLEY, R., Computer Science
SCOTT, A., Economics
SIMMONS, J., Mechanical Engineering

QUEEN MARGARET UNIVERSITY

Musselburgh, Edinburgh, EH21 6UU

Telephone: (131) 474-0000
Internet: www.qmu.ac.uk

Founded 1875, present name and status 2007

Chancellor: Sir TOM FARMER
Prin. and Vice-Chancellor: Prof. PETRA WEND
Vice-Prin. for Resources and Devt and Univ. Sec.: ROSALYN MARSHALL
Vice-Prin. for Academics: Prof. ALAN GILLORAN
Dir for Campus Services: STEVE SCOTT
Dir for Finance: MALCOLM CUTT
Dir for Human Resources: MIKE BLAIR
Dir for Registry and Secretariat: IRENE HYND

Library of 100,000 vols and 1,400 periodicals
Number of teachers: 496
Number of students: 5,892

DEANS

School of Arts and Social Sciences: Dr CHRISTINE BOVIS-CNOSSEN
School of Health Sciences: Dr FIONA COUTTS

ROBERT GORDON UNIVERSITY

Schoolhill, Aberdeen, AB10 1FR

Telephone: (1224) 262000
Fax: (1224) 263000
Internet: www.rgu.ac.uk

Founded 1750, present name and status 1992
Academic year: September to July

Chancellor: Sir IAN WOOD
Prin. and Vice-Chancellor: Prof. FERDINAND VON PRONDZYNSKI
Sec.: Dr ADRIAN GRAVES
Acad. Registrar: HILARY DOUGLAS
Chief Librarian: ELAINE DUNPHY

Library of 250,946 vols, 1,901 periodicals, 4,939 online journals
Number of teachers: 702 (full-time)
Number of students: 15,000

DEANS

Aberdeen Business School: Prof. RITA MARCELLA
Faculty of Design and Technology: Prof. JOHN WATSON
Faculty of Health and Social Care: Prof. VALERIE MAEHLE

HEADS OF SCHOOLS

Aberdeen Business School (Garthdee Rd, Aberdeen, AB10 7QE; tel. (1224) 263550; fax (1224) 263838; e-mail j.dey@rgu.ac.uk):

Accounting and Finance: ELIZABETH GAMMIE
Business and Management: MORAG HAMILTON
Information and Media: IAN M. JOHNSON
Public Administration and Law: VERONICA STRACHAN

Faculty of Design and Technology (Scott Sutherland School, Garthdee Rd, Aberdeen, AB10 7QB; tel. (1224) 263750; fax (1224) 263757; e-mail c.black@rgu.ac.uk):

School of Computing: Prof. SUSAN CRAW
School of Engineering: Prof. JOHN WATSON
Gray's School of Art: Prof. MIKE PRESS
Scott Sutherland School: Prof. ROBERT W. POLLOCK

Faculty of Health and Social Care (Garthdee Rd, Aberdeen, AB10 7QG; tel. (1224) 263050; fax (1224) 263053; e-mail s.barnett@rgu.ac.uk):

Applied Social Studies: Prof. JOYCE LISHMAN
Health Sciences: ELIZABETH HANCOCK
Life Sciences: Prof. MAUREEN MELVIN
Nursing and Midwifery: JENNIE PARRY
Pharmacy: Prof. TERENCE M. HEALEY

ROYAL SCOTTISH ACADEMY OF MUSIC AND DRAMA

100 Renfrew St, Glasgow, G2 3DB

Telephone: (141) 332-4101
Fax: (141) 332-8901
E-mail: principal@rsamd.ac.uk
Internet: www.rsamd.ac.uk

Founded 1847, present name 1968, present status 1993
Academic year: September to June

Patron: HRH Prince CHARLES
Pres.: Sir CAMERON MACKINTOSH
Chair.: Lord VALLANCE OF TUMMEL
Prin.: Prof. JOHN WALLACE
Vice-Prin.: Prof. MAGGIE KINLOCH
Number of students: 836

DEANS

School of Drama and Dance: HUGH HODGART
School of Music: HAVILLAND WILLSHIRE

UHI MILLENNIUM INSTITUTE

12B Ness Walk, Inverness, IV3 5SQ

Telephone: (1463) 279-000
Fax: (1463) 279-001
E-mail: info@uhi.ac.uk
Internet: www.uhi.ac.uk

Founded 1993, present status 2008
Private control

Rector: GARRY COUTTS
Prin.: JAMES FRASER
Vice-Prin. for Research and Enterprise: Dr JEFF HOWARTH
Vice-Prin. for Acad.: Dr CRICHTON LANG
Sec.: FIONA LARG
Librarian: GILLIAN ANDERSON
Number of students: 8,156

DEANS

Faculty of Arts, Humanities and Business: Dr NEIL SIMCO
Faculty of Science, Health and Education: IAN LESLIE

UNIVERSITY OF ABERDEEN

Telephone: (1224) 272000
Fax: (1224) 276054
E-mail: pubrel@abdn.ac.uk
Internet: www.abdn.ac.uk

Founded 1495

Chancellor: Lord WILSON OF TILLYORN
Prin. and Vice-Chancellor: Prof. IAN DIAMOND
Rector: STEPHEN ROBERTSON
Sec.: STEVE CANNON
Sr Vice-Prin.: Prof. STEPHEN LOGAN
Vice-Prin. for Culture and Communities: Prof. CHRIS GANE
Vice-Prin. for Curriculum Reform: Prof. BRYAN MACGREGOR
Vice-Prin. for Research and Commercialization: Prof. DOMINIC HOULIHAN
Vice-Prin. for Learning and Teaching: Prof. PETER MCGEORGE
Acad. Registrar: Dr GILLIAN MACKINTOSH
Librarian: CHRIS BANKS

Library: see Libraries and Archives

Number of teachers: 1,400
Number of students: 16,000

Publications: *Aberdeen University Review*, *Gaudeamus* (1 a year)

PROFESSORS

College of Arts and Social Sciences (Univ. of Aberdeen, King's College, Aberdeen, AB24 3FX; tel. (1224) 272084; fax (1224) 272082; e-mail adf076@abdn.ac.uk):

ADAMS, C. D., Land Economy
ARTER, D., Politics and Int. Relations
BEAUMONT, P. R., Law
BEBBINGTON, K. J., Accountancy
BLAIKIE, J. A. D., Sociology and Anthropology
BRIDGES, R. C., History and Economic History
BRITTON, C. M., French
BRUCE, C., Sociology
BRYDEN, J. M., Geography
BUCKLAND, R., Accountancy
BURGESS, G. J., German
CAMERON, J. R., Philosophy
CAREY-MILLER, D. L., Law
CHAPMAN, K., Geography
CLARK, B., Geography
DAWSON, P. M., Management Studies
DEVINE, T. M., Research Institute of Irish and Scottish Studies
DUFF, P. R., Law
DUKES, P., History and Economic History
DUNKLEY, J., French
EDWARDS, K. J., Geography
ELLIOTT, R. F., Economics
EVANS-JONES, R., Law
FERGUSSON, D. A. S., Divinity with Religious Studies
FORTE, A. D. M., Law
FRASER, P., Accountancy
GANE, C. H. W., Law
GRAHAM, L. G., Philosophy
HARRIS, D. R., Hispanic Studies
HARRISON, R. T., Management Studies
HEALD, D. A., Accountancy
HENDERSHOTT, P. H., Land Economy
HENDRY, L. B., Centre for Educational Research
HEWITT, D. S., English
HOESLI, M. E. R., Accountancy
HOTSON, H., Early Modern History
INGOLD, T., Sociology and Anthropology
JOHNSTONE, W., Divinity with Religious Studies
JORDAN, A. G., Politics and Int. Relations
KEATING, M. J., Politics and Int. Relations
KEMP, A. G., Economics
KIDD, M., Economics
LEBOUTTE, R. F. M. P., History
LEE, C. H., Economics
LYALL, F., Law
MACDONALD, I. R., Hispanic Studies
MACGREGOR, B. D., Land Economy
MACINNES, A. I., History
MANNINGS, D., History of Art
MATHER, A. S., Geography
MATTHEWS, E. H., Philosophy
MCKEE, L., Management Studies
MEEK, D. E., Celtic
MILLER, D., Law
MURRAY, I., English
O'BOYLE, C. J. M., Celtic
OHLMEYER, J., History
PAYNE, P. L., History and Economic History
PORTER, J. W., English (Elphinstone Institute)
ROBERTS, C., Accountancy
ROBERTSON, R., Sociology
ROWAN-ROBINSON, J. R., Law
SALMON, T. C., Politics and Int. Relations
SAUNDERS, A. M., French
SEWEL, J. B., Politics and Int. Relations
SHEEHAN, M. J., Politics and Int. Relations
SHUCKSMITH, D. M., Land Economy

SOULSBY, C., Geography
SWANSON, P., Hispanic Studies
THEODOSSIOU, I., Economics
THOMANECK, J. K. A., German
TORRANCE, I. R., Divinity with Religious Studies
URWIN, D. W., Politics and Int. Relations
VAN DER MERWE, C. G., Law
WALKER, N. C., Law
WALKER, S., Geography
WATSON, F. B., Divinity with Religious Studies
WATSON, G. J. B., English

College of Life Sciences and Medicine (Univ. of Aberdeen, Polworth Bldg, Foresterhill, Aberdeen, AB25 2ZD; tel. (1224) 552504; fax (1224) 840708; internet w3.abdn.ac.uk/medicine):

ALEXANDER, D. A., Mental Health
ASHFORD, M. L. J., Biomedical Sciences
BOOTH, I. R., Microbiology
BROWN, A. J. P., Molecular and Cell Biology
CASSIDY, J., Medicine and Therapeutics (Oncology)
CATTO, G. R. D., Medicine and Therapeutics
DOCHERTY, K., Molecular and Cell Biology (Biochemistry)
EL-OMAR, E. M., Medicine and Therapeutics
FORRESTER, J. V., Ophthalmology
FOTHERGILL, J. E., Molecular and Cell Biology (Biochemistry)
GILBERT, F. J., Radiology
GODDEN, D. J., Highlands and Islands Health Research Institute
GOLDEN, M. H. N., Medicine and Therapeutics
GOODAY, G. W., Molecular and Cell Biology
GOW, N. A. R., Molecular and Cell Biology
GRANT, A. M., Public Health
GREAVES, M., Medicine and Therapeutics (Haematology)
HAITES, N. E., Medicine and Therapeutics, and Molecular and Cell Biology
HAMILTON, W. A., Medical Microbiology
HANNAFORD, P., Primary Care
HARRIS, W. J., Molecular and Cell Biology (Genetics)
HAWKSWORTH, G. M., Biomedical Sciences, and Medicine and Therapeutics
HELMS, P. J. B., Child Health
HUHTANIEMI, I. T., Obstetrics and Gynaecology
HUKINS, D. W. L., Biomedical Physics and Bioengineering
HUTCHISON, J. D., Surgery (Orthopaedics)
KIDD, C., Biomedical Sciences (Physiology)
LITTLE, J., Medicine and Therapeutics (Epidemiology)
LOGAN, S. D., Biomedical Sciences (Neuroscience)
MACLEOD, A. M., Medicine and Therapeutics
MAUGHAN, R. J., Environmental and Occupational Medicine
MCCAIG, C. D., Biomedical Sciences
NEEDHAM, G., Medical Faculty
NORMAN, J. N., General Practice and Primary Care
ODDS, F. C., Molecular and Cell Biology
PENNINGTON, T. H., Medical Microbiology
PERTWEE, R. G., Biomedical Sciences
POPE, M. H., Medicine and Therapeutics
PRICE, D. B., General Practice and Primary Care
PROSSER, J. I., Molecular and Cell Biology
RALSTON, S. H., Medicine and Therapeutics
REES, A. J., Medicine and Therapeutics
REID, D. M., Medicine and Therapeutics
RITCHIE, L. D., General Practice and Primary Care
RUSSELL, E. M., Public Health
SEATON, A., Environmental and Occupational Medicine
SEYMOUR, D. G., Medicine and Therapeutics, and General Practice and Primary Care
SHARP, P. F., Biomedical Physics and Bioengineering
SHAW, D. J., Molecular and Cell Biology
SMITH, W. C. S., Public Health
TEMPLETON, A. A., Obstetrics and Gynaecology
VAN DER MOLEN, T., General Practice and Primary Care
WALKER, F., Pathology
WEBSTER, N. R., Medicine and Therapeutics (Anaesthesia and Intensive Care)
WHALLEY, L. J., Mental Health
WISCHIK, C. M., Mental Health

College of Physical Sciences (Univ. of Aberdeen, King's College, Aberdeen, AB24 3FX; tel. (1224) 272081; fax (1224) 272082; e-mail adf073@abdn.ac.uk):

ALEXANDER, I. J., Plant and Soil Sciences
ARCHBOLD, R. J., Mathematical Sciences
BAKER, M. J., Engineering
BOYLE, P. R., Zoology
CHANDLER, H. W., Engineering
CRAWFORD, J. E., Psychology
DELLA SALA, S. F., Psychology
DEREGOWSKI, J. B., Psychology
DUFFY, J. A., Chemistry
ENGLISH, P. R., Agriculture
FLIN, R., Psychology
FORRESTER, A. R., Chemistry
FREESTON, M. W., Computing Science
GLASSER, F. P., Chemistry
GORMAN, D. G., Engineering
GRAY, P. M. D., Computing Science
HALL, G. S., Mathematical Sciences
HOULIHAN, D. F. J., Zoology
HOWE, R. F., Chemistry
HUBBUCK, J. R., Mathematical Sciences
HUNTER, J., Computing Science
HURST, A., Geology and Petroleum Geology
INGRAM, M. D., Chemistry
JOLLIFFE, I. T., Mathematical Sciences
KILLHAM, K. S., Plant and Soil Sciences
LOGIE, R. H., Psychology
LOMAX, M. A., Agriculture
MACDONALD, D. I. M., Geology and Petroleum Geology
MEHARG, A. A., Plant and Soil Sciences
MILLER, H. G., Agriculture and Forestry
MITCHELL, C. P., Agriculture and Forestry
MORDUE, W., Zoology
NAYLOR, R. E. L., Agriculture
PENMAN, J., Engineering
PLAYER, M. A., Engineering
PRIEDE, I. G., Zoology
RACEY, P. A., Zoology
ROBINSON, D., Plant and Soil Sciences
RODGER, A. A., Engineering
SECOMBES, C. J., Zoology
SLEEMAN, D. H., Computing Science
SPEAKMAN, J. R., Zoology
SPRACKLEN, C. T., Engineering
THOMSON, K. J., Agriculture
VAS, P., Engineering
WIERCIGROCH, M., Engineering
WILLETTS, B. B., Engineering

UNIVERSITY OF ABERTAY DUNDEE

Bell St, Dundee, DD1 1HG
Telephone: (1382) 308000
Fax: (1382) 308877
E-mail: sro@abertay.ac.uk
Internet: www.abertay.ac.uk

Founded 1888 as Dundee Technical Institute, present name and status 1994

Academic year: October to June

Chancellor: Rt Hon. The Lord DOUGLAS CULLEN
Vice-Chancellor and Prin.: Prof. BERNARD KING
Vice-Prin. and Deputy Vice-Chancellor: Prof. NICHOLAS TERRY
Pro-Vice-Chancellor for Acad. Devt: Prof. STEVE OLIVIER
Pro-Vice-Chancellor for Recruitment and Student Experience: Prof. ROSITSA BATESON
Head of Information Services: MICHAEL TURPIE

Library of 120,000 vols, 400 journals
Number of teachers: 380 (230 full-time, 150 part-time)
Number of students: 5,084

HEADS OF SCHOOL

Dundee Business School: Prof. HEATHER TARBERT
School of Computing and Engineering Systems: Dr COLIN MILLER
School of Contemporary Sciences: Prof. JOHN W. PALFREYMAN
School of Social and Health Sciences: RAY LLOYD

UNIVERSITY OF DUNDEE

Dundee, DD1 4HN
Telephone: (1382) 383000
Fax: (1382) 385505
E-mail: university@dundee.ac.uk
Internet: www.dundee.ac.uk

Founded 1881 as Univ. College, Dundee, Royal Charter 1967

Academic year: September to August

Chancellor: Lord NAREN PATEL
Rector: BRIAN COX
Prin. and Vice-Chancellor: Prof. C. PETER DOWNES
Vice-Prin.: Prof. DOREEN CANTRELL (acting)
Vice-Prin.: Prof. J. CALDERHEAD
Vice-Prin.: Prof. CHRISTOPHER WHATLEY
Vice-Prin.: Prof. Dr IRENE LEIGH
Deputy Prin.: Prof. GEORGINA FOLLETT
Sec.: Dr J. MCGEORGE
Librarian: Dr RICHARD PARSONS

Library: see Libraries and Archives
Number of teachers: 3,000
Number of students: 17,000

DEANS

College of Art, Science and Engineering: Prof. ANNE ANDERSON
College of Arts and Social Sciences: Prof. CHRISTOPHER WHATLEY
College of Life Sciences: Prof. M. A. J. FERGUSON
College of Medicine, Dentistry and Nursing: Prof. IRENE LEIGH

PROFESSORS

College of Arts & Social Sciences (Tower Bldng, Dundee, DD1 4HN; tel. (1382) 384935; e-mail cassoffice@dundee.ac.uk; internet http://www.dundee.ac.uk/cass):

ANDREWS-SPEED, C., Energy Policy
BELCHER, C., Law
BENNETT, R., Developmental Biology
BONELL, M., Catchment Science
BROWN, C., Religious and Cultural History
CAMERON, P., International Energy Law and Policy
CHALKLEY, M. J., Economics
CHATTERJI, M., Applied Economics
CHURCHILL, R., Law
COLLISON, D., Accounting and Society
DAY, A., English Literature
DEWHURST, J. H. L., Economic, Social and Regional Statistics
DOBSON, A. P., Politics
FERGUSON, ., Scots Law
FINDLAY, A. M., Geography
FISCHER, M., Psychology
FYFE, N., Human Geography
GUNN, K., Creative Writing

HARRIS, R., Social Care
HASLAM, J., Business Finance
HOBER, K., International Law
HUDSON, B., Education
KELLY, T., Social Work
KITSON, P., English Literature
MCELEAVY, P., Law
MCKEAN, C., Scottish Architectural History
MCLEAN, J., Law
MOLANA, H., Economics
MONTAGNA, ., Economic Studies
POWER, D., Business Finance
RAITT, F., Law
REID, C., Environmental Law
RODRIGUES, S., Science Education
SPRAY, C., Water Science
TOMLINSON, J., Bonar Modern History
WERRITTY, A., Physical Geography
WILLIAMS, J., European Philosophy
WILLSON, P., History
WOUTERS, P., International Water Law and Policy

College of Art, Science & Engineering (Queen Mother Bldg, Dundee, DD1 4HN; tel. (1382) 386610; e-mail case@dundee.ac.uk; internet www.dundee.ac.uk/case/index.htm):

ABEL, E. W., Biomedical Engineering
ARNOTT, J. L., Communication Systems
CHAPLAIN, M. A., Mathematical Biology
COLVIN, C. M., Fine Art Photography
DAVIES, P. A., Fluid Dynamics
DONG, P., Coastal Engineering
FISHER, G. R.,
GILLESPIE, , Sculpture
HANSON, V. L., Inclusive Technologies
INNS, T. G., Design
JENG, D., Civil Engineering
JOHNSON, N. M., Numerical Analysis/Computational Mathematics
LIN, P., Numerical Analysis/Computational Mathematics
MACDONALD, M J S., History Of Scottish Art
MARTIN, T., Animal Conservation
MCKENNA, S. J., Computer Vision
MELZER, A., Foundation Director Of Imsat
MUIR WOOD, D., Geotechnical Engineering
PARTRIDGE, S., Media Art
PRESS, M., Design Policy
REED, C. A., Art And Policy
RENWICK, G. T., Assistive Systems And Healthcare Computing
RICKETTS, I. W.
ROSE, M. J., Physical Electronics
SHEMILT, T. E., Fine Art Printmaking
TRUCCO, E., Inclusive Technologies

Faculty of Education, Social Work and Community Education (Gardyne Rd, Dundee, DD5 1NY; tel. (1382) 464000; fax (1382) 464900; e-mail edusocwk@dundee.ac.uk; internet www.dundee.ac.uk/facedusoc):

BALDWIN, N., Child Care and Protection
DANIEL, D. M., Child Care and Protection
HARTLEY, J. D., Educational Theory and Policy
TOPPING, K. J., Educational and Social Research

Faculty of Engineering and Physical Sciences (Carnegie Bldg, Dundee, DD1 4HN; tel. (1382) 344190; fax (1382) 344389; e-mail engineering@dundee.ac.uk; internet www.dundee.ac.uk/facengphys):

ABEL, E. W., Biomedical Engineering
ARNOTT, J. L., Communications Systems
CHAPLAIN, M. A., Mathematical Biology
DAVIES, M. C. R., Civil Engineering
DAVIES, P. A., Fluid Dynamics
DHIR, R. K., Concrete Technology
FITZGERALD, A. G., Physics
FLETCHER, R., Mathematics
GOODMAN, T. N. T., Applied Analysis
HORNER, R. M. W., Engineering Management
NEWELL, A. F., Electronics and Microcomputer Systems
PANFILOV, A., Mathematical Biology
RICKETTS, I. W., Assistive Systems and Healthcare Computing
VARDY, A. E., Civil Engineering
WATSON, G. A., Numerical Analysis

Faculty of Law (Scrymgeour Bldg, Dundee, DD1 4HN; tel. (1382) 344185; fax (1382) 345094; e-mail lawandaccy@dundee.ac.uk; internet www.dundee.ac.uk/faclawacc):

BELCHER, C. A., Law
BISSETT-JOHNSON, A., Private Law
CAMERON, P. D., International Energy Law and Policy
FERGUSON, P. R., Scots Law
GRINYER, J. R., Accountancy
HELLIER, C. V., Accountancy and Business Finance
NIXON, W. A. J., Accountancy
PAGE, A. C., Public Law
PALMER, K. F., Mineral Policy
POUNDER, D. J., Forensic Medicine
POWER, D. M., Business Finance
REID, C. T., Environmental Law
STEVENS, P., Petroleum Policy and Economics
WALDE, T. W., International Economic, Energy and Natural Resources Law

College of Life Sciences (MSI/WTB/JBC Complex, Dow St, Dundee, DD1 4HN; tel. (1382) 385136; fax (1382) 345519; e-mail d.a.hill@dundee.ac.uk; internet www.lifesci.dundee.ac.uk):

BARTON, G. J., Bioinformatics
BIRCH, P R J, Plant Pathology
BLACK, S M, Anatomy & Forensic Anthropology
BLOW, J. J., Chromosome Maintenance
BROWN, J W S, Molecular Plant Sciences
CODD, G A, Microbiology
FAIRLAMB, A H., Wellcome Trust Building
FLAVELL, A. J., Plant Genomics
GADD, G. M., Microbiology
GILBERT, I H., Medicinal Chemistry
HALPIN, C., Plant Biology And Biotechnology
HARDIE, D. G., Cellular Signalling
HAY, R T., Molecular Biology
HOPKINS, A L, Medicinal Informatics
HUNDAL, H S., Molecular Physiology
HUNTER, W. N., Structural Biology
LAMOND, A I, Biochemistry
LILLEY, D M J, Molecular Biology
NATHKE, I S., Epithelial Biology
OWEN-HUGHES, T. A., Chromatin Structure And Dynamics
PALMER, T., Molecular Microbiology
SARGENT, F., Bacterial Physiology
SCHAAP, P., Developmental Signalling
SOAMES, M., Anatomy
STARK, M. J. R., Yeast Molecular Biology
SWEDLOW, J. R., Quantitative Cell Biology
VAN AALTEN, D. M. F., Biological Chemistry
WATTS, C., Immunobiology
WEIJER, C. J., Developmental Physiology
WILLIAMS, J. A., Developmental Biology
WYATT, P G., Drug Discovery

College of Medicine, Dentistry & Nursing (Ninewells Hospital and Medical School, Dundee, DD1 9SY; tel. (1382) 232763; fax (1382) 644267; e-mail cmdn-office@dundee.ac.uk; internet www.dundee.ac.uk/cmdn):

ABBOUD, R J, Education in Biomechanics
ANDERSON, A. S., Food Choice
ASHFORD, M. L. J., Neuroscience
BALFOUR, D. J. K., Behavioural Pharmacology
BARBOUR, R., Health and Social Care
BARRATT, C., Reproductive Medicine
BEARN, D., Orthodontics
BELCH, J. J. F., Vascular Medicine
CADDEN, S. W., Oral Biology
CLARKE, P. R., Cancer Cell Biology
CLARKSON, J. E., Clinical Effectiveness
COLHOUN, H., Public Health
CROMBIE, I. K., Public Health
DAVEY, P. G., Pharmacoeconomics
DONNAN, P. T., Epidemiology And Biostatistics
ENTWISTLE, V. A., Values In Health Care
EVANS, A., Breast Imaging
FLEMING, S., Cellular and Molecular Pathology
FREEMAN, R. E., Dental Public Health Research
GUTHRIE, B, Primary Care Medicine
HALES, T. G., Anaesthesia
HAYES, J. D., Molecular Carcinogenesis
HIOM, K., Biomedical Research Institute
HOUSTON, S., Imaging
HUME, R., Developmental Medicine
JOVANOVIC, A., Experimental Medicine
KEARNEY, N., Nursing And Midwifery
LAMBERT, J. J., Neuropharmacology
LANG, C. C., Cardiology
LIPWORTH, B. J., Allergy and Respiratory Medicine
MACDONALD, T. M., Clinical Pharmacology and Pharmacoepidemiology
MACFARLAINE, G. T., Bacteriology
MCLEAN, W. H. I., Human Genetics
MCMURDO, M. E. T., Ageing and Health
MIRES, G. J., Perinatal Health And Education
MORRIS, A. D., Diabetic Medicine
MOSSEY, P. A., Craniofacial Dev And Dentofacial Orthopaedics
MUNRO, A. J., Radiation Oncology
OGDEN, G. R., Oral and Maxillofacial Surgery
PALMER, C. N. A., Pharmacogenomics
PARKIN, I. G., Applied Clinical Anatomy
PETERS, J. A., Pharmacolog
PITTS, N. B., Dental Health
RANKIN, E. M., Cancer Medicine
REES, C., Education Research
RICKETTS, D. N. J., Cariology And Conservative Dentistry
SCHWEIGER, S., Molecular Medicine
STEELE, J. D., Neuro-Imaging
STEELE, R. J., Surgery
STONEBRIDGE, P. A., Vascular Surgery
STRUTHERS, A. D., Cardiovascular Medicine and Therapeutics
SULLIVAN, F. M., General Practice and Primary Care
TAYLOR, J. S., Family Health
THOMPSON, A. M., Surgical Oncology
WOLF, C. R., Molecular Pharmacology
WRIGHT, E. G., Experimental Haematology
WYATT, J., Health Informatics

Faculty of Duncan of Jordanstone College (Perth Rd, Dundee, DD1 4HT; tel. (1382) 345213; fax (1382) 227304; internet www.dundee.ac.uk/facdjcad):

COLVIN, C., Fine Art Photography
FISHER, G. R., Sculpture
FOLLETT, G. L. P., Design
INNS, T. G., Design
PARTRIDGE, S., Media Art
ROBB, A., Fine Art
UNWIN, S. D. A., Architecture

UNIVERSITY OF EDINBURGH

Old College, South Bridge, Edinburgh EH8 9YL

Telephone: (131) 650-1000
Fax: (131) 650-2147
E-mail: communications.office@ed.ac.uk
Internet: www.ed.ac.uk

Founded 1583
Academic year: September to June

Chancellor: HRH PRINCE PHILIP, DUKE OF EDINBURGH
Prin.: Prof. Sir TIMOTHY O'SHEA
Rector: IAIN MACWHIRTER

Sec.: Dr KIM WALDRON
Hon. Vice-Prin.: Prof. IAN HOWARD
Vice-Prin. for Academic Enhancement: Prof. DAI HOUNSELL
Vice-Prin. for Devt: YOUNG DAWKINS
Vice-Prin. for Equality and Diversity: Prof. LORRAINE WATERHOUSE
Vice-Prin.l for High Performance Computing: Prof. RICHARD KENWAY
Vice-Prin. for Int. Affairs: Prof. STEVE HILLIER
Vice-Prin. for Knowledge Management and Chief Information Officer: Prof. JEFF HAYWOOD
Vice-Prin. for Planning, Resources and Research Policy: Prof. APRIL MCMAHON
Vice-Prin. for Research Training and Community Relations: Prof. MARY BOWNES
Dir of Registry: RIO WATT
Dir of Finance: JON GORRINGE
Dir of Int. Office: ALAN MACKAY
CEO of Edinburgh Research and Innovation: DEREK WADDELL
Librarian: Prof. JEFF HAYWOOD
Library: see Libraries and Archives
Number of teachers: 2,730
Number of students: 26,951
Publications: *EDIT Magazine* (2 a year), *Scottish Affairs* (4 a year), *Scottish Studies* (1 a year), *The University of Edinburgh Journal* (2 a year)

HEADS OF COLLEGES

Edinburgh College of Art: Prof. IAN HOWARD (Prin.)
College of Humanities and Social Science: Prof. DOROTHY MIELL
College of Medicine and Veterinary Medicine: Prof. Sir JOHN SAVILL
College of Science and Engineering: Prof. NIGEL BROWN

PROFESSORS

College of Humanities and Social Science (Administration Office, 55–56 George Sq., Edinburgh, EH8 9JU; tel. (131) 650-4646; fax (131) 650-6512; internet www.hss.ed.ac.uk):

ABHYONKAR, A., Financial Markets
ADLER, M. E., Socio-Legal Studies
ALTHAUS-REID, M., Contextual Theology
ANDERSON, R. D., Modern History
ANGOLD, M. J., Byzantine History
ANSELL, J. I., Risk Management
ARCHIBALD, T. W., Business Modelling
BAILEY, P., Modern Chinese History
BANKOWSKI, Z., Legal Theory
BANNER, M. C., Ethics and Public Policy in Life Sciences
BARKER, A. W., Austrian Studies
BARNARD, A. J., Anthropology of Southern Africa
BARRINGER, J. M., Greek Art and Archaeology
BARSTAD, H. M., Hebrew and Old Testament Studies
BLOOR, D., Sociology of Science
BLOXHAM, D., Modern History
BOYLE, A. E., Public International Law
BRAY, F., Social Anthropology
BRODIE, D., Employment Law
BROWN, S. J., Ecclesiastical History
BRUCE, V., Psychology
CAIRNS, D. L., Classics
CAIRNS, J. W., Legal History
CAMPBELL, I., Scottish and Victorian Literature
CARR, C. H., Corporate Strategy
CARR, D., Philosophy of Education
CARSTEN, J. F., Social and Cultural Anthropology
CASTLES, F. G., Social and Public Policy
CLARK, A., Logic and Metaphysics
CLARK, C., Social Work Ethics
CLASON, J., Comparative Social Policy
COGLIANO, F. D., American History
COLEBROOK, C. M., Literary Theory
COLVIN, S., German
COWLING, E. G., 20th-century European Art
COX, J. L., Religious Studies
COYNE, A. R., Architectural Computing
CREE, V. E., Social Work Studies
CROOK, J. N., Business Economics
CURRIE, C., Child and Adolescent Health
DAVIDSON, R., Social History
DAWSON, J., Reformation History
DAYAN, P., French
DEARY, I. J., Differential Psychology
DELLA SALA, S., Human Cognitive Neuroscience
DEVINE, T. M., Scottish History and Palaeography
DUFFY, J. H., French
ERSKINE, A., Ancient History
FABRE, C., Political Theory
FERGUSSON, D., Divinity
FERREIRA, F., Language and Cognition
FRANSMAN, M., Economics
FROTH, S., Music
GENTZ, N., Chinese
GIEGERICH, H. J., English Linguistics
GILLIES, W., Celtic Languages, Literature, History and Antiquities
GILMORE, W. C., Int. Criminal Law
GOODE, A., Social Anthropology in Practice
GREASLEY, D. G., Economic History
GREEN, J., Medieval History
GRETTON, G. L., Law
GRIFFITHS, A., Anthropology of Law
GRIFFITHS, M., Classroom Learning
HARDING, D. W., Archaeology
HARDMAN MOORE, J. H., Political Economy
HAYWARD, T., Environmental Political Theory
HAYWOOD, J., Education and Technology
HENDERSON, J., Visual Cognition and Cognitive Neuroscience
HENLEY, J. S., Int. Management
HEYCOCK, C., Syntax
HIGGINS, P., Outdoor and Environmental Education
HILLENBRAND, C., Islamic History
HILLENBRAND, R., Islamic Art
HIMSWORTH, C. M. G., Admin. Law
HOPKINS, E. H. K., Economics
HOUNSELL, D., Higher Education
HURFORD, J. R., General Linguistics
HURTADO, L. W., New Testament Language, Literature and Theology
JACKSON, A., History
JAMIESON, L. H. A., Sociology of Families and Relationships
JEFFERY, C., Politics
JEFFERY, P. M., Sociology
JEFFERY, R., Sociology of South Asia
JEFFREYS-JONES, R., American History
JOSEPH, J. E., Applied Linguistics
KREBER, C., Teaching and Learning in Higher Education
LADD, D. R., Linguistics
LAPSLEY, I. MCL., Accountancy
LAURIE, G. T., Medical Jurisprudence
LIM, T. M., Hebrew Bible and Second Temple Judaism
LINGARD, R., Education
LOGIE, R. H., Human Cognitive Neuroscience
MACDONALD, A. J., Architectural Studies
MACINNES, J., Sociology
MACKENZIE, D. A., Sociology
MACQUEEN, H. L., Private Law
MAHER, G., Criminal Law
MAIN, B. G. M., Business Economics
MANNING, S., English Literature
MARDER, R., Midwifery
MARSHALL, D. W., Marketing and Consumer Behaviour
MCCRONE, D., Sociology
MCDOUGALL, B. S., Chinese
MCMAHON, A., English Language
MCMILLAN, J. F., History
MEEK, D. E., Scottish and Gaelic Studies
MELIA, K. M., Nursing Studies
MEYERHOFF, M., Sociolinguistics
MITCHELL, F., Management Accounting
MOLINA, A. H., Technology Strategy
MUNN, P., Curriculum Research
MUNRO, C. R., Constitutional Law
MYERS, A., Organology
NELSON, P., Music and Technology
NICHOLSON, C. E., 18th-century and Modern Literature
NORTHCOTT, M. S., Ethics
NUGENT, P., Comparative African History
NUTLEY, S., Public Management
O'DONOVAN, O., Christian Ethics and Practical Theology
OLIVER, N., Management
OSBORNE, N., Music
OSBORNE, S., Int. Public Management
OZGA, J., Educational Research
PATERSON, L., Educational Policy
PEDRESCHI, R., Architectural Technology
PELTENBURG, E. J., Archaeology
PETERSON, J., Int. Politics
PICKERING, M., Psychology of Language and Communication
POLLOCK, A., Health Policy
POWER, M. J., Clinical Psychology
PRITCHARD, D., Philosophy
PULLUM, G., General Linguistics
RAAB, C. D., Govt
RAFFE, D., Sociology of Education
RALSTON, I., Prehistoric European Archaeology
REID, K. G. C., Property Law
RIDDELL, S., Inclusion and Diversity
RIDGE, M. R., Moral Philosophy
ROBBINS, J. M. W., Hispanic Studies
RODGER, R., Economic and Social History
ROSA, P., Entrepreneurship and Family Business
SAKOVICS, J., Economic Theory
SANDERS, R., Sport Science
SCALTSAS, T., Ancient Philosophy
SCHOFIELD, J., Healthcare Management
SCOTT, A. G., European Union Studies
SHAW, J., European Institutions
SNELL, A. J., Economics and Econometrics
SORACE, A., Developmental Linguistics
SPARKS, R., Criminology
SPENCER, J., Anthropology of South Asia
STANLEY, E., Sociology
STEPHENSON, A. J. R., Modern German History
STEVENSON, R., 20th-century Literature
TAFFER, R., Finance and Investment
TETT, L., Community Education and Lifelong Learning
THOMAS, J. P., Economics
THOMSON, R., Fine Art
USHER, J., Italian
WASOFF, F., Family Policies
WATERHOUSE, L. A. M., Social Work
WEBB, J., Sociology of Organizations
WHYTE, I. B., Architectural History
WHYTE, W. J., Social Work
WILLIAMS, R., Social Research on Technology
WISHART, J. G., Developmental Disabilities in Childhood
YEARLEY, S., Sociology of Scientific Knowledge

College of Medicine and Veterinary Medicine (The Queen's Medical Research Institute, 47 Little France Crescent, Edinburgh, EH16 4TJ; tel. (131) 242-9300; fax (131) 242-9301; e-mail mvm@ed.ac.uk; internet www.mvm.ed.ac.uk):

AMOS, A., Health Promotion
AMYES, S. G. B., Microbial Chemotherapy
ANDERSON, R., Clinical Reproductive Science
ARGYLE, D., Veterinary Clinical Studies

BACKETH-MILLBURN, K. C., Sociology of Families and Health
BALL, K., Biochemistry and Cell Signalling
BARD, J., Bio-informatics and Devt
BATEMAN, D. N., Clinical Toxicology
BELL, J. E., Neuropathology
BEST, J. J. K., Medical Radiology
BHOPAL, R., Public Health
BLACKWOOD, D., Psychiatric Genetics
BOYD, K. M., Medical Ethics
BROPHY, P. J., Veterinary Anatomy and Cell Biology
CALDER, A. A., Obstetrics and Gynaecology
CAMPBELL, H., Genetic Epidemiology and Public Health
CLUTTON, E., Veterinary Anaesthesiology
CORCORAN, B. M., Veterinary Cardiopulmonary Medicine
CRAWFORD, D. H., Bacteriology
CRITCHLEY, H., Reproductive Medicine
CUMMING, A. D., Medical Education
CUNNINGHAM-BURLEY, S. J., Medical and Family Sociology
DAVIES, J., Experimental Anatomy
DENNIS, M. S., Stroke Medicine
DEWHURST, D., Student Learning (e-Learning)
DIXON, P. M., Equine Surgery
DONALDSON, K., Respiratory Toxicology
DOUGLAS, N. J., Respiratory and Sleep Medicine
DROUSFIELD, I., Leukocyte and Lung Cell Biology
DUNLOP, M. G., Coloproctology
EBMEIER, K. P., Psychiatry
ELSE, R. W., Diagnostic Veterinary Pathology
FALLON, M. T., Palliative Medicine
FAZAKERLEY, J., Virology
FEARON, K. C. H., Surgical Oncology
FFRENCH-CONSTANT, C., Multiple Sclerosis
FLEETWOOD WALKER, S. M., Sensory Neuroscience
FORBES, S. J., Transplantation and Regenerative Medicine
FOWKES, F. G. R., Epidemiology
FOX, K. A. A., Cardiology
GALLY, D. L., Microbial Genetics
GARDEN, O. J., Clinical Surgery
GHAZAL, P., Molecular Genetics and Biomedicine
GOVAN, J. R. W., Microbial Pathogenecity
GRANT, S. G. N., Molecular Neuroscience
GREENING, A. P., Pulmonary Disease
GREGORY, C. D., Inflammatory Cell Biology
GUNN-MOORE, D., Feline Medicine
HARKISS, G. D., Veterinary Immunopathology
HARMAR, A. J., Molecular Pharmacology
HARRISON, D. J., Pathology
HASLETT, C., Respiratory Medicine
HAYES, P. C., Hepatology
HECK, M., Cell Biology and Genetics
HILLIER, S. G., Reproductive Endocrinology
HOOPER, M. L., Molecular Pathology
HOPKINS, J., Veterinary Immunology
HOWIE, S. E. M., Immunopathology
HUPP, E., Cancer Research
IBBETSON, R. J., Dental Primary Care
IREDALE, J., Medicine
IRONSIDE, J. W., Clinical Neuropathology
JARMAN, A. P., Developmental Cell Biology
JODRELL, D., Cancer Therapeutics
JOHNSTONE, E. C., Psychiatry
KAUFMAN, M. H., Anatomy
LAMB, J. R., Veterinary Clinical Immunology
LAWRIE, S. M., Psychiatric Imaging
LENG, G., Experimental Physiology
LINCOLN, Q. A., Biological Tuning
LUDWIG, M., Neurophysiology
MACNEE, W., Respiratory and Environmental Medicine
MACPHERSON, S. G., Postgraduate Medical Education
MARSHALL, I., Magnetic Resonance Physics
MASON, J. I., Clinical Biochemistry
MCCULLOCH, J., Neuropharmacology
MCDICKEN, W. N., Medical Physics and Medical Engineering
MCGORUM, B. C., Equine Medicine
MCINTOSH, N., Child Life and Health
MCQUEEN, D. S., Sensory Pharmacology
MCKEEVER, D., Veterinary Clinical Science
MELTON, D. W., Somatic Cell Genetics
MIMS, R. A., Paediatric Neurology
MORRIS, R. G. M., Neuroscience
MURRAY, G. D., Medical Statistics
MURRAY, S. A., Primary Palliative Care
NASH, A. A., Veterinary Pathology
NEWBY, D., Cardiology
OWENS, D. G. C., Clinical Psychiatry
PETTIGREW, G. W., Bioenergetics
PORTEOUS, D. J., Human Molecular Genetics and Medicine
POWER, I., Anaesthetics, Critical Care and Pain
POXTON, I. R., Microbial Infection and Immunity
PRESCOTT, R. J., Health Technology Assessment
PRICE, D. J., Developmental Neurobiology
RALSTON, S. H., Rheumatology
REES, J. L., Dermatology
RHIND, S. M., Veterinary Medical Education
ROCHESTER, R. R., Cellular Neuroscience
ROSS, J. A., Liver Cell Biology
ROSSI, A., Respiratory and Inflammation Pharmacology
RUSSELL, J. A., Neuroendocrinology
SALLER, D. M., Osteoarticular Pathology
SANDERCOCK, P., Medical Neurology
SATSANGI, J., Gastroenterology
SAVILL, J. S., Experimental Medicine
SECKL, J. R., Molecular Medicine
SETHI, T. J., Respiratory and Lung Cancer Biology
SHARPE, M., Psychological Medicine and Symptoms Research
SHEIKH, A., Primary Care Research and Devt
SHIPSTON, M. J., Physiology
SIMMONDS, P., Virology
SIMPSON, A. H. R. W., Orthopaedic Surgery
SIMPSON, J. W., Canine Medecine
SMYTH, J. F., Medical Oncology
TAYLOR, D. W., Tropical Animal Health
THODAY, K. L., Veterinary Dermatology
TURNER, A. N., Nephrology
TURNER, M., Cellular Therapy
VAN HEYNINGEN, S., Learning and Teaching
WALKER, B. R., Endocrinology
WARDLAW, J. M., Applied Neuroimaging
WARLOW, C. P., Medical Neurology
WATSON, E. D., Veterinary Reproduction
WEBB, D. J., Clinical Pharmacology
WELBURN, S., Medical and Veterinary Molecular Epidemiology
WELLER, D., General Practice
WHITTLE, I. R., Surgical Neurology
WILL, R. G., Clinical Neurology
WILMUT, I., Reproductive Science
WOOLHOUSE, M. E. J., Veterinary Public Health and Quantitative Epidemiology

College of Science and Engineering (Weir Bldg, King's Bldgs, West Mains Rd, Edinburgh, EH9 3JY; tel. (131) 650-5759; fax (131) 650-5738; e-mail sciengmail@ed.ac.uk; internet www.scieng.ed.ac.uk):

ACKLAND, G. J., Computer Simulation
AITKEN, A., Protein Biochemistry
AITKEN, C. G. G., Forensic Statistics
ALLEN, J. E., Immunology
ALLSHIRE, R., Chromosome Biology
ANDERTON, X., Therapeutic Immunology
ARSLAN, T., Integrated Electronic Systems
ATKINSON, M. P., e-Science
ATTFIELD, J. P., Materials Science at Extreme Conditions
BALL, R. D., Mathematical Physics
BARLOW, P. N., Structural Biology
BARTHOLEMIE, R. J., Renewable Energy
BARTON, N. H., Evolutionary Genetics
BAXTER, R. L., Chemical Biology
BEGGS, J. D., Molecular Biology
BIALEK, J. W., Electrical Engineering
BIRD, A. P., Genetics
BISHOP, C. M., Computer Science
BLAXTER, M. L., Evolutionary Genomics
BONDI, E., Social Geography
BOULTON, G. S., Geology
BOWNES, M., Developmental Biology
BRADEN, H. W., Integrable Systems
BRADLEY, M., Chemical Biology
BRAND, P. W. J. L., Astrophysics
BRANDONI, S., Chemical Engineering
BRANFORD, D., Photonuclear Physics
BRUCE, A. D., Statistical Physics
BRYDON, I. G., Renewable Energy
BULFIELD, G., Animal Genetics
BUNDY, A. R., Automated Reasoning
BUNEMAN, P., Database Systems
CAMPBELL, D. M., Musical Acoustics
CARBERY, A., Mathematics
CATES, M., Natural Philosophy
CHAPMAN, S. K., Biological Inorganic Chemistry
CHEUNG, R., Nanoelectronics
CLARKE, P., e-Science
COOPER, J. M., Micro- and Nanosystems
CRAIN, J., Applied Physics
CROWLEY, T., Earth Systems Science
DAVIE, A. M., Mathematical Analysis
DAVIES, M., Signal Processing
DAVIS, I., Cell Biology
DONOVAN, R. J., Chemistry
DUGMORE, A. J., Geosciences
DUNLOP, J. S., Extragalactic Astronomy
EASSON, W. J., Fluid Mechanics
FAN, W., Web Data Management
FARMER, J. G., Environmental Geochemistry
FIGUEROA-O'FARRILL, J., Geometric Physics
FINNEGAN, D. J., Molecular Genetics
FISHER, R. B., Computer Vision
FITTON, J. G., Igneous Petrology
FORDE, M. C., Civil Engineering Construction
FOURMAN, M. P., Computer Systems
FRY, S. C., Plant Biochemistry
GILLESPIE, T. A., Mathematical Analysis
GONDZIS, J., Optimization
GORDON, I., Mathematics
GORYANIN, I., Systems Biology
GRACE, J., Environmental Biology
GRAHAM, C. M., Experimental Geochemistry
GRANT, P. M., Electronic Signal Processing
GRAY, D., Immunology
GYÖNGY, I. J., Probability
HALL, C., Materials
HALLIDAY, I., Physics
HARLEY, S. L., Lower Crustal Processes
HARRISON, A., Solid-State Chemistry
HARTE, B., Metaphorism
HASZELDINE, S., Sedimentary Geology
HEAVENS, A. F., Theoretical Astrophysics
HEGGIE, D. C., Mathematical Astronomy
HILLSTON, J., Quantitative Modelling
HUDSON, A. D., Developmental Genetics
HUXLEY, A., Physics, Quantum Ordering at Extreme Positions
ILLIUS, A. W., Animal Ecology
JACK, M. A., Electronic Systems
JACOBS, J. M., Cultural Geography
JERRUM, M. R., Algorithms and Complexity
KEIGHTLEY, P. D., Evolutionary Genetics
KENNEDY, A. D., Computational Science
KENWAY, R. D., Mathematical Physics
KLEIN, E., Cognitive Systems
KROON, D., Geology
LAWRENCE, A., Astronomy
LEACH, D. R. F., Molecular Genetics
LEIGH, D. A., Organic Chemistry
LEIGH BROWN, A. J., Evolutionary Genetics
LEIM-KUHLER, B., Applied Mathematics

LENAGAN, T. H., Non-commutative Algebra
LIBKIN, L., Foundations of Data Management
LOAKE, G. J., Molecular Plant Sciences
LU, Y., Structural Mechanics
MADDON, P., Physical Chemistry
MAIN, I. G., Seismology and Rock Physics
MAIZELS, R. M., Zoology
MATTHEWS, K., Parasite Biology
MCKINNON, K. I. M., Operational Research
MCLAUGHLIN, S., Electronic Communications Systems
MCMAHON, M., High Pressure Physics
MCNABB, H., Heterocyclic Chemistry
MEDVINSKY, A., Haematopoietic Stem Cell Biology
METCALFE, S. E., Environmental Change
MILLER, A. J., Systems Biology
MONCRIEFF, J., Micrometeorology
MOORE, J. D., Artificial Intelligence
MULGREW, B., Signals and Systems
MULHEIM, F., Particle Physics
MURRAY, A. F., Neural Electronics
NEE, S., Social Evolution
NELMES, R. J., Physical Crystallography
O'BOYLE, M., Computer Science
OBERLANDER, J., Epistemics
OOI, J., Particulate Solid Mechanics
OPARKA, K. J., Plant Science
PARKER, D. F., Applied Mathematics
PARSONS, S., Crystallography
PEACOCK, J. A., Cosmology
PEMBERTON, J. M., Molecular Ecology
PLAYFER, S. M., Experimental Particle Physics
PLOTKIN, G. D., Computation Theory
PONTON, J. W., Chemical and Process Systems Engineering
POON, W. C. K., Condensed Matter Physics
PUSEY, P. N., Physics
RANICKI, A. A., Algebraic Surgery
RANKIN, D. W. H., Structural Chemistry
READ, A. F., Natural History
REID, G. A., Molecular Microbiology
RENALS, S., Speech Technology
RESBOL, N. D., Fungal Cell Biology
ROBERTSON, A. H. F., Geology
ROTTER, J. M., Civil Engineering
ROUNSEVELL, M., Rural Economy and Environmental Sustainability
SANNELLA, D. T., Computer Science
SAWYER, L., Biomolecular Structure
SCHÄFER, A., Environmental Engineering
SEATON, N. A., Interfacial Engineering
SHEIKHDESLAMI, R., Chemical Process Engineering
SHOTTER, A. C., Experimental Physics
SIEGERT, M. J., Geoscience
SINGER, M., Geometry
SMOKTURNOWICZ, A., Algebra
STAEHELI, L., Geography
STEEDMAN, M., Cognitive Science
STENNING, K., Human Communications
STIRLING, C., Computation Theory
SUGDEN, D. E., Geography
SUMMERFIELD, M. A., Geomorphology
TASKER, P. A., Industrial Chemistry
TATE, A., Knowledge-based Systems
TELEMAN, C., Mathematics
TETT, S. F. B., Earth Systems Dynamics
THOMPSON, R., Environmental Geophysics
TOPHAM, N. P., Computer Systems
TORERO, J. L., Fire Safety Engineering
TREW, A. S., Computational Science
TUDHOPE, A. W., Climate Science
TYER, S. M. D., Systems Biology
UNDERHILL, J. R., Seismic Stratigraphy
UNDERWOOD, I., Electronic Displays
USAMI, A. S., Structural Engineering and Computational Mechanics
VOLBERG, A., Mathematical Sciences
WALDER, P., Theoretical Computer Science
WALKINSHAW, M. D., Structural Biochemistry
WALLACE, A. R., Renewable Energy Systems
WALTON, A. J., Microelectronic Manufacturing
WEBBER, B., Intelligent Systems
WEST, S. A., Evolutionary Ecology
WHALER, K. A., Geophysics
WHITTEMORE, C. T., Agriculture and Rural Economy
WILLIAMS, C. K. I., Machine Learning
WILLIAMS, W., Mineral Physics
WILLSHAW, D., Computational Neurobiology
WITHERS, C. W. J., Geography
WOODS, P. J., Nuclear Physics
WRIGHT, J., Mathematical Analysis
YELLOWLEES, L. J., Inorganic Electrochemistry
ZIOLKOWSKI, A. M., Petroleum Geoscience

CONSTITUENT COLLEGE

New College: Mound Pl., Edinburgh, EH1 2LX; f. 1846; Prin. Rev. Prof. A. G. AULD.

UNIVERSITY OF GLASGOW

Glasgow, G12 8QQ
Telephone: (141) 330-2000
Fax: (141) 330-4808
E-mail: media@gla.ac.uk
Internet: www.gla.ac.uk

Founded 1451, reconstituted 1577
Academic year: October to June

Chancellor: Prof. Sir KENNETH CALMAN
Prin. and Vice-Chancellor: Prof. ANTON MUSCATELLI
Pro-Vice-Prin.: Prof. JOHN COGGINS
Sr Vice-Prin. and Deputy Vice-Chancellor: ANDREA NOLAN
Vice-Prin. for Learning and Teaching: Prof. FRANK COTON
Vice-Prin. for Life Sciences and Medicine: Prof. JOHN COGGINS
Vice-Prin. for Research and Enterprise: Prof. STEVE P. BEAUMONT
Vice-Prin. for Strategy and Resources: Prof. NEAL JUSTER
Clerk of Senate: Prof. GRAHAM CAIE
Rector: CHARLES KENNEDY
Sec. of Court: DAVID NEWALL
Librarian: HELEN DURNDELL

Library: see Libraries and Archives
Number of teachers: 2,607
Number of students: 21,954

Publications: *Avenue* (2 a year), *News Review* (2 a year)

HEADS OF COLLEGES AND SCHOOLS

Arts Lab: Prof. JOHN CAUGHIE (Dir)
Business School: Prof. FARHAD NOORBAKHSH
College of Arts: Prof. MURRAY PITTOCK
College of Medical, Veterinary and Life Sciences: Prof. ANNA DOMINICZAK
College of Science and Engineering: Prof. JOHN CHAPMAN
College of Social Sciences: Prof. ANNE ANDERSON
School of Chemistry: Prof. STEPHEN CLARK
School of Computing Science: Prof. JOSEPH S. SVENTEK
School of Critical Studies: Prof. NIGEL J. LEASK
School of Culture and Creative Arts: Prof. NICHOLAS J. PEARCE
School of Education: Prof. ROBERT A. DAVIS
School of Engineering: Prof. JOHN H. MARSH
School of Geographical and Earth Sciences: Prof. TREVOR HOEY
School of Humanities/Sgoil nan Daonnachdan: Prof. SIMON J. BALL
School of Interdisciplinary Studies: Prof. DAVID CLARK (Dir)
School of Law: Prof. ROSA GREAVES
School of Life Sciences: Dr ROBERT AITKEN
School of Mathematics and Statistics: Prof. NICHOLAS A. HILL
School of Medicine: Prof. DAVID H. BARLOW
School of Modern Languages and Cultures: Prof. JOHN MACKLIN
School of Physics and Astronomy: Prof. ANDREW R. LONG
School of Psychology: Prof. ANTHONY M. BURTON
School of Social and Political Sciences: Prof. MICHAEL J. FRENCH
School of Veterinary Medicine: Prof. STUART W. REID

PROFESSORS

Faculty of Arts (6 University Gardens, Glasgow, G12 8QQ; tel. (141) 330-6319; fax (141) 330-4537; e-mail dean@arts.gla.ac.uk; internet www.arts.gla.ac.uk):

ABRAMS, L. C., Gender History
ADAMS, A. R., Emblem Studies
BISHOP, P. C., German
BLACK, C. F., Italian History
BROADIE, A., Logic and Rhetoric
BUTT, J. A., Music (Gardiner Chair)
CAIE, G. D., English Language
CARTER, A. B., Moral Philosophy
CASTILLO, S., American Literature (John Nichol Chair)
CAUGHIE, J. M., Film and Television Studies
CLANCY, T. O., Celtic
COHN, S. K., Medieval History
COWAN, E. J., Scottish History
CRONIN, R., English Literature
GERAGHTY, C., Film and TV Studies
GEYER-KORDESCH, J. M., European Natural History and Medicine
GIFFORD, D. G., Scottish Literature
GONZALEZ, M. A., Latin American Studies
GRANT, R. A., Cultural and Political Thought
GREEN, R. P., Humanity
HAIR, G. B., Music
HANSON, W. S., Roman Archaeology
HAZLETT, W. I., Ecclesiastical History
HOPKINS, D., Art History
JASPER, D., Literature and Theology
KAY, C. J., English Language
KIDD, C., Modern History (Chair)
KIRK, J., Scottish History
KNAPP, A. B., Mediterranean Archaeology
KNOWLES, D. R., Political Philosophy
LEASK, N., English Language and Literature (Regius Chair)
LEONARD, T. A., Creative Writing
MACKENZIE, A. L., Spanish (Ivy McClelland Research Chair)
MACMAHON, M. K. C., Phonetics
MALEY, W. T., Renaissance Studies
MARSHALL, W. J., Modern French Studies
MAWDSLEY, E., International History
MCDONALD, J. B., Drama (James Arnott Chair)
MCLEOD, M. D., African Studies
MOIGNARD, E. A., Classical Art and Archaeology
MORRIS, C. D., Archaeology
MOSS, M. S., Archival Studies
NEWLANDS, G. M., Divinity
NEWMAN, S. P., American Studies (Sir Denis Brogan Chair)
O'MAOLALAIGH, R., Celtic
O'DOCHARTAIGH, C. N. O., Celtic
PEACOCK, N. A., French (Marshall Chair)
READER, K. A., Modern French Studies
RIACH, A. S., Scottish Literature
ROBERTSON, P. B., Mackintosh Studies
ROSS, S., Humanities Informatics and Digital Curation
RYCROFT, M. E., Music
SCHMIDT-LEUKEL, P. H., World Religions for Peace
SMITH, J. J., English Philology
STALLEY, R. F., Ancient Philosophy

STEPHENSON, R. H., German Language and Literature; Modern Languages (William Jacks Chair)
TAYLOR, R. C., Social Policy and Social Work
THORP, N. R., History of Art
TODD, J., English Literature (Francis Hutcheson Chair)
WARD, M. G., German Language and Literature
YARRINGTON, A. W., Fine Art (Richmond Chair)

Faculty of Biomedical and Life Sciences (Room 237, West Medical Bldg, Glasgow, G12 8QQ; tel. (141) 339-8855; fax (141) 330-4758; e-mail ilbs-acstaff@bio.gla.ac.uk; internet www.gla.ac.uk/ibls/faculty/html):

BIRKBECK, T. H., Marine Microbiology
BLATT, M. R., Botany (Regius Chair)
CAMPBELL, A. M., Biochemical Immunology
CLEMENTS, J. B., Virology
COGDELL, R. J., Botany (Hooker Chair)
COGGINS, J. R., Molecular Enzymology
COOMBS, G. H., Biochemical Parasitology
CROZIER, A., Plant Biochemistry and Human Nutrition
CUSHLEY, W., Molecular Immunology
DAVIES, R. W., Biotechnology (Robertson Chair)
DOW, J. A. T., Molecular and Integrative Physiology
ELLIOTT, R. M., Molecular Virology
EVANS, D. J., Virology
FERRELL, W. R., Clinical Physiology
FURNESS, R. W., Seabird and Fishing Interactions
GILLESPIE, D. A. F., Molecular and Cell Biology
GOULD, G. W., Membrane Biology
HAGAN, P., Parasitology
HOUSLAY, M. D., Biochemistry (Gardiner Chair)
HOUSTON, D. C., Zoology
HUNTINGFORD, F. A., Functional Ecology
JENKINS, G. I., Plant Cell and Molecular Biology
KENNEDY, M. W., Infection Biology
KOLCH, W., Molecular and Cellular Biology
LA THANGUE, N. B., Biochemistry (Cathcart Chair)
LINDSAY, J. G., Medical Biochemistry
MACLEAN, M. R., Pulmonary Pharmacology
MARTIN, W., Cardiovascular Pharmacology
MAXWELL, D. J., Neuroanatomy
MCGRATH, J. C., Physiology (Regius Chair)
METCALFE, N. B., Behavioural Ecology
MILLIGAN, G., Molecular Pharmacology
MILNER-WHITE, E.J., Structural Bioinformatics
MITCHELL, T. J., Microbiology
MONAGHAN, P., Animal Ecology
MONCKTON, D. G., Human Genetics
MORRIS, B. J., Molecular Neurobiology
MUTRIE, N., Physical Activity and Health Science
NIMMO, H. G., Plant Biochemistry
PAGE, R. D., Taxonomy
PAYNE, A. P., Anatomy
PHILLIPS, R. S., Parasitology
PRICE, N. C., Protein Science
RUXTON, G. D., Theoretical Ecology
SMITH, G. L., Cardiovascular Physiology
STARK, W. M., Molecular Genetics
STONE, T. W., Pharmacology
TAYLOR, A. C., Physiological Ecology
TODD, A. J., Neuroscience
TURNER, C. M. R., Parasitology
WHITE, R. J., Gene Transcription

Faculty of Education (St Andrew's Bldg, Glasgow, G12 8QQ; tel. (141) 330-3700; fax (141) 330-3005; e-mail faculty@educ.gla.ac.uk; internet www.gla.ac.uk/faculties/education):

BARON, S., Urban Education
BARR, J. L., Adult and Continuing Education
CONROY, J. C., Religious and Philosophical Education
MCGETTRICK, B. J., Educational Studies
MCGONIGAL, J., English in Education
MENTER, I. J., Teacher Education
PETERS, M. A., Education
PREECE, J., Adult and Lifelong Education
WHITEHEAD, R. R., Theoretical Physics
WILKINSON, J. E., Education

Faculty of Engineering (James Watt South Bldg, Glasgow, G12 8QQ; tel. (141) 330-3733; fax (141) 330-4722; internet www.eng.gla.ac.uk):

ACHA, E., Electrical Power Systems
AITCHISON, J. S., Photonics
ARNOLD, J. M., Applied Electromagnetics
ASENOV, A. M., Device Modelling
BARKER, J. R., Electronics
BARLTROP, N. D. P., Naval Architecture and Ocean Engineering (John Elder Chair)
BICANIC, N. J. D., Civil Engineering (Regius Chair)
CARTMELL, M. P., Mechanical Engineering
COOPER, J. M., Bioelectronics and Bioengineering
COTON, F. N., Low Speed Aerodynamics
COWLING, M. J., Marine Technology
CUMMING, D., Microelectronics
DAS, P. K., Marine Structures
DAVIES, J. H., Physical Electronics
DE LA RUE, R. M., Optoelectronics
ERVINE, D. A., Water Engineering
GALBRAITH, R. A. M., Engineering (Shoda Chair)
HANCOCK, J. W., Mechanical Engineering
HUNT, K. J., Mechanical Engineering (Wylie Chair)
HUTCHINGS, D., Optical and Quantum Electronics
IRONSIDE, C. N., Quantum Electronics
MARSH, J. H., Optoelectronic Systems
MCINNES, C. R., Space Systems Engineering
MILLER, T. J. E., Electrical Engineering
MURRAY-SMITH, D. J., Engineering Systems and Control
O'REILLY, J., Control Engineering
SEWELL, J. I., Electronic Systems
STANLEY, C. R., Semiconductor Materials
THAYNE, I., Ultrafast Systems
VASSALOS, D., Naval Architecture
WEAVER, J. M. R., Applied Nanofabrication
WHEELER, S. J., Civil Engineering (Cormack Chair)
WILKINSON, C. D. W., Electrical Engineering (James Watt Chair)

Faculty of Information and Mathematical Sciences (Room 311, Boyd Orr Bldg, Glasgow, G12 8QQ; tel. (141) 330-4269; fax (141) 330-2359; e-mail gs@fims.gla.ac.uk; internet www.gla.ac.uk/faculties/ims):

ANDERSON, A. H., Psychology
ATKINSON, M. P., Computing Science
BOWMAN, A. W., Statistics
BREWSTER, S. A., Human Computer Interaction
BROWN, K. A., Mathematics
BURTON, A. M., Psychology
CALDER, M., Formal Methods
COHEN, S. D., Number Theory
FEARN, D. R., Applied Mathematics
FORD, I., Biostatistics
GARROD, S. C., Cognitive Psychology
GILBERT, D. R., Biomedical Informatics
HILL, N. A., Mathematics (Simson Chair)
JOHNSON, C. W., Computing Science
JONES, B. T., Psychology
KROPHOLLER, P. H., Mathematics
O'DONNELL, P.
OGDEN, R. W., Mathematics (George Sinclair Chair)
PRIDE, S. J., Mathematics
SANFORD, A. J., Psychology
SCHWEINBERGER, S. R., Psychology
SCHYNS, P. G., Visual Cognition
SCOTT, E. M., Environmental Statistics
SENN, K.S. J., Statistics
SMITH, P. F., Mathematics
SVENTEK, J., Communications Systems
TITTERINGTON, D. M., Statistics
VAN RIJSBERGEN, K.J., Computing Science
WATT, D. A., Computing Science
WEBB, J. R. L., Mathematics
WELLAND, R. C., Software Engineering

Faculty of Law and Financial Studies (5–9 Stair Bldg, The Square, Univ. of Glasgow, Glasgow, G12 8QQ; tel. (141) 330-6075; fax (141) 330-4900; e-mail faculty@law.gla.ac.uk; internet www.gla.ac.uk/faculties/law):

BEATTIE, V. A., Accounting
BURROWS, N., European Law
CRERAR, L. D., Banking Law
DANBOLT, J., Finance
DAVIDSON, F. P., Law, Commercial Law (Alexander Stone Chair)
EMMANUEL, C. R., Accountancy
FARMER, L. A., Law
GRAY, R. H., Accounting
HOLLAND, J. B., Accountancy
KINNON, D. H., Accounting (Johnstone Smith Chair)
MCLEAN, S. A., Law and Ethics in Medicine (International Bar Assoc Chair)
MCPHAIL, K., Social and Ethical Accounting
MULLEN, T. J., Law
MURDOCH, J. L., Public Law
OPONG, K. K., Finance and Accounting
ORUCU, E., Comparative Law
REES, W., Accountancy
RENNIE, R., Conveyancing
SHACKLETON, J. K., Accounting History
THOMSON, J. M., Law (Regius Chair)
TOMKINS, A., Public Law (John Millar Chair)
WOOLFSON, C. A., Labour Studies

Faculty of Medicine (Wolfson Medical Bldg, University Ave, Univ. of Glasgow, Glasgow, G12 8QQ; tel. (141) 330-5921; fax (141) 330-3360; e-mail postmaster@student.gla.ac.uk; internet www.gla.ac.uk/faculties/medicine):

AYOUB, A. F., Oral Surgery
BAGG, J., Clinical Microbiology
BAKER, A. H., Molecular Medicine
BARLOW, D. H., Reproductive Medicine
BROWN, R., Cancer Therapeutics
CASSIDY, J., Oncology
COBBE, S. M., Medical Cardiology (Walton Chair)
CONNELL, J. M. C., Endocrinology
CONNOR, J. M., Medical Genetics (Burton Chair)
COOKE, T. G., Surgery (St Mungo Chair)
COOPER, S. A., Learning Disabilities
DOMINICZAK, A. F., Cardiovascular Medicine
ELLIOTT, A. T., Clinical Physics
ESPIE, C. A., Clinical Psychology
EVANS, J. J., Applied Neuropsychology
EVANS, T. J., Molecular Microbiology
FRANKLIN, I. M., Transfusion Medicine
GARSIDE, P., Immunobiology
GEMMELL, C. G., Bacterial Infection and Epidemiology
GEORGE, W. D., Surgery (Regius Chair)
GRAHAM, G. J., Molecular and Structural Immunology
GREER, I. A., Obstetrics and Gynaecology (Muirhead Chair)
GUSTERSON, B. A., Pathology
HANLON, P. W., Public Health
HARNETT, M. M., Immune Signalling
HILLAN, E. M., Midwifery
HILLIS, W. S., Cardiovascular and Exercise Medicine
HOLE, D. J., Epidemiology and Biostatistics
HOLYOAKE, T., Experimental Haematology

JUDGE, K. F., Health Promotion Policy (HEBS Chair)
KEITH, W. N., Molecular Oncology
KENNEDY, P. G. E., Neurology (Burton Chair)
KENNY, G. N. C., Anaesthesia
LANGHORNE, P., Stroke Care
LEAN, M. E. J., Human Nutrition (Rank Chair)
LEES, K. R., Cerebrovascular Medicine
LIEW, F. Y., Immunology (Gardiner Chair)
LOWE, G. D. O., Vascular Medicine
LUMSDEN, M. A., Medical Education and Gynaecology
LYALL, F., Maternal and Fetal Health
MACDONALD, D. G., Oral Pathology
MACFARLANE, P. W., Electrocardiology
MACRAE, I. M., Neuroscience
MCCOLL, K. E. L., Gastroenterology
MCINNES, G. T., Clinical Pharmacology
MCINNES, I. B., Experimental Medicine
MCKILLOP, J. H., Medicine (Muirhead Chair)
MCMILLAN, T., Clinical Neuropsychology
MCMURRAY, J. I. V., Medical Cardiology
MILLAR, K., Behavioural Science
MORRISON, J. M., General Practice
MOWAT, A. M., Mucosal Immunology
MURRAY, T. S., General Practice
O'DWYER, P. J., Gastrointestinal Surgery
OLIVER, J. S., Forensic Toxicology
RAMPLING, R. P., Neuro-oncology
REID, J. L., Materia Medica, Medicine and Therapeutics (Regius Chair)
REID, M., Professor of Women's Health
SATTAR, N. A., Metabolic Medicine
SHEPHERD, J., Pathological Biochemistry
SMITH, L. N., Nursing Studies
STONE, D. H., Paediatric Epidemiology
STOTT, D. J., Geriatric Medicine (David Cargill Chair)
STURROCK, R. D., Rheumatology (McLeod/ Arthritis and Rheumatism Council Chair)
THOMSON, N. C., Respiratory Medicine
WATT, G. C. M., General Practice (Norrie-Miller Chair)
WEAVER, L. T., Child Health (Samson Gemmell Chair)
WELBURY, R. R., Paediatric Dentistry
WELSH, J., Palliative Medicine (Dr Olav Kerr Chair)
WHEATLEY, D. J., Cardiac Surgery
WILLISON, H. J., Neurology
WRAY, D., Oral Medicine

Faculty of Physical Sciences (Room 234, Kelvin Bldg, Univ. of Glasgow, Glasgow, G12 8QQ; tel. (141) 330-4374; fax (141) 330-4371; e-mail physci@gla.ac.uk; internet www.facps.gla.ac.uk):

BARRON, L. D., Physical Chemistry (Gardiner Chair)
BISHOP, P. M., Geography
BRIGGS, J. A., Geography
BROWN, J. C., Astrophysics, Astronomy (Regius Chair)
BROWN, R. W., Earth Sciences
CHAPMAN, J. N., Physics
COOPER, A., Biophysical Chemistry
CRAVEN, A. J., Physics
DAVIES, C. T., Physics
DOYLE, A. T., Physics
FALLICK, A. E., Isotope Geosciences
FROGGATT, C. D., Physics
GILMORE, C. J., Crystallography
HOEY, T., Numerical Geoscience
HOUGH, J., Physics
ISAACS, N. W., Protein Crystallography (Joseph Black Chair)
JACKSON, S. D., Catalysis Science
KOCOVSKY, P., Chemistry (Ramsay Chair)
LEAKE, R. E., Endocrine Oncology
LONG, A. R., Physics
PADDISON, R., Geography
PADGETT, M. J., Physics
PHILO, C., Geography
ROBERTSON, N. A., Experimental Physics
ROBINS, D. J., Bio-organic Chemistry
ROSNER, G., Natural Philosophy (Cargill Chair)
RUSSELL, M. J., Applied Geology (Dixon Chair)
SAXON, D. H., Physics (Kelvin Chair)
STRAIN, K. A., Physics
WILSON, C., Chemistry (Regius Chair)
WINFIELD, J. M., Inorganic Chemistry

Faculty of Social Sciences (Adam Smith Bldg, 40 Bute Gardens, Glasgow, G12 8RT; tel. (141) 330-0347; fax (141) 330-3547; e-mail enquiries@socsci.gla.ac.uk; internet www.gla.ac.uk/faculties/socialsciences):

ADAMS, C. D., Ian Mactaggart Chair of Property and Urban Studies
BEAUMONT, P. B., Employee Relations
BERRY, C. J., Political Theory
BURMAN, M., Criminology
CORRIN, C. A., Feminist Politics
CROWTHER, M. A., Social History
FERGUSON, H., Sociology
FRENCH, M. J., Economic History
FRISBY, D. P., Sociology
FURLONG, A., Sociology
GIRVIN, B., Comparative Politics
GOODLAD, R., Housing and Urban Studies
GORDON, E. J., Gender and Social History
HARRIS, R., Cairncross Professor of Applied Economics
HILL, M., Study of the Child (St Kentigern Chair)
KEARNS, A. J., Urban Studies
LAING, A. W., Business and Management
MACBETH, D. K., Supply Chain Management
MACDONALD, R., Bonar-Macfie Chair of Economics
MACLENNAN, D., Urban Studies, Economics and Finance (Mactaggart Chair of Urban Studies)
MALLEY, J., Economics
MCGREGOR, A. M., Housing and Urban Studies
MCKEGANEY, N. P., Drug Misuse Research
MILLER, W. L., Politics (Edward Caird Chair)
MOUTINHO, L. A., Marketing
MUSCATELLI, A., Economics (Daniel Jack Chair)
NOORBAKHSH, F., Development Economics
ORME, J. E., Social Work
PARR, J. B., Regional and Urban Economics
PATON, R. A., Management
PETCH, A. J., Nuffield Trust Professor of Community Care
PETERSON, J. C., European Politics (Jean Monnet Chair)
PHILO, G., Communications and Social Change
SCHENK, C., International Economic History
STOKES, R. G., International Industrial History
TUROK, I. N., Urban Economic Development
VIRDEE, S., Sociology
WATSON, N., Disability Studies
WEAVER, R., Entrepreneurship
WHITE, J. D., Russian and East European History
WHITE, S. L., Government
WILSON, F. M., Organizational Behaviour

Faculty of Veterinary Medicine (464 Bearsden Rd, Glasgow, G61 1QH; tel. (141) 330-5700; fax (141) 942-7215; internet www.gla.ac.uk/faculties/vet):

BARRY, J. D., Molecular Parasitology
BENNETT, D., Small Animal Clinical Studies
CAMERON, E. R., Molecular and Cellular Oncology
CAMPO, M. S., Viral Oncology
CARMICHAEL, S., Veterinary Clinical Studies
DEVANEY, E., Parasite Immunobiology
ECKERSALL, P. D., Veterinary Biochemistry
FITZPATRICK, J. L., Farm Animal Medicine
GRIFFITHS, I., Comparative Neurology
HOLMES, P. H., Veterinary Physiology
JARRETT, R. F., Molecular Pathology
LOVE, S., Equine Clinical Studies
MOTTRAM, J. C., Molecular and Cellular Parasitology
NASH, A. S., Small Animal Medicine
NEIL, J. C., Virology and Molecular Oncology
NOLAN, A., Veterinary Pharmacology
ONIONS, D. E., Veterinary Pathology
O'SHAUGHNESSY, P. J., Reproductive Biology
PALMARINI, M., Molecular Pathogenesis
PARKINS, J. J., Animal Health
REID, J., Veterinary Anaesthesia
REID, S. W. J., Veterinary Informatics and Epidemiology
ROBERTS, M., Molecular Bacteriology
STEAR, M. J., Veterinary Medicine
SULLIVAN, M., Veterinary Surgery and Diagnostic Imaging
TAIT, A., Veterinary Parasitology
TAYLOR, D. J., Veterinary Bacteriology and Public Health

Hunterian Museum and Art Gallery: (see Museums and Art Galleries)

UNIVERSITY OF ST ANDREWS

St Andrews KY16 9AJ
Telephone: (1334) 476161
Internet: www.st-and.ac.uk
Founded 1413
Chancellor: The Hon. Sir MENZIES CAMPBELL
Prin. and Vice-Chancellor: Prof. Dr LOUISE RICHARDSON
Deputy Prin. and Vice-Prin. for Research: Prof. CHRISTOPHER HAWKESWORTH
Vice-Prin. for External Relations: STEPHEN MAGEE
Vice-Prin. for Governance and Planning: Prof. RONALD PIPER
Vice-Prin. for Learning and Teaching: Prof. PAT WILLMER
Rector: KEVIN DUNION
Master of the United College: Prof. NEVILLE V. RICHARDSON
Proctor: Prof. PETER CLARK
Quaestor and Factor: DEREK WATSON
Dir of Library Services: JEREMY UPTON (acting)
Library: see Libraries and Archives
Number of teachers: 935
Number of students: 7,730

DEANS

Faculty of Arts: Prof. ROY DILLEY
Faculty of Divinity: Prof. IVOR DAVIDSON
Faculty of Medicine: Prof. HUGH MACDOUGALL
Faculty of Science: Prof. ALYSON TOBIN

PROFESSORS

Faculty of Arts:

BARTLETT, R. J., Medieval History
BEATH, J. A., Economics and Finance
BEBBINGTON, J., Management
BENTLEY, M. J., Modern History
BROADIE, S., Moral Philosophy
BROWN, K. M., Scottish History
CARRADICE, I. A., Art History
CHAMBERS, H. E., German
CRAWFORD, R., English
DAVIES, H. T. O., Management
DE GROOT, G. J., Modern History
DENNIS, N., Spanish
DUNN, D. E., English
FERGUSON, R., French

FITZROY, F. R., Economics and Finance
GIVEN-WILSON, C. J., Medieval History
GOW, P., Philosophical and Anthropological Studies
GRATWICK, A., Classical Philology
GRAY, R. H., Management
HALDANE, J. J., Moral Philosophy
HALLIWELL, F. S., Greek
HARRIES, J. D., Ancient History
HINNEBUSCH, R., International Relations
HOUSTON, R. A., Modern History
HUDSON, J., History
HUGHES-HALLETT, A., Economics and Finance
HUMFREY, P., Art History
LITTLER, C., Management Centre for Business Education
MAGDALINO, P., Medieval History
MCKIERNAN, P., Management
MCKINLAY, A., Management
NOLAN, C., Economics and Finance
PETTEGREE, A. D. M., Modern History
POLLMANN, K., Classics
PRIEST, G., Philosophy
RAPPORT, N. J., Social Anthropology
REID, G. C., Economics and Finance
RENGGER, N. J., International Relations
RHODES, N., English
ROE, N. H., English
SCOTT, H. M., Modern History
SELLERS, S. C., English
SKORUPSKI, J., Moral Philosophy
SMITH, C. J., Classics
SUTHERLAND, A. J., Economics and Finance
WALKER, W. B., International Relations
WOOLF, G. D., Classics
WRIGHT, C. J. G., Logic and Metaphysics

Faculty of Divinity:

ESLER, P. F., Divinity
HART, T. A., Divinity
PIPER, R. A., Divinity
TORRANCE, A. J., Divinity

Faculty of Medicine:

HERRINGTON, S., Medicine
HUMPHRIS, G., Medicine
MACDOUGALL, R. H., Medicine
RICHES, A., Medicine

Faculty of Science:

BALLANTYNE, C. K., Geography and Geosciences
BOYD, I., Biology
BOYLE, P. J., Geography and Geosciences
BROWN, V., Psychology
BRUCE, P. G., Chemistry
BUCKLAND, S. T., Mathematics and Statistics
BYRNE, R. W., Psychology
CAIRNS, R. A., Applied Mathematics
CAMERON, A. C., Physics and Astronomy
COLE-HAMILTON, D. J., Chemistry
DEARLE, A., Computer Science
DHOLAKIA, K., Physics and Astronomy
DRITSCHEL, D. G., Mathematics
DUNN, M. H., Photonics
FALCONER, K. J., Mathematics and Statistics
FLOWERDEW, R., Geography and Geosciences
HARWOOD, J., Biology
HOOD, A. W., Mathematics
HORNE, K. D., Physics and Astronomy
IRVINE, J. T. S., Chemistry
JOHNSTON, I. A., Comparative Physiology
KRAUSS, T. F., Physics and Astronomy
LEE, S., Physics and Astronomy
LEONHARDT, U., Physics and Astronomy
MACKENZIE, A., Physics and Astronomy
MACLEOD, M., Psychology
MAGURRAN, A. E., Biology
MEAGHER, T. R., Biology
MORRIS, R., Chemistry
NAISMITH, J. H., Chemistry
O'HAGAN, D., Chemistry
PATERSON, D. M., Biology
PERRETT, D. I., Psychology
PRIEST, E. R., Theoretical Solar Physics
RANDALL, R. E., Biology
REICHER, S., Psychology
RICHARDSON, N. V., Chemistry
RITCHIE, M. G., Biology
ROBERTS, B., Mathematics
SAMUEL, I., Physics and Astronomy
SIBBETT, W., Natural Philosophy
SILLAR, K. T., Biology
TAYLOR, G. L., Biology
TODD, C. D., Biology
WALTON, J. C., Chemistry
WHITEN, D. A., Psychology
WILLMER, P. G., Biology
WINN, P., Psychology
WOOLLINS, J. D., Chemistry

UNIVERSITY OF STIRLING

Stirling, FK9 4LA
Telephone: (1786) 473171
Fax: (1786) 463000
Internet: www.external.stir.ac.uk

Founded 1967
Academic year: September to May (two semesters)

Chancellor: Dr JAMES NAUGHTIE
Prin. and Vice-Chancellor: Prof. GERRY MCCORMAC
Deputy Prin.: Prof. GRANT JARVIE
Deputy Prin.: Prof. IAN SIMPSON
Deputy Prin.: Prof. STEVE BURT
Sec.: KEVIN CLARKE
Deputy Sec.: Dr EILEEN SCHOFIELD

Library: see Libraries and Archives
Number of teachers: 1,429
Number of students: 11,544

Publication: *Stirling Minds*.

UNIVERSITY OF STRATHCLYDE

16 Richmond St, Glasgow, G1 1XQ
Telephone: (141) 552-4400
Fax: (141) 552-0775
E-mail: rkes@strath.ac.uk
Internet: www.strath.ac.uk

Founded 1796 as Anderson's Institution, present status 1964
Academic year: September to June

Chancellor: Rt Hon. Lord HOPE OF CRAIGHEAD
Prin. and Vice-Chancellor: Prof. JIM MCDONALD
Vice-Prin.: Prof. KENNETH MILLER
Deputy Prin.: Prof. DAVID GANI
Chief Operating Officer: HUGH HALL
Chief Financial Officer: Prof. DAVID COYLE

Number of teachers: 821
Number of students: 14,800

DEANS

Faculty of Education: IAIN SMITH
Faculty of Engineering: Prof. SCOTT MACGREGOR
Faculty of Humanities and Social Sciences: Prof. TONY MCGREW
Faculty of Science: Dr IAIN HUNTER
Strathclyde Business School: Prof. SUSAN HART

PROFESSORS

ACKERMANN, F., Management Science
AINSWORTH, M., Mathematics
ALEXANDER, J., Immunology
ANDERSON, J., Bioscience
ANDONOVIC, I., Electronic and Electrical Engineering
ASHCROFT, B. K., Economics
BACHTLER, J., European Policy
BALENDRA, R., Design, Manufacture and Engineering Management
BANKS, W. M., Advanced Materials
BARNETT, S., Quantum Optics
BARON, S., Education
BATES, T., Law
BATH, M., English
BAUM, T. G., Hospitality Management
BEDFORD, T., Management Science
BELTON, V., Management Science
BINGHAM, R., Physics
BIRCH, D. J. S., Photophysics
BITITCI, U., Design, Manufacture and Engineering Management
BLACKIE, J. W. G., Scots Law
BOYD, B., Language Education
BOYLE, J. T., Mechanics of Materials
BRIDGES, A., Architecture
BROWN, C., History
BRYCE, T. G. K, Education
CARTER, S., Marketing
CHAKRABARTI, M., Social Work
CLARK, N., Environmental Studies
CLARKE, J. A., Energy Systems
COMMON, M., Environmental Studies
CONNOLLY, P., Bioengineering
CONNOR, R., Computer and Information Sciences
COOPER, C., Accounting and Finance
CORCORAN, M., Architecture
COURTNEY, J. M., Bioengineering
CRESTANI, F., Computer and Information Sciences
CROSS, R. B., Economics
CULSHAW, B., Optoelectronics
CURTICE, J., Government
DAVIES, J. B., Psychology
DONALDSON, G. B., Applied Physics
DUNLOP, J., Communications Engineering
DURRANI, T., Signal Processing
DUXBURY, G., Chemical Physics
EDEN, C., Graduate School of Business
ELPHINSTONE, M., Writing
FABB, N., English
FAIRLEY, J., Environmental Planning
FARRELL, J., Modern Languages
FERGUSON, A. I., Photonics
FINN, G., Educational Studies
FIRTH, W. J., Experimental Physics
FISCHER, C., History
FOOT, H. C., Psychology
FRASER, W. H., History
GENNARD, J., Human Resource Management
GETTINBY, G. C., Statistics
GIBB, F., Computer and Information Sciences
GORDON, G., Academic Practice
GORMAN, D., Mechanical Engineering
GRANT, C. D., Chemical Engineering
GRANT, M., Bioengineering
GRAY, T. G. F., Fracture Mechanics
GRIMBLE, M. J., Industrial Systems
GURNEY, A., Pharmacology
GURNEY, W. S. C., Mathematical Ecology
HALL, P., Chemical Engineering
HALLIDAY, J., Educational Studies
HALLING, P. J., Biocatalyst Science
HARNETT, W., Immunology
HART, S., Marketing
HARVEY, A. L., Pharmacology
HASTINGS, G., Marketing
HAYWARD, G., Signal Processing
HENDRY, A., Metallurgy and Engineering Materials
HIGHAM, D., Mathematics
HILLIER, D., Accounting and Finance
HOGWOOD, B. W., Politics
HOOD, N., Business Policy
HOWE, C., Psychology
HUDSON, S., Pharmaceutical Care
HUMES, W., Educational Studies
HUNTER, I., Molecular Microbiology
HUTTON, N., Law
HUXHAM, C., Management Science
JACKSON, M., Environmental Health
JACOBS, N., Training and Education in Prosthetics
JAROSZYNSKI, D., Physics
JOHNSON, G., Strategic Management
JOHNSON, M., Electronic and Electrical Engineering
JUDGE, D., Politics

JUSTER, N., Design and Manufacture
KANE, K., Physiology and Pharmacology
KARTVEDT, P., Architecture
KAY, N. M., Business Economics
KENDRICK, A., Childcare Initiative
KERR, W., Pure and Applied Chemistry
LANGFORD, D. A., Construction
LAW, D., Computer and Information Sciences
LEDINGHAM, K., Physics
LEITHEAD, W., Electronic and Electrical Engineering
LITTLEJOHN, D., Analytical Chemistry
LLOYD, I. J., Law
LO, K. L., Power Engineering
LOVE, J., Economics
MACDONALD, J., Power Engineering
MACDONALD, R., International Finance
MACFARLANE, C. J., Subsea Engineering
MACGREGOR, S., Electronic and Electrical Engineering
MACKAY, G., Educational Support and Guidance
MANGAN, J. A., Cultural Studies in Education
MAO, X., Statistics
MARSHALL, A., Accounting and Finance
MASON, C., Entrepreneurship
MAVER, T. W., Computer-aided Design
MCBRIDE, A., Mathematics
MCCALL, J., Education
MCGETTRICK, A. D., Computer and Information Sciences
MCGOWN, A., Civil Engineering
MCGREGOR, P., Economics
MCKEE, S., Mathematics
MCNAB, A., Electronic and Electrical Engineering
MCNICOLL, I. H., Applied Economics
MEARNS, D., Counselling Unit
MILBURN, R., Community Education
MILLAN, C. G., French Studies
MILLER, K., Employment Law
MILLS, A., Pure and Applied Chemistry
MITCHELL, J., Government
MULVEY, R. E., Inorganic Chemistry
MURDOCH, A., Mathematics
MURPHY, J., Preparative Chemistry
NICOL, A., Bioengineering
NICOLSON, D., Law
NIMMO, M., Exercise Physiology
NIXON, P., Computer and Information Sciences
NORRIE, K., Law
O'DONNELL, K., Physics
OPPO, G.-L., Physics
OSIPOV, M., Mathematics
PACIONE, M., Geography
PADGETT, S., Government
PATERSON, A. A., Law
PETHRICK, R. A., Physical Chemistry
PHELPS, A., Plasma Physics
PLEVIN, R., Physiology and Pharmacology
PYNE, N., Physiology and Pharmacology
REID, S., Veterinary Informatics
RENSHAW, E., Statistics and Modelling Science
RHODES, J., Mechanics of Materials
ROBERTSON, B., Physiology and Pharmacology
ROBERTSON, C., Statistics
ROBSON, P., Law
RODGER, B., Law
SAREN, M., Marketing
SAWDAY, J., English
SCULLION, H., Human Resource Management
SHAW, S. A., Marketing
SHERRINGTON, D. C., Polymer Chemistry
SLOAN, D. MCP., Numerical Analysis
SMITH, W. E., Inorganic Chemistry
SPIER, S., Architecture
STACK, M., Mechanical Engineering
STEPHEN, F. H., Economics
STEVENS, H., Pharmaceutical Sciences
STIMSON, W. H., Immunology
SUCKLING, C. J., Chemistry
SUMMERS, H. P., Theoretical Atomic Physics
SUPPLE, J., French
SWALES, J., Economics
THOMPSON, P., Human Resource Management
THOMSON, J., Psychology
UCHEGBU, I., Pharmaceutical Sciences
UTTAMCHANDANI, D., Electronic and Electrical Engineering
VASSALOS, D., Naval Architecture and Marine Engineering
WADSWORTH, R., Physiology and Pharmacology
WAIGH, R. D., Pharmacy
WALLS, L., Management Science
WATSON, J., Biochemistry
WEETMAN, P., Accounting and Finance
WEIR, A. D., Education
WHITTY, N., Law
WILLIAMS, H., Management Science
WILLIAMS, T., Management Science
WILSON, C. G., Pharmacy
WILSON, S., Mathematics
WOOD, R. C., Hospitality Management
WRIGHT, G., Business Administration
WRIGHT, H. D., Structural Engineering
WRIGHT, R., Business
YADAV, P. K., Accounting and Finance
YEO, E., History
YOUNG, S., Marketing
YUILL, D., European Policies

UNIVERSITY OF THE WEST OF SCOTLAND

Paisley, PA1 2BE
Telephone: (141) 848-3000
Fax: (141) 887-0812
E-mail: uni-direct@paisley.ac.uk
Internet: www.paisley.ac.uk

Founded 1897 as Paisley College of Technology, present name and status 2007
Academic year: October to June
Chancellor: Sir ROBERT SMITH
Prin. and Vice-Chancellor: Prof. SEAMUS MCDAID (acting)
Vice-Prin.: PAUL MARTIN
Deputy Prin. and Vice-Prin. for Strategy: GILL TROUP (acting)
Vice-Prin. for Teaching And Learning: Prof. MALCOLM FOLEY
Vice-Prin. for Research and Commercialisation: Prof. RODDY WILLIAMSON
Sec.: KENNETH ALEXANDER
Librarian: STUART JAMES

Number of teachers: 2,000
Number of students: 20,000

DEANS

School of Education: IAN SMITH
School of Engineering and Science: Prof. ROGER MCLEAN
School of Health, Nursing and Midwifery: Prof. JACK RAE
School of Information Communication Technologies: Dr CHRIS HALSALL
School of Media: ALEX GILKISON
School of Social Sciences: Dr TONY CLARKE
Paisley Business School: ALAN GODFREY

Colleges in Scotland

These institutions are not able to award their own degrees, but offer courses leading to a degree from a recognized body.

Aberdeen College: Gallowgate Centre, Gallowgate, Aberdeen, AB25 1BN; tel. (1224) 612-000; fax (1224) 612-001; e-mail enquiry@abcol.ac.uk; internet www.abcol.ac.uk; f. 1959; courses include English as a foreign language, EX training (electrical work in hazardous environments), interpreter/translator, agriculture, art and design, business studies, communication, electrical and electronic engineering, hospitality, journalism, mechanical engineering, offshore industries, systems analysis and design, sports coaching and development, social studies; 266 full-time teachers; 6,000 full-time, 18,000 part-time students; library: 25,000 vols; Prin. and Chief Exec. ROB WALLEN (acting).

Adam Smith College: St Brycedale Ave, Kirkcaldy, KY1 1EX; tel. (1592) 223400; fax (1592) 223402; e-mail enquiries@adamsmith.ac.uk; internet www.adamsmithcollege.ac.uk; f. 2005 by merger of Glenrothes College and Fife College; 5 campuses; offers degrees and professional devt awards in courses incl. built environment, business and management, care and social sciences, computing, creative industries, hair and befauty, languages and ESOL, sport and fitness, tourism and hospitality, engineering and renewables, science, skills for life and work; 900 staff; 35,000 teachers; Prin. Dr CRAIG THOMSON.

Al-Maktoum Institute for Arabic and Islamic Studies: 124 Blackness Rd, Dundee, DD1 5PE; tel. (1382) 908070; fax (1382) 908077; e-mail info@almi.abdn.ac.uk; internet www.almi.abdn.ac.uk; research and masters programmes in Islamic subjects; courses validated by Univ. of Aberdeen; library: 17,000 vols; Prin. Prof MALORY NYE.

Carnegie College: Halbeath Campus, Pittsburgh Rd, Dunfermline, KY11 8DY; tel. (1383) 845-010; e-mail info@carnegiecollege.ac.uk; internet www.carnegiecollege.ac.uk; f. 1899 as Lauder College; 4 campuses; courses to degree level; library: 27,000 books, DVDs, newspapers, journals; 10,000 srudents; Prin. and Chief Exec. GEOFF FENLON.

City of Glasgow College: 300 Cathedral St, Glasgow, G1 2TA; tel. (1412) 716-500; fax (1412) 716-511; e-mail info@newcampusglasgow.ac.uk; internet www.cityofglasgowcollege.ac.uk; f. 2010 by merger of Central College Glasgow, Glasgow Metropolitan College and Glasgow College of Nautical Studies; courses in accounting, advertising, art and design, business studies, computing, distribution, hairdressing and beauty therapy, librarianship, marketing, office studies, sports therapy; 1,200 teachers; 40,000 students; Prin. PAUL G. K. LITTLE.

Edinburgh College of Art: Lauriston Place, Edinburgh, EH3 9DF; tel. (131) 221-6000; fax (131) 221-6028; e-mail marketing@eca.ac.uk; internet www.eca.ac.uk; f. 1907; art, design, architecture and landscape architecture programmes at undergraduate, postgraduate and research degree level; degrees validated by Univ. of Edinburgh; library: 85,000 vols, 350 periodicals; 350 academic staff; 1,700 students; Prin. Prof. IAN HOWARD.

Free Church of Scotland College: The Mound, Edinburgh, EH1 2LS; tel. (131) 226-5286; fax (131) 220-0669; e-mail secretary@freescotcoll.ac.uk; internet www.freescotcoll.ac.uk; f. 1843; undergraduate, postgraduate and part-time courses in biblical studies, Christian theology and related disciplines; 8 teachers; Prin. JOHN L. MACKAY.

Glasgow School of Art: 167 Renfrew St, Glasgow, G3 6RQ; tel. (141) 353-4500; fax (141) 353-4746; e-mail registry@gsa.ac.uk; internet www.gsa.ac.uk; f. 1845; BA, MA and MPhil courses in Architecture, Fine Art and Design; all degree courses validated by Univ. of Glasgow; library: 80,000 vols, 59,000 slides, 250 periodicals of art, design, craft and architecture; 400 teachers; 1,900 students; Dir Prof. SEONA REID.

International Christian College: 110 St James Rd, Glasgow, G4 0PS; tel. (1415) 524-040; fax (1415) 520-808; e-mail college@icc.ac.uk; internet www.icc.ac.uk; f. 1998 by merger of Glasgow Bible College and Northumbria Bible College; undergraduate, postgraduate, certificate courses and doctoral research in Christian studies and theology; library: 45,000 vols, 180 periodical titles, 40 CD-ROMs; 20 teachers; Prin. Rev. RICHARD TIPLADY.

International Correspondence Schools Ltd: 45 Finnieston St, Glasgow, G3 8JU; tel. (141) 302-5487; internet www.icslearn.co.uk; f. 1890; distance learning courses in law, psychology, English and history, fashion textile, health and social care, business, educational studies; degrees in asscn with Univ. of East London, Anglia Ruskin Univ. and Edinburgh Napier Univ.; 36,000 students; Man. Dir SALLY PULVERTAFT.

James Watt College: Finnart Campus, Finnart St, Greenock, PA16 8HF; tel. (1475) 724433; fax (1475) 888079; e-mail enquiries@jameswatt.ac.uk; internet www.jameswatt.ac.uk; f. 1908 as James Watt Memorial College; 4 campuses; vocational courses in full-time and part-time, evening classes and open learning; Prin. and Chief Exec. SUE PINDER.

Scottish Agricultural College: Ayr Campus, Auchincruive Estate, Ayr, KA6 5HW; tel. (131) 535-4391; fax (131) 667-2601; e-mail recruitment@sac.ac.uk; internet www.sac.ac.uk/learning; f. 1900; campuses at Ayr, Aberdeen and Edinburgh (associated with Univ. of Edinburgh); undergraduate, postgraduate courses in agriculture and land based studies; library: 50,000 vols, 670 current journal titles; 250 teachers; 1,200 students; Prin. and Chief Exec. Prof. WILLIAM MCKELVEY.

Scottish Baptist College: K202, Univ. of the West of Scotland, High St., Paisley, PA1 2BE; tel. (141) 848-3988; fax (141) 848-3989; e-mail scottishbaptistcollege@uws.ac.uk; internet www.scottishbaptistcollege.org; f. 1894 as Baptist Theological College of Scotland; attached to Univ. of West of Scotland; certificate, diploma and Bachelors courses in Christian theology; Prin. Rev. Dr JIM GORDON.

Scottish Institute of Human Relations: Park Business Centre, 5 La Belle Place, Glasgow, G3 7LH; tel. (141) 332-0011; fax (141) 332-3999; e-mail info@sihr.org.uk; internet www.sihr.org.uk; f. 1971; postgraduate programmes and services for psychoanalytic, psychodynamic and systemic thinking; validated by Univ. of Strathclyde; Exec. Dir. AMANDA CORNISH.

Universities in Wales

ABERYSTWYTH UNIVERSITY

Old College, King St, Aberystwyth, Ceredigion, SY23 2AX
Telephone: (1970) 623111
Fax: (1970) 611446
E-mail: dym@aber.ac.uk
Internet: www.aber.ac.uk
Founded 1872, present status 2007
Languages of instruction: English, Welsh
Academic year: September to June
Pres.: Sir EMYR JONES PARRY
Vice-Pres: ELIZABETH FRANCE
Vice-Pres: WINSTON RODDICK
Vice-Chancellor: Prof. NOEL G. LLOYD
Pro-Vice Chancellor: Prof. ALED JONES
Pro-Vice Chancellor: Dr JOHN HARRIES
Pro-Vice Chancellor: Prof. MARTIN JONES
Registrar and Sec.: Dr CATRIN HUGHES
Library: see entry for Univ. of Wales Aberystwyth, Hugh Owen Library
Number of teachers: 813
Number of students: 10,210
Publication: *Prom* (1 a year)

DEANS

Faculty of Arts: Prof. TIM S. WOODS
Faculty of Postgraduate Studies: Prof. COLIN J. MCINNES
Faculty of Science: Prof. JOHN P. GRATTAN
Faculty of Social Sciences: Prof. LEN V. SCOTT

PROFESSORS

ALEXANDER, M. S., International Politics
ALEXANDER, N. S., School of Management and Business
BARKER, M. J., Theatre, Film and Television Studies
BARNES, D., Computer Science
BARRY, P., English and Creative Writing
BOOTH, K., International Politics
BORSAY, P., History and Welsh History
BROPHY, P., Biological, Environmental and Rural Sciences
CLARK, I., International Politics
CLARKE, A., Law and Criminology
CRAIG, H., Biological, Environmental and Rural Sciences
DRAPER, J., Biological, Environmental and Rural Sciences
DULLER, G. A. T., Geography and Earth Sciences
EDKINS, J. A., International Politics
ELLIS, D., Information Studies
ERSKINE, T. A., International Politics
EVANS, D., Mathematical and Physical Sciences
FOLEY, M., International Politics
GLASSER, N. F., Geography and Earth Sciences
GOUGH, J., Mathematical and Physical Sciences
GOUGH, R., Theatre, Film and Television Studies
GRANDE, M., Mathematical and Physical Sciences
GREAVES, G. N., Mathematics and Physical Siences
HAMBREY, M. J., Geography and Earth Sciences
HANNAH, M. G., Geography and Earth Sciences
HARDING, C., Law and Criminology
HARESIGN, W., Biological, Environmental and Rural Sciences
HARVEY, J., Art
HAYCOCK, M., Welsh Language and Literature
HUTTON, S., English and Creative Writing
KAY, D., Geography and Earth Sciences
KEAR, A., Theatre, Film and Television Studies
KING, R. D., Computer Science
LAVALLEE, D. E., Sport and Exercise Science
LEE, M. H., Computer Science
LINKLATER, A., International Politics
LUCAS, R. M., Geography and Earth Sciences
MACKLIN, M. G., Geography and Earth Sciences
MALTMAN, A. J., Geography and Earth Sciences
MAVRON, V., Mathematical and Physical Sciences
MCGUIRE, S. M., School of Management and Business
MIDMORE, P. R., School of Management and Business
MISHURIS, G., Mathematical and Physical Sciences
NEWBOLD, C. J., Biological, Environmental and Rural Sciences
O'MALLEY, T. P., Theatre, Film and Television Studies
PEARSON, M. J., Theatre, Film and Television Studies
PIOTROWICZ, R. W., Law and Criminology
POSTER, J. P., English and Creative Writing
POWELL, W., Biological, Environmental and Rural Sciences
PRICE, C. J., Computer Science
PRICE, R. D., History and Welsh History
PYKETT, L., English and Creative Writing
RABEY, D. I., Theatre, Film and Television Studies
ROWLAND, D., Law and Criminology
RUBINSTEIN, W. D., History and Welsh History
SCHOFIELD, P. R., History and Welsh History
SCULLY, R., International Politics
SHEN, Q., Computer Science
SIMS-WILLIAMS, P., Welsh Language
STEPHENS, E. C., Theatre, Film and Television Studies
SUGANAMI, H., International Politics
THOMAS, C., Biological, Environmental and Rural Sciences
TROTTER, D., European Languages
WATT, P. D., English and Creative Writing
WHEELER, N. J., International Politics
WILKINSON, M., Biological , Environmental and Rural Sciences
WILLIAMS, G. A., Law and Criminology
WILLIAMS, H. L., International Politics
WOODS, T. S., Geography & Earth Sciences
YOUNG, M., Biological, Environmental and Rural Sciences
ZWIGGELAAR, R., Computer Science

BANGOR UNIVERSITY

Bangor LL57 2DG
Telephone: (1248) 351151
Fax: (1248) 370451
Internet: www.bangor.ac.uk
Founded 1884
Academic year: September to June
Pres.: Rt Hon. Lord ELIS-THOMAS OF NANT CONWY
Vice-Chancellor: Prof. JOHN HUGHES
Deputy Vice-Chancellor: Prof. C. FERGUS LOWE
Pro-Vice-Chancellor: Prof. W. THOMAS
Pro-Vice-Chancellor for Teaching and Learning: Prof. COLIN BAKER
Pro-Vice-Chancellor for Research and Enterprise: Prof. DAVID SHEPHERD
Academic Registrar: DAVID FORDHAM (acting)
Dir of Information and Library Services: DAVID LEARMONT
Library: see entry for Univ. of Wales, Bangor, Information Services
Number of teachers: 692
Number of students: 13,600

DEANS

College of Arts and Humanities: Prof. A. M. CLAYDON
College of Business, Social Sciences and Law: Prof. PHIL MOLYNEUX (acting)
College of Education and Lifelong Learning: Prof. J. PRITCHARD
College of Health and Behavioural Sciences: Prof. OLIVER TURNBULL (acting)
College of Natural Sciences: Prof. COLIN JAGO (acting)
College of Physical and Applied Sciences: Prof. PAUL SPENCER (acting)

PROFESSORS

College of Arts and Humanities:

BROWN, A. D., English
BUSHELL, A., Modern Languages
CORNS, T. N., English
DEUCHAR, M., Linguistics and English Language
EDWARDS, J., English
FRANCIS, L., Theology and Religious Studies
HARPER, G., Creative Industries
LEWIS, A.P., Music
LYNCH, P., Welsh
MORGAN, D. D., Theology and Religious Studies
PRYCE, A. H., History and Welsh History
SCHMIDT-BESTE, T. C., Music
TANNER, D. M., History and Welsh History
THOMAS, J. A., Linguistics and English Language
WILCOX, H., English
WILLIAMS, G., Welsh

College of Business, Social Sciences and Law:

CAIN, M., Management Science
CHAKRAVARTY, S. P., Economics
DAVIS, H., Social Sciences
GARDENER, E. P. M., Banking
GODDARD, J., Financial Economics
HESTER, S., Social Sciences
JOHNSON, H., Law
MCLEAY, S. J., Treasury
MOLYNEUX, P., Banking and Finance
ROWLEY, J., Marketing and Information Management

College of Education and Lifelong Learning:

BAKER, C. R., Education
ROBERTS, H. G. FF., Education

College of Health and Behavioural Sciences:

COX, W. M., Psychology of Addictive Behaviours
GATHERCOLE, V. M., Psychology
HARDY, L., Sport, Health and Exercise Sciences
HASTINGS, R. P., Psychology
LOWE, C. F., Psychology
MADDISON, P., Sport, Health and Exercise Sciences
NOYES, J., Nursing
RAFAL, R. D., Psychology of Neuroscience and Neuropsychology
RAYMOND, J., Experimental Consumer Psychology
REES, M. R., Vascular Studies
RUSSELL, I. T., Public Health
SHAPIRO, K. L., Cognitive Neuroscience
STUART, N. S. A., Cancer Studies
TIPPER, S. P., Cognitive Science
VIHMAN, M. M., Developmental Psychology
WOODS, R. T., Clinical Psychology of the Elderly

College of Natural Sciences:

CARVALHO, G. R., Biological Sciences
DANDO, P. R., Marine Biology
DAVIES, A. G., Physical Oceanography
EDWARDS-JONES, G., Environment and Natural Resources
ELLIOTT, A. J., Ocean Sciences
FARRAR, J. F., Biological Sciences
FREEMAN, C., Biological Sciences
GODBOLD, D. L., Environment and Natural Resources
HUGHES, R. N., Biological Sciences
JONES, D. L., Environment and Natural Resources
KAISER, M. J., Ocean Sciences
PRICE, C., Environment and Natural Resources
SCOURSE, J. D., Ocean Sciences
SEED, R., Marine Ecology
SIMPSON, J. H., Ocean Sciences
STUART, N. S. A., Biological Sciences
THOMAS, D. N., Ocean Sciences
THORPE, R. S., Biological Sciences
TOMOS, A. D., Biological Sciences
WILLIAMS, P. A., Biological Sciences

College of Physical and Applied Sciences:

ASHWELL, G. J., Chemistry
BAIRD, M. S., Chemistry
HOPE, S., Computer Science
IRVINE, S. J. C., Chemistry
JOHN, N. W., Computing
KALAJI, M., Chemistry
PETHIG, R., Electronic Engineering
SHORE, K. A., Electronic Engineering
SPENCER, P. S., Electronic Engineering
TAYLOR, D. M., Electronic Engineering

CARDIFF UNIVERSITY

Cardiff, CF10 3XQ
Telephone: (29) 2087-4000
E-mail: prospectus@cardiff.ac.uk
Internet: www.cardiff.ac.uk

Founded 2004 by merger of Cardiff University (f. 1883) and University of Wales College of Medicine (f. 1931)

Academic year: September to June

Pres.: Prof. Sir MARTIN EVANS
Vice-Chancellor: Dr DAVID GRANT
Deputy Vice-Chancellor: Prof. ELIZABETH TREASURE
Pro-Vice-Chancellor for Engagement and Int.: Prof. HYWEL THOMAS
Pro-Vice-Chancellor for Education and Students: Prof. JONATHAN OSMOND
Pro-Vice-Chancellor for Estates: Prof. TIM WESS
Pro-Vice-Chancellor for Research: Prof. GRAHAM HUTCHINGS
Pro-Vice-Chancellor for Staff and Diversity: Prof. TERRY THREADGOLD
Dean of Strategic Futures and Interdisciplinary Studies: Prof. PETER HALLIGAN
Library: see entry for Cardiff University Libraries
Number of teachers: 2,922
Number of students: 28,000

HEADS OF SCHOOLS

College of Humanities and Sciences:

Architecture: Prof. PHIL JONES
Business School: Prof. GEORGE BOYNE
Chemistry: Prof. PETER KNOWLES
City and Regional Planning: Prof. CHRISTOPHER WEBSTER
Computer Science: Dr. ROGER WHITAKER
Earth and Ocean Sciences: Prof. JOHN PARKES
Engineering: Prof. HYWEL THOMAS
English, Communication and Philosophy: Prof. MARTIN KAYMAN
European Studies: Prof. DAVID BOUCHER
History, Archaeology and Religion: Prof. PETER COSS
Journalism, Media and Cultural Studies: Prof. JUSTIN LEWIS
Law School: Prof. NIGEL LOWE
Lifelong Learning: Dr RICHARD EVANS
Mathematics: Prof. A RUSSELL DAVIES
Music: Prof. DAVID WYN JONES
Physics and Astronomy: Prof. WALTER GEAR
Social Sciences: Prof. MALCOLM WILLIAMS
Welsh: Prof. SIONED DAVIES

Wales College of Medicine, Biology, Life and Health Sciences:

Biosciences: Prof. OLE PETERSEN
Dentistry: Prof. ELIZABETH TREASURE
Healthcare Studies: Prof. PATRICIA PRICE
Medicine: Prof. PAUL MORGAN
Nursing and Midwifery Studies: Prof. SHEILA HUNT
Optometry and Vision Sciences: Prof. TIM WESS
Pharmacy: Prof. GARY BAXTER
Postgraduate Medical and Dental Education: Prof. DEREK GALLEN
Psychology: Prof. DYLAN JONES

PROFESSORS

College of Humanities and Sciences

Architecture:

WESTON, R.

Business School:

BLYTON, P. R.
BOYNE, G. A.
CHANDLER, R. A.
CLARKE, R.
COLLIE, D. R.
COPELAND, L.
DAVIES, A. J.
DELBRIDGE, R. I.
EDWARDS, J. R.
EZZAMEL, M. A.
FOREMAN-PECK, J.
FOSH, P.
FOXALL, G. R.
HARRIS, L. C.
HEERY, E. J.
HINES, P. A.
HUGHES HALLET, A.
JONES, D. T.
JONES, M. J.
KNOTT, J. H.
MAKEPEACE, G. H.
MARTIN, S. J.
MATTHEWS, K. G. P.
MCNABB, R.
MELLETT, H. J.
MINFORD, A. P. L.
MORRIS, J. L.
NAIRN, M. M.
OGBONNA, E.
PEATTIE, K. J.
PEEL, M. J.
PENDLEBURY, M. W.
POOLE, M. J. F.
REED, M. I.
RHYS, D. G.
SILVER, M. S.
TOWILL, D. R.
TURNBULL, P. J.
WALKER, S. P.
WHITFIELD, K. L.
XU, X.

Chemistry:

ATTARD, G. A.
BOWKER, M.
CAVELL, K. J.
EDWARDS, P. G.
HARRIS, K. D. M.
HEWLINS, M. J. E.
JONES, C.
KNIGHT, D. W.
KNOWLES, P. J.
MCKEOWN, N. B.
ROBERTS, M. W.
WELLS, P. B.
WILLIAMS, D. R.
WIRTH, T.

City and Regional Planning:

ALDEN, J. D.
CLAPHAM, D. F.
COOKE, P. N.
GUY, C. M.
HOOPER, A. J.
LOVERING, J.
MORGAN, K. J.
MURDOCH, J. L.
PUNTER, J. V.
WEBSTER, C. J.
WILLIAMS, H. C. W. L.

Computer Science:

AVIS, N. J.
BATCHELOR, B. G.
BROWN, B. M.
GRAY, W. A.
JONES, A. J.

JONES, C. B.
MARTIN, R. R.
WALKER, D. W.

Earth and Ocean Sciences:

BOWEN, D. Q.
CARTWRIGHT, J. A.
EDWARDS, D.
HARRIS, C.
LISLE, R. J.
O'HARA, M. J.
PARKES, R. J.
PEARCE, J. A.
PEARSON, P. N.
RICKARD, D. T.
SCHULTZ, A.
WRIGHT, V. P.
ZAHN, R.

Engineering:

BARR, B. I. G.
BARROW, D. A.
BORODICH, F. M.
CHAMBERS, J. A.
EVANS, H. P.
DIMOV, S. S.
FALCONER, R. A.
HUGHES, T. G.
KARIHALOO, B. L.
LEVER, K. V.
MILES, J. C.
MORGAN, D. V.
MOSES, A. J.
PHAM, D. T.
POOLEY, F. D.
ROWE, D. M.
SNIDLE, R. W.
SYRED, N.
TASKER, P. J.
WATTON, J.
WILLIAMS, F. W.

English, Communication and Philosophy:

ATTFIELD, R.
BELSEY, C.
COUPLAND, N. J. R.
KAYMAN, M. A.
KNIGHT, S. T.
NORRIS, C. C.
SARANGI, S. K.
SKILTON, D. J.
VAN LEEUWEN, T.
WEEDON, C. M.

European Studies:

BERENDSE, G.-J.
BOUCHER, D.
BRYDEN, K. M.
COLE, A. M.
DYSON, K. H. F.
HADDOCK, B. A.
HANLEY, D. L.
JACKSON, D. A.
LOUGHLIN, J. P.

History and Archaeology:

BENTON, G.
COSS, P. R.
EDBURY, P. W.
FREESTONE, I. C.
FISHER, N. R. E.
HINES, J.
HUDSON, P.
PRINGLE, R. D.
WHITTLE, A. W. R.

Journalism, Media and Cultural Studies:

HARGREAVES, I. R.
KITZINGER, J.
LEWIS, J. W.
MILLER, B. T. A.
TAIT, R.

Law School:

CAMPBELL, I. D.
CHURCHILL, R. R.
DOE, C. N.
DOUGLAS, G. F.
FENNELL, P. W. H.
HARPWOOD, V.
HOLM, S.
LEE, R. G.
LEWIS, R. K.
LOWE, N. V.
MIERS, D. R.
MORGAN, D. M.
MURCH, M.
NELKEN, D.
SMITH, K. J. M.
THOMAS, P. A.
WELLS, C. K.
WYLIE, J. C. W.

Mathematics:

BOURENKOV, K.
EVANS, D. E.
EVANS, W. D.
HOOLEY, C.
HUXLEY, M. N.
PHILLIPS, T. N.
WICKRAMASINGHE, N. C.
ZHIGLJAVSKY, A. A.

Music:

THOMAS, A. T.
TYRELL, J.
WALSH, S.

Physics and Astronomy:

ADE, P. A. R.
BLOOD, P.
DISNEY, M. J.
GEAR, W. K.
GRIFFIN, M. J.
GRISHCHUK, L.
INGLESFIELD, J. E.
IVANOV, A. L.
SATHYAPRAKASH, B. S.
WHITWORTH, A. P.

Religious and Theological Studies:

SAMUEL, G. B.
TREVETT, C.

Social Sciences:

ADAM, B. E.
ATKINSON, P.
BROWN, P.
COLLINS, H. M.
CROZIER, W. R.
DAVIES, W. B.
DRAKEFORD, M.
EPSTEIN, D. A.
FAIRBROTHER, P.
FEVRE, R. W.
FITZ, J.
GLASNER, P. E.
LAWN, M.
LEVI, M.
MAGUIRE, E. M. W.
MOORE, L. A. R.
NICHOLS, W. A. T.
POWER, S. A. R.
PRIOR, L. F.
REES, G. M.
REES, T. L.
WALKERDINE, V.
WALTERS, D.
WILLIAMS, G. H.

Welsh:

JONES, R. O.
THOMAS, P. W.
WILLIAMS, C. H.

Wales College of Medicine, Biology, Life and Health Sciences

Biosciences:

ARCHER, C. W.
BENJAMIN, M.
BODDY, L.
BOWEN, I. D.
BRUFORD, M. W.
BUCHMAN, V.
CATERSON, B.
CLARKE, A. R.
COAKLEY, W. T.
CRUNELLI, V.
DALE, T. C.
DAVIES, A. M.
DUANCE, V. C.
DUNNETT, S. B.
ECCLES, R.
EHRMANN, M.
FOX, K. D.
FRY, J. C.
HARWOOD, A. J.
HARWOOD, J. L.
JACOB, T. J. C.
JOHN, R. A.
KAY, J.
MOXHAM, B. J.
ORMEROD, S. J.

Dentistry:

DUMMER, P. M. H., Adult Dental Health
GLANTZ, P.-O. J., Adult Dental Health
JONES, M. L., Dental Health and Development
LEWIS, M. A. O., Oral Medicine
MACKENZIE, I. C., Adult Dental Health
RICHMOND, S., Dental Health and Development
SHEPHERD, J. R., Oral Surgery and Pathology
TREASURE, E. T., Dental Public Health
WHITTAKER, D. K., Basic Dental Science
WILTON, J. M. A., Adult Dental Health

Healthcare Studies:

PALASTANGA, N.

Medicine:

BURNETT, A. K., Haematology
CAMPBELL, A. K., Medical Biochemistry
CLARKE, A. J., Medical Genetics
COOPER, D. N., Human Molecular Genetics
DAVIES, D. P., Child Health
DUERDEN, B. I., Medical Microbiology
EVANS, W. H., Medical Biochemistry
FELCE, D., Mental Handicap Research
FIANDER, A., Obstetrics and Gynaecology
FINLAY, A. Y., Dermatology
FINLAY, I. G., Palliative Care
FRENNEAUX, N. P., Cardiology
GRIFFITH, T. M., Medical Imaging
HARDING, K. G., Rehabilitation Medicine
HARMER, M., Anaesthetics and Intensive Care Medicine
HARPER, P. S., Medical Genetics
HOUSTON, H. L. A., General Practice
KRAWCZAK, M., Mathematical Genetics
LAI, F. A., Cell Signalling
LEWIS, M. J., Cardiovascular Pharmacology
MANSEL, R. E., Surgery
MASON, M., Clinical Oncology
MORGAN, B. P., Medical Biochemistry
O'DONOVAN, M. C., Psychological Medicine
OWEN, M. J., Neuropsychiatric Genetics
OWENS, D. R., Diabetes
PALMER, S. R., Epidemiology, Statistics and Public Health
PILL, R., General Practice
ROUTLEDGE, P., Clinical Pharmacology
ROWE, M., Cell Biology
SAMPSON, J. R., Medical Genetics
SCANLON, M. F., Endocrinology
SHALE, D. J., Respiratory and Communicable Diseases
SIBERT, J. R., Community Child Health
SMITH, P. J., Cancer Biology
STEPHENS, S. D. G., Audiology
THAPAR, A., Child and Adolescent Psychiatry
WHEELER, M. H., Surgery
WILES, C. M., Neurology
WILKINSON, C., General Practice
WILLIAMS, B. D., Rheumatology
WILLIAMS, G. T., Pathology
WILLIAMS, J. D., Nephrology
WOODCOCK, J. P., Bioengineering
WOODHOUSE, K. W., Geriatric Medicine
WORWOOD, M., Haematology
WYNFORD-THOMAS, D., Pathology

Nursing and Midwifery Studies:

BURNARD, P., Nursing and Midwifery Education
LYNE, P. A., Nursing Research
TUCKER, A., Nursing and Midwifery

Optometry and Vision Sciences:

MEEK, K. M. A.
ROVAMO, J. M.
WESS, T. J.
WILD, J.

Pharmacy:

AKHTAR, S.
BROADLEY, K. J.
DUNCAN, R.
LUSCOMBE, D. K.
MCGUIGAN, C.
MRSNY, R. J.
NICHOLSON, R. I.
RUSSELL, A. D.
WALKER, R. D.

Psychology:

AGGLETON, J. P.
ELLIS, H. D.
HALLIGAN, P.
HAY, D. F.
HONEY, R. C.
MANSTEAD, A. S. R.
OAKSFORD, M. R.
PAYNE, S. J.
PEARCE, J. M.
PIDGEON, N.
SMITH, A. P.
SNOWDEN, R. J.
SPEARS, R.
WRIGHT, P.

SWANSEA UNIVERSITY

Singleton Park, Swansea, SA2 8PP
Telephone: (1792) 205678
Fax: (1792) 295157
Internet: www.swan.ac.uk

Founded 1920
Academic year: September to June

Vice-Chancellor: Prof. RICHARD B. DAVIES
Pro-Vice-Chancellor for Acad. Devt: Prof. NOEL THOMPSON
Pro-Vice-Chancellor for Internationalization: Prof. IWAN DAVIES
Pro-Vice-Chancellor for Science and Engineering: Prof. IAN CLUCKIE
Pro-Vice-Chancellor for Student Experience and Acad. Quality Enhancement: Prof. ALAN SPEIGHT

Library: see Libraries and Archives
Number of teachers: 800
Number of students: 12,500

HEADS OF DEPARTMENTS

College of Arts and Humanities: Prof. JOHN SPURR
College of Engineering: Prof. JAVIER BONET
College of Human and Health Sciences: Prof. MELANIE JASPER
College of Medicine: Prof. GARETH MORGAN
College of Science: Prof. STEVE WILKS
Department of Adult Continuing Education: Prof. COLIN TROTMAN
School of Business and Economics: Prof. STEVEN COOK (acting)
School of Law: Prof. NOEL THOMPSON (acting)

UNIVERSITY OF GLAMORGAN

Pontypridd, CF37 1DL
Telephone: (1443) 480480
Fax: (1443) 654050
E-mail: enquiries@glam.ac.uk
Internet: www.glam.ac.uk

Founded 1913 as South Wales and Monmouthshire School of Mines, became Glamorgan College of Technology 1956, became Glamorgan Polytechnic 1970, later Polytechnic of Wales, present name and status 1992
Academic year: September to July

Chancellor: Rt Hon Lord MORRIS OF ABERAVON
Vice-Chancellor: Prof. JULIE LYDON
Pro-Vice-Chancellor for Acad. Devt and Quality: HELEN MARSHALL
Pro-Vice-Chancellor for Learning and Student Support: Prof. CLIVE MULLHOLLAND
Pro-Vice-Chancellor for Research: Prof. BRIAN HOBBS
Pro-Vice-Chancellor for Resources: Dr HUW WILLIAMS
Acad. Registrar: WILLIAM CALLAWAY

Library of 245,000 vols, 1,600 current periodicals
Number of teachers: 616
Number of students: 23,990

DEANS

Cardiff School of Creative and Cultural Industries: Prof. PETER ROBERTSON
Faculty of Advanced Technology: VASSILIS KONSTANTINOU
Faculty of Health, Sport and Science: Prof. DONNA MEAD
Faculty of Humanities and Social Sciences: Dr CATHERINE JONES (acting)
Glamorgan Business School: MONICA GIBSON-SWEET

UNIVERSITY OF WALES

University Registry, King Edward VII Ave, Cathays Park, Cardiff, CF10 3NS
Telephone: (29) 2037-6999
Fax: (29) 2037-6980
E-mail: uniwales@wales.ac.uk
Internet: www.wales.ac.uk

Founded 1893
Languages of instruction: English, Welsh

Chancellor: HRH Prince CHARLES, PRINCE OF WALES
Pro-Chancellor: The Most Revd Dr BARRY MORGAN, ARCHBISHOP OF WALES
Vice-Chancellor and Chief Exec.: Prof. MARC CLEMENT
Pro-Vice-Chancellor: Prof. NIGEL PALASTANGA
Sec.-Gen.: Dr LYNN E. WILLIAMS

Number of students: 80,000

Publication: *Campus*.

INSTITUTIONS AWARDING UNIVERSITY OF WALES DEGREES

Glyndŵr University

Mold Rd, Wrexham, LL11 2AW
Telephone: (1978) 290666
Fax: (1978) 290008
Internet: www.glyndwr.ac.uk

Founded 1887, present name and status 2008
Languages of instruction: English, Welsh
Academic year: September to June

Vice-Chancellor and Chief Exec.: Prof. MICHAEL SCOTT
Pro-Vice-Chancellor for Operations: Dr ALLAN HOWELLS
Pro-Vice-Chancellor for Academic Affairs: Prof. GRAEME WILKINSON

Library of 120,000 vols, DVDs, 6,000 e-journals
Number of students: 6,000

Swansea Metropolitan University

Mount Pleasant, Swansea, SA1 6ED
Telephone: (1792) 481000
Fax: (1792) 481085
E-mail: enquiry@smu.ac.uk
Internet: www.smu.ac.uk

Founded 1976 by merger of Swansea College of Art (f. 1853); Swansea College of Education (f. 1872) and Swansea Technical College (f. 1897), present name and status 2008
Languages of instruction: English, Welsh

Vice-Chancellor: Prof. DAVID WARNER
Chair.: Dr GERALD LEWIS

Library of 200,000 vols
Number of teachers: 322
Number of students: 7,000

University of Wales, Newport

Caerleon Campus, Lodge Rd, Caerleon, Newport, NP18 3QT
Telephone: (1633) 432432
Fax: (1633) 432046
E-mail: uic@newport.ac.uk
Internet: www.newport.ac.uk

Founded 1841, present name and status 1996

Vice-Chancellor: Dr PETER NOYES
Deputy Vice-Chancellor: GRAHAM ROGERS
Deputy Vice-Chancellor for Academic: Prof. STEPHEN HAGEN
Pro-Vice-Chancellor for Regional and International Development: CHRIS O'MALLEY
Pro-Vice-Chancellor for Resource Planning and Dir of Finance: DENIS JONES
Pro-Vice-Chancellor for Human Resources: BETHAN EDWARDS
Sec.: PAUL FOLAN

Number of teachers: 244
Number of students: 3,967

DEANS

School of Art, Media and Design: DEREK LAWTHER (acting)
School of Business: Dr TIM MCINTYRE-BHATTY
School of Education: Dr CARL PETERS
School of Health and Social Science: AMELIA LYONS
School of Int. Affairs: GRAHAM WOOD

University of Wales Trinity Saint David

Lampeter, Ceredigion, SA48 7ED
Telephone: (1570) 422351
Fax: (1570) 423423
Internet: www.lamp.ac.uk

Founded 1822, inc. as constituent college of Univ. of Wales 1971 and as constituent institution 1987, present name and status by merger of Trinity University College and Univ. of Wales Lampeter
Academic year: October to June

Vice-Chancellor: Prof. MEDWIN HUGHES
Pro-Vice-Chancellor for Acad.: Dr CARTIN THOMAS
Pro-Vice-Chancellor for Finance and Resources: GWYNDAF TOBIAS
Pro-Vice-Chancellor for Innovation, Skills and Community: MERI HUWS

Library: see Libraries and Archives
Number of teachers: 100
Number of students: 2,000

Publication: *Trivium*

DEANS

Faculty of Arts and Social Studies: KEVIN MATHERICK
Faculty of Education and Training: GWILYM DYFRI JONES
Faculty of Humanities: Dr MIRJAM PLANTINGA

PROFESSORS

AUSTIN, D., Archaeology
BADHAM, P., Theology and Religious Studies
BURNHAM, B. C., Archaeology
BURTON, J., History
COCKBURN, D., Philosophy
COHN-SHERBOK, D., Jewish Studies
DAVIES, D. P., Theology
EATOUGH, G., Classics
ELDRIDGE, C. C., History
FLEMING, A., Archaeology

O'LOUGHLIN, T., Theology
PRESCOTT, A., Library
ROFFE, I. M., Centre for Enterprise, Entrepreneurial and European Studies
WALKER, M. J. C., Archaeology

University of Wales Institute, Cardiff

Llandaff Campus, Western Ave, Cardiff, CF5 2SG
Telephone: (29) 2041-6070
Fax: (29) 2041-6286
E-mail: uwicinfo@uwic.ac.uk
Internet: www.uwic.ac.uk
Founded 1976, present name and status 1996
Academic year: October to July
Vice-Chancellor and Prin.: Prof. ANTHONY J. CHAPMAN
Pro-Vice-Chancellor: Prof. ROBERT BROWN
Deputy Vice-Chancellor: JACQUI HARE
Number of students: 11,000

DEANS

Cardiff School of Art and Design: Prof. GAYNOR KAVANAGH
Cardiff School of Education: PAUL THOMAS
Cardiff School of Health Sciences: Prof. ADRIAN PETERS
Cardiff School of Management: DAVID PRITCHARD
Cardiff School of Sports: DAVE COBNER

Colleges in Wales

These institutions are not able to award their own degrees, but offer courses leading to a degree from a recognized body.

Barry College: Colcot Rd, Barry, CF62 8YJ; tel. (1446) 725000; e-mail enquiries@barry.ac.uk; internet www.barry.ac.uk; 5 centres, 800 courses including construction, aircraft engineering, travel and tourism, computing, art and design; 500 staff; 10,000 students; Prin. and Chief Exec. KAY MARTIN.

Bridgend College of Further Education: Cowbridge Rd, Bridgend, CF31 3DF; tel. (1656) 302302; e-mail enquiries@bridgend.ac.uk; internet www.bridgend.ac.uk; f. 1928 as Bridgend Mining and Technical Institute; 400 courses in 20 vocational areas across 4 campuses; 15,000 students; Prin M. JONES.

Coleg Gwent: The Rhadyr, Usk, NP15 1XJ; tel. (1495) 333333; fax (1495) 333526; e-mail info@coleggwent.ac.uk; internet www.coleggwent.ac.uk; 5 campuses; provides higher education and professional qualifications courses; Prin. and Chief Exec. JIM BENNETT.

Coleg Llandrillo Cymru: Rhos, Llandudno Rd, Rhos-on-Sea, LL28 4HZ; tel. (1492) 546-666; fax (1492) 543-052; e-mail admissions@llandrillo.ac.uk; internet www.llandrillo.ac.uk; merged with Coleg Meirion-Dwyfor; 10 main campuses, 200 learning venues; 3,000 full and part-time courses; library: 40,000 vols; 1,400 teachers; 20,000 students; Prin. HUW EVANS.

Coleg Menai: Ffriddoedd Rd, Bangor, LL57 2TP; tel. (1248) 370125; fax (1248) 370052; e-mail learner.services@menai.ac.uk; internet www.menai.ac.uk; 7 learning centres; 120 programmes; partnership with Bangor Univ.; 600 teachers; 9,000 students.

Coleg Morgannwg: Cwmdare Rd, Aberdare, CF44 8ST; tel. (1685) 887500; fax (1685) 876635; e-mail college@morgannwg.ac.uk; internet www.morgannwg.ac.uk; 4 main campuses, 80 outreach centres; courses in higher national certificates, diplomas, foundation, honours degrees, postgraduate, professional qualifications; partnership with Univ. of Glamorgan, Univ. of Wales; Prin. JUDITH EVANS.

Coleg Sir Gâr/Carmarthenshire College: Graig Campus, Sandy Rd, Pwll, SA15 4DN; tel. (1554) 748-000; fax (1554) 748-170; e-mail admissions@colegsirgar.ac.uk; internet www.colegsirgar.ac.uk; 5 campuses; courses include A levels, NVQs, national diplomas, higher national certificates, foundation degrees, graduate and postgraduate programmes; 850 staff; 12,000 students; Prin. and Chief Exec. BARRY LILES.

Gower College Swansea: Tycoch Rd, Swansea, SA2 9EB; tel. (1792) 284000; fax (1792) 284074; e-mail enquiries@gowercollegeswansea.ac.uk; internet www.swancoll.ac.uk; f. 2010 by merger of Swansea College and Gorseinon College; 5 campuses; part-time and full-time degree and HND courses; all courses approved by Univ. of Glamorgan, Univ. of Wales; Prin. and Chief Exec. NICK BENNETT.

Harper Adams University College: Newport, TF10 8NB; tel. (1952) 820-280; fax (1952) 814-783; e-mail admissions@harper-adams.ac.uk; internet www.harper-adams.ac.uk; f. 1901; higher education for rural, land, animal and food-based studies; library: 50,000 books, 900 journal titles; 83 teachers; 4,000 students; Prin. Dr DAVID LLEWELLYN.

Neath Port Talbot College: Neath Campus, Dwr-y-Felin Rd, Neath, SA10 7RF; tel. (1639) 648000; fax (1639) 648009; e-mail admissions@nptc.ac.uk; internet www.nptc.ac.uk; f. 1999 by merger of Neath and Afan colleges; 8 campuses, 70 outreach centres; HNC, HND, foundation and Bachelors degree courses; library: 40,000 items; 14,000 students; Prin. and Chief Exec. MARK DACEY.

Pembrokeshire College: Haverfordwest, SA61 1SZ; tel. (1437) 753000; fax (1437) 753001; e-mail international.info@pembrokeshire.ac.uk; internet www.pembrokeshire.ac.uk; provides undergraduate and postgraduate degrees, HNDs and HNCs validated by Univ. of Glamorgan; accredited college of the univ.; 550 teachers; 8,500 students (2,000 full-time, 6,500 part-time); Prin. GLYN JONES.

Royal Welsh College of Music and Drama: Castle Grounds, Cathays Park, Cardiff, CF1 3ER; tel. (29) 2039-2854; fax (29) 2039-1301; e-mail admissions@rwcmd.ac.uk; internet www.rwcmd.ac.uk; f. 1949; national conservatoire of Wales; full- and part-time courses for performers, and degree and diploma courses validated by the Univ. of Wales; library: 50,000 books, play scripts, journals, performance scores, orchestral sets, audiovisual material and newspapers; 632 students; Prin. HILARY BOULDING.

Institute of Biological, Environmental and Rural Sciences: Aberystwyth Univ., Penglais, Aberystwyth, Ceredigion, SY23 3DA; tel. (1970) 622316; fax (1970) 622350; e-mail ibers@aber.ac.uk; internet www.aber.ac.uk/en/ibers; f. by merger of Institutes of Rural Sciences and Biological Sciences at Aberystwyth Univ.; undergraduate and postgraduate courses and research in biological, environmental and rural sciences; campuses in Gogerddan and Llanbadarn; library: 53,000 vols; 366 teachers; Dir Prof. WAYNE POWELL.

Ystrad Mynach College: Twyn Rd, Ystrad Mynach, Hengoed, CF82 7XR; tel. (1443) 816888; fax (1443) 816973; e-mail enquiries@ystrad-mynach.ac.uk; internet www.ystrad-mynach.ac.uk; f. 1959; 7 campuses; HNC/D, foundation degree, undergraduate degrees; franchised from Univ. of Wales Institute Cardiff, Univ. of Wales, Newport; 10,000 students; Prin. MALCOLM SAINSBURY.

BERMUDA

Regulatory Bodies

GOVERNMENT

Ministry of Culture and Social Rehabilitation: POB HM 788, Hamilton HM CX; Suite 304, Melbourne House, 11 Parliament St, Hamilton HM 12; tel. 296-1574; fax 295-2066; e-mail premier@gov.bm; internet www.gov.bm; Minister DALE D. BUTLER.

Ministry of Education: Dundonald Pl., 14 Dundonald St, Hamilton HM 09; tel. 278-3300; fax 278-3348; internet www.moed.bm; Minister ELVIN JAMES.

Learned Societies

GENERAL

Bermuda National Trust: POB HM 61, Hamilton HM AX; Waterville, 2 Pomander Rd, Paget PG 05; tel. 236-6483; fax 236-0617; e-mail palmetto@bnt.bm; internet www.bnt.bm; f. 1970; promotes preservation and appreciation of lands, buildings and artefacts of natural or historic interest; 4,000 mems; Pres. BILL HOLMES; Deputy Pres. SIMON VAN DE WEG; Exec. Dir JENNIFER GRAY; Curator ANDREW BAYLAY; publ. *Architectural Heritage–Bermuda* (irregular).

FINE AND PERFORMING ARTS

Bermuda Professional Photographic Association: POB 182, Southampton SN BX; tel. 238-4387; fax 295-4724; e-mail info@bermudaphotographers.com; internet www.bermudaphotographers.com; f. 1956; promotes professional photojournalism and creative photography; 26 mems.

Bermuda Society of Arts: POB HM 1202, Hamilton HM FX; The City Hall Arts Centre, 17 Church St, Hamilton; tel. 292-3824; fax 296-0699; e-mail bsoa@ibl.bm; internet www.bsoa.bm; f. c. 1950, as Society of Artists in Bermuda, present name 1956; exhibition space with 4 galleries showcasing Bermudian art and artists; 700 mems; Pres. DUNCAN HALL; Gallery Dir JULIE HASTINGS.

HISTORY, GEOGRAPHY AND ARCHAEOLOGY

Bermuda Historical Society: 13 Queen St, Hamilton HM 11; tel. 295-2487; f. 1895; promotes interest in history of Bermuda; attached museum: holds portraits, miniatures, antique furnishings, colln of early Bermuda coins and silver; attached library; 130 mems; Pres. ANDREW BERMINGHAM; Museum Curator COLIN BENBOW.

St George's Foundation: POB GE 58, St George's GE BX; Admiral's Walk, 16 Water St, St George's GE 05; tel. 297-8043; fax 297-2479; e-mail director@stgeorgesfoundation.org; internet www.stgeorgesfoundation.org; f. 1995; ind. not for profit org.; operates the St George's Historical Soc. Museum and Mitchell House (built c. 1830 purchased by St George's Historical Society 1922); contains antique furniture, paintings, porcelain and textiles; open Mondays to Thursdays and Saturdays, April–November, closed December, open Wednesdays only January–March; 150 mems; Chair. Dr KENNETH SNAITH; Pres. VIRGINIA OLANDER; Exec. Dir SHARON JACOBS; Dir of Education LEONDRA BURCHALL; Treas. HARRY WILKEN; Sec. ALISON OUTEBRIDGE.

MEDICINE

Bermuda Dental Association: POB 3059, Hamilton HM NX; tel. 236-9337; fax 236-1325; e-mail bdadental@gmail.com; internet www.bermudadental.bm; f. 1964; encourages the study of dentistry and allied sciences; promotes and maintains honour and dignity of the dental profession in Bermuda; Pres. Dr RONDA JAMES.

Bermuda Medical Society: POB HM 1023, Hamilton HM DX; King Edward VII Memorial Hospital, 7 Point Finger Rd, Paget DV 04; tel. 236-2345; fax 239-6324; f. 1970; assn of medical doctors in practice in Bermuda; 70 mems; Pres. Dr JOHN GAUGAIN; Sec. Dr GERHARD BOONSTRA.

Bermuda Pharmaceutical Association:- tel. 297-8427; e-mail admin@bpa.bm; internet www.bpa.bm; professional org; supports local pharmacists; Pres. KIRAN SHAH; Sec. (vacant); Treas. CAROLINE DICKINSON.

NATURAL SCIENCES

Biological Sciences

Bermuda Audubon Society: POB HM 1328, Hamilton HM FX; tel. 238-8628; e-mail info@audubon.bm; internet www.audubon.bm; f. 1954; environmental protection and education; 300 mems; Pres. ANDREW DOBSON; Exec. Sec. KAREN BORDER; Treas. PETER HOLMES; publ. *Newsletter* (2 a year).

Physical Sciences

Astronomical Society of Bermuda: POB HM 1046, Hamilton HM EX; tel. 236-3780; e-mail eddimac@ibl.bm; f. 1962; mem. meetings; educational activities; information provided to the media; promotes astronomy in Bermuda; 10 mems; Pres. EDDIE MCGONAGLE; Sec. and Treas. CATHIE MCGONAGLE.

Research Institutes

AGRICULTURE, FISHERIES AND VETERINARY SCIENCE

Department of Environmental Protection: POB HM 834, Hamilton HM CX; Botanical Gardens, 169 South Rd, Paget DV 04; tel. 236-4201; fax 236-7582; e-mail animals@gov.bm; internet www.gov.bm; f. 1898; management and devt of horticulture, environmental protection and Bermudan natural history; conducts research and monitors environment quality; Dir FREDERICK MING; Librarian ALISON GREEN; publ. *Envirotalk* (4 a year).

NATURAL SCIENCES

Biological Sciences

Bermuda Institute of Ocean Sciences: 17 Biological Station, Ferry Reach, St George's GE 01; tel. 297-1880; fax 297-8143; e-mail info@bios.edu; internet www.bios.edu; f. 1903 as Bermuda Biological Station for Research, present name 2006; ind. not-for-profit research instn; research in most aspects of marine sciences and oceanography and environmental sciences; courses organized during long vacation in marine invertebrates, ecology, pollution; high school and college facilities for instruction in marine sciences; attached research centres: Center for Integrated Ocean Observations (CINTOO), Int. Center for Ocean and Human Health (ICOHH); library of 20,000 vols; Chair. BRIAN DUPERREAULT; Pres. and Dir ANTHONY H. KNAP; publ. *Currents* (2 a year, print and online).

Libraries and Archives

Hamilton

Bermuda Archives: Government Admin. Bldg, 30 Parliament St, Hamilton HM 12; tel. 295-5151; fax 295-8751; internet www.gov.bm; f. 1974; repository for official, non-governmental records, private papers relating to Bermuda from 1615 to present; Dir KARLA HAYWARD.

Bermuda National Library: Par-la-Ville, 13 Queen St, Hamilton HM 11; Bermuda Youth Library, 74 Church St, Hamilton HM 12; tel. 295-2905; fax 292-8443; e-mail bdanatlib@gov.bm; internet www.bnl.bm; f. 1839, present bldg (Nat. Library) 1916; attached to Min. of Public Information Services; divs of adult and technical services operate from the Nat. Library bldg and youth services from the Youth Library; spec. colln of Bermudiana; extensive talking book and large print collns; 117,655 vols (incl. 12,700 vols at the Youth Library); Head Librarian C. JOANNE BRANGMAN; Librarian for Adult Services JULIE BEAN; Librarian for Youth Services MARLA SMITH; Librarian for Colln Management PATRICE CARVELL; publ. *Bermuda National Bibliography* (4 a year; print and online).

Museums and Art Galleries

Flatts

Bermuda Aquarium, Museum & Zoo: POB FL 145, Flatts FL BX; 40 North Shore Rd, Flatts FL 04; tel. 293-2727; fax 293-4014; e-mail info.bzs@gov.bm; internet www.bamz.org; f. 1926; live zoological colln; aquarium with large reef tank; local natural history and other exhibits; library of 3,000 vols; Prin. Curator Dr IAN WALKER; publ. *Wild* (4 a year).

Hamilton

Bermuda National Gallery: Suite 191, 48 Par-la-Ville Rd, Hamilton HM 11; City Hall Arts Centre, Church St, Hamilton; tel. 295-9428; fax 295-2055; e-mail director@bng.bm; internet www.bermudanationalgallery.com; f. 1992; attached to Bermuda Fine Art Trust; nat. art colln; Watlington Colln: spec. colln of historic European paintings; educational and social events; Chair., Bermuda Fine Art Trust GARY L. PHILLIPS; Dir LISA HOWIE; Curator SOPHIE CRESSALL.

Bermuda National Trust Museum at the Globe Hotel: POB HM 61, Hamilton HM AX; 32 York St, St George's; tel. 297-1423; fax 236-0617; e-mail palmetto@bnt.bm; internet www.bnt.bm; f. 1970, housed at the Globe Hotel built c. 1700; attached to Bermuda Nat. Trust; displays depict Bermuda's role in the American Civil War; colln of antique furniture; Dir AMANDA OUTERBRIDGE; Curator ANDREW.

Masterworks Museum of Bermuda Art: POB HM 1929, Hamilton HM HX; The Botanical Gardens 183, South Rd, Paget DV 04; tel. 236-2950; fax 236-4402; e-mail mworks@logic.bm; internet www.bermudamasterworks.com; f. 2008; not-for-profit org.; art storage facilities; classroom, main gallery and a smaller gallery dedicated to local artists; Founder and Creative Dir TOM BUTTERFIELD; Chair. MICHAEL HAMER; Treas. JUDITH HOWE-TUCKER.

Tucker House Museum: POB HM 61, Hamilton HM AX; 5 Water St, St George's; tel. 297-0545; fax 236-0617; e-mail palmetto@bnt.bm; internet www.bnt.bm; f. 1970, bldg 1750; attached to Bermuda Nat. Trust; 18th-century house with colln of Tucker family silver, china, crystal, English mahogany and Bermuda cedar furniture; Dir AMANDA OUTERBRIDGE; Curator ANDREW.

Verdmont Museum: POB HM 61, Hamilton HM AX; 6 Verdmont Lane, off Collector's Hill, Smith's Parish; tel. 236-7639; fax 236-0617; e-mail palmetto@bnt.bm; internet www.bnt.bm; f. built c. 1710, sold to the Bermuda Nat. Trust 1951; attached to Bermuda Nat. Trust; 18th-century house with period furniture; early Georgian architecture; Exec. Dir JENNIFER GRAY.

Sandys

Bermuda Arts Centre at Dockyard: POB MA 66, Mangrove Bay MA BX; tel. 234-2809; fax 234-0540; e-mail artcentre@ibl.bm; internet www.artbermuda.bm; f. 1984; not-for-profit org.; forum for local artists; art workshops; display and sale of local art work.

Bermuda Maritime Museum: POB MA 133, Sandys, MA BX; tel. 234-1333; fax 234-1735; e-mail info@bmm.bm; internet www.bmm.bm; f. 1975; area incl. fortress of Bermuda Dockyard and exhibits represent Bermuda maritime history; Exec. Dir Dr EDWARD C. HARRIS; Curator ELENA STRONG; publs *Bermuda Journal of Archaeology and Maritime History* (1 a year), *MARITimes* (members' magazine).

College

Bermuda College: POB PG 297, Paget PG BX; Stonington Ave, South Rd, Paget PG 04; tel. 236-9000; fax 239-4008; e-mail info@college.bm; internet www.college.bm; f. 1974, by merger of Bermuda Technical Institute (est. 1956), Bermuda Hotel and Catering College (est. 1965) and Academic Sixth Form Centre (est. 1967); divs of applied science and technology, business and hospitality, liberal arts, professional and career education; 52 teachers; 1,366 students; library: 30,000 vols; Pres. Dr DURANDA GREENE; Head Librarian JAMES AGEE.

CAYMAN ISLANDS

Regulatory and Representative Bodies

GOVERNMENT

Ministry of Education, Training and Employment: Royal Pl., 3rd Fl., George Town, Grand Cayman; tel. 244-2417; fax 949-9343; e-mail education@gov.ky; internet www.education.gov.ky; Min. Hon. ROLSTON M ANGLIN.

Ministry of Health, Environment, Youth, Sports and Culture: Govt Admin. Bldg, 3rd Fl., George Town, Grand Cayman; tel. 244-2318; fax 949-1790; internet www.ministryofhealth.gov.ky; Min. Hon. MARK SCOTLAND.

ACCREDITATION

Accreditation Commission on Colleges of Medicine (ACCM): see under Ireland.

Learned Societies

GENERAL

Cayman National Cultural Foundation: F. J. Harquail Cultural Centre, Harquail Dr. 17, POB 30201, Grand Cayman, KY1-1201; tel. 949-5477; fax 949-4519; e-mail admincncf@candw.ky; internet www.artscayman.org; f. 1984; facilitates and preserves cultural and artistic expression, particularly preservation and exploration of Caymanian performing, visual and literary arts; Chair. MARTYN C. W. BOULD.

National Trust for the Cayman Islands: POB 31116, Grand Cayman, KY1-1205; South Church St 558, Grand Cayman; tel. 749-1121; fax 749-1135; e-mail info@nationaltrust.org.ky; internet www.nationaltrust.org.ky; f. 1990; preserves natural environments and places of historic significance; Pres. CARLA REID; Sec. LOIS BLUMENTHAL; publ. *The Preserver* (4 a year).

FINE AND PERFORMING ARTS

Visual Arts Society of the Cayman Islands: POB 31060, Grand Cayman, KY1-1205; tel. 327-0751; internet www.visualartcayman.com; f. 1978; art appreciation, enhancement and learning; 75 mems; Chair. IVAN BURGES; Sec. SHIRLEY SCOTT.

Research Institutes

NATURAL SCIENCES

Biological Sciences

Central Caribbean Marine Institute: POB 10152, Grand Cayman KY1-1002; tel. 949-1938; e-mail info@reefresearch.org; internet www.reefresearch.org; f. 1998; sustains marine biodiversity through research, education, outreach and conservation programmes; Little Cayman research centre; Pres. Dr CARRIE MANFRINO; Sec. CHRIS HUMPHRIES; publ. *Green Guides*.

Queen Elizabeth II Botanic Park: POB 203, Grand Cayman, KY1-1701; tel. 947-3558; e-mail minfo@botanic-park.ky; internet www.botanic-park.ky; f. 1994; preserves natural environments; Gen. Man. ANDREW GUTHRIE.

Libraries and Archives

George Town

Cayman Islands National Archive: c/o Govt Admin. Bldg, Grand Cayman, KY1-9000; Archive Lane 37, George Town, Grand Cayman; tel. 949-9809; fax 949-9727; e-mail cina@gov.ky; internet www.cina.gov.ky; f. 2007; archive and records preservation, records policy unit and reprographics unit; Dir J. KIMLON SEYMOUR.

Cayman Islands Public Library Service: POB 1172, Grand Cayman, KY1-1102; Edward St 68, George Town, Grand Cayman; tel. 949-5159; fax 949-5015; e-mail foi.lib@gov.ky; internet www.cipl.gov.ky; f. 1920; 5 br. libraries and learning centre; local history reference colln; 64,025 vols; Dir JULIET LAWSON (acting).

Museums and Art Galleries

Cayman Brac

Cayman Brac Museum: POB 240, Cayman Brac, KY2-2101; tel. 948-2222; fax 948-2506; e-mail naturecayman@gov.ky; internet www.naturecayman.com; flora and fauna of the island; conserves natural environments; items of Cayman Brackers seafaring days.

George Town

Cayman Islands National Museum: POB 2189, George Town, KY1-1105; tel. 949-8368; fax 949-9309; internet www.museum.ky; f. 1990; preservation, research and dissemination of Caymanian heritage; over 8,000 items, incl. natural history specimens and rare documents; Dir DEBRA BARNES-TABORA (acting).

National Gallery of the Cayman Islands: POB 10197, Harbour Pl., Grand Cayman, KY1-1002; tel. 945-8111; fax 945-7103; internet www.nationalgallery.org.ky; f. 1997; promotes and encourages appreciation and practice of visuals arts; reference library with books and DVDs on history of art, design, and arts education and production; Chair. HENRY HARFORD; Dir NATALIE URQUHART; publ. *The Viewer* (4 a year).

Universities

ST MATTHEW'S UNIVERSITY

POB 32330, Grand Cayman, KY1-1209
Telephone: 945-3199
Fax: 945-3130
E-mail: admissions@stmatthews.edu
Internet: www.stmatthews.edu

Founded 1997
Academic year: September to August (3 semesters)
Chancellor: JOHN MARVIN
Library of 3,000 vols, 200 periodicals
Number of teachers: 280 (incl. 40 full-time)
Number of students: 1,065

DEANS

Faculty of Basic Sciences: Dr SENTHIL KUMAR
Faculty of Clinical Sciences: Dr JOHN RANDALL
Faculty of Veterinary Medicine: Dr WILLIAM WAGNER

UNIVERSITY COLLEGE CAYMAN ISLANDS

Olympic Way 168, POB 702, Georgetown, Grand Cayman, KY1-1107
Telephone: 623-8224
Fax: 949-6781
E-mail: suggestions@ucci.edu.ky
Internet: www.ucci.edu.ky

Founded 1985, present status 1987, present name 2004
State control
Academic year: September to July

Pres.: ROY BODDEN
Registrar: JOHN FREDERICK
Librarian: LUCILLE KONG

Library of 18,000 vols, 50 journals
Publication: *The Pipeline*.

Colleges

Cayman Islands Law School: POB 1568, Grand Cayman, KY1-1110; Old CIBC Bldg, 2nd–3rd Fl., George Town, Grand Cayman; tel. 945-0077; fax 946-1845; e-mail lovisa.vernon@gov.ky; internet www.lawschool.gov.ky; f. 1982; degree accredited by Univ. of Liverpool (UK); Dir MITCHELL DAVIES; Asst Dir D. BARKER.

International College of the Cayman Islands: Hirst Rd 595, POB 136, Grand Cayman, KY1-1501; tel. 947-1100; fax 947-1210; e-mail info@myicci.com; internet www.icci.edu.ky; f. 1970; Private control; undergraduate and postgraduate courses in science and business admin.; Dean SCOTT CUMMINGS.

GIBRALTAR

Regulatory Bodies

GOVERNMENT

Ministry of Culture, Heritage, Sport and Leisure: 310 Main St; tel. 20047592; fax 20052589; e-mail minculture@gibtelecom.net; internet www.gibraltar.gov.gi/culture; Min. EDWIN J. REYES; Dir of Culture YVETTE ZARB.

Ministry of Education and Training: 23 Queensway; tel. 20077486; fax 20071564; e-mail education@gibraltar.gov.gi; internet www.gibraltar.gov.gi/education-a-training; Min. CLIVE BELTRAN; Dir of Education and Training ERNEST GOMEZ.

Learned Society

NATURAL SCIENCES

Biological Sciences

Gibraltar Ornithological & Natural History Society: Field Centre, Jews' Gate, Upper Rock Nature Reserve, POB 843; tel. 20072639; fax 20074022; e-mail info@gonhs.org; internet www.gonhs.org; f. 1976; attached to Strait of Gibraltar Bird Observatory; research and conservation of nature in Gibraltar; environmental and biological education; 450 mems; Gen. Sec. Dr JOHN CORTES; publs *Alectoris* (1 a year), *Gibraltar Bird Report* (1 a year), *Gibraltar Nature News* (2 a year), *Iberis* (scientific journal).

Libraries and Archives

Gibraltar

Gibraltar Archives: 6 Convent Pl.; tel. and fax 20079461; e-mail archives@gibraltar.gov.gi; internet www.gibraltar.gov.gi/gibraltar-archives; f. 1969; attached to Min. of Culture, Heritage, Sport and Leisure; colln and preservation of public and historical records from 18th to 20th centuries; research services; liaison with schools and other instns; Archivist T. J. FINLAYSON.

Gibraltar Garrison Library: Governor's Parade; tel. 20077418; fax 20079927; e-mail gibgarlib@gibconnect.net; internet gibraltargarrisonlibrary.info; f. 1793; culture and travel; lithographs and art prints; local history colln; colln of books published in 18th and 19th centuries; 45,000 books, incl. rare vols; Trust Sec. FRED TIBBO.

John Mackintosh Hall Library: 308 Main St, POB 939; tel. 20075669; fax 20040843; e-mail gfjmh@gibraltar.gi; f. 1964; attached to European Documentation Centre; 3 exhibition galleries, theatre, reference library, information office and conf. rooms; 33,000 vols; Dir Dr GERALDINE FINLAYSON.

Museum

Gibraltar

Gibraltar Museum: 18/20 Bomb House Lane, POB 939; tel. 20074289; fax 20079158; e-mail enquiries@museum.gib.gi; internet www.gib.gi/museum; f. 1930; colln of local natural history, archaeology and palaeontology (especially Palaeolithic, Neolithic and Phoenician) and military history; displays incl. Evelegh colln (colln of miniature ordnance 1779–83), artefacts from Gibraltar's Islamic past (711–1464), medieval baths built in 1333; Dir, Heritage Div. Dr CLIVE FINLAYSON; Dir, Institute for Gibraltarian Studies GERALDINE FINLAYSON; Deputy Dir DARREN FA; publ. *Gibraltar Heritage Magazine* (2 a year).

GUERNSEY

Regulatory Bodies

GOVERNMENT

Culture and Leisure Department: Information Centre, North Esplanade, St Peter Port, GY1 2LQ; tel. (1481) 713888; e-mail enquiries@cultureleisure.gov.gg; internet www.gov.gg/ccm/navigation/culture—leisure; Min. MIKE O'HARA.

Education Department: POB 32, Grange Rd, St Peter Port, GY1 3AU; tel. (1481) 710821; fax (1481) 714475; e-mail office@education.gov.gg; internet www.education.gg; Min. CAROL STEERE.

Learned Societies

GENERAL

Alderney Society: The Alderney Society Museum, High St, St Anne, GY9 3TG; tel. (1481) 823222; e-mail info@alderneysociety.org; internet www.alderneysociety.org; f. 1966; promotes awareness and encourages historical, environmental, scientific activities relating to the Island of Alderney; 600 mems; Pres. LOUIS JEAN; publ. *Bulletin* (1 a year).

La Société Guernesiaise: Candie Gardens, St Peter Port, GY1 1UG; tel. (1481) 725093; fax (1481) 726248; e-mail societe@cwgsy.net; internet www.societe.org.gg; f. 1882; activities incl. archaeology, astronomy, botany, entomology, family history, geology, historic buildings, history and philology, marine biology, nature conservation, ornithology; also manages island's nature reserves; 2,000 mems; Pres. RODNEY COLLENETTE; Vice-Pres. (vacant); Sec. LAWNEY MARTIN; Hon. Treas. PETER BUDWIN; publs *Communiqué* (3 a year), *Transactions* (1 a year).

HISTORY, GEOGRAPHY AND ARCHAEOLOGY

Alderney Maritime Trust: POB 1, St Anne, GY9 3AA; tel. (1481) 822249; e-mail hugo@alderneywreck.com; internet www.alderneywreck.com; f. 1996 by the States of Alderney; preserves, protects and manages the historic Elizabethan shipwreck off the coast of Alderney and its contents; artefacts from the wreck are either stored or on display at the Alderney Soc. Museum; Chair. Sir NORMAN BROWSE; Excavation Dir MENSUN BOUND; Treas. DICKIN DREW.

Libraries and Archives

St Peter Port

Guille Allès Library: Market St, St Peter Port, GY1 1HB; tel. (1481) 720392; fax (1481) 712425; e-mail ga@library.gg; internet www.library.gg; f. 1882; admin. by the Guille Allès Trust to provide free library services for the community; Chief Librarian MAGGIE FALLA.

Priaulx Library: Candie Rd, St Peter Port, GY1 1UG; tel. (1481) 721998; fax (1481) 713804; e-mail info@priaulxlibrary.co.uk; internet www.priaulxlibrary.co.uk; f. 1889; based on personal colln of Osmond de Beauvoir Priaulx; also incl. archives of local newspapers on microfilm, civil and ecclesiastical records, family history files and military colln; rare vols and incunabula; local studies in French and English; 30,000 vols; Chief Librarian AMANDA BENNETT; Deputy Chief Librarian SUE LAKER.

Museums and Art Galleries

St Anne

Alderney Society Museum: The Museum, High St, St Anne, GY9 3TG; tel. (1481) 823222;

fax (1481) 824979; e-mail info@alderneymuseum.org; internet www.alderneysociety.org/museum.html; f. 1966, registered in 1993; attached to The Alderney Society; colln of 12,000 items incl. artefacts, documents, photographs; Admin. DON OAKDEN.

St Peter Port

Guernsey Museums & Galleries: Candie Gardens, St Peter Port, GY1 1UG; tel. (1481) 726518; fax (1481) 715177; internet www.museums.gov.gg; f. 1907, present status 2004; attached to Culture and Leisure Dept; history of Guernsey and its people; art gallery displays pictures of Guernsey by Guernsey painters; associated maritime and military museums at Fort Grey and Castle Cornet; Guernsey Telephone Museum; Dir Dr JASON MONAGHAN; Sr Curator ALAN HOWELL.

ISLE OF MAN

Regulatory Body

GOVERNMENT

Department of Education & Children: St George's Court, Upper Church St, Douglas, IM1 2SG; tel. (1624) 685820; fax (1624) 685834; e-mail admin@doe.gov.im; internet www.gov.im/education; Min. EDDIE TEARE; Dir J. CAIN.

Learned Societies

HISTORY, GEOGRAPHY AND ARCHAEOLOGY

Isle of Man Family History Society: Derby Lodge, Derby Rd, Peel, IM5 1HH; tel. (1624) 843105; e-mail iomfhs@manx.net; internet www.iomfhs.im; f. 1979; local genealogy and family history; attached library; Chair. ERNEST CLEATOR; Sec. PAT NICHOLSON; Treas. DAVID CHRISTIAN; publ. *Fraueyn as Banglaneyn* (Roots and Branches, 4 a year).

Isle of Man Natural History and Antiquarian Society: Ballacrye Stream Cottage, Ballaugh, IM7 5EB; tel. (1624) 897306; internet www.manxantiquarians.com; f. 1879; archaeology, geography, geology, history, literature and natural history; 500 mems; Pres. ALLISON FOX; Hon. Sec. C. J. BRYAN; Hon. Treas. IAN WRENCH; Hon. Librarian SUSAN CHAMBERS; publ. *Proceedings* (1 a year).

Research Institutes

HISTORY, GEOGRAPHY AND ARCHAEOLOGY

Centre for Manx Studies: Stable Bldg, Univ. Centre, Old Castletown Rd, Douglas, IM2 1QB; tel. (1624) 695777; fax (1624) 695783; e-mail cms@liv.ac.uk; internet www.liv.ac.uk/manxstudies; f. 1992; attached to School of Archaeology, Classics and Egyptology of Univ. of Liverpool; research in history, archaeology, culture and environment of the Isle of Man; Dir Dr HAROLD MYTUM; Admin. GILL WILSON; publ. *Studeyrys Manninagh* (Journal of Manx Studies, online).

NATURAL SCIENCES

Biological Sciences

Port Erin Marine Laboratory: Port Erin, IM9 6JA; tel. (1624) 831000; fax (1624) 831001; e-mail peml@liv.ac.uk; internet www.liv.ac.uk/www/peml/; f. 1892; attached to University of Liverpool, School of Biological Sciences; research on fish population dynamics; Dir Prof. T. A. NORTON.

Libraries and Archives

Douglas

Manx National Heritage–National Library and Archives Service: Douglas, IM1 3LY; tel. (1624) 648040; fax (1624) 648069; e-mail library@mnh.gov.im; internet www.gov.im/mnh/heritage/library/nationallibrary.xml; f. 1923; nat. library and archives of the Isle of Man; covers all aspects of Manx heritage and acts as a place of deposit for public and diocesan records; Library and Archive Services Officer PAUL WEATHERALL.

Tynwald Library: Legislative Bldgs, Finch Rd, Douglas, IM1 3PW; tel. (1624) 685520; fax (1624) 685522; e-mail library@tynwald.org.im; internet www.tynwald.org.im; f. 1975; 5,000 vols, 75 periodicals, documents issued by the Isle of Man legislature (Tynwald) and govt; Librarian G. C. HAYWOOD.

Museums and Art Galleries

Castletown

Nautical Museum: Bridge St, Castletown, IM9 1AX; internet www.gov.im/mnh/heritage/museums/nauticalmuseum.xml; f. 1951, museum bldg originates from the discovery of the 18th-century armed yacht the 'Peggy' in 1935; attached to Manx Nat. Heritage (Eiraght Ashoonagh Vannin); considered of maritime importance on the Nat. Historic Ships Register.

Cregneash

National Folk Museum at Cregneash: Cregneash Rd, Cregneash, IM9 5PX; internet www.gov.im/mnh/heritage/museums/cregneashvillage.xml; f. 1938; attached to Manx Nat. Heritage (Eiraght Ashoonagh Vannin); provides a living, working illustration of life in a typical 19th- and early 20th-century Manx upland crofting community.

Douglas

Manx Museum: Kingswood Grove, Douglas, IM1 3LY; tel. (1624) 648000; fax (1624) 648001; e-mail enquiries@mnh.gov.im; internet www.gov.im/mnh/heritage/museums/manxmuseum.xml; f. 1922; attached to Manx Nat. Heritage (Eiraght Ashoonagh Vannin); Manx history and archaeology; art and map galleries; Dir, Manx Nat. Heritage E. SOUTHWORTH.

Colleges

Isle of Man College/Colleish Ellan Vannin: Homefield Rd, Douglas, IM2 6RB; tel. (1624) 648200; fax (1624) 648201; internet www.iomcollege.ac.im; f. 1971; publicly funded instn; affiliated to Univ. of Liverpool, Liverpool Hope Univ. and Univ. of Chester, offering joint degree courses in addition to gen. further education studies; courses in adult community education, art, design and media, business, management and professional studies, computing and information technology, construction, education, training and staff devt, engineering, gen. education, hair and beauty, health and social care, heritage and Manx studies, hospitality and catering, learning services, office technology, staff devt; library: 29,000 vols; Prin. RAY SMITH; Chair. A. C. COLLISTER; Dir Prof. R. CAREY.

Isle of Man International Business School: University Centre, Old Castletown Rd, Douglas, IM2 1QB; tel. (1624) 693700; fax (1624) 665095; e-mail enquiries@ibs.ac.im; internet www.ibs.ac.im; f. 1999; attached to Dept of Education & Children; MSc courses in financial regulation and compliance management, and in international banking and finance, BA (Hons) in business studies, MBA in business management; Dir of MBA Programmes Prof. AUGUSTINE OKANLAWON.

JERSEY

Regulatory Body

GOVERNMENT

Department for Education, Sport and Culture: POB 142, Highlands Campus, St Helier, JE4 8QJ; tel. (1534) 445504; fax (1534) 445524; e-mail esc@gov.je; internet www.gov.je/esc; Min. JAMES REED.

Learned Societies

GENERAL

Société Jersiaise: 7 Pier Rd, St Helier, JE2 4XW; tel. (1534) 758314; fax (1534) 888262; e-mail societe@societe-jersiaise.org; internet www.societe-jersiaise.org; f. 1873; promotes the study of the history, archaeology, natural history, language and other fields relative to Jersey; library: Lord Coutanche Library contains books, newspapers, maps, prints, parish records and other material concerning the Channel Islands, Normandy, Brittany and southern England; 75,000 images in photographic archive; Pres. ROWLAND ANTHONY; Exec. Dir PAULINE SYVRET; publ. *Library and Photographic Archive* (online).

AGRICULTURE, FISHERIES AND VETERINARY SCIENCE

Royal Jersey Agricultural & Horticultural Society: Royal Jersey Showground, La Route de la Trinité, Trinity, JE3 5JP; tel. (1534) 866555; fax (1534) 865619; e-mail society@royaljersey.co.uk; internet www.royaljersey.co.uk; f. 1833; agricultural dept: provides a range of services to support the modern dairy industry; responsible for the management of the Jersey breed in the island; horticulture dept: promotes horticulture through talks, shows, garden competitions and general advice; Royal Jersey Showground: holds indoor and outdoor events; conference and exhibition facilities.

ECONOMICS, LAW AND POLITICS

Law Society of Jersey: POB 493, St Helier, JE4 5SZ; tel. (1534) 613920; fax (1534) 613928; e-mail ceolawsoc@gmail.com; internet www.jerseylawsociety.je; governing body of lawyers practising as advocates and solicitors of the Royal Court of Jersey; operates a fee complaints procedure; Pres. C. M. B. THACKER; Sec. S. E. FITZ; Hon. Treas. M. H. RICHARDSON; Hon. Librarian C. G. PARSLOW.

HISTORY, GEOGRAPHY AND ARCHAEOLOGY

Channel Islands Family History Society: POB 507, St Helier, JE4 5TN; e-mail cifhs@localdial.com; internet www.jerseyfamilyhistory.org; f. 1978; research colln held at Jersey Archive; Pres. JOHN NOEL; Sec. PAT NEALE; Treas. HARRY BAUDAINS; publ. *Journal* (4 a year).

Jersey Heritage: The Weighbridge, St Helier, JE2 3NF; tel. (1534) 633300; e-mail info@jerseyheritagetrust.org; internet www.jerseyheritagetrust.org; f. 1981; ind. org. funded by States of Jersey; promotes and preserves Jersey's heritage; main collns of archaeology, art, archives and social history; Chair. C. JONES; Vice-Chair. P. LE BROCQ; Dir JONATHAN CARTER.

Research Institutes

MEDICINE

Cancer Research UK Jersey: Woodlands Court, La Route des Cotils, Grouville, JE3 9AP; tel. (1534) 500420; fax (1534) 858185; e-mail jersey@cancer.org.uk; internet www.cancerresearchukjersey.org; f. 1953 as Jersey Committee; fund-raising and research into the causes of cancer, means of treating cancer more effectively and ways of reducing the incidence of cancer; Chair. ROBERT CHRISTENSEN; Treas. CAROL RAFFERTY.

Libraries and Archives

St Helier

Jersey Archive: Clarence Rd, St Helier, JE2 4JY; tel. (1534) 833333; fax (1534) 833101; e-mail archives@jerseyheritage.org; internet www.jerseyheritage.org/research-centre/jersey-archive; f. 1993; attached to Jersey Heritage; preserves records of the States of Jersey, State cttees and depts, Royal Court, Lt-Governor, parishes, churches, businesses, societies and individuals; Head of Archives and Collns LINDA ROMERIL.

Jersey Library: Halkett Pl., St Helier, JE2 4WH; tel. (1534) 448700; fax (1534) 448730; e-mail je.library@gov.je; internet www.gov.je/library; gen. lending colln, local and British newspapers and periodicals since the 18th century; Chief Librarian PAT DAVIS.

Museums and Art Galleries

Grouville

La Hougue Bie Museum: La Route de la Hougue Bie, Grouville, JE2 7UA; internet www.jerseyheritage.org; attached to Jersey Heritage; passage graves; life and history of Jersey's neolithic community.

St Helier

Jersey Museum and Art Gallery: The Weighbridge, St Helier, JE2 3NG; tel. (1534) 633300; internet www.jerseyheritage.org; attached to Jersey Heritage; history of neolithic to modern day Jersey; spec. items on display incl. Bronze Age gold torque and Millais' portrait of Lillie Langtry; works of Claude Cahun; Victorian Merchant town house with traditional gas lamps and period furniture.

Maritime Museum: New North Quay, St Helier, JE2 3ND; tel. (1534) 633372; fax (1534) 874099; e-mail info@jerseyheritagetrust.org; internet www.jerseyheritage.org; f. 1997; attached to Jersey Heritage; seafaring and navigation; displays selected objects from maritime collector and Jersey resident Tony Titterington's collns incl. a torpedo, propeller and shaft, a restored 88-mm deck gun and sonar from a German armed trawler; ship bells, bronze cannon from HMS *Determinée*, a British man-of-war wrecked off Noirmont in 1803.

Occupation Tapestry Gallery: New North Quay, St Helier, JE2 3ND; tel. (1534) 633372; internet www.jerseyheritage.org; attached to Jersey Heritage; displays 12 panels of tapestry depicting life in Jersey during the Second World War.

St Lawrence

Hamptonne Country Life Museum: La Rue de la Patente, St Lawrence, JE3 1HS; tel. (1534) 633300; internet www.jerseyheritage.org; attached to Jersey Heritage; farm bldgs and meadows; cluster of restored farmhouses and outbuildings displaying 17th-century rural life in Jersey.

Jersey War Tunnels: Les Charrières Malorey, St Lawrence, JE3 1FU; tel. (1534) 860808; fax (1534) 860886; e-mail info@jerseywartunnels.com; internet www.jerseywartunnels.com; tunnel complex fmrly known as Höhlgangsanlage 8 (Ho8); hosts a series of galleries detailing the Occupation of Jersey during the Second World War.

College

Highlands College: POB 1000, St Saviour, JE4 9QA; tel. (1534) 608608; e-mail hcwebsite@highlands.ac.uk; internet www.highlands.ac.uk; f. 1881 as naval training college, present name and status 1972; attached to Dept for Education, Sport and Culture; vocational and leisure courses; adult education service; partnership with Plymouth and London South Bank Univs; attached Univ. Centre for undergraduate and graduate study; 6,000 students; Prin. and Chief Exec. Prof. EDWARD SALLIS; Deputy Prin. Dr GARY JONES; Vice-Prin. PETER WADE (acting).

UNITED STATES OF AMERICA

The Higher Education System

Institutions of higher education predate the USA's independence from the United Kingdom in 1776, the oldest being Harvard University, which was founded in 1636. Over 500 universities and colleges were founded during the 19th century, particularly following the Morrill Land-Grants Acts of 1862 and 1890, which gave over Federal lands to the States for the purpose of establishing and funding educational institutions; the so-called 'A&M' (agricultural and mechanical) universities are among the most prominent of these institutions. There is no Federal system of higher education, which is primarily provided by State governments and private institutions. However, the Federal Department of Education is responsible for promoting education at all levels, dispensing Federal aid and enforcing civil rights statutes. The Bill of Rights of the US Constitution guarantees academic freedom at all levels. Higher education is offered by universities and two-year, four-year and community colleges. In 2005/06 there were 4,276 two-year and four-year universities and colleges, with a total enrolment of an estimated 18.2m. students in 2008 of whom 13.6m. attended public institutions and 4.6m. private institutions.

Admission to higher education is often on the basis of the High School Graduation Diploma and results in Scholastic Aptitude Tests (SATS), with institutions also applying their own criteria. Two-year Associate degrees are offered by both four-year institutions and two-year junior, technical and community colleges (junior colleges are usually privately run institutions and community colleges are funded by State or local governments). Students who have been awarded Associate degrees may transfer into four-year universities and colleges to complete full degrees. The Bachelors is the main undergraduate degree and lasts four years, consisting of two years of general education and then two years of study in a 'major' subject. Bachelors degrees in specialist or technical fields last five years. Most degrees are awarded on a 'credit-semester' basis, under which the student is required to accumulate a specified number of credits each semester in order to graduate. The minimum number of credits required for the award of the Bachelors degree is 120.

Postgraduate education in US institutions is referred to as 'graduate school' because degrees at this level are administered by university graduate schools. Admission to graduate school requires the Bachelors and an application supported by transcripts, statements of purpose and letters of recommendation. Applicants will also be required to achieve good scores in at least one of several standardized tests, depending on the subject area. Among these tests are Graduate Record Examinations, Miller Analogies Test, Graduate Management Admissions Test, Law School Admissions Test and the Medical College Admission Test. Masters degrees last between one and three years and are available on a taught or research basis, the difference being that taught degrees prepare students for professional entry and research degrees prepare students for further postgraduate studies. The PhD is the most common doctoral-level degree, and lasts between five to 10 years following the award of the Masters. The PhD consists of a period of intensive study leading to examinations before the student undertakes research for a doctoral dissertation, which is presented and defended before a panel.

There is no established Federal framework of post-secondary technical and vocational qualifications. Occupational training takes place in the workplace, and educational certificates, diplomas and degrees consist of both classroom-based learning and practical experience.

Accreditation of universities and colleges is administered by the six main regional accrediting bodies, which are recognized by the Department of Education and are members of the Council for Higher Education Accreditation. They are: Middle States Association of Colleges and Schools (MSA) , Northwest Commission on Colleges and Universities (NWCCU), North Central Association of Colleges and Schools (NCA), New England Association of Schools and Colleges, Inc. / Commission on Institutions of Higher Education (NEASC–CIHE), Southern Association of Colleges and Schools / Commission on Colleges (SACS–CC) and Western Association of Schools and Colleges / Accrediting Commission for Senior Colleges and Universities (WASC–Sr). There are also professional bodies and single-subject agencies that accredit specialist schools and individual programmes.

In 2009 President Barack Obama enacted legislation to make college more affordable by making working families eligible for a tax credit to help offset the cost of tuition and by expanding the Perkins Loan Programme. He also had plans to reform Pell Grants and the nation's student loan system by decreasing the role of private lenders and placing the responsibility on the federal Government.

Regulatory and Representative Bodies

GOVERNMENT

Department of Education: 400 Maryland Ave, SW, Washington, DC 20202; tel. (202) 401-2000; fax (202) 401-0596; internet www.ed.gov; Sec. of Education ARNE DUNCAN.

ACCREDITATION

ENIC/NARIC United States of America: United States Network for Education Information (USNEI)/US ENIC, Int. Affairs Office/OS, US Dept of Education, 400 Maryland Ave, SW, Room 6W108, Washington, DC 20202; tel. (202) 401-0430; fax (202) 401-2508; e-mail stephen.hunt@ed.gov; internet www.ed.gov/about/offices/list/ous/international/usnei/edlite-index.html; Man., USNEI Dr E. STEPHEN HUNT.

Middle States Association of Colleges and Schools: Middle States Commission on Higher Education: 3624 Market St, Philadelphia, PA 19104; tel. (267) 284-5000; e-mail info@msche.org; internet www.msche.org; f. 1887 as the College Assen of Pennsylvania, present name 1975; the Comm. is a voluntary, non-governmental, membership asscn that defines, maintains, and promotes educational excellence across instns with diverse missions, student populations and resources; it accredits degree-granting colleges and univs in the Middle States region, which includes DE, DC, MD, NJ, NY, PA, Puerto Rico, the US Virgin Islands and several locations internationally; Chair. of Commission's Exec. Cttee Dr PETER F. BURNHAM; Pres. of Comm. JEAN AVNET MORSE.

New England Association of Schools and Colleges, Inc.: Commission on Institutions of Higher Education (NEASC—CIHE): New England Asscn of Schools and Colleges, 209 Burlington Rd, Suite 201, Bedford, MA 01730-1433; tel. (781) 271-0022; fax (781) 271-0950; e-mail cihe@neasc.org; internet cihe.neasc.org; f. Asscn 1885; the Comm. is the regional accreditation agency for over 225 colleges and univs in the 6 New England states: CT, ME, MA, NH, RI and VT; 2 instns in Greece, 3 in Switzerland and 1 in Bulgaria, Bermuda and Lebanon, respectively, are also affiliated with CIHE; Chair. of Comm. JUDITH R. GORDON; Dir of Comm. Dr BARBARA E. BRITTINGHAM.

North Central Association of Colleges and Schools: Higher Learning Commission: Suite 2400, 30 North LaSalle St, Chicago, IL 60602-2504; tel. (312) 263-0456; fax (312) 263-7462; e-mail info@hlcommission.org; internet www.ncahigherlearningcommission.org; ind. corpn that accredits degree-granting educational instns in the N Central region: AR, AZ, CO, IA, IL, IN, KS, MI, MN, MO, ND, NE, OH, OK, NM, SD, WI, WV and WY; Pres. of Comm. STEVEN D. CROW; Dir of Operations BERNADETTE A. IVERS.

Northwest Commission on Colleges and Universities: Suite 100, 8060 165th Ave,

NE, Redmond, WA 98052; tel. (425) 558-4224; fax (425) 376-0596; internet www.nwccu.org; f. 1917; ind., non-profit membership org., recognized as the regional authority on educational quality and institutional effectiveness of higher education instns in the seven-state Northwest region of AK, ID, MT, NV, OR, UT and WA; it fulfills its mission by establishing accreditation criteria and evaluation procedures by which the region's 160 instns are reviewed; Pres. Dr SANDRA E. ELMAN.

Southern Association of Colleges and Schools: Commission on Colleges: 1866 southern Lane, Decatur, GA 30033; tel. (404) 679-4500; fax (404) 679-4558; internet www.sacscoc.org; recognized regional accrediting body in the 11 US Southern states (AL, FL, GA, KY, LA, MS, NC, SC, TN, TX and VA) and in Latin America for those instns of higher education that award Associate, Bachelors, Masters or doctoral degrees; Chair. of Comm. PHILIP C. STONE; Pres. of Comm. Dr BELLE S. WHEELAN.

Western Association of Schools and Colleges: Accrediting Commission for Senior Colleges and Universities: 985 Atlantic Ave, Suite 100, Alameda, CA 94501; tel. (510) 748-9001; fax (510) 748-9797; e-mail wascsr@wascsenior.org; internet www.wascsenior.org; f. Asscn 1962 to promote the welfare, interests and devt of education in the Western Region; the Comm. accredits 161 instns in CA, HI and the Pacific Basin; Chair. of Comm. SHERWOOD LINGENFELTER; Pres. and Exec. Dir RALPH A. WOLFF.

FUNDING

Alfred P. Sloan Foundation: Suite 2550, 630 Fifth Ave, New York, NY 10111; tel. (212) 649-1649; fax (212) 757-5117; internet www.sloan.org; f. 1934; makes grants for projects in science and technology, standard of living and economic performance, and education and careers in science and technology; Pres. PAUL JOSKOW.

Foundation Center: 79 Fifth Ave, New York City, NY 10003-3076; tel. (212) 620-4230; fax (212) 807-3677; internet foundationcenter.org; f. 1956; offices in Washington, DC, San Francisco, CA, Cleveland, OH, and Atlanta, GA; makes available information about philanthropic foundations; maintains a full collection of foundation reports; library of 2,500 vols, 3,250 pamphlets and articles, 500 foundation reports, computer files of foundation grants, aperture card system containing foundation IRS returns; Pres. BRADFORD K. SMITH; publs *FC Search: The Foundation Center's Database on CD-ROM* (two CDs and manual, 1 a year), *Foundation Directory* (online and 1 a year), *Foundation Grants to Individuals* (every 2 years), *Grant Guides in 30 Subjects* (1 a year), *Guide to Funding for International and Foreign Programs*, *National Directory of Corporate Giving* (1 a year).

Kellogg, W. K., Foundation: 1 Michigan Avenue, E, Battle Creek, MI 49017-4012; tel. (269) 968-1611; fax (269) 968-0413; internet www.wkkf.org; f. 1930; philanthropic nonpartisan org. administering funds for activities in the fields of youth and education, health, food systems and rural devt, and philanthropy and volunteerism, in the USA, Latin America, the Caribbean and southern Africa; Pres./CEO STERLING K. SPEIRN.

Rockefeller Foundation: 420 Fifth Ave, New York, NY 10018; tel. (212) 869-8500; fax (212) 764-3468; e-mail webmaster@rockfound.org; internet www.rockfound.org; f. 1913 to promote the well-being of mankind; makes grants in the fields of: agriculture, health, population sciences, the global environment, African initiatives, organized under the Int. Program to Support Science-Based Devt; arts and humanities; equal opportunity; school reform; offices also in San Francisco, CA, Italy, Kenya and Thailand; Chair. of Board JAMES F. ORR, III; Pres. JUDITH RODIN; Chief Operating Officer PETER MADONIA.

Woodrow Wilson International Center for Scholars: 1 Woodrow Wilson Plaza, 1300 Pennsylvania Ave, NW, Washington, DC 20004-3027; tel. (202) 691-4000; fax (202) 691-4001; internet www.wilsoncenter.org; f. 1968; non-partisan instn supported by public and private funds; provides a link between the world of ideas and the world of policy; fosters research, study, discussion and collaboration among a full spectrum of individuals concerned with policy and scholarship in nat. and world affairs; library of 20,000 vols, 250 periodicals; Pres. and Dir LEE H. HAMILTON; Chair. of Board of Trustees JOSEPH B. GILDENHORN; publ. *Wilson Quarterly*.

NATIONAL BODIES

American Association of Collegiate Registrars and Admissions Officers: Suite 520, 1 Dupont Circle, NW, Washington, DC 20036; tel. (202) 293-9161; fax (202) 872-8857; e-mail sullivanj@aacrao.org; internet www.aacrao.org; provides professional devt, guidelines and voluntary standards to be used by higher education officials regarding the best practices in records management, admissions, enrolment management, admin. information technology and student services; more than 10,000 mems in 30 countries; Pres. PAUL AUCOIN; Exec. Dir JEROME SULLIVAN; publ. *College & University* (4 a year).

American Association of Community Colleges: Suite 410, 1 Dupont Circle, NW, Washington, DC 20036; tel. (202) 728-0200; fax (202) 833-2467; internet www.aacc.nche.edu; f. 1920 as American Asscn of Junior Colleges, present name 1992; aims to build a nation of learners by advancing America's community colleges; more than 1,100 mem. instns; Pres. and CEO GEORGE R. BOGGS.

American Association of State Colleges and Universities: 5th Floor, 1307 New York Ave, NW, Washington, DC 20005-4701; tel. (202) 293-7070; fax (202) 296-5819; internet www.aascu.org; f. 1961 to improve higher education within its member institutions through cooperative planning, through studies and research on common educational problems, and through the devt of a more unified programme of action; 430 mems; Pres. Dr CONSTANTINE W. CURRIS; publ. *Public Purpose*.

American Association of University Professors: Suite 200, 1133 19th St, NW, Washington, DC 20036-3655; tel. (202) 737-5900; fax (202) 737-5526; e-mail aaup@aaup.org; internet www.aaup.org; f. 1915; 47,000 mems; Pres. CARY NELSON; Gen. Sec. GARY RHOADES; publs *AAUP Journal of Academic Freedom*, *Academe: Magazine of the AAUP* (6 a year).

American Council on Education: 1 Dupont Circle, NW, Washington, DC 20036; tel. (202) 939-9300; fax (202) 833-4760; e-mail comments@ace.nche.edu; internet www.acenet.edu; f. 1918; 1,800 mem. instns and asscns; Pres. MOLLY CORBETT BROAD; Chair. ANDREW K. BENTON; publ. *The Presidency* (3 a year).

American Federation of Teachers: 555 New Jersey Ave, NW, Washington, DC 20001; tel. (202) 879-4400; internet www.aft.org; f. 1916; represents economic, social and professional interests of classroom teachers; 1.4m. mems; Pres. EDWARD J. MCELROY; publs *AFT e-Activist Network* (electronic), *AFT Healthcare General News* (electronic, irregular), *AFT Healthcare School Nurse List* (electronic, irregular), *AFT Higher Education News from the National* (electronic), *AFT Human Rights News* (electronic, 4 a year), *AFT On Campus*, *AFT PLUS F.Y.I. Blast* (electronic, 24 a year), *AFT PSRP e-news* (electronic, 104 a year), *AFT Retiree e-news* (electronic, 20 a year), *American Academic* (higher education policy, irregular), *American Educator* (4 a year), *American Teacher* (8 a year), *Healthwire* (newspaper of the healthcare div., 6 a year), *Public Employee Advocate* (6 a year).

Association for Career and Technical Education: 1410 King St, Alexandria, VA 22314; tel. (703) 683-3111; fax (703) 683-7424; e-mail acte@acteonline.org; internet www.acteonline.org; f. 1926; Exec. Dir JAN BRAY; publ. *Techniques* (8 a year).

Association of American Colleges and Universities: 1818 R St, NW, Washington, DC 20009; tel. (202) 387-3760; fax (202) 265-9532; e-mail pub_desk@aacu.org; internet www.aacu.org; f. 1915; reinforces collective commitment to liberal education at nat. and local levels and helps individual institutions keep the quality of student learning at the core of their work; Pres. CAROL GEARY SCHNEIDER; publs *Diversity Digest* (3 a year), *Liberal Education* (4 a year), *Peer Review* (4 a year).

Association of American Universities: Suite 550, 1200 New York Ave, NW, Washington, DC 20005; tel. (202) 408-7500; internet www.aau.edu; f. 1900; 62 mems; Chair. GRAHAM B. SPANIER; Pres. ROBERT M. BERDAHL.

Association of Community College Trustees: Suite 301, 1233 20th St, NW, Washington, DC 20036; tel. (202) 775-4667; fax (202) 223-1297; e-mail acctinfo@acct.org; internet www.acct.org; promotes effective board governance through advocacy and education; Chair. LYNDA STANLEY; Pres. and CEO J. NOAH BROWN.

Association of Governing Boards of Universities and Colleges: 1133 20th St, NW, Suite 300, Washington, DC 20036; tel. (202) 296-8400; fax (202) 223-7053; e-mail info@agb.org; internet www.agb.org; f. 1921; strengthens and protects the country's unique form of institutional governance through its research, services and advocacy; Pres. RICHARD D. LEGON; Exec. Vice-Pres. SUSAN JOHNSTON; publ. *Trusteeship* (6 a year).

Center for Quality Assurance in International Education: Suite 520, 1001 North Fairfax St, Alexandria, VA 22314; tel. (703) 519-0922; fax (703) 519-0997; e-mail cqaie@cqaie.org; internet www.cqaie.org; facilitates the comparative study of nat. quality and competency assurance mechanisms to improve efforts within countries and promote mobility among nat. systems; assists countries in the devt or enhancement of quality assurance systems for higher education; promotes the globalization of the professions; monitors issues of quality in the transnational movement of higher education; Chair. CAROL BOBBY; Exec. Dir Dr MARJORIE PEACE LENN.

College Board, The: 45 Columbus Ave, New York, NY 10023-6917; tel. (212) 713-8000; internet www.collegeboard.com; f. 1900; not-for-profit membership asscn; mission is to connect students to college success and opportunity; offices in New York, Washington, DC, Albany, NY, Reston, VA, Bala Cynwyd, PA, Rosemont, IL, Waltham, MA, Duluth, GA, Tallahassee, FL, Austin, TX, San Jose, CA, Sacramento, CA, and San Juan, PR; more than 5,200 mem. schools, colleges, univs, and other educational orgs; Chair. LESTER P. MONTS; Pres. GASTON CAPERTON.

Council on International Educational Exchange: 300 Fore St, Portland, ME 04101; tel. (207) 553-4000; fax (207) 553-4299; e-mail contact@ciee.org; internet ciee .org; f. 1947 as Council on Student Travel, present name 1967; creates and administers programmes that allow high school and univ. students and educators to study and teach abroad; offices in Portland and Boston, MA; Chair. MICHAEL STOHL; Pres. and CEO STEVAN TROOBOFF.

Education Commission of the States: Suite 810, 700 Broadway, Denver, CO 80203-3442; tel. (303) 299-3600; fax (303) 296-8332; e-mail ecs@ecs.org; internet www .ecs.org; f. 1967; helps states develop effective policy and practice for public education by providing data, research, analysis and leadership; Chair. KATHLEEN SEBELIUS; Pres. ROGER SAMPSON; publs *The Progress of Education Reform* (research summaries, irregular), *ECS e-Clips* (electronic newsletter on education news, 365 a year), *ECS e-Connection* (electronic newsletter with links to key education information, 52 a year), *Citizenship Matters* (electronic newsletter on improving citizenship education in schools, 6 a year), *ECS Governance Notes* (electronic newsletter with links to key information on education governance, 6 a year), *ECS Leadership Links* (electronic newsletter with links to key information on education leadership, 6 a year), *ECS TQ Update* (electronic newsletter on improving the quality of teaching, 6 a year).

Institute of International Education: 809 United Nations Pl., New York, NY 10017; tel. (212) 883-8200; fax (212) 984-5496; e-mail info@iie.org; internet www.iie .org; f. 1919; ind. non-profit org. working to promote closer educational relations between the people of the USA and those of other countries, strengthen and link instns of higher learning globally, rescue threatened scholars and advance academic freedom, build leadership skills and enhance the capacity of individuals and orgs to address local and global challenges; offices in Washington, DC, Chicago, IL, Denver, CO, Houston, TX, San Francisco, CA, China, Egypt, Ethiopia, Hungary, India, Indonesia, Mexico, Russia, Thailand, Ukraine and Viet Nam; Chair. THOMAS S. JOHNSON; Pres. and CEO Dr ALLAN E. GOODMAN; publ. *Open Doors*.

NAFSA: Association of International Educators: 1307 New York Ave, NW, 8th Floor, Washington, DC 20005-4701; tel. (202) 737-3699; fax (202) 737-3657; e-mail inbox@ nafsa.org; internet www.nafsa.org; f. 1948 as Nat. Asscn of Foreign Student Advisers, present name 1990; promotes int. education and provides professional devt opportunities; sets and upholds standards of good practice, and provides training opportunities; 10,000 mems; Pres. JOHN K. HUDZIK; Exec. Dir and CEO MARLENE M. JOHNSON; publs *International Educator* (6 a year), *Policy Brief* (electronic, irregular).

National Academy of Education: 500 Fifth St, NW, Washington, DC 20001; tel. (202) 334-2341; fax (202) 334-2350; e-mail info@naeducation.org; internet www .naeducation.org; f. 1965; promotes the highest quality educational research and its use in policy formulation and practice; 169 mems, 17 foreign assocs; Pres. Dr SUSAN FUHRMAN; Exec. Dir GREGORY WHITE.

National Association of State Boards of Education: 2121 Crystal Dr., Suite No. 350, Arlington, VA 22202; tel. (703) 684-4000; fax (703) 836-2313; e-mail boards@nasbe.org; internet www.nasbe.org; f. 1958; works to strengthen state leadership in educational policy-making, promote excellence in the education of all students, advocate equality of access to educational opportunity, and assure continued citizen support for public education; Pres. Dr KARABELLE PIZZIGATI; Exec. Dir BRENDA L. WELBURN.

National Association of State Directors of Career Technical Education Consortium: 8484 Georgia Ave Suite 320, Silver Spring, MA 20001; tel. (301) 588-9630; fax (301) 588-9631; e-mail kgreen@careertech .org; internet www.careertech.org; f. 1920; provides leadership for career technical education's role in education, workforce preparation and economic devt; 200 mems; Pres. RICH KATT; Exec. Dir KIMBERLY A. GREEN.

National Association of State Directors of Teacher Education and Certification: 1225 Providence Rd, PMB 116, Whitinsville, MA 01588; tel. (508) 380-1202; fax (508) 278-5342; e-mail rje@nasdtec.com; internet www .nasdtec.org; f. 1928; represents professional standards boards and comms and state depts of education in all 50 states, DC, the Dept of Defense Education Activity, the US Territories, AB, BC, and ON that are responsible for the preparation, licensure, and discipline of educational personnel; promotes high standards for educators, teacher mobility across state lines, comprehensive personnel screening and a database on teacher discipline; Pres. GEORGE MAURER; Exec. Dir ROY EINREINHOFER; publs *NASDTEC KnowledgeBase* (online, constant updating), *The Communicator* (online, irregular).

National Association of State Universities and Land-Grant Colleges: Suite 400, 1307 New York Ave, NW, Washington, DC 20005-4722; tel. (202) 478-6040; fax (202) 478-6046; internet www.nasulgc.org; f. 1887; a voluntary, non-profit asscn supporting high-quality public higher education and its mem. instns as they perform their teaching, research, and public service roles; provides a forum for the discussion and devt of policies affecting higher education and the public interest; 218 mem. instns; Chair. ROBERT H. BRUININKS; Pres. PETER MCPHERSON.

National Education Association of the United States: 1201 16th St, NW, Washington, DC 20036-3290; tel. (202) 833-4000; fax (202) 822-7974; internet www.nea.org; f. 1857; 2,700,000 mems; 100,000 life mems; Pres. REG WEAVER; Dir in each State; publs *NEA Today* (8 a year), *This Active Life* (6 a year), *Thought and Action* (2 a year), *Tomorrow's Teachers* (1 a year), *NEA Almanac of Higher Education* (1 a year), *NEA Handbook* (1 a year), *Education Statistics* (1 a year).

National Society for the Study of Education: College of Education (M/C 147), Univ. of Illinois, 1040 West Harrison St, Chicago, IL 60607-7133; tel. (312) 996-4529; fax (312) 996-8134; e-mail nsse@uic.edu; internet www.nsse-chicago.org; f. 1901; 2,000 mems; Sec. DEBRA MIRETZKY.

State Higher Education Executive Officers: Suite 100, 3035 Center Green Dr., Boulder, CO 80301-2205; tel. (303) 541-1600; fax (303) 541-1639; e-mail sheeo@sheeo.org; internet www.sheeo.org; f. 1954; works to develop and sustain excellent systems of higher education; emphasizes the importance of state planning and coordination for higher education by promoting effective strategic planning and statewide coordination and governance; speaks as a nat. org. in public and private forums, promoting the interests of the states in effectively planning and financing higher education; Chair. JACK R. WARNER; Pres. Dr PAUL E. LINGENFELTER.

United States Network for Education Information: US Department of Education, 400 Maryland Ave, SW, Room 6W108, Washington, DC 20202; tel. (202) 401-0430; fax (202) 401-2508; e-mail stephen.hunt@ed .gov; internet www.ed.gov/about/offices/list/ ous/international/usnei/edlite-index.html; f. 1996; information centre under the Lisbon Convention on the Recognition of Qualifications Concerning Higher Education in the European Region, one of six UNESCO regional recognition conventions; provides guide to American and foreign systems of education to facilitate international educational mobility; Man. Dr E. STEPHEN HUNT.

Learned Societies

GENERAL

American Academy of Arts and Letters: 633 West 155th St, New York, NY 10032-1799; tel. (212) 368-5900; fax (212) 491-4615; e-mail academy@artsandletters.org; internet www.artsandletters.org; f. 1898; 250 mems; library of 25,000 vols; Pres. J. D. MCCLATCHY; Exec. Dir VIRGINIA DAJANI; publ. *Proceedings* (1 a year).

American Academy of Arts and Sciences: 136 Irving St, Cambridge, MA 02138; tel. (617) 576-5000; fax (617) 576-5050; e-mail aaas@amacad.org; internet www.amacad.org; f. 1780; ind. policy research centre; focuses on science and technology policy, global security, social policy, the humanities and culture, and education; 4,600 mems (4,000 American fellows, 600 foreign hon. mems); Chair. LOUIS W. CABOT; Pres. LESLIE C. BERLOWITZ; Sec. JERROLD MEINWALD; Treas. JOHN S. REED; publs *Bulletin* (4 a year), *Daedalus* (4 a year).

American Council of Learned Societies: 633 Third Ave, New York, NY 10017-6795; tel. (212) 697-1505; fax (212) 949-8058; e-mail grants@acls.org; internet www.acls .org; f. 1919; supports humanities research through fellowships and grants awarded to individuals, groups and institutions; represents humanities scholars and promotes the scholarly humanities in the USA and international public and policy arenas; provides a forum for learned societies to discuss and suggest improvements in scholarship, education and communication among humanities scholars; 68 mem. socs concerned with the advancement of humanistic studies in the humanities and social sciences; Pres. PAULINE YU; publ. *Occasional Paper series*.

American Philosophical Society: 104 South Fifth St, Philadelphia, PA 19106-3387; tel. (215) 440-3400; fax (215) 440-3436; internet www.amphilsoc.org; f. 1743 by Benjamin Franklin, the oldest learned society in the USA; mems are elected by the Society on the basis of distinction in any field of learning; there are five classes of membership: mathematical and physical sciences, biological sciences, social sciences, humanities, and the professions, arts and affairs; the Society meets twice a year (April, November) for symposia, lectures and presenting awards; it makes grants for research, operates a distinguished library rich in historical MSS, chiefly relating to the history of science in America (see Special Libraries), and awards prizes, including the Magellanic Premium, the oldest American scientific award; publishes several books each year and engages in community service; it owns four buildings: Philosophical Hall (1789, a National Historical Landmark), Library Hall (105 S Fifth St), Benjamin Franklin Hall (427 Chestnut St) and Richardson Hall (431 Chestnut St); the first two buildings contain numerous valuable portraits (paintings and statuary) of distinguished former members; museum and exhibition programme; 912 mems (766 US citizens, 146 foreign); Pres. BARUCH S. BLOMBERG; publs *Memoirs*, *Proceedings*, *Transactions*, *Year Book*.

Asia Foundation: POB 193223, San Francisco, CA 94119-3223 (Main Office); tel. (415) 982-4640; fax (415) 392-8863; e-mail info@asiafound.org; internet www.asiafoundation.org; f. 1954; offices in Washington, DC, and 18 Asian and Pacific island countries; assists Asian economic and social devt through private American support to Asian instns, orgs and individuals working towards constructive social change, stable political devt and equitable economic growth within their socs; provides small grants, primarily in fields of law and public admin., rural and community devt, communications and libraries, Asian regional cooperation; Books for Asia Program distributes books and journals to libraries and instns in Asia; library of 3,370 vols on current Asian and world affairs; Pres. DAVID ARNOLD; Exec. Vice-Pres. BARNETT F. BARON.

Connecticut Academy of Arts and Sciences: POB 208211, Yale University, New Haven, CT 06520-8211; tel. (203) 432-3113; fax (203) 432-5712; e-mail caas@yale.edu; internet www.yale.edu/caas; f. 1799; 400 mems; library merged with Yale University Library; Pres. FRANKLIN ROBINSON; Sec. MARGOT KOHORN; publs *A Manual of the Writings in Middle English* (irregular), *Memoirs* (irregular), *Transactions* (irregular).

English-Speaking Union of the United States: 144 E 39th St, New York, NY 10016; tel. (212) 818-1200; fax (212) 867-4177; e-mail info@esuus.org; internet www.esuus.org; f. 1920; non-profit org.; promotes communication and understanding among people of all nationalities through the medium of the English language; initiates and implements innovative educational programmes; 6,000 mems, 70 brs in USA; library of 6,000 vols; Chair. PATRICIA S. SCHROEDER; Vice-Chair. MARK STOLLAR; Pres. and Exec. Dir ALICE BOYNE; publ. *E-SU Today*.

Hispanic Society of America: 613 W 155th St, New York, NY 10032; tel. (212) 926-2234; fax (212) 690-0743; e-mail info@hispanicsociety.org; internet www.hispanicsociety.org; f. 1904; professional research staff; reference library and museum; 400 mems; Dir MITCHELL A. CODDING.

National Academies of Sciences and Engineering, Institute of Medicine and National Research Council: 2101 Constitution Ave NW, Washington, DC 20418; tel. (202) 334-2000; internet national-academies.org; f. 1863; established by Congressional charter; linked group of instns, coordinating their advice to Fed. Govt; publ. *Proceedings of the National Academy of Sciences* (52 a year).

Individual Institutions:

Institute of Medicine: 500 Fifth St, NW, Washington, DC 20001; tel. (202) 334-2352; fax (202) 334-1412; e-mail iomwww@nas.edu; internet www.iom.edu; f. 1970; 1,680 mems; Pres. HARVEY V. FINEBERG; Exec. Officer JUDITH A. SALERNO; publ. *IOM News* (4 a year).

National Academy of Engineering: 500 Fifth St, NW, Washington, DC 20001; tel. (202) 334-3200; fax (202) 334-2290; internet www.nae.edu; f. 1964; 1,622 mems; Pres. WILLIAM A. WULF; Home Sec. W. DALE COMPTON; Foreign Sec. GEORGE BUGLIARELLO; Exec. Officer LANCE DAVIS.

National Academy of Sciences: 2101 Constitution Ave NW, Washington, DC 20418; internet www.nas.edu; f. 1863; sections: mathematics; astronomy; physics; chemistry; geology; geophysics; biochemistry; cellular and developmental biology; physiology and pharmacology; cellular and molecular neuroscience; plant biology; genetics; evolutionary biology; systems neuroscience; biophysics and computational biology; engineering sciences; applied mathematical sciences; applied physical sciences; computer and information sciences; medical genetics, haematology and oncology; medical physiology and metabolism; immunology; microbial biology; anthropology; psychology; social and political sciences; economic sciences; animal, nutritional and applied microbial sciences; plant, soil and microbial sciences; environmental sciences and ecology, human environmental sciences; 2,350 mems (2,000 ordinary, 350 foreign assoc.); Pres. BRUCE ALBERTS; Home Sec. JOHN I. BRAUMAN; Foreign Sec. MICHAEL T. CLEGG.

National Research Council: 2101 Constitution Ave NW, Washington, DC 20418; internet www.national-academies.org/nrc; f. 1916 by the National Academy of Sciences as the operating arm of the National Academy of Sciences and the National Academy of Engineering; Chair., National Research Council BRUCE M. ALBERTS; Vice-Chair. WILLIAM A. WULF.

National Foundation on the Arts and the Humanities: Washington, DC 20506; f. 1965 as an independent agency in the Exec. Br. of Govt; develops and promotes a broadly conceived nat. policy of support for the humanities and the arts in the United States.

Constituent Institutions:

Federal Council on the Arts and the Humanities: Washington, DC 20506; f. 1965 to coordinate the activities of the two Endowments with related federal agencies and to carry out the federal indemnity programme; mems include the Chairmen of the two Endowments; the Secs of the Depts of Education, Interior, State, Commerce, Transportation, Housing and Urban Development, and Labor; the Commissioners of the Fine Arts Commission, Administration on Aging, and Public Buildings Service; the Administrators of the Veterans' Administration and the General Services Administration; the Dirs of the National Science Foundation, and Institute of Museum and Library Services; the Librarian of Congress; the Archivist of the United States; and the Chairman of the National Museum Services Board; mems who do not vote on indemnity include the Dir, National Gallery of Art; Sec. of the Senate; Sec., Smithsonian Institution; Member, House of Representatives.

National Council on the Arts: Washington, DC 20506; tel. (202) 682-5433; fax (202) 682-5538; f. 1964; advises the Chairman of the National Endowment for the Arts on policies, programmes and procedures and reviews applications for financial assistance; Chair. of Council is Chair. of the Arts Endowment; 20 mems (14 private citizens appointed by the President for a 6-year term, 6 *ex-officio* from Congress).

National Council on the Humanities: Washington, DC 20506; f. 1965; advises the Chair. of the Nat. Endowment for the Humanities on policies, programmes and procedures and reviews applications for financial assistance; 26 private citizen mems appointed by the Pres. for six-year terms (approx. one-third of the appointments expire every two years); Chair. of Council is Chair. of the Humanities Endowment.

National Endowment for the Arts: 1100 Pennsylvania Ave, NW Washington, DC 20506; tel. (202) 682-5400; e-mail webmgr@arts.endow.gov; internet arts.endow.gov; f. 1965 to establish and carry out a programme of grants-in-aid to non-profit groups, individuals of exceptional talent and state art agencies, which will promote progress in the arts; Chair. DANA GIOIA (acting).

National Endowment for the Humanities: 1100 Pennsylvania Ave, NW Washington, DC 20506; e-mail info@neh.gov; internet www.neh.gov; f. 1965; carries out a programme supporting projects of research, education and public activity in the humanities; Chair. JIM LEACH.

New York Academy of Sciences: 7 World Trade Center, 250 Greenwich St, 40th Fl., New York, NY 10007-2157; tel. (212) 838-0230; fax (212) 888-2894; e-mail info@nyas.org; internet www.nyas.org; f. 1817; sections of anthropology, atmospheric sciences and geology, biochemical pharmacology, chemical biology, computional biology and bioinformatics, emerging infectious diseases, environmental sciences, genome integrity, genomic medicine, history and philosophy of science, Imaging, microbiology, nanobiotechnology, neurogenerative diseases, neuroimmunology, psychology, RNAi, science education, systems biology, vision research, women investigators' network, women in science; 22,000 mems; Pres. ELLIS RUBINSTEIN; publ. *The Annals*.

North American Spanish Language Academy/Academia Norteamericana de la Lengua Española: GPO Box 349, New York, NY 10116; tel. (718) 761-0556; fax (718) 761-0556; e-mail acadnorteamerica@aol.com; f. 1973; mem. of Asociación de Academias de la Lengua Española; corresp. of Real Academia, Spain; 36 mems; Dir ODÓN BETANZOS-PALACIOS; Joint Sec. GUMERSINDO YÉPEZ; Joint Sec. GERARDO PIÑA-ROSALES; publs *Boletín* (every 2 years), *Glosas* (4 a year).

Smithsonian Institution: Washington, DC 20560; tel. (202) 357-2700; e-mail info@si.edu; internet www.si.edu; f. 1846; a museum, education and research complex for the 'increase and diffusion of knowledge' by bequest of English scientist James Smithson; 17 mems of the Board of Regents, incl. the Chief Justice of the USA and the Vice-Pres. of the USA, three mems of the Senate and of the House of Representatives, and nine citizen mems; Chancellor THE CHIEF JUSTICE OF THE UNITED STATES; Sec. (Presiding Officer) CRISTIÁN SAMPER (acting); Deputy Sec. SHEILA BURKE; Under Secs DAVID L. EVANS (Science), NED RIFKIN (Art); publs *American Art Journal*, *Archives of American Art Journal*, *Smithsonian Contributions to Anthropology*, *Smithsonian Contributions to Astrophysics*, *Smithsonian Contributions to Botany*, *Smithsonian Contributions to the Earth Sciences*, *Smithsonian Contributions to the Marine Sciences*, *Smithsonian Contributions to Paleobiology*, *Smithsonian Contributions to Zoology*, *Smithsonian Studies in Air and Space*, *Smithsonian Studies in History and Technology*.

Constituent libraries and archives; (unless indicated otherwise, each institution listed below has a separate entry in the USA chapter):

Air and Space Museum Archives: see entry for National Air and Space Museum.

American History Museum Archives Center: see entry for National Museum of American History.

Archives of American Art.

Archives of American Gardens: see entry for Smithsonian Horticulture Services Division.

Eliot Elisofon Photographic Archives: see entry for National Museum of African Art, Smithsonian Institution.

Juley Photographic Archive: see entry for Smithsonian American Art Museum and its Renwick Gallery.

National Anthropological Archives and Human Studies Film Archives: see entry for National Museum of Natural History.

Ralph Rinzler Folklife Archives and Collections: see entry for Center for Folklife and Cultural Heritage.

Smithsonian Institution Archives.

Smithsonian Institution Libraries: 22-branch library system: for details of individual libraries, see under entries for Smithsonian instns. For general details of the system, see main Smithsonian libraries entry.

Constituent museums and art galleries; (unless indicated otherwise, each institution listed below has a separate entry in the USA chapter):

Anacostia Museum and Center for African American History and Culture.

Arts and Industries Building.

Cooper-Hewitt, National Design Museums.

Freer Gallery of Art and Arthur M. Sackler Gallery.

Hirshhorn Museum and Sculpture Garden.

National Air and Space Museums.

National Museum of African Art.

National Museum of American History, Behring Center.

National Museum of the American Indian.

National Museum of Natural History.

National Portrait Gallery.

National Postal Museum.

National Zoological Park.

Smithsonian American Art Museum and the Renwick Gallery.

Smithsonian Institution Building—the Castle: see main Smithsonian entry for address and contact details.

Constituent science centres; (unless indicated otherwise, each institution listed below has a separate entry in the USA chapter):

Astrophysical Observatory (SAO): see entry for Harvard-Smithsonian Center for Astrophysics.

Carrie-Bow Marine Field Station—Caribbean Coral Reef Ecosystems (CCRE): see entry in Belize chapter.

Center for Earth and Planetary Studies.

Conservation and Research Center: see entry for Smithsonian National Zoological Park.

Environmental Research Center (SERC).

Marine Science: network of Smithsonian instns—see entries for Environmental Research Center (SERC), Marine Station at Fort Pierce, CCRE, Tropical Research Institute, National Museum of Natural History, and National Zoological Park.

Migratory Bird Center: see entry for Smithsonian National Zoological Park.

Natural History Museum Research and Collections: see entry for National Museum of Natural History.

Tropical Research Institute (STRI): see entry in Panama chapter.

Conservation research units; (unless indicated otherwise, each institution listed below has a separate entry in the USA chapter):

African Art Museum Conservation Research Department: see entry for National Museum of African Art.

Center for Materials Research and Education.

Freer and Sackler Galleries Department of Conservation and Scientific Research: see entries for Freer Gallery of Art and Arthur M. Sackler Gallery.

Cultural and scholarly programmes; (unless indicated otherwise, each institution listed below has a separate entry in the USA chapter):

Asian Pacific American Program:; f. 1997 to provide leadership and support for all Asian Pacific America (APA) activities at the Smithsonian; Dir FRANKLIN ODO.

Center for Education and Museum Studies.

Center for Folklife and Cultural Heritage.

Jerome and Dorothy Lemelson Center for the Study of Invention and Innovation.

Latino Initiatives: see entry for Smithsonian Center for Latino Initiatives.

National Science Resources Center:.

AGRICULTURE, FISHERIES AND VETERINARY SCIENCE

Agricultural History Society: Business Office: Dept of History, University of Arkansas at Little Rock, 2801 S University Ave, Little Rock, AR 72204-1099; tel. (501) 569-8782; fax (501) 569-3059; e-mail cfwilliams@ualr.edu; internet www.aghistorysociety.org; f. 1919 to encourage interest in, promote the study of, and facilitate research and publication on the history of agriculture; incorporated 1924 as a non-profit organization; 1,400 mems; Pres. ANNE EFFLAND; Exec. Sec.-Treas. C. FRED WILLIAMS; publ. *Agricultural History* (4 a year).

American Dairy Science Association: 1111 N Dunlap Ave, Savoy, IL 61874; tel. (217) 356-5146; fax (217) 398-4119; e-mail adsa@assochq.org; internet www.adsa.org; f. 1906; 4,654 mems; Pres. MICHAEL F. HUTJENS; Exec. Dir BRENDA CARLSON; publ. *Journal of Dairy Science* (12 a year).

American Forests: POB 2000, Washington, DC 20013; tel. (202) 737-1944; internet www.americanforests.org; f. 1875; 35,000 mems; Chair. KEVIN DAUGHERTY.

American Society for Horticultural Science: 113 South West St, Ste 200, Alexandria, VA 22314-2851; tel. (703) 836-4606; fax (703) 836-2024; internet www.ashs.org; f. 1903; promotes and encourages scientific research and education in all brs of horticulture; 5,000 mems; Chair. CARY MITCHELL; Pres. FREDERICK S. DAVIES; publs *Hort Science* (6 a year), *Hort Technology* (4 a year), *Journal* (6 a year).

American Society of Agricultural Engineers: 2950 Niles Rd, St Joseph, MI 49085; tel. (269) 429-0300; fax (269) 429-3852; e-mail hq@asae.org; internet www.asae.org; f. 1907; 9,000 mems; Exec. Vice-Pres. MELISSA MOORE; publs *Applied Engineering in Agriculture* (6 a year), *Agricultural Safety and Health* (4 a year), *Resource Magazine* (12 a year), *Transactions* (6 a year), *Standards* (1 a year).

American Society of Agronomy: 677 South Segoe Rd, Madison, WI 53711; tel. (608) 273-8080; fax (608) 273-2021; e-mail headquarters@agronomy.org; internet www.agronomy.org; f. 1907; 12,600 mems; Exec. Vice-Pres. ELLEN BERGFELD; publs *Agronomy Journal* (6 a year), *Crop Science* (6 a year), *Journal of Environmental Quality* (6 a year), *Journal of Natural Resources and Life Sciences Education* (1 a year), *Soil Science Society of America* (6 a year), *Soil Survey Horizons* (4 a year), *Vadose Zone* (4 a year).

American Society of Animal Science: c/o Dr Ellen Bergfeld, 1111 N Dunlap St, Savoy, IL 61874-9604; tel. (217) 356-9050; fax (217) 398-4119; internet www.asas.org; f. 1908; promotes development of sciences beneficial to animal production; 6,500 mems; Pres. Dr JAMES R. MALES; Exec. Dir Dr JEROME F. BAKER; publ. *Journal of Animal Science* (12 a year).

American Veterinary Medical Association: 1931 N Meacham Rd, Schaumburg, IL 60173-4360; tel. (847) 925-8070; fax (847) 925-1329; e-mail avmainfo@avma.org; internet www.avma.org; f. 1863; 80,000 mems; Exec. Vice-Pres. Dr W. RON DEHAVEN; library of 5,000 vols, 400 periodicals; publs *American Journal of Veterinary Research* (12 a year), *Journal of the AVMA* (26 a year).

Association for International Agricultural and Extension Education: POB 110540, Gainesville, FL 32611-0540; tel. (353) 392-0502; fax (353) 392-9585; internet www.aiaee.org; f. 1984 to provide a professional association and network of agricultural educators with the aim of improving and strengthening agricultural education programmes and institutions, especially in developing countries; c. 200 mems; Pres. JIM PHELAN; Sec. MIKE MCGIRR; publs *The Informer* (4 a year), *Journal* (4 a year).

Council for Agricultural Science and Technology: 4420 West Lincoln Way, Ames, IA 50014-3447; tel. (515) 292-2125; fax (515) 292-4512; e-mail cast@cast-science.org; internet www.cast-science.org; f. 1972; non-profit consortium of scientific socs, orgs, companies, scientists and citizens interested in public policy and the science of food and agriculture; compiles scientific information for Congress, the public, journalists and educators; 3,000 mems; Pres. TODD A. PETERSON; Exec. Vice-Pres. Dr JOHN BONNER; publs *NewsCAST*, scientific publs.

Poultry Science Association Inc.: 2441 Village Green Court, Champaign, IL 61874; tel. (217) 356-5285; fax (217) 398-4119; internet www.poultryscience.org; f. 1908; 1,300 mems; Pres. Dr MICHAEL S. LILBURN; Exec. Dir Dr JAMES W. KESSLER; publs *Journal of Applied Poultry Research* (4 a year), *Poultry Science* (12 a year).

Society of American Foresters: 5400 Grosvenor Lane, Bethesda, MD 20814-2198; tel. (301) 897-8720; fax (301) 897-3690; e-mail safweb@safnet.org; internet www.safnet.org; f. 1900; 18,000 mems; Pres. HARRY V. WIANT, Jr; Exec. Vice-Pres. WILLIAM H. BANZHAF; publs *Journal of Forestry* (12 a year), *Forestry Source* (12 a year), *Forest Science* (4 a year), *Northern Journal of Applied Forestry* (4 a year), *Southern Journal of Applied Forestry* (4 a year), *Western Journal of Applied Forestry* (4 a year).

Soil Science Society of America: c/o Ellen Bergfeld, 677 South Segoe Rd, Madison, WI 53711; tel. (608) 273-8080; fax (608) 273-2021; e-mail headquarters@soils.org; internet www.soils.org; f. 1936; 5,363 mems; Exec. Vice-Pres. ELLEN BERGFELD; publs *Journal of Environmental Quality* (6 a year), *Soil Science Society of America Journal* (6 a year).

ARCHITECTURE AND TOWN PLANNING

American Institute of Architects: 1735 New York Ave, NW, Washington, DC 20006; tel. (202) 626-7300; fax (202) 626-7547; e-mail infocentral@aia.org; internet www.aia.org; f. 1857; 74,000 mems; library of 30,400 vols; Pres. DOUGLAS L. STEIDL; publ. *AIArchitect*.

American Planning Association: 122 S Michigan Ave, Suite 1600, Chicago, IL 60603-6107; tel. (312) 431-9100; fax (312) 431-9985; internet www.planning.org; f. 1909; non-profit research, educational and professional organization for city planners and others involved in land use and community development; 30,000 mems; includes American Institute of Certified Planners (AICP); Pres. APA DAVID M. SIEGEL; Pres. AICP SUE SCHWARTZ; publs *APA Journal* (4 a year), *Planning* (12 a year), *Planning and Environmental Law* (12 a year), *PAS Memo*, *Zoning Practice* (12 a year), *Practicing Planner* (4 a year, online), *The Commissioner* (4 a year).

National Trust for Historic Preservation in the United States: 1785 Massachusetts Ave, NW, Washington, DC 20036-2117; tel. (202) 588-6000; fax (202) 588-6038; e-mail info@nthp.org; internet www.preservationnation.org; f. 1949; encourages preservation of bldgs, sites and objects significant in American history and culture; 200,000 mems; library: (at Architecture School, Univ. of Maryland, College Park) of 14,000 vols, 400 periodicals; Pres. RICHARD MOE; Exec. Vice-Pres. DAVID J. BROWN; publs *Forum*, *Historic Preservation News* (12 a year), *Preservation* (6 a year), *Preservation Law Reporter*.

Society of Architectural Historians: 1365 N Astor St, Chicago, IL 60610-2144; tel. (312) 573-1365; fax (312) 573-1141; e-mail info@sah.org; internet www.sah.org; f. 1940; 3,500 mems; Pres. THERESE O'MALLEY; First Vice-Pres. BARRY BERGDOLL; Sec. ROBERT CRAIG; publ. *Journal* (4 a year).

BIBLIOGRAPHY, LIBRARY SCIENCE AND MUSEOLOGY

American Association of Law Libraries: 53 West Jackson Blvd, Chicago, IL 60604; tel. (312) 939-4764; fax (312) 431-1097; internet www.aallnet.org; f. 1906; 5,000 mems; Pres. CLAIRE M. GERMAIN; publs *AALL Spectrum* (10 a year), *Directory of Law Libraries* (1 a year), *Index to Foreign Legal Periodicals* (4 a year), *Law Library Journal* (4 a year).

American Association of Museums: Suite 400, 1575 Eye St, NW, Washington, DC 20005; tel. (202) 289-1818; fax (202) 289-6578; internet www.aam-us.org; f. 1906; strengthens museums through leadership, advocacy, collaboration and service; programmes incl. accreditation, museum assessment, technical information service, continuing education, govt Affairs, int. programmes and AAM/ICOM; governed by a board of dirs, who are museum professionals; 21,000 mems; Pres. FORD BELL; publs *Aviso* (12 a year), *Museum* (6 a year), *The Official Museum Directory* (1 a year).

American Library Association: 50 East Huron St, Chicago, IL 10000; tel. (312) 944-6780; fax (312) 280-3255; e-mail library@ala.org; internet www.ala.org; f. 1876; promotes effective library and information services and public access to information; offers professional services and publs to mems and non-mems; 65,000 mems; library of 10,000 vols; Pres. ROBERTA STEVENS; Exec. Dir KEITH MICHAEL FIELS; publs *American Libraries* (6 a year), *Booklist* (24 a year), *Children and Libraries: The Journal of the Association for Library Service to Children (ALSC)* (3 a year), *CHOICE: Current Reviews for Academic Libraries* (12 a year), *College and Research Libraries* (6 a year), *College and Research Libraries News* (12 a year), *Documents to the People (DttP)* (4 a year), *Information Technology and Libraries (ITAL)* (4 a year), *Interface* (4 a year), *Knowledge Quest (KQ)* (5 a year), *Library Leadership & Management (LL&M)* (4 a year), *Library Resources and Technical Services (LRTS)* (4 a year), *Library Technology Reports* (6 a year), *Library Worklife: HR E-News for Today's Leaders* (12 a year), *Public Libraries* (6 a year), *RBM: A Journal of Rare Books, Manuscripts, and Cultural Heritage* (2 a year), *Reference & User Services Quarterly, (RUSQ)* (4 a year), *School Library Media Research*, *Young Adult Library Services (YALS)* (4 a year).

American Society for Information Science and Technology (ASIST): Suite 510, 1320 Fenwick Lane, Silver Spring, MD 20910; tel. (301) 495-0900; fax (301) 495-0810; e-mail asis@asis.org; internet www.asis.org; f. 1937 as American Documentation Institute, renamed American Society for Information Science 1968, current name 2000; concerned with the development of advanced methodologies and techniques that contribute to the more efficient use of information; acts as a bridge between research and development and the requirements of diverse types of information systems; comprises managers, designers and users of information systems and technology; 4,000 mems; Pres. NICHOLAS J. BELKIN; Exec. Dir RICHARD HILL; publs *Annual Proceedings*, *Annual Review of Information Science and Technology*, *Bulletin* (6 a year), *Journal*.

American Theological Library Association: 250 S Wacker Drive, Suite 1600, Chicago, IL 60606-5889; tel. (312) 454-5100; fax (312) 454-5505; e-mail atla@atla.com; internet www.atla.com; f. 1946; 1,000 mems; library of 30,000 monologue titles preserved on microfiche and microfilm, 2,000 microfilm serial titles; Exec. Dir DENNIS A. NORLIN; publs *Summary of Proceedings* (1 a year), *Theology Cataloging Bulletin* (4 a year).

Art Libraries Society of North America (ARLIS/NA): Suite 232, 329 March Rd, Box 11, Kanata, ON K2K 2E1, Canada; tel. (800) 817-0621; fax (919) 599-7027; e-mail arlisna@igs.net; internet www.arlisna.org; f. 1972; sponsors conferences and workshops, distributes publications, grants awards for art book publishing and student essays on visual librarianship; affiliated with ARLIS (UK), ARLIS (Australia—New Zealand), ARLIS (Norge), ARLIS (Norden), American Library Asscn, Visual Resources Asscn and College Art Asscn; 20 US and Canadian chapters, 1,365 mems worldwide; Pres. JEANNE M. BROWN; Exec. Dir ELIZABETH CLARKE; publs *Art Documentation* (2 a year), *ARLIS/NA Update* (6 a year), *Handbook and List of Members* (1 a year), *Occasional Papers* (irregular), *Topical Papers* (irregular).

Association for Library and Information Science Education: 65 East Wacker Place, Suite 1900 Chicago, IL 60601-7246; tel. (312) 795-0996; fax (312) 419-8950; e-mail contact@alise.org; internet www.alise.org; f. 1915; 68 institutional mems, 670 personal mems; Pres. Prof. LYNN HOWARTH; Exec. Dir KATHLEEN COMBS; publs *Journal of Education for Library and Information Science* (4 a year), *Library and Information Science Education Statistical Report* (1 a year).

Association of Academic Health Sciences Libraries: 2150 N 107th St, Suite 205, Seattle, WA 98133; tel. (206) 367-8704; fax (206) 367-8777; e-mail aahsl@sbims.com; internet www.aahsl.org; f. 1978; 149 mems; Pres. PAT THIBODEAU; Exec. Dir LOUISE MILLER; Sec.-Treas. JETT MCCANN; publ. *Annual Statistics of Medical School Libraries in the United States and Canada*.

Association of Art Museum Directors: 41 East 65th St, New York, NY 10021; tel. (212) 249-4423; fax (212) 535-5039; e-mail canagnos@aamd.org; internet www.aamd.org; f. 1916 to promote the development of a scholarly and creative role for art museums and their directors in the cultural life of the nation; to apply its members' knowledge and experience in the field of art to the promotion of the public good; to encourage communication among art museums and their directors; 168 mems; Pres. MATTHEW TEITELBAUM; Sec. ANNE HAWLEY.

Association of Research Libraries: 21 Dupont Circle, Suite 800, Washington, DC 20036; tel. (202) 296-2296; fax (202) 872-0884; e-mail arlhq@arl.org; internet www.arl.org; f. 1932; 124 institutional mems; Exec. Dir CHARLES B. LOWRY; publs *ARL Annual Salary Survey* (statistical compilation; 1 a year), *ARL Statistics* (statistical compilation, 1 a year), *Research Library Issues: A Bimonthly Report from ARL, CNI, and SPARC* (6 a year, online), *SPEC Kits* (6 a year).

Association of Vision Science Librarians: c/o Gale Oren, Kellogg Eye Center, Univ. of Michigan, 1000 Wall St, Ann Arbor, MI 48105; tel. (734) 763-9468; internet www.avsl.org; f. 1968; fosters collective and individual acquisition and dissemination of visual science information; improves services to those seeking such information; develops libraries' standards; 100 individual mems and 75 institutions; Chair. GALE OREN; Chair.-Elect and Sec. D. J. MATTHEWS; publs *Opening Day Book List* (every 2 years), *Standards for Vision Science Libraries*, *Vision Union List of Serials* (every 3 years).

Bibliographical Society of America: POB 1537, Lenox Hill Station, New York, NY 10021; tel. and fax (212) 452-2710; e-mail bsa@bibsocamer.org; internet www.bibsocamer.org; f. 1904, inc. 1927; 1,000 mems; Pres. JOHN BIDWELL; Exec. Sec. MICHELE RANDALL; publ. *Papers* (4 a year).

Bibliographical Society of the University of Virginia: POB 400152, Alderman Library, Charlottesville, VA 22904; tel. (434) 924-7013; e-mail ar3g@virginia.edu; internet etext.lib.virginia.edu/bsuva; f. 1947; int. soc. promoting the study of books, MSS, printing and the graphic arts, bibliography and textual criticism; 550 mems; Pres. G. THOMAS TANSELLE; Exec. Sec. and Treas. ANNE RIBBLE; publ. *Studies in Bibliography* (1 a year).

California Library Association: 717 20th St, Suite 200, Sacramento, CA 95814; tel. (916) 447-8541; fax (916) 447-8394; e-mail info@cla-net.org; internet www.cla-net.org; f. 1896; 2,400 mems; Exec. Dir SUSAN E. NEGREEN; Pres. DANIS KREIMEIER; publ. *California Libraries* (12 a year).

California School Library Association: 950 Glenn Drive Suite 150, Folsom, CA 95630; tel. (916) 447-2684; fax (916) 447-2695; e-mail csla@pacbell.net; internet www.schoollibrary.org; f. 1977; Exec. Dir DEIDRE BRYANT; publ. *CSLA Journal* (2 a year).

Catholic Library Association: 100 North St, Suite 224, Pittsfield, MA 01201-5178; tel. (413) 443-2252; fax (413) 442-2252; e-mail cla2@cathla.org; internet www.cathla.org; f. 1921; 1,000 mems; Exec. Dir JEAN R. BOSTLEY; publs *Catholic Library World* (4 a year),

Catholic Periodical and Literature Index (4 a year).

Council on Library and Information Resources: 1752 N St, NW, Suite 800, Washington, DC 20036; tel. (202) 939-4750; fax (202) 939-4765; internet www.clir.org; f. 1956 to develop resources and services of libraries and information services; Pres. CHARLES HENRY; publs reports (8–10 a year), *CLIR Issues* (6 a year).

Medical Library Association: Suite 1900, 65 E Wacker Pl., Chicago, IL 60601-7246; tel. (312) 419-9094; fax (312) 419-8950; internet www.mlanet.org; f. 1898; 4,500 mems; non-profit educational org.; provides information for the delivery of health care, the education of health professionals, the conduct of research, and the public's understanding of health; Exec. Dir CARLA J. FUNK; publ. *Journal* (4 a year).

Music Library Association: 8551 Research Way, Suite 180, Middleton, WI 53562; tel. (608) 836-5825; fax (608) 831-8200; internet www.musiclibraryassoc.org; f. 1931; 2,900 mems; Pres. BONNA BOETTCHER; Exec. Sec. NANCY B. NUZZO; publs *Index and Bibliography Series* (irregular), *Music Cataloging Bulletin* (12 a year), *Notes* (4 a year), *Technical Reports—Information for Music Media Specialists* (irregular).

Society of American Archivists: 17 North State St, Suite 1425, Chicago, IL 60602-3315; tel. (312) 606-0722; fax (312) 606-0728; e-mail info@archivists.org; internet www.archivists.org; f. 1936; a professional association for archivists and institutions interested in the preservation and use of archives, manuscripts and current records; 3,400 individual and institutional mems; Exec. Dir NANCY PERKIN BEAUMONT; publ. *The American Archivist* (journal).

Special Libraries Association: 331 S Patrick St, Alexandria, VA 22314-3501; tel. (703) 647-4900; fax (703) 647-4901; e-mail sla@sla.org; internet www.sla.org; f. 1909; activities: professional development, résumé referral service, employment clearing-house and career advisory service (at annual conference only), chapters and division services, book publishing, government relations, public relations; Information Resources Center provides telephone reference service; research; 14,000 mems; library of 3,000 vols; Pres. ETHEL SALONEN; Exec. Dir JANICE R. LACHANCE; publ. include *Information Outlook* (12 a year).

Theatre Library Association: c/o New York Public Library for the Performing Arts, 40 Lincoln Center Plaza, New York, NY 10023; e-mail info@tla-online.org; internet www.tla-online.org; f. 1937; annual conf. (held jtly with American Soc. for Theatre Research); symposia; annual book awards, honouring the best English-language works on live theatre and recorded performance published in the USA; 297 mems; Pres. KENNETH SCHLESINGER; Vice-Pres. NANCY FRIEDLAND BRADY; Exec. Sec. DAVID NOCHIMSON; Treas. COLLEEN REILLY; publs *Broadside* (3 a year), *Performing Arts Resources*.

ECONOMICS, LAW AND POLITICS

Academy of Political Science: 475 Riverside Drive, Suite 1274, New York, NY 10115-1274; tel. (212) 870-2500; fax (212) 870-2202; e-mail aps@psqonline.org; internet www.psqonline.org; f. 1880; 8,000 mems; Pres. and Exec. Dir DEMETRIOS CARALEY; Chair. GEORGE B. MUNROE; publ. *Political Science Quarterly*.

American Academy of Political and Social Science: 3814 Walnut St, Philadelphia, PA 19104-6197; tel. (215) 746-6500; fax (215) 573-3003; internet www.aapss.org; f. 1889; 5,000 mems; Pres. DOUGLAS S. MASSEY; Exec. Dir PHYLLIS KANISS; publ. *The Annals* (6 a year).

American Accounting Association: 5717 Bessie Drive, Sarasota, FL 34233-2399; tel. (941) 921-7747; fax (941) 923-4093; internet aaahq.org; f. 1916; professional society for educators, practitioners and students of accounting; 13,000 mems; Pres. JANE F. MUTCHLER; Exec. Dir TRACEY SUTHERLAND; publs *Accounting Horizons*, *Issues in Accounting Education*, *Surveys*, *The Accounting Review*.

American Arbitration Association: 1633 Broadway, 10th Fl, New York, NY 10019; tel. (212) 716-5800; fax (212) 716-5905; e-mail websitemail@adr.org; internet www.adr.org; f. 1926; a public-service, not-for-profit org. offering a broad range of dispute resolution services to business executives, attorneys, individual employees, trade asscns, unions, management, consumers, families, communities and all levels of govt; also conducts seminars, conferences, etc.; 5,400 mems, over 50,000 arbitrators on national panel; library of 23,500 vols, 244 periodical titles; Pres. WILLIAM K. SLATE, II; publs *Arbitration Journal*, *Arbitration Times*, *The Claims Forum*, *Forum New York*, *Lawyers' Arbitration Letter* (4 a year), *Summary of Labor Arbitration Awards*, *Arbitration in the Schools*, *Labor Arbitration in Government*, *New York No-Fault Arbitration Reports* (12 a year).

American Bar Association: 321 N Clark St, Chicago, IL 60610; tel. (312) 988-5000; internet www.abanet.org; f. 1878; 400,000 mems; library of 50,000 vols; Pres. ROBERT J. GREY; publs *Bar Leader* (6 a year), *Journal* (12 a year), *Reports* (1 a year).

American Economic Association: 2014 Broadway, Suite 305, Nashville, TN 37203-2418; tel. (615) 322-2595; fax (615) 343-7590; internet www.aeaweb.org; f. 1885 to encourage economic discussion, research and the issue of publications on economic subjects; 19,000 mems; Pres. DANIEL MCFADDEN; publs *American Economic Review*, *Papers and Proceedings*, *Journal of Economic Literature*, *Journal of Economic Perspectives*.

American Finance Association: Univ. of California Berkeley, Haas School of Business, 545 Student Services Bldg, Berkeley, CA 94720-1900; tel. and fax (510) 642-2397; e-mail pyle@haas.berkeley.edu; internet www.afajof.org; f. 1940; makes available knowledge on current devts in the field of finance; 11,000 mems; Exec. Sec. and Treas. Prof. DAVID PYLE; publ. *Journal of Finance* (6 a year).

American Judicature Society: The Opperman Center at Drake University, 2700 University Ave, Des Moines, IA 50311; tel. (515) 271-2281; fax (515) 279-3090; internet www.ajs.org; f. 1913; promotes effective admin. of justice; 6,000 mems; Pres.-Elect CAROLE WAGNER VALLIANOS; publ. *Judicature* (6 a year).

American Law Institute: 4025 Chestnut St, Philadelphia, PA 19104; tel. (215) 243-1600; fax (215) 243-1664; f. 1923; promotes the clarification and simplification of the law; research work; 3,685 mems; library of 5,000 vols; Pres. MICHAEL TRAYNOR; Dir LANCE LIEBMAN; publs *Proceedings of ALI Annual Meetings* (1 a year), *Restatements of the Law*, *Model and Uniform Codifications*.

American Law Institute-American Bar Association Committee on Continuing Professional Education: 4025 Chestnut St, Philadelphia, PA 19104; tel. (215) 243-1600; fax (215) 243-1664; internet www.ali-aba.org; f. 1947 to organize, develop and carry out a nat. programme of continuing education of the bar; library of 5,000 vols; Exec. Dir JULENE FRANKI; publs *ALI-ABA Business Law Course Materials Journal* (6 a year), *ALI-ABA Estate Planning Course Materials Journal* (6 a year), *The Practical Lawyer* (6 a year), *The Practical Litigator* (6 a year), *The Practical Real Estate Lawyer* (6 a year), *The Practical Tax Lawyer* (4 a year).

American Peace Society: 1319 18th St, NW, Washington, DC 20036-1802; f. 1828; Pres. Dr EVRON M. KIRKPATRICK; Sec. L. EUGENE HEDBERG; publ. *World Affairs* (4 a year).

American Political Science Association: 1527 New Hampshire Ave, NW, Washington, DC 20036-2106; tel. (202) 483-2512; fax (202) 483-2657; e-mail apsa@apsanet.org; internet www.apsanet.org; f. 1903; 15,000 mems; Exec. Dir MICHAEL BRINTNALL; publs *American Political Science Review* (4 a year), *Perspectives on Politics* (4 a year), *PS: Political Science and Politics* (4 a year).

American Society for Public Administration: 1301 Pennsylvania Ave NW, Suite 840, Washington, DC 20004; tel. (202) 393-7878; fax (202) 638-4952; e-mail info@aspanet.org; internet www.aspanet.org; f. 1939; 11,000 mems; nat. and regional conferences, management institutes; chapters in local centres; Exec. Dir MARY HAMILTON; publs *PA Times* (12 a year), *Public Administration Review* (6 a year).

American Society of International Law: 2223 Massachusetts Ave NW, Washington, DC 20008; tel. (202) 939-6000; fax (202) 797-7133; internet www.asil.org; f. 1906, inc. 1950; 4,300 mems; library of 22,000 vols; Pres. JAMES H. CARTER; Exec. Dir CHARLOTTE KU; publs *International Legal Materials* (6 a year), *Proceedings* (1 a year), *The American Journal of International Law* (4 a year).

American Statistical Association: 732 North Washington St, Alexandria, VA 22314-1943; tel. (703) 684-1221; fax (703) 684-2037; e-mail asainfo@amstat.org; internet www.amstat.org; f. 1839; 16,000 mems; Pres. FRITZ J. SCHEUREN; publs *Chance Magazine* (4 a year), *Journal of Agricultural, Biological and Environmental Statistics* (4 a year), *Journal of Business and Economic Statistics* (4 a year), *Journal of Computational and Graphical Statistics* (4 a year), *Journal of Educational and Behavioral Statistics* (4 a year), *Journal of the American Statistical Association* (4 a year), *Technometrics* (4 a year), *The American Statistician* (4 a year).

Association of American Law Schools: 1201 Connecticut Ave NW, Suite 800, Washington, DC 20036; tel. (202) 296-8851; fax (202) 296-8869; e-mail aals@aals.org; internet www.aals.org; f. 1900; promotes improvement of the legal profession through legal education; 165 institutional mems; Exec. Dir CARL C. MONK; publs *Directory of Law Teachers* (1 a year), *Journal of Legal Education* (4 a year), *Placement Bulletin* (irregular), *Proceedings* (1 a year).

Atlantic Council of the United States: 1101 15th St NW, 11th Fl., Washington, DC 20005; tel. (202) 463-7226; fax (202) 463-7241; e-mail info@acus.org; internet www.acus.org; f. 1961; nat., non-partisan, non-profit public policy centre that addresses the advancement of US global interests within the Atlantic and Pacific communities; the council engages the US executive and legislative branches, the nat. and int. business community, media and academia, and diplomats and other foreign leaders in an integrated programme of policy studies and round-table discussions, briefings, dialogues and conferences, designed to encourage its selected membership and other constituencies to reflect and plan for the future; funded by corporations, foundations, private individuals, and govt grants and contracts; 130 board mems, 200 councillors, 400 acad. assocs; Pres. (Finance and Admin.) DREW A. JUBERT; publs *Bulletin* (irregular), *Occasional Papers* (irregular), *Policy Papers* (irregular).

Carnegie Endowment for International Peace: 1779 Massachusetts Ave NW, Washington, DC 20036; tel. (202) 483-7600; fax (202) 483-1840; e-mail info@carnegieendowment.org; internet www.carnegieendowment.org; f. 1910; private, non-profit and non-partisan organization dedicated to advancing co-operation between nations and promoting active international engagement by the USA; 130 mems (incl. Carnegie Moscow Center); library of 8,000 vols; Pres. JESSICA T. MATHEWS; publs *Foreign Policy* (6 a year), *Pro et Contra* (1 a year).

Century Foundation: 41 East 70th St, New York, NY 10021; tel. (212) 535-4441; fax (212) 535-7534; e-mail info@tcf.org; internet www.tcf.org; f. 1919 by the late Edward A. Filene as an endowed foundation for public policy research on major economic, political and social institutions and issues; Chair. of the Board of Trustees ALAN BRINKLEY; Vice-Chair. of the Board and Chair. of Exec. Cttee JAMES A. LEACH; Pres. RICHARD C. LEONE.

Council for European Studies at Colombia University: 1203A, Int. Affairs Bldg, Columbia Univ., 420 W 118th St, Campus Mail Code 3310, New York, NY 10027; tel. (212) 854-4172; fax (212) 854-8808; e-mail ces@columbia.edu; internet www.ces.colombia.edu; f. 1970; consortium of European studies programmes at over 80 univs in the USA, Canada and Europe; affiliated with Columbia Univ.; aims to encourage greater scholarly interest in Europe, to emphasize the commonality of problems that face the nations of Europe and N America; sponsors research, information services, graduate student training; holds biennial conference in Chicago; 1,200 individual mems, 115 mem. institutions; Assoc. Dir STEFANIE GRUPP CLASBY; publ. *News from the Council for European Studies* (12 a year, electronic).

Council of State Governments: 2760 Research Park Drive, POB 11910, Lexington, KY 40511; tel. (859) 244-8000; fax (859) 244-8001; e-mail sales@csg.org; internet www.csg.org; f. 1933; offices in Washington, DC, New York, Atlanta, GA, Chicago, IL, and San Francisco, CA; a non-partisan organization established by the States for service to the States; Pres. RUTH ANN MILLER; Exec. Dir DANIEL M. SPRAGUE; publs *Book of the States* (2 a year), *CSG State Directories* (1 a year), *Spectrum* (4 a year), *State Government News* (12 a year), *Suggested State Legislation* (12 a year).

Council on Foreign Relations, Inc.: 58 East 68th St, New York, NY 10021; tel. (212) 434-9400; fax (212) 434-9800; internet www.cfr.org; f. 1921; 2,905 mems; library: Foreign Relations library of 18,000 vols, 300 periodicals, clippings files; Chair. PETER G. PETERSON; Pres. RICHARD N. HAASS; publs *Critical Issues*, *Foreign Affairs* (6 a year).

Economic History Association: c/o Dept of Economics, 500 El Camino Real, Santa Clara University, Santa Clara, CA 95053-0385; tel. (408) 554-4348; fax (408) 554-2331; e-mail eha@falcon.cc.ukans.edu; internet www.eh.net/eha; f. 1940 to encourage and promote teaching, research and publication in all fields of economic history; 1,200 individual mems; 2,210 library mems; Exec. Dir THOMAS WEISS; publ. *Journal of Economic History* (4 a year).

Federal Bar Association: Suite 444, 1220 North Fillmore St, Arlington, VA 22201; tel. (571) 481-9100; fax (571) 481-9090; e-mail fba@fedbar.org; internet www.fedbar.org; f. 1920; 16,000 mems; 99 Chapters; more than 100 committees in fields of federal law; Pres. THOMAS R. SCHUCK; publ. *The Federal Lawyer*.

Foreign Policy Association, Inc.: 470 Park Ave South, New York, NY 10016; tel. (212) 481-8100; fax (212) 481-9275; internet www.fpa.org; f. 1918; to promote citizen education in world affairs, to assist orgs, communities and educational instns, to develop programmes for citizen understanding and constructive participation in world affairs, and to advance public understanding of foreign policy problems through nat. programmes and publs of a non-partisan character based upon the principles of freedom, justice and democracy; Chair. GONZALO DE LAS HERAS; Pres. and CEO NOEL V. LATEEF; publs *Great Decisions* (1 a year), *Headline Series* (4 a year).

History of Economics Society: c/o Neil B. Niman, History of Economics Society, McConnell Hall, University of New Hampshire, Durham, NH 03824; e-mail tleonard@princeton.edu; internet historyofeconomics.org; f. 1973 to promote interest and inquiry into the history of economics and related parts of intellectual history; 300 mems in the USA and other countries; Sec. TIM LEONARD; publ. *Journal of the History of Economic Thought*.

Institute for Mediterranean Affairs, Inc.: c/o J. Yampolsky, 1800 JFK Blvd, Suite 2000, Philadelphia, PA 19103-7496; tel. (215) 545-4800; fax (207) 017-4710; est. under charter of the Univ. of the State of New York to evolve a better understanding of the historical background and contemporary political and socio-economic problems of the nations and regions that border on the Mediterranean Sea; to analyse the various tensions in the Eastern Mediterranean and to investigate the basic problems of the area; special attention is given to the Israeli–Arab conflict; 250 Academic Advisory mems; Man. Dir J. YAMPOLSKY.

Institute for Operations Research and the Management Sciences: 7240 Parkway Dr., Suite 300, Hanover, MD 21076; tel. (443) 757-3500; fax (443) 757-3515; e-mail informs@informs.org; internet www.informs.org; f. 1995 by merger of Operations Research Soc. of America (f. 1952) and Institute for Management Sciences (f. 1953); serves the scientific and professional needs of operations research educators, investigators, scientists, students, managers and consultants; nat. and int. confs for academics and professionals; 10,200 mems; Pres. RINA SCHNEUR; Pres.-Elect TERRY P. HARRISON; Exec. Dir TERESA V. CRYAN; publs *Decision Analysis* (4 a year), *Information Systems Research* (4 a year), *INFORMS Journal on Computing* (4 a year), *INFORMS Transactions on Education* (3 a year), *Interfaces* (6 a year), *Management Science* (12 a year), *Manufacturing & Service Operations Management* (4 a year), *Marketing Science* (6 a year), *Mathematics of Operations Research* (4 a year), *Operations Research* (6 a year), *Organization Science* (6 a year), *Transportation Science* (4 a year).

Society of Actuaries: 475 N Martingale Rd, Suite 600, Schaumburg, IL 60173-2226; tel. (847) 706-3500; fax (847) 706-3599; e-mail webmaster@soa.org; internet www.soa.org; f. 1949; educational, research and professional membership soc. for actuaries in life and health insurance and pension planning; spec. collns, reports and transactions from US, Canadian and int. actuarial orgs; 21,472 mems; library of 3,900 vols; Pres. DONALD SEGAL; publ. *The North American Actuarial Journal* (4 a year).

World Peace Foundation: 79 John F. Kennedy St, Cambridge, MA 02138-4952; tel. (617) 496-9812; fax (617) 491-8588; e-mail world_peace@harvard.edu; internet www.worldpeacefoundation.org; f. 1910; an operating foundation that does not give outside grants; policy-orientated studies in world affairs; Pres. ROBERT I. ROTBERG; publ. sponsors *International Organization* (4 a year).

EDUCATION

Carnegie Corporation of New York: 437 Madison Ave, New York, NY 10022; tel. (212) 371-3200; fax (212) 754-4073; internet www.carnegie.org; f. 1911 by Andrew Carnegie for the advancement and diffusion of knowledge and understanding among peoples of the USA and, with subsequent amendment of the charter, of some of the current or former British overseas Commonwealth; primary interests: education, international affairs, democracy; 17 trustees; Pres. VARTAN GREGORIAN; Chair. HELENE L. KAPLAN; publs *Carnegie Newsline*, *Carnegie Quarterly*, *Challenge Papers*, *Reporter*, *Results of Carnegie Journalism Reports*.

International Montessori Society: 9525 Georgia Ave, Suite 200, Silver Spring, MD 20910; tel. (301) 589-1127; fax (301) 589-0733; e-mail havis@imsmontessori.org; internet www.imsmontessori.org; f. 1979; supports the effective application of Montessori educational principles throughout the world; provides teacher education through correspondence; occasional workshops; mail-order book sales; audio CD and study guide of distinctive IMS technology for Montessori teaching; small library; 400 mems; Dir LEE HAVIS; publs *Montessori News* (2 a year), *Montessori Observer* (4 a year).

Philosophy of Education Society: c/o Alexander Sidorkin, PES Exec. Dir, University of Northern Colorado, McKee 208, Greeley, CO 80639; tel. (970) 351-2701; internet philosophyofeducation.org; f. 1941; 550 mems; exists to promote discussion and analysis of philosophy and education and to improve the teaching and research in philosophy and education; Pres. SUSAN LAIRD; publs *Educational Theory* (4 a year), *Philosophy of Education Newsletter* (3 a year), *Yearbook*.

FINE AND PERFORMING ARTS

American Federation of Arts: 305 East 47th St, 10th Fl., New York, NY 10017; tel. (212) 988-7700; fax (212) 861-2487; e-mail pubinfo@afaweb.org; internet www.afaweb.org; f. 1909 by act of Congress; works to strengthen the ability of museums to enrich the public's experience and understanding of art; organizes national and international travelling art exhibitions and develops educational programmes in co-operation with the museum community; Chair. BARBARA WEEDEN; Pres. GILBERT H. KINNEY; Dir JULIA BROWN; publ. *Memo to Members* (4 a year).

American Musicological Society: 6010 College Station, Brunswick, ME 04011-8451; tel. (207) 798-4243; fax (207) 789-4254; e-mail ams@ams-net.org; internet www.ams-net.org; f. 1934; 3,500 mems; Pres. ANNE WALTERS ROBERTSON; Exec. Dir ROBERT JUDD; publs *Abstracts of Papers read at the Annual Meeting* (1 a year), *Journal* (3 a year).

American Society for Aesthetics: POB 915, Pooler, GA 31322-0915; tel. (912) 748-9524; e-mail asa@armstrong.edu; internet www.aesthetics-online.org; f. 1942; research and publ. in aesthetics, criticism, and theory of the arts; 1,000 mems; Pres. Prof. PAUL GUYER; Exec. Dir Dr DABNEY TOWNSEND; publs *Journal of Aesthetics and Art Criticism* (4 a year), *ASAGE* (ASA Graduate e-journal).

American Society for Theatre Research: POB 1798, Boulder, CO 80306-1798; tel. (303) 530-1838; fax (303) 530-1839; e-mail info@astr.org; internet www.astr.org; f. 1956; serves needs of theatre and performance studies historians and fosters knowledge of the theatre in the USA and overseas; 706 mems; Pres. Prof. BRUCE MCCONACHIE; Sec. Prof. GAY GIBSON CIMA; publ. *Theatre Survey* (2 a year).

American Society of Composers, Authors and Publishers (ASCAP): 1 Lincoln Plaza, New York, NY 10023; tel. (212) 621-6000; fax (212) 595-3342; e-mail info@ascap.com; internet www.ascap.com; f. 1914; a non-profit society that issues licences for public performance of members' copyright works; 180,000 mem. songwriters, composers and music publishers; Pres. MARILYN BERGMAN; publs *ASCAP Biographical Dictionary*, *ASCAP Playback* (4 a year).

Americans for the Arts: 1 East 53rd St, New York, NY 10022; tel. (212) 223-2787; fax (212) 980-4857; internet www.artsusa.org; f. 1960 to promote the interests of the arts; 1,500 mems; library of 5,000 items; Chair. STEVEN D. SPIESS.

Center for Creative Photography: University of Arizona, 1030 N. Olive Rd, Tucson, AZ 85721-0103; tel. (520) 621-7968; fax (520) 621-9444; e-mail oncenter@ccp.arizona.edu; internet www.creativephotography.org; f. 1975; a unique resource for the study and history of photography; extensive collection of prints and other materials related to the life and works of photographers since the beginning of the 20th century; comprises a computer-catalogued archive; houses the lifetime archives of Ansel Adams, Wynn Bullock, Harry Callahan, Dean Brown, Louise Dahl-Wolfe, Andreas Feininger, Sonya Noskowiak, Aaron Siskind, Frederick Sommer, W. Eugene Smith, Edward Weston, etc.; 500 mems; library of 11,000 vols, 100 periodicals; Dean of the Libraries and the Center for Creative Photography CARLA STUFFLE; publ. *The Archive* (every 2 years).

College Art Association: 275 Seventh Ave, New York, NY 10001; tel. (212) 691-1051; fax (212) 627-2381; e-mail nyoffice@collegeart.org; internet www.collegeart.org; f. 1911 to further scholarship and excellence in the teaching and practice of art and art history; 14,000 individual, 2,000 institutional mems; Exec. Dir LINDA DOWNS; publs *Art Bulletin* (4 a year), *Art Journal* (4 a year), *CAA News*, *CAA.Reviews* (online).

Graphic Arts Information Network: Printing Industries of America, 200 Deer Run Rd, Sewickley, PA 15143-2600; tel. (412) 741-6860; fax (412) 741-2311; e-mail printing@printing.org; internet www.printing.org; f. 1924; 14,000 mems in 60 countries; library: over 6,000 vols and periodicals; non-profit scientific research and technical education org. serving the int. graphic communications community; conducts technical workshops, in-plant assessments, seminars worldwide on various aspects of graphic communications; Pres. MICHAEL MAKIN; publs *Learning Modules*, *Second Sight* (technical reports), *The Magazine* (6 a year).

National Academy of Design: 1083 Fifth Ave, New York, NY 10128; tel. (212) 369-4880; fax (212) 360-6795; e-mail info@nationalacademy.org; internet www.nationalacademy.org; f. 1825; membership composed exclusively of artists; sections: painting, sculpture, watercolour, graphic arts, architecture; attached art museum, art library and art school; 450 mems; Pres. RICHARD HAAS; Corresp. Sec. STANLEY BLEIFELD; Dir Dr CARMINE BRANAGAN; publ. *Bulletin* (2 a year).

National Sculpture Society: 75 Varick St, 11th Fl, New York, NY 10013; tel. (212) 764-5645; fax (212) 764-5651; e-mail news@nationalsculpture.org; internet www.nationalsculpture.org; f. 1893, inc. 1896; disseminates knowledge of American sculpture; promotes excellence in sculpture inspired by the natural world; 3,000 mems (incl. 320 professional mems); Pres. DAN OSTERMILLER; Exec. Dir GWEN PIER; publ. *Sculpture Review* (4 a year).

Society for Ethnomusicology: Morrison Hall 005, 1165 E Third St, Bloomington, IN 47405-3700; tel. (812) 855-6672; fax (812) 855-6673; e-mail sem@indiana.edu; internet www.ethnomusicology.org; f. 1955; 2,700 mems; Pres. GAGE AVERILL; Sec. JENNIFER POST; Exec. Dir STEPHEN STUEMPFLE; publ. *Ethnomusicology* (3 a year).

HISTORY, GEOGRAPHY AND ARCHAEOLOGY

American Antiquarian Society: 185 Salisbury St, Worcester, MA 01609-1634; tel. (508) 755-5221; fax (508) 753-3311; e-mail library@mwa.org; internet www.americanantiquarian.org; f. 1812; a learned soc. and research library concerned with American history before 1877; sponsors research, education, publs, lectures and concerts; library of 680,000 vols, 2m. MSS collns, 2m. newspaper issues, 200,300 items of graphic art; 950 mems; Pres. ELLEN S. DUNLAP.

American Association for State and Local History: 1717 Church St, Nashville, TN 37203-2991; tel. (615) 320-3203; fax (615) 327-9013; e-mail membership@aaslh.org; internet www.aaslh.org; f. 1940; successor to Conference of Historical Societies; objects: exchange of information on local and regional history and historical socs, and dissemination in scholarly and popular publs of professional material and interpretative articles; 5,900 mems; Dir of Programs BOB BEATTY; publs *History News* (4 a year, professional news), *History News Dispatch* (12 a year).

American Catholic Historical Association: The Catholic Univ. of America, Mullen Library 320, Washington, DC 20064; tel. (202) 319-5079; fax (202) 319-5079; e-mail acha@cua.edu; internet research.cua.edu/acha; f. 1919; promotes interest in the history of the Catholic Church broadly considered; research work; 890 mems; Sec. and Treas. Rev. PAUL ROBICHAUD; publ. *The Catholic Historical Review* (4 a year).

American Historical Association: 400 A St SE, Washington, DC 20003; tel. (202) 544-2422; fax (202) 544-8307; e-mail aha@historians.org; internet www.historians.org; f. 1884; 16,000 mems; Pres. Prof. ANTHONY GRAFTON; Exec. Dir JAMES R. GROSSMAN; Controller RANDY NORELL; publs *American Historical Review* (5 a year), *Perspectives* (9 a year), *Program of the Annual Meeting*.

American Irish Historical Society: 991 Fifth Ave, New York, NY 10028; tel. (212) 288-2263; fax (212) 628-7927; e-mail info@aihs.org; internet aihs.org; f. 1897; research in the history of the Irish in America; 800 mems; library of 10,000 vols; Dir WILLIAM COBERT; Chair. DONALD R. KEOUGH; Librarian Rev. JOSEPH A. O'HARE; publ. *The Recorder* (2 a year).

American Jewish Historical Society: 15 West 16th St, New York, NY 10011; tel. (212) 294-6160; fax (212) 294-6161; internet www.ajhs.org; f. 1892; collects and publishes material bearing upon the history of Jews in America; promotes the study of American-Jewish history; 3,200 mems; library of 50,000 vols, 20,000,000 MSS, contains many rare and valuable MSS since the 16th century, American-Jewish periodicals since the 18th century; Chair. Prof. JEFF GUROCK; Exec. Dir EVAN KINGSLEY; publ. *American Jewish History* (Johns Hopkins University Press).

American Numismatic Society: 75 Varick St, 11th Fl., New York, NY 10013; tel. (212) 571-4470; fax (212) 571-4479; e-mail membership@numismatics.org; internet www.numismatics.org; f. 1858; 2,000 mems; colln encompasses all periods and fields of interest; library of 100,000 vols; Pres. DONALD PARTRICK; Exec. Dir UTE WARTENBERG KAGAN; publs *American Journal of Numismatics* (1 a year), *Ancient Coins in the North American Collections* (irregular), *Magazine* (3 a year), *Numismatic Literature* (1 a year), *Numismatic Notes and Monographs* (irregular), *Numismatic Studies* (irregular), *Proceedings of the Coinage of the Americas Conference* (irregular), *Sylloge Nummorum Graecorum* (irregular), *The Collection of the American Numismatic Society* (irregular).

American Society for Eighteenth-Century Studies: Wake Forest University, Winston-Salem, NC 27109; tel. (336) 727-4694; fax (336) 727-4697; internet asecs.press.jhu.edu; f. 1969, inc. 1970; independent society; works through publications and meetings to foster interest and encourage investigation in the achievements of the 18th century in America and Europe; mems: 50 institutions, 1,077 libraries, 2,500 individuals; Pres. Prof. MARGARET ANNE DOODY; Exec. Dir BYRON R. WELLS; publs *ASECS News Circular* (4 a year), *Eighteenth-Century Studies* (4 a year), *Studies in Eighteenth-Century Culture* (1 a year).

American Society of Church History: 409 Prospect St, New Haven, CT 06511; e-mail asch@yale.edu; internet www.churchhistory.org; f. 1888, reorganized 1906; 1,500 mems; Sec. HENRY W. BOWDEN; publ. *Church History* (4 a year).

Archaeological Institute of America: 656 Beacon St, Boston, MA 02215; tel. (617) 353-9361; fax (617) 353-6550; e-mail aia@aia.bu.edu; internet www.archaeological.org; f. 1879; 8,000 mems; Pres. JANE C. WALDBAUM; Exec. Dir BONNIE R. CLENDENNING; publs *American Journal of Archaeology* (4 a year), *Archaeology* (illustrated, 6 a year), *Dig Magazine* (6 a year).

Arizona Archaeological and Historical Society: Arizona State Museum, Univ. of Arizona, Tucson, AZ 85721; internet www.statemuseum.arizona.edu/aahs/aahs.shtml; f. 1916; 1,150 mems; Pres. Dr JAMES E. AYRES; publs *Glyphs* (12 a year), *Kiva* (4 a year).

Association of American Geographers: 1710 16th St, NW, Washington, DC 20009-3198; tel. (202) 234-1450; fax (202) 234-2744; e-mail gaia@aag.org; internet www.aag.org; f. 1904; 10,700 mems; Pres. KENNETH E. FOOTE; Exec. Dir DOUGLAS RICHARDSON; publs *Annals* (5 a year), *The Professional Geographer* (4 a year).

Brooklyn Historical Society: 128 Pierrepont St, Brooklyn, NY 11201; tel. (718) 222-4111; fax (718) 222-3794; internet www.brooklynhistory.org; f. 1863; 1,250 mems; museum colln of objects relating to Brooklyn;

library of 155,000 bound vols, 100,000 graphic images, 2,000 ft of MSS, 2,000 maps and atlases; Pres. DEBORAH SCHWARTZ.

California Historical Society: 678 Mission St, San Francisco, CA 94105; tel. (415) 357-1848; fax (415) 357-1850; e-mail info@calhist.org; internet www.californiahistoricalsociety.org; f. 1871; non-profit-making instn; 3,500 mems; library of 55,000 vols, rare MSS, pamphlets and maps, 500,000 historic photographs; Exec. Dir DAVID CROSSON; Pres. Bd of Trustees JAN BERCKEFELDT; publ. *California History* (magazine, 4 a year).

Dallas Historical Society: POB 150038, Dallas, TX 75315; located at: The Hall of State at Fair Park, 3939 Grand Ave., Dallas, TX 75210; tel. (214) 421-4500; fax (214) 421-7500; internet www.dallashistory.org; f. 1922; encourages historical enquiry; collects, preserves and exhibits historical materials; the Society has the custody of the Hall of State (see under Museums and Galleries), which it operates as a museum and archive of Texas and Dallas history; 2,000 mems; library of 10,000 vols, 3,000,000 archival items, 10,000 museum artefacts and 30,000 photographs; Exec. Dir MICHAEL DUTY; Chief Operations Officer FRANK WILSON; publ. *Legacies* (published jtly with other organizations, 2 a year).

Historical Society of Pennsylvania: 1300 Locust St, Philadelphia, PA 19107; tel. (215) 732-6200; fax (215) 732-2680; e-mail hsppr@hsp.org; internet www.hsp.org; f. 1824; historical and genealogical collns; 2,300 mems; library of 600,000 vols and pamphlets, more than 19 m. MSS, 300,000 graphics; Pres. DAVID MOLTKE-HANSEN; Chair. COLIN F. MCNEIL; publs *Pennsylvania Legacies Newsmagazine* (2 a year), *The Pennsylvania Magazine of History and Biography* (4 a year).

Maryland Historical Society: 201 West Monument St, Baltimore, MD 21201-4647; tel. (410) 685-3750; fax (410) 385-2105; internet www.mdhs.org; f. 1844; 5,000 mems; museum and library: see under Museums; Pres. STANARD T. KLINEFELTER; Dir DENNIS A. FIORI; publs *Maryland Historical Magazine* (4 a year), *Maryland Magazine of Genealogy* (2 a year), *News and Notes*.

Massachusetts Historical Society: 1154 Boylston St, Boston, MA 02215-3695; tel. (617) 536-1608; fax (617) 859-0074; internet www.masshist.org; f. 1791; oldest historical society in US; library: see Libraries; Dir WILLIAM M. FOWLER; Librarian PETER DRUMMEY; publ. *Proceedings*.

Medieval Academy of America: 104 Mt Auburn St, 5th Fl., Cambridge, MA 02138; tel. (617) 491-1622; fax (617) 492-3303; e-mail speculum@medievalacademy.org; internet www.medievalacademy.org; f. 1925; promotes research, publ. and instruction in medieval records, literature, languages, art, archaeology, history, philosophy, science, life, and all other aspects of medieval civilization; 4,100 mems; Pres. ALICE-MARY TALBOT; Exec. Dir PAUL E. SZARMACH; publ. *Speculum: A Journal of Medieval Studies* (4 a year).

Minnesota Historical Society: 345 Kellogg Blvd W, St Paul, MN 55102-1906; tel. (612) 296-6126; fax (612) 297-3343; internet www.mnhs.org; f. 1849; history museum; state historic preservation office; state archives; collection of artefacts; archaeology; newspaper and audiovisual library, 78,000 cu ft of MSS; 23 historic sites; 8,000 mems; library: over 500,000 vols; Pres. DAVID A. KOCH; Dir NINA ARCHABAL; publs *Member News* (6 a year), *Minnesota History* (4 a year).

National Geographic Society: 1145 17th St NW, Washington, DC 20036; tel. (202) 857-7000; fax (202) 775-6141; internet www.nationalgeographic.com; f. 1888 for the increase and diffusion of geographic knowledge; 8,000,000 mems; library: see Libraries and Archives; Pres. and CEO JOHN M. FAHEY, Jr; publs *National Geographic* (12 a year), *National Geographic Adventure* (10 a year), *National Geographic Explorer* (classroom magazine available only in USA, 6 a year), *National Geographic Kids* (12 a year), *National Geographic Traveler* (8 a year).

New York Historical Society: 170 Central Park West, New York, NY 10024-5194; tel. (212) 873-3400; fax (212) 874-8706; internet www.nyhistory.org; f. 1804; 3,300 mems; museum of 17th–19th-century American art, antiques and history, including portraits, landscapes and genre paintings; library of 630,000 vols, 2,000,000 MSS, 10,000 maps and atlases, large collection of pre-1820 newspapers, sheet music, 20,000 broadsides, 1 m. prints and photographs; Pres. and CEO Dr LOUISE MIRRER; Dir Dr LINDA S. FERBER.

Omohundro Institute of Early American History and Culture: POB 8781, Williamsburg, VA 23187-8781; tel. (757) 221-1110; fax (757) 221-1047; e-mail ieahc1@wm.edu; internet oieahc.wm.edu; f. 1943 by the College of William and Mary and the Colonial Williamsburg Foundation; awards post-doctoral fellowships, sponsors confs, publishes 3–4 book titles annually; 1,000 assoc. mems; library of 7,000 vols, 880 periodicals, 2,000 microfilms; Dir Prof. RONALD HOFFMAN; publs *Uncommon Sense* (newsletter, 2 a year), *William and Mary Quarterly*.

Oregon Historical Society: 1200 SW Park Ave, Portland, OR 97205-2483; tel. (503) 222-1741; fax (503) 221-2035; e-mail orhist@ohs.org; internet www.ohs.org; f. 1873; 6,500 mems; library of 35,000 books, 2,000,000 photographs, 25,000 maps, MSS, thousands of pamphlets, serials and newspapers; museum artefacts from neolithic period to discovery, settlement of Oregon Country, Pacific Northwest; Dir JOHN HERMAN; publ. *Oregon Historical Quarterly* (4 a year).

Organization of American Historians: 112 N Bryan Ave, Bloomington, IN 47408; tel. (812) 855-7311; fax (812) 855-0696; e-mail oah@oah.org; internet www.oah.org; f. 1907; promotes historical study in American history; 9,300 indiv. mems, 2,400 institutional mems; Pres. DAVID A. HOLLINGER; Exec. Dir KATHERINE M. FINLEY; publs *Journal of American History* (4 a year), *OAH Magazine of History*.

Pilgrim Society: 75 Court St, Plymouth, MA 02360; tel. (508) 746-1620; fax (508) 746-3396; e-mail director@pilgrimhall.org; internet www.pilgrimhall.org; f. 1820; maintains pilgrim Hall Museum, the oldest public museum in North America; collns of pilgrim decorative arts, furnishings, prehistoric Native American collns; maintains the Nat. Monument to the forefathers; 600 mems; library of 12,000 vols and rare MSS collns dealing with the Plymouth Colony; Dir ANN BERRY.

Presbyterian Historical Society: 425 Lombard St, Philadelphia, PA 19147-1516; tel. (215) 627-1852; fax (215) 627-0509; e-mail refdesk@history.pcusa.org; internet www.history.pcusa.org; f. 1852; nat. archives of the Presbyterian Church (USA); 700 mems; library of 250,000 vols and 30,000 cu ft archive material; Exec. Dir FREDERICK J. HEUSER, JR; publ. *The Journal of Presbyterian History* (2 a year).

Renaissance Society of America: The City University of New York, 365 Fifth Ave, Room 5400, New York, NY 10011; tel. (212) 817-2130; fax (212) 817-1544; e-mail rsa@rsa.org; internet www.rsa.org; f. 1954; 2,400 individual mems, 1,100 library mems; Pres. JESSIE ANN OWENS; Exec. Dir JOHN MONFASANI; publs *Renaissance News & Notes*, *Renaissance Quarterly*.

Rhode Island Historical Society: 110 Benevolent St, Providence, RI 02906; tel. (401) 331-8575; fax (401) 351-0127; internet www.rihs.org; f. 1822; administers: John Brown House, 52 Power St: 18th-century museum house; decorative arts, furniture, paintings, silver and pewter; library: 121 Hope St, 200,000 vols; historical and genealogical; large graphics and MSS colln; Museum of Work and Culture: 42 South Main St, Woonsocket, RI; 1,700 mems; Pres. ROGER N. BEGIN; Exec. Dir BERNARD P. FISHMAN; publ. *Rhode Island History* (4 a year).

Society of American Historians: Butler Library, Box 2, Columbia University, New York, NY 10027; tel. (212) 854-5943; internet www.historians.org/affiliates/soc_am_hisn.htm; f. 1939; 350 fellows; Pres. ROBERT DALLEK; Exec. Sec. MARK C. CARNES.

Vermont Historical Society: 60 Washington St, Barre, VT 05641-4209; tel. (802) 479-8500; fax (802) 479-8510; e-mail vhs-info@state.vt.us; internet www.vermonthistory.org; f. 1838; objects: educational work in Vermont and American history; colln of books, documents and MSS relating to Vermont; publ. of historical magazines and books; maintenance of State Museum (located at: 109 State St, Montpelier, VT 05609-0901); 2,500 mems; library of 40,000 vols, early Vermont imprints; Pres. SARAH L. DOPP; Dir MARK HUDSON; publs *In Context* (4 a year), *Vermont History* (2 a year).

Western Reserve Historical Society: 10825 East Blvd, Cleveland, OH 44106; tel. (216) 721-5722; fax (216) 721-0645; f. 1867; maintains a historical museum, family and regional history library, auto-aviation museum, five historical sites; 6,400 mems; library of 235,000 vols, 25,000 vols of newspapers, 30,500 rolls of microfilm, 1,000,000 prints and photos, 6,000,000 MSS; Pres. JAMES A. SCHOFF; Exec. Dir PATRICK H. REYMANN; publ. *News* (6 a year).

Wisconsin Historical Society: 816 State St, Madison, WI 53706-1417; tel. (608) 264-6400; fax (608) 264-6404; internet www.wisconsinhistory.org; f. 1846; 1,888,000 microforms, 39,000 cu ft MSS, 49,000 cu ft public records, 25,000 maps and atlases, 1,000,000 pictures and negatives, 14,000 cinema and television films from major Hollywood studios, 2,000,000 motion picture and theatre promotional graphics; 7,200 mems; library of 1,085,000 vols, including pamphlets and government documents; Dir GEORGE VOGT; publs *Columns* (6 a year), *Wisconsin Magazine of History* (4 a year), *Wisconsin Public Documents* (6 a year).

LANGUAGE AND LITERATURE

Alliance Française: c/o French Embassy, 4101 Reservoir Rd, NW, Washington, DC 20007; tel. (202) 944-63-53; fax (202) 944-63-47; e-mail dgi@alliance-us.org; internet www.alliance-us.org; offers courses and examinations in French language and culture and promotes cultural exchange with France; attached teaching offices in Albuquerque (NM), Atlanta (GA), Austin (TX), Berkeley (CA), Beverly Hills (CA), Bloomfield Hills (MI), Bonita Springs (FL), Boston (MA), Buffalo (NY), Chicago (IL), Cincinnati (OH), Denver (CO), Doylestown (PA), Earlysville (VA), Evanston (IL), Fort Lauderdale (FL), Fresno, (CA), Greenwich (CT), Hartford (CT), Hawaii (HI), Houston (TX), Jackson (MS),

Jacksonville (FL), Kansas City (MO), Louisville (KY), Lynchburg (VA), Madison (WI), Miami (FL), Milwaukee (WI), Minneapolis-St Paul (MI), Missoula (MT), Napa (CA), Naperville (TN), New Haven (CT), New Orleans (LA), New York (NY), Newport Beach (CA), Norfolk (VA), Orlando (FL), Pasadena (CA), Philadelphia (PA), Phoenix (AZ), Pittsburg (PA), Portland (OR), Providence (RI), Sacramento (CA), Saint-Louis (MO), Salt Lake City (UT), San Antonio (TX), San Diego (CA), San Francsico (CA), San Rafael (CA), Santa Clara Valley (CA), Santa Cruz County (CA), Sarasota (FL), Saratoga (CA), Seattle (WA), Toledo (OH), Tulsa (OK), Washington, DC, White Plains (NY), Wilmington (DE), Woodbury (CT); Dir of Operations, USA PIERRE HUDELOT.

American Center of PEN: 588 Broadway, Suite 303, New York, NY 10012; tel. (212) 334-1660; fax (212) 334-2181; e-mail pen@pen.org; internet www.pen.org; f. 1922; promotes friendship and intellectual cooperation among writers, exchange of ideas and freedom of expression; confs, workshops, emergency fund for writers, translation prize; administers PEN/Nabokov Award and other literary awards; programme for inmate-writers in American prisons; 3,400 mems; library of 1,000 vols; Pres. Prof. KWAME ANTHONY APPIAH; Exec. Dir STEVEN L. ISENBERG; publs *Grants and Awards Available to American Writers* (every 2 years), *PEN America* (2 a year).

American Classical League: Miami University, Oxford, OH 45056; tel. (513) 529-7741; fax (513) 529-7742; e-mail info@aclclassics.org; internet www.aclclassics.org; f. 1919; 3,400 mems; Pres. KEN KITCHELL; Sec. TAMARA BAUER; publ. *The Classical Outlook* (4 a year).

American Comparative Literature Association: University of Texas at Austin Program in Comparative Literature, 1 University Station, B5003, Austin, TX 78712-0196; tel. (512) 471-8020; e-mail info@acla.org; internet www.acla.org; f. 1960 to further the growth of comparative literature in the USA; 1,000 mems; Pres. MARGARET HIGONNET; Sec. and Treas. ELIZABETH RICHMOND-GARZA; publ. *Comparative Literature Journal* (4 a year).

American Dialect Society: c/o Allan Metcalf, Dept of English, MacMurray College, Jacksonville, IL 62650; tel. (217) 479-7014; fax (217) 479-7013; e-mail americandialect@mac.edu; internet www.americandialect.org; f. 1889; study of the English language in N America, together with other languages or dialects of other languages influencing it or being influenced by it; sponsor of *Dictionary of American Regional English*; 350 mems; Pres. LUANNE VON SCHNEIDEMESSER; Exec. Sec. ALLAN METCALF; publ. *American Speech* (4 a year, with annual supplement).

American Philological Association: Univ. of Pennsylvania, 220S, 40th St, Suite 201E, Philadelphia, PA 19104-3512; tel. (215) 898-4975; fax (215) 573-7874; e-mail apaclassics@sas.upenn.edu; internet www.apaclassics.org; f. 1869; study of classical languages, literatures and history; 3,200 mems; Exec. Dir ADAM D. BLISTEIN; publs *Amphora* (2 a year), *Transactions* (2 a year).

British Council: c/o British Embassy, 3100 Massachusetts Ave NW, Washington, DC 20008-3600; tel. (202) 588-6500; fax (202) 588-7918; e-mail info@us.britishcouncil.org; internet www.britishcouncil.org/usa; offers courses and examinations in English language and British culture, and promotes cultural exchange with the UK; Educational Adviser ANDY MCKAY.

Goethe-Institut: 72 Spring St, 11th Fl., New York, NY 10012; tel. (212) 439-8700; fax (212) 439-8705; e-mail info@newyork.goethe.org; internet www.goethe.de/newyork; offers courses and examinations in German language and culture, and promotes cultural exchange with Germany; attached centres in Boston, MA, Chicago, IL, Los Angeles, CA, San Francisco, CA, and Washington, DC; library of 12,000 vols, 150 periodicals; Dir and Regional Dir for USA, Canada and Mexico GABRIELE BECKER.

Instituto Cervantes: 211 East 49th St, New York, NY 10017; tel. (212) 308-7720; fax (212) 308-7721; e-mail cenny@cervantes.es; internet nyork.cervantes.es; offers courses and examinations in Spanish language and culture, and promotes cultural exchange with Spain and Spanish-speaking Latin and Central America; attached centres in Albuquerque (NM) and Chicago (IL); library of 40,000 vols; Exec. Dir ANTONIO MUÑOZ MOLINA.

Linguistic Society of America: 1325 18th St NW, Suite 211, Washington, DC 20035-6502; tel. (202) 835-1714; fax (202) 835-1717; e-mail lsa@lsadc.org; internet www.lsadc.org; f. 1924; linguistic institute; annual meeting; web-based resources; cttees; fellowships; awards; 5,000 individual and institutional mems; Pres. SANDRA CHUNG; Sec. and Treas. PAUL CHAPIN; Exec. Dir ALYSON W. REED; publs *Language* (4 a year), *LSA Bulletin* (4 a year).

Modern Language Association of America: 26 Broadway, New York, NY 10004-1789; tel. (646) 576-5000; fax (646) 458-0030; e-mail info@mla.org; internet www.mla.org; f. 1883; 30,000 mems; Exec. Dir Prof. ROSEMARY G. FEAL; publs *MLA International Bibliography of Books and Articles on the Modern Languages and Literatures* (1 a year), *PMLA* (6 a year).

National Communication Association: 1765 N St NW, Washington, DC 20036; tel. (202) 464-4622; fax (202) 464-4600; internet www.natcom.org; f. 1914; 7,000 mems; Exec. Dir JAMES L. GAUDINO; publs *Communication Education* (4 a year), *Communication Monographs* (4 a year), *Critical Studies in Mass Communication* (4 a year), *Directory* (1 a year), *International and Intercultural Communication Annual*, *Journal of Applied Communication Research* (4 a year), *Quarterly Journal of Speech, Text and Performance Quarterly*, *The Communication Teacher* (4 a year).

Poetry Society of America: 15 Gramercy Park, New York, NY 10003; tel. (212) 254-9628; fax (212) 673-2352; internet www.poetrysociety.org; f. 1910; 2,000 mems; service organization for poets and readers of poetry; sponsors readings, lectures, workshops and annual prize-giving; library of 8,000 vols of American poetry; Pres. WILLIAM LOUIS-DREYFUS; Exec. Dir ALICE QUINN; publ. *Journal* (2 a year).

MEDICINE

Aerospace Medical Association: 320 S Henry St, Alexandria, VA 22314-3579; tel. (703) 739-2240; fax (703) 739-9652; internet www.asma.org; f. 1929; advancement of aerospace medicine, life sciences, bio-astronautics and environmental medicine; annual awards; 3,500 mems; Pres. Dr MARIAN SIDES; Exec. Dir JEFFREY C. SVENTEK; publ. *Aviation, Space and Environmental Medicine* (12 a year).

American Academy of Allergy, Asthma and Immunology: 555 East Wells St, Suite 1100, Milwaukee, WI 53202-3823; tel. (414) 272-6071; e-mail info@aaaai.org; internet www.aaaai.org; f. 1943; for the advancement of the knowledge and practice of allergy, asthma and immunology for optimal patient care; 6,500 mems; Pres. Dr F. ESTELLE R. SIMONS; publ. *The Journal of Allergy and Clinical Immunology*.

American Academy of Family Physicians: 11400 Tomahawk Creek, Leawood, KS 66211; tel. (913) 906-6000; fax (913) 906-6080; internet www.aafp.org; f. 1947; promotes and maintains high standards in the general/family practice of medicine; 94,000 mems; Pres. Dr MARY E. FRANK; Exec. Vice-Pres. Dr DOUGLAS E. ENLEY; publs *American Family Physician* (24 a year), *Annals of Family Medicine* (6 a year), *Caring for Hispanic Patients* (1 a year), *Family Practice Management* (10 a year).

American Academy of Ophthalmology: 655 Beach St, POB 7424, San Francisco, CA 94120-7424; tel. (415) 561-8500; fax (415) 561-8533; internet www.aao.org; f. 1896; 20,777 mems; Pres. SUSAN H. DAY; Exec. Vice-Pres. H. DUNBAR HOSKINS Jr; publs *Argus* (12 a year), *Ophthalmology*.

American Academy of Otolaryngology—Head and Neck Surgery: 1650 Diagonal Rd, Alexandria, VA 22314-2857; tel. (703) 836-4444; fax (703) 688-5100; e-mail info@entnet.org; internet www.entnet.org; f. 1896; offers more than 500 continuing medical educational courses at annual meetings and through correspondence courses throughout the USA and abroad; 12,000 US and non-US fellows, scientific and associate mems; Exec. Vice-Pres. and CEO Dr DAVID R. NIELSEN; publs *The Bulletin* (news magazine, 12 a year), *Otolaryngology—Head and Neck Surgery* (peer-reviewed scientific journal, 12 a year).

American Academy of Pediatrics: 141 Northwest Point Blvd, Elk Grove Village, IL 60007-1098; tel. (847) 434-4000; fax (847) 434-8000; e-mail kidsdocs@aap.org; internet www.aap.org; f. 1930; 60,000 mems; Pres. Dr CAROL D. BERKOWITZ; Exec. Dir Dr JERROL R. ALDEN; publs *AAP Grand Rounds* (12 a year and online), *Neoreviews* (12 a year and online), *Pediatrics* (12 a year and online), *Pediatrics in Review* (12 a year and online).

American Academy of Periodontology: 737 N Michigan Ave, Chicago, IL 60611-2690; tel. (312) 787-5518; fax (312) 787-3670; internet www.perio.org; f. 1914; 7,200 mems; Exec. Dir GERALD M. BOWERS; publ. *Journal of Periodontology* (12 a year).

American Association of Anatomists: 9650 Rockville Pike, Bethesda, MA 20814-3998; tel. (301) 634-7910; fax (301) 634-7965; e-mail exec@anatomy.org; internet www.anatomy.org; f. 1888; 2,753 mems; Pres. Dr ROBERT S. MCCUSKEY; Exec. Dir ANDREA PENDLETON; publs *Anatomical Record*, *Developmental Dynamics*, *New Anatomist*.

American Association of Immunologists: 9650 Rockville Pike, Bethesda, MD 20814; tel. (301) 634-7178; fax (301) 634-7887; e-mail infoaai@aai.org; internet www.aai.org; f. 1913; independent body for the exchange of information and advancement of knowledge in immunology and related fields; 7,000 mems; Chair. Dr BETTY DIAMOND; Exec. Dir Dr M. MICHELE HOGAN; publ. *Journal of Immunology*.

American Cancer Society, Inc.: 19 W 56th St, New York, NY 10019; internet www.cancer.org; f. 1913; voluntary health agency; library of 16,000 vols (located at 4 W 35th St, New York, NY 10001); Pres. STEPHEN F. SENER; publs *Ca-A* (cancer journal for clinicians, 6 a year), *Cancer* (24 a year), *Cancer News* (2 a year), *World Smoking & Health* (3 a year).

American College of Obstetricians and Gynecologists: 409 12th St, SW, POB 96920, Washington, DC 20090-6920; tel. (202) 638-5577; internet www.acog.org; f. 1951; 38,000 mems; Exec. Dir Dr RALPH HALE; publ. *Obstetrics and Gynecology* (12 a year).

American College of Physicians: Independence Mall West, Sixth St at Race, Philadelphia, PA 19106; internet www.acponline.org; f. 1915; 116,000 mems; Pres. CHARLES K. FRANCIS; publ. *Annals of Internal Medicine* (26 a year).

American College of Rheumatism: 1800 Century Place, Suite 250, Atlanta, GA 30345-4300; tel. (404) 633-3777; fax (404) 633-1870; internet www.rheumatology.org; 4,000 mems; Exec. Sec. ELIZABETH TINDALL.

American College of Surgeons: 633 N St Clair St, Chicago, IL 60611-3211; tel. (312) 202-5000; fax (312) 202-5001; e-mail postmaster@facs.org; internet www.facs.org; f. 1913; 63,421 fellows; Dir THOMAS R. RUSSELL; Sec. Dr KATHRYN D. ANDERSON; publs *Bulletin* (12 a year), *Journal of the American College of Surgeons* (12 a year).

American Dental Association: 211 E Chicago Ave, Chicago, IL 60611; tel. (312) 440-2547; fax (312) 440-3526; e-mail adaf@ada.org; internet www.ada.org; f. 1859; 146,000 mems; library of 50,000 vols; Exec. Dir Dr JAMES BRAMSON; publs *Journal* (12 a year), *ADA News* (26 a year), *American Dental Directory* (1 a year).

American Dietetic Association: 120 South Riverside Plaza, Chicago, IL 60606-6995; tel. (312) 899-0040; fax (312) 899-0008; e-mail membrshp@eatright.org; internet www.eatright.org; f. 1917 to improve the nutrition of human beings; to advance the science of dietetics; to promote education in these and allied fields; 70,000 mems; library of 1,000 vols; publ. *Journal* (12 a year).

American Geriatrics Society, Inc.: Suite 801, Empire State Building, 350 Fifth Ave, New York, NY 10118; tel. (212) 308-1414; fax (212) 832-8646; e-mail info@americangeriatrics.org; internet www.americangeriatrics.org; f. 1942; 6,500 mems; holds annual meeting, runs postgraduate courses; Pres. Dr MEGHAN GERETY; Exec. Vice-Pres. LINDA HIDDEMEN BARONDESS; publs *Annals of Long-term Care*, *Clinical Geriatrics*, *Geriatrics Review Syllabus*, *Journal of the American Geriatrics Society* (12 a year).

American Gynecological and Obstetrical Society: University of Virginia Health System, POB 800566, Charlottesville, VA 22908; f. 1993; 200 fellows, 92 ilfe fellows, 43 hon. fellows; Sec. Dr PAUL B. UNDERWOOD.

American Heart Association: 7272 Greenville Ave, Dallas, TX 75231; tel. (214) 373-6300; fax (214) 706-1341; internet www.americanheart.org; f. 1924; 3,629,000 mems; dedicated to the reduction of disability and death from cardiovascular diseases and stroke; supports cardiovascular research and brings its benefits to the public through professional education and community service programmes, to coordinate efforts of all medical and lay groups in combating cardiovascular diseases, and to inform the public of progress in the cardiovascular field; CEO M. CASS WHEELER; publs *Arteriosclerosis*, *Circulation*, *Circulation Research*, *Currents in Emergency Cardiac Care* (4 a year), *Hypertension*, *Stroke*, *Thrombosis and Vascular Biology*.

American Hospital Association: One N Franklin, Chicago, IL 60606; tel. (312) 422-3000; internet www.aha.org; f. 1898 to advance the health of individuals and communities; leads, represents and serves hospitals, health systems and other related organizations that are accountable to the community and committed to health improvement; 37,000 personal mems, 5,000 institutional mems; library of 63,000 vols; Pres. and Chief Operating Officer RICHARD UMBDENSTOCK; Exec. Vice-Pres NEIL J. JESUELE, RICHARD J. POLLACK; Senior Vice-Pres. and Sec. MICHAEL P. GUERIN; publs *AHA News* (52 a year), *Hospitals and Health Networks* (12 a year), *Trustee* (12 a year).

American Institute of the History of Pharmacy: Pharmacy Bldg, 777 Highland Ave, Madison, WI 53705-2222; tel. (608) 262-5378; e-mail aihp@aihp.org; internet www.pharmacy.wisc.edu/aihp; f. 1941; documentation and preservation of pharmaceutical heritage; 1,000 mems; Exec. Dir Dr GREGORY J. HIGBY; publ. *Pharmacy in History* (4 a year).

American Laryngological, Rhinological and Otological Society, Inc. (Triological Society): 555 N 30th St, Omaha, NE 68131; tel. (402) 346-5500; fax (402) 346-5300; e-mail info@triological.org; internet www.triological.org; f. 1895; 1,200 mems; Pres. Dr PATRICK E. BROOKHOUSER; Exec. Sec. Dr GERALD B. HEALY; publ. *The Laryngoscope*.

American Lung Association (ALA): 61 Broadway, New York, NY 10006; tel. (212) 315-8700; fax (212) 265-5642; internet www.lungusa.org; f. 1904; 115 affiliated associations nationally; the Medical Section of the ALA, the American Thoracic Society, has a membership of over 11,000, including some 2,000 pulmonary physicians in foreign countries; Pres. and Chief Exec. JOHN L. KIRKWOOD; Sec. JAMES M. ANDERSON; publs *American Journal of Respiratory and Critical Care Medicine*, *American Journal of Respiratory Cell and Molecular Biology* (12 a year).

American Medical Association: 515 N State St, Chicago, IL 60610-4377; tel. (312) 464-5000; internet www.ama-assn.org; f. 1847; 296,000 mems; Exec. Vice-Pres. Dr MICHAEL MAVES; publs *American Medical Directory* (irregular), *American Medical News* (52 a year), *Jama* (52 a year).

American Medical Technologists: 710 Higgins Rd, Park Ridge, IL 60068; tel. (847) 823-5169; fax (847) 823-0458; e-mail amtmail@aol.com; internet www.amt1.com; f. 1939; 29,000 mems; Pres. DAVE MCCULLOUGH; publs *AMT Events* (4 a year), *Journal of Continuing Education Topics* (3 a year).

American Neurological Association: Executive Office, 5841 Cedar Lake Rd, Suite 204, Minneapolis, MN 55416; tel. (952) 545-6284; fax (952) 545-6073; e-mail ana@llmsi.com; internet www.aneuroa.org; f. 1875; 1,000 mems; Pres. TIMOTHY A. PEDLEY; Sec. KATHLEEN B. DIGRE; publ. *Annals of Neurology*.

American Occupational Therapy Association, Inc.: 4720 Montgomery Lane, Bethesda, MD 20814; tel. (301) 652-6611; fax (301) 652-7711; e-mail ajotsis@aota.org; internet www.aota.org; f. 1917; 35,000 mems; library of 4,000 vols; Pres. CAROLYN BAUM; Exec. Dir FREDERICK P. SOMERS; publs *American Journal of Occupational Therapy* (6 a year), *OT Practice* (26 a week), *OT Week*.

American Optometric Association, Inc.: 243 N Lindbergh Blvd, St Louis, MO 63141; tel. (314) 991-4100; fax (314) 991-4101; internet www.aoanet.org; f. 1898 to promote the art and science of optometry, to improve vision care and health of the public; 31,000 mems; Pres. Dr WESLEY E. PITTMAN; publs *AOA News* (26 a year), *Optometry* (12 a year).

American Pediatric Society: 3400 Research Forest Drive, Suite B7, The Woodlands, TX 77381; tel. (281) 296-0052; fax (281) 296-0082; e-mail info@aps-spr.org; internet www.aps-spr.org; f. 1888; 855 active mems; Pres. ELIZABETH R. MCANARNEY; Exec. Dir DEBBIE ANAGNOSTELIS; publ. *Paediatric Research* (12 a year).

American Physical Therapy Association: 1111 N Fairfax St, Alexandria, VA 22314; tel. (703) 684-2782; fax (703) 684-7343; internet www.apta.org; f. 1921, inc. 1930; develops the art and science of physical therapy; represents and promotes the profession; 76,000 mems; library of 3,000 colln focus: physical rehabilitation, available to researchers by appointment only; CEO JOHN BARNES; Dir for Information Resource GINI BLODGETT BIRCHETT; publs *Physical Therapy* (12 a year), *PT in Motion Magazine* (11 a year).

American Physiological Society: 9650 Rockville Pike, Bethesda, MD 20814-3991; tel. (301) 634-7164; fax (301) 634-7241; e-mail info@the-aps.org; internet www.the-aps.org; f. 1887; 10,600 mems; Pres. Dr HANNAH V. CAREY; Exec. Dir MARTIN FRANK; publs *Advances in Physiology Education* (4 a year and online), *American Journal of Physiology (Consolidated)* (2 a year), *Cell Physiology* (online), *Endocrinology and Metabolism* (online), *Gastrointestinal and Liver Physiology* (online), *Heart and Circulatory Physiology* (online), *Journal of Applied Physiology* (12 a year and online), *Journal of Neurophysiology* (12 a year and online), *Lung Cellular and Molecular Physiology* (online), *Physiological Genomics* (online), *Physiological Reviews* (4 a year), *The Physiologist* (6 a year and online), *Physiology* (6 a year and online), *Regulatory, Integrative and Comparative Physiology* (online), *Renal Physiology* (online).

American Psychiatric Association: 1000 Wilson Blvd, Suite 1825, Arlington, VA 22209-3901; tel. (703) 907-7300; e-mail apa@psych.org; internet www.psych.org; f. 1844; 35,000 mems; library of 10,000 vols; Medical Dir MELVIN SABSHIN; publs *American Journal of Psychiatry* (12 a year), *Psychiatric News* (26 a year), *Psychiatric Services* (12 a year).

American Public Health Association: 800 I St NW, Washington, DC 20001-3710; tel. (202) 777-2742; fax (202) 777-2534; e-mail comments@apha.org; internet www.apha.org; f. 1872; interests include environment, personal health services, social factors, manpower and training in public health, global and international health; 32,000 mems; Exec. Dir Dr GEORGEN BENJAMIN; publs *American Journal of Public Health* (12 a year), *The Nation's Health* (12 a year).

American Roentgen Ray Society: 44211 Slatestone Court, Leesburg, VA 20176; tel. (703) 729-3353; fax (703) 729-4839; e-mail info@arrs.org; internet www.arrs.org; f. 1900; int. org, of physicians and scientists working in radiology and related fields; 13,000 mems; Exec. Dir SUSAN BROWN CAPPITELLI; publ. *American Journal of Roentgenology* (12 a year).

American Society for Clinical Laboratory Science: 6701 Democracy Blvd, Suite 300, Bethesda, MD 20817; tel. (301) 657-2768; fax (301) 657-2909; e-mail ascls@ascls.org; internet www.ascls.org; f. 1933; local, state and regional societies; activities include education, education and research funding, professional affairs and membership services; formerly ASMT; 13,000 mems; Pres. BARBARA BROWN; Sec. SCOTT AIKEY; publs *ASCLS Today* (12 a year), *Clinical Laboratory Science* (4 a year).

American Society for Clinical Pathology: 33 West Monroe St, Suite 1600, Chicago, IL 60603; tel. (312) 541-4999; fax (312) 541-4998; e-mail info@ascp.org; internet www.ascp.org; f. 1922; a non-profit medical society for the promotion of pathology and laboratory medicine; 140,000 mems; library of 25,500 vols; Pres. Dr DAVID KEREN; Sec. Dr FRED RODRIGUEZ, Jr; publs *American Journal of Clinical Pathology* (12 a year), *Laboratory Medicine* (12 a year), *Pathology Patterns Reviews* (2 a year).

American Society for Investigative Pathology, Inc.: 9650 Rockville Pike, Bethesda, MD 20814-3993; tel. (301) 634-7130; fax (301) 634-7990; e-mail asip@asip.org; internet www.asip.org; f. 1976; 2,500 mems; Pres. Dr STANLEY COHEN; Sec.-Treas. WILLIAM B. COLEMAN; Exec. Officer Dr MARK E. SOBEL; Dir of Finance and Operations JAMES S. DOUGLAS; publs *American Journal of Pathology* (12 a year), *The Journal of Molecular Diagnostics* (5 a year).

American Society for Microbiology: 1752 N St NW, Washington, DC 20036; tel. (202) 737-3600; fax (202) 942-9368; internet www.asm.org; f. 1899, present name 1961; 48,000 mems; Exec. Dir MICHAEL I. GOLDBERG; publs *Abstracts of the Annual Meeting* (1 a year), *Antimicrobial Agents and Chemotherapy* (12 a year), *Applied and Environmental Microbiology* (12 a year), *ASM News* (12 a year), *Clinical and Diagnostic Laboratory Immunology* (12 a year), *Clinical Microbiology Reviews* (4 a year), *Eukaryotic Cell* (12 a year), *Infection and Immunity* (12 a year), *Journal of Bacteriology* (24 a year), *Journal of Clinical Microbiology* (12 a year), *Journal of Virology* (24 a year), *Microbiology and Molecular Biology Reviews* (4 a year), *Molecular and Cellular Biology* (12 a year).

American Society for Nutritional Sciences: 9650 Rockville Pike, Bethesda, MD 20814; tel. (301) 634-7050; fax (301) 571-1892; f. 1928; develops and extends knowledge of nutrition and facilitates personal contact between investigators in nutrition and related fields of interest; 3,100 mems; Pres. Dr JOANNE LUPTON; Sec. Dr TERESA DAVIS; publs *Nutrition Notes* (4 a year), *The American Journal of Clinical Nutrition* (12 a year), *The Journal of Nutrition* (12 a year).

American Society for Pharmacology and Experimental Therapeutics, Inc.: 9650 Rockville Pike, Bethesda, MD 20814-3995; tel. (301) 634-7060; fax (301) 634-7061; e-mail info@aspet.org; internet www.aspet.org; f. 1908; holds an annual meeting on experimental biology; 4,900 mems; Exec. Officer CHRISTINE K. CARRICO; publs *Drug Metabolism and Disposition* (12 a year), *Journal of Pharmacology and Experimental Therapeutics* (12 a year), *Molecular Interventions* (6 a year), *Molecular Pharmacology* (12 a year), *Pharmacological Reviews* (4 a year), *The Pharmacologist* (4 a year).

American Society of Clinical Hypnosis: 140 N Bloomingdale Rd, Bloomingdale, IL 60108-1017; tel. (630) 980-4740; fax (630) 351-8490; internet www.asch.net; f. 1957; an ind. org. of professional people in medicine, dentistry, and psychology who share scientific and clinical interests in hypnosis; provides educational programmes to further understanding and acceptance of hypnosis as an important tool of ethical clinical medicine and scientific research; 2,400 mems; Pres. ELGAN BAKER; Exec. Dir for Governance and Policy MICHAEL WHITE; Sec. THOMAS J. BARR; publ. *The American Journal of Clinical Hypnosis* (4 a year).

American Society of Tropical Medicine and Hygiene: 60 Revere Drive, Suite 500, Northbrook, IL 60062; tel. (847) 480-9592; fax (847) 480-9282; e-mail astmh@astmh.org; internet www.astmh.org; f. 1951; 3,000 mems; Exec. Dir BRIAN MADDOX; publs *American Journal of Tropical Medicine and Hygiene* (12 a year), *Tropical Medicine and Hygiene News* (6 a year).

American Speech-Language-Hearing Association: 2200 Research Blvd, Rockville, MD 20850; tel. (301) 296-5700; fax (301) 296-8580; e-mail actioncenter@asha.org; internet www.asha.org; f. 1925; 118,000 mems; Exec. Dir ARLENE PIETRANTON; publs *American Journal of Audiology* (2 a year), *American Journal of Speech-Language Pathology* (4 a year), *ASHA* (12 a year), *Journal of Speech, Language and Hearing Research* (6 a year), *Language Speech and Hearing Services in Schools* (4 a year).

American Surgical Association: 900 Cummings Center, Suite 221-U, Beverly, MA 01915; tel. (978) 927-8330; fax (978) 524-8890; e-mail asa@prri.com; internet www.americansurgical.info; f. 1880; 1,000 mems; Pres. Dr KIRBY BLAND; Sec. Dr E. CHRISTOPHER ELLISON; publs *Annals of Surgery* (12 a year), *Transactions* (1 a year).

American Urological Association, Inc.: 1000 Corporate Blvd, Linthicum, MD 21090; tel. (410) 689-3700; fax (410) 689-3800; e-mail aua@auanet.org; internet www.auanet.org; f. 1902; 14,500 mems; Pres. Dr BRENDAN M. FOX; Sec. Dr CARL A. OLSSON; publs *AUA News* (6 a year), *The Journal of Urology* (12 a year).

Armed Forces Institute of Pathology: 6825 16th St, NW, Washington, DC 20306-6000; tel. (202) 782-2100; internet www.afip.org; 1862 as Army Medical Museum, present name 1949; it is the central laboratory of pathology for the Department of Defense serving both the military and civilian sectors in education, consultation and research in the medical, dental and veterinary sciences; research into leprosy, malaria, HIV/AIDS, sickle cell disease, radiation injury, trauma, drug toxicity and aerospace pathology; organized into: Center for Advanced Pathology, Center for Clinical Laboratory Medicine, Center for Administrative Services, Center for Education, Repository and Research Services, Office of the Armed Forces Medical Examiner and National Museum of Health and Medicine; Dir Dr FLORABEL MULLICK.

Association of American Medical Colleges: 2450 N St, NW, Washington, DC 20037-1126; tel. (202) 828-0400; fax (202) 828-1125; internet www.aamc.org; f. 1876; 126 US and 16 Canadian medical schools, more than 400 teaching hospitals and 87 academic and professional societies; Chair. Dr DEBORAH E. POWELL; publs *AAMC Curriculum Directory* (1 a year), *AAMC Directory of Medical Education* (1 a year), *AAMC Reporter* (12 a year), *Academic Medicine* (12 a year), *Medical School Admission Requirements* (1 a year).

Association of American Physicians: Harvard University, Dept of Medicine, Microbiology and Molecular Genetics, Channing Lab., 181 Longwood Ave, Boston, MA 02155; tel. (617) 277-0551; fax (617) 731-1541; internet www.aap-online.org; f. 1886; 1,200 mems; Pres. RALPH SNYDERMAN; publ. *Transactions* (1 a year).

Center for the Study of Aging and Human Development: Box 3003, Duke University Medical Center, Durham, NC 27710; tel. (919) 660-7500; fax (919) 684-8569; internet www.geri.duke.edu; f. 1955; supports and trains researchers and clinicians with emphasis on post-doctoral training in all aspects of normal ageing (gerontology) as well as diseases and disorders of human ageing (geriatrics); lectures, seminars and publications; Geriatric Evaluation and Treatment Clinic for direct service and in-service professional training; geriatric training for health professionals; co-sponsors Osher Lifelong Learning Institute; Dir HARVEY JAY COHEN.

College of Physicians of Philadelphia: 19 S 22nd St, Philadelphia, PA 19103; tel. (215) 563-3737; e-mail histref@collphyphil.org; internet www.collphyphil.org; f. 1787 to increase understanding between health professions and the general public; includes the College Library, the Mutter Museum (pathology and anatomy) and the Francis C. Wood Institute for the History of Medicine; 1,500 fellows; library of 340,000 vols; CEO MARK HOCHBERG; College Librarian and Dir, Wood Institute EDWARD T. MORMAN.

Commonwealth Fund: 1 E 75th St, New York, NY 10021; tel. (212) 606-3800; fax (212) 606-3500; e-mail cmwf@cmwf.org; internet www.cmwf.org; f. 1918 to enhance the common good through its efforts to help Americans live healthy and productive lives and to assist specific groups with serious and neglected problems; current fund initiatives include helping young people realize their potential through mentoring and educational enhancement programmes, improving health care services, promoting healthier life styles and bettering the health care of minorities; awards Harkness Fellowships, which enable future leaders of the UK, Australia and New Zealand to study social issues in the USA; Chair. of Board SAMUEL O. THIER; Pres. KAREN DAVIS.

Gerontological Society of America: 1220 L St NW, Suite 901, Washington, DC 20005; tel. (202) 842-1275; fax (202) 842-1150; e-mail geron@geron.org; internet www.geron.org; f. 1945; multidisciplinary sciences org., incl. an educational unit, AGHE (Association for Gerontology in Higher Education) and a policy institute, NAAS (National Academy on an Aging Society); 5,000 mems; Exec. Dir CAROL A. SCHUTZ; Pres. TERRY T. FULMER; publs *AGHExchange* (4 a year), *Journals of Gerontology,* (Series A: Biological Sciences and Medical Sciences; Series B: Psychological Sciences and Social Sciences), *Public Policy and Aging Report* (4 a year), *The Gerontologist*.

Industrial Health Foundation, Inc.: 34 Penn Circle West, Pittsburgh, PA 15206; f. 1935; a non-profit org. for the advancement of healthy working conditions in industry; 120 mem. cos and asscns; library of 2,000 vols; publs *Industrial Hygiene Digest* (12 a year), special technical bulletins.

John A. Hartford Foundation, Inc.: 55 East 59th St, New York, NY 10022; tel. (212) 832-7788; fax (212) 593-4913; e-mail mail@jhartfound.org; internet www.jhartfound.org; f. 1929 by John A. Hartford and George L. Hartford; ageing and health programme; Chair. of the Board NORMAN H. VOLK; Exec. Dir CORINNE H. RIEDER.

Medical Society of the State of New York: POB 9007, Westbury, New York, NY 11590; tel. (516) 488-6100; fax (516) 488-1267; e-mail mssny@mssny.org; internet www.mssny.org; f. 1807; 30,000 mems; library of 45,000 vols; Pres. Dr WILLIAM B. ROSENBLATT; Exec. Vice-Pres. WILLIAM R. ABRAMS; publs *Medical Directory of New York State* (every 2 years), *News of New York* (26 a year).

Mental Health America: 6th Fl., 2000 N Beauregard St, Alexandria, VA 22311; tel. (703) 684-7722; fax (703) 684-5968; internet www.mentalhealthamerica.net; f. 1909; 340 affiliates nationally; Pres. and CEO DAVID L. SHERN.

National Association for Biomedical Research: 818 Connecticut Ave, Suite 900, Washington, DC 2006; tel. (202) 857-0540; fax (202) 659-1902; e-mail info@nabr.org; internet www.nabr.org; f. 1979; advocates sound public policy that recognizes the vital role of humane animal use in biomedical research, higher education and product safety testing; stands for scientific community on legislative, regulatory and legal matters affecting laboratory animal research; 300 institutional mems; Pres. FRANKIE L. TRULL; Vice-Pres. MATTHEW R. BAILEY; publs *NABR Alert* (26 a year), *NABR Update* (26 a year), *State Laws*.

New York Academy of Medicine: 1216 Fifth Ave, New York, NY 10029; tel. (212) 822-7200; fax (212) 876-6620; internet www.nyam.org; f. 1847; 3,000 mems; library: see Libraries and Archives; Pres. Dr JEREMIAH A. BARONDESS.

Radiological Society of North America, Inc.: 820 Jorie Blvd, Oak Brook, IL 60523; tel. (630) 571-2670; fax (630) 571-7837; internet www.rsna.org; f. 1915; continuing medical education in radiology; 46,000 mems; Chair. Dr SARAH S. DONALDSON; Pres. Dr BURTON P. DRAYER; publs *Index to Imaging Literature* (online index of 38 journals), *RadioGraphics* (6 a year), *Radiology* (12 a year), *Radiology Legacy Collection*, *RSNA News* (12 a year).

Society of Medical Jurisprudence: POB 20678, New York, NY 10021-0073; f. 1883; investigation, study and advancement of the science of medical jurisprudence, and the attainment of a higher standard of medical testimony; members must be physicians, lawyers, chemists, forensic odontologists or health professionals of good standing in their respective professions, or teachers in approved law or medical schools; 250 mems; publ. *Proceedings* (9 a year).

NATURAL SCIENCES

General

Academy of Natural Sciences of Philadelphia: 1900 Benjamin Franklin Parkway, Philadelphia, PA 19103-1195; tel. (215) 299-1000; fax (215) 299-1028; internet www.acnatsci.org; f. 1812; natural history museum; research in systematics and evolutionary biology, ecology, limnology and geology, and environmental monitoring; 24m. specimen collections of plants, animals and fossils of world-wide scope; teaching at all levels; 200,000 mems; library: see Libraries and Archives; Pres. IAN DAVISON (acting); publs *Annual*, *Notulae Naturae*, *Occasional*, *Proceedings*.

American Association for the Advancement of Science: 1200 New York Ave, NW, Washington, DC 20005; tel. (202) 326-6400; fax (202) 789-0455; e-mail media@aaas.org; internet www.aaas.org; f. 1848; aims to advance science and serve soc. through initiatives in science policy; int. programmes; science education; 128,000 mems, 262 affiliates serving 10m. mems; Chair. Dr ALICE S. HUANG; Pres. Dr NINA V. FEDOROFF; Chief Exec. Dr ALAN I. LESHNER; publ. *Science* (52 a year).

American Society of Limnology and Oceanography: 5400 Bosque Blvd, Suite 680, Waco, TX 76710-4446; tel. (254) 399-9635; fax (254) 776-3767; internet aslo.org; f. 1936; 3,800 mems; Pres. JONATHAN COLE; publs *Limnology and Oceanography* (6 a year), *Limnology and Oceanography Bulletin* (4 a year).

Buffalo Society of Natural Sciences: 1020 Humboldt Parkway, Buffalo, NY 14211; tel. (716) 896-5200; fax (716) 897-6723; internet www.sciencebuff.org; f. 1861; administers the Buffalo Museum of Science and Tifft Nature Preserve; samples of natural life in the USA; cultures from other eras to the present; Whem Ankh: The Cycle of Life in Ancient Egypt; Dinosaurs and Company; research in anthropology, botany, entomology, geology, mycology, ornithology, palaeontology, vertebrate zoology, with collections in these fields; 11,000 mems; library of 40,000 vols; publ. *Bulletin* (irregular).

California Academy of Sciences: 55 Music Concourse Dr., Golden Gate Park, San Francisco, CA 94118; tel. (415) 379-8000; e-mail info@calacademy.org; internet www.calacademy.org; f. 1853; promotes advancement of natural sciences through public education and research; incorporated under the laws of the State of California 1871; 20,000 mems incl. 300 fellows; maintains a public museum of natural history; the Steinhart Aquarium (Dir ROBERT JENKINS); the Morrison Planetarium (Chair. STEVEN B. CRAIG), a scientific library of 100,000 vols (Librarian THOMAS MORITZ), and research departments with large scientific collections; Departments: anthropology (Curator NINA JABLONSKI), aquatic biology (Curator JOHN E. MCCOSKER), botany (Curator TOM DANIEL), entomology (Curator CHARLES GRISWOLD), exhibits (Chair. LINDA KULIK), herpetology (Curator ROBERT DREWES), ichthyology (Curator WILLIAM ESCHMEYER), invertebrate zoology and geology (Curator GARY WILLIAMS), ornithology and mammalogy (Curator LUIS BAPTISTA); Pres. Dr WILLIAM CLEMENS; Exec. Dir Dr EVELYN E. HANDLER; publs *California Wild*, *Memoirs*, *Occasional Papers*, *Pacific Discovery* (4 a year), *Proceedings*.

Chicago Academy of Sciences: 2430 N Cannon Drive, Chicago, IL 60614; tel. (773) 755-5100; internet www.chias.org; f. 1857; 2,200 mems; research colln of plants, animals, fossils and minerals; also maintains Peggy Notebaert Nature Museum, with interactive displays treating the relationship between people and nature; library: technical scientific 3,000 vols, 2,000 periodicals; Chair. PATRICK F. DALY; publs *Bulletin*, *Natural History Miscellanea*.

Cranbrook Institute of Science: 1221 N. Woodward Ave, POB 801, Bloomfield Hills, MI 48303-0801; tel. (810) 645-3259; fax (810) 645-3050; f. 1930; a non-profit-making organization with exhibits and educational programmes in astronomy, mineralogy, geology, botany, zoology, ecology, anthropology, mathematics and physics; 4,000 mems; library of 18,000 vols; Dir DANIEL E. APPLEMAN.

Franklin Institute: 222 North 20th St, Philadelphia, PA 19103; tel. (215) 448-1200; internet sln.fi.edu; f. 1824; a non-profit science centre dedicated to public science education and to advancing knowledge in the physical sciences; its committee on science and the arts awards several medals, including the Franklin Medal, for contributions to science and technology; also administers the Bower Awards for science and business; the Institute incorporates the Franklin Institute Science Museum (*q.v.*), the Fels Planetarium, The Tuttleman Omniverse Theater and the Musser Choices Forum, and houses the Benjamin Franklin National Memorial; there is an observatory open to the public; Pres. and CEO Dr DENNIS M. WINT; publ. *Journal*.

History of Science Society: 440 Geddes Hall, Univ.of Notre Dame, Notre Dame, IN 46556; tel. (574) 631-1194; fax (574) 631-1533; e-mail info@hssonline.org; internet www.hssonline.org; f. 1924; 3,500 mems; Pres. PAUL FARBER; Exec. Dir ROBERT J. MALONE; publs *Isis* (4 a year), *Osiris* (1 a year).

Maryland Science Center: 601 Light St, Baltimore, MD 21230; tel. (410) 685-2370; fax (410) 545-5974; internet www.mdsci.org; f. 1797 as Maryland Academy of Sciences, educational and scientific institution for the diffusion and explanation of scientific information to the public; new name 1976; talks, exhibits, planetarium; Pres. and CEO VAN R. REINER; publ. *Maryland Science Center News* (4 a year).

Mellon Institute: see Carnegie Mellon University under Universities and Colleges—Pennsylvania.

National Science Teachers Association: 1840 Wilson Blvd, Arlington, VA 22201-3000; tel. (703) 243-7100; internet www.nsta.org; f. 1895, reorganized 1944; advances science teaching and science education at elementary, secondary and college levels; 53,000 mems; Pres. ANNE TWEED; Exec. Dir GERALD WHEELER; publs *Journal of College Science Teaching*, *Science and Children*, *Science Scope*, *The Science Teacher*.

Ohio Academy of Science: 1500 West Third Ave, Suite 223, Columbus, OH 43212-2817; tel. (614) 488-2228; fax (614) 488-7629; e-mail oas@iwaynet.net; internet www.ohiosci.org; f. 1891; 2,000 mems; CEO LYNN E. ELFNER; publs *The Ohio Academy of Science News* (irregular), *The Ohio Journal of Science* (5 a year).

Sigma Xi, the Scientific Research Society: 3106 E NC Highway 54, POB 13975, Research Triangle Park, NC 27709; tel. (919) 549-4691; fax (919) 549-0090; e-mail memberinfo@sigmaxi.org; internet www.sigmaxi.org; f. 1886; encourages scientific research; publishes new scientific discoveries; 65,000 mems; Pres. FRANCISCO J. AYALA; Exec. Dir Dr JEROME F. BAKER; publ. *American Scientist* (6 a year).

Southern California Academy of Sciences: c/o Natural History Museum of Los Angeles County, 900 Exposition Blvd, Los Angeles, CA 90007; tel. (909) 607-2836; fax (909) 621-8588; internet scas.jsd.claremont.edu; f. 1891; annual meeting in May; papers and posters on S California science; small grants to students for research; 400 mems; Pres. JON BASKIN; Sec. DAN GUTHRIE; publs *Bulletin* (3 a year), *Memoirs* (irregular).

World Future Society: 7910 Woodmont Ave, Suite 450, Bethesda, MD 20814; tel. (301) 656-8274; fax (301) 951-0394; e-mail wfsinfo@wfs.org; internet www.wfs.org; f. 1966; private, non-profit organization promoting free discussion and study of alternative futures especially on technological and social themes; 30,000 mems; Pres. TIMOTHY C. MACK; publs *Futures Research Quarterly*, *Future Survey* (12 a year), *The Futurist* (10 a year).

Biological Sciences

American Genetic Association: 2030 SE Marine Science Dr., Newport, OR 97365; tel. (541) 272-0334; e-mail agajoh@oregonstate.edu; internet www.theaga.org; f. 1903; clearing house for information on organismal genetics; organizes and supports confs and workshops; 300 mems; Pres. Dr SCOTT V. EDWARDS; Sec. Dr LINDA STRAUSBAUGH; publ. *Journal of Heredity* (6 a year).

American Institute of Biological Sciences: 1444 I St NW, Suite 200, Washington, DC 20005; tel. (202) 628-1500; fax (202) 628-1509; internet www.aibs.org; f. 1947; mems: 34 professional societies and 6 industrial firms; 240,000 mems; Pres. MARVALEE WAKE; Exec. Dir Dr RICHARD O'GRADY; publs *BioScience* (12 a year), *Forum* (6 a year),

Membership Directory and Handbook (every 2 years).

American Malacological Society: Dept of Zoology, University of Rhode Island, Kingston, RI 02881; internet erato.acnatsci.org/ams; f. 1931; study of phylum mollusca–systematics, ecology, functional morphology, evolution; medical, neotological and palaeontological aspects; 750 mems; Pres. DIANNA K. PADILLA; Sec. PAUL CALLOMON; publs *American Malacological Bulletin* (2 a year), *AMS News* (irregular).

American Ornithologists Union: 1313 Dolly Madison Blvd, Suite 402, McLean, VA 22101; tel. (703) 790-1745; fax (703) 790-2672; e-mail aou@burkinc.com; internet www.aou.org; f. 1883; scientific study of birds; 5,000 mems; Pres. FRED COOKE; Sec. M. ROSS LEIN; publs *Check-List of North American Birds* (irregular), *The Auk* (4 a year).

American Phytopathological Society: 3340 Pilot Knob Rd, St Paul, MN 55121; tel. (651) 454-7250; fax (651) 454-0766; e-mail aps@scisoc.org; internet www.apsnet.org; f. 1908; detection and control of plant diseases; plant health management; plant management network; 5,000 mems; Pres. (vacant); Exec. Vice-Pres. STEVEN C. NELSON; Vice-Pres. for Operations AMY HOPE; publs *Phytopathology* (12 a year), *Plant Disease* (12 a year), *Molecular Plant-Microbe Interactions* (12 a year).

American Society for Photobiology: POB 1897, Lawrence, KS 66044; tel. (785) 843-1235; fax (785) 843-1287; e-mail phot@allenpress.com; internet www.pol-us.net/asp_home; f. 1972; 1,600 mems; Pres. FRANCES NOONAN; publ. *Photochemistry and Photobiology* (12 a year).

American Society of Human Genetics: 9650 Rockville Pike, Bethesda, MD 20814; tel. (301) 634-7300; e-mail society@ashg.org; internet genetics.faseb.org/genetics/ashg/ashgmenu.htm; f. 1948; 7,500 mems; Exec. Dir ELAINE STRASS; publ. *American Journal of Human Genetics* (12 a year).

American Society of Ichthyologists and Herpetologists: c/o Maureen A. Donnelly, Florida International University, Department of Biological Sciences, University Park, Miami, FL 33199; tel. (305) 348-1235; fax (305) 348-1986; e-mail asih@fiu.edu; internet www.asih.org; f. 1913; 3,500 mems (2,500 individual, 1,000 subscriber); Pres. LYNNE R. PARENTI; Sec. MAUREEN A. DONNELLY; publ. *Copeia* (4 a year).

American Society of Mammalogists: 810 E 10th St, Lawrence, KS 66044; tel. (785) 843-1235; fax (785) 843-1274; e-mail asm@aibs.org; internet www.mammalsociety.org; f. 1919, inc. 1920; 4,500 mems; object of the Society is the promotion of interest in mammalogy by holding meetings, issuing serial or other publications, and aiding research; five classes of mems, all elective: annual, life, patron, honorary and emeritus; the society is affiliated with the American Institute of Biological Sciences, the American Association for the Advancement of Science and the International Union for the Conservation of Nature; Pres. GUY CAMERON; Sec. and Treas. RONALD A. VAN DEN BUSSCHE; publs *Journal of Mammalogy* (4 a year), *Mammalian Species* (irregular).

American Society of Naturalists: 4328 Storer Hall, University of California, Davis, CA 95616-8755; tel. (530) 752-1114; e-mail rkgrosberg@ucdavis.edu; internet www.amnat.org; f. 1883; 1,835 mems; Pres. Dr RICHARD GROSBERG; Sec. Dr JUDITH L. BRONSTEIN; publ. *The American Naturalist* (12 a year).

American Society of Parasitologists: c/o Dennis J. Minchella, Dept of Biological Sciences, Purdue Univ., West Lafayette, IN 47907-2054; tel. (765) 494-8188; fax (765) 494-0876; e-mail dennism@purdue.edu; internet asp.unl.edu; f. 1924; 1,100 mems; Sec. and Treas. Dr DENNIS J. MINCHELLA; publ. *The Journal of Parasitology* (6 a year).

Biophysical Society: 9650 Rockville Pike, Room L-0512, Bethesda, MD 20814; tel. (301) 634-7114; fax (301) 634-7133; e-mail society@biophysics.org; internet www.biophysics.org; f. 1957; 7,000 mems; Pres. YALE GOLDMAN; Sec. JILL TREWHELLA; Exec. Dir ROSALBA KAMPMAN; publ. *Biophysical Journal* (12 a year).

Botanical Society of America, Inc.: POB 299, St Louis, MO 63166-0299; tel. (314) 577-9566; fax (314) 577-9515; e-mail bsa-manager@botany.org; internet www.botany.org; f. 1893; 3,000 mems; Pres. CHRISTOPHER HAUFLER; Sec. STEVE WELLER; Exec. Dir BILL DAHL; publs *American Journal of Botany* (12 a year), *Directory* (every 2 years), *Guide to Graduate Study in the US and Canada* (irregular), *Plant Science Bulletin* (4 a year).

Ecological Society of America: 1900 M St NW, Suite 700, Washington, DC 20036; tel. (202) 833-8773; fax (202) 833-8775; e-mail esahq@esa.org; internet www.esa.org; f. 1915; 8,300 mems; Exec. Dir KATHERINE S. MCCARTER; publs *Bulletin* (4 a year), *Ecology* (12 a year), *Ecological Applications* (6 a year), *Ecological Monographs* (4 a year), *Frontiers in Ecology and the Environment* (10 a year).

Entomological Society of America: 10001 Derekwood Lane, Suite 100, Lanham, MD 20706; tel. (301) 731-4535; fax (301) 731-4538; e-mail esa@entsoc.org; internet www.entsoc.org; f. 1953 by the union of the American Asscn of Economic Entomologists (f. 1889) and the fmr Entomological Soc. of America (f. 1906); 6,000 mems; Exec. Dir ANN KENWORTHY; Dir for Finance NEIL WILLOUGHBY; publs *American Entomologist* (4 a year), *Annals* (6 a year), *Anthropod Management Tests* (1 a year), *Environmental Entomology* (6 a year), *Journal of Economic Entomology* (6 a year), *Journal of Medical Entomology* (6 a year).

Environmental Mutagen Society: 1821 Michael Faraday Drive, Suite 300, Reston, VA 20190; tel. (703) 438-8220; fax (703) 438-3113; e-mail emshq@ems-us.org; internet www.ems-us.org; f. 1969; 600 mems; promotion of basic and applied studies of mutagenesis; makes an annual award; Exec. Dir TONIA MASSON; publ. *Environmental and Molecular Mutagenesis* (8 a year).

Federation of American Societies for Experimental Biology: 9650 Rockville Pike, Bethesda, MD 20814; tel. (301) 634-7000; fax (301) 634-7001; internet www.faseb.org; f. 1912; full mem. socs: American Association of Anatomists, American Association of Immunologists, American College of Sports Medicine, Biomedical Engineering Soc., American Federation for Medical Research, American Peptide Soc., American Physiological Soc., American Soc. for Biochemistry and Molecular Biology, American Soc. for Bone and Mineral Research, American Soc. for Clinical Investigation, American Soc. for Investigative Pathology, American Soc. for Nutrition, American Soc. for Pharmacology and Experimental Therapeutics, American Soc. of Human Genetics, Association of Biomolecular Resource Facilities, Biology, Environmental Mutagen Soc., Genetics Soc. of America, International Soc. for Computational Biology, Protein Soc.,Soc. for Developmental Biology; Soc. for the Study of Reproduction, Teratology Soc., The Endocrine Soc.; library of 2,500 vols; Pres. Dr WILLIAM TALMAN; Sec. and Exec. Dir Dr GUY FOGLEMAN; publ. *The FASEB Journal* (12 a year).

Genetics Society of America: 9650 Rockville Pike, Bethesda, MD 20814-3998; tel. (301) 634-7300; fax (301) 634-7079; internet www.genetics-gsa.org; f. 1932; 4,200 mems; Pres. Dr TERRY ORR-WEAVER; Sec. Dr ANITA K. HOPPER; Exec. Dir SHERRY A. MARTS; publ. *Genetics* (12 a year).

Mycological Society of America: c/o Dr Faye Murrin, Dept of Biology, Memorial University, St John's, NL A1B 3X9, Canada; tel. (709) 737-8018; fax (709) 737-3018; e-mail fmurrin@morgan.ucs.mun.ca; internet msafungi.org; f. 1931; 1,300 mems; Sec. Dr FAYE MURRIN; publs *Mycologia* (6 a year), *Mycologia Memoirs* (irregular).

National Audubon Society: 225 Varick St, 7th Fl., New York, NY 10014; tel. (212) 979-3000; fax (212) 979-3188; e-mail join@audubon.org; internet www.audubon.org; f. 1905; membership: 550,000, 518 local chapters; Dir GEOFFREY COBB RYAN; publs *Audubon* (6 a year), *Audubon Field Notes* (4 a year).

National Wildlife Federation: 11100 Wildlife Center Drive, Reston, VA 20190-5362; tel. (703) 790-4000; fax (703) 790-4075; internet www.nwf.org; f. 1936; 4 m. mems; Pres. and CEO LARRY J. SCHWEIGER; publs *Conservation Directory*, *International Wildlife Magazine*, *National Wildlife Magazine*, *Ranger Rick*, *Your Big Backyard*.

Nature Conservancy: Suite 100, 4245 North Fairfax Drive, Arlington, VA 22203-1606; tel. (800) 628-6860; e-mail comment@tnc.org; internet nature.org; f. 1951; international non-profit organization committed to preserving biological diversity by protecting lands and waters; 1m. mems; Pres. STEVEN J. MCCORMICK; publ. *Nature Conservancy* (6 a year).

Society for Developmental Biology: 9650 Rockville Pike, Bethesda, MD 20814-3998; tel. (301) 634-7815; fax (301) 634-7825; e-mail sdb@faseb.org; internet www.sdbonline.org; f. 1939; the purpose of the society is to further the study of development in all organisms and at all levels, to represent and promote communication among students of development, and to promote the field of developmental biology; 2,100 mems; Pres. JUDITH KIMBLE; publ. *Developmental Biology* (26 a year).

Society for Economic Botany: Dept of Anthropology, Univ. of Missouri, Columbia, MO 65211; tel. (314) 882-3038; internet www.econbot.org; f. 1959; 1,000 mems; Pres. BRAD BENNETT; Sec. WILL MCCLATCHEY; publ. *Economic Botany* (4 a year).

Society for Experimental Biology and Medicine: 197 W Spring Valley Ave, Maywood, NJ 07607-1727; tel. (201) 291-9080; fax (201) 291-2988; e-mail sebm@inch.com; internet www.sebm.org; f. 1903; 1,500 mems, 1,300 subscribers; Exec. Dir FELICE O'GRADY; publ. *Experimental Biology and Medicine* (11 a year).

Society of Vertebrate Paleontology: Suite 100, 111 Deer Lake Rd, Deerfield, IL 60015; tel. (847) 480-9095; fax (847) 480-9282; e-mail svp@vertpaleo.org; internet www.vertpaleo.org; f. 1941; 2,000 mems; Pres. ANNALISA BERTA; Sec. CATHERINE BADGLEY; publs *Bibliography of Fossil Vertebrates*, *Journal of Vertebrate Paleontology* (4 a year), *Palaeontologia Electronica*, *SVP News Bulletin* (3 a year).

Wildlife Conservation Society: Bronx Zoo, 2300 Southern Blvd, Bronx, NY 10460;

tel. (718) 220-5100; fax (718) 220-2685; e-mail lcorcoran@wcs.org; internet www.wcs.org; f. 1895; operates the Bronx Zoo, New York Aquarium, Central Park Zoo, Queens Zoo, Prospect Park Zoo, and c. 500 conservation field projects in over 60 nations; education programmes developed at the Bronx Zoo are in 50 states and 16 countries from K-12 grade with professional devt components; 100,000 mems; library of 6,000 vols; Chair. WARD WOODS; Pres. and CEO Dr STEVEN E. SANDERSON; publ. *Wildlife Conservation* (6 a year).

Wildlife Management Institute: 1101 14th St, NW, Suite 801, Washington, DC 20036; tel. (202) 371-1808; fax (202) 408-5059; internet www.wildlifemanagementinstitute.org; inc. 1946; Pres. STEVEN A. WILLIAMS; Exec. Vice-Pres. RICHARD E. MCCABE; publs *North American Wildlife and Natural Resources Conference Transactions* (1 a year), *Outdoor News Bulletin* (12 a year).

Wildlife Society, Inc.: 5410 Grosvenor Lane, Suite 200, Bethesda, MD 20814-2144; tel. (301) 897-9770; fax (301) 530-2471; e-mail tws@wildlife.org; internet www.wildlife.org; f. 1937; develops and promotes sound stewardship of wildlife resources and of the environments upon which wildlife and humans depend; undertakes an active role in preventing human-induced environmental degradation; increases awareness and appreciation of wildlife values; seeks the highest standards in all activities of the wildlife profession; 9,100 mems; Exec. Dir and CEO MICHAEL HUTCHINS; publs *Journal of Wildlife Management* (4 a year), *The Wildlife Professional* (mem. magazine), *Wildlife Society Bulletin* (4 a year).

Mathematical Sciences

American Mathematical Society: 201 Charles St, Providence, RI 02904; tel. (401) 455-4000; fax (401) 331-3842; e-mail ams@ams.org; internet www.ams.org; f. 1888; sponsors meetings, symposia, seminars and institutes, and provides employment services in the mathematical sciences; 32,000 mems; Exec. Dir DON MCCLURE; publs *Abstracts of Papers Presented to the American Mathematical Society* (4 a year), *Bulletin* (4 a year), *Conformal Geometry and Dynamics* (electronic only), *Current Mathematical Publications* (17–18 a year), *Employment Information in the Mathematical Sciences* (5 a year), *Electronic Research Announcements* (electronic only), *Journal* (4 a year), *Mathematical Reviews* (12 a year), *Mathematics of Computation* (4 a year), *Memoirs* (6 a year), *Notices* (11 a year), *Proceedings* (12 a year), *Representation Theory* (electronic only), *St Petersburg Mathematical Journal* (6 a year), *Sugaku Expositions* (2 a year), *Theory of Probability and Mathematical Statistics* (2 a year), *Transactions* (12 a year), *Transactions of the Moscow Mathematical Society* (1 a year).

Dozenal Society of America: 5106 Hampton Ave Suite 205, St Louis, MO 63109-3115; tel. (631) 351-7456; e-mail contact@dozens.org; internet www.dozenal.org; f. 1944 as the Duodecimal Society of America; 144 mems; library of 120 vols; Chair. Prof. JAY SCHIFFMAN; Pres. MICHAEL DE VLIEGER; publ. *Duodecimal Bulletin* (2 a year).

Mathematical Association of America, Inc.: 1529 18th St, NW, Washington, DC 20036; tel. (202) 387-5200; fax (800) 741-9415; internet www.maa.org; f. 1915; 21,000 mems; Pres. DAVID BRESSOUD; Sec. BARBARA T. FAIRES; Exec. Dir TINA H. STRALEY; publs *American Mathematical Monthly* (10 a year), *College Mathematics Journal* (5 a year), *Journal of Online Mathematics and its Applications*, *Loci*, *Mathematics Magazine* (5 a year), *Math Horizons* (4 a year).

Society for Industrial and Applied Mathematics Society: 3600 University City Science Center, Philadelphia, PA 19104; tel. (215) 382-9800; fax (215) 386-7999; e-mail siam@siam.org; internet www.siam.org; f. 1951 to promote a better understanding of how mathematics may be used in the solution of complex problems in industry; 10,000 individual mems, 500 institutional mems; Pres. MARTIN GOLUBITSKY; Sec. L. PAMELA COOK; publs *SIAM review* (4 a year), 12 specialist journals, mainly quarterly.

Physical Sciences

Acoustical Society of America: 2 Huntington Quadrangle, Melville, NY 11747-4502; tel. (516) 576-2360; fax (516) 576-2377; e-mail asa@aip.org; internet asa.aip.org; f. 1929; 6,900 mems; Pres. WILLIAM A. YOST; Exec. Dir CHARLES E. SCHMID; publs *Acoustics Research Letters Online* (4 a year), *Journal* (12 a year).

American Association of Petroleum Geologists: Box 979, Tulsa, OK 74101-0979; tel. (918) 584-2555; fax (918) 584-0469; e-mail bulletin@aapg.org; internet www.aapg.org; f. 1917; world's largest professional geoscience organization; 31,995 mems; Exec. Dir RICK FRITZ; publs *AAPG Bulletin* (12 a year), *AAPG Explorer* (12 a year), *Environmental Geosciences* (12 a year).

American Astronomical Society: 2000 Florida Ave, NW, Suite 100, Washington, DC 20009-1231; tel. (202) 328-2010; fax (202) 234-2560; e-mail aas@aas.org; internet www.aas.org; f. 1899, inc. 1928; promotes interest in astronomy; disseminates and archives the results of astronomical research; facilitates and strengthens the interactions among mems through professional meetings; supports mem. divs representing specialized research and astronomical interests; represents the goals of mems to the nation and the world; trains, mentors and supports the next generation of astronomers; promotes increased participation of historically under-represented groups in astronomy; assists mems to develop skills in fields of education and public outreach; 7,000 mems; Exec. Officer Dr KEVIN MARVEL; publs *Bulletin* (4 a year), *The Astronomical Journal* (12 a year), *The Astrophysical Journal* (36 a year).

American Chemical Society: 1155 16th St NW, Washington, DC 20036; tel. (202) 872-4600; fax (202) 872-4615; e-mail help@acs.org; internet www.chemistry.org; f. 1876; 155,000 mems; Pres. WILLIAM F. CARROLL, Jr; Exec. Dir Dr MADELEINE JACOBS; publs *Analytical Chemistry*, *Biochemistry*, *Bioconjugate Chemistry*, *Biomacromolecules*, *Chemical and Engineering News*, *Chemical Research in Toxicology*, *Chemical Reviews*, *Chemistry of Materials*, *Crystal Growth & Design*, *Energy & Fuels*, *Environmental Science & Technology*, *Journal of Chemical Information and Modeling*, *Journal of Chemical Theory and Computation*, *Journal of Combinatorial Chemistry*, *Industrial & Engineering Chemistry Research*, *Inorganic Chemistry*, *Journal of Agricultural and Food Chemistry*, *Journal of the ACS*, *Journal of Chemical & Engineering Data*, *Journal of Medicinal Chemistry*, *Journal of Organic Chemistry*, *Journal of Physical Chemistry A*, *Journal of Physical Chemistry B*, *Journal of Proteome Research*, *Langmuir*, *Macromolecules*, *Molecular Pharmaceutics*, *Nano Letters*, *Organic Letters*, *Organic Process Research & Development*, *Organometallics*.

American Crystallographic Association: c/o POB 96, Ellicott Station, Buffalo, NY 14205-0096; tel. (716) 898-8690; fax (716) 898-8695; e-mail aca@hwi.buffalo.edu; internet www.hwi.buffalo.edu/aca; f. 1949; 2,200 mems; crystallography and the application of diffraction methods to the study of the arrangement of atoms in matter; Pres. LOUIS DELBAERE; publs *Program and Abstracts* (1 a year), *Transactions* (1 a year).

American Geological Institute: 4220 King St, Alexandria, VA 22302-1502; tel. (703) 379-2480; fax (703) 379-7563; e-mail agi@agiweb.org; internet www.agiweb.org; f. 1948; comprises 49 Earth science socs; Exec. Dir P. PATRICK LEAHY; publ. *EARTH* (12 a year).

American Geophysical Union: 2000 Florida Ave NW, Washington, DC 20009-1277; tel. (202) 462-6900; fax (202) 328-0566; e-mail service@agu.org; internet www.agu.org; f. 1919; publishes journals and books; sponsors scientific meetings; sections: geodesy; seismology; atmospheric sciences; geomagnetism and paleomagnetism; ocean sciences; volcanology, Geochemistry and petrology; tectonophysics; planetary sciences; space physics and aeronomy; hydrology; 40,000 mems; Pres. JOHN A. ORCUTT; Exec. Dir A. F. SPILHAUS, Jr; publs *Earth Interactions* (electronic journal), *Eos* (52 a year), *Geochemistry, Geophysics, Geosystems* (online), *Geophysical Research Letters* (26 a year), *Global Biogeochemical Cycles* (4 a year), *International Journal of Geomagnetism and Aeronomy* (4 a year), *Journal of Geophysical Research* (7 sections, 12 a year), *Nonlinear Processes in Geophysics* (4 a year), *Paleoceanography* (6 a year), *Radio Science* (6 a year), *Reviews of Geophysics* (4 a year), *Space Weather* (4 a year), *Tectonics* (6 a year), *Virtual Choice* (online), *Water Resources Research* (12 a year).

American Institute of Chemists: 315 Chestnut St, Philadelphia, PA 19106-2702; tel. (215) 873-8224; fax (215) 925-1954; e-mail info@theaic.org; internet www.theaic.org; f. 1923; professional aspects of chemical practice, including national certification programme, involvement in governmental activities, awards, and sponsorship, through the AIC Foundation; unique programme annually to honour top college chemistry seniors; 6,000 mems; Pres. RICHARD BRADLEY; Exec. Dir SHARON DOBSON; publs *AIC Professional Directory* (12 a year), *The Chemist* (9 a year).

American Institute of Physics: 1 Physics Ellipse, College Park, MD 20740-3843; tel. (301) 209-3100; fax (301) 209-0843; e-mail aipinfo@aip.org; internet www.aip.org; f. 1931; composed of 10 mem. socs with total membership of 95,000; 18 affiliated socs, 94 corporate assocs, 550 student chapters; Niels Bohr Library;; Chair. MILDRED DRESSELHAUS; Exec. Dir and CEO MARC BRODSKY; publ. 46 publs, incl. *Physics Today*, journals, bulletins, translated Russian and Chinese journals, and secondary information services.

American Meteorological Society: c/o Dr Richard E. Hallgren, 45 Beacon St, Boston, MA 02108; tel. (617) 227-2425; fax (617) 742-8718; e-mail amsinfo@ametsoc.org; internet www.ametsoc.org; f. 1919, inc. 1920; 11,850 mems; Pres. SUSAN AVERY; Exec. Dir RONALD D. MCPHERSON; Deputy Exec. Dir KEITH L. SEITTER; publs *Bulletin of the American Meteorological Society*, *Historical Monographs*, *Journal of Applied Meteorology*, *Journal of Atmospheric and Oceanic Technology*, *Journal of Climate*, *Journal of Hydrometeorology*, *Journal of Physical Oceanography*, *Journal of the Atmospheric Sciences*, *Meteorological and Geoastrophysical Abstracts*, *Meteorological Monographs*,

Monthly Weather Review, *Weather and Forecasting*.

American Microscopical Society: Dept of Biology, Washington College, Chestertown, Maryland 21620; tel. (410) 778-2800; internet www.amicros.org; f. 1878; 695 mems and 645 subscribers; Pres. Dr VICKI PEARSE; Treas. Dr D. BRUCE CONN; publ. *Invertebrate Biology* (4 a year).

American Nuclear Society: 555 N Kensington Ave, La Grange Park, IL 60526; tel. (708) 352-6611; fax (708) 352-0499; e-mail nucleus@ans.org; internet www.ans.org; f. 1954; 17 professional divisions: fusion energy, education and training, environmental sciences, isotopes and radiation, materials science and technology, mathematics and computation, nuclear criticality safety, suel cycle and waste management, human factors, nuclear reactor safety, radiation protection and shielding, power and operations, reactor physics, robotics and remote systems technology, thermal hydraulics, biology and medicine, decommissioning, decontamination and reutilization, accelerator applications; 52 local sections, 8 overseas local sections (Japan, South Korea, Latin America, Austria, Switzerland, Italy, France, Taiwan); 51 student branches; 80 organization mems; Pres. E. JAMES REINSCH; Exec. Dir HARRY A. BRADLEY; publs *ANS News* (6 a year), *Buyers' Guide* (1 a year), *Fusion Technology* (6 a year plus supplements), *Nuclear News* (12 a year), *Nuclear Science and Engineering* (9 a year), *Nuclear Technology* (12 a year), *Transactions* (2 a year), nuclear standards.

American Pharmacists Association: 2215 Constitution Ave NW, Washington, DC 20037; tel. (202) 628-4410; fax (202) 783-2351; e-mail webmaster@aphanet.org; internet www.aphanet.org; f. 1852; 50,000 mems; library of 6,000 vols; Exec. Vice-Pres. and CEO; publs *APhA Drug Infoline* (12 a year), *Journal of Pharmaceutical Sciences* (12 a year), *Journal of the American Pharmacists Association* (6 a year), *Pharmacy Student* (6 a year), *Pharmacy Today* (12 a year).

American Physical Society: One Physics Ellipse, College Park, MD 20740; tel. (301) 209-3200; fax (301) 209-0865; e-mail exoffice@aps.org; internet www.aps.org; f. 1899; 48,000 mems; Pres. CURTIS G. CALLAN, Jr; Exec. Officer Dr KATE P. KIRBY; publs *Physical Review A-E*, *Physical Review* (in 5 series), *Physical Review Letters*, *Physical Review Special Topics–Accelerators and Beams* (12 a year), *Physical Review Special Topics–Physics Education Research*, *Physics*, *Reviews of Modern Physics*.

American Society for Biochemistry and Molecular Biology: 9650 Rockville Pike, Bethesda, MD 20814; tel. (301) 634-7145; fax (301) 634-7108; e-mail asbmb@asbmb.org; internet www.asbmb.org; f. 1906; 12,000 mems; Pres. HEIDI HAMM; Exec. Dir BARBARA A. GORDON; publs *Journal of Biological Chemistry* (52 a year), *Journal of Lipid Research* (12 a year), *Molecular and Cellular Proteomics* (12 a year).

Electrochemical Society: 65 South Main St, Pennington, NJ 08534; tel. (609) 737-1902; fax (609) 737-2743; e-mail ecs@electrochem.org; internet www.electrochem.org; f. 1902; 8,000 individual mems, 100 corporate mems; conducts two international technical meetings annually on various topics in electrochemistry, solid-state science and related fields; Exec. Dir ROQUE J. CALVO; publs *Electrochemical and Solid-State Letters* (print edn 12 a year, articles published online), *Interface* (4 a year, print and online), *Journal* (print edn 12 a year, articles published online).

Geochemical Society: Department of Earth and Planetary Sciences, Washington University, 1 Brookings Drive, St Louis, MO 63130-4899; tel. (314) 935-4131; fax (314) 935-4121; internet gs.wustl.edu; f. 1955; 1,800 mems; Pres. SUSAN BRANTLEY; Sec. JEREMY B. FEIN; publs *Geochemistry Geophysics Geosystems* (online), *Geochimica et Cosmochimica Acta*.

Geological Society of America, Inc.: POB 9140, 3300 Penrose Pl., Boulder, CO 80301-9140; tel. (303) 357-1000; fax (303) 357-1071; e-mail gsaservice@geosociety.org; internet www.geosociety.org; f. 1888; 16,000 mems; Exec. Dir JOHN W. HESS; publs *Abstracts with programs* (1 a year), *Environmental and Engineering Geoscience* (4 a year), *Geology* (12 a year), *GSA Bulletin* (12 a year), *GSA Today* (12 a year).

Microscopy Society of America: 12100 Sunset Hills Rd, Suite 130, Reston, VA 20190; tel. (703) 234-4115; fax (703) 435-4390; e-mail associationmanagement@microscopy.org; internet www.microscopy.org; f. 1942; annual meeting, presenting technical papers and exhibits; aims to increase and diffuse knowledge of microscopy and related instruments and results obtained through their use; 2,300 mems; Pres. DAVID PISTON, III; Sec. JEANETTE KILLIUS; Man. Dir PETER DOHERTY; publs *Microscopy & Microanalysis Journal* (6 a year), *Microscopy Today* (6 a year), *Proceedings* (1 a year).

Mineralogical Society of America: 3635 Concorde Pkwy Suite 500, Chantilly, 20151-1110; tel. (703) 652-9950; fax (703) 652-9951; e-mail business@minsocam.org; internet www.minsocam.org; f. 1919; mineralogy, petrology, crystallography, geochemistry; 2,700 mems; Pres. Dr DAVID L. BISH; Vice-Pres. Dr MICHAEL F. HOCHELLA, Jr; Exec. Dir J. ALEX SPEER; publs *Elements* (6 a year), *Reviews in Mineralogy and Geochemistry* (3 to 6 a year), *The American Mineralogist* (8 a year).

Oak Ridge Associated Universities, Inc.: POB 117, 130 Badger Ave, Oak Ridge, TN 37831-0117; tel. (865) 576-3000; fax (865) 576-3643; e-mail smitha@orau.gov; internet www.orau.org; f. 1946; consortium of 87 universities; promotes collaborative partnerships with universities, federal laboratories and industry; manages the Oak Ridge Institute for Science and Education for the US Department of Energy; carries out research and development, training and education, technical assistance activities for DOE and other federal and private organizations; concentrates on the following major areas: science/engineering education, worldwide emergency response and training, workforce health and safety research and training, technical training systems and environmental monitoring; manages educational programmes for undergraduate, graduate and postdoctoral students and academic staff; develops training processes that encompass the design, delivery and evaluation of training networks; performs radiological site investigations and verification surveys; manages University Radioactive Ion Beam (UNIRIB) user facility; maintains medical, training and energy/environment library; Pres. Dr RONALD D. TOWNSEND.

Optical Society of America: 2010 Massachusetts Ave, NW, Washington, DC 20036; tel. (202) 223-8130; fax (202) 223-1096; e-mail info@osa.org; internet www.osa.org; f. 1916; devoted to the advancement of optics and the service of all who are interested in any aspect of that science; 15,100 mems; Pres. Dr THOMAS BAER; CEO ELIZABETH ROGAN; publs *Journal of the Optical Society of America A* (optics, image science and vision; 12 a year), *Journal of the Optical Society of America B* (optical physics; 12 a year), *Optics and Photonics News* (12 a year), *Optics Letters* (24 a year), *Applied Optics* (36 a year), *Journal of Lightwave Technology* (12 a year), *Journal of Optical Technology* (12 a year), *Chinese Optics Letters* (12 a year), *Journal of Optical Communications and Networking (JOCN)* (12 a year), *Optics Express* (26 a year, online only), *Journal of Display Technology* (print edn 4 a year, online 12 a year).

Palaeontological Society: c/o Roger D. K. Thomas, Dept of Earth and Environment, Franklin and Marshall College, Lancaster, PA 17604-3003; tel. (717) 291-4135; fax (717) 291-4186; internet www.paleosoc.org; f. 1908 to publish and disseminate palaeontological research; 1,500 mems; 700 institutional subscribers; affiliated with the Geological Soc. of America; Pres. DOUGLAS H. ERWIN; Sec. ROGER D. K. THOMAS; publs *Journal of Paleontology* (6 a year), *Paleobiology* (4 a year), *The Paleontological Society Memoirs* (irregular), *Short Course Notes* (1 a year).

Seismological Society of America: 201 El Cerrito Plaza Professional Bldg, El Cerrito, CA 94530; tel. (510) 525-5475; fax (510) 525-7204; e-mail info@seismosoc.org; internet www.seismosoc.org; f. 1906; 1,900 mems; seismology, earthquake engineering, earthquake geology; Pres. RICK ASTER; Sec. JOE J. LITEHISER, Jr; Exec. Dir SUSAN B. NEWMAN; publs *Bulletin* (6 a year), *Seismological Research Letters* (6 a year).

Society for Sedimentary Geology (SEPM): 6128 East 38th St, Suite 308, Tulsa, OK 74135-5814; tel. (918) 610-3361; fax (918) 621-1685; internet www.sepm.org; f. 1926; 5,000 mems; Pres. J. FREDERICK SARG; Exec. Dir HOWARD HARPER; publs *Journal of Sedimentary Research* (6 a year), *PALAIOS* (6 a year).

Society of Economic Geologists: 7811 Shaffer Parkway, Littleton, CO 80127-3732; tel. (720) 981-7882; fax (720) 981-7874; e-mail seg@segweb.org; internet www.segweb.org; f. 1920; 3,500 mems; Pres. MURRAY HITZMAN; publ. *Economic Geology* (8 a year).

PHILOSOPHY AND PSYCHOLOGY

American Philosophical Association: 31 Amstel Ave, Univ. of Delaware, Newark, DE 19716; tel. (302) 831-1112; fax (302) 831-8690; e-mail apaonline@udel.edu; internet www.apaonline.org; f. 1900; promotes exchange of ideas among philosophers, encourages creative and scholarly activity in philosophy and facilitates professional work of teachers of philosophy; 11,400 mems; Chair. ANTHONY APPIAH; Exec. Dir DAVID SCHRADER.

American Psychological Association: 750 First St, NE, Washington, DC 20002-4242; tel. (202) 336-5500; internet www.apa.org; f. 1892; 155,000 mems; library of 2,500 vols; Pres. GERALD P. KOOCHER; Exec. Vice-Pres. and CEO NORMAN B. ANDERSON; publs *American Psychologist*, *APA Monitor*, *Psychological Abstracts* (12 a year), and 47 others.

Metaphysical Society of America: c/o Brian Martine, Dept of Philosophy, University of Alabama in Huntsville, AL 35899; tel. (205) 895-6555; fax (205) 895-6954; internet www.acls.org/metaphys.htm; f. 1950 to study metaphysical problems without regard to sectarian divisions; 700 mems; Pres. FREDERICK FERRE; Sec. and Treas. BRIAN MARTINE.

Philosophy of Science Association: c/o George Gale, Dept of Philosophy, University of Missouri, Kansas City, MO 64110-2499; internet philosophy.wisc.edu/psa; f. 1934 to further studies and free discussion in the field of philosophy of science; 1,000 mems; Pres. ELLIOTT SOBER; Exec. Sec. GEORGE GALE; publs *Philosophy of Science* (4 a year), *Proceedings of Biennial Meetings*.

Psychometric Society: c/o Terry Ackerman, 207 Curry Bldg, POB 26171, Univ. of N Carolina at Greensboro, Greensboro, NC 27402-6171; tel. (336) 334-3474; e-mail taackerm@uncg.edu; internet www.psychometricsociety.org; f. 1935; 800 mems; Pres. PAUL DEBOECK; Sec. TERRY ACKERMAN; publ. *Psychometrika* (4 a year).

RELIGION, SOCIOLOGY AND ANTHROPOLOGY

African Studies Association: Rutgers Univ., Douglass Campus, 132 George St, New Brunswick, NJ 08901-1400; tel. (732) 932-8173; fax (732) 932-3394; e-mail asapub@rci.rutgers.edu; internet www.africanstudies.org; f. 1957; encourages research and collects and disseminates information on Africa; 2,500 mems; Pres. ALIKO SONGOLO; Exec. Dir Dr CAROL L. MARTIN; publs *African Studies Review* (3 a year), *ASA News* (3 a year), *History in Africa* (1 a year).

American Academy of Religion: Suite 300, 825 Houston Mill Rd, Atlanta, GA 30329-4246; tel. (404) 727-3049; fax (404) 727-7959; e-mail adminasst@aarweb.org; internet www.aarweb.org; f. 1909; int. learned soc. and professional asscn of teachers and research scholars in the field of religion and religious studies; 8,500 mems; publs *Journal of the American Academy of Religion (JAAR)* (4 a year), *Religious Studies News* (4 a year).

American Anthropological Association: 2200 Wilson Blvd, Suite 600, Arlington, VA 22201-3357; tel. (703) 528-1902; fax (703) 528-3546; e-mail members@aaanet.org; internet www.aaanet.org; f. 1902; 11,000 mems; Exec. Dir WILLIAM E. DAVIS, III; publs *Abstracts of the AAA Meeting* (1 a year), *American Anthropologist* (4 a year), *American Ethnologist* (4 a year), *Annals of Anthropological Practice* (2 a year), *AnthroGuide* (1 a year), *Anthropology and Education Quarterly* (4 a year), *Anthropology and Humanism* (2 a year), *Anthropology News* (9 a year), *Anthropology of Consciousness* (2 a year), *Anthropology of Work Review* (2 a year), *AnthroSource* (2 a year), *Archeological Papers of the AAA* (1 a year), *City and Society* (3 a year), *Cultural Anthropology* (4 a year), *Culture, Agriculture, Food & the Environment* (2 a year), *Ethos* (4 a year), *General Anthropology Bulletin* (2 a year), *Journal of Latin American and Caribbean Anthropology* (2 a year), *Journal of Linguistic Anthropology* (2 a year), *Medical Anthropology Quarterly* (4 a year), *Museum Anthropology* (2 a year), *North American Dialogue* (2 a year), *PoLAR: Political and Legal Anthropology Review* (2 a year), *Transforming Anthropology* (2 a year), *Visual Anthropology Review* (2 a year).

American Counseling Association: 5999 Stevenson Ave, Alexandria, VA 22304; tel. (703) 823-9800; fax (703) 823-6862; internet www.counseling.org; f. 1952; counselling, guidance and student personnel services; divisions: American College Counseling Asscn, Asscn for Counselor Education and Supervision, National Career Development Asscn, Counseling Asscn for Humanistic Education and Development, American School Counselor Asscn, American Rehabilitation Counseling Asscn, Asscn for Assessment in Counseling, National Employment Counseling Asscn, Asscn for Multicultural Counseling and Devt, Asscn for Spiritual, Ethical and Religious Values in Counseling, Internat. Asscn of Addictions and Offender Counselors, American Mental Health Counselors Asscn, Asscn for Counselors and Educators in Government, Asscn for Adult Development and Aging, Asscn for Gay, Lesbian and Bisexual Issues in Counseling, Internat. Asscn of Marriage and Family Counselors; Asscn for Creativity in Counseling; Asscn for Specialists in Group Work; Counselors for Social Justice; publishes 16 periodicals on aspects of counselling, guidance and human devt; 43,000 mems; Pres. MARCHETA EVANS; Exec. Dir RICHARD YEP.

American Folklore Society: c/o Timothy Lloyd, Mershon Center, Ohio State Univ., 1501 Neil Ave, Columbus, OH 43201-2602; tel. (614) 292-3375; fax (614) 292-2407; internet afsnet.org; f. 1888; 2,200 mems; Pres. ELAINE LAWLESS; Exec. Dir TIMOTHY LLOYD; publ. *Journal of American Folklore* (4 a year).

American Oriental Society: Hatcher Graduate Library, University of Michigan, Ann Arbor, MI 48109-1205; e-mail jrodgers@umich.edu; internet www.umich.edu/~aos; f. 1842; 1,350 mems; library of 22,000 vols; Pres. PAUL W. KROLL; Sec. and Treas. J. RODGERS; publ. *Journal* (4 a year).

American Society for Ethnohistory: Dept of Anthropology, McGraw Hall, Cornell University, Ithaca, NY 14853; tel. (607) 277-0109; internet ethnohistory.org; f. 1954; 1,200 mems; scholarly organization devoted to the study of the histories of cultures and societies in all areas of the world; Pres. K. TSIANINA LOMAWAIMA; Sec. and Treas. CAROLYN PODRUCHNY; publ. *Ethnohistory* (4 a year).

American Sociological Association: 1430 K St NW, Suite 600, Washington, DC 20005; tel. (202) 383-9005; fax (202) 638-0882; internet www.asanet.org; f. 1905; 14,000 mems; Pres. EVELYN NAKANO GLENN; Exec. Officer SALLY T. HILLSMAN; publs *The American Sociological Review* (6 a year), *City and Community* (4 a year), *Contemporary Sociology* (6 a year), *Contexts* (4 a year), *Employment Bulletin* (12 a year), *Footnotes* (9 a year), *Journal of Health and Social Behavior* (4 a year), *Social Psychology Quarterly*, *Sociological Methodology* (1 a year), *Sociological Theory* (2 a year), *Sociology of Education* (4 a year), *Teaching Sociology* (4 a year).

Association for Asian Studies, Inc.: 1021 East Huron St, Ann Arbor, MI 48104; tel. (734) 665-2490; fax (734) 665-3801; e-mail postmaster@aasianst.org; internet www.aasianst.org; f. 1941; 8,000 mems; Pres. MARY ELIZABETH BERRY; Exec. Dir MICHAEL PASCHAL; publs *Bibliography of Asian Studies Online* (electronic database, updated 4 times a year), *Education about Asia* (3 a year), *Journal of Asian Studies* (4 a year).

Association for the Study of Afro-American Life and History, Inc.: c/o Dr Edward Beasley, 4826 Sorter Drive, Kansas City, KS 66104; tel. (913) 287-8465; internet www.dpw-archives.org/asalh.html; f. 1915; 2,200 mems; publs *The Journal of Negro History* (4 a year), *The Negro History Bulletin* (4 a year).

National Institute of Social Sciences: 161 East 91st St, New York, NY 10128-2018; tel. (212) 831-0560; f. 1899; 850 mems; Pres. J. SINCLAIR ARMSTRONG; Sec. BRUCE E. BALDING.

Pacific Sociological Association: Dept of Sociology, California State University, Sacramento, CA 95819-6005; tel. (916) 278-5254; fax (916) 278-6281; e-mail psa@csus.edu; internet www.csus.edu/psa; f. 1930; 900 mems; Exec. Dir DEAN S. DORN; publs *Sociological Perspectives* (4 a year), *The Pacific Sociologist*.

Population Association of America, Inc.: 8630 Fenton St, Suite 722, Silver Spring, MD 20910-3812; tel. (301) 565-6710; fax (301) 565-7850; e-mail info@popassoc.org; internet www.popassoc.org; f. 1931; 3,000 mems; Pres. CHARLES HIRSCHMAN; Exec. Dir STEPHANIE D. DUDLEY; publ. *Demography* (4 a year).

Population Council: 1 Dag Hammarskjold Plaza, New York, NY 10017; tel. (212) 339-0500; fax (212) 755-6052; e-mail pubinfo@popcouncil.org; internet www.popcouncil.org; f. 1952; int. non-profit NGO seeking to improve the well-being and reproductive health of current and future generations around the world and to help achieve a humane, equitable and sustainable balance between people and resources; conducts research worldwide to improve policies, programmes and products in 3 areas (HIV/AIDS; poverty, gender and youth; reproductive health); conducts fundamental biomedical research in reproduction; develops contraceptives and other products for improvement of reproductive health; conducts studies to improve the quality and outreach of services related to family planning, HIV/AIDS and reproductive health; carries out research on reproductive health and behaviour, family structure and function, causes and consequences of population growth; works to strengthen professional resources in developing countries through collaborative research, awards, fellowships and training; Pres. Dr PETER J. DONALDSON; Vice-Pres. for Corporate Affairs Div. JAMES E. SAILER; Vice-Pres. for Distinguished Scholar Dr JOHN BONGAARTS; Chief Financial Officer and Treas. SCOTT NEWMAN; Gen. Counsel and Sec. PATRICIA C. VAUGHAN; publs *Momentum* (2 a year), *Population and Development Review* (4 a year), *Population Briefs* (3 a year), *Studies in Family Planning* (4 a year).

Religious Research Association: 618 SW 2nd Ave, Galva, IL 61434-1912; tel. (309) 932-2727; fax (309) 932-2282; e-mail williamswatos@augustana.edu; internet rra.hartsem.edu; f. 1951; increases understanding of the function of religion in persons and society through application of social scientific and other scholarly methods; promotes religious research; co-operates with other socs and individuals interested in the study of religion; meets annually in conjunction with the Soc. for the Scientific Study of Religion; 600 mems; Pres. Dr JOHN A. BARTKOWSKI; Exec. Sec. Dr W. H. SWATOS, Jr; publ. *Review of Religious Research* (4 a year).

Russell Sage Foundation: 112 East 64th St, New York, NY 10065; tel. (212) 750-6000; fax (212) 371-4761; e-mail info@rsage.org; internet www.russellsage.org; f. 1907; promotes improvement of social and living conditions in the USA; supports projects on the future of work, immigration and the social psychology of cultural contact; library of 2,000 vols; Chair. MARY C. WATERS; Pres. ERIC WANNER.

Society for Applied Anthropology: POB 2436, Oklahoma City, OK 73101-2436; tel. (405) 843-5113; fax (405) 843-8553; e-mail info@sfaa.net; internet www.sfaa.net; f. 1941; application of the social and behavioural sciences to contemporary problems; 3,000 mems; Exec. Dir Dr JUDE THOMAS MAY; publs *Human Organization* (4 a year), *Practicing Anthropology* (4 a year).

Society for the Scientific Study of Religion, Inc.: Arthur L. Greil, Alfred University Division of Social Sciences Saxon Drive, Alfred, NY 14802; tel. (607) 871-2215; fax (607) 871-2085; e-mail sssr@alfred.edu; internet las.alfred.edu/~soc/sssr; f. 1949;

dedicated to research and scholarly publs relating to religious phenomena; examining the consequences of religious beliefs on individual and social behaviour, the impact of religious organizations on other institutions, and problems of continuity and change within religious groups; c. 1,500 mems; Pres. NANCY AMMERMAN; Exec. Officer LARRY GREIL; publ. *Journal* (4 a year).

Society for the Study of Evolution: c/o Charles B. Fenster, Dept of Biology, Univ. of Maryland, College Park, MD 20742; tel. (785) 843-1235; fax (785) 843-1274; internet www.evolutionsociety.org; f. 1946; promotes the study of organic evolution and the integration of the various fields of science concerned with evolution; 3,000 mems; Pres. Prof. ALLEN ORR; Exec. Vice-Pres. Prof. CHARLES B. FENSTER; publ. *Evolution* (12 a year).

TECHNOLOGY

American Ceramic Society: POB 6136, Westerville, OH 43086-6136; tel. (614) 890-4700; fax (614) 899-6109; e-mail info@ceramics.org; internet www.ceramics.org; f. 1899; 10,400 mems; library of 11,000 vols; Pres. WARREN W. WOLF; Sec. and Exec. Dir GLENN F. HARVEY; runs Ceramic Correspondence Inst.; publs *Applied Ceramic Technology* (6 a year), *Ceramic Engineering and Science Proceedings* (5 a year), *Ceramics Monthly*, *Ceramic Society Bulletin* (12 a year), *Ceramic Source* (1 a year), *Journal of the American Ceramic Society* (12 a year), *Pottery Making Illustrated* (5 a year).

American Council of Engineering Companies: 1015 15th St, NW, Washington, DC 20005-2605; tel. (202) 347-7474; fax (202) 898-0068; e-mail acec@acec.org; internet www.acec.org; f. 1956; 5,800 mems; Pres. DAVID A. RAYMOND; publs *American Consulting Engineer*, *Directory*, *Engineering Inc.*

American Institute of Aeronautics and Astronautics: 1801 Alexander Bell Drive, Suite 500, Reston, VA 20191; f. 1930; 35,000 mems; Exec. Dir CORT DUROCHER; publs *Aerospace America* (includes *AIAA Bulletin*), *AIAA Journal*, *AIAA Student Journal*, *Journal of Aerospace Computing, Information and Communication* (12 a year, online only), *Journal of Aircraft*, *Journal of Guidance, Control and Dynamics*, *Journal of Propulsion and Power*, *Journal of Spacecraft and RocketsTransfer*, *Journal of Thermophysics and Heat*.

American Institute of Chemical Engineers: 3 Park Ave, New York, NY 10016-5991; tel. (212) 591-8100; fax (212) 591-8888; e-mail xpress@aiche.org; internet www.aiche.org; f. 1908; 40,000 mems; Pres. JEFFREY J. SIIROLA; Exec. Dir JOHN SOFRANKO; publs *AIChE Journal* (12 a year), *Biotechnology Progress* (6 a year), *Chemical Engineering Progress* (12 a year), *Chemical Engineering Faculty Directory* (1 a year), *Environmental Progress* (4 a year), *Process Safety Progress* (4 a year).

American Institute of Mining, Metallurgical and Petroleum Engineers, Inc.: POB 270728, Littleton, CO 80127-0013; tel. (303) 948-4255; fax (303) 948-4260; e-mail aime@aimehq.org; internet www.aimehq.org; f. 1871; 108,000 mems via 4 mem. socs; Exec. Dir J. RICK ROLATER.

Member Societies:

Association for Iron and Steel Technology: 186 Thorn Hill Rd, Warrendale, PA 15086-7528; tel. (724) 776-6040; fax (724) 776-1880; e-mail info@aistech.org; internet www.aistech.org; 11,268 mems; Exec. Dir RONALD E. ASHBURN; publ. *Iron and Steel maker* (12 a year).

Minerals, Metals and Materials Society: 184 Thorn Hill Rd, Warrendale, PA 15086-7528; tel. (724) 776-9000; fax (724) 776-3770; e-mail tmsgeneral@tms.org; internet www.tms.org; Exec. Dir Dr WARREN HUNT; publs *B* (4 a year), *Journal of Metals* (12 a year), *Metallurgical Transactions A* (12 a year).

Society for Mining, Metallurgy and Exploration, Inc.: 8307 Shaffer Parkway, Littleton, CO 80127-7002; tel. (303) 973-9550; fax (303) 973-3845; e-mail sme@smenet.org; internet www.smenet.org; 9,836 mems; Exec. Dir DAVID L. KANAGY; publs *Minerals and Metallurgical Processing* (4 a year), *Mining Engineering* (12 a year), *Transactions* (1 a year).

Society of Petroleum Engineers: POB 833836, Richardson, TX 75083-3836; tel. (972) 952-9393; fax (972) 952-9435; e-mail postmaster@spe.org; internet www.spe.org; 60,559 mems; Exec. Dir MARK A. RUBIN; publs *Journal of Petroleum Technology* (12 a year), *Transactions*.

American Iron and Steel Institute: 1140 Connecticut Ave, NW, Suite 705, Washington, DC 20036; tel. (202) 452-7100; internet www.steel.org; f. 1908; 31 corporate mems; Pres. and CEO ANDREW G. SHARKEY.

American National Standards Institute: 25 West 43rd St, New York, NY 10036; tel. (212) 642-4900; fax (212) 398-0023; internet www.ansi.org; f. 1918; coordinates the development of voluntary national standards, approves American National Standards, and represents US interests in the ISO and the IEC; mems: 1,000 companies, organizations, academic and government bodies; Chair. Dr ROBERT W. NOTH; Pres. and CEO S. JOE BHATIA; publ. *ANSI Reporter* (12 a year).

American Society for Engineering Education: 1818 N St, NW, Suite 600, Washington, DC 20036-2479; tel. (202) 331-3500; fax (202) 245-8504; internet www.asee.org; f. 1893; promotes improvement of higher and continuing education for engineers and engineering technologists, including teaching, counselling, research, ethics, etc.; 12,000 individual mems, 500 institutional mems; Pres. SHERRA E. KERNS; Exec. Dir FRANK L. HUBAND; publs *ASEE Prism*, *Chemical Engineering Education*, *Civil Engineering Education*, *Computers in Education Journal*, *Directory of Engineering and Engineering Technology*, *Engineering Design Graphics Journal*, *Journal of Engineering Education*, *Journal of Engineering Technology*, *Journal of Industrial Engineering Design*, *Mechanical Engineering News*, *The Engineering Economist*.

American Society for Photogrammetry and Remote Sensing: 5410 Grosvenor Lane, Suite 210, Bethesda, MD 20814-2160; tel. (301) 493-0290; fax (301) 493-0208; e-mail asprs@asprs.org; internet www.asprs.org; f. 1934; aerial photography, photogrammetry, photo-interpretation, remote sensing, geographic information systems (GIS), surveying, mapping, cartography; 7,000 mems; Pres. KAREN L. SCHUCKMAN; Treas. DONALD T. LAUER; publ. *Photogrammetric Engineering and Remote Sensing* (12 a year).

American Society of Civil Engineers: 1801 Alexander Bell Drive, Reston, VA 20191-4400; tel. (703) 295-6300; fax (703) 295-6222; internet www.asce.org; f. 1852; 105,000 mems; Pres. WILLIAM P. HENRY; Exec. Dir PATRICK J. NATALE; publs *ASCE* (12 a year), *ASCE News*, *Journal of Aerospace Engineering* (4 a year), *Journal of Architectural Engineering* (4 a year), *Journal of Energy Engineering* (3 a year), *International Journal of Geomechanics* (4 a year), and 25 online journals, *Publications Information* (6 a year).

American Society of Heating, Refrigerating and Air-Conditioning Engineers, Inc.: 1791 Tullie Circle NE, Atlanta, GA 30329; tel. (404) 636-8400; fax (404) 321-5478; e-mail ashrae@ashrae.org; internet www.ashrae.org; f. 1959 by merger of the American Society of Heating and Ventilating Engineers and the American Society of Refrigerating Engineers; 55,000 mems; Sec. and Exec. Vice-Pres. JEFF H. LITTLETON; publs *ASHRAE Journal* (12 a year), *ASHRAE Handbook* (1 a year), *ASHRAE Transactions* (2 a year), *HVAC&R Research* (4 a year), *IAQ Applications* (4 a year).

American Society of Mechanical Engineers: 3 Park Ave, New York, NY 10016-5990; tel. (212) 591-7722; fax (212) 591-7674; e-mail infocentral@asme.org; internet www.asme.org; f. 1880; 120,000 mems; Pres. HARRY ARMEN; Exec. Dir VIRGIL R. CARTER; publs *Applied Mechanics Reviews* (12 a year), *Mechanical Engineering* (12 a year), *Transactions* (divided into 17 periodicals, each published 4 times a year): *Biomechanical Engineering,Dynamic Systems, Engineering for Industry, Electronic Packaging, Energy Resources Technology, Engineering for Gas Turbines and Power, Engineering Materials and Technology, Fluids Engineering, Heat Transfer Mechanisms, Journal of Applied Mechanics, Manufacturing Review Measurement and Control, Pressure Vessel Technology, Solar Energy Engineering, Tribology, Transmissions and Automationin Design, Turbomachinery, Vibration and Acoustics* (4 a year).

American Society of Naval Engineers, Inc.: 1452 Duke St, Alexandria, VA 22314-3458; tel. (703) 836-6727; fax (703) 836-7491; e-mail asnehq@navalengineers.org; internet www.navalengineers.org; f. 1888; 5,000 mems; Pres. Rear Adm. DALE GABEL; Exec. Dir Capt. (Retd) DENNIS KRUSE; publ. *Naval Engineers Journal* (4 a year).

American Welding Society: 550 NW Le Jeune Rd, Miami, FL 33126; tel. (305) 443-9353; fax (305) 443-7559; e-mail education@aws.org; internet www.aws.org; f. 1919; welding education seminars and conferences, qualification and certification, annual int. exposition; 46,000 mems; Exec. Dir R. W. SHOCK; publs *Welding Journal* (12 a year), *Inspection Trends* (4 a year), *Welding Handbook* (every 3 years), 200 welding standards, references, training guides.

ASM International: 9639 Kinsman Rd, Materials Park, OH 44073-0002; tel. (440) 338-5151; fax (440) 338-4634; e-mail cust-srv@asminternational.org; internet www.asm-intl.org; f. 1913; 43,000 mems; technical society concerned with advanced materials technology; Pres. Dr BHAKTA B. RATH; Man. Dir and Sec. STANLEY C. THEOBALD; publs *Advanced Materials and Processes* (12 a year, containing *ASM News*), *Alloy Digest* (12 a year), *Electronic Device Failure Analysis*, *International Materials Reviews* (6 a year, with Institute of Materials), *Journal of Failure Analysis and Prevention*, *Journal of Materials Engineering and Performance* (6 a year), *Journal of Phase Equilibria and Diffusion* (6 a year), *Journal of Thermal Spray Technology* (4 a year), *Metallurgical Transactions A and B (6 a year) (with TMS–AIME)* (12 a year).

Association of Consulting Chemists and Chemical Engineers, Inc.: POB 297, Sparta, NJ 07871; tel. (973) 729-6671; fax (973) 729-7088; e-mail info@chemconsult.org; internet www.chemconsult.org; f. 1928; 160 mems; Pres. Dr JOSEPH V. PORCELLI; publ. *Consulting Services Directory*.

ASTM International: 100 Barr Harbor Dr., POB C700, W Conshohocken, PA 19428-2959; tel. (610) 832-9585; fax (610) 832-9555; e-mail service@astm.org; internet www.astm.org; f. 1898; non-profit org. providing a global forum for the devt and publ. of voluntary consensus standards for materials, products, systems and services; 30,000 mems from 100 countries; Pres. JAMES THOMAS; publs *Cement, Concrete and Aggregates*, *Geotechnical Testing Journal*, *Journal of ASTM International (JAI)*, *Journal of Composites, Technology and Research*, *Journal of Forensic Sciences*, *Journal of Testing and Evaluation*.

Edison Electric Institute: 701 Pennsylvania Ave, NW, Washington, DC 20004-2696; tel. (202) 508-5000; fax (202) 508-5360; internet www.eei.org; f. 1933; mems US shareholder-owned electric power companies, int. affiliates and associates (200 US mems, 50 int. mems, 140 assoc. mems); Pres. THOMAS R. KUHN; publ. *Electric Perspectives* (6 a year).

Illuminating Engineering Society of North America: 120 Wall St, 17th Fl., New York, NY 10005; tel. (212) 248-5000; fax (212) 248-5017; e-mail ies@ies.org; internet www.ies.org; f. 1906; 8,000 mems; Exec. Vice-Pres. W. HANLEY; publs *LEUKOS* (online, 4 a year; printed compilation, 1 a year), *Lighting Design and Application* (12 a year).

Industrial Designers Society of America: 45195 Business Court, Suite 250, Dulles, VA 20166-6717; tel. (703) 707-6000; fax (703) 787-8501; e-mail idsa@idsa.org; internet www.idsa.org; f. 1965; 3,300 mems; CEO CLIVE ROUX.

Institute of Electrical and Electronics Engineers, Inc.: 3 Park Ave, 17th Floor, New York, NY 10016-5997; tel. (212) 419-7900; fax (212) 752-4929; internet www.ieee.org; f. 1884; 365,000 mems; Exec. Dir JOHN H. POWERS; publs *IEEE Potentials* (12 a year), *IEEE Spectrum/The Institute*, *Proceedings* (12 a year), *Society and Council Transactions*, etc.

Institute of Food Technologists: 525 W Van Buren, Suite 1000, Chicago, IL 60607; tel. (312) 782-8424; fax (312) 782-8348; e-mail info@ift.org; internet www.ift.org; f. 1939; 26,000 mems; Exec. Vice-Pres. BARBARA BYRD KEENAN; publs *Food Technology* (12 a year), *Journal of Food Science* (6 a year).

Institute of Industrial Engineers: 3577 Parkway Lane, Suite 200, Norcross, GA 30092; tel. (770) 449-0460; fax (770) 441-3295; internet www.iienet.org; f. 1948; 30,000 mems; Pres. ALLEN L. SOYSTER; Exec. Dir DON GREENE; publs *The Engineering Economist* (4 a year), *IIE Transactions* (12 a year), *Industrial Engineer* (12 a year), *Industrial Management* (6 a year).

Instrument Society of America (ISA): POB 12277, 67 Alexander Dr., NC 27709; tel. (919) 549-8411; fax (919) 549-8288; e-mail info@isa.org; internet www.isa.org; f. 1945; 33,000 mems; conferences and exhibitions, symposia, spec. interest divisions, training, certification, consensus standards; CEO and Exec. Dir ROB RENNER; Pres. KIM MILLER DUNN; publs *InTech* (12 a year), *ISA Directory of Instrumentation* (1 a year).

International Communication Association: c/o Michael L. Haley, Executive Director, 1730 Rhode Island NW, Suite 300, Washington, DC 20036; tel. (202) 530-9855; fax (202) 530-9851; e-mail ica@icahdq.org; internet www.icahdq.org; f. 1950 to bring together academics and professionals concerned with research and application of human communication theory; 3,200 mems; Pres. ROBERT T. CRAIG; Exec. Dir MICHAEL L. HALEY; publs *Communication Theory* (4 a year), *Human Communication Research* (4 a year), *Journal of Communication* (4 a year), *The Communication Yearbook* (1 a year).

Markle Foundation: 10 Rockefeller Pl., 16th Fl., New York, NY 10020-1903; tel. (212) 713-7600; fax (212) 765-9690; e-mail info@markle.org; internet www.markle.org; f. 1927 through an endowment given by John Markle; seeks to improve mass media and realize the potential of communications technology; addresses critical public needs, particularly in the areas of health and nat. security; collaborates with innovators and thought leaders from the public and private sectors whose expertise lies in the areas of information technology, privacy, civil liberties; 25 mems; Pres. ZOË BAIRD; Man. Dir and Chief Financial Officer KAREN BYERS; Man. Dir for Health CAROL DIAMOND.

National Society of Professional Engineers: 1420 King St, Alexandria, VA 22314-2794; tel. (703) 684-2800; fax (703) 836-4875; internet www.nspe.org; f. 1934; professional aspects of engineering; administers licensure and licensure preparation; operates a Board of Ethical Review; 60,000 mems; Pres. BOBBY E. PRICE; Exec. Dir ALBERT C. GRAY; publ. *Engineering Times* (12 a year).

Society for the History of Technology: Dept. of History, 603 Ross Hall, Iowa State University, Ames, IA 50011; tel. (515) 294-8469; fax (515) 294-6390; e-mail shot@iastate.edu; internet www.shot.jhu.edu; f. 1958; concerned with history of technological devices and processes, relations of technology with science, politics, social change, the arts and humanities, and economics; affiliated to the American Assocation for the Advancement of Science, the American Council of Learned Societies; 2,600 mems; Pres. ROSALIND WILLIAMS; Sec. AMY SUE BIX; publ. *Technology and Culture* (4 a year).

Society of Automotive Engineers, Inc.: 400 Commonwealth Drive, Warrendale, PA 15096-0001; tel. (724) 776-4841; fax (724) 772-1851; e-mail magazines@sae.org; internet www.sae.org; f. 1905; 84,000 mems; Pres. J. E. ROBERTSON; publs *Aerospace Engineering* (12 a year), *Automotive Engineering International* (12 a year), *Off-Highway Engineering* (6 a year), *SAE Handbook* (1 a year), *SAE Transactions* (1 a year), *SAE Update* (12 a year).

Society of Manufacturing Engineers: POB 930, Dearborn, MI 48121-0930; tel. (313) 271-1500; fax (313) 425-3401; internet www.sme.org; f. 1932 to advance scientific knowledge in the field of manufacturing and to apply its resources to research, writing, publishing and disseminating information; 62,000 mems; library of 7,000 vols; Pres. GENE NELSON; Exec. Dir and Gen. Man. NANCY BERG; publs *Composites in Manufacturing* (4 a year), *Electronics Manufacturing Engineering* (4 a year), *Finishing Line* (4 a year), *Forming and Fabricating* (12 a year), *Integrated Design and Manufacturing* (12 a year), *Journal of Manufacturing Processes* (4 a year), *Journal of Manufacturing Systems* (6 a year), *Machining Technology* (4 a year), *Manufacturing Engineering* (12 a year), *Molding Systems* (12 a year), *Rapid Prototyping* (4 a year), *Robotics Today* (4 a year), *Vision* (4 a year).

Society of Naval Architects and Marine Engineers: 601 Pavonia Ave, Suite 400, Jersey City, NJ 07306; tel. (201) 798-4800; fax (201) 798-4975; internet www.sname.org; f. 1893; 10,000 mems; Exec. Dir PHILIP B. KIMBALL; publs *Journal of Ship Production* (4 a year), *Journal of Ship Research* (4 a year), *Marine Technology* (4 a year), *Transactions* (1 a year).

Society of Rheology: c/o Terry Williams, American Institute of Physics, Suite 1NO1, 2 Huntington Quadrangle, Melville, NY 11747-4502; tel. (516) 576-2471; fax (516) 576-2223; internet www.rheology.org; f. 1929; 1,700 mems; Pres. FAITH A. MORRISON; Sec. ALBERT CO; publs *Journal of Rheology* (6 a year), *Rheology Bulletin* (2 a year).

Research Institutes

GENERAL

Getty Research Institute: Suite 1100, 1200 Getty Center Dr., Los Angeles, CA 90049-1688; tel. (310) 440-7335; fax (310) 440-7778; e-mail reference@getty.edu; internet www.getty.edu/research; f. 1983; an operating programme of the J. Paul Getty Trust; promotes innovative scholarship in the arts and humanities, bridging traditional academic boundaries; library of 1,000,000 vols, incl. reference rare materials, serials and auction catalogues; Dir Prof. THOMAS GAEHTGENS; Asst Dir and Co-Dir KATHLEEN SALOMON; Asst Dir and Co-Dir DAVID FARNETH; publ. *Getty Research Journal*.

National Humanities Centre: 7 Alexander Dr., POB 12256, Research Triangle Park, NC 27709; tel. (919) 549-0661; e-mail lmorgan@nationalhumanitiescenter.org; internet nationalhumanitiescenter.org; f. 1977; encourage scholarship in the humanities and enhances the usefulness and influence of the humanities in the USA; awards fellowships (40 a year) to pursue advanced post-doctoral research and writing at the Centre; organizes seminars, lectures, confs; library: reference works, bibliographical aids, microfilm catalogue; Chair. CARL PFORZHEIMER; Pres. and Dir GEOFFREY GALT HARPHAN; Sec. JOHN ADAMS.

RAND Corporation: 1776 Main St, POB 2138, Santa Monica, CA 90407-2138; tel. (310) 393-0411; fax (310) 393-4818; internet www.rand.org; f. 1948; brs in Arlington, VA, Pittsburgh, PA, New York City, NY, Cambridge (UK), Berlin (Germany), Delft (Netherlands) and Doha (Qatar); research on matters affecting the public interest; education, civil and criminal justice, health sciences, int. affairs, labour and population, science and technology, national security, information processing systems; non-profit instn receiving funds from federal, state and local government, foundations and the private sector; 718 research professionals; Pres. Dr JAMES A. THOMSON; Chair. ANN MCLAUGHLIN KOROLOGOS; publs *RAND Journal of Economics* (online), *RAND Research Review* (3 a year), *research reports*.

AGRICULTURE, FISHERIES AND VETERINARY SCIENCE

Agricultural Research Institute: 236 Massachusetts Ave NE, Suite 401, Washington, DC 20002; tel. (202) 544-5534; fax (202) 544-5749; f. 1951; 100 mems; forum for agricultural research administrators to discuss agricultural research programmes and needs; Exec. Dir RICHARD A. HERRETT; publ. *Proceedings* (1 a year).

Forest Products Society: 2801 Marshall Court, Madison, WI 53705-2295; tel. (608) 231-1361; fax (608) 231-2152; internet www.forestprod.org; f. 1947; technology transfer concerning all areas of the forest products industry; 2,000 mems in more than 30 countries; Pres. BOB LITTLE; Exec. Vice-Pres. CAROL LEWIS; publs *Forest Products Journal* (10 a year), *Journal of Forest Products*

Business Research (online), *Wood Design Focus* (4 a year).

BIBLIOGRAPHY, LIBRARY SCIENCE AND MUSEOLOGY

Getty Conservation Institute: 1200 Getty Center Dr., Suite 700, Los Angeles, CA 90049-1684; tel. (310) 440-7325; fax (310) 440-7702; e-mail gciweb@getty.edu; internet www.getty.edu/conservation; f. 1985; programme of the J. Paul Getty Trust; works for the preservation of the world's cultural heritage; library of 60,000 vols; Dir TIMOTHY P. WHALEN; Assoc. Dir JEANNE MARIE TEUTONICO; publs *Art and Archaeology Technical Abstracts* (online at aata.getty.edu/nps), *Conservation Perspectives: the GCI Newsletter* (2 a year).

Institute for Scientific Information: 3501 Market St, Philadelphia, PA 19104; internet www.isinet.com; f. 1960; periodicals library of 8,000 titles; current contents in the following editions: *Agriculture, Arts and Humanities; Biochemistry and Biophysics Citation Index Biology and Environmental Sciences; Biotechnology CitationIndex, Chemical and Earth Sciences; Chemistry Citation Index, Clinical Medicine; Engineering, Technology and Applied Sciences; Life Sciences; Materials Science Citation Index, Mathematical Science Citation Index, Neuroscience Citation Index, Physical, Social and Behavioural Sciences;*; online databases include: *Arts and Humanities Search, Computer and Mathematics Search, Current Contents Search, ISTP and B Search, ISTP Search, Research Alert Direct Scisearch, Social Scisearch,*(products available in print and in electronic form); Pres. and CEO MICHAEL TANSEY; publs *Arts and Humanities Citation Index, CompuMath Citation Index, Current Chemical Reactions, Index Chemicus, Index to Scientific Book Contents, Index to Scientific Reviews, Index to Scientific and Technical Proceedings, Index to Social Sciences and Humanities Proceedings, Science Citation Index, Social Sciences Citation Index.*

National Federation of Advanced Information Services: 1518 Walnut St, Suite 1004, Philadelphia, PA 19102-3403; tel. (215) 893-1561; fax (215) 893-1564; e-mail nfais@nfais.org; internet www.nfais.org; f. 1958; aims to serve the world's information community through education, research, and publication; 63 mem. orgs; Pres. TERENCE FORD; Exec. Dir BONNIE LAWLOR; publ. *NFAIS eNotes* (12 a year).

Smithsonian Center for Education and Museum Studies: Rm 2235, Arts and Industries Bldg, 900 Jefferson Drive, SW, Washington, DC; tel. (202) 633-1000; e-mail educate@si.edu; internet museumstudies.si.edu; interprets the collective knowledge of the Smithsonian Institution and serves as a gateway to the Institution's education resources; library: merged library of collections from the Museum Reference Center and Central Reference and Loan Services branch libraries; part of the Smithsonian Institution Libraries system; publ. *Center for Museum Studies Bulletin.*

Smithsonian Museum Conservation Institute: Museum Support Centre, 4210 Silver Hill Rd, Suitland, MD 20746; tel. (301) 238-1240; fax (301) 238-3709; e-mail mciweb@si.edu; internet www.si.edu/mci; f. 1963; research in the fields of conservation and the scientific study of colln materials; Dir Dr ROBERT J. KOESTLER.

ECONOMICS, LAW AND POLITICS

Brookings Institution: 1775 Massachusetts Ave NW, Washington, DC 20036; tel. (202) 797-6000; fax (202) 797-6004; internet www.brook.edu; f. 1916; research, education, and publishing in the fields of economics, government and foreign policy; 61 professional mems; library of 75,000 vols, 700 periodical titles, files of pamphlets and govt documents, selected UN documents; Pres. STROBE TALBOTT; Chair. JOHN L. THORNTON; publs *Brookings Papers on Economic Activity* (3 a year), *Brookings Papers on Education Policy, Brookings Trade Forum* (1 a year), *Brookings–Wharton Papers on Financial Services, Brookings–Wharton Papers on Urban Affairs, The Brookings Review* (4 a year).

Center for Strategic and International Studies (CSIS): 1800 K St NW, Washington, DC 20006; tel. (202) 887-0200; fax (202) 775-3199; internet www.csis.org; research into new challenges to national and international peace and security; helps to develop new methods of governance for the global age through programmes in technology and public policy, energy, and international trade and finance; Pres. and CEO JOHN H. HAMRE; publ. *Washington Quarterly.*

Center for the Study of Democratic Institutions: 10951 West Pico Blvd, Suite 300, Los Angeles, CA 90064; tel. (310) 474-0011; fax (310) 474-8061; e-mail nfo@npq.org; internet www.digitalnpq.org; f. 1959, fmrly Robert Maynard Hutchins Center for the Study of Democratic Institutions; Exec. Dir (vacant); publ. *New Perspectives Quarterly.*

Counterpart International, Inc.: 2345 Crystal Dr., Suite 301, Arlington, VA 22202; tel. (703) 236-1200; fax (703) 412-5035; e-mail communications@counterpart.org; internet www.counterpart.org; f. 1965 as Foundation for the Peoples of the South Pacific to develop civil society, promote economic self-sufficiency and public health and encourage sustainable environmental management; present name 1992; attached offices in New York and Los Angeles, CA; operates programmes in Armenia, Azerbaijan, Belarus, Bosnia and Herzegovina, Bulgaria, Fiji, Georgia, Guatemala, India, Iraq, Kazakhstan, Kiribati, Kyrgyzstan, Moldova, Papua New Guinea, Russia, Samoa, Senegal, Solomon Islands, Tajikistan, Tonga, Turkmenistan, Tuvalu, Ukraine, Uzbekistan, Vanuatu and Viet Nam; Pres. and CEO LELEI LELAULU.

East-West Center: 1601 East-West Rd, Honolulu, HI 96848-1601; tel. (808) 944-7111; fax (808) 944-7376; e-mail ewcinfo@eastwestcenter.org; internet www.eastwestcenter.org; f. 1960; a public, non-profit educational institution with an international board of governors; research fellows, graduate students, and professionals in government, academia and business each year work with the Center's international staff in cooperative study, training, and research; they examine major issues related to international relations, population, resources, economic development and the environment in Asia, the Pacific and the USA; Pres. Dr CHARLES E. MORRISON; publs *Asia Pacific Issues Paper* (irregular), *Observer* (4 a year).

International Center for Economic Growth: University of the Pacific, 3601 Pacifica Ave, Stockton, CA 94104; tel. (209) 946-3265; fax (209) 496-2650; internet www.iceg.com; f. 1985 to promote economic growth and human development in developing and post-socialist countries, by strengthening the capacity of local research institutes to provide project leadership; operates in conjunction with 370 mem. institutes globally; sponsors conferences and seminars; CEO ROBERT HODAM.

International Marketing Institute: 314 Hammond St, Suite 52, Chestnut Hill, MA 02467-3951; tel. (617) 552-8690; fax (617) 552-2590; f. 1960; affiliated to Boston College Graduate School of Management; int. executive devt and management training programmes in management education, with marketing as the primary focus; Exec. Dir JOSEPH B. GANNON.

Marketing Science Institute: 1000 Massachusetts Ave, Cambridge, MA 02138-5396; tel. (617) 491-2060; fax (617) 491-2065; e-mail msi@msi.org; internet www.msi.org; f. 1961; non-profit marketing consortium that stimulates, supports and reports research in order to advance marketing knowledge and practice; sponsors and publishes academic research on all areas of marketing; 65 mem. companies; Chair. GORDON A. WYNER; Exec. Dir LEIGH MCALISTER; publ. *MSI Reports* (4 a year).

National Bureau of Economic Research: 1050 Massachusetts Ave, Cambridge, MA 02138; tel. (617) 868-3900; fax (617) 868-2742; internet www.nber.org; f. 1920; fundamental qualitative analysis of the US economy; 50 dirs; Pres. and CEO MARTIN FELDSTEIN; publs *Digest* (12 a year), *NBER Reporter* (4 a year).

Scripps Foundation for Research in Population Problems and Gerontology Center: Scripps Gerontology Center, 396 Upham Hall, Oxford, OH 45056; tel. (513) 529-2914; fax (513) 529-1476; e-mail scripps@muohio.edu; internet www.scripps.muohio.edu; f. 1922; 20 mems; library of 4,000 vols; Dir SUZANNE R. KUNKEL.

EDUCATION

American Educational Research Association: 1230 17th St, NW, Washington, DC 20036-3078; tel. (202) 223-9485; fax (202) 775-1824; internet www.aera.net; f. 1916; 22,000 mems; Pres. WILLIAM TATE; publs *American Educational Research Journal, Educational Evaluation and Policy Analysis, Educational Researcher, Journal of Educational and Behavioral Statistics, Review of Educational Research, Review of Research in Education.*

Institute of Education Sciences (IES): 555 New Jersey Ave NW, Washington, DC 20208; tel. (202) 219-1385; e-mail contact.ies@ed.gov; internet ies.ed.gov; f. 2002, fmrly the Office of Educational Research and Improvement (f. 1980), which was dissolved and reinstituted as IES after the Education Sciences Reform Act 2002 was signed into law; attached to US Dept of Education; funds research studies on ways to improve academic achievement, conducts large-scale evaluations of federal education programmes and reports a wide array of statistics on the condition of education, disseminates information through 10 regional education laboratories and 10 nat. research and devt centres; Dir JOHN Q. EASTON; publ. *National Assessment of Educational Progress.*

National Science Resources Center: 901 D Street, SW, Suite 704B, Washington, DC 20024-0952; tel. (202) 633-2978; fax (202) 287-2070; internet www.nsrconline.org; f. 1985; operated by the Smithsonian Institution, National Academy of Sciences, National Academy of Engineering and Institute of Medicine to improve the teaching of science in schools; Exec. Dir SALLY GOETZ SHULER.

HISTORY, GEOGRAPHY AND ARCHAEOLOGY

Center for Reformation Research: 801 Seminary Pl., St Louis, MO 63105; tel. (314) 505-7199; f. 1957; microfilm library of original MSS and printed materials of the 15th and 16th centuries; reference library; Exec. Dir ROBERT ROSIN.

Leo Baeck Institute, Inc.: Center for Jewish History, 15 West 16th St, New York, NY 10011; tel. (212) 744-6400; fax (212) 988-1305; e-mail lbaeck@lbi.cjh.org; internet www.lbi.org; f. 1955; research and documentation on German Jewish history; exhibitions and lectures; library of 70,000 vols in German, English and Hebrew, archives of family papers, community histories, business and public records, 1,300 personal memoirs, 20,000 photographs (access to archive and library materials is available only through reading room of the Center for Jewish History); art collection; 1,100 mems; Exec. Dir CAROL KAHN STRAUSS; Head Librarian RENATE EVERS; publs *Bulletin des Leo Baeck Instituts* (in French), *Jüdischer Almanach des LBI* (in German), *LBI Yearbook*, *News*, *Overview*.

Mississippi Office of Geology: POB 2279, Jackson, MS 39225; tel. (601) 961-5500; fax (601) 961-5521; internet www.deq.state.ms.us/mdeq.nsf/page/geology_home; f. 1850; research into geology and mineral resources of the state; library of 60,000 vols; Dir MICHAEL B. E. BOGRAD; publs *Mississippi Geology*, bulletins, geologic maps.

Paleontological Research Institution: 1259 Trumansburg Rd, Ithaca, NY 14850; tel. (607) 273-6623; fax (607) 273-6620; internet www.museumoftheearth.org; f. 1932; colln of 3m. specimens; 900 mems; library of 50,000 vols; Dir Dr WARREN D. ALLMON; Assoc. Dir for Science Dr PAULA M. MIKKELSEN; publs *American Paleontologist* (4 a year), *Bulletins of American Paleontology* (2 a year), *Palaeontographica Americana* (irregular).

School for Advanced Research on the Human Experience: POB 2188, Santa Fe, NM 87504-2188; tel. (505) 954-7200; fax (505) 989-9809; internet www.sarweb.org; f. 1907; centre for advanced studies in anthropology and the humanities; grants to 6 resident scholars, incl. 1 native American, annually; native artist fellows; advanced seminars in anthropology; anthropological publs; extensive collns in south-west American Indian art; 2,000 mems; library of 6,000 vols; Pres. JAMES F. BROOKS; Chair. JEREMY SABLOFF.

LANGUAGE AND LITERATURE

Harry Ransom Humanities Research Center, The University of Texas at Austin: POB 7219, Austin, TX 78713-7219; tel. (512) 471-8944; fax (512) 471-9646; internet www.hrc.utexas.edu; f. 1957; specializes in American, British and French literature and art since 19th century; library of 1,000,000 vols, 40,000,000 MSS, 5,000,000 photographs; Dir THOMAS F. STALEY.

MEDICINE

American Association for Cancer Research, Inc.: c/o Dr Margaret Foti, 615 Chestnut St, 17th Fl., Philadelphia, PA 19106-4404; tel. (215) 440-9300; fax (215) 440-9313; e-mail meetings@aacr.org; internet www.aacr.org; f. 1907; facilitates communication and dissemination of knowledge among scientists and others dedicated to cancer research; 20,000 mems; Pres. Dr KAREN S. H. ANTMAN; CEO Dr MARGARET FOTI; publs *Cancer Epidemiology, Biomarkers & Prevention* (12 a year), *Cancer Research* (24 a year), *Clinical Cancer Research* (12 a year), *Molecular Cancer Research* (12 a year), *Molecular Cancer Therapeutics* (12 a year).

American Federation for Medical Research: 900 Cummings Center, Suite 221-U, Beverly, MA 01915; tel. (978) 927-8330; fax (978) 524-8890; e-mail afmr@prri.com; internet www.afmr.org; f. 1940; 2,500 mems; Pres. Dr FRANCIS J. MILLER; Secretary and Treasurer ROBERT J. FREISHTAT; publ. *Journal of Investigative Medicine* (8 a year).

Association for Research in Nervous and Mental Disease, Inc.: Weill Medical College of Cornell Univ., Dept of Psychiatry, 1300 York Ave, POB 171, Room F-1231, New York, NY 10065; tel. (212) 746-3770; fax (212) 746-8546; e-mail daw2026@med.cornell.edu; internet www.arnmd.org; f. 1920; annual meeting for continuing medical education credits on research topics of interest to neurologists and psychiatrists; Chair. JACK D. BARCHAS; Exec. Dir DAN WEIMAN; publ. *Clinical Neuroscience Research* (6 a year).

Association for Research in Vision and Ophthalmology, Inc.: 12300 Twinbrook Parkway, Suite 250, Bethesda, MD 20852-1606; tel. (240) 221-2900; fax (240) 221-0370; e-mail mem@arvo.org; internet www.arvo.org; f. 1928; 10,800 mems; Exec. Vice-Pres. Dr PAUL KAUFMAN; publs *Investigative Ophthalmology and Visual Science*, *Journal of Vision* (irregular).

California Pacific Medical Center Research Institute: 2340 Clay St, 5th Fl., San Francisco, CA 94115; tel. (415) 561-1601; fax (415) 561-1753; internet www.cpmc.org/professionals/research; f. 1959; non-profit research division of medical centre conducting patient-orientated research in arthritis, HIV/AIDS, cancer, including leukemia and monoclonal antibodies, heart disease, immunology and infectious diseases, artificial heart research, organ transplantation and preservation, neurology, maternal foetal medicine, child health and human development; Dir WARREN S. BROWNER.

Fox Chase Cancer Center: 333 Cottman Ave, Philadelphia, PA 19111-2497; tel. (215) 728-6900; fax (215) 728-3655; internet www.fccc.edu; f. 1926; library of 22,000 vols, including 5,000 monographs and 440 scientific journals; Pres. Dr ROBERT C. YOUNG.

Huntington Medical Research Institutes: 734 Fairmount Ave, Pasadena, CA 91105; tel. (818) 397-5436; fax (818) 397-3330; internet www.hmri.org; f. 1952; oncology, cell biology, differentiated cell culture, cancer genetics, prostatic cancer, immunotherapy, biomedical magnetic resonance spectroscopy, cardiology, development of neural prosthetic devices; Exec. Dir WILLIAM OPEL.

Jackson Laboratory: 600 Main St, Bar Harbor, Maine 04609-1500; tel. (207) 288-6000; fax (207) 288-6079; e-mail pubinfo@jax.org; internet www.jax.org; f. 1929; research in molecular genetics, cell biology, biochemistry, immunology and physiological genetics; library of 3,000 vols, 20,000 bound journals, 370 current journals, 46,000 article reprints; Dir Dr RICHARD WOYCHIK; publs *Inside the Jackson Laboratory* (4 a year), *Scientific Report* (1 a year), *Training for Research* (1 a year).

Lovelace Respiratory Research Institute: 2425 Ridgecrest Drive, SE, Albuquerque, NM 87108-5127; tel. (505) 348-9400; fax (505) 348-8541; f. 1947 to conduct biomedical research and technology development; 300 mems; library of 10,000 books and 116 current journals; Pres. and CEO ROBERT RUBIN; publ. *Advances*.

Mayo Clinic: 200 First St SW, Rochester, MN 55905; tel. (507) 284-2511; fax (507) 284-0161; internet www.mayo.edu; f. 1919; clinical medicine, medical research, graduate and undergraduate education; also located at Scottsdale, AZ, and Jacksonville, FL; library of 275,000 vols and 3,500 periodicals; Chair. Board of Trustees JAMES L. BARKSDALE; Pres. and CEO Dr DENNIS A. CORTESE; Admin. J. H. HERRELL; publ. *Mayo Clinic Proceedings* (12 a year).

Memorial Sloan-Kettering Cancer Center: 1275 York Ave, New York, NY 10021; tel. (212) 639-2000; internet www.mskcc.org; f. 1948; research in physical and biological sciences relating to cancer; postdoctoral research training in laboratory investigations with scientific staff; graduate instruction with Cornell University; Pres. Dr HAROLD VARMUS.

Menninger: 2801 Gessner Drive, POB 809045, Houston, TX 77280-9045; tel. (713) 275-5000; fax (713) 275-5117; e-mail webmaster@menninger.edu; f. 1925; non-profit mental health centre for inpatient and outpatient treatment of mental illness through preventive psychiatry, clinical treatment, research and professional education; library of 50,000 vols; Pres. and CEO IAN AITKEN; publs *Bulletin of the Menninger Clinic* (4 a year), *Menninger Perspective* (4 a year).

National Institutes of Health: US Dept of Health and Human Services, Public Health Service, Bethesda, MD 20892; tel. (301) 496-4000; fax (301) 496-0019; internet www.nih.gov; f. 1887; prin. agency of DHHS for biomedical research, research training, and biomedical communications; Nat. Library of Medicine: see Libraries and Archives; Dir Dr ELIAS A. ZERHOUNI.

Constituent Institutes:

'Eunice Kennedy Shriver' National Institute of Child Health and Human Development: Bldg 31, Room 2A32, MSC 2425, 31 Center Dr., Bethesda, MD 20892-2425; tel. (301) 496-5133; fax (301) 496-7101; internet www.nichd.nih.gov; f. 1963; supports, fosters and coordinates research and training in areas of maternal health, child health and human development, focusing on the continuing process of growth and development, biological and behavioural; also supports research in the population sciences, incl. contraceptive devt and evaluation, reproductive health, behavioural and demographic research, and medical rehabilitation; Dir Dr DUANE ALEXANDER.

National Cancer Institute: Bldg 31, Room 11A4, 31 Center Dr., Bethesda, MD 20892; tel. (301) 496-5615; fax (301) 402-0338; internet www.nci.nih.gov; f. 1937; prin. federal govt agency for cancer research; supports research into the causes, prevention, early detection and treatment of cancer, and into supportive care; cooperates with state and local health agencies and voluntary bodies; Dir Dr ANDREW C. VON ESCHENBACH.

National Eye Institute: c/o National Institutes of Health, 31 Center Dr., MSC 2510, Bethesda, MD 20892-2510; tel. (301) 496-2234; fax (301) 496-9970; internet www.nei.nih.gov; f. 1968; conducts and supports research, training, health information dissemination, and other programmes relating to blinding eye diseases, visual disorders, mechanisms of visual function, preservation of sight; special health problems and requirements of the blind; research performed in Institute's own laboratories and through contracts; supports training, and directs Nat. Eye Health Education Program; Dir Dr PAUL A. SIEVING.

National Heart, Lung and Blood Institute: POB 30105, Bethesda, MD 20824-0105; Bldg 31, Room 5A52, 31 Center Dr., MSC 2486, Bethesda, MD 20892; tel. (301) 592-8573; fax (240) 629-3246; e-mail nhlbiinfo@nhlbi.nih.gov; internet www

.nhlbi.nih.gov; f. 1948 as Nat. Heart Institute, redesignated 1969 and 1976; performs and supports research in diseases of the heart, blood vessels, lungs (exclusive of pulmonary malignancies) and blood; Dir Dr ELIZABETH NABEL.

National Human Genome Research Institute (NHGRI): Bldg 31, Room 4B09, 31 Center Dr., MSC 2152, 9000 Rockville Pike Bethesda, MD 20892-2152; tel. (301) 402-0911; fax (301) 402-2218; internet www.genome.gov; f. 1989; directs and supports work on the sequencing of the human genome; funds research on the genome's structure, function and role in health and disease; supports studies on the ethical, legal and social implications (ELSI) of genome research; Dir Dr FRANCIS S. COLLINS.

National Institute on Aging: Bldg 31, Room 5C27, 31 Center Dr., MSC 2292, Bethesda, MD 20892; tel. (301) 496-1752; fax (301) 496-1072; e-mail webmaster@nia.nih.gov; internet www.nia.nih.gov; f. 1974; conducts and supports biomedical, social and behavioural research and training related to the ageing process and diseases, and other special problems and needs of the aged; Dir Dr RICHARD J. HODES.

National Institute on Alcohol Abuse and Alcoholism (NIAAA): 5635 Fishers Lane, MSC 9304, Bethesda, MD 20892-9304; internet www.niaaa.nih.gov; f. 1970; conducts and supports research in a wide range of scientific areas, incl. genetics, neuroscience, epidemiology, health risks and benefits of alcohol consumption, prevention and treatment; Dir Dr TING-KAI LI.

National Institute of Allergy and Infectious Diseases: 6610 Rockledge Dr., MSC 6612, Bethesda, MD 20892-6612; tel. (301) 496-5717; fax (301) 402-3573; e-mail ocpostoffice@niaid.nih.gov; internet www.niaid.nih.gov; f. 1948; supports basic and translational research to prevent, diagnose and treat infectious diseases such as HIV/AIDS and other sexually transmitted infections, influenza, tuberculosis, malaria and illness from potential agents of bioterrorism; supports research on transplantation and immune-related illnesses, incl. autoimmune disorders, asthma and allergies; 14,000 mems; Dir Dr ANTHONY S. FAUCI.

National Institute of Arthritis and Musculoskeletal and Skin Diseases: 1 AMS Circle Bethesda, MD 20892-3675; tel. (301) 495-4484; fax (301) 718-6366; e-mail niamsinfo@mail.nih.gov; internet www.niams.nih.gov; f. 1986; research into the causes, treatment and prevention of arthritis and musculoskeletal and skin diseases; training of basic and clinical scientists to carry out this research; dissemination of information on progress in research; Dir Dr STEPHEN I. KATZ.

National Institute for Biomedical Imaging and Bioengineering (NIBIB): 6707 Democracy Blvd, Suite 202, Bethesda, MD 20892-5477; tel. (301) 451-6768; internet www.nibib.nih.gov; f. 2000; Dir Dr RODERIC PETTIGREW.

National Institute on Deafness and Other Communication Disorders: Bldg 31, Room 3C02, 31 Center Dr., MSC 2320, Bethesda, MD 20892-2320; tel. (301) 496-7243; fax (301) 402-0018; internet www.nidcd.nih.gov; f. 1988; supports and conducts research on the normal processes and diseases of human communication, incl. hearing, balance, smell, taste, voice, speech and language; fosters training and disseminates science-based health information; Dir Dr JAMES F. BATTEY.

National Institute of Dental and Craniofacial Research: Nat. Institutes of Health, 31 Center Dr., MSC 2290, Bethesda, MD 20892-2290; tel. (301) 496-9469; fax (301) 402-2185; internet www.nidcr.nih.gov; f. 1948; conducts and supports research and training with the aim of preventing, diagnosing and treating dental, oral and craniofacial diseases and conditions; Dir Dr LAWRENCE TABAK.

National Institute of Diabetes and Digestive and Kidney Diseases: c/o US Dept of Health and Human Services, Public Health Service, Bethesda, MD 20892; tel. (301) 496-3583; fax (301) 496-7422; e-mail niddk_inquiries@nih.gov; internet www.niddk.nih.gov; f. 1950, renamed 1986; conducts and supports research into diabetes, endocrinology, metabolic diseases, digestive diseases, nutrition, kidney and urologic diseases and haematology; information and education activities; Dir Dr ALLEN M. SPIEGEL.

National Institute on Drug Abuse (NIDA): 6001 Executive Blvd, Room 5213, Bethesda, MD 20892-9561; tel. (301) 443-1124; e-mail information@lists.nida.nih.gov; internet www.nida.nih.gov; f. 1974; Dir Dr NORA VOLKOW.

National Institute of Environmental Health Sciences: c/o US Dept of Health and Human Services, Public Health Service, Research Triangle Park, NC 27709; tel. (919) 541-1919; fax (919) 541-2260; internet www.niehs.nih.gov; f. 1969; conducts, fosters and coordinates research on the biological effects of chemical, physical and biological substances present in or introduced into the environment; Dir Dr DAVID SCHWARTZ; publ. *Environmental Health Perspectives* (12 a year).

National Institute of General Medical Sciences: c/o US Dept of Health and Human Services, Public Health Service, Bethesda, MD 20892; tel. (301) 594-2172; fax (301) 402-0156; e-mail cassmanm@nih.gov; internet www.nigms.nih.gov; f. 1962; supports a programme of research and training in the basic medical sciences; Dir Dr JEREMY M. BERG.

National Institute of Mental Health (NIMH): 6001 Executive Blvd, Room 8184, MSC 9663, Bethesda, MD 20892-9663; tel. (301) 443-4513; fax (301) 443-4279; e-mail nimhinfo@nih.gov; internet www.nimh.nih.gov; f. 1946; improves mental health through biomedical research on the mind, brain and behaviour; Dir Dr THOMAS R. INSEL.

National Institute of Neurological Disorders and Stroke: Brain Resources and Information Network (BRAIN), POB 5801, Bethesda, MD 20892-2540; tel. (301) 496-5751; fax (301) 402-2186; e-mail braininfo@ninds.nih.gov; internet www.ninds.nih.gov; f. 1950; conducts, supports, fosters and coordinates research on the causes, prevention, diagnosis and treatment of disorders of the brain and nervous system; Dir Dr STORY C. LANDIS.

National Institute of Nursing Research: c/o US Dept of Health and Human Services, Public Health Service, Bethesda, MD 20892; internet www.nih.gov/ninr; f. 1993; supports and conducts scientific research and research training to strengthen nursing practice and health care for prevention and amelioration of disease and disability; Dir Dr PATRICIA GRADY.

Naval Aerospace Medicine Institute: Pensacola, FL 32508-1047; f. 1939; training in aviation and aerospace medicine; library of 20,000 vols; Commanding Officer Capt. R. E. HAIN.

Radiation Research Society: 810 E 10th St, Lawrence, KS 66044; tel. (785) 843-1234; fax (785) 843-1274; e-mail info@radres.org; internet www.radres.org; f. 1952; 1,500 mems; Pres. PETER CORRY; Sec. and Treas. BRUCE KIMLER; publ. *Radiation Research* (12 a year).

Schepens Eye Research Institute: 20 Staniford St, Boston, MA 02114; tel. (617) 912-0100; fax (617) 912-0101; internet www.theschepens.org; f. 1950; basic and clinical research on causes, prevention and treatment of eye diseases, development of diagnostic and therapeutic devices, instruments and techniques for ophthalmology, study of the processes of vision; library of 200 vols, 100 journals; Chair. KENNETT F. BURNES; publ. *Sundial*.

Society for Pediatric Research: 3400 Research Forest Drive, Suite B7, The Woodlands, TX 77381; tel. (281) 419-0052; fax (281) 419-0082; e-mail info@aps-spr.org; internet www.aps-spr.org; f. 1929; Exec. Dir DEBBIE ANAGNOSTELIS; Exec. Sec. BRENDA PAPKE; publ. *Pediatric Research Journal*.

Southwest Foundation for Biomedical Research: POB 760549, San Antonio, TX 78425-0549; tel. (210) 258-9400; internet www.sfbr.org; f. 1941; basic research in biomedical sciences; designated in 1999 one of the regional primate research centres (Southwest Regional Primate Research Center); library of 50,000 journal vols; 6,700 books; Chair. JOHN C. KERR; Scientific Dir Dr ROBERT E. SHADE; publ. *Progress in Biomedical Research* (irregular).

Wistar Institute of Anatomy and Biology: 36th and Spruce Sts, Philadelphia, PA 19104; tel. (215) 898-3700; fax (215) 573-2097; internet www.wistar.org; f. 1892; cellular and subcellular research in human diseases; library of 10,000 vols; Dir Dr RUSSEL E. KAUFMAN.

NATURAL SCIENCES

General

Battelle Memorial Institute: 505 King Ave, Columbus, OH 43201-2693; tel. (800) 201-2011; e-mail solutions@battelle.org; internet www.battelle.org; f. 1929; serves industry and Govt in the generation, application and commercialization of technology; supports research and devt activities of clients in 30 countries; major areas of activity are health and environment, products and processes, technology management consulting, nat. security, energy; research operations in the USA and Europe; offices worldwide; library: more than 150,000 vols; Pres. and Chief Exec. JEFFREY WADSWORTH; Library Man. KEMBERLY LANG.

Carnegie Institution for Science: 1530 P St, NW, Washington, DC 20005; tel. (202) 387-6400; fax (202) 387-8092; internet www.carnegiescience.edu; f. 1902; research and education in the biological, physical, materials, earth and planetary sciences, astronomy and global ecology; 80 faculty mems; Chair. Bd of Trustees MICHAEL GELLERT; Pres. RICHARD MESERVE; publ. *Carnegie Science* (3 a year).

Attached Departments:

Department of Embryology: 3520 San Martin Dr., Baltimore, MD 21218; tel. (410) 246-3001; f. 1914; Dir ALLAN C. SPRADLING.

Department of Global Ecology: 260 Panama St, Stanford, CA 94305; tel. (650) 325-1521; f. 2002; Dir CHRISTOPHER FIELD.

Department of Plant Biology: 290 Panama St, Stanford, CA 94305; tel. (650) 325-1521; f. 1903 as Desert Laboratory; Dir CHRISTOPHER SOMERVILLE.

Department of Terrestrial Magnetism: 5241 Broad Branch Rd, NW, Washington, DC 20015; tel. (202) 478-8820; f. 1904; Dir SEAN C. SOLOMON.

Geophysical Laboratory: 5251 Broad Branch Rd, NW, Washington, DC 20015; tel. (202) 478-8900; f. 1906; Dir WESLEY HUNTRESS.

Observatories of the Carnegie Institution: 813 Santa Barbara St, Pasadena, CA 91101; tel. (626) 577-1122; internet www.obs.carnegiescience.edu; f. 1904 as Mount Wilson Observatory; Dir WENDY FREEDMAN.

Midwest Research Institute: 425 Volker Blvd, Kansas City, MO 64110; tel. (816) 753-7600; fax (816) 753-8420; e-mail info@mriresearch.org; internet www.mriresearch.org; f. 1944; 1,300 mems; specialization in chemistry, biological sciences, toxicology, health sciences, environmental sciences, engineering, energy, economics, management sciences, human services, safety, agriculture and food safety; Pres. Dr JAMES SPIGARELLI; Chair. LOUIS W. SMITH.

Smithsonian Environmental Research Center (SERC): POB 28, 647 Contees Wharf Rd, Edgewater, MD 21037; tel. (443) 482-2200; fax (443) 482-2380; internet www.serc.si.edu; f. 1965; administered by the Smithsonian Institution; multi-disciplinary instn dedicated to increasing knowledge of the biological and physical processes that sustain life on earth; scientific programmes: animal–plant interactions, bio-geochemistry, chemical ecology, ecological modelling, estuarine zoology, forest ecology, invasion studies, micro–zooplankton, phyto-plankton, plant ecophysiology, plant ecology, plant physiology, solar radiation, terrestrial animal ecology; part of the Smithsonian Marine Science Network; library: branch library of the Smithsonian Institution Libraries system: 12,500 books and bound journals, 120 current journals, collection of *Chesapeakiana*; Dir ANSON HINES; Librarian ANGELA HAGGINS.

Southern Research Institute: POB 55305, Birmingham, AL 35255-5305; tel. (205) 581-2000; fax (205) 581-2726; internet www2.southernresearch.org; f. 1941; contract scientific research in the areas of pharmaceutical discovery and development, engineering, environmental and energy-related sciences; library of 40,000 vols; Pres. and CEO ROBERT C. LONERGAN; Chair. CAROL GARRISON.

World Resources Institute: 10 G St NE, Suite 800, Washington, DC 20002; tel. (202) 729-7600; fax (202) 729-7610; e-mail front@wri.org; internet www.wri.org; f. 1982; provides information about global resources and environmental conditions, analysis of emerging issues, and development of creative yet workable policy responses; seeks to deepen public understanding by publishing a variety of reports and papers, undertaking briefings, seminars and conferences, and offering material for use in the press and on the air; Pres. JONATHAN LASH; Man. Dir MANISH BAPNA.

Biological Sciences

Boyce Thompson Institute for Plant Research, Inc.: Cornell University, Tower Rd, Ithaca, NY 14853; tel. (607) 254-1234; fax (607) 254-1242; internet bti.cornell.edu; f. 1924; non-profit affiliate of Cornell University; research on plants and human health, including molecular biology, biochemistry, plant physiology, plant pathology, entomology, air and water pollution; library of 4,700 vols; Pres. and CEO DAVID B. STERN; Vice-Pres. for Finance and Administration JOHN M. DENTES; Vice-Pres. for Research GARY BLISSARD.

Cold Spring Harbor Laboratory: POB 100, Cold Spring Harbor, NY 11724; tel. (516) 367-8397; fax (516) 367-8496; internet www.cshl.org; f. 1890, chartered under present title 1962; research on cancer biology, molecular neuroscience, structural biology, plant genetics, professional education, DNA literacy; library of 30,000 vols, spec. colln on history of science and genetics; Pres. and CEO Dr BRUCE W. STILLMAN; publs *Abstracts of Papers*, *Banbury Reports* (irregular), *Cancer Surveys*, *CSH Current Communications in Cell and Molecular Biology*, *CSH Monographs* (irregular), *Genes and Development* (6 a year), *Genome Research* (12 a year), *Learning and Memory* (6 a year), *Symposia on Quantitative Biology* (1 a year).

Marine Biological Laboratory: 7 MBL St, Woods Hole, MA 02543; tel. (508) 548-3705; fax (508) 540-6902; e-mail comm@mbl.edu; internet www.mbl.edu; f. 1888; research and teaching instn; offers courses and seminars on ecology, behaviour, developmental biology, microbiology, neurobiology, parasitology, cell and molecular biology and biological techniques, global infectious diseases; library of 150,000 vols, 3,000 periodicals; Dir and CEO GARY G. BORISY; Chair. of Board JOHN W. ROWE; publs *Biological Bulletin* (6 a year), *Catalyst Magazine* (2 a year), *Lab Notes* (4 a year).

Missouri Botanical Garden: POB 299, St Louis, MO 63166-0299; tel. (314) 577-5100; fax (314) 577-9595; internet www.mobot.org; f. 1859; botanical research, exploration, education and display, with emphases on monographic and floristic studies in N America, tropical Latin America and Africa; archives and non-book materials, herbarium colln (5.8m. vascular plants and 300,000 bryophytes); library of 175,000 vols, spec. collns: Pre-Linnaean, Linnaean, rare books; Pres. Prof. PETER RAVEN; publs *Annals* (4 a year), *Bulletin* (7 a year), *Monographs in Systematic Botany* (irregular), *Novon* (4 a year).

Moss Landing Marine Laboratories: POB 450, Moss Landing, CA 95039; tel. (831) 771-4400; fax (831) 632-4403; internet www.mlml.calstate.edu; f. 1966; research, undergraduate and postgraduate education in the marine sciences; library of 10,000 vols; Dir Dr KENNETH COALE.

Mote Marine Laboratory, Inc.: 1600 Ken Thompson Parkway, Sarasota, FL 34236-1096; tel. (941) 388-4441; fax (941) 388-4312; e-mail info@mote.org; internet www.mote.org; f. 1955; ind., non-profit marine research org.; research incl. environmental assessment, estuarine and coastal ecology, marine chemistry, toxicology, biology and behaviour of fishes, aquaculture, biomedical research, marine mammals, sea turtles and biomedical research; aquarium and environmental education programmes; library of 28,000 vols, 16,000 books and documents, 400 journal titles, 3,500 reprints; Chair. ARTHUR L. ARMITAGE; Pres. KUMAR MAHADEVAN; publs *Collected Papers* (every 3 years), *Mote Magazine* (1 a year), *Mote Technical Reports* (irregular).

New England Aquarium: Central Wharf, Boston, MA 02110; tel. (617) 973-5200; internet www.neaq.org; f. 1969; 11,000 mems; public aquarium, research programmes; library of 3,000 vols; Pres. and CEO EDMUND C. TOOMEY; publ. *Aqualog* (4 a year).

New York Botanical Garden: 200th St and Kzimiroff Blvd, Bronx, NY 10458-5126; tel. (718) 817-8632; fax (718) 220-6405; internet www.nybg.org; f. 1891; 250 acres of gardens, plant collections and wild areas, including a National Landmark conservatory; museum building includes herbarium housing some 7m. specimens; library: over 1m. items, incl. 196,000 vols; Pres. GREGORY LONG; publs *Advances in Economic Botany* (irregular), *Botanical Review* (4 a year), *Brittonia* (4 a year), *Contributions* (irregular), *Economic Botany* (4 a year), *Flora Neotropica* (irregular), *Intermountain Flora* (irregular), *Memoirs* (irregular), *North American Flora* (irregular).

Salk Institute for Biological Studies: POB 85800, San Diego, CA 92186-5800; tel. (858) 453-4100; fax (858) 552-8285; internet www.salk.edu; f. 1960; 550 mems; advanced biological research into HIV/AIDS, cancer, neuroendocrinology, developmental neurobiology, peptide biology, molecular biology, plant biology, prebiotic chemistry, language studies, neuropsychology, immunology, molecular neurobiology and neurophysiology; library of 15,000 vols; Pres. Dr RICHARD A. MURPHY.

Smithsonian Gardens: POB 37012, Capital Gallery, Suite 3300, MRC 506, Washington, DC 20013-7012; tel. (202) 633-2220; fax (202) 633-5697; e-mail gardens@si.edu; internet gardens.si.edu; f. 1972; research and educational programmes; manages grounds of the Smithsonian Institution museums and creates horticultural exhibitions; library: Archives of American Gardens: 80,000 photographic images, records of historic and contemporary American gardens; special collns: Garden Club of America (40,000 images), J. Horace McFarland (glass lantern slides and photographs), Thomas Warren Sears (glass negatives).

Smithsonian Marine Station at Fort Pierce: 701 Seaway Dr., Fort Pierce, FL 34949; tel. (772) 462-6220; fax (772) 461-8154; e-mail smswebmaster@si.edu; internet www.sms.si.edu; f. 1969; attached to Nat. Museum of Natural History of the Smithsonian Instn; research into marine biodiversity and ecosystems of Florida; Head Scientist Dr VALERIE PAUL.

Smithsonian National Zoological Park: 3001 Connecticut Ave, NW, Washington, DC 20008; tel. (202) 673-4717; e-mail nationalzoo@nzp.si.edu; internet natzoo.si.edu; f. 1889; administered by the Smithsonian Institution; animal colln of 2,800 specimens from 435 species; part of the Smithsonian Marine Science Network; Dir DAVID L. EVANS; publs *CRC World* (published by the Conservation and Research Center Foundation, 4 a year), *ZooGoer* (published by Friends of the National Zoo, 6 a year).

Attached Research Institutes:

Conservation and Research Center: *Rock Creek Research Laboratories*: National Zoo, Rock Creek Park, Washington, DC; *Front Royal Campus*: Front Royal, VA; conservation biology research: Fort Royal Campus–Geographic Information Systems (GIS), endocrine and gamete laboratories, veterinary clinic, 14 field stations; Rock Creek Research Laboratories–department of conservation biology, nutrition laboratory, department of reproductive sciences; Amazonia Science Gallery.

Smithsonian Migratory Bird Center: National Zoological Park, Washington, DC 20008; research into bird migration; Dir RUSSELL GREENBERG.

Physical Sciences

Argonne National Laboratory: 9700 South Cass Ave, Argonne, IL 60439; tel. (630) 252-2000; internet www.anl.gov; f. 1946; multipurpose research laboratory with primary focuses on basic research in the physical, life and environmental sciences, and on technology-directed research in fission, fossil and fusion energy as well as conservation and renewable energy; library of 65,000 vols and 1m. technical reports; Dir Dr ERIC ISAACS; publ. *Argonne Now* (2 a year).

Association of Universities for Research in Astronomy, Inc. (AURA): 1212 New York Ave NW, Suite 450, Washington, DC 20005; tel. (202) 483-2101; fax (202) 483-2106; e-mail dnarcisso@aura-astronomy.org; internet www.aura-astronomy.org; f. 1957; operates the Space Telescope Science Institute, Baltimore, MD, and the Nat. Optical Astronomy Observatories, Tucson, AZ, which consist of the Kitt Peak Nat. Observatory, AZ, the Nat. Solar Observatory, AZ and NM, and Cerro Tololo Inter-American Observatory, Chile; manages the Int. Gemini Project, Tucson, AZ; library of 30,000 vols; Pres. WILLIAM S. SMITH; Vice-Pres. for Admin. DEBORAH NARCISSO.

Byrd Polar Research Center: Scott Hall, Room 108, 1090 Carmack Rd, Ohio State University, Columbus, OH 43210-1002; tel. (614) 292-6531; fax (614) 292-4697; e-mail lyons.142@osu.edu; internet bprc.osu.edu; f. 1960; geology, glaciology, atmospheric sciences, pedology, history, palaeontology, geophysics and remote sensing, palaeoclimatology and environmental policy in polar regions; library of 12,000 vols; papers and memorabilia of Richard E. Byrd, Sir Hubert Wilkins and other polar explorers; Dir Dr BERRY LYONS; publs *Report* (irregular), *Technical Report* (irregular).

Case Astronomy: 10900 Euclid Ave, Cleveland, OH 44106; tel. (216) 368-3728; fax (216) 368-5203; e-mail web@astronomy.case.edu; internet astronomy.case.edu; f. 1920; astronomical research and education at Case Western Reserve University; uses a 9½" telescope on the Cleveland campus; library of 15,000 vols; Dir Prof. R. EARLE LUCK..

Attached Centre:

Burrell Schmidt Telescope: Kitt Peak National Observatory, 950 N. Cherry Ave, Tucson, AZ 85719; tel. (520) 318-8000; f. 1979; 24"/36" wide field telescope.

Center for Earth and Planetary Studies (CEPS): Smithsonian Institution, POB 37012, Nat. Air and Space Museum, MRC 315, Washington, DC 20013-7012; tel. (202) 633-2480; internet www.nasm.si.edu/ceps; f. 1974; attached to the collns and research dept of the Smithsonian Institution's Nat. Air and Space Museum (Washington, DC); research into planetary and terrestrial geology and geophysics; application of remote sensing data from Earth-orbiting satellites and space missions; designated Regional Planetary Image Facility (RPIF); colln of Space Shuttle photographs; responsible for museum galleries 'Exploring the Planets' and 'Looking at Earth'; Dept Chair. BRUCE CAMPBELL; Programme Man. PRISCILLA STRAIN.

Fermi National Accelerator Laboratory: POB 500, Batavia, IL 60510-0500; tel. (708) 840-3000; fax (708) 840-4343; e-mail fermilab@fnal.gov; internet www.fnal.gov; f. 1967; research in high energy physics; run by Universities Research Assen, Inc. for US Dept of Energy; library of 15,000 vols, 250 periodicals; Dir MICHAEL S. WITHERELL; publs *Fermilab Report*, *Symmetry* (12 a year).

Goddard Institute for Space Studies: 2880 Broadway, New York, NY 10025; tel. (212) 678-5500; fax (212) 678-5552; internet www.giss.nasa.gov; f. 1961; global climate, biogeochemical cycles, cloud studies, planetary atmospheres, global habitability; library of 15,000 vols; Dir Dr JAMES HANSEN.

Harvard–Smithsonian Center for Astrophysics (CfA): 60 Garden St, Cambridge, MA 02138; tel. (617) 495-7461; fax (617) 495-7468; internet sao-www.harvard.edu; f. 1973 as a formal collaboration between the Harvard College Observatory (f. 1839) and the Smithsonian Astrophysical Observatory (f. 1890); scientific divisions: atomic and molecular physics, high energy astrophysics, optical and infrared astronomy, radio and geoastronomy, solar, stellar and planetary sciences, theoretical astrophysics, science education; library: John G. Wolbach Library and Information Resource Center (combines libraries of the SAO and HCO) of 75,000 vols, 40,000 astronomic photographic plates; Dir IRWIN SHAPIRO.

Lamont-Doherty Earth Observatory of Columbia University: POB 1000, Palisades, NY 10964-8000; tel. (845) 359-2900; fax (845) 365-8162; e-mail director@ldeo.columbia.edu; internet www.ldeo.columbia.edu; f. 1948; research in earth and ocean sciences; library of 25,000 vols; Dir G. MICHAEL PURDY (acting); publs *List of Scientific Publications*, *Year Book*.

Lick Observatory: Mount Hamilton, CA 95140; internet mthamilton.ucolick.org; attached to the University of California, Santa Cruz Campus; f. 1888; optical astronomy and astrophysics; Dir J. S. MILLER.

Lowell Observatory: 1400 W Mars Hill Rd, Flagstaff, AZ 86001; tel. (928) 774-3358; fax (928) 774-6296; internet www.lowell.edu; f. 1894; library: astronomical research library of 12,000 vols; Dir JEFFREY HALL; Librarian LAUREN AMUNDSON; publ. *The Lowell Observer*.

Lunar and Planetary Institute: 3600 Bay Area Blvd, Houston, TX 77058; tel. (281) 486-2139; fax (281) 486-2127, e-mail info@lpi.usra.edu; internet www.lpi.usra.edu; f. 1968; library is a NASA Regional Planetary Image Facility; promotes and supports research in lunar and planetary studies; library of 56,000 vols, 210 periodicals, also photographic and cartographic data from planetary spacecraft missions; Dir STEPHEN MACKWELL; publ. *Lunar and Planetary Information Bulletin* (4 a year).

Maria Mitchell Association: The Nantucket Maria Mitchell Assen, 4 Vestal St, Nantucket, MA 02554; tel. (508) 228-9198; fax (508) 228-1031; e-mail info@mmo.org; internet www.mmo.org; f. 1902; astronomical research, research training, public lectures and viewings; manages Hinchman House Natural Science Museum, Loines Observatory, Maria Mitchell Observatory, Mitchell House (birthplace of Maria Mitchell), Science Library, Aquarium; library of 8,000 vols of rare and out-of-print natural science, astronomy, and Nantucket books; Exec. Dir Dr JANET SCHULTE; Dir for Archives and Spec. Collns and Education JASCIN N. LEONARDO FINGER; Dir for Natural Sciences and Education ANDREW MCKENNA-FOSTER; Dir for Observatories and Astronomy Dr VLADIMIR STRELNITSKI.

Mount Graham International Observatory (MGIO): 1480 W Swift Trail, Safford, AZ 85546; tel. (928) 428-2739; fax (928) 428-2854; internet mgpc3.as.arizona.edu; Dir BUDDY E. POWELL.

Constituent Centres:

Arizona Radio Observatory (ARO): Univ. of Arizona, 933 N Cherry Ave, Tucson, AZ 85721; tel. (520) 621-5290; fax (520) 621-5554; e-mail opersmt@as.arizona.edu; internet aro.as.arizona.edu; operates the Heinrich Hertz Submillimeter Telescope (HHSMT); Dir Dr LUCY ZIURYS.

Large Binocular Telescope Observatory (LBTO): Univ. of Arizona, 933 N Cherry Ave, Tucson, AZ 85721; tel. (520) 626-7088; fax (520) 626-9333; e-mail rgreen@as.arizona.edu; internet medusa.as.arizona.edu/lbto; f. 1988, operational 2007; the world's most powerful optical telescope; consists of 2 8.4-m mirrors on a common mount; a collaboration between the Italian astronomical community (represented by the Istituto Nazionale di Astrofisica—*q.v.*—the Univ. of Arizona, Arizona State Univ., Northern Arizona Univ., the LBT Beteiligungsgesellschaft in Germany, the Ohio State Univ., Research Corpn in Tucson and the Univ. of Notre Dame; Dir RICHARD F. GREEN.

Vatican Observatory Research Group (VORG): Univ. of Arizona, Tucson, AZ 85721; tel. (520) 621-3225; fax (520) 621-1532; e-mail ccorbally@as.arizona.edu; internet vaticanobservatory.org; f. 1980; attached to Vatican Observatory, Vatican City; operates the 1.8-m Alice P. Lennon Telescope with its Thomas J. Bannan Astrophysics Facility, known together as the Vatican Advanced Technology Telescope, on Mount Graham, Arizona; Vice-Dir for the Vatican Observatory for VORG Dr CHRISTOPHER J. CORBALLY.

National Astronomy and Ionosphere Center: Space Sciences Bldg, Cornell Univ., Ithaca, NY 14853-6801; tel. (607) 255-3735; fax (607) 255-8803; e-mail jtm14@cornell.edu; internet www.naic.edu; f. 1963; nat. research facility funded by the US Nat. Science Foundation and operated by Cornell Univ.; research in areas of radio and radar astronomy and in space atmospheric sciences; Arecibo Observatory: see chapter on Puerto Rico; Dir Dr DONALD B. CAMPBELL; Admin. Dir JAMES N. BLAIR; publs *Astronomical Journal* (irregular), *Astrophysical Journal* (irregular), *Astronomy and Astrophysics* (irregular), *Journal of Atmospheric and Solar-Terrestrial Physics* (irregular), *Journal of Geophysical Research* (irregular), *Publication of the Astronomical Society of the Pacific* (irregular).

National Center for Atmospheric Research (NCAR): POB 3000, Boulder, CO 80307-3000; tel. (303) 497-1000; fax (303) 497-1194; internet www.ncar.ucar.edu; f. 1960; sponsored by Nat. Science Foundation; operated by the Univ. Corpn for Atmospheric Research (UCAR); research in weather prediction, causes of climatic trends, solar processes and influences of the sun on weather and climate, convective storms and global air quality; library of 100,000 items, 900 current journals; Dir TIM KILLEEN; publs *Highlights* (every 2 years), *NCAR Scientific Report*, *UCAR* (4 a year).

National Radio Astronomy Observatory: 520 Edgemont Rd, Charlottesville, VA 22903-2475; and POB 2, Green Bank, WV 24944-0002; and POB O, Socorro, NM 87801-0387; tel. (434) 296-0221; fax (434) 296-0278; e-mail hwinter@nrao.edu; internet www.nrao.edu; f. 1956; facility of the National Science Foundation, operated under co-operative agreement by Associated Univs, Inc.; research in radio astronomy, radio astronomy electronics, design of radio telescopes; observing radio telescopes, incl. a 27-

element array of 82-ft radio telescopes in New Mexico (Very Large Array); a 10-element array of 82-ft radio telescopes located in 7 states and the US Virgin Islands (Very Long Baseline Array) dedicated to very long baseline interferometry; and a 100-m fully steerable telescope in West Virginia (Robert C. Byrd Green Bank Telescope); library of 27,000 vols; Dir FRED K. Y. LO.

National Solar Observatory: NSO Tucson, 950 N Cherry Ave, Tucson, AZ 85719-4933; NSO Sacramento Peak, POB 62, Sunspot, NM 88349-0062; tel. (520) 318-8000 (Tucson); tel. (505) 434-7000 (Sacramento Peak); internet www.nso.edu; f. 1952; operated by AURA, Inc. (*q.v.*); national centre for solar research; offers telescope use to astronomical community; 50 staff, including 11 astrophysicists; library of 8,000 vols; Dir STEPHEN L. KEIL; publs research papers.

Scripps Institution of Oceanography: Mail Code 0210, La Jolla, CA 92093-0233; tel. (858) 534-3624; fax (858) 534-5306; internet www.scripps.ucsd.edu; f. 1903; graduate school and research div. of Univ. of California, San Diego; main depts: associated univ. of california institutes: institute of geophysics and planetary physics, california space institute, center for atmospheric sciences, center for coastal studies, center for marine biotechnology and biomedicine, climate research, geosciences research, marine biology research, marine physical Llaboratory, marine research, marine life research group, physical oceanography, Scripps graduate dept; spec. facilities incl. hydraulics laboratory; operates 4 research vessels and 1 platform; public aquarium and museum; geological and biological collns; library of 225,000 vols, 3,800 periodicals; Dir Dr TONY HAYMENT; publs *Bulletin* (irregular), *Contributions* (1 a year), *Explorations* (4 a year).

Sproul Observatory: Computer Science Dept, Swarthmore College, 500 College Ave, Swarthmore, PA 19081-1397; tel. (610) 328-8272; fax (610) 328-8272; internet www.cs.swarthmore.edu; f. 1911; 61-cm long focus refractor, 61-cm reflector and echelle spectrometer; astrometry and stellar spectroscopy; library of 9,000 vols.

United States Naval Observatory: 3450 Massachusetts Ave, NW, Washington, DC 20392-5420; tel. (202) 762-1437; fax (202) 762-1461; internet www.usno.navy.mil; f. 1830; positional astronomy, astrometry, proper motions, stellar parallaxes, photometry, double stars, earth rotation, master clock, precise time measurement, celestial mechanics; library of 75,000 vols; substation at Flagstaff, AZ; Superintendent Capt. K. W. FOSTER; Scientific Dir Dr KENNETH JOHNSTON; publs *Air Almanac*, *Astronomical Almanac*, *Astronomical Papers*, *Astronomical Phenomena*, *Multi-year Interactive Computer Almanac*, *Nautical Almanac*, *NavObs Circulars*, *Time Service Bulletins*, star catalogs.

Vanderbilt Dyer Observatory: 1000 Oman Drive, Brentwood, TN 37027; tel. (615) 373-4897; fax (615) 371-3904; e-mail nancy.dwyer@vanderbilt.edu; internet www.dyer.vanderbilt.edu; f. 1953; specializes in research on local structure of the Milky Way, photo-electric photometry of eclipsing binaries and variable stars, pre-planetary discs around young stars; equipped with combination 60-cm reflecting and Baker-Schmidt telescope, 40-cm computer-controlled automatic telescope, 30-cm and 40-cm Cassegrain reflecting telescopes and 15-cm refracting telescope; library of 12,000 vols; Dir RICK CHAPPELL; publ. *IAPPP Communications* (4 a year).

Woods Hole Oceanographic Institution: Woods Hole, MA 02543; tel. (508) 548-1400; fax (508) 457-2034; e-mail information@whoi.edu; internet www.whoi.edu; f. 1930; research in physical, chemical and biological oceanography, marine geology and marine geophysics, ocean acoustics, ocean engineering and marine policy; conducts jt PhD programme with Massachusetts Inst. of Technology, postdoctoral fellowship programme and summer student fellowship programme; jt library with Marine Biological Laboratory of 150,000 vols and 5,000 periodical titles; Pres. and Dir SUSAN AVERY; publs *Abstracts of Papers* (1 a yearl), *Oceanus* (3 a year).

Yale Observatory: Yale University, Dept of Astronomy, 260 Whitney Ave, POB 208101, New Haven, CT 06520-8101; tel. (203) 432-3000; fax (203) 432-5048; internet www.astro.yale.edu; publs *Bright Star Catalogue* (and supplement), *General Catalogue of Trigonometric Stellar Parallaxes*, *Transactions*.

Yerkes Observatory: 373 W. Geneva St, Williams Bay, WI 53191; tel. (262) 245-5555; fax (262) 245-9805; internet astro.uchicago.edu/yerkes; f. 1897; research branch of the Dept of Astronomy and Astrophysics of the Univ. of Chicago; library of 25,000 books and journals; Dir Dr K. M. CUDWORTH.

PHILOSOPHY AND PSYCHOLOGY

American Society for Psychical Research, Inc.: 5 W 73rd St, New York, NY 10023; tel. (212) 799-5050; fax (212) 496-2497; e-mail aspr@aspr.com; internet www.aspr.com; f. 1885; study of paranormal phenomena such as telepathy, clairvoyance, precognition, psychokinesis, etc.; library of 15,000 vols; Exec. Dir PATRICE KEANE; Librarian JEFF TWINE; publ. *Journal* (2 a year).

RELIGION, SOCIOLOGY AND ANTHROPOLOGY

American Institutes for Research: 1000 Thomas Jefferson St, Washington, DC 20007; tel. (202) 403-5000; fax (202) 403-5001; internet www.air.org; f. 1946; independent, non-profit org. conducting research, devt, analysis and evaluation studies in the behavioural and social sciences for clients in government and the private sector; Pres. and Chief Exec. Officer SOL. H. PELAVIN.

American Research Center in Egypt (ARCE): US Office, Mailstop 1256/001/1AC, Emory University Briarcliff Campus, Atlanta, GA 30322; tel. (404) 712-9854; fax (404) 712-9849; e-mail arce@emory.edu; internet www.arce.org Cairo Office: 2 Midan Simón Bolívar, Garden City, Cairo, 11461, Egypt; tel. (2) 796-4681; fax (2) 794-8622; e-mail arce@internetegypt.com; f. 1948; independent, non-profit-making; promotes research on Egypt and the Middle East in the fields of archaeology, art, architecture, history, culture, social sciences; library: (in Cairo) of 25,000 vols; c. 1,200 mems; Pres. CAROL REDMOUNT; Assoc. Dir for US Operations SUSANNE THOMAS; Cairo Dir GERRY DEE SCOTT, III; publ. *Journal* (1 a year).

American Schools of Oriental Research: Boston University, 656 Beacon St, 5th Fl., Boston, MA 02215-2010; tel. (617) 353-6570; fax (617) 353-6575; e-mail asor@bu.edu; internet www.asor.org; f. 1900; promotes research into the cultures of the Near E and supports activities of ind. archaeological instns abroad: Albright Institute of Archaeological Research (Jerusalem, Israel), American Center of Oriental Research (Amman, Jordan), and Cyprus American Archaeological Research Institute (Nicosia, Cyprus); Pres. TIMOTHY HARRISON; publs *Bulletin* (4 a year), *Journal of Cuneiform Studies* (1 a year), *Near Eastern Archaeology* (4 a year), *The Annual*.

Arctic Studies Center: Dept of Anthropology, National Museum of Natural History, Smithsonian Institution, MRC 112, Washington, DC 20013-7012; tel. (202) 633-1887; fax (202) 357-2684; e-mail arctics@si.edu; internet www.mnh.si.edu/arctic; f. 1988; attached to Dept of Anthropology of the Smithsonian Instn's Nat. Museum of Natural History; research into peoples, history, archaeology and social change in the circumpolar regions; Dir WILLIAM W. FITZHUGH.

Regional Office:

Alaska Office: 121 West 7th Ave, Anchorage, AK 99501; tel. (907) 343-6162; fax (907) 343-6130.

Center for Advanced Study in the Behavioral Sciences: 75 Alta Rd, Stanford, CA 94305-8090; tel. (650) 321-2052; fax (650) 321-1192; e-mail info@casbs.org; internet www.casbs.org; f. 1954; Dir Dr CLAUDE M. STEELE.

Middle American Research Institute: Tulane University, New Orleans, LA 70118-5698; tel. (504) 865-5110; fax (504) 862-8778; e-mail mari@tulane.edu; internet www.tulane.edu/~mari; f. 1924; research, education and publs related to Mexico and Central America; supports publication, archaeological excavation and research in humanities and social sciences; small museum gallery; anthropological collns; Dir E. WYLLYS ANDREWS, V.

Middle East Institute: 1761 N St, NW, Washington, DC 20036-2882; tel. (202) 785-1141; fax (202) 331-8861; e-mail mideasti@mideasti.org; internet www.mideasti.org; f. 1946; a non-profit, non-advocating resource centre; promotes American understanding of the Middle East, North Africa, the Caucasus and Central Asia; coordinates cultural presentations; library of 25,000 vols; Pres. EDWARD S. WALKER, Jr; publ. *Middle East Journal* (4 a year).

Smithsonian Center for Folklife and Cultural Heritage: POB 37012, Victor Bldg, Suite 4100, MRC 953, Washington, DC 20013-7012; 750 9th St, NW, Suite 4100, Smithsonian Instn, Washington, DC 20560-0953; tel. (202) 275-1150; fax (202) 275-1119; e-mail folklife-info@si.edu; internet www.folklife.si.edu; promotes the understanding and continuity of contemporary grassroots cultures in the USA and abroad; runs Smithsonian Folklife Festival, Smithsonian Folkways Recordings, exhibitions, documentary films, symposia; library: Ralph Rinzler Folklife Archives and Collns: 17,300 commercial discs, 4,000 acetate discs, 45,000 audiotapes, 2,000 CDs, 1,000,000 stills, 2,500 video casettes, 500,000 ft of motion picture film; Moses and Frances Asch colln, consisting of recordings and material relating to Folkways Records; records and archives of the center; Dir RICHARD KURIN.

Smithsonian Center for Latino Initiatives: 900 Jefferson Drive, SW, Rm 1465, MRC 448, Washington, DC 20560-0448; tel. (202) 633-1240; fax (202) 786-2477; internet latino.si.edu; f. 1998; co-ordinates all Smithsonian-related Latino exhibitions, initiatives, research and educational programmes; library: archive of papers of Latino and Latin American artists; Dir LUBEN MONTOYA (acting).

Social Science Research Council: One Pierrepont Plaza, 15th Fl., Brooklyn, New York, NY 11021; tel. (212) 377-2700; fax (212) 377-2727; e-mail info@ssrc.org; internet www.ssrc.org; f. 1923 to advance research in the social sciences by: appointment of committees of scholars to set priorities and make plans for critical areas of social research; improvement of research training through training institutes and fellowship programmes; support of individual research through postdoctoral grants; sponsorship of research conferences, often interdisciplinary and international; sponsorship of books and other research publications that may result from these activities; Pres. CRAIG CALHOUN; publ. *Items* (4 a year).

Wenner-Gren Foundation for Anthropological Research, Inc.: 470 Park Ave South, 8th Fl., New York, NY 10016; tel. (212) 683-5000; fax (212) 683-9151; e-mail inquiries@wennergren.org; internet www.wennergren.org; f. 1941 as the Viking Fund; supports research in all brs of anthropology and closely related disciplines concerned with human origins, devt and variation; grants to aid individual research, incl. dissertation research, fellowships and post-PhD research grants; Conference Grants Program; Historical Archives Program; Professional Development Int. Fellowships and Int. Collaborative Research Grants; Pres. Dr LESLIE AIELLO; publ. *Current Anthropology* (5 a year).

TECHNOLOGY

Brookhaven National Laboratory: POB 5000, Upton, Long Island, NY 11973-5000; tel. (631) 344-8000; internet www.bnl.gov; f. 1947; operated by Brookhaven Science Assocs, under contract with the US Dept of Energy; basic and applied research by staff and visiting scientists in the fields of energy, particle accelerators, physics, medicine, biology, chemistry, applied sciences, mathematics, and the environment, including the design, development, acquisition and operation of large-scale facilities too costly or complex for an individual university; training of scientists and engineers; dissemination of scientific and technical knowledge; library of 82,000 vols; staff: 644 research, 621 professional, 759 technicians, 1,129 general; Dir Dr PRAVEEN CHAUDHARI; publs *Brookhaven Bulletin*, *Brookhaven Highlights*.

Building Research Board: 2101 Constitution Ave, NW, Washington, DC 20418; tel. (202) 334-3376; f. 1949 as a unit of the Nat. Academy of Sciences—Nat. Research Council; undertakes activities concerned with the development and application of technology to serve society's needs for the built environment: infrastructure, housing, building and related community and environmental design and development; Chair. HAROLD J. PARMELEE; Dir Dr ANDREW C. LEMER.

Combustion Institute: 5001 Baum Blvd, Suite 635, Pittsburgh, PA 15213-1851; tel. (412) 687-1366; fax (412) 687-0340; e-mail office@combustioninstitute.org; internet www.combustioninstitute.org; f. 1954; non-profit educational scientific society that promotes and disseminates research in combustion science; offices in 32 countries; Pres. Dr CHARLES K. WESTBROOK; Exec. Admin. BARBARA D. WARONEK; publs *Combustion and Flame* (12 a year), *Proceedings of The Combustion Institute* (every 2 years).

HERTY Advanced Materials Development Center: 110 Brampton Rd, Savannah, GA 31408; tel. (912) 963-2600; fax (912) 963-2614; e-mail info@herty.com; internet www.herty.com; f. 1938; non-profit contractual research and development of wood, non-wood and synthetic fibres; Pres. and CEO Dr WILLIAM G. BRUNDAGE.

Industrial Research Institute, Inc.: Suite 1102, 2200 Clarendon Blvd, Arlington, VA 22201-3331; tel. (703) 647-2580; fax (703) 647-2581; internet www.iriweb.org; f. 1938; Pres. EDWARD BERNSTEIN; publ. *Research-Technology Management* (6 a year).

Institute of Textile Technology: 2401 Research Dr., POB 8301, Raleigh, NC 27695-8301; tel. (919) 513-7704; fax (919) 882-9410; internet www.itt.edu; f. 1944; research, graduate education and open funding of applied textile research; Pres. Dr GILBERT O'NEAL; Dir, Research Dr HENRY BOYTER.

Jerome and Dorothy Lemelson Center for the Study of Invention and Innovation: National Museum of American History, Rm 1016, Smithsonian Institution, POB 37012, Washington, DC 20013-7012; tel. (202) 633-3450; fax (202) 357-4517; internet invention.smithsonian.org; f. 1995 to document, interpret and disseminate information about invention and innovation, and to encourage inventive creativity in young people; part of the Smithsonian Institution National Museum of American History; Dir ARTHUR MOLELLA.

National Aeronautics and Space Administration (NASA): 300 E St SW, Washington, DC 20546; e-mail public-inquiries@hq.nasa.gov; internet www.nasa.gov; Administrator MICHAEL D. GRIFFIN.

Main Research Centres:

Ames Research Center: NASA, Moffet Field, CA 94035; tel. (650) 604-5000; internet www1.nasa.gov/centers/ame; f. 1939; Dir Dr G. SCOTT HUBBARD.

Dryden Flight Research Center: PO Box 273, Edwards, CA 93523-0273; tel. (661) 276-3311; internet www.nasa.gov/centers/dryden; research in aeronautics and space technology; Dir KEVIN L. PETERSEN.

George C. Marshall Space Flight Center: National Aeronautics and Space Administration, AL 35812; f. 1960; Dir D. A. KING.

Glenn Research Center: NASA, 21000 Brookpark Rd, Cleveland, OH 44135; tel. (216) 433-4000; internet www.nasa.gov/centers/glenn; f. 1942; Dir JULIAN EARLS.

Goddard Space Flight Center: NASA, Greenbelt, MD 20771; tel. (301) 286-8955; fax (301) 286-1707; internet www1.nasa.gov/centers/goddard; f. 1959; space research; 3,500 mems; library of 57,000 vols, 35,000 periodicals; Dir Dr EDWARD J. WEILER.

Jet Propulsion Laboratory: 4800 Oak Grove Drive, Pasadena, CA 91109; tel. (818) 354-4321; internet www.nasa.gov/centers/jpl; centre for robotic exploration of the solar system; operated by California Institute of Technology; Dir Dr CHARLES ELACHI.

John F. Kennedy Space Center: NASA, FL 32899; internet www1.nasa.gov/centers/kennedy; f. 1962; previously Launch Operations Center; space vehicle launch facility; library of 32,000 vols, 106,000 documents and reports, 589 periodicals; 160,000 specifications and standards; Dir JAMES W. KENNEDY.

Langley Research Center: NASA, Hampton, VA 23665; internet www1.nasa.gov/centers/langley; f. 1917; Dir ROY BRIDGES.

Lyndon B. Johnson Space Center: NASA, Houston, TX 77058; tel. (281) 483-0123; internet www.nasa.gov/centers/johnson; f. 1961; responsible for the design, development and testing of manned spacecraft and associated systems, for the selection and training of astronauts and for the operation of manned space flights; operates White Sands Test Facility at Las Cruces, NM; library: Johnson Space Center Technical library of 49,000 vols, 550,000 technical reports, 600 periodicals; Dir JEFFERSON D. HOWELL, Jr.

Stennis Space Center: tel. (228) 688-3341; e-mail pao@ssc.nasa.gov; internet www.nasa.gov/centers/stennis; Dir THOMAS Q. DONALDSON.

National Institute of Standards and Technology: Gaithersburg, MD 20899-1000; and at Boulder, CO 80303-3328; tel. (301) 975-3057; fax (301) 926-1630; e-mail inquiries@nist.gov; internet www.nist.gov; f. 1901; a non-regulatory agency of the Commerce Department's Technology Administration; works with industry to develop and apply technology, measurements and standards; laboratory research focused on infrastructural technologies; Dir WILLIAM JEFFREY.

National Renewable Energy Laboratory: 1617 Cole Blvd, Golden, CO 80401-3393; tel. (303) 275-3000; fax (303) 275-4091; internet www.nrel.gov; f. 1977; a national centre for federally sponsored long-range high-risk renewable energy research and development; library of 105,000 books and reports, 350 journals; Dir Dr DAN ARVIZU; publs *AFDC Update*, *Biofuels Update*.

Southwest Research Institute: 6220 Culebra Rd, Post Office Drawer 28510, San Antonio, TX 78228-0510; tel. (210) 684-5111; fax (210) 522-3547; internet www.swri.edu; f. 1947; independent non-profit organization conducting research and development in the engineering and physical sciences for government, business and industry around the world; library of 50,000 vols; Pres. J. DAN BATES; publ. *Technology Today* (3 a year).

SRI International: 333 Ravenswood Ave, Menlo Park, CA 94025-3493; tel. (650) 859-2000; e-mail customer-service@sri.com; internet www.sri.com; f. 1946 (fmrly Stanford Research Institute); non-profit-making; centres for diversified research for industry and govt in pure and applied science and engineering; br. in Washington, DC, and other locations; overseas offices in Tokyo, Japan, Seoul, Republic of Korea, and Sharjah, UAE; Pres. and CEO CURTIS R. CARLSON.

TRI Princeton: POB 625, Princeton, NJ 08542; tel. (609) 924-3150; fax (609) 683-7836; e-mail info@triprinceton.org; internet www.triprinceton.com; f. 1930; fundamental and applied research and continuing education in the physical and engineering sciences relating to fibrous materials, films, polymers, human hair, and porous and nanoporous materials; 169 individual mems; library of 5,000 vols; Pres. Dr GAIL R. EATON; Sec. of the Bd of Trustees ELEANOR LEHMAN.

Libraries and Archives

Alabama

Birmingham Public Library: 2100 Park Pl., Birmingham, AL 35203; tel. (205) 226-3610; internet www.bplonline.org; f. 1909; 1,094,390 vols; spec. collns: Agee Cartographical Colln (incl. Joseph H. Woodward Colln), Catherine Collins Colln of Dance, Scruggs Philately Colln, Tutwiler Colln of Southern History and Literature, govt documents, archives, MSS, musical recordings, film and video; DIALOG Online Computer Reference Service, Books by Mail Service; 19 brs; Dir BARBARA SIRMANS.

University of Alabama Library: POB 870266, Tuscaloosa, AL 35487-0266; tel. (205) 348-6047; internet www.lib.ua.edu; f. 1831; regional depository for federal documents; deptl libraries for business, education, engineering, sciences; spec. collns on Alabama and Southern history and literature; 3,178,641 vols; Dean of Libraries LOUIS A. PITSCHMANN.

Alaska

Alaska State Library: POB 110571, Juneau, AK 99811-0571; tel. (907) 465-2910; fax (907) 465-2665; e-mail asl@alaska.gov; internet library.alaska.gov; f. 1900; 158,166 vols: information services 73,648 vols, historical colllns 79,969 vols, incl. 859 MSS and 526 photographic collns; 3,164 vols in Anchorage office; information service, incl. service to Alaska govt and the gen. public; historical collns; library devt; talking book centre; State Librarian and Div. Dir LINDA THIBODEAU.

Arizona

Arizona State Library, Archives and Public Records: Suite 200, 1700 West Washington, Phoenix, AZ 85007; tel. (602) 542-4035; fax (602) 542-4972; e-mail services@lib.az.us; internet www.lib.az.us; f. 1864; law, govt, Arizona and South-West history, genealogy, federal and state documents; library extension, archives, library for the blind and physically handicapped, museums, public records; 1,127,196 vols; Dir GLADYS ANN WELLS.

Phoenix Public Library: 1221 N Central, Phoenix, AZ 85004; tel. (602) 262-4636; fax (602) 495-5841; internet www.phoenixpubliclibrary.org; f. 1901; 1,735,924 vols, 4,315 periodical titles; 15 brs; audiovisual material; Arizona and South-West materials; City Librarian TONI GARVEY.

University of Arizona Library: Main Library A349, POB 210055, Tucson, AZ 85721-0055; located at: 1510 East University Blvd, Tucson, AZ 85721-0055; tel. (520) 621-2101; fax (520) 621-9733; internet www.library.arizona.edu; f. 1891; 4,844,241 vols; spec. collns: history of science, South-Western Americana and borderlands history, fine and theatre arts, British and American literature; Dir Libraries CARLA STOFFLE.

Arkansas

Arkansas History Commission Library: 1 Capitol Mall, Little Rock, AR 72201; tel. (501) 682-6900; e-mail state.archives@arkansas.gov; internet www.ark-ives.com; f. 1905; official state archives; MSS, books, microfilm, newspapers, maps, photographs; Dir Dr WENDY RICHTER.

Arkansas State Library: 1 Capitol Mall, Little Rock, AR 72201; tel. (501) 682-2053; fax (501) 682-1529; e-mail shawkes@asl.lib.ar.us; internet www.asl.lib.ar.us; f. 1979; Librarian CAROLYN ASHCRAFT.

University of Arkansas Libraries: 365 North McIlroy Ave, Fayetteville, AR 72701-4002; tel. (479) 575-4104; fax (479) 575-6656; internet www.uark.edu; spec. collns: local politics, Civil War, women's records, 100,000 pictures and photographs, maps; Dir CAROLYN ALLEN.

California

California State Library: POB 942837, Sacramento, CA 94237-0001; tel. (916) 654-0174; fax (916) 654-00641; e-mail csl-adm@library.ca.gov; internet www.library.ca.gov; f. 1850; 696,000 vols, 3,011,835 govt publs; library service to state govt; preservation of CA materials; govt document depository; law library; books for the blind, and physically handicapped service; administrator of the state and federal aid to public libraries; State Librarian SUSAN HILDRETH; publs *California Library Directory* (1 a year), *California Library Laws* (1 a year), *California Library Statistics* (1 a year), *California State Publications* (12 a year).

Hoover Institution on War, Revolution and Peace: Stanford, CA 94305; tel. (650) 723-1754; fax (650) 723-1687; internet www-hoover.stanford.edu; f. 1919; centre of documentation and research on int. and domestic political, social and economic change since beginning of the 20th century; 60m. documents, 100,000 political posters; 4,772 archival units on the causes and consequences of war and revolutionary movements, and on efforts to achieve peace; with emphasis on int. rivalries and global co-operation; research programme on political, economic and social problems in the USA; independent, within the framework of Stanford Univ.; Dir Dr JOHN RAISIAN; publs *China Leadership Monitor* (4 a year), *Education Next* (4 a year), *Hoover's Digest* (4 a year), *Policy Review* (6 a year).

Huntington Library, Art Collections and Botanical Gardens: 1151 Oxford Rd, San Marino, CA 91108; tel. (626) 405-2100; fax (626) 449-5720; e-mail publicinformation@huntington.org; internet www.huntington.org; f. 1919 by the late Henry E. Huntington as a free research library, art gallery, museum and botanical garden; 7,000,000 vols; collns incl. 500,000 rare books, 6,000,000 MSS, working reference library of 500,000 vols and 600,000 photographs; available to scholars and others engaged in research work on application to the Registrar; collns concentrate on British and American history, literature and art; particular strengths incl. English medieval and Renaissance, British drama, American colonial, American Civil War, American frontier, MSS since 19th century, early science; separate reference libraries located in the Botanical Div., the latter incl. 300,000 photographs, paintings and 6,000 British drawings; public programmes, lectures, exhibitions; See also Museums and Art Galleries; Pres. STEVEN KOBLIK; Dir Library DAVID S. ZEIDBERG; publ. *Huntington Frontiers* (2 a year).

LA Law Library (Los Angeles County Law Library): 301 West First St, Los Angeles, CA 90012-3100; tel. (213) 785-2529; fax (213) 613-1329; e-mail reference@lalawlibrary.org; internet www.lalawlibrary.org; f. 1891; brs in Compton, Long Beach, Norwalk, Pomona, Santa Monica, Torrance and Van Nuys; spec. colln 7,500 vols on Roman, canon, civil, English law; public library partnerships: Pasadena, Compton, Lancaster; self-help colln for self-represented litigants; programme for mems of the California State Bar MCLE; 750,000 vols; Exec. Dir MARCIA J. KOSLOV; Sr Dir Library Operations CATHERINE ERLANGER.

Los Angeles Public Library: 630 West Fifth St, Los Angeles, CA 90071; tel. (213) 228-7272; fax (213) 228-7069; e-mail asklapl@hotmail.com; internet www.lapl.org; f. 1872; 6,222,418 vols; 70 brs; Californiana, children's literature, cookery, genealogy, North American Indians, modern languages, orchestral scores, US patents, standards and specifications, English language, theatre, congressional documents and hearings, business and finance, corporate annual reports, video casettes, DVDs, CDs, audiobooks, telephone and trade directories; Dir Central Library ANNE CONNOR; Dir Branch Libraries CECILIA RIDDLE.

Sacramento Public Library: 828 I St, Sacramento, CA 95814; tel. (916) 264-2770; fax (916) 264-2755; e-mail contact@saclibrary.org; internet www.saclibrary.org; central library, 27 brs, 2 mobile units; 2,000,000 vols; spec. collns: Sacramento current and historical information, California colln, business colln, printing history, Sacramento area authors, art and music colln; Dir ANNE MARIE GOLD.

San Diego County Public Law Library: 1105 Front St, San Diego, CA 92101-3904; tel. (619) 531-3900; fax (619) 238-7716; e-mail refdesk@sdcpll.org; internet www.sdcpll.org; f. 1891; 346,151 vols; Dir JOHN ADKINS.

San Diego Public Library: 820 E St, San Diego, CA 92101-6478; tel. (619) 236-5800; fax (619) 236-5878; e-mail weblibrary@sandiego.gov; internet www.sandiegolibrary.org; f. 1882; 5,491,543 vols; Dir DEBORAH BARROW.

San Francisco Law Library: Rm 400, 401 Van Ness Ave, San Francisco, CA 94102; tel. (415) 554-6821; fax (415) 554-6820; internet www.sfgov.org/sfll; 246,000 vols, main library; 30,367 vols, br. libraries; 3 brs; open to public; Dir MARCIA BELL.

San Francisco Public Library: 100 Larkin St, San Francisco, CA 94102-4733; tel. (415) 557-4400; fax (415) 557-4239; e-mail info@sfpl.org; internet sfpl.org; 2,309,166 vols; City Librarian LUIS HERRERA.

Stanford University Libraries and Academic Information Resources (SULAIR): Stanford, CA 94305; tel. (650) 723-9108; e-mail ic@sulmail.stanford.edu; internet www-sul.stanford.edu; f. 1885; 7.7m. vols, incl. the Green Library (2,837,863 vols), Hoover Institution on War, Revolution and Peace (1,257,466 vols) and 45 departmental and school libraries, of which the major ones are: Lane Medical Library (371,725 vols), Robert Crown Law Library (437,896 vols), Cubberley Education Library (175,849 vols), Branner Earth Sciences Library (132,446 vols), J. Hugh Jackson Business Library (548,639 vols), Linear Accelerator Center Library (8,840 vols), Falconer Biology Library (105,106 vols), Hopkins Marine Station Library (38,478 vols), Mathematical and Computer Sciences Library (127,396 vols), Swain Chemistry Library (55,529 vols), Art and Architecture (180,933 vols), Music (108,443 vols), Archive of Recorded Sound (6,382 items), Physics (59,401 vols), Eng. (114,039 vols); spec. collns: transportation, music, British and American Literature, history of science, book arts and history of the book, children's literature, Judaica and Hebraica; Univ. Librarian and Dir of Academic Information Resources MICHAEL A. KELLER.

University of Southern California Library: Los Angeles, CA 90089-0182; tel. (213) 740-2543; fax (213) 749-1221; e-mail library@usc.edu; internet www.usc.edu/isd/libraries; f. 1880; 4m. vols, 6m. microform items, 3m. photographs, 30,000 periodicals; spec. collns: Cervantes, Lewis Carroll, Max Reinhardt; American literature; cinema and television, European philosophy; German exile literature; gerontology; int. relations; Korean studies, Latin American studies, natural history, Southern California history, Univ. Archives; Dean of Libraries CATHERINE QUINLAN.

Colorado

Denver Public Library: 10 West 14th Ave, Pkwy, Denver, CO 80204-2731; tel. (720) 865-1111; fax (303) 640-6374; internet denverlibrary.org; f. 1889; 2,455,965 items; 22 brs; specializes in Western US history, conservation of natural resources, energy and the environment, genealogy, fine printing, folk music, US 10th Mountain Div. soldiers; City Librarian SHIRLEY AMORE.

DOC Boulder Laboratories Library: 325 Broadway/MC5, Boulder, CO 80305; tel. (303) 497-3271; fax (303) 497-3890; e-mail boulderlabs.ref@noaa.gov; internet library

.bldrdoc.gov; f. 1954; attached to US Dept of Commerce; 45,000 vols, 580 current journals, 38,000 bound journal vols, 700 e-journals; Dir DOTTIE ANDERSON.

University of Colorado at Boulder Libraries: 184 UCB, Boulder, CO 80309-0184; tel. (303) 492-8705; fax (303) 492-1881; e-mail reflib@colorado.edu; internet ucblibraries.colorado.edu; f. 1876; spec. collns: mountaineering, photobooks, peace and justice, western Americana; 2,920,335 vols; Dean of Libraries JAMES F. WILLIAMS.

Connecticut

Connecticut State Library: 231 Capitol Ave, Hartford, CT 06106; tel. (860) 757-6500; fax (860) 757-6503; e-mail isref@cslib.org; internet www.cslib.org; f. 1854; Connecticut newspapers, genealogy, history, law, legislative reference, public policy, Connecticut and US govt publs; 1,139,624 vols, 1,724,681 govt docs, 32,000 cu ft of archival records and state archives; State Librarian KENDALL F. WIGGIN.

University of Connecticut Library: 369 Fairfield Way, Storrs, CT 06269-2005; tel. (860) 486-2518; fax (860) 486-0584; e-mail elibrary@uconn.edu; internet www.lib.uconn.edu; f. 1881; largest public research colln in the state; 2.9m. vols, 5,000 current print periodicals, 55,000 electronic journals, 2.8m. microforms, 7,500 reference sources, 200,000 maps and a large repository of electronic information resources; Vice-Provost for Libraries BRINLEY FRANKLIN; publ. *University of Connecticut Libraries* (6 a year).

Yale University Library: POB 208240, 130 Wall St, New Haven, CT 06520-8240; tel. (203) 432-1818; fax (203) 432-1294; e-mail smlref@yale.edu; internet www.library.yale.edu; f. 1701; 10,500,544 vols; each of the 12 undergraduate colleges has its own library; Univ. Librarian ALICE PROCHASKA.

Delaware

Delaware Division of Libraries, Department of State: 43 South DuPont Highway, Dover, DE 19901; tel. (302) 739-4748; fax (302) 739-6787; internet www.state.lib.de.us; f. 1901; spec. collns: US govt documents, talking books; State Librarian and Dir ANNE E. C. NORMAN.

District of Columbia

Archives of American Art: Reference Services/ILL, AAA, Smithsonian Institution, POB 37012, Victor Bldg, Rm 2200, MRC, 937, Washington, DC 20013-7012; *Washington, DC Center*: Suite 2200, 750 Ninth St, NW, Washington, DC 20560-0937; tel. (202) 275-2156; fax (202) 275-1955 *New York City Research Center*: 1285 Ave of the Americas, Lobby Level, New York, NY 10019; tel. (212) 399-5015; fax (212) 307-4501; e-mail yeckleyk@aaany.si.edu; internet www.aaa.si.edu; f. 1954, bureau of the Smithsonian Instn since 1970; 900 mems; 14m. items; Dir JOHN W. SMITH; publ. *Journal* (4 a year).

Department of Commerce Library: 14th and Constitution Ave, NW, Washington, DC 20230; f. 1913; 50,000 vols, 2,000 vols microform; Dir ANTHONY J. STEINHAUSER..

Independent libraries within the Dept of Commerce include:

National Oceanic and Atmospheric Administration Central Library: 1315 East-West Highway, 2nd Floor, SSMC3, Silver Spring, MD 20910; tel. (301) 713-2600; fax (301) 713-4598; e-mail library.reference@noaa.gov; internet www.lib.noaa.gov; 1m. vols; 35 libraries and information centres holding spec. collns; networks with 28 NOAA libraries; disciplines incl. weather and atmospheric sciences, oceanography, ocean engineering, nautical charting, marine ecology, marine resources, ecosystems, coastal studies, aeronomy, geodesy, cartography, mathematics and statistics; Dir NEAL KASKE.

US Census Bureau: Cen Hq Rm 1L001 Library and Information Services Br. Services, Washington, DC 20233; tel. (301) 763-2511; fax (301) 763-4407; e-mail library@census.gov; internet cww.census.gov/library; f. 1952; 250,000 vols; Project Man. CATHERINE EARLES.

Department of Justice Library: 950 Pennsylvania Ave, NW, Washington, DC 20530-0001; tel. (202) 514-3775; fax (202) 514-3546; internet www.usdoj.gov; f. 1831; 300,000 vols, principally Anglo-American legal and related materials, 1m. items of microfiche and microfilm; 11 br. libraries (total 300,000 vols); specialized areas of American law; Library Dir BLANE K. DESSY.

Department of the Interior Libraries: Washington, DC 20240.

Constituent Libraries:

Library of the US Department of the Interior: Room 1151, 1849 C St, NW, Washington, DC 20240; tel. (202) 208-5815; internet library.doi.gov; f. 1949 by merger of 8 existing interior libraries at Washington; 850,000 vols; 15,000 serials and 2,500 periodicals received; subjects incl. the conservation and devt of natural resources; automated information services; interlibrary loans service; copy facilities; open to the public; Dir VICTORIA NOZERO; publ. *Bibliographies* (available from US Nat. Technical Information Service).

US Geological Survey Library: 950 National Center, 12201 Sunrise Valley Dr., Reston, VA 20192; tel. (703) 648-4302; fax (703) 648-6373; e-mail library@usgs.gov; internet library.usgs.gov; f. 1879; 1m. vols, 500,000 maps, 270,000 pamphlets; 2,500 serial and periodical titles received; comprehensive working and research library; interlibrary loan service; open to the public; Chief for Library Services ROBERT BIER.

Department of the Treasury Library: Main Treasury Bldg, 1500 Pennsylvania Ave, NW, Washington, DC 20220; tel. (202) 622-0990; fax (202) 622-2611; f. c.1817; 74,000 vols, 495,000 microfiches and 7,800 reels of microfilm; spec. collns: taxation, public finance, int. economic affairs, Treasury history.

Department of Veterans Affairs, Headquarters Library: 19-E-2, 810 Vermont Ave, NW, Washington, DC 20420; tel. (202) 273-8523; fax (202) 273-9125; internet www.va.gov; planning, policy, devt, training, centralized support services for the VA Library Network (VALNET); this comprises 176 library services at 172 VA facilities; combined library holdings 1,398,000 vols, 145,000 audiovisual items, 75,655 journal subscriptions; Chief of VALNET GINNY DUPONT; Chief of Library CARYI KAZEN.

District of Columbia Public Library: 901 G St, NW, Washington, DC 20001; tel. (202) 727-0321; fax (202) 727-1129; internet www.dclibrary.org; f. 1896; Martin Luther King, Jr Memorial Library (central library), 26 brs, Library for the Blind and the Physically Handicapped; spec. collns: Washingtoniana, Washington Star Colln, Black Studies, Musical Scores; 2,672,488 vols; Chief Librarian GINNIE COOPER.

Dumbarton Oaks Research Library and Collection: 1703 32nd St, Washington, DC 20007; tel. (202) 339-6401; fax (202) 339-6419; e-mail dumbartonoaks@doaks.org; internet www.doaks.org; f. 1940; research library of 200,000 vols; collns of early Christian and Byzantine art, and of Pre-Columbian art of Mexico, Central and South America; research programmes in Byzantine and Pre-Columbian studies, and studies in landscape architecture; Dir EDWARD J. KEENAN; publs *Colloquium Papers* (Landscape Architecture, irregular), *Conference Proceedings* (Pre-Columbian, irregular), *Dumbarton Oaks Papers* (Byzantine, 1 a year), *Dumbarton Oaks Studies* (Byzantine, irregular), *Studies in Pre-Columbian Art and Archaeology* (irregular).

Folger Shakespeare Library: 201 E Capitol St, SE, Washington, DC 20003; tel. (202) 544-4600; fax (202) 544-4623; e-mail reference@folger.edu; internet www.folger.edu; f. 1932; administered by Trustees of Amherst College with an independent bd of governors; collns incl. original edns and reprints of Shakespeare; English Renaissance books 1475–1700; 16th and 17th-century Continental European books incl. German Reformation, festival books and Italian drama; 17th- and 18th-century Strozzi MSS; Dryden colln; 16th-, 17th- and 18th-century English plays; 250,000 play bills; 55,000 MSS since 1s6th century relating to early modern Britain, and the history of theatre and Shakespearean scholarship; 50,000 literary and theatrical prints and engravings; fellowships; Folger Institute; public and educational programmes; theatre; lectures; poetry readings; concerts; exhibitions; Dir Dr MICHAEL WHITMORE; Librarian Dr STEPHEN ENNISS; publs *Folger Magazine* (3 a year), *Shakespeare Quarterly* (4 a year).

House of Representatives Library: Cannon House Office Bldg B-18, Washington, DC 20515; tel. (202) 2265200; internet clerk.house.gov/library; f. 1792; 250,000 vols, and spec. bound collns of all House of Representatives publs since c. 1800; Librarian RAE ELLEN BEST.

Library of Congress: 101 Independence Ave, SE, Washington, DC 20540; tel. (202) 707-5000; internet www.loc.gov; f. 1800; library's priority is service to the Congress of the United States, but it now performs, in its role as the nat. library, services to other libraries, which incl.: (i) the devt of scientific schemes of classification (Library of Congress and Dewey Decimal), subject headings and cataloguing embracing the whole field of printed matter, (ii) a centralized acquisition and cataloguing programme in which publs are acquired worldwide and cataloguing data distributed to other libraries, (iii) a 755-vol. *National Union Catalog: Pre-1956 Imprints*, (iv) an inter-library loan system (only within USA); registers creative work for copyright; 29m. books and pamphlets (incl. Orientalia colln, with 139,000 vols in Hebraic, 175,000 vols in other Near Eastern languages and 2m. vols in Chinese, Japanese, Korean and languages of southern Asia, colln of 1m. vols on Hispanic and Portuguese culture, and colln of Russian literature), newspapers and periodicals, 750,000 rare books and incunabula, 45,301,000 MSS relating to American history and civilization, 4,346,000 maps, 10,316,000 microforms, colln of books and recordings for the blind and physically handicapped (copies available through co-operating regional and sub-regional libraries), folklife colln (incl. 45,000 hours of recordings dating back to 1890, and 625,000 selections of folk song, folk music, folk tales and oral history), law colln (American and foreign material), music colln (8m. items), colln of motion pictures, broadcasts and sound recordings (incl. film dating back to 1894, 720,000 moving image items, 3m. sound recordings, copyright deposits of recordings since 1972, jazz and popular music on 78-rpm discs, NBC radio colln of 75,000 broadcasts, House of Representatives debates), colln of prints and photographs (15,676,000 items, incl. early daguerreotypes); Librarian of Congress JAMES H. BILLINGTON.

Moorland-Spingarn Research Center: Howard Univ., Washington, DC 20059; tel. (202) 806-7240; fax (202) 806-6405; internet www.howard.edu/msrc; f. 1914; one of the world's largest and most comprehensive repositories for collns documenting the history and culture of people of African descent in the Americas, Africa and Europe; 200,000 vols, 650 MSS and archival collns, many thousands of microforms, sheet music, audio cassettes, transcripts, photographs, records and artefacts; Dir Dr CLIFFORD L. MUSE, Jr.

National Archives and Records Administration: Nat. Archives Bldg, 700 Pennsylvania Ave, NW, Washington, DC 20408-0001; tel. (202) 501-5400 Nat. Archives at College Park, 8601 Adelphi Rd, College Park, MD 20740-6001; tel. (301) 837-2000; fax (301) 837-0483; internet www.archives.gov; f. 1934; ensures, for citizens and federal officials, ready access to essential evidence that documents the rights of American citizens, the actions of federal officials, and the nat. experience; establishes policies and procedures for managing US Govt records and assists federal agencies in documenting their activities, administering record management programmes, scheduling records, and retiring non-current records; obtains, arranges, describes, preserves and provides access to the essential documentation of the 3 brs of govt, manages the presidential libraries system, and publishes the laws, regulations, and presidential and other public documents; assists the Information Security Oversight Office, which manages federal classification and declassification policies, and the Nat. Historical Publs and records Comm., which makes grants nationwide to help non-profit orgs identify, preserve, and provide access to materials that document American history; consists of 33 facilities nationwide, incl. 18 regional records services facilities and 10 presidential Libraries; on permanent display in the Exhibition Hall are the Declaration of Independence, the Constitution of the United States, and the Bill of Rights; Archivist of the United States DAVID S. FERRIERO; publ. *Prologue: Quarterly Journal of the National Archives and Records Administration*.

National Geographic Society Library: 1145 17th St, NW, Washington, DC 20036-4688; tel. (202) 857-7783; fax (202) 429-5731; e-mail library@ngs.org; internet www.ngslis.org; f. 1920; reference reading room open to the public for research by appointment; spec. collns: polar, natural history, exploration and discovery, soc. publs; 25,000 vols; Dir for Libraries and Information Services BARBARA PENFOLD FERRY; publs *National Geographic Explorer*, *National Geographic Kids*, *National Geographic Magazine*, *National Geographic Traveller*.

National Library of Education: 400 Maryland Ave, SW, Washington, DC 20202; tel. (800) 424-1616; fax (202) 401-0547; e-mail library@ed.gov; internet ies.ed.gov/ncee/projects/nat_ed_library.asp; f. 1870 as Bureau of Education library, present name 1994; fed. govt's primary resource centre for education information; 60,000 vols, c. 800 periodicals, the complete ERIC (Education Resources Information Center) microfiche colln, archives of official print and electronic documents published by the Dept of Education, and histories and documentation of education legislation passed by the Congress; depositary library; Dir CHRISTINA DUNN.

Navy Department Library: Washington Navy Yard, 805 Kidder Breese St, SE, Washington, DC 20374-5060; tel. (202) 433-4132; fax (202) 433-9553; e-mail navylibrary@navy.mil; internet www.history.navy.mil/library; f. 1800; 170,000 vols; Dir JEAN HORT.

Pentagon Library/WHS PLCC: 1155 Defense Pentagon, Washington, DC 20301-1155; The Pentagon Bldg, Arlington, VA 22202-3905; tel. (703) 695-1997; fax (703) 695-4009; internet www.pentagonlibrary.whs.mil; f. 1944; combines the resources of 28 fmr War Dept libraries into one central colln in the Pentagon; spec. collns on military arts and sciences, unit histories, military law; and army admin., training and technical publs; 100,000 vols, 1,800 periodicals and 1m. documents; Acquisitions Librarian RICHARD C. MAY.

Ralph J. Bunche Library of the Department of State: 2201 C St, NW, Washington, DC 20520-2442; tel. (202) 647-1099; fax (202) 647-2971; e-mail library@state.gov; f. 1789; materials relate primarily to the economic, political and social conditions in foreign areas, treaties and agreements, int. relations and diplomatic history; 400,000 vols; Chief Librarian FRANCES PERROS.

Smithsonian Institution Archives: POB 37012, MRC 507, Washington, DC 20013-7012; located at: Capital Gallery Bldg, Suite 3000, 600 Maryland Ave, Washington, DC 20024-2520; tel. (202) 357-1420; fax (202) 357-2395; e-mail osiaref@osia.si.edu; internet www.si.edu/archives; repository for the official records of the Instn since its foundation in 1846, and official repository for numerous other orgs; personal papers of noted Smithsonian staff, artists, researchers and museum founders; 14,000 cu ft of materials; Dir ANNE VAN CAMP.

Smithsonian Institution Libraries: National Museum of Natural History Bldg, POB 37012, Room 22, MRC 154, Washington, DC 20560; National Museum of Natural History Bldg, 10th and Constitution Ave, NW, Washington, DC 20560; tel. (202) 633-2240; fax (202) 786-2866; e-mail libmail@sil.si.edu; internet www.sil.si.edu; f. 1968; attached to the Smithsonian Instn; exhibition gallery and annual colln-based curated exhibition; displays in Nat. Museum of American History, Nat. Air and Space Museum and Nat. Museum of Natural History; active exhibition loan programme; 1.5m. vols in 21 brs, incl. 50,000 rare books, over 450,000 pieces of trade literature, World's Fair collection, history of science and technology; Dir Dr NANCY E. GWINN.

United States Senate Library: Russell Senate Office Bldg, Washington, DC 20510; tel. (202) 224-7106; fax (202) 224-0879; f. 1871; the work of the Senate Library is essentially that of research and reference for the use of the Senate and its cttees; prin. services rendered incl. legislative and gen. reference, automated information retrieval, Micrographics Center and photoduplication facilities; 250,000 vols, incl. spec. colln of legislative proceedings and documents from 1774; Senate Librarian LEONA FAUST; Head of Reference and Information Services ZOE DAVIS.

Wirtz Labor Library, Department of Labor: Rm N2445, 200 Constitution Ave, NW, Washington, DC 20210; tel. (202) 693-6600; fax (202) 693-6642; e-mail library@dol.gov; internet www.dol.gov/oasam/library; f. 1917; 140,000 vols, 5,000 electronic and print periodical titles; Library Dir JAMES IGOE.

Florida

Broward County Division of Libraries: 100 South Andrews Ave, Fort Lauderdale, FL 33301; tel. (954) 357-7555; internet www.broward.org/library/welcome.htm; f. 1974; 919,048 vols; consists of a flagship main library, the African-American Research Library and Cultural Center, the Alvin-Sherman Library, Research, and Information Technology Center at Nova Southeastern Univ., 5 regional libraries, 30 br. libraries and 2 reading centres; spec. collns: black heritage, Spanish language, Floridiana; main library is a depository for govt documents; Dir ROBERT E. CANNON.

Florida State University Library: 116 Honors Way, Tallahassee, FL 32306-2047; tel. (850) 644-2706; fax (850) 644-1234; internet www.lib.fsu.edu; f. 1851; 2,947,702 vols and bound serials; Dir JULIA ZIMMERMAN.

Miami-Dade Public Library System: 101 West Flagler St, Miami, FL 33130-1523; tel. (305) 375-2665; fax (305) 375-3048; internet www.mdpls.org; f. 1971; 4,142,711 vols; spec. collns incl. Florida history, Spanish books, urban affairs, genealogy; main library, 43 brs with further 13 scheduled to open; 2 mobile libraries; Dir RAYMOND SANTIAGO.

University of Florida Libraries: POB 117001, Gainesville, FL 32611-7001; tel. (352) 392-0342; fax (352) 392-7251; internet www.uflib.ufl.edu; f. 1853; 4m. vols; spec. collns: children's literature in English before 1900, contemporary American and British poetry, contemporary American creative writing, Floridiana, history of printing and book arts, Judaica, Latin Americana, New England literature before 1900, performing arts, United States Borderlands (Florida), Irish literature; Dean of Univ. Libraries JUDITH RUSSELL.

Georgia

Atlanta-Fulton Public Library: 1 Margaret Mitchell Sq., NW, Atlanta, GA 30303; tel. (404) 730-1700; internet www.af.public.lib.ga.us; f. 1867; 2,177,267 vols, 70,000 recordings and audio cassettes; 34 brs; Dir JOHN F. SZABO.

Hawaii

Hawaii State Public Library System: 44 Merchant St, Honolulu, HI 96813; tel. (808) 586-3704; fax (808) 586-3715; e-mail stlib@librarieshawaii.org; internet www.librarieshawaii.org; f. 1879 as Honolulu Library and Reading Room Association; 3,679,065 vols; 51 brs on 6 islands (Oahu, Hawaii, Maui, Kauai, Molokai, Lanai); State Librarian RICHARD BURNS.

Illinois

Abraham Lincoln Presidential Library and Museum: *Library*: 112 North 6th St, Springfield, IL; *Museum*: 212 North 6th St, Springfield, IL; tel. (217) 558-8844; fax (217) 558-8878; internet www.alplm.org; f. 2002; fmr Illinois State Historical Library (f. 1889) of 12m. items; spec. colln: Henry Horner Lincoln Colln of 46,000 items incl. 1,500 signed MSS, 10,000 books and pamphlets, 1,000 posters, 1,000 prints and photographs, Gettysburg Address, Second Inaugural Address, Anti-Slavery Statement; Exec. Dir RICK BEARD.

American Medical Association—James S. Todd Memorial Library: 515 North State St, Chicago, IL 60610; tel. (312) 464-4855; fax (312) 464-5226; e-mail amalibrary@ama-assn.org; internet www.ama-assn.org; f. 1911; 18,000 vols, 1,100 journal titles; spec. collns: history of US medicine, AMA publs; Dir SANDRA R. SCHEFRIS.

Chicago Public Library: 400 South State St, Chicago, IL 60605-1203; tel. (312) 747-4300; internet www.chipublib.org; f. 1872; 4,764,000 vols; Pres. JAYNE CARR THOMPSON.

Cook County Law Library: 2900 Richard J. Daley Center, 50 W Washington St, 29th Floor, Chicago, IL 60602; tel. (312) 603-5423; fax (312) 603-4716; internet www.co.cook.il.us/agencydetail.php?pagencyid=10; f. 1966; 350,000 vols; 7 brs; Exec. Law Librarian BENNIE MARTIN.

Illinois State Library: 300 South Second St, Springfield, IL 62701-1796; tel. (217) 782-2994; fax (217) 785-4326; internet www.cyberdriveillinois.com/departments/library/home.html; f. 1839; 5m. items and documents; State Librarian JESSE WHITE; Dir ANNE CRAIG; publs *Insight* (6 a year), *Illinois Literacy* (4 a year), *Illinois Libraries* (irregular).

John Crerar Library of the University of Chicago: 5730 South Ellis Ave, Chicago, IL 60637; tel. (773) 702-7715; fax (773) 702-3317; e-mail crerar-reference@lib.uchicago.edu; internet www.lib.uchicago.edu/e/crerar; f. 1892, merged with Univ. of Chicago 1984; 1,350,000 vols on the biomedical and physical sciences, incl. history of science and medicine; rare books and MSS from the Crerar collns are in the univ. Joseph Regenstein Library; Dirs BARBARA KERN, ANDREA TWISS-BROOKS.

Library of International Relations: 565 West Adams, Chicago, IL 60661; tel. (312) 906-5615; fax (312) 906-5685; internet library.kentlaw.edu; f. 1932, 1992 became part of Illinois Institute of Technology; supported by voluntary contributions; encourages interest and research in int. affairs; specialized library of 175,000 vols, serials and periodicals; official depository of the UN and EU; open to the public; Dir KEITH ANN STIVERSON.

Newberry Library: 60 West Walton St, Chicago, IL 60610; tel. (312) 943-9090; internet www.newberry.org; f. 1887; ind. research instn; maintains research and educational programmes in its Center for the History of Cartography, Center for the History of the American Indian, Center for Renaissance Studies, and Family and Community History Center; 1.5m. vols in the humanities, 15,000 cubic ft of MSS, with spec. collns on the American Indians, the history of printing and book arts, music, American and English history and literature, exploration and early cartography, Portugal, the Renaissance in England and Europe, European history from the Renaissance to 1815, the Philippine Islands, colonial Latin America; Pres. and Librarian DAVID SPADAFORA; Vice-Pres. for Library Services HJORDIS HALVORSON.

Northwestern University Libraries: 1970 Campus Dr., Evanston, IL 60208-2300; tel. (847) 491-7658; fax (847) 491-8306; e-mail library@northwestern.edu; internet www.library.northwestern.edu; f. 1856; 3,893,000 vols; Northwestern Univ. Library (humanities and social sciences, with spec. collns on Africa: comprehensive historically on sub-Sahara, francophone West Africa and South Africa; extensive holdings in Art Nouveau, dada, surrealism, futurism and expressionism, Samuel Johnson, siege and commune of Paris 1870–71, women's liberation movement; libraries for music and transportation); br. libraries for science-eng., geology and mathematics; professional libraries (dentistry, law, medicine) and the Schaffner Library in Chicago; Univ. Librarian SARAH M. PRITCHARD.

University of Chicago Library: 1100 E 57th St, Chicago, IL 60637-1502; tel. (773) 702-8740; fax (773) 702-6623; e-mail info@lib.uchicago.edu; internet www.lib.uchicago.edu; f. 1892; 9,837,021 vols, incl. print and electronic holdings; comprises Regenstein (humanities and social sciences), Crerar (science, medicine, technology), Harper (college), D'Angelo (law), Mansueto and 2 other libraries; Spec. Collns Research Center, incl. rare books, MSS, the Chicago Jazz Archive, Univ. Archives; E Asia, S Asia, Middle E, Slavic and E European area studies; Dir and Univ. Librarian JUDITH NADLER.

University of Illinois (Urbana-Champaign) Library: 1408 West Gregory Dr., Urbana, IL 61801; tel. (217) 333-2290; internet www.library.uiuc.edu; f. 1867; 8,840,000 vols, 7,457,000 MSS, maps, microtexts and other items; 40 departmental libraries; spec. collns in classical literature and history, English literature, incl. Milton and Shakespeare, Western US history, Lincolniana, Italian history, music, architecture, science and technology; Univ. Librarian PAULA T. KAUFMAN.

Indiana

Allen County Public Library: 900 Library Pl., POB 2270, Fort Wayne, IN 46801; tel. (260) 421-1200; fax (260) 421-1386; e-mail ask@acpl.info; internet www.acpl.lib.in.us; f. 1895; 3.7m. vols; Fred J. Reynolds Historical Genealogy Colln; 13 brs; Dir JEFFREY R. KRULL.

Indiana State Library: 140 N Senate Ave, Indianapolis, IN 46204-2296; tel. (317) 232-3675; fax (317) 232-3728; internet www.library.in.gov; f. 1825; provides library service to state govt, advice and counsel to the libraries and librarians of the state, reference service and materials for local school, public, spec., and academic libraries; genealogy and spec. research collns; Indiana history colln; service to the blind and physically handicapped; library for Indiana Acad. of Science; 1,703,621 items; Dir ROBERTA L. BROOKER; publs *Focus on Indiana Libraries* (12 a year), *Indiana Libraries* (4 a year).

Indiana University Libraries: 1320 E 10th St, Bloomington, IN 47405; tel. (812) 855-8028; fax (812) 855-2576; e-mail libref@indiana.edu; internet www.libraries.iub.edu; f. 1829; 8,677,974 vols, 39,129 linear ft MSS, 281,618 music scores, 349,004 slides, 528,923 maps and charts, 309,580 audio recordings, 106,138 serial titles (print and electronic) serials, 3,097,319 graphic materials (incl. photos), 1.1m. govt publs; Dean of Libraries BRENDA JOHNSON.

Indianapolis-Marion County Public Library: 40 East St Clair St, POB 211, Indianapolis, IN 46206; tel. (317) 269-1700; fax (317) 269-1768; internet www.imcpl.org; f. 1873; 1,815,942 vols; 22 brs, 3 bookmobiles; CEO LINDA MIELKE; publ. *Reading in Indianapolis* (12 a year).

Purdue University Libraries: 504 W State St, West Lafayette, IN 47907; tel. (765) 494-2831; fax (765) 494-0156; internet www.lib.purdue.edu; f. 1869; 2.5m. vols; 14 brs; Dean Prof. JAMES MULLINS.

University of Notre Dame Libraries: Notre Dame, IN 46556; tel. (574) 631-6258; fax (574) 631-6772; internet www.library.nd.edu; f. 1873; 2.5m. vols; spec. collns: Ambrosiana, American Catholic Studies, O'Neill Irish Music, Joyce Sports Research, medieval education, Descartes, Jacques Maritain, Dante, orchids, historical botany, Irish maps and sea charts, Irish Rebellion of 1798, Irish postage stamps; Dir JENNIFER A. YOUNGER.

Iowa

Herbert Hoover Presidential Library and Museum: 210 Parkside Dr., POB 488, West Branch, IA 52358; tel. (319) 643-5301; fax (319) 643-6045; e-mail hoover.library@nara.gov; internet hoover.archives.gov; f. 1962; administered by the Nat. Archives and Records Admin.; official and personal papers of 31st Pres. of USA; also 150 MS collns; 18,000 vols, 8,247,000 MSS, 43,000 photos, 522 hours sound recordings and 156,000 ft of film, 2,770 rolls of microfilm, 11,864 pages of oral history, 5,300 museum objects covering history since beginning of the 20th century, econ. and political science; Dir TIMOTHY WALCH; publ. *Historical Materials in the Herbert Hoover Presidential Library*.

Iowa State University Library: cnr of Osborn Dr. and Morrill Rd, Ames, IA 50011-2140; tel. (515) 294-3642; fax (515) 294-5525; internet www.lib.iastate.edu; f. 1870; 2,473,075 vols, 3,491,798 microforms, 46,798 electronic journals, 108,440 photographs and maps; spec. collns: Archives of American Agriculture, Archives of American Veterinary Medicine, American Archives of the Factual Film, Women in Science and Eng. Archives, Univ. Archives; fed. depository; books on science and technology, incl. agriculture, entomology, botany, ornithology and veterinary medicine; Dean OLIVIA M. A. MADISON.

University of Iowa Libraries: Iowa City, IA 52242-1420; tel. (319) 335-5299; fax (319) 335-5900; e-mail lib-ref@uiowa.edu; internet www.lib.uiowa.edu; f. 1847; 3,823,000 vols, 11 departmental libraries; spec. colln: Iowa Women's Archives; Univ. Librarian NANCY L. BAKER.

Kansas

Dwight D. Eisenhower Library: 200 SE Fourth St, Abilene, KS 67410; tel. (785) 263-6700; fax (785) 263-6718; e-mail eisenhower.library@nara.gov; internet www.eisenhower.archives.gov; f. 1962; MSS, presidential and personal papers related to former Pres. Eisenhower, and MSS of important persons in Eisenhower's admin. and military career; museum with 65,000 artifacts; 26m. MSS pages, 31,850 pages oral history transcripts, 28,500 vols, 333,000 still photographs, audio tapes and films; Dir KARL WEISSENBACH; publ. *Overview* (4 a year).

Kansas State Historical Society: 6425 SW Sixth St, Topeka, KS 66615-1099; tel. (913) 272-8681; fax (913) 272-8682; internet www.kshs.org; f. 1875; 300,000 vols; state archives, newspapers and census, archaeology; manuscript, photograph and maps dept, museum, folk arts dept, education dept; 3,000 mems; Exec. Dir JENNIE CHIN; publs *Kansas Heritage* (4 a year), *Kansas History: A Journal of the Central Plains* (4 a year), *Kansas Kaleidoscope* (6 a year).

Kansas State University Libraries: Manhattan, KS 66506; tel. (785) 532-7400; e-mail library@ksu.edu; internet www.lib.ksu.edu; f. 1863; 1,209,000 vols, 31,867 serials, 4m. microforms, 1,840,000 govt docs, 100,000 maps, 8,400 scores, 32,000 pieces of audio visual material, 5 brs (veterinary medical, eng., maths and Pphysics, architecture and technology and aviation); spec. collns in cookbooks, Linnaeana, Robert Graves, and Diderot's *Encyclopédie*; Dean of Libraries LORI GOETSCH; publs *KSU Library Cassette Series on Library Technology* (irregular), *Library Bibliography Series* (irregular).

University of Kansas Libraries: Suite 502, 1425 Jayhawk Blvd, Lawrence, KS 66045-7544; tel. (785) 864-8983; fax (785) 864-5311; e-mail sroyer@ku.edu; internet www.lib.ku.edu; f. 1866; 3.8m. vols, 322,000 maps, 3,370,000 microforms, 3m. graphics (mostly photographs), 30,000 sound recordings, 691,000 govt docs, 15,000 linear ft MSS; Dean of Libraries LORRAINE HARICOMBE.

Kentucky

Kentucky Department for Libraries and Archives: 300 Coffee Tree Rd, Frankfort, KY 40601; tel. (502) 564-8300; internet www.kdla.ky.gov; 116,000 vols; 3,400 films, 5,000 video cassettes; 646 periodicals; 44,000 fed. documents; State Librarian WAYNE ONKST.

Louisville Free Public Library: 301 York St, Louisville, KY 40203; tel. (502) 574-1611; fax (502) 574-1666; internet www.lfpl.org; f. 1902; 1,172,236 vols; 36,000 phono-discs, 70,000 programmes on electronic tape, operates 2 FM radio stations for music and educational programmes; 18 brs, 1 bookmobile; spec. Kentucky History Colln; houses a 'Louisville Art Gallery'; Talking Book Library for the blind and physically handicapped; Dir CRAIG BUTHOD; publ. *Library News*.

University of Kentucky Libraries: Lexington, KY 40506-0456; tel. (859) 257-0500; fax (859) 257-8379; e-mail refdesk@uky.edu; internet www.uky.edu/libraries; f. 1909; 3,537,710 vols, 44,610 current serials incl. 34,463 electronic journals, 417 licensed networked electronic resources, 260,702 maps, 1,102,510 govt documents, 2,097,143 photographs and graphic materials, 92,600 audio, film and video cassette items, 6,433,748 microforms; 14 br. and collegiate libraries; regional depository for govt publs and a depository for EU and Canadian publs, British parliamentary papers, Kentucky govt publs, and technical reports from US fed. agencies; King Library Press; univ. and audiovisual archives; large colln of Kentuckiana, spec. collns of 19th-century British literature, French and Spanish drama from 1600 to 1900, modern political manuscript collns, broadsides, ballads and chapbooks, Cortot colln of music theory, typography, history of books, Appalachian Regional Commission archives, oral history colln; Center for Digital Programs creates digital content for the Kentuckiana Digital Library, incl. electronic texts, digitized photographs, images and archival finding aids; Dean of Libraries CAROL PITTS DIEDRICHS.

Louisiana

Louisiana State University Libraries: Baton Rouge, LA 70803; tel. (225) 578-2217; fax (225) 578-6825; internet www.lib.lsu.edu; f. 1860; UN, fed. and state depositories; spec. collns incl. E. A. McIlhenny Natural History Colln, Louisiana Colln, sugar technology, Southern history, agriculture, plant pathology, petroleum, bibliography colln, aquaculture, incl. crawfish, wetlands research and marine biology; archives on Lower Mississippi Valley; 3,175,014 vols, 5,375,405 microforms; Dean JENNIFER CARGILL; publ. *Library Lectures*.

New Orleans Public Library: 219 Loyola Ave, New Orleans, LA 70112; tel. (504) 596-2550; fax (504) 596-2609; internet nutrias.org; f. 1843; 1,043,471 vols; 12 brs; spec. collns: city archives colln, civil and criminal courts colln, carnivals, maps, photographs, rare books, early sheet music, early jazz recordings and MSS; incl. African American Resource Center and Business and Science Div.; Chair. IRVIN MAYFIELD; Head of Main Public Services LINDA MARSHALL HILL.

Tulane University Libraries: 7001 Freret St, New Orleans, LA 70118; tel. (504) 865-5605; fax (504) 865-6773; internet library.tulane.edu; f. 1834; 2,331,250 vols (incl. law, medicine and 6 other collns); spec. collns on New Orleans, Louisiana and Southern US history; Latin America, architecture and jazz; Dean of the Library LANCE QUERY.

Maine

Maine State Library: 64 State House Station, Augusta, ME 04333-0064; tel. (207) 287-5600; fax (207) 287-5615; internet www.maine.gov/msl; f. 1836; 291,526 vols, 703 periodicals, 1,411 video cassettes, 250,164 govt docs; Librarian J. GARY NICHOLS.

Maryland

Enoch Pratt Free Library: 400 Cathedral St, Baltimore, MD 21201-4484; tel. (410) 396-5430; fax (410) 837-5837; internet www.pratt.lib.md.us; f. 1886; spec. collns: H. L. Mencken colln, Maryland history colln; 2,290,042 vols, 91,000 maps, 5,000 films, 19,094 video cassettes, 38,450 slides, 486 filmstrips, 34,802 recordings; Dir CARLA D. HAYDEN; publs *Menckeniana* (4 a year), *Pratt Matters* (4 a year), *Staff Reporter* (12 a year).

Johns Hopkins University Libraries: Baltimore, MD 21218; tel. (410) 516-8335; internet webapps.jhu.edu/jhuniverse/libraries; f. 1876; network of libraries incl. the Milton S. Eisenhower Library, 1 of the Sheridan libraries and the principal research library of the univ.; spec. collns in medicine, int. affairs, music and earth and space science; 2,961,160 vols; Dean of Univ. Libraries WINSTON TABB.

National Agricultural Library: Abraham Lincoln Bldg, 10301 Baltimore Ave, Beltsville, MD 20705-2351; tel. (301) 504-5755; fax (301) 504-5472; internet www.nal.usda.gov; f. 1862; agriculture and the related sciences; spec. collns: Layne R. Beaty Papers (farm radio and television broadcasting); foreign and domestic nursery seed trade catalogues; flock, herd and stud books; audio-visual colln on food and nutrition; apiculture; Forest Service and USDA Photo Colln on optical laser discs; M. Truman Fossum Colln (floriculture); James M. Gwin Colln (poultry); Charles E. North Colln (milk sanitation); Pomology Colln (original pomological art); Charles Valentine Riley Colln (entomology); plant exploration photograph colln; food and nutrition micro-computer software; MAPP colln of family life education materials; computer database (AGRICOLA) of 3m. records for books and journal articles in agriculture; information centres on agricultural trade and marketing, alternative farming systems, animal welfare, aquaculture, biotechnology, food and nutrition, plant genome, rural information, technology transfer, water quality and youth devt; 3.3m. vols; Dir Dr SIMON LIU; publs *Agriculture Libraries Information Notes* (12 a year), *Quick Bibliography* (irregular).

National Institute of Standards and Technology Research Library: West End Admin. Bldg, Rm 101 E Wing, Route 70 S and Quince Rd, Gaithersburg, MD 20899; e-mail inquiries@nist.gov; internet www.nist.gov; f. 1912; 200,000 vols, 1,000 journals; spec. collns: science, eng. and technology; Dir WILLIAM A. JEFFREY; Deputy Dir JAMES TURNER; Librarian PAUL VASSALLO.

National Institutes of Health Library: Bldg 10, Room 1L25, 10 Center Dr., Bethesda, MD 20892-1150; tel. (301) 496-2447; fax (301) 402-0254; internet nihlibrary.nih.gov; f. 1903; serves the specialized research programmes of the NIH; 70,000 books, 160,000 periodicals, 2,898 microforms; biology, medicine, health sciences, chemistry, physiology, physics; Chief Librarian SUZANNE GREFSHEIM; Librarian JEAN WEISS.

National Library of Medicine: 8600 Rockville Pike, Bethesda, MD 20894; tel. (301) 496-6308; fax (301) 496-4450; e-mail custserv@nlm.nih.gov; internet www.nlm.nih.gov; f. 1836; 7m. items; books, journals, technical reports, MSS, microfilms, photographs and images; world's largest medical library; houses old and rare medical works; materials, information and research services in all areas of biomedicine and healthcare; Dir DONALD A. B. LINDBERG; publ. *Index Medicus* (12 a year).

University of Maryland Libraries: College Park, MD 20742-7011; tel. (301) 405-0800; internet www.lib.umd.edu; f. 1856; consists of 8 campus libraries: McKeldin Library, Hornbake Library, Art Library, Architecture Library, Eng. and Physical Sciences Library, Michelle Smith Performing Arts Library, Shady Grove Library and Media Center, White Memorial (Chemistry) Library and a number of spec. collns; 3,767,653 vols; Dean PATRICIA STEELE; Man. I. DILLON.

Massachusetts

Boston Athenaeum: 10½ Beacon St, Boston, MA 02108-3777; tel. (617) 227-0270; fax (617) 227-5266; internet www.bostonathenaeum.org; f. 1807; ind. research library; 750,000 vols; history, biography, English and American literature, fine and decorative arts; spec. collns incl. confederate states imprints, books from libraries of George Washington, Gen. Henry Knox and the Adams Family, the King's Chapel Colln (1698), Gypsy literature, private press publs, 19th-century tracts, early US govt documents, maps, charts and atlases, and the Charles E. Mason print colln; Bartlett Hayes poster colln; 19th-century photographs; Head of Reference MARY WARNEMENT; Head of Reader Services WILLIAM D. HACKER.

Boston Public Library: 700 Boylston St, Boston, MA 02116; tel. (617) 536-5400; fax (617) 236-4306; e-mail info@bpl.org; internet www.bpl.org; f. 1848; the oldest free municipal library supported by public taxation in the world; 28 brs; 15m. vols; Pres. AMY RYAN.

Boston University Libraries: 771 Commonwealth Ave, Boston, MA 02215; tel. (617) 353-3704; e-mail ask@bu.edu; internet www.bu.edu/library; f. 1839; 1,920,000 vols, 28,000 periodicals; 5 major libraries: Mugar Memorial Library (7 brs humanities and social sciences), Howard Gotlieb Archival Research Center (rare books and MSS), Pappas Law Library, Medical Library, School of Theology Library; Dir ROBERT HUDSON.

Francis A. Countway Library of Medicine: 10 Shattuck St, Boston, MA 02115; tel. (617) 432-2142; fax (617) 432-0693; internet www.countway.harvard.edu; f. 1965; serves the Harvard Medical School, Harvard School of Public Health, Harvard School of Dental Medicine, Boston Medical Library and the Massachusetts Medical Soc.; 630,000 vols, 3,500 journals, 10,000 non-current biomedical journals; Dir Dr ISAAC KOHANE; Dir of Center for the History of Medicine SCOTT PODOLSKY.

Harvard University Library: Cambridge, MA 02138; tel. (617) 495-3650; fax (617) 495-0370; e-mail administration@hulmail.harvard.edu; internet hul.harvard.edu; f. 1638; 13,143,330 vols divided among c. 80 libraries; the oldest library in the USA; the central collns are housed in the Widener, Houghton, Pusey, Lamont, Hilles, Cabot Science, Harvard-Yenching, Littauer, Loeb Music, Tozzer, Fine Arts and Geological Sciences Libraries; important collns in nearly every field of learning and 4,000 vols printed before 1501; Dir ROBERT DARNTON; Harvard College Librarian NANCY CLINE; publ. *Harvard Library Bulletin*.

Massachusetts Historical Society Library: 1154 Boylston St, Boston, MA 02215; tel. (617) 536-1608; fax (617) 859-0074; e-mail library@masshist.org; internet www.masshist.org/library; f. 1791; 250,000 vols, 3,600 MSS collns; personal papers of individuals and families who lived in Massachusetts; Librarians PETER DRUMMEY, STEPHEN T. RILEY; publs *Miscellany* (4 a year), *Proceedings* (1 a year).

Massachusetts Institute of Technology Libraries: 14S 216, 77 Massachusetts Ave, Cambridge, MA 02139-4307; tel. (617) 253-5651; fax (617) 253-8894; internet libraries .mit.edu; f. 1861; 2,667,215 vols and pamphlets, 17,000 current journals, 30,000 electronic journals, 478 online databases; 5 major subject libraries, for Architecture and planning, eng., humanities, science, management and social science, as well as 5 specialized libraries and the Institute archives; Dir of Libraries ANN J. WOLPERT.

Springfield Library: 220 State St, Springfield, MA 01103; tel. (413) 263-6828; fax (413) 263-6817; e-mail askalibrarian@ springfieldlibrary.org; internet www .springfieldlibrary.org; f. 1857; 668,856 vols, 32,490 audio recordings, 20,804 video cassettes, 3,933 CD-ROMs, 296 periodicals; 6 brs; Dir EMILY BADER.

State Library of Massachusetts: 341 State House, Boston, MA 02133; tel. (617) 727-2590; fax (617) 727-5819; e-mail library .director@state.ma.us; internet www.mass .gov/lib; f. 1826; 822,083 vols; a govt and public affairs library serving the information and research needs of the exec. and legislative branches of Massachusetts state govt; depository for printed documents of the same and for selected fed. documents; collns esp. strong in public law, public affairs, state and local history; State Librarian LESLIE A. KIRWAN; publ. *Commonwealth of Massachusetts Publications Received by the State Library* (4 a year).

Worcester Public Library: 3 Salem Sq., Worcester, MA 01608; tel. (508) 799-1690; internet www.worcpublib.org; f. 1859; 586,000 vols; 3 sites: main library at Salem Sq., Frances Perkins Library at Greendale and Great Brook Valley Branch Library; largest selective depository of fed. documents in central Massachusetts; Librarian PENELOPE B. JOHNSON.

Michigan

Detroit Public Library: 5201 Woodward Ave, Detroit, MI 48202; tel. (313) 833-4036; internet www.detroitpubliclibrary.org; f. 1865; 2,655,156 vols, 163,158 maps, 754,397 microforms, 788,464 pictures, 20,000 video cassettes; spec. collns on automotive history, Burton Historical Colln (Michigan, Great Lakes and Old North-west Territory), Labor History Colln, Azalia Hackley Memorial Colln of Negro Music, Dance and Drama; 24 brs; Dir NANCY SKOWRONSKI.

Library of Michigan: 702 West Kalamazoo, POB 30007, Lansing, MI 48909-7507; tel. (517) 373-1300; fax (517)373-5700; e-mail librarian@michigan.gov; internet www .michigan.gov/libraryofmichigan; f. 1828; operates a main library and a law library; specializes in MI history, current information, public policy issues, genealogy, state and fed. govt document depositories; 2.75m. vols; State Librarian NANCY R. ROBERTSON; publs *Directory of Michigan Libraries* (online), *District Library Law, Michigan Library Statistics, Michigan Public Libraries Data Digest* (online, 1 a year).

Michigan State University Libraries: East Lansing, MI 48824-1048; tel. (517) 432-6123; fax (517) 432-3532; internet www .lib.msu.edu; f. 1855; 4.9m. vols; br. libraries within main bldg incl. Africana, Digital and Multimedia Center, Fine Arts, Govt Documents (3m. items), Map Library (200,000 maps), Spec. Collns (incl. Chicano and Boricua), Turfgrass Information Center, Vincent Voice Library; br. libraries outside main bldg incl. Biomedical and Physical Sciences Library, William C. Gast Business Library (incl. Labor and Industrial Relations Library), Engineering Library, Gull Lake Library, Int. Center Library, Law College Library, Mathematics Library, Charles W. Barr Planning and Design Library, Veterinary Medical Center Library; Dir CLIFFORD H. HAKA.

University of Michigan Libraries: 818 Hatcher South, Ann Arbor, MI 48109-1205; tel. (734) 764-9356; fax (734) 763-5080; internet www.lib.umich.edu; f. 1817; 7m. vols, incl. spec. collns in ancient papyri, early economics, early military science, Elsevier imprints, English and American drama, Frost and Faulkner collns, fine printing, French historical pamphlets (16th–17th century), imaginary voyages, music and musicology (17th–19th century); William L. Clements Library of American History; Michigan Historical Collns; Univ. Librarian PAUL N. COURANT.

Wayne State University Libraries: 5150 Anthony Wayne Dr., Detroit, MI 48202; tel. (313) 577-0243; fax (313) 577-6777; e-mail acquisitions@wayne.edu; internet www.lib .wayne.edu; 3,342,000 vols in 5 library units: the David Adamany Undergraduate Library (general), the Neef Law Library, the Purdy/ Kresge Library (arts), the Science and Engineering Library and the Shiffman Medical Library; Dean of Library Services SANDRA YEE.

Minnesota

James Jerome Hill Reference Library: 80 West 4th St, Saint Paul, MN 55102; tel. (651) 265-5500; internet www.jjhill.org; f. 1916; 240,000 vols; applied business and commerce; Dir of Library Services NICOLE MARCHAND.

Minneapolis Public Library: 250 South Marquette, Minneapolis, MN 55401; tel. (612) 630-6000; fax (612) 630-6210; e-mail askus@mplib.org; internet www.mplib.org; f. 1885; 3,271,000 vols; 15 brs; spec. collns incl. Heffelfinger Aesop's and Others' Fables, 19th-century American studies, Kittleson World War II, Minneapolis history, Mark Twain, Huttner Abolition and Anti-Slavery, Environmental Conservation Library, Foundations, US Patents, Early American Exploration and Travel, North American Indians, Spencer Natural History; Dir KATHERINE G. HADLEY.

Minnesota Historical Society Library: 345 Kellogg Blvd, W, Saint Paul, MN 55102-1906; tel. (651) 259-3300; fax (651) 296-7436; e-mail reference@mnhs.org; internet www.mnhs.org/library; f. 1849; 300,000 vols; N American history particularly relating to Minnesota and the Upper Midwest (especially travel accounts, fur trade, Scandinavian and other immigration, labour, political and church history, railway records, local history and genealogy); several million pamphlets, documents, Minnesota newspapers, films, maps, photographs, cassettes, artefacts, manuscripts, and state and local govt archives; Asst Dir for Library and Archives ROBERT HORTON.

Minnesota State Library Services: 1500 Highway 36W, Roseville, MN 55113-4266; tel. (651) 582-8791; fax (651) 582-8752; e-mail mde.lst@state.mn.us; internet education.state.mn.us/mde/learning_support/library_services; f. 1899; attached to Minnesota Dept of Education; resource and information center serving state and local govt, libraries and library support groups; administers state library programmes and federal LSTA grant programme; State Librarian and Dir NANCY WALTON (acting); publs *Minnesota Libraries, Streaming News* (12 a year).

Saint Paul Public Library: 90 West 4th St, Saint Paul, MN 55102; tel. (651) 266-7073; fax (651) 266-7060; internet www.sppl.org; f. 1882; 1,131,578 vols; 13 brs; Dir MELANIE HUGGINS.

University of Minnesota Libraries: 499 Wilson Library, 309 19th Ave South, Minneapolis, MN 55455; tel. (612) 624-4520; fax (612) 626-9353; e-mail infopoint@umn.edu; internet www.lib.umn.edu; f. 1851; 6,200,669 vols, 36,900 current journals; general and 14 deptl libraries; spec. collns: law, immigration history, social welfare history, data processing, medicine, children's literature, horticulture, literary MSS; Librarian WENDY PRADT LOUGEE.

Missouri

Harry S. Truman Library and Museum: Independence, MO 64050; tel. (816) 268-8200; fax (816) 268-8295; e-mail truman .library@nara.gov; internet www .trumanlibrary.org; f. 1957; administered by the Nat. Archives and Records Admin.; 15m. MSS, 110,000 photographs, 30,000 vols, 80,000 other printed items, sound recordings, oral history interviews, 30,000 museum objects relating to the career and admin. of Pres. Harry S. Truman (1945–53); Dir Dr MICHAEL DEVINE.

Kansas City Public Library: 14 West 10th St, Kansas City, MO 64105; tel. (816) 701-3400; fax (816) 701-3401; internet www .kclibrary.org; f. 1873; 2,007,420 vols; 10 brs; spec. historical collns incl. the Missouri Valley Collection (local history), Ramos Colln (African American history) and Western expansion materials; Dir R. CROSBY KEMPER, III.

Linda Hall Library: 5109 Cherry St, Kansas City, MO 64110-2498; tel. (816) 363-4600; fax (816) 926-8790; e-mail requests@ lindahall.org; internet www.lindahall.org; f. 1946; ind., non-profit, public access science, engineering and technology library, specializing in periodicals and scientific and technical research materials; document supplier; fee-based literature search services; collns: 1m. vols, 12,330 current periodicals, 47,425 total serial titles, 528,000 monographs, 1,550,000 govt-contracted technical reports, incl. 70,000 maps, 170,000 standards and specifications, History of Science Colln (10,000 vols), US patent and trademark colln; Pres. LISA BROWAR.

Missouri State Library: POB 387, 600 W Main St, Jefferson City, MO 65101; tel. (573) 751-3615; fax (573) 751-3612; e-mail mostlib@sos.mo.gov; internet www.sos.mo .gov/library; f. 1945; spec. colln: Missouri state docs; Wolfner Library holds; 80,000 vols, 495 periodicals, Wolfner Library of 360,000 vols and 70 periodicals; Librarian MARGARET M. CONROY; publ. *Show Me Express* (52 a year).

St Louis County Library: 1640 South Lindbergh Blvd, St Louis, MO 63131-3598; tel. (314) 994-3300; internet www.slcl.org; f. 1946; 2,028,498 vols; 20 brs and 19 bookmobiles; Dir DAN WILSON.

St Louis Public Library: 1301 Olive St, St Louis, MO 63103-2389; tel. (314) 241-2288; fax (314) 539-0393; internet www.slpl.org; f. 1865; 4,895,532 vols, 115,000 maps; 17 brs; spec. collns incl. the Julia Davis Colln (African American history and culture); genealogical sources dating from 1902; Steedman Colln (architecture); Federal Documents Depository since 1866; Exec. Dir WALLER

McGuire; publ. *Missouri Union List of Serial Publications.*

St Louis University Library: 3650 Lindell Blvd, St Louis, MO 63108; tel. (314) 977-3100; fax (314) 977-3108; e-mail piusref@slu.edu; internet libraries.slu.edu; f. 1818; spec. collns: Knights of Columbus Vatican Film Library (microfilm colln of medieval and renaissance MSS studies), univ. archives and MSS (Walter J. Ong colln, Tristan da Cunha colln), rare books (16th–19th century theology, church history, patristics, Jesuitica); 1,849,584 vols; Asst Vice-Pres. for Univ. Libraries Dr Gail M. Staines; Dir, Pius XII Memorial Library David E. Cassens; publ. *Manuscripta* (2 a year).

University of Missouri Libraries: Columbia, MO 65201-5149; tel. (573) 882-4701; fax (573) 882-8044; internet mulibraries.missouri.edu; f. 1839; 3,205,927 vols, 14,548 journals; 7 brs; spec. collns of Western historical MSS and Missouriana; Dir of Libraries James Cogswell.

Nebraska

Nebraska State Historical Society Library and Archives: 1500 R. St, Lincoln, NE 68501; tel. (402) 471-4751; fax (402) 471-8922; internet www.nebraskahistory.org; incl. Dept of Public Instruction Reports, govt and prison records, State Newspaper Project; newspapers dating back to 1854; archival collns incl. state and local govt records, incl. those of most Nebraska governors; over 500,000 photographs, incl. sod house images taken by Solomon D. Butcher; private MSS collns incl. famous Nebraskans (Willa Cather, John Falter); 50,000 vols; Assoc. Dir Andrea Faling.

Nebraska State Library: POB 98931, State Capitol Bldg, 15th and K Sts, Lincoln, NE 68509-8931; tel. (402) 471-3189; fax (402) 471-1011; e-mail library@nsc.state.ne.us; internet supremecourt.ne.gov/state-library; f. 1871; 130,000 vols; reference and research library serving Nebraska Supreme Court, Nebraska Court of Appeals, attorneys within the State of Nebraska and general public.

New Hampshire

New Hampshire State Library: 20 Park St, Concord, NH 03301-6314; tel. (603) 271-2393; fax (603) 271-6826; internet www.nh.gov/nhsl; spec. collns of historical children's books, New Hampshire govt, town records and history; 600,000 vols; State Librarian Michael C. York; publ. *Granite State Libraries* (4 a year).

New Jersey

New Jersey State Library: 185 West State St, POB 520, Trenton, NJ 08625-0520; tel. (609) 278-2640; fax (609) 278-2647; e-mail refdesk@njstatelib.org; internet www.njstatelib.org; f. 1796; 2m. vols and documents, 800 current periodicals, 750,000 items on microfiche and microfilm; State Librarian Norma E. Blake.

Newark Public Library: 5 Washington St, POB 630, Newark, NJ 07101-0630; tel. (973) 733-7779; fax (973) 733-5648; e-mail reference@npl.org; internet www.npl.org; f. 1888; collns: art, music, science, technology, business histories, US patent specifications and drawings 1790 to present, US govt documents regional depository, New Jersey documents, New Jersey history, fine printing, black studies, Newark Evening News Morgue; 8 brs; 1,180,492 vols, 924,814 catalogued non-book items, 1,696,441 uncatalogued items, 411,531 periodicals, 1,015,095 prints, pictures and art slides; Library Dir Wilma J. Grey; Prin. Librarian Jane Seiden.

Princeton University Libraries: 1 Washington Rd, Princeton, NJ 08544; tel. (609) 258-1470; fax (609) 258-0441; e-mail libhr@princeton.edu; internet libweb.princeton.edu; f. 1746; 6m. vols; spec. collns incl. 450 medieval and Renaissance codices, 10,000 Islamic MSS, cuneiform tablets, stone seals and papyri, pre-Columbian indigenous materials (especially Mayan), George Cruikshank and Aubrey Beardsley, American theatre (incl. papers of Max Gordon and Otto Kahn), archives of American publishers, especially Charles Scribner's Sons, the Morris L. Parrish Colln of Victorian Novelists, early American family papers, especially Edward Livingston and Blair-Lee, public policy papers since early 20th century, especially John Foster Dulles, Adlai Stevenson and the American Civil Liberties Union, 'Boom' period Latin American writers (incl. Mario Vargas Llosa); Univ. Librarian Karin A. Trainer; publ. *Princeton University Library Chronicle*.

Rutgers University Libraries: 169 College Ave, CAC, New Brunswick, NJ 08901-1163; tel. (732) 932-7505; fax (732) 932-7637; internet www.libraries.rutgers.edu; f. 1766; 3m. vols; 26 libraries on Rutgers campuses in Camden, Newark and New Brunswick, with spec. collns in medicine, physics, chemistry, mathematics, microbiology, art, alcohol studies, labour/management relations, urban research, law and music; Univ. Librarian Marianne Gaunt.

New Mexico

New Mexico State Library: 1209 Camino Carlos Rey, Santa Fe, NM 87505; tel. (505) 476-9700; fax (505) 476-9701; internet www.stlib.state.nm.us; f. 1929; 110 brs statewide; provides state agencies with library resources and services, and serves as a primary reference source for libraries in the state; 2m. vols; spec. collns: Southwest Resources (books, journals and newspapers on the history of the southwestern area of the USA), New Mexico Documents (publs of the various depts, agencies, commissions comprising the state govt), Federal Documents (selective depository focus on New Mexico federal agency publs); State Librarian Susan Oberlander (acting); publs *Directory of New Mexico Libraries*, *Hitchhiker* (52 a year).

New York

American Museum of Natural History Library: Central Park West at 79th St, New York, NY 10024; tel. (212) 769-5400; fax (212) 769-5009; internet library.amnh.org; f. 1869; subject areas incl. anthropology, astronomy, geology, palaeontology, zoology, exploration and travel, history of science, and museology; 487,000 vols, 21,000 periodicals, 1m. photographs, 3,000 films, 13,000 rare vols; Dir Tom Baione (acting); publs *Anthropological Papers*, *Bulletin*, *Novitates* (irregular).

Association of the Bar of the City of New York Library: 42 West 44th St, New York, NY 10036; tel. (212) 382-6666; fax (212) 302-8219; internet www.abcny.org/library; f. 1870; 600,000 vols; law; Dir Nathan A. Rosen.

Brooklyn Public Library: Grand Army Plaza, Brooklyn, NY 11238; tel. (718) 230-2100; internet www.brooklynpubliclibrary.org; f. 1897; 7,189,998 items; spec. collns incl. Brooklyn history; 58 brs, Business Library, Central Library, bookmobile; Exec. Dir Ginnie Cooper.

Buffalo and Erie County Public Library: 1 Lafayette Sq., Buffalo, NY 14203; tel. (716) 858-8900; fax (716) 858-6211; internet www.buffalolib.org; f. 1954 following merger; 3,639,922 vols; 37 brs, of which 8 are city br. libraries; Dir Bridget Quinn-Carey.

Center for Jewish History: 15 West 16th St, New York, NY 10011; tel. (212) 294-8301; fax (212) 294-8302; e-mail inquiries@cjh.org; internet www.cjh.org; f. 2000 through collaboration between American Jewish Historical Society, American Sephardi Federation, Leo Baeck Institute, Yeshiva University Museum, YIVO Institute for Jewish Research; repository for the cultural and historical legacy of the Jewish people; combined library and archive holdings of 500,000 books, 10m. documents; photographs, paintings, textiles; Chair. Bruce Slovin; Chief Operational Officer Michael S. Glickman.

Central Library of Rochester and Monroe County: 115 South Ave, Rochester, NY 14604-1896; tel. (585) 428-7300; internet www.libraryweb.org/central; f. 1912; 1,344,621 vols; audiovisual dept; pictures and photographs on 2,000 subjects; local history archive collection of MSS, directories, histories, newspapers, city and county publs; 20 brs; Dir P. Smith; publ. *Rochester History* (4 a year).

Columbia University Libraries: 535 West 114th St, New York, NY 10027; tel. (212) 854-7309; fax (212) 854-5082; e-mail lio@columbia.edu; internet www.columbia.edu/cu/lweb; f. 1754; 9.4m. vols; 23 deptl and professional school libraries with important collns in architecture, business, humanities, history, law, medicine, engineering, the sciences and social sciences; Vice-Pres. for Information Services and Univ. Librarian James G. Neal.

Cornell University Library: Ithaca, NY 14853; tel. (607) 255-4144; fax (607) 255-9091; internet www.library.cornell.edu; f. 1865; 7,298,409 vols, 7,992,461 microforms; special collections: French Revolution, East Asia, South and South-east Asia, Iceland, history of science, Dante, Petrarch, slavery, Wordsworth, witchcraft; Librarian Sarah E. Thomas.

Department of Records and Information Services: 31 Chambers St, New York, NY 10007; tel. (212) 788-8602; fax (212) 788-8614; internet www.nyc.gov/html/records/home.html; f. 1977; comprises Municipal Archives of the City of New York, City Hall Library and Municipal Records Management Division; Commissioner Brian G. Andersson.

Franklin D. Roosevelt Presidential Library: 4079 Albany Post Rd, Hyde Park, New York, NY 12538; tel. (845) 486-7760; fax (845) 486-1147; e-mail roosevelt.library@nara.gov; internet www.fdrlibrary.marist.edu; f. 1939; MSS, photographs, printed and museum materials concerning life and times of Franklin and Eleanor Roosevelt, incl. 4,700 lin. ft of the fmr's papers,and many papers of his contemporaries and associates; 17m. MSS pages, 130,000 photographs, 52,000 books, 78,000 other printed items, 34,000 museum items; administered by the National Archives and Records Administration; Dir Dr Cynthia M. Koch.

Hispanic Society of America Library: 613 West 155 St, New York, NY 10032; tel. (212) 926-2234; fax (212) 690-0743; e-mail library@hispanicsociety.org; internet www.hispanicsociety.org; f. 1904; art, history and literature of Spain, Portugal and Hispanic America; 300,000 MSS; 18,000 books printed before 1701, incl. 300 incunabula; 250,000 later books; Curator of Modern Books Edwin X. Rolon; Curator of Manuscripts and Rare Books John O'Neill.

Jewish Theological Seminary Library: 3080 Broadway, New York, NY 10027; tel. (212) 678-8080; fax (212) 678-8998; e-mail library@jtsa.edu; internet www.jtsa.edu/library.xml; f. 1903; 400,000 vols, 11,000 MSS, 35,000 leaves of Cairo Genizah, Archives, Louis Ginzberg Microfilm library (foreign colln of Hebrew MSS); incunabula; Bible, Rabbinics, Jewish history, liturgy, theology, Early Yiddish, Hebrew literature, history of science and medicine; Haggadahs; Megillot (Esther scrolls); Ketuboth (marriage contracts); prints and photographs; musical scores; microfilms; video cassettes; sound recordings; electronic resources; Librarian DAVID KRAEMER.

Medical Research Library of Brooklyn: 450 Clarkson Ave, POB 14, Brooklyn, NY 11203; tel. (718) 270-7401; fax (718) 270-7413; internet library.downstate.edu; f. 1962 as the joint library of the Academy of Medicine of Brooklyn, Inc. (f. 1845) and the State University of New York Downstate Medical Center (f. 1860); 255,000 vols; Dir of Libraries RICHARD M. WINANT.

Morgan Library: 29 East 36th St, New York, NY 10016; tel. (212) 685-0610; fax (212) 481-3484; e-mail media@morganlibrary.org; internet www.morganlibrary.org; f. 1924; public museum and research library; collns formed by Pierpont Morgan, with additions made by his son and subsequent directors; among its treasures are: Medieval and Renaissance MSS from the 5th to the 16th century; a colln of 10,000 drawings by artists since the 15th century; colln of Rembrandt prints; Pierre Matisse Gallery Archives; major monuments in the history of printing and typography, from Gutenberg and Caxton to modern times; comprehensive group of fine bindings; literary and historical MSS, incl. Dickens, Ruskin, the Brontës, Austen, Thoreau and Steinbeck; Carter Burden Colln of American Literature; colln of autograph scores, incl. works by Beethoven, Mahler, Mozart and Stravinsky; extensive Gilbert and Sullivan archive; regular public lectures and exhibitions; Dir CHARLES ELIOT PIERCE, Jr.

New York Academy of Medicine Library: 1216 Fifth Ave, New York, NY 10029; tel. (212) 876-8200; fax (212) 423-0275; e-mail library@nyam.org; internet www.nyam.org; f. 1847; 696,951 vols, 182,910 catalogued pamphlets, 275,788 catalogued illustrations and portraits, 2,700 serials; special collns: medical Americana, history of medicine, medical biography, rare medical books and incunabula, food and cookery; Pres. JO IVEY BOUFFORD; publ. *Bulletin of the New York Academy of Medicine*.

New York Law Institute Library: 120 Broadway, New York, NY 10271-0043; tel. (212) 732-8720; fax (212) 406-1204; internet www.nyli.org; f. 1828; 300,000 vols; 1,450 reels of microfilm; 16,300 microfiches; law library for practising attorneys; special collns and editions incl. George Washington's copy of the Code de Louis XIII: the Plantation Laws of Virginia, autographed by Richard Henry Lee; Librarian NANCY G. JOSEPH; publ. *New Acquisitions Bulletin*.

New York Public Library: Fifth Ave and 42nd St, New York, NY 10018; tel. (212) 930-0800; fax (212) 930-9299; e-mail nyplweb@nypl.org; internet www.nypl.org; f. 1895 by the consolidation of Astor, Tilden and Lenox Libraries; 11.3m. vols, 40,000 periodicals and newspapers, 26m. manuscripts, maps, microfilms, films, video and audio cassettes, phonorecords, prints and sheet music; spec. collns incl. Berg collection of English and American literature, Arents collection of books on tobacco and books in parts, and the Spencer collection of illustrated books; 85 local brs and 4 research centres (Humanities and Social Sciences Library, Library for the Performing Arts, Science, Industry and Business Library, Schomburg Center for Research in Black Culture) with 4.4m. vols and 5.9m. non-book items; research libraries: 10m. vols, 8m. manuscripts; Pres. PAUL LECLERC.

New York State Library: Albany, NY 12230; tel. (518) 474-5355; fax (518) 474-5279; internet www.nysl.nysed.gov; American and New York State history, law, medicine, education, technology and genealogy; MSS and special collections; US govt depository; talking book and braille library; 19m. items; State Librarian JANET WELCH; publ. *Checklist of Official Publications of the State of New York* (12 a year).

New York University Libraries: 70 Washington Square South, New York, NY 10012; tel. (212) 998-2505; fax (212) 995-4070; e-mail libweb@nyu.edu; internet www.nyu.edu/library; f. 1835; 4,057,000 vols; 9 brs: Bobst Library has 3 specialized research centres (digital projects, arts, labour history), Courant Institute of Mathematical Sciences focuses on research-level material in mathematics, computer science and related fields, Stephen Chan Library of Fine Arts houses collections in art history and archaeology, Jack Brause Real Estate Library, Frederick L. Ehrman Medical Library, the Dental Center's Waldman Memorial Library and the Law Library; Dean CAROL A. MANDEL.

Queens Borough Public Library: 89-11 Merrick Blvd, Jamaica, NY 11432; tel. (718) 990-0700; fax (718) 291-8936; e-mail webmaster@queenslibrary.org; internet queenslibrary.org; f. 1896; 9.7m. vols; spec. collns incl. Long Island history and genealogy; 500,000 pictures; 62 brs; Dir THOMAS W. GALANTE.

Syracuse University Library: 222 Waverly Ave, Syracuse, NY 13244-2010; tel. (315) 443-2573; fax (315) 443-2060; internet libwww.syr.edu; f. 1870; 2,650,000 vols; 8 campus sites (audio lab, science and technology, mathematics, physics, geology, law, architecture and African American history); special collections: Leopold von Ranke, Kipling, Crane, letters and publishing history since the early 20th century, cartoon art; Univ. Librarian SUZANNE THORIN (acting); publ. *Associates Courier* (1 a year).

Union Theological Seminary (The Burke Library): 3041 Broadway at 121st St, New York, NY 10027; tel. (212) 851-5607; fax (212) 851-5613; e-mail refdesk@uts.columbia.edu; internet www.columbia.edu/cu/lweb/indiv/burke/index.html; f. 1836; incorporates Missionary Research Library; incl. Archives of Women in Theological Scholarship; 700,000 vols, 163,000 pieces in microform, 1,500 periodical subscriptions, 1,800 audio and video cassettes; Library Dir SARA J. MYERS.

United Nations Dag Hammarskjöld Library: United Nations Plaza, New York, NY 10017; tel. (212) 963-7412; fax (212) 963-2388; e-mail unreference@un.org; internet www.un.org/depts/dhl; f. 1949, dedicated 1961; comprehensive collns of documents on the UN, specialized agencies and the League of Nations; collns of books, periodicals and govt documents on topics of concern to the UN; activities and history of the UN; int. affairs since 1918; 600,000 vols, 10,000 serials, 6.5m.documents, 80,000 maps; Head Librarian SHINICHI KUSHIMA; publs *Indices to Proceedings of the General Assembly, Security Council and Economic and Social Council*, *UN Pulse*.

United States Military Academy Library: 757 Thayer Rd, West Point, NY 10996-1711; tel. (845) 938-2230; e-mail 8lib@usma.edu; internet www.library.usma.edu; f. 1802; 500,000 bound vols; military-historical, academic, government documents, MSS, rare books and special collections; Librarian Dr BRYN GEFFERT.

University of Rochester Libraries: Rochester, NY 14627-0055; tel. (585) 275-4461; fax (585) 273-5309; internet www.lib.rochester.edu; f. 1850; 3,120,000 vols; libraries comprise the River Campus Libraries (7 deptl libraries), the Sibley Music Library at the Eastman School of Music, the Edward G. Miner Library (medicine and dentistry) and the Charlotte Whitney Allen Library at the Memorial Art Gallery; Dean RONALD DOW.

North Carolina

Duke University Library: Perkins Library, POB 90193, Durham, NC 27708-0193; tel. (919) 660-5800; fax (919) 660-5923; internet library.duke.edu; f. 1838; 5,560,966 vols, 51,827 linear ft of MSS and archives; British history and literature of 17th to 19th centuries; general European history since 1870; French Revolution; church history of Reformation; E Asia; advertising history; American and Latin American history; S Americana; women's history; history of economic thought; labour history; French, English, Italian, German Baroque and American literature; int. law; 6 br. libraries and 4 professional school libraries: Law (Ford Library), medicine, business and divinity; Univ. Librarian and Vice-Provost for Library Affairs DEBORAH JAKUBS; publ. *Duke University Libraries* (3 a year).

Public Library of Charlotte and Mecklenburg County: 310 North Tryon St, Charlotte, NC 28202; tel. (704) 336-2725; fax (704) 336-2002; internet www.plcmc.org; f. 1903; 1.5m. vols; colln of foreign-language publs, local history and genealogy; 23 br. libraries; Dir of Libraries CHARLES M. BROWN.

University of North Carolina Library: Chapel Hill, NC 27514-8890; tel. (919) 962-1301; fax (919) 843-8936; e-mail reference@unc.edu; internet www.lib.unc.edu; f. 1795; 6,526,824 vols; spec. collns on NC, S Americana, the history of the book, incunabula, 16th-century books, incl. large colln of Estienne imprints, *crónicas* of the discovery and conquest of the New World, also Johnson, Boswell, Dickens, Shaw and selected contemporary authors, Napoleon and the French Revolution, World War I and World War II materials, early Americana, Confederate imprints, Spanish, Catalan and Portuguese drama, John Murray and Smith, Elder and Co imprints, Afro-American materials, fed. and state documents, Latin America, Mazarinades, music and historical MSS; 10 departmental libraries in scientific and other fields; Institute of Govt Library; separate libraries in Law, Health Sciences, Population and a Data Library; Univ. Librarian SARAH C. MICHALAK.

North Dakota

North Dakota State Library: 604 E Boulevard Ave, Bismarck, ND 58505-0800; tel. (701) 328-4622; fax (701) 328-2040; e-mail statelib@nd.gov; internet www.library.nd.gov; f. 1907 as Public Library Commission; State Librarian HULEN BIVINS.

North Dakota State University Libraries: NDSU Dept 2080, POB 6050, Fargo, ND 58108-6050; tel. (701) 231-8753; fax (701) 231-6128; e-mail ndsu-library-librarians@listserv.nodak.edu; internet library.ndsu.edu; f. 1891; incl. Main Library, Architecture Library, Barry Library (Business), Chemistry Library, Health Sciences Library, Institute for Regional Studies and Univ. Archives, Germans for Russia Heritage Colln; 955,000 vols, 8,757 periodicals, govt documents; Dean of Libraries MICHELE M. REID.

State Historical Society of North Dakota State Archives: 612 E Boulevard Ave, Bismarck, ND 58505-0830; tel. (701) 328-2668; fax (701) 328-2650; e-mail archives@nd.gov; internet www.nd.gov/hist; f. 1905; State Archivist ANN JENKS; publs *North Dakota History* (4 a year), *Plains Talk* (4 a year).

University of North Dakota Libraries: Grand Forks, ND 58505-9000; internet www.library.und.edu; f. 1883; incl. Chester Fritz Library (US Patent and Trademark and govt publs depository), Health Sciences Library and Thormodsgard Law Library; 3m. vols, access to 30,000 e-journals; Dir for Libraries WILBUR STOLT.

Ohio

Akron-Summit County Public Library: 55 South Main St, Akron, OH 44326; tel. (330) 643-9000; internet ascpl.lib.oh.us; f. 1874; 1,118,000 vols; spec. collns in genealogy and local history; 17 brs, 1 bookmobile; Dir DAVID JENNINGS; publ. *Shelf Life*.

Case Western Reserve University Libraries: 11055 Euclid Ave, Cleveland, OH 44106-7151; tel. (216) 368-3506; fax (216) 368-6950; internet www.case.edu/dir/libraries.html; f. 1826; 1.5m. vols, more than. 1.3m. monographs, 7,363 serial titles, US Govt publs, company annual reports, newspapers, CDs, technical reports, 9,000 DVDs; Kelvin Smith Library is the main Univ. Library; other libraries are Astronomy Library, Cleveland Health Sciences Library, Allen Memorial Medical Library, Health Centre Library, Kulas Music Library, Law School Library, Lillian F. and Milford J. Harris Library; spec. collns incl. early American children's books, German literature and philology, history of medicine, history of printing, history of science and technology, environmental sciences, natural history, public housing and urban devt; Dir JOANNE EUSTIS.

Cleveland Public Library: 325 Superior Ave, Cleveland, OH 44114-1271; tel. (216) 623 2800; fax (216) 623 7015; e-mail info@cpl.org; internet www.cpl.org; f. 1869; 3,723,666 vols, 45,000 edns classical music and jazz in Naxos Music Library; 28 neighbourhood brs; home-bound services; the John G. White endowed colln of folklore, orientalia and chess; large circulating colln of video cassettes and sound recordings; services to hospitals, the homebound, the physically handicapped and the blind; telephone reference service; fee-based research service;; Dir FELTON THOMAS, Jr.

Columbus Metropolitan Library: 96 South Grant Ave, Columbus, OH 43215; tel. (614) 645-2275; fax (614) 645-2050; internet www.columbuslibrary.org; 2,815,300 vols; 20 brs; Exec. Dir PATRICK A. LOSINSKI.

Dayton Metro Library: 215 East Third St, Dayton, OH 45402; tel. (937) 463-2665; fax (937) 496-4300; internet www.daytonmetrolibrary.org; f. 1805; 1,509,623 vols, 23 brs; bookmobile service; service to homebound, elderly and blind; circulating colln of 16-mm films, records and cassettes; Exec. Dir TIMOTHY G. KAMBITSCH.

Ohio State University Libraries: 1858 Neil Ave Mall, Columbus, OH 43210-1286; tel. (614) 292-6154; fax (614) 292-7859; e-mail library@osu.edu; internet www.lib.ohio-state.edu; f. 1873; Main (Thompson) Library and 26 deptl and affiliated libraries; 5.8m. vols, 5,749,143 microforms, 35,000 serials; spec. collns incl. American fiction, theatre, cartoons and cartooning, medieval Slavic MSS on microfilm; Dir of Libraries JOSEPH J. BRANIN.

Public Library of Cincinnati and Hamilton County: 800 Vine St, Library Sq., Cincinnati, OH 45202-2009; tel. (513) 369-6900; fax (513) 369-6993; internet www.cincinnatilibrary.org; f. 1853; 4,887,372 books, 150,000 maps; US Documents Depository; spec. collns incl. local history, genealogy, theology, art, music, theatre, US patents and trademarks, Inland Rivers Library, Bibles, English-language dictionaries, Cincinnatiana, first edns of English and American authors; 41 brs; Regional Library for the Blind and Physically Handicapped; Exec. Dir KIMBER L. FENDER.

State Library of Ohio: 274 East First Ave, Columbus, OH 43201; tel. (614) 644-7061; fax (614) 466-3584; internet winslo.state.oh.us; f. 1817; 1.4m. vols; a spec. library for state govt, incl. periodicals, documents, pamphlets, services and microforms; spec. colln of management, genealogy, local history, education and health; State Librarian JO BUDLER.

Toledo-Lucas County Public Library: 325 Michigan St, Toledo, OH 43624; tel. (419) 259-5207; internet www.toledolibrary.org; f. 1970; 1.9m. vols; 18 brs; 1 outreach service; Dir CLYDE S. SCOLES.

University of Cincinnati Libraries: Cincinnati, OH 45221-0033; tel. (513) 556-1424; fax (513) 556-0325; internet www.libraries.uc.edu; f. 1819; 3,123,318 vols; comprises a general library, medical, law, deptl and branch libraries; incl. spec. collns on classics, modern Greek, medicine, fine arts, modern poetry, 18th-century literature; Dean and Univ. Librarian Dr VICTORIA MONTAVON.

Oklahoma

Oklahoma Department of Libraries: 200 NE 18th St, Oklahoma City, OK 73105-3298; tel. (405) 521-2502; fax (405) 525-7804; internet www.odl.state.ok.us; f. 1967; state archives, state and federal govt depository; Dir SUSAN C. MCVEY; Deputy Dir VICKI SULLIVAN.

University of Oklahoma Libraries: Norman, OK 73019; tel. (405) 325-4142; internet libraries.ou.edu; f. 1892; 4.9m. vols, 63,000 periodicals, 1.6m. photographs, 1.5m. maps, 50 incunabula; spec. collns in Western history, business and economic history, history of science, English, European and American literatures; Dean of Univ. Libraries SUL H. LEE.

Oregon

Multnomah County Library: 801 Southwest 10th Ave, Portland, OR 97205; tel. (503) 988-5402; fax (503) 998-5441; internet www.multcolib.org; f. 1864; 19 brs; 1,587,291 vols; Dir VAILEY OEHLKE.

Oregon State Library: 250 Winter St, NE, Salem, OR 97301-3950; tel. (503) 378-4243; fax (503) 588-7119; e-mail reference@library.state.or.us; internet www.oregon.gov/osl; f. 1905; 1,140,680 vols; provides service to state agencies and print-disabled persons; develops local library services; special collns: Oregon and Oregon authors; State Librarian JIM SCHEPPKE.

University of Oregon Libraries: 1299 Univ. of Oregon, Eugene, OR 97403-1299; tel. (541) 346-3053; fax (541) 346-3485; internet libweb.uoregon.edu; f. 1876; 3.1m. vols, 481,414 govt documents, 783,154 maps, 4.2m. microfilm units; 420,557 computer files; Dean of Libraries DEBORAH A. CARVER; Head of Licensing, Grants and Collns Analysis Assoc. Prof. DAVID C. FOWLER.

Pennsylvania

American Philosophical Society Library: 105 S 5th St, Philadelphia, PA 19106-3386; tel. (215) 440-3400; fax (215) 440-3423; internet www.amphilsoc.org; f. 1743; 300,000 vols, 8m. MSS, microfilms; spec. collns on Benjamin Franklin, Thomas Paine, history of science, genetics, quantum physics, Darwinism, American Indian linguistics; Librarian MARTIN L. LEVITT.

Carnegie Library of Pittsburgh: 4400 Forbes Ave, Pittsburgh, PA 15213-4080; tel. (412) 622-3114; fax (412) 622-6278; e-mail info@carnegielibrary.org; internet www.carnegielibrary.org; f. 1895; adjacent to Carnegie Institute; main library, library for the blind and physically handicapped; 18 local brs; 5.4m. vols, 3.3m. other materials; Pres. and Dir BARBARA K. MISTICK; Dir for External and Govt Relations KARLYN VOSS; Dir for Human Resources PAUL VANDERWIEL.

Ewell Sale Stewart Library of the Academy of Natural Sciences: 1900 Benjamin Franklin Parkway, Philadelphia, PA 19103-1195; tel. (215) 299-1040; fax (215) 299-1144; e-mail library@ansp.org; internet www.ansp.org/library; f. 1812; 200,000 vols, 2,500 current periodicals, 250,000 MSS; collns in the field of natural history since the 18th century; expedition literature, incl. the works of scientists such as Lewis and Clark, and the published journals of amateur naturalists; illustrated works in natural sciences, from the pre-Linnaean classics of Gesner, Aldrovandi and Catesby (published before 1750) to the great bird books of Gould, Audubon, Elliot and Wilson, and the flora of Redouté, Sowerby and the Bauers, to the modern masters of wildlife art, F. L. Jaques, L. A. Fuertes and Terence Shortt; Librarian DANIANNE MIZZY.

Free Library of Philadelphia: 1901 Vine St, Philadelphia, PA 19103-1189; tel. (215) 686-5322; internet www.library.phila.gov; 55 brs throughout the city; f. 1891; 7,881,335 vols; special collections include: Fleisher orchestral music; Carson history of the common law; Widener incunabula; Drinker Choral Library; Lewis Illuminated MSS, European and Oriental; History of the Automobile; Elkins Americana, Dickens, Goldsmith, Gimbel Poe; Lewis cuneiform tablets; Rosenbach children's books of the 18th to 19th centuries; children's illustrators, Beatrix Potter, Kate Greenaway, Arthur Rackham; theatre collection; map collection (over 130,000 single-sheet maps, also atlases, etc.); Pres. and Dir E. L. SHELKROT.

Pennsylvania State University Libraries: 515 Paterno Library, University Park, PA 16802; tel. (814) 865-0401; fax (814) 865-3665; e-mail s2w@psulias.psu.edu; internet www.libraries.psu.edu; f. 1859; 4,779,165 vols; 5,135,467 microforms, 461,603 maps, 1.5m. government documents, 57,235 serials; comprises a central library (Pattee Library and Paterno Library), which houses 9 subject libraries, 6 departmental brs, 12 Commonwealth College Libraries, Penn State Erie, The Behrend College, Penn State Great Valley, Penn State Abington, Abington College, Penn State Altoona, Altoona College, Berks-Lehigh Valley College, Capital College, Penn State Mont Alto, Dickinson School of Law; Special Collections Library includes: American Literature; Australian art and literature; gift books, emblem books; German literature in translation (Allison-Shelley); Joseph Priestley; Renaissance; Williamscote Library (18th-century English, history, Theology and Classics); Utopian literature; labour history; Australiana; Vance Packard; John O'Hara; Conrad Richter, Theodore Roethke, Kenneth Burke, Arnold Bennett, C. R. Carpenter; Nunzio J. Palladino Nuclear Regulatory Commission Papers; university Archives; US Steel Workers of America archives; United Mineworkers of America; Stapleton Collection of Pennsylvania Imprints; Dean of Libraries NANCY L. EATON.

State Library of Pennsylvania: 333 Market St, Harrisburg, PA 17126-1745; tel. (717) 787-2646; fax (717) 783-2070; e-mail ra-reference@state.pa.us; internet www.statelibrary.state.pa.us; f. 1745; 992,500 vols; American history, education, political science, sociology, library science, law, genealogy; Pennsylvania history, newspapers, maps, original Pennsylvania Assembly Collection; Dir CARYN CARR.

University of Pennsylvania Library: 3420 Walnut St, Philadelphia, PA 19104-6206; tel. (215) 898-7555; fax (215) 898-0559; e-mail library@pobox.upenn.edu; internet www.library.upenn.edu; f. 1750; 6,096,588 vols; central library and 14 departmental and affiliated libraries; archaeology, anthropology, Leibniz, Descartes, history of philosophy and science, Lithuanian history and literature, history of chemistry, criminology, French Revolution, Judaica, Modern Jewish history, modern Hebrew literature, Aristotelianism, Occam, Medieval history, medieval Cchurch history, Inquisition, Middle East and Islamic studies, Italian Renaissance literature, Spanish literature of the Golden Age, Shakespeareana (Furness Library), Restoration drama, 18th- and early 19th-century English fiction, Jonathan Swift, Thomas Paine, American drama, fiction, and poetry: Walt Whitman, Washington Irving, Robert Montgomery Bird, Theodore Dreiser, James Farrell; Middle-High German, Old French, Indic MSS, South Asia, History of economics, history of education, Programmschriften, Elzevir Imprints, Franklin Imprints, early Americana, the American West; Vice-Provost and Dir of Libraries H. CARTON ROGERS, III.

University of Pittsburgh Libraries: Pittsburgh, PA 15260; tel. (412) 648-7747; fax (412) 648-7887; internet www.pitt.edu/libraries.html; f. 1873; 22 separate libraries on or near main campus and 4 regional campus libraries in Bradford, Greensburg, Johnstown and Titusville; 3.7m. vols, 3.7m. micro-units; Dir RUSH MILLER.

Rhode Island

Brown University Library: Providence, RI 02912; tel. (401) 863-2167; fax (401) 863-1272; e-mail rock@brown.edu; internet dl.lib.brown.edu/libweb; f. 1764; 3,509,710 vols; incl. John D. Rockefeller, Jr. Library (research library for humanities, social sciences, fine arts), Sciences Library, Owing Music Library, John Hay Library (spec. collns, rare books, MSS archives), Art Slide Library; Univ. Librarian HARRIETTE HEMMASI.

John Carter Brown Library: POB 1894, Providence, RI 02912; tel. (401) 863-2725; fax (401) 863-3477; e-mail jcbl_information@brown.edu; internet www.jcbl.org; f. 1846; independently funded and administered centre for advanced research in history and the humanities at Brown Univ.; contains primary historical sources pertaining to the colonial period of the Americas 1492–1825; 45,000 rare books, 16,000 reference books; Dir Dr EDWARD L. WIDMER.

Providence Public Library: 150 Empire St, Providence, RI 02903; tel. (401) 455-8000; fax (401) 455-8080; e-mail pplref@provlib.org; internet www.provlib.org; f. 1876; 1m. vols; Dir M. DALE THOMPSON.

South Dakota

South Dakota State Library: Mercedes MacKay Bldg, 800 Governors Dr., Pierre, SD 57501-2294; tel. (605) 773-3131; fax (605) 773-6962; e-mail library@state.sd.us; internet www.sdstatelibrary.com; state govt publication depository; State Librarian DOROTHY M. LIEGL.

Tennessee

Jean and Alexander Heard Library, Vanderbilt University: 419 21st Ave S, Nashville, TN 37240-0007; tel. (615) 322-7110; fax (615) 343-8279; internet www.library.vanderbilt.edu/; f. 1873; housed in central, science—engineering, biomedical, divinity, education, law, management and music libraries; 2.5m. vols; Dean of Libraries CONNIE VINITA DOWELL; Dir for Collns JARED INGERSOLL (acting).

Memphis Public Library and Information Center: 3030 Poplar Ave, Memphis, TN 38111-3527; tel. (901) 725-8855; fax (901) 725-8883; internet www.memphislibrary.org; f. 1893; 4.5m. vols; CATV and colour videotaping studio; information and referral service (LINC-Library Information Center); Dir J. A. DRESCHER; publs *Kaleidoscope* (12 a year), *Staff Newsline* (12 a year).

University of Tennessee, Knoxville Libraries: 1015 Volunteer Boulevard, Knoxville, TN 37996-1000; tel. (865) 974-4351; fax (865) 974-4180; internet www.lib.utk.edu; f. 1794; 2,376,414 vols; spec. collns incl. Tennesseana, North American Indians; Dean BARBARA I. DEWEY.

Texas

Austin Public Library: 800 Guadalupe St, Box 2287, Austin, TX 78768-2287; tel. (512) 974-7444; fax (512) 974-7403; internet www.ci.austin.tx.us/library; f. 1926; 1,550,145 vols; 20 facilities; system maintains a comprehensive collection of books, magazines, newspapers, recordings, audio cassettes and video cassettes; Austin History Center contains materials on history of Austin and Travis County; Dir BRENDA BRANCH.

Dallas Public Library: 1515 Young St, Dallas, TX 75201-5499; tel. (214) 670-1400; e-mail director@dallaslibrary.org; internet www.dallaslibrary.org; f. 1901; 6,143,644 items; Dir CORRINE HILL.

Fort Worth Public Library: 500 W 3rd St, Fort Worth, TX 76102-7305; tel. (817) 871-7701; fax (817) 871-7734; internet www.fortworthlibrary.org; f. 1901; 2,066,000 vols; 15 brs; special collections: genealogy, local history, sheet music, postcards, bookplates; US and Texas govt depository; Dir Dr GLENIECE ROBINSON.

George Bush Presidential Library and Museum: 1000 George Bush Dr. West, College Station, TX 77845; tel. (979) 691-4000; fax (979) 691-4050; e-mail library.bush@nara.gov; internet bushlibrary.tamu.edu; 38m. pages of official and personal papers, 1m. photographs, 2,500 hrs of video cassettes; museum of 70,000 items relating to the life and career of President George Bush (1989–93); Dir Dr WARREN FINCH.

Houston Public Library: 500 McKinney St, Houston, TX 77002; tel. (832) 393-1313; fax (832) 393-1266; e-mail website@hpl.lib.tx.us; internet www.houstonlibrary.org; f. 1901; 4,561,000 vols; 35 brs; special collections: Bibles, Civil War, Salvation Army posters, early Houston photographs, early printing and illuminated MSS, juvenile literature, petroleum, sheet music, Texana, US and Texas depository; specializes in genealogy, art, architecture, business, management; jazz, Afro-American and Hispanic archives; Dir TONI LAMBERT.

University of Texas System Libraries: POB P, Austin, TX 78713-8916; tel. (512) 495-4350; fax (512) 495-4347; internet www.lib.utexas.edu; f. 1883; 6,835,983 vols; also Arlington, 893,155 vols; El Paso, 746,308 vols; Permian Basin, 215,945 vols; San Antonio, 367,583 vols; Health Science Center, Houston, 54,000 vols; Health Science Center, Dallas, 224,732 vols; Health Science Center, San Antonio, 173,143 vols; Medical Branch, Galveston, 291,326; Dir Dr FRED HEATH.

Utah

Family History Library of the Church of Jesus Christ of Latter-day Saints: 35 NW Temple St, Salt Lake City, UT 84150-3400; tel. (801) 240-2584; fax (801) 240-3718; e-mail fhl@ldschurch.org; internet www.familysearch.org; f. 1894; 300,000 bound vols, 2.2m. reels of microfilm, 734,000 microfiches; Dir DAVID E. RENCHER.

University of Utah Library: 295 S 1500E, Salt Lake City, UT 84112-0860; tel. (801) 581-8558; fax (801) 581-3464; internet www.lib.utah.edu; f. 1850; 2m. vols, 13,000 serial titles; special collections: archives, Middle East, MSS, rare books, Western Americana, oral history; US state and UN documents depository; Dir (vacant).

Vermont

University of Vermont Libraries: Burlington, VT 05405-0036; tel. (802) 656-2003; fax (802) 656-4038; internet library.uvm.edu; Bailey/Howe Library houses spec. collns of Vermont materials, rare books, govt documents and maps, and univ. archives; Cook Chemistry/Physics Library; Dana Medical Library; Library Reseach Annex; Dean of Libraries MAURA SAULE.

Vermont Historical Society Library: 60 Washington St, Barre, VT 05641-4209; tel. (802) 479-8500; fax (802) 479-8510; e-mail vhs-library@state.vt.us; internet www.vermonthistory.org; f. 2002; collns of books and pamphlets dating from 1770; large genealogical colln; Librarian PAUL CARNAHAN.

Vermont State Archives and Records Administration Vermont Office of the Secretary of State: 1078 US Route 2, Middlesex, Montpelier, VT 05633-7701; tel. (802) 828-3700; fax (802) 828-3710; e-mail archives@sec.state.vt.us; internet vermont-archives.org; f. 2003; Sec. of State JAMES C. CONDOS; State Archivist GREGORY SANFORD.

Virginia

Fairfax County Public Library: 12000 Government Center Parkway, Suite 324, Fairfax, VA 22035; tel. (703) 324-3100; internet www.co.fairfax.va.us/library; f. 1939; 3m. vols; 21 brs; also CD-ROMs, microfilm, audio and video cassettes, periodicals, recorded and talking books, CATV hook-up; Dir EDWIN S. CLAY, III.

Library of Virginia: 800 E Broad St, Richmond, VA 23219-8000; tel. (804) 692-3500; internet www.lva.virginia.gov; f. 1823; 700,000 vols, 834 current periodicals; Virginiana, Southern US history, Civil War, genealogy; archive colln of 55,000 cu ft; Librarian SANDRA G. TREADWAY; publ. *Virginia Cavalcade*.

Mariners' Museum Research Library and Archives: 100 Museum Dr., Newport News, VA 23606-3759; tel. (757) 591-7782; fax (757) 591-7310; e-mail library@mariner.org; internet www.mariner.org/library; f. 1933 by Archer M. and Anna H. Huntington; library of materials related to human interaction with the world's waterways; 75,000 vols, 350,000 photographs, 1m. archival items such as ships' logs, charts, manuscripts, blueprints and memorabilia; spec. collns: Edwin Levick Colln of photographs of passenger ships, yachts, and America's Cup Races; A. Aubrey Bodine Colln of images of life on the Chesapeake Bay; Chris-Craft Colln documenting the construction of boats by one of America's most important pleasure boat builders; Dir SUSAN BERG.

Patent and Trademark Office Scientific and Technical Information Center: c/o Commissioner for Patents, POB 1450, Alexandria, VA 22313-1450; c/o Commissioner for Trademarks, POB 1451, Alexandria, VA 22313-1451; tel. (800) 786-9199; e-mail usptoinfo@uspto.gov; internet www.uspto.gov; f. 1836; 200,000 vols; foreign patent documents since 1617; Program Man. HENRY ROSICKY.

Richmond Public Library: 101 East Franklin St, Richmond, VA 23219; tel. (804) 646-4256; fax (804) 646-7685; internet www.richmondpubliclibrary.org; f. 1924; 810,066 vols; Dir HARRIET HENDERSON.

University of Virginia Library: POB 400114, Charlottesville, VA 22904-4111; tel. (804) 924-3026; fax (804) 924-1431; internet www.lib.virginia.edu; f. 1819; 5,053,162 vols, 53,015 journals, 150,362 maps, 447,020 slides and photographs, 87,642 video and audio recordings, 16.7m. MSS; spec. collns incl. American history and literature, incl. McGregor Library of American History and the Barrett Library of American Literature, Massey-Faulkner colln, Streeter colln on Southeastern railways, optics, evolution, Thomas Jefferson, Scott Sporting Colln, Victorian fiction, Greek and Latin literature, music, int. law, history of printing, Gothic novels, Matthew Arnold, Jorge Luis Borges coln, Gordon colln of French books, Tibetan colln, Paul Mellon colln of Americana and Virginiana; Librarian KARIN WITTENBORG.

Washington

Seattle Public Library: 1000 4th Ave, Seattle, WA 98104-1109; tel. (206) 386-4636; internet www.spl.org; f. 1891; 1,668,000 vols; spec. collns: Aeronautics, Pacific Northwest Americana; 23 br. libraries; City Librarian SUSAN HILDRETH.

University of Washington Libraries: POB 352900, Seattle, WA 98195-2900; tel. (206) 543-0242; fax (206) 685-8727; e-mail libquest@u.washington.edu; internet www.lib.washington.edu; f. 1862; incl. Law Library (separately administered; Librarian PENNY HAZELTON), Health Sciences Library, Odegaard Undergraduate Library, East Asia Library, Spec. Collns Div. and 9 br. libraries; 7,203,156 vols, 63,221 current serials, 8,006,596 microforms; Dir and Dean, Univ. of Washington Libraries LIZABETH WILSON.

Washington State Library: POB 42460, Olympia, WA 98504-2460; tel. (360) 902-4151; fax (360) 586-7575; internet www.sos.wa.gov/library; f. 1853; spec. collns: Washington authors, Pacific Northwest, Washington state Ddocuments, Washington state newspapers, transportation, labor and industries, utilities; 167,094 vols, 1,241,503 fed. and state documents, 198,142 microfiche, 49,183 microfilms, 8,914 films, 456,320 audio and video cassettes; State Librarian Dr RAND SIMMONS (acting).

West Virginia

West Virginia University Libraries: POB 6069, Morgantown, WV 26506-6069; 1549 University Ave, Morgantown, WV 26506-6069; tel. (304) 293-4040; fax (304) 293-6638; internet www.libraries.wvu.edu; f. 1867; 1,497,710 vols; spec. collns incl. W Virginia historical art, Appalachian, Myers, rare books; 1.9m. microforms; 4m. archives; Dean FRANCES O'BRIEN.

Wisconsin

American Geographical Society Library, University of Wisconsin—Milwaukee Libraries: POB 399, Milwaukee, WI 53201-0399; 2311 E Hartford Ave, Milwaukee, WI 53211; tel. (414) 229-6282; fax (414) 229-3624; internet www.uwm.edu/libraries/agsl; f. 1851; library and map colln transferred from the Society's headquarters in New York City to the campus of the Univ. of Wisconsin—Milwaukee in 1978; specialized academic research library with emphasis on discovery and exploration, history of cartography, history of geographical thought, historical geography and geographical themes with a significant historical component; 2 research fellowship programmes available to support visiting scholars; sponsors various lecture series; home of the Map Society of Wisconsin; 222,000 vols, 512,000 maps, 10,700 atlases, 114 globes, 33,676 pamphlets, 450,000 photographs and slides, 2,450 CD-ROMs, 800 gigabytes of data storage; Curator Dr CHRISTOPHER BARUTH; publ. *Current Geographical Publications—Contents* (online).

Milwaukee Public Library: 814 West Wisconsin Ave, Milwaukee, WI 53233; tel. (414) 286-3000; fax (414) 286-2794; internet www.mpl.org; f. 1878; 3,170,711 vols; spec. collns incl. Great Lakes marine colln, Milwaukee Road archives, Omar Khayyam colln, Arkham House colln, Philosopher Press colln, cookbooks, H. G. Wells, definitive edns of collected works of British and American authors, Charles King colln, Harry Franck colln, genealogy; depository for US fed. documents, US Geologic Survey, US Defense Mapping Agency maps and US Patent Office; 12 br. libraries, Wisconsin Regional Library for the Blind and Physically Handicapped headquarters, 1 mobile library, 2 library vans; City Librarian PAULA KIELY.

University of Wisconsin Library: 728 State St, Madison, WI 53706; tel. (608) 262-3193; fax (608) 265-2754; internet www.library.wisc.edu; f. 1848; spec. collns on pharmacy, Scandinavian literature, Gaelic literature and history, modern Polish literature, history of science, history of Calvinism, socialist and labour movements; English, American, French, German, Icelandic, Irish, Spanish literature and history; 7.3m. vols; 55,000 serial titles, 6.2m. microforms, 160 linear ft of MSS, 7m. govt documents, maps, musical scores; Dir-Gen. for Library System KENNETH FRAZIER.

Museums and Art Galleries

Alabama

Alabama Museum of Natural History, University of Alabama: POB 870340, Tuscaloosa, AL 35487-0340; tel. (205) 348-7550; e-mail programs@bama.ua.edu; internet amnh.ua.edu; exhibits and collns incl. the Hodges meteorite, the only meteorite known to have struck a human being, fossils, minerals and palaeontology; Dir Dr RANDY MECREDY.

Alaska

Alaska State Museum: 395 Whittier St, Juneau, AK 99801-1718; tel. (907) 465-2901; fax (907) 465-2976; internet www.museums.state.ak.us; f. 1900, opened to the public 1920; Alaskan history, Alaska's native people, Russian America, art, natural history and ethnographic materials; state-wide assistance to museums in Alaska; Alaska State Chief Curator BRUCE KATO.

Attached Museum:

Sheldon Jackson Museum: 104 College Dr., Sitka, AK 99835-7657; tel. (907) 747-8981; fax (907) 747-3004; internet www.museums.state.ak.us; f. 1888; Alaska Native artefacts; Chief Curator GLENN COOK (acting).

Arizona

Arizona State Museum: POB 210026, Univ. of Arizona, Tucson, AZ 85721-0026; 1013 East University Blvd, Tucson, AZ 85721-0026; tel. (520) 621-6302; fax (520) 621-2976; internet www.statemuseum.arizona.edu; f. 1893; archaeology, anthropology and ethnology of Arizona and surrounding regions; research colln incl. Hohokam, Mogollon and other archaeological material, osteological remains, vertebrate zoo-archaeological and herbarial specimens, 1,500 linear ft of archive material and 250,000 photographs; collns Southwest Indian pottery, Navajo textiles; library of 50,000 vols, 1,500 periodicals; Dir BETH GRINDELL.

Arkansas

Arkansas Arts Center: POB 2137, Little Rock, AR 72203; located at: 501 East Ninth St, Little Rock, AR 72202; tel. (501) 372-4000; fax (501) 375-8053; internet www.arkarts.com; incl. Children's Theatre and Museum School; spec. colln American and European art from Renaissance to present, paintings by Diego Rivera, Odilon Redon, Francesco Bassano; sculpture by Henry Moore, Louise Nevelson, Roy Lichtenstein; prints by Rembrandt, Whistler, Dürer; contemporary crafts; library of 5,000 vols; Dir Dr ELLEN PLUMMER.

Arkansas Museum of Science and History: Suite 150, 500 President Clinton Ave, Little Rock, AR 72201; tel. (501) 396-7050; fax (501) 396-7054; e-mail erandolph@amod.org; internet www.amod.org; Egyptian sarcophagus from 6th century BC, multicultural masks, 51 species of animals; Exec. Dir NAN SELZ.

Historic Arkansas Museum: 200 East Third St, Little Rock, AR 72201; tel. (501) 324-9351; fax (501) 324-9345; e-mail info@historicarkansas.org; internet www.arkansashistory.com; f. 1939; 5 pre-Civil War houses; collns of decorative, mechanical and fine arts; Dir BILL WORTHEN.

California

Asian Art Museum of San Francisco, The Avery Brundage Collection: 200 Larkin St, San Francisco, CA 94102; tel. (415) 581-3500; fax (415) 581-4700; e-mail pr@asianart.org; internet www.asianart.org; f. 1969; museum and centre of research on outstanding collns of Chinese, Japanese, Korean, Indian, South-east Asian, Himalayan and Islamic art; library of 40,000 vols; Chair. DIXON R. DOLL.

California Palace of the Legion of Honor: Lincoln Park, 34th Ave and Clement St, San Francisco, CA 94121; tel. (415) 750-3600; fax (415) 750-7686; e-mail mediarelations@famsf.org; internet www.legionofhonor.org; f. 1924; attached to Fine Arts Museums of San Francisco; European decorative arts and paintings; ancient art; sculpture by Auguste Rodin; Achenbach Foundation for Graphic Arts has largest colln of prints and drawings in the Western USA (see also de Young Museum); Dir JOHN E. BUCHANAN, Jr; publ. *Fine Arts Magazine* (3 or 4 a year).

de Young Museum: 50 Hagiwara Tea Garden Dr., Golden Gate Park, San Francisco, CA 94118; tel. (415) 863-3330; fax (415) 750-7692; internet www.deyoungmuseum.org; f. 1895, reopened 2005; attached to Fine Arts Museums of San Francisco; collns of American art from the 17th to the 21st century; art of the native Americas, Africa and the Pacific (see also California Palace of the Legion of

Honor); Dir JOHN E. BUCHANAN, Jr; publ. *Fine Arts Magazine* (3 or 4 a year).

J. Paul Getty Museum: Suite 1000, 1200 Getty Center Dr., Los Angeles, CA 90049-1687; tel. (310) 440-7330; fax (310) 440-7751; e-mail gettymuseum@getty.edu; internet www.getty.edu; f. 1954; Greek, Roman and Etruscan antiquities, European paintings; drawings, manuscripts, decorative arts; European and American photographs, modern and contemporary European and American outdoor sculpture; conservation work and symposia; Dir DAVID BOMFORD (acting).

Getty Villa: 17985 Pacific Coast Highway, Pacific Palisades, Malibu, CA 90272; tel. (310) 440-7300; e-mail gettymuseum@getty.edu; internet www.getty.edu/museum/home.html; f. 1953, reopened in 2006 after major renovations; educational centre and museum dedicated to the study of the arts and cultures of ancient Greece, Rome and Etruria, incl. re-creation of a Roman seaside villa, the Villa dei Papiri, which was destroyed by the eruption of Vesuvius in AD 79; houses permanent colln of 44,000 Greek, Roman and Etruscan antiquities, 1,200 of which are on public display; a library and other facilities for scholars supports research and study programmes; Dir MICHAEL BRAND.

Griffith Observatory and Planetarium: 2800 East Observatory Rd, Los Angeles, CA 90027; tel. (213) 473-0800; fax (213) 473-0816; internet www.griffithobservatory.org; f. 1935; 3 main divs: the Observatory, with Zeiss twin 12-inch and 9-inch refracting telescopes and 3 solar telescopes; more than 100 exhibits; the Samuel Oschin Planetarium, with its Zeiss star projector and laser video all-dome animation; Dir Dr E. C. KRUPP; publ. *The Griffith Observer* (illustrated, 12 a year).

Huntington Library, Art Collections and Botanical Gardens: 1151 Oxford Rd, San Marino, CA 91108; tel. (626) 405-2100; fax (626) 449-5720; e-mail publicinformation@huntington.org; internet www.huntington.org; f. 1919; British and French paintings from 18th to 19th centuries (incl. full-length portraits by Reynolds, Gainsborough and Lawrence); 18th-century French sculpture, furniture and porcelain; European decorative arts from 16th to 18th centuries; American painting, furniture and decorative arts from 1730 to 1930; botanical gardens of 120 acres with 15,000 plant species; library of 500,000 rare books, 500,000 ref. books, 6m. MSS, prints, 600,000 photographs and maps; Pres. STEVEN S. KOBLIK; Dir Art Collns JOHN MURDOCH; See also Libraries and Archives; publ. *Huntington Frontiers* (2 a year).

Natural History Museum of Los Angeles County: 900 Exposition Blvd, Los Angeles, CA 90007; e-mail info@nhm.org; internet www.nhm.org; f. 1910; Western USA and American History, New World ethnology and archaeology, palaeontology, geology, mineralogy, botany, ichthyology, mammalogy, entomology, herpetology, invertebrate zoology, ornithology; active research centre in areas of living and fossil invertebrates, vertebrates, mineralogy, anthropology (Native American, pre-Columbian and Pacific) and history (CA and Southwestern); incl. Page Museum at La Brea Tar Pits and William S. Hart Museum; 15,000 mems; library of 100,000 vols; Pres. Board of Governors ED. N. HARRISON; Chair. Museum Foundation STEPHEN R. ONDERDONK; Dir JAMES L. POWELL; publs *Contributions in Science* (irregular), *Science Series* (irregular), *Terra* (6 a year).

San Diego Museum of Art: Balboa Park, POB 122107, San Diego, CA 92112-2107; 1450 El Prado, Balboa Park, San Diego, CA; tel. (619) 232-7931; fax (619) 232-9367; e-mail information@sdmart.org; internet www.sdmart.org; f. 1925; Renaissance and Baroque paintings of Spanish, Italian, Dutch, Flemish and French schools; major works by El Greco, Zurbarán, Goya, Crivelli, Tiepolo, Guardi, Rubens, Rembrandt, Ruysdael, Hals, Matisse, Braque; early and contemporary American artists; Asiatic arts and sculpture, graphics and decorative arts from many countries; Latin American art; lectures, concerts and classes; library of 27,000 vols, 12,000 periodicals; Dir DERRICK R. CARTWRIGHT.

San Diego Natural History Museum: POB 121390, San Diego, CA 92112-1390; tel. (619) 232-3821; fax (619) 232-0248; e-mail library@sdnhm.org; internet www.sdnhm.org; f. 1874 to further the knowledge of natural history and the conservation of natural resources; depts of botany, herpetology, birds and mammals, entomology, palaeontology and marine invertebrates; library of 92,000 vols, 900 journals and series; archives; Laurence Klauber Herpetology Colln; Pres. and CEO Dr MICHAEL W. HAGER; Library Dir MARGARET DYKENS; publ. *Proceedings*.

San Francisco Museum of Modern Art: 151 Third St, San Francisco, CA 94103; tel. (415) 357-4000; fax (415) 357-4037; internet www.sfmoma.org; f. 1935 by the San Francisco Art Asscn; contemporary art; permanent colln: early Modernism, Analytical Cubism, Abstract Expressionism and other major schools since the beginning of the 20th century; also German Expressionism, Modernist Mexican painting, figurative art of the San Francisco Bay area; important photography dept with colln of images since the 1840s; dept of architecture and design focusing on works by architects and designers of the Pacific region; dept of media arts incl. multimedia, videotape, film and other works created in moving-image or image-reproduction media; library of 80,000 vols, 1,860 periodicals, 56,000 monographs, catalogues raisonnés and exhibition catalogues; Dir NEAL BENEZRA.

University of California, Berkeley, Art Museum and Pacific Film Archive: 2625 Durant Ave, Berkeley, CA 94720-2250; tel. (510) 642-0808; fax (510) 642-4889; e-mail bampfa@berkeley.edu; internet www.bampfa.berkeley.edu; f. 1970; 10 exhibition galleries, sculpture garden; permanent colln of Asian and Western art; Hans Hofmann colln; 10,000 film colln and programme; serves the univ. and San Francisco Bay Area community with exhibitions, study collns, etc.; organizes and receives travelling exhibitions from major museums internationally; screens 550–600 films annually; Dir KEVIN E. CONSEY.

Colorado

Denver Art Museum: 100 W 14th Ave Parkway, Denver, CO 80204-2788; tel. (720) 865-5000; fax (720) 913-0001; e-mail info@denverartmuseum.org; internet www.denverartmuseum.org; f. 1893 as Artists' Club of Denver; exhibitions and art education programmes for children and adults; permanent collns incl. architecture, design and graphics; Asian; modern and contemporary; native art (incl. American Indian, African and Oceanic artworks); New World (incl. pre-Columbian and Spanish Colonial); painting and sculpture (incl. American and European); photography; Western American art; textile art; Dir Dr CHRISTOPH HEINRICH; Pres. CATHEY FINLON; publs *On & Off the Wall* (mems magazine, 6 a year), *Western Passages* (1 a year).

Denver Museum of Nature and Science: 2001 Colorado Blvd, Denver, CO 80205-5798; tel. (303) 322-7009; fax (303) 331-6492; e-mail feedback@dmns.org; internet www.dmns.org/main/en; f. and inc. 1900; depts of anthropology and archaeology, archives, photographic srchives, earth sciences, zoology, conservation, exhibitions, youth programmes, adult programmes; gates Planetarium, Hall of Life, IMAX theater, auditorium; library of 40,000 vols, 800 periodicals; Chief Curator Dr KIRK JOHNSON; Pres. and CEO GEORGE W. SPARKS; publ. *Museum Quarterly*.

Connecticut

Connecticut State Museum of Natural History and Archaeology Center: 2019 Hillside Rd, Storrs, CT 06269-1023; tel. (860) 486-4460; fax (860) 486-0827; internet www.cac.uconn.edu; attached to Univ. of Connecticut; Archaeological Center f. 2004; 500,000 archaeological and ethnographic items primarily of Native North and South American origin, including 19th-century Plains Indian shirts and Palaeolithic stone tools dating from over 250,000 years ago; State Archaeologist Dr NICHOLAS BELLANTONI; Dir LEANNE KENNEDY HARTY.

Discovery Museum and Planetarium: 4450 Park Ave, Bridgeport, CT 06604; tel. (203) 372-3521; fax (203) 374-1929; internet www.discoverymuseum.org; independent; f. 1958; incl. CineMuse Theater, Henry B. duPont Planetarium, Challenger Learning Center, interactive science galleries and educational programmes; Exec. Dir LINDA MALKIN; Admin. Dir LYNN HAMILTON.

Peabody Museum of Natural History: POB 208118, New Haven, CT 06520-8118; tel. (203) 432-5050; fax (203) 432-9816; internet www.peabody.yale.edu; f. 1866 by a gift of George Peabody, banker and philanthropist; affiliated with Yale Univ.; extensive collns in the fields of anthropology, meteorites, botany, palaeobotany, invertebrate palaeontology, mineralogy, vertebrate palaeontology, invertebrate zoology and vertebrate zoology, historic scientific instruments, each with its own curator; also Yale Peabody Museum Field Station; Dir MICHAEL J. DONOGHUE, publs *Bulletin*, *Discovery*, *Postilla*.

Wadsworth Atheneum Museum of Art: 600 Main St, Hartford, CT 06103; tel. (860) 278-2670; fax (860) 527-0803; e-mail info@wadsworthatheneum.org; internet www.wadsworthatheneum.org; f. 1842; early American furniture, Hudson River School landscapes, Renaissance and Baroque paintings, African-American art; Meissen and Sèvres porcelains; costume and textiles; 19th-century French and Impressionist paintings; modernist and surrealist masterpieces; MATRIX Gallery for Contemporary Art; library: Auerbach library of 40,000 vols; Dir SUSAN TALBOT.

Delaware

Winterthur, An American Country Estate (Museum, Gardens and Library): Winterthur, DE 19735; tel. (302) 888-4600; fax (302) 888-4820; e-mail webmaster@winterthur.org; internet www.winterthur.org; f. 1951; American antiquities from 1640 to 1860, 60-acre naturalistic garden; MA programme in Early American Culture and MS programme in Art Conservation, both in conjunction with Univ. of Delaware; colln of over 85,000 articles and antiques; 23,000 mems; library of 500,000 vols, MSS, microfilm, periodicals, photographs; Dir and CEO LESLIE GREENE BOWMAN; publ. *Winterthur Portfolio* (4 a year).

District of Columbia

Anacostia Museum and Center for African American History and Culture: 1901 Fort Pl., SE, Washington, DC 20020; tel. (202) 633-4020; fax (202) 287-3183; e-mail aminfo@si.edu; internet www.anacostia.si .edu; attached to the Smithsonian Instn; Dir JAMES C. EARLY (acting).

Arthur M. Sackler Gallery: Smithsonian Institution, 1050 Independence Ave, SW, Washington, DC 20560; tel. (202) 653-4880; fax (202) 357-4911; internet www.asia.si.edu; f. 1982, opened 1987; initial colln gift of Arthur M. Sackler; part of the Smithsonian Instn, and interlinked with the Freer Gallery of Art; int. loan exhibitions and displays of permanent colln, incl. ancient Egyptian art, arts of the Islamic world, Chinese art, Japanese art, Korean art and South-east Asian art; public programmes and publs aim to promote artistic and cultural traditions of Asia; joint Sackler and Freer scientific and research dept; library of 80,000 vols; Dir JULIAN RABY.

Arts and Industries Building: 900 Jefferson Dr., SW, Washington, DC; tel. (202) 633-1000; e-mail info@si.edu; internet www.si .edu/ai; f. 1881 for the inaugural ball of Pres. James A. Garfield, to host exhibits from the Centennial Exposition in Philadelphia; attached to the Smithsonian Instn; exhibitions from the Smithsonian Instn and other museums and collns; closed for renovation.

Corcoran Gallery of Art: 700 17th St, NW, Washington, DC 20006-4840; tel. (202) 639-1700; internet www.corcoran.org; f. 1869 from colln of banker William Corcoran; 14,000 items from 19th and 20th centuries; American and European painting, sculpture and photography, incl. works by Cuyp, Degas, Delacroix, Hopper, Elsworth Kelly, Monet, Picasso, Man Ray, Renoir, Rodin, Sargent, Warhol, Whistler; also houses the Corcoran Gallery of Art and Design; Dir and Pres. PAUL GREENHALGH.

Freer Gallery of Art: Jefferson Dr. at 12th St, SW, Washington, DC 20560; tel. (202) 633-4880; fax (202) 357-4911; e-mail asiainfo@asia.si.edu; internet www.asia.si .edu; f. 1923 (est. 1906), based on gift of the late Charles L. Freer, of Detroit, MI (1854–1919); part of the Smithsonian Instn, and interlinked with the Arthur M. Sackler Gallery; devoted to research and exhibition of the outstanding collns of Chinese, Japanese, Korean, Indian, Near Eastern and late 19th- to 20th-century American art; works of James McNeill Whistler; joint Sackler and Freer scientific and research dept; library of 80,000 vols, (approx. one-half in Chinese and Japanese); Dir JULIAN RABY; publs *Ars Orientalis*, *Oriental Studies*.

Hirshhorn Museum and Sculpture Garden: POB 37012 HMSG/MRC 350, Washington, DC 20013-7012; located at: Independence Ave at 7th St, SW, Washington, DC 20560; tel. (202) 633-4674; fax (202) 786-2682; e-mail hmsginquiries@si.edu; internet hirshhorn.si.edu; f. 1966; administered by the Smithsonian Instn; modern and contemporary int. art; sculpture since 19th century; library: research library of 57,000 vols, 50 serials, 13,000 slides from 900 contemporary artists; Chair. J. TOMILSON HILL.

International Spy Museum: 800 F St, NW, Washington, DC 20004; tel. (202) 393-7798; fax (202) 654-0977; e-mail other@spymuseum .org; internet www.spymuseum.org; f. 2002; history and contemporary role of espionage from a global perspective; Exec. Dir PETER EARNEST; Chief Operating Officer KAREN CORBIN.

National Air and Space Museum: 6th and Independence Ave, SW, Washington, DC 20013-7012; tel. (202) 633-1000; fax (202) 633-8174; e-mail info@si.edu; internet www .nasm.si.edu; f. 1946; administered by the Smithsonian Instn; records the nat. devt of aeronautics and astronautics; collects, preserves and displays aeronautical and astronautical equipment of historical interest and significance; provides educational material for the historical study of aeronautics and astronautics; colln contains original full-size aircraft, spacecraft, recovered space exploration vehicles, engines, instruments, flight clothing, accessories of technical, historical, and biographical interest, photographs, scale models and extensive reference data; Paul E. Garber Preservation, Restoration and Storage Facility and Steven F. Udvar-Hazy Center; includes Center for Earth and Planetary Studies (*q.v.*); library of 40,000 vols and journals; archives: 11,000 cu ft of materials, 1.7m. photographs, 700,000 ft of film, 2m. technical drawings; Dir JOHN R. DAILEY.

National Gallery of Art: 2000B South Club Dr., Landover, MD 20785; between Third and Ninth St, NW, on Constitution Ave, Washington, DC 20565; tel. (202) 737-4215; fax (202) 789-2681; internet www.nga.gov; f. 1937; ind. establishment of the US Govt; European and American paintings, sculpture and graphic arts since 12th century; photographic archives; slide colln; library of 365,000 vols, 2,321 periodicals; Pres. VICTORIA P. SANT; Dir EARL A. POWELL, III; Admin. DARRELL R. WILLSON; Admin. Librarian ROGER LAWSON; publ. *Studies in the History of Art*.

National Museum of African Art, Smithsonian Institution: 950 Independence Ave, SW, Washington, DC 20560-0708; tel. (202) 633-4649; fax (202) 357-4879; e-mail nmafaweb@nmafa.si.edu; internet africa.si .edu; f. 1964, merged with Smithsonian Instn 1979; 8,000 items from throughout Africa, incl. traditional and contemporary art; library: research facilities include the Warren M. Robbins library of 25,000 vols and the Eliot Elisofon Photographic Archives (300,000 photographic prints and transparencies, 120,000 ft of motion picture film and videotape); Dir Dr SHARON F. PATTON.

National Museum of American History: The National Mall, 14th St and Constitution Ave, NW, Washington, DC 20560; tel. (202) 633-1000; e-mail info@si.edu; internet americanhistory.si.edu; administered by the Smithsonian Instn; f. 1964; devoted to the colln, care, study and exhibition of objects that reflect the experience of the American people, incl. 3m. artefacts; programme of lectures and concerts; library: Archives Center of 700 collns; Dir BRENT D. GLASS; Curator, Archives Center JOHN A. FLECKNER.

Attached Research Institute:

Jerome and Dorothy Lemelson Center for the Study of Invention and Innovation: see separate entry.

National Museum of Natural History: POB 37012, Smithsonian Institution, NW, Washington, DC 20013-7012; tel. (202) 357-2661; fax (202) 357-4779; internet www.mnh .si.edu; f. 1846; administered by the Smithsonian Instn; depository of the nat. collns, containing more than 120m. catalogued items; it is especially rich in the natural science and anthropology of the Americas, including zoology, entomology, botany, geology, palaeontology, archaeology, ethnology and physical anthropology; also houses exhibits relating to the natural sciences and anthropology; research: 100 scientists working in 4 depts: anthropology, Mineral Sciences, palaeobiology, systematic siology; part of the Smithsonian Marine Science Network; library: Nat. Anthropological Archives: 400,000 ethnological and archaeological photographs, 20,000 works of native art, 1,200 aluminum discs recorded by J. P. Harrington; Human Studies Film Archives: 8m. ft of film and video; Dir Dr PAUL RISSER (acting); publ. *Smithsonian Contributions* (separate series for Anthropology, Botany, Earth Sciences, Palaeobiology, Zoology and Marine Sciences).

Attached Research Institutes:

Arctic Research Centre: see separate entry.

Carrie-Bow Marine Field Station—Caribbean Coral Reef Ecosystems (CCRE): see separate entry in Belize chapter.

Marine Station at Fort Pierce: see separate entry.

National Portrait Gallery: POB 37012, Victor Bldg, Suite 8300, MRC 973, Washington, DC 20013-7012; tel. (202) 633-8300; fax (202) 633-8243; e-mail npgnews@si.edu; internet npg.si.edu; administered by the Smithsonian Instn; f. 1962; portraits of persons who have made significant contributions to the history, devt or culture of the people of the USA; library of 90,000 vols; Dir MARTIN E. SULLIVAN; publ. *PROFILE* (4 a year).

National Postal Museum: 2 Massachussetts Ave, NE, Washington, DC 20002; tel. (202) 633-5555; fax (202) 633-9393; internet www.postalmuseum.si.edu; f. 1993 in the bldg of the former Washington, DC post office (1914–86); Nat. Philatelic Colln (f. 1886); controlled by the Smithsonian Instn with the support of the United States Postal Service; Nat. Philatelic Colln of 6m. items; delivery vehicles, mailboxes and mailbags, uniforms and equipment and other items of postal history; library of 40,000 vols, journals, catalogues, archival documents (part of the Smithsonian Instn Libraries system); Dir ALLEN KANE; Librarian PAUL MCCUTCHEON.

Smithsonian American Art Museum and its Renwick Gallery: 750 Ninth St, NW, Rm 3100, Washington, DC 20004; tel. (202) 633-1000; fax (202) 275-1424; e-mail americanartinfo@si.edu; internet americanart.si.edu; f. 1829; attached to Smithsonian Instn; largest colln of American art in the world; 41,000 artworks since 18th century; recently renovated museum bldg houses Lunder Conservation Center (permanent displays of the museum's preservation work) and provides information on conservation science and techniques; other centres incl. Luce Foundation Center for American Art (art storage and study centre): 3,300 objects on display, incl. a discussion of each artwork, artist biographies, audio interviews, video-clips and still images; specialized art research databases of 500,000 records, incl. Inventory of American Paintings and Sculpture; pre-1877 Art Exhibition Catalogue Index and findings from the Save Outdoor Sculpture programme; Photographic Archives of 250,000 photographs, negatives and slides; Peter A. Juley and Son colln (127,000 images documenting the work of 11,000 American artists from the 1890s to 1975); and the Water Rosenblum colln (7,500 black-and-white photographs documenting the New York art scene from 1945 to 1970); Graphic Arts Study Center (28,000 works on paper, including prints, drawings, watercolours and photographs) and the Joseph Cornell Study Center; Renwick Gallery of craft work; now part of the Donald W. Reynolds Center; library of 180,000 vols specializing in American art, history and biography; shared by the Smithsonian American Art Museum and the Nat. Portrait Gallery; Dir ELIZABETH BROUN; Chief of Art Information Resources

CHRISTINE HENNESSEY; publ. *American Art* (3 a year).

Florida

John and Mable Ringling Museum of Art/State Art Museum of Florida: 5401 Bay Shore Rd, Sarasota, FL 34243; tel. (941) 359-5700; fax (941) 359-7704; e-mail info@ringling.org; internet www.ringling.org; f. 1927, bequeathed to the State of Florida 1936; attached to Florida State Univ.; comprises Museum of Art (European, American and Non-Western art), 2 Circus Museums including the Tibbals Learning Center, home of the world's largest miniature circus, Cà d'Zan Mansion (former Ringling winter residence), Historic Asolo Theater (18th-century Venetian theatre from Asolo, Italy), 66-acre waterfront estate; library of 60,000 vols and exhibition catalogues, 100 periodicals; Exec. Dir Dr JOHN WETENHALL; Curator Dr STEPHEN BORYS (Circus Museum); Curator DEBORAH WALK (Circus Museum); Curator JOANNA WEBER (Museum of Art).

Marineland Foundation, Inc. (Marineland of Florida): 9600 Oceanshore Blvd, St Augustine, FL 32080; tel. (904) 471-1111; fax (904) 460-1330; e-mail reservations@marineland.net; internet www.marineland.net; f. 1937; incl. 2 Oceanariums, 11 marine and fresh-water exhibits; houses C. V. Whitney Laboratory; ref. library on aquatic sciences (not open to the public); Gen. Man. ROBIN B. FRIDAY, Sr.

Georgia

Roosevelt's Little White House: 401 Little White House Rd, Warm Springs, GA 31830; tel. (706) 655-5870; fax (706) 655-5872; internet www.fdr-littlewhitehouse.org; f. 1946; under direction of Georgia Dept of Natural Resources; remains as it was when Pres. Franklin Delano Roosevelt died here in 1945; exhibits and film of Roosevelt in Georgia; Franklin Delano Roosevelt Memorial Museum opened in April 2004 with expanded and updated exhibits and films; Superintendent (vacant); Volunteer Coordinator LYNN BARFIELD.

Hawaii

Bernice P. Bishop Museum: 1525 Bernice St, Honolulu, HI 96704; tel. (808) 847-3511; fax (808) 841-8968; e-mail library@bishopmuseum.org; internet www.bishopmuseum.org; f. 1889; devoted to the study of natural and cultural history in the Pacific; depts of Hawaiian and Pacific Studies (ethnology and archaeology), natural sciences (botany, entomology, zoology, ichthyology, malacology, vertebrate and invertebrate zoology), education, library and archives; lectures, films, education programmes, permanent and temporary exhibits; Richard T. Mamiya Science Adventure Center; library of 115,000 vols, 1m. historic photographs; Pres. MICHAEL T. CHINAKA; publ. *Ka'Elele* (12 a year).

Attached Institutes:

Amy B. H. Greenwell Ethnobotanical Garden: POB 1053, Captain Cook, HI 96704; tel. (808) 323-3318; fax (808) 323-2394; e-mail agg@bishopmuseum.org; 200 species of endemic, indigenous and Polynesian introduced plants; insect house; archaeological site.

Hawaii Maritime Center: Pier 7, Honolulu Harbor, Honolulu, HI 96813; tel. (808) 563-6373; maritime history; two ships, Hōkūle'a (Polynesian double-hulled canoe) and The Falls of Clyde (18th-century, 4-masted, fully rigged).

Museum of the Honolulu Academy of Arts: 900 South Beretania St, Honolulu, HI 96814-1495; tel. (808) 532-8700; fax (808) 532-8787; e-mail info@honoluluacademy.org; internet www.honoluluacademy.org; f. 1927; museum and art school; Western and Asian art collns; educational programmes for adults and young people; Doris Duke Theatre with frequent films, lectures, concerts and performances; outdoor gardens; arts festivals; guided tours/gallery talks; art classes and educational programmes for children and adults; spec. exhibitions; Robert Allerton Art Research Library; 8,865 mems; library of 45,000 vols; spec. colln 8,000 woodblock prints; Dir STEPHEN LITTLE; publ. *Calendar News* (bulletin for members, 6 a year).

Shangri La: 4055 Papu Circle, Honolulu, HI 96816; tel. (808) 734-1941; fax (808) 732-4361; e-mail mclark@ddcf.org; internet www.shangrilahawaii.org; f. 2002 as a bequest of the collector Doris Duke; 3,500 items of Islamic art and craft: architectural features, furniture, ceramics, textiles and paintings; attached to the Doris Duke Foundation for Islamic Art; library of 1,500 vols; Exec. Dir DEBORAH POPE; Curator Dr SHARON LITTLEFIELD.

Idaho

Boise Art Museum: 670 Julia Davis Dr., Boise, ID 83702; tel. (208) 345-8330; internet www.boiseartmuseum.org; private, non-profit; f. 1931 as the Boise Art Assn; regional and nat. artwork; permanent colln of 2,300 works of 20th-century American art with emphasis on artists of the Pacific Northwest, American Realism and ceramics; education programme; Exec. Dir MELANIE FALES.

Nez Perce National Historical Park: POB 1000, Lapwai, ID 83540; tel. (208) 843-7001; fax (208) 843-7003; e-mail nepe_visitor_information@nps.gov; internet www.nps.gov/nepe; attached to govt Nat. Park Service; Nez Perce (Nimiipuu) history and culture; 38 sites marking important events related to war of 1877; incl. White Bird Battlefield, Big Hole National Battlefield and Bear Paw Battlefield.

Illinois

Adler Planetarium: 1300 South Lake Shore Dr., Chicago, IL 60605-2403; tel. (312) 922-7827; fax (312) 322-2257; internet www.adlerplanetarium.org; f. 1930 by Max Adler; the circular planetarium chamber seats 280 persons, with a hemispherical dome 68 ft wide and Zeiss VI projector; the exhibition area houses one of the world's finest collns of astronomical artefacts, incl. the world's oldest known window sundial (dated 1529) and a telescope made by William Herschel; some of the oldest artefacts in the colln date back to 12th-century Persia; exhibits in astronomy and related sciences; 190-seat theatre featuring real-time interactive virtual environments; library of 5,000 vols; classrooms; photographic laboratories; solar telescope; several telescopes incl. 20-inch diam. Cassegrain reflector equipped with a charge-coupled device (in the Doane Observatory, east of the planetarium); programme incl. sky shows, classes in astronomy, navigation and telescope making; grade school programme; public observation sessions, demonstrations, lectures and films; Pres. Dr PAUL H. KNAPPENBERGER, Jr.

Art Institute of Chicago: 111 South Michigan Ave, Chicago, IL 60603-6404; tel. (312) 443-3600; e-mail webmaster@artic.edu; internet www.artic.edu; f. 1879; American painting and sculpture; European painting since 13th century, medieval and Renaissance art; prints and drawings; sculpture; Asian arts (of 5,000 years); African and Amerindian art; textiles; decorative arts; photography; architecture; School of Art; Ryerson Library (f. 1901); Burnham Library of Architecture (f. 1912); Kraft Education Centre; library of 180,000 vols and 340,000 slides on art and architecture; Dir JAMES CUNO; publs *Member Magazine* (6 a year), *Museum Studies* (2 a year).

Field Museum: 1400 South Lake Shore Dr., Chicago, IL 60605; tel. (312) 922-9410; fax (312) 427-7269; internet www.fieldmuseum.org; f. 1893; depts of anthropology, botany, geology, zoology (birds, fishes, insects, invertebrates, mammals, reptiles and amphibians); large colln of books on China, incl. several thousand in Chinese; Ornithological Section incl. many rare and illustrated vols; library of 275,000 vols; Pres. JOHN W. MCCARTER, Jr; publs *Fieldiana* (peer-reviewed publs in anthropology, botany, geology and zoology), *In The Field*.

Illinois State Museum: Spring and Edwards Sts, Springfield, IL 62706; tel. (217) 782-7386; fax (217) 782-1254; internet www.museum.state.il.us; f. 1877; natural history and anthropology (recreations of American Indian villages and natural habitats); 'At Home in the Heartland' exhibition of decorative arts in Illinois since 1750; historic and contemporary works by Illinois artists are exhibited in the fine and applied arts galleries; 'A Place for Discovery' interactive learning centre; library of 10,000 vols mainly relative to collns; Dir BONNIE W. STYLES; publs *Events and Activities* (4 a year), *Impressions* (4 a year), *The Living Museum* (4 a year).

Attached Museums and Galleries:

Dickson Mounds Museum: 10956 North Dickson Mounds Rd, Lewistown, IL 61542; tel. (309) 547-3721; fax (309) 547-3189; internet www.museum.state.il.us/ismsites/dickson; on-site archaeological museum covering 12,000 years of Illinois history; Dir Dr MICHAEL WIANT.

Illinois State Museum at Springfield: Spring and Edwards Sts, Springfield, IL 62706-5000; tel. (217) 782-7386; fax (217) 782-1254; e-mail info@museum.state.il.us; internet www.museum.state.il.us/ismsites/main/geninfo.html; natural and cultural heritage of Illinois; Dir BONNIE W. STYLES.

ISM Chicago Gallery: James R. Thompson Center, 100 W Randolph, Suite 2-100, Chicago, IL 60601-3219; tel. (312) 814-5322; fax (312) 814-3471; exhibitions of art by past and contemporary Illinois artists.

Lockport Gallery: 201 West 10th St, Lockport, IL 60441; tel. (815) 838-7400; fax (815) 838-7448; e-mail jzimmer@museum.state.il.us; internet www.museum.state.il.us/ismsites/lockport/geninfo.html; f. 1987; exhibitions of art by past and contemporary Illinois artists and artisans; Dir JIM ZIMMER.

John G. Shedd Aquarium: 1200 South Lake Shore Dr., Chicago, IL 60605; tel. (312) 939-2435; fax (312) 939-8069; e-mail contactus@sheddaquarium.org; internet www.sheddaquarium.org; f. 1930; exhibits both fresh-water and salt-water species; oceanarium re-creates a Pacific Northwest Coast environment and a Falkland Islands habitat; 90,000-gallon Coral Reef exhibit; Wild Reef re-creates a coral reef in the Philippines and offers a diverse shark habitat; Pres. and CEO TED A. BEATTIE.

Lincoln Park Zoological Gardens: 2001 N Clark St, Chicago, IL 60614; tel. (312) 742-2000; fax (312) 742-2137; e-mail webmaster@lpzoo.org; internet www.lpzoo.org; f. 1868; specimens of mammals, birds, reptiles, and amphibians; farm; specialities: great apes, primates, perching birds, snakes, big cats; spec. programmes: Farm in the Zoo, Travelling Zoo and Endangered Species educational programmes; scientific studies incl. nutrition, behaviour, reproductive biology, physiology, African, Asian and South American field work; library of 2,000 vols; Pres. and CEO KEVIN J. BELL; publ. *Lincoln Park Zoo Magazine* (3 a year).

Research Centres:

Alexander Center for Applied Population Biology:; f. 2005; research in small population biology; Population Management Centre conducts population biology-based analyses for captive populations at North American zoos; Dir Dr JOANNE EARNHARDT.

Davee Center for Epidemiology and Endocrinology:; f. 2001; studies on health in captive and wild animal populations; Dir DOMINIC A. TRAVIS.

Lester E. Fisher Center for the Study and Conservation of Apes:; f. 2004; multidisciplinary ape research and conservation programme; initiatives in animal health, epidemiology, nutrition, behaviour, population biology and conservation of wild populations and study of ape cognition, endocrinology and citizen science; Dir Dr ELIZABETH V. LONSDORF.

Museum of Science and Industry: 57th St and Lake Shore Dr., Chicago, IL 60637; tel. (773) 684-1414; fax (773) 684-7141; e-mail msi@msichicago.org; internet www.msichicago.org; f. 1933; metals, power, physics, chemistry, electronics, transportation, petroleum, food, space eng., communications and medical sciences; over 2,000 exhibit units incl. re-creation of a coal mine, German submarine, walk-through model of human heart, Colleen Moore's Fairy Castle, 'Yesterday's Main Street', actual Apollo 8 spacecraft, Henry Crown Space Center, 'Omnimax' theater, and exhibits on space exploration and energy research; Pres. and CEO DAVID MESENA.

Oriental Institute Museum: 1155 E 58th St, Chicago, IL 60637; tel. (773) 702-9514; fax (773) 702-9853; e-mail oi-museum@uchicago.edu; internet oi.uchicago.edu; f. 1919; holds 202,000 registered objects from Egypt, Iran, Iraq, Israel, Jordan, Palestinian Autonomous Areas, Sudan, Syria and Turkey; research arm supports archaeological excavations in Egypt, Iran, Sudan, Syria and Turkey; Institute has dictionary projects in Demotic Egyptian, Sumerian, Akkadian and Hittite; library of 60,000 vols; Museum Dir GEOFF EMBERLING; Head Registrar HELEN McDONALD; publ. *Journal of Near Eastern Studies*.

Indiana

Indianapolis Museum of Art: 4000 Michigan Rd, Indianapolis, IN 46208-3326; tel. (317) 923-1331; e-mail ima@ima.museum; internet www.ima-art.org; f. 1883; library of 10,000 vols; files on 28,000 artists, incl. 3,800 Indiana artists; spec. collns incl. Samuel Josefowitz Colln of Gauguin and the School of Pont-Aven, Holliday Colln of Neo-Impressionism, featuring the work of Georges Seurat and his followers, the largest colln of works by J. M. W. Turner outside the UK, a comprehensive Chinese colln, Japanese Edo-period paintings, more than 2,000 objects in the African art colln; also fashion arts, textiles and West Asian rugs; incl. Virginia B. Fairbanks Art and Nature Park and Oldfields–Lilly House and Gardens.

Indiana State Museum: 650 West Washington St, Indianapolis, IN 46204; tel. (317) 232-1637; e-mail museumcommunication@dnr.in.gov; internet www.in.gov/ism; f. 1888; cultural and natural history ranging from prehistoric fossils to current popular culture items; Dir of Collns REX GARNIEWICZ.

Iowa

Iowa Museum Association: 1116 Washington St, Cedar Falls, IA 50613; tel. (319) 239-2236; e-mail imasweet@cfu.net; internet www.iowamuseums.org; f. 1976; provides training and devt to Iowa museum professionals and volunteers, advocates support of Iowa's museums; art centres and museums, botanical gardens, children's museums, historic sites, historical socs, living history sites, nature centres, natural history museums, planetariums, science and technology centres, and zoos; 184 mems; Pres. LINDA WILLEKE; Exec. Dir CYNTHIA SWEET.

Museum of Natural History and Old Capitol Museum: 10 Macbride Hall, Iowa City, IA 52242; tel. (319) 335-0480; fax (319) 335-0653; internet www.uiowa.edu/~nathist; attached to Univ. of Iowa; spec. collns incl. geology, ecology and native cultures; giant Ice Age sloth; North American birds; Mammal Hall incl. a skeleton of an Atlantic Right Whale; Dir PAMELA TRIMPE.

University of Iowa Museum of Art: 1375 Highway 1W, 1840 Studio Arts Bldg, Iowa City, IA 52242; tel. (319) 335-1727; fax (319) 335-3677; e-mail uima@uiowa.edu; internet uima.uiowa.edu; f. 1969; attached to Univ. of Iowa; European and American art; colln of traditional African arts; 12,000-piece colln; collns and exhibitions moved to temporary locations owing to flooding: the Figge Art Museum in Davenport, Iowa, Memorial Union on the Univ. of Iowa campus, Iowa City; Provost WALLACE LOH; Sec. BETTY BREAZEALE.

Kansas

Natural History Museum, University of Kansas: Dyche Hall, 1345 Jayhawk Blvd, Lawrence, KS 66045-7561; tel. (785) 864-4540; fax (785) 864-5335; e-mail kunhm@ku.edu; internet www.nhm.ku.edu; f. 1870; attached to Univ. of Kansas Biodiversity Institute; covers 50,000 sq ft; exhibits and dioramas of the animals and plants of N America; 8m. specimens of plants and animals, from prehistoric to living species and from every continent and ocean; collns: botany, entomology, herpetology, ichthyology, ichthyology tissue, invertebrate palaeontology, invertebrate zoology, mammalogy, ornithology, palaeobotany, vertebrate palaeontology; Dir LEONARD KRISHTALKA.

Spencer Museum of Art, University of Kansas: 1301 Mississippi St, Lawrence, KS 66045-7500; tel. (785) 864-4710; fax (785) 864-3112; e-mail spencerart@ku.edu; internet www.spencerart.ku.edu; f. 1928; houses 36,000 artworks and artefacts in all media; incl. European and American art from ancient to contemporary; significant holdings of E Asian art; recently reopened 20/21 Gallery of modern and contemporary objects; spec. collns incl. medieval art; European and American paintings, sculpture and prints; photography; Japanese Edo-period painting and prints; 20th-century Chinese painting; Kansas Univ.'s ethnographic colln: incl. 10,000 Native American, African, Latin American and Australian works; runs public programmes, programmes for school children, Kansas Univ. students; objects not on view in the galleries are available by appointment; works on paper are accessible for viewing in the Print Room every Friday; organizes exhibitions of local, regional, national and int. interest; also houses Kress Foundation Dept of Art History and the Murphy Library of Art and Architecture; library of 165,000 vols in Murphy Library of Art and Architecture; Dir SARALYN REECE HARDY; publs *The Franklin D. Murphy Lecture* (1 a year), *Register* (1 a year).

Kentucky

Behringer-Crawford Museum: 1600 Montague Rd, Devou Park, Covington, KY 41011; tel. (859) 491-4003; e-mail info@bcmuseum.org; internet www.bcmuseum.org; f. 1950; regional cultural history, minerals, fossils, and American Indian artefacts, transportation objects, art collns of Harlan Hubbard, Dr Wolfgang Ritschel and Mary Bruce Sharon; Exec. Dir LAURIE RISCH; Asst Dir SARAH SIEGRIST.

Kentucky Historical Society: 100 West Broadway, Frankfort, KY 40601; tel. (502) 564-1792; e-mail khstours@ky.gov; internet history.ky.gov; incl. Thomas D. Clark Center for Kentucky History, Old State Capitol, and Kentucky Military History Museum; incl. a 'Historymobile' and 'Museums to go'.

Museums:

Kentucky Military History Museum: 125 East Main St, Frankfort, KY 40601; the Old State Arsenal, a 2-storey brick Gothic-Revival 'castle' standing on a cliff overlooking the Kentucky River and the downtown area, built in 1850, houses the weapons and equipment of the Kentucky Militia, State Guard, and other volunteer military orgs, from the Revolution to the Gulf War; collns of firearms, edged weapons, artillery, uniforms, flags, photographs, personal items.

Old State Capitol: 300 West Broadway, Frankfort, KY 40601; f. 1830; nat. historical landmark introduced Greek-Revival architecture to the USA west of the Appalachian Mountains; bldg served as capitol of the Commonwealth of Kentucky from 1830 to 1910; site of the assassination of William Goebel, the only Governor in US history to die in office as a result of assassination; re-creation of State Law Library.

Thomas D. Clark Center for Kentucky History: 100 West Broadway, Frankfort, KY 40601; prehistoric times to the present: First Kentuckians (10,000 BC to AD 1750), The Kentucky Frontier (1750–1800), The Antebellum Age (1800–60), War and Aftermath (1860–75), Continuity and Change (1875–1900), The New Century (1900–30), Depression and War (1930–50), and Many Sides of Kentucky (1950 to present); Pure Kentucky highlights the lives and contributions of famous Kentuckians through artefacts.

Louisiana

New Orleans Museum of Art: POB 19123, New Orleans, LA 70179; 1 Collins Diboll Circle, City Park, New Orleans, LA 70124; tel. (504) 658-4100; fax (504) 658-4199; e-mail gwilson@noma.org; internet www.noma.org; f. 1911; paintings, sculpture, prints, drawings, photographs and decorative arts; spec. collns incl. history of glass; 150-year colln of photographs; Japanese paintings of the Edo Period; Chinese pottery and stone sculpture; 17th- to 20th-century French paintings; Italian and Spanish paintings from Renaissance and Baroque periods; 16th- to 18th-century Low Countries paintings; tribal arts of sub-Saharan Africa; 18th- and 19th-century French porcelain; 20th-century American art and pottery; Spanish colonial Latin American paintings and sculpture; English and Continental portrait miniatures; P. C. Fabergé jewelled objects; 18th- to 20th-century American and English silver; arts of pre-Columbian Mexico, and of Central and South America; North American Indian arts; Sculpture Garden containing 50 works by Henry Moore, Fernando Botero, Elisabeth Frink, Barbara Hepworth and others; library of 20,000 vols, 70 periodicals; Dir SUSAN TAYLOR; publ. *Arts Quarterly*.

Maine

Maine Archives and Museums: POB 5024, Augusta, ME 04333; tel. (207) 441-1410; e-mail mam@gwi.net; internet www.mainemuseums.org; directory of 201 museums in Maine; Pres. EDWARD S. ALLEN.

Portland Museum of Art: 7 Congress Sq., Portland, ME 04101; tel. (207) 775-6148; fax (207) 773-7324; e-mail info@portlandmuseum.org; internet www.portlandmuseum.org; f. 1882 as Portland Soc. of Art; fine and decorative arts from 18th century housed in 3 bldgs of architectural note: Charles Shipman Payson Bldg, L. D. M. Sweat Memorial Galleries, McLellan House; Maine artists such as Winslow Homer, Marsden Hartley, Rockwell Kent, Louise Nevelson; European collns incl. works by Cassatt, Degas, Magritte, Monet, Munch, Picasso, Rodin; Dir MARK BESSIRE; Deputy Dir and Chief Curator THOMAS DENENBERG.

Maryland

Baltimore Museum of Art: 10 Art Museum Dr., Baltimore, MD 21218-3898; tel. (443) 573-1700; fax (443) 573-1582; internet www.artbma.org; f. 1914; total colln of 90,000 items; Cone Colln of post-impressionist and modern art (incl. 500 works by Matisse, and examples by Picasso, Cézanne and Van Gogh); West Wing for Contemporary Art housing 16 galleries of art since 1960s; Old Master and 19th-century European paintings and sculpture; prints, drawings and photographs since 15th century; American paintings, sculpture and decorative arts from the 17th to the 19th century; Maryland period rooms; African, Asian, Native American, and Oceanic art; 3-acre sculpture garden; library of 55,000 vols; Chair. SUZANNE F. COHEN; Dir DOREEN BOLGER; publ. *BMA Today* (members' magazine, 4 a year).

Maryland Historical Society, Museum and Library of Maryland History: 201 W Monument St, Baltimore, MD 21201; tel. (410) 685-3750; fax (410) 385-2105; internet www.mdhs.org; f. 1844; exhibits Francis Scott Key's original manuscript of The Star-Spangled Banner and the war of 1812; 3,000 paintings and miniatures; 700 pieces of furniture; sculpture, drawings, silver; ceramics; jewellery, textiles; library: library of over 90,000 vols, etc.; manuscript room incl. Calvert Papers, papers of Benjamin Henry Latrobe, over 1,300 letters and documents of the Lords Baltimore and their families, genealogical colln and many hundreds of prints and drawings; maritime colln emphasizing crafts of Chesapeake Bay; Dir ROB ROGERS; publs *Maryland Historical Magazine* (4 a year), *News and Notes* (4 a year).

Attached Museums:

Baltimore Civil War Museum: President Street Station, 601 President St, Baltimore, MD 21202; tel. (410) 385-5188.

Fells Point Maritime Museum: 1724 Thames St, Baltimore, MD 21231; tel. (410) 732-0278.

Walters Art Museum: 600 N Charles St, Baltimore, MD 21201; tel. (410) 547-9000; fax (410) 783-7969; internet www.thewalters.org; f. 1931; collns range from pre-dynastic Egypt to 20th-century Europe; Chinese, Japanese and Indian art, Ancient Egyptian, Greek and Roman art, Byzantine art, Romanesque, early Gothic art, later Gothic art, Renaissance sculpture and decorative arts, manuscript illumination, incunabula, arms and armour, old master paintings, 19th-century paintings, decorative arts; library of 120,000 vols; Dir GARY VIKAN; publs *Journal* (1 a year), *The Walters Magazine* (4 a year).

Massachusetts

Adams National Historical Park: 135 Adams St, Quincy, MA 02169-1749; tel. (617) 773-1177; fax (617) 472-7562; e-mail adam_visitor_center@nps.gov; internet www.nps.gov/adam; donated to the USA in December 1946 by the Adams Memorial Soc.; designated a nat. historic site under the admin. of the Nat. Park Service of the Dept of the Interior; built in 1731 by Major Leonard Vassall of Boston; bought by John Adams in 1787; at the end of his term, he lived in the house until his death in 1826; the house then passed to his son, John Quincy Adams, in the middle of his term as sixth Pres.; the Adams family continued to live there until 1927; the house, contents, and garden are as the Adams family left them; the separate stone library, standing in the garden, was built in 1870 by Charles Francis Adams, and contains 14,000 vols, comprising most of the libraries of John Quincy Adams and Charles Francis Adams, and some of the libraries of John Adams, Henry and Brooks Adams.

Concord Museum: 200 Lexington Rd, Concord, MA 01742; tel. (978) 369-9763; fax (978) 369-9660; e-mail cm1@concordmuseum.org; internet www.concordmuseum.org; f. 1886; history and decorative arts museum with 16 period rooms and galleries, with artefacts from Concord area; museum rooms chronicle life in Concord from Native American habitation to present; spec. collns incl. relics from the battle at N Bridge, the largest colln of Thoreau artefacts from his stay at Walden Pond, and the contents of Emerson's study; Exec. Dir PEGGY BURKE.

Harvard Art Museums: 32 Quincy St, Cambridge, MA 02138; tel. (617) 495-9400; internet www.harvardartmuseums.org; f. 1891; incorporates the Fogg Museum (Western art from the Middle Ages to the present), Busch-Reisinger Museum (art of German-speaking countries), Arthur M. Sackler Museum (ancient, Asian, Islamic and later Indian art, reinstalled with works representing the collns of all 3 museums until 2013), Straus Center for Conservation, Center for the Technical Study of Modern Art, Harvard Art Museum Archives, and the US HQ for the Archaeological Exploration of Sardis; library of 3,000 vols of conservation-related books in the Straus Centre, 3,000 linear ft of historical records and artists papers in the archives (1895–present); Dir THOMAS W. LENTZ; publ. *Next* (3 a year).

Museum of Fine Arts, Boston: 465 Huntington Ave, Boston, MA 02115-5523; tel. (617) 267-9300; fax (617) 267-0280; e-mail webmaster@mfa.org; internet www.mfa.org; f. 1870; 450,000 objects; rare and important works incl. masters of American painting, Impressionist art, Asian scrolls and Egyptian mummies; library of 350,000 vols and catalogues; Dir MALCOLM ROGERS.

Museum of Science: Science Park, Boston, MA 02114; tel. (617) 723-2500; fax (617) 589-0454; e-mail information@mos.org; internet www.mos.org; f. 1830; exhibits on astronomy, natural history, physical science, technology, medicine, etc.; educational programmes with more than 550 interactive exhibits; houses the Charles Hayden Planetarium, the Mugar Omni Theater and the Lyman Library; library of 40,000 vols and journals; Pres. and Dir IOANNIS N. MIAOULIS; publ. *Magazine* (2 a year).

Peabody Essex Museum: East India Sq., Salem, MA 01970-3738; tel. (978) 745-1876; fax (978) 744-6776; internet www.pem.org; f. 1799; maritime art and history, Asian, Oceanic, Indian, African and Native American art; American art and architecture; incl. Phillips Library; library of 400,000 vols; Dir DAN L. MONROE; publs *American Neptune* (4 a year), *Quarterly Review of Archaeology*.

Peabody Museum of Archaeology and Ethnology: Harvard Univ., 11 Divinity Ave, Cambridge, MA 02138; tel. (617) 496-1027; fax (617) 495-7535; e-mail peabody@fas.harvard.edu; internet www.peabody.harvard.edu; f. 1866 by George Peabody; works in close co-operation with the Dept of Anthropology of Harvard, and much of the research is jtly determined; since its founding more than 800 expeditions have been sent to every continent, resulting, with the addition of important gifts and purchases, in the building up of one of the most comprehensive collns of ethnology, archaeology and physical anthropology in the USA; the first scientific studies of Maya archaeology were made under its direction, and its collns from this area, and from Middle America generally, are extremely important; there are also collns of Old World archaeology; in ethnology, the material from the Pacific Islands is important, and the Museum is also rich in material representing the native tribes of Africa, of South America, and of the Plains and North-west Coast Indians of N America, where some of the objects date from the Lewis and Clark expedition of 1806; the archaeology of the south-western USA, incl. the Pueblo Indian area, is also strongly represented; the Tozzer Library, with its 250,000 vols and pamphlets, covers the entire field of anthropology; Dir WILLIAM L. FASH; publs *Papers*, *Memoirs*, *Bulletin*.

Smith College Museum of Art: Northampton, MA 01063; tel. (413) 585-2770; fax (413) 585-2782; e-mail artmuseum@smith.edu; internet www.smith.edu/artmuseum; f. 1879; collns incl. examples from most periods and cultures with spec. emphasis on European and American paintings, sculpture, drawings, prints and photographs since 17th century; Dir and Chief Curator JESSICA NICOLL.

Worcester Art Museum: 55 Salisbury St, Worcester, MA 01609; tel. (508) 799-4406; fax (508) 799-4767; e-mail information@worcesterart.org; internet www.worcesterart.org; f. 1898; 40,000-piece colln of paintings, sculptures, decorative arts, photographs, prints, drawings and new media illustrating the evolution of art from early Egyptian civilization to modern times; esp. notable are ancient Egyptian, Greek, Roman, Asian and medieval sculpture; mosaics from Antioch; a French Romanesque Chapter House; Italian and other European schools of painting from 13th century to present; American collns from 17th century to the present; pre-Columbian art; Japanese and Western prints; offers a year-round studio art and art appreciation programme; library of 45,000 vols; Dir JAMES A. WELU.

Michigan

Detroit Institute of Arts: 5200 Woodward Ave, Detroit, MI 48202; tel. (313) 833-7900; fax (313) 833-2357; internet www.dia.org; f. 1885; comprehensive fine arts colln from prehistoric to contemporary times; colln of American, Dutch, Flemish, French, Italian and German Expressionist painting; Ancient, African, Oceanic and New World cultures; Asian, Native American and Islamic art since the beginning of the 20th century; graphic arts; American and European decorative arts since the beginning of the 20th century;

theatre arts colln; library of 190,000 vols; Dir GRAHAM W. J. BEAL; publs *Bulletin of the DIA* (1 a year), *Your DIA* (12 a year).

The Henry Ford: 20900 Oakwood Blvd, Dearborn, MI 48124-5029; tel. (313) 982-6001; internet www.thehenryford.org; f. 1929; indoor and outdoor museum of US history from European settlement to the present; domestic life, agriculture and industry, leisure and entertainment, transportation and communication; historic structures; incl. Henry Ford Museum, Greenfield Village, Ford Rouge Factory Tour, IMAX Theatre and Benson Ford Research Center; library: 37,600 books, 146,000 periodicals, 18,500 trade catalogues, 9,000 linear ft of archival material incl. records of the Ford Motor Co, 1m. photographic images and 50,000 graphic items; Chair. of Board S. EVAN WEINER; Pres. and Sec. PATRICIA MOORADIAN.

Minnesota

Minneapolis Institute of Arts: 2400 Third Ave South, Minneapolis, MN 55404; tel. (612) 870-3046; fax (612) 870-3004; internet www.artsmia.org; f. 1883; library of 20,000 vols; colln of 100,000 objects representing nearly every school and period of art, incl. European and American paintings, sculpture, decorative arts, period rooms, prints and drawings, photography, Oriental, African, Oceanic, N and S American arts since 1500BC; Minnich colln of botanical, zoological and fashion prints, paintings by Poussin, Rembrandt, El Greco, Goya, Manet, Monet, Renoir, Van Gogh, Matisse; Alfred F. Pillsbury colln of ancient Chinese jades and bronzes, etc.; Dir and Pres. KAYWIN FELDMAN.

Science Museum of Minnesota: 120 West Kellogg Blvd, St Paul, MN 55102; tel. (651) 221-9444; fax (651) 221-4777; e-mail info@smm.org; internet www.smm.org; f. 1907; research in anthropology, biology, palaeontology, ethnology, zoology, archaeology, geology and geography; collns in the field of biology, anthropology, palaeontology, geology; outdoor research centre; a 300-seat omnitheatre; nature centre; Pres. ERIC JOLLY.

Walker Art Center: 1750 Hennepin, Minneapolis, MN 55403; tel. (612) 375-7600; fax (612) 375-7618; e-mail info@walkerart.org; internet www.walkerart.org; f. 1927; modern paintings, drawings, prints, sculpture, photography; extensive music, dance, film and video, theatre and education programmes; incl. Minneapolis Sculpture Garden; library of 35,000 vols; audio and film and video archive; Dir OLGA VISO.

Mississippi

Mississippi Museum of Art: 380 South Lamar St, Jackson, MS 39201; tel. (601) 960-1515; fax (601) 960-1505; internet www.msmuseumart.org; f. 1903 by Bessie Cary Lemly as the Art Study Club; 1911 became Mississippi Art Association; 1978 current name; permanent colln of 3,800 pieces with an emphasis on mid-19th and 20th-century American art; incl. paintings, sculptures, prints, drawings and photographs by Albert Bierstadt, Arthur B. Davies, Robert Henri, George Inness, Georgia O'Keeffe, Thomas Sully, J. A. M. Whistler; photographs and works on paper incl. works by Thomas Hart Benton, Alexander Calder, William Eggleston, Walker Evans, Andy Warhol, Eudora Welty; Annie Laurie Swaim Hearin Memorial Exhibition Series hosts world-class exhibitions every 2 years; educational programmes for adults and children; Dir BETSY BRADLEY.

Mississippi Museum of Natural Science: 2148 Riverside Dr., Jackson, MS 39202-1353; tel. (601) 354-7303; fax (601) 354-7227; internet www.msnaturalscience.org; an aquarium system with over 200 living species of native fish, reptiles, amphibians and aquatic invertebrates; 1,700-sq. ft greenhouse called 'The Swamp' with another 20,000-gallon aquarium, provides a home for alligators, turtles, fish and a lush native plant garden; 200-seat auditorium, library, biological archives; Exec. Dir Dr SAM POLLES.

Walter Anderson Museum of Art: 510 Washington Ave, Ocean Springs, MS 39564-4632; tel. (228) 872-3164; fax (228) 875-4494; e-mail wama@walterandersonmuseum.org; internet www.walterandersonmuseum.org; f. 1991; watercolors, drawings, oils, block prints, ceramics, and carvings by the 3 Anderson brothers; Exec. Dir GAYLE PETTY-JOHNSON.

Missouri

Kansas City Museum: 30 West Pershing Rd, Kansas City, MO 64108-2422; tel. (816) 460-2020; fax (816) 460-2260; internet www.unionstation.org/kcmuseum.cfm; f. 1939; administered by Kansas City Museum Asscn; science and technology exhibitions, American Indian artefacts, costume and textile colln, natural history exhibits, planetarium, archives and reference library; Pres. and CEO ANDI UDRIS; Exec. Vice-Pres. and Chief Financial Officer ART CHAUDRY.

Nelson-Atkins Museum of Art: 4525 Oak St, Kansas City, MO 64111; tel. (816) 751-1278; fax (816) 561-4011; internet www.nelson-atkins.org; f. 1933; depts of Asian art, prints, photography, modern and contemporary art, American art, American Indian art, European art, decorative arts, ancient art, African art, Chinese art, Japanese art, Kansas City Sculpture Park (incl. monumental bronzes by Henry Moore); works by Thomas Hart Benton; library of 147,000 vols, 500 serials; Dir MARC F. WILSON.

Saint Louis Art Museum: 1 Fine Arts Dr., Forest Park, St Louis, MO 63110-1380; tel. (314) 721-0072; fax (314) 721-6172; e-mail publicrelations@slam.org; internet www.slam.org; f. 1879; publicly owned colln of about 35,000 art objects; incl. important collns of Oceanic art, pre-Columbian art, ancient Chinese bronzes, and European and American art of the late 19th and 20th centuries, with particular strength in 20th-century German painting; library of 100,000 vols, 425 periodicals; Dir BRENT R. BENJAMIN.

Montana

Montana Historical Society Museum: POB 201201, 225 North Roberts, Helena, MT 59620-1201; tel. (406) 444-2694; e-mail mhslibrary@mt.gov; internet mhs.mt.gov/museum; f. 1865; collects, preserves, and interprets fine art, historical, archaeological and ethnological artefacts that pertain to Montana and its adjoining geographic region; incl. original Governor's Mansion and Moss Mansion historic house; research centre; State Historic Preservation Officer Dr MARK BAUMLER; publ. *Montana The Magazine of Western History* (4 a year).

Museum of the Rockies: 600 West Kagy Blvd, Bozeman, MT 59717; tel. (406) 444-2694; e-mail wwwmor@montana.edu; internet museumoftherockies.org; f. 1957, donated by Dr Caroline McGill; attached to Montana State Univ.; independent, non-profit; cultural and natural history; palaeontology colln; on-site 19th-century farm; incl. planetarium, dinosaur complex and tyrannosaurus rex; Dean and Dir SHELDON MCKAMEY.

Yellowstone Art Museum: 401 North 27th St, Billings, MT 59101; tel. (406) 256-6804; e-mail artinfo@artmuseum.org; internet yellowstone.artmuseum.org; f. 1964 as Yellowstone Arts Center; contemporary and historic art; Montana Colln of 3,000 regional artefacts; Virginia Snook Colln incl. illustrations from Will James, paintings and drawings from Joseph Henry Sharp, Charles M. Russell; Exec. Dir ROBYN G. PETERSON.

Nebraska

Nebraska State Historical Society: POB 82554, 1500 R St, Lincoln, NE 68501; tel. (402) 471-4758; fax (402) 471-3100; internet www.nebraskahistory.org; state-wide network of historical sites and museums; incl. Chimney Rock Nat. Historic Site, Fort Robinson Museum, Gerald R. Ford Conservation Center, John G. Neihardt State Historic Site, K St Govt Records Facility, Museum of Nebraska History, Neligh Mill State Historic Site, Senator George W. Norris State Historic Site, Thomas P. Kennard House Nebraska Statehood Memorial, Willa Cather State Historic Site; documentation of bldg first transcontinental railroad through Union Pacific Railroad colln; 300,000 photographs, incl. colln of sod house photographs taken by Solomon D. Butcher; library of 80,000 vols, 12,000 film and video reels, 35,000 reels of microfilm with state newspapers dating from 1854 to present; Dir and CEO MICHAEL J. SMITH; Deputy Dir LYNNE IRELAND; publs *History News* (4 a year), *Nebraska History* (4 a year).

University of Nebraska State Museum: 307 Morrill Hall, Univ. of Nebraska-Lincoln City Campus, Lincoln, NE 68588-0338; tel. (402) 472-2642; internet www.museum.unl.edu; incl. planetarium; educational programming; collns and research in following: anthropology, botany, entomology, invertebrate palaeontology, parasitology, vertebrate palaeontology, zoology; Dir PRISCILLA C. GREW.

Affiliated Museums:

Ashfall Fossil Beds State Historical Park: 6930 517th Ave, Royal, NE 68773; tel. (402) 893-2000; e-mail ashfall2@unl.edu; internet ashfall.unl.edu; fossil site of int. significance left intact for public viewing; Superintendent RICK OTTO.

Lester F. Larsen Tractor Test and Power Museum: POB 830833, Lincoln, NE 68583-0833; tel. (402) 472-8389; fax (402) 472-8367; e-mail tractormuseum2@unl.edu; internet tractormuseum.unl.edu; collects, preserves, researches and interprets the traditions and technologies of agriculture; Dir BILL SPLINTER.

Trailside Museum of Natural History: Fort Robinson State Park, Crawford, NE 69339; tel. (308) 665-2929; internet trailside.unl.edu; geological and natural history.

Nevada

Fleischmann Planetarium and Science Center: POB 272, 1650 North Virginia St, Reno, NV 89557; tel. (775) 784-4812; fax (775) 784-4822; internet planetarium.unr.nevada.edu; attached to Univ. of Nevada, Reno; f. 1964; public star shows and large-format films; Spitz SciDome digital projector; Dir Dr DEE HENDERSON.

Nevada Museum of Art: 160 W Liberty St, Reno, NV 89501; tel. (775) 329-3333; fax (775) 329-1541; internet www.nevadaart.org; f. 1931; altered landscape incl. 600 pieces of contemporary landscape photography; contemporary colln focuses on west coast and Nevada-based artists; sierra Nevada/great basin colln surveys artists' impressions of the landscape over 150 years; historical colln incl. paintings and sculptures; work-ethic themed E. L. Wiegand colln; Curator of Exhibitions and Collections ANN M. WOLF; Exec. Dir and CEO DAVID B. WALKER; Dir for Communications and Marketing RACHEL MILON; publ. *The Altered Landscape*.

Nevada State Museum and Historical Society: 700 Twin Lakes Dr., Las Vegas, NV 89107; tel. (702) 486-5205; fax (702) 486-5172; internet www.springspreserve.org/html/nsm.html; biological sciences, earth sciences, regional history; Dir DAVID MILLMAN.

New Hampshire

Currier Museum of Art: 201 Myrtle Way, Manchester, NH 03104-4393; tel. (603) 669-6144; fax (603) 669-7194; internet www.currier.org; f. 1929; art museum featuring European and American paintings, decorative arts, photographs and sculptures; permanent colln incl. works by Picasso, Matisse, Monet, O'Keeffe, Calder and Wyeth; owns Frank Lloyd Wright's 1950 Zimmerman House; year-round exhibitions, tours and classical music performances; library of 15,000 vols; Dir SUSAN STRICKLER.

New Jersey

Montclair Art Museum: 3 South Mountain Ave, Montclair, NJ 07042-1747; tel. (973) 746-5555; fax (973) 746-9118; e-mail rbausch@montclairartmuseum.org; internet www.montclairartmuseum.org; opened 1914; American art since mid-18th century, incl. paintings, sculpture, works on paper, costumes and bookplates; Native American art and artefacts; library: LeBrun library of 50,000 vols; 20,000 colour slides; Pres. WILLIAM H. TURNER, III; Dir ELLEN S. HARRIS; publ. *Members Bulletin* (6 a year).

New Mexico

Museum of New Mexico: POB 2087, Santa Fé, NM 87504-2087; internet www.museumofnewmexico.org; f. 1909; a state agency, under Bd of Regents appointed by Governor, divs in anthropology, history, fine arts, int. folk art, Indian arts and culture, state monuments located in separate buildings; library: custody of combined libraries 26,000 vols; Dir THOMAS A. LIVESAY; publ. *El Palacio* (4 a year).

Constituent Museums:

Museum of Indian Arts and Culture: 708-710 Camino Lejo, Santa Fe, NM 87505; tel. (505) 476-1250; fax (505) 476-1330; internet www.indianartsandculture.org; Native art and material culture; incl. Laboratory of Anthropology; Dir SHELBY TISDALE.

Museum of International Folk Art: 706 Camino Lejo, Santa Fe, NM 87505; tel. (505) 476-1200; fax (505) 476-1300; internet www.internationalfolkart.org; 135,000 artefacts; Dir JOYCE ICE.

New Mexico Museum of Art: 107 West Palace Ave, Santa Fe, NM 87501; tel. (505) 476-5072; fax (505) 476-5076; internet www.mfasantafe.org; f. 1917; 23,000 objects, focusing on the areas of photography and works on paper; paintings, sculpture and furniture since the beginning of the 20th century; Dir Dr MARSHA C. BOL.

New Mexico State Monuments: 725 Camino Lejo, Santa Fe, NM 87504; tel. (505) 476-1150; fax (505) 476-1127; internet www.nmmonuments.org; incl. Coronado State Monument (where Francisco Vásquez de Coronado—with 300 soldiers and 800 Indian allies from New Spain—entered the valley while looking for the fabled Seven Cities of Gold); Fort Seldon (est. in 1865 in an effort to bring peace to the south central region of present day New Mexico); Jemez State Monument (incl. stone ruins of a 500-year-old Indian village and the San José de los Jemez church dating to 1610); Lincoln (incl. 7 structures and outbuildings from 1870 and 1880s); El Camino Real International Heritage Center (commemorates El Camino Real de Tierra Adentro, the historic trade route and its impact on New Mexico); Bosque Redondo Memorial at Fort Sumner State Monument (incorporates story of how the US Army forcibly moved the Navajo and Mescalero Apache people from their traditional homelands to the land surrounding this lonely outpost).

Palace of the Governors: 105 West Palace Ave, Santa Fe, NM 87501; tel. (505) 476-5100; fax (505) 476-5104; internet www.palaceofthegovernors.org; constructed in the early 17th century as Spain's seat of govt in what is today the American South-West; chronicles the history of Santa Fe, as well as New Mexico and the wider region; Dir FRANCES LEVINE.

Wheelwright Museum of the American Indian: POB 5153, 704 Camino Lejo, Santa Fe, NM 87502; tel. (505) 982-4636; fax (505) 989-7386; e-mail info@wheelwright.org; internet www.wheelwright.org; f. 1937; access by appointment; houses collns of artefacts, archives, sound recordings and photographs, documenting Native American (especially Navajo) culture, both historic and contemporary; contemporary and traditional American Indian art; Dir JONATHAN BATKIN.

New York

Albright-Knox Art Gallery: 1285 Elmwood Ave, Buffalo, NY 14222; tel. (716) 882-8700; fax (716) 882-1958; e-mail mmorreale@albrightknox.org; internet www.albrightknox.org; f. 1862; colln of paintings since the 18th century, with emphasis on American and European contemporary artists; sculpture; prints and drawings; photographs; Dir LOUIS GRACHOS; Chief Curator Dr DOUGLAS DREISHPOON.

American Museum of Natural History: Central Park West at 79th St, New York, NY 10024-5192; tel. (212) 769-5100; internet www.amnh.org; f. 1869; divs of anthropology, invertebrate zoology, paleontology, physical sciences, vertebrate zoology; library: see Libraries and Archives; Chair. Bd of Trustees LEWIS W. BERNARD; Pres. ELLEN V. FUTTER; publs *American Museum Novitates*, *AMNH Bulletin*, *Anthropological Papers*, *Curator*, *Natural History*, *Rotunda*.

Attached Institution:

Hayden Planetarium: Rose Center for Earth and Space, 81st St and Central Park West, New York, NY 10024; f. 1935; Zeiss Star Projector and more than 250 special effects projectors are used on a 75-ft diameter dome; 9,000 stars are projected in the Planetarium heavens; new sky-show several times a year; lectures, educational courses; Chair. Dr WILLIAM A. GUTSCH, Jr.

Brooklyn Botanic Garden: 1000 Washington Ave, Brooklyn, NY 11225; tel. (718) 623-7200; fax (718) 622-7839; e-mail publicaffairsoffice@bbg.org; internet www.bbg.org; f. 1910; living colln of 12,000 species and varieties; herbarium with 200,000 specimens; education programmes, children's garden, art and horticulture classes, cultural programmes, guided tours, plant information service; library of 55,000 vols; Chair. of the Board EARL D. WEINER; Pres. SCOTT MEDBURY; publ. *Plants and Gardens News* (3 a year).

Brooklyn Children's Museum: 145 Brooklyn Ave, Brooklyn, NY 11213; tel. (718) 735-4400; fax (718) 604-7442; internet www.brooklynkids.org; f. 1899; teaching colln of more than 27,000 ethnographic objects and natural science specimens, interactive technological exhibits on science and culture; Children's Resource Library; Portable Colln Loan Program for schools; special cultural performances, participatory activities for gen. public, school classes, groups, workshops; Pres. CAROL ENSEKI.

Brooklyn Museum: 200 Eastern Parkway, Brooklyn, NY 11238; tel. (718) 638-5000; fax (718) 501-6136; e-mail information@brooklynmuseum.org; internet www.brooklynmuseum.org; f. 1823 as a library; Native American art; Peruvian textiles; pre-Columbian gold; Costa Rican sculpture; collns from Africa, Melanesia and Polynesia; collns from China, Korea, South-east Asia, Japan, India and Persia; Colonial South American art; American period rooms; sculpture garden; American and European paintings; prints and drawings; ancient art of the Near East, Egypt, Greece and Rome; American and European costumes; American glass, pewter and silver; contemporary paintings and sculpture; Elizabeth A. Sackler Center for Feminist Art, art reference library and Egyptological library; library of 170,000 vols and periodicals; Dir Dr ARNOLD L. LEHMAN.

Buffalo Museum of Science: 1020 Humboldt Parkway, Buffalo, NY 14211; tel. (716) 896-5200; fax (716) 897-6723; internet www.sciencebuff.org; f. 1861; administered by Buffalo Society of Natural Sciences; exhibition halls feature insects, dinosaurs and other fossils, birds, wild flowers and fungi, vertebrates, minerals, flora and fauna of the Niagara Frontier, life in ancient Egypt, solar system and space exploration, geology; solar and lunar observatory; loan collns, lectures, day and evening classes, etc.; library of 45,000 vols, 400 journals; Pres. and CEO CARROLL SIMON.

Cooper-Hewitt, National Design Museum, Smithsonian Institution: 2 East 91st St, New York, NY 10128; tel. (212) 849-8400; fax (212) 849-8401; e-mail info@si.edu; internet www.cooperhewitt.org; f. 1897 as the Cooper Union Museum; Smithsonian Instn; 250,000 items, incl. collns of original drawings and designs for architecture and the decorative arts; prints since 15th century; textiles, lace, woodwork and furniture, ceramics, glass, etc.; drawings and paintings by F. E. Church, W. Homer and other 19th-century American artists; exhibitions change regularly, each one focusing on aspects of contemporary or historical design; incl. Design Resource Center, a modern study facility, housing the depts of product design and decorative arts, textiles, and wallcoverings; the Center is linked to the Andrew Carnegie Mansion by the Agnes Bourne Bridge Gallery; the Library, the Drue Heinz Study Center for Drawings and Prints, and the Henry Luce Study Room for American Art are located in the Carnegie Mansion; library of 70,000 vols, incl. 6,500 rare books; Dir CAROLINE BAUMANN (acting); Curatorial Dir CARA MCCARTY.

Dia Beacon Riggio Galleries: 3 Beekman St, Beacon, NY 12508; tel. (845) 440-0100; fax (845) 440-0092; e-mail info@diaart.org; internet www.diacenter.org; f. 2003; administered by Dia Art Foundation; works by artists who have come to prominence since the early 1960s; additional site in New York, Dia Chelsea; Chair. LEONARD RIGGIO.

Frick Collection: 1 East 70th St, New York, NY 10021; tel. (212) 288-0700; fax (212) 628-4417; e-mail info@frick.org; internet www.frick.org; f. 1920; European paintings from 13th to 19th centuries; Italian Renaissance bronzes and furniture; Limoges enamels of the Renaissance; French 18th-century sculpture, furniture and porcelains; Oriental porcelains; the works of art were mostly assembled by the industrialist Henry Clay Frick; attached reference library; Dir ANNE L. POULET.

Guggenheim, Solomon R., Museum: 1071 Fifth Ave at 89th St, New York, NY 10128-0173; tel. (212) 423-3500; fax (212) 423-3650; e-mail visitorinfo@guggenheim.org; internet www.guggenheim.org; f. 1937; bldg designed by Frank Lloyd Wright; permanent colln of 6,000 works since the post-Impressionist era, augmented by the Justin K. Thannhauser Colln of Impressionist and post-Impressionist masterpieces, incl. large collns of Brancusi sculptures, Kandinsky paintings and graphics, and works by Klee, Braque, Chagall, Delaunay, Dubuffet, Léger, Marc, Mondrian and Picasso, and the Panza Colln of American Minimalist paintings and sculptures and Conceptual pieces; a continuous programme of loan exhibitions is presented, drawn from its own colln and from leading public and private collns throughout the world; library of 20,000 vols; Dir THOMAS KRENS; Sr Curator GERMANO CELANT; Chief Operating Officer MARC STEGLITZ.

Attached Museum:

Guggenheim Museum SoHo: 575 Broadway, New York, NY 10012-4233; tel. (212) 423-3500.

Hispanic Society of America Museum: Broadway, between 155th and 156th Sts, New York, NY 10032; tel. (212) 926-2234; fax (212) 690-0743; e-mail info@hispanicsociety.org; internet www.hispanicsociety.org; f. 1904; free museum concentrated on the culture of the Iberian Peninsula and Latin America: paintings, prints and drawings (14th century to present), sculpture (13th century to present), archaeology, decorative arts (ceramics, textiles, metalwork, furniture); reference library and photograph files; Dir Dr MITCHELL A. CODDING; Curator of Paintings and Drawings MARCUS BURKE; Curator of Iconography PATRICK LENAGHAN.

Jewish Museum: 1109 Fifth Ave at 92nd St, New York, NY 10128; tel. (212) 423-3200; fax (212) 423-3232; e-mail info@thejm.org; internet www.thejewishmuseum.org; f. 1904; pre-eminent instn in the USA devoted exclusively to exploring the scope and diversity of 4,000 years of Jewish art and culture; Dir HELEN GOLDSMITH MENSCHEL.

Metropolitan Museum of Art: 1000 Fifth Ave at 82nd St, New York, NY 10028–0198; tel. (212) 535-7710; internet www.metmuseum.org; f. 1870; depts of art of Africa, Oceania and the Americas, American paintings and sculpture, American decorative arts, ancient Near Eastern art, Asian art, costume institute, drawings and prints, European paintings, European sculpture and decorative arts, Greek and Roman art, Islamic art, Robert Lehman Colln, medieval art, musical instruments, photographs, twentieth-century art; 2m. works of art and 6,500 objects; library of 240,000 vols, 1,400 periodicals; photograph and slide library; Pres. EMILY K. RAFFERTY; Sr Vice-Pres. and Chief Financial Officer OLENA PASLAWSKY; Dir PHILIPPE DE MONTEBELLO; publ. *The Bulletin*.

Museum of Modern Art: 11 West 53rd St, New York, NY 10019-5497; tel. (212) 708-9400; fax (212) 708-9889; e-mail info@moma.org; internet www.moma.org; f. 1929; int. permanent colln and temporary exhibitions of paintings, drawings, prints, sculptures, industrial and graphic design, photographs, architecture and design since 1880s; large colln of American, British, French, German and Russian films, 1,200 of which are available to educational organizations; daily film showings; organizes exhibitions worldwide in all the visual arts; library of 140,000 vols; Dir GLENN D. LOWRY.

Museum of Sex: 233 Fifth Ave at 27th St, New York, NY 10016; tel. (212) 689-6337; e-mail info@museumofsex.com; internet www.museumofsex.com; f. 2002; seeks to preserve and present the history, evolution and cultural significance of human sexuality; collns on pornography and burlesque theatre; Pres. RUTH ABRAM (founder); Curator REBECCA AMES.

Museum of the City of New York: Fifth Ave at 103rd St, New York, NY 10029; tel. (212) 534-1672; fax (212) 423-0758; internet www.mcny.org; f. 1923; colln of 1.4m. paintings, sculptures, prints, photographs, costumes, toys reflecting historical and modern New York city; Dir SUSAN HENSHAW JONES.

National Cartoon Museum: POB 17M, New York, NY 10118-0069; tel. (561) 391-2200; fax (561) 391-2721; e-mail inquiry@cartoon.org; internet www.cartoon.org; f. 1974; 160,000 original drawings from the following genres: animation, comic books, comic strips, gag cartoons, illustration, editorial, cartoons, greeting cards, caricature, graphic novels, sports cartoons and computer-generated art; the colln also includes over 10,000 books on cartoons and 1,000 hours of film and tape of animated cartoons, interviews and cartoon documentaries; from May 2007 looking to relocate; Dir JEANNE GREEVER; publ. *Inklings* (4 a year).

National Museum of the American Indian, Smithsonian Institution: *George Gustav Heye Center*, 1 Bowling Green, New York, NY 10004; tel. (212) 514-3700; fax (212) 514-3800 *Cultural Resources Center*, 4220 Silver Hill Rd, Suitland, MD 20746; tel. (301) 238-1435 *NMAI on the National Mall*, Fourth St and Independence Ave, Washington, DC 20560; tel. (202) 633-1000; e-mail nin@ic.si.edu; internet www.nmai.si.edu; f. 1989 by Act of Congress; part of the Smithsonian Instn; dedicated to the preservation, study, exhibition and collection of the material culture of the Native peoples of the Western Hemisphere; 800,000 items, mostly from the colln of George Gustav Heye (1874–1957); library of 40,000 vols, 90,000 photographs and negatives; Dir W. RICHARD WEST.

Neue Galerie New York: 1048 Fifth Ave, New York, NY 10028; tel. (212) 628-6200; fax (212) 628-8824; e-mail museum@neuegalerie.org; internet www.neuegalerie.org; f. 2001; early 20th-century German and Austrian art and design; Dir RENÉE PRICE.

Paley Center for Media: 25 West 52nd St, New York, NY 10019; tel. (212) 621-6800; fax (212) 621-6700 *Museum in Los Angeles*, 465 North Beverly Dr., Beverly Hills, CA 90210; tel. (310) 786-1025; internet www.paleycenter.org; f. 1975; fmrly Museum of Television and Radio; prior to that Museum of Broadcasting; colln of 140,000 programmes and exhibition reflecting radio and television history; seminars and education programmes for groups and students; Pres. and Chief Exec. PAT MITCHELL.

Rochester Museum and Science Center: 657 East Ave, Rochester, NY 14607; tel. (585) 271-4320; fax (585) 271-5935; internet www.rmsc.org; f. 1912; hands-on exhibitions, programmes and lifelong learning courses in science and technology, the natural environment and regional cultural heritage; collns of 1.2m. objects; RMSC Preschool enrolling children ages 3 to 5 years; Strasenburgh Planetarium presenting astronomy/space science shows and giant-screen films; Cumming Nature Center, 1,900-acre environmental education facility in nearby Naples, NY; library of 25,000 vols; Pres. KATE BENNETT.

Whitney Museum of American Art: 945 Madison Ave at 75th St, New York, NY 10021; tel. (212) 570-3676; fax (212) 570-1807; e-mail feedback@whitney.org; internet www.whitney.org; f. 1930; established for the encouragement and advancement of contemporary American art; spec. exhibitions incl. Whitney biennial and historical surveys; highlights from the permanent colln of over 8,500 paintings, sculptures and works on paper; Pres. ROBERT J. HURST; Dir ADAM D. WEINBERG.

North Carolina

Morehead Planetarium and Science Center: Univ. of North Carolina at Chapel Hill, Chapel Hill, NC 27599; tel. (919) 962-1236; fax (919) 962-1238; e-mail mhplanet@unc.edu; internet www.moreheadplanetarium.org; f. 1947; educational programmes for adults and children; daily planetarium shows; digital video theatre; Star Theatre; exhibitions; Dir TODD BOYETTE; publ. *Sundial*.

North Dakota

North Dakota Museum of Art: 261 Centennial Dr., Grand Forks, ND 58202; tel. (701) 777-4195; fax (701) 777-4425; e-mail ndmoa@ndmoa.com; internet www.ndmoa.com; private, non-profit; f. 1985; contemporary, int. art in all media starting with the early 1970s; colln contemporary Native American art; Pres. LAUREL REUTER.

State Historical Society of North Dakota Museum: 612 East Boulevard Ave, Bismarck, ND 58505-0830; tel. (701) 328-2666; fax (701) 328-3710; internet www.nd.gov/hist; history, natural history, archaeology, and ethnology; 1,050,000 items ranging from a 10,000-year-old mastodon to a 1915 homesteader's claim shack to 1990s youth soccer equipment; Pres. MARVYN L. KAISER; publ. *North Dakota History: Journal of the Northern Plains* (4 a year).

Attached Museum:

Pembina State Museum: PO Box 456, Exit 215, Off Interstate 29, 805 Highway 59 Pembina, ND 58271; tel. (701) 825-6840; e-mail shspembina@nd.gov; 2 exhibition galleries; observation tower offering a grand view of the Red River Valley; preglacial fossils; bone and stone tools; frontier military forts.

Ohio

Cincinnati Art Museum: 953 Eden Park Dr., Cincinnati, OH 45202; tel. (513) 639-2951; fax (513) 721-0129; e-mail information@cincyart.org; internet www.cincinnatiartmuseum.org; f. 1881; permanent collns grouped in 88 galleries: Art of the ancient world, Near Eastern art, Far Eastern art, Medieval art, arts of Africa and the Americas, musical instruments, continental and English decorative arts, American decorative arts, European painting and sculpture, American painting and sculpture, prints, drawings and photographs, costumes and textiles; Nabataean antiquities from Khirbet Tannur; large colln of Old Master prints and modern Japanese and East European prints; contemporary art; temporary exhibitions; library of 52,000 vols, 250,000 pamphlets and clippings; Pres. J. PHILIP VOLLMER; Dir ANITA J. ELLIS (acting); publ. *CANVAS* (6 a year).

Cleveland Museum of Art: 11150 East Blvd, Cleveland, OH 44106; tel. (216) 421-7340; fax (216) 421-0411; e-mail info@clevelandart.org; internet www.clevelandart.org; inc. 1913, opened 1916; collns incl. paintings, sculpture, prints and drawings, textiles and decorative arts from the ancient world, Asia, Europe, the Americas, Africa and Oceania; library of 401,918 books and periodicals; 6m. images; Pres. ALFRED M. RANKIN; Dir TIMOTHY RUB; publ. *Cleveland Studies in the History of Art* (1 a year).

Cleveland Museum of Natural History: 1 Wade Oval Dr., University Circle, Cleveland, OH 44106-1767; tel. (216) 231-4600; fax (216) 231-5919; internet www.cmnh.org; f. 1920; comprises Natural History Museum, Shafran Planetarium, Observatory and 26 separate natural areas in northern Ohio; collns in all fields with particular emphasis on the northern half of Ohio, incl. Upper Devonian Fossil Fishes; also vertebrates, insects, shells, minerals, precious and semi-precious stones, and botanical and ethnological materials; dept of physical anthropology responsible for the discovery and naming of new species of early man, *A. afarensis*; the Museum has sponsored or participated in several expeditions to Africa, islands of the South Atlantic, Antarctica, the Azuero Peninsula of Panama and various parts of North America; many study collns, incl. herbarium, the Hamann-Todd Skeletal colln; mounted Jurassic cetiosaurid, Haplocanthosaurus; library of 60,000 vols; Exec. Dir EVALYN GATES; publs *The Explorer* (4 a year), *Kirtlandia* (scientific papers), *Tracks* (6 a year).

National Museum of the United States Air Force: 1100 Spaatz St, Wright-Patterson Air Force Base, OH 45433; tel. (937) 255-3286; e-mail nationalmuseum.usaf@wpafb.af.mil; internet www.nationalmuseum.af.mil; f. 1923; displays of historical events, individuals and materials incl. aircraft and missiles; preservation of milestones in aerospace technology; study of aviation and aerospace history; Research Center available by appointment only; Dir JOHN L. HUDSON.

Oklahoma

Oklahoma Historical Society History Center and Museum: 2401 North Laird Ave, Oklahoma, OK 73105; tel. (405) 522-5248; fax (405) 522-5402; e-mail okhc@okhistory.org; internet www.okhistorycenter.org; 50 topics and 2,000 artefacts reflecting Oklahoma's past; Dir Dr DEE HENDERSON.

Attached Museum:

Spiro Mounds Archaeological Center: 18154 1st St, Spiro, OK 74959; tel. (918) 962-2062; e-mail spiro@okhistory.org; internet www.okhistory.org; f. 1978; 150-acre site encompassing 12 southern mounds containing evidence of an Indian culture that occupied the site from AD 850 to 1450; preserves and interprets Okhlahoma prehistory and Native American culture; organizes solstice and equinox alignment tours; other museums incl. Pioneer Woman, Cherokee Strip, Chisholm Trail, State Capital Publishing House, Route 66; Dir DENNIS PETERSON.

Oregon

Jordan Schnitzer Museum of Art: 1223 University of Oregon, Eugene, OR 97403-1233; 1430 Johnson Lane, Eugene, OR 97403; tel. (541) 346-3027; fax (541) 346-0976; e-mail mnh@uoregon.edu; internet uoma.uoregon.edu; attached to Univ. of Oregon; galleries featuring American, European, Korean, Chinese and Japanese art; Gordon Gilkey Research Center; Pres. CONNIE HULING.

Museum of Natural and Cultural History: 1680 East 15th Ave, Eugene, OR 97403; tel. (541) 346-3024; fax (541) 346-5334; e-mail mnh@uoregon.edu; internet natural-history.uoregon.edu; attached to Univ. of Oregon; Native American cultural and archaeological artefacts, spanning 15,000 years; incl. cache of 10,000-year-old sagebrush bark sandals, extensive fossil collections, several hundred western Indian baskets made before 1900; Dir JOHN ERLANDSON.

Oregon Historical Society Museum: 1200 Southwest Park Ave, Portland, OR 97205; tel. (503) 222-1741; e-mail orhist@ohs.org; internet www.ohs.org; 85,000 artefacts of local history; library of 32,000 vols, 25,000 maps, 12,500 linear ft of MSS, 4,000 serials titles, 6,000 vertical files, 18,000 reels of newspaper microfilm, 8.5m. ft of film and video cassettes, 10,000 oral history tapes, 2.5m. photographs; Exec. Dir GEORGE VOGT.

Pennsylvania

American Swedish Historical Museum: 1900 Pattison Ave, Philadelphia, PA 19145; tel. (215) 389-1776; fax (215) 389-7701; e-mail info@americanswedish.org; internet www.americanswedish.org; f. 1926; contributions by Swedes and Swedish-Americans since the mid-17th century; 12 galleries dedicated to all major historical and cultural aspects of Swedish accomplishments; exhibition on New Sweden Colony (1638–1655); colln of letters, documents and designs by John Ericsson; library of 11,000 vols, primary source genealogical documents and sources; Chair. JOHN MCCANN; Exec. Dir TRACEY BECK.

Barnes Foundation Gallery, Collections and Arboretum: 300 North Latch's Lane, Merion, PA 19066-1729; tel. (610) 667-0290; fax (610) 664-4026; e-mail info@barnesfoundation.org; internet www.barnesfoundation.org; f. 1922 by Dr Albert C. Barnes; offers courses in visual literacy and the philosophy and appreciation of art; colln of 1,000 paintings, including works by El Greco, Titian, Goya, Rubens, Cézanne, Renoir, Modigliani, Soutine, Picasso, Matisse and Van Gogh; also sculpture, antique furniture and wrought iron; Arboretum, school with courses in botany, horticulture and landscape design; Teacher Institute with courses in visual arts and environmental and horticultural studies; school programmes for children from kindergarten level to grade 12; Chair. Dr BERNARD C. WATSON.

Carnegie Science Center: One Allegheny Ave, Pittsburgh, PA 15212-5850; tel. (412) 237-3400; fax (412) 237-3375; internet www.carnegiesciencecenter.org; f. 1991 to develop scientific literacy and promote participation in science and technology among the residents of Pennsylvania and neighbouring states; 400 interactive exhibits; 3 live demonstration theatres; 4-storey Imax dome theatre; interactive planetarium; 36,000-sq. ft sport science exhibition; Cold War submarine moored on Pittsburgh's Ohio River; model-railway display; working foundry; Tesla coil and Van de Graaff generator; interactive exhibits featuring robotics, cryogenics and lasers; Dir JOANNA HAAS.

Franklin Institute Science Museum: 118–128 N Broad St, Philadelphia, PA 19103; tel. (215) 448-1200; fax (215) 448-1235; internet www.fi.edu; f. 1824; planetarium, Imax Theater, 3D theatre; exhibits and demonstrations in physical sciences and technology; workshops and teacher training; Pres. and CEO Dr DENNIS M. WINT; publ. *Journal*.

Pennsylvania Academy of the Fine Arts: 118 N Broad St, Philadelphia, PA 19102; tel. (215) 972-7600; fax (215) 569-0153; internet www.pafa.org; f. 1805; colln of American paintings since 18th century, sculpture, graphics; spec. exhibitions annually; archive; library of 12,000 vols; Pres. Dr EDWARD LEWIS; Chair. DONALD R. CALDWELL; Dir EDNA S. TUTTLEMAN.

Philadelphia Museum of Art: POB 7646, Philadelphia, PA 19101-7646; tel. (215) 763-8100; fax (215) 236-4465; e-mail mpr@philamuseum.org; internet www.philamuseum.org; f. 1876; 250,000 works of art, incl. paintings, prints, sculpture and silver from medieval to contemporary times representing European, American, and Far Eastern Art; Chair. H. F. (GERRY) LENFEST; CEO GAIL HARRITY.

Attached Museum:

Rodin Museum: Benjamin Franklin Parkway at 22nd St, Philadelphia, PA 19101-7646; tel. (215) 763-8100; internet www.rodinmuseum.org; f. 1929; houses 124 sculptures; Chair. BARBARA ARONSON.

University of Pennsylvania Museum of Archaeology and Anthropology: 3260 South St, Philadelphia, PA 19104; tel. (215) 898-4000; fax (215) 898-0657; e-mail info@museum.upenn.edu; internet www.penn.museum; f. 1887; items from ancient Egypt, Mesopotamia, Africa, Asia, Polynesia, the ancient Mediterranean world and the Americas; library of 100,000 vols, archives with 300,000 photographic items and more than 600 m of textual records; Dir Dr RICHARD HODGES; publ. *Expedition* (3 a year).

Rhode Island

Haffenreffer Museum of Anthropology: 300 Tower St, Bristol, RI 02809; tel. (401) 253-8388; fax (401) 253-1198; internet www.brown.edu/facilities/haffenreffer; attached to Brown Univ.; library of 10,000 vols; 110,000 items of ethnographic and archaeological interest mainly from North America but also from Latin America, Africa, Middle East and Asia; Herbert Spinden Photographic Archive of 20,000 images and documents relating to Central American archaeology and ethnography from the early 20th century, incl. many images of important archaeological sites that have since been altered or destroyed; Kensinger Colln with 5,000 photographs and related field notes and texts from anthropologist Ken Kensinger's research with the Cashinahua of Peru in 1960s; Conti Colln has 3,000 photographs dating from the late 1950s to early 1970s taken by Rhode Island photographer Gino Conti, primarily on the Hopi, Apache and Navaho reservations, and also in Mexico; Dir SHEPARD KRECH, III.

National Museum of American Illustration: Vernon Court, 492 Bellevue Ave, Newport, RI 02840; tel. (401) 851-8949; fax (401) 851-8974; e-mail art@americanillustration.org; internet www.americanillustration.org; private, non-profit; f. 1998 by Judy and Laurence Cutler; housed in Vernon Court, an adaptation of an 18th-century French château built in 1898; American Imagist Colln of originals by Maxfield Parrish, Norman Rockwell, J. C. Leyendecker, Howard Pyle, N. C. Wyeth, Charles Dana Gibson, Henry Hutt, James Montgomery Flagg, Howard Chandler Christy, John Falter; comprises original art works, prints (open and limited edns), as well as significant memorabilia, vintage materials, artefacts (such as Rockwell's first paint box and Parrish's stippling paint brushes) and photographic materials.

South Carolina

Gibbes Museum of Art: 135 Meeting St, Charleston, SC 29401; tel. (843) 722-2706; fax (843) 720-1682; internet www.gibbesmuseum.org; f. 1905; local visual arts; 18th-, 19th- and early 20th-century paintings, works on paper (prints, drawings, watercolours, photographs), miniature portraits and sculpture; Dir ANGELA MACK.

South Carolina State Museum: 301 Gervais St, Columbia, SC 29201; tel. (803) 898-4921; e-mail publicrelations@scmuseum.org; internet www.southcarolinastatemuseum.org; f. 1988; art, cultural history, natural history, science and technology; Stringer Discovery Center; travelling exhibits; 4,000 mems; Exec. Dir WILLIAM CALLOWAY; publ. *Images* (4 a year, for museum members).

South Dakota

Museum of the South Dakota State Historical Society: 900 Governors Dr., Pierre, SD 57501-2217; tel. (605) 773-3458; fax (605) 773-6041; internet www.sdhistory.org/mus/museum.htm; 5 galleries of local history; travelling exhibitions; Dir HELEN B. LOUISE; Curators RONETTE RUMPCA, DANIEL BROSZ, KATHRYN HIGDON.

South Dakota Art Museum: Medary Ave at Harvey Dunn St, Brookings, SD 57007; tel. (605) 688-5423; fax (605) 688-4445; e-mail sdsu.sdam@sdstate.edu; internet www.southdakotaartmuseum.com; f. 1970; collns incl. Harvey Dunn, Native American Art, Marghab Linens, Paul Goble; Dir LYNN VERSHOOR.

Tennessee

American Museum of Science and Energy: 300 South Tulane Ave, Oak Ridge, TN 37830; tel. (865) 576-3200; e-mail iinformation@amse.org; internet www.amse.org; f. 1949; operated for the US Dept of Energy by Enterprise Advisory Services, Inc.; one of the world's largest energy exhibitions, with live demonstrations, computers and films on all energy forms and uses; Dir DAVID SINCERBOX.

Texas

Dallas Museum of Art: 1717 North Harwood, Dallas, TX 75201; tel. (214) 922-1200; fax (214) 954-0174; internet www.dallasmuseumofart.org; f. 1903; arts of Africa, Asia and Pacific; Indonesian textiles; architectural and shrine objects from S Asia; Egyptian antiquities; contemporary art since 1945; American art from pre-Columbian times to the mid-20th century; 19th- century and early modern European paintings and sculpture; N American and European decorative arts; Wendy and Emery Reves Colln, Faith and Charles Bybee Colln of American Furniture; prints, drawings, photographs; library: reference library of 25,000 vols, special collns: ethnography, artists' files; Dir Dr JOHN R. LANE.

Hall of State: c/o Dallas Historical Society, POB 150038, Dallas, TX 75315-0038; 3939 Grand Ave, Dallas, TX 75210; tel. (214) 421-4500; fax (214) 421-7500; internet www.dallashistory.org; f. 1936; museum and archives of Texas and Dallas history; operated by Dallas Historical Society (see Learned Societies); library of 14,000 vols, 15,000 museum artefacts and 2m. archival items; Chief Operating Officer FRANKLIN K. WILSON; Collns Dir ALAN COLSON.

Museum of Fine Arts: 1001 Bissonnet St, Houston, TX 77005; tel. (713) 639-7300; fax (713) 639-7399; internet www.mfah.org; inc. 1900; 55,000 artworks; art of the ancient world; European painting and sculpture; Far Eastern art; art of Africa, Oceania and the Americas; decorative arts; prints and drawings; film and video; modern art; photography; textiles and costume; 2 major museum bldgs, the Caroline Wiess Law Bldg and the Audrey Jones Beck Bldg; 2 facilities for the Glassell School of Art, the Studio School for Adults and the Glassell Jr School; 2 house museums that exhibit decorative arts, Bayou Bend Colln and Gardens and Rienzi; the Lillie and Hugh Roy Cullen Sculpture Garden; 18 acres of public gardens; library of 80,000 vols, 83,000 slides; Dir PETER C. MARZIO; publ. *MFA Today* (6 a year).

San Jacinto Museum of History: 1 Monument Circle, La Porte (Houston), TX 77571-9585; tel. (281) 479-2421; fax (281) 479-2428; e-mail sjm@sanjacinto-museum.org; internet www.sanjacinto-museum.org; f. 1939; exhibits revisualize the history of Texas region from 1519 to 1900; library of 25,000 vols; MSS and documents since the 15th century; Pres. PAUL G. BELL, Jr; Dir J. C. MARTIN.

Texas Memorial Museum: 2400 Trinity St, Campus of the Univ. of Texas, Austin, TX 78705; tel. (512) 471-1604; fax (512) 471-4794; internet www.utexas.edu/tmm; f. 1936; natural history of Texas, the Southwest and Latin America, minerals, fossils, palaeontology, vertebrate and invertebrate zoology, geology, entomology; Dir EDWARD C. THERIOT; publ. *Pearce-Sellards Series*.

Utah

BYU Museum of Paleontology: 1683 N Canyon Rd, Provo, UT 84602-3300; tel. (801) 422-3680; fax (801) 422-7919; internet cpms.byu.edu/esm; f. 1976; attached to Brigham Young Univ.; fossil vertebrate colln of over 17,000 specimens ranging from Devonian fish (380m. years ago) to Pleistocene mammoths and cave fossils (15,000 years ago), with primary focus on dinosaurs from the Intermountain West; Curator and Man. Dr RODNEY D. SCHEETZ.

Utah Museum of Fine Arts: 410 Campus Center Dr., Salt Lake City, UT 84112-0350; tel. (801) 581-7332; internet www.umfa.utah.edu; attached to Univ. of Utah; collns of African art, American art, American Indian art, ancient Greek and Roman art, art of the Pacific Islands, Austrian art, Cambodian art, Chinese art, decorative arts, Dutch art, Egyptian art, English art, Flemish art, French art, German art, Italian art, Japanese art, Nazi-era provenance research project, Pre-Columbian art, Scottish art, Spanish art, Thai art.

Vermont

University of Vermont Libraries: Burlington, VT 05405-0036; tel. (802) 656-2003; fax (802) 656-4038; internet library.uvm.edu; Bailey/Howe Library houses spec. collns of Vermont materials, rare books, govt docs and maps and univ. archives; Cook Chemistry/Physics Library; Dana Medical Library; Library Reseach Annex; Dean of Libraries MAURA SAULE.

Vermont Heritage Network: Wheeler House, University of Vermont, Burlington, VT 05405; tel. (802) 656-3180; e-mail vhnet@zoo.uvm.edu; internet www.uvm.edu/~vhnet; Univ. of Vermont Historic Preservation Program; 13 National Historic Landmarks, 13 state-owned historic sites, numerous underwater archaeological sites, over 100 National Register historic districts and over 8,500 bldgs listed on the National Register of Historic Places.

Vermont Museum and Gallery Alliance: c/o Lake Champlain Maritime Museum, 4472 Basin Harbor Rd, Vergennes, VT 05491; tel. (802) 475-2022; fax (802) 475-2953; e-mail vccp@sover.net; internet www.vmga.org; f. 1990; consortium of museums, galleries and historical socs.

Virginia

Colonial Williamsburg Foundation: POB 1776, Williamsburg, VA 23187-1776; tel. (757) 229-1000; fax (757) 220-7702; internet www.history.org; f. 1926; 301-acre outdoor living history museum with nearly 500 preserved, restored and reconstructed bldgs; 90 acres of period gardens and greens; demonstration of 18 historic trades; incl. DeWitt Wallace Decorative Arts Museum, Bassett Hall, Kimball Theatre and Abby Aldrich Rockefeller Folk Art Museum; library: John D. Rockefeller, Jr Library of 75,000 vols, 45,000 MSS, 55,000 architectural plans; Pres. COLIN G. CAMPBELL; publ. *Colonial Williamsburg* (3 a year).

Mariners' Museum: 100 Museum Dr., Newport News, VA 23606; tel. (757) 596-2222; fax (757) 591-7310; e-mail info@mariner.org; internet www.mariner.org; f. 1930; int. maritime colln of c. 35,000 artefacts; incl. Peter W. Ifland Colln of Navigation Instruments (169 navigation pieces covering 5 centuries), Edwin Levick Colln of 30,000 photographs (yachting events and America's Cup races), artefacts and archives of the Civil War ironclad USS Monitor; library: see Libraries and Archives; Pres. and Chief Exec. JOHN B. HIGHTOWER.

Virginia Museum of Fine Arts: 200 North Blvd, Richmond, VA 23220-4007; tel. (804) 340-1400; fax (804) 340-1548; internet www.vmfa.museum; f. 1936; state-wide network of local and regional arts orgs and loan programme offering exhibition material to affiliated groups; film programmes; permanent collns incl. Russian Imperial jewelled objects by Fabergé, ancient Greek, Roman and Byzantine objects and sculptures; Indian, Chinese, Japanese, medieval, renaissance, and baroque paintings and sculptures; Himalayan colln; Art Nouveau and Art Deco colln; European and American decorative arts, prints, sculpture and paintings; contemporary art; library of 134,500 vols; Assoc. Dir SANDRA C. RUSAK; publ. *Calendar* (6 a year).

Washington

Seattle Art Museum: 1300 First Ave, Seattle, WA 98101-2003; tel. (206) 625-8900; fax (206) 654-3135; e-mail boxoffice@seattleartmuseum.org; internet www.seattleartmuseum.org; permanent collns of Aboriginal and Oceanic art, African art, American art, ancient Mediterranean and Islamic art, decorative arts, European arts, Japanese and Korean art, modern and contemporary art, Native and Mesoamerican art, textiles.

Attached Museums:

Olympic Sculpture Park: 2901 Western Ave, Seattle, WA 98121; tel. (206) 332-1377; fax (206) 332-1371; f. 1999; waterfront site for exhibition of sculptures.

Seattle Asian Art Museum: 1400 East Prospect St, Volunteer Park, Seattle, WA 98112-3303; tel. (206) 654-3100; fax (206) 654-3191; Chinese, South Asian and South-east Asian Art.

Washington State History Museum: 1911 Pacific Ave, Tacoma, WA 98402; tel. (253) 272-3500; fax (253) 272-9518; internet www.washingtonhistory.org/wshm; Washington State Historical Soc.; Great Hall of Washington History, History Lab Learning Center; Dir PATRICIA TOBIASON; publ. *Columbia* (1 a year).

West Virginia

Huntington Museum of Art: 2033 McCoy Rd, Huntington, WV 25701; tel. (304) 529-2701; fax (304) 529-7447; internet www.hmoa.org; collns incl. folk art, prints, silver, touma, glass; Herman P. Dean Firearms; Daywood Colln; library of 20,000 vols in James D. Francis Art Library; incl. C. Fred Edwards Conservatory of subtropical plants; Exec. Dir MARGARET MARY LANE.

West Virginia State Museum and Cultural Center: Capitol Complex, 1900 Kanawha Blvd, E, Charleston, WV 25305-0300; tel. (304) 558-0220; fax (304) 558-2779; internet www.wvculture.org/agency/cultcenter.html; local art and history; also houses state archives; Dir ADAM HODGES; publ. *Artworks* (4 a year).

Wisconsin

Milwaukee Art Museum: 700 North Art Museum Dr., Milwaukee, WI 53202; tel. (414) 224-3200; fax (414) 271-7588; e-mail mam@mam.org; internet www.mam.org; f. 1957 as Milwaukee Art Center; private, non-profit; collns in ancient art, early European art, 19th-Century Art, American art to 1900, modern art, contemporary art, photography, Asian art, Haitian Colln, African art, folk, self-taught and outsider art; Brooks Stevens Archive of Industrial Design; Rogovin Colln of photographs of working-class families; Dir and CEO DAVID GORDON.

Wisconsin Historical Museum: 30 N Carroll St, Madison, WI 53703; 30 N Carroll St, Madison, WI 53703; tel. (608) 264-6555; e-mail museumstore@wisconsinhistory.org; internet www.wisconsinhistory.org/museum; attached to Wisconsin Historical Society; spec. collns incl. anthropology, business and technology, costumes and textiles, domestic life, political life; Marketing Coordinator HEATHER GROFF.

Wyoming

National Museum of Wildlife Art: 2820 Rungius Rd, Jackson Hole, WY 83002; tel. (307) 733-5771; e-mail info@wildlifeart.org; internet www.wildlifeart.org; 2,000 pieces of art portraying wildlife, dating from 2,000 BC to the present, focusing primarily on European and American painting and sculpture; colln of American art from the 19th and 20th centuries recording European exploration of the American West; spec. collns incl. Carl Rugius Colln; art library and archives; incl. National Elk Refuge; Pres. and CEO JAMES MCNUTT.

Wyoming Dinosaur Center and Dig Sites: 110 Carter Ranch Rd, Thermopolis, WY 82443; tel. (307) 864-2997; fax (307) 864-5762; e-mail wdinoc@wyodino.org; internet www.wyodino.org; museum with interpretive displays, dioramas, life-size dinosaur mounts, exhibits covering all facets of early life; fossil preparation laboratory; 60 dig sites in Warm Springs Ranch; Research Center; Casting Laboratory; Dir of Science SCOTT HARTMAN.

Wyoming State Museum: Barrett Bldg, 2301 Central Ave, Cheyenne, WY 82002; tel. (307) 777-7022; fax (307) 777-5375; e-mail wsm@state.wy.us; internet wyomuseum.state.wy.us; themed galleries: Barber Gallery, Drawn to this Land, Hands-on History Room, Living in Wyoming, RIP–Rex in Pieces, Swamped with Coal, The Wild Bunch, Wyoming's Story; travelling exhibits; Dir MANNY VIGIL.

Universities and Colleges

(Arranged alphabetically by State)

ALABAMA

ALABAMA AGRICULTURAL AND MECHANICAL UNIVERSITY

4900 Meridian St, Normal, AL 35762
POB 1357, Normal, AL 35762

Telephone: (256) 372-5245
E-mail: admissions@aamu.edu
Internet: www.aamu.edu

Founded 1875
Academic year: August to May

Pres.: Dr VIRGINIA CAPLES
Vice-Pres. for Academic Affairs: Dr VIRGINIA CAPLES
Vice-Pres. for Business and Finance: ARTHUR J. HENDERSON
Vice-Pres. for Research and Devt: Dr ROSE M. YATES
Vice-Pres. for Student Affairs: Dr JEROME ROBERTS
Registrar: Dr SHIRLEY HOUZER

Library of 339,272 vols
Number of teachers: 340
Number of students: 5,700

DEANS

Agricultural and Environmental Studies: JAMES W. SHUFORD
Arts and Sciences: JERRY R. SHIPMAN
School of Business: Dr BARBARA A. P. JONES
School of Education: Dr JOHN VICKERS, Jr
School of Engineering and Technology: Dr ARTHUR J. BOND
School of Graduate Studies: Dr CHANDRA REDDY
Univ. College: Dr THOMAS MCALPINE (acting)
J. F. Drake Memorial Learning Resources Center: Dr CLARENCE TOOMER

ALABAMA STATE UNIVERSITY

915 South Jackson St, POB 271, Montgomery, AL 36101-0271

Telephone: (205) 293-4100
Fax: (205) 834-6861
Internet: www.alasu.edu

Founded 1867 as college, attained univ. status 1969

Pres.: Dr JOE A. LEE
Vice-Pres. for Academic Affairs: Dr EVELYN WHITE
Vice-Pres. for Admin. Services: Dr LEON FRAZIER
Vice-Pres. for Fiscal Affairs: FREDDIE GALLOT
Vice-Pres. for Institutional Advancement: Dr WILLIAM BROCK
Vice-Pres. for Student Affairs: RICKY DRAKE
Dir for Univ. Relations): JULIE DEBARDELABEN

Library of 218,850 vols
Number of teachers: 415
Number of students: 5,608

Publications: *Alabama State University Bulletin* (1 a year), *ASU Today*

DEANS

College of Arts and Sciences: Dr THELMA IVERY
College of Business Admin.: Dr PERCY VAUGHN
College of Education: Dr PETE MACCHIA (acting)
Division of Aerospace Studies: Col KEITH SINGLETON
School of Graduate Studies: Dr ALLEN STEWART (acting)
School of Music: Dr HORACE B. LAMAR, Jr
Univ. College: Dr T. CLIFFORD BIBB

ATHENS STATE UNIVERSITY

300 North Beaty St, Athens, AL 35611-1999

Telephone: (205) 233-8100
Internet: www.athens.edu

Founded 1822

Pres.: Dr JERRY F. BARTLETT
Dir of Admissions: NECEDAH HENDERSON
Library Dir: ROBERT BURKHARDT

Library of 100,000 vols
Number of teachers: 69
Number of students: 3,200

DEANS

School of Arts and Sciences: (vacant)
School of Business: Dr LINDA SHONESY
School of Education: DEBRA BAIRD

AUBURN UNIVERSITY

Auburn Univ., AL 36849

Telephone: (334) 844-4000
Fax: (334) 844-6179
Internet: www.auburn.edu

Founded 1856 as The East Alabama Male College. became Alabama Agricultural and Mechanical College 1872, Alabama Polytechnic Institute 1899, present name and status 1960
Land-grant state univ.
Academic year: August to July

Pres.: Dr JAY GOGUE
Exec. Vice-Pres. and Chief Financial Officer: Dr DONALD L. LARGE, Jr
Vice-Pres. for Alumni Affairs: Dr DEBORAH SHAW
Vice-Pres. for Development: ROB WELLBAUM
Vice-Pres. for Research and Assoc. Provost: Dr JOHN M. MASON
Vice-Pres. for Students' Affairs: Dr AINSLEY CARRY
Provost: TIMOTHY BOOSINGER
Dean of Libraries: Dr BONNIE MACEWAN (acting)

Library of 3,459,542 bound vols, 2,718,948 microfilms, 39,318 current periodicals, 256,354 maps, govt documents
Number of teachers: 1,196
Number of students: 25,078

Publications: *Alabama Cooperative Extension System* (1 a year), *Auburn Magazine* (4 a year), *Auburn University Research* (1 a year), *AU Daily*, *AU Report* (24 a year), *Beyond Auburn* (4 a year), *Engineering Research Activities* (1 a year), *Facts and Figures* (every 2 years), *Glomerata* (1 a year), *Graduate & Undergraduate* (1 a year), *Southern Humanities Review* (4 a year), *The Auburn Bulletin* (1 a year), *The Auburn Plainsman* (48 a year), *The Auburn Pharmacist* (4 a year), *The Auburn Veterinarian* (4 a year), *The Circle* (4 a year), *Tiger Cub* (1 a year)

DEANS

Agriculture: Dr WILLIAM BATCHELOR
Architecture, Design and Construction: Dr VINI NATHAN
Business: Dr BILL HARDGRAVE
Education: Dr BETTY LOU WHITFORD
Engineering: Dr LARRY BENEFIELD
Forestry and Wildlife Sciences: Dr RICHARD W. BRINKER
Graduate School: Dr GEORGE FLOWERS
Human Sciences: Dr JUNE HENTON
Liberal Arts: Dr ANNE-KATRIN GRAMBERG
Nursing: Dr GREGG E. NEWSCHWANDER
Pharmacy: Dr R. LEE EVANS
Sciences and Mathematics: Dr CHARLES SAVRDA
Veterinary Medicine: Dr CALVIN JOHNSON

BIRMINGHAM-SOUTHERN COLLEGE

900 Arkadelphia Rd, Birmingham, AL 35254
Telephone: (205) 226-4600
Fax: (205) 226-4627
Internet: www.bsc.edu

Founded 1856 (Southern Univ.) and 1898 (Birmingham College); instns merged to form Birmingham-Southern College 1918

Pres.: Dr David Pollick
Provost: Dr Wayne Shew
Vice-Pres. for Admission: Sheri Salmon
Vice-Pres. for Business and Finance: Wayne Echols
Vice-Pres. for Communications: Bill Wagnon
Vice-Pres. for Devt: George L. Jenkins
Vice-Pres. for Student Affairs: Dudley Long
Librarian: Billy Pennington

Library of 250,000 vols, 57,000 govt documents, 1,030 current periodicals, 47,000 microfiches, 13,500 microfilms, audiovisual items, recordings, slides
Number of teachers: 106
Number of students: 1,425

DEANS

Div. of Behavioural and Social Sciences: Bob Slagter
Business and Graduate Programmes: Dr Tara Sudderth
Div. of Education: Clint E. Bruess
Div. of Fine and Performing Arts: Lester Seigel
Div. of Humanities: John Tatter
Div. of Science and Mathematics: Clyde Stanton

FAULKNER UNIVERSITY

5345 Atlanta Highway, Montgomery, AL 36109
Telephone: (334) 272-5820
Internet: www.faulkner.edu

Founded 1942 as Montgomery Bible College; changed name to Alabama Christian College 1953; present name 1985

Campuses at Huntsville, Birmingham, Montgomery and Mobile
Private control
Academic year: August to July

Pres.: Dr Billy D. Hilyer
Dir of Admissions: Keith Mock
Dir of Libraries: Brenda G. Turner

Library: Nichols Main Library of 100,000 vols; also George H. Jones, Jr Law Library

DEANS

Arts and Sciences: Prof. Dave Rampersad
College of Biblical Studies: Prof. Cecil May
College of Business: Prof. Dave A. Khadanga
Jones School of Law Administration: Charles Nelson

HERITAGE CHRISTIAN UNIVERSITY

POB HCU, Florence, AL 35630
E-mail: hcu@hcu.edu
Internet: www.hcu.edu

Founded 1971 as International Bible College; present name 2000
Private control
Academic year: August to July

Pres.: Dennis Jones
Academic Dean: Dr Bill Bagents
Dean of Men: Travis Harmon
Dean of Students: Dr Nathan Segars
Dean of Women: Holly Young
Registrar: Sara Goldman
Librarian: Jamie Cox

Library of 61,000 vols.

HUNTINGDON COLLEGE

1500 E Fairview Ave, Montgomery, AL 36106-2148
Telephone: (334) 833-4222
Fax: (334) 833-4347
E-mail: admiss@huntingdon.edu
Internet: www.huntingdon.edu

Founded 1854
Private control
Academic year: August to July

Pres.: J. Cameron West
Sr Vice-Pres. for Planning and Administration and Treas.: Jay Dorman
Vice-Pres. for Academic Affairs: Sidney Stubbs
Vice-Pres. for Enrolment Management: Laura Duncan
Dean of Students: Richard Jones
Dir of the Library: Eric A. Kidwell

Library of 111,610 vols
Number of teachers: 123
Number of students: 1,107

CHAIRS OF DEPTS

Biology and Chemistry: Dr Erastus C. Dudley
Business, Global Leadership and Political Science: Dr Samir R. Moussalli
Education, Human Performance and Psychology: Shelby Searcy
English and Communication Studies: Dr Jackie Trimble
History, Modern Languages and Religious Studies: Dr Frank W. Bruckner
Mathematics and Computer Science: Dr Anthony Jack Carlisle
Music, Theatre and Fine Art: Dr James W. Glass

JACKSONVILLE STATE UNIVERSITY

700 Pelham Rd North, Jacksonville, AL 36265-1602
Telephone: (256) 782-5881
E-mail: info@jsucc.jsu.edu
Internet: www.jsu.edu

Founded 1883

Pres.: Bill Meehan
Vice-Pres. for Academic and Student Affairs: Dr Rebecca O. Turner
Vice-Pres. for Admin. and Business Affairs: William Fielding (acting)
Librarian: William Hubbard

Library of 583,365 vols
Number of teachers: 384 (265 full-time, 119 part-time)
Number of students: 8,478

DEANS

College of Arts and Sciences: J. E. Wade
College of Commerce and Business Admin.: William Fielding
College of Education and Professional Studies: Dr Cynthia Harper
College of Graduate Studies and Continuing Education: William D. Carr
College of Nursing and Health Sciences: Martha Lavender

MILES COLLEGE

POB 3800, Birmingham, AL 35208
located at: 5500 Myron Massey Blvd, Fairfield, AL 35064
Telephone: (205) 929-1000
Fax: (205) 929-1453
E-mail: info@mail.miles.edu
Internet: www.miles.edu

Founded 1905
Private control
Number of students: 1,700

Pres.: Albert J. H. Sloan, II
Dean of Academic Affairs: Hattie G. Lamar
Dean of Students: Carolyn D. Ray.

OAKWOOD UNIVERSITY

7000 Adventist Blvd NW, Huntsville, AL 35896
Telephone: (256) 726-7000
Fax: (256) 726-7596
E-mail: info@oakwood.edu
Internet: www.oakwood.edu

Founded 1896, present status 2008
Private control, affiliated to Seventh-day Adventist Church
Academic year: July to June

Pres.: Dr Leslie Pollard
Provost and Sr Vice-Pres.: Dr Mervyn A. Warren
Vice-Pres. for Academic Affairs: Dr John E. Anderson
Dir of Admissions: Joyce Smith
Dir of Library Services: Paulette MacLean Johnson

Library of 119,760 vols
Number of teachers: 169 (108 full-time, 61 part-time)
Number of students: 1,915

SAMFORD UNIVERSITY

800 Lakeshore Dr., Birmingham, AL 35229
Telephone: (205) 726-2011
Fax: (205) 726-2654
E-mail: web@samford.edu
Internet: www.samford.edu

Founded 1841
Academic year: June to May

Pres.: Thomas E. Corts
Provost: J. Bradley Creed
Vice-Pres. for Business Affairs and Gen. Counsel: Joseph W. Mathews, Jr
Vice-Pres. and Dean of Students: Richard H. Franklin
Vice-Pres. for Facilities: Don M. Mott
Vice-Pres. for Univ. Relations: Michael Morgan
Librarian: Jean Thomason

Number of teachers: 252
Number of students: 4,377

Publication: *Bulletin*

DEANS

School of Business: Marlene Reed (acting)
Beeson School of Divinity: Dr Timothy F. George
School of Education: Dr Jean Ann Box (acting)
Cumberland School of Law: Dr John L. Carroll
Ida V. Moffett School of Nursing: Nena Sanders
McWhort School of Pharmacy: Dr Charles D. Sands III
Howard College of Arts and Sciences: David Chapman
Metro College: Dr Cindy Kirk
Div. of Music: Dr Milburn Price
Theatre Dept: Dr Don Sandley (Chair.)

SOUTHEASTERN BIBLE COLLEGE

2545 Valleydale Rd, Birmingham, AL 35244-2083
Telephone: (205) 970-9200
Fax: (205) 970-9207
E-mail: info@sebc.edu
Internet: www.sebc.edu

Founded 1935 as Birmingham School of the Bible; name changed to Southeastern Bible School 1943; present name 1950
Private control
Academic year: August to May

Pres.: Dr Donald W. Hawkins
Vice-Pres. for Academics: Dr Ed Glasscock

Vice-Pres. for Business Affairs: PETE WALKER
Dean of Students: RANDY HOFHEINS
Dir of Institutional Effectiveness and Research: Dr PETER REOCH
Registrar: LUCRETIA MOBBS
Dir of Library Services: REBECCA KNIGHT

Library of 35,000 vols.

SOUTHERN CHRISTIAN UNIVERSITY

POB 240240, Montgomery, AL 36124-0240
1200 Taylor Rd, Montgomery, AL 361170-3553

Telephone: (334) 387-3877
Fax: (334) 387-3878
E-mail: admissions@southernchristian.edu
Internet: www.southernchristian.edu

Founded 1967 as Alabama Christian School of Religion; present name 1991
Private control
Academic year: August to August

President: Dr REX A. TURNER
Vice-President for Academic Affairs: Dr STANLEY PATTERSON
Registrar: ELAINE TARENCE
Librarian: TERRY SHERIDAN

DEANS

College of General Studies: JAMES CRABTREE (acting)
School of Leadership and Human Services: Dr TERRY GUNNELLS
Turner School of Theology: Dr WINSTON TEMPLE (acting)

SPRING HILL COLLEGE

4000 Dauphin St, Mobile, AL 36608

Telephone: (251) 380-4000
Internet: www.shc.edu

Founded 1830
Private control
Academic year: August to May

Pres.: Rev. RICHARD P. SALMI
Provost: Dr GEORGE E. SIMS
Vice-Pres. for Business and Finance: RHONDA M. SHIRAZI
Vice-Pres. for Enrollment Management: RAMONA M. CARROCCI
Vice-Pres. for Devt: KEN HOKENSON
Vice-Pres. for Student Affairs and Dean of Students: JOSEPH W. DEIGHTON
Dir of Library Services: BRUCE WHITMAN

Library of 194,187 vols
Number of teachers: 140 (78 full-time, 62 part-time)
Number of students: 1,601

DEANS

Biology: Dr. PAUL KOHNEN
Business: Ms. GLENDA PARTRIDGE
Chemistry, Physics and Engineering: Dr. LESLI BORDAS
Communication Arts: Mr. THOMAS LOEHR
English: Dr. MICHAEL KAFFER
Fine and Performing Arts: Rev. STEPHEN CAMPBELL
Foreign Languages: Dr, COLETTE WINDISH
History: Dr. PATRICIA HARRISON
Mathematics: Dr, DANIEL CYPHERT
Nursing: Dr. MARGARET COLE
Philosophy: Dr. JOANNA FORSTROM
Political Science and Law: Dr. ALEXANDER LANDI
Psychology: Dr. ROYCE SIMPSON
Teacher Education: Dr. ANN ADAMS
Theology: Rev. CHRISTOPHER VISCARDI

STILLMAN COLLEGE

POB 1430, Tuscaloosa, AL 35403
E-mail: admissions@stillman.edu
Internet: www.stillman.edu

Founded 1876 as Tuscaloosa Institute; renamed Stillman Institute 1898; present name 1948
Private control
Academic year: August to July

Pres.: Dr ERNEST MCNEALEY
Vice-Pres. for Academic Affairs: Dr CHRISTOPHER JEFFRIES
Vice-Pres. for Fiscal Affairs: SAMA MONDEH
Vice-Pres. for Student Affairs: Dr SHARON WHITTAKER
Dean of Enrolment Management: GEORGE LEE
Dean of the Library: ROBERT J. HEATH

Library of 117,500 vols, 410 periodicals

DEANS

Arts and Sciences: Dr CHARLOTTE CARTER

TALLADEGA COLLEGE

627 West Battle St, Talladega, AL 35160

Telephone: (256) 761-6212
Fax: (256) 362-2268
E-mail: bhawkins@talladega.edu
Internet: www.talladega.edu

Founded 1867 as Swayne School, present name 1869
Private control
Academic year: August to May

Pres.: BILLY C. HAWKINS
Provost and Vice-Pres. for Academic Affairs: Dr EVELYN M. WHITE
Vice-Pres. for Admin. and Finance: Dr GERALD WILLIAMS
Vice-Pres. for Institutional Advancement: CASANDRA D. BLASSINGAME
Dean of Student Affairs: JACQUELINE PADDIO
Registrar: FLORETTA DORTCH
Librarian: JULIETTE SMITH

Library of 130,000 vols

DEANS

Division of Business and Administration: (vacant)
Division of Humanities and Fine Arts: (vacant)
Division of Natural Sciences and Mathematics: Dr CHARLIE STINSON (acting)
Eunice Walker Division of Social Sciences and Education: Dr LISA LONG

TROY STATE UNIVERSITY

Troy, AL 36082

Telephone: (334) 670-3000
Fax: (334) 670-3735
E-mail: intlprog@troyst.edu
Internet: www.troy.edu

Founded 1887
Academic year: August to May

Chancellor: Dr JACK HAWKINS, Jr
Sr Vice-Chancellor for Admin.: Dr DOUGLAS C. PATTERSON
Vice-Chancellor for Academic and Student Affairs: Dr ED ROACH
Asst to Provost: VICKIE MILES
Librarian: Dr HENRY R. STEWART

Library of 334,000 vols
Number of teachers: 265
Number of students: 5,100.

CONSTITUENT UNIVERSITIES

Troy State University, Dothan

500 Univ. Dr., Dothan, AL 36303

Telephone: (334) 9836556
Fax: (334) 9836322
Internet: dothan.troy.edu

Founded 1887 as Troy State Normal School; name changed to Troy State Teachers College 1929, Troy State College 1957, present name 1996
Academic year: August to August

Pres.: Dr BARBARA ALFORD
Exec. Sec.: KAREN MCGAHEE
Dir of Academic Records and Registrar: LYNDA SALISBURY
Dir of Continuing Education Center: MICHAEL H. TEW
Dir of Information Services: RONNIE CREEL
Dir of Student and Community Services: BOB WILLIS
Dir of Fort Rucker Location: GAYE PEACOCK
Dir of Library Services: JULIA SMITH
Number of students: 1,855 (part-time and full-time undergraduates and graduates)

DEANS

College of Arts and Sciences: Dr ALAN BELSCHES
College of Business Admin.: Dr ADAIR GILBERT
College of Education: Dr SANDRA LEE JONES

Troy State University, Montgomery

231 Montgomery St, PO Drawer 4419, Montgomery, AL 361034419
E-mail: m01admissions@troy.edu
Internet: montgomery.troy.edu
Academic year: August to May

Pres.: Dr CAMERON MARTINDALE
Vice-Pres. for Academic Affairs: Dr TERRY DIXON
Vice-Pres. for Admin. and Financial Affairs: RAY WHITE
Exec. Asst to Pres.: SANDRA GOUGE
Dean of Distance Learning: Dr MAC ADKINS
Dean of Student Affairs: Dr CHARLES WESTERN
Registrar: LYNN LEWIS
Library Dir: KAY FOWLER

DEANS

College of Arts and Sciences: Dr WILLIAM S. RICHARDSON
College of Education: Dr LEN KITCHENS
Division of Business: Dr JAMES SIMPSON

Troy State University, Phenix City

1 Univ. Pl., Phenix City, AL 36869

Telephone: (334) 448-5106
Internet: phenix.troy.edu
Academic year: August to August

Vice-Chancellor: Dr CURTIS PITTS
Dir of Admin.: KENNY MARCUM
Dir of Institutional Advancement: KATHY NINAS
Dir of Student Services and Registrar: DARLENE SCHMURR-STEWART
Academic Dean: Dr JOHN IRWIN

DEANS

College of Business Admin.: Dr CHERIE FRETWELL
College of Counselling and Psychology: Dr KATHRYN NESS
College of Education: Dr LARRY THACKER

TUSKEGEE UNIVERSITY

Tuskegee, AL 36088

Telephone: (334) 727-8011
Fax: (334) 727-5276
E-mail: admi@tuskegee.edu
Internet: www.tuskegee.edu

Founded 1881
Academic year: August to May

Pres.: Dr GIBERT ROCHON
Provost and Vice-Pres. for Academic Affairs: Dr LUTHER S. WILLIAMS
Vice-Pres. for Admissions and Enrollment Management: CYNTHIA SELLERS
Vice-Pres. for Business and Fiscal Affairs: LESLIE V. PORTER
Dean of Students: PETER J. SPEARS

Registrar: EDRICE LEFTWICH
Dir of Library Services: JUANITA ROBERTS

Library of 250,000 vols, 1,000 periodicals
Number of teachers: 266
Number of students: 3,000

DEANS

College of Agriculture and Environmental and Natural Sciences: Dr WALTER H. HILL
College of Business and Information Science: Dr TEJINDER SARA
College of Engineering, Architecture and Physical Science: Dr LEGAND L. BURGE
College of Liberal Arts and Education: Dr CARLTON E. MORRIS
College of Veterinary Medicine, Nursing and Allied Health: (vacant)

UNITED STATES SPORTS ACADEMY

1 Academy Dr., Daphne, AL 36526
Telephone: (251) 626-3303
Fax: (251) 625-1035
E-mail: academy@ussa.edu
Internet: www.ussa.edu

Founded 1972
Private control
Academic year: September to August

Pres. and CEO: Dr THOMAS P. ROSANDICH
Vice-Pres.: Dr T. J. ROSANDICH
Exec. Sec.: KRISTIE SHEPPARD
Assoc. Dean of Academic Affairs: Dr ARTHUR OGDEN
Dir of Continuing Education: BETSY SMITH
Dir of Doctoral Studies: Dr FRED CROMARTIE
Registrar: FELISHA BISHOP
Library Dir: NANCY GRAY

Library: 1m. vols

Publications: *The Academy* (2 a year), *The Sport Digest* (4 a year), *The Sport Journal* (4 a year).

UNIVERSITY OF ALABAMA

POB 870100, Tuscaloosa, AL 35487
Telephone: (205) 348-6010
Fax: (205) 348-9046
E-mail: admissions@ua.edu
Internet: www.ua.edu

Founded 1831
Academic year: August to May

Pres.: Dr ROBERT E. WITT
Provost and Vice-Pres. for Academic Affairs: Dr JUDY L. BONNER
Vice-Pres. for Financial Affairs and Treas.: LYNDA GILBERT
Vice-Pres. for Student Affairs: Dr MARGARET KING
Vice-Pres. for Univ. Advancement: ROBERT E. WITT
Dean of Libraries: LOUIS A. PITSCHMANN

Library: see Libraries and Archives
Number of teachers: 1,051
Number of students: 20,929

Publications: *Alabama Alumni Magazine* (6 a year), *Alabama Business* (12 a year), *Alabama Heritage* (4 a year), *Alabama Law Review* (12 a year), *Alabama Research Magazine* (1 a year), *Alabama Review* (4 a year), *Law and Psychology Review* (1 a year)

DEANS

College of Arts and Sciences: Dr ROBERT F. OLIN
College of Commerce and Business Admin.: Dr BARRY MASON
College of Communication and Information Sciences: E. CULPEPPER CLARK
College of Community Health Sciences: Dr EUGENE MARSH
College of Continuing Studies: Dr CAROLYN DAHL
College of Education: Dr JAMES MCLEAN
College of Engineering: Dr KEITH MCDOWELL
College of Human Environmental Sciences: Dr MILLA BOSCHUNG
Capstone College of Nursing: SARA E. BARGER
Graduate School: Dr RONALD ROGERS
Honors College: Dr ROBERT HALLI
School of Law: Dr KENNETH RANDALL
School of Social Work: Dr JAMES P. (IKE) ADAMS, Jr

UNIVERSITY OF ALABAMA AT BIRMINGHAM

1530 Third Ave ., Birmingham, AL 35294
Telephone: (205) 934-4011
Internet: main.uab.edu

Founded 1969

Pres.: Dr CAROL Z. GARRISON
Provost: Dr ELI CAPILOUTO
Vice-Pres. and Dean of the School of Medicine: Dr ROBERT RICH
Vice-Pres. for Financial Affairs and Admin.: RICHARD L. MARGISON

Library of 1,409,945 vols (Mervyn H. Sterne Library), 358,858 vols (Lister Hill Library of the Health Sciences); 2,125 current periodicals (Sterne), 1,809 current periodicals (Lister Hill)
Number of teachers: 1,988 (1,839 full-time)
Number of students: 16,516

Publications: *UAB Magazine* (4 a year), *UAB Reporter* (52 a year)

DEANS

School of Arts and Humanities: BERT BROUWER
School of Business: Dr ROBERT HOLMES (acting)
School of Dentistry: MARY LYNNE CAPILOUTO (acting)
School of Education: Dr MICHAEL FRONING
School of Engineering: LINDA C. LUCAS
School of Health Related Professions: CHARLES L. JOINER
School of Medicine: Dr ROBERT RICH
School of Natural Sciences and Mathematics: LOWELL E. WENGER
School of Nursing: Dr RACHEL Z. BOOTH
School of Optometry: AROL AUGSBURGER
School of Public Health: Dr MAX MICHAEL, III
School of Social and Behavioural Sciences: Dr TENNANT S. MCWILLIAMS
Graduate School: JAMES B. MCCLINTOCK (acting)

UNIVERSITY OF ALABAMA IN HUNTSVILLE

301 Sparkman Dr., Huntsville, AL 35899
Telephone: (256) 824-1000
Fax: (256) 890-6538
Internet: www.uah.edu

Founded 1950
Public control
Language of instruction: English
Academic year: August to July

Pres.: Dr MALCOLM PORTERA
Provost and Exec. Vice-Pres. for Academic Affairs: Dr VISTASP KARBHARI
Vice-Pres. for Diversity: DELOIS SMITH
Vice-Pres. for Finance and Administration: RAY PINNER
Vice-Pres. for Research: Dr JOHN HORACK
Vice-Pres. for University Advancement: RAY PINNER

Library of 322,645 vols, 26,610 current serial titles, 543,462 microforms, 2,677 audiovisual materials, 61,249 electronic books
Number of teachers: 480
Number of students: 7,614

DEANS

College of Business Administration: Dr CARON ST. JOHN
College of Engineering: Dr SHANKAR MAHALINGAM
College of Liberal Arts: Dr GLENN DASHER
College of Nursing: Dr C. FAY RAINES
College of Science: Dr JACK D. FIX
Graduate Studies: Dr RHONDA GAEDE

UNIVERSITY OF MOBILE

5735 College Highway, Mobile, AL 36663-0220
Telephone: (251) 675-5990
Fax: (251) 675-6293
Internet: www.umobile.edu

Founded 1961
Private control

Pres.: Dr MARK R. FOLEY
Chancellor: Dr WILLIAM K. WEAVER, Jr
Vice-Pres. for Academic Affairs: Dr AUDREY C. EUBANKS
Vice-Pres. for Business Affairs: J. STEPHEN LEE
Vice-Pres. for Institutional Advancement: MICHAEL R. BLAYLOCK
Vice-Pres. for Student Development: KIMBERLY B. LEOUSIS
Dean of Academic Services and Registrar: Dr DONALD BERRY
Dir of Library Services: JEFFREY D. CALAMETTI

Library of 64,504 vols, 143,605 microfiches, 950 periodical titles
Number of teachers: 111 full-time
Number of students: 1,987

DEANS

School of Business: Dr ANNE LOWERY
School of Christian Studies: Dr CECIL TAYLOR
School of Education: Dr LARRY V. TURNER
School of Nursing: Dr ELIZABETH M. FLANAGAN
College of Arts and Sciences: Dr CHARLES M. CLARK

UNIVERSITY OF MONTEVALLO

Montevallo, AL 35115
Telephone: (205) 665-6000
Fax: (205) 665-6003
Internet: www.montevallo.edu

Founded 1896

Pres.: PHILIP C. WILLIAMS
Provost and Vice-Pres. for Academic Affairs: Dr WAYNE C. SEELBACH
Vice-Pres. for Business Affairs: CYNTHIA S. JARRETT
Vice-Pres. for Student Affairs: Dr GLENDA E. ISENHOUR
Dir of Admissions: IRA L. GURGANUS
Dir of Libraries: ROSEMARY H. ARNESON

Library of 248,132 vols, 751,618 microfilms items, 2,523 audio-visual items, 868 current periodicals
Number of teachers: 199
Number of students: 2,935

DEANS

College of Arts and Sciences: Dr MICHAEL L. ROWLAND
College of Business: Dr NANCY BELL
College of Education: Dr BETH COUNCE
College of Fine Arts: KENNETH J. PROCTER
Graduate Studies: Dr TERRY G. ROBERSON

UNIVERSITY OF NORTH ALABAMA

Florence, AL 35632-0001
Telephone: (205) 765-4100
Fax: (205) 765-4329
Internet: www.una.edu

Founded 1830 as a private instn; became a state instn 1872

Pres.: WILLIAM G. CALE, Jr
Vice-Pres. for Academic Affairs, and Provost: Dr ROOSEVELT NEWSON
Vice-Pres. for Fiscal Affairs: Dr STEVE SMITH
Vice-Pres. for Student Affairs, and Univ. Counsel: Dr DAVID P. SHIELDS, Jr
Vice-Pres. for Univ. Advancement and Admin.: Dr G. DANIEL HOWARD
Dean of Information Technologies: Dr G. GARRY WARREN

Library of 328,456 vols, 900,000 microform items, 7,800 audiovisual items, 2,145 current periodicals
Number of teachers: 285 (201 full-time, 84 part-time)
Number of students: 5,601

DEANS

College of Arts and Sciences: Dr VAGN HANSEN
College of Business: Dr KERRY GATLIN
College of Education: Dr MARK EDWARDS
College of Nursing and Allied Health: Dr BIRDIE I. BAILEY

UNIVERSITY OF SOUTH ALABAMA

307 University Blvd, Mobile, AL 36688-0002
Telephone: (251) 460-6101
Internet: www.southalabama.edu

Founded 1963

Pres.: GORDON MOULTON
Sr Vice-Pres.: Dr PAT C. COVEY
Dean and Vice-Pres. for Medical Affairs: Dr ROBERT A. KREISBERG
Vice-Pres. for Finance: M. WAYNE DAVIS
Vice-Pres. for Student Affairs: Dr DALE T. ADAMS
Registrar: MELISSA WOLD
Dean of Libraries: Dr RICHARD J. WOOD

Library of 548,800 vols
Number of teachers: 981
Number of students: 13,538

DEANS

College of Allied Health Professions: Dr RICHARD TALBOTT
College of Arts and Sciences: Dr G. DAVID JOHNSON
Mitchell College of Business: Dr CARL C. MOORE
College of Education: Dr RICHARD HAYES MITCHELL
College of Engineering: Dr JOHN STEADMAN
College of Medicine: Dr ROBERT KREISBERG
College of Nursing: Dr DEBRA C. DAVIS
School of Computer and Information Sciences: Dr DAVID L. FEINSTEIN
School of Continuing Education and Special Programs: Dr THOMAS L. WELLS
Graduate School: Dr JUDY STOUT

UNIVERSITY OF WEST ALABAMA

Livingston, AL 35470
Telephone: (205) 652-3400
Internet: www.uwa.edu

Founded 1835

Pres.: RICHARD HOLLAND
Provost: DAVID M. TAYLOR
Vice-Pres. for Financial Affairs: T. RAIFORD NOLAND
Vice-Pres. for Institutional Advancement: CLEMIT W. SPRUIELL
Vice-Pres. for Student Affairs: DANNY BUCKALEW
Dir of the Library: MONROE C. SNIDER

Library of 250,000 vols
Number of teachers: 92
Number of students: 2,153

DEANS

College of Business: Dr HABIB BAYZARI
College of Education: Dr TOM DEVANEY
College of Liberal Arts: Dr MICHAEL A. COOKE
College of Natural Sciences and Mathematics: Dr JUDY MASSEY
Div. of Nursing: SYLVIA HOMAN (Chairperson)
School of Graduate Studies: JOE B. WILKINS, Jr.

ALASKA

ALASKA BIBLE COLLEGE

POB 289, Glennallen, AK 99588
Telephone: (907) 822-3201
Fax: (907) 822-5027
E-mail: info@akbible.edu
Internet: www.akbible.edu

Founded 1966
Private control
Academic year: August to May

Pres.: Dr GARY J. RIDLEY

Number of teachers: 10
Number of students: 45

ALASKA PACIFIC UNIVERSITY

4101 University Dr., Anchorage, AK 99508
Telephone: (907) 564-8248
Fax: (907) 562-4276
E-mail: infodesk@alaskapacific.edu
Internet: www.alaskapacific.edu

Founded 1957
Academic year: September to August

Pres.: Dr DOUGLAS MCKAY NORTH
Academic Dean: MARILYN R. BARRY
Registrar: JEANETTE BROOKS

Library of 400,000 vols, shared with Univ. of Alaska, Anchorage
Number of teachers: 80
Number of students: 689

SHELDON JACKSON COLLEGE

801 Lincoln St, Sitka, AK 99835
Telephone: (907) 747-5220
Internet: www.sheldonjackson.edu

Founded 1878 as Sitka Training School; name changed to Sheldon Jackson School 1911; present name 1966
Private control
Academic year: August to May

Pres.: Rev. Dr DAVID DOBLER
Dir of Admissions: ANDY LEE
Chief Financial Officer: JIM SHARPE
Dir of Communications: HOLLY KEEN
Dean of Academic Affairs: Dr MARY LOUISE VAN WINKLE
Dean of Student and Community Affairs: CHRIS BRYNER
Grants Administrator: CARNIELLE CALL

Library of 80,000 vols
Number of students: 250 (full-time and part-time)

UNIVERSITY OF ALASKA STATEWIDE SYSTEM

POB 755000, Fairbanks, AK 99775
Telephone: (907) 450-8000
Fax: (907) 450-8002
E-mail: sypres@alaska.edu
Internet: www.alaska.edu

Founded 1917 as Alaska Agricultural College and School of Mines; univ. status 1935; consists of 3 multi-campus 4-year univs, community college

Pres.: MARK R. HAMILTON
Vice-Pres. for Finance: JOSEPH M. BEEDLE
Vice-Pres. for Research: Dr CRAIG DORMAN
Vice-Pres. for Univ. Relations: WENDY REDMAN

Number of teachers: 2,332 (statewide)
Number of students: 32,711 (statewide)

Publs program catalogues from various units of the univ.

CONSTITUENT UNIVERSITIES

University of Alaska Anchorage: 3211 Providence Dr., Anchorage, AK 99508; tel. (907) 786-1800; Chancellor Dr ELAINE P. MAIMON.

University of Alaska Fairbanks: POB 757520, Fairbanks, AK 99775; tel. (907) 474-7581; Chancellor Dr STEPHEN JONES.

University of Alaska Southeast: 11120 Glacier Highway, Juneau, AK 99801; tel. (907) 465-6457; Chancellor JOHN PUGH.

ARIZONA

AMERICAN INDIAN COLLEGE

10020 North 15th Ave, Phoenix, AZ 85021-2199
Telephone: (602) 944-3335
Fax: (602) 943-8299
E-mail: aicadm@aicag.edu
Internet: www.aicag.edu

Founded 1957
Private control
Academic year: August to May

Pres.: Rev. JAMES V. COMER (acting)
Vice-Pres. and Academic Dean: Dr DAVID L. DEGARMO (acting)
Dean of Institutional Assessment: Dr JOSEPH J. SAGGIO (acting)
Dean of Institutional Research: JIM DEMPSEY (acting)
Dean of Students: VINCE ROUBIDEAUX (acting)
Dir of Elementary Education: Dr EVERETT PERALTA
Registrar: SANDRA M. GONZALES (acting)
Library Dir: JOHN S. ROSE (acting)

Library of 20,000 vols
Number of teachers: 21 (7 full-time, 14 part-time)
Number of students: 68

ARIZONA STATE UNIVERSITY

University Dr. and Mill Ave Tempe, AZ 85287
Telephone: (602) 965-9011
E-mail: askasu@asu.edu
Internet: www.asu.edu

Founded 1885

Pres.: Dr MICHAEL M. CROW
Exec. Vice-Pres. and Provost: ELIZABETH D. CAPALDI
Exec. Vice-Pres. and Chief Financial Officer: CAROL CAMPBELL
Vice-Pres. and Provost, Phoenix Campus: MERNOY HARRISON
Vice-Pres. and Provost, Polytechnic Campus: ALBERT MCHENRY
Vice-Pres. and Provost, West Campus: MARJORIE ZATZ
Vice-Pres. for Academic Affairs: DAVID YOUNG
Vice-Pres. for Academic Personnel: MARK SEARLE
Vice-Pres. for Admin. and Legal Affairs: PAUL WARD
Vice-Pres. for Global Engagement: ANTHONY ROCK
Vice-Pres. for Public Affairs: VIRGIL RENZULI
Vice-Pres. for Research and Economic Affairs: JONATHAN FINK
Vice-Pres. for Univ. Athletics: LISA LOVE
Vice-Pres. for Univ. Student Initiatives: JAMES RUND

Vice-Pres. and Univ. Technology Officer: ADRIAN SANNIER
Librarian: SHERRIE SCHMIDT

Library: 2.5m. vols
Number of teachers: 1,800 full-time
Number of students: 60,000

DEANS

Barrett Honors College: MARK JACOBS
Carey School of Business: ROBERT MITTELSTAEDT
College of Design: WELLINGTON REITER
College of Education: SARAH HUDELSON
College of Engineering: DEIRDRE MELDRUM
College of Fine Arts: KWANG-WU KIM
Graduate Studies: MARIA T. ALLISON
College of Human Services: JOHN HEPBURN
College of Law: PATRICIA D. WHITE
College of Liberal Arts and Sciences: QUENTIN WHEELER
College of Nursing and Healthcare Innovation: BERNADETTE MELNYK
College of Public Programs: DEBRA FRIEDMAN
College of Science and Technology: TIMOTHY LINDQUIST
College of Teacher Education and Leadership: MARI KOERNER
East College: DAVID SCHWALM
New College of Interdisciplinary Arts and Sciences: BARRY RITCHIE
School of Global Management and Leadership: GARY WAISSI
School of Journalism and Mass Communication: CHRISTOPHER CALLAHAN
School of Management and Agribusiness: PAUL PATTERSON
University College: GAIL HACKETT

GRAND CANYON UNIVERSITY

POB 11097, Phoenix, AZ 85061-1097
located at: 3300 West Camelback Rd, Phoenix, AZ 85017-3030

Telephone: (602) 249-3300
Internet: www.grand-canyon.edu

Founded 1949 as Grand Canyon College, present name 1989
Private control
Academic year: August to August

Pres.: KATHY PLAYER
Chancellor: Dr BILL R. WILLIAMS
CEO: BRIAN MUELLER
Chief Academic Officer: Dr CHERI ST. ARNOULD

Library of 155,000 vols
Number of students: 36,000

DEANS

College of Doctoral Studies: Dr HANK RADDA
College of Education: Dr KIM LA PRADA
College of Fine Arts and Production: CLAUDE PENSIS
College of Health Sciences: MARK WOODEN
College of Liberal Arts: Dr LISA ST. LOUIS
College of Nursing: Dr ANNE MCNAMARA
Ken Blanchard College of Business: Dr KEVIN BARKSDALE

NORTHERN ARIZONA UNIVERSITY

Flagstaff, AZ 86011

Telephone: (928) 523-9011
Internet: www.nau.edu

Founded 1899
Language of instruction: English
Academic year: August to May

Pres.: Dr JOHN D. HAEGER
Exec. Vice-Pres.: Dr M. J. MCMAHON
Provost and Vice-Pres. for Academic Affairs: Dr LIZ GROBSMITH
Vice-Pres. for Admin. and Finance: JENNUS BURTON
Vice-Pres. for Enrollment Management and Student Affairs: DAVID BOUSQUET
Vice-Pres. for Univ. Advancement: MASON GERETY
Vice-Provost for Undergraduate Studies: Dr KAREN PUGLIESI
Vice-Pres. for Research: Dr LAURA HUENNEKE
Univ. Librarian: CYNTHIA CHILDREY

Library of 929,089 vols, 53,775 current serial subscriptions incl. on-line serials, 378,717 microforms, 37,039 audiovisual materials, 62,811 electronic books
Number of teachers: 836
Number of students: 25,204

DEANS

College of Arts and Letters: Dr MICHAEL VINCENT
College of Education: Dr GYPSY DENZINE
College of Engineering, Forestry and Natural Sciences: Dr PAUL JAGODZINSKI
College of Social and Behavioral Sciences: Dr MICHAEL STEVENSON
Graduate College: Dr RAMONA MELLOTT
School of Health and Human Services: Dr LESLIE SCHULZ
W. A. Franke College of Business: Dr MARC CHOPIN

PRESCOTT COLLEGE

220 Grove Ave, Prescott, AZ 86301

Telephone: (877) 350-2100
E-mail: admissions@prescott.edu
Internet: www.prescott.edu

Founded 1966
Private control
Academic year: September to August

Pres.: Dr DAN GARVEY
Chief Operating Officer: STEVEN M. COREY
Dean of Adult Degree Program: Dr PAUL BURKHARDT
Dean of Master of Arts Program: Dr PAUL BURKHARDT
Dean of Resident Degree Program: Dr GRET ANTILLA
Library Dir: EILEEN CHALFOUN
Registrar: LAURIE GILBRETH

Library of 23,900 vols
Number of teachers: 60 (full-time)
Number of students: 1,100

Publications: *Alligator Juniper*, *Transitions*, *Wolfberry Sun*

Adult Degree, Resident Degree, MA and PhD courses in: abstract art, agroecology, counselling, creative writing, ecopsychology, education, environmental education and interpretation, human devt, human ecology, management, outdoor adventure and teacher education.

BRANCH CAMPUS

Prescott College Tucson Center: 2233 East Speedway Blvd, Tucson, AZ 85719; tel. (520) 319-9868; fax (520) 319-1032; Exec. Dir BILL WALTON.

SOUTHWESTERN COLLEGE

2625 East Cactus Rd, Phoenix, AZ 85032

Telephone: (602) 992-6101
E-mail: swc@swcaz.edu
Internet: www.southwesterncollege.edu

Founded 1960
Private control
Academic year: August to August

Pres.: Dr BRENT GARRISON
Exec. Vice-Pres.: DAVID M. BARNES
Vice-Pres. for Academics and Student Devt: SHERRY HAEHL
Vice-Pres. for Devt: PAUL HENDRICKS
Dir of Enrolment Management: BRIAN HAEHL
Registrar: LAMBERT CRUZ
Librarian: ALICE EICKMEYER

Undergraduate courses in biblical studies, business admin., Christian ministries, counselling, elementary and secondary education, music.

THUNDERBIRD SCHOOL OF GLOBAL MANAGEMENT

15249 North 59th Ave, Glendale, AZ 85306-6000

Telephone: (602) 9787000
E-mail: admissions@thunderbird.edu
Internet: www.thunderbird.edu

Founded 1946 as The American Institute for Foreign Trade; present name 1997
Private control
Academic year: September to August

Pres.: Dr ÁNGEL CABRERA
Chief Operating Officer and Treasurer: TIM PROPP
Senior Vice-Pres. for Academic Programs: Dr ROBERT E. WIDING
Vice-Pres. for Institutional Advancement: JOAN NEICE
Dean of Faculty: Dr F. JOHN MATHIS
Dir of Corporate Learning: BETH STOOPS

Depts of accounting, culture and languages, economics, entrepreneurship, finance, int. studies, management, marketing, operations and supply chain management

Publication: *Thunderbird International Business Review* (6 a year)

DEANS

Accounting: DALE L. DAVISON
Economics: JOHN F. MATHIS
Executive Education: DAVID BOWEN

PROFESSORS

Applied Accounting: DALE DAVISON
Applied Entrepreneurship: STEVEN STRALSER
Applied Family Business: ERNESTO POZA
Global Entrepreneurship: ROBERT HISRICH
Global Management: MARY TEAGARDEN
Int. Finance: JOHN F. MATHIS
Int. Studies: MARTIN SOURS
Management: ANDREW INKPEN
Management: CHRISTINE PEARSON
Management: DAVID BOWEN
Management: MANSOUR JAVIDAN
Management: KANNAN RAMASWAMY
Marketing: ROBERT WIDING
Risk Management: JOHN O'CONNELL
Supply Chain Management: JOSEPH CAVINATO

UNIVERSITY OF ADVANCING TECHNOLOGY

2625 West Baseline Rd, Tempe, AZ 85283-1056

Telephone: (602) 383-8228
Fax: (602) 383-8228
E-mail: admissions@uat.edu
Internet: www.uat.edu

Founded 1983 as CAD Institute; name changed to Univ. of Advancing Computer Technology 1997; present name 2002
Private control
Academic year: September to August

Pres.: DOMINIC P. PISTILLO
Vice-Pres. of Finance: ROBERT WRIGHT
Provost: DAVID B. BOLMAN
Dean of Academic Affairs: REBECCA R. WHITEHEAD
Dean of Admissions and Student Support: CHRYS PISTILLO
Dean of Institutional Accreditation: BILL PEACE
Dean of Student and Employer Affairs: MEREDITH BARHAM
Registrar: JUDITH DRAYER
Academic Librarian: SUSAN WHITE

Library of 10,000 books, CD-ROMs and video cassettes
Number of students: 1,201 (incl. 267 online, 51 graduates)
Number of teachers: 64
Technology disciplines incl. game design, game programming, artificial life programming, network security and computer forensics
Publication: *Journal of Advancing Technology* (2 a year).

UNIVERSITY OF ARIZONA

Tucson, AZ 85721
Telephone: (520) 621-2211
Fax: (602) 621-9118
E-mail: facil@listserv.arizona.edu
Internet: www.arizona.edu
Founded 1885
Academic year: August to May (two terms)
Pres.: ROBERT N. SHELTON
Senior Vice-Pres. for Business Affairs: BOB SMITH (acting)
Exec. Vice-Pres. and Provost: MEREDITH HAY
Vice-Pres. for External Relations: STEPHEN J. MACCARTHY
Vice-Pres. for Health Affairs: WILLIAM M. CRIST
Vice-Pres. for Human Resources: ALLISON VAILLANCOURT
Vice-Pres. for Legal Affairs and General Counsel: GLENN GEORGE
Vice-Pres. for Research, Graduate Studies and Economic Devt: LESLIE TOLBERT
Vice-Pres. for Student Affairs: MELISSO VITO
Dean of Univ. Libraries: CARLA STOFFLE
Library: see Libraries and Archives
Number of teachers: 2,400 (f.t.e.)
Number of students: 38,767
Publications: *Arizona Law Review*, *Arizona Quarterly* (literature), *Arizona and the West* (history, 4 a year), *Books of the Southwest*, *Bulletin*, *Business and Economic Review* (12 a year), *Hispanic American Historical Review* (4 a year), *Record*

DEANS

College of Agriculture and Life Sciences: EUGENE SANDER
College of Architecture and Landscape Architecture: JANICE CERVELLI
College of Education: RONALD W. MARX
College of Engineering: JEFF GOLDBERG
College of Fine Arts: Dr JORY HANCOCK
College of Humanities: MARY WILDNER-BASSETT
Colleges of Letters, Arts and Science: JOAQUIN RUIZ (Exec. Dean)
College of Medicine: STEVE GOLDSCHMID
College of Nursing: JOAN SHAVER
College of Optical Sciences: JAMES C. WYANT
College of Pharmacy: J. LYLE BOOTMAN
College of Science: JOAQUIN RUIZ
College of Social and Behavioral Sciences: J. P. JONES, III
Eller College of Management: PAUL PORTNEY
Graduate College: ANDREW COMRIE
Honors College: PATRICIA MACCORQUODALE
James E. Rogers College of Law: LAWRENCE PONOROFF
Mel and Enid Zuckerman College of Public Health: IMAN HAKIM
Outreach College: MIKE PROCTOR
UA South: JIM SHOCKEY (Exec. Officer)

PROFESSORS

College of Agriculture and Life Sciences:

ALLEN, R. E., Animal Science; Nutritional Sciences
AX, R. L., Animal Science; Obstetrics and Gynaecology
BEATTIE, B. R., Agricultural and Resource Economics
BOURQUE, D. P., Biochemistry; Molecular and Cellular Biology
BOWERS, W. S., Entomology
BRUSSEAU, M. L., Soil, Water and Environmental Sciences; Hydrology and Water Resources
BURAS, N., Hydrology and Water Resources
BYRNE, D. N., Entomology
CALDWELL, R. L., Soil, Water and Environmental Sciences; Communication
CATE, R. M., Family and Consumer Sciences
CHANDLER, V. L., Plant Science; Molecular and Cellular Biology
CHRISTENSON, J. A., Agricultural and Resource Economics
COATES, W. E., Arid Lands
COLBY, B. G., Agricultural and Resource Economics; Hydrology and Water Resources
COLLIER, R. J., Animal Science
COLLINS, J. K., Veterinary Science and Microbiology
CORY, D. C., Agricultural and Resource Economics
COX, D. E., Agriculture Education
DANIEL, T. C., Renewable Natural Resources; Psychology
DENISE, R. K., Animal Science
DENNEHY, T. J., Entomology
DESTEIGUER, J. E., Renewable Natural Resources
FFOLLIOTT, P. F., Watershed Management; Arid Lands
FOSTER, K. E., Arid Lands
GALBRAITH, D. W., Plant Science
GAY, L. W., Watershed Management
GERBA, C. P., Soil, Water and Environmental Sciences; Microbiology and Immunology
GIACOMELLI, G. A., Agricultural and Biosystems Engineering
GIMBLETT, H. R., Renewable Natural Resources; Landscape Architecture
GLENN, E. P., III, Soil, Water and Environmental Sciences; Wildlife and Fisheries Science
GOLL, D. E., Nutritional Sciences; Biochemistry
GUNATILAKA, L., Arid Lands
HAGEDORN, H. H., Entomology
HARTSHORNE, D. J., Nutritional Sciences; Biochemistry
HATCH, K. L., Agricultural and Biosystems Engineering
HAWES, M. C., Plant Pathology
HAWKINS, R. H., Watershed Management; Hydrology and Water Resources
HUETE, A. R., Soil, Water and Environmental Sciences
INNES, R. D., Agricultural and Resource Economics; Economics
JENSEN, M. H., Plant Science
JOENS, L. A., Veterinary Science and Microbiology
KALTENBACH, C., Animal Science
KENNEDY, C. K., Plant Pathology; Molecular and Cellular Biology
KNIGHT, J. A., Jr, Agriculture Education
LARKINS, B. A., Plant Science; Molecular and Cellular Biology
LEONARD, R. T., Plant Science
LIGHTNER, D. V., Veterinary Science and Microbiology
MCCLARAN, M. P., Range Management
MCCLURE, M. A., Plant Pathology
MCDANIEL, R. G., Plant Science
MCLAUGHLIN, S. P., Arid Lands
MCPHERSON, G. R., Renewable Natural Resources
MAIER, R. M., Soil, Water and Environmental Sciences
MANNAN, R. W., Wildlife and Fisheries Science
MARCHELLO, J. A., Animal Science; Nutritional Sciences
MARSH, S. E., Arid Lands; Geography and Regional Development; Renewable Natural Resources
MILLER, G. M., Agriculture Education
MONKE, E. A., Agricultural and Resource Economics
MORAN, N. A., Ecology and Evolutionary Biology; Entomology
PEPPER, I. L., Soil, Water and Environmental Sciences
POE, S. E., Agricultural and Biosystems Engineering
RAY, D. T., Plant Science
REID, C. P., Renewable Natural Resources
RIDLEY, C. A., Family and Consumer Sciences; Psychology
ROHRBAUGH, M. J., Family and Consumer Sciences; Psychology
ROTH, R. L., Agricultural and Biosystems Engineering
ROWE, D. C., Family and Consumer Sciences; Psychology
RUYLE, G. B., Range Management
SANDER, E. G., Biochemistry; Nutritional Sciences
SCHOWENGERDT, R., Arid Lands; Electrical and Computer Engineering; Optical Sciences
SCHURG, W. A., Veterinary Science and Microbiology; Animal Science
SHAW, W. W., Wildlife and Fisheries Science
SHIM, S., Family and Consumer Sciences
SILVERTOOTH, J. C., Soil, Water and Environment Sciences; Plant Science
SLACK, D. C., Agricultural and Biosystems Engineering
SONGER, J. G., Veterinary Science and Microbiology
STERLING, C. R., Veterinary Science and Microbiology
TABASHNIK, B., Entomology
THOMPSON, G. D., Agricultural and Resource Economics
VANETTEN, H. D., Plant Pathology
VIERLING, E., Biochemistry; Molecular and Cellular Biology
WARRICK, A. W., Soil, Water and Environmental Sciences; Hydrology and Water Resources
WHEELER, D. E., Entomology
WIERENGA, P. J., Soil, Water and Environmental Sciences
WILSON, P. N., Agricultural and Resource Economics
WOLFE, F. H., Nutritional Sciences
ZWOLINSKI, M. J., Watershed Management

College of Architecture and Landscape Architecture:

ALBANESE, C. A., Architecture
CHALFOUN, N. V., Architecture
ERIBES, R. A., Planning; Architecture
MALO, A., Architecture
MATTER, F. S., Planning; Architecture
ROSENBLOOM, S., Planning; Architecture
SAN MARTIN, I. J., Architecture
STAMM, W. P., Architecture

College of Education:

ALEAMONI, L. M., Special Education, Rehabilitation and School Psychology
AMES, W. S., Teaching and Teacher Education
ANDERS, P. L., Language, Reading and Culture
ANTIA, S. D., Special Education, Rehabilitation and School Psychology
CARTER, K. J., Teaching and Teacher Education
DOYLE, W., Teaching and Teacher Education
GOOD, T. L., Educational Psychology
GOODMAN, Y. M., Language, Reading and Culture

GRIFFEY, D. C., Physical Education
LESLIE, L., Higher Education
LEVIN, J. R., Educational Psychology
LEVIN, J. S., Higher Education
MCCARTY, T. L., Language, Reading and Culture
MAKER, C. J., Special Education, Rehabilitation and School Psychology
MISHRA, S. P., Special Education, Rehabilitation and School Psychology
MOLL, L. C., Language, Reading and Culture
MORRIS, R. J., Special Education,Rehabilitation and School Psychology
OBRZUT, J. E., Special Education, Rehabilitation and School Psychology
RHOADES, G. D., Higher Education (H)
RUIZ, R., Language, Reading and Culture
SABERS, D. L., Educational Psychology
SALES, A. P., Special Education, Rehabilitation and School Psychology
SHORT, K. G., Language, Reading and Culture
SLAUGHTER, S. A., Higher Education
STREITMATTER, J. L., Educational Psychology
TAYLOR, J. L., Educational Administration
UMBREIT, J., Special Education, Rehabilitation and School Psychology
VALMONT, W. J., Language, Reading and Culture
WOODARD, D. B., Higher Education

College of Engineering:

ARNOLD, R. G., Chemical Engineering
ASKIN, R. G., Systems and Industrial Engineering
BAHILL, A. T., Systems and Industrial Engineering
BALES, R. C., Hydrology and Water Resources
BALSA, T. F., Aerospace and Mechanical Engineering
BASSETT, R. L., Hydrology and Water Resources
BIRNIE, D. P. III, Materials Science and Engineering; Electrical and Computer Engineering
BREWS, J. R., Electrical and Computing Engineering
BUDHU, M., Civil Engineering and Engineering Mechanics
BURAS, N., Hydrology and Water Resources
CALVERT, P. D., Materials Science and Engineering
CELLIER, F. E., Electrical and Computer Engineering
CETAS, T. C., Aerospace and Mechanical Engineering; Electrical and Computer Engineering
CHAMPAGNE, F. H., Aerospace and Mechanical Engineering
CHEN, C. F., Aerospace and Mechanical Engineering
COLBY, B. G., Hydrology and Water Resources
CONTRACTOR, D., Civil Engineering and Engineering Mechanics
DAVENPORT, W. G., Materials Science and Engineering
DAVIS, D. R., Hydrology and Water Resources
DESAI, C., Civil Engineering and Engineering Mechanics
DEYMIER, P. A., Materials Science and Engineering
EHSANI, M. R., Civil Engineering and Engineering Mechanics
FASEL, H. F., Aerospace and Mechanical Engineering
FRANTZISKONIS, G. N., Civil Engineering and Engineering Mechanics
GANAPOL, B. D., Hydrology and Water Resources
HALDAR, A., Civil Engineering and Engineering Mechanics
HAWKINS, R. H., Hydrology and Water Resources
HEINRICH, J. C., Aerospace and Mechanical Engineering
HIGLE, J. L., Systems and Industrial Engineering
HISKEY, J. B., Materials Science and Engineering
JACKSON, K. A., Materials Science and Engineering; Optical Sciences
KECECIOGLU, D. B., Aerospace and Mechanical Engineering
KERSCHEN, E. J., Aerospace and Mechanical Engineering
KOSTUK, R. K., Electrical and Computer Engineering; Optical Sciences
KULATILAKE, P., Mining and Geological Engineering
KUNDU, T., Civil Engineering and Engineering Mechanics
LOURI, A., Electrical and Computer Engineering
LYNCH, D. C., Materials Science and Engineering
MADDOCK, T., III, Hydrology and Water Resources
MADENCI, E., Aerospace and Mechanical Engineering
MARCELLIN, M. W., Electrical and Computer Engineering
MIRCHANDANI, P. B., Systems and Industrial Engineering; Electrical and Computer Engineering
NEUMAN, S. P., Hydrology and Water Resources
NIKRAVESH, P. E., Aerospace and Mechanical Engineering
OHANLON, J. F., Electrical and Computer Engineering
PALUSINSKI, O. A., Electrical and Computer Engineering
PETERSON, T. W., Chemical and Environmental Engineering (H)
POIRIER, D. R., Materials Science and Engineering
PRINCE, J. L., III, Electrical and Computer Engineering
RAGHAVAN, S., Materials Science and Engineering
RAMBERG, J. S., Systems and Industrial Engineering
RAMOHALLI, K. N., Aerospace and Mechanical Engineering
REAGAN, J. A., Electrical and Computer Engineering; Optical Sciences
ROZENBLIT, J. W., Electrical and Computer Engineering
SAADATMANESH, H., Civil Engineering and Engineering Mechanics
SCHOOLEY, L. C., Electrical and Computer Engineering
SCHOWENGERDT, R., Electrical and Computer Engineering; Optical Sciences
SEN, S., Systems and Industrial Engineering
SHADMAN, F., Chemical Engineering
SHUTTLEWORTH, W. J., Hydrology and Water Resources
SIMMONS, J. H., Materials Science and Engineering; Optical Sciences
SIMON, B. R., Aerospace and Mechanical Engineering
SOROOSHIAN, S., Hydrology and Water Resources; Systems and Industrial Engineering
STERNBERG, B. K., Mining and Geological Engineering
STRICKLAND, R. N., Electrical and Computer Engineering; Optical Sciences
SUNDARESHAN, M. K., Electrical and Computer Engineering
SZIDAROVSZKY, F., Systems and Industrial Engineering; Hydrology and Water Resources
SZILAGYI, M. N., Electrical and Computer Engineering
UHLMANN, D. R., Materials Science and Engineering; Optical Sciences
VALDES, J. B., Civil Engineering and Engineering Mechanics; Hydrology and Water Resources
VARADY, R. G., Hydrology and Water Resources
VRUDHULA, S. B. K., Electrical and Computer Engineering
WANG, F., Systems and Industrial Engineering
WEINBERG, M. C., Materials Science and Engineering
WENDT, J. O. L., Chemical and Environmental Engineering
WILLIAMS, J. G., Nuclear and Energy Engineering
WILLIAMS, S. K., Materials Science and Engineering
WYGNANSKI, I. J., Aerospace and Mechanical Engineering
YEH, T.-C. J., Hydrology and Water Resources
ZEIGLER, B. P., Electrical and Computer Engineering
ZIOLKOWSKI, R. W., Electrical and Computer Engineering

College of Fine Arts:

ASIA, D. I., Music
BOELTS, J. G., Art
CALDWELL, C. B., Media Arts
CHABOT, A. M., Art
CHAMBERLAIN, B. B., Music
COOK, G. D., Music
CROFT, M. F., Art
CUTIETTA, R. A., Music
DEMING, C. J., Media Arts
DIETZ, W. D., Music
DIXON, H. W., Theatre Arts
ERVIN, T. R., Music
FAN, P., Music
FERNANDEZ, N., Music
GEOFFRION, M. M., Art
GREER, W. D., Art
HAMMAN, D. L., Music
HAMMOND, H., Art
HANCOCK, J. L., Dance
HANSON, G. I., Music
HASKELL, J. R., Music
HEDDEN, S. K., Music
HITNER, C. V., Art
JONES, H. H., Art
KASHY, J. L., Music
KIRKBRIDE, J. E., Music
KOLOSICK, J. T., Music
LOWE, M., Dance
MCLAUGHLIN, C. M., Music
MURPHY, E. W., Music
O'BRIEN, J. P., Music
PARRY, E. C., III, Art
PATTERSON, R. T., Music
POLK, A. W., Art
POWELL, G. C., Music
QUIROZ, A. J., Music
ROE, C. R., Music
ROGERS, B. J., Art
SEVIGNY, M. J., Art
TUCCI, A. D., Theatre Arts
TUNKARA, M. S., Art
WIMMER, G. E., Art
WINSLOW, D. J., Theatre Arts
ZUMBRO, N. L., Music

College of Humanities:

AIKEN, S. H., English
ARIEW, R. A., French and Italian
BABCOCK, B. A., English
BECK, J., French and Italian
BOWEN, R., English
CANFIELD, J. D., English
CHANDOLA, A. C., East Asian Studies
CHISHOLM, D. H., German Studies
CLASSEN, A., German Studies
COMPITELLO, M. A., Spanish and Portuguese
DAHOOD, R., English

DAYAN, J., English
DRYDEN, E. A., English
ENOS, T., English
EPSTEIN, W. H., English
EVANS, E. J., English
EVERS, L. J., English
FIELDER, G. E., Russian and Slavic Languages
FIORE, R. L., Spanish and Portuguese
GARRARD, J. G., Russian and Slavic Languages
GILABERT, J. J., Spanish and Portuguese
GONZALEZ, R. D., English
GUTSCHE, G. J., Russian and Slavic Languages
GYURKO, L. A., Spanish and Portuguese
HOGLE, J. E., English
HOUSTON, R. W., English
KIEFER, F. P., Jr, English
KINKADE, R. P., Spanish and Portuguese
KOLODNY, A., English
KUNNIE, J. E., African-American Studies
LEONARD, A., Jr, Classics; Near Eastern Studies
MCKNIGHT, B. E., East Asian Studies
MARTINSON, S. D., German Studies
MEDINE, P. E., English
MILLER, J. R., English
MILLER, T. P., English
MOMADAY, N. S., English
MONSMAN, G. C., English
NANTELL, J. A., Spanish and Portuguese
ORLEN, S. L., English
PENNER, J. D., English
PIALORSI, F. P., English
POVERMAN, C. E., English
PROMIS, J. M. O., Spanish and Portuguese
RAVAL, S. S., English
RIVERO, E. S., Spanish and Portuguese
SALDATE, M., IV, Education Foundations and Administration
SAVILLE-TROIKE, M., English
SCHULZ, R. A., German Studies
SCRUGGS, C. W., English
SHELTON, R. W., English
SKINNER, M. B., Classics
SOLOMON, J., Classics
SOREN, H. D., Classics
TAO, C-L. P., East Asian Studies
TAO, J-S., East Asian Studies
TAPAHONSO, L., American Indian Studies
TATUM, C. M., Spanish and Portuguese
TERPENING, R. H., French and Italian
TROIKE, R. C., English
ULREICH, J. C., Jr, English
VANCE, T. J., East Asian Studies
VOYATZIS, M. E., Classics
WAUGH, L. R., French and Italian
WILD, P. T., English
WITTIG, M. M., French and Italian; Women's Studies

Eller College of Business and Public Administration:

BLOCK, M. K., Economics
BRUCKS, M. L., Marketing
BURGOON, J. K., Communication
CHEN, H., Management Information Systems
CONNOLLY, T., Management and Policy
COX, J. C., Economics
DROR, M., Management Information Systems
DYL, E. A., Finance
FELIX, W. L., Accounting
FISHBACK, P. V., Economics
GILLILAND, S. W., Management and Policy
HECKLER, S. E., Marketing
IACOBUCCI, D. M., Marketing
ISAAC, M. R., Economics
KANTOR, S. E., Economics
LIBECAP, G. D., Economics
MCCABE, K. A., Economics
MILWARD, H. B., Public Administration and Policy; Management and Policy
NUNAMAKER, J. F., Jr, Management Information Systems
OAXACA, R. L., Economics
RAM, S., Management Information Systems
RAPORPORT, A., Management and Policy
SHENG, O. R. L., Management Information Systems
SILVERS, A. L., Public Administration and Policy
SMITH, K. R., Economics
TAYLOR, L. D., Economics
WALKER, M. A., Economics
WALLENDORF, M., Marketing
WALLER, W. S., Accounting
ZUPAN, M. A., Economics

James E. Rogers College of Law:

ANAYA, S. J.
ANDREWS, A. W.
ATWOOD, B. A.
AUSTIN, G. W.
BRAUCHER, J.
CHIORAZZI, M. G.
DOBBS, D. B.
GANTZ, D. A.
GLENNON, R. J., Jr, Law and Public Policy
HEGLAND, K. F.
HENDERSON, R. C.
KORN, J. B.
KOZOLCHYK, B.
MASSARO, T. M.
MAUET, T. A.
OBIORA, L. A.
RATNER, J. R.
SCHNEYER, T. J.
SCHUESSLER, T. L.
SILVERMAN, A.
SPECE, R. G., Jr
WEISS, E. J.
WILLIAMS, R. A., Jr
WOODS, W. D., Jr

College of Medicine:

AHMANN, F. R., Medicine; Surgery
AKPORIAYE, E., Microbiology and Immunology
ALBERTS, D. S., Medicine; Pharmacology; Public Health
ALECK, K. A., Clinical Paediatrics
ALPERT, J. S., Medicine
AMPEL, N. M., Medicine
ATWATER, A. E., Physiology
BALDWIN, A. L., Physiology
BARANKO, P. V., Clinical Professor
BARKER, S. J., Anaesthesiology
BARNES, G. R., Jr, Clinical Professor
BARRETT, H. H., Optical Sciences; Radiology
BARTON, L. L., Paediatrics
BERG, R. A., Paediatrics
BERNSTEIN, H., Microbiology and Immunology
BOWDEN, G. T., Radiation Oncology; Pharmacology and Toxicology
BOYWER, T. D., Medicine
BRANDENBURG, R. O., Medicine
BRAUN, E. J., Physiology
BUCHSBAUM, H. W., Clinical Neurology
BURT, J. M., Physiology; Surgery
BUXER, J. B., Clinical Professor
CANFIELD, L. M., Public Health
CARMONA, R. H., Clinical Surgery
CARTER, D. E., Pharmacology and Toxicology
CETAS, T. C., Radiation Oncology
CHAMBLISS, L., Clinical Obstetrics and Gynaecology
CLEWELL, W. H., Clinical Professor
COULL, B. M., Neurology; Medicine
COULTHARD, S. W., Clinical Surgery
CRAIG, A. D., Jr, Cell Biology and Anatomy
CROSS, H. E., Clinical Ophthalmology
CUNNIFF, C. M., Paediatrics; Clinical Obstetrics and Gynaecology
CUNNINGHAM, J. T., Clinical Medicine
DALLAS, W. J., Optical Sciences; Radiology
DALTON, W. S., Medicine
DANTZLER, W. H., Physiology
DASPIT, C. P., Clinical Surgery
DAVIS, T. P., Pharmacology
DELLON, A. L., Clinical Professor
DEMEURE, M. J., Surgery
DORR, R. T., Pharmacology
DRESNER, M. L., Clinical Surgery
DRYDEN, R. M., Clinical Opthalmology
DUCKWORTH, W. C., Clinical Medicine
DUNCAN, B. R., Paediatrics; Public Health
ELLIOT, J., Clinical Obstetrics and Gynaecology
ERENBERG, A., Clinical Paediatrics
ESCOBAR, P. L., Clinical Medicine
EWY, G. A., Medicine
FAGAN, T. C., Medicine
FELICETTA, J. V., Clinical Medicine
FISHBURNE, J. I., Jr, Clinical Obstetrics and Gynaecology
FLINK, I. L., Medicine
FREGOSI, R. F., Physiology
FRENCH, E. D., Pharmacology
FREUNDLICH, I. M., Clinical Professor
FRIEDMAN, R. L., Microbiology and Immunology
GALGIANI, J. N., Medicine
GANDOLFI, A. J., Anaesthesiology; Pharmacology and Toxicology
GAREWAL, H. S., Medicine
GATENBY, R. A., Radiology
GELENBERG, A. J., Psychiatry
GERNER, E. W., Radiation Oncology
GHISHAN, F. K., Paediatrics; Physiology
GILLIES, R. J., Radiology
GLATTKE, T. J., Surgery
GLEASON, D. M., Clinical Surgery
GLICKMAN, S. I., Clinical Surgery
GMITRO, A. F., Radiology; Optical Sciences
GOLDMAN, S., Surgery; Medicine
GORE, R. W., Physiology; Cell Biology and Anatomy
GRAHAM, A. R., Pathology
GRANA, W. A., Orthopaedic Surgery
GREEN, S. A., Public Health
GROGAN, T. M., Pathology
GROSS, R. A., Clinical Medicine
GROSSMAN, M., Clinical Medicine
GRUENER, R. P., Physiology
HABIB, M. P., Clinical Medicine
HADJIPAVLOU, A. G., Clinical Surgery
HALE, F. A., Clinical Family and Community Medicine
HALONEN, M. J., Pharmacology; Microbiology; Medicine
HAMEROFF, S. R., Anaesthesiology
HAMILTON, A. J., Surgery; Clinical Radiation Oncology; Psychology
HANSEN, R. C., Medicine; Paediatrics
HARRIS, D. T., Microbiology and Immunology
HATCH, K. D., Obstetrics and Gynaecology
HAUSSLER, M. R., Biochemistry
HAYNES, R. J., Clinical Surgery
HEINE, M. W., Obstetrics and Gynaecology
HENDIN, B. A., Clinical Neurology
HERMAN, R. M., Pharmacology
HERSH, E. M., Medicine; Microbiology and Immunology
HOYER, P. B., Physiology
HUNT, K. R., Clinical Radiology
HUNTER, T. B., Radiology
HUTTER, J. J., Paediatrics
ISERSON, K. V., Emergency Medicine
JOHNSON, D. G., Medicine; Pharmacology
KALIVAS, J., Clinical Medicine
KAPLAN, A. M., Clinical Paediatrics
KATZ, M. A., Medicine; Physiology
KAY, M., Microbiology and Immunology; Medicine
KERN, K. B., Medicine
KLOTZ, S. A., Medicine
LANCE, M. P., Medicine
LANE, R. D., Psychiatry
LEIBOWITZ, A. I., Clinical Medicine
LESLIE, J. B., Clinical Anaesthesiology

LEVINE, B. E., Clinical Medicine
LEVINE, N., Medicine
LEVINE, R. B., Neurobiology; Physiology
LEVY, P., Clinical Medicine
LIEN, Y-H. H., Medicine; Physiology
LISSE, J. R., Medicine
LOHMAN, T. G., Physiology
LUKAS, R. J., Pharmacology
MCCARTY, R. J., Clinical Medicine
MCCLURE, C. L., Clinical Family and Community Medicine
MCCUSKEY, R. S., Cell Biology and Anatomy; Physiology
MCDONAGH, P. F., Surgery; Physiology
MCLOONE, J. B., Clinical Psychiatry
MCMULLEN, N. T., Cell Biology and Anatomy; Neurology
MALAN, T. P., Anaethesiology
MALONE, J. M., Clinical Surgery
MARCHALONIS, J. J., Microbiology and Immunology; Pathology; Medicine
MARSHALL, J. R., Public Health; Medicine
MARSHALL, W. N., Jr, Clinical Paediatrics
MARTINEZ, F., Paediatrics
MATTOX, J. H., Public Health; Clinical Obstetrics and Gynaecology
MEISLIN, H. W., Emergency Medicine
MICHAEL, U. F., Clinical Medicine
MILLER, J. M., Ophthalmology; Optical Sciences
MILLER, T. P., Medicine
MILLS, J. L., Surgery
MOHER, L. M., Clinical Family and Community Medicine
MORGAN, W. J., Paediatrics; Physiology
MORKIN, E., Medicine; Physiology; Pharmacology
MORRISON, D. A., Medicine; Radiology
NAGLE, R. B., Pathology; Cell Biology and Anatomy; Surgery
NOLTE, J., Cell Biology and Anatomy
OBER, R. R., Clinical Ophthalmology
OLESON, J. R., Radiation Oncology
ORTIZ, A., Public Health
OTTO, C. W., Anaesthesiology
OUTWATER, E. K., Radiology
OVITT, T. W., Radiology
PALMER, C. M., Clinical Anaesthesiology
PAYNE, C. M., Microbiology and Immunology
PEIRCE, J. C., Clinical Medicine
PELLETIER, K. R., Clinical Professor
PENG, Y-M., Medicine
PETERSEN, E. A., Medicine; Family and Community Health; Public Health
PETERSEN, S. R., Clinical Professor
PHIBBS, B. P., Clinical Medicine
PINNAS, J. L., Clinical Professor
PORRECA, F., Pharmacology; Anaethesiology
PORTER, J. M., Clinical Surgery
POTTER, R. L., Psychiatry
POWIS, G., Pathology; Pharmacology
PURDON, T. F., Clinical Obstetrics and Gynaecology
PUST, R. E., Family and Community Medicine; Public Health
PUTNAM, C. W., Surgery; Pharmacology
QUAN, S. F., Medicine; Anaesthesiology
RACY, J. C., Psychiatry
RAMSAY, E. G., Surgery
RANCE, N. E., Pathology; Neurology; Cell Biology and Anatomy
RAY, C. G., Clinical Pathology
REED, K. L., Obstetrics and Gynaecology
REICHLIN, S., Medicine
REIMAN, E. M., Psychiatry
REKATE, H. L., Clinical Surgery
REYNA, V. F., Surgery; Medicine
RIMSZA, M. E., Clinical Paediatrics
RIZKALLAH, T. H., Clinical Obstetrics and Gynaecology
ROBBINS, R. A., Medicine
ROEHRIG, H., Radiology
ROESKE, W. R., Medicine; Pharmacology
ROSENFELD, P. A., Clinical Obstetrics and Gynaecology
RUNYAN, R. B., Cell Biology and Anatomy
RYAN, K. J., Pathology; Microbiology and Immunology
SABBAGH, A. H., Clinical Professor
SAMPLINER, R. E., Medicine
SANDERS, A. B., Emergency Medicine
SANOWSKI, R. A., Clinical Medicine
SATTENSPIEL, E., Clinical Obstetrics and Gynaecology
SCHIFF, M., Clinical Surgery
SCHILLER, W. R., Clinical Surgery
SCHMITZ, G. L., Clinical Surgery
SCHORR, W. F., Clinical Medicine
SCHUMACHER, M. J., Paediatrics; Medicine
SECOMB, T. W., Physiology
SEEGER, J. F., Radiology
SETHI, G. K., Surgery
SHAH, J. H., Medicine; Radiology
SHAPIRO, W. R., Clinical Neurology
SHEHAB, Z. M., Clinical Paediatrics; Clinical Pathology
SHISSLAK, C. M., Public Health; Family and Community Medicine, Psychology
SIBLEY, W. A., Neurology
SILVERMAN, H. D., Clinical Family and Community Medicine
SIPES, I. G., Pharmacology and Toxicology; Anaesthesiology
SKINNER, P. H., Family and Community Medicine
SLOVITER, R. S., Pharmacology; Neurology
SNYDER, R. W., Ophthalmology
SOBONYA, R. E., Pathology
SONNTAG, V. K. H., Clinical Surgery
SPAITE, D. W., Emergency Medicine
SPETZLER, R. F., Surgery
STERN, L. Z., Medicine
STERN, R. G., Clinical Radiology
STONE, H. H., Clinical Surgery
STUART, D. G., Physiology
SURWIT, E. A., Clinical Obstetrics and Gynaecology
SZIVEK, J. A., Orthopaedic Surgery
TAETLE, R., Medicine
TISCHLER, M. E., Biochemistry; Medicine; Physiology
TOLBERT, L. P., Neurobiology; Cell Biology and Anatomy
ULMER, D. D., Clinical Medicine
UNGER, E. C., Radiology
VALENZUELA, T. D., Emergency Medicine
VAN WYCK, D., Medicine
VILLAR, H. V., Surgery; Radiation Oncology
WEIL, A. T., Clinical Public Health
WEINSTEIN, R. S., Pathology
WEISS, B. D., Clinical Family and Community Medicine
WEISS, J. C., Clinical Paediatrics
WHITNEY, P. J., Clinical Surgery
WILLIAMS, C. L., Surgery
WILLIAMS, R. L., Clinical Paediatrics
WILLIAMS, S. K., Surgery; Physiology
WITTE, C. L., Surgery
WITTE, M. H., Surgery
WITTEN, M. L., Paediatrics
WOOLFENDEN, J. M., Radiology
WOOSLEY, R. L., Pharmacology; Medicine
WRIGHT, S. H., Physiology
YAMAMURA, H. I., Pharmacology; Biochemistry; Psychiatry
YATES, A., Clinical Family and Community Medicine
YUDELL, A., Clinical Neurology

College of Nursing:

BADGER, T. A.
GLITTENBERG, J. E.
ISENBERG, M. A.
MOORE, I. M.
PARSONS, L. C.
PHILLIPS, L. R.
REED, P. G.
VERRAN, J. A.
WOODTLI, M. A.

College of Pharmacy:

BOOTMAN, J. L., Pharmacy Practice and Science; Pharmaceutical Sciences; Public Health
CARTER, D. E., Pharmacology and Toxicology
COLE, J. R., Medicinal Chemistry; Pharmaceutical Sciences
CONSROE, P. F., Pharmacology and Toxicology
COONS, S. J., Pharmacy Practice and Science; Public Health
DRAUGALIS, J., Pharmacy Practice and Science; Pharmaceutical Sciences
GANDOLFI, A. J., Pharmacology; Pharmacology and Toxicology
HURLEY, L., Medicinal Chemistry–Pharmacology and Toxicology; Medicinal Chemistry–Pharmaceutical Sciences
JACOBSON, E. L., Pharmacology and Toxicology
JACOBSON, M. K., Medicinal Chemistry–Pharmacology and Toxicology
LIEBLER, D. C., Pharmacology and Toxicology
MCQUEEN, C. A., Pharmacology and Toxicology
MAYERSOHN, M., Pharmaceutical Sciences
MURPHY, J. E., Pharmacy Practice and Science; Pharmaceutical Sciences
NOLAN, P. E., Pharmacy Practice and Science; Pharmaceutical Sciences
REGAN, J. W., Pharmacology and Toxicology
SCHRAM, K. H., Pharmaceutical Sciences
SIPES, I. G., Pharmacology and Toxicology
SLOVITER, R. S., Pharmacology
TIMMERMANN, B., Pharmacology and Toxicology; Pharmaceutical Sciences
TONG, T. G., Pharmacy Practice and Science; Pharmacology and Toxicology
YALKOWSKY, S. H., Pharmaceutical Sciences

College of Science:

ADAMOWICZ, L., Chemistry
ANDREWS, G. R., Computer Science
ANGEL, J. R. P., Astronomy; Optical Sciences
APOSHIAN, H. V., Molecular and Cellular Biology; Pharmacology
ARMSTRONG, N. R., Chemistry; Optical Sciences
ARNETT, W. D., Astronomy
ATKINSON, G. H., Chemistry; Optical Sciences
BALDWIN, T. O., Biochemistry
BARRETT, B. R., Physics
BARTON, M. D., Geosciences
BAYLES, K. A., Speech and Hearing Science
BECK, S. L., Geosciences
BETTERTON, E. A., Atmospheric Sciences
BICKEL, W. S., Physics
BIRKY, C. W., Jr, Ecology and Environmental Biology
BOURQUE, D. P., Biochemistry; Molecular and Cellular Biology
BOWDEN, G. T., Radiation Oncology; Pharmacology and Toxicology; Molecular and Cellular Biology
BOYNTON, W. V., Lunar and Planetary Laboratory; Planetary Sciences
BREDAS, J-L. E., Chemistry
BRILLIANT, M. H., Paediatrics; Molecular and Cellular Biology
BROWER, D. L., Molecular and Cellular Biology; Biochemistry
BROWN, M. F., Chemistry; Biochemistry
BROWN, R. H., Planetary Sciences; Lunar and Planetary Laboratory; Astronomy
BURD, G. D., Molecular and Cellular Biology; Cell Biology and Anatomy; International Studies
BURROWS, A. S., Physics; Astronomy
BUTLER, R. F., Geosciences; Arizona Research Laboratories

CALDER, W. A., III, Ecology and Evolutionary Biology
CHANDLER, V. L., Plant Science; Molecular and Cellular Biology
CHASE, C. G., Geosciences
COHEN, A. S., Geosciences; Ecology and Environmental Biology
CRANFIELD, L. M., Biochemistry; Public Health
CRESS, A. E., Radiation Oncology; Molecular and Cellular Biology
CUSANOVICH, M. A., Biochemistry; Chemistry
CUSHING, J. M., Mathematics
DAVIES, R., Atmospheric Sciences
DAVIS, O. K., Geosciences
DEAN, J. S., Dendrochronology; Anthropology
DEBRAY, S. K., Computer Science
DECELLES, P. G., Geosciences
DENTON, M. B., Chemistry; Geosciences
DIECKMANN, C. L., Biochemistry; Molecular and Cellular Biology
DOWNEY, P. J., Computer Science
DRAKE, M. J., Planetary Sciences; Lunar and Planetary Laboratory; Arizona Research Laboratories; Geosciences
ENEMARK, J. H., Chemistry
ERCOLANI, N. M., Mathematics
ERICKSON, R. P., Paediatrics; Molecular and Cellular Biology
FANG, L.-Z., Physics
FARIS, W. G., Mathematics
FINK, U., Lunar and Planetary Laboratory; Planetary Sciences
FLASCHKA, H., Mathematics
FLESSA, K. W., Geosciences
FORSTER, K. I., Psychology
FRIEDLANDER, L., Mathematics
GANGULY, T., Geosciences
GARCIA, J. D., Physics
GAY, D. A., Mathematics
GEHRELS, A. M. J. T., Lunar and Planetary Laboratory; Planetary Sciences
GEHRELS, G. E., Geosciences
GLASS, R. S., Chemistry
GLATTKE, T. J., Speech and Hearing Science; Surgery
GREENBERG, R. J., Planetary Sciences; Teaching and Teacher Education
GREENLEE, W. M., Mathematics
GRIMES, W. J., Biochemistry; Molecular and Cellular Biology
GROVE, L. C., Mathematics
GUPTA, R., Computer Science
HALLICK, R. B., Biochemistry
HAUSSLER, M. R., Biochemistry
HAYNES, C. V., Geosciences
HERMAN, B. M., Atmospheric Sciences
HILDEBRAND, J. G., Neurobiology; Biochemistry
HOLLAND, A. L., Speech and Hearing Science
HRUBY, V. J., Chemistry; Arizona Research Laboratories; Biochemistry
HSIEH, K. C., Physics
HUBBARD, W. B., Lunar and Planetary Laboratory; Planetary Sciences
HUGHES HALLETT, D. J., Mathematics
HUGHES, M. K., Dendrochronology; Watershed Management
IMPEY, C. D., Astronomy
JOHNS, K. A., Physics
JOHNSON, R. A., Geosciences
JOKIPII, J. R., Planetary Sciences; Lunar and Planetary Laboratory; Astronomy
KELLER, P. C., Chemistry
KENNEDY, C. K., Plant Pathology; Molecular and Cellular Biology
KENNEDY, T. G., Mathematics; Physics
KENNICUTT, R. C., Astronomy
KRIEG, P. A., Cell Biology and Anatomy; Molecular and Cellular Biology
KUKOLICH, S. G., Chemistry
LARSON, H. P., Lunar and Planetary Laboratory; Planetary Sciences
LEAVITT, S. W., Dendrochronology
LEVERMORE, C. D., Mathematics
LEWIS, J. S., Lunar and Planetary Laboratory; Planetary Sciences
LICHTENBERGER, D. L., Chemistry
LIEBERT, J. W., Astronomy
LITTLE, J. W., Biochemistry; Molecular and Cellular Biology
LOMEN, D. O., Mathematics
LOVELOCK, D., Mathematics
LUNINE, J. I., Planetary Sciences; Lunar and Planetary Laboratory; Arizona Research Laboratories; Physics
MCCALLUM, W. G., Mathematics
MCCULLEN, J. D., Physics
MCINTYRE, L., Jr, Physics
MAIER, R., Mathematics; Physics
MARDER, S. R., Chemistry; Optical Sciences
MARKOW, T. A., Ecology and Environmental Biology
MASH, E. A., Jr., Chemistry
MAZUMDAR, S., Physics; Optical Sciences
MELIA, F., Physics; Astronomy
MELOSH, H. J., Lunar and Planetary Laboratory; Planetary Sciences; Geosciences
MENDELSON, N. H., Molecular and Cellular Biology
MICHOD, R. E., Ecology and Evolutionary Biology
MIESFELD, R. L., Biochemistry; Molecular and Cellular Biology
MITTAL, Y. D., Mathematics
MOLONEY, J. V., Mathematics; Optical Sciences
MORAN, N. A., Ecology and Environmental Biology; Entomology
MOUNT, D. W., Molecular and Cellular Biology; Ecology and Environmental Biology; Biochemistry
MULLEN, S. L., Atmospheric Sciences; Hydrology and Water Resources
MYERS, E. W., Jr, Computer Science; Molecular and Cellular Biology
NEWELL, A. C., Mathematics; Arizona Research Laboratories
O'BRIEN, D. F., Chemistry; Biochemistry
OCHMAN, H., Biochemistry; Ecology and Environmental Biology; Molecular and Cellular Biology
OVERPECK, J. T., Geosciences
PALMER, J. N., Mathematics
PARKER, R. R., Molecular and Cellular Biology; Biochemistry
PARRISH-JONES, J. T., Geosciences
PATCHETT, P. J., Geosciences; Arizona Research Laboratories
PATRASCIOIU, A. N., Physics
PEMBERTON, J. E., Chemistry
POLT, R. L., Chemistry
POMEAU, Y., Mathematics
RAFELSKI, J., Physics; Arizona Research Laboratories
RIEKE, G. H., Astronomy; Planetary Sciences; Lunar and Planetary Laboratory
RIEKE, M. J., Astronomy
ROSENZWEIG, M. L., Ecology and Evolutionary Biology
RUIZ, J., Geosciences
RUTHERFOORD, J. P., Physics
RYCHLIK, M. R., Mathematics
SALZMAN, W. R., Chemistry
SARCEVIC, I., Physics
SCADRON, M. D., Physics
SCHAFFER, W. M., Ecology and Evolutionary Biology
SCHLICHTING, R. D., Computer Science
SCHMIDT, G. D., Astronomy
SHAKED, M., Mathematics
SHUPE, M. A., Physics
SMITH, M. A., Chemistry
SNODGRASS, R. T., Computer Science
STEIN, D. L., Physics
STEVENSON, F. W., Mathematics
STRITTMATTER, P. A., Astronomy
SWETNAM, T. W., Dendrochronology
SWINDLE, T. D., Lunar and Planetary Laboratory; Planetary Sciences; Geosciences
TABOR, M., Mathematics; Applied Mathematics; Physics
THAKUR, D. S., Mathematics
THOMPSON, R. I., Astronomy
TIFFT, W. G., Astronomy
TISCHLER, M. E., Biochemistry; Medicine; Physiology
TITLEY, S. R., Geosciences
TOMASKO, M. G., Lunar and Planetary Laboratory
TOUBASSI, E., Mathematics
TOUSSAINT, W. D., Physics
VANETTEN, H. D., Plant Pathology; Molecular and Cellular Biology
VELEZ, W. Y., Mathematics
VENABLE, D. L., Ecology and Evolutionary Biology
VIERLING, E., Biochemistry; Molecular and Cellular Biology
VON HOFF, D. D., Medicine; Pathology; Molecular and Cellular Biology
WALKER, F. A., Chemistry; Biochemistry
WALLACE, T. C., Jr, Geosciences
WARD, S., Molecular and Cellular Biology; Ecology and Environmental Biology
WELLS, M. A., Biochemistry
WILLOUGHBY, S. S., Mathematics
WINFREE, A. T., Ecology and Environmental Biology
WING, W. H., Physics; Optical Sciences; Arizona Research Laboratories; International Studies
WOJTKOWSKI, M. P., Mathematics
WOOLF, N. J., Astronomy
WYSOCKI, V. H., Chemistry; Biochemistry
YELLE, R. V., Planetary Sciences; Lunar and Planetary Laboratory
ZAKHAROV, V. E., Mathematics
ZANDT, G., Geosciences
ZIURYS, L. M., Chemistry; Astronomy

College of Social and Behavioral Sciences:

ADAMS, E. C., Anthropology
ANDERSON, K. S., History
ANNAS, J. E., Philosophy
BARNES, C. A., Psychology
BASSO, E. B., Anthropology
BECHTEL, R. B., Psychology; Renewable Natural Resources
BECKER, J. V., Psychology; Psychiatry
BEEZLEY, W. H., History
BERGENSEN, A. J., Sociology
BERNSTEIN, A. E., History
BERNSTEIN, G. L., History
BEVER, T. G., Psychology; Linguistics; Cognitive Science
BONINE, M. E., Near Eastern Studies; Geography and Regional Development
BOOTZIN, R. R., Psychology; Psychiatry
BUCHANAN, A. E., Philosophy
CHALMERS, D. J., Philosophy
CHAVES, M. A., Sociology
CLARKE, J. W., Political Science
COSGROVE, R. A., History
DANIEL, T. C., Psychology; Renewable Natural Resources
DE LA TORRE, A. I., Mexican American Studies–Public Health
DEAN, J. S., Dendrochronology; Anthropology
DEMERS, R. A., Linguistics
DEUTSCH, S. J., History
DEVER, W. G., Near Eastern Studies
DINNERSTEIN, L., History
DINNERSTEIN, M., Women's Studies
DOBSON, M. V., Ophthalmology
EATON, R. M., History
ESTRADA, A. L., Mexican American Studies
FERNANDEZ, C., Sociology
FINAN, T. J., Anthropology
FISH, P. R., Anthropology
FORSTER, K. I., Psychology

FUCHS, E., Near Eastern Studies; Judaic Studies
GALASKIEWICZ, J. J., Sociology
GAMAL, A. S., Near Eastern Studies
GARCIA, J. A., Political Science
GARCIA, J. R., History
GARRETT, M. F., Psychology; Linguistics; Speech and Hearing Studies
GIBSON, L. J., Geography
GLISKY, E. L., Psychology
GLITTENBERG, J. E., Nursing; Psychiatry; Anthropology
GOLDMAN, A. I., Philosophy
GREENBERG, J. B., Anthropology
GUMERMAN, G. J., Anthropology
HAMMOND, M., Linguistics
HARNISH, R. M., Philosophy; Linguistics
HEALEY, R. A., Philosophy
HILL, J. H., Anthropology
HURT, C. D., Information Resources and Library Science; Communication
JACOB, C. S., Communication
JOHNSON, J. W., Journalism
KARANT-NUNN, S. C., History
KASZNIAK, A. W., Psychology; Psychiatry; Neurology
KENNEDY, E. J., Women's Studies; Anthropology
KING, J. E., Psychology; Anthropology
KRAMER, C., Anthropology
LANGENDOEN, D. T., Linguistics
LANSING, J. S., Anthropology
LONGACRE, W. A., Anthropology
MCNAUGHTON, B. L., Psychology; Physiology
MCPHERSON, J. M., Sociology
MALONEY, J. C., Philosophy
MARSH, S. E., Arid Lands; Geography and Regional Development
MARSTON, S., Geography and Regional Development
MARTINEZ, O., History
MISHLER, W. T., II, Political Science
MOLM, L. D., Sociology
MORBECK, M. E., Anthropology
MORILL, C. K., Sociology; Psychology; Communication
MULLIGAN, G. F., Geography and Regional Development
NADEL, L., Psychology
NADER, H., History
NICHOLS, R. L., History
NICHTER, M., Anthropology; Public Health
NORRANDER, B., Political Science
OLSEN, J. W., Anthropology
PAREZO, N. J., American Indian Studies; Anthropology
PETERSON, M. A., Psychology
PHILIPS, S. U., Anthropology
PIATTELLI-PALMARINI, M., Cognitive Science
PLANE, D., Geography and Regional Development
POLLOCK, J. L., Philosophy
RAGIN, C. C., Sociology
REID, J. J., Jr, Anthropology
ROHRBAUGH, M. J., Psychology; Family and Consumer Sciences
ROWE, D. C., Family and Consumer Sciences; Psychology
SALES, B. D., Psychology; Psychiatry; Law
SCHIFFER, M. B., Anthropology
SCHLEGEL, A. E., Anthropology
SCHMIDTZ, D. J., Philosophy; Economics
SCHWARTZ, G. E., Psychology; Psychiatry; Neurology; Medicine
SCHWARTZ, J. E., Political Science
SECHREST, L., Psychology
SHARKEY, J. E., Journalism
SHELDON, B. E., Information Resources and Library Science
SHERIDAN, T. E., Anthropology
SHOHAM, V., Psychology
SILVERS, A. L., Public Administration and Policy
SMITH, C. D., Jr, Near Eastern Studies
SMITH-LOVIN, D. L., Sociology
SNOW, D. A., Sociology
STEVENS, S. J., Research Professor
STINI, W. A., Anthropology; Family and Community Medicine; Public Health
SULLIVAN, M. P., Political Science
VOLGY, T. J., Political Science
WALKER, H. A., Sociology
WEINER, D. R., History
WELSH, W. A., Political Science; Family and Consumer Medicine
WENK, G. L., Psychology; Neurology
WILLIAMS, E. J., Political Science
WILLIAMS, J. M., Psychology
ZEGURA, S. L., Anthropology
ZEPEDA, O., Linguistics

Arizona International College:
AMEGAGO, M. M. K.
BIXBY, B. R.
BUKHARDT, P. E.
BURGESS, K. H.
CONTERIS, H. J.
DURAN-CERDA, D. M.
FERNANDO, J. L.
GRIJALVA, M. A.
HELGERT, J. P.
PELTIER, J.
POPE, E. R.
SCOTT, A. G.
SHERMAN, P. M.
SPATARO, L. P.
TAL, K.

Optical Sciences Center:
DERENIAK, E. L., Optical Sciences; Electrical and Computer Engineering
FALCO, C. M., Optical Sciences; Arizona Research Laboratories
FRIEDEN, B. R., Optical Sciences
GIBBS, H. M., Optical Sciences
MANSURIPUR, M., Optical Sciences
MARATHAY, A. S., Optical Sciences
MEYSTRE, P., Optical Sciences; Physics
PEYGHAMBARIAN, N. N., Optical Sciences; Materials Science and Engineering
POWELL, R. C., Optical Sciences; Materials Science and Engineering
SARGENT, M., III, Optical Sciences
SARID, D., Optical Sciences; Arizona Research Laboratories
SASIAN, J. M., Optical Sciences; Astronomy
SHACK, R. V., Optical Sciences
SHOEMAKER, R. L., Optical Sciences; Chemistry; Radiology
WRIGHT, E. M., Optical Sciences; Physics
WYANT, J. C., Optical Sciences; Electrical and Computer Engineering

Other academic units:
ACOSTA, J. J., Military Science Tactics
CHRISTMAN, W. E., Naval Science
DYCHE, D. D., Military Aerospace Studies
WILKINSON, R. H., Humanities Programme

ATTACHED RESEARCH INSTITUTE

Mount Graham International Observatory: operated by Steward Observatory, the research arm of the Dept of Astronomy; see separate entry under Research Institutes.

UNIVERSITY OF PHOENIX

4615 East Elwood, Phoenix, AZ 85040
Telephone: (480) 966-9577
Internet: www.phoenix.edu

Founded 1976
Private control

Pres.: Dr LAURA PALMER NOONE
Provost and Senior Vice-Pres. for Academic Affairs: CRAIG SWENSON
Senior Vice-Pres. for Public Affairs: TERRI HEDEGAARD-BISHOP
Exec. Vice-Pres.: BOB BARKER
Vice-Pres. for Finance: LARRY FLEISCHER
Vice-Pres. for University Services: NINA OMELCHENKO
CEO, Online Campus: BRIAN MUELLER
Number of teachers: 9,758
Number of students: 125,364

163 Campuses and learning centres in the USA, Canada and Puerto Rico; also Internet-based degree courses.

WESTERN INTERNATIONAL UNIVERSITY

9215 North Black Canyon Highway, Phoenix, AZ 85021

Telephone: (602) 943-2311
Fax: (602) 371-8637
E-mail: wiuinfo@apollogrp.edu
Internet: www.wintu.edu

Founded 1978
Private control

Registrar: HUE HASLIM

Campuses in China, India and Netherlands; undergraduate courses in: accounting, behavioural science, business, business admin., human resource management, information technology, int. business, management; graduate courses in: finance, information systems engineering, information technology, int. business, management, marketing.

BRANCH CAMPUSES

Chandler East Valley Campus: Suite 101, 55 North Arizona Place, Chandler, AZ 85225; tel. (602) 943-2311; fax (480) 726-3068.

Fort Huachuca Campus: Buffalo Soldier Training and Education Center/Rascon Building #52104. ATZS-HRH-E, Fort Huachuca, AZ 85613-6000; tel. (520) 459-5040; fax (520) 459-7571.

Peoria Campus: Suite 100, 14100 North 83rd Ave, Peoria, AZ 85381; tel. (602) 943-2311; fax (602) 429-1433.

Scottsdale Campus: Suite 120, 8860 East Chaparral Rd, Scottsdale, AZ 85250; tel. (602) 943-2311; fax (480) 850-1338.

ARKANSAS

ARKANSAS BAPTIST COLLEGE

1621 Dr Martin Luther King Dr., Little Rock, AR 72202

Telephone: (501) 370-4000
Internet: www.arkansasbaptist.edu
Private control

Founded 1885

Pres.: FITZ HILL
Vice-Pres.: JOHNNY JONES
Registrar: FREDDIE FOX
Librarian: SONYA BELL

DEANS

Scholars College: Dr MIRON BILLINGSLEY
School of Business and Applied Science: CONSTANCE MEADORS
School of Liberal Arts and Social Sciences: Dr NANCY GREER-WILLIAMS

ARKANSAS STATE UNIVERSITY

State Univ., AR 72467
Telephone: (870) 972-2030
Fax: (870) 972-2036
Internet: www.astate.edu

Founded 1909
Academic year: August to July

Pres.: Dr J. LESLIE WYATT
Vice-Pres. for Finance and Admin.: JENNUS L. BURTON
Vice-Pres. for Univ. Advancement: CRISTIAN MURDOCK
Chancellor: Dr ROBERT POTTS

Vice-Chancellor for Academic Affairs and Research: Dr DANIEL HOWARD
Vice-Chancellor for Student Affairs: Dr WILLIAM R. STRIPLING
Registrar: TRACY FINCH
Dean of Library: JEFF BAILEY

Library of 597,000 vols, 524,000 govt documents, 587,000 microfilm items, 21,000 audio-visual items, 1,800 periodicals
Number of teachers: 632
Number of students: 18,947 (ASU System)

Main campus in Jonesboro, also campuses in Beebe, Mountain Home, Newport, Heber Springs, Paragould; Technical Center at Marked Tree

DEANS

College of Agriculture: Dr GREGORY C. PHILLIPS
College of Business: Dr LEN FREY
College of Communications: Dr RUSSELL E. SHAIN
College of Education: Dr JOHN BEINEKE
College of Engineering: Dr DAVID B. BEASLEY
College of Fine Arts: Dr DANIEL REEVES
College of Humanities and Social Sciences: Dr CAROL O'CONNOR
College of Nursing and Health Professions: Dr SUSAN N. HANRAHAN
College of Sciences and Mathematics: Dr ANDREW SUSTICH
Univ. College: Dr LYNITA COOKSEY
Graduate School: Dr ANDREW SUSTICH
Ind. Dept of Military Science: Lt-Col JEFFERY HELMS (Chair.)
Honors College: Dr ANDREW SUSTICH

ARKANSAS TECH UNIVERSITY

1605 Coliseum Dr., Russellville, AR 72801
Telephone: (479) 968-0389
Fax: (479) 964-0839
Internet: www.atu.edu

Founded 1909, present name and status 1976

Pres.: ROBERT CHARLES BROWN
Vice-Pres. for Academic Affairs: Dr JACK HAMM
Vice-Pres. for Admin. and Finance: DAVID MOSELEY
Vice-Pres. for Devt: JAYNE W. JONES
Vice-Pres. for Student Services: GARY M. BILLER
Chancellor of Ozark Campus: Dr JO ALICE BLONDIN
Registrar: C. GLENN SHEETS
Dir of Library: BILL PARTON

Library of 142,000 vols, 810,000 microforms, 88,000 govt documents and 1,245 current periodicals
Number of teachers: 300
Number of students: 5,855

DEANS

School of Business: THOMAS P. TYLER
School of Community Education and Professional Devt: MARY ANN ROLLINS
School of Education: GLENN SHEETS
School of Liberal and Fine Arts: GEORGENA D. DUNCAN
School of Physical and Life Sciences: RICHARD R. COHOON
School of Systems Science: JOHN W. WATSON
Graduate Studies: ELDON G. CLARY, Jr.

CENTRAL BAPTIST COLLEGE

1501 College Ave, Conway, AR 72034
Telephone: (501) 329-6872
Fax: (501) 329-2941
E-mail: info@cbc.edu
Internet: www.cbc.edu

Founded 1952 as Conway Baptist College; present name 1962
Private control

Pres.: TERRY KIMBROW
Vice-Pres. for Academic Affairs: Dr GARY MCALLISTER
Vice-Pres. for Financial Affairs: DON JONES
Vice-Pres. for Student Services: SANCY FAULK
Registrar: PHYLIS HOFFMANN
Librarian: ANNE CLEMENTS

Library of 40,000 books, periodicals, tapes, CDs, video cassettes and microforms
Number of teachers: 50 full-time and part-time
Number of students: 400

Depts of behavioural sciences, bible, business, fine arts, health and physical education, literature and language arts, maths and science, social studies.

HARDING UNIVERSITY

915 East Market Ave, Searcy, AR 72149
Telephone: (501) 279-4000
Fax: (501) 279-4865
E-mail: admissions@harding.edu
Internet: www.harding.edu

Founded 1924

Pres.: DAVID B. BURKS
Vice-Pres. for Academic Affairs: NEALE T. PRYOR
Registrar: JANICE HURD
Librarian: ANN DIXON

Library of 444,382 vols, 1,397 current periodicals, maps, audio visual items, etc.
Number of teachers: 217
Number of students: 6,100

DEANS

College of Arts and Humanities: Dr DENNIS ORGAN
College of Bible and Religion: BRUCE MCLARTY
College of Business Admin.: Dr BRYAN D. BURKS
College of Education: Dr LEWIS 'TONY' FINLEY
College of Nursing: Dr CATHLEEN M. SCULTZ
College of Sciences: Dr TRAVIS THOMPSON

HENDERSON STATE UNIVERSITY

1100 Henderson St, Arkadelphia, AR 71999-0001
Telephone: (870) 230-5000
Fax: (870) 230-5147
Internet: www.hsu.edu

Founded 1890 as church-related college; became a state institution in 1929
Academic year: August to May

Pres.: Dr CHARLES D. DUNN
Vice-Pres. for Academic Affairs: Dr ROBERT E. HOUSTON
Vice-Pres. for Finance and Admin.: BOBBY G. JONES
Vice-Pres. for Student Services: GAIL STEPHENS
Vice-Pres. for Univ. and Community Relations: DORIS N. WRIGHT
Registrar: TOM GATTIN
Dir of Learning Resources: ROBERT YEHL

Library of 250,000 vols
Number of teachers: 175
Number of students: 3,636

DEANS

Ellis College of Arts and Sciences: Dr MARALYN SOMMER
Graduate School: Dr MARCK L. BEGGS
School of Business: PAUL HUO
Teachers' College: JUDY HARRISON

HENDRIX COLLEGE

1600 Washington Ave, Conway, AR 72032
Telephone: (501) 329-6811
Fax: (501) 450-1200
Internet: www.hendrix.edu

Founded 1876

Pres.: Dr J. TIMOTHY CLOYD
Provost: Dr ROBERT ENTZMINGER
Exec. Vice-Pres.: ROCK JONES
Vice-Pres. for Business and Finance: ROB YOUNG
Vice-Pres. for Enrolment: KAREN FOUST
Vice-Pres. for Student Affairs: JOYCE M. HARDIN
Registrar: XINYING WANG
Library Director: AMANDA MOORE

Depts of biology, chemistry, mathematics and computer science, physics, art, English, foreign languages, music, philosophy, religion, theatre arts and dance, economics and business, education, history, kinesiology, politics and int. relations, psychology, sociology

Library of 190,000 vols
Number of teachers: 85
Number of students: 1,094

JOHN BROWN UNIVERSITY

2000 West University St, Siloam Springs, AR 72761
Telephone: (479) 5249500
E-mail: jbuinfo@jbu.edu
Internet: www.jbu.edu

Founded 1919 as Southwestern Collegiate Institute, name changed to John E. Brown College 1920, present name 1934
Private control

Undergraduate academic divs: biblical studies, business, communication and fine arts, education, engineering and construction management, general studies, humanities and social sciences, natural sciences; depts in the graduate studies division: Christian ministry, counselling, leadership and ethics

Pres.: Dr CHARLES POLLARD
Vice-Pres. for Academic Affairs: Dr ED ERICSON, III
Vice-Pres. for Enrollment Management: DON CRANDALL
Vice-Pres. for Finance and Admin.: KIM HADLEY
Vice-Pres. for Student Devt: Dr STEPHEN BEERS
Vice-Pres. for Univ. Advancement: Dr JAMES KRALL
Dean for Graduate Studies: Dr RICHARD ELLIS
Dean for Undergraduate Studies: Dr ROBERT NORWOOD
Registrar: BECKY LAMBERT
Library Director: MARY HABERMAS

Library of 120,000 items, incl. 4,000 periodicals
Number of teachers: 187 (92 full-time, 95 part-time)
Number of students: 2,000

LYON COLLEGE

POB 2317, Batesville, AR 72503-2317
Telephone: (870) 793-9813
Fax: (870) 698-4622
Internet: www.lyon.edu

Founded 1872; name changed from Arkansas College 1994
Academic year: September to May

Pres.: WALTER B. ROETTGER
Vice-Pres. for Academic Services: JOHN M. PEEK
Vice-Pres. for Business and Finance: KENNETH J. RUETER
Vice-Pres. for Enrollment Services: DENNY G. BARDOS
Vice-Pres. for Institutional Advancement: TIMOTHY L. BRUNER
Vice-Pres. for Student Life and Dean of Students: Dr F. BRUCE JOHNSTON

Library Dir: DEAN COVINGTON
Library of 150,000 vols
Number of teachers: 45
Number of students: 540

Depts of: accounting, anthropology, art, biochemistry, biology, business administration, chemistry, computer science, economics, education, English, French, history, mathematics, music, philosophy and religion, physics, political science, psychology, Spanish, theatre.

OUACHITA BAPTIST UNIVERSITY

410 Ouachita St, Arkadelphia, AR 71998
Telephone: (870) 245-5000
Fax: (870) 245-5412
Internet: www.obu.edu

Founded 1886 as Ouachita Baptist College, present name 1965
Private control
Academic year: June to May

Pres.: REX M. HORNE, Jr
Vice-Pres. for Academic Affairs: STAN POOLE
Vice-Pres. for Communications: TRENNIS HENDERSON
Vice-Pres. for Devt: TERRY PEEPLES
Vice-Pres. for Institutional Advancement: WESLEY KLUCK
Chancellor: BEN ELROD
Dean of Students: KELDON HENLEY
Registrar: JUDY JONES
Dir for Library Services: Dr RAY GRANADE

Number of teachers: 107 full-time
Number of students: 1,504

DEANS
School of Business: BRYAN MCKINNEY
School of Christian Studies: J. DANIEL HAYS
School of Education: MERRIBETH BRUNING
School of Fine Arts: D. SCOTT HOLSCLAW
School of Humanities: JEFF ROOT
School of Natural Sciences: JOE JEFFERS
School of Social Sciences: HAL BASS

PHILANDER SMITH COLLEGE

1 Trudie Kibbe Reed Dr., Little Rock, AR 72202
Telephone: (501) 375-9845
Fax: (501) 370-5277
E-mail: registrar@philander.edu
Internet: www.philander.edu

Founded 1877 as Walden Seminary; present name 1882
Private control
Academic year: August to July

Pres.: Dr WALTER KIMBROUGH
Vice-Pres. for Academic Affairs: Dr JOHN SIMPSON
Vice-Pres. for Fiscal Affairs and Chief Financial Officer: GERALD B. COLEMAN
Vice-Pres. for Institutional Advancement: Dr DELIA ANDERSON
Vice-Pres. for Student Affairs: Dr JULIANA MOSELEY ANDERSON
Registrar: BERTHA OWENS
Dir Library Services: CHARLES ROGERS

Divs of: humanities, education, business and economics, natural and physical sciences, social sciences.

SOUTHERN ARKANSAS UNIVERSITY

100 East University, Magnolia, AR 71753-5000
Telephone: (870) 235-4000
Internet: www.saumag.edu

Founded 1911 as Third District Agricultural School; present name 1976
Academic year: August to July

Pres.: Dr DAVID RANKIN
Vice-Pres. for Academic Affairs: Dr CORBET J. LAMKIN
Vice-Pres. for Administration and General Counsel: ROGER GILES
Vice-Pres. for Finance: DARRELL MORRISON
Vice-Pres. for Student Affairs: Dr DONNA ALLEN
Dean of Students: BRIAN BERRY
Dean of Enrollment Services: SARA JENNINGS
Registrar: ED NIPPER
Library Dir: PEGGY WALTERS

Library of 150,000 vols
Number of students: 3,035

DEANS
College of Business: EARL STENNIS
College of Liberal and Performing Arts: DAVID L. CROUSE
School of Education: Dr RUBY BURGESS
School of Graduate Studies: Dr KIM BLOSS-BERNARD
School of Science and Technology: Dr JOE WINSTEAD

UNIVERSITY OF ARKANSAS

Fayetteville, AR 72701
Telephone: (479) 575-2000
Fax: (479) 575-7515
E-mail: uofa@uark.edu
Internet: www.uark.edu

Founded 1871
Academic year: August to May

Chancellor: Dr JOHN A. WHITE
Provost and Vice-Chancellor for Academic Affairs: Dr BOB SMITH
Vice-Chancellor for Finance and Admin.: Dr DONALD PETERSON
Vice-Chancellor for Govt and Community Relations: RICHARD B. HUDSON
Vice-Chancellor for Student Affairs: Dr JOHNETTA CROSS BRAZZELL
Vice-Chancellor for Univ. Advancement: Dr G. DAVID GEARHART
Dean of Students: Dr DANNY PUGH
Dir of Libraries: CAROLYN HENDERSON

Library of 1,656,907 vols
Number of teachers: 839 (main campus; 792 full-time, 47 part-time)
Number of students: 16,499 (main campus)

DEANS
Dale Bumpers College of Agricultural, Food and Life Sciences: GREG WEIDEMANN
J. W. Fulbright College of Arts and Sciences: Dr DON BOBBITT
College of Business: ANTHONY F. CHELTE
College of Education and Health Professions: Dr REED GREENWOOD
College of Engineering: ASHOK SAXENA
Graduate School: Dr COLLIS R. GEREN
School of Law: CYNDI NANCE
School of Architecture: JEFF SHANNON
School of Continuing Education: DONNIE DUTTON
Clinton School of Public Service: JAMES L. RUTHERFORD

UNIVERSITY OF ARKANSAS AT LITTLE ROCK

2801 South University Ave, Little Rock, AR 72204
Telephone: (501) 569-3000
Internet: www.ualr.edu

Founded 1927

Chancellor: Dr JOEL E. ANDERSON
Provost and Vice-Chancellor for Academic Affairs: DAVID BELCHER
Vice-Chancellor for Educational and Student Services: Dr CHARLES W. DONALDSON
Vice-Chancellor for Finance and Administration: LUCIAN SHOCKEY
Vice-Chancellor for Univ. Advancement: BILL WALKER
Dir Ottenheimer Library: BILL TRAYLOR
Dir Law Library: A. MICHAEL BEAIRD

Library of 500,000 vols, 11,000 electronic books, 28,000 journals, 3,600 periodicals
Number of teachers: 1,202 (675 full-time, 527 part-time)
Number of students: 10,889

DEANS
College of Arts, Humanities and Social Sciences: Dr DEBORAH BALDWIN
College of Business Administration: Dr WILLIAM C. GOOLSBY
College of Education: Dr ANGELA MAYNARD SEWALL
College of Professional Studies: Dr ANGELA BRENTON
College of Science and Mathematics: Dr MICHAEL LEDBETTER
Donaghey College of Information Science and Systems Engineering: Dr MARY L. GOOD
Graduate Institute of Technology: Dr M. KEITH HUDSON (Dir)
Graduate School: Dr RICHARD H. HANSON
School of Law: CHARLES W. GOLDNER, Jr.

UNIVERSITY OF ARKANSAS AT MONTICELLO

Monticello, AR 71655
Telephone: (870) 460-1026
Fax: (870) 460-1933
Internet: www.uamont.edu

Founded 1909

Chancellor: H. JACK LASSITER
Vice-Chancellor for Academic Affairs: Dr R. DAVID RAY
Vice-Chancellor for Finance and Administration: JAY JONES
Vice-Chancellor for Student Affairs: Dr CLAY E. BROWN
Registrar: Dr DEBBIE K. BRYANT
Library Dir: SANDRA CAMPBELL

Library of 500,000 items incl. books, bound periodicals, govt documents and 1,200 current periodicals
Number of teachers: 100
Number of students: 1,900

CHAIRS
Div. of Agriculture: Dr KELLY BRYANT
Div. of Computer Information Systems: Dr JIM ROIGER
Div. of Music: J. ANNETTE HALL
Div. of Nursing: Dr LARRY EUSTACE
General Studies: Dr RANELLE EUBANKS

DEANS
School of Arts and Humanities: Dr ERIN O'NEILL
School of Business: Dr LOUIS JAMES
School of Education: Dr PEGGY DOSS
School of Forest Resources: Dr RICHARD A. KLUENDER
School of Mathematics and Natural Sciences: Dr JOHN T. ANNULIS
School of Social and Behavioural Sciences: Dr VANNEISE COLLINS

UNIVERSITY OF ARKANSAS AT PINE BLUFF

1200 North University Dr., Pine Bluff, AR 71601
Telephone: (870) 575-8000
Internet: www.uapb.edu

Founded 1873

Liberal arts and land-grant institution

Chancellor: LAWRENCE A. DAVIS, Jr
Vice-Chancellor for Academic Affairs: Dr MARY E. BENJAMIN

Vice-Chancellor for Finance and Administration: JOSÉ R. ARJONA
Vice-Chancellor for Student Affairs: Dr BOBBIE A. IRVINS
Dir Library: EDWARD J. FONTENETTE
Library of 220,000 vols
Number of students: 3,710

DEANS
School of Agriculture, Fisheries and Human Sciences: Dr JACQUELINE W. MCCRAY
School of Business and Management: Dr ANDREW HONEYCUTT
School of Education: Dr CALVIN JOHNSON

UNIVERSITY OF ARKANSAS FOR MEDICAL SCIENCES

4301 West Markham St, Little Rock, AR 72205
Telephone: (501) 686-7000
Internet: www.uams.edu
Pres.: B. ALAN SUGG
Chancellor: Dr I. DODD WILSON
Exec. Vice-Chancellor: JOHN SHOCK
Vice-Chancellor for Academic Affairs and Research Admin.: Dr LARRY D. MILNE
Vice-Chancellor for Admin. and Governmental Affairs: TOM S. BUTLER
Vice-Chancellor for Campus Operations: LEO GEHRING
Vice-Chancellor for Clinical Programs: RICHARD PIERSON
Vice-Chancellor for Devt and Alumni Affairs: JOHN I. BLOHM
Vice-Chancellor for Finance: MELONY GOODHAND
Vice-Chancellor for Institutional Compliance: ROBERT BISHOP
Vice-Chancellor for Regional Programs: Dr CHARLES O. CRANFORD
Library Dir: MARY L. RYAN
Library of 46,120 vols
Number of teachers: 1,031
Number of students: 2,320

DEANS
College of Health Related-Professions: Dr RONALD H. WINTERS
College of Medicine: Dr DEBRA FISER
College of Nursing: Dr CLAUDIA P. BARONE
College of Pharmacy: Dr STEPHANIE GARDNER
College of Public Health: Dr JAMES M. RACZYNSKI
Graduate School: Dr ROBERT E. MCGEHEE

UNIVERSITY OF CENTRAL ARKANSAS

201 Donaghey Ave, Conway, AR 72035
Telephone: (501) 450-5000
Fax: (501) 450-5734
E-mail: admissions@uca.edu
Internet: www.uca.edu
Founded 1907 as Arkansas State Normal School; name changed to Arkansas State Teachers College 1925, State College of Arkansas 1967; present name 1975
Academic year: August to August
Pres.: ALLEN MEADORS
Executive Vice-Pres.: BARBARA ANDERSON
Vice-Pres. for Admin.: JACK GILLEAN
Vice-Pres. for Financial Services: PAUL MCLENDON
Vice-Pres. for Institutional Advancement and Development: KELLEY ERSTIN
Vice-Pres. for Student Services: RONNIE WILLIAMS
Provost and Dean of the Faculty: Dr A. GABRIEL ESTEBAN
Dean of Students: Dr GARY ROBERTS
Registrar: ANTHONY D. SITZ
Library Dir: ART LICHTENSTEIN
Library of 400,000 vols
Number of teachers: 382 (full-time)
Number of students: 8,481

DEANS
College of Business Administration: Dr PATRICIA CANTRELL
College of Education: Dr LARRY ROBINSON
College of Fine Arts and Communication: Dr ROLLIN POTTER
College of Health and Applied Sciences: Dr NEIL W. HATTLESTAD
College of Liberal Arts: Dr MAURICE LEE
College of Natural Science and Mathematics: Dr STEPHEN SEIDMAN
Undergraduate Studies: Dr SALLY A. RODEN
Graduate School: Dr ELAINE MCNIECE

UNIVERSITY OF THE OZARKS

415 North College Ave, Clarksville, AR 72830-2880
Telephone: (501) 979-1000
Fax: (501) 979-1355
E-mail: admiss@ozarks.edu
Internet: www.ozarks.edu
Founded 1834 as Cane Hill School; present name since 1987
Pres.: Dr RICK NIECE
Exec. Vice-Pres.: STEVE EDMISTEN
Vice-Pres. for Academic Affairs: Dr DANIEL TADDIE
Dean of Admissions and Financial Aid: JANA HART
Dean of Enrolment Management: KIM MYRICK
Dean of Students: JOE HOING
Registrar: WILMA HARRIS
Library Dir: STUART STELZER
Divs of: business, communications and govt; education; humanities and fine arts; sciences and mathematics
Library of 80,000 vols, 40,000 govt documents, 10,000 microfilms, 12,000 bound periodicals, 480 current periodicals
Number of teachers: 49
Number of students: 622

WILLIAMS BAPTIST COLLEGE

60 West Fulbright Ave, Walnut Ridge, AR 72476
Telephone: (870) 886-6741
Fax: (870) 886-3924
E-mail: admissions@wbcoll.edu
Internet: www.wbcoll.edu
Founded 1941 as Southern Baptist College; present name 1991
Private control
Pres.: Dr JEROL B. SWAIM
Academic Dean: Dr KENNETH STARTUP
Registrar: TONYA BOLTON
Dir Library: MARILYN GOODWIN
Library of 75,000 vols
Number of students: 691
Areas of study: art, education, biblical studies, biology, business administration, church music, computer information science, English, psychology, history, liberal arts, physical education, youth ministry.

CALIFORNIA

ACADEMY OF ART UNIVERSITY

79 New Montgomery St, San Francisco, CA 94105
Telephone: (415) 274-2200
E-mail: info@academyart.edu
Internet: www.academyart.edu
Founded 1929
Private control
Pres.: ELISA STEPHENS
Library Dir: KERRI SHAFFER CARTER (acting)
Library of 30,000 vols
Number of students: 6,500
Schools of advertising, animation and visual effects, architecture, computer arts: new media, digital arts and communication, fashion, fine art, graphic design, illustration, industrial design, interior architecture and design, motion pictures and television, photography.

AFI CONSERVATORY

2021 North Western Ave, Los Angeles, CA 90027-1657
Telephone: (323) 856-7628
Fax: (323) 467-4578
Internet: www.afi.com
Founded 1969
Private control
Dir and CEO: JEAN PICKER FIRSTENBERG
Chair.: HOWARD STRINGER
Dean: ROBERT MANDEL
Artistic Dirs: ROGER BIRNBAUM, FRANK PIERSON
Exec. Vice-Dean: JOE PETRICCA
Vice-Dean for Fellow Affairs: SHEILA SULLIVAN
Vice-Dean for Production and Post-Production: PHILLIP LINSON
Library of 14,000 vols, 100 journals, 5,000 film scripts, 4,000 television scripts; spec. collns Martin Scorsese, Fritz Lang, Robert Aldrich, Charles Feldman
Depts of cinematography, directing, editing, producing, production design, screenwriting; sound stage and post-production facilities.

ALLIANT INTERNATIONAL UNIVERSITY

10455 Pomerado Rd, San Diego, CA 92131-1799
Telephone: (858) 635-4000
E-mail: admissions@alliant.edu
Internet: www.alliant.edu
Founded 2001, merger of California School of Professional Psychology and United States Int. Univ.
Private control
Language of instruction: English
Academic year: August to May
6 Campuses in Fresno, Irvine, Los Angeles, Sacramento, San Diego, San Francisco; also in Mexico (Mexico City)
Pres.: Dr GEOFFREY COX
Provost and Vice-Pres. for Academic Affairs: Dr RUSS NEWMAN
Vice-Pres. for Devt and Univ. Relations: JOHN DE MICHELE
Vice-Pres. for Finance and Strategic Planning: TARUN BHATIA
Vice-Pres. for Int. Relations: TERENCE BARBER
Vice-Pres. for Admin. and Gen. Counsel: JENNIFER TREESE WILSON
Vice-Pres. for Student Affairs: JENNIFER TREESE WILSON
Vice-Pres. for Undergraduates: Dr ERIC GRAVENBERG
Chief Human Resources Officer: KRISTINA COMBS
Dir of Communications: NICOLETTE TOUSSAINT
Dir of Students: CRAIG BREWER
Univ. Librarian: SCOTT ZIMMER
Library of 136,471 vols, 10,065 online vols, 375 print journals, 4,945 electronic journals, 55 research databases, 3,007 video cassettes and DVDs, 892 audio cassettes, 4,463 psychological tests
Number of teachers: 200
Number of students: 4,236

DEANS

California School of Forensic Studies: Dr Eric Hickey
California School of Professional Psychology: Dr Morgan Sammons
Marshall Goldsmith School of Management: Jim Goodrich
San Francisco Law School: Jane Gamp
Shirley Hufstedler School of Education: Dr Karen Schuster Webb

AMERICAN BAPTIST SEMINARY OF THE WEST

2606 Dwight Way, Berkeley, CA 94704
Telephone: (510) 841-1905
Fax: (510) 841-2446
E-mail: admissions@absw.edu
Internet: www.absw.edu
Founded 1968
Private control (part of the Graduate Theological Union)
Pres.: Dr Keith A. Russell
Vice-Pres: Michelle M. Holmes
Dean of Faculty: Judy Yates Siker
Registrar: Annie Russell
Graduate areas of study: biblical studies, theology, ethics, church history, arts of ministry, history, social sciences, foreign languages, social theory, psychology, art, liturgical studies, Christian spirituality.

AMERICAN CONSERVATORY THEATER

6th Fl., 30 Grant Ave, San Francisco, CA 94108-5800
Telephone: (415) 834-3200
Internet: www.act-sf.org
Founded 1965
Private control
Language of instruction: English
Academic year: September to May
Graduate area of study: fine arts
Artistic Dir: Carey Perloff
Conservatory Dir: Melissa Smith
Exec. Dir: Ellen Richard
Producing Dir: James Haire
Library of 10,000 vols
Number of students: 1,900

AMERICAN JEWISH UNIVERSITY

15600 Mulholland Dr., Bel Air, CA 90077
Telephone: (310) 476-9777
E-mail: admissions@ajula.edu
Internet: www.ajula.edu
Founded 1947
Private control
Academic year: August to May
Pres.: Dr Robert Wexler
Sr Vice-Pres. and Provost: Dr Mark Bookman
Vice-Pres. for Academic Affairs: Dr Lois Hecht Oppenheim
Vice-Pres. for Business, Admin. and Technology: Zofia Yalovsky
Vice-Pres. and Dean for Continuing Education and Extended Univ.: Gady Levy
Vice-Pres. for Devt: Rabbi Jay Strear
Rector: Rabbi Dr Elliot Dorff
Registrar: Arnie Weisberg
Library Dir: Paul Miller
Library of 120,000 vols

DEANS

College of Arts and Sciences: Dr Paula Stern
Department of Continuing Education: Gady Levy
Fingerhut School of Education: Rami Wernik (acting)
Graduate Programmes: Nina Lieberman-Giladi
Ziegler School of Rabbinic Studies: Rabbi Bradley Shavit Artson

DIRECTORS

Graduate Programmes in Nonprofit Management: Dr Beryl Geber
Whizin Center: Dr Ronald Wolfson

ARMSTRONG UNIVERSITY

1608 Webster St, Oakland, CA 94612
Telephone: (510) 835-7900
Fax: (510) 835-1670
E-mail: au@armstrong-u.edu
Internet: www.armstrong-u.edu
Founded 1918
President: Michael T. C. Hwang
Registrar: Owais Qureshi
Librarian: Sara O'Keefe
Library of 15,000 vols
Number of teachers: 28
Number of students: 200
Graduate and undergraduate courses in accounting, international business, marketing, finance, management and computer management science.

ART CENTER COLLEGE OF DESIGN

1700 Lida St, Pasadena, CA 91103
Telephone: (626) 396-2200
Fax: (626) 405-9104
E-mail: mktngcomm@artcenter.edu
Internet: www.artcenter.edu
Founded 1930
Private control
Language of instruction: English
Academic year: September to August
Undergraduate courses in advertising, environmental design, film, fine art media, graphic design, illustration, photography and imaging, product design, transportation design; graduate courses in Film, art, industrial design, media design, criticism and theory
Pres. and CEO: Lorne Buchman
Provost: Fred Fehlau
Vice-Pres. and Chief Financial Officer: Richard Haluschak
Vice-Pres. for Int. Initiatives: Mariana Amatullo
Sr Vice-Pres. for Real Estate and Operations: George Falardeau
Chief Human Resources Officer: Nancy Duggan
Vice-Pres. for Marketing and Communications: Arwin Duffy
Vice-Pres. for Admissions: Kit Baron
Vice-Pres. for Student Gallery: Stephen L. Nowlin
Chief Officer for Student Affairs: Jeffrey Hoffman
Vice-Pres. and Library Dir: Elizabeth Galloway
Registrar: William Gartrell
Number of teachers: 375
Number of students: 1,781

AZUSA PACIFIC UNIVERSITY

901 East Alosta Ave, POB 700, Azusa, CA 91702-700
Telephone: (626) 815-6000
Internet: www.apu.edu
Founded 1899
Private Christian univ.
Pres. and CEO: Dr Jon R. Wallace
Exec. Vice-Pres.and CDO: David E. Bixby
Exec. Vice-Pres. and CIO: John C. Reynolds
Sr Vice-Pres. for Student Life and Dean of Students: Terry A. Franson
Vice-Pres. for Enrollment: Deana L. Porterfield
Vice-Pres. for Legal Affairs and Community Relations: Mark S. Dickerson
Provost: Dr Michael M. White
Vice-Provost for Academic Programs and Dean of Univ. Libraries: Dr Paul W. Gray
Vice-Provost for Graduate and Adult Programs: Paul W. Gray
Vice-Provost for Undergraduate Programs: Paul W. Gray
Library of 215,000 vols, media items, 630,000 microfilms, 1,800 serial titles, 100 online databases, 23,000 electronic titles
Number of teachers: 352
Number of students: 4,564

DEANS

Center for Adult and Professional Studies: Fred Garlett
College of Liberal Arts and Sciences: David L. Weeks
School of Behavioural and Applied Sciences: Mark Stanton
School of Business and Management: Ilene L. Smith-Bezjian
School of Education: Helen Easterling Williams
School of Music: Duane Funderburk
School of Nursing: Aja Tulleners Lesh
Haggard School of Theology: David Wright

BETHANY COLLEGE

800 Bethany Dr., Scotts Valley, CA 95066
Telephone: (831) 438-3800
Fax: (831) 438-6104
E-mail: info@fc.bethany.edu
Internet: www.bethany.edu
Founded 1919
Private Christian college, affiliated to the Assemblies of God
Academic year: August to May
Pres.: Dr Máximo Rossi, Jr
Vice-Pres. for Academic Affairs: Dr Richard Israel
Vice-Pres. for Business: John Jones
Dean of Students: Dr Sharon Anderson
Registrar: Wesley Wick
Librarian: Arnold McLellan
Library of 65,000 vols, 800 magazine and journal titles
Number of teachers: 45 (incl. 23 part-time)
Number of students: 545

DEANS

School of Arts and Sciences: Don Adkins
School of Distributed Learning: Dr James W. Stewart
School of Professional Studies: Sharon Anderson
School of Theological Studies: Dr Timothy Powell

BIOLA UNIVERSITY

13800 Biola Ave, La Mirada, CA 90639-001
Telephone: (562) 903-6000
Fax: (562) 903-4761
Internet: www.biola.edu
Founded 1908
Pres.: Dr Barry Corey
Provost and Sr Vice-Pres.: Dr Gary A. Miller
Vice-Provost for Faculty Devt and Univ. Assessment: Chris Grace
Vice-Provost for Undergraduate Education: Carol Taylor
Vice-Pres. for Financial Affairs and Information Technology: Carl W. Schreiber
Vice-Pres. for Univ. Advancement: Dr Wesley K. Willmer
Vice-Pres. for Univ. Services: Ken Bascom
Dean of Student Affairs: John W. Back

Sr Director for Enrollment Management: GREGORY VAUGHAN

Library of 270,000 vols, 1,100 current periodicals

Number of teachers: 252

Number of students: 3,447

DEANS

Crowell School of Business: LARRY D. STRAND

Fine Arts and Communication: DOUG TARPLEY

Humanities: TODD PICKETT

School of Intercultural Studies: Dr F. DOUGLAS PENNOYER

School of Professional Studies: Dr IRMA D. HILL

Rosemead School of Psychology: Dr PATRICIA L. PIKE

Science: WALT STANGL

Talbot School of Theology: Dr DAVID DIRKS

BROOKS INSTITUTE OF PHOTOGRAPHY

27 E Cota St, Santa Barbara, CA 93101

Telephone: (805) 585-8000

E-mail: admissions@brooks.edu

Internet: www.brooks.edu

Founded 1945

Private control

Pres.: JOHN CALMAN

Areas of study: photography, visual communications, visual journalism, film and video production.

CALIFORNIA BAPTIST UNIVERSITY

8432 Magnolia Ave, Riverside, CA 92504

Telephone: (951) 689-5771

Fax: (951) 351-1808

E-mail: admissions@calbaptist.edu

Internet: www.calbaptist.edu

Founded 1950

Pres.: Dr RONALD L. ELLIS

Provost: Dr JONATHAN K. PARKER

Vice-Pres. for Finance and Admin.: MARK HOWE

Vice-Pres. for Institutional Advancement: BRUCE HITCHCOCK

Vice-Pres. for Marketing and Communication: Dr MARK A. WYATT

Vice-Pres. for Student Services: KENT DACUS

Dean of Students: ANTHONY LAMMONS

Registrar: SHAWNN KONING

Dir of Library Services and Information Technology: ERICA MCLAUGHLIN

Library of 76,000 vols, 36,000 microfiches, 500 journals, 1,600 video cassettes

Number of teachers: 51 full-time

Number of students: 3,400

DEANS

College of Arts and Sciences: Dr GAYNE ANACKER

School of Behavioural Sciences: Dr H. BRUCE STOKES

School of Business: Dr ANDREW HERRITY

School of Christian Ministries: Dr DAN WILSON

School of Education: Dr MARY CRIST

School of Engineering: Dr ANTHONY DONALDSON

School of Music: Dr GARY BONNER

School of Nursing: Dr CONSTANCE L. MILTON

CALIFORNIA COLLEGE OF THE ARTS

1111 Eighth St, San Francisco, CA 94107-2247

Telephone: (415) 703-9500

Fax: (415) 703-9539

E-mail: info@cca.edu

Internet: www.cca.edu

Founded 1907

Campuses in Oakland and San Francisco

Academic year: September to May

Founded 1907

Pres.: MICHAEL ROTH

Provost: STEPHEN BEAL

Vice-Pres. of Advancement: SUSAN AVILA

Vice-Pres. of Communications: CHRIS BLISS

Vice-Pres. of Enrollment Management: SHERI MCKENZIE

Dean of Students: LIZ POINTER

Dir of Libraries: JANICE WOO

Library of 73,000 vols, 2,500 online periodicals, 500,000 images and 150,000 slides

Number of teachers: 326

Number of students: 1,400

Publication: *Design Book Review* (4 a year).

ATTACHED INSTITUTES

Center for Art and Public Life: tel. (510) 594-3763; fax (510) 594-3769; internet center .cca.edu; f. 1998; Dir Dr SONIA BASSHEVA MAÑJON.

Wattis Institute for Contemporary Arts: tel. (415) 551-9210; e-mail wattis@cca.edu; internet www.wattis.org; f. 1998; forum for presentation and discussion of local, nat. and int. contemporary culture; Dir JENS HOFFMAN.

CALIFORNIA INSTITUTE OF INTEGRAL STUDIES

1453 Mission St, San Francisco, CA 94103

Telephone: (415) 575-6100

Fax: (415) 575-1628

Internet: www.ciis.edu

Founded 1968

Pres.: JOSEPH L. SUBBIONDO

Academic Vice-Pres.: JUDIE WEXLER

Dean of Students and Alumni: RICHARD BUGGS

Dir of Communications and Marketing: VALERIE BUSH

Dir of Devt: DOROTEA REYNA

Dir of Diversity and Human Resources: L'ESA GUILLIAN

Dir of Facilities and Operations: JONATHAN MILLS

Dir of Finance: KEN ABIKO

Dir of Financial Aid: MICHAEL SZKOTAK

Dir of Information Technology Services: SCOTT CILIBERTI

Dir of Public Programs: KARIM BAER

Dir of Undergraduate Studies: MICHELLE ENG

Registrar: NANCY HAGER

Library Dir: LISE DYCKMAN

Library of 35,000 vols, 300 periodicals, 1,300 audio and video titles

Number of teachers: 55 full-time, 11 part-time

Number of students: 1,005

BA in Interdisciplinary Studies; School of Professional Psychology (1 PhD and 4 MA programmes); School of Consciousness and Transformation (7 MA and 6 PhD programmes).

CALIFORNIA INSTITUTE OF TECHNOLOGY

Mail Code 206-31, Pasadena, CA 91125

1200 East California Blvd, Pasadena, CA 91125

Telephone: (626) 395-6811

Fax: (626) 795-1547

Internet: www.caltech.edu

Founded 1891

Private control

Academic year: September to June

Pres.: Dr JEAN-LOU CHAMEAU

Provost: Dr EDWARD STOLPER

Vice-Provosts: Prof. MORY GHARIB, Prof. MELANY HUNT

Gen. Counsel: VICTORIA STRATMAN

Vice-Pres. for Business and Finance: DEAN W. CURRIE

Vice-Pres. for Devt and Institute Relations: PETER DECOURCY HERO

Vice-Pres. for Marketing and Communications: (vacant)

Vice-Pres. for Student Affairs: Prof. ANNEILA SARGENT (acting)

Dir of Admissions: RAY PRADO

Dean of Students: (vacant)

Controller and Chief Financial Accountant: MATTHEW BREWER

Sec.: MARY L. WEBSTER

Registrar: MARY NEARY MORLEY

Univ. Librarian: KIMBERLY DOUGLAS

Library of 825,498 vols

Number of teachers: 368

Number of students: 2,130

Publication: *Engineering and Science*

CHAIRMEN OF DIVISIONS

Biology: ELLIOT M. MEYEROWITZ

Chemistry and Chemical Engineering: JACQUELINE K. BARTON

Engineering and Applied Science: ARES J. ROSAKIS

Geological and Planetary Sciences: KENNETH A. FARLEY

Humanities and Social Sciences: JONATHAN N. KATZ

Physics, Mathematics and Astronomy: B. THOMAS SOIFER

PROFESSORS

ABU-MOSTAFA, Y. S., Electrical Engineering and Computer Science
ADOLPHS, R., Psychology and Neuroscience and Biology
ALLMAN, J. M., Neurobiology
ALVAREZ, R. M., Political Science
ANDERSEN, R. A., Neuroscience
ANDERSON, D. J., Biology
ANTONSSON, E. K., Mechanical Engineering
ARNOLD, F. H., Chemical Engineering and Biochemistry
ASCHBACHER, M., Mathematics
ATTARDI, G., Molecular Biology
ATWATER, H. A., Jr, Applied Physics and Materials Science
AVOUAC, J., Geology
BALTIMORE, D., Biology
BARR, A. H., Computer Science
BARTON, J. K., Chemistry
BEAUCHAMP, J. L., Chemistry
BECK, J. L., Engineering and Applied Science
BELLAN, P. M., Applied Physics
BERCAW, J. E., Chemistry
BHATTACHARYA, K., Mechanics and Materials Science
BJORKMAN, P. J., Biology
BLAKE, G. A., Cosmochemistry, Planetary Sciences, Chemistry
BORDER, K. C., Economics
BORODIN, A., Mathematics
BOSSAERTS, P. L., Finance
BRADY, J. F., Chemical Engineering and Mechanical Engineering
BRENNEN, C. E., Mechanical Engineering
BREWER, J., History and Literature
BRONNER-FRASER, M., Biology
BROWN, M. E., Astronomy
BRUCK, J., Computation and Neural Systems and Electrical Engineering
BRUNO, O. P., Applied and Computational Mathematics
BUCHWALD, J. Z., History
BURDICK, J. W., Mechanical Engineering and Bioengineering
CALEGARI, D., Mathematics
CAMERER, C. F., Economics
CAMPBELL, J. L., Chemistry and Biology

CANDES, E. J. D., Applied and Computational Mathematics
CHAMEAU, J., Civil Engineering, Environmental Science and Engineering, Mechanical Engineering
CHANDY, K. M., Computer Science
CLAYTON, R. W., Geophysics
COHEN, J. G., Astronomy
COLONIUS, T. E., Mechanical Engineering
CROSS, M. C., Theoretical Physics
CVITANIC, J., Mathematical Finance
DAVIDSON, E. H., Cell Biology
DAVIS, M. E., Chemical Engineering
DERVAN, P. B., Chemistry
DESHAIES, R., Biology
DICKINSON, M. H., Bioengineering
DIMOTAKIS, P. E., Aeronautics, Applied Physics
DJORGOVSKI, S. G., Astronomy
DOUGHERTY, D. A., Chemistry
DOYLE, J. C., Control and Dynamical Systems, Electrical Engineering and Bioengineering
DUBIN, J. A., Economics
DUNPHY, W. G., Biology
EFFROS, M., Electrical Engineering
EILER, J. M., Geochemistry
EISENSTEIN, J. P., Physics, Applied Physics
ELACHI, C., Electrical Engineering and Planetary Science
ELLIS, R. S., Astronomy
ENSMINGER, J. E., Anthropology
FARLEY, K. A., Geochemistry
FEINGOLD, M., History
FILIPPONE, B. W., Physics
FLACH, M., Mathematics
FLAGAN, R. C., Chemical Engineering, Environmental Science and Engineering
FRASER, S. E., Biology, Bioengineering
FULTZ, B. T., Materials Science and Applied Physics
GHARIB, M., Aeronautics and Bioengineering
GODDARD, W. A., III, Chemistry, Materials Science and Applied Physics
GOEREE, J. K., Economics
GOODSTEIN, D. L., Physics and Applied Physics
GOODWIN, D. G., Mechanical Engineering and Applied Physics
GRAY, H. B., Chemistry
GRETHER, D. M., Economics
GROTZINGER, J. P., Geology
GRUBBS, R. H., Chemistry
GURNIS, M. C., Geophysics
HAILE, S. M., Materials Science and Chemical Engineering
HAJIMIRI, S., Electrical Engineering
HALL, J. F., Civil Engineering
HARRISON, F. A., Physics and Astronomy
HEATH, J. R., Chemistry
HEATON, T. H., Engineering Seismology
HELMBERGER, D. V., Geophysics
HERING, J. G., Environmental Science and Engineering
HITCHCOCK, C. R., Philosophy
HITLIN, D. G., Physics
HOFFMAN, P. T., History and Social Science
HOFFMANN, M. R., Environmental Science
HOU, Y. T., Applied and Computational Mathematics
HUGHES, E. W., Physics
HUNT, M. L., Mechanical Engineering
INGERSOLL, A. P., Planetary Science
JOHNSON, W. L., Engineering and Applied Science
KAMIONKOWSKI, M., Theoretical Physics and Astrophysics
KATZ, J. N., Political Science
KECHRIS, A. S., Mathematics
KENNEDY, M. B., Biology
KIEWIET, D. R., Political Science
KIMBLE, H. J., Physics
KIRSCHVINK, J. L., Geobiology
KITAEV, A., Theoretical Astrophysics and Computer Science
KOCH, C., Computation and Neural Systems
KONISHI, M., Behavioural Biology
KORMOS-BUCHWALD, D. L., History
KORNFIELD, J. A., Chemical Engineering
KOUSSER, J. M., History and Social Science
KULKARNI, S. R., Astronomy and Planetary Science
KUPPERMANN, A., Chemical Physics
LA BELLE, J., English
LANGE, A. E., Physics
LAURENT, G. J., Biology and Computation and Neural Systems
LEDYARD, J. O., Economics and Social Sciences
LESTER, H. A., Biology
LEWIS, N. S., Chemistry
LIBBRECHT, K. G., Physics
LORDEN, G. A., Mathematics
LOW, S., Computer Science and Electrical Engineering
MCAFEE, R. P., Business Economics and Management
MCELIECE, R. J., Electrical Engineering
MCGILL, T. C., Applied Physics
MCKEOWN, R. D., Physics
MCKOY, B. V., Theoretical Chemistry
MACMILLAN, D. W. C., Chemistry
MAKAROV, N. G., Mathematics
MARCUS, R. A., Chemistry
MARSDEN, J. E., Engineering and Control and Dynamical Systems
MARTIN, A. J., Computer Science
MARTIN, D. C., Physics
MAYO, S. L., Biology and Chemistry
MEIRON, D. I., Applied and Computational Mathematics and Computer Science
MEYEROWITZ, E. M., Biology
MURRAY, R. M., Control and Dynamical Systems
NEWMAN, D. K., Geobiology and Biology
NEWMAN, H. B., Physics
OGURI, H., Theoretical Physics
OH, H., Mathematics
OKUMURA, M., Chemical Physics
ORDESHOOK, P. C., Political Science
ORTIZ, M., Aeronautics and Mechanical Engineering
PALFREY, T. R., III, Economics and Political Science
PARKER, C. S., Biochemistry
PATTERSON, P. H., Biology
PERONA, P., Electrical Engineering
PETERS, J. C., Chemistry
PHILLIPS, R., Applied Physics and Mechanical Engineering
PHILLIPS, T. G., Physics
PHINNEY, E. S., III, Theoretical Astrophysics
PIGMAN, G. W., III, English
PINE, J., Physics
PLOTT, C. R., Economics and Political Science
POLITZER, H. D., Theoretical Physics
PORTER, F. C., Physics
PRESKILL, J. P., Theoretical Physics
PRINCE, T. A., Physics
PSALTIS, D., Electrical Engineering
PULLIN, D. I., Aeronautics
RAMAKRISHNAN, D., Mathematics
RAVICHANDRAN, G., Aeronautics and Mechanical Engineering
READHEAD, A. C. S., Astronomy
REES, D. C., Chemistry
RICHARDS, J. H., Organic Chemistry and Biochemistry
ROSAKIS, A. J., Aeronautics and Mechanical Engineering
ROSENSTONE, R. A., History
ROSENTHAL, J., Economics
ROSSMAN, G. R., Mineralogy
ROTHENBERG, E., Biology
ROUKES, M. L., Physics, Applied Physics and Bioengineering
RUTLEDGE, D. B., Electrical Engineering
SALEEBY, J. B., Geology
SARGENT, A. I., Astronomy
SARGENT, W. L. W., Astronomy
SCHERER, A., Electrical Engineering, Applied Physics, and Physics
SCHRODER, P., Computer Science and Applied and Computational Mathematics
SCHULMAN, L. J., Computer Science
SCHUMAN, E. M., Biology
SCHWARZ, J. H., Theoretical Physics
SCOVILLE, N. Z., Astronomy
SEINFELD, J. H., Chemical Engineering
SHEPHERD, J. E., Aeronautics and Mechanical Engineering
SHERMAN, R. P., Economics and Statistics
SHIMOJO, S., Biology
SIEH, K. E., Geology
SIMON, B. M., Mathematics and Theoretical Physics
SOIFER, B. T., Physics
SPITZER, M. L., Law and Social Science
STEIDEL, C. C., Astronomy
STERNBERG, P. W., Biology
STEVENSON, D. J., Planetary Science
STOCK, J. M., Geology and Geophysics
STOLPER, E. M., Geology
STOLTZ, B. M., Chemistry
STONE, E. C., Physics
STRAUSS, J. H., Biology
TAI, Y., Electrical Engineering and Mechanical Engineering
THORNE, K. S., Theoretical Physics
TIRRELL, D. A., Chemistry and Chemical Engineering
TOMBRELLO, T. A., Physics
TROIAN, S., Applied Physics, Aeronautics, and Mechanical Engineering
TROMP, J., Geophysics
VAHALA, K. J., Applied Physics
VAIDYANATHAN, P. P., Electrical Engineering
VARSHAVSKY, A. J., Cell Biology
WALES, D. B., Mathematics
WANG, Z., Chemical Engineering
WEINSTEIN, A. J., Physics
WEINSTEIN, C., English
WEITEKAMP, D. P., Chemical Physics
WENNBERG, P. O., Atmospheric Chemistry and Environmental Science and Engineering
WERNICKE, B. P., Geology
WILSON, R. M., Mathematics
WISE, M. B., High Energy Physics
WOLD, B. J., Molecular Biology
WOODWARD, J. F., Philosophy
YARIV, A., Applied Physics and Electrical Engineering
YEH, N., Physics
YUNG, Y. L., Planetary Science
ZEWAIL, A. H., Chemical Physics, Physics
ZINN, K., Biology
ZMUIDZINAS, J., Physics

ATTACHED INSTITUTE

Jet Propulsion Laboratory: 4800 Oak Grove Dr., Pasadena, CA 91109; tel. (818) 354-4321; internet www.jpl.nasa.gov; planetary exploration and related research; Dir Dr CHARLES ELACHI.

CALIFORNIA INSTITUTE OF THE ARTS

24700 McBean Parkway, Valencia, CA 91355-2397
Telephone: (661) 255-1050
Fax: (661) 253-7710
E-mail: info@calarts.edu
Internet: www.calarts.edu
Founded 1961
Academic year: September to May
Pres.: STEVEN D. LAVINE
Vice-Pres. for Admin.: D. DEAN HOUCHIN
Vice-Pres. for Advancement: ARWIN DUFFY
Vice-Pres. for Spec. Projects: LYNN R. ROSENFELD
Provost: NANCY J. USCHER
Registrar: NANCY WHITTEMORE
Dean of Enrollment Management: CAROL KIM
Dean of Library: JEFFREY GATTEN
Dean of Students: YVONNE GUY

Library of 90,000 vols
Number of teachers: 201
Number of students: 1,300

Publications: *Afterall* (2 a year), *Black Clock* (2 a year), *Trepan* (1 a year)

DEANS

Art: THOMAS LAWSON
Critical Studies: NANCY WOOD
Dance: STEPHAN KOPLOWITZ
Film and Video: STEVEN ANKER
Music: DAVID ROSENBLOOM
Theatre: ERIK EHN

CALIFORNIA LUTHERAN UNIVERSITY

60 West Olsen Rd, Thousand Oaks, CA 91360-2787
Telephone: (805) 492-2411
Fax: (805) 493-3114
E-mail: cluadm@clunet.edu
Internet: www.clunet.edu

Founded 1959

Private control, affiliated with the Evangelical Lutheran Church in America

Pres.: Dr LUTHER S. LUEDTKE
Provost: Dr A. JOSEPH EVERSON
Vice-Pres. for Admin. and Finance: ROBERT ALLISON
Vice-Pres. for Student Affairs and Dean of Students: WILLIAM ROSSER
Vice-Pres. for Univ. Advancement: R. STEPHEN WHEATLY
Registrar: MARIA KOHNKE
Librarian: KENNETH PFLUEGER

Library of 110,416 vols
Number of teachers: 256 (118 full-time, 138 part-time)
Number of students: 3,021

DEANS

College of Arts and Sciences: TIMOTHY HENGST
School of Business: Dr CHARLES MAXEY
School of Education: TERENCE CANNINGS

CALIFORNIA MARITIME ACADEMY

200 Maritime Academy Dr., Vallejo, CA 94590
Telephone: (707) 654-1000
Fax: (707) 654-1001
E-mail: admission@csum.edu
Internet: www.csum.edu

Founded 1929 as California Nautical School; present name 1938; attached to specialized campus of California State Univ.

Pres.: Dr WILLIAM B EISENHARDT
Vice-Pres. for Academic Affairs: Dr DONALD ZINGALE
Vice-Pres. for Admin. and Finance: MARK NICKERSON
Vice-Pres. for Marine Programmes and Student Devt: Capt. JOHN KEEVER
Academic Dean: STEVE KRETA

Degrees in business admin., facilities engineering technology, global studies and maritime affairs, marine engineering technology, marine transportation, mechanical engineering

Library of 35,000 vols, 270 periodicals.

CALIFORNIA STATE UNIVERSITY SYSTEM

401 Golden Shore, Long Beach, CA 90802-4210
Telephone: (562) 951-400
Internet: www.calstate.edu

Co-ordinating HQ for 23 state univs

Number of teachers: 46,000
Number of students: 417,000

Chancellor: CHARLES B. REED.

CALIFORNIA POLYTECHNIC STATE UNIVERSITY

1 Grand Ave, San Luis Obispo, CA 93407
Telephone: (805) 756-1111
Fax: (805) 756-5400
E-mail: admissions@calpoly.edu
Internet: www.calpoly.edu

Founded 1901

Academic year: September to June

Pres.: WARREN J. BAKER
Provost and Vice-Pres. for Academic Affairs: LARRY KELLEY
Vice-Pres. for Student Affairs: CORNEL MORTON
Vice-Pres. for Univ. Advancement: SANDRA OGREN
Dean of Library Services: MICHAEL D. MILLER

Library of 769,180 vols and serials
Number of teachers: 1,203 , incl. part-time
Number of students: 18,722

Publications: *Cal Poly Today* (4 a year), *Mustang Daily*

DEANS

College of Agriculture: DAVID J. WEHNER
College of Architecture and Environmental Design: R. THOMAS JONES
College of Business: DAVE CHRISTY
College of Education: BONNIE KONOPAK
College of Engineering and Technology: MOHAMMAD NOORI
College of Liberal Arts: LINDA HALISKY
College of Science and Mathematics: PHILIP S. BAILEY

CALIFORNIA STATE POLYTECHNIC UNIVERSITY, POMONA

3801 W Temple Ave, Pomona, CA 91768
Telephone: (909) 869-7659
Internet: www.csupomona.edu

Founded 1938

Pres.: MICHAEL ORTIZ
Provost and Vice-Pres. for Academic Affairs: Dr MARTEN L. denBOER
Vice-Pres. for Admin. Affairs: EDWIN A. BARNES
Vice-Pres. for Instructional and Information Technology: DEBRA BRUM
Vice-Pres. for Student Affairs: Dr DOUGLAS R. FREER
Vice-Pres. for Univ. Advancement: SCOTT WARRINGTON
Registrar: MARIA L. MARTINEZ
Library Dean: GILBERT BRUM

Library of 625,000 vols, 1.42m. microforms, 13,000 maps, 2,200 periodicals
Number of teachers: 1,200
Number of students: 21,000

DEANS

College of Agriculture: LESTER C. YOUNG
College of Business Admin.: RICHARD S. LAPIDUS
College of Education and Integrative Studies: Dr PEGGY KELLY
College of Engineering: Dr EDWARD C. HOHMANN
College of Environmental Design: KYLE D. BROWN
College of Letters, Arts and Social Sciences: Dr CAROL RICHARDSON
College of Science: DONALD O. STRANEY
College of the Extended Univ.: Dr UEI-JIUN FAN
Collins School of Hospitality Management: ANDREW FEINSTEIN

CALIFORNIA STATE UNIVERSITY, BAKERSFIELD

9001 Stockdale Highway, Bakersfield, CA 93311-1022
Telephone: (661) 664-2011
Fax: (661) 664-3194
Internet: www.csub.edu

Founded 1970

Academic year: September to June

Pres.: Dr HORACE MITCHELL
Provost and Vice-Pres. for Academic Affairs: SORAYA M. COLEY
Vice-Pres. for Business and Admin. Services: MICHAEL A. NEAL
Vice-Pres. for Student Affairs: Dr SHELLEY RUELAS
Vice-Pres. for Univ. Advancement: W. MICHAEL CHERTOK
Dean of Libraries: RODNEY M. HERBSBERGER

Library of 461,829 vols, 1,128 periodicals, 55,883 govt publs, 2,696 sound recordings, 5,555 films/video cassettes
Number of teachers: 408
Number of students: 6,210

DEANS

School of Business and Public Administration: Dr HENRY LOWENSTEIN
School of Education: Dr CURT GUAGLIANONE
School of Humanities and Social Sciences: MARIA IYASERE
School of Natural Sciences, Mathematics and Engineering: (vacant)

CALIFORNIA STATE UNIVERSITY, CHICO

400 West First St, Chico, CA 95929
Telephone: (530) 898-6116
Internet: www.csuchico.edu

Founded 1887

Pres.: PAUL J. ZINGG
Provost and Vice-Pres. for Academic Affairs: SANDRA M. FLAKE
Vice-Pres. for Business and Finance: DENNIS GRAHAM
Vice-Provost for Information Resources: WILLIAM POST
Vice-Pres. for Student Affairs: DREW CALANDRELLA
Vice-Pres. for Univ. Advancement: RICHARD ELLISON
Library Services Dir: CAROLYN DUSENBURY

Library of 634,000 vols, 2m. documents
Number of teachers: 960
Number of students: 15,500

DEANS

College of Agriculture: JENNIFER RYDER FOX
College of Behavioural and Social Sciences: Dr BOB JACKSON
College of Business: Dr WILLIE HOPKINS
College of Communication and Education: Dr PHYLLIS FERNLUND
College of Engineering, Computer Science and Construction Management: Dr KENNETH N. DERUCHER
College of Humanities and Fine Arts: SARAH BLACKSTONE (acting)
College of Natural Sciences: Dr JAMES L. J. HOUPIS
School of Graduate, Int. and Sponsored Programmes: SUSAN PLACE
Graduate Studies: WILLIAM LOKER

CALIFORNIA STATE UNIVERSITY, DOMINGUEZ HILLS

1000 East Victoria St, Carson, CA 90747
Telephone: (310) 243-3696
Fax: (310) 243-3858
Internet: www.csudh.edu

Founded 1960

Pres.: Dr Boice M. Bowman
Provost and Vice-Pres. for Academic Affairs: Dr Allen Mori
Vice-Pres. for Admin. and Finance: Mary Ann Rodriguez
Vice-Pres. for Student Affairs: Dr Boice Bowman
Vice-Pres. for Univ. Advancement: Dr Justine Bell-Waters (acting)
Registrar: Gayle Ball (acting)
Dean of Univ. Library: Sandra Parham

Library of 440,000 vols, 687,800 microfilms and 2,200 current periodicals
Number of teachers: 267 full-time, 420 part-time
Number of students: 12,068

DEANS

College of Business and Public Policy: Dr James Strong
College of Education: Dr Kathleen Taira
College of Extended Education: Margaret Gordon
College of Health and Human Services: Angela Albright (acting)
College of Liberal Arts: Dr Selase Williams
College of Natural Behavioural Sciences: Dr Charles Holm

CALIFORNIA STATE UNIVERSITY, EAST BAY

25800 Carlos Bee Blvd, Hayward, CA 94542-3000
Telephone: (510) 885-3000
Fax: (510) 885-3808
Internet: www.csuhayward.edu

Founded 1957

Pres.: Mo Qayoumi
Provost and Vice-Pres. for Academic Affairs: Dr Michael Mahoney
Vice-Pres. for Admin. and Finance: Shawn Bibb
Vice-Pres. for Planning and Enrollment Management: Dr Linda Dalton
Vice-Pres. for Student Affairs: Dr Sonja Redmond
Vice-Pres. for Univ. Advancement: Robert Burt
Chief Information Officer: John Charles
Univ. Librarian: Myoung-ja Lee Kwon

Library of 700,000 vols
Number of teachers: 506
Number of students: 12,706

DEANS

School of Arts, Letters and Social Sciences: Benjamin Bowser
School of Business and Economics: John Kohl
School of Education and Allied Studies: Emily Brizendine
School of Science: Michael Leung

CALIFORNIA STATE UNIVERSITY, FRESNO

5241 North Maple Ave, Fresno, CA 93740-8027
Telephone: (559) 278-4240
Internet: www.csufresno.edu

Founded 1911 as Fresno State Normal School
Academic year: July to June

Pres.: John D. Welty
Provost and Vice-Pres. for Academic Affairs: Dr Jeronima (Jeri) Echeverria
Vice-Pres. for Admin. and CFO: Cynthia Teniente-Matson
Vice-Pres. for Student Affairs and Dean of Students: Dr Paul M. Oliaro
Vice-Pres. for Univ. Advancement: Dr Peter N. Smits
Dean of Undergraduate Studies: Dr Dennis Nef
Dean of Library Services: Peter McDonald

Library: 1m. vols
Number of teachers: 1,250
Number of students: 20,013

DEANS

College of Agricultural Sciences and Technology: Charles Boyer
College of Arts and Humanities: Vida Samiian
College of Engineering: Dr Michael Jenkins
College of Health and Human Services: Benjamin Cuellar
College of Science and Mathematics: Dr Karen Carey
College of Social Sciences: Luz Gonzalez
Craig School of Business: Doug Hensler
Div. of Graduate Studies: Diane Dickerson
Kremen School of Education and Human Development: Paul Beare

CALIFORNIA STATE UNIVERSITY, FULLERTON

800 North College Blvd, Fullerton, CA 92831-3599
Telephone: (714) 287-2011
Internet: www.fullerton.edu

Founded 1957

Pres.: Milton A. Gordon
Exec. Vice-Pres.: Judith A. Anderson
Vice-Pres. for Academic Affairs: Ephraim P. Smith
Vice-Pres. for Admin.: Willie J. Hagan
Vice-Pres. for Student Affairs: Robert L. Palmer, Jr
Vice-Pres. for Univ. Advancement: Pamela Hillman
Chief Information/Technology Officer: Amir Dabirian
Registrar: Melissa Whatley
Univ. Librarian: Richard C. Pollard

Library of 1,258,571 vols, 10,902 serials, 1,149,353 microfilm titles, 7,417 video and audio cassettes
Number of teachers: 1,852
Number of students: 36,996

DEANS

School of the Arts: Jerry Samuelson
College of Business and Economics: Anil K. Puri
College of Communications: Rick D. Pullen
College of Education: Claire C. Cavallaro (acting)
College of Engineering and Computer Science: Raman Unnikrishnan
College of Health and Human Devt: Dr Roberta E. Rikli
College of Humanities and Social Sciences: Dr Thomas P. Klammer
College of Natural Sciences and Mathematics: Steven N. Murray

CALIFORNIA STATE UNIVERSITY, LONG BEACH

1250 Bellflower Blvd, Long Beach, CA 90840-0115
Telephone: (562) 985-4111
Internet: www.csulb.edu

Founded 1949
Public control

Pres.: F. King Alexander
Provost and Sr Vice-Pres. for Academic Affairs: Don Para
Vice-Pres. for Admin. and Finance: Mary Stephens
Vice-Pres. for Student Services: Douglas W. Robinson
Vice-Pres. for Univ. Relations and Devt: Andrea Taylor
Dean of Library Services: Roman Kochan

Library of 1,096,089 vols, 1,503,457 microfilms, 35,080 non-book materials, 2,110 current periodicals
Number of teachers: 2,128 (948 full-time, 1,180 part-time)
Number of students: 33,419

DEANS

College of the Arts: Raymond Torres-Santos
College of Business Administration: Michael E. Solt
College of Continuing and Professional Education: Jeet Joshee
College of Education: Marquita Grenot-Scheyer
College of Engineering: Forouzan Golshani
College of Health and Human Sciences: Kenneth I. Millar
College of Liberal Arts: Gerry Riposa
College of Natural Sciences and Mathematics: Laura Kingsford

CALIFORNIA STATE UNIVERSITY, LOS ANGELES

5151 State University Dr., Los Angeles, CA 90032-8530
Telephone: (323) 343-3901
Fax: (323) 343-6306
E-mail: admission@calstatela.edu
Internet: www.calstatela.edu

Founded 1947

Pres.: James M. Rosser
Provost and Vice-Pres. for Academic Affairs: Herman D. Lujan
Vice-Pres. for Admin. and Finance: Steven N. Garcia
Vice-Pres. for Information Technology Services: Peter Quan
Vice-Pres. for Institutional Advancement: Kyle C. Button
Vice-Pres. for Student Affairs: Anthony R. Ross
Dean of Graduate Studies and Research: Jose L. Galvan (acting)
Dean of Undergraduate Studies: Alfredo G. Gonzalez (acting)
Univ. Librarian: Alice Kawakami (acting)

Library: 1m. vols
Number of teachers: 888
Number of students: 18,000

DEANS

College of Arts and Letters: Terry L. Allison
College of Business and Economics: Dong-Woo Lee (acting)
Charter College of Education: Mary Falvey
College of Engineering, Computer Science and Technology: Dr Keith Moo-Young
College of Health and Human Sciences: Beatrice Yorker (acting)
College of Natural and Social Sciences: Desdemona Cardoza

CALIFORNIA STATE UNIVERSITY, MONTEREY BAY

100 Campus Center, Seaside, CA 93955-8001
Telephone: (831) 582-3000
E-mail: moreinfo_prospective@csumb.edu
Internet: csumb.edu

Founded 1994
Academic year: August to May

Pres.: Dr Diane F. Harrison
Provost and Vice-Pres. for Academic Affairs: Dr Kathryn Cruz-Uribe
Vice-Pres. for Admin. and Finance: Dan Kubiak
Vice-Pres. for Devt: Dr Chris Hasegawa
Vice-Pres. for Student Affairs: Dr Susan E. Borrega
Vice-Pres. for Univ. Advancement: Steve Reed

Dir of the Library: BILL ROBNETT
Library of 65,000 vols
Number of teachers: 280
Number of students: 4,000

DEANS

College of Arts, Humanities, and Social Sciences: RENÉE R. CURRY
College of Professional Studies: Dr MARTIN TADLOCK
College of Science, Media Arts, and Technology: Dr MARSHA MOROH
College of Univ. Studies and Programmes: Dr DAVID ANDERSON

CALIFORNIA STATE UNIVERSITY, NORTHRIDGE

18111 Nordhoff St, Northridge, CA 91330
Telephone: (818) 677-1200
Fax: (818) 677-3766
E-mail: admissions@csun.edu
Internet: www.csun.edu
Founded 1958
Pres.: JOLENE KOESTER
Provost and Vice-Pres. for Faculty Affairs: LINDA BAIN
Vice-Pres. for Admin. and Finance: MOHAMMAD H. QAYOUMI
Vice-Pres. for Operations: JULIE WANKE
Vice-Pres. for Student Affairs: TERRY B. PIPER
Vice-Pres. for Univ. Advancement: JUDY C. KNUDSON
Dir of Admissions and Records: ERIC FORBES
Dean of Univ. Library: SUSAN C. CURZON
Library: 1.2m. vols, 8,000 periodicals, 3m. microforms, 60,000 pictures, 10,000 sound recordings, 6,000 films and video recordings
Number of teachers: 1,900
Number of students: 34,000

DEANS

College of Arts, Media and Communication: DAVE MOON
College of Business and Economics: MICHAEL FRONMUELLER
Michael D. Eisner College of Education: PHILIP J. RUSCHE
College of Engineering and Computer Science: S. T. MAU
College of Extended Learning: JOYCE FEUCHT-HAVIAR
College of Health and Human Development: HELEN CASTILLO
College of Humanities: ELIZABETH SAY
College of Science and Mathematics: EDWARD CARROLL
College of Social and Behavioural Sciences: STELLA THEODOULOU

CALIFORNIA STATE UNIVERSITY, SACRAMENTO

6000 J St, Sacramento, CA 95819-6056
Telephone: (916) 278-6011
Fax: (916) 278-6664
E-mail: infodesk@csus.edu
Internet: www.csus.edu
Founded 1947
Academic year: September to May
Pres.: ALEXANDER GONZALEZ
Provost and Vice-Pres. for Academic Affairs: JOSEPH F. SHELEY
Vice-Pres. for Admin.: STEPHEN G. GARCIA
Vice-Pres. for Student Affairs: LORI VARLOTTA
Vice-Pres. for Univ. Affairs: CAROLE HAYASHINO
Dir of Library Systems: CARLOS RODRIGUEZ
Library: 2m. vols
Number of teachers: 1,647 (877 full-time, 770 part-time)
Number of students: 28,558
Publications: *Calaveras Station* (4 a year), *Capitol University Journal* (2 a year)

DEANS

College of Arts and Letters: JEFFREY MASON (acting)
College of Business Administration: SANJAY VARSHNEY
College of Education: Dr VANESSA SHEARED
College of Engineering and Computer Science: EMIR JOSÉ MACARI
College of Health and Human Services: Dr MARILYN HOPKINS
College of Natural Sciences and Mathematics: LAUREL HEFFERNAN
College of Social Sciences and Interdisciplinary Studies: OTIS L. SCOTT

CALIFORNIA STATE UNIVERSITY, SAN BERNARDINO

5500 University Parkway, San Bernardino, CA 92407
Telephone: (909) 880-5000
Fax: (909) 880-5903
E-mail: moreinfo@csusb.edu
Internet: www.csusb.edu
Founded 1960
Liberal arts college with several applied programmes offering a broad range of first degrees, several teaching credentials and Masters degrees in selected fields
Pres.: ALBERT K. KARNIG
Provost and Vice-Pres. for Academic Affairs: Dr LOUIS A. FERNÁNDEZ
Vice-Pres. for Admin. and Finance: DAVID DEMAURO
Vice-Pres. for Information Resources and Technology: LORAINE M. FROST
Vice-Pres. for Student Affairs: Dr FRANK RINCÓN
Vice-Pres. for Univ. Advancement: WILLIAM AGUILAR
Univ. Librarian: JOHNNIE ANN RALPH
Library of 720,000 vols, 2,400 current periodicals and serial publications, also maps, microfilms, musical scores, CD-ROMs; depository for CA state and fed. govt documents
Number of teachers: 454
Number of students: 16,341

DEANS

College of Arts and Letters: Dr ERI YASUHARA
College of Business and Public Admin.: KAREN DILL BOWERMAN
College of Education: Dr PATRICIA ARLIN
College of Natural Sciences: Dr B. ROBERT CARLSON
College of Social and Behavioural Sciences: Dr JOHN CONLEY

CALIFORNIA STATE UNIVERSITY, SAN MARCOS

333 South Twin Oaks Valley Rd, San Marcos, CA 92096
Telephone: (760) 750-4000
E-mail: apply@csusm.edu
Internet: www.csusm.edu
Founded 1989
Academic year: September to May
Pres.: Dr KAREN D. HAYNES
Chancellor: CHARLES B. REED
Provost and Vice-Pres. for Academic Affairs: EMILY F. CUTRER
Vice-Pres. for Finance and Admin.: NEIL HOSS
Vice-Pres. for Student Affairs: Dr PAT WORDEN
Vice-Pres. for Univ. Advancement: RICK D. KEITH
Dean of Library: MARION REID
Library of 250,000 vols, 800 periodicals
Number of teachers: 190
Number of students: 7,627

DEANS

College of Arts and Sciences: Dr VICKI GOLICH
College of Business Administration: Dr DENNIS GUSEMAN
College of Education: Dr MARK BALDWIN
School of Nursing: JUDY PAPENHAUSEN
Extended Studies: JAN JACKSON
Graduate Studies: GERARDO M. GONZÁLEZ

CALIFORNIA STATE UNIVERSITY, STANISLAUS

801 West Monte Vista Ave, Turlock, CA 95382
Telephone: (209) 667-3122
Fax: (209) 667-3333
Internet: www.csustan.edu
Founded 1957
Pres.: HAMID SHIRVANI
Provost and Vice-Pres. for Academic Affairs: WILLIAM COVINO
Vice-Pres. for Business and Finance: MARY STEPHENS
Vice-Pres. for Student Affairs: STACEY MORGAN-FOSTER
Vice-Pres. for Univ. Advancement: (vacant)
Assoc. Vice-Pres. for Enrollment Management: ROGER PUGH
Dean of Admissions and Registrar: LISA BERNARDO
Dean of Library Services: CARL E. BENGSTON
Library of 361,000 vols, 2,000 current periodicals, 1.3m. microfilms, 4,700 sound and video recordings, govt documents, special colln of children's literature
Number of teachers: 495 (285 full-time; 210 part-time)
Number of students: 8,137 (6,424 undergraduate; 1,713 postgraduate)

DEANS

College of Arts, Letters and Sciences: STEPHEN THOMAS
College of Business Administration: AMIN A. ELMALLAH
College of Education: CARL BROWN
College of Human and Health Sciences: GARY NOVAK
College of Humanities and Social Sciences: MARJORIE JAASMA
College of Natural Sciences: JANE BRUNER

CALIFORNIA WESTERN SCHOOL OF LAW

225 Cedar St, San Diego, CA 92101
Telephone: (619) 239-0391
Fax: (619) 525-7092
E-mail: admissions@cwsl.edu
Internet: www.cwsl.edu
Founded 1924 as Balboa Law College; present name 1975
Private control
Academic year: August to August
Dean: Prof. STEVEN R. SMITH
Assoc. Dean for Academic Affairs: Prof. JANET M. BOWERMASTER
Assoc. Dean for Admin.: Prof. MARK I. WEINSTEIN
Asst Dean for Academic Support: MARILYN SCHEININGER
Asst Dean for Career Services: Dr LOUIS W. HELMUTH
Assoc. Dir for Diversity Services: MARION CLOETE
Assoc. Dir of Marketing and Communications: FRANKI FITTERER
Registrar: DIANE SHRAGG
Dir of Law Library: Prof. PHYLLIS C. MARION
Number of teachers: 40 (full-time)
Number of students: 1,002

Publication: *Law Review/International Law Journal* (2 a year).

CHAPMAN UNIVERSITY

1 University Dr., Orange, CA 92866
Telephone: (714) 997-6815
Internet: www.chapman.edu

Founded 1861
Private (Disciples of Christ) Liberal Arts

Pres.: Dr James L. Doti
Provost and Exec. Vice-Pres.: Dr Harry Hamilton
Exec. Vice-Pres. for Finance and Admin.: Gary Brahm
Vice-Pres. and Dean for Enrollment Services: Saskia Knight
Vice-Pres. and Dean of Students: Dr Joseph Kertes
Vice-Pres. for Univ. Advancement: Sheryl Bourgeois
Registrar: John Snodgrass
Dean of the Libraries: Charlene Baldwin

Library of 200,000 vols, 2,200 periodicals
Number of teachers: 581 (264 full-time, 317 part-time)
Number of students: 5,134

DEANS

Argyros School of Business and Economics: Dr Arthur Kraft
College of Film and Media Arts: Bob Bassett
School of Arts and Communication: Dr Myron Yeager
School of Education: Dr Don Cardinal
School of Law: Dr Parham Williams
School of Music: William Hall
Univ. College: Dr Karen Graham
Wilkinson College of Letters and Sciences: Dr Roberta Lessor

CHURCH DIVINITY SCHOOL OF THE PACIFIC

2451 Ridge Rd, Berkeley, CA 94709-1217
Telephone: (510) 204-0700
Fax: (510) 644-0712
E-mail: info@cdsp.edu
Internet: www.cdsp.edu

Founded 1893
Private control (part of the Graduate Theological Union)
Academic year: August to May

Pres. and Dean: Rev. Dr Mark Richardson
Vice-Pres. for Admin.: Steve Argyris
Vice-Pres. for Advancement: Jerry Campbell
Dean of School for Deacons: Roderick Dugliss
Dean of Students: Jan Wood
Registrar: Margo Webster

Areas of study: divinity, theological studies, arts, ministry.

CLAREMONT GRADUATE UNIVERSITY

171 East 10th St, Claremont, CA 91711
Telephone: (909) 621-8028
Fax: (909) 621-8390
Internet: www.cgu.edu

Founded 1925

Pres.: Robert Klitgaard
Provost and Vice-Pres. for Academic Affairs: Yi Feng
Vice-Pres. for Advancement: Grantland Rice
Vice-Pres. for Finance and Admin.: William L. Everhart

Library: Claremont Colleges share 4 libraries with combined holdings of 2m. vols
Number of teachers: 169 (81 full-time, 88 part-time; augmented by faculty members from the Claremont Colleges)
Number of students: 2,033
Masters and doctoral degrees in 22 professional and academic disciplines

DEANS

School of the Arts and Humanities: Patricia Easton
School of Behavioural and Organizational Sciences: Stewart Donaldson
School of Information Systems and Technology: Lorne Olfman
School of Mathematical Sciences: John Angus
School of Politics and Economics: Thomas D. Willett
School of Religion: Karen J, Torjesen
Peter F. Drucker Graduate School of Management: Ira Jackson

CLAREMONT MCKENNA COLLEGE

Claremont, CA 91711-6400
Telephone: (909) 621-8000
Internet: www.claremontmckenna.edu

Founded 1946

Liberal arts college with emphasis on business and public affairs; member of the Claremont Colleges

Pres.: Prof. Pamela Brooks Gann
Dean of the Faculty and Vice-Pres. for Academic Affairs: Gregory Hess
Vice-Pres. for Business and Admin./Treas.: Robin Aspinall
Vice-Pres. for Devt and External Relations: William Lowery
Vice-Pres. for Student Affairs: Jefferson Huang
Assoc. Vice-Pres. for Devt: Richard Watkins
Dean of Students: Mary Spellman
Registrar and Dir of Institutional Research: Elizabeth Morgan
Chief Technology Officer: Cynthia Humes

Number of teachers: 135
Number of students: 1,237

CLAREMONT SCHOOL OF THEOLOGY

1325 North College Ave, Claremont, CA 91711-3199
Telephone: (909) 447-2500
Fax: (909) 626-7062
E-mail: admission@cst.edu
Internet: www.cst.edu

Founded 1885 as Maclay College of Theology; present name 1957
Private control
Academic year: September to May

Pres.: Dr Jerry D. Campbell
Vice-Pres. for Academic Affairs and Dean: Susan Nelson
Vice-Pres. for Devt: Bronnie McNabb
Chief Financial Officer: Joan Frost
Dean of Student Life: Soomee Kim
Registrar: Jennie J. Allen
Library and IT Dir: John Dickason.

CLEVELAND CHIROPRACTIC COLLEGE

590 North Vermont Ave, Los Angeles, CA 90004
Telephone: (323) 660-6166
Fax: (323) 906-2094
E-mail: la.admissions@cleveland.edu
Internet: www.clevelandchiropractic.edu

Founded 1911 as Los Angeles branch of Ratledge System of Chiropractic Schools; present name 1955
Private control
Located on 2 campuses: Kansas City and Los Angeles

Pres.: Dr Carl S. Cleveland, III
Sr Vice-Pres. for Institutional Outreach: Dr Matthew M. Givrad
Vice-Pres. for Academic Services: Dr Ruth Sandefur
Vice-Pres. for Enrollment Management: Dennis L. Giacomino
Vice-Pres. for Finance and Admin.: John J. Sopinski
Vice-Pres. for Institutional Planning and Assessment: Gary Globe
Vice-Pres. for Research and Scholarship: Dr Cheryl Hawk

Library of 22,000 vols
Number of students: 568

Depts of basic sciences, diagnostic sciences, chiropractic sciences, clinical sciences, humanities and social sciences, physical and life sciences.

COGSWELL POLYTECHNICAL COLLEGE

1175 Bordeaux Dr., Sunnyvale, CA 94089-9772
Telephone: (408) 541-0100
Fax: (408) 747-0764
E-mail: info@cogswell.edu
Internet: www.cogswell.edu

Founded 1887
Private control
Academic year: September to May

Pres.: Dr Chester D. Haskell
Vice-Pres. for Finance and Admin.: Rejino Castaneda
Dean of College: Dr Timothy Duncan
Dean of Institutional Advancement: Bonnie Phelps
Dean of Student Life: Barb Bloom
Registrar: Jill Musick
Librarian: Bruce Dahms

Number of teachers: 48 , incl. 36 part-time
Number of students: 285 (144 full-time, 141 part-time)

Library of 12,000 vols, 100 periodicals

Areas of study: 3D animation, 3D modelling, game design, entertainment design, digital audio, software engineering, computer engineering, digital arts engineering.

COLEMAN COLLEGE

8888 Balboa Ave, San Diego, CA 92123-1506
Telephone: (858) 499-0202
Fax: (858) 499-0233
Internet: www.coleman.edu

Founded 1963
Private control

Pres.: Paul Panesar
Vice-Pres. for Academics: Jim Farmer
Vice-Pres. for Marketing: Darlene Ankton
Librarian (San Diego): Manny Bernad
Librarian (San Marcos): Donna Longstreet
Number of students: 1,000

Depts of bioinformatics, graphic design, information systems, networks and security.

BRANCH CAMPUS

San Marcos Campus: 1284 West San Marcos Blvd, San Marcos, CA 92078-4073; tel. (760) 747-3990; fax (760) 752-9808.

COLUMBIA COLLEGE HOLLYWOOD

18618 Oxnard St, Tarzana, CA 91356
Telephone: (818) 345-8414
Fax: (818) 345-9053
E-mail: info@columbiacollege.edu
Internet: www.columbiacollege.edu

Founded 1951
Private control

Pres. and CEO: Richard Kobritz
Dean of Academics: Dr James C. Lundstrom
Dean of Students: Andrew H. Kesler
Dir of Admissions: Carmen Munoz

Dir of Education Services and Registrar: STEVE MARTINEZ
Librarian: MARA BURNS

Areas of study: television/video production, cinema

Library of 10,000 vols.

CONCORDIA UNIVERSITY IRVINE

1530 Concordia West, Irvine, CA 92612-3203
Telephone: (949) 854-8002
Fax: (949) 854-6894
E-mail: admission@cui.edu
Internet: www.cui.edu

Founded 1973 as Christ College Irvine; present name 1993
Private control
Academic year: August to May

Pres.: Rev. Dr JACOB A. O. PREUS
Provost: Dr KURT J. KRUEGER
Exec. Vice-Pres. for Community and Church Relations: STEPHEN CHRISTENSEN
Exec. Vice-Pres. for Univ. Advancement: STEPHEN CHRISTENSEN
Vice-Pres. for Admin. Services: Dr MARY K. SCOTT
Vice-Pres. for Business Operations and Information Technology: ALAN K. RUDI
Vice-Pres. for Student Services: Dr GARY R. MCDANIEL
Dean of Students: Dr JOHN HOFFMAN
Registrar: KENNETH CLAVIR
Dir of Library Services: CAROLINA BARTON

Number of teachers: 74 (full-time)
Number of students: 1,650

Library of 92,000 vols

DEANS

Christ College: Dr STEVEN P. MUELLER
School of Adult Studies: Dr TIMOTHY PETERS
School of Arts and Sciences: Dr KENNETH MANGELS
School of Business: Dr JOHN ROONEY (acting)
School of Education: BARBARA MORTON
School of Theology: Rev. Dr JAMES BACHMAN

DOMINICAN SCHOOL OF PHILOSOPHY AND THEOLOGY

2301 Vine St, Berkeley, CA 94708
Telephone: (510) 849-2030
Fax: (510) 849-1372
E-mail: admissions@dspt.edu
Internet: www.dspt.edu

Founded 1850s, present name 1978
Part of the Graduate Theological Union; attached to ATS and WASC
Language of instruction: English
Academic year: September to May

Pres.: MICHAEL SWEENEY
Vice-Pres. for Admin.: PETER MACLEOD
Academic Dean: CHRISTOPHER RENZ
Registrar: TERESA OLSON

Library of 450,000 vols

Publication: *Ad Gentes*.

DOMINICAN UNIVERSITY OF CALIFORNIA

50 Acacia Ave, San Rafael, CA 94901-2298
Telephone: (415) 457-4440
Fax: (415) 485-3205
E-mail: enroll@dominican.edu
Internet: www.dominican.edu

Founded 1890 as a women's college; name changed to Dominican College of San Rafael 1917; present name 2000
Private control
Academic year: August to May

Pres.: Dr JOSEPH R. FINK
Provost: Dr KENNETH J. PORADA
Vice-Pres: DAVID BEHRS, ROGER ONO, VERN UMMEL
Dir of Library Services: CAL KURZMAN

Library of 100,000 vols, 375 periodicals
Number of teachers: 223
Number of students: 1,937 (1,391 undergraduate, 546 graduate)

DEANS

School of Arts and Sciences: MARTHA NELSON
School of Business and Leadership and School of Education: LUIS MARIA CALINGO

BRANCH CAMPUS

Ukiah Center: 2240 Old River Rd, Ukiah, CA 95482; tel. (707) 463-4800; fax (707) 463-5525; e-mail ukiah@dominican.edu; serves Lake, Mendocino and Sonoma counties; BA in strategic management, MSc in education.

FIELDING GRADUATE UNIVERSITY

2112 Santa Barbara St, Santa Barbara, CA 93105
Telephone: (805) 687-1099
E-mail: admissions@fielding.edu
Internet: www.fielding.edu

Founded 1974
Private control

Pres.: Dr RICHARD S. MEYERS
Provost: Dr ANNA DISTEFANO
Assoc. Provost for Enrollment Management: MONIQUE SNOWDEN
Assoc. Provost for Research and Learning: Dr DANIEL R. SEWELL
Vice-Pres. for Advancement: Dr ANNE KRATZ
Vice-Pres. for Human Resources and Admin.: Dr ANNA J. MCDONALD

Number of students: 1,400

DEANS

School of Educational Leadership and Change: Dr JUDY WITT
School of Human and Organization Development: Dr CHARLES MCCLINTOCK
School of Psychology: Dr RAYMOND TRYBUS

FIVE BRANCHES INSTITUTE

200 Seventh Ave, Santa Cruz, CA 95062
Telephone: (831) 476-9424
Fax: (831) 476-8928
E-mail: tcm@fivebranches.edu
Internet: www.fivebranches.edu

Founded 1984
Academic year: programme begins in August and February
Private control

Pres. and CEO: RON ZAIDMAN
Academic Dean: Prof. JOANNA ZHAO
Dir of Admissions: ELEONOR MENDELSON
Registrar: JUDY CAVIN BROWN

Library of 2,000 vols
Number of teachers: 35
Number of students: 200

Areas of study: traditional Chinese medicine, Western medicine and natural sciences, acupuncture, Chinese herbology.

BRANCH CAMPUS

San Jose Campus: Suite 5PW, 3031 Tisch Way, San Jose, CA 95128; tel. (408) 260-0208; fax (408) 261-3166; e-mail sjcampus@fivebranches.edu; Dir LYNN ABLONDI; Clinic Dir GINA HUANG.

FRANCISCAN SCHOOL OF THEOLOGY

1712 Euclid Ave, Berkeley, CA 94709-1294
Telephone: (510) 848-5232
Fax: (510) 549-9466
E-mail: info@fst.edu
Internet: www.fst.edu

Run by Province of Saint Barbara of the Order of Friars Minor; part of the Graduate Theological Union

Pres. and Rector: MARIO DICICCO
Academic Dean: Prof. FAUSTINO CRUZ
Number of students: 100

MAs in theology, divinity, ministry, arts; continuing education programme.

FRESNO PACIFIC UNIVERSITY

1717 South Chestnut Ave, Fresno, CA 93702-4709
Telephone: (209) 453-2000
Fax: (209) 453-2007
Internet: www.fresno.edu

Founded 1944
Academic year: August to May

Pres.: Dr D. MERRILL EWERT
Provost and Vice-Pres. for Academic Affairs: Dr HERMA B. WILLIAMS
Vice-Pres. and Chief Information Officer: ALAN OURS
Vice-Pres. for Advancement and Univ. Relations: MARK DEFFENBACHER
Vice-Pres. for Finance and Business Affairs: JOHN WARD
Library Dir: RICHARD RAWLS

Library of 145,000 vols
Number of teachers: 70
Number of students: 1,453

DEANS

School of Business: JANITA RAWLS
School of Education: JO ELLEN MISAKIAN
School of Humanities, Religion and Social Sciences: WILL FRIESEN
School of Natural Sciences: LORIN NEUFELD

BRANCH CAMPUSES

Bakersfield Center: Suite A, 1330 Truxtun Ave, Bakersfield, CA 93301; tel. (661) 864-1515; internet www.fresno.edu/bakersfield.

North Fresno Center: Suite 201, 5 River Place West, Fresno, CA 93720; tel. (559) 453-3440; internet www.fresno.edu/northfresno.

Visilia Center: 5429 West Cypress Ave, Visilia, CA 93277; tel. (800) 837-8648; fax (559) 622-9958; internet www.fresno.edu/visilia.

FULLER THEOLOGICAL SEMINARY

135 North Oakland Ave, Pasadena, CA 91182
Telephone: (626) 584-5498
E-mail: admiss@fuller.edu
Internet: www.fuller.edu

Founded 1947
Private control

Pres.: Dr RICHARD J. MOUW
Registrar: DAVID E. KIEFER
Library Dir: DAVID BUNDY

Library of 400,000 vols, 3,400 print and 10,000 electronic periodicals
Number of teachers: 80
Number of students: 4,300

DEANS

School of Intercultural Studies: Dr C. DOUGLAS MCCONNELL
School of Psychology: Dr WINSTON E. GOODEN
School of Theology: HOWARD LOEWEN

EXTENSION SITES

Fuller Colorado: Suite 202, 525 North Cascade Ave, Colorado Springs, CO 80903; tel. (719) 385-0085; fax (719) 385-0089; e-mail fullerco@fuller.edu; internet www.fuller.edu/cll/fco; Dir WILL STOLLER-LEE.

Fuller Northern California: POB 906, 320 Middlefield Rd, Menlo Park, CA 94026-0906; tel. (650) 321-7444; fax (650) 321-8606;

e-mail fts.nca@fuller.edu; internet www.fuller.edu/cll/fnc; Dir Dr CURT LONGACRE.

Fuller Northwest: Suite 330, Nickerson Business Park, 101 Nickerson St, Seattle, WA 98109-1621; tel. (206) 284-9000; fax (206) 284-4735; e-mail fts.nw@fuller.edu; internet www.fuller.edu/cll/fnw; Dir KIM ANDERSON.

Fuller Southern California: Suite 102, 2061 Business Center Dr., Irvine, CA 92612; tel. (949) 975-0775; fax (949) 975-0787; e-mail fts.sca@fuller.edu; internet www.fuller.edu/cll/fsc; Dir PATRICIA REXROAT.

Fuller Southwest: Suite 185, 4636 East Van Buren St, Phoenix, AZ 85008; tel. (602) 220-0400; fax (602) 220-0444; e-mail fts.sw@fuller.edu; internet www.fuller.edu/cll/fsw; Dir THOMAS PARKER.

GOLDEN GATE BAPTIST THEOLOGICAL SEMINARY

201 Seminary Dr., Mill Valley, CA 94941-3163
Telephone: (415) 380-1300
Fax: (415) 380-1302
E-mail: admissions@ggbts.edu
Internet: www.ggbts.edu

Founded 1944
Private control
Academic year: August to August

Pres.: Dr JEFF IORG
Vice-Pres. for Academic Affairs: Dr MICHAEL MARTIN
Vice-Pres. for Business and Finance: GARY GROAT
Vice-Pres. for Institutional Advancement: Dr THOMAS O. JONES
Vice-Pres. for Enrollment and Student Services: Dr ADAM GROZA
Registrar: JENNIFER PEACH
Dir of Library Services: KELLY CAMPBELL
Number of students: 2,057.

BRANCH CAMPUSES

Arizona Campus: Suite 101, 2240 N Hayden Rd, Scottsdale, AZ 852572840; tel. (480) 941-1993; fax (480) 945-4199; e-mail arc-info@ggbts.edu; Dir DAVID W. JOHNSON.

Pacific Northwest Campus: 3200 NE 109th Ave, Vancouver, WA 98682-7749; tel. (360) 882-2200; fax (360) 882-2270; e-mail pnwc-info@ggbts.edu; Dir CHRIS TURNER.

Rocky Mountain Campus: 7393 S Alton Way, Centennial, CO 80112-2372; tel. (303) 779-6431; fax (303) 779-6432; e-mail rmc-info@ggbts.edu; Dir STEPHEN G. VETETO.

Southern California Campus: Suite A, 251 S Randolph Ave, Brea, CA 92821-5705; tel. (714) 256-1311; fax (714) 256-9284; e-mail scc-info@ggbts.edu; Dir J. SAM SIMMONS.

GOLDEN GATE UNIVERSITY

536 Mission St, San Francisco, CA 94105
Telephone: (415) 442-7000
Fax: (415) 442-7807
Internet: www.ggu.edu

Founded 1901

Pres.: DAN ANGEL
Vice-Pres. for Academic Affairs: Dr BARBARA H. KARLIN
Vice-Pres. for Operations: JEFFREY V. BIALIK
Dir of Univ. Library: JANICE CARTER
Dirs of Law Library: MICHAEL DAW, MOHAMED NASRALLA

Library of 340,000 vols, 1,200 periodicals in the Law library
Number of teachers: 750
Number of students: 6,617

DEANS

School of Accounting: Dr MARY CANNING
School of Business: TERRY CONNELLY
School of Law: Dr FREDERIC WHITE
School of Taxation: Dr MARY CANNING

HARVEY MUDD COLLEGE

301 Platt Blvd, Claremont, CA 91711-5990
Telephone: (909) 621-8120
Fax: (909) 621-8360
E-mail: admissions@hmc.edu
Internet: www.hmc.edu

Founded 1955
Academic year: August to May

Mem. of the Claremont Colleges; depts of biology, chemistry, computer science, Eng., humanities and social sciences, mathematics, physics

Pres.: MARIA KLAWE
Vice-Pres. and Dean of Students: MAGGIE BROWNING
Vice-Pres. and Chief Information Officer: JOSEPH VAUGHAN
Vice-Pres. for Academic Affairs and Dean of Faculty: ROBERT CAVE
Vice-Pres. for Admin. and Finance/Treasurer: ANDREW DORANTES
Vice-Pres. for Admission and Financial Aid: THYRA BRIGGS
Vice-Pres. for College Advancement: MARC ARCHAMBAULT
Registrar: NOEL KELLER
Librarian: JOHN MCDONALD

Library: 1m. vols (shared with the Claremont Colleges)
Number of teachers: 80
Number of students: 730

HEBREW UNION COLLEGE – JEWISH INSTITUTE OF RELIGION

3077 University Ave, Los Angeles, CA 90007
Telephone: (213) 749-3424
Fax: (213) 747-6128
Internet: www.huc.edu

Founded 1954
Private control
Academic year: September to May

Teaching centres in Cincinnati, OH, New York and Jerusalem, Israel

Pres.: Rabbi DAVID ELLENSON
Provost: Norman J. COHEN ELLENSON
Vice-Pres. and Chief Admin. Officer: GREGORY N. BROWN
Vice-Pres. for Admin.: GARY G. BOKELMAN
Vice-Pres. for Devt: ERICA S. FREDERICK
Vice-Pres. for Finance: MICHAEL A. CHENEY
Vice-Pres. for Spec. Projects: Rabbi CHARLES A. KROLOFF
Vice-Pres. for Strategic Initiatives and Dean: Rabbi AARON D. PANKEN
Registrar: CAROL L. SOFER
Dir of Libraries: DAVID J. GILNER

Library of 100,000 vols

DEANS

Cincinnati: Rabbi KENNETH E. EHRLICH
Los Angeles: Dr STEVEN F. WINDMUELLER
New York: Rabbi AARON D. PANKEN
Jerusalem: Rabbi MICHAEL MARMUR

HOLY NAMES UNIVERSITY

3500 Mountain Blvd, Oakland, CA 94619-1699
Telephone: (510) 436-1000
Fax: (510) 436-1199
Internet: www.hnu.edu

Founded 1868

4-Year, coeducational liberal arts college

Pres.: Dr WILLIAM HYNES
Vice-Pres. for Academic Affairs and Dean of Faculty: LIZBETH MARTIN
Vice-Pres. for Finance and Admin.: STUART KOOP
Vice-Pres. for Institutional Advancement: DAV CVITKOVIC
Vice-Pres. for Mission Effectiveness: Dr CAROL SELLMAN
Vice-Pres. for Student Affairs: MICHAEL MILLER
Dir for Library Services: KAREN SCHEINDER
Library of 111,000 vols
Number of teachers: 121
Number of students: 1,135

HOPE INTERNATIONAL UNIVERSITY

2500 East Nutwood Ave, Fullerton, CA 92831
Telephone: (714) 879-3901
Fax: (714) 681-7451
Internet: www.hiu.edu

Founded 1928 as Pacific Bible Seminary; present name 1997
Private control

Pres.: Dr JOHN DERRY
Vice-Pres. for Academic Affairs: STEVE EDDINGTON
Vice-Pres. for Business and Finance: LAURE CLOSE
Vice-Pres. for Institutional Advancement: DAVID L. POOLE
Vice-Pres. for Student Affairs: MARK COMEAUX
Registrar: MICHAEL R. BOON
Dir of Library Services: ROBIN HARTMAN

Library of 65,000 vols
Number of teachers: 165
Number of students: 1,077

DEANS

Pacific Christian College: Dr STEVE EDDINGTON
School of Graduate Studies: Dr ALAN RABE
School of Professional Studies: Dr CHRISTOPHER A. DAVIS

HUMBOLDT STATE UNIVERSITY

1 Harpst St, Arcata, CA 95521-8299
Telephone: (707) 826-3011
E-mail: welcome@humboldt.edu
Internet: www.humboldt.edu

Founded 1913
Academic year: August to May

Pres.: ROLLIN C. RICHMOND
Provost and Vice-Pres. for Academic Affairs: RICHARD VREM
Vice-Pres. for Admin. Affairs: CARL COFFEY
Vice-Pres. for Student Affairs: STEVEN BUTLER
Vice-Pres. for Univ. Advancement: ROBERT GUNSALUS
Dean of Enrollment Management: JEAN BUTLER
Registrar: HILARY DASHIELL
Dean of the Library: SHARMON KENYON

Library of 560,000 vols
Number of teachers: 563
Number of students: 7,550

DEANS

College of Arts, Humanities and Social Sciences: ROBERT A. SNYDER
College of Natural Resources and Sciences: JAMES HOWARD
College of Professional Studies: SUSAN HIGGINS

HUMPHREYS COLLEGE

6650 Inglewood Ave, Stockton, CA 95207
Telephone: (209) 478-0800
Fax: (209) 478-8721
Internet: www.humphreys.edu

Founded 1896 as Stockton Business College; present name 1947
Private control
Academic year: September to September
Pres.: Dr ROBERT G. HUMPHREYS
Dean of Admin.: WILMA OKAMOTO-VAUGHN
Dean of Instruction: JESS BONDS
Dean of Law School: L. PATRICK PIGGOTT
Registrar: MARIA J. GARCIA-MILLER
Librarian: STANISLAV PERKNER

Areas of study: accounting, administrative management, business admin., community studies, court reporting, early childhood education, liberal arts, paralegal studies.

BRANCH CAMPUS

Modesto Campus: Suite 3A, 3600 Sisk Rd, Modesto, CA 95356; tel. (209) 543-9411; fax (209) 543-9413.

ITT TECHNICAL INSTITUTE

9680 Granite Ridge Dr., San Diego, CA 922123

Telephone: (858) 571-8500
Internet: itt-tech.edu

Founded 1981
Private control (ITT Educational Services, Inc.)
85 Technical institutes in 30 states; schools of information technology, drafting and design, electronics technology, business, school of criminal justice, health sciences
Academic year: September to September
Dir: JOHN A. BYERS
Dean: CORNELL R. HOKE
Registrar: COLLEEN HEBDING.

JESUIT SCHOOL OF THEOLOGY AT BERKELEY

1735 LeRoy Ave, Berkeley, CA 94709
Telephone: (510) 549-5000
Fax: (510) 841-8536
E-mail: admissions@jstb.edu
Internet: www.jstb.edu

Founded 1934 as Alma College; present name 1969
Private control (part of the Graduate Theological Union)
Academic year: September to May
Pres.: Dr JOSEPH P. DAOUST
Academic Dean: KEVIN BURKE
Dean of Students: JILL MARSHALL
Registrar: SHARON-GAY SMITH
Dir of the Library: BONNIE HARDWICK

Library of 684,000 holdings.

JOHN F. KENNEDY UNIVERSITY

100 Ellinwood Way, Pleasant Hill, CA 94563
Telephone: (510) 254-0200
Fax: (510) 254-6964
Internet: www.jfku.edu

Founded 1964
Pres.: Dr STEVEN STARGARDTER
Academic Vice-Pres.: IRVING BERKOWITZ
Vice-Pres. for Enrollment Services: K. SUE DUNCAN
Vice-Pres. for Human Resources: PAULA L. SWAIN
Provost: DIANA PAQUE
Registrar: ADAM J. STONE
Librarians: ANN BUCHALTER (Campbell Campus), JOHN TAYLOR (Berkeley Campus)
Dir of Law Library: STEVEN R. FELLER

Library of 68,300 vols
Number of teachers: 687
Number of students: 1,900

DEANS

School of Education and Liberal Arts: SUSAN KWOCK
School of Holistic Studies: Dr PETER ROJCEWICZ
School of Law: GEOFFREY BROWN
School of Management: CARLOS GUTIERREZ
Graduate School of Professional Psychology: Dr WILLIAM D. PARHAM

BRANCH CAMPUSES

Berkeley Campus: 2956 San Pablo Ave, Berkeley, CA 94702-2471; tel. (510) 649-0499.

Campbell Campus: 1 West Campbell Ave, Campbell, CA 95008; e-mail camp1@jfku.edu.

LA SIERRA UNIVERSITY

4500 Riverwalk Parkway, Riverside, CA 92515

Telephone: (951) 785-2000
Fax: (951) 785-2901
E-mail: info@lasierra.edu
Internet: www.lasierra.edu

Founded 1922
Academic year: September to June
Pres.: Dr LAWRENCE GERATY
Provost and Vice-Pres. for Academic Admin.: Dr WARREN C. TRENCHARD
Vice-Pres. for Advancement/Univ. Relations: JEFFRY M. KAATZ
Vice-Pres. for Enrollment Services: GENE EDELBACH
Vice-Pres. for Financial Admin.: DAVID GERGUIS
Vice-Pres. for Student Life: JENNIFER TYNER
Registrar: FAYE SWAYZE
Library Dir: KITTY SIMMONS

Number of teachers: 110 (full-time)
Number of students: 1,400

Graduate and undergraduate curricula in applied and liberal arts and sciences, business and management, education, religion

Publication: *Adventist Heritage* (4 a year)

DEANS

College of Arts and Sciences: JAMES W. BEACH
School of Business and Management: Dr JOHN THOMAS
School of Education: Dr ED BOYATT
School of Religion: Dr JOHN WEBSTER

LIFE CHIROPRACTIC COLLEGE WEST

25001 Industrial Blvd, Hayward, CA 94545
Telephone: (510) 788-4467
Fax: (510) 780-4525
Internet: www.lifewest.edu

Founded 1976 as Pacific States Chiropractic College; present name 1981
Private control
Academic year: September to June
Offers Doctor degree in Chiropractic
Pres.: Dr GERARD CLUM
Dean of College: Dr JOSEPH FERGUSON
Dean of Health Center: Dr SCOTT DONALDSON
Registrar: ARLENE BASILICO
Library Dir: ANNETTE OSENGA.

LIFE PACIFIC COLLEGE

1100 West Covina Blvd, San Dimas, CA 91773

Telephone: (909) 599-5433
Fax: (909) 599-6690
E-mail: info@lifepacific.edu
Internet: www.lifepacific.edu

Founded 1923
Private control
Academic year: August to May
Pres.: DAN R. STEWART
Vice-Pres. for Academic Affairs: Dr TERRY SAMPLES
Dir of Advancement: CARMEN QUEVEDO
Dir of Institutional Research: JASON SHIPMAN
Chief Financial Officer: JARROD KULA
Dean of Students: TIM CLARKE
Registrar: BRUCE PRIMROSE
Librarian: KEITH DAWSON

Biblical Exegesis, Children's Ministry, Counselling Ministry, Cross-Cultural Ministry, Education, Music and Worship Ministry, Pastoral Ministry, Youth Ministry.

LOMA LINDA UNIVERSITY

Loma Linda, CA 92350

Telephone: (909) 558-8161
Fax: (909) 558-0242
E-mail: admissions.app@llu.edu
Internet: www.llu.edu

Founded 1905
Pres. and CEO: B. LYN BEHRENS
Sr Vice-Pres. for Clinical Faculty: RICARDO PEVERINI
Sr Vice-Pres. for Educational Affairs: RONALD L. CARTER
Sr Vice-Pres. for Faculty Practice: DAVID WREN
Sr Vice-Pres. for Finance: STEVEN MOHR
Sr Vice-Pres. for Health Administration: DANIEL FONTOURA
Sr Vice-Pres. for Human Resource Management and Risk Management: MARK L. HUBBARD
Sr Vice-Pres. for Managed Care: ZAREH SARRAFIAN
Sr Vice-Pres. for Strategic Planning: MICHAEL H. JACKSON
Exec. Vice-Pres. for Finance and Admin./Chief Financial Officer: KEVIN J. LANG
Exec. Vice-Pres. for Hospital Affairs: RUTHITA J. FIKE
Exec. Vice-Pres. for Medical Affairs: H. ROGER HADLEY
Exec. Vice-Pres. for Univ. Affairs: RICHARD H. HART
Vice Pres./CIO for Academia: DAVID P. HARRIS
Vice Pres./CIO for Health Ministries: RICHARD HERGERT
Vice-Pres. for Allied Health Professions Education: CRAIG R. JACKSON
Vice-Pres. for Dentistry: CHARLES J. GOODACRE
Vice-Pres. for Diversity: LESLIE N. POLLARD
Vice-Pres. for Finance: VERLON STRAUSS
Vice-Pres. for Graduate Medical Education: DANIEL W. GIANG
Vice-Pres. for Graduate Studies Education: ANTHONY J. ZUCCARELLI
Vice-Pres. for Healthcare Business Devt/Govt Relations: MEL SAUDER
Vice-Pres. for Nursing Education: MARILYN M. HERMANN
Vice-Pres. for Patient Care Services: ELIZABETH J. DICKINSON
Vice-Pres. for Public Affairs: W. AUGUSTUS CHEATHAM
Vice-Pres. for Quality: JAMES PAPPAS
Vice-Pres. for Religious Education: JON PAULIEN
Vice-Pres. for Spiritual Life and Wholeness: GERALD R. WINSLOW
Dir of Libraries: CARLENE DRAKE

Library: 317,368 vols and periodicals
Number of teachers: 1,068 (full-time)
Number of students: 3,427

DEANS

School of Allied Health Professions: CRAIG R. JACKSON

School of Dentistry: Dr CHARLES J. GOODACRE
School of Medicine: Dr ROGER HADLEY
School of Nursing: Dr MARILYN HERMANN
School of Pharmacy: Dr AVIS J. ERICSON
School of Public Health: Dr JAMES KYLE
Faculty of Religion: Dr DAVID L. TAYLOR
Faculty of Science and Technology: RONALD L. CARTER
Graduate School: ANTHONY J. ZUCCARELLI

LOYOLA MARYMOUNT UNIVERSITY

1 LMU Dr., Los Angeles, CA 90045-2659
Telephone: (310) 338-2700
Internet: www.lmu.edu

Founded 1911 by Jesuit Fathers; present name 1973
Academic year: August to May

Pres.: Rev. ROBERT B. LAWTON
Chancellor: PATRICK J. CAHALAN
Sr Vice-Pres.: DAVID W. BURCHAM
Sr Vice-Pres. for Academic Affairs: Dr ERNEST T. ROSE
Sr Vice-Pres. for Admin.: LYNN SCARBOROUGH
Sr Vice-Pres. for Business and Finance: THOMAS FLEMING
Sr Vice-Pres. for Student Affairs: Dr LANE BOVE
Sr Vice-Pres. for Univ. Relations: DENNIS SLON
Vice-Pres. for Communications and Govt Relations: KATHLEEN FLANAGAN
Vice-Pres. for Devt and Alumni Relations: BEDFORD MCINTOSH
Dir of Graduate Admissions: CHAKÉ KOUYOUMJIAN
Dean of Univ. Libraries: KRISTINE BRANCOLINI

Library of 561,498 vols (289,201 main campus; 272,297 Law School)
Number of teachers: 805 (692 main campus, 113 Law School)
Number of students: 8,215 (6,804 main campus, 1,411 Law School)

DEANS

Bellarmine College of Liberal Arts: Dr MICHAEL E. ENG
College of Business Admin.: Dr JOHN T. WHOLIHAN
College of Communication and Fine Arts: Prof. BARBARA BUSSE
Frank R. Seaver College of Science and Engineering: Dr RICHARD G. PLUMB
Loyola Law School: Dr DAVID W. BURCHAM
School of Education: SHANE MARTIN
School of Film and Television: TERRI SCHWARTZ

MASTER'S COLLEGE

21726 Placerita Canyon Rd, Santa Clarita, CA 91321
Telephone: (661) 259-3540
Fax: (661) 288-1037
E-mail: enrollment@masters.edu
Internet: www.masters.edu

Founded 1927 as Los Angeles Baptist Theological Seminary; present name 1985
Private control

Pres.: Dr JOHN MACARTHUR
Sr Vice-Pres. and Provost: Dr RICHARD MAYHUE
Vice-Pres. for Academic Affairs: Dr JOHN HUGHES
Vice-Pres. for Enrollment Management: Dr PAUL BERRY
Vice-Pres. for Operations: ROBERT L. HOTTON
Vice-Pres. for Student Life: Dr MARK TATLOCK
Chief Financial Officer: BRADLEY G. WETHERELL
Dir of Library Services: JOHN STONE

Library of 143,000 vols
Number of teachers: 70
Number of students: 1,100

Areas of study: biblical studies, biological and physical science, business, communication, computer and information sciences, English, history and political studies, home economics, liberal studies, mathematics, music, physical education, teacher education, biblical counselling, divinity, theology.

MENLO COLLEGE

1000 El Camino Real, Atherton, CA 94027-4301
Telephone: (650) 543-3753
E-mail: admissions@menlo.edu
Internet: www.menlo.edu

Founded 1927 as Menlo Junior College; present name 1949
Private control

Depts of communication, liberal arts and management

Pres.: TIMOTHY HAIGHT
Provost: JAMES J. KELLY
Academic Dean: LOWELL PRATT
Dean of Library and Information Services: C. BRIGID WELCH
Number of students: 550

MENNONITE BRETHREN BIBLICAL SEMINARY

4824 East Butler Ave, Fresno, CA 93727-5097
Telephone: (559) 251-8628
Fax: (559) 251-7212
E-mail: fresno@mbseminary.edu
Internet: www.mbseminary.edu

Founded 1955
Private control
Academic year: August to August

Pres.: JIM HOLM
Academic Dean: LYNN JOST
Dean of Students: RICK BARTLETT
Chief Financial Officer: LINDA BOWMAN
Registrar: LORI JAMES
Librarian: RICHARD RAWLS

Library of 150,000 vols
Number of teachers: 11
Number of students: 143

MAs in christian ministry, divinity, intercultural mission, marriage, family and child counselling, New Testament, Old Testament, theology; diplomas in Anglican studies, christian studies, congregational care, evangelism and church planting, integration, Presbyterian studies, women in ministry.

CANADA CAMPUSES

Langley Campus: MBBS, 7600 Glover Rd, Langley, BC V2Y 1Y1, Canada; tel. (604) 513-2019; fax (604) 513-2045; e-mail langley@mbseminary.edu; internet www.acts.twu.ca.

Winnipeg Campus: MBBS, Canadian Mennonite Univ., 500 Shaftesbury Blvd, Winnipeg, MB R3P 2N5, Canada; tel. (204) 487-3300; fax (204) 487-3858; e-mail winnipeg@mbseminary.edu; internet www.ministrystudies.ca.

MILLS COLLEGE

5000 MacArthur Blvd, Oakland, CA 94613
Telephone: (510) 430-2255
Fax: (510) 430-3314
E-mail: admission@mills.edu
Internet: www.mills.edu

Founded as a seminary 1852, as a college 1885
Academic year: June to May

Liberal arts college; women only at undergraduate level; mixed at graduate level

Pres.: JANET HOLMGREN
Provost and Dean of the Faculty: MARY-ANN MILFORD
Vice-Pres. for Admin. and Finance and Treas.: ELIZABETH BURWELL
Vice-Pres. for Information Resources: RENÉE JADUSHLEVER
Vice-Pres. for Institutional Advancement: CYNTHIA BRANDT STOVER
Dean of Admission: GIULIETTA AQUINO
Dean of Student Life: KENNEDY GOLDEN (acting)

Library of 225,000 vols; spec. collns 12,000 vols and 10,000 MSS, incl. Shakespeare's First Folio, a Mozart MSS, and edn of *Alice in Wonderland* illustrated by Salvador Dali
Number of teachers: 94
Number of students: 1,400

Publications: *580 Split* (1 a year), *The Walrus* (1 a year)

DEANS

Fine Arts: MARY-ANN MILFORD
Letters: RUTH SAXTON
Natural Sciences and Education: LINDA KROLL
Social Sciences: LAURA NATHAN

MONTEREY INSTITUTE OF INTERNATIONAL STUDIES

460 Pierce St, Monterey, CA 93940
Telephone: (831) 647-4100
Fax: (831) 647-4199
E-mail: admit@miis.edu
Internet: www.miis.edu

Founded 1955
Academic year: September to June

Ind. int. graduate school

Pres.: CLARA YU
Vice-Pres. for Academic Affairs and Provost: (vacant)
Vice-Pres. for Enrollment Management: DENNIS R. JOHNSON
Vice-Pres. for Finance and Admin.: (vacant)
Vice-Pres. for Institutional Advancement: ANN JONES-WEINSTOCK
Library Dir: PETER LIU

Library of 90,000 vols, 500 periodical titles; incl. all UN publs since 1993, and dictionaries and translation resources (one-third of whole colln is in languages other than English)
Number of students: 699

DEANS

Fisher Graduate School of Int. Business: Dr ERNEST SCALBERG
Graduate School of Int. Policy Studies: EDWARD J. LAURANCE
Graduate School of Language and Educational Linguistics: RUTH LARIMER
Graduate School of Translation and Interpretation: CHUANYUN BAO

MOUNT ST MARY'S COLLEGE

Chalon Campus, 12001 Chalon Rd, Los Angeles, CA 90049-1599
Telephone: (310) 954-4000
Fax: (310) 954-4379
Internet: www.msmc.la.eduDoheny Campus, 10 Chester Pl., Los Angeles, CA 9007
Telephone: (213) 477-2500

Founded 1925

Pres.: Dr JACQUELINE POWERS DOUD
Provost and Academic Vice-Pres.: Dr ELEANOR SIEBERT
Vice-Pres. for Admin. and Finance: CHRIS K. MCALARY
Vice-Pres. for Information Support Service: LARRY SMITH

Vice-Pres. for Institutional Advancement: STEPHANIE CUBBA
Vice-Pres. for Student Affairs: JANE LINGUA
Dir of Libraries: CLAUDIA REED

Library of 140,000 vols
Number of teachers: 185
Number of students: 2,480 (1,980 undergraduates, 500 graduates)

Depts of American studies, art, biological sciences, business admin., education, English, film and social justice, gerontology, history, humanities, language and culture, music, nursing, philosophy, physical sciences and mathematics, physical therapy, political science, psychology, religious studies, social work, sociology.

NATIONAL UNIVERSITY

11255 North Torrey Pines Rd, La Jolla, CA 92037-1011
Telephone: (858) 642-8000
Fax: (858) 642-8708
Internet: www.nu.edu

Founded 1971
Private control
26 Learning centres throughout California; campuses at Carlsbad, La Mesa, Mission Valley, Rancho Bernardo, South Bay, Spectrum Business Park

Chancellor: Dr JERRY C. LEE
Vice-Chancellor for Organizational Devt: Dr GARY FROST
Provost and Vice-Pres. for Academic Affairs: Dr SHARON P. SMITH
Vice-Pres. for Admin and Business: KEVIN CASEY
Vice-Pres. for Advancement and Alumni Relations: MAGGIE T. WATKINS
Vice-Pres. for Regional Operations and Marketing: VIRGINIA BENEKE
Vice-Pres. for Strategic Planning: RICHARD C. JOY
Vice-Pres. for Student Services: Dr DOUGLAS SLAWSON
Exec. Vice-Pres.: Dr JOHN F. CADY
Dean of Graduate Studies: (vacant)
Library Dir: ANNE MARIE SECORD

Library of 200,000 vols
Number of teachers: 1,096 (140 full-time, 85 assoc., 871 adjunct)
Number of students: 17,090 (full-time)

DEANS

School of Business and Management: Dr WALI MONDAL
School of Education: Dr GLORIA JOHNSTON
School of Engineering and Technology: Dr HOWARD EVANS
School of Health and Human Sciences: (vacant)
College of Letters and Sciences: Dr DEBRA SCHNEIGER
School of Media and Communication: Dr MICHAEL MCANEAR

NAVAL POSTGRADUATE SCHOOL

1 University Circle, Monterey, CA 93943-5001
Telephone: (831) 656-2023
Fax: (831) 656-3238
Internet: www.nps.edu

Founded 1909

Pres.: Vice-Admiral DANIEL T. OLIVER
Provost and Academic Dean: Dr LEONARD A. FERRARI
Univ. Librarian: ELEANOR UHLINGER

Library of 1,063,696 vols (incl. microform)
Number of teachers: 359
Number of students: 1,500

Courses in aeronautical engineering, applied mathematics, applied physics, applied science, astronautical engineering, computer science, contract management, defence analysis, electrical engineering, engineering acoustics, engineering science, information technology management, int. resource planning and management, leadership and human resource devt, management, materials science and engineering, mechanical engineering, meteorology, meteorology and physical oceanography, modelling, operations research, physical oceanography, physics, programme management, software engineering, systems engineering, systems engineering management, systems technology, virtual environments and simulation

DEANS

Graduate School of Business and Public Policy: Dr ROBERT N. BECK
Graduate School of Engineering and Applied Sciences: Dr JAMES L. KAYS
Graduate School of Operational and Information Sciences: PETER PURDUE
School of Int. Graduate Studies: ROBERT L. ORD

NOTRE DAME DE NAMUR UNIVERSITY

1500 Ralston Ave, Belmont, CA 94002
Telephone: (650) 508-3500
Fax: (650) 508-3736
Internet: www.ndnu.edu

Founded 1851; chartered 1868

Pres.: Dr JOHN B. OBLAK
Provost: Dr JUDITH MAXWELL GREIG
Registrar: SANDRA LEE
Vice-Pres. for Campus Life: RAYMOND JONES
Vice-Pres. for Institutional Advancement: DAVID CATHERMAN
Dean of Enrollment: JARRID WHITNEY
Librarian: Dr KLAUS MUSMANN

Library of 105,910 vols
Number of teachers: 100
Number of students: 1,652

DEANS

School of Arts and Humanities: Dr GREGORY B. WHITE
School of Business and Management: GEORGE KLEMIC
School of Education and Leadership: Dr JOANNE ROSSI
School of Sciences: Dr GREGORY B. WHITE

OCCIDENTAL COLLEGE

1600 Campus Rd, Los Angeles, CA 90041
Telephone: (323) 259-2500
Fax: (323) 259-2958
Internet: www.oxy.edu

Founded 1887

Pres.: JONATHAN VEITCH
Vice-Pres. for Admin. and Finance: MICHAEL GROENER
Vice-Pres. for Admission and Financial Aid: WILLIAM D. TINGLEY
Vice-Pres. for Institutional Advancement: JON KEATES
Vice-Pres. for Legal Affairs and General Counsel: Dr SANDRA COOPER
Dean of Admission: VINCE CUSEO
Dean of the College: ERIC FRANK
Dean of Students: Dr LOUANNE KENNEDY,
Registrar: VICTOR T. EGITTO
Librarian: EMILY BERGMAN

Library of 500,000 items (books, video and audio recordings and microfilms) and 1,255 current periodicals
Number of teachers: 140
Number of students: 1,534

Courses in American studies, art history and visual arts, Asian studies, biochemistry, biology, chemistry, cognitive science, critical theory and social justice, diplomacy and world affairs, economics, education, English and comparative literary studies, English writing, environmental programmes, geology, German, Russian, and classical studies, global affairs, history, kinesiology, mathematics, music, philosophy, physics, politics, psychobiology, psychology, religious studies, sociology, Spanish and French literary studies, Theatre, women's studies/gender studies.

OTIS COLLEGE OF ART AND DESIGN

9045 Lincoln Blvd, Los Angeles, CA 90045
Telephone: (310) 665-6800
Fax: (310) 665-6821
E-mail: admissions@otis.edu
Internet: www.otis.edu

Founded 1918

Pres.: SAMUEL HOI
Provost: JOHN S. GORDON
Vice-Pres. for Admin. and Finance: CHRIS ALFORD
Vice-Pres. for Enrollment Management: SAMUEL HOI
Dean of Admissions: MARC MEREDITH
Dean of Student Affairs: MARY WARDELL
Gallery Dir: MEG LINTON
Registrar: ANNA MANZANO
Dir of Library: SUE MABERRY

Library of 25,000 vols
Number of teachers: 200
Number of students: 940

BAs in architecture/landscape/interiors, communication arts, digital media, fashion design, fine arts, interactive product design, toy design; MAs in fine arts, public practice, writing.

PACIFIC LUTHERAN THEOLOGICAL SEMINARY

2770 Marin Ave, Berkeley, CA 94708
Telephone: (510) 524-5264
Fax: (510) 524-2408
E-mail: reception@plts.edu
Internet: plts.edu

Founded 1950
Private control (part of the Graduate Theological Union)
Academic year: September to May

Pres.: Dr PHYLIS ANDERSON
Vice-Pres. for Advancement: CINDY CARROLL
Dir of Admissions: GREG SCHAEFER
Dean of Faculty: MICHAEL B. AULNE
Dean of Students and Registrar: CHERYL HEUER
Library Dir: BONNIE HARDWICK

Library of 648,163 items, 382,523 bound vols, 301,640 audiovisual materials, 18,426 reference vols, 2,559 current subscriptions
Number of teachers: 15
Number of students: 186

MAs in christian ministry, divinity, theological studies.

PACIFIC OAKS COLLEGE AND CHILDREN'S SCHOOL

5 Westmoreland Pl., Pasadena, CA 91103-3592
Telephone: (626) 397-1300
Fax: (626) 577-3502
Internet: www.pacificoaks.edu

Founded 1945

Pres.: CAROLYN DENHAM
Vice-Pres. for Advancement: ARRISTIDE J. COLLINS
Registrar: MARSHA FRANKER
Provost: LESLIE JOHNSON
Librarian: NERMINE HANNA

Library of 17,000 items

Number of teachers: 71
Number of students: 1,281
Courses in human devt, marital and family therapy, teacher education programmes.

PACIFIC SCHOOL OF RELIGION

1798 Scenic Ave, Berkeley, CA 94709-1323
Telephone: (510) 848-0528
Fax: (510) 845-8948
E-mail: psrinfo@psr.edu
Internet: www.psr.edu
Founded 1866 as Pacific Theological Seminary, present name 1916; attached to Graduate Theological Union
Private control
Academic year: September to May
Pres.: Rev. Dr WILLIAM MCKINNEY
Vice-Pres. for Academic Affairs and Dean: Dr MARY DONOVAN TURNER
Registrar: DELPHINE HWANG
Dir of Badè Museum: AARON BRODY
Library Dir: ROBERT BENETTO
Library of 700,000 vols
Number of teachers: 57 (17 core, 40 adjunct)
Number of students: 241

PACIFIC UNION COLLEGE

1 Angwin Ave, Angwin, CA 94508
Telephone: (707) 965-6311
Fax: (707) 965-6506
E-mail: enroll@puc.edu
Internet: www.puc.edu
Founded 1882
Private control, affiliated with the Seventh-day Adventist Church
Academic year: September to June
Pres.: HEATHER KNIGHT
Vice-Pres. for Academic Admin. and Academic Dean: NANCY LECOURT
Vice-Pres. for Advancement: PAM SADLER
Vice-Pres. for Financial Admin.: JOHN COLLINS
Vice-Pres. for Student Services: Dr LISA BISSELL PAULSON
Registrar: H. SUSI MUNDY
Chair of Library Services: ADUGNAW WORKU
Library of 240,000 vols
Number of teachers: 115
Number of students: 1,700
Depts of aviation, biology, business admin. and economics, chemistry, communication, computer science, education, English, exercise science, health and nutrition, history, honours, mathematics, modern languages, music, nursing, physics, psychology and social work, religion, visual arts
Publications: *College Bulletin*, *PUC Viewpoint* (4 a year).

PACIFICA GRADUATE INSTITUTE

249 Lambert Rd, Carpinteria, CA 93013
Telephone: (805) 969-3626
Fax: (805) 565-1932
E-mail: admissions@pacifica.edu
Internet: www.pacifica.edu
Pres.: Dr STEPHEN AIZENSTAT
Provost: CHARLES ASHER
Chief Financial Officer: CATHY WALKER
Dean of Academic Affairs: Dr CINDY CARTER
Dir of Admissions: WENDY OVEREND
Dir of Library Services: ERIN BARTA
Registrar: FRANCINE MATAS
Depts of clinical psychology, counselling psychology, depth psychology, depth psychotherapy, humanities, mythological studies.

PALO ALTO UNIVERSITY

1791 Arastradero Rd, Palo Alto, CA 94304
Telephone: (800) 818-6136
Fax: (650) 433-3888
E-mail: admissions@paloaltou.edu
Internet: www.paloaltou.edu
Founded 2009; fmrly Pacific Graduate School of Psychology
Pres.: Dr ALLEN D. CALVIN
Vice-Pres. for Academic Affairs: Dr WILLIAM FROMING
Registrar: NORA MARQUEZ
Undergraduate and graduate and doctoral programmes; offers business psychology, clinical psychology, neuropsychology; psychology and social action; mental health counselling.

PARDEE RAND GRADUATE SCHOOL

1776 Main St, Santa Monica, CA 90407-3208
Telephone: (310) 393-0411
Fax: (310) 451-6978
E-mail: prgs@prgs.edu
Internet: www.prgs.edu
Founded 1970
Private control
Dean: JOHN GRAHAM
Number of teachers: 100
Number of students: 92
Areas of study: policy analysis, social and behavioural sciences, science and technology, modelling and computational methods, empirical analysis, economics.

PATTEN COLLEGE

2433 Coolidge Ave, Oakland, CA 94601
Telephone: (510) 261-8500
Fax: (510) 534-4344
E-mail: admissions@patten.edu
Internet: www.patten.edu
Founded 1944
Private control
Pres.: Dr GARY MONCHER
Academic Vice-Pres. and Provost: Dr KENNETH ROMINES
Dean of Enrollment Services: ROBERT OLIVERA
Dean of Student Services: SHARON BARTA
Library Dir: ANN ZEMENS
Library of 33,000 vols, 180 periodicals
Depts of art, biblical studies, christian leadership, church ministries, communications, education, liberal studies for teaching, music, organizational management, pastoral studies, psychology, urban missions, youth ministry.

PEPPERDINE UNIVERSITY

24255 Pacific Coast Highway, Malibu, CA 90263
Telephone: (310) 506-4000
Internet: www.pepperdine.edu
Founded 1937 as college, attained univ. status 1970
Pres.: ANDREW K. BENTON
Chancellor: Dr CHARLES B. RUNNELS
Provost and Chief Academic Officer: Dr DARRYL TIPPENS
Exec. Vice-Pres. and Chief Operating Officer: GARY HANSON
Sr Vice-Pres. for Investments: JEFF PIPPIN
Sr Vice-Pres. for Planning, Information and Technology: Dr NANCY MAGNUSSON
Vice-Pres. for Advancement and Public Affairs: KEITH HINKLE
Dean of Admission and Enrollment Management: PAUL A. LONG
Dean of Int. Programs: CHARLES HALL
Dean of Libraries: MARK S. ROOSA
Dean of Student Affairs: MARK DAVIS
Library: 7 libraries with a combined colln of 1m. vols
Number of teachers: 300 full-time
Number of students: 7,603
Publication: *Pepperdine People Magazine*

DEANS

Seaver College: RICK MARRS
Graduate School of Education and Psychology: MARGARET WEBER
Graziadio School of Business and Management: LINDA A. LIVINGSTONE
School of Law: KENNETH W. STARR
School of Public Policy: JAMES R. WILBURN

PROFESSORS

Seaver College:
ADJEMIAN, C., Mathematics
ADLER, R., Marketing
ARDOIN, B., Communication
BAIM, D., Economics and Finance
BAIRD, D., History
BANKS, J., Management and Organizational Behaviour
BATCHELDER, R., Economics
BUCHANAN, R. W., Communication
CALDWELL, D. E., Social Sciences
CARROLL, L. A., English
CASEY, M. W., Communication
CHANDLER, R., Communication
CHESNUTT, R. D., Religion
CLEGG, C., English
CLOUD, D. C., Accounting
COBB, G., Music
COLLINGS, M. R., English
DAVIS, S., Biology
DOWDEY, D., German
DUNPHY, M., Physical Education
FALKNER, A., Art
FELTNER, M., Sports Medicine
GAMBILL, K., English
GANSKE, J., Chemistry
GIBONEY, S., Education
GIBSON, D., Philosophy
GOSE, M. D., Education
GREEN, D. B., Chemistry
HANCOCK, D. L., Mathematics
HART, G. W., English
HENDERSON, J., Theatre
HUGHES, R. T., Religion
KATS, L., Biology
LANGFORD, M., French
LOVE, S., Religion
LOWRY, D. N., Communication
MACRAE, H., Sports Medicine
MACRAE, P., Sports Medicine
MADDOX, R. B., Mathematics
MARRS, R. R., Religion
MARTIN, K. L., Biology
MONSMA, S., Political Science
MURRIE, M., Telecommunications
MYERS, V., English
NEILSON, G., Theatre
PARKENING, C., Music
PAYNE-PALACIO, J., Nutritional Science
PHILLIPS, W., Physics
PIASENTIN, J., Art
PULLEN, M., Music
REINECK, L., English
SESHAN, V., Management
SEXTON, R. L., Social Sciences
SHATZER, M., Communication
SHORES, D., Broadcasting
STRACHE, C. V., Physical Education
SUMMERS, M. R., Business Administration
SWARTZENDRUBER, D., Biology
THOMAS, J., English
THOMASON, P. B., Spanish
THOMPSON, D., Mathematics
TYLER, R. L., Religion
WARFORD, S., Computer Science
WEBB, G. T., Japanese Cultural History
WHITE, J. B., Chemistry

WILSON, J. F., New Testament
YATES, J. E., Organizational Behaviour and Management

School of Business and Management:
BLEUEL, W. H., Quantitative Methods
BUSKIRK, B. D., Marketing
DARDEN, C. E., Organization and Management
DUDLEY, T. J., Quantitative Methods
FLIEGE, S., Quantitative Methods
FOJTIK, C. W., Marketing
GERTMENIAN, W., Economics
GOODRICH, J., Int. Business
HAGAN, A. J., Economics
HALL, O. P., Jr, Quantitative Methods
HESSE, R., Quantitative Methods
HITCHIN, D. E., Management
HOISMAN, A. J., Behavioural Science
HUNT, C. J., Jr, Business Law
LARSON, W. G., Business Law
MALLINGER, M., Organization Behaviour
MARTINOFF, J. T., Finance
MOTAMEDI, K. K., Organization and Management
NICKLES, M. D., Economics
PENDERGHAST, T. F., Quantitative Methods
PETRO, F. A., Accounting
REISMAN, G., Economics
RICHARDSON, J. E., Marketing
RIERDAN, R. C., Behavioural Science
ROCKEY, E., Behavioural Science
SAMUELSON, B. A., Accounting
SANFORD, E., Economics
SHAFER, W., Accounting
SIEGEL, S., Technology Management
STANLEY, D. J., Finance and Accounting
STROM, W. L., Behavioural Science
VARDIABASIS, D., Economics
YOUNG, T. W., Economics

School of Education and Psychology:
ASAMEN, J. K., Psychology
COZOLINO, L. J., Psychology
FOY, D., Psychology
GARCIA, C. L., Education
HARRELL, S. P., Psychology
HEDGESPETH, J., Psychology
HIATT-MICHAEL, D., Education
HIBBS, C., Psychology
INGRAM, B., Psychology
LEVY, D. A., Psychology
LOWE, D. W., Psychology
MCCALL, C., Research Methods
MCMANUS, J. F., Education
MARTINEZ, T., Psychology
NEELY, F. W., Psychology
PAULL, R., Education
POLIN, L. G., Education
ROWE, D., Psychology
SÁNCHEZ, M., Education
SCHMIEDER-RAMIREZ, J., Education
SHAFRANSKE, E. P., Psychology
STEPHENS, R., Education

School of Law:
ALFORD, R. P.
BOST, T. G.
BOYD, K. L.
BUCHAN, L.
CALDWELL, H. M.
CHASE, C. A.
COCHRAN, R. F., Jr
COE, J. J., Jr
GAFFNEY, E. M., Jr
GASH, J. A.
GOODMAN, C. C.
GRADISHER, M. R.
GRAFFY, C. P.
JAMES, B.
KERR, C. L.
KERR, J. E.
KNAPLUND, K. S.
LEVINE, S. J.
LOWRY, L. R.
MCCRORY, J. P.
MCDERMOTT, A. X.
MCDONALD, B. P.
MCGOLDRICK, J. M., Jr
MARTIN, D. W.
MENDOZA, A.
MILLER, A.
NELSON, C. I.
OGDEN, G. L.
PERRIN, L. T.
POPOVICH, R.
PUSHAW, R. J.
ROBINSON, P.
SAXER, S. R.
SCARBERRY, M. S.
SEYMOUR, A. D.
SMITH, M. L.
WENDEL, P. T.
WESTON, M. A.

School of Public Policy:
LLOYD, G., Public Policy
MCALLISTER, E., Public Policy
MONSMA, S. V., Political Science
SEXTON, R., Economics
VAN EATON, C., Public Policy
VARDIABASIS, D., Economics
WILSON, J. Q., Public Policy

PITZER COLLEGE

1050 N Mills Ave, Claremont, CA 91711-6110
Telephone: (909) 621-8000
E-mail: admission@pitzer.edu
Internet: www.pitzer.edu

Founded 1963; attached to Claremont Colleges
Private control
Language of instruction: English
Academic year: August to May

Pres.: LAURA SKANDERA TROMBLEY
Vice-Pres. of Academic Affairs and Dean of Faculty: ALAN JONES
Vice-Pres. of Admin. and Treas.: YUET LEE
Vice-Pres. of Admission and Financial Aid: ARNALDO RODRIGUEZ
Vice-Pres. of College Advancement: DENNIS TROTTER
Vice-Pres. of Marketing and Public Relations: KIRA POPLOWSKI
Vice-Pres. of Student Affairs and Dean of Students: JIM MARCHANT
Registrar: EVA PETERS
Librarian: ALBERTA WALKER

Library: 2m. vols
Number of teachers: 75
Number of students: 950

POINT LOMA NAZARENE UNIVERSITY

3900 Lomaland Dr., San Diego, CA 92106-2899
Telephone: (619) 849-2200
Fax: (619) 849-2579
E-mail: admissions@ptloma.edu
Internet: www.pointloma.edu

Founded 1902 as Pacific Bible College; present name 1998
Private control
Academic year: August to May

Pres.: Dr BOB BROWER
Vice-Pres. for Financial Affairs: GEORGE LATTER
Vice-Pres. for Spiritual Devt: MICHAEL A. PITTS
Vice-Pres. for Student Devt: W. GORDON GOLSAN
Vice-Pres. for Univ. Advancement: DANIEL J. MARTIN
Provost and Chief Academic Officer: Dr JOHN W. HAWTHORNE
Dir of Admissions: SCOTT SHOEMAKER
Dir of Learning Services: Dr FRANK QUINN

Number of students: 2,000

Depts of art and design, biology, chemistry, communication and theatre, family and consumer sciences, history and political science, kinesiology, literature, journalism and modern languages, mathematics, information and computer sciences, music, physics and eng., psychology, sociology and social work

DEANS

Arts and Sciences: Dr DAVID L. STRAWN
Social Science and Professional Studies: Dr REBECCA A. HAVENS
Graduate and Continuing Education: Dr DARREL R. FALK

BRANCH CAMPUSES

Arcadia Campus: 225 East Santa Clara St, Arcadia, CA 91006; tel. (626) 821-8240; fax (626) 821-8249.

Bakersfield Campus: Suite 100, 2100 Chester Ave, Bakersfield, CA 93301; tel. (661) 321-3480; fax (661) 321-3489.

Mission Valley Campus: 4007 Camino Del Rio South, San Diego, CA 92108; tel. (619) 563-2818.

POMONA COLLEGE

Alexander Hall, 550 N College Ave, Claremont, CA 91711
Telephone: (909) 621-8000
Internet: www.pomona.edu

Founded 1887
Private control, mem. of the Claremont Colleges

Pres.: DAVID W. OXTOBY
Vice-Pres. for Academic Affairs and Dean of the College: CECILIA CONRAD
Vice-Pres. for Devt: CHRIS PONCE
Vice-Pres. and Dean of Students: MIRIAM FELDBLUM
Vice-Pres. and Treas.: KAREN SISSON
Dean of Admissions: BRUCE POCH
Registrar: MARGARET ADORNO

Library: 1.9m. vols
Number of teachers: 186
Number of students: 1,500

Publication: *Pomona College Magazine* (4 a year).

ST MARY'S COLLEGE OF CALIFORNIA

Moraga, CA 94575
Telephone: (925) 631-4000
Internet: www.stmarys-ca.edu

Founded 1863

Pres.: Bro. RONALD GALLAGHER
Vice-Pres. for Academic Affairs and Provost: Prof. SARA STAMPP
Vice-Pres. for Advancement and Planning: Bro. STANISLAUS SOBCZYK
Vice-Pres. for Finance: PETER MICHELL
Vice-Pres. for College Communications and Vice-Provost for Enrollment: MICHAEL BESEDA
Dean of Academic Resources: THOMAS CARTER
Vice-Provost for Academic Affairs: FRANCES SWEENEY
Vice-Provost for Student Life: SCOTT KIER

Library of 200,000 vols, 1,100 current periodicals
Number of teachers: 274
Number of students: 4,378

DEANS

School of Economics and Business Administration: Dr ROY ALLEN
School of Education: Dr NANCY L. SORENSON
School of Extended Education: Dr DEAN ELIAS
School of Liberal Arts: Dr STEPHEN WOOLPERT
School of Nursing: Dr ARLENE SARGENT
School of Science: Dr JUDD CASE

ST PATRICK'S SEMINARY AND UNIVERSITY

320 Middlefield Rd, Menlo Park, CA 94025
Telephone: (650) 325-5621
Fax: (650) 323-5447
E-mail: info@stpatricksseminary.org
Internet: www.stpatricksseminary.org

Founded 1898
Private control
Academic year: September to May

Pres. and Chancellor: Rev. GEORGE H. NIEDERAUER
Vice-Pres. and Sec.: Rev. JOHN C. WESTER
Vice-Pres. for Advancement: CHRISTOPHER GRASSO
Pres., Rector and Vice-Chancellor: Rev. GERALD S. S. BROWN
Academic Dean: DOROTHY TULLY
Dean of Students: Rev. VINCENT D. BUI
Registrar: NURIA ORTIZ
Dir of Library: Dr CECIL R. WHITE

Library of 101,400 vols, 286 periodicals.

ATTACHED INSTITUTE

Vatican II Institute for Continuing Formation: 320 Middlefield Rd, Menlo Park, CA 94025; tel. (650) 325-9122; fax (650) 325-6765; e-mail vat2ins@aol.com; internet www.stpatricksseminary.org/vatican2; f. 1972; Dir Rev. JIM MYERS.

SAMRA UNIVERSITY OF ORIENTAL MEDICINE

3rd Fl., 3000 1730 W Olympic Blvd, Los Angeles, CA 90015
Telephone: (213) 381-2221
E-mail: info@samra.edu
Internet: www.samra.edu
Private control
Languages of instruction: English, Chinese, Korean
Academic year: October to September

Pres.: Dr HYUNG JOO PARK
Vice-Pres.: Dr BYUNG S. HONG
Provost: Dr KAATSUYUKI SAKAMOTO
Registrar: ELIZABETH GOMEZ
Librarian: GAN YE

Library of 7,000 items

Areas of study: Chinese medical theory, acupuncture theory, Chinese herbology, basic sciences, anatomy, physiology.

SAMUEL MERRITT COLLEGE

370 Hawthorne Ave, Oakland, CA 94609
Telephone: (510) 869-6511
E-mail: information@samuelmerritt.edu
Internet: www.samuelmerritt.edu

Founded 1909, merged with California College of Podiatric Medicine (f. 1914) in 2002

Pres. and CEO: SHARON DIAZ
Academic Vice-Pres. and Provost: Dr SCOT FOSTER
Vice-Pres. for Enrollment and Student Services: JOHN GARTEN-SHUMAN
Vice-Pres. for Finance and Admin.: GREGORY GINGRAS
Library Dir: BARBARA RYKEN

Library of 15,000 vols, 7,740 bound periodicals, 474 current periodicals
Number of teachers: 42 (full time)
Number of students: 650

Depts of nursing, occupational therapy, physical therapy, physician assistant training, podiatric medicine

DEANS

Nursing: AUDREY BERMAN
Podiatric Medicine: AL BURNS

SAN DIEGO CHRISTIAN COLLEGE

2100 Greenfield Dr., El Cajon, CA 92019
Telephone: (619) 441-2200
Fax: (619) 590-1739
E-mail: admissions@sdcc.edu
Internet: www.sdcc.edu

Founded 1971
Private control
Academic year: September to May

Pres.: Dr PAUL AGUE
Vice-Pres. of Academic Affairs: LUNDIE CARSTENSEN
Dean of Students: STEVE JENKINS
Registrar: SUSIE PARKS
Dir of Library Services: RUTH MARTIN

Library of 65,000 vols, video cassettes, CD-ROMs and periodicals
Number of students: 403

Depts of aviation, adult professional studies (degree completion), biblical studies, business, communication, education, English, history and social science, kinesiology, mathematics, music, psychology, biological science.

SAN DIEGO STATE UNIVERSITY

5500 Campanile Dr., San Diego, CA 92182-8000
Telephone: (619) 594-5200
Internet: www.sdsu.edu

Founded 1897
Academic year: August to May

Pres.: STEPHEN L. WEBER
Provost for Academic Affairs: NANCY A. MARLIN
Vice-Pres. for Research: THOMAS R. SCOTT
Vice-Pres. for Student Affairs: JAMES R. KITCHEN
Vice-Pres. for Univ. Relations and Advancement: MARY RUTH CARLETON
Exec. Dir of Enrolment Services: SANDRA COOK
Dean of Library: CONNIE V. DOWELL

Library of 1,342,735 vols, 644,028 govt documents
Number of teachers: 1,795 (985 full-time; 810 part-time)
Number of students: 38,567 (31,665 undergraduate; 6,566 graduate; 345 doctoral)

Publications: *Fiction International* (1 a year), *Poetry International* (1 a year), *Journal of Borderlands Studies* (2 a year), *Pacific Review: A West Coast Arts Review Annual*, *Mobilization* (3 a year), *Pacific Coast Council on Latin-American Studies* (2 a year)

DEANS

Arts and Letters: PAUL WONG
Business Admin.: GAIL K. NAUGHTON
Education: LIONEL R. MENO
Engineering: DAVID T. HAYHURST
Extended Studies: WILLIAM E. BYXBEE
Health and Human Services: MARILYN NEWHOFF
Professional Studies and Fine Arts: JOYCE M. GATTAS
Sciences: STANLEY MALOY
Graduate Studies: STEVEN KRAMER
Undergraduate Studies: GEOFFREY W. CHASE
Imperial Valley Campus: STEPHEN ROEDER

SAN FRANCISCO ART INSTITUTE

800 Chestnut St, San Francisco, CA 94133
Telephone: (415) 771-7020
E-mail: sfaiinfo@sfai.edu
Internet: www.sanfranciscoart.edu

Founded 1871 as San Francisco Art Asscn; present name 1961
Private control
Academic year: August to May

Pres.: CHRIS BRATTON
Sr Vice-Pres. for Finance and Admin.: JUDY LOGAN
Dean of Academic Affairs, Sr Vice-Pres.: OKWUI ENWEZOR
Vice-Pres. for Academic Planning and Facilities: JENNIFER STEIN
Vice-Pres. for Advancement: KATHY LOWRY

Library of 26,000 vols

Areas of study: design and technology, filmmaking, liberal arts, new genres, painting, photography, printmaking, sculpture.

SAN FRANCISCO CONSERVATORY OF MUSIC

50 Oak St, San Francisco, CA 94102-6011
Telephone: (415) 864-7326
Fax: (415) 503-6299
Internet: www.sfcm.edu

Founded 1917

Pres.: COLIN MURDOCH
Vice-Pres. for Advancement: NANCY SACKSON
Dean: MARY ELLEN POOLE
Dir of Office of Admission: ALEX BROSE
Registrar: ERIKA JOHNSON
Chief Librarian: KEVIN MCLAUGHLIN

Library of 55,603 items and 38,000 scores and parts, 15,900 audio visual items, 12,500 vols, 77 periodicals
Number of teachers: 110
Number of students: 400

Depts of brass, chamber music, conducting, composition, guitar, keyboards, percussion, strings, voice, woodwinds; undergraduate and graduate degrees, postgraduate diplomas.

SAN FRANCISCO STATE UNIVERSITY

1600 Holloway Ave, San Francisco, CA 94132
Telephone: (415) 338-1111
Fax: (415) 338-2514
Internet: www.sfsu.edu

Founded 1899

Pres.: Dr ROBERT A. CORRIGAN
Provost: SUE V. ROSSER
Vice-Pres. for Academic Programme Devt: GAIL WHITAKER (acting)
Vice-Pres. for Admin. and Finance: LEROY M. MORISHITA
Vice-Pres. for Student Affairs and Dean of Students: J. E. (PENNY) SAFFOLD
Vice-Pres. for Univ. Advancement: LEE BLITCH (acting)
Registrar: SUZANNE DMYTRENKO
Univ. Librarian: DEBORAH MASTERS

Library of 1,160,869 items, incl; 2,557,985 microforms, 193,202 audiovisual items, 17,119 subscription periodicals
Number of teachers: 1,818
Number of students: 30,125

DEANS

College of Behavioural and Social Sciences: JOEL KASSIOLA
College of Business: NANCY K. HAYES (acting)
College of Creative Arts: RONALD COMPESI (acting)
College of Education: JACOB E. PEREA
College of Ethnic Studies: KENNETH P. MONTEIRO
College of Extended Learning: GAIL WHITAKER
College of Health and Human Services: DON TAYLOR (acting)
College of Humanities: PAUL SHERWIN
College of Science and Engineering: SHELDON AXLER
Graduate Div.: ANN HALLUM

SAN FRANCISCO THEOLOGICAL SEMINARY

105 Seminary Rd, San Anselmo, CA 94960
Telephone: (415) 451-2800
Fax: (415) 451-2851
E-mail: jperry@sfts.edu
Internet: www.sfts.edu
Private control (part of the Graduate Theological Union)
Pres.: Dr PHILIP W. BUTIN
Vice-Pres. for Academic Affairs and Dean of the Seminary: Dr JANA L. CHILDERS
Vice-Pres. for Finance and Admin.: BARBARA BRENNER BUDER
Vice-Pres. for Seminary and Church Relations: PETER CROUCH
Vice-Pres. for Southern California Campus: Dr DAVID TOMLINSON
Registrar: Dr POLLY COOTE
Library Dir (GTU): ROBERT BENETTO
Librarian (SFTS): MICHAEL PETERSON
Library of 365,000 vols.

BRANCH CAMPUS

Southern California Campus: 54 North Oakland Ave, Pasadena, CA 91101; tel. (626) 397-9004; fax (626) 397-9011; internet www.sfts.edu/sc.

SAN JOSÉ STATE UNIVERSITY

San José, CA 95192
Telephone: (408) 924-1000
Internet: www.sjsu.edu
Founded 1857
Pres.: DON W. KASSING
Provost and Vice-Pres. for Academic Affairs: CARMEN SIGLER
Vice-Pres. for Administration and Finance: ROSE LEE
Vice-Pres. for Student Affairs: VERIL PHILLIPS
Vice-Pres. for Univ. Advancement: FRED NAJJAR
Dean of the Univ. Library: RUTH E. KIFER
Library of 900,000 vols, 3,500 periodical titles
Number of teachers: 704 (full-time)
Number of students: 30,000

DEANS

College of Applied Sciences and Arts: BARBARA CONRY
College of Business: BRUCE MAGID
College of Education: Prof. SUSAN MEYERS
College of Engineering: BELLE WEI
College of Humanities and the Arts: KARL TOEPFER
College of Science: MICHAEL PARRISH
College of Social Sciences: TIM HEGSTROM
Continuing Education: MARK NOVAK

SANTA CLARA UNIVERSITY

Santa Clara, CA 95053

Telephone: (408) 554-4000
Internet: www.scu.edu
Founded 1851
Private control
Academic year: September to June
Pres.: MICHAEL ENGH
Provost: LUCIA ALBINO GILBERT
Vice-Pres. for Admin. and Finance: ROBERT WARREN
Vice-Pres. for Univ. Relations: JAMES PURCELL
Registrar: MONICA AUGUSTIN
Univ. Librarian: ELIZABETH SALZER
Library of 800,000 vols; law library of 370,000 vols
Number of teachers: 721 (434 full-time, 287 part-time)
Number of students: 8,758
Publications: *Explore* (journal of the Bannan Center for Jesuit Education, 4 a year), *STS Nexus* (journal of the Center for Science, Technology and Society, 2 a year)

DEANS

College of Arts and Sciences: YEE W. ATOM (acting)
School of Business: ANDREW STARBIRD (acting)
School of Education, Counselling Psychology and Pastoral Ministries: JANICE CHAVEZ, TOM POWERS
School of Engineering: GODFREY MUNGAL
School of Law: DONALD J. POLDEN

SAYBROOK GRADUATE SCHOOL AND RESEARCH CENTER

3rd Floor, 747 Front St, San Francisco, CA 94111-1920
Telephone: (415) 433-9200
Fax: (415) 433-9271
E-mail: admissions@saybrook.edu
Internet: www.saybrook.edu
Founded 1971
Academic year: September to July
Pres.: Dr LORNE M. BUCHMAN
Exec. Vice-Pres.: Dr ARTHUR C. BOHART, Jr
Vice-Pres. of Academic Affairs: DENISE SCATENA
Vice-Pres. of Marketing and Enrolment Management: SIGRID BADINELLI
Vice-Pres. of Operations, Treasurer and CFO: JOHN W. REHO
Dir of Admissions: ANN MCGEADY
Dir of Research and Library Services: ANNE-MARIE WELTEKE
Number of teachers: 114 (20 executive, 22 consulting, 72 part-time)
Number of students: 525
Publication: *International Journal of Transpersonal Studies* (1 a year)
MA and PhD programmes in psychology, human science, and organizational systems; areas of study are humanistic, transpersonal clinical inquiry and health studies, consciousness and spirituality studies, peace, conflict resolution and community development, organizational systems.

SCRIPPS COLLEGE

1030 Columbia Ave, Claremont, CA 91711
Telephone: (909) 621-8000
Internet: www.scrippscol.edu
Founded 1926
Private control, mem. of the Claremont Colleges
Pres.: FREDERICK WEIS
Vice-Pres. and Dean of Admission and Financial Aid: PATRICIA F. GOLDSMITH
Vice-Pres. and Dean of Faculty: MICHAEL D. LAMKIN
Vice-Pres. and Dean of Students: DEBRA CARLSON WOOD
Vice-Pres. for Business Affairs: JAMES MANIFOLD
Vice-Pres. for Devt and College Relations: MARTHA H. KEATES
Librarian: JUDY HARVEY SAHAK
Library of 110,000 vols in Denison Library and 10,000 in Rare Book Room
Number of teachers: 95 (69 full-time and 26 part-time)
Number of students: 859

SIMPSON UNIVERSITY

2211 College View Dr., Redding, CA 96003
Telephone: (530) 226-4606
Fax: (530) 226-4861
E-mail: registrar@simpsonu.edu
Internet: www.simpsonu.edu
Founded 1921 as Simpson Bible Institute, Simpson College 1971
Private control
Academic year: September to July
Pres.: LARRY J. MCKINNEY
Exec. Vice-Pres. and Vice-Pres. for Business Services: BRADLEY E. WILLIAMS
Vice-Pres. for Advancement: GORDON B. FLINN
Vice-Pres. for Student Devt: RICHARD BROWN
Provost: Dr STANLEY A. CLARK
Dean of Education: GLEE R. BROOKS
Dir ASPIRE Programme: PATTY TAYLOR
Registrar: WENDY RIDDLE
Dir of Library Services: LARRY L. HAIGHT
Library of 70,000 vols
Number of students: 1,216

DEANS

A. W. Tozer Theological Seminary: Dr SARAH SUMNER
School of Continuing Studies: PATTY TAYLOR
School of Education: Dr GLEE BROOKS
School of Traditional Undergraduate Studies: ROBIN DUMMER

SONOMA STATE UNIVERSITY

1801 E Cotati Ave, Rohnert Park, CA 94928
Telephone: (707) 664-2880
Fax: (707) 664-2505
Internet: www.sonoma.edu
Founded 1960
Academic year: August to June
Pres.: Dr RUBEN ARMIÑANA
CFO and Vice-Pres. for Admin. and Finance: Dr LAURENCE FURUKAWA-SCHLERETH
Vice-Pres. for Devt: PATRICIA MCNEIL
Vice-Pres. for Student Affairs and Enrollment Management: MATTHEW LOPEZ-PHILLIPS
Vice-Pres. for Univ. Affairs: DAN CONDRON
Provost and Vice-Pres. for Academic Affairs: Dr EDUARDO M. OCHOA
Library Dean: Dr BARBARA BUTLER
Library of 636,613 vols, 21,115 periodicals, 1,708,201 microforms, 29,529 audio visual items
Number of teachers: 627 (274 full-time, 353 part-time)
Number of students: 8,921

DEANS

School of Arts and Humanities: Dr WILLIAM BABULA
School of Business and Economics: Dr WILLIAM SILVER
School of Education: Dr MARY GENDERNALIK-COOPER
School of Science and Technology: Dr SAEID RAHIMI
School of Social Sciences: Dr ELAINE LEEDER

SOUTHERN CALIFORNIA COLLEGE OF OPTOMETRY

2575 Yorba Linda Blvd, Fullerton, CA 92831-1699
Telephone: (714) 449-7440
Fax: (714) 879-0481
Internet: www.scco.edu
Founded 1904
Pres.: Prof. LESLEY L. WALLS
Vice-Pres. and Dean of Academic Affairs: Prof. MORRIS S. BERMAN
Vice-Pres. and Dean of Clinical Affairs: Dr JOHN H. NISHIMOTO
Vice-Pres. for Advancement: WILLIAM E. HEATON, Jr
Vice-Pres. for Financial Affairs and CFO: LISA K. ALBERS

Vice-Pres. for Student Affairs: LORRAINE I. VOORHEES
Librarian: DONNA JEAN MATTHEWS
Library of 10,000 vols, 6,500 bound journals and 300 current periodicals
Number of teachers: 80 full- and part-time
Number of students: 381
Publications: *The Alumniscope* (4 a year), *The Reflex* (1 a year), *SCCO Admissions Catalog* (every 2 years).

SOUTHERN CALIFORNIA UNIVERSITY OF HEALTH SCIENCES

16200 E Amber Valley Dr., Whittier, CA 90604-4051
Telephone: (562) 947-8755
E-mail: admissions@scuhs.edu
Internet: www.scuhs.edu
Pres.: Dr RONALD KRAFT
Vice-Pres. for Academic Affairs: JOHN SCARINGE
Vice-Pres. for Institutional Advancement: REGINA WEBSTER
Assoc. Vice-Pres. for Student Affairs: GEOFFREY JOWETT
CFO: ROGER JENKINS

DEANS
Acupuncture and Oriental Medicine: WEN-SHUO WU
Chiropractic: TODD KNUDSEN
School of Professional Studies: DEBRA MITCHELL

SOUTHWESTERN LAW SCHOOL

3050 Wilshire Blvd, Los Angeles, CA 90010
Telephone: (213) 738-6700
Fax: (213) 383-1688
E-mail: admissions@swlaw.edu
Internet: www.swlaw.edu
Founded 1911
Private control
Academic year: August to July
Dean and CEO: BRYANT G. GARTH
Vice-Dean for Academic Affairs: AUSTEN PARRISH
Assoc. Dean for Academic Admin.: DOREEN E. HEYER
Assoc. Dean for Career Services: GARY G. GREENER
Assoc. Dean for Institutional Advancement: DEBRA L. LEATHERS
Assoc. Dean for Library Services: LINDA WHISMAN
Assoc. Dean for Research: MICHAEL B. DORFF
Assoc. Dean for Students and Diversity Affairs: NYREE GRAY
Assoc. Dean and Gen. Counsel: PATRICK PYLE
Assoc. Dean for Public Affairs: LESLIE R. STEINBERG
Asst Dir of Admissions: LISA M. GEAR
Dir of Financial Aid: PEGGY LOEWY WELLISCH
Dir of Registration and Academic Records: CAROLYN HAITH
CFO: PAUL KALUSH
Chief Information Systems Officer: BO SUZOW
Chief Operating Officer: JANICE A. MANIS
Library of 480,000 vols and vol. equivalents
Number of teachers: 56 (full-time)
Number of students: 1,050
Publications: *Journal of International Media and Entertainment Law, Southwestern Journal of International Law, Southwestern Law Review*.

STANFORD UNIVERSITY

450 Serra Mall, Stanford, CA 94305
Telephone: (650) 723-2300
Internet: www.stanford.edu
Founded 1885
Private control
Academic year: September to June
Pres.: Dr JOHN HENNESSY
Provost: Dr JOHN ETCHEMENDY
Vice-Pres. and Gen. Counsel: DEBRA ZUMWALT
Vice-Pres. for Alumni Affairs: HOWARD WOLF
Vice-Pres. for Business Affairs and CFO: RANDALL S. LIVINGSTON
Vice-Pres. for Devt: MARTIN SHELL
Vice-Pres. for Land, Bldgs and Real Estate: ROBERT REIDY
Vice-Pres. for Public Affairs: DAVID DEMAREST
Vice-Pres., Stanford Linear Accelerator Center: WILLIAM J. MADIA
Registrar: THOMAS C. BLACK
Vice-Provost for Graduate Education: PATRICIA GUMPORT
Vice-Provost for Undergraduate Education: HARRY ELAM
Vice-Provost and Dean of Research: ANN ARVIN
Univ. Librarian: MICHAEL KELLER
Library: see Libraries and Archives
Number of teachers: 1,903
Number of students: 15,666
Publications: *Journal of Law, Business and Finance* (2 a year), *Stanford Environmental Law Journal* (2 a year), *Stanford Humanities Review* (2 a year), *Stanford Journal of International Law* (2 a year), *Stanford Law Review* (6 a year), *Stanford Social Innovation Review* (4 a year)

DEANS
Graduate School of Business: ROBERT JOSS
School of Earth Sciences: PAMELA MATSON
School of Education: DEBORAH STIPEK
School of Engineering: JAMES PLUMMER
School of Humanities and Sciences: RICHARD SALLER
School of Law: LARRY KRAMER
School of Medicine: PHILIP PIZZO

DIRECTORS
Hoover Institution: JOHN RAISIAN
Stanford Linear Accelerator Center: PERSIS DRELL

PROFESSORS
AAKER, J. L., Graduate School of Business
ADLER, J. R., Jr, Neurosurgery
ADMATI, A. R., Graduate School of Business
ALBANESE, C., Surgery
ALBERS, G. W., Neurology
ALDRICH, R. W., Molecular and Cell Physiology
ALEXANDER, J. C., Law
ALEXANDER, S. R., Paediatrics
AMEMIYA, T., Economics
ANDERSEN, H., Chemistry
ANDERSON, R. U., Jr, Urology
ANDRIACCHI, T. P., Mechanical Engineering
APOSTOLIDES, J.-M., French and Italian
ARBER, D., Pathology
ARIAGNO, R. L., Paediatrics
ARVIN, A. M., Paediatrics
ATHEY, S. C., Economics
ATLAS, S. W., Radiology
ATTANASAIO, O., Economics
AYDIN, A., Geology and Environmental Sciences
AZIZ, K., Petroleum Engineering
BABCOCK, B., Law
BACHRACH, L. K., Paediatrics
BAER, U., German Studies
BAKER, B. S., Biological Sciences
BAKER, K., History
BAMBOS, N., Management Science and Engineering
BANDURA, A., Psychology
BANKMAN, A. J., Law
BARCHIESI, A., Classics
BARLEY, S., Management Science and Engineering
BARNETT, D., Materials Science and Engineering
BARNETT, W., Graduate School of Business
BARON, D. P., Graduate School of Business
BARON, E. J., Pathology
BARON, J. N., Graduate School of Business
BARRES, B. A., Neurobiology
BARSH, G. S., Paediatrics
BARTH, M. E., Graduate School of Business
BARTH, R. A., Radiology
BAUGH, J., Education
BEACH, D., Mechanical Engineering
BEASLEY, M., Applied Physics
BEAVER, W. H., Graduate School of Business
BEININ, J. S., History
BENDER, J., English
BENDOR, J., Graduate School of Business
BENITZ, W. E., Paediatrics
BERGER, K., Music
BERMAN, R. A., German Studies
BERNHARDT, E., German Studies
BERNHEIM, B. D., Economics
BERNSTEIN, B., History
BERNSTEIN, D., Paediatrics
BEROZA, G. C., Geophysics
BETTINGER, J. R., Communication
BIELEFELDT, C. W., Religious Studies
BIENENSTOCK, A. I., Stanford Synchrotron Radiation Laboratory
BIRD, D. K., Geological and Environmental Sciences
BLACK, B. S., Law
BLAND, R. D., Paediatrics
BLANDFORD, R., Stanford Linear Acceleration Center
BLASCHKE, T., Medicine
BLAU, H. M., Molecular Pharmacology
BLOCH, D. A., Health Research and Policy
BLOCK, S. M., Applied Physics
BLOOM, E., Stanford Linear Accelerator Center
BLUMENKRANZ, M. S., Ophthalmology
BOBO, L., Sociology
BOOTHROYD, J. C., Microbiology and Immunology
BORJA, R. I., Civil and Environmental Engineering
BOSKIN, M., Economics
BOWER, G. H., Psychology
BOWMAN, C., Mechanical Engineering
BOXER, S., Chemistry
BOYD, S. P., Electrical Engineering
BOYER, A. L., Radiation Oncology
BRADY, D., Graduate School of Business
BRANDEAU, M. L., Management Science and Engineering
BRATMAN, M., Philosophy
BRAUMAN, J. J., Chemistry
BRAUND, S., Classics
BRAVMAN, J. C., Materials Science and Engineering
BREIDENBACH, M., Stanford Linear Accelerator Center
BRESNAHAN, T., Economics
BRESNAN, J., Linguistics
BROCK-UTNE, J. G., Anaesthesia
BRODSKY, J. B., Anaesthesia
BRODSKY, S., Stanford Linear Accelerator Center
BROTHERSTON, J. G., Spanish and Portuguese
BROWN, G. H., English
BROWN, J. M., Radiation Oncology
BROWN, P. O., Biochemistry
BRUMFIEL, G., Mathematics
BRUNGER, A. T., Molecular and Cellular Physiology
BRUTLAG, D. L., Biochemistry
BRYK, A., Education
BUC, P. C., History
BULOW, J. I., Graduate School of Business
BUMP, D. W., Mathematics
BURCHAT, P. R., Physics
BURGELMAN, R. A., Graduate School of Business

BURKE, D. L., Stanford Linear Accelerator Center
BUTCHER, E. C., Pathology
BYER, R., Applied Physics
BYERS, T. H., Management Science and Engineering
CABRERA, B., Physics
CALLAN, E., Education
CAMARILLO, A. M., History
CAMPBELL, A. M., Biological Sciences
CANTWELL, B., Aeronautics, Astronautics
CARLSON, R., Management Science and Engineering
CARLSON, R. W., Medicine
CARLSSON, G., Mathematics
CARNOY, M., Education
CARRAGEE, E. J., Orthopaedic Surgery
CARROLL, G. R., Graduate School of Business
CARSON, C., History
CARSTENSEN, L. L., Psychology
CARTER, D., Mechanical Engineering
CARTER, S., Asian Languages
CASEY, E. B., English
CASPER, G., Law
CASPER, R., Psychiatry
CASTLE, T., English
CHAFE, C. D., Music
CHAMBERLAIN, C. P., Geological and Environmental Sciences
CHAN, P. H., Neurosurgery
CHANG, F. K., Aeronautics and Astronautics
CHAO, A. W., Stanford Linear Accelerator Center
CHERITON, D. R., Computer Science
CHIEN, Y. K., Microbiology and Immunology
CHRISTENSEN, R. M., Aeronautics and Astronautics
CHU, G., Medicine
CHU, S., Physics
CIOFFI, J. M., Electrical Engineering
CLAERBOUT, J. F., Geophysics
CLARK, E., Linguistics
CLARK, H. H., Psychology
CLAYBERGER, C. A., Paediatrics
CLEARY, M. L., Pathology
CLEMENS, B. M., Materials Science and Engineering
COHEN, H. J., Paediatrics
COHEN, M., French and Italian
COHEN, P. J., Mathematics
COHEN, R. L., Mathematics
COHEN, S. E., Anaesthesia
COHEN, S. N., Genetics
COLE, G. M., Law
COLLMAN, J. P., Chemistry
CONTI, M., Gynaecology and Obstetrics
COOK, K. S., Sociology
COOKE, J. P., Medicine
COOPER, A., Medicine
CORK, L., Comparative Medicine
CORN, W., Art, Art History
CORNELL, C. A., Civil and Environmental Engineering
COTTLE, R. W., Management Science and Engineering
COVER, T. M., Electrical Engineering
COX, D., Electrical Engineering
COX, K. L., Paediatrics
CRABTREE, G., Pathology
CRASWELL, R., Law
CROSS, P. C., Structural Biology
CUTKOSKY, M. R., Mechanical Engineering
DAHL, G. V. H., Paediatrics
DAINES, R., Law
DALLY, W. J., Electrical Engineering
DAMON, W., Education
DARLING-HAMMOND, L., Education
DAUSKARDT, R. H., Materials Science and Engineering
DAVID, P. A., Economics
DAVIS, M. M., Microbiology and Immunology
DAVIS, R., Biochemistry
DEIERLEIN, G. G., Civil and Environmental Engineering
DE KRUYFF, R. H., Paediatrics
DE MARZO, P. M., Graduate School of Business
DEMBO, A., Mathematics
DEMENT, W. C., Psychiatry
DE MICHELI, G., Electrical Engineering
DENNY, M. W., Biological Sciences
DEVINE, A., Classics
DIACONIS, P., Statistics
DILL, D. L., Computer Science
DIMOPOULOS, S., Physics
DIRZO, R., Biological Sciences
DIXON, L. J., Stanford Linear Accelerator Center
DOLAN, J., Drama
DONALDSON, S., Radiation Oncology
DONIACH, S., Applied Physics
DONOHO, D., Statistics
DORFAN, J., Stanford Linear Accelerator Center
DORFMAN, L., Neurology
DRELL, P. S., Stanford Linear Accelerator Center
DRUZIN, M. L., Obstetrics and Gynaecology
DUFFIE, J. D., Graduate School of Business
DUNBAR, R. B., Geological and Environmental Sciences
DUPUY, J.-P., French and Italian
DURBIN, P. A., Mechanical Engineering
DURHAM, W., Anthropological Sciences
DURLOFSKY, L. J., Petroleum Engineering
DUTTON, R., Electrical Engineering
EATON, J. K., Mechanical Engineering
ECKERT, P., Linguistics
EFRON, B., Statistics
EGBERT, P., Ophthalmology
EHRLICH, P. R., Biological Sciences
EISEN, A. M., Religious Studies
EISENHARDT, K. M., Management Science and Engineering
EISNER, E. W., Education
EL GAMAL, A., Electrical Engineering
ELAM, H. J., Jr, Drama
ELIASHBERG, Mathematics
ENGE, P. K., Aeronautics and Astronautics
ENGLAND, P., Sociology
ENGLEMAN, E., Pathology
EPEL, D., Biological Sciences
ERNST, W. G., Geology, Environmental Sciences
ESQUIVEL, C., Surgery
ETCHEMENDY, J. W., Philosophy
EVANS, J. M., English
EVERITT, C. W. F., Hansen Laboratory
FAINSTAT, T., Obstetrics and Gynaecology
FAJARDO, L., Pathology
FALKOW, S., Microbiology and Immunology
FARHAT, C., Mechanical Engineering
FATHMAN, C., Medicine
FAURE, B. R., Religious Studies
FAYER, M., Chemistry
FEARON, J. D., Political Science
FEE, W., Surgery
FEINSTEIN, C. B., Psychiatry
FEJER, M. M., Applied Physics
FELDMAN, D., Medicine
FELDMAN, M. W., Biological Sciences
FELSTINER, J., English
FEREJOHN, J. A., Political Science
FERGUSON, J., Cultural and Social Anthropology
FERNALD, R. D., Psychology
FERNEYHOUGH, B., Music
FERRELL, J. E., Jr, Molecular Pharmacology
FETTER, A. L., Physics
FIELD, C., Biological Sciences
FIELDS, K., English
FIKES, R. E., Computer Science
FINDLEN, P., History
FIORINA, M. P., Political Science
FIRE, A., Pathology
FISH, K. J., Anaesthesia
FISHER, G., Law
FISHER, R. S., Neurology
FISHKIN, J., Communication
FISHKIN, S. F., English
FLANAGAN, R., Graduate School of Business
FLEISHMAN, L., Slavic Languages and Literatures
FLIEGELMAN, J. W., English
FOLLESDAL, D., Philosophy
FORD, J. M., Psychiatry
FORD, R. T., Law
FORTMANN, S. P., Medicine
FOSTER, G., Graduate School of Business
FOWLER, M. B., Medicine
FRANCKE, U., Genetics
FRANK, C., Chemical Engineering
FREEDMAN, E., History
FREIDIN, G., Slavic Languages and Literature
FRIED, B., Law
FRIEDLANDER, L., English
FRIEDMAN, J. H., Statistics
FRIEDMAN, L. M., Law
FRIEDMAN, M., Philosophy
FRIES, J. F., Medicine
FROELICHER, V. F., Medicine
FULLER, G. G., Chemical Engineering
FULLER, M. T., Developmental Biology
FURTHMAYR, H., Pathology
GABA, D. M., Anaesthesia
GABRIELLI, J., Psychology
GALLI, S. J., Pathology
GAMBHIR, S., Radiology
GAMBLE, J. G., Orthopaedic Surgery
GARBER, A. M., Medicine
GARCIA-MOLINA, H., Computer Science
GARNER, C. C., Psychiatry
GARWIN, E. L., Stanford Linear Accelerator Center
GELLER, E., Anaesthesia
GIACCIA, A. J., Radiation Oncology
GIACOMINI, J. C., Medicine
GIBBONS, J. F., Electrical Engineering
GILLY, W. F., Biological Sciences
GILSON, R. J., Law
GIROD, B., Electrical Engineering
GIUDICE, L. C., Obstetrics and Gynaecology
GLADER, B. E., Paediatrics
GLASSER, T. L., Communication
GLAZER, G. M., Radiology
GLICK, I., Psychiatry
GLOVER, G. H., Radiology
GLYNN, P. W., Management Science and Engineering
GOLDSTEIN, J. L., Political Science
GOLDSTEIN, P. L., Law
GOLUB, G. H., Computer Science
GOODE, R., Surgery
GOODMAN, S. B., Functional Restoration
GORDON, D. M., Biological Sciences
GORELICK, S. M., Geological and Environmental Sciences
GORIS, M., Radiology
GOSLING, J. A., Surgery
GOTLIB, I. H., Psychology
GOULD, J., Paediatrics
GOULDER, L. H., Economics
GRAHAM, S. A., Geological and Environmental Sciences
GRANOVETTER, M., Sociology
GRAY, R., Electrical Engineering
GRECO, R. S., Surgery
GREELY, H. T., Law
GREENBERG, H., Medicine
GREENBERG, P., Medicine
GREENE, R., English
GREGG, R. C., Religious Studies
GREIF, A., Economics
GRENADIER, S. R., Graduate School of Business
GREY, T. C., Law
GROSSMAN, P. L., Education
GRUENFELD, D. H., Graduate School of Business
GRUMET, F. C., Pathology
GRUNDFEST, J. A., Law
GRUSKY, D. B., Sociology
GUIBAS, L. J., Computer Science
GUILLEMINAULT, C., Psychiatry
GUMBRECHT, J. U., French and Italian
GUMPORT, P. J., Education
HABER, S. H., History

HAERTEL, E. H., Education
HAKUTA, K., Education
HALL, R., Economics
HAMMER, L. D., Paediatrics
HAMMOND, P., Economics
HANAWALT, P. C., Biological Sciences
HANCOCK, S. L., Radiation Oncology
HANLEY, F. L., Cardiothoracic Surgery
HANNAH, D., Art, Art History
HANNAN, M., Graduate School of Business
HANRAHAN, P. M., Computer Science
HANSON, R., Mechanical Engineering
HARO, M.-P., Spanish and Portuguese
HARRIS, J. M., Geophysics
HARRIS, J. S., Electrical Engineering
HARRIS, S. E., Electrical Engineering
HARRISON, J. M., Graduate School of Business
HARRISON, R. P., French and Italian
HARSH, G. R., IV, Neurosurgery
HASTIE, T. J., Statistics
HAUSMAN, W., Management Science and Engineering
HEDMAN, G.-B., Stanford Synchrotron Radiation Laboratory
HELLER, H. C., Biological Sciences
HELLER, T. C., Law
HENDRICKSON, M. R., Pathology
HENNESSY, J., Electrical Engineering
HENSLER, D. R., Law
HENTZ, V. R., Surgery
HERFKENS, R. J., Radiology
HERSCHLAG, D., Biochemistry
HERTZENBERG, L. A., Genetics
HERZOG, T., History
HESSELINK, L., Electrical Engineering
HIMEL, T. M., Stamford Linear Accelerator Center
HINTON, S., Music
HINTZ, R., Paediatrics
HLATKY, M. A., Health Research and Policy
HODDER, I., Cultural and Social Anthropology
HODGSON, K., Chemistry
HOFFMAN, A. R., Medicine
HOLLOWAY, D., Political Science
HOPPE, R., Radiation Oncology
HORNE, R. N., Petroleum Engineering
HORNING, S. J., Medicine
HOROWITZ, L., Psychology
HOROWITZ, M. A., Electrical Engineering
HOTSON, J. R., Neurology
HOWARD, R. A., Management Science and Engineering
HOYME, H. E., Paediatrics
HSUEH, A., Obstetrics and Gynaecology
HUESTIS, W., Chemistry
HUNT, S., Medicine
INAN, U. S., Electrical Engineering
INGLE, J., Geological and Environmental Sciences
ISHII, K., Mechanical Engineering
IYENGAR, S., Communication
JACKLER, R., Otolaryngology and HNS
JACOBS, C. D., Medicine
JAFFE, R. A., Anaesthesia
JAMESON, A., Aeronautics and Astronautics
JARDETZKY, O., Molecular Pharmacology
JARDETZKY, T., Structural Biology
JAROS, J. A., Stanford Linear Accelerator Center
JEFFREY, R. B., Radiology
JOHNSTONE, I. M., Statistics
JONES, P., Biological Sciences
JOURNEL, A., Petroleum Engineering
JUEL, C., Education
KAHN, J., Electrical Engineering
KAHN, M. S., Art, Art History
KAHN, S., Stanford Linear Accelerator Center
KAISER, A. D., Biochemistry
KALLOSH, R., Physics
KAMAE, T., Stanford Linear Accelerator Center
KAPITULNIK, A., Applied Physics
KAPP, D. S., Radiation Oncology
KARL, T. L., Political Science
KARLAN, P., Law
KASEVICH, M., Physics
KATZNELSON, Y., Mathematics
KAY, M., Linguistics
KAY, M. A., Paediatrics
KAZOVSKY, L. G., Electrical Engineering
KEEFFE, E. B., Medicine
KELLEY, D. M., Mechanical Engineering
KELMAN, M. G., Law
KENDIG, J., Anaesthesia
KENNEDY, D. M., History
KERCKHOFF, S. P., Mathematics
KERNER, J. A., Paediatrics
KESSLER, D. P., Graduate School of Business
KESSLER, R., Urology
KHATIB, O., Computer Science
KHAVARI, P. A., Dermatology
KHOSLA, C. S., Chemical Engineering
KILLEN, J. D., Medicine
KIM, S. K., Developmental Biology
KING, A. C., Health Research and Policy
KINGSLEY, D. M., Developmental Biology
KIPARSKY, P., Linguistics
KIREMIDJIAN, A. S., Civil and Environmental Engineering
KIRKEGAARD, K, Microbiology and Immunology
KIRST, M., Education
KITANIDIS, P. K., Civil and Environmental Engineering
KLAUSNER, M., Law
KLEIN, R. G., Anthropological Studies
KLENOW, P., Economics
KNIGHT, R., Geophysics
KNUDSEN, E. I., Neurobiology
KOBILKA, B. K., Medicine
KOCHERLAKOTA, N., Economics
KOLLMAN, N. S., History
KOOL, E. T., Chemistry
KOPITO, R. R., Biological Sciences
KORAN, L. M., Psychiatry
KORNBERG, R. D., Structural Biology
KOSEFF, J. R., Civil and Environmental Engineering
KOSEK, J., Pathology
KOVACH, R. L., Geophysics
KRAEMER, F. B., Medicine
KRAEMER, H., Psychiatry
KRAMER, R. M., Graduate School of Business
KRANE, E. J., Anaesthesia
KRASNER, S., Political Science
KRASNOW, M. A., Biochemistry
KRAWINKLER, H., Civil and Environmental Engineering
KRAWITZ, J., Communication
KREHBIEL, K., Graduate School of Business
KRENSKY, A. M., Paediatrics
KREPS, D., Graduate School of Business
KROO, I. M., Aeronautics and Astronautics
KROSNICK, J. A., Communication
KRUGER, C. H., Mechanical Engineering
KRUMBOLTZ, J. D., Education
KRUMMEL, T. M., Surgery
KURZ, M., Economics
LABAREE, D., Education
LAI, T. L., Statistics
LAITIN, D., Political Science
LAM, M. S., Computer Science
LANE, A. T., Dermatology
LANE, B., Radiology
LATOMBE, J.-C., Computer Science
LATTIN, J. M., Graduate School of Business
LAU, L. J., Economics
LAUGHLIN, R., Physics
LAVORI, P. W., Health Research and Policy
LAW, K. H., Civil and Environmental Engineering
LAZEAR, E. P., Graduate School of Business
LECKIE, J., Civil and Environmental Engineering
LEE, H. L., Graduate School of Business
LEHMAN, I. R., Biochemistry
LEIFER, L., Mechanical Engineering
LEITH, D., Stanford Linear Accelerator Center
LEIVICK, J. R., Art and Art History
LELE, S. K., Aeronautics and Astronautics
LEMLEY, M., Law
LENOIR, T., History
LEPPER, M., Psychology
LERER, S., English
LESSIG, L., Law
LEUNG, L. L., Medicine
LEVIN, B., Linguistics
LEVITT, L. J., Medicine
LEVITT, M., Structural Biology
LEVITT, R. E., Civil and Environmental Engineering
LEVY, R., Medicine
LEVY, S., Medicine
LEWIS, M. E., Asian Languages
LI, J., Mathematics
LINDE, A., Physics
LINK, M., Paediatrics
LIOU, J., Geological and Environmental Sciences
LIPSICK, J., Pathology
LITT, I., Paediatrics
LIU, T.-P., Mathematics
LOAGUE, K., Geological and Environmental Sciences
LOEW, G. A., Stanford Linear Accelerator Center
LONG, S., Biological Sciences
LONGAKER, M. T., Surgery
LORIG, K., Medicine
LOUGEE CHAPPELL, C., History
LOWE, D. R., Geological and Environmental Sciences
LUENBERGER, D. G., Management Science and Engineering
LUNSFORD, A., English
LUTH, V., Stanford Linear Acceleration Center
LUTHY, R. G., Civil and Environmental Engineering
MCADAM, D., Sociology
MCCALL, M., Classics
MCCLUSKEY, E. J., Electrical Engineering
MCCONNELL, S. K., Biological Sciences
MACCORMACK, R., Aeronautics and Astronautics
MCDERMOTT, R., Education
MCDEVITT, H. O., Microbiology and Immunology
MCDONALD, J. G., Graduate School of Business
MCDOUGALL, I. R., Radiology
MCGINN, R. E., Management Science and Engineering
MCGUIRE, J., Dermatology
MCKAY, D., Structural Biology
MCKINNON, R. I., Economics
MCLAUGHLIN, M. W., Education
MCMAHAN, U. J., Neurobiology
MCMILLAN, R. J., Graduate School of Business
MCNICHOLS, M., Graduate School of Business
MCNUTT, M. K., Geophysics
MACURDY, T., Economics
MADIX, R. J., Chemical Engineering
MAHOOD, G. A., Geological and Environmental Sciences
MALENKA, R. C., Psychiatry
MANCALL, M., History
MANNA, Z., Computer Science
MARINA, N., Paediatrics
MARKMAN, E., Psychology
MARKUS, H., Psychology
MARMOR, M., Ophthalmology
MARTIN, J., Graduate School of Business
MARTIN, R. P., Classics
MATHESON, G. O., Orthopaedic Surgery
MATHEWS, M. V., Music
MATIN, A., Microbiology and Immunology
MATSON, P. A., Geological and Environmental Sciences
MAVKO, G. M., Geophysics
MAZZEO, R. R., Mathematics
MENDELSON, H., Graduate School of Business
MENDEZ, M. A., Law
MENDOZA, F. S., Paediatrics
MENG, T. H.-Y., Electrical Engineering

MERIGAN, T., Medicine
MEYER, T. W., Medicine
MICHELSON, P. F., Physics
MIGNOT, E., Psychiatry
MIHM, F. G., Anaesthesia
MILGRAM, R. J., Mathematics
MILGROM, P., Economics
MILLER, D. A. B., Electrical Engineering
MILLER, D. C., Cardiothoracic Surgery
MILLER, D. T., Graduate School of Business
MILLER, E., Geological and Environmental Sciences
MINTS, G., Philosophy
MITCHELL, J. C., Computer Science
MITCHELL, R. S., Cardiothoracic Surgery
MOBLEY, W. C., Neurology
MOCARSKI, E. S., Microbiology and Immunology
MOCHLY-ROSEN, D., Molecular Pharmacology
MOE, T. M., Political Science
MOERNER, W. E., Chemistry
MOIN, P., Mechanical Engineering
MOLDOWAN, J. M., Geological and Environmental Sciences
MONISMITH, S. G., Civil and Environmental Engineering
MOONEY, H. A., Biological Sciences
MOOS, R. H., Psychiatry
MORA-MANGANO, C., Anaesthesia
MORAVCSIK, J. M., Philosophy
MORETTI, F., English
MORRIS, I., Classics
MORRIS, R. E., Cardiothoracic Surgery
MOSS, R. B., Paediatrics
MOTWANI, R., Computer Science
MUNGAL, M. G., Mechanical Engineering
MURRAY, W., Management Science and Engineering
MUSEN, M. A., Medicine
MYERS, B., Medicine
MYERS, R. M., Genetics
NAIMARK, N., History
NAPEL, S. A., Radiology
NASS, C. I., Communications
NEALE, M. A., Graduate School of Business
NELSON, D. V., Mechanical Engineering
NELSON, W. J., Molecular and Cell Physiology
NETZ, R., Classics
NEWSOME, W. T., III, Neurobiology
NISHI, Y., Electrical Engineering
NISHIMURA, D. G., Electrical Engineering
NOLL, R., Economics
NUR, A., Geophysics
NUSSE, R., Developmental Biology
OAKES, D. D., Surgery
OI, J., Political Science
OKIMOTO, D. I., Political Science
OLCOTT, C., IV, Surgery
OLKIN, I., Statistics
OLSHEN, R., Health Research and Policy
OLZAK, S., Sociology
OMARY, M. B., Medicine
O'REILLY, C. A., III, Graduate School of Business
ORGEL, S., English
ORNSTEIN, D., Mathematics
ORR, F., Petroleum Engineering
ORTOLANO, L., Civil and Environmental Engineering
OSGOOD, B. G., Electrical Engineering
OSHEROFF, D., Physics
OWEN, A. B., Statistics
OYER, P. E., Cardiothoracic Surgery
PADILLA, A., Education
PALUMBI, S., Biological Sciences
PALUMBO-LIU, D. J., Comparative Literature
PAPANICOLAOU, G. C., Mathematics
PARHAM, P., Structural Biology
PARKER, G. G. C., Graduate School of Business
PARKER, P., English
PARNES, J. R., Medicine
PATE-CORNELL, E., Management Science and Engineering
PATELL, J., Graduate School of Business
PATERSON, J., Stanford Linear Accelerator Center
PAULRAJ, A., Electrical Engineering
PAULSON, B., Civil and Environmental Engineering
PEA, R., Education
PEARL, R., Anaesthesia
PEASE, R., Electrical Engineering
PECORA, R., Chemistry
PELC, N. J., Radiology
PENCAVEL, J., Economics
PERKASH, I., Urology
PERLROTH, M. G., Medicine
PERRY, J., Philosophy
PERRY, W., Management Science and Engineering
PESKIN, M., Stanford Linear Accelerator Center
PETERS, P. S., Linguistics
PETERSEN, J., Medicine
PETROSIAN, V., Physics
PFEFFER, J., Graduate School of Business
PFEFFER, S. R., Biochemistry
PFEFFERBAUM, A., Psychiatry
PFLEIDERER, P., Graduate School of Business
PHELAN, P., Drama
PHILIP, A. G. S., Paediatrics
PHILLIPS, D., Education
PHIZACKERLEY, R. P., Stanford Synchrotron Radiation Laboratory
PIANETTA, P., Stanford Synchrotron Radiation Laboratory
PINSKY, P. M., Mechanical Engineering
PIZZO, P. A., Paediatrics
PLUMMER, J., Electrical Engineering
POLAN, M., Obstetrics and Gynaecology
POLHEMUS, R., English
POLINSKY, A., Law
POLLARD, D. D., Geological and Environmental Sciences
POPP, R., Medicine
PORTEUS, E., Graduate School of Business
POWELL, W. W., Education
PRATT, M., Spanish and Portuguese
PREDMORE, M., Spanish and Portuguese
PRESCOTT, C., Stanford Linear Accelerator Center
PRINCE, D. A., Neurology
PRINZ, F. B., Mechanical Engineering
PROBER, C. G., Paediatrics
PROCTOR, R., History
QUERTERMOUS, T., Medicine
QUINN, H., Stanford Linear Accelerator Center
RABIN, R. L., Law
RABINOVITCH, M., Paediatrics
RADIN, M., Law
RAJAN, M. V., Graduate School of Business
RAKOVE, J., History
RAMIREZ, F., Education
RAMPERSAD, A., English
RAMSAUR, M. F., Drama
RECHT, L., Neurology
REEVES, B., Communication
REHM, M. R., Drama
REICHELSTEIN, S. J., Graduate School of Business
REINHARD, M., Civil and Environmental Engineering
REISS, A. L., Psychiatry
REISS, P. C., Graduate School of Business
REITZ, B., Cardiothoracic Surgery
REMINGTON, J. S., Medicine
RHINE, W. D., Paediatrics
RHODE, D. L., Law
RICE, C., Political Science
RICHTER, B., Stanford Linear Accelerator Center
RICKFORD, J., Linguistics
RIDGEWAY, C., Sociology
RIGGS, D., English
RINSKY, L. A., Orthopaedic Surgery
RISCH, N. J., Genetics
RIVERS, D., Political Science
RIZK, N. W., Medicine
ROBERTS, D. F., Communication
ROBERTS, D. J., Graduate School of Business
ROBERTS, E. S., Computer Science
ROBERTS, R. L., History
ROBERTSON, C. R., Chemical Engineering
ROBINSON, J. A., Political Science
ROBINSON, O. W., III, German Studies
ROBINSON, P., History
ROCK, S. M., Aeronautics and Astronautics
RODRIGUE, A., History
ROMANO, J., Statistics
ROMER, P., Graduate School of Business
RORTY, R., Comparative Literature
ROSALDO, R. I., Jr, Cultural and Social Anthropology
ROSENTHAL, M. H., Anaesthesia
ROSS, L., Psychology
ROTH, B., Mechanical Engineering
ROTH, R. A., Molecular Pharmacology
ROTH, W., Psychiatry
ROUGHGARDEN, J., Biological Sciences
ROUSE, R. V., Pathology
RUBIN, K., Mathematics
RUDD, P., Medicine
RUFFINELLI-ALTESOR, J., Spanish and Portuguese
RUMELHART, D. E., Psychology
RUTH, R. D., Stanford Linear Accelerator Center
SAG, I. A., Linguistics
SAGAN, S. D., Political Science
SAIDMAN, L. J., Anaesthesia
SALDIVAR, R., English
SALISBURY, J. K., Computer Science
SALONER, G., Graduate School of Business
SALVATIERRA, O., Jr, Surgery
SAMUELSON, K., Communication
SAPOLSKY, R. M., Biological Sciences
SARASWAT, K., Electrical Engineering
SARGENT, T. J., Economics
SARNOW, P., Microbiology and Immunology
SAUNDERS, M. A., Management Science and Engineering
SAUSSY, C. P. H., Comparative Literature
SCANDLING, J., Medicine
SCHATZBERG, A., Psychiatry
SCHEIDEL, W., Classics
SCHENDEL, S. A., Surgery
SCHERRER, P. H., Physics
SCHIEBERGER, L., History
SCHINDLER, R., Stanford Linear Accelerator Center
SCHNAPP, J. T., French and Italian
SCHNEIDER, S., Biological Sciences
SCHNITTGER, I., Medicine
SCHOEN, R., Mathematics
SCHOOLNIK, G. K., Medicine
SCHROEDER, J. S., Medicine
SCHUPBACH, Slavic Languages and Literatures
SCHURMAN, D., Functional Restoration
SCOTT, M. P., Developmental Biology
SEGAL, I. R., Economics
SEGALL, P., Geophysics
SELLS, P., Linguistics
SERRES, M., French and Italian
SHAFER, S. L., Anaesthesia
SHANKS, M., Classics
SHAPIRO, L., Developmental Biology
SHAQFEH, E. S. G., Chemical Engineering
SHAVELSON, R., Education
SHAW, K., Graduate School of Business
SHEEHAN, J. J., History
SHEEHAN, T., Religious Studies
SHEIKH, J. T., Psychiatry
SHEN, Z.-X., Applied Physics
SHENKER, S. H., Physics
SHORTLIFFE, L., Urology
SHOVEN, J., Economics
SHUER, L. M., Neurosurgery
SIBLEY, R. K., Pathology
SIEGMUND, D. O., Statistics
SIEMANN, R., Stanford Linear Accelerator Center
SIKIC, B. I., Medicine
SILVERBERG, G. D., Neurosurgery
SILVERMAN, N., Paediatrics

SIMON, L., Mathematics
SIMONI, R., Biological Sciences
SIMONSON, I., Graduate School of Business
SINCLAIR, R., Materials Science and Engineering
SINGH, K., Ophthalmology
SINGLETON, K., Graduate School of Business
SKEFF, K. M., Medicine
SLEEP, N., Geophysics
SMITH, S. J., Molecular and Cell Physiology
SMITH, T. I., Physics
SNIDERMAN, P., Political Science
SNIPP, C. M., Sociology
SO, S. K. S., Surgery
SOLOMON, E., Chemistry
SOMERO, G., Biological Sciences
SOMERVILLE, C., Biological Sciences
SOMMER, F. G., Radiology
SPAIN, D., Surgery
SPIEGEL, D., Psychiatry
SPRINGER, G., Aeronautics and Astronautics
SPUDICH, J. A., Biochemistry
SRINIVASAN, V., Graduate School of Business
STAMEY, T. A., Urology
STANSKI, D. R., Anaesthesia
STANSKY, P. D. L., History
STEBBINS, J., Geological and Environmental Sciences
STEELE, C. M., Psychology
STEFANICK, M., Medicine
STEINBERG, G. K., Neurosurgery
STEINER, H., Psychiatry
STEINMAN, L., Neurology
STEPHENS, S., Classics
STEVENS, D., Medicine
STEVENSON, D., Paediatrics
STIPEK, D. J., Education
STOHR, J., Stanford Synchrotron Radiation Laboratory
STREET, R. L., Civil and Environmental Engineering
STRNAD, J. F., Law
STROBER, M., Education
STROBER, S., Medicine
SULLIVAN, K., Law
SUSSKIND, L., Physics
SUSSMAN, H., Pathology
SUTTON, R. I., Management Science and Engineering
SWAIN, J., Medicine
SWARTZ, J. R., Chemical Engineering
SWEENEY, J., Management Science and Engineering
SWITZER, P., Statistics
TAKEUCHI, M. R., Art and Art History
TALLENT, E., English
TATUM, C. B., Civil and Environmental Engineering
TAYLOR, C., Psychiatry
TAYLOR, J. B., Economics
TAYLOR, K. A., Philosophy
TESSIER-LAVIGNE, M., Biological Sciences
THOMAS, E. A. C., Psychology
THOMPSON, B. H., Jr, Law
THOMPSON, D. G., Psychiatry
THOMPSON, S., Biological Sciences
TIBSHIRANI, R. J., Health Research and Policy
TINKLENBERG, J., Psychiatry
TOBAGI, F., Electrical Engineering
TOMPKINS, L., Medicine
TRIADAFILOPOULOS, G., Medicine
TROST, B., Chemistry
TRUDELL, J. R., Anaesthesia
TSIEN, R., Molecular and Cellular Physiology
TULJAPURKAR, S., Biological Sciences
TUMA, N., Sociology
TURNER, P., Art and Art History
TVERSKY, B., Psychology
TYLER, G., Electrical Engineering
UMETSU, D. T., Paediatrics
VALANTINE, H. A., Medicine
VALDES, G., Education
VAN BENTHEM, J. F., Philosophy
VAN DAM, J., Medicine
VAN HORNE, J. C., Graduate School of Business
VAN MEURS, K. P., Paediatrics
VEINOTT, A. F., Jr, Management Science and Engineering
VINOGRAD, R. E., Art and Art History
VITOUSEK, P., Biological Sciences
WAGONER, R. V., Physics
WALBOT, V., Biological Sciences
WALD, M. S., Law
WALDER, A. G., Sociology
WALDRON, K. J., Mechanical Engineering
WALKER, D., Education
WANDELL, B. A., Psychology
WANG, J., Asian Languages
WANG, P., Medicine
WANG, T. S.-F., Pathology
WARNKE, R., Pathology
WASOW, T., Linguistics
WATT, W., Biological Sciences
WAYMOUTH, R. M., Chemistry
WEBER, C., Drama
WEIN, L. M., Graduate School of Business
WEINGAST, B. R., Political Science
WEISBERG, R., Law
WEISSMAN, I., Pathology
WENDER, P., Chemistry
WEYANT, J. P., Management Science and Engineering
WHANG, S., Graduate School of Business
WHITE, B., Mathematics
WHITE, R., History
WHITMORE, I., Surgery
WHITTEMORE, A., Health Research and Policy
WHYTE, R. I., Cardiothoracic Surgery
WIDROW, B., Electrical Engineering
WILSON, D. M., Paediatrics
WINE, J., Psychology
WINEBERG, S., Education
WINOGRAD, T., Computer Sciences
WOJCICKI, S. G., Physics
WOLAK, F. A., Economics
WOLF, A., Anthropological Sciences
WOLF, B. J., Art and Art History
WOLFF, T., English
WONG, H.-S., Electrical Engineering
WONG, S.-W. S., Electrical Engineering
WOOD, A. W., Philosophy
WOOD, R., Philosophy
WOOLEY, B. A., Electrical Engineering
WRIGHT, G., Economics
XIE, Y., Sociology
YAMAMOTO, Y., Electrical Engineering
YANAGISAKO, S. J., Cultural and Social Anthropology
YARBRO-BEJARANO, Y., Spanish and Portuguese
YAU, H.-T., Mathematics
YE, Y., Management Science and Engineering
YEARLEY, L., Religious Studies
YESAVAGE, J., Psychiatry
YOCK, P. G., Medicine
ZARE, R. N., Chemistry
ZARINS, C. K., Surgery
ZHANG, S., Physics
ZIPPERSTEIN, S. J., History
ZOBACK, M., Geophysics

STARR KING SCHOOL FOR THE MINISTRY

2441 LeConte Ave, Berkeley, CA 94709-1209
Telephone: (510) 845-6232
Fax: (510) 845-6273
E-mail: starrking@sksm.edu
Internet: www.sksm.edu

Founded 1904 as Pacific Unitarian School for the Ministry; present name 1941
Private control (part of the Graduate Theological Union)
Academic year: September to May

Pres.: Rev. Dr REBECCA A. PARKER
Vice-Pres. for Academic Affairs and Dean of Faculty: Rev. Dr IBRAHIM FARAJAJÉ
Vice-Pres. for Advancement: KELLY FLOOD
Vice-Pres. for Finance and Admin.: THOMAS SMITH
Dean of Students: BECKY LEYSER
Dir of Continuing and Online Education: CATHLEEN YOUNG
Library Dir: BONNIE HARDWICK

Library of 365,000 vols.

THOMAS AQUINAS COLLEGE

10000 North Ojai Rd, Santa Paula, CA 93060
Telephone: (805) 525-4417
Fax: (805) 525-0620
E-mail: admissions@thomasaquinas.edu
Internet: www.thomasaquinas.edu

Founded 1971
Private control
Academic year: September to June

Pres.: Dr THOMAS E. DILLON
Dean: Dr MICHAEL MCLEAN
Asst Dean for Student Affairs: Dr MICHAEL LETTENEY
Vice-President for Devt and General Counsel: JOHN QUINCY MASTELLER
Registrar: SEAN COLLINS
Librarian: VILTIS JATULIS

Library of 50,000 vols
Number of teachers: 32
Number of students: 331

Publication: *The Aquinas Review* (2 a year).

THOMAS JEFFERSON SCHOOL OF LAW

2121 San Diego Ave, San Diego, CA 92110
Telephone: (619) 297-9700
Fax: (619) 294-4713
E-mail: info@tjsl.edu
Internet: www.tjsl.edu
Private control

Pres. and Dean: RUDY HASL
Library Dir: Prof. KARLA M. CASTETTER

Library of 116,537 vols.

UNIVERSITY OF CALIFORNIA

Office of the Pres., 12th Fl., 1111 Franklin St, Oakland, CA 94607-5200
Internet: www.universityofcalifornia.edu

Founded 1868

Campuses at Berkeley, Davis, Irvine, Los Angeles, Merced, Riverside, San Diego, San Francisco, Santa Barbara, and Santa Cruz

Pres.: ROBERT DYNES
Provost and Exec. Vice-Pres. for Academic Affairs: Dr WYATT R. HUME
Exec. Vice-Pres. for Univ. Affairs: BRUCE B. DARLING
Vice-Pres. for Agriculture and Natural Resources: W. R. GOMES
Vice-Pres. for Budget: LARRY HERSHMAN
Vice-Pres. for Clinical Services Devt: WILLIAM H. GURTNER
Vice-Pres. for Financial Management: ANNE BROOME
Vice-Pres. for Health Affairs: RORY HUME
Vice-Pres. for Investments: MARIE N. BERGREN
Vice-Pres. for Laboratory Admin.: S. ROBERT FOLEY
Vice-Pres. for Legal Affairs: CHARLES F. ROBINSON
Vice-Pres. for Student Affairs: JUDY K. SAKAKI

Library: see Libraries and Archives
Number of teachers: 8,776
Number of students: 208,000.

CONSTITUENT CAMPUSES

University of California, Berkeley

Berkeley, CA 94720
Telephone: (510) 642-6000
Internet: www.berkeley.edu
Founded 1868
130 Depts divided into 14 colleges and schools
Chancellor: ROBERT J. BIRGENEAU
Exec. Vice-Chancellor and Provost: GEORGE W. BRESLAUER
Vice-Chancellor for Admin. (vacant)
Vice-Chancellor for Equity and Inclusion: GIBOR BASRI
Vice-Chancellor for Facilities Services: EDWARD J. DENTON
Vice-Chancellor for Research: GRAHAM FLEMING
Vice-Chancellor for Student Affairs: HARRY LE GRANDE
Vice-Chancellor for Univ. Relations: SCOTT BIDDY
Univ. Librarian: THOMAS C. LEONARD
Number of teachers: 2,082
Number of students: 35,843

DEANS

Boalt School of Law: CHRISTOPHER F. EDLEY, Jr
College of Chemistry: RICHARD A. MATHIES
College of Engineering: SHANKAR SASTRY
College of Environmental Design: JENNIFER WOLCH
College of Letters and Science: MARK RICHARDS (Exec. Dean)
College of Natural Resources: J. KEITH GILLESS
Div. of Arts and Humanities: JANET BROUGHTON
Div. of Biological Sciences: MARK SCHLISSEL
Div. of Mathematical and Physical Sciences: MARK RICHARDS
Div. of Social Sciences: CARLA HESSE
Graduate Div.: ANDREW J. SZERI
Graduate School of Education: JUDITH WARREN LITTLE
Graduate School of Journalism: NEIL HENRY
Richard and Rhoda Goldman School of Public Policy: HENRY BRADY
School of Information: ANNALEE SAXENIAN
Undergraduate Div.: TYLER STOVALL
School of Optometry: DENNIS LEVI
School of Public Health: STEPHEN SHORTELL (acting)
School of Social Welfare: LORRAINE MIDANIK
Univ. Extension: DIANA WU
Walter A. Haas School of Business: RICHARD K. LYONS

CHAIRMEN OF DEPARTMENTS

College of Letters and Science:
African American Studies: CHARLES HENRY
Anthropology: MEG CONKEY
Art History: CHRISTOPHER HALLETT
Art Practice: HERTHA SWEET WONG
Astronomy: JAMES GRAHAM
Classics: GIOVANNI FERRARI (acting)
Comparative Literature: VICTORIA KAHN
Demography: MICHAEL HOUT
East Asian Languages and Cultures: ALAN TANSMAN
Earth and Planetary Science: ROLAND BURGMANN
Economics: GERALD ROLAND
English: SAMUEL OTTER
Ethnic Studies: THOMAS J. BIOLSI
Film and Media: ANNE NESBET
French: MICHAEL LUCEY
Gender and Women's Studies: MINOO MOALLEM
Geography: KURT CUFFEY
German: ANTON KAES
History: MARY ELIZABETH BERRY
Integrative Biology: WAYNE SOUSA
Italian Studies: STEVEN BOTTERILL
Linguistics: SHARON INKELAS
Mathematics: TED SLAMAN (acting)
Molecular and Cell Biology: G. STEVEN MARTIN
Music: BENJAMIN BRINNER
Near Eastern Studies: CAROL REDMOUNT
Philosophy: PAOLO MANCOSU
Physics: FRANCES HELLMAN
Political Science: PAUL PIERSON
Psychology: RICHARD IVRY (acting)
Rhetoric: DAVID COHEN
Scandinavian: LINDA RUGG
Slavic Languages and Literatures: IRINA PAPERNO
Sociology: TROND PETERSEN
South and Southeast Asian Studies: ALEXANDER VON ROSPATT
Spanish and Portuguese: INGACIO NAVARRETE (acting)
Statistics: BIN YU
Theater, Dance, and Performance Studies: PETER GLAZER

College of Chemistry:
Chemical and Biomolecular Engineering: JEFFREY A. REIMER
Chemistry: DAN NEUMARK

College of Engineering:
Bioengineering: MATT TIRRELL
Civil and Environmental Engineering: LISA ALVAREZ-COHEN
Electrical Engineering and Computer Sciences: COSTAS SPANOS
Industrial Engineering and Operations Research: RHONDA RIGHTER
Materials Science and Engineering: ROBERT RITCHIE
Mechanical Engineering: ALBERT PISANO
Nuclear Engineering: PER PETERSON

College of Environmental Design:
Architecture: TOM J. BURESH
City and Regional Planning: KAREN CHRISTENSEN
Landscape Architecture and Environmental Planning: LINDA JEWELL

College of Natural Resources:
Agricultural and Resource Economics: LARRY KARP
Environment Science, Policy and Management: ALLEN GOLDSTEIN
Nutritional Science and Toxicology: JOE NAPOLI
Plant and Microbial Biology: BRIAN STASKAWICZ

University of California, Davis

1 Shields Ave, Davis, CA 95616
Telephone: (530) 752-1011
Fax: (530) 752-6363
Internet: www.ucdavis.edu
Founded 1905
State control
Academic year: September to June
Chancellor: LINDA KATEHI
Provost and Exec. Vice-Chancellor: ENRIQUE LAVERNIA
Vice-Chancellor for Admin. and Resource Management: JOHN A. MEYER
Vice-Chancellor for Human Health Sciences: CLAIRE POMEROY
Vice-Chancellor for Research: BARRY M. KLEIN
Vice-Chancellor for Student Affairs: FRED WOOD
Vice-Chancellor for Univ. Relations: BEVERLY SANDEEN
Vice-Provost for Academic Personnel: BARBARA HORWITZ
Vice-Provost for Information and Educational Technology: PETER SIEGEL
Vice-Provost for Undergraduate Studies: PATRICA TURNER
Vice-Provost for Univ. Outreach and Int. Programs: WILLIAM B. LACY
Univ. Librarians: HELEN HENRY, GAIL YAKOTE (acting)
Library: see Libraries and Archives
Number of teachers: 2,558
Number of students: 32,153
Publications: *BizLawJournal.com* (online), *CA&ES Outlook* (2 a year), *Environs* (2 a year), *Journal of International Law Policy* (2 a year), *Journal of Juvenile Law and Policy* (2 a year), *Migration News* (12 a year), *The Horse Report* (4 a year), *UC Davis Law Review* (4 a year)

DEANS

College of Agricultural and Environmental Sciences: NEAL K. VAN ALFEN
College of Biological Sciences: KENNETH C. BURTIS
College of Education: HAROLD G. LEVINE
College of Engineering: BRUCE R. WHITE (acting)
College of Biological Sciences: KENNETH C. BURTIS
Div. of Humanities, Arts and Cultural Studies: JESSIE ANN OWENS
Div. of Mathematics and Physical Sciences: WINSTON KO
Div. of Social Sciences: GEORGE R. MANGUN
Graduate School of Management: STEVEN CURRALL
Graduate Studies: JEFFERY C. GIBELING
School of Law: KEVIN JOHNSON
School of Medicine: CLAIRE POMEROY
School of Veterinary Medicine: BENNIE I. OSBURN
Univ. Extension: DENNIS F. PENDLETON

CHAIRPERSONS AND DIRECTORS OF FACULTY

College of Agricultural and Environmental Sciences (150 Mrak Hall, 1 Shields Ave, Davis, CA 95616; tel. (530) 752-0108; fax (530) 752-9049; internet www.aes.ucdavis.edu):
Agricultural and Resource Economics: RICHARD HOWITT (Chair.)
Agronomy and Range Science: CHRIS VAN KESSEL (Chair.)
Animal Science: GARY ANDERSON (Chair.)
Biological and Agricultural Engineering: BRUCE HARTSOUGH (Chair.)
Entomology: ROBERT PAGE (Chair.)
Environmental Design—Design: PATRICIA HARRISON (Chair.)
Environmental Design—Landscape Architecture: HEATH SCHENKER
Environmental Horticulture: J. HEINER LIETH (Chair.)
Environmental Science and Policy: ANDREW SIH (Chair.)
Environmental Toxicology: MARION MILLER (Chair.)
Food Science and Technology: CHARLES SHOEMAKER (Chair.)
Human and Community Devt: BETH OBER (Chair.)
Land, Water and Air Resources: MICHAEL SINGER (Chair.)
Nematology: EDWARD P. CASWELL-CHEN (Chair.)
Nutrition: CARL L. KEEN (Chair.)
Plant Pathology: RICHARD M. BOSTOCK (Chair.)
Pomology: VITO POLITO (Chair.)
Division of Textiles and Clothing: SUSAN KAISER (Chair.)
Vegetable Crops: JOHN YODER (Chair.)
Viticulture and Oenology: ANDREW WATERHOUSE (Chair.)
Wildlife, Fish and Conservation Biology: DIRK VAN VUREN (Chair.)

School of Education (2077 Academic Surge Bldg, 1 Shields Ave, Davis, CA 95616; tel. (530) 752-8019; fax (530) 752-5411):

Education: HAROLD LEVIN (Dean)

College of Engineering (1050 Engineering Unit II, 1 Shields Ave, Davis, CA 95616; tel. (530) 752-0553; fax (530) 752-8058; internet engineering.ucdavis.edu):

Applied Science: RICHARD FREEMAN (Chair.)
Biological and Agricultural Engineering: BRUCE HARTSOUGH (Chair.)
Division of Biomedical Engineering: KATHERINE FERRARA
Chemical Engineering and Materials Science: ROBERT POWELL
Civil and Environmental Engineering: DEBBIE NIEMEIER (Chair.)
Computer Science: DAN GUSFIELD (Chair.)
Electrical Engineering and Computer Engineering: JONATHAN HERITAGE (Chair.)
Mechanical and Aeronautical Engineering: RIDA FAROUKI (Chair.)

School of Law (1013 King Hall, 1 Shields Ave, Davis, CA 95616; tel. (530) 752-0243; fax (530) 752-4704; internet kinghall.ucdavis .edu):

Law: REX PERSCHBACHER (Dean)

College of Letters and Science (200 Social Sciences and Humanities Bldg, 1 Shields Ave, Davis, CA 95616; tel. (530) 752-0392; fax (530) 752-3490; internet www.ls.ucdavis .edu):

African-American and African Studies: JACOB K. OLUPONA (Dir)
American Studies: MICHAEL SMITH (Dir)
Anthropology: CAROL SMITH (Chair.)
Art History and Art Studio: GINA WERFEL (Chair.)
Asian American Studies: WENDY HO (Dir)
Chemistry: WILLIAM JACKSON (Chair.)
Chicana/o Studies: ADELA DE LA TORRE (Dir)
Classics: LYNN E. ROLLER (Dir)
Communications: ROBERT BELL (Chair.)
Comparative Literature: GAIL FINNEY (Dir)
East Asian Languages and Cultures: ROBERT BORGEN (Chair.)
East Asian Studies: ROBERT BORGEN (Dir)
Economics: KEVIN HOOVER (Chair.)
English: DAVID SIMPSON (Chair.)
French and Italian: JOANN CANNON (Chair.)
Geology: LOUISE KELLOGG (Chair.)
German and Russian: WINDER MCCONNELL (Chair.)
History: DANIEL R. BROWER (Chair.)
Humanities: MICHELE YEH (Dir)
Integrated Studies: JAMES SHACKELFORD (Dir)
Int. Relations: JEANETTE MONEY (Dir)
Italian: JOANN CANNON (Chair.)
Linguistics: LENORA TIMM (Dir)
Mathematics: JOHN HUNTER (Chair.)
Medieval Studies: WINDER MCCONNELL (Dir)
Military Science: DONALD HILL
Music: ROSS BAUER (Chair.)
Native American Studies: VICTOR MONTEJO (Chair.)
Philosophy: GERALD DWORKIN (Chair.)
Physical Education: SUZANNE WILLIAMS (Dir)
Physics: WINSTON KO (Chair.)
Political Science: WALTER STONE (Chair.)
Psychology: PHILLIP SHAVER (Chair.)
Religious Studies: NAOMI JANOWITZ (Dir)
Russian: DANIEL RANCOUR-LAFERRIERE (Dir)
Sociology: MARY JACKMAN (acting) (Chair.)
Spanish and Classics: SAMUEL ARMISTEAD (Co-Chair.: ROBERT BLAKE (Co-Chair.)
Statistics: JANE-LING WANG (Chair.)
Theatre and Dance: SARAH PIA ANDERSON (Chair.)
Women and Gender Studies: JUDITH NEWTON (Dir)

Division of Biological Sciences (202 Life Sciences Addition, 1 Shields Ave, Davis, CA 95616; tel. (530) 752-0410; fax (530) 752-2604; internet www.dbs.ucdavis.edu):

Evolution and Ecology: MICHAEL TURELLI (Chair.)
Exercise Biology: CHARLES FULLER (Chair.)
Microbiology: DOUGLAS C. NELSON (Chair.)
Molecular and Cellular Biology: MICHAEL DAHMUS (Chair.)
Neurobiology, Physiology and Behaviour: LEO CHALUPA (Chair.)
Plant Biology: VENKATESAN SUNDARESAN (Chair.)

Graduate School of Management (106 AOB4, 1 Shields Ave, Davis, CA 95616; tel. (530) 752-7399; fax (530) 752-2924; e-mail gsm@ucdavis.edu; internet www.gsm.ucdavis .edu):

Management: ELIZABETH BIGGART (Dean)

School of Medicine (Med Sci 1C, Room 102 Campus, 1 Shields Ave, Davis, CA 95616; tel. (530) 752-4028; fax (530) 752-1532; internet www-med.ucdavis.edu):

Anaesthesiology and Pain Medicine: PETER MOORE (Chair.)
Biological Chemistry: LARRY HJELMELAND (Chair.)
Cell Biology and Human Anatomy: KENT ERICKSON (Chair.)
Dermatology: FU-TONG LIU (Chair.)
Epidemiology and Preventive Medicine: MARC SCHENKER (Chair.)
Family and Community Medicine: KLEA BERTAKIS (Chair.)
Human Physiology: PETER CALA (Chair.)
Internal Medicine: FRED MEYERS (Chair.)
Medical Microbiology and Immunology: SATYA DANDEKAR (Chair.)
Pharmacology: ANN BONHAM (Chair.)
Neurological Surgery: J. PAUL MUIZELAAR (Chair.)
Neurology: WILLIAM JAGUST (Chair.)
Obstetrics and Gynaecology: LLOYD H. SMITH (Chair.)
Ophthalmology: JOHN KELTNER (Chair.)
Orthopaedic Surgery: GEORGE RAB (Chair.)
Otolaryngology: HILARY BRODIE (acting) (Chair.)
Paediatrics: ANTHONY PHILLIPS (Chair.)
Pathology: RALPH GREEN (Chair.)
Physical Medicine and Rehabilitation: DAVID KILMER (Chair.)
Psychiatry: ROBERT HALES (Chair.)
Radiation Oncology: JANICE RYU (Chair.)
Radiology: JAMES BRUNBERG (Chair.)
Surgery: JAMES GOODNIGHT, Jr (Chair.)
Urology: RALPH DEVERE WHITE (Chair.)

School of Veterinary Medicine (1 Shields Ave, Davis, CA 95616; tel. (530) 752-1360; fax (530) 752-2801; internet www.vetmed .ucdavis.edu):

Anatomy, Physiology and Cell Biology: CHARLES PLOPPER (Chair.)
Medicine and Epidemiology: RICHARD W. NELSON (Chair.)
Molecular Biosciences: ALAN BUCKPITT (Chair.)
Pathology, Microbiology and Immunology: N. JAMES MACLACHLAN (Chair.)
Population Health and Reproduction: ROBERT BONDURANT (Chair.)
Surgical and Radiological Sciences: RICHARD A. LECOUTEUR (Chair.)

PROFESSORS

College of Agricultural and Environmental Sciences (150 Mrak Hall, 1 Shields Ave, Davis, CA 95616; tel. (530) 752-0107; fax (530) 752-9049; internet www.aes.ucdavis .edu):

Faculty of Agricultural and Resource Economics:

ALSTON, J. M.
CAPUTO, M. R.
CARMAN, H.
CARTER, C. A.
CHALFANT, J. A.
FARZIN, Y. H.
GREEN, R. D.
HAVENNER, A.
HEIEN, D. M.
HOWITT, R. E.
JARVIS, L. S.
MARTIN, P. L.
MORRISON PAUL, C. J.
PARIS, Q.
ROZELLE, S.
SEXTON, R. J.
SUMNER, D. A.
TAYLOR, J. E.
VOSTI, S. A.
WILEN, J. E.
WILLIAMS, J.

Faculty of Agronomy and Range Science:

DEMMENT, M. W.
DENISON, R. F.
DVORAK, J.
FOIN, T. C.
GENG, S.
GEPTS, P. L.
JERNSTEDT, J.
PHILLIPS, D. A.
PLANT, R. E.
RAINS, D. W.
RICE, K. J.
TEUBER, L. R.
TRAVIS, R. L.
VAN KESSEL, C.
WILKENS, T.

Faculty of Animal Science:

ADAMS, T. E.
ANDERSON, G. B.
BERGER, T. J.
CALVERT, C. C.
DE PETERS, E. J.
DOROSHOV, S. I.
FADEL, J. G.
FAMULA, T. R.
GALL, G. A.
HUNG, S. S.
KING, A. J.
KLASING, K. C.
LEE, Y. B.
MEDRANO, J. F.
MENCH, J. A.
MILLAM, J. R.
OBERBAUER, A. M.
PRICE, E. O.
ROSER, J. F.
WEATHERS, W. W.
WILSON, B. W.
ZINN, R. A.

Faculty of Biological and Agricultural Engineering under the College of Agricultural and Environmental Sciences:

PIEDRAHITA, R. H.
UPADHYAYA, S. K.

Faculty of Entomology:

CAREY, J. R.
CRANSTON, P. S.
DINGLE, H.
EDMAN, J. D.
EHLER, L. E.
GRANETT, J.
GULLAN, P. J.
HAMMOCK, B. D.
KARBAN, R.
KAYA, H. K.
KIMSEY, L. S.
LEAL, W. S.
PAGE, R. E.
PARRELA, M. P.
PENG, Y. S. C.

ROSENHEIM, J. A.
SCOTT, T. W.
ULLMAN, D. E.
WARD, P. S.

Faculty of Environmental Design:

GOTELLI, D. E.
HARRISON, P.
LAKY, G.
RIVERS, V. Z.
SHAWCROFT-GUARINO, B.

Faculty of Environmental Horticulture:

BARBOUR, M. G.
BERRY, A. M.
BURGER, D. W.
DURZAN, D. J.
HARDING, J. A.
LIETH, J. H.
REID, M. S.
WU, L. L.

Faculty of Environmental Science and Policy:

GOLDMAN, C. R.
HARRISON, S. P.
HASTINGS, A. M.
JOHNSTON, R. A.
ORLOVE, B. S.
QUINN, J. F.
REJMANKOVA, E.
RICHERSON, P. J.
SABATIER, P. A.
SIH, A.
WILLIAMS, S. L.

Faculty of Environmental Toxicology:

CHERR, G. N.
DENISON, M. S.
KADO, N. Y.
KNEZOVICH, J. P.
MATSUMURA, F.
MILLER-SEARS, M. G.
RICE, R. H.
SHIBAMOTO, T.
TJEERDEMA, R. S.

Faculty of Food Science and Technology:

BAMFORTH, C. W.
BANDMAN, E.
DUNGAN, S. R.
GERMAN, J. B.
GUINARD, J.
HAARD, N. F.
KROCHTA, J. M.
MCCARTHY, M. J.
OGRYDZIAK, D. M.
O'MAHONY, M. A.
PRICE, C. W.
REID, D. S.
SHOEMAKER, C. F.
SINGH, R. P.
SMITH, G. M.

Faculty of Human and Community Development:

ALDWIN, C.
BARTON, K.
BRUSH, S. B.
BRYANT, B. K.
CONGER, R. D.
GE, X.
HARPER, L. V.
KENNEY, M. F.
LACY, W. B.
MOMSEN, J.
OBER, B. A.
SMITH, M. P.
WELLS, M. J.

Faculty of Land, Air and Water Resources:

BAHRE, C. J.
BLEDSOE, C. S.
CARROLL, J. J.
CASEY, W. H.
DAHLGREN, R. A.
FLOCCHINI, R. G.
FOGG, G. E.
GRISMER, M. E.
GROTJAHN, R.
HOPMANS, J. W.
HSIAO, T. C.
LAUCHLI, A. E.
NATHAN, T. R.
PAW U, K. T.
RECK, R. A.
RICHARDS, J. M.
ROLSTON, D. E.
SCOW, K. M.
SHELTON, M. L.
SILK, M. W.
SINGER, M. J.
SOUTHARD, R. J.
USTIN, S. L.
WEARE, B. C.
ZASOSKI, R. J.

Faculty of Landscape Architecture:

ALLAN, N.
FRANCIS, M.
MACCANNELL, E. D.

Faculty of Nematology:

CASWELL-CHAN, E. P.
FERRIS, H.
JAFFEE, B. A.
NADLER, S. A.
WILLIAMSON, V. M.

Faculty of Nutrition:

ALLEN, L. H.
BROWN, K. G.
CLIFFORD, A. J.
DEWEY, K. G.
GRIVETTI, L. E.
KEEN, C. L.
LONNERDAL, B. L.
MCDONALD, R. B.
RUCKER, R. B.
SCHNEEMAN, B. O.
STERN, J. S.

Faculty of Plant Pathology:

BOSTOCK, R. M.
BRUENING, G.
COOK, D. R.
DAVIS, R. M.
DUNIWAY, J. M.
FALK, B. W.
GILBERTSON, R. L.
GILCHRIST, D. G.
GORDON, T. R.
KADO, C. I.
KIRKPATRICK, B. C.
MACDONALD, J. D.
RONALD, P. C.
TYLER, B. M.
VAN ALFEN, N.
WEBSTER, R. K.

Faculty of Pomology:

BLUMWALD, E.
BROWN, P. H.
DANDEKAR, A. M.
DEJONG, T. M.
GRADZIEL, T. M.
KADER, A. A.
LABAVITCH, J. M.
POLITO, V. S.
SHACKEL, K. A.
SHAW, D. V.
SUTTER, E. G.
WEINBAUM, S.

Faculty of Textiles and Clothing:

HSIEH, Y.
KAISER, S. B.
PAN, N.
RUCKER, M. H.

Faculty of Vegetable Crops:

BAYER, D. E.
BLOOM, A. J.
BRADFORD, K. J.
JACKSON, L. E.
MICHELMORE, R. W.
NEVINS, D. J.
QUIROS, C. F.
SALTVEIT, M. E.
YODER, J. I.

Faculty of Viticulture and Oenology:

BISSON, L. F.
BOULTON, R. B.
HEYMANN, H.
MATTHEWS, M. A.
MEREDITH, C. P.
NOBLE, A. C.
WALKER, M. A.
WATERHOUSE, A. L.
WILLIAMS, L. E.

Faculty of Wildlife, Fish and Conservation Biology:

ANDERSON, D. W.
BOTSFORD, L. W.
CARO, T. M.
CECH, J. J.
EADIE, J. M.
ELLIOTT-FISK, D. L.
MOYLE, P. B.
VAN VUREN, D.

School of Education (2077 Academic Surge Bldg, 1 Shields Ave, Davis, CA 95616; tel. (530) 752-8019; fax (530) 752-5411):

DUGDALE, S. S.
FIGUEROA, R. A.
GANDARA, P.
LEVINE, H. G.
MERINO, B. J.
MURPHY, S.
SANDOVAL, J. H.
WAGNER, J. C.
WATSON-GEGEO, K. A.
YOUNG, I. P.

College of Engineering (1050 Engineering Unit II, 1 Shields Ave, Davis, CA 95616; tel. (530) 752-0553; fax (530) 752-8058; internet engineering.ucdavis.edu):

Faculty of Biological and Agricultural Engineering under the College of Engineering:

DELWICHE, M. J.
GILES, D. K.
HARTSOUGH, B. R.
HILLS, D. J.
JENKINS, B. M.
MCCARTHY, K. L.
MILES, J. A.
RUMSEY, T. R.
SLAUGHTER, D. C.
UPADHYAYA, S. K.
WALLENDER, W. W.

Faculty of Biomedical Engineering:

BENHAM, C. J.
CHERRY, S. R.
FERRARA, K. W.
INSANA, M. F.
SAVAGEAU, M. A.
SIMON, I.

Faculty of Chemical Engineering and Materials Science:

BROWNING, N. D.
GATES, B. C.
GIBELING, J. C.
GROZA, J. R.
HIGGINS, B. G.
HOWITT, D. G.
JACKMAN, A. P.
MCCOY, B. J.
MCDONALD, K. A.
MUKHERJEE, A. K.
NAVROTSKY, A.
PALAZOGLU, A. N.
PHILLIPS, R. J.
POWELL, R. L.
RISBUD, S. H.
RYU, D. D. Y.
SHACKELFORD, J. F.
STROEVE, P.
WHITAKER, S.

Faculty of Civil and Environmental Engineering:

ARULANANDAN, K.
BOULANGER, R.
CHANG, D. P.
DAFALIAS, Y. F.
DARBY, J. L.
GINN, T.
IDRISS, I. M.
KAVVAS, M. L.
KUTTER, B. L.
LAROCK, B. E.
LUND, J. R.
MARINO, M. A.
MOKHTARIAN, P. L.
NIEMEIER, D. A.
RAMEY, M. R.
RUNDLE, J. B.
SPERLING, D.
YOUNIS, B.

Faculty of Computer Science:

BAI, Z.
BRUNO, J.
FARRENS, M. K.
GUSFIELD, D.
HAMANN, B.
JOY, K. I.
LEVITT, K. N.
MARTEL, C. U.
MATLOFF, N. S.
MUKHERJEE, B.
OLSSON, R. A.
ROGAWAY, P. W.
RUSCHITZKA, M. G.

Faculty of Electrical and Computer Engineering:

ABDEL-GHAFFAR, K. A.
BRANNER, G. R.
CHANG, T. S.
COLINGE, J. P.
CURRENT, K. W.
DING, Z.
FEHER, K.
FORD, G. E.
HALEY, S. B.
HERITAGE, J. P.
HUNT, C. E.
HURST, P. J.
KNOESEN, A.
LEVY, B. C.
LEWIS, S. H.
OKLOBDZIJA, V. G.
REDINBO, G. R.
REED, T. R.
SMITH, R. L.
SPENCER, R. R.
TIEN, N. C.
WANG, S.
YOO, S. B.

Faculty of Engineering:

MUNIR, Z. A.

Faculty of Engineering: Applied Science:

BALDIS, H. A.
CRAMER, S. P.
FREEMAN, R. R.
HWANG, D. Q.
JENSEN, N. G.
KOLNER, B. H.
KROL, D.
LAUB, A. J.
LUHMANN, N. C.
MAX, N. L.
MCCURDY, W. C.
MILLER, G. H.
OREL, A. E.
ROCKE, D. M.
RODRIGUE, G.
VEMURI, V.
YEH, Y.

Faculty of Mechanical and Aeronautical Engineering:

BAUGHN, J. W.
CHATTOT, J. J.
DAVIS, R. J.
DWYER, H. A.
FAROUKI, R. T.
FRANK, A. A.
HAFEZ, M. M.
HESS, R. A.
HUBBARD, M.
HULL, M. L.
KARNOPP, D. C.
KENNEDY, I. M.
KOLLMANN, W.
MARGOLIS, D. L.
RAVANI, B.
REHFIELD, L. W.
SARIGUL-KLIJN, N.
SHAW, B. D.
VAN DAM, C. P.
VELINSKY, S. A.
WEXLER, A. S.
WHITE, B. R.
YAMAZAKI, K.

School of Law (1013 King Hall, 1 Shields Ave, Davis, CA 95616; tel. (530) 752-0243; fax (530) 752-4704; internet www.kinghall .ucdavis.edu):

AMANN, D. M.
AYER, J. D.
BROWNSTEIN, A. E.
DOBRIS, J. C.
DOREMUS, H.
FEENEY, F. F.
GANDARA, A.
GLENNON, M. J.
GROSSMAN, G. S.
HILLMAN, R. W.
IMWINKELRIED, E. J.
JOHNSON, K. R.
JOO, T. W.
KURTZ, L. A.
LEWIS, E. A.
OAKLEY, J. B.
PERSCHBACHER, R. R.
POULOS, J. W.
REYNOSO, C.
SIMMONS, D. L.
WEST, M. S.
WOLK, B. A.
WYDICK, R. C.

College of Letters and Science (200 Social Sciences and Humanities Bldg, 1 Shields Ave, Davis, CA 95616; tel. (530) 752-0392; fax (530) 752-3440; internet www.ls.ucdavis .edu):

Faculty of African American and African Studies:

OLUPONA, J. K.
STEWART, J. O.
TURNER, P. A.

Faculty of American Studies:

BLAIR, C.
FRANKENBERG, R.
MECHLING, J. E.
SMITH, M.

Faculty of Anthropology:

BETTINGER, R. L.
BORGERHOFF-MULDER, M.
DONHAM, D. L.
HARCOURT, A. H.
JOSEPH, S.
MCHENRY, H. M.
RODMAN, P. S.
SMITH, C. A.
SMITH, D. G.
SMITH, J. S.
SRINIVAS, S.
WINTERHALDER, B. P.
YENGOYAN, A. A.

Faculty of Art History and Art Studio:

ATKINSON, C.
BILLS, T. B.
COLLINS, H. M.
HENDERSON, W.
HERSHMAN, L.
HOLLOWELL, D.
MACLEOD, D. S.
PULS, L. A.
RUDA, J.
WERFEL, G. S.

Faculty of Asian American Studies:

HAMAMOTO, D. Y.
HING, B. O.
SUE, S.

Faculty of Chemistry:

BALCH, A. L.
BRITT, R. D.
FAWCETT, W. R.
FINK, W. H.
GERVAY HAGUE, J.
JACKSON, W. M.
KAUZLARICH, S.
KELLY, P. B.
KURTH, M. J.
LAMAR, G. N.
LEBRILLA, C. B.
MEARES, C. F.
MOLINSKI, T.
NANTZ, M
NG, C. Y.
POWER, P. P.
ROCK, P. A.
SCHORE, N. E.
STUCHEBRUKHOV, A.
TINTI, D. S.
TRUE, N. S.
TUCKER, S. C.

Faculty of Chicana/o Studies:

CHABRAM-DERNE, A.
DE LA TORRE, A.
MONTOYA, M.

Faculty of Communication:

BELL, R. A.
BERGER, C. R.
MOTLEY, M. T.

Faculty of Comparative Literature:

BLANCHARD, M. E.
FINNEY, G.
LARSEN, N. A.
LU, S. H.
MURAV, H. L.
SCHEIN, S. L.
SCHIESARI, J.
SCHILDGEN, B. P.
TORRANCE, R. M.

Faculty of Comparative Research:

SKINNER, G. W.

Faculty of East Asian Languages and Cultures:

BORGEN, R.
YEH, M.

Faculty of Economics:

BONANNO, G.
CAMERON, A.
CLARK, G.
FEENSTRA, R. C.
HOOVER, K. D.
LINDERT, P. H.
MAKOWSKI, L.
OLMSTEAD, A. L.
QUINZII, M.
SHEFFRIN, S. M.
SILVESTRE, J.
WALTON, G. M.
WOO, W. T.

Faculty of English:

ABBOTT, D. P.
BYRD, W. M.
DALE, P. A.
DIEHL, J. F.
FERGUSON, M. W.
FREED, L. R.
GILBERT, S. M.
HAYS, P. L.
LANGLAND, E.
LEVIN, R. A.

LOKKE, K.
MCPHERSON, S. J.
MAJOR, C.
MORRIS, L. A.
OSBORN, M.
OWENS, L. D.
ROBERTSON, D. A.
SCHLEINER, W.
SIMMONS, S.
SIMPSON, D. E.
SNYDER, G. S.
VAN LEER, D. M.
WADDINGTON, R. B.
WATKINS, E. P.
WILLIAMSON, A. B.
ZENDER, K. F.

Faculty of French and Italian:

BLANCHARD, M. E.
CANNON, J.
DUTSCHKE, D. J.
MANOLIU, M. I.
VAN DEN ABBEELE, G.

Faculty of Geology:

CARLSON, S. J.
DAY, H. W.
DEWEY, J. F.
KELLOGG, L. H.
LESHER, C. E.
MONTAÑEZ, I. P.
MOORES, E. M.
MOUNT, J. F.
SCHIFFMAN, P.
SPERO, H. J.
TURCOTTE, D. L.
TWISS, R. J.
VERMEIJ, G.
VEROSUB, K. L.
ZIERENBERG, R. A.

Faculty of German and Russian:

BERND, C. A.
DRUZHNIKOV, Y.
MCCONNELL, W.
MENGES, K. R.
RANCOUR-LAFERRIERE, D.
SCHAEFFER, P. M.

Faculty of History:

BAUER, A. J.
BIALE, D.
BRANTLEY, C. L.
BROWER, D. R.
CADDEN, J.
HAGEN, W. W.
HALTTUNEN, K.
HOLLOWAY, T. H.
KUDLICK, C. J.
LANDAU, N. B.
MANN, S. L.
MARGADANT, T. W.
METCALF, B. O.
PRICE, D. C.
ROSEN, R. E.
SMITH, M.
SPYRIDAKIS, S.
TAYLOR, A. S.
WALKER, C. E.

Faculty of Linguistics:

BENWARE, W. A.
OJEDA, A. E.
TIMM, L. A.

Faculty of Mathematics:

BORGES, C. R.
BRAMSON, M. D.
CHEER, A. Y.
DIEDERICH, J. R.
EDELSON, A. L.
FUCHS, D. B.
GRAVNER, J.
HAAS, J.
HUNTER, J. K.
KRENER, A. J.
KUPERBERG, G. J.
MILTON, E. O.
MOGILNER, A.
MULASE, M.
NACHTERGAELE, B.
PUCKETT, E. G.
SAITO, N.
SALLEE, G. T.
SCHWARZ, A.
SHKOLLER, S.
SILVIA, E. M.
TEMPLE, J. B.
THOMPSON, A. A.
THURSTON, W. P.
TRACY, C. A.
WETS, R. J.

Faculty of Music:

BAUER, R.
BUSSE BERGER, A. M.
FRANK, A. D.
HOLOMAN, D. K.
NUTTER, D. A.
ORTIZ, P. V.
REYNOLDS, C. A.

Faculty of Native American Studies:

HERNANDEZ-AVILA, I.
LONGFISH, G. C.
MACRI, M. J.
MONTEJO, V. D.
VARESE, S.

Faculty of Philosophy:

CUMMINS, R. C.
DWORKIN, G.
GRIESEMER, J. R.
JUBIEN, M.
KING, J. C.
NEANDER, K. L.
TELLER, P.
WEDIN, M. V.
WILSON, G. M.

Faculty of Physics:

ALBRECHT, A. J.
BECKER, R. H.
CARLIP, S.
CHAU, L.
CHIANG, S.
CORRUCCINI, L. R.
COX, D. L.
FADLEY, C. S.
FONG, C.
GUNION, J. F.
KISKIS, J. E.
KLEIN, B. M.
KO, W. T.
LANDER, R.
PELLETT, D. E.
PICKETT, W. E.
SCALETTAR, R. T.
SINGH, R. R.
TRIPATHI, S. M.
YAGER, P. M.
ZHU, X.
ZIMANYI, G.

Faculty of Political Science:

HUCKFELDT, R. R.
JACKMAN, R. W.
NINCIC, M.
PETERMAN, L. I.
ROTHCHILD, D. S.
SIVERSON, R. M.
STONE, W. J.
WADE, L. L.

Faculty of Psychology:

ACREDOLO, L. P.
CAPITANIO, J. P.
COSS, R. G.
ELMS, A. C.
EMMONS, R. A.
ERICKSEN, K. P.
GOODMAN, G. S.
HARRISON, A. A.
HENRY, K. R.
HEREK, G. M.
JOHNSON, J. T.
KROLL, N. E.
KRUBITZER, L. A.
LONG, D. L.
MANGUN, G. R.
MENDOZA, S. P.
OWINGS, D. H.
PARKS, T. E.
POST, R. B.
SHAVER, P. R.
SIMONTON, D. K.
SOMMER, R.
WIDAMAN, K. F.

Faculty of Religious Studies:

JANOWITZ, N.
LAI, W. W.

Faculty of Sociology:

BLOCK, F.
COHEN, L. E.
CRAMER, J. C.
FELMLEE, D. H.
GOLDSTONE, J. A.
HALL, J. R.
JACKMAN, M. R.
JOFFE, C.
LOFLAND, L. H.
MCCARTHY, W. D.
SMITH, V. A.
WALTON, J. T.
WOLF, D. L.

Faculty of Spanish and Classics:

ARMISTEAD, S. G.
BLAKE, R. J.
GONZÁLEZ, C.
LARSEN, N. A.
ROLLER, L. E.
SCARI, R. M.
TRAILL, D. A.
VERANI, H. J.

Faculty of Statistics:

BERAN, R. J.
BURMAN, P.
JOHNSON, W. O.
MACK, Y. P.
MUELLER, H. G.
ROUSSAS, G. G.
SAMANIEGO, F. J.
SHUMWAY, R. H.
UTTS, J. M.
WANG, J.-L.

Faculty of Theatre and Dance:

ANDERSON, S. P.
IACOVELLI, J. C.
SELLERS-YOUNG, B. A.
SHANNON, P.

Faculty of Women and Gender Studies:

KUHN, A. K.
NEWTON, J.
RABINE, L. W.

Division of Biological Sciences (202 Life Sciences Addition, 1 Shields Ave, Davis, CA 95616; tel. (530) 752-0410; fax (530) 752-2604; internet www.dbs.ucdavis.edu):

Biological Science:

CHANG, E. S.

Evolution and Ecology:

CHESSON, P. L.
DOYLE, J. A.
GILLESPIE, J. H.
GOTTLIEB, L. D.
GREY, R. D.
GROSBERG, R. K.
LANGLEY, C. H.
PEARCY, R. W.
REJMANEK, M.
SANDERSON, M. J.
SCHOENER, T. W.
SHAFFER, H. B.
SHAPIRO, A. M.
STAMPS, J. A.
STANTON, M. L.
STRONG, D. R.
TOFT, C. A.
TURELLI, M.

WAINWRIGHT, P. C.

Microbiology:

ARTZ, S. W.
BAUMANN, P.
HEYER, W. D.
KOWALCZYKOWSKI, S. C.
MANNING, J. S.
MEEKS, J. C.
NELSON, D. C.
PRIVALSKY, M. L.
STEWART, V. J.
ROTH, J. R.

Molecular and Cellular Biology:

ARMSTRONG, P. B.
BASKIN, R. J.
BURTIS, K. C.
CALLIS, J.
CLEGG, J. S.
CROWE, J. H.
DAHMUS, M. E.
DOI, R. H.
ERICKSON, C. A.
ETZLER, M. E.
GASSER, C. S.
HEDRICK, J. L.
HJELMELAND, L. M.
KIGER, J. A.
LAGARIAS, J. C.
MYLES, D.
RODRIGUEZ, R. L.
SCHMID, C. W.
SHOLEY, J. M.
SEGEL, I. H.

Neurobiology, Physiology and Behaviour:

CARSTENS, E. E.
FULLER, C. A.
HORWITZ, B. A.
ISHIDA, A. T.
MULLONEY, B.
PAPPONE, P. A.
SILLMAN, A. J.
WEIDNER, W. J.
WILSON, M. C.
WOOLLEY, D. E.

Plant Biology:

DELMER, D. P.
HARADA, J. J.
LUCAS, W. J.
MURPHY, T. M.
O'NEILL, S. D.
ROST, T. L.
SINHA, N.
STEMLER, A. J.
SUNDARESEN, V.
THEG, S. M.
VANDERHOEF, L. N.

Graduate School of Management (106 AOB4, 1 Shields Ave, Davis, CA 95616; tel. (530) 752-7399; fax (530) 752-2924; e-mail gsm@ucdavis.edu; internet www.gsm.ucdacvis.edu):

BARBER, B.
BIGGART, N. W.
BUNCH, D. S.
CLARK, P. K.
GERSTNER, E.
GRIFFIN, P. A.
MAHER, M.
PALMER, D.
SMILEY, R. H.
SWAMINATHAN, A.
TOPKIS, D. M.
TSAI, C.-L.
WOODRUFF, D.

School of Medicine (Med Sci 1c, Room 102 Campus, 1 Shields Ave, Davis, CA 95616; tel. (530) 752-4028; fax (530) 752-1532; internet www-med.ucdavis.edu):

Department of Anaesthesiology and Pain Medicine:

ANTOGNINI, J. F.

Department of Biological Chemistry:

BRADBURY, E. M.
HAGERMAN, P. J.
HERSHEY, J. W.
HJELMELAND, L. M.
HOLLAND, M. J.
JUE, T.
KUNG, H.-J.
TROY LI, F. A.

Department of Cell Biology and Human Anatomy:

ERICKSON, K. L.
FITZGERALD, P.
KUMARI, V.
MEIZEL, S.
PRIMAKOFF, P.
TUCKER, R. P.

Department of Dermatology:

GRANDO, S. A.
HUNTLEY, A. C.
ISSEROFF, R. R.
LIU, F.-T.
ZIBOH, V. A.

Department of Epidemiology and Preventive Medicine:

BECKETT, L. A.
CHEN, M. S.
GOLD, E. B.
LEIGH, J. P.
SCHENKER, M. B.
WINTEMUTE, G. J.

Department of Family and Community Medicine:

BERTAKIS, K. D.
CALLAHAN, E. J.
FRANKS, P.
MELNIKOW, J.
NESBITT, T. S.
NUOVO, J.

Department of Human Physiology:

CALA, P. M.
CARLSEN, R. C.
CURRY, F. E.
O'DONNELL, M. E.
TURGEON, J. L.
WIDDICOMBE, J.
WISE, P.

Department of Internal Medicine:

ALBERTSON, T. E.
AMSTERDAM, E. A.
AOKI, T.
BERGLUND, L.
BONHAM, A. C.
COHEN, S. H.
CROSS, C. E.
DEGREGORIO, M.
DENARDO, S. J.
DEPNER, T. A.
FITZGERALD, F. T.
GANDARA, D. R.
GERSHWIN, M. E.
HALSTED, C. H.
HINSHAW, V. S.
KAPPAGODA, C. T.
KARAKAS, S. E.
KAUFMAN, M. P.
KAYSEN, G.
KRAVITZ, R.
LAM, K.
LAST, J. A.
LEUNG, J.
LOEWY, E.
MARTIN, R. B.
MATTHEWS, H. R.
MEYERS, F. J.
PARSONS, G. H.
PIMSTONE, N. R.
POLLARD, R. B.
POWELL, J. S.
PRINDIVILLE, T. P.
REDDI, A. H.
RICHMAN, C. M.
ROBBINS, J. A.
ROBBINS, R. L.
RUTLEDGE, J. C.
SCHAEFER, S.
SIEGEL, D.
SILVA, J.
STEBBINS, C. L.
ZERN, M.

Department of Medical Microbiology and Immunology:

BEAMAN, B. L.
DANDEKAR, S.
PAPPAGIANIS, D.
SYVANEN, M.
THEIS, J. H.

Medicine:

ANDERS, T. F.
SELDIN, M. F.

Department of Neurological Surgery:

BERMAN, R. F.
BOGGAN, J. E.
LYETH, B. G.
MATTHEWS, D. L.
MUIZELAAR, J. P.
SCHWARTZKROIN, P. A.

Department of Neurology:

DE CARLI, C.
GORIN, F. A.
JAGUST, W. J.
KWEE, I.
MANGUN, G. R.
MASELLI, R. A.
REMLER, M. P.
RICHMAN, D. P.
SEYAL, M.

Department of Obstetrics and Gynaecology:

BOYERS, S.
GILBERT, W. M.
OVERSTREET, J. W.
SMITH, L. H.

Department of Ophthalmology:

CHALUPA, L. M.
KELTNER, J. L.
MANNIS, M. J.
WERNER, J. S.

Department of Orthopaedic Surgery:

BENSON, D. R.
RAB, G. T.
RODRIGO, J. J.
SZABO, R. M.

Department of Otolaryngology:

DONALD, P. J.

Department of Paediatrics:

HAGERMAN, R. J.
JOAD, J. P.
MAKKER, S. P.
PHILIPPS, A. F.
SHERMAN, M. P.
STYNE, D. M.
TARANTAL, A. F.
WENMAN, W. M.

Department of Pathology:

CARDIFF, R. D.
ELLIS, W. G.
GREEN, R.
JIALAL, I.
KOST, G. J.
LARKIN, E. C.
LUCIW, P. A.

Department of Pharmacology:

BONHAM, A. C.
CHUANG, R. Y.
HENDERSON, G. L.

Department of Plastic Surgery:

STEVENSON, T. R.

Department of Psychiatry:

AMARAL, D. G.
HENDREN, R. L.
JONES, E. G.

KNAPP, P. K.
MADDOCK, R. J.
MORRISON, T. L.
ROGERS, S. J.

Department of Radiation Oncology:

BOGREN, H. G.
BOONE, J. M.
BRUNBERG, J. A.
BUONOCORE, M. H.
KATZBERG, R. W.
KUBO, H.
LATCHAW, R. E.
LINK, D. P.
MCGAHAN, J. P.
MOORE, E. H.
ROSENQUIST, C. J.
SEIBERT, J. A.
STADAINIK, R. C.
VIJAYAKUMAR, S.

Department of Surgery:

FOLLETTE, D. M.
GREENHALGH, D. G.
HOLCROFT, J. W.
SEGEL, L. D.
WISNER, D. H.
WOLFE, B. M.

Department of Urology:

DE VERE WHITE, R. W.
STONE, A. R.

School of Veterinary Medicine (tel. (530) 752-1360; fax (530) 752-2801; internet www.vetmed.ucdavis.edu):

Faculty of Anatomy, Physiology and Cell Biology:

BRUSS, M. L.
GIETZEN, D. W.
HART, B. L.
HYDE, D. M.
PINKERTON, K. E.
PLOPPER, C. G.
RAYBOULD, M. J.
STOVER, S. M.
TABLIN, F.
WU, R.

Faculty of Medicine and Epidemiology:

ARDANS, A. A.
CARLSON, G. P.
CARPENTER, T. E.
COWGILL, L. D.
FELDMAN, E. C.
GARDNER, I.
GEORGE, L. W.
HEDRICK, R. P.
HIRD, D. W.
IHRKE, P. J.
KITTLESON, M. D.
LING, G. V.
MADIGAN, J. E.
NELSON, R. W.
PEDERSEN, N. C.
SMITH, B. P.
THOMAS, W. P.
THURMOND, M. C.
WALSH, D. A.
WHITE, S. D.
WILSON, W. D.

Faculty of Molecular Biosciences:

BUCKPITT, A. R.
CORTOPASSI, G. I.
GIRI, S. N.
HANSEN, R. J.
PESSAH, I. N.
ROGERS, Q. R.
SEGALL, H. J.
VULLIET, P. R.

Faculty of Pathology, Microbiology and Immunology:

BARTHOLD, S. W.
BOYCE, W. M.
CHRISTOPHER, M. W.
CONRAD, P. A.
GERSHWIN, L. J.
HIGGINS, R. J.
LEFEBVRE, R. B.
LOWENSTINE, L. J.
MACLACHLAN, N. J.
MILLER, C. J.
MOORE, P. F.
MUNSON, L.
MURPHY, F. A.
OSBURN, B. I.
STOTT, J. L.
WILSON, D. W.
YILMA, T.
ZINKL, J. G.

Faculty of Population Health and Reproduction:

BALL, B. A.
BONDURANT, R. H.
CHOMEL, B. B.
CLIVER, D. O.
CULLOR, J. S.
FARVER, T. B.
HART, L. A.
LAM, K. M.
LASLEY, W. L.
LIU, I. K.
MURRAY, J. D.
TANNENBAUM, J.

Faculty of Surgical and Radiological Sciences:

BUYUKMIHCI, N. C.
GREGORY, C. R.
HASKINS, S. C.
HILDEBRAND, S. V.
HORNOF, W. J.
ILKIW, J.
JONES, J. H.
LECOUTEUR, R. A.
MADEWELL, B. R.
NYLAND, T. G.
O'BRIEN, T. R.
PASCOE, J. R.
PASCOE, P. J.
SNYDER, J. R.
STEFFEY, E. P.
THEON, A. P.
VASSEUR, P.
VERSTRAETE, F. J. M.
WISNER, E. R.

University of California, Irvine

Irvine, CA 92697
Telephone: (949) 824-5011
Internet: www.uci.edu
Founded 1965
State control
Chancellor: MICHAEL V. DRAKE
Exec. Vice-Chancellor and Provost: MICHAEL R. GOTTFREDSON
Vice-Chancellor for Admin. and Business Services: WENDELL C. BRASE
Vice-Chancellor for Planning and Budget: M. MICHAELS
Vice-Chancellor for Research (vacant)
Vice-Chancellor for Student Affairs (vacant)
Vice-Chancellor for University Advancement: D. G. ALDRICH, III
Univ. Librarian (vacant)
Library of 2,250,000 vols and 22,000 current periodicals
Number of teachers: 1,520
Number of students: 26,984
Publications: *New University* (student newspaper, 52 a year), *UCI* Gen. Catalogue (1 a year), *UCI Journal* (newspaper, 4 a year), *UCI News Paper* (12 a year), and numerous student publications

DEANS

Claire Trevor School of the Arts: JOSEPH S. LEWIS, III
Donald Bren School of Information and Computer Sciences: HAL STERN (acting)
Div. of Undergraduate Education: SHARON V. SALINGER
Graduate Studies: FRANCES LESLIE
Henry Samueli School of Engineering: RAFAEL L. BRAS
Paul Merage School of Business: ANDREW J. POLICANO (acting)
School of Biological Sciences: ALBERT BENNETT
School of Humanities: VICKI RUIZ
School of Law: ERWIN CHEMERINSKY
School of Medicine: RALPH V. CLAYMAN
School of Physical Sciences: JOHN C. HEMMINGER
School of Social Ecology: VALERIE JENNESS
School of Social Sciences: BARBARA DOSHER
College of Health Sciences: THOMAS C. CESARIO
Univ. Extension: GARY MATKIN

DIRECTORS AND DEPARTMENT CHAIRPERSONS

Biological Sciences:
Anatomy and Neurology: Prof. HERBERT P. KILLACKEY
Developmental and Cell Biology: Prof. ARTHUR D. LANDER
Ecology and Evolutionary Biology: Prof. ARTHUR F. BENNETT
Molecular Biology and Biochemistry: Prof. JERRY E. MANNING

Education:
DAVID BRANT (interim Chair.)

Engineering:
Biomedical Engineering: Dr STEVE C. GEORGE
Chemical Engineering and Materials Science: Prof. STANLEY B. GRANT
Civil and Environmental Engineering: Prof. MASANOBU SHINOZUKA
Electrical and Computer Engineering: Prof. ENDER AYANOGLU
Mechanical and Aerospace Engineering: Prof. DIMITRI PAPAMOSCHOU

Claire Trevor School of the Arts:
Dance: ALAN TERRICCIANO
Drama: CAMERON HARVEY
Music: ALAN TERRICCIANO (Co-Chair: CAMERON HARVEY (Co-Chair)
Studio Art: YONG SOON MIN

Humanities:
African American Studies: Dr BELINDA ROBNETT (acting)
Art History: Prof. JAMES D. HERBERT
Asian American Studies: Prof. KETU H. KATRAK
Classics: LYNN MALLY
East Asian Language and Literatures: Prof. STEVEN D. CARTER
English and Comparative Literature: Prof. STEVE MAILLOUX
English as a Second Language: ROBIN SCARCELLA
Film Studies: (vacant)
French and Italian: Prof. DAVID CARROLL
German: Prof. JENS RIECKMANN
History: Prof. KENNETH L. POMERANZ
Humanities Core Course: JOHN SMITH
Latin American Studies: JAIME E. RODRÍGUEZ
Philosophy: Prof. NICHOLAS P. WHITE
Russian Studies: Dr DRAGAN KUJUNDZIĆ
Spanish and Portuguese: Dr ANA PAULA FERREIRA
Women's Studies: Prof. INDERPAL GREWAL

Information and Computer Science:
Dr DEBRA J. RICHARDSON

Medicine:
Anaesthesiology: CYNTHIA ANDERSON
Anatomy and Neurobiology: Dr RICHARD T. ROBERTSON
Biological Chemistry: Prof. SUZANNE B. SANDMEYER

C and E Medicine: DANIEL MENZEL
Dermatology: Dr JERRY L. MCCULLOUGH
Emergency Medicine: Dr MARK I. LANGDORF
Family Medicine: JOSEPH E. SCHERGER (acting)
Medicine: ALLAN HUBBELL (acting)
Microbiology and Molecular Genetics: Dr BERT L. SEMLER
Neurological Surgery: MARIO AMMIRATI (acting)
Neurology: Dr MARK FISHER
Obstetrics and Gynaecology: Prof. THOMAS J. GARITE
Ophthalmology: Dr PETER J. MCDONNELL (acting)
Orthopaedic Surgery: Dr HARRY B. SKINNER
Otolaryngology, Head and Neck Surgery: Prof. ROGER L. CRUMLEY
Paediatrics: Dr FEIZAL WAFFARN
Pathology: Prof. MICHAEL E. SELSTED
Pharmacology: Prof. SUE PIPER DUCKLES
Physical Medicine and Rehabilitation: Prof. JEN YU
Physiology and Biophysics: Prof. JANOS LANYI
Psychiatry and Human Behaviour: SIU TANG
Radiation Oncology: NILAM RAMSINGHANI
Radiological Sciences: Prof. FONG Y. TSAI
Surgery: Prof. SAMUEL E. WILSON

Physical Sciences:
Chemistry: Prof. KENNETH J. SHEA
Earth System Science: Dr WILLIAM REEBURGH
Mathematics: Prof. BERNARD RUSSO
Physics and Astronomy: Prof. ANDREW LANKFORD

Social Ecology:
Criminology, Law and Society: Dr VALERIE JENNEESS
Environmental Analysis and Design: Prof. JONATHON E. ERICSON (acting)
Psychology and Social Behaviour: Dr CHUANSHENG CHEN
Urban Planning: Dr SCOTT BOLLENS

Social Sciences:
Anthropology: Prof. JAMES G. FERGUSON
Chicano and Latino Studies Programme: LEO CHÁVEZ
Cognitive Sciences: TED WRIGHT
Economics: MICHELLE GARFINKEL
Global Peace and Conflict Studies: WAYNE SANDHOLTZ (acting)
Linguistics: Prof. NAOKO FUKUI
Logic and Philosophy of Science: JEFFREY BARRETT
Political Science: KATHERINE TATE
Sociology: CALVIN MORRILL
Transportation Studies: MICHAEL MCNALLY (acting)

Statistics:
Prof. HAL S. STERN

University of California, Los Angeles (UCLA)

405 Hilgard Ave, Los Angeles, CA 90095-9000
Telephone: (310) 825-4321
Internet: www.ucla.edu

Founded 1919

Chancellor: GENE D. BLOCK
Exec. Vice-Chancellor and Provost: SCOTT WAUGH
Vice-Chancellor for Academic Personnel: THOMAS H. RICE
Vice-Chancellor for Admin. Affairs: SAM J. MORABITO
Vice-Chancellor for External Affairs: RHEA TURTELTAUB
Vice-Chancellor for Finance, Budget and Capital Programmes: STEVEN A. OLSEN
Vice-Chancellor for Health Sciences: A. EUGENE WASHINGTON
Vice-Chancellor for Legal Affairs: KEVIN REED
Vice-Chancellor for Research: JAMES ECONOMOU
Vice-Chancellor for Student Affairs: JANINA MONTERO
Vice-Chancellor (Graduate Studies) and Dean of Graduate Division: CLAUDIA MITCHELL-KERNAN
Univ. Librarian: GARY STRONG

Library: 8m. vols, 90,000 periodicals
Number of teachers: 4,016
Number of students: 39,252

DEANS

Anderson School of Management: JUDY OLIAN
Continuing Education and UCLA Extension: CATHY SANDEEN
David Geffen School of Medicine: A. EUGENE WASHINGTON
Div. of Humanities: TIMOTHY STOWELL
Div. of Life Sciences: VICTORIA SORK
Div. of Physical Sciences: JOSEPH RUDNICK
Div. of Social Sciences: ALESSANDRO DURANTI
Div. of Undergraduate Education: JUDITH L. SMITH
Graduate Div.: CLAUDIA MITCHELL-KERNAN
Graduate School of Education and Information Studies: AIMEE DORR
Henry Samueli School of Engineering and Applied Science: VIJAY DHIR
Int. Institute: RONALD ROGOWSKI
School of the Arts and Architecture: CHRISTOPHER WATERMAN
School of Dentistry: NO-HEE PARK
School of Law: RACHEL MORAN
School of Nursing: COURTNEY LYDER
School of Public Affairs: FRANKLIN GILLIAM, Jr
School of Public Health: LINDA ROSENSTOCK
School of Theater, Film and Television: TERI SCHWARTZ

CHAIRPERSONS OF DEPARTMENTS

Arts and Architecture (303 East Melnitz, POB 951427, Los Angeles, CA 90095-1427; tel. (310) 206-6465; fax (310) 206-8504; e-mail webmaster@arts.ucla.edu; internet www.arts.ucla.edu):
Architecture and Urban Design: Prof. RICHARD WEINSTEIN (acting)
Art: BARBARA DRUCKER
Design: VICTORIA VESNA
Ethnomusicology and Systematic Musicology: TIM RICE
Music: IAN KROUSE
World Arts and Cultures: DAVID GERE

Education and Information Studies (Moore Hall, 405 Hilgard Ave, POB 951521, Los Angeles, CA 90095-1521; tel. (310) 825-8326; fax (310) 794-4732; e-mail info@gseis.ucla.edu; internet www.gseis.ucla.edu):
Education: SANDRA GRAHAM
Information Studies: VIRGINIA WALTER

Engineering and Applied Science (7400 Boelter Hall, POB 951600, Los Angeles, CA 90095-1600; tel. (310) 825-2938; fax (310) 206-4061; e-mail mori@ea.ucla.edu; internet www.engineer.ucla.edu):
Bioengineering: Prof. CARLO D. MONTEMAGNO
Chemical Engineering: Prof. VASILOS MANOUSIOUTHAKIS
Civil and Environmental Engineering: Prof. WILLIAM W.-G. YEH
Computer Science: Prof. MILOS D. ERCEGOVAC
Electrical Engineering: Prof. YAHYA RAHMAT-SAMII
Materials Science and Engineering: Prof. MARK GOORSKY
Mechanical and Aerospace Engineering: Prof. H. THOMAS HAHN

Letters and Science (1312 Murphy Hall, POB 143801, Los Angeles, CA 90095-1438; tel. (310) 825-9009; fax (310) 825-9368; e-mail webadmin@college.ucla.edu; internet www.college.ucla.edu):
Aerospace Studies: Lt Col ANTHONY LEPPELLERE
Anthropology: DOUGLAS HOLLAN
Applied Linguistics and TESL: LYLE BACHMAN
Art History: CECELIA KLEIN
Asian Languages and Cultures: GREGORY SCHOPEN
Atmospheric Sciences: LARRY LYONS
Cesar Chavez Center: REYNALDO MACIAS
Chemistry and Biochemistry: HAROLD MARTINSON
Classics: ROBERT GURVAL
Earth and Space Sciences: DAVID JACKSON
Ecology and Evolution: VICTORIA SORK
Economics: DAVID LEVINE
English: THOMAS WORTHAM
French: FRANÇOISE LIONNET
Geography: GLEN MACDONALD
Germanic Languages: ANDREW HEWITT
History: TEOFILO RUIZ
Italian: MASSIMO CIAVOLELLA
Linguistics: TIMOTHY STOWELL
Mathematics: JAMES RALSTON
Microbiology and Molecular Genetics: JEFFREY MILLER
Military Science: Maj. SHAUN BUCK
Molecular, Cell and Developmental Biology: UTPAL BANERJEE
Musicology: ROBERT A. WALSER
Naval Science: Col STEPHEN HUBBLE
Near Eastern Languages and Cultures: WILLIAM SCHNIEDEWIND
Philosophy: CALVIN NORMORE
Physics and Astronomy: JOSEPH RUDNICK
Physiological Science: ART ARNOLD
Political Science: MICHAEL LOFCHIE
Psychology: ROBERT BJORK
Slavic Languages and Literatures: RONALD VROON
Sociology: DAVID LOPEZ
Spanish and Portuguese: JOHN DAGENAIS
Speech: NEIL MALAMUTH
Statistics: JAN DE LEEUW

Medicine (12-138 CHS, POB 951722, Los Angeles, CA 90095-1722; tel. (310) 825-6373; fax (310) 206-5046; e-mail trelease@ucla.edu; internet www.medsch.ucla.edu):
Anaesthesiology: PATRICIA KAPUR
Biological Chemistry: S. LAWRENCE ZIPURSKY
Biomathematics: ELLIOT LANDAW
Family Medicine: PATRICK DOWLING
Human Genetics: KENNETH LANGE
Medicine: ALAN FOGELMAN
Microbiology and Immunology: JEFFERY F. MILLER
Molecular and Medical Pharmacology: MICHAEL PHELPS
Neurobiology: MARIE-FRANÇOISE CHESSELET
Neurology: JOHN MAZZIOTTA
Obstetrics and Gynaecology: GAUTAM CHAUDHURI
Ophthalmology: BARTLY MONDINO
Orthopaedic Surgery: GERALD FINERMAN
Paediatrics: EDWARD MCCABE
Pathology and Laboratory Medicine: JONATHAN BRAUN
Physiology: KENNETH PHILIPSON
Psychiatry and Biobehavioural Sciences: PETER WHYBROW
Radiation Oncology: H. RODNEY WITHERS
Radiological Sciences: DIETER ENZMANN
Surgery: RONALD BUSUTTIL
Urology: JEAN DE KERNION

Public Health (16-071 CHS, POB 951772, Los Angeles, CA 90095-1772; tel. (310) 825-5524; fax (310) 825-8440; internet www.ph.ucla.edu):

Biostatistics: WILLIAM G. CUMBERLAND
Community Health Sciences: DONALD MORISKY
Environmental Health Sciences: CURTIS ECKHERT
Epidemiology: ROGER DETELS
Health Services: ROBERT KAPLAN

Public Policy and Social Research (3250 Public Policy Bldg, POB 951656, Los Angeles, CA 90095-1656; tel. (310) 825-3792; fax (310) 206-5773; e-mail emooreb@ucla.edu; internet www.sppsr.ucla.edu):
Policy Studies: MARK A. PETERSON
Social Welfare: STUART KIRK
Urban Planning: A. LOUKAITOU-SIDERIS

Theatre, Film and Television (Student Services, 103 E. Melnitz, POB 951622, Los Angeles, CA 90095-1622; tel. (310) 825-8787; fax (310) 825-3383; e-mail frontoffice@emelnitz.ucla.edu; internet www.tft.ucla.edu):
Film and Television: BARBARA BOYLE
Theatre: WILLIAM WARD

DIRECTORS OF ORGANIZED RESEARCH INSTITUTES

School of the Arts and Architecture:
Center for Intercultural Performance: Prof. JUDY MITOMA
Fowler Museum of Arts and Cultures: MARLA C. BERNS
Grunwald Center for the Graphic Arts: DAVID RODES
UCLA Hammer Museum: ANN PHILBIN

School of Dentistry:
Dental Research Institute: Dr DAVID WONG

Graduate School of Education and Information Studies:
Center for Entrepreneurial Leadership Clearinghouse on Entrepreneurship Education: Dr ARTHUR M. COHEN
Center for Int. and Devt Education: Prof. JOHN N. HAWKINS
Center for the Study of Evaluation (member of National Center for Research on Evaluation, Standards and Student Testing): Prof. EVA BAKER, Dr JOAN L. HERMAN (co-directors)
CONNECT: Center for Research and Innovation in Elementary Education: FREDERICK ERICKSON
Corrine A. Seeds University Elementary School: DONNA L. ELDER
Higher Education Research Institute: Dr ALEXANDER W. ASTIN
Teacher Education Program: ELOISE LOPEZ METCALFE

Henry Samueli School of Engineering and Applied Science:
California NanoSystems Institute (operated in collaboration with UC Santa Barbara): Prof. EVELYN HU (acting Co-Director, from UCSB: Prof. J. FRASER STODDART (acting Co-Director, from UCLA)
Center for Embedded Network Sensing: Prof. DEBORAH ESTIN
Fusion Science and Technology Center: Prof. MOHAMED ABDOU

College of Letters and Sciences:
Basic Plasma Science Facility: WALTER GEKELMAN
California Center for Population Research: DUNCAN THOMAS
Center for American Politics and Public Policy: Prof. JOEL D. ABERBACH
Center for Communications and Community: Prof. FRANKLIN D. GILLIAM, Jr
Center for Comparative Social Analysis: REBECCA EMIGH
Center for Digital Humanities: (vacant)
Center for Jewish Studies: DAVID MYERS
Center for Language, Interaction and Culture: Prof. ALESSANDRO DURANTI
Center for Medieval and Renaissance Studies: HENRY ANSGAR KELLY
Center for Modern and Contemporary Studies: Prof. VINCENT P. PECORA
Center for 17th- and 18th-Century Studies: PETER H. REILL
Center for Research in Society and Politics: MARTIN GILENS
Center for Social Theory and Comparative History: Prof. ROBERT P. BRENNER
Center for the Study of Religion: Prof. SCOTT BARTCHY
Center for the Study of Urban Poverty: Prof. ABEL VALENZUELA
Center for the Study of Women: CHRISTINE LITTLETON
Clark Library: PETER H. REILL
Cognitive Science Research Program: Prof. PHIL KELLMAN
Cotsen Institute of Archaeology: Prof. CHARLES S. STANISH
Humanities Consortium: Prof. VINCENT P. PECORA
Institute for Pure and Applied Mathematics: Dr MARK GREEN
Institute for Social Science Research: DAVID O. SEARS
Institute of Geophysics and Planetary Physics: JOHN VIDALE
Institute of Radiation and Remote Sensing: Prof. K. N. LIOU
Marine Science Center: Dr WILLIAM HAMNER
Molecular Biology Institute: Prof. STEVEN G. CLARKE
National Center for History in the Schools: Prof. GARY B. NASH
Plasma Science and Technology Institute: Prof. GEORGE J. MORALES
Stunt Ranch Santa Monica Mountains Reserve: Prof. PHILIP RUNDEL
Survey Research Center: EVE FIELDER

Anderson School of Management:
Center for Health Services Management: Prof. PAUL TORRENS
Center for Int. Business Education and Research: Prof. BHAGWAN CHOWDHRY
Center for Management in the Information Economy: Prof. UDAY KARMARKAR
Harold Price Center for Entrepreneurial Studies: ALFRED E. OSBOURNE, Jr
Information Systems Research Program: Prof. E. BURTON SWANSON
Richard S. Ziman Center for Real Estate: Prof. WALTER N. TOROUS
UCLA Anderson Forecast Center: Prof. EDWARD E. LEARNER

School of Medicine:
AIDS Institute: Prof. IRVIN CHEN
Brain Research Institute: Dr CHRISTOPHER EVANS
Crump Institute for Molecular Imaging: Dr MICHAEL PHELPS
CURE: Digestive Diseases Research Center: Prof. JUAN ENRIQUE ROZENGURT
Jonsson Comprehensive Cancer Center: Prof. PATRICIA GANZ
Jules Stein Eye Institute: Prof BARTLY J. MONDINO
Neuropsychiatric Institute: Dr PETER C. WHYBROW

School of Public Affairs:
Center for Communication Policy: JEFFREY COLE
Center for Globalization and Policy Research: HELMUT ANHEIER
Center for Health Policy Research: Prof. E. RICHARD BROWN
Center for Int. Science, Technology and Cultural Policy: LYNNE G. ZUCKER
Center for Policy Research on Aging: Dr FERNANDO TORRES-GIL
Institute of Industrial Relations: RUTH MILKMAN
Institute of Transportation Studies: Dr BRIAN TAYLOR
North American Integration and Devt Center: Dr LEO F. ESTRADA
Ralph and Goldy Lewis Center for Regional Policy Studies: Prof. PAUL ONG

DIRECTORS OF INDEPENDENT UNITS

American Indian Studies Center: Prof. HANAY GEIOGAMAH
Asian-American Studies Center: Prof. DON T. NAKANISHI
Center for African-American Studies: Prof. DARNELL M. HUNT
Chicano Studies Research Center: Prof. REYNALDO MACIAS

DIRECTORS OF INTERNATIONAL STUDIES AND OVERSEAS PROGRAMMES

Asia Institute: R. BIN WONG
Center for Chinese Studies: Prof. RICHARD BAUM
Center for European and Eurasian Studies: Prof. IVAN BEREND
Center for Japanese Studies: Prof. FRED NOTEHELFER
Center for Korean Studies: JOHN DUNCAN
Education Abroad Program: Prof. VAL RUST
Gustave Von Grunebaum Center for Near Eastern Studies: LEONARD BINDER
James C. Coleman African Studies Center: Prof. ALLEN F. ROBERTS
Language Resource Center: OLGA KAGAN
Latin American Center: Prof. CARLOS TORRES
Ronald W. Burkle Center for Int. Relations: Prof. GEOFFREY GARRETT

University of California, Merced

POB 2039, Merced, CA 95344
Telephone: (209) 228-4400
Internet: www.ucmerced.edu
Founded 2005
Chancellor: SUNG-MO (STEVE) KANG (acting)
Exec. Vice-Chancellor and Provost: KEITH E. ALLEY (acting)
Vice-Chancellor for Admin.: MARY E. MILLER
Vice-Chancellor for Research: SAMUEL TRAINA
Vice-Chancellor for Student Affairs: JANE FIORI LAWRENCE
Vice-Chancellor for Univ. Relations: JOHN GARAMENDI
Chief Information Officer: RICHARD M. KOGUT
Univ. Librarian: R. BRUCE MILLER
Number of teachers: 80
Number of students: 1,200

DEANS

School of Engineering: JEFF R. WRIGHT
School of Natural Sciences: MARIA G. PALLAVICINI
School of Social Sciences, Humanities and Arts: HANS BJÖRNSSON
Graduate Studies: SAMUEL TRAINA (acting)

ATTACHED SCHOOLS

School of Engineering: POB 2039, Merced, CA 95343; tel. (209) 228-4411; e-mail engineering@ucmerced.edu; internet eng.ucmerced.edu.

School of Natural Sciences: POB 2039, Los Angeles, CA 95344; tel. (209) 228-4309; e-mail naturalsciences@ucmerced.edu; internet naturalsciences.ucmerced.edu.

School of Social Sciences, Humanities and Arts: tel. (209) 228-7742; fax (209) 228-4007; internet ssha.ucmerced.edu.

ATTACHED RESEARCH INSTITUTES

Sierra Nevada Research Institute (SNRI): tel. (209) 724-4311; e-mail straina@ucmerced.edu; internet www.ucmerced.edu/

research/snri.asp; interdisciplinary research in natural sciences, Eng. and policy sciences; Dir Dr SAMUEL TRAINA.

World Cultures Institute: tel. (209) 724-4335; e-mail ssha@ucmerced.edu; internet www.ucmerced.edu/research/wci.asp; combines humanities, arts and social sciences to research migration and impact on established peoples and resources.

University of California, Riverside

900 University Ave, Riverside, CA 92521
Telephone: (909) 787-1012
Fax: (909) 787-3866
Internet: www.ucr.edu
Founded 1954
State control
Academic year: September to June
Chancellor: Dr FRANCE A. CÓRDOVA
Exec. Vice-Chancellor and Provost: Dr ELLEN WARTELLA
Vice-Chancellor for Academic Planning and Budget: GRETCHEN BOLAR
Vice-Chancellor for Admin.: AL DIAZ
Vice-Chancellor for Public Service and Int. Programmes: JOHN F. AZZARETTO
Vice-Chancellor for Research: Dr CHARLES F. LOUIS
Vice-Chancellor for Student Affairs: JAMES W. SANDOVAL
Vice-Chancellor for Univ. Advancement: Dr WILLIAM G. BOLT
Registrar: ELIZABETH C. BENNETT
Univ. Librarian: Dr RUTH JACKSON
Library: see Libraries and Archives
Number of teachers: 615 F.t.e.
Number of students: 15,934

DEANS

A. Gary Anderson Graduate School of Management: ANIL DEOLALIKAR
College of Humanities, Arts and Social Science: STEPHEN CULLENBERG
College of Natural and Agricultural Sciences: DONALD COOKSEY
Div. of Biomedical Sciences: CRAIG V. BYUS
Graduate Div.: DALLAS L. RABENSTEIN
Graduate School of Education: STEVEN BOSSERT
Marlan and Rosemary Burns College of Engineering: REZA ABBASCHIAN
University Extension: SHEILA DWIGHT

University of California, San Diego

9500 Gilman Dr., La Jolla, CA 92093
Telephone: (858) 534-2230
Fax: (858) 534-5355
Internet: ucsd.edu
Became part of the Univ. of California system 1960
Academic year: September to June
Chancellor (vacant)
Vice-Chancellor for Academic Affairs: PAUL DRAKE
Vice-Chancellor for External and Business Affairs: STEVEN W. RELYEA
Vice-Chancellor for Health Sciences and Dean of the School of Medicine: DAVID BRENNER
Vice-Chancellor for Marine Sciences and Dir of Scripps Institution of Oceanography: TONY HAYMET
Vice-Chancellor for Research: ARTHUR ELLIS
Vice-Chancellor for Resource Management and Planning: GARY MATTHEWS
Vice-Chancellor for Student Affairs: PENNY RUE
Provost of Revelle College: DON WAYNE
Provost of John Muir College: SUSAN SMITH (acting)
Provost of Thurgood Marshall College: ALLAN HAVIS
Provost of Earl Warren College: STEVEN ADLER
Provost of Eleanor Roosevelt College: ALAN HOUSTON
Provost of Sixth College: NAOMI ORESKES
Registrar: GABRIEL OLSEZEWSKI
Librarian: BRIAN SCHOTTLAENDER
Number of teachers: 1,205
Number of students: 29,110
Publication: *USCD Perspectives*

DEANS

Division of Arts and Humanities: SETH LERER
Division of Biological Sciences: STEVE KAY
Division of Physical Sciences: MARK THIEMENS
Division of Social Sciences: JEFF ELMAN
Graduate Studies: KIM BARRETT
Jacobs School of Engineering: FRIEDER SEIBLE
Preuss School: SCOTT BARTON (Prin.)
Rady School of Management: ROBERT SULLIVAN
School of Int. Relations and Pacific Studies: PETER COWHEY
School of Medicine: DAVID A. BRENNER
Scripps Instn of Oceanography: TONY HAYMET (Dir)
Skaggs School of Pharmacy and Pharmaceutical Sciences: PALMER TAYLOR
UCSD Extension: MARY LINDENSTEIN WALSHOK

CHAIRPERSONS OF DEPARTMENTS

Anthropology: M. SHOENINGER
Bioengineering: S. CHIEN
Cell and Developmental Biology: R. FIRTEL
Chemistry and Biochemistry: C. KUBIAK
Cognitive Science: R. BELEW
Communication: R. HORWITZ
Computer Science and Engineering: R. PATURI
Ecology, Behaviour and Evolution Biology: L. CHAO
Economics: R. CARSON
Electrical and Computer Engineering: P. YU
Ethnic Studies: R. ALVAREZ
History: J. MARINO
Linguistics: R. KLUENDER
Literature: T. KONTJE
Mathematics: B. DRIVER
Mechanics and Aerospace Engineering: P. LINDEN
Molecular Biology: J. KADONAGA
Music: J. FONVILLE
Neurobiology: W. KRISTAN
Philosophy: P. CHURCHLAND
Physics: B. MAPLE
Political Science: G. COX
Psychology: J. WIXTED
Scripps Institution of Oceanography: M. HENDERSHOTT
Sociology: A. SCULL
Structural Engineering: A. ELGAMAL
Theatre and Dance: C. OATES
Visual Arts: S. FAGIN

School of Medicine:
- Anaesthesiology: J. DRUMMOND
- Family and Medicine: R. KAPLAN
- Medicine: K. KAUSHANSKY
- Neurosciences: L. THAL
- Ophthalmology: S. BROWN
- Orthopaedics: S. GARFIN
- Paediatrics: S. MENDOZA
- Pathology: D. BAILEY
- Pharmacology: P. TAYLOR
- Psychiatry: L. JUDD
- Radiology: G. LEOPOLD
- Reproductive Medicine: T. MOORE
- Surgery: A. MOOSSA

University of California, San Francisco

3rd and Parnassus Aves, San Francisco, CA 94143
Telephone: (415) 476-9000
Fax: (415) 476-9634
Internet: www.ucsf.edu
Founded 1873
Chancellor: J. MICHAEL BISHOP
Exec. Vice-Chancellor and Provost: A. EUGENE WASHINGTON
Sr Vice-Chancellor: STEVE BARCLAY
Sr Vice-Chancellor for Finance and Admin.: JOHN PLOTTS
Sr Vice-Chancellor for Univ. Advancement and Planning: BRUCE SPAULDING
Vice-Chancellor for Medical Affairs: DAVID KESSLER
Exec. Dir Institute for Biomedical Research: REGIS KELLY
Registrar: DOUGLAS CARLSON
Librarian: KAREN BUTTER
Library of 821,492 vols
Number of teachers: 2,051
Number of students: 4,051

DEANS

School of Dentistry: JOHN FEATHERSTONE
School of Medicine: SAM HAGWOOD
School of Nursing: KATHLEEN DRACUP
School of Pharmacy: MARY-ANNE KODA-KIMBLE
Graduate Division: PATRICIA CALARCO

DIRECTORS

Center for Bioentrepreneurship and Industry Partnerships: GAIL SCHECHTER
Langley Porter Neuropsychiatric Institute: CRAIG VAN DYKE
Proctor Foundation: TODD MARGOLIS

University of California, Santa Barbara

Santa Barbara, CA 93106
Telephone: (805) 893-8000
Internet: www.ucsb.edu
Founded 1909, became part of the Univ. of California 1944
Academic year: September to June
Chancellor: HENRY T. YANG
Exec. Vice-Chancellor: GENE LUCAS
Vice-Chancellor for Admin. Services (vacant)
Vice-Chancellor for Institutional Advancement (vacant)
Vice-Chancellor for Research: MICHAEL WITHERELL
Vice-Chancellor for Student Affairs: MICHAEL D. YOUNG
Asst Chancellor for Budget and Planning: TODD G. LEE
Assoc. Vice-Chancellor for Academic Personnel: JOHN E. TALBOTT
Assoc. Vice-Chancellor for Academic Programs: RONALD W. TOBIN
Registrar: VIRGINIA K. JOHNS (acting)
Co-Acting Univ. Librarians: SHERRY DEDECKER, LUCIA SNOWHILL
Library of 3,444,662 vols, serial backfiles and govt documents, 69,327 current serials, 3,772,031 microforms, 149,150 audio and video recordings, 399,370 electronic books
Number of teachers: 1,052
Number of students: 22,218

DEANS

College of Creative Studies: BRUCE TIFFNEY
Gevirtz Graduate School of Education: JANE CLOSE CONOLEY
College of Engineering: LARRY COLDREN (acting)
Donald Bren School of Environmental Science and Management: STEVEN GAINES
Graduate Division: GALE M. MORRISON
Humanities and Fine Arts: Dr DAVID MARSHALL

Science: PIERRE WILTZIUS
Social Sciences: Dr MELVIN OLIVER
Undergraduate Education: MARY NISBET (acting)

University of California, Santa Cruz

1156 High St, Santa Cruz, CA 95064
Telephone: (831) 459-0111
Fax: (831) 459-0146
Internet: www.ucsc.edu
Founded 1962
Academic year: September to June
Chancellor: GEORGE BLUMENTHAL (acting)
Campus Provost and Exec. Vice-Chancellor: DAVID S. KLIGER
Vice-Provost for Academic Affairs: ALISON GALLOWAY
Vice-Provost and Dean of Undergraduate Education: WILLIAM A. LADUSAW
Vice-Provost and Dean of Univ. Extension: CARL E. WALSH
Vice-Chancellor for Business and Admin. Services: THOMAS M. VANI
Vice-Chancellor for Planning and Budget: MEREDITH MICHAELS
Vice-Chancellor for Research: BRUCE MARGON
Vice-Chancellor for Student Affairs: SUSAN HANSEN (acting)
Vice-Chancellor for Univ. Relations: DONNA M. MURPHY
Exec. Director of Admissions and University Registrar: KEVIN BROWNE
Univ. Librarian: VIRGINIA STEEL
Library of 1,350,000 vols, 15,000 periodicals, 800,000 microforms, 500 other items (maps, slides, audio and visual recordings)
Number of teachers: 542 (ladder-rank faculty)
Number of students: 15,013
Publication: *The Cultivar* (2 a year)

DEANS

Arts: EDWARD F. HOUGHTON
Engineering: SUNG MO (STEVE) KANG
Graduate Studies: LISA C. SLOAN
Humanities: GEORGE VAN DEN ABBEELE
Physical and Biological Sciences: STEPHEN THORSETT
Social Sciences: SHELDON KAMIENIECKI

DIRECTORS OF INSTITUTES

Geophysics and Planetary Physics: A. CHRISTINA RAVELO
Marine Sciences: GARY B. GRIGGS
Particle Physics: ABRAHAM SEIDEN
UCO/Lick Observatory: MICHAEL J. BOLTE

PROVOSTS

College Eight: ANDREW SZASZ
College Nine: CAMPBELL LEAPER
College Ten: CAMPBELL LEAPER
Cowell College: Prof. WILLIAM LADUSAW
Crown College: F. JOEL FERGUSON
Kresge College: CONN HALLINAN
Merrill College: JOHN SCHECHTER
Oakes College: PEDRO CASTILLO
Porter College: DAVID EVAN JONES
Stevenson College: MARGO HENDRICKS

UNIVERSITY OF LA VERNE

1950 Third St, La Verne, CA 91750
Telephone: (909) 593-3511
Fax: (909) 953-0965
Internet: www.ulv.edu
Founded 1891 as Lordsburg College; became La Verne College in 1917; present name 1977
9 Regional campuses
Private control
Academic year: September to June
Pres.: Dr STEPHEN MORGAN
Provost and Vice-Pres. for Academic Affairs: ROBERT NEHER
Exec. Vice-Pres.: PHILIP A. HAWKEY
Vice-Pres. for Enrollment Management: HOMA SHABAHANG
Vice-Pres. for Univ. Relations: JEAN BJERKE
Registrar: MARILYN DAVIES
Dean of Student Affairs: LORETTA RAHMANI
Librarian: TAYLOR RUHL
Library of 337,000 vols
Number of teachers: 220 (85 full-time, 135 part-time)
Number of students: 3,004

DEANS

College of Arts and Sciences: Prof. FRED YAFFE
College of Law: Prof. DONALD DUNN
School of Business and Public Management: GORDON J. BADOVICK
School of Education and Organization Leadership: LEONARD PELLICER

UNIVERSITY OF REDLANDS

1200 East Colton Ave, POB 3080, Redlands, CA 92373-0999
Telephone: (909) 793-2121
Fax: (909) 793-2029
Internet: www.redlands.edu
Founded 1907
Private
Pres.: STUART DORSEY
Chancellor: JAMES R. APPLETON
Vice-Pres. for Academic Affairs: Dr NANCY CARRICK
Sr Vice-Pres. for Finance and Admin.: PHILLIP DOOLITTLE
Vice-Pres. for Univ. Relations: RONALD STEPHANY
Registrar: CHARLOTTE LUCEY
Library Dir: JEAN SWANSON
Library of 233,882 vols
Number of teachers: 551
Number of students: 4,080
Publication: *Redlands*

DEANS

College of Arts and Sciences: Dr BARBARA JEAN MORRIS
School of Business: Dr STUART NOBLE-GOODMAN
School of Education: Dr PAM DWORAK

AFFILIATED CENTRES

Alfred North Whitehead College for Lifelong Learning: f. 1976; 2,150 students; Dean MARY BOYCE.

Johnston Center for Integrative Studies: tel. (909) 748-8615; f. 1969; 200 students; Dir Prof. KATHY OGREN.

UNIVERSITY OF SAN DIEGO

5998 Alcala Park, San Diego, CA 92110
Telephone: (619) 260-4600
E-mail: admissions@sandiego.edu
Internet: www.sandiego.edu
Founded 1949
Pres.: Dr MARY E. LYONS
Vice-Pres. and Provost: Dr JULIE SULLIVAN
Vice-Pres. for Finance and Admin.: PAUL E. BISSONNETTE
Vice-Pres. for Mission and Ministry: DANIEL DILLABOUGH
Vice-Pres. for Student Affairs: CARMEN VAZQUEZ
Vice-Pres. for Univ. Relations: Dr TIMOTHY O'MALLEY
Librarian: EDWARD STARKEY
Library of 300,000 vols and 2,200 current periodicals
Number of teachers: 508
Number of students: 7,000
Publications: *Contemporary Legal Issues* (1 or 2 a year), *Journal of International Law* (1 a year), *Law Review* (4 a year)

DEANS

College of Arts and Sciences: NICHOLAS M. HEALY
School of Business Admin.: ANDREW ALLEN
School of Law: KEVIN COLE
School of Leadership and Education Sciences: Dr PAULA A. CORDEIRO
School of Nursing and Health Sciences: Prof. SALLY BROSZ HARDIN
School of Peace Studies: WILLIAM HEADLEY

UNIVERSITY OF SAN FRANCISCO

2130 Fulton St, San Francisco, CA 94117-1080
Telephone: (415) 422-5555
Fax: (415) 422-2303
Internet: www.usfca.edu
Founded 1855
Private; Jesuit
Academic year: September to May
Pres.: STEPHEN A. PRIVETT
Provost and Vice-Pres. for Academic Affairs: Dr JAMES L. WISER
Chancellor: Rev. JOHN LO SCHIAVO
Vice-Pres. for Business and Finance: CHARLIE CROSS
Vice-Pres. for Int. Relations: STANLEY D. NEL
Vice-Pres. for Univ. Advancement: DAVID F. MACMILLAN
Vice-Pres. for Univ. Life: Dr MARGARET M. HIGGINS
Dean of Students: FELICIA J. LEE
Dean of the Univ. Library: TYRONE H. CANNON
Library of 593,543 vols
Number of teachers: 290
Number of students: 8,568
Publication: *USF Law Review* (4 a year)

DEANS

Colleges of Arts and Sciences: Dr JENNIFER E. TURPIN
College of Professional Studies: Dr LARRY G. BREWSTER
School of Business and Management: MICHAEL L. DUFFY
School of Education: Dr WALTER GMELCH
School of Law: Dr JEFFREY S. BRAND
School of Nursing: JUDITH F. KARSHNER

UNIVERSITY OF SOUTHERN CALIFORNIA

University Park Campus, Los Angeles, CA 90089
Telephone: (213) 740-2311
Internet: www.usc.edu
Founded 1880
Academic year: August to May
Pres.: C. L. MAX NIKIAS
Sr Vice-Pres. for Academic Affairs and Provost, and Vice-Pres. for Academic Planning and Budget: ELIZABETH GARRETT
Sr Vice-Pres. for Admin.: TODD R. DICKEY
Sr Vice-Pres. for Finance and Chief Financial Officer: ROBERT ABELES
Vice-Pres. for Admissions and Planning: KATHERINE HARRINGTON
Vice-Pres. for Athletic Compliance: DAVID M. ROBERTS
Vice-Pres. for Campus Devt and Facilities Management Services: JOE BACK
Vice-Pres. for Devt: COURTNEY SURLS
Vice-Pres. for Finance: MARGO STEURBAUT
Vice-Pres. for Govt and Community Relations: THOMAS S. SAYLES
Vice-Pres. for Research: RANDOLPH HALL

Vice-Pres. for Student Affairs: MICHAEL L. JACKSON
Gen. Counsel and Sec.: CAROL MAUCH AMIR
Dean of Libraries: CATHERINE QUINLAN
Library: see Libraries and Archives
Number of teachers: 3,200 (full-time)
Number of students: 35,000
Publications: *USC Chronicle*, *USC Trojan Family* (4 a year)

DEANS

Annenberg School for Communication and Journalism: ERNEST J. WILSON III
College of Letters, Arts and Sciences: HOWARD GILLMAN
Davis School of Gerontology: GERALD C. DAVISON
Gould School of Law: ROBERT K. RASMUSSEN
Keck School of Medicine: CARMEN A. PULIAFITO
Leventhal School of Accounting: RANDOLPH P. BEATTY
Marshall School of Business: JAMES G. ELLIS
Ostrow School of Dentistry: AVISHAI SADAN
Roski School of Fine Arts: ROCHELLE STEINER
Rossier School of Education: KAREN SYMMS GALLAGHER
School of Architecture: QINGYUN MA
School of Cinematic Arts: ELIZABETH M. DALEY
School of Pharmacy: R. PETE VANDERVEEN
School of Policy, Planning, and Devt: JACK H. KNOTT
School of Social Work: MARILYN L. FLYNN
School of Theatre: MADELINE PUZO
Thornton School of Music: ROBERT A. CUTIETTA
Viterbi School of Engineering: YANNIS C. YORTSOS

PROFESSORS

Distinguished and University Professors:
ARBIB, MICHAEL A., Biological Sciences and Biomedical Engineering
ARMSTRONG, LLOYD, Jr, Physics and Education
BENNIS, WARREN, Business Admin.
BRAUDY, LEO B., English and American Literature
CAPRON, ALEXANDER M., Law and Medicine
COHEN, MARSHALL, Emeritus of Philosophy and Law
COWAN, GEOFFREY, Communication Leadership
EASTERLIN, RICHARD A., Economics
FINCH, CALEB, Gerontology and Biological Sciences
GOLOMB, SOLOMON W., Electrical Engineering and Mathematics
HELLWARTH, ROBERT W., Physics
JORDAN, THOMAS, Geophysics and Earth Sciences
KINDER, MARSHA, Comparative Literature
PIKE, MALCOLM CECIL, Preventive Medicine
SHIH, JEAN C., Cell and Neurobiology
STARR, KEVIN O., History and Policy, Planning and Devt
TIERNEY, WILLIAM G., Higher Education
TOULMIN, STEPHEN E., Anthropology, Int. Relations and Religion
WATERMAN, MICHAEL S., Biological Sciences and Mathematics
ARNHEIM, NORMAN, Biological Sciences
BENNIS, WARREN, English
CORAGHESSAN BOYLE, T., English
EVERETT, PERCIVAL, Cinematic Arts
HARRIS, MARK JONATHAN, Theory and Composition
HARTKE, STEPHEN, Preventive Medicine
HENDERSON, BRIAN E., Biochemistry and Molecular Biology
JONES, PETER A., Paediatrics
KAUFMAN, FRANCINE R., Molecular Microbiology and Immunology
LAI, MICHAEL M. C., Business
LAWLER, EDWARD E., III, Medicine
LEVINE, ALEXANDRA M., Chemistry
OLAH, GEORGE A., Medicine
RAHIMTOOLA, SHAHBUDIN H., Cardiothoracic Surgery
STARNES, VAUGHN A., Pharmaceutical Sciences
WOLF, MICHAEL A., Biological Sciences and Biomedical Engineering

School of Gerontology:
BENGTSON, V. L.
BONDAREFF, W.
CRIMMINS, E.
DAVIES, K.
FINCH, C.
GATZ, M.
KNIGHT, R.
PYNOOS, J.
SCHNEIDER, E. L.
SCHNEIDER, L.
SILVERSTEIN, M.
WILBER, K.
ZELINSKI, E.

School of Law:
ALTMAN, S. A.
ARMOUR, J. D.
BICE, S. H.
BRECHT, A. O.
CAPRON, A. M.
COWAN, G.
CRUZ, D. B.
DUDZIAK, M. L.
ESTRICH, S.
FINEGAN, E. J.
GARET, R. R.
GARRETT, E.
GILLMAN, H.
GRIFFITH, T. D.
GROSS, A. J.
HADFIELD, G.
KEATING, G. C.
KLERMAN, D. M.
KURAN, T.
LEFCOE, G.
LEVINE, M. L.
LYON, T. D.
MCCAFFERY, E. J.
MARMOR, A.
MURPHY, K. J.
SAKS, E. R.
SCHOR, H. M.
SHAPIRO, M. H.
SIMON, L. G.
SLAWSON, W. D.
SMITH, E. M.
SPITZER, M. L.
STOLZENBERG, N. M.
STONE, C. D.
TALLEY, E. L.
WHITEBREAD, C. H.

School of Medicine:
ADLER, R.
AHMADI, J.
AKMAL, M.
ALKANA, R.
ANDERSON, W.
ANN, D.
APUZZO, M.
ASKANAS, V.
AZEN, S.
BAEHNER, R.
BALLARD, C.
BEART, R., Jr
BERGMAN, R.
BERNE, T.
BERNSTEIN, L.
BEYDOUN, S.
BONDAREFF, W.
BOYD, S.
BREMNER, C.
BRENNER, P.
BRINTON, R.
BROEK, D.
BUCHANAN, T.
CADENAS, E.
CAMPESE, V.
CHANDRASOMA, P.
CHUI, H.
CHUONG, C.-M.
CLARK, F.
COLLETTI, P.
CONTI, P.
COSTIN, G.
COTE, R.
CRAFT, C.
CRANDALL, E.
DANENBERG, P.
DE JUAN, E., Jr
DE MEESTER, T.
DECLERCK, Y.
DEMETRIADES, D.
DENNERT, G.
DIZEREGA, G.
DUBEAU, L.
DWYER, J.
ELKAYAM, U.
EL-SHAHAWY, M.
ENGEL, W.
EPSTEIN, A.
FARLEY, R.
FEINSTEIN, D.
FRANK, G.
GAYNON, P.
GEFFNER, M.
GIANNOTTA, S.
GILL, P.
GILLES, F.
GILLILAND, F.
GILSANZ, V.
GOMER, C.
GONG, H., Jr
GOODWIN, T.
GORAN, M.
GOVINDARAJAN, S.
GRANT, E.
GROFFEN, J.
GRUSHKIN, C.
HAHN, R.
HAILE, R.
HALLS, J.
HAMMOND, G.
HAYS, D.
HAYWOOD, L.
HEISTERKAMP, N.
HENDERSON, B.
HILL, A.
HINTON, D.
HODGMAN, J.
HODIS, H.
HOFMAN, F.
HOHN, A.
HORWITZ, D.
HSIEH, C.-L.
HUANG, H.
HUMAYUN, M.
HURVITZ, R.
ISRAEL, R.
IWAKI, Y.
JACOBS, R.
JELLIFFE, R.
JOHNSON, C.
JOHNSON, C.
JOHNSON, D.
JONES, P.
KALRA, V.
KAPLOWITZ, N.
KAPTEIN, E.
KAST, W. M.
KATKHOUDA, N.
KAUFMAN, F.
KEANE, J.
KEDES, L.
KEENS, T.
KILBURN, K.
KLONER, R.
KOHN, D.
KORSCH, B.
KOSS, M.
LAINE, L.
LAMB, H.

LAUG, W.
LAWLOR, M.
LEE, A.
LEVINE, A.
LEVY, D.
LEWIS, A.
LIEBER, M.
LIESKOVSKY, G.
LU, S.
LUMB, P.
MCCOMB, J.
MCDONOUGH, A.
MCMILLAN, M.
MCNEILL, T.
MACK, T.
MAHOUR, G.
MARKLAND, F.
MARTIN, W.
MATTINGLY, C.
MAXSON, R.
MEISELMAN, H.
MENDEZ, R.
MILLER, C.
MINCKLER, D.
MIRCHEFF, A.
MISHELL, D., Jr
MISHRA, S.
MORROW, C.
MULL, J.
MURPHREE, A.
NATHWANI, B.
NELSON, M.
NEWTH, C.
NICOLOFF, J.
NIMNI, M.
O'LEARY, D.
OU, J.-H.
PARKMAN, R.
PATTENGALE, P.
PATZAKIS, M.
PAULSON, R.
PENTZ, M.
PETERS, J. M.
PIKE, M.
PLATZKER, A.
PORTNOY, B.
POWARS, D.
PRESS, M.
PRESTON-MARTIN, S.
QUISMORIO, F.
RADIN, D.
RAHIMTOOLA, S.
RALLS, P.
RAO, N.
RASHEED, S.
REYNOLDS, C.
RICE, D.
RICHARDSON, J.
ROSS, R.
ROY, S.
ROY-BURMAN, P.
RUDE, R.
RYAN, S., Jr
SADUN, A.
SATTLER, F.
SCHECHTER, J.
SCHNEIDER, L.
SEEGER, R.
SEGALL, H.
SELBY, R.
SENER, S.
SHARMA, O.
SHERWIN, R.
SHIBATA, D.
SHIH, J.
SHOUPE, D.
SHRIVASTAVA, P.
SHULMAN, I.
SIEGEL, M.
SIEGEL, S.
SILBERMAN, H.
SILKA, M.
SILVERSTEIN, M.
SINATRA, F.
SINGH, M.
SKINNER, D.
SMITH, R.
SOHAL, R.
SOKOL, R.
STALLCUP, M.
STANLEY, P.
STARNES, V.
STELLWAGEN, R.
STOHL, W.
STOHLMAN, S.
STRAM, D.
SUSSMAN, S.
TAKAHASHI, M.
TAYLOR, C.
TENG, E.
THOMAS, D.
THORDARSON, D.
TOKES, Z.
TOLO, V.
TRICHE, T.
TSUKAMOTO, H.
VANGSNESS, T., Jr
VARMA, R.
VESELY, L.
WARBURTON, D.
WEAVER, F.
WEBER, J.
WEINBERG, K.
WEINER, L.
WEISS, M.
WETZEL, R.
WILLIAMS, R.
WOOD, B.
WOODLEY, D.
WU, P.
WU-WILLIAMS, A.
YELLIN, A.
YING, S.-Y.
YU, M.
ZEE, C.-S.
ZEIDLER, A.
ZELMAN, V.

School of Music:
BEER, H., Conducting
BERG, S., Jazz Studies
BROWN, B. A., Music History
CRAVENS, T., Winds and Percussion
CROCKETT, D., Composition
DEHNING, W., Choral and Sacred Music
GLAZE, G., Vocal Arts
GORDON, S., Keyboard Studies
HARTKE, S. N., Composition
HOPKINS, J. F., Composition
LAURIDSEN, M., II, Composition
LEONARD, R., Strings
LESEMANN, F., Composition
LIVINGSTON, L., Conducting
MASON, T. D., Jazz Studies
MCCURDY, R. C., Jazz Studies
MCINNES, D., Strings
PERRY, J., Keyboard Studies
POLLACK, D., Keyboard Studies
SCHOENFELD, E., Strings
SIMMS, B., Music History
THOMAS, W. E. L., Electro-Acoustic Media
TICHELI, F., IV, Composition
TYLER, J., Early Music Performance, Music History

School of Pharmacy:
ALKANA, R. L.
ANN, D.
BRINTON, R.
BURCKHART, G.
CADENAS, E.
CHAN, T. M.
JOHNSON, D.
SHEN, W.-C.
SHIH, J. C.
SOHAL, R.
STIMMEL, G. L.
WOLF, W.

School of Policy, Planning and Development:
BANERJEE, T.
CAIDEN, G.
COOPER, T.
FERRIS, J. M.
GABRIEL, S. A.
GIULIANO, G.
GORDON, P.
GRADDY, E.
GREENWALD, H.
HEIKKILA, E.
KREIGER, M. H.
LOPEZ-LEE, D.
MAZMANIAN, D.
MELNICK, G.
MYERS, D.
MYRTLE, R.
NEWLAND, C.
PACHON, H.
PETAK, W.
RICHARDSON, H.
SLOANE, D.
SUNDEEN, R., Jr
TANG, S.-Y.
VON WINTERFELDT, D.
WHOLEY, J. S.

School of Social Work:
BREKKE, J.
CHI, I.
ELL, K.
FLYNN, M.
JANSSON, B.
MCCROSKEY, J.
MONDROS, J.
MOR-BARAK, M.
STONER, M.
TRICKETT, P.

School of Theatre:
CARNICKE, S. M.
HOUSTON, V.
PUZO, M.

UNIVERSITY OF THE PACIFIC

3601 Pacific Ave, Stockton, CA 95211
Telephone: (209) 946-2344
E-mail: admissions@pacific.edu
Internet: www.uop.edu

Founded as California Wesleyan College 1851; name changed to Univ. of the Pacific 1852; consolidated with Napa College 1896; name changed to College of the Pacific 1911; name changed to Univ. of the Pacific 1961
Private control
Main campus in Stockton; McGeorge School of Law in Sacramento; School of Dentistry in San Francisco

Pres.: DONALD V. DEROSA
Provost: PHILIP N. GILBERTSON
Vice-Pres. for Business and Finance: PATRICK CAVANAUGH
Vice-Pres. of Student Life: ELIZABETH GRIEGO
Vice-Pres. of Univ. Advancement: TED LELAND
Assoc. Provost for Enrollment: THOMAS M. RAJALA
Assoc. Provost and CIO: LAWRENCE FREDERICK
Dean of the Library: (vacant)

Library of 281,769 vols, 1,361 periodicals, 689,462 microforms
Number of teachers: 444 (all campuses)
Number of students: 6,000 (all campuses)
Publications: *Contact Point* (Dental School), *De Minimis* (School of Law), *Pacifican*, *Pacific Historian*, *Pacific Review*

DEANS

Eberhardt School of Business: CHUCK WILLIAMS
School of Dentistry: PATRICK FERRILLO
Benerd School of Education: LYNN BECK
School of Engineering and Computer Science: RAVI JAIN
School of Int. Studies: MARGEE ENSIGN

McGeorge School of Law: Elizabeth Rindskopf Parker
Conservatory of Music: Stephen Anderson
College of the Pacific: Robert Cox
Thomas J. Long School of Pharmacy and Health Sciences: Philip Oppenheimer
Graduate School: Philip Oppenheimer

UNIVERSITY OF WEST LOS ANGELES

9920 South La Cienega Blvd, Inglewood, CA 90301-4423
Telephone: (310) 342-5200
Fax: (310) 342-5295
Internet: www.uwla.edu

Founded 1966
Private control

Campuses in West Los Angeles and the San Fernando Valley

Pres.: Robert W. Brown
Vice-Pres. for Student Affairs: Dr Robert W. Adams
Dean: George Dezes
Dir of Facilities: Ron Beatty
Dir of Library Services: Jimmy Rimonte
Dir of Operations (San Fernando Valley Campus): Pat Galasso
Dir of Student Services: Pat Myers

Library of 34,000 vols
Number of teachers: 40 (3 full-time, 37 adjunct)
Number of students: 350
Publication: *UWLA Law Review* (2 a year)

DEANS

School of Law: Basil George Dezes
School of Paralegal Studies: Marlene Amera Alhandy

VANGUARD UNIVERSITY OF SOUTHERN CALIFORNIA

55 Fair Dr., Costa Mesa, CA 92626-9601
Telephone: (714) 556-3610
Fax: (714) 957-9317
Internet: www.vanguard.edu

Founded 1920

Pres.: Murray W. Dempster
Provost: Russell Spittler
Vice-Pres. for Business and Finance: (vacant)
Vice-Pres. for Enrollment Management: Jessica Mireless
Vice-Pres. for Student Affairs: Ed Westbrook
Vice-Pres. for Univ. Advancement: Rick Hardy
Dean of Students: Linda Hartzell
Registrar: Judy Hamilton
Head Librarian: Alison English

Library of 135,500 vols, 1,053 periodicals
Number of teachers: 162 (75 full-time, 87 part-time)
Number of students: 2,300

DEANS

School of Business and Management: David Alford
School of Communication and the Arts: James L. Melton
School of Education: Jerry Ternes
School of Humanities and Social Sciences: Dr Michael D. Wilson
School of Natural Sciences and Mathematics: Dr Cecil Miller
School for Professional Studies: Dr Paul Cox
School of Psychology: Jerre L. White
School of Religion: April Westbrook

WESTERN STATE UNIVERSITY COLLEGE OF LAW

1111 North State College Blvd, Fullerton, CA 92831
Telephone: (714) 738-1000
Fax: (714) 441-1748
E-mail: adm@wsulaw.edu
Internet: www.wsulaw.edu

Founded 1966
Private control
Academic year: August to May

Dean and Pres.: Maryann Jones
Dean of Academic Affairs: Susan Keller
Dir of Criminal Law Practice Center: David Frakt
Dir of Legal Clinic: Terence W. Roberts
Library Dir: Patricia Harris O'Connor (acting)

Number of teachers: 48 (21 full-time, 27 adjunct)
Number of students: 1,157

WESTERN UNIVERSITY OF HEALTH SCIENCES

309 East Second St, Pomona, CA 91766-1854
Telephone: (909) 6236116
E-mail: admissions@westernu.edu
Internet: www.westernu.edu

Founded 1977 as College of Osteopathic Medicine of the Pacific; present name 1996
Private control

Pres.: Dr Philip Pumerantz
Provost and Chief Operating Officer: Benjamin L. Cohen
Treas. and Chief Financial Officer: Kevin D. Shaw
Sr Vice-Pres. for Executive Affairs: Dr Gary M. Gugelchuk
Vice-Pres. for Human Resources: Howard M. Pardue
Vice-Pres. for Research and Biotechnology: Steven J. Henriksen
Vice-Pres. for Student Affairs: Beverly A. Guidry
Library Dir: Patricia Vader
Number of students: 1,425

DEANS

College of Allied Health Professions: Dr Stephanie D. Bowlin
College of Graduate Nursing: Karen Hanford
College of Osteopathic Medicine of the Pacific: Clint Adams
College of Pharmacy: Dr Daniel Robinson
College of Veterinary Medicine: Dr Shirley D. Johnston

WESTMINSTER SEMINARY CALIFORNIA

1725 Bear Valley Parkway, Escondido, CA 92027
Telephone: (760) 480-8474
Fax: (760) 480-0252
E-mail: info@wscal.edu
Internet: www.wscal.edu

Founded 1980
Private control
Academic year: September to May

Pres.: Dr W. Robert Godfrey
Exec. Vice-Pres.: Steven Oeverman
Vice-Pres. for Advancement: Dawn G. Doorn
Academic Dean: Dr Dennis E. Johnson
Dean of Students: Dr Julius J. Kim
Registrar: Brian J. Mills
Library Dir: Elizabeth E. Mehne (acting)

Library of 120,000 vols, 260 periodicals
Number of teachers: 25
Number of students: 150

Areas of study: MDiv and MA in biblical studies, theological studies, historical theology, Christian studies.

WESTMONT COLLEGE

955 La Paz Rd, Santa Barbara, CA 93108
Telephone: (805) 565-6000
Fax: (805) 565-6234
E-mail: pubaffairs@westmont.edu
Internet: www.westmont.edu

Founded 1937
Private control
Academic year: August to May

Accredited by Western Asscn for Schools and Colleges, California State Board of Education

Pres.: Gayle D. Beebe
Provost: Dr Susan Harper
Executive Vice-Pres.: J. Clifton Lundberg
Vice-Pres. for Admin. and Planning: Christopher D. Call
Vice-Pres. for Advancement and Chief Information Officer: Dr Reed Sheard
Vice-Pres. for Finance: Douglas W. Jones
Vice-Pres. for Student Life and Dean of Students: Jane Hideko Higa
Dir for Library and Information Services: Debra Quast

Library of 150,000 vols
Number of teachers: 91 full-time
Number of students: 1,347

WHITTIER COLLEGE

13406 East Philadelphia, Whittier, CA 90608-4413
Telephone: (562) 907-4200
Fax: (562) 698-4067
E-mail: president@whittier.edu
Internet: www.whittier.edu

Founded 1887

Liberal arts, business and law

Pres.: Sharon Herzberger
Vice-Pres. for Academic Affairs and Dean of the Faculty: Susan D. Gotsch
Vice-Pres. for Advancement: Elizabeth Power
Vice-Pres. for Enrollment: Lisa Meyer
Vice-Pres. for Finance and Admin.: Janice A. Legoza
Dean of Whittier Law School: Neil H. Cogan
Registrar: William Gartrell
Librarian: Katherine Gill

Library of 302,000 vols, 44,000 microfilms, 715 current periodicals; spec. collns: John Greenleaf Whittier, Quakers
Number of teachers: 96 full-time
Number of students: 1,427

Publications: *Cornerstone* (6 a year), *The Rock* (4 a year), *Whittier Law Review*.

WILLIAM JESSUP UNIVERSITY

333 Sunset Blvd, Rocklin, CA 95765
Telephone: (916) 577-2200
Fax: (916) 577-2203
E-mail: sps-sj@jessup.edu
Internet: www.jessup.edu

Founded 1939 as San Jose Bible College; San Jose Christian College 1989; present name and status 2004
Private control
Academic year: September to May

Pres.: Bryce Jessup
Vice-Pres. for Academic Affairs: Dr David Nystrom
Vice-Pres. for Advancement: Joseph D. Womack
Vice-Pres. for Finance and Admin.: Gene de Young
Vice-Pres. for Student Devt and Dean of Students: Paul Blezien

Registrar: TINA PETERSEN
Library Dir: MAY WU

Library of 34,000 vols

Areas of study: Bible and theology, business administration, Christian education, English, history, intercultural studies, liberal studies, music, pastoral ministry, psychology, public policy, youth ministry.

BRANCH CAMPUS

San Jose Extension: Suite 210, 1190 Saratoga Ave, San Jose, CA 95129; tel. (408) 278-4343; fax (408) 278-4342; e-mail sps-sj@jessup.edu.

WOODBURY UNIVERSITY

7500 Glenoaks Blvd, Burbank, CA 91510-7846

Telephone: (818) 767-0888
E-mail: info@woodbury.edu
Internet: www.woodbury.edu

Founded 1884 as Woodbury Business College; present name 1974
Private control
Academic year: August to August

Pres.: Dr KENNETH R. NIELSEN
Vice-Pres. for Academic Affairs: DAVID M. ROSEN
Vice-Pres. for Enrollment Management and Univ. Marketing: DON E. ST. CLAIR
Vice-Pres. for Finance and Admin.: KEN JONES
Vice-Pres. for IT and Planning: STEVE DYER
Vice-Pres. for Univ. Advancement: RICHARD M. NORDIN
Dir of Library Services: NEDRA PETERSON
Number of students: 1,500

DEANS

School of Architecture: NORMAN MILLAR
School of Business: ANDRÈ B. VAN NIEKERK
School of Media, Culture and Design: (vacant)
Transdisciplinary Studies: DOUGLAS J. CREMER

BRANCH CAMPUS

San Diego Campus: Suite 200, 1060 Eighth Ave, San Diego, CA 92101; tel. (619) 235-2900, e-mail san.diego@woodbury.edu; Admin. Dir DEBRA ABEL.

WRIGHT INSTITUTE

2728 Durant Ave, Berkeley, CA 94704

Telephone: (510) 841-9230
Fax: (510) 841-0167
E-mail: info@wrightinst.edu
Internet: www.wrightinst.edu

Founded 1968
Private control
Academic year: September to June

Pres.: PETER DYBWAD
Dean: Dr CHARLES ALEXANDER
Registrar: GINNY MORGAN
Librarian: JASON STRAUSS

Library of 10,000 items, 125 periodicals

Area of study: clinical psychology.

COLORADO

ADAMS STATE COLLEGE OF COLORADO

208 Edgemont Blvd, Alamosa, CO 81102

Telephone: (719) 587-7011
E-mail: ascadmit@adams.edu
Internet: www.adams.edu

Founded 1923

Pres.: DAVID SVALDI
Provost: FRANK NOVOTNY
Vice-Provost for Academic Affairs: MARGARET DOELL
Vice-Pres. for Enrollment Management: GEORGIA GRANTHAM
Vice-Pres. for Finance and Administration: BILL MANSHEIM
Dean of Student Affairs: KEN MARQUEZ
Registrar: M. BELEN MAESTAS
Dir of Luther Bean Museum: KATHERINE OLANCE
Dir of Nielsen Library: DIANNE MACHADO

Library of 132,615 vols, 34,651 bound periodicals, 1,005 current periodicals, 488,675 govt publications, 1,334 maps, 2,493 audiovisual items, 732,387 microforms, 13,294 microfilms
Number of teachers: 123
Number of students: 1,455 full-time and 319 part-time

Depts of art, biology, business administration, chemistry, communications, computer science, earth sciences, English, history/government/philosophy, human performance and physical education, interdisciplinary studies, mathematics, music, nursing, physics, psychology, sociology, Spanish, teacher education, theatre.

COLORADO CHRISTIAN UNIVERSITY

8787 West Alameda Ave, Lakewood, CO 80226

Telephone: (303) 963-3000
Fax: (303) 963-3001
E-mail: admission@ccu.edu
Internet: www.ccu.edu

Founded 1989 following merger of Colorado Christian College and Colorado Baptist Univ.
Private control
Academic year: August to August

Pres.: BILL ARMSTRONG
Vice-Pres. for Academic Affairs: Dr CHERRI PARKS
Asst Vice-Pres. for Administrative Services: RON BENTON
Vice-Pres. for Business Affairs and Chief Financial Officer: DAN COHRS
Vice-Pres. for Student Development: JAMES S. MCCORMICK
Vice-Pres. for Development: Dr KEITH WRIGHT
Registrar: LINDA PERCIANTE
Library Dir: GAYLE GUNDERSON

Library of 64,855 vols
Number of teachers: 334
Number of students: 3,561

DEANS

Business and Technology Division, College of Adult and Graduate Studies: Dr MELLANI DAY
College of Adult and Graduate Studies, Curriculum and Instruction Education Division: Dr WENDY ELLIOT WENDOVER
College of Adult and Graduate Studies, Nursing and Sciences Division: Dr BARBARA J. WHITE
College of Adult and Graduate Studies, Social Sciences and Humanities Division: Dr LAVERNE K. JORDAN
School of Business and Leadership: Dr GARY EWEN
School of Education: Dr SARA DALLMAN
School of Humanities and Sciences: Dr WILLIAM R. SAXBY
School of Music: STEVEN T. TAYLOR
School of Theology: Dr SID BUZZELL

BRANCH CAMPUSES

Colorado Springs Center: Suite 150, 1125 Kelly Johnson Blvd, Colorado Springs, CO 80920; tel. (719) 528-5080.

Denver Metro Center: Suite 100, Financial Plaza II, 225 Union Blvd, Lakewood, CO 80228; tel. (303) 963-3300.

Northern Colorado Center: Suite 100, 1750 Foxtrail Dr., Loveland, CO 80538; tel. (970) 669-8700.

Western Colorado Center: Suite 220, 743 Horizon Court, Grand Junction, CO 81506; tel. (970) 242-1811.

COLORADO COLLEGE

14 East Cache La Poudre St, Colorado Springs, CO 80903

Telephone: (719) 389-6000
Fax: (719) 389-6933
E-mail: communications@coloradocollege.edu
Internet: www.coloradocollege.edu

Founded 1874

Pres.: RICHARD F. CELESTE
Vice-Pres. for Advancement: STEPHEN ELDER
Vice-Pres. for Business/Finance and Treasurer: THOMAS NYCUM
Vice-Pres. for Enrollment Management: MARK HATCH
Vice-Pres. for Information Management: RANDALL STILES
Vice-Pres. for Student Life: MIKE EDMONDS
Registrar: PHIL APODOCA
Library Dir: CAROL DICKERSON
Number of teachers: 140
Number of students: 1,850

American cultural studies, anthropology, art, Asian studies, biology, chemistry, classics, comparative literature, drama and dance, East Asian languages, economics and business, education, English, environmental science, feminist and gender studies, geology, German, history, mathematics and computer science, music, philosophy, physics, political science, psychology, religion, Romance languages, Russian, sociology, sport science, Southwest studies

DEANS

College and Faculty: SUSAN A. ASHLEY
Summer Session: LIBBY RITTENBERG

COLORADO SCHOOL OF MINES

1500 Illinois St, Golden, CO 80401-1887

Telephone: (303) 273-3000
Fax: (303) 273-3278
E-mail: presoffice@mines.edu
Internet: www.mines.edu

Founded 1874

Engineering education and applied science related to earth, energy, materials and environment

Pres.: BILL SCOGGINS
Provost and Exec. Vice-Pres.: Dr TERENCE PARKER
Exec. Vice-Pres. for Academic Affairs and Dean of the Faculty: NIGEL T. MIDDLETON
Vice-Pres. for Research and Technology Transfer: Dr JOHN POATE
Sr Vice-Pres. for Finance and Administration and Treas.: KIRSTEN VOLPI
Vice-Pres. for Institutional Advancement: PETER HAN
Vice-Pres. for Student Life: Dr DANIEL FOX
Assoc. Provost and Dean of Graduate Studies: Dr THOMAS M. BOYD
Dir for Enrollment Management: HEATHER BOYD
Chief Information Officer: DEREK WILSON
Dir for Library: JOANNE LERUD HECK

Library of 200,000 vols, 900 print journals, 30,000 electronic journals, 30,000 electronic books, 226,000 govt publications, 453,000 microforms and 172,000 maps
Number of teachers: 200

Number of students: 4,800

Publications: *Mineral Industries Bulletin*, *Quarterly of the Colorado School of Mines*.

COLORADO STATE UNIVERSITY

Fort Collins, CO 80523
Telephone: (970) 491-1101
Fax: (970) 491-0501
Internet: www.colostate.edu

Founded 1870 as The Agricultural College of Colorado, became a state institution in 1876, a land-grant college in 1879

Pres.: LARRY EDWARD PENLEY
Provost and Sr Vice-Pres.: Dr TONY FRANK
Vice-Pres. for Administrative Services: BOB RIZZUTO
Vice-Pres. for Advancement: JOYCE BERRY
Vice-Pres. for Research: WILLIAM H. FARLAND
Vice-Pres. for Student Affairs: Dr BLANCHE HUGHES
Exec. Dir of Admissions: MARY R. ONTIVEROS
Dean of Libraries: CATHERINE MURRAY-RUST

Library of 2,000,000 vols
Number of teachers: 1,400
Number of students: 23,934

DEANS

College of Agricultural Sciences: Dr MARC JOHNSON
College of Applied Human Sciences: Dr APRIL MASON
College of Business: Dr AJAY MENON
College of Engineering: Dr SANDRA WOODS
College of Liberal Arts: Dr ANN GILL
College of Natural Resources: JOSEPH T. O'LEARY
College of Natural Sciences: Dr RICK MIRANDA
College of Veterinary Medicine and Biomedical Sciences: Dr LANCE E. PERRYMAN

ASSOCIATED INSTITUTIONS

Colorado Agricultural Experiment Station: Dir LEE E. SOMMERS.

Colorado Cooperative Fish and Wildlife Research Unit: Unit Leader Prof. DAVID R. ANDERSON.

Colorado State Forest Service: Dir JAMES E. HUBBARD.

Cooperative Extension: Dir MILAN A. REWARTS.

COLORADO STATE UNIVERSITY–PUEBLO

2200 Bonforte Blvd, Pueblo, CO 81001-4901
Telephone: (719) 549-2100
Fax: (719) 549-2419
E-mail: info@colostate-pueblo.edu
Internet: www.colostate-pueblo.edu

Founded as Junior College 1933, Southern Colorado State College 1961, Univ. of Southern Colorado 1975

State control, mem. of Colorado State Univ. system

Pres.: JOSEPH A. GARCIA
Provost and Vice-Pres. for Academic Affairs: Dr RUSS MEYER
Dean of Student Life and Devt: ARROW KENNEDY
Dean of Univ. Library: RHONDA GONZALES

Library of 171,000 vols, 1,600 periodical titles, 275,000 govt documents, 21,000 audiovisual items
Number of teachers: 200
Number of students: 4,000

DEANS

Hasan School of Business: SUE HANKS
Education, Engineering and Professional Studies: Prof. HECTOR R. CARRASCO
College of Humanities and Social Sciences: ROY B. SONNEMA
College of Science and Mathematics: Prof. KRISTINA PROCTOR

COLORADO TECHNICAL UNIVERSITY

4435 North Chestnut St, Colorado Springs, CO 80907
Telephone: (719) 598-0200
Fax: (719) 598-3740
E-mail: ctucos@coloradotech.edu
Internet: www.coloradotech.edu

Private control
Academic year: October to September

Pres.: GREG MITCHELL
CEO: Dr MARIJANE AXTELL PAULSEN
Chancellor: Dr RICHARD KETTNER-POLLEY
Vice-Pres. for Academic Affairs: Dr SCOTT VAN TONNINGEN
Dir of Education: Dr CHARLES SCHROEDER
Vice-Pres. for Admissions: ROBERT LEE
Librarian: KAY BURMAN

DEANS

Computer Science, Information Technology, and Management Information Systems: Dr MARY JANE WILLSHIRE
Engineering, Technology, Mathematics, and Sciences: ALEX DWELIS
Management: Dr ERIC GOODMAN
Nursing: Dr DEB BANIK

BRANCH CAMPUSES

Colorado Technical University—Pueblo: 1025 West Sixth Street, Pueblo, CO 81003; tel. (877) 676-0200; internet pueblo.coloradotech.edu.

Denver Campus: 5775 Denver Tech Center Blvd, Greenwood Village, CO 80111-3201; tel. (303) 694-6600; fax (303) 694-6673; e-mail ctudenver@coloradotech.edu; internet www.ctudenver.com.

North Kansas City Campus: 520 East 19th Ave, North Kansas City, CO 64116; tel. (816) 472-7400; internet kc.coloradotech.edu.

Sioux Falls Campus: 3901 West 59th Street, Sioux Falls, SD 57108; tel. (605) 361-0200; fax (605) 361-5954; e-mail ctusf@coloradotech.edu; internet www.ctusiouxfalls.com.

DENVER SEMINARY

POB 100000, Denver, CO 80250-0100
located at: 6399 South Santa Fe Dr., Littleton, CO 80120
Telephone: (303) 761-2482
Fax: (303) 761-8060
E-mail: info@denverseminary.edu
Internet: www.denverseminary.edu

Founded 1950
Private control; mem. of Institute of Theological Studies
Academic year: September to May

Pres.: Dr G. CRAIG WILLIFORD
Vice-Pres. and Academic Dean: Dr RANDY MACFARLAND
Vice-Pres. for Advancement: GARY HOAG
Vice-Pres. for Enrolment Management: BOB FOMER
Vice-Pres. for Finance: JACK C. HEIMBICHNER
Chancellor: Dr VERNON C. GROUNDS
Dean of Student Services: VANESSA ANDERSON
Registrar: PAM BETKER
Dir of Library: Dr P. KEITH WELLS

Library of 166,000 vols
Number of teachers: 57
Number of students: 700

MA in counselling and Doctor of ministry.

FORT LEWIS COLLEGE

1000 Rim Dr., Durango, CO 81301-3999
Telephone: (970) 247-7010
E-mail: admission@fortlewis.edu
Internet: www.fortlewis.edu

Founded 1911
State control, mem. of Colorado State Univ. system

Pres.: Dr BRAD BARTEL
Provost and Vice-Pres. for Academic Affairs: Dr STEPHEN A. RODERICK
Vice-Pres. for Finance and Admin.: STEVEN SCHWARTZ
Vice-Pres. for Student Affairs: Dr GLENNA WITT SEXTON
Dean of Admission and Devt: SHERI R. ROCHFORD
Registrar: EDWIN JOHNSON
Dir of the Library: CHANDLER JACKSON

Library of 175,000 vols
Number of teachers: 187
Number of students: 4,441

DEANS

School of Arts, Humanities and Social Sciences: RICHARD SAX
School of Business Administration: Dr TOM HARRINGTON
School of Natural and Behavioural Sciences: Dr JOHN NIMMEMANN
General and Exploratory Studies: Dr CAROL SMITH

ILIFF SCHOOL OF THEOLOGY

2201 South Univ. Blvd, Denver, CO 80210-4798
Telephone: (303) 744-1287
Fax: (303) 777-0164
E-mail: info@iliff.edu
Internet: www.iliff.edu

Private control
Academic year: September to August

Pres.: DAVID TRICKETT
Academic Vice-Pres. and Dean of Faculty: ALBERT HERNANDEZ
Vice-Pres. for Business and Chief Fiscal Officer: KELLY MCCORMICK
Dean of Enrollment: DAVID WORLEY
Library Dir: DEBORAH CREAMER

Library of 202,250 vols, 700 periodicals
Number of teachers: 14
Number of students: 300

ITT TECHNICAL INSTITUTE

500 East 84th Ave, Thornton, CO 80229-5338
12500 East Iliff Ave, Aurora, CO 80014
Telephone: (303) 695-6317
Internet: www.itt-tech.edu

Founded 1984
Private control (ITT Educational Services, Inc.)
Academic year: September to September

Dir: RICHARD F. HANSEN
Dean: Dr PETER M. LINZMAIER
Registrar: LISA MEYERDIERKS

Depts of computer and electronics engineering, computer drafting and design, data communication systems technology, electronics and communications engineering, electronics engineering and technology, information systems security, information technology, technical project management for electronic commerce, general education.

MESA STATE COLLEGE

1100 North Ave, Grand Junction, CO 81501
Telephone: (970) 248-1020
Fax: (970) 248-1973
Internet: www.mesastate.edu

Founded 1925 as Grand Junction Junior College; present name 1988
Academic year: August to May
Pres.: TIM FOSTER
Vice-Pres. for Academic and Student Affairs: CAROL FUTHEY
Vice-Pres. for Financial and Admin. Services: PATRICK DOYLE
Dean of Students: ANDREW BRECKEL
Registrar: PATRICK HAMPTON
Dir of Library: ELIZABETH BRODAK (acting)

Library of 178,409 vols, 919 current journals, 82,375 govt docs, 12,248 audiovisual items, 17,390 maps
Number of teachers: 207
Number of students: 5,346 (3,983 full-time, 1,363 part-time)

Depts of accounting and information technology, applied technology, biological sciences, business admin., computer sciences, mathematics and statistics, fine and performing arts (art), fine and performing arts (music), fine and performing arts (theatre), human performance and wellness, languages, literature and communications, nursing and radiological sciences, physical and environmental sciences, social and behavioural sciences.

BRANCH CAMPUSES

Montrose Campus: 234 S Cascade Ave, Montrose, CO 81401; tel. (970) 249-7009; fax (970) 249-2579; Dir BEN KEEFER.

Unified Technical Education Campus: School of Applied Technology, 2508 Blichmann, Grand Junction, CO 81505; tel. (970) 255-2600.

METROPOLITAN STATE COLLEGE OF DENVER

POB 173362, Denver, CO 80217-3362
Telephone: (303) 556-2400
Internet: www.mscd.edu
Private control
Academic year: August to May

Pres.: Dr STEPHEN M. JORDAN
Provost and Vice-Pres. for Academic Affairs: Dr RODOLFO ROCHA
Vice-Pres. for Admin. and Finance: NATALIE LUTES
Vice-Pres. for Institutional Advancement: GEORGE ENGDAHL
Vice-Pres. for Information Technology: GEORGE MIDDLEMIST
Vice-Pres. for Student Services: Dr DOUGLAS SAMUELS
Registrar: THOMAS R. GRAY
Dean of Library: ALIRE CAMILA

Library: 1m. traditional print and media items
Number of teachers: 402
Number of students: 18,432

DEANS

School of Business: Dr JOHN P. COCHRAN
School of Letters, Arts and Sciences: Dr JOAN L. FOSTER
School of Professional Studies: Dr SANDRA D. HAYNES

BRANCH CAMPUSES

Metro North Campus: Suite 102, 11990 Grant St, Northglenn, CO 80233; tel. (303) 450-5111.

Metro South Campus: Suite L100, 5660 Greenwood Plaza Blvd, Greenwood Village, CO 80111; tel. (303) 721-1313.

NAROPA UNIVERSITY

2130 Arapahoe Ave, Boulder, CO 80302
Telephone: (303) 444-0202
Fax: (303) 444-0410
E-mail: infodesk@naropa.edu
Internet: www.naropa.edu

Founded 1974 by Chogyam Trungpa to combine Buddhist studies with traditional Western scholastic and artistic disciplines; based on Nalanda Univ. (5th–12th century), India

Pres.: THOMAS B. COBURN
Library Dir: MARK KILLE

Library of 26,000 vols, 100 periodicals; spec. collns incl. 15,000 original Tibetan texts in 2,200 vols, 6,000 audiocassette recordings of events held at Naropa Univ., psychology
Number of students: 1,000

BAs in contemplative psychology, early childhood education, environmental studies, interdisciplinary studies, music, religious studies, traditional eastern arts, visual arts and writing and literature, fine arts in performance; MAs in contemplative education, creative writing, divinity, environmental leadership, fine arts, Indo-Tibetan Buddhism, religious studies, counselling psychology (contemplative, somatic transpersonal), writing and poetics.

NATIONAL THEATRE CONSERVATORY

1050 13th Street, Denver, CO 80204-2154
E-mail: ntc@dcpa.org
Internet: www.denvercenter.org

Pres. of Denver Center for the Performing Arts: RANDY WEEKS
Dir of Education: DANIEL RENNER
Registrar: KATE AMBERG
Librarian: LINDA ELLER

Library of 30,000 single scripts and anthologies

Area of study: fine arts.

NAZARENE BIBLE COLLEGE

1111 Academy Park Loop, Colorado Springs, CO 80910
Telephone: (719) 884-5000
Fax: (719) 884-5199
E-mail: info@nbc.edu
Internet: www.nbc.edu

Founded 1967
Private control
Academic year: September to May

Pres.: Dr HAROLD B. GRAVES
Vice-Pres. for Academic Affairs and Extension Education: Dr DONALD E. STELTING, SR
Vice-Pres. for Enrollment and Student Development: Dr LAUREL L. MATSON
Vice-Pres. for Finance: J. MIKE ARRAMBIDE
Vice-Pres. for Online Education: Dr DAVID M. PHILLIPS
Registrar: Dr MIKE A. WORRELL
Library Dir: ANN M. ATTIG

BAs in Christian counselling, Christian educational ministries, Christian school education, ministry, music ministries, pastoral ministries.

REGIS UNIVERSITY

3333 Regis Blvd, Denver, CO 80221-1099
Telephone: (303) 458-4100
Fax: (303) 964-5473
E-mail: publicaffairs@regis.edu
Internet: www.regis.edu

Founded 1877
Private control (Society of Jesus)
Academic year: August to August

Pres.: MICHAEL J. SHEERAN
Director of Admissions: VIC DAVOLT
Dean of Libraries: IVAN GAETZ

Library of 260,000 vols, 2,500 periodicals
Number of students: 16,128

Areas of study: accounting, biochemistry, biology, business admin., Catholic studies, chemistry, Christian leadership, communication, computer science, core studies, economics education, English, environmental studies, exercise science, French, history, leadership, mathematics, music, neuroscience, nursing, peace and justice philosophy, political economy, politics, pre-med/health, pre-law, psychology, religious studies, sociology, Spanish, visual arts, women's studies

Publication: *Human Development* (2 a year).

BRANCH CAMPUSES

Aurora Campus: Suite 200, Abilene St, Boulder, CO 80011; tel. (303) 458-7420; fax (303) 964-5765.

Colorado Springs Campus: Suite 100, 7450 Campus Dr., Colorado Springs, CO 80920; tel. (303) 458-7420; fax (719) 264-7095.

Denver Tech Center Campus: Suite 100N, 7600 East Orchard Rd, Englewood, CO 80111; tel. (303) 458-7420; fax (303) 964-5053.

Fort Collins Campus: 1501 Academy Court, Fort Collins, CO 80524; tel. (970) 472-2208; fax (970) 472-2201.

Interlocken at Broomfield Campus: Suite 150, 11001 West 120th Ave, Broomfield, CO 80021; tel. (303) 458-7420; fax (303) 635-1363.

Las Vegas Campus: Suite 100, 1401 North Green Valley Parkway, Henderson, NV 89074; tel. (702) 990-0375; e-mail vegas@regis.edu.

Longmont Campus: 2101 Ken Pratt Blvd, Longmont, CO 80501; tel. (303) 458-7420.

UNITED STATES AIR FORCE ACADEMY

HQ USAFA/RRS, Suite 200, 2304 Cadet Dr., Colorado Springs, CO 80840
Telephone: (719) 333-1110
E-mail: webmaster@usafa.af.mil
Internet: www.usafa.edu

Founded 1954

Superintendent: Lt Gen. JOHN F. REGNI
Dean of Faculty: Brig. Gen. DANA H. BORN

Library of 387,000 vols
Number of teachers: 531

UNIVERSITY OF COLORADO

1800 Grant St, Suite 800, Denver, CO 80203
Telephone: (303) 860-5600
Fax: (303) 860-5610
E-mail: officeofthepresident@cu.edu
Internet: www.cu.edu

Inc. 1861, opened 1877

Pres.: BRUCE BENSON
Assoc. Vice-Pres. for Academic Affairs: KATHLEEN BOLLARD
Sr Vice-Pres. for Admin. and Chief of Staff: LEONARD DINEGAR
Vice-Pres. and Chief Financial Officer: KELLY FOX

Library: see Libraries and Archives
Number of teachers: 3,500
Number of students: 50,000

Publications: *Arctic and Alpine Research* (4 a year), *College Catalog* (1 a year), *Colorado Alumnus* (10 a year), *Colorado Business Review* (12 a year), *Colorado Engineer, Colorado Quarterly, East European Quarterly, English Language Notes, University of Colorado Law Review, and University of Colorado Studies series covering various subjects.*

CONSTITUENT CAMPUSES

University of Colorado at Boulder

Boulder, CO 80309

Telephone: (303) 492-1411
E-mail: homepage@colorado.edu
Internet: www.colorado.edu

Chancellor: PHILIP P. DISTEFANO
Provost and Exec. Vice-Chancellor for Academic Affairs: STEIN STURE
Sr Vice-Chancellor and Chief Financial Officer: RIC PORRECA
Vice-Chancellor for Admin.: FRANK BRUNO
Vice-Chancellor for Diversity, Equity and Community Engagement: SALLYE MCKEE
Vice-Chancellor for Research: RUSS MOORE
Vice-Chancellor for Student Affairs: JULIE WONG
Chief Information Officer: LAWRENCE M. LEVINE
Dean of Libraries: JAMES WILLIAMS, II

Number of teachers: 1,075
Number of students: 29,709

DEANS

College of Architecture and Planning: MARK GELERNTER
College of Arts and Sciences: TODD GLEESON
Leeds School of Business: DENNIS AHLBURG
School of Education: LORRIE SHEPARD
College of Engineering and Applied Science: ROBERT DAVIS
School of Journalism and Mass Communication: PAUL VOAKES
School of Law: DAVID H. GETCHES
College of Music: DANIEL SHER
Graduate School: JOHN STEVENSON
Continuing Education and Professional Studies: ANNE HEINZ

University of Colorado at Colorado Springs

1420 Austin Bluffs Pkwy, Colorado Springs, CO 80918

Telephone: (719) 262-3000
Internet: www.uccs.edu

Chancellor: Prof. PAMELA S. SHOCKLEY-ZALABAK
Vice-Chancellor for Academic Affairs: MARGARET BACON
Vice-Chancellor for Admin. and Finance: BRIAN D. BURNETT
Vice-Chancellor for Student Success: Prof. JAMES P. HENDERSON
Dean of Students: TAMARA MOORE
Dean of the Library: Prof. LESLIE A. MANNING

Library of 351,359 vols, 451,257 microforms, 358,019 govt docs/maps, 6,791 audio visual items, 1,441 current journals in print, and 21,000 journals online
Number of teachers: 514
Number of students: 7,600

DEANS

College of Business and Administration: Dr VENKAT K. REDDY
College of Education: MARK MALONE
College of Engineering and Applied Science: JEREMY HAEFNER
College of Letters, Arts and Sciences: Dr THOMAS M. CHRISTIENSEN
Beth-El College of Nursing and Health Sciences: Prof. CAROLE SCHOFFSTALL
Graduate School of Public Affairs: Prof. KATHLEEN M. BEATTY

University of Colorado at Denver and Health Sciences Center

POB 173364, Denver, CO 80217-3364

Telephone: (303) 556-2400
Internet: www.cudenver.edu

Chancellor: M. ROY WILSON (acting)
Vice-Chancellor for Admin. and Finance: TERESA BERRYMAN
Vice-Chancellor for Student Affairs: MARGARET B. COZZENS
Provost and Vice-Chancellor for Academic and Student Affairs: MARK ALAN HECKLER
Dean of Faculty: J. C. BOSCH
Dean of the Library: DAVID GLEIM

Number of teachers: 437 (full-time)
Number of students: 27,000

DEANS

College of Architecture and Planning: MARK GELERNTER
College of Arts and Media: KATHY MAES
Business School: SUEANN AMBRON
College of Engineering and Applied Science: Dr RENJENG SU
College of Liberal Arts and Sciences: JON HARBOR
Graduate School: JIM HAGEMAN
Graduate School of Public Affairs: Prof. KATHLEEN BEATTY
School of Education and Human Development: LYNN RHODES

UNIVERSITY OF DENVER

2199 South University Blvd, Denver, CO 80208

Telephone: (303) 871-2000
Fax: (303) 871-4000
Internet: www.du.edu

Founded 1864
Private control
Academic year: September to May

Chancellor: ROBERT COOMBE
Provost: GREGG KVISTAD
Vice-Chancellor for Business and Financial Affairs: CRAIG WOODY
Vice-Chancellor for Communications and Marketing: CAROL E. FARNSWORTH
Vice-Provost for Undergraduate Studies: SHEILA WRIGHT
Vice-Chancellor for Univ. Advancement: ED HARRIS
Vice-Provost for Graduate Studies and Research: Dr JAMES MORAN
Registrar: DENNIS BECKER
Dean and Dir of the Library: NANCY ALLEN

Library of 1,897,000 vols
Number of teachers: 500
Number of students: 4,850 undergraduates and 5,500 graduates

Arts, Humanities and Social Sciences: depts of anthropology, art and art history, economics, English, history, human communications, Judaic study, languages and literature, music (Lamont School of), mass communications and journalism studies, philosophy, political sciences, psychology, public policy studies, religious studies, sociology, theatre. Natural Sciences, Mathematics and Engineering: depts of biological sciences, chemistry and biochemistry, computer science, engineering, geography, mathematics, physics and astronomy. Daniels College of Business: depts of accountancy, ethics and legal studies, finance (Renman School of), hotel, restaurant and tourism management, information technology and electronic commerce, management, marketing, real estate and construction management, statistics and operations technology

Publications: *Denver Law Journal* (4 a year), *Denver Law Journal of International Law and Policy*, *Family Law Quarterly*, *The Centre Report* (4 a year), *The University of Denver Law Review*, *Transportation Law Journal*

DEANS

Arts, Humanities and Social Sciences: GEORGE POTTS
Daniels College of Business: KAREN NEWMAN
College of Education: Dr VIRGINIA MALONEY
School of Engineering and Computer Science: RAHMAT A. SHOURESHI
Graduate School of International Studies: TOM J. FARER
College of Law: JOSÉ ROBERTO JUÁREZ, Jr
Natural Sciences and Mathematics: JIM FOGLEMAN
Graduate School of Professional Psychology: Prof. PETER BUIRSKI
Graduate School of Social Work: CHRISTIAN E. MOLIDOR
Univ. College of Professional and Continuing Education: JAMES R. DAVIS
Women's College: LYNN M. GANGONE

ATTACHED INSTITUTE

University of Denver Research Institute.

UNIVERSITY OF NORTHERN COLORADO

Greeley, CO 80639

Telephone: (970) 351-1890
Fax: (970) 351-1837
E-mail: admissions.help@unco.edu
Internet: www.unco.edu

Founded 1889 as the State Normal School; name changed to Colorado State Teachers College 1911, to Colorado State College of Education in 1935, to Colorado State College in 1957; present name adopted in 1970
Academic year: August to May

Pres.: KAY NORTON
Sr Vice-Pres. and Provost: Dr ABE HARRAF
Sr Vice-Pres. for Finance and Admin.: MICHELLE QUINN
Vice-Pres. and Gen. Counsel: RON LAMBDEN
Registrar: NOLAN OLTJENBRUNS
Dean of Students: Dr RAUL CARDENAS
Dean of Libraries: Dr GARY PITKIN

Number of teachers: 705
Number of students: 12,711

DEANS

College of Education and Behavioural Sciences: Dr EUGENE SHEEHAN
College of Humanities and Science: DAVID CALDWELL
College of Natural and Health Sciences: DENISE BATTLES
College of Performing and Visual Arts: ANDREW SVEDLOW
Kenneth W. Montfort College of Business: DONALD GUDMUNDSON

WESTERN STATE COLLEGE OF COLORADO

600 North Adams St, Gunnison, CO 81231

Telephone: (970) 943-0120
Fax: (970) 943-7069
Internet: www.western.edu

Founded 1911

Pres.: Dr JAY W. HELMAN
Vice-Pres. for Academic Affairs: Prof. JOHN B. SOWELL
Vice-Pres. for Devt: THOMAS F. BURGGRAF
Vice-Pres. for Finance and Admin.: BRAD BACA
Vice-Pres. for Student Affairs and Dean of Students: SHERRYL HALL-PETERSON
Registrar: MARYETTE ROGERS
Dir of Library Services: ELIZABETH AVERY

Library of 435,000 vols, 700 periodicals, 1,461 video cassettes; spec. colln of books and govt docs about Colorado
Number of teachers: 143
Number of students: 2,514

Depts of art, behavioural and social sciences, business, accounting and economics, communication arts, environmental studies, languages and literature, mathematics and computer information science, music, natural and environmental sciences, recreation and exercise, and sport science.

CONNECTICUT

ALBERTUS MAGNUS COLLEGE

700 Prospect St, New Haven, CT 06511
Telephone: (203) 777-8550
E-mail: registrar@albertus.edu
Internet: www.albertus.edu
Co-educational liberal arts college
Founded 1925
Pres.: Dr JULIA M. McNAMARA
Vice-Pres. for Academic Affairs: JOHN J. DONOHUE
Vice-Pres. for Finance and Treas.: JEANNE MANN
Vice-Pres. for Institutional Advancement and Planning: ROBERT J. BUCCINO
Dean for Admissions and Financial Aid: RICHARD J. LOLATTE
Dean for Student Services: MAUREEN V. MORRISON
Registrar: EILEEN S. PERILLO
Dir of Library and Information Services: ANNE LECNEY-PANAGROSSI
Library of 100,000 vols, 650 periodical titles, 2,000 audiovisual titles
Number of teachers: 202
Number of students: 2,400

CENTRAL CONNECTICUT STATE UNIVERSITY

1615 Stanley St, New Britain, CT 06050
Telephone: (860) 832-3200
Fax: (860) 832-2522
E-mail: admissions@ccsu.edu
Internet: www.ccsu.edu
Founded 1849
State control, mem. of Connecticut State Univ. system
Academic year: September to May
Pres.: JOHN W. MILLER
Provost and Vice-Pres. for Academic Affairs: Dr CARL R. LOVITT
Chief Financial Officer: LARRY WILDER
Chief Information Officer: ROBERT E. CERNOCK
Dean of Students: JANE M. HIGGINS
Registrar: SUSAN PETROSINO
Dir of Library Services: JEANNE SOHN
Library of 665,605 vols, 3,000 current periodicals, govt docs, Polish Heritage Colln of 17,000 vols
Number of teachers: 885 (417 full-time, 468 part-time)
Number of students: 11,418 (7,427 full-time, 3,991 part-time)
BAs and MAs in a wide variety of disciplines and Sixth-Year Certificate in reading; Doctoral degree (EdD) in educational leadership

DEANS
School of Arts and Sciences: SUSAN PEASE
School of Business: CHRIS GALLIGAN (acting)
School of Education and Professional Studies: MITCHELL SAKOFS (acting)
School of Technology: ZDZISLAW KREMENS
School of Graduate Studies: PAULETTE LEMMA

CHARTER OAK STATE COLLEGE

55 Paul J. Manafort Dr., New Britain, CT 06053-2150
Telephone: (860) 832-3800
Fax: (860) 832-3999
E-mail: info@charteroak.edu
Internet: www.cosc.edu
Founded 1973
Pres.: Dr MERLE W. HARRIS
Vice-Pres. for Academic Affairs: Dr SHIRLEY M. ADAMS
Chief Financial and Admin. Officer: CLIFFOR S. WILLIAMS
Dean of Marketing and Enrolment Services: HARRY E. WHITE
Dean and Chief Information Officer: GEORGE F. CLAFFEY, Jr
Registrar: PATRICIA R. DERECH
Number of students: 2,000
Offers 4 general studies degrees in arts and sciences; professional certificates in project management, computer security, public safety admin.

CONNECTICUT COLLEGE

270 Mohegan Ave, New London, CT 06320-4196
Telephone: (860) 447-1911
Internet: www.conncoll.edu
Founded 1911
Academic year: August to May
Coeducational liberal arts college
Pres.: LEO I. HIGDON, Jr
Vice-Pres. for Advancement: GREG WALDRON
Vice-Pres. for College Relations: PATRICIA CAREY
Vice-Pres. for Finance: PAUL MARONEY
Provost and Dean of the Faculty: ROGER BROOKS
Dean of Admissions and Financial Aid: MARTHA MERRILL
Dean of College Community: ARMANDO BENGOCHEA
Dean of Freshmen: ANDREA ROSSI-REDER
Dean of Religious and Spiritual Life: CLAUDIA HIGHBAUGH
Dean of Student Life: DAVID MILSTONE
Registrar: BETH LABRIOLE
College Librarian: W. LEE HISLE
Library of 555,578 vols
Number of teachers: 162 full-time
Number of students: 1,912

EASTERN CONNECTICUT STATE UNIVERSITY

83 Windham St, Willimantic, CT 06226-2295
Telephone: (860) 465-5000
Fax: (860) 465-4485
E-mail: webmaster@easternct.edu
Internet: www.easternct.edu
Founded 1889, re-f. as Willimantic State College 1959, present name 1983
Academic year: September to May
Pres.: Dr ELSA NUÑEZ
Exec. Vice-Pres.: Dr MICHAEL PERNAL
Vice-Pres. for Academic Affairs: Dr DIMITROIS S. PACHIS
Vice-Pres. for Finance and Admin.: DENNIS A. HANNON
Vice-Pres. for Institutional Advancement: KENNETH DELISA
Vice-Pres. for Student Affairs: Dr LAURA TORDENTI
Dir of Admissions and Enrollment Management: KIMBERLY CRONE
Dean of Arts and Sciences: Dr CARMEN CID
Dean of Educational and Professional Studies: Dr PATRICIA A. KLEINE
Dean of Students: Dr PAUL BRYANT
Registrar: KATHLEEN B. FABIAN
Dir of Library Services: PATRICIA S. BANACH
Library of 311,320 vols
Number of teachers: 361 (184 full-time, 177 part-time)
Number of students: 5,095

FAIRFIELD UNIVERSITY

1073 North Benson Rd, Fairfield, CT 06824-5195
Telephone: (203) 254-4000
Fax: (203) 254-4199
Internet: www.fairfield.edu
Founded 1942
Academic year: September to May
Pres.: Rev. JEFFREY P. VON ARX
Academic Vice-Pres.: Dr ORIN L. GROSSMAN
Vice-Pres. for Finance and Treas.: WILLIAM J. LUCAS
Vice-Pres. for Student Affairs: MARK C. REED
Vice-Pres. for Univ. Advancement: STEPHANIE FROST
Dean of Students: THOMAS C. PELLEGRINO
Univ. Registrar: ROBERT C. RUSSO
Vice-Pres. for Information Services and Univ. Librarian: JAMES A. ESTRADA
Library of 325,166 vols, 888,554 microforms, 9,615 audiovisual items, 4,478 e-books, 1,796 periodicals
Number of teachers: 426 (222 full-time, 204 part-time)
Number of students: 4,008 (and 1,083 graduates

DEANS
College of Arts and Sciences: Dr TIMOTHY SNYDER
Dolan School of Business: Dr NORMAN SOLOMON
Graduate School of Education and Allied Professions: SUSAN D. FRANZOSA
School of Continuing Education: Dr EDNA F. WILSON
School of Engineering: Dr E. VAGOS HADJIMICHAEL
School of Nursing: Dr JEANNE MARIE L. NOVOTNY

HARTFORD SEMINARY

77 Sherman St, Hartford, CT 06105-2260
Telephone: (860) 509-9500
Fax: (860) 509-9509
E-mail: info@hartsem.edu
Internet: www.hartsem.edu
Founded 1913 by merger of Hartford Theological Seminary, Hartford School of Religious Education and Kennedy School of Missions; present name 1981
Private control
3 Academic centres: Center for Faith in Practice, Hartford Institute for Religion Research, Duncan Black Macdonald Center for the Study of Islam and Christian–Muslim Relations
Academic year: September to June
Pres.: Dr HEIDI HADSELL
Dean: Dr IAN MARKHAM
Registrar: KAREN ROLLINS
Library Dir: Dr STEVEN BLACKBURN
Library of 83,000 vols, 312 periodicals
Publications: *Conversations in Religion and Theology* (4 a year), *The Muslim World* (4 a year), *Reviews in Religion and Theology* (4 a year).

HOLY APOSTLES COLLEGE

33 Prospect Hill Rd, Cromwell, CT 06416-2005
Telephone: (860) 632-3010
Fax: (860) 632-3030
E-mail: rector@holyapostles.edu
Internet: www.holyapostles.edu
Founded 1956 as Holy Apostles Seminary; present name 1972
Private control
Catholic liberal arts college
Academic year: September to May

Chancellor: Most Rev. MICHAEL R. COTE
Pres. and Rector: Very Rev. DOUGLAS L. MOSEY
Academic Dean: Rev. MAURICE SHEEHAN
Vice-Pres.: Rev. JOHN HILLIER
Registrar: Dr CYNTHIA TOOLIN
Library Dir: CLARE ADAMO

Library of 60,000 vols, 200 periodicals.

PAIER COLLEGE OF ART, INC.

20 Gorham Ave Hamden, CT 06514
Telephone: (203) 287-3031
Fax: (203) 287-3021
E-mail: paier.admin@snet.net
Internet: www.paierart.com

Founded 1946
Private control

Fine arts, graphic design, illustration, interior design, photography.

POST UNIVERSITY

POB 2540, 800 Country Club Rd, Waterbury, CT 06723-2540
Telephone: (203) 596-4520
Fax: (203) 756-5810
E-mail: registrar@post.edu
Internet: www.post.edu

Founded 1890
Private control
Academic year: September to May

Pres.: Dr PATRICIA SANDERS
Vice-Pres. for Academic Affairs: Dr JEFFREY HAND
Vice-Pres. for Finance and Admin.: SCOTT T. ALLEN
Dean of Students: JOHN WALLACE
Library Dir: TRACY A. RALSTON

Library of 125,000 vols

Divs of arts, business and science.

QUINNIPIAC UNIVERSITY

275 Mount Carmel Ave, Hamden, CT 06518-1908
Telephone: (203) 282-8200
Fax: (203) 281-8906
E-mail: admissions@quinnipiac.edu
Internet: www.quinnipiac.edu

Founded 1929
Independent

Pres.: JOHN L. LAHEY
Sr Vice-Pres. for Academic and Student Affairs: KATHLEEN MCCOURT
Sr Vice-Pres. for Finance and Admin.: PATRICK HEALY
Vice-Pres. and Chief Information and Technology Officer: RICHARD FERGUSON
Vice-Pres. and Dean of Admissions: JOHN ISAAC MOHR
Vice-Pres. and Dean of Student Affairs: MANUEL CARREIRO
Vice-Pres. for Athletic Marketing and External Relations: VAL BELMONTE
Vice-Pres. for Devt and Alumni Affairs: DONALD WEINBACH
Vice-Pres. for Public Affairs: LYNN BUSHNELL
Registrar: DOROTHY LAURIA
Library Dir: CHARLES M. GETCHELL, Jr

Library of 466,000 vols
Number of teachers: 569 (248 full-time, 321 part-time)
Number of students: 7,400

DEANS

College of Liberal Arts: HANS BERGMANN
School of Business: Dr MARK A. THOMPSON
School of Communications: DAVID DONNELLY
School of Health Sciences: Dr EDWARD R. O'CONNOR
School of Law: Dr BRAD SAXTON

ATTACHED INSTITUTES

Albert Schweitzer Institute: tel. (203) 582-3144; fax (203) 582-8478; e-mail schweitzer@quinnipiac.edu; f. 1984 as Albert Schweitzer Memorial Foundation; affiliated with Quinnipiac Univ. in 2002; Dir DAVID T. IVES.

Bioanthropology Research Institute: f. 1998; research in biology, archaeology, anthropology and palaeopathology through diagnostic imaging, video endoscopy and laboratory analysis; Dirs RONALD BECKETT, WILLIAM HENNESSY.

RENSSELAER AT HARTFORD

275 Windsor St, Hartford, CT 06120-2991
Telephone: (860) 548-2400
Fax: (860) 548-7823
E-mail: info@ewp.rpi.edu
Internet: www.rh.edu

Founded 1955; attached to Rensselaer Polytechnic Institute, New York

Vice-Provost and Dean: LESTER GERHARDT
Registrar: DORIS M. MATSIKAS
Library Dir: MARY S. DIXEY

Library of 30,000 vols, 490 periodicals
Number of teachers: 135 (35 full-time, 100 part-time)
Number of students: 2,100

MAs in computer science, management, engineering, and information technology; computer science and engineering graduate certificate programmes.

SACRED HEART UNIVERSITY

5151 Park Ave, Fairfield, CT 06825-1000
Telephone: (203) 371-7999
Internet: www.sacredheart.edu

Founded 1963
Private control

Pres.: Dr ANTHONY J. CERNERA
Provost and Vice-Pres. for Academic Affairs: Dr THOMAS V. FORGET
Vice-Pres. for Enrollment Planning and Student Affairs: JAMES M. BARQUINERO
Vice-Pres. for Finance and Admin.: Dr PAUL K. MADONNA
Vice-Pres. for Human Resources: ROB HARDY
Vice-Pres. for Institutional Advancement: MARY P. YOUNG
Dean of Students: LARRY WIELK
Registrar: DOUGLAS J. BOHN
Univ. Librarian: DENNIS C. BENAMATI

Library of 180,000 vols
Number of teachers: 153 (full-time)
Number of students: 5,800 (3,400 full-time undergraduates, 800 part-time undergraduates and 1,600 graduates)

DEANS

College of Arts and Sciences: Dr CLAIRE J. PAOLINI
John F. Welch College of Business: JOHN PETILLO
College of Education and Health Professions: Dr PATRICIA WALKER
Univ. College: NANCY SIDOTI

CAMPUSES

Sacred Heart University at Griswold: Griswold High School, 267 Slater Ave, POB 399, Griswold, CT 06351; tel. (860) 376-8408.

Sacred Heart University Ireland: Diseart Institute of Education and Celtic Culture, Green St, Dingle, Ireland; e-mail irishstudies@sacredheart.edu; internet shuireland.sacredheart.edu; Irish linguistics and culture (incl. archaeology, customs, folklore, history, language, literature, music, spirituality, theology); Dir of Admissions for SHU DEANNA FIORENTINO; Academic Dir of Diseart Institute Prof. PADRAIG O FIANNACHTA.

Sacred Heart University Luxembourg: see separate entry in Luxembourg chapter.

Sacred Heart University at Stamford: Stamford Campus, 12 Omega Dr., Stamford, CT 06907; tel. (203) 323-4959; fax (203) 323-4974.

Sacred Heart University at Trumbull: 101 Oakview Dr., Trumbull, CT 06611; tel. (203) 371-7941.

Sacred Heart University in the Valley: Derby Campus, Derby High School, 8 Nutmeg Ave, Derby, CT 06418; tel. (203) 371-7831.

SAINT JOSEPH COLLEGE

1678 Asylum Ave, West Hartford, CT 06117-2791
Telephone: (860) 232-4571
Fax: (860) 231-8396
E-mail: info@sjc.edu
Internet: www.sjc.edu

Founded 1932

Pres.: Dr CAROL J. GUARDO
Vice-Pres. for Finance and Admin.: CHUCK MANN
Registrar: BRENDA R. SEBASTIANELLI
Library Dir: LINDA GEFFNER

Library of 133,700 vols
Number of teachers: 119
Number of students: 1,794

Depts of biology, chemistry, child study, counsellor education, education, English, fine and performing arts, gerontology, history and political science, human devt and family studies, int. studies, languages, liberal studies, management sciences, marriage and family therapy, mathematical sciences, nursing, nutrition and dietetics, philosophy, pre-med, psychology, religious studies, social work, sociology and economics.

SOUTHERN CONNECTICUT STATE UNIVERSITY

501 Crescent St, New Haven, CT 06515
Telephone: (203) 392-5200
Fax: (203) 392-5705
Internet: www.southernct.edu

Founded 1893
State control, mem. of the Connecticut State Univ. system

Pres.: CHERYL J. NORTON
Provost: SELASE W. WILLIAMS
Exec. Vice-Pres.: JAMES E. BLAKE
Vice-Pres. for Institutional Advancement: MEGAN A. ROCK
Vice-Pres. for Student and Univ. Affairs: RONALD HERRON
Dean of Student and Univ. Affairs: RICHARD V. FARRICIELLI
Registrar: LYNN KOHRN
Dir of Library Services: EDWARD C. HARRIS

Library of 300,000 vols
Number of teachers: 786 (403 full-time, 383 part-time)
Number of students: 12,100 (incl. 6,010 full-time undergraduates, 992 full-time graduates)

Depts of accounting, anthropology, art, biology, chemistry, communication, communication disorders, computer science, counselling and school psychology, earth science, economics and finance, educational leadership, elementary education, English, ethnic studies, exercise science, foreign languages, geography, history, information and library science, journalism, management and management information systems, marketing, marriage and family therapy, mathematics, media studies, music, nursing, philosophy, physics, political science, psychology, public health, recreation and leisure studies, school health, science education and environmental studies, social work, sociology, special education and reading, theatre, urban studies, women's studies

DEANS

School of Arts and Sciences: DONNA JEAN FREDEEN
School of Business: HENRY H. HEIN
School of Communication, Information and Library Sciences: Dr EDWARD C. HARRIS
School of Education: JAMES GRANFIELD
School of Graduate Studies: SANDRA C. HOLLEY
School of Health and Human Services: GEORGE APPLEBY

TRINITY COLLEGE

300 Summit St, Hartford, CT 06106
Telephone: (860) 297-2000
Fax: (860) 297-2257
Internet: www.trincoll.edu
Founded 1823
Independent
Pres.: JAMES F. JONES, Jr
Dean of the Faculty and Vice-Pres. for Academic Affairs: RENA FRADEN
Vice-Pres. for Alumni Relations and Communications: KATHLEEN O'CONNOR BOELHOUWER
Vice-Pres. of College Advancement: RONALD A. JOYCE
Vice-Pres. of Finance and Treas.: EARLY REESE
Vice-Pres. for Strategic Planning, Admin. and Affirmative Action: PAULA A. RUSSO
Dean of Admissions and Financial Aid: LARRY DOW
Dean of Multicultural Affairs: KARLA SPURLOCK-EVANS
Dean of Students: FREDERICK ALFORD
Librarian: RICHARD ROSS
Library of 100,000 vols, 13,000 current periodicals, 250,000 audiovisual materials, govt documents
Number of teachers: 174 (full-time)
Number of students: 2,203 (undergraduate)
Areas of study: American studies, anthropology, art history, biology, chemistry/biochemistry, classics, computer science, economics, educational studies, engineering, English, environmental science, history, int. studies, Jewish studies, mathematics, modern languages and literature, music, neuroscience, philosophy, physics, political science, psychology, public policy and law, religion, sociology, studio arts, theatre and dance, women, gender and sexuality
Publications: *Reporter*, *Review*, *Trinity Papers*, *Tripod*.

UNITED STATES COAST GUARD ACADEMY

31 Mohegan Ave, New London, CT 06320-8103
Telephone: (860) 444-8444
Internet: www.uscga.edu
Founded 1876 as School of Instruction for the Revenue Marine; present name 1915
Depts of engineering, homeland security, humanities, management, mathematics, natural science, science
Superintendent: Rear Admiral J. SCOTT BURHOE
Dean of Academics: Dr KURT J. COLELLA
Registrar: DONALD E. DYKES
Library Dir: PATRICIA DARAGAN
Library of 130,000 vols, 600 periodicals
Number of students: 975

UNIVERSITY OF BRIDGEPORT

126 Park Ave, Bridgeport, CT 06604
Telephone: (203) 576-4552
Fax: (203) 576-4941
E-mail: admit@bridgeport.edu
Internet: www.bridgeport.edu
Founded 1927
Private control
Academic year: September to May
Pres.: NEIL ALBERT SALONEN
Provost and Sr Vice-Pres. for Academic Affairs: HANS VAN DER GIESSEN
Vice-Pres. for Admin. and Finance and Treas.: Dr SUSAN D. WILLIAMS
Vice-Pres. for Enrollment Management: AUDREY ASHTON SAVAGE
Vice-Pres. for Univ. Relations: MARY-JANE FOSTER
Vice-Pres. for Int. Programmes: Dr THOMAS J. WARD
Dean of Admissions: BARBARA L. MARYAK
Dean of Student Affairs: KENNETH HOLMES
Registrar: CHRISTIAN HANSEN
Univ. Librarian: DIANE MIRVIS
Library of 293,440 vols, 1,051,159 microforms, 3,624 video and audio items, 57,006 serial subscriptions
Number of teachers: 120 full-time
Number of students: 5,155

DEANS

Acupuncture: Dr JENNIFER BRETT
College of Chiropractice: FRANK A. ZOLLI
College of Naturopathic Medicine: GURU SANDESH SINGH KHALSA
Education: Dr ALLEN P. COOK
Fones School of Dental Hygiene: Dr MARGARET H. ZAYAN
Int. College: Dr THOMAS J. WARD
School of Arts and Sciences: Dr STEPHEN HEALEY
School of Business: (vacant)
School of Continuing and Professional Studies: MICHAEL J. GIAMPAOLI
School of Education: (vacant)
School of Engineering: Dr TAREK M. SOBH
Shintaro Akatsu School of Design: RICHARD YELLE

UNIVERSITY OF CONNECTICUT

Storrs, CT 06269
Telephone: (860) 486-2000
Internet: www.uconn.edu
Founded 1881 as The Storrs Agricultural School, present name 1939
State control
Language of instruction: English
Academic year: September to May
Pres.: SUSAN HERBST
Provost and Exec. Vice-Pres. for Academic Affairs: PETER J. NICHOLLS
Exec. Vice-Pres. for Health Affairs: CATO T. LAURENCIN
Vice-Pres. and Chief Financial Officer: RICHARD GRAY
Vice-Pres. and Chief Operating Officer: BARRY M. FELDMAN
Vice-Pres. for Student Affairs: JOHN SADDLEMIRE
Assoc. Vice-Pres. for Human Resources and Payroll: DONNA MUNROE
Assoc. Vice-Pres. for Operations and Admin.: THOMAS CALLAHAN
Vice-Provost: NANCY BULL
Sr Vice-Provost and Vice-Pres. for Research: SUMAN SINGHA
Vice-Provost for Enrollment Planning and Management: LEE H. MELVIN
Vice-Provost for Graduate Education and Dean of the Graduate School: CHARLES LOWE
Library: see Libraries
Number of teachers: 1,304 (full-time)
Number of students: 30,034
Publications: *Connecticut Insurance Law Journal* (2 a year), *Connecticut Journal of International Law* (2 a year), *Connecticut Law Review* (4 a year), *Connecticut Public Interest Law Journal* (online), *MELUS* (4 a year), *The Connecticut Economy* (4 a year), *UConn* (3 a year), *University Advance* (52 during academic year)

DEANS

College of Agriculture and Natural Resources: GREGORY WEIDEMANN
College of Liberal Arts and Sciences: JEREMY TEITELBAUM
Graduate School: CHARLES LOWE
Ratcliffe Hicks School of Agriculture: CAMERON FAUSTMAN (Dir)
School of Business: P. CHRISTOPHER EARLEY
School of Dental Medicine: LAMONT MACNEIL
School of Education: THOMAS DEFRANCO
School of Engineering: MUN CHOI
School of Fine Arts: DAVID G. WOODS
School of Law: JEREMY PAUL
School of Medicine: CATO T. LAURENCIN
School of Nursing: ANNE BAVIER
School of Pharmacy: ROBERT MCCARTHY
School of Social Work: SALOME RAHEIM

PROFESSORS

College of Agriculture and Natural Resources (1376 Storrs Rd, Unit 4066, Storrs, CT 06269-4066; tel. (860) 486-2917; fax (860) 486-5113; internet www.canr.uconn.edu):

ADAMS, R. G., Jr, Entomology
BERKOWITZ, G., Plant Science
BLASIAK, M. M., Plant Science
BRAND, M. H., Plant Science
BRAVO-URETA, B. E., Agricultural Economics
BULL, N. H., Extension
BUSHMICH, S., Pathobiology
CIVCO, D. L., Natural Resources Management
CLARK, R. M., Nutritional Sciences
CLAUSEN, J. C., Natural Resources Management and Engineering
COTTERILL, R. W., Agricultural Economics
DARRE, M. J., Animal Science
FAUSTMAN, L. C., Animal Science
FERNANDEZ, M. L., Nutritional Sciences
FLETCHER, D., Animal Science
FREAKE, H. C., Nutritional Sciences
GARMENDIA, A., Pathobiology
GEARY, S. J., Pathobiology
GREGER, J., Nutritional Sciences
GUILLARD, K., Plant Science
HART, I. C., Animal Science
HOAGLUND, T. A., Animal Science
KERR, K. M., Pathobiology
KHAN, M. I., Pathology
KOO, S. I., Nutritional Sciences
LEE, L. K., Agriculture and Resource Economics
LI, Y., Plant Science
LOPEZ, R. A., Agricultural Economics
LOVE, C., Extension
MCAVOY, R. J., Plant Science
PAGOULATOS, E., Agricultural Economics
PEREZ-ESCAMILLA, R., Nutritional Sciences
POMEROY, R., Agricultural and Resource Economics
ROBBINS, G. A., Natural Resources
RODRIGUEZ, N., Nutritional Sciences
SILBART, L. K., Allied Health Sciences
SINGHA, S., Horticulture
VAN KRUININGEN, H. J., Pathobiology
WARNER, G., Natural Resources Management and Engineering
YANG, X., Animal Science

YANG, X. (H.), Natural Resources Management and Engineering
ZINN, S. A., Animal Science

College of Liberal Arts and Sciences (215 Glenbrook Rd, Unit 4098, Storrs, CT 06269-4098; tel. (860) 486-2713; fax (860) 486-0304; internet www.clas.uconn.edu):

ABE, K., Mathematics
ABIKOFF, W., Mathematics
ADAMS, E., Ecology and Evolutionary Biology
ALBERT, A. D., Molecular and Cell Biology
ANDERSON, G. J., Ecology and Evolutionary Biology
ANDERSON, S., Human Development and Family Studies
ANDERSON, S. L., Philosophy
ANSELMENT, R. A., English
AUSTIN, P. E., Economics
AZIMI, F., History
BAILEY, W. F., Chemistry
BARNES-FARRELL, J., Psychology
BARRECA, R. R., English
BASS, R., Mathematics
BASU, A. K., Chemistry
BAXTER, D. L., Philosophy
BEALL, J. C., Philosophy
BENSON, C. D., English
BENSON, D. R., Molecular and Cell Biology
BERENTSON, W., Geography
BERTHELOT, A., Modern and Classical Languages (French)
BEST, P. E., Physics
BIGGS, F., English
BIRGE, R. R., Physics
BLANK, T. O., Human Development and Family Studies
BLEI, R. C., Mathematics
BLOOM, L. Z., English
BOBALJIK, J., Linguistics
BOHLEN, W. F., Marine Sciences
BOHN, R. K., Chemistry
BOSKOVIC, Z., Linguistics
BOSTER, J. S., Anthropology
BOYER, M. A., Political Science
BRADFIELD, S., English
BROADHEAD, R. S., Sociology
BROWN, R. D., History
BUCK, R. W., Communication Sciences
BUCKLEY, R. N., History
BUCKLIN, A., Marine Sciences
CAIRA, J. N., Ecology and Evolutionary Biology
CALABRESE, A., Linguistics
CARELLO, C. A., Psychology
CARSTENSEN, F. V., Economics
CELESTIN, R., Modern and Classical Languages (French)
CHAFFIN, R., Psychology
CHAPPLE, W. D., Physiology and Neurobiology
CHAZDON, R. L., Ecology and Environmental Biology
CHEN, M. H., Statistics
CHEN, T. T., Molecular and Cell Biology
CHOI, Y. S., Mathematics
CLARK, A., Philosophy
CLIFFORD, J. G., Political Science
COELHO, C. A., Communication Sciences
COLWELL, R. K., Ecology and Evolutionary Biology
COMPRONE, J. J., English
CORMIER, V. F., Physics
COSGEL, M. M., Economics
COSTIGLIOLA, F., History
COTE, R., Physics
CRAWFORD, M., Psychology
CRIVELLO, J. F., Physiology and Neurobiology
CROMLEY, E. K., Geography
CROMLEY, R. G., Geography
CROTEAU, M. E., Journalism
DALMOLIN, E. F., Modern and Classical Languages (French)
DAM, H. G., Marine Sciences
D'ANDRELE, R., Anthropology
DASHEFSKY, A. M., Sociology
DAVID, C. W., Chemistry
DAVIS, J. A., History
DEBLAS, A. L., Physiology and Neurobiology
DESCH, C. E., Jr, Ecology and Evolutionary Biology
DEY, D. K., Statistics
DULACK, T., English
DUNNE, G. V., Physics
DUSSART, J. T., Psychology
DUTTA, N. K., Physics
EBY, C. V., English
ELDER, C. L., Philosophy
ERICKSON, P. I., Anthropology
EYLER, E. E., Physics
FARNEN, R. F., Political Science
FEIN, D. A., Psychology
FISHER, J. D., Psychology
FITZGERALD, W. F., Marine Sciences
FOWLER, C. A., Psychology
FRANK, H. A., Chemistry
FRANKLIN, W., English
FULLERTON, R. J., Jr, Aerospace Studies
GAI, M., Physics
GALLO, R. V., Physiology and Neurobiology
GIBSON, G. N., Physics
GILBERT, H. R., Communication Sciences
GINE, E., Mathematics
GLASBERG, D. S., Sociology
GLAZ, J., Statistics
GLAZ, S., Mathematics
GOGARTEN, J. P., Molecular and Cell Biology
GOMES, M. A., Modern and Classical Languages (Spanish)
GOODHEART, L. B., History
GOODSTEIN, L., Sociology
GORDON, R. B., Modern and Classical Languages (French)
GOULD, P. L., Physics
GREEN, J. A., Psychology
GROSS, R. A., History
GUENOUN, S., Modern and Classical Languages (French)
GUI, C., Mathematics
HAAS, A. H., Mathematics
HALLWOOD, C. P., Economics
HAMILTON, D. S., Physics
HANDWERKER, W. P., Anthropology
HANINK, D. M., Geography
HANSON, B. C., Political Science
HARKNESS, S., Human Development and Family Studies
HARRIS, S., English
HARVEY, C., Military Science
HASENFRATZ, R., English
HEFFLEY, D. R., Economics
HENRY, C. S., Ecology and Evolutionary Biology
HIGONETT, M. R., English
HISKES, R. P., Political Science
HOGAN, P. C., English
HOLLENBERG, D. C., English
HOLSINGER, K. E., Ecology and Evolutionary Biology
HOLZWORTH, J., Psychology
HOWELL, A. R., Chemistry
JAVANAINEN, J. M., Physics
JOESTEN, R. L., Chemistry
JOHNSON, B. T., Psychology
JONES, S. P., English
KALICHMAN, S., Psychology
KAPPERS, L. A., Physics
KENDALL, D. A., Molecular and Cell Biology
KENNY, D. A., Psychology
KHARCHENCO, V., Physics
KNECHT, D. A., Molecular and Cell Biology
KNOBLAUCH, V. L., Economics
KOLTRACHT, I., Mathematics
KOVNER, A., Physics
KREMER, J. N., Marine Sciences
KUMAR, C. V., Chemistry
KUO, L., Statistics
KUPPERMAN, J. J., Philosophy
LANGLOIS, R. N., Economics
LES, D. H., Ecology and Environmental Biology
LEWIS, C. W., Political Science
LILLO-MARTIN, D. C., Linguistics
LIN, C. A., Communication Sciences
LINNEKIN, J. S., Anthropology
LOTURCO, J. J., Physiology and Neurobiology
LOWE, C. A., Psychology
LUYSTER, R. W., Philosophy
LYNCH, M. P., Philosophy
LYNES, M. A., Molecular and Cell Biology
MCBREATY, S. A., Anthropology
MCBREEN, E., Human Development and Family Studies
MCKENNA, P. J., Mathematics
MACKINNON, R. D., Geography
MACLEOD, G. G., English
MCMANUS, G. B., Marine Sciences
MADYCH, W. R., Mathematics
MAKOWSKY, V. A., English
MALLETT, R. L., Physics
MANNHEIM, P. O., Physics
MARCUS, P. I., Molecular and Cell Biology
MARKUS, E., Psychology
MARSDEN, J., English
MASCIANDARO, F., Modern and Classical Languages (Italian)
MASON, R., Marine Sciences
MAXSON, S. C., Psychology
MEYER, M., English
MEYERS, D. T., Philosophy
MICELI, T. J., Economics
MICHEL, R. G., Chemistry
MILLER, D. B., Psychology
MILLER, R. L., English
MILLER, S. S., Modern and Classical Languages (Classics and Hebrew)
MOISEFF, A., Physiology and Neurobiology
MUKHOPADHYAY, N., Statistics
MURPHY, B., English
MUSIEK, F., Communication Sciences
NAIGLES, L. R., Psychology
NAPLES, N., Sociology
NEUMANN, M., Mathematics
NOLL, K. M., Molecular and Cell Biology
O'DONNELL, J., Marine Sciences
OLSHEVASKY, V., Mathematics
OSLEEB, J. P., Geography
PAPADIMITRAKOPOULOUS, F., Chemistry
PEASE, D. M., Physics
PETERSON, C. W., Physics
PETERSON, R. S., English
PHILLIPS, R. L., Philosophy
PICKERING, S. F., English
PRATTO, F., Psychology
RAVISHANKER, N., Statistics
RAWITSCHER, G. H., Physics
RAY, S. C., Economics
REITER, H. L., Political Science
RENFRO, J. L., Physiology and Neurobiology
RICKARDS, J. P., Psychology
RIGAZIO-DIGILIO, S., Human Development and Family Studies
ROBINSON, J., Human Development and Family Studies
ROCKWELL, R. C., Sociology
ROE, S. A., History
ROSS, S. L., Economics
RUSLING, J. F., Chemistry
SABATELLI, R., Human Development and Family Studies
SALAMONE, J. D., Psychology
SANDERS, C. R., Sociology
SCHAEFER, C. W., Ecology and Evolutionary Biology
SCHLICHTING, C. D., Ecology and Environmental Biology
SCHWENK, K., Ecology and Environmental Biology
SEGERSON, K., Economics
SEHULSTER, J. R., Psychology
SHOEMAKER, N., History
SIDNEY, S. J., Mathematics

SILANDER, J. A., Ecology and Evolutionary Biology
SILVESTRINI, B. G., History
SIMON, C. M., Ecology and Environmental Biology
SIMONSEN, W., Public Policy
SMITH, M. B., Chemistry
SMITH, W. W., Physics
SNYDER, L. B., Communication Sciences
SONSTROEM, D. A., English
SPALDING, K., History
SPIEGEL, E. S., Mathematics
STRAUSBAUGH, L. D., Molecular and Cell Biology
STWALLEY, W. C., Physics
SUIB, S. L., Chemistry
SUNG, C. S. P., Chemistry
SUPER, C. M., Human Development and Family Studies
SWADLOW, H. A., Psychology
SWANSON, M. S., Physics
TAYLOR, R. L., Sociology
TEITELBAUM, J., Mathematics
TESCHKE, C., Molecular and Cell Biology
THORSON, R. M., Ecology and Evolutionary Biology
TOLLEFSON, J. L., Mathematics
TORGERSEN, T. L., Marine Sciences
TROYER, L., Sociology
TRUMBO, S., Ecology and Evolutionary Biology
TUCHMAN, G., Sociology
TURCHIN, P., Ecology and Environmental Biology
TURVEY, M. T., Psychology
VAN DER HULST, H. G., Linguistics
VILLEMEZ, W. J., Sociology
VITALE, R. A., Statistics
WAGNER, D., Ecology and Evolutionary Biology
WALLACE, M., Sociology
WALLER, A. L., History
WANG, Y., Statistics
WEAKLIEM, D. L., Sociology
WELLS, K. D., Ecology and Evolutionary Biology
WHEELER, S. C., Philosophy
WHITLATCH, R. B., Marine Sciences
WILKENFELD, R. B., English
WILSON, R. A., Anthropology
WISENSALE, S., Human Development and Family Studies
WORCESTER, W. A., Journalism
YARISH, C., Ecology and Evolutionary Biology
YEAGLE, P. L., Molecular and Cell Biology
ZIRAKZADEH, C. E., Political Science

Ratcliffe Hicks School of Agriculture (1376 Storrs Rd, Unit 90, Storrs, CT 06269-4090; tel. (860) 486-2920; e-mail acadprog@canr.uconn.edu; internet www.canr.uconn.edu/rh).

School of Business (2100 Hillside Rd, Unit 1041, Storrs, CT 06269-1041; tel. (860) 486-2314; fax (860) 486-0889; internet www.sba.uconn.edu):

BIGGS, S. F., Accounting
CARRAFIELLO, V. A., Business Law
CLAPP, J. M., Finance
COULTER, R. H., Marketing
EARLEY, P. C., Management
FOX, K. H., Business Law
GARFINKEL, R. S., Operations Research and Information Management
GHOSH, C., Finance
GIACOTTO, C., Finance
GOES, P. B., Operations and Information Management
GOPAL, R., Operations Research and Information Management
HARDING, J., Finance
HEGDE, S. P., Finance
HUSSEIN, M. E., Accounting
JAIN, S. C., Marketing
KLEIN, L. S., Finance
KUMAR, V., Marketing
LUBATKIN, M. J., Management
MARSDEN, J. R., Operations Research and Information Management
MATHIEU, J. E., Management
NAIR, S. K., Operations Research and Information Management
O'BRIEN, T. J., Finance
POWELL, G. N., Management
SANTERRE, R., Finance
SEWALL, M. A., Marketing
SIRMANS, C. F., Finance and Real Estate
VEIGA, J. F., Management
WILLENBORG, M., Accounting

School of Dental Medicine (263 Farmington Ave, Farmington, CT 06030; tel. (860) 679-2000; internet sdm.uchc.edu):

AGAR, J., Reconstructive Sciences
BEAZOGLOU, T., Craniofacial Sciences
D'AMBROSIO, J., Oral Health and Diagnostic Services
DEALY, C., Reconstructive Sciences
DONGARI-BAGTZOGLOU, A., Oral Health and Diagnostic Services
EISENBERG, E., Oral Health and Diagnostic Sciences
FRANK, M. E., Oral Health and Diagnostic Sciences
FREILICH, M., Reconstructive Sciences
GOLDBERG, A. J., Reconstructive Sciences
GOUPIL, M., Craniofacial Sciences
HAND, A., Craniofacial Sciences
KAZEMI, R., Reconstructive Sciences
KELLY, J. R., Reconstructive Sciences
KOSHER, R., Reconstructive Sciences
LITT, M. D., Oral Health and Diagnostic Sciences
LURIE, A. G., Oral Health and Diagnostic Sciences
MACNEIL, R., Oral Health and Diagnostic Sciences
MEIERS, J., Reconstructive Sciences
MINA, M., Craniofacial Sciences
NANDA, R., Craniofacial Sciences
NEWITTER, D., Reconstructive Sciences
NICHOLS, F., Oral Health and Diagnostic Sciences
PENDRYS, D., Oral Health and Diagnostic Services
PETERSON, D. E., Oral Health and Diagnostic Sciences
REISINE, S., Oral Health and Diagnostic Sciences
ROBINSON, P., Oral Health and Diagnostic Sciences
ROSSOMANDO, E. P., Craniofacial Sciences
SAFAVI, K., Craniofacial Sciences
SHAFER, D., Craniofacial Sciences
SPANGBERG, L. S. W., Oral Health and Diagnostic Sciences
TANZER, J. M., Oral Health and Diagnostic Sciences
TAYLOR, T., Reconstructive Sciences
TRUMMEL, C. L., Oral Health and Diagnostic Sciences
UPHOLT, W., Reconstructive Sciences
ZHU, Q., Craniofacial Sciences

Neag School of Education (249 Glenbrook Rd, Unit 2064, Storrs, CT 06269-2064; tel. (860) 486-3813; fax (860) 486-0210; internet www.education.uconn.edu):

ARMSTRONG, L. E., Kinesiology
BONANNON, R., Physical Therapy
BRAY, M., Educational Psychology
BROWN, S. W., Educational Psychology
DEFRANCO, T., Curriculum and Instruction
DENEGAR, C. R., Physical Therapy
DOYLE, M. A., Curriculum and Instruction
GOODKIND, T. B., Curriculum and Instruction
HASSON, S. M., Physical Therapy
JUNDA, M. E., Educational Leadership
KARAN, O. C., Educational Psychology
KEHLE, T. J., Educational Psychology
KRAEMER, W. J., Kinesiology
LEU, D. J., Curriculum and Instruction
MCGUIRE, J. M., Educational Psychology
MARESH, C. M., Kinesiology
REAGAN, T. G., Curriculum and Instruction
REIS, S. M., Educational Psychology
SCHWAB, R. L., Educational Leadership
SHECKLEY, B. G., Educational Leadership
SMEY, J. W., Physical Therapy
STEPHENS, R., Educational Leadership
SUGAI, G., Educational Psychology
SWAMINATHAN, H., Educational Psychology

School of Engineering (261 Glenbrook Rd, Unit 2237, Storrs, CT 06269-2237; tel. (860) 486-2221; fax (860) 486-0318; internet www.enga.uconn.edu):

ACCORSI, M. L., Civil and Environmental Engineering
ACHENIE, L. E., Chemical, Materials and Biomolecular Engineering
AINDOW, M., Chemical, Materials and Biomolecular Engineering
AMMAR, R. A., Computer Science and Engineering
ANWAR, A. F. M., Electrical and Computer Engineering
BAGTZOGLOU, A., Civil and Environmental Engineering
BANSAL, R., Electrical and Systems Engineering
BAR SHALOM, Y., Electrical and Computer Engineering
BARKER, K., Computer Science and Engineering
BERGMAN, T. L., Mechanical Engineering
BRODY, H. D., Chemical, Materials and Biomolecular Engineering
CETEGEN, B., Mechanical Engineering
COOPER, D. J., Chemical, Materials and Biomolecular Engineering
DEMURJIAN, S. A., Computer Science and Engineering
DEWOLF, J. T., Civil and Environmental Engineering
ENDERLE, J. D., Electrical and Computer Engineering
ENGEL, G. L., Computer Science and Engineering and Electrical and Systems Engineering
EPSTEIN, H. I., Civil and Environmental Engineering
ERKEY, C., Chemical, Materials and Biomolecular Engineering
FAGHIRI, A., Mechanical Engineering
FOX, M. D., Electrical and Computer Engineering
FRANTZ, G. C., Civil and Environmental Engineering
IVAN, J. N., Civil Engineering
JAIN, F. C., Electrical and Computer Engineering
JAVIDI, B., Electrical and Computer Engineering
JORDAN, E. H., Mechanical Engineering
KATTAMIS, T. Z., Materials Science and Engineering
KAZEROUNIAN, K., Mechanical Engineering
LUH, P. B., Electrical and Computer Engineering
MAGNUSSON, R., Electrical and Computer Engineering
MARCUS, H. L., Chemical, Materials and Biomolecular Engineering
OLGAC, N., Mechanical Engineering
OR, D., Civil and Electrical Engineering
PATTIPATI, K. R., Electrical and Computer Engineering
PETERS, T. J., Computer Science and Engineering
PITCHUMANI, R., Mechanical Engineering
RAJASEKARAN, S., Computer Science and Engineering
REIFSNIDER, K. L., Mechanical Engineering
SAMMES, N. M., Mechanical Engineering
SHAW, L. L., Chemical, Materials and Biomolecular Engineering

SHAW, M. T., Chemical, Materials and Biomolecular Engineering
SHIN, D. G., Computer Science and Engineering
SMITH, E., Civil and Environmental Engineering
TAYLOR, G. W., Electrical and Computer Engineering
WEISS, R. A., Chemical, Materials and Biomolecular Engineering
WILLETT, P. K., Electrical and Computer Engineering
ZHANG, B., Mechanical Engineering
ZHU, Q., Electrical and Computer Engineering

Whetten Graduate Center (438 Whitney Rd Ext., Unit 1006, Storrs, CT 06269-1006; tel. (860) 486-3617; fax (860) 486-6739; e-mail gradschool@uconn.edu; internet www.grad.uconn.edu).

School of Fine Arts (875 Coventry Rd, Unit 1128, Storrs, CT 06269-1128; tel. (860) 486-3016; fax (860) 486-5845; internet www.sfa.uconn.edu):

ARM, T. E., Music
BASS, W. R., Music
CROW, L. J., Dramatic Arts
ENGLISH, G. M., Dramatic Arts
FRANKLIN, J. F., Dramatic Arts
FROGLEY, A., Music
FUCHS, K., Music
GIVENS, J., Art and Art History
MCDONALD, R. A., Dramatic Arts
MARTINEZ, A., Art
MAZZOCCA, A. N., Art
MILLER, R. F., Music
MILLS, D. L., Music
MOLETTE, C. W., Dramatic Arts
MUIRHEAD, D. D., Art
MYERS, K. M., Art and Art History
OGUIBE, O., Art and Art History
RENSHAW, J. H., Music
ROCCOBERTON, B. P. Jr, Dramatic Arts
RYKER, K., Dramatic Arts
SABATINE, J., Dramatic Arts
STANLEY, G., Music
STERN, A. S., Dramatic Arts
TALVACCHIA, B. L., Art
THORPE, J. K., Art
WOODS, D. G., Music

School of Law (55 Elizabeth St, Hartford, CT 06105-2296; tel. (860) 570-5000; fax (860) 570-5128; internet www.law.uconn.edu):

BAKER, T. E.
BARNES, R. D.
BECKER, L. E., Jr
BERGER, B.
BERMAN, P. S.
BIRMINGHAM, R. L.
CALLOWAY, D. A.
DAILEY, A. C.
DICKERSON, L.
FERNOW, T. O.
FISCHL, R. M.
GUSTAFSON, K.
JANIS, M. W.
KAY, R. S.
KIRK, D.
KURLANTZICK, L. S.
LEVIN, L. C.
LINDSETH, P.
MCCOY, P.
MCLEAN, W. E.
MORAWETZ, T. H.
OQUENDO, A. R.
ORLAND, L.
PARKER, R. W.
PAUL, J.
POMP, R. D.
SIEGELMAN, P.
STARK, J. H.
STRASSER, K. A.
TONDRO, T. J.
UTZ, S. G.
WEISBROD, C. A.
WHITMAN, R.
WILF, S.

School of Medicine (263 Farmington Ave, Farmington, CT 06030-1920; tel. (860) 679-2413; fax (860) 679-1371; internet medicine.uchc.edu):

ALBERTSON, P. C., Surgery
ALTMAN, A. J., Paediatrics
ARNOLD, A., Medicine
BABOR, T. F., Community Medicine and Health Care
BARBARESE, E., Neuroscience
BAUER, L. O., Psychiatry
BENN, P. A., Genetics and Developmental Biology
BERNSTEIN, L., Neuroscience
BIGAZZI, P. E., Pathology and Laboratory Medicine
BROWNER, B. O., Orthopaedic Surgery
BRUDER, M. E., Paediatrics
CAMPBELL, W. A., Obstetrics and Gynaecology
CARMICHAEL, G. G., Genetics and Developmental Biology
CARSON, J. H., Molecular, Microbial and Structural Biology
CHERNIAK, M. G., Medicine
CLOUTIER, M., Paediatrics
CONE, R. E., Immunology
CUSHMAN, R. A., Family Medicine
DAS, A. K., Molecular, Microbial and Structural Biology
DAS, D. K., Surgery
DECKERS, P. J., Surgery
EIPPER, E. A., Molecular, Microbial and Structural Biology
EISENBERG, S., Molecular, Microbial and Structural Biology
FEDER, H. M., Jr, Family Medicine
FEIN, A., Cell Biology
FEINSTEIN, M. B., Cell Biology
FIFIELD, J., Family Medicine
FOROUHAR, F., Pathology and Laboratory Medicine
FORTINSKY, R. H., Medicine
GOLDSCHNEIDER, I., Immunology
GRANT-KELS, J. M., Dermatology
GRASSO, J. A., Cell Biology
GREENSTEIN, R. M., Genetics and Developmental Biology
GRONOWICZ, G. F., Surgery
GROSS, J. B., Anaesthesiology
HANSEN, M., Medicine
HESSELBROCK, V. M., Psychiatry
HLA, T. R., Cell Biology
HUEY, L., Psychiatry
HURLEY, M. M., Medicine
JAFFE, L., Cell Biology
KADDEN, R. M., Psychiatry
KIM, D. O., Neuroscience
KING, S. M., Molecular, Microbial and Structural Biology
KLOBUTCHER, L. A., Molecular, Microbial and Structural Biology
KOEPPEN, B. M., Medicine
KOPPEL, D. E., Molecular, Microbial and Structural Biology
KRANZLER, H. R., Psychiatry
KREAM, B., Medicine
KREUTZER, D. L., Pathology
KUCHEL, G., Medicine
KUWADA, S., Neuroscience
LALANDE, M., Genetics and Developmental Biology
LE FRANCOIS, L., Medicine
LEVINE, J. B., Medicine
LIANG, B. T., Medicine
LIEBERMAN, J., Orthopaedic Surgery
LOEW, L. M., Cell Biology
LORENZO, J. A., Medicine
MAINS, R. E., Neuroscience
MAULIK, N., Surgery
MAXWELL, G. D., Neuroscience
MAYER, B., Genetics and Developmental Biology
MOREST, D. K., Neuroscience
MUKHOPADHYAY, B., Medicine
OLIVER, D. L., Neuroscience
O'ROURKE, J. T., Immunology
OZOLS, J., Molecular, Microbial and Structural Biology
PACHTER, J., Cell Biology
PAPPANO, A. J., Cell Biology
PELUSO, J. J., Cell Biology
PETRY, N., Psychiatry
POTASHNER, S. J., Neuroscience
RADOLF, J. D., Medicine
RAJAN, T. V., Pathology and Laboratory Medicine
RATZAN, S. K., Paediatrics
ROSENBERG, D., Medicine
RUNOWICZ, C. D., Obstetrics and Gynaecology
SANDERS, M. M., Pathology and Laboratory Medicine
SARFARAZI, M., Surgery
SCHENSUL, S., Community Medicine and Health Care
SETLOW, P., Molecular, Microbial and Structural Biology
SIMON, R. H., Surgery
SRIVASTAVA, P. K., Immunology
STEVENS, R., Community Medicine and Health Care
TENNEN, H., Community Medicine and Health Care
TRAHIOTIS, C., Neuroscience
TRESTMAN, R., Medicine
TSIPOURAS, P., Genetics and Developmental Biology
WELLER, S. K., Molecular, Microbial and Structural Biology
WHITE, B. A., Cell Biology
WHITE, W. B., Medicine
WIKEL, S. K., Immunology
WINOKUR, A., Psychiatry
WOLFSON, L. I., Neurology
WU, C. H., Medicine
WU, G. Y., Medicine

School of Nursing (231 Glenbrook Rd, Unit 2026, Storrs, CT 06269-2026; tel. (860) 486-3716; fax (860) 486-0001; internet www.nursing.uconn.edu):

BAVIER, A., Nursing
BECK, C. L., Nursing
CUSSON, R., Nursing
KOERNER, B. L., Nursing
NEAFSEY, P. J., Nursing

School of Pharmacy (372 Fairfield Rd, Unit 2092, Storrs, CT 06269-2092; tel. (860) 486-2129; fax (860) 486-4998; internet pharmacy.uconn.edu):

BURGESS, D. J., Pharmaceutics
GERALD, M. C., Pharmacology
LANGNER, R. O., Pharmacology
MCCARTHY, R. L., Pharmacy Practice
MORRIS, J. B., Toxicology
PIKAL, M. J., Pharmaceutics
WHITE, C. M., Pharmacy Practice

School of Social Work (1798 Asylum Ave, West Hartford, CT 06117; tel. (860) 570-9141; fax (860) 570-9139; internet socialwork.uconn.edu):

DAVIDSON, K. W.
FISHER, R.
GITTERMAN, A.
HEALY, L. M.
HESSELBROCK, M. N.
HUMPHREYS, N. A.
JOHNSON, H. C.

ATTACHED INSTITUTES

Alcohol Research Center: Dir VICTOR HESSELBROCK.

Asian American Studies Institute: Dir ROGER BUCKLEY.

Biotechnology Center: Dir PHILIP MARCUS.

Booth Engineering Center for Advanced Technology: Dir SANGUTHEVAR RAJASEKARAN.

Center for Applied Genetics and Technology: Dir LINDA D. STRAUSBAUGH.

Center for Biochemical Toxicology: Dir JOHN MORRIS.

Center for Conservation and Biodiversity: Co-Dirs JOHN SILANDER, DAVID WAGNER.

Center for Contemporary African Studies: Dir ELIZABETH MAHAN.

Center for Economic Education: Chair. FRED CARSTENSEN.

Center for Environmental Health: Dir CAMERON FAUSTMAN.

Center for European Studies: Dir JOHN A. DAVIS.

Center for Healthcare and Insurance Studies: Dir JEFFREY KRAMER.

Center for Immunotherapy of Cancer and Infectious Diseases: Dir PRAMOD SRIVASTAVA.

Center for International Business and Education Research: Dir SUBHASH JAIN.

Center for International Social Work Studies: Dir LYNN HEALY.

Center for Judaic Studies and Contemporary Jewish Life: Dir ARNOLD DASHEFSKY.

Center for Latin American and Caribbean Studies: Dir PETER KINGSTONE.

Center for Materials Simulation: Dir PHILIP C. CLAPP.

Center for Microbial Pathogenesis: Dir Dr STEPHEN WIKEL.

Center for Molecular Medicine: Dir Dr ANDREW ARNOLD.

Center for Oral History: Dir BRUCE STAVE.

Center for Real Estate and Urban Economic Studies: Dir C. F. SIRMANS.

Center for the Study of Parental Acceptance and Rejection: Dir RONALD P. ROHNER.

Connecticut Center for Economic Analysis: Dir FRED CARSTENSEN.

Connecticut Global Fuel Cell Center: Dir KENNETH REIFSNIDER.

Connecticut Small Business Development Center: Dir RICHARD CHENEY.

Connecticut Transportation Institute: Dir LISA AULTMAN-HALL.

Electrical Insulation Research Center: Dir STEVEN BOGGS.

Environmental Research Institute: Dir JOHN C. CLAUSEN.

Food Marketing Policy Center: Dir RONALD COTTERILL.

Health Policy and Primary Care Research Center: Dir Dr HOWARD L. BAILIT.

Institute for African-American Studies: Dir JEFFREY OGBAR.

Institute for Social Inquiry (and The Roper Center for Public Opinion Research): Dir DAVID WEAKLIEM.

Institute for the Advancement of Political Social Work Practice: Dir NANCY A. HUMPHREYS.

Institute for Violence Reduction: Dir (vacant).

Institute of Materials Science: Dir HARRIS MARCUS.

Institute of Public Affairs: Dir KENNETH DAUTRICH.

Institute of Public Service International: Dir MARIA-TERESA LEPELEY.

Institute of Water Resources: Dir GLEN WARNER.

Insurance Law Center: Dir TOM BAKER.

Labor Education Center: Dir MARK SULLIVAN.

Marine Science and Technology Center: Dir ANN BUCKLIN.

National Research Center on the Gifted and Talented: Dir JOSEPH RENZULLI.

National Undersea Research Center: Dir IVAR BABB.

Northeastern Research Center for Wildlife Diseases: Dir HERBERT VAN KRUININGEN.

Pappanikou Center for Developmental Disabilities: Dir MARY BETH BRUDER.

Puerto Rican and Latino Studies Institute: Dir BLANCA SILVESTRINI (acting).

Small Business Institute: Dir JOHN F. VEIGA.

UNIVERSITY OF HARTFORD

200 Bloomfield Ave, West Hartford, CT 06117

Telephone: (860) 768-5234
Fax: (860) 768-4378
Internet: www.hartford.edu

Founded 1877
Private control
Academic year: July to June

Pres.: Dr WALTER HARRISON
Provost: LYNN PASQUERELLA
Asst Provost and Dean of Faculty Devt: H. FREDERICK SWEITZER
Vice-Pres. for Finance and Admin.: AROSHA JAYAWICKREMA
Vice-Pres. for Institutional Advancement: DONALD RIZZO
Vice-Pres. for Student Affairs: J. LEE PETERS
Vice-Pres. for Univ. Relations: JOHN J. CARSON
Registrar: DOREEN LAY
Assoc. Provost and Dean of Undergraduate Studies: GUY C. COLARULLI
Dean of Admissions: RICHARD ZEISER
Dean of Graduate Studies: PETER DIFFLEY
Dir of Libraries and Learning Resources: RANDI ASHTON-PRITTING

Library of 606,154 vols
Number of teachers: 336 full-time, 591 part time
Number of students: 7,366 (5,695 undergraduate, 1,671 postgraduate)

DEANS

Hartford Art School: Dr POWER BOOTHE
College of Arts and Sciences: Dr JOSEPH VOELKER
Barney School of Business: JAMES W. FAIRFIELD-SONN
College of Education, Nursing and Health Professions: Dr RALPH MUELLER
College of Engineering, Technology and Architecture: LOUIS T. MANZIONE
Hartt School: AARON FLAGG
Hillyer College: Dr DAVID GOLDENBERG

UNIVERSITY OF NEW HAVEN

300 Boston Post Rd, West Haven, CT 06516

Telephone: (203) 932-7000
Fax: (203) 932-3060
E-mail: adminfo@newhaven.edu
Internet: www.newhaven.edu

Founded 1920

Pres.: STEVEN H. KAPLAN
Provost and Sr Vice-Pres. for Academic Affairs: Dr DAVID P. DAUWALDER
Vice-Pres. for Enrollment Management: JAMES MCCOY
Vice-Pres. for Facilities: THOMAS BEEBE
Vice-Pres. for Finance: GEORGE SYNODI
Vice-Pres. for Univ. Advancement: RICHARD TUCHMAN
Librarian: HANKO DOBI

Library of 250,460 vols, 158,159 documents
Number of teachers: 599 (170 full-time, 429 part-time)
Number of students: 5,113

Publication: *Essays in Arts and Sciences*

DEANS

College of Arts and Sciences: Dr RONALD H. NOWACZYK
Henry C. Lee College of Criminal Justice and Forensic Sciences: Dr RICHARD WARD
School of Business: Dr RICHARD HIGHFIELD
Tagliatela College of Engineering: Dr BARRY FARBROTHER

WESLEYAN UNIVERSITY

229 High St, Middletown, CT 06459

Telephone: (860) 685-2000
Fax: (860) 685-3000
Internet: www.wesleyan.edu

Founded 1831
Academic year: September to May

Pres.: Dr MICHAEL S. ROTH
Vice-Pres. for Academic Affairs and Provost: JOSEPH W. BRUNO
Vice-Pres. and Chief Investment Officer: THOMAS P. KANNAM
Vice-Pres. for Diversity and Strategic Partnerships: SONIA B. MAÑJON
Vice-Pres. for Finance and Admin.: JOHN C. MEERTS
Vice-Pres. for Student Affairs: MICHAEL J. WHALEY
Vice-Pres. for Univ. Relations: BARBARA-JAN WILSON
Dean of Admissions and Financial Aid: NANCY HARGRAVE MEISLAHN
Univ. Librarian: PATRICIA TULLY

Library: more than 1.2m. vols
Number of teachers: 300
Number of students: 3,149 (undergraduates and postgraduates)

Publications: *Annual Catalog*, *History and Theory*

DEANS

Arts and Humanities: KRISHNA R. WINSTON
Natural Sciences and Mathematics: DAVID BODZNICK
Social Sciences and Interdisciplinary Programmes: DONALD J. MOON

WESTERN CONNECTICUT STATE UNIVERSITY

181 White St, Danbury, CT 06810

Telephone: (203) 837-8210
Internet: www.wcsu.edu

Founded 1903
State control, mem. of Connecticut State Univ. System
Academic year: August to May

Pres.: JAMES W. ROACH
Provost and Vice-Pres. for Academic Affairs: Dr LINDA RINKER
Vice-Pres. for Student Affairs: WALTER B. BERNSTEIN
Dean of Students: WALTER CRAMER
Registrar: IRENE DUFFY
Dir of Library Services: RALPH HOLIBAUGH

Number of teachers: 518 (200 full-time and 318 part-time)
Number of students: 6,086 (4,208 full-time and 1,878 part-time)

DEANS

Ancell School of Business: ALLEN MORTON
School of Arts and Sciences: LINDA VANDENGOAD
School of Professional Studies: LYNNE CLARK

School of Visual and Performing Arts: CAROL A. HAWKES
Graduate Studies: Dr ELLEN D. DURNIN

BRANCH CAMPUS

WestConn at Waterbury: Founders Hall 129, 750 Chase Parkway, Waterbury, CT 06708; tel. (203) 596-8777; fax (203) 596-8793; e-mail durnine@wcsu.edu; programmes in management and nursing; Dean Dr ELLEN DURNIN.

YALE UNIVERSITY

POB 208232, New Haven, CT 06520-8232
Telephone: (203) 432-1333
Internet: www.yale.edu
Founded 1701, named Yale College 1718, transition to univ. status from 1810 to 1861
Private control
Pres.: Dr RICHARD CHARLES LEVIN
Provost: Dr PETER SALOVEY
Vice-Pres. and Gen. Counsel: Dr DOROTHY K. ROBINSON
Vice-Pres. and Sec.: Dr LINDA KOCH LORIMER
Vice-Pres. for Devt: INGEBORG THERESIA REICHENBACH
Vice-Pres. for Finance and Business Operations: SHAUNA RYAN KING
Vice-Pres. for Human Resources and Admin.: MICHAEL A. PEEL
Vice-Pres. for New Haven and State Affairs and Campus Devt: Dr BRUCE D. ALEXANDER
Vice-Pres. for West Campus Planning and Program Devt: Dr MICHAEL J. DONOGHUE
Librarian: FRANK TURNER
Library: see Libraries and Archives
Number of teachers: 3,619
Number of students: 11,416
Publications: *American Journal of Science, American Scientist, Bulletin of Art Gallery Associates, Journal of American Oriental Society, Journal of Biological Chemistry, Journal of Industrial Ecology, Journal of Music Theory, Journal of the History of Medicine and Allied Sciences, Library Gazette, Technical Brief (Drama School), Theatre Magazine, Yale Alumni Magazine, Yale Divinity News, Yale Forest School News, Yale French Studies, Yale Human Rights and Development Law Journal, Yale Journal of Biology and Medicine, Yale Journal of Criticism, Yale Journal of Ethics, Yale Journal of International Law, Yale Journal of Law and Feminism, Yale Journal of Law and the Humanities, Yale Journal on Regulation, Yale Law and Policy Review, Yale Law Journal, Yale Literary Magazine, Yale Review, Yale Scientific Magazine*

DEANS

School of Architecture: ROBERT A. M. STERN
School of Art: ROBERT STORR
Divinity School: HAROLD W. ATTRIDGE
School of Drama: JAMES BUNDY
School of Engineering and Applied Science: T. KYLE VANDERLICK
School of Forestry and Environmental Studies: PETER CRANE
Law School: ROBERT C. POST
School of Management: SHARON M. OSTER
School of Medicine: ROBERT J. ALPERN
School of Music: ROBERT BLOCKER
School of Nursing: MARGARET GREY
School of Public Health: PAUL D. CLEARY
Graduate School of Arts and Sciences: JON BUTLER
Yale College: MARY MILLER

PROFESSORS

(Some staff serve in more than one faculty)

School of Architecture:

ALEXLEY, J. W.
BEEBY, T. H., Architectural Design
BLOOMER, K. C., Architectural Design
GARVIN, A., Urban Planning and Devt
HAYDEN, D., Architecture and Urbanism
KOETTER, F. H.
PLATTUS, A. J.
PURVES, A., Architectural Design
STERN, R. A. M.

School of Art:

BARTH, F., Painting and Printmaking
BENSON, R. M., Photography
DE BRETTEVILLE, S. L., Graphic Design
LYTLE, W. R., Painting
PAPAGEORGE, T., Photography
REED, R. J., Jr, Painting and Printmaking
STOCKHOLDER, J., Sculpture

Faculty of Arts and Sciences (Yale College and Graduate School):

ACKERMAN, B., Law and Political Science
ADAIR, R. K., Physics
ADAMS, M. McC., Philosophy, Religious Studies
ADAMS, R. M., Philosophy
ADORNO, R., Spanish
AGNEW, J.-C., American Studies and History
ALEXANDER, J. C., Sociology
ALEXANDROV, V. E., Slavic Languages and Literatures
ALHASSID, Y., Physics
ALTMAN, S., Biology
ALTONJI, J., Economics
AMANAT, A., History
ANDERSON, S. R., Linguistics
ANDREW, D., Comparative Literature, Film Studies
ANDREWS, D. W. K., Economics and Statistics
ANGULIN, D., Computer Science
APPADURAI, A., Int. Studies
APPELQUIST, T. W., Physics
AUSTIN, D. J., Chemistry
AVNI, O., French
BAILYN, C., Astronomy, Physics
BALTAY, C., Physics and Astronomy
BANAC, I., History
BARRON, A., Statistics
BATISTA, V. S., Chemistry
BEALS, R. W., Mathematics
BENHABIB, S., Philosophy, Political Science
BERCOVICI, D., Geology and Geophysics
BERNER, R. A., Geology and Geophysics
BERNSTEIN, I. B., Mechanical Engineering and Physics
BERRY, S. T., Economics
BERS, V., Classics
BEWLEY, T. F., Economics
BLOCH, R. H., French
BLOOM, H. I., English Language and Literature
BLOOM, P., Psychology and Linguistics
BOBZIEN, S., Philosophy
BOORMAN, S. A., Sociology
BÖWERING, G. H., Religious Studies
BRACKEN, P., Management and Political Science
BRAINARD, W. C., Economics
BRAUND, S. M., Classics
BRISMAN, L., English Language and Literature
BRODHEAD, R. H., American Studies, English Language and Literature
BROMLEY, D. A., Physics
BROMWICH, D., English Language and Literature
BROOKS, P., Comparative Literature and French
BROWN, D. J., Economics
BROWN, T. H., Psychology and Physiology
BROWNELL, K. D., Psychology
BRUDVIG, G., Chemistry
BURGER, R. L., Anthropology
BUSHKOVITCH, P. A., History
BUSS, L. W., Ecology and Evolutionary Biology, Geology and Geophysics
BUTLER, J., History and American Studies, Religious Studies
CAMERON, D. R., Political Science
CAMPBELL, J., English Language and Literature
CARBY, H. V., African American Studies and American Studies
CASSON, A. W., Mathematics
CASTEN, R., Physics
CHANG, J. T., Statistics
CHANG, K.-I. S., East Asian Languages and Literatures
CHANG, R. K., Applied Physics, Physics and Electrical Engineering
CHU, B.-T., Mechanical Engineering
CLARK, K., Comparative Literature and Slavic Languages and Literatures
COIFMAN, R. R., Mathematics and Computer Science
COLEMAN, J., Philosophy
CRABTREE, R. H., Chemistry
CROSS, R. J., Jr, Chemistry
CROTHERS, D. M., Chemical Engineering, Chemistry and Molecular Physics and Biochemistry
DAVIS, D., Sociology
DE LA MORA, J. F., Mechanical Engineering
DELLAPORTA, S., Biology
DEMOS, J. P., Religious Studies, Near Eastern Languages and Civilizations, and History
DENNING, M., American Studies
DE ROSE, K., Philosophy
DEVORET, M., Applied Physics and Physics
DIMOCK, W. C., American Studies, English Language and Literature
DONOGHUE, M. J., Ecology and Environmental Biology
DORSEY, J., Computer Science
DOUDNA, J., Molecular Biophysics and Biochemistry
DUDLEY, K., American Studies
DUNCAN, J., Diagnostic Radiology, Electrical Engineering
DUVAL, E. M., French
EIRE, C. M. N., History and Religious Studies
EISENSTAT, S. C., Computer Science
ELIMELECH, M., Chemical Engineering
ENGEL, E., Economics
ENGELMAN, D. M., Molecular Biophysics and Biochemistry
ENGELSTEIN, L., History
ERRINGTON, J. J., Anthropology, East Asian Languages and Literatures
EVENSON, R. E., Economics
FAIR, R. C., Economics
FALLER, J. W., Jr, Chemistry
FARAGHER, J. M., American Studies, History
FEIGELBAUM, J., Computer Science
FEIT, W., Mathematics
FELMAN, S., French and Comparative Literature
FISCHER, M. J., Computer Science
FLAVELL, R. A., Immunobiology and Biology
FLEURY, P., Engineering and Applied Physics, Physics
FOLTZ, W. J., African Studies and Political Science
FOSTER, B. R., Near Eastern Languages and Civilizations
FRAADE, S. D., Religious Studies
FRANK, R., English Language and Literature
FREEDMAN, P. H., History
FRENKEL, I. B., Mathematics
FRY, P. H., English Language and Literature
GADDIS, J. L., History
GAREN, A., Molecular Biophysics and Biochemistry
GARLAND, H., Mathematics
GAUTHIER, J. A., Geology and Geophysics
GEANAKOPLOS, J., Economics

GELERNTNER, D., Computer Science
GERBER, A., Political Science
GHOSH, S., Molecular Biophysics and Biochemistry
GILMORE, G., African American Studies, History
GILROY, P., Sociology and African American Studies
GIRVIN, S. M., Physics and Applied Physics
GLIER, I., Germanic Languages and Literatures
GOLDBERG, P., Economics
GOLDBLATT, H., Medieval Slavic Languages and Literatures
GOLDSMITH, M. H., Biology
GOLDSMITH, T. H., Biology
GOLDSTEIN, L. M., Linguistics
GOMEZ, A., Mechanical Engineering
GONZÁLEZ ECHEVERRÍA, R. O., Hispanic and Comparative Literatures
GOODYEAR, S. S., English Language and Literature
GORDON, R. B., Geology and Geophysics
GORDON, R. W., History, Law
GRAEDEL, T., Geology and Geophysics
GREEN, D., Political Science
GRIFFITH, E. H., African and African American Studies
GRINDLEY, N. D. F., Molecular Biophysics and Biochemistry
GROBER, R., Applied Physics and Physics
GRUENDLER, B., Near Eastern Languages and Civilizations
GUICHARNAUD, J. E., French
GUINNANE, T., Economics and History
GUTAS, D., Near Eastern Languages and Civilizations
HALLER, G. L., Chemical Engineering and Chemistry
HAMADA, K., Economics
HAMILTON, A. D., Chemistry
HAMLIN, C., Germanic Languages and Literatures and Comparative Literature
HAMMER, L., English Language and Literature
HANSEN, V., History
HARMS, R. W., African Studies, History
HARRIES, K., Philosophy
HARRIS, J., Physics
HARSHAV, B., Comparative Literature
HARTIGAN, J. A., Statistics
HARTWIG, J. F., Chemistry
HAYDEN, D., American Studies
HAYES, C., Religious Studies
HENRICH, V. E., Applied Sciences, Physics
HERSEY, G. L., History of Art
HICKEY, L. J., Geology and Geophysics
HILL, A., Anthropology
HOLE, F., Anthropology
HOLFORD, T., Public Health and Statistics
HOLLOWAY, J. S., History
HOLMES, F. L., History
HOMANS, M. B., English, Women's and Gender Studies
HORN, L. R., Linguistics
HORVÁTH, C. G., Chemical Engineering
HUDAK, P., Computer Science
HYMAN, P. E., Modern Jewish History
IACHELLO, F., Physics and Chemistry
INSLER, S., Linguistics
JACKSON, K. D., Spanish and Portuguese
JACOBS, C., Comparative Literature
JACOBSON, M. F., African American Studies, American Studies, History
JAYNES, G. D., Economics, African Studies and African American Studies
JESHION, R., Philosophy
JOHNSON, M. A., Chemistry
JOHNSON, M. K., Psychology
JONES, P. W., Mathematics
JORGENSEN, W. L., Chemistry
JOSEPH, G. M., History
KAGAN, D., Classics and History
KAGAN, S., Classics, Philosophy
KAMENS, E., East Asian Languages and Literatures
KANKEL, D. R., Biology
KARATO, S., Geology and Geophysics
KAVANAGH, T., French
KAZDIN, A. E., Psychology
KEANE, M., Economics
KEIL, F. C., Psychology and Linguistics
KELLY, W. W., Anthropology
KENNEDY, P. M., History
KENNEY, J., Astronomy
KEVLES, D. J., History
KIERNAN, B. F., History
KLEIN, M. J., History of Science and Physics
KLEINER, D. E. E., Classics and History of Art
KLEVORICK, A. K., Economics
KONIGSBERG, W., Molecular Biophysics and Biochemistry
KUTZINSKY, V. M., English Language and Literature, African American Studies and American Studies
LAFRANCE, M., Psychology, Women's and Gender Studies
LANG, S., Mathematics
LARSON, R. B., Astronomy
LAWLER, T., English Language and Literature
LAYTON, B. R., Religious Studies and Near Eastern Languages and Civilizations
LEE, R., Mathematics
LEVIN, R. C., Economics
LIFTON, R., Medicine, Genetics, Molecular Biophysics and Biochemistry
LONG, M. B., Mechanical Engineering and Applied Physics
MA, T.-P., Electrical Engineering and Applied Physics
MCDERMOTT, D. V., Computer Science
MACDOWELL, S. W., Physics
MACNAB, R. M., Molecular Biophysics and Biochemistry
MANDELBROT, B. B., Mathematics
MANLEY, L. G., English Language and Literature
MARCUS, I. G., Jewish History
MARGULIS, G. A., Mathematics
MARMOR, T., Public Management and Political Science
MARTIN, D., Religious Studies
MATTHEWS, J. F., History and Classics
MAYER, E., Anthropology
MAYHEW, D. R., Political Science
MAZZOTTA, G., Italian
MENDELSOHN, R., Economics, Forestry and Enviromental Studies, Management
MENOCAL, M. R., Spanish
MERRIMAN, J. M., History
MILLER, C. L., French, and African and African American Studies
MILLER, G., Molecular Bophysics and Biochemistry
MOCHRIE, S., Physics and Applied Physics
MONTGOMERY, D., History
MOORE, P. B., Chemistry and Molecular Biophysics and Biochemistry
MOOSEKER, M. S., Biology and Cell Biology
MORGAN, R. P., Theory of Music
MORRIS, S., Economics
MORSE, A. S., Computer Science, Electrical Engineering
MUSSER, C., American Studies, Film Studies
NALEBUFF, B., Economics
NARENDRA, K. S., Electrical Engineering
NOVICK, A., Ecology and Environmental Biology
ORNSTON, L. N., Biology
ORSZAG, S. A., Mathematics
OUTKA, G., Philosophy and Christian Ethics
PARK, J., Geology and Geophysics
PARKER, P. D. M., Physics
PATTERSON, A., English Language and Literature
PATTERSON, L., English Language and Literature
PEARCE, D. G., Economics
PETERSON, L. H., English Language and Literature
PEUCKER, B., Germanic Languages and Literatures
PFEFFERLE, L. D., Chemical Engineering
PHILLIPS, P. C. B., Economics and Statistics
PIATETSKI-SHAPIRO, I., Mathematics
PLANTINGA, L. B., History of Music
POLAK, B., Economics
POLLARD, D. B., Statistics and Mathematics
POWELL, J. R., Ecology and Environmental Biology
PROBER, D. E., Applied Physics, Physics
QUINT, D. L., English and Comparative Literature
RAE, D. W., Political Science and Management
RANIS, G., Int. Economics
RAWSON, C., English Language and Literature
READ, N., Physics and Applied Physics
REED, M. A., Electrical Engineering and Applied Physics
REGAN, L. J., Molecular Biophysics and Biochemistry
RILEY, M. A., Ecology and Environmental Biology
ROACH, J. R., Theatre and English
ROBINSON, F. C., English
ROEDER, S., Biology
ROEMER, J. E., Economics, Political Science
ROGERS, J., English Language and Literature
ROKHLIN, V., Computer Science and Mathematics
ROSE-ACKERMAN, S., Jurisprudence, Law and Political Science
ROSENBAUM, J. L., Biology
ROSENBLUTH, F. M., Political Science
ROSNER, D. E., Chemical Engineering
RUDDLE, F. H., Biology and Genetics
RUSSETT, B. M., Political Science and Int. Relations
RUSSETT, C. E., History
RYE, D. M., Geology and Geophysics
SACHDEV, S., Physics and Applied Physics
SALOVEY, P., Epidemiology and Public Health, Psychology
SALTZMAN, W. M., Chemical Engineering
SAMMONS, J. L., Germanic Languages and Literatures
SANDWEISS, J., Physics
SANNEH, L., History, Divinity
SAUNDERS, M., Chemistry
SCARF, H. E., Economics
SCHEFFLER, H. W., Anthropology
SCHEPARTZ, A., Chemistry
SCHMIDT, M. P., Physics
SCHULTZ, M. H., Computer Science
SCHULZ, T. P., Economics and Demography
SCHWARTZ, S. B., History
SCOTT, J. C., Political Science and Anthropology
SEILACHER, A., Geology and Geophysics
SHANKAR, R., Physics and Applied Physics
SHAPIRO, I., Political Science
SHIN, S.-J., Philosophy
SHUBIK, M., Economics
SHULMAN, R. G., Chemistry, Molecular Biophysics and Biochemistry
SILBERSCHATZ, A., Computer Science
SIMPSON, W. K., Near Eastern Languages and Civilizations
SINGER, J. L., Psychology
SIU, H. F., Anthropology
SKINNER, B. J., Geology and Geophysics
SKOWRONEK, S., Political Science and Social Science
SMITH, R. B., Geology and Geophysics
SMITH, S. B., Political Science
SMOOKE, M. D., Mechanical Engineering
SNYDER, M., Molecular Biophysics and Biochemistry
SOFIA, S., Astronomy

SÖLL, D. G., Molecular Biophysics and Biochemistry, Biology and Chemistry
SOMMERFIELD, C. M., Physics
SPENCE, J. D., History
SREENIVASAN, K. R., Mechanical Engineering, Physics and Applied Physics
SRINIVASAN, T. N., Economics
STEITZ, T. A., Chemistry, Molecular Biophysics and Biochemistry
STEPTO, R. B., English, African American Studies, American Studies
STERNBERG, R. J., Psychology and Education
STIMSON, H. M., Linguistics, East Asian Languages and Literatures
STONE, A. D., Physics and Applied Physics
STOUT, H. S., History, Religious Studies and American Studies, American Christianity
STROBEL, S., Molecular Biophysics and Biochemistry
SUMMERS, W. C., History of Medicine and Science, Molecular Biophysics and Biochemistry, Therapeutic Radiology
SUNDER, S., Accounting, Economics and Finance
SZELENYI, I., Sociology
SZWED, J. F., Anthropology, African and African American Studies and American Studies
THOMPSON, R. F., African American Studies and History of Art
TREAT, J., East Asian Languages and Literatures
TRUMPENER, K., English and Comparative Literature
TULLY, J. C., Chemistry, Physics and Applied Physics
TUREKIAN, K. K., Geology and Geophysics
TURNER, F. M., History
TURNER, H. A., Jr, History
UDRY, C., Economics
URRY, C. M., Physics and Astrophysics
VACCARO, P. H., Chemistry
VAISNYS, J. R., Ecology and Environmental Biology, Electrical Engineering
VALENTINE, A. M., Chemistry
VALESIO, P., Italian
VALIS, N., Spanish and Portuguese
VAN ALTENA, W. F., Astronomy
VENCLOVA, T., Slavic Languages and Literatures
VERONIS, G., Geology and Geophysics
VRBA, E. S., Geology and Geophysics
WAGNER, A. R., Psychology
WAGNER, G. P., Ecology and Environmental Biology
WALZ, J. Y., Chemical Engineering
WARD, D. C., Genetics, Molecular Biophysics and Biochemistry
WARNER, J. H., American Studies, History, History of Medicine
WATTS, D. P., Anthropology
WEINSTEIN, S., Religious Studies, Buddhist Studies and East Asian Languages and Literatures
WEISS, H., Near Eastern Archaeology, Near Eastern Languages and Civilizations, and Anthropology
WELSH, A., English Language and Literature
WETTLAUFER, J., Geology and Geophysics, Physics
WEXLER, L., American Studies
WHEELER, S., Law and the Social Sciences
WIKSTROM, L. L., Chemical Engineering
WILSON, R., Religious Studies
WINTER, J., History
WOOD, J. L., Chemistry
WOODALL, J. M., Electrical Engineering
WRIGHT, C. M., History of Music
WRIGHTSON, K., History
WYMAN, R. J., Biology
WYNN, K., Psychology
YEAZELL, R. B., English Language and Literature
ZELLER, M. E., Physics
ZIEGLER, F. E., Chemistry
ZIGLER, E. F., Psychology
ZILM, K. W., Chemistry
ZINN, R. J., Astronomy
ZUCKER, S. W., Computer Science and Electrical Engineering
ZUCKERMAN, G. J., Mathematics

Divinity School:

ADAMS, M. MC., Historical Theology
ATTRIDGE, H. W., New Testament
BARTLETT, D. L., Preaching and Christian Communication
COLLINS, A. Y., Old Testament Interpretation and Criticism
DITTES, J. E., Pastoral Theology and Psychology
FARLEY, M. A., Christian Ethics
FASSLER, M. E., Music History and Liturgy
KELSEY, D. H., Theology
MURRAY, T., Organ
OGLETREE, T. W., Theological Ethics
OUTKA, G., Philosophy and Christian Ethics
SANNEH, L. O., Missions and World Christianity and History
SPINKS, B. D., Liturgical Studies
STOUT, H. S., American Religious History
VOLF, M., Systematic Theology
WILSON, R. R., Old Testament and Religious Studies

School of Drama:

BUNDY, J.

School of Forestry and Environmental Studies:

ASHTON, M. S., Silviculture and Forest Ecology
BERLYN, G. P., Anatomy and Physiology of Trees
BREWER, G. D., Resource Policy and Management
BURCH, W. R., Jr, Natural Resource Management
DOVE, M. R., Social Ecology
ESTY, D. C., Environmental Law and Policy
GRAEDEL, T. E., Industrial Ecology
GREGOIRE, T. G., Forest Management
KELLERT, S. R., Social Ecology
LYONS, J. R., Natural Resource Management
MENDELSOHN, R., Forest Policy
MONTAGNINI, F., Tropical Forestry
OLIVER, C. D., Forest Policy
REPETTO, R., Economics and Sustainable Devt
SCHMITZ, O. J., Population and Community Ecology
SICCIAMA, T. G., Forest Ecology
SPETH, J. G., Environmental Policy and Sustainable Devt
WARGO, J. P., Environmental Risk Analysis, Political Science

School of Law:

ACKERMAN, B. A., Law and Political Science
AMAR, A. R., Law
AYRES, I., Law
BALKIN, J. M., Constitutional Law and the First Amendment
BRILMAYER, L., Int. Law
BURT, R. A., Law
CARTER, S. L., Law
CHUA, A. L., Law
COLEMAN, J. L., Jurisprudence and Philosophy
CURTIS, D. E., Law
DALTON, H. L., Law
DAMASKA, M. R., Law
DAYS, D. S., III, Law
DEUTSCH, J. G., Law
DIGNAM, B., Law
DUKE, S. B., Law
ELLICKSON, R. C., Property and Urban Law
ESTY, D. C., Environmental Law and Policy
FISS, O. M., Law
GEWIRTZ, P. D., Constitutional Law
GOLDSTEIN, A. S., Law
GORDON, R. W., Law and Legal History
GRAETZ, M. J., Law
HANSMANN, H. B., Law
KAHAN, D. M., Law
KAHN, P. W., Law and the Humanities
KLEVORICK, A. K., Law and Economics
KOH, H. H., Int. Law
LANGBEIN, J. H., Law and Legal History
LUCHT, C. L., Law
MASHAW, J. L., Law
PETERS, J. K., Law
POTTENGER, J. L., Law
PRIEST, G. L., Law and Economics
REISMAN, W. M., Int. Law
RESNIK, J., Law
ROMANO, R., Law
ROSE, C. M., Law and Organization
ROSE-ACKERMAN, S., Jurisprudence (Law School and Dept of Political Science)
RUBENFELD, J., Law
SCHUCK, P. H., Law
SCHULTZ, V., Law and Social Sciences
SIEGEL, R., Law
SIMON, J. G., Law
SOLOMON, R. A., Law
STITH, K., Law
WEDGWOOD, R., Law
WHITMAN, J. Q., Comparative and Foreign Law
WIZNER, S., Law
YOSHINO, K., Law

Yale School of Management:

BRACKEN, P., Management and Political Science
BREWER, G. D., Resource Policy and Management
CHEN, ZH., Finance
CHEVALIER, J. A., Finance and Economics
DHAR, R., Marketing
FEINSTEIN, J., Economics
GARSTKA, S., Practice of Management
GARTEN, J. E., Practice of Int. Trade and Finance
GOETZMANN, W., Management and Finance Studies
IBBOTSON, R., Practice of Finance
INGERSOLL, J. E., Jr, Int. Trade and Finance
KAPLAN, E., Management Sciences, Public Health
LI, L., Production Management
LÓPEZ-DE-SILANES, F., Finance and Economics
MACAVOY, P., Management Studies
MARMOR, T. R., Public Policy and Management
NALEBUFF, B., Economics and Management
OSTER, S. M., Management and Entrepreneurship
POLAK, B., Economics and Management
RAE, D. W., Management
ROUWENHORST, K. G., Finance
SCOTT MORTON, F. M., Economics
SEN, S. K., Organization, Management and Marketing
SHUBIK, M. S., Mathematical Institutional Economics
SPIEGEL, M., Finance
SUNDER, S., Accounting, Economics and Finance
SWERSEY, A. J., Operations Research
VROOM, V. H., Organization and Management, Psychology
WELCH, I., Finance
WITTINK, D. R., Management and Marketing

School of Medicine:

AGHAJANIAN, G. K., Psychiatry and Pharmacology
ANDERSON, K. S., Pharmacology
ANDIMAN, W. A., Paediatrics and Epidemiology and Public Health
ANDREWS, N. W., Cell Biology, Microbial Pathogenesis

ANDRIOLE, V. T., Internal Medicine
ANYAN, W. R., Paediatrics
ARONSON, P. S., Internal Medicine and Cellular and Molecular Physiology
ASKENASE, P. W., Internal Medicine
BAKER, M. D., Emergency Medicine, Paediatrics
BALTIMORE, R. S., Paediatrics, Infectious Diseases and Epidemiology and Public Health
BARASH, P. G., Anaesthesiology
BARNSTABLE, C. J., Neurobiology, Ophthalmology and Visual Science
BARON, R., Orthopaedics and Rehabilitation, Internal Medicine and Cell Biology
BARTOSHUK, L. M., Surgery
BATSFORD, W. P., Internal Medicine
BEARDSLEY, G. P., Paediatric Haematology and Pharmacology
BEHRMAN, H. R., Obstetrics and Gynaecology
BELSKY, J. L., Internal Medicine
BERLINER, N., Genetics and Internal Medicine
BIA, F. J., Medicine and Laboratory Medicine
BIA, M. J., Medicine
BINDER, H. J., Cellular and Molecular Physiology, Digestive Diseases and Internal Medicine
BLATT, S. J., Psychiatry and Psychology
BOLOGNIA, J. L., Dermatology
BOOSS, J., Neurology and Laboratory Medicine
BORON, W. F., Cellular and Molecular Physiology
BOTHWELL, A., Immunobiology
BOTTOMLY, H. K., Immunobiology and Molecular, Cellular and Developmental Biology
BOULPAEP, E. L., Cellular and Molecular Physiology
BOWERS, M. B., Jr, Psychiatry
BOYER, J. L., Digestive Diseases, Internal Medicine
BRACKEN, M. B., Epidemiology and Public Health, Chronic Disease Epidemiology, Neurology
BRASH, D. E., Genetics, Therapeutic Radiology
BRAVERMAN, I. M., Dermatology
BROADUS, A. E., Internal Medicine and Cellular and Molecular Physiology
BROWN, T. H., Cellular and Molecular Physiology, Psychology
BUCALA, R., Medicine
BUNNEY, B. S., Psychiatry and Pharmacology
BURRELL, M. I., Diagnostic Radiology
BURROW, G. N., Obstetrics and Gynaecology
BYRNE, T. N., Neurology and Medicine
CABIN, H., Internal Medicine
CADMAN, E. C., Internal Medicine
CAPLAN, M., Cellular and Molecular Physiology
CARPENTER, T. O., Endocrinology, Paediatrics
CARTER, D., Pathology
CENTRELLA, M., Surgery
CHAMBERS, S. K., Obstetrics and Gynaecology
CHANDLER, W. K., Cellular and Molecular Physiology
CHASE, H. S., Jr, Medicine
CHENG, Y.-C., Pharmacology
CHOI, Y., Laboratory Medicine, Pathology
CLEARY, J. P., Internal Medicine
CLEMAN, M., Internal Medicine
COCA-PRADOS, M., Ophthalmology and Visual Science
COHEN, L. B., Cellular and Molecular Physiology
COHEN, L. S., Internal Medicine
COLEMAN, D., Medicine
COLLINS, J. G., Anaesthesiology
COOLEY, L., Cell Biology, Genetics
COONEY, L. M., Jr, Internal Medicine
COSTA, J. C., Pathology
CRAFT, J., Immunobiology, Medicine
CRESSWELL, P., Immunobiology
CULLEN, M. R., Medicine, Occupational and Environmental Medicine, Public Health
CURTIS, A. M., Diagnostic Radiology
DANNIES, P. S., Pharmacology
DAW, N. W., Ophthalmology and Visual Science
DE CAMILLI, P. V., Cell Biology
DEISSEROTH, A. B., Internal Medicine
DE LUCA, V. A., Internal Medicine
D'ESCOPO, N. D., Internal Medicine
DE VITA, V. T., Internal Medicine
DI MAIO, D., Genetics
DOBBINS, J. W., Internal Medicine
DONABEDIAN, R. K., Laboratory Medicine
DU BOIS, A. B., Epidemiology and Public Health, and Cellular and Molecular Physiology
DUFFY, T. P., Internal Medicine
DUNCAN, C. C., Neurosurgery and Paediatrics
DUNCAN, J., Diagnostic Radiology
EDBERG, S. C., Internal Medicine, Laboratory Medicine
EHRENKRANZ, R. A., Neonatology, Obstetrics and Gynaecology, Paediatrics
EHRENWERTH, J., Anaesthesiology
EHRLICH, B., Pharmacology and Cellular and Molecular Biology
ELEFTERIADES, J. A., Surgery
ELIAS, J. A., Medicine
FARBER, L. R., Internal Medicine
FERRO-NOVICK, S., Cell Biology
FINKELSTEIN, F. O., Internal Medicine
FISCH, D., Epidemiology of Microbial Diseases
FISCHER, D. S., Internal Medicine
FISCHER, J. J., Therapeutic Radiology
FLAVELL, R., Immunobiology, Molecular, Cellular and Developmental Biology
FLOCH, M. H., Internal Medicine
FLYNN, S. D., Pathology, Surgery
FORBUSH, B., III, Cellular and Molecular Physiology
FORGET, B. G., Medicine and Genetics
FORMAN, B. H., Internal Medicine
FORREST, J. N., Jr, Medicine
FRIEDLAENDER, G. E., Orthopaedics and Rehabilitation
FRIEDLAND, G. H., Epidemiology, Medicine
GALÁN, J., Cell Biology, Microbial Pathogenesis
GEIBEL, J. P., Surgery
GENEL, M., Paediatrics
GHOSH, S., Immunobiology, Molecular Biophysics and Biochemistry, Molecular, Cellular and Developmental Biology
GIEBISCH, G. H., Cellular and Molecular Physiology
GIFFORD, R. H., Internal Medicine
GLAZER, P. M., Therapeutic Radiology and Genetics
GLICKMAN, M. G., Diagnostic Radiology and Surgery
GOLDMAN-RAKIC, P., Neurobiology, Neurology
GOLDSTEIN, S. A. N., Cellular and Molecular Physiology, Paediatrics
GONZALEZ, C., Ophthalmology and Visual Science, Paediatrics
GORE, J. C., Diagnostic Radiology
GORELICK, F., Internal Medicine, Digestive Diseases and Cell Biology
GREEN, B., Surgery
GREENFELD, D. G., Psychiatry
GREER, C., Neurobiology, Neurosurgery
GRIFFITH, B., Laboratory Medicine
GRIFFITH, E. E. H., Psychiatry
GROSS, I., Neonatology, Obstetrics and Gynaecology, Paediatrics
GROSZMANN, R. J., Digestive Diseases, Internal Medicine
GUSBERG, R. J., Surgery
HAFFTY, B. G., Therapeutic Radiology
HAYSLETT, J. P., Medicine
HEALD, P. W., Dermatology
HEBERT, S. C., Cellular and Molecular Physiology, Medicine
HENDLER, E. D., Internal Medicine
HENINGER, G. R., Psychiatry
HERBERT, P. N., Internal Medicine
HIERHOLZER, W. J., Internal Medicine and Epidemiology
HINES, R. L., Anaesthesiology
HOCKFIELD, S., Neurology
HOFFER, P. B., Diagnostic Radiology
HOFFMAN, J. F., Cellular and Molecular Physiology
HOLBROOK, N. J., Geriatrics
HOLFORD, T. R., Epidemiology and Public Health
HORWICH, A. L., Genetics and Paediatrics
HOSTETTER, M. K., Paediatrics
IANNINI, P. B., Internal Medicine
INNIS, R. B., Psychiatry and Pharmacology
INOUYE, S. K., Geriatrics
INSOGNA, K. L., Internal Medicine
JACOBS, S. C., Psychiatry
JACOBY, R. O., Comparative Medicine
JAFFE, C. C., Diagnostic Radiology and Internal Medicine
JAMIESON, J. D., Cell Biology
JANEWAY, C., Immunobiology and Molecular, Cellular and Developmental Biology
JATLOW, P. I., Laboratory Medicine and Psychiatry
JOINER, K. A., Internal Medicine, Cell Biology and Infectious Diseases
JOKL, P., Orthopaedics and Rehabilitation
KACZMAREK, L. K., Cellular and Molecular Physiology and Pharmacology
KAETZ, H. W., Internal Medicine
KAIN, Z., Anaesthesiology, Paediatrics
KANTOR, F. S., Internal Medicine
KAPADIA, C. R., Internal Medicine
KASHGARIAN, M., Pathology and Molecular, Cellular and Developmental Biology
KASL, S. V., Chronic Disease Epidemiology
KAVATHAS, P., Genetics, Immunobiology, Laboratory Medicine
KELLER, M. S., Diagnostic Radiology and Paediatrics
KENNEY, J. D., Internal Medicine
KICKBUSCH, I. S., Epidemiology and Public Health
KIDD, K. K., Genetics, Molecular, Cellular and Developmental Biology, and Psychiatry
KIER, E. L., Diagnostic Radiology
KIM, J. H., Pathology
KINDER, B. K., Surgery
KLIGER, A. S., Internal Medicine
KOCSIS, J. D., Neurology
KOPF, G. S., Surgery
KOSTEN, T. R., Psychiatry
KRUMHOLZ, H. M., Epidemiology and Public Health, Internal Medicine
KRYSTAL, J. H., Psychiatry
LAMOTTE, R. H., Anaesthesiology
LANDRY, M., Laboratory Medicine
LANNIN, D. R., Surgery
LAWSON, J. P., Diagnostic Radiology, Orthopaedics and Rehabilitation
LEADERER, B. P., Public Health, Environmental Studies
LEDER, S. B., Surgery
LEFFELL, D. J., Dermatology
LENTZ, T. L., Cell Biology
LESSER, R. L., Neurology, Ophthalmology and Visual Science
LEVANTHAL, J. M., Nursing, Paediatrics and Child Study Center
LEVINE, R. A., Laboratory Medicine
LEVINE, R. J., Internal Medicine
LEVITIN, H., Internal Medicine
LEVY, L. L., Neurology
LEVY, S. R., Neurology
LIFTON, R. P., Medicine and Genetics

LISTER, G., Jr, Paediatrics and Anaesthesiology
LORBER, M. I., Surgery
LYTTON, B., Surgery, Urology
MCCARTHY, P., Paediatrics, Nursing
MCCARTHY, S., Diagnostic Radiology
MCCLENNAN, B. L., Diagnostic Radiology
MCCORMICK, D., Neurology
MCGLASHAN, T. H., Psychiatry
MCMAHON-PRATT, D., Epidemiology of Microbial Diseases
MCPHEDRAN, P., Laboratory Medicine and Internal Medicine
MADRI, J. A., Pathology
MAHNENSMITH, R., Medicine
MAHONEY, M. J., Genetics, and Obstetrics and Gynaecology, and Paediatrics
MAKUCH, R. W., Epidemiology and Public Health
MALAWISTA, S. E., Medicine
MARCHESI, S. L., Pathology and Laboratory Medicine
MARCHESI, V. T., Pathology, Cell Biology
MARIEB, N. J., Internal Medicine
MARKS, L. E., Environmental Health Sciences
MARSH, J. C., Internal Medicine
MATTHAY, R. A., Medicine
MAZURE, C. M., Psychiatry
MELLMAN, I. S., Cell Biology and Immunobiology
MENT, L. R., Paediatrics and Neurology
MERIKANGAS, K. R., Chronic Disease Epidemiology, Psychiatry
MERSON, M. H., Epidemiology and Public Health
MILLER, I. G., Jr Epidemiology and Public Health, Molecular Biophysics and Biochemistry, Paediatrics
MILLER, P. L., Anaesthesiology
MILSTONE, L. M., Dermatology
MOCZYDLOWSKI, E. G., Cellular and Molecular Physiology, Pharmacology
MODLIN, I. M., Surgery
MOGHADDAM, B., Neurobiology, Psychiatry
MOOSEKER, M., Cell Biology
MORROW, J. S., Molecular, Cellular and Developmental Biology, Pathology
MOSER, M., Internal Medicine
MOYER, M. S., Paediatrics
NAIM, A., Psychiatry
NAIR, S., Internal Medicine
NATH, R., Therapeutic Radiology
NOVICK, P., Cell Biology
O'MALLEY, S. S., Psychiatry
PATTON, C. L., Epidemiology of Microbial Diseases
PELKER, R. R., Orthopaedics and Rehabilitation
PERILLIE, P. E., Internal Medicine
PERSING, J. A., Surgery and Neurosurgery
PESCHEL, R. E., Therapeutic Radiology
PEZZIMENTI, J. F., Internal Medicine
PIEPMEIER, J. M., Neurosurgery
POBER, J. S., Pathology, Dermatology and Immunobiology
QUAGLIARELLO, V. J., Medicine
RABINOVICI, R., Surgery
RADDING, C. M., Genetics and Molecular Biophysics and Biochemistry
RAFFERTY, T. D., Anaesthesiology
RAKIC, P., Neurology and Neurobiology
RAPPEPORT, J., Internal Medicine
RASTEGAR, A., Medicine
REDMOND, D. E., Jr, Psychiatry and Neurosurgery
RENSHAW, T., Orthopaedics and Rehabilitation
RICHARDS, F. F., Internal Medicine
RISCH, H. A., Chronic Disease Epidemiology
ROCKWELL, S. C., Pharmacology, Therapeutic Radiology
ROEDER, S., Genetics, Molecular, Cellular and Developmental Biology
ROSE, J. K., Pathology and Cell Biology
ROSENBAUM, S., Anaesthesiology
ROSENFIELD, A. T., Diagnostic Radiology
ROSENHECK, R. A., Epidemiology and Public Health, Psychiatry
ROTH, R. H., Jr, Psychiatry and Pharmacology
ROUNSAVILLE, B. J., Psychiatry
RUDDLE, F., Genetics, Molecular, Cellular and Developmental Biology
RUDDLE, N. H., Epidemiology of Microbial Diseases, Immunobiology
RUDNICK, G., Pharmacology
SACKS, F. L., Internal Medicine
SANTOS-SACCHI, J., Surgery
SARTORELLI, A. C., Pharmacology
SASAKI, C. T., Surgery
SCHATZ, D., Immunobiology
SCHLESSINGER, J., Pharmacology
SCHOEN, R., Internal Medicine
SCHOTTENFELD, R. S., Psychiatry
SCHWARTZ, I. R., Surgery
SCHWARTZ, P. E., Obstetrics and Gynaecology
SEASHORE, J. H., Surgery
SEASHORE, M. R., Genetics, Paediatrics
SEGAL, S. S., Cellular and Molecular Physiology
SESSA, W. C., Pharmacology
SHAPIRO, E. D., Epidemiology and Public Health, Paediatrics, Nursing
SHAW, C., Diagnostic Radiology
SHAYWITZ, A. E., Neurology, Paediatrics
SHAYWITZ, S. E., Paediatrics
SHERTER, C. B., Internal Medicine
SHERWIN, R. S., Internal Medicine
SHULMAN, G. I., Internal Medicine, and Cellular and Molecular Physiology
SIEGEL, N. J., Medicine, Paediatrics
SIGWORTH, F. J., Cellular and Molecular Physiology
SILVERMAN, D., Anaesthesiology
SINATRA, R., Anaesthesiology
SIVARAJAN, M., Anaesthesiology
SLAYMAN, C. L., Cellular and Molecular Physiology
SLAYMAN, C. W., Genetics and Cellular and Molecular Physiology
SLEDGE, W. H., Psychiatry
SMITH, B. R., Internal Medicine, Laboratory Medicine, Paediatrics
SNOW, D. L., Psychiatry
SNYDER, E. L., Laboratory Medicine
SPENCER, D. D., Neurosurgery
SPENCER, S. S., Neurology
SPIRO, H. M., Internal Medicine
STERN, D. F., Pathology
STITT, J. T., Cellular and Molecular Physiology, Epidemiology and Environmental Health Sciences
STRITTMATTER, S. M., Neurobiology, Neurology
SULAVIK, S. B., Internal Medicine
SUMMERS, W. C., Therapeutic Radiology, Molecular Biophysics and Biochemistry, and Genetics
SUMPIO, B. E., Surgery
TAMBORLANE, W. V., Paediatrics
TATTERSALL, P., Laboratory Medicine and Genetics
TAYLOR, K. J., Diagnostic Radiology
TIGELAAR, R. E., Dermatology and Immunobiology
TINETTI, M., Medicine, Epidemiology and Public Health
TOULOUKIAN, R. J., Paediatrics, Surgery
TRAUBE, M., Digestive Diseases, Internal Medicine
UDELSMAN, R., Surgery
ULLU, E., Cell Biology, Medicine
VAN DEN POL, A., Neurosurgery
WACKERS, F. J., Diagnostic Radiology and Medicine
WALSH, T. J., Neurology, Ophthalmology and Visual Science
WARD, D. C., Genetics, Molecular Biophysics and Biochemistry
WARDLAW, S. C., Laboratory Medicine
WARREN, G., Cell Biology
WAXMAN, S. G., Neurology, Neurobiology
WEISS, R. M., Surgery, Urology
WEISSMAN, S. M., Genetics and Internal Medicine
WESTCOTT, J. A., Diagnostic Radiology
WHITE, R. I., Jr, Diagnostic Radiology
WRIGHT, F. S., Internal Medicine and Cellular and Molecular Physiology
ZARET, B. L., Diagnostic Radiology, Medicine
ZELTERMAN, D., Epidemiology and Public Health
ZONANA, H. V., Psychiatry

School of Music:

AGAWU, K., Theory of Music
AKI, S., Violin
BERMAN, B., Piano
BRESNICK, M. I., Composition
CHOOKASIAN, L., Voice and Opera
DUFFY, T. C.
FASSLER, M. E.
FORTE, A., Theory of Music
FRANK, C., Piano
GOTTLIEB, G., Percussion
HARTH, S., Violin
HAWKSHAW, P., History of Music
LADERMAN, E., Composition
LEVINE, J., Viola
MURRAY, T., Organ
OUNDJIAN, P., Violin
PARISOT, A. S.
REPHANN, R.
ROSAND, E., History of Music
ROSEMAN, R., Oboe
RUFF, W. H., Jr.
SHIFRIN, D., Clarinet
SMITH, L. L.
SWALLOW, J. W., Brass and Ensemble Performance
TIRRO, F. P.
YARICK-CROSS, D., Voice

School of Nursing:

BURST, H. V., Nursing
DIERS, D. K., Nursing
DIXON, J. K., Nursing
FUNK, M., Nursing
GILLISS, C. L., Nursing
GREY, M., Nursing
KNAFL, K. A., Nursing
KNOPF, M. T., Oncology Nursing
KRAUSS, J. B., Nursing
MILONE-NUZZO, P., Nursing
MINARKI, P., Nursing
WILLIAMS, A., Nursing

DELAWARE

DELAWARE STATE UNIVERSITY

1200 N. Dupont Highway, Dover, DE 19901-2277

Telephone: (302) 857-6290

Internet: www.desu.edu

Founded 1891

Pres.: CLAIBOURNE D. SMITH (acting)
Provost and Vice-Pres. for Academic Affairs: Dr HARRY L. WILLIAMS
Vice-Pres. for Business and Finance: DONALD L. HENRY
Vice-Pres. for Devt and Univ. Relations: CAROLYN S. CURRY
Vice-Pres. for Enrollment Management and Student Affairs: (vacant)
Dean of Graduate Studies and Research: Dr HAZELL REED
Registrar: GLENN T. PARKER
Dir of Admissions: LAWITA G. CHEATHAM
Head Librarian: VIVIAN H. ROYSTER

Library of 205,400 vols, 22,000 microbooks, 12,635 microform reels, 14,871 audio-visual items, 3,367 bound periodicals

Number of teachers: 168
Number of students: 3,200

DEANS

College of Agriculture and Related Sciences: Dr KENNETH W. BELL
College of Education and Sport Sciences: Prof. DORIS E. WOOLEDGE (acting)
College of Humanities and Social Sciences: Prof. BRADLEY SKELCHER
School of Management: Prof. PATRICK R. LIVERPOOL
School of Professional Studies: Dr JACQUELYNE W. GORUM

GOLDEY-BEACOM COLLEGE

4701 Limestone Rd, Wilmington, DE 19808
Telephone: (302) 998-8814
E-mail: admissions@gbc.edu
Internet: www.gbc.edu

Founded 1886 as Wilmington Commercial College; present name 1951
Private control
Academic year: August to August
Pres.: MOHAMMAD ILYAS
Dean of Admissions: (vacant)
Dean of Information Technology: EMILY JACKSON

Areas of study: accounting, accounting and information systems, business admin., computer information systems.

UNIVERSITY OF DELAWARE

Newark, DE 19716
Telephone: (302) 831-2000
Internet: www.udel.edu

Founded 1833 from the Newark Acad. founded in 1765; chartered 1769
Pres.: Dr DAVID P. ROSELLE
Provost: Dr DANIEL RICH (acting)
Exec. Vice-Pres. and Univ. Treas.: DAVID E. HOLLOWELL
Vice-Pres. and Univ. Sec.: PIERRE D. HAYWARD
Vice-Pres. for Admin.: Dr MAXINE COLM
Vice-Pres. for Devt and Alumni Relations: ROBERT R. DAVIS
Vice-Pres. for Information Technologies: SUSAN J. FOSTER
Vice-Pres. and Univ. Treas.: STEPHEN M. GRIMBLE
Dir of Libraries: SUSAN BRYNTESON

Library: 2.6m. vols, 3.3m. microforms
Number of teachers: 1,089
Number of students: 21,289

DEANS

College of Agriculture and Natural Resources: Prof. ROBIN MORGAN
College of Arts and Science: Prof. TOM APPLE
College of Business and Economics: Prof. MICHAEL J. GINZBERG
College of Engineering: Prof. ERIC W. KALER
College of Health and Nursing Sciences: Prof. BETTY J. PAULANKA
College of Human Services, Education and Public Policy: Prof. TIMOTHY K. BARENKOV (acting)
College of Marine Studies: Dr NANCY M. TARGETT

PROFESSORS

ABRAMS, B. A., Economics
ACKERMAN, B. P., Psychology, Linguistics
ADAMS, F., Philosophy
ADVANI, S. G., Mechanical Engineering
AGARWAL, S. K., Mechanical Engineering
AGUIRRE, B. E., Sociology and Criminal Justice
ALCHON, S. A., History
ALLEN, H. E., Civil Engineering
ALLMENDINGER, D. F., Jr, History
AMER, P. D., Computer and Information Sciences, Electrical and Computer Engineering
AMES, D. L., Urban Affairs and Public Policy, Geography
ANDERSEN, M. L., Sociology and Criminal Justice, Women's Studies
ANDERSON, L. G., Marine Studies, Economics
ANDREWS, D. C., English
ANGELL, T. S., Mathematical Sciences
ARCE, G. R., Electrical and Computer Engineering, Marine Studies
ARDIS, A. L., English
ARENSON, M. A., Music
ATHANASSOGLOU-KALLMYER, N., Art History
BACH, R. D., Chemistry and Biochemistry
BACHMAN, R, Sociology and Criminal Justice
BADIEY, M., Marine Studies
BARNEKOV, T. K., Urban Affairs and Public Policy
BAROUDI, J., Accounting and Management Information Systems
BARR, S. M., Bartol Research Institute
BARTEAU, M. A., Chemical Engineering, Chemistry and Biochemistry
BEAR, G. G., Education
BEASLEY, J. C., English
BEEBE, T. P., Jr, Chemistry and Biochemistry
BELLAMY, D. P., Mathematical Sciences
BENNETT, J., English
BENNETT, R. B., English
BERIS, A. N., Chemical Engineering
BERNHARDT, S. A., Writing
BERNSTEIN, J. A., History
BEST, J., Sociology and Criminal Justice
BIEBER, J. W., Bartol Research Institute
BIEDERMAN, K., Finance
BILINSKY, Y., Political Science and International Relations
BINDER-MACLEOD, S. A., Physical Therapy
BLITS, J. H., Education, Political Science and Int. Relations
BOLTON, R. C., Art
BONCELET, C. G., Electrical and Computer Engineering
BOULD, S., Sociology and Criminal Justice, Individual and Family Studies, Women's Studies
BOYER, J. S., Marine Biochemistry and Biophysics, Plant and Soil Sciences
BOYLAN, A. M., History, Women's Studies
BRAUN, T. E. D., Comparative Literature, Foreign Languages and Literatures
BRICKHOUSE, N., Education
BRILL, T. B., Chemistry and Biochemistry
BROADBRIDGE, P., Mathematical Sciences
BROCK, D. H., English
BROCKMANN, R. J., English
BROWN, F., English
BROWN, H. E., Art, Art Conservation, Art History, Museum Studies
BROWN, J. L., Foreign Languages and Literatures
BROWN, R. F., Philosophy
BROWN, R. P., Theatre
BROWN, S. D., Chemistry and Biochemistry
BROWNING, J. E., Theatre
BROWNING, W. L., Theatre
BUCHANAN, T. S., Mechanical Engineering
BUCKMASTER, D. A., Accounting and Management Information Systems
BURMEISTER, J. L., Chemistry and Biochemistry
BURNSIDE, J., Animal and Food Sciences, Biological Sciences
BUTKIEWICZ, J. L., Economics
BYRNE, J. M., Urban Affairs and Public Policy, Marine Studies
CALLAHAN, D. F., History
CALLAHAN, R. A., History
CAMPBELL, L. L., Biological Sciences
CARBERRY, M. S., Computer and Information Sciences, Linguistics
CARON, D. M., Entomology and Applied Ecology
CAROTHERS, M. L., Art
CARR, C. L., Music
CARROLL, R. B., Plant and Soil Sciences
CARSON, D., Biological Sciences
CASE, J., Computer and Information Sciences
CAVINESS, B. F., Computer and Information Sciences, Mathematical Sciences
CHAJES, M. J., Civil and Environmental Engineering
CHAPMAN, H. P., Art History
CHEN, J. G., Chemical Engineering, Materials Science and Engineering
CHOU, T. W., Mechanical Engineering
CHUI, S.-T., Bartol Research Institute
CHURCH, T. M., Marine Studies, Chemistry and Biochemistry
CICALA, G. A., Psychology
CINCIN-SAIN, B., Marine Studies, Political Science and International Relations, Urban Affairs and Public Policy
COGBURN, L. A., Animal and Food Sciences
COHEN, L. H., Psychology
COLE, P., Linguistics
COLLINS, G. E., Computer and Information Sciences
COLLINS, N. E., Bioresources Engineering
COLMAN, R. F., Chemistry and Biochemistry
COLTON, D. L., Mathematical Sciences
COOK-IOANNIDIS, P., Mathematical Sciences
CORNELL, H. V., Biological Sciences
COTUNGA, N., Nutrition and Diatetics
COURTRIGHT, J. A., Communications
CURTIS, J. C., History
CURTIS, L. A., Biological Sciences, Marine Studies
CUSTER, J. F., Anthropology
DAVIS, S., Political Science and International Relations
DAVISON, R. A., English
DAWSON, C., English
DEAN, J. M., English
DEBESSAY, A., Accounting and Management Information Systems
DEINER, P. L., Individual and Family Studies
DE LEON, P. A., Biological Sciences
DEL FATTORE, J., English, Legal Studies
DEMICCIO, F. J., Hotel, Restaurant and Institutional Management
DENSON, C. D., Chemical Engineering
DENTEL, S. K., Civil and Environmental Engineering
DEXTER, S. C., Marine Studies, Materials Science and Engineering
DHURJATI, P., Chemical Engineering
DI LORENZO, T. M., Psychology
DIRENZO, G., Sociology and Criminal Justice
DOHMS, J. E., Immunology and Microbiology
DONALDSON-EVANS, M. P., Foreign Languages and Literatures
DOREN, D. J., Chemistry and Biochemistry
DUGGAN, L. G. J., History
DURBIN, P. T., Philosophy, Urban Affairs and Public Policy
DYBOWSKI, C. R., Chemistry and Biochemistry
EBERT, G. L., Mathematical Sciences
EISENBERGER, R. W., Psychology
ELIAS, J. G., Electrical and Computer Engineering
ELSON, C. M., Legal Studies, Corporate Governance
EPIFANIO, C., Marine Studies
ERMANN, M. D., Sociology and Criminal Justice
EVANS, D. H., Chemistry and Biochemistry
EVENSON, P. A., Bartol Research Institute
FAGHRI, A., Civil and Environmental Engineering
FANELLI-KUCZMARSKI, M. T., Nutrition and Diatetics
FARACH-CARSON, M. C., Biological Sciences
FERRETTI, R., Education, Psychology
FITZMAURICE, C., Theatre
FLYNN, P. D., English
FOU, C.-M., Physics and Astronomy
FRETT, J. J., Plant and Soil Sciences
FUHRMANN, J. J., Plant and Soil Sciences

GAERTNER, S. L., Psychology
GAFFNEY, P. M., Marine Studies
GAISSER, T. K., Bartol Research Institute
GALLAGHER, J. L., Marine Studies
GALVIN, M. E., Materials Science and Engineering
GAO, G.-R., Electrical and Computer Engineering
GARLAND, H., Business Administration
GARVINE, R. W., Marine Studies, Civil and Environmental Engineering
GATES, B. T., English, Women's Studies
GEHRLEIN, W. V., Business Administration
GELB, J., Jr, Animal and Food Sciences
GEMPESHAW, C. M., II, Economics, Food and Resource Economics
GIBSON, A. E., Art History
GILBERT, R. P., Mathematical Sciences, Marine Studies, Computer and Information Sciences
GILLESPIE, J. W., Jr, Materials Science and Engineering
GINZBERG, M. J., Accounting and Management Information Systems, Business Administration
GLASS, B. P., Geology, Marine Studies
GLUTTING, J. J., Education
GLYDE, H. R., Physics and Astronomy
GOLDSTEIN, L. F., Political Science and Int. Relations
GOLINKOFF, R. M., Education, Linguistics, Psychology
GOODMAN, S., English
GREEN, P., Plant and Soil Sciences
GREENBERG, M. D., Mechanical Engineering
GRIFFITHS, L., Animal and Food Sciences
GRUBB, F., Economics, History
HAAS, K. C., Sociology and Criminal Justice
HABER, C., History
HADJIPANAYIS, G., Physics and Astronomy
HALIO, J. L., Communications, Comparative Literature, English, Theatre
HALL, H. B., Philosophy
HALL, S. J., Health and Exercise Sciences
HALLENBECK, D. J., Mathematical Sciences
HALPRIN, A., Physics and Astronomy
HAMILTON, C., Nutrition and Diatetics
HAMPEL, R., Education
HANEY, M. H., Electrical and Computer Engineering
HANS, V. P., Sociology and Criminal Justice
HAREVEN, T. K., Individual and Family Studies, History
HASLETT, B. J., Communications, Psychology, Women's Studies
HASLETT, D. W., Philosophy
HASTINGS, S. E., Food and Resource Economics
HAUS, H.-U., Theatre
HAWK, J. A., Plant and Soil Sciences
HAYES, E. R., Nursing
HELMLING, S., English
HERMAN, B. L., Art History, History
HERMAN, D., Music
HEWITT, K. H., Military Science
HEYRMAN, C. L., History
HIEBERT, J., Education
HIGGINBOTHAM, E., Sociology and Criminal Justice
HILDEBRANDT, D. J., Music
HOFFECKER, C. E., History
HOFFMAN, J. E., Psychology
HOFFMAN, S. D., Economics, Women's Studies
HOFSTETTER, F., Education
HOLMES, L. W., Art
HOOVER, D. G., Animal and Food Sciences
HOUGH-GOLDSTEIN, J. A., Entomology and Applied Ecology
HSIAO, G. C., Mathematical Sciences
HUANG, C. P., Civil and Environmental Engineering, Marine Studies
HUDDLESTON, M. W., Political Science and Interntional Relations, Urban Affairs and Public Policy
HUNSPERGER, R. G., Electrical and Computer Engineering
HURT, J. J., History
IH, C. S., Electrical and Computer Engineering, Marine Studies
ILVENTO, T. W., Food and Resource Economics
INCIARDI, J. A., Sociology and Criminal Justice
INGERSOLL, D. E., Political Science and International Relations
INTRAUB, H., Psychology
IZARD, C., Psychology
JACKSON, M. D., English
JAIN, M. K., Chemistry and Biochemistry
JOHNSON, H. B., Black American Studies, History
JOHNSON, M. V., Chemistry and Biochemistry
JONES, J. M., Psychology
JONES, S. K., Accounting and Management Information Systems
JORDAN, R. R., Geology
KALER, E. W., Chemical Engineering
KALKSTEIN, L. S., Geography
KALLAL, M. J., Consumer Studies
KAPLAN, D. W., Education
KARLSON, R. H., Biological Sciences
KEELER, C., Animal and Food Sciences
KENNEDY, J. A., Mathematical Sciences
KERR, A. D., Civil and Environmental Engineering
KERRANE, K., English
KIKUCHI, S., Civil and Environmental Engineering
KIRBY, J. T., Civil and Environmental Engineering, Marine Studies
KIRCHMAN, D. L., Marine Studies
KIRWAN, A. D., Jr, Marine Studies
KITTO, S. L., Plant and Soil Sciences
KLEMAS, V. V., Marine Studies, Electrical and Computer Engineering
KLINZING, D. G., Individual and Family Studies
KLOCKARS, C. B., Sociology and Criminal Justice
KMIEC, E. B., Biological Sciences
KOBAYASHI, N., Civil and Environmental Engineering, Marine Studies
KOFORD, K. J., History, Economics, Political Science and International Relations
KOLCHIN, P. R., History
KOLODZEY, J., Electrical and Computer Engineering
KRAFT, J. C., Geology, Marine Studies
KUNG, L., Animal and Food Sciences
KUSHMAN, J. E., Consumer Studies
LAMBRECHT, M., Nursing
LANE, R., Art
LATHROP, T. A., Foreign Languages and Literatures
LAZENBIK, F., Mathematical Sciences
LEATHERS, D. J., Geography
LEAVENS, P. B., Geology
LEITCH, T. M., English
LEJA, M., English
LEMIEUX, B., Plant and Soil Sciences
LENHOFF, A. M., Chemical Engineering
LESHCHINSKY, P. E., Civil and Environmental Engineering
LEUNG, C. N., Physics and Astronomy
LEWIS, K. A., Business
LI, W., Mathematical Sciences
LINK, C. R., Economics
LLOYD, E. L., Computer and Information Sciences
LUTHER, G. W., Marine Studies, Chemistry and Biochemistry, Civil and Environmental Engineering
MACDONALD, J., Physics and Astronomy
MCINNIS, J. B., Comparative Literature, Foreign Languages and Literatures, Women's Studies
MAGEE, J., Political Science and International Relations
MANGONE, G. J., Legal Studies, Marine Studies
MANRAI, A. K., Business Administration
MANRAI, L., Business Administration
MARKS, C. C., Black American Studies, Sociology and Criminal Justice
MARTIN, R. E., Geology
MASON, C. E., Entomology and Applied Ecology
MASON, D. M., Food and Resource Economics
MASTERSON, F. A., Psychology
MATTHAEUS, W. H., Bartol Research Institute
MAY, G., History
MELL, D. C., English
MEYER, D. H., History
MEYER, W. H., Political Science and International Relations
MILLER, G. E., English
MILLER, J. B., Economics
MILLER, M. J., Political Science and International Relations
MILLER, S., Sociology and Criminal Justice, Women's Studies
MILLS, D. L., Electrical and Computer Engineering
MONK, P. B., Mathematics
MOODY, W. B., Education, Mathematical Sciences
MORGAN, R. W., Agriculture and Food Sciences, Biology, Chemistry and Biochemistry
MORRISON, J. L., Consumer Studies
MULLAN, D. J., Bartol Research Institute
MULLIGAN, J., Economics
MUNSON, M. S. B., Chemistry and Biochemistry
MURRAY, F. B., Education, Psychology
NANDAKUMAR, R., Education
NASHED, M. Z., Mathematical Sciences, Electrical Engineering
NEES, L. P., Art History
NEEVES, R. E., Health and Exercise Science
NELSON, F. E., Geography
NELSON, M., English
NELSON, P., Food and Resource Economics
NESS, N. F., Bartol Research Institute
NEWTON, J. E., Black American Studies
NICHOLS, R. D., Art
NIGG, J. M., Sociology and Criminal Justice
NORTHMORE, D. P. M., Psychology
OLIVER, J. K., Political Science and International Relations, Marine Studies
O'NEILL, J. B., Economics
OPILA, R. L., Materials Science and Engineering
OWOCKI, S. P., Bartol Research Institute
PALKOVITZ, R. J., Individual and Family Studies
PALLEY, M. L., Political Science and International Relations, Women's Studies
PALMER, L. M., Philosophy, Women's Studies
PARSONS, G. R., Marine Studies, Economics
PAULANKA, B. J., Nursing
PAULY, T. H., English
PERSE, E. M., Communications
PETERS, D. L., Individual and Family Studies, Urban Affairs and Public Policy
PETERSON, L. W., Music
PFAELZER, J., English
PIFER, E. I., Communications, Comparative Literature, English
PIKA, J. A., Political Science and International Relations
PILL, W. G., Plant and Soil Sciences
PITTEL, S., Bartol Research Institute
PIZZOLATO, T. D., Plant and Soil Sciences
PIZZUTO, J. E., Geology
PONG, D., History
POPE, C. R., Animal and Food Sciences
POTTER, L. D., English
PRODAN, J. C., Music
PURNELL, L., Nursing
RABOLT, J. F., Materials Science and Engineering
RAFFEL, J. A., Urban Affairs and Public Policy, Political Science and International Relations
RATHS, J., Education
REEDY, C. L., Museum Studies, Art History, Urban Affairs and Public Policy

REIDEL, L., Theatre
REYNOLDS, H. T., Political Science and International Relations, Urban Affairs and Public Policy
RHEINGOLD, A. L., Chemistry and Biochemistry
RICH, D., Urban Affairs and Public Policy, Political Science and International Relations
RICHARDS, J. G., Health and Exercise Sciences
RICHARDS, M. P., English
RIDGE, D., Chemistry and Biochemistry
RITTER, W. F., Bioresources Engineering
ROBBINS, C., Sociology and Criminal Justice
ROBBINS, S. L., Theatre
ROBINSON, C. E., English
ROE, P. G., Anthropology
ROSELLE, D. P., Mathematics
ROSENBERGER, J. K., Microbiology
ROTH, R. R., Entomology and Applied Ecology
RUARK, G., English
RUSSELL, T. W. F., Chemical Engineering
SAFER, E. B., English
SANDLER, S. I., Chemical Engineering, Chemistry and Biochemistry
SANIGA, E. M., Business Administration
SATINOFF, E., Psychology
SAUNDERS, B. D., Computer and Information Sciences, Mathematical Sciences
SAYDAM, T., Computer and Information Sciences
SCARPITTI, F. R., Sociology and Criminal Justice
SCHWARTZ, L. W., Mechanical Engineering, Mathematical Sciences
SCHWARTZ, N. B., Anthropology
SCHWEDA-NICHOLSON, N. L., Legal Studies, Linguistics
SCHWEITZER, R. L., Economics
SEIDMAN, L. S., Economics
SELEKMAN, J. A., Nursing
SETHI, A. S., Computer and Information Sciences
SETTLE, R. F., Economics
SETTLES, B. H., Individual and Family Studies
SHAFI, M., Foreign Languages and Literatures
SHAFI, Q., Bartol Research Institute
SHARNOFF, M., Physics and Astronomy
SHARP, J. H., Marine Studies
SHIPMAN, H. L., Physics and Astronomy
SIDEBOTHAM, S. E., History
SIGNORIELLI, N., Communications
SIMMONS, D. T., Biological Sciences
SIMONS, R. F., Psychology
SIMS, J. T., Plant and Soil Sciences
SKOPIK, S. D., Biological Sciences
SLOYER, C. W., Jr, Mathematical Sciences
SMITH, J. L., Nutrition and Diatetics
SNIDER, O. S., Animal and Food Sciences
SNYDER-MACKLER, L., Physical Therapy, Philosophy
SOLES, J. R., Political Science and International Relations
SPARKS, D. L., Civil and Environmental Engineering, Chemistry and Biochemistry, Plant and Soil Sciences
SPINSKI, V., Art
STANEV, T., Bartol Research Institute
STARK, C., English
STARK, R. M., Mathematical Sciences, Civil and Environmental Engineering
STETSON, M. H., Biological Sciences
STONER, J. H., Art Conservation
ST PIERRE, E. K., Accounting and Management Information Systems
STRAIGHT, R., Arts
STRASSER, S., History
STRECKFUSS, R. J., Music
SVENDSEN, I. A., Civil and Environmental Engineering, Marine Studies
SWASEY, J. E., Plant and Soil Sciences
SWEENEY, S. R., Theatre
SYLVES, R. T., Political Science and Int. Relations, Marine Studies, Urban Affairs and Public Policy
SZALEWICZ, K., Physics and Astronomy
SZERI, A. Z., Mechanical Engineering
TABER, D. F., Chemistry and Biochemistry
TALLAMY, D. W., Entomology and Applied Ecology
TARGETT, N. M., Marine Studies
TARGETT, T. E., Marine Studies
THEOPOLD, K. H., Chemistry and Biochemistry
THIBAULT, B., Foreign Languages and Literatures
THORPE, C., Chemistry and Biochemistry
TIERNEY, K. J., Sociology and Criminal Justice
TILMON, H. D., Food and Resource Economics
TOENSMEYER, U. C., Food and Resource Economics
TOLLES, B. F., Jr, Art History, History, Museum Studies
TURKEL, G. M., Sociology and Criminal Justice
ULLMAN, W. J., Marine Studies, Geology
UNGER, D. G., Individual and Family Studies
UNRUH, K., Physics and Astronomy
VARMA, R. D., Economics
VASILAS, B. L., Plant and Soil Sciences
VENEZKY, R., Education, Computer and Information Sciences, Linguistics
VICKERY, C. E., Nutrition and Diatetics
VINSON, J. R., Mechanical Engineering; Marine Studies
VUKELICH, C., Individual and Family Studies
WAGNER, N. J., Chemical Engineering
WAGNER, R. C., Biological Sciences
WALKER, J. H., Theatre
WALKER, J. M., English
WARREN, R., Urban Affairs and Public Policy; Political Science and International Relations
WATSON, G. H., Physics and Astronomy
WEBSTER, F., Marine Studies
WEDEL, A. R., Communications, Linguistics, Foreign Languages and Literatures
WEHMILLER, J. F., Geology, Marine Studies
WEISS, J. J., Art
WHITE, C. E., Jr, Accounting and Management Information Systems
WHITE, H. B., III, Chemistry and Biochemistry
WILDER, M. S., Urban Affairs and Public Policy
WILKINS, D. J., Mechanical Engineering
WILLMOTT, C. J., Geography, Marine Studies
WIRTH, M. J., Chemistry and Biochemistry
WOLTERS, R. B., History
WONG, K.-C., Marine Studies
WOOD, T. K., Entomology and Applied Ecology
WOOL, R. P., Chemical Engineering
YAGODA, B., English
YAN, X.-H., Marine Studies
ZINN, M. A., Music
ZIPSER, R. A., Foreign Languages and Literatures
ZUCKERMAN, M., Psychology

WESLEY COLLEGE

120 North State St, Dover, DE 19901
Telephone: (302) 736-2300
E-mail: info@wesley.edu
Internet: www.wesley.edu

Founded 1873 as Wilmington Conference Acad.; present name 1978
Private control
Academic year: August to May

Pres.: Dr SCOTT D. MILLER
Exec. Vice-Pres. and Provost: Dr BETTE S. COPLAN
Vice-Pres. for Institutional Advancement: KEVIN J. LOFTUS
Dean of Students: Dr KENNETH C. WALDROP
Registrar: PETER MEDWICK
Library Dir: SUSAN MATUSAK

Library of 460,000 vols
Number of students: 2,400

DEANS

School of Arts and Sciences: Dr PAUL J. DE GATEGNO
School of Professional Studies: Dr CHRISTOPHER MALONE

WIDENER UNIVERSITY SCHOOL OF LAW

Delaware Campus: POB 7474, 4601 Concord Pike, Wilmington, DE 19803-0474
Harrisburg Campus: POB 69381, 3800 Vartan Way, Harrisburg, PA 17106-9381

Telephone: (302) 477-2100 (Delaware); (717) 541-3900 (Harrisburg)
E-mail: meanderson@mail.widener.edu
Internet: www.law.widener.edu

Founded 1971
Academic year: August to May

Pres.: JAMES HARRIS
Dean: LINDA L. AMMONS

Number of teachers: 198 (78 full-time, 120 part-time)
Number of students: 1,600

Publications: *Delaware Journal of Corporate Law* (2 a year), *Widener Law Journal* (1 a year), *Widener Law Review* (1 a year).

DISTRICT OF COLUMBIA

AMERICAN UNIVERSITY

4400 Massachusetts Ave, NW, Washington, DC 20016

Telephone: (202) 885-1000
Fax: (202) 885-3265
E-mail: president@american.edu
Internet: www.american.edu

Chartered 1893

Pres.: CORNELIUS KERWIN
Provost: SCOTT BASS
Vice-Pres. of Campus Life: GAIL SHORT HANSON
Vice-Pres. of Enrollment Services: SHARON ALSTON (acting)
Vice-Pres. of Finance and Treas.: DONALD L. MYERS
Vice-Pres. of Int. Affairs: ROBERT A. PASTOR
Vice-Pres. and Univ. Counsel: MARY E. KENNARD
Vice-Pres. of Univ. Relations: ALBERT R. CHECCIO
Dean of Academic Affairs: KAY MUSSELL (acting)
Dean of Students: (vacant)
Registrar: LINDA BOLDEN-PITCHER
Univ. Librarian: WILLIAM MAYER

Library of 763,000 vols, 3,300 print periodicals, 1m. microforms, 8,759 films and videos, 34,000 sound recordings, 12,850 musical scores
Number of teachers: 594 full-time
Number of students: 11,224

DEANS

College of Arts and Sciences: (vacant)
Kogod College of Business Administration: Dr RICHARD DURAND
School of Communication: LARRY KIRKMAN
School of International Service: LOUIS GOODMAN
School of Public Affairs: WILLIAM M. LEOGRANDE (acting)
Washington College of Law: CLAUDIO GROSSMAN

CATHOLIC UNIVERSITY OF AMERICA

620 Michigan Ave, NE, Washington, DC 20064

Telephone: (202) 319-5000
Internet: www.cua.edu

Founded 1887
Private control
Academic year: September to August

Pres.: JOHN GARVEY
Provost: Dr JAMES BRENNAN
Vice-Pres. for Enrollment Management: Dr W. MICHAEL HENDRICKS
Vice-Pres. for Finance and Treas.: CATHY WOOD
Vice-Pres. for Student Life: SUSAN PERVI
Vice-Pres. for Univ. Devt: ROBERT SULLIVAN ROBERT M. SULLIVAN
Vice-Pres. for Univ. Relations and Chief of Staff: FRANK PERSICO
Registrar: ADRIANA FARELLA
Dir of Libraries: STEPHEN CONNAGHAN

Library: 1.5m. vols.
Number of teachers: 746
Number of students: 6,967

Publications: *Catholic Biblical Quarterly*, *Catholic University Law Review*, *CUA Magazine*, *Journal of Religion & Spirituality in Social Work: Social Thought*, *New Catholic Encyclopedia*, *Review of Metaphysics*, *The Catholic Historical Review* (4 a year), *U.S. Catholic Historian*

DEANS

Benjamin T. Rome School of Music: Dr GRAYSON WAGSTAFF
Columbus School of Law: VERYL MILES
Metropolitan College: Dr SARA THOMPSON
Nat. Catholic School of Social Service: Dr JAMES R. ZABORA
School of Architecture and Planning: RANDALL OTT
School of Arts and Sciences: Dr LAWRENCE R. POOS
School of Engineering: Dr CHARLES C. NGUYEN
School of Library and Information Science: Dr INGRID HSIEH-YEE
School of Nursing: Dr PATRICIA MCMULLEN
School of Philosophy: Rev. Dr KURT PRITZL
School of Theology and Religious Studies: KEVIN IRWIN

CORCORAN COLLEGE OF ART AND DESIGN

500 17th St, NW, Washingon, DC 20006-4804

Telephone: (202) 639-1801
E-mail: admissions@corcoran.org
Internet: www.corcoran.edu
Private control

Dean: CHRISTINA DE PAUL

Library of 26,000 vols.

OTHER CAMPUSES

Georgetown Campus: 1801 35th St, NW, Washington, DC 20007; tel. (202) 298-2541.

H St Campus: 1705 H St, NW, Washington, DC 20006.

DOMINICAN HOUSE OF STUDIES

487 Michigan Ave, NE, Washington, DC 20017-1585

Telephone: (202) 529-5300
Fax: (202) 636-1700
Internet: www.dhs.edu

Founded 1905
Private control
Academic year: August to May

Chancellor: Very Rev. CARLOS AZPIROZ
Vice-Chancellor: Very Rev. DOMINIC IZZO
Pres.: Very Rev. REGINALD WHITT
Vice-Pres. and Academic Dean: Fr GABRIEL O'DONNELL
Registrar: TOBIAS NATHE
Dir of Library: Rev. KEVIN MCGRATH

Library of 79,000 vols
Number of teachers: 19
Number of students: 67

GALLAUDET UNIVERSITY

800 Florida Ave, NE, Washington, DC 20002

Telephone: (202) 651-5000
E-mail: public.relations@gallaudet.edu
Internet: www.gallaudet.edu
Academic year: August to May

Founded 1864

Pres.: Dr ROBERT R. DAVILA
Provost: Dr STEPHEN WEINER
Vice-Pres. for Admin. and Finance: PAUL KELLY
Dean of Pre-College: (vacant)
Dean of Student Affairs: CARL PRAMUK
Librarian: (vacant)

Library of 200,000 vols
Number of teachers: 253
Number of students: 2,000

Publications: *Gallaudet Today* (2 a year), *Perspectives in Education and Deafness* (4 a year), *World Around You* (4 a year)

DEANS

College of Arts and Sciences: Dr JANE DILLEHAY
Graduate School and Professional Programmes: Dr THOMAS ALLEN

ATTACHED INSTITUTE

Gallaudet Research Institute: research into deafness; Dir MICHAEL KARCHMER.

GEORGE WASHINGTON UNIVERSITY

2121 I St, NW, Washington, DC 20052

Telephone: (202) 994-1000
Fax: (202) 994-9025
Internet: www.gwu.edu

Founded 1821
Private control
Academic year: September to May

Pres.: STEVEN KNAPP
Sr Vice-Pres. and Sr Vice-Provost for Student and Academic Support Services: ROBERT A. CHERNAK
Exec. Vice-Pres. and Treas.: LOUIS H. KATZ
Provost and Exec. Vice-Pres. for Academic Affairs: STEVEN LERMAN
Vice-Pres. for Advancement: MICHAEL MORSBERGER
Vice-Pres. for Research: LEO CHALUPA
Asst Vice-Pres. for DC Relations: BERNARD DEMCZUK
Vice-Provost for Health Affairs: JEFF AKMAN
Sr Vice-Pres. and Gen. Counsel: BETH NOLAN
Asst Vice-Pres. for Academic Planning, Institutional Research and Assessment: CHERYL BEIL
Registrar: ELIZABETH ADMUNDSON
Univ. Librarian: JACK A. SIGGINS

Library: 2m. vols
Number of teachers: 2,226
Number of students: 25,135

DEANS

College of Professional Studies: KATHLEEN BURKE
Columbian College of Arts and Sciences: MARGUERITE BARRATT
Elliott School of Int. Affairs: MICHAEL BROWN
Graduate School of Education and Human Devt: MICHAEL FEUER
Law School: GREG MAGGS
School of Business and Public Management: DOUG GUTHRIE
School of Engineering and Applied Science: DAVID DOLLING
School of Medicine and Health Services: JEFF AKMAN
School of Public Health and Health Sciences: LYNN GOLDMAN
School of Nursing: JEAN JOHNSON

PROFESSORS

(Some professors serve in more than one school)

Columbian School of Arts and Sciences and Elliott School of International Affairs:

ABRAMSON, F. P., Pharmacology, Chemistry
ABRAVANEL, E., Psychology
ADAMS, G. M., Int. Affairs
ALBRIGHT, J. W., Microbiology and Immunology
ALLEN, C. J., Anthropology, Int. Affairs
ANDERSON, J. C., Art
ARNDT, R. A., Physics
ARTERTON, F. C., Political Management
ASKARI, H. G., Business, Int. Affairs
ATKIN, M. A., History
AUSTIN, J. F., Sociology
AZAR, I., Spanish and Human Sciences
BAGINSKI, F. E., Mathematics
BAILEY, J. M., Biochemistry and Molecular Biology
BECKER, W. H., History and Int. Affairs
BELL, D., Anthropology
BERKOWITZ, E. D., History
BERMAN, B. L., Physics
BHALA, R., Law, Int. Affairs
BLACK, A. M., History and Int. Affairs
BLOSSOM, N. H., Interior Design
BORRIELLO, J., Psychology
BOULIER, B. L., Economics
BRADLEY, M. D., Economics, Int. Affairs
BRISCOE, W. J., Physics
BROCK, G. W., Telecommunications
BROWN, N. J., Political Science, Int. Affairs
BURNS, J. R., Zoology
CARESS, E. A., Chemistry
CAWS, P. J., Philosophy
CHAVES, J., Chinese
CHIAPPINELLI, V. A., Basic Science, Pharmacology, Neurological Surgery
CHURCHILL, R. P., Philosophy
CORDES, J. J., Economics and Int. Affairs
COSTIGAN, C. C., Design
COTTROL, R. J., Law, History, Sociology
DAVIS, H., Strategic Management and Int. Affairs
DEERING, C. J., Political Science
DONALDSON, R. P., Biology
DUNNING, R. M., Jr, Economics
EAST, M. A., Int. Affairs and Political Science
ETZIONI, A., Sociology
FALK, J. E., Operations Research
FEIGELBAUM, H. B., Political Science, Int. Affairs
FERRER, J., Jr, Business, Int. Affairs
FISHER, E. A., Classics
FRIEDLER, G., Engineering and Applied Science, Statistics
FUERTH, L., Int. Affairs
GALLO, L. L., Biochemistry and Molecular Biology
GANZ, R. N., Jr, English
GARNER, N. C., Theatre
GASTWIRTH, J. L., Statistics and Economics
GLICK, I. I., Mathematics
GOLDFARB, R. S., Economics
GOLDSTEIN, A. L., Biochemistry and Molecular Biology
GOW, D. D., Anthropology, Int. Affairs
GRIFFITH, W. B., Philosophy
GRINKER, R. R., Anthropology, Int. Affairs, Human Sciences
GUENTHER, R. J., Music
GUPTA, M. M., Mathematics
HARDING, H., Int. Affairs, Political Science
HARTMANN, H., Women's Studies

HENIG, J. R., Political Science
HILTEBEITEL, A. J., Religion, Human Sciences
HOLMES, D. E., Clinical Psychology
HORTON, J. O., American Civilization and History
HOTEZ, P. J., Microbiology, Tropical Medicine, Global Health, Int. Affairs
HOWE, G. W., Psychology
INDERFURTH, K. F., Int. Affairs
JACOBSON, L. B., Theatre
JOHNSON, K. E., Anatomy
JUDSON, H. F., History
JUNGHENN, H. D., Mathematics
KAMINSKI, G. L., Economics, Int. Affairs
KATZ, I. J., Mathematics
KENNEDY, D. K., History, Int. Affairs
KENNEDY, K. A., Pharmacology and Genetics
KENNEDY, R. E., Jr, European History
KIM-RENAUD, Y. K., Korean Language and Culture, Int. Affairs
KING, M. M., Chemistry
KLAMER, A., Economics, Int. Affairs
KLARÉAN, P. F., History, Int. Affairs
KNOWLTON, R. E., Biology
KUIPERS, J. C., Anthropology, Int. Affairs, Human Sciences
KUMAR, A., Biochemistry, Molecular Biology and Genetics
KWOKA, J. E., Jr, Economics
LABADIE, P. A., Economics
LACHIN, J. M., III, Statistics, Biostatistics
LADER, M. P., Art
LADISCH, S., Paediatrics, Biochemistry and Molecular Biochemistry
LAKE, J. L., Photography
LEHMAN, D. R., Physics
LENGERMANN, P. M., Sociology
LEWIS, J. F., Geology
LILLIEFORS, H. W., Statistics
LINEBAUGH, C. W., Speech and Hearing, Medicine
LIPSCOMB, D. L., Biology
LOGSDON, J. M., Political Science, Int. Affairs
LONGSTRETH, R. W., American Civilization
LUDLOW, G., French, Int. Affairs
MCALEAVEY, D. W., English
MCCLINTOCK, C., Political Science, Int. Affairs
MCGRATH, D. C., Jr, Geography, Urban and Regional Planning
MADDOX, J. H., English
MAHMOUD, H. M., Statistics
MANDEL, H. G., Pharmacology
MANHEIM, J. B., Political Communications and Political Science
MAXIMON, L. C., Physics
MAZZUCHI, T. A., Operations Research, Engineering Management
MERGEN, B. M., American Civilization
MILLAR, J. R., Economics and Int. Affairs
MILLER, B. D., Anthropology, Int. Affairs
MILLER, J. A., English, American Studies
MILLER, J. C., Psychology
MILLER, J. H., Chemistry
MOLINA, S. B., Art
MUFTIC, S., Computer Science
NASR, S. H., Islamic Studies
NAU, H. R., Political Science and Int. Affairs
NAYAK, T. K., Statistics
OFFERMAN, L. R., Psychology
OZDOGAN, T., Ceramics
PACKER, R. K., Biology
PALMER, P. M., American Civilization, Women's Studies
PARKE, W. C., Physics
PARSONS, D. O., Economics
PASTER, G. K., English
PATIERNO, S. R., Pharmacology, Genetics
PECK, L. L., History
PELZMAN, J., Economics and Int. Affairs
PERRY, D. C., Pharmacology
PETERSON, R. A., Psychology, Psychiatry and Behavioural Sciences
PEUSNER, K. D., Anatomy
PLOTZ, J. A., English, Human Sciences
POPPEN, P. J., Psychology
POST, J. M., Psychiatry, Political Psychology, Int. Affairs
PRZYTYCKI, J. H., Mathematics
RAMAKER, D. E., Chemistry
RASKIN, M., Policy Studies
REDDAWAY, P., Political Science and Int. Affairs
REICH, B., Political Science and Int. Affairs
REICH, W., Int. Affairs, Ethics and Human Behaviour
REISS, D., Psychiatry and Behavioural Science, Medicine, Psychology
RIBUFFO, L. P., History
ROBINSON, E. A., Jr, Mathematics
ROBINSON, L. F., Art
ROBLES, F., Int. Marketing, Int. Affairs
ROSENAU, J. N., Int. Affairs
ROTHBLAT, L. A., Psychology, Anatomy
ROWE, W. F., Forensic Sciences
ROWLEY, D. A., Chemistry
RYCROFT, R. W., Int. Science and Technology Policy, Int. Affairs
SACHAR, H. M., History, Int. Affairs
SALAMON, L. B., English, Human Sciences
SAPERSTEIN, M. E., Jewish History
SASHKIN, M., Human Resource Devt
SCHAFFNER, R. F., Medical Humanities, Philosophy
SCHWANDT, D. R., Human Resource Devt
SCOTT, D. W., Microbiology and Immunology, Anatomy and Cell Biology
SEAVEY, O. A., English
SHAMBAUGH, D. L., Political Science and Int. Affairs
SHAO, X.-Q., Anthropology
SIGELMAN, C. K., Psychology
SIGELMAN, L., Political Science
SINGPURWALLA, N. D., Operations Research, Statistics
SMITH, S. C., Economics, Int. Affairs
SODARO, M. J., Political Science and Int. Affairs
SOLAND, R. M., Operations Research
SPECTOR, R. H., History and Int. Affairs
SQUIRES, G. D., Sociology
STEINHARDT, R., Law, Int. Affairs
STEN, C. W., English
STEPHENS, G. C., Geology
STERLING, C. H., Media and Public Affairs, Telecommunication
THIBAULT, J. F., French, Human Sciences
THORNTON, R. C., History and Int. Affairs
TROPEA, J. L., Sociology
TROST, R. P., Economics
TUCH, S. A., Sociology
ULLMAN, D. H., Mathematics
VANDERHOEK, J. Y., Biochemistry and Molecular Biology
VERTER, J. L., Statistics
VLACH, J. M., American Civilization, Anthropology
VON BARGHAHN-CALVETTI, B. A., Art
WADE, A. G., Theatre
WALLACE, D. D., Jr, Religion
WALLACE, R. A., Sociology
WALSH, R. J., Anatomy and Cell Biology
WARREN, C., Communication
WATSON, H. S., Economics
WEGLICKI, W. B., Medicine, Physiology
WEINER, R. J., Int. Business, Int. Affairs
WEITZER, R., Sociology
WERLING, L. L., Pharmacology
WILLIAMS, R. L., Naval Science
WINSLOW, E. K., Behavioural Sciences
WIRTZ, P. W., Management Science, Psychology
WITHERS, M. R., Dance
WOLCHIK, S. L., Political Science and Int. Affairs
WOOD, B., Human Origins, Human Evolutionary Anatomy
WOODWARD, W. T., Painting
WRIGHT, J. F., Jr, Drawing and Graphics
YEIDE, H. E., Jr, Religion
YEZER, A., Economics
ZIOLKOWSI, J. E., Classics

School of Business and Public Management:

ACHROL, R. S., Marketing
ADAMS, W. C., Public Admin.
ARTERTON, F. C., Political Management
BABER, W. R., Accountancy
BAGCHI, P. K., Business Admin.
BARNHILL, T. M., Finance
CARSON, J. H., Management Science
CHERIAN, E. J., Information Systems
CHITWOOD, S. R., Public Admin.
COYNE, J. P., Management Science
DAVIS, H. J., Strategic Management
DIVITA, S. F., Marketing
DYER, R. F., Business Admin.
FOLKERTS, J., Media and Public Affairs
FORMAN, E. H., Management Science
GLASCOCK, J. L., Finance
GRANGER, M. J., Management Science
HALAL, W. E., Management Science
HANDORF, W. C., Finance
HARMON, M. M., Public Admin.
HARVEY, J. B., Management Science
HAWKINS, D. E., Tourism Studies, Tourism Policy, Medicine
HILMY, J., Accountancy
INFELD, D. L., Public Admin., Health Services Management and Policy
JAQUES, E., Management Science
KEE, J. E., Public Admin.
KLOCK, M. S., Finance
KUMAR, K. R., Accountancy
LAUTER, G. P., Int. Business
LENN, D. J., Strategic Management and Public Policy
LOBUTS, J. F., Jr, Management Science
MCSWAIN, C. J., Public Admin.
MADDOX, L. M., Business Admin.
MANHEIM, J. B., Media and Public Affairs, Political Science
NEWCOMER, K. E., Public Admin.
PAIK, C.-M., Accountancy and Quantitative Methods
PARK, Y. S., International Business
PERRY, J. H., Jr, Business Admin.
PHILLIPS, S. M., Finance
RAU, P. A., Business Admin.
ROBERTS, S. V., Media and Public Affairs
ROBLES, F., Int. Marketing and Int. Affairs
SHELDON, D. R., Accountancy
SOYER, R., Management Science
STERLING, C. H., Media and Public Affairs, Telecommunication
STERN, C., Media and Public Affairs
TRACHTENBERG, S. J., Public Admin.
UMPLEBY, S. A., Management Science
WEINER, R. J., Int. Business and Int. Affairs
WIRTZ, P. W., Management Science, Psychology
WORTH, M. J., Nonprofit Management

School of Engineering and Applied Science:

BERKOVICH, S. Y., Engineering and Applied Science
BOCK, P. S., Engineering
BRIER, G. R., Engineering Management
CARROLL, R. L., Jr, Engineering and Applied Science
CHOI, H.-A., Engineering and Applied Science
COOPER, P. A., Engineering
DEASON, J. P., Engineering Management, Systems Engineering
DELLA TORRE, E., Engineering and Applied Science
DIGGES, K. H., Engineering and Applied Science
EDELSON, B. L., Engineering
EISNER, H., Engineering Management
FELDMAN, M. B., Engineering and Applied Science

Frieder, G., Engineering and Applied Science, Statistics
Garris, C. A., Engineering
Gilmore, C. M., Engineering and Applied Science
Haque, M. I., Engineering and Applied Science
Harrald, J. R., Engineering Management
Harrington, R. J., Engineering and Applied Science
Helgert, H. J., Engineering and Applied Science
Heller, R. S., Engineering and Applied Science
Hoffman, L. J., Engineering and Applied Science
Jones, D. L., Engineering
Kahn, W. K., Engineering and Applied Science
Kaufman, R. E., Engineering
Kyriakopoulos, N., Engineering
Lang, R. H., Engineering and Applied Science
Lee, J. D.-Y., Engineering and Applied Science
Liebowitz, H., Engineering and Applied Science
Loew, M. H., Engineering
Mahmood, K., Engineering
Martin, C. D., Engineering and Applied Science
Maurer, W. D., Engineering and Applied Science
Mazzuchi, T. A., Operations Research, Engineering Management
Meltzer, A. C., Engineering and Applied Science
Murphree, E. L., Jr, Engineering Management, Systems Engineering
Myers, M. K., Engineering and Applied Science
Nagel, D. J., Engineering
Narahari, B., Engineering and Applied Science
Pardavi-Horvath, M., Engineering and Applied Science
Pelton, J. N., Engineering
Pickholtz, R. L., Engineering and Applied Science
Post, J. M., Engineering Management, Political Psychology, Int. Affairs, Psychiatry and Behavioural Sciences
Roper, W. E., Engineering and Applied Science
Sandusky, R. R., Jr, Engineering and Applied Science
Sarkani, S., Engineering Management, Systems Engineering
Sibert, J. L., Engineering and Applied Science
Szu, H., Engineering
Tolson, R. H., Engineering and Applied Science
Tong, T. W., Mechanical Engineering
Vojcic, B. R., Engineering and Applied Science
Wasylkiwskyj, W., Engineering and Applied Science
Waters, R. C., Engineering Management
Youssef, A., Engineering and Applied Science
Zaghloul, M. E., Engineering and Applied Science

Law School:

Adelman, M. J.
Banzhaf, J. F., III
Barron, J. A.
Benitez, A. M.
Bhala, R.
Block, C. D.
Bratton, W. W.
Brown, K. B.
Butler, P.
Cahn, N. R.
Carter, W. B.
Cheh, M. M.
Clark, B. R.
Craver, C. B.
Cunningham, L. E.
Dienes, C. T.
Friedenthal, J. H.
Gabaldon, T. A.
Gutman, J. S.
Izumu, C. L.
Johnston, G. P.
Jones, S. R.
Kovacic, W. E.
Lee, C.
Lees, F. J.
Lerner, R. L.
Lupu, I. C.
Lyman, J. P.
Maggs, G. E.
Meier, J. S.
Meyer, P. H.
Mitchell, L. E.
Morgan, T. D.
Pagel, S. B.
Park, R. E.
Peroni, R. J.
Peterson, T. D.
Pierce, R. J., Jr
Raven-Hansen, P.
Reitze, A. W., Jr
Robinson, D., Jr
Saltzburg, S. A.
Schechter, R. E.
Schwartz, J. I.
Selmi, M.
Siegel, J. R.
Sirulnik, E. S.
Sohn, L. B.
Solomon, L. D.
Spanogle, J. A.
Steinhardt, R. G.
Strand, J. H.
Trangsrud, R. H.
Turley, J. R.
Tuttle, R.
Wilmarth, A. E., Jr
Young, M. K.
Zubrow, L. E.

School of Medicine and Health Sciences:

Abramson, F. P., Pharmacology, Chemistry
Adelson, E., Medicine
Advani, M., Psychiatry and Behavioural Sciences
Ahlgren, J. D., Medicine, Pharmacology
Albert, M., Medicine
Albright, J., Microbiology and Tropical Medicine
Amiri, S., Paediatrics
Ammerman, B., Neurological Surgery
Apud, J., Psychiatry and Behavioural Sciences
Arling, B., Medicine
Arons, B., Psychiatry and Behavioural Sciences
Ascensao, J., Medicine
August, G. P., Paediatrics
Bachman, L., Anaesthesiology, Critical Care Medicine, Paediatrics
Bailey, J. M., Biochemistry and Molecular Biology
Bank, W. O., Radiology and Neurological Surgery
Baraf, H., Medicine
Barnhill, R., Dermatology, Pathology
Barr, N., Surgery, Health Care Sciences
Barry, P., Medicine, Health Care Sciences
Barth, W. F., Medicine
Batshaw, M., Paediatrics
Battey, J., Surgery
Battle, C., Paediatrics
Becker, A., Obstetrics and Gynaecology
Becker, K. L., Medicine and Physiology, Experimental Medicine
Belman, A. B., Urology and Paediatrics
Bennett, H., Paediatrics
Berberian, B. J., Dermatology
Berenson, R., Health Care Sciences
Bernad, P., Neurology
Bernstein, L., Medicine
Berry, G., Paediatrics
Bigelow, L., Psychiatry and Behavioural Sciences
Blank, A., Psychiatry and Behavioural Sciences
Borenstein, D., Medicine
Borum, M., Medicine
Bowles, L. T., Surgery
Braun, M., Dermatology
Brill, D., Medicine
Brill, W., Medicine
Bronsther, O., Surgery
Brown, B., Psychiatry and Behavioural Sciences
Brown, H., Ophthalmology
Bukrinsky, M., Microbiology and Tropical Medicine
Bulas, D., Radiology, Paediatrics
Burman, K., Medicine
Burns, W., Pathology
Burris, B., Psychiatry
Byrne, J., Paediatrics, Epidemiology and Biostatistics
Byron, H., Ophthalmology
Cahan, J., Surgery, Health Care Sciences
Callender, C., Surgery
Campos, J. M., Paediatrics, Pathology, Microbiology and Tropical Medicine
Canter, J., Surgery
Caputy, A., Neurological Surgery
Carlson, D., Obstetrics and Gynaecology
Cawley, J., Prevention and Community Health, Health Care Sciences
Chamberlain, J., Paediatrics
Chandra, R., Pathology, Paediatrics
Chang, P., Medicine
Chatoor-Koch, I. M., Psychiatry and Behavioural Sciences and Paediatrics
Cheng, T. O., Medicine
Chertoff, J., Psychiatry and Behavioural Sciences
Chiappinelli, V., Pharmacology and Neurological Surgery
Chin, M., Anaesthesiology and Critical Care Medicine
Chodoff, P., Psychiatry and Behavioural Sciences
Chused, J., Psychiatry and Behavioural Sciences, Paediatrics
Cogen, P., Neurological Surgery, Paediatrics
Cohen, G. D., Health Care Sciences, Psychiatry and Behavioural Sciences
Cohen, L., Paediatrics
Cohen, M., Surgery
Cohen-Mansfield, J., Health Care Sciences, Prevention and Community Health
Colberg-Poley, A., Paediatrics, Biochemistry and Molecular Biology
Coleman, R., Paediatrics
Coleman, R., Psychiatry and Behavioural Sciences
Colice, G., Medicine
Comas-Diaz, L., Psychiatry and Behavioural Sciences
Cook, C., Pathology
Cooney, F., Neurological Surgery
Cooper, B., Medicine
Corso, P., Surgery
Cotlove, E., Psychiatry and Behavioural Sciences
Cowan, C., Ophthalmology
Cox, G., Emergency Medicine
Cytryn, L., Psychiatry and Behavioural Sciences
D'Angelo, L. J., Paediatrics, Prevention and Community Health, Medicine
Daniel, D., Psychiatry and Behavioural Sciences
Danovitch, S., Medicine
Davis, D., Psychiatry and Behavioural Sciences

DAVIS, D. O., Radiology, Neurology and Neurological Surgery
DAVIS, G., Microbiology and Tropical Medicine
DENNIS, M., Neurological Surgery
DEPALMA, L., Pathology, Anatomy and Cell Biology
DIAMOND, D., Psychiatry and Behavioural Sciences
DIAMOND, R., Medicine
DLUHY, J., Psychiatry and Behavioural Sciences
DOMAN, D., Medicine
DOPPELHEUER, J., Obstetrics and Gynaecology
DOSA, S., Medicine
DRUY, E. M., Radiology
DUBEY, A., Obstetrics and Gynaecology
DUFOUR, D. R., Pathology
DYER, C., Psychiatry and Behavioural Sciences
EATON, J., Psychiatry and Behavioural Sciences
ECONOMOPOULOS, B., Anaesthesiology and Critical Care Medicine
EDELSON, R., Neurology
EDELSTEIN, S., Emergency Medicine, Anaesthesiology and Critical Care Medicine
EICHELBERGER, M. R., Surgery and Paediatrics
EIG, B., Paediatrics
EIN, D., Medicine
EIN, T., Obstetrics and Gynaecology
EIST, H., Psychiatry and Behavioural Sciences
ELLWOOD, L., Health Care Sciences
EL-MOHANDES, A., Prevention and Community Health, Paediatrics, Obstetrics and Gynaecology
ERSHLER, W., Medicine
EVANS, F. B., Psychiatry and Behavioural Sciences
FAIRBANKS, D., Surgery
FALK, N., Medicine, Health Care Sciences
FALK, R., Obstetrics and Gynaecology
FEIGIN, D., Radiology
FELDMAN, B., Surgery, Health Care Sciences, Paediatrics
FELDMAN, I., Surgery
FIELDS, A., Anaesthesiology and Critical Care Medicine
FINKELSTEIN, J. D., Medicine
FISCHER, R., Medicine
FRAM, D., Psychiatry and Behavioural Sciences
FRANK, J., Psychiatry and Behavioural Sciences
FRASER, C., Pharmacology, Microbiology and Tropical Medicine
FUCHS, M., Medicine
GAARDER, K., Psychiatry and Behavioural Sciences
GAASTERLAND, D., Ophthalmology
GAHRES, E., Obstetrics and Gynaecology
GALLO, L., Biochemistry and Molecular Biology
GALLO, V., Paediatrics, Pharmacology
GEELHOED, G. W., International Medicine and Surgery
GEORGE, D., Psychiatry and Behavioural Sciences
GERSHEN, B., Medicine
GIAUME, C., Anatomy and Cell Biology
GILBERT, C., Obstetrics and Gynaecology
GILLANDERS, R., Obstetrics and Gynaecology
GILLMAN, R., Psychiatry and Behavioural Sciences
GINDOFF, P. R., Obstetrics and Gynaecology
GINSBERG, A. L., Medicine
GIORDANO, J. M., Surgery
GLASER, B., Ophthalmology
GLASSMAN, L., Radiology
GLATT, M., Paediatrics, Psychiatry and Behavioural Sciences
GOLD, M., Medicine
GOLDSTEIN, A., Biochemistry and Molecular Biology
GOLDSTEIN, H., Medicine
GOLDSTEIN, K., Medicine
GOLDSTEIN, S., Medicine
GOODENHOUGH, D. J., Radiology
GOODMAN, S., Psychiatry and Behavioural Sciences
GOODWIN, F., Psychiatry and Behavioural Sciences
GORDIN, F., Medicine
GORDON, G., Psychiatry and Behavioural Sciences
GORELICK, K., Psychiatry and Behavioural Sciences
GRAETER, J., Orthopaedic Surgery
GRANATIR, W., Psychiatry and Behavioural Sciences
GRAVITZ, M., Psychiatry and Behavioural Sciences
GREENBERG, L. W., Paediatrics
GREENE, C., Paediatrics
GREENSPAN, S., Psychiatry and Behavioural Sciences, Paediatrics
GRIFFITH, J. L., Psychiatry and Behavioural Sciences, Neurology
GROSS, P., Urology
GROSS, R., Psychiatry and Behavioural Sciences
GROSSMAN, J. H., Obstetrics and Gynaecology, Microbiology and Tropical Medicine, Prevention and Community Health
GUIDOTTI, T., Environmental Occupational Health, Medicine
GULYA, A., Surgery
GUNTHER, S. F., Orthopaedic Surgery
GUTIERREZ, G., Medicine, Anaesthesiology and Critical Care Medicine
HAAS, M., Psychiatry and Behavioural Sciences
HAAS, S., Orthopaedic Surgery
HAIDER, R., Medicine
HANNALLAH, R. S., Anaesthesiology and Critical Care Medicine, Paediatrics
HARISIADIS, L. A., Radiology
HARSHBARGER, J., Pathology
HARTMAN, G., Surgery, Paediatrics
HASSAN, M., Obstetrics and Gynaecology
HAUDENSCHILD, C. C., Pathology and Medicine
HAWLEY, R., Anatomy and Cell Biology
HECKMAN, B., Medicine
HEINTZE, A., Obstetrics and Gynaecology
HELLER, N., Psychiatry and Behavioural Sciences
HELMKAMP, B., Obstetrics and Gynaecology
HENSON, D., Pathology
HERER, G. R., Paediatrics
HERSH, S., Psychiatry and Behavioural Sciences, Paediatrics
HILL, M. C., Radiology
HOFFMAN, D., Epidemiology and Biostatistics, Global Health
HOFFMAN, E., Paediatrics, Biochemistry and Molecular Biology
HOLBROOK, P. R., Anaesthesiology and Critical Care Medicine, Paediatrics
HOLLAND, C. A., Paediatrics
HOPPING, S., Surgery
HOTEZ, P., Microbiology and Tropical Medicine, Global Health, Epidemiology and Biostatistics
HOWARD, W. J., Medicine
HOWE, G., Psychiatry and Behavioural Sciences
HSIA, J., Medicine
HURLEY, J., Paediatrics
HUTTON, J., Surgery
ISSA, F., Psychiatry and Behavioural Sciences
JAAFAR, M., Ophthalmology, Paediatrics
JACOBSEN, F., Psychiatry and Behavioural Sciences
JACOBSON, J., Neurological Surgery
JAFFE, E., Pathology
JANATI, A., Neurology
JEROME, M., Obstetrics and Gynaecology
JOHNSON, F., Pathology
JOHNSON, K., Anatomy and Cell Biology, Obstetrics and Gynaecology
JOSEPH, D., Psychiatry and Behavioural Sciences
JOSEPH, J., Paediatrics, Epidemiology and Biostatistics
JOSHI, P., Psychiatry and Behavioural Sciences, Paediatrics
KAFKA, J., Psychiatry and Behavioural Sciences
KALINER, M., Medicine
KAMANI, N., Paediatrics
KAO, G., Dermatology
KAPIKIAN, A., Paediatrics
KAPLAN, K., Psychiatry and Behavioural Sciences, Paediatrics
KAPLAN, R., Anaesthesiology and Critical Care Medicine, Paediatrics
KARCHER, D., Pathology
KATZ, A., Pathology
KATZ, B., Ophthalmology
KATZ, N., Surgery
KATZ, R., Dermatology, Paediatrics
KATZ, R. J., Medicine and Emergency Medicine
KATZ, S., Urology
KAUFMAN, R., Engineering, Anatomy and Cell Biology
KAUFMAN, R., Medicine
KELLEHER, J., Physiology and Experimental Medicine
KELLY, J. J., Neurology and Neurological Surgery
KENNEDY, K., Pharmacology, Genetics
KESHISHIAN, J., Surgery
KHOURY, A., Obstetrics and Gynaecology
KIMMEL, P. L., Medicine
KIRBY, E., Psychiatry and Behavioural Sciences
KIRKPATRICK, J., Surgery
KLINE, P., Medicine
KNELLER, M., Radiology
KNOLL, S., Surgery
KOBRINE, A., Neurological Surgery
KOCH, E., Obstetrics and Gynaecology
KOENIG, K., Emergency Medicine
KOVAL, N., Medicine
KOZLOFF, L., Surgery
KREBS, H., Obstetrics and Gynaecology
KRESSEL, B., Medicine
KUEHL, K., Paediatrics
KUMAR, A., Biochemistry and Molecular Biology, Genetics
KUSHNER, D. C., Radiology and Paediatrics
KUSHNER, E., Psychiatry and Behavioural Sciences
LACHER, D., Pathology
LADISCH, S., Paediatrics, Biochemistry and Molecular Biology
LAKSHMAN, R., Medicine, Biochemistry and Molecular Biology
LANDAU, B., Psychiatry and Behavioural Sciences, Paediatrics
LANDO, H., Medicine
LANE, H., Medicine
LARSEN, J. W., Jr, Obstetrics and Gynaecology
LAURENO, R., Neurology
LAWS, E., Neurological Surgery
LAZAR, S., Psychiatry and Behavioural Sciences
LAZARUS, A., Obstetrics and Gynaecology
LE GOLVAN, P., Pathology
LEATHERBURY, L., Paediatrics
LEFKOWITZ, L., Paediatrics, Health Care Sciences
LEMP, M., Ophthalmology
LEVI, L., Psychiatry and Behavioural Sciences
LEVINE, P., Epidemiology and Biostatistics, Medicine

LEVITT, R., Obstetrics and Gynaecology
LEVY, L., Radiology
LEW, S., Medicine
LEWIS, J., Medicine
LEWIS, R., Orthopaedic Surgery
LIEBERMAN, E., Psychiatry and Behavioural Sciences
LIEBERMAN, M., Medicine
LINDSAY, J., Medicine
LIOTTA, L., Pathology
LIPSIUS, S., Psychiatry and Behavioural Sciences, Obstetrics and Gynaecology
LIPSON, A., Medicine
LITOVITZ, T., Emergency Medicine
LITTMAN, B., Obstetrics and Gynaecology
LOO, T., Pharmacology
LOWE, J., Paediatrics
LUBAN, N. C., Paediatrics and Pathology
LUKE, J., Pathology
LURIE, N., Medicine
LYNN, D. J., Health Care Sciences and Medicine
MCAFEE, J., Radiology
MACDONALD-GINZBURG, M. G., Paediatrics
MCDOWELL, R., Paediatrics
MCGILL, W. A., Anaesthesiology and Critical Care Medicine, Paediatrics
MACHT, S., Surgery
MCKNEW, D., Paediatrics
MADDOX, J., Obstetrics and Gynaecology
MAHDAVI, I., Paediatrics
MAJD, M., Radiology and Paediatrics
MALAWER, M. M., Orthopaedic Surgery
MANDEL, H. G., Pharmocology
MANDLER, R., Neurology and Neurological Surgery
MANYAK, M. J., Urology, Microbiology and Tropical Medicine
MARINOFF, S., Obstetrics and Gynaecology
MARLOW, J., Obstetrics and Gynaecology
MARTIN, D., Obstetrics and Gynaecology
MARTIN, G. R., Paediatrics
MASTERS, E. C., Obstetrics and Gynaecology
MASTROYANNIS, C., Obstetrics and Gynaecology
MASUR, H., Medicine
MAYER, T., Emergency Medicine
MECKLENBURG, F., Obstetrics and Gynaecology
MERIKANGAS, J., Psychiatry and Behavioural Science
MEYER, J., Medicine
MIDGLEY, F. M., Surgery and Paediatrics
MILLER, G., Psychiatry and Behavioural Sciences
MILOWE, I., Paediatrics
MOAK, J. P., Paediatrics
MONDZAC, A., Medicine
MOODY, S., Anatomy and Cell Biology
MOSKOVITZ, P., Orthopaedic Surgery, Neurological Surgery
MUFARRIJ, I., Obstetrics and Gynaecology
MULLAN, F., Health Care Sciences, Paediatrics, Prevention and Community Health
MURPHY, R., Ophthalmology
NACHNANI, G., Medicine
NASHEL, D., Medicine
NASR, M., Psychiatry and Behavioural Sciences
NAWAB, E., Obstetrics and Gynaecology
NEVIASER, R. J., Orthopaedic Surgery
NEWMAN, K., Surgery, Paediatrics
NEWMAN, M., Medicine
NG, L., Neurology
NICKLAS, R., Medicine
NICOLAS, J., Paediatrics, Pharmacology
NIERMAN, W., Biochemistry and Molecular Biology
NIGRA, T., Dermatology, Paediatrics
NOWAK, J., Psychiatry and Behavioural Sciences
OBOLER, A., Medicine
OCHSENSCHLAGER, D. W., Paediatrics and Emergency Medicine
O'KIEEFE, D., Medicine
OLDFIELD, E., Neurological Surgery
OMMAYA, A., Neurological Surgery
O'NEILL, J., Ophthalmology
ORENSTEIN, J., Pathology
ORKIN, B., Surgery
PACKER, R. J., Neurology and Paediatrics
PALOMBI, J., Psychiatry and Behavioural Sciences, Paediatrics
PAN, J., Obstetrics and Gynaecology
PARENTI, D., Medicine, Microbiology and Tropical Medicine
PARKER, P., Paediatrics
PARKS, M., Ophthalmology, Paediatrics
PATEL, R. I., Anaesthesiology and Critical Care Medicine, Paediatrics
PATIERNO, S., Pharmacology, Genetics, Environmental Occupational Health
PAWLSON, L. G., Healthcare Sciences, Medicine, Health Services Management and Policy
PEDREIRA, F., Paediatrics
PEEBLES, P., Paediatrics
PEELE, R., Psychiatry and Behavioural Sciences
PERMAN, G., Psychiatry and Behavioural Sciences
PERRY, D., Pharmacology
PETROVITCH, C., Anaesthesiology and Critical Care Medicine
PEUSNER, K., Anatomy and Cell Biology
PHILLIPS, M., Medicine
PILLAI, M., Medicine
PLATIA, E. V., Medicine
POLIS, M., Emergency Medicine
POLLACK, M. M., Anaesthesiology and Critical Care Medicine, Paediatrics
POST, J., Psychiatry and Behavioural Sciences
POTOLICCHIO, S. J., Neurology and Neurological Surgery
POTTER, B. M., Radiology and Paediatrics
POVAR, G., Health Care Sciences, Medicine
POWERS, D., Obstetrics and Gynaecology
PRINCIPATO, J., Surgery
PROTOS, P., Obstetrics and Gynaecology
PULASKI, P., Neurology
PUMPHREY, R., Surgery
PUTNAM, J., Medicine
PYATT, R., Radiology
RABSON, A., Pathology
RAIS-BAHRMANI, K., Paediatrics
RANKIN, J., Psychiatry and Behavioural Sciences
RANKIN, R., Psychiatry and Behavioural Sciences
RAPOPORT, J., Psychiatry and Behavioural Sciences, Paediatrics
RATNER, R., Psychiatry and Behavioural Sciences
REAMAN, G. H., Paediatrics
REICH, W., Psychiatry and Behavioural Sciences
REISS, D., Psychiatry and Behavioural Sciences, Medicine and Psychology
RESTAK, R., Neurology
RICKLES, F., Medicine, Paediatrics
RIEGELMAN, R., Epidemiology and Biostatistics, Medicine, Health Care Sciences
RIEGER, R., Paediatrics, Psychiatry and Behavioural Sciences
ROBBINS, D. C., Medicine
ROBERTSON, W. W., Orthopaedic Surgery
ROBINOWITZ, C., Psychiatry and Behavioural Sciences
ROBINSON, L., Psychiatry and Behavioural Sciences
RODRIGUEZ-GARCIA, R., Global Health, Prevention and Community Health, International Affairs
ROSENBAUM, S., Health Policy, Health Services Management and Leadership, Health Care Sciences
ROSENBERG, J., Medicine
ROSENBLUM, S., Psychiatry and Behavioural Sciences
ROSENQUIST, G. C., Paediatrics
ROSENSTEIN, J., Anatomy and Cell Biology, Neurological Surgery
ROSS, M., Obstetrics and Gynaecology
ROTHMAN, B., Obstetrics and Gynaecology
ROTSZTAIN, A., Medicine
RUBOVITS-SEITZ, P., Psychiatry and Behavioural Sciences
RUCKMAN, R. N., Paediatrics
RUDZKI, C., Medicine
RUSHTON, H. G., Urology and Paediatrics
SADIN, H., Medicine
SARIN, P., Environmental Occupational Heath, Biochemistry and Molecular Biology
SCALETTAR, R., Medicine
SCHECHTER, G. P., Medicine
SCHEER, J., Health Care Sciences
SCHLEIN, P., Medicine
SCHNEIDER, M., Medicine
SCHWARTZ, A., Pathology
SCHWARTZ, R., Paediatrics, Health Care Sciences
SCOTT, D., Immunology, Anatomy and Cell Biology
SCOTT, J., Emergency Medicine
SCOTT, S., Medicine
SEIBEL, N., Paediatrics
SEIDES, S., Medicine
SEKHAR, L. N., Neurological Surgery
SEMERJIAN, H., Urology
SEVER, J. L., Paediatrics, Microbiology and Tropical Medicine, Obstetrics and Gynaecology
SHARGEL, M., Medicine
SHESSER, R. F., Emergency Medicine, Medicine, Environmental Occupational Health
SHORE, M., Paediatrics
SHORT, B. L., Paediatrics
SHRIER, D., Psychiatry and Behavioural Sciences, Paediatrics
SIDAWY, A. N., Surgery
SIDAWY, M., Pathology
SILBER, T. J., Paediatrics, Global Health, Prevention and Community Health
SILVA, C., Surgery
SILVER, S., Pathology, Prevention and Community Health, Medicine
SIMON, D., Medicine
SIMON, G. L., Medicine, Biochemistry and Molecular Biology, Microbiology and Tropical Medicine
SIMON, J., Obstetrics and Gynaecology
SINGH, N., Paediatrics, Health Care Sciences, Global Health
SLUZKI, C., Psychiatry and Behavioural Sciences
SLY, R. M., Paediatrics
SMITH, L., Surgery
SMITH, M., Emergency Medicine
SMOLLER, B., Psychiatry and Behavioural Sciences
SOLDIN, S. J., Paediatrics, Pathology
SOLOMON, F., Psychiatry and Behavioural Sciences
SOREL, E., Psychiatry and Behavioural Sciences
SOUTHBY, R., Global Health, Health Care Sciences, Health Policy
SPAGNOLO, S. V., Medicine
STAR, R., Medicine
STARK, W., Psychiatry and Behavioural Sciences, Paediatrics
STEIN, M., Psychiatry and Behavioural Sciences, Paediatrics
STEINBERG, W. M., Medicine
STEINFELD, H., Medicine
STERN, M., Psychiatry and Behavioural Sciences
STEVENS, C., Psychiatry and Behavioural Sciences
STOCK, M., Medicine and Health Care Sciences
STOCKTON, W., Psychiatry and Behavioural Sciences

STONE, A., Health Care Sciences, Medicine
STOPAK, B., Neurological Surgery
STOPAK, S., Ophthalmology
STRASSBURGER, F., Paediatrics
STRICKLAND, D., Biochemistry and Molecular Biology
TAUBER, L., Neurological Surgery
TAUBIN, J., Medicine, Health Care Sciences
TAVASSOLI, F., Pathology
TAYLOR, D., Psychiatry and Behavioural Sciences
TETTE, A., Surgery
THOMAS, J., Psychiatry and Behavioural Sciences
THOMPSON, A., Medicine
TIEVSKY, G., Radiology
TRAMONT, E., Medicine
TROUT, H., Surgery
TRUJILLO, N., Medicine
TSOKOS, G., Paediatrics
TUAZON, C. U., Medicine
TUCHMAN, M., Paediatrics, Biochemistry and Molecular Biology
TURNER, M., Dermatology
USHER, M., Psychiatry and Behavioural Sciences
VAN BREDA, A., Radiology
VANDERHOEK, J., Biochemistry and Molecular Biology
VARGHESE, P. J., Medicine and Paediatrics
VELASQUEZ, M. T., Medicine
VENBRUX, A., Radiology, Surgery
VIRMANI, R., Pathology
WALETZKY, J., Psychiatry and Behavioural Sciences
WALKER, G., Biochemistry and Molecular Biology
WALSH, R., Anatomy and Cell Biology, Neurological Surgery
WARGOTZ, E., Pathology
WARREN, N., Dermatology
WARTOFSKY, L., Medicine
WATKIN, D., Medicine
WEGLICKI, W. B., Medicine, Physiology and Experimental Medicine
WEINBERGER, D., Psychiatry and Behavioural Sciences
WEINSTEIN, S., Neurology, Paediatrics
WEISS, H., Medicine
WEISS, L., Medicine
WELBORN, L. G., Anaesthesiology and Critical Care Medicine, Paediatrics
WERLING, L., Pharmacology, Neurological Surgery
WHERRY, D., Surgery
WHITE, P. H., Medicine and Paediatrics
WILKINSON, R., Medicine
WILLIAMS, C. M., Dermatology and Pathology
WILLIAMS, J. F., Anaesthesiology and Critical Care Medicine, Health Services Management and Policy
WILLIAMS, M., Pathology
WILLIAMS, S., Obstetrics and Gynaecology
WINKLES, J., Biochemistry and Molecular Biology
WISNESKI, L., Medicine
WITTENBERG, R., Psychiatry and Behavioural Sciences
WOLFE, M., Medicine
WOLIN, S., Psychiatry and Behavioural Sciences
WOLMAN, S., Pathology
WOOD, B., Anthropology, Anatomy and Cell Biology
WRIGHT, D. C., Neurological Surgery
YODAIKEN, R., Pathology, Health Care Sciences
YOO, D., Medicine
YU, G., Urology
ZAJTCHUK, R., Surgery
ZALAL, G. H., Surgery and Paediatrics
ZALESKE, D., Orthopaedic Surgery, Paediatrics
ZEMAN, R., Radiology
ZIMMERMAN, M., Ophthalmology
ZINNER, J., Psychiatry and Behavioural Sciences

School of Public Health and Health Services:

BILES, B., Health Policy
BORZI, P., Health Policy
BOYD, N. R., Prevention and Community Health
CAWLEY, J. F., Prevention and Community Health
D'ANGELO, L. J., Prevention and Community Medicine
DARR, K. J., Health Services Management and Leadership
EASTAUGH, S. R., Health Services Management and Leadership
EL-MOHANDES, A., Prevention and Community Medicine
GREENBERG, W., Health Economics
GUIDOTTI, T. L., Environmental and Occupational Health
HIDALGO, J., Health Policy
HIRSCH, R. P., Epidemiology and Biostatistics
LACHIN, J., Epidemiology and Biostatistics
LEVINE, P. H., Epidemiology and Biostatistics, Environmental and Occupational Health
MICHAELS, D., Environmental and Occupational Health
MILLER, W. C., Exercise Science
PAUP, D. C., Exercise Science
RIEGELMAN, R. K., Epidemiology and Biostatistics
RODRIGUEZ-GARCIA, R., Center for International Health
ROSSELLO, P., Global Health
SARIN, P., Environmental and Occupational Health
SOUTHBY, R. M. F., Global Health, Health Policy
SULLIVAN, P. A., Exercise Science
WINDSOR, R. A., Prevention and Community Medicine

Graduate School of Education and Human Development:

CASTLEBERRY, M. S., Special Education
CONFESSORE, G. J., Higher Education Administration
CUMMINGS, W. K., International Education
DEW, D. W., Counselling, Psychiatry and Behavioural Sciences
EL-KHAWAS, E. H., Education Policy
FERRANTE, R., Education
FREUND, M. B., Special Education
FUTRELL, M. H., Education
HEDDESHEIMER, J. C., Counselling, Psychiatry and Behavioural Sciences
HOARE, C. H., Human Devt and Human Resource Devt
HOLMES, D. H., Education
HOWERTON, E. B., Jr, Education
IANACONE, R. N., Special Education
KOCHHAR-BRYANT, C. A., Special Education
LINKOWSKI, D. C., Counselling, Psychology and Behavioural Sciences
LYNCH, S. H., Teacher Preparation, Special Education
MAZUR, A. J., Special Education
MULLER, R. O., Educational Research
PALEY, N. B., Elementary Education
PARATORE, S. R., Education
ROTBERG, I. C., Education Policy
SASHKIN, M., Human Resource Devt
SCHWANDT, D. R., Human Resource Devt
SHOTEL, J. R., Special Education
TAYMANS, J. H., Special Education
WATSON, A., Higher Education Admin.
WEST, L. L., Special Education
WHITAKER, R., Higher Education

GEORGETOWN UNIVERSITY

37th and O Sts, NW, Washington, DC 20057
Telephone: (202) 687-0100
Internet: www.georgetown.edu

Founded in 1789 as the first Catholic univ. in the USA

Pres.: JOHN J. DEGIOIA
Provost: JAMES J. O'DONNELL
Sr Vice-Pres. and Chief Admin. Officer: SPIROS DIMOLITSAS
Sr Vice-Pres., Chief Financial Officer, and Treas.: CHRIS AUGOSTINI
Sr Vice-Pres. for Strategic Devt: DANIEL R. PORTERFIELD
Exec. Vice-Pres. and Exec. Dean of the School of Medicine: HOWARD FEDEROFF
Exec. Vice-Pres. and Dean of Law Center: WILLIAM TREANOR
Vice-Pres. and Chief Human Resources Officer: MARY ANN MAHIN
Vice-Pres. for Facilities and Student Housing: KAREN S. FRANK
Vice-Pres. for Financial Planning and Analysis: DAVID RUBINSTEIN
Vice-Pres. and Gen. Univ. Counsel: STEPHANIE TSACOUMIS
Vice-Pres. for Alumni and Univ. Relations: R. BARTLEY MOORE
Vice-Pres. for Institutional Diversity and Equity: ROSEMARY KILKENNY
Vice-Pres. for Mission and Ministry: Fr PHILIP L. BOROUGHS
Vice-Pres. for Student Affairs and Dean of Students: TODD A. OLSON
Vice-Pres. of Technology Commercialization: CLAUDIA CHERNEY STEWART
Vice-Pres. for Univ. Safety: ROCCO DELMONACO, Jr
Registrar: JOHN Q. PIERCE, IV
Librarian: ARTEMIS G. KIRK

Library of 2,123,000 vols
Number of teachers: 1,957 (1,268 full-time, 689 part-time)
Number of students: 15,318

Publications: *American Criminal Law Review*, *Domesday Book*, *Entrecaminos*, *Georgetown Immigration Law Journal*, *Georgetown International Environmental Law Review*, *Georgetown Journal of Gender and the Law*, *Georgetown Journal of International Affairs*, *Georgetown Journal of Legal Ethics*, *Georgetown Journal on Poverty Law & Policy*, *Georgetown Law Journal* (6 a year), *Georgetown Magazine* (4 a year), *Georgetown Medical Bulletin* (3 a year), *Georgetown Public Policy Review*, *Gnovis*, *Hoya Review*, *The Blue and Gray* (26 a year), *Law and Policy in International Business* (3 a year), *The Hoya* (104 a year), *The Voice* (52 a year), *The Anthem*, *The Tax Lawyer*

DEANS

Georgetown College: CHESTER L. GILLIS
Graduate School of Arts and Sciences: TIMOTHY A. BARBARI
Law Center: T. ALEXANDER ALEINIKOFF
McDonough School of Business: Dr GEORGE G. DALY
Walsh School of Foreign Service: ROBERT L. GALLUCCI
School of Medicine: STEPHEN RAY MITCHELL (Dean for Medical Education)
School of Nursing and Health Studies: JULIE A. DELOIA
School of Continuing Studies: ROBERT L. MANUEL

PROFESSORS

Edmund A. Walsh School of Foreign Service:

ALBRIGHT, M.
ANDERSON, J.
BAILEY, J.
CANZONERI, M.
CHICKERING, R.
CROCKER, C.
CUDDINGTON, J.

CUMBY, R. E.
ESPOSITO, J. L.
GALLUCCI, R. L.
HADDAD, Y. Y.
HOWE, H. M.
HUDSON, M. C.
IKENBERRY, G. J.
KEELY, C. B.
KLINE, J. M.
KROGH, P. F.
LAKE, A.
LANGAN, J.
LIEBER, R.
MCHENRY, D.
MCNEILL, J. R.
MIKELL, G.
MORAN, T. H.
PIRTLE, C. E.
RAMO, F.
REARDON-ANDERSON, J.
STENT, A.
STITES, R.
STOWASSER, B.
SUBIRATS, J.
TABAK, F.
TILLMAN, S. P.
TUCKER, N. B.
VALENZUELA, A.
VIKSNINS, G. J.
VOLL, J.
WEISS, C.
WINTERS, F. X.
YOST, C.

Law School:

ABERNATHY, C. F.
ALEINIKOFF, T. A.
AREEN, J. C.
BABCOCK, H.
BAUMAN, J. D.
BLOCH, S. L.
BLOCHE, M. G.
BYRNE, J. P.
CAMPBELL, A. J.
CARTER, B. E.
CASHIN, S. D.
CHUSED, R. H.
COHEN, J. E.
COHEN, S. B.
COHN, S. L.
COLE, D. D.
COOK, A. E.
COPACINO, J. M.
DASH, S.
DIAMOND, R. D.
DINH, V. D.
DONAHOE, D. R.
DRINAN, R. F.
EDELMAN, P. B.
ERNST, D. R.
FEINERMAN, J. V.
FELDBLUM, C. R.
FELDMAN, H. L.
GINSBURG, M. D.
GOLDBERG, S. P.
GOLDBLATT, S. H.
GOSTIN, L. O.
GOTTESMAN, M. H.
GULATI, G. M.
GUSTAFSON, C. H.
HAFT, R. J.
HAY, A. M.
HEINZERLING, L.
JACKSON, J. H.
JACKSON, V. C.
JORDAN, E. C.
KATYAL, N. K.
KING, P. A.
KOPLOW, D. A.
LANGEVOORT, D. C.
LAWRENCE, C. R., III
LAZARUS, R. J.
LUBAN, D. J.
MACKLIN, L. W. S.
MATSUDA, M. J.
MENKEL-MEADOW, C. J.
MLYNIEC, W. J.
MURPHY, J. G., Jr
NORTON, E. H.
OAKLEY, R. L.
OLDHAM, J. C.
O'SULLIVAN, J. R.
PAGE, J. A.
PEARLMAN, R. A.
PELLER, G.
PERDUE, W. C.
PITOFSKY, R.
QUINN, K. P.
RAMSFIELD, J. J.
REGAN, M. C., Jr
ROE, R. L.
ROSS, S. D.
ROTHSTEIN, P. F.
SALOP, S. C.
SCHOTLAND, R. A.
SCHRAG, P. G.
SCHWARTZ, W. F.
SEIDMAN, L. M.
SPANN, G. A.
STROMSETH, J. E.
STUMBERG, R. K.
TAGUE, P. W.
TARULLO, D. K.
THOMAS, J. R.
TUSHNET, M. V.
VÁZQUEZ, C. M.
VUKOWICH, W. T.
WASSERSTROM, S. J.
WEIDENBRUCH, P. P., Jr
WEISS, E. B.
WERRO, F.
WEST, R. L.
WILLIAMS, W. W.

McDonough School of Business:

AGGARWAL, R.
ANDREASEN, A. R.
BIES, R. J.
BRENKERT, G. G.
COOKE, T. B.
DROMS, W. G.
ERNST, R.
FEKRAT, M. A.
FERDOWS, K.
GRANT, R.
JOHANSSON, J. K.
LEVY, M. B.
MCCABE, D. M.
MAYO, J. W.
MAZZOLA, J. B.
MICELI, M. P.
NOLLEN, S. D.
ORD, J. K.
PARKER, R. S.
POWERS, J. J., Jr
QUINN, D. P.
REINSCH, L.
STATEN, M. E.
THOMAS, R. J.
WALKER, D. A.

School of Nursing and Health Studies:

BAIGIS, J.
EVANS, C.
FILERMAN, G.
RAMEY, C.
RAMEY, S.

Undergraduate School:

AGGARWAL, R., School of Business
ALATIS, J. E., Linguistics and Modern Greek
ALBRECHT, J. W., Economics
ALBRIGHT, M. K., Practice of Diplomacy
ANDERLINI, L., Economics
ANDREASEN, A. R., School of Business
ASTARITA, T., History
BABB, V., English
BAIGIS, J., Nursing
BAILEY, J. J., Government and School of Foreign Service
BARNES, S. H., Govt and School of Foreign Service
BARROWS, E. M., Biology
BATES, R. D., Jr, Chemistry
BEAUCHAMP, T. L., Philosophy
BENKE, G., Mathematics
BENSKY, R. D., French
BETZ, P. F., English
BIES, R. J., School of Business
BRADLEY, Rev. D. J. M., Philosophy
BRENKERT, G. G., School of Business
BROUGH, J. B., Philosophy
BROWN, D. M., History
BYRNES, A. S., German
CALVERT, S., Psychology
CALVEZ, J.-Y., Government
CANZONERI, M. B., Economics and School of Foreign Service
CAREY, G. W., Government
CHANG, D.-C., Mathematics
CHAPMAN, G. B., Biology
CHAPMAN, T., School of Nursing and Health Studies
CHICKERING, R., History and School of Foreign Service
CIMA, G. G., English
COLLINS, J. B., History
COLLINS, S. M., Economics
COOKE, T. B., School of Business
CROCKER, C. A., Strategic Studies in School of Foreign Service
CUDDINGTON, J. T., Economics and School of Foreign Service
CUMBY, R. E., International Business Diplomacy
CURRAN, R. E., History
CURRIE, J. F., Physics
DAVIS, W., Philosophy
DENNING, D. E., Computer Science
DROMS, W.M G., School of Business
ENGLER, H., Mathematics
ERNST, R., School of Business
ESPOSITO, J. L., Center for Muslim–Christian Understanding
EVANS, M. D., Economics
FASOLD, R. H W., Linguistics
FEKRAT, M. A., School of Business
FERDOWS, K.A, School of Business
FILERMAN, G., Health Studies
FINKEL, N. J., Psychology
GALE, I., Economics
GALLUCCI, R. L., School of Foreign Service
GIBERT, S. P., Government
GLAVIN, J. J., English
GODSON, R., Government
GOLDFRANK, D. M., History
GOMEZ-LOBO, A., Philosophy
GOODMAN, A. E., School of Foreign Service
GORMLEY, W. T., Government and Public Policy
GRANT, R. M., School of Business
GUSTAFSON, T., Government
HADDAD, Y. Y., School of Foreign Service
HALL, C. M., Sociology
HAUGHT, J. F., Theology
HEELAN, P. A., Philosophy
HENDERSON, E. J., Biology
HILTON, A. H., Art
HIRSH, J. C., English
HOLMER, J. M., English
HOWARD, D. V., Psychology
HUDSON, M. C., Arab Studies
IKENBERRY, G. J., School of Foreign Service
IRIZARRY, E. D., Spanish
JANKOWSKY, K. R., German
JOHANSSON, J. K., School of Business
JOHNSON, R. M., History
JOYNER, C. C., Government
KALYANASUNDARAM, B., Computer Science
KAZIN, M., History
KELTNER, B., School of Nursing and Health Studies
KERTESZ, M., Chemistry
KING, T. M., Theology
KIRKPATRICK, J. J.
KLINE, J. M., School of Foreign Service
KONÉ, A., French
KORD, S. T., German

KROGH, P. F., School of Foreign Service
KUHN, S. T., Philosophy
LAGNESE, J. E., Mathematics
LAKE, A., School of Foreign Service
LARUBIA-PRADO, F., Spanish
LEVY, M. B., School of Business
LIEBER, R. J., Govt
MCAULIFFE, J. D., Georgetown College
MCCABE, D. M., School of Business
MCDONALD, W. F., Sociology
MCHENRY, D. F., School of Foreign Service
MCKEOWN, E., Theology
MCNAMARA, D., Sociology
MCNEILL, J. R., School of Foreign Service and History
MCNELIS, P. D., Economics and School of Foreign Service
MADDOX, L. B., English
MARTIRE, D. E., Chemistry
MARULLO, S., Sociology
MASSOUD-MOGHADDAM, F., Psychology
MAZZOLA, J. B., School of Business
MICELI, M. P., School of Business
MIKELL, G., Sociology and School of Foreign Service
MORAN, T. H., Int. Business Diplomacy
MORRIS, M. A., Slavic Languages
MUJICA, B. L., Spanish
MURPHY, G. R., German
NEALE, J. H., Biology
NISHIOKA, D. J., Biology
NOLLEN, S. D., School of Business
O'BRIEN, G., English
ORD, J. K., School of Business
PARKER, R. S., School of Business
PARROTT, W. G., Psychology
PFORDRESHER, J. C., English
PHILLIPS, D. A., Psychology
POPE, M. T., Chemistry
PRELINGER, E. A., Art
PUTO, C. P., School of Business
QUINN, D., School of Business
RAGUSSIS, M., English
RAMEY, C. T., School of Nursing and Health Studies
RAMEY, S. L., School of Nursing and Health Studies
RAPPAPORT, J., Spanish and School of Foreign Service
REARDON-ANDERSON, J., School of Foreign Service
REINSCH, N. LAMAR, Jr, School of Business
ROBINSON, D. N., Psychology
ROSENBLATT, J. P., English
ROSHWALD, A., History
RUEDY, J. D., History
RYDING, K. C., Arabic
SANDEFUR, J. T., Jr, Mathematics
SCHALL, J. V., Govt
SCHIFFRIN, D., Linguistics
SCHURER, W., School of Business
SCHWARTZ, M., Economics
SCOLLON, R. T., Linguistics
SERENE, J. W., Physics
SEVERINO, R., Italian
SHAHID, I., Arabic
SHERMAN, N.
SITTERSON, J. C., Jr, English
SLEVIN, J. F., English
SMITH, B. R., English
STEINBERG, D. I., School of Foreign Service
STENT, A., Govt
STITES, R., History and School of Foreign Service
STOWASSER, B., Arabic and School of Foreign Service
SWEENEY, R. J., School of Business
SZITTYA, P. R., English
TAMBASCO, A. J., Theology
TANNEN, D.
TAYLOR, D. W., Biology
THOMAS, R. J., School of Business
TUCKER, J. E., History
TUCKER, N. B., School of Foreign Service and History
VALENZUELA, A., Government
VEATCH, R. M., Philosophy
VELAUTHAPILLAI, M., Computer Science
VERECKE, W., Philosophy
VIKSNINS, G. J., Economics and School of Foreign Service
VOLL, J. O., School of Foreign Service and History
VROMAN, S., Economics
WALKER, D. A., School of Business
WALTERS, L. B., Jr, Philosophy
WAYNE, S. J., Govt
WEISS, C., School of Foreign Service
WEISS, R. G., Chemistry
WILCOX, W. C., Govt
WINTERS, F. X., School of Foreign Service
YANG, D. C., Chemistry
YOST, C. A., School of Foreign Service

HOWARD UNIVERSITY

2400 Sixth St, NW, Washington, DC 20059
Telephone: (202) 806-6100
Fax: (202) 806-5934
Internet: www.howard.edu

Founded 1867
Private control
Academic year: August to May (2 terms)

Pres.: Dr SIDNEY RIBEAU
Sr Vice-Pres.: Dr HASSAN MINOR
Sr Vice-Pres. and Chief Financial Officer: ROBERT TAROLA
Sr Vice-Pres. for Health Sciences: Dr EVE HIGGINBOTHAM
Sr Vice-Pres. and Sec.: ARTIS G. HAMPSHIRE-COWAN
Exec. Vice-Pres. and Chief Operating Officer: TROY STOVALL
Vice-Pres. for Research and Compliance: Dr FLORENCE BONNER
Vice-Pres. for Development and Alumni Affairs: NESTA BERNARD
Vice-Pres. for Student Affairs: Dr BARBARA GRIFFIN
Provost and Chief Academic Officer: Dr JAMES WYCHE
Gen. Counsel: NORMA LEFTWICH
Dir of Libraries: MOHAMED MEKKAWI

Library: 1.9m. vols
Number of teachers: 2,051
Number of students: 10,987

Publications: *Howard Journal of Communications* (4 a year), *Howard Law Review* (4 a year), *Journal of Negro Education* (4 a year), *Journal of Religious Thought* (2 a year), *The Capstone* (weekly during academic terms)

DEANS

College of Arts and Sciences: Dr JAMES DONALDSON
College of Dentistry: Dr LEO E. ROUSE
College of Medicine: Dr ROBERT TAYLOR
College of Pharmacy, Nursing and Allied Health Sciences: Dr BEATRICE ADDERLY-KELLY
Graduate School: Dr CHARLES BETSEY
School of Business: Dr BARRON HARVEY
School of Communications: (vacant)
School of Divinity: Dr ALTON POLLARD III
School of Education: Dr LESLIE FENWICK
School of Engineering, Architecture and Computer Sciences: Dr JAMES MITCHELL
School of Law: Dr KURT L. SCHMOKE
School of Social Work: Dr CUDORE L. SNELL

NATIONAL DEFENSE INTELLIGENCE COLLEGE

200 MacDill Blvd, Washington, DC 20340-5100
Telephone: (202) 231-3319
E-mail: jmic@dia.mil
Internet: www.dia.mil/college

Founded 1962 as Defense Intelligence School, renamed Joint Military Intelligence College 1993, present name 2006
Pres.: DAVID R. ELLISON
Provost: Dr TERESA J. DOMZAL
Dir of Office of Institutional Research: Dr TARA E. MCNEALY
Library: 2.5m. items.

STRAYER UNIVERSITY

Suite 300, 1133 15th St, NW, Washington, DC 20005
Telephone: (202) 408-2400
Fax: (202) 289-1831
E-mail: washington@strayer.edu
Internet: www.strayer.edu

Founded 1892 as Strayer Business College; present name 1998
Private control (Strayer Education, Inc.)
Academic year: September to September

Pres. and CEO: ROBERT S. SILBERMAN
Provost and Academic Dean: Dr J. CHRIS TOE
Campus Man.: ED DOBSON

Library of 32,000 vols (combined holdings)
Number of teachers: 575 (125 full-time, 450 adjunct)
Number of students: 16,500

Areas of study: accounting, business admin., information technology.

BRANCH CAMPUSES

Alexandria Campus: 2730 Eisenhower Ave, Alexandria, VA 22314; tel. (703) 329-9100; fax (703) 3299602; e-mail alexandria@strayer.edu; Campus Man. OSCAR MAMARIL.

Anne Arundel Campus: 1520 Jabez Run, Suite 100, Millersville, MD 21108; tel. (410) 923-4500; e-mail annearundel@strayer.edu; Campus Man. JAMES DERDOCK.

Arlington Campus: 2121 15th St, North, Arlington, VA 22201; tel. (703) 892-5100; fax (703) 769-2677; e-mail arlington@strayer.edu; Campus Man. DAN JACKSON.

Cary Campus: Suite 105, 3200 Gateway Centre Blvd, Morrisville, NC 27560; tel. (919) 466-1150; e-mail cary@strayer.edu; Campus Man. DIANNA ANDERSON.

Chamblee Campus: Suite 100, 3055 Northeast Expressway, Atlanta, GA 30341; tel. (770) 454-9270; fax (770) 457-6958; e-mail chamblee@strayer.edu; Campus Man. AYANNA MARTIN.

Chesapeake Campus: Suite 400, 700 Independence Parkway, Chesapeake, VA 23320; tel. (757) 382-9900; e-mail chesapeake@strayer.edu; Campus Man. MICHAEL CAMDEN.

Chesterfield Campus: Suite 100, 2820 Waterford Lake Dr., Midlothian, VA 23112; tel. (804) 763-6300; fax (804) 763-6304; e-mail chesterfield@strayer.edu.

Cobb County Campus: Suite 700, 3101 Towercreek Parkway, Atlanta, GA 30339; tel. (770) 612-2170; fax (770) 956-7241; e-mail cobbcounty@strayer.edu; Campus Man. HAROON MOKEL.

Fredericksburg Campus: 4500 Plank Rd, Fredericksburg, VA 22407; fax (540) 785-8808; e-mail fredericksburg@strayer.edu; Campus Man. CLARY ORSBOURNE.

Greensboro Campus: Suite 400, 4900 Koger Blvd, Greensboro, NC 27404; tel. (336) 315-7800; fax (336) 315-7830; e-mail greensboro@strayer.edu; Campus Man. TONYA WILLIAMS.

Greenville Campus: Suite 300, 555 North Pleasantburg Dr., Greenville, SC 29607; tel. (864) 232-4700; fax (864) 235-5739; e-mail greenville@strayer.edu; Campus Man. KRISTA LIMER.

Henrico Campus: 11501 Nuckols Rd, Glen Allen, VA 23059; tel. (804) 527-1000; e-mail henrico@strayer.edu.

King of Prussia Campus: Suite G 50, 234 Mall Blvd, King of Prussia, PA 19406; tel. (610) 992-1700; fax (610) 992-9777; e-mail kingofprussia@strayer.edu; Campus Man. CHARLES BAUKMAN.

Loudoun Campus: Suite 200, 45150 Russell Branch Parkway, Ashburn, VA 20147; tel. (703) 729-8800; fax (703) 729-8820; e-mail loudoun@strayer.edu; Campus Man. BRENDA EVANS.

Lower Bucks County Campus: Suite 100, 3600 Horizon Blvd, Trevose, PA 19453; tel. (215) 953-5999; fax (215) 953-9464; e-mail bucks@strayer.edu; Campus Man. FATIMA ARUKWE.

Manassas Campus: 9990 Battleview Parkway, Manassas, VA 20109; tel. (703) 330-8400; fax (703) 330-8135; e-mail manassas@strayer.edu; Campus Man. MARLON PRINCE.

Montgomery Campus: Suite 300, 20030 Century Blvd, Germantown, MD 20874; tel. (301) 540-8066; e-mail montgomery@strayer.edu; Campus Man. ROBERT SCHULTZ.

Nashville Campus: Suite 200, 30 Rachel Dr., Nashville, TN 37214; tel. (615) 871-2260; fax (615) 391-5330; e-mail nashville@strayer.edu; Campus Man. TONYA YANCY.

Newport News Campus: Suite 100, 813 Diligence Dr., Newport News, VA 23606; tel. (757) 873-3100; e-mail newportnews@strayer.edu; Campus Man. CONSTANCE ARTER.

North Charlotte Campus: Suite 150, 8335 IBM Dr., Charlotte, NC 28262; tel. (704) 717-2380; e-mail northcharlotte@strayer.edu; Campus Man. CARTER SMITH.

North Raleigh Campus: Suite 3214, 3200 Spring Forest Rd, Raleigh, NC 27616; tel. (919) 878-9900; fax (919) 878-6625; e-mail northraleigh@strayer.edu; Campus Man. CHERRY CLARK.

Owings Mills Campus: Suite 100, 500 Redland Court, Owings Mills, MD 21117; tel. (443) 394-3339; e-mail owingsmills@strayer.edu; Campus Man. PAULA KHANAL.

Prince George's Campus: 4710 Auth Pl., 1st Floor, Suitland, MD 20746; tel. (301) 423-3600; fax (301) 423-3999; e-mail princegeorges@strayer.edu; Campus Man. SANA CHAUDRY.

Shelby Oaks Campus: Suite 100, 6211 Shelby Oaks Dr., Memphis, TN 38134; tel. (901) 383-6750; fax (901) 373-8700; e-mail shelbyoaks@strayer.edu; Campus Man. DARYL DANIELS.

South Charlotte Campus: Suite 700, 2430 Whitehall Park Dr., Charlotte, NC 28273; tel. (704) 587-5360; e-mail southcharlotte@strayer.edu; Campus Man. HELEN HOUSER.

Takoma Park Campus: 6830 Laurel St, NW, Washington, DC 20012; tel. (202) 722-8100; fax (202) 722-8108; e-mail takomapark@strayer.edu; Campus Man. KAVITA FREEMAN.

Tampa East Campus: Suite 450, 6302 East Martin Luther King Blvd, Tampa, FL 33619; tel. (813) 663-0100; fax (813) 626-2245; e-mail tampaeast@strayer.edu; Campus Man. ROBIN LEWIS-GAGE.

Tampa Westshore Campus: Suite 100, 4902 Eisenhower Blvd, Tampa, FL 33634; tel. (813) 882-0100; e-mail tampawestshore@strayer.edu; Campus Man. DEB SAWYER.

Thousand Oaks Campus: Suite 1100, 2620 Thousand Oaks Blvd, Memphis, TN 38118; tel. (901) 369-0835; fax (901) 565-9400; e-mail thousandoaks@strayer.edu; Campus Man. MARK WILLIAMS.

White Marsh Campus: 9409 Philadelphia Rd, Baltimore, MD 21237; tel. (410) 238-9000; fax (410) 238-9099; e-mail whitemarsh@strayer.edu; Campus Man. RUTH BUTLER.

Woodbridge Campus: 13385 Minnieville Rd, Woodbridge, VA 22192; tel. (703) 878-2800; fax (703) 878-2993; e-mail woodbridge@strayer.edu; Campus Man. FRANK HANCOCK.

TRINITY COLLEGE

125 Michigan Ave, NE, Washington, DC 20017

Telephone: (202) 884-9000
Fax: (202) 884-9229
E-mail: president@trinitydc.edu
Internet: www.trinitydc.edu

Founded 1897

Roman Catholic liberal arts college for women, sponsored by Sisters of Notre Dame de Namur

Pres.: Dr PATRICIA MCGUIRE
Exec. Vice-Pres. and Chief Financial Officer: RAYMOND V. BARBIC
Vice-Pres. for Academic Affairs: SUE BLANSHAN
Vice-Pres. for Institutional Advancement: ANN PAULEY
Dean of Education: SUELLEN MEARA
Dean of Student Services: MICHELE BOWIE
Registrar: MARVA BOSWELL
Dir of Library: KAYE GAPEN

Library: over 200,000 vols
Number of teachers: 59 full-time
Number of students: 1,500

Publications: *Alumnae Journal*, *Trinilogue*, *Trinity College Record*, *Trinity Times*, *Trinity Today*

DEANS

College of Arts and Sciences: Dr LORETTA MAY SHPUNT
School of Education: Dr GLORIA GRANTHAM
School of Professional Studies: Dr SARA MURRAY THOMPSON

UNIVERSITY OF THE DISTRICT OF COLUMBIA

4200 Connecticut Ave, NW, Washington, DC 20008

Telephone: (202) 274-5000
Internet: www.udc.edu

Founded 1851; a public urban land-grant univ. organized on 3 campuses from existing colleges; first degree programmes

Pres.: Dr ALLEN L. SESSOMS
Provost and Vice-Pres. for Academic Affairs: GRAEME BAXTER
Vice-Pres. for Student Affairs: JANICE BORLANDOE (acting)
Vice-Pres. for Univ. Relations: BOBBY W. AUSTIN
Chief of Staff and Vice-Pres. of Operations: STAN JACKSON

Number of students: 9,660

DEANS

College of Arts and Sciences: Dr RACHEL PETTY
David A. Clarke School of Law: Dr KATHERINE S. BRODERICK
School of Business and Public Admin.: Dr CHARLES MAHONE
School of Engineering and Applied Sciences: Dr BEN O. LATIGO

WASHINGTON THEOLOGICAL UNION

6896 Laurel St, NW, Washington, DC 20012

Telephone: (202) 726-8800
Fax: (202) 726-1716
E-mail: pr@wtu.edu
Internet: www.wtu.edu

Founded 1968 as Coalition of Religious Seminaries, present name 1969

Private control
Academic year: August to May

Pres.: Rev. FREDERICK J. TILLOTSON
Vice-Pres. for Academic Affairs and Academic Dean: Dr C. COLT ANDERSON
Dir for Institutional Advancement: JOAN KNETEMANN
Registrar: Rev. BARTHOLOMEW MERELLA
Dir of Library: ALEXANDER MOYER

Library of 130,000 vols
Number of students: 250

WESLEY THEOLOGICAL SEMINARY

4500 Massachusetts Ave, NW, Washington, DC 20016

Telephone: (202) 885-8600
Fax: (202) 885-8605
E-mail: admiss@wesleysem.edu
Internet: www.wesleyseminary.edu

Founded 1882 as Westminster Theological Seminary, present name 1958

Private control
Academic year: August to May

Pres.: Rev. Dr DAVID F. MCALLISTER-WILSON
Vice-Pres. for Devt: VOLLIE MELSON
Vice-Pres. for Finance and Admin.: JUNE R. STOWE
Vice-Pres. for Int. Relations: KYUNGLIM SHIN LEE
Dean: BRUCE C. BIRCH
Registrar: MITCHELL BOND
Dir of Library: BILL FAUPEL

Number of students: 660.

ATTACHED RESEARCH INSTITUTES

Churches' Center for Theology and Public Policy: tel. (202) 885-8648; e-mail cctpp@wesleysem.edu; internet www.cctpp.org; Dir Rev. BARBARA G. GREEN.

G. Douglass Lewis Center for Church Leadership: tel. (202) 885-8757; e-mail lewiscenter@wesleyseminary.edu; internet www.churchleadership.com; Dir Dr LOVETT H. WEEMS, Jr.

Henry Luce III Center for Arts and Religion: tel. (202) 885-8608; e-mail artsandreligion@wesleysem.edu; internet www.luceartsandreligion.org; Dir CATHERINE ANDREWS KAPIKIAN.

FLORIDA

BAPTIST COLLEGE OF FLORIDA

5400 College Dr., Graceville, FL 32440-1898

Telephone: (850) 263-3261
E-mail: admissions@baptistcollege.edu
Internet: www.baptistcollege.edu

Founded 1943 as Baptist Bible Institute; present name 2000

Private control
Academic year: August to July

Pres.: Dr THOMAS A. KINCHEN
Sr Vice-Pres.: Dr R. C. HAMMACK
Vice-Pres. for Institutional Advancement: CHARLES R. PARKER
Dir of Devt: KYLE S. LUKE
Dir of Library Services: JOHN E. SHAFFETT, Jr

Number of students: 600

Areas of study: child devt, music, residential child care, teacher education, theology.

BARRY UNIVERSITY

11300 NE Second Ave, Miami Shores, FL 33161-6695

Telephone: (305) 899-3000

Fax: (305) 899-3100
E-mail: admissions@mail.barry.edu
Internet: www.barry.edu

Founded 1940
Academic year: August to May

Pres.: Sister LINDA BEVILACQUA
Provost: Dr LINDA M. PETERSON
Sr Vice-Pres. for Business and Finance: D. BRUCE EDWARDS
Vice-Pres. for Institutional Advancement: ANN E. PATON
Vice-Pres. for Legal Affairs: JOHN WALKER
Vice-Pres. for Student Services: Dr MICHAEL J. GRIFFIN
Registrar: CYNTHIA CHRUSZCZYK
Library Dir: KENNETH VENET

Library of 950,000 vols, 2,880 periodicals, 541,560 microforms
Number of teachers: 311 full-time
Number of students: 8,650

DEANS

College of Arts and Sciences: Dr KAREN CALLAGHAN
College of Health Sciences: Dr PEGGE BELL
School of Adult and Continuing Education: Dr CAROL-RAE SODANO
School of Business: Dr TOMISLAU MANDAKOVIĆ
School of Education: Dr TERRY PIPER
School of Graduate Medical Science: Dr JOHN NELSON
School of Human Performance and Leisure Sciences: (vacant)
School of Law: Dr LETICIA DIAZ
School of Social Work: Dr DEBRA MCPHEE

BETHUNE-COOKMAN COLLEGE

640 Dr Mary McLeod Bethune Blvd, Daytona Beach, FL 32114-3099
Telephone: (386) 481-2000
Fax: (386) 481-2010
E-mail: bronson@cookman.edu
Internet: www.bethune.cookman.edu

Founded 1904
United Methodist Church
Academic year: August to April

Pres.: Dr TRUDIE KIBBE REED
Provost/Vice-Pres. for Academic Affairs: WILLIAM D. LINDSEY
Vice-Pres. for Admin. and Finance: E. DEAN MONTGOMERY
Vice-Pres. for Governmental Relations: JOHNSON AKINLEYE
Vice-Pres. for Institutional Advancement: STEPHEN SHAFER
Vice-Pres. for Student Affairs: RAY SHACKLEFORD (acting)
Registrar: ANN THOMAS
Dir of Library Learning: TASHA LUCAS-YOUMANS

Library of 175,483 vols
Number of teachers: 192 (150 full-time, 42 part-time)
Number of students: 2,895 (2,677 full-time, 218 part-time)

Publication: *Undergraduate Research Journal* (1 a year)

DEANS OF SCHOOLS

Arts and Humanities: Dr JOHNSON O. AKINLEYE
Business: Dr AUBREY E. LONG
Education: Dr LORRAIN DANIELS-DAY
General Studies: Dr LOIS S. FENNELLY
Natural Sciences, Engineering and Mathematics: Dr THEODORE R. NICHOLSON, Sr
Nursing: Dr ALMA Y. DIXON
Social Sciences: Dr SHEILA Y. FLEMMING

CLEARWATER CHRISTIAN COLLEGE

3400 Gulf-to-Bay Blvd, Clearwater, FL 33759-4595
Telephone: (727) 726-1153
Fax: (727) 726-8597
E-mail: admissions@clearwater.edu
Internet: www.clearwater.edu

Founded 1966
Private control
Academic year: August to May

Areas of study: biblical studies, business, education, fine arts, humanities, sciences

Pres.: Dr RICHARD A. STRATTON
Chancellor: Dr ARTHUR E. STEELE
Vice-Pres. for Academic Affairs: Dr MARY DRAPER
Vice-Pres. for Financial and Administrative Affairs: RANDY LIVINGSTON
Vice-Pres. for Student Affairs: RYAN DUPEE
Registrar: TOM CANNON
Dir of Library: ELIZABETH WERNER

Library of 100,000 vols
Number of teachers: 51 (incl. 32 full-time)
Number of students: 561

ECKERD COLLEGE

4200 54th Ave, S, St Petersburg, FL 33711
Telephone: (727) 867-1166
E-mail: admissions@eckerd.edu
Internet: www.eckerd.edu

Founded 1958 as Florida Presbyterian College
Academic year: August to May
Liberal arts college

Pres.: Dr DONALD R. EASTMAN, III
Vice-Pres. and Dean of Faculty: Dr LLOYD W. CHAPIN
Chief Financial Officer: CHRIS BRENNAN
Vice-Pres. for Advancement: MATTHEW BISSET
Vice-Pres. for Church Relations: BENJAMIN J. JACOBSON
Dean of Students: Dr JAMES ANNARELLI
Dir of Admissions: JOHN SULLIVAN
Dir of Library Services: Dr DAVID WENDERSON

Number of teachers: 102 (full-time)
Number of students: 1,631

EDWARD WATERS COLLEGE

1658 Kings Rd, Jacksonville, FL 32209-6199
Telephone: (904) 470-8200
Fax: (904) 470-8048
Internet: www.ewc.edu
Private control

Pres.: Dr OSWALD P. BRONSON, Sr
Vice-Pres. for Academic Affairs: Dr EMMANUEL O. OKAFOR
Registrar: ANGELA FREEMAN
Library Dir: EVELYN BROWN

Areas of study: biology, business admin., communications, computer information systems, criminal justice, elementary education, gerontology, hotel, hospitality and tourism management, mathematics, music education, physical education, political science, psychology, religion and philosophy, sociology.

EMBRY-RIDDLE AERONAUTICAL UNIVERSITY

600 South Clyde Morris Blvd, Daytona Beach, FL 32114-3900
Telephone: (386) 226-6100
E-mail: dbadmit@erau.edu
Internet: www.embryriddle.edu

Founded 1926 as Embry-Riddle School of Aviation; present name 1970
Private control
Academic year: September to August

Pres.: Dr JOHN P. JOHNSON
Provost and Chief Academic Officer: Dr JOHN JOHNSON
Vice-Pres. and Chief Business Officer: ROBERT JOST
Vice-Pres. and Chief Financial Officer: ERIC WEEKES
Vice-Pres. for Devt: PAT RAMSEY
Vice-Pres. for Global Planning and Program Devt: JOHN METZNER
Vice-Pres. for Univ. Relations: KEN STACKPOLE
Chief Information Officer: CINDY BIXLER
Chancellor of Daytona Beach Campus: Dr TOM CONNOLLY
Chancellor of Prescott Campus: DANIEL CARRELL

Number of teachers: 227 (full-time)
Number of students: 4,776

Areas of study: arts and sciences, aviation, business, engineering

DEANS

College of Arts and Sciences: Dr RODNEY PIERCEY
College of Aviation: Dr TIM BRADY
College of Business: Dr DAN PETREE
College of Engineering: Dr REDA MANKBADI

CAMPUSES

Embry-Riddle Aeronautical University—Prescott, Arizona Campus

3700 Willow Creek Rd, Prescott, AZ 86301-3720
Telephone: (928) 777-6600
Fax: (928) 777-6606
E-mail: pradmit@erau.edu
Internet: www.erau.edu
Private control
Academic year: September to August

Chancellor: NORVAL POHL

Number of teachers: 100 (full-time)
Number of students: 1,674 (1,630 undergraduate, 44 postgraduate)

DEANS

College of Arts and Sciences: Dr RICHARD BLOOM
College of Aviation: Dr JACKIE LUEDTKE
College of Engineering: Dr DON RABERN

Embry-Riddle Aeronautical University—Worldwide

600 South Clyde Morris Blvd, Daytona Beach, FL 32114-3900
Telephone: (386) 226-6910
E-mail: ecssc@erau.edu
Internet: www.embryriddle.edu

Chancellor: MARTIN SMITH
Central Regional Dean: Dr BRUCE ROTHWELL
Eastern Regional Dean: Dr BERNARD CORDIAL
Int. Regional Dean: Dr DONNA ROBERTS
Western Regional Dean: Dr KATHERINE MORAN

Number of teachers: 137 (full-time)
Number of students: 25,290 (19,527 undergraduate, 5,763 undergraduate)

Comprises the Center for Distance Learning and the College of Career Education; operates in the USA and Europe.

FLAGLER COLLEGE

POB 1027, St Augustine, FL 32085-1027
Telephone: (904) 829-6481
Fax: (904) 826-0094
E-mail: admiss@flagler.edu
Internet: www.flagler.edu

Founded 1968
Private control
Academic year: September to April

Language of instruction: English
Chancellor: Dr WILLIAM L. PROCTOR
Pres.: Dr WILLIAM ABARE
Vice-Pres. for Business Services: KENNETH RUSSOM
Vice-Pres. for Enrollment: MARC WILLIAR
Dean of Academic Affairs: PAULA MILLER
Dean of Student Services: DANIEL STEWART
Registrar: MIRIAM ROBERSON
Library Dir: MICHAEL GALLEN
Library of 193,729 vols, holdings: 85,654 printed, 69,158 microform, 3,499 audiovisual, 34,940 electronic items, 470 periodicals
Number of students: 2,500

FLORIDA AGRICULTURAL AND MECHANICAL UNIVERSITY

Tallahassee, FL 32307
Telephone: (904) 599-3000
Internet: www.famu.edu
Founded 1887
Pres.: JAMES AMMONS
Provost and Vice-Pres. for Academic Affairs: Dr DEBRA AUSTIN
Vice-Pres. for Admin.: Dr ROBERT D. CAROLL
Vice-Pres. for Research: Dr KEITH H. JACKSON
Vice-Pres. for Univ. Devt and Public Affairs: Col (Retd) RONALD JOE
Librarian: LAUREN B. SAPP
Library of 505,490 vols, 6,000 current periodicals, 131,500 microforms, 73,000 non-print items; depository for US govt publications; consists of the main library and 4 br. libraries in the fields of architecture, eng., journalism and graphic communication, and science
Number of teachers: 532
Number of students: 12,161

DEANS
College of Arts and Sciences: Dr ARTHUR C. WASHINGTON
College of Education: Dr MELVIN GADSON
College of Engineering Sciences, Technology and Agriculture: Dr BOBBY R. PHILLS
College of Pharmacy and Pharmaceutical Sciences: HENRY LEWIS, III
FAMU/FSU College of Engineering: CHING-JEN CHENG
School of Allied Health Sciences: Dr JACQUELINE B. BECK
School of Architecture: RODNER WRIGHT
School of Business and Industry: Dr SYBIL C. MOBLEY
School of General Studies: Dr BARBARA BARNES
School of Graduate Studies, Research and Continuing Education: Dr THEODORE HEMMINGWAY
School of Journalism, Media and Graphic Arts: ROBERT RUGGLES
School of Nursing: Dr MARGARET W. LEWIS

FLORIDA ATLANTIC UNIVERSITY

777 Glades Rd, Boca Raton, FL 33431
Telephone: (561) 297-3000
Internet: www.fau.edu
Founded 1961
State control
Campuses in Boca Raton, Davie, Fort Lauderdale, Jupiter and Port St. Lucie; also Open Univ. and Continuing Education Div. (Fort Lauderdale), Harbor Branch Marine Sciences Building (Fort Pierce) and SeaTech (ocean engineering research and graduate education centre, Dania Beach)
Pres.: FRANK T. BROGAN
Univ. Provost and Chief Academic Officer: Dr JOHN PRITCHETT
Vice-Provost and Chief Information Officer: JASON BALL
Sr Vice-Pres. for Student Affairs: Dr EMANUEL NEWSOME
Vice-Pres. for Research: Dr LARRY LEMANSKI
Vice-Pres. for Univ. Advancement: ANN PATON
Univ. Architect and Vice-Pres.: ROBERT FRIEDMAN
Campus Vice-Pres., Broward Campuses: Dr JOYANNE C. STEPHENS
Campus Vice-Pres., Jupiter: Dr KRISTEN O. MURTAUGH
Campus Vice-Pres., Treasure Coast: Dr GERALD F. LAFFERTY
Registrar: HARRY E. DEMIK
Dir of Libraries: Dr WILLIAM MILLER
Library of 665,000 volumes
Number of teachers: 778
Number of students: 25,000
Publication: *Journal of the Fantastic in the Arts*

DEANS
Charles E. Schmidt College of Science: Dr NATHAN W. DEAN
Christine E. Lynn College of Nursing: Dr ANNE BOYKIN
College of Architecture, Urban and Public Affairs: Dr ROSALYN CARTER
College of Business: Dr BRUCE MALLEN
College of Education: Dr GREGORY F. ALOIA
College of Engineering: Dr KARL K. STEVENS (acting)
Dorothy F. Schmidt College of Arts and Letters: Dr WILLIAM CORVINO
Harriet L. Wilkes Honors College: Dr WILLIAM P. MECH
Open Univ. and Continuing Education: Dr ELY MEYERSON

FLORIDA CHRISTIAN COLLEGE

1011 Bill Beck Blvd, Kissimmee, FL 34744
Telephone: (407) 847-8966
Fax: (407) 847-3925
E-mail: fcc@fcc.edu
Internet: www.fcc.edu
Founded 1975
Private control
Academic year: August to May
Pres.: HAROLD ARMSTRONG
Exec. Vice-Pres.: J. R. (TONY) BUCHANAN
Vice-Pres. for Finance: DAVID L. MCNEELY
Vice-Pres. for Institutional Advancement: WILLIAM K. BEHRMAN
Vice-Pres. for Student Life: TERRY ALLCORN
Librarian: LINDA STARK
Number of teachers: 28
Number of students: 250

DEANS
Management Enrollment: PHILIP VINCENT

FLORIDA GULF COAST UNIVERSITY

10501 FGCU Blvd S, Fort Myers, FL 33965-6565
Telephone: (239) 590-1000
Fax: (239) 590-1059
E-mail: oar@fgcu.edu
Internet: www.fgcu.edu
Founded 1991
Academic year: August to May
Pres.: DICK PEGNETTER
Provost and Vice-Pres. for Academic Affairs: BONNIE L. YEGEDIS
Vice-Pres. for Admin. Services: CURTIS BULLOCK
Vice-Pres. for Univ. Advancement: TOM HEALY
Dean of Graduate Studies and Continual Learning: W. JACK CROCKER
Dean of Instructional Technology: KATHLEEN DAVEY
Dean of Planning and Evaluation: JOSEPH L. RAVELLI
Dean of Student Affairs: JOE SHEPARD
Dir of Library Services: KATHLEEN HOETH
Number of students: 5,300

DEANS
College of Arts and Sciences: JOSE BARRETO
College of Business: RICHARD PEGNETTER
College of Education: LAWRENCE W. BYRNES
College of Health Professions: DENISE HEINEMAN
College of Professional Studies: JOHN MCGAHA

FLORIDA INSTITUTE OF TECHNOLOGY

150 West University Blvd, Melbourne, FL 32901-6975
Telephone: (321) 674-8030
Fax: (321) 674-8004
E-mail: admission@fit.edu
Internet: www.fit.edu
Founded 1958
Academic year: August to May
Pres.: Dr ANTHONY JAMES CATANESE
Exec. Vice-Pres. and Chief Operating Officer: T. DWAYNE MCCAY
Deputy Chief Operating Officer: Dr RAYMOND BONHOMME
Vice-Pres. for Academic Affairs: Dr GORDON NELSON
Vice-Pres. and Chief Financial Officer: JACK ARMUL
Vice-Pres. for Marketing and Communication: WESLEY SUMNER
Vice-Pres. for Research: Dr FREDRIC HAM
Vice-Pres. for Student Affairs: Dr RANDY ALFORD
Registrar: CHARLOTTE YOUNG
Dir of Admission: MICHAEL J. PERRY
Dir of Libraries: Dr CELINE LANG
Number of teachers: 664 (238 full-time, 426 part-time)
Number of students: 8,985

DEANS
College of Aeronautics: Dr WINSTON SCOTT
College of Engineering: Dr THOMAS WAITE
College of Psychology and Liberal Arts: Dr MARY BETH KENKEL
College of Science: Dr HAMID RASSOUL
Nathan M. Bisk College of Business: Dr ROBERT NIEBUHR
School of Extended Graduate Studies: Dr RONALDO L. MARSHALL

FLORIDA INTERNATIONAL UNIVERSITY

University Park, Miami, FL 33199
Telephone: (305) 348-2000
Internet: www.fiu.edu
Founded 1965; part of the State Univ. System of Florida
Pres.: MODESTO A. MAIDIQUE
Provost and Exec. Vice-Pres. for Academic Affairs: RONALD M. BERKMAN
Vice-Provost for Academic Affairs at Biscayne Bay Campus: DAMIAN FERNANDEZ
Sr Vice-Pres.: PAUL GALLAGHER (acting)
Sr Vice-Pres. for Finance and Chief Operating Officer: Dr KENNETH A. JESSELL
Vice-Pres. for Advancement: HOWARD R. LIPMAN
Vice-Pres. for External Relations: DALE CHAPMAN WEBB
Vice-Pres. for Research: GEORGE WALKER
Vice-Pres. for Student Affairs and Undergraduate Education: (vacant)

Vice-Pres. for Univ. Technology Services and Chief Information Officer: (vacant)
Exec. Dir: ANTONIE DOWNS

Library: 1.5m. vols, 9,700 current periodicals, maps, microforms, govt documents, archives, rare books
Number of teachers: 1,100 (full-time)
Number of students: 34,000

DEANS
College of Arts and Sciences: Dr ARTHUR W. HERRIOTT
College of Business Admin.: JOYCE J. ELAM (Exec. Dean)
College of Education: LINDA P. BLANTON
College of Engineering: VISH PRASAD
College of Health and Urban Affairs: Prof. RONALD BERKMAN
School of Journalism and Mass Communication: J. ARTHUR HEISE

FLORIDA MEMORIAL UNIVERSITY

15800 North West 42nd Ave, Miami, FL 33054
Telephone: (305) 626-3600
Internet: www.fmuniv.edu

Founded 1879

Pres.: Dr KARL S. WRIGHT
Provost: Dr SANDRA THOMPSON
Vice-Pres. for Business and Fiscal Affairs: WILLIE KEMP
Vice-Pres. for Office of Institutional Advancement: Dr BARBARA EDWARDS
Vice-Pres. for Student Affairs: Dr HAROLD R. CLARKE, Jr
Dir of Information Management and Technology: PAMELA TENNELL

Library of 116,678 vols, 700 current periodicals
Number of teachers: 100
Number of students: 2,242

FLORIDA METROPOLITAN UNIVERSITY

Suite 400, 6 Hutton Centre Dr., Santa Ana, FL 92707
Telephone: (714) 427-3000
Fax: (714) 427-5111
Internet: fmu.edu

Founded 1995
Private control (Corinthian Colleges, Inc.)

Chair. and CEO: DAVID G. MOORE
Pres. and Chief Operating Officer: ANTHONY DIGIOVANNI
Sr Vice-Pres. for Academic Affairs: Dr MARY H. BARRY
Number of students: 11,000 (all campuses)
Areas of study: accounting, business admin., commercial art, computers, criminal justice, film and video, healthcare, hospitality, int. business, legal assistant/paralegal, management, marketing, network admin.

BRANCH CAMPUSES

Brandon Campus

3924 Coconut Palm Dr., Tampa, FL 33619
Telephone: (813) 621-0041
Fax: (813) 623-5769

Academic Dean: NEIL WERTLEY
Dean of Students: DOLLY BROWN
Registrar: INGRID ZEKAN
Library Dir: MADELINE LOCK.

Jacksonville Campus: 8226 Phillips Highway, Jacksonville, FL 32256; tel. (904) 731-4949; fax (904) 731-0599; f. 2000.

Lakeland Campus: Suite 110, 995 East Memorial Blvd, Lakeland, FL 33801; tel. (863) 686-1444; fax (863) 688-9881.

Melbourne Campus: 2401 North Harbor City Blvd, Melbourne, FL 32935; tel. (321) 253-2929; fax (321) 255-2017.

North Orlando Campus: 5421 Diplomat Circle, Orlando, FL 32810; tel. (407) 628-5870; fax (407) 628-1344; f. 1953 as Jones College.

Orange Park Campus: 805 Wells Rd, Orange Park, FL 32073; tel. (904) 264-9122; f. 2003.

Pinellas Campus: Suite 200, 2471 McMullen Booth Rd, Clearwater, FL 33759; tel. (727) 725-2688; fax (727) 796-3722.

Pompano Beach Campus: 225 North Federal Highway, Pompano Beach, FL 33062; tel. (954) 783-7339; fax (954) 568-2008.

South Orlando Campus: 2411 Sand Lake Rd, Orlando, FL 32809; tel. (407) 851-2525; fax (407) 851-1477.

Tampa Campus: 3319 West Hillsborough Ave, Tampa, FL 33614; tel. (813) 879-6000; fax (813) 871-2483.

FLORIDA SOUTHERN COLLEGE

111 Lake Hollingsworth Dr., Lakeland, FL 33801-5698
Telephone: (863) 680-4111
Internet: www.flsouthern.edu

Founded 1885
Private control
Academic year: August to May

Pres.: Dr ANNE B. KERR
Vice-Pres. and Dean of the College: Dr SUSAN P. CONNER
Vice-Pres. and Dean of Enrollment Management: Dr ROBERT B. PALMER
Vice-Pres. for Advancement: Dr ROBERT H. TATE
Vice-Pres. for Finance: V. TERRY DENNIS
Vice-Pres. for Student Life: Dr CAROLE R. OBERMEYER
Library Dir: ANDREW L. PEARSON

Library of 192,684 vols
Number of teachers: 109
Number of students: 2,487 (1,841 full-time, 646 part-time)

FLORIDA STATE UNIVERSITY

Tallahassee, FL 32306
Telephone: (904) 644-1234
Internet: www.fsu.edu

Founded 1851 as the Seminary W of the Suwannee River, and later became the Florida State College, became the Florida State College for Women 1905, became co-educational again and attained univ. status 1947
Academic year: August to April (2 semesters)

Chancellor of the State Univ. System: CHARLES REED
Pres.: T. K. WETHERELL
Provost and Vice-Pres. for Academic Affairs: LAWRENCE ABELE
Sr Vice-Pres. for Finance and Admin.: JOHN R. CARNAGHI
Vice-Pres. for Research: RAYMOND E. BYE, Jr
Vice-Pres. for Student Affairs: WINSTON E. SCOTT
Vice-Pres. for Univ. Relations: BEVERLEY B. SPENCER
Dean of the Faculties and Deputy Provost: STEVE EDWARDS
Dean of Graduate Studies: DIANNE F. HARRISON (acting)
Dean of Panama City Campus: EDWARD WRIGHT
Dean of Undergraduate Studies: SANDRA RACKLEY
Registrar: MAXWELL CARRAWAY
Dir of Univ. Libraries: RANDALL M. MACDONALD

Library: see Libraries and Archives
Number of teachers: 1,956
Number of students: 36,683
Publication: *Bulletin*

DEANS
College of Arts and Sciences: DONALD FOSS
College of Business: MELVIN T. STITH
College of Communication: JOHN K. MAYO
College of Criminology and Criminal Justice: DANIEL MAIER-KATKIN
College of Education: RICHARD C. KUNKEL
College of Human Sciences: PENNY A. RALSTON
College of Information Studies: JANE B. ROBBINS
College of Law: DONALD J. WEIDNER
College of Medicine: JOSEPH E. SCHERGER
College of Motion Picture, Television and Recording Arts: RAYMOND FIELDING
College of Music: JON R. PIERSOL
College of Social Sciences: MARIE COWART
College of Social Work: BRUCE THYER
College of Visual Arts, Theatre and Dance: SALLY E. MCRORIE
FAMU-FSU College of Engineering: CHING-JEN CHEN
School of Nursing: KATHERINE P. MASON

HOBE SOUND BIBLE COLLEGE

POB 1065, Hobe Sound, FL 33475
Telephone: (772) 546-5534
Fax: (772) 545-1422
E-mail: hobesoundbiblecollege@hsbc.edu
Internet: www.hsbc.edu

Founded 1960
Private control
Academic year: August to June

Pres.: P. DANIEL STETLER
Academic Dean: Dr CLIFFORD W. CHURCHILL
Dir of Admissions: JUDY FAY
Dir of Finance: KEN LITZINGER
Deans of Men: JOHN S. JONES, GEORGE VERNON
Dean of Women: LOUISE CROUSE
Registrar: ANN FRENCH
Librarian: WILLIAM SNIDER.

HODGES UNIVERSITY

2655 Northbrooke Dr., Naples, FL 34119
Telephone: (239) 513-1122
E-mail: admit@internationalcollege.edu
Internet: www.hodges.edu

Founded 1990 as International College, present name and status 2007
Private control
Academic year: September to August

Pres.: TERRY P. MCMAHAN
Exec. Vice-Pres. for Academic Affairs: JEANETTE BROCK
Vice-Pres. for Information Technology: DAVE RICE
Vice-Pres. for Institutional Advancement: LOUIS TRAINA
Vice-Pres. for Student Devt: RON BOWMAN
Vice-Pres. for Student Enrollment Management: RITA LAMPUS
Vice-Pres. for Student Records' Management: CAROL MORRISON
Registrar: JENNA KAISER
Dir of Library: CAROLYNN VOLZ
Number of students: 2,040.

BRANCH CAMPUS
Fort Myers Campus: 4501 Colonial Blvd, Fort Myers, FL 33966; tel. (239) 482-0019.

JACKSONVILLE UNIVERSITY

2800 University Blvd, N Jacksonville, FL 32211-3394
Telephone: (904) 256-8000

Internet: www.ju.edu
Founded 1934
Pres.: KERRY D. ROMESBURG
Sr Vice-Pres. for Academic Affairs: Dr LOIS S. BECKER
Sr Vice-Pres. for Enrollment Management: MIRIAM KING
Vice-Pres. for Finance and Admin.: Dr WILLIAM CROSBY
Registrar: CAROLYN A. BARRETT
Librarian: THOMAS H. GUNN
Library of 572,000 vols
Number of teachers: 233 (116 full-time, 117 part-time)
Number of students: 2,123

JONES COLLEGE

5353 Arlington Expressway, Jacksonville, FL 32211-5588
Telephone: (904) 743-1122
E-mail: info@jones.edu
Internet: www.jones.edu
Founded 1918
Private control
Academic year: September to August
Pres.: Dr DAVID SWANN
Dean: CALVIN SLATTER
Areas of study: allied health management, business admin., computer information systems, interdisciplinary studies, legal asst (paralegal), medical asst.

BRANCH CAMPUSES

Miami Campus: Suite 200, 11430 North Kendall Dr., Kendall Summit, Miami, FL 33176; tel. (305) 275-9996; Dir and Dean SARAH FRIDAY.

West Campus: 1195 Edgewood Ave, S Jacksonville, FL 32205; tel. (904) 743-1122; Dir and Dean DEE THORNTON.

LYNN UNIVERSITY

3601 North Military Trail, Boca Raton, FL 33431
Telephone: (561) 237-7000
E-mail: admission@lynn.edu
Internet: www.lynn.edu
Founded 1962 as Marymount College, present name 1991
Private control
Academic year: September to May
Pres. and CEO: Dr KEVIN M. ROSS
Chief of Staff: Dr JASON WALTON
Senior Vice-President for Institutional Advancement: Dr LANSING BAKER
Dean of Admin.: THOMAS HEFFERMAN
Sr Vice-Pres. for Enrollment Management: Dr KARLA STEIN
Vice-Pres. and Exec. Asst to the Pres.: ANTHONY J. CASALE
Vice-Pres. for Academic Affairs: Dr KATHLEEN CHEEK-MILBY
Vice-Pres. for Business and Finance: LAURIE LEVINE
Vice-Pres. for Corporate Devt: Dr ROBERT LEVINSON
Vice-Pres. for Endowment and Planned Giving: JOHN J. GALLO
Library Dir: CHARLES L. KUHN
Library of 235,648 items (incl. books, periodicals, video cassettes and microforms)

DEANS

College of Arts and Sciences: Dr GREGG COX
College of Business and Management: Dr RALPH NORCIO
College of Education, Health and Human Services: Dr RICHARD B. COHEN
College of Hospitality Management: Dr JOSEPH A. ROONEY
College of Int. Communication: Dr IRVING R. LEVINE
College of Professional, Adult and Continuing Education: Dr CINDY L. SKARUPPA
Conservatory of Music: Dr CLAUDIO JAFFÉ
School of Aeronautics: Major JEFFREY C. JOHNSON

NEW COLLEGE OF FLORIDA

5800 Bay Shore Rd, Sarasota, FL 34243-2109
Telephone: (941) 487-5000
E-mail: admissions@ncf.edu
Internet: www.ncf.edu
Founded 1960
Public control
Academic year: August to May
Pres.: Dr GORDON E. MICHALSON, Jr
Provost and Vice-Pres. of Academic Affairs: Dr CHARLENE CALLAHAN
Vice-Pres. for Admin. and Finance: JOHN U. MARTIN
Dean of Student Affairs: WENDY BASHANT
Dean of Enrollment Services and Information Technology: KATHLEEN KILLION
Registrar: KATHY ALLEN
Dean of the Library: Dr BRIAN DOHERTY
Library of 279,206 vols, 1,174 current serials received, 525,736 microforms, 700 electronic books, 2,658 audio materials, 4,210 video cassettes
Number of teachers: 94
Number of students: 825

PROFESSORS

Division of Humanities:
- CARRASCO, M. E., Art History
- CUOMO, G. R., German Language and Literature
- EDIDIN, A. Z., Philosophy
- HASSOLD, C., Art History
- LANGSTON, D. C., Philosophy and Religion
- MICHALSON, G. E., Humanities

Division of Natural Sciences:
- BEULIG, A., Biology
- DEMSKI, L. S., Biology
- GILCHRIST, S., Biology
- LOWMAN, M., Biology and Environmental Studies
- RUPPEINER, G., Physics
- SCUDDER, P., Chemistry

Division of Social Sciences:
- ANTHONY, A. P., Art History
- DOENECKE, J., History
- ELLIOTT, C., Economics
- LEWIS, E., Political Science
- STROBEL, F., Economics
- VESPERI, M. D., Anthropology

NOVA SOUTHEASTERN UNIVERSITY

3301 College Ave, Fort Lauderdale-Davie, FL 33314-7796
Telephone: (954) 262-7300
Fax: (954) 262-3800
E-mail: ron@nova.edu
Internet: www.nova.edu
Founded 1964
Academic year: July to June
Chancellor and CEO: RAY FERRERO, Jr
Chancellor of Health Professions Division: Dr FREDERICK LIPPMAN
Pres. and Chief Operating Officer: Dr GEORGE L. HANBURY, II
Provost and Vice-Pres. for Academic Affairs: FRANK DE PIANO
Assoc. Provost: Dr MARGARET MALMBERG
Vice-Pres. for Community and Govt Affairs: Dr LARRY A. CALDERON
Vice-Pres. for Financial Operations: W. DAVID HERON
Vice-Pres. for Institutional Advancement: Dr JOANNE FERCHLAND-PARELLA
Vice-Pres. for Legal Affairs: JOEL BERMAN
Vice-Pres. for Information Services and Univ. Librarian: LYDIA ACOSTA
Dean for Student Affairs: Dr BRAD WILLIAMS
Registrar: ELAINE POFF
Library: 1.4m. vols
Number of teachers: 723
Number of students: 28,741 (15,146 full-time, 13,595 part-time)
Publications: *ILSA Journal of International and Comparative Law* (3 a year), *International Travel Law Journal* (3 a year), *Internet Journal of Allied Health Sciences and Practice* (6 a year), *Nova Law Review* (3 a year), *Peace and Conflict Studies* (2 a year), *The Qualitative Report* (4 a year)

DEANS

Center for Psychological Studies: Dr KAREN GROSBY
College of Allied Health: Dr RICHARD DAVIS
College of Dental Medicine: Dr ROBERT UCHIN
College of Medical Sciences: Dr HAROLD LAUBACH
College of Optometry: Dr DAVID LOSHIN
College of Osteopathic Medicine: Dr ANTHONY S. SILVAGNI
College of Pharmacy: Dr ANDRES MALAVE
Farquhar College for Arts and Sciences: Dr DONALD ROSENBLUM
Fischler School of Education and Human Services: Dr H. WELLS SINGLETON (Dean and Provost)
Graduate School of Computer and Information Sciences: Dr LEO IRAKLIOTIS
Graduate School of Humanities and Social Sciences: Dr HONGGANG YANG
Mailman Segal Centre for Human Development: Dr RONI LIEDERMAN
Oceanographic Center: Dr RICHARD DODGE
Shepard Broad Law Center: ATHORNIA STEELE
Univ. School: Dr JEROME CHERMAK
Wayne Huizenga School of Business and Entrepreneurship: Dr MICHAEL FIELDS

PALM BEACH ATLANTIC UNIVERSITY

POB 24708, West Palm Beach, FL 33416-4708
901 South Flagler Dr., West Palm Beach, FL 33401
Telephone: (561) 803-2000
E-mail: admit@pba.edu
Internet: www.pba.edu
Founded 1968
Private control
Academic year: August to May
Pres.: Dr DAVID W. CLARK
Provost: Dr JOSEPH A. KLOBA
Vice-Pres. and Chief Financial Officer: GEORGE GALL
Vice-Pres. for Devt: WILLIAM M. B. FLEMING, Jr
Vice-Pres. for Enrollment Services: BUCKLEY A. JAMES
Vice-Pres. for Student Devt: Dr MARY ANN SEARLE
Library Dean: Dr J. RAY DOERKSEN
Library of 259,877 vols
Number of teachers: 253
Number of students: 3,066

DEANS

School of Arts and Sciences: Dr JEFFREY W. STOUT
School of Business: Dr ROBERT MYERS
School of Communication and Media: Dr JOSEPH WEBB
School of Continuing Education: Dr PAM SIGAFOOSE
School of Education and Behavioral Studies: Dr DONA THORNTON

School of Ministry: Dr KENNETH L. MAHANES
School of Music and Fine Arts: Dr LLOYD MIMS
School of Nursing: Dr LINDA MILLER
School of Pharmacy: Dr SCOTT A. SWIGART

RINGLING COLLEGE OF ART AND DESIGN

2700 North Tamiami Trail, Sarasota, FL 342345895
Telephone: (941) 3515100
Fax: (941) 3597517
E-mail: admissions@ringling.edu
Internet: www.ringling.edu
Founded 1931 by John Ringling
Private control
Academic year: August to May
Pres.: Dr LARRY R. THOMPSON
Vice-Pres. for Devt and Alumni Relations: LANCE BURCHETT
Vice-Pres. for Finance and Admin.: TRACY WAGNER
Vice-Pres. for Institutional Advancement: (vacant)
Dean of Admissions: AMY FISHER
Dean of Students: Dr TAMMY S. WALSH
Dir of Library Services: KATHLEEN LIST
Library: Verman Kimbrough Memorial Library of 55,000 vols, 6,100 DVDs, video cassettes, videodiscs and multimedia titles on CD-ROM, 350 periodicals and 127,000 35-mm slides
Number of teachers: 130
Number of students: 1,100

ROLLINS COLLEGE

1000 Holt Ave, Winter Park, FL 32789
Telephone: (407) 646-2000
Fax: (407) 646-2600
E-mail: contact@rollins.edu
Internet: www.rollins.edu
Founded 1885
Academic year: September to May
Pres.: LEWIS M. DUNCAN
Vice-Pres. for Academic Affairs and Provost: Dr ROGER N. CASEY
Vice-Pres. for Business and Finance and Treas.: GEORGE H. HERBST
Vice-Pres. for Institutional Advancement: CYNTHIA R. WOOD
Dean of Admissions and Enrollment: DAVID G. ERDMANN
Dean of Faculty: HOYT EDGE
Dean of Student Affairs: DONNA A. LEE
Dean of the Hamilton Holt School: SHARRON CARRIER
Dir of Libraries: JONATHAN MILLER
Library of 303,000 vols, 1,600 current periodicals
Number of teachers: 195
Number of students: 3,835 .
Publications: *Alumni Record* (4 a year), *Brushing* (1 a year), *Sandspur* (52 a year).

ST JOHN VIANNEY COLLEGE SEMINARY

2900 South West 87th Ave, Miami, FL 33165-3244
Telephone: (305) 223-4561
Fax: (305) 223-0650
E-mail: info@sjvcs.edu
Internet: www.sjvcs.edu
Founded 1959 as St John Vianney Seminary; present name 1977
Rector and Pres.: Very Rev. MICHAEL G. CARRUTHERS
Dean of Students: Rev. JOSÉ ALVAREZ
Academic Dean: Dr RAMON J. SANTOS
Registrar: BONNIE DE ANGULO
Library Dir: MARIA RODRIGUEZ
Library of 50,000 vols
Number of teachers: 22

ST LEO UNIVERSITY

POB 6665, Saint Leo, FL 33574-6665
Telephone: (352) 588-8200
Fax: (352) 588-8654
Internet: www.saintleo.edu
Founded 1889
Private control
Academic year: August to May
Pres.: Dr ARTHUR F. KIRK, Jr
Sr Exec. Asst to the Pres.: MARCIA MALIA
Vice-Pres. for Academic Affairs: MARIBETH DURST
Vice-Pres. for Business Affairs and Chief Financial Officer: FRANK MEZZANINI (acting)
Vice-Pres. for Enrollment and Online Learning: KATHRYN MCFARLAND
Vice-Pres. for Student Affairs: Dr EDWARD DADEZ
Dir of Univ. Advancement: DAVID OSTRANDER
Registrar: KAREN HATFIELD
Librarian: BRENT SHORT
Library of 152,584 vols
Number of teachers: 906
Number of students: 15,565

DEANS

School of Arts and Sciences: MARY SPOTO
School of Business: Dr MICHAEL NASTANSKI
School of Education and Social Services: Dr CAROL WALKER

ST THOMAS UNIVERSITY

16401 North West 37th Ave, Miami Gardens Miami, FL 33054
Telephone: (305) 628-2546
Fax: (305) 628-6591
E-mail: signup@stu.edu
Internet: www.stu.edu
Founded 1947 in Cuba, moved to present location 1961
Private control (Roman Catholic church)
Academic year: August to May
Pres.: Mgr FRANKLYN M. CASALE
Provost and Chief Academic Officer: Dr GREGORY CHAN
Vice-Pres. for Admin. Affairs and Treas.: TERRENCE O'CONNOR
Vice-Pres. for Student Affairs: Dr SARAH SHUMATE
Vice-Pres. for Univ. Advancement: BEVERLY S. BACHRACH
Asst Vice-Pres. for Academic Affairs: Dr SUSAN ANGULO
Dean of Academic Support: BARBARA SINGER
Dean of Graduate Studies: Dr JOSEPH A. IANNONE
Dean of Law School: ALFREDO GARCIA
Dean of Undergraduate Studies: Dr GUIYOU HUANG
Registrar: IRAIDA ACEBO
Library Dir: Dr L. BRYAN COOPER
Library of 215,000 vols
Number of teachers: 131 (72 full-time, 59 part-time)
Number of students: 2,500
Publication: *St Thomas Law Review* (1 a year).

ATTACHED RESEARCH INSTITUTES

Human Rights Institute.
Institute of Pastoral Ministries.

ST VINCENT DE PAUL REGIONAL SEMINARY

10701 South Military Trail, Boynton Beach, FL 33436-4899
Telephone: (561) 732-4424
Fax: (561) 737-2205
Internet: www.svdp.edu
Founded 1963
Academic year: August to May
Rector, Pres. and Dean of Formation: Rev. Mgr KEITH BRENNAN
Vice-Rector and Dean of Academic Formation: Rev. STEVEN O'HALA
Dean of Pastoral Formation: Rev. Mgr MICHAEL MCGRAW
Dean of Spiritual Formation: Rev. MICHAEL MUHR
Treas. and Dir of Office of Institutional Research and Evaluation: KEITH PARKER
Library Dir: ARTHUR G. QUINN
Library of 72,000 vols
Number of teachers: 30

SCHILLER INTERNATIONAL UNIVERSITY - FLORIDA

(For general information, see entry for Schiller International University in Germany chapter)

300 East Bay Dr., Largo, FL 33770
Telephone: (727) 736-5082
Fax. (727) 736-2623
E-mail: admissions@schiller.edu
Internet: www.schiller.edu
Academic year: September to June
Vice-Pres. and Dir: Dr CHRISTOPH LEIBRECHT
Number of teachers: 40
Number of students: 250

SOUTHEASTERN UNIVERSITY OF THE ASSEMBLIES OF GOD

1000 Longfellow Blvd, Lakeland, FL 33801
Telephone: (863) 667-5000
Fax: (863) 667-5200
E-mail: info@secollege.edu
Internet: www.secollege.edu
Founded 1935
Private control
Academic year: August to May
Pres.: Dr MARK RUTLAND
Vice-Pres. for Academic Affairs: Dr ROBERT W. HERRON, Jr
Vice-Pres. for Devt: Dr JAMES L. DAVIS
Vice-Pres. for Finance and Admin.: JOHN KAUTZ, III
Vice-Pres. for Student Devt: Dr ROBERT CROSBY
Student Worship and Ministry Arts Dir: Dr WAYNE H. LEE, Jr
Registrar: Rev. GLENN PEARL
Dir of Library Services: GRACE VEACH
Library of 100,000 vols
Number of teachers: 52
Number of students: 1,076

STETSON UNIVERSITY

421 North Woodland Blvd, DeLand, FL 32723
Telephone: (904) 822-7000
Fax: (904) 822-8925
E-mail: jward@stetson.edu
Internet: www.stetson.edu
Founded 1883 as DeLand Academy, DeLand Univ. 1887, present name 1889
Academic year: August to May
Pres.: Dr H. DOUGLAS LEE
Chancellor: Dr POPE A. DUNCAN
Sr Vice-Pres. and Chief Operating Officer: Dr JAMES R. BEASLEY

Vice-Pres. and Dean of College of Law: Dr W. GARY VAUSE
Vice-Pres. of Enrollment Growth: DEBORAH THOMPSON
Vice-Pres. of Facilities Management: DAVID S. NOYES
Vice-Pres. of Finance: SALLY A. DOWLING
Vice-Pres. of Information Technology: Dr SHAHRAM AMIRI
Vice-Pres. of Univ. Relations: F. MARK WHITTAKER

Library of 330,000 vols and 245,000 govt documents
Number of teachers: 196 (excl. College of Law)
Number of students: 3,255 (2,505 in DeLand, 750 at College of Law in St Petersburg)
Publications: *Commons* (2 a year), *Stetson University Magazine* (2 a year), *The Cupola* (4 a year), *The Stetson University Bulletin* (1 a year)

DEANS

College of Arts and Sciences: Dr GRADY W. BALLENGER
College of Law: Dr W. GARY VAUSE
School of Business Administration: Dr STUART MICHELSON
School of Music: Dr JAMES E. WOODWARD

UNIVERSITY OF CENTRAL FLORIDA

POB 160000, Orlando FL 32816
4000 Central Florida Blvd, Orlando, FL 32816
Telephone: (407) 823-3000
Fax: (407) 823-5625
E-mail: admission@mail.ucf.edu
Internet: www.ucf.edu
Founded 1963 as Florida Technological Univ., present name 1978

Pres.: JOHN C. HITT
Provost and Exec. Vice-Pres.: Dr TERRY L. HICKEY
Vice-Provost and Dean of Graduate Studies: PATRICIA J. BISHOP
Vice-Pres. and Chief of Staff: Dr BETH BARNES
Vice-Pres. for Admin. and Finance: WILLIAM F. MERCK, II
Vice-Pres. for Devt and Alumni Relations: ROBERT J. HOLMES, Jr
Vice-Pres. for Research: Dr M. J. SOILEAU
Vice-Pres. for Student Devt and Enrollment Services: MARIBETH EHASZ
Vice-Pres. for Univ. Relations: Dr DANIEL C. HOLSENBECK
Registrar: Dr DENNIS J. DULNIAK
Dir of Univ. Libraries: BARRY B. BAKER

Library of 1,459,775 vols, 9,866 current periodicals, 2,372,416 microforms, 35,233 audiovisual items
Number of teachers: 1,308 (1,050 full-time, 258 part-time)
Number of students: 38,598

DEANS

Burnett Honors College: Dr ALLYN MACLEAN STEARMAN
College of Arts and Sciences: Dr KATHRYN SEIDEL
College of Business Admin.: Dr THOMAS KEON
College of Education: Dr SANDRA ROBINSON
College of Engineering and Computer Science: Dr MARTIN P. WANIELISTA
College of Health and Public Affairs: Dr BELINDA MCCARTHY

UNIVERSITY OF FLORIDA

Gainesville, FL 32611
Telephone: (352) 392-3261
Internet: www.ufl.edu
Founded 1853

Pres.: Dr JAMES BERNARD MACHEN
Provost and Sr Vice-Pres. for Academic Affairs: JUDITH RUSSELL
Sr Vice-Pres. for Agricultural and Natural Resources: Dr JIMMY G. CHEEK
Sr Vice-Pres. for Health Affairs: Dr DOUGLAS J. BARRETT
Vice-Pres. and Gen. Counsel: JAMIE LEWIS KEITH
Vice-Pres. for Devt and Alumni Affairs: PAUL A. ROBELL
Vice-Pres. for Human Resource Services: KYLE CAVANAUGH
Vice-Pres. for Research: WINFRED M. PHILLIPS
Vice-Pres. for Student Affairs: PATRICIA TELLES-IRVIN
Vice-Pres. for Univ. Relations: JANE ADAMS
Univ. Registrar: STEPHEN J. PRITZ, Jr
Dean of Univ. Libraries: JUDITH RUSSELL

Library: see Libraries
Number of teachers: 1,654
Number of students: 47,993
Publications: *Florida Historical Quarterly*, *Journal of Politics*, *Latin American Studies Association Newsletter*, *Southern Folklore Quarterly*, *University of Florida Law Review*

DEANS

College of Agricultural and Life Sciences: WAYNE SMITH
College of Dentistry: TERESA DOLAN
College of Design, Construction and Planning: JAY M. STEIN
College of Education: CATHERINE EMIHOVICH
College of Engineering: CAMMY ABERNATHY
College of Fine Arts: DONALD E. MCGLOTHLIN
College of Health and Human Performance: JILL VARNES
College of Health Professions: Prof. ROBERT G. FRANK
College of Journalism and Communications: TERRY HYNES
College of Liberal Arts and Sciences: NEIL SULLIVAN
College of Medicine: C. CRAIG TISHER
School of Natural Resources and Environment: NANCY PETERSON
College of Nursing: KATHLEEN A. LONG
College of Veterinary Medicine: JOSEPH A. DIPIETRO
Continuing Education: JAMES W. KNIGHT
Institute of Food and Agricultural Sciences: LARRY ARRINGTON (acting) (Extension: RICHARD L. JONES (Research)
Graduate School: KENNETH GERHARDT
Levin College of Law: ROBERT JERRY
Warrington College of Business: JOHN KRAFT

UNIVERSITY OF MIAMI

Coral Gables, FL 33124
Telephone: (305) 284-2211
Internet: www.miami.edu
Founded 1925 (chartered)
Private control
Academic year: September to May (2 terms)

Pres.: DONNA E. SHALALA
Provost and Exec. Vice-Pres.: THOMAS J. LEBLANC
Sr Vice-Pres. for Business and Finance: JOSEPH T. NATOLI
Sr Vice-Pres. for Medical Affairs: PASCAL J. GOLDSCHMIDT
Vice-Pres. and Gen. Counsel and Sec. of the Univ.: AILEEN M. UGALDE
Vice-Pres. for Finance and Treas.: JOHN R. SHIPLEY
Asst Vice-Pres. for Business Services: HUMBERTO M. SPEZIANI
Vice-Pres. for Enrollment Management and Continuing Studies: PAUL M. OREHOVEC
Vice-Pres. for Govt Affairs: RODOLFO J. FERNANDEZ
Vice-Pres. for Human Resources: NERISSA E. MORRIS
Assoc. Vice-Pres. for Information Technology: JACK J. GEORGE
Vice-Pres. for Medical Admin. and Chief Operating Officer: WILLIAM J. DONELAN
Vice-Pres. for Student Affairs: PATRICIA A. WHITELY
Sr Vice-Pres. for Univ. Advancement and External Affairs: SERGIO M. GONZALEZ
Univ. Librarian: WILLIAM D. WALKER

Library: 3.3m. vols
Number of teachers: 2,987 (2,558 full-time, 429 part-time)
Number of students: 15,657
Publications: *Ibis* (1 a year), *Journal of Inter-American Studies* (4 a year), *The Miami Hurricane* (student newspaper, 104 a year), *World Affairs* (4 a year)

DEANS

College of Arts and Sciences: LEONIDAS BACHAS
College of Engineering: Dr JAMES TIEN
Graduate School: Dr TERRI SCANDURA
Rosenstiel School of Marine and Atmospheric Sciences: Dr RONI AVISSAR
School of Architecture: ELIZABETH PLATER-ZYBERK
School of Business Admin.: Dr BARBARA KAHN
School of Communication: SAM L. GROGG
School of Education: Dr ISAAC PRILLELTENSKY
School of Law: PATRICIA WHITE
School of Medicine: Dr PASCAL J. GOLDSCHMIDT
School of Music: Dr SHELTON G. BERG
School of Nursing: NILDA P. PERAGALLO

UNIVERSITY OF NORTH FLORIDA

4567 St Johns Bluff Rd, S Jacksonville, FL 32224-2645
Telephone: (904) 620-1000
Internet: www.unf.edu

Pres.: Prof. JOHN A. DELANEY
Provost: Dr GERARD GIORDANO
Vice-Pres. and Chief of Staff: Dr THOMAS S. SERWATKA
Vice-Pres. for Admin. and Finance: SHARI SHUMAN (acting)
Vice-Pres. for Institutional Advancement: Dr PIERRE N. ALLAIRE
Vice-Pres. for Student Affairs: Dr MAURICIO GONZALEZ
Dean of the Div. of Continuing Education: ROBERT WOOD
Dean of Library: SHIRLEY HALLBLADE

Library of 761,595 vols, 3,271 current periodicals, 69,180 audiovisual items, 7,067 maps, 1.3m. microforms
Number of teachers: 520 (full-time)
Number of students: 14,666

DEANS

College of Arts and Sciences: Prof. MARK E. WORKMAN
College of Business Admin.: Prof. EARLE C. TRAYNHAM
College of Computing Sciences and Engineering: Prof. NEAL S. COULTER
College of Education and Human Services: Dr LARRY DANIEL
College of Health: Prof. PAMELA S. CHALLY

UNIVERSITY OF SOUTH FLORIDA

4202 East Fowler Ave, SVC 1034, Tampa, FL 33620
Telephone: (813) 974-2000
E-mail: info@admin.usf.edu
Internet: www.usf.edu
Founded 1956, classes commenced 1960
State control

Academic year: September to April (semester system) and summer sessions

Pres.: Dr JUDY LYNN GENSHAFT
Provost and Vice-Pres. for Academic Affairs: Dr RENU KHATOR
Exec. Vice-Pres. and Chief Financial Officer: CARL CARLUCCI
Vice-Pres. for Admin. Affairs: RICKARD C. FENDER
Vice-Pres. for Health Sciences: Dr ROBERT M. DAUGHERTY
Vice-Pres. for Public Affairs: Dr MARK LONO
Vice-Pres. for Research: Dr ROBERT CHANG
Vice-Pres. of Student Affairs: Dr JUDITH MENINGALL
Vice-Pres. for Univ. Advancement: JO ANN ALESSANDRINI
Vice-Pres. and Campus Chief Exec. Officer, St Petersburg: Dr RALPH C. WILCOX
Vice-Pres. and Campus Chief Exec. Officer, Sarasota/Manatee: Dr LAUREY STRIKER
Vice-Pres. and Campus Chief Exec. Officer, Lakeland: Dr L. PRESTON MERCER
Registrar: LINDA ERICKSON

Library of 1,698,386 vols, 15,263 current periodicals, 4,194,897 microforms
Number of teachers: 1,754 (1,594 full-time, 160 part-time)
Number of students: 39,262

DEANS

College of Arts and Sciences: Dr RENU KHATOR
College of Business Admin.: ROBERT L. ANDERSON
College of Education: Dr HAROLD R. KELLER
College of Engineering: Dr LOUIS MARTIN-VEGA
College of Marine Science: Dr PETER R. BETZER
College of Medicine: Dr ROBERT DAUGHERTY (acting)
College of Nursing: Dr PATRICIA BURNS
College of Public Health: Dr LAURENCE BRANCH
College of Visual and Performing Arts: RON JONES
School of Architecture and Community Design: STEPHEN D. SCHREIBER (Dir)

UNIVERSITY OF TAMPA

401 W Kennedy Blvd, Tampa, FL 33606-1490
Telephone: (813) 253-3333
Fax: (813) 258-7398
E-mail: admissions@ut.edu
Internet: www.ut.edu

Founded 1931
Private control
Academic year: June to May

Pres.: Dr RONALD L. VAUGHN
Vice-Pres. for Admin. and Finance: RICHARD OGOREK
Vice-Pres. for Devt and Univ. Relations: DANIEL GURA
Vice-Pres. for Enrollment and Admissions: DENNIS NOSTRAND
Vice-Pres. for Operations and Planning: Dr LINDA W. DEVINE
Dean of Students: ROBERT M. RUDAY
Dir of Macdonald-Kelce Library: MARLYN R. PETHE

Library of 275,297 vols, 46,306 periodicals, 49,301 microforms, 7,335 audiovisual items, 32,536 electronic books, spec. collns, partial depository for US govt documents
Number of teachers: 260 full-time
Number of students: 6,434 full-time

Publication: *Tampa Review* (2 a year)

DEANS

College of Arts and Letters: Dr HAIG MARDIROSIAN
College of Natural and Health Sciences: Dr JAMES GORE
College of Social Sciences, Mathematics and Education: Dr ANNE GORMLY
John H. Sykes College of Business: Dr FRANK GHANNADIAN

UNIVERSITY OF WEST FLORIDA

11000 University Parkway, Pensacola, FL 32514
Telephone: (850) 474-2230
Fax: (850) 474-3360
E-mail: admissions@uwf.edu
Internet: www.uwf.edu

Founded 1963
State control
Academic year: August to August

Pres.: Dr JOHN C. CAVANAUGH
Provost: SANDRA FLAKE
Exec. Vice-Pres.: HAROLD M. WHITE, Jr
Vice-Pres. for Admin. Affairs: Dr ALBERT HARTLEY
Vice-Pres. for Devt: (vacant)
Vice-Pres. for Student Affairs: DEBORAH LYNN FORD
Registrar: ANN DZIADON
Dean of Libraries: DANA SALLY

Library of 700,000 vols
Number of teachers: 343
Number of students: 9,800

DEANS

College of Arts and Sciences: Dr JANE HALONEN
College of Business: Prof. EDWARD RANELLI
College of Professional Studies: Dr DON CHU

BRANCH CAMPUS

Fort Walton Beach Campus: 1170 Martin Luther King Blvd, Fort Walton Beach, FL 32547; tel. (850) 863-6569; Vice-Provost Dr WESLEY LITTLE.

WARNER SOUTHERN COLLEGE

13895 Highway 27, Lake Wales, FL 33859
Telephone: (863) 638-1426
Fax: (863) 638-1472
E-mail: admissions@warner.edu
Internet: www.warner.edu

Founded 1968
Private control
Academic year: August to May

Pres.: Dr GREGORY V. HALL
Exec. Vice-Pres. and Chief Academic Officer: Dr WILLIAM M. RIGEL, Jr
Vice-Pres. for Advancement: DORIS B. GUKICH
Vice-Pres. for Church Relations: Dr DAVID REAMES
Dean of Enrollment Management: DAWN RAFOOL
Dean of Students: JANICE L. ROBILLARD
Library Dir: SHERILL HRRIGER

Library of 100,000 vols
Number of students: 1,040

DEANS

School of Arts and Science: Dr JAMES R. CHRISTOPH
School of Business: Dr CYNTHIA ROBINSON

WEBBER INTERNATIONAL UNIVERSITY

POB 96, 1201 North Scenic Highway, Babson Park, FL 33827
Telephone: (836) 638-1431
Fax: (836) 638-2823
E-mail: admissions@webber.edu
Internet: www.webber.edu

Founded 1927
Private control

Pres.: Dr WILLIAM B. LOGAN
Exec. Vice-Pres. and Chief Academic Officer: Dr H. KEITH WADE
Dean of Students: Dr FREDERICK ATHERTON
Registrar and Financial Aid Dir: KATHY WILSON

Number of teachers: 44 (19 full-time, 25 adjunct)
Number of students: 650

Offers BSc courses in accounting, business admin., finance, hospitality, marketing, management, pre-law, sport management; other courses include general MBAs and MBAs with a sport management major.

GEORGIA

AGNES SCOTT COLLEGE

141 East College Ave, Decatur, GA 30030
Telephone: (404) 471-6000
Fax: (404) 471-6067
E-mail: info@agnesscott.edu
Internet: www.agnesscott.edu

Founded 1889; attached to Southern Asscn of Colleges and Schools (SACS)
Private control
Academic year: August to May

Pres.: ELIZABETH KISS
Vice-Pres. for Academic Affairs and Dean of College: Prof. CAROLYN STEFANCO
Vice-Pres. for Business and Finance: JOHN P. HEGMAN
Vice-Pres. for Institutional Advancement: ROBERT PARKER
Vice-Pres. for Student Life and Dean of Students: DONNA A. LEE
Dir and Dean of Admissions: ALEXA GAERA
Registrar: ANGIE DEWBERRY
Dir of Library Services: ELIZABETH BAGLEY

Library of 234,470 vols, 50,386 e-books, 23,354 audiovisual items, 28,598 current periodicals
Number of teachers: 109
Number of students: 917

ALBANY STATE UNIVERSITY

504 College Dr., Albany, GA 31705
Telephone: (229) 430-4600
Internet: asuweb.asurams.edu/asu

Founded 1903

Pres.: Dr EVERETTE J. FREEMAN
Dir of Admissions and Financial Aid: FRED SUTTLES
Vice-Pres. for Academic Affairs: Dr ELLIS SYKES
Librarian: Dr LAVERNE L. MCLAUGHLIN

Library of 161,000 vols
Number of teachers: 150
Number of students: 2,405

AMERICAN INTERCONTINENTAL UNIVERSITY

3330 Peachtree Rd, NE, Atlanta, GA 30326-1016
Telephone: (404) 965-5712
Fax: (404) 965-5701
Internet: www.aiuniv.edu

Multi-campus, nat. and int. (see www.aiustudyabroad.com) instn offering residential, correspondence and online (see www.aiuonline.edu) assoc., Bachelors and graduate degrees

Pres.: Dr GREG WASHINGTON.

NATIONAL CAMPUSES

AIU–Buckhead

3330 Peachtree Rd, NE, Atlanta, GA 30326-1016

Telephone: (404) 965-5712
Fax: (404) 965-5701
Internet: www.aiubuckhead.com

Undergraduate degree programmes: fashion, int. business, interior design, media production, visual communication.

AIU–Dunwoody

6600 Peachtree Rd, 500 Embassy Row, Atlanta, GA 30328

Internet: www.aiudunwoody.com

Assoc. degree programmes: business admin., visual communications; Bachelors degree programmes: enterprise management, information technology, visual communications; graduate degree programmes: global technology management, information technology.

AIU–Fort Lauderdale

8151 West Peters Rd, Suite 1000, Plantation, FL 33324

Internet: www.aiufortlauderdale.com

Assoc. degree programmes: business admin., int. business; Bachelors degree programmes: enterprise management, information technology, visual communication; graduate degree programmes: global technology, management information technology.

AIU–Los Angeles

12655 West Jefferson Blvd, Los Angeles, CA 90066

Telephone: (310) 302-2000
Fax: (310) 302-2002
Internet: www.aiula.com

Founded 1970

Number of teachers: 137
Number of students: 1,800

Assoc. degree programmes: business admin., fashion design, fashion marketing, int. business, media production, visual communication; Bachelors degree programmes: business admin., criminal justice, fashion design, fashion marketing, fashion marketing and design, information technology, int. business, interior design, visual communication; graduate programmes: global technology management, information technology, instructional technology..

INTERNATIONAL CAMPUSES

AIU–London: see separate entry in UK chapter.

The American University in Dubai: see separate entry in UAE chapter.

ARMSTRONG ATLANTIC STATE UNIVERSITY

11935 Abercorn St, Savannah, GA 31419

Telephone: (912) 927-5277
E-mail: adm-info@armstrong.edu
Internet: www.armstrong.edu

Founded 1935
Academic year: August to May

Pres.: LINDA M. BLEICKEN
Vice-Pres. and Dean of Faculty: ELLEN V. WHITFORD
Vice-Pres. for Business and Finance: JAMES BRIGNATI
Vice-Pres. for Student Affairs: VICKI L. MCNEIL
Registrar: KIM WEST
Librarian: BEN LEE

Library of 800,000 items
Number of teachers: 250
Number of students: 5,700

DEANS

College of Arts and Sciences: Dr ED WHEELER
College of Education: Dr JANE MCHANEY
College of Health Professions: Dr BARRY ECKERT
School of Computing: Dr RAYMOND GREENLAW
School of Graduate Studies: MICHAEL E. PRICE

ART INSTITUTE OF ATLANTA

6600 Peachtree Dunwoody Rd, 100 Embassy Row, Atlanta, GA 30328-1649

Telephone: (770) 394-8300
Fax: (770) 394-0008
E-mail: aiaadm@aii.edu
Internet: www.artinstitutes.edu/atlanta/

Founded 1949 as Massey Business College; present name 1975
Private control
Academic year: October to September

Pres.: JANET S. DAY
Vice-Pres. of Admin. and Financial Services: CHRISTOPHER J. FERRELL
Vice-Pres. of Admissions: DONNA SCOTT
Vice-Pres. of Human Resources: JOSELYN C. CASSIDY
Dean of Academic Affairs: Dr SALLY PARSONSON
Dean of Student Affairs: JAMES PETTY
Registrar: MARDI RICHARDSON
Library Dir: GAYLE MEIER

Number of teachers: 150
Number of students: 2,650

DIRECTORS

Culinary Arts: JAMES W. PAUL
Gen. Education: Dr HEATHER OLSON
Graphic Design: LARRY STULTZ
Illustration and Design: DAN L. HENDERSON
Interactive Media Design: Dr AMEETA JADAV
Interior Design: PAUL M. BLACK
Media Arts and Animation: LEE CROWE
Photographic Imaging: (vacant)
Video Production and Digital Media Production: ROB ALBERTSON

ATLANTA CHRISTIAN COLLEGE

2605 Ben Hill Rd, East Point, GA 30344

Telephone: (404) 761-8861
E-mail: kwagner@acc.edu
Internet: www.acc.edu

Founded 1928
Private control
Academic year: August to May

Pres.: DEAN COLLINS
Vice-Pres. for Academic Affairs: Dr DENNIS E. GLENN
Vice-Pres. for Admin.: S. TODD WEAVER
Vice-Pres. for Devt: (vacant)
Vice-Pres. for Student Devt: R. SIDNEY TILLER, Jr
Registrar: KATHLEEN D. DAVID
Library Dir: MICHAEL L. BAIN

Library of 55,500 vols

Depts of biblical studies, business, education, human relations, humanities and general studies, music.

AUGUSTA STATE UNIVERSITY

2500 Walton Way, Augusta, GA 30904-2200

Telephone: (706) 737-1444
E-mail: admissions@aug.edu
Internet: www.aug.edu

Founded 1783 as Acad. of Richmond County; present name 1996
Academic year: August to July

Pres.: Dr WILLIAM A. BLOODWORTH, Jr
Vice-Pres. for Academic Affairs: Dr SAMUEL SULLLIVAN
Vice-Pres. for Business Operations: DAN WHITFIELD
Vice-Pres. for Student Services and Dean of Students: Dr JOYCE A. JONES
Vice-Pres. for Univ. Advancement: ELIZABETH B. HOUSE DEAN (acting)
Registrar and Dir of Admissions: KATHERINE H. SWEENEY
Library Dir: Dr WILLIAM N. NELSON

Library of 475,000 vols
Number of teachers: 200
Number of students: 5,000

DEANS

College of Business Admin.: JACKSON K. WIDENER, Jr
College of Education: Dr THOMAS E. DEERING (acting)
Pamplin College of Arts and Sciences: Dr M. E. PETTIT (acting)

BERRY COLLEGE

2277 Martha Berry Highway, NW, Mount Berry, GA 30149

Telephone: (706) 232-5374
Internet: www.berry.edu

Founded 1902

Pres.: Dr STEPHEN R. BRIGGS
Provost: Dr THOMAS E. DASHER
Vice-Pres. for Student Affairs and Dean of Students: DEBBIE E. HEIDA
Vice-Pres. for Finance: BRIAN ERB
Vice-Pres. for Institutional Advancement: BETTYANN M. O'NEILL
Dean of Admissions: RICHARD DANA PAUL
Registrar: LINDA A. TENNANT
Library Dir: MAUREEN K. MORGAN

Library of 184,829 vols, 495,679 microfiche vols, 104,871 govt documents, 507 compact discs, 1,365 current periodicals
Number of teachers: 126
Number of students: 2,075 (1,846 undergraduate, 229 graduate)

DEANS

Campbell School of Business: Dr KRISHNA S. DHIR
Charter School of Education and Human Sciences: Dr JACQUELINE M. MCDOWELL

BEULAH HEIGHTS BIBLE COLLEGE

POB 18145, 892 Berne Street, SE, Atlanta, GA 30316

Telephone: (404) 627-2681
Fax: (404) 627-0702
E-mail: admissionsinfo@beulah.org
Internet: www.beulah.org

Founded 1918
Private control
Academic year: August to May

Pres.: Dr BENSON M. KARANJA
Vice-Pres. and Dean of Academics: Dr JAMES B. KEILLER
Vice-Pres. for Finance: MAXINE MARKS
Vice-President for Institutional Effectiveness and Operations: MONIQUE BAUCHAM
Vice-Pres. for Student Devt: WESLEY B. WILSON
Registrar and Dean of Admissions: JACQUELYN B. ARMSTRONG
Dir of Library Service: PRADEEP K. DAS

Number of teachers: 35
Number of students: 677

BREWTON-PARKER COLLEGE

Highway 280, 201 David-Eliza Fountain Circle, POB 197, Mount Vernon, GA 30445

Telephone: (912) 583-2241

Fax: (912) 583-4498
E-mail: admissions@bpc.edu
Internet: www.bpc.edu
Founded 1904 as Union Baptist Institute; present name 1978
Private control
Academic year: August to June
Pres.: Dr David R. Smith
Provost: Dr Ron Melton
Vice-Pres. for College Advancement: Pamela Davis
Vice-Pres. for Enrollment Services: Dr Cindy Skaruppa
Chief Financial Officer: Samuel T. Moore
Dean of Students: Sherrie Helms
Library Dir: Ann C. Turner
Number of teachers: 52
Number of students: 1,136
Depts of business, education, humanities, intercollegiate athletics, mathematics and natural sciences, music, religion and philosophy, social and behavioural sciences
Publication: *Oracle* (1 a year).

CLARK ATLANTA UNIVERSITY

223 James P. Brawley Dr., SW, Atlanta, GA 30314-4389
Telephone: (404) 880-8000
Internet: www.cau.edu
Founded 1988, following consolidation of Atlanta Univ. (founded 1865) and Clark College (founded 1869); member of Atlanta Univ. Center
Pres.: Dr Walter D. Broadnax
Provost and Vice-Pres. for Academic Affairs: Dr Dorcas D. Bowles
Exec. Vice-Pres.: Dr George E. Ross
Vice-Pres. for Enrollment Services and Student Affairs: Darrin Rankin
Vice-Pres. for Finance and Admin.: Bobby E. Young
Gen. Counsel: Lance Dunnings
Dean of the School of Arts and Sciences: Dr Shirley Williams-Kirksey
Dean of Graduate Studies: Dr William Boone
Dean of Undergraduate Studies: Dr Alexia Henderson
Dir of Library Services (Atlanta Univ. Center): Dr Elaine Sloan
Library of 500,000 vols, 800,000 microforms, 300,000 govt documents, 50,000 bound periodicals, 5,000 compact discs
Number of teachers: 300
Number of students: 4,813 (3,864 undergraduate, 949 graduate)

DEANS

School of Arts and Sciences: Dr Charles W. Washington
School of Business: Dr Edward Davis
School of Education: Dr Ernest J. Middleton
School of Library and Information Studies: Dr Arthur C. Gunn
School of Social Work: Dr Dorcas D. Bowles

CLAYTON COLLEGE AND STATE UNIVERSITY

2000 Clayton State Blvd, Morrow, GA 30260
Telephone: (678) 466-4000
E-mail: csu-info@clayton.edu
Internet: www.clayton.edu
Founded 1969 as Clayton Junior College; present name 1996
Academic year: August to May
Pres.: Dr Thomas K. Harden
Provost and Vice-Pres. for Academic Affairs: Dr Sharon E. Hoffman
Vice-Pres. for Business and Operations: David Heflin
Vice-Pres. for External Relations: Robert L. Stephens, Jr
Vice-Pres. for Information Technology and Services: Dr John Bryan (acting)
Vice-Pres. for Student Affairs: Dr Brian Haynes
Registrar: Rebecca Gmeiner
Library Dir: Gordon Baker
Number of teachers: 130
Number of students: 5,000

DEANS

College of Information and Mathematical Sciences: Dr Charles Ford (acting)
School of Arts and Sciences: Dr Ray Wallace
School of Business: Dr Judith Planecki
School of Health Sciences: Dr Linda F. Samson
School of Technology: Dr Art Rossner (acting)

COLUMBIA THEOLOGICAL SEMINARY

701 S Columbia Dr., Decatur, GA 30031
Telephone: (404) 378-8821
Fax: (404) 377-9696
Internet: www.ctsnet.edu
Founded 1828
Academic year: September to May
Pres.: Laura S. Mendenhall
Exec. Vice-Pres. and Dean of Faculty: D. Cameron Murchison
Vice-Pres. for Advancement Services: C. J. Drymon
Vice-Pres. for Business and Finance: Martin Sadler
Vice-Pres. for Institutional Advancement: Richard DuBose
Dean and Vice-Pres. for Lifelong Learning: Dent C. Davis
Dean of Students and Vice-Pres. for Student Services: John E. White
Registrar: Linda Sabo
Library Dir: Sara Myers
Number of teachers: 36
Number of students: 500

COLUMBUS STATE UNIVERSITY

4225 University Ave, Columbus, GA 31907
Telephone: (706) 507-8800
E-mail: pr@colstate.edu
Internet: www.colstate.edu
Founded 1958
Academic year: August to June
Pres.: Dr Timothy Mescon
Provost and Vice-Pres. for Academic Affairs: Dr Inessa Levi
Vice-Pres. for Business and Finance: Tom Helton
Vice-Pres. for Student Affairs: Dr Gina Sheeks
Vice-Pres. for Univ. Advancement: Dr Kayron Laska
Dean of Students: Aaron Reese
Registrar: Lori Gibbon
Dir of Libraries: Callie B. McGinnis
Library of 375,000 vols
Number of teachers: 429 (252 full-time and 177 part-time)
Number of students: 8,000

DEANS

College of Arts and Letters: Dr James McHenry, Jr (acting)
College of Education: Dr David Rock
College of Science: Dr Glenn Cleveland
D. Abbott Turner College of Business: Dr Linda Hadley
Univ. College: Beverly M. Davis (acting)

EMMANUEL COLLEGE

POB 129, Franklin Springs, GA 30639
located at: 181 Springs St, Franklin Springs, GA 30639
Telephone: (706) 245-7226
Fax: (706) 245-4424
E-mail: mail@emmanuelcollege.edu
Internet: www.emmanuelcollege.edu
Founded 1919 as Franklin Springs Institute; present name 1939
Private control
Academic year: August to May
Pres.: Dr David R. Hopkins
Vice-Pres. and Academic Dean: Craig Edwards
Dean of Students: Tim Harrison
Registrar: Debra F. Grizzle
Head Librarian: Richard Dupont
Library of 50,000 vols
Number of students: 800
Schools of business, christian ministries, developmental studies, education, humanities, natural sciences and mathematics, social and behavioural sciences.

EMORY UNIVERSITY

Atlanta, GA 30322
Telephone: (404) 727-6123
Internet: www.emory.edu
Founded 1836 as Emory College, present status 1915
Private control
Language of instruction: English
Academic year: August to May
Pres.: James W. Wagner
Provost and Exec. Vice-Pres. for Academic Affairs: Earl Lewis
Exec. Vice-Pres. for Finance and Admin.: Michael J. Mandl
Exec. Vice-Pres. for Health Affairs: Wright Caughman
Sr Vice-Pres. and Gen. Counsel: Steve Sencer
Sr Vice-Pres. and Dean of Campus Life: John L. Ford
Sr Vice-Pres. for Devt and Alumni Relations: Susan Cruse
Vice-Pres. and Deputy to the Pres.: Gary S. Hauk
Vice-Pres. and Sec. of the Univ.: Rosemary M. Magee
Vice-Pres. for Communications and Marketing: Ron Sauder
Vice-Provost and Dean of the Graduate School: Lisa A. Tedesco
Vice-Provost for Univ. Libraries: Rick Luce
Registrar: Tom Millen
Library: Libraries with 3,619,651 vols
Number of teachers: 2,868 (full-time)
Number of students: 13,381
Publications: *Bankruptcy Developments Journal* (2 a year), *Emory International Law Review* (2 a year), *Emory Law Journal* (4 a year), *Emory Magazine* (4 a year), *Emory Medicine* (3 a year), *Emory Nursing* (2 a year), *Goizueta Business Magazine* (3 a year), *New Vico Studies* (1 a year), *Public Health Magazine* (2 a year)

DEANS

Candler School of Theology: Janice Love
Emory College of Arts and Sciences: Robin Forman
Graduate School: Linda A. Tedesco
Nell Hodgson Woodruff School of Nursing: Linda McCauley
Oxford College (Oxford): Stephen H. Bowen
Roberto C. Goizueta Business School: Lawrence Benveniste
Rollins School of Public Health: James W. Curran
School of Law: David Partlett

School of Medicine: THOMAS J. LAWLEY

PROFESSORS

AABERG, T. M., Ophthalmology
ABRAMOWITZ, A., Political Science
ABRAMOWSKY, C. R., Pathology
ABRAMS, H. E., Law
ADAMSON, W. L., History
AGNEW, R. S., Sociology
ALARCON, R., Psychiatry/Behavioural Sciences
ALAVI, M., Information Strategy
ALBRECHT, T. E., Music
ALDRIDGE, D. P., Sociology
ALEXANDER, F. S., Law
ALEXANDER, G. E., Neurology
ALEXANDER, R. W., Medicine
ALLITT, P., History
AN-NA'IM, A., Law
ANSARI, A. A., Pathology
ANSEL, J. C., Dermatology
ARMELAGOS, G., Anthropology
ARTHUR, T. C., Law
AUSTIN, H., Epidemiology
BAJAJ, K., Physics
BARLETT, P., Anthropology
BARON, M., Radiology
BARROW, D., Neurosurgery
BARSALOU, L., Psychology
BAUERLEIN, M., English
BAUMGARTNER, B. R., Radiology
BEARD, L., Accounting
BECKER, E. R., Health Policy and Management
BEDERMAN, D. J., Law
BEIK, W., History
BENSTON, G. J., Finance
BERMAN, H. J., Law
BERNSTEIN, A., Law
BERNSTEIN, K. E., Pathology
BERRY, A. J., Anaesthesiology
BESSEMBINDER, H., Finance
BLACK, M., Political Science
BLAKE, D. A., Pharmacology
BLUMENTHAL, D. R., Judaic Studies
BONDI, R. C., Church History
BONNEFIS, P., French and Italian
BOOTHE, R., Psychology
BORING, J. R., III, Epidemiology
BOSS, J., Microbiology/Immunology
BOSTWICK, J., III, Plastic Surgery
BOSWELL, T. E., Sociology
BRACHMAN, P., International Health
BRAITHWAITE, R., Behavioural Science and Health Education
BRANCH, W. T., General Medicine
BRANN, A. W., Neurology, Paediatrics
BRIGHT, D. F., Classics and Comparative Literature
BROGAN, D. J., Biostatistics
BROWN, P. J., Anthropology
BROWN, W. V., Medicine (Lipids)
BROWNLEY, M. W., English
BRYAN, J. A., Pathology
BUGGE, J. M., English
BUSS, M. J., Religion
BUZBEE, W., Law
CALABRESE, R., Biology
CARNEY, W. J., Law
CARPENTER, L., English
CARR, D., Philosophy
CARTER, E. B., Biology
CARUTH, C., English
CASARELLA, W. J., Radiology
CATLIN, P. A., Rehabilitation Medicine
CAUGHMAN, S. W., Dermatology
CHAKRABORTY, H., Biostatistics
CHEN, R. L., Physics
CHENG, X., Biochemistry
CHIMOWITZ, M. I., Neurology
CHIRINKO, R., Economics
CHOPP, R., Systematic Theology
CHURCH, R., Ophthalmology
CLEMENTS, S. D., Cardiology
CLOUD, A. M., Law
COHEN, C., Pathology
COLE, J. A., Anthropology
COMPANS, R. W., Microbiology/Immunology
CONN, D. L., Rheumatology
CONN, P. J., Pharmacology
COOK, D. A., Film Studies
COOPER, R., Practice of Cost Management, Accounting
COPE, T., Physiology
CORNISH, J. D., Paediatrics
COURTRIGHT, P., Asian Studies
CRAVER, J. M., Cardiothoracic Surgery
CURRAN, J. M., Public Health
DANNER, D. J., Genetics
DAVIS, D. C., Medicine
DAVIS, L. W., Oncology
DAVIS, M., Psychiatry/Behavioural Sciences
DAVIS, P., Radiology
DE WAAL, F. B. M., Psychology, Primate Behaviour
DEANGRADE, J. R., Orthopaedics
DECONCINI, B., Religion
DELONG, M. R., Neurology
DICLEMENTE, R. J., Behavioural Science and Health Education
DIGIROLAMO, M., Medicine (Geriatrics)
DILORIO, C., Behavioural Science and Health Education
DINGLEDINE, R. J., Pharmacology
DOERNBERG, R. L., International Legal Studies
DOETSCH, P., Biochemistry
DONHAM, D. L., Anthropology
DOUGLAS, J. S., Medicine (Cardiology)
DUFFUS, D. A., Mathematic and Computer Science
DUKE, M., Psychology
DUNBAR, S., Adult and Elder Health
DUNCAN, M., Law
EATON, D. C., Physiology
ECKMAN, J. R., Haematology/Oncology
EDELHAUSER, H., Ophthalmology
EDMONDSON, D. E., Biochemistry
ELMER, W. A., Biology
ELSAS, L. J., II, Medical Genetics, Paediatrics
EMORY, E., Psychology
ENGELHARD, G., Educational Studies
ENGLAND, P., Physical Education
ENGLISH, A. W., Cell Biology
EPSTEIN, M., Russian and East Asian Languages and Culture
FALEK, A., Psychiatry/Behavioural Sciences
FAMILY, F., Physics
FARLEY, M. M., Infectious Diseases
FELICIANO, D. V., Surgery, Trauma/Critical Care
FELNER, J. M., Medicine (Cardiology)
FINK, A. S., General Surgery
FINNERTY, V. M., Biology
FIVUSH, R., Psychology
FLANDERS, W. D., Epidemiology
FLANNERY, J., Performing Arts
FLEMING, L. L., Orthopaedics
FLYNN, T. R., Philosophy
FONG, P., Physics
FOSTER, F. S., English
FOTION, N., Philosophy
FOWLER, J., Theology
FOX-GENOVESE, E., History
FRANCH, R., Medicine (Cardiology)
FRANKEL, B., Psychiatry/Behavioural Sciences
FREER, R. D., Law
FYFE, D., Paediatrics
GARCIA, E. V., Radiology
GARROW, D. J., Law
GELLER, R. J., Paediatrics
GIDDENS, D., Medical School Administration
GILES, M. W., Political Science
GOLDSMITH, D., Chemistry
GOODING, L. R., Microbiology/Immunology
GOODMAN, M., Radiology
GOULD, K., Primate Research
GOULD, R., Mathematic and Computer Science
GOUZOULES, H., Psychology
GOZANSKY, N. E., Law
GRAVANIS, M. B., Pathology
GREENAMYRE, T. J., Neurology
GREENE, D. K., History
GRIFFIN, J. B., Psychiatry/Behavioural Sciences
GRINDON, A. J., Pathology
GROSSNIKLAUS, H., Ophthalmology
GRUBER, W., English
GUNN, R. B., Physiology
GUNNEMANN, J., Social Ethics, Theology
GUTTERMAN, M., Law
GUTTIERREZ-MOUAT, R., Spanish
GUYTON, R., Cardiothoracic Surgery
HABER, M. J., Biostatistics
HAHN, C., Educational Studies
HALLORAN, M. E., Biostatistics
HANSON, S. R., Biomedical Engineering
HARARI, J., French and Italian
HARTGRAVES, A., Accounting
HARTLE, A., Philosophy
HARTZELL, H. C., Cell Biology
HATCHER, R. A., Gynaecology/Obstetrics
HAY, P., Law
HAYES, J. H., Theology (Old Testament)
HEAVEN, M., Chemistry
HERMAN, C., Pathology
HERRON, C., French and Italian
HICKS, A., Sociology
HILL, C. L., Chemistry
HOGUE, C., Epidemiology
HOLIFIELD, E. B., Theology
HOLLADAY, C. R., Theology (New Testament)
HOLLAND, B., Psychiatry/Behavioural Sciences
HOLTZMAN, S. G., Pharmacology
HOPKINS, L. C., Neurology
HOROWITZ, I. R., Gynaecology/Obstetrics
HUDSON, T., Radiology
HUG, C. C., Academic Affairs
HUMPHREY, D. R., Physiology
HUNTER, H. O., Law
HUNTER, R. J., Theology
HUTTON, W. C., Orthopaedics
HUYNH, B. H., Physics
INSEL, T. R., Psychiatry/Behavioural Sciences
IRVINE, J., Educational Studies
IUVONE, P. M., Pharmacology
JAFFE, S. L., Psychiatry/Behavioural Sciences
JENSEN, P., Pathology
JINKS-ROBERTSON, S., Biology
JOHNSON, L. T., Theology
JOHNSON, R., Chemistry
JOHNSON, T. C., Health, Physical Education and Dance
JOHNSTON, J. H., English
JONES, D. P., Biochemistry
JONES, E., Cardiothoracic Surgery
JONES, G., Biology
JORDAN, M., Religion
JOSEPH, R., Political Science
JOYNER, R. W., Paediatrics
JUDOVITZ, D., French and Italian
JUSTICE, J. B., Chemistry
KAHN, R. A., Biochemistry
KALAIDJIAN, W., English
KANTER, K. R., Cardiothoracic Surgery
KAPP, J., Ophthalmology
KARP, I., Liberal Arts, African Studies
KASLOW, N., Psychiatry/Behavioural Sciences
KAUFMAN, M. J., Chemistry
KAUFMAN, S., Radiology
KELLER, J. W., Radiation Oncology
KELLERMANN, A., Emergency Medicine
KERTZ, C. L., Accounting
KINKADE, J. M., Biochemistry
KLEHR, H., Politics and History
KLEIN, L., Gynaecology/Obstetrics
KLEINBAUM, D., Epidemiology
KLUGMAN, K. P., International Health
KNAUFT, B. M., Anthropology
KOHLI, A., Marketing
KONNER, M. J., Anthropology
KONSYNSKI, B., Business
KOVAC, S. R., Gynaecology/Obstetrics
KUHAR, M. J., Pharmacology
KULL, A., Law

KUSHNER, H., Science and Society
KUTNER, M., Biostatistics
KUTNER, N., Rehabilitation Medicine
LAMBETH, J. D., Biochemistry
LANGBERG, J. J., Cardiology, Electrophysiology
LAUER, S., Oncology, Paediatrics
LAWLEY, T. J., Medical School Administration
LAWRENCE, E. C., Medicine
LESSER, J., History, Latin American and Caribbean Studies
LETZ, R., Behavioural Science and Health Education
LEVEY, A. I., Neurology
LEVIN, B., Biology
LEVINSON, R. M., Medicine
LEVY, R., Psychiatry/Behavioural Sciences
LEWIS, W., Pathology
LIEBESKIND, L. S., Chemistry
LIN, M. C., Physical Chemistry
LINVILLE, K. B., Academic Affairs
LIOTTA, D. C., Chemistry
LIPSTADT, D., Judaic Studies
LIVINGSTON, D., Philosophy
LOLLAR, J. S., Haematology/Oncology
LONG, R. A., African Studies
LONG, T., Theology
LONGINI, I. M., Biostatistics
LOWE, W. J., Theology
LUCCHESI, J., Biology
LUSKIN, M. B., Cell Biology
LUTZ, L. J., Family and Preventive Medicine
LYNN, D., Chemistry
MABERLY, G., International Health
MCCAREY, B. E., Ophthalmology
MCCAULEY, R., Philosophy
MCDOWELL, J. J., Psychology
MCGINLEY, P. H., Radiation/Oncology
MCGOWAN, J. E., Epidemiology
MACON, E. J., Medicine
MCQUAIDE, M. M., Sociology
MADARA, J. L., Pathology
MAHAVIER, W. S., Mathematics and Computer Science
MAJMUDAR, B., Pathology
MAKKREEL, R. A., Philosophy
MANDELL, A. J., Psychiatry/Behavioural Sciences
MANSOUR, K., Cardiothoracic Surgery
MARSHALL, F. F., Urology
MARTIN, L. G., Radiology
MARTIN, R. C., Religion
MARTORELL, R., International Health
MARZILLI, L. G., Chemistry
MATTOX, D. E., Otolaryngology
MAYTON, W. T., Law
MEINERT, W. J., Family and Preventive Medicine
MERRILL, A. H., Biochemistry
MILLER, J. I., Cardiothoracic Surgery
MILLER, M., Law
MILLER, S. B., General Medicine
MINNEMAN, K. P., Pharmacology
MITCH, W. E., Medicine (Renal)
MOHANTY, J. N., Philosophy
MORAN, C., Microbiology/Immunology
MORGAN, E. T., Pharmacology
MOROKUMA, K., Chemistry
MORRIS, D. C., Cardiology
MURRAY, J., Adult and Elder Health
MUTH, R. D., Economics
NAHMIAS, A. J., Infectious Diseases, Paediatrics
NASSAR, V. H., Pathology
NAURIGHT, L. P., Adult and Elder Health
NEILL, D. B., Psychology
NEMEROFF, C., Psychiatry/Behavioural Sciences
NEWBY, G., Middle Eastern Studies
NEWSOM, C. A., Old Testament
NEYLAN, J. F., Medicine
NICHOLS, T. R., Physiology
NOE, B., Cell Biology
NOWICKI, S., Psychology
O'DAY, G. R., Theology
OLIKER, V., Mathematics and Computer Science
OLIVER, H. P., Religion
O'SHEA, H. S., Adult and Elder Health
OUSLANDER, J. G., Geriatric Medicine
PACKARD, R., International Health, History
PADWA, A., Chemistry
PARTIN, C., Health, Physical Education and Dance
PASCAL, R. R., Pathology
PASTOR, R., International Relations/Political Science
PATTERSON, R., Philosophy
PATTERSON, R. E., Cardiology
PEDERSON, L., English
PENNELL, J. N., Law
PERKOWITZ, S., Physics
PESKOWITZ, M., Religion
PETERSEN, K. W., Cell Biology
PETTIGREW, R., Radiology
PHILLIPS, L. S., Endocrinology
PINTER, M., Physiology
PLOTSKY, P. M., Psychiatry/Behavioural Sciences
PLUMMER, A., Medicine
POHL, J., Medicine
POLING, C. V., Art History
POLLET, R. J., Medicine
POMERANTZ, G., Journalism
POWELL, M. L., Nursing
POWNALL, G., Accounting
RAMBUSS, R., English
RAMOS, H. S., General Medicine
RANDALL, H. W., Gynaecology/Obstetrics
REAL, L., Biology
RECTOR, A. M., Law
REED, W. L., English
REMINGTON, T. F., Political Science
RICHEY, R., Theology
RICKETTS, R., Surgery, Paediatrics
RIMLAND, D., Infectious Diseases
ROARK, J., History
ROBBINS, V., Religion
ROCHAT, P., Psychology
ROCK, J. A., Gynaecology/Obstetrics
RODL, V., Mathematics and Computer Science
ROSENBERG, A., Psychiatry/Behavioural Sciences
ROTHENBERG, R. B., Family and Preventive Medicine
RUBIN, P. H., Economics
RUBINSON, R., Sociology
RUDOLPH, H., English
RYAN, P. B., Environmental and Occupational Health
SALAM, A., Surgery (Vascular)
SALE, W. S., Cell Biology
SALIERS, D. E., Theology
SALMON, M. E., Nursing
SALTMAN, R. B., Health Policy and Management
SANDS, J. M., Medicine
SARAL, R., Medicine
SCHAFFER, B. K., Economics
SCHINAZI, R. F., Paediatrics
SCHISLER, C., Music History
SCHMID, R., Mathematics and Computer Science
SCHUCHARD, R., English
SCOTT, J., Cell Biology
SCOTT, J. R., Microbiology/Immunology
SEBEL, P., Anaesthesiology
SEWELL, C. W., Pathology
SHAFER, W. M., Microbiology/Immunology
SHANOR, C. A., Law
SHAPIRO, M. M., Psychology
SHAPIRO, W., Political Science
SHAPPELL, R., Physical Education
SHARP, E., Nursing
SHERMAN, S., Genetics
SHETH, J., Marketing
SHORE, B., Anthropology
SHULMAN, J. A., Medicine
SHURE, D., Biology
SIDELL, N., Gynaecology/Obstetrics
SILVERMAN, M. E., Medicine
SIMONS, J. W., Medicine
SITTER, J. E., English
SKANDALAKIS, J. E., Surgical Anatomy and Technique
SLATER, N. W., Classics
SMITH, G. R., Law
SMITH, K., Haematology/Oncology
SMITH, L. E., Theology
SMITH, R. B., III, Surgery
SNAREY, J., Human Development and Ethics, Psychology
SOCOLOW, S. M., History, Latin American and Caribbean Studies
SOLOMON, A. R., Dermatology
SPITZNAGEL, J. K., Microbiology/Immunology
SPRAWLS, P., Radiological Services
SRIVASTAVA, R., Marketing
STEIN, D., Emergency Medicine
STEIN, D. G., Psychology
STEIN, K. W., Middle East Research
STERK, C. E., Behavioural Science and Health Education
STERN, B. J., Neurology
STERNBERG, P., Ophthalmology
STOKES, D., Biology
STONE, J., Medicine
STRICKLAND, O., Nursing
STULTING, R. D., Ophthalmology
SUNDERAM, V. S., Mathematics and Computer Science
SUNG, Y. F., Anaesthesiology
SYBERS, R. G., Radiology
SYMBAS, P., Cardiothoracic Surgery
TARCAN, Y., Radiology
TAYLOR, A., Nuclear Medicine, Radiology
TERRELL, T. P., Law
THOMAS, L.-G., III, Business Organization and Management
THORPE, K. E., Health Policy and Management
TIPTON, S. M., Theology
TORRES, W. E., Radiology
TUNE, L., Psychiatry/Behavioural Sciences
TUSA, R., Neurology
VAN DER VYVER, J., International Law
VANDALL, F. J., Law
VARADY, T., Law
VERENE, D. P., III, Philosophy
VINTEN-JOHANSEN, J., Cardiothoracic Surgery
VON WURTTEMBERG, A., Sanskrit
WAINER, B. E., Pathology, Geriatric Medicine
WALKER, E., Psychology
WALKER, H. K., Medicine
WALKER, T. G., Political Science
WALLEN, K., Psychology, Primate Research
WALLER, J. L., Anaesthesiology
WALTER, P. F., Medicine
WALTMAN, P., Mathematics and Computer Science
WARING, G. O., Ophthalmology
WARREN, S., Genetics
WATTS, N. B., Endocrinology
WATTS, R. L., Neurology
WAYMIRE, G., Marketing
WEATHERS, D. R., Pathology
WEBER, C. J., General Surgery
WEINTRAUB, W. S., Medicine
WEISS, B., Pathology
WEISS, J., Psychiatry/Behavioural Sciences
WEISS, S. A., Pathology
WENGER, N. K., Medicine
WHITE, D. F., Liberal Arts
WHITE, S., History
WHITESIDES, T. E., Orthopaedics
WILCOX, W. D., Paediatrics
WILKINSON, K. D., Biochemistry
WILLIAMS, W. H., Cardiothoracic Surgery
WILSON, M., Primate Research
WINOGRAD, E., Psychology
WITTE, J., Law
WOLF, S. L., Rehabilitation Medicine
WOOD, J. G., Cell Biology
WOOD, W. C., Surgical Oncology
WORKOWSKI, K. A., Infectious Diseases
WORTHMAN, C., Anthropology

YOUNG, J., Epidemiology
YOUNG, L., Physiology
ZAIDAN, J. R., Anaesthesiology
ZIEGLER, H. K., Microbiology/Immunology
ZUMPE, D., Psychiatry/Behavioural Sciences

FORT VALLEY STATE UNIVERSITY

1005 State University Dr., Fort Valley, GA 31030-4313
Telephone: (478) 825-6211
Fax: (478) 825-6394
Internet: www.fvsu.edu

Founded 1895
Academic year: July to June

Pres.: KOFI LOMOTEY
Vice-Pres. for Academic Affairs: Dr DOROTHY CONTEH
Vice-Pres. for Business and Finance: E. THOMAS OLIVER
Registrar: SHAREE LAWRENCE
Librarian: Dr CAROLE R. TAYLOR

Library of 191,806 vols
Number of teachers: 147
Number of students: 3,000

DEANS

Agriculture and Allied Programs: Dr FRED HARRISON
Arts and Sciences: Dr LAWRENCE WANG
Education, Graduate and Special Academic Programs: Dr CURTIS MARTIN

GEORGIA COLLEGE AND STATE UNIVERSITY

Milledgeville, GA 31061
Telephone: (478) 445-5004
Internet: www.gcsu.edu

Chartered in 1889 as Georgia Normal and Industrial College; name changed 1922 to Georgia State College for Women and 1961 to The Woman's College of Georgia; became co-educational instn in 1967 under the name of Georgia College; assumed present name when designated as Georgia's public liberal arts univ. in 1996

Pres.: Dr DOROTHY LELAND
Vice-Pres. for Academic Affairs and Dean of Faculties: Dr ANNE V. GORMLY
Vice-Pres. for Institutional Research and Enrolment Management: Dr PAUL JONES
Vice-Pres. for Student Affairs and Dean of Students: Dr BRUCE HARSBARGER
Vice-Pres. for Univ. Advancement: AMY NITSCHE
Dean of School of Health Sciences: Dr SANDRA GANGSTEAD
Dean of School of Liberal Arts and Sciences: Dr BETH RUSHING
Univ. Librarian: WILLIAM A. RICHARDS

Library of 190,000 vols, 23,500 print and electronic periodicals, partial depository for US govt documents
Number of teachers: 277
Number of students: 5,800

DEANS

School of Business: Dr JO ANN JONES
School of Education: Dr JANET FIELDS
School of Health Sciences: Dr JIMMY H. ISHEE
School of Liberal Arts and Sciences: Dr BETH RUSHING

GEORGIA INSTITUTE OF TECHNOLOGY

Atlanta, GA 30332
Telephone: (404) 894-2000
Internet: www.gatech.edu
Public control
Academic year: August to May

Chartered 1885

Pres.: G. P. PETERSON
Exec. Vice-Pres. for Admin. and Finance: STEVEN SWANT
Provost and Vice-Pres. for Academic Affairs: RAFAEL BRAS
Vice-Pres. for Devt: BARRETT CARSON
Vice-Pres. for Institute Diversity: Dr ARCHIE ERVIN
Exec. Vice-Pres. for Research: STEPHEN CROSS
Vice-Pres. for Student Affairs: WILLIAM SCHAFER
Vice-Pres. of Communications and Marketing: MICHAEL WARDEN
Sr Vice-Provost for Academic Affairs: ANDERSON SMITH
Exec. Dir of Govt and Community Relations: DENE SHEHEANE
Registrar: RETA PIKOWSKY
Dir of Libraries: CATHERINE MURRARY-RUST

Library of 4,634,954 vols, 1,449,328 govt documents, 2,804,720 technical reports, 198,288 maps, 8,167,358 patents, 28,686 electronic journals
Number of teachers: 935
Number of students: 20,291

Publications: *Blue Print*, *Georgia Tech Fact Book*, *Research Horizons*, *The Technique*

DEANS

College of Architecture: Prof. ALAN BALFOUR
College of Computing: Prof. ZVI GALIL
College of Engineering: Dr DON P. GIDDENS
College of Management: Prof. STEVE SALBU
College of Sciences: Prof. PAUL HOUSTON
Ivan Allen College of Liberal Arts: Prof. JACQUELINE JONES-ROYSTER

GEORGIA SOUTHERN UNIVERSITY

POB 8104, Statesboro, GA 30460
Telephone: (912) 478-4636
Fax: (912) 478-0325
E-mail: admissions@georigasouthern.edu
Internet: www.georgiasouthern.edu

Founded 1906
Academic year: August to July

Pres.: Dr BROOKS A. KEEL
Vice-Pres. for Business and Finance: JOSEPH W. FRANKLIN
Vice-Pres. for Student Affairs and Enrollment Management: Dr TERESA ELAINE THOMPSON
Vice-Pres. for Univ. Advancement: WILLIAM I. GRIFFIS
Registrar: MIKE DEAL
Dean of the Library: W. BEDE MITCHELL

Library of 541,535 vols
Number of teachers: 720 (626 full-time, 94 part-time)
Number of students: 14,371

GEORGIA SOUTHWESTERN STATE UNIVERSITY

800 Wheatley St, Americus, GA 31709
E-mail: gswapps@canes.gsw.edu
Internet: www.gsw.edu

Founded 1906 as Third Agricultural and Mechanical School; present name 1996
Academic year: August to May

Pres.: Dr KENDALL BLANCHARD
Vice-Pres. for Academic Affairs and Dean of Faculty: Dr CATHY L. ROZMUS
Vice-Pres. for Business and Finance: Dr C. ALAN PARKS
Vice-Pres. for Student Affairs: Dr SAMUEL T. MILLER
Vice-Pres. for Dir of Univ. Relations: STEPHEN SNYDER
Dean of Students: GAYE S. HAYES
Registrar: DONJA TRIPP
Dean of the Library: VERA WEISSKOPF

Library of 190,000 vols
Number of teachers: 108
Number of students: 2,239 (1,969 undergraduate, 270 graduate)

DEANS

School of Arts and Sciences: Dr WILLIAM WYSOCHANSKY
School of Business Admin.: Dr JOHN G. KOOTI
School of Computer and Information Sciences: Dr BORIS V. PELTSVERGER
School of Education: Dr MARY GENDERNALIK COOPER
School of Nursing: Dr MARIA R. WARDA

GEORGIA STATE UNIVERSITY

University Plaza, POB 2000, Atlanta, GA 30303
Telephone: (404) 651-2000
Internet: www.gsu.edu

Founded 1913
Academic year: August to May

Pres.: Dr CARL V. PATTON
Provost and Vice-Pres. for Academic Affairs: Dr RONALD J. HENRY
Vice-Pres. for Devt: NANCY PETERMAN
Vice-Pres. for External Affairs: THOMAS C. LEWIS
Vice-Pres. for Finance and Admin.: JERRY RACKLIFFE
Vice-Pres. for Research: Dr ROBIN MORRIS
Vice-Pres. for Student Services: DOUGLASS COVEY
Asst Vice Pres. for Enrollment Services and Registrar: CHERISE PETERS (acting)
University Librarian: CHARLENE HURT

Library of 1,476,610 vols, 9,832 current periodicals, 2,540,014 microforms, 25,155 audiovisual items, 57,716 e-books, 807,224 US govt documents
Number of teachers: 1,046
Number of students: 26,134

Publications: *CHHS E-Newsletter* (2 a year), *CPS Newsletter* (1 a year), *EPS Newsletter* (2 a year), *Eudora Welty Newsletter* (2 a year), *GSU Review* (2 a year), *Health and Human Review* (2 a year), *International Journal of Bioinformatics Research* (4 a year), *Law Review* (4 a year), *Robinson Business Beat* (9 a year), *South Atlantic Review* (irregular), *State of Business Magazine* (3 a year), *Studies in Literary Imagination* (2 a year), *The Briefing* (1 a year), *The Forecast for the Nation* (4 a year)

DEANS

Andrew Young School of Policy Studies: Dr ROY BAHL (acting)
College of Arts and Sciences: Dr LAUREN ADAMSON
College of Education: Dr RONALD COLARUSSO
College of Health and Human Sciences: Dr SUSAN KELLEY
College of Law: Dr STEVEN KAMINSHINE (acting)
Dean J. Mack Robinson College of Business: Dr H. FENWICK HUSS

ATTACHED RESEARCH INSTITUTES

Institute of Int. Business: Suite 800, 35 Broad St, Atlanta, GA; tel. (404) 651-4057; e-mail iib@gsu.edu; internet www.iib.gsu.edu; Dir Dr JOAN GABEL.

Institute of Public Health: Georgia State University, PO Box 3995, Atlanta, GA; tel. (404) 651-4133; fax (404) 651-1559; e-mail publichealth@gsu.edu; internet publichealth.gsu.edu; Dir Dr MICHAEL ERIKSON.

Ron Brown Institute: Co-Dirs ROY BAHL, JOHN HICKS.

The Gerontology Institute: tel. (404) 651-2692; fax (404) 651-4272; e-mail gerontology@gsu.edu; internet www.gsu.edu/gerontology; Dir Prof. FRANK J. WHITTINGTON.

INTERDENOMINATIONAL THEOLOGICAL CENTER

700 Martin Luther King, Jr Dr., Atlanta, GA 303144143
Telephone: (404) 527-7700
E-mail: info@itc.edu
Internet: www.itc.edu
Founded 1958
Academic year: September to May
Pres.: Dr MICHAEL A. BATTLE.

KENNESAW STATE UNIVERSITY

1000 Chastain Rd, Kennesaw, GA 30144
Telephone: (770) 423-6300
E-mail: ksuadmit@kennesaw.edu
Internet: www.kennesaw.edu
Founded 1963 as Kennesaw Junior College; present name 1996
Academic year: August to May
Pres.: Dr DANIEL S. PAPP
Provost and Vice-Pres. for Academic Affairs: Dr LENDLEY C. BLACK
Vice-Pres. for Operations: RANDY C. HINDS
Vice-Pres. for Student Success and Enrollment Services: Dr NANCY S. KING
Vice-Pres. for Univ. Advancement: WESLEY K. WICKER
Dean of Graduate Studies: Dr TERESA M. JOYCE
Dean of Undergraduate and Univ. College: Dr MARY LOU FRANK
Dean of Division of Continuing Education: BARBARA S. CALHOUN
Registrar: WILLIAM L. HAMRICK
Library Dir: DAVID EVANS
Library of 600,000 vols and govt publs
Number of teachers: 537
Number of students: 18,000

DEANS

Bagwell College of Education: Dr YIPING WAN
Coles College of Business: Dr TIM MESCON
College of the Arts: JOSEPH MEEKS
College of Health and Human Services: Dr RICHARD SOWELL
College of Humanities and Social Sciences: Dr HELEN S. RIDLEY
College of Science and Mathematics: Dr LAURENCE I. PETERSON

LAGRANGE COLLEGE

601 Broad St, LaGrange, GA 30240
Telephone: (706) 880-8005
Fax: (706) 880-8358
Internet: www.lagrange.edu
Founded 1831
Academic year: September to May
Pres.: Dr FRANK STUART GULLEY
Exec. Vice-Pres. for Admin.: PHYLLIS D. WHITNEY
Vice-Pres. for Academic Affairs and Dean: Dr JAY K. SIMMONS
Vice-Pres. and Dean for Student Life and Retention: Dr LINDA R. BUCHANAN
Dir for Enrollment Management and Admissions: WELLS SHEPARD
Registrar: JIMMY HERRING
Library Dir: LOREN PINKERMAN
Library of 138,000 vols
Number of teachers: 70
Number of students: 1,000

LIFE UNIVERSITY

1269 Barclay Circle, Marietta, GA 30060
Telephone: (770) 426-2884
Fax: (770) 426-2895
E-mail: admissions@life.edu
Internet: www.life.edu
Founded 1974 as Life Chiropractic College; present name 1997
Private control
Pres.: Dr GUY F. RIEKEMAN
Provost: Dr BRIAN MCAULAY
Vice-Pres. for Operations and Finance: BILL JARR
Vice-Pres. for Univ. Advancement: BARRY NICKELSBERG
Dean for College of Arts and Sciences: Dr JERRY HARDEE
Registrar: BRIAN SHERES
Number of teachers: 126
Number of students: 1,242

DEANS

College of Arts and Sciences: Dr SAM DEMONS (acting)
College of Chiropractic Science: Dr ROBERT M. SCOTT

MEDICAL COLLEGE OF GEORGIA

1120 15th St, Augusta, GA 30912
Telephone: (706) 721-0211
Internet: www.mcg.edu
Founded 1828 as Medical Academy of Georgia
Part of univ. system of Georgia
Pres.: Dr DANIEL W. RAHN
Provost: Dr BARRY D. GOLDSTEIN
Vice-Pres. for Admin.: Dr J. MICHAEL ASH
Vice-Pres. for Decision Support: DEB BARSHAFSKY
Vice-Pres. for Enrolment and Student Services: Dr MICHAEL H. MILLER
Vice-Pres. for Finance: DIANE C. WRAY
Vice-Pres. for Information Technology: BETH BRIGDON
Vice-Pres. for Legal Affairs: ANDREW R. H. NEWTON
Vice-Pres. for Research: FRANK A. TREIBER
Vice-Pres. for Univ. Advancement: BRIAN R. GINN, Jr
Registrars: Dr MIKE MILLER, RITA GARNER
Dir of Libraries: TAMERA LEE
Library of 219,984 vols, 1,232 current periodicals, 980 audiovisual titles
Number of teachers: 2,023 (590 full-time, 119 part time, 1,314 volunteer)
Number of students: 1,939
Publication: *Scope*

DEANS

Allied Health Sciences: Dr SHELLEY MISHOE
Dentistry: Dr BRAD J. POTTER
Medicine: Dr DAVID M. STERN
Nursing: Dr MARLENE ROSENKOETTER
Graduate Studies: Dr MATTHEW J. KLUGER

MERCER UNIVERSITY

1400 Coleman Ave, Macon, GA 31207-0001
Telephone: (912) 752-2700
Fax: (912) 752-4124
Internet: www.mercer.edu
Chartered 1833
Private control (Baptist)
Pres.: WILLIAM D. UNDERWOOD
Exec. Vice-Pres. for Finance and Admin.: Dr JAMES S. NETHERTON
Sr Vice-Pres. for Univ. Advancement and External Affairs: EMILY P. MYERS
Vice-Pres. and Dean of Students: Dr DOUGLAS R. PEARSON
Exec. Vice-Pres. and Provost: HORACE W. FLEMING
Library of 243,000 vols, 1,000 current periodicals, 4,400 audio items, US govt documents
Number of teachers: 1,291
Number of students: 7,300
Publications: *Discoveries*, *Inside Mercer*, *The Business Advisor*, *The Law Letter*, *The Mercer Engineer*, *The Mercerian*, *TIFToday*

DEANS

College of Liberal Arts: Prof. RICHARD C. FALLIS
Eugene W. Stetson School of Business and Economics: DAVID SHIELDS
Georgia Baptist College of Nursing: Dr SUSAN S. GUNBY
Law: Prof. MICHAEL SABBATH
McAfee School of Theology: Prof. R. ALAN CULPEPPER
Medicine: Dr ANN JOBE
Pharmacy (Atlanta): Prof. HEWITT W. 'TED' MATTHEWS
School of Engineering: Prof. M. DAYNE ALDRIDGE
Tift College of Education: Prof. RICHARD T. SIETSEMA

MOREHOUSE COLLEGE

830 Westview Dr., SW, Atlanta, GA 30314
Telephone: (404) 681-2800
Internet: www.morehouse.edu
Founded 1867; member of Atlanta Univ. Center
Pres.: Dr WALTER E. MASSEY
Provost and Sr Vice-Pres. for Academic Affairs: DAVID V. TAYLOR
Vice-Pres. for Business and Finance: KEITH APPLETON
Vice-Pres. for Campus Operations: ANDRÉ BERTRAND
Vice-Pres. for Institutional Advancement: PHILLIP HOWARD
Library Dir: LORETTA PARHAM
Library of 650,000 vols
Number of teachers: 238 (176 full-time, 62 part-time)
Number of students: 3,000
Publication: *Journal of Negro History*.

MOREHOUSE SCHOOL OF MEDICINE

720 Westview Dr., SW, Atlanta, GA 30310-1495
Telephone: (404) 752-1500
Internet: www.msm.edu
Founded 1975 as School of Medicine at Morehouse College; present name 1981
Private control
Academic year: July to May
Pres.: Dr JOHN E. MAUPIN
Dean and Sr Vice-Pres. for Academic Affairs: Dr EVE J. HIGGINBOTHAM
Vice-Pres. for Finance: ELI H. PHILLIPS
Vice-Pres. for Human Resources: SYLVIA D. NEALY
Exec. Dir for Marketing and Communications: CHERIE A. RICHARDSON
Chief Information Officer: ERIC L. JACKSON
Registrar: RODDRICK JONES
Library of 73,572 vols
Number of teachers: 204
Number of students: 217

MORRIS BROWN COLLEGE

634 Martin Luther King Dr., SW, Atlanta, GA 30314
Telephone: (404) 220-0270
Fax: (404) 659-4315
Internet: www.morrisbrown.edu
Founded 1881; member of Atlanta Univ. Center and United Negro College Fund
Pres.: Dr CHARLES E. TAYLOR (acting)
Vice-Pres. for Academic Affairs: Dr REGINALD LINDSEY (acting)

Vice-Pres. for Admin. and Operations: JIM MARING
Vice-Pres. for Devt: OLIVER DELK
Vice-Pres. for Fiscal Affairs: DENISE SMITH-MOORE
Vice-Pres. for Legal Affairs: DIONYSIA JOHNSON-MASSIE
Vice-Pres. for Student Affairs: Dr LEVITA SMALL
Registrar: LUCILE WILLIAMS

Library of 797,684 vols
Number of teachers: 143
Number of students: 2,154

Publications: *Bulletin*, *Wolverine Observer* (12 a year).

NORTH GEORGIA COLLEGE AND STATE UNIVERSITY

82 College Circle, Dahlonega, GA 30597
Telephone: (706) 864-1400
Fax: (706) 864-1478
E-mail: admissions@ngcsu.edu
Internet: www.ngcsu.edu

Founded 1873
Academic year: August to May

Pres.: DAVID POTTER
Vice-Pres. for Academic Affairs: Dr LINDA ROBERTS-BETSCH
Vice-Pres. for Business and Finance: FRANK J. MCCONNELL
Vice-Pres. for Institutional Advancement: BRUCE HOWERTON
Vice-Pres. for Student Affairs: Dr CHARLES SCHRODER
Registrar: JASON K. PRUITT
Dir of Library Services: SHAWN TONNER

Library of 175,330 vols (incl. old periodicals, electronic documents and govt documents), 550 paper periodicals, 100 microform periodicals, 15,978 electronic periodicals, 1,487 audiovisual items, 92 CD-ROMs
Number of teachers: 362
Number of students: 4,552

Publication: *Honores: The NGCSU Journal of Undergraduate Research* (2 a year)

DEANS

Arts and Letters: Dr ROBERT LYMAN
Business and Govt: Dr GERALD SKELLY
Education: Dr BOB MICHAEL
Natural and Health Sciences: Dr THOMAS FOX

OGLETHORPE UNIVERSITY

4484 Peachtree Rd, NE, Atlanta, GA 30319
Telephone: (404) 261-1441
Fax: (404) 364-8500
E-mail: admission@oglethorpe.edu
Internet: www.oglethorpe.edu

Founded 1835
Academic year: September to May

Pres.: LAWRENCE SCHALL
Registrar: TANYA CRUMP
Provost: WILLIAM O. SHROPSHIRE
Vice-Pres. for Business and Finance: MARILYN FOWLÉ
Vice-Pres. for Devt: PETER A. ROONEY
Dir of the Library: ANNE A. SALTER

Library of 150,000 bound vols
Number of teachers: 116
Number of students: 1,230

Publications: *The Flying Petrel* (4 a year), *The Stormy Petrel* (26 a year), *The Tower* (2 a year), *Yamacraw* (1 a year).

PAINE COLLEGE

1235 15th St, Augusta, GA 30901-3182
Telephone: (706) 821-8200
Internet: www.paine.edu

Founded 1882

Pres.: Dr SHIRLEY A. R. LEWIS
Vice-Pres. for Academic Affairs: Dr CURTIS E. MARTIN
Vice-Pres. for Admin. and Fiscal Affairs: FREDDIE L. JOHNSON
Vice-Pres. for Institutional Devt: JUDITH LITTLE
Registrar: CAROLYN MARTIN
Dir of Library: SUZETTE HOLLINS

Library of 73,000 vols
Number of teachers: 74
Number of students: 900

Publications: *The Lion* (1 a year), *The Paineite* (2 to 4 a year), *The Paine Magazine* (4 a year), *The Windowpaine* (12 a year).

PIEDMONT COLLEGE

Demorest, GA 30535
Telephone: (706) 778-3000
Internet: www.piedmont.edu

Founded 1897
Academic year: August to May

Pres.: Dr W. RAY CLEERE
Vice-Pres. for Academic Affairs: Dr JAMES MELLICHAMP
Admissions: CINDY PETERSON
Registrar: LINDA WOFFORD
Librarian: ROBERT GLASS

Library of 100,000 vols
Number of teachers: 100
Number of students: 2,700

REINHARDT COLLEGE

7300 Reinhardt College Circle, Waleska, GA 30183-2981
Telephone: (770) 720-5600
Fax: (770) 720-5602
E-mail: admissions@reinhardt.edu
Internet: www.reinhardt.edu

Founded 1883 as Reinhardt Academy; present name 1911
Private control
Academic year: August to May

Pres.: Dr J. THOMAS ISHERWOOD
Vice-Pres. for Academic Affairs and Dean of the College: Dr ROBERT L. DRISCOLL
Vice-Pres. for Finance and Admin.: JAMES T. HAKES
Vice-Pres. for Institutional Advancement and External Affairs: JOELLEN WILSON
Vice-Pres. for Student Affairs and Dean of Students: Dr ROGER LEE
Library Dir: MICHAEL MARTINEZ

Library of 52,556 vols and bound periodicals
Number of teachers: 60 full-time
Number of students: 1,060

DEANS

McCamish School of Business: Dr DAVID W. CHOWN
Price School of Education: Dr THOMAS REED
School of Arts and Humanities: Dr WAYNE GLOWKA
School of Communication Arts and Music: PEG O'CONNOR
School of Mathematics and Sciences: WILLIAM DE ANGELIS

BRANCH CAMPUS

N Fulton Center: 4100 Old Milton Parkway, Suite 250, Alpharetta, GA 30005-4442; tel. (770) 7209191; fax (770) 4750263; e-mail nfmail@reinhardt.edu; Asst Dean for Extended Academic Studies Dr DONALD D. WILSON, Jr.

SAVANNAH COLLEGE OF ART AND DESIGN

POB 77300, Atlanta, GA 30357-1300
Telephone: (404) 253-2700
Fax: (404) 253-3466
E-mail: scadatl@scad.edu
Internet: www.scad.edu

Founded 1905
Incorporates the Atlanta College of Art and Design; additional campus in Lacoste, France
Private control
Academic year: August to May

Pres.: PAULA S. WALLACE
Vice-Pres. for Academic Services: JOE SEIPEL
Vice-Pres. for Business and Finance: TIMOTHY A. SPAETH
Vice-Pres. for Enrollment Management: LUCY LEUSCH
Vice-Pres. for Institutional Advancement: ELIZABETH CHAPMAN
Vice-Pres. for Student Services: DAVID PUGH
Head Librarian: MELISSA MCDONALD

Library of 25,000 vols, 180 periodicals, 90,000 slides
Number of teachers: 73
Number of students: 425

SAVANNAH STATE UNIVERSITY

3219 College St, Savannah, GA 31404
Telephone: (912) 356-2240
Fax: (912) 356-2998
E-mail: ssu.inquiries@tigerpaw.savstate.edu
Internet: www.savstate.edu

Founded 1890
Academic year: August to May

Pres.: Dr JULIUS S. SCOTT, Jr
Vice-Pres. for Academic Affairs: Dr JANE MCBRIDE-GATES
Vice-Pres. for Business and Finance: ELAINE CAMPBELLE
Vice-Pres. for Institutional Advancement: LARION WILLIAMS
Vice-Pres. for Student Affairs: Dr RANDY GUNTER
Library Dir: MARY JO FAYOYIN

Library of 188,068 items
Number of teachers: 160
Number of students: 2,300

SHORTER UNIVERSITY

315 Shorter Ave, Rome, GA 30165-4298
Telephone: (706) 291-2121
Fax: (706) 236-1515
E-mail: admissions@shorter.edu
Internet: www.shorter.edu

Founded 1873
Private control
Language of instruction: English
Academic year: August to May

Pres.: Dr HAROLD E. NEWMAN
Provost: Dr L. CRAIG SHULL
Chief Financial Officer: STEPHANIE OWENS
Vice-Pres. for Student Affairs: Dr. DEBRA FAUST
Dir of Institutional Advancement: SUZANNE SCOTT
Registrar: MELISSA TARRANT
Dir of Admissions: Dr JOHN HEAD
Dean of Libraries: Dr DEBORAH MEYER

Library of 144,475 vols
Number of teachers: 85
Number of students: 3,775

DEANS

College of Adult and Professional Programs: Dr BARBARA FINN
College of Arts and Sciences: Dr SABRENA PARTON
College of Business: Dr ROBERT DARVILLE

School of Education: Dr SANDRA LESLIE
School of Fine and Performing Arts: Dr ALAN WINGARD
School of Nursing: Dr VANICE ROBERTS
School of Science and Mathematics: Dr CRAIG ALLEE

SOUTHERN POLYTECHNIC STATE UNIVERSITY

1100 S Marietta Parkway, Marietta, GA 30060-2896
Telephone: (678) 915-7778
Fax: (678) 915-7483
E-mail: admissions@spsu.edu
Internet: www.spsu.edu
Founded 1948 as The Technical Institute; present name 1996
Part of Univ. System of Georgia
Academic year: August to August
Pres.: Dr LISA A. ROSSBACHER
Vice-Pres. for Academic Affairs: Dr ZVI SZAFRAN
Vice-Pres. for Business and Finance: PATRICK R. McCORD
Vice-Pres. for Student and Enrollment Services: Dr RON R. KOGER
Library Dir: Dr JOYCE WHITE MILLS
Library of 105,000 vols
Number of teachers: 150
Number of students: 4,000

DEANS

Extended Univ.: DAWN RAMSEY
School of Architecture, Civil Engineering Technology, and Construction: Dr WILSON BARNES
School of Arts and Sciences: Dr ALAN GABRIELLI
School of Computing and Software Engineering: Dr MICHAEL MURPHY
School of Engineering Technology and Management: Dr C. WAYNE UNSELL

SPELMAN COLLEGE

350 Spelman Lane, SW, Atlanta, GA 30314-4399
Telephone: (404) 681-3643
Fax: (404) 223-1428
Internet: www.spelman.edu
Founded 1881; member of Atlanta Univ. Center
Pres.: Dr BEVERLEY DANIEL TATUM
Provost: Dr JOHNNELLA BUTLER
Vice-Pres. for Business and Financial Affairs and Treasurer: ROBERT D. FLANAGAN, Jr
Vice-Pres. for Institutional Advancement: A. TRISA LONG PASCHAL
Vice-Pres. for Media and Information Technology: ELLIS RAINEY
Vice-Pres. for Student Affairs: Dr SHERRY L. TURNER
Assoc. Provost for Liberal Arts and Education: Dr RONNIE TRIBBLE
Assoc. Provost for Science Programs and Mathematics: Dr SYLVIA T. BOZEMAN
Academic Dean: Dr CYNTHIA NEAL SPENCE
Registrar: Dr FRED BUDDY
Number of teachers: 156
Number of students: 2,139

STATE UNIVERSITY OF WEST GEORGIA

1601 Maple St, Carrollton, GA 30118
Telephone: (678) 839-5000
Internet: www.westga.edu
Founded 1906; sr college status 1957, univ. status 1995
State (Public)
Language of instruction: English
Academic year: August to July
Accredited by Comm. on Colleges of the S Asscn of Colleges and Schools, AACSB Int., American Chemical Soc., Comm. on Collegiate Nursing Education Computing Accreditation, Comm. of the Accreditation Board for Engineering and Technology, Ccl for Humanistic Transpersonal Psychology, Nat. Asscn of Schools of Music, Nat. Asscn of Schools of Art and Design, Nat. Asscn of Schools of Theatre, Nat. Asscn of Schools of Public Affairs and Admin., Nat. Ccl for Accreditation of Teacher Education Orgs in which the Univ. holds institutional membership incl. the American Ccl on Education, the American Asscn of State Colleges and Univs, the American Asscn of Colleges for Teacher Education, the Conf. of S Graduate Schools, the Georgia Asscn of Colleges, the Nat. Asscn for Foreign Student Affairs, the Nat. Business Education Asscn, and the Nat. Collegiate Honors Ccl.
Pres.: Dr BEHERUZ N. SETHNA
Vice-Pres. for Academic Affairs: Dr SANDRA STONE
Vice-Pres. for Business and Finance: JAMES SUTHERLAND
Vice-Pres. for Student Services: Dr MELANIE McCLELLAN
Vice-Pres. for Univ. Advancement: MICHAEL RUFFNER
Registrar: DONNA HALEY
Dir of Admissions: Dr ROBERT S. JOHNSON
Dir of Libraries: LORENE FLANDERS
Library of 536,446 vols, 16,131 current serials subscriptions (paper, microform, electronic), 1m. microforms, 11,643 audiovisual items
Number of teachers: 551 (428 full-time, 123 part-time)
Number of students: 11,252 (undergraduate: 7,833 full-time, 1,397 part-time; graduate: 468 full-time, 1,554 part-time)
Publications: *Graduate Catalog* (1 a year), *Just the Facts*, *Under Graduate Catalog* (1 a year), *Studies in the Social Sciences* (1 a year), *University of West Georgia Fact Book*, *West Georgia College Faculty Research Review* (1 a year), *West Georgia Fact Book* (1 a year)

DEANS

College of Arts and Sciences: Dr GEORGE K. KIEH
College of Education: Dr KIM METCALF
Graduate School: Dr CHARLES CLARK
Honors College: Dr DONALD WAGNER
Richards College of Business: Dr FAYE McINTYRE
School of Nursing: Dr KATHRYN GRAMS

THOMAS UNIVERSITY

1501 Millpond Rd, Thomasville, GA 31792
Telephone: (229) 226-1621
Fax: (229) 226-1653
E-mail: admissions@thomasu.edu
Internet: www.thomasu.edu
Founded 1950 as Birdwood Junior College; present name 2000
Private control
Academic year: August to May
Pres.: Dr GARY BONVILLIAN
Vice-Pres. for Academic Affairs: KIM ESTEP
Vice-Pres. for Finance and Admin.: ALLEN TOWNS
Vice-Pres. for Institutional Advancement: RICHARD MUNROE
Academic Dean: ANN M. LANDIS
Registrar: DEBBIE WHITE
Dir of Library Services: GARY COOPER
Library of 49,153 vols
Number of teachers: 61
Number of students: 5,509
Depts of arts and sciences, business, counselling and rehabilitation, education, human services, justice studies, nursing, social work.

TOCCOA FALLS COLLEGE

107 N Chapel Dr., POB 800777, Toccoa Falls, GA 30598
Telephone: (706) 886-6831
Fax: (706) 282-6005
E-mail: president@tfc.edu
Internet: www.tfc.edu
Founded 1907
Private control
Schools of arts and sciences: communication, counselling psychology, humanities and natural sciences; school of Christian ministries: Bible studies, Christian education, theology, world missions; school of professional studies: business admin., music, teacher education
Academic year: August to May
Pres.: Dr W. WAYNE GARDNER
Provost: BARBARA K. BELLEFEUILLE
Vice-Pres. for Academic Affairs: Dr W. BRIAN SHELTON
Vice-Pres. for Finance: GREGG SCHULTE
Vice-Pres. for Institutional Advancement: (vacant)
Vice-Pres. for Student Devt: LEE YOWELL
Dir for Spiritual Formation: Dr JEFFREY GANGEL
Registrar: KELLY VICKERS
Dir for Library Services and Information Technology: PATRICIA FISHER
Number of teachers: 71
Number of students: 767

DEANS

School of Arts and Sciences: Dr KIERAN CLEMENTS
School of Christian Ministries: Dr W. BRIAN SHELTON
School of Professional Studies: Dr THOMAS COUNCIL

UNIVERSITY OF GEORGIA

Athens, GA 30602
Telephone: (706) 542-3000
Internet: www.uga.edu
Founded 1785
Pres.: MICHAEL F. ADAMS
Sr Vice-Pres. for Academic Affairs and Provost: ARNETT C. MACE, Jr
Sr Vice-Pres. for External Affairs: TOM S. LANDRUM
Sr Vice-Pres. for Finance and Admin.: TIM BURGESS
Vice-Pres. for Instruction: DELMER D. DUNN
Vice-Pres. for Instruction: JERE W MOREHEAD
Vice-Pres. for Public Service and Outreach: ARTHUR DUNNING
Vice-Pres. for Research: DAVID LEE
Vice-Pres. for Student Affairs: RODNEY BENNETT
Registrar: REBECCA MACON
Univ. Librarian: Dr WILLIAM G. POTTER
Library of 3,955,004 vols
Number of teachers: 2,984
Number of students: 33,878
Publications: *Environmental Ethics* (4 a year), *Fact Book* (1 a year), *Georgia Economic Outlook* (1 a year), *Georgia Historical Quarterly* (4 a year), *Georgia Journal of College Student Affairs* (2 a year), *Georgia Journal of Ecological Anthropology* (1 a year), *Georgia Journal of International and Comparative Law* (3 a year), *Georgia Magazine* (4 a year), *Georgia Museum of Art Bulletin* (1 a year), *Georgia Pharmacist Magazine* (1 a year), *Georgia Pharmacist Quarterly* (4 a year), *Georgia*

Preceptor (4 a year), *Georgia Science Teacher* (3 a year), *Impact Interactive* (a service-learning magazine project, 1 a year), *Journal of Agribusiness* (2 a year), *Journal of Business Research* (12 a year), *Journal of Public Service and Outreach* (3 a year), *Journal of Research and Development in Education* (4 a year), *State and Local Government Review* (3 a year), *Teaching Georgia Government* (3 a year), *The Aesculapian* (4 a year), *The Georgia Advocate* (3 a year), *The Georgia Review* (4 a year), *Toxicology Digest* (4 a year)

DEANS

C. Herman and Mary Virginia Terry College of Business: Dr P. GEORGE BENSON
College of Agricultural and Environmental Sciences: Dr GALE A. BUCHANAN
College of Education: Dr LOUIS A. CASTENELL, Jr
College of Environment and Design: Dr JOHN F. CROWLEY
College of Family and Consumer Sciences: Dr SHARON Y. NICKOLS
College of Pharmacy: Dr SVEIN OIE
Daniel B. Warnell School of Forest Resources: Dr JAMES SWEENEY (acting)
Franklin College of Arts and Sciences: Dr WYATT W. ANDERSON
Graduate School: Dr MAUREEN GRASSO
Henry W. Grady College of Journalism and Mass Communication: Dr JOHN SOLOSKI
School of Law: Dr DAVID E. SHIPLEY
School of Public and Int. Affairs: Dr THOMAS P. LAUTH
School of Social Work: Dr LARRY NAKERUD
School of Veterinary Medicine: Dr KEITH W. PRASSEE

VALDOSTA STATE UNIVERSITY

1500 N Patterson St, Valdosta, GA 31698
Telephone: (229) 245-6517
Internet: www.valdosta.edu

Founded 1906

Pres.: Dr RONALD M. ZACCARI
Vice-Pres. for Academic Affairs: Dr LOUIS H. LEVY
Vice-Pres. for Finance and Admin.: JAMES L. BLACK
Vice-Pres. for Student Affairs: Dr KURT J. KEPPLER
Vice-Pres. for Univ. Advancement: SCOTT H. SYKES (acting)
Dir of Human Resources and Employee Devt: Dr DENISE BOGART
Registrar: GERALD B. WRIGHT
Librarian: Dr GEORGE R. GAUMOND

Library of 395,000 vols
Number of teachers: 500
Number of students: 10,000

Publication: *The Journal of Southwest Georgia History* (4 a year)

DEANS

College of Arts and Sciences: Dr SHARON GRAVETT (acting)
College of Education: Dr THOMAS REED, III (acting)
College of Nursing: Dr MARYANN REICHENBACH
College of the Arts: Dr JOHN GASTON (acting)
Division of Social Work: Dr MARTHA M. GIDDINGS
Graduate School: Dr ERNESTINE CLARK
Harley Labgdale, Jr College of Business Admin.: Dr KENNETH A. STANLEY

WESLEYAN COLLEGE

4760 Forsyth Rd, Macon, GA 31210
Telephone: (478) 477-1110
Fax: (478) 757-4030
Internet: www.wesleyancollege.edu

Founded 1836
Academic year: August to May

Pres.: RUTH A. KNOX
Vice-Pres. for Academic Affairs and Dean of the College: DELMAS S. CRISP, Jr
Vice-President for Admin. and Marketing: C. STEPHEN FARR
Vice-Pres. for Enrollment Services and Student Affairs: PATRICIA M. GIBBS
Vice-Pres. for Finance and Treas.: RICHARD P. MAIER
Vice-Pres. for Institutional Advancement: DEBORAH JONES SMITH
Librarian: CATHERINE LEE

Library of 142,579 vols
Number of teachers: 79
Number of students: 715

HAWAII

BRIGHAM YOUNG UNIVERSITY, HAWAII CAMPUS

55–220 Kulanui St, Laie, Oahu, HI 96762
Telephone: (808) 293-3211
Internet: www.byuh.edu

Founded 1955

Pres.: Dr ERIC B. SHUMWAY
Vice-Pres. for Academics: KEITH J. ROBERTS
Vice-Pres. for Admin. Services: MICHAEL B. BLISS
Vice-Pres. for Student Affairs: ILILELI T. KONGAIKA
Vice-Pres. for Univ. Advancement: V. NAPUA BAKER
Chief Information Officer: JIM NILSON
Asst to Pres.: WILLIAM G. NEAL
Registrar: VERNELLE LAKATANI
Librarian: DOUGLAS BATES

Library of 163,000 vols
Number of teachers: 109
Number of students: 2,400

DEANS

Center for Instructional Technology and Outreach: ROBERT HAYDEN
College of Arts and Sciences: W. JEFFERY BURROUGHS
School of Business: CLAYTON HUBNER
School of Computing: BRET ELLIS
School of Education: JOHN BAILEY

ATTACHED RESEARCH INSTITUTE

Institute of Polynesian Studies: Dir Dr VERNICE WINEERA; publ. *Pacific Studies* (4 a year).

CHAMINADE UNIVERSITY OF HONOLULU

3140 Waialae Ave, Honolulu, HI 96816-1578
Telephone: (808) 735-4711
Fax: (808) 735-4870
E-mail: admissions@chaminade.edu
Internet: www.chaminade.edu

Founded 1955
Academic year: August to May

Pres.: SUE WESSELKAMPER
Exec. Vice-Pres. and Provost: Bro. BERNARD PLOEGER
Vice-Pres. for Finance and Facilities: DANIEL GILMORE
Dean of Enrollment Management: JOY BOUEY
Dean of Students: GRISSEL BENITEZ-HODGE
Dean of Information Services and Library: LARRY OSBORNE
Registrar: JOHN MORRIS

Library of 75,000 vols
Number of teachers: 245
Number of students: 2,800

Publications: *Aulama*, *Chaminade Literary Review* (2 a year)

DEANS

Behavioral Science: ROBERT SANTEE
Education: DAVID JELINEK
Humanities and Fine Arts: DAVID L. COLEMAN
Natural Sciences and Mathematics: LEE M. GOFF
Professional Studies: SCOTT SCHROEDER

HAWAII PACIFIC UNIVERSITY

1164 Bishop St, Honolulu, HI 96813
Telephone: (808) 544-0200
Fax: (808) 544-9323
E-mail: admissions@hpu.edu
Internet: www.hpu.edu

Founded 1965
Academic year: September to June

Pres.: CHATT G. WRIGHT
Sr Vice-Pres. for Academic Affairs: JOHN FLECKLES
Vice-Pres. for Community Relations: NANCY ELLIS
Vice-Pres. for Enrollment Management: SCOTT STENSRUD
Vice-Pres. for Human Resources: LINDA KAWAMURA
Vice-Pres. for Research: ALISSA ARP
Vice-Pres. for Student Support Services: JEFFREY PHILPOTT
Registrar: KELLY NASHIRO-YOSHIDA
Librarian: KATHLEEN CHEE

Library of 180,000 vols and 11,000 periodicals
Number of teachers: 587
Number of students: 7,800

Colleges of business, communication, int. studies, liberal arts, natural sciences, nursing, professional studies

Publications: *Hawaii Pacific Review* (1 a year), *Kalamalama* (12 a year), *The Voice* (2 a year), *Wanderlust* (1 a year).

BRANCH CAMPUS

Windward Campus: 45–045 Kamehameha Highway, Kaneohe, HI 96744-5297.

UNIVERSITY OF HAWAII

2444 Dole St, Honolulu, HI 96822
Telephone: (808) 956-8207
Fax: (808) 956-5286
Internet: www.hawaii.edu

Founded 1907, Univ. of Hawaii 1920
Central admin. for Univ. of Hawaii System
Academic year: August to May

10 Campuses: 3 univs and 7 community colleges in Hawaii, Honolulu, Kapiolani, Kauai, Leeward, Maui, Windward

Pres.: DAVID MCCLAIN
Vice-Pres. for Admin.: SAM CALLEJO
Vice-Pres. for Academic Planning and Policy: LINDA JOHNSRUD
Vice-Pres. for Budget and Finance: HOWARD TODO
Vice-Pres. for Community Colleges: JOHN MORTON
Vice-Pres. for Information Technology: DAVID LASSNER
Vice-Pres. for Legal Affairs and Univ. Gen. Counsel: DAROLYN LENDIO
Vice-Pres. for Research: JAMES GAINES
Librarian: DIANE PERUSHEK

Library: 3m. vols
Number of teachers: 3,310
Number of students: 45,994

Publications: *Asian Perspectives* (archaeology for Asia and the Pacific, 2 a year), *Asian Theatre Journal* (journal of the Asscn for Asian Performance, 2 a year),

Buddhist–Christian Studies (journal of the Soc. for Buddhist–Christian Studies, 1 a year), *Biography* (interdisciplinary biographical scholarship, 4 a year), *The Contemporary Pacific* (island affairs, 2 a year), *China Review International* (reviews of scholarly literature in Chinese studies, 2 a year), *Journal of World History* (journal of the World History Asscn, 4 a year), *Ka Ho'oilina* (journal of Hawaiian language sources, 2 a year), *Korean Studies* (multidisciplinary journal on Korea and Koreans abroad, 2 a year), *Manoa* (new writing from America, the Pacific and Asia, 2 a year), *Oceanic Linguistics* (current research on languages of the Oceanic area, 2 a year), *Pacific Science* (biological and physical sciences of the Pacific region, 4 a year), *Philosophy East & West* (comparative philosophy, 4 a year), *Journal of Modern Literature in Chinese* (bilingual, 2 a year), *Yearbook of the Association of Pacific Coast Geographers* (1 a year), *Yishu* (contemporary Chinese art, 4 a year).

CONSTITUENT CAMPUSES

University of Hawaii at Hilo

200 West Kawili St, Hilo, HI 96720-4091
Telephone: (808) 974-7414
Fax: (808) 933-0861
E-mail: uhhadm@hawaii.edu
Internet: www.uhh.hawaii.edu

Founded 1941 as Hawaii Vocational School; present name 1970
Academic year: August to May
Chancellor: Dr Rose Y. Tseng
Number of teachers: 230
Number of students: 3,457

DEANS

College of Agriculture, Forestry and Natural Resource Management: William Mokahi Steiner
College of Arts and Sciences: Randy Hirokawa
College of Business and Economics: Marcia Sakai
College of Pharmacy: John M. Pezzuto
Ka Haka 'Ula O Ke'elikolani (College of Hawaiian Language): Kalena Silva (Dir)

University of Hawaii at Manoa

2500 Campus Rd, Honolulu, HI 96822
Telephone: (808) 956-8111
Internet: manoa.hawaii.edu

Founded 1907
Academic year: August to May
Chancellor: Denise Konan
Number of teachers: 1,695
Number of students: 20,600

DEANS

College of Arts and Humanities: Judith R. Hughes
College of Business Administration: David McClain
College of Education: Dr Randy A. Hitz
College of Engineering: Dr Wai-Fah Chen
College of Languages, Linguistics and Literature: Joseph H. O'Mealy
College of Natural Sciences: Charles Hayes
College of Social Sciences: Richard Dubanoski
College of Tropical Agriculture and Human Resources: Andrew Hashimoto
Graduate Division: Alan Teramura
Outreach College: Peter Tanaka
School of Architecture: Raymond Yeh
School of Hawaiian, Asian and Pacific Studies: Edgar A. Porter
School of Law: Lawrence Foster
School of Medicine: Dr Edwin C. Cadman
School of Nursing and Dental Hygiene: Barbara Molina Kooker
School of Ocean and Earth Science and Technology: C. Barry Raleigh
School of Social Work: Dr Jon K. Matsuoka
School of Travel Industry Management: Dr Pauline J. Sheldon

University of Hawaii – West O'ahu

96-129 Ala Ike, Pearl City, HI 96782
Telephone: (808) 454-4700
Fax: (808) 453-6075
Internet: westoahu.hawaii.edu

Founded 1976
Academic year: August to May
Divs of humanities, professional studies, social sciences
Chancellor: Gene Awakuni
Number of teachers: 41
Number of students: 740

IDAHO

ALBERTSON COLLEGE OF IDAHO

2112 Cleveland Blvd, Caldwell, ID 83605
Telephone: (208) 459-5011
Fax: (208) 454-2077
E-mail: admissions@albertson.edu
Internet: www.albertson.edu

Founded 1891
Academic year: September to June
Pres.: Dr Robert Hoover
Vice-Pres. for Academic Affairs: Dr Mark Smith
Vice-Pres. for Advancement: Robert Hoover
Dir of Admissions: Charlene Brown
Dean of Student Affairs: Paul Bennion
Vice-Pres. for Admin. and Finance: Chris Anton
Exec. Dir of Devt: Michael Vandervelden
Library Dir: Christine Schutz
Library of 183,756 vols, 75,000 govt documents, 27,535 microforms, 797 current periodicals, 1,117 audiovisual items
Number of teachers: 60 (full-time)
Number of students: 761 (undergraduate)
Publications: *Catalog* (1 a year), *Quest* (3 a year).

BOISE BIBLE COLLEGE

8695 West Marigold St, Boise, ID 83714
Telephone: (208) 376-7731
Fax: (208) 376-7743
E-mail: rknudsen@boisebible.edu
Internet: www.boisebible.edu

Founded 1945
Private control
Academic year: July to June
Pres.: Dr Charles A. Crane
Academic Dean: Charles H. Faber
Student Dean: Neil Kluckow
Dir of Admissions: Martin Flaherty
Dir of Devt: David Davolt
Librarian: Nadene Mack
Library of 32,500 vols
Number of teachers: 15
Number of students: 175

BOISE STATE UNIVERSITY

1910 University Dr., Boise, ID 83725
Telephone: (208) 426-1000
Internet: www.boisestate.edu

Founded 1932
Pres.: Robert W. Kustra
Provost and Vice-Pres. for Academic Affairs: Sona Andrews
Vice-Pres. for Finance and Admin.: Stacy A. Pearson
Vice-Pres. for Student Affairs: Michael Laliberte
Registrar: Kris Marie Collins
Dean of Univ. Libraries: Marilyn Moody
Library of 576,682 vols books, 1,441,447 microforms, 2,548 current periodicals, newspapers and other serials, 92,353 bound periodicals, 101,446 maps, 99,433 US govt documents, 6,330 linear ft of MSS, 42,639 non-print materials
Number of teachers: 1,136 (617 full-time, 519 part-time)
Number of students: 19,540

DEANS

College of Applied Technology: Vera McCrink
College of Arts and Sciences: Dr Martin Schimpf
College of Business and Economics: Dr Patrick Shannon
College of Education: Dr Diane Boothe
College of Engineering: Dr Cheryl Schrader
College of Health Science: Dr Tim Dunnagan
College of Social Sciences and Public Affairs: Dr Melissa Lavitt
Extended Studies: Mark Wheeler
Graduate College: Dr Jack Pelton
Honors College: Dr Craig Hammons (Dir)

IDAHO STATE UNIVERSITY

921 South Eighth Ave, Pocatello, ID 83209
Telephone: (208) 236-0211
Fax: (208) 236-4000
Internet: www.isu.edu

Founded 1901
Pres.: Arthur C. Vailas
Provost and Vice-Pres. for Academic Affairs: Robert A. Wharton
Vice-Pres. for Financial Services: Ken Prolo
Vice-Pres. for Institutional Advancement: Dr Kent Tingley
Vice-Pres. for Student Affairs: Dr Lee E. Krehbiel
Registrar: Ross Ruchti
Librarian: Kay Flowers
Library of 995,525 vols (incl. books, bound periodicals and govt documents), 34,428 microfilms, 1,847,083 microfiches and microcards, 44,257 maps and 2,938 current periodicals
Number of teachers: 770
Number of students: 12,739

DEANS

College of Arts and Sciences: James R. 'Dick' Pratt
College of Business: William E. Stratton
College of Education: Larry B. Harris
College of Engineering: Jau Kunze
College of Health Professions: Linda C. Hatzenbuehler
College of Pharmacy: Joseph Steiner
College of Technology: Rayane J. Marsh
Graduate Studies: Paul Tate

LEWIS-CLARK STATE COLLEGE

500 Eighth Ave, Lewiston, ID 83501
Telephone: (208) 792-5272
Fax: (208) 792-2822
E-mail: admissions@lcsc.edu
Internet: www.lcsc.edu

Founded 1893 as Lewiston State Normal School; present name 1971
Academic year: August to May
Offers academic, professional-technical and community college support programmes
Pres.: Dr Dene Kay Thomas
Provost and Vice-Pres. for Academic Affairs: Dr J. Anthony Fernandez
Vice-Pres. for Admin. Services: Chet Herbst
Dean of Student Services: Andrew Hanson

Registrar: LEILANI ANDERSON
Dir of Library Services: SUSAN NIEWENHOUS

Library of 251,000 vols
Number of teachers: 180
Number of students: 3,325

DEANS

Academic Programmes: Dr CHRISTINE PHARR
Community Programmes: KATHY MARTIN
School of Technology: Dr ROB LOHRMEYER

NORTHWEST NAZARENE UNIVERSITY

623 Holly St Nampa, ID 83686-5897
Telephone: (208) 467-8011
Fax: (208) 467-8645
Internet: www.nnu.edu

Founded 1913

Pres.: Dr RICHARD A. HAGOOD
Vice-Pres. for Academic Affairs: MARK PITTS
Vice-Pres. for Enrollment and Marketing: ERIC FORSETH
Registrar: NANCY AYERS
Dir of Library Services: SHARON BULL

Library of 120,000 vols, 850 current periodicals, 600,000 vols of microforms, non-print materials and govt documents
Number of teachers: 105 (full-time)
Number of students: 1,700 (1,200 undergraduate, 500 graduate)

UNIVERSITY OF IDAHO

875 Perimeter Dr., Moscow, ID 83844
Moscow Campus: 709 S Deakin Ave, Moscow, ID 83843

Telephone: (208) 885-6326
Fax: (208) 885-9119
E-mail: admissions@uidaho.edu
Internet: www.uidaho.edu

Chartered 1889

Pres.: DUANE NELLIS
Provost: DOUGLAS D. BAKER
Vice-Provost for Student Affairs: BRUCE M. PITMAN
Vice-Pres. for Finance and Admin.: LLOYD MUES
Vice-Pres. for Research: JOHN TRACY
Vice-Pres. for Univ. Advancement: CHRIS MURRAY
Registrar: RETA PIKOWSKY
Dean of the Library: LYNN BAIRD

Library of 936,738 vols, 105,493 microforms, 642,199 govt documents, 786,882 govt documents on microfiche, 207,087 maps and 5,305 current periodicals
Number of teachers: 814
Number of students: 11,027

DEANS

College of Agriculture and Life Sciences: Dr LARRY BRANEN
College of Business and Economics: BYRON DANGERFIELD
College of Education: JEANNE CHRISTIANSEN
College of Engineering: DAVE THOMPSON
College of Forestry, Wildlife and Range Sciences: STEVEN DALEY LAURSEN
College of Law: Dr DONALD L. BURNETT, Jr
College of Letters, Arts and Social Sciences: JOE ZELLER
College of Science: EARL BENNETT

ILLINOIS

ADLER SCHOOL OF PROFESSIONAL PSYCHOLOGY

Suite 2100, 65 East Wacker Place, Chicago, IL 60601-7298

Telephone: (312) 201-5900
Fax: (312) 201-5917
E-mail: information@adler.edu
Internet: www.adler.edu

Founded 1952 as Alfred Adler Institute of Chicago; present name 1991
Private control
Academic year: June to June

Campus in Vancouver, Canada

Pres.: RAYMOND E. CROSSMAN
Vice-Pres. for Academic Affairs: Dr FRANK GRUBA-MCCALLISTER
Vice-Pres. for Admin.: JO BETH CUP
Vice-Pres. for IT and Finance: JOEL POMERENK
Dir of Institute on Social Exclusion: Dr LINDA TODMAN
Dir of Library Services: KERRY COCHRANE
Dir of Psychological Services Centre: Dr DAN BARNES

Library of 10,000 vols
Number of teachers: 30

ARGOSY UNIVERSITY

13th Fl., Michigan Plaza, 205 N Michigan Ave, Chicago, IL 60601

Telephone: (312) 899-9900
Fax: (312) 899-1938
Internet: www.argosy.edu

Campuses: Atlanta, Georgia; Chicago, Illinois; Dallas, Texas; Denver, Colorado, Honolulu, Hawaii; Inland Empire, Nashville, Tennessee; Orange County, California; Phoenix, Arizona; San Diego, San Francisco Bay Area, California; Santa Monica, Sarasota, Florida; Schaumburg, Illinois; Seattle, Washington; Tampa, Florida; Twin Cities (Minneapolis and St Paul), Minnesota; Washington, DC

Founded 2001 following merger of American Schools of Professional Psychology, Medical Institute of Minnesota and Univ. of Sarasota
Private control

Pres.: Dr CRAIG D. SWENSON

Colleges of business and information technology, education and human devt, health sciences, psychology and behavioural sciences.

AUGUSTANA COLLEGE

639 38th St, Rock Island, IL 61201

Telephone: (309) 794-7000
Fax: (309) 794-7422
Internet: www.augustana.edu

Founded 1860
Academic year: September to May

Pres.: STEVEN C. BAHLS
Dean of the College: JEFF ABERNATHY
Dean of Enrollment: (vacant)
Dean of Students: EVELYN S. CAMPBELL
Registrar: LIESL FOWLER
Dir of the Library: CARLA TRACY

Library of 244,368 vols
Number of teachers: 184 (135 full-time, 49 part-time)
Number of students: 2,300

Courses in accounting, art, art education, art history, biochemistry, biology, business admin., chemistry, classics, communication sciences and disorders, computer science/mathematics, earth science teaching, economics, elementary and secondary education, English, French, geography, geology, German, history, mathematics, pre-medicine, music, music education, music performance, philosophy, physics, political science, psychology, religion, Scandinavian, sociology, Spanish, speech communication, studio art, theatre.

AURORA UNIVERSITY

347 South Gladstone Ave, Aurora, IL 60506-4892

Telephone: (630) 892-6431
Fax: (630) 844-5463
E-mail: admission@aurora.edu
Internet: www.aurora.edu

Founded 1893 as Mendota Seminary; present name 1985
Private control
Academic year: September to May

Pres.: REBECCA L. SHERRICK
Vice-Pres. for Admin.: THOMAS HAMMOND
Vice-Pres. for Advancement: THEODORE PARGE
Vice-Pres. for Enrollment: DONNA DESPAIN
Vice-Pres. for Finance: DAVE EISINGER
Vice-Pres. for George Williams Campus: WILLIAM B. DUNCAN
Vice-Pres. for Student Life: MICHAEL MOSER
Provost: ANDREW P. MANION
Registrar: LYNN HAYES
Library Dir: JOHN LAW

Library of 110,000 vols and multimedia materials
Number of teachers: 155
Number of students: 4,300

DEANS

College of Arts and Sciences: Dr LORA DELACEY
College of Education: DONALD WOLD
College of Professional Studies: MICK CARROLL
School of Experiential Leadership: Dr RITA YERKES

BRANCH CAMPUS

George Williams College of Aurora University: 350 Constance Blvd, POB 210, Williams Bay, WI 53191-0210; tel. (262) 245-5531; fax (262) 245-8505; Academic Dean LINDA OLBINSKI.

BENEDICTINE UNIVERSITY

5700 College Rd, Lisle, IL 60532-0900

Telephone: (630) 829-6000
E-mail: admissions@ben.edu
Internet: www.ben.edu

Founded 1887 as St Procopius College
Private control
Academic year: September to May

Pres.: Dr WILLIAM J. CARROLL
Provost and Vice-Pres. of Academic Affairs: Dr DONALD B. TAYLOR
Exec. Vice-Pres.: CHARLES GREGORY
Vice-Pres. for Business and Financial Services: ALLAN GOZUM
Assoc. Vice-Pres. for Enrollment: KARL GIBBONS
Assoc. Vice-Pres. for Student Affairs: MARCO MASINI
Exec. Dir of Marketing and Communications: MERCY ROBB

Library of 126,000 vols, 14,000 periodicals, 90 databases
Number of teachers: 426
Number of students: 5,759 (3,355 undergraduate, 2,404 graduate)

Publication: *Voices Magazine* (3 a year)

DEANS

College of Business: Dr SANDRA GILL
College of Education and Health Services: Dr ALAN GORR
College of Liberal Arts: Dr MARÍA DE LA CÁMARA
College of Science: Dr RALPH MEEKER
Margaret and Harold Moser College of Adult and Professional Studies: Dr MICK CARROLL

BLACKBURN COLLEGE

700 College Ave, Carlinville, IL 62626
Telephone: (217) 854-3231
Fax: (217) 854-3713
Internet: www.blackburn.edu

Founded 1837
Academic year: August to May

Pres.: Miriam R. Pride
Provost: Jeffery Aper
Dean of Enrollment Management: John Malin
Dean of Students: Heidi Heinz
Registrar: Dianna Ruyle
Head Librarian: Carol Schaefer

Library of 81,250 vols
Number of teachers: 46 (31 full-time, 15 part-time)
Number of students: 600

Depts of accounting, art, biology, business and economics, chemistry, communications, computer science, criminal justice, education, engineering, English, history, mathematics, medical technology, performing arts, philosophy and religion, physical education, physics, political science, pre-law, pre-professional, psychology, Spanish.

BRADLEY UNIVERSITY

1501 West Bradley Ave, Peoria, IL 61625
Telephone: (309) 676-7611
Internet: www.bradley.edu

Founded 1897
Ind. comprehensive univ.

Pres.: Joanne Glasser
Provost and Vice-Pres. for Academic Affairs: Dr Robert Bolla
Vice-Pres. for Advancement: Patrick Vickerman
Vice-Pres. for Business Affairs: Gary Anna
Vice-Pres. for Student Affairs: Dr Alan Galsky
Registrar: Katherine M. Beaty
Exec. Dir of Library: Barbara A. Galik

Library of 1.2m. items, incl. 510,297 books, bound periodicals and govt documents; 787,169 microforms
Number of teachers: 300
Number of students: 5,855 (5,057 undergraduate, 798 graduate)

DEANS

College of Education and Health Sciences: Dr Joan Sattler
College of Engineering and Technology: Dr Richard T. Johnson
College of Liberal Arts and Sciences: Dr Claire Etaugh
Foster College of Business Admin.: Dr Rob Baer
Graduate School: Dr Kurt Field
Slane College of Communications and Fine Arts: Dr Jeffrey H. Huberman

CATHOLIC THEOLOGICAL UNION

5401 South Cornell Ave, Chicago, IL 60615-5698
Telephone: (773) 324-8000
E-mail: admissions@ctu.edu
Internet: www.ctu.edu

Founded 1968
Private control
Academic year: September to June

Pres.: Donald Senior
Vice-Pres. and Academic Dean: Gary Riebe-Estrella
Vice-Pres. for Admin. and Finance: Michael W. Connors
Registrar: María de Jesús Lemus
Library Dir: Mary H. Ocasek

Library of 150,000 vols, 500 periodicals

Depts of biblical literature and languages, cross-cultural ministries, historical and doctrinal studies, spirituality and pastoral care, word and worship

Publication: *New Theology Review*.

CHICAGO SCHOOL OF PROFESSIONAL PSYCHOLOGY

2nd Floor, 47 West Polk Street, Chicago, IL 60605
Telephone: (312) 329-6600
Fax: (312) 644-3333
E-mail: admissions@thechicagoschool.edu
Internet: www.thechicagoschool.edu

Founded 1979
Private control
Academic year: October to August

Pres.: Dr Michael Horowitz
Vice-Pres. for Academic Affairs: Dr Pat Breen
Vice-Pres. for Admin.: Tamara Rozhon
Vice-Pres. for Finance: Jeff Keith
Registrar: Ana del Castillo
Dir of Library Services: Indu Aggarwal

Applied behaviour analysis, clinical psychology graduate programme, counselling psychology graduate programmes, forensic psychology graduate programmes, industrial organizational and business psychology programmes, school psychology, continuing professional education.

CHICAGO STATE UNIVERSITY

9501 South King Dr., Chicago, IL 60628-1598
Telephone: (773) 995-2000
Internet: www.csu.edu

Founded 1867
State control
Academic year: August to May (2 terms)

Pres.: Wayne Watson
Provost and Vice-Pres. for Academic Affairs: Beverley J. Anderson
Sr Vice-Pres. for Admin. and External Affairs: Sylvius S. Moore, Jr
Vice-Pres. for Planning, Research and Sponsored Programs: Linda Petty
Vice-Pres. for Student Affairs: Michael Battle
Asst Vice-Pres. for Academic Personnel: Debrah H. Jefferson
Registrar: Lois M. Davis
Dean of Library and Learning Resources: Lawrence McCrank

Number of teachers: 282
Number of students: 9,500

Publications: *Illinois Schools Journal*, *Tempo* (26 a year), *Reflections* (12 a year), *CSU Excellence Magazine* (2 a year)

DEANS

College of Arts and Sciences: Rachel Lindsey
College of Business: Farhad Simyar
College of Education: Sandra Westbrooks
College of Health Sciences: Joseph Balogun
Continuing Education and Non-Traditional Degree Programs: Cecilia Bowie
Graduate Studies: Anitra Ward
Honors College: Richard G. Milo

CHICAGO THEOLOGICAL SEMINARY

5757 South University Ave, Chicago, IL 60637
1164 East 58th St, Chicago, IL 60637
Telephone: (773) 752-5757
Fax: (773) 752-0905
E-mail: info@ctschicago.edu
Internet: www.ctschicago.edu

Founded 1855
Private control

Offers postgraduate courses in arts, divinity, sacred theology, and doctoral courses in ministry and philosophy

Pres.: Dr Alice Hunt
Vice-Pres. for Devt: Chris Dorsey
Vice-Pres. for Finance and Admin.: Stephen Manning
Academic Dean: Dr Ken Stone
Registrar: Cheryl Miller
Library Dir: Rev. Dr Neil Gerdes

Library of 110,000 vols.

COLUMBIA COLLEGE

600 South Michigan Ave, Chicago, IL 60605
Telephone: (312) 663-1600
E-mail: admissions@colum.edu
Internet: www.colum.edu

Founded 1890

Pres.: Dr Warwick L. Carter
Provost and Sr Vice-Pres. for Academic Affairs: Dr Steven Kapelke
Vice-Pres. and General Counsel: Annice M. Kelly
Vice-Pres. for Academic Affairs: Louise Love
Vice-Pres. for Business Affairs and Chief Financial Officer: R. Michael DeSalle
Vice-Pres. for Campus Environment: Alicia Berg
Vice-Pres. for Institutional Advancement: Eric Winston
Vice-Pres. for Student Affairs: Mark Kelly
Assoc. Vice-Pres. and Chief of Staff: Paul Chiaravalle
Dean of Students: Sharon Wilson-Taylor
Library Dir: Conrad Winkie (acting)

Library of 225,000 vols, 2,000 current periodicals, 13,000 films and video cassettes, 12,000 slides, CDs; spec. collns incl. artists' books, history of black music, history of photography, film and television scripts, music scores, and pop-up and spec. format books
Number of teachers: 1,167
Number of students: 10,850 (10,200 undergraduate, 650 graduate)

DEANS

School of Fine and Performing Arts: Leonard Lehrer (acting)
School of Graduate and Continuing Education: Keith Cleveland (acting)
School of Liberal Arts and Sciences: Dominic Pacyga (acting)
School of Media Arts: Doreen Bartoni (acting)

CONCORDIA UNIVERSITY

7400 Augusta St, River Forest, IL 60305-1499
Telephone: (708) 771-8300
Internet: www.cuchicago.edu

Founded 1864
Private control
Academic year: August to May

Pres.: Dr John F. Johnson
Sr Vice-Pres. for Academics: Dr Manfred B. Boos
Sr Vice-Pres. for Univ. Advancement: Dr Alan C. Klaas
Sr Vice-Pres. for Univ. Planning: Alan E. Meyer
Vice-Pres. for Admin.: Dr Dennis Witte
Vice-Pres. for Enrollment and Marketing: Evelyn Burdick
Vice-Pres. for Finance and Chief Financial Officer: Tom W. Hallett
Vice-Pres. for Student Life and Leadership: Jeffrey C. Hynes
Registrar: Constance K. Pettinger
Dir of Library Services: Yana V. Serdyuk

Library of 160,000 vols, 237 periodicals, 480,000 ERIC microfiche documents
Number of students: 3,710 (1,074 undergraduate, 2,636 graduate)

DEANS

College of Arts and Sciences: Dr GARY E. WENZEL
College of Education: Dr JANE BUERGER
College of Graduate and Innovative Programs: Dr THOMAS JANDRIS

ATTACHED COLLEGE

West Suburban College of Nursing: 3 Erie Court, Oak Park, IL 60302; tel. (708) 763-6530; internet www.wscn.edu/; Chancellor Dr REBECCA A. JONES.

DEPAUL UNIVERSITY

Chicago, IL 60604
Telephone: (312) 362-8000
Internet: www.depaul.edu
Chartered as Saint Vincent's College 1898, as DePaul Univ. 1907
Campuses at Lincoln Park, Loop, Naperville, O'Hare, Oak Forest, Rolling Meadows
Pres.: Rev. DENNIS H. HOLTSCHNEIDER
Chancellor: Rev. JOHN T. RICHARDSON
Provost: Dr HELMUT P. EPP
Exec. Vice-Pres.: Dr SCOTT L. SCARBOROUGH
Sr Vice-Pres. for Advancement: MARY C. FINGER
Sr Vice-Pres. for Enrollment Management and Marketing: Dr DAVID H. KALSBEEK
Sr Exec. for Presidential Operations: JAY BRAATZ (acting)
Sec. of the Univ.: Rev. EDWARD R. UDOVIĆ
Vice-Pres. and Gen. Counsel: JOSÉ D. PADILLA
Vice-Pres. for Community, Govt and Int. Affairs: J. D. BINDENAGEL
Vice-Pres. for Devt: JOHN BERGHOLZ
Vice-Pres. for Facility Operations: ROBERT JANIS
Vice-Pres. for Finance: ROBERT L. KOZOMAN
Vice-Pres. for Human Resources: WILLIAM SEITHEL
Vice-Pres. for Information Services: VINCENT J. KELLEN
Vice-Pres. for Institutional Diversity and Equity: ELIZABETH F. ORTIZ
Vice-Pres. for Public Relations and Communications: CHERYL PROCTER-ROGERS
Vice-Pres. for Student Affairs: JAMES R. DOYLE
Treas.: DAVID O. DABNEY
Registrar: NANCY GALL
Dir of Libraries: LINDA MORRISSETT
Library of 906,794 vols
Number of teachers: 1,521
Number of students: 23,149
Publications: *Business Law Journal* (2 a year), *De Paul Magazine* (4 a year), *De Paulia* (52 a year), *Journal of Art and Entertainment* (2 a year), *Journal of Health and Hospital Law* (12 a year), *Law Review* (2 a year), *Newsline* (12 a year), *Philosophy Today* (4 a year)

DEANS

College of Commerce: Dr RAY WHITTINGTON
College of Law: Dr GLEN WEISSENBERGER
College of Liberal Arts and Sciences: Dr CHARLES S. SUCHAR
School of Computer Science, Telecommunications and Information Systems: Dr DAVID MILLER
School of Education: Dr CLARA M. JENNINGS
School of Music: Dr DONALD E. CASEY
School for New Learning: Dr SUSANNE DUMBLETON
Theatre School: JOHN CULBERT

DEVRY UNIVERSITY

1 Tower Lane, Oakbrook Terrace, IL 60181
Telephone: (630) 571-7700
E-mail: info@devry.edu
Internet: www.devry.edu
Founded 2002 following merger of DeVry Institutes (f. 1931 as DeForest Training School) and Keller Graduate School of Management (f. 1973 as CBA Institute)
Private control (a division of DeVry, Inc.)
Academic year: November to October
Chairman: DENNIS J. KELLER
President: DAVID J. PAULDINE
Chief Exec. Officer: DANIEL HAMBURGER
Number of students: 47,000 (incl. online)
11 Campuses in Illinois, 23 in the USA and 1 in Canada.
Areas of undergraduate study: business admin., computer engineering technology, computer information systems, electronics and computer technology, electronics engineering technology, information technology, network systems admin., technical management, telecommunications management.

GRADUATE SCHOOL

Keller Graduate School of Management
1 Tower Lane, Oakbrook Terrace, IL 60181-4624
Telephone: (630) 574-1960
Fax: (630) 574-1969
Internet: www.keller.edu
Academic year: September to June
53 Centres in 16 states
Chair. and CEO: DENNIS J. KELLER
Pres. and Chief Operating Officer: RONALD L. TAYLOR
Vice-Pres. for Enrollment Management and Dean: Dr TIMOTHY H. RICORDATI
Academic Dean of Admin. and Accreditation: Dr SHERRIL HOEL
Dean of Curriculum: DAVID OVERBYE
Registrar: SANDRA BRANICK
Dir of Libraries: MARIS ROZE
Number of students: 9,000 (incl. online)

DIRECTORS

Accounting and Financial Management: SETH LEVINE
Business Admin.: JOHN HEINEMANN
Human Resource Management: Dr ROMUALD A. STONE
Information Systems Management: AMITA SUHRID
Project Management: Dr FRANK CESARIO
Public Admin.: Dr FRANK CESARIO
Telecommunications Management: AMITA SUHRID

DOMINICAN UNIVERSITY

River Forest, IL 60305
Telephone: (708) 366-2490
Fax: (708) 366-5360
Internet: www.dom.edu
Founded 1901
Academic year: May to April
Pres.: DONNA M. CARROLL
Sr Vice-Pres. for Admin.: AMY MCCORMACK
Vice-Pres. for Academic Affairs: CHERYL JOHNSON-OLIM
Vice-Pres. for Enrollment: PAMELA JOHNSON
Vice-Pres. for Institutional Advancement: STEPHEN KUHN
Vice-Pres. for Mission and Ministry: DIANE KENNEDY
Registrar: MARILYN GERKEN BENAKIS
Academic Dean: MOLLY BURKE
Dean of Students: TRUDI GOGGIN
Assoc. Dean for Information Services: INEZ RINGLAND
Library of 320,000 vols
Number of teachers: 201
Number of students: 2,500
Publication: *World Libraries* (2 a year)

DEANS

Brennan School of Business: MOLLY BURKE
College of Arts and Sciences: Dr JEFFREY CARLSON
Graduate School of Library and Information Science: Prof. SUSAN ROMAN
Graduate School of Social Work: MARK RODGERS
Institute for Adult Learning: BRIAN J. WATKINS (Exec. Dir)
School of Education: Sister COLLEEN MCNICHOLAS

EAST-WEST UNIVERSITY

816 South Michigan Ave, Chicago, IL 60605
Telephone: (312) 939-0111
Fax: (312) 939-0083
E-mail: info@eastwest.edu
Internet: www.eastwest.edu
Founded 1978
Private control
Academic year: September to August
Chancellor: Dr M. WASIULLAH KHAN
Provost: Dr MADHU JAIN
Dean of Enrollment Management: MAZIN SAFAR
Registrar: AMAL MATARI
Librarian: Dr EKKEHARD-TEJA WILKE
Number of teachers: 43 full-time
Number of students: 1,128
Depts of behavioural and social sciences, biology and physical science, business admin., computer and information science, criminal justice, electronics and engineering technology, English and communications, mathematics, pre-medical, pre-nursing

DIRECTORS

Behavioural Sciences: Dr FARID MUHAMMED
Biological and Physical Sciences Program and Electroneurodiagnostic Technology Program: Dr VERONICA DRANTZ
Business Admin.: Dr ROBERT GOODMAN
Computer Science: Dr INJOO JEONG
Electronics Engineering: BADRINATH MIRMIRA
English and Communications: Dr LARRY GORMAN
History: Dr EKKEHARD-TEJA WILKE
Mathematics: Dr SUPHA PHINAITRUP

EASTERN ILLINOIS UNIVERSITY

600 Lincoln Ave, Charleston, IL 61920-3099
Telephone: (217) 581-5000
Internet: www.eiu.edu
Founded 1895
Academic year: August to June
Pres.: LOUIS V. HENCKEN
Provost and Vice-Pres. for Academic Affairs: Dr BLAIR M. LORD
Vice-Pres. for Business Affairs: JEFF COOLEY
Vice-Pres. for External Relations: Dr JILL F. NILSEN
Vice-Pres. for Student Affairs: Dr DANIEL P. ADLER
Dean of Enrollment Management: FRANK HOHENGARTEN
Dean of Library Services: Dr ALLEN LANHAM
Number of teachers: 659 (585 full-time, 74 part-time)
Number of students: 10,963

DEANS

College of Arts and Humanities: JAMES JOHNSON
College of Education and Professional Studies: DIANE H. JACKMAN

College of Sciences: Dr MARY ANNE HANNER
Graduate School, Research and Int. Programs: Dr ROBERT AUGUSTINE
Honors College: Dr BONNIE IRWIN
Lumpkin College of Business and Applied Sciences: DIANE HOADLEY
School of Continuing Education: Dr WILLIAM C. HINE

ELMHURST COLLEGE

190 Prospect Ave, Elmhurst, IL 60126
Telephone: (630) 617-3500
Fax: (630) 617-3282
E-mail: admit@elmhurst.edu
Internet: elmhurst.edu

Founded 1871
Private control
Language of instruction: English
Academic year: August to May

Depts of art, biology, business and economics, chemistry, communication arts and sciences, computer science and information systems, education, English, foreign languages and literatures, geography and geosciences, history, kinesiology, mathematics, music, nursing, philosophy, physics, political science, psychology, sociology, theology and religion, urban studies

Pres.: S. ALAN RAY
Vice-Pres. of Academic Affairs and Dean of the Faculty: ALZADA J. TIPTON
Vice-Pres. and Chief Information Officer: JAMES KULICH
Vice-Pres. for Communication and Public Affairs: JAMES WINTERS
Vice-Pres. for Devt: MEG HOWES
Vice-Pres. for Financial Affairs: DENISE P. JONES
Dean of Admission and Financial Aid: GARY ROLD
Dean of Students: EILEEN SULLIVAN
Librarian: SUSAN SWORDS STEFFEN

Library of 320,000 vols
Number of teachers: 136
Number of students: 3,400

EUREKA COLLEGE

300 East College Ave, Eureka, IL 61530
Telephone: (309) 467-3721
Fax: (309) 467-6386
Internet: www.eureka.edu

Founded 1855
Academic year: August to May

Provost and Dean: PHILIP CAVALIER
Pres.: DAVID J. ARNOLD
Vice-Pres. for Admissions and Marketing and Dean of Admissions and Financial Aid: BRIAN SAJKO
Vice-Pres. for Finance and Facilities: MARC PASTERIS
Vice-Pres. for Student Services: KENNETH BAXTER
Asst Dean for Records: SCOTT WIGNALL
Library Dir: VIRGINIA MCCOY

Library of 75,000 vols, 330 current periodicals
Number of teachers: 44
Number of students: 520

Divs of business, education, fine and performing arts, humanities, science and mathematics, social sciences.

GARRETT-EVANGELICAL THEOLOGICAL SEMINARY

2121 Sheridan Rd, Evanston, IL 60201
Telephone: (847) 866-3900
Fax: (847) 866-3957
E-mail: seminary@garrett.edu
Internet: www.garrett.edu

Founded 1853 as Garrett Biblical Institute; present name 1974
Private control (United Methodist Church)
Academic year: September to July

Pres.: PHILIP AMERSON
Vice-Pres. for Business and Financial Affairs: ARNOLD HENNING
Vice-Pres. for Devt: DAVID HEETLAND
Assoc. Vice-Pres. of Student Affairs: PAMELA LIGHTSEY
Academic Dean: LALLENE RECTOR
Dir of Academic Studies and Registrar: VINCE MEGLOTHIN-ELLER
Librarian: Dr BETH SHEPPARD

Library of 300,000 vols
Number of teachers: 36

Masters programmes: arts, divinity, theological studies; Doctorate programmes: ministry, philosophy.

GOVERNORS STATE UNIVERSITY

1 University Parkway, University Park, IL 60466-0975
Telephone: (708) 534-5000
Fax: (708) 534-8399
E-mail: gsunow@govst.edu
Internet: www.govst.edu

Founded 1969

Pres.: STUART I. FAGAN
Provost: PEGGY WOODWARD
Exec. Vice-Pres.: GEBEYEHU EJIGU
Vice-Pres. for Institutional Advancement: JAMES BRITT
Registrar: ADRIENNA TROTTER
Dean of Library Services: DIANE DATES CASEY

Library of 375,000 vols.
Number of teachers: 300
Number of students: 6,200

DEANS

College of Arts and Sciences: ERIC V. MARTIN
College of Business and Public Admin.: Dr WILLIAM A. NOWLIN
College of Education: STEVEN RUSSELL
College of Health Professions: Dr LINDA SAMSON

ATTACHED INSTITUTE

Institute for Public Policy and Administration: Dir JOHN W. SWAIN

GREENVILLE COLLEGE

315 E College Ave, Greenville, IL 62246
Telephone: (618) 664-2800
Internet: www.greenville.edu

Founded 1892
Academic year: July to June

Depts of art, biology, chemistry, communication, criminal justice, digital media, education, health, history and political science, language, literature and culture, management, mathematics, media promotions, music, music business, philosophy, physical education and recreation, physics, psychology, religion, social work, sociology, theatre

Pres.: LARRY LINAMEN
Provost: RANDALL BERGEN
Vice-Pres. for Advancement: WALTER FENTON
Vice-Pres. for Enrollment: MICHAEL RITTER
Vice-Pres. for Finance and CEO: DANA FUNDERBURK
Vice-Pres. for Student Devt: NORMAN HALL
Registrar: MICHELLE SUSSENBACH

Library of 114,059 vols
Number of teachers: 163 (68 full-time, 95 part-time)
Number of students: 1,605
Publication: *Record* (1 a year).

HARRINGTON INSTITUTE OF INTERIOR DESIGN

2nd Floor, 200 West Madison St, Chicago, IL 60606-3433
Telephone: (877) 939-4975
Fax: (312) 939-8005
Internet: www.interiordesign.edu

Founded 1931
Private control

Pres.: PATRICK W. COMSTOCK

Library of 22,000 vols
Number of teachers: 70
Number of students: 508

Courses in communication design, digital photography, interior design.

ILLINOIS COLLEGE

1101 West College Ave, Jacksonville, IL 62650
Telephone: (217) 245-3030
Fax: (217) 245-3034
Internet: www.ic.edu

Founded 1829

Pres.: Dr AXEL D. STEUER
Vice-Pres. for Academic Affairs and Dean of the College: Dr ELIZABETH TOBIN
Vice-Pres. for Advancement: ROBERT J. LANE
Vice-Pres. for Business Affairs: FRANK G. WILLIAMS
Vice-Pres. for Enrollment: SCOTT BELOBRAJDIĆ
Vice-Pres. for Student Affairs: Dr MALINDA L. CARLSON
Registrar: Dr GLEN W. CLATTERBUCK
Librarian: MARTIN H. GALLAS

Library of 164,000 vols
Number of teachers: 52
Number of students: 975

Divs of humanities, natural science, social sciences.

ILLINOIS COLLEGE OF OPTOMETRY

3241 South Michigan Ave, Chicago, IL 60616
Telephone: (312) 949-7400
E-mail: admissions@ico.edu
Internet: www.ico.edu

Founded 1872
Private control
Academic year: August to May

Pres.: Dr AROL AUGSBURGER
Vice-Pres. and Dean for Academic Affairs: Dr KENT DAUM
Vice-Pres. for Business and Finance: JOHN W. BUDZYNSKI
Vice-Pres. for Compliance and Risk Management: VALERIE LYNN CONRAD
Vice-Pres. for Devt: DAVID KORAJCZYK
Vice-Pres. for Human and Physical Resources: LAURA ROUNCE
Vice-Pres. for Patient Care Services: Dr LEONARD V. MESSNER
Registrar: LAVERN YOUNG
Dir of Learning Resources: GERALD DUJSIK

Library of 22,000 vols
Number of teachers: 87 (54 full-time, 33 part-time)
Number of students: 600

Degrees offered: Doctor of Optometry, Bachelor of Science in Visual Science; in conjunction with the Univ. of Chicago, Master of Science, Doctor of Philosophy.

ILLINOIS INSTITUTE OF TECHNOLOGY

3300 South Federal St, Chicago, IL 60616-3793
Telephone: (312) 567-3000
Internet: www.iit.edu

Formed 1940 by consolidation of Armour Institute of Technology (founded 1892), Lewis Institute (founded 1896)

Pres.: Dr JOHN L. ANDERSON
Sr Vice-Pres. and Provost: Dr ALLEN S. MYERSON
Vice-Pres. for Enrollment and General Counsel: MARY ANN ROWAN
Vice-Pres. for Institutional Advancement: BETSY HUGHES
Vice-Pres. for Int. Affairs: Prof. DARSH WASAN
Dean of Student Affairs: DOUG GEIGER
Registrar: REBECCA NICHOLES
Dean of Libraries: CHRISTOPHER STEWART

4 Libraries with 522,000 vols
Number of teachers: 551 (295 full-time, 256 part-time)
Number of students: 6,199

Publications: *Employee Rights and Employment Policy, Seventh Circuit Review* (2 a year)

DEANS

Armour College of Engineering: HAMID ARASTOOPOUR
Center for Professional Devt: ROBERT CARLSON (Dir)
Chicago-Kent College of Law: Prof. HARLD J. KRENT
College of Architecture: DONNA ROBERTSON
College of Science and Letters: F. R. MCMORRIS
Graduate College: Dr ALI CINAR
Institute of Design: PATRICK WHITNEY (Dir)
Institute of Psychology: Dr M. ELLEN MITCHELL (Dir)
Stuart School of Business: Dr HARVEY KAHALAS

AFFILIATED INSTITUTES

Center for Law and Financial Markets: Chair. Dr JOHN A. WING.

Center for the Study of Ethics in the Professions: Dir Dr VIVIAN WEIL.

IIT Research Institute: f. 1936.

Institute for Science, Law and Technology: Dir Prof. LORI B. ANDREWS.

Institute of Gas Technology: f. 1941.

Pritzker Institute of Biomedical Science and Engineering: Dir Dr VINCENT TURITTO.

ILLINOIS STATE UNIVERSITY

Normal, IL 61790
Telephone: (309) 438-5677
E-mail: admissions@illinoisstate.edu
Internet: illinoisstate.edu

Founded 1857

Pres.: Dr AL BOWMAN
Vice-Pres. and Provost: Dr SHERI NOREN EVERTS
Vice-Pres. for Finance and Planning: Dr DANIEL LAYZELL
Vice-Pres. for Student Affairs: STEVE ADAMS
Vice-Pres. for Univ. Advancement: ERIN MINNÉ
Dean of Univ. Libraries: Dr SOHAIR F. WASTAWY

Library of 1,603,102 vols, 73,111 current periodicals (printed and electronic)
Number of teachers: 1,184
Number of students: 20,762 (on-campus)

DEANS

College of Applied Science and Technology: Dr JEFFERY A. WOOD
College of Arts and Sciences: Dr JAMES PAYNE
College of Business: Dr SCOTT D. JOHNSON
College of Education: Dr DEBORAH J. CURTIS
College of Fine Arts: Dr JAMES MAJOR (acting)
Mennonite College of Nursing: Dr JANET KREJCI

ILLINOIS WESLEYAN UNIVERSITY

1312 Park St, Bloomington, IL 61702
Telephone: (309) 556-1000
Fax: (309) 556-3411
Internet: www.iwu.edu

Founded 1850
Private control
Academic year: August to May

Pres.: RICHARD F. WILSON
Provost and Dean of the Faculty: BETH CUNNINGHAM
Assoc. Provost: ROGER H. SCHNAITTER
Vice-Pres. for Business and Finance: KENNETH C. BROWNING
Vice-Pres. for Univ. Advancement: RICHARD WHITLOCK
Dean of Admissions: J. R. RUOTI
Dean of Student Affairs: JAMES MATTHEWS
Assoc. Dean of the Faculty: FRANK BOYD
Registrar and Asst Provost: JACK FRICK
Librarian: KRISTIN VOGEL (acting)

Number of teachers: 143
Number of students: 2,100

Publication: *Illinois Wesleyan University Quarterly*

Schools of music, theatre, art and nursing.

JOHN MARSHALL LAW SCHOOL

315 S Plymouth Court, Chicago, IL 60604
Telephone: (312) 427-2737
E-mail: admission@jmls.edu
Internet: www.jmls.edu

Founded 1899
Private control
Academic year: August to May

Dean: JOHN E. CORKERY (acting)
Assoc. Dean for Academic Affairs: RALPH RUEBNER
Assoc. Dean for Admin.: JAMES J. KREMINSKI
Assoc. Dean for Admission and Student Affairs: Dr WILLIAM B. POWERS
Assoc. Dean for Advanced Studies and Research: KATIE KENNEDY
Asst Dean for Institutional Affairs: JOHN M. MCNAMARA
Assoc. Dean for Outreach and Planning: RORY DEAN SMITH
Registrar: JODIE PANARIELLO NEEDHAM
Library Dir: JUNE LIEBERT (acting)

Library of 360,000 vols
Number of teachers: 57
Number of students: 1,444 (1,234 undergraduate, 210 graduate)

Advocacy and dispute resolution, global legal studies, tax, employee benefits, fair housing, information technology and privacy, intellectual property, int. business and trade, real estate.

JUDSON COLLEGE

1151 North State St, Elgin, IL 60123-1498
Telephone: (847) 628-2500
Fax: (847) 695-0712
Internet: www.judsoncollege.edu

Founded 1963

Pres.: Dr JERRY B. CAIN
Chancellor: Dr HARM A. WEBER
Provost and Vice-Pres. for Academic Affairs: Dr DALE H. SIMMONS
Senior Vice-Pres. for Advancement and Marketing: Dr C. NEAL DAVIS
Vice-Pres. and Sr Dean for Graduate, Adult and Continuing Education: Dr C. JIM ROHE
Vice-Pres. for Business Affairs: LAINE MALMQUIST
Vice-Pres. for Enrollment Services: PHILIP C. GUTH
Vice-Pres. for Student Devt: LEANN PAULEY HEARD
Registrar: ELAINE SUITTS
Library Dir: LARRY C. WILD

Library of 91,000 vols
Number of teachers: 103 (40 full-time, 63 part-time)
Number of students: 883

Programmes in art, design and architecture, business, Christian religion, philosophy and ministry, communication arts, education, exercise and sports sciences, music, science and mathematics, social sciences.

KENDALL COLLEGE

900 North Branch St, Chicago, IL 60662
Telephone: (312) 752-2000
Fax: (312) 752-2057
E-mail: admissions@kendall.edu
Internet: www.kendall.edu

Founded 1934 as Evanston Collegiate Institute; present name 1950
Private control
Academic year: November to October

Pres.: Dr NIVINE MEGAHED
Registrar: BRAD BERGERON
Dir of Devt: CHARLES JONES
Dir of Enrollment Management: KATIE KILLIAN
Dir of Finance and Business Services: DAVID DONENBERG
Dir of Library Services: IVA FREEMAN

Library of 35,000 vols
Number of teachers: 32
Number of students: 560

DEANS

Education: Dr MARTI WATSON GARLETT
Hospitality Management: JEFFREY CATRETT
School of Business: SASCHA COCRON
School of Culinary Arts: CHRIS KOETKE

KNOX COLLEGE

2 East South St, Galesburg, IL 61401-4999
Telephone: (309) 341-7000
Fax: (309) 341-7090
E-mail: admission@knox.edu
Internet: www.knox.edu/knox

Founded 1837

Pres.: ROGER L. TAYLOR
Vice-Pres. for Academic Affairs and Dean of College: LAWRENCE B. BREITBORDE
Vice-Pres. for Advancement: BEVERLY HOLMES
Vice-Pres. for Enrollment and Dean of Admission: PAUL STEENIS
Vice-Pres. for Finance and Treasurer: THOMAS B. AXTELL
Vice-Pres. for Student Devt and Dean of Students: XAVIER ROMANO
Librarian: JEFFREY DOUGLAS

Library of 295,922 vols
Number of teachers: 94
Number of students: 1,351

Publications: *Catch*, *Knox Bulletin*, *Knox Magazine* (4 a year).

LAKE FOREST COLLEGE

555 North Sheridan Rd, Lake Forest, IL 60045
Telephone: (847) 234-3100
Fax: (847) 735-6291
Internet: www.lakeforest.edu

Founded 1857
Academic year: August to May

Pres.: STEPHEN D. SCHUTT

Provost and Dean of the Faculty: JANET McCRACKEN
Vice-Pres. for Admissions and Career Services: WILLIAM J. MOTZER, Jr
Vice-Pres. for Alumni and Devt: JAMES P. THOMPSON
Vice-Pres. for Business Affairs: LESLIE T. CHAPMAN
Registrar: RUTHANE BOPP
Dean of Students: BETH TYLER
Librarian: JAMES R. CUBIT

Library of 265,000 vols, incl. 40,000 rare and spec. colins
Number of teachers: 117
Number of students: 1,413
4-Year liberal arts college.

LAKE FOREST GRADUATE SCHOOL OF MANAGEMENT

1905 West Field Court, Lake Forest, IL 60045-4824
Telephone: (847) 234-5005
Fax: (847) 295-3656
Internet: www.lfgsm.edu

Founded 1946
Private control
Academic year: August to June

Pres. and CEO: JOHN N. POPOLI
Exec. Vice-Pres. and Dean for Degree Programs: BRUCE J. SUCH
Exec. Vice-Pres. for Corporate Education Programs: KATHLEEN M. LECK
Vice-Pres. for Alumni Relations: JOAN STELTMANN
Vice-Pres. for Enterprise Advancement: JOAN M. STELTMANN
Vice-Pres. for Finance, Technology and Admin.: MALCOLM C. DOUGLAS
Vice-Pres. for Marketing and Communications: CURTIS P. WANG
Registrar: CHRISTINE L. PERLSTROM

Number of teachers: 120 (all adjunct faculty)
Number of students: 825.

BRANCH CAMPUSES

Chicago Campus: Federal Reserve Bank of Chicago, Suite 100, 230 South LaSalle St, Chicago, IL 60604; tel. (312) 435-5330; fax (312) 435-5333.

Schaumburg Campus: Motorola Galvin Center, 1295 East Algonquin Rd, Schaumburg, IL 60196; tel. (847) 576-1212; fax (847) 576-1213.

LEWIS UNIVERSITY

1 University Parkway, Romeoville, IL 60446-2200
Telephone: (815) 838-0500
Fax: (815) 838-9456
Internet: www.lewisu.edu

Founded 1932

Pres.: Br JAMES GAFFNEY
Provost: STEPHANY SCHLACHTER
Exec. Vice-Pres.: WAYNE DRAUDT
Vice-Pres. for Business and Finance: ROBERT C. DEROSE
Vice-Pres. for Enrollment Management: RAYMOND KENNELLY
Vice-Pres. for Student Services: JOSEPH FALESE
Vice-Pres. for Univ. Advancement: DANIEL J. ALLEN
Dean of Admissions: ANDREW SISON
Registrar: ROBERT KEMPIAK
Library Dir: LAURA PATTERSON

Library of 145,000 vols, 600 current periodicals, 2,500 video cassettes
Number of teachers: 140 (full-time)
Number of students: 4,400 (3,400 undergraduate, 1,000 graduate)

DEANS

College of Arts and Sciences: Dr BONNIE BONDAVALLI
College of Business: Dr RAMI KHASAWNEH
College of Education: Dr JEANETTE M. MINES
College of Nursing and Health Professions: Dr PEGGY RICE

LINCOLN CHRISTIAN UNIVERSITY

100 Campus View Dr., Lincoln, IL 62656
Telephone: (217) 732-3168
Fax: (888) 522-5228
E-mail: admissions@lincolnchristian.edu
Internet: www.lincolnchristian.edu

Founded 1944
Private control
Academic year: August to May

Pres.: Dr KEITH H. RAY
Provost: Dr CLAY ALAN HAM
Vice-Pres. for Finance: ANDREA SHORT
Vice-Pres. for Student Devt.: BRIAN MILLS
Vice-Pres. for Univ. Advancement: GORDON VENTURELLA
Assoc. Vice-Pres. for Alumni Devt: LYNN LAUGHLIN
Academic Dean for School of Undergraduate Studies: Dr NEAL WINDHAM
Seminary Academic Dean: Dr DINELLE FRANKLAND
Academic Dean of the School of Adult & Graduate Studies: Dr TOM TANNER
Registrar: SHAWN SMITH
Library Dir: NANCY OLSON

Library of 108,000 vols
Number of teachers: 48
Number of students: 1,164

LOYOLA UNIVERSITY CHICAGO

6525 North Sheridan Rd, Chicago, IL 60626
Telephone: (312) 915-6000
Internet: www.luc.edu

Founded 1870 as St Ignatius College; incorporated as Loyola Univ. 1909
Academic year: August to May

Pres.: Rev. MICHAEL J. GARANZINI
Pres. for the Medical Center: Dr ANTHONY L. BARBATO
Provost: Dr JOHN FRENDREIS
Vice-Pres. and Chief Information Officer: SUSAN M. MALISCH
Vice-Pres. and Gen. Counsel: ELLEN KANE MUNRO
Vice-Pres. for Admin.: Dr MARJORIE BEANE
Vice-Pres. for Advancement: JONATHAN HEINTZELMAN
Vice-Pres. for Facilities: PHILIP KOSIBA
Vice-Pres. for Finance: WILLIAM G. LAIRD
Vice-Pres. for Human Resources: THOMAS KELLY
Vice-Pres. for Public Affairs: PHILIP D. HALE
Vice-Pres. for Strategic Planning: WAYNE MAGDZIARZ
Vice-Pres. for Student Services: Rev. RICHARD P. SALMIE
Vice-Pres. for Univ. Ministry: LUCIEN ROY
Dean of Libraries: ROBERT SEAL

Library: 1.4m. vols
Number of teachers: 1,600
Number of students: 13,759

Publications: *Loyola Law, Loyola Magazine, Loyola World, Stritch M.D.*

DEANS

College of Arts and Sciences: Dr ISIAAH CRAWFORD (acting)
Graduate School: Dr SAMUEL ATTOH
School of Business Admin.: Dr ABOL JALLIVAND
School of Education: Dr DAVID PRASSE
School of Law: DAVID YELLEN
School of Social Work: Dr JACK WALL

LUTHERAN SCHOOL OF THEOLOGY AT CHICAGO

1100 East 55th St, Chicago, IL 60615
Telephone: (773) 256-0700
Fax: (773) 256-0782
E-mail: admissions@lstc.edu
Internet: www.lstc.edu

Founded 1962 from merger of 4 seminaries
Private control
Academic year: September to May

Pres.: JAMES KENNETH ECHOLS
Vice-Pres. for Advancement: MARK VAN SCHARREL
Vice-Pres. for Operations: BOB BERRIDGE
Registrar: PATRICIA A. BARTLEY
Dir of Library: CHRISTINE WENDEROTH

Library of 400,000 items

Publication: *Currents in Theology and Mission* (4 a year)

Areas of study incl. biblical studies, environmental ministry and interfaith, religion and science, urban ministry.

MCCORMICK THEOLOGICAL SEMINARY

5460 South University Ave, Chicago, IL 60615
Telephone: (773) 947-6300
Fax: (773) 947-6273
E-mail: info@mccormick.edu
Internet: www.mccormick.edu

Founded 1829 as Indiana Seminary; present name 1884
Private control (associated with the Presbyterian Church)
Academic year: September to June

Pres.: Rev. Dr CYNTHIA M. CAMPBELL
Vice-Pres. for Academic Affairs and Dean of Faculty: DAVID ESTERLINE
Vice-Pres. for Finance and Operations: DANA PETERSON
Vice-Pres. for Seminary Relations and Devt: WALTER VERDOOREN
Vice-Pres. for Student Affairs: MARY PAIK
Registrar: JANE BRAWLEY
Dir of Library: CHRISTINE WENDEROTH

Library of 400,000 items
Number of teachers: 28

MCKENDREE COLLEGE

701 College Rd, Lebanon, IL 62254
Telephone: (618) 537-4481
E-mail: mebornheimer@mckendree.edu
Internet: www.mckendree.edu

Founded 1828 as Lebanon Seminary; present name 1830
Private control
Academic year: August to May

Pres.: Dr JAMES M. DENNIS
Provost and Dean of the College: Dr GERALD A. DUFF
Vice-Pres. for Admin. and Finance: ROBERT G. MCKINNON
Vice-Pres. for Admissions: MARK CAMPBELL
Vice-Pres. for College Relations: Dr SUSAN S. SCRIBNER
Vice-Pres. for Devt: VICTORIA DOWLING
Vice-Pres. for Student Affairs: Dr TODD A. REYNOLDS
Academic Dean, Kentucky Centers: Dr ROBERT A. GERVASI
Registrar: GRETCHEN D. FRICKE
Librarian: LIZ VOGT

Library of 70,000 vols
Number of teachers: 66
Number of students: 2,000

Divs of business, education, computer science, humanities, language, literature and communications, nursing, science and mathematics, social science.

BRANCH CAMPUSES

Center at Scott AFB: 375 MSS/DPE, 604 Tyler St (Room 73), Scott AFB, IL 622255420; tel. (618) 256-2006; fax (618) 744-0635.

Louisville Campus: 11850 Commonwealth Dr., Louisville, KY 40299; tel. (502) 266-6696; fax (502) 267-4340.

Radcliff Campus: 1635 West Lincoln Trail Blvd. Radcliff, KY 40160; tel. (270) 351-5003; fax (502) 267-4340.

MACMURRAY COLLEGE

447 East College Ave, Jacksonville, IL 62650
Telephone: (217) 479-7000
Fax: (217) 245-0405
Internet: www.mac.edu

Founded 1846

Pres.: Dr LAWRENCE D. BRYAN
Vice-Pres. for Academic Affairs and Dean of College: DAVID FITZ
Vice-Pres. and Chief Financial Officer: WENDY LITTLE
Vice-Pres. and Chief Information Officer: MORRIS RANG, III
Vice-Pres. for Enrollment Management: RHONDA CORS
Vice-Pres. for Institutional Advancment: ERIC J. GREEN
Vice-Pres. for Student Affairs: SALLY CAYAN
Library Dir: SUSAN EILERING

Library of 130,000 vols, 200 periodicals
Number of teachers: 53
Number of students: 715

Publications: *MacMurray College News*, *Montage*

Depts of art, biology, business and accounting, chemistry, criminal justice, education, English and theatre, history and political science, modern languages, music, nursing, philosophy and religion, physics and mathematics, psychology, social work.

MEADVILLE LOMBARD THEOLOGICAL SCHOOL

5701 South Woodlawn Ave, Chicago, IL 60637
Telephone: (773) 753-1323
Fax: (773) 256-3006
Internet: www.meadville.edu

Founded 1844
Private control (affiliated with the Unitarian Universalist Assn)
Academic year: September to June

Pres.: LEE BARKER
Vice-Pres. for Enrollment and Student Services: JOHN TOLLEY
Vice-Pres. for Finance and Admin.: DEBORAH BIEBER
Vice-Pres. for Institutional Advancement: JOAN WHITE
Registrar: (vacant)
Librarian: Rev. Dr NEIL W. GERDES

Library of 100,000 vols
Number of teachers: 9
Number of students: 101

MIDWESTERN UNIVERSITY

555 31st St, Downers Grove, IL 60515
Telephone: (630) 969-4400
E-mail: admissil@midwestern.edu
Internet: www.midwestern.edu

Founded 1993 following merger of 3 colleges
Private control
Academic year: September to May

Pres. and CEO: Dr KATHLEEN H. GOEPPINGER
Exec. Vice-Pres. and Chief Operating Officer: Dr ARTHUR G. DOBBELEARE
Sr Vice-Pres. and Chief Financial Officer: GREGORY J. GAUS
Vice-Pres. for Business Services: DEAN P. MALONE
Vice-Pres. for Clinical Education: GEORGE T. CALEEL
Vice-Pres. for Human Resources and Admin.: ANGEL L. MARTY
Vice-Pres. for Univ. Relations: KAREN D. JOHNSON
Dean of Students: Dr TERESA DOMBROWSKI

DEANS

Basic Sciences: Dr JOHN R. BURDICK
College of Dental Medicine: RICHARD J. SIMONSEN
College of Health Sciences: Dr DENNIS J. PAULSON
College of Pharmacy: Dr MARY W. L. LEE

BRANCH CAMPUS

Glendale, Arizona Campus: 19555 North 59th Ave, Glendale, AZ 85308; tel. (623) 572-3200; e-mail admissaz@midwestern.edu; Dean of Students Dr ROSS J. KOSINSKI

DEANS

College of Osteopathic Medicine: JAMES W. COLE
College of Pharmacy: Dr ANNE Y. F. LIN

MILLIKIN UNIVERSITY

1184 West Main St, Decatur, IL 62522-2084
Telephone: (217) 424-6211
Fax: (217) 424-3993
Internet: www.millikin.edu

Founded 1901
Academic year: August to May

Pres.: DOUGLAS E. ZEMKE
Vice-Pres. for Academic Affairs: JAMIE CORNSTOCK
Vice-Pres. for Business Affairs: RONALD RECK
Vice-Pres. for Univ. Devt: PEGGY S. LUY
Vice-Pres. of Enurement: RICH DUNSWORTH
Registrar: WALTER WESSEL
Dean of Student Life and Academic Devt: DAVID WOMACK
Dir of the Library: KARIN BOREI

Number of teachers: 249
Number of students: 2,499

Publications: *Collage* (1 a year), *The Decaturian* (26 a year), *Millikin University Quarterly*, *Quarterly Economic and Financial Forecast*

DEANS

College of Arts and Sciences: Dr RALPH CZERWINSKI
College of Fine Arts: BARRY PEARSON
College of Professional Studies: Dr KATHY BOOKER
Tabor School of Business: Dr JAMES DAHL

MONMOUTH COLLEGE

700 East Broadway, Monmouth, IL 61462
Telephone: (309) 457-2131
Fax: (309) 457-2310
E-mail: info@monm.edu
Internet: www.monm.edu

Founded 1853

Pres.: Dr MAURI DITZLER
Vice-Pres. for Academic Affairs and Dean of the Faculty: JANE JAKOUBEK
Vice-Pres. for Advancement: J. LANCE CAVANAUGH
Vice-Pres. for Finance and Business: DONALD GLADFELTER
Vice-Pres. for Student Life and Dean of Students: JACQUELYN CONDON
Registrar: SUSAN DAGIT
Library Dir: J. RICHARD SAYRE

Library of 300,000 vols
Number of teachers: 82 (full-time)
Number of students: 1,097

MOODY BIBLE INSTITUTE

820 North LaSalle Blvd, Chicago, IL 60610
Telephone: (312) 329-4000
E-mail: pr@moody.edu
Internet: www.moody.edu

Founded 1886 as Chicago Evangelization Society; present name 1900
Private control
Academic year: August to May

Pres.: Dr PAUL NYQUIST
Provost and Dean of Education: CHARLES DYER
Exec. Vice-Pres. and Chief Operating Officer: EDWARD CANNON
Vice-Pres. and Dean of Graduate School: JOHN JELINEK
Vice-Pres. and Dean of Undergraduate School: (vacant)
Vice-Pres. and General Counsel: STEPHEN OAKLEY
Vice-Pres. for Educational Resources: BILL BLOCKER
Vice-Pres. for Student Services: THOMAS SHAW
Registrar: TIMOTHY C. WIEGERT
Library Dir: JAMES PRESTON.

MEDICINE SHIELD COLLEGE PROGRAM AMERICAN INDIAN ASSOCIATION OF ILLINOIS/NATIVE AMERICAN EDUCATIONAL SERVICES

5751 N. Richmond, Chicago, IL 60659
Telephone and fax (773) 338-8320
E-mail: dpwiese@aol.com
Internet: www.chicago-american-indian-edu.org

Founded 1974, present name and status 2007; attached to Eastern Illinois Univ.
Private control
Languages of instruction: English, Ojibwe, Lakota
Academic year: August to May
Areas of study: general studies, public policy, with emphasis on tribal knowledge, community service, community devt and leadership

Pres.: DORENE WIESE
Dean of AIAI Campus: LOLA HILL
Registrar: Dr MELANIE CLOUD
Head Librarian: MELANIE CLOUD

Library of 10,000 items
Number of teachers: 8
Number of students: 30

NATIONAL–LOUIS UNIVERSITY

Chicago Campus, 122 South Michigan Ave, Chicago, IL 60603
Telephone: (312) 621-9650
Fax: (312) 621-3057
E-mail: nluinfo@nl.edu
Internet: www.nl.edu

Founded 1886

Campuses in Skokie, Lisle, Wheeling and Elgin (Illinois), Milwaukee and Beloit (Wisconsin), Tampa (Florida), Washington, McLean (Virginia) and Nowy Sacz (Poland)

Pres.: RICHARD J. PAPPAS
Provost: KATHRYN J. TOORDEMAN
Vice-Pres. for Communications: CHRISTIAN ANDERSON
Vice-Pres. for Devt: REBECCA STIMSON
Vice-Pres. for Enrollment and Student Services: LARRY POLSELLI
Vice-Pres. for Human Resources: THOMAS BERGMANN
Vice-Pres. for Operational Services: WILLIAM ROBERTS
Registrar: KENNETH GILSON

Dean of Library: KATHLEEN WALSH
Library of 125,000 vols
Number of teachers: 745 (320 full-time, 425 part-time)
Number of students: 14,166 (4,057 undergraduate, 10,109 graduate)

DEANS

College of Arts and Sciences: Dr MARTHA CASAZZA
College of Management and Business: Dr RICHARD MAGNER
Nat. College of Education: Dr ALISON HILSABECK

NATIONAL UNIVERSITY OF HEALTH SCIENCES

200 East Roosevelt Rd, Lombard, IL 60148
Telephone: (630) 629-2000
Internet: www.nuhs.edu
Founded 1906 as Nat. School of Chiropractic; present name 2000
Private control
Pres.: Dr JAMES WINTERSTEIN
Vice-Pres. for Academic Services: Dr CHRISTINA NICHOLSON
Vice-Pres. for Business Services: RON MENSHING
Registrar: KEITH WEROSH
Librarian: JOYCE WHITEHEAD
Library of 15,000 vols

DEANS

College of Allied Health Sciences: Dr RANDY SWENSON
College of Professional Studies: Dr KEITH SMITH
Lincoln College of Post-Professional, Graduate and Continuing Education: Dr JONATHAN SOLTYS

NORTH CENTRAL COLLEGE

30 N Brainard St, Naperville, IL 60540
Telephone: (630) 637-5100
Fax: (630) 637-5121
Internet: www.noctrl.edu
Founded 1861
Academic year: September to June
Liberal arts college
Pres.: Dr HAROLD WILDE
Vice-Pres. for Academic Affairs and Dean of Faculty: Dr R. DEVADOSS PANDIAN
Vice-Pres. for Business Affairs: PAUL H. LOSCHEIDER
Vice-Pres. for Enrollment Management and Student Affairs: LAURIE HAMEN
Vice-Pres. for Institutional Advancement: RICK SPENCER
Librarian: CAROLYN SHEEHY
Library of 170,000 vols
Number of teachers: 133 full-time, 119 part-time
Number of students: 2,416 full-time, 382 part-time

NORTH PARK UNIVERSITY

3225 West Foster Ave, Chicago, IL 60625-4895
Telephone: (773) 244-6200
Internet: www.northpark.edu
Founded 1891
Pres.: Dr DAVID L. PARKYN
Exec. Vice-Pres. of Academic Affairs and Dean of Seminary: Dr JOHN E. PHELAN, Jr
Vice-Pres. for Estate Planning Services: LEROY M. JOHNSON
Vice-Pres. for Univ. Relations, Communications and Devt: DANIEL TEPKE
Academic Dean: CHARLES PETERSON
Dean of Enrollment: MARK OLSON
Registrar: AARON SCHOOF
Library Dir: SARAH ANDERSON
Library of 443,665 vols
Number of teachers: 125 full-time
Number of students: 2,900

NORTHEASTERN ILLINOIS UNIVERSITY

5500 North St Louis Ave, Chicago, IL 60625-4699
Telephone: (773) 583-4050
Fax: (773) 442-4900
Internet: www.neiu.edu
Founded 1961
Pres.: Dr SALME H. STEINBERG
Provost and Vice-Pres. for Academic Affairs: LAWRENCE P. FRANK
Vice-Pres. for Finance and Admin.: MARK D. WILCOCKSON
Vice-Pres. for Student Affairs: Dr MELVIN C. TERRELL
Exec. Dir of Marketing and Communications: TERRY M. BUSH
Dir for Admissions and Records: MIRIAM RIVERA
Dir of Devt and Alumni Affairs: LEONARD IAQUINTA
Dean of Students: Dr MICHAEL T. KELLY
Univ. Librarian: BRADLEY BAKER
Library of 651,005 vols (and Regional Archives Depository)
Number of teachers: 488 (325 full-time, 163 part-time)
Number of students: 12,000

DEANS

College of Arts and Sciences: KATIE L. FORIHAN
College of Business and Management: Dr VARKEY K. TITUS
College of Education: MAUREEN D. GILLETTE
Graduate College: Dr JANET FREDERICKS (acting)

NORTHERN BAPTIST THEOLOGICAL SEMINARY

660 E Butterfield Rd, Lombard, IL 60148
Telephone: (630) 620-2180
Fax: (630) 620-2190
E-mail: admissions@seminary.edu
Internet: www.seminary.edu
Founded 1913
Private control
Pres.: Dr ALISTAIR BROWN
Dean of Academic Affairs: Dr KAREN WALKER FREEBURG
Exec. Dir of External Relations: GREG HENSON
Registrar: MARILYN MAST HEWITT
Dean of Academic Administration and Library Dir: BLAKE WALTER
Library of 53,200 vols, 282 periodical titles
Number of teachers: 15
Number of students: 200

NORTHERN ILLINOIS UNIVERSITY

1425 W Lincoln Highway, DeKalb, IL 60115-2854
Telephone: (815) 753-1000
Fax: (815) 753-8686
E-mail: admissions@niu.edu
Internet: www.niu.edu
Founded 1895
Academic year: August to May
Pres.: JOHN G. PETERS
Exec. Vice-Pres. and Provost: RAYMOND W. ALDEN, III
Exec. Vice-Pres. for Finance and Facilities: EDDIE R. WILLIAMS
Vice-Pres. for Admin. and Univ. Outreach: ANNE C. KAPLAN
Vice-Pres. for Devt and Univ. Relations: MICHAEL P. MALONE
Vice-Pres. for Research and Graduate Studies: LISA C. FREEMAN
Vice-Pres. for Student Affairs: BRIAN HEMPHILL
Dean of Univ. Libraries: PATRICK J. DAWSON
Library: 2m. vols, 1,343,933 govt documents, 21,267 current periodicals, 3,000,087 microfilm units
Number of teachers: 1,292
Number of students: 24,397 (incl. 2,177 extension)
Publications: *Applied and Computational Control, Signals, and Circuits* (1 a year), *Crossroads: An Interdisciplinary Journal of Southeast Asian Studies* (2 a year), *George Eliot – George Henry Lewes Studies* (1 or 2 a year), *International Economic Journal* (4 a year), *International Journal of Sociology of the Family* (2 a year), *International Review of Modern Sociology* (2 a year), *Journal of Political and Military Sociology* (2 a year), *Names: A Journal of Onomastics* (4 a year), *Popular Music and Society* (4 a year), *Style* (4 a year), *The Journal of Burma Studies* (1 a year), *Thresholds in Education* (4 a year)

DEANS

College of Business: DENISE D. SCHOENBACHLER
College of Education: LEMUEL W. WATSON
College of Engineering and Engineering Technology: PROMOD VOHRA (acting)
College of Health and Human Sciences: SHIRLEY A. RICHMOND
College of Law: JENNIFER ROSATO
College of Liberal Arts and Sciences: CHRISTOPHER MCCORD
College of Visual and Performing Arts: RICH HOLLY
Graduate School: BRADLEY BOND (acting)

NORTHWESTERN UNIVERSITY

633 Clark St, Evanston, IL 60208
Telephone: (847) 491-3741
E-mail: webmaster@northwestern.edu
Internet: www.northwestern.edu
Founded 1851
Private control
Academic year: September to June
Pres.: MORTON O. SCHAPIRO
Provost: DANIEL I. LINZER
Sr Vice-Pres. for Business and Finance: EUGENE S. SUNSHINE
Vice-Pres. and Chief Investment Officer: WILLIAM H. MCLEAN
Vice-Pres. and Gen. Counsel: THOMAS G. CLINE
Vice-Pres. for Admin. and Planning: MARILYN MCCOY
Vice-Pres. for Alumni Relations and Devt: SARAH R. PEARSON
Vice-Pres. for Information Technology: MORTEZA A. RAHIMI
Vice-Pres. for Research: JOSEPH T. WALSH, Jr
Vice-Pres. for Student Affairs: WILLIAM J. BANIS
Vice-Pres. for Univ. Relations: ALAN K. CUBBAGE
Registrar: SUZANNE M. W. ANDERSON
Librarian: SARAH M. PRITCHARD
Library: see Libraries and Archives
Number of teachers: 3,096 full-time
Number of students: 16,337 full-time
Publications: *Journal of Criminal Law and Criminology* (4 a year), *Northwestern Observer* (52 a year), *Northwestern Perspective* (4 a year), *Northwestern University Journal of International Law and*

Business (3 a year), *Tri-Quarterly* (3 a year), *The Reporter* (4 a year), *Northwestern University Law Review* (4 a year)

DEANS

Feinberg School of Medicine: J. LARRY JAMESON
Graduate School: ANDREW B. WACHTEL
J. L. Kellogg School of Management: SUNIL CHOPRA
Robert R. McCormick School of Engineering and Applied Science: JULIO OTTINO
Medill School of Journalism: JOHN LAVINE
School of Communication: BARBARA J. O'KEEFE
School of Continuing Studies: THOMAS F. GIBBONS
School of Education and Social Policy: PENELOPE L. PETERSON
School of Law: DAVID E. VAN ZANDT
Henry and Lee Bienen School of Music: TONI-MARIE MONTGOMERY
Judd A. and Marjorie Weinberg College of Arts and Sciences: SARAH MANGELSDORF
Northwestern Univ. in Qatar: JOHN MARGOLIS

OLIVET NAZARENE UNIVERSITY

1 University St, Bourbonnais, IL 60914-2345
Telephone: (815) 939-5011
Internet: www.olivet.edu

Founded 1907

Pres.: Dr JOHN C. BOWLING
Vice-Pres. for Academic Affairs and Academic Dean: Dr GARY STREIT
Vice-Pres. for Finance: Dr DOUGLAS PERRY
Vice-Pres. for Institutional Advancement: BRIAN ALLEN
Vice-Pres. for Student Devt and Dean of Students: Rev. WALTER (WOODY) WEBB
Registrar: JIM KNIGHT
Dean of Admissions: JOHN MONGERSON
Library Dir: KATHY BOYENS

Library of 160,000 vols, 900 current periodicals, 100,000 other items (maps, pamphlets, sheet-music, microforms, govt documents)
Number of teachers: 100
Number of students: 4,400

DEANS

College of Arts and Sciences: Dr GREGG CHENOWETH
School of Education: Dr JAMES UPCHURCH
School of Graduate and Continuing Studies: Dr CAROL MAXSON
School of Professional Studies: Dr FRAN REED
School of Theology and Christian Ministry: Dr CARL LETH

PRINCIPIA COLLEGE

Elsah, IL 62028-9799
Telephone: (618) 374-2131
Fax: (618) 374-5122
E-mail: registrar@prin.edu
Internet: www.prin.edu/college

Founded 1910

Pres.: Dr JONATHAN W. PALMER
Dean of Academics: Dr SCOTT SCHNEBERGER
Registrar: PATRICIA W. LANGTON
Dean of Enrollment Management: BRIAN MCCAULEY
Librarian: CAROL STOOKEY

Library of 125,000 vols
Number of teachers: 95
Number of students: 550

QUINCY UNIVERSITY

1800 College Ave, Quincy, IL 62301-2699
Telephone: (217) 222-8020
Fax: (217) 228-5479
Internet: www.quincy.edu

Founded 1860; chartered 1873

Pres.: Dr ROBERT GERVASI (acting)
Sr Vice-Pres. for Academic and Student Affairs: Dr DAVID SCHACHTSIEK
Vice-Pres. for Business and Finance: CHARLES DAVIS
Registrar: BARB. WELLMAN
Dean of Library and Information Resources: PAT TOMCZAK

Library of 210,000 vols
Number of teachers: 153
Number of students: 1,424

DEANS

Div. Behavioral and Social Sciences: Dr WENDY BELLER (Chair.)
Div. Fine Arts and Communication: Dr BARBARA SCHLEPPENBACH (Chair.)
Div. Humanities: Dr TERRENCE RIDDELL (Chair.)
Div. Science and Technology: Dr E. JOSEPH EMEKA (Chair.)
School of Business: Dr CYNTHIA HALIEMUN
School of Education: Dr ANN BEHRENS
School of Professional Studies: Dr DAVID SCHACHTSIEK

ROBERT MORRIS UNIVERSITY

401 S State St, Chicago, IL 60605
Telephone: (312) 935-6800
Fax: (312) 935-6819
E-mail: enroll@robertmorris.edu
Internet: www.robertmorris.edu

Founded 1965
Private control

Pres.: MICHAEL P. VIOLLT
Provost: MABLENE KRUEGER
Sr Vice-Pres. for Enrollment Management: CATHERINE LOCKWOOD
Sr Vice-Pres. for Resource Admin.: DEBORAH BRODZINSKI
Vice-Pres. for Business Affairs: RONALD M. ARNOLD
Vice-Pres. for External Affairs: MARIE GIACOMELLI
Vice-Pres. for Human Resources: NICOLE R. SKALUBA
Vice-Pres. for Information Systems: LISA CONTRERAS
Vice-Pres. for Marketing: CONNNIE ESPARZA
Vice-Pres. for Student Affairs: ANGELA JORDAN
Registrar: STELLA MACH
Institutional Library Dir: SUE DUTLER

Library of 185,059 vols in 5 campus libraries
Number of students: 3,519

DEANS

Div. of Science and Humanities: PAULA DIAZ
Institute of Art and Design: JANICE KAUSHAL
School of Business Admin.: LARRY NIEMAN
School of Computer Studies: Dr KAYED AKKAWI
School of Nursing and Health Studies: Dr JANET HAGGERTY DAVIS

BRANCH CAMPUSES

Bensenville Campus: 1000 Tower Lane, Bensenville, IL 60106; tel. (630) 787-7800; fax (630) 787-7802.

DuPage Campus: 905 Meridian Lake Dr., Aurora, IL 60504; tel. (630) 375-8020; fax (630) 375-8000.

Lake County Campus: 1507 Waukegan Rd, Waukegan, IL 60085; tel. (847) 578-6000; fax (847) 578-7110.

Orland Park Campus: 43 Orland Sq. and 82 Orland Sq., Orland Park, IL 60462; tel. (708) 226-3800; fax (708) 226-3873.

Peoria Campus: 211 Fulton St, Peoria, IL 61602; tel. (309) 636-8600; fax (309) 636-8602.

Springfield Campus: 3101 Montvale Dr., Springfield, IL 62704; tel. (217) 793-2500; fax (217) 793-4210.

ROCKFORD COLLEGE

5050 East State St, Rockford, IL 61108
Telephone: (815) 226-4000
Fax: (815) 226-4119
Internet: www.rockford.edu

Co-educational college founded 1847

Pres.: Dr RICHARD KNEEDLER
Exec. Vice-Pres. and Dean of College: Dr STEPHANIE QUINN
Vice-Pres. for College Devt: JOHN MCNAMARA
Vice-Pres. for Student Life: HENRY ESPENSEN
Library Dir: KAREN TIBBETTS

Library of 130,000 vols and 500 current periodicals
Number of teachers: 133 (83 full-time, 50 part-time)
Number of students: 1,100

Depts of anthropology and sociology, art and art history, biology, chemistry/biochemistry, computer science, economics, business and accounting, education, English, history, mathematics, modern and classical languages, nursing, performing arts, philosophy, physical education, physics, political science, psychology

Publications: *Decus* (3 a year), *Rockford Report* (4 a year).

ROOSEVELT UNIVERSITY

430 South Michigan Ave, Chicago, IL 60605
Telephone: (312) 341-3800
Internet: www.roosevelt.edu

Founded 1945
Private control

Pres.: Dr CHARLES R. MIDDLETON
Provost and Exec. Vice-Pres.: PAMELA TROTMAN REID
Vice-Provost for Research and Graduate Dean: JANETT TRUBATCH
Sr Vice-Pres. for Finance and Operations: JOHN ALLERSON
Vice-Pres. and Dean of Albert A. Robin Campus: Dr ANTONIA POTENZA
Vice-Pres. for Enrollment and Student Services: MARY E. HENDRY
Vice-Pres. for Governmental Relations: J. MICHAEL DURNIL
Vice-Pres. for Human Resources: GRETCHEN VAN NATTA
Vice-Pres. for Institutional Advancement: THOMAS MINAR
Vice-Pres. for Technology and Chief Information Officer: J. BRADLEY REESE
Registrar: MICHAEL D. FORD
Librarian: MARY BETH RIEDNER

Library of 374,000 vols
Number of teachers: 500
Number of students: 7,400

Publications: *Business and Society*, *Roosevelt University Magazine*

DEANS

Chicago College of Performing Arts: Dr JAMES GANDRE
College of Arts and Science: Dr LYNN Y. WEINER
College of Education: Dr JAMES GANDRA
Evelyn T. Stone Univ. College: Dr DOUGLAS G. KNERR
Walter E. Heller College of Business Administration: Dr GORDON L. PATZER

ROSALIND FRANKLIN UNIVERSITY OF MEDICINE AND SCIENCE

3333 Green Bay Rd, North Chicago, IL 60064
Telephone: (847) 578-3000
Internet: www.rosalindfranklin.edu

Founded 1967 as Univ. of Health Sciences/The Chicago Medical School following the merger of Chicago Medical School (f. 1912), School of Graduate and Postdoctoral Studies (f. 1968) and School of Related Health Sciences (f. 1970); renamed Finch Univ. of Health Sciences/The Chicago Medical School 1994; incorporated Dr William M. Scholl College of Podiatric Medicine (f. 1912) 2001; present name 2004
Private control
Academic year: July to June

Pres.: K. MICHAEL WELCH
Exec. Vice-Pres. and Chief Operating Officer: MARGOT SURRIDGE
Vice-Pres. for Academic Affairs: TIMOTHY HANSEN
Vice-Pres. for Institutional Advancement: PRISCILLA KHOURY
Vice-Pres. for Medical Affairs: ARTHUR J. ROSS, III
Vice-Pres. for Research: Dr MICHAEL P. SARRAS, Jr
Vice-Pres. for Strategic Devt: NABIH RAMADAN
Vice-Pres. for Univ. Relations: NANCY GARN
Registrar: CINDY FRIESEN
Dir of Library: BONNIE WATSON

Library of 119,000 vols

DEANS

Chicago Medical School: Dr ARTHUR J. ROSS
College of Health Professions: Dr WENDY RHEAULT
Dr William M. Scholl College of Podiatric Medicine: Dr TERENCE ALBRIGHT
School of Graduate and Postdoctoral Studies: Dr MICHAEL P. SARRAS, Jr

RUSH UNIVERSITY

Suite 440, 600 South Paulina St, Chicago, IL 60612
Telephone: (312) 942-5000
Internet: www.rushu.rush.edu

Founded 1972
Private control
Academic year: September to June (3 terms)

Pres.: Dr LARRY J. GOODMAN
Vice-Pres. for Academic Resources: Dr JOHN E. TRUFANT
Registrar: WILLIAM F. KARNOSCAK
Library Dir: Dr TRUDY GARDNER

Library of 59,451 vols, 2,003 periodicals
Number of teachers: 2,900
Number of students: 1,452

DEANS

College of Health Sciences: Dr HERB MILLER (acting)
College of Nursing: Dr MELANIE C. DREHER
Graduate College: Dr PAUL M. CARVEY
Rush Medical College: THOMAS A. DEUTSCH (acting)

SAINT ANTHONY COLLEGE OF NURSING

5658 E State St, Rockford, IL 61108-2468
Telephone: (815) 395-5091
Fax: (815) 227-2275
E-mail: info@sacn.edu
Internet: www.sacn.edu

Founded 1915 as Saint Anthony School of Nursing; present name 1990
Private control
Academic year: August to May; attached to Asscn of College of Nursing, N Central Asscn of Colleges and Univs

Dean and Pres.: Dr TERESE ANN BURCH
Assoc. Dean for Graduate Affairs: Dr CHARLOTTE SANFORD (acting)
Assoc. Dean for Support Services: NANCY SANDERS
Assoc. Dean for Undergraduate Affairs: Dr ELIZABETH CARSON
Dir of Learning Resource Center: HEATHER KLEPITSCH

Library of 2,700 vols; 200 print and more than 1,000 online periodicals
Number of teachers: 17 F.t.e.
Number of students: 178

SAINT FRANCIS MEDICAL CENTER COLLEGE OF NURSING

511 NE Greenleaf St, Peoria, IL 61603-3783
Telephone: (309) 655-2596
Fax: (309) 655-3648
Internet: www.sfmccon.edu

Founded 1905 as Saint Francis Hospital School of Nursing; present name 1985
Private control
Accredited by American Asscn of Colleges of Nursing, American Asscn of Collegiate Registrars and Admission Officers, American College Health Asscn, American Hospital Asscn, Catholic Health Asscn, Illinois Asscn of Colleges of Nursing, Illinois Asscn of Student Financial Aid Administrators, Midwest Association of Student Financial Aid Administrators, Nat. Asscn of Student Financial Aid Administrators, Nat. League for Nursing, Nat. League for Nursing Accrediting Comm., Nurse Educators of Illinois, Higher Learning Comm.—a Comm. of the N Central Asscn of Colleges and Schools
Academic year: August to May

Pres.: Dr LOIS J. HAMILTON
Dean, Undergraduate Program: Dr PATRICIA STOCKERT
Dean, Graduate Program: Dr JANICE BOUNDY
Assoc. Dean of Institutional Research: MARY C. SHOEMAKER
Asst Dean of Student Services: KEVIN STEPHENS
Dir of Admissions/Registrar: JANICE FARQUHARSON
Student Finance Coordinator, Financial Assistance: NANCY PERRYMAN
Coordinator of Student Accounts and Business Services: LAURA SIMMONS
Librarian: KARL GIBSON

Library of 7,556 vols, 1,840 periodicals, 123 professional journals
Number of teachers: 32 full-time, 12 part-time
Number of students: 452 undergraduate (333 undergraduate, 119 graduate)

Offers BSc and MSc in Nursing and RN accelerated path to BScN.

ST JOHN'S COLLEGE

421 North Ninth St, Springfield, IL 62702
Telephone: (217) 525-5628
Fax: (217) 757-6870
E-mail: college@st-johns.org
Internet: www.st-johns.org/education/schools/nursing

Founded 1886
Private control

Pres.: Dr JANE SCHACHTSIEK

Number of teachers: 18
Number of students: 93

SAINT XAVIER UNIVERSITY

3700 West 103rd St, Chicago, IL 60655
Telephone: (773) 298-3000
Fax: (773) 779-9061
E-mail: admission@sxu.edu
Internet: www.sxu.edu

Founded 1846
Academic year: August to May

Pres.: Dr JUDITH A. DWYER
Provost: Dr DOMINICK HART
Vice-Pres. for Business and Finance: SUSAN L. PIROS
Vice-Pres. for Student Affairs: JOHN P. PELRINE, Jr
Vice-Pres. for Univ. Advancement: Dr STEVEN J. MURPHY
Vice-Pres. for Univ. Mission and Heritage: Dr SUSAN M. SANDERS
Vice-Pres. for Univ. Relations: ROBERT C. TENCZAR
Vice-Pres. for Univ. Research: Dr KATHLEEN CARLSON
Librarian: MARK VARGAS

Library of 123,325 vols
Number of teachers: 187
Number of students: 5,648

DEANS

College of Arts and Sciences: Dr KATHLEEN ALAIMO
Graham School of Management: Dr JOHN E. EBER
School for Continuing and Professional Studies: Dr LESLIE M. PETTY
School of Education: Dr BEVERLY GULLEY
School of Nursing: Dr ANNE R. BAVIER

BRANCH CAMPUS

Orlando Park Campus: Orlando Park, IL 60467; tel. (708) 802-6200.

SCHOOL OF THE ART INSTITUTE OF CHICAGO

37 South Wabash, Chicago, IL 60603
Telephone: (312) 629-6100
Fax: (312) 263-0141
E-mail: admiss@saic.edu
Internet: www.saic.edu

Founded 1866
Academic year: September to May

Pres.: WELLINGTON REITER

Library: libraries with 325,000 vols, 450,000 slides, 4,000 video cassettes, films, sound recordings
Number of teachers: 160 full-time and 400 part-time
Number of students: 2,588 (2,008 undergraduate, 580 graduate)

Depts of architecture, art education, art history, art and technology studies, ceramics, design for emerging technologies, fashion design, fiber and material studies, film, video and new media, liberal arts, painting and drawing, performance, photography, print media, sculpture, sound, visual communication, visual and critical studies, writing.

SEABURY-WESTERN THEOLOGICAL SEMINARY

2122 Sheridan Rd, Evanston, IL 60201
Telephone: (847) 328-9300
Fax: (847) 328-9624
E-mail: seabury@seabury.edu
Internet: www.seabury.edu

Founded 1933 following merger of Seabury Divinity School (f. 1858) and Western Theological Seminary (f. 1883)
Private control (Episcopal Church)
Academic year: September to June

Dean and Pres.: GARY HALL

Vice-Pres. for Advancement and Admin.: ELIZABETH BUTLER
Academic Dean: RUTH A. MYERS
Registrar: PEGGY PEARSON
Librarian: NEWLAND F. SMITH, III

Library of 300,000 vols
Number of students: 92

Degrees in congregational devt, divinity, theological studies, preaching.

SOUTHERN ILLINOIS UNIVERSITY CARBONDALE

Carbondale, IL 62901
Telephone: (618) 453-2341
Fax: (618) 453-5362
E-mail: ltripp@siu.edu
Internet: www.siuc.edu

Founded 1869
State control

Chancellor: Dr RITA CHENG
Pres.: Dr GLENN POSHARD
Vice-Chancellor for Administration and Finance: KEVIN D. BAME
Provost and Sr Vice-Chancellor: Dr GARY MINISH
Vice-Chancellor for Institutional Advancement: RICKEY N. MCCURRY
Vice-Chancellor for Research and Graduate Dean: JOHN A. KOROPCHAK
Exec. Dir for Finance: KEVIN D. BAME

Library of 3,203,455 vols, 58,246 current serials, 4,633,365 microform units, 312,153 govt documents
Number of students: 20,037

DEANS

College of Agricultural Sciences: TODD WINTERS
College of Applied Sciences and Arts: TERRY OWENS
College of Business: J. DENNIS CRADIT
College of Education and Human Services: KENNETH TEITELBAUM
College of Engineering: LIZETTE CHEVALIER
College of Liberal Arts: ALAN VAUX
College of Mass Communication and Media Arts: GARY KOLB
College of Science: JAY MEANS
School of Law: CYNTHIA FOUNTAINE
School of Medicine: J. KEVIN DORSEY

SOUTHERN ILLINOIS UNIVERSITY EDWARDSVILLE

Edwardsville, IL 62026-1151
Telephone: (618) 650-2000
Fax: (618) 650-3837
E-mail: vandegr@siue.edu
Internet: www.siue.edu

Founded 1957
State control
Academic year: August to May

Chancellor: VAUGHN VANDEGRIFT
Provost and Vice-Chancellor for Academic Affairs: ANN M. BOYLE
Vice-Chancellor for Admin.: KENNETH NEHER
Vice-Chancellor for Student Affairs: NARBETH EMMANUEL
Vice-Chancellor for Univ. Relations and Chief Exec. Officer of the SIUE Foundation: PATRICK D. HUNDLEY
Dean of the Lovejoy Library: REGINA MCBRIDE

Library of 810,217 vols, 1,676,670 microforms, 13,472 current periodicals, 30,379 audiovisual items
Number of teachers: 878 (627 full-time, 251 part-time)
Number of students: 14,133

Publications: *Papers on Language and Literature*, *Sou'wester*

DEANS

College of Arts and Sciences: Dr ALDEMARO ROMERO
Graduate School: Dr JERRY WEINBERG
School of Business: Dr GARY GIAMARTINO
School of Dental Medicine: Dr ANN M. BOYLE
School of Education: Dr BETTE S. BERGERON
School of Engineering: Dr HASAN SEVIM
School of Nursing: Dr MARCIA MAURER
School of Pharmacy: Dr GIREESH GUPCHUP

SPERTUS INSTITUTE OF JEWISH STUDIES

618 South Michigan Ave, Chicago, IL 60605
Telephone: (312) 322-1700
E-mail: college@spertus.edu
Internet: www.spertus.edu

Founded 1924
Private control

Dean of Spertus College: Dr DEAN BELL

Library of 110,000 vols; spec. colln 1,500 rare books dating from 15th 20th centuries; Chicago Jewish Archives.

TELSHE YESHIVA–CHICAGO

3535 West Foster Ave, Chicago, IL 60625
Telephone: (773) 463-7738
Private control

Pres.: Rabbi AVRAHAM LEVIN
Number of students: 74

Areas of study: rabbinical and Talmudic education.

TRINITY CHRISTIAN COLLEGE

6601 West College Dr., Palos Heights, IL 60463-0929
Telephone: (708) 597-3000
E-mail: admissions@trnty.edu
Internet: www.trnty.edu

Founded 1959
Private control
Academic year: August to May

Pres.: Dr STEVEN TIMMERMANS
Provost: Dr ELIZABETH A. RUDENGA
Vice-Pres. for Admissions and Marketing: PETER HAMSTRA
Vice-Pres. for Devt: LARRYL HUMME
Vice-Pres. for Finance and Admin.: EUN AHN
Vice-Pres. for Student Devt: GINNY CARPENTER
Dean of Academic Services: Dr BURTON J. ROZEMA
Registrar: S. DEAN ELLENS
Library Dir: MARCILLE FREDERICK

Library of 68,000 vols
Number of students: 1,310

Programmes of study in accounting, art and design, biology, business, business communication, chemistry, church and ministry leadership, communication arts, computer science, economics, education, English, exercise science, geology, Greek, history, information systems, mathematics, music, nursing, philosophy, physical education, physics, political science, psychology, science, social work, sociology, Spanish, special education, theology.

TRINITY INTERNATIONAL UNIVERSITY

2065 Half Day Rd, Deerfield, IL 60015
Telephone: (847) 945-8800
Fax: (847) 317-8097
Internet: www.tiu.edu

Founded 1995 following merger of Trinity Evangelical Divinity School and Trinity College; Trinity Graduate School formed 1997; Trinity Law School (formerly Simon Greenleaf School of Law) joined 1998

Campuses in California, Illinois and Florida

Chancellor: KENNETH L. MEYER
Pres.: GREGORY L. WAYBRIGHT
Exec. Vice-Pres.: JEANETTE L. HSIEH
Sr Vice-Pres. for Academic Affairs: JAMES STAMOOLIS
Sr Vice-Pres. for Business and Finance: MIKE PICHA
Sr Vice-Pres. for Education: TITE TIÉNOU
Sr Vice-Pres. for Enrollment: ROGER L. KIEFFER
Sr Vice-Pres. for Information Technology: STEVE GEGGIE
Sr Vice-Pres. for Institutional Advancement: PAUL MAURER
Sr Vice-Pres. for Planning and Enrollment: ROGER L. KIEFFER
Sr Vice-Pres. for Student Affairs: WILLIAM O. WASHINGTON
Vice-Pres. for Communications and Marketing: GARY CANTWELL
Vice-Pres. for Institutional and Auxiliary Services: LYLE ERSTAD
Registrar: ROBERT M. BOSANAC
Univ. Librarian: ROBERT H. KRAPOHL

Library of 233,000 bound vols, 170,000 microform vols, 2,000 current periodicals; 2 major microform collns of English literature from 15th–17th centuries; items from collns of Dr Carl F. H. Hentry and Dr Wilbur Smith

Publication: *Trinity Journal* (2 a year).

CONSTITUENT COLLEGES

Trinity College

E-mail: tcadmissions@tiu.edu
Internet: www.tiu.edu/college

Depts of athletic training, biblical and religious studies, bioethics, business, education, history, human performance and wellness, interdisciplinary studies, language, literature and communication, music, philosophy, psychology and sociology, science

Dean: Dr JEANETTE L. HSIEH

DIRECTORS

School of Biblical and Religious Studies: Assoc. Prof. JAMES W. MOHLER
School of Human Performance and Wellbeing: Assoc. Prof. TIMOTHY J. VOSS
School of Humanities: Assoc. Prof. STEVEN D. FRATT
School of Language, Literature and Communications: Assoc. Prof. LOIS C. FLEMING
School of Science and Technology: Assoc. Prof. ANGELO G. RENTAS
School of Social Sciences: Prof. PAUL A. TWELKER

PROFESSORS

GRADDY, W. E., English
MOULDER, W. J., Biblical Studies
POINTER, S. R., History
SATRE, P. J., Music

Trinity Evangelical Divinity School

E-mail: tedsadm@tiu.edu
Internet: www.tiu.edu/divinity

Dean: TITE TIÉNOU
Theological Librarian: KEITH P. WELLS
Number of students: 1,800 (post-graduate)

PROFESSORS

AVERBECK, R. E., Old Testament and Semitic Languages
BEITZEL, B. J., Old Testament and Semitic Languages
CANNELL, L. M., Educational Ministries

CARSON, D. A., New Testament
COLE, G. A., Biblical and Systematic Theology
ELMER, D. H., Educational Ministries
FEINBERG, P. D., Biblical and Systematic Theology
HIEBERT, P. G., Mission and Anthropology
HOFFMEIER, J. K., Old Testament and Ancient Near Eastern History and Archaeology
KILNER, J. F., Bioethics and Contemporary Culture
NETLAND, H. A., Mission and Evangelism
NYQUIST, J. W., Mission and Evangelism
OSBORNE, G. R., New Testament
SENTER, M. H., Educational Ministries
VANGEMEREN, W. A., Old Testament and Semitic Languages
WOODBRIDGE, J. D., Church History and the History of Christian Thought
YOUNGER, K. L., Jr, Old Testament, Semitic Languages and Near Eastern History

Trinity Graduate School

E-mail: tgsadm@tiu.edu
Internet: www.tiu.edu/graduate
Dean: JOYCE A. SHELTON
Number of teachers: 46
Number of students: 163 (Deerfield, California and South Florida campuses)

PROFESSORS

KILNER, J. F., Bioethics and Contemporary Culture
TIÉNOU, T., Theology of Mission

Trinity Law School/Trinity California Campus

2200 North Grand Ave, Santa Ana, CA 92705
Telephone: (714) 796-7100
Fax: (714) 796-7190
Internet: www.tiu.edu/law
Dean: DONALD R. MCCONNELL
Law and Humanities Librarian (vacant)
Library: Law library, 50,000 vols incl. primary sources of federal and California law, also int. human rights colln of 3,000 vols and periodicals
Number of students: 158

ATTACHED INSTITUTE

Bannockburn Institute for Christianity and Contemporary Culture:

Constituent centres:

Center for Bioethics and Human Dignity: Dir Dr JOHN F. KILNER.

Center for Family Life: Dir Dr CHARLES SELL.

Center for Human Rights and Freedom: Dir WINSTON FROST.

Center for Theological Understanding: Dir Dr DOUG SWEENEY.

Center of the Foundations of the Law: Dir MYRON STEEVES.

UNIVERSITY OF CHICAGO

5801 South Ellis Ave, Chicago, IL 60637
Telephone: (773) 702-1234
Internet: www.uchicago.edu
Founded 1890
Academic year: September to June
Pres.: ROBERT J. ZIMMER
Provost: THOMAS F. ROSENBAUM
Vice-Pres. and Chief Investment Officer: MARK A. SCHMID
Vice-Pres. and Dean of College Admissions and Financial Aid: JAMES G. NONDORF
Vice-Pres. and Gen. Counsel: BETH A. HARRIS
Vice-Pres. and Sec. of the Univ.: DAVID B. FITHIAN
Vice-Pres. for Admin. and Chief Financial Office: NIM CHINNIAH
Vice-Pres. for Alumni Relations and Devt: THOMAS J. FARRELL
Vice-Pres. for Campus Life and Dean of Students in the Univ.: KIMBERLY GOFF-CREWS
Vice-Pres. for Civic Engagement: ANN MARIE LIPINSKI
Vice-Pres. for Communications: JULIE PETERSON
Vice-Pres. for Financial Planning for Science: LAWRENCE J. FURNSTAHL
Vice-Pres. for Medical Affairs and Dean of the Biological Sciences Division and the Pritzker School of Medicine: EVERETT E. VOKES
Vice-Pres. for Research and Nat. Laboratories: DONALD H. LEVY
Vice-Pres. for Strategic Initiatives: DAVID A. GREENE
Registrar: THOMAS BLACK
Dir of Libraries: JUDITH NADLER
Library: see Libraries
Number of teachers: 2,211
Number of students: 15,626
Publications: *American Art: Smithsonian American Art Museum* (3 a year), *American Journal of Education* (4 a year), *American Journal of Human Genetics* (12 a year), *American Journal of Sociology* (6 a year), *American Naturalist* (12 a year), *Astronomical Journal* (12 a year), *Astrophysical Journal* (36 a year and a monthly supplement), *Classical Philology* (4 a year), *Clinical Infectious Diseases* (24 a year), *Comparative Education Review* (4 a year), *Crime and Justice* (1 a year), *Critical Inquiry* (4 a year), *Current Anthropology* (5 a year), *Economic Development and Cultural Change* (4 a year), *Elementary School Journal* (5 a year), *Ethics: An International Journal of Social, Political, and Legal Philosophy* (4 a year), *History of Religions* (4 a year), *International Journal of American Linguistics* (4 a year), *International Journal of Plant Sciences* (6 a year), *Isis* (4 a year, plus *Current Bibliography* as 5th issue), *Journal of the American Musicological Society* (3 a year), *Journal of British Studies* (4 a year), *Journal of Business* (4 a year), *Journal of Consumer Research: An Interdisciplinary Quarterly*, *Journal of Geology* (6 a year), *Journal of Infectious Diseases* (24 a year), *Journal of Labor Economics* (4 a year), *Journal of Law & Economics* (2 a year), *Journal of Legal Studies* (2 a year), *Journal of Modern History* (4 a year), *Journal of Near Eastern Studies* (4 a year), *Journal of Political Economy* (6 a year), *Journal of Religion* (4 a year), *Law & Social Inquiry* (4 a year), *Library Quarterly*, *Modern Philology* (4 a year), *Ocean Yearbook* (1 a year), *Osiris* (1 a year), *Philosophy of Science* (5 a year), *Physiological and Biochemical Zoology* (6 a year), *Publications of the Astronomical Society of the Pacific* (12 a year), *Quarterly Review of Biology*, *Signs: Journal of Women in Culture and Society* (4 a year), *Social Service Review* (4 a year), *Supreme Court Economic Review* (1 a year), *Supreme Court Review* (1 a year), *Winterthur Portfolio: A Journal of American Material Culture* (3 a year)

DEANS

Biological Sciences Div. and the Pritzker School of Medicine: Dr EVERETT E. VOKES
Booth School of Business: (vacant)
Divinity School: MARGARET M. MITCHELL
Graham School of General Studies: DANIEL SHANNON
Humanities: MARTHA T. ROTH
Law School: MICHAEL H. SCHILL
Physical Sciences: ROBERT A. FEFFERMAN
Harris School of Public Policy: COLM O'MUIRCHEARTAIGH
Social Sciences: JOHN MARK HANSEN
School of Social Service Admin.: NEIL GUTERMAN
The College: JOHN W. BOYER

UNIVERSITY OF ILLINOIS

Urbana, IL 61801
Telephone: (217) 333-1000
Fax: (217) 333-5733
E-mail: uipres@uillinois.edu
Internet: www.uillinois.edu
Founded 1867 (chartered)
State control
Pres.: MICHAEL J. HOGAN
Vice-Pres. for Academic Affairs: MRINALINI CHATTA RAO
Vice-Pres. for Health Affairs.: JOE G. N. GARCIA
Vice-Pres. for Research: LAWRENCE B. SCHOOK
Chief Financial Officer and Vice-Pres.: WALTER K. KNORR
Library: see Libraries and Archives
Number of teachers: 5,654 (full-time)
Number of students: 76,886.

CONSTITUENT CAMPUSES

University of Illinois at Chicago

601 South Morgan St, Chicago, IL 60607-7128
Telephone: (312) 413-3350
Fax: (312) 413-3393
Internet: www.uic.edu
Founded 1894
Chancellor: SYLVIA MANNING
Provost and Vice-Chancellor for Academic Affairs: R. MICHAEL TANNER
Vice-Chancellor for Admin.: JOSEPH MUSCARELLA
Vice-Chancellor for Devt: PENELOPE HUNT
Vice-Chancellor for External Affairs: WARREN CHAPMAN
Vice-Chancellor for Human Resources: JOHN LOYA
Vice-Chancellor for Research: ERIC A. GISLASON
Vice-Chancellor for Student Affairs: BARBARA HENLEY
Univ. Librarian: MARY CASE (acting)
Library: 1.9m. vols
Number of teachers: 2,413
Number of students: 24,530

DEANS

College of Applied Health Sciences: CHARLOTTE (TOBY) TATE
College of Architecture and the Arts: JUDITH R. KIRSHNER
College of Business Admin.: STEFANIE LENWAY
College of Dentistry: BRUCE GRAHAM
College of Education: VICTORIA CHOU
College of Engineering: PRITH BANNERJEE
College of Liberal Arts and Sciences: CHRISTOPHER M. COMER (acting)
College of Medicine: JOSEPH A. FLAHERTY
College of Medicine at Peoria: RODNEY LORENZ (Regional Dean)
College of Medicine at Rockford: MARTIN LIPSKY (Regional Dean)
College of Medicine at Urbana-Champaign: BRADFORD S. SCHWARTZ (acting) (Regional Dean)
College of Nursing: JOAN SHAVER
College of Pharmacy: JERRY L. BAUMAN

College of Urban Planning and Public Affairs: ROBIN HAMBLETON
Graduate College: CLARK HULSE
Honors College: LON KAUFMAN
Jane Addams College of Social Work: CREASIE FINNEY HAIRSTON
School of Public Health: SYLVIA FURNER SUSAN C. M. SCRIMSHAW

University of Illinois at Springfield

1 University Plaza, Springfield, IL 62703
Telephone: (217) 206-6600
Internet: www.uis.edu
Chancellor: RICHARD RINGEISEN
Provost and Vice-Chancellor for Academic Affairs: HARRY J. BERMAN
Vice-Chancellor for Student Affairs: L. CHRISTOPHER MILLER
Librarian: JANE TREADWELL
Number of students: 4,500

DEANS

College of Business and Management: RONALD MCNEIL
College of Education and Human Services: Dr LARRY STONECIPHER
College of Liberal Arts and Sciences: MARGOT I. DULY
College of Public Affairs and Admin.: (vacant)

University of Illinois at Urbana-Champaign

901 W Illinois St, Urbana, IL 61801
Telephone: (217) 333-1000
E-mail: admissions@illinois.edu
Internet: www.uiuc.edu
More than 80 centres, laboratories, and institutes on the Urbana-Champaign campus that perform research for govt agencies and industry
Chancellor and Provost: ROBERT EASTER
Vice-Chancellor for Academic Affairs and Vice-Provost: RICHARD WHEELER
Vice-Chancellor for Institutional Advancement: JAMES SCHROEDER
Vice-Chancellor for Public Engagement: STEVEN SONKA
Vice-Chancellor for Research: RAVISHANKAR (RAVI) IYER
Vice-Chancellor for Student Affairs: RENEE C. ROMANO
Number of teachers: 3,078
Number of students: 41,918

DEANS

College of Agricultural, Consumer and Environmental Sciences: ROBERT J. HAUSER
College of Applied Health Sciences: TANYA M. GALLAGHER
College of Business: LARRY DEBROCK
College of Communications: RON YATES
College of Education: MARY KALANTZIS
College of Engineering: ILESANMI ADESIDA
College of Fine and Applied Arts: ROBERT B. GRAVES
College of Law: BRUCE P. SMITH
College of Liberal Arts and Sciences: RUTH V. WATKINS
College of Media: JAN SLATER
College of Medicine at Urbana-Champaign: BRADFORD S. SCHWARTZ
College of Veterinary Medicine: HERB WHITELEY
Graduate College: DEBASISH (DEBA) DUTTA
Graduate School of Library and Information Science: JOHN UNSWORTH
Institute of Aviation: TOM W. EMANUEL (Dir)
School of Labor and Industrial Relations: JOEL CUTCHER-GERSHENFELD
School of Social Work: WYNNE KORR

PROFESSORS

College of Agricultural, Consumer and Environmental Sciences:
AHERIN, R. A., Farm Safety
ANSELIN, L. E., Econometrics, Regional Economics
BAHR, J. M., Reproductive Physiology
BAIANU, I. C., Food Chemistry
BANWART, W. L., Soil Chemistry
BARRICK, R. K., Human and Community Devt
BARRY, P. J., Agricultural Finance
BELLER, A. H., Family Economics
BELOW, F. E., Plant Physiology
BERENBAUM, M. R., Insect Ecology
BERGER, L. L., Ruminant Nutrition
BLASCHEK, H. P., Food Microbiology
BOAST, C. W., Soil Physics
BODE, L. E., Power and Machinery
BOHNERT, H. J., Molecular Biology and Genomics of Plant Stress
BRADEN, J. B., Natural Resource and Environmental Economics
BREWER, M. S., Food Science
BRISKIN, D. P., Plant Physiology, Plant Biochemistry
BULLOCK, D. G., Crop Production and Biometry
BURIAK, P., Technical Systems Management
CAMPION, D. R., Animal Growth and Devt
CARR, T. R., Meat Science
CHASSY, B. M., Food Microbiology and Biotechnology
CHERYAN, M., Processing, Food and Biochemical Engineering
CHICOINE, D. L., State and Local Govt Finance
CHOW, P., Wood Science
CHRISTIANSON, L. L., Structures and Environment
CLARK, J. H., Ruminant Nutrition
COOKE, P. S., Veterinary Biosciences, Morphology
D'ARCY, C. J., Virology
DARMODY, R. G., Pedology
DAVID, M. B., Biogeochemistry
DAWSON, J. O., Tree Physiology
DIAMOND, A. M., Human Nutrition
DOCAMPO, R., Microbiology and Immunology
DONG, F. M., Food Science and Human Nutrition
DONOVAN, S. M., Nutrition
DRACKLEY, J. K., Nutrition
DUDLEY, J. W., Plant Genetics
EASTER, R. A., Animal Nutrition
ECKHOFF, S. R., Food and Bioprocess Engineering
ELLIS, M., Swine Nutrition
ENDRESS, A. G., Environmental Stress Physiology
ERDMAN, J. W., Nutrition
FAHEY, G. C., Animal Sciences, Nutritional Biochemistry
FARRAND, S. K., Molecular Biology
FAULKNER, D. B., Beef Extension
GARCIA, P., Agricultural Marketing and Price Analysis
GASKINS, H. R., Animal Sciences
GERTNER, G. Z., Forest Biometrics
GOOD, D. L., Agricultural Marketing
GRAY, M. E., Integrated Pest Management and Extension
GROSSMAN, M., Genetics
GROSSMAN, M. R., Agricultural Law
HANSEN, L. G., Pharmacology and Toxicology
HARPER, J. G., Agricultural Education
HAUSER, R. J., Agricultural Marketing and Price Analysis
HEICHEL, G. H., Plant Physiology
HELFERICH, W. G., Nutrition, Food Toxicology
HESS, R. A., Morphology/Toxicology
HIRSCHI, M. C., Soil and Water Extension
HOEFT, R. G., Soil Fertility and Extension
HOLLIS, G. R., Swine Extension
HURLEY, W. L., Lactation
HUTJENS, M. F., Dairy Extension
HYMOWITZ, T., Plant Genetics and Genetic Engineering
IRWIN, M. E., Int. Entomology
IRWIN, S. H., Agricultural Marketing and Price Analysis
ISSERMAN, A. M., Rural Economic Devt
JEFFERY, E. H., Toxicology, Food Science and Human Nutrition, Veterinary Biosciences
JONES, R. L., Soil Mineralogy and Ecology
JUVIK, J. A., Plant Genetics
KALITA, P. K., Soil and Water Association
KELLEY, K. W., Animal Sciences
KESLER, D. J., Reproductive Physiology
KOLB, F. L., Small Grain Breeding and Genetics
KORBAN, S. S., Plant Genetics
KRAMER, L. F., Applied Family Studies
KUHLENSCHMIDT, M. S., Microbiology
LARSON, R. A., Environmental Chemistry
LARSON, R. W., Family Ecology
LAYMAN, D. K., Nutrition
LEWIN, H. A., Biotechnology
LILA, M. A., Plant Physiology
LINS, D. A., Finance
LITCHFIELD, J. B., Food and Bioprocess Engineering
LONG, S. P., Photosynthesis and Environmental Sciences
MCKEITH, F. K., Meat Science
MACKIE, R. I., Animal Sciences, Microbiology
MARTIN, S. E., Food Microbiology
MERCHEN, N. R., Animal Sciences, Ruminant Nutrition
MILLER, G. Y., Veterinary Pathobiology
MORGANOSKY, M. A., Consumer and Retail Marketing
MORRIS, S. A., Processing Association
MULVANEY, R. L., Soil Fertility, Soil Chemistry, Soil Microbiology
MURPHY, M. R., Animal Sciences, Ruminant Nutrition
NAFZIGER, E. D., Crop Production and Extension
NELSON, R. L., Plant Genetics
NIBLACK, T. L., Cyst Nematode Management and Extension
NOEL, G. R., Nematology
NOVAKOFSKI, J. E., Animal Sciences, Meat Science
O'BRIEN, W. D., Electrical and Computer Engineering
OLSON, K. R., Soil Conservation, Soil Management, Pedology
ORT, D. R., Plant Physiology
PARRETT, D. F., Meat Animal Evaluation
PARSONS, C. M., Poultry Nutrition and Management
PATAKY, J. K., Epidemiology
PAUL, A. J., Small Animal Extension and Medicine
PAULSEN, M. R., Food and Bioprocess Engineering
PECK, T. R., Soil Chemistry and Extension
PERLMAN, A. L., Speech and Hearing
PERSHING, R. L., Power and Machinery
PETTIGREW, J. E., Animal Sciences, Swine Nutrition
PLECK, E. H., Human and Community Devt, History
PLECK, J. H., Human Devt and Family Studies
PLEWA, M. J., Plant Genetics/Environmental Mutagens
PORTIS, A. R., Plant Biochemistry
PUEPPKE, S. G., Plant Pathology
RAHEEL, M., Textiles and Clothing
REBEIZ, C. A., Plant Biochemistry and Plant Physiology

ROLFE, G. L., Forest Ecology and Environmental Studies
SALAMON, S. B., Community Studies, Family Studies
SCHMIDT, S. J., Food Chemistry
SCHOOK, L. B., Comparative Genomics
SHANKS, R. D., Genetics
SHAPIRO, C. H., Human and Community Devt
SINGLETARY, K. W., Nutrition
SKIRVIN, R. M., Horticulture
SMITH, R. D., Epidemiology and Preventive Medicine
SOFRANKO, A. J., Rural Sociology
SONKA, S. T., Agricultural Management
SPOMER, L. A., Plant Physiology
STEFFEY, K. L., Forage and Field Crop Insects and Extension
STUCKI, J. W., Soil Chemistry
SWANSON, B. E., Int. Agricultural Education, Int. Extension Technology Transfer
TIAN, L., Power and Machinery Association
TRUPIN, S. R., Obstetrics and Gynaecology
UCHTMANN, D. L., Agricultural Law
UNNEVEHR, L. J., Agricultural Marketing and Policy
VAN ES, J. C., Rural Sociology
VODKIN, L. O., Soybean Genetics and Genetic Engineering
WALLIG, M. A., Veterinary Pathobiology
WANSINK, B. C., Marketing and Agricultural Economics
WAX, L. M., Plant Physiology and Weed Science
WEATHERHEAD, P. J., Behavioural Ecology
WEIGEL, R. M., Epidemiology and Preventive Medicine
WEINZIERL, R. A., Fruit, Vegetable, and Livestock Insects
WHEELER, M. B., Reproductive Physiology
WHITE, B. A., Microbiology
WHITE, D. G., Fungal Diseases of Corn
WIDHOLM, J. M., Plant Physiology and Genetic Engineering
WILKINSON, H. T., Turfgrass Diseases
WILLIAMS, D. J., Horticulture
ZHANG, Q., Power and Machinery Association

College of Applied Health Studies:
BOILEAU, R. A., Kinesiology
CHAMBERS, R. D., Speech and Hearing Science
CHODZKO-ZAJKO, W., Kinesiology
FESENMAIER, D. R., Leisure Studies
GALLAGHER, T. M., Speech and Hearing Science
GOOLER, D. M., Speech and Hearing Science
HENGST, J., Speech and Hearing Science
IWAMOTO, G., Kinesiology
JOHNSON, C. J., Speech and Hearing Science
KUEHN, D. P., Speech and Hearing Science
LANSING, C. R., Speech and Hearing Science
MCAULEY, E., Kinesiology
O'ROURKE, T., Community Health
PERLMAN, A. L., Speech and Hearing Science
PROCTOR, F. A., Speech and Hearing Science
REIS, J., Community Health
SCHIRO-GEIST, C., Community Health
WATKIN, K. L., Speech and Hearing Science
WATKINS, R. V., Speech and Hearing Science
YAIRI, E., Speech and Hearing Science

College of Business:
ABDEL-KHALIK, A. R., Accountancy
ALSTON, L. J., Economics
ARNOULD, R. J., Economics
BAER, W., Economics
BECK, P. J., Accountancy
BERA, A. K., Economics
BERNHARDT, D., Economics
BLAIR, C., Management Science/Process Management
BLAIR, C. E., Business Admin.
BROWN, C. E., Accountancy
BRUECKNER, J. K., Economics
CHAN, L. K. C., Finance
CHENG, J. L., Business Admin., Int. Business
CHHAJED, D., Business Admin., Program Management Science/Process Management
CHO, I. K., Economics
COLWELL, P. F., Finance and Real Estate Research
CONLEY, J. P., Economics
D'ARCY, S. P., Finance
DEBROCK, L., Economics
ENGELBRECHT-WIGGANS, R., Business Admin., Management Science/Process Management
FINNERTY, J. E., Finance
GAHVARI, F., Economics
GENTRY, J. A., Finance
GIERTZ, J. F., Economics
GOTTHEIL, F. M., Economics
GRIFFIN, A., Business Admin., Marketing
GRINOLS, E. L., Economics
HALPERIN, R. M., Accountancy
HESS, J. D., Business Admin.
IKENBERRY, D., Finance
JEGADEESH, N., Finance
KAHN, C. M., Finance and Economics
KANNAN, S., Finance
KINDT, J., Business Law
KLEINMUNTZ, D. N., Business Admin., Strategic Management
KOENKER, R., Economics
KRASA, S., Economics
KWON, Y. K., Accountancy
LAKONISHOK, J., Finance
LANSING, P., Business Admin., Business Law
LEBLEBICI, H., Business Admin., Organizational Behaviour
LINS, D. A., Finance, Agricultural and Consumer Economics
LYNGE, M. J., Jr, Finance
MONAHAN, G. E., Business Admin., Management Science/Process Management
MONROE, K. B., Marketing
NEAL, L. D., Economics
NEUMANN, F. L., Accountancy Executive Leadership
NORTHCRAFT, G., Organizational Behaviour
OLDHAM, G., Organizational Behaviour
PEARSON, N. D., Finance
PENNACCHI, G. G., Finance
QUALLS, W. J., Business Admin., Marketing
RASHID, S., Economics
RESEK, R. W., Economics
ROSZKOWSKI, M. E., Business Admin., Business Law
SETH, A., Business Admin., Strategic Management
SHAFER, W. J., Economics
SHAVITT, S., Business Admin., Marketing
SHAW, M. J., Commerce and Business Admin., Marketing
SOLOMON, I., Accountancy
SUDHARSHAN, D., Business Admin., Marketing
TAUB, B., Economics
VILLAMIL, A. P., Economics
WANSINK, B., Marketing
WEISBACH, M. S., Finance
WILLIAMS, S. R., Economics
WON, Y., Accountancy
YANNELIS, N. C., Economics
ZIEBART, D. A., Accountancy

College of Communications:
BREWER, W. F., Psychology
CHRISTIANS, C., Communications
DASH, L., Journalism
DAVIS, S., Folklore and Folklife
DELIA, J. G., Communication and Human Relations
DENZIN, N., Sociology
DESSER, D., Cinema Studies, Speech Communication
GAINES, W., Journalism
HARRINGTON, W., Journalism
HELLE, S., Advertising and Journalism
LIEBOVICH, L. W., Mass Communications
MCCARTHY, C., Education, Curriculum Theory
MCCHESNEY, R. W., Library and Information Science
MERRITT, R. L., Int. Relations, Political Science
NERONE, J., Media Studies
O'GUINN, T., Advertising and Business Admin.
PRESS, A., Media Studies, Speech Communication
RICH, R., Law, Political Science
ROTZOLL, K., Advertising
SCHILLER, D., Communication, Library and Information Science
SRULL, T., Advertising
TREICHLER, P. A., Linguistics, Criticism and Interpretive Theory
WILLIAMS, B., Political Science
YATES, R., Journalism

College of Education:
ALEXANDER, K.
ANDERSON, R.
ANDERSON, T.
ARMBRUSTER, B.
BAROODY, A.
BARRERA, R.
BRAGG, D.
BRESLER, L.
BURBULES, N.
CHADSEY, J.
CLIFT, R.
CORDOVA-WENTLING, R. M.
CZIKO, G.
FEINBERG, W.
GARCIA, G.
GREENE, J.
HALLE, J.
HARRIS, V.
HUNTER, R.
IKENBERRY, S. R.
JOHNSON, S.
LEVIN, J.
LOEB, J.
MCCLURE, E.
MCCOLLUM, J.
MCCONKIE, G.
MIRON, L.
PERRY, M.
RENZAGLIA, A.
RIZVI, F.
ROUNDS, J.
RUSCH, F.
SCHWANDT, T.
STAHL, S.
TRAVERS, K.
TRENT, W.
WARD, J.
WESTBURY, I.
WILLIS, A.

College of Engineering:
ABELSON, J. R., Materials Science and Engineering
ADRIAN, R. J., Mechanical and Industrial Engineering, Theoretical and Applied Mechanics
AGHA, G., Computer Science
AHERIN, R., Agricultural Engineering
AHUJA, N., Engineering
ALKIRE, R. C., Chemical and Biomolecular Engineering
AREF, H., Physics, Theoretical and Applied Mechanics
AVERBACK, R. S., Materials Science and Engineering

AXFORD, R., Nuclear, Plasma and Radiological Engineering
BALACHANDAR, S. B., Theoretical and Applied Mechanics
BASAR, T., Electrical and Computer Engineering
BAYM, G. A., Physics
BECK, D. H., Physics
BERGMAN, L. A., Aeronautical and Astronautical Engineering
BLAHUT, R., Electrical and Computer Engineering
BRAATZ, R. D., Chemical and Biomolecular Engineering
BRAGG, M. B., Aeronautical and Astronautical Engineering
BREWSTER, M. Q., Mechanical and Industrial Engineering
BUCKIUS, R. O., Mechanical and Industrial Engineering
BUCKMASTER, J. D., Aeronautical and Astronautical Engineering, Theoretical and Applied Mechanics
BULLARD, C. W., Mechanical and Industrial Engineering
BURIAK, P., Agricultural Engineering
BURTON, R. L., Aeronautical and Astronautical Engineering
CAHILL, D. G., Materials Science and Engineering
CAMPBELL, E., Computer Science
CARLSON, D. E., Theoretical and Applied Mechanics
CEPERLEY, D. M., Physics
CHANG, Y.-C., Physics
CHEW, W., Engineering
CHIANG, T.-C., Physics
CHRISTIANSON, L., Agricultural Engineering
CLEGG, R. M., Physics
COLEMAN, J., Electrical and Computer Engineering
CONRY, T. F., General Engineering
CONWAY, B. A., Aeronautical and Astronautical Engineering
COOK, H. E., Gen. Engineering
COOPER, S. L., Physics
CRAIG, J., Mechanical and Industrial Engineering
DANTZIG, J. A., Mechanical and Industrial Engineering
DAVIS, W. J., Gen. Engineering
DEBEVEC, P. T., Physics
DEJONG, G., Computer Science
DEVOR, R. E., Mechanical and Industrial Engineering
ECKHOFF, S., Agricultural Engineering
ECKSTEIN, J. N., Physics
ECONOMY, J., Materials Science and Engineering
EHRLICH, G., Materials Science and Engineering
ERREDE, S. M., Physics
FENG, M., Electrical and Computer Engineering
FERREIRA, P. M., Mechanical and Industrial Engineering
FLYNN, C. P., Physics
FRADKIN, E. H., Physics
GEIL, P. H., Materials Science and Engineering
GEORGIADIS, J. G., Mechanical and Industrial Engineering
GLADDING, G. E., Physics
GOLDBART, P. M., Physics, Gen. Engineering
GOLDENFELD, N. D., Physics
GOLLIN, G. D., Physics
GRANICK, S., Chemical and Biomolecular Engineering, Materials Science and Engineering, Physics
GRATTON, E., Physics
GREENE, J. E., Materials Science and Engineering, Physics
GREENE, L. H., Physics
GRUEBELE, M. H., Physics
HABER, R. B., Theoretical and Applied Mechanics
HAJEK, B., Engineering
HAN, J., Computer Science
HEATH, M. T., Computer Science
HERTZOG, D. W., Physics
HESS, K., Physics
HIGDON, J. J. L., Chemical and Biomolecular Engineering
HIRSCHI, M., Agricultural Engineering
HODDESON, L., Physics
HOLONYAK, N., Physics
HRNJAK, P. S., Mechanical and Industrial Engineering
HUANG, T., Electrical Engineering
HUANG, Y. Y., Mechanical and Industrial Engineering, Theoretical and Applied Mechanics
HWU, W.-M., Electrical and Computer Engineering
IYER, R., Engineering
JACOBI, A. M., Mechanical and Industrial Engineering
JACOBSON, S. H., Mechanical and Industrial Engineering
JAMISON, R. D., Materials Science and Engineering
JONES, B. G., Nuclear, Plasma and Radiological Engineering, Mechanical and Industrial Engineering
KALE, L., Computer Science
KAPOOR, S. G., Mechanical and Industrial Engineering
KATZ, S., Physics
KERKHOVEN, T., Computer Science
KIM, K., Nuclear, Plasma and Radiological Engineering
KLEIN, M. V., Physics
KOGUT, J. B., Physics
KRIER, H., Mechanical and Industrial Engineering
KRIVEN, W. M., Materials Science and Engineering
KUMAR, P., Electrical and Computer Engineering
KUSHNER, M., Engineering
KUSHNER, M. J., Physics
KUSHNER, M. K., Chemical and Biomolecular Engineering
KWIAT, P. G., Physics
LAMB, F. K., Physics
LAWRENCE, F. V., Jr, Materials Science and Engineering
LECKBAND, D. E., Chemical and Biomolecular Engineering
LEE, K. D., Aeronautical and Astronautical Engineering
LEGGETT, A. J., Physics
LISS, TONY M., Physics
LOTH, E., Aeronautical and Astronautical Engineering
MAKRI, N., Physics
MARTIN, R. M., Physics
MASEL, R. I., Chemical and Biomolecular Engineering
MEDANIC, J. V., Gen. Engineering
MESEGUER, J., Computer Science
MILEY, G. H., Nuclear, Plasma and Radiological Engineering
MOSER, R. D., Theoretical and Applied Mechanics
MOUSCHOVIAS, T. C., Physics
MUNSON, D., Jr, Electrical and Computer Engineering
NAHRSTEDT, K., Computer Science
NAMACHCHIVAYA, N. S., Aeronautical and Astronautical Engineering
NAYFEH, M. H., Physics
NEWELL, T. A., Mechanical and Industrial Engineering
OONO, Y., Physics
PADUA, D., Computer Science
PANDHARIPANDE, V. R., Physics
PATEL, J., Engineering
PAULSEN, M., Agricultural Engineering
PAYNE, D. A., Materials Science and Engineering
PEARLSTEIN, A. J., Mechanical and Industrial Engineering, Theoretical and Applied Mechanics
PENG, J.-C., Physics
PHILLIPS, J. W., Theoretical and Applied Mechanics
PHILLIPS, P. W., Physics
PHILLIPS, W. R. C., Theoretical and Applied Mechanics
PINES, D., Physics
PITT, L., Computer Science
PONCE, J., Computer Science
PRICE, R. L., Gen. Engineering
PRUSSING, J. E., Aeronautical and Astronautical Engineering
REED, D., Computer Science
REIS, H. L. M., Gen. Engineering
RIAHI, D. N., Theoretical and Applied Mechanics
ROBERTSON, I. M., Materials Science and Engineering
ROBINSON, I. K., Physics
ROCKETT, A., Materials Science and Engineering
ROGERS, J. A., Materials Science and Engineering
RUZIĆ, D. N., Nuclear, Plasma and Radiological Engineering
SALAMON, M. B., Physics
SCHULTEN, K. J., Physics
SCHWEIZER, K. S., Chemical and Biomolecular Engineering, Materials Science and Engineering
SEEBAUER, E. G., Chemical and Biomolecular Engineering
SEHITOGLU, H., Mechanical and Industrial Engineering
SELEN, M. A., Physics
SENTMAN, L. H., Aeronautical and Astronautical Engineering
SHA, L., Computer Science
SHAPIRO, S. L., Physics
SINGER, C., Nuclear, Plasma and Radiological Engineering
SKEEL, R. D., Computer Science
SLICHTER, C. P., Physics
SNIR, M., Computer Science
SOCIE, D. F., Mechanical and Industrial Engineering
SOTTOS, N. R., Theoretical and Applied Mechanics
SPONG, M. W., Gen. Engineering
STACK, J. D., Physics
STEWART, D. S., Theoretical and Applied Mechanics
STONE, M., Physics
STUBBINS, J. F., Nuclear, Plasma and Radiological Engineering
SULLIVAN, J. D., Physics
THALER, J. J., Physics
THOMAS, B. G., Mechanical and Industrial Engineering
THURSTON, D. L., Gen. Engineering
TORRELLAS, J., Computer Science
TORTORELLI, D. A., Mechanical and Industrial Engineering, Theoretical and Applied Mechanics
TUCKER, C. L., III, Mechanical and Industrial Engineering
VAN HARLINGEN, D. J., Physics
VANKA, S. P., Mechanical and Industrial Engineering
WAH, B., Electrical and Computer Engineering
WALKER, J. S., Mechanical and Industrial Engineering
WATSON, W. D., Physics
WEAVER, J. H., Materials Science and Engineering, Physics
WEAVER, R. L., Theoretical and Applied Mechanics
WEISSMAN, M. B., Physics
WHITE, S. R., Aeronautical and Astronautical Engineering

WILTZIUS, P., Materials Science and Engineering, Physics
WISS, J. E., Physics
WOLFE, J. P., Physics
ZUKOSKI, C. F., Chemical and Biomolecular Engineering

College of Fine and Applied Arts:
ALBRECHT, J. G., Architecture
ALEXANDER, R., Music
ALI, M. M., Architecture
ANDERSON, J. R., Architecture
ANTHONY, K. H., Architecture
ARENDS, M., Industrial Design
BASKINGER, M., Graphic Design
BELLAFIORE, V., Landscape Architecture
BOGNAR, B., Architecture
BULLOCK, W., Industrial Design
CAMERON, M., Music
CARLSON, W., Glass
CONLIN, K. F., Theatre
DALHEIM, E., Music
DI VIRGILIO, N., Music
DRY, C., Architecture
EWALD, M., Music
FINEBERG, J., Art History
FORREST, C. W., Urban and Regional Planning
GARNER, J. S., Architecture
GOGGIN, N., Narrative Media
GRAVES, R., Theatre
GRUCZA, L., Painting
HARKNESS, T., Landscape Architecture
HARRIS, J. B., Theatre
HEDEMAN, A. D., Art History
HEDLUND, R., Music
HEILES, W., Music
HILL, J. W., Music
HOBSON, I., Music
HOPKINS, L., Landscape Architecture
HOPKINS, L. D., Urban and Regional Planning
HOSTETTER, E., Art History
ISSERMAN, A., Urban and Regional Planning
JAKLE, J., Landscape Architecture
KEENE, J. F., Music
KENDRICK, B., Painting
KEYS, H., Theatre
KIM, M. K., Architecture
KIM, T. J., Urban and Regional Planning
KINDERMAN, W., Music
KNAAP, G. J., Urban and Regional Planning
KOVATCH, R., Ceramics
KRAMER, K., Music
MCFARQUHAR, R., Theatre
MACHALA, K., Music
MARTENS, C., Foundation
METTEM, A., Foundation
NETTLES, B., Photography
OUSTERHOUT, R. G., Architecture
PERKINS, K. A., Theatre
PLUMMER, H. S., Architecture
RICHTMEYER, D., Music
ROMM, R., Music
ROWAN, D., Printmaking
SCHAFFER, P., Music
SCHWARTZ, R., Painting
SIENA, J., Music
SILVER, C., Urban and Regional Planning
SOCHA, D., Printmaking
SQUIERM, J., Narrative Media
STOLTZFUS, F., Music
STONE, S., Music
SULLIVAN, D., Theatre
THEIDE, B. J., Metals
TIPEI, S., Music
TURINO, T., Music
VAN LAARM, T., Painting
WADLEIGH, R., Dance
WARD, T. R., Music
WARFIELD, J. P., Architecture
WESCOAT, J. L., Landscape Architecture
WILLIAMS, B., Urban and Regional Planning
WYATT, S. A., Music

College of Law:
BALL, C. A.
BELL, G.
BOYLE, F. A.
COLOMBO, J. D.
DAVEY, W. J.
FINKIN, M. W.
FREYFOGLE, E. T.
GEERDES, C. E.
HARRIS, O. F., Jr
HURD, H. M.
KAPLAN, R. L.
KINPORTS, K.
LEIPOLD, A. D.
MCADAMS, R. H.
MAGGS, P. B.
MEYER, D. D.
PAINTER, R. W.
PFANDER, J. E.
REYNOLDS, L. A.
RIBSTEIN, L. E.
RICH, R. F.
ROSS, S. F.
SHOBEN, E. W.
TABB, C. J.
TARR, N. W.
TERRY, C. T.
ULEN, T. S.

College of Liberal Arts and Sciences:
ACCAD, E., French
ADELMAN, G., English
ALEXANDER, S., Mathematics
ALKIRE, R. C., Chemical and Biomolecular Engineering
ANGIONE, R. J., Astronomy
AUGSPURGER, C., Animal Biology, Plant Biology
BAILLARGEON, R., Psychology
BARON, D., English
BASS, J. D., Geology
BASSETT, T. J., Geography
BATZLI, G. O., Animal Biology
BAYM, G. A., Physics
BAYM, N., English
BEAK, P., Chemistry
BEARD, K., Atmospheric Sciences
BELFORD, R. L., Chemistry
BELMONT, A. S., Cell and Structural Biology, Biophysics
BERENBAUM, M. R., Entomology
BERNDT, B. C., Mathematics
BEST, P. M., Molecular and Integrative Physiology, Biophysics, Neuroscience and Bioengineering
BETHKE, C. M., Geology
BLAKE, D. B., Geology
BLAKE, N., Comparative Literature, Slavic Languages and Literature
BOCK, J. K., Psychology
BOHN, P. W., Chemistry
BOHNERT, H., Plant Biology and Crop Sciences
BOURGAIN, J., Mathematics
BRAATZ, R. D., Chemical and Biomolecular Engineering
BRECHIN, S., Sociology
BREWER, D. J., Anthropology
BREWER, W. F., Psychology
BRISKIN, D., Natural Resources and Environmental Sciences, Plant Biology
BRISTOL, E., Slavic Languages and Literature
BROWNE, G. M., Classics
BUDESCU, D., Psychology
BUSH, D. R., Plant Biology
CALDER, W. M., III, Classics
CAPWELL, C., Music
CARMEN, I. H., Political Science
CARRINGER, R. L., Cinema Studies, English
CASSELL, A. K., Italian and Comparative Literature
CHAI, L., English
CHEESEMAN, J., Plant Biology
CHEN, W.-P., Geology
CHENG, C.-C., East Asian Languages and Culture
CHU, Y.-H., Astronomy
CLARK, R. A., Speech Communication
CLEGG, R. M., Physics and Biophysics
COATES, R. M., Chemistry
COHEN, N. J., Psychology
CONLEY, T. M., Speech Communication
CONTRACTOR, N., Speech Communication
CROFTS, A. R., Biochemistry
CRONAN, J. E., Microbiology, Biochemistry
DADE, E. C., Mathematics
D'ANGELO, J. P., Mathematics
DELCOMYN, F., Entomology
DELEY, H., French
DELIA, J. G., Speech Communication
DELL, G. S., Psychology
DELUCIA, E., Plant Biology
DENMARK, S. E., Chemistry
DENZIN, N., Cinema Studies
DESSER, D., Cinema Studies
DEVRIES, A. L., Animal Biology
DIENER, E. F., Psychology
DLOTT, D. D., Chemistry
DRASGOW, F., Psychology
DUTTA, S., Mathematics
FAGYAL, Z., French
FENG, A. S., Molecular and Integrative Physiology, Biophysics, Bioengineering, and Neuroscience
FITZGERALD, L., Psychology
FOSSUM, R. M., Mathematics
FRANCIS, G. K., Mathematics
FRAZZETTA, T. H., Animal Biology
FRIEDMAN, P., English
FRITZSCHE, P., History
FÜREDI, Z., Mathematics
GABRIEL, M., Psychology
GARBER, P. A., Anthropology
GARCIA, P., Agricultural Economics
GARRETT, P., English
GENNIS, R. B., Biochemistry, Chemistry, Biophysics
GERLACH, U. H., Germanic Languages and Literature
GERLT, J. A., Biochemistry, Chemistry and Biophysics, Basic Medical Science
GEWIRTH, A. A., Chemistry
GIROLAMI, G. S., Chemistry
GLASER, M., Biochemistry, Basic Medical Sciences
GOLATO, P., French
GOLD, P. E., Psychology
GOODMAN, D. G., East Asian Languages and Culture
GOTTLIEB, A., Anthropology
GRAHAM, P., English
GRANICK, S., Chemical and Biomolecular Engineering
GRAY, M. E., Entomology
GRAYSON, D. R., Mathematics
GREENOUGH, W. T., Psychology
GROVE, D., Anthropology
GRUEBELE, M., Chemistry
GUIBBOR, A., English
GUMPORT, R. I., Biochemistry, Basic Medical Sciences
HABOUSH, W., Mathematics
HADLEY, A. O., French
HANNON, B. M., Geography
HAWISHER, G. E., English
HE, X., Statistics
HELLER, W., Psychology
HELMAN, S. I., Molecular and Integrative Physiology, Biophysics, and Bioengineering
HENSON, C. W., Mathematics
HEWINGS, G. J. D., Geography
HIGDON, J. J. L., Chemical and Biomolecular Engineering
HILDEBRAND, A. J., Mathematics
HINKKANEN, A., Mathematics
HITCHINS, K., History
HOCK, H. H., Linguistics
HSUI, A. T., Geology

HUALDE, J. I., Linguistics and Spanish, Italian, and Portuguese
HUBERT, L., Psychology
IBEN, I., Jr, Physics
IMREY, P., Statistics
IRWIN, D., Psychology
IRWIN, M. E., Entomology
IVANOV, S. V., Mathematics
JACOBSON, H., Classics
JAEGER, C. S., Cinema Studies
JAEGER, S., Comparative Literature
JAHER, F. C., Cinema Studies
JAHIEL, E., Cinema Studies, French
JAKLE, J. A., Geography
JAKOBSSON, E., Molecular and Integrative Physiology, Biochemistry, Biophysics, Bioengineering, and Neuroscience
JOCKUSCH, C. G., Mathematics
JOHNSON, D. L., Geography
JURASKA, J., Psychology
KALINKE, M. E., Germanic Languages and Literature
KATZ, S., Mathematics
KATZENELLENBOGEN, B. S., Molecular and Integrative Physiology
KATZENELLENBOGEN, J. A., Chemistry
KELLER, J. D., Anthropology
KELLY, B., English
KEMPER, B. W., Molecular and Integrative Physiology, Cell and Structural Biology
KIBBEE, D., French
KIM, C. W., Linguistics, East Asian Languages and Culture
KIRKPATRICK, R. J., Geology
KLEMPERER, W. G., Chemistry
KLEPINGER, L. L., Anthropology
KLUEGEL, J., Sociology
KNOTT, J. H., Political Science
KOENKER, D. P., History
KOSTOCHKA, A. V., Mathematics
KRAMER, A., Psychology
KRANZ, D. M., Biochemistry
KUKLINSKI, J. H., Political Science
LAMB, F. K., Physics
LAUGHLIN, P. R., Psychology
LAUTERBUR, P. C., Chemistry
LECKBAND, D. E., Chemistry, Chemical and Biomolecular Engineering
LEHMAN, F. K., Anthropology
LEWIS, R. B., Anthropology
LIEBERMAN, L., English
LISY, J. M., Chemistry
LOEB, P. A., Mathematics
LOTZ, H. P., Mathematics
LOVE, J. L., History
MCCARTHY, T., Philosophy
MCDONALD, J. D., Chemistry
MCDONALD, R., Psychology
MCKIM, R., Religious Studies, Philosophy
MCLAFFERTY, S., Geography
MCLINDEN, L., Mathematics
MCMAHAN, J., Philosophy
MAHER, P., Philosophy
MAK, M., Atmospheric Sciences
MAKRI, N., Chemistry
MALL, L., French
MALPELI, J. G., Psychology
MANGELSDORF, S., Psychology
MARDEN, J., Statistics
MARSHAK, S., Geology
MARTINSEK, A., Statistics
MASEL, R. I., Chemical and Biomolecular Engineering
MATHY, J.-P., French, Comparative Literature
MICHELSON, B., English
MILES, J. B., Mathematics
MILLER, G., Psychology
MILLER, P., Psychology
MILLER, P. J., Speech Communication
MOHR, R., Philosophy
MOORE, J. S., Chemistry
MORGAN, J. L., Linguistics
MORRISSEY, J. H., Biochemistry
MORTIMER, A., French
MOUSCHOVIAS, T., Physics and Astrophysics
MURAV, H., Slavic Languages and Literature, Comparative Literature
MUSUMECCI, A., Italian
NARDULLI, P. F., Political Science
NEDERVEEN-PIETERSE, J., Sociology
NEELY, C., English
NIKOLAEV, I., Mathematics
NUZZO, R., Chemistry
O'KEEFE, D. J., Speech Communication
OLDFIELD, E., Chemistry
ONO, K., Asian American Studies
ORDAL, G. W., Biochemistry, Basic Medical Science
ORT, D. R., Plant Biology
PACKARD, J., East Asian Languages and Culture
PAHRE, R., Political Science
PAIGE, K. N., Animal Biology
PALENCIA-ROTH, M., Comparative Literature
PALMORE, J. I., Mathematics
PANDHARIPANDE, R., Linguistics, Religious Studies, Sanskrit, Comparative Literature
PANDHARIPANDE, V., Physics
PARK, D., Psychology
PARKER, R. D., English
PHILLIPS, P. W., Physics
PHILLIPS, T. L., Plant Biology
PILLAY, A., Mathematics
PINDERHUGHES, D. M., Political Science, Afro-American Studies
PINES, D., Physics and Electrical and Computer Engineering
PITARD, W. T., Religious Studies
PORTON, G. G., Religious Studies, History, Comparative Literature
POWERS, R., English
PRESS, A., Speech Communication
QUIRK, P. J., Political Science
RAPPAPORT, J., Psychology
RAUBER, R., Atmospheric Sciences
RAUCHFUSS, T. B., Chemistry
REZNICK, B., Mathematics
RHOADS, B. L., Geography
RICH, R. F., Political Science
ROBERTSON, H. M., Entomology
ROBINSON, D. J. S., Mathematics
ROBINSON, G. E., Entomology, Political Science
ROBINSON, S. K., Animal Biology
ROBINSON, W., Atmospheric Sciences
ROEDIGER, D., Afro-American Studies
ROGERS, J. A., Chemistry
RONCADOR, S. M., Brazilian, Portuguese and Lusophone Literatures
ROSENBLATT, J., Mathematics
ROSS, B., Psychology
ROTMAN, J., Mathematics
ROY, E., Psychology
RUAN, Z.-J., Mathematics
SAHINIDIS, N. V., Chemical and Biomolecular Engineering
SANSONE, D., Classics
SCHACHT, R., Philosophy
SCHEELINE, A., Chemistry
SCHEHR, L., French
SCHLESINGER, M., Atmospheric Sciences
SCHULER, M. A., Cell and Structural Biology, Biochemistry
SCHULTEN, K., Chemistry
SCHUPP, P., Mathematics
SCHWEIZER, K. S., Chemistry, Chemical and Biomolecular Engineering
SEEBAUER, E. G., Chemical and Biomolecular Engineering
SEIGLER, D. S., Plant Biology
SHAFTER, A. W., Astronomy
SHAPIRO, M., English
SHAPIRO, S. L., Physics and Astronomy
SHAPLEY, J. R., Chemistry
SHAPLEY, P. A., Chemistry
SHEARER, C. A., Plant Biology
SHERWOOD, O. D., Molecular and Integrative Physiology
SHOBEN, E. J., Psychology
SIMPSON, D., Statistics
SLIGAR, S. G., Chemistry
SMITH, S. G., Chemistry
SNIEZEK, J. A., Psychology
SOFFER, O., Anthropology
SOUSA, R., Portuguese, Spanish and Comparative Literature
SRULL, T. K., Psychology
STEFFEY, K. L., Entomology
STILLINGER, N. B., English
STOLARSKY, K. B., Mathematics
SULLIVAN, Z., English
SUSLICK, K. S., Chemistry
SWANSON, D. L., Political Science, Speech Communication
SWEEDLER, J. V., Chemistry
TALBOT, E. J., French
TEARE, S., Electrical Engineering
THOMPSON, L. A., Astronomy
THOMPSON, J., English
TOBY, R. P., East Asian Languages and Culture
TODOROVA, M., History
TUMANOV, A. E., Mathematics
ULLOM, S. V., Mathematics
UNNEVEHR, L., Agricultural and Consumer Economics
VALENTE, J., English
VAN DEN DRIES, L., Mathematics
WALLACE, J., Philosophy
WALSH, J., Atmospheric Sciences
WASSERMAN, S., Psychology, Statistics
WATSON, W. D., Physics and Astronomy
WATTS, E., English
WEATHERHEAD, P. J., Animal Biology, Natural Resources, Environmental Sciences
WEBBINK, R. F., Astronomy
WEINZIERL, R. A., Entomology
WEISSBERG, R., Political Science
WEST, D. B., Mathematics
WHITT, G. S., Animal Biology
WHITTEN, N. E., Jr, Anthropology
WICKENS, C., Psychology
WIECKOWSKI, A., Chemistry
WILCOX, J., Spanish
WILHELMSON, R., Atmospheric Sciences
WILSON, B. J., Speech Communication
WOESE, C. I., Microbiology and Animal Biology
WRAIGHT, C. A., Biochemistry and Plant Biology
WRIGHT, D., English
WRIGHT, R., Germanic Languages and Literature, Cinema Studies
WU, J.-M., Mathematics
WUEBBLES, D. J., Atmospheric Sciences
YU, G. T., Political Science
ZIMMERMAN, S. C., Chemistry
ZINNES, D., Political Science
ZUKOSKI, C. F., Chemical and Biomolecular Engineering

College of Medicine:

BAKER, D. H., Internal Medicine
BELMONT, A. S., Cell and Structural Biology
BEST, P. M., Molecular and Integrative Physiology, Physiology, Biophysics, Bioengineering and Neuroscience
BOILEAU, R. A., Internal Medicine
BUETOW, M. K., Paediatrics and Adolescent Health
CLEGG, R. M., Physics and Biophysics
CRASS, J. R., Internal Medicine
CROFTS, A. R., Biochemistry and Biophysics
CRONAN, J. E., Microbiology, Biochemistry and Microbiology
DONCHIN, E., Internal Medicine
ENSRUD, E. R., Internal Medicine
ERDMAN, J. W., Jr, Internal Medicine
ESSEX-SORLIE, D. L., Internal Medicine
FARRAND, S., Microbiology and Plant Pathology
FENG, A. S., Physiology, Biophysics, Bioengineering and Neuroscience

FREEDMAN, P., Internal Medicine
GARDNER, J. F., Microbiology
GELFAND, V. I., Cell and Structural Biology
GENNIS, R. B., Biochemistry, Chemistry, Biophysics
GERLT, J. A., Biochemistry, Chemistry and Biophysics, Basic Medical Sciences
GILLETTE, M. U., Cell and Structural Biology
GILLETTE, R., Molecular and Integrative Physiology, Biophysics
GLASER, M., Biochemistry and Biophysics
GREENOUGH, W. T., Psychiatry, Cell and Structural Biology, Psychology and Psychiatry
GUMPORT, R. I., Biochemistry, Basic Medical Sciences
HELMAN, S. I., Physiology, Biophysics and Bioengineering
JAKOBSSON, E., Physiology, Biochemistry, Biophysics
JEFFERY, E., Pharmacology
KATZENELLENBOGEN, B. S., Cell and Structural Biology, Molecular and Integrative Physiology
KAUFMAN, S. J., Cell and Structural Biology
KEMPER, B. W., Cell and Structural Biology, Pharmacology, Molecular and Integrative Physiology
KIRBY, R. W., Internal Medicine
KRANZ, D. M., Biochemistry
LAYMAN, D. K., Internal Medicine
LEVY, A., Pathology
MARSHALL, W. P., Internal Medicine
MILLER, C. G., Microbiology
MILLER, G. A., Psychiatry
MORRISSEY, J. H., Biochemistry
NELSON, R. A., Internal Medicine
OLSEN, G., Microbiology and Biophysics
ORDAL, G. W., Biochemistry, Basic Medical Science
POLLARD, J. W., Internal Medicine
PRABHUDESAI, M., Pathology
RAMIREZ, V. D., Physiology and Neuroscience
ROBBINS, A. W., Internal Medicine
ROBERTSON, H. M., Cell and Structural Biology, Entomology
ROBINSON, G. E., Cell and Structural Biology, Entomology
RUEDA, J. L., Psychiatry
SALYERS, A., Microbiology
SCHULER, M. A., Cell and Structural Biology, Biochemistry, Plant Biology
SCHWARTZ, B. S., Biochemistry
SHAPIRO, D. J., Biochemistry
SHERWOOD, O. D., Physiology
SIEGEL, I. A.
SLIGAR, S. G., Biochemistry, Chemistry, Physiology and Biophysics, Medicine
SWITZER, R. L., Biochemistry, Basic Medical Sciences
WEYHENMEYER, J., Pathology
WILLIAMS, B., Pathology
WOESE, C. R., Microbiology
WRAIGHT, C. A., Biochemistry, Biophysics, Plant Biology

College of Veterinary Medicine:

ANDREWS, J. J., Veterinary Pathobiology
ARDEN, W. A., Veterinary Clinical Medicine
BEASLEY, V. R., Veterinary Biosciences
BENSON, G. J., Veterinary Clinical Medicine, Veterinary Anaesthesiology and Comparative Medicine
CAMPBELL, K. L., Veterinary Clinical Medicine
CLARKSON, R. B., Veterinary Clinical Medicine, Veterinary Biosciences
COOKE, P. S., Veterinary Biosciences
DOCAMPO, R., Veterinary Pathobiology
GOETZ, T. E., Veterinary Clinical Medicine
GROSS, D. R., Veterinary Biosciences
HANSEN, L. G., Veterinary Biosciences
HASCHEK-HOCK, W. M., Veterinary Pathobiology
HESS, R. A., Veterinary Biosciences
JOHNSON, A. L., Veterinary Clinical Medicine
KITRON, U. D., Veterinary Pathobiology
KUHLENSCHMIDT, M. S., Veterinary Pathobiology
LOCK, T. F., Veterinary Clinical Medicine
MANOHAR, M., Veterinary Biosciences
MARRETTA, S. M., Veterinary Clinical Medicine
MEERDINK, G. L., Toxicology
MILLER, G. Y., Veterinary Pathobiology, Veterinary Clinical Medicine
OTT, R. S., Veterinary Clinical Medicine, Veterinary Medicine Administration
PAUL, A. J., Veterinary Pathobiology
RAFFE, M. R., Veterinary Clinical Medicine
SCHANTZ, S. L., Veterinary Biosciences
SEGRE, M., Veterinary Pathobiology
SISSON, D. D., Veterinary Clinical Medicine
SMITH, R. D., Veterinary Pathobiology
TRANQUILLI, W. J., Veterinary Clinical Medicine
TROUTT, H. F., Veterinary Clinical Medicine
VALLI, V. E. O., Veterinary Pathobiology
VIMR, E. R., Veterinary Pathobiology
WALLIG, M. A., Veterinary Pathobiology
WEIGEL, R. M., Veterinary Pathobiology
WHITELEY, H. E., Veterinary Pathobiology
ZACHARY, J. F., Veterinary Pathobiology

Institute of Labor and Industrial Relations:

DRASGOW, F.
FEUILLE, P.
LAWLER, J.
LEROY, M.
MARTOCCHIO, J.
NORTHCRAFT, G.
OLDHAM, G.
OLSON, C.

UNIVERSITY OF ST FRANCIS

500 Wilcox St, Joliet, IL 60435
Telephone: (815) 740-3400
Fax: (815) 740-5032
E-mail: information@stfrancis.edu
Internet: www.stfrancis.edu

Founded 1920
Private control
Academic year: August to May

Pres.: Dr MICHAEL J. VINCIGUERRA
Provost and Vice-Pres. for Academic Affairs: Dr FRANK PASCOE
Vice-Pres. for Admin. and Finance: ROBERT TENUTA
Vice-Pres. for Admission and Enrollment Services: CHARLES M. BEUTEL
Vice-Pres. for Mission Integration and Min.: MARY ELIZABETH IMLER
Dir of Libraries: TERRY COTTRELL

Library of 134,400 vols
Number of teachers: 302
Number of students: 3,255

DEANS

College of Arts and Sciences: Dr ROBERT KASE
College of Business and Health Administration: Dr MIKE LAROCCO
College of Education: Dr JOHN GAMBRO
College of Nursing: Dr CAROL WILSON

UNIVERSITY OF ST MARY OF THE LAKE – MUNDELEIN SEMINARY

1000 East Maple Ave, Mundelein, IL 60060
Telephone: (847) 566-6401
E-mail: info@usml.edu
Internet: www.vocations.org
Private control

Rector and Pres.: Very Rev. DENNIS LYLE
Vice-Pres. for Facilities: STAN RYS
Vice-Pres. for Finance: JOHN LEHOCKY
Library Dir: LORRAINE OLLEY

Library of 180,000 vols
Publication: *Chicago Studies* (3 a year).

VANDERCOOK COLLEGE OF MUSIC

3140 South Federal St, Chicago, IL 60616
Telephone: (312) 225-6288
Fax: (312) 225-5211
Internet: www.vandercook.edu
Private control

Pres.: Dr CHARLES MENGHINI
Dean of Undergraduate Studies: KAYE CLEMENTS
Dean of Graduate Studies: RUTH RHODES
Registrar: CAROLYN BERGHOFF
Library Dir: DON WIDMER

Number of teachers: 6
Number of students: 230

WESTERN ILLINOIS UNIVERSITY

710 West University Dr., Macomb, IL 61455-1380
Telephone: (309) 295-1414
Fax: (309) 298-2400
E-mail: info@wiu.edu
Internet: www.wiu.edu

Founded 1899
Academic year: August to May

Pres.: Dr AL GOLDFARB
Provost and Academic Vice-Pres.: Dr JOE RALLO
Vice-Pres. for Admin. Services: JACQUELINE THOMPSON
Vice-Pres. for Advancement and Public Services: Dr DAN HENDRICKS
Vice-Pres. for Student Services: Dr W. GARRY JOHNSON
Dean of Univ. Libraries: Dr PHYLIS C. SELF

Library of 1,150,000 vols
Number of teachers: 648
Number of students: 13,206

Publication: *Essays in Literature*

DEANS

College of Arts and Sciences: Dr INESSA LEVI
College of Business and Technology: Dr TOM EREKSON
College of Education and Human Services: Dr BONNIE SMITH-SKRIPPS
College of Fine Arts and Communication: Dr PAUL KREIDER
School of Graduate Studies: Dr BARBARA A. BAILY

WHEATON COLLEGE

501 College Ave, Wheaton, IL 60187-5593
Telephone: (630) 752-5000
Fax: (630) 752-5555
Internet: www.wheaton.edu

Founded 1860
Private control
Academic year: August to May

Pres.: Dr PHILIP RYKEN
Provost: Dr STANTON JONES
Sr Vice-Pres. for Finance: Dr DALE A. KEMP
Vice-Pres. for Advancement and Alumni Relations: Dr R. MARK DILLON
Vice-Pres. for Student Devt: Dr PAUL CHELSEN
Dean of Student Care and Service: Dr MELANIE J. HUMPHREYS
Registrar: PEGGY KING
Librarian: LISA RICHMOND

Library of 1,113,924 items, 7,833 current periodicals
Number of teachers: 291 (198 full-time, 93 part-time)

Number of students: 2,768 (2,386 undergraduate, 382 graduate)
Publications: *Kodon Literary Magazine* (3 a year), *Record* (52 a year), *Tower* (1 a year)

DEANS

Conservatory, Arts, and Communication: Dr MICHAEL WILDER
Graduate School: Dr JEFFREY MOSHIER
Humanities and Theological Studies: Dr JILL PELÁEZ BAUMGAERTNER
Information and Technology: Dr GARY N. LARSON
Natural and Social Sciences: Dr DOROTHY F. CHAPPELL

INDIANA

ANDERSON UNIVERSITY

Anderson, IN 46012
Telephone: (765) 649-9071
Fax: (765) 641-3851
E-mail: matas@anderson.edu
Internet: www.anderson.edu
Founded 1917
Academic year: August to May
Pres.: Dr JAMES L. EDWARDS
Vice-Pres. for Academic Affairs and Dean: Dr CARL H. CALDWELL
Vice-Pres. for Advancement: ROBERT L. COFFMAN
Vice-Pres. for Enrollment Management and Information Systems: Dr MICHAEL COLLETTE
Vice-Pres. for Finance and Treas.: SENA LANDEY
Vice-Pres. for Student Life and Dean of Students: BRENT BAKER
Registrar: ARTHUR LEAK
Dir of Univ. Libraries: JANET BREWER
Library of 210,000 vols
Number of teachers: 140
Number of students: 2,500

DEANS

College of Science and Humanities: D. BLAKE JANUTOLO
College of the Arts: JEFFREY E. WRIGHT
Falls School of Business: TERRY TRUITT
School of Education: DIANA N. ROSS (Chair.)
School of Theology: Dr DAVID SEBASTIAN

ASSOCIATED MENNONITE BIBLICAL SEMINARY

3003 Benham Ave, Elkhart, IN 46517-1999
Telephone: (574) 295-3726
Fax: (574) 295-0092
E-mail: admissions@ambs.edu
Internet: www.ambs.edu
Private control
Pres.: Dr SARA WENGER SHENK
Academic Dean: REBECCA SLOUGH
Registrar: IRENE KOOP
Librarian: EILEEN K. SANER
Library of 109,000 vols
Number of teachers: 15
Number of students: 180.

BRANCH CAMPUS

Great Plains Campus: 2517 Main St, POB 306, North Newton, KS 67117; tel. (316) 283-6300; Dir Dr LOIS Y. BARRETT.

BALL STATE UNIVERSITY

Muncie, IN 47306
Telephone: (765) 289-1241
E-mail: askbsu@bsu.edu
Internet: www.bsu.edu
Founded 1918
Academic year: August to May
President: Dr BLAINE A. BROWNELL
Provost and Vice-President for Academic Affairs: BEVERLY J. PITTS
Vice-President for Business Affairs: THOMAS J. KINGHORN
Vice-President for Informational Technology: Dr H. O'NEAL SMITHERMAN
Vice-President for Student Affairs and Enrollment Management: Dr DOUGLAS F. MCCONKEY
Vice-President for University Advancement: Dr DON L. PARK
Registrar: THOMAS BILGER
Dean of University Libraries: ARTHUR W. HAFNER
Library: 1.5m. items (inc. microfilms and audiovisual items), 4,000 current periodicals
Number of teachers: 836 (full-time)
Number of students: 18,000
Publications: *Ball State Monographs* (irregular), *Indiana Mathematics Teacher* (2 a year), *International Journal of Social Education, Odyssey* (1 a year), *Proceedings of the Indiana Academy of Social Sciences* (1 a year), *Teacher Educator* (4 a year)

DEANS

College of Applied Sciences and Technology: Dr NANCY KINGSBURY
College of Architecture and Planning: Prof. JOSEPH BILELLO
College of Business: Prof. LYNNE RICHARDSON
College of Communication, Information, and Media: Prof. SCOTT R. OLSON
College of Fine Arts: Prof. ROBERT A. KVAM
College of Sciences and the Humanities: Prof. DONALD E. VAN METER
Teachers' College: ROY A. WEAVER
University College: Dr B. THOMAS LOWE

BETHANY THEOLOGICAL SEMINARY

615 Nat. Rd W, Richmond, IN 47374-4019
Telephone: (765) 983-1800
Fax: (765) 983-1840
E-mail: contactus@bethanyseminary.edu
Internet: www.bethanyseminary.edu
Founded 1905 as Bethany Bible School, present name 1963
Private control
Academic year: August to May
Pres.: RUTHANN KNECHEL JOHANSEN
Academic Dean: RICK GARDNER
Number of teachers: 17
Number of students: 64.

BRANCH CAMPUS

Susquehanna Valley Satellite: 1 Alpha Dr., Elizabethtown College, Elizabethtown, PA 17022-2298; tel. (717) 361-1450.

BETHEL COLLEGE

1001 W McKinley Avenue, Mishawaka, IN 46545
Telephone: (260) 259-8511
Fax: (260) 257-3335
E-mail: info@bethelcollege.edu
Internet: www.bethelcollege.edu
Founded 1947
Private control
Academic year: August to May
Pres.: Dr STEVEN R. CRAMER
Sr Vice-Pres.: Dr DENNIS D. ENGBRECHT
Vice-Pres. and Chief Fiscal Officer: JOHN R. MYERS
Vice-Pres. for Academic Services: JAMES B. STUMP
Vice-Pres. for College Relations: C. ROBERT LAURENT
Vice-Pres. for Devt: TERRY ZEITLOW
Registrar: STEPHEN J. MATTESON
Dir of Library Services: Dr CLYDE R. ROOT
Number of teachers: 219
Number of students: 2,100

DEANS

Office of Graduate Studies: Dr BRADLEY D. SMITH
School of Adult Studies: JOHN R. MOW
School of Arts and Sciences: Dr ALESHA D. SEROCZYNKSI
School of Business and Social Science: Dr NORMAN R. SPIVEY
School of Education: Dr CANDICE C. HOLLINGSEAD
School of Nursing: Dr RUTH E. DAVIDHIZAR
School of Religion and Philosophy: Dr TERENCE D. LINHART

BUTLER UNIVERSITY

4600 Sunset Ave, Indianapolis, IN 46208
Telephone: (317) 940-8000
Fax: (317) 940-9930
Internet: www.butler.edu
Founded 1855
Private control
President: BOBBY FONG
Provost and Senior Vice-President for Academic Affairs: BILL BERRY
Vice-President for University Advancement: CAMERON A. MCGUIRE
Registrar: SONDREA OZOLINS
Dean of Libraries: LEWIS MILLER
Number of teachers: 255 (full-time)
Number of students: 4,326

DEANS

College of Business Administration: Dr RICHARD FETTER
College of Education: Dr BOB RIDER
College of Liberal Arts and Sciences: Dr PAUL HANSON
College of Pharmacy and Health Sciences: Dr PATRICIA A. CHASE
Jordan College of Fine Arts: Dr PETER ALEXANDER

CALUMET COLLEGE OF ST JOSEPH

2400 New York Ave, Whiting, IN 46394
Telephone: (219) 473-7770
Fax: (219) 473-4259
E-mail: admissions@ccsj.edu
Internet: www.ccsj.edu
Founded 1951
Academic year: September to August
President: Dr DENNIS C. RITTENMEYER
Registrar: DIANA FRANCIS
Librarian: JOANN ARNOLD
Library of 115,874 vols
Number of teachers: 60
Number of students: 1,300

CHRISTIAN THEOLOGICAL SEMINARY

1000 W 42nd St, Indianapolis, IN 46208
Telephone: (317) 924-1331
Fax: (317) 923-1961
E-mail: communications@cts.edu
Internet: www.cts.edu
Private control
Academic year: September to May
President: Dr EDWARD L. WHEELER
Vice-President and Academic Dean: Dr CAROLYN HIGGINBOTHAM
Vice-President for Finance: DEAN RAMGA
Vice-President for Seminary Advancement/Development: ANN UPDEGRAFF SPLETH
Library Dir: LORNA SHOEMAKER
Number of teachers: 44
Number of students: 300

CONCORDIA THEOLOGICAL SEMINARY

6600 N Clinton Street, Fort Wayne, IN 46825-4996
Telephone: (260) 452-2100
Fax: (260) 452-2121
Internet: www.ctsfw.edu

Founded 1847
Private control
Academic year: September to May

President: DEAN O. WENTHE
Academic Dean: WILLIAM C. WEINRICH
Director of Library and Information Services: ROBERT ROETHEMEYER

Library of 150,000 items
Number of teachers: 29
Number of students: 389

Publication: *Concordia Theological Quarterly* (4 a year).

DEPAUW UNIVERSITY

313 S Locust St, Greencastle, IN 46135
Telephone: (765) 658-4800
Fax: (317) 658-4177
Internet: www.depauw.edu

Founded 1837 as Indiana Asbury Univ.; present name 1884
Academic year: August to May

Pres.: Dr BRIAN W. CASEY
Exec. Vice-Pres. and Dean of the Faculty: Dr NEAL ABRAHAM
Vice-Pres. for Admission and Financial Aid: STEFANIE NILES
Vice-Pres. for Devt and Alumni Relations: LISA HOLLANDER
Vice-Pres. for Finance and Admin.: BRAD A. KELSHEIMER
Vice-Pres. for Student Services: CINDY BABINGTON
Registrar: Dr KENNETH J. KIRKPATRICK
Dir of Libraries: RICK PROVINE

Library of 351,677 vols
Number of teachers: 281 (217 full-time, 64 part-time)
Number of students: 2,298

EARLHAM COLLEGE

Richmond, IN 47374
Telephone: (765) 983-1200
Fax: (765) 983-1560
E-mail: admissions@earlham.edu
Internet: www.earlham.edu
Academic year: August to May

Founded 1847
Private control

Pres.: DOUGLAS BENNETT
Vice-Pres. for Academic Affairs and Academic Dean: GREG MAHLER
Vice-Pres. for Business Affairs: RICHARD K. SMITH
Vice-Pres. for Institutional Advancement: JAMES MCKEY
Librarian: SCOTT SILVERMAN

Library of 400,834
Number of teachers: 101
Number of students: 1,181

DEANS

College: GREG MAHLER
Earlham School of Religion: JAY MARSHALL

FRANKLIN COLLEGE

Franklin, IN 46131
Telephone: (317) 738-8000
Fax: (317) 736-6030
Internet: www.franklincollege.edu

Founded 1834
Academic year: August to May

Chancellor: (vacant)
Pres.: JAMES MOSELEY
Vice-Pres. for Academic Affairs and Dean of the College: DAVID BRAILOW
Vice-Pres. for Business and Finance: LARRY GRIFFITH
Vice-Pres. for Enrollment and Student Affairs: ALAN HILL
Vice-Pres. for Institutional Advancement: MYRON DAVIS
Dean of Students: ELLIS HALL
Head Librarian: RONALD SCHUETZ

Library of 126,345 vols
Number of teachers: 100
Number of students: 994

GOSHEN COLLEGE

Goshen, IN 46526
Telephone: (219) 535-7000
Fax: (219) 535-7660
E-mail: admission@goshen.edu
Internet: www.goshen.edu

Founded 1894

President: SHIRLEY H. SHOWALTER
Provost and Exec. Vice-Pres.: JOHN D. YORDY
Vice-Pres. for Academic Affairs and Dean: ANITA STALTER
Vice-Pres. for Institutional Advancement: ANDREA COOK
Vice-Pres. for Multicultural Education: ZENABE ABEBE
Vice-Pres. for Student Life and Dean of Students: BILL BORN
Registrar: STANLEY MILLER
Library Dir: LISA GUEDEA CARREÑO

Library of 155,000 vols
Number of teachers: 112 (82 full-time, 30 part-time)
Number of students: 1,000

Publication: *Mennonite Quarterly Review*.

GRACE COLLEGE AND THEOLOGICAL SEMINARY

200 Seminary Dr., Winona Lake, IN 46590
Telephone: (574) 372-5100
Fax: (574) 372-5263
E-mail: admissions@grace.edu
Internet: www.grace.edu
Private control
Language of instruction: English
Academic year: August to July

Pres.: Dr RONALD E. MANAHAN
Provost: Dr WILLIAM J. KATIP
Registrar: STEVE CARLSON
Dir for Library Services: WILLIAM DARR

Library of 140,000 vols
Number of teachers: 118
Number of students: 1,773

HANOVER COLLEGE

Hanover, IN 47243
Telephone: (812) 866-2151
Internet: www.hanover.edu

First instruction 1827; chartered 1829
Private control (Presbyterian)

President: RUSSELL L. NICHOLS
Vice-President and Dean of Academic Affairs: JANE JAKOUBEK
Vice-President for Administrative Affairs: TERRY A. PHILLIPS
Vice-President for Business Affairs: FRANK G. WILLIAMS
Vice-President for Development: RICK HASKINS
Vice-President for Student Life: DENNIS MCDONALD
Associate Dean of Academic Affairs and Registrar: JON ENRIQUEZ
Director of Duggan Library: KENNETH E. GIBSON

Library of 215,000 vols, 284,000 documents, 4,500 audiovisual items
Number of teachers: 71
Number of students: 1,050

HUNTINGTON COLLEGE

2303 College Ave, Huntington, IN 46750
Telephone: (219) 356-6000
Fax: (219) 359-4086
Internet: www.huntington.edu

Founded 1897
Academic year: September to May

Pres.: Dr G. BLAIR DOWDEN
Vice-Pres. and Dean of the College: Dr RONALD J. WEBB
Vice-Pres. for Advancement: NED J. KISER
Vice-Pres. for Business and Finance: THOMAS W. AYERS
Vice-Pres. for Student Development: Dr A. NORRIS FRIESEN
Dean of Enrollment: JEFF BERGGREN
Registrar: SARAH J. HARVEY
Director of Library Services: ROBERT E. KAEHR

Library of 164,000 items, 550 current periodicals, 14,000 bound periodical vols, 50,000 govt documents
Number of teachers: 68
Number of students: 942

INDIANA INSTITUTE OF TECHNOLOGY

1600 E Washington Blvd, Fort Wayne, IN 46803
Telephone: (260) 422-5561
Fax: (260) 422-7696
Internet: www.indianatech.edu

Founded 1930
Private control
Language of instruction: English

Schools of business, computer science, criminal sciences, engineering

President: Dr ARTHUR E. SNYDER
Librarian: CONNIE SCOTT

Library of 33,000 volumes
Number of teachers: 50
Number of students: 3,400

INDIANA STATE UNIVERSITY

Terre Haute, IN 47809
Telephone: (812) 237-6311
Fax: (812) 237-2291
Internet: web.indstate.edu

Founded 1865
Academic year: August to May

President: Dr LLOYD W. BENJAMIN, III
Provost and Vice-Pres. for Academic Affairs: C. JACK MAYNARD
Gen. Counsel and Sec. of the Univ.: MELONY A. SACOPULOS
Vice-Pres. for Business Affairs and Finance: GREGG S. FLOYD
Vice-Pres. for Enrollment Management, Marketing and Communication: JOHN E. BEACON
Vice-Pres. for Student Affairs and Dean of Students: D. THOMAS RAMEY
Registrar and Data and Technology Man.: SHARON GICK
Dean of Library Services: ALBERTA COMER

Library of 1,344,592 vols
Number of teachers: 446 full-time
Number of students: 10,543

Publications: *Cognitive Technology* (2 a year), *Folklore Historian* (1 a year), *Grassland* (1 a year), *Indiana English* (3 a year), *Midwestern Folklore* (2 a year), *The Hoosier Science Teacher* (4 a year), *The Indiana Council of Teachers of Mathemat-*

ics Journal—Mathematics Teacher (2 a year), *Tonic* (1 a year)

DEANS

College of Arts and Sciences: Dr THOMAS G. SAUER
College of Business: Dr NANCY MERRITT
College of Education: Dr BRADLEY V. BALCH
College of Nursing, Health and Human Services: Dr RICHARD WILLIAMS
College of Technology: Dr BRADFORD SIMS
School of Graduate Studies: Dr JOLYNN S. KUHLMAN

INDIANA UNIVERSITY

Bloomington, IN 47405
Telephone: (812) 855-4848
Internet: www.indiana.edu
Founded 1820 as a state seminary, opened 1824, became Indiana College 1828, attained university status 1838, became state university 1852
Pres.: GERALD L. BEPKO
Vice-Pres. and Chief Admin. Officer: J. TERRY CLAPACS
Vice-Pres. and Chief Financial Officer: JUDITH G. PALMER
Vice-President for Academic Affairs: SHARON S. BREHM
Vice-President for Information Technology: MICHAEL A. MCROBBIE
Vice-President for Long-Range Planning: GERALD L. BEPKO
Vice-President for Public Affairs and Government Relations: WILLIAM STEPHAN
Vice-President for Research and Dean of the Graduate School: GEORGE E. WALKER
Vice-President for Student Development and Diversity: CHARLIE HELMS
Dean of University Libraries: SUZANNE THORIN
Number of students: 98,710 (all campuses).

CONSTITUENT CAMPUSES

Indiana University Bloomington

107 S Indiana Ave, Bloomington, IN 47405-7000
Telephone: (812) 855-4848
Internet: www.iub.edu
Provost and Exec. Vice-Pres.: KAREN HANSON
Vice-Provost for Enrollment Management: DAVID JOHNSON
Vice-Provost for Faculty and Academic Affairs: THOMAS GIERYN
Vice-Provost for Research: SARITA SONI
Vice-Provost for Undergraduate Education: SONYA STEPHENS
Dean of Students: HAROLD GOLDSMITH
Registrar: ROLAND A. COTÉ
Dir of Student Enrollment Services: JAMES KENNEDY
Librarian: BRENDA JOHNSON
Library: see Libraries and Archives
Number of teachers: 1,539
Number of students: 41,756
Publications: *American Historical Review* (5 a year), *American Journal of Semiotics* (4 a year), *Anthropological Linguistics* (4 a year), *Business Horizons* (6 a year), *Folklore Research Journal* (3 a year), *Indiana Business Review* (6 a year), *Indiana Law Journal* (4 a year), *Indiana Magazine of History* (4 a year), *Indiana Slavic Studies* (1 a year), *Indiana University Mathematics Journal* (4 a year), *Journal of American History* (4 a year), *Journal of Asian History, Journal of Chemical Physics* (52 a year), *Journal of Mathematical Physics* (12 a year), *Journal of Slavic Linguistics* (2 a year), *Journal of the Experimental Analysis of Behavior* (6 a year), *Phi Delta Kappan* (10 a year), *University Bulletin* (30 a year), *Victorian Studies* (4 a year)

DEANS

College of Arts and Sciences: DAVID ZARET
Hutton Honors College: MATTHEW AUER
Kelley School of Business: DANIEL SMITH
School of Continuing Studies: DANIEL CALLISON
School of Education: Prof. GERARDO GONZÁLEZ
School of Health, Physical Education and Recreation: ROBERT GOODMAN
School of Informatics and Computing: ROBERT SCHNABEL
School of Journalism: BRADLEY HAMM
Maurer School of Law: Prof. LAUREN ROBEL (acting)
School of Library and Information Science: (vacant): BLAISE CRONIN
School of Medical Sciences: JOHN WATKINS
Jacobs School of Music: GWYN RICHARDS
School of Nursing: JOYCE KROTHE
School of Optometry: SARITA SONI
School of Public and Environmental Affairs: JOHN GRAHAM
School of Social Work: KATHY BYERS
Graduate School: JAMES WIMBUSH

CHAIRPERSONS OF DEPARTMENTS

College of Arts and Sciences:
- African American and African Diaspora Studies: Prof. JOHN H. STANFIELD, II (acting)
- Anthropology: Dr RICHARD R. WILK
- Apparel Merchandising and Interior Design: Prof. REED BENHAMOU
- Astronomy: Prof. RICHARD H. DURISEN
- Biology: JEFFREY D. PALMER
- Central Eurasian Studies: Dr ELLIOT H. SPERLING
- Chemistry: Prof. DAVID E. CLEMMER
- Classical Studies: Prof. WILLIAM HANSEN (acting)
- Communication and Culture: Prof. ROBERT L. IVIE
- Comparative Literature: Prof. OSCAR S. KENSHUR
- Criminal Justice: Dr KIP SCHLEGEL
- East Asian Languages and Cultures: Prof. RICHARD RUBINGER
- Economics: Prof. JAMES A. WALKER
- English: Prof. STEPHEN MYERS WATT
- Folklore and Ethnomusicology: Prof. JOHN H. MCDOWELL
- French and Italian: Dr ANDREA CICCARELLI
- Geography: Prof. DANIEL C. KNUDSEN
- Geological Sciences: Prof. CHRISTOPHER G. MAPLES
- Germanic Studies: Prof. KARI ELLEN GADE
- History: Prof. JOHN BODNAR (acting)
- History and Philosophy of Science: WILLIAM ROYALL NEWMAN (acting)
- Linguistics: Prof. STEVEN L. FRANKS
- Mathematics: Prof. DANIEL P. MAKI
- Near Eastern Languages and Cultures: Prof. M. NAZIF SHAHRANI
- Philosophy: Prof. MARK KAPLAN
- Physics: Prof. STEVEN E. VIGADOR
- Political Science: Prof. JEFFREY A. HART
- Psychology: Prof. JOSEPH E. STEINMETZ
- Religious Studies: RICHARD B. MILLER
- Slavic Languages and Literatures: Prof. RONALD FELDSTEIN
- Sociology: Prof. ROBERT VICTOR ROBINSON
- Spanish and Portuguese: Prof. CONSUELO LOPEZ-MORILLAS
- Speech and Hearing Sciences: Prof. PHIL J. CONNELL
- Telecommunications: Prof. WALTER GANTZ
- Theatre and Drama: Prof. RONALD WAINSCOTT
- West European Studies: PETER BONDANELLA

Kelley School of Business:
- Accounting and Information Systems: Prof. JAMIE PRATT
- Business Communication: Dr SUE VARGO
- Business Economics and Public Policy: Prof. MICHELE FRATIANNI
- Business Law: Prof. ARLEN W. LANGVARDT
- Finance: Prof. ROBERT C. KLEMKOSKY
- Management: Prof. PATRICIA P. MCDOUGALL
- Marketing: Prof. DAN SMITH
- Operations and Decision Technology: Prof. MUNIRPALLAM A. VENKATARAMANAN

School of Education:
- Counselling and Educational Psychology: Prof. DANIEL J. MUELLER
- Curriculum and Instruction: Prof. SUSAN M. KLEIN
- Educational Leadership and Policy Studies: Prof. BARRY BULL
- Instructional Systems Technology: ELIZABETH BOLING
- Language Education: Dr MARTHA NYIKOS

School of Health, Physical Education and Recreation:
- Applied Health Science: Prof. MOHAMMAD RAHIM TORABI
- Kinesiology: Prof. JOHN B. SHEA
- Recreation and Park Administration: Dr LYNN MARIE JAMIESON

School of Music:
- Ballet: VIRGINIA CESBRON
- Bands: RAY E. CRAMER
- Brass: F. MICHAEL HATFIELD
- Choral Conducting: JAN. D. HARRINGTON
- Composition: Prof. CLAUDE BAKER
- Early Music Institute: PAUL D. HILLIER
- Harp: SUSANN MCDONALD
- Instrumental Conducting: IMRE ZOLTAN PALLO
- Jazz: DAVID N. BAKER
- Music Education: Prof. MICHAEL SCHWARTZKOPF
- Music (in General Studies): Prof. MARY GOETZE
- Musicology: Prof. A. PETER BROWN
- Music Theory: Dr ERIC J. ISAACSON
- Organ: CHRISTOPHER YOUNG
- Percussion: GERALD CARLYSS
- Strings: LAWRENCE P. HURST
- Theory: MARY H. WENNERSTROM
- Woodwinds: HOWARD KLUG

DIRECTORS OF RESEARCH INSTITUTES

African American Arts Institute: Dr CHARLES E. SYKES
American Indian Studies Research Institute: Prof. RAYMOND J. DEMALLIE
Anthropological Center for Training & Research on Global Environmental Change (ACT): Prof. EMILIO MORAN
Borish Center for Ophthalmic Research: Prof. B. SARITA SONI, Prof. GERALD E. LOWTHER
Center for Design Process: C. THOMAS MITCHELL
Center for Econometric Model Research: R. JEFFREY GREEN, MORTON MARCUS
Center for Economic Education: (vacant)
Center for Electronic and Computer Music: Prof. JEFFREY HASS
Center for English Language Training: MARLIN HOWARD
Center for Genomics and Bioinformatics: PETER CHERBAS
Center for Geospatial Data Analysis: EDWIN HARTKE
Center for Health and Safety Studies: JAMES W. CROWE
Center for Human Growth: Dr THOMAS L. SEXTON
Center for Italian Studies: ANDREA CICCARELLI

Center for Latin American and Caribbean Studies: JEFFREY GOULD
Center for Postsecondary Research and Planning: ASHTON ALEY HALL
Center for Public Sector Labor Relations: RICHARD S. RUBIN
Center for Reading and Language Studies: ROGER C. FARR
Center for Research and Development in Language Instruction: ALBERT VALDMAN
Center for Research into the Anthropological Foundations of Technology (CRAFT): NICHOLAS TOTH, KATHY SCHICK
Center for Research on Concepts and Cognition: Prof. DOUGLAS HOFSTADTER
Center for Social Informatics: Prof. ROB KLING
Center for Studies of Law in Action: Prof. KIP SCHLEGEL, Dr BARRY K. LOGAN
Center for Survey Research: JOHN M. KENNEDY
Center for the History of Medicine: ANN G. CARMICHAEL, ELLEN DWYER
Center for the Integrative Study of Animal Behavior (CISAB): EMILIA P. MARTINS
Center for the Study of Institutions, Populations and Environmental Change (CIPEC): Dr EMILIO MORAN, Dr ELINOR OSTROM
Center for the Study of Law and Society: LEE LUSKIN
Center for the Study of the College Fraternity: RICHARD N. MCKAIG
Center for the Study of Global Change: BRIAN WINCHESTER
Center on Aging and Aged: BARBARA A. HAWKINS
Chemical Informatics Center: GARY WIGGINS
Committee for Research and Development in Language Instruction: ALBERT VALDMAN
Computational Fluid Dynamics Laboratory: Prof. AKIN ECER
Creole Institute: Albert VALDMAN
Early Music Institute: PAUL HILLIER (acting)
East Asian Studies Center: GEORGE M. WILSON
East Asian Summer Language Institute: YASUKO ITO WATT
Environmental Systems Applications Center: WILLIAM W. JONES
ERIC Clearinghouse for Social Studies/Social Science Education: JOHN PATRICK
Folklore Institute: JOHN MCDOWELL
Glenn A. Black Laboratory of Archaeology: Prof. CHRIS PEEBLES
High School Journalism Institute: Prof. JACK DVORAK
Howard Hughes Medical Institute Research Laboratory: THOMAS C. KAUFMAN
Indiana Business Research Center: MORTON J. MARCUS
Indiana Center for Evaluation: Dr KIM K. METCALF
Indiana Education Policy Center: JONATHAN PLUCKER
Indiana Institute on Disability and Community: Dr DAVID M. MANK
Indiana Geological Survey: JOHN STEINMETZ
Indiana Molecular Biology Institute: Dr RUDOLF A. RAFF
Indiana University Art Museum: ADELHEID GEALT
Indiana University Cyclotron Facility: Prof. JOHN M. CAMERON
Indiana University Molecular Structure Center: JOHN C. HUFFMAN
Inner Asian and Uralic National Resource Center: WILLIAM FIERMAN
Institute for Advanced Study: Prof. MARY ELLEN BROWN
Institute for Child Study: RUSSELL SKIBA
Institute for Development Strategies: DAVID B. AUDRETSCH
Institute for Drug Abuse Prevention: WILLIAM J. BAILEY, Prof. MOHAMMAD R. TORABI
Institute for Family and Social Responsibility: Prof. MAUREEN A. PIROG, Dr KATHARINE V. BYERS
Institute for Neural Systems and Plasticity: GEORGE V. REBEC
Institute for Scientific Computing and Applied Mathematics: ROGER TEMAM
Institute for Study of Developmental Disabilities: DAVID MANK
Institute for Study of Human Capabilities: Prof. CHARLES WATSON
Institute for the Study of Labor in Society (ISLS): JEFF VINCENT
Institute for the Study of Russian and Eurasian Education: BEN EKLOF, HOWARD MEHLINGER
Institute for Urban Transportation: GEORGE M. SMERK
Institute of German Studies: MARC WEINER
Institute of Social Research: DAVID JAMES
International Development Institute: CHARLES RAEFSNYDER
Jewish Studies Center: ALVIN H. ROSENFELD
Johnson Center for Entrepreneurship and Innovation: ELIZABETH J. GATEWOOD
Kinsey Institute for Research in Sex, Gender, and Reproduction: Prof. JOHN BANCROFT
Laboratory Animal Resources: RUSSELL L. SCHMIDT
Latin American Music Center: CARMEN TÉLLEZ
Leisure Research Institute: LYNN M. JAMIESON
Mathematics Education Development Center: FRANK K. LESTER, Jr
Medieval Studies Institute: LAWRENCE M. CLOPPER
National Center on Accessibility: GARY ROBB
National Center for Recreation Resources: BRUCE HRONEK
National Clearinghouse for United States–Japan Studies: C. FREDERICK RISINGER
National Institute on Global Environment Change—Midwest Regional Center: J. C. RANDOLPH
Nuclear Theory Center: J. TIMOTHY LONDERGAN
Philanthropy and Americans Outdoors Program: BRUCE HRONEK
Polish Studies Center: BILL JOHNSTON
Population Institute for Research and Training: Prof. GEORGE ALTER
Poynter Center for the Study of Ethics and American Institutions: DAVID H. SMITH
Reading Practicum Center: ANNABEL NEWMAN
Research Institute for Inner Asian Studies (RIFIAS): DEVIN DEWEESE
Rural Center for AIDS/STD Prevention (RCAP): Prof. WILLIAM L. YARBER
Russian and East European Institute: Prof. DAVID RANSEL
School of Business Division of Research: MORTON MARCUS
School of Business Institute for Research on the Management of Information Systems: JO BASEY
Seismic Laboratory: MICHAEL W. HAMBURGER
Social Studies Development Center: JOHN J. PATRICK
Telecommunications Management Institution: BOB AFFE
Transportation Research Center: STEPHEN MCDONALD
Underwater Science: CHARLES BEEKER
West European National Resource Center: PETER BONDANELLA
William Hammond Mathers Museum: GEOFFREY W. CONRAD
Workshop in Political Theory and Policy Analysis: ELINOR OSTROM, VINCENT OSTROM

Indiana University East

Richmond, IN 47374
Telephone: (317) 966-8261
Internet: www.iue.edu
Chancellor: DAVID J. FULTON
Library Director: GORDON LYNN HUFFORD
Number of students: 2,480

Indiana University at Kokomo

Kokomo, IN 46902
Telephone: (317) 453-2000
Internet: www.iuk.edu
Chancellor: RUTH J. PERSON
Vice-Chancellor for Academic Affairs: STUART GREEN
Number of students: 2,772

Indiana University Northwest

Gary, IN 46408
Telephone: (219) 980-6700
Internet: www.iun.edu
Chancellor: BRUCE BERGLAND
Executive Vice-Chancellor for Academic Affairs: MARILYN VASQUEZ
Vice-Chancellor for Student Affairs: ERNEST SMITH
Library Director: ROBERT MORAN
Library of 200,000 vols, 200,000 govt documents
Number of students: 5,149

Indiana University at South Bend

South Bend, IN 46634
Telephone: (574) 520-5005
Internet: www.iusb.edu
Chancellor: Dr UNA RAE MECK
Library Dir: MICHELE RUSSO
Number of students: 7,457

DEANS

College of Liberal Arts and Sciences: Dr ELIZABETH DUNN
College Health Sciences: Dr MARY JO REGAN-KUBINSKI
Raclin School of the Arts: MARVIN CURTIS
School of Business and Economics: Dr ROBERT DUCOFFE
School of Education: Dr DAVID HORVATH
School of Public and Environmental Affairs: Dr LEDA MCINTYRE HALL
School of Social Work: Dr MARILYNNE RAMSEY (Dir)

Indiana University Southeast

New Albany, IN 47150
Telephone: (812) 945-2731
Internet: www.ius.edu
Chancellor: SANDRA R. PATTERSON-RANDLES
Vice-Chancellor of Academic Affairs: GILBERT ATNIP
Vice-Chancellor for Administrative Affairs: STEPHEN J. TAKSAR
Vice-Chancellor for Student Affairs: Dr RUTH C. GARVEY-NIX
Director of Library Services: C. MARTIN ROSEN
Library of 585,000 vols and microforms, 1,200 current periodicals
Number of students: 6,716

DEANS

Division of Nursing: Dr LILLIAN E. YEAGER
School of Education: GLORIA MURRAY
School of Natural Sciences: Prof. BAHMAN (BEN) E. NASSIM
School of Social Sciences: CLIFF STATEN

Indiana University—Purdue University at Fort Wayne

2101 E Coliseum Blvd, Fort Wayne, IN 46805-1499
Telephone: (260) 481-6812
Internet: www.ipfw.edu
Chancellor: MICHAEL A. WARTELL

Vice-Chancellor for Academic Affairs: SUSAN B. HANNAH
Vice-Chancellor for Financial Affairs: WALTER J. BRANSON
Vice-Chancellor for Student Affairs: FRANK L. BORELLI
Registrar: KEVIN M. BROWNE
Library Dir: JUDITH L. VIOLETTE

Library of 300,000 vols, 1,700 current periodicals, 150,000 govt publications, microforms, audiovisual items

Number of students: 6,463

DEANS

Division of Continuing Studies: Dr MICHAEL STOCKSTILL (Exec. Dir)
Division of Labour Studies: MARK A. CROUCH (Dir)
Division of Organizational Leadership and Supervision: Dr KIMBERLY S. MCDONALD (Co-ordinator)
Division of Public and Environmental Affairs: Dr WILLIAM G. LUDWIN
Medical Education: Prof. BARTH H. RAGATZ (Dir)
School of Arts and Sciences: Prof. EVANGELOS COUFOUDAKIS
School of Business and Management Studies: Prof. JOHN WELLINGTON
School of Education: Prof. ROBERTA B. WIENER
School of Engineering, Technology and Computer Science: Prof. G. ALLEN PUGH
School of Health Sciences: Prof. JAMES E. JONES
School of Visual and Performing Arts: Prof. BENJAMIN CHRISTY

Indiana University—Purdue University at Indianapolis

Indianapolis, IN 46202
Telephone: (317) 274-4417
Internet: www.iupui.edu

Chancellor: Dr WILLIAM M. PLATER (acting)
Exec. Vice-Chancellor and Dean of the Faculties: Dr WILLIAM M. PLATER
Vice-Chancellor for Administration and Finance: ROBERT E. MARTIN
Vice-Chancellor for External Affairs: CHERYL G. SULLIVAN
Vice-Chancellor for Planning and Institutional Improvement: Dr TRUDY W. BANTA
Vice-Chancellor for Research and Graduate Education: Dr MARK L. BRENNER
Vice-Chancellor for Student Life and Diversity: KAREN WHITNEY

Number of students: 29,025

DEANS

Herron School of Art: VALERIE EICKMEIER
Kelley School of Business: Prof. JOHN M. HASSELL (Acting Assoc. Dean)
School of Allied Health Sciences: Prof. MARK SOTHMANN
School of Dentistry: Prof. LAWRENCE I. GOLDBLATT
School of Education: GERARDO GONZALES
School of Engineering and Technology: H. ONER YURTSEVEN
School of Informatics: Dr DARRELL L. BAILEY
School of Journalism: Prof. JAMES W. BROWN
School of Law: Prof. ANTHONY A. TARR
School of Liberal Arts: Prof. HERMAN J. SAATKAMP, Jr
School of Library and Information Science: Prof. BLAISE CRONIN
School of Medicine: Prof. D. CRAIG BRATER
School of Nursing: Prof. ANGELA BARRON MCBRIDE
School of Physical Education and Tourism Management: Prof. P. NICHOLAS. KELLUM
School of Science: Prof. DAVID L. STOCUM
School of Social Work: MICHAEL PATCHNER

CHAIRS OF DEPARTMENTS

Kelley School of Business:
- Accounting and Information Systems: JAMES H. PRATT
- Business Economics and Public Policy: MICHELE FRATIANNI
- Business Law: TERRY M. DWORKIN
- Distance Education: RICHARD J. MAGJUKA
- Finance: ROBERT H. JENNINGS
- Management: HARVEY HEGARTY
- Marketing: FRANKLIN ACITO
- Masters of Professional Accountancy: WILLIAM R. KULSRUD
- Operations and Decision Technologies: MUNIRPALLAM A. VENKATARAMANAN
- Undergraduate Program: GLEN A. LARSEN

School of Allied Health Sciences:
- Clinical Laboratory Science: LINDA M. KASPER (Dir)
- Cytotechnology: WILLIAM N. CRABTREE (Dir)
- Health Information Administration: DANITA FORGEY (Dir)
- Health Sciences Education: Dr KAREN E. GABLE (Dir)
- Histotechnology: GLENDA F. HOYE (Dir)
- Nutrition and Dietetics: Prof. JACQUELYNN M. O'PALKA (Dir)
- Occupational Therapy: CELESTINE HAMANT (Dir)
- Paramedic Sciences: LEON H. BELL (Dir)
- Physical Therapy: Dr WILLIAM S. QUILLEN (Dir)
- Radiation Therapy: DONNA K. DUNN (Dir)
- Radiologic Sciences: EMILY M. HERNANDEZ (Dir)
- Respiratory Therapy: Prof. DEBORAH L. CULLEN (Dir)
- Therapeutic Outcomes Research: Prof. NEIL OLDRIDGE

School of Dentistry:
- Endodontics: CECIL E. BROWN, Jr (acting)
- Oral Biology: Prof. ARDEN G. CHRISTEN (acting)
- Oral Facial Development: Prof. JAMES K. HARTSFIELD
- Oral Pathology, Medicine and Radiology: Prof. SUSAN L. ZUNT (acting)
- Oral Surgery and Hospital Dentistry: Dr WILLIAM C. HINE, Jr (acting)
- Periodontics and Allied Dental Programs: Prof. E. BRADY HANCOCK
- Preventative and Community Dentistry: Prof. DOMENICK T. ZERO
- Restorative Dentistry: Prof. E. STEVEN DUKE

School of Engineering and Technology:
- Biomedical Engineering Program: Prof. EDWARD J. BERBARI (Dir)
- Computer Technology: Prof. THOMAS HO
- Construction Technology: Prof. ERDOGAN SENER
- Electrical and Computer Engineering: Prof. RUSSEL C. EBERHART (acting)
- Electrical and Computer Engineering Technology: Prof. MARVIN NEEDLER
- Mechanical Engineering: Prof. HASAN AKAY
- Mechanical Engineering Technology: Prof. JACK ZECHER
- Organizational Leadership and Supervision: CLIFFORD GOODWIN

School of Liberal Arts:
- Anthropology: JEANETTE DICKERSON-PUTMAN
- Communication Studies: Prof. JOHN PARRISH-SPROWL
- Economics: Dr ROBERT SANDY
- English: Prof. CHRISTIAN KLOESEL
- Foreign Languages and Cultures: Prof. GABRIELLE BERSIER
- Geography: Dr TIMOTHY S. BROTHERS
- History: Dr PHILIP V. SCARPINO
- Medical Humanities: Prof. WILLIAM H. SCHNEIDER (Dir)
- Museum Studies: Dr ELIZABETH KRYDER-REID
- Philanthropic Studies: EUGENE TEMPEL (Exec. Dir, Center on Philanthropy)
- Philosophy: Prof. MICHAEL B. BURKE
- Political Science: Prof. JOHN MCCORMICK
- Religious Studies: Prof. ROWLAND A. SHERRILL
- Sociology: Dr DAVID A. FORD

School of Medicine:
- Anaesthesia: Dr ROBERT K. STOELTING
- Anatomy and Cell Biology: Prof. DAVID B. BURR
- Biochemistry and Molecular Biology: Prof. ROBERT A. HARRIS
- Cellular and Integrative Physiology: Dr RODNEY RHOADES
- Dermatology: Dr JEFFREY B. TRAVERS
- Emergency Medicine: Prof. ROLAND B. MCGRATH
- Experimental Oncology Laboratory: GEORGE WEBER (Dir)
- Family Medicine: Prof. DOUGLAS B. MCKEAG
- Medical and Molecular Genetics: Dr GAIL HABEGGER VANCE
- Medicine: Prof. DAVID W. CRABB
- Microbiology and Immunology: Prof. HAL E. BROXMEYER
- Neurology: Prof. JOSÉ BILLER
- Obstetrics and Gynaecology: Prof. FREDERICK B. STEHMAN
- Ophthalmology: Prof. ROBERT D. YEE
- Orthopaedic Surgery: Prof. STEPHEN B. TRIPPEL
- Otolaryngology–Head and Neck Surgery: Prof. RICHARD T. MIYAMOTO
- Paediatrics: Prof. RICHARD L. SCHREINER
- Pathology and Laboratory Medicine: Prof. JOHN N. EBLE
- Pharmacology and Toxicology: Prof. MICHAEL R. VASKO
- Physical Medicine and Rehabilitation: RALPH M. BUSCHBACHER (acting)
- Physiology and Biophysics: RODNEY A. RHOADES
- Psychiatry: Dr CHRISTOPHER MCDOUGLE
- Public Health: Dr STEPHEN J. JAY
- Radiation Oncology: Prof. MARCUS E. RANDALL
- Radiology: Prof. VALERIE P. JACKSON
- Surgery: Prof. JAY L. GROSFELD
- Urology: Prof. MICHAEL O. KOCH

School of Nursing:
- Adult Health: JUANITA KECK
- Environments for Health: Prof. DANIEL J. PESUT
- Family Health: Prof. SHARON SIMS

School of Physical Education and Tourism Management:
- Physical Education: BETTY JONES
- Tourism, Conventions and Events Management: LINDA R. BROTHERS

School of Science:
- Biology: NORMAN D. LEES
- Chemistry: Prof. FRANKLIN A. SCHULTZ
- Computer Science: Prof. MATHEW J. PALAKAL
- Geology: ANDREW P. BARTH
- Mathematical Sciences: Prof. BENZION BOUKAI
- Physics: Prof. GAUTAM VEMURI
- Psychology: Prof. JOHN GREGOR FETTERMAN

INDIANA WESLEYAN UNIVERSITY

4201 S Washington St, Marion, IN 46953
Telephone: (765) 674-6901
Fax: (765) 677-2499
Internet: www.indwes.edu

Founded 1920

Academic year: September to April
Pres.: Dr JAMES BARNES
Vice-Pres. for Academic Affairs: Dr HENRY SMITH
Vice-Pres. for Financial Affairs: ELVIN WEINMANN
Librarian: SHEILA CARLBLOM
Library of 133,396 vols
Number of teachers: 121
Number of students: 3,027

ITT TECHNICAL INSTITUTE

9511 Angola Court, Indianapolis, IN 46268-1119
Telephone: (317) 875-8640
Internet: www.itt-tech.edu
Private control
President: Dr LARRY L. GRAPHMAN
Number of students: 1,690
Areas of study: automated manufacturing technology, computer and electronics engineering technology, computer drafting and design, computer visualization technology, computer-aided drafting and design technology, electronics engineering technology, information systems security, information technology–computer network systems, information technology–multimedia, information technology–software applications and programming, information technology–web development, technical project management for electronic commerce; more than 100 campuses.

MANCHESTER COLLEGE

604 E College Ave, North Manchester, IN 46962
Telephone: (260) 982-5000
Internet: www.manchester.edu
Founded 1889
Four-year liberal arts and professional studies
Pres.: JO YOUNG SWITZER
Exec. Vice-Pres.: Dr DAVID F. MCFADDEN
Vice-Pres. and Dean for Academic Affairs: GLENN SHARFMAN
Vice-Pres. for Financial Affairs and Treas.: JACK GOCHENAUR
Vice-Pres. for Student Devt: BETH SWEITZER-RILEY
Registrar: LILA D. HAMMER
Dir of the Library: ROBIN J. GRATZ
Library of 160,000 vols
Number of teachers: 72 full-time
Number of students: 1,054
Publications: *Manchester Magazine* (4 a week), *The Oak Leaves* (26 a year), *The Aurora* (1 a year).

MARIAN COLLEGE

3200 Cold Spring Rd, Indianapolis, IN 46222-1997
Telephone: (317) 955-6000
Fax: (317) 955-6448
E-mail: regis@marian.edu
Internet: www.marian.edu
Founded 1851
Baccalaureate liberal arts college
Academic year: August to May
President: DANIEL J. ELSENER
Chief Advancement Officer: ANN RUNYON
Dean for Academic Affairs: Dr C. EDWARD BALOG
Dean for Student Affairs: WILLIAM H. WOODMAN
Chief Financial Officer: RUSSELL GLASSBURN
Librarian: KELLEY GRIFFITH
Library of 135,000 vols
Number of teachers: 77 (full-time)
Number of students: 1,427

MARTIN UNIVERSITY

2171 Avondale Place, Indianapolis, IN 46218
Telephone: (317) 543-3243
Fax: (317) 543-4790
Internet: www.martin.edu
Founded 1977
Private control
President: Dr ALGEANIA FREEMAN
Number of teachers: 33
Number of students: 1,000
Academic divisions: business and management, human sciences, liberal arts, religious studies, science and mathematics.

OAKLAND CITY UNIVERSITY

138 N Lucretia St, Oakland City, IN 47660
Telephone: (800) 737-5125
Fax: (812) 749-1433
E-mail: ocuadmit@oak.edu
Internet: www.oak.edu
Founded 1885
Private control
Academic year: August to May
Pres.: Dr RAY G. BARBER
Provost: Dr MICHAEL ATKINSON
Vice-Pres. for Admin. and Finance: Dr ROBERT E. YEAGER
Dir of Advancement: BRIAN BAKER
Registrar: BETTY BURNS
Library Dir: Dr DENISE J. PINNICK
Number of teachers: 32
Number of students: 2,310 (2,165 undergraduate, 145 graduate)

DEANS

Chapman Seminary: Dr DOUGLAS LOW
School of Arts and Sciences: Dr CLAUDINE CUTCHINE
School of Business: (vacant)
School of Education: Dr MARY JO BEAUCHAMP

PURDUE UNIVERSITY

West Lafayette, IN 47907
Telephone: (765) 494-4600
Fax: (765) 494-7875
E-mail: webmaster@purdue.edu
Internet: www.purdue.edu
Founded 1869; instruction commenced 1874
State control
Academic year: August to May
Chancellor: MICHAEL A. WARTELL
Pres.: FRANCE A. CÓRDOVA
Exec. Vice-Pres. for Academic Affairs and Provost: TIMOTHY D. SANDS
Exec. Vice-Pres. for Business and Finance, Treas.: ALPHONSO V. DIAZ
Sr Vice-Pres., Treas. and Chief Operating Officer: JOSEPH B. HORNETT
Sr Vice-Pres. for Business Services and Asst Treas.: JAMES S. ALMOND
Vice-Pres. for Devt: ROBIN BELLINGER
Vice-Pres. for Ethics and Compliance: ALYSA CHRISTMAS ROLLOCK
Vice-Pres. for Human Resources: LUIS E. LEWIN
Vice-Pres. for Information Technology and Chief Information Officer: GERARD MCCARTNEY
Vice-Pres. for Marketing and Media: TERI LUCIE THOMPSON
Vice-Pres. for Physical Facilities: ROBERT MCMAINS
Vice-Pres. for Research: RICHARD O. BUCKIUS
Registrar: ROBERT A. KUBAT
Dean of Libraries: JAMES L. MULLINS
Dean of Students: L. TONY HAWKINS
Library: see Libraries and Archives
Number of teachers: 3,768
Number of students: 67,968 (39,697 at West Lafayette campus, 28,271 at regional campuses)
Publications: *Inside Purdue*, *Perspective*, *University Bulletins*

DEANS

College of Agriculture: JAY AKRIDGE
College of Consumer and Family Sciences: DENNIS A. SAVAIANO
College of Education: MARYANN SANTOS DE BARONA
College of Engineering: LEAH H. JAMIESON
College of Health and Human Sciences: CHRISTINE M. LADISCH
College of Liberal Arts: IRWIN WEISER
School of Management and Krannert Graduate School of Management: JERRY LYNCH
College of Pharmacy: CRAIG K. SVENSSON
College of Science: JEFF ROBERTS
College of Technology: DENNIS R. DEPEW
Graduate School: M. J. T. SMITH
School of Veterinary Medicine: WILLIE M. REED

UNIVERSITY BRANCHES

Purdue University Calumet

2200 169th Street, Hammond, IN 463232094
Telephone: (219) 989-2400
Fax: (219) 989-2775
E-mail: adms@calumet.purdue.edu
Internet: www.calumet.purdue.edu
Chancellor: HOWARD COHEN
Vice-Chancellor for Academic Affairs: NABIL A. IBRAHIM
Vice-Chancellor for Admin. Services: GARY H. NEWSOM
Vice-Chancellor for Advancement: DOLORES M. STEUER-WAGNER
Vice-Chancellor for Student Services and Dean of Students: LEO A. BRYANT
Exec. Dean of the Graduate School: DANIEL DUNN
Registrar: ANNE AGOSTO-SEVERA
Library Dir: KATHRYN H. CARPENTER
Library of 264,000 vols
Number of teachers: 247
Number of students: 8,863 (7,920 undergraduate, 943 graduate)

DEANS

School of Education: Dr ROBERT RIVERS
School of Engineering, Mathematics and Science: Dr MICHAEL GEALT
School of Liberal Arts and Social Sciences: Dr DANIEL DUNN
School of Management: Dr SHOMIR SIL
School of Nursing: Dr PEGGY GERARD
School of Technology: DENNIS KORCHEK

Purdue University North Central

1401 S U.S. 421, Westville, IN 46391
Telephone: (219) 8720527
Fax: (219) 7855355
E-mail: admissions@pnc.edu
Internet: www.pnc.edu
Founded 1967
Chancellor: Dr JAMES B. DWORKIN
Vice-Chancellor for Academic Affairs: Dr L. EDWARD BEDNAR
Vice-Chancellor for Admin.: Dr G. WILLIAM BACK
Vice-Chancellor for Devt: JOSEPH K. GOEPFRICH
Registrar: GEORGE ROYSTER
Library Dir: K. R. JOHNSON
Number of teachers: 244
Number of students: 3,657 (3,635 undergraduate, 22 graduate)

ROSE-HULMAN INSTITUTE OF TECHNOLOGY

5500 Wabash Ave, Terre Haute, IN 47803
Telephone: (812) 877-1511
Fax: (812) 877-8001
E-mail: webmaster@rose-hulman.edu
Internet: www.rose-hulman.edu

Founded 1874

Pres.: Gerald S. Jakubowski
Vice-Pres. for Academic Affairs and Dean of the Faculty: Prof. Arthur B. Western
Assoc. Vice-Pres. for Business and Finance: Robert A. Coons
Registrar: Timothy Prickel
Dir of the Library: John Robson

Library of 70,000 vols, 22,000 vols of periodicals, 1,500 NASA and NATO documents
Number of teachers: 172
Number of students: 1,832

Publication: *Bulletin* (every 2 years).

SAINT JOSEPH'S COLLEGE

Rensselaer, IN 47978
Telephone: (219) 866-6000
E-mail: admissions@saintjoe.edu
Internet: www.saintjoe.edu

Founded 1889

President: Dr Ernest R. Mills, III
Registrar: Carol Burns
Librarian: Catherine Saylers

Library of 150,000 vols
Number of teachers: 64
Number of students: 974

SAINT MARY-OF-THE-WOODS COLLEGE

Saint Mary-of-the-Woods, IN 47876
Telephone: (812) 535-5151
Fax: (812) 535-5010
E-mail: smeier@smwc.edu
Internet: www.smwc.edu

Founded 1840
Academic year: August to May

Pres.: Dr David Behrs
Co-Chancellors: Dr Barbara Doherty, Dr Jeanne Knoerle
Chief Academic Officer: Dr Chris Bahr
Dir of Academic Records and Institutional Research: Susan Meier
Librarian: Judith Tribble

Library of 151,000 vols
Number of teachers: 67
Number of students: 881 f.t.e.

Publication: *Aurora* (literary journal, 2 a year)

CHAIRS OF DEPARTMENTS

Business: Dr Jennie Mitchell
Education: Debra Hardin
English, Journalism and Language: Terry McCammon
Mark Hulman George School of Equine Studies: Dr Christine Stewart Marks
Performing and Visual Arts: Pat Jancosek
Science, Mathematics and Computer Information Systems: Dr Ellen Cunningham
Social and Behavioural Science: Dr Glenna Simons
Theology and Philosophy: Dr Robert Watts

SAINT MARY'S COLLEGE

Notre Dame, IN 46556
Telephone: (219) 284-4000
E-mail: admission@saintmarys.edu
Internet: www.saintmarys.edu

Founded 1844

Pres.: Dr Marilou Eldred
Vice-Pres. and Dean of Faculty: Dr Dorothy M. Feigl
Vice-Pres. for College Relations: (vacant)
Vice-Pres. for Fiscal Affairs: Daniel F. Osberger
Vice-Pres. for Student Affairs: Dr Linda L. Timm
Registrar: Lorraine A. Kitchener

Library of 195,424 vols
Number of students: 1,435 full-time

Publications: *Blue Mantle*, *Chimes* (1 a year), *Courier*.

SAINT MEINRAD SEMINARY AND SCHOOL OF THEOLOGY

200 Hill Dr., St Meinrad, IN 47577
Telephone: (812) 357-6611
Fax: (812) 357-6964
E-mail: theology@saintmeinrad.edu
Internet: www.saintmeinrad.edu

Private control

President and Rector: Fr Denis Robinson
Academic Dean: Dr Robert Alvis

Library of 170,000 vols
Number of teachers: 31
Number of students: 136

TAYLOR UNIVERSITY

236 W Reade Ave, Upland, IN 46989-1001
Telephone: (317) 998-2751
Fax: (317) 998-4925
E-mail: admissions_u@taylor.edu
Internet: www.taylor.edu

Founded 1846
Private interdenominational Christian liberal arts college; campuses in Upland and Fort Wayne
Academic year: September to May (three terms)

Pres.: Dr David J. Gyertson
Chancellor: Dr Jay Kesler
Exec. Vice-Pres. and Provost: Dr Daryl Yost
Vice-Pres. for Admin. and Planning: Steve Bedi
Registrar: LaGatha Adkison
Dir of Admissions: Stephen Mortland
Librarian: Dan Bowell

Library of 235,114 vols
Number of teachers: 153
Number of students: 2,400 (Upland campus 1,900, Fort Wayne campus 500)

Publications: *Profile*, *Taylor Club News*, *Taylor University Magazine*.

TRINE UNIVERSITY

1 University Ave, Angola, IN 46703-1764
Telephone: (260) 665-4100
Fax: (260) 665-4292
E-mail: admit@trine.edu
Internet: www.trine.edu

Founded 1884 as Tri-State Normal College; present name 2008
Private control

Pres.: Dr Earl D. Brooks, II
Sr Vice-Pres.: Michael R. Bock
Vice-Pres. for Academic Affairs: Dr David R. Finley
Vice-Pres. for Alumni and Devt: Raymond Stuckey
Vice-Pres. for Enrollment Management: Scott J. Goplin
Vice-Pres. for Finance: Jody Greer
Registrar: Debbie Helmsing
Library Director: Kristina Brewer

Number of teachers: 65
Number of students: 1,480

DEANS

Allen School of Engineering and Technology: Dr David Finley
Ketner School of Business: Dr Jeffery Sherlock
School of Arts and Sciences: Dr Dolores Tichenor
School of Education: Dr Suzanne Van-Wagner

BRANCH CAMPUSES

Trine University—Angola North: 498 E Harcourt Rd, Angola, IN 46703; tel. (260) 624-2420; fax (260) 624-2380; e-mail trinenorth@trine.edu; Dir David Wagner.

Trine University—Fort Wayne: 9910 Dupont Circle Drive E, Suite 130, Fort Wayne, IN 46825; tel. (260) 483-4949; fax (260) 482-8553; e-mail trinefw@trine.edu; Dir of Criminal Justice Program Dr Thomas Beckner.

Trine University—Merrillville: 8400 Louisiana St, Merrillville, IN 46410; tel. (219) 942-9712; fax (219) 942-7935; e-mail trinem@trine.edu; Dir David Vrbanich.

Trine University—South Bend/Mishiwaka: 4101 Edison Lakes Parkway, Suite 250, Mishiwaka, IN 46545; tel. (574) 243-0500; fax (574) 243-0600; e-mail trinesb@trine.edu; Office Man. Emily Bay.

UNIVERSITY OF EVANSVILLE

1800 Lincoln Ave, Evansville, IN 47722
Telephone: (812) 479-2000
Fax: (812) 479-2320
E-mail: webmaster@evansville.edu
Internet: www.evansville.edu

Founded 1854
Academic year: August to May

Pres.: Dr Thomas A. Kazee
Vice-Pres. for Academic Affairs: Dr Susan Kupisch
Vice-Pres. for Institutional Advancement: John Barner
Vice-Pres. for Fiscal Affairs: Jeffrey Wolf
Dean of Students: Dana Clayton
Dir of Adult Education: Carla Doty
Dir of Univ. Relations: Lucy Himstedt
Registrar: Amy Brandebury
Univ. Librarian: William Louden

Number of teachers: 192
Number of students: 2,400

DEANS

College of Arts and Sciences: Dr Susan Calovini
College of Education and Health Sciences: Dr Lynn R. Penland
College of Engineering and Computer Science: Dr Philip Gerhart
School of Business Admin.: Dr Stephen Standifird

UNIVERSITY OF INDIANAPOLIS

1400 East Hanna Ave, Indianapolis, IN 46227
Telephone: (317) 788-3368
Internet: www.uindy.edu

Founded 1902

Pres.: Dr Jerry Israel
Sr Vice-Pres. and Provost: Dr Everette Freeman
Vice-Pres. for Business and Treasurer: Kendall L. Hottell
Vice-Pres. for Enrollment: Mark T. Weigand
Vice-Pres. for Institutional Advancement: Michael J. Ferin
Vice-Pres. for Student Affairs: David W. Wantz
Registrar: Dr Mary Beth Bagg

Dean of Extended Programs: Dr PAT JEFFERSON BIBLY
Coordinator of Graduate Business Programmes: Dr RENEE WACHTER
Dir of Admissions: RON WILKS
Librarian: Dr PHILIP H. YOUNG

Library of 180,000 vols
Number of teachers: 165 full-time
Number of students: 4,300

UNIVERSITY OF NOTRE DAME

Notre Dame, IN 46556
Telephone: (574) 631-5000
E-mail: admissions@nd.edu
Internet: www.nd.edu

Founded 1842
Academic year: August to May

Pres.: Rev. JOHN I. JENKINS
Provost: Dr THOMAS G. BURISH
Vice-Pres. and Sr Assoc. Provost for Budget and Planning: CHRISTINE MAZIAR
Vice-Pres. and Assoc. Provost for Faculty Affairs: DON POPE-DAVIS
Vice-Pres. and Assoc. Provost for Undergraduate and Int. Studies: DENNIS JACOBS
Exec. Vice-Pres.: JOHN F. AFFLECK-GRAVES
Vice-Pres. for Business Operations: JAMES J. LYPHOUT
Vice-Pres. for Finance: JOHN A. SEJDINAJ
Vice-Pres. for Public Affairs and Communication: JANET M. BOTZ
Vice-Pres. for Research: ROBERT J. BERNHARD
Vice-Pres. for Student Affairs: Rev. THOMAS P. DOYLE
Vice-Pres. for Univ. Relations: LOUIS M. NANNI
Vice-Pres. and Gen. Counsel: MARIANNE CORR
Vice-Pres. and Chief Investment Officer: SCOTT C. MALPASS
Registrar: HAROLD L. PACE
Dir of Admissions: ROBERT MUNDY
Dir of Libraries: SUSAN OHMER
Archivist: WENDY CLAUSON SCHLERETH

Library: see Libraries
Number of teachers: 1,055
Number of students: 11,817

Publications: *Academy of Management Review*, *American Midland Naturalist*, *Bullan*, *Journal of College and University Law*, *Journal of Legislation*, *Journal of Multicultural Counseling and Development*, *Nineteenth-Century Contexts*, *Notre Dame Journal of Formal Logic*, *Notre Dame Journal of Law, Ethics and Public Policy*, *Notre Dame Law Review*, *Notre Dame Philosophical Review*, *Notre Dame Review*, *Religion and Literature*, *Review of Politics*, *Technical Review*, *The American Journal of Jurisprudence*

DEANS

College of Arts and Letters: JOHN T. MCGREEVY
College of Engineering: PETER KILPATRICK
College of Science: GREGORY CRAWFORD
First Year of Studies: HUGH R. PAGE, Jr
Graduate School: GREGORY STERLING
Law School: NELL NEWTON
Mendoza College of Business: Dr CAROLYN Y. WOO
School of Architecture: MICHAEL N. LYKOUDIS

PROFESSORS

College of Arts and Letters:

ALDOUS, J., Sociology
AMERIKS, K., Philosophy
ANADON, J., Romance Languages and Literatures
APPLEBY, R. S., History
ARNOLD, P., Political Science
AUNE, D. E., Theology
AYO, N., Liberal Studies
BARBER, S. A., Political Science
BARTELL, E., Economics
BIDDICK, K., History
BLACHLY, A., Music
BLANTZ, T. E., History
BOBIK, J., Philosophy
BORKOWSKI, J. G., Psychology
BOULTON, M. B., Romance Languages and Literatures
BOWER, C., Music
BRADLEY, K. R., Classics
BRADSHAW, P. F., Theology
BROGAN, J. V., English
BRUNS, G. L., English
BURRELL, D. B., Philosophy
BUSTAMANTE, J. A., Psychology, Sociology
BUTTIGIEG, J. A., English
CACHEY, T., Romance Languages and Literatures
CARDENAS, G., Psychology
CRAFTON, D., Film, Television and Theatre
CRAMER, C., Music
CUMMINGS, E. M., Psychology
CUNNINGHAM, L. S., Theology
DALEY, S. J., Theology
DALLMAYR, F., Political Theory
DAMATTA, R., Anthropology
DAVID, M., Philosophy
DAY, J. D., Psychology
DELANEY, C. F., Philosophy
DEPAUL, M., Philosophy
DETLEFSEN, M., Philosophy
DOODY, M. A., English Literature
DOUGHERTY, J. P., English
DOUTHWAITE, J., Romance Languages and Literatures
DOWTY, A., Political Science
DUNNE, J. S., Theology
DUTT, A., Economics
DYE, K., Music
EMERY, K., Jr, Program of Liberal Studies
FLINT, T., Philosophy
FOX, C. B., English
FRANCIS, M. J., Political Science
FREDDOSO, A. J., Philosophy
FREDMAN, S., English
FRESE, D., English
GERNES, S. G., English
GERSH, S., Medieval Studies
GIBBONS, L., English, Film, Television and Theatre
GODMILOW, J., Film, Television and Theatre
GUTTING, G., Philosophy
HAIMO, E. T., Music
HALLINAN, M. W., Sociology
HALTON, E., Sociology
HAMBURG, G., History
HAMLIN, C., History
HART, K., English
HERO, R. E., Political Science
HIGGINS, P., Music
HOLLAND, P. D., Film, Television and Theatre
HÖSLE, V., German and Russian Languages and Literatures
HOWARD, D. A., Philosophy
HOWARD, G. S., Psychology
JAKSIC, I., History
JEMIELITY, T. J., English
JENSEN, R., Economics
JOHANSEN, R. C., Political Science
JOHNSON, M., Theology
JOY, L. S., Philosophy
KAVENY, M., Theology
KIM, K., Economics
KLINE, E. A., English
KOMMERS, D. P., Political Science
KREMER, W. J., Art, Art History and Design
KRIEG, R. A., Theology
KSELMAN, T., History
LAPIDGE, M., English
LEAHY, W. H., Economics
LOPEZ, G., Political Science
LOUX, M. J., Philosophy
MCADAMS, A. J., Political Science
MCBRIEN, R. P., Theology
MCINERNY, R., Philosophy
MCKENNA, J. J., Anthropology
MAINWARING, S., Political Science
MANIER, E., Philosophy
MANN, G. L., English
MARSDEN, G. M., History
MARULLO, T., German and Russian Languages and Literature
MATTHIAS, J. E., English
MAXWELL, S. E., Psychology
MEIER, J. P., Theology
MOODY, P., Political Science
MURRAY, D., History
NEYREY, S. J., Theology
NICGORSKI, W. J., Political Science, Program of Liberal Studies
NOBLE, T., Medieval Institute
NORTON, R. E., German and Russian Languages and Literatures
O'BRIEN O'KEEFFE, K., English
O'DONNELL, G., Political Science
O'REGAN, C., Theology
O'ROURKE, W. A., English
PILKINTON, M. C., Film, Television and Theatre
PLANTINGA, A., Philosophy
POPE-DAVIS, D., Psychology
POWER, F. C., Liberal Studies, Psychology
PROFIT, V. B., German and Russian Languages and Literatures
ROCHE, M., German Language and Literature, Philosophy
ROOS, J., Political Science
ROS, J., Economics
ROSENBERG, C., Art, Art History and Design
SAYERS, V., English
SAYRE, K. M., Philosophy
SCHLERETH, T. J., American Studies
SCHMUHL, R., American Studies
SCULLY, T. R., Political Science
SEIDENSPINNER-NÚÑEZ, D., Romance Languages and Literatures
SHEERIN, D., Classics, Theology
SHRADER-FRECHETTE, K., Philosophy, Biological Sciences
SKURSKI, R., Economics
SLAUGHTER, T., History
SLOAN, P. R., Liberal Studies
SMYTH, J., History
STERBA, J., Philosophy
STERLING, G. E., Theology
SWARTZ, T., Economics
TURNER, J., History
ULRICH, E., Theology
VALENZUELA, J. S., Sociology
VANDEN BOSSCHE, C., English
VANDERKAM, J. C., Theology
VAYRYNEN, R., Political Science
WALSHE, A. P., Political Science
WALTON, J., English
WATSON, S., Philosophy
WEGS, R., History
WEIGERT, A., Sociology
WEITHMAN, P., Philosophy
WELLE, J., Romance Languages and Literatures
WERGE, T., English
WHITMAN, T., Psychology
YOUENS, S., Music
ZIAREK, E., English

College of Engineering

Department of Aerospace and Mechanical Engineering:

ATASSI, H. M., Aero-acoustics
BATILL, S. M., Design
CORKE, T. C., Fluid Mechanics
DUNN, P. F., Particle Dynamics
INCROPERA, F. P., Heat Transfer
JUMPER, E. J., Aerodynamics
MUELLER, T. J., Fluid Mechanics
NELSON, R. C., Aerodynamics
OVAERT, T., Manufacturing
PAOLUCCI, S., Fluid Mechanics
RENAUD, J. E., Design

SEN, M., Heat Transfer
SKAAR, S. B., Control
THOMAS, F. O., Fluid Mechanics

Department of Chemical Engineering:

BRENNECKE, J. F.
CHANG, H.-C.
KANTOR, J. C.
LEIGHTON, D. T.
MCCREADY, M. J.
MCGINN, P. J.
MILLER, A. E.
SCHMITZ, R. A.
STADTHERR, M. A.
STRIEDER, W. C.
VARMA, A.
WOLF, E. E.

Department of Civil Engineering and Geological Sciences:

BURNS, P. C.
KAREEM, A.
SILLIMAN, S. E.
TAYLOR, J. I.

Department of Computer Science and Engineering:

BOWYER, K.
CHEN, D. Z.
KOGGE, P. M.
UHRAN, J., Jr

Department of Electrical Engineering:

ANTSAKLIS, P. J.
BAUER, P. H.
BERNSTEIN, G. H.
COLLINS, O.
COSTELLO, D. J.
FUJA, T. E.
HUANG, Y.-F.
LENT, C. S.
MERZ, J. L.
POROD, W.
ROSENTHAL, J.
SAIN, M. K.
SEABAUGH, A. C.
STEVENSON, R. L.

College of Science:

ALBER, M. S., Mathematics
APRAHAMIAN, A., Physics
ARNOLD, G. B., Physics
ASMUS, K.-D., Chemistry and Biochemistry
BARABASI, A.-L., Physics
BASU, S. C., Chemistry and Biochemistry
BELOVSKY, G. E., Biological Sciences
BENDER, H. A., Biological Sciences
BERRY, H. G., Physics
BESANSKY, N. J., Biological Sciences
BIGI, I. I., Physics
BLACKSTEAD, H. A., Physics
BOTTEI, R. S., Chemistry and Biochemistry
BUECHLER, S. A., Mathematics
BUNKER, B. A., Physics
CAO, J., Mathematics
CASON, N. M., Physics
COLLINS, F. H., Biological Sciences
CONNOLLY, F. X., Mathematics
CREARY, X., Chemistry and Biochemistry
DOBROWOLSKA-FURDYNA, M., Physics
DUMAN, J., Biological Sciences
DWYER, W. G., Mathematics
FAYBUSOVICH, L. E., Mathematics
FEHLNER, T. P., Chemistry and Biochemistry
FRASER, M. J., Jr, Biological Sciences
FRAUENDORF, S. G., Physics
FURDYNA, J. K., Physics
GARG, U., Physics
GOERRES, J., Physics
HAHN, A. J., Mathematics
HELLENTHAL, R., Biological Sciences
HELQUIST, P., Chemistry and Biochemistry
HIMONAS, A. A., Mathematics
HOWARD, A., Mathematics
HU, B., Mathematics
HYDE, D. R., Biological Sciences
HYDER, A. K., Research Physics
JACOBS, D. C., Chemistry and Biochemistry
JOHNSON, A. L., Biological Sciences
JOHNSON, W. R., Physics
JONES, G. L., Physics
KNIGHT, J. F., Mathematics
KOLATA, J. J., Physics
KULPA, C. F., Biological Sciences
LAMBERTI, G. A., Biological Sciences
LAPPIN, A. G., Chemistry and Biochemistry
LEPRAPPIER, F., Mathematics
LIVINGSTON, A. E., Physics
LODGE, D. M., Biological Sciences
LOSECCO, J. M., Physics
MARINO, J. P., Chemistry and Biochemistry
MATHEWS, G. J., Physics
MEISEL, D., Chemistry and Biochemistry
MERZ, J. L., Physics
MIGLIORE, J. C., Mathematics
MILLER, M. J., Chemistry and Biochemistry
NEWMAN, K. E., Physics
NOWAK, T. L., Chemistry and Biochemistry
O'TOUSA, J. E., Biological Sciences
PAONI, N., Chemistry and Biochemistry
RETTIG, T. W., Physics
ROSENTHAL, J. J., Mathematics
RUCHTI, R. C., Physics
SAPIRSTEIN, J. R., Physics
SCHEIDT, W. R., Chemistry and Biochemistry
SERIANNI, A. S., Chemistry and Biochemistry
SEVERSON, D. W., Biological Sciences
SEVOV, S., Chemistry and Biochemistry
SHAW, M.-C., Mathematics
SHEPHARD, W. D., Physics
SHRADER-FRECHETTE, K., Biological Sciences
SMITH, B. D., Chemistry and Biochemistry
SMYTH, B., Mathematics
SNOW, D. M., Mathematics
SOMMESE, A. J., Mathematics
STANTON, N. K., Mathematics
STOLZ, S. A., Mathematics
TAYLOR, L. R., Mathematics
TENNISWOOD, M. P., Biological Sciences
WARCHOL, J., Physics
WAYNE, M. R., Physics
WELSH, J. E. J., Biological Sciences
WIESCHER, M. C. F., Physics
WILLIAMS, E. B., Mathematics
WONG, P.-M., Mathematics
XAVIER, F., Mathematics

Law School:

BARRETT, M.
BAUER, J. P.
BENNETT, G.
BLAKEY, G. R.
BRADLEY, G. V.
DUTILE, F. N.
GUNN, A.
GURULE, J.
JACOBS, R. F.
KAVENY, M. C.
KELLENBERG, C. L.
KOMMERS, D. P.
MENDEZ, J. E.
MOONEY, C. A.
O'HARA, P.
PHELPS, T. G.
PRATT, W. F., Jr
RODES, R. E., Jr
SECKINGER, J. H.
SHELTON, D. L.
SMITHBURN, E.
TIDMARSH, J.

Mendoza College of Business:

AFFLECK-GRAVES, J., Finance and Business Economics
BRETZ, R., Management and Administrative Sciences
CONLON, E. J., Management and Administrative Sciences
COSIMANO, T. F., Finance and Business Economics
ENDERLE, G., Marketing
ETZEL, M. J., Marketing
FRECKA, T. J., Accountancy
GRESIK, T., Finance and Business Economics
GUILTINAN, J. P., Marketing
GUNDLACH, G. T., Marketing
HARTVIGSEN, D. B., Management and Administrative Sciences
HUANG, R. D., Finance and Business Economics
KEANE, J. G., Management and Administrative Sciences
KEATING, B. P., Finance and Business Economics
KENNEDY, J. J., Marketing
KRAJEWSKI, L., Management and Administrative Sciences
MCDONALD, W. D., Finance and Business Economics
MATTA, K. F., Management and Administrative Sciences
MILANI, K. W., Accountancy
MITTELSTAEDT, H. F., Accountancy
MORRIS, M. H., Accountancy
MURPHY, P. E., Marketing
NICHOLS, W. D., Accountancy
RAMANAN, R., Accountancy
REILLY, F. K., Finance and Business Economics
RICCHIUTE, D. N., Accountancy
RUESCHHOFF, N. G., Accountancy
SCHAEFER, T., Accountancy
SCHULTZ, P., Finance and Business Economics
SHEEHAN, R. G., Finance and Business Economics
SIMON, D. T., Accountancy
TAVIS, L. A., Finance and Business Economics
URBANY, J., Marketing
VECCHIO, R. P., Management and Administrative Sciences
WILKIE, W. L., Marketing
WITTENBACH, J. L., Accountancy

School of Architecture:

AMICO, R.
CROWE, N.
LYKOUDIS, M.
SMITH, T. G.
WESTFALL, C . W.

UNIVERSITY OF SAINT FRANCIS

2701 Spring St, Fort Wayne, IN 46808-3994
Telephone: (260) 399-7999
Fax: (260) 434-8152
E-mail: admis@sf.edu
Internet: www.sf.edu

Founded 1890
Private control
Academic year: August to May

Pres.: Sister M. ELISE KRISS
Provost: Dr ROLF DANIEL
Exec. Vice-Pres.: Dr STACY ADKINSON
Vice-Pres. for Finance: RICHARD BIENZ
Vice-Pres. for Student Life: SHARON MEJEUR
Vice-Pres. for Univ. Relations: Dr DONALD SCHENKEL
Registrar: FRANK CONNOR
Dir for Library Services: KARLA ALEXANDER

Number of teachers: 142
Number of students: 2,165

DEANS

Health Sciences: Dr NANCY GILLESPIE
Professional Studies: Dr JANE SWISS

UNIVERSITY OF SOUTHERN INDIANA

8600 University Blvd, Evansville, IN 47712-3596
Telephone: (812) 464-8600
Fax: (812) 465-7154

E-mail: enroll@usi.edu
Internet: www.usi.edu

Founded 1965 as the Evansville Campus of Indiana State University, current name and independent status 1985

State control

Academic year: August to May

President: Dr LINDA L. M. BENNETT
Provost and Vice-President for Academic Affairs: (vacant)
Vice-President for Business Affairs: MARK ROZEWSKI
Vice-President for Government and University Relations: CYNTHIA S. BRINKER
Vice-President for Student Affairs: Dr ROBERT W. PARRENT

Number of teachers: 255
Number of students: 9,675

DEANS

Bower-Suhrheinrich School of Education and Human Services: Dr THOMAS PICKERING
Pott School of Science and Engineering: Dr JEROME R. CAIN
School of Business: Dr PHIL FISHER
School of Liberal Arts: IAIN L. CRAWFORD
School of Nursing and Health Professions: Dr NADINE COUDRET

VALPARAISO UNIVERSITY

Valparaiso, IN 46383
Telephone: (219) 464-5000
Fax: (219) 464-5381
E-mail: university.relations@valpo.edu
Internet: www.valpo.edu

Founded 1859

President: ALAN F. HARRE
Provost and Vice-President for Academic Affairs: Dr ROY AUSTENSEN
Vice-President for Administration and Finance: CHARLEY GILLESPIE
Vice-President for Admissions, Financial Aid and Marketing: KATHARINE WEHLING
Vice-President for Institutional Advancement: RICHARD MADDOX
Dean of Students: TIMOTHY JENKINS
Dean of Graduate and Continuing Education: DAVID ROWLAND
Registrar: ANN TROST
Librarian: RICHARD A. AMRHEIN

Library of 451,000 vols
Number of teachers: 228
Number of students: 3,603

DEANS

Christ College: MARK SCHWEIHN
College of Arts and Sciences: ALBERT TROST
College of Business Administration: KARL REICHARDT (acting)
College of Engineering: KRAIG J. OLEJNICZAK
College of Nursing: JANET BROWN

WABASH COLLEGE

Crawfordsville, IN 47933
Telephone: (765) 361-6100
E-mail: admissions@wabash.edu
Internet: www.wabash.edu

Founded 1832

Pres.: Dr PATRICK E. WHITE
Treasurer and Chief Financial Officer: LARRY B. GRIFFITH
Dean of Admissions and Financial Aid: STEVEN J. KLEIN
Dean of College: GARY A. PHILLIPS
Dean of College Advancement: JOSEPH R. EMMICK
Dean of Students: MICHAEL P. RATERS
Registrar: JULIE OLSEN
Librarian: JOHN LAMBORN

Library of 260,000 vols, 18,783 current periodicals, 162,000 govt documents, 15,739 audiovisual titles
Number of teachers: 89
Number of students: 883

IOWA

ALLEN COLLEGE

1825 Logan Ave, Waterloo, IA 50703
Telephone: (319) 226-2000
Fax: (319) 226-2020
E-mail: allencollegeadmissions@ihs.org
Internet: www.allencollege.edu

Founded 1925 as Allen Memorial Hospital Nurses Training School; present name 1989

Private control

Chancellor: Dr JERRY D. DURHAM
Dean of Academic Affairs: Dr SUSAN DAWSON
Dir of Student Services: JOANNA RAMSDEN-MEIER
Library/Media Services Coordinator: MELISSA KANE

Number of teachers: 23
Number of students: 220

Faculties of nursing, radiography

CHAIRMEN OF ACADEMIC PROGRAMMES

Nursing: Dr NANCY KRAMER (BSc: Dr DIANE YOUNG (MSc)
Radiography: PEGGY FORTSCH

ASHFORD UNIVERSITY

400 North Bluff Blvd, Clinton, IA 52732
Telephone: (563) 242-4023
E-mail: admissions@ashford.edu
Internet: www.ashford.edu

Founded 1918 as Mount St Clare College; Franciscan Univ. 2002; present name 2005

Private control

Pres.: Dr MICHAEL E. KAELKE
Chancellor: Dr JANE MCAULIFFE
Exec. Vice-Pres. for College Relations and Mission Effectiveness: MARY ANN PHELAN
Academic Dean: Dr WILLIAM C. LOWE
Dean of Student Affairs: GARY COOPER
Library Dir: FLORA S. LOWE

Library of 101,000 vols, 650 periodicals, 70,000 microforms, 700 audiovisual titles
Number of teachers: 52 (26 full-time, 26 part-time)
Number of students: 495 (461 undergraduate, 34 graduate)

BAs in accounting, art (visual), biology, business admin., business education, clinical cytotechnology, clinical laboratory science, computer graphic design, computer science, criminal justice, elementary education, health and human services management, information systems, liberal arts, nuclear medicine technology, psychology, social justice, social science, sports and recreation management

DEANS

College of Education: Dr JOEN ROTTLER
School of Arts and Sciences: Dr WILLIAM LOWE

DIVISION CHAIRS

Business Div.: Dr M. DIANE CORNILSEN
Education Div.: Dr LOIS J. YOCUM
Fine Arts Div.: Dr ROBERT A. ENGELSON
Humanities Div.: THERESA JUDGE
Science Div.: Dr JOHN W. ZIMMERMAN
Social Science Div.: Dr GARY HEATH

BRIAR CLIFF UNIVERSITY

POB 2100, Sioux City, IA 51104-0100
3303 Rebecca St, Sioux City, IA 51104-2324
Telephone: (712) 279-5200
Fax: (712) 279-1632
E-mail: admissions@briarcliff.edu
Internet: www.briarcliff.edu

Founded 1930 as Briar Cliff College; present name 2001

Private control

Academic year: September to May

Pres.: BEVERLY A. WHARTON
Provost/Vice-Pres. and Academic Dean: Dr THOMAS V. BOEKE
Vice-Pres. for Enrollment Management: SHARISUE WILCOXON
Vice-Pres. for Finance: RUTH BITTNER
Vice-Pres. for Institutional Advancement: PHYLLIS M. CONNER
Dean of Students: CALVIN J. BRINKERHOFF
Registrar: BEV AHRENS
Library Dir: RACHEL CROWLEY

Number of teachers: 51
Number of students: 1,000

Programmes in accounting, art, biology, business administration, chemistry, computer science, criminal justice, elementary education, English, environmental science, graphic design, health, physical education, and recreation, history, human resource management, mass communications, management information systems, mathematics, medical technology, music, new media, nursing, political science, psychology, radiological technology, secondary education, social research, social work, Spanish, sports science, theatre, theology, writing.

BUENA VISTA UNIVERSITY

610 W Fourth St, Storm Lake, IA 50588
Telephone: (712) 749-2351
Fax: (712) 749-2037
E-mail: library@bvu.edu
Internet: www.bvu.edu

Founded 1891

Academic year: September to May

Programmes in accounting, art, arts management, athletic training, biology, business economics, business education, chemistry, communication and graphic design, communication and performance studies, computer science, computer science/mathematics, corporate communication, criminology and criminal justice, elementary education, English, exercise science (teaching emphasis), finance and banking, general science, history, int. business, management, management information systems, marketing, mathematics, media studies, music, philosophy and religion, physics, political science, psychology, public admin., social science, social work, Spanish

Pres.: FREDERICK V. MOORE
Vice-Pres. for Academic Affairs: Dr DAVID EVANS
Vice-Pres. for Business Services: ELIZABETH MERTEN
Vice-Pres. for Enrollment: MARCIA NANCE
Vice-Pres. for Institutional Advancement: KENNETH CONVERSE
Vice-Pres. for Student Services and Dean of Students: KEITH BETTS
Univ. Librarian: JAMES R. KENNEDY

Library of 146,000 vols
Number of teachers: 80 full-time
Number of students: 2,607

CENTRAL COLLEGE

812 University, Pella, IA 50219
Telephone: (877) 462-3687
Fax: (641) 628-5983

E-mail: admission@central.edu
Internet: www.central.edu

Founded 1853

4-Year liberal arts college; programmes in accounting, actuarial science, anthropology, art, athletic training, biology, business management, chemistry, communication studies, computer science, economics, elementary education, English, environmental studies, exercise science, french, general studies, German studies, history, information systems, international management, international studies, linguistics, mathematics, mathematics/computer science, music, music education, natural science, philosophy, physics, political science, psychology, religion, secondary education, social science, sociology, Spanish, theatre; pre-professional programmes: architecture, chiropractics, dentistry, engineering, law, medicine, nursing, occupational therapy, optometry, pharmacy, physical therapy, podiatric medicine, veterinary medicine; attached to Reformed Church

Academic year: August to May

Pres.: Dr Mark Putnam
Vice-Pres. for Academic Affairs: Dr Mary Strey
Vice-Pres. for Finance and Administration and Treas.: Jim Galbally
Vice-Pres. for Student Enrollment Management: Carol Williamson
Library Dir: Natalie H. Hutchinson

Library of 199,538 vols
Number of teachers: 89
Number of students: 1,600

Publications: *The Central Bulletin*, *The Central Ray*.

CLARKE COLLEGE

1550 Clarke Dr., Dubuque, IA 52001-3198

Telephone: (563) 588-6300
Fax: (563) 588-6789
E-mail: clarke-info@clarke.edu
Internet: www.clarke.edu

Founded 1843

Academic year: August to May

Pres.: Dr Joanne M. Burrows
Provost and Vice-Pres. for Academic Affairs: Joan Lingen
Vice-Pres. for Business and Finance and Treasurer: Deanna McCormick
Vice-Pres. for Information Technology: Pat Maddux
Vice-Pres. for Institutional Advancement: Melba Rodriguez
Vice-Pres. for Student Life and Enrollment Management: Kathleen Zanger
Registrar: Kristi Droessler
Library Dir: Nancy Carroll

Library of 121,000 vols
Number of teachers: 120
Number of students: 1,201

Depts of accounting and business admin., art and art history, athletic training, biology, chemistry, communication, computer science, drama and speech, education, history/political science, language and literature, mathematics, music, nursing, philosophy, physical therapy, psychology, religious studies, social work.

COE COLLEGE

1200 First Ave, NE, Cedar Rapids, IA 52402

Telephone: (319) 399-8500
Fax: (319) 399-8816
E-mail: admission@coe.edu
Internet: www.coe.edu

Founded 1851
Private control
Academic year: August to May

Majors in accounting, African-American studies, American studies, art, Asian studies, athletic training, biochemistry, biology, business admin., chemistry, computer science, economics, education, English, English as a second language, environmental science, French, French studies, gender studies, general science, German, German studies, historical studies, history, interdisciplinary, literature, mathematics, molecular biology, music, nursing, philosophy, physical education, physics, political science, pre-professional programmes, psychology, public relations, religion, sociology, Spanish, Spanish studies, speech, theatre arts, writing

Pres.: James R. Phifer
Vice-Pres. for Academic Affairs and Dean of Faculty: Marie Baehr
Vice-Pres. for Admin. Services: John Grundig
Vice-Pres. for Advancement: Richard Meisterling
Vice-Pres. for Enrollment and Admin.: Michael White
Vice-Pres. for Student Affairs: Lou Stark
Registrar: Dr Evelyn Moore
Dir of Library Services: Jill Jack

Library of 300,000 vols, 1,100 current periodicals, 10,000 microforms, 16,000 audiovisual items, 33,500 print and online periodicals
Number of teachers: 80
Number of students: 1,300

Publication: *Courier* (4 a year).

CORNELL COLLEGE

600 First St, SW, Mount Vernon, IA 52314-1098

Telephone: (319) 895-4477
Fax: (319) 895-4492
E-mail: admission@cornellcollege.edu
Internet: www.cornellcollege.edu

Founded 1853

Pres.: Dr Leslie H. Garner, Jr
Sr Vice-Pres. for Alumni and College Advancement: Terry Gibson
Vice-Pres. for Academic Affairs and Dean of the College: Brenda Tooley
Vice-Pres. for Business Affairs and Treasurer: Mark Zinkula
Vice-Pres. for Enrollment and Dean of Admissions: Jonathan Stroud
Vice-Pres. for Student Affairs: John Harp
Registrar: Jackie Wallace
Librarian: Dr Jean Donham

Library of 190,000 vols
Number of teachers: 82
Number of students: 1,000

Depts of art, biology, chemistry, computer science, economics and business, education, English, geology, history, kinesiology, languages, mathematics, music, philosophy, physics, politics, psychology, religion, sociology and anthropology, theatre and communications studies.

DES MOINES UNIVERSITY

3200 Grand Ave, Des Moines, IA 50312-4198

Telephone: (515) 271-1400
Fax: (515) 271-1578
E-mail: webmaster@dmu.edu
Internet: www.dmu.edu

Founded 1898 as Dr S. S. Still College of Osteopathy
Private control

Pres. and CEO: Terry Branstad
Exec. Vice-Pres. and Chief Operating Officer: Stephen Dengle
Vice-Pres. for Academic Admin.: Dr Robert M. Yoho
Vice-Pres. for Planning and Technology: Dr William Appelgate
Vice-Pres. for Student Services: Mary Ann Zug
Registrar: Kathy L. Scaglione
Library Dir: Larry D. Marquardt

Library of 23,000 medical vols, 29,000 bound journals
Number of students: 1,306

DEANS

College of Health Sciences: Dr Jodi L. Cahalan
College of Osteopathic Medicine and Surgery: Dr Kendall Reed
College of Podiatric Medicine and Surgery: Dr Robert M. Yoho
Univ. Research: Dr Bryan Larsen

DIVINE WORD COLLEGE

102 Jacoby Drive, POB 380, Epworth, IA 52045-0380

Telephone: (319) 876-3353
E-mail: dwcinfo@dwci.edu
Internet: www.dwci.edu

Founded 1931 as St Paul's Mission House; present name 1964
Private control
Academic year: August to May

Pres.: Rev. Michael Hutchins
Vice-Pres. for Academic Affairs: Dr James Russett
Vice-Pres. for Devt: Mark Singsank
Vice-Pres. for Finance: Linda Weidemann
Vice-Pres. for Formation and Dean of Students: Rev. Khien Mai Luu
Vice-Pres. for Recruitment and Admissions: Len Uhal
Registrar: Deborah Hirsch
Library Dir: Daniel Boice

BAs in cross-cultural studies, philosophy.

DORDT COLLEGE

498 Fourth Ave, NE, Sioux Center, IA 51250

Telephone: (712) 722-6000
Fax: (712) 722-1185
E-mail: public-relations@dordt.edu
Internet: www.dordt.edu

Founded 1955

Languages of instruction: English, Dutch, Spanish, Latin

Academic year: August to May

Pres.: Dr Carl Zylstra
Vice-Pres. for Academic Affairs: Dr Rockne McCarthy
Vice-Pres. for Business: Arlan Nederhoff
Vice-Pres. for College Advancement: John Baas
Vice-Pres. for Student Services: Ken Boersma
Exec. Dir of Admissions: Quentin Van Essen
Registrar: Jim Bos
Dir of Library Services: Sheryl Taylor

Library of 306,000 vols
Number of teachers: 80 full-time
Number of students: 1,250

Publication: *Pro Rege* (4 a year).

DRAKE UNIVERSITY

2507 University Ave, Des Moines, IA 50311-4505

Telephone: (515) 271-2011
Fax: (515) 271-3977
Internet: www.drake.edu

Founded 1881
Private control
Academic year: September to May (2 semesters)

Pres.: Dr David E. Maxwell
Provost: Ronald J. Troyer

Vice-Pres. for Admission and Financial Aid: TOM DELAHUNT
Vice-Pres. for Alumni and Devt: JOHN SMITH
Vice-Pres. for Business and Finance: VICTORIA PAYSEUR
Exec. Dir of Marketing and Communications: DEBRA K. LUKEHART
Dean of Students: Dr SENTWALI BAKARI
Registrar: NANCY GEIGER
Dean of Cowles Library: RODNEY HENSHAW
Dir of Law Library: JOHN EDWARDS

Library of 471,209 vols, 2,000 periodicals, 96,147 govt documents, 855 audiovisual items
Number of teachers: 417 (237 full-time, 180 part-time)
Number of students: 5,150 (3,577 undergraduate, 1,573 postgraduate)

Publications: *Drake Law Review*, *Drake Update*

DEANS

College of Arts and Sciences: Dr JOHN M. BURNEY
College of Business and Public Admin.: CHARLIE EDWARDS
College of Pharmacy and Health Sciences: RAYLENE ROSPOND
Law School: Prof. C. PETER GOPLERUD, III
School of Education: JAN MCHILL
School of Journalism and Mass Communication: CHARLES EDWARDS

EMMAUS BIBLE COLLEGE

2570 Asbury Rd, Dubuque, IA 52001
Telephone: (563) 588-8000
Fax: (563) 588-1216
E-mail: info@emmaus.edu
Internet: www.emmaus.edu
Private control
Academic year: August to May

Programmes in biblical studies, ministry studies, professional studies

Pres.: KENNETH A. DAUGHTERS
Chancellor: Dr DANIEL H. SMITH
Vice-Pres. for Admin.: KENNETH W. MURRAY
Dean for Academic Affairs: LISA L. BEATTY
Dean for Biblical Studies: DAVID J. MACLEOD
Dean for Student Affairs: JONATHAN W. GLOCK
Registrar: KATHRYN L. VAN DINE
Librarian: JOHN H. RUSH

Number of teachers: 25
Number of students: 283

FAITH BAPTIST BIBLE COLLEGE AND THEOLOGICAL SEMINARY

1900 NW Fourth St, Ankeny, IA 50023
Telephone: (515) 964-0601
Fax: (515) 964-1638
E-mail: admissions@faith.edu
Internet: www.faith.edu
Private control
Academic year: August to May
Language of instruction: English

Divs of Christian studies, Bible and theology, gen. education

Pres.: Dr JAMES MAXWELL
Vice-Pres. for Academic Services and Dean of College: Dr JOHN HARTOG
Vice-Pres. for Enrolment and Constituent Services: PATRICK ODLE
Dean of Seminary: Dr ERNIE SCHMIDT
Dean of Students: SHON LUNDBERG
Registrar: DAVID STOUT
Head Librarian: JOHN HARTOG

Library of 67,000 vols, 430 periodicals
Number of teachers: 34
Number of students: 325

GRACELAND UNIVERSITY

1 University Pl., Lamoni, IA 50140
Telephone: (641) 784-5423
Fax: (641) 784-5480
E-mail: admissions@graceland.edu
Internet: www.graceland.edu
Founded 1895
Academic year: August to May

Pres.: Dr JOHN D. SELLARS
Vice-Pres. for Academic Affairs and Dean of Faculty: PARRIS R. WATTS
Vice-Pres. for Business and Admin. Services: JANICE TIFFANY
Vice-Pres. for Enrollment Management: LOUISE CUMMINGS-SIMMONS
Vice-Pres. for Institutional Advancement: KELLY EVERETT
Exec. Dir for Information Systems: KAM MAHI
Dir for Admissions: KEVIN BROWN
Registrar: JOYCE LIGHTHILL
Librarian: DIANE E. SHELTON

Library of 114,249 vols
Number of teachers: 93 (full-time)
Number of students: 2,271 (undergraduate and graduate)

DEANS

College of Liberal Arts and Studies: Dr GARY HEISSERER
School of Business: Dr STEVEN L. ANDERS
School of Education: Dr TAMMY EVERETT
School of Nursing: Dr CLAUDIA HORTON
Seminary: Dr DON COMPIER

BRANCH CAMPUS

Independence Campus: 1401 W Truman Rd, Independence, MO 64050-3434; tel. (816) 833-0524; school of nursing; business admin., education, religion courses.

GRAND VIEW COLLEGE

1200 Grandview Ave, Des Moines, IA 50316
Telephone: (515) 263-2800
Fax: (515) 263-6095
E-mail: admissions@gvc.edu
Internet: www.gvc.edu
Founded 1896
Private control
Academic year: August to May

Pres.: KENT L. HENNING
Provost and Vice-Pres. for Academic Affairs: Dr RONALD L. TAYLOR
Vice-Pres. for Admin. and Finance: SCOTT BOCK
Vice-Pres. for Advancement: WILLIAM BURMA
Vice-Pres. for Enrollment Management: DEBBIE M. BARGER
Dean, College for Professional and Adult Learning: KAREN ANDERSON
Dir of Admissions: DIANE JOHNSON
Registrar: ELLEN M. STRACHOTA
Library Dir: SANDRA H. KEIST

Number of teachers: 180 (incl. 95 part-time)
Number of students: 1,750

HEADS OF ACADEMIC DIVISIONS

Humanities: KAYLENE RUBY
Natural Sciences: Dr DIANE DOIDGE
Nursing: Dr JEAN LOGAN
Social Sciences: Dr A. KATHLEEN PETERSON

GRINNELL COLLEGE

Grinnell, IA 50112-1690
Telephone: (641) 269-4000
Fax: (641) 269-3408
E-mail: askgrin@grinnell.edu
Internet: www.grinnell.edu
Founded 1846

Pres.: RUSSELL K. OSGOOD
Vice-Pres. and Treas. of the College: DAVID S. CLAY
Vice-Pres. for Academic Affairs and Dean of the College: Dr JIM SWARTZ
Vice-Pres. for College and Alumni Relations: MICKEY MUNLEY
Vice-Pres. for College Services: JOHN W. KALKBRENNER
Vice-Pres. for Institutional Planning: MARCI SORTOR
Vice-Pres. for Student Services: THOMAS CRADY
Dean of Admission and Financial Aid: JAMES M. SUMNER
Registrar: GERALD S. ADAMS
Librarian: RICHARD FYFFE

Library: 1m. vols, 5,100 current periodicals, govt documents
Number of teachers: 141
Number of students: 1,460

Depts of anthropology, art, biology, chemistry, Chinese/Japanese, classics, computer science, economics, education, English, French, German, history, mathematics and statistics, music, philosophy, physical education, physics, political science, psychology, religious studies, Russian, sociology, Spanish, theatre.

IOWA STATE UNIVERSITY

Ames, IA 50011
Telephone: (515) 294-4111
E-mail: admissions@iastate.edu
Internet: www.iastate.edu
Founded 1858

Pres.: Prof. GREGORY GEOFFROY
Exec. Vice-Pres. and Provost: ELIZABETH HOFFMAN
Vice-Pres. for Business and Finance: WARREN R. MADDEN
Vice-Pres. for Extension and Outreach: JACK M. PAYNE
Vice-Pres. for Research and Economic Devt: JOHN A. BRIGHTON
Vice-Pres. for Student Affairs: THOMAS L. HILL
Dean of Library Services: OLIVIA MADISON

Library of 2,348,646 vols, 29,681 current periodicals, 3,380,573 microforms, 780,839 photographs and slides, 46,493 films and videos, 11,562 audio items, 130,008 maps and aerial photographs, 14,042 linear ft of manuscripts and archives
Number of teachers: 1,709
Number of students: 26,000

Publications: *Ethos*, *Inquiry*, *Inside Iowa State*, *Iowa State Daily*, *Iowa State University Veterinarian*, *Iowa Stater*, *Marston Muses*, *Outlook*, *The Agriculturist*, *The Gentle Doctor*, *The Iowa Engineer*, *IVisions*

DEANS

College of Agriculture: WENDY WINTERSTEEN
College of Business: Prof. LABH S. HIRA
College of Design: LUIS RICO-GUTIERREZ
College of Engineering: JONATHAN WICKERT
Graduate College: DAVID K. HOLGER
College of Human Sciences: PAM WHITE
College of Liberal Arts and Sciences: MICHAEL B. WHITEFORD
College of Veterinary Medicine: JOHN U. THOMSON

ATTACHED RESEARCH INSTITUTES AND CENTRES

Ames Laboratory of US Department of Energy: Dir Prof. THOMAS J. BARTON.

Analog and Mixed-Signal VLSI Design Center: Dir Prof. ROBERT J. WEBER.

Carrie Chapman Catt Center for Women and Politics: Dir Dr DIANNE G. BYSTROM.

Center for Advanced Technology Development: Dir MARK LAURENZANO.

Center for Agricultural and Rural Development: Dir Prof. BRUCE BABCOCK.

Center for Agricultural History: Dir Prof. R. DOUGLAS HURT.

Center for Crops Utilization Research: Prof. LAWRENCE A. JOHNSON.

Center for Designer Crops: Dir BASIL J. NIKOLAU.

Center for Designing Foods to Improve Nutrition: Dir Prof. DIANE BIRT.

Center for Family Policy.

Center for Historical Studies of Technology and Science: Dir ALAN MARCUS.

Center for Indigenous Knowledge for Agricultural and Rural Development: Dir MIKE WARREN.

Center for Industrial Research and Service: Dir RONALD A. COX.

Center for International Agricultural Finance: Dir Prof. NEIL E. HARL.

Center for Nondestructive Evaluation: Dir R. BRUCE THOMPSON.

Center for Physical and Computational Mathematics: Dir BRUCE N. HARMON (acting).

Center for Plant Genomics: Dir Prof. PATRICK S. SCHNABLE.

Center for Plant Responses to Environmental Stresses: Dir CHARLOTTE R. BRONSON.

Center for Plant Transformation and Gene Expression: Dir Prof. PATRICK S. SCHNABLE.

Center for Survey Statistics and Methodology: Dir SARAH NUSSER.

Center for Sustainable Environmental Technologies: Dir Prof. ROBERT C. BROWN.

Center for Teaching Excellence: Dir CORLY BROOKE.

Center for Technology in Learning and Teaching: Dir ANN THOMPSON.

Center for Transportation Research and Education: Dir STEVE ANDRLE.

Computational Fluid Dynamics Center: Man. Prof. JOHN TANNEHILL.

Electric Power Research Center: Dir VIJAY VITTAL.

Food and Agricultural Policy Research Institute: Dir JOHN C. BEGHIN.

Food Safety Consortium.

Industrial Relations Center: Dir Prof. PETER F. ORAZEM.

Institute for Design Research and Outreach: Dir MARK ENGELBRECHT.

Institute for International Cooperation in Animal Biologics (IICAB): Exec. Dir Dr JAMES ROTH.

Institute for Physical Research and Technology: Dir Prof. THOMAS J. BARTON.

Institute for Social and Behavioral Research: Dir CAROLYN CUTRONA.

Interdisciplinary Research Institute for Social Science (IRISS): Dir KIRK WOLTER.

Iowa Energy Center: Dir FLOYD E. BARWIG (acting).

Iowa Lakeside Laboratory: Dir Dr ARNOLD VAN DER VALK.

Iowa Pork Industry Center: Dir JOHN MABRY.

Iowa Space Grant Consortium: Dir WILLIAM J. BYRD.

Laurence H. Baker Center for Bioinformatics and Biological Statistics: Dir ROBERT L. JERNIGAN.

Leopold Center for Sustainable Agriculture: Dir Prof. FREDERICK L. KIRSCHENMANN.

Microanalytical Instrumentation Center: Dir MARC PORTER.

Microelectronics Research Center: Dir Prof. VIKRAM L. DALAL.

Midwest Agribusiness Trade Research and Information Center (MATRIC): Exec. Dir BRUCE A. BABCOCK.

NASA Food Technology Commercial Space Center: Dir Dr TONY POMETTO, III.

National Soil Tilth Laboratory: Dir Dr JERRY HATFIELD.

North Central Regional Aquaculture Center.

North Central Regional Center for Rural Development: Dir Dr CORNELIA BUTLER FLORA.

Raymond F. Baker Center for Plant Breeding: Dir KENDALL R. LAMKEY.

Research Institute for Studies in Education: Dir Dr JACKIE BLOUNT.

Seed Science Center: Dir MANJIT K. MISRA.

Veterinary Medical Research Institute: Dir RICHARD F. ROSS.

Water Resources Research Institute: Dir STEVE MELVIN.

IOWA WESLEYAN COLLEGE

601 North Main, Mount Pleasant, IA 52641
Telephone: (319) 385-8021
E-mail: wnj@iwc.edu
Internet: www.iwc.edu

Founded 1842

Pres.: WILLIAM JOHNSTON
Vice-Pres. for Academic Affairs: NANCY ERICKSON
Vice-Pres. of Devt: JOHN HELD
Registrar: ED KROPA
Dean of Enrollment Management: CARY OWENS
Library Dir: PAULA KINNEY

Library of 108,427 vols
Number of teachers: 42
Number of students: 849

Divs of business, education, fine arts, human studies, language and literature, nursing, science, mathematics and computer studies.

LORAS COLLEGE

1450 Alta Vista, Dubuque, IA 52004-0178
Telephone: (563) 588-7100
E-mail: admissions@loras.edu
Internet: www.loras.edu

Founded 1839

Pres.: JAMES E. COLLINS
Provost: CHERYL R. JACOBSEN
Vice-Pres. for Institutional Advancement: PAMELA S. GERAD
Vice-Pres. for Finance and Admin. Services: STEVE SCHMALL
Vice-Pres. for Enrollment Management: LISA BUNDERS
Dean of Students: ARTHUR W. SUNLEAF
Dean of Campus Spiritual Life: Fr JOHN HAUGEN
Registrar: MARY K. WECK
Librarian: ROBERT F. KLEIN

Library of 440,000 vols, 8,000 current periodicals
Number of teachers: 141
Number of students: 1,683

Courses in accounting, art-studio, athletic training, archaeology/cultural interpretation, biochemistry, biology, business, business finance, business management, business marketing, Catholic studies, chemistry, computer science, criminal justice, economics, electromechanical engineering, elementary education, English literature, English writing, gender studies, Greek and Roman studies, history, integrated visual arts, int. studies, iIish studies, management information systems, mathematics, media studies, music/music education, philosophy, physics-applied, politics, psychology, public relations, publishing, religious studies, social work, sociology, Spanish, sport management, sport science, theatre, world literature.

LUTHER COLLEGE

700 College Dr., Decorah, IA 52101-1045
Telephone: (563) 387-2000
Fax: (563) 387-2158
Internet: www.luther.edu

Founded 1861

Pres.: Dr RICHARD L. TORGERSON
Vice-Pres. and Dean for Student Life: ANN HIGHUM
Vice-Pres. for Academic Affairs and Dean of the College: WILLIAM CRAFT
Vice-Pres. for Devt: KEITH CHRISTENSEN
Vice-Pres. for Enrollment and Marketing: (vacant)
Vice-Pres. for Finance and Admin.: DIANE TACKE
Registrar: LIANG CHEE WEE
Librarian: JANE KEMP

Library of 340,000 vols
Number of teachers: 191 full-time
Number of students: 2,600

Majors/minors in accounting, African studies, anthropology, art, arts management, athletic training, biblical languages, biology, business (management), chemistry, classical studies, classics, communication studies, computer science, economics, education, English, environmental studies, French, German, Greek, health, history, int. management studies, Latin, Latin American studies, management, management information systems, mathematics, mathematics/statistics, museum studies, music, music management, nursing, philosophy, physical education, physics, political science, psychology, religion, resource management, Russian studies, Scandinavian studies, social work, sociology, Spanish, speech/theatre, sports management, theatre/dance management, women's and gender studies.

MAHARISHI UNIVERSITY OF MANAGEMENT

Fairfield, IA 52557
Telephone: (641) 472-7000
Fax: (641) 472-1179
E-mail: admissions@mum.edu
Internet: www.mum.edu

Founded 1971 as Maharishi International Univ.; present name 1995
Private control
Academic year: August to July

Pres.: Dr BEVAN MORRIS
Exec. Vice-Pres.: Dr CRAIG PEARSON
Chief Admin. Officer: DAVID STREID
Exec. Dir of Institutional Advancement: BRADFORD MYLETT
Dean of Admissions: RON BARNETT
Dean of Faculty: CATHERINE GORINI
Dean of Men: DAVID POHLMAN
Dean of Women: SUSAN RUNKLE
Registrar: TOM ROWE
Library Dir: MARTIN SCHMIDT

Library of 144,000 vols
Number of teachers: 102
Number of students: 901

DEANS

College of Arts and Sciences: SAM BOOTHBY
College of Computer Science and Mathematics: GREGORY GUTHRIE
Graduate School: Dr FRED TRAVIS

MORNINGSIDE COLLEGE

1501 Morningside Ave, Sioux City, IA 51106
Telephone: (712) 274-5000
Fax: (712) 274-5101
E-mail: msadm@morningside.edu
Internet: www.morningside.edu

Founded 1894

Pres.: JOHN C. REYNDERS
Vice-Pres. for Academic Affairs and Dean of the College: WILLIAM C. DEEDS
Vice-Pres. for Business and Finance: RONALD A. JORGENSEN
Vice-Pres. for Institutional Advancement: TOM RICE
Vice-Pres. for Student Services: TERRI CURRY
Registrar: MARY PESHEK
Dean of Enrollment: ROBBIE ROHLENA
Dir of Library Services: DARIA BOSSMAN

Library of 117,330 vols, 3,575 sound recordings, 8,869 micofilm, 76,285 microfiche
Number of teachers: 75
Number of students: 1,122

Depts of art, biology, business admin., chemistry, computer and application programming, computer science, corporate communication, education, engineering physics, English, history, mass communication, mathematics, music, nursing, philosophy, political science, psychology, religious studies, Spanish, theatre

CHAIRPERSONS OF ACADEMIC DIVISIONS

Behavioural and Health Science: CAROL SEARLS
Business Admin. and Communication: DOUGLAS LIVERMORE
Education: GLENNA TREVIS
Fine Arts: LANCE LEHMBERG
Humanities: GAIL AMENT
Natural Sciences and Mathematics: DOUG SWAN

MOUNT MERCY COLLEGE

1330 Elmhurst Dr., NE, Cedar Rapids, IA 52402-4798
Telephone: (319) 363-1323
Fax: (319) 363-5270
Internet: www.mtmercy.edu

Founded 1928
Private control
Academic year: August to May

Pres.: Dr CHRISTOPHER R. L. BLAKE
Vice-Pres. for Academic Affairs: A. BUELANE DAUGHERTY
Vice-Pres. for Enrollment and Student Services: PHILIP C. ADAMS, III
Vice-Pres. for Finance: BARBARA PARKS POOLEY
Vice-Pres. for Institutional Advancement: DEBORAH K. GREEN
Registrar: LORI HEYING
Dir of Library Services: MARILYN MURPHY

Library of 128,000 vols
Number of teachers: 142
Number of students: 1,486

Depts of applied philosophy, art, biology, business admin. (accounting, management, marketing, interdisciplinary), communication, computer information systems, computer science, criminal justice, education, English, health services, history, int. studies, mathematics, medical technology, music, nursing, political science, pre-professional programmes, psychology, religious studies, social work, sociology, speech/drama, urban and community services.

NORTHWESTERN COLLEGE

101 Seventh St, SW, Orange City, IA 51041-1996
Telephone: (712) 707-7100
Fax: (712) 707-7247
E-mail: admissions@nwciowa.edu
Internet: www.nwciowa.edu

Founded 1882
Academic year: August to May

Pres.: Dr BRUCE G. MURPHY
Provost: Dr JASPER LESAGE
Vice-Pres. for Advancement: JAY WIELENGA
Vice-Pres. for External Relations: RON DE JONG
Vice-Pres. for Financial Affairs: DOUG BEUKELMAN
Vice-Pres. for Student Devt: JOHN G. BROGAN
Chaplain: Rev. HARLAN VANOORT
Registrar: CHARLIE COUCH
Dir of Library: DOUG ANDERSON

Library of 185,000 items
Number of teachers: 86 full-time and 46 part-time
Number of students: 1,225

Depts of art, biology, business/economics, chemistry, communications, computer science, education, English/writing and rhetoric, foreign languages, history, humanities, kinesiology, mathematics, music, nursing, philosophy, physics, political science, psychology, religion/Christian education, social work, sociology, theatre and speech.

PALMER CHIROPRACTIC UNIVERSITY SYSTEM

723 Brady St, Davenport, IA 52803
Telephone: (563) 884-5500
Fax: (563) 884-5505
Internet: www.palmer.edu

Founded 1897 as Palmer School and Cure, present name 1991
Private control

Chair. Board of Trustees: VICKIE A. PALMER
Vice-Chair.: TREVOR V. IRELAND
Sec.: KENT M. FORNEY.

CONSTITUENT COLLEGES

Palmer College of Chiropractic

1000 Brady St, Davenport, IA 52803
Telephone: (563) 884-5656
Fax: (563) 884-5414
E-mail: pcadmit@palmer.edu
Internet: www.palmer.edu

Chancellor: Dr DENNIS MARCHIORI
Pres.: Dr DONALD KERN
Vice-Pres. for Academic Affairs: Dr BRIAN J. MCAULAY
Vice-Pres. for Alumni, Devt and Student Affairs: GARY M. MOHR
Vice-Pres. for Education and Research Devt: Dr KEVIN MCCARTHY
Vice-Pres. for Marketing and Recruitment: C. RANDALL HEUSTON
Vice-Pres. for Operations and Finance: WILLIAM JARR
Vice-Pres. for Professional and Int. Affairs: Dr DAVID B. KOCH
Vice-Pres. for Research: Dr WILLIAM MEEKER
Registrar: MINDY LEAHY
Dir of Libraries: DENNIS PETERSON

Library of 50,000 vols

Publication: *Streams from the Fountainhead* (2 a year).

Palmer College of Chiropractic–Florida

4777 City Centre Parkway, Port Orange, FL 32129
Telephone: (386) 763-2709
Fax: (386) 763-2620
E-mail: pccf_admiss@palmer.edu
Internet: www.palmer.edu
Academic Dean: Dr GLORIA NILES.

Palmer College of Chiropractic–West

90 East Tasman Dr., San Jose, CA 95134
Telephone: (408) 944-6000
Fax: (408) 944-6032
E-mail: pccw_admiss@palmer.edu
Internet: www.palmer.edu

Founded 1978 as Northern California College of Chiropractic, present name 1980

Academic Dean: Dr KEVIN MCCARTHY.

ST AMBROSE UNIVERSITY

518 West Locust St, Davenport, IA 52803-2898
Telephone: (319) 333-6000
Fax: (319) 333-6243
Internet: www.sau.edu

Founded 1882
Private control (Roman Catholic church)

Pres.: Dr EDWARD J. ROGALSKI
Vice-Pres. for Academic Affairs: Dr LORRAINE RODRIGUES-FISHER
Vice-Pres. for Advancement: Dr EDWARD LITTIG
Vice-Pres. for Enrollment Management and Student Services: Dr JAMES LOFTUS
Vice-Pres. for Finance: Dr EDWARD HENKHAUS
Library Dir: MARY HEINZMAN

Library of 143,334 vols
Number of teachers: 299
Number of students: 3,780 (2,829 undergraduate, 951 graduate)

DEANS

College of Arts and Sciences: Dr ARON R. AJI
College of Business: Dr RICHARD DIENESCH
College of Education and Health Sciences: Dr ROBERT RISTOW
College of Professional Studies: Dr LEWIS SANBORNE

SIMPSON COLLEGE

701 N C St, Indianola, IA 50125-1297
Telephone: (515) 961-6251
Fax: (515) 961-1498
E-mail: admiss@simpson.edu
Internet: www.simpson.edu

Founded 1860
Academic year: August to May

Depts of art, biology and environmental science, business admin. and economics, chemistry and physics, communication studies, computer science, Dunn Library, education, English, foreign languages, Hawley Academic Resource Center, history, mathematics, music, philosophy and religion, physical education, political science, psychology, social sciences, student support services, theatre arts, women's studies

Pres.: JOHN W. BYRD
Vice-Pres. and Dean for Academic Affairs: STEVE GRIFFITHS
Vice-Pres. for Business and Finance: KEN BIRKENHOLTZ
Vice-Pres. for College Advancement: BOB LANE
Vice-Pres. for Enrollment: DEB TIERNEY
Vice-Pres. for Information Services and Chief Information Officer: KELLEY BRADDER
Vice-Pres. for Student Devt and Dean of Students: JIM THORIUS
Registrar: JOHN BOLAN
Librarian: CYD DYER

Library of 155,761 vols
Number of teachers: 87
Number of students: 1,950

Publications: *The Simpson Magazine* (4 a year), *Viewbook* (1 a year).

BRANCH CAMPUSES

Ankeny Campus: Suite 800, Southeast Tones Dr., West Des Moines, IA 50021; tel. (515) 965-9355; fax (515) 286-6195.

West Des Moines Campus: Suite 2E, 3737 Westown Parkway, West Des Moines, IA 50265; tel. (515) 223-8842; fax (515) 961-1887.

UNIVERSITY OF DUBUQUE

2000 University Ave, Dubuque, IA 52001
Telephone: (319) 589-3000
Internet: www.dbq.edu

Founded 1852

Pres.: Rev. Dr JEFFREY F. BULLOCK
Sr Vice-Pres. for Advancement: JOHN PUOTINEN
Sr Vice-Pres. for Finance and Auxiliary Services: RENNIE ROOT
Vice-Pres. and Dean of the Seminary: BRADLEY LONGFIELD
Vice-Pres. for Academic Affairs: JOHN STEWART
Vice-Pres for Enrollment Management, Marketing, and Univ. Relations: SUSAN SMITH, PETER SMITH
Dean of Student Life: Dr PETER GITAU
Library Dir: MARY ANN KNEFEL

Library of 165,000 vols, 25,000 microtext items, 9,000 vols in spec. collns, 700 current periodicals
Number of students: 1,000

Schools of business, liberal arts, professional programmes, theological seminary.

UNIVERSITY OF IOWA

2222 Old Highway 218 South, Iowa City, IA 52242-1602
Telephone: (319) 335-3549
Fax: (319) 335-0807
Internet: www.uiowa.edu

Founded 1847
State control
Academic year: August to May (2 terms and summer session)

Pres.: GARY FETHKE
Exec. Vice-Pres. and Provost: MICHAEL J. HOGAN
Sr Vice-Pres. and Treas.: DOUGLAS K. TRUE
Vice-Pres. for Legal Affairs and Gen. Counsel: MARCUS MILLS
Vice-Pres. for Medical Affairs: JEAN E. ROBILLARD
Vice-Pres. for Research: MEREDITH HAY
Vice-Pres. of Student Services and Dean of Students: PHILLIP E. JONES
Registrar: LAWRENCE LOCKWOOD
Univ. Librarian: NANCY L. BAKER

Library of 4,626,626 vols, also manuscript and special collns
Number of teachers: 1,679 (tenured and tenure-track faculty)
Number of students: 29,979 (20,738 undergraduate, 5,388 graduate, 3,853 professional)
Publications: *Journal of Communication Inquiry* (4 a year), *Iowa Law Review* (5 a year), *Syllecta Classica* (1 a year), *The Iowa Review* (3 a year), *Walt Whitman Quarterly Review* (4 a year)

DEANS

College of Dentistry: DAVID C. JOHNSEN
College of Education: SANDRA BOWMAN DAMICO
College of Engineering: P. BARRY BUTLER
College of Law: CAROLYN JONES
College of Liberal Arts and Sciences: LINDA MAXSON
College of Nursing: MARTHA CRAFT-ROSENBERG
College of Pharmacy: JORDAN L. COHEN
College of Public Health: JAMES A. MERCHANT
Graduate College: JOHN C. KELLER
Henry B. Tippie College of Business: WILLIAM C. HUNTER
Roy J. and Lucille A. Carver College of Medicine: JEAN E. ROBILLARD

UNIVERSITY OF NORTHERN IOWA

1227 W 27th St, Cedar Falls, IA 50614
Telephone: (319) 273-2311
Fax: (319) 273-3509
Internet: www.uni.edu

Founded 1876
Public control
Academic year: July to June

Pres.: Dr BENJAMIN ALLEN
Exec. Vice-Pres. and Provost: Dr GLORIA GIBSON
Vice-Pres. for Student Affairs: Dr TERRENCE HOGAN
Vice-Pres. for Admin. and Financial Services: TOM SCELLHARDT
Dir of Univ. Relations: JAMES O'CONNOR
Dir of Admissions: CHRISTIE KANGAS
Dean of Students: JON BUSE
Registrar: PHILIP PATTON

Library of 1,239,107 vols, 262,832 govt docs, 1,125,075 microforms, 41,425 maps, 17,330 audio recordings, 176,036 periodicals, 44,350 electronic journals, 15 newspapers
Number of teachers: 824 (623 full-time, 201 part-time)
Number of students: 13,201
Publications: *American Journal of Undergraduate Research* (4 a year), *Argumentation and Advocacy* (4 a year), *Business and Society* (4 a year), *Iowa Council for the Social Studies (ICSS) Journal*, *Iowa Journal of Communication* (4 a year), *Journal of Assessment and Accountability in Educator Preparation*, *Journal of Contemporary Ethnography* (6 a year), *Journal of Economics* (2 a year), *The North American Review* (5 a year), *Universitas* (2 a year)

DEANS

College of Business Admin.: Dr FARZAD MOUSSAVI
College of Education: Dr DWIGHT WATSON
College of Humanities and Fine Arts: Dr JOEL HAACK
College of Natural Sciences: Dr JOEL HAACK
College of Social and Behavioural Science: Dr PHILIP MAUCERI
Continuing Education and Special Programs: KENT JOHNSON
Graduate College: Dr MIKE LICARI
Library: MARILYN MERCADO

UPPER IOWA UNIVERSITY

605 Washington, POB 1857, Fayette, IA 52142
Telephone: (563) 425-5200
Fax: (563) 425-5271
E-mail: admissions@uiu.edu
Internet: www.uiu.edu

Founded 1857
Academic year: August to May

Pres.: Dr ALAN WALKER
Sr Vice-Pres. for Business Services: DONALD AUNGST
Sr Vice-Pres. for Residential Univ.: Dr EDWARD OGLE
Registrar: HOLLY STREETER
Library Dir: BECKY WADIAN

Library of 155,108 vols
Number of teachers: 574
Number of students: 5,799

BAs in arts and science; MAs in business admin., education, public admin.

VENNARD COLLEGE

POB 29, University Park, IA 52595
2300 Eighth Ave East, University Park, IA 52595
Telephone: (641) 673-8391
Fax: (641) 673-8365
E-mail: admiss@vennard.edu
Internet: www.vennard.edu

Founded 1910 as Chicago Evangelistic Institute; present name 1959
Private control
Academic year: August to May

Pres.: Dr BRUCE MOYER
Vice-Pres. for Academic Affairs and Academic Dean: Dr ROBERT W. BAGLEY
Vice-Pres. for Business: JEFF STRONG
Vice-Pres for Student Affairs and Dean of Students: LARRY OLSON
Registrar: DEANNE DOLL
Librarian: (vacant)

Number of teachers: 12
Number of students: 100

Areas of study: Bible/theology, business management, Christian ministries, Christian education, computer technology and communications, elementary education, general education, multidisciplinary studies, music, pastoral ministries, professional education, psychology and human relations, secondary education, world missions, youth ministries.

WARTBURG COLLEGE

100 Wartburg Blvd, Waverly, IA 50677
Telephone: (319) 352-8200
Fax: (319) 352-8514
Internet: www.wartburg.edu

Founded 1852
Academic year: September to June

Pres.: DARREL D. COLSON
Vice-Pres. for Academic Affairs and Dean of Faculty: Dr FEROL MENZEL
Vice-Pres. for Enrollment Management: Dr EDITH J. WALDSTEIN
Vice-Pres. for Institutional Advancement: SCOTT LEISINGER
Vice-Pres. for Student Life and Dean of Students: Dr ALEXANDER SMITH
Dir of Financial Aid: JENNIFER SASSMAN
Registrar: SHEREE COVERT
Librarian: KAREN LEHMAN

Library of 130,000 vols
Number of teachers: 160
Number of students: 1,769

Depts of accounting, art, art education, biochemistry, biology, business admin., chemistry, church music, communication arts, communication design, communication studies, community sociology, computer information systems, computer science, economics, education, engineering science, English, exploring, fitness management, history, interdepartmental major, int. relations, mathematics, medical technology, modern languages, music education, music performance, music therapy, philosophy, physical education, physics, political science, psychology, religion, social work, sociology, writing.

WARTBURG THEOLOGICAL SEMINARY

333 Wartburg Pl., POB 5004, Dubuque, IA 52004-5004
Telephone: (563) 589-0200
Fax: (563) 589-0333
E-mail: admissions@wartburgseminary.edu
Internet: www.wartburgseminary.edu

Founded 1854
Private control

Pres.: DUANE LARSON

Vice-Pres. for Finance and Operations: ANDREW WILLENBORG
Vice-Pres. for Mission Support: Rev. KEN GIBSON
Dean of Students and Enrollment Services: Rev. M DEWAYNE TEIG
Registrar: KEVIN ANDERSON
Dir of Libraries: SUSAN EBERTZ

Library of 84,500 vols
Number of teachers: 21
Number of students: 190

MAs in arts, diaconal ministry, divinity, sacred theology, theology, devt and Evangelism.

WILLIAM PENN UNIVERSITY

201 Trueblood Ave, Oskaloosa, IA 52577
Telephone: (641) 673-1076
Fax: (641) 673-1385
E-mail: admissions@wmpenn.edu
Internet: www.wmpenn.edu

Founded 1873 as Penn College; present name 2000
Private control
Academic year: August to May

Pres.: Dr RICHARD E. SOURS
Vice-Pres. for Advancement: STEPHEN NOAH
Vice-Pres. for Enrollment Management: JOHN OTTOSSON
Dean of Students: GARY GARVIS
Registrar: PATRICK MCADAMS
Librarian: JULIE HANSEN

Number of teachers: 55
Number of students: 1,400

DEANS

College of Arts, Sciences and Professional Studies: Dr FREDERICK ALLEN
College for Working Adults: Dr LEE BASH

CHAIRMEN OF ACADEMIC DIVISIONS

Applied Technology: JIM DROST
Business Admin.: LONNY L. WILSON
Education: PAMELA MARTIN
Health and Life Sciences: JAMES NORTH
Humanities: DAVID L. MAJOR
Social and Behavioral Sciences: L. FREDERICK ALLEN

KANSAS

BAKER UNIVERSITY

POB 65, Baldwin City, KS 66006-0065
Telephone: (785) 594-6451
Fax: (785) 594-8425
E-mail: admission@bakeru.edu
Internet: www.bakeru.edu

Founded 1858 (chartered)
United Methodist
Academic year: varies by programme

Accredited by N Central Asscn, Higher Learning Comm.; Nat. Ccl for the Accreditation of Teacher Education; Kansas State Dept of Education; Comm. on Collegiate Nursing Education, Kansas State Board of Nursing; Asscn of Collegiate Business Schools and Programs (College of Arts and Sciences); Nat. Asscn of Schools of Music

Pres.: PATRICIA N. LONG
Vice-Pres. for Endowment and Planned Giving: JERRY WEAKLEY
Vice-Pres. for Enrollment Management: LOUISE CUMMINGS-SIMMONS
Vice-Pres. for Information Technology: SIMON MAXWELL
Vice-Pres. for Univ. Advancement: LYN LAKIN
Provost: RANDY PEMBROOK
Univ. Min.: IRA DESPAIN
Dean of Student Affairs: CASSY BAILEY
Chief Operations Officer: SUSAN LINDAHL
Dir of Library Services: KAY BRADT

Library of 108,652 vols 399 periodicals
Number of teachers: 500 (94 full-time, 406 part-time)
Number of students: 2,993 F.t.e.

DEANS

College of Arts and Sciences: RAND ZIEGLER
Education: PEGGY HARRIS
Nursing: KATHLEEN HARR
School of Professional and Graduate Studies: (vacant)

BARCLAY COLLEGE

607 North Kingman, Haviland, KS 67059
Telephone: (620) 862-5252
Fax: (620) 862-5242
E-mail: admission@barclaycollege.edu
Internet: www.barclaycollege.edu

Founded 1917 as Kansas Central Bible Training School; present name 1990
Private control

Divs of biblical studies, general studies, liberal arts

Pres.: ROYCE FRAZIER
Librarian: EMILY HARKNESS

Library of 62,000 vols
Number of teachers: 30
Number of students: 194

BENEDICTINE COLLEGE

1020 N Second St, Atchison, KS 66002-1499
Telephone: (913) 367-5340
Fax: (913) 367-6566
Internet: www.benedictine.edu

Founded 1858, name changed 1971 as result of merger of College of St Benedict's and Mount St Scholastica College
Private control
Language of instruction: English
Academic year: August to May

Depts of arts and communication, business and public policy, education, health, humanities, science and mathematics, social and behavioural science

Pres.: STEPHEN D. MINNIS
Vice-Pres. for Academic Affairs and Dean of College: KIMBERLY J. SHANKMAN
Dean of Students: JOE WURTZ
Vice-Pres. for Advancement: KELLY J. VOWELS
Chief Financial Officer: RONALD OLINGER
Library Dir: STEVEN GROMATZKY

Library of 320,000 vols, 340 current periodicals
Number of teachers: 52
Number of students: 1,488

BETHANY COLLEGE

421 N First St, Lindsborg, KS 67456
Telephone: (785) 227-3311
Fax: (785) 227-2860
Internet: www.bethanylb.edu

Founded 1881
Private control
Academic year: August to July

Depts of accounting, anthropology, art, biology, business, chemistry, communication, computer science, criminal justice, economics, education, English, geography, German, history, health physical education/athletic training, mathematics, music, philosophy, physics, political science, psychology, religion, social work, Spanish, spec. education, Swedish, theatre

Pres.: Dr EDWARD LEONARD
Provost and Dean: Dr EUGENE BALES
Registrar: JILL MEGREDY
Librarian: DENISE CARSON

Library of 115,000 vols
Number of teachers: 54
Number of students: 622

BETHEL COLLEGE

300 E 27th St, North Newton, KS 67117
Telephone: (316) 283-2500
E-mail: admissions@bethelks.edu
Internet: www.bethelks.edu

Founded 1887
Private control

Pres.: PERRY WHITE
Vice-Pres. for Academic Affairs: BRAD BORN
Vice-Pres. for Admissions: TODD MOORE
Vice-Pres. for Advancement: SONDRA KOONTZ
Vice-Pres. for Business Affairs: ALLEN WEDEL
Vice-Pres. for Student Life: CHAD CHILDS
Registrar: RODNEY FREY
Co-Dir of Libraries: GAIL NILES STUCKY
Co-Dir of Libraries: BARBARA THIESEN
Co-Dir of Libraries: JOHN THIESEN

Library of 125,000 vols
Number of teachers: 60 (40 full-time, 20 part-time)
Number of students: 476

Publications: *Context*, *Mennonite Life*.

EMPORIA STATE UNIVERSITY

1200 Commercial St, Emporia, KS 66801-5087
Telephone: (620) 341-1200
Fax: (316) 341-5073
Internet: www.emporia.edu

Founded 1863, univ. status 1976

Pres.: MICHAEL R. LANE
Vice-Pres. for Academic Affairs: Dr JOHN O. SCHWENN
Vice-Pres. for Student Affairs: JAMES E. WILLIAMS
Dean of Graduates: ROBERT GROVER
Dean of the Library: JOYCE DAVIS

Library of 711,000 vols
Number of students: 6,006 (4,476 undergraduate, 1,530 postgraduate)

Publications: *ESU Business World* (4 a year), *Flint Hills Review*, *Kansas School Naturalist* (4 a year), *Spotlight* (4 a year)

DEANS

College of Liberal Arts and Sciences: RODNEY SOBIESKI
School of Business: ROBERT HITE
School of Library and Information Management: ANN O'NEILL
Teachers' College: TERESA MEHRING

FORT HAYS STATE UNIVERSITY

600 Park St, Hays, KS 67601-4099
Telephone: (785) 628-4000
Internet: www.fhsu.edu

Founded 1902
Public control
Academic year: August to May

Pres.: Dr EDWARD H. HAMMOND
Provost: LAWRENCE V. GOULD (acting)
Vice-Pres. for Administration and Finance: MIKE BARNETT
Vice-Pres. for Student Affairs: Dr TISA MASON
Assoc. Vice-Pres. for Student Affairs and Registrar: Dr JOEY LINN
Library Dir: JOHN ROSS

Library of 300,000 vols, 500,000 vols in govt document section,
Number of teachers: 300
Number of students: 12,131

Publications: *Leader*, *Reveille*

DEANS

College of Arts and Sciences: PAUL W. FABER

College of Business and Leadership: MARK BANNISTER
College of Education and Technology: ROB SCOTT
College of Health and Life Sciences: JEFF BRIGGS
Graduate Studies and Research: STEVEN TROUT
Virtual College: DENNIS KING

FRIENDS UNIVERSITY

2100 West University St, Wichita, KS 67213
Telephone: (316) 295-5000
Fax: (316) 295-5060
E-mail: learn@friends.edu
Internet: www.friends.edu
Founded 1898
Academic year: July to June
Pres.: Dr BIFF GREEN
Vice-Pres. for Academic Affairs: Dr JOHN YODER
Vice-Pres. for Admin. and Finance: RANDALL C. DOERKSEN
Vice-Pres. for Univ. Advancement: HERVEY WRIGHT, III
Assoc. Vice-Pres. for Student Affairs: CYNTHIA JACOBSON
Registrar: MARCIA MORTON
Librarian: DAVID PAPPAS
Library of 100,000 vols
Number of teachers: 79
Number of students: 2,749
Publication: *Focus* (4 a year)

DEANS

College of Adult and Professional Studies: Dr VICKI BERGKAMP
College of Business, Arts, Sciences, and Education: Dr WAYNE HOWDESHELL
Graduate School: Dr AL SABER

KANSAS STATE UNIVERSITY

Manhattan, KS 66506
Telephone: (785) 532-6151
Fax: (785) 532-6393
E-mail: kstateag@ksu.edu
Internet: www.ksu.edu
Founded 1863
Pres.: Dr JON WEFALD
Vice-Provost for Academic Services and Technology: ELIZABETH A. UNGER
Vice-Provost for Research: Prof. R. W. TREWYN
Vice-Pres. for Admin. and Finance: Dr THOMAS M. RAWSON
Vice-Pres. for Institutional Advancement: ROBERT KRAUSE
Dean of Libraries: LORI A. GOETSCH
Library: see Libraries
Number of teachers: 1,197
Number of students: 23,000
Publications: *K-State Engineer Magazine* (2 a year), *K-Stater* (5 a year)

DEANS

College of Agriculture: FRED CHOLICK
College of Architecture: DENNIS LAW
College of Arts and Sciences: STEPHEN WHITE
College of Business Administration: Prof. YAR EBADI
College of Education: MICHAEL C. HOLEN
College of Engineering: RICHARD R. GALLAGHER
College of Human Ecology: VIRGINIA MOXLEY
College of Technology and Aviation: DENNIS KUHLMAN
College of Veterinary Medicine: RALPH C. RICHARDSON
Continuing Education: ELIZABETH A. UNGER
Graduate School: Prof. R. W. TREWYN

KANSAS WESLEYAN UNIVERSITY

100 East Claffin Ave, Salina, KS 67401-6196
Telephone: (785) 827-5541
Fax: (785) 827-0927
E-mail: admissions@kwu.edu
Internet: www.kwu.edu
Founded 1886
Private control, affiliated with the United Methodist Church
Pres.: PHILIP KERSTETTER
Vice-Pres. and Academic Dean: Dr MIKE MITCHELL
Vice-Pres. for Finance and Admin.: WAYNE SCHNEIDER
Vice-Pres. for Institutional Advancement: DARIN RUSSELL
Dir of Admissions: JIM ALLEN
Dir of Enrollment and Financial Services: GLENNA ALEXANDER
Registrar: DENISE HOEFFNER
Dir of Library Services: RUTH COX
Library of 75,938 vols
Number of teachers: 45 (40 full-time, 5 part-time)
Number of students: 800

MCPHERSON COLLEGE

1600 East Euclid, POB 1402, McPherson, KS 67460
Telephone: (620) 241-0731
Fax: (620) 241-8443
E-mail: admiss@mcpherson.edu
Internet: www.mcpherson.edu
Founded 1887 as McPherson College and Institute; present name 1898
Private control
Academic year: September to May
Pres.: RON HOVIS
Vice-Pres. for Advancement: MICHAEL P. SCHNEIDER
Provost and Dean of Faculty: Dr LAURA EELLS
Dean of Students: LAMONTE ROTHROCK
Dir of Library and Media Services: Dr SUSAN TAYLOR
Number of teachers: 42
Number of students: 440
Depts of art, behavioural science, business, English, health, physical education and recreation, history, mathematics and information technology, modern language, music, natural sciences, philosophy and religion, teacher education, technology, theatre.

MANHATTAN CHRISTIAN COLLEGE

1415 Anderson Ave, Manhattan, KS 66502
Telephone: (785) 539-3571
Fax: (785) 539-0832
E-mail: admit@mccks.edu
Internet: www.mccks.edu
Founded 1927 as Christian Workers' Univ.; present name 1971
Private control
Academic year: August to May
Pres.: KEVIN INGRAM
Vice-Pres. for Academic Affairs: RANDY INGMIRE
Vice-Pres. for Business Affairs: LORI JO STANFIELD
Vice-Pres. for Institutional Advancement: VERN HENRICKS
Vice-Pres. for Student Life: Dr RICK L. WRIGHT
Librarian: MARY ANN LITTRELL
Library of 40,000 vols
Number of teachers: 24
Number of students: 406
Depts of Bible and theology, general studies, practical ministries.

MID-AMERICA NAZARENE UNIVERSITY

2030 E College Way, Olathe, KS 66062-1899
Telephone: (913) 782-3750
Fax: (913) 791-3290
E-mail: info@mnu.edu
Internet: www.mnu.edu
Founded 1966
Private control
Academic year: August to April
Pres.: ED ROBINSON
Vice-Pres. for Academic Affairs and Dean: Dr STEPHEN RAGAN
Vice-Pres. for Enrollment Devt: (vacant)
Vice-Pres. for Finance: KEVIN GILMORE
Vice-Pres. for Student Devt: RANDY BECKUM
Vice-Pres. for Univ. Advancement: Dr JASON DRUMMOND
Registrar: JAMES GARRISON
Librarian: Dr RODNEY BIRCH
Library of 400,000 items
Number of teachers: 123
Number of students: 1,778

CHAIRPERSONS

College of Liberal Arts and Sciences: Dr CYNTHIA L. PETERSON
School of Business: Dr ROY ROTZ
School of Christian Ministry and Formation: Dr JAMES O. EDLIN
School of Education and Counseling: Dr LINDA ALEXANDER
School of Nursing and Health Science: SUSAN LARSON

NEWMAN UNIVERSITY

3100 McCormick Ave, Wichita, KS 67213-2097
Telephone: (316) 942-4291
Fax: (316) 942-4483
E-mail: admissions@newmanu.edu
Internet: www.newmanu.edu
Founded 1933 as Sacred Heart Junior College; present name 1998
Private control
Pres.: Dr NOREEN M. CARROCCI
Provost and Vice-Pres. for Academic Affairs: Dr B. LEE COOPER
Vice-Pres. for Enrollment Management: KIM MILLER JACOBS
Vice-Pres. for Finance and Admin.: MARK B. DRESSELHAUS
Vice-Pres. for Institutional Advancement: THOMAS E. BORREGO
Registrar: SHIRLEY RUEB
Library Dir: JOSEPH FORTE
Number of teachers: 191
Number of students: 2,071

DEANS

School of Applied Social Sciences: Dr MICHAEL SMITH
School of Arts and Humanities: NYALLS HARTMAN
School of Business: Dr JOSEPH GOETZ
School of Education: Dr GREGORY MOSS
School of Science, Nursing and Allied Health: Dr JOAN FELTS

OTTAWA UNIVERSITY

1001 South Cedar St, Ottawa, KS 66067
Telephone: (785) 242-5200
Fax: (785) 229-1020
E-mail: admiss@ottawa.edu
Internet: www.ottawa.edu
Founded 1865
Academic year: June to May
Mesa, Phoenix and Tempus campuses in Arizona; Indiana, Kansas City and Wisconsin campuses

Pres.: Dr FREDERICK R. SNOW
Exec. Vice-Pres.: Dr JAMES BILLICK
Vice-Pres. for Enrollment Management: SUSAN BACKOFEN
Provost: Dr BARBARA DINEEN
Provost, Kansas City: Dr TERREL W. HAINES
Provost, Arizona: Dr DONNA LEVENE
Dir, Milwaukee: Dr DONALD CLAUSER
Registrar: KAREN ADAMS
Dir of Library Services: GLORIA CREED-DIKEOGU
Library of 84,000 vols, 186 periodicals
Number of teachers: 65
Number of students: 2,503 full-time

PITTSBURG STATE UNIVERSITY

1701 South Broadway, Pittsburg, KS 66762
Telephone: (620) 231-7000
Fax: (620) 235-6192
Internet: www.pittstate.edu
Founded 1903
Pres.: STEVEN A. SCOTT
Vice-Pres. for Admin. and Campus Life: JOHN D. PATTERSON
Vice-Pres. for Univ. Advancement: J. BRADFORD HODSON
Registrar: DEBBIE GREVE
Dean of Learning Resources: ROBERT WALTER
Library of 545,000 vols
Number of teachers: 325
Number of students: 6,500

DEANS
College of Arts and Sciences: Dr LYNETTE OLSON
College of Education: Dr JAMES C. CHRISTMAN
College of Technology: Dr BRUCE DALLMAN
Graduate Studies: Dr OLIVER HENSLEY
Kelce College of Business: Dr J. RUSSELL HARDIN

SAINT MARY COLLEGE

4100 South Fourth St, Leavenworth, KS 66048-5082
Telephone: (913) 682-5151
Fax: (913) 758-6140
E-mail: admiss@stmary.edu
Internet: www.stmary.edu
Founded 1923
Private control (Roman Catholic church)
Academic year: August to July
Pres.: Dr DIANE STEELE
Vice-Pres. and Dean for Academic Affairs: Dr SANDRA VAN HOOSE
Vice-Pres. for Finance and Admin. Services: DALE L. CULVER
Vice-Pres. for Student Life: KEITH R. HANSEN
Vice-Pres. and Dean of Overland Park: RONALD LOGAN
Registrar: WANDA OWEN
Dean of Students: KEITH HANSEN
Librarian: PENELOPE LONERGAN
Library of 118,195 vols
Number of teachers: 43
Number of students: 826

SOUTHWESTERN COLLEGE

100 College St, Winfield, KS 67156-2499
Telephone: (620) 229-6000
Fax: (620) 229-6224
Internet: www.sckans.edu
Founded 1885
Academic year: August to May
Pres.: Dr W. RICHARD MERRIMAN, Jr
Vice-Pres. for Academic Affairs and Dean of Faculty: J. ANDREW SHEPPARD
Vice-Pres. for Institutional Advancement: PAUL M. BEAN
Registrar: STACY TOWNSLEY
Dir of Admission: TODD N. MOORE
Library Dir: VERONICA MCASEY
Library of 70,000 vols, 11,000 e-books
Number of teachers: 50 full-time
Number of students: 1,401 (691 full-time, 710 part-time)
Professional, liberal arts and general, teacher preparatory college.

STERLING COLLEGE

125 West Cooper, Sterling, KS 67579
Telephone: (620) 278-2173
Fax: (620) 278-3188
Internet: www.sterling.edu
Founded 1887
Pres.: Dr DOUGLAS BRUCE
Vice-Pres. of Academic Affairs: TROY PETERS
Vice-Pres. for Institutional Advancement: MARK SARVER
Vice-Pres. for Student Life: TINA WOHLER
Registrar: JANET CAYWOOD
Library Dir: BETTY CALDERWOOD
Library of 85,000 vols
Number of teachers: 32
Number of students: 490
Majors incl. art and graphic design, athletic training, biology, business admin., chemistry, Christian ministries, communication and theatre arts, culinary arts, elementary education, English, exercise science, graphic design and effects, history, ind. interdisciplinary, mathematics, music, music education, psychology, religious and philosophical studies.

TABOR COLLEGE

400 South Jefferson, Hillsboro, KS 67063
Telephone: (620) 947-3121
Fax: (620) 947-2676
E-mail: admissions@tabor.edu
Internet: www.tabor.edu
Founded 1908
Academic year: August to May
Pres.: LARRY NIKKEL
Vice-Pres. of Academics and Student Devt: Dr LAWRENCE RESSLER
Vice-Pres. for Advancement: JIM ELLIOTT
Vice-Pres. for Business and Finance: KIRBY FADENRECHT
Vice-Pres. for Enrollment Management: RUSTY ALLEN
Registrar: DEANNE DUERKSEN
Dean of Student Devt: ERIC CODDING
Dir of Library Services: ROBIN OTTOSON
Library of 80,000 vols
Number of teachers: 65
Number of students: 586
Liberal arts college.

UNITED STATES ARMY COMMAND AND GENERAL STAFF COLLEGE

1 Reynolds Ave, Fort Leavenworth, KS 66027-1352
E-mail: leav-cgscregistrar@conus.army.mil
Internet: www-cgsc.army.mil
Founded 1882 as School of Application for Cavalry and Infantry; present name 1947
Academic year: August to June
Deputy Commandant: Brig.-Gen. JAMES HIRAI
Librarian: EDWIN B. BURGESS.

UNIVERSITY OF KANSAS

Room 230, 1450 Jayhawk Blvd, Lawrence, KS 66045
Telephone: (785) 864-2700
Fax: (785) 864-4120
E-mail: chancellor@ku.edu
Internet: www.ku.edu
Founded 1864
State univ., under the Kansas Board of Regents
Academic year: August to May
Chancellor: BERNADETTE GRAY-LITTLE
Provost and Exec. Vice-Chancellor: JEFFREY S. VITTER
Sr Vice-Provost for Scholarly Support: DON STEEPLES
Vice-Provost for Academic Affairs: BARBARA ROMZEK
Vice-Provost for Faculty Devt: MARY LEE HUMMERT
Vice-Provost for Finance: DIANE GODDARD
Vice-Provost for Scholarly Support: DON STEEPLES
Vice-Provost for Student Success: MARLESA RONEY
Vice-Chancellor and Dean for Edwards Campus: Dr ROBERT M. CLARK
Vice-Chancellor for Research and Graduate Studies: STEVE WARREN
Chief Information Officer: DIANE GODDARD
Registrar: CINDY DERRITT
Dean of Libraries: LORRAINE HARICOMBE
Library: 4.3m. vols, 73,613 periodicals, 3.7m. microforms
Number of teachers: 2,460
Number of students: 30,004
Publications: *American Studies Journal*, *Auslegung*, *Chimères*, *Indigenous Nations Studies Journal*, *Journal of Applied Behavior Analysis*, *Journal of Dramatic Theory and Criticism*, *Journal of Kansas Entomological Society*, *Journal of Public Administration Research and Theory*, *Journal of Social and Clinical Psychology*, *Kansas Academy of Science Transactions*, *Kansas Journal of Law and Public Policy*, *Kansas Law Review*, *La Coronica: A Journal of Medieval Spanish Language and Literature*, *Latin American Theatre Review*, *Middle School Journal*, *The Nabokovian*, *Paleontological Contributions*, *Research Opportunities in Renaissance Drama*, *Russkii Tekst*, *Slovene Linguistic Studies*, *Social Thought and Research*, *Treatise on Invertebrate Paleontology*, *Yearbook of German-American Studies*

DEANS
College of Liberal Arts and Sciences: DANNY ANDERSON
Graduate Studies: SARA ROSEN
School of Architecture, Design and Planning: (vacant)
School of Business: WILLIAM FUERST
School of Education: RICK GINSBERG
School of Engineering: Dr STUART R. BELL
School of Journalism and Mass Communications: ANN M. BRILL
School of Law: GAIL B. AGRAWAL
School of Music: ROBERT WALZEL
School of Pharmacy: KENNETH L. AUDUS
School of Social Welfare: MARY ELLEN KONDRAT

ATTACHED MEDICAL CENTRE

Kansas University Medical Center
3901 Rainbow Blvd, Kansas City, KS 66160
Telephone: (913) 588-5000
Fax: (913) 588-1412
Internet: www.kumc.edu
Founded 1905
Exec. Vice-Chancellor: Dr BARBARA ATKINSON
Sr Vice-Chancellor for Academic and Student Affairs: KAREN MILLER
Vice-Chancellor for Academic Affairs: Dr ALLEN B. RAWITCH
Vice-Chancellor for Admin.: EDWARD PHILLIPS
Vice-Chancellor for Planning and Policy: MARCI NELSON

Vice-Chancellor for Research: Dr PAUL TERRANOVA
Number of teachers: 890
Number of students: 3,178

DEANS

Graduate Studies: Dr ALLEN B RAWITCH
School of Allied Health: Prof. KAREN MILLER
School of Medicine: Dr BARBARA F. ATKINSON (Exec. Dean)
School of Nursing: Dr KAREN MILLER

WASHBURN UNIVERSITY

1700 Southwest College, Topeka, KS 66621
Telephone: (785) 670-1010
Fax: (785) 670-1048
E-mail: webmaster@washburn.edu
Internet: www.washburn.edu
Founded 1865
Academic year: August to May
Pres.: Dr JERRY B. FARLEY
Vice-Pres. for Academic Affairs and Provost: Dr RON WASSERSTEIN
Vice-Pres. for Admin. and Treas.: WANDA HILL
Vice-Pres. for Student Life: Dr WANDA HILL
Dean of Univ. Library: Dr GARY SCHMIDT
Registrar: Dr WANDA DOLE
Library of 315,293 vols
Number of teachers: 300
Number of students: 6,626
Publications: *Alumni Magazine*, *Circuit Rider*, *KAW*, *Washburn Review*, *Washburn Update*

DEANS

College of Arts and Sciences: Dr GORDON MCQUERE
Division of Continuing Education: Dr TIM PETERSON
Law: WILLIAM RICH
School of Applied Studies: Dr WILLIAM S. DUNLAP
School of Business: Dr DAVID SOLLARS
School of Nursing: Dr CYNTHIA HORNBERGER

WICHITA STATE UNIVERSITY

1845 Fairmont St, Wichita, KS 67260
Telephone: (316) 978-3456
Fax: (316) 978-3174
Internet: www.wichita.edu
Founded 1894 as Fairmount College (Congregational), control transferred to City of Wichita 1926, added to the Kansas state higher education system 1964
Pres.: Dr DONALD L. BEGGS
Vice-Pres. and Gen. Counsel: TED D. AYRES
Vice-Pres. for Academic Affairs and Research: Dr GARY L. MILLER
Vice-Pres. for Admin. and Finance: ROBERT D. LOWE
Vice-Pres. for Campus Life and Univ. Relations: WADE ROBINSON
Dean of Univ. Libraries: PAL RAO
Library of 1,085,000 vols, 1,096,000 microforms, 14,270 current periodicals, 495,000 govt documents, 4,000 linear ft of archives and MSS
Number of teachers: 520 (479 full-time, 41 part-time)
Number of students: 15,000
Publications: *Sunflower*, *Wichita State Alumni News*, *Wichita State University Magazine*

DEANS

Barton School of Business: Dr JOHN M. BEEHLER
College of Education: JON ENGELHARDT
College of Engineering: ZULMA TORO-RAMOS
College of Fine Arts: RODNEY E. MILLER
College of Health Professions: Prof. PETER A. COHEN
College of Liberal Arts and Sciences: WILLIAM D. BISCHOFF
Graduate School: SUSAN KOVAR

KENTUCKY

ALICE LLOYD COLLEGE

100 Purpose Rd, Pippa Passes, KY 41844
Telephone: (606) 368-2101
Fax: (606) 368-2125
E-mail: enrolments@alc.edu
Internet: www.alc.edu
Founded 1923
Private control
Academic year: August to May
Pres.: JOE A. STEPP
Vice-Pres. for Academic Affairs: MARYLEE JAMES
Vice-Pres. for Admin.: JAMES STEPP
Vice-Pres. for Business Affairs: DAVID JOHNSON
Registrar: THELMARIE THORNSBERRY
Library Dir: ANDREW BUSROE
Number of teachers: 32
Number of students: 508

CHAIRS OF ACADEMIC DIVISIONS

Humanities: RICHARD KENNEDY
Natural Science and Mathematics: Dr PAUL YEARY

ASBURY COLLEGE

1 Macklem Dr., Wilmore, KY 40390
Telephone: (859) 858-3511
E-mail: pr@asbury.edu
Internet: www.asbury.edu
Founded 1890
Private control
Academic year: August to May
Pres.: Dr WILLIAM C. CROTHERS
Provost: Dr JOHN S. KULAGA
Vice-Pres. for Business Affairs: Dr CHARLIE D. FISKEAUX
Vice-Pres. for Institutional Advancement: ROBERT T. BRIDGES
Vice-Pres. for Student Devt: Dr W. JOSEPH BROCKINTON
Registrar: Dr TIMOTHY L. THOMAS
Dir of Library Services: DOUGLAS J. BUTLER
Library of 155,000 vols
Number of teachers: 155
Number of students: 1,218 (1,155 undergraduate, 63 graduate)

ASBURY THEOLOGICAL SEMINARY

204 North Lexington Ave, Wilmore, KY 40390
Telephone: (859) 858-3581
Internet: www.asburyseminary.edu
Founded 1923
Private control
Academic year: September to May
Pres.: ELLSWORTH KALAS
Vice-Pres. for Academic Affairs and Provost: Dr BILL ARNOLD
Vice-Pres. for Community Life: Rev. JOHN DAVID WALT
Vice-Pres. for Finance and Admin.: BRYAN BLANKENSHIP
Vice-Pres. for Florida Campus: Dr J. STEVEN HARPER
Vice-Pres. for Seminary Advancement: RONNIE JONES
Exec. Dir of Libraries: PAUL TIPPEY
Library of 247,000 items
Number of teachers: 62
Number of students: 1,778.

BRANCH CAMPUS

Florida Campus: 8401 Valencia College Lane, Orlando, FL 32825; tel. (407) 482-7564.

BELLARMINE UNIVERSITY

2001 Newburg Rd, Louisville, KY 40205-0671
Telephone: (502) 272-8000
Fax: (502) 272-8033
E-mail: admissions@bellarmine.edu
Internet: www.bellarmine.edu
Founded 1950
Private control
Language of instruction: English
Academic year: August to May
Pres.: Dr JOSEPH J. MCGOWAN
Provost: Dr DORIS TEGART
Vice-Pres. for Academic Affairs: Dr CAROLE PFEFFER
Vice-Pres. for Student Affairs: Dr FRED RHODES
Vice-Pres. for Communications and Public Affairs: HUNT C. HELM
Vice-Pres. for Devt and Alumni Relations: GLENN KOSSE
Vice-Pres. for Enrollment Management: SEAN J. RYAN
Dean of Graduate Admissions: SARA YOUNT
Dean of Students: HELEN-GRACE RYAN
Dean of Undergraduate Admissions: TIMOTHY STURGEON
Library Dir: JOHN STEMMER
Library of 93,000 vols
Number of teachers: 228 (138 full-time, 90 part-time)
Number of students: 3,132

DEANS

Allan and Donna Lansing School of Nursing and Health Sciences: Dr SUSAN H. DAVIS
Annsley Frazier Thornton School of Education: Dr ROBERT COOTER
Bellarmine College of Arts and Sciences: Dr BILL FENTON
Centre for Regional Environmental Studies: Dr ROBERT KINGSOLVER
Rubel School of Business: Dr DANIEL L. BAUER
School of Communication (Dir): ED MANASSAH
School of Continuing and Professional Studies: Dr MICHAEL MATTEI

BEREA COLLEGE

101 Chestnut St, Berea, KY 40404
Telephone: (859) 985-3000
Fax: (859) 985-3915
Internet: www.berea.edu
Founded 1855
Academic year: September to May
Pres.: Dr LARRY D. SHINN
Academic Vice-Pres. and Provost: CAROLYN NEWTON
Vice-Pres. for College Relations and Devt: WILLIAM LARAMEE
Vice-Pres. for Finance: JEFFREY AMBURGEY
Vice-Pres. for Labor and Student Life: GAIL WOLFORD
Vice-Pres. for Operations and Sustainability: STEVE KARCHER
Academic Vice-Pres. and Dean of the Faculty: STEPHANIE P. BROWNER
Dir of Library Services: ANNE CHASE
Library of 450,000 vols
Number of teachers: 144
Number of students: 1,500

BRESCIA UNIVERSITY

717 Frederica St, Owensboro, KY 42301-3023
Telephone: (270) 685-3131
E-mail: admissions@brescia.edu

Internet: www.brescia.edu

Founded 1925 as Mount Saint Joseph Jr College for Women; present name 1998

Private control

Academic year: August to May

Pres.: Sr VIVIAN M. BOWLES
Vice-Pres. for Academic Affairs and Academic Dean: JAMES AHERN
Dir of Library Services: Sr JUDITH NELL RINEY

Number of teachers: 60
Number of students: 840

CHAIRMEN OF ACADEMIC DIVISIONS

Educational Studies: Sr SHARON SULLIVAN
Fine Arts: Sr MARY DIANE TAYLOR
Humanities: Dr ELLEN DUGAN-BARRETTE
Mathematics and Natural Sciences: Sr MICHELE MOREK
Social and Behavioural Sciences: (vacant)
William H. Thompson School of Business: Dr JULIE JOHNSON

CAMPBELLSVILLE COLLEGE

1 University Dr., Campbellsville, KY 42718-2799

Telephone: (800) 264-6014
Fax: (800) 789-5020
E-mail: admissions@campbellsville.edu
Internet: www.campbellsville.edu

Founded 1906

Affiliated with the Kentucky Baptist Convention

Pres.: Dr MICHAEL V. CARTER
Vice-Pres. for Academic Affairs: Dr FRANKLIN D. CHEATHAM
Vice-Pres. for Church and External Relations: JOHN E. CHOWNING
Vice-Pres. for Communications and Marketing: MARCUS C. WHITT
Vice-Pres. for Devt: Dr ALAN MEDDERS
Vice-Pres. for Finance and Admin.: OTTO TENNANT, Jr
Dir of Library Services: Dr JOHN RUSSELL BIRCH, Jr

Library of 95,000 vols
Number of teachers: 45
Number of students: 1,800

CENTRE COLLEGE

Danville, KY 40422

Telephone: (859) 238-5200
Fax: (859) 236-5373
Internet: www.centre.edu

Founded 1819

Pres.: JOHN ROUSH
Vice-Pres. and Dean of Student Life: RANDY HAYS
Vice-Pres. and Treas.: JOHN CUNY
Registrar: TIM CULHAN
Library Dir: STAN CAMPBELL

Library of 373,682 vols and 28,296 periodicals
Number of teachers: 114
Number of students: 1,200

CLEAR CREEK BAPTIST BIBLE COLLEGE

300 Clear Creek Rd, Pineville, KY 40977

Telephone: (606) 337-3196
Fax: (606) 337-2372
E-mail: ccbbc@ccbbc.edu
Internet: www.ccbbc.edu

Founded 1926 as Clear Creek Mountain Springs, Inc.; present name 1986

Private control

Academic year: August to May

Pres.: Dr DONNIE FOX
Academic Dean: Dr MALCOLM HESTER
Registrar: MARY LOU WALZER
Dir of Library Services: MARGE CUMMINGS

Library of 37,000 vols
Number of teachers: 22
Number of students: 174

EASTERN KENTUCKY UNIVERSITY

521 Lancaster Ave, Richmond, KY 40475-3102

Telephone: (859) 622-1000
Fax: (859) 622-1020
E-mail: marc.whitt@eku.edu
Internet: www.eku.edu

Founded 1906

Academic year: August to May

Pres.: Dr DOUG WHITLOCK
Provost and Vice-Pres. for Academic Affairs and Research: Dr JANNA VICE
Vice-Pres. for Financial Affairs and Treas.: DEBORAH NEWSOM
Vice-Pres. for Student Affairs: Dr JAMES CONNEELY
Vice-Pres. for Univ. Advancement: JIM CLARK
Vice-Pres. for Univ. Advancement: JOSEPH FOSTER
Dir of Govt Relations: TINA DAVIS
Registrar: CARRIE COOPER
Dean of Libraries: CARRIE COOPER

Library of 837,945 vols, 3,565 current periodicals, 1,410,522 current periodicals
Number of teachers: 575 (full-time)
Number of students: 16,500

DEANS

Arts and Sciences: Dr DOMINIC HART
Business and Technology: Dr ROBERT ROGOW
Education: Dr LARRY SEXTON (acting)
Graduate Studies: Dr BANKOLE THOMPSON
Health Sciences: Dr DAVID GALE
Law Enforcement: Dr GARY CORDNER

GEORGETOWN COLLEGE

Georgetown, KY 40324-1696

Telephone: (502) 863-8011
Fax: (502) 868-8891
E-mail: pr@georgetowncollege.edu
Internet: www.georgetowncollege.edu

Founded 1787

Private control

Academic year: July to June

Pres.: Dr WILLIAM H. CROUCH, Jr
Vice-Pres. and Treas.: JAMES MOAK Jr
Provost and Academic Dean: Dr ROSEMARY ALLEN
Vice-Pres. for Enrollment Management: GARVEL KINDRICK
Vice-Pres. for Institutional Advancement: ROY LOWDENBACK
Vice-Pres. for Student Life and Dean of Students: TODD GAMBILL
Library Dir: MARY MARGARET LOWE
Dean of Education: YOLANDA CARTER

Library of 183,572 vols, 733 current periodicals, 4,064 audiovisual items
Number of teachers: 113
Number of students: 1,851

KENTUCKY CHRISTIAN UNIVERSITY

100 Academic Parkway, Grayson, KY 41143-2205

Telephone: (606) 474-3000
Fax: (606) 474-3154
Internet: www.kcu.edu

Founded 1919 as Christian Normal Institute; as Kentucky Christian College 1944; present name 2004

Private control

Academic year: August to May

Pres.: Dr KEITH P. KEERAN
Chancellor: Dr L. PALMER YOUNG
Exec. Vice-Pres.: JOHN L. DUNDON
Sr Vice-Pres. and Provost: Dr JEFF METCALF
Vice-Pres. for Academic Affairs: Dr JEFF METCALF
Vice-Pres. for Business and Finance: Dr TIM NISCHIN
Vice-Pres. for Enrollment Management: SANDRA DEAKINS
Vice-Pres. for Student Life: Dr SHERRY L. CURTIS
Registrar: GEORGE W. WAGGONER, III
Library Dir: THOMAS SCOTT

Library of 80,000 vols
Number of teachers: 32
Number of students: 580

KENTUCKY MOUNTAIN BIBLE COLLEGE

POB 10, Vancleve, KY 41385-0010
855 Kentucky Highway 541, Vancleve, KY 41385-0010

Telephone: (606) 666-5000
Fax: (606) 666-7744
E-mail: kmbc@kmbc.edu
Internet: www.kmbc.edu

Founded 1931 as Kentucky Mountain Bible Institute; present name 1989

Private control

Academic year: August to May

Pres.: Dr PHILIP SPEAS
Exec. Vice-Pres. and Vice-Pres. for Academic Affairs: THOMAS LORIMER
Business Man.: DOUG DUNN
Vice-Pres. for Business Affairs: DOUG DUNN
Vice-Pres. for Devt: JOHN NEIHOF
Registrar: CATY NELSON
Librarian: PAT BOWEN

Library of 26,000 vols
Number of teachers: 16
Number of students: 85

KENTUCKY STATE UNIVERSITY

400 East Main St, Frankfort, KY 40601

Telephone: (502) 597-6000
E-mail: admissions@kysu.edu
Internet: www.kysu.edu

Founded 1886

Academic year: August to May

Pres.: Dr MARY EVANS SIAS
Vice-Pres. for Academic Affairs and Provost: STEFANIE WATSON
Vice-Pres. for External Relations and Devt: HINFRED MCDUFFIE
Vice-Pres. for Finance and Admin.: (vacant): KATHY WILSON
Vice-Pres. for Student Affairs: Dr RUBYE JONES
Dir of Libraries: SHEILA A. STUCKEY
Dir of Records, Registration and Admissions: JAMES BURRELL

Library of 304,000 vols
Number of teachers: 149
Number of students: 2,315

KENTUCKY WESLEYAN COLLEGE

3000 Frederica St, Owensboro, KY 42301

Telephone: (270) 926-3111
Fax: (270) 926-3196
E-mail: admitme@kwc.edu
Internet: www.kwc.edu

Founded 1858

Academic year: August to May

Pres.: Dr ANNE CAIRNS FEDERLEIN
Vice-Pres. for Advancement: RONALD S. MCCRACKEN
Vice-Pres. for Finance: CINDRA K. STIFF
Dean of Admission and Financial Aid: CLAUDE M. BACON
Dean of the College: Dr M. MICHAEL FAGAN
Dean of Student Life: SCOTT E. KRAMER

Dir of Library: PATRICIA MCFARLING
Library of 85,085 vols, 315 periodicals
Number of teachers: 69
Number of students: 636 (606 full-time, 30 part-time)

LEXINGTON THEOLOGICAL SEMINARY

631 South Limestone St, Lexington, KY 40508
Telephone: (859) 252-0361
Fax: (859) 281-6042
E-mail: admissions@lextheo.edu
Internet: www.lextheo.edu

Founded 1865 as College of the Bible, present name 1965
Private control

Pres.: JAMES P. JOHNSON
Vice-Pres. for Advancement: JAMES M. WRAY, Jr
Registrar: SHARON WARNER
Librarian: BARBARA PFEIFLE

Number of teachers: 6
Number of students: 90

LINDSEY WILSON COLLEGE

210 Lindsey Wilson St, Columbia, KY 42728
Telephone: (270) 384-2126
Fax: (270) 384-8200
E-mail: info@lindsey.edu
Internet: www.lindsey.edu

Founded 1903 as Lindsey Wilson Training School; present name 1923
Private control
Academic year: August to May

Pres.: WILLIAM T. LUCKEY, Jr
Chancellor: JOHN B. BEGLEY
Vice-Pres. for Admin. and Finance: ROGER DRAKE
Vice-Pres. for Advancement: RON HEATH
Vice-Pres. for Student Services and Enrollment Management: DEAN ADAMS
Provost and Dean of Faculty: JOHN RIGNEY
Registrar: SUE COOMER
Library Dir: PHILIP HANNA

Library of 496,000 items
Number of teachers: 58
Number of students: 1,585

CHAIRMEN OF ACADEMIC DIVISIONS

Business and Computer Information Systems: JOHN HOWERY
Education: ROBERT BROWN
Human Services and Counselling: JOHN RIGNEY
Humanities and Fine Arts: TIM SMITH
Mathematics and Natural Sciences: ROBERT SHUFFETT
Social and Behavioral Sciences: (vacant)

LOUISVILLE PRESBYTERIAN THEOLOGICAL SEMINARY

1044 Alta Vista Rd, Louisville, KY 40205
Telephone: (502) 895-3411
Fax: (502) 895-1096
E-mail: admissions@lpts.edu
Internet: www.lpts.edu
Private control

Pres.: DEAN K. THOMPSON
Dean: DAVID C. HESTER
Library Dir: DOUGLAS GRAGG

Library of 160,000 vols
Number of teachers: 24
Number of students: 200

PROFESSORS

ADENEY, FRANCES S., Evangelism and Global Mission
BOS, JOHANNA W. H., Bible and Old Testament
COOK, CAROL J., Pastoral Care and Counselling
ELWOOD, CHRISTOPHER, Historical Theology
GARRETT, SUSAN R., New Testament
HESTER, DAVID C., Ministry
JOHNSON, KATHRYN L., Historical Theology and Church History
PAUW, AMY PLANTINGA, Doctrinal Theology
REISTROFFER, DIANNE, Ministry
SAWYER, DAVID R., Ministry
SOARDS, MARION L., New Testament
THOMPSON, DEAN K., Ministry
TOWNSEND, LOREN L., Pastoral Ministry, and Pastoral Care and Counselling
TULL, PATRICIA KATHLEEN, Old Testament
WIGGER, J. BRADLEY, Christian Education
WILLIAMSON, SCOTT C., Theological Ethics

MID-CONTINENT COLLEGE

99 Powell Rd, Mayfield, KY 42066
Telephone: (270) 247-8521
Fax: (270) 247-3115
E-mail: mcc@midcontinent.edu
Internet: www.midcontinent.edu

Founded 1949
Private control

Pres.: Dr ROBERT IMHOFF
Provost and Vice-Pres. for Academic Affairs: Dr ALLAN L. BEANE
Exec. Vice-Pres. for Admin. and Student Affairs: CHARLES W. FORD
Vice-Pres. for Business Operations: ANDY STRATTON
Vice-Pres. for Devt: Dr LARRY STEWART
Registrar: YVONNE YATES
Library Dir: Dr RAYMOND E. CARROLL

Library of 30,000 vols, 200 periodicals, 1,600 audiovisual items
Number of students: 786

DEANS

Baptist College of Arts and Sciences: Dr STEPHEN WILSON
Baptist College of the Bible: Dr JAMES CECIL

MIDWAY COLLEGE

512 East Stephens St, Midway, KY 40347
Telephone: (859) 846-4421
Fax: (859) 846-5817
Internet: www.midway.edu

Founded 1847 as Kentucky Female Orphan School; present name 1978
Private control
Academic year: August to May

Pres.: Dr WILLIAM B. DRAKE, Jr
Vice-Pres. for Academic Affairs: (vacant)
Vice-Pres. for Business Affairs: LYEN CREWS
Vice-Pres. for College Relations and Devt: JUDY MARCUM
Vice-Pres. and Dean of Enrollment Management: Dr JAMES WOMBLES
Vice-Pres. and Assoc. Dean of School for Career Devt: Dr WILLIAM BROWN
Provost and Dean of Women's College: SARAH H. LAWS
Registrar: P. EDWARD PRESLER
Dir of Library Services: CATHY REILENDER

Number of teachers: 48 full-time, 112 assoc. staff
Number of students: 1,200

CHAIRMEN OF ACADEMIC DIVISIONS

Business Studies and Organizational Management: Dr FRANK FLETCHER
Equine Studies: Dr SALLY HAYDON
Liberal Studies: Dr JUDITH HATCHETT
Mathematics and Science: Dr JOHN SASSER
Nursing: Dr PATTY RYAN
Teacher Education: (vacant)

MOREHEAD STATE UNIVERSITY

150 University Blvd, Morehead, KY 40351
Telephone: (606) 783-2221
Fax: (606) 783-2678
E-mail: webmaster@moreheadstate.edu
Internet: www.moreheadstate.edu

Founded 1922
Academic year: August to May

Pres.: Dr WAYNE D. ANDREWS
Provost and Exec. Vice-Pres. for Academic Affairs: MICHAEL MOORE
Vice-Pres. for Admin. and Fiscal Services: MICHAEL WALTERS
Vice-Pres. for Devt: BARBARA A. ENDER
Vice-Pres. for Planning, Budgets and Technology: BETH G. PATRICK
Vice-Pres. for Student Life: MADONNA WEATHERS
Vice-Pres. for Univ. Relations: KEITH KAPPES
Registrar: LORETTA B. LYKINS
Dean of Library Services: ELSIE PRITCHARD

Library of 441,203 vols, 2,546 periodicals
Number of teachers: 440 (320 full-time, 120 part-time)
Number of students: 8,171 (5,849 full-time, 2,322 part-time)

DEANS

Caudill College of Humanities: Dr MICHAEL SEELIG
College of Business: Dr ROBERT ALBERT
College of Education: Dr DAN BRANHAM
College of Science and Technology: Dr GERALD DEMOSS
Institute for Regional Analysis and Public Policy: Dr DAVID RUDY

MURRAY STATE UNIVERSITY

102 Curris Centre, Murray, KY 42071
Telephone: (270) 762-3011
Fax: (270) 809-3413
E-mail: admissions@murraystate.edu
Internet: www.murraystate.edu

Founded 1922
Public control
Academic year: August to May

Pres.: RANDY J. DUNN
Provost and Vice-Pres. for Academic Affairs: Dr BONNIE S. HIGGINSON
Vice-Pres. for Finance and Admin. Services: THOMAS W. DENTON
Vice-Pres. for Institutional Advancement: JAMES F. CARTER
Vice-Pres. for Student Affairs: Dr DONALD E. ROBERTSON
Dean of Libraries: ADAM MURRAY

Library of 401,663 vols of monographs, 124,175 vols of periodicals, 215,649 govt documents
Number of teachers: 559 (402 full-time, 157 part-time)
Number of students: 10,416

DEANS

Academic Outreach and Continuing Education: Dr BRIAN VAN HORN
College of Business and Public Affairs: Dr TIMOTHY TODD
College of Education: Dr RENEE CAMPOY
College of Health Sciences and Human Services: Dr JAMES BROUGHTON
College of Humanities and Fine Arts: Dr TED BROWN
College of Science, Engineering and Technology: Dr STEPHEN H. COBB
School of Agriculture: Dr TONY BRANNON

NORTHERN KENTUCKY UNIVERSITY

Nunn Dr., Highland Heights, KY 41099
Telephone: (859) 572-5220
Fax: (859) 572-5566

E-mail: admitnku@nku.edu
Internet: www.nku.edu

Founded 1968 as Northern Kentucky State College; present name 1976
State control
Academic year: August to May

Pres.: Dr JAMES C. VOTRUBA
Vice-Pres. for Academic Affairs and Provost: Dr GAIL W. WELLS
Vice-Pres. for Admin. and Finance: W. MICHAEL BAKER
Vice-Pres. for Govt and Community Relations: JOSEPH E. WIND
Vice-Pres. for Legal Affairs and Gen. Counsel: SARA L. SIDEBOTTOM
Vice-Pres. for Planning, Policy and Budget: SUE HODGES MOORE
Vice-Pres. for Student Affairs: Dr MARK G. SHANLEY
Vice-Pres. for Univ. Advancement: GERARD A. ST AMAND
Registrar: KIMBERLY K. TAYLOR
Assoc. Provost of Libraries: ARNE ALMQUIST

Library of 342,642 vols
Number of teachers: 648 (full-time)
Number of students: 13,743

DEANS

Chase College of Law: Dr GERARD A. ST AMAND
College of Arts and Sciences: Dr PHILLIP SCHMIDT
College of Business: Dr MICHAEL R. CARRELL
College of Education: RACHELLE BRUNO
College of Professional Studies: J. PATRICK MOYNAHAN

PIKEVILLE COLLEGE

147 Sycamore St, Pikeville, KY 41501
Telephone: (606) 218-5250
Fax: (606) 218-5269
Internet: www.pc.edu

Founded 1889
Academic year: August to July

Pres.: MICHAEL LOONEY
Vice-Pres. for Academic Affairs and Dean of the College: THOMAS R. HESS
Librarian: KAREN EVANS

Library of 72,673 vols
Number of teachers: 57
Number of students: 1,013 (762 undergraduate, 251 postgraduate)

SOUTHERN BAPTIST THEOLOGICAL SEMINARY

2825 Lexington Rd, Louisville, KY 40280
Telephone: (502) 897-4011
Fax: (502) 899-1770
E-mail: admissions@sbts.edu
Internet: www.sbts.edu

Founded 1859
Private control
Academic year: August to May

Pres.: Dr R. ALBERT MOHLER, Jr
Sr Vice-Pres. for Academic Admin.: Dr RUSSELL D. MOORE
Sr Vice-Pres. for Institutional Admin.: R. CLARK LOGAN
Sr Vice-Pres. for Institutional Relations: DOUGLAS C. WALKER, III
Vice-Pres. for Student Services: DANIEL E. HATFIELD
Registrar: NORMAN CHUNG
Librarian and Assoc. Vice-Pres. for Academic Resources: BRUCE L. KEISLING

Library of 900,000 items
Number of teachers: 130
Number of students: 2,890

Publication: *Southern Baptist Journal of Theology* (4 a year).

SPALDING UNIVERSITY

845 South Third St, Louisville, KY 40203
Telephone: (502) 585-9911
Fax: (502) 585-7158
E-mail: info@spalding.edu
Internet: www.spalding.edu

Founded 1814

Pres.: Dr JO ANN ROONEY
Sr Vice-Pres. for Academic Affairs: RANDY L. STRICKLAND
Vice-Pres. for Finance: LARRY ROMINE
Vice-Pres. for Univ. Advancement: JEFFREY L. ASHLEY
Dean of Students: RICHARD HUDSON
Dir of Admissions: CHRIS HART
Asst Dir of Financial Aid: KRYSTAN LIVELY
Library Dir: JACKIE LENARZ

Library of 200,000 vols, 22,000 bound journals, 450 current periodical subscriptions
Number of teachers: 147 (81 full-time, 66 part-time)
Number of students: 1,585

DEANS

College of Arts and Sciences: (vacant)
College of Professional Studies: Dr JUDITH PLAWECKI

SULLIVAN UNIVERSITY

3101 Bardstown Rd, Louisville, KY 40205
Telephone: (502) 456 6505
Fax: (502) 454-4880
E-mail: admissions@sullivan.edu
Internet: www.sullivan.edu

Founded 1962 as Sullivan Business College; present name 2000
Private control
Academic year: September to September (4 quarters)

Pres.: Dr THOMAS F. DAVISSON
Exec. Vice-Pres. and CEO: Dr STEPHEN COPPOCK
Dean of Graduate School: Dr JEFFREY JOHNSON
Library Dir: CHARLES BROWN

Library of 20,000 vols
Number of teachers: 38
Number of students: 2,001

Areas of study: business, business admin., childhood education, computer technology, hospitality, legal studies.

BRANCH CAMPUSES

Fort Knox Campus: 63 Quartermaster St, Fort Knox, KY 40121-0998; tel. (502) 942-8500; fax (502) 942-3640.

Lexington Campus: 2355 Harrodsburg Rd, Lexington, KY 40504; tel. (859) 276-4357; fax (859) 276-1153.

THOMAS MORE COLLEGE

333 Thomas More Parkway, Crestview Hills, KY 41017-3495
Telephone: (859) 341-5800
Fax: (859) 344-3345
E-mail: admissions@thomasmore.edu
Internet: www.thomasmore.edu

Founded 1921
Private control
Academic year: June to May

Pres.: Sister MARGARET A. STALLMEYER
Vice-Pres. for Academic Affairs: Dr BRADLEY BIELSKI
Vice-Pres. for Finance: PETER W. AAMODT
Vice-Pres. for Institutional Advancement: CATHY L. SILVERS
Vice-Pres. for Student Services: MATTHEW H. WEBSTER
Registrar: KELLY GOYETTE
Dir of Library: JAMES M. MCKELLOGG

Library of 112,103 vols
Number of teachers: 148 (73 full-time, 75 part-time)
Number of students: 1,886

TRANSYLVANIA UNIVERSITY

300 North Broadway, Lexington, KY 40508-1797
Telephone: (859) 233-8300
E-mail: admissions@transy.edu
Internet: www.transy.edu

Founded 1780 as Transylvania Seminary; inc. as Transylvania Univ. 1799

Pres.: CHARLES L. SHEARER
Vice-Pres. and Dean of the College: WILLIAM F. POLLARD
Vice-Pres. for Devt: MARK V. BLANKENSHIP
Vice-Pres. for Finance and Business: MARC A. MATHEWS
Dean of Students: MICHAEL K. VETTER
Dir for Admissions: BRADLEY L. GOAN
Registrar: JAMES M. MILLS
Librarian: SUSAN M. BROWN

Library of 130,000 vols
Number of teachers: 96
Number of students: 1,100

UNION COLLEGE

310 College St, Barbourville, KY 40906-1499
Telephone: (606) 546-4151
Fax: (606) 546-1217
Internet: www.unionky.edu

Founded 1879
Academic year: July to June

Pres.: EDWARD DE ROSSET
Vice-Pres. for Academic Affairs: Dr THOMAS J. MCFARLAND
Vice-Pres. for Advancement: DENISE WAINSCOTT
Dean of Admissions and Financial Aid: ANDRE WASHINGTON
Athletics Dir: DARIN WILSON
Dean of Education: Dr ROBERT SWANSON
Dean of Student Life: DEBBIE D'ANNA
Registrar: KATHY WEBB
Head Librarian: TARA L. COOPER

Library of 162,646 vols, 439,794 microforms
Number of teachers: 54
Number of students: 1,069 (637 undergraduate, 432 postgraduate)

UNIVERSITY OF KENTUCKY

Lexington, KY 40506
Telephone: (606) 257-9000
Fax: (606) 257-4000
Internet: www.uky.edu

Founded 1865
Academic year: August to May

Pres.: Dr LEE T. TODD, Jr
Provost: KUMBLE R. SUBBASWAMY (acting)
Exec. Vice-Pres. for Finance and Admin.: FRANK A. BUTLER
Exec. Vice-Pres. for Health Affairs: MICHAEL KARPF
Vice-Pres. for Commercialization and Economic Devt: LEN HELLER
Vice-Pres. for Facilities Management: BOB WISEMAN
Vice-Pres. for Information Technology: EUGENE R. WILLIAMS
Vice-Pres. for Institutional Advancement: TERRY B. MOBLEY
Vice-Pres. for Institutional Research, Planning and Effectiveness: Dr CONNIE A. RAY
Vice-Pres. for Planning, Budget and Policy: ANGELA S. MARTIN
Vice-Pres. for Student Affairs: Dr PATRICIA S. TERRELL
Gen. Counsel: BARBARA W. JONES (acting)

Assoc. Provost for Academic Affairs: Dr DAVID WATT
Assoc. Provost for Int. Affairs: Dr DAVID BETTEZ (acting)
Assoc. Provost for Multicultural and Academic Affairs: Dr LAURETTA BYARS
Assoc. Provost for Undergraduate Education: Dr PHILIP J. KRAEMER
Dean of the Graduate School: Dr JEANNINE BLACKWELL (acting)
Dir of Admissions and Univ. Registrar: DONALD E. WITT
Dir of UK Art Museum: KATHY WALSH-PIPER
Dean of Libraries: CAROL PITTS DIEDRICHS

Library: see Libraries and Archives
Number of teachers: 1,209 full-time
Number of students: 25,397

Publications: *Alzheimer's Disease Review* (4 a year), *Colloquia Germanica* (4 a year), *Disclosure (Lexington)* (1 a year), *Esprit Createur* (4 a year), *Growth and Change* (urban and regional policy, 4 a year), *Kentucky Law Journal* (4 a year), *Kentucky Review* (2 a year), *Retiarius: commentarii periodici Latini* (1 a year)

DEANS

College of Agriculture: Dr M. SCOTT SMITH
College of Arts and Sciences: Dr STEVEN L. HOCH
College of Business and Economics: Dr DEVANTHAN SUDHARSHAN
College of Communications and Information Studies: Dr J. DAVID JOHNSON
College of Dentistry: Dr SHARON P. TURNER
College of Design: DAVID MOHNEY
College of Education: Dr JAMES G. CIBULKA (acting)
College of Engineering: Dr THOMAS W. LESTER
College of Fine Arts: Dr ROBERT SHAY
College of Health Sciences: Dr THOMAS C. ROBINSON
College of Law: ALLAN WALKER VESTAL
College of Medicine: Dr JAY A. PERMAN
College of Nursing: Dr CAROLYN A. WILLIAMS
College of Pharmacy: Dr KENNETH B. ROBERTS
College of Social Work: Dr KAY S. HOFFMAN

UNIVERSITY OF LOUISVILLE

Louisville, KY 40292
Telephone: (502) 852-5555
E-mail: admitme@louisville.edu
Internet: www.louisville.edu

Founded 1798

Pres.: Dr JAMES RAMSEY
Univ. Provost: Dr SHIRLEY C. WILLIHNGANZ (acting)
Vice-Pres. for Advancement: KEITH INMAN
Vice-Pres. for External Affairs: Dr DAN HALL
Vice-Pres. for Finance: MICHAEL J. CURTIN
Vice-Pres. for Health Affairs: LARRY N. COOK
Vice-Pres. for Information Technology: RONALD MOORE
Vice-Pres. for Research: MANUEL MARTINEZ
Vice-Pres. for Student Affairs: TOM JACKSON, Jr (acting)
Registrar: KATHLEEN OTTO
Dean of Univ. Libraries: Prof. HANNELORE RADER (acting)

Library: 2m. vols
Number of teachers: 1,154
Number of students: 21,089

Publications: *The Cardinal*, *Inside U of L*

DEANS

College of Arts and Sciences: JAMES F. BRENNAN
College of Business and Public Admin.: ROBERT L. TAYLOR
College of Education and Human Devt: Dr JOHN F. WELSH (acting)
Graduate School: RONALD M. ATLAS
Kent School of Social Work: TERRY SINGER (acting)
Louis D. Brandeis School of Law: Prof. LAURA F. ROTHSTEIN
School of Dentistry: Dr JOHN N. WILLIAMS
School of Medicine: Dr JOEL A. KAPLAN
School of Music: Dr CHRISTOPHER DOANE
School of Nursing: Dr MARY MUNDT (acting)
School of Public Health and Information Sciences: Dr RICHARD D. CLOVER (acting)
Speed Scientific School (Engineering): Dr THOMAS HANLEY

UNIVERSITY OF THE CUMBERLANDS

6191 College Station Dr., Williamsburg, KY 40769
Telephone: (606) 549-2200
E-mail: admiss@ucumberlands.edu
Internet: www.ucumberlands.edu

Founded 1889

Pres.: JIM TAYLOR
Vice-Pres. for Academic Affairs: Dr LARRY COCKRUM
Vice-Pres. for Business Affairs and Treas.: BARRY POYNTER
Vice-Pres. for Institutional Advancement: SUE WAKE
Vice-Pres. for Student Services: MICHAEL COLGROVE
Registrar: EMILY MEADORS
Dir of the Library: JANICE WREN

Library of 155,000 vols
Number of teachers: 112
Number of students: 1,743

WESTERN KENTUCKY UNIVERSITY

1906 College Heights Blvd, Bowling Green, KY 42101
Telephone: (270) 745-0111
E-mail: western@wku.edu
Internet: www.wku.edu

Founded 1906

Pres.: Dr GARY A. RANSDELL
Provost and Vice-Pres. for Academic Affairs: Dr BARBARA G. BURCH
Vice-Pres. for Finance and Admin.: Dr JAMES RAMSEY
Vice-Pres. for Information Technology: Dr RICHARD H. KIRCHMEYER
Vice-Pres. for Institutional Advancement: THOMAS S. HILES
Vice-Pres. for Student Affairs and Campus Services: Dr GERALD E. TICE
Registrar: FREIDA EGGLETON
Dean of Libraries: Dr MICHAEL BINDER

Library of 1,060,000 vols
Number of teachers: 599
Number of students: 16,579

DEANS

Bowling Green Community College: Dr FRANK D. CONLEY
College of Arts, Humanities and Social Sciences: Dr DAVID LEE
College of Education and Behavioural Sciences: Dr KAREN I. ADAMS
College of Science, Technology and Health: Dr MARTIN HOUSTON
Gordon Ford College of Business: Dr ROBERT W. JEFFERSON
Graduate Studies, Research and Extended Programs: Dr ELMER GRAY

LOUISIANA

CENTENARY COLLEGE OF LOUISIANA

POB 41188, Shreveport, LA 71134-1188
Telephone: (318) 869-5011
Internet: www.centenary.edu

Founded 1825

Academic year: June to May

Pres.: B. DAVID ROWE
Dean of Student Life: LORI BRADSHAW
Registrar: GARY YOUNG
Dir of Library Services: CHRISTY WRENN

Number of teachers: 74
Number of students: 1,017

DILLARD UNIVERSITY

1555 Poydras St, 12th Floor New Orleans, LA 70112
Telephone: (504) 571-2160
E-mail: admissions@dillard.edu
Internet: www.dillard.edu

Founded 1869

Pres.: Dr MARVALENE HUGHES
Dean of Academic Affairs: Dr KASSIE FREEMAN
Vice-Pres. for Business and Finance: SIDNEY H. EVANS, Jr
Vice-Pres. for Enrollment Management: DARRIN RANKIN
Vice-Pres. for Institutional Advancement and Devt: LOVE COLLINS, III
Vice-Pres. for Student Affairs: JANICE L. BARTLEY
Registrar: CHARLES SAUNDERS
Dean of Library: TOMMY S. HOLTON

Library of 105,128 vols, 295 current periodicals, 1,150 microfilms, 320 audiovisual items
Number of teachers: 139 full-time
Number of students: 1,953.

ATTACHED CENTRE

National Center for Black–Jewish Relations.

LOUISIANA COLLEGE

1140 College Dr., Pineville, LA 71359
Telephone: (318) 487-7011
E-mail: admissions@lacollege.edu
Internet: www.lacollege.edu

Founded 1906

College of liberal arts and sciences under auspices of the Louisiana Baptist Convention

Pres.: Dr JOE AQUILLARD
Vice-Pres. for Academic Affairs: Dr GLENN SUMRALL
Vice-Pres. for Business Affairs and Chief Financial Officer: RANDALL HARGIS
Vice-Pres. for Student Devt: Dr PEGGY PACK
Registrar: ALAN MOBLEY
Dean of Students: LORI THAMES
Dir of Library: W. TERRY MARTIN

Library of 135,000 vols, 199,000 govt documents, music scores, audiovisual items
Number of teachers: 109
Number of students: 1,204

LOUISIANA STATE UNIVERSITY SYSTEM

3810 West Lakeshore Dr., Baton Rouge, LA 70808
Telephone: (225) 388-2111
Internet: www.lsusystem.lsu.edu

Founded 1860

Academic year: August to July

Pres.: Dr WILLIAM L. JENKINS.

CONSTITUENT UNIVERSITIES

Louisiana State University

Baton Rouge, LA 70803
Telephone: (504) 388-3202
Fax: (504) 388-5982
E-mail: admissions@lsu.edu

Internet: www.lsu.edu
Founded 1860
Chancellor: Dr SEAN O'KEEFE
Exec. Vice-Chancellor and Provost: Dr HAROLD SILVERMAN
Vice-Provost for Academics and Planning: FRANK K. CARTLEDGE
Vice-Provost for Equity, Diversity and Community Outreach: KATRICE ALBERT
Vice-Chancellor for Finance and Admin. Services: Dr JERRY BAUDIN
Vice-Chancellor for Research and Economic Devt (vacant)
Vice-Chancellor for Strategic Initiatives: Dr ISIAH M. WARNER
Vice-Chancellor for Student Life and Academic Services: Dr F. NEIL MATHEWS
Chancellor of Law Center: JOHN J. COSTONIS
Chancellor of LSU Agriculture Center: Dr PAUL COREIL
Dean of Students: Dr KEVIN S. PRICE
Dean of Univ. Libraries: JAMES G. NEAL
Registrar: ROBERT K. DOOLOS
Library: 2.9m. vols
Number of teachers: 1,300 (full-time)
Number of students: 30,000

DEANS

College of Agriculture: Dr KENNETH KOONCE
College of Art and Design: KENNETH E. CARPENTER
College of Arts and Sciences: Dr M. JANE COLLINS
College of Basic Sciences: Dr HAROLD SILVERMAN
College of Education: Dr BARBARA FUHRMANN
College of Engineering: Dr PIUS J. EGBELU
College of Music and Dramatic Arts: Dr RONALD ROSS
Division of Continuing Education: Dr DANIEL C. WALSH
E. J. Ourso College of Business Admin.: THOMAS D. CLARK, Jr
Graduate School: Dr KEVIN M. SMITH
Honors College: Dr BILLY M. SEAY
Manship School of Mass Communication: Dr JOHN M. HAMILTON
School of Library and Information Science: Dr BETH M. PASKOFF
School of Social Work: Dr STEVEN R. ROSE (Interim Dir)
School of the Coast and Environment: Dr RUSSELL L. CHAPMAN
School of Veterinary Medicine: Dr MICHAEL GROVES
Univ. College: Dr CAROLYN C. COLLINS

Louisiana State University. at Alexandria

8100 Highway 71, S, Alexandria, LA 71302-9633
Telephone: (318) 473-6444
E-mail: info@lsua.edu
Internet: www.lsua.edu
Founded 1960
Chancellor: Dr ROBERT CAVANAUGH
Provost and Vice-Chancellor for Academic and Student Affairs: Dr THOMAS ARMSTRONG
Vice-Chancellor for Business Affairs: VIRGIL STANFORD
Dir of the Library: ALBERT TATE
Library of 120,000 vols
Number of students: 2,404

HEADS OF DIVISIONS

Div. of Business Admin.: Dr JAMES K. BREYLEY
Div. of Liberal Arts: Dr GREG GORMANOUS
Div. of Nursing and Health Sciences: Dr SANDRA TUCKER
Div. of Sciences: Dr FRED BECKERDITE

Louisiana State University Eunice

POB 1129, Eunice, LA 70535
Telephone: (337) 457-7311
Fax: (337) 546-6620
Internet: www.lsue.edu
Founded 1964
Academic year: August to July
Chancellor: Dr WILLIAM J. NUNEZ, III
Vice-Chancellor for Academic Affairs: Dr STEPHEN GUEMPEL
Vice-Chancellor for Business Affairs: ARLENE C. TUCKER
Vice-Chancellor for Student Affairs: JUDY DANIELS
Dir of Continuing Education: DAVID PULLING
Dir of the Library: GERALD PATOUT
Library of 100,000 vols
Number of teachers: 85
Number of students: 3,431

HEADS OF DIVISIONS

Business, Technology, and Health Studies: DOROTHY MCDONALD
Liberal Arts: Dr LUCIANE BERG
Sciences: Dr RENEE ROBICHAUX

Louisiana State University at Shreveport

One University Pl., Shreveport, LA 71115
Telephone: (318) 797-5000
Internet: www.lsus.edu
Founded 1965
Chancellor: Dr VINCENT J. MARSALA
Provost and Vice-Chancellor for Academic Affairs: Dr STUART MILLS (acting)
Vice-Chancellor for Business Affairs: MICHAEL T. FERRELL
Vice-Chancellor for Student Affairs: Dr GLORIA RAINES
Vice-Chancellor for Univ. Devt: GLENDA ERWIN
Registrar and Dir of Admissions: MICKY P. DIEZ (acting)
Dean of the Library: Dr ALAN D. GABEHART
Library of 250,000 vols, 2,000 periodicals
Number of students: 4,100
Publications: *Bulletin of the Museum of Life Sciences* (2 a year), *North Louisiana Historical Journal* (4 a year)

DEANS

College of Business Admin.: Dr CHARLOTTE A. JONES
College of Education: (vacant)
College of Liberal Arts: Dr MERRELL KNIGHTEN
College of Sciences: Dr WILLIAM A. VEKOVIUS
Continuing Education and Public Service: Dr DONNA AUSTIN
Graduate Studies: Dr PATRICIA F. DOERR

University of New Orleans

2000 Lakeshore Dr., New Orleans, LA 70148
Telephone: (504) 280-6000
Fax: (504) 280-6872
E-mail: pr@uno.edu
Internet: www.uno.edu
Metropolitan campus of the Louisiana State Univ. System; founded 1956 by Act 60 of Louisiana State Legislature
Chancellor: Dr TIMOTHY P. RYAN
Vice-Chancellor for Academic and Student Affairs and Provost: FREDERICK BARTON
Vice-Chancellor for Campus Services: JOEL CHAITLIN
Vice-Chancellor for Financial Services, Comptroller and Chief Financial Officer: LINDA K. ROBISON
Vice-Chancellor for Governmental Affairs and Athletic Dir: ROBERT W. BROWN
Vice-Chancellor for Research and Sponsored Programs: Dr ROBERT C. CASHNER
Vice-Chancellor for Univ. Advancement: SHARON WHITE GRUBER
Univ. Registrar: KATHLEEN PLANTE
Dean of Admissions: RONALD MAGIORE
Dean of Library Services: Dr SHARON MADER
Library of 800,000 vols, 3,000 current periodicals, 2m. microforms, govt documents
Number of teachers: 455
Number of students: 16,262
Publications: *Metropolitan Report* (4 a year), *New Orleans Real Estate Market Survey* (2 a year), *Review of Business and Economics Research* (2 a year), *Statistical Abstract of Louisiana* (3 a year)

DEANS

College of Business Admin.: Dr JOHN C. GARDNER
College of Education and Human Devt: Dr JAMES MEZA, Jr
College of Engineering: JOHN N. CRISP
College of Liberal Arts: Prof. FREDERICK BARTON
College of Sciences: Dr JOE M. KING
College of Urban and Public Affairs: Prof. ALAN F. J. ARTIBISE
Graduate School: Dr ROBERT C. CASHNER
Metropolitan College: ROBERT L. DUPONT.

OTHER CONSTITUENT INSTITUTIONS

Louisiana State University Agricultural Center

101 Efferson Hall, Baton Rouge, LA 70803
Telephone: (225) 578-4161
Fax: (225) 578-4143
Internet: www.lsuagcenter.com
Chancellor: WILLIAM B. RICHARDSON.

Louisiana State University Health Sciences Center, New Orleans

New Orleans, LA 70112-2784
Telephone: (504) 568-4800
Internet: www.lsuhsc.edu
Chancellor: Dr LARRY H. HOLLIER
Number of students: 2,500

DEANS

School of Allied Health: Dr JOHN R. SNYDER
School of Dentistry: Dr ERIC J. HOVLAND
School of Graduate Studies: Prof. JOSEPH M. MOERSCHBAECHER, III
School of Medicine: Prof. JAMES P. O'LEARY (acting)
School of Nursing: Dr ELIZABETH A. HUMPHREY

Louisiana State University Health Sciences Center, Shreveport

1501 Kings Highway, Shreveport, LA 71103-4228
Telephone: (318) 675-5000
Internet: www.sh.lsuhsc.edu
Chancellor: Dr JOHN C. MCDONALD.

Paul M. Hebert Law Center

202 Law Center, Baton Rouge, LA 70803-1000
Telephone: (225) 578-8646
Fax: (225) 578-8647
E-mail: admissions@law.lsu.edu
Internet: www.law.lsu.edu
Chancellor: JOHN COSTONIS.

Pennington Biomedical Research Center

6400 Perkins Rd, Baton Rouge, LA 70808
Telephone: (225) 763-2500
Internet: www.pbrc.edu
Exec. Dir: Dr CLAUDE BOUCHARD.

LOYOLA UNIVERSITY

6363 St Charles Ave, New Orleans, LA 70118
Telephone: (504) 865-2011
E-mail: publaff@loyno.edu
Internet: www.loyno.edu

Founded 1905 as Loyola College; chartered as Univ. 1912

Pres.: Rev. KEVIN WM. WILDES
Provost and Vice-Pres. for Academic Affairs: Dr WALTER HARRIS, Jr
Vice-Pres. for Finance and Admin.: RHONDA DELRIE CARTWRIGHT
Vice-Pres. for Institutional Advancement: VICTORIA A. FRANK
Vice-Pres. for Student Affairs: Dr M. L. (CISSY) PETTY
Dean of Admissions and Enrollment Management: DEBORAH STIEFFEL
Dean of Libraries: MARY LEE SWEAT
Dean of Univ. Ministry: KURT BINDEWALD

Library of 255,000 vols; law library of 123,000 vols
Number of teachers: 275
Number of students: 5,500
Publications: *Loyola Law Review*, *Loyola Magazine*, *New Orleans Review*

DEANS

City College: Dr MARCEL DUMESTRE
College of Arts and Sciences: Dr FRANK E. SCULLY Jr
College of Business Admin.: Dr J. PATRICK O'BRIEN
College of Music: Dr EDWARD J. KVET
School of Law: Dr JAMES M. KLEBBA (acting)

NEW ORLEANS BAPTIST THEOLOGICAL SEMINARY

3939 Gentilly Blvd, New Orleans, LA 70126
Telephone: (504) 282-4455
Fax: (504) 816-8023
Internet: www.nobts.edu
Private control

Pres.: Dr CHARLES S. KELLEY, Jr
Vice-Pres. for Business Affairs: L. CLAY CORVIN
Provost: Dr STEVE W. LEMKE
Dean of Libraries: Dr JEFF GRIFFIN

Library of 266,000 vols
Number of teachers: 102
Number of students: 1,926 (full-time)

NOTRE DAME SEMINARY

2901 South Carrolton Ave, New Orleans, LA 70118-4391
Telephone: (504) 866-7426
Fax: (504) 866-3119
E-mail: registrar@nds.edu
Internet: www.nds.edu

Founded 1923
Private control

Chancellor: THE ARCHBISHOP OF NEW ORLEANS
Pres. and Rector: Very Rev. PATRICK J. WILLIAMS
Academic Dean: Rev. JOSE I. LAVASTIDA
Registrar: MARGARET BREAUX
Library Dir: GEORGE DANSKER

Library of 94,000 vols
Number of teachers: 30
Number of students: 154 (full-time)

OUR LADY OF HOLY CROSS COLLEGE

4123 Woodland Dr., New Orleans, LA 70131-7399
Telephone: (504) 394-7744
Fax: (504) 391-2421
E-mail: admissions@olhcc.edu
Internet: www.olhcc.edu

Founded 1916
Academic year: August to July

Pres.: Rev. ANTHONY J. DE CONCILIIS
Vice-Pres. of Academic Affairs: Dr EDWARD J. DUPAY
Registrar: Sister ANN MARTINEZ
Librarian: Sister HELEN FONTENOT

Library of 201,807 vols
Number of teachers: 116 (45 full-time, 71 part-time)
Number of students: 1,450

SAINT JOSEPH SEMINARY COLLEGE

St Benedict, LA 70457
Telephone: (985) 867-2238
Fax: (985) 327-1085
E-mail: acdean@sjasc.edu
Internet: www.sjasc.edu
Private control

Pres.-Rector: Rev. GREGORY BOQUET
Dean of Academic Affairs: Dr JUDE LUPINETTI
Library Dir: BONNIE BESS WOOD

Number of teachers: 26
Number of students: 194

SOUTHERN UNIVERSITY SYSTEM

J. S. Clark Admin. Bldg, Baton Rouge, LA 70813
Telephone: (225) 771-4500
Internet: www.sus.edu

Founded 1880

Pres.: Dr RALPH SLAUGHTER
Vice-Pres. for Academic and Student Affairs: PRESS L. ROBINSON
Vice-Pres. for Finance and Business Affairs: TOLOR E. WHITE.

CONSTITUENT INSTITUTIONS

Southern Univ. and A & M College

Baton Rouge, LA 70813
Telephone: (225) 771-4500
Internet: www.subr.edu

Chancellor: EDWARD R. JACKSON
Vice-Chancellor for Academic Affairs: Dr JOHNNY TOLLIVER
Vice-Chancellor for Finance and Admin.: FLANDUS MCCLINTON, Jr
Vice-Chancellor for Student Affairs: LYNN DICKERSON
Number of students: 9,172

Southern University at New Orleans

6801 Press Dr., New Orleans, LA 70126
Telephone: (225) 286-5314
Internet: www.suno.edu

Chancellor: Dr VICTOR UKPOLO
Number of students: 4,000

Southern University at Shreveport

3050 Martin Luther King, Jr Dr., Shreveport, LA 71107
Telephone: (318) 674-3300
E-mail: admissions@susla.edu
Internet: www.susla.edu

Chancellor: Dr RAY L. BELTON
Vice-Chancellor for Academic Affairs: Dr RUBY EVANS
Vice-Chancellor for Community and Workforce Devt: JANICE R. STEED
Vice-Chancellor for Fiscal Affairs: BENJAMIN W. PUGH
Vice-Chancellor for Student Affairs: Dr SHARON F. GREEN
Librarian: Dr ORELLA BRAZILE
Number of students: 1,229

CHAIRS OF DIV.

Academic Outreach Programs: GWENDOLYN LEWIS
Allied Health Sciences: HAYWOOD JOINER
Behavioural Sciences: ROSALYN HOLT
Business Studies: GEORGE LEWIS, III
Humanities: JUNE PHILLIPS
Science and Technology: Dr BARRY HESTER

TULANE UNIVERSITY OF LOUISIANA

6823 St Charles Ave, New Orleans, LA 70118
Telephone: (504) 865-5000
E-mail: pr@tulane.edu
Internet: www2.tulane.edu

Founded 1834 as Medical College of Louisiana; became Tulane Univ. of Louisiana 1884

Pres.: SCOTT S. COWEN
Sr Vice-Pres. for Academic Affairs, Provost and Chief Information Officer: PAUL BARRON
Sr Vice-Pres. for External Affairs: YVETTE M. JONES
Sr Vice-Pres. for Operations and Chief Financial Officer: ANTHONY P. LORINO
Sr Vice-Pres. for the Health Sciences: ALAN MILLER
Vice-Pres. and Chief of Staff: ANNE P. BAÑOS
Vice-Pres. for Clinical Affairs, Tulane Univ. Health Sciences Center: ALAN M. MILLER
Vice-Pres. for Enrollment Management and Institutional Research and Registrar: EARL RETIF
Vice-Pres. for Human Resources: ANDREW HICK
Vice-Pres. for Student Affairs and Dean of Students: CYNTHIA CHERREY
Vice-Pres. for Tulane Univ. Health Sciences Center: JAMES J. CORRIGAN
Gen. Counsel: VICTORIA JOHNSON
Dean of Libraries and Academic Information Resources: LANCE QUERY
Library: see Libraries
Number of teachers: 1,988
Number of students: 12,381

DEANS

A. B. Freeman School of Business: JAMES W. MCFARLAND
Faculty of the Liberal Arts and Sciences: TERESA S. SOUFAS (acting)
Graduate School: MICHAEL HERMAN
Law School: LAWRENCE PONOROFF
Newcomb College: CYNTHIA J. LOWENTHAL
School of Architecture: DONALD GATZKE
School of Engineering: NICHOLAS J. ALTIERO
School of Medicine: IAN LOGAN TAYLOR
School of Public Health and Tropical Medicine: PIERRE BUEKENS (acting)
School of Social Work: RON MARKS
Tulane College: T. R. KIDDER
Univ. College: RICHARD A. MARKSBURY

UNIVERSITY OF LOUISIANA SYSTEM

Suite 7-300, 1201 N Third St, Baton Rouge, LA 70802
Telephone: (225) 342-6950
E-mail: sclausen@uls.state.la.us
Internet: www.uls.state.la.us

Founded 1974
Number of students: 83,000 at 8 univs
Pres.: Dr SALLY CLAUSEN.

CONSTITUENT INSTITUTIONS

Grambling State University

403 Main St, Grambling, LA 71245
Telephone: (318) 247-3811
Fax: (318) 274-6172
E-mail: admissions@gram.edu
Internet: www.gram.edu

Founded 1901
Academic year: August to May
Pres. (vacant)

Provost and Vice-Pres. for Academic Affairs: Dr ROBERT M. DIXON
Vice-Pres. of Finance: BILLY OWENS
Registrar and Exec. Dir: KAREN C. LEWIS
Dir of Library Services: Dr ROSEMARY N. MOKIA (acting)

Library of 294,000 vols
Number of teachers: 250
Number of students: 4,716

Louisiana Tech University

Ruston, LA 71272
Telephone: (318) 257-0211
Internet: www.latech.edu

Founded chartered as Louisiana Industrial Institute and College 1894; name changed to Louisiana Industrial Institute 1898; became Louisiana Polytechnic Institute 1921; present name and status 1970

Pres.: DANIEL D. RENEAU
Vice-Pres. for Academic Affairs: KENNETH REA
Vice-Pres. for Admin. Services: JERRY DREWETT
Vice-Pres. for Finance and Admin.: JOSEPH R. THOMAS, Jr
Vice-Pres. for Student Affairs: Dr JAMES M. KING
Vice-Pres. for Univ. Advancement: CORRE STEGALL
Registrar: BOB VENTO
Dean of Library Services: WALTER WICKER

Library of 400,000 vols, 500,000 microforms, 2,250,000 govt documents
Number of teachers: 400
Number of students: 10,000

DEANS

College of Admin. and Business: Dr SHIRLEY P. REAGAN
College of Applied and Natural Sciences: Dr JAMES D. LIBERATOS
College of Education: Dr JO ANN DAUZAT
College of Engineering and Science: Dr LESLIE GUICE, Jr
College of Liberal Arts: Dr EDWARD C. JACOBS
Graduate School and Univ. Research: TERRY MCCONATHY

McNeese State University

4205 Ryan St, Lake Charles, LA 70609
Telephone: (337) 475-5000
Fax: (337) 475-5012
Internet: www.mcneese.edu

Founded 1939
Academic year: August to May

Pres.: Dr ROBERT D. HEBERT
Registrar: STEPHANIE B. TARVER
Librarian: NANCY L. KHOURY

Number of teachers: 285
Number of students: 8,000
Publications: *The Log* (1 a year), *The McNeese Arena* (1 a year), *The McNeese Review* (1 a year), *The McNeese Update* (3 a year)

DEANS

College of Business: Dr BRENDA BIRKETT
College of Education: Dr WAYNE FETTER
College of Engineering and Technology: Dr CARROLL KARKALITS
College of Liberal Arts: Dr RAY MILES
College of Nursing: Dr PEGGY L. WOLFE
College of Science: Dr GEORGE F. MEAD, Jr
Graduate School: Dr GEORGE MEAD

Nicholls State University

Thibodaux, LA 70310
Telephone: (985) 446-8111
Internet: www.nicholls.edu

Founded 1948 as a junior college of Louisiana State Univ., became Francis T. Nicholls State College 1956, univ. status 1970

Pres.: Dr STEPHEN T. HULBERT
Exec. Vice-Pres.: LARRY HOWELL
Vice-Pres. for Academic Affairs: Dr ALLAYNE BARRILLEAUX
Assoc. Vice-Pres. for Finance and Chief Financial Officer: MIKE NAQUIN,
Vice-Pres. for Institutional Advancement: Dr DAVID E. BOUDREAUX
Vice-Pres. for Student Affairs and Enrollment Services: Dr EUGENE A. DIAL, Jr
Library Dir: CAROL A. MATHIAS

Library of 400,000 vols and periodicals and 380,000 microforms
Number of teachers: 278 (full-time)
Number of students: 7,093

DEANS

College of Arts and Sciences: Dr BADIOLLAH ASRABADI
College of Business Admin.: Dr SHAWN MAULDIN
College of Education: Dr J. STEVEN WELSH
College of Nursing and Allied Health: Dr SUE WESTBROOK
Graduate Studies: Dr BETTY KLEEN
University College: Dr ALBERT DAVIS

Northwestern State University

Natchitoches, LA 71497
Telephone: (318) 357-6441
Fax: (318) 357-4223
Internet: www.nsula.edu

Founded 1884 as state normal school, univ. status 1970
Academic year: June to June

Pres.: Dr RANDALL J. WEBB
Provost and Vice-Pres. for Academic Affairs: Dr TOM HANSON
Vice-Pres. for Business Affairs and Controller: CARL JONES
Vice-Pres. for External Affairs: JERRY D. PIERCE
Vice-Pres. for Student Affairs: Dr PATRICE MOULTON (acting)
Vice-Pres. for Univ. Affairs: JOHN DILWORTH
Registrar: LILLIE BELL
Librarian: THOMAS FLEMING

Library of 320,000 vols
Number of teachers: 300
Number of students: 8,600
Publication: *Southern Studies* (4 a year)

DEANS

College of Business: Dr STEPHEN ELLIOTT (acting)
College of Education: Dr VICKIE GENTRY (acting)
College of Liberal Arts: Dr DONALD HATLEY
College of Nursing: Dr NORMAN PLANCHOCK
College of Science and Technology: Dr AUSTIN TEMPLE
Graduate Studies and Research: Dr STEVEN HORTON
Univ. College: Dr SUE WEAVER

Southeastern Louisiana University

SLU 10752, Hammond, LA 70402
Telephone: (985) 549-2000
Fax: (985) 549-5882
E-mail: admissions@selu.edu
Internet: www.selu.edu

Founded 1925 as college, present status 1970
Academic year: June to May

Pres.: Dr JOHN CRAIN
Provost and Vice-Pres. for Academic Affairs: Dr TAMMY BOURG
Vice-Pres. for Admin. and Finance: STEPHEN SMITH
Vice-Pres. for Student Affairs: Dr MARVIN L. YATES
Vice-Pres. for Univ. Advancement: WENDY J. LAUDERDALE
Library Dir: ERIC JOHNSON

Library of 362,419 vols, 3,526 serial subscriptions, 817,379 microforms, 50,487 audiovisual materials, 65,560 E-books, 240,920 govt documents
Number of teachers: 613 (513 full-time, 100 part-time)
Number of students: 15,351
Publications: *Economic Reporter* (4 a year), *Louisiana Literature* (2 a year), *Nineteenth Century Studies* (1 a year), *The Pick* (2 a year)

DEANS

College of Arts, Humanities and Social Sciences: Dr KAREN FONTENOT
College of Business: Dr RANDY SETTOON
College of Education and Human Devt: Dr BILL NEAL
College of Nursing and Health Studies: Dr ANN CARRUTH
College of Science and Technology: Dr DANIEL MCCARTHY
Enrollment Management: Dr JEFF RHODES
Office of Research and Graduate Studies: Dr JERALD AINSWORTH

PROFESSORS

ALESSI, H., Counseling and Human Development
BEAUBOUEF, T., Computer Science and Industrial Technology
BEDELL, J., English
BELL, J., History and Political Science
BLACKWOOD, C., Visual Arts
BOND, E., Nursing
BOND, W., Biological Sciences
BONNETTE, J., Computer Science and Industrial Technology
BOSTIC, M., Computer Science and Industrial Technology
BUDDEN, M., Marketing and Supply Chain Management
CANNON, G., Mathematics
CAPPEL, S., Management
CARR, S., Teaching and Learning
CARRUTH, A., Nursing
CARRUTH, P., Accounting
CHILDERS, G., Biological Sciences
COPE, R., Marketing and Supply Chain Management
CROTHER, B., Biological Sciences
DEALWIS, T., Mathematics
DOUGHTY, M., Chemistry and Physics
DRANGUET, C., History and Political Science
DUGGAL, R., Business Administration and Finance
ELLIOTT, C., Teaching and Learning
FAUST, J., English
FELLOM, M., Music and Dramatic Arts
FICK, T., English
FONT, W., Biological Sciences
FORREST, B., History and Political Science
FREDELL, J., English
FULWILER, J., Educational Leadership and Technology
GERMAN, H., English
GOLD, E., English
GONZALEZ-PEREZ, M., History and Political Science
GUTTHY, A., Foreign Languages and Literature
HIGGINBOTHAM, T., Computer Science and Industrial Technology
HOLMES, L., Chemistry and Physics
HSING, Y., Business Administration and Finance
HYDE, B., Nursing
JAMAL, A., Marketing and Supply Chain Management
JONES, M., Marketing and Supply Chain Management
KABZA, L., Mathematics

KEARNEY, M., English
KEDDY, P., Biological Sciences
KEOWN, G., Visual Arts
KING, P., Management
KOLB, K., Foreign Languages and Literature
KRAEMER, R., Kinesiology and Health Studies
LANE, K., Educational Leadership and Technology
LEWIS, B., Sociology and Criminal Justice
LI, S., Mathematics
LONGMAN, D., General Studies
LOUTH, R., English
MCALLISTER, C., English
MCALLISTER, H., Psychology
MCKAY, S., Marketing and Finance
MARSHALL, M., Foreign Languages and Literature
MEEKER, B., Nursing
MERINO, D., Mathematics
MIRANDO, J., Communication
MUNCHAUSEN, L., Chemistry and Physics
NAQUIN, M., Kinesiology and Health Studies
NELSON, E., Biological Sciences
NEUERBURG, K., Mathematics
NORTON, W., Biological Sciences
OESCHER, J., Education Leadership and Technology
PARENT, F., Sociology and Criminal Justice
PARTRIDGE, M., Teaching and Learning
PEDERSEN, K., Mathematics
PHILLIPS, C., Management
PRYOR, S., Nursing
RAMSEY, R., Management
REYES, E., Mathematics
RIEDEL, M., Sociology and Criminal Justice
ROLLING, P., Counselling and Human Development
SCHEPKER, S., Music and Dramatic Arts
SCHULDT, B., Marketing and Supply Chain Management
SHAFFER, G., Biological Sciences
STIEGLER, L., Communication Sciences and Disorders
SUBER, S., Music and Dramatic Arts
SYNOVITZ, L., Kinesiology and Health Studies
TITARD, P., Accounting
TRAVER, A., Accounting
VOLDMAN, Y., Music and Dramatic Arts
WADLINGTON, E., Teaching and Learning
WAIKAR, A., Marketing and Supply Chain Management
WALTER, J., English
WHITE, M., Biological Sciences
WYLD, D., Management
YEARGAIN, J., Management

University of Louisiana at Lafayette

104 University Circle, Lafayette, LA 70504-1732
Telephone: (337) 482-1000
Fax: (337) 482-6195
Internet: www.louisiana.edu

Founded 1898 as Southwestern Louisiana Industrial Institute, became Southwestern Louisiana Institute 1921 and Univ. of Southwestern Louisiana 1960, present name 1999
Academic year: June to May

Pres.: Dr RAY
Registrar: DEWAYNE BOWIE
Librarian: Dr CHARLES TRICHE

Library of 976,202 vols
Number of teachers: 699
Number of students: 16,561

Publications: *Attakapas Gazette* (4 a year), *Louisiana History* (4 a year), *Southwestern Review* (1 a year).

University of Louisiana at Monroe

700 University Ave, Monroe, LA 71209
Telephone: (318) 342-1000
Fax: (318) 342-5161
Internet: www.ulm.edu

Founded 1931 as college, attained univ. status 1970

Pres.: Dr JAMES E. COFER, Sr
Provost and Vice-Pres. for Academic Affairs: Dr STEPHEN RICHTERS
Vice-Pres. for Business Affairs: DAVE NICKLAS
Vice-Pres. for Student Affairs: Dr WAYNE BRUMFIELD
Vice-Pres. for Univ. Advancement: Dr DON SKELTON
Registrar: CARLETTE M. BROWDER
Dean of the Library: DONALD R. SMITH

Library of 633,818 vols, incl. 193,935 govt documents, 2,939 current periodicals, 555,603 microformat vols
Number of teachers: 521
Number of students: 9,400

DEANS

College of Arts and Sciences: Dr CARLOS FANDAL
College of Business Admin.: Dr RONALD BERRY
College of Education and Human Devt: Dr LUKE THOMAS
College of Health Sciences: Dr JAN CORDER
College of Pharmacy: Dr F. LAMAR PRITCHARD
Graduate Studies and Research: Dr VIRGINIA EATON (Dir)

XAVIER UNIVERSITY OF LOUISIANA

1 Drexel Dr., New Orleans, LA 70125
Telephone: (504) 486-7411
Internet: www.xula.edu

Founded 1915

Pres.: NORMAN C. FRANCIS
Sr Vice-Pres. for Admin.: CALVIN TREGRE
Sr Vice-Pres. for Sponsored Programs: Dr GENE D'AMOUR
Vice-Pres. for Academic Affairs: ELIZABETH A. BARRON
Vice-Pres. for Fiscal Affairs: EDWARD J. PHILLIPS
Vice-Pres. for Institutional Advancement: KENNETH ANTHONY ST CHARLES
Vice-Pres. for Student Services: JOSEPH K. BYRD
Dean of Admissions: WINSTON D. BROWN
Librarian: ROBERT E. SKINNER

Library of 120,000 vols
Number of teachers: 226 (full-time)
Number of students: 3,994

DEANS

College of Arts and Sciences: Dr KENNETH G. BOUTTE
College of Pharmacy: Dr WAYNE HARRIS
Graduate School: Dr ALVIN J. RICHARD

MAINE

BANGOR THEOLOGICAL SEMINARY

2 College Circle, POB 411, Bangor, ME 04402-0411
Telephone: (207) 942-6781
Fax: (207) 990-1267
E-mail: fgilbride@bts.edu
Internet: www.bts.edu

Founded 1814
Private control
Academic year: September to May

Pres.: Dr WILLIAM C. IMES
Vice-Pres. for Advancement: REBECCA WRIGHT
Academic Dean: GLENN MILLER
Registrar: DANIELLE R. LAVINE
Librarian: LORRAINE MCQUARRIE

Library of 124,000 vols
Number of teachers: 50
Number of students: 70 (full-time).

BRANCH CAMPUS

Portland Campus: 159 State St, Portland, ME 04101; tel. (207) 774-5212; fax (207) 874-2214; Dir REBECCA WRIGHT.

BATES COLLEGE

2 Andrews Rd, Lewiston, ME 04240
Telephone: (207) 786-6255
Fax: (207) 786-6025
E-mail: www@bates.edu
Internet: www.bates.edu

Founded 1855
Academic year: September to May

Pres.: ELAINE TUTTLE HANSEN
Vice-Pres. for Academic Affairs and Dean of Faculty: Dr JILL REICH
Vice-Pres. for College Advancement: VICTORIA M. DEVLIN
Vice-Pres. for External Affairs: WILLIAM C. HISS
Vice-Pres. for Finance and Admin.: TERRY J. BECKMANN
Dean of Admissions: WYLIE L. MITCHELL
Dean of Students: TEDD R. GOUNDIE
Librarian: EUGENE WIEMERS

Library of 568,750 vols
Number of teachers: 203
Number of students: 1,738

Depts of anthropology, art and visual culture, biology, chemistry, economics, education, English, geology, German and Russian studies, history, mathematics, music, philosophy and religion, physical education, physics and astronomy, politics, psychology, Romance languages and literatures, sociology, theatre and rhetoric.

BOWDOIN COLLEGE

Brunswick, ME 04011
Telephone: (207) 725-3000
Fax: (207) 725-3123
Internet: www.bowdoin.edu

Founded 1794

Pres.: BARRY MILLS
Sr Vice-Pres. for Finance and Admin. and Treas.: S. CATHERINE LONGLEY
Sr Vice-Pres. for Investments: PAULA J. VOLENT
Sr Vice-Pres. for Planning and Devt and Chief Devt Officer: WILLIAM A. TORREY
Vice-Pres. for Communications and Public Affairs: SCOTT W. HOOD
Dean for Academic Affairs: CRISTLE C. JUDD
Dean of Student Affairs: TIM FOSTER
Registrar: CHRISTINE BROOKS COTE
Librarian: SHERRIE BERGMAN

Library of 940,000 vols
Number of teachers: 158
Number of students: 1,710

Academic programmes in Africana studies, anthropology, art history, art history and archaeology, art history and visual arts, Asian studies, biochemistry, biology, chemical physics, chemistry, classical studies, computer science, computer science and mathematics, dance, economics, education, English, English and theatre, environmental studies, Eurasian and Eastern European studies, film studies, French, gay and lesbian studies, gender and women's studies, geology, geology and chemistry, geology and physics, German, government and legal studies, history, Italian, Latin American studies, mathematics, mathematics and economics, music, neuroscience, philosophy, physics and astronomy, psychology, religion, Romance languages, Russian, sociology, Spanish, theatre, visual arts

Publications: *Bowdoin Magazine* (4 a year), *Bowdoin Forum* (int. affairs, 1 a year).

COLBY COLLEGE

4000 Mayflower Hill, Waterville, ME 04901-8840
Telephone: (207) 859-4000
Fax: (207) 859-4055
E-mail: admissions@colby.edu
Internet: www.colby.edu

Founded 1813
Private control
Academic year: September to May
Languages of instruction: French, Spanish, Italian

Accredited by the New England Asscn of Colleges and Univs; depts of admin. science, African studies, African-American studies, American studies, anthropology, art, biology, chemistry, classics, computer science, creative writing, East Asian studies, economics, education, English, environmental studies, French and Italian, geology, German, govt, history, int. studies, Jewish studies, Latin American studies, mathematics, music, philosophy, physical education, physics and astronomy, psychology, religious studies, Russian, science, technology and soc., sociology, Spanish, theatre and dance, women's, gender and sexuality studies

Pres.: WILLIAM D. ADAMS
Vice-Pres. for Academic Affairs and Dean of Faculty: LORI KLETZER
Vice-Pres. for Admin.: DOUGLAS C. TERP
Vice-Pres. for College Relations: (vacant)
Vice-Pres. of Student Affairs and Dean of Students: JAMES S. TERHUNE
Dean of Admissions and Financial Aid: PARKER J. BEVERAGE
Registrar: ELIZABETH N. SCHILLER
Librarian: CLEMENT P. GUTHRO

Library of 926,000 vols, 18,000 serial titles, 24,000 audiovisual items, 300,000 microforms, 186,000 electronic books
Number of teachers: 183 (full-time)
Number of students: 1,825

Publications: *Colby* (4 a year), *Colby Library Quarterly*, *Colby Perspective*.

ATTACHED RESEARCH INSTITUTES

Goldfarb Center for Public Affairs and Civic Engagement: internet www.colby.edu/goldfarb.

Oak Institute for the Study of International Human Rights: internet www.colby.edu/oak.

COLLEGE OF THE ATLANTIC

105 Eden St, Bar Harbor, ME 04609
Telephone: (207) 288-5015
Fax: (207) 288-4126
E-mail: inquiry@coa.edu
Internet: www.coa.edu

Founded 1969
Private control
Academic year: September to June

Pres.: DAVID HALES
Dean of Admission: SARAH BAKER
Dean of Devt: LYNN BOULGER
Admin. Dean: ANDREW GRIFFITHS
Registrar: DAVID BALDWIN
Library Dir: JANE HULTBERG

Library of 36,000 vols, 475 periodicals
Number of teachers: 25
Number of students: 300

Areas of study: arts and design, environmental sciences, human studies.

HUSSON COLLEGE

1 College Circle, Bangor, ME 04401
Telephone: (207) 941-7100
Fax: (207) 941-7935
E-mail: admit@husson.edu
Internet: www.husson.edu
Private control
Academic year: September to May
Pres.: Dr WILLIAM H. BEARDSLEY
Dean: JOHN RUBINO
Librarian: AMY AVERRE

Number of teachers: 70
Number of students: 2,000 (1,600 undergraduate, 400 graduate)

Areas of study: accounting, biology, business admin., computer information systems, criminal justice, education, English, nursing, occupational therapy, paralegal studies, physical therapy, psychology, science and humanities.

MAINE COLLEGE OF ART

97 Spring St, Portland, ME 04101
Telephone: (207) 775-3052
Fax: (207) 772-5069
E-mail: info@meca.edu
Internet: www.meca.edu
Private control

Pres.: JAMES BAKER
Exec. Vice-Pres.: BETH ELICKER
Vice-Pres. for Academic Affairs and Dean of the College: SHARON PORTELANCE
Vice-Pres. for Advancement and College Relations: TIM KANE
Vice-Pres. for Enrollment: RICK LONGO
Registrar: ANNE DENNISON
Library Dir: MOIRA STEVEN

Library of 30,000 vols, 100 periodicals, 52,000 slides
Number of teachers: 53
Number of students: 314.

ATTACHED RESEARCH INSTITUTE

Institute of Contemporary Art: Porteous Bldg, 522 Congress St, Portland, ME 04101; tel. (207) 879 5742; fax (207) 780 0816; e-mail ica@meca.edu; Dir LAUREN FENSTERSTOCK.

MAINE MARITIME ACADEMY

Castine, ME 04420-5000
Telephone: (207) 326-2206
E-mail: admissions@mma.edu
Internet: www.mainemaritime.edu

Founded 1941
State control

Depts of arts and sciences, engineering, physical education; Corning School of Ocean Studies; Loeb-Sullivan School of Int. Business and Logistics; Thompson School of Marine Transportation
Academic year: September to April

Pres.: Dr WILLIAM BRENNAN
Provost and Academic Dean: Dr JOHN BARLOW
Vice-Pres. for Finance, Admin. and Govt Affairs: RICHARD R. ERICSON
Registrar: TOM SAWYER
Dir of Library Services: BRENT HALL

Library of 99,614 vols, 326 periodicals, 5,093 maps
Number of teachers: 55
Number of students: 850

SAINT JOSEPH'S COLLEGE

278 Whites Bridge Rd, Standish, ME 04084-5263
Telephone: (207) 892-6766
Fax: (207) 893-7861
E-mail: info@sjcme.edu
Internet: www.sjcme.edu

Founded 1912

Pres.: Dr JOSEPH LEE
Vice-Pres. of Academic Affairs and Dean of College: Dr RANDALL KING
Dean of Admissions: VINCENT J. KLOSKOWSKI
Librarian: NATALIE HUTCHINSON

Library: over 50,000 vols
Number of teachers: 96 (53 full-time; 43 part-time)
Number of students: 5,128 (750 full-time; 446 part-time; 3,932 external)

Academic programmes in biology, business admin., chemistry, classics, communications, criminal justice, elementary education, English, environmental science, environmental studies, exercise science fitness, exercise science specialist, history, literature and American culture, marine science, mathematics, nursing, philosophy, physical education teaching, political science, psychology, sociology, sports management, theology.

THOMAS COLLEGE

180 West River Rd, Waterville, ME 04901-5097
Telephone: (207) 859-1111
Fax: (207) 859-1114
E-mail: its@thomas.edu
Internet: www.thomas.edu

Founded 1894
Private control
Academic year: September to May

Pres.: Dr GEORGE SPANN
Vice-Pres. for Academic Affairs: Dr THOMAS EDWARDS
Vice-Pres. for Financial Affairs and Treas.: BETH GIBBS
Vice-Pres. for Information Services: CHRISTOPHER RHODA
Dean of Enrollment Management: JAMES LOVE
Dean of Institutional Advancement: FRAN DAY
Dean of Student Affairs: LISA DESAUTELS-POLIQUIN
Registrar: VALERIE SIROIS
Library Dir: LISA AURIEMMA

Library of 30,000 vols
Number of students: 594

FACULTY CHAIRS

Arts and Sciences: JUDY HANSEN-CHILDERS
Business: JAMES LIBBY

UNITY COLLEGE

90 Quaker Hill Rd, Unity, ME 04988
Telephone: (207) 948-3131
Fax: (207) 948-6277
E-mail: admissions@unity.edu
Internet: www.unity.edu

Founded 1965
Private control
Academic year: September to May

Pres.: Dr DAVID C. GLENN-LEWIN
Vice-Pres. for Finance: ROGER R. JOLIN
Dir of College Advancement and Vice-Pres.: MARTHA NORDSTROM
Dean for Student Affairs: GARY ZANE
Registrar: HOLLY A. HEIN
Library Dir: ROBERT DOAN

Library of 40,000 vols
Number of teachers: 33
Number of students: 508

CHAIRMEN OF ACADEMIC DIVISIONS

Environmental Programs: Dr JERRY CINNAMON
Liberal Studies: PATRICIA CLARK (acting)

UNIVERSITY OF MAINE SYSTEM

16 Central St, Bangor, ME 04401
Telephone: (207) 973-3201
Fax: (207) 973-3296
E-mail: moreinfo@maine.edu

Internet: www.maine.edu
Founded 1968
Number of students: 34,700 total across 7 univs
Chancellor: Richard L. Pattenaude
Vice-Chancellor for Academic and Student Affairs: James Breece.

CONSTITUENT INSTITUTIONS

University of Maine

Orono, ME 04469
Telephone: (207) 581-1110
E-mail: umainetoday@umaine.edu
Internet: www.umaine.edu
Founded 1865
Pres.: Robert A. Kennedy
Sr Vice-Pres. for Academic Affairs and Provost: Edna Szymanski
Vice-Pres. for Admin. and Finance: Janet E. Waldron
Vice-Pres. for Devt: Barbara M. Beers
Vice-Pres. for Research: Dr Michael J. Eckardt
Dean of Students: Robert Dana
Number of teachers: 608
Number of students: 12,000
Publications: *Agricultural Experimental Station Publications, Bulletin, Co-operative Extension Bulletins, Maine Studies, Technology Experiment Station Publications*

DEANS

College of Business, Public Policy and Health: Dr Virginia Gibson (acting)
College of Education and Human Devt: Robert Cobb
College of Engineering: Prof. Dana Humphrey
College of Liberal Arts and Sciences: Dr Rebecca Eilers
College of Natural Sciences, Forestry and Agriculture: Edward Ashworth

University of Maine at Augusta

46 University Dr., Augusta, ME 04330-9410
Telephone: (207) 621-3000
Fax: (207) 621-3116
E-mail: umaar@maine.edu
Internet: www.uma.edu
Founded 1965
Pres.: Dr Richard Randall
Exec. Vice-Pres. and Provost: Joshua Nadel
Vice-Pres. for Admin.: Sheri Stevens
Vice-Pres. for Finance: Laurie Pruett
Dean of Extended Campus Learning: Dr Thomas E. Abbott
Dean of Students: Kathleen Dexter
Dean of University College of Bangor: Gillian Jordan
Number of teachers: 100 (full-time)
Number of students: 6,000

DEANS

College of Arts and Humanities: Margaret Danielson
College of Mathematics and Professional Studies: Frank B. Bean
College of Natural and Social Sciences: Grace M. Leonard

BRANCH CAMPUS

University College of Bangor: 1 University Dr., Bangor, ME 04401-4331; tel. (207) 262-7800.

University of Maine at Farmington

224 Main St, Farmington, ME 04938
Telephone: (207) 778-7000
Fax: (207) 778-8193
E-mail: umfadmit@maine.edu
Internet: www.umf.maine.edu
Founded 1864 as college, univ. status 1970
Pres.: Theodora J. Kalikow
Vice-Pres. for Academic Affairs and Provost: Allen H. Berger
Vice Pres. for Admin.: Ryan Low
Vice-Pres. for Student and Community Services: F. Celeste Branham
Dir of Admissions: Jamie Marcus
Dir of Library: Franklin D. Roberts
Library of 105,000 vols
Number of teachers: 125
Number of students: 2,000

DEANS

College of Arts and Sciences: Robert L. Lively
College of Education, Health and Rehabilitation: Katherine W. Yardley

University of Maine at Fort Kent

23 University Dr., Fort Kent, ME 04743
Telephone: (207) 834-7500
Fax: (207) 834-7503
E-mail: umfkadm@maine.edu
Internet: www.umfk.maine.edu
Academic year: September to May
Founded 1878
Pres.: Richard W. Cost
Vice-Pres. for Academic Affairs: Rachel E. Albert
Vice-Pres. for Admin.: John D. Murphy
Registrar: Donald M. Raymond
Dean of Information Services and Library Dir: Sharon M. Johnson
Library of 69,574 vols
Number of teachers: 59
Number of students: 1,339

CHAIRMEN OF ACADEMIC DIVISIONS

Arts and Humanities: Scott T. Brickman
Education: Bruno Hicks
Natural and Behavioural Sciences: Raymond T. Albert
Nursing: Dr Rachel E. Albert

University of Maine at Machias

9 O'Brien Ave, Machias, ME 04654-1397
Telephone: (207) 255-1200
Fax: (207) 255-4864
Internet: www.umm.maine.edu
Founded 1909
Academic year: September to May
Pres.: Dr Cynthia E. Huggins
Vice-Pres. for Academic Affairs: Stuart Swain (acting)
Registrar: Mary Stover
Librarian: Marianne Thibodeau
Library of 94,000 vols
Number of teachers: 52
Number of students: 1,300

CHAIRMEN OF ACADEMIC DIVISIONS

Arts and Letters: Dr Randall Kindleberger
Environmental and Biological Science: Sherrie Sprangers
Professional Studies: Dr William J. Eckhart, Jr

University of Maine at Presque Isle

181 Main St, Presque Isle, ME 04769-2888
Telephone: (207) 768-9400
Fax: (207) 768-9608
E-mail: admissions@umpi.edu
Internet: www.umpi.edu
Academic year: September to May
Founded 1903
Pres.: Dr Donald N. Zillman
Vice-Pres. for Academic Affairs: Dr Michael Sonntag
Vice-Pres. for Admin. and Finance: Charles Bonin
Dean of Students: Christine Corsello
Admissions Dir: Erin Benson
Registrar: Kathy Davis
Library Dir: Greg Curtis
Library of 458,500 items
Number of students: 1,455
Depts of business and int. studies; English, communication and fine art; exercise science/physical education, recreation/leisure services, athletic training, and health; psychology, social work, and criminal justice; teacher education; world languages, science and mathematics; liberal studies, bachelors of applied science and honours programmes.

University of Southern Maine

POB 9300, Portland, ME 04104-9300
Telephone: (207) 780-4141
Fax: (207) 780-4933
Internet: www.usm.maine.edu
Founded 1878
Academic year: September to May
Pres.: Dr Joseph Wood
Vice-Pres. for Univ. Advancement: Elizabeth Shorr
Registrar: Steven Rand
Dir of Admission: Scott Steinberg
Librarian: David Nutty
Library of 484,000 volumes
Number of teachers: 351
Number of students: 11,000

DEANS

College of Arts and Sciences: Devinder M. Malhotra
College of Education and Human Devt: Betty Lou Whitford
College of Nursing and Health Professions: Brian J. Toy
Muskie School of Public Service: William H. Foster
School of Applied Science, Engineering and Technology: John R. Wright
School of Business: James Shaffer
School of Law: Peter Pitegoff

UNIVERSITY OF NEW ENGLAND

11 Hills Beach Rd, Biddeford, ME 04005
Telephone: (207) 283-0171
Fax: (207) 282-6379
E-mail: admissions@une.edu
Internet: www.une.edu
Founded 1939 as College Séraphique; present name 1978; merged with Westbrook College (f. 1831) 1996
Private control
Academic year: September to May
Pres.: Dr Danielle N. Ripich
Provost and Vice-Pres. for Academic Affairs: Dr Jacque Carter
Vice-Pres. for Business and Finance: Bernard G. Chretien
Vice-Pres. for Enrollment Management: Alan Liebrecht
Vice-Pres. for Institutional Advancement: Harley G. Knowles
Vice-Pres. for Student Affairs: Barbara J. Hazard
Dean of Library Services: Andrew J. Golub
Number of teachers: 148
Number of students: 3,800

DEANS

College of Arts and Sciences: Dr Alfred H. Fuchs
College of Health Professions: Dr David M. Ward
College of Osteopathic Medicine: Jacquelyn B. Cawley
College of Pharmacy: Dr John F. Cormier

BRANCH CAMPUS

Westbrook College Campus: 716 Stevens Ave, Portland, ME 04103; tel. (207) 797-7261.

MARYLAND

BALTIMORE INTERNATIONAL COLLEGE

Commerce Exchange, 17 Commerce St, Baltimore, MD 21202-3230
Telephone: (410) 752-4710
Fax: (410) 752-3730
E-mail: admissions@bic.edu
Internet: www.bic.edu
Founded 1972
Private control
Areas of study: business and management, culinary arts
Pres.: Dr EDGAR SCHICK
Library of 11,000 vols
Number of students: 510

CAPITOL COLLEGE

11301 Springfield Rd, Laurel, MD 20708
Telephone: (301) 369-2800
Fax: (301) 953-1442
E-mail: admissions@capitol-college.edu
Internet: www.capitol-college.edu
Private control
Pres.: Dr MICHAEL T. WOOD
Dir of Library Services: RICK A. SAMPLE
Library of 10,000 vols
Number of teachers: 57
Number of students: 801 (630 undergraduate, 171 graduate)
Areas of study: computer engineering, computer engineering technology, computer science, electrical engineering, electronic commerce management, electronics engineering technology, information architecture, information systems management, management of information technology, management of telecommunication systems, network security, software and internet applications, software engineering, telecommunications engineering technology.

COLLEGE OF NOTRE DAME OF MARYLAND

4701 North Charles St, Baltimore, MD 21210
Telephone: (410) 532-5330
Fax: (410) 532-6287
E-mail: admiss@ndm.edu
Internet: www.ndm.edu
Founded 1873
Private control
Pres.: Dr MARY PAT SEURKAMP
Dir of Admissions: LUCAS J. SIFUENTES
Number of teachers: 105
Number of students: 2,935 (1,338 undergraduate; 1,597 graduate)

GOUCHER COLLEGE

1021 Dulaney Valley Rd, Baltimore, MD 21204
Telephone: (410) 337-6000
E-mail: communications@goucher.edu
Internet: www.goucher.edu
Founded 1885
Pres.: SANFORD J. UNGAR
Vice-Pres. and Dean of Students: GAIL EDMONDS
Registrar: PATRICIA KELLY
Vice-Pres. for Finance: TOM PHIZACKLEA
Librarian: NANCY MAGNUSON
Number of teachers: 173
Number of students: 2,350
Publications: *Donnybrook Fair*, *Goucher College Catalog*, *Preface*, *President's Bulletin*, *Quindecim*, *The Goucher Quarterly*.

HOOD COLLEGE

401 Rosemont Ave, Frederick, MD 21701-8575
Telephone: (301) 663-3131
Fax: (301) 694-7653
Internet: www.hood.edu
Founded 1893
Academic year: August to May
Pres.: Dr RONALD VOLPE
Provost and Dean of the Faculty: Dr ROBERT FUNK
Sr Vice-Pres. for Finance and Admin. and Treas.: WILLIAM GEARHART
Vice-Pres. for Institutional Advancement: NANCY GILLECE
Vice-Pres. for Student Life and Dean of Students: OLIVIA WHITE
Registrar: NANETTE MARKEY
Library Dir: JAN SAMET O'LEARY
Library of 175,000 vols
Number of teachers: 143 (73 full-time, 70 adjunct)
Publications: *Graduate Bulletin*, *Hood Magazine* (4 a year)

DEANS

Academic Affairs: TOM SAMET
Graduate School: ANN BOYD

JOHNS HOPKINS UNIVERSITY

3400 North Charles St, Baltimore, MD 21218
Telephone: (410) 516-8000
Internet: www.jhu.edu
Founded 1876
Private control
Academic year: September to June
Pres.: RONALD J. DANIELS
Provost and Sr Vice-Pres. for Academic Affairs: LLOYD B. MINOR
Sr Vice-Pres. for Finance and Admin.: JAMES T. MCGILL, Jr
Vice-Pres. and Gen. Counsel: STEPHEN S. DUNHAM
Vice-Pres. for Devt and Alumni Relations: MICHAEL C. EICHER
Vice-Pres. for Finance and Treasurer: MICHAEL STRINE
Vice-Pres. for Govt and Community Affairs: THOMAS S. LEWIS
Vice-Pres. for Human Resources: CHARLENE MOORE HAYES
Vice-Pres. for Medicine: EDWARD D. MILLER
Registrar: HEDY SCHAEDEL
Library: see Libraries
Number of teachers: 519
Number of students: 6,782

DEANS

School of Advanced Int. Studies: JESSICA P. EINHORN (acting)
School of Arts and Sciences: MICHELA GALLAGHER
Carey Business School: YASH P. GUPTA
School of Education: MARIALE HARDIMAN
School of Engineering: NICHOLAS P. JONES
School of Medicine: EDWARD D. MILLER
School of Nursing: MARTHA N. HILL (acting)
School of Public Health: MICHAEL J. KLAG
Peabody Institute: JEFFREY SHARKEY (Dir)
Applied Physics Laboratory: RICHARD T. ROCA (Dir)

PROFESSORS

Bloomberg School of Public Health:

ALEXANDER, C. S., Population and Family Health Sciences
ANDERSON, G. F., Health Policy and Management
ANTHONY, J. C., Mental Hygiene
ARMENIAN, H. K., Epidemiology
BAKER, S. P., Health Policy and Management
BAKER, T. D., Int. Health
BEATY, T. H., Epidemiology
BECKER, S., Population and Family Health Sciences
BERTRAND, J. T., Population and Family Health Sciences
BLACK, R., Int. Health
BREITNER, J. C. S., Mental Hygiene
BRENNER, M. H., Health Policy and Management
BREYSSE, P., Environmental Health Sciences
BROOKMEYER, R., Biostatistics
BROWN, T. R., Biochemistry and Molecular Biology
BRYANT, F. R., Biochemistry and Molecular Biology
BURKE, D. S., Int. Health
CABALLERO, B., Int. Health
CELENTANO, D., Epidemiology
CHANDRASEGARAN, S., Environmental Health Sciences
CHOW, L., Population and Family Health Sciences
COHEN, B. H., Epidemiology
COMSTOCK, G. W., Epidemiology
CULOTTA, V., Environmental Health Sciences
DANNENBERG, A. M., Environmental Health Sciences
DIENER-WEST, M., Biostatistics
EATON, W. W., Mental Hygiene
ENSMINGER, M. E., Health Policy and Management
FADEN, R., Health Policy and Management
FEINLEIB, M., Epidemiology
FITZGERALD, R. S., Environmental Health Sciences
GIELEN, A., Health Policy and Management
GILMAN, R., Int. Health
GOLDBERG, A. M., Environmental Health Sciences
GOLDMAN, L., Environmental Health Sciences
GORDIS, L., Epidemiology
GOSTIN, L., Health Policy and Management
GRAY, R. H., Population and Family Health Sciences
GRIFFIN, D. E., Molecular Microbiology and Immunology
GROOPMAN, J. D., Environmental Health Sciences
GROSSMAN, L., Biochemistry and Molecular Biology
GUILARTE, T. R., Environmental Health Sciences
GUYER, B., Population and Family Health Sciences
HALSEY, N., Int. Health
HARDWICK, J. M., Molecular Microbiology and Immunology
HELZLSOUER, K., Epidemiology
HENDERSON, D. A., Int. Health
HILL, K. H., Population and Family Health Sciences
HUANG, P. C., Biochemistry
JAKAB, G. J., Environmental Health Sciences
KASPER, J. A., Health Policy and Management
KATZ, J., Int. Health
KENSLER, T. W., Environmental Health Sciences
KETNER, G. W., Molecular Microbiology and Immunology
KIM, Y. J., Population and Family Health Sciences
KLEEBURGER, S., Environmental Health Sciences

KRAG, S. S., Biochemistry and Molecular Biology
KUMAR, N., Molecular Microbiology and Immunology
LAWRENCE, R. S., Health Policy and Management
LEAF, P. J., Mental Hygiene
LEVIN, D. E., Biochemistry
LIANG, K. Y., Biostatistics
LINKS, J. M., Environmental Health Sciences
MACKENZIE, E. J., Health Policy and Management
MCMACKEN, R., Biochemistry and Molecular Biology
MARGOLIK, J., Molecular Microbiology and Immunology
MARKHAM, R., Molecular Microbiology and Immunology
MATANOSKI, G. M., Epidemiology
MEINERT, C. L., Epidemiology
MILLER, P. S., Biochemistry and Molecular Biology
MITZNER, W. A., Environmental Health Sciences
MORLOCK, L., Health Policy and Management
MORROW, R., Int. Health
MOSLEY, W. H., Population and Family Health Sciences
MUÑOZ, A., Epidemiology
NATHANSON, C. A., Population and Family Health Sciences
NAVARRO, V., Health Policy and Management
NELSON, K., Epidemiology
PAIGE, D. M., Population and Family Health Sciences
PICKART, C. M., Biochemistry
PIERCE, N. F., Int. Health
PIOTROW, P. T., Population and Family Health Sciences
POWE, N. R., Epidemiology
REINKE, W. A., Int. Health
RISBY, T., Environmental Health Sciences
ROHDE, C. A., Biostatistics
ROSE, N. R., Molecular Microbiology and Immunology
ROTER, D., Health Policy and Management
ROYALL, R. M., Biostatistics
SACK, D., Int. Health
SACK, R. B., Int. Health
SALKEVER, D. S., Health Policy and Management
SAMET, J., Epidemiology
SANTOSHAM, M., Int. Health
SCHOENRICH, E. H., Health Policy and Management
SCHWARTZ, B., Environmental Health Sciences
SCOCCA, J. J., Biochemistry
SCOTT, A. L., Molecular Microbiology and Immunology
SHAH, K. V., Molecular Microbiology and Immunology
SOMMER, A., Epidemiology
SPANNHAKE, E., Environmental Health Sciences
STARFIELD, B., Health Policy and Management
STEINHOFF, M., Int. Health
STEINWACHS, D. M., Health Policy and Management
STRICKLAND, P. T., Environmental Health Sciences
STROBINO, D. M., Population and Family Health Sciences
SZKLO, M., Epidemiology
TERET, S. P., Health Policy and Management
TIELSCH, J. M., Int. Health
TONASCIA, J., Biostatistics
TRPIS, M., Molecular Microbiology and Immunology
TRUSH, M. A., Environmental Health Sciences
TS'O, P. O. P., Biochemistry and Molecular Biology
TSUI, A. O., Population and Family Health Sciences
WAGNER, H. N., Environmental Health Sciences
WANG, M., Biostatistics
WEINER, J. P., Health Policy and Management
WEST, K., Int. Health
WRIGHT, W. W., Biochemistry and Molecular Biology
YAGER, J., Environmental Health Sciences
ZABIN, L. S., Population and Family Health Sciences
ZEGER, S., Biostatistics
ZIRKIN, B., Biochemistry and Molecular Biology

Carey School of Business:

AGRESTI, W., Business Studies
ANIKEEF, M., Business Studies
DADA, M., Business Studies
LIEBOWITZ, J., Business Studies
PHAN, P., Business Studies

Faculty of Medicine:

ABELOFF, M. D., Oncology, Medicine
ACHUFF, S. C., Medicine
ADKINSON, N. F., Jr, Medicine
ADLER, R., Ophthalmology and Neuroscience
AGNEW, W. S., Physiology and Neuroscience
AGRE, P. C., Biological Chemistry and Medicine
AMBINDER, R. F., Oncology, Pathology, Pharmacology and Molecular Science
AMZEL, L. M., Biophysics and Biophysical Chemistry
ANHALT, G. J., Dermatology and Pathology
ASKIN, F. B., Pathology
ATOR, N. A., Psychiatry
AUGUST, J. T., Pharmacology and Molecular Sciences, Oncology
BARBARAN, J. M., Neuroscience, Psychiatry
BARKER, L. R., Medicine
BARTLETT, J. G., Medicine
BAUGHMAN, K. L., Medicine
BAUMGARTNER, W. A., Surgery and Cardiac Surgery
BAYLESS, T. M., Medicine
BAYLIN, S. B., Oncology and Medicine
BEACHY, P. A., Molecular Biology and Genetics
BECKER, D. M., Medicine
BECKER, L. C., Medicine
BELL, W. R., Medicine
BERG, J. M., Biophysics and Biophysical Chemistry
BIGELOW, G. E., Psychiatry and Behavioural Sciences
BOCHNER, B. S., Medicine
BOEKE, J. D., Molecular Biology and Genetics
BOITNOTT, J. K., Pathology
BOROWITZ, M. J., Pathology, Oncology
BOTTOMLEY, P. A., Radiology and Radiological Science, Nuclear Magnetic Resonance Research, Biomedical Engineering and Medicine
BRANDT, J., Psychiatry
BREAKEY, W. R., Psychiatry
BREM, H., Neurological Surgery, Oncology
BRESSLER, N. M., Ophthalmology
BRESSLER, S. B., Ophthalmology
BRIEGER, G. H., History of Science, Medicine and Technology
BRINKER, J. A., Medicine
BROONER, R. K., Psychiatry
BRUSHART, T. M., Orthopaedic Surgery, Surgery, Plastic Surgery and Neurology
BULKLEY, G. B., Surgery
BURDICK, J. F., Surgery
BURGER, P. C., Pathology, Oncology Center, Neurological Surgery
BURKE, P. J., Oncology Center, Medicine
BURTON, J. R., Medicine
CALKINS, H. G., Medicine and Paediatrics
CAMERON, J. L., Surgery, Oncology
CAMPBELL, J. N., Neurological Surgery
CAMPOCHIARO, P. A., Ophthalmology and Neuroscience
CAPUTE, A. J., Paediatrics
CARSON, B. S., Neurological Surgery, Oncology, Paediatrics and Plastic Surgery
CARTER, H. B., Urology and Oncology
CASELLA, J. F., Paediatrics, Oncology Center
CASERO, R. J., Jr, Oncology
CATALDO, M. F., Psychiatry and Paediatrics
CHAISSON, R. E., Medicine
CHAKRAVARTI, A., Medicine and Paediatrics
CHAN, D. W., Pathology, Oncology, Radiology and Radiological Science, Urology
CHANDRA, N., Medicine
CHANG, A. Y., Oncology
CHAO, E. Y., Orthopaedic Surgery and Biomedical Engineering
CHARACHE, P., Pathology, Oncology, Medicine
CHATTERJEE, S. B., Paediatrics
CIVIN, C. I., Oncology, Paediatrics
CLEMENTS, J. E., Comparative Medicine, Neurology and Pathology
COFFEY, D. S., Urology, Oncology, Pharmacology and Molecular Sciences
COLE, P. A., Pharmacology and Molecular Sciences
COLOMBANI, P. M., Surgery, Paediatric Surgery, Oncology
CORDEN, J. L., Molecular Biology and Genetics
CORNBLATH, D. R., Neurology
COTTER, R. J., Pharmacology and Molecular Sciences, Biophysics and Biophysical Chemistry
CRAIG, N. L., Molecular Biology and Genetics
CRAIG, S. W., Biological Chemistry and Pathology
CUMMINGS, C. W., Otolaryngology—Head and Neck Surgery, Oncology
CUTTING, G. R., Paediatrics and Medicine
DANG, C. V., Medicine, Oncology, Pathology
DANNALS, R. F., Radiology, Radiological Science and Nuclear Medicine
DAVIDSON, N. E., Oncology
DAWSON, T., Neurology and Neuroscience
DE JUAN, E., Jr, Ophthalmology
DELATEUR, B. J., Physical Medicine and Rehabilitation
DENCKLA, M. B., Neurology and Paediatrics
DEPAULO, J. R., Psychiatry
DESIDERIO, S. V., Molecular Biology and Genetics
DEVREOTES, P. N., Biological Chemistry, Cell Biology and Anatomy
DICELLO, J. F., Oncology
DIEHL, A. M., Medicine
DIETZ, H. C., Paediatrics
DONEHOWER, R. C., Oncology and Medicine
DONOWITZ, M., Medicine
DOVER, G. J., Paediatrics and Oncology
DRACHMAN, D. B., Neurology and Neuroscience
EGGLESTON, P. A., Paediatrics
EISELE, D. W., Otolaryngology—Head and Neck Surgery, Anaesthesiology, Critical Care Medicine, Oncology and Urology
ENGLUND, P. T., Biological Chemistry
EPSTEIN, J. I., Pathology, Oncology, Urology
EROZAN, Y. S., Pathology
ETTINGER, D. S., Oncology, Medicine
FAJARDO, L. L., Radiology and Radiological Science, Diagnostic Radiology and Oncology
FEINBERG, A. P., Medicine and Oncology
FINKELSTEIN, D., Ophthalmology

FISHMAN, E. K., Radiology and Radiological Science, Diagnostic Radiology, Oncology
FORASTIERE, A. A., Oncology, Otolaryngology—Head and Neck Surgery
FORTUIN, N. J., Medicine
FOX, H. E., Gynaecology and Obstetrics
FRASSICA, F. J., Orthopaedic Surgery and Oncology
FREEMAN, J. M., Neurology and Paediatrics
FRIED, L. P., Medicine
FROST, J. J., Radiology and Radiological Science, and Nuclear Medicine and Neuroscience
FUCHS, P. A., Otolaryngology—Head and Neck Surgery, Biomedical Engineering and Neuroscience
GARCIA, J. G., Medicine
GEARHART, J. D., Gynaecology and Obstetrics, Comparative Medicine and Physiology
GEARHART, J. P., Urology and Paediatrics
GERSTENBLITH, G., Medicine
GIARDIELLO, F. M., Medicine, Oncology, Pathology
GIBSON, D. W., Pharmacology and Molecular Sciences
GOLDBERG, M. F., Ophthalmology
GOLDSTEIN, G. W., Neurology and Paediatrics
GORDIS, L., Paediatrics
GORDON, B., Neurology
GOTTSCH, J. D., Ophthalmology
GREEN, W. R., Ophthalmology and Pathology
GREENOUGH, W. B., III, Medicine
GREIDER, C. W., Molecular Biology and Genetics, Oncology
GRIFFIN, J. W., Neurology, Neuroscience and Pathology
GRIFFITH, L. S., Medicine
GRIFFITHS, R. R., Psychiatry and Neuroscience
GROSSMAN, S. A., Oncology, Medicine and Neurological Surgery
GUGGINO, W. B., Physiology and Paediatrics
GUYTON, D. L., Ophthalmology
HALPERIN, H. R., Medicine, Biomedical Engineering
HAMILTON, R. G., Medicine
HANDLER, J. S., Medicine
HANLEY, D. F., Neurology, Anaesthesiology and Critical Care Medicine
HAPONIK, E. F., Medicine
HARMON, J. W., Surgery
HARRIS, J. C., Jr, Psychiatry and Paediatrics
HART, G. W., Biological Chemistry
HAWKINS, B. S., Ophthalmology
HAYWARD, G. S., Pharmacology and Molecular Sciences, Oncology and Pathology
HAYWARD, S. D., Pharmacology and Molecular Sciences, Oncology and Pathology
HELLMAN, D. B., Medicine
HENDRY, S. H., Neuroscience
HEPTINSTALL, R. H., Pathology
HESS, A. D., Oncology and Pathology
HOLTZMAN, N. A., Paediatrics
HRUBAN, R. H., Pathology, Oncology
HUBBARD, A. L., Cell Biology, Anatomy and Physiology
HUGANIR, R. L., Neuroscience
HUGGINS, G. R., Gynaecology and Obstetrics
HUNGERFORD, D. S., Orthopaedic Surgery
HUTCHINS, G. M., Pathology
ISAACS, J. T., Oncology and Urology
ISAACS, W. B., Urology, Oncology
JABS, D. A., Ophthalmology and Medicine
JABS, E. W., Paediatrics, Medicine, Surgery and Plastic Surgery
JACKSON, J. B., Pathology
JASINSKI, D. R., Medicine
JOHNS, R. A., Anaesthesiology and Critical Care Medicine
JOHNS, R. J., Medicine
JOHNSON, K. O., Neuroscience and Biomedical Engineering
JOHNSON, R. T., Neurology, Molecular Biology, Genetics and Neuroscience
JOHNSTON, M. V., Neurology and Paediatrics
JONES, B., Radiology and Radiological Sciences, Diagnostic Radiology
JONES, R. J., Oncology
KAN, J. S., Paediatrics
KASHIMA, H. K., Otolaryngology—Head and Neck Surgery, Oncology
KASS, D. A., Medicine and Biomedical Engineering
KAVOUSSI, L. R., Urology
KELEN, G. D., Emergency Medicine
KELLY, T. J., Jr, Molecular Biology and Genetics
KICKLER, T. S., Pathology, Oncology and Medicine
KIM, K. S., Paediatrics
KINZLER, K. W., Oncology
KIRSCH, J. R., Anaesthesiology and Critical Care Medicine
KLAG, M. J., Medicine
KLEIN, A. S., Surgery
KOCH, W., Otolaryngology, Oncology
KOEHLER, R. C., Anaesthesiology and Critical Care Medicine
KOSTUIK, J., Orthopaedic Surgery and Neurological Surgery
KUNCL, R. W., Neurology
KURMAN, R. J., Gynaecology and Obstetrics, Pathology
KWITEROVICH, P. O., Jr, Paediatrics and Medicine
LADENSON, P. W., Medicine, Oncology and Pathology
LANE, M. D., Biological Chemistry
LAWSON, E. E., Paediatrics
LEDERMAN, H. M., Paediatrics
LEE, S., Molecular Biology and Genetics
LENZ, F. A., Neurological Surgery
LEONG, K. W., Biomedical Engineering
LESSER, R. P., Neurology, Neurological Surgery
LEVINE, D. M., Medicine
LEVINE, M. A., Paediatrics and Medicine
LI, G., Emergency Medicine
LICHTENSTEIN, L. M., Medicine
LIETMAN, P. S., Medicine, Paediatrics, Pharmacology and Molecular Sciences
LILLEMOE, K. D., Surgery
LIU, J., Pharmacology and Molecular Sciences, Neuroscience
LONG, D. M., Neurological Surgery
LOUGHLIN, G. M., Paediatrics
LYKETSOS, C. G., Psychiatry
MCARTHUR, J. C., Neurology
MCCARTHY, E. F., Jr, Pathology, Orthopaedic Surgery
MCCAUL, M. E., Psychiatry
MACGLASHAN, D. W., Medicine
MCHUGH, P. R., Psychiatry
MCKHANN, G. M., Neurology and Neuroscience
MCKUSICK, V. A., Medicine
MCMILLAN, J. A., Paediatrics
MALONEY, P. C., Physiology
MANN, R. B., Pathology, Oncology
MANSON, P. N., Surgery and Plastic Surgery
MARBAN, E., Medicine and Physiology
MASSOF, R. W., Ophthalmology
MAUGHAN, W. L., Medicine and Biomedical Engineering
MAUMENEE, I. E., Ophthalmology
MERZ, W. G., Pathology
MEYER, R. A., Neurological Surgery and Biomedical Engineering
MEZEY, E., Medicine
MIGEON, B. R., Paediatrics
MIGEON, C. J., Paediatrics
MILDVAN, A. S., Biological Chemistry
MILLER, E. D., Anaesthesiology and Critical Care Medicine
MILLER, N. R., Ophthalmology and Neurology, Neurological Surgery
MINOR, L. B., Otolaryngology—Head and Neck Surgery, Biomedical Engineering, Neuroscience
MOLLIVER, M. E., Neuroscience and Neurology
MONTELL, C., Biological Chemistry and Neuroscience
MONTZ, F. J., Gynaecology and Obstetrics, Oncology
MOORE, T. H., Medicine
MORAN, T. H., Psychiatry
MOSER, H. W., Neurology and Paediatrics
MOSTWIN, J. L., Urology
MUNSTER, A. M., Surgery and Plastic Surgery
MURPHY, D. B., Cell Biology and Anatomy
MURPHY, P. A., Medicine and Molecular Biology and Genetics
NAIDU, S., Neurology, Paediatrics
NATARAJAN, V., Medicine
NATHANS, J., Molecular Biology and Genetics, Neuroscience and Ophthalmology
NESS, P. M., Pathology and Medicine
NICHOLS, D. G., Anaesthesiology, Critical Care Medicine
NIPARKO, J. K., Otolaryngology—Head and Neck Surgery
NORTH, R., Neurological Surgery, Anaesthesiology and Critical Care Medicine
PARDOLL, D. M., Oncology, Medicine and Pathology
PARTIN, A., Urology
PEARLSON, G. D., Psychiatry
PEDERSEN, P. L., Biological Chemistry
PERLER, B. A., Surgery
PERMUTT, S., Medicine
PETRI, M., Medicine
PIANTADOSI, S., Oncology
PITHA-ROWE, P. M., Oncology
PLOTNICK, L., Paediatrics
POPEL, A. S., Biomedical Engineering
POWE, N. R, Medicine
PRICE, D. L., Pathology, Neurology and Neuroscience
QUIGLEY, H. A., Ophthalmology
QUINN, T. C., Medicine
RABINS, P. V., Psychiatry
RACUSEN, L., Pathology
RAJA, S. N., Anaesthesiology and Critical Care Medicine
REED, R. R., Molecular Biology and Genetics and Neuroscience
REEVES, R. H., Physiology
REPKA, M. X., Ophthalmology, Paediatrics
RICHARDSON, M. A., Otolaryngology—Head and Neck Surgery
RIGAMONTI, D., Neurological Surgery, Radiology and Radiological Science, Neuroradiology
RONNETT, G. V., Neuroscience, Neurology
ROSE, G. D., Biophysics and Biophysical Chemistry
ROSE, K. D., Cell Biology and Anatomy
ROSENSTEIN, B. J., Paediatrics
ROSENTHAL, D. L., Pathology, Gynaecology and Obstetrics, Oncology
ROSS, C. A., Psychiatry and Neuroscience
ROTHSTEIN, J. D., Neurology and Neuroscience
ROWE, P. C., Paediatrics
RUFF, C. B., Cell Biology, Anatomy and Orthopaedic Surgery
RYUGO, D. K., Otolaryngology—Head and Neck Surgery, Neuroscience
SACHS, M. B., Biomedical Engineering and Neuroscience, Otolaryngology—Head and Neck Surgery
SAUDEK, C. D., Medicine
SAUDER, D. N., Dermatology
SCHACHAT, A. P., Ophthalmology and Oncology

SCHEIN, O. D., Ophthalmology
SCHLEIMER, R. P., Medicine
SCHMIDT, C. W., Jr, Psychiatry
SCHNAAR, R. L., Pharmacology, Molecular Sciences and Neuroscience
SCHNECK, J., Pathology
SCHRAMM, L. P., Biomedical Engineering and Neuroscience
SCHWARZ, K., Paediatrics
SCIUBBA, J. J., Otolaryngology—Head and Neck Surgery, Dermatology, Pathology
SEMENZA, G. L., Paediatrics
SHAPER, J. H., Oncology
SHAPIRO, E. P., Medicine
SHAPIRO, T. A., Medicine
SHARKIS, S. J., Oncology
SHORTLE, D. R., Biological Chemistry, Biophysics and Biophysical Chemistry
SHOUKAS, A. A., Biomedical Engineering
SIDRANSKY, D., Otolaryngology - Head and Neck Surgery, Urology, Oncology, Pathology
SIEGELMAN, S. S., Radiology and Radiological Science
SILICIANO, R. F., Medicine
SINGER, H. S., Neurology and Paediatrics
SLAVNEY, P. R., Psychiatry and Medicine
SMITH, K. D., Paediatrics
SMITH, P. L., Medicine
SNYDER, S. H., Neuroscience, Pharmacology, Molecular Sciences and Psychiatry
SOLLNER-WEBB, B. T., Biological Chemistry
SOMMER, A., Ophthalmology
SPIVAK, J. L., Medicine and Oncology
SPONSELLER, P. D., Orthopaedic Surgery
STARK, W. J., Jr, Ophthalmology
STITZER, M. L., Psychiatry
STRAIN, E. C., Psychiatry
SYLVESTER, J. T., Medicine
TALALAY, P., Pharmacology and Molecular Sciences
TEAFORD, M. F., Cell Biology and Anatomy
TERRY, P. B., Medicine
THAKOR, N. V., Biomedical Engineering
THOMAS, G. H., Paediatrics and Pathology
TOMASELLI, G. F., Medicine
TRAILL, T. A., Medicine
TRAYSTMAN, R. J., Anaesthesiology and Critical Care Medicine
TSO, M. D., Ophthalmology and Pathology
UNDEM, B. J., Medicine
VALLE, D. L., Paediatrics and Ophthalmology
VAN ZIJL, P. C., Radiology and Radiological Sciences, Nuclear Magnetic Resonance, Biophysics and Biophysical Chemistry
VOGELSANG, G. B., Oncology
VOGELSTEIN, B., Oncology and Pathology
VON DER HEYDT, R., Neuroscience
WALLACH, E. E., Gynaecology and Obstetrics
WALSER, M., Pharmacology and Molecular Sciences and Medicine
WALSH, P.C., Urology
WAND, G. S., Medicine, Psychiatry
WATKINS, L., Jr, Surgery and Cardiac Surgery
WEISHAMPEL, D. B., Cell Biology and Anatomy
WEISS, J. L., Medicine
WEST, S., Ophthalmology
WHARAM, M. D., Jr, Oncology, Paediatrics, Radiology and Radiological Science and Neurological Surgery
WIGLEY, F. M., Medicine
WILLIAMS, G. M., Surgery
WINCHURCH, R. A., Surgery
WINKELSTEIN, J. A., Paediatrics, Medicine and Pathology
WINSLOW, R. L., Biomedical Engineering
WISE, R. A., Medicine
WOLBERGER, C., Biophysics and Biophysical Chemistry
WONG, D. F., Radiology and Radiological Science, and Nuclear Medicine
WORLEY, P. F., Neuroscence and Neurology
YARDLEY, J. H., Pathology
YASTER, M., Anaesthesiology and Critical Care Medicine
YAU, K., Neuroscience and Ophthalmology
YEO, C. J., Surgery and Oncology
YOLKEN, R. H., Paediatrics
YOUNG, E. D., Biomedical Engineering and Neuroscience, Otolaryngology—Head and Neck Surgery
YOUSEM, D. M., Radiology and Radiological Science, Neuroradiology
YUE, I. D., Biomedical Engineering and Neuroscience
ZACUR, H. A., Gynaecology and Obstetrics
ZEE, D. S., Neurology and Neuroscience, Ophthalmology and Otolaryngology—Head and Neck Surgery
ZEIMER, R., Ophthalmology
ZEITLIN, P. L., Paediatrics
ZERHOUNI, E. A., Radiology and Radiological Science, Diagnostic Radiology and Biomedical Engineering
ZIEVE, P. D., Medicine
ZINK, C., Comparative Medicine and Pathology
ZWEIER, J. L., Medicine

G. W. C. Whiting School of Engineering:

ANANDARAJAH, A., Civil Engineering
ANDREOU, A. G., Electrical and Computer Engineering
AWERBUCH, B., Computer Science
BALL, W. P., Geography and Environmental Engineering
BETENBAUGH, M. J., Chemical Engineering
BOLAND, J., Geography and Environmental Engineering
BOUWER, E. J., Geography and Environmental Engineering
BRUSH, G. S., Geography and Environmental Engineering
BUSCH-VISHNIAC, I. J., Mechanical Engineering
CAMMARATA, R., Materials Science and Engineering
CHEN, S., Mechanical Engineering
CHIRIKJAN, G., Mechanical Engineering
DAVIDSON, F. M., Electrical and Computer Engineering
DONOHUE, M., Chemical Engineering
DOUGLAS, A. S., Mechanical Engineering
ELLIS, J. H., Geography and Environmental Engineering
FILL, J. A., Mathematical Sciences
GERMAN, D., Mathematical Sciences
GOODRICH, M. T., Computer Science
GOUTSIAS, J. I., Electrical and Computer Engineering
GREEN, R. E., Jr, Materials Science and Engineering
HAGER, G. D., Computer Science
HAN, S.-P., Mathematical Sciences
HANKE, S., Geography and Environmental Engineering
HEMKER, K. J., Mechanical Engineering
HOBBS, B. F., Geography and Environmental Engineering
IGUSA, T., Civil Engineering
JELINEK, F., Electrical and Computer Engineering
JONES, N. P., Civil Engineering
JOSEPH, R. I., Electrical and Computer Engineering
KAPLAN, A. E., Electrical and Computer Engineering
KATZ, J., Mechanical Engineering
KATZ, J. L., Chemical Engineering
KHURGIN, J. B., Electrical and Computer Engineering
KNIO, O., Mechanical Engineering
KOSARAJU, S. R., Computer Science
MASSON, G. M., Computer Science
MENEVEAU, C. V., Mechanical Engineering
MEYER, G. G. L., Electrical and Computer Engineering
MILLER, M., Biomedical Engineering
MILLER, M. I., Electrical and Computer Engineering
NAIMAN, D. Q., Mathematical Sciences
O'MELIA, C. R., Geography and Environmental Engineering
PANG, J.-S., Mathematical Sciences
PARLANGE, M. B., Geography and Environmental Engineering
PAULAITIS, M. E., Chemical Engineering
PRIEBE, C. E., Mathematical Sciences
PRINCE, J. L., Electrical and Computer Engineering
PROSPERETTI, A., Mechanical Engineering
RAMESH, K. T., Mechanical Engineering
REVELLE, C., Geography and Environmental Engineering
RUGH, W. J., Electrical and Computer Engineering
SCHEINERMAN, E. R., Mathematical Sciences
SCHOENBERGER, E. J., Geography and Environmental Engineering
SEARSON, P. C., Materials Science and Engineering
SHARPE, W. N., Jr, Mechanical Engineering
SMITH, S. F., Computer Science
STEBE, K., Chemical Engineering
STONE, A. T., Geography and Environmental Engineering
TAYLOR, R. H., Computer Science
WEINERT, H. L., Electrical and Computer Engineering
WIERMAN, J. C., Mathematical Sciences
WILCOCK, P. R., Geography and Environmental Engineering
WOLFF, L. B., Computer Science
WOLMAN, M. G., Geography and Environmental Engineering

Paul H. Nitze School of Advanced Int. Studies (1730 Massachusetts Ave, Washington, DC 20036):

AJAMI, F., Middle East Studies
BARRET, S., Int. Relations
BODNAR, G., Int. Finance
CALLEO, D. P., European Studies
COHEN, E. A., Strategic Studies
CORDEN, W. M., Int. Economics
DORAN, C. F., Canadian Studies and Int. Relations
FRANK, I., Int. Economics
FUKUYAMA, F., Political Economy
GLEIJESES, P., US Foreign Policy and Latin American Studies
GOODELL, G. E., Int. Devt
GRILLI, E., Int. Economics
JACKSON, K. D., Asian and South East Asia Studies
LAMPTON, D. M., Asian Studies
MANDELBAUM, M., US Foreign Policy
PARROTT, B., Russian and Eurasian Studies
PEARSON, C. S., Int. Economics
RIEDEL, J. C., Int. Economics
ROETT, R., Latin American Studies and Western Hemisphere Programs
THAYER, N. B., Asian Studies
WEDGEWOOD, J. D., Int. Law and Organization
ZARTMAN, I. W., African Studies

School of Nursing:

ALLEN, J., Preventive Cardiology
BERK, R. A., Psychometrics and Statistics
CAMPBELL, J., Community Health
DONALDSON, S., Physiology and Biophysics
FRALIC, M., Nursing Management
GASTON-JOHANSSON, F., Research Utilization and Pain
HILL, M., Adult Health

Zanvyl Krieger School of Arts and Sciences:

ACHINSTEIN, P., Philosophy
ALEXANDER, K., Sociology
ANDERSON, A., English
ANDERSON, W., Romance Languages and Literatures
ARRIGHI, G., Sociology

BAGGER, J., Physics and Astronomy
BALL, G., Psychology
BALL, L., Economics
BARNETT, B., Physics and Astronomy
BECKWITH, S., Physics and Astronomy
BEEMON, K., Biology
BELL, D., History
BENNETT, C. L., Physics and Astronomy
BERRY, S., History
BESSMAN, M., Biology
BETT, R., Philosophy
BLUMENFELD, B. J., Physics and Astronomy
BOARDMAN, J. M., Mathematics
BOWEN, K., Chemistry
BRAND, L., Biology
BRIEGER, G., History of Science, Medicine and Technology
BROHOLM, C., Physics and Astronomy
BROOKS, J., History
BRYAN, B. M., Near Eastern Studies
BURZIO, L., Cognitive Science
CAMERON, S., English
CAMPE, R., German
CARROLL, C., Economics
CASTRO-KLARÉN, S., Romance Languages and Literatures
CHERLIN, A., Sociology
CHIEN, C.-L., Physics and Astronomy
CHIEN, C.-Y., Physics and Astronomy
CONE, R. A., Biophysics
CONNOLLY, W., Political Science
COOPER, J., Political Science
COOPER, J. S., Near Eastern Studies
CORCES, V., Biology
CRENSON, M., Political Science
CUMMINGS, M., Political Science
DAGDIGIAN, P., Chemistry
DAS, V., Anthropology
DAVID, S., Political Science
DAVIDSEN, A., Physics and Astronomy
DEFAUX, G., Romance Languages and Literatures
DEMPSEY, C., History of Art
DETIENNE, M., Classics
DIETZE, G., Political Science
DITZ, T., History
DIXON, S., Writing Seminars
DOERING, J., Chemistry
DOMOKOS, G., Physics and Astronomy
DRAPER, D., Chemistry
DRAPER, D., Biophysics and Chemistry
EBERT, J. D., Biology
EDIDIN, M., Biology
EGETH, H., Psychology
FALK, A., Physics and Astronomy
FAMBROUGH, D., Biology
FELDMAN, G., Physics and Astronomy
FELDMAN, P., Physics and Astronomy
FERGUSON, F., English
FERRY, J., Earth and Planetary Sciences
FISHER, G. W., Earth and Planetary Sciences
FLATHMAN, R. C., Political Science
FORD, H., Physics and Astronomy
FORNI, P., Romance Languages and Literatures
FORSTER, E., Humanities Center
FREIRE, E., Biology, Biophysics
FRIED, M., Humanities Center, History of Art
GALAMBOS, L. P., History
GALLAGHER, M., Psychology
GARVEN, G., Earth and Planetary Sciences
GERSOVITZ, M., Economics
GINSBERG, B., Political Science
GOLDBERG, J., English
GONZÁLEZ, E., Romance Languages and Literatures
GORDON, R., Sociology
GREENE, J., History
GROSSMAN, A., English
GROSSMAN, J., Political Science
HARDIE, L. A., Earth and Planetary Sciences
HARRINGTON, J., Economics
HECKMAN, T., Physics and Astronomy
HEDGECOCK, E., Biology
HENRY, R., Physics and Astronomy
HERTZ, N., Humanities Center
HOLLAND, P., Psychology
HOYT, M. A., Biology
HUANG, R. C., Biology
IRWIN, J., Writing Seminars
JOHNSON, M., History
JUSCZYK, P., Psychology
KAGAN, R., History
KARGON, R. H., History of Science, Medicine and Technology
KARLIN, K., Chemistry
KARNI, E., Economics
KATZ, R., Political Science
KECK, M., Political Science
KESSLER, H., History of Art
KHAN, M. A., Economics
KINGSLAND, S., History of Science, Medicine and Technology
KNIGHT, F., History
KOHN, M., Sociology
KOLYVAGIN, V., Mathematics
KOVESI-DOMOKOS, S., Physics and Astronomy
KROLIK, J., Physics and Astronomy
LANDAU, B., Cognitive Science
LATTMAN, E., Biophysics
LEE, Y. C., Biology
LEE, Y. K., Physics and Astronomy
LEGENDRE, G., Cognitive Science
LESLIE, S., History of Science, Medicine and Technology
LEYS, R., Humanities Center
LYKKEN, J., Physics and Astronomy
MCCARTER, P. K., Jr, Near Eastern Studies
MCCARTY, R., Biology
MCCLOSKEY, M., Cognitive Science
MCGARRY, J., Writing Seminars
MACCINI, L., Economics
MACKSEY, R., Humanities Center
MAGUIRE, H., History of Art
MARSH, B., Earth and Planetary Sciences
MELION, W., History of Art
MEYER, G., Chemistry
MINICOZZI, W. P., Mathematics
MOFFITT, R., Economics
MOON, M., English
MOOS, H. W., Physics and Astronomy
MORAVA, J., Mathematics
MORGAN, P., History
MOUDRIANAKIS, E., Biology
NÄGELE, R., German
NEUFELD, D., Physics and Astronomy
NEWMAN, S., Introduction to Policy Analysis (Policy Studies)
NICHOLS, S., Humanities Center
NICHOLS, S., Romance Languages and Literature
NIRENBERG, D., History
NORMAN, C., Physics and Astronomy
OLSON, P. L., Earth and Planetary Sciences
ONO, T., Mathematics
OSBORN, T., Earth and Planetary Sciences
PAGDEN, A., History
PANDEY, G., Anthropology
PAULSON, R., English
PEVSNER, A., Physics and Astronomy
POLAND, D., Chemistry
POSNER, G. H., Chemistry
PRIVALOV, P., Biology
REICH, D., Physics and Astronomy
ROBBINS, M., Physics and Astronomy
ROSEMAN, S., Biology
ROSS, D., History
ROWE, W., History
RUSSELL-WOOD, A. J. R., History
RUSSO, E., Romance Languages and Literature
RYNASIEWICZ, R., Philosophy
SALAMON, L., Political Science
SCHLEIF, R., Biology
SCHROER, T., Biology
SCHWARTZ, G. M., Near Eastern Studies
SHALIKA, J., Mathematics
SHAPIRO, A., Classics
SHEARN, A., Biology
SHIFFMAN, B., Mathematics
SHOKUROV, V. A., Mathematics
SIEBER, H., Romance Languages and Literatures
SILVERSTONE, H. J., Chemistry
SISSA, G., Classics
SMOLENSKY, P., Cognitive Science
SOGGE, C., Mathematics
SPIEGEL, G., History
SPRUCK, J., Mathematics
STANLEY, S., Earth and Planetary Sciences
STEPHENS, W., Romance Languages and Literatures
STROBEL, D., Earth and Planetary Sciences
SVERJENSKY, D., Earth and Planetary Sciences
SWARTZ, M., Physics and Astronomy
SZALAY, A., Physics and Astronomy
TESANOVIC, Z., Physics and Astronomy
TOWNSEND, C., Chemistry
VEBLEN, D., Earth and Planetary Sciences
VISHNIAC, E., Physics and Astronomy
WALKER, J. C., Physics and Astronomy
WALKOWITZ, J., History
WALTERS, R., History
WEISS, D., History of Art
WENTWORTH, R., Mathematics
WESTBROOK, R., Near Eastern Studies
WILLIAMS, M., Philosophy
WILSON, G., Philosophy
WILSON, W. S., Mathematics
WOLF, S., Philosophy
WOODSON, S. A., Biophysics
WYSE, R., Physics and Astronomy
YANTIS, S., Psychology
YARKONY, D., Chemistry
YOUNG, H. P., Economics
ZELDICH, S., Mathematics
ZUCKER, S., Mathematics

LOYOLA UNIVERSITY MARYLAND

4501 North Charles St, Baltimore, MD 21210-2699

Telephone: (410) 617-2000
Fax: (410) 617-2176
Internet: www.loyola.edu

Founded 1852
Private control
Academic year: August to May

Pres.: Rev. BRIAN F. LINNANE
Vice-Pres. for Academic Affairs: TIMOTHY SNYDER
Vice-Pres. for Admin.: TERRENCE SAWYER
Vice-Pres. for for Advancement: MEGAN GILLICK
Vice-Pres. for Business and Finance: THOMAS KINGSTON
Vice-Pres. for Enrollment Management and Communications: MARC M. CAMILLE
Vice-Pres. for Student Devt and Dean of Students: Dr SUSAN M. DONOVAN

Number of teachers: 561
Number of students: 6,000 (3,700 undergraduate, 2,300 graduate)

DEANS

College of Arts and Sciences: Dr JAMES BUCKLEY
School of Education: Dr PETER C. MURRELL, Jr
Sellinger School of Business and Management: Dr KARYL B. LEGGIO
S. J. Loyola College: Rev. JAMES MIRACKY

MCDANIEL COLLEGE

2 College Hill, Westminster, MD 21157-4390

Telephone: (410) 848-7000
Fax: (410) 857-2729
E-mail: pio@mcdaniel.edu
Internet: www.mcdaniel.edu

Founded 1867 as Western Maryland College, present name 2002

Private control
Academic year: August to June
Liberal arts; Masters degrees; training for teachers of the deaf
Pres.: ROGER N. CASEY
Provost and Dean of the Faculty: THOMAS M. FALKNER
Vice-Pres. for Admin. and Finance: ETHAN A. SEIDEL
Vice-Pres. for Enrollment Management and Dean of Admissions: FLORENCE W. HINES
Vice-Pres. for Institutional Advancement: RICHARD G. KIEF
Dean and Vice-Pres. for Student Affairs: BETH R. GERL
Registrar: JAN KIPHART
Chief Information Officer and Library Dir: JESSAME FERGUSON
Library of 200,000 vols
Number of teachers: 135
Number of students: 2,360

MARYLAND INSTITUTE, COLLEGE OF ART

1300 Mt Royal Ave, Baltimore, MD 21217
Telephone: (410) 669-9200
Fax: (410) 669-9206
E-mail: pr@mica.edu
Internet: www.mica.edu
Founded 1826
Pres.: FRED LAZARUS, IV
Vice-Pres. and Dean for Admission and Financial Aid: THERESA LYNCH BEDOYA
Provost and Vice-Pres. for Academic Affairs: RAYMOND V. ALLEN
Vice-Pres. for Advancement: MICHAEL FRANCO
Librarian: MARJORIE CHENOWETH
Library of 51,000 vols
Number of teachers: 178
Number of students: 1,143

MORGAN STATE UNIVERSITY

1700 East Coldspring Lane, Baltimore, MD 21251
Telephone: (443) 885-3333
E-mail: info@morgan.edu
Internet: www.morgan.edu
Founded 1867
Public control
Academic year: August to May
Pres.: Dr DAVID WILSON
Academic Provost and Vice-Pres. for Academic Affairs: Dr T. JOAN ROBINSON
Vice-Pres. for Finance and Management: RAYMOND VOLLMER
Vice-Pres. for Institutional Advancement: CHERYL Y. HITCHCOCK
Vice-Pres. for Planning and Information Technology: Dr JOSEPH POPOVICH
Vice-Pres. for Student Services: A. RECARDO PERRY
Dir of Library: KAREN A. ROBERTSON
Library of 350,042 vols
Number of teachers: 1,500
Number of students: 8,200

DEANS

College of Liberal Arts: Dr BURNEY HOLLIS
School of Business and Management: Dr OTIS THOMAS
School of Education and Urban Studies: Dr PATRICIA WELCH
School of Engineering: Dr EUGENE M. DELOATCH
School of Graduate Studies: Dr FRANK MORRIS
School of Mathematics and Natural Sciences: T. JOAN ROBINSON

MOUNT SAINT MARY'S UNIVERSITY

Emmitsburg, MD 21727
Telephone: (410) 447-6122
Fax: (301) 447-5755
E-mail: postmaster@msmary.edu
Internet: www.msmary.edu
Founded 1808
Pres.: THOMAS H. POWELL
Vice-Pres. for Academic Affairs: Dr DAVID REHM
Registrar: JOHN C. GILL
Dir of Library: Dr D. STEPHEN ROCKWOOD
Library of 200,000 vols
Number of teachers: 120 (98 full-time, 22 part-time)
Number of students: 1,798
Publication: *Mountaineer Briefing* (4 a year)

DEANS

School of Business: WILLIAM G. FORGANG
School of Education and Human Services: BARBARA MARTIN PALMER
School of Natural Science and Mathematics: DAVID W. BUSHMAN
College of Liberal Arts: JOSHUA P. HOSCHCHILD

ST JOHN'S COLLEGE

60 College Ave, Annapolis, MD 21401
Telephone: (410) 626-2522
Fax: (410) 269-7916
E-mail: admissions@sjca.edu
Internet: www.stjohnscollege.edu
Founded as King William's School 1696
Private control
Academic year: August to May
For Santa Fe campus, see under New Mexico
Pres.: CHRISTOPHER B. NELSON
Vice-Pres. for Advancement: BARBARA GOYETTE
Dean: PAMELA KRAUS
Treas.: BRONTE JONES
Registrar: DANIEL CROWE
Dir of Admissions: JOHN CHRISTENSEN
Dir of Alumni Relations: JO ANN MATTSON
College Librarian: CATHERINE DIXON
Library of 100,000 vols
Number of teachers: 69
Number of students: 450
Publication: *The Review* (3 a year).

ST MARY'S COLLEGE OF MARYLAND

18952 E Fisher Rd, St Mary's City, MD 20686-3001
Telephone: (240) 895-2000
Fax: (240) 895-5001
E-mail: admissions@smcm.edu
Internet: www.smcm.edu
Founded 1840
Academic year: August to May
Pres.: Dr JOSEPH URGO
Vice-Pres. for Academic Affairs and Dean of Faculty: Dr BETH RUSHING
Vice-Pres. for Advancement: Dr MAUREEN SILVA
Vice-Pres. for Business and Finance: Dr TOM BOTZMAN
Dean of Admissions and Financial Aid: Dr WESLEY JORDAN
Dean of Students: Dr LAURA BAYLESS
Dir of Library: Dr CELIA RABINOWITZ
Library of 200,000 vols
Number of teachers: 142
Number of students: 2,060
Publications: *The Mulberry Tree* (2 a year), *The Point News* (student newspaper).

ST MARY'S SEMINARY AND UNIVERSITY

5400 Roland Ave, Baltimore, MD 21210-1994
Telephone: (410) 864-4000
E-mail: admissions@stmarys.edu
Internet: www.stmarys.edu
Founded 1791
Pres. and Rector: Father TOM HURST
Vice-Rector: Rev. GLADSTONE STEVENS
Vice-Pres. for Advancement and Admin.: ELIZABETH L. VISCONAGE
Vice-Pres. for Finance: RICHARD G. CHILDS
Registrar and Dir of Information Services: PATRICIA GREGA
Libraries of 95,281 vols
Number of teachers: 45 (21 full-time, 24 part-time)
Number of students: 276 (75 full-time, 201 part-time)
Publications: *Catalogues*, *St Mary's Bulletin* (4 a year).

SOJOURNER-DOUGLASS COLLEGE

200 North Central Ave, Baltimore, MD 21202
Telephone: (410) 276-0306
Fax: (410) 276-1810
Internet: www.sdc.edu
Private control
Pres.: Dr CHARLES W. SIMMONS
Provost and Vice-Pres. for Academic and Student Affairs: Dr MARIAN STANTON
Vice-Pres. for Admin. and Fiscal Affairs: DONALD HUTCHINS
Number of teachers: 44
Number of students: 444
Areas of study: admin., human and social resources, human growth and devt.

BRANCH CAMPUSES

Annapolis Campus: Suite 302, 49 Old Solomons Island Rd, Annapolis, MD 21401; tel. (410) 897-1244; fax (410) 897-1245; Dir Dr CHARLESTINE FAIRLEY.

Bahamas Campus: Gold Circle House, 2nd Floor, East Bay St, Nassau; tel. (242) 394-8570; fax (242) 394-8623; Dir DORIS CARROLL.

Cambridge Campus: 824 Fairmount Ave, Cambridge, MD 21613; tel. (410) 943-1171; fax (410) 943-1976; Dir ENEZ GRUBB.

Prince George's County Campus: Suite 11, 8200 Professional Pl., Lanham, MD 20785; tel. (301) 459-8686; fax (301) 459-2023; Dir Dr BERNARD GROSS.

Salisbury Campus: Salisbury Mall, 351 Civic Ave, Unit B-17, Salisbury, MD 21804; tel. (410) 572-5640; fax (410) 572-5642; Dir (vacant).

UNIFORMED SERVICES UNIVERSITY OF THE HEALTH SCIENCES

4301 Jones Bridge Rd, Bethesda, MD 20814
Telephone: (301) 295-3101
E-mail: admissions@mxa.usuhs.mil
Internet: www.usuhs.mil
Founded 1972
Pres.: Dr CHARLES S. RICE
Vice-Pres. for Exec. Affairs: CHARLES R. MANNIX
Vice-Pres. for Research: Dr STEVEN KAMINSKY
Vice-Pres. for Teaching and Research Support: Dr VERNON D. SCHINSKI
Assoc. Registrar: LINDA A. PORTER
Number of teachers: 332 (on campus)
Number of students: 896

DEANS

F. Edward Hébert School of Medicine: Dr LARRY W. LAUGHLIN

Graduate Education: Dr CINDA J. HELKE (Assoc. Dean)
Graduate School of Nursing: Dr PATRICIA HINTON WALKER

UNITED STATES NAVAL ACADEMY

Annapolis, MD 21402-5000
Telephone: (410) 293-1000
Fax: (410) 293-3735
Internet: www.usna.edu

Founded 1845
Public
Academic year: August to May
Superintendent: Vice Admiral JEFFREY L. FOWLER
Commandant of Midshipmen: Capt. MATHEW L. KLUNDER
Academic Dean and Provost: WILLIAM C. MILLER
Vice-Academic Dean: MICHAEL C. HALBIG
Dean of Admissions: BRUCE LATTA
Dir of Athletics: CHET GLADCHUK
Registrar: Dr MICHAEL CHAMBERLAIN
Dir of Museum: Dr J. SCOTT HARMON
Librarian: RICHARD HUME WERKING

Library of 701,505 vols
Number of teachers: 574
Number of students: 4,350 midshipmen
Publications: *Lucky Bag*, *Shipmate* (online), *Trident*

DIVISION DIRECTORS

Athletics: CHET GLADCHUK
Engineering and Weapons: Capt. DOUGLAS H. RAU
Humanities and Social Sciences: Col KENNETH A. INMAN
Mathematics and Science: Capt. SCOTT S. PUGH
Professional Devt: Capt. RICHARD THAYER

UNIVERSITY OF MARYLAND SYSTEM

3300 Metzerott Rd, Adelphi, MD 20783-1690
Telephone: (301) 445-2740
Fax: (301) 445-4761
E-mail: webnotes@usmd.edu
Internet: www.usmd.edu

Founded 1988 by the merger of the 5 Univ. of Maryland instns and 6 mems of the State Univ. and College System of Maryland
Number of students: 130,000 across 13 instns
Chancellor: Dr WILLIAM ENGLISH KIRWAN.

CONSTITUENT UNIVERSITIES

Bowie State University

14000 Jericho Park Rd, Bowie, MD 20715
Telephone: (301) 860-4000
Internet: www.bowiestate.edu

Founded 1865
Academic year: September to May

Pres.: Dr MICKEY L. BURNIM
Provost and Vice-Pres. for Academic Affairs: Dr PATRICIA P. RAMSEY
Vice-Pres. for External Relations: MAITLAND DADE
Vice-Pres. for Finance and Admin.: Dr KARL B. BROCKENBROUGH

Library of 352,795 vols
Number of teachers: 346 (190 full-time, 156 part-time)
Number of students: 5,415

DEANS

School of Arts and Sciences: Dr COSMAS NWOKEAFOR
School of Business: Dr MATHIAS MBAH
School of Education: Dr VERNON POLITE
School of Graduate Studies and Continuing Education: Dr DIANNE KRECHMAR (acting)
School of Professional Studies: Dr JOYCE BOWLES

CHAIRS OF DEPARTMENTS

School of Arts and Sciences (New Sciences Bldg, Dean's Office 315, 14000 Jericho Park Rd, Bowie, MD 20715; tel. (301) 860-3320; fax (301) 860-3325):
- Communications: Dr CHUCKA ONWUMECHILLI
- Computer Science: Dr SADANAND SRIVASTAVA
- English and Modern Languages: Dr SIDNEY WALKER
- Fine and Performing Arts: Dr CLARENCE KNIGHT
- History and Govt: Dr WILLIAM LEWIS
- Mathematics: Dr NELSON PETULANTE
- Natural Sciences: Dr ELAINE DAVIS

School of Business (Milk Bldg, Dean's Office, Room 301, 14000 Jericho Park Rd, Bowie, MD 20715; tel. (301) 860-3592; fax (301) 860-3644):
- Financial and Economic Accounting: Dr SAMUEL DUAL
- Management Information System: Dr DAVID ANYIWO
- Management, Marketing and Public Admin.: Dr SHELTON RHODES

School of Education (CLT Bldg, Dean's Office, Room 226, 14000 Jericho Park Rd, Bowie, MD 20715; tel. (301) 860-3230; fax (301) 860-3234):
- Counseling: Dr RHONDA JETER
- Educational Leadership: Dr BARBARA JACKSON
- Teaching, Learning and Professional Devt: Dr BARBARA SMITH

School of Professional Studies (CLT Bldg, Dean's Office, Room 321, 14000 Jericho Park Rd, Bowie, MD 20715; tel. (301) 860-4700; fax (301) 860-4702):
- Behavioural Sciences and Human Services: Dr ELLIOTT PARRIS
- Nursing: Dr JOSEPHINE MCCASKELL
- Psychology: Dr CHERYL BLACKMAN
- Social Work: Dr DORIS POLSTON

Coppin State University

2500 W North Ave, Baltimore, MD 21216-3698
Telephone: (410) 951-3000
Fax: (410) 523-7351
E-mail: admissions@coppin.edu
Internet: www.coppin.edu

Founded 1900, part of Univ. of Maryland System
Academic year: August to May

Pres.: Dr REGINALD S. AVERY
Provost and Vice-Pres. for Academic Affairs: Dr SADIE GREGORY
Vice-Pres. for Admin. and Finance: WILLIAM H. FEATHERSTONE
Vice-Pres. for Information Technology: Dr AHMED M. EL-HAGGAN (acting)
Vice-Pres. for Institutional Advancement: JAMES L. ROBERTS (acting)
Vice-Pres. for Student Life: Dr EARL JENKINS
Dir of Institutional Research: Dr OYEBANJO LAJUBUTU
Dir of University Relations: URSULA BATTLE
Dir of Library: Dr MARY E. WANZA
Registrar: Dr MARGARET W. TURNER

Library of 81,742 vols, 286,929 microform titles, 705 current periodicals
Number of teachers: 238
Number of students: 4,200
Publication: *Journal of Minority Affairs* (1 a year)

DEANS

Faculty of Arts and Sciences: Dr JACQUELINE BRICE-FINCH
Faculty of Education: Dr LEONTYE L. LEWIS
Faculty of Graduate Studies: Dr MARY E. OWENS
Faculty of Nursing: Dr MARCELLA A. COPES
Honors College: RON L. COLLINS, Sr

Frostburg State University

101 Braddock Rd, Frostburg, MD 21532
Telephone: (301) 687-4000
Fax: (301) 687-4737
Internet: www.frostburg.edu

Founded 1898

Pres.: Dr JONATHAN C. GIBRALTER
Provost and Vice-Pres. for Academic Affairs: Dr STEPHEN J. SIMPSON
Vice-Pres. for Admin. and Finance: DAVID ROSE
Vice-Pres. for Economic Devt: STEPHEN SPAHR
Vice-Pres. for Student and Educational Services: Dr THOMAS L. BOWLING
Registrar: MORRIS H. WILLEY
Dir of Admissions: PATRICIA E. GREGORY
Dir of the Library: DAVID M. GILLESPIE

Library of 423,782 vols
Number of teachers: 305
Number of students: 5,295

Salisbury University

1101 Camden Ave, Salisbury, MD 21801
Telephone: (410) 543-6000
Fax: (410) 677-5025
Internet: www.salisbury.edu

Founded 1925
Academic year: August to May

Pres.: Dr JANET DUDLEY-ESHBACH
Provost: Dr TOM JONES
Registrar: JACQUELINE M. MAISEL
Vice-Pres. of Business and Finance: GREIG MITCHELL
Vice-Pres. of Student Affairs: Dr ELLEN NEUFELDT
Vice-Pres. for Univ. Advancement: Dr ROSEMARY THOMAS
Dean of Enrollment Management: JANE DANÉ
Dean of Libraries and Instructional Resources: Dr ALICE H. BAHR

Library of 254,151 vols, 4,467 audiovisual items
Number of teachers: 494 (314 full-time, 180 part-time)
Number of students: 6,942
Publication: *Literature/Film Quarterly* (4 a year).

Towson University

8000 York Rd, Towson, MD 21252-0001
Telephone: (410) 704-2000
E-mail: admissions@towson.edu
Internet: www.towson.edu

Founded 1866
Academic year: September to May

Pres.: BOB CARET
Registrar: DAVID DECKER
Dir of Admissions: LOUISE SHULACK (acting)
Provost and Vice-Pres. for Academic Affairs: MARCIA G. WELSH
Vice-Pres. for Admin. and Finance: JAMES SHEEHAN
Vice-Pres. for Student Affairs: DEB MORIARTY
Vice-Pres. for Univ. Advancement: Dr GARY RUBIN
Univ. Librarian: DEBORAH NOLAN

Library of 573,000 vols
Number of teachers: 678
Number of students: 15,105
Publications: *Metropolitan Universities: an International Forum* (4 a year), *Tower*

Echoes (1 a year), *Towson Journal of International Affairs*, *Transitions* (1 a year).

University of Baltimore

1420 N Charles St, Baltimore, MD 21201
Telephone: (410) 837-4200
E-mail: intladms@ubalt.edu
Internet: www.ubalt.edu

Founded 1925

Pres.: ROBERT L. BOGOMOLNY
Provost and Sr Vice-Pres. for Academic Affairs: WIM WIEWEL
Sr Vice-Pres. for Admin. and Finance: HARRY SCHUCKEL
Vice-Pres. for Institutional Advancement: THERESA SILANSKIS
Dir of Library: STEVE LABASH

Library of 400,000 vols
Number of teachers: 167
Number of students: 5,000

DEANS

Robert G. Merrick School of Business: JOHN HATFIELD
School of Law: JOHN SEBENT
Yale Gordon College of Liberal Arts: CARL STENBENG

DEPARTMENT CHAIRS

Robert G. Merrick School of Business:
Accounting: Dr KAREN FOR TIN
Economics and Finance: Dr SINAN CEBENOYAN
Information and Quantitative Sciences: Dr MARILYN OBLAK
Management: Dr SUSAN ZACUR
Marketing: Dr R. STIFF

Yale Gordon College of Liberal Arts:
Criminal Justice: Dr JEFFERY SENSE
English and Communications Design: Dr STEPHEN MATANLE
Govt and Public Admin.: Dr L. THOMAS
History and Philosophy: Dr JEFFERY SAWYER
Psychology: Dr BILL CLEWELL

University of Maryland, Baltimore

522 W Lombard St, Baltimore, MD 21201
Telephone: (410) 706-3100
Internet: www.umaryland.edu

Founded 1807

Schools of dentistry, law, medicine, nursing, pharmacy, social work, Univ. of Maryland Medical System, Univ. of Maryland Graduate School.

Pres.: Dr DAVID J. RAMSAY
Vice-Pres. for Admin. and Finance: JAMES HILL

Library of 613,407 vols
Number of students: 5,975

University of Maryland, Baltimore County

1000 Hilltop Circle, Baltimore, MD 21250
Telephone: (410) 455-1000
Internet: www.umbc.edu

Founded 1963

Academic year: September to May

Pres.: FREEMAN A. HRAQBOWSKI, III
Provost and Sr Vice-Pres. for Academic Affairs: ARTHUR T. JOHNSON
Vice-Pres. for Admin. and Finance: LYNNE SCHAEFER
Vice-Pres. for Institutional Advancement: SHELDON K. CAPLIS
Vice-Pres. for Research and Dean of the Graduate School: SCOTT A. BASS
Vice-Pres. for Student Affairs: CHARLES J. FEY
Gen. Counsel: DAVID GLEASON
Dean of Art, Humanities and Sciences: JOHN W. JEFFRIES

Library of 763,045 vols and 4,108 journals
Number of teachers: 835
Number of students: 10,265

Publications: *Graduate Catalog* (every 2 years), *Undergraduate Catalog*.

University of Maryland, College Park

College Park, MD 20742-5260
Telephone: (301) 405-1000
Fax: (301) 314-9443
Internet: www.umd.edu

Founded 1856
State control
Academic year: September to May

Colleges of agriculture and natural resources; arts and humanities; behavioural and social sciences; computer, mathematical and physical sciences; education; information studies; journalism; life sciences schools: architecture; business; engineering; public health; public policy

Pres.: Dr WALLACE D. LOH
Provost and Sr Vice-Pres. for Academic Affairs: Dr ANN WYLIE
Vice-Pres. for Admin. Affairs: FRANK BREWER
Vice-Pres. for Student Affairs: Dr LINDA M. CLEMENT
Dean of Graduate School: Dr CHARLES CARAMELLO
Registrar: CHUCK WILSON
Dean of Libraries: Dr PATRICIA STEELE

Library of 3,930,013 vols
Number of students: 37,641

DEANS

Agriculture and Natural Resources: Dr CHENG-I WEI
Architecture, Planning and Preservation: DAVID CRONRATH
Arts and Humanities: JAMES HARRIS
Behavioural and Social Sciences: Dr JOHN TOWNSHEND
Business: ANAND ANANDALINGAM
Computer, Mathematical and Natural Sciences: STEPHEN HALPERIN
Education: DONNA WISEMAN
Engineering: DARRYLL PINES
Graduate School: CHARLES CARAMELLO
Information Studies: Dr JENNIFER PREECE
Journalism: KEVIN KLOSE
Public Health: ROBERT GOLD
Public Policy: DONALD KETTL
Undergraduate Studies: DONNA HAMILTON

University of Maryland Eastern Shore

1 Backbone Rd, Princess Anne, MD 21853
Telephone: (410) 651-2200
Fax: (410) 651-6105
Internet: www.umes.edu

Founded 1886

Pres.: Dr THELMA B. THOMPSON
Vice-Pres. for Academic Affairs: Dr CHARLES WILLIAMS
Vice-Pres. for Admin. Affairs: Dr RONNIE HOLDEN
Vice-Pres. for Student Life and Enrollment Management: QUENTIN JOHNSON
Vice-Pres. for Technology and Commercialization: Dr RONALD G. FORSYTHE
Dir of Library: SHELIA BAILEY

Library of 161,000 vols
Number of teachers: 212
Number of students: 3,166

University of Maryland University College

3501 University Blvd, E, Adelphi, MD 20783
Fax: (301) 985-7678
E-mail: umucinfo@info.umuc.edu
Internet: www.umuc.edu

Founded 1947

Pres.: Dr SUSAN C. ALDRIDGE
Provost and Chief Academic Officer: Dr GREG VON. LEHMEN (acting)
Vice-Pres. for Admin. and CFO: GEORGE SHOERBERGER
Vice-Pres. for the Dept of Defense Relations: JOHN F. JONES, Jr
Vice-Pres. and Dir of UMUC Asia: Dr WILLIAM BECK
Vice-Pres. and Dir of UMUC Europe: Dr ALLEN J. BERG
Vice-Pres. and Gen. Counsel: RACHEL E. ZELKIND
Vice-Pres. for Information Technology and Chief Information Officer: J. ROBERT SAPP
Vice-Pres. for the Office of Planning: JAVIER MIYARES

Number of teachers: 2,189 worldwide
Number of students: 90,000 worldwide

DEANS

Graduate Studies: Dr MICHAEL FRANK
Undergraduate Programs: Dr MARIE CINI.

OTHER CONSTITUENT INSTITUTIONS

University of Maryland Biotechnology Institute

9600 Gudelsky Dr., Rockville, MD 20850
Telephone: (240) 314-6000
Fax: (240) 314-6255
Internet: www.umbi.umd.edu

Pres.: JENNIE C. HUNTER-CEVERA.

University of Maryland Center for Environmental Science

POB 775, Cambridge, MD 21613
Telephone: (410) 228-9250
Internet: www.ca.umces.edu

Pres.: Prof. DONALD F. BOESCH.

VILLA JULIE COLLEGE

1525 Greenspring Valley Rd, Stevenson, MD 21153-0641
Telephone: (410) 486-7001
E-mail: admissions@mail.vjc.edu
Internet: www.vjc.edu

Founded 1947
Private control
Academic year: August to May

Pres.: Dr KEVIN J. MANNING
Exec. Vice-Pres. and Chief Financial Officer: TIMOTHY M. CAMPBELL
Vice-Pres. for Academic Affairs and Dean: Dr PAUL D. LACK
Vice-Pres. for Institutional Advancement: STEVENSON W. CLOSE, Jr
Registrar: TRACY R. BOLT
Dir of Library Services: PATTI RICKERT-WILBUR

Library of 100,000 vols
Number of students: 2,410

DIRECTORS

Arts and Humanities: (vacant)
Business and Paralegal Studies: PATRICIA M. TURNBAUGH
Education and Social Sciences: Dr DEBORAH S. KRAFT
Information Technology: STEVEN R. ENGHORN
Nursing and Allied Health: Dr JUDITH A. FEUSTLE
School of Graduate and Professional Studies (Baltimore): Dr JEAN BLOSSER
Science and Mathematics: Dr SUSAN T. GORMAN

WASHINGTON ADVENTIST UNIVERSITY

7600 Flower Ave, Takoma Park, MD 20912
Telephone: (301) 891-4000
Fax: (301) 891-4167
E-mail: info@wau.edu
Internet: www.wau.edu

Founded 1904

Private (Seventh-Day Adventist) liberal arts university

Pres.: Dr WEYMOUTH SPENCE
Provost: SUSAN SCHARFFENBERG
Vice-Pres. for Advancement and Alumni Relations: BRUCE PEIFER
Vice-Pres. for Finance: PATRICK FARLEY
Vice-Pres. for Student Life and Retention: JEAN WARDEN
Registrar: Dr EMILE JOHN
Librarian: LEE WISEL

Library of 127,000 vols
Number of teachers: 47
Number of students: 1,212

Publications: *The Academic Bulletin*, *The Columbia Journal* (2 a year), *Golden Memories*, *Montage* (1 a year), *Reunion* (2 a year).

WASHINGTON BIBLE COLLEGE/ CAPITAL BIBLE SEMINARY

6511 Princess Garden Parkway, Lanham, MD 20706
Telephone: (301) 552-1400
Fax: (301) 552-2775
E-mail: admissions@bible.edu
Internet: www.bible.edu

Founded 1938 by merger of 3 Bible institutes; present name 1956
Private control

Pres.: Dr LARRY A. MERCER
Library Dir: JAMES S. STAMBAUGH

Library of 92,000 items
Number of teachers: 26
Number of students: 670

WASHINGTON COLLEGE

300 Washington Ave, Chestertown, MD 21620-1197
Telephone: (410) 778-2800
Fax: (410) 778-7850
Internet: www.washcoll.edu

Founded 1782

Pres.: BAIRD TIPSON
Provost and Dean of the College: CHRISTOPHER AMES
Sr Vice-Pres. for Finance and Management: JAMES MANARO
Exec. Vice-Pres.: JOSEPH L. HOLT
Vice-Pres. for Admissions and Enrollment Management: KEVIN COVENEY
Vice-Pres. for College Advancement: BETH HERMAN
Vice-Pres. for College Relations and Marketing: MEREDITH DAVIES HADAWAY
Vice-Pres. for Student Affairs and Dean of Students: MELA DUTKA
Registrar: JENNIFER BERSHON
Dir of Library: RUTH SHOGE

Library of 200,000 vols
Number of teachers: 149
Number of students: 1,275

MASSACHUSETTS

AMERICAN INTERNATIONAL COLLEGE

100 State St, Springfield, MA 01109
Telephone: (413) 737-7000
E-mail: inquiry@aic.edu
Internet: www.aic.edu

Founded 1885

Pres.: VINCENT M. MANIACI
Exec. Vice-Pres. for Academics: GREGORY T. SCMUTTE
Exec. Vice-Pres. for Admin.: RICHARD BEDARD
Vice-Pres. for Admissions: PETER J. MILLER
Vice-Pres for Institutional Advancement: JOHN T. SHORT
Registrar: JUDITH SYNER
Librarian: F. KNOWLTON UTLEY

Library of 189,000 vols
Number of teachers: 167 (84 full-time, 83 part-time)
Number of students: 1,350 undergraduates, 539 graduates

DEANS

Arts and Sciences: Dr VICKIE L. HESS
Business Administration: Dr JOHN W. ROGERS
Graduate and Continuing Education: Dr ROLAND E. HOLSTEAD
Health Sciences: Dr CAROL JOBE
Psychology and Education: Dr GREGORY T. SCHMUTTE

AMHERST COLLEGE

Amherst, MA 01002-5000
Telephone: (413) 542-2000
E-mail: info@amherst.edu
Internet: www.amherst.edu

Founded 1821; chartered 1825
Academic year: September to May

Pres.: ANTHONY W. MARX
Dir of Public Affairs: SPETER ROONEY
Registrar: KATHLEEN M. GOFF
Dean of Admission and Financial Aid: THOMAS H. PARKER
Dean of the Faculty: GREGORY S. CALL
Dean of Students: BENSON LIEBER

Library of 1 m. vols, 12,000 video cassettes/ DVDs, 5,000 online and 2,500 print journals
Number of teachers: 194
Number of students: 1,683

Depts of American studies, anthropology and sociology, Asian languages and civilizations, astronomy, biology, black studies, chemistry, classics, economics, English, European studies, fine arts, French, geology, German, history, law, jurisprudence, and social thought, mathematics and computer science, music, neuroscience, philosophy, physical education and athletics, physics, political science, psychology, religion, Russian, Spanish, theater and dance, women's and gender studies.

ANDOVER NEWTON THEOLOGICAL SCHOOL

210 Herrick Rd, Newton Centre, MA 02459
Telephone: (617) 964-1100
Fax: (617) 965-9756
E-mail: admissions@ants.edu
Internet: www.ants.edu
Private control
Academic year: September to May

Founded 1807; attached to Boston Theological Institute

Pres.: Rev. NICK CARTER
Vice-Pres. for Academic Affairs and Dean of the Faculty: WILLIAM R. HERZOG
Vice-Pres. for Finance and Operations: ROBERT MACDONALD
Vice-Pres. for Institutional Advancement: PRISCILLA DECK
Registrar: NAYDA AQUILA
Dirs: S. DIANA YOUNT, JEFFREY L. BRIGHAM

Library of 230,000 vols
Number of teachers: 91
Number of students: 480

ANNA MARIA COLLEGE

50 Sunset Lane Paxton, MA 01612
Telephone: (800) 344-4586
E-mail: admissions@annamaria.edu
Internet: www.annamaria.edu

Founded 1946

Pres.: JACK P. CALARESO
Academic Dean: Dr CYNTHIA M. PATTERSON
Dean of Students: Dr JOSEPH FARRAGHER
Dir of Institutional Advancement: BRIDGET HAVARD
Registrar: Sister ROLLANDE QUINTAL
Library Dir: RUTH PYNE

Library of 95,000 vols
Number of teachers: 150
Number of students: 1,915

Divs of business, law and public policy, environmental, natural and technological sciences, fine arts, humanities and int. studies, human devt and human services.

ASSUMPTION COLLEGE

500 Salisbury St, Worcester, MA 01609-1296
Telephone: (508) 767-7000
Fax: (508) 756-1780
E-mail: admiss@assumption.edu
Internet: www.assumption.edu

Founded 1904
Augustinians of the Assumption (Roman Catholic)
Language of instruction: English
Academic year: September to May

Divs of art and music, business studies, economics and global studies, education, English, modern and classical languages and cultures, history, human services and rehabilitation studies, mathematics and computer science, natural sciences, philosophy, political science, psychology, social and rehabilitation services, sociology and anthropology, theology

Exec. Dir: DAWN THISTLE
Pres.: FRANCESCO CESAREO
Vice-Pres. for Mission: Fr DENNNIS GALLAGHER
Dir of Public Affairs: RENE BUISSON
Provost: FRANCIS LAZARUS
Assoc. Provost: LOUISE CARROLL KEELEY
Registrar: DAVID W. AALTO
Dir of Library Services: DAWN THISTLE

Library of 220,545 vols
Number of teachers: 284
Number of students: 2,724

Publication: *Assumption College Magazine* (4 a year).

ATLANTIC UNION COLLEGE

338 Main St, POB 1000, S Lancaster, MA 01561-1000
Telephone: (978) 368-2000
Fax: (978) 368-2015
E-mail: enrolment@auc.edu
Internet: www.auc.edu

Founded 1882

Depts of art, business, computer science and mathematics, education, English, history, music, natural science, nursing, physical education, religion and theology, social work, vegetarian culinary arts

Pres.: GEORGE BABCOCK
Sr Vice-Pres. for Academic Admin.: BORDES HENRY-SATURNE
Vice-Pres. for Advancement: HEBE SOARES
Vice-Pres. for Enrollment Services: WAYNE DUNBAR
Vice-Pres. for Finance: JAMES SEGAR

Vice-Pres. for Student Services: JOHN F. MENTGES
Registrar: ROGER BOTHWELL
Dir of Library Services: MONICA K. MCCARTER
Library of 119,000 vols
Number of teachers: 53
Number of students: 623

BABSON COLLEGE

231 Forest St, Babson Park, Wellesley, MA 02457-0310
Telephone: (781) 235-1200
Fax: (617) 239-5614
E-mail: ugradadmission@babson.edu
Internet: www.babson.edu
Founded 1919
Pres.: BRIAN M. BAREFOOT
Provost: Dr SHAHID ANSARI
Vice-Pres. for Admin.: MARY ROSE
Dean of Admissions: GRANT GOSSELIN
Vice-Pres. for College Marketing: F. SCOTT TIMMINS
Vice-Pres. for Devt and Alumni Affairs: PETER RAMSEY
Vice-Pres. for Finance: HENRY DENEAULT
Librarian: HOPE N. TILLMAN
Library of 132,024 vols
Number of teachers: 151
Number of students: 3,342

DEANS

Babson Executive Education: ELAINE EISENMAN
F. W. Olin Graduate School of Business: MARK RICE
Undergraduate School: Dr DENNIS HANNO

BARD COLLEGE AT SIMON'S ROCK

84 Alford Rd, Great Barrington, MA 01230
Telephone: (413) 528-0771
Fax: (413) 528-7365
E-mail: admin@simons-rock.edu
Internet: www.simons-rock.edu
Founded 1966
Private control
Academic year: August to May
Pres.: LEON BOTSTEIN
Provost and Vice-Pres.: MARY MARCY
Dean of Academic Affairs: SAM RUHMKORFF
Vice-Pres. for Early College Policies and Programs: U BA WIN
Registrar: HEIDI-BETH ROTHBERG
Library Dir: JOAN GOODKIND
Library of 71,000 items
Number of teachers: 40
Number of students: 400
Divs of arts, languages and literature, science, mathematics and computing, social studies.

BAY PATH COLLEGE

588 Longmeadow St, Longmeadow, MA 01106
Telephone: (413) 565-1000
Fax: (413) 565-1103
E-mail: contact@baypath.edu
Internet: www.baypath.edu
Founded 1897
Private control
Language of instruction: English
Academic year: August to May
Accounting, biology, biotechnology, business administration, child psychology, communications, criminal justice, early childhood education, elementary education, forensic psychology, forensic science, interior design, legal studies, liberal studies, management, marketing, occupational therapy, paralegal, psychology
Pres.: Dr CAROL A. LEARY
Provost and Vice-Pres. for Academic Affairs: Dr MELISSA MORRIS-OLSON
Vice-Pres. for Finance and Admin. Services: MICHAEL GIAMPIETRO
Vice-Pres. for Institutional Advancement: KATHY BOURQUE
Registrar: LAURA K. LANDER
Dir of Library and Information Services: MICHAEL MORAN
Library of 42,300 vols, 150 periodicals, 3,400 items of video, audio, microfilm and CD-ROM
Number of teachers: 68
Number of students: 2,116

BENTLEY COLLEGE

175 Forest St, Waltham, MA 02154
Telephone: (781) 891-2000
Fax: (781) 891-2569
Internet: www.bentley.edu
Founded 1917
Pres.: GLORIA LARSON
Provost and Vice-Pres. for Academic Affairs: ROBERT D. GALLIERS
Vice-Pres. for Business and Finance, and Treas.: PAUL CLEMENTE
Vice-Pres. for Devt, Corporate and Alumni Affairs: ROBERT H. MINETTI
Vice-Pres. for Information Technology: TRACI A. LOGAN
Vice-Pres. for Marketing, Communication and Enrollment: SANDRA T. KING
Vice-Pres. for Student Affairs: KATHLEEN L. YORKIS
Library Dir: PHIL KNUTEL
Library of 192,566 vols
Number of teachers: 271 full-time
Number of students: 3,994 undergraduate, 1,256 graduate
Publication: *Business in the Contemporary World* (4 a year)

DEANS

Arts and Sciences: CATHERINE A. DAVY
Business and the McCallum Graduate School: MARGRETHE H. OLSON

BERKLEE COLLEGE OF MUSIC

1140 Boylston St, Boston, MA 02215-3695
Telephone: (617) 266-1400
Fax: (617) 536-2632
E-mail: admissions@berklee.edu
Internet: www.berklee.edu
Founded 1945 as Schillinger House of Music; present name 1973
Ind. control
Academic year: September to May
Pres.: ROGER BROWN
Sr Vice-Pres. for Academic Affairs: LAWRENCE J. SIMPSON
Sr Vice-Pres. for Admin. and Finance and Sec./Treas.: DAVID R. HORNFISCHER
Sr Vice-Pres. for Institutional Advancement: DEBORAH GROZEN BIERI
Vice-Pres. for Academic Affairs: LARRY A. MONROE
Vice-Pres. for Admin.: JOHN ELDERT
Vice-Pres. for Berklee Media: DAVID KUSEK
Vice-Pres. for Cultural Diversity: MYRA HINDUS
Vice-Pres. for External Affairs: TOM RILEY
Vice-Pres. for Finance: AMELIA KOCH
Vice-Pres. for Information Technology: DAVID S. MASH
Vice-Pres. for Institutional Advancement: DAVID M. MCKAY
Vice-Pres. for Student Affairs and Dean of Students: LAWRENCE E. BETHUNE
Library Dir: GARY HAGGERTY
Library of 20,000 vols, 11,500 recordings, 17,000 musical scores, 6,000 lead sheets
Number of teachers: 460
Number of students: 3,800

DEANS

Music Technology Div.: STEPHEN CROES
Professional Education Div.: LAWRENCE MCCLELLAN, Jr
Professional Performance Div.: MATT MARAVUGLIO
Professional Writing Div.: KARI H. JUUSELA

BLESSED JOHN XXIII NATIONAL SEMINARY

558 South Ave, Weston, MA 02493-2699
Telephone: (781) 899-5500
Fax: (781) 899-9057
E-mail: seminary@blessedjohnxxiii.edu
Internet: www.blessedjohnxxiii.edu
Founded 1964
Private control
Academic year: September to May
Roman Catholic professional and graduate theological instn
Rector and Pres.: Rev. PETER J. UGLIETTO
Academic Dean and Registrar: Rev. WILLIAM B. PALARDY
Dean of Students: Rev. THOMAS F. SCHMITT
Library Dir: Sister JACQUELINE MILLER
Library of 63,000 vols
Number of teachers: 20
Number of students: 73

BOSTON ARCHITECTURAL COLLEGE

320 Newbury St, Boston, MA 02115
Telephone: (617) 262-5000
Fax: (617) 585-0111
E-mail: info@the-bac.edu
Internet: www.the-bac.edu
Founded 1889 as Boston Architectural Club, present name 1944
Private control
Areas of study incl. architecture, interior design, landscape design
Pres.: Dr THEODORE LANDSMARK
Provost: JULIA HALEVY
Exec. Vice-Pres.: JAMES T. DUNN
Vice-Pres. for Finance and Admin.: KATHY ROOD
Dean of Research and Assessment: HERB CHILDRESS
Registrar: ANN ROYALL
Library Dir: SUSAN LEWIS
Library of 45,700 vols, 45,000 slides, 7,000 images
Number of teachers: 485
Number of students: 1,091 (612 undergraduate, 479 graduate)

BOSTON COLLEGE

140 Commonwealth Ave, Chestnut Hill, MA 02467
Newton Campus, 885 Centre St, Newton Centre, MA 02459
Telephone: (617) 552-8000
Fax: (617) 552-0798
Internet: www.bc.edu
Founded 1863 by the Soc. of Jesus
Private control
Academic year: September to May
Pres.: Rev. WILLIAM P. LEAHY
Provost and Dean of Faculty: CUTBERTO GARZA
Exec. Vice-Pres.: P. KEATING
Financial Vice-Pres. and Treas.: PETER C. MCKENZIE
Vice-Pres. for Facilities Management: T. DEVINE
Vice-Pres. for Human Resources: L. SULLIVAN

Vice-Pres. for Information Technology: M. MOORE
Vice-Pres. for Student Affairs: C. PRESLEY
Dir of Libraries: JEROME YAVARKOVSKY

Library of 2,594,750 vols
Number of teachers: 1,215 (full time 737, part time 478)
Number of students: 14,640
Publications: *Boston College Environmental Affairs Law Review* (4 a year), *Boston College International and Comparative Law Review* (2 a year), *Boston College Law Review* (5 a year), *Boston College Third World Law Journal* (2 a year), *Catholic Education: A Journal of Inquiry and Practice*, *Journal of Educational Change*, *Journal of Technology, Learning, and Assessment*, *Learning Disability Quarterly*, *Lonergan Workshop Journal* (1 a year), *Philosophy and Social Criticism* (6 a year), *Religion and the Arts* (4 a year), *The Community, Work and Family Journal*, *The Journal of Corporate Citizenship*, *Uniform Commercial Code Reporter-Digest* (4 a year)

DEANS

College of Advancing Studies: ALBERTO GODENZI
College of Arts and Sciences: PATRICK MANEY
Graduate School of Arts and Sciences: PATRICK MANEY
Graduate School of Social Work: ALBERTO GODENZI
Law School: JOHN H. GARVEY
School of Education: JOSEPH O'KEEFE
School of Management: ANDREW C. BOYNTON
School of Nursing: BARBARA HAZARD

PROFESSORS

College of Arts and Sciences (140 Commonwealth Ave, Chestnut Hill, MA 02467; tel. (617) 552-3270; fax (617) 552-1383):

ANDERSON, J., Economics
ANNUNZIATO, A., Biology
ARNOTT, R., Economics
ASH, A., Mathematics
BAGLIVO, J., Mathematics
BANUAZIZI, A., Psychology
BARTH, J. R., English
BEDELL, K., Physics
BELSLEY, D., Economics
BERGER, P., Fine Arts
BERNAUER, J. W., Philosophy
BLAKE, R., Fine Arts
BLANCHETTE, O., Philosophy
BODENHEIMER, R., English
BOMBOLAKIS, E. G., Geology and Geophysics
BROIDO, D. A., Physics
BROWN, S., Theology
BROWNELL, H., Psychology
BRUCKNER, M. T., Romance Languages
BRUELL, C., Political Science
BUCKLEY, M., Theology
BUNIE, A., History
BURGESS, D., Biology
BYRNE, P. H., Philosophy
CAHILL, L., Theology
CARPENTER, D. E., Romance Languages
CLARKE, M. J., Chemistry
CLEARY, J. J., Philosophy
CLOONEY, F. X., Theology
CLOTE, P., Biology
COBB-STEVENS, R., Philosophy
COX, D., Economics
CRANE, M., English
CRONIN, J., History
DAVIDOVITS, P., Chemistry
DERBER, C., Sociology
DI BARTOLO, B., Physics
DIETRICH, D., Theology
EASTON, R., Psychology
EBEL, J. E., Geology and Geophysics
EGAN, H., Theology
EYKMAN, C., German Studies
FAULKNER, R. K., Political Science
FLANAGAN, J. F., Philosophy
FLEMING, R., History
FOURKAS, J. T., Chemistry
FRIEDBERG, S., Mathematics
GARCIA, J., Philosophy
GOIZUETA, R., Theology
GOLLOP, F. M., Economics
GOTTSCHALK, P., Economics
GRAY, P., Psychology
GROOME, T. H., Theology
GUILLEMIN, J., Sociology
HACHEY, T. E., History
HAFNER, D. L., Political Science
HASKIN, D., English
HEINEMAN, J., History
HEPBURN, J. C., Geology and Geophysics
HERBECK, D., Communications
HESSE-BIBER, S., Sociology
HIBBS, T., Philosophy
HIMES, M., Theology
HOFFMAN, C., Biology
HOLLENBACH, D., Theology
HOLMSTROM, L. L., Sociology
HOVEYDA, A. H., Chemistry
IRELAND, P., Economics
KANTROWITZ, E. R., Chemistry
KARP, D. A., Sociology
KEARNEY, R., Philosophy
KELLY, C. J., Political Science
KELLY, T. R., Chemistry
KEMPA, K., Physics
KENNEDY, T. F., Music
KENNEY, M., Mathematics
KIRSCHNER, D. A., Biology
KRAUS, M., Economics
KREEFT, P. J., Philosophy
LAMB, M., Theology
LANDY, M., Political Science
LEE, T. O., Music
LEWBEL, A., Economics
LEWIS, P., English
LIEM, R., Psychology
LOWRY, R., Sociology
LYDENBERG, R., English
MCFADDEN, D. L., Chemistry
MCLAUGHLIN, L. W., Chemistry
MADIGAN, A., Philosophy
MANNING, R., History
MARIANI, P., English
MATELSKI, M., Communications
MATSON, S., English
MEISSNER, W., Theology
MELNICK, R. S., Political Science
MEYERHOFF, G. R., Mathematics
MICHALCZYK, J., Fine Arts
MILLER, S. J., Chemistry
MUNNELL, A. H., Finance
MUSKAVITCH, M., Biology
NAUGHTON, M., Physics
NETZER, N., Fine Arts
NORTHRUP, D., History
NUMAN, M., Psychology
PARIS, J. J., Theology
PERKINS, P., Theology
PFOHL, S. J., Sociology
PHILIPPIDES, D. M. L., Classics
QUINN, J., Economics
RASMUSSEN, D. M., Philosophy
REEDER, M., Mathematics
REINERMAN, A. J., History
RESLER, M., German Studies
RESTUCCIA, F., English
RICHARDSON, A., English
RICHARDSON, W. J., Philosophy
RINTALA, M., Political Science
ROBERTS, M. F., Chemistry
ROSS, R. S., Political Science
ROY, D. C., Geology and Geophysics
RUSSELL, J. A., Psychology
SARDELLA, D. J., Chemistry
SCHERVISH, P. G., Sociology
SCHIANTARELLI, F., Economics
SCHLOZMAN, K. L., Political Science
SCHOR, J., Sociology
SCHRADER, R., English
SCOTT, L. T., Chemistry
SCOTT-JONES, D., Psychology
SEGAL, U., Economics
SEYFRIED, T., Biology
SHELL, S., Political Science
SHOLL, M. J., Psychology
SMITH, J. H., Mathematics
SMYER, M., Psychology
SNAPPER, M. L., Chemistry
TAMINIAUX, J., Philosophy
TAYLOR, D., English
THIE, P. R., Mathematics
VALETTE, R. M., Romance Languages
VAUGHAN, D., Sociology
WEILER, P., History
WILLIAMSON, J. B., Sociology
WILSON, C. P., English
WILT, J., English
WINNER, E., Psychology
WOLFE, A., Political Science
WOLFF, L., History

Graduate School of Social Work (140 Commonwealth Ave, Chestnut Hill, MA 02467; tel. (617) 552-4020; fax (617) 552-2374):

BLYTHE, B.
GODENZI, A.
IATRIDIS, D. S.
KAYSER, K.
MALUCCIO, A. N.

Law School (885 Centre Street, Newton Center, MA 02459; tel. (617) 552-4340; fax (617) 552-2851):

AULT, H. J.
BARON, C. H.
BLOOM, R. M.
BRODIN, M. S.
BROWN, G. D.
COQUILLETTE, D. R.
CUNNINGHAM, L.
FITZGIBBON, S. T.
GOLDFARB, P.
HILLINGER, I. M.
HOWE, R.-A. W.
KATZ, S. N.
KOHLER, T. C.
MCMORROW, J. A.
PLATER, Z. J. B.
REPETTI, J. R.
ROGERS, J. S.
SOIFER, A.
SPIEGEL, M.
WELLS, C.
WIRTH, D. A.
YEN, A. C.-C.

School of Education (140 Commonwealth Ave, Chestnut Hill, MA 02467; tel. (617) 552-4200; fax (617) 552-0812):

AIRASIAN, P. W.
ALTBACH, P. G.
BLUSTEIN, D.
BRABECK, M. M.
BRISK, M. E.
CASEY, M. B.
COCHRAN-SMITH, M.
DACEY, J. S.
DUDLEY-MARLING, C.
HANEY, W. M.
HARGREAVES, A.
HAUSER-CRAM, P.
HELMS, J. E.
LADD, G. T.
LERNER, J. V.
LYKES, M. B.
MADAUS, G. F.
MULLIS, I. V. S.
PINE, G. J.
PULLIN, D. C.
SHIRLEY, D. L.
STARRATT, R. J.
TWOMEY, E.
WALSH, M. E.
YOUN, E. I. K.

School of Management (140 Commonwealth Ave, Chestnut Hill, MA 02467; tel. (617) 552-8420; fax (617) 552-2593):

BARTUNEK, J., Organization Studies
CAMPANELLA, F. B., Finance
CLOTE, P., Computer Science
CRONIN, M., Operations and Strategic Management
FERSON, W. E., Finance
GIPS, J., Computer Science
GRAVES, S., Operations and Strategic Management
HOLDERNESS, C. G., Finance
KANE, E. J., Finance
MARCUS, A., Finance
NIELSEN, R., Organization Studies
O'BRIEN, C., Business Law
PARKER, F. J., Business Law
RAELIN, J., Operations and Strategic Management
RINGUEST, J., Operations and Strategic Management
RITZMAN, L., Operations and Strategic Management
SAFIZADEH, M. H., Operations and Strategic Management
STRAUBING, H., Computer Science
TAGGART, R., Finance
TEHRANIAN, H., Finance
TORBERT, W. R., Organization Studies
TWOMEY, D. P., Business Law
WADDOCK, S., Operations and Strategic Management
WILSON, G. P., Accounting
WOODSIDE, A., Marketing
WRIGHT, A., Accounting

School of Nursing (140 Commonwealth Ave, Chestnut Hill, MA 02467; tel. (617) 552-4250; fax (617) 552-0745):

BURGESS, A. W.
DUFFY, M. E.
FRY, S. T.
HAWKINS, J. W.
JONES, D. A.
MUNRO, B. H.
ROY, Sr, C.
VESSEY, J. A.
WARDLE, M. G.

BOSTON COLLEGE SCHOOL OF THEOLOGY AND MINISTRY

140 Commonwealth Ave, Chestnut Hill, MA 02467-3800
9 Lake St, Brighton, MA 02135-3841
Telephone: (617) 552-6501
Fax: (617) 552-0811
E-mail: stmadmissions@bc.edu
Internet: www.bc.edu/schools/stm
Founded 2008, by merger of Weston Jesuit School of Theology and Institute of Religious Education and Pastoral Ministry
Private control
Academic year: August to DecemberJanuary to August (2 semesters)
Library of 2,440,000 vols
Dean: RICHARD CLIFFORD
Dir for Admissions: SEAN PORTER.

BOSTON CONSERVATORY

8 The Fenway, Boston, MA 02215
Telephone: (617) 536-6340
Fax: (617) 912-9101
E-mail: admissions@bostonconservatory.edu
Internet: www.bostonconservatory.edu
Founded 1867
Private control
Academic year: September to May
Pres.: RICHARD ORTNER
Dean of the Conservatory: MICHAEL NASH
Vice-Pres. for Admin. Services and Dean of Students: CARMEN GRIGGS
Registrar: GREGORY KARAS
Library Dir: JENNIFER HUNT
Library of 40,000 vols
Number of teachers: 160
Number of students: 500

DIRECTORS

Dance Div.: YASUKO TOKUNAGA
Liberal Arts Dept: JUDSON EVANS
Music Div.: KARL PAULNACK
Theater Div.: NEIL DONOHOE

BOSTON UNIVERSITY

1 Silber Way, Boston, MA 02215
Telephone: (617) 353-2000
Fax: (617) 353-2053
Internet: www.bu.edu
Founded 1839, chartered 1869
Private control
Academic year: September to May (2 semesters), June to August (summer session)
Pres.: ROBERT A. BROWN
Chief of Staff: ELIZABETH GREEN
Provost: DAVID K. CAMPBELL
Exec. Vice-Pres.: JOSEPH P. MERCURIO
Vice-Pres. for Admin. Services: PETER FIEDLER
Vice-Pres. for Auxiliary Services: PETER CUSATO
Vice-Pres. for Devt and Alumni Relations: SCOTT NICHOLS
Vice-Pres. for Enrollment and Student Affairs: LAURIE POHL
Vice-Pres., Chief Financial Officer and Treasurer: MARTIN HOWARD
Vice-Pres. and Gen. Counsel: TODD KLIPP
Vice-Pres. for Global Operations and Deputy Gen. Counsel: WILLIS WANG
Vice-Pres. for Govt and Community Affairs: EDWARD KING
Vice-Pres. for Information Services and Technology: TRACY SCHROEDER
Vice-Pres. for Marketing and Communications: STEPHEN BURGAY
Vice-Pres. for Operations: GARY NICKSA
Vice-Pres. and Assoc. Provost for Research: ANDREI RUCKENSTEIN
Registrar: FLORENCE BERGERON
Dir of Library: ROBERT HUDSON
Library: see Libraries and Archives
Number of teachers: 4,178
Number of students: 32,557
Publications: *Arion*, *Boston University Law Review*, *Journal of Education*, *Journal of Field Archaeology*

DEANS

College and Graduate School of Arts and Sciences: VIRGINIA SAPIRO
College of Communication: TOM FIEDLER
College of Engineering: KENNETH LUTCHEN
College of Fine Arts: BENJAMIN JUAREZ
College of General Studies: LINDA WELLS
Sargent College of Health and Rehabilitation Sciences: GLORIA S. WATERS
Goldman School of Dental Medicine: JEFFREY HUTTER
School of Education: HARDIN COLEMAN
School of Hospitality Admin.: JAMES STAMAS
School of Law: MAUREEN O'ROURKE
School of Management: LOUIS LATAIF
School of Medicine: KAREN ANTMAN
School of Public Health: ROBERT MEENAN
School of Social Work: GAIL STEKETEE
School of Theology: MARY MOORE
Metropolitan College and Extended Education: JAY HALFOND

BRANDEIS UNIVERSITY

415 S St, Waltham, MA 02454-9110
Telephone: (781) 736-2000
Fax: (781) 736-8699
E-mail: admissions@brandeis.edu
Internet: www.brandeis.edu
Founded 1948
Private control
Language of instruction: English
Academic year: August to May
Pres.: Dr FREDERICK LAWRENCE
Provost and Sr Vice-Pres. for Academic Affairs: Dr MARTY WYNGAARDEN KRAUSS
Exec. Vice-Pres. and Chief Operating Officer: JEFFREY APFEL
Sr Vice-Pres. for Communications and External Affairs: ANDREW GULLY
Sr Vice-Pres. of Institutional Advancement: NANCY K. WINSHIP
Asst Vice-Pres. for Students and Enrollments: KEENYN MCFARLANE
Vice-Pres. and Vice-Provost for Libraries and Information Technology: PERRY HANSON
Library of 1,202,159 vols, 55,988 current serial subscriptions, 959,292 microforms, 43,105 audiovisual materials, 352,502 e-books
Number of teachers: 506 (363 full-time, 143 part-time)
Number of students: 5,642 (3,341 undergraduate, 2,301 graduate)

DEANS

Graduate Professional Studies: SYBIL SMITH (Exec. Dir)
Graduate School of Arts and Sciences: Dr MALCOLM WATSON
Heller School for Social Policy and Management: Dr LISA LYNCH
Int. Business School: Dr BRUCE MAGID
School of Arts and Sciences: Dr ADAM JAFFE

BRIDGEWATER STATE COLLEGE

131 Summer St, Bridgewater, MA 02325
Telephone: (508) 531-1000
Fax: (508) 697-1707
Internet: www.bridgew.edu
Founded 1840
Pres.: Dr DANA MOHLER-FARIA
Provost and Vice-Pres. for Academic Affairs: NANCY KLENIEWSKI
Dir of Libraries: MICHAEL A. SOMMERS
Library of 352,500 vols
Number of teachers: 259
Number of students: 8,400

DEANS

School of Arts and Sciences: Dr HOWARD B. LONDON
School of Business: CATHERINE MORGAN
School of Education and Allied Studies: Dr ANNA BRADFIELD
School of Graduate Studies: Dr WILLIAM S. SMITH (acting)

CAMBRIDGE COLLEGE

1000 Massachusetts Ave, Cambridge, MA 02138-5304
Telephone: (617) 868-1000
Fax: (617) 349-3561
E-mail: admit@cambridgecollege.edu
Internet: www.cambridgecollege.edu
Founded 1971
Private control
Academic year: September to August
Founder and Chancellor: EILEEN M. BROWN
Pres.: MAHESH C. SHARMA
Exec. Vice-Pres.: Dr EZAT PARNIA
Vice-Pres. for Academic Affairs: Dr JOSEPH C. REED
Vice-Pres. for College Affairs: Dr JOSEPH DAISY
Vice-Pres. for Finance, Admin. and Student Services: JENNIFER TONNESON
Number of teachers: 718

Number of students: 8,300

DEANS OF GRADUATE STUDIES

Counselling Psychology: Dr NITI SETH
School of Education: Dr ANTHONY DEMATTEO
School of Management: Dr EZAT PARNIA

BRANCH CAMPUSES

Cambridge College California: Suite 100, 337 North Vineyard Ave, Ontario, CA 91764; tel. (909) 635-0250; fax (909) 635-0253; Dir GREGORY WHITE.

Cambridge College Georgia: Suite 1000, Lamar Bldg, 753 Broad St, Augusta, GA 30901; tel. (706) 821-3965; fax (706) 821-3793; Dir SHARLOTTE EVANS.

Chesapeake Campus: Suite 300, 1403 Greenbrier Parkway, Chesapeake, VA 23320; tel. (757) 424-0333; fax (757) 424-1140; e-mail chesapeake@cambridgecollege.edu; Dir JIM WALDMAN.

Lawrence Campus: Lawrence Center, 60 Island St, Lawrence, MA 01840-1835; tel. (978) 738-0502; fax (978) 738-9655; e-mail lawrence@cambridgecollege.edu; Dir DOLORES C. CALAF.

Puerto Rico Center: Suite 1400, Hato Rey Center Building, 268 Ponce de Leon Ave, San Juan, PR 00918; tel. (787) 296-1101; e-mail puertorico@cambridgecollege.edu.

Springfield Campus: 570 Cottage St, Springfield, MA 01104; tel. (413) 747-0204; fax (413) 747-0613; e-mail springfield@cambridgecollege.edu; Dir PATRICIA CRUTCHFIELD.

CLARK UNIVERSITY

950 Main St, Worcester, MA 01610-1477
Telephone: (508) 793-7711
E-mail: admissions@clarku.edu
Internet: www.clarku.edu

Founded 1887
Academic year: September to May

Pres.: DAVID ANGEL
Provost and Vice-Pres. for Academic Affairs: (vacant)
Exec. Vice-Pres.: JAMES E. COLLINS
Vice-Pres. for Govt and Community Affairs: JOHN FOLEY
Vice-Pres. for Planning and Budget: ANDREA MICHAELS
Vice-Pres. for Univ. Advancement: C. ANDREW MCGADNEY
Assoc. Provost and Dean of College: WALTER WRIGHT
Dean of Admissions and Financial Aid: DON HONEMAN
Dean of Graduate Studies and Research: NANCY BUDWIG
Registrar: JANE RENO
Librarian: GWENDOLYNE ARTHUR

Library of 584,350 vols
Number of teachers: 172 full-time
Number of students: 2,115

Publications: *Clark University News*, *Economic Geography*, *Idealistic Studies*.

COLLEGE OF THE HOLY CROSS

1 College St, Worcester, MA 01610
Telephone: (508) 793-2011
Fax: (508) 793-3030
Internet: www.holycross.edu

Founded 1843

Pres.: Rev. MICHAEL MCFARLAND
Sr Vice-Pres.: FRANK VELLACCIO
Vice-Pres. for Academic Affairs and Dean of the College: TIMOTHY R. AUSTIN
Vice-Pres. for Devt and Alumni Relations: MICHAEL PERRY
Vice-Pres. for Student Affairs and Dean of Students: JACQUELINE D. PETERSON
Dir of Library Services: JAMES E. HOGAN

Library of 550,000 vols
Number of teachers: 239
Number of students: 2,790

Depts of African studies, American sign language/deaf studies, Asian studies, biochemistry, biological psychology, biology, chemistry, Chinese, classics, economics and accounting, education, engineering, English, environmental studies, French, German, gerontology studies, graduate studies, history, Italian, Latin American and Latino studies, mathematics and computer science, medieval and renaissance studies, modern languages and literatures, music, naval science (NROTC), peace and conflict studies, philosophy, physics, political science, prebusiness, prelaw, premedical and predental studies, psychology, religious studies, Russian, Russian and Eastern European studies, science coordinator, sociology and anthropology, Spanish, studies in world literature, theatre, visual arts, women's and gender studies

Publications: *Interfaces* (bilingual, illustrated, 2 a year), *Fosforo* (bilingual, literature, art, ideas), *The Holy Cross Journal of Law and Public Policy* (1 a year).

CURRY COLLEGE

1071 Blue Hill Ave, Milton, MA 02186
Telephone: (617) 333-0500
Fax: (617) 333-6860
E-mail: curryadm@curry.edu
Internet: www.curry.edu

Founded 1879 as School of Elocution and Expression; present name 1943
Private control
Academic year: September to May

Pres.: Dr KENNETH K. QUIGLEY, Jr
Vice-Pres. of Academic Affairs: SUSAN W. PENNINI
Dean of Academic Affairs: LISA IJIRI
Registrar: SALLY A. BUCKLEY
Library Dir: JANE LAWLESS

Number of teachers: 76
Number of students: 3,880

Depts of applied technology communication, education, fine and applied arts, humanities, interdisciplinary studies, management, natural sciences and mathematics, nursing, politics and history, psychology, sociology and criminal justice.

EASTERN NAZARENE COLLEGE

23 East Elm Ave, Quincy, MA 02170
Telephone: (617) 745-3700
Fax: (617) 745-3929
E-mail: admissions@enc.edu
Internet: www.enc.edu

Founded 1900
Academic year: September to May

Pres.: Dr CORLIS MCGEE
Vice-Pres. for Academic Affairs: Dr NANCY ROSS
Vice-Pres. for Enrollment: JEFFREY A. WELLS
Vice-Pres. for Finance: PETER CAREY
Vice-Pres. for Student Devt: VERNON WESLEY
Registrar: MEREDITH BAKER
Dir of Library Services: SUSAN WATKINS

Library of 126,465 vols
Number of teachers: 52
Number of students: 1,100

Depts of biology, business, chemistry, communication arts, computer sciences, criminal justice, education, engineering, English, environmental science, general studies, govt, health sciences, history, int. studies, liberal arts, mathematics, movement arts, music, philosophy, physics, pre-law, pre-medical, pre-nursing, pre-physical therapy, psychology, religion, social work, sociology.

ELMS COLLEGE

291 Springfield St, Chicopee, MA 01013-2839
Telephone: (413) 594-2761
Fax: (413) 592-4871
Internet: www.elms.edu

Founded 1928
Liberal arts college

Pres.: Dr JAMES H. MULLEN, Jr
Vice-Pres. for Academic Affairs: Dr WALTER C. BREAU
Vice-Pres. for Finance and Admin.: BRIAN DOHERTY
Vice-Pres. for Institutional Advancement: MARYANNE ROONEY
Vice-Pres. for Student Affairs: DAWN M. ELLINWOOD
Registrar: LAURA LANDER
Dir of Library: PATRICIA BOMBARDIES

Library of 103,000 vols, 684 periodicals
Number of teachers: 68
Number of students: 1,191

Divs of business and law, education, health sciences, humanities and fine arts, natural sciences and mathematics, social sciences.

EMERSON COLLEGE

120 Boylston St, Boston, MA 02116-4624
Telephone: (617) 824-8500
Internet: www.emerson.edu

Founded 1880

Pres.: Dr JACQUELINE W. LIEBERGOTT (acting)
Vice-Pres. and Gen. Counsel: CHRISTINE HUGHES
Vice-Pres. for Academic Affairs: LINDA MOORE
Vice-Pres. for Admin. and Finance: DAVID A. ELLIS
Vice-Pres. for Information Technology: WILLIAM GILLIGAN
Vice-Pres. for Institutional Advancement: DONALD C. MAIN
Vice-Pres. for Public Affairs: DAVID ROSEN
Registrar: WILLIAM F. DEWOLF
Dir of Library: ROBERT FLEMING

Library of 125,000 vols
Number of teachers: 225
Number of students: 3,900

Publications: *Berkeley Beacon* (2 a week), *Emerson Review* (2 a year), *Omnivore* (2 a year)

DEANS

Graduate Studies: DONNA SCHROTH (Dir)
Institute for Liberal Arts and Interdisciplinary Studies: DAVID BOGEN (Dir)
Professional Studies and Spec. Programs: HANK W. ZAPPALA (Dir)
School of Arts: GRAFTON NUNES
School of Communication: JANIS ANDERSEN

EMMANUEL COLLEGE

400 The Fenway, Boston, MA 02115
Telephone: (617) 735-9715
Fax: (617) 735-9801
E-mail: enroll@emmanuel.edu
Internet: www.emmanuel.edu

Founded 1919

Pres.: Sister JANET EISNER
Vice-Pres. for Devt and Alumnae Relations: Sister ANNE DONOVAN (acting)
Vice-Pres. for Finance and Admin.: NEIL BUCKLEY
Vice-Pres. for Govt and Community Relations: SARAH WELSH
Vice-Pres. for Operations and Information Technology: JOHN AVERSA

Vice-Pres. for Programs and Partnerships in Education: Sally Dias
Vice-Pres. of Student Affairs: Patricia Rissmeyer
Library Dir: Dr Susan von Daum Tholl (acting)
Library of 134,000 vols
Number of teachers: 80
Number of students: 1,800
Depts of American studies, art, biology, chemistry and physics, economics, education, English, environmental science, foreign languages, global studies, graduate studies, history, individualized major, information technology, management, mathematics, nursing, performance arts, philosophy, physics, political science, psychology, religious studies, sociology, women's studies

DEANS

Arts and Sciences: Dr Nancy Northrup

EPISCOPAL DIVINITY SCHOOL

99 Brattle St, Cambridge, MA 02138
Telephone: (617) 868-3450
Fax: (617) 864-5385
E-mail: admissions@eds.edu
Internet: www.eds.edu
Private control
Academic year: September to May
Pres. and Dean: Rt Rev. Steven Charleston
Academic Dean: Sheryl Kujawa-Holbrook
Registrar: Lisa Howell
Library Dir: Esther A. Griswold
Library of 232,000 vols
Number of teachers: 22
Number of students: 68 (full-time)
Master of Divinity, MA in Theological Studies, Doctor of Ministry, Certificates in Theological Studies.

FITCHBURG STATE COLLEGE

160 Pearl St, Fitchburg, MA 01420-2697
Telephone: (978) 345-2151
Fax: (978) 665-3693
E-mail: mriccards@fsc.edu
Internet: www.fsc.edu
Founded 1894
Academic year: September to June
Pres.: Dr Robert V. Antonucci
Vice-Pres. for Academic Affairs: Dr Michael Fiorentino, Jr
Vice-Pres. for Finance and Admin.: Sheila Sykes
Library Dir: Robert Foley
Library of 229,000 vols, 478,000 microforms, 1,000 periodicals
Number of teachers: 171
Number of students: 7,000
Depts of behavioural sciences, biology/chemistry, business admin., communications media, computer science, education, English/speech/theater, exercise and sport science, geo/physical sciences, industrial technology, interdisciplinary studies/humanities/music, mathematics, nursing, social science

DEANS

Education: Elaine E. Francis
Graduate and Continuing Education: Catherine Canney

FRAMINGHAM STATE COLLEGE

100 State St, Framingham, MA 01701-9101
Telephone: (508) 620-1220
Fax: (508) 626-4592
E-mail: fscfeedback@framingham.edu
Internet: www.framingham.edu
Founded 1839
Pres.: Dr Timothy J. Flanagan
Vice-Pres. for Academic Affairs: Dr Robert A. Martin
Vice-Pres. for Admin. and Finance: John J. Horrigan
Dean of Students: Susanne H. Conley
Librarian: Bonnie Mitchell (acting)
Library of 344,185 vols
Number of teachers: 290
Number of students: 6,093
Depts of art and music, biology, chemistry and food science, communication arts, computer science, consumer sciences, economics and business admin., education, English, geography, govt, history, mathematics, modern languages, nursing, physics and earth science, psychology and philosophy, sociology.

GORDON COLLEGE

255 Grapevine Rd, Wenham, MA 01984
Telephone: (978) 927-2300
Fax: (978) 524-3704
E-mail: info@gordon.edu
Internet: www.gordon.edu
Founded 1889; merged with Barrington College, RI, 1985
Pres.: R. Judson Carlberg
Provost: Mark L. Sargent
Sr Vice-Pres. for Finance and Admin.: James R. MacDonald
Vice-Pres. for Advancement, Communications and Technology: Dan Tymann
Vice-Pres. for Devt: Robert Grinnell
Vice-Pres. for Enrollment: Silvio Vazquez
Dean of Students: Barry J. Loy
Registrar: Carol Herrick
Dir of Library Services: Myron Schirer-Suter
Library of 190,000 vols
Number of teachers: 75
Number of students: 1,375
Divs of fine arts, education, humanities, natural sciences, mathematics and computer science, social and behavioural sciences.

GORDON-CONWELL THEOLOGICAL SEMINARY

130 Essex St, South Hamilton, MA 01982
Telephone: (978) 646-4300
Fax: (978) 468-6691
E-mail: info@gcts.edu
Internet: www.gordonconwell.edu
Founded 1969 following merger of Conwell School of Theology (f. 1884) and Gordon Divinity School (f. 1889)
Private control
Academic year: September to May
Pres.: Dr Haddon W. Gordon-Conwell
Exec. Vice-Pres.: Robert S. Landrebe
Academic Dean: Barry H. Corey
Dean of Enrollment Management and Registrar: William B. Levin
Dean of Students: Lise Schlueter
Head Librarian: Freeman Barton
Library of 250,000 vols
Number of teachers: 48
Number of students: 986.

BRANCH CAMPUSES

Center for Urban Ministerial Education, Boston Campus: 90 Warren St, Roxbury, MA 02119; tel. (617) 427-7293; fax (617) 541-3432; e-mail cumeinfo@gcts.edu; Dean Dr Alvin Padilla.

Charlotte Campus: 14542 Choate Circle, Charlotte, NC 28273-5596; tel. (704) 527-9909; fax (704) 527-8577; e-mail charinfo@gcts.edu; Dean Dr Sidney L. Bradley.

HAMPSHIRE COLLEGE

893 West St, Amherst, MA 01002
Telephone: (413) 549-5471
Fax: (413) 582-5584
E-mail: admissions@hampshire.edu
Internet: www.hampshire.edu
Founded 1965
Private control
Pres.: Ralph J. Hexter
Vice-Pres. and Dean of Faculty: Aaron Berman
Vice-Pres. for Finance and Admin.: Johan Brongers
Dean of Student Services: R. Michelle Green
Dir of Admissions: Karen S. Parker
Librarian: Gai Carpenter
Library of 111,000 vols
Number of teachers: 100
Number of students: 1,100

DEANS

Cognitive Science: Neil Stillings
Humanities, Arts and Cultural Studies: Susan Tracy
Interdisciplinary Arts: William Brayton
Natural Science: Charlene D'Avanzo
Social Science: Barbara Yngvesson

HARVARD UNIVERSITY

Massachusetts Hall, Cambridge, MA 02138
Telephone: (617) 495-1000
Internet: www.harvard.edu
Founded 1636; charter signed 1650
Academic year: September to June
Pres.: Drew Gilpin Faust
Provost: Dr Steven E. Hyman
Exec. Vice-Pres.: Katherine N. Lapp
Vice-Pres. for Admin.: Tom Vautin
Vice-Pres. for Finance: Dan Shore
Vice-Pres. and Gen. Counsel: Robert Iuliano (acting)
Vice-Pres. for Human Resources: Marilyn Hausammann
Dir of Univ. Library: Robert Darnton
Number of teachers: 12,100 (2,100 non-medical, 10,000 medical)
Number of students: 20,000

DEANS

Faculty of Arts and Sciences: Michael D. Smith
Graduate School of Arts and Sciences: Allan M. Brandt
Harvard Business School: Nitin Nohria
Harvard College: Evelynn Hammonds
Continuing Education and Univ. Extension: Michael Shinagel
Harvard School of Dental Medicine: R. Bruce Donoff
Graduate School of Design: Mohsen Mostafavi
Harvard Divinity School: William A. Graham
Harvard Graduate School of Education: Kathleen McCartney
School of Engineering and Applied Sciences: Cherry A. Murray
Kennedy School of Government: David T. Ellwood
Harvard Law School: Martha Minow
Harvard Medical School: Jeffrey S. Flier
Harvard School of Public Health: Julio Frenk
Radcliffe Institute for Advanced Study: Barbara J. Grosz

PROFESSORS

Faculty of Medicine (Office of the Committee on Admissions, 25 Shattuck St, Boston, MA 02115; tel. (617) 432-1550; e-mail admissions_office@hms.harvard.edu; internet www.hms.harvard.edu):

ABBAS, A. K., Pathology
ABBOTT, W. M., Surgery
ADAMS, D. F., Radiology
ADELSTEIN, S. J., Medical Biophysics
AISENBERG, A. C., Medicine
AKINS, C. W., Surgery
ALBERT, M. S., Psychiatry
ALI, H. H., Anaesthesia
ALONSO, A. W., Psychiatry
ALPER, C., Paediatrics
ALT, F. W., Genetics
ANDERSON, E., Comparative Anatomy
APPLEBURY, M. L., Ophthalmology
ARKY, R., Medicine
ARNAOUT, M. A., Medicine
ARNDT, K. A., Dermatology
ATHANASOULIS, C. A., Radiology
AUSIELLO, D. A., Medicine
AUSTEN, K. F., Medicine
AUSTEN, W. G., Surgery
AUSUBEL, F., Genetics
AVRUCH, J., Medicine
BACH, F., Surgery
BADEN, H., Dermatology
BAIM, D., Medicine
BALDESSARINI, R. J., Psychiatry
BARBIERI, R., Obstetrics, Gynaecology and Reproductive Biology
BARLOW, C. F., Neurology
BARNETT, G. O., Medicine
BARSAMIAN, E. M., Surgery
BARSKY, A. J., III, Psychiatry
BEAL, M. F., Neurology
BEAN, B. P., Neurobiology
BEARDSLEE, W., Psychiatry
BECKWITH, J. R., Microbiology and Molecular Genetics
BELFER, M. L., Psychiatry
BENACERRAF, B. R., Obstetrics, Gynaecology and Reproductive Biology
BENDER, W. W., Biological Chemistry, Molecular Pharmacology
BENES, F. M., Psychiatry
BENJAMIN, T. L., Pathology
BERKOWITZ, R. S., Obstetrics, Gynaecology and Reproductive Biology
BERNFIELD, M., Paediatrics
BERSON, E. L., Ophthalmology
BIEDERMAN, J., Psychiatry
BIGGERS, J., Cell Biology
BIRD, E. D., Neuropathology
BISTRIAN, B. R., Medicine
BLACK, P. M., Neurosurgery
BLENIS, J., Cell Biology
BLOCH, K. J., Medicine
BONVENTRE, J. V., Medicine
BORUS, J. F., Psychiatry
BRADY, T., Radiology
BRANDT, A. M., History of Medicine
BRAUNWALD, E., Medicine
BREAKEFIELD, X. O., Neurology
BRENNAN, T., Medicine
BRENNER, B., Medicine
BRENNER, M. B., Medicine
BREWSTER, D., Surgery
BROTMAN, A. W., Psychiatry
BROWN, E. M., Medicine
BRUGGE, J. S., Cell Biology
BUCHANAN, J. R., Medicine
BUCKLEY, M. J., Surgery
BUNN, H. F., Medicine
BURAKOFF, S. J., Paediatrics
BURGESON, R. E., Dermatology
BURROWS, P. E., Radiology
CANELLOS, G. P., Medicine
CANTLEY, L. C., Medicine
CANTOR, H. I., Pathology
CAPLAN, D. N., Neurology
CAREY, M. C., Medicine
CARPENTER, C. B., Medicine
CASSEM, E. H., Psychiatry
CAVINESS, V. S., Jr, Child Neurology and Mental Retardation
CEPKO, C. L., Genetics
CHABNER, B., Medicine
CHEN, L. B., Pathology
CHIN, W. W., Medicine
CHRISTIANI, D. C., Medicine
CHURCH, G. H., Genetics
CHYLACK, L. T., Jr, Ophthalmology
CLAPHAM, D. E., Neurobiology
CLEARY, P. D., Medical Sociology
CLEVELAND, R. H., Radiology
CLOUSE, M. E., Radiology
COEN, D. M., Biological Chemistry, Molecular Pharmacology
COHEN, B. M., Psychiatry
COHEN, J. B., Neurobiology
COHN, L. H., Surgery
COLDITZ, G. A., Medicine
COLE, J. O., Psychiatry
COLEMAN, C. N., Radiation Oncology
COLES, R., Psychiatry and Medical Humanities
COLLIER, R. J., Microbiology and Molecular Genetics
COLLINS, J. J., Surgery
COLLINS, P., Pathology
COLODNY, A. H., Surgery
COLVIN, R. B., Pathology
COMPTON, C. C., Pathology
COOPER, G. M., Pathology
COREY, D. P., Neurobiology
CORSON, J. M., Pathology
COSIMI, A. B., Surgery
COTRAN, R., Pathology
COYLE, J. T., Psychiatry
CRONE, R., Anaesthesia
CROWLEY, W. F., Jr, Medicine
CRUM, C. P., Pathology
CRUMPACKER, C., Medicine
DAGGETT, W. M., Surgery
D'AMORE, P. A., Ophthalmology
DATTA, S., Anaesthesiology
DAVID, J. R., Medicine
DAVIDOVITCH, Z., Orthodontics
DAVIS, K. R., Radiology
DAWSON, D. M., Neurology
DELBANCO, T., Medicine
DEMLING, R. H., Surgery
DESANCTIS, R. W., Medicine
DESROSIERS, R. C., Microbiology, Molecular Genetics
DEUEL, T. F., Medicine
DEWOLF, W. C., Surgery
DIAMANDOPOULOS, G. T., Pathology
DOGON, I. L., Operative Dentistry
DONAHOE, P. K., Surgery
DONOFF, R. B., Oral and Maxillofacial Surgery
DORF, M. E., Pathology
DORSEY, J. L., Medicine
DORWART, R., Psychiatry
DOUGLASS, C. W., Dental Care Administration
DOWLING, J. E., Ophthalmology
DRAZEN, J. M., Medicine
DRETLER, S. P., Surgery
DRYJA, T. P., Jr, Ophthalmology
DVORAK, A. M., Pathology
DVORAK, H. F., Pathology
DZAU, V. J., Medicine
EARLS, F. J., III, Child Psychiatry
EBERLEIN, T. J., Surgery
EDELMAN, R., Radiology
EISENSTEIN, B., Medicine
EPSTEIN, A., Medicine
EPSTEIN, F., Medicine
ERIKSSON, E., Surgery
EZEKOWITZ, R. A. B., Paediatrics
FEDERMAN, D. D., Medicine and Medical Education
FEIN, R., Medical Economics
FINBERG, R. W., Medicine
FINK, M., Surgery
FISCHBACH, G. D., Neurobiology
FISHMAN, M. C., Medicine
FLEISHER, G. R., Paediatrics
FLETCHER, C., Pathology
FLETCHER, R., Ambulatory Care and Prevention
FLETCHER, S., Ambulatory Care and Prevention
FLIER, J. S., Medicine
FOLKMAN, M. J., Paediatric Surgery
FOSTER, C. S., Ophthalmology
FOX, I. H., Medicine
FRAENKEL, D. G., Microbiology
FRANK, R., Health Economics in Health Care Policy
FREI, E., III, Medicine
FRIED, M. P., Otology and Laryngology
FRIEDMAN, E., Ophthalmology
FRIGOLETTO, F. D., Jr, Obstetrics and Gynaecology
FURIE, B., Medicine
FURSHPAN, E. J., Neurobiology
GALABURDA, A., Neurology and Neuroscience
GALLI, J. J., Pathology
GARNICK, M. B., Medicine
GEHA, R. S., Paediatrics
GELBER, R. D., Paediatrics
GELMAN, S., Anaesthesia
GIMBRONE, M. A., Pathology
GIPSON, I. K., Ophthalmology
GLICKMAN, R. M., Medicine
GLIMCHER, L. H., Medicine
GLIMCHER, M. J., Orthopaedic Surgery
GOETINCK, P. F., Dermatology
GOITEIN, M., Radiation Therapy
GOLDBERG, A. L., Cell Biology
GOLDBERG, I. H., Pharmacology
GOLDHABER, P., Periodontology
GOLDMAN, H., Pathology
GOLDMAN, P., Biological Chemistry and Molecular Pharmacology
GOLDMANN, D. A., Paediatrics
GOLDSTEIN, D. P., Obstetrics, Gynaecology and Reproduction
GOLDWYN, R. M., Surgery
GOOD, B. J., Medical Anthropology
GOOD, M. J. D., Social Medicine
GOODENOUGH, D. A., Anatomy and Cell Biology
GOODMAN, H. M., Genetics
GOYAL, R. K., Medicine
GRAGOUDAS, E., Ophthalmology
GREEN, H., Cell Biology
GREENBERG, M. E., Neurology, Neuroscience
GREENBERG, R. M., Psychiatry
GREENE, R. E., Radiology
GREENES, R. A., Radiology
GRIFFIN, J., Medicine
GRILLO, H. C., Surgery
GRISCOM, N. T., Radiology
GROOPMAN, J. E., Medicine
GROWDON, J. H., Neurology
GRUNEBAM, H. U., Psychiatry
GUNDERSON, J. G., Psychiatry
GUREWICH, V., Medicine
GUSELLA, J. F., Genetics
GUTHEIL, T. G., Psychiatry
HABENER, J. F., Medicine
HABER, E., Medicine
HALES, C. A., Medicine
HALL, F. M., Radiology
HALL, J. E., Orthopaedic Surgery
HANDIN, R. I., Medicine
HARLOW, E. E., Genetics
HARRIS, J. R., Radiation Oncology
HARRIS, N. L., Pathology
HARRIS, W. H., Orthopaedic Surgery
HARRISON, S. C., Biological Chemistry and Molecular Biology
HAUSER, S. T., Psychiatry
HAVENS, L. L., Psychiatry
HAY, D. I., Oral Biology
HAY, E. D., Embryology
HAYES, W. C., Biomechanics
HAYNES, H. A., Dermatology
HEALY, G. B., Otolaryngology
HECHTMAN, H. B., Surgery
HEDLEY-WHYTE, E. T., Pathology
HEDLEY-WHYTE, J., Anaesthesia and Respiratory Therapy

HEMLER, M., Pathology
HENDREN, W. H., III, Paediatric Surgery
HENNEKENS, C. H., Ambulatory Care and Prevention
HERNDON, J. H., Orthopaedic Surgery
HERZOG, D. B., Psychiatry
HIATT, H. H., Medicine
HICKEY, P. R., Anaesthesia
HIROSE, T., Ophthalmology
HIRSCH, M. S., Medicine
HOBSON, J. A., Psychiatry
HOGLE, J. M., Biological Chemistry and Molecular Pharmacology
HOLLENBERG, N. K., Radiology
HOLMES, G. L., Neurology
HOLMES, L. B., Paediatrics
HORTON, E. S., Medicine
HOWLEY, P. M., Comparative Pathology
HUBEL, D. H., Neurophysiology
HUNT, R. D., Comparative Pathology
IEZZONI, L. I., Medicine
INGWALL, J. S., Medicine
INUI, T. S., Ambulatory Care and Prevention
ISSELBACHER, K. J., Medicine
IZUMO, S., Medicine
JACOBSON, A. M., Psychiatry
JAIN, R. K., Radiation Oncology
JAKOBIEC, F. A., Ophthalmology
JANDL, J. H., Medicine
JELLINCK, M. S., Paediatrics
JENIKE, M. A., Psychiatry
JOHNSON-POWELL, G., Child Psychiatry
JOLESZ, F. A., Radiology
JONAS, R., Surgery
JONES, H. R., Neurobiology
JOSEPHSON, M., Medicine
KABAN, L. B., Oral and Maxillofacial Surgery
KAHN, C. R., Medicine
KARCHMER, A. W., Medicine
KARNOVSKY, M. J., Pathological Anatomy
KASPER, D. L., Medicine
KASSER, J. R., Orthopaedic Surgery
KAUFMAN, D. S., Medicine
KAZEMI, H., Medicine
KESSLER, R., Health Care Policy
KHANTZIAN, E., Psychiatry
KHURI, S. F., Surgery
KIEFF, E. D., Medicine
KINET, J. P., Pathology
KING, G. L.
KINGSTON, R., Genetics
KIRSCHNER, M. W., Medicine and Cell Biology
KISSIN, I., Anaesthesia
KITZ, R. J., Research and Teaching in Anaesthetics and Anaesthesia
KLAGSBRUN, M., Surgery
KLEINMAN, A. M., Medical Anthropology
KLIBANSKI, A., Medicine
KNIPE, D. M., Microbiology and Molecular Genetics
KOLODNER, R. D., Biological Chemistry and Molecular Pharmacology
KOLTER, R. G., Microbiology and Molecular Genetics
KOMAROFF, A. L., Medicine
KOSIK, K. S., Neurology
KRANE, S. M., Clinical Medicine
KRAVITZ, E. A., Neurobiology
KRESSEL, H. Y., Radiology
KRIS, A., Psychiatry
KRONENBERG, H. M., Medicine
KUFE, D. W., Medicine
KUNKEL, L. M., Genetics
KUPPER, T., Dermatology
LAING, F. C.
LAMONT, J. T., Medicine
LARSEN, P. R., Medicine
LEBOWITZ, R. L., Radiology
LEDER, P., Genetics
LEFFERT, R. D., Orthopaedic Surgery
LESSELL, S., Ophthalmology
LETVIN, N., Medicine
LEVITON, A., Neurology
LEVITSKY, S., Surgery
LI, F. P., Medicine
LIANG, M., Medicine
LIBBY, P., Medicine
LIBERMAN, M. C., Physiology
LIN, E. C. C., Microbiology and Molecular Genetics
LIPSITT, D. R., Psychiatry
LIVINGSTON, D. M., Medicine
LIVINGSTONE, M. S., Neurobiology
LOCK, J. E., Paediatrics
LOEFFLER, J. S., Radiation Oncology
LOGERFO, F. W., Surgery
LOVEJOY, F. H., Jr, Paediatrics
LOWENSTEIN, E., Anaesthesia
LUX, S. E., IV, Paediatrics
MCCARLEY, R. W., Psychiatry
MCCORMICK, M. C., Paediatrics
MCDOUGAL, W. S., Surgery
MCINTOSH, K., Paediatrics
MACK, J. E., Psychiatry
MCKEON, F. D., Cell Biology
MCLOUD, T. C., Radiology
MCNEIL, B. J., Health Care Policy
MANKIN, H. J., Orthopaedic Surgery
MANNICK, J. A., Surgery
MANSCHRECK, T. C., Psychiatry
MARGOLIES, M. N., Surgery
MARTIN, J. B., Neurology
MARTYN, J. A. J., Anaesthesia
MASLAND, R. H., Neuroscience
MATTHYSSE, S., Psychiatry
MAY, J., Surgery
MAYER, J. E., Jr, Surgery
MAYER, R. J., Medicine
MEKALANOS, J. J., Microbiology and Molecular Genetics
MELLO, N. K., Psychology
MENDELSON, J. H., Psychiatry
MEYER, J. E., Radiology
MIHM, M. C., Jr, Dermatopathology
MILLER, K. W., Anaesthesiology
MIRIN, S. M., Psychiatry
MISHLER, E. G., Social Psychology
MITCHISON, T. J., Cell Biology
MODELL, A. H., Psychiatry
MOELLERING, R. C. Jr, Medical Research
MONACO, A. P., Surgery
MONGAN, J., Health Care Policy
MONTGOMERY, W. W., Otolaryngology
MONTMINY, M., Cell Biology
MOORE, G. T., Ambulatory Care and Prevention
MORGAN, J. P., Medicine
MORRIS, C. N., Health Care Policy
MORSE, W. H., Psychobiology
MORTON, C. C., Obstetrics and Gynaecology
MOSKOWITZ, M. A., Neurology
MULLIGAN, R., Genetics
MURPHY, J. M., Psychiatry
NADELSON, C., Psychiatry
NADLER, L. M., Medicine
NADOL, J. B., Jr, Otolaryngology
NATHAN, D. G., Paediatrics
NEEDLEMAN, H. L., Paediatric Dentistry
NEER, E. J., Medicine
NESSON, H. R., Medicine
NEUTRA, M. R., Paediatrics
NEWBURGER, J. W., Paediatrics
NEWHOUSE, J. P., Health Care Policy
NOTMAN, M. T., Psychiatry
NOVELLINE, R. A., Radiology
OJEMANN, R. G., Surgery
OLSEN, B. R., Anatomy
ORKIN, S. H., Paediatrics
PALFREY, J. S., Paediatrics
PARRISH, J. A., Dermatology
PAUL, D. L., Neurobiology
PENNEY, J. B., Jr, Neurology
PEPPERCORN, M. A., Medicine
PERRIMON, N., Genetics
PFEFFER, M. A., Medicine
PIER, G. B., Pathology
PINKUS, G. S., Pathology
PIZZO, P., Paediatrics
PLATT, O., Paediatrics
PLOEGH, H. L., Pathology
PODOLSKY, D. K., Medicine
POSS, R., Orthopaedic Surgery
POTTER, D. D., Neurobiology
POTTS, J. T., Jr, Clinical Medicine
POUSSAINT, A. F., Psychiatry
RABKIN, M. T., Medicine
RANDO, R. R., Biological Chemistry and Molecular Pharmacology
RAO, A., Pathology
RAPOPORT, T. A., Cell Biology
RAVIOLA, E., Neurobiology
REICH, P., Psychiatry
REID, L., Pathology
REINHERZ, E. L., Medicine
REMOLD, H. G., Medicine
REPPERT, S. M., Paediatrics
RETIK, A. B., Surgery
RICHARDSON, C. C., Biological Chemistry and Molecular Pharmacology
RICHIE, J. P., Surgery
RIORDAN, J. F., Biochemistry
RITZ, J., Medicine
ROBERTS, T. M., Pathology
ROBINSON, D. R., Medicine
ROSEN, F. S., Paediatrics
ROSEN, S. S., Pathology
ROSENBERG, R. D., Medicine
ROSENBLATT, M., Molecular Medicine
ROSENTHAL, D. I., Radiology
ROSENTHAL, D. S., Medicine
ROSNER, B. A., Medicine
ROTHENBERG, A., Psychiatry
RUDERMAN, J. V., Anatomy and Cell Biology
RUSSELL, P. S., Surgery
RUVKUN, G. B., Genetics
SACHS, B. P., Obstetrics, Gynaecology and Reproductive Medicine
SACHS, D. H., Surgery
SAITO, H., Biological Chemistry and Molecular Pharmacology
SALLAN, S. E., Paediatrics
SALZMAN, C., Psychiatry
SAMUELS, M. A., Neurology
SAPER, C. B., Neurology
SCHIFF, I., Gynaecology
SCHILDKRAUT, J. J., Psychiatry
SCHLOLLSMAN, S. F., Medicine
SCHNEEBERGER, E. E., Pathology
SCHNIPPER, L. E., Medicine
SCHOEN, F. J., Pathology
SCHUR, P. H., Medicine
SCOTT, R. M., Surgery
SEED, B., Genetics
SEIDMAN, C. E., Medicine
SEIDMAN, J. G., Genetics
SELKOE, D. J., Neurology
SELMAN, R. L., Psychology
SELTZER, S. E., Radiology
SELWYN, A., Medicine
SERHAN, C. N., Anaesthesia
SHANNON, D. C., Paediatrics
SHEFFER, A. L., Medicine
SHIPLEY, W. U., Radiation Therapy
SHKLAR, G., Oral Pathology
SHORE, M. F., Psychiatry
SIDMAN, R. L., Neuropathology
SILBERT, J. E., Medicine
SILEN, W., Surgery
SILVER, P. A., Biological Chemistry and Molecular Pharmacology
SIMEONE, J. F., Radiology
SIMON, B., Psychiatry
SKILLMAN, J. J., Surgery
SKLAR, J. L., Pathology
SLEDGE, C. B., Orthopaedic Surgery
SMITH, A. R., Radiation Oncology
SOBER, A. J., Dermatology
SODROSKI, J. G., Pathology
SONIS, S. T., Oral Medicine and Oral Pathology
SOUBA, W. W., Surgery
SPEALMAN, R. D., Psychobiology
SPECTOR, M., Orthopaedic Surgery
SPEIZER, F. E., Medicine

SPIEGELMAN, B. M., Biological Chemistry and Molecular Pharmacology
SPIRO, R. G., Biological Chemistry
SPRINGER, T. A., Pathology
STEER, M. L., Surgery
STEINMAN, T. I., Medicine
STERN, R. S., Dermatology
STILES, C. D., Microbiology and Molecular Genetics
STONE, A. A., Law and Psychiatry
STOSSEL, T. P., Medicine
STREILEIN, J. W., Ophthalmology
STREWLER, G. J., Medicine
STRICHARTZ, G. R., Anaesthesia
STROM, T. B., Medicine
STRUHL, K., Biological Chemistry and Molecular Pharmacology
SUIT, H. D., Radiation Oncology
SUKHATME, V. P., Medicine
SWARTZ, M. N., Medicine
SZOSTAK, J. W., Genetics
TABIN, C. J., Genetics
TASHJIAN, A. H., Jr, Biological Chemistry and Molecular Pharmacology
TAUBMAN, M. A., Oral Biology
TAYLOR, G. A., Radiology
TERHORST, C. P., Medicine
THIBAULT, G. E., Medicine
THIER, S. O., Medicine and Health Care Policy
THRALL, J. H., Radiology
TILNEY, N. L., Surgery
TOMKINS, R. G., Surgery
TOSTESON, D. C., Cell Biology
TREVES, S. T., Radiology
TSUANG, M. T., Psychiatry
TYLER, H. R., Neurology
UTIGER, R. D., Medicine
VACANTI, J. P., Surgery
VAILLANT, G. E., Psychiatry
VAN PRAAGH, R., Pathology
VOLPE, J. J., Neurology
WAGNER, G., Biological Chemistry and Molecular Pharmacology
WALKER, W. A., Nutrition and Paediatrics
WALSH, C. T., Biological Chemistry and Molecular Pharmacology
WARSHAW, A. L., Surgery
WEINBERG, A. N., Medicine
WEINBERGER, S. E., Medicine
WEINBLATT, M. E., Medicine
WEINER, H. L., Neurology
WEINSTEIN, H. J., Paediatrics
WEINSTEIN, M. C., Medicine
WEIR, G. C., Medicine
WEISS, S. T., Medicine
WEISSMAN, B. N., Radiology
WELLER, P. F., Medicine
WEYMAN, A. E., Medicine
WHITE, A. A., III, Orthopaedic Surgery
WHITTEMORE, A., Surgery
WILLETT, W. C., Medicine
WILLIAMS, G. H., Medicine
WILMORE, D. W., Surgery
WILSON, T. H., Cell Biology
WINKELMAN, J. W., Pathology
WINSTON, F. M., Genetics
WITTENBERG, J., Radiology
WOHL, M. E., Paediatrics
WOLF, G. L., Radiology
WOLF, M. A., Medicine
WOLFF, C., Anaesthesia
WOLFF, P. H., Psychiatry
WRAY, S. H., Neurology
YARMUSH, M., Surgery
YOUNG, A. B., Neurology
YOUNG, R. H., Pathology
YUNIS, E. J., Pathology
ZAPOL, W. M., Anaesthesia
ZERVAS, N. T., Neurosurgery
ZETTER, B. R., Surgery
ZINNER, M., Surgery

Graduate School of Arts and Sciences (University Hall, Cambridge, MA 02138; tel. (617) 495-1566; internet www.fas.harvard.edu):

ABERNATHY, F. H., Mechanical Engineering
ALESINA, A., Economics and Government
ALEXIOU, M., Modern Greek Studies, Comparative Literature
ALT, J. E., Government
ANDERSON, D., Applied Mathematics
ANDERSON, J. G., Atmospheric Chemistry
ASHTON, P. S., Forestry
AZIZ, M., Materials Science
BARANCZAK, S., Polish Language and Literature
BAR-YOSEF, O., Prehistoric Archaeology
BATES, R. H., Government
BAZZAZ, F. A., Biology
BENHABIB, S., Government
BENSON, L. D., English Literature
BERCOVITCH, S., English and American Literature and Language, Comparative Literature
BERG, H. C., Molecular and Cellular Biology, Physics
BIAGIOLI, M., History of Science
BIEWENER, A., Biology
BISSON, T. N., Medieval History
BLACKBOURN, D., History
BLIER, S., History of Art and Architecture
BLOXHAM, J., Geophysics
BOBO, L., Sociology and Afro-American Studies
BOIS, Y.-A., Modern Art
BOL, P., Chinese History
BOLITHO, H., Japanese History
BOSS, K. J., Biology
BOSSERT, W. H., Science
BOTT, R., Mathematics
BOYM, S., Slavic Languages and Literatures, Comparative Literature
BRANDT, A., History of Science
BRANTON, D., Biology
BRINKMANN, R., Music
BROCKETT, R. W., Electrical Engineering and Computer Science
BRYSON, W., History of Art and Architecture
BUELL, L., English
BURGARD, P., German
BUTLER, J. N., Applied Chemistry
CAMERON, A., Astrophysics
CAMPBELL, J. Y., Applied Economics
CARAMAZZA, A., Psychology
CATON, S., Contemporary Arab Studies
CAVANAGH, P., Psychology
CAVANAUGH, C., Biology
CAVES, R. E., Political Economy
CHAMBERLAIN, G., Economics
CHANDRA, P., Indian and South Asian Art
CHEATHAM, T. E., Computer Science
COATSWORTH, J., Latin American Affairs
COELHO, J.-F., Portuguese Language and Literature, Comparative Literature
COHEN, L., History
COLEMAN, K., Latin
COLEMAN, S. R., Science
COLTON, T., Government and Russian Studies
CONLEY, T., Romance Languages and Literature
COOPER, R., International Economics
COREY, E. J., Organic Chemistry
COTT, N. F., History
CRAIG, A. M., History
CRANSTON, E. A., Japanese Literature
CROMPTON, A. W., Natural History
CUTLER, D., Economics
DAMROSCH, L., Literature
DAVIDOVSKY, M., Music
DAWSON, M., Government
DEMPSTER, A. P., Theoretical Statistics
DEVORE, B. I., Biological Anthropology
DOMINGUEZ, J. I., International Affairs
DONOGHUE, D., English and American Literature and Language
DONOGHUE, M., Biology
DOWLING, J., Natural Sciences
DUFFY, J., Byzantine Philology and Literature

DZIEWONSKI, A. M., Science
ECK, D. L., Comparative Religion and Indian Studies
ECKERT, C., Korean History
EHRENREICH, H., Science
EKSTROM, G., Geology and Geophysics
ELKIES, N., Mathematics
ELLISON, P., Anthropology
ENGELL, J., English and Comparative Literature
EPPS, B., Romance Languages and Literature
ERIKSON, R. L., Cellular and Developmental Biology
EVANS, A., Materials Engineering
EVANS, D. A., Chemistry
FANGER, D. L., Literature
FARRELL, B., Meteorology
FASH, W., Central American and Mexican Archaeology and Ethnology
FELDMAN, G., Science
FELDSTEIN, M. S., Economics
FERGUSON, N., History
FERNANDEZ-CIFUENTE, L., Romance Languages and Literatures
FIDO, F., Romance Languages and Literatures
FIELD, G. B., Applied Astronomy
FISHER, D., Physics
FISHER, P. J., English and American Literatures
FLEMING, D. H., American History
FLIER, M., Ukrainian Philology
FORD, P., Celtic Languages and Literatures
FRANKLIN, M., Physics
FREEMAN, R. B., Economics
FRIEDEN, J., Government
FRIEDMAN, B. M., Political Economy
FRIEND, C., Chemistry
FUDENBERG, D., Economics
GABRIELSE, G., Physics
GALISON, P., History of Science and of Physics
GARBER, M., English
GATES, H., Humanities
GAYLORD, M., Romance Languages and Literatures
GELBART, W. M., Molecular and Cellular Biology
GEORGI, H. M., Physics
GIENAPP, W., History
GILBERT, D., Psychology
GILBERT, W.
GLASHOW, S. L., Physics
GLAUBER, R. J., Physics
GOLDFARB, W., Modern Mathematics and Mathematical Logic
GOLDIN, C., Economics
GOLOVCHENKO, J., Physics
GORDON, A., History
GORDON, R. G., Chemistry
GRABOWICZ, G. G., Ukrainian Literature
GRAHAM, W. A., History of Religion and Islamic Studies
GREEN, J. R., Political Economy
GREENBLATT, S., English and American Literature and Language
GRILICHES, Z., Economics
GRINDLAY, J. E., Astronomy
GROSS, B. H., Mathematics
GROSZ, B., Computer Science
GUIDOTTI, G., Biochemistry
GUILLORY, J., English
GUTHKE, K. S., German Art and Culture
GUZZETTI, A. F., Visual Arts
HACKMAN, J., Social and Organizational Psychology
HALL, P., Government
HALPERIN, B. I., Mathematics and Natural Philosophy
HANKINS, J., History
HARDACRE, H., Japanese Religions and Society
HARRINGTON, A., History of Science
HARRINGTON, J. J., Environmental Engineering

HARRIS, J. C., English and Folklore
HARRIS, J. D., Mathematics
HARRIS, J. M., Jewish Studies
HARRISON, S. C., Biochemistry and Molecular Biology
HART, O., Economics
HARTL, D., Biology
HASTINGS, J., Natural Sciences
HEIMERT, A. E., American Literature
HEINRICHS, W. P., Arabic
HELLER, E., Physics
HELPMAN, E., Economics
HENRICHS, A. M., Greek Literature
HERSCHBACH, D. R., Science
HERZFELD, M., Anthropology
HIGGINBOTHAM, E. B., Afro-American Studies, History
HIGONNET, P. L.-R., French History
HO, Y. C., Engineering and Applied Mathematics
HOFFMAN, P., Geology
HOFFMANN, S. H.
HOLLAND, H. D., Geology
HOLM, R. H., Chemistry
HOOLEY, J., Psychology
HOROWITZ, P., Physics
HOWE, R., Engineering
HUEHNERGARD, J. D., Semitic Philology
HUTCHINSON, J. W., Applied Mechanics
HUTH, J., Physics
IRIYE, A., American History
JACOB, D., Atmospheric Chemistry, Environmental Engineering
JACOBSEN, E., Chemistry
JACOBSEN, S. B., Geochemistry
JAFFE, A. M., Mathematics and Theoretical Science
JARDINE, A., Romance Languages and Literatures
JASANOFF, J., Linguistics
JENKINS, F., Zoology and Biology
JOHNSON, B., Law and Psychiatry in Society
JONES, C. P., Classics and History
JONES, R. V., Applied Physics
JORGENSON, D. W., Economics
KAFADAR, C., Turkish Studies
KAGAN, J., Psychology
KAISER, W. J., English and Comparative Literature
KALAVREZOU, I., Byzantine Art
KATZ, L., Economics
KAZHDAN, D., Mathematics
KEENAN, E. L., History
KELLY, T., Music
KELMAN, H. C., Social Ethics
KIELY, R. J., English
KILLIP, C., Visual and Environmental Studies
KILSON, M. L., Government
KING, G., Government
KIRBY, W., History
KIRSHNER, R. P., Astronomy
KISHLANSKY, M., History
KLECKNER, N., Biochemistry and Molecular Biology
KLEINMAN, A. M., Medical Anthropology
KLEMPERER, W. A., Chemistry
KNOLL, A., Biology
KOERNER, J., History of Art and Architecture
KORNAI, J., Economics
KORSGAARD, C., Philosophy
KOSSLYN, S. M., Psychology
KRONAUER, R. E., Mechanical Engineering
KRONHEIMER, P., Mathematics
KUGEL, J. L., Classical and Modern Jewish and Hebrew Literature and Comparative Literature
KUHN, P. A., History and East Asian Languages and Civilizations
KUNG, H., Electrical Engineering and Computer Science
KUNO, S., Linguistics
LAMBERG-KARLOVSKY, C. C., Archaeology and Ethnology
LANGER, E. J., Psychology
LEE, L., Chinese Literature
LEVIN, R., Music
LEVINE, N., History of Art and Architecture
LEWALSKI, B., History and Literature, English Literature
LEWIN, D. B., Music
LEWIS, H. R., Computer Science
LEWONTIN, R. C., Biology
LIEBER, C., Chemistry
LIEBERSON, S., Sociology
LIEM, K., Ichthyology
LOCKWOOD, L. H., Music
LOEB, A., Astronomy
LOSICK, R. M., Biology
MCCANN, D., Korean Literature
MCCARTHY, J. J., Biological Oceanography
MCCORMICK, M., History
MCDONALD, C., Romance Languages and Literatures
MCELROY, M. B., Environmental Studies
MACFARQUHAR, R., History and Political Science
MACHINIST, P., Hebrew and Other Oriental Languages
MCMAHON, A., Molecular and Cellular Biology
MCMAHON, T. A., Applied Mechanics and Biology
MCMULLEN, C., Mathematics
MCNALLY, R., Personality Psychology
MAHER, B. A., Psychology of Personality
MAIER, C. S., European Studies
MALMSTAD, J., Slavic Languages and Literatures
MANIATIS, T. P., Molecular and Cellular Biology
MANKIW, N. G., Economics
MANSFIELD, H. C., Government
MARGLIN, S. A., Economics
MARSDEN, P. V., Sociology
MARTIN, L., Government
MARTIN, P. C., Pure and Applied Physics
MASKIN, E. S., Economics
MAY, E. R., American History
MAYBURY-LEWIS, D. H., Anthropology
MAZUR, B., Mathematics
MAZUR, E., Physics
MEDOFF, J. L., Labour and Industry
MEISTER, M., Molecular and Cellular Biology
MELTON, D. A., Molecular and Cellular Biology
MENDELSOHN, E. I., History of Science
MESELSON, M. S., Natural Sciences
MITCHELL, R., Applied Biology
MITCHELL, S. A., Scandinavian and Folklore
MITTEN, D. G., Classical Art and Archaeology
MORALEJO, S., Fine Arts
MORAN, R., Philosophy
MORRIS, C., Statistics
MOTTAHEDEH, R., History
MURDOCH, J. E., History of Science
MYERS, A., Chemistry and Chemical Biology
NAGY, G. J., Classical Greek Literature and Comparative Literature
NAKAYAMA, K., Psychology
NARAYAN, R., Astronomy
NECIPOGLU, G., Islamic Art
NELSON, D. R., Physics
NOZICK, R., Philosophy
O'CATHASAIGH, T., Irish Studies
O'CONNELL, R. J., Geophysics
OETTINGER, A., Applied Mathematics, Information Resources Policy
OWEN, E., Middle East History
OWEN, S.
OZMENT, S. E., Ancient and Modern History
PALUMBI, S., Biology
PARK, K., History of Science, Women's Studies
PARSONS, C., Philosophy
PATTERSON, O., Sociology
PAUL, W., Applied Physics
PEARSALL, D. A., English Literature
PEDERSON, S., History
PERALTA, E., Molecular Neurobiology
PERKINS, D. H., Political Economy
PERRY, E., Government
PERSHAN, P. S., Applied Physics
PERTILE, L., Romance Languages and Literature, Comparative Literature
PETERSON, P., Government
PFISTER, D. H., Systematic Botany
PHARR, S. J., Japanese Politics
PIERCE, N., Biology
PIERSON, P., Government
PILBEAM, D. R., Social Sciences
PINNEY, G., Classical Archaeology and Art
PRENTISS, M., Physics
PRESS, W. H., Astronomy, Physics
PUTNAM, H. W.
PUTNAM, R. D., Political Science
RABIN, M. O., Computer Science
RANDS, B., Music
RENTSCHLER, E., German
RESKIN, B., Sociology
RICE, J. R., Engineering Sciences and Geophysics
ROBERTSON, E., Molecular and Cellular Biology
ROBINSON, A. R., Geophysical Fluid Dynamics
ROGERS, P. P., Environmental Engineering
ROSEN, S., National Security and Military Affairs
ROSENTHAL, R., Social Psychology
RUBIN, D. B., Statistics
RUBIN, J., Japanese Humanities
RUDENSTINE, N., English and American Literature and Language
RUSSELL, J., Armenian Studies
RUVOLO, M., Anthropology
RYAN, J. L., German and Comparative Literature
SACKS, G. E., Mathematical Logic
SACKS, P., English and American Literature and Language
SANDEL, M. J., Government
SCANLON, T., Natural Religion, Moral Philosophy and Civil Policy
SCARRY, E., Aesthetics and the General Theory of Value
SCHACTER, D., Psychology
SCHMID, W., Mathematics
SCHOR, N., Romance Languages and Literature
SCHREIBER, S. L., Chemistry
SEGAL, C., Classics
SEN, A., Economics, Philosophy
SEPTIMUS, B., Jewish History and Sephardic Civilization
SHAKHNOVICH, E., Chemistry and Chemical Biology
SHAPIRO, I. I.
SHEARMAN, J.
SHELEMAY, K., Music
SHELL, M., English and Comparative Literature
SHEPSLE, K., Government
SHIEBER, S., Computer Science
SHLEIFER, A., Economics
SILVERA, I. F., Natural Sciences
SIMON, E., Germanic Languages and Literature
SIU, Y. T., Mathematics
SKJAERVO, P., Iranian
SKOCPOL, T. R., Government, Sociology
SOLBRIG, O. T., Biology
SOLLORS, W., English Literature, Afro-American Studies
SOMMER, D., Romance Languages and Literatures
SØRENSEN, A. B., Sociology
SPAEPEN, F. A., Applied Sciences
STAGER, L., Archaeology of Israel
STEINKELLER, P., Assyriology
STERNBERG, S. Z., Mathematics

STEVENS, P. F., Biology
STILGOE, J. R., History of Landscape
STONE, H. A., Applied Mathematics, Chemical Engineering
STONE, P. J., Psychology
STROMINGER, J. L., Biochemistry
SULEIMAN, S. R., Civilization of France, Comparative Literature
SZPORLUK, R., Ukrainian History
TAI, H., Sino-Vietnamese History
TAMBIAH, S. J., Anthropology
TARRANT, R. J., Latin Language and Literature
TATAR, M. M., German
TAUBES, C. H., Mathematics
TAYLOR, R. L., Mathematics
THERNSTROM, S., History
THOMAS, R., Greek and Latin
THOMPSON, D., Political Philosophy
TINKHAM, M., Physics
TODD, W. M., Slavic Languages and Literatures, Comparative Literature
TOMLINSON, P. B., Biology
TROMP, J., Geophysics
TU, W.-M., Chinese History and Philosophy
TUCK, R., Government
ULRICH, L., Early American History
VAFA, C., Physics
VAIL, H., History
VALIANT, L. G., Computer Science and Applied Mathematics
VAN DER KUIJP, L., Tibetan and Himalayan Studies
VAN DER MERWE, N. J., Scientific Archaeology
VENDLER, H.
VERBA, S.
VERDINE, G., Bio- and Organic Chemistry
VOGEL, E. F., Social Sciences
WANG, J. C., Biochemistry and Molecular Biology
WARREN, K., Anthropology
WATERS, M., Sociology
WATKINS, C. W., Linguistics and Classics
WATSON, J., Chinese Society
WEITZMAN, M., Economics
WESTERVELT, R., Physics
WHITE, S. H., Psychology
WHITESIDES, G. M., Chemistry
WILLIAMSON, J. G., Economics
WILSON, R., Physics
WINSHIP, C., Sociology
WINTER, I. J., Fine Arts
WISSE, R., Yiddish Literature and Comparative Literature
WITZEL, E., Sanskrit
WOFSEY, S., Atmospheric and Environmental Studies
WOLFF, C., Music
WOMACK, J., Latin American History and Economics
WOOLLACOTT, R. M., Biology
WRANGHAM, R., Anthropology
WU, T. T., Applied Physics
YALMAN, N. O., Social Anthropology and Middle Eastern Studies
YANG, W., Electrical Engineering and Computer Science
YAU, S., Mathematics
ZIOLKOWSKI, J., Medieval Latin and Comparative Literature

Graduate School of Design (Office of Admissions, 419 Gund Hall, 48 Quincy St, Cambridge, MA 02138; tel. (617) 495-5453; e-mail admissions@gsd.harvard.edu; internet www.gsd.harvard.edu):

ALTSHULER, A., Urban Policy and Planning
BAIRD, G., Architecture
FORMAN, R. T. T., Landscape Ecology
GOMEZ-IBAÑEZ, J. A., Urban Planning and Public Policy
HARGREAVES, G., Landscape Architecture
HAYS, M., Architectural Theory
KOOLHAAS, R., Architecture and Urban Design
KRIEGER, A., Urban Design
MACHADO, R., Architecture and Urban Design
MONEO, J. R., Architecture
MORI, T., Architecture
PEISER, R., Real Estate Development
POLLALIS, S. N., Design Technology and Management
ROWE, P. G., Architecture and Urban Design
SCHODEK, D. L., Architectural Technology
SILVETTI, J. S., Architecture
SMITH, C., Architectural History
STEINITZ, C. F., Landscape Architecture and Planning
STILGOE, J. R., History of Landscape Development
VAN VALKENBURGH, M., Landscape Architecture
VIGIER, F. C., Regional Planning

Graduate School of Education (Admissions, 111 Longfellow Hall, Cambridge, MA 021388; tel. (617) 495-3414; e-mail gseadmissions@harvard.edu; internet www.gse.harvard.edu/admissions):

CHAIT, R.
DUCKWORTH, E. R.
ELGIN, C. Z.
ELMORE, R. F.
FISCHER, K. W.
GARDNER, H. E.
HARRIS, P.
JOHNSON, S. M.
JUEL, C.
KORETZ, D.
LAWRENCE-LIGHTFOOT, S.
LIGHT, R. J.
MCCARTNEY, K.
MURNANE, R.
MURPHY, J. T.
ORFIELD, G., Education and Social Policy
PERKINS, D.
REUBEN, J.
SELMAN, R. L.
SINGER, J. D.
SNOW, C. E.
SUÁREZ-OROZCO, M.
WILLETT, J. B.

Harvard Business School (Communications Office, Harvard Business School, Soldiers Field, Boston, MA 02163; tel. (617) 495-6000; e-mail news@hbs.edu; internet www.hbs.edu):

AMABILE, T. M., Entrepreneurial Management
APPLEGATE, L. M., General Management
AUSTIN, J. E., Business, Government and International Economy
BADARACCO, J. L., General Management
BAKER, G. P., III, Organizations and Markets
BALDWIN, C. Y., Organizations and Markets
BARTLETT, C. A., General Management
BARTON, D. A., Technology and Operations Management
BEER, M., Organizational Behaviour
BELL, D. E., Marketing
BOWEN, H. K., Technology and Operations Management
BOWER, J. L., General Management
BRADLEY, S. P., Competition and Strategy
BRANDENBERGER, A. M., Competition and Strategy
BRUNS, W. J., Jr, Accounting and Control
CASH, J. I., Jr, Service Management
CAVES, R. E., Competition and Strategy
CHRISTENSEN, C. J., Control
CLARK, K. B., Dean of the Faculty
CRANE, D. B., Finance
CRUM, M. C., Finance
DATAR, S., Accounting and Control
DEIGHTON, J. A., Marketing
DESHPANDÉ, R., Marketing
FERGUSON, N., Business, Government and the International Economy
FROOT, K. A., Finance
FRUHAN, W. E., Jr, Finance
GABARRO, J. J., Organizational Behaviour
GARVIN, D. A., General Management
GHEMAWAT, P., Competition and Strategy
GREYSER, S. A., Marketing
HAMMOND, J. H., Technology and Operations Management
HAWKINS, D. F., Accounting and Control
HAYES, R. H., Technology and Operations Management
HEALY, P. M., Accounting and Control
HERZLINGER, R. E., Accounting and Control
HILL, L. A., Organizational Behaviour
IANSITI, M., Technology and Operations Management
IBARRA, H., Organizational Behaviour
JENSEN, M. C., Organizations and Markets
KANTER, R. M., General Management
KAPLAN, R. S., Accounting and Control
KESTER, W. C., Finance
KOHLBERG, E., Competition and Strategy
KOTTER, J. P., Organizational Behaviour
LIGHT, J. O., Finance
LORSCH, J. W., Organizational Behaviour
MCCRAW, T. K., Business, Government and International Economy
MCFARLAN, F. W., General Management
MCKENNEY, J. L., Management Information Systems
MASON, S. P., Finance
MERTON, R. C., Finance
MEYER, R. F., Managerial Economics
MILLS, D. Q., Human Resource Management
MONTGOMERY, C. A., Competition and Strategy
NOHRIA, N., Organizational Behaviour
NOLAN, R. L., General Management
PAINE, L. S., General Management
PALEPU, K. G., Accounting and Control
PEROLD, A. F., Finance
PIPER, T. R., Finance
PISANO, G., Technology and Operations Management
PODOLNY, J.
PORTER, M. E., Competition and Strategy
QUELCH, J.
RANGAN, V. K., Marketing
REILING, H. B., Finance
ROTEMBERG, J. J., Business, Government and International Economy
ROTH, A. E., Negotiation and Decision Making.
RUBACK, R. S., Finance
SAHLMAN, W. A., Entrepreneurial Management
SALTER, M. S., Organizations and Markets
SASSER, W. E., Jr., Service Management
SCHLESINGER, L. A., Service Management
SCOTT, B. R., Business, Government and International Economy
SEBENIUS, J. K., Negotiation and Decision Making
SHAPIRO, R. D., Technology and Operations Management
SILK, A. J., Marketing
SIMONS, R. L., Accounting and Control
SLOANE, C. S., Organizational Behaviour
STEVENSON, H. H., Entrepreneurial Management
STOBAUGH, R. B., Production and Operations Management
TEDLOW, R. S., Business, Government and International Economy
TUFANO, P., Finance
TUSHMAN, M. L., Organizational Behaviour
UPTON, D. M., Technology and Operations Management
VIETOR, R. H. K., Business, Government and International Economy
WELLS, L. T., Jr, Business, Government and International Economy

WHEELWRIGHT, S. C., Technology and Operations Management
YOFFIE, D. B., Competition and Strategy
YOSHINO, M. Y., General Management
ZALTMAN, G., Marketing
ZUBOFF, S., Organizational Behaviour

Harvard Divinity School (Office of Admissions and Financial Aid, Room 214, 14 Divinity Ave, Cambridge, MA 02138; tel. (617) 495-5796; e-mail admissions@hds.harvard.edu; internet www.hds.harvard.edu):

AHMED, L., Women's Studies in Religion
BOVON, F., New Testament
COAKLEY, S., Theology
COX, H. G., Theology
CURRASCO, D., Religion, America and Anthropology
DYCK, A., Ethics
ECK, D., Comparative Religion
FIORENZA, F. S., Roman Catholic Theological Studies
GOMES, P. J., Christian Morals
GRAHAM, W., Middle Eastern Studies
GYATSO, J., Comparative Religion
HALL, D. D., American Religious History
HANSON, P. D., Hebrew Bible/Old Testament
KING, K. L., New Testament Studies and Gnosticism
LEVENSON, J. D., Jewish Studies
ORSI, R., History of Religion
SCHÜSSLER FIORENZA, E., New Testament and Ministerial Studies
SULLIVAN, L., History of Religion
THIEMANN, R. F., Theology

Harvard Law School (1563 Massachusetts Avenue, Cambridge, MA 02138; tel. (617) 495-3100; e-mail jdadmiss@law.harvard.edu; internet www.law.harvard.edu):

ALFORD, W.
ANDREWS, W. D.
BARTHOLET, E., Public Interest
BEBCHUK, L. A., Law, Economics, Finance
BELLOW, G.
BREWER, S.
CHARNY, D.
CLARK, R. C.
DERSHOWITZ, A. M.
DESAN, C.
DONAHUE, C.
EDLEY, C. F.
ELHAUGE, E.
FALLON, R. H.
FIELD, M.
FISHER, W.
FRUG, G. E.
GLENDON, M. A.
GUINIER, L.
HALPERIN, D. I.
HANSON, J.
HAY, B. L.
HERWITZ, D. R.
HEYMANN, P. B.
HORWITZ, M. J., Legal History
JACKSON, H.
KAPLOW, L.
KAUFMAN, A. L.
KENNEDY, D. M.
KENNEDY, D. W., General Jurisprudence
KENNEDY, R. L.
KRAAKMAN, R. H.
LESSIG, L.
MANSFIELD, J. H.
MARTIN, H. S.
MELTZER, D. J.
MICHELMAN, F. I.
MILLER, A. R.
MINOW, M.
MNOOKIN, R.
NESSON, C. R.
OGLETREE, C., Jr
PARKER, R. D.
RAKOFF, T. D., Administrative Law
RAMSEYER, M.
ROSENBERG, M. D.
SANDER, F. E. A.
SARGENTICH, L. D.
SCOTT, H. S., International Financial Systems
SHAPIRO, D. L.
SHAVELL, S. M., Law and Economics
SINGER, J. W.
SLAUGHTER, A.-M.
STEIHER, C.
STEINER, H. J.
STONE, A. A., Law and Psychiatry
TRIBE, L. H., Constitutional Law
UNGER, R. M.
VAGTS, D. F., International Law
VISCUSI, W. K.
VORENBERG, J.
WARREN, A. C.
WARREN, E.
WEILER, J. H. H.
WEILER, P. C.
WEINREB, L. L.
WESTFALL, D.
WHITE, L.
WILKINS, D. B.
WOLFMAN, B.

Harvard School of Dental Medicine (Office of Admissions, DMD, 188 Longwood Ave, Boston, MA 02115; tel. (617) 432-1443; e-mail hsdm_admissions@hsdm.harvard.edu; internet www.hsdm.harvard.edu):

DOGON, I. L., Restorative Dentistry
DONOFF, R. B., Oral and Maxillofacial Surgery
DOUGLASS, C. W., Oral Health Policy and Epidemiology
GOLDHABER, P., Periodontology
HAY, D. I., Oral Biology
KABAN, L. B., Oral and Maxillofacial Surgery
OLSEN, B. R., Oral Biology
SHKLAR, G., Oral Pathology
SONIS, S. S., Oral Medicine and Diagnostic Sciences
TAUBMAN, M. A., Oral Biology

Harvard School of Public Health (Harvard School of Public Health, Admissions Office, 677 Huntington Ave, Boston, MA 02115; tel. (617) 432-1031; e-mail admisofc@hsph.harvard.edu; internet www.hsph.harvard.edu):

ALONSO, W., Population and International Health
BERKMAN, L. F., Health and Social Behaviour
BLENDON, R. J., Health Policy and Management
BLOOM, D. E., Population and International Health
BRAIN, J. D., Environmental Health
BRENNAN, T. A., Health Policy and Management
CHEN, L. C., Population and International Health
CHRISTIANI, D. C., Environmental Health
COOK, E. F., Epidemiology
DAVID, J. R., Tropical Public Health
DEGRUTTOLA, V. G., Biostatistics
DEMPLE, B. F., Toxicology
DYCK, A. J., Population and International Health
EARLS, F. J., Maternal and Child Health
EPSTEIN, A. M., Health Policy and Management
ESSEX, M. E., Cancer Biology
FINEBERG, H. V., Administration
FREDBERG, J. J., Environmental Health
GLIMCHER, L. H., Cancer Biology
GOLDMAN, P., Nutrition
GRAHAM, J. D., Health Policy and Management
HARN, D. A., Tropical Public Health
HARRINGTON, D. P., Biostatistics
HARRINGTON, J. J., Environmental Health
HEMENWAY, D., Health Policy and Management
HILL, A. G., Population and International Health
HSIAO, W. C., Health Policy and Management
KELSEY, K. T., Environmental Health
KOUTRAKIS, P., Environmental Health
LAGAKOS, S. W., Biostatistics
LAIRD, N. M., Biostatistics
LEE, T., Immunology and Infectious Diseases
LEVINS, R., Population and International Health
LI, F. P., Epidemiology
LITTLE, J. B., Cancer Biology
MCCORMICK, M. C., Maternal and Child Health
MONSON, R. R., Epidemiology and Environmental Health
MUELLER, N. E., Epidemiology
MURRAY, C., Population and International Health
NEWHOUSE, J. P., Health Policy and Management
PAGANO, M., Biostatistics
PIESSENS, W. F., Tropical Public Health
PROTHROW-STITH, D. B., Health Policy and Management
REICH, M. R., Population and International Health, and Health Policy and Management
ROBERTS, M. J., Health Policy and Management
ROBINS, J. M., Epidemiology and Biostatistics
RYAN, L. M., Biostatistics
SAMSON, L. D., Molecular and Cellular Toxicology
SMITH, T. J., Environmental Health
SORENSON, G., Health and Social Behaviour
SPEIZER, F. E., Environmental Health
SPENGLER, J. D., Environmental Health
SPIELMAN, A., Tropical Public Health
STAMPFER, M. J., Nutrition and Epidemiology
TARLOV, A., Health Policy and Management
TASHJIAN, A. H., Jr, Toxicology
TRICHOPOULOS, D. V., Epidemiology
WALKER, A. M., Epidemiology
WARE, J. H., Biostatistics
WEI, L. J., Biostatistics
WEINSTEIN, M. C., Health Policy, Management and Biostatistics
WILLETT, W. C., Epidemiology and Nutrition
WIRTH, D. F., Tropical Public Health
ZELEN, M., Biostatistics

J. F. Kennedy School of Government (Admissions, Harvard University, 119 Belfer, Cambridge, MA 2138; tel. (617) 495-1155; e-mail ksg_admissions@harvard.edu; internet www.ksg.harvard.edu/apply):

ALLISON, G. T., Government
ALTSHULER, A., Urban Policy and Planning
APPLBAUM, A., Ethics and Public Policy
AVERY, C., Public Policy
BANE, M. J., Domestic Social Policy
BORJAS, G., Immigration
CARTER, A. B., International and National Security
CLARK, W. C., International Science, Public Policy and Human Development
DOTY, P. M., Public Policy
ELLWOOD, D., Income Support and Social Welfare Policy
FRANKEL, J., Capital Formation and Growth
GERGEN, D., Public Management and Leadership
GOLDSMITH, S., Practice of Public Management
GOMEZ-IBANEZ, J. A., Public Policy and Urban Policy
GRINDLE, M. S., International Development

HAUSMANN, R., Practice of Economic Development
HOGAN, W., Public Policy and Management
HOLDREN, J., Science and Energy Policy
IGNATIEFF, M., Human Rights Practice
JASANOFF, S., Science and Public Policy
JENCKS, C., US Domestic Social Policy
JUMA, C., Practice of International Development
KALT, J., International Political Economy
KELMAN, S. J., Public Management
KEYSSAR, A., History and Social Policy
LAWRENCE, R. Z., International Trade
LEONARD, H., Public Management
LIGHT, R., Education
MANSBRIDGE, J., Democratic Governance
MOORE, M. H., Criminal Justice Policy and Management
NEWHOUSE, J. P., Health Policy and Management
NEWMAN, K., Sociology of Labour Markets
NYE, J., International Affairs and Democratic Governance
ORREN, G. R., Public Policy
PATTERSON, T., Press and Politics
PORTER, R., Business and Government
PUTNAM, R., Democratic Governance
RODRIK, D., International Trade and Development
ROSENSWEIG, M., Public Policy
RUGGIE, J., International Affairs
SAICH, A., International Affairs
SCHAUER, F., First Amendment
SPARROW, M., Practice of Public Management
STAVINS, R. N., Environmental Economics
THOMPSON, D., Political Philosophy
VELASCO, A., International Finance and Development
WILSON, W. J., Urban Sociology
WISE, D., Political Economy
ZECKHAUSER, R. J., Political Economy

HEBREW COLLEGE

160 Herrick Rd, Newton Centre, MA 02459
Telephone: (617) 559-8600
Fax: (617) 559-8601
E-mail: admissions@hebrewcollege.edu
Internet: www.hebrewcollege.edu

Founded 1921
Languages of instruction: English, Hebrew
Academic year: September to May

Pres.: Rabbi DANIEL LEHMANN
Vice-Pres. for Devt: MICHAEL GILBERT
Provost: Dr BARRY MESCH
Registrar: MARILYN JAYE
Library Dir: HARVEY SUKENIC

Library of 100,000 vols
Number of teachers: 43
Number of students: 200

DEANS

Hebrew College Online: NATHAN EHRLICH
Rabbinical School: Rabbi SHARON COHEN ANISFELD
School of Jewish Music: JOSHUA JACOBSON (acting)
Shoolman Graduate School of Jewish Education: INA REGOSIN

HELLENIC COLLEGE–HOLY CROSS GREEK ORTHODOX SCHOOL OF THEOLOGY

50 Goddard Ave, Brookline, MA 02445-7496
Telephone: (617) 731-3500
Fax: (617) 850-1460
E-mail: admissions@hchc.edu
Internet: www.hchc.edu
Private control

Pres.: Rev. NICHOLAS C. TRIANTAFILOU
Chief Operating Officer: JAMES D. KARLOUTSOS
Dean of Hellenic College: DEMETRIOS KATOS
Dean of Holy Cross: Fr THOMAS FITZGERALD
Registrar: ALBA PAGAN
Library Dir: Very Rev. Dr Archimandrite JOACHIM COTSONIS

Library of 75,000 vols
Number of teachers: 15
Number of students: 209 (77 undergraduate, 132 graduate)

HULT INTERNATIONAL BUSINESS SCHOOL

1 Education St, Cambridge, MA 02141
Telephone: (617) 746-1990
Fax: (617) 746-1991
E-mail: admissions@hult.edu
Internet: www.hult.edu

Founded 1964 as Arthur D. Little School of Management
Private control

Pres. and Chair.: STEPHEN HODGES
Dean of Academic Affairs: RICHARD JOSEPH
Registrar: NICOLE GREGOIRE
Librarian: JOHN WALSH

Number of teachers: 38
Number of students: 59

LASELL COLLEGE

1844 Commonwealth Ave, Newton, MA 02466
Telephone: (617) 243-2000
Fax: (617) 796-4343
E-mail: info@lasell.edu
Internet: www.lasell.edu

Founded 1851
Private control
Academic year: September to May

Pres.: MICHAEL B. ALEXANDER
Vice-Pres. for Academic Affairs: JAMES OSTROW
Vice-Pres. for Enrollment Management: KATHLEEN M. O'CONNOR
Library Dir: ALLYSON GRAY

Library of 55,000 vols
Number of teachers: 331
Number of students: 1,200

DEANS

Graduate and Professional Studies: MARK SCIEGAI
School of Allied Health and Sports Studies: Dr LISA BORTMAN
School of Arts and Sciences: Dr STEVEN BLOOM
School of Business and Information Technology: Dr K. BREWER DORAN
Undergraduate Education: STEVEN BLOOM

LESLEY UNIVERSITY

29 Everett St, Cambridge, MA 02138-2790
Telephone: (617) 868-9600
Fax: (617) 349-8717
E-mail: info@lesley.edu
Internet: www.lesley.edu

Founded 1909
Academic year: September to May

Pres. and Provost: MARGARET A. MCKENNA
Vice-Pres. for Admin.: MARY LOU BATT
Vice-Pres. for Budgeting and Financial Planning: ML DYMSKI
Vice-Pres. for Finance: BERNICE BRADIN
Vice-Pres. for Urban Initiatives: WILLIAM DANDRIDGE
Dean of Faculty: WILLIAM STOKES
Registrar: MELISSA JANOT
Dir of Libraries: PATRICIA PAYNE

Library of 100,000 vols
Number of teachers: 500
Number of students: 11,259 (1,702 undergraduate, 9,557 postgraduate)

Publication: *Journal of Pedagogy, Pluralism and Practice* (irregular)

DEANS

Art Institute of Boston: TERRENCE KEENEY
Graduate School of Arts and Social Sciences: JULIA HALEVY
Lesley College: SHAUN MCNIFF
School of Education: MARIO BORUNDA

MASSACHUSETTS COLLEGE OF ART

621 Huntington Ave, Boston, MA 02215
Telephone: (617) 232-1555
Fax: (617) 232-0050
Internet: www.massart.edu

Founded 1873

Pres.: Dr KATHERINE SLOAN
Sr Vice-Pres. for Academic Affairs: Dr JOHANNA BRANSON
Vice-Pres. for Admin. and Finance: KURT STEINBERG
Vice-Pres. for Institutional Advancement: RICHARD MACMILLAN
Vice-Pres. for Student Devt: MAUREEN KEEFE
Library Dir: PAUL DOBBS

Library of 95,000 vols
Number of teachers: 216
Number of students: 1,432 and 617 continuing education students

MASSACHUSETTS COLLEGE OF LIBERAL ARTS

375 Church St, North Adams, MA 01247
Telephone: (413) 662-5000
Fax: (413) 662-5580
Internet: www.mcla.mass.edu

Founded 1894

Pres.: Dr MARY K. GRANT
Vice-Pres. for Academic Affairs: Dr STEVE GREEN
Vice-Pres. for Admin. and Finance: Dr JAMES STAKENAS
Vice-Pres. for Enrollment and External Relations: DENISE RICHARDELLO
Dean of Academic Affairs: Dr MONICA NESET JOSLIN
Dir of Career Services: SHARRON ZAVATTARO
Registrar: ANDREA DEMAYO (acting)
Library Dir: LINDA M. KAUFMANN (acting)

Library of 172,000 vols, 500 print periodicals, 300,000 microforms, 4,000 online journals

Depts of arts management, biology, business admin., chemistry, computer science and information systems, education, English/communications, environmental studies, fine and performing arts, history, political science and geography, interdisciplinary studies, mathematics, modern languages, philosophy, physical education, physics, psychology, sociology, anthropology and social work, women's studies.

MASSACHUSETTS COLLEGE OF PHARMACY AND HEALTH SCIENCES

179 Longwood Ave, Boston, MA 02115-5896
Telephone: (617) 732-2800
Fax: (617) 732-2801
Internet: www.mcphs.edu

Founded 1823
Private control

Pres.: CHARLES F. MONAHAN, Jr
Vice-Pres. for Academic Affairs and Provost: Dr MICHELLE M. KALIS (acting)
Assoc. Vice-Pres. for External Relations: Dr GEORGE E. HUMPHREY
Vice-Pres. for Finance and Admin.: RICHARD J. LESSARD
Vice-Pres. for Legal Affairs: Dr ROBERT W. HOLMES, Jr
Registrar: MARJORIE MCMAHON

Dean of Students: Jean Joyce-Brady
Dean of Library: Richard Kaplan

Library of 30,000 vols, 800 periodicals
Number of teachers: 157
Number of students: 3,200

DEANS

Forsyth School of Dental Hygiene: (vacant)
School of Arts and Sciences: Dr David E. Tanner
School of Health Sciences: Dr James Blagg
School of Nursing: (vacant)
School of Pharmacy, Boston: Dr Douglas J. Pisano
School of Pharmacy, Worcester/Manchester: Dr Michael J. Malloy
School of Radiologic Sciences: Dr K. Cyrus Whaley (acting)

BRANCH CAMPUSES

Manchester Campus: 1260 Elm St, Manchester, NH 03101-1305; tel. (603) 314-0210; fax (603) 314-0303.

Worcester Campus: 19 Foster St, Worcester, MA 01608-1715; tel. (508) 890-8855; fax (508) 890-8515.

MASSACHUSETTS INSTITUTE OF TECHNOLOGY

77 Massachusetts Ave, Cambridge, MA 02139-4307
Telephone: (617) 253-1000
Fax: (617) 253-8000
Internet: web.mit.edu
Founded 1861
Private control
Academic year: September to May

Pres.: Susan Hockfield
Chancellor: W. Eric L. Grimson
Provost: L. Rafael Reif
Exec. Vice-Pres. and Treas.: Theresa Stone
Vice-Pres. for Finance: Israel Ruiz
Vice-Pres. for Human Resources: Alison Alden
Vice-Pres. for Institute Affairs and Corporation Sec.: Kirk Kolenbrander
Vice-Pres. for Research and Associate Provost: Claude Canizares
Vice-Pres. for Resource Devt: Jeffrey Newton
Vice-Pres. and Gen. Counsel: R. Gregory Morgan
Dir of Lincoln Laboratory: Eric Evans
Assoc. Provosts for Faculty Equity: Wesley Harris, Barbara Liskov
Assoc. Provosts: Philip S. Khoury, Martin Schmidt
Dean of Graduate Education: Christine Ortiz
Dean of Undergraduate Education: Daniel Hastings
Dean of Student Life: Chris Colombo
Registrar: Mary R. Callahan
Dir of Libraries: Ann J. Wolpert

Library of 3,119,157 vols
Number of teachers: 1,017
Number of students: 10,566
Publications: *MIT Bulletin* (1 a year), *Sloan Management Review* (4 a year), *Technology Review* (6 a year)

DEANS

Harvard-MIT Division of Health Sciences and Technology: David Cohen (Dir: Ram Sasisekharan (Dir)
School of Architecture and Planning: Adèle Naudé Santos
School of Engineering: Ian A. Waitz
School of Humanities, Arts and Social Sciences: Deborah Fitzgerald
School of Science: Marc Kastner
Sloan School of Management: David Schmittlein

PROFESSORS

(Some professors serve in more than one department)

School of Architecture and Planning (77 Massachusetts Ave, Room 7-231, Cambridge, MA 02139-4307; tel. (617) 253-4401; fax (617) 253-9417; internet sap.mit.edu):

Department of Architecture:

Anderson, S., History and Architecture
Beinart, J., Architecture
Chang, Y. H., Architecture (Head)
De Monchaux, J., Architecture and Urban Planning
Dennis, M., Architecture
Glicksman, L. R., Building Technology
Jarzombek, M., History and Architecture
Jonas, J., Visual Arts
Jones, C., History of Art
Knight, T., Design and Computation
Mitchell, W. J., Architecture, Media Arts and Sciences
Norford, L., Building Technology
Rabbat, N., History of Architecture
Santos, A. N., Architecture and Urban Planning
Spirn, A. W., Landscape Architecture and Planning
Stiny, G., Design and Computation
Wampler, J., Architecture
Wescoat, J., Architecture
Wodiczko, K., Visual Arts

Department of Urban Studies and Planning:

Amsden, A., Political Economy
Ciochetti, B. A., Practice of Real Estate
Clay, P., Urban Studies and Planning
Davis, D., Political Sociology
Ferreira, J., Urban Studies and Operations Research
Fogelson, R. M., Urban Studies and History
Frenchman, D., Urban Design
Gakenheimer, R., Urban Planning
Geltner, D., Real Estate Finance
Keyes, L. C., City and Regional Planning
Levy, F. S., Urban Economics
McDowell, C., Practice of Community Development
Osterman, P., Human Resources and Management
Polenske, K. R., Regional Political Economy and Planning
Rein, M., Social Policy
Sanyal, B., Urban and Regional Planning
Spirn, A., Landscape Architecture and Planning
Susskind, L. E., Urban and Environmental Planning
Tendler, J., Political Economy
Vale, L. J., Urban Design and Planning (Head)
Wheaton, W. C., Urban Economics

Program in Media Arts and Sciences:

Gershenfeld, N., Media Arts and Sciences
Ishii, H., Media Arts and Sciences
Machover, T., Music and Media
Maeda, J., Design and Computation
Mitchell, W. J., Architecture and Media Arts and Sciences
Negroponte, N. P., Media Technology
Pentland, A. P., Media Arts and Sciences
Picard, R., Media Arts and Sciences
Resnick, M., Media Arts and Sciences and Learning Research (Head)
Vercoe, B., Media Arts and Sciences

School of Engineering (77 Massachusetts Ave, Room 1-206, Cambridge, MA 02139-4307; tel. (617) 253-3291; fax (617) 253-8549; internet web.mit.edu/engineering):

Department of Aeronautics and Astronautics:

Crawley, E. F., Aeronautics and Astronautics and Engineering Systems
Deyst, J. J., Aeronautics and Astronautics
Drela, M., Aeronautics and Astronautics
Epstein, A. H., Aeronautics and Astronautics
Greitzer, E. M., Aeronautics and Astronautics
Hall, S. R., Aeronautics and Astronautics
Hansman, R. J., Aeronautics and Astronautics and Engineering Systems
Harris, W. L., Aeronautics and Astronautics
Hastings, D. E., Aeronautics and Astronautics, Engineering Systems
Hoffman, J. A., Practice of Astronautics
How, J. P., Aeronautics and Astronautics
Lagacé, P. A., Aeronautics and Astronautics, Engineering Systems
Leveson, N. G., Aeronautics and Astronautics, Engineering Systems
Liebeck, R., Practice of Aerospace Engineering
Martínez-Sánchez, M., Aeronautics and Astronautics
Newman, D. J., Aeronautics and Astronautics, Engineering Systems
Nightingale, D. J., Practice of Aeronautics and Astronautics and Engineering Systems
Odoni, A. R., Aeronautics and Astronautics and Civil and Environmental Engineering
Peraire, J., Aeronautics and Astronautics
Waitz, I. A., Aeronautics and Astronautics (Head)
Widnall, S. E., Aeronautics and Astronautics and Engineering Systems
Williams, B. C., Aeronautics and Astronautics
Young, L. R., Astronautics, Health Sciences and Technology

Department of Biological Engineering:

Belcher, A. M., Materials Science and Biological Engineering
Chakraborty, A., Chemical Engineering, Chemistry and Biological Engineering
Dedon, P. C., Toxicology and Biological Engineering
DeLong, E. F., Environmental and Biological Engineering
Dewey, C. F., Jr, Mechanical Engineering and Biological Engineering
Essigman, J. M., Chemistry, Toxicology and Biological Engineering
Fox, J. G., Toxicology
Griffith, L. G., Biological and Mechanical Engineering
Grodzinsky, A. J., Electrical, Mechanical and Biological Engineering
Kamm, R. D., Biological and Mechanical Engineering
Klibanov, A. M., Chemistry and Biological Engineering
Langer, R. S., Chemical and Biomedical Engineering
Lauffenburger, D. A., Biological Engineering, Biology and Chemical Engineering (Head)
Lodish, H. F., Biology and Biological Engineering
Matsudaira, P. T., Biology and Biological Engineering
Samson, L. D., Toxicology and Biological Engineering
Sasisekharan, R., Biological Engineering and Health Sciences and Technology
Schauer, D. B., Biological Engineering and Comparative Medicine
So, P. T., Mechanical and Biological Engineering
Suresh, S., Materials Science and Bioengineering
Tannenbaum, S. R., Toxicology and Chemistry
Thilly, W. G., Toxicology
Tidor, B., Bioengineering and Computer Science

WITTRUP, K. D., Chemical Engineering and Bioengineering
YANNAS, I. V., Polymer Science and Bioengineering

Department of Chemical Engineering:

ARMSTRONG, R. C., Chemical Engineering
BARTON, P., Chemical Engineering
BLANKSCHTEIN, D., Chemical Engineering
CHAKRABORTY, A., Chemical Engineering, Chemistry and Biological Engineering
COHEN, R. E., Chemical Engineering
COLTON, C. K., Chemical Engineering
COONEY, C. L., Chemical and Biochemical Engineering
DEEN, W. M., Chemical Engineering
GLEASON, K. K., Chemical Engineering
HAMMOND, P., Chemical Engineering
HATTON, T. A., Chemical Engineering Practice
JENSEN, K. F., Chemical Engineering (Head)
LANGER, R. S., Chemical and Biomedical Engineering
LAUFFENBURGER, D. A., Biological Engineering, Chemical Engineering and Biology
MCRAE, G. J., Chemical Engineering
RUTLEDGE, G. C., Chemical Engineering
SAWIN, H. H., Chemical and Electrical Engineering
SMITH, K. A., Chemical Engineering
STEPHANOPOULOS, G., Chemical Engineering
STEPHANOPOULOS, GRE., Chemical Engineering
TESTER, J. W., Chemical Engineering
TROUT, B., Chemical Engineering
WANG, D. I. C., Chemical Engineering
WITTRUP, K. D., Chemical Engineering and Biological Engineering

Department of Civil and Environmental Engineering:

BARNHART, C., Civil and Environmental Engineering
BEN-AKIVA, M., Civil and Environmental Engineering
BRAS, R. L., Civil and Environmental Engineering and Earth, Atmospheric and Planetary Sciences
BUYUKOZTURK, O., Civil and Environmental Engineering
CHISHOLM, S., Civil and Environmental Engineering and Biology
CONNOR, J. J., Jr, Civil and Environmental Engineering
DELONG, E., Civil and Environmental Engineering and Biological Engineering
DE NEUFVILLE, R. L., Civil and Environmental Engineering, Engineering Systems
EINSTEIN, H. H., Civil and Environmental Engineering
ELTAHIR, E., Civil and Environmental Engineering
ENTEKHABI, D., Civil and Environmental Engineering
GIBSON, L., Materials Science and Engineering, Civil and Environmental Engineering and Mechanical Engineering
GSCHWEND, P., Civil and Environmental Engineering
HEMOND, H. F., Civil and Environmental Engineering
JAILLET, P., Civil and Environmental Engineering (Head)
KAUSEL, E., Civil and Environmental Engineering
LARSON, R. C., Civil and Environmental Engineering and Engineering Systems
LERMAN, S. R., Civil and Environmental Engineering
MCLAUGHLIN, D. B., Civil and Environmental Engineering
MADSEN, O. S., Civil and Environmental Engineering
MARKS, D. H., Civil and Environmental Engineering, Engineering Systems
MEI, C. C., Civil and Environmental Engineering
MOAVENZADEH, F., Civil and Environmental Engineering, Engineering Systems
NEPF, H., Civil and Environmental Engineering
ODONI, A. R., Aeronautics and Astronautics and Civil and Environmental Engineering
ROOS, D., Engineering Systems and Civil and Environmental Engineering
SHEFFI, Y., Civil and Environmental Engineering, Engineering Systems
SIMCHI-LEVI, D., Civil and Environmental Engineering, Engineering Systems
SUSSMAN, J. M., Civil and Environmental Engineering, Engineering Systems
ULM, F.-J., Civil and Environmental Engineering
VENEZIANO, D., Civil and Environmental Engineering
WHITTLE, A. J., Civil and Environmental Engineering
WILSON, N. H. M., Civil and Environmental Engineering

Department of Electrical Engineering and Computer Science:

ABELSON, H., Computer Science and Engineering
AGARWAL, A., Computer Science and Engineering
AKINWANDE, A., Electrical Engineering
ANTONIADIS, D., Electrical Engineering
ARVIND, Computer Science and Engineering
BAGGEROER, A. B., Engineering and Mechanical Engineering
BERS, A., Electrical Engineering
BERTSEKAS, D. P., Electrical Engineering
BERWICK, R. C., Computer Science and Engineering and Computational Linguistics
BHATIA, S., Electrical Engineering and Health Sciences and Technology
BONING, D., Electrical Engineering and Computer Science
BRAIDA, L. B. D., Electrical Engineering and Health Sciences and Technology
BROOKS, R. A., Computer Science and Engineering
CHAN, V. W. S., Electrical Engineering
CHANDRAKASAN, A., Electrical Engineering
DAHLEH, M. A., Electrical Engineering
DAVIS, R., Computer Science and Engineering
DEL ALAMO, J. A., Electrical Engineering
DEVADAS, S., Electrical Engineering and Computer Science
DRESSELHAUS, M. S., Electrical Engineering and Physics
FONSTAD, C. G., Jr, Electrical Engineering
FREEMAN, D. M., Computer Science and Engineering
FUJIMOTO, J. G., Electrical Engineering
GALLAGER, R. G., Electrical Engineering
GIFFORD, D. K., Computer Science and Engineering
GOLDWASSER, S., Computer Science and Engineering
GRAY, M. L., Medical and Electrical Engineering
GRAY, P. E., Electrical Engineering
GRIMSON, W. E. L., Medical Engineering (Head)
GRODZINSKY, A. J., Electrical, Mechanical and Biological Engineering
GUTTAG, J. V., Computer Science and Engineering
HENNIE, F. C., III, Computer Science and Engineering
HORN, B. K., Computer Science and Engineering
HOYT, J. L., Electrical Engineering
HU, Q., Electrical Engineering
IPPEN, E. P., Electrical Engineering and Physics
JAAKKOLA, T. S., Computer Science and Engineering
JACKSON, D. N., Computer Science and Engineering
KAASHOEK, M. F., Computer Science and Engineering
KAEBLING, L. P., Computer Science and Engineering
KAERTNER, F. X., Electrical Engineering
KARGER, D. R., Computer Science and Engineering
KASSAKIAN, J. G., Electrical Engineering
KIRTLEY, J. L., Jr, Electrical Engineering
KOLODZIEJSKI, L. A., Electrical Engineering
LANG, J. H., Electrical Engineering
LEE, H.-S., Electrical Engineering
LEEB, S. B., Electrical and Mechanical Engineering
LEISERSON, C. E., Computer Science and Engineering
LIM, J. S., Electrical Engineering
LISKOV, B. H., Engineering
LOZANO-PÉREZ, T., Computer Science and Engineering
LYNCH, N. A., Software Science and Engineering
MAGNANTI, T. L., Management Science and Electrical Engineering
MARK, R. G., Health Sciences and Technology and Electrical Engineering and Computer Science
MEDARD, M., Electrical Engineering
MEGRETSKI, A., Electrical Engineering
MEYER, A. R., Computer Science and Engineering
MICALI, S., Computer Science and Engineering
MINSKY, M. L., Media Arts and Sciences and Computer Science and Engineering
MITTER, S. K., Electrical Engineering and Engineering Systems
MOSES, J., Computer Science and Engineering and Engineering Systems
OPPENHEIM, A. V., Engineering
ORLANDO, T. P., Electrical Engineering
PARKER, R. R., Electrical Engineering and Nuclear Science and Engineering
PARRILO, P., Electrical Engineering and Computer Science
PEAKE, W. T., Electrical and Bioengineering
PENFIELD, P. L., Jr, Electrical Engineering
RAM, R. J., Electrical Engineering
REIF, L. R., Emerging Technology
RIVEST, R. L., Computer Science and Engineering
ROBERGE, J. K., Electrical Engineering
RUBINFELD, R., Computer Science and Engineering
RUS, D. L., Computer Science and Engineering
SAWIN, H. H., Chemical Engineering and Electrical Engineering
SCHINDALL, J. E., Practice
SCHMIDT, M. A., Electrical Engineering
SHAPIRO, J. H., Electrical Engineering
SMITH, A. C., Electrical Engineering
SMITH, H. I., Electrical Engineering
SODINI, C. G., Electrical Engineering
STAELIN, D. H., Electrical Engineering
STEVENS, K. N., Electrical Engineering and Health Sciences and Technology
SUDAN, M., Computer Science and Engineering
SUSSMAN, G. J., Electrical Engineering
SZOLOVITS, P., Computer Science and Engineering and Health Sciences and Technology
TELLER, S., Computer Science and Engineering
TIDOR, B., Electrical Engineering and Computer Science and Biological Engineering

TROXEL, D. E., Electrical Engineering
TSITSIKLIS, J. N., Electrical Engineering and Computer Science
VERGHESE, G. C., Electrical Engineering
WARD, S. A., Computer Science and Engineering
WARDE, C., Electrical Engineering
WHITE, J. K., Electrical Engineering
WILLSKY, A. S., Electrical Engineering
WILSON, G. L., Electrical and Mechanical Engineering
WINSTON, P. H., Engineering
WORNELL, G. W., Electrical Engineering
WYATT, J. L., Electrical Engineering
ZAHN, M., Electrical Engineering
ZUE, V. M., Electrical Engineering and Computer Science

Department of Materials Science and Engineering:

ALLEN, S. M., Physical Metallurgy
BALLINGER, R., Materials Science and Engineering and Nuclear Science and Engineering
BELCHER, A. M., Materials Science and Engineering and Biological Engineering
CARTER, W. C., Materials Science and Engineering
CEDER, G., Materials Science and Engineering
CHIANG, Y.-M., Ceramics
CIMA, M., Engineering
CLARK, J. P., Materials Systems
EAGAR, T. W., Materials Engineering and Materials Systems
FITZGERALD, E. A., Materials Science and Engineering
GIBSON, L., Materials Science and Engineering, Civil and Environmental Engineering and Mechanical Engineering
HOBBS, L. W., Materials Science and Nuclear Science and Engineering
HOSLER, D., Archaeology and Ancient Technology
JENSEN, K. F., Chemical Engineering, Materials Science and Engineering
KIMERLING, L. C., Materials Science and Engineering
LECHTMAN, H., Archaeology and Ancient Technology
MAYES, A. M., Polymer Physics
ROSS, C., Materials Science
RUBNER, M. F., Materials Science and Engineering
SADOWAY, D. R., Metallurgy
SURESH, S., Materials Science and Engineering and Mechanical Engineering
THOMAS, E. L., Materials Science and Engineering (Head)
THOMPSON, C. V., Materials Science and Engineering
TULLER, H. L., Ceramics and Electronic Materials
WUENSCH, B. J., Ceramics
YIP, S., Nuclear Science and Materials Science Engineering

Department of Mechanical Engineering:

ABEYARATNE, R., Mechanics
AKYLAS, T. R., Mechanical Engineering
ANAND, L., Mechanical Engineering
ASADA, H., Engineering
BAGGEROER, A., Mechanical, Ocean and Electrical Engineering
BATHE, K.-J., Mechanical Engineering
BOYCE, M. C., Mechanical Engineering (Head)
BRISSON, J. G., II, Mechanical Engineering
CHEN, G., Mechanical Engineering
CHENG, W. K., Mechanical Engineering
CHRYSSOSTOMIDIS, C., Ocean Science and Engineering and Mechanical and Ocean Engineering
CHUN, J. H., Mechanical Engineering
CRAVALHO, E. G., Mechanical Engineering
D'ARBELOFF, A., Practice of Mechanical Engineering and Management
DEWEY, C. F., Jr, Mechanical Engineering and Bioengineering
DUBOWSKY, S., Mechanical Engineering and Aeronautics and Astronautics
GHONIEM, A. F., Mechanical Engineering
GIBSON, L., Materials Science and Engineering and Mechanical Engineering and Environmental Engineering
GLICKSMAN, L., Mechanical Engineering and Architecture
GOSSARD, D. C., Mechanical Engineering
GRAVES, S., Mechanical Engineering and Management
GRIFFITH, L., Teaching Innovation, Mechanical and Biological Engineering
GRODZINSKY, A. J., Mechanical, Electrical and Biological Engineering
GUTOWSKI, T. G., Mechanical Engineering
HARDT, D. E., Mechanical Engineering
HART, D., Mechanical Engineering
HEYWOOD, J. B., Mechanical Engineering
HOGAN, N. J., Mechanical Engineering and Brain and Cognitive Science
HUNTER, I. W., Mechanical Engineering
KAMM, R. D., Mechanical and Biological Engineering
KAZIMI, M. S., Mechanical and Nuclear Engineering
LANGER, R. S., Mechanical, Chemical and Biological Engineering
LEEB, S. B., Mechanical and Electrical Engineering and Computer Science
LEONARD, J. J., Mechanical and Ocean Engineering
LIEHARD, J., Mechanical Engineering
LLOYD, S., Mechanical Engineering
MCKINLEY, G. H., Teaching Innovation and Mechanical Engineering
MAKRIS, N. C., Mechanical and Ocean Engineering
MARCUS, H., Marine Systems
MEI, C. C., Engineering, Mechanical and Civil Engineering
MIKIC, B. B., Mechanical Engineering
MILGRAM, J., Mechanical and Ocean Engineering
PARKS, D. M., Mechanical Engineering
PATERA, A. T., Engineering
PATRIKALAKIS, N. M., Engineering, Mechanical and Ocean Engineering
ROWELL, D., Mechanical Engineering
SACHS, E. M., Mechanical Engineering
SCHMIDT, H., Mechanical and Ocean Engineering
SCLAVOUNOS, P., Mechanical Engineering and Naval Architecture
SEERING, W. P., Mechanical Engineering
SLOCUM, A., Mechanical Engineering
SLOTINE, J.-J. E., Mechanical Engineering and Brain and Cognitive Sciences
SMITH, J. L., Jr, Mechanical Engineering
SO, P. T., Mechanical and Biological Engineering
SURESH, S., Biological Engineering and Materials Science and Engineering
TRIANTAFYLLOU, M., Mechanical and Ocean Engineering
TRUMPER, D. L., Mechanical Engineering
VANDIVER, J. K., Mechanical and Ocean Engineering
VEST, C. M., Mechanical Engineering
WALLACE, D., Mechanical Engineering
WELSH, M. S., Practice of Naval Construction and Engineering
WIERZBICKI, T., Applied Mechanics
WILLIAMS, J. H., Jr, Teaching Excellence, Mechanical Engineering and Writing and Humanistic Studies
WILSON, G. L., Electrical and Mechanical Engineering
YANNAS, I. V., Mechanical Engineering, Polymer Science and Biological Engineering
YOUCEF-TOUMI, K., Mechanical Engineering
YUE, D. K.-P., Engineering, Mechanical and Ocean Engineering

Department of Nuclear Science and Engineering:

APOSTOLAKIS, G., Nuclear Science and Engineering and Engineering Systems
BALLINGER, R. G., Nuclear Science and Engineering and Materials Science and Engineering
CORY, D. G., Nuclear Science and Engineering
FREIDBERG, J. P., Nuclear Science and Engineering
GOLAY, M. W., Nuclear Science and Engineering
HOBBS, L. W., Materials Science and Nuclear Science and Engineering
HUTCHINSON, I. H., Nuclear Science and Engineering (Head)
KADAK, A. C., Practice, Nuclear Science and Engineering
KAZIMI, M. S., Nuclear Engineering and Mechanical Engineering
LESTER, R. K., Nuclear Science and Engineering
PARKER, R. R., Electrical Engineering and Nuclear Science and Engineering
YANCH, J. C., Nuclear Science and Engineering
YIP, S., Nuclear Science and Engineering and Materials Science and Engineering

Engineering Systems Division:

ALLEN, T. J., Management and Engineering Systems
APOSTOLAKIS, G., Engineering Systems
BARNHART, C., Civil and Environmental Engineering and Engineering Systems
CARROLL, J., Behavioural and Policy Sciences and Engineering Systems
CLARK, J. P., Materials Systems and Engineering Systems
CRAWLEY, E. F., Aeronautics and Astronautics and Engineering Systems
CUSUMANO, M., Management and Engineering Systems
DE NEUFVILLE, R., Civil and Environmental Engineering and Engineering Systems
EAGAR, T. W., Materials Engineering and Engineering Systems
EPPINGER, S. D., Management Science and Engineering Systems
FINE, C., Management and Engineering Systems
GRAVES, S. C., Management and Engineering Systems
HANSMAN, J., Aeronautics and Astronautics and Engineering Systems
HARDT, D. E., Mechanical Engineering and Engineering Systems
HASTINGS, D., Aeronautics and Astronautics and Engineering Systems
KOCHAN, T. A., Management and Engineering Systems
LAGACÉ, P. A., Aeronautics and Astronautics and Engineering Systems
LARSON, R., Civil and Environmental Engineering and Engineering Systems
LEVESON, N., Aeronautics and Astronautics and Engineering Systems
LLOYD, S., Mechanical Engineering and Engineering Systems
MADNICK, S., Information Technology and Engineering Systems
MARKS, D. H., Civil and Environmental Engineering and Engineering Systems
MINDELL, D., History of Engineering and Manufacturing and Engineering Systems
MITTER, S., Electrical Engineering and Engineering Systems
MOAVENZADEH, F., Civil and Environmental Engineering and Engineering Systems
MONIZ, E., Physics and Engineering Systems

MOSES, J., Computer Science and Engineering Systems
NEWMAN, D. J., Aeronautics and Astronautics and Engineering Systems
ROOS, D., Civil and Environmental Engineering and Engineering Systems (Co-Dir)
SEERING, W. P., Mechanical Engineering and Engineering Systems
SHEFFI, Y., Engineering Systems and Civil and Environmental Engineering (Head)
SIMCHI-LEVI, D., Civil and Environmental Engineering and Engineering Systems
STERMAN, J., Management and Engineering Systems
SUSSMAN, J. M., Civil and Environmental Engineering and Engineering Systems
UTTERBACK, J., Management and Innovation and Engineering Systems
WELSCH, R., Statistics and Management Science and Engineering Systems
WIDNALL, S., Aeronautics and Astronautics and Engineering Systems

School of Humanities, Arts, and Social Sciences (77 Massachusetts Ave, Room E51-255, Cambridge, MA 02139-4307; tel. (617) 253-3450; e-mail www-shss@mit.edu; internet web.mit.edu/shass):

Department of Economics:

ACEMOGLU, K. D., Economics
ANGELETOS, G.-M., Economics
ANGRIST, J., Economics
AUTOR, D., Economics
BANERJEE, A., Economics
BLANCHARD, O. J., Economics
CABALLERO, R., Economics (Head)
CHERNOZHUKOV, V., Economics
DIAMOND, P. A., Economics
DUFLO, E., Poverty Alleviation and Development Economics
ELLISON, G., Economics
FINKELSTEIN, A., Economics
GIBBONS, R. S., Management and Economics
GREENSTONE, M., Environmental Economics
GRUBER, J., Economics
HARRIS, J. E., Economics
HAUSMAN, J. A., Economics
HOLMSTRÖM, B. R., Economics (Head)
JOSKOW, P. L., Economics and Management
NEWEY, W. K., Economics
PIORE, M. J., Political Economy
POTERBA, J. M., Economics
ROSE, N., Economics
ROSS, S., Finance and Economics
SCHMALENSEE, R. L., Management and Economics
SNYDER, J., Political Science and Economics
TEMIN, P., Economics
THUROW, L. C., Management and Economics
TOWNSEND, R., Economics
WERNING, I., Economics
WHEATON, W. C., Economics and Urban Studies

Department of Linguistics and Philosophy:

BYRNE, A., Philosophy
CHOMSKY, N. A., Linguistics
FLYNN, S., Second Language Acquisition
FOX, D., Linguistics
GIBSON, E. A., Cognitive Science
HASLANGER, S., Philosophy
HEIM, I., Linguistics
HOLTON, R., Philosophy
IATRIDOU, S., Linguistics
KENSTOWICZ, M., Linguistics
LANGTON, R., Philosophy
MCGEE, V., Philosophy
MIYAGAWA, S., Japanese Language and Culture, Linguistics
O'NEIL, W., Linguistics
PESETSKY, D., Linguistics
SINGER, I., Philosophy
STALNAKER, R., Philosophy
STERIADE, D., Linguistics
VON FINTEL, K., Linguistics
WEXLER, K. N., Psychology and Linguistics
YABLO, S., Philosophy

Department of Political Science:

ANSOLABEHERE, S. D., Political Science
BERGER, S., Political Science
CHOUCRI, N., Political Science
LOCKE, R. M., Entrepreneurship and Political Science
PIORE, M. J., Political Economy and Political Science
POSEN, B. R., Political Science
SAMUELS, R. J., Political Science
SNYDER, J. M., Political Science and Economics
STEWART, C., III, Political Science (Head)
VAN EVERA, S. W., Political Science

Foreign Languages and Literatures Section:

DE COURTIVRON, I., French Studies (Head)
GARRELS, E., Spanish and Latin American Studies
MIYAGAWA, S., Japanese Language and Culture, Linguistics
TURK, E. B., French Studies and Film
WANG, J., Chinese Languages and Culture

History Section:

DOWER, J. W., History
FOGELSON, R. M., History and Urban Studies
KHOURY, P. S., History
MCCANTS, A. E. C., History (Head)
MAIER, P., History
RITVO, H., History
SMITH, M. R., History of Technology
WOOD, E. A., History

Literature Section:

BUZARD, J., Literature (Head)
DONALDSON, P. S., Literature
HENDERSON, D., Literature
HILDEBIDLE, J., Literature
JENKINS, H., III, Comparative Media Studies and Literature
KIBEL, A. C., Literature
PERRY, R., Literature and Women's Studies
TAPSCOTT, S. J., Literature
THORBURN, D., Literature
URICCHIO, W., Comparative Media Studies

Music and Theater Arts Section:

BRODY, A., Theater Arts
CHILD, P., Music
DEFRANTZ, T., Theater Arts
HARBISON, J., Music
HARRIS, E. T., Music
LINDGREN, L., Music
SONENBERG, J., Theater Arts
THOMPSON, M. A., Music
VERCOE, B., Media Arts and Sciences
ZIPORYN, E., Music

Program in Anthropology:

FISCHER, M. M. J., Anthropology and Science and Technology Studies
HOWE, J., Anthropology
JACKSON, J. E., Anthropology
SILBEY, S., Sociology and Anthropology (Head)

Program in Comparative Media Studies:

JENKINS, H., III, Humanities, Comparative Media Studies and Literature
URICCHIO, W., Comparative Media Studies

Program in Science, Technology and Society:

FISCHER, M. M. J., Humanities
FITZGERALD, D. K., History of Technology
MANNING, K. R., Rhetoric and the History of Science
MINDELL, D. A., History of Engineering and Manufacturing, Engineering Systems (Dir)
POSTOL, T. A., Science, Technology and Nat. Security Policy
SMITH, M. R., History of Technology
TURKLE, S. R., Social Studies of Science and Technology
WILLIAMS, R. H., History of Science and Technology

Program in Writing and Humanistic Studies:

KANIGEL, R., Science Writing
LEVENSON, T., Science Writing
MANNING, K. R., Rhetoric and the History of Science
PARADIS, J., Writing (Program Head)
WILLIAMS, J. H., Engineering
WILLIAMS, R. H., History of Science and Technology

School of Science (77 Massachusetts Ave, Room 6-123, Cambridge, MA 02139; tel. (617) 253-8900; fax (617) 253-8901; internet web.mit.edu/science):

Department of Biology:

AMON, A., Biology
BAKER, T., Biology
BARTEL, D. P., Biology
BELL, S., Biology
CHEN, J., Biology
CHISHOLM, S. W., Civil and Environmental Engineering and Biology
CONSTANTINE-PATON, M., Biology
FINK, G. R., Genetics
GERTLER, F., Biology
GROSSMAN, A. D., Biology
GUARENTE, L. P., Biology
HOPKINS, N. H., Biology
HORVITZ, H. R., Biology
HOUSMAN, D. E., Cancer Research and Biology
HYNES, R. O., Cancer Research
IMPERIALI, B., Chemistry and Biology
JACKS, T. E., Biology
JAENISCH, R., Biology
KAISER, C., Biology (Head)
KING, J. A., Biology
KRIEGER, M., Biology, Molecular Genetics
LANDER, E., Biology
LAUFFENBURGER, D., Bioengineering, Chemical Engineering and Biology
LEES, J. A., Biology
LINDQUIST, S., Biology
LODISH, H. F., Biology and Bioengineering
MATSUDAIRA, P., Biology and Bioengineering
NEWMAN, D. K., Biology
ORR-WEAVER, T., Biology
PAGE, D., Biology
PARDUE, M. L., Biology
PLOEGH, H., Biology
QUINN, W., Neurobiology
RAJBHANDARY, U. L., Molecular Biology
RICH, A., Biophysics
SAMSON, L., Toxicology and Biological Engineering
SAUER, R. T., Biology
SHARP, P. A., Biology
SHENG, M., Neuroscience
SINSKEY, A. J., Microbiology
SIVE, H. L., Biology
SOLOMON, F., Biology
STEINER, L. A., Immunology
STUBBE, J., Chemistry and Biology
TONEGAWA, S., Biology and Neuroscience
WALKER, G. C., Biology
WEINBERG, R. A., Cancer Research
WILSON, M., Neurobiology
YOUNG, R. A., Biology

Department of Brain and Cognitive Sciences:

ADELSON, E. H., Visual Sciences
BEAR, M., Neuroscience
BERWICK, R. C., Computational Linguistics
BIZZI, E., Brain Sciences and Human Behaviour
BROWN, E. N., Computational Neuroscience and Health Sciences and Technology

CHOROVER, S. L., Psychology
CONSTANTINE-PATON, M., Biology
CORKIN, S. H., Behavioural Neuroscience
DESIMONE, R., Neuroscience
GABRIELI, J., Health Sciences and Technology and Cognitive Neuroscience
GIBSON, E., Cognitive Sciences
GRAYBIEL, A. M., Neuroanatomy
HEIN, A., Experimental Psychology
HOCKFIELD, S., Neuroscience
HOGAN, N., Mechanical Engineering
KANWISHER, N. G., Cognitive Neuroscience
MILLER, E. K., Visual Neuroscience
POGGIO, T. A., Brain Sciences and Human Behaviour
POTTER, M. C., Psychology
PRELAC, D., Management
QUINN, W. G., Neurobiology
RICHARDS, W. A., Cognitive Sciences
SCHILLER, P. H., Medical Engineering and Medical Physics
SCHNEIDER, G. E., Neuroscience
SEUNG, H. S., Computational Neuroscience
SHENG, M. H.-T., Neurobiology
SLOTINE, J.-J. E., Mechanical Engineering and Information Sciences
SUR, M., Neuroscience (Head)
TONEGAWA, S., Biology and Neuroscience
TSAI, L.-H., Neuroscience
WEXLER, K. N., Psychology and Linguistics
WILSON, M., Neuroscience
WURTMAN, R. J., Neuropharmacology

Department of Chemistry:

BAWENDI, M. G., Chemistry
BUCHWALD, S. L., Chemistry
CEYER, S. T., Chemistry
CUMMINS, C. C., Chemistry
DANHEISER, R. L., Chemistry
DEUTCH, J. M., Chemistry
DRENNAN, C. L., Chemistry
ESSIGMANN, J. M., Chemistry and Toxicology
FIELD, R. W., Chemistry
FU, G. C., Chemistry
GRIFFIN, R. G., Chemistry
IMPERIALI, B., Chemistry and Biology
KLIBANOV, A. M., Chemistry and Bioengineering
LIPPARD, S. J., Chemistry
NELSON, K. A., Chemistry
NOCERA, D. G., Energy Chemistry
PETERS, J. C., Chemistry
SCHROCK, R. R., Chemistry
SILBEY, R. J., Chemistry
STUBBE, J., Chemistry and Biology
SWAGER, T. M., Chemistry (Head)
TANNENBAUM, S. R., Chemistry and Toxicology
TOKMAKOFF, A., Chemistry

Department of Earth, Atmospheric and Planetary Sciences:

BINZEL, R. P., Planetary Sciences
BOWRING, S. A., Geology
BOYLE, E. A., Ocean Geochemistry
BURCHFIEL, B. C., Geology
ELLIOT, J. L., Planetary Astronomy and Physics
EMANUEL, K. A., Atmospheric Science
ENTEKHABI, D., Civil and Environmental Engineering and Earth, Atmospheric and Planetary Sciences
EVANS, J. B., Geophysics
FLIERL, G. R., Oceanography
FREY, F. A., Geochemistry
GROVE, T. L., Geology
HAGER, B. H., Earth Sciences
HERRING, T. A., Geophysics
LINDZEN, R. S., Meteorology
MARSHALL, J., Atmospheric and Oceanic Sciences
MORGAN, F. D., Geophysics
PLUMB, R. A., Meteorology
PRINN, R. G., Atmospheric Chemistry
RIZZOLI, P. M., Physical Oceanography
ROTHMAN, D. H., Geophysics
ROYDEN, L., Geology and Geophysics
SUMMONS, R. E., Geobiology
TOKSÖZ, M. N., Geophysics
VAN DER HILST, R., Geophysics
WISDOM, J., Planetary Sciences
WUNSCH, C. I., Physical Oceanography
ZUBER, M. T., Planetary Sciences and Geophysics (Head)

Department of Mathematics:

ARTIN, M., Mathematics
BENNEY, D. J., Applied Mathematics
BERGER, B., Applied Mathematics
BEZRUKAVNIKOV, R., Mathematics
CHENG, H., Applied Mathematics
COLDING, T. H., Mathematics
DUDLEY, R. M., Mathematics
EDELMAN, A., Applied Mathematics
ETINGOF, P. I., Mathematics
FREEDMAN, D. Z., Applied Mathematics
GOEMANS, M., Applied Mathematics
GUILLEMIN, V. W., Mathematics
HELGASON, S., Mathematics
JERISON, D. S., Mathematics
KAC, V., Mathematics
KLEIMAN, S., Mathematics
KLEITMAN, D. J., Applied Mathematics
LEIGHTON, F. T., Applied Mathematics
LUSZTIG, G., Mathematics
MCKERNAN, J., Mathematics
MATTUCK, A. P., Mathematics
MELROSE, R. B., Mathematics
MILLER, H. R., Mathematics
MROWKA, T., Mathematics
POONEN, B., Mathematics
ROGERS, H., Jr, Mathematics
ROSALES, R. R., Applied Mathematics
SEIDEL, P., Mathematics
SHEFFIELD, S., Mathematics
SHOR, P., Applied Mathematics
SINGER, I. M., Mathematics
SIPSER, M., Applied Mathematics (Head)
STAFFILANI, G., Mathematics
STANLEY, R. P., Applied Mathematics
STRANG, W. G., Mathematics
STROOCK, D. W., Mathematics
TOOMRE, A., Applied Mathematics
VOGAN, D. A., Jr, Mathematics

Department of Physics:

ASHOORI, R., Physics
BECKER, U. J., Physics
BELCHER, J. W., Physics
BENEDEK, G. B., Physics and Biological Physics
BERTOZZI, W., Physics
BERTSCHINGER, E., Physics (Head)
BUSZA, W., Physics
CANIZARES, C. R., Physics
CHAKRABARTY, D., Physics
CHEN, M., Physics
COPPI, B., Physics
DRESSELHAUS, M. S., Physics and Electrical Engineering
ELLIOT, J. L., Earth, Atmospheric and Planetary Sciences and Physics
FARHI, E., Physics
FELD, M. S., Physics
FISHER, P. H., Physics
FREEDMAN, D., Mathematics and Physics
GREYTAK, T. J., Physics
GUTH, A. H., Physics
HEWITT, J. N., Physics
IPPEN, E. P., Electrical Engineering and Physics
JACKIW, R. W., Physics
JAFFE, R. L., Physics and Science
JOANNOPOULOS, J. D., Physics
JOSS, P. C., Physics
KARDAR, M., Physics
KASTNER, M., Physics
KETTERLE, W., Physics
KOWALSKI, S. B., Physics
LEE, P. A., Physics
LEVITOV, L., Physics
LEWIN, W. H. G., Physics
LITSTER, J. D., Physics
MATTHEWS, J. L., Physics
MILNER, R. G., Physics
MONIZ, E. J., Physics
NEGELE, J. W., Physics
PORKOLAB, M., Physics
PRITCHARD, D. E., Physics
RAJAGOPAL, K., Physics
RAPPAPORT, S. A., Physics
REDWINE, R. P., Physics
SCHECHTER, P., Astrophysics
SEUNG, H. S., Computational Neuroscience and Physics
TAYLOR, W., Physics
TING, S. C. C., Physics
WEN, X.-G., Physics
WILCZEK, F., Physics
WYSLOUCH, B., Physics
ZWIEBACH, B., Physics

Whitaker College of Health Sciences and Technology (77 Massachusetts Ave, Room E25-519, Cambridge, MA 02139; tel. (617) 258-4418; fax (617) 253-7498; internet hst.mit.edu):

BENEDEK, G. B., Physics and Biological Physics and Health Sciences and Technology
BRAIDA, L. D., Electrical Engineering and Health Sciences and Technology
COHEN, R. J., Biomedical Engineering
CRAVALHO, E. G., Mechanical Engineering and Health Sciences and Technology
EDELMAN, E. R., Health Sciences and Technology
GABRIELI, J., Health Sciences and Technology, Brain and Cognitive Sciences
GEHRKE, L., Health Sciences and Technology
GRAY, M. L., Medical and Electrical Engineering
HOUSMAN, D. E., Biology
LANGER, R. S., Chemical and Biomedical Engineering and Health Sciences and Technology
MARK, R. G., Health Sciences and Technology and Electrical Engineering and Computer Science
SINSKEY, A. J., Biology and Health Sciences and Technology
SZOLOVITS, P., Computer Science and Engineering and Health Sciences and Technology
WURTMAN, R. J., Neuropharmacology and Health Sciences and Technology
YOUNG, L. R., Astronautics and Health Sciences and Technology

Harvard-MIT Division of Health Sciences and Technology

BHATIA, S. N., Health Sciences and Technology, and Electrical Engineering and Computer Science
BROWN, E. N., Health Sciences and Technology, and Computational Neuroscience
FREEMAN, D. M., Electrical Engineering
LANGER, R. S., Chemical and Biomedical Engineering, and Health Sciences and Technology
SASISEKHARAN, R., Biological Engineering, and Health Sciences and Technology

Sloan School of Management (50 Memorial Dr., Cambridge, MA 02142; tel. (617) 253-2659; internet mitsloan.mit.edu):

ANCONA, D. G., Management
ASQUITH, P., Finance
BARNETT, A. I., Operations Research and Management and Management Science
BERNDT, E. R., Applied Economics
BERTSIMAS, D., Management
BITRAN, G. R., Management
BRYNJOLFSSON, E., Management Science
CARROLL, J. S., Management
COX, J. C., Finance
CUSUMANO, M. A., Management
EPPINGER, S. D., Management

Fernández, R. M., Management
Fine, C. H., Management
Freund, R. M., Management Science
Gibbons, R. S., Management
Graves, S. C., Management
Hauser, J. R., Marketing
Henderson, R. M., Management
Holmstrom, B. R., Economics and Management
Johnson, S., Entrepreneurship
Joskow, P. L., Economics and Management
Kochan, T. A., Management
Kothari, S. P., Accounting
Lessard, D. R., Int. Management
Little, J. D. C., Marketing
Lo, A. W., Finance
Locke, R., Entrepreneurship
Madnick, S. E., Information Technology and Engineering Systems
Magnanti, T. L., Management Science and Electrical Engineering
Malone, T. W., Management
Myers, S. C., Financial Economics
Orlikowski, W. J., Communication Sciences
Orlin, J. B., Management
Osterman, P., Human Resources and Management
Pindyck, R. S., Finance and Economics
Prelec, D., Management
Roberts, E. B., Management
Ross, S. A., Financial Economics
Schmalensee, R. L., Management and Economics
Schmittlein, D. C., Management
Simester, D., Management Science
Sterman, J., Computer Studies
Stoker, T. M., Management and Economics
Thurow, L. C., Management and Economics
Urban, G. L., Management
Utterback, J., Management and Innovation
Van Maanen, J. E., Management
von Hippel, E. A., Management
Wang, J., Finance
Watts, R. L., Accounting
Welsch, R. E., Statistics and Management Science
Wernerfelt, B., Management
Yates, J., Management

MASSACHUSETTS MARITIME ACADEMY

101 Academy Dr., Buzzards Bay, MA 02532
Telephone: (508) 830-5000
Fax: (508) 830-5077
E-mail: admissions@maritime.edu
Internet: www.maritime.edu

Founded 1891 as Massachusetts Nautical Training School; present name 1942

Pres.: (vacant)
Vice-Pres. for Academic Affairs: Bradley Lima
Vice-Pres. for Admin. and Finance: Michael A. Joyce
Vice-Pres. for Student Services: Allen Hansen
Dir of Admissions: Roy Fulgueras
Library Dir: Susan Berteaux

Number of teachers: 52
Number of students: 770

Depts of engineering, humanities, int. maritime business, marine safety and environmental protection, marine transportation, science and mathematics, social science.

MERRIMACK COLLEGE

315 Turnpike St, North Andover, MA 01845
Telephone: (978) 837-5000
Fax: (978) 837-5222
Internet: www.merrimack.edu

Founded 1947
Academic year: September to May

Pres.: Richard J. Santagati
Registrar: Jennifer DiSteffano
Dir of Library: Barbara Lachance

Library of 118,083 vols, 1,069 current periodicals
Number of teachers: 139
Number of students: 2,000

DEANS

Girard School of Business and Int. Commerce: Robert Cuomo
Liberal Arts: Michael Rossi
Science and Engineering: (vacant)

MGH INSTITUTE OF HEALTH PROFESSIONS

Charleston Navy Yard, 36 First Ave, Boston, MA 02129-4557
Telephone: (617) 726-2947
Fax: (617) 726-3716
E-mail: admissions@mghihp.edu
Internet: www.mghihp.edu

Founded 1980
Academic year: September to August

Pres.: Ann W. Caldwell
Academic Dean: Kevin Kearns

Library of 50,000 vols
Number of teachers: 79
Number of students: 665 (498 full-time)

Divs of clinical investigation, communication sciences and disorders, medical imaging, nursing, physical therapy

DIRECTORS OF GRADUATE PROGRAMS

Clinical Investigation: Dr Paul Boepple
Communication Sciences and Disorders: Dr Kevin P. Kearns
Medical Imaging: Dr Richard Terrass
Nursing: Dr Margery Chisholm
Physical Therapy: Dr Leslie Portney

MONTSERRAT COLLEGE OF ART

23 Essex St, POB 26, Beverly, MA 01915
Telephone: (978) 922-8222
Fax: (978) 921-4241
E-mail: admiss@montserrat.edu
Internet: www.montserrat.edu
Private control
Academic year: September to May

Pres.: Dr Stephen D. Immerman
Dean of Admissions and Enrollment Management: Rick Longo
Dean of College Relations: Jo Broderick
Dean of Faculty and Academic Affairs: Laura Tonelli
Dean of Student Services: Brian Bicknell
Registrar: Theresa Skelly
Library Dir: Cheri Coe

Library of 12,000
Number of teachers: 60
Number of students: 403

Divs of art education, foundation, graphic design, illustration, interdisciplinary, liberal arts, painting and drawing, photo and video, printmaking, sculpture.

MOUNT HOLYOKE COLLEGE

50 College St, South Hadley, MA 01072
Telephone: (413) 538-2000
Fax: (413) 538-2391
E-mail: admission@mtholyoke.edu
Internet: www.mtholyoke.edu

Founded 1837
Academic year: September to May

Pres.: Joanne V. Creighton
Treas.: Mary Jo Maydew
Assoc. Dean of College and Dean of Students: H. Elizabeth Braun
Dean of College: Lee Bowie
Dean of Faculty: Donal O'Shea
Dean of Studies: Joseph Cohen
Registrar: Monica Augustin
Chief Information Officer and Dir of Library, Information and Technology Services: Patricia Albanese

Library of 700,000 vols
Number of teachers: 206
Number of students: 2,100

Divs of humanities, science and mathematics, social sciences

Publication: *Alumnae Quarterly*.

MOUNT IDA COLLEGE

777 Dedham St, Newton, MA 02459
Telephone: (617) 928-4553
Fax: (617) 928-4507
E-mail: admissions@mountida.edu
Internet: www.mountida.edu

Founded 1899
Private control
Academic year: August to May

Pres.: Carol J. Matteson
Vice-Pres. for Academic Affairs: Dr Lance W. Carluccio
Vice-Pres. for Devt: Christopher S. Mosher
Vice-Pres. for Enrollment Management and Marketing: Philip A. Conroy, Jr
Vice-Pres. for Finance and Admin.: David Healy
Vice-Pres. for Student Affairs: Dr Elizabeth True
Registrar: Maureen Moriarty
Dean of Academic Services: Alyce Curtis
Dean of Information Technology and Learning Resources: Marge Lippincott

Library of 120,000 titles
Number of teachers: 100
Number of students: 1,429

Schools of animal science, arts and sciences, business, design.

NEW ENGLAND COLLEGE OF OPTOMETRY

424 Beacon St, Boston, MA 02115
Telephone: (617) 266-2030
E-mail: admissions@neco.edu
Internet: www.neco.edu

Founded 1894 as Klein School of Optics; present name 1976
Private control
Academic year: September to May

Pres.: Elizabeth Chen
Vice-Pres. and Dean of Academic Affairs: Dr Steven Koevary
Vice-Pres. and Dean of Students, Admin. and Alumni: Dr Terrance B. Neylon
Vice-Pres. for Clinical Care and Services: Dr Barry J. Barresi
Vice-Pres. for Devt: Larry Raff
Vice-Pres. for Finance and Admin.: Carol DeCourcey
Vice-Pres. for Professional Services: Roger Wilson
Dir of Admissions: Taline Farra
Registrar: Glenda Underwood
Dir of Library Services: Cindy Hutchison

Number of teachers: 77
Number of students: 425

Depts of biomedical science and disease, community care, specialty and advanced care, vision science.

NEW ENGLAND CONSERVATORY OF MUSIC

290 Huntington Ave, Boston, MA 02115
Telephone: (617) 585-1101
Fax: (617) 585-1115
E-mail: admission@newenglandconservatory.edu
Internet: www.newenglandconservatory.edu

Founded 1867
Academic year: September to May

Pres.: TONY WOODCOCK
Provost: ROBERT DODSON
Dean of College: TOM NOVAK
Registrar: ROBERT WINKLEY
Dir of Libraries: JEAN MORROW

Library: Spaulding Library contains 85,000 vols (books, scores, periodicals); the Firestone Library contains 60,000 sound and video recordings
Number of teachers: 216
Number of students: 770
Publications: *Journal for Learning through Music* (1 a year), *Notes* (2 a year).

NEW ENGLAND LAW-BOSTON

154 Stuart St, Boston, MA 02116
Telephone: (617) 422-7210
Fax: (617) 422-7201
E-mail: admit@nesl.edu
Internet: www.nesl.edu

Founded 1908 as Portia Law School, present name 2008
Private control
Academic year: August to May

Dean: JOHN F. O'BRIEN
Dir of Admissions: MICHELLE L'ETOILE
Library Dir: Prof. ANNE M. ACTON

Library of 321,000 vols
Number of teachers: 37 full-time, 50 part-time
Number of students: 800 full-time, 335 part-time
Publications: *New England Journal of Comparative and International Law*, *New England Law Review*.

NICHOLS COLLEGE

POB 5000, Dudley, MA 01571
Telephone: (508) 213-1560
Fax: (508) 213-2225
E-mail: admissions@nichols.edu
Internet: www.nichols.edu

Founded 1815

Business admin. and liberal arts

Pres.: Dr SUSAN WEST ENGELKEMEYER
Provost and Sr Vice-Pres.: ALAN REINHARDT
Vice-Pres. and Dean of Student Services: BRIAN MCCOY
Vice-Pres. for Admin.: MICHAEL STANTON
Vice-Pres. for College Advancement: WILLIAM PIECZYNSKI
Vice-Pres. for Enrollment and Marketing: TOM CAFARO
Vice-Pres. for Information Technology: KEVIN BRASSARD
Registrar: BETIN ROBICHAUD
Dir of Library: JIM DOUGLAS

Library of 67,000 vols
Number of teachers: 50
Number of students: 1,343 undergraduates, 249 graduates

NORTHEASTERN UNIVERSITY

360 Huntington Ave, Boston, MA 02115
Telephone: (617) 373-2000
Internet: www.northeastern.edu

Founded 1898

Pres.: Dr JOSEPH AOUN
Sr Vice-Pres. for Enrollment and Student Life: PHILOMENA MANTELLA
Sr Vice-Pres. for Exec. Affairs: MARK PUTNAM
Sr Vice-Pres. for External Affairs: MICHAEL ARMINI
Vice-Pres. and Dean for Student Affairs: E. EDWARD KLOTZBIER
Vice-Pres. for Marketing and Communications: BRIAN KENNY
Provost: STEPHEN DIRECTOR
Dean of Admissions: RONNE PATRICK
Dean of Library: EDWARD A. WARRO

Library of 966,923 vols, 126,190 e-books, 2.3m. microforms, 1,950 serial titles, 23,684 audio and video items, 150,029 govt documents
Number of teachers: 1,965 (984 full-time, 981 part-time)
Number of students: 25,376 (19,541 full-time, 5,835 part-time)

DEANS

Bouvé College of Health Sciences: STEPHEN R. ZOLOTH
College of Arts, Media and Design: BRUCE RONKIN
College of Business Administration: Prof. THOMAS MOORE
College of Computer and Information Science: LARRY FINKELSTEIN
College of Criminal Justice: JACK R. GREENE
College of Engineering: DAVID LUZZI
School of Law: EMILY SPIELER
College of Science: BRUCE RONKIN
College of Social Science: BRUCE RONKIN
School of Technological Entrepreneurship: PAUL ZAVRACKY

OLIN COLLEGE OF ENGINEERING

Olin Way, Needham, MA 02492-1200
Telephone: (781) 292-2300
E-mail: info@olin.edu
Internet: www.olin.edu

Founded 1997
Private control; funded by F. W. Olin Foundation
Academic year: August to May

Pres.: RICHARD K. MILLER
Vice-Pres. for Admin. and Finance: STEPHEN P. HANNABURY
Vice-Pres. for External Relations and Dean of Admission: CHARLES S. NOLAN
Vice-Pres. for Innovation and Research: SHERRA E. KERNS
Provost and Dean of Faculty: MICHAEL MOODY (acting)
Dean of Student Life: ROGER C. CRAFTS
Registrar: LINDA CANAVAN
Library Dir: DIANNA MAGNONI

Number of teachers: 37
Number of students: 304
Publication: *Journal of Asynchronous Learning Networks* (2–4 a year)

PROFESSORS

BOURNE, J., Electrical and Computer Engineering
DONIS-KELLER, H., Biology and Art
HOLT, S. S., Physics
KERNS, D., Electrical Engineering
KERNS, S., Electrical and Computer Engineering
MILLER, R., Mechanical Engineering
PRATT, G., Electrical and Computer Engineering

PINE MANOR COLLEGE

400 Heath St, Chestnut Hill, MA 02467
Telephone: (617) 731-7000
Fax: (617) 731-7199
E-mail: admission@pmc.edu
Internet: www.pmc.edu

Founded 1911 as a post-secondary div. of Dana Hall School; present name and status 1977
Private control
Academic year: September to May

Pres.: Dr GLORIA NEMEROWICZ
Dean of the College: Dr NIA LANE CHESTER
Vice-Pres. for Finance and Business: BETSY ESPE
Vice-Pres. for Institutional Advancement: SUSAN WEBBER
Registrar: KERRY BOYD
Dean of Student Life: DENISE ALLEYNE
Library Dir: MARILYN SMITH BREGOLI

Library of 70,000 vols
Number of teachers: 66
Number of students: 491

Majors in biology, business admin., communication, economic and financial systems, English, history, liberal studies, management, psychology, social and political systems, visual arts.

REGIS COLLEGE

235 Wellesley St, Weston, MA 02493-1571
Telephone: (781) 768-7000
Fax: (781) 768-8339
Internet: www.regiscollege.edu

Founded 1927
Academic year: September to June

Pres.: MARY JANE ENGLAND
Vice-Pres. for Academic Affairs: PAULA HARBECKE
Vice-Pres. for Enrollment and Marketing: R. JOSEPH BELLEVANCE, Jr
Vice-Pres. for Finance and Business: THOMAS G. PISTORINO
Vice-Pres. for Student Affairs: LYNN TRIPP COLEMAN
Registrar: Sister PATRICIA MCDONOUGH
Dir of Library: LYNN TRIPLETT

Library of 133,000 vols
Number of teachers: 145
Number of students: 1,138
Publications: *Alumnae Bulletin*, *Hemetera*, *Regis Today*.

ST JOHN'S SEMINARY

127 Lake Street, Brighton, MA 02135
Telephone: (617) 254-2610
Fax: (617) 787-2336
E-mail: rjsullivan@rcab.org
Internet: www.sjs.edu

Founded 1884
Private control
Academic year: September to May

Rector: Rev. JOHN A. FARREN
Vice-Rector: Rev. STEPHEN DONOHOE
Dean of Students: Rev. CHRISTOPHER K. O'CONNOR
Dean of Faculty: Rev. STEPHEN SALOCKS
Librarian: Rev. Mgr LAURENCE W. MCGRATH

Library of 159,000 vols
Number of teachers: 22
Number of students: 80 (full-time)

SALEM STATE COLLEGE

352 Lafayette St, Salem, MA 01970
Telephone: (978) 542-6000
E-mail: college.relations@salemstate.edu
Internet: www.salemstate.edu

Founded 1854

Pres.: Dr NANCY D. HARRINGTON
Vice-Pres. for Academic Affairs: Dr DIANE R. LAPKIN
Vice-Pres. for Admin. and Finance: JOSEPH DONOVAN
Vice-Pres. for Institutional Advancement: CYNTHIA MCGURREN

Exec. Vice-Pres. for Student Life: STANLEY P. CAHILL
Dean of Students: JAMES G. STOLL
Dean of Library: SUSAN E. CIRILLO

Library of 225,000 vols
Number of teachers: 301
Number of students: 5,400

Depts of accounting and finance, art, biology, business, cartography and GIS, chemistry, communications, computer science, criminal justice, economics, education, English, fire science, foreign languages, geography, geology, history, interdisciplinary studies, management, marketing and decision sciences, mathematics, music, nursing, occupational therapy, philosophy, physics, political science, psychology, speech communication, social work, Spanish, sociology, sport, fitness and leisure studies, theatre

DEANS

School of Arts and Sciences: ANITA SHEA
School of Business: K. BREWER DORAN
Schools of Human Services: NEAL DECHILLO

SCHOOL OF THE MUSEUM OF FINE ARTS

230 The Fenway, Boston, MA 02115
Telephone: (617) 267-6100
Fax: (617) 424-6271
E-mail: admissions@smfa.edu
Internet: www.smfa.edu
Academic year: September to May

Dean of Admissions: SUSAN CLAIN
Dean of Faculty: LORNE FALK
Dean of the School: DEBORAH H. DLUHY
Provost and Dir of Devt: DAN POTEET

Library of 130,000 vols
Number of teachers: 140
Number of students: 1,124

SIMMONS COLLEGE

300 The Fenway, Boston, MA 02115
Telephone: (617) 521-2000
Fax: (617) 521-3199
E-mail: ugadm@simmons.edu
Internet: www.simmons.edu

Founded 1899

Pres.: HELEN DRINAN
Sr Vice-Pres. for Admin. and Planning: STEFANO FALCONI
Sr Vice-Pres. and Treas.: HUMBERTO GONÇALVES
Vice-Pres. for Advancement: KRISTINA SCHAEFFER
Vice-Pres. for Marketing and Admission: CHERYL HOWARD
Provost: CHARLENA SEYMOUR
Registrar: DONNA DOLAN
Dir of Libraries: DAPHNE HARRINGTON

Number of teachers: 548 (231 full-time, 317 part-time)
Number of students: 5,003

Publications: *Abafazi*, *Essays and Studies*, *Now*, *Simmons News*, *Simmons Review*

DEANS

College of Arts and Sciences: DIANE RAYMOND (acting)
School of Health Studies: GERALD KOOCHER
School of Management: DEBORAH MERRILL-SANDS
School of Social Work: STEFAN KRUG
Graduate School of Library and Information Sciences: MICHELE CLOONAN

SMITH COLLEGE

Northampton, MA 01063
Telephone: (413) 584-2700
Fax: (413) 585-2123
E-mail: admission@smith.edu
Internet: www.smith.edu

Founded 1871
Academic year: September to May

Pres.: CAROL CHRIST
Provost and Dean of the Faculty: SUSAN BOURQUE
Vice-Pres. for Advancement: PATRICIA JACKSON
Dean of the College: MAUREEN A. MAHONEY
Dean of Students: JULIANNE OHOTNICKY
Registrar: TRICIA O'NEILL
Dir of Libraries: CHRISTOPHER LORING

Library of 1,200,000 vols
Number of teachers: 303 (287 full-time, 16 part-time)
Number of students: 2,781 (2,682 undergraduate women, 99 postgraduate men and women)

Publications: *Alumnae Quarterly*, *Bulletin of the Museum of Art* (irregular), *Meridians*.

SOUTHERN NEW ENGLAND SCHOOL OF LAW

333 Faunce Corner Rd, North Dartmouth, MA 02747
Telephone: (508) 998-9600
E-mail: admissions@snesl.edu
Internet: www.snesl.edu
Private control
Academic year: August to May

Chancellor: Hon. FRANCIS J. LARKIN
Dean: Dr ROBERT V. WARD, Jr
Registrar: CAROL VIDAL
Library Dir: SPENCER CLOUGH
Number of students: 227

SPRINGFIELD COLLEGE

263 Alden St, Springfield, MA 01109-3797
Telephone: (413) 748-3000
Fax: (413) 748-3746
Internet: www.spfldcol.edu

Founded 1885
Academic year: August to May

Pres.: Dr RICHARD B. FLYNN
Vice-Pres. for Academic Affairs: Dr JEAN WYLD
Vice-Pres. for Finance and Admin.: JOHN MAILHOT
Vice-Pres. for Institutional Advancement: DAVID FRABONI
Vice-Pres. for Student Affairs: Dr DAVID G. BRAVERMAN
Registrar: IRENE RIOS
Librarian: ANDREA TAUPIER

Library of 187,358 vols, 25,586 bound periodicals
Number of teachers: 205 full-time
Number of students: 5,090 (incl. satellite campuses)

DEANS

School of Arts, Science and Professional Studies: Dr MARY HEALEY
School of Health, Physical Education, and Recreation: Dr WILLIAM J. CONSIDINE
School of Health Sciences and Rehabilitation Studies: Dr WILLIAM M. SUSMAN
School of Human Services: Dr ROBERT WILLEY
School of Social Work: Dr FRANCINE J. VECCHIOLLA

STONEHILL COLLEGE

320 Washington St, Easton, MA 02357
Telephone: (508) 565-1000
Fax: (508) 565-1500
Internet: www.stonehill.edu

Founded 1948
Academic year: September to May

Pres.: Rev. MARK T. CREGAN
Vice-Pres. for Academic Affairs: KATIE CONBOY
Vice-Pres. for Advancement: FRANCIS X. DILLON
Vice-Pres. for Finance: JEANNE FINLAYSON
Vice-Pres. for Mission: Rev. JOHN DENNING
Vice-Pres. for Student Affairs: Rev. GEORGE B. MULLIGAN
Dean of Faculty: KAREN TALENTINO
Registrar: JOHN PESTANA
Dir of Library: ED HYNES

Library of 194,587 vols
Number of teachers: 230 (126 full-time, 104 part-time)
Number of students: 2,617

Depts of admin., history, history and philosophy of science, int. studies, Irish studies, labour studies, mathematics, Middle Eastern/Asian studies, military science, philosophy, physics, political science, psychology, public admin., religious studies, sociology and criminology, theatre arts, writing programme.

SUFFOLK UNIVERSITY

8 Ashburton Place, Boston, MA 02108-2770
Telephone: (617) 573-8000
Fax: (617) 573-8353
Internet: www.suffolk.edu

Founded 1906

Pres.: DAVID J. SARGENT
Provost and Academic Vice-Pres.: PATRICIA MAGUIRE MESERVEY
Vice-Pres. for Advancement: KATHRYN M. BATTILLO
Vice-Pres. for Enrollment and Int. Programs: MARGUERITE DENNIS
Vice-Pres. for Govt and Community Affairs: JOHN A. NUCCI
Vice-Pres. and Treas.: FRANCIS X. FLANNERY
Dean of College: KENNETH S. GREENBERG
Dean of Students: NANCY C. STOLL
Registrar of Colleges: MARY M. LALLY
Registrar of Law School: LORRAINE D. COVE
Dir of Libraries: EDMUND HAMANN

Libraries of 241,000 vols, 2,070 periodicals, 396,250 microform units
Number of teachers: 400
Number of students: 6,203

Publications: *Suffolk Journal*, *Suffolk Law Review*, *The Advocate*, *Transnational Law Journal*, *Venture*

DEANS

Colleges of Arts and Sciences: KENNETH S. GREENBERG
Law School: ALFRED C. AMAN, Jr
Sawyer Business School: WILLIAM J. O'NEILL, Jr

TUFTS UNIVERSITY

Medford, MA 02155
Telephone: (617) 628-5000
Internet: www.tufts.edu
Private

Founded 1852
Academic year: September to May

Pres.: LAWRENCE S. BACOW
Provost and Sr Vice-Pres.: JAMSHED BHARUCHA
Exec. Vice-Pres.: PATRICIA L. CAMPBELL
Vice-Pres. for Finance and Treas.: THOMAS S. MCGURTY
Vice-Pres. for Human Resources: KATHLEEN CRONIN
Vice-Pres. for Information Technology and Chief Information Officer: DAVID KAHLE
Vice-Pres. for Operations: RICHARD W. REYNOLDS

Vice-Pres. for Univ. Advancement: BRIAN K. LEE
Vice-Pres. for Univ. Relations: MARY R. JEKA
Dean of Student Affairs: BRUCE REITMAN
Dean of Student Services: PAUL STANTON
Dean of Admissions and Enrollment Management: LEE COFFIN
Dir of Tisch Library: JO-ANN MICHALAK

Library of 1,192,935 vols, contained in 4 libraries on 3 campuses
Number of teachers: 1,233
Number of students: 9,273

Publications: *International Journal of Middle East Studies*, *Tufts Health and Nutrition Letter*, *Tufts Journal*, *Tufts Medicine*, *Tufts Veterinary Medicine* (2 a year)

DEANS

Cummings School of Veterinary Medicine (Grafton): DEBORAH T. KOCHEVAR
Fletcher School of Law and Diplomacy (Medford): STEPHEN W. BOSWORTH
Friedman School of Nutrition Science and Policy (Boston): EILEEN T. KENNEDY
Graduate School of Arts and Sciences (Medford): LYNNE PEPALL
Jonathan M. Tisch College of Citizenship and Public Service (Medford): ROBERT M. HOLLISTER
Sackler School of Graduate Biomedical Sciences (Boston): NAOMI ROSENBERG
School of Arts and Sciences (Medford): VICKIE SULLIVAN
School of Dental Medicine (Boston): LONNIE H. NORRIS
School of Engineering (Medford): LINDA M. ABRIOLA
School of Medicine (Boston): HARRIS BERMAN

PROFESSORS

ADELMAN, L., Pathology
ADLER, D., Psychiatry
AFSAR, M., Electrical and Computer Engineering
ALEXANDER, S., Paediatric Dentistry
ALONSO, J., Romance Languages
AMATO, R., Paediatrics
AMBADDY, N., Psychology
AMMONS, E., English
AMPOLA, M., Paediatrics
ARIAS, I., Physiology
AUNER, J., Music
AZZOUNI, J., Philosophy
BACHOVCHIN, W., Biochemistry
BACOW, L., Public Health and Family Medicine
BAGHDIANTZ-MCCABE, I., History
BANKOFF, M., Radiology
BANKS, H., Orthopaedic Surgery
BARRETT, D., Urology
BAUM, J., Ophthalmology
BEINFELD, M., Pharmacology and Experimental Therapeutics
BELSKY, M., Orthopaedic Surgery
BERESFORD, J., Obstetrics and Gynaecology
BERG, J., Clinical Sciences
BERKMAN, E., Medicine
BERMAN, H., Public Health and Family Medicine
BERNSTEIN, J., Music
BERRY, J., Political Science
BHARUCHA, J., Neuroscience
BIANCHI, D., Paediatrics
BIERBAUM, B., Orthopaedic Surgery
BIRKETT, D., Surgery
BLACHER, R., Psychiatry
BLOOMQUIST, E., Physiology
BLUMENTHAL, S., Psychiatry
BOGHOSIAN, B., Mathematics
BORGERS, C., Mathematics
BOUDREAU, F., Obstetrics and Gynaecology
BOYER, M., Public Health and Family Medicine
BRATT, R., Urban and Environmental Policy and Planning
BRAWERMAN, G., Biochemistry
BRIDGES, R., Biomedical Sciences
BRISS, B., Orthodontics
BRODER, M., Medicine
BRODY, C., Computer Science
BRONSON, R., Biomedical Sciences
BROWN, B., Paediatrics
BROWN, W., Neurology
BROWN, W., Psychiatry
BULLOCK, P., Biochemistry
BURKMAN, R., Obstetrics and Gynaecology
BUSHNELL, E., Psychology
CALLOW, A., Surgery
CAMER, S., Surgery
CAMILLI, A., Molecular Biology and Microbiology
CARPINITO, G., Urology
CARTER, B., Radiology
CASSADY, J., Radiation Oncology
CASTELLOT, J., Anatomy and Cellular Biology
CAVAZOS, L., Public Health and Family Medicine
CEBE, P., Physics and Astronomy
CELLI, B., Medicine
CEPEDA, M., Anaesthesiology
CETRULO, C., Obstetrics and Gynaecology
CHAPMAN, R., Prosthodontics and Operative Dentistry
CHAPRA, S., Civil and Environmental Engineering
CHARM, S., Biochemistry
CHECHILE, R., Psychology
CHELMOW, D., Obstetrics and Gynaecology
CHEN, J., General Dentistry
CHEW, F., Biology
CHOI, I., Radiology
CHONG, F., Pathology
COCHRAN, B., Physiology
COCHRANE, D., Biology
COE, N., Surgery
COFFIN, J., Microbiology—Basic Science
COHEN, L., Psychiatry
CONKLIN, J., Sociology
CONNOLLY, N., Anaesthesiology
COOK, R., Psychology
COOPER, A., Pathology
COSGROVE, G., Neurosurgery
COTTER, S., Clinical Sciences
CRANE, G., Classics
CRAVEN, D., Medicine
CRISCITIELLO, M., Medicine
DAMASSA, D., Anatomy and Cellular Biology
DARLING, D., Radiology
DAVIS, J., Paediatrics
DAWSON-HUGHES, B., Medicine
DENNETT, D., Philosophy
DESFORGES, J., Medicine
DEVIGNE, R., Political Science
DEWALD, R., Chemistry
DICE, J., Physiology
DIGGES, D., English
DODMAN, N., Clinical Sciences
DOGEL, Y., Pathology
DOHERTY, R., Prosthodontics and Operative Dentistry
DRACHMAN, V., History
DRAPKIN, M., Medicine
DUCIBELLA, T., Obstetrics and Gynaecology
DUKER, J., Ophthalmology
DUNLAP, K., Neuroscience
DWYER, J., Medicine
EASTERBROOKS, A., Child Development
EDGERS, L., Civil and Environmental Engineering
ENGELKING, L., Biomedical Sciences
ENGELKING, L., Physiology
ENGELMAN, R., Surgery
EPSTEIN, L., Psychiatry
EPSTEIN, S., Medicine
ERNST, S., Biology
ESTES, N., Medicine
FANBURG, B., Medicine
FEIG, L., Biochemistry
FEINGOLD, D., Dermatology
FELDMAN, D., Child Development
FERNANDEZ-ARMESTO, F., History
FERRONE, J., Orthopaedic Surgery
FIELDING, R., Medicine
FLAX, M., Pathology
FLORES, A., Paediatrics
FLYNN, C., English
FLYTZANI-STEPHANOPOULOS, M., Chemical Engineering
FOLSTEIN, M., Psychiatry
FORD, L., Physics and Astronomy
FORGAC, M., Physiology
FOSTER, E., Pathology
FRANK, E., Physiology
FRANTZ, I., Paediatrics
FREEMAN, R., Surgery
FREIDBERG, S., Neurosurgery
FRIEDBERG, R., Pathology
FRIEDMAN, L., Medicine
FRIEDMANN, P., Surgery
FRISKEN, S., Computer Science
FYLER, J., English
GAASCH, W., Medicine
GALBURT, R., Oral and Maxillofacial Surgery
GALPER, J., Medicine
GANDA, K., General Dentistry
GANG, D., Pathology
GARLICK, J., Cell, Molecular, Developmental Biology
GARVEN, G., Geology
GASARIAN, G., Romance Languages
GELFAND, J., Medicine
GEORGAKIS, C., Chemical Engineering
GERMAIN, M., Medicine
GILL, M., Psychiatry
GITTLEMAN, S., German, Russian, Asian Languages and Literatures
GOLDBERG, E., Microbiology—Basic Science
GOLDBERG, M., Orthopaedic Surgery
GOLDENBERG, D., Medicine
GOLDIN, B., Public Health and Family Medicine
GOLDSTEIN, G., Physics and Astronomy
GONZALEZ, F., Mathematics
GOODMAN, E., Paediatrics
GORBACH, S., Public Health and Family Medicine
GORSON, K., Neurology
GOTTLIEB, A., Dermatology
GRACE, N., Medicine
GRADY, G., Medicine
GREEN, D., Endodontics
GREENBLATT, D., Pharmacology and Experimental Therapeutics
GREIF, R., Mechanical Engineering
GUERTIN, R., Physics and Astronomy
GUNTHER, L., Physics and Astronomy
GUSS, D., Anthropology
GUTIERREZ, M., Mathematics
HAAS, T., Chemistry
HAHN, M., Mathematics
HALL, S., Anaesthesiology
HAMMER, N., Prosthodontics and Operative Dentistry
HAMMER, R., Psychiatry
HAMPF, F., Radiology
HAND, R., Medicine
HANNENBERG, A., Anaesthesiology
HARDER, D., Psychology
HARRINGTON, J., Medicine
HARTMANN, E., Psychiatry
HARTNELL, G., Radiology
HASSELBLATT, B., Mathematics
HAWLEY, C., Periodontology
HAYDON, P., Neuroscience
HAYES, C., Public Health and Community Service
HEIJIN, C., Psychiatry
HENNEMAN, P., Emergency Medicine
HERMAN, I., Physiology
HERN, D., Prosthodontics and Operative Dentistry
HESKETH, P., Medicine
HIBBERD, P., Medicine
HIGBY, D., Medicine
HIGGENS, T., Medicine
HILL, N., Medicine
HINDS, P., Radiation Oncology

HINES, E., Civil and Environmental Engineering
HIRATA, H., German, Russian, Asian Languages and Literatures
HIRAYAMA, H., Prosthodontics and Operative Dentistry
HOLCOMB, P., Psychology
HOMER, M., Radiology
HOPWOOD, J., Electrical and Computer Engineering
HOWE, E., Romance Languages
HSU, L., Psychiatry
HUBER, B., Pathology
HUGHES, W., Physiology
HUVOS, A., Medicine
INOUYE, C., German, Russian, Asian Languages and Literatures
IOANNIDES, Y., Economics
ISBERG, R., Microbiology—Basic Science
ISLAM, S., Civil and Environmental Engineering
JACKENDOFF, R., Philosophy
JACKSON, F., Neuroscience
JACOB, M., Neuroscience
JACOB, R., Computer Science
JACOBSON, S., Anatomy and Cellular Biology
JALAL, A., History
JANKOWSKI, J., Psychiatry
JAY, D., Physiology
JENNINGS, J., Urban and Environmental Policy and Planning
JENSEN, H., Paediatrics
JIANG, L., Medicine
JOHNSON, V., German, Russian, Asian Languages and Literatures
JONES, E., Paediatrics
JOSEPH, P., Sociology
KACHANOV, M., Mechanical Engineering
KAHN, M., Oral Pathology
KANAREK, R., Psychology
KAPLAN, D., Biomedial Engineering
KARAS, R., Medicine
KARMODY, C., Otolaryngology/Head and Neck Surgery
KASSIRER, J., Medicine
KAUER, J., Neuroscience
KEANE, T., Psychiatry
KENLER, K., Obstetrics and Gynaecology
KENNEY, P., Surgery
KENNISON, R., Obstetrics and Gynaecology
KENNY, J., Chemistry
KILARU, P., Anaesthesiology
KILMER, M., Mathematics
KISLIUK, R., Biochemistry
KLAPHOLZ, H., Obstetrics and Gynaecology
KLAUBER, G., Urology
KLINGEMANN, H., Medicine
KONSTAM, M., Medicine
KOPELMAN, R., Medicine
KOPIN, A., Medicine
KOSCH, P., Paediatrics
KOSOWSKY, B., Medicine
KREAM, R., Pharmacology
KRETSCHMAR, C., Paediatrics
KRIMSKY, S., Urban and Environmental Policy and Planning
KRINSKY, N., Biochemistry
KROLL, A., Ophthalmology
KULIG, J., Paediatrics
KUMAMOTO, C., Molecular Biology and Microbiology
KUMAR, K., Chemistry
KUMAR, M., Biomedical Sciences
LANG, K., Physics and Astronomy
LASSER, R., Electrical and Computer Engineering
LAU, J., Medicine
LAURENT, P., History
LAURENZI, G., Medicine
LECHAN, R., Medicine
LEE, M., Medicine
LEIVILLE-WEBSTER, C., Clinical Sciences
LERNER, R., Child Development
LEUPP, G., History
LEVESQUE, P., Anaesthesiology
LEVEY, A., Medicine
LEVINE, H., Medicine
LEVY, S., Molecular Biology and Microbiology
LEWIS, S., Biology
LIBERTINO, J., Urology
LICHTENSTEIN, A., Public Health and Family Medicine
LINSENMAYER, T., Anatomy and Cellular Biology
LIPTZIN, B., Psychiatry
LISCUM, L., Physiology
LITVAK, J., English
LO, T., Radiation Oncology
LOPEZ, M., Surgery
LUNDY, L., Obstetrics and Gynaecology
MCCARTHY, H., Surgery
MCCARTHY, J., Orthopaedic Surgery
MCCAULEY, R., Radiology
MACDONNELL, K., Medicine
MACKEY, W., Surgery
MADIAS, N., Medicine
MADOFF, M., Public Health and Family Medicine
MAHLER, D., Anaesthesiology
MALAMY, M., Microbiology—Basic Science
MALCHOW, H., History
MANN, W., Physics and Astronomy
MANNO, V., Mechanical Engineering
MARCHANT, D., Obstetrics and Gynaecology
MARRONE, S., History
MAZZOTTI, J., Romance Languages
MEHTA, N., General Dentistry
MEIRI, K., Anatomy and Cellular Biology
MEISSNER, H., Paediatrics
MENDELSOHN, M., Medicine
METCALF, G., Economics
MEYDANI, S., Immunology
MICZEK, K., Psychiatry
MICZEK, K., Psychology
MILLER, E., Electrical and Computer Engineering
MILLER, K., Medicine
MILNER, L., Paediatrics
MIRKIN, S., Biology
MIRKIN, S., Genetics
MITCHELL, G., Obstetrics and Gynaecology
MOORE, C., Microbiology—Basic Science
MOREHEAD, J., Anatomy and Cellular Biology
MORGAN, J., Medicine
MULHOLLAND, D., History
MUNSAT, T., Neurology
MURPHY, R., Medicine
MUST, A., Public Health and Family Medicine
NAGINSKI, I., Romance Languages
NAIMI, S., Medicine
NALEBUFF, E., Orthopaedic Surgery
NAPIER, A., Physics and Astronomy
NAPIER, S., German, Russian, Asian Languages and Literatures
NASRAWAY, S., Surgery
NAVAB, F., Medicine
NEUMANN, P., Medicine
NEWBERG, A., Radiology
NIELSEN, H., Paediatrics
NITECKI, Z., Mathematics
NOLLER, K., Obstetrics and Gynaecology
NOONAN, J., Electrical and Computer Engineering
NORMAN, G., Economics
NORTON, R., Medicine
O'DONNELL, K., Surgery
O'DONNELL, T., Surgery
O'GRADY, J., Obstetrics and Gynaecology
OHMAN, J., Medicine
O'LEARY, D., Radiology
OLIVER, W., Physics and Astronomy
ORDOVAS, J., Genetics
OSTRANDER, S., Sociology
OTIS, C., Pathology
OXENKRUG, G., Psychiatry
PAGE, D., Surgery
PAIS, V., Urology
PALMER, C., Public Health and Community Service
PANDIAN, N., Medicine
PANJWANI, N., Ophthalmology
PAPAGEORGE, M., Oral and Maxillofacial Surgery
PAPAS, A., General Dentistry
PATTERSON, J., Medicine
PAUKER, S., Medicine
PAUL, R., Radiology
PAYNE, D., Surgery
PECHENIK, J., Biology
PENNINCK, D., Clinical Sciences
PEPPER, M., Public Health and Family Medicine
PEREIRA, B., Medicine
PERRIN, E., Paediatrics
PERRIN, M., Pathology
PERRONE, R., Medicine
PLAUT, A., Medicine
POLAK, J., Radiology
PORTNEY, K., Political Science
PREIS, D., Electrical and Computer Engineering
QUINTO, E., Mathematics
RABINOVICI, R., Surgery
RABSON, A., Pathology
RANKIN, C., Endodontics
REECE, R., Paediatrics
REED, J., Biology
REICHLIN, S., Medicine
REID, P., Classics
REITER, E., Paediatrics
REUBEN, S., Anaesthesiology
REUTER, K., Radiology
REYNOLDS, R., Anaesthesiology
RICHARD, M., Philosophy
RICHARDS, D., Economics
RICHMOND, J., Orthopaedic Surgery
RIDGE, J., Geology
ROAF, E., Anaesthesiology
ROBBINS, A., Public Health and Family Medicine
ROBERTS, P., Surgery
ROGERS, C., Mechanical Engineering
ROHRER, R., Surgery
ROMERO, C., German, Russian, Asian Languages and Literatures
ROMERO, L., Biology
ROSE, D., Medicine
ROSENBERG, I., Physiology
ROSENBERG, M., Oral and Maxillofacial Surgery
ROSENBERG, N., Pathology
ROSENBLATT, M., Physiology
ROWLAND, T., Paediatrics
RUBENSTEIN, J., Medicine
RUBY, L., Orthopaedic Surgery
RUSH, J., Clinical Sciences
RUSSELL, R., Medicine
SABIN, T., Neurology
SADEGHI-NEJAD, A., Paediatrics
SADOWSKY, N., Radiology
SAFAII, H., Pathology
SAHAGIAN, G., Physiology
SAIGAL, A., Mechanical Engineering
SAMO, R., Radiology
SANAYEI, M., Civil and Environmental Engineering
SAPERSTEIN, G., Environmental and Population Health
SAWKAT, A., Pharmacology and Experimental Therapeutics
SCHAEFER, E., Medicine
SCHALLER, J., Paediatrics
SCHLIEMANN, A., Education
SCHMIDT, K., Anaesthesiology
SCHNEPS, J., Physics and Astronomy
SCHOETZ, D., Surgery
SCHOLZ, F., Radiology
SCHREIBER, J., Paediatrics
SCHULTZ, M., Chemistry
SCHWARTZ, A., Clinical Sciences
SEDDON, J., Ophthalmology
SELKER, H., Medicine
SENELICK, L., Drama and Dance
SHADER, R., Pharmacology
SHAUGHNESSY, A., Public Health and Family Medicine
SHEN, E., Pathology

SHIKORA, S., Surgery
SHOEMAKER, C., Biomedical Sciences
SHUCART, W., Neurosurgery
SIEGEL, E., Biology
SILBERMAN, E., Psychiatry
SILVA, J., Medicine
SINGH, I., Prosthodontics and Operative Dentistry
SKIEST, D., Medicine
SLIWA, K., Physics and Astronomy
SMITH, G., Philosophy
SMITH, L., Obstetrics and Gynaecology
SMITH, T., Political Science
SNYDMAN, D., Medicine
SONENSCHEIN, A., Microbiology—Basic Science
SONNENSCHEIN, C., Anatomy and Cellular Biology
SORBERA, R., Oral and Maxillofacial Surgery
SORGER, K., Pathology
SOTO, A., Anatomy and Cellular Biology
SOUVAINE, D., Computer Science
SPOLAORE, E., Economics
STEARNS, N., Medicine
STECHENBERG, B., Paediatrics
STEER, M., Surgery
STELLER, M., Obstetrics and Gynaecology
STOLOW, R., Chemistry
STRAUSS, G., Medicine
STROM, J., Medicine
SUNG, N., Chemical Engineering
SYLVIA, W., Jr, Prosthodontics and Operative Dentistry
TALAMO, B., Neuroscience
TARLOV, S., Neuroscience
TAYLOR, H., Psychology
TEIXIDOR I BIGAS, M., Mathematics
TERES, D., Medicine
TERRES, G., Physiology
TERRONO, A., Orthopaedic Surgery
THEOHARIDES, T., Pharmacology and Experimental Therapeutics
THORLEY-LAWSON, D., Pathology
TICKLE-DEGNEN, L., Occupational Therapy
TILLMAN, H., General Dentistry
TISCHLER, A., Pathology
TOBIN, R., Physics and Astronomy
TRIMMER, B., Biology
TSICHLIS, P., Medicine
TUERK, I., Urology
TURKSOY-MARCUS, R., Obstetrics and Gynaecology
TURNER, R., Orthopaedic Surgery
TWITCHELL, T., Neurology
TZIPORI, S., Biomedical Sciences
UEDA, R., History
UMLAS, J., Pathology
VALAES, T., Paediatrics
VAN ETTEN, R., Medicine
VILENKIN, A., Physics and Astronomy
VOGEL, R., Civil and Environmental Engineering
WAIT, R., Surgery
WALT, D., Chemistry
WANKE, C., Medicine
WAX, F., Dermatology
WAZER, D., Radiation Oncology
WECHSLER, J., Art and Art History
WEILER, K., Education
WEINER, A., Oral Diagnostic
WEINSTOCK, J., Medicine
WEISS, R., Mathematics
WERTLEIB, D., Child Development
WIDMER, G., Biomedical Sciences
WILL KUO, L., Orthodontics
WILSON, I., Medicine
WILSON, J., English
WINN, P., History
WITTENBERG, S., Medicine
WLEZIEN, R., Mechanical Engineering
WOLF, M., Child Development
WOLFE, L., Paediatrics
WONG, J., Medicine
WORTIS, H., Pathology
WRIGHT, A., Microbiology—Basic Science
WU, J., Neurosurgery
YEE, A., Biochemistry
YUCEL, E., Radiology
ZAMENHOF, R., Radiation Oncology
ZINMAN, L., Urology

CAMPUSES

Boston Campus: 136 Harrison Ave, Boston, MA 02111; Schools of Medicine, Dental Medicine, Sackler School of Graduate Biomedical Services, Jean Mayer USDA Human Nutrition Research Center on Aging.

Medford/Somerville Campus: Medford, MA 02155; School of Arts and Sciences, School of Engineering, Fletcher School, Gerald J. and Dorothy R. Friedman School of Nutrition Science and Policy, Jonathan M. Tisch College of Citizenship and Public Service.

North Grafton Campus: 22 Westboro Rd, North Grafton, MA 01536; Cummings School of Veterinary Medicine.

UNIVERSITY OF MASSACHUSETTS

225 Franklin St, 33rd Fl., Boston, MA 02110
333 S St, Suite 400, Shrewsbury, MA 01545-4169
Telephone: (617) 287-7000
Internet: www.massachusetts.edu
Founded 1863
Comprises campuses at Amherst, Boston, Dartmouth and Lowell, University of Massachusetts Medical School and UMassOnline (online undergraduate and graduate degree programmes)
Pres.: JACK WILSON
Exec. Vice-Pres.: JAMES JULIAN
Vice-Pres. for Economic Devt: THOMAS CHMURA
Vice-Pres. for Information Services, Chief Information Officer and CEO, UMassOnline: DAVID GRAY
Vice-Pres. for Management and Fiscal Affairs and Treas.: STEPHEN LENHARDT
Vice-Pres. for Univ. Advancement: KATHERINE V. SMITH
Sec. to the Board of Trustees: BARBARA DEVICO
Number of students: 60,000 across 5 campuses.

CONSTITUENT UNIVERSITIES

University of Massachusetts Amherst

Amherst, MA 01003
Telephone: (413) 545-0111
Fax: (413) 545-2328
Internet: www.umass.edu
Founded 1863 as Massachusetts Agricultural College, Massachusetts State College 1931, present status 1947
Academic year: September to June
Chancellor: JOHN V. LOMBARDI
Provost and Sr Vice-Chancellor for Academic Affairs: JAMES V. STAROS
Vice-Chancellor for Admin. and Finance: JOYCE HATCH
Vice-Chancellor for Student Affairs: MIKE GARGANO
Vice-Provost for Outreach: SHARON L. FROSS
Vice-Provost for Research: PAUL KOSTECKI
Dean of Students: JO-ANNE T. VANIN
Dir of Libraries: JAY SCHAFER
Library of 5,800,000 vols
Number of teachers: 1,169
Number of students: 25,593
Publication: *The Massachusetts Review* (4 a year)

DEANS

College of Engineering: MICHAEL F. MALONE
College of Humanities and Fine Arts: JOEL MARTIN
College of Natural Resources and the Environment: CLEVE E. WILLIS
College of Natural Sciences and Mathematics: GEORGE M. LANGFORD
College of Social and Behavioral Sciences: JANET RIFKIN
Commonwealth College: PRISCILLA CLARKSON
Graduate School: SANDY PETERSON
Isenberg School of Management: SOREN BISGAARD
School of Education: CHRISTINE B. MCCORMICK
School of Nursing: EILEEN T. BRESLIN
School of Public Health and Health Sciences: JOHN CUNNINGHAM

ASSOCIATED INSTITUTE

Stockbridge School of Agriculture: Amherst, MA 01003; tel. (413) 545-2222; fax (413) 577-0242; e-mail stockbridgeschool@nre.umass.edu; internet www.umass.edu/stockbridge; f. 1918; Dir MARTHA G. BAKER.

University of Massachusetts Boston

100 Morrissey Blvd, Boston, MA 02125-3393
Telephone: (617) 287-6000
Fax: (617) 265-6040
E-mail: enrollment.info@umb.edu
Internet: www.umb.edu
Founded 1964
Public control
Language of instruction: English
Academic year: September to June
Chancellor: J. KEITH MOTLEY
Provost and Sr Vice-Chancellor for Academic Affairs: WINSTON LANGLEY
Vice-Chancellor for Admin. and Finance: ELLEN M. O'CONNOR
Vice-Chancellor for Athletics and Recreation, Special Projects and Programs: CHARLIE TITUS
Vice-Chancellor for Enrollment Management: KATHLEEN S. TEEHAN
Vice-Chancellor for Student Affairs: PATRICK K. DAY
Vice-Chancellor for Univ. Advancement: GINA CAPPELLO
Vice-Provost for Information Technology: ANNE SCRIVENER AGEE
Library of 600,000 vols
Number of teachers: 1,038
Number of students: 15,430

DEANS

College of Education and Human Development: FELICIA WILCZENSKI
College of Liberal Arts: DONNA KUIZENGA
College of Management: PHILIP L. QUAGLIERI
College of Nursing and Health Sciences: GREER GLAZER
College of Public and Community Service: CARROY U. FERGUSON
College of Science and Mathematics: ANDREW GROSOVSKY
John W. McCormack Graduate School of Policy Studies: STEPHEN CROSBY
University College: PHILIP DI SALVIO

University of Massachusetts Dartmouth

285 Old Westport Rd, N Dartmouth, MA 02747-2300
Telephone: (508) 999-8000
Fax: (508) 999-8901
Internet: www.umassd.edu
Public
Founded 1895
Language of instruction: English
Academic year: September to May
Chancellor: Dr JEAN F. MACCORMACK
Vice-Chancellor for Academic Affairs: Dr ANTHONY J. GARRO
Dir of Undergraduate Admissions: MICHAEL LYNCH

Registrar: Dr CARNELL JONES
Dean of Library Services: SHARON WEINER
Library of 468,216 vols
Number of teachers: 644 (375 full-time, 269 part-time)
Number of students: 9,432
Publications: *Portuguese Literary and Cultural Studies* (1 a year), *TEMPER* (literary review, 1 a year)

DEANS
Charlton College of Business: Dr EILEEN PEACOCK
College of Arts and Sciences: Dr WILLIAM HOGAN
College of Engineering: Dr ROBERT PECK
College of Nursing: Dr JAMES A. FAIN
College of Visual and Performing Arts: Dr MICHAEL D. TAYLOR
Professional and Continuing Education: Dr SUSAN LANE
School of Education, Public Policy and Civic Engagement: Dr ISMAEL RAMERIZ-SOTO
School of Law: Dr ROBERT WARD
School of Marine Science and Technology: Dr AVIJIT GANGOPADHYAY

University of Massachusetts Lowell

1 University Ave, Lowell, MA 01854
Telephone: (978) 934-4000
Fax: (978) 934-3000
Internet: www.uml.edu
Founded 1975, by merger of Lowell State College and Lowell Technological Institute, present name 1991
Public control
Language of instruction: English
Academic year: September to June
Chancellor: MARTY MEEHAN
Exec. Vice-Chancellor: JACQUELINE MOLONEY
Provost: AHMED ABDELAL
Vice-Chancellor for Admin., Finance and Facilities: JOANNE YESTRAMSKI
Vice-Chancellor for Advancement: EDWARD CHIU
Library of 354,922 vols
Number of teachers: 683 (405 full-time, 278 part-time)
Number of students: 14,702 (8,691 undergraduate, 3,426 graduate, 2,585 continuing education)
Publication: *New Solutions* (environmental and occupational health policy, 4 a year)

DEANS
Education: ANITA GREENWOOD
Engineering: JOHN TING
Fine Arts, Humanities and social Sciences: NINA COPPENS
Health and Environment: SHORTIE McKINNEY
School of Marine Sciences: ROBERT GAMACHE
Sciences: ROBERT TAMARIN

University of Massachusetts Medical School

55 Lake Avenue N, Worcester, MA 01655
Telephone: (508) 856-2000
E-mail: publicaffairs@umassmed.edu
Internet: www.umassmed.edu
Founded 1962
Chancellor: Dr MICHAEL F. COLLINS
Vice-Chancellor: EDWARD J. KEOHANE
Vice-Chancellor and Chief Operating Officer: JOYCE A. MURPHY
Vice-Chancellor for Devt: CHARLIE J. PAGNAM
Vice-Chancellor for Faculty Admin.: Dr JUDITH K. OCKENE
Vice-Chancellor for Operations: ROBERT E. JENAL
Vice-Chancellor for Research: JOHN L. SULLIVAN
Vice-Chancellor for Univ. Relations: ALBERT SHERMAN
Dean and Exec. Deputy Chancellor: TERRY R. FLOTTE
Dir of Library Services: ELAINE R. MARTIN
Number of teachers: 810
Number of students: 741

DEANS
Graduate School of Biomedical Sciences: Dr ANTHONY CARRUTHERS (acting)
Graduate School of Nursing: Dr PAULETTE SEYMOUR ROUTE
School of Medicine: Dr TERRY R. FLOTTE

WELLESLEY COLLEGE

106 Central St, Wellesley, MA 02481
Telephone: (781) 283-1000
Fax: (781) 283-3650
E-mail: publicinfo@wellesley.edu
Internet: www.wellesley.edu
Chartered 1870; opened 1875
Private
Accredited by New England Assen of Schools and Colleges; American Chemical Soc.
Pres.: H. KIM BOTTOMLY
Vice-Pres. for Admin. and Planning: PATRICIA M. BYRNE
Vice-Pres. for Finance and Treas.: ANDREW B. EVANS
Vice-Pres. for Information Services and College Librarian: MICHELINE JEDREY
Asst Vice-Pres. for Public Affairs: MARY ANN HILL
Dean of Admissions: JENNIFER DESJARLAIS
Dean of the College: ANDREW SHENNAN
Dean of Students: DEBRA DEMEIS (acting)
Library of 874,000 vols, 32,000 sound and video recordings, 16,000 maps
Number of teachers: 326 (251 full-time, 75 part-time)
Number of students: 2,344 (2,190 full-time, 154 part-time)

ASSOCIATE DEANS
Prof. JOANNE BERGER-SWEENEY, Prof. ADELE WOLFSON

WENTWORTH INSTITUTE OF TECHNOLOGY

550 Huntington Ave, Boston, MA 02115-5998
Telephone: (617) 989-4590
Fax: (617) 989-4591
E-mail: admissions@wit.edu
Internet: www.wit.edu
Private control
Academic year: August to May
Founded 1904
Pres.: Dr ZORICA PANTIC
Vice-Pres. of Academic Affairs and Provost: RUSSELL PINIZZOTTO
Vice-Pres. for Business and Finance: JOHN P. HEINSTADT
Registrar: MATTHEW BURKE
Library Dir: WALTER PUNCH
Number of teachers: 134
Number of students: 3,636
Depts of architecture, civil, construction and environment, computer science and systems, design and facilities, electronics and mechanics, humanities, management, social sciences.

WESTERN NEW ENGLAND COLLEGE

1215 Wilbraham Rd, Springfield, MA 01119
Telephone: (413) 782-3111
Fax: (413) 782-1746
E-mail: ugradmis@wnec.edu
Internet: www.wnec.edu
Founded 1919
Pres.: ANTHONY S. CAPRIO
Provost and Vice-Pres. for Academic Affairs: JERRY A. HIRSCH
Vice-Pres. for Devt and Alumni Relations: BEVERLY DWIGHT
Vice-Pres. for Enrollment Management: CHARLES R. POLLOCK
Vice-Pres. for Finance and Admin.: DAVID P. KRUGER
Vice-Pres. for Marketing and External Affairs: BARBARA A. CAMPANELLA
Vice-Pres. for Student Affairs and Dean of Students: RICHARD M. DIRUZZA
Assoc. Dean for Library and Information Resources: BARBARA WEST
Library of 510,000 vols
Number of teachers: 164 full-time
Number of students: 4,000

DEANS
School of Arts and Sciences: SAEED GHAHRAMANI
School of Business: JULIE SICILIANO
School of Engineering: CARL RATHMANN
School of Law Admin.: ARTHUR R. GAUDIO

WESTFIELD STATE COLLEGE

POB 1630, Westfield, MA 01086-1630
577 Western Ave, Westfield, MA 01086
Telephone: (413) 572-5300
E-mail: admissions@wsc.ma.edu
Internet: www.wsc.ma.edu
Founded 1838
Pres.: BARRY MALONEY
Sr Vice-Pres. for Academic Affairs: Dr JOAN A. RASOOL
Vice-Pres. for Admin. and Finance: NICK A. WOJTOWICZ
Vice-Pres. for Advancement and College Relations: ROBERT ZIOMEK
Vice-Pres. for Student Affairs: Dr ARTHUR J. JACKSON
Library Dir: CATHERINE DOYLE
Library of 136,000 vols
Number of teachers: 170
Number of students: 3,200
Majors in art, biology, business management, computer information systems, computer science, criminal justice, economics, education, English, environmental sciences, French, general science, history, mass communication, mathematics, movement science, multicultural and ethnic studies, music, philosophy, political science, psychology, regional planning, social work, sociology, Spanish, theatre arts, women's studies.

WHEATON COLLEGE

26 East Main St, Norton, MA 02766
Telephone: (508) 286-8200
Fax: (508) 285-8270
E-mail: info@wheatoncollege.edu
Internet: www.wheatoncollege.edu
Founded 1834
Pres.: RONALD A. CRUTCHER
Provost: MOLLY EASO SMITH
Vice-Pres. for Enrollment and Marketing: GAIL BERSON
Vice-Pres. for Finance and Operations: RODERICK G. WALLICK
Vice-Pres. for Library and Information Services: TERRY METZ
Dean of Students: SUE ALEXANDER
Library of 352,700 vols
Number of teachers: 140
Number of students: 1,550
Depts of African studies, African American studies, diaspora studies, American studies, ancient studies, anthropology, art history, studio art, Asian studies, astronomy, biochemistry, biology, chemistry, classics, com-

puter science, devt studies, economics, education, English, environmental science, environmental studies, family studies, French, German, Greek, Hispanic studies, history, int. relations, Italian studies, Latin, Latin American studies, legal studies, management, mathematics, mathematics and computer science, mathematics and econ., music, philosophy, physics and astronomy, political science, psychobiology, psychology, public policy studies, religion, Russian and Russian studies, sociology, statistics, theatre studies and dance, urban studies, women's studies

Publications: *Quarterly Magazine*, *Wheaton Matters*.

WHEELOCK COLLEGE

200 The Riverway, Boston, MA 02215
Telephone: (617) 879-2000
Internet: www.wheelock.edu

Founded 1888

Pres.: Jackie Jenkins-Scott
Vice-Pres. for Academic Affairs: Suzanne Pasch
Vice-Pres. and Chief Financial Officer: Anne Marie Martorana
Vice-Pres. for Institutional Advancement and Devt: Linda Welter
Dean of Students: Susan Antonelli
Assoc. Vice-Pres. for Academic Resources and Library Dir: Albie Johnson

Library of 85,000 vols
Number of teachers: 65 (full-time)
Number of students: 1,640

Academic programmes in arts and sciences, child life, child and family studies, education, juvenile justice and youth advocacy, social work

Publications: *Bulletin*, *Magazine*.

WILLIAMS COLLEGE

Williamstown, MA 01267
Telephone: (413) 597-3131
E-mail: admission@williams.edu
Internet: www.williams.edu

Chartered as free school 1791; college charter granted 1793

Pres.: Adam Faulk
Vice-Pres. for Operations: Stephen P. Klass
Vice-Pres. for Strategic Planning and Institutional Diversity: Mike Reed
Provost: William J. Lenhart
Dean of the Faculty: William G. Wagner
Dean of the College: Karen Mill
Dir of Admission: Dick Nesbitt
Registrar: Charles R. Toomajian, Jr
Librarian: David M. Pilachowski

Library of 885,000 vols, 61,000 rare books, 30,500 paper and electronic periodicals, 480,000 microtexts, 30,000 sound recordings, 11,000 video cassettes, 368,000 govt documents
Number of teachers: 312
Number of students: 2,100

Depts of American studies, anthropology, art, Asian studies, astronomy, astrophysics, biology, chemistry, Chinese, classics, comparative literature, computer science, economics, English, French, geosciences, German, history, Japanese, literary studies, mathematics and statistics, music, philosophy, physics, political economy, political science, psychology, religion, Russian, sociology, Spanish, theatre, women's and gender studies.

WORCESTER POLYTECHNIC INSTITUTE

100 Institute Rd, Worcester, MA 01609-2280
Telephone: (508) 831-5000
Fax: (508) 831-5753
Internet: www.wpi.edu

Founded 1865
Academic year: August to May

Pres.: Dennis D. Berkey
Exec. Vice-Pres.: Jeffrey S. Solomon
Provost and Vice-Pres. for Academic Affairs: John A. Orr
Vice-Pres. for Enrollment Management: Kristin Ruth Tichenor
Vice-Pres. for Information Technology: Thomas J. Lynch
Vice-Pres. for Marketing and Communications: Christopher Hardwick
Vice-Pres. for Student Affairs: Janet Begin Richardson
Registrar: Alaina Wiehn
Librarian: Helen M. Shuster

Library of 225,000 vols
Number of teachers: 324
Number of students: 3,903

Areas of study incl. engineering and computer science, liberal arts, management, pre-professional studies, sciences.

WORCESTER STATE COLLEGE

486 Chandler St, Worcester, MA 01602-2597
Telephone: (508) 929-8000
Fax: (508) 929-8191
E-mail: admissions@worcester.edu
Internet: www.worcester.edu

Founded 1874
Academic year: September to May

Pres.: Janelle C. Ashley
Vice-Pres. of Academic Affairs: Dorothy Escribano
Library Dir: Donald Hochstetler

Library of 149,662 vols
Number of teachers: 170
Number of students: 5,369

Depts of biology, business admin./economics, communication, computer science, criminal justice, education, health sciences, history/political science, languages and literature, mathematics, nursing, philosophy, physical and earth sciences, psychology, sociology, visual and performing arts

Publication: *Journal of Graduate Research* (1 a year).

ATTACHED RESEARCH INSTITUTES

Center for Effective Instruction.
Center for Health Professions.
Intergenerational Urban Institute.

MICHIGAN

ADRIAN COLLEGE

110 South Madison St, Adrian, MI 49221-2575
Telephone: (517) 265-5161
Fax: (517) 264-3856
Internet: www.adrian.edu

Founded 1859
Academic year: September to May

Pres.: Dr Jeffrey R. Docking
Exec. Vice-Pres.: Richard A. Creehan
Vice-Pres. for Business Affairs and Treas.: Jerry L. Wright
Vice-Pres. for Institutional Advancement: Ronald L. Reeves
Registrar: Cynthia Kojima
Librarian: Noelle Keller

Library of 147,080 vols
Number of teachers: 71
Number of students: 1,600

Depts of accounting and business, art and design, biology, chemistry, communication arts and sciences, earth science, economics, English, environmental science/studies, exercise science/physical education, history, interior design, mathematics, modern languages and cultures, music, philosophy/religion, physics, political science, psychology, sociology, social work and criminal justice, teacher education, theatre.

ALBION COLLEGE

611 E Porter St, Albion, MI 49224
Telephone: (517) 629-1000
Fax: (517) 629-0509
Internet: www.albion.edu

Founded 1835
Private control
Language of instruction: English
Academic year: August to May

Depts of American studies, anthropology and sociology, art, art history, athletic training, biology, chemistry, computer science, earth science, economics and management, English, ethnic studies, French, geological sciences, German, history, int. studies, mathematics, music, philosophy, physical education, physics, political science, psychology, public policy, religious studies, Spanish, speech communication, theatre, women's and gender studies

Pres.: Donna M. Randall
Provost: Dr Susan Conner
Vice-Pres. for Student Affairs and Dean of Students: Dr Sally J. Walker
Registrar: Drew Dunham
Librarian: John Kondelik

Library of 357,416 vols, 19,605 microforms, 51,316 video cassettes and audiovisual items, 124,171 e-books
Number of teachers: 130
Number of students: 1,602

ALMA COLLEGE

614 W Superior St, Alma, MI 48801
Telephone: (989) 463-7111
Fax: (989) 463-7057
E-mail: admissions@alma.edu
Internet: www.alma.edu

Founded 1886
Private liberal arts college; attached to Higher Learning Comms; mem. of the N Central Assen of Colleges and Secondary Schools

Pres.: Dr Saundra J. Tracy
Provost and Vice-Pres. for Academic Affairs: Michael Selmon
Vice-Pres. for Enrollment: Karen Klumpp
Vice-Pres. for Student Life: Nick Piccolo
Library Dir: Carol Zeile

Library of 275,000 vols
Number of teachers: 142 (90 full-time; 52 part-time)
Number of students: 1,400

Depts of humanities, natural sciences, social sciences.

ANDREWS UNIVERSITY

Berrien Springs, MI 49104
Telephone: (269) 471-7771
Fax: (269) 471-3228
E-mail: enroll@andrews.edu
Internet: www.andrews.edu

Founded 1874
Academic year: August to May

Pres.: Niels-Erik Andreasen
Provost: (vacant)
Vice-Pres. for Enrollment: Stephen Payne
Vice-Pres. for Financial Admin.: Lawrence Schalk
Vice-Pres. for Student Services: Frances Faehner

Vice-Pres. for Univ. Advancement: DAVID A. FAEHNER
Registrar: Dr EMILIO GARCIA-MARENKO
Librarian: LARRY ONSAGER

Library of 1,513,179 vols
Number of teachers: 298
Number of students: 3,195

Publication: *Andrews University Seminary Studies* (2 a year)

DEANS

College of Arts and Sciences: KEITH E. MATTINGLY
College of Technology: VERLYN BENSON
Division of Architecture: CAREY CARSCALLEN
Graduate Studies: LYNDON G. FURST
School of Business: CHARLES H. TIDWELL, Jr (acting)
School of Education: JAMES JEFFERY
SDA Theological Seminary: DENIS FORTIN

AQUINAS COLLEGE

1607 Robinson Rd, SE, Grand Rapids, MI 49506-1799

Telephone: (616) 632-8900
Fax: (616) 732-4589
Internet: www.aquinas.edu

Founded 1886

Pres.: C. EDWARD BALOG
Vice-Pres. for Devt: JULIE RIDENOUR (Devt)
Vice-Pres. for Finance and Operations: WILLIAM SHEFFERLY (Devt)
Vice-Pres for Planning and Enrollment: MICHAEL KELLER
Chancellor: Sister MARY AQUINAS WEBER
Registrar: CECELIA MESLER

Library of 110,000 vols, 991 periodicals and over 16,000 non-print items
Number of teachers: 192 (90 full-time, 102 part-time)
Number of students: 2,500

Publications: *Aquinas Magazine* (4 a year), *Presidential Perspectives* (2 a year).

AVE MARIA COLLEGE

300 West Forest Ave, Ypsilanti, MI 48197

Telephone: (734) 337-4100
Fax: (734) 337-4140
E-mail: admissions@avemaria.edu
Internet: www.avemaria.edu

Founded 1998
Private control
Academic year: September to April

Pres.: NICOLAS J. HEALY
Chancellor: THOMAS S. MONAGHAN
Chief Financial Officer: PAUL RONEY
Vice-Pres. for Academic Affairs: JOHN E. SITES
Vice-Pres. for Student Affairs and Dean of Students: DANIEL DENTINO
Registrar: MARIA HERBEL
Librarian: SARAH BEITING

Number of teachers: 28 (12 full-time, 16 adjunct)
Number of students: 109

Depts of biology and chemistry, classics and early Christian literature, economics, history, literature, mathematics and physics, philosophy, politics, sacred music, theology.

AVE MARIA SCHOOL OF LAW

3475 Plymouth Rd, Ann Arbor, MI 48105-2550

Telephone: (734) 827-8040
Fax: (734) 622-0123
E-mail: info@avemarialaw.edu
Internet: www.avemarialaw.edu

Founded 1999
Private control
Academic year: August to May

Dean and Pres.: Dr BERNARD DOBRANSKI
Assoc. Dean for Academic Affairs: EUGENE R. MILHIZER
Dir of Admissions: MICHELE CONNOR
Registrar: ANGELA KOJIRO
Library Dir: JANICE SELBERG

Library of 400,000 vols and other items

Publication: *Law Review*.

CALVIN COLLEGE

3201 Burton SE, Grand Rapids, MI 49546

Telephone: (616) 526-6000
Fax: (616) 526-8551
E-mail: info@calvin.edu
Internet: www.calvin.edu

Founded 1876
Academic year: September to May

Pres.: Dr GAYLEN J. BYKER
Vice-Pres. for Admin., Finance and Information Services: HENRY E. DEVRIES, II
Vice-Pres. for Enrollment and External Relations: THOMAS MCWHERTOR
Vice-Pres. for Student Life: SHIRLEY HOOGSTRA
Provost: CLAUDIA BEVERSLUIS
Registrar: THOMAS STEENWYK
Dir of the Library: GLENN A. REMELTS

Library of 700,000 vols
Number of teachers: 349 (284 full-time, 65 part-time)
Number of students: 4,200

Publications: *Fides et Historia* (2 a year), *Turkish Studies Association Bulletin* (2 a year).

AFFILIATED RESEARCH CENTRES

Calvin Center for Christian Scholarship: 1855 Knollcrest Circle SE, Grand Rapids, MI 49546-4402; tel. (616) 526-6049; fax (616) 526-6681; e-mail jbratt@calvin.edu; Dir Dr JAMES BRATT.

H. H. Meeter Center for Calvin Studies: 1855 Knollcrest Circle SE, Grand Rapids, MI 49546-4402; tel. (616) 526-7081; fax (616) 526-6470; e-mail meeter@calvin.edu; Dir Dr KARIN MAAG.

Institute of Christian Worship: 1855 Knollcrest Circle SE, Grand Rapids, MI 49546-4402; tel. (616) 526-6088; Dir Dr JOHN WITVLIET.

Paul Henry Institute for Christianity and Politics: e-mail smid@calvin.edu; Dir Dr CORWIN SMIDT.

Social Research Center: Dir Dr MARK REGNERUS.

CALVIN THEOLOGICAL SEMINARY

3233 Burton St SE, Grand Rapids, MI 49546

Telephone: (616) 957-6036
Fax: (616) 957-8621
E-mail: admissions@calvinseminary.edu
Internet: www.calvinseminary.edu
Private control (Christian Reformed Church in North America)

Founded 1876

Pres.: Dr CORNELIUS PLANTINGA, Jr
Vice-Pres. for Academic Affairs: Dr HENRY DE MOOR
Vice-Pres. for Admin.: Dr DUANE KELDERMAN
Registrar: JOAN BEELEN
Librarian: PAUL FIELDS

Number of teachers: 28
Number of students: 222 (full-time)

CENTRAL MICHIGAN UNIVERSITY

Mount Pleasant, MI 48859

Telephone: (989) 774-4000
Fax: (989) 774-3665
E-mail: cmuline@cmich.edu
Internet: www.cmich.edu
Academic year: August to May

Founded 1892

Pres.: MICHAEL RAO
Provost and Vice-Pres.: E. GARY SHAPIRO
Vice-Pres. for Devt and Alumni Relations: MICHAEL LETO
Vice-Pres. for Finance and Admin. Services: GEORGE ROSS
Vice-Pres. for Govt Relations and Public Affairs: KATHLEEN M. WILBUR
Registrar: KAREN HUTSLAR
Dean of Students: BRUCE ROSCOE
Dean of Libraries: THOMAS J. MOORE

Number of teachers: 739
Number of students: 27,452

Publication: *Michigan Historical Review* (2 a year)

DEANS

College of Business Administration: D. MICHAEL FIELDS
College of Communication and Fine Arts: SUE ANN MARTIN
College of Education and Human Services: KAREN ADAMS
College of Graduate Studies: ROGER COLES
College of Health Professions: TOM MASTERSON
College of Humanities and Social and Behavioural Sciences: PAMELA GATES
College of Science and Technology: ROBERT KOHRMAN

CLEARY UNIVERSITY

3601 Plymouth Rd, Ann Arbor, MI 48105

Telephone: (734) 332-4477
Fax: (734) 332-4646
E-mail: admissions@cleary.edu
Internet: www.cleary.edu

Founded 1883 as The Cleary School of Penmanship; present name 2002
Private control
Academic year: September to June

Pres.: THOMAS P. SULLIVAN
Provost and Vice-Pres. for Academic Affairs: Dr VINCE LINDER
Vice-Pres. for Admin. and Finance: JUDITH WALKER
Exec. Dir and Chief Information Officer: DAVID BOWERS

Number of teachers: 33
Number of students: 1,000

Area of study: business admin.

BRANCH CAMPUS

Livingston Campus: 3750 Cleary Dr., Howell, MI 48843; tel. (517) 548-3670; fax (517) 552-7805.

COLLEGE FOR CREATIVE STUDIES

201 East Kirby, Detroit, MI 48202-4034

Telephone: (313) 664-7400
Fax: (313) 827-2739
E-mail: admissions@ccscad.edu
Internet: www.ccscad.edu

Founded 1906 as Detroit Society of Arts and Crafts; present name 2001
Private control
Academic year: September to May

Pres.: RICHARD L. ROGERS
Academic Dean: IMRE MOLNAR
Vice-Pres. for Admin. and Finance: ANNE BECK
Vice-Pres. for Institutional Advancement: NANCY J. NELSON
Registrar: NADINE HAGOORT
Librarian: BETH WALKER

Library of 30,000 vols, 100,000 slides, 188,000 current periodicals

Number of teachers: 207
Number of students: 1,307

CONCORDIA UNIVERSITY – ANN ARBOR

4090 Geddes Rd, Ann Arbor, MI 48105
Telephone: (734) 995-7300
Fax: (734) 995-4610
E-mail: admission@cuaa.edu
Internet: www.cuaa.edu
Founded 1963 as Concordia Lutheran Junior College
Private control
Academic year: September to May
Pres.: Rev. Dr Thomas R. Ahlersmeyer
Exec. Vice-Pres. and Vice-Pres. for External Relations: Steve DeBoer
Registrar: Tim Taylor
Library Dir: Kevin J. Brandon
Number of teachers: 47
Number of students: 770

DEANS

Haab School of Business and Management: Dr F. K. Marsh
School of Adult and Continuing Education: Dr Jeanette Sprik
School of Arts and Sciences: Dr Robert McCormick
School of Education: Dr Timothy Frusti

CORNERSTONE UNIVERSITY

1001 East Beltline Ave NE, Grand Rapids, MI 49525
Telephone: (616) 949-5300
Fax: (616) 222-1418
E-mail: admissions@cornerstone.edu
Internet: www.cornerstone.edu
Private control
Campuses in Kalamazoo and Zeeland; Asia Baptist Theological Seminary in Singapore
Pres.: Dr Rex M. Rogers
Exec. Vice-Pres. for Advancement: Paul Baker
Provost: Bayard Baylis
Sr Vice-Pres. for Operations and Chief Financial Officer: Marc Fowler
Vice-Pres. for Cornerstone Univ. Radio: Lee Geysbeek
Vice-Pres. for Student Devt: Tom Emigh
Dean of Enrollment Management: Brent Rudin
Registrar: Gail Duhon
Library Dir: Fred Sweet
Number of teachers: 64
Number of students: 1,900 (1,200 undergraduates, 700 graduates)

DEANS

School of Arts and Sciences: Dr Timothy Detwiler
School of Professional Studies: Davis Berryman

ATTACHED INSTITUTE

Grand Rapids Theological Seminary: tel. (616) 222-1422; fax (616) 222-1502; e-mail grts@cornerstone.edu.

CRANBROOK ACADEMY OF ART

39221 Woodward Ave, POB 801, Bloomfield Hills, MI 48303-0801
Telephone: (248) 645-3300
Fax: (248) 646-0046
Internet: www.cranbrookart.edu
Founded 1904
Dir: Gerhardt Knodel
Dean of Admissions: Katharine Willman
Registrar: Katharine Willman
Librarian: Judith Dyki
Library of 25,000 vols
Number of teachers: 10 full-time
Number of students: 150
Graduate education in the visual arts, architecture and design, leading to Master of Architecture and Master of Fine Arts degree in ceramics, fibre, 2-D design, 3-D design, metalsmithing, painting, photography, print media, sculpture.

DAVENPORT UNIVERSITY

415 East Fulton, Grand Rapids, MI 49503
Telephone: (616) 451-3511
Fax: (616) 732-1142
Internet: www.davenport.edu
Founded 1866 as Grand Rapids Business College; present name 2000
Private control
Academic year: September to August
30 Campuses throughout Michigan and northern Indiana
Pres.: Randolph K. Flechsig
Exec. Vice-Pres. for Academics and Provost: Dr Thomas H. Brown
Exec. Vice-Pres. for Advancement: Dr Barbara A. Mieras
Exec. Vice-Pres. for Finance: Michael Volk
Exec. Vice-Pres. for Univ. Relations and Communications: Kim Bruyn
Vice-Pres. for Human Resources and Organizational Devt: David Veneklase
Number of teachers: 1,200
Number of students: 13,048 (all campuses; 12,956 undergraduate, 92 graduate)
Areas of study: business, allied health, nursing, technology.

EASTERN MICHIGAN UNIVERSITY

Ypsilanti, MI 48197
Telephone: (734) 487-1849
Fax: (734) 487-7170
Internet: www.emich.edu
Founded 1849
Academic year: September to April
Pres.: Don Loppnow
Provost and Vice-Pres. for Academic Affairs: Don Loppnow
Vice-Pres. for Business and Finance: Patrick Doyle
Vice-Pres. for Enrollment Services: Courtney McAnuff
Vice-Pres. for Student Affairs: Jim Vick
Vice-Pres. for Univ. Relations: Juanita Reid
Dean of Students: Greg Peoples
Registrar: Joy Garrett
Univ. Librarian: (vacant)
Library of 600,000 vols, 129,847 periodicals
Number of teachers: 675
Number of students: 25,000

DEANS

Arts and Science: Linda Pritchard
Business: Earl Potter
Continuing Education: David Clifford
Education: Jerry Robbins
Graduate School: Robert Holkebeer
Human Services: Elizabeth C. King
Technology: John Dugger

FERRIS STATE UNIVERSITY

1201 S State St, CSS 301, Big Rapids, MI 49307
Telephone: (231) 591-2450
Fax: (231) 591-2423
E-mail: international@ferris.edu
Internet: www.ferris.edu
Founded 1884
Public control
Academic year: August to May
Pres.: David Eisler
Vice-Pres. for Academic Affairs: Thomas Oldfield
Vice-Pres. for Admin. and Finance: Richard Duffett
Vice-Pres. for Student Affairs: Daniel Burcham
Dean of Student Life: Leroy Wright
Dean of Instructional Services and Library: Leah Nixon
Library of 370,000 vols and periodicals
Number of teachers: 530
Number of students: 13,865

DEANS

College of Allied Health Sciences: Dr Julie Coon
College of Arts and Sciences: Dr Reinhold Hill
College of Business: Dr David M. Nicol
College of Education and Human Services: Dr Michelle Johnston
College of Pharmacy: Dr Stephen Durst
College of Technology: Dr Ron McKean
Michigan College of Optometry: Dr Michael Cron
University College: Dr William Potter

GRACE BIBLE COLLEGE

POB 910, 1011 Aldon St SW, Grand Rapids, MI 49509
Telephone: (616) 538-2330
Fax: (616) 538-0599
E-mail: info@gbcol.edu
Internet: www.gbcol.edu
Founded 1939 as Milwaukee Bible Institute; present name 1961
Private control
Pres.: Ken Kemper
Academic Dean: Paul Sweet
Vice-Pres. for Advancement and Devt: Bryan J. Walker
Vice-Pres. for Business and Finance: Randy Helm
Vice-Pres. for Community Life: Brian Sherstad
Number of teachers: 29
Number of students: 149

GRAND VALLEY STATE UNIVERSITY

1 Campus Dr., Allendale, MI 49401-9401
Telephone: (616) 331-5000
Internet: www.gvsu.edu
State control
Academic year: August to April
Pres.: Thomas J. Haas
Provost and Vice-Pres. for Academic Affairs: Dr Gayle R. Davis
Vice-Provost for Health Affairs: Dr Jean M. Nagelkerk
Vice-Provost and Dean of Students: Dr H. Bart Merkle
Vice-Pres. for Devt: Maribeth G. Wardrop
Vice-Pres. for Finance and Admin.: Jim Bachmeier
Vice-Pres. for Planning and Equity: Dr Patricia Oldt
Vice-Pres. for Inclusion and Equity: Dr Jeanne J. Arnold
Vice-Pres. for Univ. Relations: Matthew E. McLogan
Univ. Counsel: Thomas A. Butcher
Registrar: Lynn Blue
Library Dir: Lynell DeWind
Library of 750,000 vols
Number of teachers: 837
Number of students: 24,541

DEANS

College of Community and Public Service: Dr George Grant, Jr
College of Education: Dr Elaine Collins

College of Health Professions: Dr ROY H. OLSSON, Jr
College of Interdisciplinary Studies: Dr WENDY J. WENNER
College of Liberal Arts and Sciences: Dr FREDERICK J. ANTCZAK
Kirkhof College of Nursing: Dr CYNTHIA A. MCCURREN
Padnos College of Engineering and Computing: Dr PAUL D. PLOTKOWSKI
Seidman College of Business: Dr H. JAMES WILLIAMS

BRANCH CAMPUSES

Annis Water Resources Institute: 740 West Shoreline Dr., Muskegon, MI 49441; tel. (231) 728-3601; internet www.gvsu.edu/wri.

Meijer Campus: 515 South Waverly Rd, Holland, MI 49423; tel. (616) 394-4848; internet www.gvsu.edu/learn/holland; Exec. Dir SIMONE JONAITIS.

Muskegon Center: 221 S Quaterline Rd, Muskegon, MI 49442; tel. (231) 777-0505; internet www.gvsu.edu/learn/muskegon.

Richard M. DeVos Center: 401 W Fulton St, Grand Rapids, MI 49504; tel. (616) 331-5000.

Traverse City Center: 2200 Dendrinos Dr., Suite 101, Traverse City, MI 49684; tel. (231) 995-1785; internet www.gvsu.edu/learn/traverse.

GREAT LAKES CHRISTIAN COLLEGE

6211 West Willow Highway, Lansing, MI 48917
Telephone: (517) 321-0242
Fax: (517) 321-5902
E-mail: glcc@glcc.edu
Internet: www.glcc.edu

Founded 1949 as Great Lakes Bible College; present name 1992
Private control
Academic year: August to May

Pres.: LAWRENCE L. CARTER
Vice-Pres. for Academic Affairs: Dr MARK CHRISTIAN
Vice-Pres. for Finance and Operations: WILLIAM D. BROSSMANN
Vice-Pres. for Institutional Advancement: PHILIP E. BEAVERS
Registrar: JEDDIE ELLIS
Librarian: JAMES ORME

Library of 52,000 vols
Number of teachers: 14
Number of students: 192

Areas of study: Bible/theology, Christian education, Christian ministries, cross-cultural ministry, family life education, history, interpersonal and organizational communication, music, psychology/counselling, youth ministry.

HILLSDALE COLLEGE

Hillsdale, MI 49242
Telephone: (517) 437-7341
Fax: (517) 437-3923
E-mail: admissions@hillsdale.edu
Internet: www.hillsdale.edu

Founded 1844

Pres.: LARRY P. ARNN
Provost: Dr ROBERT BLACKSTOCK
Vice-Pres. for Admin.: RICHARD PEWE
Vice-Pres. for External Affairs: DOUGLAS JEFFREY
Vice-Pres. for Finance and Treas.: H. KENNETH COLE
Vice-Pres. for Institutional Advancement: JOHN CERVINI
Vice-Pres. for Student Affairs: DIANE PHILIPP
Registrar: DOUGLAS MCARTHUR
Librarian: DAN KNOCH

Library of 209,000 vols
Number of teachers: 115
Number of students: 1,300

Publication: *Imprimis* (12 a year)

Areas of study incl. accounting, art, biology, chemistry, classical studies, computational mathematics, economics, education (elementary and secondary), English, financial management, French, German, history, marketing management, mathematics, music, philosophy, physical education, physics, political science, psychology, religion, Spanish, speech and theatre.

HOPE COLLEGE

POB 9000, Holland, MI 49422-9000
Telephone: (616) 395-7000
Fax: (616) 395-7922
Internet: www.hope.edu

Founded 1866
Academic year: August to May

Pres.: Dr JAMES E. BULTMAN
Vice-Pres. and Chief Financial Officer: TOM BYLSMA
Vice-Pres. for Admissions: WILLIAM C. VANDERBILT
Vice-Pres. for College Advancement: SCOTT WOLTERINK
Vice-Pres. of Student Devt and Dean of Students: Dr RICHARD FROST
Provost: Dr JAMES N. BOELKINS
Registrar: JON J. HUISKEN
Dir of Libraries: KELLY JACOBSMA

Library of 370,000
Number of teachers: 203
Number of students: 3,230

DEANS

Arts and Humanities: Dr WILLIAM D. REYNOLDS
Natural Sciences: Dr MOSES N. F. LEE
Social Sciences: Dr RICHARD RAY

KALAMAZOO COLLEGE

1200 Academy St, Kalamazoo, MI 49006-3295
Telephone: (269) 337-7000
Fax: (269) 337-7251
Internet: www.kzoo.edu

Founded 1833 as Michigan and Huron Institute; name changed to Kalamazoo Literary Institute 1837, to Kalamazoo College 1855
Academic year: September to June

Pres.: EILEEN WILSON-OYELARAN
Provost: MICKEY MCDONALD
Vice-Pres. for Advancement: VICTORIA GORRELL
Vice-Pres. for Business and Finance: JAMES E. PRINCE
Vice-Pres. for Enrollment: JOELLEN SILBERMAN
Dir of Library: STACY NOWICKI

Library of 330,000 vols
Number of teachers: 89
Number of students: 1,379

Divs of fine arts, foreign languages, humanities, natural sciences and mathematics, physical education, social sciences.

KETTERING UNIVERSITY

1700 West Third Ave, Flint, MI 48504-4898
Telephone: (810) 762-9500
Internet: www.gmi.edu

Founded 1919

Pres.: STANLEY R. LIBERTY
Vice-Pres. for Academic Affairs and Provost: MICHAEL HARRIS
Vice-Pres. for Admin. and Finance: SUSAN BOLT
Vice-Pres. for Human Resources: LINDA PETERSON
Vice-Pres. for Information Technology: JIM HAMILTON
Vice-Pres. for Univ. Advancement: DENNIS WASHINGTON
Dir of Library Services: CHARLES D. HANSON

Library of 100,000 vols, 540 periodicals
Number of teachers: 135
Number of students: 3,200

Depts of business, engineering and science.

KUYPER COLLEGE

3333 East Beltline NE, Grand Rapids, MI 49525
Telephone: (616) 222-3000
E-mail: admissions@kuyper.edu
Internet: www.kuyper.edu

Founded 1939 as Reformed Bible Institute
Private control
Academic year: August to April

Pres.: Dr NICHOLAS V. KROEZE
Vice-Pres. for Academic Admin.: Dr MELVIN J. FLIKKEMA
Vice-Pres. for Enrollment: LARISSA LIGHTHISER
Academic Dean and Registrar: Dr BEN A. MEYER
Dir of Library Services: DIANNE ZANDBERGEN

Library of 55,000 vols
Number of teachers: 38
Number of students: 299

Areas of study: Bible and theology, cross-cultural studies, educational ministries, general education, liberal arts, physical education, pre-seminary studies, professional education, social work, youth ministry.

LAKE SUPERIOR STATE UNIVERSITY

650 West Easterday Ave, Sault Ste Marie, MI 49783
Telephone: (906) 632-6841
Fax: (906) 635-2111
E-mail: admissions@lssu.edu
Internet: www.lssu.edu

Founded 1946 as Sault Ste Marie Br. of Michigan College of Mining and Technology; present name 1987
State control
Academic year: September to May

Pres.: Dr RODNEY L. LOWMAN
Vice-Pres. for Academic Affairs and Provost: Dr BRUCE T. HARGER
Vice-Pres. for Enrollment Services: WILLIAM EILOLA
Vice-Pres. for Finance: JOSEPH HERBIG
Vice-Pres. for Student Affairs: KEN PERESS
Vice-Pres. for Univ. Relations and Marketing: WILLIAM CRAWFORD
Registrar: NANCY NEVE
Dean of Library: Dr FREDRICK A. MICHELS

Library of 130,000 vols
Number of teachers: 111
Number of students: 3,077

DEANS

College of Arts, Letters and Social Sciences: JAMES R. BLASHILL
College of Business and Economics: Dr VARKEY K. TITUS
College of Natural and Health Sciences: Dr MICHAEL P. DONOVAN
College of Natural and Mathematical Sciences: ANTHONY BLOSE
Great Lakes Academy: Dr MELVIN L. WAISANEN
School of Engineering and Technology: MORRIE WALWORTH

School of Nursing and Health Sciences: STEVEN E. MERRILL

LAWRENCE TECHNOLOGICAL UNIVERSITY

21000 West Ten Mile Rd, Southfield, MI 48075-1058
Telephone: (248) 204-4000
Fax: (248) 204-3727
E-mail: admissions@ltu.edu
Internet: www.ltu.edu

Founded 1932
Private control
Academic year: August to May

Pres.: Dr LEWIS N. WALKER
Provost: Dr MARIA J. VAZ
Vice-Pres. for Finance and Admin.: LINDA L. HEIGHT
Vice-Pres. for Univ. Advancement: STEPHEN E. BROWN
Registrar: HOLLY A. DIAMOND
Dean of Students: KEVIN FINN
Admissions Dir: JANE T. ROHRBACK
Library Dir: GARY R. COCOZZOLI

Number of teachers: 452
Number of students: 5,000

Publication: *Prism* (1 a year)

DEANS

College of Architecture and Design: GLEN S. LEROY
College of Arts and Sciences: Dr HSIAO-PING MOORE
College of Engineering: Dr LAIRD E. JOHNSTON
College of Management: Dr LOUIS A. DEGENNARO

ATTACHED RESEARCH INSTITUTE

Center for Innovative Materials Research (CIMR): tel. (248) 204-2556; fax (248) 204-2568; e-mail nabil@ltu.edu; f. 2005; Dir Dr NABIL F. GRACE.

MADONNA UNIVERSITY

36600 Schoolcraft Rd, Livonia, MI 48150-1173
Telephone: (734) 432-5300
Fax: (734) 432-5393
E-mail: muinfo@madonna.edu
Internet: www.madonna.edu

Founded 1947
Academic year: September to July

Pres.: Sister Dr ROSE MARIE KUJAWA
Vice-Pres. for Academic Admin.: ERNEST NOLAN
Vice-Pres. for Finance and Operations: LEONARD A. WILHELM
Vice-Pres. for Student Services: Sister NANCY MARIE JAMROZ
Vice-Pres. for Univ. Advancement: ANDREA NODGE
Dir of Library Services: JOANNE LUMMETTA

Library of 163,678 vols
Number of teachers: 274
Number of students: 4,000

Publication: *Madonna Mind* (2 a year)

DEANS

College of Arts and Humanities: Dr KATHLEEN MARTIN O'DOWD
College of Education: Dr ROBERT KIMBALL
College of Nursing and Health: Dr TERESA L. C. THOMPSON
College of Science and Mathematics: Dr TED F. BIERMANN
College of Social Sciences: Dr KAREN ROSS
Graduate Studies: Dr EDITH RALEIGH
Outreach and Distance Learning: Dr JAMES NOVACK
School of Business: Dr STUART ARENDS

MARYGROVE COLLEGE

8425 West McNichols Rd, Detroit, MI 48221
Telephone: (313) 927-1200
Fax: (313) 927-1345
E-mail: info@marygrove.edu
Internet: www.marygrove.edu

Founded 1905
Academic year: September to April

Pres.: Dr DAVID J. FIKE
Provost: EDWARD THOMPSON
Vice-Pres. for Finance and Admin.: HANK CHASE
Vice-Pres. for Institutional Advancement: BARBARA HILL
Dean of Enrollment Services: SALLY JANACEK
Dir of Institutional Research and Assessment: (vacant)
Registrar: KIMBERLY SANDERS

Library of 84,015 vols, 371 periodicals
Number of teachers: 56 full-time, 8 part-time, 70 adjuncts, 90 mentors
Number of students: 8,432 (780 undergraduate, 7,652 postgraduate)

Publication: *Maxis Review* (1 a year)

Liberal arts college; 2- and 4-year undergraduate courses; Masters courses; continuing education programme

DEANS

Arts and Sciences: Dr JUDITH HEINEN
Continuing Education: SHERRY LEFTON (Asst Dean)
Fine Arts: ROSE DE SLOOVER
Professional Studies: Dr KURT SMITH

MICHIGAN JEWISH INSTITUTE

25401 Coolidge Highway, Oak Park, MI 48237-1304
Telephone: (248) 414-6900
Fax: (248) 414-6907
E-mail: info@mji.edu
Internet: www.mji.edu

Founded 1994
Private control
Academic year: September to August

Pres., Chief Financial Officer and Vice-Pres. of Financial Affairs: Rabbi KASRIEL SHEMTOV
Vice-Pres. of Institutional Advancement and Dean of Academic Affairs: Dr T. HERSHEL GARDIN
Registrar: FRAN HERMAN

Areas of study: computer information systems, business and information systems, Judaic studies.

MICHIGAN STATE UNIVERSITY

East Lansing, MI 48824
Telephone: (517) 355-6560
Fax: (517) 355-4670
E-mail: presmail@msu.edu
Internet: www.msu.edu

Founded 1855; the first college for teaching scientific agriculture and the forerunner of the American system of land-grant colleges
State control
Academic year: August to May (2 terms)

Pres.: LOU ANN K. SIMON
Provost and Vice-Pres. for Academic Affairs: KIM A. WILCOX
Vice-Pres. for Finance and Operations and Treas.: FRED POSTON
Vice-Pres. for Global Engagement and Strategic Projects: JOHN HUDZIK
Vice-Pres. for Governmental Affairs: STEVEN WEBSTER
Vice-Pres. for Legal Affairs and Gen. Counsel: ROBERT NOTO
Vice Pres. for Research and Graduate Studies: J. IAN GRAY
Vice-Pres. for Student Affairs and Services: LEE JUNE
Vice-Pres. for Univ. Devt: CHARLES WEBB
Vice-Pres. for Univ. Relations: TERRY DENBOW
Registrar: NICOLE G. ROVIG (acting)
Dir of Libraries: CLIFFORD H. HAKA

Library: see Libraries and Archives
Number of teachers: 4,500
Number of students: 45,520

Publications: *Centennial Review*, *MSU Alumni Magazine*, *MSU News Bulletin*

DEANS

Agriculture and Natural Resources: JEFFREY D. ARMSTRONG
Arts and Letters: KAREN A. WURST
Communication Arts and Sciences: CHARLES SALMON
Education: CAROLE AMES
Eli Broad College of Business and Eli Broad Graduate School of Management: ROBERT B. DUNCAN
Engineering: SATISH UDPA
Human Medicine: MARSHA D. RAPPLEY (acting)
James Madison College: SHERMAN GARNETT
Law: CLIFF F. THOMSON (acting)
Lyman Briggs College: ELIZABETH SIMMONS
Music: JAMES FORGER
Natural Science: ESTELLE MCGROARTY
Nursing: MARY MUNDT
Osteopathic Medicine: WILLIAM D. STRAMPEL
Social Science: MARIETTA BABA
Veterinary Medicine: CHRISTOPHER M. BROWN
Honors College: RONALD FISHER
Residential College in Arts and Humanities: STEPHEN L. ESQUITH (acting)

PROFESSORS

(C = Chairman of Department)

(Departments may be attached to more than one college)

College of Nursing:

ALLEN, G. D.
COLLINS, C.
GIFT, A. G.
GIVEN, B. A.
ROTHERT, M. L. (Dean)

Department of Accounting:

ARENS, A. A. (C)
BUZBY, S. L.
DILLEY, S. C.
GRAY, J.
HAKA, S.
MCCARTHY, W. E.
MEAD, G. C.
O'CONNOR, M. C.
OUTSLAY, E.
SHIELDS, M. D.
SOLLENBERGER, H. M.
WARD, D. D.

Department of Advertising:

PRATT, C.
REECE, B. B.
SALMON, C.
VANDENBERGH, B. G. (C)

Department of Agricultural Economics:

BATIE, S. S.
BERNSTEN, R. H.
BLACK, J. R.
CRAWFORD, E.
HAMM, L. G. (C)
HARSH, S. B.
HARVEY, L. R.
HILKER, J. H.
HOEHN, J.
KELSEY, M. P.
LEHOLM, A. G.
MOSER, C. H.
MYERS, R. J.
NOTT, S. B.
PIERSON, T. R.

RICKS, D. J.
ROBISON, L. J.
SCHMID, A. A.
SCHWAB, G.
STAATZ, J. M.
VAN RAVENSWAAY, E.
WEBER, M.

Department of Agricultural Engineering:
BAKKER-ARKEMA, F. W.
BICKERT, W. G.
BROOK, R.
GERRISH, J.
LOUDON, T. L.
MROZOWSKI, T.
SEGERLIND, L. J.
SRIVASTAVA, A. (C)
STEFFE, J. F.
SURBROOK, T. C.
VAN EE, G. R.
VON BERNUTH, R.

Department of American Thought and Language:
ABRAHAMS, E. C.
BECKWITH, G. M.
BRATZEL, J. N.
BRESNAHAN, R. J.
BUNGE, N. L.
CHAMBERLAIN, W.
COOPER, D. D.
D'ITRI, P. A.
ELLISTON, S. F.
HOPPENSTAND, G. C.
LADENSON, J. R.
LUNDE, E.
MCKINLEY, B. E.
NOVERR, D. A. (acting C)
ROUT, K.
SOMERS, P. P., Jr
STEINBERG, M.
THOMAS, F. R.
ZIEWACZ, L. E.

Department of Animal Science:
ALLEN, M. S.
AULERICH, R. J.
BEEDE, D. K.
BENSON, M. E.
BUCHOLTZ, H. F.
BURSIAN, S.
DENNIS BANKS, B.
ERICKSON, R. W.
FERRIS, T. A.
FOGWELL, R.
HAWKINS, D. R.
HOGBERG, M. G. (C)
IRELAND, J.
MELLENBERGER, R. W.
RAHN, A. P.
RITCHIE, H. D.
RUST, S. R.
SHELLE, J. E.
VARGHESE, S. K.
YOKOYAMA, M. T.

Department of Anthropology:
CHARTKOFF, J.
CLELAND, C. E.
CLIMO, J.
DERMAN, W.
DWYER, D.
GALLIN, B.
GOLDSTEIN, L. G. (C)
LOVIS, W. A.
POLLARD, H. P.
ROBBINS, L. H.
SAUER, N.
SPIELBERG, J.
WHITEFORD, S.

Department of Art:
BANDES, S. J.
DEUSSEN, P. W.
FAGAN, J. E.
FUNK, R.
GLENDINNING, P.
KILBOURNE, W. G.
KUSZAI, J. J.
LAWTON, J. L.
MACDOWELL
STANFORD, L. O.
TARAN, I. Z.
VANLIERE, E. N.
WOLTER, K. H.

Department of Audiology and Speech Sciences:
CASBY, M.
EULENBERG, J. B.
MOORE, E. J.
PUNCH, J. L. (C)
RAKERD, B. S.
SMITH, L. L.
STOCKMAN, I. G.

Department of Biochemistry and Molecular Biology:
BIEBER, L. L.
FERGUSON-MILLER, S.
FRAKER, P. J.
GREEN, P. G.
HOLLINGSWORTH, R. I.
KAGUNI, J. M.
KAGUNI, L. S.
KINDEL, P. K.
KROOS, L. R.
MCCORMICK, J. J.
MCGROARTY, E. J.
MCINTOSH, L.
MAHER, V. M.
PREISS, J.
RAIKHEL, N. V.
REVZIN, A.
SCHINDLER, M. S.
SMITH, W. L. (C)
TRIEZENBERG, S. J.
WANG, J. L.
WATSON, J. T.
WILSON, J. E.

Department of Botany and Plant Pathology:
DEZOETEN, G. A.
EKERN, F. F.
EWERS, F. W.
FULBRIGHT, D. W.
HAMMERSCHMIDT, R. (C)
HART, L. P.
HOLLENSEN, R.
JONES, A. L.
KEEGSTRA, K. G.
KENDE, H.
KLOMPARENS, K. L.
MURPHY, P. G.
NADLER, K. D.
OHLROGGE, J. B.
POFF, K. L.
SAFIR, G. R.
SEARS, B.
TAGGART, R.
VARGAS, J. M., Jr
WALTON, J. D.
WEBBER, P. J.
WOLK, C. P.
ZEEVAART, J. A. D.

Department of Chemical Engineering:
BERGLUND, K.
DALE, B. (C)
DRZAL, L. T.
HAWLEY, M. C.
JAYARAMAN, K.
MILLER, D. J.
NARAYAN, R.
PETTY, C. A.
WORDEN, R. M.

Department of Chemistry:
ALLISON, J.
BABCOCK, G. T.
CHANG, C. K.
CROUCH, S. R.
CUKIER, R. I.
DUNBAR, K.
FROST, J.
HARRISON, J. F.
HUNT, K. C.
HUNT, P. M.
KANATZIDES, M. G.
LEROI, G. E.
MCGUFFIN, V. L.
MCHARRIS, W. C.
MORRISSEY, D. J.
PINNAVAIA, T. J.
RATHKE, M. W.
REUSCH, W. H.
MALECZKA, R. (C)
WAGNER, P. J.
WULFF, W. D.

Department of Civil and Environmental Engineering:
BALADI, G.
DAVIS, M. L.
HARICHANDRAN, R. S. (C)
HATFIELD, F.
LYLES, R. W.
MCKELVEY, F.
SOROUSHIAN, P.
TAYLOR, W. C.
VOICE, T. C.

Department of Communication:
ATKIN, C. K. (C)
BOSTER, F. J.
DONOHUE, W.
SMITH, S. W.

Department of Computer Science and Engineering:
CHUNG, M.-J.
DILLON, L. K.
GREENBERG, L.
HUGHES, H. D.
JAIN, A. K.
MUTKA, M. (C)
NI, L. M.
PRAMANIK, S.
STOCKMAN, G. C.
WEINSHANK, D. J.
WOJCIK, A. S.

Department of Counseling, Educational Psychology and Special Education:
AMES, C.
BECKER, B. J.
CLARK, C. M.
CREWE, N. M.
DICKSON, W. P.
ENGLERT, C. S.
FLODEN, R. E.
HAPKIEWICZ, W. C.
JUNE, L. N.
LEAHY, M. J.
LOPEZ, F. G.
MEHRENS, W. A.
PALAS, A. M.
PERNELL, E.
PHILLIPS, S. E.
PRAWAT, R. (C)
RECKASE, M. D.
SCHMIDT, W. H.
SMITH, G.
SPIRO, R. J.
STEWART, D. A.
YELON, S. L.

Department of Crop and Soil Sciences:
BOYD, S. A.
CHRISTENSON, D. R.
CRUM, J. R.
FOSTER, E. F.
FREED, R. D.
GOODMAN, E.
HARWOOD, R. R.
JACOBS, L. W.
JOHNSTON, T. J. (acting C)
KELLS, J. D.
KELLY, J. D.
LEEP, R. H.
LEMME, G. D.
LENSKI, R. E.
MOKMA, D. L.
PAUL, E. A.

PENNER, D.
PIERCE, F. J.
RENNER, K. A.
RITCHIE, J. T.
ROBERTSON, G. P.
SMUCKER, A. J. M.
THOMASHOW, M.
TIEDJE, J. M.
WARNCKE, D. D.

Department of Economics:

ALLEN, B. T.
BAILLIE, R. T.
BALLARD, C. L.
BIDDLE, J. E.
BOYER, K. D.
BROWN, B. W.
CHOI, J. P.
DAVIDSON, C.
FISHER, R. C.
GODDEERIS, J. H. (C)
HOLZER, H. J.
KREININ, M. E.
LIEDHOLM, C. E.
LINZ, S. J.
MACKEY, M. C.
MARTIN, L. W.
MATUSZ, S. J.
MENCHIK, P. L.
MEYER, J.
NEUMARK, D. B.
OBST, N. P.
PECCHENINO, R. A.
SCHMIDT, P. J.
SEGERSTROM, P. S.
STRAUSS, J. A.
WILSON, J. D.
WOODBURY, S. A.
WOOLDRIDGE, J.

Department of Educational Administration:

CHURCH, R. L.
CUSICK, P. A. (C)
DAVIS, M.
FAIRWEATHER, J.
GRANDSTAFF, M. E.
IGNATOVICH, F. R.
KAAGAN, S. S.
MOORE, K. M.
PLANK, D. N.
ROMANO, L. G.
SIMON, L. A. K.
SYKES, G.
TURNER, M.
WEILAND, S.

Department of Electrical and Computer Engineering:

ASMUSSEN, J., Jr (C)
DELLER, J.
FISHER, P. D.
FOUKE, J. M.
KHALIL, H.
NYQUIST, D. P.
PIERRE, P. A.
REINHARD, D. K.
ROTHWELL, E. J.
SALAM, F. M.
SCHLUETER, R. A.
SHANBLATT, M.
SIEGEL, M.
TUMMALA, R. L.
WEY, C.-L.

Department of English:

ATHANASON, A. N.
BANKS, J. S.
BRUNNER, D. D.
CRANE, M.
DEWHURST, C. K.
DULAI, S. S.
FISHBURN, K. R.
GASS, S. M.
GOCHBERG, D. S.
GOODSON, A. C.
GROSS, B. E.
HARROW, K.
HILL, J. L.
JOHNSEN, W.
LANDRUM, L. N.
LUDWIG, J. B.
MCCLINTOCK, J. I.
MCGUIRE, P. C.
MARTIN, R. A.
MATHESON, L. M.
MEINERS, R. K.
O'DONNELL, P. J. (C)
PAANANEN, V. N.
PENN, W. S.
POGEL, N.
ROBINSON, R. F.
ROSENBERG, D. M.
SEATON, J.
SKEEN, A. C.
SMITHERMAN, G.
STALKER, J. C.
STOCK, P. L.
TAVORMINA, M. T.
UPHAUS, R. W.
VINCENT, W. A.
WAKOSKI, D.
WHALLON, W.
WILSON, M.

Department of Entomology:

AYERS, G. S.
BESAW, L. C.
BIRD, G. W.
DELFOSSE, E. S. (C)
GAGE, S.
GRAFIUS, E. J.
HOLLINGWORTH, R. M.
MERRITT, R. W.
MILLER, J. R.
POSTON, F. L.
RAIKHEL, A.
SCRIBER, J. M.
SMITLEY, D. R.
STEHR, F. W.
VANTASSELL, E.
WHALON, M. E.
ZABIK, M. J.

Department of Epidemiology:

PARETH, N. (C)
PATHAK, P. K.

Department of Family and Child Ecology:

AMES, B. D.
BARRATT, M. S.
BOBBITT, N.
BOGER, R.
GRIFFORE, R.
IMIG, D. R.
IMIG, G. L.
JOHNSON, D. J.
KEITH, J. G.
KOSTELNIK, M. (C)
LUSTER, T. J.
MCADOO, H. P.
MILLER, J. R.
PHENICE, L.
SCHIAMBERG, L. B.
SODERMAN, A. K.
TAYLOR, C. S.
WALKER, R.
WHIREN, A. P.
YOUATT, J. P.

Department of Family and Community Medicine:

AGUWA, M. I. (C)
BORDINAT, S. M.
CUMMINGS, M.
KURTZ, M.
PAPSIDERO, J.

Department of Family Practice:

ALEXANDER, E.
BRODY, H.
GERARD, R.
GIVEN, C. W.
HICKNER, J.
OGLE, K. S.
PATHAK, D. R.
WHITTIER, H. L.

Department of Finance:

BOOTH, G. G. (C)
GRUNEWALD, A. E.
HENRY, J. B.
KHANNA, N.
LASHBROOKE, E. C., Jr
O'DONNELL, J. L.
RAINEY, J. F.
SIMONDS, R. R.
STENZEL, P.

Department of Fisheries and Wildlife:

BATIE, R. E.
D'ITRI, F.
DOBSON, T. A.
GARLING, D. L.
JOHNSON, D. I.
PEYTON, R. B.
PRINCE, H. H.
TAYLOR, W. W. (C)

Department of Food Science and Human Nutrition:

BENNINK, M. R.
BOND, J. T.
BOOREN, A. M.
CASH, J. N.
CHENOWETH, W. L.
GRAY, I. J.
HEGARTY, P. V.
HOERR, S. M.
LINZ, J. E.
PESTKA, J. J.
ROMSOS, D. R.
SMITH, D. M.
SONG, W. O.
UEBERSAX, M. A. (C)
ZABIK, M.
ZILE, M. H.

Department of Forestry:

DICKMANN, D. I.
KEATHLEY, D. E. (C)
KIELBASO, J. J.
KOELLING, M. R.
MCDONOUGH, M.
POTTER-WITTER, K. L.

Department of Geography:

CAMPBELL, D. J.
CHUBB, M.
COREY, K. E.
GROOP, R. E. (C)
HAMLIN, R.
HARMAN, J. R.
HINOJOSA, R.
LIM, G.-C.
MANSON, G. A.
MEHRETU, A.
OLSON, J. M.
SCHAETZL, R. J.
SKOLE, D. L.
THOMAS, J.
WILLIAMS, J.
WITTICK, R. I.

Department of Geological Sciences:

ANSTEY, R. L.
CAMBRAY, F. W.
FUJITA, K.
LARSON, G. J.
LONG, D. T.
SIBLEY, D. F.
TROW, J. W.
VELBEL, M. A. (C)
VOGEL, T. A.

Department of History:

ANDERSON, J. R.
EADIE, J. W.
FISHER, A.
GLIOZZO, C. A.
HINE, D. C.
LAURENCE, R. R.
LEVINE, P. D.
MARCUS, H. G.
MOCH, L. P.
RADDING, C. M.

REED, H. A.
ROBINSON, D. W.
SCHOENL, W. J.
SIEGELBAUM, L. H. (C)
SILVERMAN, H.
STEWART, G. T.
SWEENEY, J. M.
THOMAS, R. W.
THOMAS, S. J.
VIETH, J. K.
WILBUR, E.

Department of Horticulture:
BIERNBAUM, J. A.
CAMERON, A. C.
CARLSON, W. H.
DILLEY, D. R.
FLORE, J. A.
HANCOCK, J. F.
HANSON, E. J.
HEINS, R. D.
HERNER, R. C.
HOWELL, G. S.
IEZZONI, A. F.
LOESCHER, W. H. (C)
NAIR, M.
PERRY, R. L.
SINK, K. C.
WIDDERS, I. E.
ZANDSTRA, B. H.

Department of Human Environment and Design:
SONTAG, M. S.
STERNQUIST, B.
STEWART, D. G. (C)

Department of Internal Medicine:
HUGHES, M. J.
OTTEN, R. F.
PYSH, J. J.
RISTOW, G. E.

Department of Kinesiology:
DUMMER, G.
FELTZ, D. L. (C)
HAUBENSTRICKER, J. L.
MALINA, R. M.
PIVARNIK, J. M.

Department of Large Animal Clinical Sciences:
AMES, N. K.
BAKER, J. C.
BARTLETT, P. C.
CARON, J. P.
DERKSEN, F. J. (C)
HERDT, T.
HOLLAND, R. E.
KANEENE, J. B.
KING, L. J.
LLOYD, J. W.
MATHER, E. C.
NACHREINER, R. F.
NICKELS, F. A.
ROBINSON, N. E.
ROOK, J. S.
SEARS, P. M.
SPRECHER, D. J.
STICK, J. A.
STRAW, B. E.

Department of Linguistics and Germanic, Slavic, Asian and African Languages:
ABBOTT, B. K.
BELGARDT, R.
FALK, J. S.
HUDSON, G.
JUNTUNE, T. W.
LIN, Y.-H.
LOCKWOOD, D. G.
MCCONEGHY, P.
PAULSELL, P.
PETERS, G. F. (C)
PRESTON, D.
SENDICH, M.
WILKINS, W. K.
WURST, K. A.

Department of Management:
BARRICK, M.
HOLLENBECK, J. R.
MOCH, M. K.
RUBIN, P. A.
WAGNER, J. A., III (C)

Department of Marketing and Supply Chain Management:
ALLEN, J. W.
BOWERSOX, D. J.
CALANTONE, R. J.
CAVUSGIL, S. T.
CLOSS, D.
DROGE, C. L.
HARRELL, G. D.
MELNYK, S. A.
NARASIMHAN, R.
NASON, R. W. (C)
SONG, X.-X. M.
VICKERY, S. K.
WILSON, R. D.

Department of Materials Science and Mechanics:
ALTIERO, N. J. (C)
CASE, E. D.
CLOUD, G. L.
GRUMMON, D. S.
HUBBARAD, R. P.
LIU, D.
MUKHERJEE, K.
PENCE, T. J.
SOUTAS-LITTLE, R. W.
SUBRAMANIAN, K. N.

Department of Mathematics:
AKBULUT, S.
BAO, P.
BLAIR, D. E.
BROWN, W. C.
CHEN, B.-Y.
DRACHMAN, B.
DUNNINGER, D. R.
FINTUSHEL, R. A.
FRAZIER, M. W.
HALL, J. I.
HESTENES, M.
HILL, R. O.
IVANOV, N.
KUAN, W. E.
KURTZ, J. C.
LAMM, P. K.
LAPPAN, G.
LAPPAN, P. A. (C)
LI, T. Y.
LO, C. Y.
LUDDEN, G. D.
MCCARTHY, J. D.
MACCLUER, C. R.
MASTERSON, J. J.
MEIERFRANKENFELD, U.
MORAN, D. A.
NEWHOUSE, S. E.
OW, W. H.
PALMER, E. M.
PARKER, T. H.
PLOTKIN, J. M.
ROTTHAUS, C.
SAGAN, B. E.
SCHUUR, J. D.
SEEBECK, C. L.
SENK, S. L.
SHAPIRO, J. H.
SLEDD, W. T.
SONNEBORN, L. M.
SREEDHARAN, V. P.
TREIL, S.
ULRICH, B.
VOLBERG, A.
WALD, J. W.
WANG, C.-Y.
WEIL, C. E.
WINTER, D. L.
WINTER, M. J. K.
WOLFSON, J. G.
WONG, P. K.

ZEIDAN, V. M.
ZHOU, Z.

Department of Mechanical Engineering:
FOSS, J. F.
LLOYD, J. R.
MCGRATH, J.
MEDICK, M. A.
RADCLIFFE, C. J.
ROSENBERG, R. C. (C)
SCHOCK, H. J.
SHAW, S. W.
SHIK, T.
THOMPSON, B. S.
WICHMAN, I. S.

Department of Medicine:
ABELA, G. S.
DIMITROV, N. V.
DIPETTE, D. J. (C)
GOSSAIN, V. V.
HASSOUNA, H. I.
HOLMES-ROVNER, M.
HOPPE, R.
JONES, J. W.
MAYLE, J. E.
NEIBERG, A. D.
PENNER, J. A.
ROSENMAN, K. D.
SCHWARTZ, K. A.
SMITH, R. C.
STEIN, G. E.
SWANSON, G. M.
WANG, D. H.

Department of Microbiology and Molecular Genetics:
BAGDASARIAN, M.
BERTRAND, H.
BREZNAK, J. A.
BRUBAKER, R. R.
CONRAD, S. E.
CORNER, T.
DAZZO, F.
DEBRUIJN, F. J.
DODGSON, J. B. (C)
ESSELMAN, W.
FLUCK, M. M.
GARRITY, G. M.
HAUG, A.
HAUSINGER, R. P.
JACKSON, J. H.
KIERSZENBAUM, F.
MAES, R. K.
MULKS, M. H.
ORIEL, P. J.
PATTERSON, M. J.
PATTERSON, R.
REDDY, C. A.
REUSCH, R. N.
SNYDER, L. R.
VELICER, L. F.
WALKER, R. D.

Department of Obstetrics, Gynecology and Reproductive Biology:
MARSHALL, J. F. (C)
VASILENKO, P.

Department of Osteopathic Manipulative Medicine:
RECHTIEN, J. J. (acting C)
REYNOLDS, H.
WARD, R. C.

Department of Osteopathic Surgical Specialities:
BECKMEYER, H. E.
HARDING, S. A. (C)
HAUT, R. C.
HOGAN, M. J.
JACOBS, A. W.

Department of Park, Recreation and Tourism Resources:
BRISTOR, J. L.
FRIDGEN, J. (C)
HOLECEK, D. F.
RASMUSSEN, G. A.

STYNES, D. J.
VAN DER SMISSEN, B.

Department of Pathology:
BELL, T. G.
HARKEMA, J. R.
KREHBIEL, J.
LOVELL, K. L.
MACKENZIE, C.
MULLANEY, T. P.
PADGETT, G. A.
REED, W. M. (acting C)
RHEUBEN, M. B.
TVEDTEN, H.
WILLIAMS, C. S. F.
YAMINI, B.

Department of Pediatrics:
BREITZER, G. M.
MAGEN, M.
SCHNEIDERMAN, D. O.

Department of Pediatrics and Human Development:
CHANG, C. C.
FISHER, R.
GORDON, R.
KALLEN, D. J.
KAUFMAN, D. B.
KULKARNI, R.
KUMAR, A.
MURRAY, D. L.
NETZLOFF, M. L.
SCOTT-EMUAKPOR, A.
SEAGULL, E. A.
SPARROW, A. W. (C)
TROSKO, J. E.

Department of Pharmacology and Toxicology:
ATCHISON, W. D.
BARMAN, S.
BENNETT, J. L.
BRASELTON, W. E., Jr
FINK, G. D.
FISCHER, L. J.
GALLIGAN, J. J.
GEBBER, G. L.
GOODMAN, J. I.
KAMINSKI, N. E.
MOORE, K. E. (C)
ROTH, R. A.
THORNBURG, J.

Department of Philosophy:
ANDRE, J. A.
ASQUITH, P. D. (C)
BENJAMIN, M.
ESQUITH, S. L.
FLECK, L. M.
FRYE, M.
GARELICK, H. M.
HALL, R. J.
HANNA, J. F.
KOCH, D. F.
KOTZIN, R. H.
LAWSON, B. E.
MCCRACKEN, C. J.
MILLER, B.
PETERSON, R. T.
TOMLINSON, T.

Department of Physical Medicine and Rehabilitation:
HALLGREN, R.
HINDS, W. C.
KAUFMAN, D.
STANTON, D. F.

Department of Physics and Astronomy:
ABOLINS, M. A.
AUSTIN, S. M.
BALDWIN, J. A.
BASS, J.
BAUER, W. W.
BENENSON, W.
BERZ, M. M.
BORYSOWICZ, J.
BROCK, R. L. (C)
BROMBERG, C. M.
BROWN, B. A.
DANIELEWICZ, P.
DUXBURY, P. M.
DYKMAN, M. I.
GALONSKY, A. I.
GOLDING, B.
HARRISON, M. J.
HARTMANN, W. M.
HUSTON, J. W.
KASHY, E.
LINNEMAN, J. T.
LYNCH, W. G.
MAHANTI, S. D.
POLLACK, G. L.
POPE, B. G.
PRATT, W. P., Jr
PUMPLIN, J. C.
REPKO, W. W.
SHERRILL, B. M.
SIGNELL, P. S.
SIMKIN, S. M.
SMITH, H. A.
STEIN, R. F.
THOENNESSEN, M.
THORPE, M. F.
TOMANEK, D.
TUNG, W. K.
WEERTS, H. J.
WESTFALL, G. D.
ZELENVINSKY, V.

Department of Physiology:
ADAMS, T.
HASLAM, S. Z.
HEIDEMANN, S.
HOOTMAN, S. R.
JUMP, D. B.
KREULEN, D. L.
MEYER, R. A.
PETROPOULOS, E. A.
RIEGLE, G. D.
ROOT-BERNSTEIN, R. S.
SPARKS, H.
SPIELMAN, W. S. (C)
TIEN, H. T.
ZIPSER, B.

Department of Political Science:
ABRAMSON, P. R.
ALLEN, W. B.
BRATTON, M.
FINIFTER, A. W.
HALL, M. G.
HAMMOND, T. H.
HULA, R. C.
KNOTT, J. H.
MELZER, A.
OSTROM, C. W., Jr
ROHDE, D. W.
SILVER, B. D.
STEIN, B. N.
WAGMAN, J.
WEINBERGER, J. W. (C)

Department of Psychiatry:
BIELSKI, R. J.
COLENDA, C. (C)
OSBORN, G. G.
ROSEN, L. W.
STOFFELMAYR, B.
VAN EGEREN, L. F.
WERNER, A.
WILLIAMS, D. H.

Department of Psychology:
ABELES, N.
BARCLAY, A. M.
BOGAT, G. A.
CALDWELL, R. A.
CARR, T. H.
DAVIDSON, W., II
FERREIRA, M. F.
FITZGERALD, H. E.
FORD, J. K.
HARRIS, L. J.
HENDERSON, J. M.
HUNTER, J. E.
ILGEN, D. R.
JACKSON, L. A.
KARON, B. P.
KERR, N. L.
KOSLOWSKI, S. W.
LEVINE, R. L.
LOMBARDI, V. L.
MESSE, L. A.
NUNEZ, A. A.
PAULUS, G. S.
SCHMITT, N. W. (C)
SISK, C. L.
STOLLAK, G. E.
VON EYE, A. A.
WOOD, G. (C)
ZACKS, J. L.
ZACKS, R. T.

Department of Radiology:
FALLS, W. M.
GOTTSCHALK, A.
HALPERT, R. D.
JOHNSON, J. I.
POTCHEN, E. J. (C)
ROSS, L. M.
WALKER, B. E.

Department of Religious Studies:
GREENE, J. T.
VERSLUIS, A.
WELCH, A. T.

Department of Resource Development:
BARNES-MCCONNELL, P.
BRONSTEIN, D. A.
DERSCH, E.
FEAR, F. A.
KAKELA, P. J.
KAMRIN, M. A.
NICKEL, P. E.
ROWAN, G.
SCHULTINK, G.
WRIGHT, D.

Department of Romance and Classical Languages:
COLMEIRO, J. F.
DONOHOE, J. I.
FIORE, R. L.
FRANCESE, J.
GRAY, E. F.
JOSEPHS, H.
KOPPISCH, M.
MANSOUR, G. P.
MARINO, N. F.
PORTER, L. M. (acting C)
SNOW, J. T.
TYRRELL, W. B.

Department of Small Animal Clinical Sciences:
ARNOCZKY, S. P.
BRADEN, T. D.
DECAMP, C. E.
EVANS, A. T.
EYSTER, G. E.
FLO, G. L.
HAUPTMAN, J.
JOHNSON, C.
MOSTOSKY, U. V.
PROBST, C. W. (C)
ROSSER, E. J.
SCHALL, W. D.
WALSHAW, R.

Department of Sociology:
BOKEMEIER, J.
BROMAN, C. L.
BUSCH, L. M.
CONNER, T. L. (C)
GALLIN, R. S.
GOLD, S. J.
HAMILTON, R. S.
HILL, R. C.
JOHNSON, N. E.
KAPLOWITZ, S.
MANNING, P. K.
PERLSTADT, H.
RUMBAUT, R. G.

SHLAPENTOKH, V.
VANDERPOOL, C. K.
WILEY, D.
ZINN, M. B.

Department of Statistics and Probability:
ERICKSON, R. V.
FABIAN, V.
FELDMAN, D.
GARDINER, J. C.
GILLILAND, D. C.
HANNAN, J. F.
KOUL, H. L.
LEPAGE, R. D.
MANDREKAR, V.
PAGE, C. F.
RAMAMOORTHI, R. V.
SALEHI, H. (C)
STAPLETON, J.

Department of Surgery:
DEAN, R. E. (C)
HARKEMA, J.
OSUCH, J. R.
TOLEDO, L. H.

Department of Teacher Education:
ALLEMAN, J. E.
ANDERSON, C. W.
ANDERSON, K.
ANDERSON, L. M.
BADER, L. A.
BARNES, H. L.
BOOK, C.
BROPHY, J. E.
CHERRYHOLMES, C.
EDWARDS, P. A.
FEATHERSTONE, J.
FERRINI-MUNDY, J.
FLORIO-RUANE, S.
GALLAGHER, J. J.
JOYCE, W. W.
KENNEDY, M. M.
KOZIOL, S. M. (C)
LABAREE, D. F.
LANIER, J. E.
LANIER, P. E.
LITTLE, T.
NEMSER, S. F.
PEARSON, P. D.
PURCELL-GATES, V.
PUTNAM, J. G.
RIETHMILLER, P. L.
ROEHLER, L. R.
SCHWILLE, J. R.
SEDLAK, M. W.
WEST, B. B.
WHEELER, C.

Department of Telecommunication:
BIOCCA, F. A.
GREENBERG, B. S.
HEETER, C. J.
LA ROSE, R. J.
LEVY, M. R. (C)
LITMAN, B. R.
MODY, B.
MUTH, T. A.
STEINFIELD, C.
WILDMAN, S. S.
WILLIAMS, G. A.

Department of Theatre:
DURR, D. L. (C)
RUTLEDGE, F. C.
RUTLEDGE, G.
SCHUTTLER, G.

Department of Zoology:
AGGARWAL, S. K.
ATKINSON, J. W.
BAND, R. N.
BEAVER, D. L.
BROMLEY, S. C.
BURTON, T. M. (C)
BUSH, G. L.
CATHEY, B.
CLEMENS, L. G.
COOPER, W. E.
DYER, F. C.
EILAND, L. C.
GIESY, J. P.
HALL, D. J.
HILL, R. W.
HOLEKAMP, K. E.
HUGGETT, R. J.
MUZZALL, P. M.
PEEBLES, C.
ROBBINS, L. G.
SNIDER, R. J.
STEVENSON, R. J.
STRANEY, D.
WEBBER, M. M.

Division of Human Pathology:
JONES, M.
KUMAR, K.
SANDER, C. M.
SIEW, S.

James Madison College:
AYOOB, M.
BANKS, R. F.
DORR, R. F.
GARNETT, S. W. (Dean)
GRAHAM, N. A.
HOEKSTRA, D. J.
RUBNER, M.
SCHECHTER, M.
SEE, K. O.
WALTZER, K.
ZINMAN, M. R.

Lyman Briggs School:
EBERT-MAY, D. (Dir)
INGRAHAM, E. C.
MERCURO, N.
SAYED, M. M. A.
SIMPSON, W. A.
SPEES, S. T.

National Superconducting Cyclotron Laboratory:
BLOSSER, H. G.
GELBKE, C. K. (Dir)
HANSEN, P. G.
YORK, R. C.

Office of Medical Education Research and Development:
ABBETT, W. S.
ANDERSON, W. A. (Dir)
FARQUAR, L. J.
HENRY, R. C.
MOLIDOR, J. B.

School of Criminal Justice:
BONNER, R. W.
BYNUM, T. S.
CARTER, D. L.
HORVATH, F. S.
HUDZIK, J. K.
MASTROFSKI
MORASH, M. A. (Dir)
NALLA, M. K.
SIEGEL, J.
SMITH, C. E.
STEWART, C. S.

School of Hospitality Business:
CICHY, R. (Dir)
KASAVANA, M. L.
KNUTSON, B. J.
NINEMEIER, J. D.
SCHMIDGALL, B. H.

School of Journalism:
BOSSEN, H. S.
COTE, W. E.
DAVENPORT, L. D.
DETJEN, J. T.
FICO, F.
LACY, S. R. (acting Dir)
MOLLOY, J. D.
SOFFIN, S. I.
SPANIOLO, J. D.

School of Labor and Industrial Relations:
BLOCK, R. N.
CURRY, T. H. (Dir)
KOSSEK, E. E.
KRUGER, D. H.
MOORE, M. L. (Dir)
REVITTE, J.
SMITH, P. R.
TOBEY, S. H.
VANDE VORD, N.
WOLKINSON, B. W.

School of Music:
CARMAN, O. W.
CATRON, D. L.
DAN, R. M.
DONAKOWSKI, C.
ELL, F. W.
FORGER, D. M.
FORGER, J. B. (Dir)
GREGORIAN, L.
HUTCHESON, J. T.
JOHNSON, M. E.
JOHNSON, T. O.
KRATUS, J. K.
LEBLANC, A.
LULLOFF, J. P.
MOON, Y. H.
NEWMAN, R.
OLSON, C.
RUGGIERO, C. H.
SINDER, P. N.
SMITH, C. K.
STOLPER, D.
TIMS, F. C.
VERDEBR, E. L.
VERDEBR, W.
VOTAPEK, R. J.
WARD, B. W.
WHITWELL, J. L.
ZARA, M.

School of Packaging:
BURGESS, C. J.
DOWNES, T. W.
GIACIN, J. R.
HARTE, B. (Dir)
HUGHES, H. A.
LOCKHART, H. E.
SELKE, S. E. M.

School of Social Work:
ANDERSON, G. R. (Dir)
DUANE, E. A.
FREDDOLINO, P. P.
HAROLD, R. D.
HERRICK, J. M.
LEVANDE, D. I.
WHITEMAN, V. L.

Centers and Other Administrative Units:
BLINN, L. V.
BOWMAN, H. E.
CARROLL, T. W.
KAUFMAN, G.
LOPUSHINSKY, T.
NERENZ, D. R.
NOVICKI, D. J.
ROSENTHAL, W. H.
SIERRA, L.
VORRO, J.
WILLIAMS, J. G.

Medical Technology Program:
DAVIS, G. L.

Undergraduate University Division:
CURRY, B. P. (Dir)

Urban Affairs Programs:
DARDEN, J. T. (Dean)
LANG, M.
SCHWEITZER, J. H.
THORNTON, D. (acting Dean)

W. K. Kellogg Biological Station:
GROSS, K. L.
KLUG, M. J. (Dir)
KNEZEK, B. D.
MITTELBACH, G. G.
TESSIER, A. J.

MICHIGAN TECHNOLOGICAL UNIVERSITY

1400 Townsend Dr., Houghton, MI 49931-1295

Telephone: (906) 487-1885
E-mail: mtu4u@mtu.edu
Internet: www.mtu.edu

Founded 1885; fmrly Michigan College of Mining and Technology
Academic year: August to April

Pres.: Dr GLENN D. MROZ
Provost and Vice-Pres. for Academic Affairs: Dr LESLEY LOVETT-DOUST
Vice-Pres for Govt Relations and Sec. of Board of Control: Dr DALE TAHTINEN
Vice-Pres. for Research: DAVID D. REED
Vice-Pres. for Student Affairs: Dr LES COOK
Chief Financial Officer and Treas. of Board of Control: DANIEL GREENLEE
Head of Keweenaw Research Center: Dr JAY MELDRUM
Dir of Library: PHYLLIS JOHNSON

Number of teachers: 417
Number of students: 6,738

Publication: *Catalog*.

NORTHERN MICHIGAN UNIVERSITY

1401 Presque Isle Ave, Marquette, MI 49855

Telephone: (906) 227-1000
Fax: (906) 227-2204
Internet: www.nmu.edu

Founded 1899
Academic year: August to May

Pres.: LESLIE E. WONG
Provost and Vice-Pres. for Academic Affairs: SUSAN J. KOCH
Vice-Pres. for Finance and Admin.: MICHAEL J. ROY
Dean of Academic Information Services: DARLENE WALCH
Dir of Admissions: GERRI DANIELS

Library of 522,000 vols, 530,000 govt docs
Number of teachers: 481
Number of students: 8,347

DEANS

College of Arts and Sciences: Dr MICHAEL BROADWAY
College of Business: Dr JAMAL RASHED
College of Professional Studies: Dr PAUL LANG

NORTHWOOD UNIVERSITY

4000 Whiting Dr., Midland, MI 48640-2398

Telephone: (989) 837-4200
Fax: (989) 837-4490
E-mail: miadmit@northwood.edu
Internet: www.northwood.edu

Founded 1959
Private control
Academic year: September to May

Pres. and CEO: KEITH A. PRETTY
Provost of Michigan Campus: DAVID LONG
Exec. Vice-Pres. and Chief Academic and Operating Officer: Dr JOHN JASINSKI
Vice-Pres. for Finance and Treas.: DONALD E. HUNKINS
Vice-Pres. for Graduate and Special Programs: TIMOTHY G. NASH
Vice-Pres. for Marketing and Enrollment Management: JOHN YOUNG
Vice-Pres. for Univ. Advancement: THOMAS KAVANAGH, Jr
Library Dir: SANDRA POTTS

Library of 50,000 vols
Number of teachers: 61
Number of students: 1,775

Areas of study: arts, business admin.

BRANCH CAMPUSES

Florida Campus: 2600 North Military Trail, West Palm Beach, FL 33409-2911; tel. (561) 478-5500; fax (561) 640-3328; e-mail fladmit@northwood.edu; internet www.northwood.edu/fl; Provost JOHN H. HAYNIE; 661 students.

Texas Campus: 1114 West FM 1382, Cedar Hill, TX 75104-1204; tel. (972) 291-1541; fax (972) 291-3824; e-mail txadmit@northwood.edu; Provost Dr KEVIN G. FEGAN; 1,601 students.

OAKLAND UNIVERSITY

Telephone: (248) 370-2100
Internet: www.oakland.edu

Founded 1957
State control
Academic year: September to August (2 semesters, 2 sessions)

Pres.: Dr GARY D. RUSSI
Vice-Pres. for Academic Affairs: VIRINDER MOUDGIL
Vice-Pres. for Finance and Admin.: JOHN W. BEAGHAN
Vice-Pres. for Student Affairs: MARY BETH SNYDER
Vice-Pres. for Univ. Relations and Exec. Dir of OU Foundation: SUSAN DAVIES GOEPP
Gen. Counsel and Sec. to Board of Trustees: VICTOR A. ZAMBARDI
Librarian: JULIE VOELCK

Number of teachers: 434 full-time
Number of students: 16,902

DEANS

College of Arts and Sciences: RONALD A. SUDOL
Graduate Study and Research: RONALD OLSON
School of Business Administration: MOHAN TANNIRU
School of Educational and Human Service: MARY L. OTTO
School of Engineering and Computer Science: PIETER FRICK
School of Health Sciences: KENNETH HIGHTOWER
School of Nursing: LINDA THOMPSON-ADAMS

OLIVET COLLEGE

320 South Main St, Olivet, MI 49076

Telephone: (616) 749-7000
Fax: (616) 749-7121
Internet: www.olivetcollege.edu

Founded 1844

Pres.: Dr DONALD L. TUSKI
Vice-Pres. for Academic Affairs: NORMA CURTIS
Vice-Pres. for Admin.: LARRY COLVIN
Vice-Pres. and Chief Financial Officer: MARK DERUITER
Vice-Pres. and Dean of Student Life: Dr LINDA LOGAN
Vice-Pres. for Enrollment Management: LARRY VALLAR
Vice-Pres. for Institutional Advancement: MARK VEICH
Dir for Institutional Advancement: TODD HIBBS
Dir of Library: JANE REITER

Library of 90,000 vols, 180 periodicals
Number of students: 825

Depts of business admin., education, health, physical education, recreation and sport (HPERS), humanities, natural and physical science, mathematics and computer science, social science, visual and performing arts.

ROCHESTER COLLEGE

800 West Avon Rd, Rochester Hills, MI 48307

Telephone: (248) 218-2000
Fax: (248) 650-6060
Internet: www.rc.edu

Founded 1959 as North Central Christian College; present name 1997
Private control
Academic year: August to May

Pres.: Prof. RUBEL SHELLY
Exec. Vice-Pres. and Chief Financial Officer: ALAN B. WAITES
Vice-Pres. of Academic Affairs: BRIAN L. STOGNER
Vice-Pres. for Devt: KLINT PLEASANT
Vice-Pres. for Enrollment Services and Marketing: LARRY D. NORMAN
Vice-Pres. for Human Resources and Special Projects and Alumni Relations: KELVIN BROWN
Vice-Pres. for Student Services: CANDACE CAIN
Registrar: CATHY MACKENZIE
Library Dir: ALLIE KELLER

Number of teachers: 37
Number of students: 600

DEANS

College of Arts and Sciences: Dr JENNIFER HAMILTON
College of Business and Professional Studies: Dr JEFFEREY A. SIMMONS

SACRED HEART MAJOR SEMINARY

2701 Chicago Blvd, Detroit, MI 48206

Telephone: (313) 883-8500
Fax: (313) 868-6440
E-mail: information@shms.edu
Internet: www.aodonline.org/shms

Founded 1919 as Sacred Heart Seminary; present name 1988
Private control

Rector and Pres.: Rev. Mgr JEFFREY M. MONFORTON
Vice-Rector and Dean of Seminarians: Fr MICHEL BYRNES
Dean of Institute for Ministry: PATRICIA RENNIE
Dean of Studies: Fr TODD LAJINESS
Library Dir: KAREN RAE MEHAFFEY

Library of 110,000 vols
Number of teachers: 39
Number of students: 2,030

SAGINAW VALLEY STATE UNIVERSITY

7400 Bay Rd, University Center, MI 48710

Telephone: (989) 964-4000
E-mail: admissions@svsu.edu
Internet: www.svsu.edu

Founded 1963
State control
Academic year: August to August

Pres.: Dr ERIC R. GILBERTSON
Vice-Pres. for Academic Affairs: DONALD J. BACHAND
Vice-Pres. for Admin. and Business Affairs: JIM MULADORE
Vice-Pres. for Student Services and Enrollment Management: ROBERT MAUROVICH
Library Dir: LINDA FARYNK

Library of 232,770 print items, 404,458 non-print items; 651 current subscriptions to print journals; 23,090 e-journals
Number of teachers: 294
Number of students: 9,837 (7,747 undergraduates, 1,574 graduates, 516 other teacher certification, non-degree, special-ist).

DEANS

College of Arts and Behavioral Sciences: MARY HEDBERG
College of Business and Management: MARWAN A. WAFA
College of Education: STEVE BARBUS
College of Science, Engineering and Technology: RONALD WILLIAMS
Crystal M. Lange College of Nursing and Health Sciences: JANALOU BLECKE

SIENA HEIGHTS UNIVERSITY

Telephone: (517) 263-0731
Fax: (517) 264-7702
Internet: www.sienaheights.edu

Founded 1919
Academic year: August to May

Pres.: Sister Dr PEG ALBERT
Vice-Pres. of Advancement: JERE L. RIGHTER
Academic Dean: Dr SHARON WEBER
Dean of College for Professional Studies: DEBORAH CLARKE
Dean of Graduate Studies and Lifelong Learning: Dr ROBERT W. GORDON
Dean of Students: TRUDY MCSORLEY
Dir of Admissions and Enrollment: KEVIN KUCERA
Chief Financial Officer: J. LEE JOHNSON
Registrar: AMY SMITH
Librarian: (vacant)

Library of 136,082 vols
Number of teachers: 220
Number of students: 2,161

Divs of business and management, computing, mathematics and sciences, humanities, social and behavioural science, visual and performing arts, teacher education

Publications: *Reflections* (3 a year), *Spectra* (6 a year).

SPRING ARBOR UNIVERSITY

106 East Main St, Spring Arbor, MI 49283
Telephone: (517) 750-1200
Fax: (517) 750-2108
E-mail: admissions@arbor.edu
Internet: www.arbor.edu

Founded 1873

Pres.: GERALD E. BATES
Vice-Pres. for Academic Affairs: BETTY J. OVERTON-ADKINS
Vice-Pres. for Enrollment Services: MATT S. OSBORNE
Vice-Pres. for Student Devt and Learning: KIM K. HAYWORTH
Vice-Pres. for Technology Services: REED A. SHEARD
Vice-Pres. for Univ. Advancement: JAY E. MANSUR

Library of 120,300 vols
Number of teachers: 80
Number of students: 4,000

THOMAS M. COOLEY LAW SCHOOL

POB 13038, Lansing, MI 48901
300 South Capitol Ave, Lansing, MI 48933
Telephone: (517) 371-5140
Fax: (517) 334-5718
E-mail: admissions@cooley.edu
Internet: www.cooley.edu

Founded 1972
Private control
Academic year: September to August

Pres. and Dean: DON LEDUC
Vice-Pres. for Finance and Chief Operating Officer: WILLIAM SCHOETTLE
Assoc. Dean for Enrollment and Student Services: Dr PAUL ZELENSKI
Assoc. Dean of Faculty: CHARLES CERCONE
Assoc. Dean for Grand Rapids Univ. Campus: MARION HILLIGAN
Assoc. Dean for Library and Instructional Support: DUANE STROJNY
Assoc. Dean for Rochester/Oakland Univ. Campus: JOHN NUSSBAUMER
Assoc. Dean for Students and Professionalism: AMY TIMMER

Library of 550,000 vols
Number of teachers: 257 (87 full-time, 154 part-time, 16 additional)
Number of students: 3,606

Publications: *Art and Museum Law Journal*, *Journal of Practical and Clinical Law*, *Thomas M. Cooley Law Review*.

UNIVERSITY OF DETROIT MERCY

POB 19900, 4001 West McNichols Rd, Detroit, MI 48219-0900
Telephone: (313) 993-1000
E-mail: admissions@udmercy.edu
Internet: www.udmercy.edu

Founded 1877 as Detroit College and chartered as such 1881; chartered as univ. 1911; merged with Mercy College of Detroit in 1990

Pres.: Rev. GERARD L. STOCKHAUSEN
Vice-Pres. for Academic Affairs and Provost: PAMELA ZARKOWSKI
Vice-Pres. for Business and Finance: VINCENT ABATEMARCO
Exec. Vice-Pres.: MICHAEL JOSEPH
Dean of Student Life: MONICA LEONARD
Registrar: DIANE M. PRAET
Dean of Libraries: MARGARET AUER

Library of 508,000 vols
Number of teachers: 295
Number of students: 5,600

DEANS

College of Business Admin.: HOSSEIN NIVI
College of Engineering and Science: LEO C. HANIFIN
College of Health Professions: SUZANNE MELLON
College of Liberal Arts and Education: CHARLES E. MARSKE
School of Architecture: STEPHEN VOGEL
School of Dentistry: H. ROBERT STEIMAN
School of Law: MARK GORDON

UNIVERSITY OF MICHIGAN

Ann Arbor, MI 48109
Telephone: (734) 764-1817
E-mail: info@umich.edu
Internet: www.umich.edu

Founded 1817
Public control
Language of instruction: English
Academic year: September to April

Pres.: MARY SUE COLEMAN
Provost and Exec. Vice-Pres. for Academic Affairs: Prof. PHILIP HANLON
Exec. Vice-Pres. and Chief Financial Officer: TIMOTHY P. SLOTTOW
Exec. Vice-Pres. for Medical Affairs: ORA HIRSCH PESCOVITZ
Vice-Pres. for Communications: DAVID R. LAMPE
Vice-Pres. for Devt: JERRY A. MAY
Vice-Pres. for Govt Relations: CYNTHIA H. WILBANKS
Vice-Pres. for Research: Dr STEPHEN R. FORREST
Vice-Pres. for Student Affairs: E. ROYSTER HARPER
Vice-Pres. and Gen. Counsel: SUELLYN SCARNECCHIA
Vice-Pres. and Sec.: SALLY J. CHURCHILL
Univ. Registrar: PAUL ROBINSON
Exec. Dir of Admissions: THEODORE L. SPENCER
Univ. Librarian: PAUL N. COURANT

Library: see Libraries and Archives
Number of teachers: 5,965
Number of students: 41,924

Publications: *Amicus*, *Dividend*, *Emergence*, *Espanol*, *Findings*, *Innovator*, *LSA Magazine*, *Medicine at Michigan*, *Michigan Alumnus* (4 a year), *Michigan Engineer*, *Michigan Quarterly Review*, *Montage*, *Movement*, *Muse*, *Ongoing*, *Portico*, *SI Information*, *State & Hill*, *Stewards*, *The University of Michigan Today* (4 a year)

DEANS

College of Architecture and Urban Planning: MONICA PONCE DE LEON
College of Engineering: DAVID C. MUNSON, Jr
College of Literature, Science and the Arts: TERRENCE J. MCDONALD
College of Pharmacy: FRANK J. ASCIONE
Law School: EVAN CAMINKER
Medical School: JAMES O. WOOLLISCROFT
School of Art and Design: BRYAN ROGERS
School of Business: ROBERT J. DOLAN
School of Dentistry: PETER POLVERINI
School of Education: DEBORAH BALL
School of Graduate Studies: JANET WEISS
School of Information: JEFFREY MACKIE-MASON
School of Kinesiology: RONALD ZERNICKE
School of Music, Theatre and Dance: CHRISTOPHER KENDALL
School of Natural Resources and Environment: ROSINA M. BIERBAUM
School of Nursing: KATHLEEN M. POTEMPA
School of Public Health: MARTIN PHILBERT
School of Public Policy: SUSAN M. COLLINS
School of Social Work: LAURA LEIN

PROFESSORS

Gerald Ford School of Public Policy (Joan and Sanford Weill Hall, 735 S State St, Ann Arbor, MI 48109-3091; tel. (734) 764-3490; fax (734) 763-9181; internet www.fordschool.umich.edu):

AXELROD, R.
CHAMBERLIN, J.
COHEN, D.
COLLINS, S.
CORCORAN, M.
COURANT, P.
DANZIGER, S.
DANZIGER, S.
DEARDORFF, A.
DINARDO, J.
DOMINGUEZ, K.
GERBER, E.
HALL, R.
HOUSE, J.
JACOB, B.
LEVITSKY, M.
RABE, B.
SIMON, C.
SVEJNAR, J.

College of Architecture and Urban Planning (tel. (734) 764-1300; fax (734) 763-2322; internet www.tcaup.umich.edu):

BURESH, T.
CONSTANT, C.
DEWAR, M.
FISHMAN, R.
GILES, H.
GROAT, L.
HILL, E.
KELBAUGH, D.
LEINBERGER, C.
LEVINE, J.
MURRAY, M.
PONCE DE LEON, M.
RAY, M.
THOMAS, J.
WINEMAN, J.

College of Engineering (tel. (734) 647-7000; fax (734) 647-7001; internet www.engin.umich.edu):

ADRIAENS, P., Civil and Environmental Engineering
ARMSTRONG, T., Industrial Operations
ARRUDA, E., Mechanical Engineering
ASHTON-MILLER, J., Biomedical Engineering
ASHTON-MILLER, J., Mechanical Engineering
ASSANIS, D., Mechanical Engineering
ATKINS III, D., COE EECS—CSE Division
ATREYA, A., Mechanical Engineering
ATREYA, S., Atmospheric, Oceanic and Space Science.
ATZMON, M., Nuclear Engineering and Radiological Science
AUSTIN, T., COE EECS—CSE Division
BARBER, J., Mechanical Engineering
BARKER, J., Atmospheric, Oceanic and Space Science.
BAVEJA, S., COE EECS—CSE Division
BECK, R., Naval Architecture and Marine Dept
BERNITSAS, M., Naval Architecture and Marine Dept
BERNSTEIN, D., Aerospace Engineering
BHATTACHARYA, P., COE EECS—ECE Division
BIELAJEW, A., Nuclear Engineering and Radiological Science
BLAAUW, D., COE EECS—CSE Division
BLAAUW, D., COE EECS—ECE Division
BORENSTEIN, J., Mechanical Engineering
BOUGHER, S., Atmospheric, Oceanic and Space Science.
BOYD, I., Aerospace Engineering
BOYD, J., Atmospheric, Oceanic and Space Science
BOZER, Y., Industrial Operations
BULKLEY, J., Civil and Environmental Engineering
BURNS, M., Chemical Engineering
CAIN, C., Biomedical Engineering
CARROLL, M., Atmospheric, Oceanic and Space Science.
CECCIO, S., Mechanical Engineering
CESNIK, C., Aerospace Engineering
CHAO, X., Industrial Operations
CHEN, P., COE EECS—CSE Division
COMBI, M., Space Physics Research Lab
DAHM, W., Aerospace Engineering
DASKIN, M., Industrial Operations
DOWLING, D., Mechanical Engineering
DOWNAR, T., Nuclear Engineering and Radiological Science
DRAKE, R., Atmospheric, Oceanic and Space Science.
DRISCOLL, J., Aerospace Engineering
DUENYAS, I., Industrial Operations
DURFEE, E., COE EECS—CSE Division
EL-TAWIL, S., Civil and Environmental Engineering
ENGLAND, A., COE EECS—ECE Division
FESSLER, J., COE EECS—ECE Division
FISK, L., Atmospheric, Oceanic and Space Science.
FLEMING, R., Nuclear Engineering and Radiological Science
FOGLER, H., Chemical Engineering Dept
FORREST, S., COE EECS—ECE Division
FREUDENBERG, J., COE EECS—ECE Division
FRIEDMANN, P., Aerospace Engineering
GALLIMORE, A., Aerospace Engineering
GALVANAUSKAS, A., COE EECS—ECE Division
GHOSH, A., Materials Science and Engineering
GIANCHANDANI, Y., COE EECS—ECE Division
GILCHRIST, B., COE EECS—ECE Division
GILGENBACH, R., Nuclear Engineering and Radiological Science
GLOECKLER, G., Atmospheric, Oceanic and Space Science
GLOTZER, S., Chemical Engineering
GOLDMAN, R., Materials Science and Engineering.
GOMBOSI, T., Atmospheric, Oceanic and Space Science
GREEN, P., Materials Science and Engineering.
GRIZZLE, J., COE EECS—ECE Division
GROSH, K., Mechanical Engineering
GROTBERG, J., Biomedical Engineering
GULARI, E., Chemical Engineering
HALLORAN, J., Materials Science and Engineering.
HANSEN, W., Civil and Environmental Engineering
HAYES, J., COE EECS—CSE Division
HAYES, K., Civil and Environmental Engineering
HERO III, A., COE EECS—ECE Division
HERRIN, G., Industrial Operations
HE, Z., Nuclear Engineering and Radiological Science
HISKENS, I., COE EECS—ECE Division
HOLLAND, J., COE EECS—CSE Division
HOLLISTER, S., Biomedical Engineering
HOLLOWAY, J., Nuclear Engineering and Radiological Science
HONEYMAN, P., COE EECS—CSE Division
HRYCIW, R., Civil and Environmental Engineering
HULBERT, G., Mechanical Engineering
HU, S., Mechanical Engineering
IOANNOU, P., Civil and Environmental Engineering
ISLAM, M., COE EECS—ECE Division
JAGADISH, H., COE EECS—CSE Division
JAHANIAN, F., COE EECS—CSE Division
JONES, J., Materials Science and Engineering.
KABAMBA, P., Aerospace Engineering
KANICKI, J., COE EECS—ECE Division
KANNATEY-ASIBU JR, E., Mechanical Engineering
KANTOWITZ, B., Industrial Operations
KATOPODES, N., Civil and Environmental Engineering
KAVIANY, M., Mechanical Engineering
KEARFOTT, K., Nuclear Engineering and Radiological Science
KEYSERLING, W., Industrial Operations
KIEFFER, J., Materials Science and Engineering.
KIERAS, D., COE EECS—CSE Division
KIKUCHI, N., Mechanical Engineering
KIPKE, D., Biomedical Engineering
KIVELSON, M., Atmospheric, Oceanic and Space Science.
KOLMANOVSKY, I., Aerospace Engineering
KOREN, Y., Mechanical Engineering
KOTA, S., Mechanical Engineering
KOTOV, N., Chemical Engineering
KOZYRA, J., Space Physics Research Lab
KRUSHELNICK, K., Nuclear Engineering and Radiological Science
KUIPERS, B., COE EECS—CSE Division
KUO, A., Mechanical Engineering
KUSHNER, M., COE EECS—ECE Division
LAFORTUNE, S., COE EECS—ECE Division
LAINE, R., Materials Science and Engin.
LAIRD, J., COE EECS—CSE Division
LARSEN, E., Nuclear Engineering and Radiological Science
LARSON, R., Chemical Engineering Dept
LAU, Y., Nuclear Engineering and Radiological Science
LEE, J., Nuclear Engineering and Radiological Science
LIKER, J., Industrial Operations
LINDERMAN, J., Chemical Engineering Dept
LI, V., Civil and Environmental Engineering
LOVE, B., Materials Science and Engineering
LOVE, N., Civil & Environmental Engineering
MARTIN, W., Nuclear Engineering and Radiological Sci
MAZUMDER, J., Mechanical Engineering
MAZUMDER, P., COE EECS—CSE Division
MCCLAMROCH, N., Aerospace Engineering
MEADOWS, G., Naval Architecture and Marine Dept
MEERKOV, S., COE EECS—ECE Division
MEYHOFER, E., Mechanical Engineering
MICHALOWSKI, R., Civil and Environmental Engineering
MICHIELSSEN, E., COE EECS—ECE Division
MOGHADDAM, M., COE EECS—ECE Division
MOLDWIN, M., Atmospheric, Oceanic and Space Science
MORTAZAWI, A., COE EECS—ECE Division
MUDGE, T., COE EECS—CSE Division
MUNSON JR, D., COE EECS—ECE Division
MURTY, K., Industrial Operations
NAJAFI, K., COE EECS—ECE Division
NEUHOFF, D., COE EECS—ECE Division
NI, J., Mechanical Engineering
NOLL, D., Biomedical Engineering
NORRIS, T., COE EECS—ECE Division
OLSEN, L., COE Technical Communications
PAN, J., Mechanical Engineering
PAN, X., Materials Science and Engineering
PANG, S., COE EECS—ECE Division
PAPAEFTHYMIOU, M., COE EECS—CSE Division
PAPALAMBROS, P., Mechanical Engineering
PENG, H., Mechanical Engineering
PENNER, J., Atmospheric, Oceanic and Space Science
PERKINS, N., Mechanical Engineering
PERLIN, M., Naval Arch and Marine
POLLACK, M., COE EECS—CSE Division
POWELL, K., Aerospace Engineering
PRAKASH, A., COE EECS—CSE Division
RAND, S., COE EECS—ECE Division
RASKIN, L., Civil and Environmental Engineering
RENNO, N., Atmospheric, Oceanic and Space Science
ROBERTSON, R., Materials Science and Engineering.
ROE, P., Aerospace Engineering
ROMEIJN, H., Industrial Operations
ROOD, R., Atmospheric, Oceanic and Space Science
RUF, C., Atmospheric, Oceanic and Space Science
SAIGAL, R., Industrial Operations
SAKALLAH, K., COE EECS—CSE Division
SAMSON, P., Atmospheric, Oceanic and Space Science.
SARABANDI, K., COE EECS—ECE Division
SASTRY, A., Mechanical Engineering
SAVAGE, P., Chemical Engineering
SCHULTZ, W., Mechanical Engineering
SCHWANK, J., Chemical Engineering
SCOTT, R., Mechanical Engineering
SEIFORD, L., Industrial Operations
SHIH, A., Mechanical Engineering
SHIN, K., COE EECS—CSE Division
SHYY, W., Aerospace Engineering
SICK, V., Mechanical Engineering
SILLMAN, M., Space Physics Research Laboratory
SINGH, J., COE EECS—ECE Division
SMITH, J., Materials Science and Engineering.
SMITH, R., Industrial Operations
SOLOMON, M., Chemical Engineering
SOLOWAY, E., COE EECS—CSE Division
STARK, W., COE EECS—ECE Division
STEEL, D., COE EECS—ECE Division
STEFANOPOULOU, A., Mechanical Engineering
STEIN, J., Mechanical Engineering

STOUT, Q., COE EECS—CSE Division
SUN, J., Naval Architecture and Marine Dept
TENEKETZIS, D., COE EECS—ECE Division
TERRY JR, F., COE EECS—ECE Division
THOMPSON JR, L., Chemical Engineering Dept
THOULESS, M., Mechanical Engineering
TILBURY, D., Mechanical Engineering
TRIANTAFYLLIDIS, N., Aerospace Engineering
TROESCH, A., Naval Architecture and Marine Dept
ULABY, F., COE EECS—ECE Division
ULSOY, A., Mechanical Engineering
VAN LEER, B., Aerospace Engineering
VLAHOPOULOS, N., Naval Architecture and Marine Dept
WAAS, A., Aerospace Engineering
WANG, H., Chemical Engineering
WANG, K., Mechanical Engineering
WANG, L., Nuclear Engineering and Radiological Science
WAS, G., Nuclear Engineering and Radiological Science
WEHE, D., Nuclear Engineering and Radiological Science
WELLMAN, M., COE EECS—CSE Division
WIGHT, J., Civil and Environmental Engineering
WINEMAN, A., Mechanical Engineering
WINFUL, H., COE EECS—ECE Division
WINICK, K., COE EECS—ECE Division
WISE, K., COE EECS—ECE Division
WOOLDRIDGE, M., Mechanical Engineering
WRIGHT, S., Civil and Environmental Engineering
YAGLE, A., COE EECS—ECE Division
YALISOVE, S., Materials Science and Engineering.
YANG, R., Chemical Engineering
ZIFF, R., Chemical Engineering
ZURBUCHEN, T., Atmospheric, Oceanic and Space Science

College of Literature, Science and the Arts (tel. (734) 764-0322; fax (734) 764-2697; internet www.lsa.umich.edu):

ABEL, R., Screen Arts and Cultures
ADAMS, F., Physics
ADAMS, J., Molecular Cellular and Developmental Biology
ADAMS, W., Economics
AHBEL-RAPPE, S., Classical Studies
AKERLOF, C., Physics
AKHOURY, R., Physics
ALEXANDER, W., English Language and Literature
AL-HASHIMI, H., Biophysics
AL-HASHIMI, H., Chemistry
ALLEN, J., Physics
ALLER, H., Astronomy
AMIDEI, D., Physics
ANDERSON, B., Sociology
ANDERSON, E., Philosophy
ANTONUCCI, T., Psychology
AWKWARD, M., CAAS
AWKWARD, M., English Language and Literature
AXELROD, R., Political Science
AXINN, W., Sociology
BANASZAK HOLL, M., Chemistry
BARBER, J., Sociology
BARDAKJIAN, K., Near Eastern Studies
BARDAKJIAN, K., Slavic Languages and Literature
BARDWELL, J., Molecular Cellular and Developmental Biology
BARRETT, D., Mathematics
BARSKY, R., Economics
BARVINOK, A., Mathematics
BASS, H., Mathematics
BAUMILLER, T., Geological Sciences
BECCHETTI JR, F., Physics
BECKMAN, G., Near Eastern Studies
BEDDOR, P., Linguistics
BEHAR, R., Anthropology
BELOT, G., Philosophy
BENDER, R., Molecular Cellular and Developmental Biology
BERMAN, P., Physics
BERRIDGE, K., Psychology
BERRY, P., Ecology and Evolutionary Biology
BINETTI, V., Romance Languages and Literature
BIRO, M., History of Art
BLAIR, S., English Language and Literature.
BLASS, A., Mathematics
BLOCH, A., Mathematics
BLUM, J., Geological Sciences
BOCCACCINI, G., Near Eastern Studies
BOLAND, J., Linguistics
BOLAND, J., Psychology
BONK, M., Mathematics
BONNER, M., Near Eastern Studies
BORGERS, T., Economics
BOUND, J., Economics
BRANDWEIN, P., Political Science
BRATER, E., English Language and Literature
BREGMAN, J., Astronomy
BRICK, H., History
BRIGHT, C., History
BROOKS III, C., Biophysics
BROOKS III, C., Chemistry
BROWN, C., Economics
BRUSATI, C., History of Art
BRUSATI, C., Women's Studies
BURNS JR, D., Mathematics
BURNS, N., Political Science
BUSHMAN, B., Communication Studies
CAIN, A., Psychology
CALVET, N., Astronomy
CAMERON, H., Classical Studies
CAMPBELL, M., Physics
CANARY, R., Mathematics
CANNING, K., History
CARON, D., Romance Languages and Literature
CASA, F., Romance Languages and Literature
CASTON, V., Philosophy
CHANG, C., History
CHEN, Z., Chemistry
CHUPP, T., Physics
CLARKE, R., Physics
CLARK, S., Molecular Cellular and Developmental Biology
COHEN, C., UG: Residential College
COLE, J., History
COLEMAN, M., Chemistry
COLLINS, D., Classical Studies
CONLON, J., Mathematics
COPPOLA, B., Chemistry
CORCORAN, M., Political Science
COUCOUVANIS, D., Chemistry
COURANT, P., Economics
CROCKER, J., Psychology
CURLEY, E., Philosophy
DAVIES, P., English Language and Literature
DEARDORFF, A., Economics
DEBACKER, S., Mathematics
DELBANCO, N., English Language and Literature
DELORIA, P., American Culture
DELORIA, P., History
DENVER, R., Molecular Cellular and Developmental Biology
DERKSEN, H., Mathematics
DESHPANDE, M., Asian Languages and Cultures
DESHPANDE, M., Linguistics
DILLARD, A., CAAS
DISCH, L., Political Science
DISCH, L., Women's Studies
DOERING, C., Mathematics
DOLGACHEV, I., Mathematics
DOMINGUEZ, K., Economics
DOUGLAS, S., Communication Studies
DOWD, G., American Culture
DOWD, G., History
DUAN, C., Molecular Cellular and Developmental Biology
DUANMU, S., Linguistics
DUNLAP, P., Ecology and Evolutionary Biology
DUREN, P., Mathematics
DWORKIN, S., Linguistics
DWORKIN, S., Romance Languages and Literature
ECCLES, J., Psychology
ELEY, G., History
ELLIS, N., Psychology
ELLISON, J., American Culture
ELLSWORTH, P., Psychology
ENDELMAN, T., History
EPSTEIN, S., Linguistics
ESTABROOK, G., Ecology and Evolutionary Biology
EVRARD, A., Physics
EWING, R., Geological Sciences
FALLER, L., English Language and Literature
FEATHERMAN, D., Sociology
FEELEY-HARNIK, G., Anthropology
FIERKE, C., Chemistry
FINE JR, J., History
FINK, W., Ecology and Evolutionary Biology
FISHER, D., Geological Sciences
FLANNERY, K., Anthropology
FLORIDA, N., Asian Languages and Cultures
FOMIN, S., Mathematics
FORNAESS, J., Mathematics
FRANCIS, A., Chemistry
FRANZESE JR, R., Political Science
FREEDMAN, J., American Culture
FREEDMAN, J., English Language and Literature
FREESE, K., Physics
FRICKE, T., Anthropology
FRIER, B., Classical Studies
FULTON, W., Mathematics
GAGOS, T., Classical Studies
GAINES, K., CAAS
GAINES, K., History
GARBRAH, K., Classical Studies
GARCIA SANTO-TOMAS, E., Romance Languages and Literature
GAZDA, E., History of Art
GELMAN, S., Psychology
GERDES, D., Physics
GERE, A., English Language and Literature
GIBBARD, A., Philosophy
GIDLEY, D., Physics
GINGERICH, P., Geological Sciences
GITELMAN, Z., Political Science
GLICK, G., Chemistry
GOLDBERG, D., Ecology and Evolutionary Biology
GOLDENBERG, E., Political Science
GOLDSTEIN, L., English Language and Literature
GONZALEZ, R., Psychology
GOODISON, L., CAAS
GOODISON, L., English Language and Literature
GOODMAN, D., History
GOODMAN, D., Women's Studies
GOODSON III, T., Chemistry
GRAHAM-BERMANN, S., Psychology
GREGERSON, L., English Language and Literature
GRIESS JR, R., Mathematics
GROVES, R., Sociology
GUNNING, S., American Culture
GUNNING, S., CAAS
GUNNING, S., English Language and Literature
GUTMANN, M., History
HALL, R., Political Science
HALPERIN, D., English Language and Literature

HANCOCK, D., History
HANLON, P., Mathematics
HANNOOSH, M., Romance Languages and Literature
HARTMANN, L., Astronomy
HEATH, J., Linguistics
HERBERT, S., Classical Studies
HERRERO-OLAIZOLA, A., Romance Languages and Literature.
HERRMANN, A., English Language and Literature
HERRMANN, A., Women's Studies
HERWITZ, D., Comparative Literature
HERWITZ, D., History of Art
HERWITZ, D., Philosophy
HINES JR, J., Economics
HOCHSTER, M., Mathematics
HOLLAND, J., Psychology
HOUSE, J., Sociology
HOWARD, J., American Culture
HOWARD, J., English Language and Literature
HSING, T., Statistics
HUESMANN, L., Communication Studies
HUME, R., Molecular Cellular and Developmental Biology
HUNTER, M., Ecology & Evolutionary Biology
HUTCHINGS, V., Political Science
INGLEHART, R., Political Science
IRVINE, J., Anthropology
ITO, K., Asian Languages and Cultures
JACKSON, J., Psychology
JACKSON, J., Political Science
JACKSON, S., Near Eastern Studies
JACKSON, T., Mathematics
JACOBSON, D., Philosophy
JANKO, R., Classical Studies
JI, L., Mathematics
JONIDES, J., Psychology
JONSSON, M., Mathematics
JORDAN, A., English Language and Literature.
JOYCE, J., Philosophy
JUSTER, S., History
KANE, G., Physics
KAPLAN, S., Psychology
KARLSEN, C., History
KARNI, S., Mathematics
KEANE Jr, E., Anthropology
KEATING, D., Psychology
KEENER, R., Statistics
KELLER-COHEN, D., Linguistics
KELLEY, M., American Culture
KELLEY, M., History
KENNEDY, R., Chemistry
KESLER, S., Geological Sciences
KILIAN, L., Economics
KIMBALL, M., Economics
KIMELDORF, H., Sociology
KINDER, D., Political Science
KITAYAMA, S., Psychology
KIVELSON, V., History
KLING II, G., Ecology and Evolutionary Biology
KLIONSKY, D., Molecular Cellular and Developmental Biology
KNYSH, A., Near Eastern Studies
KOLLMAN, K., Political Science
KONDRASHOV, A., Ecology and Evolutionary Biology
KOPELMAN, R., Chemistry
KOREEDA, M., Chemistry
KOTTAK, C., Anthropology
KRASNY, R., Mathematics
KRISCH, J., Physics
KRIZ, I., Mathematics
KUWADA, J., Molecular Cellular and Developmental Biology
LAGARIAS, J., Mathematics
LAITNER, J., Economics
LAMBROPOULOS, V., Classical Studies
LAMBROPOULOS, V., Comparative Literature
LAM, D., Economics
LANGE, R., Geological Sciences
LARSON, K., English Language and Literature
LAZARSFELD, R., Mathematics
LEE, F., Psychology
LEGASSICK, T., Near Eastern Studies
LEHMAN, J., Ecology and Evolutionary Biology
LEVINE, D., Political Science
LEVINSON, M., English Language and Literature.
LEWIS, R., Psychology
LIEBERMAN, V., History
LINDNER, R., History
LIN, S., Asian Languages and Cultures
LOEB, L., Philosophy
LOHMANN, K., Geological Sciences
LOPEZ Jr, D., Asian Languages and Cultures
LORD, C., Psychology
LORENZON, W., Physics
LOVE, T., Psychology
LUBMAN, D., Chemistry
LUMA, J., Psychology
LUPIA, A., Political Science
MACDONALD, M., History
MADDOCK, J., Molecular Cellular and Developmental Biology
MANNHEIM, B., Anthropology
MARCUS, J., Anthropology
MAREN, S., Psychology
MARKOVITS, A., Germanic Languages and Literature.
MARKOVITS, A., Political Science
MARKUS, G., Political Science
MARSH, E., Chemistry
MASUZAWA, T., Comparative Literature
MASUZAWA, T., History
MATEO, M., Astronomy
MATZGER, A., Chemistry
MCCRACKEN, P., Romance Languages and Literature.
MCCRACKEN, P., Women's Studies
MCDONALD, T., History
MCKAY, T., Physics
MEBANE Jr, W., Political Science
MEBANE Jr, W., Statistics
MEGGINSON, R., Mathematics
MERLIN, R., Physics
MEYER, D., Psychology
MEYERHOFF, M., Chemistry
MICHAILIDIS, G., Statistics
MICHALOWSKI, P., Near Eastern Studies
MILLER, P., Mathematics
MITANI, J., Anthropology
MIZRUCHI, M., Sociology
MONTGOMERY, H., Mathematics
MONTGOMERY, J., Chemistry
MOORE, D., History
MORANTZ-SANCHEZ, R., History
MORRIS, M., Chemistry
MORRISON, F., Psychology
MORROW, J., Political Science
MOSS, T., English Language and Literature
MRAZEK, R., History
MUKASA, S., Geological Sciences
MURPHY, S., Statistics
MUSTATA, M., Mathematics
MYERS, P., Ecology and Evolutionary Biology
NADELHOFFER, K., Ecology and Evolutionary Biology
NAGATA, D., Psychology
NAIR, V., Statistics
NEAL, H., Physics
NESSE, R., Psychology
NEUMAN, W., Communication Studies
NEWMAN, M., Physics
NISBETT, R., Psychology
NORICH, A., English Language and Literature
NORNES, M., Asian Languages and Cultures
NORNES, M., Screen Arts and Cultures
NOVAK, W., History
NUSSBAUM, R., Ecology and Evolutionary Bio
OCONNOR, B., Ecology and Evolutionary Biology
O'FOIGHIL, D., Ecology and Evolutionary Biology
OLSON, S., Psychology
ORR, B., Physics
O'SHEA, J., Anthropology
OWEN, R., Geological Sciences
OWUSU, M., Anthropology
OYSERMAN, D., Psychology
PACHELLA, R., Psychology
PAGE, S., Political Science
PAIGE, J., Sociology
PASCUAL, M., Ecology and Evolutionary Biology
PAULSON, W., Romance Languages and Literature
PECORARO, V., Chemistry
PEDRAZA, S., Sociology
PENNER-HAHN, J., Biophysics
PENNER-HAHN, J., Chemistry
PERLMUTTER, M., Psychology
PERNICK, M., History
PETERSON, C., Psychology
PICHERSKY, E., Molecular Cellular and Developmental Biology
PITCHER, M., CAAS
POTTER, D., Classical Studies
POTTS, A., History of Art
POWERS, M., History of Art
PRASAD, G., Mathematics
PRICE, R., Psychology
QIAN, J., Physics
RABKIN, E., English Language and Literature
RAILTON, P., Philosophy
RAITHEL, G., Physics
RAMAMOORTHY, A., Biophysics
RAMAMOORTHY, A., Chemistry
RAMIREZ-CHRISTENSEN, E., Asian Languages and Cultures
RAMMUNY, R., Near Eastern Studies
RAUCH, J., Mathematics
RAYMOND, P., Molecular Cellular and Developmental Biology
REUTER-LORENZ, P., Psychology
RHODE, P., Economics
RICHSTONE, D., Astronomy
RILES, J., Physics
ROBERTSON, J., Anthropology
ROBINSON, T., Psychology
ROHANI, P., Ecology and Evolutionary Biology
ROHANI, P., Study of Complex Systems
RONEN, O., Slavic Languages and Literature
ROOT, M., History of Art
ROSENBERG, W., History
ROTHMAN, E., Statistics
RUAN, Y., Mathematics
RUETSCHE, L., Philosophy
RUFF, L., Geological Sciences
SALANT, S., Economics
SAMEROFF, A., Psychology
SANDELANDS, L., Psychology
SANDER, L., Physics
SARTER, M., Psychology
SAVIT, R., Physics
SAXONHOUSE, A., Political Science
SCANNELL, G., Communication Studies
SCHIEFELBEIN JR, J., Molecular Cellular and Developmental Biology
SCHOENFELDT, M., English Language and Literature
SCHULENBERG, J., Psychology
SCHWARZ, N., Psychology
SCODEL, R., Classical Studies
SCOTT, G., Mathematics
SCOTT, R., History
SEARS, E., History of Art
SEIFERT, C., Psychology
SELLERS, R., Psychology
SENSION, R., Chemistry
SHAMMAS, A., Comparative Literature

SHAMMAS, A., Near Eastern Studies
SHAPIRO, M., Economics
SHIPAN, C., Political Science
SIEBERS, T., English Language and Literature
SIEGFRIED, S., History of Art
SIEGFRIED, S., Women's Studies
SILVERMAN, R., CAAS
SILVERMAN, R., History of Art
SIMON, C., Mathematics
SINOPOLI, C., Anthropology
SKLAR, L., Philosophy
SLEMROD, J., Economics
SMEREKA, P., Mathematics
SMITH, J., Psychology
SMITH, J., Economics
SMITH, K., Mathematics
SMITH, L., Economics
SMITH, S., English Language and Literature
SMITH, S., Women's Studies
SMOCK, P., Sociology
SMOLLER, J., Mathematics
SMUTS, B., Psychology
SOMERS, M., Sociology
SPATZIER, R., Mathematics
SPETH, J., Anthropology
STAFFORD, F., Economics
STAM, A., Political Science
STEIN, H., CAAS
STEINMETZ, G., Germanic Languages and Literature.
STEINMETZ, G., Sociology
STEMBRIDGE, J., Mathematics
STENSONES, B., Mathematics
STEWART, A., Psychology
STEWART, A., Women's Studies
SULLIVAN, T., Sociology
SUNY, R., History
SVEJNAR, J., Economics
TANG, X., Asian Languages and Cultures
TANG, X., Comparative Literature
TARDIF, T., Psychology
TARLE, G., Physics
TERRENATO, N., Classical Studies
TESAR, L., Economics
TESSLER, M., Political Science
THOMASON, R., Linguistics
THOMASON, R., Philosophy
THOMASON, S., Linguistics
THORNTON, A., Sociology
THORNTON III, J., History
THUN, R., Physics
TOMAN, J., Slavic Languages and Literature
TONOMURA, H., History
TRAUB, V., English Language and Literature
TRAUB, V., Women's Studies
TRAUGOTT, M., Communication Studies
TRAUTMANN, T., History
TSEBELIS, G., Political Science
TUCKER, P., Ecology and Evolutionary Biology
UHER, C., Physics
URIBE-AHUMADA, A., Mathematics
VAN DAM, R., History
VANDERMEER, J., Ecology and Evolutionary Biology
VAN DER PLUIJM, B., Geological Sciences
VAN DER VOO, R., Geological Sciences
VAN KEKEN, P., Geological Sciences
VEDEJS, E., Chemistry
VERSHYNIN, R., Mathematics
VICINUS, M., English Language and Literature
VINOVSKIS, M., History
VOLLING, B., Psychology
VON ESCHEN, P., American Culture
VON ESCHEN, P., History
WALD, A., English Language and Literature
WALTER, L., Geological Sciences
WALTER, N., Chemistry
WALTON JR, H., Political Science
WALTON, K., Philosophy
WANG, N., Statistics
WASSERMAN, A., Mathematics
WEBB, P., Ecology and Evolutionary Biology
WEISSKOPF, T., Economics
WELLMAN, H., Psychology
WELLS, J., Physics
WERNER, E., Ecology and Evolutionary Biology
WHALLON JR, R., Anthropology
WHATLEY, W., Economics
WILLIAMS, M., Anthropology
WILLIAMS, R., English Language and Literature
WILLIS, R., Economics
WILSON, M., Ecology and Evolutionary Biology
WINTER, D., Psychology
WINTER, D., Mathematics
WOLPOFF, M., Anthropology
WRIGHT, H., Anthropology
WU, S., Mathematics
XIE, Y., Sociology
YAEGER, P., English Language and Literature
YAEGER, P., Women's Studies
YATES, J., Psychology
YBARRA, O., Psychology
YOCUM, C., Molecular Cellular and Developmental Biology
YOFFEE, N., Anthropology
YOFFEE, N., Near Eastern Studies
YOUNG, V., Mathematics
ZHANG, J., Ecology and Evolutionary Biology
ZHANG, J., Psychology
ZHANG, Y., Geological Sciences
ZHOU, B., Physics
ZUCKER, R., Psychology

College of Pharmacy (tel. (734) 764-7312; fax (734) 763-2022; internet www.umich.edu/~pharmacy):

AMIDON, G. E.
AMIDON, G. L.
ASCIONE, F.
BAGOZZI, R.
BERARDI, R.
CRIPPEN, G.
JOHNSON, C.
LARSEN, S.
LEE, K.
MOSBERG, H.
MUELLER, B.
SCHWENDEMAN, S.
SHERMAN, D.
SHIMP, L.
SHOWALTER, H.
SMITH, D.
WELAGE, L.
WOODARD, R.
YANG, V.

Law School (tel. (734) 764-0514; fax (734) 763-9375; internet www.law.umich.edu):

ALVAREZ, A.
AVI-YONAH, R.
BAGENSTOS, S.
BARR, M.
BENY, L.
CAMINKER, E.
CLARK, S.
COOPER, E.
CRANE, D.
CRAWFORD, S.
CROLEY, S.
DUQUETTE, D.
EISENBERG, R.
ELLSWORTH, P.
EVANS, A.
FRIEDMAN, R.
FRIER, B.
FROST, P.
GROSS, S.
HALBERSTAM, D.
HATHAWAY, J.
HERZOG, D.
HINES JR, J.
HORWITZ, J.
KAHN, D.
KATZ, E.
KHANNA, V.
KRIER, J.
LAYCOCK, D.
LITMAN, J.
LOGUE, K.
MACKINNON, C.
MCCORMACK, B.
MENDELSON, N.
MILLER, W.
MORAN, D.
NOVAK, W.
PARSON, E.
PAYTON, S.
POTTOW, J.
PRIMUS, R.
PRITCHARD, A.
RADIN, M.
RATNER, S.
REGAN, D.
REIMANN, M.
REINGOLD, P.
RINE, N.
SANTACROCE, D.
SCARNECCHIA, S.
SCHLANGER, M.
SCHNEIDER, C.
SCHROTH, A.
SCOTT, R.
WAGGONER, L.
WEST, M.
WHITE, J.
WHITMAN, C.

Ross School of Business (tel. (734) 763-5796; fax (734) 763-7804; internet www.bus.umich.edu):

ADRIAENS, P.
AHUJA, G.
ANDERSON, E.
ASHFORD, S.
BAGOZZI, R.
BAKER, W.
BATRA, R.
BROCKBANK, J.
BUCHMUELLER, T.
CAMERON, K.
CAPOZZA, D.
DAVIS, G.
DEGRAFF, J.
DOLAN, R.
DUENYAS, I.
DUTTON, J.
FEINBERG, F.
FORNELL, C.
GLADWIN, T.
GORDON, M.
HINES JR, J.
HOPP, W.
IMHOFF JR, E.
INDJEJIKIAN, R.
JACKSON, W.
KAUL, G.
KENNEDY, R.
KIM, E.
KINNEAR, T.
KRISHNA, A.
KRISHNAN, M.
LAFONTAINE, F.
LANEN, W.
LENK, P.
LI, H.
LIM, L.
LOVEJOY, W.
LUNDHOLM, R.
LYON, T.
MANCHANDA, P.
MASTEN, S.
MUIR, D.
NARAYANAN, M.
OSWALD, L.
PRAHALAD, C.
QUINN, R.

RAMASWAMY, V.
SANDELANDS, L.
SCHIPANI, C.
SCHRIBER, T.
SEVERANCE, D.
SEYHUN, H.
SIEDEL III, G.
SLEMROD, J.
SPREITZER, G.
SUSLOW, V.
SUTCLIFFE, K.
SVEJNAR, J.
TALBOT, F.
TICHY, N.
WALSH, J.
WEICK, K.
WEISS, J.
WESTPHAL, J.
ZHANG, L.
ZIMMERMAN, M.

School of Art and Design (2000 Bonisteel Blvd, Ann Arbor, MI 48109-2069; tel. (734) 764-0397; fax (734) 936-0463; internet www.art-design.umich.edu):

COGSWELL JR, J.
HERWITZ, D.
INUZUKA, S.
JACKSON, W.
JACOBSEN, C.
LEONARD, J.
MARINARO, L.
MOSS, T.
NUNOO-QUARCOO, F.
OVERMYER JR, R.
PORTER, M.
RODEMER, C.
ROGERS, B.
SMITH, S.
WEST, E.

School of Dentistry (tel. (734) 763-6933; internet www.dent.umich.edu):

BAGRAMIAN, R.
BAYNE, S.
BRADLEY, R.
BROOKS, S.
CLARKSON, B.
EBER, R.
FASBINDER, D.
FEINBERG, S.
FRANCESCHI, R.
GIANNOBILE, W.
HELMAN, J.
HEYS, D.
HOLLAND, G.
HU, J.
JOHNSON, L.
KAPILA, S.
KOHN, D.
KREBSBACH, P.
LANTZ, M.
LOPATIN, D.
MA, P.
MCCAULEY, L.
MCDONALD, N.
MCNAMARA JR, J.
MISTRETTA, C.
NOR, J.
O'BRIEN, W.
PETERS, M.
POLVERINI, P.
RAZZOOG, M.
RICHARDS, P.
SIMMER, J.
STEFANAC, S.
TAICHMAN, R.
TAYLOR, G.
WANG, H.
WOOLFOLK, M.
YAMAN, P.

School of Education (610 E University Ave, Ann Arbor, MI 48109-1259; tel. (734) 764-7563; internet www.soe.umich.edu):

BALL, D.
BASS, H.
BATES, P.
BLUMENFELD, P.
BOWMAN, P.
BURKHARDT, J.
CARLISLE, J.
COHEN, D.
COOK, C.
CRAIG, H.
DESJARDINS, S.
GERE, A.
JACOB, B.
KING, P.
KRAJCIK, J.
LAMPERT, M.
LARSEN-FREEMAN, D.
LEE, V.
MCCALL, B.
MILLER, K.
MIREL, J.
MOJE, E.
MOSS, P.
NEUMAN, S.
PALINCSAR, A.
PETERS, C.
REX, L.
ROWAN, B.
SCHLEPPEGRELL, M.
SELLERS, R.
SILVER, E.
SONGER, N.
ST JOHN, E.
STONE III, C.
WIXSON, K.

School of Kinesiology (tel. (734) 647-9856; fax (734) 647-2808; internet www.kines.umich.edu):

BORER, K.
CARTEE, G.
CORNWELL, T.
EDINGTON, D.
FORT, R.
KATCH, V.
ROSENTRAUB, M.
ULRICH, B.
ULRICH, D.
ZERNICKE, R.

School of Information (1085 S University Ave, 304 West Hall, Ann Arbor, MI 48109-1107; tel. (734) 964-9376; fax (734) 764-2475; e-mail info@umich.edu; internet www.si.umich.edu):

ACKERMAN, M.
ATKINS III, D.
BLOUIN JR, F.
CHEN, Y.
COHEN, M.
CRAWFORD, S.
DURRANCE, J.
FINHOLT, T.
KING, J.
MARKEY, K.
MASON, J.
POLLACK, M.
RADEV, D.
RESNICK, P.
VAN HOUWELING, D.

School of Music, Theatre and Dance (E. V. Moore Bldg, 1100 Baits Dr., Ann Arbor, MI 48109-2085; tel. (734) 764-0584; internet www.music.umich.edu):

AARON, R.
BLACKSTONE, J.
BORDERS, J.
CULVER, R.
DAUGHERTY, M.
DEYOUNG JR, G.
DICKERSON, G.
ELLIOTT, A.
EVERETT, W.
FOGEL, J.
FREDRICKSEN, E.
FULCHER, J.
GANNETT, D.
GENNE, B.
GORDON, C.
GREENE, A.
GUCK, M.
HAITHCOCK, M.
JENNINGS, A.
KAENZIG, F.
KANE, A.
KATZ, M.
KENDALL, C.
KERR, P.
KIBBIE, J.
KIESLER, K.
KING, N.
KORSYN, K.
LAM, J.
MASON, M.
MCCARTHY, M.
MEAD, A.
MONTS, L.
NAGEL, L.
NEVILLE-ANDREWS, J.
PARMENTIER, E.
POGGI, G.
RUSH, S.
RUSH, S.
SARATH, E.
SCHOENFIELD, P.
SCHOTTEN, Y.
SHENG, B.
SHIPPS, S.
SIMONI, M.
SINTA, D.
SKELTON, J.
SPARLING, P.
STEIN, L.
UDOW, M.
VERRETT, S.
WEST, S.
WILEY, R.
WOODS, L.

School of Natural Resources and Environment (Dana Bldg, 440 Church St, Ann Arbor, MI 48109-1041; tel. (734) 764-6453; fax (734) 936-2195; internet www.snre.umich.edu):

AGRAWAL, A.
ALLAN, J.
BIERBAUM, R.
BROWN, D.
BRYANT JR, B.
BULKLEY, J.
BURTON, G.
DIANA, J.
GLADWIN, T.
GRESE, R.
HOFFMAN, A.
HUNTER, M.
KAPLAN, R.
KEOLEIAN, G.
LOW, B.
LYON, T.
MOHAI, P.
MOORE, M.
NASSAUER, J.
PARSON, E.
PERFECTO, I.
SCAVIA, D.
WEBB, P.
WILEY, M.
YAFFEE, S.
ZAK, D.

School of Nursing (Room 1160 400, North Ingalls, Ann Arbor, MI 48109-5482; tel. (734) 764-7185; fax (734) 936-3644; e-mail sn-osams@umich.edu; internet www.nursing.umich.edu):

ALGASE, D.
BOYD, C.
KALISCH, B.
KALISCH, P.
KETEFIAN, S.
LARSON, J.
LOVELAND-CHERRY, C.
NORTHOUSE, L.
POHL, J.
POTEMPA, K.

PRESSLER, S.
REDMAN, R.
SAMPSELLE, C.
SCISNEY-MATLOCK, M.
STEIN, K.
TITLER, M.
VILLARRUEL, A.
WILLIAMS, R.

School of Public Health (1415 Washington Heights, 1700 SPH I, Ann Arbor, MI 48109-2029; tel. (734) 763-5454; fax (734) 763-5455; e-mail sph.web@umich.edu; internet www.sph.umich.edu):

ABECASIS, G.
ALEXANDER, J.
BATTERMAN, S.
BOEHNKE, M.
BUCHMUELLER, T.
CHATTERS, L.
CLARK, N.
CONNELL, C.
DIEZ ROUX, A.
FOXMAN, B.
FRANZBLAU, A.
FRIES, B.
GALEA, S.
GERONIMUS, A.
GOOLD, S.
GRAZIER, K.
GRIFFITH, J.
HARLOW, S.
HARRIS, C.
HIRTH, R.
HU, H.
ISRAEL, B.
JACOBSON, P.
JANZ, N.
KALBFLEISCH, J.
KARDIA, S.
KAZANJIAN, P.
KEELER, G.
KOOPMAN, J.
KRAUSE, N.
LANTZ, P.
LEPKOWSKI, J.
LIANG, J.
LITTLE, R.
LOCH-CARUSO, R.
LONGWORTH, Z.
MCLAUGHLIN, C.
MEADOWS, P.
MONTO, A.
MORGENSTERN, H.
NEIGHBORS, H.
NORTON, E.
NRIAGU, J.
PETERSON, K.
PEYSER, P.
PHILBERT, M.
RAGHUNATHAN, T.
RESNICOW, K.
RICHARDSON, R.
ROBINS, T.
SHOPE, J.
SMITH, D.
SONG, P.
SOWERS, M.
STRECHER, V.
TAYLOR, J.
TSODIKOV, A.
VILLARRUEL, A.
WARNER, K.
WHEELER, J.
WILSON, M.
ZELLERS, E.
ZIMMERMAN, M.

School of Social Work (1080 S University Ave, Ann Arbor, MI 48109-1106; tel. (734) 764-3309; fax (734) 936-1961; internet www.ssw.umich.edu):

BURGIO, L.
CHECKOWAY, B.
DANZIGER, S.
DELVA, J.
DUNKLE, R.
FALLER, K.
GANT, L.
GOLDMAN, K.
GUTIERREZ, L.
INGERSOLL-DAYTON, B.
LEIN, L.
OYSERMAN, D.
POWELL, T.
ROOT, L.
SAUNDERS, D.
SIEFERT, K.
TAYLOR, R.
TOLMAN, R.
TROPMAN, J.
TUCKER, D.

BRANCH CAMPUSES

University of Michigan–Dearborn

4901 Evergreen Rd, Dearborn, MI 48128-1491
Telephone: (313) 593-5000
Fax: (313) 593-5452
Internet: www.umd.umich.edu
Founded 1959
Academic year: September to August
Chancellor: DANIEL LITTLE
Provost and Vice-Chancellor for Academic Affairs: SUSAN W. MARTIN
Vice-Chancellor for Business Affairs: ROBERT G. BEHRENS
Vice-Chancellor for Enrollment Management and Student Life: DONNA L. MCKINLEY
Vice-Chancellor for Govt Relations: EDWARD J. BAGALE
Vice-Chancellor for Institutional Advancement: THOMAS A. BAIRD
Number of students: 8,215

DEANS

Arts, Sciences and Letters: KATHRYN ANDERSON-LEVITT
Education: PAUL ZIONTS
Engineering: SUBRATA SENGUPTA
Management: KIM SCHATZEL

University of Michigan–Flint

302 E Kearsley Flint, MI 48502-1950
Telephone: (313) 762-3000
Fax: (313) 762-3687
E-mail: admissions@umflint.edu
Internet: www.flint.umich.edu
Founded 1956
61 Bachelors programmes, 7 Masters programmes
State control
Academic year: July to June
Chancellor: RUTH PERSON
Provost and Vice-Chancellor for Academic Affairs: JACK KAY
Vice-Chancellor for Admin.: DAVID BARTHELMES
Vice-Chancellor for Institutional Advancement: Dr KRISTEN SKIVINGTON
Vice-Chancellor for Student Services and Enrollment Management: MARY-JO SEKELSKY
Registrar: KAREN ARNOULD
Librarian: BOB HOUBECK
Library of 865,795 vols
Number of teachers: 372 full-time
Number of students: 6,188

DEANS AND DIRECTORS

College of Arts and Sciences: D. J. TRELA
Graduate Programs: DEAN VAHID
School of Education and Human Services: SUSANNE CHANDLER
School of Health Professions and Studies: AUSTIN AGHO
School of Management: Dr JOHN A. HELMUTH

WALSH COLLEGE OF ACCOUNTANCY AND BUSINESS ADMINISTRATION

POB 7006, 3838 Livernois Rd, Troy, MI 48007-7006
Telephone: (248) 689-8282
Fax: (248) 689-0938
E-mail: admissions@walshcollege.edu
Internet: www.walshcollege.edu
Founded 1922 as Walsh Institute of Accountancy; present name 1968
Private control
Academic year: September to September
Pres. and CEO: STEPHANIE W. BERGERON
Exec. Vice-Pres. and Chief Academic Officer: Dr ROBERT L. MINTER
Vice-Pres. for Finance: HELEN C. KIEBA-TOLKSDORF
Vice-Pres. for Human Resources and Admin.: ELIZABETH A. BARNES
Registrar: KAREN HILLEBRAND
Library Dir: J. CAMPBELL
Library of 26,000 vols
Number of students: 3,147 (1,122 undergraduate, 2,025 graduate).

BRANCH CAMPUSES

Novi Campus: 41500 Gardenbrook Rd, Novi, MI 48375-1313; tel. (248) 349-5454; fax (248) 349-7449.

University Center at Macomb Community College: 44575 Garfield Rd, Clinton Township, MI 48038-1139; tel. (586) 723-1500; fax (586) 723-1501.

St Clair County Community College: 323 Erie St, Port Huron, MI 48061-5015; tel. (810) 984-3881.

Wayne County Community College District: 19305 Vernier Rd, Harper Woods, MI 48225; tel. (313) 886-2425.

WAYNE STATE UNIVERSITY

Detroit, MI 48202
Telephone: (313) 577-5743
Fax: (313) 577-2198
E-mail: emoen@oia.wayne.edu
Internet: www.wayne.edu
Founded as univ. 1933; oldest antecedent college 1868
State control
Academic year: August to May
Pres.: IRVIN D. REID
Vice-Pres., Treas. and Chief Financial Officer: JOHN L. DAVIS
Provost and Vice-Pres. for Academic Affairs: NANCY BARRETT
Exec. Vice-Pres. and Chief of Staff: ANDREA DICKSON
Vice-Pres. and Gen. Counsel: LOUIS LESSEM
Vice-Pres. for Govt Affairs: HARVEY HOLLINS, III
Vice-Pres. for Research: GLORIA HEPPNER
Dean of Univ. Libraries: SANDRA G. YEE
Number of teachers: 2,636
Number of students: 33,091

DEANS

College of Education: PAULA C. WOOD
College of Engineering: RALPH H. KUMMLER
College of Fine, Performing and Communication Arts: SHARON L. VASQUEZ
College of Liberal Arts and Sciences: ROBERT L. THOMAS
College of Nursing: BARBARA K. REDMAN
College of Pharmacy and Health Sciences: BEVERLY J. SCHMOLL
Graduate School: HILARY RATNER
Law School: FRANK H. WU
School of Business Administration: RICHARD GABRYS
School of Medicine: ROBERT M. MENTZER
School of Social Work: PHYLLIS I. VROOM

PROFESSORS

College of Education

Admin. and Organizational Studies:

BRANDENBURG, D.
DEMONT, R.
GIPSON, J. H.
MORRISON, G.
RICHEY, R.

Teacher Education:

BALE, J.
KAPLAN, L.
PETERSON, J. M.
RONEY, R.
SMITH, G.
WHITIN, D.

Theoretical and Behavioural Foundations:

HILLMAN, S.
MARCOTTE, D.
MARKMAN, B. S.
PIETROFESA, J.
SAWILOWSKY, S.

College of Engineering

Chemical Engineering:

GULARI, E.
HUANG, Y.
NG, K.
PUTATUDNA, S.
ROTHE, E. W.

Civil Engineering:

AKTAN, H. M.
DATTA, T. K.
FU, G.
MILLER, C.

Electrical and Computer Engineering:

AUNER, G.
ERLANDSON, R.
HASSOUN, M.
HUANG, C.
LIN, F.
SILVERSMITH, D.
SINGH, H.
SIY, P.
WANG, L.
YING, H.

Industrial and Manufacturing Engineering:

PLONKA, F.
SINGH, N.

Mechanical Engineering:

BERDICHEVSKY, V.
GIBSON, R.
IBRAHIM, R.
MAI, M.-C.
RIVIN, E.
SINGH, T.
TAN, C.-A.
TARAZA, D.
WHITMAN, A. B.
WU, S.
YANG, K.-H.

College of Fine, Performing and Communication Arts

Art and Art History:

HEGARTY, J.
JACKSON, M.
MARTIN, R.
NAWARA, J.
ROBARE, D.
ROSAS, M.
WILLIAMS, P.
ZAJAC, J.

Communication:

SEEGER, M.

Music:

MARKOU, K.

Theatre:

CALARCO, J.
KAUSHANSKY, L.
MAGIDSON, D.
PULLIN, N.
SCHRAEDER, T.
THOMAS, J.

College of Liberal Arts

Africana Studies:

BOYD, M. (H)
HUTCHFUL, E.

Anthropology:

MONTILUS, G.
SANKAR, A.

Classics, Greek and Latin:

MCNAMEE, K.

Criminal Justice:

STACK, S.
ZALMAN, M.

Economics:

BRAID, R.
LEE, L.
ROSSANA, A.
SPURR, S.

English:

BARTON, E.
BRILL, L.
BURGOYNE, R.
COLEMBA, H.
HARRIS, W.
LANDRY, D.
LELAND, C.
LINDBERG, K.
MAROTTI, A.
RAY, R.
SCRIVENER, M.
SKLAR, E.
VLASOPOLOS, A.
WASSERMAN, R.

History:

BUKOWCZYK, J.
FAUE, E.
HYDE, C.
RAUCHER, A.
SMALL, M.

Humanities:

COGAN, M.

Philosophy:

GRANGER, H.
LOMBARD, L.
MCKINSEY, T.
YANAL, R.

Political Science:

ABBOTT, P. R.
BLEDSOE, T.
DOWNING, R. G.
ELDER, C.
FINO, S.
PARRISH, C.

Romance Languages and Literatures:

DITOMMASO, A.
HIGUERO, F.
STIVALE, C.

Sociology:

ESHLEMAN, J. R.
GELFAND, D.
HANKIN, J.
SENGSTOCK, M.
WARSHAY, L.

College of Lifelong Learning

Interdisciplinary Studies Program:

ARONSON, A. R.
BAILS, J. G.
GLABERMAN, M.
KLEIN, J.
MAIER, C. L.
RASPA, R. N.
SCHINDLER, R.
WRIGHT, R. H.

College of Nursing

AROIAN, K.
HOUGH, E.
NIES, M.
OERMANN, M.
PIPER, B. A.
RICE, V.

College of Pharmacy and Health Sciences

Anaesthesia:

COOK, K. A.
CRAWFORTH, K. L.
HAGLUND, V. L.
MANGAHAS, P.
WALCZYK, M. L.
WORTH, P. A.

Clinical Laboratory Science:

ALDRIGE, G.
CASTILLO, J. B.
HARAKE, B.
WALLACE, A. M.

Mortuary Science:

BURDA-MASTROGIANIS, L.
FRADE, P.
FRITTS-WILLIAMS, M. L.
HUNTOON, R.

Occupational and Environmental Health Sciences:

BASSETT, D.
BHALLA, D.
KERFOOT, E. J.
TAFFE, B.
WARNER, P. O.

Occupational Therapy:

BROWN, K.
ESDAILE, S.
LUBORSKY, M.
LYSACK, C.
POWELL, N.

Pharmaceutical Sciences:

ABRAMSON, H.
BOLARIN, D.
COMMISSARIS, R.
CORCORAN, G. B.
FULLER, G. C.
GIBBS, R.
HIRATA, F.
LINDBLAD, W.
LOUIS-FERDINAND, R. T.
PITTS, D. K.
SVENSSON, C. K.
WORMSER, H.
WOSTER, P. M.

Pharmacy Practice:

CAPPELLETTY, D.
EDWARDS, D. J.
FAGAN, S.
JABER, L. A.
KALE-PRADHAN, P. B.
KEYS, P.
MILLER, M.
MOSER, L. R.
MUNZENBERGER, P. J.
RHONEY, D.
RYBAK, M. J.
SCHUMANN, W.
SINGH, R.
SLAUGHTER, R. L.
SMITH, G. B.
SMYTHE, M. A.
STEVENSON, J. G.
TISDALE, J. E.
VIVIAN, J. C.
WILSON, J.

Physical Therapy:

AMUNDSEN, L.
CARLSON, C.
DROVIN, J.
DUNLEAVY, K.
MCNEVIN, N.
TALLEY, S.

Physician Assistant Studies:

FRICK, J.
NORMILE, H.
SIDDIQUE, M.
TODD, K.

WORMSER, H.

Radiation Therapy Technology:

CHADWELL, D.
KEMPA, A.

College of Science

Biology:

ARKING, R.
FREEMAN, D.
GREENBERG, M.
HEBERLEIN, G.
HOUGH, R.
MIZUKAMI, H.
MOORE, W. S.
SMITH, P. D.
TAYLOR, J.

Chemistry:

BHAGWAT, A.
CHA, J.-K.
LINVELDT, R.
MCCLAIN, W.
MONTGOMERY, J.
POOLE, C.
RABAN, J. P.
ROMANO, L.
RORABCHER, D.
SCHLEGEL, H.

Computer Science:

GOEL, N.
REYNOLDS, R.

Mathematics:

BACHELIS, G. F.
BRENTON, L.
CHOW, P.-L.
COHN, W.
GLUCK, D. H.
HANDEL, D.
KHAN, S.
KHASMINSKII, R.
KLEIN, J.
KOROSTELEV, A.
LIANG, T.
MAGAARD, K.
MAKAR-LIMANOV, L.
MALCOLMSON, P.
MENALDI, J. L.
MORDUKHOVICH, B.
OKOH, F.
RHEE, C.
SCHOCHET, C. L.
SCHREIBER, B. H.
SUN, T.-C.
YIN, G.
ZHANG, Z.

Nutrition and Food Science:

JEN, C.
KLURFELD, D. M.
SHELEF, L.

Physics:

BELLWIED, R.
CHANG, J. J.
CORMIER, T.
DUNIFER, G.
KARCHIN, P.
KAUPPILA, W. E.
KEYES, P. H.
KUO, P. K.
MORGAN, C.
NAIK, R.
SAPERSTEIN, A. M.
STEIN, T. S.

Psychology:

ALEXANDER, S.
COSCINA, D.
FIRESTONE, I. J.
FITZGERALD, J.
KAPLAN, K.
KILBEY, M. M.
LABOUVIE-VIEF, G.
LEVY, S.
URBERG, K.
WEISFELD, G.

College of Urban, Labour and Metropolitan Affairs

Clarence Hillberry Prof. of Urban Affairs:

GALSTER, G.

Coleman A. Young Prof. of Urban Affairs:

YOUNG, A. H.

Geography and Urban Planning:

BOYLE, R. M.
RESSE, L.
SINCLAIR, R.

Urban and Labor Studies:

BATES, T.
BROWN, D. R.
COOKE, W.
MASON, P.
SMOCK, S. M.
WOLMAN, H.
YOUNG, H.

Law School:

BROWN, K.
BURNHAM, W.
CALKINS, S.
DANNIN, E.
FRIEDMAN, J. M.
HENNING, P.
LITMAN, J.
MCINTYRE, M. J.
MOGK, J.
SCHENK, A.

School of Business Administration

Accounting:

BILLINGS, B.
REINSTEIN, A.
SPAULDING, A.
VOLZ, W.

Finance and Business Economics:

HAMILTON, J.
SOMERS, T.
SPENCER, M.

Management:

MARTIN, J. E.
OSBORN, R. N.

Marketing:

BELTRAMINI, R.
CANNON, H.
JACKSON, G.
KELLY, J.
RIORDAN, E.
RYMER, J.
YAPRAK, A.

School of Medicine

Anaesthesiology:

BROWN, E. (H)

Anatomy:

BERNSTEIN, M.
GOODMAN, M.
GOSHGARIAN, H.
HAZLETT, L.
LASKER, G.
MAISEL, H.
MEYER, D.
MITCHELL, J. A.
MIZERES, N. J.
POURCHO, R.
RAFOLS, J.
ROHER, A.
SKOFF, R.

Audiology:

RINTELMANN, W. F. (H)

Biochemistry:

BROOKS, S.
BROWN, R. K.
EDWARDS, B.
EVANS, D.
JOHNSON, R.
LEE, C. P.
ROSEN, B.
ROWND, R.
VINOGRADOV, S.

Cardiology:

KLONER, R.
WYNNE, J.

Community Medicine:

WALLER, J.

Dermatology and Syphilology:

BIRMINGHAM, D.
HASHIMOTO, K.

Family Medicine:

DALLMAN, J.
GALLAGHER, R. E.
WERNER, P.

Immunology and Microbiology:

BERK, R.
BOROS, D. L.
BROWN, W. J.
DEGUISTI, D.
HAZLEH, L.
JEFFRIES, C.
KAPLAN, J.
KONG, Y.-C.
LEFFORD, M.
LEON, M.
LEVIN, S.
LISAK, R.
MONTGOMERY, P. C.
PALCHAUDHURI, S.
SOBEL, J.
SUNDICK, R.
SWANBORG, R. H.
WEINER, L. M.

Internal Medicine:

AL-SARRAF, M.
BAGCHI, N.
BERGSMAN, K. L.
BISHOP, C. R.
BRENNAN, M.
CLAPPER, I.
CORBETT, T.
FERNÁNDEZ-MADRID, F. B.
GRUNBERGER, G.
HEILBRUN, L.
HEPPNER, G.
KESSEL, D.
LERNER, S.
LEWIS, B. M.
LUM, L.
LYNNE-DAVIS, P.
MCDONALD, F.
MACK, R.
MAJUMDAR, A.
MARSH, J.
MIGDAL, S.
MILLER, R.
MUTCHNICK, M.
NAKEFF, A.
PRASAD, A. S.
PURI, P.
RESNICK, L.
SAMSON, M.
SANTEN, R.
SENSENBRENNER, L.
SOBEL, J.
SOWERS, J.
SPEARS, J.
TALMERS, F.
TRANCHIDA, L.
VAITKEVICIUS, V.
VALDIVIESO, M.
VALERIOTE, F.
WYNNE, J.

Neurology:

BENJAMINS, J. A.
CHUGANI, H.
DORE-DUFFY, P.
LEWITT, P.
LISAK, R.
NIGRO, M.

Neurosurgery:

DIAZ, F. G.
THOMAS, L. M.

Obstetrics and Gynaecology:

ABEL, E.
AGER, J.
BEHRMAN, S. J.
BERMAN, R.
COTTON, D.
DEPPE, G.
EVANS, M.
FREEDMAN, R.
LANCASTER, W.
MAMMEN, E.
MARIONA, F.
MILLER, O.
MOGHISSI, K.
POLAND, M.
ROMERO, R.
SACCO, A. G.
SHERMAN, A.
SOBEL, J.
SOKOL, R.
STRYKER, J.
SUBRAMANIAN, M.

Ophthalmology:

ESSNER, E.
FRANK, R. N.
JAMPEL, R. S.
PUKLIN, J.
SHICHI, H.
SHIN, D.
SPOOR, T.

Orthopaedic Surgery:

FITZGERALD, R.
MANOLI II, A.
RYAN, J.

Otolaryngology:

COHN, A. M.
DRESCHER, D.
DWORKIN, J.
JACOBS, J.
MATHOG, R. H.

Paediatrics:

BEN-YOSEPH, Y.
BRANS, Y. W.
CASH, R.
CHUGANI, H.
COHEN, S.
COLLINS, J.
DAJANI, A. S.
EPSTEIN, M.
FAROOKI, Z.
FLEISCHMANN, L.
GRUSKIN, A.
GUTAI, J.
KAPLAN, J.
KAUFFMAN, R.
LUM, L.
LUSHER, J.
NIGRO, M.
OSTREA, E.
PINSKY, W. W.
RAUMDRANATH, Y.
ROBIN, A.
SAMAIK, A.
SARNAIK, A.
SENSENBRENNER, L.
SHANKARIAN, G.
SLOVIS, T.

Pathology:

BEDROSSIAN, C.
BROWN, W.
CRISSMAN, J.
DALE, E.
EVANS, M.
GIACOMELLI, F. E.
HONN, K.
KURKINEN, M.
MAMMEN, E.
MILLER, D.
PALUTKE, M.
PERRIN, E. V.
RAZ, A.
SHEAHAN, D.
SPITZ, W. U.
THIBERT, R.
WEINER, L.
WIENER, J.
ZAK, B.

Pharmacology:

ANDERSON, G.
BANNON, M.
CHOPRA, D.
DUTTA, S.
GOLDMAN, H.
HIRATA, F.
HOLLENBERG, P. F.
KESSEL, D.
MARKS, B.
NOVAK, R.
SLOANE, B.
WAKADE, A.

Physiology:

BARRACO, R.
CHURCHILL, P. C.
DUNBAR, J. C.
FOA, P.
GALA, R.
HONG, F. T.
LAWSON, D.
MCCOY, L. E.
MAMMEN, E.
NYBOER, J.
PENNEY, D.
PHILLIS, J. W.
RAM, J.
RILLEMA, J. A.
SEEGERS, W.
WALZ, D. A. (H)

Psychiatry:

BANNON, M.
FISCHHOFF, J.
FREEDMAN, R.
GALLOWAY, M.
KAPATOS, G.
KUHN, D.
LEWITT, P.
LUBY, E.
LYCAKI, H.
POHL, R.
ROSENBAUM, A.
ROSENZWEIG, N.
SARWER-FONER, G.
SCHORER, C.
SITARAM, N.
UHDE, T.

Radiation Oncology:

HERSKOVIC, A. M.
HONN, K. V.
MARUYAMA, Y.
ORTON, C. G.
PORTER, A.

Radiology:

KLING, G.
SOULEN, R.
WOLLSCHLAEGER, G.

Surgery:

BERGUER, R.
FROMM, D.
KLEIN, M.
LEDGERWOOD, A. M.
LUCAS, C.
PHILIPPART, A.
ROSENBERG, J. C.
SILVA, Y. J.
STEPHENSON, L.
SUGAWA, C.
WALT, A. J.
WEAVER, A. W.
WILSON, R. F.

Urology:

JAFFER, D.
MONTIE, J.
PERLMUTTER, A. D.
PONTES, J.

School of Social Work:

BEVERLY, C.
BRANDALL, J.
MOXLEY, D.

University Libraries

Library and Information Science:

ALBRITTON, R. L.
BAKER, L. M.
BROWN-SYED, C. L.
EZELL, C. L.
FIELD, J. J.
HOLLEY, R.
JOHNSON, N. B.
MIKA, J.
NEAVILL, G. B.
POWELL, R.
SPITERI, L. F.

ATTACHED RESEARCH INSTITUTES

Barbara Anne Karmanos Cancer Institute: 4100 John R., Detroit, MI 48201; e-mail info@karmanos.org; internet www.karmanos.org; CEO JOHN C. RUCKDESCHEL.

Bioengineering Center: 818 West Hancock, Detroit, MI 48201; tel. (313) 577-0252; fax (313) 577-8333; e-mail king.yang@wayne.edu; internet www.bioengineeringcenter.org; attached to College of Engineering; Dir Dr KING H. YANG.

Center to Advance Palliative-Care Excellence: 247 Cohn Bldg, 5557 Cass Ave, Detroit, MI 48202; tel. (313) 577-0907; e-mail renatak@wayne.edu; internet www.capewayne.org; Dir Dr ROBERT J. ZALENSKI.

Center for Automotive Research: attached to College of Engineering; Dir Dr NAEIM HENEIN.

Center for Chicano-Boricua Studies: attached to College of Liberal Arts and Sciences; Dir Dr JORGE CHINEA.

Center for Fine Arts and Public Policy: e-mail cappwsu@wayne.edu; internet www.capp-wsu.org; Dir NICOLE YOUNG.

Center for Health Research: attached to College of Nursing; Dir JUDITH FLOYD.

Center for Molecular Medicine and Genetics: internet cmmg.biosci.wayne.edu; attached to School of Medicine; Dir LAWRENCE I. GROSSMAN.

Center for Peace and Conflict Studies: tel. (313) 577-3453; fax (313) 577-8269; e-mail ab3440@wayne.edu; attached to College of Liberal Arts and Sciences; Dir Dr FREDERIC PEARSON.

Center for the Study of Citizenship: tel. (313) 577-2593; fax (313) 577-6987; e-mail m.kruman@wayne.edu; Dir MARC W. KRUMAN.

Center for Urban Studies: tel. (313) 577-5209; e-mail ad5122@wayne.edu; internet www.cus.wayne.edu; Dir LYKE THOMPSON.

Cohn-Haddow Center for Judaic Studies: tel. (313) 577-2679; fax (313) 577-8136; e-mail aa2690@wayne.edu; internet www.judaicstudies.wayne.edu; Dir Dr DAVID WEINBERG.

C. S. Mott Center for Human Growth and Development: Dir ROBERT J. SOKOL.

Developmental Disabilities Institute: tel. (313) 577-2654; fax (313) 577-3770; internet ddi.wayne.edu; Dir Dr BARBARA LEROY.

Douglas A. Fraser Center for Workplace Issues: tel. (313) 577-2100; e-mail w.cooke@wayne.edu; internet www.frasercenter.wayne.edu; Dir WILLIAM COOKE.

Humanities Center: Dir Dr WALTER EDWARDS.

Institute of Environmental Health Science: tel. (313) 577-0100; fax (313) 577-0082; internet www.iehs.wayne.edu; Dir RAYMOND NOVAK.

Institute of Gerontology: tel. (313) 577-2297; fax (313) 875-0127; e-mail ioginfo@

wayne.edu; internet www.iog.wayne.edu; attached to Graduate School; Dir PETER LICHTENBERG.

Institute for Information Technology and Culture: tel. (313) 874-7010; fax (313) 874-5977; internet www.iitc.wayne.edu; Dir ALLEN BATTEAU.

Institute for Learning and Performance Improvement: tel. (313) 577-6674; e-mail d.brandenburg@wayne.edu; internet www.ilpi.wayne.edu; attached to College of Education; Dir DALE BRANDENBURG.

Institute for Manufacturing Research: tel. (313) 577-2970; fax (313) 577-7743; internet www.imr.wayne.edu; Dir JOHN OLIVER.

Institute for Organizational and Industrial Competitiveness: attached to School of Business Admin.; Dir LARRY L. FOBES.

Institute for Scientific Computing: attached to College of Science; Dir VIPIN CHAUDHARY.

Labor Studies Center: tel. (313) 577-2191; fax (313) 577-7726; e-mail laborschool@wayne.edu; internet www.laborstudies.wayne.edu; Dir HAL STACK.

Ligon Research Center of Vision: 4717 St Antoine, Detroit, MI 48201; tel. (313) 577-9136; e-mail ligoncenter@med.wayne.edu; internet www.kresgeeye.org/ligon; attached to Kresge Eye Institute; Dir GARY ABRAMS.

Manufacturing Information Systems Center: tel. (313) 577-7837; fax (313) 577-4880; attached to School of Business Admin.; Dir ARIK RAGOWSKY.

Merill-Palmer Institute: tel. (313) 872-1790; fax (313) 875-0947; e-mail mpsi@wayne.edu; internet www.mpsi.wayne.edu; Dir LAURA MCCLOSKEY.

WESTERN MICHIGAN UNIVERSITY

1903 W Michigan Ave, Kalamazoo, MI 49008-5200

Telephone: (269) 387-1000
E-mail: ask-wmu@wmich.edu
Internet: www.wmich.edu

Founded 1903
State control
Language of instruction: English
Academic year: July to June

Pres.: JOHN M. DUNN
Provost and Vice-Pres. for Academic Affairs: TIMOTHY J. GREENE
Sr Vice-Pres. for Advancement and Legislative Affairs: GREGORY J. ROSINE
Sr Vice Pres. For Business and Finance: LOWELL P. RINKER
Vice-Pres. for Business and Finance: LOWELL RINKER
Vice-Pres. for Devt: BUD BENDER
Vice-Pres. for Legal Affairs and Gen. Counsel: CAROL L. J. HUSTOLES
Vice-Pres. for Research: DANIEL M. LITYNSKI
Vice-Pres. for Student Affairs and Dean of Students: DIANE K. ANDERSON
Registrar: BARBARA T. MCKINNEY
Dean of Univ. Libraries: JOSEPH G. REISH

Library: 4.9m. vols, 37,826 periodical titles
Number of teachers: 1,435
Number of students: 24,576

Publications: *Accent on Alumni* (4 a year), *Analysis of Verbal Behaviour* (1 a year), *Behavior Analyst* (2 a year), *Caribe* (jtly with Western Michigan Univ. in Kalamazoo, Univ. of Northern Florida in Jacksonville and Marquette Univ. of Milwaukee, 2 a year), *Cistercian Institute Publications* (1 a year), *Comparative Drama* (4 a year), *Gatherings* (2 a year), *Journal of Comparative Religion* (online), *Journal of Sociology and Social Welfare* (4 a year), *Medieval Prosopography* (2 a year), *Medieval Review* (online), *Mid-American Journal of Business* (4 a year), *Old English Newsletter* (4 a year), *Old English Newsletter—Subsidia* (1 a year), *Proceedings of the Heraclitean Society* (1 a year), *Reading Horizons Journal* (4 a year), *Studies in Iconography* (1 a year), *Studies in Medieval Culture* (series of vols, 1 a year), *Teaching Ethics Journal: The Journal for the Society for Ethics Across the Curriculum* (1 a year), *The Hilltop Review: A Journal of Western Michigan University Graduate Research* (2 a year), *The Parkview Edition* (2 a year), *Third Coast* (2 a year), *WMU Magazine* (2 a year), *WMU Research Magazine* (2 a year), *Yearbook of Langland Studies* (1 a year)

DEANS

College of Arts and Sciences: THOMAS L. KENT
College of Aviation: DAVID M. POWELL
College of Education and Human Development: GARY L. WEGENKE
College of Engineering and Applied Sciences: ANTHONY J. VIZZINI
College of Fine Arts: MARGARET M. MERRION
College of Health and Human Services: EARLIE M. WASHINGTON
Graduate College: LEWIS PYENSON
Haworth College of Business: AJAY A. SAMANT
Lee Honors College: NICOLAS A. ANDREADIS (acting)

WESTERN THEOLOGICAL SEMINARY

101 East 13th St, Holland, MI 49423

Telephone: (616) 392-8555
Fax: (616) 392-2072
E-mail: admissions@westernsem.edu
Internet: www.westernsem.edu

Founded 1866
Private control
Academic year: September to May

Pres.: Dr TIMOTHY BROWN
Dean and Vice-Pres. of Academic Affairs: Dr LEANNE VAN DYK
Vice-Pres. for Advancement and Communications: KENNETH NEEVEL
Vice-Pres. for Finance: NORMAN DONKERSLOOT
Dir of Admissions: Dr MARK POPPEN
Registrar: PAT DYKHUIS
Librarian: PAUL M. SMITH

Library of 100,000 vols
Number of teachers: 18
Number of students: 189

MINNESOTA

AUGSBURG COLLEGE

2211 Riverside Ave, Minneapolis, MN 55454

Telephone: (612) 330-1000
Fax: (612) 330-1649
E-mail: enroll@augsburg.edu
Internet: www.augsburg.edu

Founded 1869

Pres.: PAUL C. PRIBBENOW
Registrar: WAYNE KALLERSTAD
Dir of Library: JANE ANN NELSON

Library of 180,000 vols
Number of teachers: 305 (125 full-time, 180 part-time)
Number of students: 3,785

Areas of study: accounting, American Indian studies, biology, business admin., chemistry, communication studies, computer science, economics, education, engineering, finance, health education, history, int. relations, management information systems, marketing, mathematics, medieval studies, metro-urban studies, modern languages, music, philosophy, physical education, physics, political science, psychology, religion, sociology, theatre arts, women's studies

Publication: *Augsburg College Now* (4 a year).

BETHEL UNIVERSITY

3900 Bethel Dr., St Paul, MN 55112-6999

Telephone: (651) 638-6230
Fax: (651) 638-6008
E-mail: buadmissions-cas@bethel.edu
Internet: www.bethel.edu

Founded 1871

School of the churches of the Baptist General Conference

Liberal arts coeducational Christian college, offering Baccalaureate and Masters degree, and graduate theological seminary

3 Seminaries in St Paul, San Diego, CA and Willow Grove, PA

Pres.: JAMES H. BARNES, III
Exec. Vice-Pres. for Devt: BRUCE W. ANDERSON
Sr Vice-Pres. for Communications and Marketing: SHERIE J. LINDVALL
Sr Vice-Pres. for Finance and Admin.: KATHLEEN J. NELSON
Sr Vice-Pres. for Strategic Planning and Research: JOSEPH D. LALUZERNE
Seminary Provost: LELAND V. ELIASON
Registrar: KATRINA CHAPMAN
Library Dir: BOB SUDERMAN

Library of 528,000 vols, 18,720 electronic books, 32,000 online journals, 4,000 microform serials, 26,000 audiovisual items
Number of teachers: 237 (207 at colleges and graduate school, 30 at seminary)
Number of students: 6,300

CARLETON COLLEGE

1 N College St, Northfield, MN 55057

Telephone: (507) 222-4000
Fax: (507) 222-4204
Internet: www.carleton.edu

Founded 1866
Independent
Academic year: September to June

Depts of African-American studies; American studies; Arabic; archaeology; art and art history; Asian languages and literatures; Asian studies; biochemistry; biology; chemistry; cinema and media studies; classical languages; cognitive science; computer science; cross cultural studies; economics; educational studies; English; environmental studies; European studies; French and Francophone studies; geology; German; Hebrew; history; international relations; Latin American studies; linguistics; literary and cultural studies; mathematics; medieval and renaissance studies; music; neuroscience; philosophy; physics and astronomy; political science; physical education, athletics and recreation; psychology; religion; Russian; sociology and anthropology; Spanish; theatre and dance; women's and gender studies; off-campus studies, pre-med and summer academic programmes

Pres.: STEVEN G. POSKANZER
Vice-Pres. and Treas.: FREDERICK ROGERS
Dean of the College: BEVERLY NAGEL
Dean of Students: HUDLIN WAGNER
Registrar: ROGER LASLEY
Librarian: SAM DEMAS

Library of 563,581 vols of books, 446,089 electronic books, 39,060 electronic journals, 11,886 spec. colln, 278,138 vols of govt docs, 12,490 media colln
Number of teachers: 235
Number of students: 1,980

COLLEGE OF SAINT BENEDICT

37 South College Ave, Saint Joseph, MN 56374-2099
Telephone: (320) 363-5011
Fax: (320) 363-5050
E-mail: admission@csbsju.edu
Internet: www.csbsju.edu

Chartered 1887

Catholic liberal arts college for women partnered with Saint John's Univ. for men; co-educational classes and social activities available to students on both campuses

Pres.: MARY E. LYONS
Chief of Staff: SONJA GIDLOW
Provost: RITA KNUESEL
Vice-Pres. for Finance and Admin.: SUSAN PALMER
Vice-Pres. for Institutional Advancement: MARY GELLER
Vice-Pres. for Student Devt: MARY GELLER
Dir of Libraries and Media: KATHY PARKER

Library of 535,400 vols
Number of teachers: 359 (294 full-time, 65 part-time)
Number of students: 3,928
Publications: *Diotima*, *Independent*, *Saint Benedict's Today*, *Studio I*.

COLLEGE OF ST CATHERINE

2004 Randolph Ave, St Paul, MN 55105
Telephone: (651) 690-6000
Fax: (651) 690-6024
E-mail: admission@stkate.edu
Internet: www.stkate.edu

Founded 1905

Roman Catholic liberal arts college for women

Pres.: ANDREA J. LEE
Sr Vice-Pres. for Academic and Student Affairs: COLLEEN HEGRANES (acting)
Vice-Pres. for External Relations: MARJORIE MATHISON
Vice-Pres. for Finance and Admin.: TAMMY MCGEE
Librarian: CAROL JOHNSON

Library of 252,107 vols
Number of teachers: 268
Number of students: 5,246

DEANS

Arts and Sciences: Dr ALAN SILVA
Health Professions: Dr MARGARET MCLAUGHLIN
Professional Studies: SUSAN COCHRANE

BRANCH CAMPUS

Minneapolis Campus: 601 25th Ave South, Minneapolis, MN 55454; tel. (651) 690-7700.

COLLEGE OF ST SCHOLASTICA

1200 Kenwood Ave, Duluth, MN 55811-4199
Telephone: (218) 723-6000
Fax: (218) 723-5991
E-mail: admissions@css.edu
Internet: www.css.edu

Founded 1912

Private (Roman Catholic) liberal arts college; graduate programmes in educational media, exercise physiology and education, management, nursing, occupational therapy, physical therapy, science and mathematics education; campuses at Brainerd, St Cloud, St Paul and Rochester
Academic year: September to August

Pres.: Dr LARRY GOODWIN
Vice-Pres. for Academic Affairs: BETH DOMHOLDT
Vice-Pres. for Enrollment Management: BRIAN DALTON
Vice-Pres. for Extended and Graduate Studies: COLLETTE GARRITY
Vice-Pres. for Finance: PATRICK FLATTERY
Vice-Pres. for Institutional Advancement: DEL CASE
Vice-Pres. for Student Life and Dean of Students: COLLETTE GARRITY
Registrar: GEORGE BEATTIE
Librarian: KEVIN MCGREW

Library of 127,400 vols
Number of teachers: 166 (126 full-time, 40 part-time)
Number of students: 2,200

DEANS

School of Arts and Letters: TAMMY OSTRANDER
School of Business and Technology: BOB SHERMAN
School of Education: JO OLSEN
School of Extended Studies: CATHY CARTER
School of Health Sciences: RONDELL BERKELAND
School of Nursing: MARTHA WITRAK
School of Sciences: LAWRENCE MCGAHEY

COLLEGE OF VISUAL ARTS

344 Summit Ave, St Paul, MN 55102
Telephone: (651) 224-3416
Fax: (651) 224-8854
E-mail: info@cva.edu
Internet: www.cva.edu
Private control

Pres. and Chief Academic Officer: ANN LEDY
Vice-Pres. and Chief Operations Officer: SUSAN SHORT
Dir of Admissions: JANE NORDHORN
Registrar: LOIS CANEDAY
Library Dir: KATHRYN HEUER

Library of 5,000 vols, 27,500 slides
Number of teachers: 65
Number of students: 250

CONCORDIA COLLEGE

901 South 8th St, Moorhead, MN 56562
Telephone: (218) 299-4000
Fax: (218) 299-3947
Internet: www.cord.edu

Founded 1891

Pres.: Dr PAMELA M. JOLICOEUR
Vice-Pres. for Academic Affairs: Dr MARK KREJCI
Vice-Pres. for Business Affairs: WERNER GOLLING
Vice-Pres. for Devt: LINDA BROWN
Vice-Pres. for Enrollment: OMAR CORREA
Registrar: CAROLE STALHEIM
Librarian: SHARON HOVERSON

Library of 328,349 vols
Number of teachers: 225
Number of students: 2,814

CONCORDIA UNIVERSITY, ST PAUL

275 Syndicate St N, St Paul, MN 55104-5494
Telephone: (651) 641-8230
Fax: (651) 603-6320
E-mail: admission@csp.edu
Internet: www.csp.edu

Founded 1893
Academic year: August to May
Lutheran Church—Missouri Synod

Pres.: Dr ROBERT HOLST
Exec. Vice-Pres.: Dr CHERYL CHATMAN
Vice-Pres. for Academic Affairs: LONN MALY
Vice-Pres. for Admin.: Dr ERIC LAMOTT
Vice-Pres. for Finance: MICHAEL DORNER
Vice-Pres. for Univ. Advancement: KEITH STOUTH
Librarian: Dr CHARLOTTE KNOCHE

Library of 152,000 vols
Number of teachers: 344 (83 full-time, 261 part-time)
Number of students: 2,842

DEANS

College of Arts and Sciences: Dr MARILYN REINECK
College of Business and Organizational Leadership: Dr BRUCE CORRIE
College of Education: DON HELMSTETTER
College of Vocation and Min.: Dr DAVID LUMPP

CROSSROADS COLLEGE

920 Mayowood Rd SW, Rochester, MN 55902
Telephone: (507) 288-4563
Fax: (507) 288-9046
E-mail: info@crossroadscollege.edu
Internet: www.crossroadscollege.edu

Founded 1913 as Int. Christian Bible College Asscn, present name 2002
Private control
Academic year: August to May

Areas of study: biblical and classical languages, Christian education, counselling psychology, general ministry, intercultural studies, music ministry, pastoral leadership, youth and family studies, youth studies

Pres.: MICHAEL KILGALLIN
Vice-Pres. for Academics: CLAUDIO DIVINO
Vice-Pres. for Admin. and Finance: ROGER LANGSETH
Vice-Pres. for Advancement: BRADLEY STOLDT
Vice-Pres. for Student Devt: TIM MCKINNEY
Registrar: ROBERT DAMON
Dir of Library: JIM GODSEY

Library of 37,000 vols
Number of teachers: 21
Number of students: 170

CROWN COLLEGE

8700 College View Dr., St Bonifacius, MN 55375
Telephone: (952) 446-4142
Fax: (952) 446-4149
E-mail: info@crown.edu
Internet: www.crown.edu
Private control
Academic year: August to May

Pres.: Dr RICK MANN
Exec. Vice-Pres.: MIKE SOHM
Vice-Pres. for Academic Affairs: SCOTT MOATS
Vice-Pres. for Advancement: JIM RIGHTLER
Vice-Pres. for Enrollment Services: BRAD KISSELL
Vice-Pres. for Finance and Operations: DAVID TARRANT
Vice-Pres. for Student Devt: DWIGHT A. CARLBLOM
Registrar: CHERYL FISK
Dir of Library and Media Services: DENNIS INGOLGSLAND

Library of 100,000 vols, 70,000 microform vols, 30,000 electronic vols
Number of teachers: 57
Number of students: 1,300

GUSTAVUS ADOLPHUS COLLEGE

800 West College Ave, St Peter, MN 56082
Telephone: (507) 933-8000
Fax: (507) 933-7041
Internet: www.gustavus.edu

Founded 1862
Academic year: September to June

Pres.: JAMES L. PETERSON
Provost and Vice-Pres. for Academic Affairs: Dr MARY E. MORTON
Registrar: KRISTIANNE REINHOLTZEN
Academic Deans: MARIANGELA MAGUIRE, ERIC ELIASON

Librarian: DAN MOLLNER
Library of 245,000 vols
Number of teachers: 200
Number of students: 2,500
Divs of education, fine arts, humanities, natural sciences and mathematics, social sciences.

HAMLINE UNIVERSITY

1536 Hewitt Ave, St Paul, MN 55104-1284
Telephone: (612) 523-2800
Internet: www.hamline.edu
Founded 1854
Related to the United Methodist Church
Pres.: LINDA HANSON
Vice-Pres. for Academic and Student Affairs: DAVID STERN
Vice-Pres. for Finance: DOUGLAS ANDERSON
Vice-Pres. for Univ. Relations: DANIEL LORITZ
Dean of Students: ALAN SICKBERT
Registrar for Admin.: CHRIS MILLER
Registrar for Law and Graduate Schools: LAURIE HERBRAND
Dirs of Arts Library: DIANE CLAYTON JULIE ROCHAT
Dirs of Law Library: FRANCES SINGH, RANDY SNYDER
Library of 230,000 vols
Number of teachers: 152
Number of students: 2,228

DEANS

College of Liberal Arts: FERNANDO DELGADO
Graduate School of Education: CANDACE BURNS
Graduate School of Liberal Studies: MARY ROCKCASTLE
Graduate School of Management: JULIAN SCHUSTER
School of Law: JON GARON

LUTHER SEMINARY

2481 Como Ave, St Paul, MN 55108
Telephone: (651) 641-3456
Fax: (651) 523-1609
Internet: www.luthersem.edu
Private control
Academic year: September to May
Pres.: RICHARD H. BLIESE
Exec. Dir and Vice-Pres. for Seminary Relations: KATHY HANSEN
Vice-Pres. for Admin. and Finance: DONALD LEWIS
Academic Dean: DAVID J. LOSE
Registrar: DIANE DONCITS
Dir of Library Services: DAVID STEWART
Number of teachers: 46
Number of students: 836
Offers Masters degrees in arts, divinity, sacred music, social work.

MACALESTER COLLEGE

1600 Grand Ave, St Paul, MN 55105-1899
Telephone: (612) 696-6000
Fax: (612) 696-6500
E-mail: lundin@macalester.edu
Internet: www.macalester.edu
Founded 1874
Liberal arts college
Pres.: BRIAN C. ROSENBERG
Vice-Pres. for Admin. and Finance: DAVID WHEATON
Vice-Pres. for Advancement: THOMAS P. BONNER
Vice-Pres. for Student Affairs: LAURIE B. HAMRE
Dean of Faculty and Provost: DIANE MICHELFELDER
Dean of Students: JIM HOPPE
Chief Investment Officer: CRAIG H. AASE
Registrar: JAYNE NIEMI
Library Dir: TERESA FISHEL
Library of 400,000 vols
Number of teachers: 186 (full-time)
Number of students: 1,895
Publication: *Macalester Today* (4 a year).

MARTIN LUTHER COLLEGE

1995 Luther Court, New Ulm, MN 56073-3300
Telephone: (507) 354-8221
Fax: (507) 354-8225
E-mail: mlcadmit@mlc-wels.edu
Internet: www.mlc-wels.edu
Founded 1995 following merger of Dr Martin Luther College (f. 1884) and Northwestern College (f. 1865)
Private control (Wisconsin Evangelical Lutheran Synod)
Academic year: August to May
Pres.: Rev. MARK G. ZARLING
Vice-Pres. for Academics: Dr DAVID O. WENDLER
Vice-Pres. for Admin.: Prof. STEVEN R. THIESFELDT
Vice-Pres. for Enrollment Management: Prof. PHILIP M. LEYRER
Vice-Pres. for Student Life: JEFFREY L. SCHONE
Registrar: GWEN KRAL
Number of teachers: 67
Number of students: 712

DEANS

Educational Ministry: Prof. KURT WITTMERSHAUS
Pastoral Ministry: Prof. DANIEL BALGE

MINNEAPOLIS COLLEGE OF ART AND DESIGN

2501 Stevens Ave, Minneapolis, MN 55404
Telephone: (612) 874-3700
Fax: (612) 874-3704
E-mail: admissions@mcad.edu
Internet: www.mcad.edu
Founded 1886
Academic year: September to May
Pres.: MICHAEL O'KEEFE
Dir of Admissions: BRAD NUORALA
Dir of Continuing Studies: BRENDA GRACHER
Treas.: JAMES HOSETH
Dean of Liberal Studies: MARY MCDUNN
Dean of Student Affairs: SUSAN CALMENSON
Dean of Studio Programmes: TOM DE BIASO
Library Dir: SUZANNE DEGLER
Library of 60,000 vols
Number of teachers: 65
Number of students: 600

MINNESOTA STATE COLLEGES AND UNIVERSITIES

501 World Trade Center, 30 East 7th St, St Paul, MN 55101
Telephone: (612) 296-8012
Fax: (612) 297-5550
Internet: www.mnscu.edu
Founded 1995
Academic year: August to May
Incorporates 32 colleges and univs, incl. 25 two-year colleges and 7 state univs
Chancellor: JAMES H. MCCORMICK
Sr Vice-Chancellor for Academic and Student Affairs: LINDA BAER
Vice-Chancellor for Human Resources: BILL TSCHIDA
Deputy to the Chancellor and Chief of Staff: JANICE FITZGERALD
Number of students: 225,000 (system-wide).

CONSTITUENT UNIVERSITIES

Alexandria Technical College

1601 Jefferson St, Alexandria, MN 56308
Telephone: (320) 762-0221
Fax: (320) 762-4501
Internet: www.alextech.edu
Pres.: KEVIN KOPISCHKE
Number of students: 2,145

Anoka Technical College

1355 West Highway 10, Anoka, MN 55303
Telephone: (763) 576-4700
Fax: (763) 576-4715
Internet: www.anokatech.edu
Pres.: ANNE WEYANDT
Number of students: 1,559

Anoka-Ramsey Community College

Coon Rapids Campus, 11200 Mississippi Blvd, NW, Coon Rapids, MN 55433
Telephone: (763) 433-1840
Fax: (763) 433-1841
Internet: www.anokaramsey.edu
Pres.: PATRICK JOHNS.

Bemidji State University

1500 Birchmont Dr. NE, Bemidji, MN 56601-2699
Telephone: (218) 755-2001
Fax: (218) 755-4048
E-mail: admissions@bemidjistate.edu
Internet: www.bemidjistate.edu
Founded 1919
Aligned with Northwest Technical College
Pres.: Dr JON QUISTGAARD
Dean of Library Services (vacant)
Library of 250,000 vols, 900 periodicals
Number of teachers: 220 full-time
Number of students: 4,991

DEANS

College of Arts and Letters: NANCY ERICKSON
College of Professional Studies: CAROL NIELSEN
College of Social and Natural Sciences: RANAE WOMACK

Central Lakes College

Brainerd Campus, 501 West College Dr., Brainerd, MN 56401
Telephone: (218) 855-8000
Fax: (218) 855-8057
Internet: www.clcmn.edu
Pres.: LARRY LUNDBLAD
Number of students: 2,362

Century College

3300 Century Ave, White Bear Lake, MN 55110
Telephone: (651) 779-3200
Fax: (651) 779-3417
Internet: www.century.edu
Pres.: LARRY LITECKY
Number of students: 6,133

Dakota County Technical College

1300 East 145th St, Rosemount, MN 55068-2999
Telephone: (651) 423-8200
Fax: (651) 423-8775
Internet: www.dctc.edu
Pres.: RONALD E. THOMAS
Number of students: 2,245

Fond du Lac Tribal and Community College

2101 14th St, Cloquet, MN 55720
Telephone: (218) 879-0800

Fax: (218) 879-0728
Internet: www.fdltcc.edu
Pres.: DON DAY
Number of students: 1,121

Hennepin Technical College

Brooklyn Park Campus, 9000 Brooklyn Blvd, Brooklyn Park, MN 55445-2399
Telephone: (763) 488-2500
Fax: (763) 448-2944
Internet: www.hennepintech.edu
Pres.: KATHRYN JEFFERY
Number of students: 3,642

Inver Hills Community College

2500 80th St, E, Inver Grove Heights, MN 55076
Telephone: (651) 450-8500
Fax: (651) 450-8679
Internet: www.inverhills.edu
Pres.: CHERYL FRANK
Number of students: 3,380

Lake Superior College

2101 Trinity Rd, Duluth, MN 55811-3399
Telephone: (218) 733-7600
Fax: (218) 723-4921
Internet: www.lsc.edu
Pres.: KATHLEEN NELSON
Number of students: 3,505

Metropolitan State University

700 East Seventh St, St Paul, MN 55106
Telephone: (616) 793-1300
Fax: (616) 772-7738
Internet: www.metrostate.edu
Founded 1971
Colleges of arts and sciences, management, professional studies
Pres.: WILSON G. BRADSHAW
Librarian: DAVID BARTON
Number of teachers: 684 (132 full-time, 552 part-time)
Number of students: 8,868

Minneapolis Community and Technical College

1501 Hennepin Ave, Minneapolis, MN 55403
Telephone: (612) 659-6000
Fax: (612) 659-6310
Internet: www.minneapolis.edu
Pres.: PHILLIP DAVIS
Number of students: 5,013

Minnesota State College—Southeast Technical

Winona Campus, POB 409, 1250 Homer Rd, Winona, MN 55987-0409
Telephone: (507) 453-2700
Fax: (507) 453-2755
Internet: www.southeastmn.edu
Pres.: JIM JOHNSON
Number of students: 1,558

Minnesota State Community and Technical College

Fergus Falls Campus, 1414 College Way, Fergus Falls, MN 56537
Telephone: (218) 736-1500
Fax: (218) 736-1511
Internet: www.minnesota.edu
Pres.: ANN VALENTINE
Number of students: 4,414

Minnesota State University, Mankato

228 Wiecking Center, Mankato, MN 56001-6062
Telephone: (507) 389-1866
Fax: (507) 389-2227
E-mail: thehub@mnsu.edu
Internet: www.mnsu.edu
Founded 1868
Academic year: August to May
Pres.: Dr RICHARD DAVENPORT
Vice-Pres. for Academic Affairs: Dr SCOTT R. OLSEN
Vice-Pres. for Finance and Admin.: RICK STRAKA
Vice-Pres. for Student Affairs: Dr PATRICIA SWATFAGER-HANEY
Vice-Pres. for Technology: MARILYN DELMONT
Vice-Pres. for Univ. Advancement: DAVID WILLIAMS
Registrar: DAVID GJERDE
Dean of Library Services: JOAN ROCA
Library of 693,973 vols
Number of teachers: 600
Number of students: 14,000

DEANS

College of Allied Health and Nursing: KAYE HERTH
College of Arts and Humanities: JANE F. EARLEY
College of Business: SCOTT JOHNSON
College of Education: MICHAEL A. MILLER
College of Science, Engineering and Technology: JOHN E. FREY
College of Social and Behavioural Sciences: JOHN ALESSIO

Minnesota State University Moorhead

1104 Seventh Ave, S, Moorhead, MN 56563
Telephone: (218) 236-2011
Fax: (218) 236-2168
Internet: www.mnstate.edu
Founded 1887
Academic year: August to May
Pres.: Dr EDNA MORA SZYMANSKI
Vice-Pres. for Academic Affairs (vacant)
Vice-Pres. for Admin. Affairs: Dr DAN KIRK
Vice-Pres. for Student Affairs: WARREN WIESE
Registrar: JAYNE WASHBURN
Library of 595,000 books and periodicals
Number of teachers: 547
Number of students: 7,400

DEANS

College of Arts and Humanities: TIM BORCHERS
College of Business and Industry: DAVID CROCKETT
College of Education and Human Services: TERI WALSETH
College of Social and Natural Sciences: MICHELLE MALOTT

Minnesota West Community and Technical College

Granite Falls Campus, 1593 11th Ave, Granite Falls, MN 56241
Telephone: (320) 564-4511
Fax: (320) 564-2318
Internet: www.mnwest.edu
Pres.: RONALD A. WOOD
Number of students: 2,154

Normandale Community College

9700 France Ave, S, Bloomington, MN 55431
Telephone: (952) 487-8200
Fax: (952) 487-8101
Internet: www.normandale.edu
Pres.: JOSEPH OPATZ
Number of students: 6,108

North Hennepin Community College

7411 85th Ave, N, Brooklyn Park, MN 55445
Telephone: (763) 424-0702
Fax: (763) 424-0929
Internet: www.nhcc.edu
Pres.: ANN WYNIA
Number of students: 4,283

Northland Community and Technical College

Thief River Falls Campus, 1101 Highway 1, E, Thief River Falls, MN 56701
Telephone: (218) 681-0701
Fax: (218) 681-0724
Internet: www.northlandcollege.edu
Pres.: ANNE TEMTE
Number of students: 2,785

Pine Technical College

900 Fourth St, SE, Pine City, MN 55063
Telephone: (320) 629-5100
Fax: (320) 629-5101
Internet: www.pinetech.edu
Pres.: ROBERT MUSGROVE
Number of students: 422

Ridgewater College

Hutchinson Campus, 2 Century Ave, SE, Hutchinson, MN 55350
Telephone: (320) 222-5202
Fax: (320) 222-5212
Internet: www.ridgewater.edu
Pres.: DOUGLAS ALLEN
Number of students: 3,292

Riverland Community College

Austin Campus, 1900 Eighth Ave, NW, Austin, MN 55912
Telephone: (507) 433-0600
Fax: (507) 433-0370
Internet: www.riverland.edu
Pres.: TERRENCE LEAS
Number of students: 2,421

Rochester Community and Technical College

851 30th Ave, SE, Rochester, MN 55904-4999
Telephone: (507) 285-7210
Fax: (507) 285-7108
Internet: www.rctc.edu
Pres.: DON SUPALLA
Number of students: 4,383

St Cloud State University

720 Fourth Ave, S, St Cloud, MN 56301-4498
Telephone: (612) 255-2122
E-mail: scsu4u@stcloudstate.edu
Internet: www.stcloudstate.edu
Founded 1869, univ. status in 1975
Pres.: EARL H. POTTER, III
Vice-Pres. for Academic Affairs: BARBARA GRACHEK
Dean of Library: KRISTI TORNQUIST
Library of 569,000 vols
Number of teachers: 650
Number of students: 16,000

DEANS

College of Business: DIANA LAWSON
College of Education: KATE M. STEFFENS
College of Fine Arts and Humanities: ROLAND SPECHT-JARVIS
College of Science and Engineering: DAVID DEGROOTE
College of Social Sciences: SHARON E. COGDILL

St Cloud Technical College

1540 Northway Dr., St Cloud, MN 56303-1240
Telephone: (320) 308-5000
Fax: (320) 308-5058
Internet: www.sctc.edu
Pres.: JOYCE HELENS
Number of students: 2,738

Saint Paul College—A Community and Technical College

235 Marshall Ave, St Paul, MN 55102
Telephone: (651) 846-1600
Fax: (651) 846-1451
Internet: www.saintpaul.edu

Pres.: DONOVAN SCHWICHTENBERG
Number of students: 3,012

South Central College

Faribault Campus, 1225 SW Third St, Faribault, MN 55021
Telephone: (507) 334-3965
Fax: (507) 332-5888
Internet: www.southcentral.edu

Pres.: KEITH STOVER
Number of students: 2,514

Southwest Minnesota State University

1501 State St, Marshall, MN 56258-1598
Telephone: (507) 537-7021
Fax: (507) 537-7154
Internet: www.southwestmsu.edu

Founded 1963
Academic year: August to May

Pres.: Dr DAVID C. DANAHAR
Provost: Dr BETH WETHERBY
Vice-Pres. for Advancement: Dr VINCENT PELLEGRINO
Library Dir: SANDRA FUHR

Library of 160,000 vols
Number of teachers: 162
Number of students: 5,500

DEANS

College of Arts, Letters and Sciences: Dr BETSY DESY
College of Business, Education and Professional Studies: Dr DONNA BURGRAFF
Distance Learning: Dr GERALD TOLAND

Winona State University

POB 5838, Winona, MN 55987
Telephone: (507) 457-5000
Fax: (507) 457-2415
Internet: www.winona.edu

Founded 1858
Academic year: August to May

Pres.: JUDITH A. RAMALEY
Vice-Pres. for Academic Affairs: SALLY JOHNSTONE
Vice-Pres. for Finance and Admin. Services: SCOTT ELLINGHUYSEN (acting)
Vice-Pres. for Student Life and Devt: CONNIE GORES
Vice-Pres. for Univ. Advancement: JAMES C. SCHMIDT
Dean of Library: LARRY HARDESTY

Library of 262,692 vols, 772,500 microforms
Number of teachers: 350
Number of students: 7,500

DEANS

College of Business: BILL MUROHY
College of Education: SALLY STANDIFORD
College of Liberal Arts: TROY PAINO
College of Nursing and Health Science: TIMOTHY M. GASPAR
College of Science and Engineering: JEFFREY R. ANDERSON (acting)

NORTH CENTRAL UNIVERSITY

910 Elliot Ave, Minneapolis, MN 55404
Telephone: (612) 343-4400
E-mail: info@northcentral.edu
Internet: www.northcentral.edu

Founded 1930 as North Central Bible Institute; present name 1998
Private control

Pres.: Dr GORDON ANDERSON
Vice-Pres. for Academic Affairs: Dr THOMAS BURKMAN
Vice-Pres. for Business and Finance: CHERYL BOOK
Vice-Pres. for Student Devt: MIKE NOSSER
Vice-Pres. for Univ. Relations: NATE RUCH
Registrar: KRISTA HERRERA
Librarian: Dr JOHN DAVENPORT

Library of 70,000 vols
Number of teachers: 88
Number of students: 1,204

NORTHWESTERN COLLEGE

3003 Snelling Ave N, St Paul, MN 55113-1598
Telephone: (651) 631-5100
E-mail: admissions@nwc.edu
Internet: www.nwc.edu
Private control
Academic year: August to May

Pres.: Dr ALAN CURETON
Provost and Vice-Pres. for Academic Affairs: Dr ALFORD H. OTTLEY
Dean of Faculty: Dr MARK D. BADEN
Registrar: ANDREW L. SIMPSON
Library Dir: RUTH MCGUIRE

Library of 100,000 vols
Number of teachers: 117
Number of students: 3,000

Areas of study: art and graphic design, Bible and theological studies, business, Christian ministries, communication, education, English and literature, history and related fields, modern languages and cultures, music, psychology, science and mathematics.

NORTHWESTERN HEALTH SCIENCES UNIVERSITY

2501 West 84th St, Bloomington, MN 55431
Telephone: (952) 888-4777
E-mail: admit@nwhealth.edu
Internet: www.nwhealth.edu
Private control

Pres.: MARC ZIEGLER
Provost: MICHAEL WELLES
Registrar: RUTH ANN MARKS
Dir of Library Services: DELLA SHUPE
Number of students: 1,000

Incl. College of Chiropractic, Minnesota College of Acupuncture and Oriental Medicine, School of Massage Therapy, Integrative Health and Wellness Certificate Program.

OAK HILLS CHRISTIAN COLLEGE

1600 Oak Hills Rd SW, Bemidji, MN 56601
Telephone: (218) 751-8670
Fax: (218) 751-8825
E-mail: oakhills@oakhills.edu
Internet: www.oakhills.edu

Founded 1946 as Oak Hills Christian Training School; present name 1998
Private control

Provost and Academic Dean: STEVE HOSTETTER
Vice-Pres. for Advancement: PAMELA MAGAWA
Dean of Student Life: GALE STRUTHERS
Registrar: MARY HANNAH
Librarian: KEITH BUSH

Library of 23,000 vols
Number of teachers: 20
Number of students: 175

Areas of study: biblical studies, Christian ministries, general education.

SAINT JOHN'S UNIVERSITY

Collegeville, MN 56321
Telephone: (320) 363-2011
Fax: (320) 363-2778
E-mail: admission@csbsju.edu
Internet: www.csbsju.edu

Founded 1857

Private liberal arts college for men; partnered with the College of Saint Benedict for women

Pres.: Fr ROBERT KOOPMANN
Academic Dean: JOE DESJARDINS
Vice-Pres. for Finance and Admin.: DICK ADAMSON
Vice-Pres. for Institutional Advancement: ROB CULLIGAN
Vice-Pres. for Student Devt: Fr DOUG MULLIN
Dir of Libraries and Media: KATHY PARKER

Library of 310,000 vols, 121,244 microforms, 658,438 govt docs, 71,720 current serial titles, 116,741 e-books
Number of teachers: 147 full-time, 30 part-time
Number of students: 2,020

SAINT MARY'S UNIVERSITY

700 Terrace Heights, Winona, MN 55987
Telephone: (507) 452-4430
Fax: (507) 457-1633
Internet: www.smumn.edu

Founded 1912

Pres.: Bro. LOUIS DE THOMASIS
Provost: Dr JEFFREY HIGHLAND
Vice-Pres. for Academic Affairs: THOMAS C. MANS
Vice-Pres. for Communication and Marketing: BOB CONOVER
Vice-Pres. for Financial Affairs: CYNTHIA MAREK
Vice-Pres. and Gen. Counsel: ANN E. MERCHLEWITZ
Librarian: Bro. RICHARD LEMBERG

Library of 180,000 vols, 750 periodicals
Number of teachers: 94
Number of students: 5,500

DEANS

School of the Arts: MICHAEL CHARRON
School of Business: THOMAS MARPE
School of Education: JANE ANDERSON

ST OLAF COLLEGE

1520 St Olaf Ave, Northfield, MN 55057-1098
Telephone: (507) 786-2222
Fax: (507) 786-3986
Internet: www.stolaf.edu

Founded 1874
Academic year: September to May

Pres.: DAVID R. ANDERSON
Provost and Dean of College: JAMES MAY
Vice-Pres. and Dean of Enrollment: MICHAEL KYLE
Vice-Pres. and Treas.: ALAN NORTON
Vice-Pres. for Advancement and College Relations: MICHAEL STITSWORTH
Vice-Pres. for Student Life and Dean of Students: GREG KNESER
Dir of the Library: (vacant)

Library of 685,000 vols
Number of teachers: 365
Number of students: 3,073

Areas of study incl. fine arts, humanities, interdisciplinary and general studies, natural sciences and mathematics, social and applied science

Publication: *St Olaf*.

UNITED THEOLOGICAL SEMINARY OF THE TWIN CITIES

3000 Fifth St NW, New Brighton, MN 55112-2598
Telephone: (651) 633-4311
Fax: (651) 633-4315

Internet: www.unitedseminary.edu
Private control
Pres.: KITA MCVAY
Dean: RICHARD D. WEIS
Vice-Pres. for Finance and Admin.: JUDY LANGE
Registrar: SUSAN HASTINGS
Library Dir: SUSAN K. EBBERS
Library of 83,000 vols
Number of teachers: 27
Number of students: 112 (full-time)

UNIVERSITY OF MINNESOTA

100 Church St, SE, Minneapolis, MN 55455
Telephone: (612) 625-5000
Fax: (612) 624-6369
E-mail: feedback@tc.umn.edu
Internet: www.umn.edu
Founded 1851
State control
Academic year: September to May
Pres.: ROBERT H. BRUININKS
Sr Vice-Pres. for Academic Affairs and Provost: E. THOMAS SULLIVAN
Sr Vice-Pres. for Health Sciences: FRANK B. CERRA
Sr Vice-Pres. for System Academic Admin.: ROBERT J. JONES
Vice-Pres. and Chief Financial Officer: RICHARD PFUTZENREUTER
Vice-Pres. and Chief Information Officer: STEPHEN CAWLEY
Vice-Pres. and Chief of Staff: KATHRYN BROWN
Vice-Pres. for Human Resources: CAROL CARRIER (acting)
Vice-Pres. for Research: R. TIMOTHY MULCAHY
Vice-Pres. for Scholarly and Cultural Affairs: STEVEN ROSENSTONE
Vice-Pres. for Univ. Relations: KAREN HIMLE
Vice-Pres. for Univ. Services: KATHLEEN O'BRIEN
Gen. Counsel: MARK ROTENBERG
Librarian: WENDY P. LOUGEE
Library: see Libraries
Number of teachers: 4,105
Number of students: 67,364 system-wide (51,659 Twin Cities campus)

DEANS

Carlson School of Management: ALISON DAVIS-BLAKE
College of Biological Sciences: ROBERT ELDE
College of Continuing Education: MARY NICHOLS
College of Design: THOMAS FISHER
College of Education and Human Devt: JEAN QUAM
College of Food, Agricultural and Natural Resource Sciences: ALLEN LEVINE
College of Liberal Arts: JAMES A. PARENTE, Jr
College of Pharmacy: MARILYN K. SPEEDIE
College of Science and Engineering: STEVEN L. CROUCH
College of Veterinary Medicine: TREVOR R. AMES (acting)
Graduate School: HENNING SCHROEDER
Law School: DAVID WIPPMAN
Medical School: FRANK B. CERRA
School of Dentistry: PATRICK LLOYD
School of Nursing: CONNIE DELANEY
School of Public Health: JOHN FINNEGAN, Jr
Humphrey (Hubert H.) Institute of Public Affairs: J. BRIAN ATWOOD

PROFESSORS

Accounting (3-122 Carlson School of Management, 321 19th Ave, S, Minneapolis, MN 55455; tel. (612) 624-6506; fax (612) 626-1335; e-mail balston@esom.umn.edu; internet www.csom.umn.edu/facultydepartments/departments/accounting/welcometoaccounting/welcometoaccounting.cfm):

AMERSHI, A.
DICKHAUT, J.
JOYCE, E.
KANODIA, C.
RAYBURN, J.

Adult Psychiatry (F-282/2A W, 2450 Riverside Ave, Minneapolis, MN 55455; tel. (612) 273-9800; fax (612) 273-9779):

CARROLL, M.
ECKERT, E.
EL-FAKAHANY, E.
HARTMAN, B.
HATSUKAMI, D.
KROLL, J.
MACKENZIE, T.
SCHULTZ, C.

Aerospace Engineering and Mechanics (107 Akerman Hall, 110 Union St, SE, Minneapolis, MN 55455; tel. (612) 625-8000; fax (612) 626-1558; e-mail dept@aem.umn.edu; internet www.aem.umn.edu):

BALAS, G.
BEAVERS, G. S.
CANDLER, G. V.
FOSDICK, R. L.
GARRARD, W. L.
LEO, P.
WILSON, T. A.

African-American and African Studies (808 Social Sciences Bldg, 267 19th Ave, S, Minneapolis, MN 55455; tel. (612) 624-9847; internet www.afroam.umn.edu):

FARAH, C.
ISAACMAN, A. F.
MCCURDY, R.
NIMTZ, A.
PORTER, P. W.
SCOTT, E.

Agricultural, Food and Environmental Education (320 Vocational and Technical Education Bldg, 1954 Buford Ave, St Paul, MN 55108; tel. (612) 624-2221; fax (612) 625-2798; internet education.umn.edu/wcfe/afee):

KRUEGER, R.
PETERSON, R.

Agronomy and Plant Genetics (411 Borlang Hall, 1991 Upper Burford Circle, St Paul, MN 55108; tel. (612) 625-7773; fax (612) 625-1268; e-mail agro@coates.umn.edu; internet www.agro.agri.umn.edu):

BECKER, R. L.
CARDWELL, V. B.
DURGAN, B. R.
EHLKE, N. J.
GENGENBACH, B. G.
GRONWALD, J. W.
GUNSOLUS, J. L.
HARDMAN, L. L.
HICKS, D. R.
JONES, R. J.
JUNG, H. J.
LUESCHEN, W. E.
ORF, J. H.
PHILLIPS, R. L.
RINES, H. W.
SHEAFFER, C. C.
SIMMONS, S. R.
SOMERS, D. A.
STUTHMAN, D. D.
VANCE, C. P.
WYSE, D. L.

American Studies (104 Scott Hall, 72 Pleasant St, SE, Minneapolis, MN 55455; tel. (612) 624-4190; fax (612) 624-3858; e-mail amstdy@umn.edu; internet cla.umn.edu/american/american.html):

MAY, E. T.
MAY, L.
NOBLE, D.
PRELL, R. E.
YATES, G. G.

Anaesthesiology (B-515 Mayo Memorial Bldg (MMC 294), 420 Delaware St, SE, Minneapolis, MN 55455; tel. (612) 624-9990; fax (612) 624-2363; internet www.anesthesiology.umn.edu):

BEEBE, D. S.
BELANI, K. G.
IAIZZO, P. A.
PALAHNIUK, R. J.

Animal Science (305 Haecker Hall, 1364 Eckles Ave, St Paul, MN 55108; tel. (612) 624-9752; fax (612) 625-5789; internet www.ansci.umn.edu):

CROOKER, B. A.
DAYTON, W. R.
EL HALAWANI, M. E.
FOSTER, D. N.
HANSEN, L. B.
HATHAWAY, M. R.
HAWTON, J. D.
HUNTER, A. G.
JOHNSON, D. G.
JOHNSTON, L. J.
LINN, J. G.
MARX, G. D.
NOLL, S. N.
O'GRADY, S. M.
OSBORN, J. W.
PONCE DE LEÓN, F. A.
RENEAU, J. K.
SEYKORA, A.
SHURSON, G. C.
STERN, M. D.
WHEATON, J. E.
WHITE, M. E.

Anthropology (395 Hubert H. Humphrey Center, 301 19th Ave, S, Minneapolis, MN 55453; tel. (612) 625-3400; fax (612) 625-3095; internet www.cla.umn.edu/anthropology):

GIBBON, G.
GUDEMAN, S.
INGHAM, J. M.
MILLER, F. C.
RAHEJA, G. G.
WELLS, P.

Applied Economics (231 Classroom-Office Bldg, 1994 Buford Ave, St Paul, MN 55108; tel. (612) 625-1222; fax (612) 625-6245; e-mail depthead@dept.agecon.umn.edu; internet www.apec.umn.edu):

APLAND, J. D.
EASTER, K. W.
EIDMAN, V. R.
GARTNER, W. C.
KING, R. P.
KINSEY, J. L.
LEVINS, R. L.
MORSE, G. W.
OLSEN, K. D.
PARLIAMENT, C. D.
PEDERSON, E. D.
POLASKY, S.
ROE, T. L.
RUNGE, C. F.
RUTTEN, V. W.
SCHUH, G. E.
SENAUER, B. H.

Architecture (89 Church St, SE, Minneapolis, MN 55455; tel. (612) 626-9068; fax (612) 625-7525; e-mail calainfo@tc.umn.edu; internet www.cala.umn.edu/architecture.html):

FISHER, T.
LAVINE, L.
ROBINSON, J. W.
ROCKCASTLE, G.
SATKOWSKI, L.

Art (208 Art Bldg, 216 21st Ave, Minneapolis, MN 55455; tel. (612) 625-8096; fax (612) 625-7881; e-mail artdept@tc.umn.edu; internet artdept.umn.edu):

BETHKE, K. E.

HOARD, C. C.
KATSIAFICAS, D.
MORGAN, C.
PHARIS, M.
PORTRATZ, W. E.
ROSE, T. A.

Art History (338 Heller Hall, 271 19th Ave, S, Minneapolis, MN 55455; tel. (612) 624-4500; fax (612) 626-8679; internet www.arthist.umn.edu):

ASHER, F. M.
COOPER, F.
MCNALLY, S.
MARLING, K. A. R.
POOR, R. J.
WEISBERG, G.

Astronomy (356 Tate Lab of Physics, 116 Church St, SE, Minneapolis, MN 53455; tel. (612) 624-0211; fax (612) 626-2029; internet www.astro.umn.edu):

DAVIDSON, K. D.
DICKEY, J. M.
GEHRZ, R. D.
HUMPHREYS, R. M.
JONES, T.
JONES, T. W.
KUHI, L.
RUDNICK, L.
SKILLMAN, E.
WOODWARD, P. R.

Biochemistry, Molecular Biology and Biophysics (6-155 Jackson Hall, 321 Church St, SE, Minneapolis, MN 55455; tel. (612) 625-6100; fax (612) 625-2163; e-mail bmbb@biosci.cbs.umn.edu; internet www.cbs.umn.edu/bmbb):

ALLEWELL, N. M.
ANDERSON, J. S.
ARMITAGE, I. M.
BANASZAK, L. J.
BARRY, B. A.
BERNLOHR, D. A.
BLOOMFIELD, V. A.
CONTI-FINE, B. M.
DAS, A.
DEMPSEY, M. E.
FLICKINGER, M. C.
FUCHS, J. A.
HOGENKAMP, H. P. C.
HOOPER, A. B.
HOWARD, J. B.
KOERNER, J. F.
LA PORTE, D. C.
LIPSCOMB, J. D.
LIVINGSTON, D. M.
LOUIS, C. F.
LOVRIEN, R. E.
MAYO, K. H.
NELSESTUEN, G. L.
OEGEMA, T. R.
OHLENDORF, D. H.
SANDERS, M. M.
SCHOTTEL, J. S.
THOMAS, D. D.
TOWLE, H. C.
TSONG, T.
VAN NESS, B. G.
WACKETT, L. P.

Bioethics (N-504 Boynton, 410 Church St, SE, Minneapolis, MN 55455; tel. (612) 624-9440; fax (612) 624-9108; e-mail bioethx@umn.edu; internet www.bioethicsd.umn.edu):

BEBEAU, M.
BURK, D.
CRANFORD, R.
KANE, R.
MAYO, D.

Biomedical Engineering (7-105 Basic Sciences and Biomedical Engineering, 312 Church St, SE, Minneapolis, MN 55455; tel. (612) 626-3332; fax (612) 626-6583; internet www1.umn.edu/bme):

POLLA, D.
SIEGEL, R.
TRANQUILLO, R.

Biostatistics (A-460 Mayo Bldg (MMC 303), 420 Delaware St, Minneapolis, MN 55455; tel. (612) 624-4655; fax (612) 626-0660; internet www.biostat.umn.edu):

CARLIN, B.
CONNETT, J.
DUNSMUIR, W.
GOLDMAN, A.
LE, C.
LOUIS, T.
NEATON, J.
TWEEDIE, R.

Biosystems and Agricultural Engineering (213 Biosystems and Agricultural Engineering, 1390 Eckles Ave, St Paul, MN 55108; tel. (612) 625-7733; fax (612) 624-3005; e-mail bae@gaia.bae.umn.edu; internet www.bae.umn.edu):

BHATTACHARYA, M.
CLAYTON, C. J.
JACOBSEN, L. D.
JANNI, K. A.
MOREY, R. V.
NIEBER, J. L.
RUAN, R.
WILCKE, W. F.

Biotechnology Institute (240 Gortner Lab of Biochemistry, 1479 Gortner Ave, St Paul, MN 55108; tel. (612) 624-6774; fax (612) 625-1700; e-mail bti@biosci.cbs.umn.edu; internet biosci.cbs.umn.edu/bti):

BROOKER, R.
FLICKINGER, M.
SADOWSKY, M.
SHERMAN, D.
SRIENC, F.
URRY, D.
WACKETT, L.

Business and Industry Education (425 Vocational and Technical Education Bldg, 1954 Buford Ave, St Paul, MN 55108; tel. (612) 624-3004; fax (612) 624-4720; internet education.umn.edu/wcfe/bie):

BROWN, J.
LAMBRECH, J.
LEWIS, T.
MCLEAN, G.
PUCEL, D.

Chemical Engineering and Materials Science (151 Amundson Hall, 421 Washington Ave, SE, Minneapolis, MN 55455; tel. (612) 625-1313; fax (612) 626-7246; e-mail jjmurphy@tc.umn.edu; internet www.cems.umn.edu):

BATES, F.
CARETTA, R.
CARR, R. W.
CARTER, B.
CHELIKOWSKY, J. R.
CUSSLER, E. L.
DAVIS, H. T.
DERBY, J.
EVANS, D. F.
GEANKOPLIS, C. J.
GERBERICH, W. W.
HU, W. S.
KELLER, K. H.
MCCORMICK, A.
MACOSKO, C. W.
PALMSTROM, C.
SCHMIDT, L. D.
SCRIVEN, L. E.
SEIDEL, R.
SHORES, D. A.
SMYRL, W. H.
SRIENC, F.
TRANQUILLO, R.
WARD, M. D.

Chemistry (139 Smith Hall, 207 Pleasant St, SE, Minneapolis, MN 55455; tel. (612) 624-6000; fax (612) 6626-7541; internet www.chem.umn.edu):

BARANY, G.
BLOOMFIELD, V. A.
CARR, P. W.
CRAMER, C. J.
DAVIS, H. T.
ELLIS, J. E.
GENTRY, W. R.
GLADFELTER, W. L.
GRAY, G. R.
HOYE, T.
KASS, S.
LEOPOLD, K.
LIPSKY, S.
LODGE, T.
MANN, K. R.
MILLER, L. L.
NOLAND, W. E.
PIGNOLET, L. H.
QUE, L.
RAFTERY, M.
STANKOVICH, M. T.
TOLMAN, W.
TRUHLAR, D. G.

Child Development (51 E River Rd, Minneapolis, MN 55455; tel. (612) 624-0526; fax 612 624-6373; e-mail icd@umn.edu; internet education.umn.edu/icd):

BAUER, P.
COLLINS, W. A.
CRICK, N.
EGELAND, B. R.
GUNNAR, M. R.
MARATSOS, M. P.
MASTEN, A. S.
NELSON, C.
PICK, A. D.
PICK, H. L., Jr
SROUFE, L. A.
WEINBERG, R. A.
YONAS, A.

Civil Engineering (122 Civil Engineering Bldg, 500 Pillsbury Dr., SE, Minneapolis, MN 55455; tel. (612) 625-5522; fax (612) 626-7750; e-mail cive@umn.edu; internet www.ce.umn.edu):

ARNDT, R. E. A.
BREZONIK, P. L.
CROUCH, S. L.
DETOURNAY, E.
DRESCHER, A.
FOUFOULA-GEORGIOU, E.
FRENCH, C. W.
GULLIVER, J. S.
MICHALOPOULOS, P.
PARKER, G. N.
SEMMENS, M. J.
STEFAN, G.
STOLARSKI, H. K.
STRACK, O. D. L.
VOLLER, V. R.

Classical and Near Eastern Studies (305 Folwell Hall, 9 Pleasant St, SE, Minneapolis, MN 55455; tel. (612) 625-5353; fax (612) 624-4894; e-mail cnes@umn.edu; internet cnes.cla.umn.edu):

BELFIORE, E.
CLAYTON, T.
COOPER, F.
DOUGLAS, S.
MCNALLY, S.
OLSON, T.
SONKOWSKY, R. P.
STAVROU, T.

Classical Civilization Programme (330 Folwell Hall, 9 Pleasant St, SE, Minneapolis, MN 55455; tel. (612) 625-7565):

AKEHURST, F. R.
BELFIORE, E.
CLAYTON, T.
COOPER, F.
LIBERMAN, A.
SONKOWSKY, R.
TRACY, J.
WILSON, L.

Clinical and Population Sciences (225 Veterinary Teaching Hospitals, 1352 Boyd Ave/ 1365 Gortner Ave, St Paul, MN 55108; tel. (612) 625-7755; fax (612) 625-6241; e-mail amesx001@tc.umn.edu; internet www.cvm.umn.edu):

AMES, T. R.
BLAHA, T. C.
FAHNING, M. L.
FARNSWORTH, R. J.
FETROW, J. P.
JOO, H. S.
MOLITOR, T. M.
MORRISON, R. B.
PIJOQAN, C. J.
PULLEN, M. M.
SEGUIN, B. E.
TURNER, T. A.

Clinical Pharmacology (6-120 Jackson Hall, 321 Church St, SE, Minneapolis, MN 55455; tel. (612) 625-9997; fax (612) 625-8408; internet www.pharmacology.med.umn.edu):

HOLZMAN, J. L.
HUNNINGHAKE, D.
PENTEL, P.
YEE, D.

Cognitive Sciences (205 Elliot Hall, 75 East River Rd, Minneapolis, MN 55455; tel. (612) 625-9367; fax (612) 626-7253; e-mail ccs@cogsci.umn.edu; internet www.cogsci.umn.edu):

CHILDERS, T.
GEORGOPOULOS, A.
GINI, M.
GUNDEL, J.
JOHNSON, P.
KERSTEN, D.
LEGGE, G.
MARATSOS, M.
NELSON, C.
OVERMIER, B.
PICK, A.
PICK, H.
SAMUELS, J.
SPEAKS, C.
UGURBIL, K.
VAN DEN BROEK, P.
VIEMEISTER, N.
WADE, M.
YONAS, A.

Communication Disorders (115 Shevlin Hall, 164 Pillsbury Dr., SE, Minneapolis, MN 55455; tel. (612) 624-3322; fax (612) 624-7586; e-mail cdis@tc.umn.edu; internet www.cdis.umn.edu):

CARNEY, A. E.
REICHLE, J. E.
SPEAKS, C. E.
WINDSOR, J.

Communication Studies (225 Ford Hall, 221 Church St, SE, Minneapolis, MN 55455; tel. (612) 624-5800; internet www.comm.umn.edu):

BROWNE, D. R.
CAMPBELL, K.
HEWES, D.
SCHIAPPA, E.

Community Health Education (300 W Bank Office Bldg, 1300 52nd St, Minneapolis, MN 55455; tel. (612) 624-1878; fax (612) 624-0315; internet www.epi.umn.edu):

FORSTER, J.
GARRAD, J.
JEFFREY, R. W.
LANDO, H. A.
LUEPKER, R. V.
LYTLE, P.
MCGOVERN, P.
PERRY, C. L.
PIRIE, P. L.
VENMGA, R.
WAGENAAR, A. C.

Computer Science and Engineering (4-192 Electrical Engineering/Computer Science, 200 Union St, SE, Minneapolis, MN 55455; tel. (612) 625-4002; fax (612) 625-0572; internet www.cs.umn.edu):

BOLEY, D. L.
DU, D.
DU, D. Z.
FOX, D.
GINI, M. L.
JANARDAN, R.
KUMAR, V.
NORBERG, A. L.
PAPANIKOLOPOULOUS, W.
PARK, H.
SAAD, Y.
SHEKHAR, S.
SHRAGOWITZ, E.
SRIVASTAVA, J.
TRIPATHI, A. R.
YEW, P.

Counselling and Student Personnel Psychology (129 Burton Hall, 178 Pittsburgh Dr., SE, Minneapolis, MN 55455; tel. (612) 624-6827; fax (612) 625-4063; e-mail cspp-adm@umn.edu; internet www.education.umn.edu/edpsych/cspp):

HUMMEL, T.
ROMANO, J.
SKOVHOLT, T.
VEACH, P.

Cultural Studies and Comparative Literature (350 Folwell Hall, 9 Pleasant St, SE, Minneapolis, MN 55455; tel. (612) 624-8099; fax (612) 626-0228; internet cscl.cla.umn.edu):

BRENNAN, T.
LEPPERT, R.
MOWITT, J.
SARLES, H. B.
SCHULTE-SASSE, J.

Curriculum and Instruction (125 Peik Hall, 159 Pillsbury Dr., SE, Minneapolis, MN 55455; tel. (612) 625-6372; fax (612) 624-8277; e-mail ciinfo@umn.edu; internet www.education.umn.edu/ci):

AVERY, P.
BEACH, R. W.
COGAN, J.
DILLON, D.
GRAVES, M.
JOHNSON, R.
LAMBRECHT, J.
LAWRENZ, F.
MANNING, J. C.
O'BRIEN, D.
POST, T.
TAYLOR, B.

Dental Research Center for Biomaterials and Biomechanics (16-212 Malcolm Moos Health Sciences Tower, 515 Delaware St, SE, Minneapolis, MN 55455; tel. (612) 625-0950; fax (612) 626-1484):

COMBE, E.
DOUGLAS, W.

Dermatology (4-240 Phillips-Wangensteen Bldg, 516 Delaware St, SE, Minneapolis, MN 55455; tel. (612) 625-8625; fax (612) 624-6678; internet www.dermatology.umn.edu):

HORDINSKY, M.
KING, R.

Design, Housing, and Apparel (240 McNeal Hall of Home Econ., 1985 Buford Ave, St Paul, MN 55108; tel. (612) 624-9700; fax (612) 624-2750; internet dha.che.umn.edu):

ANGELL, W.
DELONG, M.
EICHER, J.
GUERIN, D.
JOHNSON, K.

Ecology, Evolution, and Behaviour (100 Ecology Bldg, 1987 Upper Buford Circle, St Paul, MN 55108; tel. (612) 625-5200; fax (612) 624-6777; internet www.cbs.umn.edu/eeb):

ALSTAD, D.
BARNWELL, F.
BEATTY, J.
CORBIN, K.
CURTSINGER, J.
CUSHING, E.
LANYON, S.
MEGARD, R.
MORROW, P.
NEUHAUSER, C.
PACKER, C.
PUSEY, A.
REGAL, P.
SHAW, R.
SINIFF, D.
STARFIELD, A.
STERNER, R. W.
TILMAN, G. D.
ZINK, R.

Economics (1035 Walter W Heller Hall, 271 19th Ave, S, Minneapolis, MN 55455; tel. (612) 625-6353; fax (612) 624-0209; e-mail econdept@econ.umn.edu; internet www.econ.umn.edu):

ALLEN, B.
BOLDRIN, M.
CHARI, V. V.
CHIPMAN, J. S.
ECKSTEIN, Z.
FELDMAN, R. D.
FOSTER, E.
HOLMES, T.
HURWICZ, L.
JONES, L.
KEHOE, T.
KOCHERLAKOTA, N.
MCLENNAN, A.
PRESCOTT, E. C.
RICHTER, M. K.
RUSTICHOTRI, A.
RUTTAN, V.
SCHUH, G. E.
SWAN, C.
WERNER, J.

Education for Work and Community (425 Vocational and Technical Education Bldg, 1954 Buford Ave, St Paul, MN 55108; tel. (612) 624-3004; fax (612) 624-4720; internet education.umn.edu/wcfe/wcfe):

BROWN, J.
KRUEGER, R.
LEWIS, T.
PETERSON, R.
THOMAS, R.

Educational Policy and Administration (330 Wulling Hall, 86 Pleasant St, SE, Minneapolis, MN 55455; tel. (612) 624-1006; fax (612) 624-3377; e-mail edpagrad@umn.edu; internet www.education.umn.edu/edpa):

AMMENTORP, W. M.
CHAPMAN, D. W.
COGAN, J. J.
FRY, G. W.
HEARN, J. C.
LEWIS, D. R.
LEWIS, T.
SEASHORE, R.

Educational Psychology (204 Burton Hall, 178 Pillsbury Dr., SE, Minneapolis, MN 55455; tel. (612) 624-1698; fax (612) 624-8241; e-mail epsy-adm@umn.edu; internet www.education.umn.edu/edpsych):

BART, W. M.
BRUININKS, R.
CHRISTENSON, S.
DAVISON, M. L.
DENO, S.
HARWELL, M.
HUMMEL, T.

HUPP, S.
JOHNSON, D. W.
LAWRENZ, F.
MCCONNELL, S.
MCEVOY, M.
MARUYAMA, G.
PELLEGRINI, A.
ROMANO, J.
SAMUELS, S. J.
SKOVHOLT, T. M.
TENNYSON, R.
VAN DEN BROEK, P.
VEACH, P. M.
YSSELDYKE, J.

Electrical and Computer Engineering (4-178 Electrical Engineering/Computer Science, 200 Union St, SE, Minneapolis, MN 55455; tel. (612) 625-3300; fax (612) 625-4583; internet www.ece.umn.edu):

COHEN, P. I.
GEORGIOU, T.
GIANNAKIS, G.
GOPINATH, A.
KAVEH, M.
KIEFFER, J. C.
KIEHL, R.
KINNEY, L. L.
KUMAR, K. S. P.
LEE, E. B.
LEGER, J.
LILJA, D.
MAZIAR, C.
MOHAN, N.
MOON, J.
NATHAN, M.
PARHI, K.
PERIA, W. T.
POLLA, D.
ROBBINS, W. P.
RUDEN, P.
TANNENBAUM, A.
TEWFIK, A.
WOLLENBERG, B. F.

Emergency Medicine (A-624 Mayo Memorial Bldg (MMC 911), 420 Delaware St, SE, Minneapolis, MN 55455; tel. (612) 626-6911; fax (612) 626-2352):

AMSTERDAM, J.
CLINTON, J.
KNOPP, R.
LING, L.
RUIZ, E.

English (207 Lind Hall, 207 Church St, SE, Minneapolis, MN 55455; tel. (612) 625-3363; fax (612) 624-8228; internet english.cla.umn .edu):

BALES, K.
BRENNAN, T.
BRIDWELL-BOWLES, L.
BROWNE, M. D.
CLAYTON, T.
ELFENBEIN, A.
ESCURE, G.
FIRCHOW, P. E.
GARNER, S.
GRIFFIN, E. M.
HALEY, D.
HAMPL, P. M.
HANCHER, M.
HIRSCH, G.
KENDALL, C.
MINER, V.
MOWITT, J.
RABINOWITZ, P.
REED, P. J.
ROSS, D.
ROTH, M.
SOLOTAROFF, R.
SPRENGNETHER, M.
WEINSHEIMER, J.

English as a Second Language (214 Nolte Center for Continuing Education, 315 Pillsbury Dr., SE, Minneapolis, MN 55455; tel. (612) 624-3331; fax (612) 624-4579; e-mail eatarone@tc.umn.edu; internet www.iles .umn.edu/esl.htm):

COHEN, A.
TARONE, E.

Entomology (219 Hodson Hall, 1980 Folwell Ave, St Paul, MN 55108; tel. (612) 624-3636; fax (612) 625-5299; e-mail entodept@tc.umn .edu):

ANDOW, D. A.
ASCERNO, M. E.
HIEMPEL, G. E.
HOLZENTHAL, R. W.
HUTCHINSON, W. G.
KURTTI, T. J.
MESCE, R. D.
MOON, R. D.
OSTLIE, K. R.
RADCLIFFE, E. B.
RAGSDALE, D. W.
WALGENBACH, D. D.

Environmental and Occupational Health (1260 Mayo Memorial Bldg (MMC 807), 420 Delaware St, SE, Minneapolis, MN 55455; tel. (612) 626-0900; fax (612) 626-4837; internet www.umn.edu/eoh):

GERBERICH, S.
SEXTON, K.
SWACKHAMER, D.
TOSCANO, W.
VESLEY, D.

Epidemiology (300 West Bank Office Bldg, 1300 52nd St, Minneapolis, MN 55455; tel. (612) 624-1878; fax (612) 624-0315; internet www.epi.umn.edu):

BROWN, J. E.
CROW, R. S.
FINNEGAN, J. R.
FOLSOM, A. R.
FORSTER, J. L.
GARRAD, J.
GLASSER, S. P.
HIMES, J. M.
JACOBS, D. R.
JEFFEREY, R. W.
LANDO, H. A.
LUEPKER, R. V.
MCGOVERN, P.
MENOTTI, A.
PERRY, C. L.
PIRIE, P. L.
SHAHAR, E.
STORY, M. T.
VENINGA, R.
WAGENAAR, A. C.

Experimental and Clinical Pharmacology (7-159 Weaver-Densford Hall, 308 Harvard St, SE, Minneapolis, MN 55455; tel. (612) 626-9937; fax (612) 625-9931; internet www .pharmacy.umn.edu):

CLOYD, J. C.
FLETCHER, C. V.
GROSS, C.
GUAY, D. R.
HANLON, J. T.
LACKNER, J. E.
MANN, K. J.
ROTSCHAFER, J. C.
ZASKE, D. E.

Family Education (325 Vocational and Technical Education Bldg, 1954 Buford Ave, St Paul, MN 53708; tel. (612) 624-3010; fax (612) 625-6798; internet education.umn.edu/ wcfe/fe):

THOMAS, R.

Family Practice and Community Health (6-240 Phillips-Wangensteen Bldg, 516 Delaware St, SE, Minneapolis, MN 55455; tel. (612) 624-2622; fax (612) 624-5930; internet www.med.umn.edu/fp):

BLAND, C. J.
COLEMAN, E.
GJEROINGEN, D.
KEENAN, J.
SIMON ROSSER, B. R.

Family Social Science (290 McNeal Hall of Home Econ., 1985 Buford Ave, St Paul, MN 55108; tel. (612) 625-1900; fax (612) 625-4227; internet fsos.che.umn.edu):

BAUER, J.
BOSS, P.
DANES, S.
DETZNER, D.
DOHERTY, W.
GROTEVANT, H. D.
HOGAN, M. J.
MADDOCK, J.
RETTIG, K.
ROSENBLATT, P.
TURNER, W.

Finance (3-122 Carlson School of Management, 321 19th Ave, S, Minneapolis, MN 55455; tel. (612) 624-2888; fax (612) 626-1335; internet www.csom.umn.edu):

ALEXANDER, G.
BENVENISTE, L.
BOYD, J.
LEVINE, R.
NANTELL, T.

Fisheries and Wildlife (200 Hodson Hall, 1980 Folwell Ave, St Paul, MN 55455; tel. (612) 624-3600; fax (612) 625-5299; internet www.fw.umn.edu):

ADELMAN, I.
ANDERSON, D.
COHEN, Y.
COOPER, J.
CUTHBERT, F.
KAPUSCINSKI, A.
PERRY, J.
SMITH, D.
SORENSEN, P.
SPANGLER, G.

Food Science and Nutrition (225 Food Science and Nutrition, 1334 Eckles Ave, St Paul, MN 55108; tel. (612) 624-1290; fax (612) 625-5272; e-mail fscn@mail.coafes.umn .edu; internet fscn.che.umn.edu):

ADDIS, P. B.
BRADY, L. J.
CSALLANY, A. S.
FULCHER, R. G.
LABUZA, T. P.
MCKAY, L. L.
REINECCIUS, G. A.
SLAVIN, J. L.
SMITH, D. E.
TATINI, S. R.
VICKERS, Z. M.
WARTHESEN, J. J.

Forest Resources (115 Green Hall, 1530 North Cleveland Ave, St Paul, MN 53108; tel. (612) 624-3400; fax (612) 625-5212; e-mail fr@forestry.umn.edu; internet www .cnr.umn.edu/fr):

ANDERSON, D. H.
BAUER, M. E.
BAUGHMAN, M. J.
BLINN, C. R.
BROOKS, K. N.
BURK, T. E.
EK, A. R.
ELLEFSON, P. B.
PERRY, J. A., II
REICH, P. B.
ROSE, D. W.

French and Italian (260 Folwell Hall, 9 Pleasant St, SE, Minneapolis, MN 55455; tel. (612) 624-4308; fax (612) 624-6021; e-mail frit@umn.edu; internet cla.umn.edu/ frit):

AKEHURST, F. R. P.
NOAKES, S.
PAGANINI, M.

General College (25 Appleby Hall, 128 Pleasant St, SE, Minneapolis, MN 55455; tel. (612) 625-3339; fax (612) 625-0704; internet www.gen.umn.edu):

BROTHEN, T. F.
COLLINS, T. G.
GIDMARK, J. B.
HIGHBEE, J. H.
MOORE, R. C.
ROBERTSON, D. F.
YAHNKE, R. E.

Genetics, Cell Biology and Development (6-160 Jackson Hall, 321 Church St, SE, Minneapolis, MN 55455; tel. (612) 624-3110; fax (612) 626-6140; e-mail gcd@mail.med.umn.edu; internet www.gcd.med.umn.edu):

BAUER, G. E.
BERMAN, J. G.
BERRY, S.
BROOKER, R. J.
ERLANDSEN, S. L.
FAN, D. P.
FARAS, A. H.
GOLDSTEIN, S. F.
HACKETT, P. B.
HAMILTON, D. W.
HERMAN, R. K.
HERMAN, W. S.
JOHNSON, R. G.
KING, R. A.
KURIYAMA, P. A.
LEFEBVRE, P. A.
LINCK, R. W.
MCIVOR, R. S.
MAGEE, P. T.
O'CONNOR, M. B.
ORR, H. T.
SILFLOW, C. D.
SIMMONS, M. J.
SNUSTAD, D. P.
SORENSON, R. L.
VANNESS, B. G.

Geography (414 Social Sciences Bldg, 267 19th Ave, S, Minneapolis, MN 55455; tel. (612) 625-6080; fax (612) 624-1044; e-mail geog@geog.umn.edu; internet www.geog.umn.edu):

ADAMS, J. S.
BROWN, D. A.
GERSMEHL, P. J.
HART, J. F.
HSU, M. L.
LEITNER, H.
MCMASTER, R. B.
MARTIN, J. A.
SAMATOR, A. I.
SCOTT, E. P.
SHEPPARD, E. S.
SKAGGS, R. H.

Geology and Geophysics (108 Pilsbury Hall, 310 Pilsbury Dr., SE, Minneapolis, MN 55455; tel. (612) 624-1333; fax (612) 625-3819; e-mail geology@umn.edu; internet www.geo.umn.edu):

ALEXANDER, E. C., Jr
BANERJEE, S. K.
EDWARDS, R. L.
HUDLESTON, P.
ITO, E.
KOHLSTEDT, D.
KOHLSTEDT, S. G.
MOREY, G. B.
MOSHOWITZ, B.
MURTHY, V. R.
PAOLA, C.
PFANNKUCH, H. O.
SEYFRIED, W. E., Jr
SOUTHWICK, D.
STOUT, J.
TEYSSIER, C.
YUEN, D.

German, Scandinavian, and Dutch (205 Folwell Hall, 9 Pleasant St, SE, Minneapolis, MN 55455; tel. (612) 625-2080; fax (612) 624-8297; internet www.folwell.umn.edu/gsd):

FIRCHOW, E. S.
HASSELMO, N.
HOUE, P.
JOERES, R. B.
LIBERMAN, A.
PARENTE, J., Jr
SCHULTE-SASSE, J.
STOCKENSTRÖM, G.
TERAOKA, A.
ZIPES, J.

Gerontology (D-312 Mayo Memorial Bldg (MMC 197), 420 Delaware St, SE, Minneapolis, MN 55455; tel. (612) 624-3904; fax (612) 624-8448; e-mail coa@tc.umn.edu; internet www.umn.edu/coa):

AHLBURG, D.
BORN, D.
BOSS, P.
BOULT, C.
CLOYD, J.
CURTSONGER, J.
DETZNER, D.
DIFABIO, R.
DURFEE, W.
DYSKEN, M.
EUSTIS, N.
FELDMAN, B.
GARRARD, J.
GERSHEENSON, C.
GUAY, D.
HANCOCK, P.
HANLON, J.
HELLER, L.
KANE, R.
KANE, R.
KELLER, L.
KIVNICK, H.
LACKNER, T.
LARSON, A.
LE, C.
MCGUE, M.
MEYERS, S.
MILES, S.
PARK, R.
QUAM, J.
SCHONDEMEYER, S.
SEYBOLD, V.
SNYDER, M.
SWIONTKOWSKI, M.
THOMAS, D.
WADE, M.
WYMAN, J.
ZIMMERMAN, S.

Healthcare Management (3-140 Carlson School of Management, 321 19th Ave, S, Minneapolis, MN 55455; tel. (612) 624-8814; internet www.csom.umn.edu/facultydepartments/departments/healthcaremgmt/healthcaremgmt.cfm):

BEGUN, J.
CHRISTIANSON, J.
WECKWERTH, V.

Health Ecology (15-136 Malcolm Moos Health Sciences Tower, 515 Delaware St, SE, Minneapolis, MN 55455; tel. (612) 625-1191; fax (612) 626-6096; e-mail tlpash@maroon.tc.umn.edu; internet www.umn.edu/dental/department/prevsei/div_hecology.html):

BEBEAU, M.
BORN, D.
DIANGELIS, A.
MARTENS, L.

Health Informatics (777 Mayo Memorial Bldg (MMC 511), 420 Delaware St, SE, Minneapolis, MN 55455; tel. (612) 625-8440; fax (612) 625-7166; e-mail grad@email.labmed.umn.edu; internet www.hinf.umn.edu):

CONNELLY, D.
FINKELSTEIN, S.
GATEWOOD, L.
SPEEDIE, S.

Health Informatics Graduate Programme (777 Mayo Memorial Bldg (MMC 511), 420 Delaware St, SE, Minneapolis, MN 55455; tel. (612) 625-8440; fax (612) 625-7166; e-mail grad@email.labmed.umn.edu; internet www.hinf.umn.edu):

CONNELLY, D.
ELLIS, L.
FAN, D.
FINKELSTEIN, S.
FRICTON, J.
GATEWOOD, L.
HARRIS, I.
JOHNSON, P.
MCQUARRIE, D.
PATTERSON, R.
SPEEDIE, S.
WHOLEY, D.
WILCOX, G.

Health Services Research and Policy, Division of (15-200 Phillips-Wangensteen Bldg, 516 Delaware St, SE, Minneapolis, MN 55455; tel. (612) 624-6151; fax (612) 624-2196; e-mail ihsr@umn.edu; internet www.hsr.umn.edu):

CHRISTIANSON, J.
DOWD, B.
FELDMAN, R.
GARRARD, J.
HANLON, J.
KANE, R.
KANE, R.
KRALEWSKI, J.
LURIE, N.
MCBEAN, M.
MOSCOVICE, I.
NYMAN, J.
SWIONTKOWSKI, M.
VENNIGA, R.

History (614 Social Sciences Bldg, 267 19th Ave, S, Minneapolis, MN 55455; tel. (612) 624-2800; fax (612) 624-7096; internet www.hist.umn.edu):

ALTHOLZ, J. L.
BACHRACH, B. S.
BERMAN, H.
EVANS, J.
EVANS, S.
FARMER, E. L.
GOOD, D.
ISAACMAN, A. F.
MCCAA, R.
MAYNES, M. J.
MENARD, R. R.
MUNHOLLAND, J. K.
NOONAN, T. S.
PHILLIPS, C.
PHILLIPS, W.
REYERSON, K.
RUGGLES, S.
SAMAHA, J.
STAVROU, T. G.
THAYER, J. A.
TRACY, J. D.
VECOLI, R. J.
WALTNER, A.

History of Medicine (511A Diehl Hall, 505 Essex St, SE, Minneapolis, MN 55455; tel. (612) 624-4416; fax (612) 625-7938; internet www.med.umn.edu/history/home.htm):

EYLER, J. M.

History of Science and Technology (381 Tate Lab of Physics, 116 Church St, SE, Minneapolis, MN 55455; tel. (612) 624-7069; fax (612) 624-4578; internet www.physics.umn.edu):

BEATTY, J.
KOHLSTEDT, S. G.
NORBERG, A. L.
SEIDEL, R. W.
SHAPIRO, A. E.

Hormel Institute (801 16th Avenue, NE, Austin, MN 55912; tel. (507) 433-8804; fax (507) 437-9606; internet www.smig.net/hi):

BROCKMAN, H. L.
BROWN, R. E.
DONG, Z.
KISS, Z.
SCHMID, H. H. O.

Horticultural Science (305 Alderman Hall, 1970 Rolwell Ave, St Paul, MN 55108; tel. (612) 624-5300; fax (612) 624-4941; internet www.hort.agri.umn.edu):

BECKER, R. L.
BROWN, D. L.
COHEN, J. D.
GARDNER, G. M.
HOOVER, E. E.
LI, P. H.
LUBY, J. J.
MARKHART, A. H., III
OLIN, P. J.
PELLETT, H. M.
PRESTON, D.
ROSEN, C. J.
SOWOKINOS, J. R.
WHITE, D. B.
WILDUNG, D. K.

Human Genetics (4-122 Malcolm Moos Health Sciences Tower, 515 Delaware St, SE, Minneapolis, MN 55455; tel. (612) 624-8111; fax (612) 626-7031; internet www.ihg.med.umn.edu):

BERRY, S.
CONKLIN, K.
HACKETT, P.
KERSEY, J.
KING, R.
MCIVOR, R. S.
MOSER, K.
ORR, H.
SOMIA, M.
VANNESS, B.
WHITLEY, C.

Human Resource Development and Adult Education (425 Vocational and Technical Education Bldg, 1954 Buford Ave, St Paul, MN 55108; tel. (612) 624-3004; fax (612) 624-4720; internet education.umn.edu/wcfe/hrd/default.html):

BROWN, J.
LEWIS, T.
MCLEAN, G.
PUCEL, D.
SWANSON, R.

Human Sexuality (180 West Bank Office Bldg, 1300 52nd St, Minneapolis, MN 55455; tel. (612) 625-1500; fax (612) 626-8311):

COLEMAN, E.
ROSSER, S.

Humphrey (Hubert H.) Institute of Public Affairs (300 Hubert H. Humphrey Center, 301 19th Ave, S, Minneapolis, MN 55455; tel. (612) 625-9505; fax (612) 625-3513; internet www.hhh.umn.edu):

ADAMS, J.
ARCHIBALD, S.
BRANDL, J.
BRYSON, J.
EUSTIS, N.
FENNELLY, K.
HOENACK, S.
KAPSTEIN, E.
KELLER, K.
KENNEY, S.
KLEINER, M.
KUDRLE, R.
MARKUSEN, A.
MYERS, S. L., Jr
SCHUH, G. E.

Industrial Relations (3-300 Carlson School of Management, 321 19th Ave, S, Minneapolis, MN 55455; tel. (612) 624-2500; fax (612) 624-8360; internet www.irc.csom.umn.edu):

AHLBURG, D.
ARVEY, R.
BEN-NER, A.
BOGNANNO, M.
FOSSUM, J.
REMINGTON, J.
SCOVILLE, J.
WHITMAN, A.
ZAIDI, M.

Information and Decision Sciences (3-365 Carlson School of Management, 321 19th Ave, S, Minneapolis, MN 55455; tel. (612) 624-8030; fax (612) 626-1316; internet www.csom.umn.edu):

ADAMS, C. R.
CHERVANY, N. L.
CURLEY, S.
DAVIS, G. B.
JOHNSON, P. E.
KAUFFMAN, R. J.

Jewish Studies Center (339 Folwell Hall, 9 Pleasant St, SE, Minneapolis, MN 55455; tel. (612) 624-4914):

BACHRACH, B.
BERMAN, H.
BRUSTEIN, W.
PRELL, R. V.-E.
ZIPES, J.

Journalism and Mass Communication (111 Murphy Hall, 206 Church St, SE, Minneapolis, MN 55455; tel. (612) 625-9824; fax (612) 626-8251; internet sjmc.umn.edu):

DICKEN-GARCIA, H.
FABER, R. J.
FANG, I. E.
HANSEN, K. A.
KIRTLEY, J. E.
LEE, C. C.
ROBERTS, N. L.
SULLIVAN, D.
WACKMAN, D. B.

Kinesiology (220 Cooke Hall, 1900 University Ave, SE, Minneapolis, MN 55455; tel. (612) 625-5300; fax (612) 625-7700; internet education.umn.edu/kls/kinesiology/default.html):

KANE, J.
LEON, A.
WADE, M.

Laboratory Medicine and Pathology (D-242 Mayo Memorial Bldg (MMC 609), 420 Delaware St, SE, Minneapolis, MN 55455; tel. (612) 625-9171; fax (612) 625-0617; internet www.borg.labmed.umn.edu/ateam.html):

AHMED, K.
APPLE, F.
BALFOUR, H. J.
BROWN, D. M.
CLARK, B.
ECKFELDT, J.
ELLIS, L.
FERRIERI, P.
FINKELSTEIN, S.
FURCHT, L. T.
GARRY, V.
GATEWOOD, L. C.
HALBERG, F.
HAUS, E.
HECHT, S.
HORWITZ, C.
JESSURUN, J.
KERSEY, J. H.
LEBIEN, T.
MCCARTHY, J.
MCCULLOUGH, J. J.
MCIVOR, S.
MALEJKA-GIGANTI, D.
MANIVEL, C.
MESCHER, M.
ORR, H.
RAO, G.
ROSE, A.
SHIMIZU, Y.
STANLEY, M.
TSAI, M.
WATTENBERG, L.
WELLS, C.
WHITE, J.
WILSON, M.

Landscape Architecture (1425 University Ave, SE, Minneapolis, MN 55455; tel. (612) 625-6860; fax (612) 625-0710; internet www.cala.umn.edu/landscape_architecture/landscape.html):

NECKAR, L.
PITT, D.

Law (285 Mondale Hall, 229 19th Ave, S, Minneapolis, MN 55455; tel. (612) 625-1000; fax (612) 625-2011; internet www.law.umn.edu):

ADAMS, E.
BEFORT, S.
BURK, P.
BURKHART, A.
CHEN, J.
COOPER, L. J.
DRIPPS, D.
ERICKSON, M.
FARBER, D. A.
FELD, B. C.
FELLOWS, M. L.
FRASE, R. S.
GIFFORD, D. J.
KELLY, B.
KOEPPEN, B.
MARSHALL, D. P.
MATHESON, J.
MORRISON, F. L.
MUNDSTOCK, G.
OKEDIJI, R.
PAULSEN, M.
POWELL, J.
SAMAHA, A.
SCHOETTLE, F.
SHARPE, C.
STEIN, R. A.
TONRY, M. H.
WEISS, F.
WEISSBRODT, D. S.
WOLF, S.
YOUNGER, J.
YUDOF, M.

Life Course Center (1014 Social Sciences Bldg, 267 19th Ave, S, Minneapolis, MN 55455; tel. (612) 624-6333; fax (612) 624-7020; internet www.soc.umn.edu/research/aboutlcc.htm):

KRUTTSCHNITT, C.
LASLETT, B.
MALMQUIST, C.
MORTIMER, J.
STRYKER, R.

Limnological Research Center (220 Pillsbury Hall, 310 Pillsbury Dr., SE, Minneapolis, MN 55455; tel. (612) 624-7005; fax (612) 625-3819; internet lrc.geo.umn.edu):

BANERJEE, S. K.
CUSHING, E. J.
EDWARDS, L.
ITO, E.
JOHNSON, T. C.
MEGARD, R. O.

Linguistics (214 Nolte Center for Continuing Education, 315 Pillsbury Dr., SE, Minneapolis, MN 55455; tel. (612) 624-3331; fax (612) 624-4579; e-mail umling@tc.umn.edu):

GUNDEL, J.

Marketing and Logistics Management (3-150 Carlson School of Managment, 321 19th Ave, S, Minneapolis, MN 55455; tel. (612) 624-5055; fax (612) 624-8804; internet www.csom.umn.edu/wwwpages/depts/mktg/mktgdept.htm):

HOUSTON, M.
JOHN, D.
JOHN, G.
LOKEN, B.
MEYERS-LEVY, J.
ROERING, K.
RUEKERT, R.
WALKER, O.

Mathematics (127 Vincent Hall, 206 Church St, SE, Minneapolis, MN 55455; tel. (612) 625-2004; fax (612) 626-2017; e-mail dpt@math.umn.edu; internet www.math.umn.edu):

ADAMS, S.
AGARD, S.
ANDERSON, G.
ARNOLD, D.
ARONSON, D.
BAXTER, J.
BOBKOV, S.
BRAMSON, M.
CALDERER, M. C.
COCKBURN, B.
FESHBACH, M.
FRISTEDT, B.
GARRETT, P.
GOLDMAN, J.
GRAY, L.
GULLIVER, R.
HARRIS, M.
HEJHAL, D.
JAIN, N.
JODEIT, M.
KAHN, D.
KEYNES, H.
KRYLOV, N.
LITTMAN, W.
LOWENGRUB, J.
LUSKIN, M.
LYUBEZNIK, G.
MCCARTHY, C.
MCGEHEE, R.
MARDEN, A.
MESSING, W.
MEYERS, N.
MILLER, W., Jr
MOECKEL, R.
NI, W.-M.
ODLYZKO, A.
OLVER, P.
OTHMER, H.
POLACIK, P.
PRIKRY, K.
REINER, V.
REITICH, F.
REJTO, P.
ROBERTS, J.
SAFONOV, M.
SANTOSA, F.
SELL, G.
SPERBER, S.
STANTON, D.
STORVICK, D.
WEBB, P.
WHITE, D.

Mechanical Engineering (1100 Mechanical Engineering, 111 Church St, SE, Minneapolis, MN 55455; tel. (612) 625-0705; fax (612) 626-1854; e-mail mech-eng-info@me.umn.edu; internet www.me.umn.edu):

ARORA, S. R.
BAR-COHEN, A.
DAVIDSON, J.
DONATH, M.
DURFEE, W.
ERDMAN, A. G.
GIRSHICK, S.
HEBERLEIN, J.
KITTLESON, D. B.
KLAMECHI, B.
KUEHN, T. H.
KULACKI, F.
KVÅLSETH, T. O.
LEWIS, J.
MCMURRY, P. H.
MARPLE, V. A.
PUI, D.
RAMALINGAM, S.
RAMSEY, J. W.
SIMON, T. W.
SPARROW, E. M.
STARR, P.
STELSON, K.
STRYKOWSKI, P.
TAMMA, K.

Medical Biotechnology (7-105 Basic Sciences and Biomedical Engineering, 312 Church St, SE, Minneapolis, MN 55455; tel. (612) 626-2366; fax (612) 625-1121; internet www.med.umn.edu/imb):

FURCHT, L.
MCCARTHY, J.
MCCULLOUGH, J.
RAO, G.

Medical Technology (15-170 Phillips-Wangensteen Bldg, 516 Delaware St, SE, Minneapolis, MN 55455; tel. (612) 625-9490; fax (612) 625-5901; e-mail medtech@tc.umn.edu):

TSAI, M.
WELLS, C.

Medicinal Chemistry (8-101 Weaver-Densford Hall, 308 Harvard St, SE, Minneapolis, MN 55455; tel. (612) 624-9919; fax (612) 624-0139; internet www.pharmacy.umn.edu):

ABUL-HAJJ, Y. J.
HANNA, P. E.
HECHT, S. S.
JOHNSON, R. L.
NAGASAWA, H. T.
PORTOGHESE, P. S.
REMMEL, R. P.
SHIER, W. T.
SPEEDIE, M. K.
VINCE, R.

Medicine (100 Philips-Wangensteen Bldg, 516 Delaware St, SE, Minneapolis, MN 55455; tel. (612) 625-7140):

ANAND, I.
ASINGER, R.
BACHE, R.
BANTLE, J.
BEHRENS, T.
BENDITT, D.
BILLINGTON, C.
BITTERMAN, P.
BLUMENTHAL, M.
BOND, J.
CHESLER, E.
CHRISTIANSON, J.
COHN, J. N.
COLLINS, A.
CROSSLEY, K.
DANIELS, B.
DAVIES, S.
DUANE, W.
FROHNERT, P.
FROM, A.
GEORGOPOULOS, A.
GLASSER, S.
GOLDSMITH, S.
GOODMAN, J.
GRAY, R.
GRIMM, R.
HAASE, A.
HEBBEL, R.
HERTZ, M.
HOLTZMAN, J.
HOSTETTER, T.
HOWE, R.
HUNNINGHAKE, D.
INGBAR, D.
JANOFF, E.
JOHNSON, G.
JOHNSON, J.
KAHN, J.
KASISKE, B.
KEANE, W.
KENNEDY, H.
KING, R.
KUBO, S.
LAKE, J.
LEDERLE, F.
LEVINE, A.
LEVITT, M. D.
LUEPKER, R.
LUIKART, S.
LURIE, N.
MCCLAVE, P.
MAHOWALD, M.
MARIASH, C.
MARINI, J.
MESSNER, R.
MILES, S.
MILLER, J.
MILLER, L.
MILLER, W.
MOLDOW, C.
MUELLER, D.
NICHOL, K.
NIEWOEHNER, D.
NUTTALL, F. O.
PALLER, M.
PENTEL, P.
PETERSON, B.
PETERSON, P. K.
PIERACH, C.
POPKIN, M.
RAIJ, L.
RAO, K.
RAVDIN, J.
ROSENBERG, A.
ROSENBERG, M.
RUBINS, H.
SABATH, L. D.
SIMON, G.
SKUBITZ, K.
STEER, C.
TAYLOR, A.
UGURBIL, K.
VERCELLOTTI, G.
VERFAILLIE, C.
WEIR, E. K.
WEISDORF, D.
WHITE, C.
WILLIAMS, D.
WILSON, R.
WOLF, S.
YEE, D.

Microbial Biochemistry and Biotechnology (156 Gortner Laboratory, 1479 Gortner Ave, St Paul, MN 55108; tel. (612) 625-3785; fax (612) 625-5780; internet www.cbs.umn.edu/bmbb):

ANDERSON, J. S.
FLICKINGER, M. C.
HOOPER, A. B.
SCHOTTEL, J. L.

Microbiology (1460 Mayo Memorial Bldg (MMC 196), 420 Delaware St, SE, Minneapolis, MN 55455; tel. (612) 624-6190; fax (612) 626-0623; e-mail micro@lenti.med.umn.edu; internet www.microbiology.med.umn.edu):

BERMAN, J.
CLEARY, P. P.
DUNNY, G.
DWORKIN, M.
FARAS, A. J.
HAASE, A.
HANSON, R.
JENKINS, M.
JOHNSON, R. C.
MAGEE, P. T.
PLAGEMANN, P. G. W.
SCHLIEVERT, P. M.
SHERMAN, D.

Molecular and Cellular Therapy (D-242 Mayo Memorial Bldg (MMC 609), 420 Delaware St, SE, Minneapolis, MN 55455; tel. (612) 626-3272; fax (612) 625-0617; internet www.mbbnet.umn.edu/institutes/cmct):

McCULLOUGH, J.
MILLER, J.

Molecular Biology (6-155 Jackson Hall, 321 Church St, SE, Minneapolis, MN 55455; tel. (612) 625-6100; fax (612) 625-2163; internet www.cbs.umn.edu/bmbb):

DAS, A.
FUCHS, J. A.
LAPORTE, D. C.
LIVINGSTON, D. M.
SANDERS, M. M.
TOWLE, H. C.
VANNESS, B. G.

Music (100 Donald N. Ferguson Hall, 2106 4th St, S, Minneapolis, MN 55455; tel. (612) 624-5740; fax (612) 626-2200; internet www.music.umn.edu):

ANDERSON, J.
ASHWORTH, T.
BALDWIN, D.
BRAGINSKY, A.
CHERLIN, M.
GARRETT, M.
GRAYSON, D.
HAACK, P.
JACKSON, D.
KIRCHHOFF, C.
KONKOLL, K.
LANCASTER, T.
LUBET, A.
McCURDY, R.
MAURICE, G.
O'REILLY, S.
REMENIKOVA, T.
SHOCKLEY, R.
SUTTON, V.
WARE, D. C.
WELLER, L.
ZAIMONT, J. L.

Naval Science (203 Armory Bldg, 15 Church St, SE, Minneapolis, MN 55455; tel. (612) 625-6677; fax (612) 624-5030; e-mail nrotc@umn.edu; internet www.umn.edu/nrotc):

FREY, W.

Neurology (12-100 Phillips-Wangensteen Bldg (MMC 295), 516 Delaware St, SE, Minneapolis, MN 55455; tel. (612) 625-9900; fax (612) 625-7950; internet www.neurology.umn.edu):

ANSARI, K.
ASHE, K.
CRANFORD, R.
ETTINGER, M.
GEORGOPOULOS, A.
IADECOLA, C.
KENNEDY, W. R.
KLASSEN, A. C.
KNOPMAN, D.
KRIEL, R.
LOCKMAN, L.
MAHOWALD, M.
MORIARTY, G.
NELSON, C.
PARRY, G.
RAMIREZ-LASSEPAS, M.
ROSS, E. M.
ROTTENBERG, D.
SHAPIRO, E.
TRUWITT, C.
WIRTSCHAFTER, J.

Neuroscience (6-145 Jackson Hall, 321 Church St, SE, Minneapolis, MN 55455; tel. (612) 626-6800; fax (612) 626-5009; internet www.neurosci.umn.edu):

CARROLL, M.
ELDE, R.
EL-FAKAHANY, E.
ENGELAND, W.
FLANDERS, M.
GEORGOPOULOS, A.
GIESLER, G., Jr
IADECOLA, C.
JUHN, S.
LARSON, A.
LETOURNEAU, P.
LEVINE, A.
McLOON, S.
MANTYH, P.
MILLER, R.
NEWMAN, E.
POPPELE, R.
SANTI, P.
SEYBOLD, V.
SOECHTING, J.
SORENSON, P.
SPARBER, S.
UGURBIL, K.
WILCOX, G.

Neurosurgery (D-429 Mayo Memorial Bldg (MMC 96), 420 Delaware St, SE, Minneapolis, MN 55455; tel. (612) 624-6666; fax (612) 624-0644; internet www.neuro.umn.edu):

EFANGE, S. M. N.
HALL, W. A.
KUCHARCZYK, J.
LOW, W. C.
MAXWELL, R. E.
ROCKSWOLD, G. L.
WIRTSCHAFTER, J. D.

Nuclear Medicine (2-449 Fairview Univ. Medical Center (MMC 292), 420 Delaware St, SE, Minneapolis, MN 55455; tel. (612) 273-4092; fax (612) 273-1950; internet www.med.umn.edu/radiology):

ANDERSON, Q.
EFRANGE, S.
GOMES, M.

Nursing (6-101 Weaver-Densford Hall, 308 Harvard St, SE, Minneapolis, MN 55455; tel. (612) 624-9600; fax (612) 626-2359; internet www.nursing.umn.edu):

BEARINGER, L.
DISCH, J.
EDWARDSON, S.
GROSS, C.
HODGE, F.
LEONARD, B.
WYMAN, J.

Obstetrics, Gynaecology and Women's Health (12-211 Malcolm Moos Health Sciences Tower, 515 Delaware St, SE, Minneapolis, MN 55455; tel. (612) 626-3111; fax (612) 626-0665; internet www.med.umn.edu/obgyn):

CARSON, L.
DE JONGE, C.
GAZIANO, E. P.
KNOX, G. E.
LEUNG, B. S.
MARTENS, M. G.
OKAGAKI, T.
POTISH, R.
RAMAKRISHAN, S.
THOMPSON, T. R.
TROFATTER, K. F.
TWIGGS, L. B.

Operations and Management Science (3-150 Carlson School of Management, 321 19th Ave, S, Minneapolis, MN 55455; tel. (612) 624-7010; fax (612) 624-8804; internet carlsonschool.umn.edu/csom/deptinfo.html):

ANDERSON, J. C.
CHERVANY, N.
HILL, A. V.
NACHTSHEIM, C.
SCHROEDER, R. G.

Ophthalmology (9th Fl., Phillips-Wangensteen Bldg, 516 Delaware St, SE, Minneapolis, MN 55455; tel. (612) 625-4400; fax (612) 626-3119; internet www.med.umn.edu/ophthalmology):

DOUGHMAN, D. J.
GREGERSON, D. S.
KRACHMER, J. H.
NELSON, J. D.
SUMMERS, C. G.
WIRTSCHAFTER, J. D.

Oral Sciences (17-252 Malcolm Moos Health Sciences Tower, 515 Delaware St, SE, Minneapolis, MN 55455; tel. (612) 624-9123; fax (612) 626-2651; internet www1.umn.edu/dental/department/oralsci/dep_oral.html):

ANDERSON, D. L.
COMBE, E.
DELONG, R.
DOUGLAS, W. H.
GERMAINE, G. R.
LILJEMARK, W. F.
ROHRER, M.
SCHACHTELE, C. F.
SHAPIRO, B. L.

Orthodontics (6-320 Malcolm Moos Health Sciences Tower, 515 Delaware St, SE, Minneapolis, MN 55455; tel. (612) 625-5110; fax (612) 626-2571):

SPEIDEL, T. M.

Orthopaedic Surgery (350 Variety Club Research Center, 401 E River Rd, Minneapolis, MN 55455; tel. (612) 625-1177; fax (612) 625-6032):

LEWIS, J. L.
OEGEMA, T., Jr
OGILVIE, J.
SWIONTKOWSKI, M.
THOMPSON, R. C., Jr

Otolaryngology (8-240 Phillips-Wangensteen Bldg (MMC 396), 516 Delaware St, SE, Minneapolis, MN 55455; tel. (612) 625-3200; fax (612) 625-2101):

ADAMS, G.
GIEBINK, G. S.
JUHN, S. K.
MAISEL, R.
MARGOLIS, R.
NELSON, D.
SANTI, P.

Paediatric Dentistry (6-150 Malcolm Moos Health Sciences Tower, 515 Delaware St, SE, Minneapolis, MN 55455; tel. (612) 624-1985; fax (612) 629-2900; internet www.umn.edu/dental/department/prevsci/div_pediatric.html):

BEIRAGHI, S.
MOLLER, K.
TILL, M.

Paediatrics (13-118 Phillips Wangensteen Bldg, 516 Delaware St, SE, Minneapolis, MN 55455; tel. (612) 624-3113; fax (612) 626-6601):

BALFOUR, H.
BELANI, K.
BERRY, S.
BLAZAR, B.
BLUM, R.
BLUMENTHAL, M.
BROWN, D. M.
CHAVERS, B.
CLAWSON, C. C.
FERRIERI, P.
FISH, A.
GEORGIEFF, M.
GIEBINK, G. S.
HULL, H.
INGBAR, D.
JOHNSON, D.
KAPLAN, E.
KASHTAN, C.
KERSEY, J.
KIM, Y.
KING, R.
KOHEN, D.
KRIEL, R.
LOCKMAN, L.
MAMMEL, M.
MAUER, S. M.
MOLLER, J.
NELSON, C.
NEVINS, T.
OGILVIE, J.

RAMSAY, N.
REMAFEDI, G.
RESNICK, M.
ROBISON, L.
SHAPIRO, E.
SHARP, H.
SINAIKO, A.
STORY, M.
SUMMERS, G.
THOMPSON, T.
TRUWIT, C.
WAGNER, J.
WANGENSTEEN, O. D.
WARWICK, W.
WHITE, J.
WHITLEY, C.

Periodontology (7-368 Malcolm Moos Health Sciences Tower, 515 Delaware St, SE, Minneapolis, MN 55455; tel. (612) 625-5400; fax (612) 626-2652; internet www.umn.edu/dental/department/prevsci/div_perio.html):

BAKDASH, B.
HERZBERG, M. C.
PHILSTROM, B. L.
WOLFF, L. F.

Pharmaceutical Care and Health Systems (7-159 Weaver-Densford Hall, 308 Harvard St, SE, Minneapolis, MN 55455; tel. (612) 626-9938; e-mail tesda001@tc.umn.edu; internet www.pharmacy.umn.edu):

CIPOLLE, R. J.
MORLEY, P. C.
SCHONDELMEYER, S. W.
STRAND, I. M.
WEAVER, L. C.

Pharmaceutics (9-177 Weaver-Densford Hall, 308 Harvard St, SE, Minneapolis, MN 55455; tel. (612) 624-5151; fax (612) 626-2125; internet www.pharmacy.umn.edu/resgrad/pceutics/pharmaceuticshome.html):

BRAECKMAN, R.
FREY II, W. H.
GRANT, D. J. W.
RESCIGNO, A.
SAWCHUK, R. J.
SIEGEL, R. A.
SURYANARAYANAN, R. G.

Pharmacology (6-120 Jackson Hall, 321 Church St, SE, Minneapolis, MN 55455; tel. (612) 625-9997; fax (612) 625-8408; internet www.pharmacology.med.umn.edu):

BEATTIE, C. W.
CONTI-FINE, B.
EL-ZAKAHANY, E.
HANNA, P. E.
HOLTZMAN, J. L.
HUNNINGHAKE, D. B.
LAW, P.
LEE, H. C.
LOH, H. H.
PENTEL, P. R.
SINAIKO, A. R.
SLADEK, N. E.
SPARBER, S. B.
THAYER, A.
WILCOX, G. L.
WOOD, W. G.
YEE, D.
ZIMMERMAN, B. G.

Philosophy (831 Walter W. Heller Hall, 271 19th Ave, S, Minneapolis, MN 55455; tel. (612) 625-6563; fax (612) 624-8380; internet philosophy.umn.edu):

BOWIE, N.
DAHL, N. O.
EATON, M. M.
GIERE, R.
GUNDERSON, K.
HANSON, W. H.
HELLMAN, G.
HOPKINS, J. S.
KAC, M.
LEWIS, D.
LONGINO, H.
OWENS, J.
PETERSON, S.
SAVAGE, C. W.
SCHEMAN, N.
WALLACE, J. R.

Philosophy of Science (746 Walter W. Heller Hall, 271 19th Ave, S, Minneapolis, MN 55455; tel. (612) 625-6635; fax (612) 626-8380; internet www.mcps.umn.edu):

GIERE, R.
GUNDERSON, K.
HANSON, W.
HELLMAN, G.
LONGINO, H.
SAVAGE, C. W.
SHAPIRO, A.
STUEWER, R.

Physical Medicine and Rehabilitation (500 Boynton (MMC), Minneapolis, MN 55455; tel. (612) 626-4050; fax (612) 624-6686; internet www.mcps.umn.edu):

DI FABIO., R.
PATTERSON, R.

Physics and Astronomy (148 Tate Lab of Physics, 116 Church St, SE, Minneapolis, MN 55455; tel. (612) 624-7375; fax (612) 624-4578; internet www.physics.umn.edu):

BROADHURST, J. H.
CAMPBELL, C. E.
CATTELL, C.
CUSHMAN, P.
DAHLBERG, E. D.
ELLIS, P. J.
GOLDMAN, A. M.
GROSBERG, A.
HALLEY, J. W.
HELLER, K. J.
HUANG, C. C.
KAKALIOS, J.
KAPUSTA, J. I.
LARKIN, A.
LYSAK, R. L.
MARSHAK, M. L.
PEPIN, R. O.
PETERSON, E. A.
POLING, K.
RUDAZ, S.
RUDDICK, K.
RUSACK, R.
SHIFMAN, M.
SHKLOVSKII, B.
VAINSHTEIN, A.
VALLS, O. T.
VOLOSHIN, M.
WALSH, T. F.

Physiology (6-125 Jackson Hall, 321 Church St, SE, Minneapolis, MN 55455; tel. (612) 625-5902; fax (612) 625-5149; internet physiology.med.umn.edu):

DI SALVO, J.
IAIZZO, P.
LEVITT, D.
LOW, W.
O'GRADY, S.
OSBORN, J.
WANGENSTEEN, O. D.
WEIR, K. E.

Plant Biology (220 Biological Sciences Center, 1445 Gortner Ave, St Paul, MN 55108; tel. (612) 625-1234; fax (612) 625-1738; e-mail pbio@ux.acs.umn.edu; internet www.cbs.umn.edu/plantbio/pbio):

BIESBOER, D. D.
BRAMBL, R.
CHARVAT, L.
GLEASON, F. K.
KOUKKARI, W. L.
MCLAUGHLIN, D. J.
OLSZEWSKI, N. E.
SNUSTAD, P. D.
VANDENBOSCH, K.
WETMORE, C. M.
WICK, S.

Plant Pathology (495 Borlaug Hall, 1991 Upper Buford Circle, St Paul, MN 55108; tel. (612) 625-8200; fax (612) 625-9728; internet www.plpa.agri.umn.edu):

BLANCHETTE, R. A.
GROTH, J. V.
JONES, R. K.
KINKEL, L. L.
KRUPA, S. V.
LARSEN, P. O.
LOCKHART, B. E.
MACDONALD, D. H.
NYVALL, R. F.
PERCICH, J. A.
PFLEGER, F. L.
WINDELS, C. E.
YOUNG, N. D.
ZEYEN, R. J.

Political Science (1414 Social Sciences Bldg, 267 19th Ave, S, Minneapolis, MN 55455; tel. (612) 624-4144; fax (612) 626-7599; internet www.polisci.umn.edu):

DIETZ, M.
DUVALL, R.
FARR, J.
FLANIGAN, W. H.
FOGELMAN, E.
JACOBS, L.
KVAVIK, R.
NIMITZ, A.
ROSENSTONE, S.
SCOTT, T. M.
SHIVELY, W. P.

Psychiatry Research (628 Diehl Hall (MMC 392), 505 Essex St, SE, Minneapolis, MN 55455; tel. (612) 626-4034; fax (612) 624-8939):

CARROLL, M. E.
EL-FAKAHANY, E.
HATSUKAMI, D.

Psychological Foundations of Education (206 Burton Hall, 178 Pillsbury Drive, SE, Minneapolis, MN 55455; tel. (612) 624-6083; fax (612) 624-8241; internet www.coled.umn.edu/edpsych/default.html):

BART, W.
DAVISON, M.
HARWELL, H.
JOHNSON, D.
LAWRENZ, F.
MARUYAMA, G.
PELLEGRINI, A.
SAMUELS, S. J.
TENNYSON, R.
VAN DEN BROEK, P.

Psychology (N-218 Elliot Hall, 75 East River Rd, Minneapolis, MN 55455; tel. (612) 625-4042; fax (612) 626-2079; internet www.psych.umn.edu):

BORGIDA, E.
BOUCHARD, T. J.
BURKHARDT, D. A.
BUTCHER, J. N.
CAMPBELL, J. P.
CUDECK, R.
DAVIS, E. R.
DUNETTE, M.
FOX, P.
GARMEZY, N.
HANSEN, J. I.
KERSTEN, D.
LEON, G. R.
LYKKEN, D.
MCGUE, M.
MATOWIDLOS, S.
MOTOWIDLO, S.
OVERMIER, J. B.
PATRICK, C.
SACKETT, D.
SNYDER, M.
TELLEGEN, A.
VIEMEISTER, N. F.

WEISS, D. J.

Public Health Administration (D-359 Mayo Memorial Bldg (MMC 97), 420 Delaware St, SE, Minneapolis, MN 55455; tel. (612) 625-9480; fax (612) 624-5920; internet www.hsr.umn.edu):

McBEAN, M.
VENINGA, R.

Public Health Nutrition (300 W Bank Office Bldg, 1300 52nd St, Minneapolis, MN 55455; tel. (612) 624-1818; fax (612) 624-0315; internet www.epi.umn.edu):

BROWN, J. E.
HIMES, J. H.
JEFFERY, R. W.
LUEPKER, R. V.
PERRY, C.
STORY, M. T.

Radiology (2-300 Fairview Univ. Medical Center (MMC 292), 420 Delaware St, SE, Minneapolis, MN 55455; tel. (612) 273-6004; fax (612) 273-1470; internet www.med.umn.edu/radiology):

EFANGE, S.
GARWOOD, M.
HU, X.
HUNTER, D.
JEROSCH-HERALD, M.
KIEFFER, S.
KIM, S.
KUCHARCZYK, J.
REINKE, D.
RITENOUR, E. R.
STEENSON, C.
STILLMAN, A.
TRUWIT, C.
UGURBIL, K.

Recreation and Sports Studies (220 Cooke Hall, 1900 University Ave, SE, Minneapolis, MN 55455; tel. (612) 625-5300; fax (612) 626-7700; internet www.kls.umn.edu):

KANE, M. J.
McAVOY, L.

Regulatory Biochemistry (374 Gortner Lab, 1479 Gortner Ave, St Paul, MN 55108; tel. (612) 624-3622; internet www.cbs.umn.edu/bmbb):

BERNLOHR, D. A.
CONTI-FINE, B. M.
DEMPSEY, M. E.
KOERNER, J. F.
LOUIS, C. F.
NELSESTUEN, G. L.
OEGEMA, T. G.
RAFTERY, M. A.

Rhetoric (4 Classroom Office Bldg, 1994 Buford Ave, St Paul, MN 55108; tel. (612) 624-3445; fax (612) 624-3617; internet www.rhetoric.umn.edu):

BECKER, S.
BERKEKOTTER
GROSS, A. G.
LAY, M. M.
McDOWELL, E. E.
MARCHAND, W. M.
MIKELONIS, V. M.
WAHLSTROM, B. J.
WHARTON, W. K.

Rural Sociology and Community Analysis (230 Peters Hall, 1404 Gortner Ave, St Paul, MN 55108; tel. (612) 625-4779; fax (612) 625-3746; internet ssw.che.umn.edu/centers.htm#crsca):

McTAVISH, D.
MENANTEAU, D.
MEYERS, S. S.

St Anthony Falls Laboratory (2 Third Ave, SE, Minneapolis, MN 55414; tel. (612) 627-4010; fax (612) 627-4609; internet www.umn.edu/safl):

ARNDT, R.
FARELL, C.
FOUFOULA-GEORGIOU, E.
GULLIVER, J.
PAOLA, C.
PARKER, G.
SONG, C.
STEFAN, H.
VOLLER, V.

School Psychology (344 Elliot Hall, 75 E River Rd, Minneapolis, MN 55455; tel. (612) 624-4156; fax (612) 624-0879; internet education.umn.edu/edpsych):

CHRISTENSON, S.
McCONNELL, S.
YSSELDYKE, J.

Scientific Computation (Graduate Programme) (7-125 Weaver Densford Hall, 308 Harvard St, SE, Minneapolis, MN 55455; tel. (612) 626-2601; fax (612) 626-4429):

ANDERSON, R.
BOLEY, D.
CANDLER, G.
CHELIKOWSKY, J.
COCKBURN, B.
CRAMER, C.
DERBY, J.
EBNER, T.
FONTOULA-GEORGIO, E. F.
FRIEDMAN, A.
KERSTEN, D.
KUMAR, V.
LOWENGRUB, J.
LUSKIN, M.
NIEBER, J.
OTHMER, H.
PARK, H.
PATANKAR, S.
SAAD, Y.
SCRIVEN, L. E.
SELL, G.
SONG, C.
SRIVASTAVA, J.
STECH, H.
THOMAS, D.
TIERNEY, L.
TRUHLAR, D.
TWETIK, A. H.
VOLLER, V.
WILCOX, G.
WOODWARD, P.
YUEN, D.

Slavic and Central Asian Languages and Literatures (214 Nolte Center for Continuing Education, 315 Pillsbury Dr., SE, Minneapolis, MN 55455; tel. (612) 624-3331; fax (612) 624-4579; e-mail iles@umn.edu):

BASHIRI, I.
JAHN, G.

Small Animal Clinical Sciences (C-339 Veterinary Teaching Hospitals, 1352 Boyd Ave and 1365 Gortner Ave, St Paul, MN 55108; tel. (612) 625-7744; fax (612) 624-0751):

ARMSTRONG, P. J.
BISTNER, S.
FEENEY, D.
HARDY, R.
JESSEN, C.
KLAUSNER, J.
LIPOWITZ, A.
OSBORNE, C.
POLZIN, D.
REDIG, P.
WALLACE, L.

Social Administrative and Clinical Pharmacy (7-155 Weaver-Densford Hall, 308 Harvard St, SE, Minneapolis, MN 55455; tel. (612) 624-2973; fax (612) 625-9931; internet www.pharmacy.umn.edu):

CIPOLLE, R. J.
GARRARD, J. M.
GATEWOOD, L. C.
LANGLEY, P. C.
MORLEY, P. C.
SCHONDELMEYER, S. W.
SPEEDIE, S. M.
STRAND, L. M.
WEAVER, L. C.
WECKWERTH, V. E.
ZASKE, D. E.

Social Work (105 Peters Hall, 1404 Gortner Ave, St Paul, MN 55108; tel. (612) 625-1220; fax (612) 624-3744; internet ssw.che.umn.edu):

BAIZERMAN, M.
BEKER, J.
EDLESON, J.
GILGUN, J.
HOLLISTER, D.
KIVNICK, H.
MENANTEAU, D.
MEYERS, S.
QUAM, J.
ROONEY, R.
UMBREIT, M.
WELLS, S.

Sociology (909 Social Sciences Bldg, 267 19th Ave, S, Minneapolis, MN 55455; tel. (612) 624-4300; fax (612) 624-7020; internet www.soc.umn.edu):

AMINZADE, R.
ANDERSON, J.
ANDERSON, R. E.
GALASKIEWICZ, J.
KNOKE, D.
KRUTTSCHNITT, C.
LASLETT, B.
LEIK, R. K.
MALMQUIST, C.
MARINI, M.
MORTIMER, J.
NELSON, J. I.
STRYKER, R.

Soil, Water, and Climate (439 Borlaug Hall, 1991 Upper Buford Circle, St Paul, MN 55108; tel. (612) 625-1244; fax (612) 625-2208; internet www.soils.agri.umn.edu):

ALLAN, D. L.
ANDERSON, J. L.
BAKER, J. M.
BLOOM, P. R.
CLAPP, C.
COOPER, T. H.
DOWDY, R. H.
GRAHAM, P. H.
GUPTA, S. C.
HALBACH, T. R.
KOSKINEN, W. C.
LAMB, J. A.
MALZER, G.
MOLINA, J. A.
MONCRIEF, J. F.
MULLA, D. J.
NATER, E. A.
RANDALL, G. W.
REHM, G. W.
REICOSKY, D. C.
ROBERT, P. C.
ROSEN, C. J.
RUSSELLE, M. P.
SADOWSKI, M. J.
SCHMITT, M. A.
SEELEY, M. W.

Spanish and Portuguese (34 Folwell Hall, 9 Pleasant St, SE, Minneapolis, MN 55455; tel. (612) 625-5858; fax (612) 625-3549; internet spansport.cla.umn.edu):

JARA, R.
SPADACCINI, N.
VIDAL, H.

Special Education Programs (227 Burton Hall, 178 Pillsbury Drive, SE, Minneapolis, MN 55455; tel. (612) 624-2342; fax (612) 626-9627; internet education.umn.edu/edpsych):

DENO, S.
HUPP, S.
McEVOY, M.

Statistics (313 Ford Hall, 224 Church St, SE, Minneapolis, MN 55455; tel. (612) 625-8046; fax (612) 624-8858; internet www.stat.umn.edu):

BINGHAM, C.
CHALONER, K.
COOK, R. D.
DICKEY, J.
EATON, M. L.
GEISSER, S.
GEYER, C.
HAWKINS, D.
MEEDEN, G.
OEHLERT, G.
SUDDERTH, W. D.
TIERNEY, L.
WEISBERG, S.

Strategic Management and Organization (3-353 Carlson School of Management, 321 19th Ave, S, Minneapolis, MN 55455; tel. (612) 624-5232; fax (612) 626-1316; internet www.csom.umn.edu/wwwpages/depts/smo):

BROMILEY, P.
ERICKSON, W. B.
LENWAY, S.
MAITLAND, I.
MARCUS, A.
NICHOLS, M.
SAPIENZA, H.
VAN DE VEN, A.

Structural Biology and Biophysics (140 Gortner Laboratory, 1479 Gortner Ave, St Paul, MN 55108; tel. (612) 625-6100; e-mail bmbb@biosci.cbs.umn.edu; internet www.cbs.umn.edu/bmbb):

ARMITAGE, I. M.
BANASZAK, L. J.
BARRY, B. A.
BLOOMFIELD, V. A.
HOGENKAMP, H. P.
HOWARD, J. B.
LIPSCOMB, J. D.
LOVRIEN, R. E.
MAYO, K. H.
OHLENDORF, D. H.
THOMAS, D. D.
TSONG, T. Y.

Surgery (11-100 Phillips-Wangensteen Bldg (MMC 195), 516 Delaware St, SE, Minneapolis, MN 55455; tel. (612) 625-1400; fax (612) 625-8496; internet www.surg.umn.edu):

BOLMAN, R. M., III
BUCHWALD, H.
CERRA, F.
CUNNINGHAM, B.
DALMASSO, A.
DRIES, D.
DUNN, D.
ENGELAND, W.
EYLER, J.
FOKER, J.
GOODALE, R. L.
GRUESSNER, R.
LAKE, J.
LEE, J. T.
LEVINE, A.
LYTE, M.
MCQUARRIE, D. G.
MATAS, A.
MILLER, L.
MOLINA, E.
PARK, S.
PAYNE, W.
RODRIGUEZ, J.
ROTHENBERGER, D. A.
SAKO, Y.
SHUMWAY, S.
SUTHERLAND, D.
WARD, H.
WELLS, C.

Surgical Sciences (11-100 Phillips-Wangensteen (MMC 195), 516 Delaware St, SE, Minneapolis, MN 55455; tel. (612) 625-1400):

DALMASSO, A.
ENGELAND, W.
EYLER, J.
WELLS, C.

Theatre Arts and Dance (580 Rarig Center, 330 21st Ave, S, Minneapolis, MN 55455; tel. (612) 625-6699; fax (612) 625-6334; e-mail theatre@umn.edu; internet cla.umn.edu/theater):

BROCKMAN, C. L.
KOBIALKA, M.
REID, B.

Therapeutic Radiology/Radiation Oncology (M-26 Masonic Cancer Center (MMC 494), 424 Harvard St, SE, Minneapolis, MN 55455; tel. (612) 626-6146; fax (612) 624-5445; internet www.ahc.umn.edu):

LEE, C. K.
LEVITT, S. H.
POTISH, R. A.
SONG, C. W.
VALLERA, D.

TMJ/Orofacial Pain (6-320 Malcolm Moos Health Sciences Tower, 515 Delaware St, SE, Minneapolis, MN 55455; tel. (612) 624-3130; fax (612) 626-0138):

FRICTON, J.

Toxicology Graduate Programme (244 Veterinary Diagnostic Lab, 1333 Gortner Ave, St Paul, MN 55108; tel. (612) 625-8787; fax (612) 624-8707; internet www.mvdl.umn.edu):

ABUL-HAJJ, Y.
BROWN, D.
CARLSON, R.
DISALVO, J.
DREWES, L.
HANNA, P.
MURPHY, M.
NAGASAWA, H.
NIEMI, G.
PROHASKA, J.
SCHOOK, L.
SPARBER, S.
WALLACE, K.

Urban Studies (348 Social Sciences Bldg, 267 19th Ave, S, Minneapolis, MN 55455; tel. (612) 626-1626; fax (612) 624-1044; internet urbanstudies.cla.umn.edu):

ADAMS, J. S.
FISHER, T.
GALASKIEWICZ, J.
LEITNER, H.
RUNGE, C. F.
SCOTT, T.
SHEPPARD, E.

Urologic Surgery (A-597 Mayo Memorial Bldg (MMC 394), 420 Delaware St, SE, Minneapolis, MN 55455; tel. (612) 625-9933):

HULBERT, J.

Veterinary Diagnostic Medicine (277 Veterinary Diagnostic Lab, 1333 Gortner Ave, St Paul, MN 55108; tel. (612) 625-8787; internet www.mvdl.umn.edu):

COLLINS, J.
GOYAL, S.
HAYDEN, D.
KURTZ, H.
O'BRIEN, T.
WALSER, M.

Veterinary Pathobiology (205 Veterinary Science, 1971 Commonwealth Ave, St Paul, MN 55108; tel. (612) 625-5255; fax (612) 625-5203; internet www.cvm.umn.edu):

BEITZ, A. J.
BEY, R. F.
BROWN, D. R.
FLETCHER, T. F.
GALLANT, E. M.
HALVORSON, D. A.
LARSON, A. A.
MAHESWARAN, S. K.
MURTAUGH, M. M.
NAGARAJA, K. V.
SHARMA, J. M.
STROMBERG, B. E.
WEISS, D. J.

Women's Studies (425 Ford Hall, 277 Church St, SE, Minneapolis, MN 55455; tel. (612) 624-6006; fax (612) 624-3573; internet womenstudy.cla.umn.edu):

KAMINSKY, A.
LONGINO, H.
SCHEMAN, N.

Wood and Paper Science (203 Kaufert Lab of Forest Products and Wood Science, 2004 Folwell Ave, St Paul, MN 55108; tel. (612) 625-5200; fax (612) 625-6286; internet www.cnr.umn.edu/wps):

BOWYER, J.
MASSEY, J.
SARKANEN, S.
SCHMIDT, E.

Work, Community and Family Education (Adm 210 Vocational and Technical Education Bldg, 1954 Buford Ave, St Paul, MN 55108; tel. (612) 625-3757; fax (612) 624-2231; e-mail wcfe@umn.edu; internet education.umn.edu/wcfe):

BROWN, J.
LAMBRECHT, J.
LEWIS, T.
MCLEAN, G.
PETERSON, R.
PUCEL, D.
SWANSON, R.
THOMAS, R.

OTHER CAMPUSES

University of Minnesota, Crookston

2900 University Ave, Crookston, MN 56716
Telephone: (218) 281-8020
Fax: (218) 281-8050
E-mail: umcinfo@umn.edu
Internet: www1.crk.umn.edu
Founded 1966
Academic year: August to May
Chancellor: CHARLES H. CASEY
Sr Vice-Chancellor for Academic and Student Affairs: THOMAS BALDWIN
Registrar: ROBERT NELSON
Dir of Centre for Sustainability: Prof. W. DANIEL SVEDARSKY
Dir of Library Services: OWEN WILLIAMS
Number of teachers: 55 full time, 46 part time
Number of students: 2,279

PROFESSORS

ALI, ADEL, Computer Software Technology and Information Technology Management
BRORSON, S., Marketing and Management
DEL VECCHIO, R., Agriculture and Natural Resources
GELLER, J., Sociology
KNOWLTON, D., Art and Sciences
MARX, G., Agricultural, Food, and Environmental Sciences
NEET, S., Art and Sciences
PETERSON, W. C., Art and Sciences
PETERSON, W., Mathematics
SELZLER, B., Art and Sciences
SVEDARSKY, W. D., Natural Resources
WINDELS, C., Agricultural, Food and Environmental Sciences

University of Minnesota, Duluth

1049 University Dr., Duluth, MN 55812
Telephone: (218) 726-8000
Fax: (218) 726-6186
E-mail: sknill@d.umn.edu
Internet: www.d.umn.edu
Founded 1895

Academic year: September to May
Chancellor: KATHRYN A. MARTIN
Vice-Chancellor for Academic Admin.: VINCENT MAGNUSON
Vice-Chancellor for Academic Support and Student Life: BRUCE GILDSETH
Vice-Chancellor for Finance and Operations: GREGORY FOX
Vice-Chancellor for Univ. Relations: WILLIAM WADE
Number of teachers: 431
Number of students: 10,366

DEANS

College of Education and Human Service Professions: PAUL N. DEPUTY
College of Liberal Arts: LINDA KRUG
College of Science Engineering: JAMES P. RIEHL
Duluth School of Medicine: RICHARD ZIEGLER
Labovitz School of Business and Economics: KJELL R. KNUDSEN (acting)
School of Fine Arts: JACK BOWMAN

PROFESSORS

ADAMS, S. J., English
ANDERSON, A. C., Music
ANDERSON, C., Economics
ANDREWS, I. T., Biology
BACIG, T., Sociology—Anthropology
BARTLETT, E., Women's Studies
BELOTE, L., Sociology—Anthropology
BRUSH, G., Art
BRUSH, L., Art
BURNS, S. G., Electrical and Computer Engineering
CAPLE, R., Chemistry
CARLSON, H., Education
CARLSON, R. M., Chemistry
CASTLEBERRY, S., Management Studies
CROUCH, D., Computer Science
DAS, A., Psychology
DEPUTY, P. N., Communication Sciences and Disorders
DREWES, L., Biochemistry and Molecular Biology
DUFF, T., Finance and Management Information Sciences
DURGUNOGLA, A. Y., Psychology
EISENBERG, R. M., Pharmacology
ELLIOT, B. A., Behavioural Sciences
ELLIOT, B. A., Family Medicine
EVANS, J., Chemistry
FALK, D., Social Work
FEROZ, E., Accounting
FETZER, J., Philosophy
FIRLING, C., Biology
FLEISCHMAN, W., Sociology—Anthropology
FUGELSO, M., Industrial Engineering
FULKROD, J., Chemistry
GALLIAN, J. A., Mathematics and Statistics
GORDON, R., Psychology
GRANT, J. A., Geological Sciences
GREEN, R., Mathematics and Statistics
HAFFERTY, F., Behavioural Sciences
HARRISS, D. K., Chemistry
HEDIN, T., Art
HEDMAN, S., Biology
HELLER, L. J., Medical and Molecular Physiology
HILLER, J., Physics
HOLST, T., Geological Sciences
JAMES, B., Mathematics and Statistics
JAMES, K. L., Mathematics and Statistics
JANKOFSKY, K. P., English
JESSWEIN, W. A., Economics
JOHNSON, T., Industrial Engineering
JOHNSON, T. C., Geological Sciences
JORDAN, T. F., Physics
KARIM, M. R., Biology
KENDALL, L. A., Industrial Engineering, MSc in Engineering Management
KLEMER, A., Biology
KLUEG, J., Art
KNOPP, L. M., Jr, Geography
KRAMER, J., Social Work
KRITZMIRE, J., Music
LAUNDERGAN, J. C., Sociology—Anthropology
LETTENSTROM, D., Art
LEY, E., Health, Physical Education and Recreation
LICHTY, R. W., Economics
LIEVANO, R., Finance and Management Information Sciences
LINDEKE, R., Industrial Engineering
LINN, M. D., Composition
LIU, Z., Mathematics and Statistics
MCCARTHY, D. A., Education
MCCLURE, B., Psychology
MAGNUSON, V. R., Chemistry
MAIOLO, J. C., English
MARCHESE, R., Sociology—Anthropology
MARTIN, K. A., Theatre
MAYO, D., Philosophy
MERRIER, P., Finance and Management Information Sciences
MILLER, K., Psychology
MILLER-CLEARY, L., English
MIZUKO, M. I., Communications Sciences and Disorders
MORTON, R., Geological Sciences
NEWSTROM, J. W., Management Studies
OJAKANGAS, R. W., Geological Sciences
PASTOR, J., Biology
PETERSON, J. M., Economics
PIERCE, J. L., Management Studies
POE, D., Chemistry
PROHASKA, J., Biochemistry and Molecular Biology
RAAB, R. L., Economics
RED HORSE, J. G., American Indian Studies
REGAL, J., Pharmacology
REGAL, R., Mathematics and Statistics
RICHARDS, C., Biology
RIEHL, J. P., Chemistry
RILEY, K., Composition
ROUFS, T. G., Sociology—Anthropology
RUBENFELD, S., Management Studies
SEVERSON, A. R., Anatomy and Cell Biology
SEYBOLT, R., Foreign Languages and Literatures
SHARP, P., Political Science
SHEHADEH, N., Electrical and Computer Engineering
SHEPHARD, M., Social Work
SMITH, D., Sociology—Anthropology
STACHOWITZ, M., Electrical and Computer Engineering
STECH, H., Mathematics and Statistics
STEINNES, D. N., Economics
STORCH, N. T., History
STUECHER, U., Psychology
SUNNAFRANK, M., Communication
SYDOR, M., Physics
THOMPSON, L. C., Chemistry
TRACHTE, G., Pharmacology
TROLANDER, J., Women's Studies
TROLANDER, J. A., History
TSAI, B., Chemistry
WALLACE, K., Biochemistry and Molecular Biology
WARD, P., Pathology and Laboratory Medicine
WEGREN, T., Music
WOLD, S., Music
WONG, S., Finance and Management Information Sciences
ZEITZ, E., Foreign Languages and Literatures
ZHDANKIN, V., Chemistry
ZIEGLER, R., Medical Microbiology and Immunology

University of Minnesota, Morris

600 E Fourth St, Morris, MN 56267
Telephone: (320) 589-6035
Fax: (320) 589-6051
E-mail: petersdk@mrs.umn.edu
Internet: www.morris.umn.edu
Founded 1959
Academic year: August to May
Chancellor: JACQUELINE JOHNSON
Vice-Chancellor for Academic Affairs: JUDY A. KUECHLE
Vice-Chancellor for Finance: GARY STREI
Vice-Chancellor for Student Affairs: SANDRA OLSON-LOY
Library Dir: LEANN DEAN
Number of teachers: 128
Number of students: 1,927

PROFESSORS

AHERN, W. H., History
CABRERA, V., Modern Languages
CARLSON, J. A., Music
COTTER, J., Geology
DEMOS, V. P., Sociology
FRENIER, M. D., History
GARARASO, P., Philosophy
GOOCH, V., Biology
GUYOTTE, R., History
HINDS, H. E., Jr, History
HOPPE, D. M., Biology
INGLE, J. S., Art Studio
KISSOCK, C. M., Education
KLINGER, E., Psychology
LEE, J., Political Science
LEE, M.-L., Modern Languages
LOPEZ, A. A., Computer Science
NELLIS, J. G., Art Studio
O'REILLY, M. F., Mathematics
PAYNE, T. R., Theatre Arts
PETERSON, F. W., Art History
PURDY, D. H., English
SCHUMAN, S., English
SUNGUR, E., Mathematics
TOGEAS, J. B., Chemistry
VAN ALSTINE, J. B., Geology

University of Minnesota, Rochester

855 30th Ave, SE, Rochester, MN 55904
Fax: (507) 280-2820
Internet: www.r.umn.edu
Founded 1959
Academic year: August to May
PhD, MA and BA in adult education/human resource devt, business, education, fine arts, health sciences, interpreting, nursing, public health, social work, technology
Provost: DAVID L. CARL
Vice-Provost for Health Sciences: CHUCK CHRISTIANSEN.

UNIVERSITY OF ST THOMAS

2115 Summit Ave, St Paul, MN 55105
Telephone: (651) 962-5000
Fax: (651) 962-6504
E-mail: admissions@stthomas.edu
Internet: www.stthomas.edu
Founded 1885
Academic year: September to May
Pres.: Rev. DENNIS DEASE
Exec. Vice-Pres: Dr MARK DIENHART, Dr THOMAS ROCHON
Vice-Pres. for Business Affairs and Chief Financial Officer: MARK VANSGARD
Vice-Pres. for Information Resources and Technologies: Dr SAMUEL LEVY
Vice-Pres. for Mission: Dr GENE SCAPANSKI
Vice-Pres. for Student Affairs: JANE CANNEY
Vice-Pres. for Univ. and Govt Relations: DOUG HENNES
Registrar: PAUL J. SIMMONS
Librarian: DANIEL GJELTEN
Library of 615,000 vols, 2,200 periodicals
Number of teachers: 782
Number of students: 10,721
Publications: *Logos: A Journal of Catholic Thought and Culture* (4 a year), *New Hibernia Review* (4 a year)

DEANS

College of Arts and Sciences: Dr MARISA KELLY
Graduate School of Professional Psychology: Dr I. DAVID WELCH
Opus College of Business: Dr CHRISTOPHER PUTO
School of Education: Dr SUSAN HUBER
School of Engineering: Dr RONALD BENNETT
School of Law: THOMAS MENGLER
School of Social Work: Dr BARBARA SHANK

WALDEN UNIVERSITY

Minneapolis, MN 55401
Telephone: (866) 492-5336
Internet: www.waldenu.edu

Founded 1970

Pres.: JONATHAN A. KAPLAN
Provost: Dr DENISE DEZOLT
Registrar: LAURA ANN FOREST

DEANS

College of Education: Dr SUSAN E. SAXTON (acting)
College of Social, Behavioural and Health Sciences: Dr GARY J. BURKHOLDER

WILLIAM MITCHELL COLLEGE OF LAW

875 Summit Ave, St Paul, MN 55105-3076
Telephone: (651) 227-9171
Fax: (651) 290-6414
E-mail: admissions@wmitchell.edu
Internet: www.wmitchell.edu

Founded 1900
Private control
Academic year: August to May

Pres. and Dean: ERIC S. JANUS
Vice-Pres. for Finance: NANCY KIN
Vice-Pres. for Human Resources: MARY GALE
Vice-Pres. for Information Technology Services: JAMES VILLARS
Vice-Pres. for Institutional Advancement: LINDA KEILLOR BERG
Registrar: JIM STEVENS
Library Dir: MARY ANN ARCHER

Number of teachers: 40 full-time faculty, 50 adjunct faculty
Number of students: 1,100

Publication: *William Mitchell Law Review* (4 a year).

ATTACHED INSTITUTE

Tobacco Law Center: 875 Summit Ave, Saint Paul, MN 55105; Exec. Dir DOUG BLANKE

PROFESSORS

BYRNE, A.
COLBERT, B.
DUBE, D.
EASLEY, A.
ERLINDER, P.
HAUGEN, P.
HAYDOCK, R.
HAYNSWORTH, H.
HEIDENREICH, D.
HOGG, J.
IIJIMA, A.
JANUS, E.
JORDAN, M.
JUERGENS, A.
KIRWIN, K.
KLASS, A.
KLEINBERGER, D.
KNAPP, P.
KRISHNAN, J.
KUNZ, C.
LEVINE, R.
LOGAN, W.
MOY, C.
MURPHY, R.
OH, P.
OLIPHANT, R.
PANNIER, R.
PORT, K.
PRINCE, D.
RADSAN, J.
ROBERTS, E.
ROY, D.
SCALLEN, E.
SCHAUMANN, N.
SCHMEDMAN, D.
SONSTENG, J.
STEENSON, M.
VER PLOEG, C.
VER STEEGH, N.
WINER, A.

MISSISSIPPI

ALCORN STATE UNIVERSITY

1000 ASU Dr., Alcorn State, MS 39096-7500
Telephone: (601) 877-6100
Fax: (601) 877-2975
Internet: www.alcorn.edu

Founded 1871
Academic year: August to May

Pres.: Dr M. CHRISTOPHER BROWN, II
Vice-Pres. for Academic Affairs: Dr SAMUEL L. WHITE
Vice-Pres. for Finance and Administrative Services: CAROLYN HINTON
Vice-Pres. for Devt and Marketing: STEPHEN MCDANIEL
Vice-Pres. for Student Affairs: GERALD PEOPLES
Registrar: Dr ALICE GILL
Librarian: JESSIE ARNOLD

Library of 269,858 vols
Number of teachers: 226
Number of students: 3,682

Publications: *Alcorn* (univ. magazine), *Alcornite* (1 a year), *Alcorn State University Catalogue* (every 2 years), *ASU Today* (4 a year).

BELHAVEN COLLEGE

1500 Peachtree St, Jackson, MS 39202
Telephone: (601) 968-5940
Fax: (601) 968-8946
E-mail: admission@belhaven.edu
Internet: www.belhaven.edu

Founded 1883
Academic year: August to May

Pres.: Dr ROGER PARROTT
Sr Vice-Pres. and Provost: Dr DANIEL C. FREDERICKS
Vice-Provost and Dean of the Graduate School: (vacant)
Vice-Pres. for Campus Operations: TOM PHILLIPS
Vice-Pres. for Institutional Advancement and Admin.: KEVIN RUSSELL
Vice-Pres. for Student Learning: Dr PAMELA JONES
Chief Financial Officer: VIRGINIA HENDERSON
Dir of Admissions: SUZANNE SULLIVAN
Dir of Library: CRYSTAL STAMPS-ETHERIDGE

Library of 108,042 vols
Number of teachers: 195 (51 full-time, 144 adjunct)
Number of students: 1,883

BLUE MOUNTAIN COLLEGE

POB 160, Blue Mountain, MS 38610
Telephone: (662) 685-4771
Fax: (662) 685-4776
Internet: www.bmc.edu

Sr liberal arts college for women, with co-ordinate programme for men in church-related vocations

Founded 1873
Academic year: August to May

Pres.: BETTYE R. COWARD
Vice-Pres. for Academic Affairs: SHARON ENZOR
Academic Dean: GARTH E. RUNION
Dir of Admissions: MARIA TEEL
Dean of Students: REBECCA BENNETT
Business Man.: PAM PHARR
Registrar: SHEILA FREEMAN
Dir of Library Services: SUE ETHERIDGE

Library of 60,500 vols
Number of teachers: 30
Number of students: 438

DELTA STATE UNIVERSITY

Highway 8, Cleveland, MS 38733
Telephone: (662) 846-3000
E-mail: president@deltastate.edu
Internet: www.deltastate.edu

Founded 1924

Pres.: Dr JOHN M. HILPERT
Vice-Pres. for Univ. Relations: Dr MICHELLE ROBERTS
Provost and Vice-Pres. for Academic Affairs: Dr BILLY MOREHEAD
Registrar: JOHN ELLIOTT
Dir of Library Services: JEFF SLAGELL

Library of 360,000 vols
Number of teachers: 270
Number of students: 4,000

JACKSON STATE UNIVERSITY

1400 J. R. Lynch St, Jackson, MS 39217
Telephone: (601) 968-2121
E-mail: jsumedia@jsums.edu
Internet: www.jsums.edu

Founded 1877

Pres.: Dr RONALD MASON, Jr
Chief of Staff: EVOLA BATES
Sr Vice-Pres. for Finance and Operations: TROY A. STOVALL
Vice-Pres. for Academic Affairs and Student Life: VELVELYN B. FOSTER
Vice-Pres. for Information Management: Dr WILLIE G. BROWN
Vice-Pres. for Research and Federal Relations: Dr FELIX A. OKOJIE
Dir of Libraries: Dr LOU H. SANDERS

Library of 376,566 vols
Number of students: 6,224

Publications: *Alumni Newsletter* (4 a year), *Blue and White Flash* (4 a year)

DEANS

College of Business: Dr GLENDA GLOVER
College of Education and Human Development: Dr DANIEL WATKINS
College of Liberal Arts: Dr DOLLYE ROBINSON
College of Public Service: Dr GWENDOLYN PRATER
College of Science, Engineering and Technology: Dr MARK HARDY
Graduate Dean: Dr DORRIS ROBINSON-GARDNER

MAGNOLIA BIBLE COLLEGE

822 S Huntington St, Kosciusko, MS 39090
Telephone: (662) 289-2896
Fax: (662) 289-1850
Internet: www.magnolia.edu

Founded 1976
Private control
Academic year: August to July

Pres.: Dr GARVIS SEMORE
Academic Dean: JOHN F. GARDNER
Dean of Students: SHAWN L. HARDIN
Dir of Admissions: TRAVIS BROWN

Number of teachers: 8

Number of students: 55

MILLSAPS COLLEGE

1701 North State St, Jackson, MS 39210-0001
Telephone: (601) 974-1000
E-mail: communications@millsaps.edu
Internet: www.millsaps.edu
Founded 1890
Pres.: Dr FRANCES LUCAS
Dean of Faculty: Dr RICHARD SMITH
Librarian: THOMAS HENDERSON
Library of 209,900 vols
Number of teachers: 92
Number of students: 1,154

MISSISSIPPI COLLEGE

200 South Capitol St, Clinton, MS 39058
Telephone: (601) 925-3000
Internet: www.mc.edu
Founded 1826
Pres.: Dr LEE ROYCE
Vice-Pres. for Academic Affairs: Dr RON HOWARD
Vice-Pres. for Admin. and Govt Relations: Dr STEVE STANFORD
Vice-Pres. for Advancement: DANNY RUTLAND
Vice-Pres. for Enrollment Management and Student Affairs: Dr JIM TURCOTTE
Vice-Pres. for Planning and Assessment: Dr DEBBIE NORRIS
Chief Financial Officer: DONNA LEWIS
Library Dir: KATHLEEN HUTCHISON
Library of 234,000 vols
Number of teachers: 150 (incl. 75 part-time)
Number of students: 3,800

MISSISSIPPI STATE UNIVERSITY

POB 5325, Mississippi State, MS 39762
Telephone: (662) 325-2323
Internet: www.msstate.edu
Founded 1878
Pres.: ROBERT H. FOGLESONG
Vice-Pres. for Academic Affairs and Provost: PETER RABIDEAU
Vice-Pres. for Agriculture, Forestry and Veterinary Medicine: VANCE WATSON
Vice-Pres. for Devt and Alumni: JOHN RUSH
Vice-Pres. for Research and Economic Devt: KIRK SCHULZ (acting)
Vice-Pres. for Student Affairs: WILLIAM KIBLER
Chief of Staff and Chief Financial Officer: MICHAEL J. MCGREVEY
Registrar: BUTCH STOKES
Dean of Libraries: FRANCES COLEMAN
Library of 873,000 vols, 2.1m. microforms, 8,464 records and tapes, 7,500 periodicals
Number of teachers: 1,032
Number of students: 16,206

DEANS

Agriculture and Home Economics: WILLIAM R. FOX
Architecture: JOHN MCRAE
Arts and Sciences: FRANK E. SAAL
Business and Industry: HARVEY S. LEWIS
Continuing Education: BILL SMITH
Education: WILLIAM H. GRAVES
Engineering: WAYNE BENNETT
Forestry: JOHN E. GUNTER
Veterinary Medicine: DWIGHT MERCER

MISSISSIPPI UNIVERSITY FOR WOMEN

Columbus, MS 39701
Telephone: (662) 329-4750
Fax: (662) 329-7297
Internet: www.muw.edu
Founded 1884
First state-supported college exclusively for women to be founded in the USA
Academic year: August to May
Pres.: Dr CLAUDIA LIMBERT (acting)
Provost and Vice-Pres. for Academic Affairs: TOM RICHARDSON
Vice-Pres. for Finance and Admin.: NORA MILLER
Vice-Pres. for Institutional Advancement: GARY BOUSE
Vice-Pres. for Student Services: BUCKY WESLEY
Asst to the Pres.: PERRY SANSING
Dir of Library: GAIL GUNTER
Library of 426,900 vols
Number of teachers: 128
Number of students: 3,314

HEADS OF DIVISIONS

Business and Communications: ANNE BALAZS
Culinary Arts Institute: SARAH LABENSKY
Education and Human Sciences: HAL JENKINS
Fine and Performing Arts: MICHAEL GARRETT
Health and Kinesiology: JO SPEARMAN
Humanities: BRIDGET PIESCHEL
Nursing: SHEILA ADAMS
Science and Mathematics: NANCY BRYSON

MISSISSIPPI VALLEY STATE UNIVERSITY

14000 Highway 82, W, Itta Bena, MS 38941-1400
Telephone: (662) 254-9041
E-mail: admsn@mvsu.edu
Internet: www.mvsu.edu
Founded 1946
Pres.: Dr LESTER C. NEWMAN
Vice-Pres. for Academic Affairs: W. ERIC THOMAS
Registrar: DARRELL L. JAMES
Library Dir: Dr ANNIE PAYTON
Library of 125,000 vols
Number of teachers: 112
Number of students: 2,168

REFORMED THEOLOGICAL SEMINARY

5422 Clinton Blvd, Jackson, MS 39209
Telephone: (601) 923-1600
Fax: (601) 923-1654
E-mail: rts.jackson@rts.edu
Internet: www.rts.edu
Founded 1966
Private control
Chancellor: Dr ROBERT C. CANNADA, Jr
Pres. (Jackson Campus): Dr GUY RICHARDSON
Chief Devt Officer: Rev. LYN PEREZ
Registrar: Dr PAUL LONG, Jr
Library Dir: Rev. KENNETH ELLIOTT
Library of 150,000 vols
Number of teachers: 105
Number of students: 600.

BRANCH CAMPUSES

Atlanta Campus

3585 Northside Parkway, NW, Atlanta, GA 30327-2309
Telephone: (404) 995-8484
Fax: (404) 995-8997
E-mail: admissions.atlanta@rts.edu
Founded 1996
Exec. Vice-Pres. of Extensions: JOHN T. SOWELL.

Boca Raton Campus

2400 Yamato Rd, Boca Raton, FL 33431
Telephone: (561) 994-5000
Fax: (561) 995-5005
E-mail: admissions.boca@rts.edu
Exec. Dir: Dr BUZ MCNUTT.

Charlotte Campus

2101 Carmel Rd, Charlotte, NC 28226-6399
Telephone: (704) 366-5066
Fax: (704) 366-9295
E-mail: rts.charlotte@rts.edu
Founded 1992
Pres.: Dr RIC CANNADA
Vice-Pres. for Devt: CHARLIE DUNN
Registrar: ANGELA BOYD
Library Dir: Rev. KENNETH MCMULLEN
Library of 46,000 vols.

Orlando Campus

1231 Reformation Dr., Oviedo, FL 32765
Telephone: (407) 366-9493
Fax: (407) 366-9425
E-mail: rts.orlando@rts.edu
Founded 1989
Pres.: Dr FRANK A. JAMES, III
Vice-Pres. for Devt: JOHNNY MASTRY
Registrar: LANNY CONLEY
Library Dir: JOHN MUETHER
Library of 75,000 vols.

Virtual Campus

2101 Carmel Rd, Charlotte, NC 28226
Telephone: (704) 366-4853
Fax: (704) 366-9295
E-mail: distance.education@rts.edu
Founded 1998
Pres.: Dr ANDREW J. PETERSON.

Washington DC Campus

12500 Fairlakes Circle, Suite 325, Fairfax, VA 22033
Telephone: (703) 222-7871
Fax: (703) 738-7389
E-mail: admissions.washington@rts.edu
Founded 1997
Exec. Dirs: Dr FRANK E. YOUNG, HUGH WHELCHEL
Number of students: 250

RUST COLLEGE

150 Rust Ave, Holly Springs, MS 38635
Telephone: (662) 252-8000
Fax: (662) 252-6107
E-mail: admissions@rustcollege.edu
Internet: www.rustcollege.edu
Founded 1866
Private control
Academic year: August to April
Pres.: Dr DAVID L. BECKLEY
Vice-Pres.: Dr ISHMELL H. EDWARDS
Academic Dean: Dr MARIAN Y. TALLEY
Dean for Student Affairs: ERIC W. JACKSON
Registrar: CLARENCE E. SMITH
Head Librarian: ANITA W. MOORE
Library of 120,000 vols
Number of teachers: 59
Number of students: 1,029

SOUTHEASTERN BAPTIST COLLEGE

4229 Highway 15, N, Laurel, MS 39440
Telephone: (601) 426-6346
Fax: (601) 426-6347
E-mail: info@southeasternbaptist.edu
Internet: www.southeasternbaptist.edu
Founded 1948
Private control
Academic year: August to July
Pres.: MEDRISK SAVELL
Librarian: AMY HINTON

Number of students: 63
Areas of study: business admin. and management, Bible studies, gen. studies.

TOUGALOO COLLEGE

500 West Country Line Rd, Tougaloo, MS 39174
Telephone: (601) 977-7700
Fax: (601) 977-7739
Internet: www.tougaloo.edu
Founded 1869
Private liberal arts college, affiliated with Disciples of Christ and United Church of Christ
Pres.: Dr BEVERLEY WADE HOGAN
Vice-Pres. for Academic Affairs, and Provost: Dr ABDUL TURAY
Vice-Pres. for Facilities Management: KELLE MENOGAN, Sr
Vice-Pres. for Finance and Admin.: Dr CYNTHIA MELVIN
Vice-Pres. for Institutional Advancement: EDWINA HARRIS HAMBY
Library of 139,600 vols
Number of teachers: 73
Number of students: 916
Publications: *The Harambee* (12 a year), *Tougaloo News* (3 a year).

UNIVERSITY OF MISSISSIPPI

POB 1848, University, MS 38677-1848
Telephone: (662) 915-7211
Fax: (662) 915-7486
E-mail: ipdebt@olemiss.edu
Internet: www.olemiss.edu
The School of Medicine, the School of Dentistry, the School of Nursing and the School of Health Related Professions are constituents of the Univ. of Mississippi Medical Center, located in Jackson, Mississippi
Founded 1844
Chancellor: ROBERT C. KHAYAT
Pres. and Chief Exec. Officer of the Univ. Foundation: WENDELL WEAKLEY
Provost, and Vice-Chancellor for Academic Affairs: CAROLYN STATON
Vice-Chancellor for Finance and Admin.: LARRY SPARKS
Vice-Chancellor for Research and Sponsored Programs: ALICE M. CLARK
Vice-Chancellor for Student Life: Dr THOMAS D. WALLACE (acting)
Registrar: CHARLOTTE FANT (acting)
Dean of Libraries: JULIA ROLES
Library: 1.3m. vols
Number of teachers: 595
Number of students: 11,000
Publications: *Catalogues* (Graduate School), *Law School*, *Medical Center*, *Summer Session*, *Undergraduate*

DEANS

Accountancy: Dr JAMES W. DAVIS
Business Admin.: Dr RANDY BOXX
Education: Dr JIM CHAMBLESS
Engineering: Dr ALLIE M. SMITH
Graduate School: Dr MICHAEL R. DINGERSON
Law School: Dr SAMUEL M. DAVIS
Liberal Arts: Dr H. DALE ABADIE
Pharmacy: Dr KENNETH B. ROBERTS

UNIVERSITY OF MISSISSIPPI MEDICAL CENTER

2500 North State St, Jackson, MS 39216
Telephone: (601) 984-1080
Fax: (601) 984-1079
E-mail: bbishop@registrar.umsmed.edu
Internet: www.umc.edu
Founded 1955
State control
Chancellor: ROBERT KHAYAT
Vice-Chancellor for Health Affairs: DANIEL W. JONES
Assoc. Vice-Chancellor for Academic Affairs: Dr HELEN TURNER
Assoc. Vice-Chancellor for Admin. Affairs: DAVID POWE
Assoc. Vice-Chancellor for Research: Dr JOHN E. HALL
Registrar: BARBARA WESTERFIELD
Library Dir: ADA M. SELTZER
Number of teachers: 587
Number of students: 1,778 (603 undergraduate, 1,175 graduate)

DEANS

School of Dentistry: Dr JAMES R. HUPP
School of Graduate Studies: Dr ING K. HO
School of Health-Related Professions: JACK R. GORDY
School of Medicine: Dr A. WALLACE CONERLY, Sr
School of Nursing: Dr ANNE PEIRCE

UNIVERSITY OF SOUTHERN MISSISSIPPI

118 College Dr., POB 5001, Hattiesburg, MS 39406-0001
Telephone: (601) 266-5001
Fax: (602) 266-5756
E-mail: shelby.f.thames@usm.edu
Internet: www.usm.edu
Founded 1910
Pres.: Dr SHELBY F. THAMES
Provost of Hattiesburg Campus: DARRELL JAY
Provost of Gulf Coast Campus: (vacant)
Vice-Pres. for Research and Economic Devt: Dr CECIL D. BURGE
Vice-Pres. for Student Affairs: JOSEPH S. PAUL
Assoc. Vice-Pres. for Research and Economic Devt: JULIAN ALLEN
Chief Financial Officer: JOE MORGAN
Dean of Univ. Admissions: Dr KRISTI MOTTER
Univ. Librarian: EDWARD MCCORMACK
Library: 1.3m. vols
Number of teachers: 687
Number of students: 14,810
Publications: *Journal of Mississippi History*, *Mississippi Review*, *Southern Quarterly*

DEANS

Arts and Letters: Dr ELLIOTT A. POOD
Business and Economic Devt: Dr HAROLD DOTY
Education and Psychology: Dr W. LEE PIERCE
Graduate Studies: Dr BRADLEY G. BOND
Honours College: Dr KENNETH PANTON
Health: Dr PETER FOS
Science and Technology: Dr REX FRANKLIN GANDY

WESLEY COLLEGE

POB 1070, 111 Wesley Circle, Florence, MS 39073
Telephone: (601) 845-2265
Fax: (601) 845-2266
E-mail: admissions@wesleycollege.edu
Internet: www.wesleycollege.com
Founded 1944 as Congregational Methodist Bible School; present name 1975
Private control
Pres.: LANCE SHERER
Number of teachers: 4
Number of students: 105
Areas of study: biblical literature, Christian education, missions, Christian ministries, gen. education, pastoral ministries, youth ministries.

WILLIAM CAREY COLLEGE

498 Tuscan Ave, Hattiesburg, MS 39401-5499
Telephone: (601) 318-6051
Fax: (601) 318-6454
Internet: www.wmcarey.edu
Founded 1906
Chancellor: JAMES W. EDWARDS
Pres. and Chief Exec.: R. TOMMY KING
Vice-Pres. for Academic Affairs: CLOYD L. EZELL, Jr
Vice-Pres. for Advancement: ARGILE A. SMITH, Jr
Vice-Pres. for Business Affairs: JOE RILEY
Vice-Pres. for Institutional Effectiveness and Planning: BENNIE R. CROCKETT, Jr
Vice-Pres. for Student Services: BRENDA F. WALDRIP
Dean of Enrollment Management: WILLIAM N. CURRY
Registrar: GAYLE KNIGHT
Dir of Library Services: PATRICIA H. FURR
Library of 127,000 resources
Number of teachers: 80 full-time
Number of students: 2,172

MISSOURI

AQUINAS INSTITUTE OF THEOLOGY

23 South Spring Ave, St Louis, MO 63108
Telephone: (314) 256-8800
Fax: (314) 256-8888
E-mail: info@ai.edu
Internet: www.ai.edu
Founded 1925
Private control
Academic year: August to May
Pres.: Dr CHARLES E. BOUCHARD
Vice-Pres. and Academic Dean: Dr GREG HEILLE
Dean of Students: RON KNAPP
Registrar: JANEL ESKER
Librarian: SALLY GUNTER
Number of teachers: 35
Number of students: 145 (full-time)

ASSEMBLIES OF GOD THEOLOGICAL SEMINARY

1435 N Glenstone Ave, Springfield, MO 65802-2131
Telephone: (417) 268-1000
Fax: (417) 268-1001
E-mail: agts@agts.edu
Internet: www.agts.edu
Founded 1972 as Assemblies of God Graduate School; present name 1984
Private control
Academic year: September to July
Pres.: Dr BYRON D. KLAUS
Academic Dean: STEPHEN LIM
Dir of Library Services: JOSEPH F. MARICS, JR
Number of teachers: 15
Number of students: 550

A. T. STILL UNIVERSITY OF HEALTH SCIENCES

800 West Jefferson St, Kirksville, MO 63501
Telephone: (660) 626-2391
Fax: (660) 626-2672
E-mail: admissions@atsu.edu
Internet: www.atsu.edu
Founded 1892 as Kirksville College of Osteopathic Medicine; present name 1993
Private control
Academic year: August to June
Pres.: Dr JAMES J. MCGOVERN

Vice-Pres. for Academic Affairs and Dean of Kirksville College of Osteopathic Medicine: PHILIP SLOCUM
Vice-Pres. for Institutional Advancement: ROBERT L. BASHAM (acting)
Dean of School of Health Management: Dr JON PERSAVICH
Library Dir: DOUG BLANSIT
Library of 80,000 vols, 4,500 audiovisual items
Number of teachers: 100
Number of students: 1,328.

BRANCH CAMPUS

Mesa Campus: 5850 East Still Circle, Mesa, AZ 85206; tel. (480) 219-6000; incl. Arizona School of Dentistry and Oral Health, the Arizona School of Health Sciences and the School of Osteopathic Medicine; Provost Dr CRAIG M. PHELPS; Dean of Arizona School of Dentistry and Oral Health Dr JACK DILLENBERG; Dean of Arizona School of Health Sciences Dr RANDY DANIELSEN.

AVILA COLLEGE

11901 Wornall Rd, Kansas City, MO 64145
Telephone: (816) 501-3603
Fax: (816) 942-3362
E-mail: admissions@mail.avila.edu
Internet: www.avila.edu
Founded 1916
Pres.: RON SLEPITZA
Registrar: DAVE DEITCH
Librarian: KATHLEEN FINEGAN
Library of 74,658 vols, 500 periodicals
Number of teachers: 65
Number of students: 2,000

BAPTIST BIBLE COLLEGE AND GRADUATE SCHOOL

628 East Kearney, Springfield, MO 65803
Telephone: (417) 268-6060
Fax: (417) 268-6694
Internet: www.baptist.edu
Founded 1950
Private control
Academic year: August to May
Pres.: Dr MIKE RANDALL
Vice-Pres.: Dr RICK CARTER
Chancellor: Dr LELAND KENNEDY
Academic Dean: Dr BILL DOWELL, JR
Dean of Students: RAY ADAMS
Registrar: Dr JOSEPH GLEASON
Dir of Library: TONY GARRETT
Library of 52,000 vols
Number of teachers: 28
Number of students: 805 (746 undergraduate, 59 graduate)

CALVARY BIBLE COLLEGE AND THEOLOGICAL SEMINARY

15800 Calvary Rd, Kansas City, MO 64147-1341
Telephone: (816) 322-0110
Fax: (816) 331-4474
E-mail: admissions@calvary.edu
Internet: www.calvary.edu
Founded 1961, following merger of Kansas City Bible College (f. 1932) and Midwest Bible College (f. 1938); Calvary Theological Seminary (f. 1966) as Graduate Div. of Calvary Bible College, present name 1992
Private control
Language of instruction: English
Academic year: August to May
Pres.: Dr JAMES CLARK
Vice-Pres. and Academic Dean: Dr TEDDY BITNER
Vice-Pres. and Dean of Seminary: Dr THOMAS BAURAIN
Dean of Students: STEVE BAIRD
Vice-Pres. of Operations: RANDY L. GRIMM
Registrar: LARRY SPRY
Librarian: HANNAH BITNER
Library of 62,000 vols
Number of teachers: 39
Number of students: 332 (282 undergraduate, 50 graduate)

CENTRAL BIBLE COLLEGE

3000 North Grant Ave, Springfield, MO 65803
Telephone: (417) 833-2551
Fax: (417) 833-0854
E-mail: info@cbcag.edu
Internet: www.cbcag.edu
Founded 1922
Private control (General Council of the Assemblies of God)
Academic year: August to April
Pres.: Dr GARY A. DENBOW
Vice-Pres. for Academic Affairs: Dr DAVID ARNETT
Vice-Pres. for College Advancement: Rev. RICHARD L. HARDY
Vice-Pres. for Operations: Rev. CHARLENE S. PETERSON
Vice-Pres. for Student Devt: Rev. JIM P. VIGIL
Librarian: LYNN ANDERSON
Library of 156,000 vols
Number of teachers: 39
Number of students: 805

CENTRAL CHRISTIAN COLLEGE OF THE BIBLE

911 E Urbandale Dr., Moberly, MO 65270
Telephone: (660) 263-3900
Fax: (660) 263-3936
E-mail: iwant2be@cccb.edu
Internet: www.cccb.edu
Founded 1957
Private control
Language of instruction: English
Academic year: August to May
Areas of study: biblical research, Christian counselling, Christian education, Christian mins, cross-cultural min., preaching, youth and family min.; min. certificates: certificate of biblical knowledge, children's min., TESOL, worship leader
Pres.: Dr RON OAKES
Chancellor: LLOYD M. PELFREY
Vice-Pres. of Academics: DAVID B. FINCHER
Vice-Pres. of Student Devt: RICHARD REXRODE
Registrar: FAITH M. AXTON
Librarian: PATTY AGEE
Number of teachers: 25
Number of students: 315

CENTRAL METHODIST UNIVERSITY

411 Central Methodist Sq., Fayette, MO 65248
Telephone: (660) 248-3391
Internet: www.centralmethodist.edu
Founded 1854
Academic year: August to May
Pres.: Dr MARIANNE INMAN
Dean of the College: Dr ROGER KUGLER
Librarian: CYNTHIA DUDENHOFFER
Library of 100,000 vols
Number of teachers: 60
Number of students: 3,000
College of Liberal Arts and Sciences; College of Graduate and Extended Studies
Publications: *Collegian*, *Inscape*, *The Talon*.

CLEVELAND CHIROPRACTIC COLLEGE

10850 Lowell Ave, 2nd Fl., Overland Park, Kansas, MO 66210
Telephone: (913) 234-0744
Fax: (913) 234-0906
E-mail: kc.admissions@cleveland.edu
Internet: www.cleveland.edu
Founded 1922 as Central Chiropractic College; present name 1924
Private control
Academic year: September to August
Pres.: Dr CARL S. CLEVELAND, III
Exec. Vice-Pres. and Chief Academic Officer: Dr DONNA BROADSTREET
Dean of Instruction: Dr RUTH SANDEFUR
Registrar: (vacant)
Library Dir: MARCIA M. THOMAS
Library of 14,800 vols
Number of students: 502.

BRANCH CAMPUS

Los Angeles Campus: 590 North Vermont Ave, Los Angeles, CA 90004; tel. (323) 660-6166; fax (323) 906-2094; e-mail la.admissions@cleveland.edu.

COLLEGE OF THE OZARKS

Point Lookout, MO 65726
Telephone: (417) 334-6411
Fax: (417) 335-2618
E-mail: admiss4@cofo.edu
Internet: www.cofo.edu
Founded 1906
Academic year: August to May
Pres.: Dr JERRY C. DAVIS
Vice-Pres.: Dr HOWELL KEETER
Chief Financial Officer: CHARLES F. HUGHES
Registrar: FRAN FOMAN
Dir of Alumni Affairs: HELEN YOUNGBLOOD
Dir of Financial Aid: KYLA MCCARTY
Dir of Public Relations: ELIZABETH ANDREWS
Library of 119,000 vols
Number of teachers: 115
Number of students: 1,345
Depts of accounting, agriculture, art, biology, business admin., chemistry, computer sciences, criminal justice, education, English, family and consumer sciences, foreign languages, graphic arts, history, hotel and restaurant management, mass communications, mathematics-physics, military science, music, nursing, philosophy and religion, physical education, political science, psychology, sociology, speech communication, technology, theatre
Publication: *Ozark Visitor* (4 a year).

COLUMBIA COLLEGE

1001 Rogers St, Columbia, MO 65216
Telephone: (573) 875-8700
Fax: (573) 875-7209
E-mail: admissions@ccis.edu
Internet: www.ccis.edu
Founded 1851 as Christian Female College; present name 1970
Private control
Academic year: August to July
Pres.: Dr GERALD T. BROUDER
Exec. Vice-Pres. and Dean for Academic Affairs: Dr TERRY B. SMITH
Chief Financial Officer: BRUCE BOYER
Chief Information Officer: KEVIN PALMER
Library Dir: JANET CARUTHERS
Library of 63,988 vols
Number of teachers: 63
Number of students: 24,681
Areas of study: art, business admin., computer and mathematical sciences, criminal justice admin. and human services, educa-

tion, history and social sciences, humanities, science

23 Extension campuses throughout the USA.

CONCEPTION SEMINARY COLLEGE

POB 501, Conception, MO 64433
Telephone: (660) 944-2821
Fax: (660) 944-2800
E-mail: communications@conception.edu
Internet: www.conception.edu

Founded 1886 as College of New Engelberg; present name 1972

Private control (Conception Abbey)

Pres. and Rector: SAMUEL RUSSELL
Library Dir: Bro. THOMAS SULLIVAN

Number of teachers: 32
Number of students: 80

CONCORDIA SEMINARY

801 Seminary Pl., St Louis, MO 63105
Telephone: (314) 505-7000
Fax: (314) 505-7001
E-mail: csladmis@aol.com
Internet: www.csl.edu

Founded 1839

Private control (Lutheran Church—Missouri Synod)

Academic year: September to May

Pres.: Rev. Dr DALE A. MEYER
Vice-Pres. for Academic Affairs: Dr ANDREW H. BARTELT
Vice-Pres. for Financial Planning and Admin.: MICHAEL A. LOUIS
Registrar: MARYANN HAYTER
Dir of Library Services: DAVID O. BERGER

Library of 230,000 vols
Number of teachers: 55
Number of students: 534 (full-time)

COVENANT THEOLOGICAL SEMINARY

12330 Conway Rd, St Louis, MO 63141
Telephone: (314) 434-4044
Fax: (314) 434-4819
Internet: www.covenantseminary.edu

Founded 1956

Private control (Presbyterian Church in America)

Academic year: September to May

Pres.: Dr BRYAN CHAPELL
Vice-Pres. for Academics and Dean of Faculty: Dr SEAN MICHAEL LUCAS
Assoc. Dean of Students: Dr TASHA CHAPMAN
Library Dir: JAMES C. PAKALA

Library of 68,000 vols
Number of teachers: 42
Number of students: 435 (full-time)

CULVER-STOCKTON COLLEGE

1 College Hill, Canton, MO 63435
Telephone: (573) 288-6000
Fax: (573) 288-6611
Internet: www.culver.edu

Founded 1853

Academic year: August to May

Pres.: DICK D. VALENTINE
Vice-Pres. for Academic Affairs and Dean of College: Dr R. JOSEPH DIEKER
Registrar: MARJORIE ELLISON
Librarian: SHARON UPCHURCH

Library of 164,266 vols
Number of teachers: 50
Number of students: 828

Academic programmes in accounting, art, art education, arts management, athletic training, biology, business administration, communication, criminal justice, elementary education, English, finance, history and political science, management, management information systems, mathematics, music, music education, nursing, physical education, psychology, recreation management, religion and philosophy, secondary education, speech and theatre education, theatre

Publications: *Chronicle* (4 a year), *Ex Scientia* (1 a year).

DRURY UNIVERSITY

900 North Benton Ave, Springfield, MO 65802
Telephone: (417) 873-7879
Fax: (417) 873-7435
E-mail: drury@drury.edu
Internet: www.drury.edu

Founded 1873

Liberal arts college

Pres.: TODD PARNELL
Vice-Pres. for Academic Affairs and Dean of College: CHARLES TAYLOR
Vice-Pres. for Admin. Services: KENNETH JOHNSON
Vice-Pres. for Institutional Advancement: PETER RADECKI
Dean of Admissions: DAWN HILES
Dean of Students: Dr TIJUANA JULIAN
Registrar: GALE BOUTWELL
Librarian: STEVE STOAN

Library of 160,000 vols
Number of teachers: 118 f.t.e.
Number of students: 1,600

EDEN THEOLOGICAL SEMINARY

475 East Lockwood Ave, St Louis, MO 63119-3192
Telephone: (314) 961-3627
Fax: (314) 918-2535
E-mail: dwindler@eden.edu
Internet: www.eden.edu
Private control

Pres.: Rev. Dr DAVID M. GREENHAW
Vice-Pres. for Devt: STELLA SCHOEN
Academic Dean: Rev. Dr DEBORAH KRAUSE
Registrar: MICHELLE WOBBE
Library Dir: Rev. ALLEN W. MUELLER

Library of 86,000 vols
Number of teachers: 24
Number of students: 131 (full-time)

EVANGEL UNIVERSITY OF THE ASSEMBLIES OF GOD

1111 North Glenstone, Springfield, MO 65802
Telephone: (417) 865-2815
Fax: (417) 865-9599
Internet: www.evangel.edu

Founded 1955

Academic year: September to May

Pres.: Dr ROBERT H. SPENCE
Vice-Pres. for Academic Affairs: Dr GLENN BERNET
Vice-Pres. for Business and Finance: GEORGE CRAWFORD
Vice-Pres. for Enrollment Management: ANDY DENTON
Vice-Pres. for Institutional Advancement: JIM WILLIAMS
Vice-Pres. for Student Devt: DAVID BUNDRICK
Registrar: CATHY WILLIAMS
Library Dir: WOODVALL MOORE

Library of 120,000 vols
Number of students: 1,525

Depts of behavioural sciences, business, communication, education, health, physical education and recreation, humanities, music, sciences and technology, social sciences, theology.

FONTBONNE UNIVERSITY

6800 Wydown Blvd, St Louis, MO 63105
Telephone: (314) 862-3456
Fax: (314) 889-1451
Internet: www.fontbonne.edu

Founded 1917

Pres.: DENNIS GOLDEN
Vice-Pres. and Dean for Academic Affairs: Dr NANCY BLATTNER
Exec. Vice-Pres. for Strategy and Operations: GREGORY TAYLOR
Vice-Pres. for Finance and Admin.: GARY ZACK
Vice-Pres. for Institutional Advancement and Devt: Dr WILLIAM J. ROTHWELL
Vice-Pres. for Student Affairs: RANDI WILSON
Assoc. Vice-Pres. for Enrollment Management: PEGGY MUSEN
Registrar: MAZIE MOORE
Librarian: SHARON MCCASLIN

Library of 90,020 vols, 510 periodicals
Number of teachers: 105 (45 full-time, 60 part-time)
Number of students: 1,990

HANNIBAL-LAGRANGE COLLEGE

2800 Palmyra Rd, Hannibal, MO 63401
Telephone: (573) 221-3675
Fax: (573) 221-6594
Internet: www.hlg.edu
Private control

Pres.: Dr WOODROW W. BURT
Vice-Pres. for Academic Affairs: Dr GARRY M. BRELAND
Vice-Pres. for Collegiate Affairs: Dr L. THOMAS HUFTY
Vice-Pres. for Enrollment Management: RAYMOND W. CARTY
Vice-Pres. for Institutional Advancement: CONNIE BENSON
Registrar: DARLA THOMASON
Library Dir: JULIE A. ANDRESEN

Library of 118,000 vols
Number of teachers: 46
Number of students: 1,150

HARRIS-STOWE STATE UNIVERSITY

3026 Laclede Ave, St Louis, MO 63103
Telephone: (314) 340-3366
Fax: (314) 340-3399
E-mail: admissions@hssu.edu
Internet: www.hssu.edu

Founded 1857, present name and status 2005

Pres.: Dr HENRY GIVENS, Jr
Exec. Vice-Pres. for Business and Financial Affairs: CONSTANCE GULLY
Vice-Pres. for Academic Affairs: Dr DWYANE SMITH
Exec. Dir of Enrollment Management: LASHANDA BOONE
Dir of Communications, Marketing and Alumni Affairs: NISA SCHMITZ
Dir of Information Technology: JAMES FOGT
Registrar: CHAUVETTE MCELMURRY
Librarian: BARBARA NOBLE

Library of 87,000 vols
Number of teachers: 82
Number of students: 1,980

DEANS

Anheuser-Busch School of Business: FATEMEH ZAKERY
College of Arts and Sciences: LATEEF ADELANI
College of Education: LATISHA SMITH

KANSAS CITY ART INSTITUTE

4415 Warwick Blvd, Kansas City, MO 64111-1820
Telephone: (816) 472-4852
E-mail: info@kcai.edu

Internet: www.kcai.edu
Founded 1885
Academic year: August to May
4-Year college of art and design
Pres.: KATHLEEN COLLINS
Exec. Vice-Pres. for Admin.: RON CATTELINO
Vice-Pres. for Academic Affairs: MARK SALMON
Vice-Pres. for Advancement: PAM SIBERT
Vice-Pres. for Communications: ANNE CANFIELD
Vice-Pres. for Enrollment Management: BAMBI BURGARD
Chief Information Officer: LARRY DICKERSON
Registrar: ANDREA KHAN
Library Dir: M. J. POEHLER
Library of 30,000 vols and 111,160 slides
Number of students: 650

KANSAS CITY UNIVERSITY OF MEDICINE AND BIOSCIENCES

1750 Independence Ave, Kansas City, MO 64106-1453
Telephone: (816) 283-2000
Fax: (816) 283-2484
E-mail: admissions@kcumb.edu
Internet: www.kcumb.edu
Founded 1916 as Kansas City College of Osteopathy and Surgery; as Univ. of Health Sciences 1980; present name and structure 2004
Private control
Academic year: August to July
Pres. and CEO: Dr KAREN L. PLETZ
Vice-Pres. for Academic Affairs, Provost and Dean of College of Osteopathic Medicine: Dr SANDRA K. WILLSIE
Exec. Vice-Pres. and Chief Operating Officer: RICHARD K. HOFFINE
Exec. Vice-Pres. for Institutional Devt and Corporate Planning: DOUGLAS C. DALZELL
Dir of Library: MARILYN J. DEGEUS
Number of teachers: 48
Number of students: 900

KENRICK-GLENNON SEMINARY

5200 Glennon Dr., St Louis, MO 63119
Telephone: (314) 792-6100
Fax: (314) 792-6500
E-mail: wojcicki@kenrick.edu
Internet: www.kenrick.edu
Founded 1898
Liberal arts college exclusively for candidates for Roman Catholic priesthood
Academic year: August to May
Pres. and Rector: Mgr TED L. WOJCICKI
Dir of Devt: SETH JANSEN
Rector of Cardinal Glennon College: Rev. TIMOTHY P. CRONIN
Academic Dean: Rev. DONALD E. HENKE
Dean of Students: Rev. EDWARD JAMES RICHARD
Registrar: MARY ANN AUBIN
Librarian: Dr ANDREW J. SOPKO
Library of 80,000 vols
Number of students: 110 (30 undergraduate, 80 graduate)

LINCOLN UNIVERSITY

820 Chestnut St, Jefferson City, MO 65101
Telephone: (573) 681-5000
Fax: (573) 681-5566
E-mail: president@lincolnu.edu
Internet: www.lincolnu.edu
Founded 1866
Academic year: August to July
Pres.: Dr CAROLYN R. MAHONEY
Vice-Pres. for Academic Affairs and Provost: Dr ANNETTE DIGBY
Vice-Pres. for Admin. and Finance: CURTIS CREAGH
Vice-Pres. for Student Affairs: CONSTANCE WILLIAMS
Vice-Pres. for Univ. Advancement: IDA SIMON
Dir of Univ. Relations: BRIAN GRAVES
Librarian: ELIZABETH WILSON
Library of 164,800 vols
Number of teachers: 179
Number of students: 3,347

DEANS

College of Business and Professional Studies: Dr KOJO QUARTEY
College of Liberal Arts, Education and Journalism: Dr PATRICK HENRY
College of Natural Sciences, Mathematics and Technology: Dr MICHAEL HEARD
School of Graduate Studies and Continuing Education: Dr LINDA BICKEL

LINDENWOOD UNIVERSITY

209 South Kingshighway, St Charles, MO 63301
Telephone: (636) 949-4982
E-mail: international@lindenwood.edu
Internet: www.lindenwood.edu
Academic year: August to May
Pres.: Dr JAMES D. EVANS
Provost: ARLENE TAICH
Dean of the College and Dean of Admissions and Financial Aid: DAVID R. WILLIAMS
Dean of Students: JOHN CREER
Librarian: ELIZABETH MACDONALD
Library of 132,000 books and pamphlets
Number of teachers: 100
Number of students: 5,000
Divs of arts, communications, education, human services, humanities, management, sciences.

LOGAN COLLEGE OF CHIROPRACTIC

1851 Schoettler Rd, Chesterfield, MO 63017-5529
Telephone: (636) 227-2100
Fax: (636) 207-2424
E-mail: loganadm@logan.edu
Internet: www.logan.edu
Founded 1935
Private control
Academic year: September to April
Pres.: Dr GEORGE A. GOODMAN
Vice-Pres. for Academic Affairs: Dr PATRICK M. BROWNE
Vice-Pres. for Admin. Affairs: SHARON K. KEHRER
Vice-Pres. for Institutional Advancement: PATRICIA C. JONES
Chief Financial Officer: PATRICIA MARCELLA
Library of 12,500 vols, 260 journals, 23,050 media items
Number of teachers: 45 full-time and 42 part-time
Number of students: 1,001

MARYVILLE UNIVERSITY OF SAINT LOUIS

13550 Conway Rd, St Louis, MO 63141
Telephone: (314) 529-9300
Fax: (314) 542-9085
E-mail: admissions@maryville.edu
Internet: www.maryville.edu
Founded 1872
Academic year: August to May
Pres.: Dr MARK LOMBARDT
Vice-Pres. for Academic Affairs: Dr BRIAN P. NEDWEK
Vice-Pres. for Admin. and Finance: Dr LARRY HAYS
Vice-Pres. for Enrollment: Dr BETH TRIPLETT
Vice-Pres. for Institutional Advancement: JAMES FORST
Registrar: STEPHANIE ELFRINK
Librarian: Dr EUGENIA MCKEE
Library of 269,764 items
Number of teachers: 283
Number of students: 3,055

DEANS

College of Arts and Sciences: Dr DANIEL SPARLING
John E. Simon School of Business: Dr PAMELA HORWITZ
School of Education: Dr SAM HAUSFATHER
School of Health Professions: Dr CHARLES J. GULAS

MIDWESTERN BAPTIST THEOLOGICAL SEMINARY

5001 North Oak Trafficway, Kansas City, MO 64118
Telephone: (816) 414-3700
Fax: (816) 414-3799
E-mail: admissions@mbts.edu
Internet: www.mbts.edu
Founded 1957
Private control (Southern Baptist Convention)
Academic year: August to July
Pres.: Dr R. PHILIP ROBERTS
Vice-Pres. for Academic Devt: THOR MADSEN
Vice-Pres. for Admin.: ANTHONY W. ALLEN
Vice-Pres. for Institutional Advancement: Rev. MARTY HARKEY
Vice-Pres. for Institutional Effectiveness: RODNEY HARRISON
Vice-Pres. for Student Devt: Dr ALAN BRANCH
Registrar: DAVID RICHARDS
Librarian: CRAIG KUBIC
Library of 115,000 vols
Number of teachers: 30
Number of students: 253 (full-time)

MISSOURI BAPTIST UNIVERSITY

1 College Park Dr., Creve Coeur, MO 63141-8698
Telephone: (314) 434-1115
Fax: (314) 434-7596
E-mail: admissions@mobap.edu
Internet: www.mobap.edu
Founded 1957 as campus extension of Hannibal-LaGrange College; present name 1999
Private control
Academic year: August to April
Pres.: Dr R. ALTON LACEY
Provost/Vice-Pres. for Academic Affairs: Dr ARLEN R. DYKSTRA
Vice-Pres. for Institutional Advancement: KEITH ROSS
Vice-Pres. for Student Devt: Dr ANDY CHAMBERS (acting)
Chief Financial Officer: KEN REVENAUGH
Dir of Library Services: NITSA HINDELEH
Number of teachers: 151
Number of students: 3,496 (all campuses).

BRANCH CAMPUSES

Franklin County Extension: 45 Silo Plaza Dr., Union, MO 63084; tel. (636) 583-6600; fax (636) 583-6608; e-mail fc@mobap.edu; Dean Dr ROBERTA ROSS-FISHER.

Jefferson College Extension: 1000 Viking Dr., Hillsboro, MO 63050; tel. (636) 797-3000 ext. 242; fax (636) 789-5103; e-mail jc@mobap.edu; Dean AMBER HENRY.

Troy/Wentzville Campus: 75 College Campus Dr., Moscow Mills, MO 63362; tel. (636) 366-4363; fax (636) 356-4119; e-mail tw@mobap.edu; Dean MARY SUE THOMPSON.

MISSOURI SOUTHERN STATE UNIVERSITY

3950 East Newman Rd, Joplin, MO 64801-1595
Telephone: (417) 625-9399
Fax: (417) 659-4497
E-mail: admissions@mssu.edu
Internet: www.mssu.edu
Founded 1937 as Joplin Junior College; as Missouri Southern State College 1965; present name and status 2003
State control
Academic year: June to May
Pres.: Dr TERRI AGEE (acting)
Vice-Pres. for Academic Affairs: Dr RICHARD J. MCCALLUM
Vice-Pres. for Business Affairs: Dr THERESA A. AGEE
Vice-Pres. for Lifelong Learning: Dr JACK G. SPURLIN
Registrar: CHERYL DOBSON
Library Dir: WENDY L. MCGRANE
Number of teachers: 289
Number of students: 5,899

DEANS
School of Arts and Sciences: Dr JOHN P. MESSICK
School of Business Administration: BRAD A. KLEINDL
School of Education: GLENN COLTHARP
School of Technology: Dr TIA M. STRAIT

MISSOURI STATE UNIVERSITY

901 South National, Springfield, MO 65804
Telephone: (417) 836-5000
Fax: (417) 836-6777
E-mail: info@missouristate.edu
Internet: www.missouristate.edu
Founded 1905
Pres.: Dr MICHAEL T. NIETZEL
Provost: Dr BELINDA MCCARTHY
Dean of Library Services: KAREN HORNY
Library of 609,852 vols, 827,099 govt docs, 871,618 units of microform, 29,373 audio visual titles, 184,580 maps, 4,750 current periodicals
Number of teachers: 816 (649 full-time, 167 part-time)
Number of students: 16,439

DEANS
College of Arts and Letters: Dr CAREY ADAMS
College of Business Admin.: Dr RONALD R. BOTTIN
College of Education: Dr DAVID L. HOUGH
College of Health and Human Services: Dr HELEN REID
College of Humanities and Public Affairs: Dr LORENE H. STONE
College of Natural and Applied Sciences: Dr TAMERA JAHNKE
Graduate College: Dr FRANK EINHELLIG

MISSOURI VALLEY COLLEGE

500 East College, Marshall, MO 65340
Telephone: (660) 831-4000
Fax: (660) 831-4039
Internet: www.moval.edu
Founded 1889
Pres.: Dr BONNIE L. HUMPHREY
Chief Academic Officer: Dr EARL F. WELLBORN, JR
Registrar: MARSHA LASHLEY
Librarian: PAMELA REEDER
Library of 70,000 vols
Number of teachers: 85
Number of students: 1,351

DEANS
Education, Health and Human Services: KARLA BRUNTZEL
Mathematics and Sciences: CHARLES ED LESLIE

MISSOURI WESTERN STATE UNIVERSITY

4525 Downs Dr., St Joseph, MO 64507
Telephone: (816) 271-4200
E-mail: admission@missouriwestern.edu
Internet: www.missouriwestern.edu
Founded 1915 as St Joseph Junior College, present name 1969, present status 2005
State control
Academic year: August to May
Pres.: Dr ROBERT A. VARTABEDIAN
Vice-Pres. and Provost: Dr JEANNE DAFFRON
Vice-Pres. for Financial Planning and Admin.: MEL KLINKNER
Vice-Pres. for Univ. Advancement: DAN NICOSON
Registrar: SUSAN BRACCIANO
Library Dir: JULIA SCHNEIDER
Library of 202,000 vols
Number of teachers: 200
Number of students: 5,200

DEANS
Liberal Arts and Sciences: Dr MURRAY NABORS
Professional Studies: (vacant)

NAZARENE THEOLOGICAL SEMINARY

1700 East Meyer Blvd, Kansas City, MO 64131
Telephone: (816) 268-5400
Fax: (816) 268-5500
E-mail: enroll@nts.edu
Internet: www.nts.edu
Founded 1945
Private control
Academic year: August to May
Pres.: Dr RON BENEFIEL
Dean of Admin.: Dr MARTY BUTLER
Dean of the Faculty: Dr ROGER HAHN
Registrar: PAMELA ASHER
Librarian: DEBRA L. BRADSHAW
Library of 140,000 vols, 520 periodicals
Number of teachers: 27
Number of students: 350 (full-time)
Publication: *The Tower*.

NORTHWEST MISSOURI STATE UNIVERSITY

800 University Dr., Maryville, MO 64468
Telephone: (660) 562-1212
Fax: (660) 562-1993
E-mail: admissions@nwmissouri.edu
Internet: www.nwmissouri.edu
Founded 1905
Pres.: Dr JOHN JASINSKI
Provost: Dr DOUG DUNHAM
Vice-Pres. for Finance: STACY CARRICK
Vice-Pres. for Information Systems: Dr JOHN T. RICKMAN
Vice-Pres. for Institutional Advancement: ORRIE COVERT
Vice-Pres. for Student Affairs: JACKIE ELLIOTT
Vice-Pres. for Univ. Relations: Dr TIM MCMOHAN
Registrar: LINDA GIRARD
Dir of Libraries: GREGORY HADDOCK
Library of 221,200 vols
Number of teachers: 227
Number of students: 6,280

DEANS
College of Arts and Sciences: Dr CHARLES MCADAMS
College of Business and Professional Studies: Dr THOMAS BILLESBACH
College of Education and Human Services: Dr MAX RUHL
Graduate School: GREGORY HADDOCK
Missouri Academy: Dr CLEO SAMUDZI

PARK UNIVERSITY

8700 NW River Park Dr., Parkville, MO 64152
Telephone: (816) 741-2000
Fax: (816) 741-4911
Internet: www.park.edu
Founded 1875
4-Year, liberal arts college; 43 campuses in 21 states
Pres.: Dr BEVERLEY BYERS-PEVITTS
Provost and Sr Vice-Pres.: Dr MICHAEL DROGE
Vice-Pres. for Academic Affairs: Dr MARILYN BARTELS
Vice-Pres. for Distance Learning: Dr THOMAS W. PETERMAN
Vice-Pres. for Finance and Admin.: DORLA WATKINS
Vice-Pres. for Student Services: CLARINDA H. CREIGHTON
Vice-Pres. for Univ. Advancement: CAREN HANDLEMAN
Vice-Pres. and Gen. Counsel: ROGER HERSHEY
Librarian: ANN SCHULTIS
Library of 130,900 vols, 775 periodicals
Number of teachers: 100
Number of students: 1,194

ROCKHURST UNIVERSITY

1100 Rockhurst Rd, Kansas City, MO 64110
Telephone: (816) 501-4000
Fax: (816) 501-4588
Internet: www.rockhurst.edu
Founded 1910
Academic year: August to May
Pres.: Rev. THOMAS B. CURRAN
Vice-Pres. for Academic Affairs and Student Devt: Dr WILLIAM HAEFELE
Vice-Pres. for Business and Finance: GUY SWANSON
Vice-Pres. for Mission and Min.: Rev. KEVIN CULLEN
Vice-Pres. for Univ. Advancement: Dr JANE LAMPO
Registrar: MINDA THROWER
Librarian: LAURIE HATHMAN
Library of 115,615 vols
Number of teachers: 208
Number of students: 2,765

DEANS
College of Arts and Sciences: Dr SHIRLEY SCRITCHFIELD
School of Graduate and Professional Studies: Dr JEFFREY R. BREESE
Helzberg School of Management: Dr JAMES DALEY
Research College of Nursing: Dr NANCY O. DEBASIO

SAINT LOUIS CHRISTIAN COLLEGE

1360 Grandview Dr., Florissant, MO 63033
Telephone: (314) 837-6777
Fax: (314) 837-8291
E-mail: admissions@slcconline.edu
Internet: www.slcconline.edu
Founded 1956
Private control
Academic year: July to June
Pres.: Dr GUTHRIE VEECH

Academic Dean: MICHAEL CHAMBERS
Dean of Students: CHRISTINE CABLE
Registrar: CINDY BINGAMON
CFO/COO: Dr JUDITH LINCOLN

Library of 40,298 vols
Number of teachers: 9
Number of students: 301

ST LOUIS COLLEGE OF PHARMACY

4588 Parkview Pl., St Louis, MO 63110-1088
Telephone: (314) 367-8700
E-mail: admissions@stlcop.edu
Internet: www.stlcop.edu

Founded 1864
Private control

Pres.: Dr THOMAS F. PATTON
Vice-Pres. for Academic Affairs: Dr WENDY DUNCAN-HEWITT
Vice-Pres. for Advancement: BRETT SCHOTT
Vice-Pres. for Enrollment Services: GLORIA J. VERTREES
Vice-Pres. for Finance: GARY G. TORRENCE
Vice-Pres. for Information Technology: F. CHAD SHEPHERD
Vice-Pres. for Marketing and Communications: MARCUS LONG
Vice-Pres. for Student Affairs: Dr KIMBERLY J. KILGORE
Registrar: PENELOPE MYERS BRYANT
Librarian: PATRICK HENDERSHOT

Library of 54,000 vols
Number of teachers: 108
Number of students: 854 (788 undergraduate, 66 graduate)

DIRECTORS

Arts and Sciences: Dr KIMBERLY J. KILGORE
Pharmacy: Dr WENDY DUNCAN-HEWITT

SAINT LOUIS UNIVERSITY

1 Grand Blvd, St Louis, MO 63103
Telephone: (314) 977-2500
Fax: (314) 977-3412
E-mail: admitme@slu.edu
Internet: www.slu.edu

Founded 1818; chartered 1832
Private control
Academic year: September to May (2 terms)

Pres.: Rev. LAWRENCE H. BIONDI
Provost: JOE WEIXLMANN
Vice-Pres. for Business and Finance: ROBERT WOODRUFF
Vice-Pres. for Community Relations: JEFF FOWLER
Vice-Pres. for Devt and Univ. Relations: THOMAS KEEFE
Vice-Pres. for Enrollment and Academic Services: BOYD BRADSHAW
Vice-Pres. for Facilities Management and Civic Affairs: KATHLEEN BRADY
Vice-Pres. for Human Resources: KEN FLEISCHMANN
Vice-Pres. for Information Technology Services: VIRGINIA HENSON
Vice-Pres. for Madrid Campus: FRANK REALE
Vice-Pres. for Mission and Ministry: FRANK REALE
Vice-Pres. for Student Devt: KENT PORTERFIELD
Gen. Counsel: WILLIAM KAUFFMAN
Registrar: JOHN-HERBERT JAFFRY
Dir of Libraries: GAIL M. STAINES

Library: see Libraries and Archives
Number of teachers: 3,121 (1,301 full-time, 1,820 part-time)
Number of students: 12,733

Publications: *African American Review*, *Boulevard*, *Forum for Social Economics*, *Gerontology: Social Science*, *Institute of Jesuit Sources*, *Journal of Health Law*, *Journal of Herpetology*, *Journal of Urban Affairs*, *Manuscripta*, *Pageoph*, *Policy History*, *Public Law Review*, *Review for Religious*, *Saint Louis University Law Journal*, *Studies in the Spirituality of Jesuits*, *The Modern Schoolman*, *Theology Digest*, *Warsaw Trans Atlantic Law Journal*

DEANS

College of Arts and Sciences: DONALD G. BRENNAN
College of Education and Public Service: JOHN WATZKE
College of Philosophy and Letters: GARTH L. HALLETT
Doisy College of Health Sciences: CHARLOTTE ROYEEN
Graduate School: DONALD G. BRENNAN
John Cook School of Business: ELLEN F. HARSHMAN
Parks College of Engineering, Aviation and Technology: MANOJ PATANKAR
School of Law: JEFFREY E. LEWIS
School of Medicine: PHILIP O. ALDERSON
School of Nursing: TERI A. MURRAY
School of Professional Studies: MARLA BERG-WEGER
School of Public Health: HOMER SCHMITZ
School of Social Work: JOHN WATZKE
Madrid Campus: FRANK REALE

PROFESSORS

ABELL, B. F., Meteorology
AL-JUREIDINI, S. B., Paediatrics
ALBERT, S. G., Internal Medicine
ALDRIDGE, R. D., Biology
AMINE, L. S., Marketing
AMON, E., Obstetrics and Gynaecology
ANDERSON, E. L., Internal Medicine
ANDERSON, R. O., Communication
ARMBRECHT, H. J., Internal Medicine
ARTAL, R., Obstetrics and Gynaecology
ASPINWALL, N., Biology
AZZAM, F. J., Anaesthesiology
BACON, B. R., Internal Medicine
BAJAJ, S. P., Internal Medicine
BALDASSARE, J. J., Pharmacological and Physiological Sciences
BALFOUR, I. C., Paediatrics
BANKS, W. A., Internal Medicine
BARBER, M. D., Philosophy
BARENKAMP, S. J., Paediatrics
BARMANN, L. F., American Studies
BARRY, R. C., Paediatrics
BASTANI, B., Internal Medicine
BAUDENDISTEL, L. J., Anaesthesiology
BELLONE, C. J., Molecular Microbiology and Immunology
BELSHE, R. B., Internal Medicine
BENOFY, L. P., Physics
BENOIT, R. P., English
BENTLEY, D. W., Internal Medicine
BERNHARDT, P., Biology
BIONDI, L. H., Modern Languages
BJERREGAARD, P., Internal Medicine
BLASKIEWICZ, R. J., Obstetrics and Gynaecology
BOHMAN, J. P., Philosophy
BOLLA, R. I., Biology
BRENNAN, D. G., Communication Sciences and Disorders
BRENNAN, W. C., Social Work
BRESLIN, R. D., Educational Leadership and Higher Education
BROCKHAUS, R. H., Management
BROWN, W. W., Internal Medicine
BROWNSON, R. C., Community Health
BUCHOLZ, R. D., Surgery
BULLER, R. M., Molecular Microbiology and Immunology
BURDGE, R. E., Orthopaedic Surgery
BURGIN, R. W., Communication
BURKE, W. J., Neurology
BURTON, F. R., Internal Medicine
CANTWELL, J. C., Mathematics and Mathematical Computer Science
CASE, M. E., Pathology
CERVENKA, P. A., Law
CHAITMAN, B. R., Internal Medicine
CHAPNICK, B. M., Pharmacological and Physiological Sciences
CHARRON, W. C., Philosophy
CHEN, S.-C., Paediatrics
CHINNADURAI, G., Molecular Virology
CHOATE, J. W., Obstetrics, Gynaecology and Women's Health
CHU, J.-Y., Paediatrics
CHUNG, H. D., Pathology
COHEN, J. D., Internal Medicine
COOPER, M. H., Anatomy and Neurobiology
COSCIA, C., Biochemistry and Molecular Biology
COUNTE, M. A., Health Administration
CREER, M. H., Pathology
CRITCHLOW, D. T., History
CROSSLEY, D. J., Geophysics
CUMMINGS, S. B., Public Policy Studies
CZYSZ, P. A., Aerospace Engineering
DAHMS, T. E., Anaesthesiology
DAVENPORT, G., Psychology
DELESPESSE, J. B., Aerospace Studies (ROTC)
DEMELLO, D. E., Pathology
DEUEL, R. K., Neurology
DIBISCEGLIE, A., Internal Medicine
DIECK, H. A., Chemistry
DIXIT, V. V., Physics
DORE, I. I., Law
DORSETT, D., Biochemistry and Molecular Biology
DOWDY, J., Mathematics and Mathematical Computer Science
DOYLE, J. P., Philosophy
DOYLE, R. E., Comparative Medicine
DUCKRO, P. N., Community and Family Medicine
DUNSFORD, J. E., Law
ELICEIRI, G. L., Pathology
ELLSWORTH, M. L., Pharmacological and Physiological Sciences
FARRIS, B. E., Jr, Sociology
FEMAN, S. S., Ophthalmology
FERGUSON, D. J., Orthodontics
FERMAN, M. A., Aerospace and Mechanical Engineering
FETE, T. J., Paediatrics
FIORE, A. C., Surgery
FISHER, J. T., Theological Studies
FITCH, C. D., Internal Medicine
FITZGIBBON, S. A., Law
FLETCHER, J. W., Internal Medicine
FLICK, L. H., Community Health
FLIESLER, S. J., Ophthalmology
FORD, C. E., Mathematics and Mathematical Computer Science
FORRESTER, T., Pharmacological and Physiological Science
FRANKOWSKI, S., Law
FREESE, R. W., Mathematics and Mathematical Computer Science
GALE, J. B., Paediatrics
GANNON, P., Psychiatry and Human Behaviour
GARCIA, P., Modern Languages
GARVIN, P. J., Surgery
GIBBONS, J. L., Psychology
GILNER, F. H., Psychology
GILSINAN, J. F., Public Policy Studies
GOLDMAN, R. L., Law
GOLDNER, J. A., Law
GOLDSTEIN, J. K., Law
GORSE, G. J., Internal Medicine
GRADY, M. P., Educational Studies
GRAFF, R. J., Surgery
GRAHAM, M. A., Pathology
GRANDGENETT, D. P., Molecular Virology
GREANEY, T. L., Law
GREEN, MAURICE, Molecular Virology
GREEN, MICHAEL, Molecular Microbiology and Immunology
GRIFFING, G. T., Internal Medicine
GROSSBERG, G. T., Psychiatry and Human Behaviour
GUITHUES, H. J., Finance

HAIRE-JOSHU, D. L., Community Health
HALLETT, G. L., Philosophy
HAMRICK, L. C., Modern Languages
HANDAL, P. J., Psychology
HARRIS, S. G., Mathematics and Mathematical Computer Science
HEANEY, R. M., Internal Medicine
HEBDA, J. J., Mathematics and Mathematical Computer Science
HEIBERG, E., Radiology
HERRMANN, R. B., Geophysics, Earth and Atmospheric Sciences
HITCHCOCK, J. F., History
HOMAN, S. M., Community Health
HOOVER, R. G., Pathology
HORVATH, F. L., Physician Assistant Education
HOWARD, A. J., Law
HRUBETZ, J., Nursing
HUANG, J. S., Biochemistry and Molecular Biology
HUGHES, H. M., Psychology
JANNEY, C. G., Pathology
JENNINGS, J. P., Accounting
JOHNSON, F. E., Surgery
JOHNSON, R. G., Surgery
JOHNSON, S. H., Law
JOHNSON, T. H., Modern Languages
JOIST, J. H., Pathology
JOS, C. J., Psychiatry and Human Behaviour
KALLIONGIS, J. E., Mathematics and Mathematical Computer Science
KAMINSKI, D. L., Surgery
KAO, M. S., Obstetrics and Gynaecology
KARUNAMOORTHY, S. N., Aerospace and Mechanical Engineering
KATZ, B. M., Research Methodology
KATZ, J. A., Management
KAUFMAN, N. H., Law
KAVANAUGH, J. F., Philosophy
KEENAN, W. J., Paediatrics
KEITHLEY, J. P., Accounting
KELLOGG, R. T., Psychology
KENNEDY, D. J., Internal Medicine
KERN, M. J., Internal Medicine
KIM, S. H., Finance
KIM, Y. S., Pharmacological and Physiological Sciences
KIMMEY, J. R., Community Health
KLEIN, C., Biochemistry and Molecular Biology
KNUEPFER, M. M., Pharmacological and Physiological Sciences
KNUTSEN, A. P., Paediatrics
KOLMER, E., American Studies
KORN, J. H., Psychology
KORNBLUTH, J., Pathology
KOWERT, B. A., Chemistry
KRAMER, T. J., Psychology
KURZ, R. S., Health Administration
KWAK, N. K., Decision Sciences and MIS
KWON, I. W., Decision Sciences and MIS
LABOVITZ, A. J., Internal Medicine
LAGUNOFF, D., Pathology
LANE, B. C., Theological Studies
LANG, J. M., Psychiatry and Human Behaviour
LECHNER, A. J., Pharmacological and Physiological Sciences
LEGUEY-FEILLEUX, J. R., Political Science
LEIPPE, M. R., Psychology
LEVARY, R. R., Decision Sciences and MIS
LEWIS, J. E., Law
LIN, Y. J., Meteorology, Earth and Atmospheric Sciences
LIU, M.-S., Pharmacological and Physiological Sciences
LOMPERIS, T. J., Political Science
LONGO, W. E., Surgery
LONIGRO, A. J., Internal Medicine
LUISIRI, A., Radiology
LYNCH, R. E., Paediatrics
MCCLURE, H. L., Aviation Science
MCGOWAN, J. R., Accounting
MCGUIRE, R. A., Communication Sciences and Disorders
MCLEOD, F. G., Theological Studies
MCSWEENEY, M., Nursing Research
MAGILL, G., Health Care Ethics
MALONE, L. J., Jr, Chemistry
MANCINI, M. J., American Studies
MANOR, D., Aerospace and Mechanical Engineering
MARGOLIS, R. B., Psychiatry and Human Behaviour
MARSKE, C. E., Sociology
MARTIN, D. S., Radiology
MARTIN, K. J., Internal Medicine
MATTFELDT-BEMAN, M., Nutrition and Dietetics
MATUSCHAK, G. M., Internal Medicine
MAYDEN, R. L., Biology
MEDOFF, J., Biology
MENGEL, M. B., Community and Family Medicine
METHENY, N. A., Adult and Gerontological Nursing
MEYER, A. E., Communication
MILLER, D. D., Internal Medicine
MILLER, D. K., Internal Medicine
MILLER, S. W., Marketing
MITCHELL, B. J., Geophysics, Earth and Atmospheric Sciences
MOBERG, T. F., Research Methodology
MODRAS, R. E., Theological Studies
MOISAN, T. E., English
MONTELEONE, J. A., Paediatrics
MONTELEONE, P. L., Paediatrics
MOORADIAN, A. D., Internal Medicine
MOORE, J. T., Meteorology, Earth and Atmospheric Sciences
MOORE, T. L., Internal Medicine
MORLEY, J. E., Internal Medicine
MUNZ, D. C., Psychology
MURDICK, N. L., Educational Studies
MURPHY, D. T., Modern Languages
MURRAY, R. L. E., Mental Health, Family, Community, and Systems Nursing
NAGABHUSHAN, B. L., Aerospace and Mechanical Engineering
NAUNHEIM, K. S., Surgery
NEEDHAM, C. A., Law
NEVINS, F. M., Law
NIKOLAI, R. J., Orthodontics
NOFFSINGER, J. E., Paediatrics
NOGUCHI, A., Paediatrics
O'BRIEN, J. C., Law
O'CONNOR, D. M., Paediatrics
OHAR, J. A., Internal Medicine
OLIVER, J. M., Psychology
ORDOWER, H. M., Law
O'TOOLE, M. L., Obstetrics and Gynaecology
PADBERG, W. H., Social Work
PALETTA, C. E., Surgery
PANNETON, W. M., Anatomy and Neurobiology
PARKER, G. E., Management
PAULY, J. J., Communication
PERMAN, W. H., Radiology
PERRY, E. I., History
PERRY, H. M., Internal Medicine
PERRY, L. C., History
PERRY, S. A., Adult and Gerontological Nursing
PETERSON, G. J., Surgery
PETRUSKA, P. J., Internal Medicine
PIERRON, R. L., Orthopaedic Surgery
POLLARD, C. A., Community and Family Medicine
PUNZO, V. C., Philosophy
PURO, S., Political Science
RAHMAN, H., Electrical Engineering
RANA, W.-U.-Z., Anatomy and Neurobiology
RAO, G. V., Earth and Atmospheric Sciences
RAO, P. S., Paediatrics
RAVINDRA, K., Aerospace and Mechanical Engineering
RAY, R., Internal Medicine
REBORE, R. W., Educational Leadership and Higher Education
REESE, C., Mental Health, Family, Community and Systems Nursing
REIMERS, H. J., Internal Medicine
RENARD, G. J., Jr, Theological Studies
ROHLIK, J., Law
ROMEIS, J. C., Health Services Research
ROSS, M. J., Psychology
ROY, T. S., Radiation Oncology
RUCKDESCHEL, R. A., Social Work
RUDDY, T. M., History
RUH, M. F., Pharmacological and Physiological Sciences
RUH, T. S., Pharmacological and Physiological Sciences
RYERSE, J. S., Pathology
SALIMI, Z., Radiology
SALINAS-MADRIGAL, L., Pathology
SALSICH, P. W., Jr, Law
SAMSON, W. K., Pharmacological and Physiological Sciences
SANCHEZ, J. M., History
SANTHANAM, T. S., Physics
SCALZO, A. J., Paediatrics
SCHLAFLY, D. L., Jr, History
SCHMITZ, H. H., Health Administration
SCHMITZ, P. G., Internal Medicine
SCHULZE, I. T., Molecular Microbiology and Immunology
SCOTT, J. F., English
SEITZ, N. E., Finance
SELHORST, J. B., Neurology
SEVERSON, J. G., Jr, Biology
SHANER, M. C., Management
SHAPIRO, M. J., Surgery
SHEA, W. M., Theological Studies
SHIELDS, J. B., Radiology
SHIPPEY, T. A., English
SILBERSTEIN, M. J., Radiology
SILVERBERG, A. B., Internal Medicine
SLAVIN, R. G., Internal Medicine
SLY, W. S., Biochemistry and Molecular Biology
SMITH, G. S., Surgery
SMITH, K., Jr, Surgery
SOTELO-AVILA, C., Pathology
SPAZIANO, V. T., Chemistry
SPRAGUE, R. S., Internal Medicine
STACEY, L. M., Physics
STANTON, C. M., Educational Leadership and Higher Education
STARK, W., Biology
STEINHARDT, G. F., Urology, Surgery
STEVENS, T. C., Mathematics and Mathematical Computer Science
STOEBERL, P. A., Management
STOLZER, A. J., Aviation Science
STRATMAN, H. G., Internal Medicine
STRETCH, J. J., Social Work
STUMP, D. V., English
STUMP, E. A., Philosophy
SWANSTROM, T., Public Policy Studies
SWIERKOSZ, E. M., Pathology
TAIT, R. C., Psychiatry and Human Behaviour
TAN, Y., Anatomy and Neurobiology
TERRY, N., Law
THACKER, W. D., Physics
THOMAS, C. W., Biomedical Engineering
THOMAS, D. R., Internal Medicine
TOCE, S. S., Paediatrics
TOLBERT, D. L., Anatomy and Neurobiology
TOMAZIC, T. J., Research Methodology
TREADGOLD, W., History
TRUE, W. R., Community Health
TSAU, C. M., Mathematics and Mathematical Computer Science
TUCHLER, D. J., Law
ULTMANN, M. H., Paediatrics
VAGO, S., Sociology
VAN DER BERG, S., English
VIRGO, K. S., Surgery
VOGLER, C. A., Pathology
VOGLER, G. A., Comparative Medicine
WACKER, W. D., Mathematics and Mathematical Computer Science
WALENTIK, C. A., Paediatrics
WARREN, K. F., Political Science
WATSON, S., Law

WEBB, K., Community and Family Medicine
WEBER, T. R., Surgery
WEBSTER, R. O., Internal Medicine
WEINBERGER, A. M., Law
WEIXLMANN, J., English
WELCH, P. J., Economics
WERNET, S. P., Social Work
WESTFALL, T. C., Pharmacological and Physiological Sciences
WHITING, R. B., Internal Medicine
WHITMAN, B., Paediatrics
WILLIAMS, D. R., Law
WILLMORE, L. J., Jr, Neurology
WINN, H. N., Obstetrics and Gynaecology
WOLD, W. S. M., Molecular Microbiology and Immunology
WOLINSKY, F. D., Health Administration
WOLVERSON, M. K., Radiology
WONGSURAWAT, N., Internal Medicine
WOOD, E. G., Paediatrics
WOOD, T. T., Art and Art History
YEAGER, F., Finance
YOUNG, P. A., Anatomy and Neurobiology
ZAHM, D. S., Anatomy and Neurobiology
ZASSENHAUS, H. P., Molecular Microbiology and Immunology
ZENSER, T. V., Internal Medicine

SAINT PAUL SCHOOL OF THEOLOGY

5123 East Truman Rd, Kansas City, MO 64127
Telephone: (816) 483-9600
Fax: (816) 483-9605
E-mail: spst@spst.edu
Internet: www.spst.edu
Private control
Pres.: Dr MYRON F. MCCOY
Vice-Pres. for Academic Affairs and Dean: PAMELA D. COUTURE
Registrar: NICOLE SCHOENHALS
Dir of Library and Information Services: LOGAN S. WRIGHT
Library of 81,000 vols
Number of teachers: 41
Number of students: 325

SOUTHEAST MISSOURI STATE UNIVERSITY

1 University Plaza, Cape Girardeau, MO 63701
Telephone: (314) 651-2000
Fax: (314) 651 5061
Internet: www.semo.edu
Founded 1873
Pres.: Dr KENNETH W. DOBBINS
Provost: Dr JANE STEPHENS
Dir of Admissions: DEBORAH BELOW
Registrar: SANDRA HINKLE
Dir of Library: ED BUIS
Library of 430,000 vols, 287,000 govt docs and 1.2m. microforms
Number of teachers: 401
Number of students: 9,534

DEANS
College of Business and University Int. Programs: GERALD MCDOUGALL
College of Education: SUE SHEPARD
College of Health and Human Services: LORETTA PRATER
College of Liberal Arts: CHRIS MCGOWAN
College of Science and Mathematics: CHRIS MCGOWAN
School of Graduate Studies: FRED JANZOW
School of Polytechnic Studies: RANDALL SHAW
School of Univ. Studies and Academic Information Services: DAVID STARRETT

SOUTHWEST BAPTIST UNIVERSITY

1600 University Ave, Bolivar, MO 65613
Telephone: (417) 328-5281
Fax: (417) 326-1514
E-mail: admitme@sbuniv.edu
Internet: www.sbuniv.edu
Founded 1878 as Southwest Baptist College; present name 1981
Private control
Pres.: Dr C. PAT TAYLOR
Provost: Dr GORDON DUTILE
Vice-Pres. for Admin.: RON MAUPIN
Vice-Pres. for Enrollment Management: Dr STEPHANIE MILLER
Vice-Pres. for Information and Technology Services: Dr BOB MCGLASSON
Vice-Pres. for Univ. Relations: Dr R. STANTON NORMAN
Registrar: JOHN CREDILLE
Dean of Library Services: ED WALTON (acting)
Library of 129,000 vols
Number of teachers: 106
Number of students: 3,700 (all campuses: 2,700 undergraduate, 1,000 graduate)

DEANS
College of Business and Computer Science: Dr DAVID WHITLOCK
College of Science and Mathematics: (vacant)
Courts Redford College of Theology and Church Vocations: Dr RODNEY REEVES
Geneva Casebolt College of Music, Arts and Letters: Dr WILLIAM BROWN
Lewis E. Schollian College of Education and Social Science: Dr LINDA WOODERSON
St John's College of Nursing and Health Sciences: Dr JENNIFER WILSON

BRANCH CAMPUSES
SBU-Mountain View: POB 489, Mountain View, MO 65548;209 West 1st St, Mountain View, MO 65548; tel. (417) 934-2999; Dir LARRY PRICE.
SBU-Salem: 501 South Grand, Salem, MO 65560; tel. (573) 729-7071; Dir MIKE SHELTON.
SBU-Springfield: 4431 South Fremont, Springfield, MO 65804; tel. (417) 841-5049.

STEPHENS COLLEGE

1200 E Broadway, Columbia, MO 65215
Telephone: (800) 876-7207
Fax: (573) 876-7165
E-mail: info@stephens.edu
Internet: www.stephens.edu
Founded 1833
Academic year: August to May
Pres.: Dr DIANNE LYNCH
Vice-Pres. for Academic Affairs: MARY HASSINGER
Vice-Pres. for Devt: CAROL JULIAN
Vice-Pres. for Finance and Admin.: LINDI OVERTON
Vice-Pres. for Enrollment Management: CHRIS COLLIER
Registrar: LINDA SHARP
Library Dir: CORRIE HUTCHISON
Library of 134,672 vols
Number of teachers: 56 full-time
Number of students: 864

TRUMAN STATE UNIVERSITY

100 E Normal, Kirksville, MO 63501
Telephone: (660) 785-4000
Fax: (660) 785-7456
E-mail: admissions@truman.edu
Internet: www.truman.edu
Founded 1867; fmrly Northeast Missouri State Univ. (until 1996)
Academic year: August to May
Pres.: Dr DARRELL KRUEGER
Provost and Vice-Pres. for Academic Affairs: Dr TROY PAINO
Registrar: Dr MARTY EISENBERG
Dean of Library: RICHARD COUGHLIN
Library of 483,718 vols
Number of teachers: 358
Number of students: 5,842

DEANS
College of Arts and Sciences: Dr DOUGLAS DAVENPORT
School of Business: Dr RENÉE WACHTER
School of Health Sciences and Education: Dr SAM MINNER

UNIVERSITY OF CENTRAL MISSOURI

Warrensburg, MO 64093
Telephone: (660) 543-4111
Fax: (660) 543-8517
E-mail: admit@ucmo.edu
Internet: www.ucmo.edu
Academic year: August to May
Founded 1871
Pres.: Dr AARON PODOLEFSKY
Provost: Dr MICHAEL GRELLE
Vice-Pres. of Admin. and Finance: Dr BETTY ROBERTS
Librarian: MOLLIE DINWIDDIE
Library: 1.3m. vols, 2,500 newspaper and periodical subscriptions, 829,100 microforms
Number of teachers: 449
Number of students: 10,700

DEANS
College of Arts, Humanities and Social Sciences: GERSHAM NELSON
College of Education: MIKE WRIGHT
College of Health and Human Services: RICK SLUDER
College of Science and Technology: ALICE GREIFE
Harmon College of Business Administration: JOAN MANSFIELD
Honors College: PETER VISCUSI

UNIVERSITY OF MISSOURI SYSTEM

Columbia, MO 65211
Telephone: (573) 882-2011
Fax: (573) 882-2721
E-mail: mu4u@missouri.edu
Internet: www.umsystem.edu
Founded 1839
Pres.: GORDON H. LAMB
Sr Vice-Pres. for Academic Affairs: STEPHEN W. LEHMKUHLE
Vice-Pres. for Finance and Admin.: NATALIE KRAWITZ
Vice-Pres. for Govt Relations: STEVE KNORR
Vice-Pres. for Human Resources: R. KENNETH HUTCHINSON
Vice-Pres. for Information Systems: GARY K. ALLEN
Library: see Libraries and Archives
Number of teachers: 7,478
Number of students: 63,783.

CONSTITUENT CAMPUSES

University of Missouri—Columbia

Columbia, MO 65211
Telephone: (573) 882-2121
E-mail: mu4u@missouri.edu
Internet: www.missouri.edu
Founded 1839
State control
Academic year: August to May
Chancellor: BRADY DEATON
Provost: BRIAN FOSTER
Vice-Chancellor for Admin. Services: JACQUELYN JONES
Vice-Chancellor for Devt and Alumni Relations: DAVID HOUSH

Vice-Chancellor for Student Affairs: CATHY SCROGGS
Registrar: BRENDA SELMAN
Dir of Admissions: BARBARA RUPP
Number of teachers: 4,545
Number of students: 32,415

DEANS

College of Agriculture, Food and Natural Resources: THOMAS PAYNE
College of Arts and Sciences: MICHAEL O'BRIEN
College of Business: JOAN GABEL
College of Education: DANIEL CLAY
College of Engineering: JAMES E. THOMPSON
College of Human Environmental Sciences: STEPHEN JORGENSEN
College of Veterinary Medicine: NEIL OLSON
Graduate School: GEORGE JUSTICE
School of Health Professions: RICHARD OLIVER
School of Journalism: DEAN MILLS (acting)
School of Law: R. LAWRENCE DESSEM
School of Medicine: ROBERT CHURCHILL
School of Nursing: JUDITH FITZGERALD MILLER

University of Missouri—Kansas City

5100 Rockhill Rd, Kansas City, MO 64110
Telephone: (816) 235-1000
E-mail: admit@umkc.edu
Internet: www.umkc.edu
Founded 1929
State control
Academic year: August to July
Chancellor: GUY H. BAILEY
Provost and Vice-Chancellor for Academic Affairs: MARVIN R. QUERRY
Vice-Chancellor for Admin. Affairs: RICHARD L. ANDERSON
Vice-Chancellor for Student Affairs and Enrollment Management: MELVIN C. TYLER
Vice-Chancellor for Univ. Advancement: JOHN AMATO
Registrar: WILSON BERRY
Dir of Admissions: MELVIN TYLER
Dean of Libraries: SHARON L. BOSTICK
Library of 868,000 vols, 1.5m. microforms
Number of teachers: 1,653
Number of students: 14,213

DEANS

College of Arts and Sciences: KAREN VORST
Conservatory of Music and Dance: JAMES MOBBERLEY
Henry W. Bloch School of Business and Public Administration: HOMER EREKSON
School of Biological Sciences: LAWRENCE DREYFUS
School of Computing and Engineering: KHOSROW SOHRABY
School of Dentistry: MICHAEL J. REED
School of Education: LINDA L. EDWARDS
School of Graduate Studies: RONALD A. MACQUARRIE
School of Law: ELLEN SUNI
School of Medicine: BETTY M. DREES
School of Nursing: LORA LACEY-HAUN
School of Pharmacy: ROBERT W. PIEPHO

Missouri University of Science and Technology

106 Parker Hall, 300 W 13th St, Rolla, MO 65409-1060
Telephone: (573) 341-4114
Fax: (573) 341-6306
E-mail: admissions@mst.edu
Internet: www.mst.edu
Founded 1870, fmrly Univ. of Missouri–Rolla
State control
Academic year: August to July
Chancellor: JOHN F. CARNEY, III
Provost and Exec. Vice-Chancellor: WARREN KENT WRAY
Vice-Chancellor for Admin. Services: STEVE MALOTT
Vice-Chancellor for Student Affairs: DEBRA ROBINSON
Vice-Chancellor for Univ. Advancement: CONNIE EGGERT
Registrar: LAURA STOLL
Dean of Enrollment Management: JAY GOFF
Library Dir: ANDREW STEWART
Library of 388,000 vols
Number of teachers: 461
Number of students: 4,549

University of Missouri—St Louis

1 University Blvd, St Louis, MO 63121-4400
Telephone: (314) 516-5000
Fax: (314) 516-5378
E-mail: admissions@umsl.edu
Internet: www.umsl.edu
Founded 1963
State control
Academic year: August to July
Chancellor: Prof. THOMAS F. GEORGE
Provost and Vice-Chancellor for Academic Affairs: Prof. GLEN H. COPE
Vice-Chancellor for Advancement: MARTIN F. LEIFELD
Vice-Chancellor for Managerial and Technological Services: JAMES M. KRUEGER
Vice-Provost for Research Admin.: Prof. NASSER ARSHADI
Vice-Provost for Student Affairs: CURTIS C. COONROD
Dir of Admissions: ALAN BYRD
Dir of Office of Equal Opportunity and Diversity: Prof. DEBORAH J. BURRIS
Registrar: LINDA SILMAN
Dean of Libraries: CHRISTOPHER DAMES
Library: 1.2m. vols, 1.2m. govt documents, 1.3m. microfilm units, 3,966 audiovisual units, 1,190 electronic books
Number of teachers: 1,289 (495 full-time, 794 part-time)
Number of students: 16,802
Publication: *Theory and Society Journal*

DEANS AND DIRECTORS

College of Arts and Sciences: RONALD YASBIN
College of Business Administration: N. KEITH WOMER
College of Education: KATHLEEN HAYWOOD
College of Fine Arts and Communication: JAMES RICHARDS
College of Nursing: JULIANN G. SEBASTIAN
College of Optometry: LARRY J. DAVIS
Continuing Education: WILLIAM T. WALKER
Graduate School: JUDITH WALKER DE FELIX
Honours College: ROBERT M. BLISS
School of Social Work: LOIS H. PIERCE
UMSL/WU Joint Undergraduate Engineering Program: JOSEPH A. O'SULLIVAN

PROFESSORS

ALTHOF, W., Educational Psychology
ANDERSON, K. C., Art and Art History
BERKOWITZ, M. W., Educational Psychology
BIRD, A., Business Administration
BOHAN, R. L., Art and Art History
BREAUGH, J., Business Administration
BURSIK, R. J., Criminology and Criminal Justice
CALSYN, R. J., Psychology
CAMPBELL, J. F., Business Administration
CARROLL, J. C., English
CHICKOS, J., Chemistry
CHUI, C., Mathematics and Computer Science
COCHRAN, J. A., Educational Leadership Policy
COKER, A. A., Theatre and Dance
COOK, S., English
COREY, J. Y., Chemistry
COSMOPOULOS, M., Anthropology
COTTONE, R. R., Counseling (College of Education)
CURRY, G. D., Criminology and Criminal Justice
DIBOOGLU, S., Economics
EBEST, S. B., English
ESBENSEN, F. A., Criminology and Criminal Justice
EVEN, Y., Art and Art History
EYSSELL, T. H., College of Business Administration
FEIGENBAUM, S. K., Economics
FLORES, R. A., Physics and Astronomy
FRIEDLANDER, R. J., Mathematics and Computer Science
FUNG, H. G., Business Administration
GERTEIS, L. S., History
GILLINGHAM, J. R., History
GOKEL, G. W., Center for Nanoscience
GRADY, F. W., English
GRANGER, C. R., Biology
HANDEL, P. H., Physics and Astronomy
HARBACH, B. C., Music
HARRIS, M. M., Business Administration
HARRIS, W. R., Chemistry
HENSON, B. L., Physics and Astronomy
HUNT, J. H., Biology
HURLEY, A., History
JANSON, M. A., Business Administration
JIANG, Q., Mathematics and Computer Science
JONES, E., Political Science
JOSHI, K., Business Administration
KELLOGG, E. A., Biology
KYLE, W. C., Education—Teaching and Learning
LACITY, M. C., Business Administration
LANKFORD, E. L., Art and Art History
LAURITSEN, J. L., Criminology and Criminal Justice
LAWRENCE, E. C., Business Administration
LEE, R. K., Nursing
LEVENTHAL, J. J., Physics and Astronomy
LOISELLE, B. A., Biology
LUI, J., Center for Nanoscience
MCPHAIL, T. L., Theatre and Dance
MARQUIS, R. J., Biology
MARTINICH, J. S., Business Administration
MITCHELL, R. H., History
MOSS, F. E., Physics and Astronomy
MUNDY, R. A., Center for Transportation Studies
MUNSON, R., Philosophy
MURRAY, J. Y., College of Business Administration
MURRAY, M. D., Theatre and Dance
MUSHABEN, J. M., Political Science
NAUSS, R. M., Business Administration
O'BRIEN, J. J., Chemistry
OHALLMHURAIN, G., Music
PARKER, P. G., Biology
PATTERSON, M. L., Psychology
PECK, C. K., Optometry
POPE, M. L., Counseling (College of Education)
RAO, A. P., Mathematics and Computer Science
RAY, R. J., Music
RICHARDS, J., Music
RICHARDSON, L. I., Educational Leadership and Policy
RICKLEFS, R. E., Biology
ROBERTSON, D. B., Political Science
ROCHESTER, J. M., Political Science
RONEN, D., Business Administration
ROSE, D. C., Economics
ROSENFELD, R. B., Criminology and Criminal Justice
ROSS, S. A., Philosophy
ROWAN, S. W., History
SABHERWAL, R., Business Administration
SAUL, E. W., Teaching and Learning
SAUTER, V. L., Business Administration
SCHWANTES, C. A., History
SCHWARTZ, H. E., English
SEGAL, U. A., Social Work

SHERRADEN, M. S., Social Work
SHYMANSKY, J. A., Teaching and Learning
SILVA, G. E., Political Science
SIMMONS, P. E., Teaching and Learning
SMITH, L. D., College of Business Administration
SORENSEN, R. L., Economics
SPILLING, C., Chemistry
STEIN, L., Political Science
STEVENS, P. F., Biology
TANG, M. Z., Biology
TAYLOR, G. T., Psychology
TOULIATOS, D. H., Music
VANDENBERG, B. R., Psychology
WALL, E. W., English
WANG, X., Biology
WHITE, L. H., Economics
WILKENS, L. A., Biology
WILKING, B. A., Physics and Astronomy
WILLIAMS, L. V., Foreign Languages and Literature
WILLMAN, F., Music
WINKLER, A. E., Economics
WOLFE, P., English
WRIGHT, R. T., Criminology and Criminal Justice
YOUNGER, D., Art and Art History
ZARUCCHI, J. M., Art and Art History
ZENI, J. E., English

WASHINGTON UNIVERSITY IN SAINT LOUIS

Campus Box 1089, 1 Brookings Dr., Saint Louis, MO 63130
Telephone: (314) 935-6000
Fax: (314) 935-4290
E-mail: admissions@wustl.edu
Internet: www.wustl.edu

Founded 1853 as Eliot Seminary; charter altered to Washington Univ. 1857
Private control
Academic year: August to May

Chancellor: MARK S. WRIGHTON
Exec. Vice-Chancellor: EDWARD S. MACIAS
Exec. Vice-Chancellor: DAVID T. BLASINGAME
Exec. Vice-Chancellor: HENRY S. WEBBER
Exec. Vice-Chancellor for Gen. Counsel: MICHAEL R. CANNON
Exec. Vice-Chancellor for Medical Affairs: LARRY J. SHAPIRO
Vice-Chancellor for Finance: BARBARA A. FEINER
Vice-Chancellor of Govt and Community Relations: PAMELA S. LOKKEN
Vice-Chancellor for Human Resources: ANN B. PRENATT
Vice-Chancellor for Public Affairs: M. FREDERIC VOLKMANN
Vice-Chancellor for Research: EVAN D. KHARASCH
Vice-Chancellor for Scholarly Resources: SHIRLEY K. BAKER
Vice-Chancellor for Students: JAMES E. MCLEOD
Spec. Asst to the Chancellor for Academic Affairs: GERHILD S. WILLIAMS
Dean of Libraries: SHIRLEY K. BAKER

Number of teachers: 1,487 (916 full-time, 571 part-time)
Number of students: 13,575 (11,422 full-time, 2,153 part-time)

DEANS

Arts and Sciences: GARY S. WIHL
George Warren Brown School of Social Work: EDWARD F. LAWLOR
Graduate School of Arts and Sciences: RICHARD J. SMITH
Olin Business School: MAHENDRA R. GUPTA
Sam Fox School of Design and Visual Arts: CARMON COLANGELO
School of Engineering: RALPH S. QUATRANO
School of Law: KENT D. SYVERUD
School of Medicine: LARRY J. SHAPIRO

WEBSTER UNIVERSITY

470 East Lockwood Ave, St Louis, MO 63119-3194
Telephone: (314) 968-6900
Fax: (314) 968-7117
E-mail: admit@webster.edu
Internet: www.webster.edu

Founded 1915
Academic year: August to May

Pres.: Dr RICHARD S. MEYERS
Registrar: DON MORRIS
Dean of Univ. Library: LAURA REIN

Library of 299,000 vols
Number of teachers: 2,273 (173 full-time, 2,100 part-time)
Number of students: 20,964

DEANS

College of Arts and Sciences: DAVID CARL WILSON
Leigh Gerdine College of Fine Arts: (vacant)
School of Business and Technology: Dr BENJAMIN OLA AKANDE
School of Communications: DEBRA CARPENTER
School of Education: BRENDA PFYFE

WESTMINSTER COLLEGE

Fulton, MO 65251
Telephone: (573) 642-3361
Fax: (573) 642-6356
E-mail: masekp@westminster-mo.edu
Internet: www.westminster-mo.edu

Founded 1851
Academic year: August to May

Pres.: FLETCHER M. LAMKIN
Sr Vice-Pres. and Dean of Faculty: Dr GEORGE B. FORSYTHE
Vice-Pres. and Dean of Student Life: JOHN COMERFORD
Registrar: PHYLLIS MASEK
Librarian: ANGELA GERLING

Library of 121,073 vols
Number of teachers: 60
Number of students: 700

WILLIAM JEWELL COLLEGE

500 College Hill, Liberty, MO 64068
Telephone: (816) 781-7700
Fax: (816) 415-5027
Internet: www.jewell.edu

Founded 1849
Academic year: September to May

Pres.: DAVID L. SALLEE
Vice-Pres. for Academic Affairs and Dean: JOHN WESTLIE
Vice-Pres. for Advancement: CHAD JOLLY
Vice-Pres. for Enrollment and Student Affairs: RICK WINSLOW
Vice-Pres. for Finance and Operations: RON DEMPSEY
Vice-Pres. for Institutional Effectiveness: ANNE DEMA
Registrar: STEVE SCHWEGLER
Librarian: Dr HUGH STOCKS

Library of 260,119 vols
Number of teachers: 128
Number of students: 1,500

WILLIAM WOODS UNIVERSITY

1 University Ave, Fulton, MO 65251
Telephone: (573) 642-2251
Fax: (573) 592-1146
E-mail: admissions@williamwoods.edu
Internet: www.williamwoods.edu
Private control

Founded 1870
Academic year: August to May

Accredited by Higher Learning Comm.; mem. of North Central Assn

Pres.: Prof. Dr JAHNAE H. BARNETT
Vice-Pres. and Dean of Academic Affairs: Dr SHERRY MCCARTHY
Vice-Pres. for Advancement: SCOTT GALLAGHER
Vice-Pres. for Finance and Admin.: Dr BOB FESSLER
Vice-Pres. and Dean of Graduate and Professional Studies: MICHAEL WESTERFIELD
Dean of Admissions: SARAH MUNNS
Dean of Student Life: VENITA MITCHELL
Chief Financial Officer: CALE FESSLER
Library Dir: ERLENE DUDLEY

Library of 160,000 vols
Number of teachers: 52 full-time, 300 part-time
Number of students: 3,500

DEANS

Arts: Prof. AIMEE SAPP
Behavioural and Social Sciences: Assoc. Prof. SHAWN HULL
Business and Economics: Assoc. Prof. DAVID FORSTER
Education: Prof. BETSY TUTT
Equestrian Studies: Assoc. Prof. CLAUDIA STARR
Human Performance: Assoc. Prof. ANTHONY LUNGSTRUM
Science and Humanities: Assoc. Prof. KATRICIA PIERSON

MONTANA

CARROLL COLLEGE

1601 North Benton Ave, Helena, MT 59625
Telephone: (406) 447-4300
Fax: (406) 447-4533
Internet: www.carroll.edu

Founded 1909
Academic year: August to May

Pres.: Dr THOMAS TREBON
Vice-Pres. for Institutional Advancement: Dr RICHARD ORTEGA
Vice-Pres for Student Life: LYNN C. ETCHART, Dr JIM D. HARDWICK
Academic Dean: JOHN SCHARF
Registrar: MARY PAT DUTTON
Librarian: LOIS FITZPATRICK

Library of 94,000 vols
Number of teachers: 85
Number of students: 1,400

MONTANA STATE UNIVERSITY

Bozeman, MT 59717
Telephone: (406) 994-0211
Fax: (406) 994-2893
Internet: www.montana.edu

Founded 1893

Pres.: Dr WADED CRUZADO
Vice-Pres. for Admin. and Finance: CRAIG ROLOFF
Vice-Pres. for Research, Creativity and Technology Transfer: THOMAS MCCOY
Vice-Pres. for Student Affairs and Dean of Students: Dr ALLEN YARNELL
Registrar and Dir of Admissions: CHARLES NELSON
Dean of Library: BRUCE MORTON

Number of students: 10,700

DEANS OF COLLEGES

Agriculture: THOMAS MCCOY
Arts and Architecture: JERRY BANCROFT
Business: MICHAEL OWEN
Education, Health and Human Development: LARRY BAKER
Engineering: DAVID F. GIBSON
Graduate Studies: JOSEPH FEDOCK
Letters and Science: JAMES MCMILLAN
Nursing: LEA ACORD

MONTANA STATE UNIVERSITY – BILLINGS

Billings, MT 59101
Telephone: (406) 657-2011
Fax: (406) 657-2299
E-mail: admissions@msubillings.edu
Internet: www.msubillings.edu

Founded 1927
Academic year: September to May

Chancellor: RONALD P. SEXTON
Provost and Vice-Chancellor for Academic Affairs: Dr GEORGE WHITE
Vice-Chancellor for Admin. Affairs: TERRIE IVERSON
Vice-Chancellor for Student Affairs: STACY KLIPPENSTEIN
Library Dir: JANE HOWELL

Library of 281,258 vols
Number of teachers: 226
Number of students: 4,300

MONTANA STATE UNIVERSITY—NORTHERN

POB 7751, Havre, MT 59501
Telephone: (406) 265-3700
E-mail: admissions@msun.edu
Internet: www.msun.edu

Founded 1929

Chancellor: ALEX CAPDEVILLE
Registrar: STEVE JAMRUSZKA
Library Dir: VICKI GIST

Library of 84,000 vols
Number of teachers: 80
Number of students: 1,800

Baccalaureate courses in arts and sciences, business, nursing, teacher education, technology; Masters courses in education.

MONTANA TECH OF THE UNIVERSITY OF MONTANA

1300 West Park St, Butte, MT 59701
Telephone: (406) 496-4101
Fax: (406) 496-4705
E-mail: enrollment@mtech.edu
Internet: www.mtech.edu

Founded 1893
Public control
Academic year: June to May

Chancellor: Dr FRANK GILMORE
Vice-Chancellor for Academic Affairs: Dr DOUG ABBOTT
Vice-Chancellor for Administration and Finance: MAGGIE PETERSON
Vice-Chancellor for Development and Student Services: MIKE JOHNSON
Dean of Students: PAUL BEATTY
Dir of Admissions: TONY CAMPEAU
Dir of Library: ANN ST CLAIR

Number of teachers: 214
Number of students: 2,864

Publications: *Catalog*, *MNews*, *The Technocrat*

DEANS

College of Letters, Sciences, and Professional Studies: Dr DOUG COE
College of Technology: Dr JOHN GARIC
School of Mines and Engineering: Dr PETE KNUDSEN

ROCKY MOUNTAIN COLLEGE

1511 Poly Dr., Billings, MT 59102
Telephone: (406) 657-1000
Fax: (406) 259-9751
E-mail: admissions@rocky.edu
Internet: www.rocky.edu

Founded 1878
Academic year: August to May

Pres.: Dr MICHAEL MACE (acting)
Vice-Pres. for Academic Affairs: ANTHONY PILTZ
Dir of Library: WILLIAM KEHLER

Library of 86,600 vols
Number of teachers: 83 (45 full-time, 38 part-time)
Number of students: 800

UNIVERSITY OF GREAT FALLS

1301 20th St, S, Great Falls, MT 59405
Telephone: (406) 761-8210
Fax: (406) 791-5393
Internet: www.ugf.edu

Founded 1932

Liberal arts college; 4-year and 2-year degree courses in education, human services, professional counselling

Pres.: EUGENE J. MCALLISTER
Provost and Academic Vice-Pres.: Dr RICHARD MCDOWELL
Dir of Admissions and Records: R. HENSLEY
Dir of Library: DAVID BIBB

Library of 97,353 vols
Number of teachers: 80
Number of students: 1,400

UNIVERSITY OF MONTANA

32 Campus Dr., Missoula, MT 59812
Telephone: (406) 243-0211
Fax: (406) 243-2797
Internet: www.umt.edu

Founded 1893

Pres. and Provost: GEORGE M. DENNISON
Vice-Pres. for Admin. and Finance: ROBERT DURINGER
Assoc. Vice-Pres. for Research and Devt: DANIEL J. DWYER
Vice-Pres. for Student Affairs: TERESA BRANCH
Registrar: DAVID MICUS
Dean of Students: Dr CHARLES COUTURE
Dean of Libraries: BONNIE ALLEN

Library of 700,000 vols, 77,600 US govt documents
Number of teachers: 450
Number of students: 13,019

DEANS

College of Arts and Sciences: GERALD FETZ
College of Technology: PAUL WILLIAMSON
School of Business Administration: LARRY D. GIANCHETTA
School of Education: PAUL ROWLAND
School of Fine Arts: SHIRLEY HOWELL
School of Forestry: PERRY BROWN
School of Journalism: JERRY BROWN (acting)
School of Law: IRMA RUSSELL
School of Pharmacy and Allied Health Services: DAVID FORBES
Graduate School: DAVID STROBEL
Div. of Continuing Education: SHARON ALEXANDER

UNIVERSITY OF MONTANA WESTERN

710 S Atlantic St, Dillon, MT 59725
Telephone: (406) 683-7331
Fax: (406) 683-7493
E-mail: admissions@umwestern.edu
Internet: www.umwestern.edu

Founded 1893
State control
Academic year: September to June

Chancellor: Dr RICHARD STOREY
Asst to the Chancellor: SHELLY KESSEL
Provost and Vice-Chancellor for Academic Affairs: Dr KARL ULRICH
Asst Provost: Dr BRIAN PRICE
Vice-Chancellor for Admin. and Finance: SUSAN BRIGGS
Dir of Devt/ Alumni Affairs: AMBERLY PAHUT
Registrar: JASON KARCH
Library Dir: MICHAEL SCHULZ

Number of teachers: 50
Number of students: 1,100

NEBRASKA

BELLEVUE UNIVERSITY

1000 Galvin Rd South, Bellevue, NE 68005
Telephone: (402) 293-2000
Fax: (402) 293-2020
E-mail: pr@bellevue.edu
Internet: www.bellevue.edu

Founded 1966
Private control

Pres.: Dr JOHN B. MULLER
Provost: MARY HAWKINS
Vice-Pres. for Admin.: GERALD BLASIG
Vice-Pres. for Devt Programs: DOROTHY D. MORROW
Vice-Pres. for Marketing and Strategic Initiatives: MIKE ECHOLS
Registrar: PHILLIP E. CHAPMAN
Library Dir: ROBIN BERNSTEIN

Library of 90,000 vols
Number of teachers: 62
Number of students: 3,913

DEANS

College of Arts and Sciences: Dr THERESE MICHELS
College of Business: Dr DONNA N. MCDANIEL
College of Distributed Learning: Dr CHRISTINE M. BEISCHEL
College of Information Technology: Dr DANNY J. CREAGAN
College of Professional Studies: CHARLES KATER

CHADRON STATE COLLEGE

1000 Main St, Chadron, NE 69337
Telephone: (308) 432-6000
Fax: (308) 432-6464
Internet: www.csc.edu

Founded 1911
Academic year: August to May

Pres.: Dr JANIE C. PARK
Vice-Pres. for Academic and Student Affairs: Dr LOIS VEATH
Vice-Pres. for Admin. and Finance: DALE GRANT
Vice-Pres. for Enrollment Management and Student Services: Dr R. RANDY RHINE
Registrar: DALE WILLIAMSON
Librarian: MILTON WOLF

Library of 190,666 vols
Number of teachers: 101 full-time
Number of students: 3,206

DEANS

School of Arts and Sciences: Dr CHARLES SNARE
School of Business, Economics, Applied and Mathematical Sciences: Dr GARY A. WHITE
School of Education, Human Performance, Counseling, Psychology and Social Work: Dr MARGARET R. CROUSE

CLARKSON COLLEGE

101 South 42nd St, Omaha, NE 68131-2739
Telephone: (402) 552-3100
Fax: (402) 552-6057
E-mail: admiss@clarksoncollege.edu
Internet: www.clarksoncollege.edu
Private control

Pres.: Dr DELOIS WEEKERS
Vice-Pres. for Enrollment Management and Campus Life Operations: TONY DAMEWOOD

Vice-Pres. for Institutional Assessment, Research and Quality: JEFF EHRLICH
Registrar: MICHELE STIRTZ
Dir of Library Services: NANCY RALSTON

Number of teachers: 26
Number of students: 789 (652 undergraduate, 137 graduate)

DIRECTORS

School of Allied Health and Health Care Business: ELLEN COLLINS
School of Nursing: MARLA ERBIN-ROESMANN
School of Professional Devt: JUDI DUNN

COLLEGE OF SAINT MARY

7000 Mercy Rd, Omaha, NE 68106-2377
Telephone: (402) 399-2405
Fax: (402) 399-2341
E-mail: enroll@csm.edu
Internet: www.csm.edu

Founded 1923
Private control
Academic year: August to August

Pres.: Dr MARYANNE STEVENS
Vice-Pres. for Academic Affairs: Dr MARTIN SELLERS
Vice-Pres. for Enrollment: DIANE LEE
Vice-Pres. for Financial Services: DEBBIE KAY WARD
Vice-Pres. for Institutional Advancement: RUTH HENNEMAN
Vice-Pres. for Student Devt: Dr MARTHA BROWN
Registrar: DEBBIE NUGEN
Library Dir: FAYE COUTURE

Number of teachers: 54
Number of students: 1,000

Divs of arts and sciences, health care professions, professional studies, graduate studies.

BRANCH CAMPUS

Lincoln Campus: Suite 403, 4600 Valley Rd, Lincoln, NE 68510; tel. (402) 489-2900; e-mail lincoln@csm.edu; Dir DENICE ARCHER-GALUSHA.

CONCORDIA UNIVERSITY—NEBRASKA

800 N Columbia Ave, Seward, NE 68434
Telephone: (402) 643-3651
Fax: (402) 643-4073
E-mail: info@cune.edu
Internet: www.cune.edu

Founded 1894
Academic year: August to May

Pres.: Dr BRIAN L. FRIEDRICH
Provost: Rev. Dr JENNY MUELLER-ROEBKE
Vice-Pres. for Finance and Operations: DAVID KUMM
Vice-Pres. for Institutional Advancement: PETER KENOW
Vice-Pres. for Enrollment Management, Student Life and Athletics: SCOTT SEEVERS
Registrar: EDWIN SIFFRING
Dir of Library Services: PHIL HENDRICKSON

Library of 230,000 vols
Number of teachers: 65
Number of students: 1,200

Publication: *Issues in Christian Education* (3 a year).

CREIGHTON UNIVERSITY

Omaha, NE 68178
Telephone: (402) 280-2700
Internet: www.creighton.edu

Founded 1878, chartered 1879; attached to Soc. of Jesus
Private control
Academic year: August to May

Pres.: Rev. JOHN P. SCHLEGEL
Vice-Pres. for Academic Affairs: Prof. PATRICK J. BORCHERS
Vice-Pres. for Admin.: JOHN L. WILHELM
Vice-Pres. for Finance: JAN D MADSEN
Vice-Pres. for Health Sciences: Dr CAM E. ENARSON
Vice-Pres. for Information Technology: BRIAN A. YOUNG
Sr Vice-Pres. for Operations and Treas.: DONALD R. FREY
Vice-Pres. for Student Services and Dean of Students: Dr JOHN CERNECH
Vice-Pres. and Gen. Counsel: Rev. ANDREW F. ALEXANDER
Vice-Pres. for Univ. Relations: AMS S. BONES
Registrar: JOHN A. KRECEK
Dir of Alumni Memorial Library: MICHAEL LACROIX

Library of 916,571 vols, 1.9m. microforms
Number of teachers: 976
Number of students: 7,662

Publications: *Creighton Law Review* (4 a year), *Creighton University Magazine* (4 a year)

DEANS

Arts and Sciences: Dr ROBERT LUEGER
Business Admin.: Dr ANTHONY R. HENDRICKSON
Dentistry: Dr WAYNE W. BARKMEIER
Graduate School: GAIL JENSEN
Law: Prof. MARIANNE CULHANE
Medicine: ROWEN K. ZETTERMAN
Nursing: ELEANOR HOWELL
Pharmacy and Health Professions: CHRIS J. BRADBURY
Univ. College and Summer Sessions: BARBARA J. BRADEN

PROFESSORS

ABEL, P., Pharmacology
AGRAWAL, D., Biomedical Sciences
ALLEN, R., Pathology
ANDERSON, R., Internal Medicine
ANDERSON, T., Law School Instruction
BAECHLE, T., Exercise Sciences
BEISEL, K., Biomedical Sciences
BERTONI, J., Neurology
BEWTRA, C., Pathology
BHATIA, S., Adult and Child Psychiatry
BIRMINGHAM, E., Law School Instruction
BROCK, D., Education
BRUMBACK, R., Pathology
BUCKO, R., Sociology
CARLSON, J., Philosophy
CASALE, T., Internal Medicine
CASEY, M., Obstetrics and Gynaecology
CHENG, S., Mathematics and Computer Sciences
CHERNEY, M., Physics
CHIOU, R., Urological Surgery
CHU, C., Adult Psychiatry
CIPOLLA, S., Physics
CLARK, T., Political Science and International Relations
CULLEN, D., Internal Medicine
DALLON, C., Law School Instruction
DEWAN, N., Internal Medicine
DICKEL, C., Education
DOWD, JR, F., Pharmacology
ECKERSON, J., Exercise Sciences
FEEZELL, R., Philosophy
FENNER, G., Law School Instruction
FILIPI, C., General Surgery
FITZGIBBONS, JR, R., General Surgery
FLECKY, M., Fine and Performing Arts
FLEMING, A., Obstetrics and Gynaecology
FLETCHER, S., Paediatric Cardiology
FORSE, R., General Surgery
FRITZSCH, B., Biomedical Sciences
GAINES, R., General Surgery
GALLAGHER, J., Internal Medicine
GATALICA, Z., Pathology
GOSS, E., MacAllister Chair
GREEN, J., Law School Instruction
GREENSPOON, L., Klutznick Chair
HADDAD, A., Center for Health Policy and Ethics
HALLWORTH, R., Biomedical Sciences
HAMM, M., Graff Chair in Catholic Theology
HARMLESS, J., Theology
HARPER, C., Sociology
HAUSER, R., Theology
HE, Z., Biomedical Sciences
HEANEY, R., University Chair
HOPP, R., Paediatric Allergy
HULCE, M., Chemistry
KELLY, M., Law School Instruction
KROGSTAD, J., Accounting
LANSPA, S., Internal Medicine
LAPPE, J., Internal Medicine
LEAK, G., Psychology
LOGGIE, B., Surgery Oncology
LOVAS, S., Biomedical Sciences
LYNCH, H., Preventive Medicine
MCGUIRE, M., Orthopaedic Surgery
MCLAUGHLIN WITTEBORT, B., Biomedical Sciences
MACK, R., Law School Instruction
MALIK, D., Mathematics and Computer Sciences
MALINA, B., Theology
MANGRUM, R., Yossem Chair
MATTSON, B., Chemistry
MELILLI, K., Law School Instruction
MOHIUDDIN, S., Internal Medicine
MOOSS, A., Cardiology Education
MORDESON, J., Mathematics and Computer Sciences
MORSE, E., Law School Instruction
MUELLER, J., Theology
MURPHY, R., Biomedical Sciences
MURRAY, J., Philosophy
MURRAY, T., Pharmacology
MURTHY, V., Economics and Finance
NAIR, C., Cardiology Education
NAIR, P., Computer Science
NATH, R., McGraw Chair
NEUMEISTER, K., Law School Instruction
O'BRIEN, J., Internal Medicine
O'KEEFE IV, J., Theology
PEARSON, E., Law School Instruction
PETTY, F., Psychiatry Research
PETZEL, D., Biomedical Sciences
QUINN, T., Biomedical Sciences
RAVAL, V., Accounting
RECKER, R., Internal Medicine
RENDELL, M., Internal Medicine
RENO, R., Theology
RICH, E., Internal Medicine
ROY-HEWITSON, L., Modern Languages and Literatures
SARMA, D., Pathology
SEGER, J., Physics
SIMKINS, R., Theology
SPENCER, B., English
STEPHENS, W., Philosophy
STONE, N., Psychology
SUGIMOTO, J., Cardiac Surgery
SULLIVAN, P., Psychiatry Research
TEPLY, L., Law School Instruction
VOLKMER, R., Law School Instruction
WELIE, J., Center for Health Policy and Ethics
WHITE, M., Law School Instruction
WHITE, R., Philosophy
WHITTEN, R., Law School Instruction
WILLIAMS, M., Cardiology
WILSON, D., Forensic Psychiatry
WINGENDER, J., Economics and Finance
WORKMAN, J., Management and Marketing
WRIGHT, W., Kenefick Chair in Humanities
YEE, J., Biomedical Sciences
ZACH, T., Paediatric Newborn Medicine
ZACHARIAS, G., English
ZEHNDER, J., Environmental and Atmospheric Sciences

DANA COLLEGE

2848 College Dr., Blair, NE 68008
Telephone: (402) 426-9000
Fax: (402) 426-7225
E-mail: admissions@dana.edu
Internet: www.dana.edu

Founded 1884
Academic year: September to May

Pres.: Dr JANET S. PHILIPP
Vice-Pres. for Academic Affairs and Dean of College: Dr RAYMOND RUSSIN
Vice-Pres. for Institutional Advancement: DEAN BARD
Exec. Vice-Pres. and Chief Financial Officer: ROBERT SCHMOLL
Registrar: MELINDA STONER
Dean: Dr BRIAN VIETS
Dir of Library Services: THOMAS NIELSEN

Library of 160,000 vols, 7,000 periodicals
Number of teachers: 75
Number of students: 637

Areas of study incl. accounting, art, biology, business administration, chemistry, chemistry for secondary teachers, corporate communication, community journalism, criminal justice, English, history, integrated studies, international studies, management information systems, mathematics, musical theatre, psychology, religion, social work, Spanish, sport management, vocal music, youth ministry.

DOANE COLLEGE

1014 Boswell, Crete, NE 68333
Telephone: (402) 826-2161
Fax: (402) 826-8600
E-mail: admissions@doane.edu
Internet: www.doane.edu

Founded 1872

Campuses at Lincoln and Grand Island

Pres.: JONATHAN BRAND
Vice-Pres. for Academic Affairs: MAUREEN F. FRANKLIN
Vice-Pres. for Advancement: JOHN R. LOTHROP
Vice-Pres. for Enrollment Management and Student Leadership: KIM JACOBS
Vice-Pres. for Finance and Admin.: JULIE SCHMIDT
Vice-Pres. for Information Services: MIKE CARPENTER
Registrar: DENISE ELLIS
Librarian: DONNA DURENA

Library of 221,435 vols
Number of teachers: 104
Number of students: 3,200.

ATTACHED INSTITUTE

Midwest Institute for International Studies: Dir MAUREEN FRANKLIN.

GRACE UNIVERSITY

1311 South 9th St, Omaha, NE 68108-3629
Telephone: (402) 449-2800
Fax: (402) 341-9587
E-mail: info@graceuniversity.edu
Internet: www.graceuniversity.edu

Founded 1943 as Grace Bible Institute; present name 1995
Private control

Pres.: Dr JAMES P. ECKMAN
Academic Vice-Pres. and Dean of Faculty: Dr KARL E. PAGENKEMPER
Vice-Pres. for Finance and Operations: KEVIN SHULTZ
Vice-Pres. for Student Services: Dr JARED BURKHOLDER
Vice-Pres. for Univ. Devt: KATHY LARSEN
Registrar: KRIS J. UDD
Library Dir: STANLEY V. UDD
Number of teachers: 15
Number of students: 578 (509 undergraduate, 69 graduate)

HASTINGS COLLEGE

710 North Turner, Hastings, NE 68902-0269
Telephone: (402) 463-2402
Internet: www.hastings.edu

Founded 1882

Pres.: Dr PHILLIP DUDLEY
Vice-Pres. for Academic Affairs: Dr RICH LLOYD
Vice-Pres. for Enrollment/College Relations: SAM RENNICK
Vice-Pres. for Financial Affairs: DENIS KRIENERT
Vice-Pres. for Student Affairs: RON CHESBROUGH
Registrar: DAN PETERS
Librarian: ROBERT NEDDERMAN

Library of 115,000 vols
Number of teachers: 69
Number of students: 1,060

Depts of art, biology, chemistry, communication arts, computer science, English, foreign languages and literatures, history, humanities, mathematics, music, nursing, philosophy, physical education, physics, political science, psychology, sociology, teacher education, theatre.

MIDLAND LUTHERAN COLLEGE

900 N Clarkson St, Fremont, NE 68025
Telephone: (402) 941-6250
Fax: (402) 721-0250
E-mail: boyle@mlc.edu
Internet: www.mlc.edu

Founded 1883
Academic year: August to May
Undergraduate, liberal arts college

Pres.: Dr STEPHEN E. FRITZ
Vice-Pres. for Academic Affairs: Dr HENRY SMORYNSKI
Vice-Pres. for Admin.: SARAH KOTTICH
Vice-Pres. for Student Devt: VANCE VALERIO
Registrar: APRIL PEROLIO
Dir of Library: Dr THOMAS E. BOYLE

Library of 114,000 vols
Number of teachers: 55
Number of students: 850

NEBRASKA CHRISTIAN COLLEGE

12550 South 114th St, Papillion, NE 68046
Telephone: (402) 935-9400
Fax: (402) 935-9500
E-mail: admissions@nechristian.edu
Internet: www.nechristian.edu

Founded 1944
Private control

Pres.: RICHARD MILLIKEN
Chief Academic Officer: Dr SHANE WOOD
Registrar: TIM SNYDER
Librarian: LINDA LU LLOYD

Number of teachers: 24
Number of students: 162

Areas of study incl. Biblical studies, Christian education, church music, deaf ministries, family life ministry, general studies, missions, pastoral ministries, youth ministries.

NEBRASKA WESLEYAN UNIVERSITY

5000 St Paul Ave, Lincoln, NE 68504-2794
Telephone: (402) 466-2371
Fax: (402) 465-2179
E-mail: admissions@nebrwesleyan.edu
Internet: www.nebrwesleyan.edu

Founded 1887

Pres.: FREDERIK OHLES
Vice-Pres. for Academics: GEORGIANNE MASTERA
Vice-Pres. for External Relations: PATTY KARTHAUSER
Vice-Pres. for Finance: CLARK CHANDLER
Vice-Pres. for Student Life: SARA BOATMAN
Registrar: PATRICIA GRAFELMAN HALL
Univ. Librarian: JOHN MONTAG

Library of 200,000 vols
Number of teachers: 109
Number of students: 1,601 undergraduates; 204 graduates

Depts of art, biology, business, accounting and economics, chemistry, communication and theatre arts, education, English, health and human performance, health sciences, history, mathematics and computer science, modern languages, music, physics, political science, psychology, religion and philosophy, sociology/anthropology/social work.

PERU STATE COLLEGE

POB 10, 600 Hoyt St, Peru, NE 68421
Telephone: (402) 872-3815
E-mail: admissions@oakmail.peru.edu
Internet: www.peru.edu

Founded 1867

Pres.: Dr BEN E. JOHNSON
Vice-Pres. for Academic and Student Affairs: Dr TODD DREW
Vice-Pres. for Admin. and Finance: LINDA JACOBSEN
Librarian: PEG O'ROURKE

Library of 600,000 vols
Number of teachers: 47
Number of students: 1,745

DEANS

Graduate Studies: GREG GALARDI (Dir)
School of Arts and Sciences: Dr PATRICK FORTNEY
School of Education: Dr JODI KUPPER
School of Professional Studies: BRUCE BATTERSON

UNION COLLEGE

3800 S 48th St, Lincoln, NE 68506
Telephone: (402) 486-2600
Fax: (402) 486-2895
E-mail: ucinfo@ucollege.edu
Internet: www.ucollege.edu

Founded 1891
Academic year: August to May

Divs of business and computer science, fine arts, health sciences, human devt, humanities, religion, science and mathematics

Pres.: DAVID SMITH
Vice-Pres. for Academic Admin.: MALCOLM RUSSELL
Vice-Pres. for Advancement: LUANN DAVIS
Vice-Pres. for Enrollment and Student Financial Affairs: NADINE NELSON
Vice-Pres. for Financial Admin.: GARY BOLLINGER
Vice-Pres. for Spiritual Life: RICH CARLSON
Registrar: MICHELLE YOUNKIN
Library Dir: SABRINA RILEY

Library of 112,283 vols
Number of teachers: 73
Number of students: 951

UNIVERSITY OF NEBRASKA

Telephone: (402) 472-2111
Fax: (402) 472-1237
Internet: www.nebraska.edu

Founded 1869

Pres.: JAMES B. MILLIKEN

Exec. Vice-Pres. and Provost: LINDA PRATT
Vice-Pres. for Business and Finance: DAVID LECHNER
Vice-Pres. and Gen. Counsel: RICHARD R. WOOD
Vice-Pres. for Univ. Affairs: PETE KOTSIOPULOS.

CONSTITUENT CAMPUSES

University of Nebraska at Kearney

905 W 25th St, Kearney, NE 68849-0601
Telephone: (308) 865-8441
Fax: (308) 865-8157
Internet: www.unk.edu

Founded 1903

Chancellor: DOUGLAS A. KRISTENSEN
Sr Vice-Chancellor for Academic Affairs and Student Life: Dr FINNIE MURRAY
Vice-Chancellor for Business and Finance: Dr RANDAL HAACK
Vice-Chancellor for Univ. Relations: KATHLEEN SMITH
Dean of Student Life: PETER LONGO
Registrar: KIM SCHIPPOREIT
Dean of Libraries: JANET WILKE
Library of 228,625 vols
Number of teachers: 360 (full-time)
Number of students: 8,045

DEANS

College of Business and Technology: BRUCE FORSTER
College of Education: ED SCANTLING
College of Fine Arts and Humanities: Dr WILLIAM JURMA
College of Graduate Studies and Research: KENYA TAYLOR
College of Natural and Social Sciences: Dr FRANCIS HARROLD

University of Nebraska at Lincoln

201 Canfield Admin. Bldg, Lincoln, NE 68588-0419
Telephone: (402) 472-7211
Fax: (402) 472-5110
Internet: www.unl.edu

Founded 1869

Chancellor: HARVEY PERLMAN
Sr Vice-Chancellor for Academic Affairs: Dr ELLEN WEISSINGER
Vice-Chancellor for Business and Finance: CHRISTINE A. JACKSON
Vice-Chancellor for Research and Economic Devt: Dr PREM PAUL
Vice-Chancellor for Student Affairs: Dr JUAN FRANCO
Vice-Pres. and Vice-Chancellor for Institute of Agriculture and Natural Resources: Dr RONNIE GREEN
Dean of Libraries: JOAN R. GIESECKE
Library: 2.9m. vols, 44,000 periodicals in Don L. Love Memorial Library, 6 branch libraries, Marvin and Virginia Schmid Law Library
Number of teachers: 1,732 (full-time)
Number of students: 24,491
Publications: *Nebraska Journal of Economics and Business, Nebraska Law Review, Prairie Schooner, University of Nebraska—Lincoln Daily Nebraskan, University of Nebraska Studies*

DEANS

College of Agricultural Sciences and Natural Resources: Dr STEVEN S. WALLER
College of Architecture: Dr WAYNE DRUMMOND
College of Arts and Sciences: DAVID MANDERSCHEID
College of Business Administration: Dr DONDE PLOWMAN
College of Education and Human Sciences: Dr MARJORIE KOSTELNIK
College of Engineering: Dr JAMES O'HANLON
College of Fine and Performing Arts: Dr GIACOMO M. OLIVA
College of Journalism and Mass Communications: Dr GARY KEBBEL
College of Law: Dr SUSAN POSER
Graduate Studies: KIMBERLY ESPY

University of Nebraska at Omaha

6001 Dodge St, Omaha, NE 68182
Telephone: (402) 554-2100
Fax: (402) 554-3555
Internet: www.unomaha.edu

Founded 1908

Chancellor: Dr JOHN CHRISTIANSEN
Vice-Chancellor for Academic and Student Affairs: SHERI ROGERS (acting)
Vice-Chancellor for Admin.: WADE ROBINSON
Dir of Admissions: JOLENE ADAMS
Dean of Univ. Library: STEPHEN SHORB
Library of 623,000 vols, 1.7m. micro-material items
Number of teachers: 519
Number of students: 15,899

DEANS

College of Arts and Sciences: Dr SHELTON HENDRICKS
College of Business Administration: Dr LOU POL
College of Communication, Fine Arts and Media: GAIL BAKER
College of Education: Dr JOHN LANGAN
College of Information Science and Technology: HESHAM ALI
College of Public Affairs and Community Service: Dr B. J. REED
International Studies and Programs: THOMAS E. GOUTTIERRE

University of Nebraska Medical Center

600 S 42nd St, Omaha, NE 68198
Telephone: (402) 559-4200
Fax: (402) 559-4396
Internet: www.unmc.edu

Founded 1880

Chancellor: Dr HAROLD M. MAURER
Vice-Chancellor for Academic Affairs: Dr RUBENS J. PAMIES
Vice-Chancellor for Business and Finance: DONALD S. LEUENBERGER
Vice-Chancellor for External Affairs: BOB BARTEE
Vice-Chancellor for Research: Dr THOMAS ROSENQUIST
Library Dir: Dr NANCY N. WOELFL
Library of 241,363 vols
Number of teachers: 689
Number of students: 2,703

DEANS

College of Dentistry: Dr JOHN REINHARDT
College of Medicine: Dr JOHN J. GOLLAN
College of Nursing: Dr VIRGINIA TILDEN
College of Pharmacy: Dr CLARENCE UEDA
College of Public Health: Dr JAY NOREN
Graduate Studies: Dr RUBENS J. PAMIES
School of Allied Health Professions: Dr KYLE P. MEYER

ATTACHED INSTITUTIONS

Eppley Institute for Research in Cancer and Allied Diseases: tel. (402) 559-4090; internet www.unmc.edu/eppley; Dir Dr KENNETH COWAN.

Munroe-Meyer Institute for Genetics and Rehabilitation: tel. (402) 559-6402; fax (402) 559-5737; internet www.unmc.edu/dept/mmi; Dir Dr BRUCE A. BUEHLER.

WAYNE STATE COLLEGE

1111 Main St, Wayne, NE 68787
Telephone: (402) 375-7000
E-mail: admit1@wsc.edu
Internet: www.wsc.edu

Founded 1910
State control
Accredited by Higher Learning Comm. of the N Central Asscn of Colleges and Schools; The Nat. Ccl for Accreditation of Teacher Education (NCATE); Int. Assembly of Collegiate Business Education (IACBE); Nat. Asscn of Schools of Art and Design (NASAD)

Pres.: CURT FRYE
Vice-Pres. for Academic Affairs: Dr BOB MCCUE
Vice-Pres. for Admin. and Finance: JEAN DALE
Vice-Pres. and Dean of Students: Dr JEFF CARSTENS
Vice-Pres. for Devt: PHYLLIS CONNER
Dir of College Relations: JAY COLLIER
Librarian: DAVE GRABER
Library of 250,686 vols
Number of teachers: 155
Number of students: 3,052

DEANS

Arts and Humanities: JAMES O'DONNELL
Business and Technology: VAUGHN BENSON
Education and Counseling: NEIL SCHNOOR, JEAN BLOMENKAMP
Natural and Social Sciences: JON DALAGER

YORK COLLEGE

1125 E 8th St, York, NE 68467
Telephone: (402) 363-5600
Fax: (402) 363-5623
E-mail: enroll@york.edu
Internet: www.york.edu

Founded 1890
Private control
Academic year: August to May

Pres.: Dr STEVE ECKMAN
Vice-Pres. for Finance and Operations: TODD SHELDON
Dean of Academic Affairs: Dr L. RAY MILLER, II
Dean of Students: Dr SHANE MOUNTJOY
Dir of Admissions: WILLIE SANCHEZ
Registrar: TOD J. MARTIN
Library Dir: KEN GUNSELMAN
Number of teachers: 49
Number of students: 488

NEVADA

NEVADA SYSTEM OF HIGHER EDUCATION

2601 Enterprise Rd, Reno, NV 89512
Telephone: (775) 784-4905
Fax: (775) 784-5049
Internet: www.nevada.edu

Chancellor: JAMES E. ROGERS.

CONSTITUENT INSTITUTIONS

Nevada State College

1125 Nevada State Dr., Henderson, NV 89002
Telephone: (775) 992-2000
Fax: (775) 992-2226
E-mail: students@nsc.nevada.edu
Internet: www.nsc.nevada.edu

Founded 2002

Pres.: Dr FRED J. MARYANSKI.

University of Nevada, Las Vegas

4505 S Maryland Parkway, Las Vegas, NV 89154

Telephone: (702) 895-3011
E-mail: admissions@unlv.edu
Internet: www.unlv.edu

Founded 1957
Academic year: August to May

Pres.: DAVID B. ASHLEY
Exec. Vice-Pres. and Provost: MICHAEL BOWERS
Vice-Pres. for Finance: GERRY BOMOTTI
Vice-Pres. for Student Life: Dr REBECCA MILLS
Assoc. Vice-Pres. for Community Relations: SCHYLER RICHARDS
Sr Assoc. Vice-Pres. for Devt: NANCY STROUSE
Registrar: JEFF HALVERSON
Dean of Libraries: PATRICIA A. IANNUZZI

Library: 3m. vols
Number of teachers: 1,199 (752 full-time, 447 part-time)
Number of students: 28,000

DEANS

College of Business: Dr RICHARD FLAHERTY
College of Education: Dr GENE HALL
College of Engineering: Dr RONALD SACK
College of Extended Studies: Dr PAUL AIZLEY
College of Fine Arts: Dr JEFF KOEP
College of Graduate Studies: Dr PAUL FERGUSON
College of Health Sciences: Dr CAROLYN SABO
College of Hotel Administration: Dr STUART MANN
College of Law: Dr RICHARD MORGAN
College of Liberal Arts: Dr JAMES FREY
College of Sciences: Dr PETER STARKWEATHER
College of Urban Affairs: Dr MARTHA WATSON
Honors College: Dr SUE REIMOND

ATTACHED INSTITUTE

Desert Research Institute: 2215 Raggio Parkway, Reno, NV 89512; tel. (775) 673-7300; internet www.dri.edu; offices and laboratories in Reno, Las Vegas and Boulder City; research in energy, atmospheric environment, water resources, ecology, anthropology, socio-economics and demography; Pres. Dr STEPHEN G. WELLS.

University of Nevada, Reno

1664 N Virginia St, Reno, NV 89557-0208

Telephone: (775) 784-4700
Fax: (775) 784-1300
E-mail: gradadmissions@unr.edu
Internet: www.unr.edu

Founded 1874
Academic year: August to May

Pres.: MILTON D. GLICK
Exec. Vice-Pres. and Provost: JOHN FREDERICK
Vice-Pres. for Admin. and Finance: RONALD ZUREK
Vice-Pres. for Devt and Alumni Relations: JOHN CARUTHERS
Vice-Pres. for Information Technology and Dean of Libraries: STEVEN D. ZINK
Vice-Pres. for Marketing and Communications: CINDY POLLARD
Vice-Pres. for Research: MARSHA READ
Vice-Pres. for Student Services: SHANNON ELLIS
Registrar: MELISSA N. CHOROSZY

Library: 1.1m. vols
Number of teachers: 985
Number of students: 15,950

Publication: *Electronic Journal of Science Education* (4 a year)

DEANS

College of Agriculture: DAVID THAWLEY
College of Business Admin.: H. MIKE REED
College of Education: WILLIAM SPARKMAN
College of Engineering: TED E. BATCHMAN
College of Human and Community Sciences: JEAN PERRY
College of Liberal Arts: ERIC HERZIK
College of Science: DAVID WESTFALL
School of Journalism: COLE CAMPBELL
School of Medicine: JOHN MCDONALD
Graduate School: MARSHA READ
Mackay School of Mines: ROBERT TARANIK (Dir)
Orvis School of Nursing: PATSY RUCHALA (Dir)

SIERRA NEVADA COLLEGE

999 Tahoe Blvd, Incline Village, NV 89451-9500

Telephone: (775) 831-1314
Fax: (775) 831-1347
E-mail: admission@sierranevada.edu
Internet: www.sierranevada.edu

Founded 1969
Private control
Academic year: August to May

Pres.: ROBERT C. MAXSON
Provost and Exec. Vice-Pres.: LYNN GILLETTE
Registrar: ROSEANNA BEENK
Library Dir: ELIZABETH MARKLE

Number of teachers: 130
Number of students: 997 (352 undergraduate, 645 graduate)

NEW HAMPSHIRE

COLBY-SAWYER COLLEGE

541 Main St, New London, NH 03257

Telephone: (603) 526-3000
Fax: (603) 526-3452
Internet: www.colby-sawyer.edu

Founded 1837 as New London Acad.; present name 1975
Private control
Academic year: September to May

Pres.: THOMAS C. GALLIGAN, Jr
Academic Vice-Pres. and Dean of Faculty: DEBORAH A. TAYLOR
Vice-Pres. for Admin.: DOUGLAS C. ATKINS
Vice-Pres. for Advancement: ELIZABETH A. CAHILL
Vice-Pres. for Enrollment Management: GREGORY W. MATTHEWS
Vice-Pres. for Student Devt and Dean of Students: DAVID A. SAUERWEIN
Treas.: DOUGLAS W. LYON
Registrar: CAROLE H. PARSONS
Librarian: CARRIE THOMAS

Number of teachers: 118
Number of students: 898

DANIEL WEBSTER COLLEGE

20 University Dr., Nashua, NH 03063-1300

Telephone: (603) 577-6000
Fax: (603) 577-6001
E-mail: info@dwc.edu
Internet: www.dwc.edu

Founded 1965
Private control
Academic year: August to May

Pres.: ROBERT E. MYERS
Provost and Vice-Pres. of Academic Affairs: Dr MICHAEL FISHBEIN
Vice-Pres. for Advancement and Alumni Affairs: GAIL M. GARCEAU
Vice-Pres. for Business, Finance and Operations: THOMAS N. DICONZA
Vice-Pres. for Student Affairs and Dean of Students: SUSAN C. ELSASS
Registrar: DIANE MCCANN THOMAS
Library Dir: (vacant)

Library of 34,000 vols
Number of teachers: 60
Number of students: 1,200

DARTMOUTH COLLEGE

Hanover, NH 03755

Telephone: (603) 646-1110
Fax: (603) 646-2850
E-mail: contact@dartmouth.edu
Internet: www.dartmouth.edu

Founded 1769
Private control

Pres.: JIM YONG KIM
Chief of Staff: DAVID SPALDING
Exec. Vice-Pres. and Chief Financial Officer: STEVEN KADISH
Provost: CAROL FOLT (acting)
Sr Vice-Pres. for Advancement: CAROLYN PELZEL
Vice-Pres. for Campus Planning and Facilities: LINDA SNYDER
Vice-Pres. for Communication: DIANA PEARSON
Vice-Pres. and Chief Human Resources Officer: TRACI NORDBERG
Vice-Pres. and Chief Information Officer: ELLEN WAITE-FRANZEN
Vice-Provost for Research: MARTIN WYBOURNE
Registrar: MEREDITH H. BRAZ
Dean of Admissions and Financial Aid: MARIA LASKARIS
Dean of Libraries: JEFFREY L. HORRELL (acting)

Number of teachers: 995
Number of students: 5,987

Publications: *Encrucijada* (online), *Linguistic Discovery* (online)

DEANS

College: SYLVIA SPEARS (acting)
Faculty: CAROL FOLT (acting)
Graduate Studies: BRIAN POGUE
Medical School: WILLIAM GREEN (acting)
Thayer School of Engineering: JOSEPH HELBLE (acting)
Tuck School of Business: PAUL DANOS

PROFESSORS

Note: some professors serve in more than one department

Humanities

Department of African and African-American Studies:

ALVERSON, H. S., Anthropology
AMADIUMI, I., Religion
COOK, W., English
HALL, R. L., Sociology
KASFIR, N. M., Govt
LANGFORD, G. M., Biology
PEASE, D. L., English
SPITZER, L., History
WALKER, K., French and Italian
WILDER, C., History

Department of Art History:

JORDAN, J., Modern Art
KENSETH, J., Renaissance and Baroque Art

Department of Asian and Middle Eastern Languages and Literatures:

ALLAN, S., Chinese
GLINERT, L., Hebrew

Department of Classics:

BRADLEY, E. M., Greek and Latin Literature, Roman and Early Christian Art and Architecture
RUTTER, J. B., Classical Art and Archaeology, Archaeology of the Aegean
SCOTT, W. C., Greek and Latin Literature, Classical Drama, Homer

TATUM, J., Greek and Latin Literature, Ancient Fiction, the Classical Tradition, Roman Comedy

Department of Comparative Literature:

COOK, W., English
CREWE, J., English
GAYLORD, A. T., English
GEMUNDEN, G., German
GLINERT, J. A., Asian, Middle Eastern Languages and Literature
GREEN, M. J., French and Italian
HEFFERNAN, J. W., English
HIGGINS, L. A., French and Italian
HIRSCH, M., French and Italian
JEWELL, K. J., French and Italian
KOPPER, J. M., Russian
KRITZMAN, L. D., French and Italian
LAWRENCE, A., Film

Department of English:

BOOSE, L., English
COOK, W., English
CREWE, J., English and Comparative Literature
GAYLORD, A., English
HEBERT, E., English
HEFFERNAN, J. A. W., English
HUNTINGDON, C., English
MCKEE, P., English
MATHIS, C., English and Creative Writing
RENZA, L., English
SACCIO, P., English and Shakespearean Studies
SILVER, B. R., English
SLEIGH, T., English
TRAVIS, P. W., English
WYKES, P., English

Department of Film and Television Studies:

LAWRENCE, A.

Department of French and Italian:

GREEN, M.
HIGGINS, L.
HIRSCH, M.
JEWELL, K.
KRITZMAN, L. D.
RASSIAS, J.
WALKER, K. L.

Department of German:

DUNCAN, B., German Language
GEMÜNDEN, G., German, Comparative Literature
SCHER, S. P., German, Comparative Literature

Department of Linguistics and Cognitive Science:

ALVERSON, H. S., Anthropology
DUNBAR, K., Education and Psychology
DUNCAN, B., German
GLINERT, L. H., AMELL
GRENOBLE, L., Russian
HUGHES, H. C., Psychology
JAHNER, E. A., English and Native American Studies
MOOR, J. H., Philosophy
PETTITO, L. A., Education and Psychology
SCHERR, B. P., Russian
SINNOTT-ARMSTRONG, W. P., Philosophy
SORENSEN, R. A., Philosophy
TAUBE, J., Psychology
TRAVIS, P. W., English
WALKER, K. L., French and Italian
WOLFORD, G. L., Psychology

Department of Music:

APPLETON, J. H.
O'NEAL, M.
PINKAS, S.

Department of Philosophy:

DRIVER, J.
GERT, B.
MOOR, J. H.
SINNOTT-ARMSTRONG, W.
SORENSEN, R.

Department of Religion:

ACKERMAN, S.
AMADIUME, I., African Religions
FRANKENBERRY, N., Philosophy of Religion, Women and Religion, Science and Religion
GREEN, R. M., Religious Ethics, Business Ethics
HENRICKS, R. G., Religions of China

Department of Russian:

GRENOBLE, L.
KOPPER, J.
LOSEFF, L.
SCHERR, B.

Department of Spanish and Portuguese:

BUENO-CHAVEZ, R.
PASTOR, B.

Department of Studio Art:

FRANK MOSS, B., IV
RANDALL, C.
THOMPSON, E.

Department of Theatre:

CRICKARD, L.
GAFFNEY, P.
GRENOBLE, L.
SPICER, M.

Women and Gender Studies:

ACKERMAN, S., Religion
AMADIUMI, I., Religion
BOOSE, L. E., English
DARROW, M. H., History
DOMOSH, M., Geography
FOWLER, L. L., Govt
FRANKENBERRY, N. K., Religion
GARROD, A. G., Education
GREEN, M. J., French and Italian
HIGGINS, L. A., French and Italian
HIRSCH, M., French and Italian
JEWELL, K. J., French and Italian
LAWRENCE, A., Film
SILVER, B. R., English
SPITZER, L., History

Science

Department of Biological Sciences:

BERGER, E. M., Molecular Genetics, Cell Biology
FOLT, C. L., Aquatic Ecology
GILBERT, J. J., Ecology, Aquatic Biology
GUERINOT, M. L., Molecular Genetics, Microbiology
HOLMES, R. T., Animal Behaviour, Ecology
LANGFORD, G. M., Cell Biology
MCCLUNG, C. R., Molecular Genetics
MCPEEK, M. A., Community Ecology, Evolution
PEART, D. R., Population and Community Ecology, Forest Ecology
SLOBODA, R. D., Cell Biology, Neurobiology
WITTERS, L. A., Human Biology, Endocrinology/Metabolism

Department of Chemistry:

BELBRUNO, J. J.
BRAUN, C. L.
CANTOR, R. S.
DITCHFIELD, R.
GRIBBLE, G. W.
HUGHES, R. P.
JACOBI, P. A.
LEMAL, D. M.
LIPSON, J. E. G.
SODERBERG, R. H.
SPENCER, T. A.
WILCOX, D. E.
WINN, J. S.

Department of Computer Science:

DONALD, B. R.
DRYSDALE, R. L., III
KOTZ, D. F.
MAKEDON, F. S.
ROCKMORE, D.

Department of Environmental Studies:

FRIEDLAND, A.
HOWARTH, R.
SHEPHERD, J.
VIRGINIA, R.

Department of Mathematics:

ARKOWITZ, M. A.
BAUMGARTNER, J. E.
BICKEL, T. F.
BOGART, K. P.
DOYLE, P.
GORDON, C. S.
GROSZEK, M.
LAHR, C. D.
POMERANCE, C. B.
ROCKMORE, D. N.
SHEMANSKE, T. R.
WALLACE, D. I.
WEBB, D. L.
WILLIAMS, D. P.

Department of Physics and Astronomy:

FESEN, C. G.
FESEN, R. A.
GLEISER, M.
HUDSON, M. K.
LABELLE, J. W.
LAWRENCE, W. E.
MONTGOMERY, D. C.
MOOK, D. E.
THORSTENSEN, J. R.
WEGNER, G. A.
WYBOURNE, M. N.

Social Sciences

Department of Anthropology:

ALVERSON, H.
EICKELMAN, D. F.
ENDICOTT, K.
KAN, S.
NICHOLS, D. L.

Department of Economics:

BLANCHFLOWER, D. G.
FISCHEL, W. A.
GUSTMAN, A. L.
IRWIN, D. A.
KOHN, M.
MARION, N. P.
SAMWICK, A. A.
SCOTT, J. T.
SKINNER, J.
STAIGER, D. O.
VENTI, S. F.

Department of Education:

DUNBAR, K.
GARROD, A.
PETITTO, L. A.

Department of Geography:

DOMOSH, M.
MAGILLIGAN, F. J.
WRIGHT, R. A.

Department of Government:

FOWLER, L. L.
FREEDMAN, J. O.
KASFIR, N. M.
LEBOW, R. N.
MASTANDUNO, M.
SA'ADAH, M. A.
WINTERS, R. F.

Department of History:

CALLOWAY, C.
CROSSLEY, P. K.
DARROW, M.
ERMARTH, H. M.
GARTHWAITE, G. R.
NAVARRO, M.
NELSON, J. B.
SHEWMAKER, K. E.
SPITZER, L.
WHELAN, H. W.
WILDER, C. S.
WRIGHT, J.

Department of Latin American, Latino and Caribbean Studies:

BUENO-CHAVEZ, R., Spanish and Portuguese
NAVARRO, M., History
NICHOLS, D. L., Anthropology
PASTOR, B., Spanish and Portuguese
WALKER, K. L., French and Italian
WRIGHT, R., Geography

Department of Native American Studies:

CALLOWAY, C. G.
KAN, S.
NICHOLS, D. L.

Department of Psychological and Brain Sciences:

DUNBAR, K., Cognitive Psychology
GAZZANIGA, M. S., Cognitive Neuroscience
GRAFTON, S., Functional Brain Imaging
HEATHERTON, T. F., Experimental Social Neuroscience, Personality and Motivation
HUGHES, H. C., Electrophysiological and Psychophysical Studies of Sensory Processing in Humans
HULL, J. G., Structure of Self-knowledge and Function of Self-regulatory Systems
JERNSTEDT, G. C., Learning, Instructional Design Theory, Evaluation Research
KLECK, R. E., Experimental Social Communication Processes
MACRAE, C. N., Social Cognition
MORRIS, W. N., Mood and Emotion
PETITTO, L. A., Cognitive Psychology and Psycholinguistics
TAUBE, J. S.
WOLFORD, G. L.

Department of Sociology:

CAMPBELL, J. L.
HALL, R. L.
PARSA, M.

Dartmouth Medical School (1 Rope Ferry Rd, Hanover, NH 03755-1404; tel. (603) 650-1200; fax (603) 650-1202; internet www.dartmouth.edu/dms):

ADDANTE, R. R., Oral-Maxillofacial Surgery and Anaesthesiology
AHLES, T. A., Psychiatry
ALTO, W. A., Community and Family Medicine
AMBROS, V. R., Genetics
AUBUCHON, J. P., Pathology and Haematology-Oncology
BALDWIN, J. C., Surgery
BANKER, B. Q., Pathology
BARLOWE, C. K., Biochemistry
BARON, J. A., General Internal Medicine and Community and Family Medicine
BARTELS, S. J., Psychiatry
BARTLETT, D., Physiology
BATALDEN, P. B., Paediatrics and Community and Family Medicine
BAUGHMAN, R. D., Dermatology
BEISSWENGER, P. J., Medicine
BERGER, B. J., Psychiatry
BERMAN, S. A., Medicine
BERNAT, J. L., Neurology
BERNINI, P. M., Surgery (Orthopaedics)
BIRD, H. H., Anaesthiology
BLACK, W. C., Radiology
BOYLE, W. E., Paediatrics and Community and Family Medicine
BRINCKERHOFF, C. E., Medicine and Biochemistry
BRINCK-JOHNSER, T., Pathology
BROOKS, J. G., Paediatrics
BROWN, F. E., Plastic Surgery
BURCHARD, K. W., Surgery and Anaesthesiology
BYOCK, I. R., Anaesthiology
BZIK, D. J., Microbiology and Immunology
CAMPBELL, D. G., Surgery (Ophthalmology)
CARPENTER, S. J., Anatomy
CENDRON, M., Surgery
CHAMBERS, W. F., Anatomy
CHANG, T. Y., Biochemistry
CHEUNG, A., Microbiology and Immunology
CLENDENNING, W. E., Medicine
COHEN, J. A., Medicine
COLACCHIO, T. A., Surgery
COLE, C. N., Biochemistry and Genetics
COLE, M. D., Pharmacology and Toxicology
COMPTON, D. A., Biochemistry
CORNELL, C. J., Haematology-Oncology and Paediatrics
CORNELL, G. G., Medicine
CORSON, J. A., Psychiatry
CORWIN, H. L., Medicine and Anaesthesiology
CRAIG, R. W., Pharmacology, Toxicology
CRICHLOW, R. W., Surgery
CROMWELL, L. D., Radiology and Neurosurgery
CRONENWETT, J. L., Surgery
CROW, H. C., Radiology
DARNALL, R. A., Paediatrics and Physiology
DAUBENSPECK, A., Physiology
DELEO, J. A., Anaesthesiology
DIETRICH, A. J., Community and Family Medicine
DMITROVSKY, E., Pharmacology and Toxicology
DONEGAN, J. O., Otolaryngology
DOW, R. W., Surgery
DRAKE, R. E., Psychiatry; Community and Family Medicine
DUHAIME, A.-C., Surgery
DUNLAP, J. C., Genetics and Biochemistry
EASTMAN, A., Pharmacology and Toxicology
EDWARDS, W. H., Paediatrics
EISENBERG, B. L., Surgery
ERNSTOFF, L. T., Haematology-Oncology
ERNSTOFF, M. S., Haematology-Oncology
FANGER, M. W., Microbiology and Immunology
FEJES-TOTH, A. N., Physiology
FEJES-TOTH, G., Physiology
FERM, V. H., Anatomy
FISHER, E. S., Community and Family Medicine
FLOOD, A. B., Community and Family Medicine
FRANK, J. E., Paediatrics
FREY, W. G., Medicine
FRIEDMAN, M. J., Psychiatry, Pharmacology and Toxicology
FROMM, H., Gastroenterology
GALLAGHER, J. D., Anaesthesiology
GALTON, V. A., Physiology
GLASS, D. D., Anaesthesiology
GOODMAN, D. C., Paediatrics
GORMLEY, E. A., Surgery
GOSSELIN, R. E., Pharmacology and Toxicology
GRAFTON, S. T., Medicine
GREEN, A. I., Psychiatry
GREEN, R. L., Psychiatry
GREEN, W. R., Microbiology and Immunology
GREENBERG, R., Community and Family Medicine
GUYRE, P. M., Physiology
HAMILTON, J. W., Pharmacology, Toxicology
HARBAUGH, R. E., Surgery (Neurosurgery) and Radiology
HARBURY, H. A., Biochemistry
HARTMAN, G. S., Anaesthiology
HAZARD, R. G., Orthopaedics
HEAD, J. M., Surgery
HEANEY, J. A., Surgery
HENDERSON, J. V., Community and Family Medicine
HENDERSON, L. P., Physiology
HICKEY, W. F., Pathology
HOFNAGEL, D., Paediatrics
HOLMES, G. L., Medicine
HUG, E. B., Medicine
INSELBURG, J. W., Microbiology
ISRAEL, M. A., Paediatrics and Genetics
JACOBS, N. J., Microbiology
KARAGAS, M., Community and Family Medicine
KARL, R. C., Surgery
KASPER, L. H., Medicine
KELLEY, M. L., Medicine
KERRIGAN, C. L., Surgery
KING, B. H., Psychiatry
KLAUS, S. N., Medicine
KLEIN, R. Z., Paediatrics
KOOP, C. E., Surgery
KORC, M., Medicine
KOVAL, K. J., Orthopaedics
LANE, F. W., Medicine
LAYTON, W. M., Anatomy
LEITER, J. C., Physiology and Medicine
LEVIN, D. L., Paediatrics and Anaesthesiology
LEVINE, G. M., Community and Family Medicine
LEWIS, L. D., Medicine
LIENHARD, G. E., Biochemistry
LITTLE, G. A., Paediatrics; Obstetrics and Gynaecology
LLEWELLYN-THOMAS, H. A., Community and Family Medicine
LONGNECKER, D. S., Pathology
LOROS, J. J., Biochemistry and Genetics
LUBIN, M., Microbiology
MCALLISTER, T. W., Psychiatry
MCCANN, F. V., Physiology
MCCOLLUM, R. W., Community and Family Medicine
MCDANIEL, M. D., Anatomy
MCINTYRE, D. R., Medicine
MAHLER, D. A., Medicine
MANGANIELLI, P. D., Obstetrics and Gynaecology
MARON-PADILLA, M., Pathology
MARRIN, C. A. S., Surgery
MAUE, R. A., Medicine
MAURER, L. H., Medicine
MAYOR, M. B., Surgery (Orthopaedics)
MEMOLI, V. A., Pathology
MODLIN, J. F., Paediatrics
MOESHLER, J. B., Paediatrics
MOGIELNICKI, R. P., General Internal Medicine
MOHANDAS, T. K., Pathology
MUESER, K. T., Psychiatry; Community and Family Medicine
MUNCK, A. U., Physiology
NAITOVE, A., Surgery
NATTIE, E. E., Physiology
NELSON, E. C., Community and Family Medicine
NELSON, W. H., Psychiatry
NEMIAH, J. C., Psychiatry
NIERENBERG, D. W., Pharmacology and Toxicology
NODA, L. H., Biochemistry
NOELLE, R. J., Microbiology and Immunology
NOLL, W. W., Paediatrics
NORDGREN, R. E., Paediatrics
NORTH, W. G., Physiology
NUGENT, W. C., Surgery
NYE, R. E., Physiology
O'CONNOR, G. T., Community and Family Medicine
O'DONNELL, J. F., Medicine
ONION, D. K., Community and Family Medicine
OXMAN, T. E., Psychiatry; Community and Family Medicine
PAYSON, H. E., Psychiatry
PEARLMAN, J. D., Medicine
PFEFFERKORN, E. R., Microbiology
PLUME, S. K., Surgery
QUILL, T. J., Anaesthesiology
RAVARIS, C. L., Psychiatry
REGAN-SMITH, M. G., Rheumatology; Community and Family Medicine
REEVES, A. G., Medicine
RIGBY, W. F. C., Microbiology and Immunology;

ROBERTS, D. W., Surgery (Neurosurgery)
ROEBUCK, W. D., Pharmacology and Toxicology
ROGERS, C. C., Medicine
ROLETT, E. L., Medicine
ROSENBERG, S. D., Psychiatry
ROTHSTEIN, R. I., Medicine
ROUS, S. N., Surgery
ROZYCKI, A. A., Paediatrics
RUECKERT, F., Surgery
ST GERMAIN, D. L., Medicine
ST JOHN, W. M., Physiology
SANDERS, J. H., Surgery
SARGENT, J. D., Paediatrics
SATEIA, M. J., Psychiatry
SAUNDERS, R. L., Surgery
SAYKIN, A. J., Psychiatry
SCHNED, A. R., Pathology
SCHWARTZMAN, J. D., Pathology
SCORNIK, O. A., Biochemistry
SILBERFARB, P. M., Psychiatry and Medicine
SIMONS, M., Cardiology; Pharmacology and Toxicology
SKINNER, J. S., Community and Family Medicine
SMITH, B. D., Obstetrics and Gynaecology
SMITH, R. P., Pharmacology and Toxicology
SOBEL, R., Psychiatry
SOKOL, H. W., Physiology
SOLOW, C., Psychiatry
SORENSON, G. D., Pathology
SPECK, N. A., Biochemistry
SPENCER, S. K., Dermatology and Surgery (Dermatology)
SPIEGEL, P. K., Radiology
SPIELBERG, S. P., Paediatrics
STANTON, B. A., Physiology
STAUFFER, M. W., Pathology
STOKES, D. C., Paediatrics
STRICKLER, J. C., Medicine
STYS, S. J., Obstetrics and Gynaecology (Maternal-Foetal Medicine)
SUTTON, J. E., Surgery
SWARTZ, H. M., Radiology; Community and Family Medicine; Physiology
TOSTESON, A. N., Community and Family Medicine
TOSTESON, T. D., Community and Family Medicine
TRUMPOWER, B. L., Biochemistry
VALTIN, H., Physiology
VAN LEEUWIN, D. J., Medicine
VARNUM, J. W., Hospital Administration
VIDAVER, R. M., Psychiatry
VON REYN, C. F., Medicine
WADE, W. F., Microbiology
WALLACE, A. G., Medicine
WALSH, D. B., Surgery
WASSON, J. H., Community and Family Medicine
WEINSTEIN, J. N., Surgery (Orthopaedics); Community and Family Medicine
WELCH, H. G., Community and Family Medicine
WENNBERG, J. E., Community and Family Medicine
WICKNER, W. T., Biochemistry
WILKINSON, R. H., Radiology
WILLIAMSON, P. D., Medicine
WIRA, C. R., Physiology
YEAGER, M. P., Anaesthesiology
YEO, K.-T. J., Pathology
YOUNG, R. D., Obstetrics and Gynaecology
ZACHARSKI, L. R., Medicine
ZUBKOFF, M., Community and Family Medicine
ZWOLAK, R. M., Surgery

Thayer School of Engineering (internet engineering.dartmouth.edu/thayer):

BAKER, I.
CUSHMAN-ROISIN, B.
CYBENKO, G.
GARMIRE, E.
GRAEVE, R. J.
HUTCHINSON, C. E.
KANTROWITZ, A. R.
KENNEDY, F. E.
LOTKO, W.
LYNCH, D. R.
PAULSEN, K. D.
PETRENKO, V. F.
RICHTER, H. J.
SCHULSON, E. M.
STRATTON, W. D.
TAYLOR, S.
WYMAN, C. E.

Tuck School of Business Administration (tel. (603) 646 8825; fax (603) 646-1308; e-mail tuck.school@dartmouth.edu; internet www.tuck.dartmouth.edu):

ARGENTI, P. A., Management and Corporate Communication
BAKER, K. R., Management
BERNARD, A., Int. Economics
BLAYDON, C. C., Management
DANOS, P., Business Admin.
DAVENI, R. A., Strategic Management
ECKBO, B. E., Finance
FINKELSTEIN, S., Management
FRENCH, K. R., Finance
GOVINDARAJAN, V., Int. Business
GREENHALGH, L., Management
HANSEN, R. G., Business Admin.
HELFAT, C. E., Strategy and Technology
JOHNSON, M. E., Operations Management
JOYCE, W. F., Strategy and Organizational Theory
KELLER, K. L., Marketing
KELLER, P. A., Management
LAPORTA, R., Finance
MASSEY, J. A., Int. Business
MUNTER, M. M., Management Communication
NESLIN, S. A., Marketing
POWELL, S. G., Business Admin.
PYKE, D. F., Business Admin.
ROGALSKI, R. J., Investments
SHANK, J. K., Managerial Accounting and Management Control
STICKNEY, C. P., Management
ZUBKOFF, M., Health Economics and Management

ATTACHED RESEARCH INSTITUTES

Institute of Arctic Studies: internet www.dartmouth.edu/~arctic; Dir ROSS VIRGINIA.

Institute for Security Technology Studies: e-mail info@ists.dartmouth.edu; internet www.ists.dartmouth.edu; f. 2000; Dir DAVID KOTZ.

Nelson A. Rockefeller Center for the Social Services: internet www.dartmouth.edu/~rocky; Dir ANDREW SAMWICK.

FRANKLIN PIERCE COLLEGE

40 University Dr., Rindge, NH 03461-0060
Telephone: (603) 899-4000
Fax: (603) 899-4394
E-mail: admissions@fpc.edu
Internet: www.fpc.edu

Founded 1962
Private control
Academic year: September to May

Pres.: Dr GEORGE J. HAGERTY
Provost and Vice-Pres. for Academic Affairs: MICHAEL BELL
Vice-Pres. for College Relations: EVELYN BUCHANAN
Vice-Pres. for Finance and Planning: JOHN MIMS
Vice-Pres. for Student Admin. Services: CAROLE MONROE
Registrar: Dr SUSAN R. CHAMBERLIN
Dir of Library Services: (vacant)

Library of 120,000 vols
Number of teachers: 65
Number of students: 1,489.

BRANCH CAMPUSES

Concord Campus: 5 Chenell Dr., Concord, NH 03301-5753; tel. (603) 228-1155; fax (603) 229-4580; Dir MAJOR W. WHEELOCK, III.

Keene Campus: 17 Bradco St, Keene, NH 03431-3900; tel. (603) 357-0079; fax (603) 899-1062; Dir ANDREA M. BRODE.

Lebanon Campus: 24 Airport Rd, West Lebanon, NH 03784; tel. (603) 298-5549; fax (603) 899-1065; Dir RONALD E. BIRON.

Manchester Campus: 670 North Commercial St, Manchester, NH 03101; tel. (603) 626-4972; fax (603) 626-4815; Dir LORAINE HOBAUSZ.

Portsmouth Campus: 73 Corporate Dr., Portsmouth, NH 03801-2847; tel. (603) 433-2000; fax (603) 899-1067; Dir M. DERMOT O'BRIEN.

FRANKLIN PIERCE LAW CENTER

2 White St, Concord, NH 03301
Telephone: (603) 228-1541
Fax: (603) 228-1074
E-mail: admissions@piercelaw.edu
Internet: www.piercelaw.edu

Founded 1973
Private control
Academic year: August to April

Pres. and Dean: JOHN D. HUTSON
Treas.: BRUCE BURNS
Vice-Pres. for Finance and Admin.: ERIC NORMAN
Law Librarian: Dr JUDITH GIRE

Library: colln dedicated to property law
Number of students: 450
Publications: *IDEA: The Intellectual Property Law Review*, *Pierce Law Review*.

NEW ENGLAND COLLEGE

24 Bridge St, Henniker, NH 03242
Telephone: (603) 428-2000
Fax: (603) 428-7230
E-mail: admission@nec.edu
Internet: www.nec.edu

Founded 1946
Academic year: September to May

Pres.: Dr MICHELE PERKINS
Vice-Pres. for Academic Affairs and Dean of Faculty: ED COOPER
Vice-Pres. for Finance and Operations: KEVIN CORMIER
Vice-Pres. for Institutional Advancement: WILLIAM HARROLD
Vice-Pres. for Student Devt and Dean of Student Affairs: E. JOSEPH PETRICK
Registrar: FRANK L. HALL
Librarian: KATHERINE VAN WEELDEN

Library of 103,000 vols
Number of teachers: 76 (51 full-time, 25 part-time)
Number of students: 1,000

Depts of art and art history, biology, business admin., chemistry, communication, computer technology, criminal justice, economics, education, English, environmental science, health and sports science, history, kinesiology and sport science, mathematics, music, philosophy, political science, psychology, sociology and social work, sport and recreational management, theatre, women's studies, writing

Publication: *Entelechy International: A Journal of Contemporary Ideas* (1 a year).

RIVIER COLLEGE

420 South Main St, Nashua, NH 03060
Telephone: (603) 888-1311
Fax: (603) 897-8883
E-mail: rivadmit@rivier.edu

Internet: www.rivier.edu
Founded 1933
Academic year: September to May
Pres.: WILLIAM FARRELL
Vice-Pres. for Academic Affairs: Sister THERESE LAROCHELLE
Vice-Pres. for Academic Outreach: Dr JOSEPH ALLARD
Vice-Pres. for Enrollment Management: DAVID BOISVERT
Vice-Pres. for Finance and Admin.: JOSEPH A. FAGAN
Vice-Pres. for Student Devt: LINDA JANSKY
Academic Dean: Dr ALBERT DECICCIO
Librarian: DAN SPEIDEL
Library of 128,473 vols
Number of teachers: 172 (65 full-time, 107 part-time)
Number of students: 2,375 (905 full-time, 1,470 part-time)

SAINT ANSELM COLLEGE

100 St Anselm Dr., Manchester, NH 03102-1310
Telephone: (603) 641-7000
Fax: (603) 641-7116
E-mail: admission@anselm.edu
Internet: www.anselm.edu
Founded 1889
Liberal arts college with a baccalaureate programme in nursing
Pres.: Fr JONATHAN DEFELICE
Exec. Vice-Pres.: Dr SUZANNE K. MELLON
Vice-Pres. for Academic Affairs and Dean of the College: Fr AUGUSTINE KELLY
Vice-Pres. for Student Affairs: Dr JOSEPH M. HORTON
Registrar: MARY ANN ERICSON
Librarian: JOSEPH W. CONSTANCE, Jr
Library of 190,000 vols
Number of teachers: 155 (117 full-time, 38 part-time)
Number of students: 2,019

SOUTHERN NEW HAMPSHIRE UNIVERSITY

2500 North River Rd, Manchester, NH 03106
Telephone: (603) 668-2211
E-mail: info@snhu.edu
Internet: www.snhu.edu
Private control
Pres.: Dr PAUL J. LEBLANC
Vice-Pres. for Academic Affairs: Dr PATRICIA A. LYNOTT
Vice-Pres. for Enrollment Management: BRAD POZNANSKI
Vice-Pres. for Institutional Advancement: DONALD BREZINSKI
Vice-Pres. for Marketing and Communications: MARTHA RUSH-MUELLER
Vice-Pres. for Operations and Finance: WILLIAM MCGARRY
Vice-Pres. for Student Affairs: Dr SCOTT KALICKI
Registrar: Dr RICHARD OUELLETTE
Dean of Univ. Library: KATHY GROWNEY
Number of teachers: 100
Number of students: 1,900 undergraduate, 1,800 graduate and 2,700 continuing education students

DEANS

Continuing Education: ELLEN RYDER GRIFFIN
School of Business: Dr MARTIN J. BRADLEY
School of Community Economic Development: Dr MICHAEL SWACK
School of Education: (vacant)
School of Hospitality, Tourism and Culinary Management: WILLIAM PETERSEN
School of Liberal Arts: Dr KAREN ERICKSON

THOMAS MORE COLLEGE OF LIBERAL ARTS

6 Manchester St, Merrimack, NH 03054
Telephone: (603) 880-8308
Fax: (603) 880-9280
E-mail: admissions@thomasmorecollege.edu
Internet: www.thomasmorecollege.edu
Founded 1978
Private control
Academic year: September to May
Pres.: JEFFREY O. NELSON
Dean of the College: Dr MARY K. MUMBACH
Registrar: CHRISTOPHER BLUM
Librarian: SAMUEL SCHMITT
Number of teachers: 9
Number of students: 89
Depts of literature, philosophy, political science
Publication: *Second Spring: An International Journal of Faith and Culture* (2 a year).

UNIVERSITY SYSTEM OF NEW HAMPSHIRE

Dunlap Center, 25 Concord Rd, Durham, NH 03824-3545
Telephone: (603) 862-1800
Fax: (603) 862-0908
E-mail: usnh.chancellor@unh.edu
Internet: www.usnh.unh.edu
Chancellor: Dr STEPHEN J. RENO
Vice-Chancellor and Treas.: Dr EDWARD R. MACKAY
Number of students: 30,000 at 4 constituent instns.

CONSTITUENT INSTITUTIONS

Granite State College

18 Old Suncook Rd, Concord, NH 03301
Telephone: (603) 228-3000
Fax: (603) 513-1389
E-mail: ask.granite@granite.edu
Internet: www.granite.edu
Founded 1972 as School of Continuing Studies, later named the College for Lifelong Learning, present name 2005
State control
Majors in applied technology, behavioural science, business management, criminal justice, early childhood education, self-design; courses offered at more than 50 locations across New Hampshire
Academic year: July to June
Pres.: Dr KAROL LACROIX
Dean of Academic Affairs: SHEILA TAYLOR-KING
Dir of Planning and Finance: LISA SHAWNEY
Registrar: KAREN KING
Number of teachers: 398
Number of students: 3,500

Keene State College

229 Main St, Keene, NH 03435
Telephone: (603) 352-1909
E-mail: admissions@keene.edu
Internet: www.keene.edu
Founded 1909
Academic year: September to May
Schools of arts and humanities, interdisciplinary programmes, professional and graduate studies, sciences and social sciences
Pres.: Dr HELEN F. GILES-LEE
Provost and Vice-Pres. for Academic Affairs: Dr EMILE NETZHAMMER
Vice-Pres. for Finance and Planning: JAY V. KAHN
Vice-Pres. for Student Affairs: Dr CORINNE KOWPAK
Dean of Library: IRENE HEROLD
Registrar: TOM RICHARD
Library of 258,181 vols
Number of teachers: 181
Number of students: 4,081

Plymouth State University

Plymouth, NH 03264
Telephone: (603) 535-5000
Fax: (603) 535-2654
E-mail: plymouthadmit@plymouth.edu
Internet: www.plymouth.edu
Founded 1871
Academic year: September to May
Depts of art, biological sciences, business, chemical, earth, atmospheric and physical sciences, communication and media studies, computer science and technology, criminal justice, education, English, health and human performance, interdisciplinary studies, languages and linguistics, mathematics, music, theatre, and dance, philosophy, psychology, social sciences, social work, women's studies
Pres.: SARAH JAYNE STEEN
Provost and Vice-Pres. for Academic Affairs: Dr JULIE N. BERNIER
Vice-Pres. for Financial Affairs: WILLIAM R. CRANGLE
Vice-Pres. for Student Affairs: RICHARD T. HAGE
Exec. Dir of Univ. Relations: STEPHEN BARBA
Registrar: MATTHEW BURKHART
Librarian: DAVID BERONA
Library of 306,314 vols
Number of teachers: 170 full-time
Number of students: 6,800
Publications: *Anthology of Teachers' Writing* (1 a year), *Centripetal* (2 a year), *The New Hampshire Journal of Education* (1 a year), *Writing across the Curriculum* (1 a year).

University of New Hampshire

Durham, NH 03824
Telephone: (603) 862-1234
Fax: (603) 862-3853
E-mail: telecom@unh.edu
Internet: www.unh.edu
Founded 1866 as New Hampshire College of Agriculture and the Mechanic Arts, present name 1923, merger with State Colleges at Plymouth and Keene 1963, in 1985 Merrimack Valley College (f. 1967) became the Univ. of New Hampshire at Manchester, a br. campus
Public control
Language of instruction: English
Academic year: September to May
Pres.: MARK HUDDLESTON
Provost and Exec. Vice-Pres. for Academic Affairs: JOHN ABER
Vice-Pres. for Finance and Admin.: DICK CANNON
Vice-Pres. for Student and Academic Services: MARK RUBINSTEIN
Dir of Admissions: ROBERT MCGANN
Dir of Financial Aid: SUSAN ALLEN
Dean of Cooperative Extension: JOHN PIKE
Registrar: KATHRYN P. FORBES
Librarian: SHERRY VELLUCCI
Library of 2,147,343 vols
Number of teachers: 1,008 (621 full-time, 387 part-time)
Number of students: 15,155 (12,485 undergraduate, 2,670 graduate)
Publications: *Inquiry* (undergraduate research journal), *Main Street Magazine*, *Portuguese Studies Review*, *Seafare* (jtly with Univ. of Maine)

DEANS

Arthur Greenberg Graduate School: HARRY RICHARDS

College of Engineering and Physical Sciences: JOSEPH KLEWICKI
College of Health and Human Services: BARBARA ARRINGTON
College of Liberal Arts: KENNETH FULD
College of Life Sciences and Agriculture: THOMAS BRADY
University of New Hampshire at Manchester: KRISTEN WOOLEVER
Whittemore School of Business and Economics: DANIEL INNIS

NEW JERSEY

CALDWELL COLLEGE

9 Ryerson Ave, Caldwell, NJ 07006
Telephone: (973) 618-3000
Fax: (973) 618-3600
E-mail: admissions@caldwell.edu
Internet: www.caldwell.edu

Founded 1939
Academic year: August to May

Pres.: Sister PATRICE WERNER
Vice-Pres. and Dean for Academic Affairs: Dr PAUL R. DOUILLARD
Vice-Pres. for Enrollment Management: JOSEPH L. POSILLICO
Exec. Dir of Library: PETER PANOS

Library of 142,356 vols
Number of teachers: 184
Number of students: 2,219 (1,599 full-time)

CENTENARY COLLEGE

400 Jefferson St, Hackettstown, NJ 07840-9930
Telephone: (908) 852-1400
Fax: (908) 979-4359
E-mail: admissions@centenarycollege.edu
Internet: www.centenarycollege.edu

Founded 1867
Private control

Pres.: Dr KENNETH L. HOYT
Vice-Pres. for Academic Affairs: BARBARA-JAYNE LEWTHWAITE
Vice-Pres. for Admin.: Dr JOHN A. SHAYNER
Vice-Pres. for Business and Finance: JOHN SOMMER
Vice-Pres. for College Relations: DEBRA ALBANESE
Vice-Pres. for Enrollment Management: DIANE P. FINNAN
Vice-Pres. for Information Systems: NORMAN W. RANKIS
Dean of Students: Rev. DAVID JONES
Registrar: ELISE BAYSE
Library Dir: NANCY MADACSI

Number of teachers: 40
Number of students: 970

COLLEGE OF NEW JERSEY

2000 Pennington Rd, POB 7718, Ewing, NJ 08628-0718
Telephone: (609) 771-1855
Internet: www.tcnj.edu

Founded 1855

Pres.: R. BARBARA GITENSTEIN
Provost and Vice-Pres. for Academic Affairs: CAROL BRESNAHAN
Vice-Provost: MARK KINSELICA
Vice-Pres. for Admin. and Finance: PETER L. MILLS
Vice-Pres. for Devt and Alumni Affairs: JOHN MARCY
Vice-Pres. for Student Life: JAMES M. NORFLEET
Registrar: FRANK COOPER
Dean of the Library and Information Services: TARAS PAVLOVSKY

Library of 564,000 vols
Number of teachers: 746
Number of students: 6,949 (6,458 full-time)

DEANS

School of Arts and Communication: Dr JOHN LAUGHTON
School of Business: Dr WILLIAM KEEP (acting)
School of Culture and Society: BENJAMIN RIFKIN
School of Education: Dr WILLIAM BEHRE
School of Engineering: STEVEN SCHREINER
School of Nursing, Health, and Exercise Science: Dr SUSAN BAKEWELL
School of Technology: Dr ROBERT BITTNER
Graduate Studies: Dr SUZANNE PASCH
Sachs School of Science: JEFFERY OSBORN

COLLEGE OF SAINT ELIZABETH

2 Convent Rd, Morristown, NJ 07960-6989
Telephone: (973) 290-4000
E-mail: apply@cse.edu
Internet: www.cse.edu

Founded 1899
Autonomous
Language of instruction: English
Academic year: August to May

Pres.: Sister FRANCIS RAFTERY
Vice-Pres. and Dean for Academic Affairs: JAMES S. DLUGOS
Vice-Pres. for Finance and Admin. and Treas.: MARIA CAMMARATA
Vice-Pres. for Institutional Advancement: (vacant)
Library Dir: AMIRA UNVER

Library of 188,000 vols
Number of teachers: 250
Number of students: 2,112

DREW UNIVERSITY

36 Madison Ave, Madison, NJ 07940
Telephone: (973) 408-3000
Fax: (973) 408-3080
Internet: www.drew.edu

Founded 1867
Private control
Language of instruction: English
Academic year: September to May

Pres.: ROBERT WEISBUCH
Provost and Academic Vice-Pres.: PAMELA GUNTER-SMITH
Vice-Pres. for Admin.: MARGARET E. L. HOWARD
Vice-Pres. for Advancement: CHRISTOPHER BIEHN
Vice-Pres. for Finance and Business Affairs: HOWARD BUXBAUM
Registrar: HORACE TATE
Dean of Libraries: ANDREW D. SCRIMGEOUR

Number of teachers: 157 (full-time faculty)
Number of students: 2,760

Publication: *Drew Magazine* (alumni magazine, 3 a year)

DEANS

College of Liberal Arts: JONATHAN LEVIN
Graduate School: RICHARD GREENWALD
Theological School: KAH-JIN JEFFREY KUAN

FAIRLEIGH DICKINSON UNIVERSITY

Teaneck, NJ 07666
Telephone: (201) 692-2000
E-mail: global@fdu.edu
Internet: www.fdu.edu

Founded 1942

Campuses at Madison, NJ 07940 (tel. (973) 443-8500); Teaneck, NJ 07666 (tel. (201) 692-2000); and Wroxton, Oxon., UK

Pres.: Dr J. MICHAEL ADAMS
Exec. Vice-Pres.: CARL VIOLA
Sr Vice-Pres. for Academic Affairs: Dr WILLARD GINGERICH
Vice-Pres. for Institutional Advancement and Enrollment Management: BERNADETTE MILLONDE
Univ. Librarian: JAMES MARCUM

Library of 650,000 vols
Number of teachers: 669
Number of students: 11,000

Publications: *FDU Magazine*, *Journal of Psychology and the Behavioral Sciences*, *The Literary Review*

DEANS

Becton College of Arts and Sciences (Florham-Madison Campus): Dr BARBARA SALMORE
Edward Williams College (Teaneck-Hackensack Campus): KENNETH T. VEHRKENS
Silberman College of Business Administration: Dr LEO ROGERS
Univ. College (Teaneck-Hackensack Campus): Dr JOHN SNYDER

FELICIAN COLLEGE

262 South Main St, Lodi, NJ 07644-2117
Telephone: (201) 559-6000
Fax: (201) 559-6188
E-mail: admissions@inet.felician.edu
Internet: www.felician.edu

Campuses at Lodi and Rutherford

Founded 1923 as Immaculate Conception Normal School; present name 1967
Private control

Pres.: Sister THERESA MARY MARTIN
Registrar: JUNE FINN

Number of teachers: 30
Number of students: 1,790

Divs of arts and sciences, nursing and allied health, teacher education.

GEORGIAN COURT UNIVERSITY

900 Lakewood Ave, Lakewood, NJ 08701-2697
Telephone: (732) 364-2700
Fax: (732) 987-2000
E-mail: admissions@georgian.edu
Internet: www.georgian.edu

Founded 1908 as Mount Saint Mary College and Acad.; present name 1924
Private control
Academic year: September to May

Pres.: Dr ROSEMARY E. JEFFRIES
Dir of Public Information and Univ. Communications: GAIL H. TOWNS

Library of 148,000 vols, 780 journals
Number of teachers: 309
Number of students: 3,189

DEANS

School of Arts and Humanities: LINDA JAMES
School of Business: JOSEPH M. MONAHAN
School of Education: JACQUELINE E. KRESS
School of Sciences and Mathematics: LINDA JAMES

INSTITUTE FOR ADVANCED STUDY

Einstein Dr., Princeton, NJ 08540
Telephone: (609) 734-8000
Fax: (609) 924-8399
Internet: www.ias.edu

Founded 1930
Private control

Post-doctoral research in the fields of mathematics, natural sciences, historical studies and social sciences

Academic year: September to April (2 terms)

Chair. of the Board of Trustees: CHARLES SIMONYI

Dir: PETER GODDARD
Librarian: MARCIA TUCKER
Librarian: MOMOTA GANGULI

Library of 150,000 vols
Number of teachers: 43

PROFESSORS

School of Historical Studies:
- BOWERSOCK, G.
- BYNUM, C.
- CRONE, P.
- DI COSMO, N.
- ISRAEL, J.
- VON STADEN, H.

School of Mathematics:
- BOMBIERI, E.
- BOURGAIN, J.
- DELIGNE, P.
- GRIFFITHS, P. A.
- LANGLANDS, R.
- MACPHERSON, R.
- SPENCER, T.
- VOEVODSKY, V.
- WIGDERSON, A.

School of Natural Sciences:
- ADLER, S.
- BAHCALL, J.
- GOLDREICH, P.
- LEVINE, A. J.
- MALDACENA, J.
- SEIBERG, N.
- WITTEN, E.

School of Social Science:
- MASKIN, E.
- SCOTT, J.
- WALZER, M.

KEAN UNIVERSITY

1000 Morris Ave, Union, NJ 07083
Telephone: (908) 527-2000
E-mail: admitme@kean.edu
Internet: www.kean.edu

Founded 1855, present name 1997
Academic year: September to June

Pres.: Dr DAWOOD FARAHI
Vice-Pres. of Academic Affairs: Dr JOSÉ QUILES (acting)
Vice-Pres. of Student Services: JANICE MURRAY-LAURY (acting)

Library of 350,000 vols
Number of teachers: 1,047 (372 full-time, 11 part-time, 664 adjunct)
Number of students: 13,050

Colleges of arts, humanities and social sciences, business and public admin., education, natural, applied and health sciences, Nathan Weiss graduate studies.

MONMOUTH UNIVERSITY

400 Cedar Ave, West Long Branch, NJ 07764-1898
Telephone: (732) 571-3400
E-mail: gradadm@monmouth.edu
Internet: www.monmouth.edu

Founded 1933
Ind., coeducational, non-sectarian, comprehensive univ.

Pres.: PAUL G. GAFFNEY, II
Provost and Vice-Pres. for Academic Affairs: THOMAS PEARSON
Vice-Pres. for Enrollment Management: ROBERT D. MCCAIG
Librarian: SUSAN KUYHENDALL

Library of 252,500 vols, 1,250 periodicals
Number of teachers: 397 full-time and part-time
Number of students: 5,311 (4,037 undergraduate; 1,274 graduate)

MONTCLAIR STATE UNIVERSITY

Upper Montclair, NJ 07043
Telephone: (973) 655-4000
Fax: (973) 655-5455
E-mail: undergraduate.admissions@montclair.edu
Internet: www.montclair.edu

Founded 1908
Liberal arts and professional studies
Academic year: September to May

Pres.: Dr SUSAN A. COLE
Sr Vice-Pres. for Admin.: (vacant)
Vice-Pres. for Academic Affairs and Provost: RICHARD A. LYNDE
Vice-Pres. for Finance and Treas.: DONALD C. CIPULLO
Vice-Pres. for Human Resources: JUDITH T. HAIN
Vice-Pres. for Student Devt and Campus Life: Dr KAREN PENNINGTON
Vice-Pres. for Univ. Advancement: Dr THOMAS HAYNES
Asst Vice-Pres. for Facilities Operations: TIM CAREY
Dean of Library Services: JUDITH LIN HUNT

Library of 459,034 vols
Number of teachers: 1,275 (509 full-time, 766 part-time)
Number of students: 16,736

NEW BRUNSWICK THEOLOGICAL SEMINARY

17 Seminary Pl., New Brunswick, NJ 08901-1196
Telephone: (732) 247-5241
Fax: (732) 249-5412
E-mail: info@nbts.edu
Internet: www.nbts.edu

Founded 1784
Private control
Academic year: September to May

Pres.: GREG A. MAST
Dean: VIRGINIA WILES
Dir of Library: CHRISTOPHER BRENNAN

Library of 150,000 vols, 300 periodicals
Number of teachers: 40
Number of students: 280.

ATTACHED RESEARCH INSTITUTE

Center for Reformed Church Studies: Dir Rev. Dr JOHN W. COAKLEY.

NEW JERSEY CITY UNIVERSITY

2039 Kennedy Blvd, Jersey City, NJ 07305-1597
Telephone: (201) 200-2000
Fax: (201) 200-2044
E-mail: admissions@njcu.edu
Internet: www.njcu.edu

Founded 1927 as New Jersey State Normal School; present name and status 1998
Academic year: September to May

Pres.: Dr CARLOS HERNÁNDEZ
Library Dir: GRACE F. BULAONG

Number of teachers: 170
Number of students: 7,700

DEANS

College of Arts and Sciences: (vacant)
College of Education: Dr MURIEL RAND
College of Professional Studies: Dr SANDRA BLOOMBERG

NEW JERSEY INSTITUTE OF TECHNOLOGY

University Heights, Newark, NJ 07102-1982
Telephone: (973) 596-3000
Fax: (973) 642-4380
E-mail: information@njit.edu
Internet: www.njit.edu

Founded 1881

Pres.: ROBERT A. ALLENKIRCH
Provost and Sr Vice-Pres. for Academic Affairs: PRISCILLA P. NELSON
Sr Vice-Pres. for Admin. and Treas.: HENRY A. MAUERMEYER
Sr Vice-Pres. for Research and Devt: Dr DONALD H. SEBASTIAN
Vice-Pres. for Academic and Student Services: JOEL BLOOM
Vice-Pres. for Univ. Advancement: CHARLES R. DEES, Jr
Gen. Counsel: HOLLY STERN
Librarian: RICHARD T. SWEENEY

Library of 181,000 vols
Number of teachers: 587 (354 full-time, 233 part-time)
Number of students: 7,837

DEANS

Albert Dorman Honors College: JOEL BLOOM
College of Computing Sciences: STEPHEN SEIDMAN
College of Engineering: ANGELO PERNA (acting)
College of Science and Liberal Arts: Dr G. MÜLLER JONAKAIT
School of Architecture: URS GAUCHAT
School of Management: MARK SOMERS
Graduate Studies: RONALD KANE

PRINCETON THEOLOGICAL SEMINARY

64 Mercer St, POB 821, Princeton, NJ 08542-0803
Telephone: (609) 921-8300
Fax: (609) 924-2973
E-mail: admissions@ptsem.edu
Internet: www.ptsem.edu

Founded 1812
Private control

Pres.: IAIN R. TORRANCE
Sr Vice-Pres., Chief Operating Officer and Treas.: JOHN W. GILMORE
Vice-Pres. for Information Technology: ADRIAN BACKUS
Vice-Pres. for Investment and Chief Investment Office: JUDITH W. HEAGSTEDT
Vice-Pres. for Seminary Relations: ROSEMAY MITCHELL
Dean of Academic Affairs: Prof. DARRELL L. GULDER
Dean of Continuing Education: JOYCE C. TUCKER
Dean of Student Affairs: NANCY LAMMERS GROSS
Registrar: DAVID WALL
Librarian: Dr STEPHEN D. CROCCO

Number of teachers: 50
Number of students: 746

PRINCETON UNIVERSITY

Princeton, NJ 08544
Telephone: (609) 258-3000
Internet: www.princeton.edu

Founded 1746 as the College of New Jersey, became Princeton Univ. 1896
Academic year: September to May

Pres.: SHIRLEY M. TILGHMAN
Provost: CHRISTOPHER EISGRUBER
Vice-Pres. and Sec.: ROBERT K. DURKEE
Exec. Vice-Pres.: MARK BURSTEIN
Vice-Pres. for Campus Life: CYNTHIA CHERREY
Vice-Pres. for Devt: ELIZABETH BOLUCH WOOD
Vice-Pres. for Facilities: MICHAEL E. MCKAY
Vice-Pres. for Finance and Treas.: CAROLYN N. AINSLIE
Vice-Pres. for Human Resources: LIANNE SULLIVAN-CROWLEY

Vice-Pres. for Information Technology and Chief Information Officer: BETTY LEYDON
Gen. Counsel: PETER G. MCDONOUGH
Registrar: POLLY WINFREY GRIFFIN
Librarian: KARIN TRAINER

Library: see Libraries and Archives
Number of teachers: 1,132
Number of students: 7,802

Publications: *Annals of Mathematics* (6 a year), *Library Chronicle, Population Index* (4 a year), *Princeton University Bulletin* (10 a year), *World Politics* (4 a year)

DEANS

Admission: JANET LAVIN RAPELYE
College: NANCY WEISS MALKIEL
Faculty: DAVID P. DOBKIN
Graduate School: WILLIAM B. RUSSEL
Religious Life and Chapel: ALISON L. BODEN
Research: A. J. STEWART SMITH
School of Architecture: STANLEY T. ALLEN
School of Engineering and Applied Science: H. VINCENT POOR
Undergraduate Students: KATHLEEN DEIGNAN
Woodrow Wilson School of Public and International Affairs: CHRISTINA PAXSON

PROFESSORS

ABBATE, C., Music
ABREU, D. J., Economics
ACTON, F. S., Electrical Engineering and Computer Science
ADELMAN, J. I., Latin American Studies
AGAWU, V. K., African Studies
AIT-SAHALIA, Y., Economics
AIZENMAN, M., Physics
AKSAY, I., Chemical Engineering
ALLEN, L. C., Chemistry
ALTMANN, J., Ecology and Evolutionary Biology
APPIAH, K., Afro-American Studies
ARMSTRONG, C. M., Art and Archaeology
ARNOLD, R. D., Politics and Public Affairs
ASHENFELTER, O. C., Economics
ATKINS, S. D., Classics
AUSTIN, R. H., Physics
AXTMANN, R. C., Chemical Engineering
BABBITT, M. B., Music
BABBY, L. H., Slavic Language and Literature
BAGLEY, R. W., Art and Archaeology
BAHCALL, N., Astrophysical Science
BARTELS, L. M., Public and International Affairs
BAUMOL, W. J., Economics
BELLOS, D. M., Romance Languages and Literatures
BENABOU, R. J.-M., Economics and Public Affairs
BENACERRAF, P., Philosophy
BENDER, M. L., Geosciences
BENTLEY, G. E., English Literature
BENZIGER, J. B., Chemical Engineering
BERMAN, S. L., Comparative Literature
BERNANKE, B., Economics and Public Affairs
BERNASEK, S. L., Chemistry
BERNHEIM, B. D., Economics
BERRY, C. H., Economics and Public Affairs
BHATT, R. N., Electrical Engineering
BILLINGTON, D. P., Civil Engineering
BLINDER, A. S., Economics
BOCARSLY, A. B., Chemistry
BOGDONOFF, S. M., Aeronautical, Mechanical and Aerospace Engineering
BOLTON, P., Finance, Economics
BONINI, W. E., Geophysics and Geological Engineering, Civil Engineering
BOON, J. A., Anthropology
BOYER, M. C., Architecture
BRACCO, F., Mechanical and Aerospace Engineering
BRADFORD, D. F., Economics and Public Affairs
BRANSON, W. H., Economics and International Affairs
BROACH, J. R., Molecular Biology
BROADIE, S. W., Philosophy
BRODSKY LACOUR, C. J., Comparative Literature
BROMBERT, V. H., Romance Languages and Literatures and Comparative Literature
BROWDER, W., Mathematics
BROWN, C. F., Jr, Comparative Literature
BROWN, G. L., Mechanical and Aerospace Engineering
BROWN, P. F., Art and Archaeology
BROWN, P. R., History
BUNNELL, P. C., History of Photography and Modern Art; Art and Archaeology
BURGESS, J. P., Philosophy
CALAPRICE, F. P., Physics
CALLAN, C. G., Jr, Physics
CAMPBELL, B. A., Psychology
CAR, R., Chemistry
CARMONA, R. A., Operations Research and Financial Engineering
CARRASACO, D., Religion
CASE, A. C., Economics and Public Affairs
CATES, G. D., Jr, Physics
CAVA, R. J., Chemistry
CELIA, M. A., Civil and Environmental Engineering
CHAIKIN, P. M., Physics
CHAMPLIN, E. J., Humanities; Classics
CHANCES, E. B., Slavic Languages and Literatures
CHANG, S. Y. A., Mathematics
CHASE, A. M., Biology
CHAZELLE, B. M., Computer Science
CHENG, S. I., Aeronautical Engineering
CHILDS, W. A. P., Art and Archaeology
CHOU, C.-P., East Asian Studies
CHOU, S. Y., Engineering
CHOW, G. C., Economics, Political Economy
CHRISTODOULOU, D., Mathematics
CINLAR, E., Civil Engineering
CLARK, D., Computer Sciences
CLINTON, J. W., Near Eastern Studies
COALE, A. J., Economics and Public Affairs
COFFIN, D. R., Art and Archaeology
COHEN, M. R., Near Eastern Studies
COLE, M. D., Molecular Biology
COLLCUTT, M. C., East Asian Studies
CONWAY, J. H., Applied and Computational Mathematics
COOPER, J., Psychology
COOPER, J. M., Philosophy
CORNGOLD, S. A., Germanic Languages
ÇOX, E. C., Biology
CURČIĆ, S., Art and Archaeology
CURSCHMANN, M. J. H., Germanic Languages
DAHLEN, F. A., Geological and Geophysical Sciences
DANIELSON, M. N., Politics and Public Affairs
DANSON, L. N., English
DARLEY, J. M., Psychology
DARNTON, R. C., History
DAUBECHIES, I. C., Mathematics
DAVIDSON, R. C., Astrophysical Sciences
DAVIES, H. M., Religion
DEATON, A. S., Economics and International Affairs
DEBENEDETTI, P. G., Engineering
DIAMOND, M. L., Religion
DÍAZ-QUIÑONES, A., Romance Languages and Literatures
DI BATTISTA, M. A., English and Comparative Literature
DICKINSON, B. W., Electrical Engineering
DIIULIO, J. J., Politics and Public Affairs
DILLIARD, I., Journalism and Public Relations
DIMAGGIO, P. J., Sociology
DISMUKES, G. C., Chemistry
DIXIT, A. K., Economics and International Affairs
DOBBIN, F. R., Sociology
DOBKIN, D. P., Electrical Engineering and Computer Science
DOIG, J. W., Politics and Public Affairs
DOYLE, M. W., Public and International Affairs
DRAINE, B. T., Astrophysical Sciences
DRYER, F. L., Mechanical and Aerospace Engineering
EBERT, R. P., Germanic Languages and Literatures
EMERSON, C. G., Slavic Languages and Literatures
ENGELSTEIN, L., History
ENQUIST, L. W., Molecular Biology
ERMOLAEV, H., Slavic Languages and Literatures
ESPENSHADE, T. J., Sociology
EVANS, A. G., Engineering
FAGLES, R., Comparative Literature
FALK, R. A., International Law, Politics, and International Affairs
FALTINGS, G., Mathematics
FARBER, H. S., Economics
FEENEY, D. C., Classics
FEFFERMAN, C., Mathematics
FISCH, N. J., Astrophysical Sciences
FISKE, S. T., Psychology
FITCH, V. L., Physics
FLEMING, J. V., English and Comparative Literature
FLINT, S. J., Molecular Biology
FLOUDAS, C. A., Chemical Engineering
FORCIONI, A., Comparative Literature
FORD, A. L., Classics
FORREST, S. R., Electrical Engineering
FOSTER, H. F., Art and Archaeology
FRANKFURT, H. G., Philosophy
FRASSICA, P., Romance Languages and Literatures
FREEDMAN, R. W. B., Comparative Literature
FREIDIN, R. A., Council of the Humanities
FRESCO, J. R., Life Sciences
FRIEDBERG, A. L., Politics and International Affairs
GAGER, J. G., Jr, Religion
GANDELSONAS, M. I., Architecture
GARON, S. M., History and East Asian Studies
GARVEY, G., Politics
GEDDES, R. L., Architecture
GEISON, G. L., History and History of Science
GEORGE, R. P., Jurisprudence
GIBBS, N., Journalism and Council of Humanities
GIRGUS, J. S., Psychology
GLASSMAN, I., Mechanical and Aerospace Engineering
GLUCKSBERG, S., Psychology
GOLDMAN, M. P., English
GOLDMAN, N. J., Demography and Public Affairs
GOLDSTON, R. J., Astrophysical Sciences
GOODMAN, J., Astrophysical Sciences
GOSSMAN, J. L., Romance Languages and Literatures
GOTT, J. R., III, Astrophysical Sciences
GOULD, E., Psychology
GOULD, J. L., Biology
GOWA, J., Politics
GOWIN, E. W., Council of the Humanities and Visual Arts
GRAF, F., Classics
GRAFTON, A. T., History
GRANT, P., Biology
GRAVES, M., Architecture
GREENSTEIN, F. I., Politics
GROSS, C. G., Psychology
GROSSMAN, G. M., Economics and Business Policy
GROTH, E. J., III, Physics
GROVES, J. T., Chemistry
GRUNER, S. M., Physics
GUL, F. R., Economics
GUNN, J. E., Astronomy
GUNNING, R. C.
GUTMANN, A., Politics
HAHN, B., Germanic Languages and Literatures
HALDANE, F. D. M., Physics

HAMMOUDI, A., Anthropology and Near East Studies
HAMORI, A. P., Near Eastern Studies
HANIOGLU, M. S., Near Eastern Studies
HAPPER, W., Physics
HARMAN, G. H., Philosophy
HARTOG, H. A., History
HELD, I. M., Geological and Geophysical Sciences, Atmospheric and Oceanic Sciences
HERBST, J. I., Politics and International Affairs
HIMMELFARB, M., Religion
HINDERER, W., Germanic Languages and Literatures
HOCHSCHILD, J. L., Politics and Public Affairs
HOEBEL, B. G., Psychology
HOFFMANN, L.-F., Romance Languages
HOLLANDER, R. B., Jr, European and Comparative Literature
HOLLISTER, L. S., Geological and Geophysical Sciences
HOLMES, P. J., Mechanical and Aerospace Engineering
HONORE, B. E., Economics
HOPFIELD, J. J., Molecular Biology
HORN, H. S., Biology
HOWARTH, W. L., English
HSIANG, W.-C., Mathematics
HUET, M.-H., Romance Languages and Literatures
ISSAWI, C., Near Eastern Studies
ITZKOWITZ, N., Near Eastern Studies
JACOBS, B. L., Psychology
JAFFE, P. R., Civil and Environmental Engineering
JAHN, R. G., Aerospace Sciences
JAMES, H., History
JAMESON, A., Mechanical and Aerospace Engineering
JEFFREY, P., Music
JENNINGS, M. W., Germanic Languages and Literatures
JHA, N. K., Electrical Engineering
JOHNSON, C. L., English
JOHNSON, M., Psychology
JOHNSON-LAIRD, P. N., Psychology
JOHNSTON, M., Philosophy
JONES, M., Chemistry
JORDON, W. C., History
KAHN, A., Electrical Engineering
KAHN, V. A., English and Comparative Literature
KAHNEMAN, D., Psychology
KASTER, R. A., Latin Language and Literature
KATEB, G., Politics
KATZ, N. M., Mathematics
KAUFMANN, T. D., Art and Archaeology
KELLER, G., Geological and Geophysical Sciences
KELLER, S., Sociology
KELLEY, S., Politics
KENEN, P. B., Economics and International Finance
KEVREKIDIS, Y. G., Chemical Engineering
KINCHLA, R. A., Psychology
KING, E. L., Language, Literature, and Civilization of Spain
KLAINERMAN, S., Mathematics
KLEBANOV, I. R., Mathematical Physics
KNAPP, G. R., Astrophysical Sciences
KNOEPFLMACHER, U. C., English
KOBAYASHI, H., Electrical Engineering and Computer Science
KOCHEN, S. B., Mathematics
KOHLI, A., Politics and International Affairs
KOHN, J. J., Mathematics
KOLLAR, J., Mathematics
KOMUNYAKAA, Y., Council of the Humanities and Creative Writing
KORNHAUSER, A. L., Civil Engineering
KOSTIN, M. D., Chemical Engineering
KRIPKE, S., Philosophy
KROMMES, J. A., Astrophysical Sciences
KUNG, S.-Y., Electrical Engineering
LAKE, P. G., History
LAM, S.-H., Mechanical and Aerospace Engineering
LAMB, J., English
LAMONT, M., Sociology
LANGE, V., Modern Languages
LANGLOIS, J. D., Jr, East Asian Studies
LANSKY, P., Music
LA PAUGH, A. S., Computer Science
LAU, N.-C., Geosciences and Atmospheric and Oceanic Sciences
LAW, C. K., Mechanical and Aerospace Engineering
LEE, P. C. Y., Civil Engineering
LEE, R. B.-L., Engineering
LEHMANN, K. K., Chemistry
LEIBLER, S., Physics and Molecular Biology
LERNER, R., Architecture
LEVIN, S. A., Ecology and Evolutionary Biology
LEWIS, D. K., Philosophy
LEWIS, J. P., Economics and International Affairs
LI, K., Computer Science
LIEB, E. H., Mathematical Physics
LINK, E. P., East Asian Studies
LIPTON, R. J., Computer Science
LITTMAN, M. G., Mechanical and Aerospace Engineering
LIU, B., Electrical Engineering
LONGUENESSE, B. M., Philosophy
LOWRY, H. N., Ottoman and Modern Turkish Studies
LYON, S. A., Electrical Engineering
MCDONALD, K. T., Physics
MACEDO, S. J., Politics
MACKEY, S., Music
MCLANAHAN, S. S., Sociology and Public Affairs
MCLENDON, G. L., Chemistry
MCPHERSON, J. M., History
MAHLMAN, J. D., Geological and Geophysical Sciences, and Atmospheric and Oceanic Sciences
MAHONEY, M. S., History and History of Science
MAKINO, S., East Asian Studies
MALIK, S., Electrical Engineering
MALKIEL, B. G., Economics
MALKIEL, N. W., History
MAMAN, A., French, Romance Languages and Literatures
MARLOW, D. R., Physics
MARTIN, E., Anthropology
MARTIN, R. B., English
MATHER, J. N., Mathematics
MEYER, H., Art and Archaeology
MEYERS, P. D., Physics
MILES, R. B., Mechanical and Aerospace Engineering
MILLER, D. T., Psychology
MILLER, G. A., Psychology
MILLER, H. K., English
MITCHELL, L. C., English
MODARRESSI, H., Near Eastern Studies
MOREL, F. M., Geosciences
MORGAN, W. J., Geophysics
MULDOON, P. B., Humanities
MULVEY, J. M., Civil Engineering
MURRIN, J. M., History
NAQUIN, S., History
NASH, S. C., Romance Languages and Literature
NEHAMAS, A., Humanities, Philosophy and Comparative Literature
NELSON, J., Mathematics
NEWTON, A., Molecular Biology
NOLET, A. M., Geological and Geophysical Sciences
NORD, D. E., English
NORD, P. G., History
OBER, J., Classics
ONG, N.-P., Physics
ORLANSKI, I., Geological and Geophysical Sciences, and Atmospheric and Oceanic Sciences
OSTRIKER, J. P., Astrophysical Sciences
PACALA, S., Ecology
PACZYNSKI, B., Astrophysical Sciences
PAGE, L. A., Jr, Physics
PAGELS, E. H., Religion
PAINTER, N. I., History
PANAGIOTOPOULOS, A. Z., Chemical Engineering
PAVEL, T., Comparative Literature, and Romance Languages and Literatures
PAXSON, C. H., Economics and Public Affairs
PEEBLES, P. J. E., Physics
PETERSON, L. I., Computer Science
PETERSON, W. J., East Asian Studies
PHILANDER, S. G. H., Geological and Geophysical Sciences
PHINNEY, R. A., Geological and Geophysical Sciences
PINTO, J. A., Art and Archaeology
PIROUÉ, P. A., Physics
PLAKS, A. H., East Asian Studies
POLYAKOV, A., Physics
POOR, H. V., Electrical Engineering
PORTES, A., Sociology
POWELL, W. B., Civil Engineering
POWERS, H. S., Music
PRAKASH, G., History
PRENTICE, D. A., Psychology
PREVOST, J.-H., Civil Engineering
PRUCNAL, P. R., Electrical Engineering
PRUDHOMME, P. R., Chemical and Electrical Engineering
RABB, T. K., History
RABINBACH, A. G., History
RABITZ, H. A., Chemistry
RABOTEAU, A. J., Religion
REINHARDT, U. E., Economics and Public Affairs, and Political Economy
RICHARDSON, J., English
RIGOLOT, F., Romance Languages and Literatures
ROCHE, T. P., Jr, English
RODGERS, D. T., History
RODRIGUEZ-ITURBE, I., Civil and Environmental Engineering
ROMER, T., Politics and Public Affairs
ROSE, M. D., Molecular Biology
ROSEN, H. S., Economics
ROSEN, L., Anthropology
ROSENTHAL, H., Social Sciences
ROTHSCHILD, M., Economics and Public Affairs
ROYCE, B. S. H., Mechanical and Aerospace Engineering
ROZMAN, G. F., Sociology
RUBENSTEIN, A., Economics
RUBENSTEIN, D. I., Ecology and Evolutionary Biology
RUSSEL, W. B., Chemical Engineering
RYSKAMP, C. A., English
SARMIENTO, J. L., Geological and Geophysical Sciences
SARNAK, P. C., Mathematics
SAVILLE, D. A., Chemical Engineering
SCANLON, R. H., Civil Engineering
SCHAFER, P., Jewish Studies
SCHEDL, P. D., Molecular Biology
SCHEINKMAN, J. A., Economics
SCHERER, G. W., Civil and Environmental Engineering
SCHMIDT, L. E., Religion
SCHOWALTER, W. R., Engineering and Applied Science
SCHUPBACH, G. M., Molecular Biology
SCHUTT, C. E., Chemistry
SCHWARTZ, J., Chemistry
SCHWARTZ, S. C., Electrical Engineering
SCOLES, G., Chemistry
SEAWRIGHT, J. L., Council of Humanities
SEDGEWICK, R., Computer Science
SEMMELHACK, M. F., Chemistry
SEYMOUR, P. D., Mathematics, and Applied and Computational Mathematics
SHAFIR, E. B., Psychology
SHAPIRO, H. T., Economics and Public Affairs
SHAYEGAN, M., Electrical Engineering

SHEAR, T. L., Jr, Classical Archaeology
SHENK, T. E., Molecular Biology
SHIMIZU, Y., Art and Archaeology
SHOWALTER, E., English
SIGMUND, P. E., Politics
SILHAVY, T. J., Molecular Biology
SILVER, L. M., Molecular Biology
SIMS, C. A., Economics
SINAI, Y. G., Mathematics
SINGER, B. H., Public and International Affairs
SINGER, P. A. D., Bioethics
SITNEY, P. A., Council of Humanities
SLABY, S. M., Civil Engineering
SMITH, A. J., Physics
SMITH, J. A., Civil and Environmental Engineering
SMITH, J. C. O., Humanities
SMITH, J. W., Philosophy
SMITH, N., English
SMITS, A., Mechanical and Aerospace Engineering
SMOLUCHOWSKI, R., Solid State Sciences
SOANES, S., Philosophy
SOBOYEJO, W. O., Mechanical and Aerospace Engineering
SOCOLOW, R. H., Mechanical and Aerospace Engineering
SONER, H. M., Engineering and Finance
SOOS, Z. G., Chemistry
SPIRO, T. G., Chemistry
SPITZER, L., Jr, Astronomy
SROLOVITZ, D. J., Mechanical and Aerospace Engineering
STANSELL, M. C., History
STARR, P., Sociology
STEIGLITZ, K., Computer Science
STEIN, E. M., Mathematics
STEIN, S. J., History
STEINBERG, M., Biology
STEINHARDT, P. J., Physics
STENGEL, R. F., Mechanical and Aerospace Engineering
STOCK, J. B., Molecular Biology
STOUT, J. L., Religion
STURM, J. C., Electrical Engineering
SUCKEWER, S., Mechanical and Aerospace Engineering
SULEIMAN, E. N., Politics
SUNDARESAN, S., Chemical Engineering
SUO, Z., Mechanical and Aerospace Engineering
SUPPE, J. E., Geological and Geophysical Sciences
SURTZ, R. E., Romance Languages and Literatures
TARJAN, R. E., Computer Science
TATE, C. C., English
TAYLOR, H. F., Sociology
TAYLOR, J. H., Physics
TEISER, S. F., Buddhist Studies
TEYSSOT, G. M., Architecture
TIENDA, M., Demographic Studies
TIGNOR, R. L., History
TORQUATO, S., Civil Engineering
TOWNSEND, C. E., Slavic Languages and Literatures
TREISMAN, A., Psychology
TREMAINE, S. D., Astrophysical Sciences
TROTTER, H. F., Mathematics
TRUSSELL, T. J., Economics and Public Affairs
TSUI, D. C., Electrical Engineering
TUKEY, J. W., Science, Statistics
TURNER, E. L., Astrophysical Sciences
UDOVITCH, A. L., Near Eastern Studies
UITTI, K. D., Modern Languages, Romance Languages and Literatures
ULLMAN, R., International Affairs
VAN FRAASSEN, B. C., Philosophy
VAN HOUTEN, F. B., Geological and Geophysical Sciences
VANMARCKE, E., Civil Engineering
VERDU, S., Electrical Engineering
VERLINDE, H. L., Physics
VOLKER, P. A., International and Economic Policy
VON GOELER, S. E., Astrophysical Sciences
VON HIPPEL, F. N., Public and International Affairs
WACHTEL, M. A., Slavic Languages and Literatures
WAGNER, S., Electrical Engineering
WALLACE, W. L., Sociology
WARD, B. B., Geosciences
WARREN, S., Chemistry
WATSON, G. S., Statistics
WATSON, M. W., Economics and Public Affairs
WEI, J., Chemical Engineering
WEIGERT, M., Molecular Biology
WEINAN, E., Mathematics
WEISS, T. R., English and Creative Writing
WEITZMANN, K., Art and Archaeology
WEST, C., Afro-American Studies
WEST, C. R., Religion
WESTERGAARD, P. T., Music
WESTERN, B., Sociology
WHITE, L. T., Politics
WHITWELL, J. C., Chemical Engineering
WIESCHAUS, E. F., Biology
WIGHTMAN, A. S., Mathematical Physics
WILENTZ, R. S., History
WILES, A. J., Mathematics
WILKINSON, D. T., Physics
WILLIAMS, E. S., Humanities
WILLIG, R. D., Economics and Public Affairs
WILLIS, J. R., Near Eastern Studies
WILMERDING, J., American Art; Art and Archaeology
WILSON, J. F., Religion
WOLFSON, S. J., English
WOLPERT, J., Geography, Public Affairs and Urban Planning
WOOD, E. F., Civil Engineering
WOOD, M. G., English
WOODFORD, M. D., Economics and Banking
WUTHNOW, R. J., Sociology
YAO, A. L.-L., Computer Science
YU, Y. S., East Asian Studies
ZAKIAN, V. A., Molecular Biology
ZEITLIN, F. I., Classics
ZELIZER, V. A., Sociology
ZIOLKOWSKI, T. J., Germanic Languages and Literatures, and Comparative Literature

RAMAPO COLLEGE OF NEW JERSEY

505 Ramapo Valley Rd, Mahwah, NJ 07430-1680
Telephone: (201) 684-7500
Internet: www.ramapo.edu

Founded 1969
Academic year: September to May

Pres.: Dr PETER PHILIP MERCER
Provost and Vice-Pres. for Academic Affairs: Dr BETH E. BARNETT
Vice-Pres. for Institutional Advancement: CATHLEEN DAVEY
Vice-Pres. for Student Affairs: Dr PAMELA M. BISCHOFF
Dean of Students: NANCY MACKIN
Registrar: CYNTHIA BRENNAN
Librarian: ELIZABETH SIECKE

Number of teachers: 187
Number of students: 5,459 (5,148 undergraduate, 311 postgraduate)

DEANS

School of Administration and Business: Dr FREDERIC CHAMPLIN
School of American and Int. Studies: Dr JENNEFER MAZZA
School of Contemporary Arts: STEVE PERRY
School of Social Science and Human Services: Dr HENRY VANCE DAVIS
School of Theoretical and Applied Science: Dr ERIC KARLIN

RICHARD STOCKTON COLLEGE OF NEW JERSEY

POB 195, Pomona, NJ 08240
Telephone: (609) 652-1776
Internet: www.stockton.edu

Founded 1969 as Richard Stockton State College; present name 1993
Academic year: September to May

Pres.: Dr HERMAN J. SAATKAMP, Jr
Provost and Exec. Vice-Pres. for Academic Affairs: DAVID CARR
Vice-Pres. for Admin. and Finance: CHARLES E. KLEIN
Vice-Pres. for Student Affairs: Dr JOSEPH J. MARCHETTI
Dean of Students: THOMASA GONZALEZ
Registrar: JOSEPH J. LOSASSO
Library Dir: DAVID PINTO

Number of teachers: 343 (216 full-time, 127 part-time)
Number of students: 6,459

DEANS

Arts and Humanities: KENNETH J. DOLLARHIDE
General Studies: G. JAN COLIJN
Natural Sciences and Mathematics: DENNIS WEISS
Professional Studies: MARC LOWENSTEIN
Social and Behavioural Sciences: WILLIAM C. JAYNES, IV
Graduate and Continuing Professional Education: DEBRA ISRAEL

RIDER UNIVERSITY

2083 Lawrenceville Rd, Lawrenceville, NJ 08648-3099
Telephone: (609) 896-5000
Fax: (609) 896-8029
Internet: www.rider.edu

Founded 1865

Pres.: Dr MORDECHAI ROZANSKI
Vice-Pres. for Academic Affairs and Provost: Dr DONALD A. STEVEN
Assoc. Vice-Pres. for Student Affairs: Dr ANTHONY CAMPBELL
Vice-Pres. for Univ. Advancement: JONATHAN MEER
Dean of Univ. Libraries: F. WILLIAM CHICKERING

Library of 417,000 vols
Number of teachers: 200
Number of students: 5,790

ROWAN UNIVERSITY

201 Mullica Hill Rd, Glassboro, NJ 08028
Telephone: (856) 256-4000
Fax: (856) 256-4929
E-mail: webmaster@rowan.edu
Internet: www.rowan.edu

Founded 1923 as Glassboro Normal School; became New Jersey State Teachers' College at Glassboro 1937, Glassboro State College 1958 and Rowan College of New Jersey 1992; present name and status 1997
Academic year: July to June

Pres.: Dr DONALD J. FARISH
Exec. Vice-Pres. and Provost: Dr ALI A. HOUSHMAND
Registrar: MURIEL A. J. FRIERSON
Dean of Library Services: GREGORY POTTER

Library of 339,000 vols
Number of teachers: 350
Number of students: 9,368

RUTGERS, THE STATE UNIVERSITY OF NEW JERSEY

57 US Highway 1, New Brunswick, NJ 08901-8554
Telephone: (732) 445-4636
Internet: www.rutgers.edu

Founded as Queen's College by Royal Charter 1766; name changed to Rutgers College 1825, Rutgers Univ. 1924; designated by legislature as State Univ. of New Jersey 1945 and 1956
Academic year: September to May

Pres.: RICHARD L. MCCORMICK
Exec. Vice-Pres. for Academic Affairs: Dr PHILIP FURMANSKI
Exec. Vice-Pres. for Devt and Alumni Relations: CAROL P. HERRING
Sr Vice-Pres. for Finance and Admin.: BRUCE C. FEHN
Sr Vice-Pres. and Gen. Counsel: JONATHAN R. ALGER
Vice-Pres. for Alumni Relations: DONNA THORNTON
Vice-Pres. for Continuous Education and Outreach: RAPHAEL J. CAPRIO
Vice-Pres. for Enrollment Management: COURTNEY O. MCANUFF
Vice-Pres. for Public Affairs: JEANNINE F. LARUE
Vice-Pres. for Research and Graduate and Professional Education: MICHAEL J. PAZZANI
Vice-Pres. for Student Affairs: GREGORY S. BLIMLING
Vice-Pres. for Undergraduate Education: BARRY QUALLS
Vice-Pres. for Univ. Budgeting: NANCY S. WINTERBAUER
Vice-Pres. for Univ. Relations: KIM MANNING
Sec.: LESLIE A. FEHRENBACH
Camden Campus Chancellor: Dr WENDELL PRITCHETT
Newark Campus Chancellor: Dr STEVEN DINER
Univ. Librarian: MARIANNE GAUNT

Library: see Libraries and Archives
Number of teachers: 4,150
Number of students: 54,600 (incl. 14,100 postgraduate students)

Publications: *Academic Questions*, *Child Welfare*, *Journal for the History of Ideas*, *Journal for International Law*, *Journal of Research in Crime and Delinquency*, *Labor Studies Journal*, *North–South*, *Plant Molecular Biology Reporter*, *Public Budgeting and Finance*, *Public Productivity and Management Review*, *Raritan Review*, *Society*, *The American Sociologist*, *Women's Studies* (4 a year)

DEANS

Camden Campus:
Arts and Sciences: MARGARET MARSH
Law: RAYMAN SOLOMON
Graduate School: MARGARET MARSH
School of Business: JAISHANKAR GANESH

New Brunswick Campus:
Applied and Professional Psychology: STANLEY B. MESSER
Busch Campus: THOMAS PAPATHOMAS
College Ave. Campus: MATTHEW K. MATSUDA
George H. Cook Campus: RICHARD LUDESCHER
Douglass College: HARRIET DAVIDSON
Edward J. Bloustein School of Planning and Public Policy: JAMES W. HUGHES
Ernest Mario School of Pharmacy: CHRISTOPHER J. MOLLOY
Graduate School: JEROME J. KUKOR (acting)
Graduate School of Education: RICHARD DE LISI
Graduate School of Applied and Professional Psychology: STANLEY B. MESSER
Livingston College: LEA P. STEWART
Mason Gross School of the Arts: GEORGE B. STAUFFER
Rutgers Business School (Newark and New Brunswick): MICHAEL R. COOPER
Social Work: RICHARD L. EDWARDS
School of Arts and Sciences: DOUGLAS GREENBERG (Exec. Dean)
School of Communication and Information: JORGE REINA SCHEMENT
School of Engineering: THOMAS FARRIS
School of Environmental and Biological Sciences: ROBERT M. GOODMAN (Exec. Dean)
School of Management and Labour Relations: DAVID L. FINEGOLD
Univ. College Community: SUSAN J. SCHURMAN

Newark Campus:
Arts and Sciences: PHILIP L. YEAGLE
Criminal Justice: TODD CLEAR
Graduate School: GARY ROTH
Law: JOHN J. FARMER, Jr
Nursing: WILLIAM L. HOLZEMER
Public Affairs and Admin.: MARC HOLZER
Rutgers Business School (Newark and New Brunswick): MICHAEL R. COOPER

SAINT PETER'S COLLEGE

2641 Kennedy Blvd, Jersey City, NJ 07306-5997
Telephone: (201) 761-6000
Internet: www.spc.edu

Founded 1872

Pres.: Dr EUGENE J. CORNACCHIA
Assoc. Vice-Pres. for Enrollment and Academic Admin.: Dr VIRGINIA BENDER
Academic Dean: MARYLOU LAM
Dir of Admissions: JOE GIGLIO
Registrar and Dir of Enrollment Services: STEVEN E. SMITH
Library Dir: CHARLES J. MYERS

Library of 282,000 vols
Number of teachers: 360 (118 full-time, 242 part-time)
Number of students: 4,698 (3,477 full-time, 1,221 part-time)

Undergraduate courses in business studies, humanities, nursing, sciences; masters courses in accountancy, education, int. business, management, management information systems, nursing.

SETON HALL UNIVERSITY

South Orange, NJ 07079
Telephone: (973) 761-9000
Fax: (973) 275-2040
E-mail: thehall@shu.edu
Internet: www.shu.edu

Founded 1856
Academic year: August to May

Pres.: Dr GABRIEL ESTEBAN
Exec. Vice-Pres. and Provost: Dr LARRY ROBINSON
Exec. Vice-Pres. for Admin.: Sr PAULA M. BULEY
Vice-Pres. for Finance and Technology: DENNIS GARBINI
Vice-Pres. for Mission and Ministry: Mgr ANTHONY ZICCARDI
Vice-Pres. for Student Affairs: Dr LAURA WANKEL
Vice-Pres. for University Advancement: Dr JOSEPH SANDMAN
Vice-Pres. and Gen. Counsel: CATHERINE KIERNAN

Library of 640,000 vols
Number of teachers: 909 (446 full-time, 463 part-time)
Number of students: 9,836

Publications: *Journal of Diplomacy and International Relations* (2 a year), *Mid-Atlantic Journal of Business* (3 a year), *The Chesterton Reveiw* (4 a year), *The Journal of Global Health Governance* (2 a year)

DEANS

College of Arts and Sciences: Dr JOAN GUETTI
College of Education and Human Services: Dr JOSEPH DE PIERRO
College of Nursing: Dr PHYLLIS HANSELL
Immaculate Conception School of Theology: Mgr ROBERT COLEMAN
School of Health and Medical Sciences: Dr BRIAN SHULMAN
School of Law: PATRICK HOBBS
Stillman School of Business: Dr JOYCE STRAWSER
Whitehead School of Diplomacy and International Relations: JOHN MENZIES

STEVENS INSTITUTE OF TECHNOLOGY

Castle Point on Hudson, Hoboken, NJ 07030-5991
Telephone: (201) 216-5000
Internet: www.stevens-tech.edu

Founded 1870

Pres.: HAL RAVECHE
Provost and Univ. Vice-Pres.: GEORGE KORFIATIS
Vice-Pres. for Devt and Univ. Communications: MARJORIE J. EVERITT
Vice-Pres. for Finance, Chief Financial Officer and Treas.: STEFANO FALCONI
Vice-Pres. for Univ. Enrollment and Admin.: MAUREEN WEATHERALL
Vice-Pres. for Univ. Research and Enterprise Devt: HELENA S. WISNIEWSKI
Dean of Admissions and Financial Aid: DANIEL S. GALLAGHER
Dean of Graduate Studies: CHARLES L. SUFFEL

Library of 105,000 vols
Number of teachers: 230
Number of students: 1,700 (1,200 undergraduates, 500 full-time graduate)

THOMAS EDISON STATE COLLEGE

101 West State St, Trenton, NJ 08608-1176
Telephone: (888) 442-8372
Fax: (609) 984-8447
E-mail: info@tesc.edu
Internet: www.tesc.edu

Founded 1972

Pres.: Dr GEORGE A. PRUITT
Vice-Pres. and Provost: WILLIAM J. SEATON

Number of students: 10,233

Areas of study: arts, applied science and technology, business admin., health sciences, human services, nursing.

WESTMINSTER CHOIR COLLEGE OF RIDER UNIVERSITY

101 Walnut Lane, Princeton, NJ 08540-3899
Telephone: (609) 921-7100
Internet: www.rider.edu/westminster

Founded 1926

Pres.: Dr MORDECHAI ROZANSKI
Vice-Pres. and Provost: Dr DONALD A. STEVEN
Dir and Dean: ROBERT L. ANNIS
Registrar: SUSAN A. STEFANICK
Librarian: WILLIAM F. CHICKERING

Library of 67,000 vols; books, music scores and periodicals; 5,400 choral music titles in performance quantities; choral music reference; colln of over 80,000 titles; over 23,000 sound and video recordings.
Number of teachers: 117

Number of students: 335 undergraduates and 115 graduates

WILLIAM PATERSON UNIVERSITY OF NEW JERSEY

300 Pompton Rd, Wayne, NJ 07470

Telephone: (973) 720-2000

Internet: www.wpunj.edu

Founded 1855

Academic year: September to June

Pres.: Dr ARNOLD SPEERT

Exec. Vice-Pres. and Provost: Dr CHERNOH SESAY

Vice-Pres. for Admin. and Finance: STEPHEN BOLYAI

Vice-Pres. for Institutional Advancement: SANDRA DELLER

Dean of Student Devt: GLEN SHERMAN

Registrar: MARK EVANGELISTA

Librarian: Dr JOHN GABOURY

Library of 303,545 vols

Number of teachers: 358

Number of students: 9,945

DEANS

College of Arts and Communication: OFELIA GARCIA

College of Business: Dr JESS BORONICO

College of Education: Dr LESLIE AGARD-JONES

College of Humanities and Social Science: Dr ISABEL TIRADO

College of Science and Health: Dr ESWAR PHADIA

NEW MEXICO

COLLEGE OF SANTA FE

1600 St Michael's Dr., Santa Fe, NM 87505

Telephone: (505) 473-6133

Fax: (505) 473-6127

E-mail: admissions@csf.edu

Internet: www.csf.edu

Founded 1859 by the Lasallian Brothers, a teaching order of the Catholic Church

Pres.: Dr STUART KIRK

Vice-Pres. for Academic Affairs: JOHN ALLEN

Vice-Pres. for Institutional Advancement: MARCIA SULLIVAN

Dean of Enrollment Management: JEFF MILLER

Dir of Libraries: PEG JOHNSON

Library of 160,000 vols in Fogelson Library; also two spec. libraries, Chase Art History Library and Beaumont and Nancy Newhall Library

Number of teachers: 80 full-time

Number of students: 1,950 (750 full-time, 1,200 part-time)

Courses in art, business admin., contemporary music, creative writing and literature, documentary studies, education, humanities and interdisciplinary studies, moving image arts, performing arts, politics, psychology, science and conservation studies.

EASTERN NEW MEXICO UNIVERSITY

1500 South Ave K, Portales, NM 88130

Telephone: (505) 562-1011

E-mail: enrollment.services@enmu.edu

Internet: www.enmu.edu

Founded 1934

Pres.: Dr STEVEN GAMBLE

Vice-Pres. for Academic Affairs: Dr ROBERT VARTABEDIAN

Vice-Pres. for Business Affairs: SCOTT SMART

Vice-Pres. for Student Affairs: Dr GARY MUSGRAVE

Vice-Pres. for Univ. Relations and Enrollment Services: RONNIE BIRDSONG

Registrar: EUGENE ADLER

Dean of Information Services: ART LEIBLE

Dir of Library: MELVETA WALKER

Library of 699,847 vols

Number of teachers: 262

Number of students: 4,000

DEANS

College of Business: Dr JOHN GROESBECK

College of Education and Technology: Dr JERRY HARMON

College of Fine Arts: Dr MICHAEL SITTON

College of Liberal Arts and Sciences: Dr MARY FANELLI AYALA

Graduate School: Dr PHILIP SHELLEY

NEW MEXICO HIGHLANDS UNIVERSITY

POB 9000, Las Vegas, NM 87701

Telephone: (505) 425-7511

Fax: (505) 454-3069

Internet: www.nmhu.edu

Founded 1893

Academic year: August to May

Pres.: Dr JAMES A. FRIES

Vice-Pres. for Academic Affairs: GILBERT RIVERA

Vice-Pres. for Finance and Admin. Services: STEVE WILSON

Vice-Pres. for Student Affairs: JUDY CORDOVA

Registrar: JOHN COCA

Librarian: RUBEN ARAGON

Number of teachers: 120

Number of students: 2,300

NEW MEXICO STATE UNIVERSITY

POB 30001, Las Cruces, NM 88003-8001

Telephone: (505) 646-0111

Fax: (505) 646-1517

Internet: www.nmsu.edu

Founded 1888 as Las Cruces College, as New Mexico College of Agriculture and Mechanic Arts 1899, present name and status 1960

Academic year: August to May

Pres.: BARBARA COUTURE

Exec. Vice-Pres. and Provost: (vacant)

Sr Vice-Pres. for Planning, Physical Resources and Univ. Relations: BENJAMIN WOODS

Vice-Pres. for Business and Finance: JENNIFER TAYLOR

Vice-Pres. for Economic Devt: GARREY CARRUTHERS

Vice-Pres. for Research, Graduate Studies and Int. Programmes: VIMAL CHAITANYA

Vice-Pres. for Univ. Advancement: REBECCA DUKES

Dir of Library Services: DAN KAMMER

Library: 1m. vols, plus 431,225 bound and unbound govt docs and 1.3m. microforms

Number of teachers: 1,700

Number of students: 27,150

DEANS

Graduate School: LINDA LACEY

College of Agriculture and Home Economics: LOWELL CATLETT

College of Arts and Sciences: GREGORY FANT

College of Business Admin. and Economics: GARREY CARRUTHERS

College of Education: ROBERT MOULTON

College of Engineering: STEVEN CASTILLO

College of Health and Social Services: JEFFREY BRANDON

ATTACHED RESEARCH INSTITUTES

Institute for Energy and the Environment: internet iee.nmsu.edu; Dir (vacant).

Physical Science Laboratory: tel. (505) 646-9200; e-mail director@psl.nmsu.edu; internet www.psl.nmsu.edu; Dir JAY JORDAN.

Southwest Technical Development Institute: tel. (575) 646-1049; fax (575) 646-3841; e-mail tdi@nmsu.edu; Dir RUDI SCHOENMACKERS.

Space Grant Consortium: tel. (505) 646-6414; fax (505) 646-7791; e-mail nmsgc@nmsu.edu; internet spacegrant.nmsu.edu; Dir Dr PAT HYNES.

Water Resources Research Institute: e-mail nmwrri@wrri.nmsu.edu; internet wrri.nmsu.edu; Dir KARL WOOD.

WERC: tel. (575) 646-2038; fax (575) 646-5474; e-mail werc@nmsu.edu; internet www.werc.net; Dir ABBAS GHASSEMI.

NEW MEXICO TECH

801 Leroy Pl., Socorro, NM 87801

Telephone: (575) 835-5011

Internet: www.nmt.edu

Founded 1889

Pres.: DANIEL H. LOPEZ

Vice-Pres. for Academic Affairs: PETER GERITY

Vice-Pres. for Admin. and Finance: LONNIE G. MARQUEZ

Vice-Pres. for Research and Economic Devt: VAN D. ROMERO

Vice-Pres. for Student and Univ. Relations and Dean of Students: RICARDO MAESTAS

Library Dir: OWEN ELLARD

Library of 600,000 vols

Number of students: 1,800.

ATTACHED RESEARCH CENTRES

New Mexico Institute of Mining and Technology: tel. (575) 835-5420; fax (575) 835-6333; internet geoinfo.nmt.edu; Dir PETER A. SCHOLLE.

ST JOHN'S COLLEGE

1160 Camino Cruz Blanca, Santa Fe, NM 87501-4599

Telephone: (505) 984-6000

Fax: (505) 984-6003

Internet: www.sjcsf.edu

Founded 1964

Pres.: MIKE PETERS

Dean: VICTORIA MORA

Registrar: MARLINE MARQUEZ SCALLY

Library Dir: JENNIFER SPRAGUE

Library of 60,000 vols

Number of teachers: 61

Number of students: 450

For Annapolis br. see under Maryland.

SOUTHWESTERN COLLEGE

POB 4788, Santa Fe, NM 87507

Telephone: (877) 471-5756

E-mail: info@swc.edu

Internet: www.swc.edu

Founded 1976 as Quimby College

Pres.: Dr JAMES MICHAEL NOLAN

Vice-Pres.: KATHERINE M. NINOS

Academic Dean: Dr ANTONIO NUNEZ

Registrar: ANDREA PACHECO

Librarian: LESLIE MONSALVE-JONES

Masters programmes in art therapy, counselling; certificate programmes in action methods, art therapy, grief counselling, school counselling.

UNIVERSITY OF NEW MEXICO

Albuquerque, NM 87131

Telephone: (505) 277-0111

Internet: www.unm.edu

Founded 1889
State control
Academic year: August to May

Pres.: Dr DAVID J. SCHMIDLY
Exec. Vice-Pres. for Academic Affairs and Provost: VIOLA FLOREZ
Vice-Pres. for Enrollment Management: TERRY BABBITT
Vice-Pres. for Institutional Diversity: RITA MARTINEZ-PURSON
Vice-Pres. for Research: TERRY YATES
Vice-Pres. for Student Affairs: ELISIO TORRES
Dean of Libraries: FRAN WILKINSON

Library: 1m. vols
Number of teachers: 1,250
Number of students: 25,009

DEANS

Graduate Studies: CHUCK FLEDDERMAN
Continuing Education: RITA MARTINEZ-PURSON
College of Arts and Sciences: VERA NORWOOD
College of Education: VIOLA FLOREZ
College of Engineering: JOSEPH CECCHI
College of Fine Arts: CHRISTOPHER MEAD
College of Nursing: KAREN CARLSON
College of Pharmacy: JOHN PIEPER
Univ. College: PETER WHITE
School of Architecture and Planning: RIC RICHARDSON (acting)
School of Law: SUELLYN SCARNECCHIA
Anderson Schools of Management: AMY WOHLERT (acting)
School of Medicine: JEFFREY GRIFFITH

PROFESSORS

ABDALLA, R. N., Art and Art History
ABRAMS, J., Medicine
ADAMSON, G. W., Special Education
AHLUWALIA, H. S., Physics and Astronomy
AHMED, N., Electrical and Computer Engineering
ALLEN, F. S., Chemistry
ALTENBACH, J. S., Biology
ALVERSON, D. C., Paediatrics
ANGEL, E. S., Electrical and Computer Engineering
ANGEL, R. M., Music
ANSPACH, J. F., Law
ATENCIO, A. C., Physiology
ATTERBOM, H. A., Health Promotion, Physical Education and Leisure Programmes
AVASTHI, P., Medicine
BACA, O. G., Biology
BAKER, W. E., Mechanical Engineering
BANKHURST, A. D., Medicine
BARBO, D. M., Obstetrics and Gynaecology
BARROW, T. F., Art and Art History
BARTLETT, L. A., English
BARTON, L. M., Biology
BASSALLECK, B., Physics and Astronomy
BASSO, K. H., Anthropology
BAWDEN, G. L., Anthropology
BEAR, D. G., Cell Biology
BEENE, L., English
BENNAHUM, D. A., Medicine
BENNAHUM, J., Theatre and Dance
BENNETT, M. D., Family and Community Medicine
BENZEL, E. C., Surgery
BERGEN, J. J., Spanish and Portuguese
BERGMAN, B. E., Law
BICKNELL, J. M., Neurology
BILLS, G. D., Linguistics
BIRKHOLZ, G. A., Nursing
BLACK, W. C., III, Pathology
BLACKWELL, P. J., Educational Foundations
BORDEN, T. A., Surgery
BORN, J. L., Pharmacy
BOWES, S., Educational Administration
BOYER, C. P., Mathematics and Statistics
BROGAN, J., Civil Engineering
BROOKSHIRE, D. S., Economics
BROWDE, M. B., Law
BROWN, F. L., Jr, Public Administration
BROWN, J., Biology
BRUECK, S. R. J., Electrical and Computer Engineering
BRYANT, H. C., Physics and Astronomy
BUCHNER, M. A., Mathematics and Statistics
BULLERS, W. I., Jr, Management
BURCHIEL, S. W., Pharmacy
BURNESS, H. S., Economics
BURR, S. L., Law
BURRIS, B. H., Sociology
BUSS, W., Pharmacology
BYBEE, J. L., Linguistics
CAHILL, K. E., Physics and Astronomy
CAPUTI, J. E., American Studies
CARDENAS, A. J., Spanish and Portuguese
CARLOW, T. J., Neurology
CAVES, C. M., Physics and Astronomy
CECCHI, J. L., Chemical and Nuclear Engineering
CHAMPOUX, J. E., Management
CHANDLER, C., Physics and Astronomy
CHANG, B. K., Medicine
CHAPDELAINE, M., Music
CHENG, J., Electrical and Computer Engineering
CHRISTENSEN, R. R., Mathematics and Statistics
CIVIKLY-POWELL, J. M., Communications and Journalism
CLARK, J. M., Music
CLOUGH, D. H., Nursing
COES, D. V., Management
COFER, L. F., Psychology
COHEN, E. B., Law Library
COLTON, D. L., Educational Administration
CONDON, J. C., Communication and Journalism
CONNELL-SZASZ, M., History
CORCORAN, G. B., Pharmacy
CORDOVA, I. R., Educational Administration
COUGHLIN, R., Sociology
COUTSIAS, E. A., Mathematics and Statistics
CRAVEN, D. L., Art and Art History
CRAWFORD, M. H., Medicine
CURET, L. B., Obstetrics and Gynaecology
DAIL, W. G., Jr, Anatomy
DAMICO, H., English
DATYE, A. K., Chemical and Nuclear Engineering
DAVIDSON, R., Librarianship
DAVIS, G. L., American Studies
DAVIS, L., Neurology
DAVIS, M., Radiology
DEKEYSER, J., Music
DELANEY, H. D., Psychology
DESIDERIO, R. J., Law
DEVRIES, R. C., Electrical and Computer Engineering
DICKINSON, W. E., Surgery
DIELS, J.-C. M., Physics and Astronomy
DIETERLE, B., Physics and Astronomy
DILLARD, J. F., Management
DINIUS, A., Dental Programme
DODSON, T. A., Music
DORATO, P., Electrical and Computer Engineering
DOUGHER, M. J., Psychology
DRENNAN, J., Orthopaedics
DUBAN, S. L., Paediatrics
DUMARS, C., Law
DUNCAN, M. H., Paediatrics
DURYEA, P. J., Education
DUSZYNSKI, D. W., Biology
EATON, R. P., Medicine
EFROMOVICH, S., Mathematics and Statistics
EL-GENK, M. S., Chemical and Nuclear Engineering
ELIAS, L., Medicine
ELLIOTT, P. C., Management
ELLIS, J. W., Law
ELLISON, J. A., Mathematics and Statistics
ENGELBRECHT, G. A., Counselling and Family Studies
ENKE, C. G., Chemistry
ERIBES, R. A., Architecture and Planning
ESTRIN, J. A., Anaesthesiology
ETULAIN, R., History
EVANS, W., Theatre and Dance
EWING, R. C., Earth Sciences
FEENEY, D., Psychology
FEINBERG, E. A., Art and Art History
FELBERG, L., Music
FIELD, F. R., Training and Learning Technologies
FINLEY, D., Physics and Astronomy
FISCHER, M. R., English
FISHBURN, W. R., Counselling and Family Studies
FLEMING, R. E., English
FLETCHER, M. P., General Library
FLEURY, P. A., Electrical and Computer Engineering
FORMAN, W. B., Medicine
FOUCAR, M. K., Pathology
FRANDSEN, K. D., Communication and Journalism
FRITZ, C. G., Law
FROELICH, J. W., Anthropology
FRONECH, D. K., Electrical and Computer Engineering
FRY, D., Surgery
GAINES, B., English
GALEY, W. R., Jr, Physiology
GALLAGHER, P. J., English
GARCIA, F. C., Political Science
GARRY, P. J., Pathology
GEISSMAN, J. W., Earth Sciences
GELL-MAN, M., Physics and Astronomy
GERDES, D. C., Modern and Classical Languages
GIBSON, A. G., Mathematics and Statistics
GILFEATHER, F., Mathematics and Statistics
GISSER, M., Economics
GLEW, R. H., Biochemistry
GLUCK, J. P., Psychology
GOMEZ-PALACIO, I., Law
GONZALES, R. A., Law
GONZALES-BERRY, E., Modern and Classical Languages
GOODMAN, R., Philosophy
GORDON, W. C., Psychology
GOSZ, J. R., Biology
GRANT, D., Management
GREENBERG, R. E., Paediatrics
GRIFFIN, L. E., Health Promotion, Physical Education and Leisure Programmes
GWIN, M. C., English
HAALAND, K. Y., Psychiatry
HADLEY, W. M., Pharmacy
HAHN, B., Art and Art History
HAIMAN, F. S., General Honours
HALL, G. E., Law
HALL, J., Civil Engineering
HALL, L. B., History
HARJO, J., Engineering
HARRIS, F., Political Science
HARRIS, M., Educational Foundations
HARRIS, R. J., Psychology
HART, F. M., Law
HARTSHORNE, M. F., Radiology
HASHIMOTO, F., Medicine
HAWKINS, C., Electrical and Computer Engineering
HEFFRON, W. A., Family and Community Medicine
HEGGEN, R. J., Civil Engineering
HENNEY, J. E., Medicine
HERMANN, M. S. G., Law
HERZON, F. S., Surgery
HEYWARD, V., Health Promotion, Physical Education and Leisure Programmes
HIGGINS, P. A., Nursing
HINTERBICHLER, K., Music
HOLDER, R. W., Chemistry
HOLLAN, J. D., Computer Science
HUACO, G. A., Sociology
HUMPHRIES, S., Jr, Electrical and Computer Engineering
JAFFE, I. S., Theatre and Dance
JAIN, R., Electrical and Computer Engineering

JAMSHIDI, M., Electrical and Computer Engineering
JEWELL, P. F., Surgery
JOHNSON, D. M., English
JOHNSON, G. V., Biology
JOHNSON, J. D., Paediatrics
JOHNSON, P. J., Psychology
JOHN-STEINER, V. P., Education
JONES, D., English
JOOST-GAUGIER, C., Art and Art History
JORDAN, S. W., Pathology
JUNGLING, K. C., Electrical and Computer Engineering
KARLSTROM, K. E., Earth Sciences
KARNI, S., Electrical and Computer Engineering
KASSICIEH, S. K., Management
KAUFFMAN, D., Chemical and Nuclear Engineering
KAUFMAN, A., Family, Community and Emergency Medicine
KEITH, S. J., Psychiatry
KELLEY, R. O., Anatomy
KELLY, H. W., Pharmacy
KELLY, S. G., Law
KELSEY, C. A., Radiology
KELSEY, C. W., Education
KENDALL, D. L., Electrical and Computer Engineering
KENKRE, V. M., Physics and Astronomy
KERN, R. W., History
KEY, C. R., Pathology
KISIEL, W., Pathology
KLEIN, C., Geology
KLEPPER, D. J., Medicine
KLINE, W., Education
KODRIC-BROWN, A., Biology
KOGOMA, T., Cell Biology
KORNFELD, M., Pathology
KOSTER, F. T., Medicine
KOVNAT, R., Law
KUCHARZ, W., Mathematics and Statistics
KUDO, A. M., Geology
KUES, B. S., Earth Sciences
LAFREE, G., Sociology
LAMPHERE, L., Anthropology
LANCASTER, J. B., Anthropology
LEWIS, S. L., Nursing
LIGON, J. D., Biology
LINDEMAN, R. D., Medicine
LINNELL, J., Theatre and Dance
LIPSCOMB, M. F., Pathology
LIPSKI, J., Modern Languages
LONG, V., Counselling and Family Studies
LOPEZ, A. S., Law
LORENZ, J., Mathematics and Statistics
LOTFIELD, R. B., Biochemistry
LOVE, E. B., Librarianship
LUCKASSON, R. A., Special Education
LUGER, G. F., Computer Science
LUMIA, R., Mechanical Engineering
LUTZ, W., Chemical and Nuclear Engineering
MCCARTHY, D. M., Medicine
MCCLELLAND, C. E., III, History
MCCONNELL, T. S., Pathology
MCCULLOUGH-BRABSON, E., Music
MCDANIEL, M., Psychology
MCFARLANE, D. R., Public Administration
MCGRAW, J., Physics and Astronomy
MCGUFFEE, L. J., Pharmacology
MACIEL, D. R., History
MCIVER, J. K., Physics and Astronomy
MCLAUGHLIN, J. C., Pathology
MCNAMARA, P. A., Sociology
MCNEIL, J., Electrical and Computer Engineering
MCPHERSON, D., English
MACPHERSON, W. T., Law
MAKI, G., Electrical and Computer Engineering
MALOLEPSY, J., Theatre and Dance
MANN, B. M., Mathematics and Statistics
MARTINEZ, J. G. R., Special Education
MATHEWSON, A. D., Law
MATTHEWS, J. A. J., Physics and Astronomy
MATTHEWS, O. P., Geography
MATWIYOFF, N. A., Cell Biology
MAY, G. W., Civil Engineering
MAY, P. A., Sociology
MEIZE-GROCHOWSKI, R., Nursing
MELADA, I. P., English
MENNIN, S. P., Anatomy
MERKX, G. W., Sociology
METTLER, F. A., Jr, Radiology
MIGNEAULT, R., Librarianship
MILLER, W. R., Psychology
MILSTEIN, M. M., Educational Administration
MOLD, C., Microbiology
MONEIM, M. S., Orthopaedics
MORAIN, S. A., Geography
MORET, B. M., Computer Science
MORRIS, D. M., Surgery
MORRIS, M. M., Education
MORROW, C., Chemistry
MOSELEY, P. L., Medicine
MURATA, G. H., Medicine
MURPHY, S. J., Paediatrics
NIEMCZYK, T. M., Chemistry
NORDHAUS, R. S., Architecture and Planning
NORWOOD, J. M., Law
NORWOOD, V. L., American Studies
NURNBERG, H. G., Psychiatry
NUTTALL, H. E., Jr, Chemical and Nuclear Engineering
OBENSHAIN, S. S., Paediatrics
OCCHIALINO, M., Law
OGILBY, P. R., Chemistry
OLIVER, J. M., Pathology
OLLER, J. W., Jr, Linguistics
OMDAHL, J. L., Biochemistry
OMER, G., Jr, Orthopaedics
ONDRIAS, M. R., Chemistry
ONNEWEER, C., Mathematics and Statistics
ORRISON, W. W., Radiology
ORTIZ, A. A., Anthropology
ORTIZ, J. V., Chemistry
OVERTURF, G. D., Paediatrics
OWENS, L. D., English
PABISCH, P. K., Foreign Languages and Literature
PADILLA, R. S., Dermatology
PAINE, R. T., Jr, Chemistry
PANITZ, J. A., Physics and Astronomy
PAPADOPOULOS, E. P., Chemistry
PAPIKE, J. J., Geology
PAPILE, L. A., Paediatrics
PARK, S. M., Chemistry
PARKMAN, A. M., Management
PARNALL, T., Law
PARTRIDGE, L. D., Physiology
PATHAK, P. T., Mathematics and Statistics
PEABODY, D. S., Cell Biology
PECK, R. E., English
PEREZ-GOMEZ, J. R., Music
PETERSON, S. L., Pharmacy
PHAM, C., Economics
PIPER, J., Music
PORTER, J., History
PREDOCK-LINNELL, J., Theatre and Dance
PRICE, R. M., Physics and Astronomy
PRINJA, A. K., Chemical and Nuclear Engineering
PRIOLA, D. V., Physiology
PYLE, R. R., Medicine
QUENZER, R. W., Medicine
RABINOWITZ, H., History
RADOSEVICH, R. R., Management
RAIZADA, V., Medicine
RAZANI, A., Mechanical Engineering
REBOLLEDO, T. D., Modern Languages
REED, W. D., Medicine
REES, B. L., Nursing
REEVES, T. Z., Public Administration
REHDER, R. R., Management
REID, R. A., Management
REMMER, K. L., Political Science
REYES, P., Biochemistry
RICHARDS, C. G., Mechanical Engineering
RIENSCHE, L. L., Comm. Disorders
ROBBINS, R. G., History
ROBIN, D. M., Foreign Languages and Literature
RODERICK, N. F., Chemical and Nuclear Engineering
RODRIGUEZ, A., Modern and Classical Languages
ROEBUCK, J., History
ROGERS, E. M., Communication and Journalism
ROLL, S., Psychology
ROMERO, L. M., Law
ROSENBERG, G. A., Neurology
ROSS, H. L., Sociology
ROSS, T. J., Civil Engineering
ROTH, P. B., Emergency Medicine
RUEBUSH, B. K., Psychiatry and Psychology
RUYBAL, S. E., Nursing
SAIERS, J. H., Medicine
SAIKI, J. H., Medicine
SALAND, L. C., Anatomy
SALVAGGIO, R., American Studies
SANTLEY, R. S., Anthropology
SARTO, G. E., Obstetrics and Gynaecology
SAVAGE, D. D., II, Pharmacology
SCALES, A. C., Law
SCALETTI, J. V., Microbiology
SCALLEN, T. J., Biochemistry
SCHADE, D. S., Medicine
SCHARNHORST, G. F., English and American Studies
SCHAU, C. G., Educational Foundations
SCHREYER, H. L., Mechanical Engineering
SCHUELER, G. F., Philosophy
SCHUETZ, J. E., Communication
SCHULTZ, C., Management
SCHUYLER, M. R., Medicine
SCHWARTZ, R. L., Law
SCHWERIN, K. H., Anthropology
SCOTT, P. B., Curriculum and Instruction in Multicultural Teacher Education
SEARLES, R. P., Medicine
SEMO, E., History
SEVERINO, S. K., Psychiatry
SHAHINPOOR, M., Mechanical Engineering
SHAMA, A., Management
SHANE, D. L., Nursing
SHELTON, S. P., Civil Engineering
SHIPMAN, V. C., Counseling and Family Studies
SHOMAKER, D. J., Nursing
SHULTIS, C. L., Music
SIBBITT, W. L., Jr, Medicine
SIEMBIEDA, W. J., Architecture and Planning
SIMONSON, D. G., Management
SKIPPER, B. J., Family, Community and Emergency Medicine
SKLAR, D. P., Emergency Medicine
SKLAR, L. A., Pathology
SMITH, B. T., Computer Science
SMITH, D. D., Special Education
SMITH, D. M., Chemical and Nuclear Engineering
SMITH, H. L., Management
SMITH, M. M., Counseling and Family Studies
SMITH, P. J., Special Education
SMITH, W. S., Jr, Foreign Languages and Literature
SNYDER, R. D., Neurology
SONNENBERG, A., Medicine
SOUTHALL, T. W., Art and Art History
SRUBEK, J., Art Education
STARR, G. P., Mechanical Engineering
STEINBERG, S. L., Mathematics and Statistics
STONE, A. P., Mathematics and Statistics
STRAUS, L. G., Anthropology
STRICKLAND, R. G., Medicine
STURM, F. G., Philosophy
SUMMERS, J. W., Cell Biology
SUTHERLAND, R. J., Psychology
SWINSON, D., Physics and Astronomy
SZASZ, F. M., History
TANDBERG, W. D., Emergency Medicine
TAYLOR, A. P., Architecture and Planning
TAYLOR, S. A., Law
THOMPSON, D. E., Mechanical Engineering
THOMSON, B. M., Civil Engineering
THORNHILL, A. R., Biology

THORSON, J. L., English
TIANO, S. B., Sociology
TOLMAN, J. M., Modern and Classical Languages
TOOLSON, E. C., Biology
TRINKAUS, E., Anthropology
TROTTER, J. A., Anatomy
TROUP, G. M., Pathology
TROUTMAN, W. G., Pharmacy
TUASON, V. B., Psychiatry
TURAN, M., Architecture and Planning
TURNER, P. H., Counseling and Family Studies
TYLER, M., Music
TZAMALOUKAS, A., Medicine
UHLENHUTH, E. H., Psychiatry
USCHER, N. J., Music
USEEM, B., Sociology
UTTON, A. E., Law
VALDES, N., Sociology
VANDERJAGT, D., Biochemistry
VAN DONGEN, R. D., Curriculum and Instruction in Multicultural Teacher Education
VOGEL, K. G., Biology
WALDMAN, J. D., Paediatrics
WALKER, B. R., Physiology
WALTERS, E. A., Chemistry
WANG, M.-L., Civil Engineering
WATERMAN, R. E., Anatomy
WEIGLE, M. M., Anthropology
WEISS, G. K., Physiology
WEISS, J. R., Nursing
WERNLEY, J. A., Surgery
WHEELAND, R. G., Dermatology
WHIDDEN, M. B., English
WHITE, P., English
WIESE, W., Family, Community and Emergency Medicine
WILDIN, M. W., Mechanical Engineering
WILKINS, E. S., Chemical and Nuclear Engineering
WILLIAMS, R. H., Electrical and Computer Engineering
WILLIAMSON, M. R., Radiology
WILLIAMSON, S. L., Radiology
WILLMAN, C. L., Pathology
WINOGRAD, P., Law
WITEMEYER, H., English
WOFSY, C., Mathematics and Statistics
WOLF, S. S., Law
WOLFE, D. M., Physics and Astronomy
WOLFE, J. D., Theatre and Dance
WOOD, C. J., Education Administration
WOOD, J. E., Mechanical Engineering
WOOD, W. F., Music
WOODWARD, L. A., Geology
WORRELL, R. V., Orthopaedics
WRIGHT, J. B., Library
YAGER, J., Psychiatry
YATES, T. L., Biology
ZAGER, P. G., Medicine
ZANNES, E., Communication and Journalism
ZEILIK, M., II, Physics and Astronomy
ZIMMER, W. J., Mathematics and Statistics
ZONGOLOWICZ, H. M.
ZUMWALT, R. E., Pathology

BRANCH CAMPUSES

Gallup Campus: 200 College Rd, Gallup, NM 87301; tel. (505) 863-7500; internet www.gallup.unm.edu; 3,000 students; Dean of Instruction CHRISTINE MARLOWE; depts of applied technology, arts and letters, business management and technology, education, mathematics and sciences, social science.

Los Alamos Campus: 400 University Dr., Los Alamos, NM 87544; tel. (505) 662-5919; fax (505) 662-0344; internet www.la.unm.edu; Dean of Instruction CEDRIC PAGE; Dir of Library DENNIS DAVIES-WILSON; depts of applied science and engineering, arts and social sciences, business, computer studies and IT, mathematics.

Taos Campus: 115 Civic Plaza Dr., Taos, NM 87571; tel. (505) 737-6200; e-mail askalobo@unm.edu; internet taos.unm.edu; Dean of Instruction JAMES GILROY; depts of arts and culture, business and computer technology, holistic health and human services, professions and liberal arts, sciences, trades and industry.

Valencia Campus: 280 La Entrada, Los Lunas, NM 87031; tel. (505) 925-8580; Dean of Instruction REINALDO GARCIA; offers assoc. degrees, certificate and credential programmes.

UNIVERSITY OF THE SOUTHWEST

6610 Lovington Highway, Hobbs, NM 88240
Telephone: (575) 392-6561
Fax: (575) 392-6006
E-mail: admissions@csw.edu
Internet: www.csw.edu

Campus at Hobbs

Founded 1962
Private control

Pres.: Dr GARY A. DILL
Vice-Pres. for Academic Services: Dr DENNIS ATHERTON
Vice-Pres. for Admin. Services: DEE MOONEY
Dean of Arts and Sciences: BARBARA MCGRATH
Dean of Business: TOM WILSON
Dean of Education: MARY HARRIS

Number of teachers: 50
Number of students: 590

Depts of arts and sciences, business admin., education.

WESTERN NEW MEXICO UNIVERSITY

POB 680, Silver City, NM 88062
Telephone: (505) 538-6011
Fax: (505) 538-6155
E-mail: admissions@wnmu.edu
Internet: www.wnmu.edu

Founded 1893

Pres.: Dr JOHN COUNTS
Provost and Vice-Pres. for Academic Affairs: Dr FAYE VOWELL
Vice-Pres. for Business Affairs: SHERRI BAYS (acting)
Vice-Pres. for Institutional Advancement: LINDA KAY JONES (acting)
Vice-Pres. for Student Affairs: Dr PHILLIP J. FARREN
Registrar: BETSY MILLER
Librarian: Dr GILDA ORTEGO (acting)

Library of 388,193 vols
Number of teachers: 65
Number of students: 2,527 (1,592 full-time, 935 part time); 598 graduates

DEANS

School of Applied Technology: ANTONIO MACIAS
School of Education: PARTICIA MANZANARES-GONZALES
School of Health Sciences and Human Performance: GWEN CASSEL

NEW YORK

ADELPHI UNIVERSITY

Garden City, NY 11530
Telephone: (516) 877-3000
Internet: www.adelphi.edu

Founded 1896
Academic year: August to May

Pres.: Dr ROBERT A. SCOTT
Provost and Sr Vice-Pres. for Academic Affairs: (vacant)
Vice-Pres. for Enrollment and Student Affairs: ANGELA B. PROTO
Vice-Pres. for Univ. Advancement: CHRISTIAN P. VAUPEL
Dean of Univ. Libraries: CHARLES SIMPSON

Library of 650,000 vols, 805,000 microforms
Number of teachers: 706 (239 full-time, 467 part-time)
Number of students: 7,932

DEANS

Arts and Sciences, Graduate and Undergraduate: GAYLE INSLER
School of Business: ANTHONY LIBERTELLA
School of Education: RONALD FEINGOLD
School of Nursing: PATRICK COONAN
School of Social Work: ANDREW SAFYER
Institute of Advanced Psychological Studies: LOUIS PRIMAVERA
Honors College: RICHARD GARNER

ALBANY COLLEGE OF PHARMACY

106 New Scotland Ave, Albany, NY 12208-3492
Telephone: (518) 445-7200
E-mail: info@acp.edu
Internet: www.acp.edu

Founded 1881

Pres. and Dean: JAMES J. GOZZO
Assoc. Dean for Academic Affairs: HOWARD D. COLBY
Asst Dean for Student Affairs: PACKY MCGRAW
Dir of Finance and Business Affairs: WILLIAM M. CRONIN
Dir of Admissions: CARLY T. CONNERS
Dir of Library Services: SUE IWANOWICZ

Number of teachers: 95
Number of students: 1,240

ALBANY LAW SCHOOL

80 New Scotland Ave, Albany, NY 12208-3494
Telephone: (518) 445-2311
Fax: (518) 445-2315
E-mail: admissions@albanylaw.edu
Internet: www.albanylaw.edu

Founded 1851
Academic year: July to June

Chair. of Board of Trustees: HARRY L. ROBINSON
Pres. and Dean: THOMAS F. GUERNSEY
Registrar: JOANN FITZSIMMONS
Assoc. Dean and Dir of Library: ROBERT T. BEGG

Library of 620,000 vols
Number of teachers: 71 (42 full-time, 29 adjunct)
Number of students: 755

ALBANY MEDICAL COLLEGE

43 New Scotland Ave, Albany, NY 12208
Telephone: (518) 445-5544
Internet: www.amc.edu

Founded 1839

Dean: Dr VINCENT VERDILE
Dir of Admissions: JOANNE H. NANOS
Librarian: SHERRY HARTMAN

Library of 150,000 vols
Number of teachers: 111
Number of students: 542 medical, 198 graduate

ALFRED UNIVERSITY

1 Saxon Dr, Alfred, NY 14802-1232
Telephone: (607) 871-2111
Fax: (607) 871-2339
E-mail: communications@alfred.edu
Internet: www.alfred.edu

Founded 1836

Private control
Language of instruction: English
Academic year: August to May

Pres.: CHARLES M. EDMONDSON
Provost and Vice-Pres. for Academic Affairs: WILLIAM HALL
Vice-Pres. for Business and Finance and Treas.: GIOVINA LLLOYD
Vice-Pres. for Univ. Relations: STAN COLLA
Dir for Admissions: CORRY D. UNIS
Dir for Enrollment Operations and Research: KAREN L. JOHNSON
Dean of Libraries: STEPHEN S. CRANDALL

Library of 300,000 vols
Number of teachers: 156
Number of students: 2,300 (full-time and part-time undergraduates and graduates)

Publications: *Alfred Reporter*, *Fiat Lux*, *Kanakadea*, *University Catalogue*

DEANS

College of Business: Dr NANCY EVANGELISTA (acting)
College of Liberal Arts and Sciences: Dr MARY MCGEE
School of Art and Design: LESLIE BELLAVANCE
Graduate School: Dr NANCY EVANGELISTA (Dir)
Inamori School of Engineering: Dr DOREEN EDWARDS

BANK STREET COLLEGE OF EDUCATION

610 W 112th St, New York, NY 10025-1898
Telephone: (212) 875-4400
Fax: (212) 875-4759
E-mail: collegepubs@bankstreet.edu
Internet: www.bankstreet.edu

Founded 1916
Academic year: September to July

Pres.: Dr ELIZABETH D. DICKEY
Vice-Pres. for Finance and Admin.: FRANK NUARA
Vice-Pres. for Institutional Advancement: JOHN BORDEN
Dean of Children's Programmes Div.: ALEXIS S. WRIGHT
Dean of Continuing Education: FERN KHAN
Dean of Graduate School: JON SNYDER
Dir of Library: KRISTIN FREDA

Library of 123,215 vols
Number of teachers: 125
Number of students: 1,052

BARD COLLEGE

POB 5000, Annandale-on-Hudson, NY 12504
Telephone: (845) 758-6822
E-mail: admission@bard.edu
Internet: www.bard.edu

Founded 1860

Pres.: LEON BOTSTEIN
Registrar: PETER GADSBY
Dean: DAVID SHEIN
Dir of Admissions: MARY BACKLUND
Dir of Libraries: JEFFREY KATZ

Library of 280,000 vols
Number of teachers: 224
Number of students: 1,681

BORICUA COLLEGE

3755 Broadway, New York, NY 10032
Telephone: (212) 694-1000
E-mail: acruz@boricuacollege.edu
Internet: www.boricuacollege.edu

Campuses in Manhattan and Brooklyn

Founded 1974
Private control

Pres.: VICTOR G. ALICEA
Vice-Pres. and Dean of Academic Affairs, Manhattan Campus: SHIVAJI SENGUPTA
Vice-Pres. and Dean of Academic Affairs, Brooklyn Campus: MARIA MONTES MORALES
Library Dir: LIZA RIVERA

Number of teachers: 40
Number of students: 1,190

BROOKLYN LAW SCHOOL

250 Joralemon St, Brooklyn, NY 11201
Telephone: (718) 625-2200
E-mail: admitq@brooklaw.edu
Internet: www.brooklaw.edu

Founded 1901
Private control
Academic year: August to May

Dean: JOAN G. WEXLER
Assoc. Dean for Academic Affairs: LAWRENCE M. SOLAN
Assoc. Dean for Devt: MICHAEL A. GERBER
Assoc. Dean for Student Affairs: BERYL R. JONES-WOODIN
Registrar: SUZANNE M. DENNIS

Number of students: 1,510

CANISIUS COLLEGE

2001 Main St, Buffalo, NY 14208-1098
Telephone: (716) 888-2200
Fax: (716) 888-3230
E-mail: admissions@canisius.edu
Internet: www.canisius.edu

Founded 1870
Private control
Language of instruction: English

Pres.: Rev. JOHN HURLEY
Vice-Pres. for Academic Affairs: Dr SCOTT CHADWICK
Vice-Pres. for Business and Finance: PAT RICHEY
Assoc. Vice-Pres. for College Relations: DEBRA PARK
Vice-Pres. for Student Affairs: ELLEN CONLEY
Assoc. Vice-Pres for Library and Information Services: Dr JOEL COHEN

Library of 425,000 vols
Number of teachers: 499 (224 full-time, 275 part-time)
Number of students: 5,111

DEANS

Richard J. Wehle School of Business: ANTONE ALBER
School of Education and Human Services: MICHAEL PARDALES

CAZENOVIA COLLEGE

22 Sullivan St, Cazenovia, NY 13035
Telephone: (315) 655-7000
E-mail: admissions@cazenovia.edu
Internet: www.cazcollege.edu

Founded 1824 as Seminary of the Genesee Conference; present name 1982
Private control
Academic year: September to May

Pres.: Dr MARK JOHN TIERNO
Exec. Vice-Pres.: SUSAN A. BERGER
Vice-Pres. for Academic Affairs: DONALD MCCRIMMON
Vice-Pres. for Institutional Advancement: CAROL M. SATCHWELL
Vice-Pres. for Student Devt: C. JOSEPH BEHAN
Registrar: J. ZACHARY KELLEY
Library Dir: STANLEY KOZACZKA

Library of 90,000 vols
Number of teachers: 154 (54 full-time, 100 part-time)
Number of students: 976 full-time

Areas of study: art and design, business and management, education, humanities, natural sciences, social and behavioural sciences.

CHRIST THE KING SEMINARY

711 Knox Rd, E Aurora, NY 14052
Telephone: (716) 652-8900
Fax: (716) 652-8903
E-mail: cksacad@cks.edu
Internet: www.cks.edu

Founded 1857
Private control

Pres. and Rector: Rev. PETER J. DRILLING
Vice-Rector: Rev. GREGORY M. FAULHABER
Academic Dean: Dr DENNIS A. CASTILLO
Library Dir: TERESA LUBIENECKI

Library of 160,000 vols
Number of teachers: 25 (18 full-time, 7 adjunct)
Number of students: 96 full-time

CITY UNIVERSITY OF NEW YORK

535 East 80th St, New York, NY 10021
Telephone: (212) 794-5555
Internet: www.cuny.edu

Founded 1847

Public instn comprising 10 sr colleges, listed below, a graduate school and univ. center, a law school, a medical school, a technical college and 6 community colleges: Borough of Manhattan Community College, Bronx Community College, Hostos Community College, Kingsborough Community College, Fiorello H. La Guardia Community College and Queensborough Community College

Chancellor: MATTHEW GOLDSTEIN

Library: Combined libraries of 6m. vols.

CONSTITUENT COLLEGES AND SCHOOLS

Baruch College

1 Bernard Baruch Way, New York, NY 10010
Telephone: (646) 312-1000
Internet: www.baruch.cuny.edu

Founded 1919

Pres.: STAN ALTMAN

Number of teachers: 500 (full-time)
Number of students: 15,500

Brooklyn College

2900 Bedford Ave, Brooklyn, NY 11210
Telephone: (718) 951-1000
Internet: www.brooklyn.cuny.edu

Founded 1930

Pres.: CHRISTOPHER M. KIMMICH

Number of teachers: 496 (full-time)
Number of students: 14,964

City College

Convent Ave and 138th St, New York, NY 10031
Telephone: (212) 650-7000
Internet: www.ccny.cuny.edu

Founded 1847

Pres.: GREGORY H. WILLIAMS

Number of teachers: 457 (full-time)
Number of students: 12,083

City University School of Law at Queens College

65-21 Main St, Flushing, NY 11367
Telephone: (718) 575-4200
Internet: www.law.cuny.edu

Founded 1973

Dean: MICHELLE J. ANDERSON

Number of teachers: 28 (full-time)
Number of students: 467

College of Staten Island

2800 Victory Blvd, Staten Island, NY 10314
Telephone: (718) 982-2000
Fax: (718) 982-2500
E-mail: admissions@csi.cuny.edu
Internet: www.csi.cuny.edu

Founded 1976 by amalgamation of Staten Island Community College and Richmond College
Language of instruction: English
Academic year: August to May (2 semesters)

Pres.: Dr TOMAS D. MORALES
Chief Librarian: Dr WILMA L. JONES

Library of 243,000 vols, 110,400 e-books, 250 print journals, 42,800 e-journals, 140 e-resources, 3,000 films and videos, 5,000 sound recordings
Number of teachers: 358 (full-time), 596 (part-time)
Number of students: 13,858 , FTEs 10,652

Graduate School and University Center

365 Fifth Ave, New York, NY 10016-4309
Telephone: (212) 817-7000
Internet: www.gc.cuny.edu

Founded 1961

Pres.: WILLIAM P. KELLY

Number of teachers: 334 (full-time)
Number of students: 3,813

Hunter College

695 Park Ave, New York, NY 10065
Telephone: (212) 772-4000
Internet: www.hunter.cuny.edu

Founded 1870

Pres.: JENNIFER J. RAAB

Number of teachers: 488 (full-time)
Number of students: 19,689

John Jay College of Criminal Justice

899 10th Ave, New York, NY 10019
Telephone: (212) 237-8000
Internet: www.jjay.cuny.edu

Founded 1964

Pres.: JEREMY TRAVIS

Number of teachers: 256 (full-time)
Number of students: 10,834

Lehman College

Bedford Park Blvd, W, Bronx, NY 10468
Telephone: (212) 960-8000
Internet: www.lehman.cuny.edu

Founded 1931

Pres.: RICARDO R. FERNANDEZ

Number of teachers: 266 (full-time)
Number of students: 9,283

Medgar Evers College

1650 Bedford Ave, Brooklyn, NY 11225
Telephone: (718) 951-5000
Internet: www.mec.cuny.edu

Founded 1969

Pres.: EDISON O. JACKSON

Number of teachers: 127 (full-time)
Number of students: 5,063

New York City College of Technology

Office of the President, Namm 319, 300 Jay St, Brooklyn, NY 11201
Telephone: (718) 260-5000
E-mail: connect@citytech.cuny.edu
Internet: www.citytech.cuny.edu

Founded 1946 as the New York State Institute for Applied Arts and Sciences, present name 2001
State control
Language of instruction: English
Academic year: August to June

Pres.: Dr RUSSELL K. HOTZLER (acting)
Vice-Pres. for Admin. and Finance: MIGUEL CAIROL
Vice-Pres. for Enrollment and Student Affairs: MARCELA KATZ ARMOZA
Provost and Vice-Pres. for Academic Affairs: BONNE AUGUST
Chief Librarian: DARROW WOOD

Library of 313,000 vols, 60,000 periodical titles
Number of teachers: 415 (full-time)
Number of students: 15,404

Publications: *Journal of Urban Technology*, *Perspectives*, *2 Bridges Review* (online).

Queens College

65-30 Kissena Blvd, Flushing, NY 11367
Telephone: (718) 997-5000
Internet: www.qc.edu

Founded 1937

Pres.: JAMES L. MUYSKENS
Provost and Vice-Pres. for Academic Affairs: JAMES STELLAR

Number of teachers: 514 (full-time)
Number of students: 16,381

Sophie Davis School of Biomedical Education

160 Convent Ave, Room H-107, New York, NY 10031
Telephone: (212) 650-5275
Fax: (212) 650-6696
Internet: med.cuny.edu

Founded 1984

Dean: STANFORD A. ROMAN, Jr.

York College

94-20 Guy R. Brewer Blvd, Jamaica, NY 11451
Telephone: (718) 262-2000
Internet: www.york.cuny.edu

Founded 1966

Pres.: Dr MARCIA C. KEIZS

Number of teachers: 144 (full-time)
Number of students: 6,030

CLARKSON UNIVERSITY

8 Clarkson Ave, Potsdam, NY 13699-5500
Telephone: (315) 268-6400
Fax: (315) 268-7993
E-mail: admission@clarkson.edu
Internet: www.clarkson.edu

Founded 1896

Pres.: TONY COLLINS
Vice-Pres. for Business and Financial Affairs and Treas.: BRUCE T. H. KNILL
Dean of Admissions: SUZANNE A. LIBERTY
Registrar: LYNN BROWN
Library Dir: NATALIA STAHL

Library of 229,000 vols, 272,000 microforms
Number of teachers: 172, incl. 48 full professors
Number of students: 2,670

Publication: *Clarkson*

DEANS

Graduate School: (vacant)
Liberal Studies: JERRY GRAVANDER
School of Business: VICTOR P. PEASE
School of Engineering: ANTHONY G. COLLINS
School of Science: JAMES H. THORP, III
Student Life: MICHAEL E. COOPER
Summer Session and Spec. Programmes: STEPHEN NEWKOFSKY

COLGATE ROCHESTER CROZER DIVINITY SCHOOL

1100 South Goodman St, Rochester, NY 14620-2589
Telephone: (585) 271-1320
Fax: (585) 340-9644
E-mail: admissions@crcds.edu
Internet: www.crds.edu

Founded 1970 by merger of 3 theological seminaries, 1 missionary training school and 1 theological school
Private control
Academic year: September to May

Pres.: Dr EUGENE C. BLAY
Vice-Pres. for Academic Life and Dean of Faculty: Dr CHRISTOPHER H. EVANS
Vice-Pres. for Enrollment Services: MELISSA MORRAL
Vice-Pres. for Institutional Advancement: PATRICK HANLEY
Registrar: GORDON CHAPMAN
Library Dir: MARGE NEAD

Library of 30,000 vols
Number of teachers: 8

COLGATE UNIVERSITY

13 Oak Dr., Hamilton, NY 13346
Telephone: (315) 228-1000
Fax: (315) 228-7798
Internet: www.colgate.edu

Founded 1819; chartered as Madison Univ. 1846, name changed to Colgate Univ. 1890
Academic year: August to May

Pres.: REBECCA S. CHOPP
Vice-Pres. for Business and Finance: DAVID HALE
Vice-Pres. for Communications and Public Relations: CHARLIE MELICHAR
Controller: THOMAS O'NEILL
Registrar: GRETCHEN B. HERRINGER
Dean of the College: DEAN JOHNSON
Dean of Faculty: LYLE ROELOFS
Dir of Graduate Programmes: SUSAN KAPLAN
Librarian: JUDITH NOYES

Library of 700,102 vols
Number of teachers: 343 (267 full-time; 76 part-time)
Number of students: 2,750

COLLEGE OF MOUNT SAINT VINCENT

6301 Riverdale Ave, Riverdale, NY 10471
Telephone: (718) 405-3267
E-mail: admissions.office@mountsaintvincent.edu
Internet: www.mountsaintvincent.edu

Founded 1847

Pres.: CHARLES L. FLYNN, Jr
Vice-Pres. for Student Affairs and Dean of Students: ADELE GATENS
Dir of Library: EDWARD O'HARA

Library of 149,000 vols
Number of teachers: 80
Number of students: 1,150

COLLEGE OF NEW ROCHELLE

29 Castle Pl., New Rochelle, NY 10805
Telephone: (914) 654-5000
Fax: (914) 654-5980
E-mail: admission@cnr.edu
Internet: www.cnr.edu

Founded 1904

Pres.: Dr STEPHEN J. SWEENEY
Sr Vice-Pres. for Academic Affairs: Dr JOAN E. BAILEY

Vice-Pres. for College Advancement: BRENNA SHEENAN MAYER
Vice-Pres. for Financial Affairs: JUDITH A. HUNTINGTON
Dean of the Library: Dr JAMES T. SCHLIEFER

Library of 200,000 vols
Number of teachers: 774
Number of students: 6,475

DEANS

School of Arts and Sciences: Dr C. J. DENNE
School of New Resources: BESSIE BLAKE
School of Nursing: CONNIE VANCE
Graduate School: LAURA ELLIS

COLLEGE OF SAINT ROSE

432 Western Ave, Albany, NY 12203-1490
Telephone: (518) 454-5111
Fax: (518) 454-2013
E-mail: admit@mail.strose.edu
Internet: www.strose.edu

Founded 1920
Academic year: September to May

Pres.: R. MARK SULLIVAN
Registrar: JUDITH KELLY
Provost and Vice-Pres. for Academic Affairs: Dr DAVID SZCZERBACKI
Vice-Pres. for Enrollment Management: MARY M. GRONDAHL
Vice-Pres. of Finance and Admin.: MARCUS BUCKLEY
Vice-Pres. of Institutional Advancement: KARIN CARR
Dir of Library Services: PETER KOONZ

Library of 209,899 vols
Number of teachers: 452
Number of students: 4,980

COLUMBIA UNIVERSITY

2960 Broadway, New York, NY 10027-6902
Telephone: (212) 854-1754
Fax: (212) 932-0418
Internet: www.columbia.edu

Founded as King's College 1754; inc. in 1784 and name changed to Columbia College by order of the Supreme Court of State of New York; in 1912, title changed to Columbia Univ.
Private control
Academic year: September to May

Pres.: LEE C. BOLLINGER
Provost: CLAUDE M. STEELE
Sr Exec. Vice-Pres.: ROBERT KASDIN
Exec. Vice-Pres. and Sec. of the Univ.: JEROME DAVIS
Exec. Vice-Pres. for Communications: DAVID M. STONE
Exec. Vice-Pres. for Devt and Alumni Relations: SUSAN FEAGIN
Exec. Vice-Pres. for Facilities: JOSEPH A. IENUSO
Exec. Vice-Pres. for Finance: ANNE SULLIVAN
Exec. Vice-Pres. for Govt and Community Affairs: MAXINE GRIFFITH
Exec. Vice-Pres. for Research: DAVID HIRSH
Exec. Vice-Pres. for Student and Admin. Services: JEFFREY F. SCOTT
Gen. Counsel: JANE E. BOOTH
Exec. Vice-Pres. for Arts and Sciences and Dean of the Faculty: NICHOLAS B. DIRKS
Vice-Pres. for Information Services and Univ. Librarian: JAMES G. NEAL

Library: see Libraries and Archives
Number of teachers: 3,566
Number of students: 25,459 (7,584 undergraduate, 17, 875 postgraduate and professional)

Publications: *Chemical Highlights*, *Columbia Human Rights Law Review*, *Columbia Journal of Environmental Law*, *Columbia Journal of Transnational Law*, *Columbia Journal of World Business*, *Columbia Journalism Review*, *Columbia Law Review*, *Columbia Studies in the Classical Tradition*, *Critical Texts*, *Current Musicology*, *Germanic Review*, *Global Political Assessment*, *Journal of Art and the Law*, *Journal of International Affairs*, *Journal of the Ancient Near Eastern Society*, *Journal of Philosophy*, *Johnsonian News Letter*, *Prospects: The Annual for American Cultural Studies*, *Renaissance Quarterly*, *Revista Hispánica Moderna*, *Romanic Review*, *Semiotext(e)*, *Studies in American Indian Literature*, *The Astronomical Journal*, *Translation*

DEANS

Faculty of Arts and Sciences: NICHOLAS B. DIRKS
Columbia College: MICHELE MOODY-ADAMS
Graduate School of Architecture, Planning and Preservation: MARK WIGLEY
Graduate School of Arts and Sciences: HENRY C. PINKHAM
Graduate School of Business: R. GLENN HUBBARD
Graduate School of Journalism: NICHOLAS LEMANN (acting)
School of the Arts: CAROL BECKER
School of Continuing Education: KRISTINE A. BILLMYER
College of Dental Medicine: ALLAN J. FORMICOLA
Fu Foundation School of Engineering and Applied Science: FENIOSKY PEÑA-MORA
School of General Studies: PETER J. AWN
School of International and Public Affairs: JOHN H. COATSWORTH
Law School: DAVID M. SCHIZER
Medical Center: LEE GOLDMAN
School of Nursing: BOBBIE BERKOWITZ
Mailman School of Public Health: LINDA P. FRIED
School of Social Work: JEANETTE C. TAKAMURA

PROFESSORS

Anaesthesiology:
FINCK, A. D.
FINSTER, M.
HILLEL, Z.
HYMAN, A. I.
MORISHIMA, H. O.
ORNSTEIN, E.
PANG, L.
PANTUCK, E. J.
SMILEY, R. M.
STONE, J. G.
THYS, D. M.
TRINER, L.
WEISSMAN, C.
YOUNG, W. L.

Anatomy and Cell Biology:
AMBRON, R.
APRIL, E. W.
BELLVE, A. R.
BRANDT, P.
BULINSKI, J. C.
GERSHON, M. D.
KESSIN, R. H.
ROLE, L. W.
SILVERMAN, A.-J.
TENNYSON, V. M. S.
TORAN-ALLERAND, C. D.

Anthropology:
ALLAND, A., Jr
COHEN, M. L.
COMBS-SCHILLING, M. E.
D'ALTROY, T.
HOLLOWAY, R. L.
MELNICK, D.
NEWMAN, K.
SKINNER, E. P.
TAUSSIG, M.

Applied Physics:
BOOZER, A. H.
CHU, C. K.
HERMAN, I. P.
MARSHALL, T. C.
MAUEL, M.
NAVRATIL, G.

Architecture, Planning and Preservation:
FRAMPTON, K.
GRAVA, S.
HERDEG, K.
HOLL, S.
MCINTYRE, L.
MCLEOD, M.
MARCUSE, P.
PLUNZ, R.
POLSHEK, J. S.
SASSEN, S. J.
SCLAR, E.
STERN, R. A. M.
TSCHUMI, B.
WRIGHT, G.

Art History and Archaeology:
BALLON, H. M.
BECK, J. H.
BERGDOLL, B. G.
BRILLIANT, R.
CONNORS, J.
FREEDBERG, D.
KRAUSS, R.
MIDDLETON, R.
MURASE, M. C.
MURRAY, S.
MYCK, A.
PASZTORY, E.
REFF, T.
ROSAND, D.
STALEY, A.

Arts:
FORMAN, M., Film
INSDORF, A., Film
SARRIS, A., Film

Astronomy:
APPLEGATE, J.
BAKER, N.
HALPERN, J. P.
HELFAND, D.
PATTERSON, J.
PRENDERGAST, K. H.
SPIEGEL, E. A.
VAN GORKOM, J.

Biochemistry and Molecular Biophysics:
FEIGELSON, P.
GOFF, S.
GOLD, A. M.
GOLDBERGER, R. F.
GOTTESMAN, M. E.
GREENWALD, I. S.
HENDRICKSON, W. A.
HIRSH, D. I.
HONIG, B.
JESSELL, T.
KRASNA, A. I.
SRINIVASAN, P. R.

Biological Sciences:
BOCK, W. J.
CHALFIE, M.
CHASIN, L. A.
COHEN, D. H.
KELLEY, D. B.
MACAGNO, E. R.
MANCINELLI, A.
MANLEY, J.
POLLACK, R.
POO, M.
PRIVES, C. L.
TZAGOLOFF, A.
ZUBAY, G. L.

Business:
ADLER, M.
ARZAC, E. R.
BARTEL, A.

BROCKNER, J.
BURTON, J. C.
CAPON, N.
DONALDSON, J.
EDWARDS, F.
FEDERGRUEN, A.
GIOVANNINI, A.
GLASSERMAN, P.
GLOSTEN, L. R.
GREEN, L.
GREENWALD, B. C. N.
GUPTA, S.
HARRIGAN, K.
HARRIS, T.
HEAL, G.
HOLBROOK, M.
HORTON, R.
HUBBARD, R. G.
HUBERMAN, G.
HULBERT, J. M.
ICHNIOWSKI, B. E.
KOHLI, R.
KOLESAR, P.
LEFF, N.
LEHMANN, D.
LICHTENBERG, F. R.
MELUMAD, N. D.
MISHKIN, F.
NOAM, E.
OHLSON, J.
PATRICK, H.
SELDEN, L.
SEXTON, D.
STARR, M.
SUNDARESAN, S.
THOMAS, J. K.
TUSHMAN, M.
WARREN, E. K.
WILKINSON, M.
ZIPKIN, P.

Chemical Engineering and Applied Chemistry:
CHEH, H. Y.
DURNING, C.
GRYTE, C.
LEONARD, E. F.
O'SHAUGHNESSY, B.
SPENCER, J.

Chemistry:
BENT, B. E.
BERNE, B. J.
BERSOHN, R.
BRESLOW, R.
DANISHEFSKY, S. J.
EISENTHAL, K. B.
FLYNN, G. W.
FRIESNER, R.
KATZ, T. J.
NAKANISHI, K.
PARKIN, G. F. R.
PECHUKAS, P.
STILL, W. C.
TURRO, N. J.
VALENTINI, J.

Civil Engineering and Engineering Mechanics:
DASGUPTA, G.
DIMAGGIO, F. L.
FRIEDMAN, M. B.
GJELSVIK, A.
GRIFFIS, F. H.
MEYER, C.
STOLL, R. D.
TESTA, R. B.
VAICAITIS, R.

Classics:
BAGNALL, R. S.
CAMERON, A.
COULTER, J. A.
SAID, S.
TARÁN, L.
ZETZEL, J.

Computer Science:
AHO, A. V.
ALLEN, P. K.
FEINER, S. K.
GALIL, Z.
GROSS, J. L.
KAISER, G.
KENDER, J.
MCKEOWN, K.
STOLFO, S.
TRAUB, J. F.
UNGER, S.
WOZNIAKOWSKI, M.
YEMINI, Y.

Dental and Oral Surgery:
CANGIALOSI, T. J.
DAVIS, M. J.
EFSTRATIADIS, S. S.
FORMICOLA, A. J.
HASSELGREN, B. G.
HILLS, H. L.
ISRAEL, H. A.
KAHN, N.
KLYVERT, M.
LAMSTER, I. B.
MOSS-SALENTIJN, L.
MYERS, R.
ODRICH, J.
ROSER, S. M.
TROUTMAN, K. C.
ZEGARELLI, D. J.

Dermatology:
BICKERS, D. R.

East Asian Languages and Cultures:
ANDERER, P.
HYMES, R.
LEDYARD, G. K.
SHIRANE, H.
SMITH, H. D., II
WANG, D. D.-W.
ZELIN, M.

Economics:
BHAGWATI, J.
BLOOM, D.
CHICHILNISKY, G.
CLARIDA, R.
DESAI, P.
DHRYMES, P.
DUTTA, P. K.
ERICSON, R.
FINDLAY, R.
HAYASHI, F.
LANCASTER, K.
MUNDELL, R.
PHELPS, E.
SACHS, J. D.
WATTS, H.
WELLISZ, S. H.

Electrical Engineering:
ACAMPORA, A.
ANASTASSIOU, D.
DIAMENT, P.
HEINZ, T.
LAZAR, A.
MEADOWS, H. E.
OSGOOD, R.
SCHWARTZ, M.
SEN, A. K.
STERN, T. E.
TEICH, M. C.
TSIVIDIS, Y.
WANG, W.
YANG, E. S.
ZUKOWSKI, C. A.

English and Comparative Literature:
BLOUNT, M.
DAMROSCH, D.
DELBANCO, A.
DOUGLAS, A.
EDEN, K.
FERGUSON, R.
FERRANTE, J.
HANNING, R.
HOWARD, J.
KASTAN, D.
KOCH, J. K.
KROEBER, K.
MARCUS, S.
MEISEL, M.
MENDELSON, E.
MILLER, D. A.
MIROLLO, J. V.
MORETTI, F.
O'MEALLY, R. G.
PETERS, J. S.
QUIGLEY, A.
ROSENBERG, J. D.
ROSENTHAL, M.
SEIDEL, M.
SHAPIRO, J.
SPIVAK, G. C.
STADE, G.
TAYLER, E. W.
YERKES, D.

French and Romance Philology:
BLOCH, R. H.
COMPAGNON, A.
CONDE, M.
FORCE, P.
LOTRINGER, S.
MAY, G.
MITTERAND, H.
RIFFATERRE, M.

Genetics and Development:
BESTOR, T.
CARLSON, M.
COSTANTINI, F.
EFSTRATIADIS, A.
GILLIAM, T. C.
OTT, J.
PAPAIOANNOU, V.
ROTHSTEIN, R. J.
SCHON, E. A.
STERN, C. D.
STRUHL, G.
WARBURTON, D.
WOLGEMUTH, D.

Geological Sciences:
BROECKER, W. S.
CHRISTIE-BLICK, N.
FAIRBANKS, R. G.
GORDON, A. L.
HAYES, D. E.
HAYS, J. O.
LANGMUIR, C.
MENKE, W.
MUTTER, J.
OLSEN, P.
RICHARDS, P. G.
SCHLOSSER, P.
SCHOLZ, C.
SIMPSON, H. J.
SYKES, L. R.
WALKER, D.

Germanic Languages:
ANDERSON, M. M.
HUYSSEN, A.
MULLER, H.
VON MUCKE, D. E.

History:
BILLOWS, R.
BLACKMAR, E.
BRINKLEY, A.
BULLIET, R.
BUSHMAN, R.
BYNUM, C.
CANNADINE, D.
DE GRAZIA, V.
DEAK, I.
FIELDS, B.
FONER, E.
GLUCK, C.
GOREN, A. A.
HAIMSON, L.
HARRIS, W. V.

HOWELL, M.
JACKSON, K. T.
KLEIN, H. S.
LYNCH, H. R.
MALEFAKIS, E. E.
MARABLE, M.
PAXTON, R.
ROTHMAN, D.
SCHAMA, S.
SHENTON, J. P.
SMIT, J. W.
STANISLAWSKI, M.
STEPAN, N.
STERN, F.
VON HAGEN, M. L.
WOLOCH, I.
WORTMAN, R.
WRIGHT, M.
YERUSHALMI, Y. H.

Industrial Engineering and Operations Research:
BIENSTOCK, D.
GALLEGO, G.
GOLDFARB, D.
KLEIN, M.
PINEDO, M.
SIGMAN, K.
YAO, D. D.-W.

International and Public Affairs:
MOLZ, R. K.
NELSON, R. R.
RODRIK, D.

Italian:
BAROLINI, T.
REBAY, L.

Journalism:
BELFORD, B.
BENEDICT, H.
CAREY, J. W.
GARLAND, P.
GOLDSTEIN, K. K.
ISAACS, S. D.
KONNER, J.

Krumb School of Mines:
BESHERS, D. N.
DUBY, P. F.
HARRIS, C. C.
SOMASUNDARAN, P.
THEMELIS, N. J.
YEGULALP, T. M.

Law:
BARENBERG, M.
BERGER, C. J.
BERGER, V.
BERMANN, G.
BLACK, B. A.
BLACK, B. S.
BLASI, V.
BRIFFAULT, R.
CHIRELSTEIN, M.
COFFEE, J. C.
CRENSHAW, K. W.
DAMROSCH, L.
EDGAR, H. S. H.
EDWARDS, R.
FARNSWORTH, E. A.
FINEMAN, M.
FLETCHER, G.
GARDNER, R.
GILSON, R. J.
GINSBURG, J. C.
GOLDBERG, V. P.
GOLDSCHMID, H. J.
GORDON, J. N.
GREENAWALT, R. K.
GREENBERG, J.
HOOVER, J.
JONES, W. K.
KORN, H. L.
LEEBRON, D. W.
LIEBMAN, J.
LIEBMAN, L.
LYNCH, G.
MOGLEN, E.
MONAGHAN, H.
NARASIMHAN, S.
NEUMAN, G. L.
PARKER, K. E.
RABB, H. S.
RAPACZYNSKI, A.
ROE, M. J.
SABEL, C. F.
SMIT, H.
SOVERN, M.
STONE, R.
STRAUSS, P. L.
THOMAS, K.
UVILLER, H. R.
WILLIAMS, P. J.
YOUNG, M.
YOUNG, W. F., Jr

Mathematics:
BASS, H.
FRIEDMAN, R.
GALLAGHER, P. X.
GOLDFELD, D.
JACQUET, H. M.
JORGENSEN, T.
KARATZAS, I.
KURANISHI, M.
MORGAN, J.
PHONG, D.
PINKHAM, H. C.

Mechanical Engineering:
CHEVRAY, R.
FREUDENSTEIN, F.
LONGMAN, R. W.
MODI, V.

Medicine:
AL-AWQATI, Q.
APPEL, G. B.
BAER, L. R.
BANK, A.
BIGGER, J. T.
BILEZIKIAN, J. P.
BUTLER, V. P., Jr
CALDWELL, L. P.
CANFIELD, R. E.
CANNON, P. J.
CHESS, L.
CIMINO, J. J.
CLAYTON, P. D.
CORTELL, S.
FIELD, M.
FRANCIS, C. K.
FRANTZ, A. G.
GIARDINA, E.-G.
GINSBURG, H. N.
GOLDBERG, I. J.
GRIECO, M. H.
HOLT, P. R.
JACOBS, T. P.
KEMP, H., Jr
LEGATO, M. J.
LEIFER, E.
LINDENBAUM, J.
LOEB, J.
MELCHER, G.
MORRIS, T. Q.
MORSE, J. E.
NEU, H. C.
PHILLIPS, G. B.
PI-SUNYER, F. X.
ROSNER, W.
SCHWARTZ, M. J.
TABAS, I. A.
TALL, A.
TAPLEY, D. F.
TAUB, R. N.
THOMSON, G. E.
TURINO, G. M.
WARDLAW, S.
WEINSTEIN, I. B.
WEISFELDT, M. L.
WEISS, H. J.

Microbiology:
CALAME, K. L.
FIGURSKI, D.
MITCHELL, A. P.
RACANIELLO, V. R.
SHORE, D. M.
SHUMAN, H. A.
SILVERSTEIN, S. J.
YOUNG, C.

Middle East and Asian Languages and Cultures:
BURRILL, K. R. F.
MADINA, M.
MIRON, D.
PRITCHETT, F.
RICCARDI, T.
SALIBA, G.
VAN DE MIEROOP, M.

Music:
BENT, I.
CHRISTENSEN, D.
EDWARDS, G.
FRISCH, W.
KRAMER, J.
LERDAHL, A. W.
PERKINS, L.
SISMAN, E.
TUCKER, M. T.

Neurological Surgery:
BRISMAN, R.
HOUSEPIAN, E. M.
MCMURTRY, J.
QUEST, D. O.
STEIN, B. M.

Neurology:
BRUST, J. C. M., Jr
COTE, L. J.
DE VIVO, D. C.
DI MAURO, S.
EMERSON, R. G.
FAHN, S.
GHEZ, C.
GOLD, A. P.
HALSEY, J., Jr
HAUSER, W. A.
KARLIN, A.
LATOV, N.
LOVELACE, R. E.
MAYEUX, R.
MOHR, J. P.
PEDLEY, T.
PENN, A. S.
ROWLAND, L. P.
SCHWARTZ, J.
SCIARRA, D.
STERN, Y.
WEXLER, N.

Nursing:
FULMER, T. T.
MUNDINGER, M. O.

Obstetrics and Gynaecology:
BOWE, E. T.
FERIN, M.
HEMBREE, W. C.
JAGIELLO, G.
LOBO, R. A.
NEUWIRTH, R. S.
TIMOR, I. E.
WILLIAMS, S. B.

Ophthalmology:
BEHRENS, M.
BITO, L.
DONN, A.
FARRIS, R. L.
FORBES, M.
GOURAS, P.
L'ESPERANCE, F., Jr
MOORE, S.
SPALTER, H.
SPECTOR, A.
SRINIVASAN, B.
TROKEL, S.
WORGUL, B. V.
YANNUZZI, L. A.

Orthopaedic Surgery:
DICK, H.
EFTEKHAR, N.
FIELDING, J. W.
GRANTHAM, S. A.
LAI, W. M.
MOW, V. C.
RATCLIFFE, A.
SHELTON, M. L.

Otolaryngology:
BLITZER, A.
CLOSE, L. G.
KHANNA, S. M.

Paediatrics:
COOPER, L. Z.
CUNNINGHAM, N.
DECKELBAUM, R. J.
DELL, R. B.
DRISCOLL, J. M.
GERSHON, A. A.
GERSONY, W. M.
HEAGARTY, M.
JACOBS, J.
KRONGRAD, E.
LEBLANC, W.
LEVINE, L.
MELLIN, G. W.
MELLINS, R. B.
NICHOLSON, J. F.
PIOMELLI, S.
SITARZ, A.
STARK, R.
WETHERS, D. L.
WINCHESTER, R. J.

Pathology:
AXEL, R.
DALLA-FAVERA, R.
GELLER, L. M.
GOLDMAN, J. E.
GREENE, L. A.
KAUFMAN, M.
KOHN, D. F.
LEFKOWITCH, J. H.
LIEM, R. K. H.
MASON, C. A.
PERZIN, K. H.
RICHART, R. M.
SHELANSKI, M. L.
SUCIU-FOCA, N.

Pharmacology:
BOYDEN, P.
GOLDBERG, D. J.
GRAZIANO, J. H.
HOFFMAN, B. F.
ROBINSON, R. B.
ROSEN, M. R.
SIEGELBAUM, S. A.
WIT, A. L.

Philosophy:
ALBERT, D.
BEROFSKY, B.
BILGRAMI, A.
GAIFMAN, H.
GOEHR, L. D.
LARMORE, C.
LEVI, I.
POGGE, T.
SIDORSKY, D.

Physical Education and Intercollegiate Athletics:
ROHAN, J. P.

Physics:
APRILE, E.
CHRIST, N. H.
GYULASSY, M.
HAILEY, C. J.
HARTMANN, S.
KAHN, S. M.
LEE, T. D.
LEE, W.
MUELLER, A.
NAGAMIYA, S.
RUDERMAN, M. A.
SCHWARTZ, M.
SCIULLI, F.
SHAEVITZ, M. H.
TUTS, P. M.
UEMURA, Y.
WEINBERG, E.
WILLIS, W. J.
ZAJC, W. A.

Physiology and Cellular Biophysics:
BLANK, M.
DODD, J.
FISCHBARG, J.
KANDEL, E. R.
LOW, M. G.
SCHACHTER, D.
SILVERSTEIN, S. C.
STERN, D.

Political Science:
ANDERSON, L.
BALDWIN, D.
BERNSTEIN, T. P.
BETTS, R. K.
BIALER, S.
CHALMERS, D. A.
COHEN, J. L.
CURTIS, G. L.
ELSTER, J.
FRANKLIN, J. H.
HAMILTON, C. V.
JERVIS, R. L.
JOHNSTON, D. C.
KATZNELSON, I. I.
KESSELMAN, M. J.
LEGVOLD, R.
MILNER, H.
NATHAN, A. N.
ROTHSCHILD, J.
RUGGIE, J.
SCHILLING, W. R.
SHAPIRO, R. Y.
SNYDER, J.
WESTIN, A. F.

Psychiatry:
BENNETT, R.
DEVANAND, D.
DOHRENWEND, B.
DUNTON, H. D.
EHRHARDT, A. A.
ENDICOTT, J.
ERLENMEYER-KIMLING, L.
FIEVE, R. R.
FISCHMAN, M. W.
FOLEY, A. R.
GLASSMAN, A. H.
GORMAN, J. M.
GURLAND, B. J.
HOFER, M.
JAFFE, J.
KLEBER, H. D.
KLEIN, D. F.
KLEIN, R. G.
KUPFERMANN, I.
PARDES, H.
PROHOVNIK, I.
RAINER, J.
RYAN, J.
SACKEIM, H. A.
SHAFFER, D.
SPITZER, R.
TAMIR, H.
WEISSMAN, M. M.

Psychology:
COOPER, L. A.
DWECK, C. S.
GALANTER, E. H.
GIBBON, J.
GRAHAM, N.
HIGGINS, E. T.
HOOD, D. C.
KRANTZ, D.
KRAUSS, R.
MATIN, L.
METCALFE, J.
MISCHEL, W.
TERRACE, H. S.

Public Health:
BAYER, R.
BRANDT-RAUF, P. W.
BROWN, L.
CHALLENOR, B. D.
COLOMBOTOS, J. L.
DAVIDSON, A.
DESPOMMIER, D. D.
FLEISS, J. L.
HASHIM, S. A.
HOWE, G. R.
KANDEL, D.
LEVIN, B.
LINK, B. G.
LO, S.-H.
MCCARTHY, J.
OTTMAN, R.
PEARSON, T. A.
PERERA, F. P.
ROSENFIELD, A. G.
SANTELLA, R. P.
SISK, J. E.
STRUENING, E. L.
TSAI, W.-Y.

Radiation Oncology:
AMOLS, H. I.
BRENNER, D. J.
GEARD, C.
HALL, E.
HEI, T. K.
SCHIFF, P. B.

Radiology:
ABLOW, R. C.
ALDERSON, P. O.
BERDON, W.
ESSER, P.
FELDMAN, F.
HILAL, S.
KING, D. L.
NEWHOUSE, J. H.
NICKOLOFF, E. L.
SILVER, A. J.

Rehabilitation Medicine:
DOWNEY, J. A.
EDELSTEIN, J. E.
LIEBERMAN, J. S.
MYERS, S. J.
NEUHAUS, B. E.
THORNHILL, H.

Religion:
AWN, J.
LINDT, G.
PROUDFOOT, W.
RUPP, G.
SOMERVILLE, R.
THURMAN, R.
WEISS-HALIVNI, D.

Slavic Languages:
BELKNAP, R. L.
GASPAROV, B.
MAGUIRE, R. A.
MILLER, F. J.
POPKIN, C.
REYFMAN, I.

Social Work:
AKABAS, S.
BLACK, R. B.
CLOWARD, R. A.
FELDMAN, R.
GARFINKEL, I.
GITTERMAN, A.
HESS, M. M.
IVANOFF, A.
KAMERMAN, S. B.
KIRK, S.
MCGOWAN, B.
MEYER, C. H.
MONK, A.
MULLEN, E. J.
POLSKY, H.

SCHILLING, R. F.
SCHINKE, S.
SIMON, B. L.
SOLOMON, R.

Sociology:
COLE, J. R.
GANS, H.
LITWAK, E.
RUGGIE, M.
SILVER, A. A.
SPILERMAN, S.
WHITE, H.

Spanish and Portuguese:
ALAZRAKI, J.
GRIEVE, P. E.
MARTINEZ-BONATI, F.
SILVER, P. W.
SOBEJANO, G.

Statistics:
DE LA PENA, V.
HEYDE, C. C.

Surgery:
ALTMAN, R. P.
CHIU, D. T. W.
FORDE, K.
HARDY, M. A.
HUGO, N.
LO GERFO, P.
MARKOWITZ, A.
NOWYGROD, R.
QUAEGEBEUR, J. M.
REEMTSMA, K.
ROSE, E. A.
SMITH, C. R.
SPOTNITZ, H. M.
STOLAR, C. J. H.
TILSON, M. D.

Urology:
BUTTYAN, R.
HENSLE, T. W.
OLSSON, C. A.
PUCHNER, P. J.
ROMAS, N. S.

AFFILIATED COLLEGES

Barnard College: 606 W 120th St, New York, NY 10027; private liberal arts for women; Pres. DEBORA L. SPAR.

Teachers' College, Columbia University: 525 W 120th St, New York, NY 10027; private, professional, graduate only; Pres. ARTHUR ELLIOTT LEVINE.

ATTACHED INSTITUTES AND CENTRES

Accounting Research Center: Dirs TREVOR HARRIS, NAHUM MELUMAD.

Center for Chinese Business Studies: Dir HOKE SIMPSON.

Center for Chinese Legal Studies: Dir R. RANDLE EDWARDS.

Center for Climate Research: Dir WALLACE BROECKER.

Center for Human Resource Management Studies: Dir ANN BARTEL.

Center for International Business Education: Dir KATHRYN HARRIGAN.

Center for Israel and Jewish Studies: Dir YOSEF H. YERUSHALMI.

Center for Japanese Economy and Business: Dir HUGH PATRICK.

Center for Japanese Legal Studies: Dir MICHAEL K. YOUNG.

Center for Law and the Arts: Dir JOHN M. KERNOCHAN.

Center for Law and Economic Studies: Dirs VICTOR P. GOLDBERG, JEFFREY N. GORDON.

Center for Molecular Recognition: Dir ARTHUR KARLIN.

Center for Neurobiology and Behavior: Dir JOHN KOESTER (acting).

Center for Population and Family Health: Dir JAMES MCCARTHY.

Center for Preservation Research: Dir MARTIN WEAVER.

Center for Psychoanalytic Training and Research: Dir ROGER MACKINNON.

Center for Radiological Research: Dir ERIC J. HALL.

Center for Research in Arts and Culture: Dir JOAN JEFFRI.

Center for Telecommunications Research: Dir ANTHONY ACAMPORA.

Center for the Social Sciences: Dir HARRISON WHITE.

Center for the Study of Futures Markets: Dir FRANKLIN R. EDWARDS.

Center for the Study of Geriatrics and Gerontology: Dir BARRY J. GURLAND.

Center for the Study of Human Rights: Dir J. PAUL MARTIN.

Center for the Study of Innovation and Entrepreneurship: Dir MICHAEL TUSHMAN.

Center for the Study of Operations: Dir MARTIN K. STARR.

Center for the Study of Society and Medicine: Dir DAVID J. ROTHMAN.

Columbia Institute for Tele-Information: Dir ELI NOAM.

Columbia-Presbyterian Cancer Center: Dir I. BERNARD WEINSTEIN.

Donald Keene Center of Japanese Culture: Dir HARUO SHIRANE.

East Asian Institute: Dir MADELEINE ZELIN.

Executive Leadership Research Center: Dir DONALD HAMBRICK.

Fritz Reiner Center: Dir ALFRED LERDAHL.

George T. Delacorte Center for Magazine Journalism: Dir (vacant).

Gertrude H. Sergievsky Center: Dir RICHARD P. MAYEUX.

Harriman Institute: Dir MARK VON HAGEN.

Herbert and Florence Irving Center for Clinical Research: Dir HENRY N. GINSBERG.

Institute for Marketing: Dir DONALD LEHMANN.

Institute for Not-for-Profit Management: Dir RAYMOND D. HORTON.

Institute for Research on Women and Gender: Dir VICTORIA DE GRAZIA.

Institute of African Studies: Dir GEORGE C. BOND.

Institute of Cancer Research: Dir MAXWELL E. GOTTESMAN.

Institute of Comparative Medicine: Dir DENNIS S. KOHN.

Institute of Human Nutrition: Dir RICHARD J. DECKELBAUM.

Institute of Latin American and Iberian Studies: Dir DOUGLAS CHALMERS.

Institute of War and Peace Studies: Dir JACK L. SNYDER.

Institute on Aging: Dir ABRAHAM MONK.

Institute on East Central Europe: Dir JOHN S. MICGIEL.

Institute on Western Europe: Dir GLENDA G. ROSENTHAL.

International Institute for the Study of Human Reproduction: Dir GEORGIANA JAGIELLO.

Lamont-Doherty Earth Observatory: Dir JOHN C. MUTTER (acting).

Legislative Drafting Research Fund: Dir RICHARD BRIFFAULT.

Management Institute: Dir E. KIRBY WARREN.

Middle East Institute: Dir RICHARD W. BULLIET.

Parker School of Foreign and Comparative Law: Dir HANS SMIT.

Southern Asian Institute: Dir PHILIP K. OLDENBURG.

Temple Hoyne Buell Center for the Study of American Architecture: Dir JOAN OCKMAN.

CONCORDIA COLLEGE

171 White Plains Rd, Bronxville, NY 10708
Telephone: (914) 337-9300
Fax: (914) 395-4500
E-mail: admission@concordia-ny.edu
Internet: www.concordia-ny.edu

Founded 1881
Private control
Academic year: August to May

Pres.: Dr VIJI GEORGE
Chief Financial Officer: DENNIS LONNERGAN
Vice-Pres. for Institutional Advancement: PAUL GRAND PRÉ
Chief Academic Officer: SHERRY J. FRASER
Dean of Students: JOHN M. BAHR
Registrar: MARK E. BLANCO
Library Dir: BRENDA BURROUGHS

Number of teachers: 30
Number of students: 635

Areas of study: arts management, behavioural sciences, biology, business admin., education, educational services, English, environmental science, history, interdisciplinary studies, int. studies, mathematics, music, religious studies, social work.

COOPER UNION FOR THE ADVANCEMENT OF SCIENCE AND ART

30 Cooper Sq., New York, NY 10003-7120
Telephone: (212) 353-4100
Internet: www.cooper.edu

Founded 1859
Academic year: September to May

Pres.: GEORGE CAMPBELL, Jr
Chair. of Trustees: MARK EPSKIN
Vice-Pres. for Business Affairs and Treas.: T.C. WESTCOTT
Vice-Pres. for External Affairs: RONNI DENES
Dean of Admissions: MITCHELL LIPTON
Library Dir: ULLA VOLK

Library of 136,711 vols
Number of teachers: 228
Number of students: 990

Publication: *At Cooper Union*

DEANS

Faculty of Humanities and Social Sciences: WILLIAM GERMANO
School of Architecture: ANTHONY VIDLER
School of Art: SASKIA BOS
School of Engineering: SIMON BEN-AVI (acting)

CORNELL UNIVERSITY

Ithaca, NY 14853
Telephone: (607) 255-2000
E-mail: info@cornell.edu
Internet: www.cornell.edu

Founded 1865
State and private control
Academic year: September to May

Pres.: DAVID J. SKORTON
Provost: KENT FUCHS
Provost for Medical Affairs: ANTONIO M. GOTTO, Jr

Univ. Counsel and Sec. of the Corpn: JAMES J. MINGLE
Vice-Pres. for Alumni Affairs and Devt: CHARLES T. PHLEGAR
Vice-Pres. for Facilities Services: KYU-JUNG WHANG
Vice-Pres. for Finance and Chief Financial Officer: JOANNE M. DESTEFANO
Vice-Pres. for Govt and Community Relations: STEPHEN PHILIP JOHNSON
Vice-Pres. for Human Resources: MARY G. OPPERMAN
Vice-Pres. for Planning and Budget: ELMIRA MANGUM
Vice-Pres. for Student and Academic Services: SUSAN H. MURPHY
Vice-Pres. for Univ. Communications: THOMAS W. BRUCE
Vice-Pres. for Univ. Relations: GLENN C. ALTSCHULER
Sr Vice-Provost for Academic Affairs: JOHN A. SICILIANO
Sr Vice-Provost for Research: ROBERT A. BUHRMAN
Sr Vice-Provost: RONALD SEEBER
Vice-Provost for Int. Relations: ALICE N. PELL
Vice-Provost for Undergraduate Education: LAURA BROWN
Vice-Provost: BARBARA A. KNUTH
Dean of Univ. Faculty: WILLIAM FRY
Dean of Students: KENT L. HUBBELL
Univ. Librarian: ANNE R. KENNEY

Library: see Libraries and Archives
Number of teachers: 2,908
Number of students: 21,325

Publications: *Administrative Science Quarterly* (academic), *Agricultural Finance Review* (academic), *Andean Past* (academic), *Animal Life* (newspaper), *Bird Scope* (newsletter), *Cat Watch* (newsletter), *Colloqui: Cornell Journal of Planning and Urban Issues* (academic), *Communique (Ithaca)* (academic), *Cornell Alumni* (magazine), *Cornell Biennial Electrical Engineering Conference* (academic), *Cornell Chronicle* (newspaper), *Cornell Daily Sun* (newspaper), *Cornell East Asia Series* (academic), *Cornell Engineering* (magazine), *Cornell Enterprise* (magazine), *Cornell Field Crops and Soils Handbook* (bulletin), *Cornell Focus* (academic), *Cornell Hotel and Restaurant Administration Quarterly* (academic), *Cornell Hotel School* (magazine), *Cornell International Industrial and Labor Relations Reports* (monograph), *Cornell International Law Journal* (academic), *Cornell Journal of Architecture* (academic), *Cornell Journal of Law and Public Policy* (academic), *Cornell Law Forum* (academic), *Cornell Law Review* (academic), *Cornell Linguistic Contributions* (monograph), *Cornell Linguistic Dissertations* (monograph), *Cornell Lunatic* (magazine), *Cornell Medicine* (bulletin), *Cornell Modern Indonesia Project Publications* (academic), *Cornell Nutrition Conference for Feed Manufacturers* (proceedings), *Cornell Phonetics Laboratory* (working papers), *Cornell Plantations Magazine* (academic), *Cornell Recommendations for Commercial Florist Crops* (bulletin), *Cornell Recommendations for Commercial Turfgrass Management* (academic), *Cornell Recommendations for Field Crops* (bulletin), *Cornell Recommendations for Pest Control for Commercial Production and Maintenance of Trees and Shrubs* (bulletin), *Cornell Science and Technology Magazine* (academic), *Cornell Studies in Industrial and Labor Relations* (monograph), *Cornell Working Papers in Linguistics* (academic), *Cornellian* (newspaper), *Dog Watch* (academic), *Epoch (Icatha)* (contemporary literature), *Feline Health Topics* (newsletter), *Food and Fitness Advisor* (newsletter), *Human Ecology (Ithaca)* (magazine), *Indonesia* (academic), *Industrial and Labor Relations Review* (academic), *Journal of Empirical Legal Studies* (academic), *Living Bird* (academic), *N K A* (contemporary African art), *Pest Management Recommendations for Commercial Vegetable and Potato Production* (bulletin), *Philosophical Review* (academic), *RLG DigiNews* (newsletter), *Traces (Ithaca)* (cultural theory and translation), *Window (New York)* (newspaper), *Women's Health Advisor* (newsletter), *Working Papers in Planning* (working papers)

DEANS

College of Agriculture and Life Sciences: KATHRYN J. BLOOR
College of Architecture, Art and Planning: KENT KLEINMAN
College of Arts and Sciences: G. PETER LEPAGE
College of Engineering: LANCE R. COLLINS
College of Human Ecology: ALAN D. MATHIOS
College of Veterinary Medicine: MICHAEL I. KOTLIKOFF
Faculty of Computing and Information Science: DANIEL P. HUTTENLOCHER
Graduate School: BARBARA A. KNUTH
Graduate School of Medical Sciences: DAVID P. HAJJAR
Johnson Graduate School of Management: L. JOSEPH THOMAS
Law School: STEWART J. SCHWAB
School of Continuing Education and Summer Sessions: GLENN C. ALTSCHULER
School of Hotel Administration: MICHAEL D. JOHNSON
School of Industrial and Labor Relations: HARRY C. KATZ

PROFESSORS

Africana Studies and Research Center (310 Triphammer Rd, Cornell Univ., Ithaca, NY 14853; tel. (607) 255-4625; fax (607) 255-0784; internet www.asrc.cornell.edu):

EDMONDSON, L.
HARRIS, R.
HASSAN, S.
TURNER, J.

College of Architecture, Art and Planning (129 Sibley Dome, Ithaca, NY 14853; tel. (607) 255-9110; e-mail aapdean@cornell.edu; internet www.aap.cornell.edu):

Architecture:

GOEHNER, W.
GREENBERG, D. P.
HASCUP, G.
HUBBELL, K.
MOSTAFAVI, M.
OTTO, C. F.
RICHARDSON, H.
WELLS, J.

Art:

KORD, V.
LOCEY, J.
SPECTOR, F.
SQUIER, J. L.
WALKINGSTICK, K.

City and Regional Planning:

AZIS, I.
BENERIA, L.
BOOTH, R.
CHRISOPHERSON, S.
CLAVEL, P.
DRENNAN, M.
FORESTER, J.
GOLDSMITH, W.
LEWIS, D.
OLPADWALA, P.
REARDON, K.

College of Arts and Sciences (172 Golden Smith Hall, Ithaca, NY 14853; tel. (607) 255-4833; e-mail as_admissions@cornell.edu; internet www.arts.cornell.edu):

Anthropology:

GREENWOOD, D.
HENDERSON, J.
HOLMBERG, D.
MARCH, K.
SANGREN, P.
SIEGEL, J.
SMALL, M.

Asian Studies:

DE BARY, B.
GOLD, D.
GUNN, E.
MINKOWSKI, C.
SAKAI, N.
TAYLOR, K.

Astronomy:

CAMPBELL, D.
CHERNOFF, D.
CORDES, J.
GIERASCH, P.
GIOVANELLI, R.
GOLDSMITH, P.
HAYNES, M.
HERTER, T.
HOUCK, J.
NICHOLSON, P.
SQUYRES, S.
STACEY, G.
TERZIAN, Y.
VEVERKA, J.
WASSERMAN, I.

Chemistry and Chemical Biology:

ABRUNA, H.
BAIRD, B.
BEGLEY, T.
BURLITCH, J.
CARPENTER, B.
COATES, G.
COLLUM, D.
DAVIS, H.
DISALVO, F.
EALICK, S.
EZRA, G.
FAY, R.
FREED, J.
GANEM, B.
HINES, M.
HOFFMANN, R.
HOUSTON, P.
LEE, S.
LORING, R.
MEINWALD, J.
SOGAH, D.
WIDOM, B.
WOLCZANSKI, P.

Classics:

AHL, F.
CLINTON, K.
COLEMAN, J.
NUSSBAUM, A.
PELLICCIA, H.
PUCCI, P.
RAWLINGS, H., III
RUSTEN, J.

Comparative Literature:

CARMICHAEL, C.
COHEN, W.
KENNEDY, W.
MONROE, J.

Ecology and Systematics:

ELLNER, S.
GREENE, H.
HAIRSTON, N., Jr
KENNEDY, K.
POWER, A.
PROVINE, W.

Economics:

BASU, K.

BLUME, L.
COATE, S.
DAVIS, T.
EASLEY, D.
HONG, Y.
KIEFER, N.
LYONS, T.
MAJUMDAR, M.
MASSON, R.
MITRA, T.
POSSEN, U.
SHELL, K.
VOGELSANG, T.
WAN, H., Jr

English:

BOGEL, F.
BROWN, L.
CHASE, C.
CHEYFITZ, E.
CULLER, J.
FULTON, A.
GILBERT, R.
HERRIN, W.
HILL, T.
HITE, M.
JANOWITZ, P.
JEYIFO, B.
MCCALL, D.
MCCLANE, K., Jr
MCMILLIN, H.
MOHANTY, S.
MORGAN, R.
MURRAY, T.
PARKER, A.
SAMUELS, S.
SAWYER, P.
SCHWARZ, D.
SHAW, H.
SIEGEL, S.
SPILLERS, H.
VAUGHN, S.
WETHERBEE, W., III

German Studies:

ADELSON, L.
GROOS, A., Jr
HOHENDAHL, P.
KITTLER, W.
MARTIN, C.

Government:

BENSEL, R.
BUCK-MORSS, S.
BUNCE, V.
EVANGELISTA, M.
HERRING, R.
KATZENSTEIN, M.
KATZENSTEIN, P.
KRAMNICK, I.
LOWI, T.
MEBANE, W.
PONTUSSON, J.
RABKIN, J.
RUBENSTEIN, D.
SANDERS, M.
SHEFTER, M.
TARROW, S.
VANDEWALLE, N.

History:

ALTSCHULER, G.
BLUMIN, S.
CARON, V.
COCHRAN, S.
DEAR, P.
GREENE, S.
HULL, I.
HYAMS, P.
KAMMEN, M.
KAPLAN, S.
KOSCHMANN, J.
LACAPRA, D.
LOGEVALL, F.
MOORE, R.
NAJEMY, J.
NORTON, M.
PETERSON, C.
POLENBERG, R.
STEINBERG, M.
STRAUSS, B.
WASHINGTON, M.

History of Art:

KUNIHOLM, P.
LAZZARO, C.
RAMAGE, A.

Linguistics:

BOWERS, J.
COLLINS, C.
DIESING, M.
HARBERT, W.
MCCONNELL-GINET, S.
ROOTH, M.
ROSEN, C.
WHITMAN, J.
ZEC, D.

Mathematics:

BARBASCH, D.
BILLERA, L.
BROWN, K.
CHASE, S.
CONNELLY, R.
DENNIS, R. K.
DURRETT, R.
DYNKIN, E.
GROSS, L.
GUCKENHEIMER, J.
HATCHER, A.
HENDERSON, D.
HUBBARD, J.
HWANG, J. T.
ILIACHENKO, I.
KAHN, P.
LAWLER, G.
NERODE, A.
NUSSBAUM, M.
SALOFF-COSTE, L.
SCHATZ, A.
SEN, S.
SHORE, R.
SMILLIE, J.
SPEH, B.
STILLMAN, M.
STRICHARTZ, R.
THURSTON, W.
VOGTMANN, K.
WAHLBIN, L.
WEST, J.

Molecular Biology and Genetics:

AGUADRO, C.
BRETSCHER, A.
BROWN, W.
CLARK, A.
FEIGENSON, G.
HESS, G.
HINKLE, P.
HUFFAKER, T.
WILSON, D.
WOLFNER, M.

Music:

BILSON, M.
HARRIS-WARRICLE, R.
HSU, J.
ROSEN, D.
SIERRA, R.
STUCKY, S.
WEBSTER, J., Jr
ZASLAW, N.

Near Eastern Studies:

BRANN, R.
OWEN, D.
POWERS, D.

Neurobiology and Behaviour:

BASS, A.
FETCHO, J.
HOWLAND, H.
HOY, R.
SEELEY, T.
SHERMAN, P.

Philosophy:

BOYD, R.
FINE, G.
IRWIN, T.
MACDONALD, S.
MILLER, R.
MOODY-ADAMS, M.
STURGEON, N.

Physics:

ALEXANDER, J.
AMBEGAOKAR, V.
ASHCROFT, N.
BERKELMAN, K.
BODENSCHATZ, E.
CASSEL, D.
DAVIS, J.
DUGAN, G.
ELSER, V.
FITCHEN, D.
GALIK, R.
GINSPARG, P.
GRUNER, S.
HAND, L.
HARTILL, D.
HENLEY, C.
HOFFSTAETTER, G.
LECLAIR, A.
LEE, D.
LEPAGE, G.
MCEUEN, P.
MERMIN, N.
NEUBERT, M.
PARPIA, J.
PATTERSON, J.
RALPH, D.
RICHARDSON, R.
RUBIN, D.
SETHNA, J.
SIEVERS, A., III
STEIN, P.
TALMAN, R.
TEUKOLSKY, S.
THORNE, R.
TYE, S.-H.
YAN, T.-M.
YORK, J.

Plant Biology:

TURGEON, E. G.

Programme on Ethics and Public Life:

SHUE, H.

Psychology:

BEM, D.
BEM, S.
CUTTING, J.
DARLINGTON, R.
DEVOOGD, T.
DUNNING, D.
EDELMAN, S.
FINLAY, B.
GILOVICH, T.
HALPERN, B.
JOHNSTON, R.
KRUMHANSL, C.
MAAS, J.
NEISSER, U.
REGAN, E.

Romance Studies:

BERGER, A.
CASTILLO, D.
GREENBERG, M.
KLEIN, R.
LEWIS, P.
LONG, K.
MIGIEL, M.
RESINA, J.

Russian Literature:

CARDEN, P.
POLLACK, N.
SENDEROVICH, S.
SHAPIRO, G.

Science and Technology Studies:

LYNCH, M.

PINCH, T.
REPPY, J.
ROSSITER, M.

Sociology:

HARRIS, D.
HECKATHORN, D.
MACY, M.
NEE, V.
STRANG, D.
SWEDBERG, R.

Theatre, Film and Dance:

BATHRICK, D.
FELDSHUH, D.
GAINOR, J.
GOETZ, K.
LEVITT, B.

College of Engineering (Engineering-Swanson Center, 102 Hollister Hall, Ithaca, NY 14853-3501; tel. (607) 255-5008; fax (607) 255-0971; e-mail engr_admissions@cornell.edu; internet www.engineering.cornell.edu):

Applied and Engineering Physics:

BROCK, J.
BUHRMAN, R.
COOL, T.
CRAIGHEAD, H.
GAETA, A.
KUSSE, B.
LINDAU, M.
LOVELACE, R.
SILCOX, J.
WEBB, W.
WISE, F.

Chemical Engineering:

ARCHER, L.
CLANCY, P.
COHEN, C.
KOCH, D.
OLBRICHT, W.
SHULER, M.
STEEN, P.

Civil and Environmental Engineering:

BRUTSAERT, W.
GOSSETT, J.
GRIGORIU, M.
HOVER, K.
INGRAFFEA, A.
KULHAWY, F.
LION, L.
LIU, P.
LOUCKS, D.
MEYBURG, A.
NOZICK, L.
O'ROURKE, T.
PEKOZ, T.
SANSALONE, M.
SCHULER, R.
SHOEMAKER, C.
STEDINGER, J.
TURNQUIST, M.

Computer Sciences:

ARMS, W.
BAILEY, G.
BIRMAN, K.
COLEMAN, T.
CONSTABLE, R.
ELBER, R.
GRIES, D.
HALPERN, J.
HOPCROFT, J.
HUTTENLOCHER, D.
KEDEM, K.
KOZEN, D.
PINGALI, K.
SCHNEIDER, F.
TARDOS, E.
VAN LOAN, C.
VAVASIS, S.

Earth and Atmospheric Sciences:

ALLMENDINGER, R.
BARAZANGI, M.
BROWN, L.
CATHLES, L.
CISNE, J.
GREENE, C.
ISACKS, B.
JORDAN, T.
KAY, R.
KAY, S.
PHIPPS MORGAN, J.
RHODES, F.
WHITE, W.

Electrical Engineering:

BERGER, T.
CHIANG, H.-D.
EASTMAN, L.
FARLEY, D., Jr
FINE, T.
FUCHS, W.
HAAS, Z.
HAMMER, D.
JOHNSON, C., Jr
KELLEY, M.
KINTNER, P., Jr
KLINE, R.
PARKS, T.
POLLOCK, C.
SEYLER, C.
SHEALY, J.
SPENCER, M.
TANG, C.-L.
THOMAS, R.
TIWARI, S.
TONG, L.
WICKER, S.

Materials Science and Engineering:

AST, D.
BLAKELY, J.
DIECKMANN, R.
GIANNELIS, E.
OBER, C.
RUOFF, A.
SASS, S.
VAN DOVER, R.

Mechanical and Aerospace Engineering:

AVEDISIAN, C.
BARTEL, D.
CAUGHEY, D.
COLLINS, L.
DAWSON, P.
GEORGE, A.
GOULDIN, F.
LEIBOVICH, S.
LOUGE, M.
MOON, F.
POPE, S.
TORRANCE, K.
WARHAFT, Z.
WILLIAMSON, C.
ZABARAS, N.

Operations Research and Industrial Engineering:

BLAND, R.
JACKSON, P.
LEWIS, A.
MUCKSTADT, J.
PROTTER, P.
RENEGAR, J.
RESNICK, S.
ROUNDY, R.
RUPPERT, D.
SAMORODNITSKY, G.
SHMOYS, D.
TODD, M.
TROTTER, L., Jr
TURNBULL, B.
WILLIAMSON, D.

Theoretical and Applied Mechanics:

BURNS, J.
CADY, K.
HEALEY, T.
HUI, CH.-Y.
JENKINS, J.
MUKHERJEE, S.
PHOENIX, S.
RAND, R.
RUINA, A.
SACHSE, W.
STROGATZ, S.
ZEHNDER, A.

Joan and Sanford I. Weill Medical Division (1300 York Ave, New York, NY 10021; tel. (212) 821-0560; fax (212) 821-0576; e-mail cumc_admissions@med.cornell.edu; internet www.med.cornell.edu):

Anaesthesiology:

AMAR, D., Anaesthesiology
DESIDERIO, D., Anaesthesiology
DINNER, M., Anaesthesiology (Clinical)
HALPERN, N. A., Anaesthesiology (Clinical)
HARRISON, N., Anaesthesiology (Pharmacology)
HEMMINGS, H. C., Jr, Anaesthesiology
KELLY, R. E., Anaesthesiology (Clinical)
LIEN, C. A., Anaesthesiology (Clinical)
MALHOTRA, V., Anaesthesiology (Clinical)
SAVARESE, J., Anaesthesiology
THOMAS, S. J., Anaesthesiology
THORNE, A. C., Anaesthesiology (Clinical)
WILSON, R. S., Anaesthesiology
YAO., F.-S. F., Anaesthesiology (Clinical)

Biochemistry:

BOSKEY, A. L., Biochemistry
BRESLOW, E. M. G., Biochemistry
COOPER, A. J. L., Biochemistry
MCGRAW, T. E., Biochemistry
MAXFIELD, F. R., Biochemistry
MENON, A. K., Biochemistry
NOVOGRODSKY, A., Biochemistry
ROBERTSON, H. D., Biochemistry
RUBIN, A. L., Biochemistry
RYAN, T. A., Biochemistry
STENZEL, K. H., Biochemistry
TATE, S. S., Biochemistry
WU, H., Biochemistry

Cardiothoracic Surgery:

ADKINS, M. S., Cardiothoracic Surgery (Clinical)
ALTORKI, N. K., Cardiothoracic Surgery
ISOM, O. W., Cardiothoracic Surgery
KRIEGER, K. H., Cardiothoracic Surgery
LARAGH, J. H., Medicine
TORTOLANI, A. J., Cardiothoracic Surgery (Clinical)

Cell and Developmental Biology:

BACHVAROVA, R. F., Cell and Developmental Biology
FISCHMAN, D. A., Cell and Developmental Biology
HAJJAR, K. A., Cell and Developmental Biology
MIKAWA, T., Cell and Developmental Biology
SATO, T. N., Cell and Developmental Biology

Dermatology:

GRANSTEIN, R. D., Dermatology
HALPERN, A. C., Dermatology
VARGHESE, M. C., Dermatology

Genetic Medicine:

RAFII, S., Genetic Medicine

Medicine:

ALLISON, J. P., Medicine (Immunology)
AUGUST, P., Medicine
BAJORIN, D. F., Medicine
BARDES, C. L., Medicine (Clinical)
BASSON, C. T., Medicine
BERMAN, E., Medicine (Clinical)
BOCKMAN, R. S., Medicine
BORER, J. S., Medicine
BOSL, G. J., Medicine
BROWN, A. E., Medicine
CARMEL, R., Medicine
CASPER, E. S., Medicine
CHANDRA, P., Medicine (Clinical)
CHARLSON, M. E., Medicine
CHEIGH, H., Medicine (Clinical)

CLARKSON, B. D., Medicine
CROW, M. K., Medicine
CRYSTAL, R. G., Medicine
DANNENBERG, A. J., Medicine
DEVEREUX, R. B., Medicine
DOSIK, H., Medicine
ETINGIN, O. R., Medicine
FAHEY, T. J., Jr, Medicine (Clinical)
FEIN, O. T., Medicine (Clinical)
FELDMAN, E. J., Medicine
FINNS, J. J., Medicine
FLOMENBAUM, N. E., Medicine (Clinical)
FUKS, Z. Y., Medicine (Radiation Oncology)
GIBOFSKY, A., Medicine (Clinical)
GOLDE, D. W., Medicine
GORDON, B., Medicine (Clinical)
GOTTO, A. M., Jr, Medicine
GROEGER, J. S., Medicine (Clinical)
HAYES, J. G., Medicine
HEMPSTEAD, B. L., Medicine
HOUGHTON, A. N., Medicine
IMPERATO-MCGINLEY, J. L., Medicine
IVANSHKIV, L. B., Medicine
JACOBS, J. L., Medicine (Clinical)
JACOBSON, I. M., Medicine (Clinical)
JOHNSON, W. D., Medicine
KAGEN, L. J. A., Medicine
KELSEN, D. P., Medicine
KEMENY, N. E., Medicine
KIEHN, T. E., Medicine (Clinical and Clinical Microbiology)
KLEIN, H., Medicine
KLIGFIELD, P. D., Medicine
KOLESNICK, R. N., Medicine
KRIS, M. G., Medicine
KROWN, S. E., Medicine
KURTZ, R. C., Medicine (Clinical)
LACHS, M. S., Medicine
LAURENCE, J. C., Medicine
LERMAN, B. B., Medicine
LIPKIN, M., Medicine
LIVINGSTON, P. O., Medicine
LOCKSHIN, M. D., Medicine
MCCORMICK, B., Medicine (Radiation Oncology)
MARCUS, A. J., Medicine
MARKENSON, J. A., Medicine (Clinical)
MARKS, P. A., Medicine
MAYER, K., Medicine (Clinical)
MESSINEO, F., Medicine (Clinical)
MEYER, B. R., Medicine (Clinical)
MINSKY, B., Medicine (Radiation Oncology)
MOORE, A., Medicine (Clinical)
MOTZER, R. J., Medicine
MURRAY, H. W., Medicine
NACHMAN, R. L., Medicine
NANUS, D. M., Medicine (Haematology, Oncology)
NIMER, S. D., Medicine
NORTON, L., Medicine
OETTGEN, H. F., Medicine
OFFIT, K., Medicine
OKIN, P. M., Medicine
PAGET, S. A., Medicine
PAMER, E. G., Medicine
PAPE, J. W., Medicine
PECKER, M. S., Medicine (Clinical)
PFISTER, D. G., Medicine
PORTLOCK, C. S., Medicine (Clinical)
POSNETT, D. N., Medicine
PRITCHETT, R. A. R., Medicine (Clinical)
RAHAL, J. J., Medicine
RIGGIO, R. R., Medicine (Clinical)
RIVLIN, R. S., Medicine
ROBBINS, R. J., Medicine
ROBERTS, R. B., Medicine
ROMAN, M. J., Medicine
ROSEN, N., Medicine
ROSENFELD, I., Medicine (Clinical)
SAAL, S. D., Medicine (Clinical)
SALMON, J. E., Medicine
SALTZ, L. B., Medicine
SCHEIDT, S., Medicine (Clinical)
SCHEINBERG, D. A., Medicine
SCHER, H. I., Medicine
SCHUSTER, M. W., Medicine (Clinical)
SEPKOWITZ, K. A., Medicine
SHIKE, M., Medicine
SILVER, R. T., Medicine
SMITH, K. A., Medicine
SPRIGGS, D. R., Medicine
STEINBERG, C. R., Medicine (Clinical)
STEINGART, R. M., Medicine
STOVER, D. E., Medicine (Clinical)
STRAUS, D. J., Medicine (Clinical)
SUTHANTHIRAN, M., Medicine
THOMAS, H. M., III, Medicine (Clinical)
WADLER, S., Medicine
WEINSTEIN, A. M., Medicine
WEKSLER, B. B., Medicine
WEKSLER, M. E., Medicine
WHITE, D. A., Medicine
WINAWER, S. J., Medicine
WITTES, R., Medicine
WUEST, D. L., Medicine (Pathology in Clinical)
YAHALOM, J., Medicine (Radiation Oncology)

Microbiology and Immunology:

BARANY, F., Microbiology and Immunology
BROT, N., Microbiology and Immunology
COICO, R., Microbiology and Immunology (Education)
DING, A., Microbiology and Immunology
FALCK-PEDERSEN, E., Microbiology and Immunology
HOLLOMAN, W. K., Microbiology and Immunology
MOORE, J. P., Microbiology and Immunology
NAQI, S. A., Microbiology and Immunology (Education)
NATHAN, C., Microbiology and Immunology

Neurological Surgery:

GUTIN, P. H., Neurological Surgery
STEIG, P. E., Neurological Surgery

Neurology and Neuroscience:

APPEL, S. H., Neurology
BAKER, H., Neuroscience
BEAL, M. F., Neurology and Neuroscience
BLASBERG, R. G., Neurology
BLASS, J., Neurology and Neuroscience
BROOKS, D. C., Neurology and Neuroscience (Anatomy)
CARONNA, J. J., Neurology (Clinical)
DANNON, M. J., Neurology (Clinical)
DEANGELIS, L. M., Neurology (Clinical)
FOLEY, K. M., Neurology and Neuroscience
GIBSON, G. E., Neuroscience
IADECOLA, C., Neurology and Neuroscience
LABAR, D. R., Neurology and Neuroscience
LATOV, N., Neurology and Neuroscience
MCDOWELL, F. H., Neurology and Neuroscience
MILNER, T. A., Neuroscience
PASTERNAK, G. W., Neurology and Neuroscience
PETITO, F. A., Neurology (Clinical)
PICKEL, V. M., Neuroscience
POLLACK, C. P., Neurology (Clinical)
POSNER, J. B., Neurology and Neuroscience
RATAN, R. R., Neurology and Neuroscience
ROSS, M. E., Neurology and Neuroscience
RUBIN, M., Neurology (Clinical)
VICTOR, J. D., Neurology and Neuroscience
VOLPE, B. T., Neurology and Neuroscience
WAGNER, J. A., Neurology and Neuroscience

Obstetrics and Gynaecology:

CAPUTO, T. A., Obstetrics and Gynaecology (Clinical)
CHERVENAK, F. A., Obstetrics and Gynaecology
GOSDEN, R. G., Obstetrics and Gynaecology
LIU, H.-C., Obstetrics and Gynaecology (Reproductive Medicine)
POST, R. C., Obstetrics and Gynaecology (Clinical)
ROSENWAKS, Z., Obstetrics and Gynaecology
SAXENA, B. B., Obstetrics and Gynaecology (Endocrinology)
SPITZER, M., Obstetrics and Gynaecology (Clinical)
WITKIN, S. S., Obstetrics and Gynaecology (Immunology)

Ophthalmology:

ABRAMSON, D. H., Ophthalmology
COLEMAN, D. J., Ophthalmology
RODRIGUEZ-BOULAN, E. J., Ophthalmology (Cell and Developmental Biology)
SILVERMAN, R. H., Ophthalmology (Computer Science)

Orthopaedic Surgery:

BURKE, G. W., Orthopaedic Surgery (Clinical)
CORNELL, C. N., Orthopaedic Surgery (Clinical)
CRAIG, E. V., Orthopaedic Surgery (Clinical)
HEALEY, J. H., Orthopaedic Surgery
HELFET, D. L., Orthopaedic Surgery
LANE, J. M., Orthopaedic Surgery
LASKIN, R. S., Orthopaedic Surgery (Clinical)
PELLICI, P. M., Orthopaedic Surgery (Clinical)
ROOT, L., Orthopaedic Surgery (Clinical)
SALVATI, E. A., Orthopaedic Surgery (Clinical)
SCULCO, T. P., Orthopaedic Surgery (Clinical)
TORZILLI, P. A., Orthopaedic Surgery (Applied Biomechanics)
WARREN, R. F., Orthopaedic Surgery
WEILAND, A. J., Orthopaedic Surgery (Plastic)
WICKIEWICZ, T. L., Orthopaedic Surgery (Clinical)
WILSON, P. D., Jr, Orthopaedic Surgery
WINDSOR, R. E., Orthopaedic Surgery (Clinical)
WOLFE, S. W., Orthopaedic Surgery
WRIGHT, T. M., Orthopaedic Surgery (Applied Biomechanics)

Otorhinolaryngology:

SELESNICK, S. H., Otorhinolaryngology

Paediatrics:

BROMBERG, K., Paediatrics
BUSSEL, J. B., Paediatrics
CHUTORIAN, A. B., Paediatrics
COOPER, R. S., Ophthalmology
CUNNINGHAM-RUNDLES, S., Paediatrics (Immunology)
GERMAN, J. L., Paediatrics
GERSONY, W. M., Paediatrics
GIARDINA, P. V., Paediatrics (Clinical)
GLASS, L., Paediatrics
GREENWALD, B. M., Paediatrics (Clinical)
HILGARTNER, M. W., Paediatrics
KLEIN, A. A., Paediatrics (Clinical)
KOSOFSKY, B., Paediatrics
KRAUSS, A. N., Paediatrics (Clinical)
LEHMAN, T. J. A., Paediatrics (Clinical)
LOUGHLIN, G. M., Paediatrics
MENDEZ, H. A., Paediatrics (Clinical)
MOSCONA, A., Paediatrics
O'REILLY, R. J., Paediatrics
PERLMAN, J. M., Paediatrics
RAJEGOWDA, B., Paediatrics (Clinical)
RUBIN, D. H., Paediatrics (Clinical)
SOLOMON, G. E., Paediatrics (Clinical/Neurology)
STEINHERZ, P. G., Paediatrics

Pathology and Laboratory Medicine:

AKHTAR, M., Pathology and Laboratory Medicine
ALONSO, D. R., Pathology and Laboratory Medicine
BAERGEN, R., Pathology and Laboratory Medicine (Clinical)
BARRIOS, R., Pathology and Laboratory Medicine

BULLOUGH, P. G., Pathology and Laboratory Medicine
BURKE, M. D., Pathology and Laboratory Medicine
CAGLE, P. T., Pathology and Laboratory Medicine
CHADBURN, A., Pathology and Laboratory Medicine
CHAGANTI, R. S. K., Pathology and Laboratory Medicine (Genetics)
CHEN, Y. T., Pathology and Laboratory Medicine
CHEN-KIANG, S., Pathology and Laboratory Medicine
ELLENSON, L. H., Pathology and Laboratory Medicine
HAJJAR, D. P., Pathology and Laboratory Medicine
HODA, S. A. F., Pathology and Laboratory Medicine (Clinical)
HUVOS, A. G., Pathology and Laboratory Medicine
JONES, J. G., Pathology and Laboratory Medicine
KLIMSTRA, D. S., Pathology and Laboratory Medicine
KNOWLES, D. M., Pathology and Laboratory Medicine
LAND, G. A., Pathology and Laboratory Medicine (Clinical)
LAVI, E., Pathology and Laboratory Medicine
LEONARD, D. G. B., Pathology and Laboratory Medicine
LIEBERMAN, M. W., Pathology and Laboratory Medicine
LIPMAN, N. S., Pathology and Laboratory Medicine (Veterinary Medicine)
MCNUTT, N. S., Pathology and Laboratory Medicine
MODY, D. R., Pathology and Laboratory Medicine
MULLER, W. A., Pathology and Laboratory Medicine
PEERSCHKE, E. I. B., Pathology and Laboratory Medicine
PETROVIC, L. M., Pathology and Laboratory Medicine
REUTER, V. E., Pathology and Laboratory Medicine
ROSEN, P. P., Pathology and Laboratory Medicine
ROSENBLUM, M., Pathology and Laboratory Medicine
SALEEM, A., Pathology and Laboratory Medicine (Clinical)
SESHAN, S. V., Pathology and Laboratory Medicine (Clinical)
TRUONG, L. D., Pathology and Laboratory Medicine (Clinical)
WOLF, C. F. W., Pathology and Laboratory Medicine (Clinical)

Pharmacology:

BUCK, J., Pharmacology
GROSS, S. S., Pharmacology
GUDAS, L. J., Pharmacology
INTURRISI, C., Pharmacology
LEVI, R., Pharmacology
OKAMOTO, M., Pharmacology
REIDENBERG, M. M., Pharmacology
RIFKIND, A. B., Pharmacology
SZETO, H. H., Pharmacology
TOTH, M., Pharmacology

Physiology and Biophysics:

ANDERSEN, O. S., Physiology and Biophysics
GARDNER, D., Physiology and Biophysics
GRAFSTEIN, B., Physiology and Biophysics
HUANG, X., Physiology and Biophysics
MAACK, T., Physiology and Biophysics
MEHLER, E. L., Physiology and Biophysics
PALMER, L. G., Physiology and Biophysics
RAMIREZ, F., Physiology and Biophysics
ROUX, B., Physiology and Biophysics
WEINSTEIN, H., Physiology and Biophysics
WINDHAGER, E. E., Physiology and Biophysics

Psychiatry:

ADDONIZIO, G. C., Psychiatry (Clinical)
ALEXOPOULOS, G. S., Psychiatry
AUCHINCLOSS, E. L., Psychiatry (Clinical)
BARCHAS, J. D., Psychiatry
BREITBART, W., Psychiatry
BRUCE, M. L., Psychiatry (Sociology)
CAMPBELL, S. S., Psychiatry (Psychology)
CASEY, B. J., Psychiatry (Developmental Psychobiology)
CLARKIN, J. F., Psychiatry (Clinical Psychology)
FERRANDO, S. J., Psychiatry (Clinical)
FRIEDMAN, R. A., Psychiatry (Clinical)
GEARY, N. D., Psychiatry (Psychology)
GIBBS, J. A., Jr, Psychiatry
HALMI, K. A., Psychiatry
HERTZIG, M. E., Psychiatry
HOLLAND, J. C. B., Psychiatry
KERNBERG, O. F., Psychiatry
KERNBERG, P. F., Psychiatry
KOCSIS, J. H., Psychiatry
LEDERBERG, M. S., Psychiatry (Clinical)
LEON, A. C., Psychiatry (Biostatistics)
MATTSON, M. R. A., Psychiatry (Clinical)
MEYERS, B. S., Psychiatry
PARDES, H., Psychiatry
PFEFFER, C. R., Psychiatry
POSNER, M. I., Psychiatry (Psychology)
SACKS, M. H., Psychiatry
SCHULBERG, H. C., Psychiatry (Psychology)
SHAMOIAN, C. A., Psychiatry (Clinical)
TARDIFF, K., Psychiatry
WILSON, P. G., Psychiatry (Clinical)
YOUNG, R. C., Psychiatry

Public Health:

BEGG, C. B., Public Health (Biostatistics)
BOTVIN, G. J., Public Health (Psychology)
DRUSIN, L. M., Public Health (Clinical)
FINKEL, M. L., Public Health (Clinical)
MILLMAN, R. B., Public Health
MUSHLIN, A. I., Public Health
RUCHLIN, H. S., Public Health (Economics)

Radiology:

ABRAMSON, S. J., Radiology (Clinical)
ADLER, R., Radiology
AMOLS, H. I., Radiology (Physics)
ANDERSON, L. L., Radiology (Physics)
AUH, Y. H., Radiology
BECKER, D. V., Radiology
BRILL, P., Radiology
CARAVELLI, J. F., Radiology (Clinical)
COHEN, M. A., Radiology (Clinical)
DECK, M. D. F., Radiology
DERSHAW, D. D., Radiology
DIVGI, C. R., Radiology
FINN, R. D., Radiology (Physics)
GAMSU, G., Radiology
GOBIN, Y. P., Radiology
GOLDSMITH, S. J., Radiology
HANN, L. E., Radiology
HEELAN, R. T., Radiology
HEIER, L. A., Radiology (Clinical)
HENSCHKE, C. I., Radiology
HERZOG, R. J., Radiology
HRICAK, H., Radiology
KOUTHCER, J. A., Radiology
KROL, G., Radiology (Clinical)
LARSON, S., Radiology
LI, G. C., Radiology (Biophysics)
LIBERMAN, L., Radiology
LING, C. C., Radiology (Physics)
MCCAULEY, D., Radiology (Clinical)
NORI, D., Radiology (Clinical)
PANICEK, D. M., Radiology
PAVLOV, H., Radiology
POTTER, M. R., Radiology
PRINCE, M. R., Radiology
ROSEN, N. S., Radiology (Clinical)
ROSENBLATT, R., Radiology (Clinical)
SOS, T. A., Radiology
SOSTMAN, H. D., Radiology
STRAUSS, H. W., Radiology
VALLABHAJOSULA, S., Radiology (Radiopharmacy)
WINCHESTER, P., Radiology
YANKELEVITZ, D. F., Radiology
ZAIDER, M., Radiology (Physics)
ZIMMERMAN, R. D., Radiology

Rehabilitation Medicine:

LIEBERMAN, J. S., Rehabilitation Medicine
O'DELL, M. W., Rehabilitation Medicine (Clinical)

Surgery:

BAINS, M. S., Surgery (Clinical)
BARIE, P. S., Surgery
BARONE, J. E., Surgery (Clinical)
BESSEY, P. Q., Surgery
BLUMGART, L. H., Surgery
BRENNAN, M. F., Surgery
CHASSIN, J. L., Surgery (Clinical)
CODY, H. S., III, Surgery (Clinical)
CORDEIRO, P. G., Surgery
EISENBERG, M. M., Surgery
FONG, Y., Surgery
GAGNER, M., Surgery
HURYN, J. M., Surgery (Clinical Oral and Maxillofacial Surgery)
ISRAEL, H. A., Surgery (Clinical)
KENT, K. C., Surgery
LAQUAGLIA, M. P., Surgery
MICHELASSI, F., Surgery
MILSOM, J. W., Surgery
OSBORNE, M. P., Surgery
PETREK, J. A., Surgery
PIZZI, W. F., Surgery (Clinical)
RUSCH, V. W., Surgery
SHAH, J. P., Surgery (Clinical)
SHAHA, A. R., Surgery
SMITH, B. H., Surgery (Clinical)
STAIANO-COICO, L., Surgery (Microbiology)
STOLAR, C. J., Surgery
STUBENBORD, W. T., Surgery
WISE, L., Surgery
WONG, G. Y., Surgery (Statistics)
WONG, W. D., Surgery
YURT, R. W., Surgery

Urology:

BANDER, N. H., Urology
GOLDSTEIN, M., Urology
GUILLONNEAU, B., Urology
HERR, H. W., Urology
SCARDINO, P. T., Urology
SCHLEGEL, P. N., Urology
SHEINFELD, J., Urology
SOGANI, P. C., Urology (Clinical)
VAUGHAN, E. D., Urology

Johnson Graduate School of Management (Sage Hall, Ithaca, NY 14853; tel. (607) 255-4526; fax (607) 255-0065; e-mail mba@cornell.edu; internet www.johnson.cornell.edu):

BENDANIEL, D.
BIERMAN, H., Jr
BLOOMFIELD, R.
DYCKMAN, T.
FRANK, R.
HART, S.
HASS, J.
HILTON, R.
ISEN, A.
JARROW, R.
LEE, C.
LIBBY, R.
MCADAMS, A.
MCCLAIN, J.
MICHAELY, R.
NELSON, M.
O'HARA, M.
ORMAN, L.
RAO, V.
RUSSO, J.
SMIDT, S.
SWAMINATHAN, B.
SWIERINGA, R.
THOMAS, L.
WALDMAN, M.

Law School (Myron Taylor Hall, Ithaca, NY 14853-4901; tel. (607) 255-0565; e-mail lawadmit@law.mail.cornell.edu; internet www.lawschool.cornell.edu):

ALEXANDER, G.
BARCELO, J., III
CLERMONT, K. M.
CLYMER, S.
EISENBERG, T.
FARINA, C.
GARVEY, S.
GERMAIN, C.
GREEN, R.
HAY, G. A.
HEISE, M.
HENDERSON, J., Jr
HILLMAN, R.
HOLDEN-SMITH, B.
JOHNSON, S. L.
LASSER, M.
LEHMAN, J.
MARTIN, P. W.
NDULO, M.
RACHLINSKI, J.
RILES, A.
ROSSI, F. F.
SCHWAB, S.
SHERWIN, E.
SHIFFRIN, S.
SILICIANO, J.
SIMSON, G. J.
SUMMERS, R. S.
TAYLOR, W.
WIPPMAN, D.

New York State College of Agriculture and Life Sciences (260 Roberts Hall, Ithaca, NY 14853-4203; tel. (607) 255-2241; e-mail als_admissions@cornell.edu; internet www.cals.cornell.edu):

Animal Science:

AUSTIC, R.
BAUMAN, D.
BELL, A.
BLAKE, R.
BUTLER, W.
CHASE, L.
CURRIE, W.
EVERETT, R.
FOX, D.
GALTON, D.
GOREWIT, R.
HINTZ, H.
JOHNSON, P.
OLTENACU, P.
PARKS, J.
PELL, A.
POLLAK, E.
QUAAS, R.
THONNEY, M.

Applied Economics and Management:

BARRETT, C.
BILLS, N.
BOISVERT, R.
CHAPMAN, L.
CHRISTY, R.
CONRAD, J.
KAISER, H.
KANBUR, R.
KNOBLAUCH, W.
LADUE, E.
LEE, D.
LESSER, W.
MCLAUGHLIN, E.
MOUNT, T.
NOVAKOVIC, A.
RAJ, S.
SCHULZE, W.
STREEFER, D.
TAUER, L.
WANSINK, B.
WHITE, G.

Biological and Environmental Engineering:

ALBRIGHT, L.
ANESHANSLEY, D.
COOKE, J.
DATTA, A.
GEBREMEDHIN, K.
HAITH, D.
JEWELL, W.
PARLANGE, J.-Y.
SCOTT, N.
SPANSWICK, R.
STEENHUIS, T.
TIMMONS, M.
WALKER, L.
WALTER, M.

Communication:

BOOTH, J.
GAY, G.
OSTMAN, R.
WALTHER, J.

Crop and Soil Sciences:

CHERNEY, J.
COX, W.
DEGLORIA, S.
DUXBURY, J.
FICK, G.
MCBRIDE, M.
OBENDORF, R.
SETTER, T.
VAN ES, H.

Developmental Sociology:

BROWN, D.
EBERTS, P.
FELDMAN, S.
GEISLER, C.
GURAK, D.
HIRSCHL, T.
LYSON, T.
MCMICHAEL, P.
PFEFFER, M.

Earth and Atmospheric Sciences:

COLUCCI, S.
COOK, K.
RIHA, S.
WILKS, D.

Ecology and Evolutionary Biology:

CHABOT, B.
DHONDT, A.
FEENY, P.
FITZPATRICK, J.
HARRISON, R.
HARVELL, C.
HOWARTH, R.
MCCLURE, P.
MARKS, P.
MORIN, J.
ROOT, R.
WINKLER, D.

Education:

CAFFARELLA, R.
CAMP, W.

Entomology:

AGNELLO, A.
HOFFMANN, M.
LIEBHERR, J.
NYROP, J.
PECKARSKY, B.
REISSIG, W.
ROELOFS, W.
RUTZ, D.
SCOTT, J.
SHELTON, A.
SHIELDS, E.
SODERLUND, D.
STRAUB, R.
TINGEY, W.

Food Science:

ACREE, T.
BARBANO, D.
BATT, C.
BRADY, J., Jr
DURST, R.
GRAVANI, R.
HANG, Y.
HOTCHKISS, J.
HRADZINA, G.
LAWLESS, H.
LEE, C.
MILLER, D.
REGENSTEIN, J.
RIZVI, S.
SIEBERT, K.

Horticultural Sciences:

BROWN, S.
HARMAN, G.
LAKSO, A.
POOL, R.
REISCH, B.
TAYLOR, A.

Horticulture:

BASSUK, N.
BELLINDER, R.
BRIDGEN, M.
GOOD, G.
MILLER, W.
PETROVIC, A.
PRITTS, M.
WAKKINS, C.
WEILER, T.
WIEN, H.
WOLFE, D.

International Programmes:

UPHOFF, N.

Landscape Architecture:

ADLEMAN, M.
GLEASON, K.
GOTTFRIED, H.
TRANCIK, R.
TROWBRIDGE, P.

Microbiology:

GHIORSE, W.
HELMANN, J.
WINANS, S.
ZINDER, S.

Molecular Biology and Genetics:

CALVO, J.
FOX, T.
GOLDBERG, M.
HANSON, M.
HENRY, S.
KEMPHUES, K.
LIS, J.
MACINTYRE, R.
ROBERTS, J.
SHALLOWAY, D.
TYE, B.
VOGT, V.
WU, R.

Natural Resources:

DECKER, D.
FAHEY, T.
GILLETT, J.
HULLAR, T.
KNUTH, B.
KRASNY, M.
LASSOIE, J.
MILLS, E.

Neurobiology and Behaviour:

ADLER, K.
BRADBURY, J.
EISNER, T.
EMLEN, S.
HARRIS-WARRICK, R.
HOPKINS, C.
VEHRENCAMP, S.
WALCOTT, C.

Nutrition:

BENSADOUN, A.
LEVITSKY, D.
NOY, N.
PINSTRUP-ANDERSON, P.

Plant Biology:

BATES, D.
CREPET, W.
DAVIES, P.
DOYLE, J.

NASRALLAH, J.
NASRALLAH, M.
NIKLAS, K.
RODRIGUEZ, E.

Plant Breeding:

COFFMAN, W. R.
EARLE, E.
JOHN, M.
KRESOVICH, S.
MCCOUCH, S.
MUTSCHLER, M.
SORRELLS, M.
TANKSLEY, S.
VIANDS, D.

Plant Pathology:

ABAWI, G.
ALDWINCKLE, H.
BEER, S.
BERGSTROM, G.
BURR, T.
COLLMER, A.
DILLARD, H.
FRY, W.
HOCH, H.
HUDLER, G.
KOELLER, W.
LAZAROWITZ, S.
LORBEER, J.
LORIA, R.
MARTIN, G.
MILGROOM, M.
ROSENBERGER, D.
SEEM, R.
WILCOX, W.
ZITTER, T.

New York State College of Human Ecology (Martha Van Rensselaer Hall, Ithaca, NY 14853; tel. (607) 255-2216; fax (607) 255-3794; e-mail humec_admissions@cornell.edu; internet www.human.cornell.edu):

Design and Environmental Analysis:

BECKER, F.
ESHELMAN, P.
EVANS, G.
HEDGE, A.
JENNINGS, J.
LAQUATRA, J., Jr
SIMS, W.

Human Development and Family Studies:

BRUMBERG, J.
CECI, S.
COCHRAN, M.
DEPUE, R.
ECKENRODE, J.
GABARINO, J.
HAMILTON, S.
LUST, B.
PILLEMER, K.
ROBERTSON, S.
SAVIN-WILLIAMS, R.
WILLIAMS, W.

Nutrition:

BISOGNI, C.
BRANNON, P.
BRENNA, J.
GARZA, C.
HAAS, J.
HABICHT, J.-P.
OLSON, C.
PELTO, G.
RASMUSSEN, K.
SAHN, D.
STIPANUK, M.

Policy Analysis and Management:

AVERY, R.
BATTISTELLA, R.
BURKHAUSER, R.
GERNER, J.
KENTEL, D.
MATHIOS, A.
PARROT, A.
PETERS, H.
TROCHIM, W.
WHITE, W.

Textiles and Apparel:

CHU, CH.-CH.
LEMLEY, A.
LOKER, S.
NETRAVALI, A.
OBENDORF, S.

New York State College of Industrial and Labour Relations

Collective Bargaining:

DANIEL, C.
GROSS, J.
HURD, R.
KAHN, L.
KATZ, H.
KURUVILLA, S.
LIPSKY, D.
SALVATORE, N.
TURNER, L.

Employment and Disability Institute:

BRUYERE, S.

Human Resource Studies:

BRIGGS, V., Jr
DYER, L.
SNELL, S.
WRIGHT, P.

Labour Economics:

ABOWD, J.
BLAU, F.
BOYER, G.
EHRENBERG, R.
FIELDS, G.
HUTCHENS, R.
SMITH, R.

Organizational Behaviour:

BACHARACH, S.
HAMMER, T.
LAWLER, E.
TOLBERT, P.

Social Statistics:

DICICCIO, T.
WELLS, M.

New York State College of Veterinary Medicine (Ithaca, NY 14853-6401; tel. (607) 253-3000; fax (607) 253-3709; e-mail vet_admissions@cornell.edu; internet www.vet.cornell.edu):

Biomedical Sciences:

BEYENBACH, K.
DELAHUNTA, A.
FARNUM, C.
FORTUNE, J.
GILMOUR, R., Jr
HOUPT, K.
KOTLIKOFF, M.
LOEW, E.
MINOR, R.
NODEN, D.
QUARONI, A.
SCHIMENTI, J.
SCHLAFER, D.
SUAREZ, S.
SUMMERS, B.
YEN, A.

Clinical Sciences:

AINSWORTH, D.
BARR, S.
CENTER, S.
DIVERS, T.
DUCHARME, N.
FUBINI, S.
GILBERT, R.
GLEED, R.
HACKETT, R.
HORNBUCKLE, W.
KALLFELZ, F.
KOLLIAS, G., Jr
LUDDERS, J.
MILLER, W.
MOISE, N.
NIXON, A.
PAGE, R.
RANDOLPH, J.
SCOTT, D.
SMITH, D.
TENNANT, B.

Microbiology, Immunology and Parasitology:

ANTCZAK, D.
APPLETON, J.
BAINES, J.
BLOOM, S.
BOWMAN, D.
BOWSER, P.
DIETERT, R.
LUST, G.
MCGREGOR, D.
MARSH, J.
PARRISH, C.
RUSSELL, D.
SCHAT, K.

Molecular Medicine:

CERIONE, R.
GUAN, J.
OSWALD, R.
PAULI, B.
SCHWARK, W.
SHARP, G.
WEILAND, G.

Population Medicine and Diagnostic Services:

CHANG, Y.-F.
ERB, H.
GROHN, Y.
MOHAMMED, H.
SCHUKKEN, Y.
TORRES, A.
WHITE, M.

School of Hotel Administration (Statler Hall, Ithaca, NY 14853; tel. (607) 255-9393; fax (607) 255-4179; e-mail sha_student_svcs@cornell.edu; internet www.hotelschool.cornell.edu):

BROWNELL, J.
CORGEL, J.
DITTMAN, D.
ENZ, C.
GELLER, A.
HINKIN, T.
KIMES, S.
MUTKOSKI, S.
PENNER, R.
REDLIN, M.
SIGUAW, J.
THOMPSON, G.

CULINARY INSTITUTE OF AMERICA

1946 Campus Dr., Hyde Park, NY 12538-1499

Telephone: (845) 452-9600
Internet: www.ciachef.edu

Campuses at: Hyde Park, NY, and St Helena, CA.

Founded 1946 as New Haven Restaurant Institute, present name 1951
Private control

Pres.: Dr TIM RYAN
Vice Pres. for Enrollment Management: DRUSILLA BLACKMAN
Sr Vice-Pres. for Finance and Admin.: CHARLES A. O'MARA
Vice-Pres. for Academic Affairs: Dr. PETER RAINSFORD
Vice-Pres. for Greystone and Continuing Education: MARK ERICKSON
Vice-Pres. for Human Resources: DAVID JASKIEWICZ
Vice-Pres. for Marketing and Strategy: BRUCE D. HILLENBRAND
Library of 84,000 vols
Number of teachers: 150
Number of students: 2,900

DAEMEN COLLEGE

4380 Main St, Amherst, NY 14226
Telephone: (716) 839-3600
Fax: (716) 839-8516
E-mail: admissions@daemen.edu
Internet: www.daemen.edu

Founded 1947 as Rosary Hill College; name changed 1976

Liberal arts and sciences

Pres.: Dr MARTIN J. ANISMAN
Dean: EDWIN CLAUSEN

Library of 135,000 vols
Number of teachers: 120
Number of students: 1,900

DAVIS COLLEGE

400 Riverside Dr., Johnson City, NY 13790
Telephone: (607) 729-1581
Fax: (607) 729-2962
E-mail: info@davisny.edu
Internet: www.davisny.edu

Founded 1900 as a Bible institute; Practical Bible College 1993; present name 2004
Private control
Academic year: August to May

Pres.: Dr GEORGE D. MILLER, III
Exec. Vice-Pres.: Dr GARY SMITH
Vice-Pres. for Academic Affairs: Dr GILBERT PARKER
Vice-Pres. for Business Affairs: SPENCER KEY
Vice-President for Institutional Advancement: MARSHALL SORBER
Vice-Pres. for Student Devt: RICK CRAMER
Librarian: Dr GERALD FRANZ

Number of teachers: 16
Number of students: 300

DOMINICAN COLLEGE

470 Western Highway, Orangeburg, NY 10962
Telephone: (845) 359-7800
Fax: (845) 359-2313
E-mail: admissions@dc.edu
Internet: www.dc.edu

Founded 1952
Private control
Academic year: August to May

Pres.: Sis. MARY EILEEN O'BRIEN
Chancellor for External Affairs: Sis. KATHLEEN SULLIVAN
Vice-Pres. for Academic Affairs and Academic Dean: JOHN F. M. FLYNN
Vice-Pres. for Enrollment Management: BRIAN G. FERNANDES
Vice-Pres. for Financial Affairs: CATHLEEN KENNY
Vice-Pres. for Institutional Advancement: DOROTHY CHRISTINE FILORAMO
Vice-Pres. for Student Devt and Dean of Students: DOHN E. HARSHBARGER
Registrar: MARY MCFADDEN
Head Librarian: JOHN BARRIE

Library of 102,000 vols
Number of teachers: 40
Number of students: 1,855

DIRECTORS

Allied Health Div.: Dr Sis. BERYL HERDT
Arts and Sciences Div.: Dr WILLIAM HURST
Business Admin. Div.: JOHN SPILLNER
Nursing Div.: Dr MAUREEN CREEGAN
Social Sciences Div.: Dr BARBARA SOCOR
Teacher Education Div.: Dr MARIE PAGLIARO

DOWLING COLLEGE

Idle Hour Blvd, Oakdale, NY 11769
Telephone: (631) 244-3000
Fax: (631) 563-9681
E-mail: admissions@dowling.edu
Internet: www.dowling.edu

Founded 1968
Private control

Schools of arts and science, aviation, business, education

Pres.: ROBERT J. GAFFNEY
Provost: Dr LINDA ARDITO

Number of teachers: 450
Number of students: 7,000 (undergraduate and postgraduate)

D'YOUVILLE COLLEGE

320 Porter Ave, Buffalo, NY 14201-9985
Telephone: (716) 829-8000
Internet: www.dyc.edu

Founded 1908 by the Grey Nuns of the Sacred Heart

Pres.: Sister DENISE A. ROCHE
Sr Vice-Pres.: RICHARD WIESEN
Vice-Pres. for Student Affairs: ROBERT P. MURPHY
Registrar: DION DALY
Dir of Admissions: RONALD H. DANNECKER
Librarian: MARC BAYER

Library of 127,000 vols
Number of teachers: 85
Number of students: 1,900

First degree courses in business, education, humanities, management, natural sciences, nursing, occupational therapy, pre-professional programmes, social sciences; graduate degrees in community health, nursing, occupational therapy, physical therapy, physician assistance.

ELMIRA COLLEGE

1 Park Pl., Elmira, NY 14901
Telephone: (607) 735-1800
E-mail: admissions@elmira.edu
Internet: www.elmira.edu

Founded 1855
Private control
Academic year: September to June

Pres.: Dr THOMAS K. MEIER
Academic Vice-Pres.: Dr BRYAN D. REDDICK
Vice-Pres. and Dean of Student Life: JULIANNE BAUMANN
Vice-Pres. for Devt and Dean: SHERRI TROCINO
Vice-Pres., Dir of Athletics and Health Services and Dean: PATRICIA THOMPSON
Dir of Library: ELIZABETH WAVLE

Library of 335,506 vols
Number of teachers: 78
Number of students: 1,200 full-time

Publications: *New Novel Review* (1 a year), *Quarry Farm Papers* (irregular).

EXCELSIOR COLLEGE

7 Columbia Circle, Albany, NY 12203-5159
Telephone: (518) 464-8500
E-mail: admissions@excelsior.edu
Internet: www.excelsior.edu

Pres.: JOHN F. EBERSOLE
Provost and Chief Academic Officer: DANA OFFERMAN
Number of students: 20,485

FIVE TOWNS COLLEGE

305 North Service Rd, Dix Hills, NY 11746-5871
Telephone: (631) 424-7000 ext 110
E-mail: info@ftc.edu
Internet: www.fivetowns.edu

Founded 1972
Private control

Pres.: Dr STANLEY G. COHEN
Vice-Pres. and Provost: DAVID M. COHEN
Number of teachers: 83
Number of students: 1,038

FORDHAM UNIVERSITY

Fordham Rd, Bronx, NY 10458
Telephone: (718) 817-1000
Fax: (718) 817-4925
E-mail: publicaff@fordham.edu
Internet: www.fordham.edu

Founded 1841 by Rt Rev. John Hughes, first Roman Catholic Archbishop of New York, as St John's College; inc. as a univ. 1846; name changed to Fordham Univ. 1907
Academic year: July to June

Pres.: Rev. JOSEPH M. MCSHANE
Sr Vice-Pres. and Chief Financial Officer: JOHN J. LORDAN
Vice-Pres. for Academic Affairs: JUDITH MILLS
Vice-Pres. for Admin.: BRIAN J. BYRNE
Vice-Pres. for Devt and Univ. Relations: ALBERT R. CHECCIO
Vice-Pres. for Enrollment: PETER A. STACE
Vice-Pres. for Finance: FRANK SIMIO
Vice-Pres. for Student Affairs: JEFFREY L. GRAY
Vice-Pres. for Technology: FRANK SIRIANNI
Vice-Pres. for Univ. Mission and Min.: Rev. JOSEPH QUINN
Registrar: KENNETH POKROWSKI
Dir of Libraries: Dr JAMES MCCABE

Library: 2m. vols
Number of teachers: 1,064
Number of students: 15,253

Publications: *International Philosophical Quarterly*, *Traditio* (1 a year)

DEANS

College of Business Admin.: Dr SHARON SMITH
Fordham College of Liberal Studies: Dr MICHAEL GILLAN
Fordham College at Lincoln Center: Rev. ROBERT GRIMES
Fordham College at Rose Hill: Dr BRENNAN O'DONNELL
Graduate School of Arts and Sciences: Dr NANCY BUSCH
Graduate School of Business Admin.: Dr SHARON SMITH
Graduate School of Education: Dr REGIS BERNHARDT
School of Law: WILLIAM TREANOR
Graduate School of Religion and Religious Education: Rev. VINCENT M. NOVAK
Graduate School of Social Service: Dr PETER VAUGHAN

HAMILTON COLLEGE

198 College Hill Rd, Clinton, NY 13323
Telephone: (315) 859-4011
Fax: (315) 859-4648
E-mail: admission@hamilton.edu
Internet: www.hamilton.edu

Founded 1793 as Hamilton-Oneida Academy; chartered as Hamilton College 1812
Academic year: September to May

Pres.: JOAN HINDE STEWART
Dean of Students: NANCY THOMPSON (acting)

Library of 500,000 vols
Number of teachers: 180
Number of students: 1,775

HARTWICK COLLEGE

1 Hartwick Dr., Oneonta, NY 13820-4020
Telephone: (607) 431-4000
Fax: (607) 431-4154
E-mail: admissions@hartwick.edu
Internet: www.hartwick.edu

Founded 1797
Private liberal arts college
Academic year: September to May

Pres.: Dr MARGARET L. DRUGOVICH
Vice-Pres. for Enrolment Management: DAVID B. CONWAY
Vice-Pres. for Finance and Chief Financial Officer: GEORGE ELLSBECK
Vice-Pres. for Institutional Advancement: JIM BROSCHART
Vice-Pres. for Student Affairs: Dr MEG NOWAK
Dir for Library: DAVID HEYDUK

Library of 355,776 vols
Number of teachers: 195 (103 full-time, 92 part-time)
Number of students: 1,473

HOBART AND WILLIAM SMITH COLLEGES

Geneva, NY 14456-3397
Telephone: (315) 781-3000
Fax: (315) 781-3400
E-mail: admissions@hws.edu
Internet: www.hws.edu

Liberal arts colleges
Founded 1822 (Hobart), 1908 (William Smith)
Academic year: September to May

Pres.: MARK D. GEARAN
Provost: TERESA AMOTT
Treas.: PETER POLINAK
Librarian: P. W. CRUMLISH

Library of 387,650 vols
Number of teachers: 207
Number of students: 1,928

Publications: *The Pulteney St Survey*, *The Seneca Review*

DEANS

Hobart: CLARENCE BUTLER
William Smith: DEBRA K. DEMEIS

HOFSTRA UNIVERSITY

144 Hofstra Univ., Hempstead, NY 11549-1000
Telephone: (516) 463-6800
Fax: (516) 463-6096
Internet: www.hofstra.edu

Founded 1935

Pres.: STUART RABINOWITZ
Provost and Sr Vice-Pres. for Academic Affairs: Dr HERMAN A. BERLINER
Sr Vice-Pres. for Planning and Admin.: Dr M. PATRICIA ADAMSKI
Vice-Pres. for Business Devt: RICHARD V. GUARDINO, Jr
Vice-Pres. for Devt: ALAN J. KELLY
Vice-Pres. for Financial Affairs and Treas.: CATHY HENNESSY
Vice-Pres. for Information Technology: ROBERT W. JUCKIEWICZ
Vice-Pres. for Legal Affairs: DOLORES FREDRICH
Vice-Pres. for Student Affairs: SANDRA S. JOHNSON
Vice-Pres. for Univ. Relations: MELISSA KANE CONNOLLY
Assoc. Dean of Students: LYNDA O'MALLEY
Dean of Library and Information Services: Dr DANIEL R. RUBEY (acting)
Dir of Intercollegiate Athletics: JACK HAYES

Library: 1.1m. vols
Number of teachers: 1,256
Number of students: 13,000

DEANS

Frank G. Zarb School of Business: Dr RALPH POLIMENI
School of Communication: Dr SYBIL DELGAUDIO
School of Education and Allied Human Services: Dr JAMES R. JOHNSON
School of Law: AARON TWERSKI
College of Liberal Arts and Sciences: Dr BERNARD J. FIRESTONE (acting)
New College and School for Univ. Studies: DAVID C. CHRISTMAN
Univ. College of Continuing Education: ROSANN KELLY

HOUGHTON COLLEGE

1 Willard Ave, Houghton, NY 14744
Telephone: (585) 567-9200
E-mail: admission@houghton.edu
Internet: www.houghton.edu

Founded 1883

Pres.: SHIRLEY MULLEN
Academic Dean: RON MAHURIN
Vice-Pres. for Finance: EFRAIN RIVERA
Vice-Pres. for Student Life: SHARRA HYNES
Vice-Pres. for Enrollment Management: WAYNE MACBETH
Dir of Records: MARGE AVERY
Dir of Library: DAVID STEVICK

Library of 246,000 vols
Number of teachers: 95
Number of students: 1,250.

BRANCH CAMPUS

Houghton College Suburban Campus: 910 Union Rd, West Seneca, NY 14224; tel. (716) 674-6363; Coordinator JOHN DURBIN.

IONA COLLEGE

715 N Ave, New Rochelle, NY 10801-1890
Telephone: (914) 633-2000
Fax: (914) 633-2018
E-mail: admissions@iona.edu
Internet: www.iona.edu

Founded 1940

Pres.: JAMES A. LIGOURI
Provost and Vice-Pres. for Academic Affairs: WARREN ROSENBERG
Vice-Pres. for Finance and Admin.: MARIE THORNTON
Vice-Provost for Student Devt: CHARLES CARLSON
Dir of Libraries: RICK PALLADINO

Library of 309,518 vols, 1,760 periodicals
Number of students: 4,303

DEANS

Dean of Columba School: Dr GLORIA MOLDOW
School of Arts and Sciences: WARREN ROSENBERG
School of Business: NICHOLAUS BEUTELL

ITHACA COLLEGE

100 Job Hall, Ithaca, NY 14850
Telephone: (607) 274-3124
Fax: (607) 274-1900
E-mail: admission@ithaca.edu
Internet: www.ithaca.edu

Founded 1892

Pres.: PEGGY R. WILLIAMS
Provost and Vice-Pres. for Academic Affairs: KATHLEEN ROUNTREE
Registrar: CHRISTOPHER KNAUER
Dean of Admissions: LARRY METZGER
College Librarian: LISABETH CHABOT

Library of 611,176 bound vols, and microforms, 2,541 periodical serial subscriptions
Number of teachers: 670 (460 full-time, 210 part-time)
Number of students: 6,409

Publication: *Ithaca College Quarterly*

DEANS

Athletics: ELIZABETH A. ALDEN
Roy H. Park School of Communications: THOMAS BOHN
School of Business: ROBERT ULLRICH
School of Health Sciences and Human Performance: RICHARD MILLER
School of Humanities and Sciences: HOWARD ERLICH
School of Music: ARTHUR OSTRANDER

JEWISH THEOLOGICAL SEMINARY

3080 Broadway, New York, NY 10027
Telephone: (212) 678-8000
Fax: (212) 678-8947
Internet: www.jtsa.edu

Founded 1886
Private control

Chancellor and Pres. of the Faculties: ARNOLD EISEN
Vice-Chancellor and Chief Operating Officer: Dr MICHAEL B. GREENBAUM
Vice-Chancellor for Institutional Advancement: CAROL DAVIDSON
Vice-Chancellor for Rabbinic Devt: Rabbi WILLIAM H. LEBEAU
Provost: Dr ALAN COOPER
Vice-Pres. for Student Affairs: JOSEPH A. BRODIE
Dean of Academic Affairs: Dr STEPHEN GARFINKEL
Library Dir: NAOMI M. STEINBERGER (acting).

JUILLIARD SCHOOL

60 Lincoln Center Plaza, New York, NY 10023
Telephone: (212) 799-5000
E-mail: admissions@juilliard.edu
Internet: www.juilliard.edu

Founded 1905

Pres.: JOSEPH W. POLISI
Provost and Dean: ARA GUZELIMIAN
Registrar: ELIZABETH BRUMMETT

Library of 68,000 music scores and 20,000 vols; record library: 25,000 long-playing records, CDs and tape recordings, 1,200 video cassettes
Number of teachers: 305 (incl. pre-college and evening div.)
Number of students: 1,425 (incl. pre-college and evening div.)

KEUKA COLLEGE

Keuka Park, NY 14478
Telephone: (315) 279-5000
Fax: (315) 279-5216
E-mail: admissions@mail.keuka.edu
Internet: www.keuka.edu

Founded 1890
Academic year: August to May

Pres.: Dr JOSEPH G. BURKE
Exec. Vice-Pres.: CAROLANNE MARQUIS
Dean of Admissions and Financial Aid: CLAUDINE NINESTINE
Dir of Library: DEBORAH COOVER

Library of 85,000 vols
Number of teachers: 64
Number of students: 1,521

4-Year liberal arts college.

LIM COLLEGE

12 E 53rd St, New York, NY 10022
Telephone: (212) 752-1530
Fax: (212) 750-3432
E-mail: admissions@limcollege.edu
Internet: www.limcollege.edu

Founded 1939
Private control
Academic year: August to July

Pres.: ELIZABETH S. MARCUSE

Exec. Vice-Pres.: LINDA HARRIS PAOLILLO
Assoc. Vice-Pres. for Academic Affairs: Dr JACQUELINE LEBLANC
Dean of Graduate Studies and Continuing Education: MILAN MILASINOVIĆ
Sr Vice-Pres. of Finance and Operation and Treas.: MICHAEL DONOHUE
Assoc. Vice-Pres. for Student Affairs: MICHAEL SACHS
Asst Dean of Admissions: KRISTINA ORTIZ
Dir of Library Services: GEORGE SANCHEZ

Library of 65,000 vols
Number of teachers: 187
Number of students: 1,570

LE MOYNE COLLEGE

1419 Salt Springs Rd, Syracuse, NY 13214-1399
Telephone: (315) 445-4100
Fax: (315) 445-4540
Internet: www.lemoyne.edu

Founded 1946
Academic year: August to May

Pres.: Rev. CHARLES J. BEIRNE
Provost and Academic Vice-Pres.: Dr JOHN SMARRELLI, Jr
Dir of Admissions: DENNIS NICHOLSON
Dir of Library: JAMES SIMONIS

Library of 242,233 vols
Number of teachers: 300
Number of students: 3,487

LONG ISLAND UNIVERSITY

700 Northern Blvd, Brookville, NY 11548-1326
Telephone: (516) 299-2000
Fax: (516) 299-2072
E-mail: attend@liu.edu
Internet: www.liu.edu

Founded 1926

Pres.: Dr DAVID J. STEINBERG
Vice-Pres. for Academic Affairs: Dr JEFFREY KANE
Vice-Pres. for Finance and Treas.: ROBERT N. ALTHOLZ
Vice-Pres. for Legal Services and Univ. Counsel: Dr ELAINE M. CROSSON
Vice-Pres. for Planning: Dr DANIEL J. RODAS
Vice-Pres. for Univ. Relations: RICHARD W. GORMAN
Provost for Brooklyn Campus: Dr GALE STEVENS HAYNES
Provost for C. W. Post Campus: Dr PAUL H. FORESTELL

Library: Libraries with 2.3.m. vols
Number of teachers: 1,205 full-time
Number of students: 23,540

MANHATTAN COLLEGE

Manhattan College Parkway, Riverdale, NY 10471
Telephone: (718) 862-8000
Fax: (718) 862-8014
Internet: www.manhattan.edu

Founded as Acad. of the Holy Infancy 1853; chartered as Manhattan College 1863
Private, co-educational

Pres. and Treas.: Bro. Dr THOMAS J. SCANLAN
Provost and Exec. Vice-Pres.: Dr WELDON JACKSON
Vice-Pres. for Advancement: JAMES H. HEISEY
Vice-Pres. for Finance: JOHN DALY
Vice-Pres. for Student Services: Bro. Dr ROBERT C. BERGER
Bursar: MARIA T. BREWSTER
Director of Institutional Research: Dr SUSANNE M. TUMELTY
Registrar: PHYLLIS T. BAGLEY
Dir of Library: HARRY WELSH

Library of 240,000 vols
Number of teachers: 390
Number of students: 3,070
Publications: *Engineer*, *Humanist* (1 a year), *Vistas*

DEANS

Arts: Dr MARY ANN O'DONNELL
Business: Dr JAMES SUAREZ
Education: Dr WILLIAM MERRIMAN
Engineering: Dr RICHARD HEIST
Science: Dr EDWARD BROWN
Graduate Division: Dr JAMES SUAREZ

MANHATTAN SCHOOL OF MUSIC

120 Claremont Ave, New York, NY 10027
Telephone: (212) 749-2802
E-mail: administration@msmnyc.edu
Internet: www.msmnyc.edu

Founded 1917

Pres.: Dr ROBERT SIROTA
Vice-Pres. Emeritus: RICHARD ADAMS
Vice-Pres. for External Affairs: SUSAN EBERSOLE
Vice-Pres. for Finance and Admin.: PAUL KELLEHER

Library: Libraries with 95,000 vols
Number of teachers: 250
Number of students: 850

MANHATTANVILLE COLLEGE

Purchase, NY 10577
Telephone: (914) 323-5464
Fax: (914) 694-1732
E-mail: admissions@mville.edu
Internet: www.manhattanville.edu

Founded 1841
Academic year: September to May

Pres.: RICHARD A. BERMAN
Provost: (vacant)

Number of teachers: 75 (full-time)
Number of students: 2,600 (1,600 full-time undergraduates, 1,000 graduates)
Publication: *Inkwell* (1 a year).

MARIST COLLEGE

3399 North Rd, Poughkeepsie, NY 12601
Telephone: (845) 575-3000
E-mail: admissions@marist.edu
Internet: www.marist.edu

Founded 1929

Pres.: DENNIS J. MURRAY
Exec. Vice-Pres.: Dr R. MARK SULLIVAN
Vice-Pres. for Academic Affairs: Dr MARC VAN DER HEYDEN
Vice-Pres. for Admissions and Enrollment: HARRY WOOD
Vice-Pres. for Business Affairs: ANTHONY CAMPILII
Vice-Pres. for College Advancement: SHAILEEN KOPEC
Vice-Pres. for Information Services: CARL GERBERICH
Vice-Pres. for Student Affairs: GERARD COX
Registrar: JUDY IVANKOVIĆ
Librarian: JOHN MCGINTY

Library of 120,000 vols
Number of teachers: 250
Number of students: 4,025

MARYMOUNT MANHATTAN COLLEGE

221 East 71st St, New York, NY 10021
Telephone: (212) 517-0400
Internet: marymount.mmm.edu

Founded 1936, chartered 1961

Pres.: Dr JUDSON SHAVER
Vice-Pres. for Academic Affairs and Dean of the College: DAWN R. WEBER
Vice-Pres. for Finance and Admin.: PAUL CIRAULO
Vice-Pres. for Institutional Advancement: MARGARET MINSON
Vice-Pres. for Student Affairs and Enrollment Management: JIM HUNDREISER

Library of 85,000 vols
Number of teachers: 142
Number of students: 2,185 (1,500 full-time, 685 part-time)

MEDAILLE COLLEGE

18 Agassiz Circle, Buffalo, NY 14214
Telephone: (716) 880-2000
Fax: (716) 884-0291
Internet: www.medaille.edu

Founded 1875 as Sisters of St Joseph Institute; present name 1967
Private control
Academic year: September to June

Pres.: Dr RICHARD T. JURASEK
Academic Dean: JOSEPH E. SAVARESE
Registrar: KATHLEEN LAZAR
Library Dir: ILONA MIDDLETON

Number of teachers: 175
Number of students: 1,401

MERCY COLLEGE

555 Broadway, Dobbs Ferry, NY 10522
Internet: www.mercy.edu

Campuses in: Dobbs Ferry, Bronx, Manhattan, White Plains, Yorktown

Founded 1950
Private control
Academic year: September to May

Pres.: Dr KIMBERLY R. CLINE
Provost and Vice-Pres. for Academic Affairs: Dr MICHAEL B. SPERLING
Library Dir: Prof. W. BRUCE FULTON
Number of students: 10,400

METROPOLITAN COLLEGE OF NEW YORK

431 Canal St, New York, NY 10013
Telephone: (212) 343-1234
Fax: (212) 343-7399
E mail: admissions@metropolitan.edu
Internet: www.metropolitan.edu

Founded 1964 as Women's Talent Corps; present name 2002
Academic year: September to August

Pres.: VINTON THOMPSON
Sr Vice-Pres. and Chief Financial Officer: VINCENT MASSARO
Dean of Students: DONA SOSA
Registrar: NOREEN SMITH
Library Dir: LOU ACIERNO

Number of teachers: 190
Number of students: 1,650

DEANS

Audrey Cohen School for Human Services and Education: Dr RUTH LUGO
School of Management: Dr HUMPHREY CROOKENDALE

MOLLOY COLLEGE

1000 Hempstead Ave, Rockville Centre, NY 11571-5002
Telephone: (516) 678-5000
E-mail: suffolk@molloy.edu
Internet: www.molloy.edu

Founded 1955
Private control

Pres.: Dr DREW BOGNER
Vice-Pres. for Academic Affairs and Dean of Faculty: Dr VALERIE COLLINS

Vice-Pres. for Advancement: EDWARD THOMPSON
Vice-Pres. for Enrollment Management: LINDA ALBANESE
Vice-Pres. for Finance: MICHAEL MCGOVERN
Vice-Pres. for Mission: Sr DOROTHY FITZGIBBONS
Vice-Pres. for Planning, Research and Information Technology: Dr JOAN MERLO
Vice-Pres. for Student Affairs: ROBERT HOULIHAN
Library Dir: ROBERT MARTIN
Number of teachers: 209
Number of students: 2,500

MOUNT SAINT MARY COLLEGE

330 Powell Ave, Newburgh, NY 12550
Telephone: (845) 561-0800
Fax: (845) 562-6762
E-mail: admissions@msmc.edu
Internet: www.msmc.edu
Founded 1960
Accredited by Board of Regents of the Univ. of the State of NY, Middle States Comm. on Higher Education, Nat. Ccl of Accreditation of Teacher Education, Comm. on Collegiate Nursing Education
Private control, not-for-profit
Pres.: Fr KEVIN MACKIN OFM
Vice-Pres. for Academic Affairs: IRIS TURKENKOPF
Vice-Pres. for College Advancement: BRYAN MALONEY
Vice-Pres. for Finance and Admin.: CATHLEEN KENNY
Vice-Pres. for Facilities and Operations: JIM RAIMO
Dean of Enrollment Management: ROBERT DEMPSEY
Dean of Students: HARRY STEINWAY
Registrar: DARLENE BENZENBERG
Head Librarian: BARBARA PETRUZZELLI
Library of 90,247 vols and 28,743 online subscriptions
Number of teachers: 76 full-time, 141 part-time, 129 F.t.e.
Number of students: 2,067 undergraduates, 493 graduates

CHAIRPERSONS

Division of Arts and Letters: Sister CATHERINE WALSH
Division of Business: DAVID RANT
Division of Education: Dr REVA COWAN
Division of Mathematics and Computer Science: Dr MAUREEN MARKEL
Division of Natural Sciences: Dr LYNN MAELIA
Division of Nursing: Dr ELIZABETH SCANNELL-DESCH
Division of Religion and Philosophy: Dr ED TEALL
Division of Social Sciences: Dr MARGARET BUSSIGEL

NAZARETH COLLEGE

4245 East Ave, Rochester, NY 14618-3790
Telephone: (716) 389-2525
Fax: (716) 586-2452
Internet: www.naz.edu
Founded 1924
Pres.: ROBERT A. MILLER
Vice-Pres. for Academic Affairs: DENNIS SILVA
Registrar: NANCY GREAR
Library Dir: SCOTT SMITH (acting)
Library of 266,000 vols, 2,004 serials
Number of teachers: 143
Number of students: 3,062
Publication: *Verity*

DEANS

College of Arts and Sciences: MICHAEL RENNER
College of Health and Human Services: SHIRLEY SZEKERES

ATTACHED RESEARCH INSTITUTES

Center for International Study: Exec. Dir GEORGE EISEN.

Center for Teaching Excellence: Dir DIANE ENERSON.

NEW SCHOOL UNIVERSITY

66 West 12th St, New York, NY 10011
Telephone: (212) 229-5600
Fax: (212) 229-5330
Internet: www.newschool.edu
Founded 1919
Pres.: BOB KERREY
Provost: ARJUN APPADURAI
Exec. Vice-Pres.: JAMES MURTHA
Vice-Pres. for Communications and External Affairs: NANCY DONNER
Vice-Pres. for Devt: KRISTIN SORENSON
Vice-Pres. and Gen. Counsel: GREGGORY K. SPENCE
Sec. of the Corpn: ROBERT A. GATES
Library: 4.1m. vols
Number of teachers: 1,818
Number of students: 23,000 (8,000 undergraduates, 15,000 students in continuing education)
Publications: *Philosophy Journal*, *Social Research*, *World Policy Journal*

DEANS

Eugene Lang College: NEIL GORDON
Graduate Faculty of Political and Social Science: BENJAMIN LEE
Mannes College of Music: JOEL LESTER
Milano Graduate School: FRED P. HOCHBERGER
New School Adult Division: ANN-LOUISE SHAPIRO
New School University Jazz and Contemporary Music Programme: MARTIN MUELLER
Parsons School of Design: FRED P. HOCHBERG

NEW YORK CHIROPRACTIC COLLEGE

2360 State Route 89, Seneca Falls, NY 13148
E-mail: camsonline@nycc.edu
Internet: www.nycc.edu
Private control
Pres.: Dr FRANK J. NICCHI
Number of students: 720

NEW YORK COLLEGE OF PODIATRIC MEDICINE

1800 Park Ave, New York, NY 10035
Telephone: (212) 410-8000
Fax: (212) 722-4918
E-mail: admissions@nycpm.edu
Internet: www.nycpm.edu
Founded 1911 as New York School of Chiropody; present name 1972
Private control
Academic year: July/August to May
Pres. and CEO: LOUIS L. LEVINE
Dean and Vice-Pres. for Academic Affairs: Dr MICHAEL J. TREPAL
Vice-Pres. for Admin.: JOEL A. STURM
Vice-Pres. for Finance: ALAN SHOIOCK
Vice-Pres. for Information Technology and Operations: WILLIAM H. GRAHAM
Vice-Pres. for Medical and Professional Affairs: Dr MARK H. SWARTZ
Librarian: THOMAS P. WALKER
Number of teachers: 119
Number of students: 283

NEW YORK INSTITUTE OF TECHNOLOGY

POB 8000, Old Westbury, NY 11568-0800
Telephone: (516) 686-7516
Fax: (516) 686-7613
E-mail: admissions@nyit.edu
Internet: www.nyit.edu
Founded 1955
Academic year: September to May
Pres.: EDWARD GUILIANO
Chief Financial Officer and Treas.: JOSEPH COOK, III
Vice-Pres. for Academic Affairs and Dean of Faculty: ALEXANDRA W. LOGUE
Vice-Pres. for Campus Operations: RAJENDRA SINGH
Vice-Pres. for Devt: THOMAS MAURIELLO
Vice-Pres. for Health Sciences and Medical Affairs: BARBARA ROSS-LEE
Vice-Pres. for Student Affairs: JOSEPH FORD
Library of 206,758 vols, 2,745 periodicals
Number of teachers: 847 (283 full-time, 564 part-time)
Number of students: 9,629 (5,718 undergraduate, 2,764 postgraduate, 1,147 first-time professionals)

NEW YORK LAW SCHOOL

57 Worth St, New York, NY 10013
Telephone: (212) 431-2100
E-mail: admissions@nyls.edu
Internet: www.nyls.edu
Founded 1891
Private control
Academic year: August to May
Dean and Pres.: Prof. RICHARD A. MATASAR
Assoc. Dean for Academic Affairs: Dr JETHRO K. LIEBERMAN
Assoc. Dean for Faculty Devt: Dr STEPHEN ELLMANN
Assoc. Dean for Finance and Admin.: Dr FRED DEJOHN
Assoc. Dean for Institutional Advancement: BARBARA I. LESHINSKY
Assoc. Dean for Professional Devt: Dr CAROL BUCKLER
Assoc. Dean for Public Affairs: ALTAGRACIA LEVAT
Assoc. Dean for Spec. Projects: JOAN FISHMAN
Library Dir: Dr JOYCE SALTALAMACHIA
Number of teachers: 155 (62 full-time, 93 adjunct)
Number of students: 1,400

NEW YORK MEDICAL COLLEGE

Valhalla, NY 10595
Telephone: (914) 594-4000
Internet: www.nymc.edu
Founded 1860
Private control
Pres.: Dr KARL P. ADLER
Provost: Dr RALPH A. O'CONNELL
Registrar: Dr JUDITH A. EHREN
Assoc. Dean of Library: DIANA CUNNINGHAM
Library of 149,000 vols, 2,100 journal titles
Number of teachers: 2,800 (1,350 full-time; 1,450 part-time and voluntary)
Number of students: 1,660

DEANS

School of Medicine: Dr RALPH A. O'CONNELL
School of Public Health: Dr ROBERT W. AMLER
Graduate School of Basic Medical Sciences: Dr FRANCIS L. BELLONI

NEW YORK SCHOOL OF INTERIOR DESIGN

170 E 70th St, New York, NY 10021
Telephone: (212) 472-1500

Fax: (212) 472-3800
E-mail: admissions@nysid.edu
Internet: www.nysid.edu

Founded 1916
Private control
Academic year: June to May

Number of teachers: 90
Number of students: 750

NEW YORK THEOLOGICAL SEMINARY

475 Riverside Drive, Suite 500, New York, NY 10115
Telephone: (212) 870-1211
Fax: (212) 870-1236
E-mail: online@nyts.edu
Internet: www.nyts.edu

Founded 1900 as Bible Teachers' College; present name 1965
Private control

Pres.: Prof. DALE T. IRVIN
Vice-Pres.: Dr LAURA PIRES-HESTER
Academic Dean: Dr DALE T. IRVIN
Registrar: SU KANG
Librarian: ELEANOR SOLER

Number of teachers: 35
Number of students: 287

NEW YORK UNIVERSITY

70 Washington Square South, New York, NY 10012
Telephone: (212) 998-1212
Internet: www.nyu.edu

Founded 1831
Private
Academic year: September to May

Pres.: JOHN SEXTON
Provost: DAVID W. MCLAUGHLIN
Exec. Vice-Pres.: MICHAEL ALFANO
Sr Vice-Pres. for Health: ROBERT BERNE
Chair of Faculty Advisory Cttee on Academic Priorities: RICHARD FOLEY
Chief of Staff and Deputy to the Pres.: DIANE C. YU
Sr Vice-Pres., Gen. Counsel and Sec. of the Univ.: BONNIE BRIER
Sr Vice-Pres. for Univ. Relations and Public Affairs: LYNNE P. BROWN
Counsellor to the Pres.: NORMAN DORSEN
Sr Vice-Pres. for Devt and Alumni Relations: DEBRA A. LAMORTE
Sr Vice-Pres. for Finance and Budget: MARTIN S. DORPH
Sr Vice-Pres. for Operations: ALISON LEARY
Vice-Pres. for Admin. and Chief of Staff to the Exec. Vice-Pres.: STEVEN DONOFRIO
Vice-Pres. for Budget and Financial Planning: ANTHONY JIGA
Vice-Pres. for Enrollment Management: RANDALL DEIKE
Vice-Pres. for Financial Operations and Treasurer: ROSEMARIE A. LOFFREDO
Vice-Pres. for Global Security and Crisis Management: JULES A. MARTIN
Vice-Pres. for Global Technology: THOMAS A. DELANEY
Vice-Pres. for Govt Affairs and Civic Engagement: ALICIA D. HURLEY
Vice-Pres. for Human Resources: CATHERINE CASEY
Vice-Pres. for Information Technology: MARILYN MCMILLAN
Vice-Pres. for Public Affairs: JOHN BECKMAN
Vice-Pres. for Public Resource Admin.: RICHARD N. BING
Vice-Pres. for Student Affairs: MARC L. WAIS
Sr Vice-Provost for Academic Policies: PIERRE HOHENBERG
Sr Vice-Provost for Engineering and Technology: ELIZABETH DIANNE REKOW
Sr Vice-Provost for Planning: RON ROBIN
Sr Vice-Provost for Research: PAUL HORN
Sr Vice-Provost for Undergraduate Education and Univ. Life: LINDA G. MILLS
Sr Vice-Provost: K. R. SREENIVASAN
Vice-Provost for Academic Affairs: JANE TYLUS
Vice-Provost for Faculty Affairs: FRANCES WHITE
Vice-Provost for Globalization and Multicultural Affairs: ULRICH BAER
Vice-Provost for Int. Education and Outreach: CAROL BRANDT
Assoc. Provost for Academic Financial Planning and Fiscal Affairs: CATHERINE DELONG
Assoc. Provost for Academic Operations Planning: CAROL KLAPERMAN MORROW
Assoc. Provost for the Arts: THOMAS CROW
Assoc. Provost for Undergraduate Academic Affairs: MATTHEW SANTIROCCO
Registrar: ROGER PRINTUP
Dean of Libraries: CAROL A. MANDEL

Library: see Libraries and Archives
Number of teachers: 3,100
Number of students: 50,917

Publications: *Annual Survey of American Law* (4 a year), *Environmental Law Journal* (3 a year), *Inquiry* (1 a year), *Journal of Accounting, Auditing and Finance* (4 a year), *Journal of Int. Financial Management and Accounting* (3 a year), *Journal of Int. Law and Politics* (4 a year), *Journal of Legislation and Public Policy* (2 a year), *Law Review* (6 a year), *Moot Court Casebook* (1 a year), *Review of Law and Social Change* (6 a year), *TDR: a Journal of Performance Studies* (4 a year), *Victorian Literature and Culture* (2 a year), *Washington Square* (2 a year), *Women and Performance: a Journal of Feminist Theory* (2 a year), *Wordsworth Circle* (4 a year)

DEANS

College of Arts and Science: MATTHEW S. SANTIROCCO
College of Dentistry: CHARLES N. BERTOLAMI
Gallatin School of Individualized Study: SUSANNE L. WOFFORD
Graduate School of Arts and Science: CATHARINE R. STIMPSON
Leonard N. Stern School of Business: PETER BLAIR HENRY
Mount Sinai School of Medicine (affiliated): DENNIS S. CHARNEY
NYU School of Medicine and Postgraduate Medical School: ROBERT I. GROSSMAN
Robert F. Wagner Graduate School of Public Service: ELLEN SCHALL
School of Continuing and Professional Studies: ROBERT S. LAPINER
School of Law: RICHARD L. REVESZ
Silver School of Social Work: LYNN VIDEKA
Steinhardt School of Culture, Education and Human Development: MARY M. BRABECK
Tisch School of the Arts: MARY SCHMIDT CAMPBELL
Courant Institute of Mathematical Sciences: LESLIE GREENGARD (Dir)
Institute for the Study of the Ancient World: ROGER BAGNALL (Dir)
Institute of Fine Arts: PATRICIA LEE RUBIN (Dir)

PROFESSORS

College of Arts and Science (100 Washington Square East, New York, NY 10003; internet www.nyu.edu/cas):

AARONSON, D., Psychology
AFFRON, C., French
ALEXANDER, J. J. G., Fine Arts
ALLEN, L. R., Psychology
AMENTA, E., Sociology
ANDERSEN, S. M., Psychology
ANDERSON, H. M., Spanish and Portuguese Languages and Literatures
AVELLANEDA, M., Mathematics
AVERILL, G., Music
AZMITIA, E. C., Biology, Neural Science
BACIC, Z., Chemistry
BAER, N. S., Conservation, Fine Arts
BAILEY, R., Music
BAKER, P. R., History
BALTIN, M. R., Linguistics
BARGH, J. A., Psychology
BAUMOL, W. J., Economics
BEAUJOUR, M., French
BEIDELMAN, T. O., Anthropology
BENDER, T., History
BENHABIB, J., Political Economy, Economics
BERENSON, E., History, French Studies
BERGER, M., Computer Science
BERMAN, S. M., Mathematics
BISHOP, T., French Literature, Comparative Literature
BLOCK, N., Philosophy, Psychology
BLOOM, H., English and American Literature, English
BOGHOSSIAN, P., Philosophy
BOGOMOLOV, F. A., Mathematics
BONFANTE, L., Classics
BOORMAN, S. H., Music
BRAMS, S. J., Politics
BRANDT, K. W.-G., Fine Arts
BRANDT, R. A., Physics
BRATHWAITE, K., Comparative Literature
BROWN, H. H., Jr, Physics
BROWN, J., Fine Arts
BROYDE, S., Biology
BRUNER, J., Psychology
BUDICK, B., Physics
BUENO DE MESQUITA, B., Politics
BURNS, F. J., Environmental Science
BURROWS, D. L., Music
BURROWS, W. E., Journalism and Mass Communication
CALHOUN, C. J., Sociology
CANARY, J. W., Chemistry
CANTOR, N. F., History, Comparative Literature, Sociology
CAPLIN, A., Economics
CAPPELL, S., Mathematics
CARNEVALE, P., Psychology
CARRASCO, M., Psychology and Neuroscience
CARRUTHERS, M. J., Literature
CHAIKEN, S., Psychology
CHAUDHURI, U., English
CHAZAN, R., Modern Jewish History
CHEEGER, J., Mathematics
CHELKOWSKI, P. J., Middle Eastern Studies
CHILDRESS, W. S., Mathematics
CHIOLES, J., Comparative Literature
CHUSID, M., Music
CLASTER, J. N., History
COHEN, B. S., Environmental Medicine
COHEN, J.-L., History of Architecture
COHEN, S. F., Russian Studies and History
COLE, R., Computer Science
COLLINS, C., English
COONS, E. E., Psychology, Neural Science
CORRADI, J. E., Sociology
CORUZZI, G. M., Biology
COSTA, M., Environmental Science
COSTELLO, J. R., Linguistics
DASH, J. M., French
DEIFT, P., Mathematics
DESPLAN, C., Biology
DEWAR, R. B. K., Computer Science
DIAWARA, M., Comparative Literature
DINER, H. R., American Jewish History, Hebrew and Judaic Studies, History
DINSHAW, C., English
DJEBAR, A., French
DOCTOROW, E. L., American Letters, English
DONOGHUE, D., English and American Letters
DOUBROVSKY, S., French
DOWNS, G. W., Jr, Politics
DUSTER, T., Sociology

DWORKIN, R., Law, Philosophy
EISLER, C., Fine Arts
ELBOURNE, P. D., Linguistics
ELLIS, M. H., Fine Arts
ENGEL, D., Holocaust Studies, Hebrew and Judaic Studies, and History
EVANS, H. L., Environmental Science
FAIRCHILD, S., Conservation
FARRAR, G., Physics
FELDMAN, S. M., Neural Science, Psychology
FELDMAN, Y. S., Hebrew Culture and Education
FERNANDEZ, R., Economics
FIELD, H. H., Philosophy
FINE, K., Philosophy
FLINN, C. J., Economics
FRECCERO, J., Italian, Comparative Literature
FRYDMAN, R., Economics
FURMANSKI, P., Biology
GALE, D., Economics
GANS, P. J., Chemistry
GARABEDIAN, P. R., Mathematics
GARLAND, D., Sociology
GATELY, D., Economics
GEACINTOV, N. E., Chemistry
GERSON, K., Sociology
GERSON, S., French
GERTLER, M., Economics
GILMAN, E. B., English
GILSENAN, M., Humanities, Middle Eastern Studies, Anthropology
GINSBURG, F., Anthropology
GITLIN, T., Journalism and Mass Communication, Education, Sociology
GOLDSTEIN, G. R., Dental Materials Science
GOLLWITZER, P. M., Psychology
GOODMAN, J., Mathematics
GOTTLIEB, A., Computer Science
GREENBERG, D. F., Sociology
GREENGARD, L., Mathematics
GREENLEAF, F. P., Mathematics
GRIFFIN, D., English
GRISHMAN, R., Computer Science
GROMOV, M., Mathematics
GROSS, J. T., Politics
GUILLORY, J., English
GURLAND, R. H., Philosophy
GUY, G. R., Linguistics
HAMEIRI, E., Mathematics
HANSEN, D., Ancient Middle Eastern Art and Archaeology
HARDIN, R., Politics
HARLEY, N. H., Environmental Science
HAROOTUNIAN, H., History
HARPER, P. B., English, American Studies
HARRINGTON, C., Politics
HARRISON, T., Anthropology
HAUSNER, M., Mathematics
HAVERKAMP, A., English
HAWKEN, M. J., Neural Science, Psychology
HEEGER, D. J., Psychology and Neural Science
HEILMAN, M., Psychology
HENDIN, J. G., English
HEYDEBRAND, W., Sociology
HEYNS, B., Sociology
HOFER, H., Mathematics
HOFFERT, M. I., Physics
HOFFMAN, M., Psychology
HOLLIER, D., French
HOROWITZ, R., Sociology
HOY, P. C., English
HSIUNG, J. C., Politics
HUGGINS, P., Physics
HULL, R. W., History
HÜPPAUF, B. R., German
HYMAN, I., Fine Arts
IVRY, A. L., Modern Jewish Thought, Hebrew and Judaic Studies, Middle Eastern Studies
JACOBY, L., Psychology
JAEGER, R. J., Environmental Science
JASSO, G., Sociology
JAVITCH, D., Comparative Literature, Italian
JOHNSON, P., History
JOLLY, C. J., Anthropology
JOVANOVIC, B., Economics
JUDT, A., European Studies, History
KALLENBACH, N. R., Chemistry
KAMM, F. M., Philosophy, Law
KAPLAN, F. E. S., Museum Studies
KAPLAN, M. A., Hebrew and Judaic Studies
KARCHIN, L., Music
KAYNE, R. S., Linguistics
KAZEMI, F., Politics, Middle Eastern Studies
KEDEM, Z. M., Computer Science
KELLEY, R. D. G., History
KINNELL, G., Creative Writing, English
KIRSHENBLATT-GIMBLETT, B., Performance Studies, Hebrew and Judaic Studies
KOHN, R. V., Mathematics
KOPCKE, G., Humanities
KRABBENHOFT, K., Spanish and Portuguese Languages and Literatures
KRAUSKOPF, J., Neural Science, Psychology
KRINSKY, C., Fine Arts
KRISER, D. B., Anthropology
KULICK, D., Anthropology
KUPPERMAN, K., History
LANDAU, S., Fine Arts
LANDY, M. S., Psychology, Neural Science
LAX, P. D., Mathematics
LEDOUX, J. E., Neural Science and Psychology
LEGEROS, R. Z., Dental Materials Science
LEHMAN, E. W., Sociology
LENNIE, P., Neural Science
LEVINE, B. A., Bible and Ancient Near Eastern Studies, Hebrew and Judaic Studies
LEVY, P. M., Physics
LIN, F.-H., Mathematics
LIPPMANN, M., Environmental Science
LOCKMAN, Z., Middle Eastern Studies, History
LOCKRIDGE, L. S., English
LOW, A., English
LOWENSTEIN, J. H., Physics
LUKES, S. M., Sociology
LYNCH, O. M., Urban Anthropology
MCCHESNEY, R. D., Middle Eastern Studies
MCKEAN, H. P., Mathematics
MCLAUGHLIN, D. W., Mathematics
MCNELIS, E. J., Chemistry
MAGNUSON, P. A., English
MAJDA, A. J., Mathematics
MANIN, B., Politics
MANOFF, R. K., Journalism and Mass Communication
MARINCOLA, M. D., Conservation
MARMOR, M., Environmental Medicine
MARSHALL, P., English
MARTIN, E., Anthropology
MARTÍNEZ, H. S., Spanish and Portuguese Languages and Literatures
MATHEWS, T. F., History of Art
MATTHEWS, T. J., Psychology, Neural Science
MATTINGLY, P., History
MAYNARD, J., English
MEAD, L. M., Politics
MEISEL, P., English
MICHELSON, A., Cinema Studies
MINCER, A., Physics
MISHRA, B., Computer Science
MITCHELL, C., Politics
MITCHELL, T., Politics, Middle Eastern Studies
MITSIS, P., Hellenic Culture and Civilization, Classics
MOLLOY, S., Spanish and Portuguese Languages and Literatures, Comparative Literature
MORTON, R. B., Politics
MOVSHON, J. A., Neural Science, Psychology
MURPHY, G. L., Psychology
MURPHY, L. B., Law, Philosophy
MYERS, F. R., Anthropology
NADIRI, M. I., Economics
NAGEL, T., Philosophy
NELKIN, D., Sociology
NEMETHY, P., Physics
NEWMAN, C. M., Mathematics
NICOLE, E., French
NIRENBERG, L., Mathematics
NOCHLIN, L., Modern Art
NOLAN, M., History
NYARKO, Y., Economics
O'CONNOR, D., Ancient Egyptian Art
OLDS, S., English
OLIVA, L. J., European Studies, History
OLLMAN, B., Politics
ORDOVER, J. A., Economics
OVERTON, M., Computer Science
PEACHIN, M., Classics
PEACOCKE, C., Philosophy
PELLI, D. G., Psychology, Neural Science
PERCUS, J. K., Mathematics, Physics
PERSELL, C. H., Sociology
PESKIN, C. S., Mathematics
PETERS, F. E., Middle Eastern Studies, Religious Studies, History
PINES, M. S., Dental Materials Science
PNUELI, A., Computer Science
POLLACK, R., Mathematics
POOVEY, M., English
PORRATI, M., Physics
POSNER, D., Fine Arts
POSNOCK, R., English
POSTAL, P. M., Linguistics
PRATT, M. L., Spanish and Portuguese
PRZEWORSKI, A., Politics
RAMSEY, J. B., Economics
RANDALL, R. S., Politics
RAPP, R., Anthropology
RAY, D., Economics
REGALADO, N. F., French
REIMERS, D. E., History
REISS, C. S., Biology
REISS, T. J., Comparative Literature
RICHARDSON, J., Philosophy
RICHARDSON, R. W., Physics
RINZEL, J., Neural Science, Mathematics
ROBINSON, E. J., Physics
ROELOFS, H. M., Politics
ROESNER, E. H., Music
RONELL, A., Germanic Languages and Literatures, Comparative Literature
ROSENBERG, L., Physics
ROSENBLUM, R., Modern European Art
ROSS, A., Comparative Literature
ROSS, K., Comparative Literature
ROSSMAN, T. G., Environmental Science
RUBLE, D. N., Psychology
RUDDICK, W., Philosophy
SAMMONS, J. T., History
SANDLER, L., Art History
SANTIROCCO, M. S., Classics
SARNAK, P., Mathematics
SCALLY, R. J., History, Classics
SCHAIN, M., Politics, French Studies
SCHECHNER, R., Performance Studies
SCHIEFFELIN, B. B., Anthropology
SCHIFFER, S., Philosophy
SCHIFFMAN, L. H., Hebrew and Judaic Studies
SCHLESINGER, R. B., Environmental Science
SCHLICK, T., Chemistry, Mathematics
SCHONBERG, E., Computer Science
SCHOTTER, A., Economics
SCHUCKING, E. L., Physics
SCHULMAN, A., Dental Materials Science
SCHUSTER, D. I., Chemistry
SCHWARTZ, J. T., Computer Science
SCHWEITZER, A., Humanities, Spanish and Portuguese Languages and Literatures, Comparative Literature
SCOTT, W., Biology
SCULLI, J., Physics
SEEMAN, N. C., Chemistry
SEIDMAN, E., Psychology
SEIGEL, J., History

SENNETT, R., Sociology, History
SHAPLEY, R. M., Sciences, Neural Science, Biology, Psychology
SHASHA, D., Computer Science
SHATAH, J., Mathematics
SHELLEY, M., Mathematics
SHINN, M., Psychology
SHOHAT, E., Art and Public Policy, Middle Eastern Studies
SHORE, R. E., Environmental Science
SHROUT, P., Psychology
SIDER, D., Classics
SIEBURTH, R., Comparative Literature, French
SIFAKIS, G. M., Hellenic Culture and Civilization, Classics
SILVER, K., Fine Arts, French Studies
SINGLER, J. V., Linguistics
SIRLIN, A., Physics
SKLAR, R., Cinema Studies
SMITH, M. S., Hebrew and Judaic Studies
SNODGRASS, J. G., Psychology
SOKAL, A. D., Physics
SOLOMON, S. D., Journalism and Mass Communication
SORENSEN, R. A., Philosophy
SOUCEK, P., Islamic Art
SPENCER, J. H., Computer Science, Mathematics
STAM, R., Cinema Studies
STEHLIN, S. A., History
STEPHENS, M., Journalism and Mass Communication
STIMPSON, C. R., Arts and Science
STOTZKY, G., Biology
STROKE, H. H., Physics
SUBIRATS, E., Spanish and Portuguese Languages and Literatures
SULLIVAN, E., Fine Arts
SZABOLCSI, A., Linguistics
TAYLOR, D., Performance Studies, Spanish
TING, L., Mathematics
TRACHTENBERG, M., History of Fine Arts
TROPE, Y., Psychology
TURNER, R., Art and Humanities
TYLER, T. R., Psychology
ULEMAN, J. S., Psychology
UNGER, I., History
UNGER, P., Philosophy
VARADHAN, S. R. S., Science, Mathematics
VITZ, E. B., French
VITZ, P. C., Psychology
VOLOGODSKII, A. V., Chemistry
WALEY-COHEN, J., History
WALKOWITZ, D., History
WEINEN, E., Mathematics
WEITZNER, H., Mathematics
WELKOWITZ, J., Psychology
WHITE, R., Anthropology
WIDLUND, O. B., Computer Science
WILSON, C. A., Economics
WILSON, S. R., Chemistry
WOLFF, E. N., Economics
WOLFSON, E., Hebrew Studies, Religious Studies
WRIGHT, M. H., Computer Science
XIN, Z., Mathematics
YAP, C. K., Computer Science
YAU, H.-T., Mathematics
YELLIN, V. F., Music
YOUNG, M. B., History
YÚDICE, G., Spanish and Portuguese and American Studies
ZASLAVSKY, G. M., Physics, Mathematics
ZHANG, J. Z. H., Chemistry
ZWANZIGER, D., Physics, Mathematics

College of Dentistry (345 East 24th St, New York, NY 10010; tel. (212) 998-9800; internet www.nyu.edu/dental):

BAHN, S., Biological Sciences, Medicine and Surgery
BRAL, M., Periodontics
CALAMIA, J., Restorative and Prosthodontics
CAUFIELD, P. W., Cariology and Operative Dentistry
GLICKMAN, R., Oral Maxillofacial Surgery
GOLDSTEIN, G., Prosthodontics
GUTTENPLAN, J., Basic Sciences (Biochemistry)
KATZ, R., Epidemiology and Health Promotion
KINNALLY, K., Basic Sciences
KIREMIDJIAN-SCHUMACHER, L., Basic Sciences
KUFTINEC, M., Orthodontics
LEGEROS, R., Implant Dentistry and Restorative and Prosthodontic Sciences
PINES, M., Biomaterials
REKOW, D., Basic Sciences and Craniofacial Biology and Orthodontics
ROSENBERG, P., Endodontics
ROY, M., Basic Sciences
SCHERER, W., Reconstructive and Comprehensive Care
SHIP, J. A., Oral Medicine
SINGH, I., Basic Sciences
SPIELMAN, A., Basic Science and Craniofacial Biology
TARNOW, D., Implant Dentistry
TERRACIO, L., Basic Sciences and Craniofacial Biology
VERNILLO, A., Oral Pathology

Leonard N. Stern School of Business (Henry Kaufman Management Center, 44 West Fourth St, New York, NY 10012; tel. (212) 998 0100; internet www.stern.nyu.edu):

BALACHANDRAN, K. R., Accounting and Operations Management
BARDES, P., Accounting and Finance
BARTOV, E., Accounting, Business Ethics
BILDERSEE, J. S., Accounting
BRIEF, R., Statistics and Accounting
HIPSCHER, A., Accounting, Taxation and Business Law
JONES, S., Accounting, Taxation and Business Law
LIVNAT, J., Accounting
MORAN, M. J., Accounting
NICHOLS, C. W., Business Ethics
RONEN, J., Accounting
SORTER, G. H., Accounting and Law
WIESEN, J., Accounting, Taxation and Business Law
ZICKLIN, L., Accounting

Robert F. Wagner Graduate School of Public Service (4 Washington Square North, New York, NY 10003; tel. (212) 998-7400; internet www.nyu.edu/wagner):

BERNE, R., Public Policy and Financial Management
BOISE, W. B., Public Administration
BOUFFORD, J. I., Health Policy and Public Service
BRECHER, C. M., Public and Health Administration
CHERKASKY, M., Health Policy and Management
FINKLER, S. A., Public and Health Administration, Accounting, and Financial Management
KOVNER, A., Public and Health Management
KROPF, R., Health Management
LEW, J. J., Public Administration
LIGHT, P., Public Service
MOSS, M., Urban Policy and Planning
RODWIN, V. G., Health Policy and Management
SCHALL, E., Health Policy and Management
SCHILL, M. H., Law and Urban Planning
SPARROW, R. L., Public Management
STAFFORD, W. W., Public Policy and Planning
STIEFEL, L., Economics
ZIMMERMAN, R., Planning and Public Administration

School of Law (110 West 3rd St, New York, NY 10012; internet www.law.nyu.edu):

ADLER, A. M., Law
ADLER, B. E., Law
ALLEN, W. T., Law and Business
ALSTON, P., Law
AMSTERDAM, A. G., Law
ANGELOS, C., Law
ARLEN, J., Law
BEEN, V. L., Law
BENKLER, Y., Law
BILLMAN, B. D., Law
BURNS, S. E., Clinical Law
CALDWELL, P. M., Law
CHASE, O. G., Law
CHEVIGNY, P. G., Law
COHEN, J. A., Law
CUNNINGHAM, N. B., Law
DAINES, R. M., Law
DALE, H. P., Philanthropy and the Law
DAVIS, P. C., Lawyering and Ethics
DORSEN, N., Law
DREYFUSS, R. C., Law
DWORKIN, R. M., Law
ESTREICHER, S., Law
EUSTICE, J. S., Taxation
FIRST, H., Law
FOX, E. M., Trade Regulation
FRIEDMAN, B., Law
GALOWITZ, P., Law
GARLAND, D. W., Law
GEISTFELD, M., Law
GILLERS, S., Law
GILLETTE, C. P., Contract Law
GOLOVE, D. M., Law
GUGGENHEIM, M. F., Clinical Law
HERSHKOFF, H., Law
HERTZ, R. A., Clinical Law
HOLMES, S. T., Law
JACOBS, J. B., Constitutional Law and the Courts
KAHAN, M., Law
KINGSBURY, B., Law
KORNHAUSER, L. A., Law
LAW, S. A., Law
LEVINSON, D., Law
LÓPEZ, G., Clinical Law
LOWENFELD, A. F., International Law
MAGUIGAN, H., Clinical Law
MALMAN, L. L., Law
MARTELL, L. A., Law
MERON, T., Law
MILLER, G. P., Law
MORAWETZ, N., Clinical Law
MURPHY, L., Law
NAGEL, T., Law
NELSON, W. E., Law
NEUBORNE, B., Law
NOBLE, R. K., Law
PILDES, R. H., Law
PRICE, M. K., Law
REID, J. P., Law
REVESZ, R. L., Law
RICHARDS, D. A. J., Law
SAGER, L., Law
SCHENK, D. H., Taxation
SCHILL, M. H., Law and Urban Planning
SCHMOLKA, L. L., Law
SCHULHOFER, S. J., Law
SCOTT, H. S., Law
SEXTON, J., Law
SHAVIRO, D. N., Law
SIEGEL, S., Law
SILBERMAN, L. J., Law
SORTER, G. H., Law
STEINES, J. P., Jr, Law
STEWART, R. B., Law
TAYLOR-THOMPSON, K. A., Clinical Law
THOMPSON, A. C., Law
UPHAM, F. K., Law
WEILER, J. H. H., Law
ZIMMERMAN, D. L., Law

School of Medicine (550 First Ave, New York, NY 10016; tel. (212) 263-7300; internet www.med.nyu.edu):

ABADIR, A. R., Anaesthesiology
ABELE, M. G., Radiology
ABRAMS, S., Psychiatry
ABRAMSON, S. B., Medicine, Rheumatology, Pathology
ADESNIK, M. B., Cell Biology
AIGES, H. W., Paediatrics
AL-ASKARI, S., Urology
ALBANO, A. M., Psychiatry
ALBOM, M. J., Dermatology
AMELAR, R. D., Urology
ANGRIST, B. M., Psychiatry
ARGYROS, T. G., Medicine
ARKEL, Y. S., Obstetrics and Gynaecology
ARLOW, J. A., Psychiatry
ARONOFF, M. S., Psychiatry
ARTMAN, M., Paediatric Surgery, Pharmacology
ASTON, S. J., Surgery
AUERBACH, R., Dermatology
AXEL, L., Radiology
AXELROD, F. B., Dysautonomia Treatment, Neurology
AYVAZIAN, L. F., Medicine
BAKER, R. G., Physiology, Neuroscience
BALDWIN, D. S., Medicine, Nephrology
BALLARD, H. S., Medicine
BARKIN, L., Psychiatry
BARRON, B. A., Obstetrics and Gynaecology
BASCH, R. S., Pathology
BASILICO, C., Microbiology
BAUMANN, F. G., Surgery
BEASLEY, R. W., Surgery, Plastic and Reconstructive Surgery
BEATTIE, C. N., Anaesthesiology
BECKER, J. A., Radiology
BELASCO, J. G., Microbiology
BELMAN, S., Environmental Medicine
BEN-YISHAY, Y., Rehabilitation Medicine
BENJAMIN, V., Neurosurgery
BERANBAUM, S. L., Radiology
BERCZELLER, P. H., Medicine
BERG, P., Medicine
BERGER, M. M., Psychiatry
BERKELEY, A. S., Obstetrics and Gynaecology
BERNSTEIN, R. L., Anaesthesiology
BHANOT, O. S., Environmental Medicine
BHARDWAJ, N., Medicine Physiology, Neuroscience Pharmacology
BIRNBAUM, B. A., Radiology
BLANCK, T. J. J., Anaesthesiology, Physiology, Neuroscience
BLASER, M., Internal Medicine, Microbiology
BLAUGRUND, S. M., Otolaryngology
BLOCK, J. M., Neurology
BLUM, H. P., Psychiatry
BLUM, M., Medicine, Endocrinology, Radiology
BODIAN, E. L., Dermatology
BOGART, B. I., Cell Biology
BORKOWSKY, W., Paediatrics
BOSLAND, M. C., Environmental Medicine, Urology
BOUFFORD, J. I., Paediatrics
BOXER, R. A., Paediatrics
BOYD, A. D., Surgery, Cardiothoracic Surgery
BRANCACCIO, R. R., Dermatology
BRODIE, J. D., Psychiatry
BROOME, J. D., Pathology
BROTMAN, A. W., Psychiatry
BROWN, E. R., Neurosurgery
BROWN, J. W., Neurology
BRUNO, M. S., Clinical Medicine
BUDMAN, D. R., Medicine, Oncology
BURAKOFF, S. J., Medicine, Oncology
BURDEN, S. J., Pharmacology
BURDOCK, E. I., Psychiatry
BURNS, F. J., Environmental Medicine
BUYON, J. P., Medicine, Rheumatology
BYSTRYN, J.-C., Dermatology
CAHILL, K. M., Medicine
CALANOG, A. M., Obstetrics and Gynaecology
CANCRO, R., Psychiatry
CAPAN, L., Anaesthesiology
CARR, R. E., Ophthalmology
CASTELLANOS, F. X., Child and Adolescent Psychiatry, Clinical Radiology
CHALFIN, L. S., Psychiatry
CHANDRA, M. M., Paediatrics
CHANDRA, R., Radiology
CHAO, M. V., Cell Biology
CHARAP, M. H., Medicine, General Medicine
CHARLES, N. C., Ophthalmology
CHARNEY, A. N., Medicine, Nephrology
CHASSIN, J. L., Surgery
CHESLER, M., Neurosurgery, Physiology and Neuroscience
CHESS, S., Psychiatry
CHIORAZZI, N., Medicine, Infectious Diseases and Immunology, Pathology
CHIU, D. T., Surgery, Plastic and Reconstructive Surgery
CITROME, L. L., Psychiatry
CLAPS, A. A., Paediatrics
COBRINIK, R., Paediatrics
COHEN, B. S., Environmental Medicine
COHEN, I. J., Ophthalmology
COHEN, N. L., Otolaryngology
COHEN, T., Medicine
COLLINS, A. H., Psychiatry
COLOMBO, A., Medicine
COLTRERA, J. T., Psychiatry
COOPER, J. S., Radiation Oncology
COOPER, N. S., Pathology
COOPER, P. R., Neurosurgery, Orthopaedic Surgery
COPLAN, N. L., Medicine
COSTA, M., Environmental Medicine, Pharmacology
COSTA E SILVA, J. A., Psychiatry
COWAN, N. J., Biochemistry
CRONSTEIN, B. N., Medicine, Rheumatology, Pathology, Pharmacology
CULLIFORD, A. T., Surgery, Cardiothoracic Surgery
CURTIN, J. P., Obstetrics and Gynaecology
D'AMICO, R. A., Ophthalmology
DANCIS, J., Paediatrics
DANILOWICZ, D. A., Paediatrics
DANTUONO, L. M., Obstetrics and Gynaecology
DAUM, F., Paediatrics
DAVID, R., Paediatrics
DAVIES, E. A., Paediatrics
DAVIS, J. E., Urology
DE LEON, M. J., Psychiatry
DEBROVNER, C. H., Obstetrics and Gynaecology
DEFENDI, V., Oncology, Pathology
DEGNAN, T. J., Medicine, Oncology
DELISI, L. E., Psychiatry
DELPHIN, E. S., Anaesthesiology
DEMOPOULOS, R. I., Pathology
DEPASQUALE, N. P., Medicine
DEUTSCH, B. G., Psychiatry
DEVINSKY, O., Neurology
DEWEY, S. L., Psychiatry
DHAWAN, V., Neurology
DILLER, L., Rehabilitation Medicine
DODICK, J. M., Ophthalmology
DOLGIN, M., Medicine, Cardiology
DRLICA, K. A., Microbiology
DUBIN, L., Urology
DUBNAU, D., Microbiology
DUBOIS, M. Y., Anaesthesiology
DUSTIN, M. L., Pathology
EBERSTEIN, A., Rehabilitation Medicine
EIDELBERG, D., Neurology, Neurosurgery
ELSBACH, P., Medicine
ENG, K., Surgery
EVANS, H. L., Environmental Medicine
FANTL, J. A., Obstetrics and Gynaecology
FARBER, S. J., Medicine, Nephrology
FARCON, E. M., Urology
FARCY, J.-P. C., Orthopaedic Surgery
FEINBERG, A. W., Medicine, Geriatrics
FEINER, H. D., Pathology
FERRIS, S. H., Psychiatry
FINGER, P. T., Ophthalmology
FINLAY, J. L., Paediatrics, Neurosurgery
FINLAY, J. R., Ophthalmology
FIRESTEIN, S. K., Psychiatry
FISCHEL, R. E., Psychiatry
FISHER, A. A., Dermatology
FISHER, M. M., Paediatrics
FISHER, Y. L., Ophthalmology
FISHMAN, G. I., Medicine, Cardiology, Physiology and Neuroscience, Pharmacology
FLOWER, R. W., Ophthalmology
FORMENTI, S. C., Medical Oncology
FOSTER, J. R., Psychiatry
FOX, A. C., Medicine, Cardiology
FRANCES, R. J., Psychiatry
FRANGIONE, B., Pathology, Psychiatry
FRANK, J., Cell Biology
FRANKEL, V. H., Orthopaedic Surgery
FRANKS, A. G., Jr, Dermatology
FREEDBERG, I. M., Dermatology, Cell Biology
FREEDMAN, M. L., Medicine, Geriatrics
FRENKEL, K., Environmental Medicine, Pathology
FRIEDMAN, H. S., Medicine
FRIEDMAN-KIEN, A. E., Dermatology
FROST, J. O., Otolaryngology
FURMANSKI, P., Pathology
GABRIEL, H. P., Psychiatry
GALANTER, M., Psychiatry
GALLOWAY, A. C., Surgery, Cardiothoracic Surgery
GARAY, S. M., Medicine, Pulmonary and Critical Care
GARDNER, E. P., Physiology and Neuroscience
GENIESER, N. B., Radiology
GEORGE, A. E., Radiology
GERONEMUS, R. G., Dermatology
GITTELMAN, M. I., Psychiatry
GLENN, J., Psychiatry
GLICKMAN, R. M., Medicine
GODSON, G. N., Biochemistry
GOLDBERG, E., Neurology
GOLDBERG, J. D., Environmental Medicine
GOLDBERGER, M., Psychiatry
GOLDFRANK, L. R., Medicine, Emergency Medicine, Surgery
GOLDRING, R. M., Medicine, Pulmonary and Critical Care
GOLDSTEIN, N., Psychiatry
GOLDSTEIN, S. R., Obstetrics and Gynaecology
GOLIMBU, C. N., Radiology
GOLIMBU, M. N., Urology
GOLOMB, F. M., Surgery, Surgical Oncology
GONEN, O., Radiology
GOODGOLD, A. L., Neurology, Radiology
GOPINATHAN, G., Neurology
GOUGE, T. H., Surgery
GRANT, A. D., Orthopaedic Surgery
GREBB, J. A., Psychiatry
GRECO, G. J., Ophthalmology
GREEN, M. R., Psychiatry
GREENE, J. B., Medicine
GREENSTEIN, V. C., Ophthalmology
GREGERSEN, P. K., Medicine, Rheumatology, Pathology
GRIECO, A. J., Medicine, General Medicine
GRIFO, J. A., Obstetrics and Gynaecology
GROSSI, E. A., Surgery, Cardiothoracic Surgery
GROSSMAN, R. I., Radiology, Neurosurgery, Neurology, and Physiology and Neuroscience
GROSSMAN, S., Psychiatry
GRUEN, P. H., Psychiatry
GUYER, D. R., Ophthalmology
HAGIN, R. A., Psychiatry
HAJDU, S. I., Pathology
HALPERIN, J. J., Neurology
HALPERT, E., Psychiatry
HARIN, A., Paediatrics
HARLAP, S., Obstetrics and Gynaecology

HARLEY, N. H., Environmental Medicine
HARPER, R. G., Paediatrics, Obstetrics and Gynaecology
HARRIS, H. W., Medicine, Pulmonary and Critical Care
HARRIS, M. N., Surgery, Surgical Oncology
HARRISON, R. M., Ophthalmology
HAZZI, C. G., Medicine
HEITLER, M. S., Paediatrics
HELPERN, J. A., Radiology, Psychiatry, Physiology and Neuroscience
HILLER, J. M., Psychiatry
HILLMAN, D. E., Physiology and Biophysics
HILZ, M. J., Neurology, Medicine
HIRSCH, C. S., Forensic Medicine, Pathology
HIRSCHHORN, R., Medicine, Genetics, Cell Biology, Paediatrics
HOFFMAN, I. R., Medicine
HOLZMAN, R. S., Medicine, Infectious Diseases and Immunology, Environmental Medicine
HOOD, R. M., Surgery
HORNBLASS, A., Ophthalmology
HOROWITZ, L., Medicine
HOROWITZ, M. H., Psychiatry
HORWITZ, S. T., Obstetrics and Gynaecology
HSU, L. Y.-F., Paediatrics, Obstetrics and Gynaecology
IOACHIM, H. L., Pathology
ISRAEL, J. S., Anaesthesiology
ITIL, T., Psychiatry
ITOH, M., Rehabilitation Medicine
JACOBS, A. J., Obstetrics and Gynaecology
JACOBS, D. R., Medicine
JACOBS, J. B., Otolaryngology
JACOBS, T. J., Psychiatry
JAFAR, J. J., Neurosurgery
JAFFE, W. L., Orthopaedic Surgery
JAHSS, M. H., Orthopaedic Surgery
JAVITT, D. C., Psychiatry
JAVITT, N. B., Medicine, Gastroenterology, Paediatrics
JELINEK, J. E., Dermatology
JELINEK, W. R., Biochemistry
JIMENEZ, A. C., Rehabilitation Medicine
JOHANSON, K.-E., Urology
JOHN, E. R., Psychiatry
JONAS, S., Neurology
JONG, A. Y., Psychiatry
JOYNER, A. L., Cell Biology, Physiology and Neuroscience
KAHN, E. I., Surgical Pathology, Clinical Paediatrics
KAHN, M. L., Cardiology
KALOGERAKIS, M. G., Psychiatry
KAMHOLZ, S. L., Medicine
KAMM, F. M., Medicine
KANOF, N. B., Dermatology
KANTOR, T. G., Medicine
KAPLAN, L. A., Pathology
KAPLAN, M. H., Medicine, Infectious Diseases and Immunology
KAPLAN, S. J., Clinical Psychiatry
KARPATKIN, M. H., Paediatrics
KARPATKIN, S., Medicine, Haematology
KATZ, J. L., Clinical Psychiatry
KATZ, L. A., Medicine, Nephrology
KATZ, S., Medicine
KATZ, S. E., Psychiatry
KEEGAN, A. F., Radiology
KEILL, S. L., Psychiatry
KELLY, P. J., Neurosurgery
KENAN, S., Orthopaedic Surgery
KENNEDY, J. T., Medicine
KERMANI, E. J., Psychiatry
KESSLER, R. E., Surgery
KHATAMEE, M. A., Obstetrics and Gynaecology
KING, S. A., Psychiatry
KITTREDGE, R. D., Radiology
KLEIN, H. L., Biochemistry, Medicine
KLEIN, I. L., Medicine, Endocrinology, Cell Biology
KLEIN, R. G., Psychiatry
KLEINBERG, D. L., Medicine, Endocrinology
KOCHEN, J. A., Paediatrics
KOHAN, S. L., Obstetrics and Gynaecology
KOLODNY, E. H., Neurology
KOMISAR, A., Otolaryngology
KOPF, A. W., Dermatology
KOPLEWICZ, H. S., Child and Adolescent Psychiatry, Clinical Paediatrics
KORELITZ, B. I., Medicine
KOVAL, K. J., Orthopaedic Surgery
KOZ, G., Psychiatry
KRAMER, E. L., Radiology
KRAMER, F. R., Microbiology
KRAMER, M., Psychiatry
KRASINSKI, K. M., Paediatrics, Environmental Medicine
KRASNER, R. C. J., Medicine
KREIBICH, G., Cell Biology
KREIS, W., Medicine, Oncology
KREY, L. C., Obstetrics and Gynaecology, Cell Biology
KRONZON, I., Medicine, Cardiology
KUHNS, T. R., Ophthalmology
KUMMER, F., Orthopaedic Surgery
KUPERSMITH, M. J., Neurology, Ophthalmology
KUSCHNER, M., Pathology, Environmental Medicine
LAJTHA, A. L., Psychiatry
LANE, M. E., Rehabilitation Medicine
LANYI, V. F., Rehabilitation Medicine
LASKA, E. M., Psychiatry
LASKIN, M., Psychiatry
LAVKER, R. M., Dermatology
LEE, M. H. M., Rehabilitation Medicine
LEE-HUANG, S., Biochemistry
LEGGIADRO, R. J., Paediatrics
LEHMAN, W. B., Orthopaedic Surgery
LEHMANN, R., Cell Biology
LEHNEIS, H. R., Rehabilitation Medicine
LEITMAN, B. S., Radiology
LEPOR, H., Urology, Pharmacology
LESSER, G. T., Medicine
LEVIN, R. I., Medicine, Cardiology
LEVINE, B. B., Medicine, Infectious Diseases and Immunology
LEVINE, D. N., Neurology
LEVINE, I. S., Psychiatry
LEVITZ, M., Obstetrics and Gynaecology
LEVY, D. E., Molecular Pathology
LEW, A., Psychiatry
LEWIS, D. O., Psychiatry
LIFSHITZ, K., Psychiatry
LIFSHITZ, M. S., Pathology
LILLESKOV, R. K., Psychiatry
LINDENMAYER, J.-P., Psychiatry
LIPKIN, G., Dermatology
LIPKIN, M., Jr, Medicine, Primary Care
LIPPMANN, M., Environmental Medicine
LISMAN, R., Ophthalmology
LITTMAN, D. R., Molecular Immunology, Pathology and Microbiology
LLINAS, R., Physiology and Neuroscience
LOCKWOOD, C. J., Obstetrics and Gynaecology
LOFTUS, T. A., Psychiatry
LOVECCHIO, J. L., Obstetrics and Gynaecology
LOWENSTEIN, J., Medicine, Nephrology
LUNTZ, M. H., Ophthalmology
LUSSKIN, R., Orthopaedic Surgery
LYNFIELD, J., Paediatrics
MA, D. M., Rehabilitation Medicine
MCCARTHY, J. G., Plastic Surgery
MAGRAMM, I., Ophthalmology
MAHONEY, C. J., Forensic Medicine
MALACH, M., Medicine
MANGER, W. M., Medicine
MANGIARDI, J. R., Neurosurgery
MANHEIMER, E. D., Medicine
MANNUZZA, S., Psychiatry
MARCOS, L. R., Psychiatry
MARGOLIS, R. U., Pharmacology
MARGOULEFF, D., Medicine, Nuclear Medicine
MARKOWITZ, J. F., Paediatrics
MARMOR, M., Environmental Medicine, Medicine, Pulmonary and Critical Care
MARSHALL, C. H., Radiology
MAS, F. G., Psychiatry
MASDEU, J. C., Neurology
MATTSSON, A., Psychiatry
MEGIBOW, A. J., Radiology
MEHL, S. J., Medicine
MEISELAS, L. E., Medicine, General Medicine
MEISLIN, A. G., Paediatrics
MERLINO, J. P., Psychiatry
MERUELO, D., Pathology
MESSITE, J., Environmental Medicine
MEYERSON, A. T., Psychiatry
MICHELIS, M. F., Medicine
MILANO, A. M., Medicine
MINDICH, L., Microbiology
MINUCHIN, P. P., Psychiatry
MINUCHIN, S., Psychiatry
MITNICK, H. J., Medicine
MONTEAGUDO, A., Obstetrics and Gynaecology
MORALES, P. A., Urology
MOSCATELLI, D. A., Cell Biology
MOSES, J. W., Medicine
MOSKOWITZ, P. K., Internal Medicine
MUGGIA, F. M., Oncology
NACHTIGALL, L. E., Obstetrics and Gynaecology
NACHTIGALL, R. H., Medicine
NAFTCHI, N. E., Rehabilitation Medicine
NAIDICH, D. P., Radiology
NAIDICH, J. B., Radiology
NARINS, R. S., Dermatology
NASS, R. D., Neurology
NEOPHYTIDES, A. N., Neurology
NEUBAUER, P. B., Psychiatry
NEWMAN, D., Psychiatry
NEZIROGLU, F. A., Psychiatry
NICHOLSON, C., Physiology and Neuroscience
NIXON, R. A., Psychiatry, Cell Biology
NORDIN, M., Orthopaedic Surgery, Environmental Medicine
NOVICK, R. P., Microbiology, Medicine, Pulmonary and Critical Care
NOZ, M. E., Radiology
NUSSENZWEIG, R. S., Medical and Molecular Parasitology
NUSSENZWEIG, V., Pathology
OBSTBAUM, S. A., Ophthalmology
O'HARE, D. B., Paediatrics
OLIVA-LOPEZ, E., Environmental Medicine
OPLER, L. A., Psychiatry
ORENTREICH, N., Dermatology
ORGEL, S., Psychiatry
ORLOW, S. J., Paediatric Dermatology
ORRIS, L., Environmental Medicine
ORT, P. J., Orthopaedic Surgery
OSTRER, H., Paediatrics, Pathology, Medicine
OVARY, Z., Pathology
PACHTER, H. L., Surgery
PACKER, S., Ophthalmology
PAHWA, S., Paediatrics
PANKOVICH, A. M., Orthopaedic Surgery
PAPERNIK, D. S., Psychiatry
PARISIEN, J. S., Orthopaedic Surgery
PARKS, W. P., Paediatrics, Microbiology
PASTERNACK, B. S., Environmental Medicine
PEARSON, J., Pathology
PELCOVITZ, D., Psychiatry
PELLICER, A. G., Pathology
PEPPER, B., Psychiatry
PERRY, R. I., Psychiatry
PESELOW, E. D., Psychiatry
PHILLIPS, R. A., Medicine
PHILLIPS-QUAGLIATA, J. M., Pathology
PINE, D. S., Psychiatry
PINTER, A., Microbiology
PLAINE, L., Urology
POMARA, N., Psychiatry
PORGES, R. F., Obstetrics and Gynaecology
PORTNOW, S. L., Psychiatry

POSNER, M. A., Orthopaedic Surgery
POST, R. C., Obstetrics and Gynaecology
POTMESIL, M., Radiology
POTTASH, A. C., Psychiatry
PRINCE, A. M., Pathology
QUARTERMAIN, D., Neurology, Physiology and Neuroscience
RACKOW, E., Medicine, Cardiology
RAFII, M., Radiology
RAICHT, R. F., Medicine, Gastroenterology
RAMSAY, D. L., Clinical Dermatology
RAUSEN, A. R., Paediatrics
RAYNOR, R. B., Neurosurgery
REEM, G. H., Pharmacology
REES, T. D., Surgery, Plastic and Reconstructive Surgery
REICH, T., Experimental Surgery
REISBERG, B., Psychiatry
RICHARDSON, M. A., Psychiatry
RIFKIN, D. B., Medicine and Cell Biology
RIGEL, D. S., Dermatology
RILES, T. S., Surgery
ROBBINS, E. S., Psychiatry
ROBBINS, H., Orthopaedic Surgery
ROBINS, P., Dermatology
ROGERS, B. O., Surgery
ROM, W. N., Jr, Medicine and Environmental Medicine
RON, D., Medicine, Endocrinology
ROSENBERG, Z. S., Radiology
ROSENBLUTH, J., Physiology and Neuroscience
ROSENFELD, D. L., Obstetrics and Gynaecology
ROSES, D. F., Surgery
ROSNER, R., Psychiatry
ROSSMAN, T. G., Environmental Medicine
ROTHSTEIN, A. A., Psychiatry
ROTROSEN, J. P., Psychiatry
ROUBIN, G. S., Medicine
ROVIT, R. L., Neurosurgery
ROWAN, R. L., Urology
ROY, A., Psychiatry
RUBERMAN, W., Environmental Medicine
RUBIN, S. E., Ophthalmology
RUDY, B., Physiology and Neuroscience, Biochemistry
RUOFF, M., Medicine
SABATINI, D. D., Cell Biology
SADOCK, B. J., Psychiatry
SADOCK, V. A., Psychiatry
SALZER, J. L., Neurology, Cell Biology
SAMUELS, H. H., Pharmacology and Medicine
SARNO, J. E., Jr, Rehabilitation Medicine
SARNO, M. T., Rehabilitation Medicine
SAXE, D. H., Surgery
SCHACHNE, L., Ophthalmology
SCHACHT, R. G., Paediatrics
SCHARFMAN, M. A., Psychiatry
SCHERR, L., Medicine, General Medicine
SCHLOSSMAN, A., Ophthalmology
SCHMIDT-SAROSI, C. L., Obstetrics and Gynaecology
SCHNEIDER, R. J., Microbiology
SCHOENFELD, M., Psychiatry
SCHREIBER, S. S., Clinical Medicine
SCHWARTZ, S., Medicine
SEDLIS, E., Paediatrics
SEIPLE, W. H., Ophthalmology
SHAPIRO, E., Urology
SHAW, L. N., Psychiatry
SHENGOLD, L. L., Psychiatry
SHORE, R. E., Environmental Medicine
SHUPACK, J. L., Dermatology
SIDTIS, J. J., Psychiatry
SIEGEL, C., Psychiatry
SIEGEL, I. M., Experimental Ophthalmology
SILBER, A., Psychiatry
SILVER, J., Medicine, Molecular Medicine, Pathology
SILVER, J. M., Psychiatry
SILVERBERG, M., Paediatrics
SILVERMAN, M. A., Psychiatry
SIMMS, H. H., Surgery
SIMON, E. J., Psychiatry, Pharmacology
SIMPSON, J. I., Physiology and Neuroscience
SINGER, M. H., Psychiatry
SKOLNICK, P., Psychiatry
SLABY, A. E., Psychiatry
SLAKTER, J. S., Ophthalmology
SLIPP, S., Psychiatry
SMALL, A. M., Psychiatry
SMITH, B. F., Ophthalmology
SMITH, I., Microbiology
SMITH, R. C., Psychiatry
SNYDER, C. A., Environmental Medicine
SOBERMAN, R. J., Medicine, Nephrology
SOLOMON, J. J., Environmental Medicine
SOLOWEY, A. C., Surgery
SOTER, N. A., Dermatology
SPATZ, M., Urology
SPEISER, P. W., Clinical Paediatrics
SPENCER, F. C., Surgery
SPEYER, J. L., Medicine, Oncology
SPITZER, M., Clinical Obstetrics and Gynaecology
SPRITZ, N., Medicine, Endocrinology
STEIGBIGEL, N. H., Medicine
STEINETZ, B. G., Environmental Medicine
STENSON, S. M., Ophthalmology
STERN, A., Pharmacology
STONE, E. A., Psychiatry
STONE, S. M., Paediatrics
SUGIMORI, M., Physiology and Neuroscience
SUN, T.-T., Dermatology
SUNSHINE, A., Medicine
SUSSMAN, N., Psychiatry
SVERDLIK, S. S., Rehabilitation Medicine
TAINTOR, Z. C., Psychiatry
TANCREDI, L. R., Psychiatry
TANG, M.-S., Environmental Medicine, Pathology Medicine
TAPPER, M. L., Medicine
TEEBOR, G. W., Pathology, Environmental Medicine
TESSLER, A. N., Urology
TESTA, N. N., Orthopaedic Surgery
THOMAS, A., Psychiatry
TICE, D. A., Surgery
TIMOR, I. E., Obstetrics and Gynaecology
TOBIAS, H., Medicine
TOLK, C. S., Psychiatry
TOMATIS, L., Environmental Medicine
TONIOLO, P. G., Environmental Medicine, Obstetrics and Gynaecology
TRUJILLO, M., Psychiatry
TUCHMAN, M., Medicine
TUNICK, P. A., Medicine, Cardiology
TZIMAS, N. A., Orthopaedic Surgery
VADASZ, C., Psychiatry
VALENTINE, F. T., Medicine, Infectious Diseases and Immunology
VANDERBERG, J. P., Medical and Molecular Parasitology
VAZQUEZ, C. I., Psychiatry
VILCEK, J. T., Microbiology
VINCIGUERRA, V. P., Medicine, Oncology
VOGEL, S. A., Psychiatry
VOLAVKA, J., Psychiatry
VORONTSOV, M. A., Physiology and Neuroscience
WAISMAN, J., Pathology
WALKER, P. S., Orthopaedic Surgery
WALLACH, R. C., Obstetrics and Gynaecology
WALLACH, S., Medicine
WALTZMAN, S. B., Otolaryngology
WAN, L. S., Obstetrics and Gynaecology
WANG, B. C., Anaesthesiology
WAPNIR, R. A., Paediatrics, Biochemistry
WARNER, R. S., Urology
WARSHAW, L. J., Environmental Medicine
WEINBERG, H. J., Neurology
WEINBERG, S., Dermatology
WEINSTEIN, H. C., Psychiatry
WEISSMANN, G., Medicine, Rheumatology
WELSH, H. K., Psychiatry
WEST, A. B., Pathology
WIKLER, N. S., Clinical Medicine
WILKES, B. M., Medicine, Nephrology
WISHNICK, M. M., Paediatrics
WITKOVSKY, P., Experimental Ophthalmology, Physiology and Neuroscience
WOLFF, B. B., Psychiatry
YANNUZZI, L. A., Ophthalmology
YARYURA-TOBIAS, J. A., Psychiatry
YOUNG, B. K., Obstetrics and Gynaecology
YOUNG, L. Y., Environmental Medicine
YUVIENCO, F. P., Urology
ZAVALA, F., Medical and Molecular Parasitology
ZELIKOVSKY, G., Urology
ZIDE, B. M., Surgery, Plastic and Reconstructive Surgery
ZIFF, E. B., Biochemistry
ZIMMON, D. S., Medicine, Gastroenterology
ZOLLA-PAZNER, S. B., Pathology
ZUCKER-FRANKLIN, D., Medicine, Haematology
ZUCKERMAN, J. D., Orthopaedic Surgery

Silver School of Social Work (1 Washington Square North, New York, NY 10003; internet www.nyu.edu/socialwork):

ANASTAS, J. W.
DANE, B.
ENGLAND, S.
FESTINGER, T. B.
GOLDSTEIN, E. G.
HOLDEN, G.
LANDSBERG, G.
MEENAGHAN, T. M.
MILLS, L. G.
MISHNE, J.
PADGETT, D.
SEINFELD, J.
STRAUSSNER, S. L.

Steinhardt School of Culture, Education and Human Development (82 Washington Square East, New York, NY 10003; tel. (212) 998-5030; internet www.nyu.edu/education):

CAROTHERS, S. C., Teaching and Learning
KOVNER, C., Nursing
MCCLOWRY, S., Nursing
MAYHER, J. S., English Education
MILLER, M. C., Culture and Communication
NORMAN, E., Nursing
RICHARDSON, R., Higher Education
STAGE, F., Higher Education

Tisch School of the Arts (721 Broadway, New York, NY 10003; internet www.nyu.edu/tisch):

CAMPBELL, M. S., Art and Public Policy
CANEMAKER, J., Film and Television
COOPER, P., Film and Television
DANCYGER, K., Film and Television
FROST, E. C., Film, Television, and Radio
JENKIN, L., Dramatic Writing
KIMBRELL, M. A., Acting and Directing Studies
KIRSHENBLATT-GIMBLETT, B., Performance Studies
MARTIN, R., Art and Public Policy
MICHELSON, A., Cinema Studies
MILLER, T., Cinema Studies
NEIPRIS, J., Dramatic Writing
SCHECHNER, R., Performance Studies
SHOHAT, E., Art and Public Policy
SKLAR, R., Cinema Studies
SMITH, A. D., Performance Studies
STAM, R., Cinema Studies
STONEY, G. C., Film
TAYLOR, D., Performance Studies
WILLIS, D., Photography and Imaging

Courant Institute of Mathematical Sciences (251 Mercer St, New York, NY 10012; tel. (212) 998-3000; internet www.cims.nyu.edu):

AROUS, G. B., Mathematics
AVELLANEDA, M. M., Mathematics
BERGER, M. J., Computer Science and Mathematics

BERMAN, S. M., Mathematics
BOGOMOLOV, F. A., Mathematics
CAPPELL, S. E., Mathematics
CHANG, C.-S., Research Mathematics
CHILDRESS, W. S., Mathematics
COLDING, T. H., Mathematics
COLE, R. J., Computer Science
DEIFT, P. A., Mathematics
DEWAR, R. B. K., Computer Science
GARABEDIAN, P. R., Mathematics
GOODMAN, J. B., Mathematics
GOTTLIEB, A., Computer Science
GREENGARD, L., Mathematics and Computer Science
GREENLEAF, F. P., Mathematics
GRISHMAN, R., Computer Science
GROMOV, M., Mathematics
HAMEIRI, E., Mathematics
HAUSNER, M., Mathematics
HOFER, H., Mathematics
KEDEM, Z. M., Computer Science
KOHN, R. V., Mathematics
LIN, F.-H., Mathematics
MCKEAN, H. P., Mathematics
MCLAUGHLIN, D. W., Mathematics and Neural Science
MAJDA, A. J., Mathematics
MISHRA, B., Computer Science and Mathematics
NEWMAN, C. M., Mathematics
NOVIKOFF, A. B. J., Mathematics
OVERTON, M. L., Computer Science and Mathematics
PERCUS, J. K., Mathematics and Physics
PERLIN, K., Computer Science
PESKIN, C. S., Mathematics
PNUELI, A., Computer Science
POLLACK, R., Mathematics and Computer Science
RINZEL, J., Neural Science and Mathematics
SAGER, N., Natural Language Processing
SARNAK, P., Mathematics
SCHLICK, T., Chemistry, Mathematics, and Computer Science
SCHONBERG, E., Computer Science
SCHWARTZ, J. T., Computer Science and Mathematics
SHASHA, D. E., Computer Science
SHATAH, J. M. I., Mathematics
SHELLEY, M. J., Mathematics and Neural Science
SOKAL, A., Physics and Mathematics
SPENCER, J. H., Mathematics and Computer Science
STRAUSS, H. R., Computational Plasma Physics
TERZOPOULOS, D., Computer Science and Mathematics, Science
VARADHAN, S. R. S., Mathematics, Science
WEITZNER, H., Mathematics
WIDLUND, O. B., Computer Science and Mathematics
WRIGHT, M. H., Computer Science
YAP, C. K., Computer Science
YAU, H.-T., Mathematics
YOUNG, L.-S., Mathematics
ZASLAVSKY, G., Physics and Mathematics

Institute of Fine Arts (1 East 78th St, New York, NY 10021; tel. (212) 992-5800; fax (212) 992-5807; e-mail ifa.program@nyu.edu; internet www.nyu.edu/gsas/dept/fineart):

ALEXANDER, J. J. G., Fine Arts
BAER, N. S., Conservation
BROWN, J., Fine Arts
COHEN, J.-L., History of Architecture
EISLER, C., Fine Arts
ELLIS, M. H., Conservation
FAIRCHILD, S., Fine Arts
HANSEN, D. P., Fine Arts
KOPCKE, G. H., Humanities
MARINCOLA, M., Conservation
MATHEWS, T. F., History of Art
NOCHLIN, L., Modern Art
O'CONNOR, D., Ancient Egyptian Art
POSNER, D., Fine Arts
ROSENBLUM, R., Modern European Art, Fine Arts
SANDLER, L. F., Fine Arts
SOUCEK, P. P., Islamic Art
STORR, R., Modern Art
SULLIVAN, E. J., Fine Arts
TRACHTENBERG, M., History of Fine Arts
VARNEDOE, J. K. T., History of Art
WALLACE, L. A., Ancient Egyptian Art
WEIL-GARRIS BRANDT, K., Fine Arts
WESTERMANN, M., Fine Arts

NIAGARA UNIVERSITY

NY 14109
Telephone: (716) 285-1212
Internet: www.niagara.edu

Founded 1856

Pres.: Rev. JOSEPH L. LEVESQUE
Exec. Vice-Pres. and Vice-Pres. for Academic Affairs: Dr BONNIE ROSE
Dean of Admissions and Records: GEORGE C. PACHTER
Dean of Student Affairs: JOSEPH H. CUDA
Dir of Libraries: DAVID SCHOEN

Library of 279,793 vols
Number of teachers: 323
Number of students: 3,689

Publications: *Index* (12 a year), *Niagaran* (1 a year)

DEANS

Arts and Sciences: Dr NANCY MCGLEN
Business Administration: Dr JOHN A. HELMUTH (acting)
Education: Dr DEBRA COLLEY
Hospitality and Tourism Management: Dr GARY D. PRATZEL

NYACK COLLEGE

Nyack, NY 10960-3698
Telephone: (845) 358-1710
Fax: (845) 358-1751
E-mail: admissions@nyack.edu
Internet: www.nyack.edu

Founded 1882
Academic year: September to May

Pres.: Dr DAVID E. SCHROEDER
Provost and Vice-Pres. for Academic Affairs: DAVID F. TURK
Exec. Vice-Pres. and Treas.: DAVID C. JENNINGS
Vice-Pres. for Advancement: SHINO JOHN
Vice-Pres. for Student Devt: EARL MILLER
Registrar: SUE HO
Librarian: LINDA POSTON

Library of 133,000 vols
Number of teachers: 288 (107 part-time, 181 full-time)
Number of students: 2,908

PACE UNIVERSITY

1 Pace Plaza, New York, NY 10038
Telephone: (212) 346-1200
Internet: www.pace.edu

Founded 1906

Campuses in New York City, Westchester and White Plains

Pres.: STEPHEN J. FRIEDMAN
Univ. Registrar: STEVEN L. JOHNSON
Univ. Librarian: WILLIAM J. MURDOCK (acting)

Library of 938,158 vols, 5,100 periodicals
Number of teachers: 1,200
Number of students: 15,000

POLYTECHNIC INSTITUTE OF NEW YORK UNIVERSITY

6 MetroTech Center, Brooklyn, NY 11201
Telephone: (718) 260-3600
Fax: (718) 260-3136
E-mail: inquiry@poly.edu
Internet: www.poly.edu

Founded 1854, fmrly Polytechnic Univ.

Campuses at Brooklyn, Melville and Westchester

Pres.: JERRY MACARTHUR HULTIN
Provost: Dr ELIZABETH DIANNE REKOW
Vice-Pres. for Academic Affairs: Dr RICHARD S. THORSEN
Vice-Pres. for Devt and Univ. Relations: DAWN B. DUNCAN
Vice-Pres. for Finance and Admin.: T. C. WESTCOTT
Chief of Staff: JI MI CHOI
Dir of Library Services: JANA STEVENS-RICHMAN

Number of teachers: 142 full-time
Number of students: 3,983

PRATT INSTITUTE

200 Willoughby Ave, Brooklyn, NY 11205
Telephone: (718) 636-3600
Fax: (718) 636-3785
Internet: www.pratt.edu

Founded 1887
Academic year: September to May

Pres.: Dr THOMAS F. SCHUTTE
Vice-Pres. for Finance: EDMUND RUTKOWSKI
Vice-Pres. for Institutional Advancement: TODD GALITZ
Vice-Pres. for Student Life: Dr HELEN MATUSOUR-AYRES
Provost: PETER BARNA
Registrar: LISLE HENDERSON
Dir of Libraries: PATRICIA CUTRIGHT

Library of 177,198 vols
Number of teachers: 867
Number of students: 4,280

Publications: *Gateway* (26 a year), *Prattfolio* (4 a year), *Pratt Institute Bulletin*, *Prattler* (26 a year), *Prattonia* (1 a year)

DEANS

Center for Professional and Continuing Education: CHARLES MUNSTER
Graduate School of Information and Library Science: Dr TULA GIANNINI
School of Architecture: TOM HANRAHAN
School of Art and Design: CONCETTA STEWART
School of Liberal Arts and Sciences: Dr ANDREW BARNES

RENSSELAER POLYTECHNIC INSTITUTE

110 8th St, Troy, NY 12180-3590
Telephone: (518) 276-6000
Fax: (518) 276-6003
E-mail: admissions@rpi.edu
Internet: www.rpi.edu

Founded 1824

Pres.: Dr SHIRLEY ANN JACKSON
Vice-Pres. for Admin.: TOM YURKEWECZ
Vice-Pres. for Finance: VIRGINIA GREGG
Vice-Pres. for Govt Relations: LARRY SNAVLEY
Vice-Pres. for Human Resources and Institute Diversity: (vacant)
Vice-Pres. for Institute Advancement: ROBBEE KOSAK
Vice-Pres. for Student Life: DAVID HAVILAND
Provost: G. DOYLE DAVES (acting)
Dir of Office of Contracts and Grants: RICHARD SCAMMELL
Registrar: SHARON KUNKEL
Librarian: H. LORETTA EBERT

Library of 475,000 vols, 3,117 periodicals

Number of teachers: 374 full-time
Number of students: 6,509 (5,920 full-time, 589 part-time)

DEANS AND DIRECTORS

Architecture: ALAN BALFOUR
Engineering: JAMES TIEN (acting)
Humanities and Social Sciences: FAYE DUCHIN
Management: JOSEPH ECKER
Science: G. DOYLE DAVES
Undergraduate and Continuing Education: JACK WILSON

ROBERTS WESLEYAN COLLEGE

Rochester, NY 14624-1997
Telephone: (585) 594-6000
Fax: (585) 594-6371
E-mail: admissions2@roberts.edu
Internet: www.roberts.edu

Founded 1866
Academic year: September to May

Pres.: JOHN A. MARTIN
Vice-Pres. for Academic Devt: BURTON R. JONES
Vice-Pres. for Admissions and Marketing: LINDA KURTZ
Vice-Pres. for Devt: PETER L. MCCOWN
Vice-Pres. and Treas.: JAMES E. CUTHBERT
Registrar: WESLEY VANDERHOOF
Dir of Financial Aid: STEPHEN FIELD
Librarian: ALFRED C. KROBER

Library of 115,921 vols
Number of teachers: 76
Number of students: 1,428

Publication: *Roberts Today* (4 a year).

ROCHESTER INSTITUTE OF TECHNOLOGY

1 Lomb Memorial Dr., Rochester, NY 14623-5603
Telephone: (585) 475-2411
Internet: www.rit.edu

Founded 1829 as the Rochester Athenaeum

Pres.: Dr ALBERT J. SIMONE
Provost and Vice-Pres. for Academic Affairs: Dr STANLEY MCKENZIE
Vice-Pres. for Devt and Alumni Relations: LAUREL PRICE JONES
Vice-Pres. for Enrollment Management and Career Services: Dr JAMES MILLER
Vice-Pres. for Finance and Admin.: Dr JAMES WATTERS
Vice-Pres. for Student Affairs: Dr MARY-BETH COOPER
Sec. of the Institute and Asst to the Pres.: Dr FRED W. SMITH
Librarian: CHANDRA MCKENZIE

Library of 400,000 vols
Number of teachers: 1,347
Number of students: 15,300

Publications: *Admissions Bulletin* (1 a year), *Application*, *Graduate Bulletin* (1 a year), *The University Magazine* (3 a year), *Undergraduate Bulletin* (1 a year)

DEANS

College of Applied Science and Technology: WILEY R. MCKINZIE
College of Business: Dr THOMAS HOPKINS
College of Imaging Arts and Sciences: Dr JOAN STONE
College of Liberal Arts: Dr ANDREW MOORE
College of Science: Dr IAN GATLEY
B. Thomas Golisano College of Computing and Information Sciences: Dr JORGE DIAZ-HERRERA
Kate Gleason College of Engineering: Dr HARVEY PALMER
National Technical Institute for the Deaf: Dr T. ALAN HURWITZ

ROCKEFELLER UNIVERSITY

1230 York Ave, New York, NY 10065
Telephone: (212) 327-8000
Fax: (212) 327-7974
E-mail: pubinfo@rockefeller.edu
Internet: www.rockefeller.edu

Founded 1901; became a graduate univ. in 1954; name changed from Rockefeller Institute to Rockefeller University in 1965

Pres.: Sir PAUL NURSE
Vice-Pres. for Academic Affairs: MICHAEL W. YOUNG
Vice-Pres. for Devt: MAREN E. IMHOFF
Vice-Pres. for Educational Affairs: SIDNEY STRICKLAND
Vice-Pres. for Finance and Treas.: JAMES H. LAPPLE
Vice-Pres. for Human Resources: VIRGINIA HUFFMAN
Vice-Pres. for Medical Affairs: BARRY S. COLLER
Vice-Pres. for Scientific and Facility Operations: JOHN TOOZE
Vice-Pres. and Chief Investment Officer: LISA DANZIG
Vice-Pres. and Gen. Counsel: HARRIET RABB
Corporate Sec.: JANE RENDALL (acting)
Librarian: PATRICIA E. MACKEY

Library of 230,000 vols
Number of teachers: 250 professors, 69 heads of laboratories
Number of students: 398 (148 graduates, 250 research fellows)

Publications: *Journal of Cell Biology* (12 a year), *Journal of Clinical Investigation* (12 a year), *Journal of Experimental Medicine* (12 a year), *Journal of General Physiology* (12 a year).

SAGE COLLEGES

45 Ferry St, Troy, NY 12180
Telephone: (518) 244-2000
Fax: (518) 244-6880
Internet: www.sage.edu

Founded 1916

Pres.: Dr SUSAN C. SCRIMSHAW
Vice-Pres. for Academic Affairs: Dr D'ANN CAMPBELL
Vice-Pres. for External Relations: Dr DAVID MARCELL
Vice-Pres. for Finance and Admin.: WILLIAM BECKMAN
Asst Vice-Pres. for Admissions: MICHAEL SPOSILI
Dir of Libraries: KINGSLEY GREENE

Library of 350,000 vols, 1,200 periodicals
Number of teachers: 139 (92 full-time; 47 part-time)
Number of students: 1,000 full-time

Comprises Russell Sage College, Sage College of Albany and Sage Graduate School.

ST BONAVENTURE UNIVERSITY

St Bonaventure, NY 14778
Telephone: (716) 375-2000
Fax: (716) 375-2005
Internet: www.sbu.edu

Founded 1858

Chair. of Board of Trustees: SUSAN R. GREEN
Pres.: Sr MARGARET CARNEY
Vice-Pres. for Academic Affairs: Dr FRANK E. SAAL
Vice-Pres. for Business: BRENDA MCGEE SNOW
Vice-Pres. for Student Life: GEORGE F. SOLAN
Vice-Pres. for Univ. Relations: DAVID P. FERGUSON
Registrar: HEATHER L. JACKSON
Librarian: PAUL SPAETH

Number of teachers: 160
Number of students: 2,552

Publications: *Bonadieu*, *Bonaventure*, *Cithara*, *Cord*, *Franciscan Studies*, *Laurel*, *The Works of William of Ockham*

DEANS

School of Arts and Sciences: Dr STEPHEN STAHL
School of Business: Dr MICHAEL J. FISCHER
School of Education: Dr PEGGY Y. BURKE
School of Franciscan Studies: Sr MARGARET CARNEY
School of Graduate Studies: Dr MICHAEL J. FISCHER
School of Journalism and Mass Communication: Dr LEE COPPOLA
Clare College: Dr MICHAEL V. CHIARELLO

ST FRANCIS COLLEGE

180 Remsen St, Brooklyn Heights, NY 11201
Telephone: (718) 522-2300
Internet: www.stfranciscollege.edu

Chartered 1884

Pres.: BRENDAN J. DUGAN
Registrar: (vacant)
Librarian: WENDELL GUY

Library of 177,000 vols
Number of teachers: 155
Number of students: 2,136 (1,633 full-time; 503 part-time)

ST JOHN FISHER COLLEGE

3690 East Ave, Rochester, NY 14618
Telephone: (585) 385-8000
Fax: (585) 385-8386
E-mail: admissions@sjfc.edu
Internet: www.sjfc.edu

Founded 1948
Private control

Pres.: Dr DONALD E. BAIN
Provost and Dean: Dr RONALD J. AMBROSETTI
Vice-Pres. for Enrollment Management and External Relations: GERARD J. ROONEY
Vice-Pres. for Financial Affairs: JOHN P. PECCHIA
Registrar: JULIE THOMAS
Librarian: KAREN JUNKER

Number of students: 3,100

ST JOHN'S UNIVERSITY, NEW YORK

8000 Utopia Parkway, Queens, NY 11439
Telephone: (718) 990-2000
Fax: (718) 990-5723
E-mail: admhelp@stjohns.edu
Internet: www.stjohns.edu

Campuses at Queens, Staten Island, Manhattan, Oakdale and Rome (Italy)

Founded 1870, chartered 1871; re-chartered by Regents of the Univ. of the State of New York 1906
Academic year: September to May

Pres.: Rev. DONALD J. HARRINGTON
Exec. Vice-Pres. and Treasurer: JAMES PELLOW
Exec. Vice-Pres. for Student Services: Rev. MICHAEL J. CARROLL
Provost: Dr JULIE UPTON
Sr Vice-Pres. for Student Life: Dr SUSAN L. EBBS
Vice-Pres. and Sec. to the Univ.: Dr DOROTHY E. HABBEN
Vice-Pres. for Academic Support Services: Dr ANDRÉ MCKENZIE
Vice-Pres. for Administrative Services: JOHN P. CONNOLLY , Jr
Vice-Pres. for Enrollment Management: GLENN SKLARIN
Vice-Pres. for Govt and Community Relations: JOSEPH SCIAME

Vice-Pres. for Human Resources: MARY T. HARPER
Vice-Pres. for Institutional Advancement: Rev. BERNARD TRACEY
Vice-Pres. for International Relations: Dr CECILIA CHANG
Vice-Pres. for Planning and Information Technology: Dr FRANK SIRIANNI
Vice-Pres. for Property Management: CLARE T. CROSSLEY
Vice-Pres. for University Ministry: Rev. JAMES J. MAHER
Vice-Pres. for Univ. Services: DENNIS P. MCAULIFFE
Vice-Pres. of Office of Student Service: JOHN P. CONNOLLY, Jr
Dean of Libraries: Dr JAMES BENSON
Library: 1.7m. vols, 6,000 periodical subscriptions
Number of teachers: 1,111
Number of students: 18,478
Publications: *Bankruptcy Law Review*, *Journal of Legal Commentary*, *Law Review/Catholic Lawyer*, *New York International Law Review*, *Recipe*, *Res Gestae*, *St John's Today*, *Sequoya Art and Literary Magazine*, *The Forum*, *The Mission Yearbook*, *The Spectator*, *The Stormfront*, *The Torch*, *Vincentian*

DEANS
College of Pharmacy and Allied Health Professions: Dr ROBERT MANGIONE
College of Professional Studies: Dr KATHLEEN VOUTÉ MACDONALD
Metropolitan College: Dr MARY MULVIHILL (acting)
Peter J. Tobin College of Business: PETER J. TOBIN
St John's College of Liberal Arts and Sciences: Dr JEFFERY FAGEN (acting)
School of Education and Human Services: Dr JERROLD ROSS
School of Law: Judge JOSEPH W. BELLACOSA

BRANCH CAMPUSES
Oakdale Campus: 500 Montauk Highway, Oakdale, NY 11769; tel. (631) 218-7700; e-mail gradhelp@stjohns.edu; Dir BRIAN BROWNE.
Rome Campus (Italy): Via Marcantonio Colonna 21A, 00192 Rome, Italy; tel. 06-393842; fax 06-39384200; e-mail info@stjohns.edu; Vice-Pres. for Rome Campus Rev. MICHAEL J. CARROLL.
Staten Island Campus: 300 Howard Ave, Staten Island, NY 10301; tel. (718) 390-4500; e-mail siadmhelp@stjohns.edu; Sr Vice-Pres. for the Staten Island Campus Rev. JAMES F. KIERNAN.

ST JOSEPH'S COLLEGE

245 Clinton Ave, Brooklyn, NY 11205
Telephone: (718) 636-6800
Internet: www.sjcny.edu
Campuses in: Brooklyn and Long Island
Founded 1916 as St Joseph's College for Women; present name 1970
Private control
Pres.: Sr ELIZABETH A. HILL
Dir of Library, Brooklyn: WILLIAM MENG
Number of teachers: 400
Number of students: 5,393

SAINT JOSEPH'S SEMINARY

201 Seminary Ave, Yonkers, NY 10704-1896
Telephone: (914) 968-6200
Fax: (914) 376-2019
E-mail: sjs@dunwoodie.edu
Internet: www.archny.org/seminary/st-josephs-seminary-dunwoodie
Founded 1896
Private control
Rector: Most Rev. GERALD T. WALSH
Academic Dean: Rev. KEVIN P. O'REILLY
Registrar: Sr MARY FRANCES MILLS
Dir of Library Services: Sr MONICA WOOD
Number of teachers: 22 (12 full-time, 10 part-time)

ST LAWRENCE UNIVERSITY

23 Romoda Dr., Canton, NY 13617
Telephone: (315) 229-5011
E-mail: lcania@stlawu.edu
Internet: www.stlawu.edu
Founded 1856
Academic year: August to May
Pres.: WILLIAM L. FOX
Vice-Pres. and Dean: THOMAS COBURN
Vice-Pres. for Admin. Operations: THOMAS COAKLEY
Vice-Pres. for Business Affairs: KATHRYN MULLANEY
Vice-Pres. for Finance: KATHRYN MULLANEY
Vice-Pres. for Student Affairs: MARCIA LOU PETTY
Vice-Pres. for Univ. Advancement: MICHAEL ARCHIBALD
Sec.: ANGELA M. JOHNSTON
Registrar: CAROLYN FILIPPI
Librarian: BART HARLOE
Library of 522,722 vols
Number of teachers: 192
Number of students: 1,958 (undergraduate)
Publications: *Gridiron* (1 a year), *Hill News* (52 a year), *Laurentian* (1 a year), *St Lawrence Magazine* (4 a year).

ST THOMAS AQUINAS COLLEGE

125 Route 340, Sparkill, NY 10976
Telephone: (845) 398-4100
E-mail: admissions@stac.edu
Internet: www.stac.edu
Founded 1952
Private control
Pres.: Dr MARGARET MARY FITZPATRICK
Sr Vice-Pres.: Dr L. JOHN DURNEY, III
Vice-Pres.: ANNE DONINI
Provost and Vice-Pres. for Academic Affairs: Dr LEE D. BADGETT
Vice-Pres. for Financial Affairs: MANUEL D. FERNANDES
Vice-Pres. and Dean of Student Affairs: Dr WALTER SCHNEIDER
Registrar: MILDRED ALEXIOU
Library Dir: SUZANN M. WEEKLY
Number of students: 2,200

ST VLADIMIR'S ORTHODOX THEOLOGICAL SEMINARY

575 Scarsdale Rd, Crestwood, NY 10707-1699
Telephone: (914) 961-8313
Fax: (914) 961-4507
E-mail: info@svots.edu
Internet: www.svots.edu
Founded 1938
Academic year: September to May
Dean: Fr JOHN BEHR
Chancellor: Fr CHAD HATFIELD
Assoc. Dean of Academic Affairs: Dr JOHN BARNET
Assoc. Dean of Student Affairs: Fr STEVEN BELONICK
Librarian: ELEANA SONNIE SILK
Number of teachers: 16
Number of students: 105
Publication: *The Quarterly*.

SARAH LAWRENCE COLLEGE

1 Mead Way, Bronxville, NY 10708
Telephone: (914) 337-0700
Internet: www.slc.edu
Provisional charter 1926; absolute charter 1931
Pres.: KAREN LAWRENCE
Vice-Pres. for Finance and Planning: JOHN BERNSON
Dean of Admission and Financial Aid: AMY ABRAMS
Dean of College: PAULINE WATTS
Dean of Studies and Student Life: ALLEN J. GREEN (acting)
Dir of Public Relations: DIANE FUSILLI
Registrar: DANIEL LICHT
Library of 200,000 vols
Number of teachers: 238
Number of students: 1,111
Publications: *Sarah Lawrence Literary Review*, *Sarah Lawrence Magazine*, *Sarah Lawrence Tribune*.

SCHOOL OF VISUAL ARTS

209 East 23 St, New York, NY 10010-3994
Telephone: (212) 592-2000
Fax: (212) 725-3587
E-mail: admissions@sva.edu
Internet: www.schoolofvisualarts.edu
Founded 1947
Private control
Academic year: September to May
Pres.: DAVID RHODES
Exec. Vice-Pres.: ANTHONY P. RHODES
Provost: CHRISTOPHER CYPHERS
Registrar: JON TODD
Library Dir: ROBERT LOBE
Number of students: 7,047 (3,189 undergraduate, 358 postgraduate, 3,500 continuing education)

SEMINARY OF THE IMMACULATE CONCEPTION

440 W Neck Rd, Huntington, NY 11743
Telephone: (631) 423-0483
Fax: (631) 423-2346
E-mail: info@icseminary.edu
Internet: www.icseminary.edu
Founded 1926
Private control
Number of teachers: 14

SIENA COLLEGE

515 Loudon Rd, Loudonville, NY 12211-1462
Telephone: (518) 783-2300
Fax: (518) 783-4293
E-mail: website@siena.edu
Internet: www.siena.edu
Founded 1937
Independent liberal arts college
Pres.: Fr KEVIN MULLEN
Vice-Pres. for Academic Affairs: Dr DOUGLAS ASTOLFI
Vice-Pres. for Devt: Dr GREGORY J. STAHL
Vice-Pres. for Finance and Admin.: ANTHONY G. PONDILLO
Vice-Pres. for Student Affairs: Rev. JOHN FRAMBES
Dean of Residential and Judicial Services: JEANNE OBERMAYER
Dir of Admissions: EDWARD J. JONES
Library Dir: TIMOTHY G. BURKE
Library of 244,564 vols, 33,206 other items
Number of teachers: 255 (171 full-time; 84 part-time)
Number of students: 3,436 (2,669 full-time; 767 part-time)

SKIDMORE COLLEGE

815 North Broadway, Saratoga Springs, NY 12866

Telephone: (518) 580-5000
E-mail: info@skidmore.edu
Internet: www.skidmore.edu

Founded 1903, chartered 1922

Pres.: PHILIP A. GLOTZBACH
Vice-Pres. for Business Affairs and Treas.: KARL W. BROEKHUIZEN
Vice-Pres. for Devt and Alumni Affairs: CHRISTINE R. HOEK
Dean of Enrollment and College Relations: KENT H. JONES
Dean of the Faculty: PHYLLIS A. ROTH
Dean of Spec. Programmes: DONALD J. MCCORMACK
Dean of Student Affairs: JOSEPH A. TOLLIVER
Dir of Admissions: MARY LOU BATES
Dir of Skidmore Univ. Without Walls: CORNEL J. REINHART
Librarian: PEGGY SEIDEN

Library of 420,000 vols
Number of teachers: 241 (full-time)
Number of students: 2,400

STATE UNIVERSITY OF NEW YORK

System Admin., State University Plaza, Albany, NY 12246

Telephone: (518) 443-5355
Internet: www.suny.edu

Founded 1948

Chancellor: ROBERT L. KING
Provost and Vice-Chancellor for Academic Affairs: PETER D. SALINS
Univ. Counsel and Vice-Chancellor for Legal Affairs: D. ANDREW EDWARDS
Sr Vice-Chancellor for Finance and Business: BRIAN T. STENSON
Vice-Chancellor and Sec. of the Univ.: JOHN J. O'CONNOR
Vice-Chancellor for Business and Industry Relations: WAYNE DIESEL
Vice-Chancellor for Community Colleges: CAROL EATON
Vice-Chancellor and Chief of Staff: ELIZABETH CAPALDI
Vice-Chancellor and Chief Financial Officer: DAVID RICHTER
Chief Operating Officer: RICHARD P. MILLER

Number of teachers: 29,922 full-time
Number of students: 409,886 full-time.

UNIVERSITY CENTRES

University at Albany

1400 Washington Ave, Albany, NY 12222

Telephone: (518) 442-5435
Fax: (518) 442-5383
E-mail: ugadmissions@albany.edu
Internet: www.albany.edu

Founded 1844
Academic year: August to May

Pres.: GEORGE M. PHILIP
Provost and Vice-Pres. for Academic Affairs: JERYL L. MUMPOWER
Vice-Pres. for Finance and Business: KATHRYN LOWERY
Vice-Pres. for Research and Dean of Graduate Studies: JERYL L. MUMPOWER
Vice-Pres. for Student Affairs: JAMES P. DOELLEFELD
Vice-Pres. for Univ. Advancement: ROBERT ASHTON

Number of teachers: 964
Number of students: 16,751

Binghamton University

POB 6000, Binghamton, NY 13902-6000

Telephone: (607) 777-2000
Fax: (607) 777-4000
E-mail: webmaster@binghamton.edu
Internet: www.binghamton.edu

Founded 1946
Public control
Academic year: August to May

Pres.: C. PETER MAGRATH
Provost and Vice-Pres. for Academic Affairs: JEAN-PIERRE MILEUR
Vice-Pres. for Admin.: JAMES VANVOORST
Vice-Pres. for External Affairs: MARCIA CRANER
Vice-Pres. for Student Affairs: BRIAN ROSE

Library of 2,428,777 vols
Number of teachers: 845
Number of students: 14,895

DEANS

College of Community and Public Affairs: PATRICIA INGRAHAM
Decker School of Nursing: JOYCE FERRARIO
Graduate School: NANCY E. STAMP
Harpur College of Arts and Sciences: DONALD G. NIEMAN
School of Education: S. G. GRANT
School of Management: UPINDER DHILLON
Watson School of Engineering and Applied Sciences: KRISHNASWAMI SRIHARI

University at Buffalo

Buffalo, NY 14260

Telephone: (716) 645-2400
Fax: (716) 645-2895
Internet: www.buffalo.edu

Founded 1846
Academic year: August to May

Pres.: JOHN BARCLAY SIMPSON
Provost: ROBERT J. GENCO
Senior Vice-Pres.: ROBERT J. WAGNER
Vice-Pres. for Health Affairs: MICHAEL BERNARDINO
Vice-Pres. for Public Service and Urban Affairs: MARY H. GRESHAM
Vice-Pres. for Research: DALE M. LANDI
Vice-Pres. for Student Affairs: DENNIS R. BLACK
Vice-Pres. for Univ. Advancement and Devt: JENNIFER MCDONOUGH

Number of teachers: 2,149
Number of students: 24,830

Stony Brook University

Stony Brook, NY 11794

Telephone: (631) 632-6000
Internet: www.stonybrook.edu

Founded 1957
Academic year: August to May

Pres.: SAMUEL L. STANLEY, Jr
Provost and Vice-Pres. for Academic Affairs: ERIC W. KALER
Vice-Pres. for Economic Devt: YACOV SHAMASH
Vice-Pres. for Facilities and Services: BARBARA CHERNOW
Vice-Pres. for Finance and Admin.: KAROL KAIN GRAY
Vice-Pres. for Research: JOHN HARMEN MARBURGER, III

Number of teachers: 2,200
Number of students: 24,692

HEALTH SCIENCE CENTERS

Health Science Center at Brooklyn: 450 Clarkson Ave, Brooklyn, NY 11203; Pres. JOHN C. LA ROSA.

Health Science Center at Syracuse: Syracuse, NY 13210; Pres. GREGORY L. EASTWOOD.

UNIVERSITY COLLEGES

State University College at Brockport: NY 14420; Officer-in-Charge TIMOTHY J. FLANAGAN.

State University College at Buffalo: NY 14222; Pres. MURIEL A. HOWARD.

State University College at Cortland: NY 13045; Pres. ERIK J. BITTERBAUM.

State University College at Fredonia: NY 14063; Pres. DENNIS L. HEFNER.

State University College at Geneseo: NY 14454; Pres. CHRISTOPHER C. DAHL.

State University College at New Paltz: NY 12561; Pres. STEVEN POSKANZER.

State University College at Old Westbury: NY 11568; Pres. CALVIN O. BUTTS, III.

State University College at Oneonta: NY 13820; Pres. ALAN B. DONOVAN.

State University College at Oswego: NY 13126; Pres. DEBORAH FLEMMA STANLEY.

State University College at Plattsburgh: NY 12901; Pres. JOHN ETTLING.

State University College at Potsdam: NY 13676; Pres. JOHN A. FALLON, III.

State University College at Purchase: NY 10577; Pres. THOMAS J. SCHWARZ.

State University Empire State College: Saratoga Springs, NY 12866; Pres. JOSEPH B. MOORE.

COLLEGES OF TECHNOLOGY

State University of New York College of Technology at Alfred: Alfred, NY 14802; Pres. UMA GUPTA.

State University of New York College of Technology at Canton: Canton, NY 13617; Pres. JOSEPH L. KENNEDY.

State University of New York College of Agriculture and Technology at Cobleskill: Cobleskill, NY 12043; Pres. THOMAS J. HAAS.

State University of New York College of Technology at Delhi: Delhi, NY 13753-1190; Pres. CANDACE S. VANCKO.

State University of New York College of Technology at Farmingdale: Farmingdale, NY 11735; Pres. Dr JONATHAN GIBRALTER.

State University of New York College of Agriculture and Technology at Morrisville: Morrisville, NY 13408-0636; Pres. RAYMOND W. CROSS.

SPECIALIZED COLLEGES

State University Institute of Technology at Utica/Rome: POB 3050, Utica, NY 13504-3050; Pres. MASON H. SOMERVILLE.

State University of New York College of Environmental Science and Forestry: Syracuse, NY 13210; Pres. CORNELIUS B. MURPHY.

State University of New York College of Optometry at New York City: 100 E 24th St, New York, NY 10010; Pres. ALDEN N. HAFFNER.

State University of New York Maritime College: Fort Schuyler, Bronx, NY 10465; Pres. JOHN R. RYAN.

SYRACUSE UNIVERSITY

Syracuse, NY 13244

Telephone: (315) 443-1870
E-mail: gradinfo@syr.edu
Internet: www.syr.edu

Founded 1870

Chancellor and Pres.: Dr KENNETH A. SHAW
Vice-Chancellor for Academic Affairs: Dr DEBORAH FREUND
Exec. Asst to the Chancellor: GRETCHEN GOLDSTEIN
Sr Vice-Pres. for Business and Finance: LOUIS MARCOCCIA

Sr Vice-Pres. for Giving Programs: Dr THOMAS HARBLIN
Sr Vice-Pres. for Human Services and Govt Relations: ELEANOR WARE
Sr Vice-Pres. for Institutional Advancement: Dr JOHN SELLARS
Sr Vice-Pres. and Dean for Student Affairs: BARRY L. WELLS
Vice-Pres. for Enrollment Management and Continuing Education: DAVID SMITH
Vice-Pres. for Research and Computing: Dr BEN WARE
Exec. Dir of Govt Relations: ELIZABETH ROUGEUX
Dean of Admissions and Financial Aid: SUSAN DONOVAN
Registrar: MAUREEN BREED
Univ. Librarian: PETER GRAHAM
Library: see Libraries and Archives
Number of teachers: 1,386
Number of students: 18,600

Publications: *Symposium* (on foreign languages and literature, 4 a year), *Syracuse Law Review* (4 a year), *Syracuse University Magazine* (3 a year), *Syracuse University Record* (52 a year)

DEANS

College of Arts and Sciences: Dr CATHRYN NEWTON
College of Engineering and Computer Science: Dr ERIC SPINA
College of Human Services and Health Professionals: BRUCE LAGAY
College of Law: Prof. DAAN BRAVEMAN
College of Visual and Performing Arts: CAROLE BRZOZOWSKI
University College: CHARLES BARLETTA
Utica College: Dr MICHAEL SIMPSON
School of Architecture: Dr MARK ROBBINS
School of Education: Dr LOUISE WILKINSON
School of Information Studies: Dr RAYMOND F. VON DRAN
School of Management: SANDY HURD
Graduate School: Dr JOHN MERCER
Maxwell Graduate School of Citizenship and Public Affairs: Dr MITCHELL WALLERSTEIN
S. I. Newhouse School of Public Communications: Dr DAVID RUBIN
Hendricks Memorial Chapel: THOMAS WOLFE
Summer Sessions: CHARLES BARLETTA

AFFILIATED INSTITUTIONS

All-University Gerontology Center.

Center for Computer Applications and Software Engineering.

Center for Membrane Science.

Center for Northeast Parallel Architectures.

Center of Hispanic Studies: f. 1945; cooperates closely with the faculties of geography and history.

Center on Human Policy.

Communications Research Center.

Division of International Programs Abroad.

Global Affairs Institute.

Institute for Energy Research.

Institute for Sensory Research.

TOURO COLLEGE

27–33 West 23 St, New York, NY 10010
Telephone: (212) 463-0400
Fax: 212) 627-9144
Internet: www.touro.edu

Campuses in: Manhattan, Brooklyn, Queens, Long Island, California, Florida, Nevada, Israel, Italy and Germany

Founded 1970
Private control
Pres.: Dr BERNARD LANDER
Sr Provost: ALAN KADISH
Library Dir: JACQUELINE A. MAXIN
Number of teachers: 247
Number of students: 8,950

UNIFICATION THEOLOGICAL SEMINARY

30 Seminary Dr., Barrytown, NY 12507
Telephone: (845) 752-3000
Fax: (845) 752-3016
E-mail: admissions@uts.edu
Internet: www.uts.edu

Founded 1975
Private control
Academic year: August to May
Pres.: Dr RICHARD A. PANZER
Vice-Pres.: (vacant)
Academic Dean: Dr KATHY WININGS
Dean of Students: PAUL RAJAN
Dean of New York City Extension Center: Dr KATHY WININGS
Registrar: UTE DELANEY
Library Dir: Dr KEISUKE NODA
Library of 55,000 vols
Publication: *Journal of Unification Studies* (1 a year).

UNION COLLEGE

807 Union St, Schenectady, NY 12308
Telephone: (518) 388-6000
Internet: www.union.edu

Founded 1795; oldest non-denominational college in USA
Pres.: STEPHEN C. AINLAY
Vice-Pres. for Academic Affairs and Dean of Faculty: THERESE MCCARTY
Vice-Pres. for Admissions, Financial Aid and Enrollment: MATTHEW J. MALATESTA
Vice-Pres. for Alumni Affairs: JOSEPH L. MAMMOLA
Vice-Pres. for College Relations: STEPHEN A. DARE
Vice-Pres. for Finance and Admin.: DIANE T. BLAKE
Registrar: PENELOPE S. ADEY
Library Dir: THOMAS MCFADDEN
Library of 624,475 vols
Number of teachers: 207 (full-time)
Number of students: 2,192 (full-time, degree-seeking)

Publications: *Catalogue*, *Chronicle* (college weekly), *Concordiensis* (student weekly), *Idol* (student literary magazine), *Sentinel* (political magazine), *Union Book* (Sr Year Book), *Union College* (Alumni)

DEANS

Faculty: THERESE MCCARTY
Students: STEPHEN LEAVITT

UNION THEOLOGICAL SEMINARY

3041 Broadway, New York, NY 10027
Telephone: (212) 662-7100
E-mail: contactus@uts.columbia.edu
Internet: www.uts.columbia.edu

Founded 1836
Private control
Academic year: September to May
Pres.: Rev. Dr SERENE JONES
Exec. Vice-Pres.: MARY E. MCNAMARA
Academic Dean: ROSEMARY SKINNER KELLER
Dean of Academic Admin.: JAMES A. HAYES
Dir of Admissions and Registrar: DAVID L. MCDONAGH
Library Dir: SARA J. MYERS
Number of teachers: 46
Number of students: 245

UNITED STATES MERCHANT MARINE ACADEMY

Kings Point, NY 11024-1699
Telephone: (516) 773-5000
Fax: (516) 773-5509
E-mail: admissions@usmma.edu
Internet: www.usmma.edu

Founded 1943
Academic year: July to June
Superintendent: Vice-Admiral JOSEPH D. STEWART
Chief of Staff: Capt. ROBERT SAFARIK
Academic Dean: Dr WARREN F. MAZEK
Commandant of Midshipmen: Capt. ROBERT ALLEE
Dir of Office of External Affairs: Capt. DONALD FERGUSON
Library: Dr GEORGE BILLY
Number of teachers: 81 instructors
Number of students: 950 midshipmen

UNITED STATES MILITARY ACADEMY

West Point, NY 10996
Telephone: (914) 938-4011
E-mail: webmail@usma.edu
Internet: www.usma.edu

Founded 1802
Superintendent: Lt-Gen. FRANKLIN L. HAGENBECK
Commandant of Cadets: Brig.-Gen. ROBERT J. ST ONGE, Jr
Dean of the Academic Board: Brig.-Gen. FLETCHER M. LAMKIN, Jr
Dir of Admissions: Col MICHAEL L. JONES
Librarian: JOSEPH BARTH
Library of 500,000 vols
Number of instructors: 562
Number of cadets: 4,112.

UNIVERSITY OF ROCHESTER

Rochester, NY 14627
Telephone: (585) 275-2121
Fax: (716) 275-0359
Internet: www.rochester.edu

Founded 1850
Private control
Academic year: September to May (two terms)
Pres.: JOEL SELIGMAN
Provost and Exec. Vice-Pres.: RALPH KUNCL
Sr Vice-Pres. and Robert L. and Mary L. Sproull Dean of the Faculty of Arts, Sciences and Engineering: PETER LENNIE
Sr Vice-Pres. and Chief Advancement Officer: JAMES D. THOMPSON
Sr Vice-Pres. and Gen. Counsel: SUE S. STEWART
Sr Vice-Pres. for Admin. and Finance, Chief Financial Officer and Treas.: RONALD J. PAPROCKI
Sr Vice-Pres. for Health Sciences: BRADFORD C. BERK
Vice-Pres. and Gen. Sec.: PAUL J. BURGETT
Vice-Pres. for Communications: BILL MURPHY
Sr Vice-Pres. for Institutional Resources: DOUGLAS W. PHILLIPS
Dean of Research: PAUL SLATTERY
Registrar: NANCY SPECK
Dean of River Campus Libraries: SUSAN GIBBONS
Library: see Libraries
Number of teachers: 1,331
Number of students: 9,423

DEANS

Eastman School of Music: DOUGLAS LOWRY
Graduate Studies: WENDI HEINZELMAN
Memorial Art Gallery: GRANT HOLCOMB (Dir)

School of Arts and Sciences: JOANNA B. OLMSTED
School of Engineering and Applied Sciences: ROBERT CLARK
School of Medicine and Dentistry: MARK B. TAUBMAN
School of Nursing: KATHY PARKER
Simon Graduate School of Business Admin.: MARK ZUPAN
The College: RICHARD FELDMAN
Warner Graduate School of Education and Human Devt: RAFFAELLA BORASI

VASSAR COLLEGE

Poughkeepsie, NY 12604
Telephone: (845) 437-7000
Internet: www.vassar.edu
Founded 1861
Academic year: September to May
Pres.: CATHERINE BOND HILL
Vice-Pres. for Devt: CATHERINE BAER
Vice-Pres. for Finance and Treas.: ELIZABETH EISMEIER
Dir of College Relations: SUSAN DEKREY
Dean of the College: CHRISTOPHER F. ROELLKE
Dean of the Faculty: JONATHAN L. CHERETTE
Dean of Students: DAVID H. BROWN
Dir of Libraries: SABRINA PAPE
Library of 830,235 vols
Number of teachers: 293
Number of students: 2,389

VAUGHN COLLEGE OF AERONAUTICS AND TECHNOLOGY

86-01 23rd Ave, Flushing, NY 11369
Telephone: (718) 429-6600
Fax: (718) 429-0256
E-mail: admissions@vaughn.edu
Internet: www.vaughn.edu
Founded 1932 as Casey Jones School of Aeronautics; present name 1986
Private control
Pres.: Dr JOHN C. FITZPATRICK
Number of teachers: 119
Number of students: 1,308

WAGNER COLLEGE

1 Campus Rd, Staten Island, NY 10301
Telephone: (718) 390-3100
Fax: (718) 390-3105
E-mail: webmaster@wagner.edu
Internet: www.wagner.edu
Founded 1883
Pres.: Dr RICHARD GUARASCI
Dean of Admissions: ANGELO ARAIMO
Librarian: Y. JOHN AUH
Library of 285,000 vols
Number of teachers: 100 (full-time)
Number of students: 2,229

WEBB INSTITUTE

298 Crescent Beach Rd, Glen Cove, NY 11542-1398
Telephone: (516) 671-2213
Fax: (516) 674-9838
E-mail: inquiry@webb-institute.edu
Internet: www.webb-institute.edu
Founded 1889
Academic year: August to June
Pres.: Admiral ROBERT OLSEN
Dir of Enrollment Management: WILLIAM G. MURRAY
Library Dir: PATRICIA PRESCOTT
Library of 50,000 vols
Number of teachers: 14 (10 full-time, 4 adjunct)
Number of students: 74

WELLS COLLEGE

170 Main St, Aurora, NY 13026
Telephone: (315) 364-3266
Fax: (315) 364-3227
E-mail: admissions@wells.edu
Internet: www.wells.edu
Founded 1868
Women's liberal arts college
Academic year: August to May
Pres.: LISA MARSH RYERSON
Vice-Pres. and Treas.: DIANE HUTCHINSON
Dean of Students: SUSAN RYAN
Dean of the College: ELLEN HALL
Dir of Admissions: SUSAN SLOAN
Registrar: KARLA LEYBOLD-TAYLOR
Librarian: JERI VARGO
Library of 248,130 vols
Number of teachers: 55
Number of students: 352
Publication: *Wells College Express* (4 a year).

YESHIVA UNIVERSITY

500 W 185th St, New York, NY 10033
Telephone: (212) 960-5400
Fax: (212) 960-0055
E-mail: webmaster@yu.edu
Internet: www.yu.edu
Founded 1886
Independent control
Languages of instruction: English, Hebrew
Pres.: Dr RICHARD M. JOEL
Vice-Pres. for Academic Affairs: S. R. GELMAN
Vice-Pres. for Business Affairs: S. E. SOCOL
Vice-Pres. for Devt: D. T. FORMAN
Vice-Pres. for Medical Affairs: D. P. PURPURA
Vice-Pres. for Univ. Affairs: H. C. DOBRINSKY
Dir of Public Relations: D. M. ROSEN
Gen. Counsel: M. H. BOCKSTEIN
Dean of Univ. Libraries: P. BERGER
Library: 6 libraries with 1m. vols
Number of teachers: 1,100
Number of students: 6,335
Publications: *Yeshiva University Review*, *Yeshiva University Today*

DEANS

Albert Einstein College of Medicine: D. P. PURPURA
Azrieli Graduate School of Jewish Education and Administration: Y. S. HANDEL
Benjamin N. Cardozo School of Law: P. R. VERKUIL
Bernard Revel Graduate School and Harry Fischel School for Higher Jewish Studies: A. HYMAN
Ferkauf Graduate School of Psychology: L. J. SIEGEL
Irving I. Stone Beit Midrash Program: M. D. SHMIDMAN
Isaac Breuer College of Hebraic Studies: M. D. SHMIDMAN
James Striar School of General Jewish Studies: M. D. SHMIDMAN
Stern College for Women: K. BACON
Sue Golding Graduate Division of Medical Sciences: A. M. ETGEN
Sy Syms School of Business: H. NIERENBERG
Wurzweiler School of Social Work: S. R. GELMAN
Yeshiva College: N. T. ADLER
Yeshiva Program and Mazer School of Talmudic Studies: Z. CHARLOP

NORTH CAROLINA

APPALACHIAN STATE UNIVERSITY

Boone, NC 28608
Telephone: (828) 262-2000
Internet: www.appstate.edu
Founded 1899; attached to Univ. of North Carolina
Chancellor: Dr KENNETH E. PEACOCK
Provost and Exec. Vice-Chancellor: Dr STANLEY R. AESCHLEMAN
Registrar: DON RANKINS
Univ. Librarian: MARY REICHEL
Library of 800,000 vols
Number of teachers: 619
Number of students: 15,117

BARBER-SCOTIA COLLEGE

145 Cabarrus Ave W, Concord, NC 28025
Telephone: (704) 789-2900
Fax: (704) 789-2958
Internet: www.b-sc.edu
Founded 1867
Pres.: DAVID OLAH
Vice-Pres. for Academic Affairs: ALEXANDER ERWIN
Vice-Pres. for Fiscal Affairs: NEMICHAND JAIN
Vice-Pres. for Institutional Advancement: EUGENE C. PERRY
Vice-Pres. for Student Affairs: ERIC JACKSON
Registrar: EMMA WITHERSPOON
Librarian: MINORA HICKS
Library of 68,374 vols
Number of teachers: 36
Number of students: 500

BARTON COLLEGE

POB 5000, Wilson, NC 27893-7000
Telephone: (252) 399-6300
Fax: (252) 399-6571
Internet: www.barton.edu
Founded 1902
Private (Disciples of Christ)
Academic year: September to May
Pres.: Dr NORVAL C. KNETEN
Vice-Pres. for Academic Affairs: Dr TERRENCE M. GRIMES
Vice-Pres. for Admin. and Finance: RICHARD A. MARSHALL
Dir of Library: RODNEY LIPPARD
Library of 150,000 vols
Number of teachers: 82
Number of students: 1,300

BELMONT ABBEY COLLEGE

100 Belmont-Mt Holly Rd, Belmont, NC 28012
Telephone: (704) 825-6700
Fax: (704) 825-6670
Internet: www.belmontabbeycollege.edu
Founded 1876
Academic year: August to May
Pres.: Dr WILLIAM K. THIERFELDER
Vice-Pres. for Academic Affairs: Dr DEAN DE LA MOTTE
Vice-Pres. for Business Affairs: JAMES SCHUPPENHAUER
Vice-Pres. for Institutional Advancement: Dr JOHN MARSHALL
Vice-Pres. for Student Affairs: KAREN VAN NORMAN
Dean of Admissions and Dir of Financial Aid: ANNE STEVENS
Dir of Public Relations: THERESA SOWERS MCKINNEY
Library of 150,000 vols
Number of teachers: 50
Number of students: 1,000
Publications: *Agora*, *Crossroads*.

BENNETT COLLEGE

Greensboro, NC 27401-3239
Telephone: (336) 273-4431
Internet: www.bennett.edu

Founded 1873 (reorganized 1926)
Pres.: Dr JOHNNETTA BETSCH COLE
Dir of Admissions: LINDA TORRENCE
Vice-Pres. for Academic Affairs and Student Devt: Dr DONNA H. OLIVER
Library Dir: JOAN WILLIAMS
Library of 100,000 vols
Number of teachers: 46
Number of students: 607

CAMPBELL UNIVERSITY

POB 488, Buie's Creek, NC 27506
Telephone: (910) 893-1200
Fax: (910) 893-1424
Internet: www.campbell.edu
Founded 1887
Pres.: Dr JEREMY M. WALLACE
Chancellor: Dr NORMAN ADRIAN WIGGINS
Vice-Pres. for Academic Affairs and Provost: Dr DWAINE GREENE
Vice-Pres. for Business and Treas.: JIM ROBERTS
Vice-Pres. for Institutional Advancement: Dr JACK BRITT
Vice-Pres. for Student Life: Dr DENNIS BAZEMORE
Dir of Library Services: Dr RONNIE W. FAULKNER
Library of 478,772 vols
Number of teachers: 428 (175 full-time, 253 part-time)
Number of students: 9,220
Publication: *Pine Burr* (year book)

DEANS

School of Arts and Sciences: Dr MARK L. HAMMOND
School of Business: Dr CHRISTIAN ZINKHAN
School of Education: Dr KAREN P. NERY
School of Law: WILLIS P. WHICHARD
School of Pharmacy: Dr RONALD W. MADDOX
Divinity School: Dr MICHAEL G. COGDILL

CATAWBA COLLEGE

2300 W Innes St, Salisbury, NC 28144
Telephone: (704) 637-4111
Internet: www.catawba.edu
Founded 1851
Private control
Pres.: Dr JOSEPH OXENDINE
Provost: Dr RICK STEPHENS
Registrar: P. CAROL GAMBLE
Vice-Pres. for Enrollment Management: LOIS WILLIAMS
Library Dir: STEVEN MCKINZIE
Library of 200,000 vols
Number of teachers: 115
Number of students: 1,250

DEANS

School of Arts and Sciences: Dr STEVE COGGIN
School of Business: Dr JAMES SLATE
School of Education: Dr JAMES STRINGFIELD
School of Evening and Graduate Studies: Dr EDITH BOLICK
School of Performing Arts: Dr WOODROW HOOD

CHOWAN UNIVERSITY

1 University Pl., Murfreesboro, NC 27855
Telephone: (252) 398-6500
Fax: (252) 398-1190
E-mail: admissions@chowan.edu
Internet: www.chowan.edu
Founded 1848 as Chowan Baptist Female Institute, present name 2006
Private control
Academic year: 2 semesters plus summer school
Pres.: Dr M. CHRISTOPHER WHITE
Provost and Vice-Pres. for Academic Affairs: Dr DANNY B. MOORE
Vice-Pres. of Business Affairs: DONNIE CLARY
Vice-Pres. of Devt: JOHN TAYLOE
Vice-Pres. of Human Resources: JOHN HINTON
Vice-Pres. of Student Affairs: RANDY HARRELL
Vice-Pres. of Student Enrollment: CHAD HOLT
Dir of Athletics: DENNIS HELSEL
Registrar: DONNA WOODARD
Librarian: GEORGIA WILLIAMS
Library of 230,000 vols, 29,000 periodicals
Number of teachers: 56 (full-time)
Number of students: 1,200

DEANS

School of Business: Dr LINDA MILES
School of Education: Dr BRENDA TINKHAM
School of Liberal Arts: Dr LARRY FRAZIER

DAVIDSON COLLEGE

209 Ridge Rd, Davidson, NC 28036
Telephone: (704) 894-2000
Fax: (704) 894-2005
Internet: www.davidson.edu
Founded 1837
Academic year: August to May
Pres.: JOHN W. KUYKENDALL, Sr
Vice-Pres. for Academic Affairs and Dean of the Faculty: CLARK G. ROSS
Vice-Pres. for Business and Finance: ED KANIA
Vice-Pres. for College Relations: EILEEN KEELEY
Dir of Alumni Relations: PETER WAGNER
Dean of Admissions and Financial Aid: CHRISTOPHER J. GRUBER
Registrar: Dr HANSFORD M. EPES
Dir of Library: JILL GREMMELS
Library of 600,000 vols
Number of teachers: 152
Number of students: 1,922
Publications: *Davidson Journal* (4 a year), *Hobart Park* (literary, 1 a year), *Oak Row Report* (12 a year).

DUKE UNIVERSITY

Durham, NC 27708
Telephone: (919) 684 8111
Internet: www.duke.edu
Founded 1838 as Union Institute Soc. in Randolph County, NC; became Trinity College 1851; moved to Durham 1892; present name 1924
Academic year: September to August
Pres.: RICHARD H. BRODHEAD
Exec. Vice-Pres.: TALLMAN TRASK, III
Provost: PETER LANGE
Chancellor for Health Affairs: VICTOR J. DZAU
Provost: PETER LANGE
Vice-Pres. for Information Technology and Chief Information Officer: TRACY FUTHEY
Vice-Pres. and Univ. Sec.: RICHARD RIDDELL
Vice-Pres. for Public Affairs and Govt Relations: MICHAEL J. SCHOENFELD
Vice-Pres. for Alumni Affairs and Devt: ROBERT SHEPARD
Vice-Pres. for Finance and Treasurer: B. HOFLER MILAM
Vice-Pres. for Human Resources: KYLE CAVANAUGH
Vice-Pres. for Student Affairs: LARRY MONETA
Vice-Pres. and Gen. Counsel: PAMELA J. BERNARD
Vice-Pres. and Vice-Provost for Global Strategy and Programs: GREG JONES
Vice-Pres. and Dir of Athletics: KEVIN M. WHITE
Vice-Pres., Office for Institutional Equity: BENJAMIN REESE
Vice-Pres., Durham and Regional Affairs: PHAIL WYNN, Jr
Registrar: BRUCE CUNNINGHAM
Univ. Librarian and Vice-Provost for Library Affairs: DEBORAH JAKUBS
Number of teachers: 1,752
Number of students: 13,662
Publications: *American Literary Scholarship* (1 a year), *American Literature* (4 a year), *American Speech* (4 a year), *boundary 2* (3 a year), *Camera Obscura* (3 a year), *Common Knowledge* (2 a year), *Comparative Studies of South Asia, Africa and the Middle East* (2 a year), *Duke Gifted Letter* (4 a year), *Duke Mathematical Journal* (15 a year), *Eighteenth-Century Life* (3 a year), *Environmental History* (4 a year), *Ethnohistory* (4 a year), *French Historical Studies* (4 a year), *GLQ: A Journal of Lesbian and Gay Studies* (4 a year), *Hispanic American Historical Review* (4 a year), *History of Political Economy* (4 a year), *Journal of Health Politics, Policy and Law* (6 a year), *Journal of Medieval and Early Modern Studies* (3 a year), *Lesbian and Gay Studies Newsletter* (3 a year), *Mediterranean Quarterly* (4 a year), *Modern Language Quarterly* (4 a year), *Nepantla: Views from the South* (3 a year), *Pedagogy* (3 a year), *Poetics Today* (4 a year), *positions* (3 a year), *Public Culture* (3 a year), *Radical History Review* (3 a year), *Social Science History* (4 a year), *Social Text* (4 a year), *South Atlantic Quarterly* (4 a year), *Theater* (3 a year), *Transition* (4 a year)

DEANS

Trinity College of Arts and Sciences: ALVIN L. CRUMBLISS
Fuqua School of Business: BLAIR SHEPPARD
Divinity School: RICHARD HAYS
Pratt School of Engineering: THOMAS C. KATSOULEAS
Nicholas School of the Environment: WILLIAM L. CHAMEIDES
Graduate School: JO RAE WRIGHT
School of Law: DAVID F. LEVI
School of Medicine: NANCY C. ANDREWS
School of Nursing: CATHERINE L. GILLISS
Sanford School of Public Policy: BRUCE R. KUNIHOLM

PROFESSORS

ABOU-DONIA, M. B., Pharmacology and Cancer Biology
ADDISON, W. A., Obstetrics and Gynaecology
AERS, D., English
AGARWAL, P. K., Computer Science
AKWARI, O. E., Surgery
ALBALA, D. M., Surgery
ALDRICH, J., Political Science
ALLARD, W. K., Mathematics
ALLEN, N. B., Medicine
ANDERSON, E. E., Surgery
ANDERSON, P. A. W., Paediatrics
ANDERSON, R. W., Surgery
ANDERSON, W. B., Ophthalmology
ANDREWS, E., Slavic Languages and Literature
ANLYAN, W. G., Surgery
ANSCHER, M. S., Radiation Oncology
APPLEWHITE, J. W., English
ASHER, S. R., Psychology, Social and Health Sciences
ASHTON, R. H., Business Administration
AUGUSTINE, G. J., Jr, Neurobiology
AVISSAR, R., Civil and Environmental Engineering
BAILLIE, J., Medicine
BAKER, H. A., English
BAKER, P. A., Earth and Ocean Sciences
BALDWIN, S. W., Chemistry
BARANGER, H. U., Physics
BARBER, R. T., Marine Sciences

BARR, R. C., Biomedical Engineering
BARTLETT, J. A., Medicine
BARTLETT, K., Law
BASHORE, T. M., Medicine
BASSETT, F. H., III, Surgery
BEALE, J. T., Mathematics
BEALE, S. S., Law
BECKWITH, S., English
BEEN, M. D., Biochemistry
BEHAR, V. S., Medicine
BEHRINGER, R. P., Physics
BEJAN, A., Mechanical Engineering
BELL, D. F., Romance Studies
BENFEY, P. N., Biology
BENNETT, G. V., Cell Biology
BENNETT, P. B., Anaesthesiology
BERATAN, D. N., Chemistry
BERCHUCK, A., Obstetrics and Gynaecology
BERGER, J. O., Statistics
BERTOZZI, A. L., Mathematics
BETTMAN, J. R., Business Administration
BIERMANN, A. W., Computer Science
BIGNER, D. D., Pathology
BISSET, G. S., III, Radiology
BLAND, K. P., Religion
BLAZER, D. G., Psychiatry and Behavioural Sciences
BLUMENTHAL, J. A., Psychiatry and Behavioural Sciences
BOATWRIGHT, M. T., Classical Studies
BOLLERSLEV, T., Economics
BOLLINGER, R. R., Surgery
BOLOGNESI, D. P., Surgery
BONAVENTURA, C. J., Marine Sciences
BONAVENTURA, J., Marine Sciences
BONK, J. F., Chemistry
BORCHARDT, F. L., Germanic Languages
BOSSEN, E. H., Pathology
BOULDING, W. F., Business Administration
BOWIE, J. D., Radiology
BOYLE, J. D. A., Law
BRADFORD, W. D., Pathology
BRADLEY, M., Business Administration
BRADY, D. J., Electrical and Computer Engineering
BRANDON, R. N., Philosophy
BREEDEN, D. T., Business Administration
BRIZEL, D. M., Radiation Oncology
BRODIE, H. K. H., Psychiatry and Behavioural Sciences
BROWN, A. S., Electrical and Computer Engineering
BROWN, H. L., Obstetrics and Gynaecology
BRUZELIUS, C., Art and Art History
BRYANT, R., Mathematics
BUCKLEY, E. G., Ophthalmology
BUCKLEY, P. J., Pathology
BUCKLEY, R. H., Paediatrics
BUEHLER, A., Health, Physical Education and Recreation
BURCH, W. M., Jr, Medicine
BURIAN, P. H., Classical Studies
BURNS, B. J., Psychiatry and Behavioural Sciences
BURTON, R. M., Business Administration
BUTTERS, R. R., English
CALIFF, R. M., Medicine
CARIN, L., Electrical and Computer Engineering
CARON, M. G., Cell Biology
CARRINGTON, P. D., Law
CARROLL, B. A., Radiology
CARTER, J. H., Psychiatry and Behavioural Sciences
CARTMILL, M., Biological Anthropology and Anatomy
CASEY, P. J., Pharmacology and Cancer Biology
CHAFE, W. H., History
CHAO, N. J., Medicine
CHEN, Y., Paediatrics
CHIKARAISHI, D. M., Neurobiology
CHRISTENSEN, N. L., Earth and Environmental Sciences
CHRISTIE, G. C., Law
CLARK, E. A., Religion
CLARK, J. S., Biology
CLARK, R. L., Mechanical Engineering
CLARKE-PEARSON, D. L., Obstetrics and Gynaecology
CLAY, D., Classical Studies
CLEMENTS, D. A., III, Paediatrics
CLIPP, E. C., Nursing
CLOTFELTER, C., Public Policy Studies
CLUM, J. M., Theatre Studies
COBB, F. R., Medicine
COCKS, F. H., Mechanical Engineering
COFFMAN, T. M., Medicine
COHEN, H. J., Medicine
COHEN, W. M., Business Administration
COHN, J. A., Medicine
COIE, J. D., Psychology, Social and Health Sciences
COLEMAN, R. E., Radiology
COLEMAN, W. J., Business Administration
COLVIN, O. M., Medicine
COOK, D. R., Anaesthesiology
COOK, P. J., Public Policy Studies
COOKE, M., Asian and African Language and Literature
COREY, G. R., Medicine
CORLISS, B., Earth and Ocean Sciences
COSTANZO, P. R., Psychology, Social and Health Sciences
COSTELLO, E. J., Psychiatry and Behavioural Sciences
COX, J. D., Law
CRAWFORD, J., Medicine
CRENSHAW, J. L., Divinity
CROVITZ, H. F., Psychiatry and Behavioural Sciences
CROWDER, L. B., Marine Sciences
CROWLEY, T. J., Earth and Ocean Sciences
CRUMBLISS, A. L., Chemistry
CULLEN, B. R., Molecular Genetics and Microbiology
CULP, J. M., Law
DAVIDSON, C. N., English
DAVIDSON, J. R., Psychiatry and Behavioural Sciences
DAVIS, N. G., Classical Studies
DAWSON, J. R., Immunology
DE BELLIS, M. D., Psychiatry and Behavioural Sciences
DELLINGER, W. E., Law
DELONG, G. R., Paediatrics
DE MARCHI, N., Economics
DEMOTT, D., Law
DENEEF, A. L., English
DESANCTIS, G., Business Administration
DEWHIRST, M. W., Radiation Oncology
DI GIULIO, R. T., Earth and Environmental Sciences
DIPRETE, T. A., Sociology
DODGE, K. A., Public Policy Studies
DOWELL, E. H., Mechanical Engineering
ECKERMAN, C. O., Psychological and Brain Sciences
EDELSBRUNNER, H., Computer Science
EDWARDS, G. S., Physics
EFIRD, J. M., Divinity
ELLINWOOD, E. H., Jr, Psychiatry and Behavioural Sciences
ELLIS, C. S., Computer Science
ENDOW, S. A., Cell Biology
ENGLISH, P. C., History
EPSTEIN, D. L., Ophthalmology
ERICKSON, C. J., Psychological and Brain Sciences
ERICKSON, H. P., Cell Biology
EVERETT, R. O., Law
FAIR, R. B., Electrical and Computer Engineering
FALLETTA, J. M., Paediatrics
FARMER, J. C., Surgery
FEINGLOS, M. N., Medicine
FISCHER, G. W., Business Administration
FISH, P. G., Political Science
FISHER, S. R., Surgery
FITZPATRICK, D., Neurobiology
FLANAGAN, O., Philosophy
FLEISHMAN, J., Law
FLOYD, C. E., Jr, Radiology
FOREMAN, J. W., Paediatrics
FORWARD, R. B., Marine Sciences
FRANCES, A. J., Psychiatry and Behavioural Sciences
FRANCIS, J., Business Administration
FRANK, M. M., Paediatrics
FREEMARK, M. S., Paediatrics
FRIEDMAN, A. H., Surgery
FRIEDMAN, H. S., Paediatrics
FRIEDMAN, M., Biomedical Engineering
FULKERSON, W. J., Jr, Medicine
GAINES, J. M., Literature
GARCIA-BLANCO, M. A., Molecular Genetics and Microbiology
GARCI-GOMEZ, M., Romance Studies
GARG, D. P., Mechanical Engineering
GASPAR, B., History
GAVINS, R., History
GELFAND, A., Statistics
GEORGE, L. K., Sociology
GEORGE, S. L., Biostatistics and Bioinformatics
GEORGIADE, G. S., Surgery
GEREFFI, G., Sociology
GILBOA, E., Surgery
GILLESPIE, M. A., Political Science
GILLIAM, B., Music
GLANDER, K. E., Biological Anthropology and Anatomy
GLOWER, D. D., Jr, Surgery
GOCKERMAN, J. P., Medicine
GOLDBERG, R. N., Paediatrics
GOLDING, M. P., Philosophy
GOLDSCHMIDT, P. J., Medicine
GOLDSTEIN, L. B., Medicine
GOODMAN, P. C., Radiology
GOODWIN, C. D., Economics
GOODWYN, L. C., History
GOSHAW, A. T., Physics
GRABOWSKI, H. G., Economics
GRAHAM, D. A., Economics
GRANT, A. O., Medicine
GRANT, J. P., Surgery
GRANT, R. W., Political Science
GREENBERG, C. S., Medicine
GREENFIELD, J. C., Jr, Medicine
GREENLEAF, A. L., Biochemistry
GREENSIDE, H., Physics
GREER, M. R., Romance Studies
GRIECO, J., Political Science
GRIFFITHS, P. A., Mathematics
HAAGEN, P. H., Law
HAFF, P. K., Earth and Ocean Sciences
HAIN, R., Mathematics
HALL, K. C., Mechanical Engineering
HALL, R. P., III, Medicine
HALL, W. C., Neurobiology
HALL, W. G., Psychological and Brain Sciences
HALPERIN, E. C., Radiation Oncology
HAMILTON, J. A., Psychology, Social and Health Sciences
HAMILTON, J. D., Medicine
HAMMES, G. G., Biochemistry
HAMMOND, C. B., Obstetrics and Gynaecology
HAN, M. Y., Physics
HANEY, A. F., Obstetrics and Gynaecology
HARER, J., Mathematics
HARMAN, C. M., Mechanical Engineering
HARRELSON, J. M., Surgery
HARVEY, C. R., Business Administration
HAUERWAS, S. M., Divinity
HAVIGHURST, C. C., Law
HAYNES, B. F., Medicine
HAYS, R. B., Divinity
HEALY, R. G., Earth and Environmental Sciences
HEINZ, E. R., Radiology
HEITMAN, J. B., Molecular Genetics and Microbiology
HEITZENRATER, R. P., Divinity
HELMS, C. A., Radiology
HERRUP, C. B., History
HERSHFIELD, M. S., Medicine
HERTZBERG, B. S., Radiology

HILL, G. B., Obstetrics and Gynaecology
HILL, R. L., Biochemistry
HILLERBRAND, H. J., Religion
HINTON, D. E., Earth and Environmental Sciences
HOCHMUTH, R. M., Mechanical Engineering
HOFFMAN, M. R., Pathology
HOLLOWAY, K., English
HOROWITZ, D. L., Law
HOUGH, J. F., Political Science
HOWELL, C. R., Physics
HSIEH, D. A., Business Administration
HSIEH, T., Biochemistry
HUANG, A. T., Medicine
HUBER, J. C., Business Administration
HYLANDER, W. L., Biological Anthropology and Anatomy
JAFFE, G. J., Ophthalmology
JAFFE, S., Music
JAMESON, F., Literature
JASZCZAK, R. J., Radiology
JENNINGS, R. B., Pathology
JENTLESON, B. W., Public Policy Studies
JIRTLE, R. L., Radiation Oncology
JOHNSON, G. A., Radiology
JOHNSON, K. M., Engineering
JOHNSON, V. E., Statistics
JOINES, W. T., Electrical and Computer Engineering
JONES, L. G., Divinity
JONES, R. H., Surgery
JONES, T., Law
KAMAKURA, W. A., Business Administration
KANE, W. H., Medicine
KAPLAN, A., Romance Studies
KARSON, J. A., Earth and Ocean Sciences
KATUL, G. G., Earth and Environmental Sciences
KATZ, D. F., Biomedical Engineering
KATZ, L. C., Neurobiology
KAY, R. F., Biological Anthropology and Anatomy
KEEFE, F. J., Psychiatry and Behavioural Sciences
KEENE, J. D., Molecular Genetics and Microbiology
KELLER, T. F., Business Administration
KELLEY, A. C., Economics
KELSOE, G. H., Immunology
KEOHANE, N. O., Political Science
KEOHANE, R., Political Science
KERN, F. H., Anaesthesiology
KIEHART, D. P., Biology
KILLENBERG, P. G., Medicine
KIMBROUGH, K. P., Economics
KINNEY, T. R., Paediatrics
KIRBY, M. L., Paediatrics
KISSLO, J. A., Medicine
KITSCHELT, H. P., Political Science
KLINTWORTH, G. K., Pathology
KOCH, W. J., Surgery
KOONZ, C., History
KORNBERG, A., Political Science
KORT, W. A., Religion
KRAMER, R. A., Earth and Environmental Sciences
KREDICH, N. M., Medicine
KREUZER, K. N., Biochemistry
KRISHNAN, K. R. R., Psychiatry and Behavioural Sciences
KROLIK, J. L., Electrical and Computer Engineering
KUHN, C. M., Pharmacology and Cancer Biology
KUNIHOLM, B. R., Public Policy Studies
KUO, P. C., Surgery
KURTZBERG, J., Paediatrics
KYLE, A. S., Business Administration
LADD, H., Public Policy Studies
LAHUSEN, T., Literature
LAND, K. C., Sociology
LANGE, D. L., Law
LANGE, P., Political Science
LAUGHHUNN, D. J., Business Administration
LAVINE, M. L., Statistics
LAWLER, G. F., Mathematics
LAWRENCE, B. B., Religion
LAYTON, H., Mathematics
LEE, P. P., Ophthalmology
LEFKOWITZ, R. J., Medicine
LEIGHT, G. S., Surgery
LEIGHTEN, P., Art and Art History
LENTRICCHIA, F., Literature
LEVIN, L. S., Surgery
LEWIN, A. Y., Business Administration
LEWIS, D. V., Paediatrics
LIDDLE, R. A., Medicine
LIN, N., Sociology
LIND, E. A., Business Administration
LINNEY, E. A., Molecular Genetics and Microbiology
LISCHER, R., Divinity
LIVINGSTONE, D. A., Biology
LOCHMULLER, C. H., Chemistry
LOCKHEAD, G. R., Psychological and Brain Sciences
LOGUE, P. E., Psychiatry and Behavioural Sciences
LONGINO, M., Romance Studies
LOONEY, J. G., Psychiatry and Behavioural Sciences
LOWE, J. E., Surgery
LYERLY, H. K., Surgery
LYLES, K. W., Medicine
LYNCH, J. G., Business Administration
MCCANN, R. L., Surgery
MCCARTHY, G., Radiology
MCCLAIN, P. D., Political Science
MCCLAY, D. R., Biology
MCCUEN, B. W., Ophthalmology
MCDONNELL, D. P., Pharmacology and Cancer Biology
MCELROY, M. B., Economics
MCGOVERN, F. E., Law
MCGOWN, L., Chemistry
MCINTOSH, T. J., Cell Biology
MACINTYRE, N. R., Medicine
MCLENDON, R. E., Pathology
MCNAMARA, J. O., Sr, Neurobiology
MCPHAIL, A. T., Chemistry
MADDEN, D. J., Psychiatry and Behavioural Sciences
MAHONEY, E. P., Philosophy
MALIN, P. E., Earth and Environmental Sciences
MARCH, J. S., Psychiatry and Behavioural Sciences
MARCUS, J., Divinity
MARINOS, P. N., Electrical and Computer Engineering
MARK, D. B., Medicine
MARK, J. B., Anaesthesiology
MARKS, L. B., Radiation Oncology
MARTINEZ, S., Radiology
MASON, R. M., Surgery
MASSEY, J. M., Medicine
MASSOUD, H. Z., Electrical and Computer Engineering
MATCHAR, D. B., Medicine
MAUSKOPF, S., History
MEANS, A. R., Pharmacology and Cancer Biology
MECK, W. H., Psychological and Brain Sciences
MEDINA, M. A., Civil and Environmental Engineering
METZLOFF, T. B., Law
MEYERS, C. L., Religion
MEYERS, E. M., Religion
MICKIEWICZ, E., Public Policy Studies
MIGNOLO, W., Literature
MILLER, M. A., History
MILLS, E., Pharmacology and Cancer Biology
MITCHELL, W. G., Business Administration
MODRICH, P. L., Biochemistry
MOI, T., Literature
MOON, R. E., Anaesthesiology
MOORE, J. O., Medicine
MOORMAN, C., Business Administration
MOREIRAS, A., Romance Studies
MORGAN, S. P., Sociology
MORRIS, J. J., Medicine
MORRIS, M., Law
MORRISON, D. R., Mathematics
MOSTELLER, R. P., Law
MUDIMBE, V., Literature
MUELLER, B., Physics
MUNGER, M. C., Political Science
NADLER, J. V., Pharmacology and Cancer Biology
NEEDHAM, D., Mechanical Engineering
NELSON, R. C., Radiology
NEVINS, J. R., Molecular Genetics and Microbiology
NEWGARD, C. B., Pharmacology and Cancer Biology
NEWMAN, M. F., Anaesthesiology
NICKLAS, R. B., Biology
NICOLELIS, M. A., Neurobiology
NIJHOUT, H. F., Biology
NIOU, E. S., Political Science
NOLTE, L. W., Electrical and Computer Engineering
NOWICKI, S., Biology
NUNLEY, J. A., II, Surgery
O'BARR, W. M., Cultural Anthropology
OH, S., Physics
OLSEN, E. A., Medicine
O'RAND, A. M., Sociology
OREN, R., Earth and Environmental Sciences
ORR, L., Romance Studies
OSTBYE, T., Community and Family Medicine
PALETZ, D. L., Political Science
PALMER, R. A., Chemistry
PALMER, R. G., Physics
PAPPAS, T. N., Surgery
PARDON, W. L., Mathematics
PARKERSON, G. R., Community and Family Medicine
PATZ, E. F., Radiology
PAULSON, D. F., Surgery
PAULSON, E. K., Radiology
PAYNE, C. M., History
PAYNE, J. W., Business Administration
PERFECT, J. R., Medicine
PERICAK-VANCE, M. A., Medicine
PETER, R. H., Medicine
PETROSKI, H., Civil and Environmental Engineering
PHILLIPS, H. R., III, Medicine
PIANTADOSI, C. A., Medicine
PIMM, S. L., Earth and Environmental Sciences
PIRRUNG, M. C., Chemistry
PISETSKY, D. S., Medicine
PIZZO, S. V., Pathology
POPE, D., English
PORTER, J. A., English
POWELL, H. J., Law
POWELL, R. J., Art and Art History
PREMINGER, G. M., Surgery
PRICE, D. E., Political Science
PRICE, E. R., English
PROSNITZ, L. R., Radiation Oncology
PROVENZALE, J. M., Radiology
PUROHIT, D., Business Administration
PURVES, D., Neurobiology
PUTALLAZ, M., Psychology, Social and Health Sciences
QUARLES, L. D., Medicine
QUILLIGAN, M., English
QUINN, N., Cultural Anthropology
RADTKE, R. A., Medicine
RADWAY, J. A., Literature
RAETZ, C. R. H., Biochemistry
RAJAGOPALAN, K. V., Biochemistry
RAMUS, J. S., Marine Sciences
RAUSHER, M. D., Biology
RAVIN, C. E., Radiology
RECKHOW, K. H., Earth and Environmental Sciences
REDDY, W. M., History
REED, M. C., Mathematics
REEDY, M. K., Cell Biology
REICHERT, W. M., Biomedical Engineering
REICHMAN, J. H., Law
REIF, J. H., Computer Science
REINSMOEN, N. L., Pathology

RELLER, L. B., Pathology
REMMER, K. L., Political Science
REPPY, W. A., Law
REYNOLDS, J. F., Biology
RICHARDS, J. F., History
RICHARDSON, C. J., Earth and Environmental Sciences
RICHARDSON, D. C., Biochemistry
RICHARDSON, J. S., Biochemistry
RICHTER, D. D., Earth and Environmental Sciences
RIGSBY, K. J., Classical Studies
ROBBOY, S. J., Pathology
ROCKEY, D. C., Medicine
ROCKMAN, H. A., Medicine
ROGGLI, V. L., Pathology
ROLAND, A., History
ROLLESTON, J. L., Germanic Languages
ROSE, D., Computer Science
ROSENBERG, A., Philosophy
ROTH, S., Psychology, Social and Health Sciences
ROWE, T. D., Law
RUBIN, D. C., Psychological and Brain Sciences
RYAN, T. J., Medicine
SABISTON, D. C., Surgery
SACKS, J., Statistics
ST CLAIR, E. W., Medicine
SAMULSKI, T. V., Radiation Oncology
SANDERS, D. B., Medicine
SANDERS, E. P., Religion
SANDERS, S. P., Paediatrics
SANFORD, D. H., Philosophy
SCHAEFFER, D. G., Mathematics
SCHANBERG, S. M., Pharmacology and Cancer Biology
SCHIFFMAN, S. S., Psychiatry and Behavioural Sciences
SCHLESINGER, W. H., Biology
SCHMALBECK, R. L., Law
SCHMECHEL, D. E., Medicine
SCHOEN, C. L., Mathematics
SCHOMBERG, D. W., Obstetrics and Gynaecology
SCHROEDER, C., Law
SCHULMAN, K. A., Medicine
SCHWAB, S. J., Medicine
SCHWARCZ, S. L., Law
SCHWARTZ, D. A., Medicine
SCHWARTZ-BLOOM, R. D., Pharmacology and Cancer Biology
SCHWINN, D. A., Anaesthesiology
SEIGLER, H. F., Surgery
SEXTON, D. J., Medicine
SHATZMILLER, J., History
SHAUGHNESSY, E. J., Mechanical Engineering
SHAW, A. J., Biology
SHAW, B. R., Chemistry
SHELBURNE, J. D., Pathology
SHENOLIKAR, S., Pharmacology and Cancer Biology
SHEPPARD, B. H., Business Administration
SHERWOOD, A., Psychiatry and Behavioural Sciences
SIEDOW, J. N., Biology
SIEGEL, L. M., Biochemistry
SIEGLER, I. C., Psychiatry and Behavioural Sciences
SIMEL, D. L., Medicine
SIMON, J. D., Chemistry
SIMON, S. A., Neurobiology
SIMONS, E. L., Biological Anthropology and Anatomy
SIMPSON, I. H., Sociology
SLOAN, F. A., Economics
SLOTKIN, T. A., Pharmacology and Cancer Biology
SMITH, B. C., Philosophy
SMITH, B. H., Literature
SMITH, K. K., Biology
SMITH, P. K., Surgery
SMITH, S. W., Biomedical Engineering
SMITH, T. P., Radiology
SNYDERMAN, R., Medicine
SOPER, J. T., Obstetrics and Gynaecology
SPENNER, K. I., Sociology
SPICER, L. D., Radiology
SPRAGENS, T. A., Political Science
SPRITZER, C. E., Radiology
STADDON, J. E. R., Psychological and Brain Sciences
STAELIN, R., Business Administration
STAMLER, J. S., Medicine
STANLEY, D. K., Classical Studies
STEEGE, D. A., Biochemistry
STEINMETZ, D. C., Divinity
STERN, M. A., Mathematics
STEWART, P., Romance Studies
STILES, G. L., Medicine
STRANDBERG, V. H., English
STRAUMAN, T. J., Psychology, Social and Health Sciences
STRITTMATTER, W. J., Medicine
STROHBEHN, J. W., Biomedical Engineering
SUGARMAN, J., Medicine
SULLENGER, B. A., Surgery
SULLIVAN, K. M., Medicine
SUKIN, K. J., Literature
SURWIT, R. S., Psychiatry and Behavioural Sciences
SVETKEY, L. P., Medicine
SWARTZ, M. S., Psychiatry and Behavioural Sciences
TAN, T. Y., Mechanical Engineering
TAUCHEN, G. E., Economics
TAYLOR, C. R., Economics
TEDDER, T. F., Immunology
TELEN, M. J., Medicine
TERBORGH, J. W., Earth and Environmental Sciences
THOMAS, J., Romance Studies
THOMAS, J. E., Physics
THOMPSON, J. H., History
THOMPSON, R. J., Psychology, Social and Health Sciences
THOMPSON, W. M., Radiology
TIRYAKIAN, E. A., Sociology
TODD, R. L., Music
TOONE, E. J., Chemistry
TORGOVNICK, M., English
TORNOW, W., Physics
TOWER, E., Economics
TRAHEY, G. E., Biomedical Engineering
TRANGENSTEIN, J. A., Mathematics
TREEM, W. R., Paediatrics
TRIVEDI, K. S., Electrical and Computer Engineering
TRUSKEY, G. A., Biomedical Engineering
TURNER, B. S., Nursing
TURNER, D. A., Surgery
TYREY, E. L., Obstetrics and Gynaecology
ULSHEN, M. H., Paediatrics
UNDERKUFFLER, L. S., Law
URBANIAK, J. R., Surgery
UYENOYAMA, M. K., Biology
VAN ALSTYNE, W. W., Law
VANCE, J. M., Medicine
VAN ROMPAY, L., Religion
VAN SCHAIK, C., Biological Anthropology and Anatomy
VENAKIDES, S., Mathematics
VERNON, J. M., Economics
VIDMAR, N. J., Law
VILGALYS, R. J., Biology
VISWANATHAN, S., Business Administration
VOGEL, S., Biology
VON RAMM, O. T., Biomedical Engineering
WACKER, G. A., Divinity
WAINWRIGHT, G., Divinity
WALLACH, M. A., Psychological and Brain Sciences
WALTER, R. L., Physics
WALTHER, P. J., Surgery
WANG, P. P., Electrical and Computer Engineering
WARE, R. E., Paediatrics
WARNER, D. S., Anaesthesiology
WEBSTER, G. D., Surgery
WEBSTER, R. E., Biochemistry
WEINBERG, J. B., Medicine
WEINER, R. D., Psychiatry and Behavioural Sciences
WEINERTH, J. L., Surgery
WEINHOLD, K. J., Surgery
WEINTRAUB, E. R., Economics
WEISTART, J. C., Law
WELLER, H. R., Physics
WELLS, S. A., Surgery
WEST, M., Statistics
WHALEY, R. E., Business Administration
WHARTON, A. W., Art and Art History
WHITE, R. A., Biology
WIENER, J. B., Law
WILBUR, R. L., Biology
WILKINS, R. H., Surgery
WILKINSON, W. E., Biostatistics and Bioinformatics
WILLIAMS, C. L., Psychological and Brain Sciences
WILLIAMS, K. J., English
WILLIAMS, R. B., Psychiatry and Behavioural Sciences
WILLIAMS, R. S., Medicine
WILLIMON, W. H., Divinity
WILSON, J., Sociology
WILSON, J. A. P., Medicine
WILSON, K. H., Medicine
WILSON, R. L., Nursing
WINKLER, R. L., Business Administration
WITT, R. G., History
WOLBARSHT, M. L., Psychological and Brain Sciences
WOLFE, W. G., Surgery
WOLPERT, R. L., Statistics
WONG, D. B., Philosophy
WOOD, P. H., History
WRIGHT, J. R., Cell Biology
YANG, W., Chemistry
YARGER, W. E., Medicine
YOUNG, S. L., Medicine
ZALUTSKY, M. R., Radiology
ZHOU, X., Mathematics
ZHOU, X., Sociology
ZIPKIN, P. H., Business Administration

EAST CAROLINA UNIVERSITY

East Fifth St, Greenville, NC 27858-4353
Telephone: (252) 328-6131
Internet: www.ecu.edu

Founded 1907
Constituent instn of the Univ. of North Carolina system

Chancellor: STEVE BALLARD
Provost and Vice-Chancellor for Academic Affairs: JAMES L. SMITH
Vice-Chancellor for Admin. and Finance: KEVIN SEITZ
Vice-Chancellor for Univ. Advancement: MICHAEL B. DOWDY
Registrar: ANGELA R. ANDERSON
Dir of Admissions: DONALD C. JOYNER
Dir of Academic Library Services: LARRY BOYER

Library: 1.3m. vols
Number of teachers: 1,529
Number of students: 22,767

Publications: *The Children's Folklore Review* (2 a year), *Tar River Poetry* (2 a year), *Technical Communication* (4 a year), *The North Carolina Folklore Journal* (2 a year), *The North Carolina Literary Review* (1 a year).

ELIZABETH CITY STATE UNIVERSITY

1704 Weeksville Rd, Elizabeth City, NC 27909
Telephone: (252) 335-3400
Fax: (252) 335-3731
E-mail: infoline@mail.ecsu.edu
Internet: www.ecsu.edu

Founded 1891 as a normal school; present name 1969

Academic year: August to May
Chancellor: WILLIE J. GILCHRIST
Provost and Vice-Chancellor for Academic Affairs: RONALD BLACKMON
Vice-Chancellor for Business and Finance: GREGORY DAVID
Vice-Chancellor for Institutional Advancement: RICHARD LUCAS, Jr
Vice-Chancellor for Student Affairs: Dr ANTHONY BROWN
Number of teachers: 99
Number of students: 2,330

ELON UNIVERSITY

Elon, NC 27244
Telephone: (336) 278-2000
Fax: (336) 278-7699
E-mail: interadm@elon.edu
Internet: www.elon.edu
Founded 1889
Related to the United Church of Christ
Academic year: September to May
Pres.: LEO M. LAMBERT
Provost: GERALD L. FRANCIS
Dean and Univ. Librarian: KATE D. HICKEY
Library of 240,000 vols
Number of teachers: 270 (201 full-time, 69 part-time)
Number of students: 4,138

FAYETTEVILLE STATE UNIVERSITY

1200 Murchison Rd, Fayetteville, NC 28301-4298
Telephone: (919) 672-1111
Internet: www.uncfsu.edu
Founded 1867 as the Howard School, attained univ. status 1969
Part of Univ. of North Carolina System
Chancellor: T. J. BRYAN
Provost and Vice-Chancellor for Academic Affairs: JON YOUNG
Vice-Chancellor for Business and Finance: LATONYA HANKINS
Vice-Chancellor for Institutional Advancement: STEPHEN MCDANIEL
Vice-Chancellor for Student Affairs: OLIVIA CHAVIS
Registrar: SARAH BAKER
Librarian: BOBBY WYNN
Library of 500,000 vols
Number of teachers: 210 full-time
Number of students: 5,307

GARDNER-WEBB UNIVERSITY

POB 997, Boiling Springs, NC 28017
110 South Main St, Boiling Springs, NC 28017
Telephone: (704) 406-4000
E-mail: admissions@gardner-webb.edu
Internet: www.gardner-webb.edu
Founded 1905 as Boiling Springs High School; present name 1993
Private control
Academic year: August to May
Pres.: Dr A. FRANK BONNER
Vice-Pres. and Provost of Academics: Dr BEN C. LESLIE
Vice-Pres. for Advancement: RALPH DIXON, Jr
Vice-Pres. for Athletics: CHUCK BURCH
Vice-Pres. for Business and Finance: MIKE W. HARDIN
Vice-Pres. and Dean of Student Devt: BRUCE MOORE
Vice-Pres. for Enrollment Management: JACK BUCHANAN
Registrar: STEPHEN SAIN
Library Dir: VALERIE PARRY
Number of teachers: 133 full-time
Number of students: 4,000

GREENSBORO COLLEGE

815 W Market St, Greensboro, NC 27401-1875
Telephone: (336) 272-7102
Fax: (336) 271-6634
E-mail: admissions@gborocollege.edu
Internet: www.gborocollege.edu
Founded 1838
Academic year: August to May
Pres.: Dr C. BRENT DEVORE
Vice-Pres. for Academic Affairs: PAUL LESLIE
Assoc. Vice-Pres. for Technology: PAMELA MCKIRDY
Dir of Admissions: TIMOTHY JACKSON
Library of 140,000 vols
Number of teachers: 103
Number of students: 1,300

GUILFORD COLLEGE

5800 West Friendly Ave, Greensboro, NC 27410
Telephone: (336) 316-2000
Fax: (336) 316-2949
Internet: www.guilford.edu
Founded 1837
Private (Society of Friends) co-educational liberal arts college
Academic year: August to May
Pres.: KENT JOHN CHABOTAR
Vice-Pres. for Academic Affairs and Academic Dean: MARTHA H. COOLEY
Vice-Pres. for Advancement: MIKE POSTON
Vice-Pres. for Enrollment and Campus Life: RANDY DOSS
Vice-Pres. for Finance and Admin.: JERRY BOOTHBY
Dean for Campus Life: AARON FETROW
Library Dir: MARY ELLEN CHIJIOKE
Library of 220,000 vols
Number of teachers: 132
Number of students: 1,400
Publications: *Journal of Undergraduate Mathematics* (2 a year), *Journal of Undergraduate Research in Physics* (2 a year), *The Southern Friend* (2 a year).

HIGH POINT UNIVERSITY

833 Montlieu Ave, High Point, NC 27262-3598
Telephone: (336) 841-9000
Fax: (336) 841-4599
Internet: www.highpoint.edu
Founded 1924
Provost and Vice-Pres. for Academic Affairs: DENNIS G. CARROLL
Vice-Pres. for Enrollment: ANDY BILLS
Registrar: DIANA LEE ESTEY
Dir of Library Services: DAVID L. BRYDEN
Library of 310,000 vols
Number of teachers: 166 full-time
Number of students: 3,400

JOHN WESLEY COLLEGE

2314 North Centennial St, High Point, NC 27265
Telephone: (336) 889-2262
Fax: (336) 889-2261
E-mail: admissions@johnwesley.edu
Internet: www.johnwesley.edu
Founded 1903 as Greensboro Bible and Literary School; closed 1931; re-opened 1932 as People's Bible School; present name 1956
Private control
Academic year: August to May
Pres.: Dr BRIAN DONLEY
Registrar: STEVE QUESENBERRY
Academic Dean: Dr JOHN LINDSEY
Dir of Library Services: APRIL LINDSEY
Number of teachers: 18 (6 full-time, 12 part-time)
Number of students: 145

JOHNSON C. SMITH UNIVERSITY

100–152 Beatties Ford Rd, Charlotte, NC 28216
Telephone: (704) 378-1000
Fax: (704) 372-5746
Internet: www.jcsu.edu
Founded 1867
Pres.: Dr DOROTHY COWSER YANCY
Vice-Pres. for Academic Affairs: Dr MARILYN SUTTON-HAYWOOD
Vice-Pres. for Finance: GERALD HECTOR
Vice-Pres. for Institutional Advancement: KENNETH WESTARY
Vice-Pres. for Student Affairs: JEFFREY SMITH
Dir of Admissions: JOCELYN BIGGS
Dir of Honors College: Dr SHANNA BENJAMIN
Registrar: MOSES JONES
Dir of Library: FAYE PRIESTLY
Library of 113,000 vols
Number of teachers: 80 , incl. 10 professors
Number of students: 1,427

LEES-MCRAE COLLEGE

POB 128, Banner Elk, NC 28604
Telephone: (828) 898-5241
Fax: (828) 898-8814
E-mail: admissions@lmc.edu
Internet: www.lmc.edu
Founded 1900 as a girls' school; present name 1931
Private control
Academic year: August to May
Pres.: Dr DAVID W. BUSHMAN
Provost and Dean of the Faculty: Dr DEBRA THATCHER
Vice-Pres. for Business Affairs and Treasurer: SCOTT MCKINNEY
Vice-Pres. for Enrollment Management: BILL SLIWA
Dir of Libraries: RUSSELL TAYLOR
Library of 99,138 print vols, 22,750 electronic books, 484 print periodicals, 9,364 electronic periodicals
Number of teachers: 73
Number of students: 700 (undergraduate)

CHAIRS OF ACADEMIC DIVISIONS

Business and Social Sciences: Dr KATHERINE LOGAN
Education and Physical Education: Dr PETE CAMPBELL
Humanities: Dr JOHN F. KEENER
Performing Arts: Dr JANET BARTON SPEER
Science and Mathematics: Dr GENE SPEARS

LENOIR-RHYNE COLLEGE

Hickory, NC 28603
Telephone: (828) 328-1741
Fax: (828) 328-7368
E-mail: admissions@lrc.edu
Internet: www.lrc.edu
Founded 1891
Private control (Evangelical Lutheran Church in America)
Academic year: August to May
Pres.: WAYNE B. POWELL
Academic Vice-Pres. and Dean: LARRY HALL
Vice-Pres. and Dean for Student Affairs: ANITA JOHNSON GWIN
Vice-Pres. of Enrollment Management: RACHEL NICHOLS
Library of 156,000 vols
Number of students: 1,624

LIVINGSTONE COLLEGE

701 West Monroe St, Salisbury, NC 28144
Telephone: (704) 638-5500
Internet: www.livingstone.edu

Founded 1879
Academic year: August to May

Pres.: Dr JIMMY R. JENKINS, Sr (acting)
Vice-Pres. for Academic Affairs: Dr BERTHA TAYLOR ESCOFFERY
Vice-Pres. for Business and Finance: PETAGAYE SHAW
Vice-Pres. for Institutional Advancement: Rev. ANTHONY DAVIS
Vice-Pres. for Student Affairs: Dr STANLEY ELLIOTT
Librarian: MELISSA SMITH

Library of 80,000 vols
Number of teachers: 71
Number of students: 1,000

Publications: *Alumni Bulletin* (4 a year), *Bears' Tale* (1 a year), *The Livingstonian* (1 a year).

MARS HILL COLLEGE

100 Athletic St, Mars Hill, NC 18754
Telephone: (828) 689-1208
E-mail: admissions@mhc.edu
Internet: www.mhc.edu

Founded 1856

Pres.: Dr DAN LUNSFORD
Vice-Pres. for Academic and Student Affairs: Dr NINA POLLARD
Vice-Pres. for Institutional Advancement: ALEX MILLER (acting)

Library of 90,000 vols
Number of teachers: 85
Number of students: 1,200

First degree courses in arts, music, science, social work.

MEREDITH COLLEGE

3800 Hillsborough St, Raleigh, NC27607-5298
Telephone: (919) 760-8600
Fax: (919) 760-2874
Internet: www.meredith.edu

Founded 1891

Pres.: MAUREEN A. HARTFORD
Registrar: JODY HAMILTON-DAVIS
Dir of Admissions: HEIDI FLETCHER
Dean of Library Information Services: LAURA DAVIDSON

Library of 137,000 vols
Number of teachers: 261 (112 full-time, 149 part-time)
Number of students: 1,991

METHODIST UNIVERSITY

5400 Ramsey St, Fayetteville, NC 28311-1498
Telephone: (910) 630-7000
Fax: (910) 630-7317
E-mail: pmcevoy@methodist.edu
Internet: www.methodist.edu

Founded 1956
Private control
Academic year: August to May

Pres.: Dr BEN HANCOCK
Vice-Pres. for Academic Affairs and Dean of Univ.: DELMAS S. CRISP, Jr
Vice-Pres. for Business Affairs: GENE T. CLAYTON
Vice-Pres. for Devt: ROBIN DAVENPORT

Library of 111,224 vols, 45,000 non-book holdings
Number of teachers: 214 , incl. full-time and part-time
Number of students: 2,400

DEANS

School of Arts and Humanities: Dr EMILY WRIGHT
School of Graduate Studies: Dr LORI BROOKMAN
School of Public Affairs: Dr BOINTA BELCASTRO
School of Science and Human Development: Dr TAN CHAN

MONTREAT COLLEGE

310 Gaither Circle, POB 1267, Montreat, NC 28757
Telephone: (828) 669-8012
Fax: (828) 669-0120
E-mail: admissions@montreat.edu
Internet: www.montreat.edu

Campuses at Asheville, Black Mountain, Charlotte

Founded 1916
Private control
Academic year: August to May

Pres.: Dr DAN STRUBLE
Vice-Pres. and Dean of Academics: Dr ABBY FAPETU
Vice-Pres. for Finance and Information Technology: Dr DIRK WILMOTH
Vice-Pres. for Institutional Advancement: Dr JERRY BOBILYA
Dean of Admissions and Financial Aid: LISA LANKFORD
Dean of Students: CHARLES LANCE
Registrar: KEITH KARRIKER
Library Dir: ELIZABETH PEARSON

Number of teachers: 89
Number of students: 1,036

MOUNT OLIVE COLLEGE

634 Henderson St, Mount Olive, NC 28365
Telephone: (919) 658-2502
Fax: (919) 658-7180
E-mail: admissions@moc.edu
Internet: www.moc.edu

Founded 1951 as Mount Allen Junior College, present name 1970
Private control
Academic year: August to May

Pres.: Dr PHILIP P. KERSTETTER

Number of teachers: 316 (88 full-time, 228 part-time)
Number of students: 3,569

NORTH CAROLINA AGRICULTURAL AND TECHNICAL STATE UNIVERSITY

1601 East Market St, Greensboro, NC 27411
Telephone: (919) 334-7500
Internet: www.ncat.edu

Founded 1891; attached to Univ. of North Carolina

Chancellor: STANLEY F. BATTLE
Vice-Chancellor for Academic Affairs: HAROLD MARTIN
Vice-Chancellor for Business/Finance: CHARLES MCINTYRE
Vice-Chancellor for Devt and Univ. Relations: ROBERT P. JENNINGS
Vice-Chancellor for Student Affairs: SULLIVAN WELBORNE
Registrar: DORIS GRAHAM
Librarian: WALTRENE CANADA

Library of 416,000 vols
Number of teachers: 813
Number of students: 11,103

NORTH CAROLINA CENTRAL UNIVERSITY

Durham, NC 27707
Telephone: (919) 530-6100
Fax: (919) 530-7976
Internet: www.nccu.edu

Founded 1910
State control, linked to the Univ. of N Carolina
Academic year: August to May

Chancellor: CHARLIE NELMS
Vice-Chancellor for Financial Affairs: CHARLES O'DUOR
Provost and Vice-Chancellor for Academic Affairs: BEVERLY JONES
Vice-Chancellor for Institutional Advancement: LATANYA D. AFOLAYAN
Vice-Chancellor for Student Affairs: ROLAND GAINES
Registrar: Dr JEROME GOODWIN
Dir of Library Services: Dr THEODOSIA SHIELDS

Library of 850,000 vols
Number of teachers: 388
Number of students: 6,521

Publications: *Bulletins*, *Campus Echo*, *Ex Umbra*

DEANS

College of Arts and Sciences: Dr BERNICE JOHNSON
Univ. College: Dr BEVERLY W. JONES
School of Business: Dr H. JAMES WILLIAMS
School of Education: Dr CECELIA STEPPE-JONES
School of Graduate Studies: Dr PERCY MURRAY
School of Law: JANICE MILLS
School of Library and Information Science: Dr BENJAMIN F. SPELLER

NORTH CAROLINA WESLEYAN COLLEGE

3400 North Wesleyan Blvd, Rocky Mount, NC 27804-9906
Telephone: (252) 985-5100
Fax: (252) 977-3701
Internet: www.ncwc.edu

Founded 1956

Co-educational, church-related, liberal arts college

Pres.: JAMES A. GRAY, III
Vice-Pres. for Academic Affairs and Dean of the College: Dr JAY STUBBLEFIELD

Library of 100,000 vols
Number of teachers: 70
Number of students: 1,500

Publications: *Bishop Beat* (online, 12 a year), *Bulletin* (4 a year).

PFEIFFER UNIVERSITY

Misenheimer, NC 28109
Telephone: (704) 463-1360
Fax: (704) 463-1363
E-mail: admis@pfeiffer.edu
Internet: www.pfeiffer.edu

Founded 1885
Private (Methodist) control
Academic year: August to May

Pres.: Dr CHARLES M. AMBROSE
Chief Operating Officer and Exec. Vice-Pres.: DAVID OLIVE
Vice-Pres. for Academic Affairs: Dr PHILIP OTT
Vice-Pres. for Advancement: SHON HERRICK
Vice-Pres. for Enrollment Management: DAVID M. SMITH
Vice-Pres. for Finance: ROBIN LESLIE
Library Coordinator: LARA LITTLE

Library of 129,000 vols
Number of teachers: 65 full-time
Number of students: 2,027

QUEENS UNIVERSITY OF CHARLOTTE

1900 Selwyn Ave, Charlotte, NC 28274
Telephone: (704) 337-2200
Fax: (704) 337-2517
Internet: www.queens.edu

Founded 1857 as Charlotte Female Institute; re-named Seminary for Girls 1891; became part of new Presbyterian Female College 1896; re-named Queens College 1912; present name and status 2002
Academic year: August to May

Liberal arts college, undergraduate and postgraduate programmes; Presbyterian (USA) affiliation

Pres.: Dr PAMELA L. DAVIES
Vice-Pres. for Academic Affairs: Dr J. NORRIS FREDERICK
Vice-Pres. for Admin. and Operations: LAURIE GUY
Vice-Pres. for Enrollment Management: Dr BRIAN RALPH (acting)
Vice-Pres. for Univ. Advancement: PATTON MCDOWELL, III
Librarian: Dr CAROL W. JORDAN

Library of 150,000 vols
Number of teachers: 85 (61 full-time, 24 part-time)
Number of students: 1,550
Publication: *Odyssey* (4 a year).

ROANOKE BIBLE COLLEGE

715 North Poindexter St, Elizabeth City, NC 27909
Telephone: (252) 334-2000
Fax: (252) 334-2071
E-mail: admissions@roanokebible.edu
Internet: www.roanokebible.edu

Founded 1948
Private control

Pres.: Dr D. CLAY PERKINS
Vice-Pres. for Academic Affairs: S. ELIZABETH BONDURANT
Vice-Pres. for Devt: E. HOWARD AMLAND
Vice-Pres. for Finance: JAMES R. CORMODE
Vice-Pres. for Student Life: GARRETT D. LEWIS
Registrar: JOAN U. SAWYER
Dir of Library Services: L. FRANK DODSON

Number of teachers: 17
Number of students: 194

ST ANDREWS PRESBYTERIAN COLLEGE

1700 Dogwood Mile, Laurinburg, NC 28352
Telephone: (910) 277-5555
Fax: (910) 277-5020
E-mail: info@sapc.edu
Internet: www.sapc.edu

Founded 1896
Private control
Academic year: August to May

Pres.: PAUL BALDASARE
Vice-Pres. for Academic Affairs and Dean of the College: Dr ROBERT J. HOPKINS
Vice-Pres. for Admin. and Finance: JOHN HARLAN
Vice-Pres. for Enrollment and Student Services: Rev. GLENN T. BATTEN
Registrar: DEBORAH A. SMITH
Library Dir: RITA DURSI JOHNSON

Library of 111,064 vols
Number of teachers: 45
Number of students: 741
Publication: *Cairn* (1 a year).

SAINT AUGUSTINE'S COLLEGE

1315 Oakwood Ave, Raleigh, NC 27610
Telephone: (919) 516-4000
Internet: www.st-aug.edu

Founded 1867
Private control
Academic year: August to May

Pres.: Dr DIANNE BOARDLEY SUBER
Vice-Pres. of Institutional Advancement: MARC A. NEWMAN
Library Dir: LINDA SIMMONS-HENRY

Number of teachers: 100
Number of students: 1,600

SALEM ACADEMY AND COLLEGE

601 South Church St, Winston-Salem, NC 27108-0548
Telephone: (336) 721-2600
Fax: (336) 917-5339
Internet: www.salem.edu

Founded 1772
Private control

Pres.: Dr SUSAN E. PAULY
Vice-Pres. for Academic Affairs: ANN MCELANEY-JOHNSON
Dir of Admin.: ANNA BECK GALLIMORE
Dean of Students: KRISPIN W. BARR
Dir of Libraries: Dr ROSE A. SIMON

Library of 128,500 vols
Number of teachers: 84
Number of students: 1,002

SHAW UNIVERSITY

118 East South St, Raleigh, NC 27601
Telephone: (919) 546-8200
Fax: (919) 546-8301
E-mail: admissions@shawu.edu
Internet: www.shawu.edu

Founded 1865

Pres.: Dr CLARENCE G. NEWSOME
Academic Dean: JAMES TERRY ROBERSON, Jr
Exec. Vice-Pres.: MARTEL PERRY
Registrar: GENE PAGE
Librarian: TOM CLARK

Library of 122,413 vols
Number of teachers: 242
Number of students: 2,565

SOUTHEASTERN BAPTIST THEOLOGICAL SEMINARY

POB 1889, Wake Forest, NC 27588
120 S Wingate St, Wake Forest, NC 27587
Telephone: (919) 761-2100
E-mail: president@sebts.edu
Internet: www.sebts.edu

Founded 1950
Private control
Academic year: August to May

Pres.: Dr DANIEL AKIN
Sr Vice-Pres. for Academic Admin. and Dean of the Faculty: Dr KENNETH KEATHLEY
Sr Vice-Pres. for Business Admin.: RYAN R. HUTCHINSON
Vice-Pres. for Institutional Advancement: DENNIS DARVILLE
Vice-Pres. for Institutional Effectiveness and Assessment: TRAVIS WRIGHT
Vice-Pres. for Student Services: Dr MARK LIEDERBACH
Registrar: SHELDON H. ALEXANDER
Library Dir: SHAWN C. MADDEN

Number of teachers: 80
Number of students: 1,500

UNIVERSITY OF NORTH CAROLINA

POB 2688, Chapel Hill, NC 27515-2688
Telephone: (919) 962-1000
Fax: (919) 962-2751
Internet: www.northcarolina.edu

Multi-campus univ. composed of 16 instns: Univ. of NC at Asheville, Univ. of NC at Chapel Hill, Univ. of NC at Greensboro, Univ. of NC at Charlotte, Univ. of NC at Wilmington, NC State Univ. at Raleigh, Appalachian State Univ., East Carolina Univ., Elizabeth City State Univ., Fayetteville State Univ., NC Agricultural and Technical State Univ., NC Central Univ., NC School of the Arts, Univ. of NC at Pembroke, Western Carolina Univ., Winston-Salem State Univ. (*q.v.*)

Pres.: ERSKINE BOWLES
Sr Vice-Pres. for Academic Affairs: HAROLD L. MARTIN
Vice-Pres. and Gen. Counsel: LESLIE J. WINNER
Vice-Pres. for Academic Planning: ALAN R. MABE
Vice-Pres. for Fed. Relations: KIMREY RHINEHARDT
Vice-Pres. for Finance: ROBERT NELSON
Vice-Pres. for Govt Relations: ANDY WILLS
Vice-Pres. for Institutional Research: SCOTT JENKINS
Vice-Pres. for Information Resources and Chief Information Officer: ROBYN R. RENDER
Sec. of the Univ.: BART CORGNATI.

CONSTITUENT UNIVERSITIES

University of North Carolina at Asheville

1 University Heights, Asheville, NC 28804-3299
Telephone: (828) 251-6600
E-mail: admissions@unca.edu
Internet: www.unca.edu

Founded 1927 as Buncombe County Jr College 1927, later as Asheville-Biltmore College, present status 1969

Chancellor: Dr ANNE PONDER
Vice-Chancellor for Academic Affairs: Dr JANE FERNANDES
Vice-Chancellor for Finance and Operations: JOHN PIERCE
Vice-Chancellor for Student Affairs: Dr BILL HAGGARD
Registrar: DEBBIE RACE
Univ. Librarian: JAMES R. KUHLMAN

Library of 275,323 vols
Number of teachers: 216
Number of students: 3,700

Publication: *unc asheville magazine*.

University of North Carolina at Chapel Hill

Chapel Hill, NC 27599
Telephone: (919) 962-2211
E-mail: unchelp@admissions.unc.edu
Internet: www.unc.edu

Founded and chartered 1789, opened 1795; present status 1931
Academic year: August to May

Chancellor: HOLDEN THORP
Exec. Vice-Chancellor and Provost: BRUCE CARNEY
Exec. Assoc. Provost: RONALD P. STRAUSS
Vice-Chancellor for Finance and Admin.: RICHARD MANN
Vice-Chancellor for Human Resources: BRENDA MALONE
Vice-Chancellor for Information Technology: LARRY CONRAD
Vice-Chancellor for Medical Affairs: WILLIAM ROPER
Vice-Chancellor for Research and Economic Devt: TONY WALDROP
Vice-Chancellor for Student Affairs: MARGARET JABLONSKI
Vice-Chancellor for Univ. Advancement: MATTHEW KUPEC
Vice-Chancellor and Gen. Counsel: LESLIE STROHM

Asst Provost and Univ. Registrar: CHRISTOPHER DERICKSON
Asst Provost for Institutional Research and Assessment: LYNN E. WILLIFORD
Univ. Librarian: SARAH C. MICHALAK
Library: see Libraries and Archives
Number of teachers: 3,221
Number of students: 28,916
Publications: *Baseline* (3 a year), *Centerpieces* (12 a year), *Current Contents* (4 a year), *Dear Colleague* (2 a year), *Social Science Newsletter* (4 a year), *Southern Economic Journal* (4 a year), *The High School Journal* (4 a year)

DEANS

College of Arts and Sciences: KAREN GIL
Eshelman School of Pharmacy: ROBERT BLOUIN
General College: CAROLYN CANNON
Graduate School: STEVEN MATSON
Gillings School of Global Public Health: BARBARA K. RIMER
Kenan-Flagler Business School: JAMES W. DEAN, Jr
School of Dentistry: JOHN STAMM
School of Education: BILL MCDIARMID
School of Govt: MICHAEL R. SMITH
School of Information and Library Science: GARY MARCHIONINI
School of Journalism and Mass Communication: JEAN FOLKERTS
School of Law: JOHN CHARLES BOGER
School of Medicine: WILLIAM L. ROPER
School of Nursing: KRISTEN M. SWANSON
School of Social Work: JACK RICHMAN
Summer School: JAN JOHNSON YOPP
William and Ida Friday Center for Continuing Education: NORMAN LOEWENTHAL (Dir)

PROFESSORS

Allied Medical Programmes:
MITCHELL, M. M.
MITCHELL, R. U.
PETERS, R. W.
SAKATA, R.
YODER, D. E.

American Studies Curriculum:
ALLEN, R. C.
KASSON, J. S.

Anaesthesiology:
BOYSEN, P. G.
GHIA, J. N.
KAFER, E. R.
MUELLER, R. A.
NORFLEET, E. A.
SPIELMAN, F. J.
SPRAGUE, D. H.
VAUGHAN, R. W.

Anthropology:
CRUMLEY, C. L.
EVENS, T. M.
FINKLER, K.
HOLLAND, D. C.
JOHNSON, N. B.
LARSEN, C. S.
LUTZ, C. A.
PEACOCK, J. L., III
STEPONAITIS, V. P.
WINTERHALDER, B.

Art:
FOLDA, J. T., III
GRABOWSKI, S. E.
KINNAIRD, R. W.
MARKS, A. S.
NOE, J. L.
SHERIFF, M. D.
STURGEON, C.
ZABOROWSKI, D. J.

Biochemistry:
CAPLOW, M.
CARTER, C. W., Jr
CHANEY, S. G.
ERREDE, B. J.
HERMANS, J.
LEE, D. C.
LENTZ, B. R.
MARZLUFF, W. F.
MEISSNER, G. W.
MORELL, P.
NAYFEH, S. N.
SANCAR, A.
SWANSTROM, R. I.
TIDWELL, P. F.
TRAUT, T. W.
VAN DYKE, T. A.
WOLFENDEN, R. V.

Biology:
BLOOM, K. S.
BOLLENBACHER, W. E.
DICKISON, W. C.
FEDUCCIA, J. A.
GENSEL, P. G.
GILBERT, L. I.
HARRIS, A. K., Jr
MATSON, S. W.
MATTHYSSE, A. G.
PARKS, C. R.
PEET, R. K.
PETES, T. D.
PRINGLE, J. R.
QUATRANO, R. S.
SALMON, E. D.
SCOTT, T. K.
STAFFORD, D. W.
STIVEN, A. E.
WHITE, P. S.
WILEY, R. H., Jr

Biomedical Engineering Programme:
LUCAS, C. N.
TSUI, B. M.

Biostatistics:
DAVIS, C. E.
HELMS, R. W.
KALSBEEK, W. D.
KOCH, G. G.
KUPPER, L. L.
MARGOLIN, B. H.
QUADE, D. E.
SEN, P. K.
SUCHINDRAN, C. M.
SYMONS, M. J.

Business Administration:
ALDER, R. S.
ANDERSON, C. R.
ARMSTRONG, G. M.
BATEMAN, T. S.
BAYUS, B. L.
BETTIS, R. A.
BLOCHER, E. J.
BLOOM, P. N.
COLLINS, J. H.
CONRAD, J. S.
EDWARDS, J. R.
ELVERS, D. A.
EVANS, J. P.
FISCHER, W. A.
HARTZELL, D. J.
KASARDA, J. D.
KLOMPMAKER, J. E.
LANDSMAN, W. R.
MCENALLY, R. W.
MANN, R. A.
MARUCHECK, A. E.
NEEBE, A. W.
PEIRCE, E. R.
PERREAULT, W. D., Jr
PRINGLE, J. J.
RAVENSCRAFT, D. J.
RENDLEMAN, R. J.
ROBERTS, B. S.
RONDINELLI, D. A.
ROSEN, B.
RUBIN, D. S.
SHAPIRO, D. L.
SULLIVAN, R. S.
TILLMAN, R.
WAGNER, H. M.
WHYBARK, D. C.

Cell Biology and Anatomy:
BURRIDGE, K. W. T.
GRANGER, N. A.
HACKENBROCK, C. R.
HENSON, O. W., Jr
HERMAN, B.
JACOBSON, K. A.
KOCH, W. E.
LAUDER, J. M.
LEMASTERS, J. J.
MONTGOMERY, R. L.
O'RAND, M. G.
PENG, H. B.
PETRUSZ, P.
RUSTIONI, A.
SADLER, T. W.
SULIK, K. K.

Chemistry:
BAER, T.
BROOKHART, M. S.
BUCK, R. P.
COKE, J. L.
CRIMMINS, M. T.
DESIMONE, J. M.
ERICKSON, B. W.
EVANS, S. A., Jr
IRENE, E. A.
JICHA, D. C.
JOHNSON, C. S., Jr
JORGENSON, J. W.
KROPP, P. J.
MEYER, T. J.
MILLER, R. E.
MURRAY, R. W.
PEDERSEN, L. G.
SAMULSKI, E. T.
SORRELL, T. N.
SPREMULLI, L. L.
TEMPLETON, J. L.
THOMPSON, N. L.
WIGHTMAN, R. M.

City and Regional Planning:
GODSCHALK, D. R.
GOLDSTEIN, H. A.
KAISER, E. J.
LACEY, L.
LUGER, M. I.
MALIZIA, E. E.
MOREAU, D. H.
ROHE, W. M.

Classics:
BROWN, E. L.
HOUSTON, G. W.
LINDERSKI, J.
MACK, S.
RACE, W. H.
RECKFORD, K. J.
SAMS, G. K.
STADTER, P. A.
WEST, W. C., III
WOOTEN, C. W.

Communication Studies:
BALTHROP, V. W.
COX, J. R., Jr
DYSON, M. E.
GROSSBERG, L.
HORNE, G. C.
KINDEM, G. A.
LONG, B. W.
ROSENFELD, L. B.
WOOD, J. T.

Comparative Literature:
FURST, L. R.

Computer Science:
BROOKS, F. P., Jr
FUCHS, H.
HALTON, J. H.
MAGO, G. A.
PIZER, S. M.

PLAISTED, D. A.
SMITH, J. B.
WEISS, S. F.

Curriculum, African and Afro-American Study:
NYANG'ORO, J. E.
SELASSIE, B. H.

Curriculum, Asian Studies:
SEATON, J. P.

Curriculum, Linguistics and Non-West Languages:
HENDRICK, R. J.
MELCHERT, H. C.
TSIAPERA, M.

Curriculum, Public Policy Analysis:
DILL, D. D.
STEGMAN, M. A.

Dentistry:
ARNOLD, R. R.
AUKHIL, I.
BAWDEN, J. W.
BAYNE, S. C.
BECK, J. D.
BURKES, E. J.
CRENSHAW, M. A.
HANKER, J. S.
HERSHEY, H. G.
HEYMANN, H. O.
HUNT, R. J.
HUTCHENS, L. H., Jr
JENZANO, J. W.
KUSY, R. P.
MCIVER, F. T.
MURRAH, V. A.
OFFENBACHER, S.
OLDENBURG, T. R.
PROFFIT, W. R.
ROBERSON, T. M.
SHUGARS, D. A.
SIMPSON, D. M.
STAMM, J. W.
STRAUSS, R. P.
TROPE, M.
TULLOCH, J. F. C.
TURVEY, T. A.
VANN, W. F., Jr
WARREN, D. W.
WHITE, R. P.
WHITE, R. P., Jr
WILLIAMS, R. C.
WRIGHT, J. T.
YAMAUCHI, M.
WOOD, M. T.

Dermatology:
BRIGGAMAN, R. A.
FINE, J. D.
O'KEEFE, E. J.

Developmental Disabilities Training Institute:
BAROFF, G. S.

Dramatic Art:
BARRANGER, M. S.
HAMMOND, D. A.
OWEN, R. A.
RAPHAEL, B. N.
TURNER, C. W.

Economics:
AKIN, J. S.
BENAVIE, A.
BLACK, S. W., III
BLAU, D. M.
CONWAY, P. J.
DARITY, W. A., Jr
FIELD, A. J., Jr
FRIEDMAN, J. W.
FROYEN, R. T.
GALLANT, A. R.
GALLMAN, R. E.
GUILKEY, D. K.
MROZ, T. A.
MURPHY, J. L.
ROSEFIELDE, S. S.
SALEMI, M. K.
STEWART, J. F.
TARASCIO, V. J.
TAUCHEN, H. V.

Education:
BALLEW, J. H.
BRANTLEY, J. C.
BROWN, D.
BROWN, F.
BURKE, W. I.
COOP, R. H.
CUNNINGHAM, J.
DAY, B. D.
FITZGERALD, W. J.
FRIERSON, H. T.
GALASSI, J. P.
GALLAGHER, J. J.
HENNIS, R. S.
HUNTER, R. C.
LILLIE, D. L.
MARSHALL, C.
MORRISON, J. L.
NOBLIT, G. W.
ODOM, S. L., Jr
PALMER, W.
PRYZWANSKY, W. B.
SIMEONSON, R. J.
SPIEGEL, D. L.
STEDMAN, D. J.
STUCK, G. B.
TOM, A. R.
UNKS, G.
WARE, W. B.
WASIK, B. H.
WHITE, K. P.

Emergency Medicine:
TINTINALLI, J. E.

English:
ANDREWS, W. L.
AVERY, L. G.
BETTS, D. W.
DESSEN, A. C.
EBLE, C. C.
FLORA, J. M.
GLESS, D. J.
GREENE, J. L.
GURA, P. F.
HARMON, W. R.
HARRIS, T.
HENDERSON, M. G.
HOBSON, F. C., Jr
KENNEDY, E. D.
KING, J. K.
LENSING, G. S., Jr
LINDEMANN, E.
LUDINGTON, C. T., Jr
MCGOWAN, J. P.
MOSKAL, J.
O'NEILL, P. P.
PATTERSON, D. W.
RAPER, J. R.
RUST, R. D.
SHAPIRO, A. R.
TAYLOR, B. W.
THOMPSON, J. P.
THORNTON, W.
WAGNER-MARTIN, L. C.
WHISNANT, D. E.
WITTING, J. S.
ZUG, C. G., III

Environmental Science and Engineering:
ANDREWS, R. N.
CHRISTAKOS, G.
CHRISTMAN, R. F.
CRAWFORD-BROWN, D. J.
DIGIANO, F. A.
FOX, D. L.
GLAZE, W. H.
GOLD, A.
JEFFRIES, H.
KAMENS, R. M.
LAURIA, D. T.
LEITH, D.
MILLER, C. T.
PFAENDER, F.
RAPAPORT, S. M.
REIST, P. C.
SINGER, P. C.
SOBSEY, M. D.
SWENBERG, J. A.
WATSON, J. E., Jr
WHITTINGTON, D.

Epidemiology:
HEISS, G.
HULKA, B.
IBRAHIM, M. A.
SAVITZ, D. A.
SEED, J. R.

Family Medicine:
CURTIS, P.
FIELDS, K. B.
GWYTHER, R. E.
LEA, J. W.
OLSON, P. R.
REEB, K. G.
SLOANE, P. D.

Geography:
BAND, L. E.
BIRDSALL, S. S.
FLORIN, J. W.
GESLER, W. M.
GREENLAND, D. E.
JOHNSON, J. H., Jr
MEADE, M.
MORIARTY, B. M.
PALM, R. I.
ROBINSON, P. J.
WALSH, S. J.
ZONN, L. E.

Geology:
BENNINGER, L. K.
CARTER, J. G.
DENNISON, J. M.
FULLAGAR, P. D.
POWELL, C. A.
TEXTORIS, D. A.

German:
KOELB, C. T.
MEWS, S. E.
PIKE, D. C.
ROBERGE, P. T.

History:
BARNEY, W. L.
BULLARD, M. M.
CHOJNACKI, S. J.
FILENE, P. G.
FINK, L. R.
FLETCHER, W. M.
GRIFFITHS, D. M.
HALL, J. D.
HARRIS, B. J.
HEADLEY, J. M.
HIGGINBOTHAM, R. D.
HUNT, M. H.
JARAUSCH, K. H.
KASSON, J. F.
KESSLER, L. D.
KOHN, R. H.
KRAMER, L. S.
LOTCHIN, R. W.
MCNEIL, G. R.
MCVAUGH, M. R.
MATHEWS, D. G.
NELSON, J. K.
PEREZ, L. A.
PFAFF, R. W.
SEMONCHE, J. E.
SOLOWAY, R. A.
TALBERT, R. J.
WATSON, H. L.
WILLIAMSON, J. R.

Information and Library Science:
CHATMAN, E. A.
DANIEL, E. H.
MORAN, B. B.

SHAW, W. M., Jr

Institute of Government:

ALLRED, S.
BELL, A. F. II
BRANNON, J. G.
CAMPBELL, W. A.
CLARKE, S. H.
DELLINGER, A. M.
DRENNAN, J. C.
FARB, R. L.
FERRELL, J. S.
JOYCE, R. P.
LAWRENCE, D. M.
LINER, C. D.
LOEB, B. F., Jr
MASON, J.
MESIBOV, L. L.
OWENS, D. W.
SMITH, M. R.
VOGT, A. J.
WHITAKER, G. P.

Journalism:

BLANCHARD, M. A.
BOWERS, T. A.
BROWN, J. D.
COLE, R. R.
ELAM, A. R.
LAUTERBORN, R. F.
LINDEN, T. R.
MEYER, P. E.
SHAVER, M. A.
SHAW, D. L.
SIMPSON, R. H.
STEVENSON, R. L.
STONE, C. S., Jr
WALDEN, R. C.

Law:

BILIONIS, L. D.
BLAKEY, W.
BOGER, J. C.
BROOME, L. L.
BROUN, K. S.
BROWN, C. N.
BRYAN, P. L.
BYRD, R. G.
CALMORE, J. O.
CLIFFORD, D. F., Jr
CONLEY, J. M.
CORRADO, M. L.
CRAIN, M. G.
DAYE, C. E.
GIBSON, S. E.
HASKELL, P. G.
HAZEN, T. L.
HORNSTEIN, D. T.
KALO, J. J.
LINK, R. C.
LOEWY, A. H.
MARKHAM, J. W.
MCUSIC, M. S.
ORTH, J. V.
ROSEN, R. A.
SHARP, S. B.
TURNIER, W. J.
WEGNER, J. W.
WEISBURD, A. M.
YARBROUGH, M. V.
ZELENAK, L. A.

Law Library:

GASAWAY, L. N.

Leisure Studies and Recreation Administration:

HENDERSON, K. A.

Marine Sciences:

BANE, J. M., Jr
FRANKENBERG, D.
HAY, M. E.
KOHLMEYER, J. J.
MARTENS, C. S.
NEUMANN, A. C.
PAERL, H. W.
PETERSON, C. H.
SCHWARTZ, F. J.
WELLS, J. T.
WERNER, P. E.

Maternal and Child Health Care:

BUEXENS, P.
KOTCH, J. B.
KOTELCHUCK, M.
TSUI, A. O.
UDRY, J. R.

Mathematics:

ASSANI, I.
BRYLAWSKI, T. H.
CIMA, J. A.
DAMON, J. N.
EBERLEIN, P. B.
FOREST, M. G.
GEISSINGER, L. D.
GOODMAN, S. E.
GRAVES, W. H.
HAWKINS, J. M.
KERZMAN, N.
KUMAR, S.
PETERSEN, K. E.
PFALTZGRAFF, J. A.
PLANTE, J. F.
PROCTOR, R. A.
SCHLESSINGER, M.
SMITH, W. W.
STASHEFF, J.
TAYLOR, M. E.
VARCHENKO, A.
WAHL, J. M.
WILLIAMS, M.
WOGEN, W. R.

Medical Allied Health Prof.:

BAILEY, D.
LEGRYS, V. A.
SAKATA, R.
YODER, D. E.

Medicine:

BERKOWITZ, L. R.
BERNARD, S. A.
BONDURANT, S.
BOUCHER, R. C., Jr
BOZYMSKI, E. M.
BRENNER, D. A.
BROMBERG, P. A.
CAREY, T. S.
CLEMMONS, D. R.
COHEN, M. S.
COHEN, P. L.
COLINDRES, R. E.
DEHMER, G. J.
DONOHUE, J. F.
DROSSMAN, D. A.
EARP, H. S., III
FALK, R. J.
FINN, W. F.
GABRIEL, D. A.
GETTES, L. S.
GONZALEZ, J. J.
GREGANTI, M. A.
GRIGGS, T. R.
HEIZER, W. D.
HOOLE, A. J.
HUANG, E. S.
KIZER, J. S.
KNOWLES, M. R.
LANE, T. W.
LIU, E. T.
MATTERN, W. D.
MITCHELL, B. S.
NUZUM, C. T.
ONTJES, D. A.
ORRINGER, E. P.
PAGANO, J. S.
RANSOHOFF, D. F.
ROBERTS, H.
ROGERS, C. S.
RUTALA, W. A.
SANDLER, R. S.
SARTOR, R. B.
SHEA, T. C.
SIMPSON, R. J., Jr
SMITH, S. C., Jr
SPARLING, P. F.
UNGARO, P. C.
WHITE, G. C., II
WILLIAMS, M. E.
WILLIS, P. W.
WINFIELD, J. B.
YOUNT, W. J.

Microbiology and Immunology:

BACHENHEIMER, S. L.
BOTT, K. F.
CANNON, J. G.
CLARKE, S. H.
EDGELL, M. H.
FRELINGER, J. A.
GILLIGAN, P. H.
GRIFFITH, J.
HAUGHTON, G.
HUTCHISON, C. A.
JOHNSTON, R. E.
KLAPPER, D. G.
NEWBOLD, J. E.
RAAB-TRAUB, N.
TING, J. P.
WYRICK, P. B.

Microelectronics—Chemistry:

IRENE, E. A.

Music:

BONDS, M. E.
FINSON, J. W.
KETCH, J. E.
MCKINNON, J. W.
NADAS, J. L.
NEFF, S.
OEHLER, D. L.
SMITH, B.
WARBURTON, T. A.
ZENGE, M. W.

Neurology:

GREENWOOD, R. S.
HALL, C. D.
HOWARD, J. N.
MANN, J. D.
SUZUKI, K.

Nursing:

DALTON, J. B.
DAVIS, D. H.
DOUGHERTY, M. C.
FOGEL, C. I.
FREUND, C. M.
FUNK, S. G.
GOEPPINGER, J.
HARRELL, J. S.
KJERVIK, D. K.
MILES, M. S.
MILIO, N.
MISHEL, M. H.
SANDELOWSKI, M. J.

Obstetrics and Gynaecology:

DROEGEMUELLER, W.
FOWLER, W. C., Jr
FRITZ, M. A.
GRANADOS
HASKILL, J. S.
PARISI, Y. M.
STEEGE, J. F.
WALTON, L. A.

Operations Research:

FISHMAN, G.
PROVAN, J. S.
STIDHAM, S., Jr
TOLLE, J. W.

Ophthalmology:

COHEN, K. L.
EIFRIG, D. E.
GRIMSON, B. S.
PEIFFER, R. L., Jr

Paediatrics:

AYLSWORTH, A. S.
BOSE, C. L.
CARSON, J. L.
COLLIER, A. M.

COOPER, H. A.
D'ERCOLE, A. J.
FERNALD, G. W.
FRENCH, F. S.
HAMRICK, H.
HENDERSON, F. W.
HENRY, G. W.
INGRAM, D. L.
KRAYBILL, E. N.
LAWSON, E. E.
LEIGH, M. W.
LEVINE, M. D.
LODA, F. A.
LOHR, J. A.
ROBERTS, K. B.
SCHALL, S. A.
SIMMONS, M. A.
STILES, A. D.
UNDERWOOD, L. E.
WILLIAMS, R. G.
WILSON, E. M.
WOOD, R. E.

Pathology and Laboratory Medicine:
ANDERSON, N. N.
BELLINGER, D. A.
BENTLEY, S. A.
BOULDIN, T. W.
CHAPMAN, J. F.
CROSS, R. E.
FARBER, R. A.
FOLDS, J. D.
FORMAN, D. T.
GRISHAM, J. W.
HAMMOND, J. E.
JENNETTE, J. C.
KAUFMAN, D. G.
LORD, S. T.
MAEDA, N.
REISNER, H. M.
SILVERMAN, L. M.
SMITH, G. J.
SMITHIES, O.
SUZUKI, K. I.
TIDWELL, R. R.
TOPAL, M. D.
WEISSMAN, B. E.

Pharmacology:
CREWS, F. T.
DER, C. J.
DUDLEY, K. H.
GATZY, J. T., Jr
GOZ, B.
HARDEN, T. K.
JULIANO, R. L.
KOLE, R.
MCCARTHY, K. D.
SCARBOROUGH, G. A.
THURMAN, R. G.

Pharmacy:
BROUWER, K. R.
CAMPBELL, W. H.
COCOLAS, G. H.
ECKEL, F. M.
HADZIJA, B. W.
HALL, I. H.
HARTZEMA, A. G.
LEE, K. H.
PIEPER, J. A.
THAKKER, D. R.

Philosophy:
ANTONY, L. M.
BLACKBURN, S. W.
BOXILL, B. R.
HILL, T. E., Jr
HOOKER, M.
LONG, D. C.
LYCAN, W. G.
MUNSAT, S. M.
POSTEMA, G. J.
RESNIK, M. D.
ROSENBERG, J. F.
SAYRE-MCCORD, G. D.
SCHLESINGER, G.
SMYTH, R. A.

Physical Education, Exercise and Sport Science:
BILLING, J. E.
HYATT, R. W.
MCMURRAY, R. G.
MUELLER, F. O.
PRENTICE, W. E., Jr
SILVA, J. M.

Physics/Astronomy:
CARNEY, B. W.
CHRISTIANSEN, W. A.
CLEGG, T. B.
DOLAN, L. A.
DY, K. S.
FRAMPTON, P. H.
HERNANDEZ, J.
KARWOWSKI, H. J.
LUDWIG, E. J.
MCNEIL, L. E.
NG, Y. J.
ROSE, J. A.
ROWAN, L. G.
SCHROEER, D.
THOMPSON, W. J.
VAN DAM, H.
YORK, J. W., Jr

Physiology:
ARENDSHORST, W. J.
FABER, J. E.
FAREL, P. B.
FAUST, R. G.
FROEHNER, S. C.
LIGHT, A. R.
LUND, P. K.
MCILWAIN, D. L.
OXFORD, G. S.
PERL, E. R.
REID, L. M.
SEALOCK, R. W.
STUART, A. E.
WHITSEL, B. L.

Political Science:
BEYLE, T. L.
CONOVER, P. J.
HARTLYN, J.
HUBER, E. H.
LOWERY, D. L.
MARKS, G. W.
PHAY, R. E.
RABINOWITZ, G.
RICHARDSON, R. J.
SCHOULTZ, L. G.
SCHWARTZ, J.
SEARING, D. D.
STEINER, J.
STEPHENS, J. D.
STIMSON, J. A.
WHITE, J. W.
WRIGHT, D. S.

Psychiatry:
BREESE, G. R., Jr
GOLDEN, R. N.
HOUPT, J. L.
JANOWSKY, D. S.
LIEBERMAN, J. A.
LIGHT, K. C.
MCCARTNEY, C. F.
MAILMAN, R. B.
MARCUS, L. M.
MESIBOV, G. B.
STABLER, B.
VAN BOURGONDIE, M. E.
WHITT, J. K.

Psychology:
BAUCOM, D. H.
CAIRNS, R. B.
CHAMBLESS, D. L.
DYKSTRA-HYLAND, L. A.
ECKERMAN, D. A.
FILLENBAUM, S.
GRAY-LITTLE, B.
HOLLINS, M.
INSKO, C. A.
JOHNSON, E. S.
ORNSTEIN, P.
SCHOPLER, J. H.
SHINKMAN, P. G.
THISSEN, D. M.
THOMPSON, V. D.
WALLSTEN, T. S.
YOUNG, F. W.

Public Health:
ROPER, W. L.

Health Behaviour and Health Education:
BAUMAN, K. E.
DEVELLIS, B. M.
EARP, J. L.
MUTRAN, E.
SORENSON, J.
STECKLER, A. B.

Health Policy and Administration:
JAIN, S.
KALUZNY, A. D.
KILPATRICK, K. E.
ROZIER, R. G.
VENEY, J. E.
ZELMAN, W. N.

Nutrition:
ANDERSON, J. J.
COLEMAN, R. A.
KOHLMEIER, L.
POPKIN, B. M.
ZEISEL, S. H.

Public Health Nursing:
ATWOOD, J. R.
SALMON, M. E.

Radiation Oncology:
CHANEY, E. L.
LEADON, S. A.
RALEIGH, J. A.
ROSENMAN, J. G.
TEPPER, J. E.
VARIA, M. A.

Radiology:
JAQUES, P. F.
JOHNSTON, R. E.
KWOCK, L.
LEE, J. K.
MCCARTNEY, W. H.
MITTELSTAEDT, C. A.
MAURO, M. A.

Religious Studies:
ERNST, C. W.
HALPERIN, D. J.
KAUFMAN, P. I.
SASSON, J. M.
TYSON, R. W., Jr
VAN SETERS, J.

Romance Languages:
BANDERA, C.
CASADO, P. G.
CERVIGNI, D. S.
CILVETI, A. L.
CLARK, F. M.
DOMINGUEZ, F. A.
HAIG, I. R. S., II
ILLIANO, A.
KING, L. D.
MALEY, C. A.
MASTERS, G. M.
RECTOR, M. P.
SALGADO, M. A.
SHERMAN, C. L.
VOGLER, F. W.

Slavic Languages:
DEBRECZENY, P.
JANDA, L. A.
LEVINE, M. G.

Social Medicine:
CHURCHILL, L. R.
CROSS, A. W.
DE FRIESE, G. H.
ESTROFF, S. E.

MADISON, D. L.
MORRISSEY, J. P.
RUNYAN, D. K.

Social Work:
BOWEN, G. L.
COOKE, P. W.
DOBELSTEIN, A. W.
EDWARDS, R. L.
FRASER, M. W.
GALINSKY, M. J.
HENLEY, H. C.
NELSON, G. M.
ORTHNER, D. K.
USHER, C. L.
WEIL, M. O.

Sociology:
ALDRICH, H. E.
BEARMAN, P. S.
BLAU, J. R.
ELDER, G. H.
ENTWISLE, B.
KALLEBERG, A. L.
KLEINMAN, S.
NEILSEN, F. D.
OBERSCHALL, A. R.
REED, J. S., Jr
RINDFUSS, R. R.
SIMPSON, R. L.
UHLENBERG, P.

Statistics:
ADLER, R.
CARLSTEIN, E.
CHAKRAVARTI, I. M.
KALLIANPUR, G.
KARR, A. F.
KELLY, D. G.
LEADBETTER, M. R.
MARRON, J. S.
SIMONS, G.
SMITH, R. L.

Surgery:
BAKER, C. C.
BLIGHT, A. R.
BUNZENDAHL, H.
BURNHAM, S. J.
CARSON, C. C., III
HALL, J. W., III
KEAGY, B. A.
MANDEL, S. R.
MAXWELL, J. G.
MEYER, A. A.
NAKAYAMA, D. K.
OLLER, D. W.
PECK, M. D.
PILLSBURY, H. C., III
PRAZMA, J.
SHELDON, G. F.
SHOCKLEY, W. M.
SLOAN, G. M.
STAREK, P. J.
WEISSLER, M. C.
WILCOX, B. R.

Women's Studies Programme:
BURNS, E. J.
HOFFERT, S. D.

University of North Carolina at Charlotte

9201 University City Blvd, Charlotte, NC 28223-0001
Telephone: (704) 687-8622
Fax: (704) 687-6483
E-mail: unccadm@uncc.edu
Internet: www.uncc.edu

Founded 1946 as an extension centre of the Univ. of North Carolina, later Charlotte College, made a degree-granting instn in 1963, present status 1965
Public control
Academic year: August to May

Chancellor: Dr PHILIP L. DUBOIS
Vice-Chancellor for Academic Affairs and Provost: Dr JOAN F. LORDEN
Vice-Chancellor for Business Affairs: ELIZABETH A. HARDIN
Vice-Chancellor for Development and Alumni Relations: NILES F. SORENSON
Vice-Chancellor for Student Affairs: Dr ARTHUR JACKSON
Univ. Registrar: CHRISTOPHER KNAUER
Univ. Librarian: STANLEY WILDER

Library of 1,087,642 vols, 46,966 serial subscriptions, 2,189,037 microforms, 18,468 video and audio material
Number of teachers: 1,108
Number of students: 25,063 (19,755 undergraduates, 5,308 graduates)

DEANS

Belk College of Business: Dr CLAUDE C. LILLEY
College of Arts and Architecture: KENNETH A. LAMBLA
College of Computing and Informatics: Dr MIRSAD HADZIKADIĆ
College of Education: Dr MARY LYNNE CALHOUN
College of Health and Human Services: Dr JANE NEESE
College of Liberal Arts and Sciences: Dr NANCY GUTIERREZ
William States Lee College of Engineering: Dr ROBERT E. JOHNSON

University of North Carolina at Greensboro

1000 Spring Garden St, Greensboro, NC 27403
Telephone: (336) 334-5000
Internet: www.uncg.edu

Founded 1891 as a normal college, present status 1931, present name 1963
Academic year: August to May

Chancellor: PATRICIA A. SULLIVAN
Provost and Vice-Chancellor for Academic Affairs: Dr A. EDWARD UPRICHARD
Vice-Chancellor for Business Affairs: READE TAYLOR
Vice-Chancellor for Information Technology: Dr JAMES H. CLOTFELTER
Vice-Chancellor for Student Affairs: Dr CAROL DISQUE
Vice-Chancellor for Univ. Advancement: Dr PATRICIA W. STEWART
Registrar: ELLEN H. ROBBINS
Dir of Library: DORIS D. HULBERT

Library: 2.5m. vols
Number of teachers: 812 (631 full-time, 181 part-time)
Number of students: 12,731

DEANS

Bryan School of Business and Economics: Dr JAMES K. WEEKS
College of Arts and Sciences: Dr TIMOTHY D. JOHNSTON
School of Education: Dr DALE H. SCHUNK
School of Health and Human Performance: Dr DAVID H. PERRIN
School of Human Environmental Sciences: Dr LAURA S. SIMS
School of Music: Dr JOHN J. DEAL
School of Nursing: Dr LYNNE G. PEARCEY

University of North Carolina at Pembroke

POB 1510, Pembroke, NC 28372-1510
Telephone: (910) 521-6000
Internet: www.uncp.edu

Founded 1887 as college, present status 1969
Academic year: August to May

Chancellor: Dr KYLE R. CARTER
Provost and Vice-Chancellor for Academic Affairs: Dr KENNETH D. KITTS
Vice-Chancellor for Advancement: TERESA OXENDINE
Vice-Chancellor for Business Affairs: R. NEIL HAWK
Vice-Chancellor for Enrollment Management: JACKIE CLARK
Vice-Chancellor for Student Affairs: Dr DIANE JONES
Registrar: SHARON KISSICK
Dir of Athletics: DANIEL KENNEY
Dean of Library Services: Dr ELINOR FOSTER

Library of 385,294 vols
Number of teachers: 553
Number of students: 6,944

Publication: *UNCP Today* (alumni magazine)

DEANS

Graduate Studies: Dr SARA SIMMONS
School of Arts and Sciences: Dr MARTIN SLANN
School of Business: Dr CAMMIE HUNT
School of Education: Dr LEAH FIORETINO

North Carolina State University at Raleigh

Raleigh, NC 27695
Telephone: (919) 515-2191
Fax: (919) 515-7740
E-mail: undergrad_admissions@ncsu.edu
Internet: www.ncsu.edu

Founded 1887 as North Carolina College of Agriculture and Mechanic Arts, present name 1965
State control
Language of instruction: English
Academic year: August to May

Chancellor: Dr W. RANDOLPH. WOODSON
Provost and Exec. Vice-Chancellor: WARWICK ARDEN
Vice-Chancellor for Finance and Business: CHARLES D. LEFFLER
Vice-Chancellor for Research and Graduate Studies: Dr TERRL LOMAX
Vice-Chancellor for Student Affairs: THOMAS H. STAFFORD, Jr
Vice-Chancellor for Univ. Advancement: NEVIN KESSELER
Vice-Chancellor and Gen. Counsel: EILEEN GOLDGEIER
Registrar: Dr LOUIS D. HUNT
Vice-Provost and Dir of Libraries: SUSAN K. NUTTER

Library: 4.1m. vols, bound journals and fed. govt publs, 63,271 periodicals, 69,223 serials
Number of teachers: 2,078
Number of students: 33,819

DEANS

College of Agriculture and Life Sciences: Dr .JOHNNY WYNNE
College of Design: MARVIN J. MALECHA
College of Education: Dr JOSE PICART
College of Engineering: LOUIS MARTIN-VEGA
College of Humanities and Social Sciences: JEFFAQ BRADEN
College of Management: Dr IRA R. WEISS
College of Natural Resources: Dr ROBERT BROWN
College of Physical and Mathematical Sciences: Dr DANIEL L. SOLOMON
College of Textiles: Dr A. BLANTON GODFREY
College of Veterinary Medicine: DAVID BRISTOL
Undergraduate Academic Programmes: JOHN AMBROSE

University of North Carolina at Wilmington

Wilmington, NC 28403-5931
Telephone: (910) 962-3000
Fax: (910) 962-3038
Internet: www.uncw.edu

Founded 1947 as Wilmington College, a county instn under the control of the New Hanover County Board of Education, present status 1969
Public control
Academic year: August to May

Chancellor: ROSEMARY DEPAOLO
Provost and Vice-Chancellor for Academic Affairs: CATHY BARLOW
Vice-Chancellor for Business Affairs: CHARLES MAIMONE
Vice-Chancellor for Student Affairs: PATRICIA LEONARD
Vice-Chancellor for Univ. Advancement: MARY GORNTO
Librarian: SARAH WATSTEIN

Library of 1,004,592 vols
Number of teachers: 899
Number of students: 13,071

WAKE FOREST UNIVERSITY

1834 Wake Forest Rd, Winston-Salem, NC 27106
Telephone: (336) 758-5000
Fax: (336) 758-6074
E-mail: admissions@wfu.edu
Internet: www.wfu.edu

Founded 1834
Private control
Academic year: August to May

Pres.: Dr NATHAN O. HATCH
Provost: WILLIAM C. GORDAN
Sr Vice-Pres. and Chief Financial Officer: NANCY D. SUTTENFIELD
Vice-Pres. for Admin.: MATTHEW S. CULLINAN
Vice-Pres. for Univ. Advancement: JAMES R. BULLOCK
Librarian: RHODA K. CHANNING

Library of over 1.36m. vols
Number of teachers: 1,740 (1,158 full-time, 582 part-time)
Number of students: 6,500 (4,300 undergraduates; 2,200 graduate and professional students)

DEANS

College: DEBBIE L. BEST
Wayne Calloway School of Business and Accountancy: JACK E. WILKERSON, Jr
Divinity School: BILL J. LEONARD
School of Law: ROBERT K. WALSH
School of Medicine: WILLIAM B. APPLEGATE
Graduate School of Arts and Sciences: GORDON A. MELSON
Babcock Graduate School of Management: AJAY PATEL
International Center for Computer Enhanced Learning: DAVID G. BROWN

PROFESSORS

Graduate School of Arts and Sciences:

ABRAMSON, J. S., Paediatrics
ADAMS, M. R., Comparative Medicine
AKMAN, S. A., Cancer Biology, Internal Medicine
ALTMAN, D. G., Public Health Sciences
ANDERSON, J. P., Education
ASCHNER, M., Physiology and Pharmacology
BAREFIELD, J. P., History
BASS, D. A., Medicine
BAXLEY, J. V., Mathematics
BECK, R. C., Psychology
BERRY, M. J., Health and Exercise Science
BEST, D. L., Psychology
BO, W. J., Neurobiology and Anatomy
BOND, M. G., Neurobiology and Anatomy
BORWICK, S. H., Music
BOWDEN, D. W., Biochemistry
BOYD, S. B., Religion
BROSNIHAN, K. B., Physiology and Pharmacology
BROWN, D. G., Economics
BROWNE, C. L., Biology
BROWNE, R. A., Biology
BRUNSO-BECHTOLD, J. K., Neurobiology and Anatomy
BUCKALEW, V. M., Jr, Medicine (Nephrology)
BURKE, G. L., Public Health Sciences
BUSIJA, D. W., Physiology and Pharmacology
BYINGTON, R. P., Public Health Sciences
CARMICHAEL, R. D., Mathematics
CHILDERS, S. R., Physiology and Pharmacology
CHILTON, F. H., Internal Medicine
CLAIBORNE, H. A., Jr, Biochemistry
CLARKSON, T. B., Jr, Comparative Medicine
COLLINS, J. E., Religion
CONNER, W. E., Biology
COTTON, N., English
CRAMER, S. D., Cancer Biology, Internal Medicine
CROUSE, J. R., III, Medicine (Endocrinology and Metabolism)
CUNNINGHAM, C. C., Biochemistry
CUNNINGHAM, P. M., Education
CURRAN, J. F., Biology
DANIEL, L. W., Biochemistry
DEADWYLER, S. A., Physiology
DESHAZER, M. K., English
DIMOCK, R. V., Jr, Biology
DURANT, R. H., Paediatrics and Public Health Sciences
EISENACH, J. C., Anaesthesia
ESCH, G. W., Biology
ESCOTT, P. D., History
ESPELAND, M. A., Public Health Sciences (Biostatistics)
ETTIN, A. V., English
EURE, H. E., Biology
FELDMAN, S. R., Dermatology, Pathology
FERRARIO, C. M., Surgical Sciences
FRANKEL, A. E., Medicine and Cancer Biology
FREY, D. E., Economics
FURBERG, C. D., Medicine and Public Health Sciences
GLADDING, S. T., Education
GRANT, K. A., Physiology and Pharmacology, Comparative Medicine
HALL, M. A., Law and Public Health Sciences
HAMILTON, W. S., Russian
HANS, J. S., English
HAYASHI, F. K., Mathematics and Computer Science
HAZEN, M. D., Communication
HEARN, T. K., Jr, Philosophy
HENDRICKS, J. E., Jr, History
HINZE, W. L., Chemistry
HOLZWARTH, G. M., Physics
HOLZWARTH, N. A. W., Physics
HOWARD, F. T., Mathematics
HUGHES, M. L., History
HUTSON, S. M., Biochemistry
HYDE, M. J., Communication Ethics
JARRETT, D. B., Physiology and Pharmacology
JOHNSTON, W. D., English
KAMMER, G. M., Internal Medicine
KAPLAN, J. R., Comparative Medicine, Anthropology
KERR, W. C., Physics
KIMBALL, C. A., Religion
KIRKMAN, E. E., Mathematics
KOMAN, L. A., Orthopaedics
KONDEPUDI, D. K., Chemistry
KUBERSKI, P., English
KUCERA, L. S., Microbiology
KUHN, R. E., Biology
KUZMANOVICH, J., Mathematics
LANE, H. C., Biology
LEARY, M. R., Psychology
LEONARD, W. J., Divinity School
LITCHER, J. H., Education
LIVELY, M. O., Biochemistry
LONGINO, C. F., Sociology, Public Health Sciences
LORENTZ, W. B., Jr, Paediatrics
LYLES, D. S., Microbiology and Immunology
MCCALL, C. E., Medicine (Infectious Disease), Microbiology and Immunology
MCMILLAN, J. J., Communication
MCPHAIL, L. C., Biochemistry
MAINE, B. G., English
MARGITIC, M. R., Romance Languages
MARTIN, D. R., Accountancy
MARTIN, J. A., Jr, Religion
MATTHEWS, G. E., Physics
MAY, J. G., Mathematics
MEIS, P. J., Obstetrics and Gynaecology
MELSON, G. A., Chemistry
MESSIER, S. P., Health and Exercise Science
MILLER, H. S., Medicine
MILNER, J. O., Education
MIZEL, S. B., Microbiology and Immunology
MORAN, P. R., Radiology
MORGAN, T. M., Public Health Sciences
MOSS, W. M., English
NADER, M. A., Physiology and Pharmacology
NIELSEN, L. N., Education
NOFTLE, R. E., Chemistry
O'FLAHERTY, J. T., Medicine
OPPENHEIM, R. W., Anatomy
OVERING, G. R., English
OWEN, J., Medicine
PARKS, J. S., Pathology
PLEMMONS, R. J., Mathematics and Computer Science
PORRINO, L. J., Physiology and Pharmacology
PRINEAS, R., Public Health Sciences
REIFLER, B. V., Psychiatry
REJESKI, W. J., Health and Exercise Science
RIBISL, P. M., Health and Exercise Science
RICH, S. S., Public Health Sciences
RICHMAN, C. L., Psychology
ROBERTS, D. C. S., Physiology and Pharmacology
ROSE, J. C., Physiology, Obstetrics and Gynaecology
RUBIN, B. K., Paediatrics, Physiology, and Pharmacology
RUDEL, L. L., Comparative Medicine, Biochemistry
ST CLAIR, R. W., Pathology (Physiology)
SAMSON, H. H., III, Physiology and Pharmacology, Comparative Medicine
SHAPERE, D., Philosophy and History of Science
SHERERTZ, R. J., Medicine
SHIHABI, Z. K., Pathology (Clinical Chemistry)
SHIVELY, C. A., Comparative Medicine, Psychology
SHUMAKER, S. A., Public Health Sciences
SIGAL, G., English
SILVER, W. L., Biology
SIMONELLI, J. M., Anthropology
SINCLAIR, M. L., History
SMITH, E., Sociology, American Ethnic Studies
SMITH, J. E., Physiology and Pharmacology
SMITH, J. H., History
SMITH, M. S., Art
SMITH, P. B., Biochemistry
SONNTAG, W. E., Physiology
SORCI-THOMAS, M., Comparative Medicine
STEIN, B. E., Neurobiology and Anatomy
STRANDHOY, J. W., Pharmacology
SWOFFORD, R. L., Chemistry
TAYLOR, T. C., Accountancy
THOMAS, M. J., Biochemistry
TOOLE, J. F., Neurology
TORTI, F. M., Cancer Biology, Internal Medicine
TOWER, R. B., Jr, Taxation

TRIBLE, P., Religion
VALBUENA, O., English
VAN DE RIJN, I., Microbiology and Immunology
VELEZ, R., Internal Medicine
WAGNER, W. D., Comparative Medicine
WASILAUSKAS, B. L., Pathology (Clinical Microbiology)
WEAVER, D. S., Anthropology
WEBBER, R. L., Dentistry, Medical Engineering
WEIGL, P. D., Biology
WEINBERG, R. B., Internal Medicine
WELKER, M. E., Chemistry
WELLS, B. R., Romance Languages
WHEELER, K. T., Jr, Radiology
WILKERSON, J. E., Jr, Accounting
WILLIAMS, A. J., History
WILLIAMS, J. K., Comparative Medicine
WILLIAMS, R. T., Physics
WILLINGHAM, M. C., Pathology
WILSON, E. G., English
WOODALL, J. N., Anthropology
WOODWARD, D. J., Physiology and Pharmacology
WYKLE, R. L., Biochemistry

Graduate School of Management:

BALIGA, B. R., Management
FLYNN, B. B., Operations Management
HARRIS, F. H. DE B., Managerial Economics and Finance
MEREDITH, J. R., Management
NARUS, J. A., Business Marketing
PATEL, A., Finance
RESNICK, B. G., Banking and Finance
SHOESMITH, G. L., Economics
SMUNT, T. L., Management

School of Business and Accountancy:

AKINC, U., Production and Operations Management
EWING, S., Management and Statistics
HARRISON, K., Management
JURAS, P., Academic Excellence
KNIGHT, L., Accounting
MARTIN, D., Financial Accounting
ROBIN, D., Business Ethics
TAYLOR, T., Accounting
TOWER, R., Taxation
WILKERSON, J., Accounting

School of Law:

ANDERSON, C. B.
BILLINGS, R. B.
CASTLEMAN, D. R.
CORBETT, L. H., Jr
COVINGTON, I. B., III
CURTIS, M. K.
DAVIS, T.
FOY, H. M., III
GREBELDINGER, S. K.
HALL, M. A.
HERRING, B. O. H.
LOGAN, D. A.
MEWHINNEY, K.
MONTAQUILA, S. R.
NEWMAN, J. S.
PALMITER, A. R.
PARKER, D. L.
PARKER, J. W.
PARKER, M. F.
PEEPLES, R. A.
REYNOLDS, S.
ROBERTS, P. J.
ROBERTS, T. E.
ROSE, C. P., Jr
ROSE, S.
SCHNEIDER, R. C., Jr
SHORES, D. F.
STEELE, T. M.
TAYLOR, M. H.
WALKER, G. K.
WALSH, R. K.
WRIGHT, R. F., Jr
ZICK, K. A., II

School of Medicine:

ABRAMSON, J. S., Paediatrics
ADAMS, M. R., Comparative Medicine
ADAMS, P. L., Internal Medicine (Nephrology)
ADCOCK, E. W., III, Paediatrics
AKMAN, S. A., Cancer Biology, Internal Medicine (Haematology/Oncology)
ALTMANN, D. G., Public Health Sciences (Social Sciences and Health Policy)
APPLEGATE, R. J., Internal Medicine (Cardiology)
APPLEGATE, W. B., Internal Medicine
ARGENTA, L. C., Surgical Sciences (Plastic/Reconstructive)
ASCHNER, M., Physiology and Pharmacology
ASSIMOS, D. G., Surgical Sciences (Urology)
BASS, D. A., Internal Medicine (Pulmonary Critical Care Medicine)
BECHTOLD, R. E., Radiological Sciences (Radiology)
BLEECKER, E. R., Internal Medicine (Pulmonary Critical Care Medicine)
BO, W. J., Neurobiology and Anatomy
BOND, M. G., Neurobiology and Anatomy
BOWDEN, D. W., Biochemistry
BOWTON, D. L., Anaesthesiology, Internal Medicine (Pulmonary Critical Care Medicine)
BROSNIHAN, K. B., Surgical Sciences (General)
BRUNSO-BECHTOLD, J. K., Neurobiology and Anatomy
BUCKALEW, V. M., Jr, Internal Medicine (Nephrology)
BURKART, J. M., Internal Medicine (Nephrology)
BURKE, G. L., Public Health Sciences
BUSIJA, D. W., Physiology and Pharmacology
BUSS, D. H., Pathology
BUTTERWORTH, J. F., IV, Anaesthesiology
BYINGTON, R., Public Health Sciences (Epidemiology)
CHALLA, V. R., Pathology
CHENG, C.-P., Internal Medicine (Cardiology)
CHEW, F. S., Radiological Sciences (Radiology)
CHILDERS, S. R., Physiology and Pharmacology
CHILES, C., Radiological Sciences (Radiology)
CHILTON, F. L., Internal Medicine (Pulmonary Critical Care Medicine)
CLAIBORNE, A., Biochemistry
CLARKSON, T. B., Comparative Medicine
COATES, M. L., Family and Community Medicine
COOPER, M. R., Internal Medicine (Haematology/Oncology)
COVITZ, W., Paediatrics
CROUSE, J. R., III, Internal Medicine (Endocrinology/Metabolism)
CUNNINGHAM, C. C., Biochemistry
CURL, W. W., Surgical Sciences (Orthopaedics)
DANIEL, L. W., Biochemistry
DEAN, R. H., Surgical Sciences (General)
DENTON, W. H., Psychiatry and Behavioural Medicine
DEWAN, D. M., Obstetric Anaesthesiology
DILLARD, R. G., Paediatrics
DIXON, R. L., Radiological Sciences (Radiology)
DIZ, D. I., Surgical Sciences (General), Physiology and Pharmacology
DONOFRIO, P. D., Neurology (Neuromuscular Diseases)
DURANT, R. H., Paediatrics, Public Health Sciences
DYER, R. B., Radiological Sciences (Radiology)
EISENACH, J. E., Obstetric Anaesthesiology
ELSTER, A. D., Radiological Sciences (Radiology)
ERNEST, J. M., III, Obstetrics and Gynaecology (Maternal/Fetal Medicine)
ESPELAND, M. A., Public Health Sciences (Biostatistics)
FELDMAN, S. R., Pathology
FERRARIO, C. M., Surgical Sciences (General)
FERREE, C. R., Radiation Oncology
FLEISCHER, A. B., Jr, Dermatology
FRANKEL, A. E., Cancer Biology, Internal Medicine (Haematology/Oncology)
FURBERG, C. D., Public Health Sciences
GARRISON, R. S., Dentistry
GARVIN, A. J., Pathology
GEISINGER, K. R., Pathology
GELFAND, D. W., Radiological Sciences (Radiology)
GIVNER, L. G., Paediatrics
GMEINER, W. H., Biochemistry
GOOD, D. C., Neurology
GREVEN, C. M., Surgical Sciences (Orthopaedics)
GREVEN, K. M., Radiation Oncology
HALL, M., Public Health Sciences (Social Sciences and Health Policy)
HAMMON, J. W., JR., Surgical Sciences (Cardiothoracic)
HANSEN, K. J., Surgical Sciences (General)
HARLE, T. S., Radiological Sciences (Radiology)
HARRIS, M. B., Surgical Sciences (Orthopaedics)
HENKEL, C. K., Neurobiology and Anatomy
HERRINGTON, D. M., Internal Medicine (Cardiology)
HILL, I. D., Paediatrics
HUDSPETH, A. S., Surgical Sciences (Cardiothoracic)
HURD, D. D., Internal Medicine (Haematology/Oncology)
HUTSON, S. M., Biochemistry
JANEWAY, R., Neurology
JOHNSON, C. A., Paediatrics
JORIZZO, J. L., Dermatology
KAMMER, G. M., Internal Medicine (Rheumatology)
KAPLAN, J. R., Comparative Medicine, Anthropology
KELLEY, A. E., Psychiatry and Behavioural Medicine (Child/Adolescent Psychiatry)
KELLY, D. L., Jr, Surgical Sciences (Ophthalmology)
KOMAN, L. A., Surgical Sciences (Orthopaedics)
KON, N., Surgical Sciences (Cardiothoracic)
KOUFMAN, J. A., Surgical Sciences (Otolaryngology)
KREMKAU, F. W., Medical Ultrasound
KROWCHUK, D. P., Paediatrics, Dermatology
KUCERA, L. S., Microbiology and Immunology
LAWLESS, M. R., Paediatrics
LICHSTEIN, P. R., Internal Medicine
LINK, K. M., Radiological Sciences (Radiology)
LITTLE, W. C., Internal Medicine (Cardiology)
LIVELY, M. O., III, Biochemistry
LONGINO, C. F., Jr, Public Health Sciences (Epidemiology)
LORENTZ, W. B., Paediatrics
LYLES, D. S., Microbiology and Immunology
MCCALL, C. E., Microbiology and Immunology, Internal Medicine (Infectious Diseases)
MCCALL, W. V., Psychiatry and Behavioural Medicine
MCCULLOUGH, D. L., Surgical Sciences (Urology)
MCGUIRT, W. F., Sr, Surgical Sciences (Otolaryngology)

MACH, R. H., Radiological Sciences (Radiology), Physiology and Pharmacology
MCPHAIL, L. C., Biochemistry
MARKS, M. W., Surgical Sciences (Plastic/Reconstructive)
MAYNARD, C. D., Radiological Sciences (Radiology)
MEIS, P. J., Obstetrics and Gynaecology (Maternal/Fetal Medicine), Family and Community Medicine
MEREDITH, J. Q., Surgical Sciences (General)
MEYERS, D. A., Paediatrics
MICHIELUTTE, R. L., Family and Community Medicine
MILLER, A. A., Internal Medicine (Haematology/Oncology)
MILLER, M. E., Public Health Sciences (Biostatistics)
MIZEL, S. B., Microbiology and Immunology
MOODY, D. M., Radiological Sciences (Radiology)
MORGAN, T. M., Public Health Sciences (Biostatistics)
MORTON, K. A., Radiological Sciences (Radiology)
MOSKOVITZ, J., Public Health Sciences
MUELLER-HEUBACH, E., Obstetrics and Gynaecology
NELSON, L. H., III, Obstetrics and Gynaecology (Maternal/Foetal Medicine)
NELSON, T. E., Anaesthesiology
OBER, K. P., Internal Medicine (Endocrinology/Metabolism)
O'FLAHERTY, J. T., Internal Medicine (Haematology/Oncology)
OPPENHEIM, R., Neurobiology and Anatomy
O'SHEA, T. M. D., Paediatrics
OTT, D. J., Radiological Sciences (Radiology)
OWEN, J., Internal Medicine (Haematology/Oncology)
PARKS, J. S., Comparative Medicine
PAUCA, A. L., Anaesthesiology
PEACOCK, J. E., Jr, Internal Medicine (Haematology/Oncology)
PEGRAM, P. S., Internal Medicine (Haematology/Oncology)
PENNELL, T. C., Surgical Sciences (General)
PETROZZA, P. H., Anaesthesiology
POEHLING, G. G., Surgical Sciences (Orthopaedics)
PONS, T., Surgical Sciences (Neurosurgery), Physiology and Pharmacology
POWELL, B. L., Internal Medicine (Haematology/Oncology)
PRIELIPP, R. C., Anaesthesiology
PRINEAS, R. J., Public Health Sciences (Epidemiology)
QUANDT, S. A., Public Health Sciences (Epidemiology)
RAPP, S. R., Psychiatry and Behavioural Medicine (Geriatric Medicine)
RAUTAHARJU, P. M., Public Health Sciences
REIFLER, B. V., Psychiatry and Behavioural Medicine
RICH, S. S., Public Health Sciences
RILEY, W. A., Neurology
ROGERS, L. F., Radiological Sciences (Radiology)
ROHR, M. S., Surgical Sciences (General)
ROSE, J. C., Obstetrics and Gynaecology (Maternal/Fetal Medicine)
ROUFAIL, W. M., Internal Medicine (Gastroenterology)
ROY, R. C., Anaesthesiology
ROYSTER, R. L., Anaesthesiology
RUBIN, B. K., Paediatrics, Physiology and Pharmacology
RUDEL, L. L., Comparative Medicine, Biochemistry
ST CLAIR, R. W., Pathology
SANGÜEZA, O. P., Pathology
SARTIANO, G. P., Internal Medicine (Haematology/Oncology)
SCUDERI, P. E., Anaesthesiology
SHAW, E. G., Radiation Oncology
SHERERTZ, R. J., Internal Medicine (Infectious Diseases), Microbiology and Immunology
SHIHABI, Z. K., Pathology
SHIVELY, C. A., Comparative Medicine
SHUMAKER, S. A., Public Health Sciences (Social Sciences and Health Policy)
SIMON, J. L., Paediatrics
SINAL, S. H., Paediatrics, Family and Community Medicine
SLUSHER, M. M., Surgical Sciences (Ophthalmology)
SMITH, J. E., Physiology and Pharmacology
SMITH, P. B., Biochemistry
STEIN, B. E., Neurobiology and Anatomy
STRANDHOY, J. W., Physiology and Pharmacology
SUMNER, T. E., Radiological Sciences (Radiology)
TEGELER, C. H., IV, Neurology
THOMAS, M. J., Biochemistry
THOMPSON, J. N., Surgical Sciences (Otolaryngology)
TOOLE, J. F., Neurology
TORTI, F. M., Cancer Biology, Internal Medicine (Haematology/Oncology)
TROOST, B. T., Neurology
TYTELL, M., Neurobiology and Anatomy
VAN DE RIJN, I., Microbiology and Immunology
VEILLE, J.-C., Obstetrics and Gynaecology (Maternal/Fetal Medicine)
VELEZ, R., Internal Medicine
WAGNER, W. D., Comparative Medicine
WALKER, F. O., Neurology (Neuromuscular Diseases)
WARD, W. G., Surgical Sciences (Orthopaedics)
WASILAUSKAS, B. L., Pathology
WEBB, L. X., Surgical Sciences (Otolaryngology)
WEBBER, R. L., Radiological Sciences (Medical Engineering), Dentistry
WEINBERG, R. B., Internal Medicine (Gastroenterology)
WHEELER, K. T., Jr, Radiological Sciences (Radiology)
WILLIAMS, J. K., Comparative Medicine
WILLINGHAM, M. C., Pathology
WOOD, F. B., Neurology (Neuropsychology)
WOODWARD, D. J., Physiology and Pharmacology
WYKLE, R. L., Biochemistry
ZAGORIA, R. J., Radiological Sciences (Radiology)
ZAMKOFF, K. W., Internal Medicine (Haematology/Oncology)

Divinity School:
KIMBALL, C. A., Religion
LEONARD, W. J., Church History
TRIBLE, P., Religion
TUPPER, E. F., Theology

WARREN WILSON COLLEGE

POB 9000, Asheville, NC 28815
701 Warren Wilson Rd, Swannanoa, NC 28778
Telephone: (828) 298-3325
Fax: (828) 298-1440
E-mail: admit@warren-wilson.edu
Internet: www.warren-wilson.edu
Private control
Academic year: August to May
Pres.: SANDY PFEIFFER
Vice-Pres. for Academic Affairs and Dean of the College: JOHN CASEY
Vice-Pres. for Business and Treas.: LARRY R. MODLIN
Vice-Pres. for College Relations: CARLA E. SUTHERLAND
Registrar: CHRISTA BRIDGMAN
Library Dir: CHRISTINE RICHERT NUGENT

Number of teachers: 70
Number of students: 777 (full-time)

WESTERN CAROLINA UNIVERSITY

Cullowhee, NC 28723
Telephone: (828) 227-7211
Fax: (828) 227-7202
Internet: www.wcu.edu
Founded 1889
Linked to the Univ. of North Carolina
Chancellor: JOHN W. BARDO
Provost: KYLE CARTER
Vice-Chancellor for Advancement and External Affairs: CLIFTON METCALF
Vice-Chancellor for Student Affairs: ROBERT CARUSO
Sr Dir of Admissions: CHRIS PARRISH
Registrar: LARRY HAMMER (acting)
Assoc. Dir of Library: ELOISE HITCHCOCK
Library of 436,041 vols
Number of teachers: 335
Number of students: 6,619

WINGATE UNIVERSITY

POB 159, Wingate, NC 28174
Telephone: (704) 233-8000
Fax: (704) 233-8110
E-mail: admit@wingate.edu
Internet: www.wingate.edu
Founded 1896
Private control
Academic year: August to May
Pres.: Dr JERRY E. MCGEE
Exec. Vice-Pres. and Chief Financial Officer: CHARLES TAYLOR
Vice-Pres. for Academic Affairs: Dr MARTHA S. ASTI
Vice-Pres. for Resource Devt: VINT TILSON
Vice-Pres. and Athletic Dir: STEVE POSTON
Registrar: LOURDES SILVA
Library Dir: AMEE ODOM
Number of teachers: 107
Number of students: 1,799

DEANS
College of Arts and Sciences: Dr DONALD MERRILL
School of Business and Economics: JOSEPH GRAHAM
School of Education: Dr ROBERT SHAW
School of Pharmacy: Dr ROBERT SUPERNAW

WINSTON-SALEM STATE UNIVERSITY

601 South Martin Luther King, Jr Dr., Winston-Salem, NC 27110
Telephone: (336) 750-2000
Fax: (336) 750-2049
E-mail: chancellorsoffice@wssu.edu
Internet: www.wssu.edu
Founded 1892
Academic year: August to May
Linked to the Univ. of North Carolina
Chancellor: Dr MICHELLE HOWARD-VITAL
Vice-Chancellor for Finance and Admin.: ROBERT L. BOTLEY
Vice-Chancellor for Student Affairs and Enrollment Services: Dr MELODY C. PIERCE
Vice-Chancellor for Univ. Advancement: LEE WEAVER RICHARDSON
Dir of Library Services: Dr MAE L. RODNEY
Library of 158,858 vols
Number of teachers: 199
Number of students: 6,000

NORTH DAKOTA

JAMESTOWN COLLEGE

600 College Lane, Jamestown, ND 58405
Telephone: (701) 252-3467
Fax: (701) 253-4318
E-mail: admissions@jc.edu
Internet: www.jc.edu

Founded 1883
Private control
Academic year: August to May

Pres.: ROBERT S. BADAL
Dir of Admissions: JUDY ERICKSON
Librarian: Mrs PHYLLIS BRATTON

Library of 117,000 vols
Number of teachers: 60
Number of students: 1,100

Depts of art, biology, business, accounting and economics, chemistry, communication, computer science and technology, criminal justice, English, fine arts, foreign language, health and physical education, history, mathematics, music, nursing, psychology, religion and philosophy, teacher education, theatre.

NORTH DAKOTA UNIVERSITY SYSTEM

Dept 215, 10th Fl., State Capitol 600 East Boulevard Ave, Bismarck, ND 58505-0230
Telephone: (701) 328-2960
Fax: (701) 328-2961
E-mail: ndus.office@ndus.edu
Internet: www.ndus.edu

Chancellor: WILLIAM G. GOETZ
Vice-Chancellor for Academic and Student Affairs: MICHEL HILLMAN
Vice-Chancellor for Administrative Affairs: LAURA GLATT
Vice-Chancellor for Strategic Planning: MARSHA KROTSENG
Dean of Libraries: JAMES COUNCIL

Number of teachers: 4,000.

CONSTITUENT UNIVERSITIES

Dickinson State University

291 Campus Dr., Dickinson, ND 58601-4896
Telephone: (701) 483-2507
Fax: (701) 483-2006
E-mail: dsu.hawks@dsu.nodak.edu
Internet: www.dickinsonstate.edu

Founded 1918

Pres. (vacant)
Vice-Pres. for Academic Affairs: Dr RICH BRAUHN
Vice-Pres. for Business Affairs: ALVIN BINSTOCK
Vice-Pres. for Student Devt: Dr GEORGE S. McLELLAN
Registrar: MARSHALL MELBYE
Library Dir (vacant)

Library of 164,000 vols, 21,000 periodicals
Number of teachers: 106
Number of students: 1,601

DEANS

College of Arts and Sciences: Dr RICHARD D. BRAUHN
College of Education, Business and Applied Sciences: Dr DOUGLAS A. LAPLANTE

Mayville State University

330 Third St NE, Mayville, ND 58257-1299
Telephone: (701) 786-2301
Fax: (701) 786-4748
E-mail: help_desk@mayvillestate.edu
Internet: www.mayvillestate.edu

Founded 1889

Pres.: GARY HAGEN
Vice-Pres. for Academic Affairs: KEITH STENEHJEM
Vice-Pres. for Business Affairs: STEVEN BENSEN
Vice-Pres. for Student Affairs and Institutional Research: RAYMOND GERSZEWSKI
Registrar: MARY IVERSON
Librarian: SARAH BATESEL

Library of 83,964 vols
Number of teachers: 61
Number of students: 832

Minot State University

500 University Ave, Minot, ND 58707-0001
Telephone: (701) 858-3000
E-mail: msu@minotstateu.edu
Internet: www.minotstateu.edu

Founded 1913

Pres.: Dr DAVID FULLER
Vice-Pres. for Academic Affairs: Dr GARY RABE
Vice-Pres. for Admin. and Finance: RON DORN
Vice-Pres. for Advancement: MARV SEMRAU
Vice-Pres. for Student Affairs: Dr RICHARD JENKINS
Registrar: Dr NANCY HALL
Librarian: SHEILA COLLINS

Library of 335,000 vols
Number of teachers: 220
Number of students: 3,200

Additional campus in Bottineau offers Associate in Science (AS), Associate in Arts (AA), and Associate of Applied Science (AAS) degrees.

DEANS

Center for Extended Learning: Dr KRIS WARMOTH
College of Arts and Sciences: Dr CONRAD DAVIDSON
College of Business: Dr JOANN LINRUD
College of Education and Health Sciences: Dr NEIL NORDQUIST
Graduate School: Dr LINDA CRESAP

North Dakota State University

12th Ave N, Fargo, ND 58105
Telephone: (701) 231-8011
Internet: www.ndsu.edu

Founded 1890

Pres.: Dr JOSEPH A. CHAPMAN
Vice-Pres. for Academic Affairs: CRAIG SCHNELL
Vice-Pres. for Finance and Admin.: JOHN C. ADAMS
Vice-Pres. for Information Technology: BONNIE NEAS
Vice-Pres. for Research, Creative Activities and Technology Transfer: PHILIP BOUDJOUK
Vice-Pres. for Student Affairs: PRAKASH MATHEW
Vice-Pres. for Univ. Relations: KEITH D. BJERKE
Registrar: KRISTI WOLD-MCCORMICK
Librarian: PAMELA DRAYSON

Library of 506,444 vols
Number of teachers: 550
Number of students: 10,000

DEANS

College of Agriculture, Food Systems, and Natural Resources: KEN GRAFTON
College of Arts, Humanities and Social Sciences: THOMAS RILEY
College of Business: RONALD D. JOHNSON
College of Engineering and Architecture: GARY R. SMITH
College of Human Development and Education: VIRGINIA CLARK JOHNSON
College of Pharmacy, Nursing and Allied Sciences: CHARLES D. PETERSON
College of Science and Mathematics: KEVIN MCCAUL

University of North Dakota

University Station, Grand Forks, ND 58202
Telephone: (701) 777-2011
Fax: (701) 777-3650
E-mail: university_relations@und.edu
Internet: www.und.edu

Founded 1883
Academic year: August to May

Pres.: CHARLES KUPCHELLA
Provost and Vice-Pres. for Academic Affairs: GREG WEISENSTEIN
Vice-Pres. for Finance and Operations: ROBERT GALLAGER
Vice-Pres. for Health Affairs: H. DAVID WILSON
Vice-Pres. for Research: GARY E. JOHNSON
Vice-Pres. for Student and Outreach Services: ROBERT BOYD
Librarian: WILBUR STOLT

Library: 1.1m. vols, also e-books, microforms, audiovisual items
Number of teachers: 610
Number of students: 13,034

DEANS

Aerospace Sciences: BRUCE A. SMITH
Arts and Sciences: MARTHA A. POTVIN
Business and Public Admin.: DENNIS J. ELBERT
Education and Human Devt: DAN RICE
Engineering and Mines: JOHN WATSON
Graduate School: JOSEPH BENOIT
Law: PAUL LEBEL
Nursing: CHANDICE COVINGTON

Valley City State University

101 College St SW, Valley City, ND 58072
Telephone: (701) 845-7990
Fax: (701) 845-7245
Internet: www.vcsu.edu

Founded 1890

Pres.: Dr ELLEN E. CHAFFEE
Vice-Pres. for Academic Affairs: Dr JOE BESSIE
Vice-Pres. for Business Affairs: TRUDY COLLINS
Vice-Pres. for Student Affairs: GLEN SCHMALZ
Registrar: MONTE JOHNSON
Librarian: DONNA JAMES

Library of 80,000 vols
Number of teachers: 56
Number of students: 1,077

Divs of business and information technology, communication arts and social science, education and graduate studies, fine arts, mathematics, science and health and physical education.

There are five two-year colleges offering associate and trade/technical degrees.

TRINITY BIBLE COLLEGE

50 South Sixth Ave, Ellendale, ND 58436
Telephone: (701) 349-3621
Fax: (701) 349-5443
E-mail: president@trinitybiblecollege.edu
Internet: www.trinitybiblecollege.edu

Founded 1948 as Lakewood Park Bible School; present name 1983
Private control
Academic year: August to May

Pres.: (vacant)
Vice-Pres. for Academic Affairs: Dr MICHAEL DUSING
Vice-Pres. for College Relations: Rev. STEVEN TVEDT
Dean of Students: LAURA GERLING

Registrar: Rev. DAN KUNO
Dir of Library: PHYLLIS KUNO
Number of teachers: 25
Number of students: 280

UNIVERSITY OF MARY

7500 University Dr., Bismarck, ND 58504
Telephone: (701) 255-7500
Fax: (701) 255-7687
E-mail: marauder@umary.edu
Internet: www.umary.edu
Founded 1955 as Mary College, present name 1986
Private control
Academic year: August to May
Pres.: Fr JAMES P. SHEA
Vice-Pres. for Academic Affairs: Dr DIANE FLADELAND
Vice-Pres. for Enrollment Services: BRENDA KASPARI
Vice-Pres. for Financial Affairs: BRENT WININGER
Vice-Pres. for Public Affairs: NEAL KALBERER
Vice-Pres. for Student Devt: Dr TIM SEAWORTH
Library Dir: CHERYL BAILEY
Library of 70,000 vols, 600 periodicals
Number of teachers: 101
Number of students: 2,977

DEANS

School of Arts and Sciences: Dr. DAVID FLEISCHACKER
School of Business: Dr. SHANDA TRAISER
School of Education and Behavioral Sciences: Dr. ROD JONAS
School of Health Sciences: Dr. JODI ROLLER

OHIO

AIR FORCE INSTITUTE OF TECHNOLOGY

2950 Hobson Way, OH 45433-7765
Telephone: (937) 255-6565
Fax: (937) 656-7600
E-mail: pa@afit.edu
Internet: www.afit.edu
Founded 1919
Commandant: Brig.-Gen. PAULA G. THORNHILL
Dir of Admissions: EDWARD HART
Library Dir: JAMES T. HELLING
Library of 120,000 vols
Number of teachers: 134 civilian, 126 military

DEANS

Civil Engineering and Services School: Col BARRY S. MINES
Graduate School of Engineering: Dr MARLIN U. THOMAS
School of Systems and Logistics: Col DIANA J. SCHULZ

ANTIOCH UNIVERSITY

150 E South College, Yellow Springs, OH 45387-1635
Telephone: (937) 769-1340
Fax: (937) 769-1350
Internet: www.antioch.edu
Founded 1852
Academic year: July to June
Chancellor: TONI A. MURDOCH
Vice-Chancellor and Chief Financial Officer: THOMAS A. FAECKE
Vice-Chancellor for Univ. Academic Affairs: Dr LAURIEN ALEXANDRE
Vice-Chancellor for Univ. Advancement: GRADY JONES
Number of teachers: 273
Number of students: 5,023

PRESIDENTS

Antioch Univ. Los Angeles: NEAL KING
Antioch Univ. Midwest: MICHAEL FISHBEIN
Antioch Univ. New England: DAVID CARUSO
Antioch Univ. Santa Barbara: NANCY LEFFERT
Antioch Univ. Seattle: CASSANDRA MANUELITO-KERKVLIET

ART ACADEMY OF CINCINNATI

1125 Jackson St, Cincinnati, OH 45202
Telephone: (513) 562-6262
Fax: (513) 562-8778
E-mail: admissions@artacademy.edu
Internet: www.artacademy.edu
Founded 1869 as McMicken School of Design; present name 1887
Private control
Academic year: August to May
Pres.: GREGORY ALLGIRE SMITH
Academic Dean: KEITH KUTCH
Dir of Admissions: JOHN WADDELL
Registrar: SUE HUTCHENS
Number of teachers: 15
Number of students: 250

ASHLAND UNIVERSITY

401 College Ave, Ashland, OH 44805
Telephone: (419) 289-5055
Fax: (419) 289-5999
E-mail: enrollme@ashland.edu
Internet: www.ashland.edu
Founded 1878
Academic year: August to May
Pres.: Dr FREDERICK J. FINKS
Provost: Dr FRANK E. PETTIGREW
Registrar: KAREN A. LITTLE
Dir of Libraries: WILLIAM B. WEISS
Library of 265,000 vols
Number of teachers: 205
Number of students: 6,459
Publication: *River Teeth* (2 a year)

DEANS

College of Arts and Sciences: (vacant)
College of Business and Economics: Dr KHUSHWANT K. S. PITTENGER
College of Education: Dr ANN CONVERSE SHELLY
Graduate School: Dr W. GREGORY GERRICK

ATHENAEUM OF OHIO

6616 Beechmont Ave, Cincinnati, OH 45230
Telephone: (513) 231-2223
Fax: (513) 231-3254
E-mail: ath@mtsm.org
Internet: www.mtsm.org
Founded 1829
Private control (Roman Catholic)
Academic year: September to June
Pres. and Rector: Rev. EDWARD P. SMITH
Vice-Pres. for Finance and Admin.: DENNIS K. EAGAN
Dean: Dr TERRANCE D. CALLAN
Dean of Spec. Studies: Dr TERRANCE D. CALLAN
Registrar: MICHAEL E. SWEENEY
Librarian: TRACY KOENIG
Library of 77,000 vols
Number of teachers: 58
Number of students: 252

BALDWIN-WALLACE COLLEGE

275 Eastland Rd, Berea, OH 44017-2088
Telephone: (440) 826-2900
E-mail: info@bw.edu
Internet: www.bw.edu
Founded 1845
Private control (United Methodist Church)
Pres.: RICHARD W. DURST
Sr Vice-Pres.: RICHARD L. FLETCHER
Vice-Pres. for Academic Affairs and Dean of College: Dr MARY LOU HIGGERSON
Vice-Pres. for Enrollment Management: SUSAN DILENO
Vice-Pres. for Finance and Admin.: THOMAS LEE
Vice-Pres. for Student Affairs: Dr TRINA DOBBERSTEIN
Vice-Pres. for Univ. Advancement: WILLIAM J. SPIKER
Dir of Libraries: Dr PATRICK SCANLAN
Library of 210,000 vols
Number of teachers: 164 full-time
Number of students: 4,242

BLUFFTON UNIVERSITY

1 University Dr., Bluffton, OH 45817-2104
Telephone: (419) 358-3000
Fax: (419) 358-3323
E-mail: admissions@bluffton.edu
Internet: www.bluffton.edu
Founded 1899 as Bluffton College, present name and status August 2004
Private control
Academic year: August to May
Pres.: JIM HARDER
Vice-Pres. and Academic Dean: SALLY WEAVER SOMMER
Vice-Pres. for Enrollment Management and Student Life: ERIC FULCOMER
Vice-Pres. for Fiscal Affairs: WILLIS J. SOMMER
Vice-Pres. for Institutional Advancement: JIM HARDER
Librarian: MARY JEAN JOHNSON
Library of 160,000 vols
Number of teachers: 70
Number of students: 1,191
Depts of art, communication and theatre, economics, business admin. and accounting, education, English and language, family and consumer sciences, health/physical education and recreation, history and religion, information technology, mathematics, music, sciences, social and behavioural sciences, technology-related programmes.

BOWLING GREEN STATE UNIVERSITY

Bowling Green, OH 43403
Telephone: (419) 372-2531
Internet: www.bgsu.edu
Founded 1910
Academic year: August to May
Pres.: Dr CAROL A. CARTWRIGHT
Senior Vice-Pres. and Provost for Academic Affairs: Dr KENNETH BORLAND (acting)
Vice-Pres. for Finance and Admin.: SHERIDEEN S. STOLL
Vice-Pres. for Student Affairs: EDWARD G. WHIPPLE
Vice-Pres. for Univ. Advancement: THOMAS HILES
Library: 6m. vols, recordings, documents and other materials
Number of teachers: 918
Number of students: 21,000
Publications: *Journal of Popular Culture* (4 a year), *Key* (1 a year), *Philosopher's Index* (4 a year)

DEANS

Arts and Sciences: Dr SIMON MORGAN-RUSSELL
Business Admin.: RODNEY K. ROGERS

Education and Human Development: Dr BRAD COLWELL
Graduate College: Dr DEANNE SNAVELY
Health and Human Services: LINDA PETROSINO
Musical Arts: RICHARD KENNELL
Technology: Dr JOSEPH FRIZADO

CAPITAL UNIVERSITY

Columbus, OH 43209-2394
Telephone: (614) 236-6011
Fax: (614) 236-6147
Internet: www.capital.edu
Founded 1850
Lutheran institution
Academic year: August to May (two terms)
Pres.: Dr DENVY A. BOWMAN
Provost and Vice-Pres. for Academic Affairs: RON ST PIERRE
Vice-Pres. for Business and Finance: SUSAN TATE
Vice-Pres. for Student Affairs: BETTY M. LOVELACE
Registrar: STACEY JONES
Librarian: BELLEN FERNANDEZ
Number of teachers: 201
Number of students: 3,825

DEANS

Arts and Sciences: RICHARD ASHBROOK
Conservatory of Music: ROCKY J. REUTER
Law School: JACK GUTTENBERG
School of Nursing: ELAINE HAYES

CASE WESTERN RESERVE UNIVERSITY

10900 Euclid Ave, Cleveland, OH 44106
Telephone: (216) 368-2000
Fax: (216) 368-4325
Internet: www.case.edu
Founded 1967 from the Western Reserve Univ. (f. 1826 as College) and the Case Institute of Technology (f. 1880 as Case School of Applied Science)
Private control
Academic year: August to May
Pres.: BARBARA R. SNYDER
Provost and Exec. Vice-Pres.: W. A. BAESLACK III
Sr Vice-Pres. for Admin.: JOHN WHEELER
Sr Vice-Pres. for Finance and Chief Financial Officer: JOHN SIDERAS
Sr Vice-Pres. for Univ. Relations and Devt: BRUCE LOESSIN
Deputy Provost and Vice-Pres. for Academic Programmes: LYNN T. SINGER
Vice-Pres. for Campus Planning and Facilities Management: STEPHEN M. CAMPBELL
Vice-Pres. for Campus Services: DICK JAMIESON
Vice-Pres. for Commercial Devt: RUSSELL BERUSCH
Vice-Pres. for Enrollment: RICK BISCHOFF
Vice-Pres. for Financial Planning: DONALD STEWART
Vice-Pres. for Govt Relations: DAVID BELL
Vice-Pres. for Human Resources: CAROLYN GREGORY
Vice-Pres. for Inclusion, Diversity and Equal Opportunity: MARILYN SANDERS MOBLEY
Vice-Pres. for Information Technology Services and Chief Information Officer: LEV S. GONICK
Vice-Pres. for Research and Technology Management: MARK COTICCHIA
Vice-Pres. for Student Affairs: GLENN NICHOLLS
Vice-Pres. for Univ. Planning: CHRISTINE ASH
Vice-Pres. for Univ. Relations: LARA KALAFATIS
Gen. Counsel: COLLEEN TREML
Chief Investment Officer: SALLY J. STALEY
Univ. Registrar: AMY S. HAMMETT
Dir of Univ. Library: ARNOLD HIRSHON
Number of teachers: 2,745
Number of students: 9,738

DEANS

College of Arts and Sciences: CYRUS TAYLOR
School of Dental Medicine: JEROLD GOLDBERG
School of Law: ROBERT H. RAWSON, Jr
School of Medicine: PAMELA BOWES DAVIS
Case School of Engineering: NORMAN TIEN
Frances Payne Bolton School of Nursing: MAY L. WYKLE
Mandel School of Applied Social Sciences: GROVER GILMORE
Weatherhead School of Management: MOHAN REDDY
School of Graduate Studies: CHARLES ROZEK
Undergraduate Studies: JEFFREY WOLCOWITZ

PROFESSORS

Arts and Sciences (tel. (216) 368-4413; internet www.case.edu/artsci):

ADAMS, H., Art History and Art
AKERIB, D., Physics
ALEXANDER, J., Mathematics
ANDERSON, A. B., Chemistry
BARKLEY, M. D., Chemistry
BEAL, T., Religion
BEALL, C. M., Anthropology
BROWN, R., Physics
BURKE, M., Biology
CALVETTI, D., Mathematics
CAPLAN, A. I., Biology
CARRIER, D., Art History and Art
CHIEL, H. J., Biology
CHOTTINER, G. S., Physics
CULLIS, C. A., Biology
DANNEFER, W. D., Sociology
DEACOSTA, A. D., Mathematics
DEIMLING, G. T., Sociology
DETTERMAN, D. K., Psychology
DUFFIN, R. W., Music
DUNBAR, R. C., Chemistry
FAGAN, J. F., III, Psychology
FARRELL, D. E., Physics
GAINES, A. D., Anthropology
GARNER, P. P., Chemistry
GILMORE, G. C., Psychology
GOLDSTEIN, M. C., Anthropology
GREENE, R. L., Psychology
GREKSA, L. P., Anthropology
GRUNDY, K. W., Political Science
GUP, T. S., English
GURARIE, D., Mathematics
HAAS, P. J., Religion
HAMMACK, D. C., History
HEFLING, S. E., Music
HELZE, M., Classics
HURLEY, M. G., Mathematics
IKELS, C., Anthropology
JENKINS, J. H., Anthropology
KAHANA, E., Sociology
KASH, K., Physics
KENNEY, M. E., Chemistry
KIM, C.-T., Philosophy
KOONCE, J. F., Biology
KORBIN, J. E., Anthropology
KOTELENEZ, P., Mathematics
KOWALSKI, K. L., Physics
KRAUSS, L. M., Physics
LAMBRECHT, W., Physics
LANDAU, E. G., Art History and Art
LANGER, J., Mathematics
LATHERS, M., Modern Languages and Literature
LEE, D. H., Mathematics
LEITMAN, M. J., Mathematics
LOADER, C., Statistics
LUCK, R. E., Astronomy
MCCALL, P. L., Geological Sciences
MCHALE, V. E., Political Science
MARLING, W. H., English
MATEESCU, G. D., Chemistry
MATISOFF, G., Geological Sciences
NEILS, J., Art History and Art
OLSZEWSKI, E. J., Art History and Art
ORLOCK, J. M., Theatre Arts
OVERHOLSER, J. C., Psychology
PEARSON, A. J., Chemistry
PETSCHEK, R. G., Physics
PROTASIEWICZ, J., Chemistry
RITZMANN, R. E., Biology
ROCKE, A. J., History
ROSENBLATT, C. S., Physics
RUHL, J. E., Physics
RUSS, S. W., Psychology
SALOMON, R. G., Chemistry
SAVIN, S. M., Geological Sciences
SAYRE, L. M., Chemistry
SCHERSON, D. A., Chemistry
SCHUELE, D. E., Physics
SEDRANSK, J., Statistics
SETTERSTEN, R., Jr, Sociology
SIEBENSCHUH, W. R., English
SINGER, D. A., Mathematics
SINGER, K. D., Physics
STARKMAN, G. D., Physics
STEINBERG, T. L., History
STOLLER, E. P., Sociology
STONUM, G. L., English
STRAUSS, M. E., Psychology
STUEHR, J. E., Chemistry
SUN, J., Statistics
SZAREK, S. J., Mathematics
TAYLOR, C. C., Physics
TAYLOR, P., Physics
TURNER, M., Cognitive Science
URBACH, F. L., Chemistry
VACHASPATI, T., Physics
WERNER, E., Mathematics
WHITBECK, C., Philosophy
WHITE, J., Political Science
WILSON, R. G., Theatre Arts
WOODMANSEE, M. A., English
WOYCZYNSKI, W. A., Statistics
WU, T.-S., Mathematics
ZULL, J. E., Biology

School of Dentistry (tel. (216) 368-3200; internet dental.case.edu):

BISSADA, N., Periodontics
GOLDBERG, J. S., Oral and Maxillofacial Surgery
OCCHIONERO, R. L., Dentistry
SAWYER, D. R., Oral Diagnosis and Radiology
WOTMAN, S., Community Dentistry

School of Law (11075 East Blvd, Cleveland, OH 44106; tel. (216) 368-3600; fax (216) 368-1042; e-mail lawadmissions@case.edu; internet law.case.edu):

AUSTIN, A. D., II
CHISOLM, L. B.
CHODOSH, H. E.
COFFEY, R. J.
DENT, G. W., Jr
DURCHSLAG, M. R.
ENTIN, J. L.
GABINET, L.
GERHART, P. M.
GIANNELLI, P. C.
HESSLER, K.
JENSEN, E. M.
KATZ, L. R.
KING, H. T., Jr
KORNGOLD, G.
KOSTRITSKY, J. P.
KU, R. S. R.
LAWRY, R. P.
LEATHERBERRY, W. C.
LIPTON, J. P.
MCKINNEY, L. W.
MCMUNIGAL, K. C.
MARGOLIS, K. R.
MEHLMAN, M. J.
MORRISS, A. P.
NANCE, D. A.
NARD, C. A.
NETH, S.
SCHARF, M. P.

SHANKER, M. G.
SHARPE, C. W.
SOUTHWORTH, A.
STRASSFELD, R. N.

School of Medicine (tel. (216) 368-2820; e-mail casemed@case.edu; internet casemed.case.edu):

AACH, R. D., Medicine
ABDUL-KARIM, F., Pathology
ADLER, D., Cardiology
AGARWAL, A., Surgery
AGICH, G. J., Medicine
AGLE, D., Psychiatry
ALTHOF, S., Urology
ALTOSE, M. D., Medicine
ANDERSON, J. M., Pathology
ANDERSON, V., Biochemistry and Chemistry
ARAFAH, B., Molecular Endocrinology
ARNOLD, J. E., Otolaryngology
ARON, D. C., Endocrinology and Hypertension
ARROLIGA, A., Medicine
ASKARI, A. D., Medicine
ATAYA, K., Reproductive Biology
BAHLER, R. C., Medicine
BALEY, J. E., Paediatrics
BANERJEE, A., Virology
BARNETT, G., Surgery
BERGER, M., Paediatrics
BERGER, N., Medicine, Biochemistry
BERMAN, B., Paediatrics
BINDER, L. S., Emergency Medicine
BINSTOCK, R. H., Bioethics, Ageing, Health and Society
BLUMER, J. L., Paediatrics and Pharmacology
BODNAR, D., Urology
BOHLMAN, H., Orthopaedics
BOOM, W. H., Infectious Disease
BOOTHMAN, D. A., Radiation Oncology
BORDEN, E., Molecular Medicine
BROUHARD, B. H., Paediatrics
BROZOVICH, F. V., Medicine and Physiology
BRUNENGRABER, H., Nutrition
BUCKLEY, P., Psychiatry
BUDD, G., Medicine
BUKOWSKI, R., Medicine
BURNEY, E., Ophthalmology
CALABRASE, J. R., Psychiatry
CAMPBELL, J., Family Medicine
CAREY, P., Biochemistry
CAREY, W. D., Medicine
CARLIN, C., Physiology and Biophysics
CARLSON, M. D., Cardiology
CARTER, S. G., Medicine
CASCORBI, H. F., Anaesthesiology
CATALANO, P. M., Reproductive Biology
CATHCART, M., Molecular Medicine
CAVANAUGH, P., Molecular Medicine
CEBUL, R. D., Medicine
CHAO, J., Family Medicine
CHISHOLM, G., Molecular Medicine
CHWALS, W. J., Surgery
CLARK, G. S., Medicine
COHEN, A. R., Neurosurgery
COHEN, M. L., Pathology
COLE-KELLY, K., Family Medicine
CONNORS, A., Medicine
COOPER, K. D., Dermatology
COOPERMAN, D. R., Orthopaedics
CRABB, J. W., Molecular Medicine
CROMER, B. A., Paediatrics
CULP, L. A., Molecular Biology and Microbiology
CUTTLER, L., Paediatrics and Pharmacology
CZINN, S. J., Paediatrics
DAHMS, B. B., Pathology
DAHMS, W., Paediatrics
DAROFF, R., Neurology
DAVIS, B. R., Dermatology
DAVIS, P. B., Paediatrics, Physiology and Biophysics, Molecular Biology and Microbiology
DAWSON, N. V., Medicine
DEARBORN, D., Paediatrics
DEBANNE, S., Epidemiology and Biostatistics
DEHASETH, P., Biochemistry
DELANEY, C., Surgery
DELGARDO, P. L., Psychiatry
DELL'OSSO, L., Neurology
DENERIS, E., Neuroscience
DENNIS, V. W., Medicine
DEVEREAUX, M., Neurology
DICORLETO, P. E., Physiology and Biophysics
DIMARCO, A. F., Physiology and Biophysics
DIERKER, L. J., Reproductive Biology
DISTELHORST, C. W., Haematology, Oncology
DOERSCHUK, C., Paediatrics
DRAKE, R., Surgery
DREICER, R., Medicine
DRISCOLL, D., Molecular Medicine
DROTAR, D., Paediatrics
DUBYAK, G. R., Physiology, Biophysics
DUERK, J. L., Radiology
ECKERT, R., Physiology
ELDER, J. S., Urology
ELLIS, S., Medicine
ELSTON, R. C., Epidemiology and Biostatistics
EMANCIPATOR, S. N., Pathology
EMERMAN, C. L., Emergency Medicine
ERNHART, C., Psychiatry
ERZURUM, S. C., Medicine
ESCLAMADO, R., Surgery
ESTAFANOUS, F., Anaesthesiology
EVANS, H., Radiation Oncology
FAIRCHILD, R. L., Surgery
FALCONE, T., Surgery
FANAROFF, A. A., Paediatrics
FARAH, M. G., Cardiology
FINDLING, R., Psychiatry
FINKE, J., Molecular Medicine
FIOCCHI, C., Gastroenterology Medicine
FOX, J. E. B., Physiology and Biophysics
FOX, P., Molecular Medicine
FRANCIS, G., Medicine
FRATIANNE, R. B., Surgery
FRIEDLAND, R., Neurology
GAMBETTI, P., Pathology
GANAPATHI, R., Medicine
GENUTH, S. M., Endocrinology and Hypertension
GERSON, S. L., Haematology and Oncology
GHANNOUM, M. A., Dermatology
GILL, I., Surgery
GOLDBERG, V. M., Orthopaedics
GOLDBLUM, J., Pathology
GOLDING, L., Molecular Medicine
GOLDSTONE, J., Surgery
GORDON, N. H., Bioethics
GORODESKI, G. I., Reproductive Biology
GRAHAM, A. V., Family Medicine
GRAHAM, L., Surgery
GRAHAM, R. C., Medicine
GREENFIELD, E., Orthopaedics
GREENSPAN, N. S., Pathology
GUDKOV, A. V., Biochemistry
HAAGA, J. R., Radiology
HACK, M., Paediatrics
HALL, G., Pathology
HAMILTON, T., Molecular Medicine
HAMPEL, N., Surgery
HANSON, R. W., Biochemistry
HAQQI, T. M., Medicine
HARDING, C. V., III, Pathology
HARDY, R. W., Neurosurgery
HART, W. R., Pathology
HARTE, P., Genetics
HASCALL, V. C., Biochemistry
HATZOGLOU, M., Nutrition
HAUGHEL-DE-MOUZON, S., Reproductive Biology
HAXHIU, M., Paediatrics
HAZEN, S., Molecular Medicine
HENDERSON, J. M., Surgery
HENSON, L., Anaesthesiology
HERRUP, K., Alzheimer Centre
HESTON, W., Molecular Medicine
HINES, J. D., Medicine
HODGSON, J., Medicine
HOFFMAN, G. S., Medicine
HOIT, B., Cardiology
HOLLYFIELD, J., Molecular Medicine
HOPFER, U., Physiology and Biophysics
HOPPEL, C. H., Pharmacology
HORWITZ, R. I., Medicine
HORWITZ, S. M., Psychiatry
HOSKINS, L. C., Gastroenterology Medicine
HOWE, P., Physiology and Biophysics
HRICIK, D. E., Nephrology Medicine
HUANG, S., Ophthalmology
HUGHES, G., Surgery
HUNDERT, E., Bioethics
ISMAIL-BEIGI, F., Endocrinology, Hypertension
JACOBBERGER, J. W., Cancer Research Center
JACOBS, M. R., Pathology
JACOBSEN, D., Molecular Medicine
JENTOFT, J. E., Biochemistry
JONES, S. W., Physiology
JUNIGRO, D., Molecular Medicine
KAISERMAN-ABRAMOF, I., Anatomy
KALHAN, S. C., Paediatrics
KAMINSKI, H. J., Neurology
KAPLAN, D. R., Pathology
KARN, J., Molecular Biology and Microbiology
KARNIK, S., Molecular Medicine
KASHANI, J. H., Psychiatry
KASS, L., Pathology
KATIRJI, M. B., Neurology
KATZ, D. M., Neurosciences
KAZURA, J. W., International Health
KEITH, M. W., Orthopaedics
KERCSMAR, C. M., Paediatrics
KERN, J. A., Pulmonary and Critical Care
KERN, T. S., Clinical and Molecular Endocrinology
KERR, D., Paediatrics
KHAN, M. A., Medicine
KIKANO, G. E., Family Medicine
KINSELLA, T. J., Radiation Oncology
KLEIN, A., Medicine
KLEIN, E., Paediatrics
KODISH, E., Surgery
KOWAL, J., Geriatric Medicine
KUMAR, M. L., Paediatrics
KUNZE, D. L., Neurosciences
KURSH, E., Surgery
KUSHNER, I., Medicine
LAMANNA, J. C., Anatomy
LAMM, M. E., Pathology
LANDAU, B. R., Endocrinology and Hypertension
LANDIS, D. M., Neurology and Neurosciences
LANDMESSER, L., Neurosciences
LANDRETH, G., Neurology and Neurosciences
LANZIERI, C. F., Radiology
LARNER, A., Molecular Medicine
LASEK, R. J., Bio-architectonics
LASS, J. H., Ophthalmology
LATSON, L. A., Paediatrics
LAUER, M. S., Medicine
LAVERTU, P., Otolaryngology
LAZARUS, H., Haematology and Oncology
LEDERMAN, M., Infectious Disease
LEHMANN, P. V., Pathology
LEIGH, R. J., Neurology
LEVIN, K., Medicine
LEVINE, A. D., Gastroenterology Medicine
LEVITAN, N., Haematology and Oncology
LEWIS, H., Surgery
LIEBERMAN, I., Surgery
LIEBMAN, J., Paediatrics
LIEDKE, C. M., Paediatrics
LINCOFF, A., Medicine
LIU, J., Reproductive Biology
LOUE, S., Epidemiology and Biostatistics
LOWE, J., Pathology

LÜDERS, H. O., Medicine
LUSE, D., Biochemistry
LUST, W. D., Neurological Surgery
MACIUNAS, R. J., Neurosurgery
MCCULLOUGH, A. J., Medicine
MCFADDEN, E. R., Jr, Pulmonary and Critical Care
MCHENRY, C. R., Surgery
MCLAIN, R., Surgery
MACKLIN, W. B., Neurosciences
MACKNIN, M., Paediatrics
MACLIS, R., Medicine
MAGUIRE, M. E., Pharmacology
MALANGOLI, M., Surgery
MALEMUD, C. J., Rheumatology Medicine
MANSOUR, E. G., Surgery
MARCHANT, K., Pathology
MARCUS, R. E., Orthopaedics
MARKOWITZ, S., Haematology, Oncology
MARSOLAIS, E. B., Orthopaedics
MARTIN, P. J., Physiology and Biophysics
MARTIN, R. J., Paediatrics
MASARYK, T. J., Radiology
MAVISSAKALIAN, M., Psychiatry
MAYBERG, M. R., Surgery
MEDOF, M. E., Pathology
MENON, M., Urology
MERCER, B. M., Reproductive Medicine
MERRICK, W. C., Biochemistry
MIEYAL, J. J., Pharmacology
MILLER, C., Surgery
MILLER, R., Neurosciences
MILLER, R. T., Medicine
MODIC, M., Radiology
MONNIER, V. M., Pathology
MONTAGUE, D., Surgery
MONTENEGRO, H. D., Pulmonary and Critical Care
MOORE, J. J., Paediatrics
MORGAN, P. G., Anaesthesiology
MOSKOWITZ, R. W., Rheumatology Medicine
MULLEN, K. D., Medicine
MURRAY, P., Anaesthesiology
MUSCHLER, G., Surgery
NADEAU, J. H., Genetics
NAGARAJ, R., Ophthalmology
NAGY, L., Nutrition
NAIR, R., Cardiology
NEARMAN, H. S., Anaesthesiology
NEDRUD, J. G., Pathology
NEUHAUSER, D., Epidemiology and Biostatistics
NEWMAN, C., Surgery
NILSEN, T. W., Molecular Biology
NILSON, J. H., Pharmacology
NOSEK, T., Physiology and Biophysics
NOVIC, A. C., Surgery
O'HARA, P., Surgery
OLEINICK, N., Radiation Oncology
OLNESS, K. N., Paediatrics
OURIEL, K., Surgery
PEACHEY, N., Molecular Medicine
PEARLMAN, E., Ophthalmology
PELLETT, P., Molecular Medicine
PERRY, G., Pathology
PETOT, G., Nutrition
PILAR, G., Neurosciences
PIÑA, I. L., Medicine
PLOW, E. F., Molecular Medicine
PONSKY, J. L., Surgery
POST, S. G., Bioethics
PRABHAKAR, N. R., Physiology and Biophysics
PRAYSON, R. A., Pathology
PRESTON, D. C., Neurology
PRETLOW, T. G., II, Pathology
PRETLOW, T. P., Pathology
QIN, J., Pharmacology
RANSOHOFF, R., Molecular Medicine
RATCHESON, R. A., Neurosurgery
REDLINE, R. W., Pathology
REDLINE, S., Paediatrics
REED, M. D., Paediatrics
REINHART, W., Ophthalmology
REMICK, S. C., Medicine
RESNICK, M. I., Urology
RESNICK, P., Psychiatry
RICANATI, E. S., Medicine
RICE, L. B., Infectious Disease
RICE, T., Surgery
RIMM, A. A., Epidemiology and Biostatistics
RONIS, R., Psychiatry
ROSE, P. G., Reproductive Biology
ROSS, J., Radiology
ROTE, N. S., Reproductive Biology
ROTH, B. L., Biochemistry
RUDICK, R. A., Medicine
RUFF, R., Neurology
SAGAR, S., Neurology
SAHGAL, V., Medicine
SALATA, R. A., Infectious Disease
SALZ, H., Genetics
SAMOLS, D., Biochemistry
SCARPA, A., Physiology and Biophysics
SCHER, M., Paediatric Neurology
SCHILLING, W. P., Physiology and Biophysics
SCHLUCHTER, M. D., Paediatrics
SCHUBERT, A., Anaesthesiology
SCHULAK, J. A., Surgery
SCHWARTZ, S., Genetics
SEDENSKY, M. M., Anaesthesiology
SEDOR, J. R., Medicine
SEDWICK, W. D., Haematology and Oncology
SEFTEL, A., Urology
SEGRAVES, R. T., Psychiatry
SELMAN, W. R., Neurosurgery
SEN, G. C., Physiology and Biophysics
SEN, S., Molecular Medicine
SHAFFER, J. W., Orthopaedics
SHU, S., Surgery
SHUCK, J., Anatomy, Surgery
SCHURIN, S., Paediatrics
SIEGEL, R. E., Pharmacology
SILVER, J., Neurosciences
SILVERMAN, R. H., Biochemistry
SILVERSTEIN, R., Molecular Medicine
SIMINOFF, L. A., Bioethics
SINGER, L. T., Paediatrics
SIVAK, M. V., Gastroenterology Medicine
SIVIT, C. J., Radiology
SMITH, C. E., Anaesthesiology
SMITH, C. K., Family Medicine
SMITH, J., Molecular Medicine
SMITH, M. A., Pathology
SMITH, M. C., Nephrology Medicine
SODEE, D. B., Radiology
SPIRNAK, J. P., Surgery
STANCIN, T., Paediatrics
STANGE, K. C., Family Medicine
STANLEY, W., Physiology and Biophysics
STANTON-HICKS, M., Anaesthesiology
STARK, G. R., Genetics
STAVNEZER, E., Biochemistry
STELLATO, T. A., Surgery
STERN, R., Paediatrics
STOLLER, J. K., Medicine
STORK, E. K., Paediatrics
STRAUSS, M., Otolaryngology
STROHL, K. P., Anatomy, Pulmonary and Critical Care
STROME, M., Surgery
SUPER, D. M., Paediatrics
SUREWICZ, W. K., Physiology and Biophysics
SY, M.-S., Pathology
TAKAOKA, Y., Surgery
TARR, R. W., Radiology
TARTAKOFF, A. M., Pathology
TAVILL, A. S., Medicine
TAYLOR, H. G., Paediatrics
TETZLAFF, W., Anaesthesiology
THOMPSON, G. H., Orthopaedics
TOMASHEFSKI, J. F., Pathology
TOOSSI, Z., Infectious Disease
TOPOL, E. J., Medicine
TRAPP, B., Neurosciences
TUBBS, R. R., Pathology
TUCKER, H. M., Otolaryngology
TUOHY, V., Molecular Medicine
VERTES, V., Medicine
WALDO, A. L., Cardiology
WALSH, R. A., Medicine
WALSH-SUKYS, M. C., Paediatrics
WEBER, P., Surgery
WEISS, M., Biochemistry
WEISS, M. F., Medicine
WESSELS, B. W., Radiation Oncology
WHITE, R. J., Surgery
WHITEHOUSE, F. W., Medicine
WHITEHOUSE, P. J., Bioethics, Neurology, Neuroscience, and Psychiatry
WILBER, J. H., Orthopaedics
WILKOFF, B., Medicine
WILLIAMS, B. R. G., Genetics
WISE, J., Molecular Biology and Microbiology
WISH, J. B., Nephrology Medicine
WISNIESKI, J., Medicine
WOLPAW, D., General Internal Medicine
WRIGHT, J., Hypertension Medicine
YANG, Y.-C., Pharmacology
YEN-LIEBERMAN, B., Pathology
YOMTOVIAN, R. A., Pathology
YOUNG, J., Medicine
YOUNGNER, S. J., Bioethics
ZAHKA, K. G., Paediatrics
ZIGMOND, R. E., Neurosciences
ZINS, J., Surgery
ZOLLINGER, R. M., Surgery
ZYZANSKI, S. J., Family Medicine

Case School of Engineering (tel. (216) 368-4436; internet www.engineering.case.edu):

ADAMS, M. L., Mechanical and Aerospace Engineering
ALEXANDER, J. I. D., Mechanical and Aerospace Engineering
BAER, E., Macromolecular Science and Engineering
BALLARINI, R., Engineering Mechanics
BEER, R., Electrical Engineering and Computer Science
BLACKWELL, J., Macromolecular Science and Engineering
CAWLEY, J. D., Materials Science and Engineering
CRAGO, P. E., Biomedical Engineering
DAVY, D. T., Mechanical and Aerospace Engineering
DURAND, D. M., Biomedical Engineering
EDWARDS, R. V., Chemical Engineering
ERNST, F., Materials Science and Engineering
FEKE, D. L., Chemical Engineering
GASPARINI, D. A., Structural Engineering
GREBER, I., Mechanical and Aerospace Engineering
HEUER, A. H., Materials Science and Engineering
HILTNER, A., Macromolecular Science and Engineering
ISHIDA, H., Macromolecular Science and Engineering
JAMIESON, A. M., Macromolecular Science and Engineering
JENNINGS, A. A., Environmental Engineering
KADAMBI, J. R., Mechanical and Aerospace Engineering
KAMOTANI, Y., Mechanical and Aerospace Engineering
LACKS, D. J., Chemical Engineering
LANDAU, U., Chemical Engineering
LANDO, J. B., Macromolecular Science and Engineering
LEWANDOWSKI, J. J., Materials Science and Engineering
LITT, M., Macromolecular Science and Engineering
LIU, C.-C., Chemical Engineering
LOPARO, K. A., Electrical Engineering and Computer Science
MALAKOOTI, B., Electrical Engineering and Computer Science

MANAS-ZLOCZOWER, I., Macromolecular Science and Engineering
MANN, J. A., Jr, Chemical Engineering
MANSOUR, J. M., Mechanical and Aerospace Engineering
MARCHANT, R. E., Biomedical Engineering
MEHREGANY, M., Electrical Engineering and Computer Science
MESAROVIC, M. D., Electrical Engineering and Computer Science
MICHAL, G. M., Materials Science and Engineering
MULLEN, R. L., Engineering Mechanics
NEWMAN, W. S., Electrical Engineering and Computer Science
OSTRACH, S., Mechanical and Aerospace Engineering
OZSOYOGLU, G., Electrical Engineering and Computer Science
OZSOYOGLU, Z. M., Electrical Engineering and Computer Science
PAPACHRISTOU, C. A., Electrical Engineering and Computer Science
PAYER, J. H., Materials Science and Engineering
PECKHAM, P. H., Biomedical Engineering
PINTAURO, P. N., Chemical Engineering
PIROUZ, P., Materials Science and Engineering
PRAHL, J. M., Mechanical and Aerospace Engineering
QUINN, R. D., Mechanical and Aerospace Engineering
QUTUBUDDIN, S., Chemical Engineering
SAADA, A. S., Geotechnical Engineering
SAIDEL, G. M., Biomedical Engineering
SAVINELL, R. F., Chemical Engineering
TABIB-AZAR, M., Electrical Engineering and Computer Science
T'IEN, J. S., Mechanical and Aerospace Engineering
WELSCH, G. E., Materials Science and Engineering
WHITE, L., Electrical Engineering and Computer Science
WILSON, D., Biomedical Engineering
ZAWODZINSKI, T., Chemical Engineering

Frances Payne Bolton School of Nursing (tel. (216) 368-4700; internet fpb.case.edu):

ANDERSON, G., Nursing
ANDREWS, C., Nursing
FITZPATRICK, J. J., Nursing
GARY, F. A., Nursing
GOOD, M., Nursing
LUDINGTON, S. M., Paediatric Nursing
MOORE, S., Nursing
ROBERTS, B. L., Gerontological Nursing
WYKLE, M. L., Gerontological Nursing

Mandel School of Applied Social Sciences (11235 Bellflower Rd, Cleveland, OH 44106; tel. (216) 368-2290; e-mail msassweb@case.edu; internet msass.case.edu):

BIEGEL, D. E., Social Work Practice, Psychiatry and Sociology
CHATTERJEE, P., Social Work
COULTON, C. J., Social Work and Urban Poverty
FLEISHER, M., Violence Prevention, Research and Education
GINGERICH, W. J., Social Work
GROZA, V., Social Work
HOKENSTAD, M. C., Jr, International Social Work
MAHONEY, G., Families and Communities
SINGER, M. I., Social Work, Youth Violence
WELLS, K., Social Work, Child Welfare
YOUNG, D. R., Non-profit Management

Weatherhead School of Management (tel. (216) 368-2030; internet weatherhead.case.edu):

ANVARI, M., Finance
ARAM, J. D., Management Policy
BALLOU, R. H., Operations
BOLAND, R., Information Systems
BOYATZIS, R. E., Organizational Behaviour
BRICKER, R., Accountancy
CARLSSON, B., Economics
CHATTERJEE, S., Management Policy
COLLOPY, F., Information Systems
COOPERRIDER, D., Organizational Behaviour
ERDILEK, A., Economics
FINE, S., Banking and Finance
FOGARTY, T., Accountancy
GERHART, P. F., Labour and Human Resource Policy
HELPER, S., Economics
HISRICH, R. D., Entrepreneurial Studies
KOLB, D. A., Organizational Behaviour
LYNN, L. H., Management Policy
LYYTINEN, K., Information Systems
NEILSEN, E. H., Organizational Behaviour
OSBORNE, R. L., Practice of Management
PEARSON, D., Practice of Accountancy
POZA, E. J., Practice of Family Business
PREVITS, G. J., Accountancy
REBITZER, J. B., Economics
RITCHKEN, P. H., Banking and Finance
ROOMKIN, M., Labour and Human Resource Policy
SALIPANTE, P. F., Jr, Labour and Human Resource Policy
SALKIN, H. M., Operations
SHANE, S. A., Economics
SILVERS, J. B., Banking and Finance
SINGH, J., Marketing
SOBEL, M. J., Operations
VANDENBOSCH, B., Information Systems
VONK, T., Labour and Human Resource Policy

CEDARVILLE UNIVERSITY

251 N Main St, Cedarville, OH 45314
Telephone: (937) 766-7700
Fax: (937) 766-7575
E-mail: admissions@cedarville.edu
Internet: www.cedarville.edu

Founded 1887 as Cedarville College; present name 2000
Private control
Academic year: August to May

Pres.: Dr WILLIAM E. BROWN
Chancellor: Dr PAUL H. DIXON
Academic Vice-Pres.: Dr ROBERT MILLIMAN
Vice-Pres. for Business: JOHN C. ANGLEA
Vice-Pres. for Christian Ministries: ROBERT K. ROHM
Vice-Pres. for Enrollment Management: JOHN S. GREDY
Vice-Pres. for Student Life: Dr CARL RUBY
Registrar: FRAN CAMPBELL
Dean of Library Services: LYNN A. BROCK

Number of teachers: 185 (full-time)
Number of students: 3,006

Publication: *Journal of Biblical Integration in Business* (1 a year)

DEANS

School of Biblical and Theological Studies: Dr THOMAS HUTCHISON
School of Humanities: STEVEN WINTEREGG
School of Natural and Applied Sciences: Dr STANLEY BACZEK
School of Pharmacy: (vacant)
School of Social Sciences and Human Performance: Dr PAMELA DIEHL JOHNSON

CENTRAL STATE UNIVERSITY

Wilberforce, OH 45384
Telephone: (937) 376-6142
Fax: (937) 376-6141
E-mail: info@centralstate.edu
Internet: www.centralstate.edu

Founded 1887

Pres.: JOHN W. GARLAND
Provost and Vice-Pres. for Academic Affairs: Dr JULIETTE B. BELL
Registrar: LARRY CANNON
Librarian: JOHNNY JACKSON

Library of 195,000 vols, 844,000 microfilms, 900 periodicals
Number of teachers: 80
Number of students: 1,400

DEANS

College of Arts and Sciences: Dr WILLIE HOUSTON
College of Business and Industry: Dr C. H. SHOWELL
College of Education: Dr ROBERT MOORE

CINCINNATI CHRISTIAN UNIVERSITY

POB 04320, 2700 Glenway Ave, Cincinnati, OH 45204
Telephone: (513) 244-8100
Fax: (513) 244-8140
E-mail: ccuadmissions@ccuniveristy.edu
Internet: www.ccuniversity.edu

Founded 1924 as Cincinnati Bible Seminary by merger of McGarvey Bible College (f. 1923) and Cincinnati Bible Institute (f. 1923); Cincinnati Bible College and Seminary 1987; present name and status 2004
Private control
Academic year: August to May

Pres.: Dr DAVID FAUST
Exec. Vice-Pres.: J. EDWARD RAUCH
Vice-Pres. for Institutional Advancement: FRAN ANDERSON
Academic Dean of College: Dr JON A. WEATHERLY
Academic Dean of Seminary: J. MICHAEL SHANNON
Registrar: DON THOMASON
Library Dir: JAMES H. LLOYD

Library of 150,000 vols
Number of teachers: 40
Number of students: 920

CINCINNATI COLLEGE OF MORTUARY SCIENCE

645 W North Bend Rd, Cincinnati, OH 45224-1462
Telephone: (513) 761-2020
Fax: (513) 761-3333
E-mail: generalinfo@ccms.edu
Internet: www.ccms.edu

Founded 1882 as Cincinnati School of Embalming; present name 1966
Private control

Pres.: KAREN GILES
Academic Dean: DAVID W. TACKETT
Registrar: DANA WILLIAMS
Library Dir: MICHAEL WELLS

Number of teachers: 6
Number of students: 120

CLEVELAND INSTITUTE OF ART

11141 E Blvd, Cleveland, OH 44106-1710
Telephone: (216) 421-7000
Fax: (216) 421-7438
E-mail: admiss@cia.edu
Internet: www.cia.edu

Founded 1882
Private control
Academic year: August to May

Pres.: GRAFTON NUNES
Sr Vice-Pres. for Institutional Advancement: R. MICHAEL COLE
Vice-Pres. for Business Affairs: AL ZVOSEC
Vice-Pres. for Marketing and Communications: MARK INGLIS
Registrar: KAREN HUDY
Library Dir: CRISTINE ROM

Number of teachers: 100
Number of students: 534

CLEVELAND INSTITUTE OF MUSIC

11021 East Blvd, Cleveland, OH 44106
Telephone: (216) 791-5000
Fax: (216) 791-3063
E-mail: admission@cim.edu
Internet: www.cim.edu
Founded 1920
Academic year: August to May
Pres.: DAVID CERONE
Dean: CATHERINE JARJISIAN
Dir of Admissions: WILLIAM FAY
Registrar: HALLIE MOORE
Library Dir: JEAN TOOMBS
Number of teachers: 100
Number of students: 400

CLEVELAND STATE UNIVERSITY

2121 Euclid Ave, Cleveland, OH 44115-2214
Telephone: (216) 687-2000
Fax: (216) 687-9366
E-mail: admissions@csuohio.edu
Internet: www.csuohio.edu
Founded 1964
Pres.: Dr MICHAEL SCHWARTZ
Provost and Sr Vice-Pres. for Academic Affairs: MARY JANE SAUNDERS
Vice-Pres. for Admin.: MICHAEL DRONEY
Vice-Pres. for Business Affairs and Finance: JOHN J. BOYLE
Vice-Pres. for Economic Devt: EDWARD HILL
Vice-Pres. for Institutional Diversity: NJERI NURU-HOLM
Vice-Pres. for Univ. Advancement: PETER ANAGNOSTOS
Dir of Libraries: GLENDA THORNTON
Library of 856,978 vols, 4,005 periodicals, 625,191 microforms
Number of teachers: 808 (531 full-time, 277 part-time)
Number of students: 15,600

DEANS

Cleveland-Marshall College of Law: GEOFFREY S. MEARNS
College of Education and Human Sciences: JAMES MCLOUGHLIN
College of Graduate Studies: VERA VOGELSAUG-COMBS
College of Liberal Arts and Social Sciences: GREGORY M. SADLEK
College of Science: BETTE BONDER
Continuing Education: BARBARA HANNIFORD
Fenn College of Engineering: BAHMAN GHORASHI
Maxine Goodman Levin College of Urban Affairs: EDWARD HILL
Nance College of Business Admin.: ROBERT F. SCHERER

COLLEGE OF MOUNT ST JOSEPH

5701 Delhi Rd, Cincinnati, OH 45233-1670
Telephone: (513) 244-4200
Fax: (513) 244-4601
Internet: www.msj.edu
Founded 1920
Private control
Language of instruction: English
Depts of art and design, behavioural sciences, biology, business admin., chemistry and physical sciences, education, health sciences, humanities, mathematics, music, Project Excel, religious and pastoral studies
Pres.: Dr ANTHONY ARETZ
Vice-Pres. for Institutional Advancement: MARK DI STASI
Academic Dean: Dr ALAN DECOURCY
Dir of Admissions: PEGGY MINNICH
Dean of Students: Dr DOUGLAS K. FRIZZELL
Registrar: PATSY KENNER
Dir of Library Services: PAUL JENKINS
Library of 96,000 vols
Number of teachers: 233
Number of students: 2,594

COLLEGE OF WOOSTER

1189 Beall Ave, Wooster, OH 44691
Telephone: (330) 263-2000
Fax: (330) 263-2427
Internet: www.wooster.edu
Founded 1866 by the Presbyterian Church (USA)
Academic year: August to May
Pres.: GRANT H. CORNWELL
Provost: CAROYLN NEWTON
Vice-Pres. for Devt: SARA L. PATTON
Vice-Pres. for Enrollment and College Relations: SCOTT FRIEDHOFF
Vice-Pres. for Finance and Business: LAURIE STICKELMAIER
Dean of Students: KURT C. HOLMES
Sec.: ANGELA JOHNSTON
Registrar: SUZANNE BATES
Dir of Libraries: MARK CRISTEL
Library of 645,818 vols
Number of teachers: 132 full-time
Number of students: 1,854

COLUMBUS COLLEGE OF ART AND DESIGN

107 N Ninth St, Columbus, OH 43215
Telephone: (614) 224-9101
Fax: (614) 222-4040
Internet: www.ccad.edu
Founded 1879 as Columbus Art School; present name 1959
Private control
Academic year: August to August
Provost: Dr ANEDITH NASH
Library of 50,000 vols, 275 periodicals
Number of teachers: 180
Number of students: 1,500

DEANS

Fine Arts: JULIE TAGGART
Industrial/Interior Design: CARL GARANT
Liberal Arts: Dr EDWARD LATHY
Media Studies: RON SAKS
Visual Communications: RICHARD ASCHENBRAND

DEFIANCE COLLEGE

701 North Clinton St, Defiance, OH 43512
Telephone: (419) 784-4010
E-mail: admissions@defiance.edu
Internet: www.defiance.edu
Founded 1850 as Defiance Female Seminary; present name 1903
Pres.: GERALD WOOD
Vice-Pres. for Academic Affairs and Academic Dean: Dr CATHARINE O'CONNELL
Vice-Pres. for Enrollment Management: MIKE SUZO
Vice-Pres. for Finance and Management: LOIS MCCULLOUGH
Vice-Pres. for Institutional Advancement: RICH PEJEAU
Vice-Pres. for Student Engagement and Dean of Students: KENNETH WETSTEIN
Vice-Pres. for Strategic Planning and Marketing: SUSAN PSCODNA
Registrar: BEVERLY HARRINGTON
Dir of Library Services: ANN BIBLE
Library of 90,000 vols
Number of teachers: 86
Number of students: 1,030

DENISON UNIVERSITY

Granville, OH 43023-0603
Telephone: (740) 587-0810
Fax: (740) 587-6417
E-mail: admissions@denison.edu
Internet: www.denison.edu
Founded 1831
Private control
Academic year: September to May
Pres.: DALE KNOBEL
Provost: BRADLEY BATEMAN
Vice-Pres. and Dir of Admissions: PERRY ROBINSON
Vice-Pres. for Finance and Management: SETH PATTON
Vice-Pres. for Student Affairs and Dean of Students: LAUREL KENNEDY
Vice-Pres. for Institutional Advancement: JULIA HOUPT
Assoc. Provost: KIMBERLY COPLIN
Assoc. Provost: SUSAN GARCIA
Assoc. Provost: TONI KING
Library of 462,409 vols, 360,324 documents, 963 periodicals, 26,000 audio recordings, 123,029 microforms, 46m. items available electronically through OhioLINK, 140 research databases, 6,236 annual vols
Number of teachers: 212
Number of students: 2,162
Publications: *Denisonian* (26 a year), *Denison Journal of Biological Science* (1 a year), *Denison Journal of Geosciences* (1 a year), *Denison Journal of Religion* (1 a year), *Denison Magazine* (4 a year).

FRANCISCAN UNIVERSITY OF STEUBENVILLE

1235 University Blvd, Steubenville, OH 43952
Telephone: (740) 283-3771
Fax: (740) 284-5456
Internet: www.franciscan.edu
Founded 1946
Academic year: August to May
Pres.: Rev. TERENCE HENRY
Chancellor: Rev. MICHAEL SCANLAN
Exec. Vice-Pres.: Dr ROBERT FILBY
Vice-Pres. for Academic Affairs: TOM WILSON
Vice-Pres. for Community Relations: Rev. RICHARD DAVIS
Vice-Pres. for Enrollment: JOEL RECZNIK
Vice-Pres. for Finance: DAVID SKIVIAT
Vice-Pres. for Mission Effectiveness: Rev. DAVID PIVONKA
Vice-Pres. for Student Life: DAVID SCHMIESING
Library Dir: WILLIAM JAKUB
Library of 234,631 vols
Number of teachers: 224 (113 full-time, 111 part-time)
Number of students: 2,088 undergraduates and 403 graduates
Publication: *Fides Quaerens Intellectum* (4 a year).

FRANKLIN UNIVERSITY

201 South Grant Ave, Columbus, OH 43215
Telephone: (614) 797-4700
Fax: (614) 356-9019
E-mail: info@franklin.edu
Internet: www.franklin.edu
Founded 1902 as School of Commerce under YMCA sponsorship; present name 1933
Private control
Pres.: Dr DAVID R. DECKER
Sr Vice-Pres. for Strategic Relationships and Initiatives: LINDA M. STEELE
Vice-Pres. for Academic Relations: Dr SHIRLEY PALUMBO

Vice-Pres. for Academics and Curriculum Devt: Dr EDWARD W. HOLZAPFEL, Jr
Vice-Pres. for Admin.: EVELYN LEVINO
Number of students: 10,000

HEBREW UNION COLLEGE - JEWISH INSTITUTE OF RELIGION

3101 Clifton Ave, Cincinnati, OH 45220-2488
Schools at Cincinnati, Los Angeles and New York (USA) and Jerusalem (Israel)
Telephone: (513) 221-1875
Internet: www.huc.edu
Founded 1875
Academic year: August to June
Pres.: Dr DAVID ELLENSON
Vice-Pres. for Academic Affairs: Dr MICHAEL MARMUR
Vice-Pres. for Admin.: GARY R. BOCKELMAN
Vice-Pres. for Finance: SANDRA MILLS
Vice-Pres. for Spec. Projects: CHARLES A. KROLOFF
Dean of Cincinnati School: Rabbi KENNETH EHRLICH
Dean of Los Angeles School: Dr JOSHUA HOLO
Dean of New York School: Rabbi SHIRLEY IDELSON
Dean of Jerusalem School: Rabbi NAAMAH KELMAN
Dir of Libraries: Dr DAVID J. GILNER
Library of 500,000 vols and 3,000 codices
Number of teachers: 130
Number of students: 780
Publications: *American Jewish Archives*, *Hebrew Union College Annual*, *Studies in Bibliography and Booklore*.

HEIDELBERG COLLEGE

310 East Market St, Tiffin, OH 44883-2462
Telephone: (419) 448-2000
Fax: (419) 448-2124
Internet: www.heidelberg.edu
Founded 1850
Academic year: August to May
Pres.: Dr F. DOMINIC DOTTAVIO
Vice-Pres. for Academic Affairs and Dean of College: DAVID A. WEININGER
Vice-Pres. for Admin.: JEANNINE CURNS
Vice-Pres. for Enrollment and Marketing: THANDABANTU MACEO
Vice-Pres. for Institutional Advancement: RITA LOCKE
Vice-Pres. for Student Affairs and Dean of Students: Dr JIM TROHA
Registrar: AMANDA STEELE
Dir of Library Services: EDWARD KRAKORA
Library of 200,000 vols
Number of teachers: 102 (72 full-time, 30 part-time)
Number of students: 1,500

DEANS
Arts and Sciences: Dr VICKI B. OHL
Graduate and Professional Studies: Dr MICHAEL G. PRATT

HIRAM COLLEGE

POB 67, Hiram, OH 44234
Telephone: (330) 569-3211
Fax: (330) 569-5944
E-mail: interal@hiram.edu
Internet: www.hiram.edu
Founded 1850
Private control
Academic year: August to May
Pres.: THOMAS V. CHEMA
Vice-Pres. and Dean of the College: KATHERINE FEATHER
Vice-Pres. and Dean of Students: ERIC R. RIEDEL
Registrar: JENNIFER MCDONOUGH
Librarian: DAVID EVERETT
Library of 210,269 vols; govt depository in receipt of approx. 7,000 federal documents annually; mem. of OhioLINK—information network of 74 educational instns and state libraries with shared colln of 44.5m. items
Number of teachers: 70
Number of students: 1,200
Publication: *Hiram Poetry Review* (2 a year).

JOHN CARROLL UNIVERSITY

Telephone: (216) 397-1886
Fax: (216) 397-4256
Internet: www.jcu.edu
Founded 1886
Private control (Roman Catholic affiliated)
Academic year: September to May
Pres.: Rev. ROBERT NIEHOFF
Academic Vice-Pres.: Dr JOHN DAY
Vice-Pres. for Enrolment: BRIAN G. WILLIAMS
Vice-Pres. for Finance and Admin. Services: RICHARD MAUSSER
Vice-Pres. for Student Affairs: Dr MARK MCCARTHY
Vice-Pres. for Univ. Advancement: DOREEN KNAPP RILEY
Registrar: KATHLEEN DI FRANCO
Dir of Library: Dr JEANNE SOMERS
Library of 770,000 vols
Number of teachers: 210 (full-time)
Number of students: 3,800

DEANS
College of Arts and Sciences: (vacant)
School of Business: Dr KAREN SCHUELE (acting)

KENT STATE UNIVERSITY

Kent, OH 44242
Telephone: (330) 672-3000
Internet: www.kent.edu
Founded 1910
Academic year: July to June
7 Regional campuses in Ashtabula, East Liverpool, Geauga, Salem, Stark, Trumbull and Tuscarawas
Pres.: LESTER A. LEFTON
Sr Vice-Pres. for Academic Affairs and Provost: ROBERT G. FRANK
Sr Vice-Pres. for Admin.: DAVID K. CREAMER
Vice-Pres. for Enrollment Management and Student Affairs: HAROLD GOLDSMITH
Vice-Pres. for Human Resources: CAROLYN PIZZUTO
Vice-Pres. for Information Services: EDWARD G. MAHON
Vice-Pres. for Institutional Advancement: EUGENE J. FINN
Vice-Pres. for Regional Devt: PATRICIA A. BOOK
Vice-Pres. for Univ. Relations: KATHY L. STAFFORD
Dean of Libraries and Media Services: Dr MARK WEBER
Library: 2.3m. vols
Number of teachers: 1,097
Number of students: 36,000

DEANS AND DIRECTORS
College of Architecture and Environmental Design: STEVEN FONG
College of Arts: TIMOTHY J. L CHANDLER
College of Arts and Sciences: JERRY FEEZEL
College of Business Admin.: Dr GEORGE STEVENS
College of Communication and Information: Dr JAMES GAUDINO
College and Graduate School of Education, Health and Human Services: Dr DAVID ENGLAND
College of Nursing: Dr LAURA COX DZUREC
College of Technology: Dr A. RAJ CHOWDHURY
Honors College: DON WILLIAMS

ATTACHED INSTITUTES
Applied Linguistics Center: Dir Dr GREG SHREVE.
Center for International and Comparative Programs: tel. (330) 672-7980; fax (330) 672-4025; e-mail mrubin@kent.edu; internet www.kent.edu/cicp; Dir Dr MARK RUBIN.
Kent State University Museum: tel. (330) 672-3450; e-mail museum@kent.edu; internet dept.kent.edu/museum; costume and decorative art; 20,000 items; Dir Dr JEAN DRUESEDOW.
Liquid Crystal Institute: tel. (330) 672-2654; internet www.lci.kent.edu; Dir Dr OLEG LAVRENTOVICH.

KENYON COLLEGE

Gambier, OH 43022-9623
Telephone: (740) 427-5000
E-mail: admissions@kenyon.edu
Internet: www.kenyon.edu
Founded 1824
Pres.: S. GEORGIA NUGENT
Provost: GREGORY P. SPAID
Vice-Pres. for College Relations: SARAH KAHRL
Vice-Pres. for Finance: JOSEPH G. NELSON
Dir of Admissions: C. DARRYL UY
Dean of Admissions: JENNIFER DELAHUNTY BRITZ
Dean of Students: TAMMY GOCIAL
Vice-Pres. for Library and Information Services: MICHAEL ROY
Library of 977,846 vols
Number of teachers: 176
Number of students: 1,467
Depts of fine arts, humanities, natural sciences, social sciences.

LAKE ERIE COLLEGE

391 West Washington St, Painesville, OH 44077
Telephone: (440) 942-3872
Fax: (440) 375-7005
E-mail: admissions@lec.edu
Internet: www.lec.edu
Founded 1856
Private control
Academic year: August to May
Pres.: MICHAEL VICTOR
Vice-Pres. for Admin. and Finance: JANA HOLWICK
Vice-Pres. for Enrollment Management and Student Affairs: JANA HOLWICK
Vice-Pres. for Institutional Advancement: SCOTT EVANS
Dean of Students: BILLIE DUNNE
Registrar: BARBARA ARILSON
Dir of Admissions: ERIC FELVER
Library Dir: CHRISTOPHER BENNETT
Library of 100,000 vols
Number of teachers: 34
Number of students: 650 undergraduates, 325 graduates
Depts of education, equine studies, fine arts, languages and communication, management studies, science and mathematics, social sciences.

MALONE COLLEGE

515 25th St NW, Canton, OH 44709
Telephone: (330) 471-8100
Fax: (330) 471-8478
E-mail: admissions@malone.edu
Internet: www.malone.edu

Founded 1892

Pres.: Dr GARY STREIT
Vice-Pres. for Academic Affairs: Dr PATRICIA LONG
Exec. Vice-Pres. for Admin.: RICHARD A. PAKEL
Vice-Pres. for Enrollment Management: JOHN A. CHOPKA
Vice-Pres. for Student Devt: JOHN A. CHOPKA
Dir of Library Services: STANFORD TERHUNE

Library of 170,000 vols
Number of teachers: 89 (full-time)
Number of students: 2,239

DEANS

School of Arts and Sciences: Dr RUTH C. MILES
School of Business: A. SMITH
School of Continuing Studies: MARJORIE CARLSON HURST
School of Education: Dr CHRISTINE A. KROL
School of Nursing: Dr LORETTA M. REINHART
School of Theology: LARRY REINHART

MARIETTA COLLEGE

215 Fifth St, Marietta, OH 45750
Telephone: (740) 376-4643
Fax: (740) 376-4896
E-mail: admit@marietta.edu
Internet: www.marietta.edu

Founded 1797
Private control
Academic year: August to May

Pres.: JEAN A. SCOTT
Provost and Dean of Faculty: RITA SMITH KIPP
Vice-Pres. for Admin. and Finance: DAN BRYANT
Vice-Pres. for Advancement: LORI LEWIS
Vice-Pres. for Enrollment Management: DAVID RHODES
Vice-Pres. for Student Life and Dean of Students: LON VICKERS
Librarian: DOUGLAS ANDERSON

Library of 250,000 vols, 450 print and 4,000 online periodicals
Number of teachers: 80 (full time)
Number of students: 1,350

Courses in Asian and int. studies, computer science, economics, environmental science, fine arts, int. business, liberal arts and sciences, management and accounting, petroleum engineering, sports medicine.

METHODIST THEOLOGICAL SCHOOL IN OHIO

3081 Columbus Pike, Delaware, OH 43015
Telephone: (740) 363-1146
E-mail: admit@mtso.edu
Internet: www.mtso.edu

Founded 1958
Private control
Academic year: August to May

Pres.: JAY RUNDELL
Academic Dean: JOHN KAMPEN
Registrar: SUSAN LAMPHERE
Library Dir: Dr PAUL SCHRODT

Library of 130,000 vols
Number of teachers: 22
Number of students: 250

MIAMI UNIVERSITY

501 E High St, Oxford, OH 45056
Telephone: (513) 529-1809
Fax: (513) 529-3841
Internet: www.muohio.edu

Founded 1809
State control

Pres.: DAVID HODGE
Provost and Exec. Vice-Pres. for Academic Affairs: JEFFREY HERBST
Vice-Pres. for Finance and Univ. Services: RICHARD NORMAN
Vice-Pres. for Information Technology: JOHN REID CHRISTENBERRY
Vice-Pres. for Student Affairs: RICHARD NAULT
Vice-Pres. for Univ. Advancement: JAYNE WHITEHEAD
Registrar: DAVE SAUTER
Librarian: JUDITH SESSIONS

Library: 3m. vols, 110,000 maps, 26,000 recordings, 20,000 journals, magazines and newspapers and more than 3m. pieces of microfilm
Number of teachers: 849 full-time
Number of students: 16,900

DEANS

College of Arts and Science: KAREN SCHILLING
Farmer School of Business: ROGER JENKINS
Graduate School: BRUCE J. COCHRANE
School of Education and Allied Professions: CARINE M. FEYTEN
School of Engineering and Applied Science: MAREK DOLL
School of Fine Arts: JAMES LENTINI
School of Interdisciplinary Studies: WILLIAM GRACIE

BRANCH CAMPUSES

Hamilton Campus: 1601 University Blvd, Hamilton, OH 45011; tel. (513) 785-3000; internet www.ham.muohio.edu; Dean G. MICHAEL PRATT; 3,500 .

Middletown Campus: Middletown, OH 45042; tel. (513) 727-3200; internet www .mid.muohio.edu; Dean Dr G. MICHAEL PRATT; 2,700 .

MOUNT UNION COLLEGE

1972 Clark Ave, Alliance, OH 44601
Telephone: (330) 821-5320
E-mail: info@muc.edu
Internet: www.muc.edu

Founded 1846

Pres.: Dr RICHARD F. GIESE
Vice-Pres. for Academic Affairs and Dean of College: Dr PATRICIA DRAVES
Vice-Pres. for Business Affairs and Treas.: PATRICK HEDDLESTON
Vice-Pres. for College Advancement: JIM PIATT
Vice-Pres. for Enrollment Services: AMY A. TOMKO
Vice-Pres. for Public Affairs and Marketing: HARRY P. PAIDAS
Registrar: STUART TERRASS
Librarian: ROBERT R. GARLAND

Number of teachers: 90 (full-time)
Number of students: 1,847

MOUNT VERNON NAZARENE UNIVERSITY

800 Martinsburg Rd, Mount Vernon, OH 43050
Telephone: (740) 392-6868
Fax: (740) 397-2769
Internet: www.mvnu.edu

Founded 1968
Private control

Pres.: Dr DANIEL J. MARTIN
Vice-Pres. for Academic Affairs and Academic Dean: RANDIE TIMPE
Vice-Pres. for Campus Ministries: GARY M. SIVEWRIGHT
Vice-Pres. for Finance: JEFF SPEAR
Vice-Pres. for Univ. Relations: J. KEITH NEWMAN
Library Dir: EDYTHE FEAZEL

Library: 38m. vols
Number of teachers: 133 (full-time)
Number of students: 2,670

DEANS

School of Arts and Humanities: Dr BARNEY COCHRAN
School of Business: Dr TOMAS PARKS
School of Education and Professional Studies: Dr STEVE RAGAN
School of Natural and Social Sciences: Dr ROBERT KASPER
School of Nursing and Health Sciences: Dr TERESA WOOD
School of Theology and Philosophy: Dr C. JEANNE SERRÃO

MUSKINGUM COLLEGE

163 Stormont St, New Concord, OH 43762
Telephone: (740) 826-8211
Fax: (740) 826-8196
Internet: www.muskingum.edu

Founded 1837
Church-related, liberal arts college

Pres.: (vacant)
Vice-Pres. for Academic Affairs: PAUL F. REICHARDT
Vice-Pres. for Enrollment: JEFF ZELLERS
Vice-Pres. for Institutional Advancement: JOHN SHORROCK
Vice-Pres. for Student Affairs and Dean of Students: JANET HEETER-BASS
Registrar: DANIEL WILSON
Librarian: SHEILA ELLENBERGER

Library of 215,000 vols, 600 periodicals, 140,000 microforms
Number of teachers: 82
Number of students: 1,700

MYERS UNIVERSITY

3921 Chester Ave, Cleveland, OH 44114
Telephone: (216) 391-6937
Fax: (216) 696-6430
E-mail: admissions@myers.edu
Internet: www.myers.edu

Founded 1848 as Folsom's Business College; present name 2001
Private control

Pres.: Dr RICHARD SCALDINI
Vice-Pres., Chief Financial Officer and Treas.: ERIC W. DAMON
Vice-Pres. for Academic Affairs: Dr JOYCE A. BANJAC
Vice-Pres. for Enrollment Management: RON BROWN
Dean of Student Affairs: ELENA GRIGORE
Registrar: TIFFINEY PAYTON
Library Dir: RICHARD BRHEL

Number of teachers: 15
Number of students: 1,150

Degrees in arts, business admin., management, science.

NORTHEASTERN OHIO UNIVERSITIES COLLEGE OF MEDICINE

POB 95, 4209 State Route 44, Rootstown, OH 44272-0095
Telephone: (330) 325-2511
E-mail: admission@neoucom.edu
Internet: www.neoucom.edu

Founded 1973
Pres. and Dean: Dr LOIS MARGARET NORA
Sr Vice-Pres. for Academic Affairs: Dr MARK A. PENN
Vice-Pres. for Admin. and Finance: RICHARD J. EPLAWY
Vice-Pres. for Institutional Advancement: M. SUE DREITZLER
Dir of Information Center: THOMAS C. ATWOOD
Number of students: 420
Depts of anatomy, behavioural sciences, community health sciences, emergency medicine, family medicine, general surgery, geriatric medicine/gerontology, internal medicine, microbiology, immunology and biochemistry, neurobiology, obstetrics/gynaecology, orthopaedic surgery, paediatrics, pathology, pharmaceutical sciences, pharmacy practice, physiology and pharmacology, psychiatry, radiology, urology.

NOTRE DAME COLLEGE

4545 College Rd, Cleveland, OH 44121-4293
Telephone: (216) 373-5355
Fax: (216) 373-5278
E-mail: admissions@ndc.edu
Internet: www.notredamecollege.edu
Founded 1922
Academic year: September to May
Pres.: Dr ANDREW P. ROTH
Vice-Pres. for Academic Affairs: MISSY BRECKENRIDGE
Vice-Pres. for Assessment, Planning and Human Resources: NANCY BAIRD
Vice-Pres. for Enrollment: DAVID A. ARMSTRONG
Vice-Pres. for Finance and Admin.: JOHN C. PHILLIPS
Librarian: KAREN ZOLLER
Library of 877,773 vols
Number of teachers: 94 full-time
Number of students: 887
Courses in art, business admin., biology, chemistry, communications, criminology, education, English, environmental science, history/political science, intelligence analysis, mathematics, nursing, psychology, sports management, theology

OBERLIN COLLEGE

173 West Lorain St, Oberlin, OH 44074
Telephone: (440) 775-8121
Internet: www.oberlin.edu
Founded 1833
Academic year: September to May
Pres.: MARVIN KRISLOV
Provost: ALFRED MACKAY
Vice-Pres. for College Relations: ALAN MORAN
Vice-Pres. for Devt and Alumni Affairs: ERNEST ISEMINGER
Vice-Pres. for Finance: RONALD WATTS
Dean of Studies: KATHRYN STUART
Registrar: ELIZABETH CLERKIN
Dir of Libraries: RAY ENGLISH
Library: 1.3m. vols
Number of teachers: 250
Number of students: 2,900

DEANS

College of Arts and Sciences: JEFFREY WITMER (acting)
Conservatory of Music: DAVID STULL

OHIO CHRISTIAN UNIVERSITY

1476 Lancaster Pike, Circleville, OH 43113
Telephone: (740) 474-8896
Fax: (740) 477-7755
E-mail: enroll@ohiochristian.edu
Internet: www.ohiochristian.edu
Founded 1948
Private control
Academic year: September to May
Pres.: Dr MARK A. SMITH
Academic Dean: Dr JOE BROWN
Dir of Institutional Advancement: JAMES SCHROEDER
Dean of Students: LARRY OLSON
Registrar: SHIRLEY POLLARD
Librarian: DAVID TIPTON
Number of teachers: 25
Number of students: 350

OHIO COLLEGE OF PODIATRIC MEDICINE

6000 Rockside Woods Blvd, Independence, OH 44131
Telephone: (216) 231-3300
Fax: (216) 231-0453
Internet: www.ocpm.edu
Founded 1916
Private control
Academic year: August to May
Pres.: THOMAS MELILLO
Exec. Vice-Pres.: DAVID NICOLANTI
Vice-Pres. and Dean of Academic Affairs: Dr VINCENT J. HETHERINGTON
Dean of Student Affairs: LOIS LOTT
Registrar: DAVID PUTMAN
Librarian: DONNA PERZESKI
Number of students: 430

OHIO DOMINICAN COLLEGE

1216 Sunbury Rd, Columbus, OH 43219
Telephone: (614) 253-2741
Fax: (614) 252-0776
E-mail: admissions@ohiodominican.edu
Internet: www.ohiodominican.edu
Four-year co-educational liberal arts college
Founded 1911 as College of St Mary of the Springs; name changed 1968
Academic year: September to May (two terms and a summer session)
Pres.: Rev. JAMES A. GRIFFIN
Vice-Pres. for Academic Affairs: MARY TODD
Vice-Pres. for Student Devt: JAMES CARIDI
Vice-Pres. for Univ. Resources: RONALD SEIFFERT
Registrar: SHIRLEY MCBRAYER
Dir of the Library: JIM LADEN
Library of 106,000 vols
Number of teachers: 130
Number of students: 2,100

OHIO NORTHERN UNIVERSITY

525 South Main St, Ada, OH 45810
Telephone: (419) 772-2000
Fax: (419) 772-1932
Internet: www.onu.edu
Founded 1871
Private control (United Methodist)
Academic year: September to May
Pres.: Dr KENDALL L. BAKER
Vice-Pres. for Academic Affairs: Dr ANNE LIPPERT
Vice-Pres. for Financial Affairs: JOHN GREEN
Vice-Pres. for Student Affairs: ALICE-KAY HILDERBRAND
Vice-Pres. for Univ. Advancement: THOMAS STEVICK
Dean of Students: ADRIANE THOMPSON-BRADSHAW
Registrar: R. G. CARPENTER
Librarian: P. LOGSDON
Library of 500,000 vols
Number of teachers: 200
Number of students: 2,870

DEANS

Arts and Sciences: ROBERT A. MANZER
Business Admin.: Dr JAMES W. FENTON
Engineering: Dr ERIC T. BAUMGARTNER
Law: Dr DAVID C. CRAGO
Pharmacy: Dr JON E. SPRAGUE

OHIO STATE UNIVERSITY

Enarson Hall, 154 W 12th Ave, Columbus, OH 43210
Telephone: (614) 292-4373
Fax: (614) 292-1885
Internet: www.osu.edu
Founded 1870
Campuses at Lima, Mansfield, Marion and Newark
Pres.: Dr E. GORDON GEE
Exec. Vice-Pres. and Provost: Dr JOSEPH A. ALUTTO
Sr Vice-Pres. for Admin. and Planning: JEFF KAPLAN
Sr Vice-Pres. for Alumni Relations: ARCHIE GRIFFIN
Sr Vice-Pres. for Business and Finance and Chief Financial Officer: GEOFFREY CHATAS
Sr Vice-Pres. for Devt: PETER WEILER
Sr Vice-Pres. for Govt Affairs: CURT STEINER
Sr Vice-Pres. for Health Sciences: STEVEN G. GABBE
Sr Vice-Pres. for Outreach and Engagement: JOYCE BEATTY
Sr Vice-Pres. for Univ. Communications: TOM KATZENMEYER
Sr Vice-Pres. and Gen. Counsel: CHRISTOPHER M. CULLEY
Vice-Pres. for Human Resources: LARRY M. LEWELLEN
Vice-Pres. for Research: CAROLINE WHITACRE
Vice-Pres. for Strategic Enrollment Planning: M. DOLAN EVANOVICH
Vice-Pres. for Student Life: JAVAUNE ADAMS-GASTON
Vice-Pres.: BOBBY D. MOSER
Chief Information Officer: KATHLEEN STARKOFF
Dir of Univ. Libraries: CAROL DIEDRICHS
Library: see Libraries and Archives
Number of teachers: 5,292 (f.t.e.)
Number of students: 63,217 (of whom 50,014 at the main campus)
Publications: *American Periodicals* (2 a year), *Journal of Higher Education* (6 a year), *Journal of Money, Credit and Banking* (6 a year), *The Leibniz Review* (Mansfield Campus, 1 a year), *Narrative* (3 a year), *Ohio State Journal of Criminal Law* (2 a year), *Ohio State Journal on Dispute Resolution* (4 a year), *Ohio State Law Journal* (6 a year), *Theory into Practice* (4 a year)

DEANS

College of Arts and Sciences: JOSEPH E. STEINMETZ (Exec. Dean)
Max M. Fisher College of Business: CHRISTINE A. POON (acting)
College of Dentistry: CAROLE A. ANDERSON
College of Education and Human Ecology: CHERYL L. ACHTERBERG
College of Engineering: GREGORY N. WASHINGTON
College of Food, Agricultural and Environmental Sciences: BOBBY D. MOSER
Moritz College of Law: ALAN C. MICHAELS
College of Medicine: WILEY W. SOUBA, Jr
College of Nursing: ELIZABETH R. LENZ
College of Optometry: MELVIN D. SHIPP
College of Pharmacy: ROBERT W. BRUEGGEMEIER
College of Public Health: STANLEY A. LEMESHOW
College of Social Work: TOM GREGOIRE
College of Veterinary Medicine: LONNIE KING

Graduate School: PATRICK S. OSMER

ACADEMIC DIRECTORS

School of Allied Medical Professions: STEPHEN L. WILSON
School of Architecture: ROBERT S. LIVESEY
School of Biomedical Science: WOLFGANG SADEE
School of Communication: CARROLL J. GLYNN
School of Educational Policy and Leadership: ROBERT LAWSON
School of Music: MELLASENAH MORRIS
School of Natural Resources: JERRY M. BIGHAM
School of Physical Activities and Educational Services: DONNA L. PASTORE
School of Public Health: STANLEY A. LEMESHOW
School of Public Policy and Management: BERT A. ROCKMAN
School of Teaching and Learning: PETER V. PAUL

DEPARTMENTS, ACADEMIC FACULTIES, DIVISION DIRECTORS

Accounting and Management Information Systems: J. RICHARD DIETRICH
Aerospace Engineering: MEYER J. BENZAKEIN
African-American and African Studies: KENNETH W. GOINGS
Agricultural, Environmental and Development Economics: ALAN J. RANDALL
Air Force and Aerospace Studies: Col MICHAEL J. HUHN
Anaesthesiology: MICHAEL B. HOWIE
Animal Sciences: JAMES E. KINDER
Anthropology: CLARK S. LARSEN
Art: ARDINE K. NELSON
Art Education: PATRICIA L. STUHR
Astronomy: PATRICK S. OSMER
Aviation: NAWAL K. TANEJA
Biochemistry: RICHARD P. SWENSON
Biomedical Informatics: JOEL H. SALTZ
Chemical Engineering: STUART L. COOPER
Chemistry: PRABIR K. DUTTA
Civil and Environmental Engineering, and Geodetic Science: OLIVER G. MCKEE, III
Comparative Studies: DAVID G. HORN
Computer Science and Engineering: STUART ZWEBEN
Consumer Sciences: GONG-SOOG HONG
Dance: L. SCOTT MARSH
East Asian Languages and Literatures: MARI NODA
Economics: MASANORI HASHIMOTO
Electrical and Computer Engineering: FUSUN OZGUNER
Emergency Medicine: DOUGLAS A. RUND
English: VALERIE B. LEE
Entomology: DAVID DENLINGER
Evolution, Ecology and Organismal Biology: RALPH E. J. BOERNER
Family Medicine: MARYJO WELKER
Finance: ANIL MAKHIJA
Food, Agricultural and Biological Engineering: THOMAS L. BEAN
Food Science and Technology: KENNETH LEE
French and Italian: DIANE W. BIRCKBICHLER
Geography: MORTON E. O'KELLY
Geological Sciences: E. SCOTT BAIR
Germanic Languages and Literature: ANNA A. GROTANS (acting)
Greek and Latin: DAVID A. HAHM
History: KENNETH J. ANDRIEN
History of Art: MARK D. FULLERTON (acting)
Horticulture and Crop Science: STEPHEN C. MYERS
Human and Community Resource Development: ROBERT J. BIRKENHOLZ
Human Development and Family Science: ALBERT J. DAVIS
Human Nutrition: MARK L. FAILLA
Industrial, Interior and Visual Communication Design: WAYNE E. CARLSON
Industrial, Welding and Systems Engineering: JOHN C. LIPPOLD
Internal Medicine: MICHAEL R. GREVER
Linguistics: PETER W. CULICOVER
Management and Human Resources: DAVID B. GREENBERGER
Management Sciences: PETER T. WARD
Marketing and Logistics: ROBERT E. BURNKRANT
Materials Science and Engineering: JOHN E. MORRAL
Mathematics: PETER D. MARCH
Mechanical Engineering: KRISHNASWAMY SRNIVASAN
Medieval and Renaissance Studies: BARBARA HANAWALT
Melton Center for Jewish Studies: TAMAR RUDAVSKY
Mershon Center for International Security Studies: RICHARD K. HERRMANN
Microbiology: JOHN N. REEVE
Molecular and Cellular Biochemistry: CHARLES R. HILLE
Molecular Genetics: LEE F. JOHNSON
Molecular Virology, Immunology and Medical Genetics: CARLO M. CROCE
Near-Eastern Languages and Cultures: RICHARD DAVIS
Neurological Surgery: ENNIO A. CHIOCCA
Neurology: JOHN T. KISSEL
Neuroscience: MICHAEL S. BEATTIE
Obstetrics and Gynaecology: LARRY J. COPELAND
Ohio State University Extension: BARBARA G. LUDWIG
Ophthalmology: THOMAS F. MAUGER
Orthopaedics: GARY D. BOS
Otolaryngology: DAVID E. SCHULLER
Paediatrics: THOMAS N. HANSEN
Pathology: MICHAEL G. BISSELL
Pharmacology: WOLFGANG SADEE
Philosophy: GEORGE S. PAPPAS
Physical Medicine and Rehabilitation: WILLIAM S. PEASE
Physics: WILLIAM F. SAAM
Physiology and Cell Biology: MUTHU PERIASAMY
Plant, Cellular and Molecular Biology: FRED D. SACK
Plant Pathology: RANDALL C. ROWE
Political Science: PAUL A. BECK
Psychiatry: RUDU SAVEANU
Psychology: GIFFORD WEARY
Radiology: MICHAEL KNOPP
Slavic and East European Languages and Literatures: DANIEL E. COLLINS
Sociology: ROBERT L. KAUFMAN
Spanish and Portuguese: FERNANDO UNZUETA
Speech and Hearing Science: ROBERT A. FOX
Statistics: DOUGLAS A. WOLFE
Surgery: E. CHRISTOPHER ELLISON
Theatre: LESLEY K. FERRIS
Veterinary Biosciences: MICHAEL D. LAIRMORE
Veterinary Clinical Sciences: ROBERT G. SHERDING
Veterinary Hospital: RICHARD BEDNARSKI
Veterinary Preventive Medicine: KENT H. HOBLET
Women's Studies: LINDA M. MIZEJEWSKI

BRANCH CAMPUSES

Agricultural Technical Institute: 1328 Dover Rd, Wooster, OH 44691-4000; tel. (330) 287-1331; e-mail ati@osu.edu; internet www.ati.osu.edu; f. 1972; 2-year courses; Dir STEPHEN P. NAMETH.

Ohio Agricultural Research and Development Center: 2120 Fyffe Rd, Colombus, OH 43210; tel. (330) 263-3701; fax (330) 263-3688; e-mail oardc@osu.edu; internet www.oardc.ohio-state.edu; Dir STEVEN A. SLACK.

Ohio State University at Lima: 4240 Campus Dr., Lima, OH 45804; tel. (419) 995-8600; fax (419) 995-8483; internet www.lima.ohio-state.edu; f. 1959; 2- and 4-year courses; Dean and Dir JOHN R. SNYDER.

Ohio State University at Mansfield: 1680 University Dr., Mansfield, OH 44906; tel. (419) 755-4011; internet www.mansfield.ohio-state.edu; f. 1958; Dean and Dir EVELYN B. FREEMAN.

Ohio State University at Marion: 142A Morrill Hall, 1465 Mt Vernon Ave, Marion, OH 43302-5895; tel. (614) 389-9133; internet www.marion.ohio-state.edu; f. 1957; 2- and 4-year courses; Dean and Dir GREGORY S. ROSE.

Ohio State University at Newark: 1170 University Dr., Newark, OH 43055-1797; tel. (740) 366-9333; internet www.newark.osu.edu; f. 1957; 2- and 4-year courses; Dean and Dir WILLIAM L. MACDONALD.

Stone Laboratory: 1314 Kinnear Rd, Colombus, OH 43212-1156; tel. (614) 292-8949; fax (614) 292-4364; internet ohioseagrant.osu.edu/stonelab; Dir JEFFERY M. REUTTER.

OHIO UNIVERSITY

Athens, OH 45701
Telephone: (740) 593-1000
Fax: (614) 593-4229
Internet: www.ohiou.edu

Founded 1804; the first land-grant college in the USA; main campus in Athens, regional campuses in Chillicothe, Ironton, Lancaster, St Clairsville, Zanesville

Pres.: Dr RODERICK J. MCDAVIS
Exec. Vice-Pres. and Provost: Dr PAMELA BENOIT
Vice-Pres. for Finance and Admin.: WILLIAM R. DECATUR
Vice-Pres. for Research: JAMES RANKIN
Vice-Pres. for Student Affairs: KENT J. SMITH
Vice-Pres. for Univ. Advancement: HOWARD R. LIPMAN
Registrar: DEBRA M. BENTON
Librarian: JAN MAXWELL

Library: 2m. vols
Number of teachers: 1,600
Number of students: 27,386

Publications: *Milton Quarterly*, *Ohio Review*

DEANS

Arts and Sciences: BENJAMIN OGLES
Business Administration: GLENN CORLETT
Communications: GREGORY SHEPHERD
Education: RENEE MIDDLETON
Engineering and Technology: DENNIS IRWIN
Fine Arts: CHARLES MCWEENY
Health and Human Services: GARY S. NEIMAN
Honours Tutorial College: C. ANN FIDLER
Osteopathic Medicine: JOHN BROSE
University College: DAVID DESCUTNER

OHIO WESLEYAN UNIVERSITY

61 S Sandusky St, Delaware, OH 43015
Telephone: (740) 368-2000
Fax: (740) 368-3374
E-mail: owupr@owu.edu
Internet: www.owu.edu

Founded 1842 by Methodist Episcopal Church, chartered 1842

Academic year: August to May

Depts of ancient, medieval, and renaissance studies, Black world studies, botany-microbiology, chemistry, E Asian studies, economics, education, English, environmental studies, fine arts, geology and geography, health professions advising, history, humanities-classics, int. studies, journalism, Latin American studies, mathematics and computer science, modern foreign languages, music, neuroscience, philosophy, physical education, physics and astronomy, politics and government, psychology, religion, sociology-anthropology, theatre and dance, urban studies, women's and gender studies, zoology

Pres.: Rock Jones
Provost: David O. Robbins
Vice-Pres. for Financial and Administration Affairs and Treas.: Eric Algoe
Vice-Pres. for Univ. Relations: James Kenny
Dean of Academic Affairs: Charles L. Stinemetz
Dean of Students: Kimberlie Goldsberry
Registrar: Shelly McMahon
Librarian: Theresa Byrd

Number of teachers: 138 full-time
Number of students: 1,850

Publications: *Civic Arts Review* (4 a year), *Zumari: a Journal of Black World Studies* (2 a year).

OTTERBEIN COLLEGE

Westerville, OH 43081
Telephone: (614) 890-3000
Fax: (614) 823-1200
E-mail: uotterb@otterbein.edu
Internet: www.otterbein.edu

Founded 1847
Private control
Academic year: September to August

Pres.: C. Brent De Vore
Vice-Pres. for Academic Affairs and Academic Dean: Abíódún Gòkè-Paríólá
Registrar: Karen Eckelbarger
Dir of Admissions: Cass Johnson
Dir of the Library: Lois Szudy

Library of 200,000 vols
Number of teachers: 140
Number of students: 3,200

Depts of art, business, accounting and economics, chemistry and biochemistry, communication, education, English, equine science, foreign languages, health and sport sciences, history and political science, life and earth science, mathematics, computer science and actuarial science, music, nursing, physics and astronomy, psychology, religion and philosophy, sociology, theatre and dance

Publications: *Aegis Humanities Journal* (1 a year), *Journal of Teacher Initiated Research* (1 a year).

SAINT MARY SEMINARY AND GRADUATE SCHOOL OF THEOLOGY

28700 Euclid Ave, Wickliffe, OH 44092-2585
Telephone: (440) 943-7600
Fax: (440) 943-7577
E-mail: mal@dioceseofcleveland.org
Internet: www.stmarysem.edu

Founded 1848 as a diocesan seminary; present name 1968
Private control
Academic year: August to May

Pres.-Rector: Rev. Thomas W. Tifft
Academic Dean: Dr Ed Kaczuk (acting)
Dean of Students: (vacant)
Registrar: Paulette Begin
Librarian: Alan Rome

Library of 60,000 vols, 340 periodicals
Number of teachers: 20
Number of students: 130

SHAWNEE STATE UNIVERSITY

940 Second St, Portsmouth, OH 45662-4344
Telephone: (740) 351-3205
Fax: (740) 351-3416
E-mail: to_ssu@shawnee.edu
Internet: www.shawnee.edu

Founded 1986
Academic year: September to June

Pres.: Dr Rita Rice Morris
Vice-Pres. for Academic Affairs and Provost: Dr Michael Field
Vice-Pres. for Finance and Admin.: Elinda C. Boyles
Vice-Pres. for Student Affairs: Dr Jim Settle
Library Dir: Tess Midkiff

Number of teachers: 120
Number of students: 3,600

DEANS

College of Arts and Sciences: Dr Timothy E. Scheurer
College of Professional Studies: Dr Jim Kadel

SIEGAL COLLEGE OF JUDAIC STUDIES

26500 Shaker Blvd, Cleveland, OH 44122
Telephone: (216) 464-4050
Fax: (216) 464-5827
E-mail: info@siegalcollege.edu
Internet: www.siegalcollege.edu

Founded 1963
Private control
Languages of instruction: English, Hebrew

Pres.: Dr Seymour Kopelowitz
Provost: Brian Amkraut
Library Dir: Jean Lettofsky

Library of 40,000 vols, 160 periodicals
Number of teachers: 20
Number of students: 30

TIFFIN UNIVERSITY

155 Miami St, Tiffin, OH 44883
Telephone: (419) 447-6443
Fax: (419) 443-5006
E-mail: info@tiffin.edu
Internet: www.tiffin.edu

Founded 1888
Private control
Academic year: August to May

12 Regional campuses

Pres.: Paul Marion
Vice-Pres. for Academic Affairs: Dr Charles Christensen
Vice-Pres. for Enrollment Management: Ron Schumacher
Vice-Pres. for Devt: Michael Grandillo
Registrar: Alice Nichols
Library Dir: Frances A. Fleet

Number of teachers: 133
Number of students: 4,615

DEANS

School of Arts and Sciences: Dr Jan Samoriski
School of Business: Dr Lillian Schumacher
School of Criminal Justice and Social Sciences: Tim Shaw

TRINITY LUTHERAN SEMINARY

2199 E Main St, Columbus, OH 43209-2334
Telephone: (614) 235-4136
E-mail: admissions@trinitylutheranseminary.edu
Internet: www.trinitylutheranseminary.edu

Founded 1830 as Evangelical Lutheran Theological Seminary, present name 1978
Private control
Academic year: September to May

Pres.: Mark R. Ramseth
Dean of Academic Affairs: James M. Childs, Jr
Registrar: Carol M. Dixon
Librarian: Ray A. Olson

Number of teachers: 20
Number of students: 250

Publication: *Trinity Seminary Review* (2 a year).

UNION INSTITUTE & UNIVERSITY

440 East McMillan St, Cincinnati, OH 45206-1925
Telephone: (513) 861-6400
Fax: (513) 861-4887
E-mail: admissions@tui.edu
Internet: www.tui.edu

Founded 1964
Private control

Academic centres in Cincinnati, Florida, Los Angeles, Sacramento, Brattleboro, Montpelier

Pres.: Roger H. Sublett
Provost: Roger Sublett
Vice-Pres. and Dean of Graduate Studies: Richard Green
Vice-Pres. and Dean of Undergraduate Studies: Richard Hansen
Vice-Pres. of Devt and Univ. Relations: Kristine Howland
Chief Financial Officer: Edward Walton
Registrar: Lew Rita Moore
Librarian: Matthew Pappathan

Library of 50,000 books, 2,000 periodicals
Number of teachers: 230
Number of students: 2,800.

CONSTITUENT COLLEGE

Vermont College

Montpelier Campus, 36 College St, Montpelier, VT 05602
Telephone: (802) 828-8500

Founded 1834 as the Vermont Seminary; acquired by Union Institute & University 2001.

UNITED THEOLOGICAL SEMINARY

4501 Denlinger Rd, Trotwood, OH 45426
Telephone: (937) 529-2201
Fax: (937) 529-2292
E-mail: utscom@united.edu
Internet: www.united.edu

Campuses at Dayton and Buffalo (NY)
Private control

Pres.: G. Edwin Zeiders
Vice-Pres. for Academic Affairs and Academic Dean: Wendy J. Deichmann Edwards
Vice-Pres. for Admin. and Treas.: Anne Brown
Registrar: Martha M. Anderson
Library Dir: Sarah D. Brooks Blair

Library of 150,000 vols
Number of teachers: 12
Number of students: 170 (full-time)

UNIVERSITY OF AKRON

302 Buchtel Common, Akron, OH 44325-3101
Telephone: (330) 972-6349
Fax: (330) 972-8604
E-mail: international@uakron.edu
Internet: www.uakron.edu

Founded 1870 by Ohio Universalist Convention, became municipal univ. of Akron 1913, present title 1926, became state univ. 1967
Public control
Language of instruction: English
Academic year: August to May

Pres.: Luis M. Proenza
Sr Vice-Pres. and Provost and Chief Operating Officer: William Sherman
Vice-Pres. and Chief of Staff: Candace Campbell-Jackson
Vice-Pres. and Gen. Counsel: Ted A. Mallo
Vice-Pres. for Capital Planning and Facilities Management: Ted Curtis

Vice-Pres. for Finance and Admin.: DAVID J. CUMMINS
Vice-Pres. for Information Technology: JIM SAGE
Vice-Pres. for Research: GEORGE R. NEWKOME
Vice-Pres. for Public Affairs and Devt: JOHN LA GUARDIA
Vice-Pres. for Student Affairs: CHARLES J. FEY
Dean of Univ. Libraries: CHERYL KERN-SIMIRENKO

Library: 2.9m. vols
Number of teachers: 2,555
Number of students: 27,758
Publication: *University of Akron Press*

DEANS

Buchtel College of Arts and Sciences: CHAND K. MIDHA
College of Business Administration: RAVI KROVI
College of Creative and Professional Arts: CHAND K. MIDHA
College of Education: MARK D. SHERMIS
College of Engineering: GEORGE K. HARITOS
College of Health Sciences and Human Services: JAMES M. LYNN
College of Nursing: N. MARGARET WINEMAN
College of Polymer Science and Polymer Engineering: STEPHEN Z. CHENG
Graduate School: GEORGE R. NEWKOME
Honours College: DALE H. MUGLER
School of Law: MARTIN H. BELSKY
Wayne College: JOHN P. KRISTOFCO

UNIVERSITY OF CINCINNATI

2624 Clifton Ave, Cincinnati, OH 45221
Telephone: (513) 556-6000
Fax: (513) 556-2340
Internet: www.uc.edu

Founded 1819 as Cincinnati College; renamed Univ. of Cincinnati (a municipal instn) 1870; became a municipally sponsored state-affiliated instn 1968; joined State of Ohio Univ. system 1977
Academic year: September to June

Pres.: NANCY ZIMPHER
Sr Vice-Pres. and Provost: JANE E. HENNEY
Sr Vice-Pres. and Provost for Baccalaureate and Graduate Education: ANTHONY PERZEGIAN
Sr Vice-Pres. for Admin. and Finance: MONICA RIMAI
Vice-Pres. for Devt and Alumni Relations: MICHAEL W. CARROLL
Vice-Pres. for Finance: JAMES D. PLUMMER
Vice-Pres. for Govt Relations and Univ. Communications: GREGORY J. VEHR
Vice-Pres. for Information Technology: FREDERICK H. SIFF
Vice-Pres. for Research: SANDRA DEGEN
Vice-Pres. for Student Affairs: MITCHEL D. LIVINGSTON
Dean and Univ. Librarian: VICTORIA MONTAVON

Library: see Libraries
Number of teachers: 3,481 (2,149 full-time, 1,332 part-time)
Number of students: 33,823 (26,165 undergraduate, 6,685 postgraduate, 973 professional)
Publications: *Freedom Center Journal*, *Journal of Crime and Justice* (2 a year)

DEANS

Clermont College: JAMES F. MCDONOUGH
College-Conservatory of Music: WARREN E. GEORGE
College of Allied Health Sciences: ELIZABETH C. KING
College of Applied Science: RICHARD NEWROCK
College of Arts and Sciences: VALERIE GRAY HARDCASTLE
College of Business: WILL MCINTOSH
College of Design, Architecture, Art and Planning: (vacant)
College of Education, Criminal Justice and Human Services: LAWRENCE J. JOHNSON
College of Engineering: CARLO D. MONTEMAGNO
College of Law: LOUIS D. BILLIONIS
College of Medicine: DAVID M. STERN
College of Nursing: ANDREA R. LINDELL
College of Pharmacy: DANIEL ACOSTA
Graduate School: NEVILLE G. PINTO
Raymond Walters College: DOLORES Y. STRAKER
School of Social Work: SOPHIA DZIEGIELEWSKI

PROFESSORS

Clermont College (4200 Clermont College Dr., Batavia, OH 45103-1749; tel. (513) 732-5200; fax (513) 732-5275; internet www.ucclermont.edu):

BENOIT, M., Academic Service
DEJONG, M. F., Art
FANKHAUSER, D. B., Biology and Chemistry
HEIMBOLD, B. L., English
LONG, L. L., Academic Service
MURDOCH, G., Academic Service
WOLFF, G., English

College-Conservatory of Music (POB 210003, Cincinnati, OH 45221-0003; tel. (513) 556-6638; fax (513) 556-3330; internet www.ccm.uc.edu):

ADAMS, D., Performance Studies
ANDERSON, S. V., History and Composition
BERG, A., Opera and Musical Theatre
BLACK, W. D., Keyboard
BOYER-ALEXANDER, R., Music Education
CALLAHAN, C., Performance Studies
CHILDS, S. G., Opera and Musical Theatre
DEKANT, R., Performance Studies
DOAN, G. R., Music Education
FAABORG, K. K., Opera and Musical Theatre
FINNEY, T., Opera and Musical Theatre
FISHER, L. W., Performance Studies
FRASER, M., Opera and Musical Theatre
GAGE, J. H., Opera and Musical Theatre
GARDNER, R. C., Performance Studies
GARNER, B. A., Performance Studies
GARY, R., Keyboard
GIESBRECHT, P. M. B., Performance Studies
GRIFFITHS, K., Keyboard
HALE, N. K., Opera and Musical Theatre
HANANI, Y., Performance Studies
HASHIMOTO, E., Keyboard
HOFFMAN, J., History and Composition
HONN, B., Performance Studies
IWASAKI, C. N., Dance
LEMAN, J. W., Ensembles and Conducting
MCGRAW, W., Performance Studies
METZ, D., Music Education
MORRIS, R., Keyboard
OTTE, A. C., Performance Studies
PENDLE, K., History and Composition
PLYLER, S. J., Opera and Musical Theatre
PRIDONOFF, E. A., Keyboard
RIVERS, E., Ensembles and Conducting
SABLINE, O., Dance
SASSMANNSHAUS, K., Performance Studies
SHORTT, P., Opera and Musical Theatre
STUCKY, M. H., Performance Studies
TOCCO, J. V., Keyboard
UMFRID, T., Opera and Musical Theatre
WAXLER, S., Opera and Musical Theatre
WEINSTOCK, F. M., Keyboard
WING, L., Music Education
WINTHER, R. K., Ensembles and Conducting
WOLFRAM, M., Broadcasting
ZIEROLF, R. L., History and Composition

College of Allied Health Sciences (POB 670394, Cincinnati, OH 45267-0394; tel. (513) 558-7495; fax (513) 558-7494; internet www.cahs.uc.edu):

CREAGHEAD, N., Communication Sciences
FALCIGLIA, G., Health Sciences
KRETSCHMER, L. W., Rehabilitation Sciences
LEE, L., Communication Sciences and Disorders
NEILS-STRUNJAS, J., Communication Sciences and Disorders
WALLACE, G. J., Communication Sciences and Disorders
WEILER, E. M., Rehabilitation Sciences

College of Applied Science (2220 Victory Parkway, Cincinnati, OH 45206-2839; tel. (513) 556-6567; fax (513) 556-5056; internet www.uc.edu/cas):

BILL, H. L., Construction Science
BORONKAY, T. G., Mechanical Engineering Technology
BROWN, M. A., Humanities
DORSEY, R. W., Construction Science
DURBIN, D. J., Construction Science
GEONETTA, S. C., Humanities
GILLIGAN, L. G., Mathematics
KREPPEL, M. C., Humanities
MEAL, L., Chemical Technology
SUCKARIEH, G. G., Construction Science
SULLIVAN, J. F., Mathematics

College of Arts and Sciences (POB 210037, Cincinnati, OH 45221-0037; tel. (513) 556-5860; fax (513) 556-0142; internet asweb.artsci.uc.edu):

ALEXANDER, J. J., Chemistry
ALEXANDER, J. K., History
ARDEN, H. M., Romance Languages and Literatures
ARNER, R., English
ATKINSON, M., English
AULT, B. S., Chemistry
BACON, S. M., Romance Languages
BEAVER, D., History
BECK, T. L., Chemistry
BENNETT, S., Political Science
BERRY, C. A., Economics
BERRYMAN-FINK, C. L., Communication Arts
BISHOP, G. F., Political Science
BOBST, A. M., Chemistry
BOGEN, D. H., English
BOWMAN, S., Judaic Studies
BRETT, C. E., Geology
BRISKIN, M., Geology
BRYC, W., Mathematical Sciences
BURLEW, A. K. H., Psychology
CAMERON, B. N., Biological Sciences
CARUSO, J., Biological Sciences
CHALKLEY, R., Mathematical Sciences
CHANG, T. C., Mathematical Sciences
CHIMEZIE, A., Afro-American Studies
COHEN, G., Classics
COLLINS, P. H., Afro-American Studies
DANIELS, R., History
DAVIS, J. L., Classics
DAY, R. A., Chemistry
DEDDENS, J. A., Mathematical Sciences
DRURY, J. P., English
DUMAS, H. S., Mathematical Sciences
DURST, R. K., English
ELDER, A. A., English
ELDER, R. C., Chemistry
ENDORF, R. J., Physics
ERWAY, L. C., Biological Sciences
ESPOSITO, F. P., Physics
FAIRHURST, G., Communication Arts
FEINBERG, W. E., Sociology
FENICHEL, H., Physics
FISHBEIN, H., Psychology
FISHER, J. W., Mathematical Sciences
FRENCH, D. A., Mathematical Sciences
FRIEDRICHSMEYER, S. L., Germanic Languages
GALLO, J., Economics
GAUKER, C. P., Philosophy

GERMAN, R., Biological Sciences
GLENN, J. H., Germanic Languages
GODDARD, H. C., Economics
GODSHALK, W. L., English
GOTOFF, H. C., Classics
GRASHA, A. F., Psychology
GROVER, J. E., Geology
GUTZWILLER, R. J., Classics
HALPERIN, R., Anthropology
HALPERN, H. P., Mathematical Sciences
HALSALL, B., Chemistry
HAMILTON, J. F., Romance Languages and Literatures
HEINEMAN, W., Chemistry
HERMAN, E., Economics
HERRON, D. A., Mathematical Sciences
HINKEL, J. M., Geography
HODGES, T., Mathematical Sciences
HONECK, R. P., Psychology
HORN, P. S., Mathematical Sciences
HUDGINS, A. L., English
HUETHER, C., Biological Sciences
HUFF, W. D., Geology
HUGHES, J., English
ISAAC, B. L., Anthropology
JAMISON-HALL, A., Afro-American Studies
JARRELL, M. S., Physics
JAYASIMHULU, K., Chemistry
JENSEN, W. B., Chemistry
JOHNSON, R. A., Physics
JOINER, W. C. H., Physics
JOST, L. J., Philosophy
KAFTAL, V., Mathematical Sciences
KANE, T. C., Biological Sciences
KANESHIRO, E., Biological Sciences
KAPLAN, F., Chemistry
KARP, R., Biological Sciences
KILINC, A. I., Geology
KING, T., Mathematical Sciences
KINOSHITA, K., Physics
KLEIN, E. B., Psychology
KORMAN, P., Mathematical Sciences
KREISHMAN, G., Chemistry
LANGMEYER, D., Psychology
LEAKE, L., Mathematical Sciences
LECLAIR, T. E., English
LEFTWICH, H. M., Economics
LEUNG, A., Mathematical Sciences
LOWELL, T. V., Geology
LUNDGREN, D., Sociology
MA, M., Physics
MCCORD, C. K., Mathematical Sciences
MCEVOY, J., Philosophy
MANSOURI, F., Physics
MARGOLIS, M. S., Political Science
MARK, H. B., Jr, Chemistry
MARK, J. E., Chemistry
MARTIN, J., Philosophy
MAUME, D. J., Sociology
MAYER, W., Economics
MAYNARD, J. B., Geology
MEADOWS, B. T., Physics
MEEKS, F., Chemistry
MELTON, R. S., Psychology
MEYER, D. L., Geology
MEYER, K. R., Mathematical Sciences
MEYER, R. R., Biological Sciences
MEYERS, W., Psychology
MICHELINI, A. N., Classics
MILLER, A., Political Science
MILLER, A. I., Geology
MILLER, M. C., Biological Sciences
MINDA, C. D., Mathematical Sciences
MITRO, J., Mathematical Sciences
MUKKADA, A. J., Biological Sciences
MURIO, D. A., Mathematical Sciences
MURRAY, J. M., History
NASH, D. B., Geology
NAVEH, G. O. S., Judaic Studies
NIGRO, K. V., Romance Languages
OSTERBURG, J., Mathematical Sciences
PELIGRAD, C., Mathematical Sciences
PELIGRAD, M., Mathematical Sciences
PELIKAN, S., Mathematical Sciences
PERSON, L. S., English
PINHAS, A. R., Chemistry
PINSKI, F., Physics
PORTE, M., Communication Arts
RALESCU, D., Mathematical Sciences
RAMUSACK, B. N., History
RAWLINGS, E. I., Psychology
RESNIK, D., Pharmacological Sciences
RICHARDSON, R., Philosophy
RIDGWAY, T. H., Chemistry
ROBINSON, J., Philosophy
RODER, W., Geography
ROLWING, R., Mathematical Sciences
ROMERO, A., Romance Languages and Literatures
RUBENSTEIN, J., English
RUSSELL, J., Physics
SABOURIN, T. C., Community Arts
SAGE, M. M., Classics
SAKMYSTER, T., History
SCARBOROUGH, V. L., Anthropology
SCHADE, R., Germanic Languages and Literature
SCHULTZ, L. M., English
SCHUMSKY, D. A., Psychology
SELISKAR, C., Chemistry
SELYA, R. M., Geography
SHAPIRO, H., History
SITKO, M. L., Physics
SIVAGANESAN, S., Mathematical Sciences
SLOTKIN, E., English
SMITH, H., History
SNIDER, J. A., Biological Sciences
SOKOLOFF, M. D., Physics
SPRAGUE, E. D., Chemistry
STAFFORD, H., Geography
STEVER, J. A., Political Science
STOJANOVIC, S., Mathematical Sciences
STUTZ, R. M., Psychology
SULLIVAN, A. P., Anthropology
SURANYI, P., Physics
TEPPERMAN-ELDER, K., Biological Sciences
THAYER, J., Chemistry
TOLLEY, H. B., Political Science
TUAN, T.-F., Physics
TWINAM, A., History
UETZ, G. W., Biological Sciences
UNGAR, G. S., Mathematical Sciences
VESPRANI, G. J., Psychology
VIALET, M. E., Romance Languages
VREDEVELD, G. M., Economics
WALBERG, G., Classics
WARM, J., Psychology
WEISS, G. M., Mathematical Sciences
WELLINGTON, D. C., Economics
WHITMORE, H. W., Economics
WIJEWARDHANA, L. C. R., Physics
WILSON, R. M., Chemistry
WINGET, G., Biological Sciences
WOLFE, J. D., Political Science
WRIGHT, D. J., Mathematical Sciences
YORK, A. D., English
ZANDVAKILI, S., Economics
ZHANG, B., Mathematical Sciences
ZHANG, F., Physics
ZHANG, S., Mathematical Sciences

College of Business (POB 210020, Cincinnati, OH 45221-0020; tel. (513) 556-7002; fax (513) 556-4891; e-mail business@uc.edu; internet www.business.uc.edu):

ALLEN, C. T., Marketing
ANDERSON, D. R., Quantitative Analysis and Information Systems
ANGLE, H., Management
BAKER, N. R., Quantitative Analysis and Information Systems
BURNS, D., Accounting
CAMM, J. D., Quantitative Analysis and Information Systems
COMER, J., Marketing
CURRY, D. J., Marketing
DEAN, M., Marketing
DWYER, F. R., Marketing
EVANS, J. R., Quantitative Analysis and Information Systems
GELTNER, D. M., Finance
HENDERSON, G. V., Finance
KARDES, F., Marketing
KELTON, W. D., Quantitative Analysis and Information Systems
KIM, Y. H., Finance
LEVY, M. S., Quantitative Analysis and Information Systems
MACHLEIT, R., Marketing
MACKLIN, M. C. W., Marketing
MAGAZINE, M., Quantitative Analysis and Information Systems
MILLER, N. G., Finance
SALE, T., Accounting
SWEENEY, D. J., Quantitative Analysis and Information Systems
WALKER, M. C., Finance
WYATT, S. B., Finance

College of Design, Architecture, Art and Planning (POB 210016, Cincinnati, OH 45221-0016; tel. (513) 556-4933; fax (513) 556-3288; internet www.daap.uc.edu):

BARRY, R. J., Planning
BOTTONI, J., Design
BURLEIGH, K., Art
BURNHAM, R., Architecture and Interior Design
CARTWRIGHT, R., Art
EDELMAN, D. J., Planning
ELLISON, C. E., Planning
ENGELBRECHT, L. C., Art
ENSTICE, W. E., Art
GOSLING, D., Planning
HANCOCK, J. E., Architecture and Interior Design
HERRMANN, F. H., Art
HILDEBRANDT, H. P., Architecture and Interior Design
MANN, D. A., Architecture and Interior Design
MEACHAM, G. M., Design
NILAND, D. L., Architecture and Interior Design
PREISER, W., Architecture and Interior Design
PROBST, R., Design
PUHALLA, D. M., Design
RIESS, J. B., Art
ROMANOS, M. C., School of Planning
SAILE, D., Architecture and Interior Design
SALCHOW, G. R., School of Design
SIMMONS, G. B., Architecture and Interior Design
SMITH, D. L., Architecture and Interior Design
STEVENS, J. A., Art
STEWART, J. P., Art
STRICEVIC, G., Art
TUCKER, M., Art
VARADY, D., Planning
WOODHAM, D., Art
WOOL, M., Design

College of Education, Criminal Justice and Human Services (POB 210002, Cincinnati, OH 45221-0002; tel. (513) 556-2335; fax (513) 556-2483; internet www.cech.uc.edu):

AMSPAUGH-CORSON, L. B., Curriculum and Instruction
BARNETT, D. W., School Psychology and Counselling
BAUER, A. M., Early Childhood and Special Education
BERLOWITZ, M. J., Educational Foundation
CHAMLIN, L. B., Criminal Justice
COLLINS, R. L., Educational Foundation
CONYNE, R. K., School Psychology and Counselling
COOK, E. P., School Psychology and Counselling
COTTRELL, R., Health and Nutrition Sciences
CULLEN, F. T., Criminal Justice
DORSEY, A., Early Childhood and Special Education
EKVALL, S., Health and Nutrition Sciences
EVERS, N. A., Educational Administration

FOWLER, T. W., Curriculum and Instruction
GORDON, J. S., Curriculum and Instruction
GRADEN, J. L., School Psychology and Counselling
KRETSCHMER, R., Early Childhood and Special Education
KRZYWKOWSKI, L. V., Educational Foundation
LATESSA, E. J., Criminal Justice
LENTZ, F. E., School Psychology and Counselling
MARKLE, G. C., Curriculum and Instruction
MATRIANO, E., Curriculum and Instruction
NAYLOR, D., Curriculum and Instruction
O'REILLY, P., Educational Foundation
STEVENS, J., Educational Foundation
SWAMI, P., Curriculum and Instruction
TRAVIS, L. F., Criminal Justice
TRUAX, R. R., Early Childhood and Special Education
VANVOORHIS, P., Criminal Justice
WAGNER, D. I., Health and Nutritional Sciences
WILSON, B., Health and Nutritional Sciences
WILSON, F. R., School Psychology and Counselling
YAGER, G. G., School Psychology and Counselling
ZINS, J., Early Childhood and Special Education

College of Engineering (POB 210018, Cincinnati, OH 45221-0018; tel. (513) 556-5417; fax (513) 556-5007; internet www.eng.uc.edu):

ABDALLAH, S. A., Aerospace Engineering and Engineering Mechanics
AGRAWAL, D. P., Electrical and Computer Engineering and Computer Science
ALLEMANG, R. J., Mechanical and Industrial Engineering
BERMAN, K. A., Computer Science
BISHOP, P. L., Civil and Environmental Engineering
BOERIO, F. J., Materials Science and Engineering
BOOLCHAND, P., Electrical and Computer Engineering
BOYD, J. T., Electrical and Computer Engineering
BROWN, D. L., Mechanical and Industrial Engineering
BUCHANAN, R. C., Materials Science and Engineering
BUTLER, D. L., Aerospace Engineering and Engineering Mechanics
CAHAY, M. M., Electrical and Computer Engineering and Computer Science
CARTER, H. W., Electrical and Computer Engineering
CHRISTENSON, J., Mechanical and Industrial Engineering
CLARSON, S. J., Materials Science and Engineering
DEGOUVEA-PINTO, N. R., Chemical Engineering
FAN, H. H., Electrical and Computer Engineering
FRANCO, J. V., Electrical and Computer Engineering and Computer Science
FRIED, J. R., Chemical Engineering
GERNER, F. M., Mechanical, Industrial and Nuclear Engineering
GHIA, K. N., Aerospace Engineering and Engineering Mechanics
GHIA, U., Mechanical and Industrial Engineering
GOVIND, R., Chemical Engineering
GROOD, E. S., Aerospace Engineering and Engineering Mechanics
GUTMARK, E. J., Aerospace Engineering and Engineering Mechanics
HALL, E. L., Mechanical and Industrial Engineering
HAMED, A., Aerospace Engineering and Engineering Mechanics
HERSHEY, D., Chemical Engineering
HUSTON, R. L., Mechanical and Industrial Engineering
HWANG, S.-T., Chemical Engineering
JAIN, R. K., Civil and Environmental Engineering
JAYARAMAN, N., Materials Science and Engineering
JENG, S. M., Aerospace Engineering and Engineering Mechanics
KAO, Y. K., Chemical Engineering
KEENER, T. C., Civil and Environmental Engineering
KHANG, S. J., Chemical Engineering
KHOSLA, P. K., Aerospace Engineering and Engineering Mechanics
KINMAN, R. N., Civil and Environmental Engineering
KOSEL, P. B., Electrical and Computer Engineering
KRANTZ, W., Chemical Engineering
KROLL, R. J., Aerospace Engineering and Engineering Mechanics
KUKRETI, A. R., Civil and Environmental Engineering
LIN, R. Y., Materials Science and Engineering
MANTEI, T. D., Electrical and Computer Engineering
MITAL, A., Mechanical and Industrial Engineering
NAGY, P., Aerospace Engineering and Engineering Mechanics
NAYFEH, A. H., Aerospace Engineering and Engineering Mechanics
PANT, P. D., Civil and Environmental Engineering
PAUL, J. L., Computer Science
POOL, M. J., Materials Science and Engineering
PRATSINIS, S. E., Chemical Engineering
PURDY, G. B., Computer Science
QUO, P. C., Mechanical and Industrial Engineering
RALESCU, A. L., Electrical and Computer Engineering and Computer Science
RAMAMOORTHY, P., Electrical and Computer Engineering
RICHARDSON, D., Aerospace Engineering and Engineering Mechanics
ROENKER, K. P., Electrical and Computer Engineering
SCARPINO, P. V., Civil and Environmental Engineering
SCHAEFER, D. W., Materials Science and Engineering
SCHLIPF, J. S., Electrical and Computer Engineering and Computer Science
SCHMIDT, D. S., Computer Science
SEKHAR, J. A., Materials Science and Engineering
SHELL, R. L., Mechanical and Industrial Engineering
SINGH, R. N., Materials Science and Engineering
SLATER, G., Aerospace Engineering and Engineering Mechanics
STECKL, A., Electrical and Computer Engineering
SUIDAN, M. T., Civil and Environmental Engineering
VAN OOIJ, W. J., Materials Science and Engineering
VASUDEVAN, V. K., Materials Science and Engineering
VEMURI, R., Electrical and Computer Engineering and Computer Science
WEE, W. G., Electrical and Computer Engineering

College of Law (POB 210040, Cincinnati, OH 45221-0040; tel. (513) 556-6805; fax (513) 556-2391; internet www.law.uc.edu):

BIANCALANA, J.
BROWN, D. A.
CARON, P.
CHIN, G. J.
EISELE, T. D.
LASSITER, C.
LETSOU, P. V.
LOCKWOOD, B. B.
MANK, B. C.
NAGY, D. M.
RANDS, W.
SCHNEIDER, R.
SOLIMINE, M. E.
VAN ALSTINE, M. P.
WEISSENBERGER, G.

College of Medicine (POB 670555, Cincinnati, OH 45267-0555; tel. (513) 558-7391; fax (513) 558-1165; internet www.med.uc.edu):

ALEXANDER, J. W., Surgery
ALLOWAY, R. R., Internal Medicine
ASBURY, T., Ophthalmology
ASHRAF, M., Pathology and Laboratory Medicine
AZIZKHAN, R. G., Surgery
BALASUBRAMANIAM, A., Surgery
BANKS, R. O., Molecular and Cellular Physiology
BAUGHMAN, R. P., Internal Medicine
BEHBEHANI, M. M., Molecular and Cellular Physiology
BEN-JONATHAN, N., Cell Biology
BERNSTEIN, D. I., Internal Medicine
BHATTACHARYA, A., Environmental Health
BIBLER, M. R., Internal Medicine
BORNSCHEIN, R. L., Environmental Health
BOWER, R. H., Surgery
BRACKEN, R. B., Surgery
BRACKENBURY, R. W., Cell Biology
BRENEMAN, J. C., Radiology
BUNCHER, C. R., Environmental Health
CAVALLO, T., Pathology and Laboratory Medicine
CHATTERJEE, M., Internal Medicine
CHATTERJEE, S. K., Internal Medicine
CHERNUS, L., Psychiatry
CLARK, C. S., Environmental Health
CLARK, K. E., Obstetrics and Gynaecology
CLEMENS, T. L., Internal Medicine
COTTON, R., Otolaryngology
COX, J. A., Surgery
CRAWFORD, A. H., Orthopaedic Surgery
CROCKER, D. J., Surgery
CRUTCHER, K. A., Neurosurgery
CUPPOLETTI, J., Molecular and Cellular Physiology
DANIELS, A. S., Psychiatry
DECOURTEN-MYERS, G. M., Pathology
DEDMAN, J. R., Molecular and Cellular Physiology
DEEPE, G. S., Internal Medicine
DIETRICH, R. N., Environmental Health
DIXON, K., Environmental Health
DOETSCHMAN, T. C., Molecular Genetics and Biochemistry
DONOVAN, E. F., Paediatrics
DORN, G. W., Internal Medicine
DRAKE, R. L., Cell Biology
DUNSKER, S. B., Neurosurgery
ECKMAN, M. H., Internal Medicine
ELSON, H. R., Radiology
FAGIN, J. A., Internal Medicine
FEINBERG, J., Internal Medicine
FERNANDEZ-ALLOA, M., Radiology
FINKELMAN, F. D., Internal Medicine
FIRST, M. R., Internal Medicine
FISCHER, C. G., Anaesthesiology
FOON, K. A., Internal Medicine
FRAME, P. T., Internal Medicine
FRANCO, R. S., Internal Medicine
GALLA, J. H., Internal Medicine
GASS, M. L., Obstetrics and Gynaecology
GERSON, M. C., Internal Medicine
GHOSN, S., Pathology and Laboratory Medicine
GIANNELLA, R. A., Internal Medicine
GOTHELF, E. J., Family Medicine

GRERNER, A. L., Neurosurgery
GRUENSTEIN, E. I., Molecular Genetics and Biochemistry
GRUNENWALD, P. W., Internal Medicine
GRUPP, I. L., Pharmacology and Cell Biophysics
HANTO, D. W., Surgery
HASSELGREN, P., Surgery
HAWKINS, H. H., Radiology
HEATON, C. L., Radiology
HECK, J. E., Family Medicine
HENTHORN, R. W., Internal Medicine
HERMAN, J. P., Psychiatry
HILLARD, P. A., Obstetrics and Gynaecology
HORSEMAN, N., Molecular and Cellular Physiology
HOUR, J. L., Internal Medicine
HUI, D. Y., Pathology and Laboratory Medicine
HURST, J. M., Surgery
HUSSEINZADEH, N., Obstetrics and Gynaecology
IP, W. S., Cell Biology
IVEY, T. D., Surgery
JARRELL, J. L., Environmental Health
KANT, S., Internal Medicine
KAO, W. W. Y., Ophthalmology
KECK, P. E., Psychiatry
KEITH, R. W., Otolaryngology
KELLER, J. T., Neurosurgery
KHADADAD, G., Neurosurgery
KHAN, S. A., Cell Biology
KOTAGAL, U. R., Paediatrics
KRANIAS, E. G., Pharmacy and Cell Biophysics
LABARBERA, A. R., Obstetrics and Gynaecology
LEHMAN, M. N., Cell Biology
LEIKAUF, G. D., Environmental Health
LEMASTERS, G., Environmental Health
LEVY, R. C., Emerging Medicine
LIEBERMAN, M. A., Molecular Genetics and Biochemistry
LIGGETT, S. B., Internal Medicine
LIND, L. J., Anaesthesiology
LINGREL, J. B., Molecular Genetics and Biochemistry
LIU, J. H., Obstetrics and Gynaecology
LOCKEY, J. E., Environmental Health
LOWE, E. E., Anaesthesiology
LOWER, E., Internal Medicine
LUDKE, R. L., Family Medicine
MCCALL, J. E., Anaesthesiology
MCELROY, S. L., Psychiatry
MAGGIO, J. E., Pharmacology and Cell Biophysics
MALIK, I. A., Internal Medicine
MARCIANI, R. D., Surgery
MARGOLIS, C. F., Family Medicine
MATHIEU, A., Anaesthesiology
MATLIB, M. A., Pharmacology and Cell Biophysics
MICHAEL, J. G., Molecular Genetics and Biochemistry
MICKELSON, J. K., Internal Medicine
MILLARD, R., Pharmacology and Cell Biophysics
MILLHORN, D. E., Molecular and Cellular Physiology
MONTAUK, S. L., Family Medicine
MORRIS, R. E., Cell Biology
MOULTON, J. S., Radiology
MUHLEMAN, A. F., Internal Medicine
MUNDA, R., Surgery
MYATT, L., Obstetrics and Gynaecology
MYER, C., Otolaryngology
NEALE, H. W., Surgery
NEBERT, D. W., Environmental Health
NELSON, R. D., Pharmacology and Cell Biophysics
NEWMAN, S. L., Internal Medicine
NORLUND, J., Dermatology
NORMAN, A. B., Psychiatry
OGLE, C. K., Surgery
OPPENHEIMER, S., Paediatrics
OTTEN, E. J., Emergency Medicine
PAI, U. T., Anaesthesiology
PAUL, R. J., Molecular and Cellular Physiology
PENSAK, M. L., Otolaryngology
PERIASAMY, M., Internal Medicine
PESCE, A. J., Pathology and Laboratory Medicine
PHERO, J. C., Anaesthesiology
PIKE, J. W., Molecular and Cellular Physiology
POREMBKA, D. T., Anaesthesiology
PRIVITERA, M. D., Neurology
PUGA, A., Environmental Health
RASHKIN, M. C., Internal Medicine
RATNER, N., Cell Biology
REIF, M. C., Internal Medicine
RICE, C. H., Environmental Health
RICER, R. E., Family Medicine
ROUAN, G. W., Internal Medicine
SAELINGER, C., Molecular Genetics and Biochemistry
SAMAHA, F. J., Neurology
SCHWARTZ, A., Surgery
SEIDEN, A. M., Otolaryngology
SHARP, F. R., Neurology
SHELDON, C. A., Surgery
SHUKIA, R., Environmental Health
SHULL, B. E., Molecular Genetics and Biochemistry
SHUMRICK, D. A., Otolaryngology
SHUMRICK, K. A., Otolaryngology
SIDDIGI, T. A., Obstetrics and Gynaecology
SIDMAN, C. L., Molecular Genetics and Biochemistry
SIEGEL, E. G., Emergency Medicine
SINGH, S., Internal Medicine
SMITSON, W. S., Psychiatry
SOLEIMANI, M., Internal Medicine
SOLOMKIN, J. S., Surgery
SPINNATO, J. A., Obstetrics and Gynaecology
STAMBROOK, P. J., Cell Biology
STEICHEN, J. J., Paediatrics
STEMMERMAN, G. N., Pathology and Laboratory Medicine
STONE, W. N., Psychiatry
STRAKOWSKI, S. M., Psychiatry
STRIKER, T. W., Anaesthesiology
STRINGER, J. R., Molecular Genetics and Biochemistry
SUBBIAH, M. T. R., Internal Medicine
SUSZKIW, J. B., Molecular and Cellular Pathology
TABOR, M. W., Environmental Health
TAMI, T. A., Otolaryngology
TOMSICK, T. A., Radiology
TROTT, A., Emergency Medicine
TSO, P. P. W., Pathology and Laboratory Medicine
VANLOVEREN, H. R., Neurosurgery
WALZER, P. D., Internal Medicine
WANDER, A. H., Ophthalmology
WARDEN, G. D., Surgery
WARSHAW, G. A., Family Medicine
WARSHAWSKY, D., Environmental Health
WEISS, A. A., Molecular Genetics and Biochemistry
WEXLER, L., Internal Medicine
WHITSETT, J. A., Paediatrics
WILLEKE, K., Environmental Health
WONES, R. G., Internal Medicine
WOODLE, E. S., Surgery
WOODS, S. C., Psychiatry
YATANI, A., Pharmacology and Cell Biophysics
YEH, H.-S., Neurosurgery
YOUNKER, D., Anaesthesiology
YU, L, Cell Biology
ZEMLAN, F., Psychiatry

College of Nursing (POB 670038, Cincinnati, OH 45267-0038; tel. (513) 558-5500; fax (513) 558-3600; internet www.nursing.uc.edu):

BUNYAN, R. M., Medical Surgical Nursing
DRISCOLL, R. A., Mental Health Nursing
DYEHOUSE, J. M., Physical and Mental Health Nursing
HERN, M. J., Parent-Child Nursing
KENNER, C. A., Parent-Child Nursing
MARTIN, M. T., Medical Surgical Nursing
MILLER, E. L., Medical Surgical Nursing
SOMMERS, M., Medical Surgical Nursing
WERNER, E. E., Medical Surgical Nursing
WILSON, C. R., Parent-Child Nursing

College of Pharmacy (POB 670004, Cincinnati, OH 45267-0004; tel. (513) 558-3784; fax (513) 558-4372; internet pharmacy.uc.edu):

BOTTORFF, M. B.
CACINI, W.
CAPERELLI, C. A.
CONRAD, W. F.
JANG, R.
SAKR, A.
SHENOUDA, L. S.
SKAU, K. A.
WARNER, V. D.
WICKETT, R. R.
WUEST, J. R.

Raymond Walters College (9555 Plainfield Rd, Blue Ash, OH 45236-1096; tel. (513) 745-5600; fax (513) 745-8300; internet www.rwc.uc.edu):

ALLYANG, G. C., Behavioural Science
BAUGHIN, J. H., Foreign Languages
BAUMAN, D. H., Administration
BROD, E. F., Foreign Languages
CALLAN, J., Business and Commerce
CEBULA, J. E., History
CHISKO, A. M., Mathematics and Physics
COOPER-FREYTAG, L., Biological Sciences
DAVIS, L. K., Mathematics and Physics
FLAVIN, L. A., English
GARNETT, W. B., Biological Sciences
GOODMAN, E., History
HAGERTY, R. E., Communications and Visual Art
HANSEN, B. L., English
HEHMAN, R. G., Business and Commerce
LEAKE, J. A., History
LUTHER, P. A., English
MARSH, C. W., Mathematics, Physics
RNO, J., Mathematics, Physics
ROOS, M. E., English
SCHIERLING, J. M., Dental Hygiene
SCHLECHT, P. A., Nursing
SCHULTZ, J. A., Biological Sciences
SULKES, S., English
TAYLOR, R. N., Business and Commerce
WEINGARTNER, E. L., Nursing
WHEELER, S. G., History
YAKALI, E., Chemistry

School of Social Work (POB 21018, Cincinnati, OH 45221-0108; tel. (513) 556-4615; fax (513) 556-2077; internet www.uc.edu/socialwork):

BORKIN, J.
SUNDERLAND, S. C.

University College (POB 210047, Cincinnati, OH 45221-0047; tel. (513) 556-1646; fax (513) 556-3007; internet www.ucollege.uc.edu):

CROCKER-LAKNESS, J. W., Language Arts
DZIECH, B., Language Arts
GARRETT, M. P., Language Arts
GRIESINGER, W. S., Humanities and Social Science
KAHN, S. R., Business and Commerce
MEEM, D. T., Language Arts
MURDOCH, N. H., Humanities and Social Science
NAPOLI, D., Humanities and Social Science
RUSH, S., Humanities and Social Science
SUMMERLIN, L., Language Arts
WHITE, L. M., Language Arts

UNIVERSITY OF DAYTON

300 College Park, Dayton, OH 45469
Telephone: (937) 229-1000

E-mail: info@udayton.edu
Internet: www.udayton.edu
Founded 1850
Private control
Language of instruction: English
Academic year: August to May
Pres.: DANIEL J. CURRAN
Provost: JOSEPH E. SALIBA
Vice-Pres. for Finance and Administrative Services: THOMAS E. BURKHARDT
Registrar: TOM WESTENDORF
Vice-Pres. and Dir of Athletics: TIM WABLER
Vice-Pres. for Enrollment Management: SUNDAR KUMARASAMY
Vice-Pres for Human Resources: JOYCE CARTER
Vice-Pres. for Research and Exec. Dir: MICKEY MCCABE
Vice-Pres. for Student Devt and Dean of Students: ANNETTE T. SCHMELING
Vice-Pres. for Univ. Advancement: DEBORAH READ
Dean of Libraries: KATHLEEN M. WEBB
Library of 1,313,112 vols
Number of teachers: 831
Number of students: 10,909
Publication: *Law Review*

DEANS

Admission: ROBERT F. DURKLE
College of Arts and Sciences: PAUL H. BENSON
Graduate School: F. THOMAS EGGEMEIER
School of Business Admin.: MATTHEW SHANK
School of Education and Allied Professions: KEVIN R. KELLY
School of Engineering: TONY E. SALIBA
School of Law: LISA KLOPPENBERG

DIRECTORS

Admissions: MYRON H. ACHBACH
Continuing Education and Spec. Programs: JULIE L. MITCHELL
Research Institute: JOHN LELAND

UNIVERSITY OF FINDLAY

1000 North Main St, Findlay, OH 45840
Telephone: (419) 422-8313
Fax: (419) 424-4822
Internet: www.findlay.edu
Founded 1882
Pres.: Dr DEBOW FREED
Vice-Pres. for Academic Affairs: Dr DANIEL J. MAY
Vice-Pres. for Business Affairs: (vacant)
Vice-Pres. for Devt: DAVID P. FERGUSON
Vice-Pres. for Student Services: DAVID W. EMSWELLER
Registrar: TONY G. GOEDDE
Librarian: ROBERT W. SCHIRMER
Library of 127,000 vols
Number of teachers: 128
Number of students: 4,018

UNIVERSITY OF RIO GRANDE

218 North College Ave, Rio Grande, OH 45674-3131
Telephone: (740) 245-5353
E-mail: admissions@rio.edu
Internet: www.rio.edu
Private control
Academic year: August to May
Pres.: Dr GREG SOJKA
Provost and Vice-Pres. for Academic Affairs: Dr BARBARA HATFIELD
Vice-Pres. for Admin. Services: PAUL HARRISON
Vice-Pres. for Enrollment Management and Institutional Advancement: DEAN BROWN
Vice-Pres. for Finance: RANDY ELDRIDGE
Library Dir: J. DAVID MAUER
Library of 92,839 vols, 319 periodicals, 443,590 microforms, 25,000 federal govt docs
Number of teachers: 85
Number of students: 2,081

DEANS

College of Liberal Arts and Sciences: Dr BARRY THOMPSON
College of Professional Studies: Dr KRISHNA KOOL

UNIVERSITY OF TOLEDO

2801 West Bancroft, Toledo, OH 43606-3390
Telephone: (419) 530-2696
Fax: (419) 530-4504
Internet: www.utoledo.edu
Founded 1872 as Toledo Univ. of Arts and Trades; became municipal univ. 1883, state univ. 1967
Pres.: Dr LLOYD JACOBS
Sr Vice-Pres. for Finance and Strategy: DANIEL J. MORISSETE
Provost for Academic Affairs: ROSEMARY R. HAGGETT
Provost and Exec. Vice-Pres. for Health Affairs: WILLIAM LOGIE
Vice-Pres. for Admin.: WILLIAM LOGIE
Vice-Pres. for Enrollment, Marketing and Communications: LAWRENCE J. BURNS
Vice-Pres. for Govt Relations: WILLIAM MCMILLEN
Vice-Pres. for Institutional Advancement: C. VERNON SNYDER
Vice-Pres. for Student Affairs: KAYE PATTEN WALLACE
Dean of Libraries: JOHN GABOURY
Library: 1m. vols
Number of teachers: 1,316 (614 full-time; 702 part-time)
Number of students: 20,307

DEANS

College of Arts and Sciences: Dr YUEH-TING LEE
College of Business Administration: Dr THOMAS GUTTERIDGE
College of Education: THOMAS J. SWITZER
College of Engineering: Dr NAGI G. NAGANATHAN
College of Health Science and Human Service: MARGARET F. TRABAND
College of Law: DOUGLAS E. RAY
College of Medicine: JEFFREY P. GOLD
College of Nursing: JERI A. MILSTEAD
College of Pharmacy: Dr JOHNNIE L. EARLY, II
Graduate School: JAMES FRY
University College Programmes: DENNIS LETTMAN

PROFESSORS

College of Arts and Sciences

Anthropology:

METRESS, S.

Art:

ATTIE, D.
BASTIAN, D.
BELL-AMES, L.
ELLOIAN, P.
GUIP, D.

Astronomy:

ANDERSON, L.
BOPP, B. W.
WITT, A. N.

Biology:

GOLDMAN, S. L.
JOHNSON, K.
KOMUNIECKI, P.
KOMUNIECKI, R. W.
LEE, H. H.
PRIBOR, D. B.
TRAMER, E. J.
WHEELOCK, M. J.

Chemistry:

CHRYSOCHOOS, J.
DAVIES, J. A.
DOLLIMORE, D.
EDWARDS, J. G.
FUNK, M. O., Jr
GANO, J. E.
PINKERTON, A. A.

Communications:

BENJAMIN, J. B.
KNECHT, R. J.
RUSSELL, C. G.
WILCOX, E. M.

Economics:

LESAGE, J.
MAGURA, M.
ROY, R.
WEISS, S. J.

English:

ABU-ABSI, S.
BARDEN, T.
BOENING, J.
DESSNER, L. J.
FREE, W. N.
LIPMAN, J.
REISING, R.
RUDOLPH, R. S.
SAUNDERS, J.
SZUBERLA, G. A.
WIKANDER, M. H.

Foreign Languages:

FEUSTLE, J. A.
NORMAND, G. M.
O'NEAL, W. J.
SCANLAN, T. M.
SCHAUB, U. T.

Geography:

FRANCKOWIAK, E. N.
MURACO, W. A.

Geology:

CAMP, M.
HARRELL, J.
HATFIELD, C.
PHILLIPS, M. W.

History:

BRITTON, D.
CAVE, A. A.
GLAAB, C. N.
HOOVER, W. D.
LINEBAUGH, P.
LONGTON, W. H.
LORA, R. G.
MENNING, C.
NATSOULAS, T.
O'NEAL, W.
RAY, R. D.
SMITH, R. F.
THOMPSON, G. E.
WILCOX, L. D.

Mathematics:

BENTLEY, H. L.
CARLSON, D.
KERTZ, G. J.
KUMMER, M.
LIN, E. B.
NAGISETTY, R. V.
PETTET, M. R.
SCHWARZ, F.
SHIELDS, P. C.
STEINBERG, S. A.
VAYO, H. W.
WENTE, H. C.
WHITE, D.
WOLFF, H. E.

Music:

DEYARMAN, R. M.
JEX, D.
KIHSLINGER, M. R.
RENZI, F. A.
RONDELLI, B.

VAN DER MERWE, R. A.
WEBSTER, R. M.

Nursing:

FABISZAK, A.

Philosophy:

BLATZ, C.
CAMPBELL, J.

Physics:

BOHN, R. G.
COMPAAN, A. D.
CURTIS, L. J.
ELLIS, D. G.
IWAMOTO, N.
JAMES, P. B.
KVALE, T.
LEE, S.
SIMON, H. J.
THEODOSIOU, C.
WILLIAMSON, W.

Political Science:

LINDEEN, J. W.
RANDALL, R.
WEISFELDER, R. F.

Psychology:

ARMUS, H.
ELLIOTT, R. K., Jr
HAAF, R. A.
HEFFNER, H.
HEFFNER, R.
HOROWITZ, I. A.
MCKEEVER, W. F.
PALMER, A.
SLAK, S.

Sociology:

ALKALIMAT, A.
KART, C. S.
KING, J. A.
METRESS, S.
MORRISSEY, M.

Theater:

HILL, J.
WATERMEIER, D. J.

College of Business Administration

Accounting:

FINK, P. R.
GAFFNEY, D. J.
LAVERTY, B.
RAGUNATHAN, B.
SAFTNER, D.
SCHROEDER, N.

Finance:

SMOLEN, G. E.

Information Systems and Operations Management:

AHMED, M. U.
KAMBUROWSKI, J.
KUNNATHUR, A.
MARCHAL, W. G.
RACHAMADUGU, R.
RAGHUNATHAN, T.
RAO, S. S.
SASS, C. J.
SMITH, A.
SUNDARARAGHAVAN, P. S.
VONDEREMBSE, M. A.

Management:

BEEMAN, D. R.
BHATT, B. J.
DOLL, W. J.
KIM, K. I.
LONGNECKER, C.
NYKODYM, N.
SIMONETTI, J. L.
SPIRN, S.
TIMMINS, S. A.

Marketing:

DEKORTE, M. J.
FLASCHNER, A. B.
KOZLOWSKI, P. J.
LIM, J.
OKOROAFO, S.
THUONG, L.
ZALLOCCO, R.

College of Education

Counsellor and Human Services Education:

PIAZZA, N.
RITCHIE, M.
WENDT, R. N.

Educational Administration and Supervision:

BALDWIN, G.
MERRITT, D.
PIPER, J.
RUSCH, E.
SULLIVAN, R.

Educational Psychology, Research and Social Foundation:

DAVISON, D. C.
DUNN, T. G.
GRAY, W. M.
HUDSON, L. M.
HURST, J.
JURS, S.
LOPEZ, T.
ZIMMER, J.

Educational Technology:

ELSIE, L. J.
PATTERSON, A. C.

Elementary and Early Childhood Education:

AHERN, J.
BALZER, D. M.
CARR, E.
COOKE, G. E.
CRYAN, J. R.
DEBRUIN, J. E.
GRESS, J. R.
KOONTZ, F.
MCFARLAND, S. L.
SANDMAN, A.
SHIRK, G. B.

Health Promotion and Human Performance:

ANDRES, F. F.
ARMSTRONG, C.
DROWATZKY, J.
FULTON, G. B.
GRENINGER, L. O.
METRESS, E.
OLSSON, R.
PRICE, J. H.
RANCK, S. L.

Secondary Education:

DEMEDIO, D.
NATSOULAS, A.

Special Education:

BENJAMIN, B.
CARROLL, M. E.
MCINERNEY, W.

Vocational Education:

PIPER, J.

College of Engineering

Bioengineering:

CIOS, K.
DHAWAN, A.
FARISON, J.
FOURNIER, R.
LU, S.-Y.
MIKHAIL, W. E.

Chemical Engineering:

ABRAHAM, M.
CHANG, L.
DISMUKES, J.
JABARIN, S.

Civil Engineering:

ANGELBECK, D. I.
FU, K. C.
GUPTA, J.
KUMAR, A.
MOSTAGHEL, N.

Electrical Engineering:

ALAM, M.
ELTIMSAHY, A. H.
GHANDAKLY, A. A.
KING, R.
KWATRA, S. C.
LEDGARD, H.
SALARI, E.
SELIGA, T.
SMITH, E.
STUART, T. A.

Mechanical Engineering:

AFJEH, A.
BENNETT, R.
CHEN, F.
FATEMI, A.
HEFZY, M.
IREY, R. K.
KEITH, T. G.
KRAMER, S. N.
MCNICHOLS, R.
NAGANATHAN, N.
NG TSUNG, M.
WHITE, P.
WOLFE, K. R.

College of Law:

ANDERSON, R. W.
BERKOWITZ, R. L.
BOURGUIGNON, H. J.
CAMPBELL, B. A.
CHAPMAN, D. K.
CLOSIUS, P. J.
CRANDALL, T.
FRIEDMAN, H.
HARRIS, D.
HOPPERTON, R. J.
KADENS, M.
KENNEDY, B.
KLEIN, J. M.
LEAFFER, M. A.
MARTYN, S. R.
MERRITT, F. S.
MORAN, G. P.
RAITT, R.
RAY, D. E.
RICHMAN, W. M.
RIPPS, S. R.
STEINBOCK, D. J.
TIERNEY, J.

Library

Library Administration:

BALDWIN, J. F.
HOGAN, A. D.
SHERIDAN, L.

Technological Media:

KALMBACH, J. A.

College of Pharmacy:

ALEXANDER, K.
BACHMANN, K. A.
BILLUPS, N. F.
BLACK, C. D.
DOLLIMORE, D.
ERHARDT, P.
HINKO, C.
HUDSON, R. A.
LIVELY, B. T.
MESSER, W.
PARKER, G.
SHERMAN, G. P.

University Community and Technical College

Business Technologies:

DETTINGER, J. F.
LAWSHE, C. J.
POSTA, B.
RUDDY, M.

Engineering Technologies:

GALLAGHER, R.
KAMM, J.
KIME, E.
SOLAREK, D.

General Studies:

GERLACH, J.
GLEN, M.
KRAUSE, T. J.
MILLER, K. J.

Health and Human Services:

LEWTON, J.
SULLIVAN, J.
TRABAND, M.
WEDDING, M. E.

Law Enforcement Technologies:

ROSSI, R.
TELB, J.

Technical Science and Mathematics:

GRECO, D.
PALMER, J.
STEIN, R. D.

URBANA UNIVERSITY

579 College Way, Urbana, OH 43078
Telephone: (937) 484-1400
E-mail: admiss@urbana.edu
Internet: www.urbana.edu

Founded 1850
Private control

Pres.: ROBERT HEAD
Vice-Pres. for Academic Affairs: THOMAS FAUQUET
Vice-Pres. for Enrollment Management: JAMES SAGONA
Vice-Pres. for Institutional Advancement: BOB KELLER
Dean of Students: JAMES WEISGERBER
Registrar: KATHY YODER
Library Dir: BARBARA MACKE

Number of teachers: 81
Number of students: 1,300

DEANS

College of Business: Dr HERSCHEL PURDUE
College of Social and Behavioral Sciences: Dr ALICE E. SIDDLE
School of Adult and Continuing Education: WILLIAM D. BLIZZARD

URSULINE COLLEGE

2550 Lander Rd, Pepper Pike, Cleveland, OH 44124
Telephone: (440) 449-4203
Fax: (440) 646-8318
E-mail: admission@ursuline.edu
Internet: www.ursuline.edu

Founded 1871
Academic year: August to May

Pres.: Sr DIANA STANO
Vice-Pres. for Academic Affairs: Dr JOANNE PODIS
Vice-Pres. for Institutional Advancement: KEVIN GLADSTONE
Vice-Pres. for Student Affairs: DEANNE HURLEY
Registrar: LEAH SULLIVAN
Librarian: BETSEY BELKIN

Library of 120,000 vols
Number of teachers: 125
Number of students: 1,600

DEANS

Breen School of Nursing: CHRISTINE WYND
School of Arts and Sciences: CHRISTINE DEVINNE
School of Graduate Studies: ALISON BENDERS
School of Professional Studies: MARILYN BUTLER

WALSH UNIVERSITY

2020 East Maple St, NW, North Canton, OH 44720
Telephone: (330) 490-7090
Internet: www.walsh.edu

Campuses at North Canton, Akron and Medina
Private control

Pres.: RICHARD JUSSEAUME
Provost and Vice-Pres. for Academic Affairs: LAURENCE F. BOVE
Vice-Pres. for Academic Projects: NANCY BLACKFORD
Vice-Pres. for Business and Finance: PHILIP DANIELS
Vice-Pres. for Enrollment Management: BRETT FRESHOUR
Vice-Pres. for Student Affairs: DALE S. HOWARD
Vice-Pres. for Univ. Advancement: BRIDGETTE NEISEL
Registrar: EDNA MCCULLOH
Librarian: SARAH R. SIPE

Number of teachers: 65
Number of students: 2,500

Depts of business and economics, communication, education, humanities, language and letters, nursing, physical therapy, social and behavioural sciences.

WILBERFORCE UNIVERSITY

Telephone: (937) 376-2911
Fax: (937) 376-2627
Internet: www.wilberforce.edu

Founded 1856
Academic year: August to May

Pres.: Rev. Dr FLOYD H. FLAKE
Vice-Pres. for Research Devt: ABHAY TRIVEDI
Registrar: GAIL LASH

Library of 68,000 vols
Number of teachers: 72
Number of students: 998

WILMINGTON COLLEGE

1870 Quaker Way, Wilmington, OH 45177
Telephone: (937) 382-6661
Fax: (937) 382-7077
E-mail: admission@wilmington.edu
Internet: www.wilmington.edu

Founded 1870
Private control
Academic year: August to May

Pres.: DANIEL A. DIBIASIO
Vice-Pres. for Academic Affairs: JAMES REYNOLDS
Vice-Pres. for Business and Finance: THOMAS M. JENKINS
Vice-Pres. for College Advancement: EDWARD F. LEONARD
Vice-Pres. for Enrollment Management: MARK DENNISTON
Vice-Pres. for External Programmes: IRIS KELSON
Dean of Students: SIGRID B. SOLOMON
Registrar: KAREN M. GARMAN
Dir of Library: JEAN MULHERN

Library of 110,000 vols
Number of teachers: 65 full-time
Number of students: 1,183

Programmes in accounting, agriculture, art, athletic training, biology, business admin., chemistry and physics, communication arts, criminal justice, education, English, environmental science, equine studies, history, mathematics, music, psychology, religion and philosophy, social and political studies, social work, Spanish, sports management and health/PE, theatre.

WINEBRENNER THEOLOGICAL SEMINARY

950 North Main St, Findlay, OH 45840
Telephone: (419) 434-4200
Fax: (419) 434-4267
E-mail: admissions@winebrenner.edu
Internet: www.winebrenner.edu

Founded 1942
Private control
Academic year: August to May

Pres.: Dr DAVID E. DRAPER
Vice-Pres. for Academic Advancement: Dr M. JOHN NISSLEY
Registrar: SHARI BRANDEBERRY
Dir of Library Services: MARGARET HIRSCHY

Library of 38,000 vols, 145 periodicals
Number of teachers: 17
Number of students: 130

WITTENBERG UNIVERSITY

POB 720, Ward St at North Wittenberg Ave, Springfield, OH 45501-0720
Telephone: (937) 327-6231
Fax: (937) 327-6340
E-mail: admission@wittenberg.edu
Internet: www.wittenberg.edu

Founded 1842
Private control
Academic year: August to May

Pres.: MARK H. ERICKSON
Provost: KENNETH W. BLADH
Vice-Pres. for Business and Finance: DARRELL KITCHEN
Dir of Admissions: BRAD POCHARD
Registrar: JACK CAMPBELL
Dir of Library: DOUGLAS LEHMAN

Library of 367,000 vols, 1,500 periodicals
Number of teachers: 239 (170 full-time, 69 part-time)
Number of students: 2,100

Programmes in Africana studies, American studies, art, biochemistry and molecular biology, biology, chemistry, communication, community education, computer science, dance, East Asian studies, economics, education, engineering, English, environmental studies, forestry, geography, geology, global studies, health/fitness/sport, history, languages, management, marine biology, mathematics, music, nursing, occupational therapy, philosophy, physics, political science, pre-law, pre-medicine, psychology, religion, Russian area studies, sociology, theatre and dance, urban studies, women's studies

Publications: *Pholeos: Journal of the Wittenberg Speleological Society*, *Wittenberg University East Asian Studies Journal*.

WRIGHT STATE UNIVERSITY

3640 Colonel Glenn Highway, Dayton, OH 45435
Telephone: (937) 775-3333
Fax: (937) 775-3301
E-mail: registrar@wright.edu
Internet: www.wright.edu

Founded 1967

Pres.: Dr DAVID HOPKINS
Provost: Dr STEVEN R. ANGLE
Sr Vice-Pres. for Curriculum and Instruction: Dr LILLIE P. HOWARD
Exec. Vice-Pres. for Planning: Dr ROBERT J. SWEENEY
Vice-Pres. for Business and Fiscal Affairs and Univ. Treas.: Dr MATTHEW V. FILIPIC
Vice-Pres. for Research and Graduate Studies: Dr JOHN A. BANTLE
Vice-Pres. for Student Affairs: Dr DAN ABRAHAMOWICZ
Vice-Pres. for Univ. Advancement: MARCIA G. MUELLER

Registrar: GAIL FRED
Librarian: STEPHEN FOSTER

Library of 696,000 vols
Number of teachers: 676 full-time
Number of students: 11,878 full-time

DEANS

College of Business: BERKWOOD M. FARMER
College of Education and Human Services: GREGORY BERNHARDT
College of Engineering and Computer Service: BOR Z. JANG
College of Liberal Arts: CHARLES S. TAYLOR
College of Nursing and Health: PATRICIA MARTIN
College of Science and Mathematics: (vacant)
Lake Campus: JAMES E. SAYER
School of Graduate Studies: JOSEPH A. THOMAS
School of Medicine: HOWARD PART
School of Professional Psychology: JOHN R. RUDISILL
Univ. College: ANITA CURRY-JACKSON

ATTACHED INSTITUTE

Asian/Hispanic/Native American Center: Dir MAI NGUYEN.

Bolinga Black Cultural Resources Center: Dir Dr YVONNE SEON.

Center for Urban and Public Affairs: Dir JACK L. DUSTIN.

Child Development Center: Dir (vacant).

XAVIER UNIVERSITY

3800 Victory Parkway, Cincinnati, OH 45207
Telephone: (513) 745-3000
Fax: (513) 745-4223
Internet: www.xu.edu

Founded 1831
Private control
Academic year: August to May

Pres.: Rev. MICHAEL J. GRAHAM, S. J.
Vice-Pres. and Provost for Academic Affairs: ROGER A. FORTIN
Vice-Pres. for Admin.: Dr JOHN F. KUCIA
Vice-Pres. for Financial Admin.: MARIBETH AMYOT
Vice-Pres. for Information Resources and Chief Information Officer: DAVID DODD
Vice-Pres. for Student Enrollment: TERRY RICHARDS
Vice-Pres. for Univ. Relations: GARY R. MASSA
Vice-Provost for Diversity: CHERYL NUÑEZ
Assoc. Vice-Pres. for Information Resources: ROBERT COTTER

Library of 374,000 vols
Number of teachers: 334
Number of students: 7,019

DEANS

College of Arts and Sciences: Dr JANICE B. WALKER
College of Social Science, Health and Education: Dr MARK MEYERS
Williams College of Business: Dr ALI MALEKZADEH

YOUNGSTOWN STATE UNIVERSITY

One University Plaza, Youngstown, OH 44555
Telephone: (330) 941-3000
Fax: (330) 742-1998
Internet: www.ysu.edu

Founded 1908
State control
Academic year: September to August (four terms)

Pres.: Dr DAVID C. SWEET
Vice-Pres. for Academic Affairs and Provost: Dr IKRAM KHAWAJA
Vice-Pres. for Finance and Admin.: EUGENE P. GRILLI
Vice-Pres. for Student Affairs: Dr CYNTHIA E. ANDERSON
Dir of Library: PAUL J. KOBULNICKY

Library of 492,300 titles
Number of teachers: 732
Number of students: 12,222

DEANS

College of Business Administration: Dr BETTY JO LICATA
College of Education: PHILIP GINETTI
College of Fine and Performing Arts: Dr BRYAN DEPOY
College of Health and Human Services: Dr JOSEPH MOSCA
College of Liberal Arts and Social Sciences: Dr SHEARLE FURNISH
College of Science, Technology, Engineering and Mathematics: Dr MARTIN ABRAHAM
School of Graduate Studies and Research: Dr PETER J. KASVINSKY

OKLAHOMA

EAST CENTRAL UNIVERSITY

1100 East 14th St, Ada, OK 74820
Telephone: (580) 332-8000
Internet: www.ecok.edu

Founded 1909

Pres.: Dr RICHARD RAFES
Provost and Vice-Pres. for Academic Affairs: Dr DUANE C. ANDERSON
Registrar: PAMLA ARMSTRONG
Librarian: ADRIANNA LANCASTER

Library of 275,000 vols
Number of teachers: 168
Number of students: 4,378

DEANS

College of Education and Psychology: Dr BILL OSBORNE
College of Health and Sciences: Dr BRUCE WEEMS
College of Liberal Arts and Social Sciences: Dr SCOTT BARTON
School of Business: Dr WILLIAM C. CHAPMAN
School of Graduate Studies: Dr RICK WETHERILL

LANGSTON UNIVERSITY

POB 728, Langston, OK 73050
Telephone: (405) 466-3428
Fax: (405) 466-3391
E-mail: admissions@lunet.edu
Internet: www.lunet.edu

Founded 1897
Academic year: August to May
Campuses at Tulsa and Oklahoma City

Pres.: Dr JOANN W. HAYSBERT
Vice-Pres. for Academic Affairs: Dr JEAN B. MANNING
Vice-Pres. for Devt and Institutional Advancement: Dr RODERICK SMOTHERS
Vice-Pres. for Fiscal Affairs: ANGELA KELSO-WATSON
Vice-Pres. for Student Affairs: Dr VALADIMIR APPEANING
Dir of Univ. Libraries: NJAMBI KAMOCHE

Number of teachers: 143
Number of students: 3,482

DEANS

School of Agriculture and Applied Sciences: Dr MARVIN BURNS
School of Arts and Sciences: Dr CLYDE MONTGOMERY
School of Business: Dr SOLOMON S. SMITH
School of Education and Behavioral Sciences: Dr DARNELL WILLIAMS
School of Nursing and Health Professions: Dr CAROLYN T. KORNEGAY
Physical Therapy: Dr MILAGROS JORGE
Honours Programme: Dr JO ANN CLARK

MID-AMERICA CHRISTIAN UNIVERSITY

3500 SW 119th St, Oklahoma City, OK 73170
Telephone: (405) 691-3800
E-mail: info@macu.edu
Internet: www.macu.edu

Founded 1953 as South Texas Bible Institute; present name 2003
Private control
Academic year: August to May

Pres.: Dr JOHN FOZARD
Vice-Pres. for Academic Affairs: Dr RON RODDY
Vice-Pres. for Student Affairs: DERRY EBERT
Registrar: DEBORAH SHOEMAKE
Library Dirs: MICHAEL FOOTE, ELISSA PATADAL

Number of teachers: 59
Number of students: 600

DEANS

College of Adult/Graduate Studies: Dr SHIRLEY RODDY
College of Arts and Sciences: JULIA CARPENTER

NORTHEASTERN STATE UNIVERSITY

600 North Grand Ave, Tahlequah, OK 74464-2399
Telephone: (918) 456-5511
Fax: (918) 458-2015
E-mail: nsuinfo@nsuok.edu
Internet: www.nsuok.edu

Founded 1888 (state purchase 1909)
Academic year: August to July

Pres.: Dr LARRY B. WILLIAMS
Vice-Pres. for Academic Affairs: Dr DALTON BIGBEE
Vice-Pres. for Admin.: KIM CHERRY (acting)
Vice-Pres. for Univ. Relations: Dr NEAL WEAVER
Registrar: BILL NOWLIN
Dir of Library: Dr ALLEN MCKIEL

Library of 500,000 vols
Number of teachers: 290 full-time
Number of students: 8,750

DEANS

College of Business and Technology: Dr JOHN SCHLEEDE
College of Education: Dr KAY GRANT
College of Liberal Arts: Dr PAUL WESTBROOK
College of Optometry: DOUGLAS K. PENISTEN
College of Science and Health Professions: Dr MARTIN VENNEMAN
Graduate College: Dr THOMAS JACKSON
Muskogee Campus and Weekend College: Dr TIM MCELROY

BRANCH CAMPUSES

Broken Arrow Campus: 3100 East New Orleans, Broken Arrow, OK 74014; tel. (918) 449-6000; internet www.nsuba.edu.

Muskogee Campus: 2400 West Shawnee, Muskogee, OK 74401; tel. (918) 683-0040; internet www.nsuok.edu/muskogee.

NORTHWESTERN OKLAHOMA STATE UNIVERSITY

709 Oklahoma Blvd, Alva, OK 73717-2799
Telephone: (580) 327-1700
Fax: (580) 327-1881
E-mail: recruit@nwosu.edu
Internet: www.nwosu.edu

Founded 1897

Academic year: August to May
Pres.: Dr Janet Cunningham
Exec. Vice-Pres.: Dr Steve Lohmann
Vice-Pres. for Admin.: David Pecha
Registrar: Cynthia Nighswonger
Dir of Libraries: Susan Jeffries

Library of 500,000 vols (incl. microforms)
Number of teachers: 168
Number of students: 2,013

DEANS

School of Arts and Sciences: Dr Mike Knedler
School of Professional Studies: Dr James Brown

BRANCH CAMPUSES

Enid Campus: 2929 East Randolph, Enid, OK 73701; tel. (580) 213-3103; Dean Dr Cheryl Evans.

Woodward Campus: 2220 Oklahoma Ave, Woodward, OK 73801; tel. (580) 256-0047; Dean Dr Deena Fisher.

OKLAHOMA BAPTIST UNIVERSITY

500 W University, Shawnee, OK 74804
Telephone: (405) 878-2850
Fax: (405) 878-2069
E-mail: info@okbu.edu
Internet: www.okbu.edu

Founded 1910

Pres.: Dr David W. Whitlock
Sr Vice-Pres. for Academic Affairs: Debbie Blue
Exec. Vice-Pres. for Business and Admin. Services: Randy Smith
Vice-Pres. for Devt: Bill W. Holley
Provost: Dr Stan Norman
Dean of Enrollment Management: Trent Argo
Dean of Library Sciences: Dr Richard Cheek
Dean of Students: Bobby Canty
Dir of Admissions: Bruce Perkins
Dir of Graduate School: Dr Scott Harris

Library of 220,000 vols, 310,000 microforms
Number of teachers: 113
Number of students: 1,764

DEANS

College of Arts and Sciences: Dr Pam Robinson
College of Fine Arts: Dr Paul Hammond
School of Business: Dr Dan Reeder
School of Christian Service: Dr Mark McClellan
School of Nursing: Dr Lana Bolhouse

OKLAHOMA CHRISTIAN UNIVERSITY

POB 11000, Oklahoma City, OK 11000-1100
2501E Memorial Rd, Edmond, OK 73013
Telephone: (405) 425-5000
Fax: (405) 425-5090
Internet: www.oc.edu

Founded 1950

Campuses in Oklahoma City and Portland, OR
Private control
Academic year: August to April

Pres.: Dr Mike E. O'Neal
Exec. Vice-Pres. and Chief Operating Officer: Alfred Branch
Vice-Pres. for Academic Affairs: Dr Allison Garrett
Vice-Pres. for Advancement: Dr John deSteiguer
Vice-Pres. for Finance: Jeff Bingham
Vice-Pres. for Univ. Outreach: Nathan Mellor
Dean of Students: Neil Arter
Registrar: Mickey D. Banister
Library Dir: Tamie Willis

Library of 110,000 vols and media, 30,000 electronic books, access to 8,000 periodicals in electronic or print format
Number of teachers: 105
Number of students: 2,200

DEANS

College of Arts and Sciences: Dr David Lowry
College of Biblical Studies: Dr Lynn McMillon
College of Professional Studies: Dr Phil Lewis

OKLAHOMA CITY UNIVERSITY

2501 N Blackwelder, Oklahoma City, OK 73106
Telephone: (405) 2008-5000
Fax: (405) 521-5264
Internet: www.okcu.edu

Founded 1904
Language of instruction: English
Academic year: August to July

Pres.: Dr Robert Henry
Provost and Vice-Pres. for Academic Affairs: Dr Susan Barber (acting)
Vice-Pres. for Student Affairs: Rick Hall
Vice-Pres. for Univ. Advancement: (vacant)
Vice-Pres. for Univ. and Church Relations: Rev. Margaret A. Ball
Registrar: Charles L. Monnot
Librarian: Dr Victoria Swinney

Library of 520,953 vols, 975,580 microfilms, 12,000 video and audio items
Number of teachers: 352
Number of students: 3,770

DEANS

College of Arts and Sciences: Dr Mark Y. A. Davies
School of Adult and Continuing Education: Dr Leo Werneke
School of Business: Dr Steve Agee
School of Dance: John Bedford
School of Law: Dr Lawrence K. Hellman
School of Music: Mark Parker
School of Nursing: Dr Marvel L. Williamson
School of Religion: Dr Sharon Betsworth
School of Theatre: (vacant)

OKLAHOMA PANHANDLE STATE UNIVERSITY

POB 430, Goodwell, OK 73939
Telephone: (580) 349-2611
Fax: (580) 349-2302
E-mail: opsu@opsu.edu
Internet: www.opsu.edu

Founded 1909
Academic year: August to May

Pres.: David A. Bryant
Vice-Pres. for Academic Affairs: Wayne E. Manning
Vice-Pres. for Fiscal Affairs: Larry Peters
Registrar: Bobby Jenkins
Librarian: Evlyn Schmidt

Library of 91,000 vols
Number of teachers: 69
Number of students: 1,400

DEANS

Agriculture: Peter Camfield
Business and Technology: Diane Murphey
Development Studies: Carolyn McCargish
Education: R. Wayne Stewart
Liberal Arts: Sarah Jane Richter
Science, Mathematics and Nursing: Justin K. Collins

OKLAHOMA STATE UNIVERSITY

Stillwater, OK 74078
Telephone: (405) 744-5000
Fax: (405) 744-5285
E-mail: admit@okstate.edu
Internet: www.okstate.edu

Founded 1890
Academic year: August to May

Pres.: Dr Marlene Strathe
Provost and Sr Vice-Pres.: (vacant)
Vice-Pres. for Admin. and Finance: Dr David C. Bosserman
Vice-Pres. for Enrollment Management: Albert N. Colom
Vice-Pres. for Institutional Diversity: Dr Cornell Thomas
Vice-Pres. for Research and Technology Transfer: Dr Stephen W. McKeever
Vice-Pres. for Student Affairs: Dr Lee Bird
Registrar: Joan Payne
Dean of Libraries: Sheila Johnson

Library of 2,470,138 vols
Number of teachers: 1,060
Number of students: 23,571

Publications: *International Fire Service Journal of Leadership and Management* (4 a year), *Journal of Computer Information Systems* (4 a year), *The Review of Regional Studies* (3 a year)

DEANS

Center for Veterinary Health Sciences: Dr Michael D. Lorenz
College of Agricultural Sciences and Natural Resources: Dr Robert E. Whitson
College of Arts and Sciences: Dr Peter Sherwood
College of Education: Dr Pamela Fry
College of Engineering, Architecture and Technology: Dr Karl N. Reid, Jr
College of Human Environmental Sciences: Dr Patricia K. Knaub
Graduate College: Dr Gordon Emslie
School of Business: Dr Sara M. Freedman

OKLAHOMA WESLEYAN UNIVERSITY

2201 Silver Lake Rd, Bartlesville, OK 74006
Telephone: (918) 335-6200
Fax: (918) 335-6229
E-mail: info@okwu.edu
Internet: www.okwu.edu

Founded 1910 as Colorado Springs Bible College, present name 2001
Private control
Academic year: August to July

Pres.: Dr Everett Piper
Vice-Pres. for Academic Affairs: Dr Robert M. Meyers
Vice-Pres. for Adult and Graduate Studies: Brett Andrews
Vice-Pres. for Institutional Devt: Dr Randy Thompson
Vice-Pres. for Student Life: Kyle White
Registrar: Becky Tupper
Library Dir: Wendell Thompson

Number of teachers: 70
Number of students: 960

ORAL ROBERTS UNIVERSITY

7777 South Lewis Ave, Tulsa, OK 74171
Telephone: (918) 495-6161
Fax: (918) 495-6033
E-mail: admissions@oru.edu
Internet: www.oru.edu

Founded 1965
Academic year: August to May

Chancellor: G. Oral Roberts
Pres.: Dr Richard L. Roberts
Exec. Vice-Pres. and Provost for Academic Affairs: Dr Mark Lewandowski
Exec. Vice-Pres. for Finance and Operations: David Elsworth
Vice-Pres. for Academic Admin.: Dr Ralph Fagin

Vice-Pres. for Information Technology and Communication Systems: MIKE BERNARD
Vice-Pres. for Partner Communications: COLEEN BARKER
Vice-Pres. for Univ. Relations and Devt: DAVID WAGNER
Registrar: DAVID FULMER

Library: 1m. vols
Number of teachers: 275
Number of students: 5,723

DEANS

Arts and Cultural Sciences: Dr WENDY SHIRK
Business: Dr MARSHAL WRIGHT
Education: Dr DAVID HAND
Nursing: Dr KENDA JEZEK
Science and Engineering: Dr DOMINIC HALSMER
Theology and Missions: Dr THOMSON MATHEW

PHILLIPS THEOLOGICAL SEMINARY

901 North Mingo Rd, Tulsa, OK 74116
Telephone: (918) 610-8303
Fax: (918) 610-8404
E-mail: myrna.jones@ptstulsa.edu
Internet: www.ptstulsa.edu

Founded 1906 as College of the Bible; present name 1995
Private control

Pres.: Dr WILLIAM TABBERNEE
Exec. Vice-Pres.: Dr JOHN M. IMBLER
Vice-Pres. for Academic Affairs and Dean: Dr DON A. PITTMAN
Registrar: LINDA ASHLOCK
Library Dir: SANDY SHAPOVAL

Number of teachers: 15
Number of students: 185

SOUTHEASTERN OKLAHOMA STATE UNIVERSITY

1405 North Fourth St, Durant, OK 74701
Telephone: (580) 745-2000
Internet: www.sosu.edu

Founded 1909, refounded under present name 1974
Academic year: August to May (and summer session)

Pres.: Dr MICHAEL TURNER
Exec. Vice-Pres.: Dr DOUGLAS N. MCMILLAN
Library Dir: Dr SHARON MORRISON

Library of 180,000 vols
Number of students: 4,000

DEANS

Graduate and Univ. Studies: Dr DOUG MCMILLAN
School of Arts and Sciences: Dr C. W. MANGRUM
School of Business: Dr BUDDY GASTER
School of Education and Behavioural Sciences: Dr ED MAUZEY

SOUTHERN NAZARENE UNIVERSITY

6729 NW 39th Expressway, Bethany, OK 73008
Telephone: (405) 789-6400
Fax: (405) 491-6381
E-mail: admissions@snu.edu
Internet: www.snu.edu

Founded 1899
Church control
Academic year: August to June (two summer sessions and two terms)

Pres.: Dr LOREN P. GRESHAM
Provost: Dr PATRICK ALLEN
Dean of Graduate and Professional Studies: Dr DAVIS BERRYMAN
Dean of Undergraduate College: Dr MARTHA BANZ
Registrar: WESLEY C. LEE
Librarian: JAN REINBOLD

Library of 105,000 vols, 13,000 periodicals, 339,000 microform items
Number of teachers: 120
Number of students: 2,200

SOUTHWESTERN CHRISTIAN UNIVERSITY

7210 NW 39th Expressway, Bethany, OK 73008
Telephone: (405) 789-7661
Fax: (405) 495-0078
E-mail: admissions@swcu.edu
Internet: www.swcu.edu

Founded 1946 as Southwestern Bible College; present name 2001
Private control

Pres.: ED HUCKEBY
Dean of Academic Affairs: CHARLES S. CHITWOOD
Dean of Graduate School: GARNET E. PIKE
Dean of Student Devt: MICHAEL POTTER
Registrar: JEAN PERDUE
Library Dir: MARILYN HUDSON

Number of teachers: 24
Number of students: 150

SOUTHWESTERN OKLAHOMA STATE UNIVERSITY

100 Campus Dr., Weatherford, OK 73096
Telephone: (580) 772-6611
Fax: (580) 774-3795
Internet: www.swosu.edu

Founded 1901
Public control
Language of instruction: English
Academic year: July to June

Pres.: RANDY BEUTLER
Vice-Pres. for Admin. and Finance: TOM FAGAN
Registrar: DANIEL ARCHER
Librarian: JON SPARKS

Library of 242,406 vols
Number of teachers: 222
Number of students: 5,226

DEANS

College of Arts and Sciences: Dr RADWAN AL-JARRAH
College of Pharmacy: Dr DENNIS THOMPSON
College of Professional and Graduate Studies: KEN ROSE

UNIVERSITY OF CENTRAL OKLAHOMA

100 North University Dr., Edmond, OK 73034
Telephone: (405) 974-2000
Fax: (405) 359-5841
Internet: www.ucok.edu

Founded 1890

Pres.: W. ROGER WEBB
Exec. Vice-Pres.: STEVE KREIDLER
Vice-Pres. for Academic Affairs: Dr WILLIAM J. RADKE
Vice-Pres. for Enrollment Management: Dr MYRON L. POPE
Vice-Pres. for Student Affairs: Dr KATHRYN GAGE
Dir of Univ. Library: Dr BONNIE MCNEELY

Library of 706,000 vols
Number of teachers: 400
Number of students: 14,000

DEANS

College of Arts, Media and Design: Dr JOHN CLINTON
College of Business Administration: Dr MICHAEL SHIRLEY (acting)
College of Education and Professional Studies: Dr JAMES MACHELL
College of Liberal Arts: Dr PAM WASHINGTON
College of Mathematics and Science: Dr JOHN BARTHELL
Graduate Studies and Research: Dr GEORGE AVELLANO

UNIVERSITY OF OKLAHOMA

660 Parrington Oval, Norman, OK 73019-0390
Telephone: (405) 325-0311
E-mail: publicaffairs@ou.edu
Internet: www.ou.edu

Founded 1890; opened 1892

Campuses at Norman, Oklahoma City and Tulsa
State control
Academic year: August to May (summer session June and July)

Pres.: DAVID L. BOREN
Sr Vice-Pres. and Provost: NANCY L. MERGLER
Chief Information Officer and Vice-Pres. for Information Technology: DENNIS AEBERSOLD
Vice-Pres. and Gen. Counsel: JOSEPH HARROZ
Vice-Pres. for Admin. and Exec. Affairs: NICHOLAS S. HATHAWAY
Vice-Pres. for Health Affairs: DEWAYNE ANDREWS
Vice-Pres. for Public Affairs: CATHERINE F. BISHOP
Vice-Pres. for Research: T. H. LEE WILLIAMS
Vice-Pres. for Student Affairs and Dean of Students: CLARKE STROUD
Vice-Pres. for Technology Devt: ANIL GOLLAHALLI
Vice-Pres. for Univ. Devt: PAUL MASSAD (acting)
Vice-Pres. for Univ. Governance: CHRIS A. PURCELL
Dean of Univ. Libraries: SUL H. LEE

Number of teachers: 1,138 (920 full-time, 218 part-time)
Number of students: 24,887

Publications: *American Indian Law Review* (2 a year), *Genre: Forms of Discourse and Culture* (4 a year), *Oklahoma Business Bulletin* (12 a year), *Oklahoma Law Review* (4 a year), *Papers on Anthropology* (2 a year), *World Literature Today* (4 a year)

DEANS

College of Architecture: BOB G. FILLPOT
College of Arts and Sciences: PAUL B. BELL
College of Atmospheric and Geographic Sciences: JOHN T. SNOW
College of Business: KENNETH R. EVANS
College of Earth and Energy: LARRY GRILLOT
College of Education: JOAN K. SMITH
College of Engineering: THOMAS L. LANDERS
College of Fine Arts: EUGENE ENRICO
College of Journalism and Mass Communication: JOE FOOTE
College of Law: ANDREW M. COATS
College of Liberal Studies: JAMES P. PAPPAS
Graduate College: T. H. LEE WILLIAMS
Honors College: ROBERT DAVIS-UNDIANO
Univ. College: DOUGLAS GAFFIN

CAMPUSES

University of Oklahoma Health Sciences Center

POB 26901, Oklahoma City, OK 73190
Telephone: (405) 271-4000
Fax: (405) 271-3151
Internet: www.ouhsc.edu

Founded 1900
Academic year: June to May

Sr Vice-Pres. and Provost: Dr JOSEPH SERRETTI
Vice-Pres. for Admin. Affairs: KENNETH ROWE
Vice-Pres. for Research: JOSEPH L. WARNER

Number of teachers: 800
Number of students: 4,000

DEANS

College of Allied Health: KEVIN RUDEEN
College of Dentistry: STEPHEN K. YOUNG
College of Medicine: DEWAYNE ANDREWS
College of Nursing: CAROLE ANN KENNER
College of Pharmacy: JOLAINE REIERSON DRAUGALIS
College of Public Health: GARY RASKOB
Graduate College: JAMES J. TOMASEK

University of Oklahoma—Tulsa

4502 East 41st St, Tulsa, OK 74135-2515
Telephone: (918) 660-3000
Internet: tulsa.ou.edu

Pres.: GERARD P. CLANCY
Library Dir: STEWART M. BROWER

DEANS

College of Medicine: GERARD P. CLANCY
Graduate College: WILLIAM O. RAY

UNIVERSITY OF SCIENCE AND ARTS OF OKLAHOMA

POB 82345, Chickasha, OK 73018-0001
Telephone: (405) 224-3140
Fax: (405) 521-6244
Internet: www.usao.edu

Founded 1908
State-supported college

Pres.: JOHN FEAVER
Vice-Pres. for Academic Affairs: SANDERS HUGUENIN
Vice-Pres. for Admin. Affairs: TERRY WINN
Vice-Pres. for Business and Finance: MICHAEL COPONITI
Vice-Pres. for Univ. Advancement: MICHAEL NEALEIGH
Dean of Students: ELOY CHAVEZ
Librarian: KELLY BROWN

Library of 97,000 vols
Number of teachers: 55
Number of students: 1,393

Divs of arts and humanities, business and social studies, education and speech language pathology, mathematics, science and physical education, teacher education programme.

UNIVERSITY OF TULSA

800 South Tucker Dr., Tulsa, OK 74104
Telephone: (918) 631-2000
Fax: (918) 631-2622
E-mail: elisso@utulsa.edu
Internet: www.utulsa.edu

Founded as Henry Kendall College under Presbyterian control 1894, reorganized and name changed to Univ. of Tulsa 1920; became non-denominational 1928
Independent control
Academic year: August to May

Pres.: Dr STEADMAN UPHAM
Provost and Vice-Pres. for Academic Affairs: ROGER N. BLAIS
Vice-Pres. for Business and Finance: KEVAN BUCK
Vice-Pres. for Enrollment and Student Services: ROGER SOROCHTY
Dean of Students: YOLANDA D. TAYLOR
Registrar: GINNA LANGSTON
Dean of Libraries: ADRIAN W. ALEXANDER

Number of teachers: 406
Number of students: 4,072

Publications: *James Joyce Quarterly*, *Nimrod International Journal*, *Tulsa Studies in Women's Literature*

DEANS

College of Business Admin.: A. GALE SULLENBERGER
College of Engineering and Natural Sciences: STEVEN J. BELLOVICH
College of Law: JANET KOVEN LEVIT
Graduate School: JANET A. HAGGERTY
Henry Kendall College of Arts and Sciences: D. THOMAS BENEDIKTSON

PROFESSORS

ADAMS, C. W., Law
ALLISON, G. D., Law
ARNOLD, M. T., Law
ASHENAYI, K., Electrical Engineering
BAILEY, G. A., Anthropology
BELSKY, M. H., Law
BENEDIKTSON, D. T., Languages
BERRY, J. O., Psychology
BEY, R. P., Finance
BLAIR, D. M., Law
BRADLEY, J. C., History
BROWN, C. R., Biological Sciences
BUCHOLTZ, B. K., Law
BUCKLEY, T. H., History
BURGESS, R. C., Finance
BURSTEIN, A. M., History
CAGLEY, J. W., Management and Marketing
CAIRNS, T. W., Mathematics and Computer Science
CHIANG, W. C., Operations Management
COLLIER, G. E., Biological Science
COLLINS, J. M., Finance
CONSTANDA, C., Mathematics and Computer Science
COOK, D. B., Theatre
CRAVENS, K. S., Accounting
CULLEM, C. M., Law
DE ALMEIDA, H. B., English
DIAZ, J. C., Mathematics and Computer Science
DONALDSON, R. H., Political Science
DOTY, D. R., Mathematics and Computer Science
DUGGER, W. M., Economics
DURHAM, M. O., Electrical Engineering
EISENACH, E. J., Political Science
FINKELMAN, P., Law
GAMBLE, R. F., Computer Science
GASTON, S. K., Nursing
GILPIN, G. H., English
HAGGERTY, J. A., Geosciences
HANSSON, R. O., Psychology
HENNESSEE, P. A., Accounting
HENRY, D. O., Anthropology
HENSHAW, J. M., Mechanical Engineering
HICKS, J. F., Law
HIPSHER, W. L., Education
HITTINGER, F. R., Philosophy and Religion
HOLLAND, T. L., Law
HOLLINGSWORTH, W. G., Law
HORNE, T. A., Political Science
HOWARD, R. E., Chemistry
HOWLAND, J. A., Philosophy
HUIE, M. C., Law
HYATTE, R. L., Languages
JENSEN, J. K., Communication
KANE, G. R., Electrical Engineering
KELKAR, B. G., Petroleum Engineering
KESTNER, J. A., English
KRAIGER, K., Psychology
LACEY, L. J., Law
LAIRD, H. A., English
LAMPTON, J. D., Art
LANGENKAMP, R. D., Law
LAWLESS, R. W., Mathematical Sciences and Quantitative Methods
LEVETIN, E. A., Biological Science
LEWICKI, P., Psychology
LIMAS, V. J., Law
LINDSTROM, L. C., Anthropology
LUKS, K. D., Chemical Engineering
MANNING, F. S., Chemical Engineering
MANSFIELD, M. E., NELPI, Law
MARTIN, B. C., Nursing
MICHAEL, P. J., Geosciences
MILLER, G. P., Physics
MISKA, S. Z., Petroleum Engineering
MONCRIEF, D. L., Communication
MONROE, R. J., Finance
NEIDELL, L. A., Management and Marketing
NORBERG, A. H., Music
ODELL, G. H., Anthropology
PARKER, J. C., Law
PRICE, G. L., Chemical Engineering
RAHE, P. A., History
REDNER, R. A., Mathematics and Computer Science
REEDER, R. L., Biological Science
REYNOLDS, A. C., Petroleum Engineering
RONDA, J. P., History
ROYSTER, J. V., Law
RUSSELL, R. A., Management Information Systems
RYBICKI, E. F., Mechanical Engineering
SAMIEE, S., Management and Marketing
SARICA, C., Petroleum Engineering
SCHOENEFELD, D. A., Mathematics and Computer Science
SEN, S., Computer Science
SHADLEY, J. R., Mechanical Engineering
SHENOI, S., Mathematics and Computer Science
SHIRAZI, S. A., Mechanical Engineering
SHOHAM, O., Petroleum Engineering
SMITH, P. C., Management
SOREM, J. R., Mechanical Engineering
STEIB, S., Economics
SUBLETTE, K. L., Chemical Engineering
SULLENBERGER, A. G., Management Information Systems and Operations Management
TAI, H. M., Electrical Engineering
TAKACH, N. E., Chemistry
TATUM, M. L., Law
TAYLOR, G. O., English
TEETERS, D. C., Chemistry
THOMAS, J. C., Law
TIPTON, S. M., Mechanical Engineering
TOMLINS, C. B., Art
URBAN, T. L., Operations Management
VOZIKIS, G. S., Bovaird Chair
WAINWRIGHT, R. L., Mathematics and Computer Science
WAITS, K., Law
WATSON, J. G., English
WHALEN, M. E., Anthropology
WILSON, L. C., Theatre
YASSER, R. L., Law
YEVTUSHENKO, Y. A., English
ZEDALIS, R. J., NELPI

OREGON

ART INSTITUTE OF PORTLAND

1122 Northwest Davis St, Portland, OR 97209
Telephone: (503) 228-6528
E-mail: aipdadm@aii.edu
Internet: www.aipd.artinstitutes.edu

Private control
Academic year: October to June

Pres.: Dr STEVEN GOLDMAN
Dir of Admin.: ANGELA BOSTOCK
Dir of Learning Resources: NANCY THURSTON
Registrar: ROBERT TUFTS

Number of teachers: 33 full-time, 60 adjunct per quarter
Number of students: 1,538

CONCORDIA UNIVERSITY

2811 Northeast Holman St, Portland, OR 97211
Telephone: (503) 288-9371
E-mail: admissions@cu-portland.edu

Internet: www.cu-portland.edu
Founded 1905 as a four-year acad.; present name 1995
Private control
Academic year: August to May
Pres.: Dr CHARLES E. SCHLIMPERT
Provost and Chief Operating Officer: Dr MARK WAHLERS
Dean of Students: Dr GLENN SMITH
Registrar: MICKIE BUSH
Librarian: BRENT MAI
Number of teachers: 60
Number of students: 1,600

DEANS
College of Education: Dr JOSEPH MANNION
College of Theology, Arts and Sciences: Dr CHARLES J. KUNERT
School of Management: Dr ANN WIDMER

CORBAN COLLEGE

5000 Deer Park Dr., SE, Salem, OR 97317-9392
Internet: www.corban.edu
Founded 1935 as Bible Institute; Western Baptist College 1978; present name 2005
Private control
Academic year: August to April
Pres.: RENO R. HOFF
Provost: LINDA L. SAMEK
Vice-Pres. for Advancement: MICHAEL BATES
Vice-Pres. for Business: CHRIS D. ERICKSON
Vice-Pres. for Marketing: J. STEVEN HUNT
Vice-Pres. for Student Life: NANCY HEDBERG
Dean of Education: D. MATTHEW LUCAS
Number of teachers: 60
Number of students: 900
Publication: *Corban News* (4 a year).

EASTERN OREGON UNIVERSITY

1 University Blvd, La Grande, OR 97850
Telephone: (541) 962-3672
Fax: (541) 962-3113
E-mail: dheinzma@eou.edu
Internet: www.eou.edu
Founded 1929
Academic year: July to June
Pres.: Dr KHOSROW FATEMI
Provost and Vice-Pres. for Academic Affairs: JOHN MILLER
Vice-Pres. for Business, Finance and Facilities: VIRGINIA KEY
Vice-Pres. for Student Affairs: Dr SHELDON NORD
Dean of College of Arts and Sciences: MARILYN LEVINE
Dean of Colleges of Education and Business: MICHAEL JAEGER
Dean of Div. of Distance Education: MICHAEL CANNON
Dir of Libraries: KAREN CLAY
Library of 154,000 vols
Number of teachers: 170
Number of students: 3,338

DEANS
School of Arts and Sciences: SARAH WITTE
School of Education and Business Programs: MICHAEL JAEGER
Distance Education: Dr MICHAEL CANNON

EUGENE BIBLE COLLEGE

2155 Bailey Hill Rd, Eugene, OR 97405
E-mail: admissions@ebc.edu
Internet: www.ebc.edu
Private control
Academic year: September to June
Pres.: Dr DAVID COLE
Academic Dean: Dr LARRY BURKE
Registrar: Dr JAMES WICK
Librarian: N. PRISCILLA CAMERON
Number of teachers: 15
Number of students: 175

GEORGE FOX UNIVERSITY

Newberg, OR 97132-2697
Telephone: (503) 538-8383
Fax: (503) 537-3830
Internet: www.georgefox.edu
Founded 1891
Academic year: September to April
Pres.: Dr ROBIN E. BAKER
Dir of Enrollment Services: DALE SEIPP
Provost: PATRICK ALLEN
Vice-Pres. for Advancement: SHARI SCALES
Vice-Pres. for Finance: MICHAEL GOINS
Vice-Pres. for Marketing Communications: ROB WESTERVELT
Vice-Pres. for Student Life: BRAD LAU
Librarian: MERRILL JOHNSON
Library of 200,000 vols
Number of teachers: 379
Number of students: 3,484
Publications: *George Fox Journal* (3 a year), *Life* (4 a year).

LEWIS AND CLARK COLLEGE

0615 SW Palatine Hill Rd, Portland, OR 97219
Telephone: (503) 768-7000
Fax: (503) 768-7055
E-mail: iso@lclark.edu
Internet: www.lclark.edu
Founded 1867
Pres.: BARRY GLASSNER
Dean of College of Arts and Sciences: JANE HUNTER
Dean of Graduate School: SCOTT FLETCHER
Dean of Law School: ROBERT KLONOFF
Vice-Pres. for Business and Finance: CARL B. VANCE
Vice-Pres. for Institutional Advancement: GREG VOLK
Registrar: DIANE CRABTREE
Dir of Library: JAMES KOPP
Library of 477,010 vols
Number of teachers: 191
Number of students: 3,500
Publication: *Journal*.

LINFIELD COLLEGE

900 SE Baker St, McMinnville, OR 97128-6894
Telephone: (503) 883-2213
Fax: (503) 883-2630
E-mail: admission@linfield.edu
Internet: www.linfield.edu
Founded 1849
Academic year: September to May
Pres.: Dr THOMAS L. HELLIE
Assoc. Vice-Pres.: BONNIE SAUCIER
Vice-Pres. for Academic Affairs: Dr SUSAN AGRE-KIPPENHAN
Vice-Pres. for College Relations: BRUCE WYATT
Vice-Pres. for Finance and Admin.: W. GLENN FORD
Vice-Pres. for Student Affairs: SUSAN HOPP
Vice-Pres. for Enrollment Services: DAN PRESTON
Registrar: EILEEN BOURASSA
Library of 135,000 vols
Number of teachers: 273 (138 full-time, 135 part-time)
Number of students: 2,313 (full-time)

MARYLHURST UNIVERSITY

17600 Pacific Highway, POB 261, Marylhurst, OR 97036-0261
Telephone: (503) 636-8141
Fax: (503) 636-9526
E-mail: admissions@marylhurst.edu
Internet: www.marylhurst.edu
Private control
Pres.: Dr JUDITH JOHANSEN
Provost: Dr DAVID PLOTKIN
Vice-Pres. for Finance and Admin.: MICHAEL LAMMERS
Vice-Pres. for Human Resources: JANET WILLIAMS
Vice-Pres. for Univ. Advancement: DAVID DICKSON
Number of teachers: 265
Number of students: 1,802

MULTNOMAH BIBLE COLLEGE

8435 Northeast Glisan St, Portland, OR 97220
Telephone: (503) 255-0332
Fax: (503) 254-1268
E-mail: admiss@multnomah.edu
Internet: www.multnomah.edu
Founded 1936 as Multnomah School of the Bible; present name 1994
Private control
Academic year: August to May
Pres.: Dr DANIEL R. LOCKWOOD
Academic Dean and Vice-Pres.: Dr WAYNE STRICKLAND
Vice-Pres. and Dir of Information Systems: Dr JOE WONG
Dean of Student Services: MATTHEW RYGG
Registrar: Prof. AMY STEPHENS
Dir of Library: Dr PHILIP JOHNSON
Number of teachers: 33
Number of students: 595

NORTHWEST CHRISTIAN COLLEGE

828 East 11th Ave, Eugene, OR 97401
Telephone: (541) 343-1641
Fax: (541) 343-9159
E-mail: admissions@nwcc.edu
Internet: www.nwcc.edu
Founded 1895
Academic year: September to June
Pres.: DAVID W. WILSON
Vice-Pres. for Academic Affairs: DENNIS LINDSAY
Library Dir: STEVE SILVER
Library of 65,000 vols
Number of teachers: 21
Number of students: 500

OREGON HEALTH SCIENCES UNIVERSITY

3181 Southwest Sam Jackson Park Rd, Portland, OR 97239-3098
Telephone: (503) 494-8311
Internet: www.ohsu.edu
Pres.: Dr PETER O. KOHLER
Chief Financial Officer: BRADLEY N. KING
Exec. Vice-Pres.: STEVEN D. STADUM
Library of 180,000 vols

DEANS
School of Dentistry: JACK CLINTON
School of Medicine: MARK RICHARDSON
School of Nursing: SANDY THEIS

OREGON STATE UNIVERSITY

Corvallis, OR 97331
Telephone: (541) 737-0123
Fax: (541) 737-2400
E-mail: osuadmit@oregonstate.edu

Internet: oregonstate.edu
Founded 1858
State control
Academic year: September to June
Pres.: EDWARD J. RAY
Provost and Exec. Vice-Pres.: SABAH U. RANDHAWA
Vice-Pres. for Finance and Admin.: MARK E. MCCAMBRIDGE
Vice-Pres. for Research: JOHN M. CASSADY
Vice-Pres. for Univ. Advancement: LUANNE LAWRENCE
Vice-Provost for Academic Affairs and Int. Programmes: REBECCA L. JOHNSON
Vice-Provost for Student Affairs: LARRY D. ROPER
Registrar: BARBARA S. BALZ
Univ. Librarian: KARYLE BUTCHER
Library of 1,403,451 vols, 1,905,093 microfilms
Number of teachers: 1,231
Number of students: 19,162
Publications: *Beaver* (1 a year), *Oregon Agricultural Progress* (3 a year), *Oregon Stater* (3 a year), *Prism* (literary magazine, 1 a year), *Research OSU* (1 a year)

DEANS

College of Agricultural Sciences: SONNY RAMASWAMY
College of Business: ILLENE K. KLEINSORGE
College of Engineering: RONALD L. ADAMS
College of Forestry: HAL SALWASSER
College of Health and Human Sciences: TAMMY M. BRAY
College of Liberal Arts: KAY F. SCHAFFER
College of Oceanic and Atmospheric Sciences: MARK R. ABBOTT
College of Pharmacy: WAYNE A. KRADJAN
College of Science: SHERMAN H. BLOOMER
College of Veterinary Medicine: HOWARD P. GELBERG
Graduate School: SALLY K. FRANCIS
School of Education: SAM STERN
Univ. Honours College: JON A. HENDRICKS

PACIFIC NORTHWEST COLLEGE OF ART

1241 Northwest Johnson, Portland, OR 97209
Telephone: (503) 226-4391
Fax: (503) 226-3587
E-mail: admissions@pnca.edu
Internet: www.pnca.edu
Private control
Academic year: September to May
Pres.: Dr THOMAS MANLEY
Vice-Pres. for Academic Affairs: GREG WARE
Vice-Pres. for Finance and Admin.: NANCY BARROWS
Dir of Advancement: SUZANNE HASHIM
Registrar: JENNIFER DEKALB
Library Dir: RACHEL MENDEZ
Number of teachers: 50
Number of students: 300

PACIFIC UNIVERSITY

College Way, Forest Grove, OR 97116
Telephone: (503) 352-6151
Internet: www.pacificu.edu
Founded 1849
Pres.: LESLEY HALLICK
Vice-Pres. for Academic Affairs: WILLARD M. KNIEP
Registrar: TANIA M. HAND
Dir of Admissions: JON-ERIK LARSEN
Library Management Team Coordinator: ALEX TOTH
Library of 135,360 vols, 130,086 US documents, 1,670 Oregon documents
Number of teachers: 79 (full-time)
Number of students: 1,750 (full-time)

PORTLAND STATE UNIVERSITY

POB 751, Portland, OR 97207-0751
Telephone: (503) 725-6411
Fax: (503) 725-4882
E-mail: askadm@mail_pdx.edu
Internet: www.pdx.edu
Founded 1946
Academic year: September to June
Pres.: Prof. MICHAEL REARDON
Provost and Vice-Pres. for Academic Affairs: ROY KOCH
Vice-Pres. for Finance and Admin.: LINDSAY DESROCHERS
Vice-Provost and Dean of Extended Studies: MICHAEL BURTON
Vice-Provost for Graduate Studies and Research: WILLIAM FEYERHERM
Vice-Provost for Student Affairs: DAN FORTMILLER
Dir of Financial Aid: PHILLIP RODGERS
Dir of Institutional Research and Planning: KATHI KETCHESON
Assoc. Vice-Pres. for Information Technology: MARK GREGORY
Dir of Library: HELEN SPALDING
Library of 1,805,336 vols
Number of teachers: 1,260
Number of students: 24,284

DEANS

College of Liberal Arts and Sciences: MARVIN KAISER
College of Urban and Public Affairs: LAWRENCE WALLACK
School of Business Administration: SCOTT DAWSON
School of Engineering and Applied Science: ROBERT DRYDEN
School of Extended Studies: MICHAEL BURTON
School of Fine and Performing Arts: ROBERT SYLVESTER
Graduate School of Education: PHYLLIS EDMUNDSON
Graduate School of Social Work: KRISTINE NELSON

REED COLLEGE

3203 Southeast Woodstock Blvd, Portland, OR 97202-8199
Telephone: (503) 771-1112
Fax: (503) 777-7769
Internet: www.reed.edu
Founded 1908
Pres.: COLIN S. DIVER
Vice-Pres. and Dean of Student Services: MARY CATHERINE KING
Vice-Pres. and Treas.: EDWIN O. MCFARLANE
Vice-Pres. for College Relations: HUGH PORTER
Registrar: NORA MCLAUGHLIN
Dean of Admissions: PAUL MARTHERS
Dean of the Faculty: PETER J. STEINBERGER
Dir of Computing and Information Systems: ETHAN J. BENATAN
Dir of Institutional Research: JON W. RIVENBURG
Librarian: VICTORIA HANAWALT
Library of 490,000 vols
Number of teachers: 132
Number of students: 1,396

SOUTHERN OREGON UNIVERSITY

1250 Siskiyou Blvd, Ashland, OR 97520
Telephone: (541) 552-6111
Fax: (541) 552-6337
Internet: www.sou.edu
Founded 1926
Academic year: September to June
Pres.: MARY CULLINAN
Registrar: MICHAEL CORCORAN
Provost: EDWIN L. BATTISTELLA
Library Dir: TERESA MONTGOMERY
Library of 375,000 vols incl. bound periodicals, 200,000 govt documents, 600,000 items on microfilm
Number of teachers: 288
Number of students: 5,478

UNIVERSITY OF OREGON

Eugene, OR 97403-1242
Telephone: (541) 346-3111
Fax: (541) 346-2537
E-mail: fdyke@oregon.uoregon.edu
Internet: www.uoregon.edu
Founded 1872
State control
Academic year: September to June
Pres.: DAVE FROHNMAYER
Sr Vice-Pres. and Provost: LINDA P. BRADY
Vice-Pres. for Academic Affairs: RUSSELL S. TOMLIN
Vice-Pres. for Finance and Admin.: FRANCES DYKE
Vice-Pres. for Public and Govt Affairs: MICHAEL REDDING
Vice-Pres. for Research: RICHARD W. LINTON
Vice-Pres. for Student Affairs: MICHAEL E. EYSTER
Registrar: HERBERT R. CHERECK
Dean of Libraries: DEBORAH CARVER
Library: see Libraries
Number of teachers: 1,168
Number of students: 17,207
Publications: *Bulletin of the Museum of Natural History*, *Comparative Literature*, *Governmental Research Bulletins*, *Imprint Oregon*, *Northwest Review*, *Oregon Business Review* (4 a year), *Oregon Law Review*

DEANS

Graduate School: MARIAN FRIESTAD
College of Arts and Sciences: JOE A. STONE
College of Business Administration: DALE MORSE
College of Education: MARTIN KAUFMAN
School of Architecture and Allied Arts: ROBERT MELNICK
School of Journalism: TIMOTHY GLEASON
School of Law: RENNARD STRICKLAND
School of Music: ANNE DHU MCLUCAS

PROFESSORS

ACRES, A. J., Art History
AGUIRRE, C. A., History
AIKENS, C. M., Anthropology
ALBAUM, G. S., Business
ALBERTGALTIER, A., Romance Languages
ALLEY, H. M., Honours College
ALPERT, L. J., Fine Arts
ALTMANN, B., Romance Languages
ANDERSON, F. W., Mathematics
ANDERSON, M. C., Psychology
ANDERSON, S. C., German
ANDERSON-INMAN, L., Education Policy and Management
AOKI, K., Law
ARIOLA, Z., Computer and Information Science
ASH, A. D., Political Science
AXLINE, M. D., Law
AYRES, W. S., Anthropology
BALDWIN, D. A., Psychology
BALDWIN, J. H., Planning Public Policy Management
BAMBURY, J. E., Architecture
BARACCHI, C., Philsophy
BARKAN, A., Biology
BARNES, B. A., Mathematics
BARNHARD, R. J., Chemistry
BARR, S. A., Dance
BARTLEIN, P., Geography

BARTON, R. F., Theatre Arts
BAUGH, W. H., Political Science
BAUMGOLD, D. J., Political Science
BAYLESS, M. J., English
BELITZ, D., Physics
BENDER, S. W., Law
BENGSTON, M. C., Fine Arts
BENNETT, R. W., Music
BENZ, M. R., Education Policy and Management
BERK, G. P., Political Science
BEST, R. J., Business
BEUDERT, M. C., Music
BIERSACK, A., Anthropology
BIRN, R. F., History
BIVINS, T. H., Journalism
BJERRE, C., Law
BLANDY, D. E., Arts and Admin.
BLONIGEN, B. A., Economics
BOGEL, C. J., Art History
BOLTON, C. R., Recreation and Tourist Management
BONDS, A. B., Theatre Arts
BONINE, J. E., Law
BOREN, J. L., English
BOROVSKY, Z. P., German
BOSS, J. F., III, Music
BOTHUN, G. D., Physics
BOTVINNIK, B., Mathematics
BOUSH, D. M., Business
BOWDITCH, P. L., Classics
BOWERMAN, B. A., Biology
BOYNTON, S. L., Music
BRADSHAW, W. E., Biology
BRANCHAUD, B. P., Chemistry
BRAU, J. E., Physics
BRICK, H., History
BRICKER, D. D., Special Education
BRODIE, D. W., Law
BROKAW, C. J., History
BROWN, G. Z., Architecture
BROWN, S. T., East Asian Languages
BROWN, W. B., Business
BROX, R. M., Romance Languages
BULLIS, M. D., Education Policy and Management
BURRIS, V. L., Sociology
BUSTAMANTE, C. J., Chemistry
BYBEE, C. R., Journalism
BYRD, B. K., Labour Education Center
CALHOON, K. S., German
CALIN, F. G., Romance Languages
CAMPBELL, E. A., Music
CAPALDI, R. A., Biology
CARMICHAEL, H. J., Physics
CARNINE, D. W., Education Policy and Management
CARPENTER, G. M., Recreation and Tourism Management
CARPENTER, K. L., Linguistics
CARROLL, G. C., Biology
CARTER, L. R., Sociology
CARTIER, C. L., Geography
CARTWRIGHT, V., Architecture
CASHMAN, K. V., Geological Sciences
CASTENHOLZ, R. W., Biology
CASTILLO, D., Romance Languages
CHALMERS, J. M., Business
CHANDLER, V. L., Biology
CHANEY, R. P., Anthropology
CHATFIELD, S. J., Dance
CHENG, N. YEN-WEN, Architecture
CINA, J., Chemistry
CLARK, R., Music
CLARK, S., English
COGAN, F. B., Honours College
COHEN, J. D., Physics
COHEN, S. E., Geography
COLEMAN, E. L., II, English
COLLIN, R. M., Law
COLLINS, P. F., Psychology
CONERY, J. S., Computer and Information Science
CONLEY, D. T., Education Policy and Management
CORNER, D. B., Architecture
CRAIG, J. P., Dance
CROSSWHITE, J. R., English
CRUMB, D. R., Music
CRUZ, J., Romance Languages
CSONKA, P. L., Physics
CUNY, J., Computer and Information Science
DAHLQUIST, F. W., Chemistry
DANN, L. Y., Business
DARST, R. G., Political Science
DAVIE, W. E., Philosophy
DAVIES, P. H., Creative Writing
DAVIS, H., Architecture
DAVIS, R. L., Romance Languages
DAWSON, J. I., Political Science
DEGGE, R. M., Arts and Admin.
DELANCEY, S. C., Linguistics
DELGUERCIO, D. G., Business
DENNIS, M., History
DESCUTNER, J. W., Dance
DESHPANDE, N. G., Physics
DEVRIES, P. J., Biology
DIAMOND, I., Political Science
DICKMAN, A. W., Biology
DIETHELM, J. K., Landscape Architecture
DISHION, T. J., Special Education
DOERKSEN, D. P., Music
DOERKSEN, P. F., Music
DOLEZAL, M.-L., Art History
DORSEY, R. J., Geological Science
DOUGLAS, S. A., Computer and Information Science
DOWD, C. R., Music
DOWNES, B. T., Planning Public Policy Management
DOXSEE, K. M., Chemistry
DREILING, M. C., Sociology
DUFEK, J. S., Exercise and Movement Sciences
DUFF, S. F., Architecture
DUGAW, D. M., English
DUNCAN, I. H., English
DURRANT, S., East Asian Languages
DYER, M. N., Mathematics
DYKE, T. R., Chemistry
EARL, J. W., English
EDSON, C. H., Education Policy and Management
EISEN, J. S., Biology
ELLIS, C. J., Economics
EMLET, R. B., Biology
ENGELKING, P. C., Chemistry
EPPLE, J. A., Romance Languages
EPPS, G., Law
EPSTEIN, M., East Asian Languages
ERLANDSON, J. M., Anthropology
ETTINGER, L. F., Arts and Admin.
EVANS, G. W., Economics
EXTON, D., Chemistry
FAGOT, B. I., Psychology
FAIR, L. J., History
FANG, Y., Business
FARLEY, A. M., Computer and Information Science
FARWELL, M. R., English
FICKAS, S. F., Computer and Information Science
FIGLIO, D. N., Economics
FISHLEN, M. B., East Asian Languages
FLYNN, G. C., Chemistry
FORD, K. J., English
FORELL, C. A., Law
FOSTER, J. B., Sociology
FRACCHIA, J. G., Honours College
FRANK, D. A., Honours College
FRANKLIN, J. D., Journalism
FRAZIER, G. V., Business
FREINKEL, L. A., English
FREY, R. E., Physics
FREYD, J. J., Psychology
FRIESTAD, M. S., Business
FRISHKOFF, P., Business
FRY, G., International Studies
FUJII, N., East Asian Languages
FULLER, L. O., Sociology
GAGE, J. T., English
GALE, M. K., Planning Public Policy Management
GALL, M. D., Education Policy and Management
GARCIA-PABON, L., Romance Languages
GARY, S. N., Law
GASSAMA, I. J., Law
GAST, W. G., Architecture
GENASCI, D. B., Architecture
GEORGE, K. M., Anthropology
GEORGE, O., English
GERBER, T. P., Sociology
GERNON, H., Business
GERSTEN, R. M., Special Education
GILKEY, P. B., Mathematics
GILLAND, W. G., Architecture
GIRLING, C. L., Landscape Architecture
GIVON, T., Linguistics
GLADHART, A., Romance Languages
GLASER, S. R., Business
GLEASON-RICKER, M. M., Education Policy and Management
GLOVER, E., Special Education
GOBLE, A. E., History
GOLDMAN, M. S., Sociology
GOLDMAN, P., Education Policy and Management
GOLDRICH, D., Political Science
GOLDSCHMIDT, S. M., Education Policy and Management
GOLES, G. G., Geological Sciences
GOOD, R. H. III, Special Education
GOODMAN, D., History
GORDON-LICKEY, B., Psychology
GORDON-LICKEY, M., Psychology
GOULD, E., Romance Languages
GRAFF, R. J., Fine Arts
GRAY, J., Biology
GRAY, J. A., Economics
GREENE, F. D., Law
GREENE, R. A., Comparative Literature
GREENLAND, D. E., Geography
GREGORY, S., Physics
GRIFFITH, O. H., Chemistry
GROSENICK, J. K., Education Policy and Management
GRUDIN, R., English
GWARTNEY, P., Sociology
HACKMAN, R. M., Academic Affairs
HALEY, M. M., Chemistry
HANES, J. E., History
HARBAUGH, W. T., Economics
HARFORD, W. T., Business
HARRIS, L. J., Law
HARVEY, S. M., Anthropology
HASKETT, R. S., History
HATON, D. S., Music
HAUSHALTER, G. D., Business
HAWKINS, D. I., Business
HAWLEY, D. K., Chemistry
HAWN, A. W., Architecture
HAYDOCK, R., Physics
HAYNES, S. E., Economics
HECKER, S. F., Labour Education Center
HELPHAND, K. I., Landscape Architecture
HERRICK, D. R., Chemistry
HESSLER, J. M., History
HIBBARD, J., Planning Public Policy Management
HIBBARD, M. J., Planning Public Policy Management
HICKMAN, R. C., Fine Arts
HILDRETH, R. G., Law
HINTZMAN, D. L., Psychology
HO, S., Architecture
HODGES, S. D., Psychology
HOKANSON, K. E., Comparative Literature
HOLCOMB, J. M., Fine Arts
HOLLAND, M. J., Law
HOLLANDER, J. A., Sociology
HONGO, G. K., Creative Writing
HORNER, R. H., Center on Human Devt
HOSAGRAHAR, J., Architecture
HOUSWORTH, E. A., Mathematics
HOWARD, D. R., Business
HUDSON, B. S., Chemistry

HUHNDORF, S. M., English
HULSE, D. W., Landscape Architecture
HUMMER, T. R., Creative Writing
HUMPHREYS, E. D., Geological Sciences
HURWIT, J. M., Art History
HURWITZ, R., Music
HUTCHINSON, J., Chemistry
HYMAN, R., Psychology
IMAMURA, J. N., Physics
ISENBERG, J., Mathematics
JACOBS, D., Political Science
JACOBSON, J. L., Law
JACOBSON-TEPFER, E., Art History
JAEGER, M. K., Classics
JEWETT, W. J., Architecture
JOHNSON, B. R., Landscape Architecture
JOHNSON, D. C., Chemistry
JOHNSON, L. B., Fine Arts
JOHNSON, L. T., Architecture
JOHNSON, M. L., Philosophy
JOHNSTON, A. D., Geological Sciences
JONES, B. J. K., Arts and Admin.
JONES, S. I., Landscape Architecture
KAHLE, L. R., Business
KAMEENUI, E. J., Education Policy and Management
KANAGY, R., East Asian Languages
KANTOR, W. M., Mathematics
KARLYN, K., English
KATAOKA, H. C., East Asian Languages
KAYS, M. A., Geological Sciences
KEANA, J. F. W., Chemistry
KELLETT, R. W., Architecture
KELLMAN, M. E., Chemistry
KELSKY, K. L., Anthropology
KEMPNER, K. M., Education Policy and Management
KESSLER, L. J., Journalism
KEVAN, S. D., Physics
KEYES, P. A., Architecture
KIMBALL, R. A., History
KIMBLE, D. P., Psychology
KIMMEL, C. B., Biology
KING, R. D., Business
KINTZ, L. C., English
KIRKPATRICK, L. C., Law
KLESHCHEV, A., Mathematics
KLOPPENBERG, L. A., Law
KLUG, G. A., Exercise and Movement Sciences
KOCH, R. M., Mathematics
KOHL, S. W., East Asian Languages
KOKIS, G., Fine Arts
KOLPIN, V. W., Economics
KOREISHA, S. G., Business
KRAMER, D. F., Music
KRAUS, R. C., Political Science
KRUSOE, S., Fine Arts
KYR, R. H., Music
LAFER, G. C., Labour Education
LANDE, R., Biology
LARSON, S., Music
LARSON, S. J., English
LARSON, W. A., East Asian Languages
LASKAYA, C. A., English
LAUX, D. L., Creative Writing
LAVERY, R. M., Journalism
LAWRENCE, M. S., Law
LEAHY, J. V., Mathematics
LEE, C.-R., Creative Writing
LEES, C. A., English
LEFEVRE, H. W., Physics
LEONG, A., Russian
LESAGE, J. L., English
LEVI, D. S., Philosophy
LIBERMAN, K. B., Sociology
LIBESKIND, S., Mathematics
LIN, H., Mathematics
LIVELYBROOKS, D. W., Physics
LO, V. M., Computer and Information Science
LOCKERY, S. R., Biology
LONERGAN, M., Chemistry
LONG, J. W., Chemistry
LOVINGER, R. J., Landscape Architecture
LOWENSTAM, S. D., Classics
LUCKTENBERG, K., Music
LUEBKE, D. M., History
LUKACS, J. R., Anthropology
LUKS, E. M., Computer and Information Science
LYNCH, M. R., Biology
LYONS, R. M., Creative Writing
LYSAKER, J. T., Philosophy
MCCOLE, J. J., History
MCDOWELL, P. F., Geography
MCGOWEN, R. E., History
MCKERNIE, G., Theatre Arts
MCLAUCHLAN, G., Sociology
MCWHIRTER, B. T., Behaviour and Communication Sciences
MCWHIRTER, E. H., Behaviour and Communication Sciences
MADDEX, J. P., Jr, History
MADRIGAL, R., Business
MAITLAND-GHOLSON, J. C., Arts and Admin.
MALLE, B. F., Psychology
MALLINCKRODT, B. S., Counselling Psychology
MALONY, A., Computer and Information Science
MALSCH, D. L., Linguistics
MANCE, A. M., English
MANGA, M., Geological Sciences
MARCUS, A. H., Chemistry
MARROCCO, R. T., Psychology
MARTIN, G. M., Music
MARTINS, E., Biology
MATE, M., History
MATHAS, A., German
MATSUNAGA, S. R., Business
MATTHEWS, B. W., Physics
MATTHEWS, K. M., Architecture
MAURO, R., Psychology
MAVES, L. C., Jr, Music
MAXWELL, A., Journalism
MAY, B. D., Romance Languages
MAY, G. A., History
MEDLER, J. F., Political Science
MEEKS-WAGNER, D. R., Biology
MELONE, N. P., Business
MERSKIN, D. L., Journalism
MEYER, A. D., Business
MEYER, G. W., Computer and Information Science
MIKKELSON, W. H., Business
MILLS, P. K., Business
MITCHELL, R. B., Political Science
MOHR, J. C., History
MONROE, S. M., Psychology
MOONEY, R. J., Law
MOORE, J. R., Music
MOORE, R. S., Music
MORENO-BLACK, G., Anthropology
MORGEN, S. L., Sociology
MORROGH, A., Art History
MORSE, D. C., Business
MOSES, L., Psychology
MOSS, M. L., Anthropology
MOSSBERG, T. W., Physics
MOURSUND, D. G., Education Policy and Management
MOURSUND, J. P., Counselling Psychology
MOWDAY, R. T., Business
MOYE, G. W., Architecture
MURPHY, A. B., Geography
MYAGKOV, M. G., Political Science
NATELLA, D. C., Fine Arts
NEAL, L. L., Recreation and Tourism Management
NEVILLE, H., Psychology
NICHOLSON, K., Art History
NICOLS, J., History
NIPPOLD, M. A., Special Education
NOVKOV, J. L., Political Science
O'BRIEN, R. M., Sociology
O'CONNELL, K. R., Fine Arts
O'FALLON, J. M., Law
O'KEEFE, T., Business
ORBELL, J. M., Political Science
OSTERNIG, L. R., Exercise and Movement Sciences
OSTLER, J., History
OVERLEY, J. C., Physics
OWEN, H. J., Music
OWEN, S. W., Music
PAGE, C. J., Chemistry
PAINTER, R. W., Law
PALMER, T. W., Mathematics
PAN, Y., Business
PARIS, M. L., Law
PARK, K., Physics
PARTCH, M. M., Business
PASCOE, P. A., History
PAUL, K. H., Fine Arts
PAYNE, D. L., Linguistics
PENA, R. B., Architecture
PEPPIS, P. W., English
PETING, D. L., Architecture
PETTINARI, J. A., Architecture
PHILLIPS, N. C., Mathematics
PICKETT, B. S., Fine Arts
PIELE, P. K., Education Policy and Management
POLOGE, S., Music
PONDER, S. E., Journalism
PONTO, R. D., Music
POPE, B. C., Women's Studies
POPE, D. A., History
POSNER, M. I., Psychology
POSTLETHWAIT, J. H., Biology
POVEY, D. C., Planning Public Policy Management
POWELL, D. T., Fine Arts
PRATT, S. L., Philosophy
PRENTICE, M. H., Fine Arts
PROSKUROWSKI, A., Computer and Information Science
PROUDFOOT, R. C., International Studies
PSAKI, F. R., Romance Languages
PYLE, F. B., III, English
RACETTE, G. A., Business
RAISKIN, J. L., Women's Studies
RAMIREZ, E. C., Theatre Arts
RAMSING, K. D., Business
RAVITS, M. A., Women's Studies
RAYFIELD, G. W., Physics
RAYMER, M. G., Physics
RECKER, G. W., Music
REED, M. H., Geological Sciences
REMINGTON, S. J., Physics
RETALLACK, G. J., Geological Sciences
REYNOLDS, J. S., Architecture
RIBE, R. G., Landscape Architecture
RICE, J. L., Russian
RICE, J. M., Geological Sciences
RICE, K. S., Physical Education and Recreation Services
RICHARDS, L. E., Business
RICHMOND, G. L., Chemistry
ROBERTS, W. M., Biology
ROBINSON, D. M., Journalism
ROCHA, E., Planning Public Policy Management
ROCKETT, G. W., English
RONDEAU, J. F., History
ROSE, J., Theatre Arts
ROSS, K. A., Mathematics
ROSSI, W. J., English
ROTH, L. M., Art History
ROTHBART, M., Psychology
ROTHBART, M. K., Psychology
ROWE, G. E., English
ROWELL, J., Architecture
RUSH, K. L., Behaviour and Communication Sciences
RUSSIAL, J. T., Journalism
RUSSO, M. V., Business
RYAN, C. C., Philosophy
RYAN, W. E., II, Journalism
SABRY, A., Computer and Information Science
SADOFSKY, H., Mathematics
SANG, T., East Asian Languages
SARANPA, K., German
SAUCIER, G. T., Psychology
SAYRE, G. M., English
SCHACHTER, J., Linguistics
SCHOMBERT, J. M., Physics

SCHULTZ, K. L., German
SCHUMAN, D., Law
SCHWARZ, I. E., Special Education
SEGALL, Z., Computer and Information Science
SEITZ, G. M., Mathematics
SELKER, E. U., Biology
SERCEL, P. C., Physics
SHANKMAN, S., English
SHANKS, A. L., Institute of Marine Biology
SHAO, Q. M., Mathematics
SHAPIRO, L., Biology
SHELTON, B. S., Mathematics
SHERER, P. D., Business
SHERIDAN, G. J., Jr, History
SHERMAN, S. R., English
SHINN, M. R., Special Education
SHURTZ, N. E., Law
SIERADSKI, A. J., Mathematics
SILVA, E. C., Economics
SILVERMAN, C. T., Anthropology
SIMMONS, D. C., Education Policy and Management
SIMMONS, W. S., Art History
SIMONDS, P. E., Anthropology
SIMONS, A. D., Psychology
SIMONSEN, W. S., Planning Public Policy Management
SINGELL, L. D., Jr, Economics
SISLEY, B. L., Physical Education and Recreation Services
SKALNES, L., Political Science
SLOVIC, P., Psychology
SMITH, J. R., Business
SMITH, M. E., Music
SOHLBERG, M. M., Behavioural and Communication Sciences
SOHLICH, W. F., Romance Languages
SOKOLOFF, D. R., Physics
SOPER, D. E., Physics
SOUTHWELL, P., Political Science
SPALTENSTEIN, J. N., Mathematics
SPRAGUE, G. F., Jr, Biology
SPRAGUE, K. U., Biology
STAHL, F. W., Biology
STAVITSKY, A. G., Journalism
STEEVES, H. L., Journalism
STEIN, A. J., Sociology
STEIN, R. L., English
STEINHARDT, V., Music
STEVENS, K. A., Computer and Information Science
STEVENS, T. H., Chemistry
STEVENSON, R. C., English
STOCKARD, A. J., Sociology
STOLET, J., Dance
STONE, J. A., Economics
STORMSHAK, E. A., Behaviour and Communication Sciences
STRAKA, L. M., Music
STROM, D. M., Physics
SUGAI, G. M., Education Policy and Management
SUNDT, R. A., Art History
SUTTMEIER, R. P., Political Science
SWAN, P. N., Law
SZURMUK, M., Romance Languages
TAKAHASHI, T. T., Biology
TAN, Y., Fine Arts
TAYLOR, M. E., Psychology
TAYLOR, Q., Jr, History
TEDARDS, A. B., Music
TEICH, N., English
TERBORG, J. R., Business
TERWILLIGER, N. B., Biology
THALLON, R., Architecture
THEODOROPOULOS, C., Architecture
THOMA, M. A., Economics
THOMAS, S., Mathematics
THOMPSON, A. C., Religious Studies
TICE, J. T., Architecture
TINDAL, G., Education Policy and Management
TIRAS, S. L., Business
TOKUNO, K., Religious Studies
TOMLIN, R., Linguistics
TONER, J., Physics
TOOMEY, D. R., Geological Sciences
TROMBLEY, R., Music
TUAN, M. H. C., Sociology
TUANA, N., Philosophy
TUBLITZ, N. J., Biology
TUCKER, D. M., Psychology
TYLER, D. R., Chemistry
UDOVIC, J. D., Biology
UNGSON, G. R., Business
UPSHAW, J. R., Journalism
UTSEY, G. F., Architecture
UTSEY, M. D., Architecture
VAKARELIYSKA, C., Russian
VANDENNOUWELAND, A., Economics
VANHEECKEREN, J., Business
VAN HOUTEN, D. R., Sociology
VAN SCHEEUWIJCK, M., Music
VARGAS, M., Music
VERSACE, G. T., Music
VETRI, D. R., Law
VITULLI, M. A., Mathematics
VLATTEN, A., German
VONHIPPEL, P. H., Chemistry
WACHTER, C. L., Music
WAFF, H. S., Geological Sciences
WAGLE, K. E., Fine Arts
WALKER, H. M., Center on Human Devt
WALKER, P. A., Geography
WANG, H., Physics
WANTA, W. M., Journalism
WARPINSKI, T. L., Fine Arts
WASKO, J., Journalism
WATSON, J. C., Theatre Arts
WEEKS, E. C., Planning Public Policy Management
WEEKS, J. C., Biology
WEINSTEIN, M. G., Business
WEISS, A. M., International Studies
WEISS, J., Romance Languages
WEISS, M. R., Exercise and Movement Sciences
WEISS, R. L., Psychology
WELCH, M. C., Architecture
WELDON, R. J., Geological Sciences
WELKE, B. Y., History
WESTERFIELD, M., Biology
WESTLING, L. H., English
WESTLING, W. T., Law
WESTON, J. A., Biology
WHEELER, T. H., Journalism
WHITELAW, W. E., Economics
WHITLOCK, C. L., Geography
WIDENOR, M. R., Labour Education Center
WILLIAMS, J. P., Music
WILLIAMS, J. R., Theatre Arts
WILLIS, J. H., III, Biology
WILSON, C. B., Computer and Information Science
WILSON, M. C., Classics
WILSON, W. W., Economics
WIXMAN, R., Geography
WOJCIK, D. N., English
WOLFE, A. S., East Asian Languages
WOLFE, J. M., Mathematics
WONHAM, H. B., English
WOOD, A. M., Biology
WOOD, M. C., Law
WOOD, M. E., English
WOOLLACOTT, M. H., Exercise and Movement Sciences
WRIGHT, C. R. B., Mathematics
WRIGHT, P. L., Business
WYBOURNE, M. N., Physics
XU, D., Mathematics
XU, Y., Mathematics
YOUNG, J. E., Architecture
YOUNG, M. T., Computer Science
YOUNG, P. D., Anthropology
YUZVINSKY, S., Mathematics
ZILIAK, J. P., Economics
ZIMMER, L. K., Architecture
ZIMMERMAN, R. L., Physics
ZINBARG, R., Psychology
ZUCK, O. V., German

ATTACHED INSTITUTES

Advanced Science and Technology Institute: Dir ROBERT MCQUATE.

Center for Asian and Pacific Studies: Dir STEPHAN DURRANT.

Center for Housing Innovation: Dir DONALD B. CORNER.

Center for the Study of Women in Society: Dir SANDRA MORGEN.

Center for the Study of Work, Economy and Community: Dir DONALD VAN HOUTEN.

Chemical Physics Institute: Dir DAVID HERRICK.

Computational Intelligence Research Laboratory: Dir DAVID ETHERINGTON.

Computational Science Institute: Dirs JOHN S. CONERY, JANICE CLUNY.

Institute for Community Arts: Dir DOUG BRANDY.

Institute for Sustainable Environment: Dir JOHN BALDWIN.

Institute of Cognitive and Decision Sciences: Dir SARAH DOUGLAS.

Institute of Molecular Biology: Dir FREDERICK DAHLQUIST.

Institute of Neurosciences: Dir MONTE WESTERFIELD.

Institute of Theoretical Science: Dir DAVISON SOPER.

Institute on Violence and Destructive Behavior: Dir HILL WALKER.

International Institute for Sports and Human Performance: Dir HENRIETTE HEINY.

Materials Science Institute: Dir DAVID JOHNSON.

Oregon Center for Optics: Dir MICHAEL RAYMER.

Oregon Humanities Center: Dir STEVEN SHANKMAN.

Oregon Institute of Marine Biology: Dir LYNDA SHAPIRO.

Solar Energy Center: Dir JOHN S. REYNOLDS.

UNIVERSITY OF PORTLAND

5000 North Willamette Blvd, Portland, OR 97203

Telephone: (503) 943-8000
Fax: (503) 943-7399
Internet: www.up.edu

Founded 1901
Private control
Language of instruction: English
Academic year: August to May

Pres.: Rev. E. WILLIAM BEAUCHAMP
Provost: Brother DONALD J. STABROWSKI
Vice-Pres. for Financial Affairs: ROY F. HEYNDERICKX
Vice-Pres. for Student Services: JOHN T. GOLDRICK
Vice-Pres. for Univ. Relations: Rev. THOMAS P. DOYLE
Registrar: BOBBI LINDAHL
Univ. Librarian: DREW HARRINGTON

Library of 360,000 vols
Number of teachers: 175
Number of students: 3,263

DEANS

Graduate School: Dr PATRICIA L. CHADWICK
College of Arts and Sciences: Dr MARLENE MOORE
School of Business Administration: Dr LAWRENCE LEWIS
School of Education: Sr MARIA CIRIELLO
School of Engineering: Dr ZIA YAMAYEE
School of Nursing: Dr TERRY MISENER

PROFESSORS

ADRANGI, B., Business Admin.
ALBRIGHT, R. J., Engineering
ARWOOD, E., Education
ASARNOW, H., English and Foreign Languages
ASKAY, R., Philosophy
BAILLIE, J., Philosophy
BOWEN, E., Drama
DOYLE, R. O., Music
DRAKE, B. H., Business Admin.
DUFF, R., Psychology and Social Science
FALLER, T., Philosophy
FAVERO, T., Biology
FREED, E., Business Admin.
GAYLE, B., Communication Studies
GRITTA, P. R., Business Admin.
HODDICK, J. P., Theatre
HOSINSKI, T., Theology
HOUCK, B., Biology
INAN, A., Engineering
KHAN, K. H., Engineering
KLESYNSKI, K., Music
KOLMES, S., Biology
LINCOLN, S., Chemistry
LUM, L., Mathematics and Computer Science
MALE, J., Engineering
MASSON, L., English
MONTO, M., Sociology
MURTY, D., Engineering
RUTHERFORD, H. R., Theology
SHANK, T., Business
SHERRER, C., English and Foreign Languages
SNOW, M., Physics
UTLAUT, M., Physics
WYNNE, A., Nursing

WARNER PACIFIC COLLEGE

2219 Southeast 68th Ave, Portland, OR 97215
Telephone: (503) 517-1000
Fax: (503) 517-1350
E-mail: admiss@warnerpacific.edu
Internet: www.warnerpacific.edu

Founded 1937
Academic year: August to May

Pres.: Dr JAY A. BARBER, Jr
Vice-Pres., Chief Operating Officer and Treas.: WAYNE PEDERSON
Vice-Pres. for Academic Affairs and Dean of Faculty: COLE DAWSON
Vice-Pres. for Institutional Advancement: ANDREA COOK
Registrar: TORI CUMMINGS
Gen. Library Admin.: ALICE KIENBERGER

Library of 53,000 vols
Number of teachers: 35
Number of students: 740

WESTERN OREGON UNIVERSITY

345 North Monmouth Ave, Monmouth, OR 97361
Telephone: (503) 838-8000
Fax: (503) 838-8474
E-mail: fultzk@wou.edu
Internet: www.wou.edu

Founded 1856 as Monmouth Univ.; present name 1997
Academic year: September to June

Pres.: Dr JOHN P. MINAHAN
Provost and Vice-Pres. for Academic Affairs: Dr JEM SPECTAR
Vice-Pres. for Student Affairs: Dr GARY L. DUKES
Registrar: NANCY FRANCE

Number of teachers: 150
Number of students: 4,850

DEANS

College of Education: Dr HILDA ROSSELLI
College of Liberal Arts and Sciences: Dr JAMES CHADNEY

WESTERN SEMINARY

5511 Southeast Hawthorne Blvd, Portland, OR 97215
Telephone: (503) 517-1800
E-mail: western@westernseminary.edu
Internet: www.westernseminary.edu

Campuses at Portland (OR) and San Jose (CA)
Private control
Academic year: September to April

Pres.: Dr BERT E. DOWNS
Academic Dean and Provost: Dr RANDAL R. ROBERTS
Vice-Pres. for Advancement: DUANE STOREY
Dean of Student Devt and Registrar: Dr ROBERT W. WIGGINS
Library Dir: Dr ROBERT A. KRUPP

Number of teachers: 40
Number of students: 675

WESTERN STATES CHIROPRACTIC COLLEGE

2900 Northeast 132nd Ave, Portland, OR 97230-3099
Telephone: (503) 256-3180
Fax: (503) 251-5723
E-mail: admissions@wschiro.edu
Internet: www.wschiro.edu

Founded 1904 as Marshes' School and Cure; present name 1967
Private control
Academic year: September to June

Pres.: Dr JOSEPH E. BRIMHALL

Number of teachers: 35
Number of students: 400

WILLAMETTE UNIVERSITY

900 State St, Salem, OR 97301
Telephone: (503) 370-6300
E-mail: communications@willamette.edu
Internet: www.willamette.edu

Founded 1842

Pres.: M. LEE PELTON
Registrar: THOMAS H. HIBBARD
Dir of Library: RICHARD BREEN

Library of 285,000 vols, 1,355 periodicals
Number of teachers: 145 (full-time)
Number of students: 2,300

Publications: *Atkinson Graduate School of Management Bulletin*, *College of Law Bulletin*, *Willamette College of Law Journal*, *Willamette Scene*, *Willamette University Bulletin*

DEANS

College of Law: ROBERT M. ACKERMAN
College of Liberal Arts: LAWRENCE D. CRESS
George H. Atkinson Graduate School of Management: DALE WEIGHT

PENNSYLVANIA

ALBRIGHT COLLEGE

POB 15234, Reading, PA 19612-5234
Telephone: (610) 921-2381
Fax: (610) 921-7530
Internet: www.albright.edu

Founded 1856

Pres.: LEX O. MCMILLAN, III
Dir of Admissions: GREGORY EICHHORN
Library Dir: ROSEMARY DEEGAN

Library of 240,000 vols
Number of teachers: 103
Number of students: 1,650

ALLEGHENY COLLEGE

520 N Main St, Meadville, PA 16335
Telephone: (814) 332-3100
Internet: www.allegheny.edu

Founded 1815
Academic year: September to May

Pres.: JAMES H. MULLEN, Jr
Dean: LINDA C. DEMERITT
Vice-Pres. for Devt and Alumni Affairs: MARJORIE KLEIN
Vice-Pres. for Finance and Planning: DAVID W. MCINALLY
Assoc. Vice-Pres. for Finance and Planning: LARRY K. LEE
Registrar: ANNE E. SHEFFIELD
Dir of Library: LINDA BILLS

Library of 922,540 vols
Number of teachers: 145 full-time
Number of students: 2,193

Publications: *Allegheny Magazine* (3 a year), *Allegheny Review* (1 a year), *Center for Economic and Environmental Development Newsletter*, *Civic Engagement Newsletter*, *Film Criticism* (3 a year), *Kaldron* (1 a year), *The Soapbox* (1 a year)

PROFESSORS

BARRY, MICHAEL J., Mathematics
BENSEL, TERRENCE, Environment Science
BOWDEN, RICHARD D., Environmental Science
BUCK, SUE, Art
BULMAN, JAMES C., English
BYWATER, WILLIAM G., Jr, Philosophy and Religious Studies
CASLER, STEPHEN D., Economics
CHIEN, ALEC F.-L., Music
CROSS, JEFFREY D., Psychology
CUPPER, ROBERT D., Computer Science
D'AMICO, DIANE, English
DELAMARTER, WILLIAM A., Psychology
DODGE, COURTENAY B., Modern and Classical Languages
ENSBERG, PETER, Modern and Classical Languages
GEFFEN, AMARA B., Art
GOLDSTEIN, DONALD, Economics
HEPLER, LOWELL E., Music
HEUCHERT, J. W. P., Psychology
HOLLAND, GLENN S., Philosophy and Religious Studies
JAMISON, WARD M., Music
KEELEY, MICHAEL N., Communication Arts/Theatre
LO BELLO, ANTHONY J., Mathematics
LYONS, STEPHEN M., History
MANIATES, MICHAEL F., Political Science
MICHAELS, LLOYD, English
MILLER, DAVID C., English
MUMME, RONALD L., Biology
NESSET, KIRK, English
OLSON, CARL, Philosophy and Religious Studies
OSTROFSKY, MILTON L., Biology
OZORAK, ELIZABETH W., Psychology
PALLANT, ERIC. T., Environmental Science
QUINN, LAURA, English
RAHMAN, SHAFIQUR M., Physics
RANKIN, SUSAN M., Biology
RICHTER, JOCHEN H., Modern and Classical Languages
ROLAND, GEORGE S., Art
SCHWARTZ, ROBERT K., Geology
SEDDIG, ROBERT G., Political Science
SERRA, MARTIN J., Chemistry
SHAPIRO, BARRY M., History
SHEA, DANIEL M., Political Science
SHEFFIELD, ANN E., Chemistry
SMITH, BRUCE J., Political Science
STATMAN, DAVID, Physics
TAMASHIRO, HOWARD, Political Science
TRECKEL, PAULA A., History
WILLEY, DANIEL R., Physics
WISSINGER, SCOTT A., Biology

WOLFE, PHILLIP J., Modern and Classical Languages

ALVERNIA COLLEGE

400 Saint Bernardine St, Reading, PA 19607-1799
Telephone: (610) 796-8220
E-mail: admissions@alvernia.edu
Internet: www.alvernia.edu
Founded 1958
Private control
Academic year: August to May
Pres.: Dr THOMAS F. FLYNN
Provost: Dr SHIRLEY J. WILLIAMS
Registrar: BEKI STEIN
Dean of Library and Educational Services: Dr MARTHA M. SMITH
Number of teachers: 65
Number of students: 2,136

AMERICAN COLLEGE

270 Bryn Mawr Ave, Bryn Mawr, PA 19010
Telephone: (610) 526-1000
Fax: (610) 526-1465
E-mail: studentservices@theamericancollege.edu
Internet: www.theamericancollege.edu
Founded 1927
Ind., non-traditional, distance-education instn; professional diplomas and designations, graduate degrees in the financial sciences and management
Private control (non-profit public charity)
Pres. and CEO: Dr LAURENCE BARTON
Sr Vice-Pres.: STEPHEN D. TARR
Exec. Vice-Pres.: Prof. H. KING MCGLAUGHON
Vice-Pres. for Academics and Dean: WALT J. WOERHEIDE
Vice-Pres. for Finance and Admin.: NEAL R. FEGELY
Vice-Pres. for Marketing: KEITH E. HICKERSON
Vice-Pres. for Sales: JACK C. HONDROS
Assoc. Vice-Pres. for Information Technology: EDWARD M. MCEVOY
Assoc. Vice-Pres. for Institutional Assessment: Dr JOHN W. BAJTELSMIT
Exec. Dir of Online Learning: BILLY L. WILLIAMS
Librarian: JUDITH L. HILL
Library of 13,000 vols, 600 periodicals
Number of teachers: 20
Number of students: 35,000 (part-time and non-resident)

ARCADIA UNIVERSITY

450 South Easton Rd, Glenside, PA 19038-3295
Telephone: (215) 572-2900
Fax: (215) 572-0240
E-mail: admiss@arcadia.edu
Internet: www.arcadia.edu
Founded 1853
Academic year: September to May
Pres.: Dr JERRY M. GREINER
Registrar: BILL ELNICK
Vice-Pres. for Technology and Chief Information Officer: PARAM BEDI
Library of 136,900 vols, 56,940 microforms
Number of teachers: 304
Number of students: 3,600
Publications: *Arcadia Bulletin*, *Arcadia Herald*, *Landmarks*.

BAPTIST BIBLE COLLEGE AND SEMINARY

538 Venard Rd, Clarks Summit, PA 18411
Telephone: (570) 586-2400
E-mail: info@bbc.edu
Internet: www.bbc.edu
Private control
Academic year: August to May
Pres.: JAMES JEFFERY
Seminary Dean and Vice-Pres. for Seminary Academics: HOWARD BIXBY
Vice-Pres. for Alumni Services and Summer Ministries: JIM HUCKABY
Vice-Pres. for Business and Finance: HAL CROSS
Vice-Pres. for College Academics: Dr BARRY PHILLIPS
Vice-Pres. for College and Graduate School Academics: JIM LYTLE
Vice-Pres. for Communications: TOM GATTORNA
Vice-Pres. for Enrollment Management: GLENN AMOS
Vice-Pres. for Institutional Advancement: Dr DENNIS TOCCI
Vice-Pres. for Student Devt: Dr FRIEDIE LOESCHER
Number of teachers: 47
Number of students: 1,142 (983 undergraduate, 159 postgraduate)

BRYN ATHYN COLLEGE OF THE NEW CHURCH

2695 College Dr., POB 717, Bryn Athyn, PA 19009
Telephone: (267) 502-2400
Fax: (267) 502-2593
E-mail: admissions@brynathyn.edu
Internet: www.brynathyn.edu
Founded 1887
Private control
Academic year: August to May
Pres.: Dr CHRISTOPHER M. CLARK
Dean: Dr CHARLES W. LINDSAY
Library Dir: CARROLL C. ODHNER
Number of teachers: 39
Number of students: 150

BRYN MAWR COLLEGE

Bryn Mawr, PA 19010-2899
Telephone: (610) 526-5000
E-mail: info@brynmawr.edu
Internet: www.brynmawr.edu
Founded 1885
Academic year: September to May
Pres.: NANCY J. VICKERS
Provost: KIMBERLY E. CASSIDY
Dean of Admissions: JENNIFER RICKARD
Chief Admin. Officer: JERRY BERENSON
Dir of Libraries: ELLIOTT SHORE
Library: 1m. vols
Number of teachers: 176
Number of students: 1,790
Publications: *Bryn Mawr Classical Review* (online), *Bryn Mawr Review of Comparative Literature* (1 a year)

DEANS

Graduate School of Arts and Sciences: DALE KINNEY
School of Social Work and Social Research: MARCIA L. MARTIN
Undergraduate College: KAREN TIDMARSH

BUCKNELL UNIVERSITY

Telephone: (570) 577-2000
Fax: (570) 577-3760
E-mail: admisssions@bucknell.edu
Internet: www.bucknell.edu
Founded 1846
Private control
Language of instruction: English
Accredited by Middle States Asscn of Colleges and Schools Comm. on Higher Education, Accreditation Board for Engineering and Technology (ABET), Nat. Asscn of Schools of Music (NASM), PA Dept of Education, American Chemical Soc. (ACS)
Academic year: August to May
Pres.: Dr JOHN C. BRAVMAN
Vice-Pres. for Devt: SCOTT ROSEVEAR
Vice-Pres. for Finance and Admin.: DAVID SURGALA
Vice-Pres. for Enrollment Management: KURT THIEDE
Dean of Student Life: Dr LINDA LOCHER
Dir for Information Services and Resources: PARAM BEDI
Library of 818,837 vols
Number of teachers: 374 (354 full-time, 20 part-time)
Number of students: 3,615 3,488 full-time undergraduates, 20 part-time and 66 full-time graduate students, 41 part-time
Publication: *Aperçus*

DEANS

College of Arts and Sciences: Dr GEORGE C. SHIELDS
Dean of College of Engineering: Dr KEITH BUFFINTON

CABRINI COLLEGE

610 King of Prussia Rd, Radnor, PA 19087-3698
Telephone: (610) 902-8100
Fax: (610) 902-8539
E-mail: admit@cabrini.edu
Internet: www.cabrini.edu
Founded 1957 by the Missionary Sisters of the Sacred Heart
Academic year: August to May
Coeducational liberal arts and sciences college, offering undergraduate and graduate programmes
Pres.: Dr MARIE ANGELELLA GEORGE
Vice-Pres.: Dr JONNIE GUERRA
Vice-Pres. for Enrollment Management: DENNIS KELLY
Vice-Pres. for Institutional Advancement: SHARON LOMAN
Vice-Pres. for Student Devt: Dr CHRISTINE LYSIONEK
Sr Assoc. Dir for Admin. Services: STEPHEN COLFER
Dean for Graduate and Professional Studies: Dr DENNIS DOUGHTERY
Dir for Admin. Services: HEATHER CARDAMONE
Dir for Admissions: CHARLES SPENCER
Library Dir: Dr ROBERTA JACQUET
Library of 87,000 vols
Number of teachers: 194 (56 full-time, 138 part-time)
Number of students: 3,514 (1,554 undergraduate, 1,960 graduate)

CARLOW COLLEGE

3333 Fifth Ave, Pittsburgh, PA 15213
Telephone: (412) 578-6000
E-mail: admissions@carlow.edu
Internet: www.carlow.edu
Founded 1929
Academic year: August to May
Pres.: Dr MARY HINES
Exec. Dir of Corporate and Foundation Relations: BRUCE SEILING
Provost and Vice-Pres. for Academic Affairs: Dr GARY SMITH
Vice-Pres. for Advancement: Dr PAT JOYCE
Vice-Pres. for Institutional Relations: ANN RAGO

Vice-Pres. for Student Affairs: Dr CAROL A. GRUBER
Dean of Enrollment Management: CAROL DESCAK
Dir of Admissions: CHRISTINE DEVINE
Dir of Adult Degree Center and Graduate Admissions: SUSAN SHUTTER
Librarian: ELAINE MISKO
Library of 123,927 vols
Number of teachers: 255
Number of students: 2,070

CARNEGIE MELLON UNIVERSITY

5000 Forbes Ave, Pittsburgh, PA 15213
Telephone: (412) 268-2000
Fax: (412) 268-7838
Internet: www.cmu.edu
Founded 1900
Private control
Academic year: August to May
Pres.: JARED L. COHON
Provost: MARK KAMLET
Vice-Pres. of Finance and Chief Financial Officer: DEBORAH MOON
Vice-Pres. of Univ. Advancement: ROBBEE BAKER-KOSAK
Vice-Pres. for Campus Affairs: MICHAEL MURPHY
Vice-Pres. for Research: RICHARD MCCULLOUGH
Dean of University Libraries: GLORIANA ST. CLAIR
Library of 961,507 vols
Number of teachers: 1,368
Number of students: 11,371

DEANS AND DIRECTORS

Carnegie Institute of Technology: PRADEEP KHOSLA
College of Fine Arts: HILARY ROBINSON
College of Humanities and Social Sciences: JOHN LEHOCZKY
H. John Heinz III College: MARK KAMLET
Hunt Institute for Botanical Documentation: ROBERT W. KIGER (Dir)
Institute for Software Research: WILLIAM SCHERLIS (Dir)
Mellon College of Science: FRED GILMAN
School of Computer Science: RANDY BRYANT
Tepper School of Business: KENNETH B. DUNN

PROFESSORS

Carnegie Institute of Technology (tel. (412) 268-2481; fax (412) 268-6421; internet www.cit.cmu.edu):
AKAY, A., Mechanical Engineering
AMON, C., Mechanical Engineering
ANDERSON, J., Chemical Engineering
BAUMANN, D. M. B., Mechanical Engineering
BHAGAVATULA, V., Electrical and Computer Engineering
BIEGLER, L. T., Chemical Engineering
BIELAK, J., Civil Engineering
CAGAN, J., Mechanical Engineering
CARLEY, L. R., Electrical and Computer Engineering
CASASENT, D., Electrical and Computer Engineering
CHIGIER, N. A., Mechanical Engineering
CRAMB, A., Materials Science Engineering
DAVIDSON, C., Civil Engineering
DOMACH, M., Chemical Engineering
DZOMBAK, D. A., Civil Engineering
FRUEHAN, R. J., Materials Science Engineering
GABRIEL, K. S., Electrical and Computer Engineering
GARRETT, J. H., Civil Engineering
GARRISON, W. M., Jr, Materials Science Engineering
GELLMAN, A., Chemical Engineering
GREVE, D. W., Electrical and Computer Engineering
GRIFFIN, J. H., Mechanical Engineering
GROSSMANN, I. E., Chemical Engineering
HENDRICKSON, C. T., Civil Engineering
HOBURG, J. F., Electrical and Computer Engineering
JHON, M. S., Chemical Engineering
KHOSLA, P., Electrical and Computer Engineering
KIM, H. S., Electrical and Computer Engineering
KROGH, B., Electrical and Computer Engineering
KRYDER, M. H., Electrical and Computer Engineering
KUMTA, P., Materials Science Engineering
LAMBETH, D. N., Electrical and Computer Engineering
LAUGHLIN, D. E., Materials Science Engineering
MCHENRY, M., Materials Science Engineering
MCMICHAEL, F. C., Civil Engineering
MALY, W., Electrical and Computer Engineering
MORGAN, M. G., Engineering and Public Policy
MOURA, J. M., Electrical and Computer Engineering
NEUMAN, C. P., Electrical and Computer Engineering
OPPENHEIM, I. J., Civil Engineering
PIEHLER, H. R., Materials Science Engineering
PILEGGI, L., Electrical and Computer Engineering
POWERS, G., Chemical Engineering
PRIEVE, D. G., Chemical Engineering
REHAK, D. R., Civil Engineering
ROHRER, G., Materials Science Engineering
ROLLETT, T., Materials Science Engineering
RUBIN, E. S., Engineering and Public Policy
RUTENBAR, R., Electrical and Computer Engineering
SAIGAL, S., Civil Engineering
SCHLESINGER, E., Electrical and Computer Engineering
SHEN, J., Electrical and Computer Engineering
SIDES, P. J., Chemical Engineering
SINCLAIR, G. B., Mechanical Engineering
SIRBU, M. A., Engineering and Public Policy
SKOWRONSKI, M., Materials Science Engineering
SMALL, M. J., Civil Engineering
STANCIL, D. D., Electrical and Computer Engineering
STEIF, P. S., Mechanical Engineering
STERN, R., Electrical and Computer Engineering
STROJWAS, A., Electrical and Computer Engineering
TALUKDAR, S., Electrical and Computer Engineering
THOMAS, D. E., Jr, Electrical and Computer Engineering
WESTERBERG, A. W., Chemical Engineering
WHITE, L. R., Chemical Engineering
WHITE, R., Electrical and Computer Engineering
WICKERT, J., Mechanical Engineering
WYNBLATT, P., Materials Science Engineering
YAO, S.-C., Mechanical Engineering
YDSTIE, B. E., Chemical Engineering
ZHU, J., Electrical and Computer Engineering

College of Fine Arts (tel. (412) 268-2349; internet www.cmu.edu/cfa):
AKIN, O., Architecture
ANDERSON, B. J. B., Drama
ANDERSON, C. R., Drama
BALADA, L. I., Music
BALLAY, J. M., Design
BAXTRESSER, J., Music
BECKLEY, J., Art
BELLAN-GILLEN, P., Art
BENNETT, R., Art
BOYARSKI, D., Design
BUCHANAN, R., Design
BURGESS, L., Art
CARDENES, A., Music
COOPER, W. D., Architecture
FLEMMING, U., Architecture
FRISCH, P., Drama
HARTKOPF, V., Architecture
IZQUIERDO, J.-P., Music
JOHNSTON, B., Drama
JOSEPH, A., Music
KEELING, K., Sr, Music
KING, E., Art
KRISHNAMURTI, R., Architecture
KUMATA, C., Art
LEE, S., Architecture
LEHANE, G., Drama
LOFTNESS, V., Architecture
MAHDAVI, A., Architecture
MAIER, J., Art
MARINELLI, D., Drama
MENTZER, M., Design
MIDANI, A., Drama
OLDS, H. T., Art
PREKOP, M., Art
SLAVICK, S., Art
STITT, M., Drama
SWINEHART, R. O., Design
THOMAS, M., Music
VOGEL, C. M., Design
WADSWORTH, D. H., Drama
WEIDNER, M., Art

College of Humanities and Social Sciences (tel. (412) 268-2830; internet hss.cmu.edu):
ANDERSON, J. R., Psychology
BALAS, E., History
BICCHIERI, C., Philosophy
CARLEY, K. M., Social and Decision Sciences
CARPENTER, J., Psychology
CARRIER, D. S., Philosophy
CLARK, M., Psychology
COHEN, S. A., Psychology
COHEN, W., Social and Decision Sciences
COSTANZO, G., English
DANIELS, J., English
DAVIS, O. A., Social and Decision Sciences
DAWES, R., Social and Decision Sciences
EDDY, W. F., Statistics
FEINBERG, S. E., Statistics
FISCHHOFF, B., Social and Decision Sciences
FLOWER, L. S., English
FREED, B. F., Modern Languages
GLYMOUR, C., Philosophy
GREENHOUSE, J., Statistics
HAYES, A. L., English
HAYES, J. R., Psychology
HOPPER, P., English
HOUNSHELL, D. A., History and Social and Decision Sciences
JOHNSTONE, B., English
JUST, M. A., Psychology
KADANE, J. B., Statistics
KASS, R. E., Statistics
KAUFER, D., English
KEECH, W., Social and Decision Sciences
KELLY, K. T., Philosophy
KENNEDY, A., English
KLAHR, D., Psychology
KLATZKY, R., Psychology
KLEPPER, S., Social and Decision Sciences
KNAPP, P., English
KOTOVSKY, K., Psychology
LEHOCZKY, J. P., Statistics
LINDEMANN, M., History
LOEWENSTEIN, G., Social and Decision Sciences
LYNCH, K., History

McClelland, J., Psychology
MacWhinney, B., Psychology
Masters, H., English
Miller, D. W., History
Miller, J. H., Social and Decision Sciences
Modell, J., History
Reder, L., Psychology
Resnick, D. P., History
Roeder, K., Statistics
Scheier, M. F., Psychology
Schervish, M., Statistics
Schlossman, B. F., Modern Languages
Schlossman, S., History
Seidenfeld, T., Philosophy
Shumway, D., English
Sieg, W., Philosophy
Siegler, R. S., Psychology
Spirtes, P. L., Philosophy
Steinberg, E. R., English
Sutton, D., History
Tarr, J. A., History
Trotter, J., History
Tucker, G. R., Modern Languages
Wasserman, L., Statistics

Mellon College of Science (tel. (412) 268-5124; fax (412) 268-3268; internet www.cmu.edu/mcs):

Andrews, P. B., Mathematical Sciences
Berry, G. C., Chemistry
Brown, W. E., Biology
Collins, T., Chemistry
Feenstra, R., Physics
Ferguson, T., Physics
Fonseca, I., Mathematical Sciences
Franklin, G. B., Physics
Frieze, A., Physics
Garoff, S., Physics
Gilman, F., Physics
Greenberg, J., Mathematical Sciences
Griffiths, R. B., Physics
Griffiths, R. E., Physics
Gurtin, M. E., Mathematical Sciences
Hackney, D., Biology
Heath, D. C., Mathematical Sciences
Ho, C., Biology
Hollinger, J. O., Biology
Holman, R. F., Physics
Hrusa, W. J., Mathematical Sciences
Jones, E. W., Biology
Kaplan, M., Chemistry
Karol, P., Chemistry
Kinderlehrer, D., Mathematical Sciences
Kisslinger, L. S., Physics
Kraemer, R. W., Physics
Levine, M. J., Physics
Li, L.-F., Physics
Llinás, M., Chemistry
McClure, W. R., Biology
McCullough, R., Chemistry
Majetich, S., Physics
Matyjaszewski, K., Chemistry
Mizel, V. J., Mathematical Sciences
Münck, E., Chemistry
Nagle, J. F., Physics
Nicolaides, R. A., Mathematical Sciences
Owen, D. R., Mathematical Sciences
Patterson, G. D., Chemistry
Russ, J. S., Physics
Schäffer, J. W., Mathematical Sciences
Schumacher, R. A., Physics
Sekerka, R. F., Physics
Shreve, S. E., Mathematical Sciences
Staley, S. W., Chemistry
Statman, R., Mathematical Sciences
Stewart, R. F., Chemistry
Suter, R., Physics
Swendsen, R. H., Physics
Ta'asan, S., Mathematical Sciences
Tartar, L., Mathematical Sciences
Vogel, H., Physics
Waggoner, A., Biology
Walkington, N. J., Mathematical Sciences
Widom, M., Physics
Williams, J. F., Biology
Williams, W. O., Mathematical Sciences
Woolford, J., Biology
Young, H., Physics

Graduate School of Industrial Administration (tel. (412) 268-2266; internet www.gsia.cmu.edu):

Argote, L., Organizational Behaviour
Balas, E., Industrial Admin. and Mathematics
Baybars, I., Industrial Admin.
Cornuejols, G. P., Operations Research and Mathematics
Dunn, D., Industrial Admin. and Statistics
Epple, D., Economics
Goodman, P. S., Industrial Admin. and Psychology
Green, R. C., Financial Economics
Hooker, J., Jr, Industrial Admin.
Ijiri, Y., Industrial Admin.
Kekre, S., Industrial Admin.
Kydland, F. E., Economics
Lave, L. B., Economics
McCallum, B. T., Economics
Meltzer, A. H., Economics, Industrial Admin. and Public Policy
Miller, R., Economics
Mukhopadhyay, T., Information Systems
Shaw, K., Economics
Spatt, C. S., Economics and Finance
Spear, S., Economics
Srinivasan, K., Industrial Admin.
Srivastava, S., Economics and Finance
Tayur, S.
Thompson, G. L., Industrial Admin. and Mathematics
Williams, J., Industrial Admin.
Zin, S., Economics and Finance

H. J. Heinz School of Public Policy and Management (tel. (412) 268-2164; fax (412) 268-7036; internet www.heinz.cmu.edu):

Barcock, L. C., Economics
Blumstein, A., Urban Systems and Operations Research
Caulkins, J. P., Operations Research
Duncan, G., Statistics
Florida, R., Public Policy and Management
Gaynor, M. S., Economics and Health Policy
Gorr, W., Public Policy and Management Information Systems
Krackhardt, D. M., Organizations and Public Policy
Krishnan, R., Management Science and Information Systems
Larkey, P. D., Public Policy and Decision-making
Nagin, D., Management
Rousseau, D., Organization Behaviour
Stewman, S., Sociology and Demography
Strauss, R. P., Economics and Public Policy
Taylor, L., Economics and Public Policy

School of Computer Science (tel. (412) 268-8525; fax (412) 268-5576; e-mail scs@cs.cmu.edu; internet www.cs.cmu.edu):

Blelloch, G. E., Computer Science
Bryant, R. E., Computer Science
Carbonell, J. G., Computer Science
Clark, E. M., Jr, Computer Science
Faloutsos, C. N., Computer Science
Harper, R. W., Computer Science
Herbert, M., Robotics
Kanade, T., Robotics
Kiesler, S., Human–Computer Interaction
Kraut, R. E., Human–Computer Interaction
Lee, P., Computer Science
Mason, M. T., Computer Science
Miller, G. L., Computer Science
Mitchell, T. M., Computer Science
Morris, J., Computer Science
Pausch, R. F., Human–Computer Interaction
Reddy, R., Computer Science
Reynolds, J. C., Computer Science
Satyanarayanen, M., Computer Science
Scott, D. F., Computer Science, Mathematics and Philosophy
Shaw, M., Computer Science
Siewiorek, D., Human–Computer Interaction
Sleator, D. D., Computer Science
Waibel, A., Language Technologies
Wing, J., Computer Science

CEDAR CREST COLLEGE

100 College Dr., Allentown, PA 18055
Telephone: (610) 437-4471
Fax: (610) 437-5955
Internet: www.cedarcrest.edu

Founded 1867
Private control

Liberal arts college for women

Pres.: Jill Leauber Sherman
Library Dir: Mary Beth Freeh

Library of 133,763 vols
Number of teachers: 72
Number of students: 1,527

Publications: *Alumnae Magazine*, *Catalog and Promotional Brochures*, *Exchange* (4 a year).

CHATHAM UNIVERSITY

Woodland Rd, Pittsburgh, PA 15232
Telephone: (412) 365-1290
Fax: (412) 365-1609
E-mail: admissions@chatham.edu
Internet: www.chatham.edu

Founded 1869
Private control
Academic year: August to May

Comprised of Chatham College for Women housing academic and co-curricular programmes for undergraduate women; College for Graduate Studies for women and men offering Masters and doctoral programmes in art and architecture, business, counselling psychology, health sciences and nursing, teaching, and writing; College for Continuing and Professional Studies providing online and hybrid undergraduate and graduate degree programmes for women and men, certificate programmes and community programming

Pres.: Dr Esther L. Barazzone
Vice-Pres. for Academic Affairs: Dr Laura Armesto
Vice-Pres. for Enrollment Management: Wendy Beckemeyer
Vice-Pres. for Finance and Admin.: Walt Fowler
Vice-Pres. for University Advancement: Richard Donovan
Vice-Pres for Student Affairs: Dr Zauyah Waite
Library Dir: Jill Ausel

Library of 87,962 vols, 700 subscriptions to online and print periodicals
Number of teachers: 247
Number of students: 1,868

DEANS

School of Sustainability and Environment: Dr David Hassenzahl

CHESTNUT HILL COLLEGE

9601 Germantown Ave, Philadelphia, PA 19118
Telephone: (215) 248-7000
Fax: (215) 248-7056
Internet: www.chc.edu

Founded 1924

Pres.: Carol Jeab Vale

Sr Vice-Pres. and Vice-Pres. for Academic Affairs: WILLIAM T. WALKER
Vice-Pres. for Institutional Advancement: KENNETH M. HICKS
Librarian: MARY JO LARKIN
Library of 135,554 vols
Number of teachers: 120
Number of students: 1,543

COLLEGE MISERICORDIA

301 Lake St, Dallas, PA 18612
Telephone: (570) 674-6400
E-mail: admiss@misericordia.edu
Internet: www.misericordia.edu
Founded 1924
Private control
Academic year: August to May
Pres.: Dr MICHAEL A. MACDOWELL
Dean of Students: JEAN MESSAROS
Registrar: EDWARD LAHART
Library Dir: BARBARA BURD
Number of teachers: 145
Number of students: 2,358

CURTIS INSTITUTE OF MUSIC

1726 Locust St, Philadelphia, PA 19103
Telephone: (215) 893-5252
Fax: (215) 893-9065
E-mail: info@curtis.edu
Internet: www.curtis.edu
Founded 1924
Academic year: September to May
Pres. and Dir: ROBERTO DIAZ
Vice-Pres. for Devt: ELIZABETH A. WRIGHT
Exec. Vice-Pres. for Finance and Admin.: ELIZABETH WARSHAWER
Dean: ROBERT FITZPATRICK
Registrar: PAUL BRYAN
Head Librarian: ELIZABETH WALKER
Library of 60,000 vols, musical scores and recordings
Number of teachers: 82 (mainly part-time)
Number of students: 169

DELAWARE VALLEY COLLEGE OF SCIENCE AND AGRICULTURE

Doylestown, PA 18901
Telephone: (215) 345-1500
Fax: (215) 345-8916
E-mail: leamer@devalcol.edu
Internet: www.devalcol.edu
Founded 1896
Academic year: August to May
Pres.: JOSEPH S. BROSNAN
Vice-Pres for Academic Affairs and Dean of Faculty: Dr DOROTHY A. PRISCO
Vice-Pres. for Institutional Advancement: JASON KETTER
Registrar: ROBERT P. MORAN
Library Dir: PETER KUPERSMITH
Library of 73,600 vols
Number of teachers: 81
Number of students: 1,380

DESALES UNIVERSITY

2755 Station Ave, Center Valley, PA 18034-9568
Telephone: (610) 282-1100
E-mail: admiss@desales.edu
Internet: www.desales.edu
Founded 1964 as Allentown College of St Francis de Sales; present name 2001
Private control
Academic year: August to May
Pres.: Fr BERNARD O'CONNOR
Sr Vice-Pres.: Rev. ALEXANDER T. POCETTO
Provost and Vice-Pres. for Academic Affairs: Dr KAREN DOYLE WALTON
Vice-Pres. for Admin., Finance and Technology: WILLARD H. CRESSMAN
Vice-Pres. for Institutional Advancement: THOMAS L. CAMPBELL
Vice-Pres. for Program and Strategic Devt: Dr MOHAMED LATIB
Registrar: THOMAS MANTONI
Library Dir: DEBORAH MALONE
Number of teachers: 60
Number of students: 2,225 (1,445 undergraduate, 780 postgraduate and evening)

DICKINSON COLLEGE

POB 1773, Carlisle, PA 17013-2896
Telephone: (717) 243-5121
Fax: (717) 245-1899
Internet: www.dickinson.edu
Founded 1783
Academic year: August to May
Pres.: WILLIAM G. DURDEN
Dean of Students: APRIL VARI
Registrar: KAREN WEIKEL
Dir of Library: ELEANOR MITCHELL
Number of teachers: 210
Number of students: 2,321
Publications: *Frontiers* (1 a year), *Glossen* (3 or 4 a year and online), *John & Mary's Journal* (published by Friends of the Library), *The Dickinson Review* (1 a year).

DREXEL UNIVERSITY

3141 Chestnut St, Philadelphia, PA 19104
Telephone: (215) 895-2000
Fax: (215) 895-1414
E-mail: enroll@drexel.edu
Internet: www.drexel.edu
Founded 1891 as Drexel Institute of Art, Science and Industry; present name and status 1970; assumed full control of the collective instns fmrly known as MCP Hahnemann Univ. (previously Allegheny Univ. of the Health Sciences) in 2002
Private control
Academic year: September to August
Pres.: JOHN FRY
Provost and Sr Vice-Pres. for Academic Affairs: Dr MARK GREENBERG
Vice-Provost for Research: Dr DEBORAH CRAWFORD
Sr Vice-Pres. for Finance and Treas.: THOMAS J. ELZEY
Sr Vice-Pres. for Institutional Advancement: ELIZABETH A. DALE
Sr Vice-Pres. for Student Life and Admin. Services: JAMES R. TUCKER
Sr Vice-Pres. and General Counsel: MICHAEL J. EXLER
Sr Vice-Pres. and Exec. Dir: KENNETH BLANK
Vice-Pres. for Govt and Community Relations: DAVID E. WILSON
Vice-Pres. for Information Resources and Technology: Dr JOHN A. BIELEC
Vice-Pres. and Comptroller: SUSAN WILMER
Dir of Libraries: JANE G. BRYAN
Library of 611,143 vols
Number of teachers: 1,760 (1,044 full-time, 716 part-time)
Number of students: 17,000 (incl. 11,613 undergraduate, 5,387 postgraduate)
Publications: *BMa: The Sonia Sanchez Literary Review*, *Drexel Law Review*, *Drexel Med Journal*, *Journal of Culture and Retail* (1 or 2 a year), *Maya Literary Magazine*, *The Smart Set*

DEANS

Antoinette Westphal College of Media Arts and Design: ALLEN SABINSON
Bennett S. LeBow College of Business: Dr GEORGE P. TSETSEKOS
College of Arts and Sciences: Dr DONNA MURASCO
College of Engineering: Dr SELCUK GUCERI
College of Information Science and Technology: Dr DAVID E. FENSKE
College of Nursing and Health Professions: Dr GLORIA F. DONNELLY
Drexel Univ. College of Medicine: Dr RICHARD V. HOMAN
Earle Mack School of Law: ROGER J. DENNIS
Goodwin College of Professional Studies: Dr WILLIAM F. LYNCH
Pennoni Honours College: Dr D. B. JONES
School of Public Health: Dr MARLA GOLD

DIRECTORS

Athletics: Dr ERIC ZILLMER
School of Biomedical Engineering, Science and Health Systems: Dr BANU ONARAL
School of Education: Dr MARK GREENBURG

DUQUESNE UNIVERSITY

600 Forbes Ave, Pittsburgh, PA 15282
Telephone: (412) 396-6000
E-mail: president@duq.edu
Internet: www.duq.edu
Founded 1878; chartered 1911
Private control
Language of instruction: English
Academic year: August to May
Pres.: Dr CHARLES J. DOUGHERTY
Provost and Academic Vice-Pres.: Dr RALPH L. PEARSON
Exec. Vice-Pres. for Student Life: Rev. SEAN M. HOGAN
Vice-Pres. for Institutional Advancement: JOHN PLANTE
Vice-Pres. for Management and Business: STEPHEN A. SCHILLO
Registrar: PATRICIA JAKUB
Librarian: Dr LAVERNA SAUNDERS
Library of 723,919 vols, 328,312 microforms
Number of teachers: 874 (414 full-time, 460 part-time)
Number of students: 9,722
Publications: *Classical World* (4 a year), *Duquesne Law Review* (4 a year)

DEANS

School of Education: Dr RICK R. MCCOWN
School of Law: NICHOLAS P. CAFARDI
School of Leadership and Professional Advancement: Dr BENJAMIN HODES
School of Music: Dr EDWARD KOCHER
School of Nursing: Dr EILEEN ZUNGOLO
Bayer School of Natural and Environmental Sciences: Dr DAVID SEYBERT
Mylan School of Pharmacy: Dr R. PETE VANDERVEEN
Palumbo School of Business Administration: JAMES C. STALDER
Rangos School of Health Sciences: Dr GREGORY H. FRAZER
McAnulty College and Graduate School of Liberal Arts: Dr FRANCESCO C. CESAREO

EASTERN UNIVERSITY

1300 Eagle Rd, St Davids, PA 19087-3696
Telephone: (610) 341-5800
Fax: (610) 341-1377
Internet: www.eastern.edu
Founded 1932 as a dept of Eastern Baptist Theological Seminary; became a separate instn as Eastern Baptist College 1952; renamed Eastern College 1972; present name and status 2001
Academic year: August to May
Pres.: BRYAN STEVENSON
Exec. Vice-Pres.: HAROLD HOWARD
Chief Academic Officer, and Academic Dean of Undergraduates: DAVID FRASER
Chief Operating Officer: A. WESLEY BRYAN

Academic Dean (Campolo School): VIVIAN NIX-EARLY
Academic Dean for Graduate and Professional Students: EFRAIN RAMIREZ
Academic Dean for Honours College: ALLEN GUELZO
Academic Dean for Junior College: SARA MILES
Vice-Pres. for Enrollment Management: LEONARD JAMISON
Vice-Pres. for Student Devt: THEODORE J. CHAMBERLAIN
Librarian: JAMES L. SAUER
Library of 260,000 vols, 6,000 online journals
Number of teachers: 335
Number of students: 3,700

ELIZABETHTOWN COLLEGE

One Alpha Dr., Elizabethtown, PA 17022-2298
Telephone: (717) 361-1000
Internet: www.etown.edu
Founded 1899
Pres.: THEODORE E. LONG
Provost: SUSAN TRAVERSO
Vice-Pres. for Advancement: DAVID C. BEIDLEMAN
Library of 180,000 vols
Number of teachers: 125
Number of students: 1,900

EVANGELICAL THEOLOGICAL SEMINARY

121 S College St, Myerstown, PA 17067
Telephone: (717) 866-5775
Fax: (717) 866-4667
E-mail: admissions@evangelical.edu
Internet: www.evangelical.edu
Founded 1953, fmrly known as Evangelical School of Theology
Private control
Accredited by Middle States Asscn and the Asscn of Theological Schools
Academic year: two semesters
Pres.: MICHAEL W. SIGMAN
Vice-Pres. for Academic Affairs and Dean of Faculty: JOHN V. TORNFELT
Vice-Pres. for Business and Finance: KEVIN C. HENRY
Vice-Pres. for Continuing Education: CRAIG E. SIDER
Vice-Pres for Institutional Advancement: ANN E. STEEL
Dean of Admissions: TOM M. MAIELLO
Registrar: ELLIS I. KIRK
Head Librarian: TERRY M. HEISEY
Library of 80,000 bound vols; 550 periodical titles, Pense Archaeological Museum, artefacts from the Neolithic Period to the late Christian era
Number of teachers: 15
Number of students: 200

FRANKLIN AND MARSHALL COLLEGE

POB 3003, Lancaster, PA 17604-3003
Telephone: (717) 291-3911
Fax: (717)-291-4183
Internet: www.fandm.edu
Private control
Language of instruction: English
Franklin College founded in 1787, Marshall College founded in 1836; merged in 1853
Pres.: JOHN A. FRY
Dean: KENT TRACHTE
Provost: ANN STEINER
Librarian: PAMELA SNELSON
Library of 523,323 vols, 29,096 periodicals
Number of teachers: 217
Number of students: 2,147

GANNON UNIVERSITY

109 University Sq., Erie, PA 16541-0001
Telephone: (814) 871-7000
Internet: www.gannon.edu
Founded 1925
Pres.: Dr ANTOINE M. GARIBALDI
Provost and Vice-Pres. for Academic Affairs: Dr KEITH TAYLOR
Dean of Devt: WARD MCCRACKEN
Library Dir: KEN BRUNDAGE
Library of 263,600 vols, 39,346 periodicals
Number of teachers: 360 (200 full-time, 160 part-time)
Number of students: 4,238

GENEVA COLLEGE

3200 College Ave, Beaver Falls, PA 15010
Telephone: (724) 846-5100
Fax: (724) 847-6687
E-mail: geneva@geneva.edu
Internet: www.geneva.edu
Founded 1848
Academic year: August to May
Pres.: Dr KENNETH A. SMITH
Chief Financial Officer: MIKE FOX
Vice-Pres. for Academic Affairs: Dr KENNETH P. CARSON
Vice-Pres. for Marketing: EDGARDO VENCIO
Vice-Pres. for Operations: JIM PRINCE
Registrar: ANDREA KORCAN-BUZZA
Library Dir: JOHN DONCEVIC
Library of 250,000 vols, incl. microforms
Number of teachers: 90
Number of students: 2,000

GETTYSBURG COLLEGE

300 North Washington St, Gettysburg, PA 17325
Telephone: (717) 337-6000
Fax: (717) 337-6008
E-mail: admiss@gettysburg.edu
Internet: www.gettysburg.edu
Founded 1832 as Pennsylvania College; present name 1921
Academic year: August to May
Pres.: KATHERINE HALEY WILL
Provost: JANET MORGAN RIGGS
Vice-Pres. for College Life and Dean of Students: JULIE L. RAMSEY
Dir of Admissions: GAIL SWEEZEY
Library of 350,000 vols
Number of teachers: 174
Number of students: 2,200
Publication: *Gettysburg Review*.

GRATZ COLLEGE

7605 Old York Rd, Melrose Park, PA 19027
Telephone: (215) 635-7300
Fax: (215) 635-7399
E-mail: enroll@gratz.edu
Internet: www.gratzcollege.edu
Founded 1895
Private control
Language of instruction: English
Academic year: September to May
Pres.: Dr JONATHAN ROSENBAUM
Dean for Academic Affairs: Dr JERRY M. KUTNICK
Library Dir: ELIEZER M. WISE
Library of 95,000 vols
Number of teachers: 15
Number of students: 150

GROVE CITY COLLEGE

100 Campus Dr., Grove City, PA 16127
Telephone: (724) 458-2000
E-mail: admissions@gcc.edu
Internet: www.gcc.edu
Founded 1876
Private control
Academic year: August to May
Pres.: Dr RICHARD G. JEWELL
Provost and Vice-Pres. for Academic Affairs: Dr WILLIAM P. ANDERSON, Jr
Vice-Pres. for Financial Affairs: ROGER K. TOWLE
Vice-Pres. for Institutional Advancement: THOMAS J. PAPPALARDO
Vice-Pres. for Operations: THOMAS W. GREGG
Vice-Pres. for Student Life: Dr JEAN-NOEL THOMPSON
Dean of Int. Studies, Graduate Advancement and Faculty Devt: Dr CHARLES W. DUNN
Registrar: JOHN G. INMAN
Library Dir: DIANE H. GRUNDY
Number of teachers: 115
Number of students: 2,250

DEANS

School of Arts and Letters: Dr JOHN A. SPARKS
School of Science and Engineering: JOSEPH F. GONCZ, Jr

GWYNEDD-MERCY COLLEGE

1325 Sumneytown Pike, POB 901, Gwynedd Valley, PA 19437-0901
Telephone: (215) 646-7300
E-mail: admissions@gmc.edu
Internet: www.gmc.edu
Campuses at Gwynedd Valley and Fort Washington
Founded 1948 as Gwynedd-Mercy Junior College; present name 1963
Private control
Pres.: Dr KATHLEEN OWENS
Vice-Pres. for Academic Affairs: Dr DENISE WILBUR
Vice-Pres. for Enrollment Management: JAMES ABBUHL
Vice-Pres. for Finance and Admin.: KEVIN O'FLAHERTY
Vice-Pres. for Institutional Advancement: GERALD MCLAUGHLIN
Vice-Pres. for Student Services: Dr CHERYL LYNN HORSEY
Registrar: THERESA ANDERSON
Library Dir: KATHLEEN MULROY
Number of teachers: 193
Number of students: 2,429

DEANS

School of Allied Health Professions: LINDA REILLY
School of Arts and Sciences: (vacant)
School of Business and Computer Information Sciences: JOANNE TROTTER
School of Education: LORRAINE CAVALIERE
School of Nursing: ANDREA HOLLINGSWORTH

HAVERFORD COLLEGE

370 Lancaster Ave, Haverford, PA 19041-1392
Telephone: (610) 896-1000
Fax: (610) 896-1224
E-mail: admission@haverford.edu
Internet: www.haverford.edu
An ind. coeducational liberal arts college
Founded 1833 by the Soc. of Friends
Academic year: September to May
Pres.: Dr STEPHEN EMERSON
Treas. and Vice-Pres. for Admin. and Finance: G. RICHARD WYNN

Vice-Pres. for Institutional Advancement: MICHAEL KIEFER
Dean of Admissions: JESS H. LORD
Registrar: LEE WATKINS
Dean of College: MARTHA DENNEY
Librarian: TERRY SNYDER

Library of 595,522 vols
Number of teachers: 139 (119 full-time, 20 part-time)
Number of students: 1,169

Publication: *Haverford Magazine* (3 a year).

HOLY FAMILY UNIVERSITY

Grant and Frankford Ave, Philadelphia, PA 19114
Telephone: (215) 637-7700
Fax: (215) 281-1022
E-mail: admissions@holyfamily.edu
Internet: www.holyfamily.edu

Founded 1954
Academic year: October to May (two semesters)

Pres.: Sister Dr FRANCESCA ONLEY
Dir of Undergraduate Admissions: LAUREN CAMPBELL
Dir of Library Services: LORI SCHWABENBAUER

Library of 106,000 vols
Number of teachers: 256
Number of students: 2,100

Publications: *Familogue* (1 a year), *Folio*, *Mosaic*, *The Family Tree*, *Tri-Lite*

Degree programmes in business admin., education, fire science admin., interdisciplinary programmes, liberal arts, mathematics, medical imaging, science, medical technology, nursing. Masters programmes in computer communications management, counselling psychology, criminal justice, education, human resources, nursing.

IMMACULATA UNIVERSITY

1145 King Rd, Immaculata, PA 19345
Telephone: (610) 647-4400
Fax: (610) 251-1668
Internet: www.immaculata.edu

Founded 1920 as Villa Maria College; became Immaculata College 1929; present name and status 2002

Pres.: Sis. R. PATRICIA FADDEN
Registrar: JANICE BATES
Dir of Admissions: REBECCA BOWLBY
Library Dir: JEFFREY ROLLISON

Library of 115,000 vols
Number of teachers: 164
Number of students: 2,391

JUNIATA COLLEGE

1700 Moore St, Huntingdon, PA 16652
Telephone: (814) 641-3000
Fax: (814) 641-3199
E-mail: info@juniata.edu
Internet: www.juniata.edu

Founded 1876
Private control
Academic year: August to May

Pres.: Dr THOMAS R. KEPPLE, Jr
Provost and Vice-Pres. for Student Devt: JAMES LAKSO
Vice-Pres. for Advancement and Marketing: JOHN HILLE
Vice-Pres. and Chief Information Officer: RAY CHAMBERS
Vice-Pres. for Finance and Operations: WILLIAM ALEXANDER
Registrar: ATHENA FREDERICK
Library Dir: JOHN MUMFORD

Number of teachers: 120
Number of students: 1,356 (full-time)

KING'S COLLEGE

Wilkes-Barre, PA 18711
Telephone: (570) 208-5900
Fax: (570) 825-9049
E-mail: admissions@kings.edu
Internet: www.kings.edu

Founded 1946
Academic year: August to May

Pres.: Rev. Dr THOMAS J. O'HARA
Registrar: DANIEL CEBRICK
Dean of Enrollment Management: TERESA PECK
Library Dir: Dr TERRENCE MECH

Library of 182,658 vols
Number of teachers: 230 (130 full-time, 100 part-time)
Number of students: 2,356

LA ROCHE COLLEGE

9000 Babcock Blvd, Pittsburgh, PA 15237-5898
Telephone: (412) 367-9300
E-mail: admsns@laroche.edu
Internet: www.laroche.edu
Private control

Pres.: Sis. CANDACE INTROCASO
Vice-Pres. for Academic Affairs: Dr HOWARD ISHIYAMA
Vice-Pres. for Admin. Services: GEORGE ZAFFUTO
Vice-Pres. for Devt: JANET DENNIS
Vice-Pres. for Institutional Relations: KEN SERVICE
Registrar: LUCILLE ADKINS
Library Dir: LAVERNE P. COLLINS

Number of teachers: 155
Number of students: 1,280 (1,150 undergraduate, 130 postgraduate)

LA SALLE UNIVERSITY

1900 West Olney Ave, Philadelphia, PA 19141
Telephone: (215) 951-1000
Fax: (215) 951-1892
Internet: www.lasalle.edu

Founded 1863

Pres.: MICHAEL J. MCGINNISS
Provost: RICHARD A. NIGRO
Dean of Admissions: ROBERT G. VOSS
Library Dir: JOHN BAKY

Library of 375,000 vols
Number of teachers: 478 (218 full-time; 260 part-time)
Number of students: 6,130 (3,200 Day Div., 1,800 Evening Div., 1,300 Graduate Div.)

Publications: *Four Quarters* (4 a year), *La Salle Bulletin* (4 a year), *La Salle Magazine* (4 a year).

LAFAYETTE COLLEGE

Easton, PA 18042
Telephone: (610) 330-5100
E-mail: admissions@lafayette.edu
Internet: www.lafayette.edu

Founded 1826
Private control
Academic year: August to May

Pres.: DANIEL H. WEISS
Provost and Dean of the Faculty: WENDY L. HILL
Sec., Board of Trustees: EDWARD W. AHART
Registrar: FRANCIS A. BENGINIA
Clerk of the Faculty: SUSAN NILES
Dir of Libraries and Academic Information Resources: NEIL J. MCELROY

Library of 502,603 vols
Number of teachers: 208
Number of students: 2,400

Publications: *Lafayette Alumni News Magazine* (3 a year), *The Lafayette* (Student newspaper, 52 a year).

LANCASTER BIBLE COLLEGE

901 Eden Rd, POB 83403, Lancaster, PA 17608-3403
Telephone: (717) 569-7071
E-mail: admissions@lbc.edu
Internet: www.lbc.edu
Private control

Pres.: Dr PETER W. TEAGUE
Vice-Pres. for Academic Affairs: Dr RAY A. NAUGLE
Library Dir: GERALD E. LINCOLN

Number of teachers: 80
Number of students: 1,126 (854 undergraduate, 272 postgraduate)

LEBANON VALLEY COLLEGE

Annville, PA 17003-1400
Telephone: (717) 867-6100
Fax: (717) 867-6018
Internet: www.lvc.edu

Founded 1866
Academic year: August to May

Pres.: STEPHEN C. MACDONALD
Registrar: PATRICIA A. KALEY
Vice-Pres. for Academic Affairs and Dean of Faculty: MICHAEL GREEN (acting)
Vice-Pres. for Enrollment: BILL BROWN
Dir of Library: FRANK MOLS

Library of 178,288 vols, 23,709 microfilms and recordings
Number of teachers: 96 full-time
Number of students: 1,567 full-time

LEHIGH UNIVERSITY

27 Memorial Dr., W, Bethlehem, PA 18015-3089
Telephone: (610) 758-3000
Fax: (610) 758-3154
Internet: www.lehigh.edu

Founded 1865
Language of instruction: English
Academic year: August to May

Pres.: ALICE P. GAST
Provost and Vice-Pres. for Academic Affairs: MOHAMMED S. EL-AASSER
Sr Vice-Provost for Institutional Research: STEPHEN J. DEVLIN
Vice-Provost for Library and Technology Services: BRUCE M. TAGGART
Vice-Provost for Student Affairs: JOHN W. SMEATON
Vice-Pres. for Advancement: BONNIE N. DEVLIN
Vice-Pres. for Finance and Admin.: MARGARET F. PLYMPTON
Vice-Pres. for Univ. Relations: BRADLEY M. DREXLER
Assoc. Vice-Pres. for Govt Relations: WILLIAM D. MICHALERYA
Registrar: BRUCE S. CORRELL

Library of 1,324,500 vols
Number of teachers: 393
Number of students: 6,479

DEANS

College of Arts and Sciences: Dr BOBB CARSON
College of Business and Economics: RICHARD M. DURAND
College of Education: SALLY A. WHITE
College of Engineering and Applied Science: MOHAMED S. EL-AASSER

PROFESSORS

College of Arts and Sciences (tel. (610) 758-3300):

ABEL, J. H., Biological Sciences
ALHADEFF, J., Chemistry
BARKEY, H., Int. Relations
BAYLOR, M., History
BEARN, G., Philosophy
BEHE, M., Biological Sciences
BEIDLER, P., English
BICKHARD, M., Psychology
BORSE, G., Physics
BROSS, A., English
CARRELL-SMITH, K., History
CARSON, R., Earth and Environmental Sciences
CHABUT, M.-H., Modern Languages and Literature
COLON, F., Political Science
CUNDALL, D., Biological Sciences
DAVIS, D., Mathematics
DELEO, G., Physics
DOBRIC, V., Mathematics
DOTY, A., English
DUFFY, I., History
EISENBERG, B., Mathematics
EVENSON, E., Earth and Environmental Sciences
FERGUS, J., English
FIFER, E., English
FOLK, R., Physics
FRIEDMAN, S., Journalism
GALLAGHER, E., English
GANS, L., Art and Architecture
GATEWOOD, J., Sociology and Anthropology
GHOSH, B. K., Mathematics
GIRARDOT, N., Religion
GOLDMAN, S., Philosophy
GORNEY, C., Journalism
GUNTON, J., Physics
HEINDEL, N. D., Chemistry
HERRENKOHL, R., Sociology and Anthropology
HICKMAN, P., Physics
HUANG, W.-M., Mathematics
HUENNEKENS, J., Physics
HYLAND, D., Psychology
ITZKOWITZ, M., Biological Sciences
KANOFSKY, A., Physics
KHABBAZ, S., Mathematics
KIM, Y., Physics
KING, J. P., Mathematics
KLIER, K., Chemistry
KODAMA, K., Earth and Environmental Sciences
KRAFT, K., Religion
KRAWIEC, S., Biological Sciences
KRITZ, A., Physics
KROLL, B., English
LARSEN, J., Chemistry
LASKER, J., Sociology and Anthropology
LULE, J. F., Journalism
MCCLUSKEY, G. E., Mathematics
MCINTOSH, J., Sociology and Anthropology
MALT, B., Psychology
MARKLEY, N. G., Mathematics
MASON, D., Art and Architecture
MATTHEWS, R., Political Science
MELTZER, A. S., Earth and Environmental Sciences
MENON, M. R., International Relations
MILET, J., Theatre
MOON, B., International Relations
MORGAN, E., Political Science
MUNDHENK, R., English
MYERS, P. B., Earth and Environmental Sciences
NYBY, J. G., Biological Sciences
OLSON, L., Political Science
OU-YANG, D., Physics
PANKENIER, D., Modern Languages and Literature
PETERS, T., Art and Architecture
PHILLIPS, C. R., History
RAPOSA, M., Religion
REGEN, S. L., Chemistry
RICHTER, M., Psychology
RIPA, A., Theatre
ROSENWEIN, R., Sociology and Anthropology
SAEGER, J. S., History
SALATHE, E., Mathematics
SALERNI, P., Music
SAMETZ, S., Music
SANDS, J., Biological Sciences
SCHRAY, K., Chemistry
SCOTT, W. R., History
SILBERSTEIN, L., Religion
SIMMONS, G. W., Chemistry
SIMON, N., Biological Sciences
SIMON, R., History
SINE, N., Music
SMALL, D., Sociology and Anthropology
SMOLANSKY, O., International Relations
SODERLUND, J., History
STANLEY, L., Mathematics
STAVOLA, M., Physics
STEFFEN, L., Religion
STENGLE, G. A., Mathematics
STEWART-GAMBINO, H., Political Science
TANNENBAUM, N., Sociology and Anthropology
TOULOUSE, J., Physics
TRAISTER, B., English
USSLER, C., Art and Architecture
VIERA, R., Art and Architecture
WEINTRAUB, S. H., Mathematics
WEISS, R., Philosophy
WEISSLER, L. E. C., Religion
WILLIAMSON, C., Earth and Environmental Sciences
WOLFGANG, L., Modern Languages and Literature
WRIGHT, B., Religion
WYLIE, R., International Relations
YUKICH, J., Mathematics
ZAKNIC, I., Art and Architecture
ZEITLER, P., Earth and Environmental Sciences
ZEROKA, D., Chemistry

College of Business and Economics (tel. (610) 758-3400):

ARONSON, J. R., Business and Economics
BARSNESS, R. W., Management
BUELL, S. G., Finance
DEARDEN, J. A., Economics
DURAND, R. M., Management and Marketing
FALCINELLI, D. F., Marketing and Management
HYCLAK, T. J., Economics
KING, A. E., Economics
KISH, R. J., Finance
KOLCHIN, M. G., Management
KUCHTA, R., Management and Marketing
LARGAY, J. A., III, Accounting
MUNLEY, V. G., Economics
NATION, G. A., III, Law and Business
NAYAR, N., Finance
O'BRIEN, A. P., Economics
PAUL, J. W., Accounting
SHERER, S. A., Management and Technology
SINCLAIR, K. P., Accounting
SIVAKUMAR, K., International Marketing and Logistics
SMACKEY, B. M., Marketing and Manufacturing Systems Engineering
STEVENS, J. E., Management
TAYLOR, L. W., Economics
THORNTON, R. J., Economics
ZIRKEL, P. A., Education and Law

College of Education (tel. (610) 758-3225):

BAMBARA, L. M., Special Education
CATES, W. M., Instructional Design and Devt
COLE, C., Psychology
DUPAUL, G., Psychology
JITENDRA, A., Special Education
MILLER, D. N., Psychology
SHAPIRO, E., Psychology
ZIRKEL, P., Education and Law

College of Engineering and Applied Science (tel. (610) 758-4025):

BLYTHE, P. A., Chemical Engineering, Mechanical Engineering and Mechanics
BOULT, T. E., Computer Science and Engineering
BROWN, F. T., Mechanical Engineering and Mechanics
CARAM, H. S., Chemical Engineering
CARGILL, G. S., III, Materials Science and Engineering
CHAN, H. M., Materials Science and Engineering
CHARLES, M., Chemical Engineering
CHAUDHURY, M. K., Chemical Engineering
CHEN, J. C., Chemical Engineering
CHRISTODOULIDES, D., Electrical and Computer Engineering
COULTER, J. P., Mechanical Engineering and Mechanics
DECKER, D. R., Electrical and Computer Engineering
DELPH, T. J., Mechanical Engineering and Mechanics
EADES, J. A., Materials Science and Engineering
EL-AASSER, M. S., Chemical Engineering
FARRINGTON, G. C., Chemical Engineering
FISHER, J. W., Civil and Environmental Engineering
FREY, D. R., Electrical and Computer Engineering
FRITCHMAN, B. D., Electrical and Computer Engineering
GARDINER, K. M., Industrial and Systems Engineering
GROOVER, M. P., Industrial and Systems Engineering
GULDEN, S. L., Computer Science and Engineering
HARLOW, D. G., Mechanical Engineering and Mechanics
HARMER, M. P., Materials Science and Engineering
HARTRANFT, R. J., Mechanical Engineering and Mechanics
HATALIS, M., Electrical and Computer Engineering
HEINDEL, N. D., Chemistry
HERTZBERG, R. W., Materials Science and Engineering
HILLMAN, D. J., Computer Science and Engineering
HSU, J. T., Chemical Engineering
HWANG, J. C. M., Electrical and Computer Engineering
JAIN, H., Materials Science and Engineering
JOHNSON, S. H., Mechanical Engineering and Mechanics
KALNINS, A., Mechanical Engineering and Mechanics
KAY, E. J., Computer Science and Engineering
KAZAKIA, J. Y., Mechanical Engineering and Mechanics
KLEIN, A., Chemical Engineering
KORTH, H., Computer Science and Engineering
KOSTEM, C. N., Civil and Environmental Engineering
LARSEN, J. W., Chemistry
LENNON, G. P., Civil and Environmental Engineering
LEVY, E. K., Mechanical Engineering and Mechanics
LU, L.-W., Civil and Environmental Engineering
LUCAS, R. A., Mechanical Engineering and Mechanics
LUYBEN, W. L., Chemical Engineering
MCAULAY, A. D., Electrical and Computer Engineering

McHugh, A., Chemical Engineering
Macpherson, A. K., Mechanical Engineering and Mechanics
Marder, A. R., Materials Science and Engineering
Nagel, R. N., Computer Science and Engineering
Neti, S., Mechanical Engineering and Mechanics
Nied, H. F., Mechanical Engineering and Mechanics
Notis, M. R., Materials Science and Engineering
Ochs, J. B., Mechanical Engineering and Mechanics
Odrey, N. G., Industrial and Systems Engineering
Ou-Yang, H. D., Physics
Regen, S. L., Chemistry
Roberts, R., Mechanical Engineering and Mechanics
Rockwell, D. O., Mechanical Engineering and Mechanics
Sawyers, K. N., Mechanical Engineering and Mechanics
Schiesser, W. E., Chemical Engineering
Schray, K. J., Chemistry
Sengupta, A. K., Chemical Engineering, Civil and Environmental Engineering
Silebi, C. A., Chemical Engineering
Simmons, G. W., Chemistry
Smith, C. R., Mechanical Engineering and Mechanics
Sorensen, R. M., Civil and Environmental Engineering
Sperling, L. H., Chemical Engineering, Materials Science and Engineering
Stenger, H. G., Jr, Chemical Engineering
Tarby, S. K., Materials Science and Engineering
Tzeng, K. K., Electrical and Computer Engineering
Varley, E., Mechanical Engineering and Mechanics
Voloshin, A. S., Mechanical Engineering and Mechanics
Wachs, I. E., Chemical Engineering
Walker, J. D. A., Mechanical Engineering and Mechanics
Wei, R. P., Mechanical Engineering and Mechanics
Weisman, R. N., Civil and Environmental Engineering
White, M. H., Electrical and Computer Engineering
Williams, D. B., Materials Science and Engineering
Wilson, J. L., Civil and Environmental Engineering
Wu, S. D., Industrial and Systems Engineering
Zimmers, E. W., Jr, Industrial and Systems Engineering

LINCOLN UNIVERSITY

1570 Baltimore Pike, POB 179, PA 19352
Telephone: (610) 932-8300
Fax: (610) 932-8316
Internet: www.lincoln.edu
Founded 1854
Academic year: August to April
Pres.: Dr Ivory V. Nelson
Vice-Pres. for Academic Affairs: Dr Grant Venerable, II
Vice-Pres. for Devt and External Relations: Michael B. Hill
Vice-Pres. for Fiscal Affairs: Howard Merlin
Vice-Pres. for Student Affairs and Enrollment Management: Dr William Bynum
Registrar: James Simington
Library Dir: Neal Carson
Library of 185,000 vols
Number of teachers: 102 (full-time)
Number of students: 2,084

LUTHERAN THEOLOGICAL SEMINARY AT GETTYSBURG

61 Seminary Ridge, Gettysburg, PA 17325
Telephone: (717) 334-6286
Fax: (717) 334-3469
E-mail: info@ltsg.edu
Internet: www.ltsg.edu
Founded 1826
Private control
Academic year: September to May
Pres.: Rev. Michael L. Cooper-White
Dean: Rev. Dr Robin J. Steinke
Registrar: Rev. Dr Marty Stevens
Library Dir: Briant Bohleke
Library of 185,000 vols; part of Combined Libraries of the E Cluster of Lutheran Seminaries
Number of teachers: 22
Number of students: 270
Publications: *Seminary Ridge Review* (2 a year), *Seminary Views* (3 a year).

LUTHERAN THEOLOGICAL SEMINARY AT PHILADELPHIA

7301 Germantown Ave, Philadelphia, PA 19119-1794
Telephone: (215) 248-4616
Fax: (215) 248-4577
E-mail: admissions@ltsp.edu
Internet: www.ltsp.edu
Founded 1864
Private control
Pres.: Rev. Dr Philip D. W. Krey
Exec. Dir: Glenn Miller
Dean: Paul Rajashekar
Registrar: René Diemer
Library Dir: Karl Krueger
Number of teachers: 35
Number of students: 220 (full-time)

LYCOMING COLLEGE

700 College Pl., Williamsport, PA 17701
Telephone: (717) 321-4000
Fax: (717) 321-4337
Internet: www.lycoming.edu
Founded 1812
Pres.: James E. Douthat
Provost and Dean: Thomas A. Griffiths
Registrar: Mary Savoy
Dir of Library Services: Janet McNeil Hurlbert
Library of 178,400 vols
Number of teachers: 92 (full-time)
Number of students: 1,546

MARYWOOD UNIVERSITY

2300 Adams Ave, Scranton, PA 18509
Telephone: (570) 348-6211
Internet: www.marywood.edu
Founded 1915
Pres.: Sis. Anne Munley
Vice-Pres. for Academic Affairs: Peter Cimbolic
Vice-Pres. for Student Life: Raymond P. Heath
Vice-Pres. for Univ. Advancement: Clayton N. Pheasant
Dir of Library: Cathy Schappert
Library of 216,191 vols
Number of teachers: 294
Number of students: 2,926

MERCYHURST COLLEGE

501 East 38th St, Erie, PA 16546-0001
Telephone: (814) 824-2000
Internet: www.mercyhurst.edu
Founded 1926
Private control
Academic year: September to May
Pres.: Dr Thomas J. Gamble
Exec. Vice-Pres. for Admin.: Dr Heidi Hosey
Vice-Pres. for Academic Affairs: Dr Barbara A. Behan
Vice-Pres. for Finance: Jane M. Kelsey
Vice-Pres. for Institutional Advancement: Gary L. Bukowski
Registrar: Sis. Patricia Whalen
Dean of Libraries: Kenneth Brundage
Number of teachers: 124
Number of students: 3,080

MESSIAH COLLEGE

1 College Ave, Grantham, PA 17027
Telephone: (717) 766-2511
Fax: (717) 691-6025
Internet: www.messiah.edu
Founded 1909
Private control
Academic year: September to May
Pres.: Dr Kim S. Phipps
Provost: Dr Randall G. Basinger
Vice-Pres. for Advancement: Barry G. Goodling
Vice-Pres. for Finances: Dr Lois J. Voigt
Vice-Pres. for Operations: Kathrynne G. Shafer
Vice-Pres. of Enrollment Management: John Chopka
Vice-Provost and Dean of Students: Dr Kristin M. Hansen-Kieffer
Vice-Provost and Dean of Curriculum: Dr William Strausbaugh
Library of 292,272 vols
Number of teachers: 281 (175 full-time, 106 part-time)
Number of students: 2,808 (2,739 full-time, 69 part-time)
Publication: *The Bridge*

DEANS

School of Arts: Richard E. Roberson
School of Business, Education and Social Sciences: Susan Hasseler
School of Humanities: Peter K. Powers
School of Science, Engineering and Health: W. Ray Norman

MOORE COLLEGE OF ART AND DESIGN

20th St and The Parkway, Philadelphia, PA 19103-1179
Telephone: (215) 568-4515
Fax: (215) 568-8017
E-mail: info@moore.edu
Internet: www.moore.edu
Founded 1848
Private control
Academic year: August to May
Pres.: Dr Happy Craven Fernandez
Vice-Pres. for Finance and Admin.: William L. Hill, II
Academic Dean: Dona Lantz
Dean of Students: Joan Stevens
Registrar: Dianne Runyon
Library Dir: Sharon Watson-Mauro
Number of teachers: 55
Number of students: 500

MORAVIAN COLLEGE

1200 Main St, Bethlehem, PA 18018
Telephone: (610) 861-1300
Fax: (610) 861-1445
Internet: www.moravian.edu
Founded 1742; men first admitted 1807
Academic year: August to May
Pres.: Dr Christopher M. Thomforde

Vice-Pres. for Academic Affairs and Dean of Faculty: CURTIS A. KEIM
Vice-Pres. for Admin.: DENNIS A. DOMCHEK
Vice-Pres. for Institutional Advancement: PETER CAPUTO
Vice-Pres. for Planning and Enrollment: BERNARD J. STORY
Vice-Pres. for Student Affairs and Dean of Students: BEVERLY J. KOCHARD
Dean of Student Life: ROBERT R. WINDOLPH

Library of 220,000 vols
Number of teachers: 88
Number of students: 1,234

MUHLENBERG COLLEGE

2400 Chew St, Allentown, PA 18104
Telephone: (484) 664-3200
Fax: (484) 664-3234
Internet: www.muhlenberg.edu

Founded 1848

Pres.: PEYTON RANDOLPH HELM
Provost: Dr JOHN RAMSAY
Dean of Admissions and Financial Aid: CHRIS HOOKER-HARING
Dean of Students: KAREN GREEN
Library Dir: JOYCE HOMMEL

Library of 290,000 vols
Number of teachers: 161
Number of students: 2,150

NEUMANN COLLEGE

1 Neumann Dr., Aston, PA 19014-1298
Telephone: (610) 459-0905
Fax: (610) 459-1370
E-mail: neumann@neumann.edu
Internet: www.neumann.edu

Founded 1965 as Our Lady of Angels College; present name 1980
Private control

Pres.: Dr ROSALIE M. MIRENDA
Vice-Pres. for Academic Affairs: GERALD P. O'SULLIVAN
Vice-Pres. for Enrollment Management and Student Affairs: DENNIS MURPHY
Vice-Pres. for Finance and Admin.: DAVID W. BROWNLEE
Vice-Pres. for Institutional Advancement and College Relations: HENRY A. SUMNER
Vice-Pres. for Mission and Ministry Affairs: Sr MARGUERITE O'BEIRNE
Library Dir: JOHN MICHAEL POWELL

Number of teachers: 158
Number of students: 2,221 (1,853 undergraduate, 368 postgraduate)

PALMER THEOLOGICAL SEMINARY

6 East Lancaster Ave, Wynnewood, PA 19096
Telephone: (610) 896-5000
Fax: (610) 649-3834
E-mail: semadmis@eastern.edu
Internet: www.palmerseminary.edu

Founded 1925 as Eastern Baptist Theological Seminary, present name 2005
Private control

Seminary Pres.: WALLACE CHARLES SMITH
Univ. Pres.: DAVID R. BLACK
Vice-Pres. and Academic Dean: ELOUISE RENICH FRASER
Vice-Pres. of Finance and Chief Operating Officer: ANUP KAPUR
Registrar: CRAIG MILLER
Library Dir: MELODY MAZUK

Number of teachers: 55
Number of students: 700

PENNSYLVANIA STATE SYSTEM OF HIGHER EDUCATION

Office of the Chancellor, Dixon Univ. Center, 2986 North Second St Harrisburg, PA 17110
Telephone: (717) 720-4010
Fax: (717) 720-4011
Internet: www.passhe.edu

Chancellor: Dr JUDY G. HAMPLE
Number of students: 107,000 total at 14 univs.

CONSTITUENT INSTITUTIONS

Bloomsburg University of Pennsylvania

400 East Second St, Bloomsburg, PA 17815
Telephone: (717) 389-4000
Internet: www.bloomu.edu

Founded 1839

Pres.: Dr JESSICA KOZLOFF
Provost: Dr WILSON BRADSHAW
Registrar: K. SCHNURE
Librarian (vacant)

Library of 376,800 vols
Number of teachers: 396
Number of students: 7,500

Courses in arts and sciences, business, computer and information science, nursing and medical imaging, teacher education.

California University of Pennsylvania

250 University Ave, California, PA 15419-1394
Telephone: (412) 938-4000
Internet: www.cup.edu

Founded 1852

Pres.: Dr ANGELO ARMENTI, Jr
Dean of Admissions and Academic Records: NORMAN HASBROUCK
Dean of Library Services: WILLIAM L. BECK

Library of 739,395 vols (405,667 microforms)
Number of teachers: 311
Number of students: 5,850

Publications: *Contribution to Scholarship* (1 a year), *Graduate Catalog* (2 a year), *Undergraduate Catalog* (2 a year)

DEANS

College of Education and Human Services: Dr STEPHEN PAVLAK
College of Liberal Arts: JESSE CIGNETTI
School of Graduate Studies and Research: Dr GEORGE CRANE
School of Science and Technology: Dr RICHARD HART

Cheyney University of Pennsylvania

Cheyney and Creek Rds, Cheyney, PA 19319-0200
Telephone: (610) 399-2220
Fax: (610) 399-2415
E-mail: admissions@cheyney.edu
Internet: www.cheyney.edu

Founded 1837
Academic year: August to May

Pres.: W. CLINTON PETTUS
Dir of Enrollment Management: JAMES BROWN
Provost: TETA V. BANKS
Librarian: LUT NERO

Library of 238,699 vols
Number of teachers: 102
Number of students: 1,821

Clarion University of Pennsylvania

Clarion, PA 16214
Telephone: (814) 393-2000
E-mail: info@clarion.edu
Internet: www.clarion.edu

Founded 1867
Academic year: August to May

Pres.: DIANE L. REINHARD
Provost: JOSEPH P. GRUNENWALD
Vice-Pres. for Devt and Student Affairs: HARRY E. TRIPP
Vice-Pres. for Finance and Admin.: W. PAUL BYLASKA
Dir of Admissions: WILLIAM D. BAILEY
Dir of Libraries: HOWARD F. MCGINN

Library of 363,000 vols
Number of teachers: 364
Number of students: 6,300

East Stroudsburg University of Pennsylvania

200 Prospect St, East Stroudsburg, PA 183301-2999
Telephone: (570) 422-3211
Internet: www.esu.edu

Founded 1893 as East Stroudsburg Normal School; present name 1983
Academic year: August to May

Pres.: Dr ROBERT J. DILLMAN
Provost and Vice-Pres. for Academic Affairs: Dr EVELYN C. LYNCH
Vice-Pres. for Finance and Admin.: RICHARD A. STANESKI
Vice-Pres. for Student Affairs: VALERIE M. HODGE
Vice-Pres. for Univ. Advancement: Dr ISAAC W. SANDERS
Registrar: GEORGIA PRELL
Library Dir: DAVID G. SCHAPPERT

Number of teachers: 274
Number of students: 6,291 (5,176 undergraduate, 1,115 postgraduate)

DEANS

School of Arts and Sciences: Dr BONNIE NEUMANN
School of Graduate Studies and Research: Dr JAMES A. FAGIN
School of Health Sciences and Human Performance: Dr MARK J. KILKER
School of Professional Studies: Dr SAM HAUSFATHER

Edinboro University of Pennsylvania

219 Meadville St, Edinboro, PA 16444
Telephone: (814) 732-2000
Fax: (814) 732-2880
E-mail: eup_admissions@edinboro.edu
Internet: www.edinboro.edu

Founded 1857
Academic year: August to May

Pres.: Dr JEREMY D. BROWN
Provost and Vice-Pres. for Academic Affairs: Dr PHILIP GINNETTI
Vice-Pres. for Finance and Admin.: GORDON HERBST
Vice-Pres. for Student Affairs and Student Success: Dr KAHAN SABLO
Asst Vice-Pres. for Admissions: TERRENCE CARLIN
Assoc. Vice-Pres. for Univ. Libraries: Dr DONALD DILMORE

Library of 500,152 vols
Number of teachers: 407
Number of students: 8,642

DEANS

Graduate Studies and Research: Dr ALAN BIEL
School of Education: Dr JOEL ERION
School of Liberal Arts: Dr TERRY L. SMITH

Indiana University of Pennsylvania

Indiana, PA 15705
Telephone: (412) 357-2100
Internet: www.iup.edu

Founded 1875 as Indiana State Normal School

State control
Academic year: September to May (two sessions)
Pres.: Dr LAWRENCE K. PETTIT
Provost and Vice-Pres. for Academic Affairs: Dr MARK J. STASZKIEWICZ
Vice-Pres. for Admin. and Finance: C. EDWARD RECESKI
Vice-Pres. for Institutional Advancement: Dr JOAN FISHER
Vice-Pres. for Student Affairs: Dr HAROLD GOLDSMITH
Dean of Admissions: WILLIAM NUNN
Dean of Graduate School: Dr JAMES PETERSON
Dir of Libraries and Media Resources: Dr RENA FOWLER

Library of 806,332 vols
Number of teachers: 738
Number of students: 13,410

DEANS

College of Business: Dr ROBERT C. CAMP
College of Education: Dr JOHN BUTZOW
College of Fine Arts: Dr MICHAEL J. HOOD
College of Human Ecology and Health Sciences: Dr CARLENE ZONI
College of Humanities and Social Sciences: Dr BRENDA CARTER
College of Natural Sciences and Mathematics: Dr JOHN ECK
Graduate School: Dr JAMES PETERSON
School of Continuing Education: Dr NICHOLAS E. KOLB
International Studies: Dr PATRICK CARONE

Kutztown University of Pennsylvania

POB 730, Kutztown, PA 19530
Telephone: (610) 683-4102
Fax: (610) 683-4693
E-mail: officeofthepresident@kutztown.edu
Internet: www.kutztown.edu

Founded 1866
State control
Academic year: September to May

Pres.: Dr F. JAVIER CEVALLOS
Provost and Vice-Pres. for Academic Affairs: Dr CARLOS VARGAS-ABURTO
Vice-Provost for Information Technology: RICHARD ZERA
Vice-Pres. for Admin. and Finance: GERALD L. SILBERMAN
Vice-Pres. for Student Affairs: Dr CHARLES WOODARD
Vice-Pres. for Univ. Advancement: Dr PRUDENCE PRECOURT
Dir of Admissions: Dr WILLIAM STAHLER
Registrar: MICHELLE HUGHES
Librarian: Dr BARBARA DARDEN

Library of 415,000 vols
Number of teachers: 540
Number of students: 10,393

DEANS

College of Business: Dr WILLIAM DEMPSEY
College of Education: Dr DARRELL GARBER (acting)
College of Liberal Arts and Sciences: Dr ANNE ZAYAITZ (acting)
College of Visual and Performing Arts: Dr WILLIAM MOWDER

Lock Haven University of Pennsylvania

Lock Haven, PA 17745
Telephone: (717) 893-2000
Fax: (717) 893-2432
Internet: www.lhup.edu

Founded 1870
Academic year: August to May

Pres.: Dr CRAIG D. WILLIS
Dir of Admissions: JAMES REESER
Dir of Library Services: TARA FULTON

Library of 352,369 vols
Number of teachers: 224
Number of students: 3,945

Publication: *Lock Haven International Review* (1 a year).

Mansfield University of Pennsylvania

Mansfield, PA 16933
Telephone: (717) 662-4000
Internet: www.mansfield.edu

Founded 1857
Academic year: September to May

Pres.: JOHN R. HALSTEAD
Provost: PETER KELLER
Dir of Enrollment Services: BRIAN BARDEN
Dir of Library Service and Instructional Resources: LARRY NESBIT
Dir of Student Records: CAROL ALEXANDER

Library of 222,650 vols
Number of teachers: 170
Number of students: 3,500

Millersville University of Pennsylvania

POB 1002, Millersville, PA 17551-0302
Telephone: (717) 872-3011
Fax: (717) 871-2147
Internet: www.millersville.edu

Founded 1855
Academic year: September to August

Associate, Baccalaureate and Masters degree programmes in business, liberal arts and sciences, professional studies, teacher education

Pres.: Dr FRANCINE G. MCNAIRY
Registrar: CANDACE A. DEEN
Assoc. Provost for Enrollment: DOUGLAS ZANDER
Dir for Univ. Library: Dr MAJORIE WARMKESSEL

Library of 1,106,025 vols incl. microfilm/microfiche
Number of teachers: 431 (299 full-time, 132 part-time)
Number of students: 8,729 (7,604 undergraduate, 1,125 postgraduate)

Shippensburg University of Pennsylvania

1871 Old Main Dr., Shippensburg, PA 17257-2299
Telephone: (717) 477-7447
Fax: (717) 477-1273
E-mail: admiss@ship.edu
Internet: www.ship.edu

Founded 1871
Academic year: August to May

Pres.: ANTHONY F. CEDDIA
Provost and Vice-Pres. for Academic Affairs: PATRICIA SPAKES
Assoc. Provost: JAMES COOLSEN
Vice-Pres. for Admin. and Finance: DONALD WILKINSON
Vice-Pres. for Student Affairs: GEORGE F. HARPSTER, Jr
Dean of Academic Programmes and Services: MARIAN SCHULTZ
Dean of Admissions: JOSEPH CRETELLA
Dean of Library and Media Services: HECTOR MAYMI-SUGRANES

Library of 1,804,005 items
Number of teachers: 393 (365 instructional)
Number of students: 7,607

Publication: *Proteus: A Journal of Ideas* (2 a year)

DEANS

College of Arts and Sciences: SARA GROVE
College of Business: STEPHEN HOLOVIAK
College of Education and Human Services: ROBERT B. BARTOS

Slippery Rock University of Pennsylvania

Slippery Rock, PA 16057
Telephone: (724) 738-9000
Fax: (724) 738-2098
E-mail: asktherock@sru.edu
Internet: www.sru.edu

Founded 1889
Academic year: June to May

Pres.: Dr ROBERT M. SMITH
Provost and Vice-Pres. for Academic Affairs: Dr WILLIAM F. WILLIAMS
Vice-Pres. for Finance and Admin. Affairs: Dr CHARLES CURRY
Vice-Pres. for Student Affairs and Dean of Students: Dr CONSTANCE FOLEY
Vice-Pres. for Univ. Advancement: BARBARA ENDER
Dir of Academic Records and Summer School: ELIOTT BAKER
Dir of Admissions: W. C. VANCE
Dir of Graduate Admissions: ANGELA PIVERETTO
Dir of Int. Initiatives: PAMELA FRIGOT
Dir of Library Services: PHILIP TRAMDACK

Library of 513,194 vols, 500 periodicals, 1,537,645 microforms
Number of teachers: 432
Number of students: 8,458

Publications: *Ginger Hill* (1 a year), *Saxigena* (1 a year), *The Rock* (4 a year)

DEANS

College of Business, Information and Social Sciences: Dr BRUCE RUSSELL
College of Education: Dr KATHLEEN STRICKLAND
College of Health, Environment and Sciences: Dr SUSAN HANNAM
College of Humanities, Fine and Performing Arts: Dr EVA TSUQUIASHI-DADDESIO

West Chester University of Pennsylvania

West Chester, PA 19383
Telephone: (610) 436-1000
Internet: www.wcupa.edu

Founded 1871

Pres.: Dr MADELEINE WING ADLER
Dir of Admissions: Ms MARSHA HAUG
Librarian: F. Q. HELMS

Library of 500,000 vols
Number of teachers: 670 (539 full-time, 131 part-time)
Number of students: 11,344

Publications: *College Literature*, *Serpentine*.

PENNSYLVANIA STATE UNIVERSITY

University Park, PA 16802
Telephone: (814) 865-4700
Internet: www.psu.edu

Founded 1855
Academic year: August to May

Pres.: GRAHAM SPANIER
Exec. Vice-Pres. and Provost: RODNEY A. ERICKSON
Sr Vice-Pres. for Devt and Alumni Relations: RODNEY P. KIRSCH
Sr Vice-Pres. for Finance and Business/Treas.: ALBERT G. HORVATH
Sr Vice-Pres. for Health Affairs: HAROLD L. PAZ
Vice-Pres. and Dean for Undergraduate Education: ROBERT N. PANGBORN
Vice-Provost for Academic Affairs: BLANNIE BOWEN
Vice-Pres. for Admin.: THOMAS G. POOLE
Vice-Pres. for Commonwealth Campuses: JOHN J. ROMANO
Vice-Pres. for Educational Equity: W. TERRELL JONES

Vice-Pres. for Outreach: CRAIG D. WEIDEMANN
Vice-Pres. for Research and Dean of the Graduate School: HENRY C. FOLEY
Vice-Pres. for Student Affairs: DAMON SIMS
Vice-Pres. for Univ. Relations: WILLIAM M. MAHON III
Vice-Pres. and Gen. Counsel: CYNTHIA BALDWIN
Dean of Libraries and Scholarly Communications: BARBARA I. DEWEY

Library: see Libraries
Number of teachers: 5,944 (full-time)
Number of students: 87,163 (all locations)
Campuses: University Park (admin. hub), Abington, Altoona, Beaver, Berks, Brandywine, Dickinson School of Law, DuBois, Erie (Behrend College), Fayette, Great Valley, Greater Allegheny, Harrisburg, Hazleton, Lehigh Valley, Milton S. Hershey Medical Center and College of Medicine, Mont Alto, New Kensington, Pennsylvania College of Technology, Schuylkill, Shenango, Wilkes-Barre, Worthington Scranton, York

DEANS

College of Agricultural Sciences: BRUCE MCPHERON
College of Arts and Architecture: BARBARA O. KORNER
College of Communications: DOUGLAS A. ANDERSON
College of Earth and Mineral Sciences: WILLIAM E. EASTERLING
College of Education: DAVID H. MONK
College of Engineering: DAVID N. WORMLEY
College of Health and Human Development: ANN C. CROUTER
College of Information Sciences and Technology: DAVID HALL
College of the Liberal Arts: SUSAN WELCH
Dickinson School of Law, Carlisle: PHILIP J. MCCONNAUGHAY
Graduate School: HENRY C. FOLEY
Hershey Medical Center: HAROLD L. PAZ
Pennsylvania College of Technology, Penn College: DAVIE J. GILMOUR (Pres.)
School of Int. Affairs: TIYANJANA MALUWA (Dir)
School of Nursing: PAULA MILONE-NUZZO
Schreyer Honors College: CHRISTIAN BRADY
Smeal College of Business: JAMES B. THOMAS
The Eberly College of Science: DANIEL J. LARSON

PROFESSORS

(Some professors serve in more than one department)

College of Agricultural Sciences (201 Agricultural Admin. Bldg, University Park, PA 16802; internet www.cas.psu.edu):

Agricultural and Biological Engineering:

BUFFINGTON, D. E., Agricultural Engineering
ELLIOT, H. A., Agricultural Engineering
GRAVES, R. E.
HEINEMANN, P. H., Systems Modelling
JARRETT, A. R.
MANBECK, H. B.
MURPHY, D. J., Agricultural Engineering
PURI, V. M., Agricultural Engineering
WALKER, P. N.
YOUNG, R. E.

Agricultural Economics and Rural Sociology:

ABLER, D. G., Agricultural, Environmental and Regional Economics and Demography
ALTER, T. R., Agricultural Economics
BAILEY, K. W., Agricultural Economics
BECKER, J. C., Agricultural Economics
BEIERLEIN, J. G., Agricultural Economics
BLANDFORD, D., Agricultural Economics
DUNN, J. W., Agricultural Economics
EPP, D. J., Agricultural Economics
FISHER, A. N. P., Agricultural and Environmental Economics
HANSON, G. D., Agricultural Economics
HARPER, J. K., Agricultural and Environmental Economics
HYMAN, D. W., Public Policy and Community Systems
JENSEN, L. I., Rural Sociology and Demography
LULOFF, A. E., Rural Sociology
MOORE, H. L., Agricultural Economics
SACHS, C., Rural Sociology
SHORTLE, J. S., Agricultural Economics
SMITH, S. M., Agricultural Economics
STEFANOU, S. E., Agricultural Economics
STOKES, C. S., Rural Sociology
VAN HORN, J. E., Rural Sociology
WEAVER, R. D., Agricultural Economics
WILLITS, F. K., Rural Sociology
ZOUMAS, B., Agribusiness

Agricultural and Extension Education:

BOWEN, B. E., Agricultural and Extension Education
CAREY, H. A., Extension Information
FLANAGAN, C. A., Agricultural and Extension Education
LEWIS, R. B., 4-H Youth
SCANLON, D. C., Agricultural and Extension Education
THOMSON, J. S., Agricultural Communications
YODER, E. P., Agricultural and Extension Education

Crop and Soil Sciences:

BEEGLE, D. B., Agronomy
CIOLKOSZ, E. J., Soil Genesis and Morphology
CURRAN, W. S., Weed Science
FRITTON, D. D., Soil Physics
HALL, M. H., Agronomy
HATLEY, O. E., Agronomy
KOMARNENI, S., Clay Mineralogy
KRUEGER, C. R., Agronomy
LANYON, L. E., Soil Science and Management
PENNYBACKER, B. W., Agronomy
PETERSEN, G. W., Soil and Land Resources
SYLVIA, D., Soil Microbiology
TURGEON, A. J., Turfgrass Management
WATSCHKE, T. L., Turfgrass Science

Dairy and Animal Science:

BAUMRUCKER, C. R., Animal Nutrition-Physiology
CASH, E. H., Animal Science
ETHERTON, T. D., Animal Nutrition
HAGEN, D. R., Animal Science
HEALD, C. W., Dairy Science
HEINRICHS, A. J., Dairy and Animal Science
HENNING, W. R., Animal Science
KEPHART, K. B., Animal Science
KILLIAN, G. J., Reproductive Physiology
MULLER, L. D., Dairy Science
O'CONNOR, M. L., Dairy Science
VARGA, G. A., Animal Science
VASILATOS-YOUNKEN, R., Endocrine Physiology and Nutrition

Entomology:

CALVIN, D.
FELTON, G.
FRAZIER, J. L., Entomology
HELLER, P. R., Entomology
HULL, L. A., Entomology
KIM, K. C., Entomology
MCPHERON, B.
MULLIN, C. A., Entomology
SCHULTZ, J. C., Entomology

Food Science:

ANANTHESWARAN, R. C., Food Science
BEELMAN, R. B., Food Science
FLOROS, J. D., Food Science
HOOD, L. F., Food Science
MARETZKI, A. N., Food Science and Nutrition
THOMPSON, D. B., Food Science

Horticulture:

ARTECA, R. N., Horticultural Physiology
BROWN (EVENSON), K. M., Post-harvest Physiology
CRAIG, R., Plant Breeding
CRASSWELLER, R. M., Tree Fruit
EISSENSTAT, D. M., Woody Plant Physiology
FERRETTI, P. A., Vegetable Crops
GUILTINAN, M. J., Plant Molecular Biology
HEUSER, C. W., Horticultural Physiology
HOLCOMB, E. J., Floriculture
KOIDE, R. T., Horticultural Ecology
KUHNS, L. J., Ornamental Horticulture
ORZOLEK, M. D., Horticulture

Plant Pathology:

AYERS, J. E.
CHRIST, B. J., Potato Breeding and Diseases
COLE, H., Jr, Agricultural Sciences
DAVIS, D. D.
GILDOW, F. E., Virus-vector Biology
FLORES, H. E.
LUKEZIC, F. L.
MACNAB, A. A.
MOORMAN, G. W., Plant Pathology
PELL, E. J., Agriculture
ROMAINE, C. P., Plant Viruses
ROYSE, D. J., Plant Pathology
SKELLY, J. M.
STEWART, E. L., Plant Pathology
TRAVIS, J. W.

Poultry Science:

ELKIN, R. G., Nutritional Biochemistry
LEACH, R. M., Jr, Poultry Science
VASILATOS-YOUNKEN, R., Metabolic Endocrinology

School of Forest Resources:

ABRAMS, M. D., Forestry
BLANKENHORN, P. R., Wood Technology
BOWERSOX, T. W., Silviculture
BROOKS, R. P., Wildlife and Wetlands
DEWALLE, D. R., Forest Hydrology
GERHOLD, H. D., Forest Genetics
LYNCH, J. A., Forest Hydrology
MCCORMICK, L. H., Forest Resources
MCKINSTRY, R. B., Forestry and Environmental Resource Management
SAN JULIAN, G., Wildlife Resources
SHARPE, W. E., Forest Resources
SMITH, P. M., Wood Products Marketing
STAUFFER, J. R., Ichthyology
STEINER, K. C., Forest Biology
YAHNER, R. H., Wildlife Management

Veterinary Science:

GRIEL, L. C., Jr
HUTCHINSON, L. J.
OMIECINSKI, C.
PERDEW, G. H.
REDDY, C. C.
SHAW, D. P.
SORDILLO, L. M.
WOJCHOWSKI, D. M.

College of Arts and Architecture (Office of the Dean, 111 Arts Bldg, University Park, PA 16802; tel. (814) 865-2591; fax (814) 865-7140; internet www.artsandarchitecture.psu.edu):

Architecture:

HAIDER, J., Architecture
KALISPERIS, L. N., Architecture
LUCAS, J. P., Architecture

Art History:

CUTLER, A.

Integrative Arts:

HAMPTON, G., Art Education and Integrative Arts
LANG, G., Art and Integrative Arts

Landscape Architecture:

DICKIE, G.
JONES, D. R.

ORLAND, B.

School of Music:

ARMSTRONG, D. C., Music
BROYLES, M., Music and American History
CARR, M. A., Music
DOSSE, M., Music
SMITH, S. H., Music
THOMPSON, K. P., Music Education
TRINKLEY, W. B., Music
WILLIAMS, E. V., Music
YODER, M. D., Music

School of Theatre:

CARTER, D. H.
GIBSON, A. A.
LEONARD, R. E.
NICHOLS, R.

School of Visual Arts:

AMATEAU, M., Art and Women's Studies
GRAVES, K., Art
HAMPTON, G., Art and Art Education
LANG, G., Art
LEUPP, L. G., Art
MADDOX, J., Art
PORTER, S., Art
SOMMESE, L. B., Art
STEPHENSON, J. E., Art
WILSON, B. G., Art Education

College of Communications (Dean's Office, 201 Carnegie, University Park, PA 16802; internet www.psu.edu/dept/comm):

Advertising and Public Relations:

BAUKUS, R. A., Communications (non-professorial Head)

Film/Video and Media Studies:

BARTON, R. L., Media Studies
COHEN, J., Communications
DAVIS, D., Communications
NICHOLS, J. S., Communications

Journalism:

BERNER, R. T., Journalism and American Studies
CURLEY, J., Communications
FOREMAN, G., Communications
RICHARDS, R. D., Journalism and Law

Telecommunications:

FRIEDEN, R. M., Cable Telecommunications
SCHEMENT, J. R., Telecommunications
TAYLOR, R. D., Telecommunications Studies and Law

College of Earth and Mineral Sciences (; internet www.ems.psu.edu):

Energy and Geo-Environmental Engineering:

ADEWUMI, M., Petroleum and Natural Gas Engineering
BISE, C. J., Mining Engineering and Industrial Health and Safety
CHANDER, S., Mineral Processing and Geo-Environmental Engineering
ELSWORTH, D., Energy and Geo-Environmental Engineering
ERTEKIN, T., Petroleum and Natural Gas Engineering
GRADER, A., Petroleum and Natural Gas Engineering
OSSEO-ASARE, K., Metals Science and Engineering and Geo-Environmental Engineering
PARIZEK, R., Geosciences and Geo-Environmental Engineering
SCARONI, A., Energy and Geo-Environmental Engineering
SCHOBERT, H. H., Fuel Science
WYNGAARD, J. C., Meteorology, Mechanical Engineering, and Geo-Environmental Engineering
YOUNG, G., Meteorology and Geo-Environmental Engineering

Geography:

CARLETON, A. M.
DOWNS, R. M.
ERICKSON, R. A., Geography and Business Admin.
GLASMEIER, A. K., Geography and Regional Planning
HOLDSWORTH, D. W.
KNIGHT, C. G.
MACEACHREN, A. M., Geography
PEUQUET, D. J., Geography
YARNAL, B. M.

Geosciences:

ALEXANDER, S. S., Geophysics
ALLEY, R. B., Geosciences
ARTHUR, M. A., Geosciences
BARRON, E. J., Geosciences
BRANTLEY, S. L., Geosciences
CUFFEY, R. J., Palaeontology
DEINES, P., Geochemistry
EGGLER, D. H., Petrology
ENGELDER, T. E., Geosciences
FURLONG, K. P., Geosciences
GRAHAM, E. K., Geophysics
KASTING, J. F., Geosciences and Meteorology
KERRICK, D. M., Petrology
KUMP, L. R., Geosciences
OHMOTO, H., Geochemistry
PARIZEK, R. R., Geology
SLINGERLAND, R. L., Geology
VOIGHT, B., Geology
WHITE, W. B., Geochemistry

Materials Science and Engineering:

ADAIR, J. H., Materials Science and Engineering
ALLARA, D. L., Polymer Science and Chemistry
BROWN, P., Ceramic Science and Engineering
CHEN, L.-Q., Materials Science and Engineering
CHUNG, T.-C., Polymer Science
COLBY, R. H., Polymer Science
COLEMAN, M. M., Polymer Science
DEBROY, T., Metallurgy
GREEN, D. J., Ceramic Science and Engineering
HARRISON, I. R., Polymer Science
HOWELL, P. R., Metallurgy
KOSS, D. A., Metallurgy
KUMAR, S. K., Materials Science and Engineering
LANAGAN, M., Materials Science and Engineering
MACDONALD, D. D., Materials Science and Engineering
MESSING, G. L., Ceramic Science and Engineering
OSSEO-ASARE, K., Metallurgy
PAINTER, P. C., Polymer Science
PANTANO, C. G., Materials Science and Engineering
PICKERING, H. W., Metallurgy
RUNT, J. P., Polymer Science
RUZYLLO, J., Electrical Engineering and Materials Science
SCHLOM, D. G., Materials Science and Engineering
SINGH, J., Materials Science and Engineering
SPEAR, K. E., Ceramic Science
TRESSLER, R. E., Materials Science and Engineering
TROLIER-MCKINSTRY, S., Ceramic Science

Meteorology:

BANNON, P.
BRUNE, W. H.
CAHIR, J. J.
CARLSON, T. N.
DUTTON, J. A.
FRANK, W. M.
FRITSCH, J. M.
KASTING, J. F., Geosciences and Meteorology
KLEIT, A. N., Economics
LAMB, D.
THOMSON, D. W.
WYNGAARD, J. C.
YOUNG, G. S., Meteorology and Geo-environmental Engineering

College of Education (tel. (814) 863-2216; e-mail jdeitrich@psu.edu; internet www.ed.psu.edu):

Adult Education, Instructional Systems, and Workforce Education and Development:

ASKOV, E. N., Education
DWYER, F., Instructional Systems
GRAY, K. C., Education
PASSMORE, D. L., Education
ROTHWELL, W. J., Workforce Education and Devt

Counsellor Education, Counselling Psychology, and Rehabilitation Services:

HERBERT, J. T., Counsellor Education
HERR, E. L., Education
KEAT, D. B., II, Education and Counselling Psychology
NILES, S. G., Counsellor Education
SLANEY, R. B., Counselling Psychology

Curriculum and Instruction:

BLUME, G. W., Mathematics Education
CARLSEN, W. S., Science Education
GIROUX, H.
HEID, M. K., Mathematics Education
JOHNSON, J. E.
NELSON, M. R., Education and American Studies
NOLAN, J. F., Jr, Curriculum and Supervision
RUBBA, P. A., Jr
SHANNON, P.
SIMON, M. A., Mathematics Education
SOTO, L., Language and Literacy
YAWKEY, T. C.

Education Policy Studies:

BAKER, D. P., Education
BOYD, W. L., Educational Admin.
EVENSEN, D., Education
GEIGER, R., Education
HARTMAN, W., Education
HENDRICKSON, R. M., Education
NICELY, R., Jr, Education
PRAKASH, M. S., Education
STEFKOVICH, J. A., Education
TERENZIN, P., Education
TIPPECONNIC, J., III, Education
VOLKWEIN, J. F., Education

Educational and School Psychology and Special Education:

GAJAR, A. H., Special Education
HALE, R. L., Education
HUGHES, C. A., Education
MEYER, B. J. F., Educational Psychology
ROBERTS, D. M., Educational Psychology
RUHL, K. L., Special Education
SALVIA, J. A., Special Education
SUEN, H. K., Educational Psychology
WATKINS, M., Education (School Psychology)

College of Engineering (101 Hammond, University Park, PA 16802; internet www.engr.psu.edu):

Acoustics:

ATCHLEY, A. A.
BLOOD, I. M., Communication Disorders
BRENTNER, K. S., Aerospace Engineering
FRANK, T. A., Communication Disorders
GARRETT, S. L.
HETTCHE, L. R., Engineering Research
KOOPMANN, G. H., Mechanical Engineering
LAMANCUSA, J. S., Mechanical Engineering
LAUCHLE, G. C.
LESIEUTRE, G. A., Aerospace Engineering
LONG, L. N., Aerospace Engineering
MCLAUGHLIN, D. K., Aerospace Engineering
MAYNARD, J. D., Physics
MORRIS, P. J., Aerospace Engineering

SHUNG, K. K., Bioengineering
STERN, R., Applied Science and Mechanics
THOMSON, D. W., Meteorology
TITTMANN, B. R., Engineering Science and Mechanics

Aerospace Engineering:

CAMCI, C., Aerospace Engineering
LESIEUTRE, G. A., Aerospace Engineering
LONG, L.
MCLAUGHLIN, D. K.
MAUGHMER, M. D., Aerospace Engineering
MELTON, R. G., Aerospace Engineering
MICCI, M. M.
MORRIS, P. J.

Agricultural and Biological Engineering:

BUFFINGTON, D. E., Agricultural Engineering
ELLIOT, H. A., Agricultural Engineering
GRAVES, R. E.
HEINEMANN, P. H., Systems Modelling
JARRETT, A. R.
MANBECK, H. B.
MURPHY, D. J., Agricultural Engineering
PURI, V. M., Agricultural Engineering
WALKER, P. N.
YOUNG, R. E.

Architectural Engineering:

BEHR, R. A.
BURNETT, E. F. P., Architectural and Civil Engineering
GESCHWINDER, L. F.
MUMMA, S. A.

Bioengineering:

ALLCOCK, H. R., Chemistry
BROWN, P. W., Materials Science and Engineering
CURTIS, W. R., Chemical Engineering
FREIVALDS, A., Industrial and Manufacturing Engineering
GESELOWITZ, D. B., Bioengineering
HIGGINS, W. E., Electrical and Computer Engineering
KENNEY, E. S., Nuclear Engineering
LIPOWSKY, H. H., Bioengineering and Engineering Science
ROSE, J. L., Engineering Design and Manufacturing
ROSENBERG, G., Bioengineering and Surgery
RUNT, J. P., Polymer Sciences
SNYDER, A. J., Surgery and Bioengineering
TARBELL, J. M., Chemical Engineering and Bioengineering
ULTMAN, J. S., Chemical Engineering
ZELIS, R., Medicine and Cellular and Molecular Physiology

Chemical Engineering:

BEN-JEBRIA, A.
BORHAN, A.
CURTIS, W.
DANNER, R. P.
DUDA, J. L.
FICHTHORN, K.
FOLEY, H. C.
NAGARAJAN, R.
NEDWICK, R.
TARBELL, J. M.
ULTMAN, J. S.
VANNICE, M. A.
VRENTAS, J. S.
ZYDNEY, A. L.

Civil and Environmental Engineering:

ANDERSON, D. A.
BURNETT, E. F. P., Architectural and Civil Engineering
GOULIAS, K. G.
JOVANIS, P. P.
KILARESKI, W. P.
KRAUTHAMMER, T.
LOGAN, B. E.
MATSON, J. V.
MILLER, A. C.
REGAN, R. W., Sr
SCANLON, A.
THOMAS, H. R.
WANG, M. C.

Computer Science and Engineering
(joint department with the Eberly College of Science)

ACHARYA, R.
BARLOW, J.
DAS, C.
FENG, T.-Y.
GILES, C. L.
HIGGINS, W.
HURSON, A. R.
IRWIN, M. J.
KASTURI, R.
KUMARA, S.
LA PORTA, T.
LONG, L. N.
METZNER, J. J.
MILLER, D. A.
MILLER, W. C.
PALAMIDESSI, C.
SARASWAT, V. A.
YEN, J.

Electrical Engineering:

AYDIN, K., Electrical Engineering
BOSE, N. K., Electrical Engineering
BREAKALL, J. K.
BURTON, L. C., Electrical and Computer Engineering
CROSKEY, C. L.
CROSS, L. E., Electrical Engineering
FERRARO, A. J., Electrical Engineering
GILDENBLAT, G., Electrical Engineering
HALL, D. L.
HIGGINS, W.
JACKSON, T. N., Electrical Engineering
JENKINS, K., Electrical Engineering
KAVEHRAD, M.
KHOO, I. C., Electrical Engineering
KURTZ, S. K., Electrical Engineering
LEE, K. Y., Electrical Engineering
LUEBBERS, R. J., Electrical Engineering
MATHEWS, J. D., Electrical Engineering
METZNER, J., Electrical Engineering
MILLER, D. L., Electrical Engineering
MITCHELL, J. D., Electrical Engineering
MITTRA, R., Electrical Engineering
PHILBRICK, C. R., Electrical Engineering
PHOHA, S., Electrical and Computer Engineering
RUSSELL, D., Electrical Engineering
RUZYLLO, J., Electrical Engineering and Materials Science and Engineering
SZNAIER, M., Electrical Engineering
UCHINO, K., Electrical Engineering
WRONSKI, C. R., Microelectronic Materials and Devices
YU, F. T. S., Electrical Engineering
ZHANG, Q., Electrical Engineering

Engineering Science and Mechanics:

AMATEAU, M. F., Engineering Science and Mechanics
ASHOK, S., Engineering Science
AWADLEKARIM, O. O., Engineering Science and Mechanics
BAKIS, C. E.
CONWAY, J. C., Engineering Mechanics
ENGEL, R. S.
FONASH, S. J., Engineering Science
GERMAN, R. M., Materials
HAYEK, S. I., Engineering Mechanics
LAKHTAKIA, A.
LENAHAN, P. M., Engineering Science and Mechanics
MCGRATH, R. T.
MCNITT, R. P., Engineering Science and Mechanics
MESSIER, R. F., Engineering Science and Mechanics
PANGBORN, R. N., Engineering Mechanics
QUEENEY, R. A., Engineering Mechanics
ROSE, J. L., Engineering Design and Manufacturing
SALAMON, N. L., Engineering Science and Mechanics
TITTMANN, B. R., Engineering
TODD, J. A., Engineering Science and Mechanics
URQUIDI-MACDONALD, M.
VARADAN, V. K., Engineering Science and Mechanics
VARADAN, V. V., Engineering Science and Mechanics, and Electrical Engineering
VENTSEL, E. S., Engineering Science
WRONSKI, C. R., Microelectronic Devices and Materials

Industrial and Manufacturing Engineering:

CAVALIER, T. M.
CHANDRA, M. J.
COHEN, P. H.
ENSCORE, E. E.
FREIVALDS, A.
JOSHI, S. B.
KUMARA, S.
RAVINDRAN, A.
RUUD, C. O.
VENTURA, J. A.
VOIGHT, R. C.
WYSK, R. A.

Mechanical and Nuclear Engineering:

BARATTA, A. J.
BELEGUNDU, A. D.
BRASSEUR, J. G.
CATCHEN, G. L.
CHEUNG, F. B.
CIMBALA, J. M.
HARRIS, T. A.
HOCHREITER, L.
JESTER, W. A.
KOOPMAN, G. H.
KULAKOWSKI, B. T.
KULKARNI, A. K.
KUO, K. K.
LAMANCUSA, J. S.
LITZINGER, T. A.
MODEST, M. F.
PEREZ-BLANCO, H.
RAY, A.
SANTAVICA, D. A.
SANTORO, R. J.
SETTLES, G. S.
SINHA, A.
SOMMER, H. J., III
THYNELL, S. T.
TRETHEWY, M. W.
TURNS, S. R.
WEBB, R. L.
YANG, V.
YAVUZKURT, S.

School of Engineering Technology and Commonwealth Engineering:

HAGER, W. R.

College of Health and Human Development (Office of the Dean, 201 Henderson Bldg, University Park, PA 16802-6501; tel. (814) 865-1428; fax (814) 865-3282; e-mail healthhd@psu.edu; internet www.hhdev.psu.edu):

Biobehavioural Health:

AHERN, F. M.
AIRHIHENBUWA, C. O., Biobehavioural Health
BEARD, J. L., Nutrition Science
BECHTEL, L. J., Biobehavioural Health
CAVANAGH, P. R., Locomotion Studies, Biobehavioural Health, Medicine and Orthopaedics
FINKELSTEIN, J. W.
GRAHAM, J. W., Biobehavioural Health and Human Devt
GRANGER, D. A., Biobehavioural Health, Human Devt and Family Studies
JONES, B. C., Biobehavioural Health and Pharmacology

KOZLOWSKI, L. T.
MCCLEARN, G. E., Biobehavioural Health and Psychology
NEWELL, K. M., Biobehavioural Health and Kinesiology
NICHOLSON, M. E., Health Education and Biobehavioural Health
ROLLS, B. J., Biobehavioural Health
SUSMAN, E. J., Biobehavioural Health, Human Devt and Nursing
VICARY, J. R.
VOGLER, G. P., Biobehavioural Health

Communication Disorders:

BLOOD, G. W.
BLOOD, I. M.
FRANK, T. A.
LIGHT, J. C.
PROSEK, R. A.

Health Policy and Administration:

BRANNON, D.
KEMPER, P.
SHEA, D. G.
SHORT, P. F.
YESALIS, C. E.
YU, L. C.

Hotel, Restaurant and Recreational Management:

CALDWELL, L., Leisure Studies
CHICK, G., Hotel, Restaurant and Recreation Management (Leisure Studies)
GODBEY, G. C., Leisure Studies
LEE, R. D., Public Admin.
SHAFER, E. L., Environmental Management and Tourism

Human Development and Family Studies:

BARRY, K., Human Devt
BIRCH, L. L.
BURGESS, R. L.
BURTON, L. M., Sociology and Human Devt
COLLINS, L. M.
CROUTER, A. C., Human Devt
D'AUGELLI, A. R., Human Devt
EDELBROCK, C. S., Behavioural Health
GREENBERG, M. T.
MCHALE, S. M., Human Devlopment
SCHAIE, K. W., Human Devt and Psychology
STIFTER, C. A.
VONDRACEK, F. W.
WILLIS, S. L.
ZARIT, S. H., Human Devt

Kinesiology:

BUCKLEY, W. E., Exercise and Sport Science and Health Education
CAVANAUGH, P. R., Locomotion Studies
ECKHARDT, R. B., Kinesiology
FARRELL, P. A., Physiology
GRAHAM, G. M., Kinesiology
KENNEY, W. L., Physiology and Kinesiology
KRETCHMAR, R. S., Exercise and Sport Science
LARSSON, L. G., Physiology and Clinical Neurophysiology
LATASH, M. L., Kinesiology
MARTIN, P. E., Kinesiology
NEWELL, K. M., Kinesiology and Biobehavioural Health
ZATSIORSKY, V., Kinesiology

Nursing:

BROWN, R.
PRESTON, D.

Nutrition:

ACHTERBERG, C. L.
BAUMRUCKER, C. R., Animal Nutrition, Physiology
BEARD, J. L.
BERLIN, C. M., Jr, Paediatrics, Pharmacology
BIRCH, L. L.
CONNOR, J. R.
ETHERTON, T. D., Animal Nutrition
GREEN, M. H., Nutrition Science
JEFFERSON, L. S., Jr
KRIS-ETHERTON, P. M., Nutrition Science
LEACH, R. M., Jr
MARETZKI, A. N., Food Science and Nutrition
MASTRO, A. M., Microbiology and Cell Biology
REDDY, C. C.
ROLLS, B. J., Nutrition and Biobehavioural Health
ROSS, A. C., Nutrition and Veterinary Science
SMICIKLAS-WRIGHT, H.
THOMPSON, D. B.
VASILATOS-YOUNKEN, R.
YEH, Y.-Y.

College of the Liberal Arts (110 Sparks Bldg, University Park, PA 16802; tel. (814) 865-7691; internet www.la.psu.edu):

African and African-American Studies:

MCBRIDE, D., African-American History
MENGISTEAB, K.
SPENCER, R. C., African-American History

American Studies:

CLARKE, D. C.

Anthropology:

DURRENBERGER, E.
HIRTH, K. G.
MILNER, G. R.
RICHTSMEIER, J. T.
SANDERS, W. T.
SNOW, D. R.
WALKER, A.
WEBSTER, D. L.
WEISS, K. M., Anthropology and Genetics
WOOD, J. W.

Classics and Ancient Mediterranean Studies:

BALDI, P. H., Linguistics and Classics
HALPERN, B., Ancient History and Religious Studies
KNOPPERS, G.
PETERSEN, W., Religious Studies
REDFORD, D. B.

Communication Arts and Sciences (Speech Communication):

BENSON, T. W.
BROWNE, S. H.
GOURAN, D. S.
HECHT, M.
HOGAN, J.
NUSSBAUM, J. F.
PARROTT, R. L.

Comparative Literature:

BEEBEE, T. O., Comparative Literature and German
BEGNAL, M., English and Comparative Literature
CHENEY, P., English and Comparative Literature
ECKHARDT, C. D., English and Comparative Literature
EDWARDS, R. R., English and Comparative Literature
GROSSMAN, K., French
HALE, T. A., African, French, and Comparative Literature
KADIR, D., Comparative Literature
LIMA, R. F., Spanish and Comparative Literature
MAKWARD, C. P., French and Women's Studies
STOEKL, A., French and Comparative Literature
STRASSER, G. F., German and Comparative Literature

Crime, Law and Justice:

AUSTIN, R. L., Theory of Crime and Deviancy
BERNARD, T. J.
BLOCK, A. A.
FELSON, R., Crime
KRAMER, J. H., Sociology and Admin. of Justice
MILLER, L. L.
OSGOOD, D. W.
RUBACK, R. B.
SILVER, E.
STEFFENSMEIER, D., Sociology and Crime, Law and Justice
ULMER, J. T.

Economics:

BIERENS, H. J.
BOND, E. W.
CHATTERJEE, K., Economics and Management Science
FELLER, I.
ICKES, B. W.
JORDAN, J. S.
KLEIN, P. A.
KRISHNA, K.
KRISHNA, V.
LOMBRA, R. E.
MARSHALL, R. C.
NELSON, J. P.
ROBERTS, B.-Y.
ROBERTS, M. J.
SHAPIRO, D., Economics and Women's Studies
SJÖSTRÖM, J. T.
TYBOUT, J. R.
WALLACE, N.

English:

BECKER, R., English and Women's Studies
BEGNAL, M. H., English and Comparative Literature
BELL, B.
BIALOSTOSKY, D.
BUCKALEW, R.
CHENEY, P., English and Comparative Literature
CLAUSEN, C.
ECKHARDT, C. D., English and Comparative Literature
EDWARDS, R., English and Comparative Literature
GANNON, R.,
GILYARD, K.
HARRIS, S. K.
HUME, K.
HUME, R. D.
NEALON, J.
SELZER, J. L.
SQUIER, S. M., Women's Studies and English
WEST, J. L. W., III
WOODBRIDGE, L.

French:

BRAGGER, J. D.
GREENBERG, W. N.
GROSSMAN, K. M.
HALE, T. A., African, French and Comparative Literature
LACY, N. J.
MAKWARD, C. P., French and Women's Studies
STOEKL, A., French and Comparative Literature

Germanic and Slavic Languages and Literature:

BEEBEE, O. B., Comparative Literature and German
GENTRY, F. G.
NAYDAN, M. M.
SCHURER, E.
STRASSER, G. F., German and Comparative Literature

History and Religious Studies:

CROSS, G. S., Modern European History
DERICKSON, A., Labour History
FINKE, R., Sociology and Religious Studies
HALPERN, B., Ancient History and Jewish Studies
HSIA, R., History and Religious Studies
JENKINS, P., Religious Studies and History

KNOPPERS, G., Religious Studies
LANDES, J. B., Women's Studies and History
MCMURRY, S. A., American History
MOSES, W. J., American History
NEELY, M. E., American Civil War
PENCAK, W. A., American History
PETERSEN, W., Religious Studies
PREBISH, C., Religious Studies
PROCTOR, R. N., History of Science
ROEBER, A. G., Early Modern History and Religious Studies
ROSE, A. C., American History and Religious Studies
ROSE, P. L., European History, Jewish Studies
RUGGIERO, G., Renaissance History
SCHIEBINGER, L. L., History of Science
SWEENEY, J. R., Medieval European History

Jewish Studies:

BLOCK, A., Admin. of Justice
HALPERN, B., Ancient History and Religious Studies
KNOPPERS, G., Religious Studies
ROSE, P. L., European History, Jewish Studies

Labour Studies and Industrial Relations:

CLARK, P. F.
DERICKSON, A., Labour Studies and History
DRAGO, R.
GOURAN, D. S., Communications Arts and Sciences
FILIPPELI, R. L.
ROGERS, J. K.
STEWART, J. B.

Latin American Studies:

GONZALEZ-PEREZ, A., Spanish
HIRTH, K., Anthropology
LIMA, R., Spanish and Comparative Literature
NICHOLS, J. S., Communications
PEAVLER, T. J., Spanish
SNOW, D., Anthropology
WEBSTER, D., Anthropology

Linguistics and Applied Language Studies:

BALDI, P. H., Linguistics and Classics
GOLOMBEK, P., English as a Second Language
JOHNSON, K. E., Applied Linguistics
KROLL, J., Psychology and Applied Linguistics
LANTOLF, J. P., Spanish and Applied Linguistics
SAVIGNON, S. J., Applied Linguistics

Philosophy:

COLAPIETRO, V.
CONWAY, D. W.
GROSHOLZ, E. R.
JACQUETTE, D. L.
SALLIS, J.
SCOTT, C. E.
STUHR, J. J.
TUANA, N.

Political Science:

BAUMGARTNER, F.
BREMER, S.
EISENSTEIN, J.
HARKAVY, R. E.
LAPORTE, R., Jr, Public Admin. and Political Science
WELCH, S.

Psychology:

BERENBAUM, S.
BIERMAN, K. L.
BORKOVEC, T. D.
CARLSON, R.
CLEVELAND, J. N.
COLE, P. M.
CRNIC, K. A.
FARR, J. L.
JACOBS, R. R.
JOHNSON, E.
KROLL, J. F.
LIBEN, L. S.
MARK, M. M.
MURPHY, K. R.
NELSON, K. E.
RAY, W. J.
ROSENBAUM, D. A.
SHIELDS, S. A., Women's Studies and Psychology
STERN, R. M.
THOMAS, H.

Sociology:

BAKER, D. P., Education and Sociology
BOOTH, A.
BURTON, L., Human Devt and Sociology
CLEMENTE, F. A.
DE JONG, G. F.
FARKAS, G., Sociology and Demography
FELSON, R., Crime, Law, Justice and Sociology
FINKE, R., Sociology and Religious Studies
FIREBAUGH, G.
HAYWARD, M. D.
JOHNSON, D. R., Sociology and Human Devt and Family Studies
KRAMER, J., Sociology, Crime, Law and Justice
LANDALE, N. S., Sociology and Demography
LEE, B. A.
MCCARTHY, J. D.
MORRIS, M. W.
NELSEN, H. M.
OSGOOD, D. W., Crime, Law, Justice and Sociology
RUBACK, R. B., Crime, Law, Justice and Sociology
SCHOEN, R., Family Sociology and Demography
SICA, A.
STEFFENSMEIER, D. J., Sociology and Crime, Law and Justice

Spanish, Italian and Portuguese:

GONZALEZ-PEREZ, A., Spanish
LANTOLF, J., Spanish and Applied Linguistics
LIPSKI, J. M., Spanish and Linguistics

Women's Studies:

LANDES, J. B., Women's Studies and History
MANSFIELD, P. K., Women's Studies and Health Education
SQUIER, S. M., Women's Studies and English

Abington College (1600 Woodland Rd, Abington, PA 19001; tel. (215) 881-7300; fax (215) 881-7317; internet www.abington.psu.edu):

Division of Arts and Humanities:

KLIGER, H., Communications and Jewish Studies
MILLER, L., English
MUSTAZZA, L., English and American Studies
SMITH, J. F., English and American Studies
STUTMAN, S., English

Division of Science and Engineering:

AYOUB, A., Mathematics
JOHNSON, K., Mathematics
MOORE, G., Chemistry
REDLIN, L., Mathematics
SCHUSTER, I., Chemistry

Division of Social and Behavioural Sciences:

SMITH, J., English and American Studies

Altoona College (3000 Ivyside Park, Altoona, PA 16601; tel. (814) 949-5000; internet www.aa.psu.edu):

Division of Arts and Humanities:

MARSHALL, I. S., English
MOORE, D. W., English
WOLFE, M., History

Division of Education, Human Development and Social Sciences:

BECHTEL, L. J., Biobehavioural Health

Behrend College, Penn State Erie (5091 Station Rd, Erie, PA 16563; tel. (814) 898-6000; internet www.pserie.psu.edu):

School of Business:

PATTERSON, R., Accountancy
VOSS, J. A., Accountancy

School of Humanities and Social Sciences:

BALDWIN, D., English
FERNANDEZ-JIMENEZ, J., Spanish
FRANKFORTER, A. D., European History
GAMBLE, J. K., Political Science and International Law
GEORGE, D. H., English and Women's Studies
MORRIS, G. L., American Literature
PORAC, C., Psychology
WOLFE, K., French
WOLFORD, C., English, Business

School of Science:

LARSON, R., Mathematics (Calculus)

Berks–Lehigh Valley College (*Berks campus*: Tulpehocken Rd, POB 7009, Reading, PA 19610-6009
Lehigh Valley campus: 8380 Mohr Lane, Fogelsville, PA 18051-9999; tel. (610) 396-6000 (Berks), (610) 285-5220 (Lehigh Valley); fax (610) 285-5220 (Lehigh Valley), internet www.bklv.psu.edu):

BARTKOWIAK, R. A., Engineering
FIFER, K., English
GREENBERG, W., French
LITVIN, D. B., Physics
LODWICK, K. L., History
MILAKOFSKY, L., Chemistry
RILEY, M., English

Capital College, Harrisburg and Schuylkill (*Harrisburg campus*: 777 W Harrisburg Pike, Middletown, PA 17057-4846
Schuylkill campus: 200 University Drive, Schuylkill Haven, PA 17972-2208; tel. (717) 948-6250 (Harrisburg), (570) 385-6000 (Schuylkill); fax (570) 385-3672 (Schuylkill); internet www.cl.psu.edu):

ANSARY, O., Engineering
ASWAD, A., Engineering
BLUMBERG, M., Management
BRONNER, S. J., American Studies and Folklore
CARDAMONE, M. J., Physics
CHEN, Y. F., Civil Engineering
CHISHOLM, R. F., Management
CIGLER, B. A., Public Policy and Admin.
COLE, C. A., Engineering
COUCH, S. R., Sociology
CULPAN, R., Management
DISHNER, E. K., Education
FOXX, R., Psychology
HANES, M. L., Education
KAYNAK, E., Marketing
MAHAR, W. J., Humanities and Music
MILLS, P., Business Admin.
PETERSON, S. A., Public Affairs
PLANT, J. F., Public Policy and Admin.
RABIN, J. M., Public Admin. and Public Policy
RAY, G., Engineering
RICHMAN, I., American Studies and History
SACHS, H. G., Biology
STEPHENS, J. L., Speech Communications
YAVERBAUM, G. J., Information Systems
ZIEGENFUSS, J. T., Management and Health Care Systems

Commonwealth College (111 Old Main, University Park, PA 16802-1501; tel. (814) 863-0327); internet www.cwc.psu.edu):

Arts and Humanities Division:

CLEMENT, P., History
GINSBERG, R., Philosophy
PLUHAR, E., Philosophy

Business and Economics Division:
KUCUKEMIROGLU, O., Accounting
Engineering Division:
WALTERS, R.
WEED, M.
English Division:
COLLISON, G.
FRUSHELL, R.
JARRETT, J.
MCCARTHY, W.
PRICE, R. A.
SORKIN, A.
Mathematics Division:
BARSHINGER, R.
DAWSON, J.
GOMEZ-CALDERON, J.
HELOU, C.
HORWITZ, A.
IVANOV, A.
NOURI, M.
ZEMYAN, S.
Science Division:
BITTNER, E., Chemistry
BLACK, R., Biology
BURSEY, C., Biology
CAMARDA, H., Physics
DE ROSA, M., Chemistry
FEHLNER, J., Chemistry
HARRISON, E., Chemistry
HOULIHAN, J., Physics
KHAN, A., Chemistry
MARICONDI, C., Chemistry
MILLER, D., Physics
MONROE, J., Physics
OBERMYER, R., Physics
SARAFIAN, H., Physics
SUBRAMANIAM, G., Chemistry
VISWANATHAN, N., Chemistry
WINTER, T., Physics
WOLFE, C., Biology
Social Sciences and Education Division:
BALL, R., AOJ
CIMBALA, S., Political Science
GERGEN, M., Psychology
GRESSON, A., Curriculum and Instruction
JOHNSON, J., Psychology

College of Medicine, Hershey (Penn State Milton S. Hershey Medical Center, 500 University Drive, Hershey, PA 17033; tel. (717) 531-8521; internet www.hmc.psu.edu):
Behavioural Science:
JONES, M. B.
NORGREN, R.
Biochemistry and Molecular Biology:
BHAVANANDAN, V. P.
BOND, J. S.
GOWDA, D. C.
HOPPER, A. K.
HOPPER, J. E.
SCHENGRUND, C.-L.
Cellular and Molecular Physiology:
FLOROS, J.
JEFFERSON, L. S., Jr
LANG, C. H.
LANOUE, K. F.
PEGG, A. E.
QUINN, P. G.
RANNELS, D. E.
VARY, T. C.
Comparative Medicine:
GRIFFITH, J. W.
LANG, C. M.
Health Evaluation Sciences:
CHINCHILLI, V. M.
LLOYD, T.
ORKIN, F. K.
YOUNG, M. J.
Humanities:
BALLARD, J. O., Medicine and Humanities
HAWKINS, A. H., Humanities
HUFFORD, D., Humanities, Behavioural Science and Family and Community Medicine
Microbiology and Immunology:
CHORNEY, M. J., Microbiology and Immunology, Paediatrics
COURTNEY, R. J.
HOWETT, M. K.
ISOM, H. C.
MEYERS, C. M.
SUN, S.-C.
TEVETHIA, M. J.
TEVETHIA, S. S.
WIGDAHL, B.
WILLS, J. W.
Neuroscience and Anatomy:
CONNOR, J. R.
MILNER, R. J.
SIMPSON, I. A.
ZAGON, I. S.
Ophthalmology:
AMINLARI, A., Clinical Ophthalmology
GARDNER, T. W., Ophthalmology, Cellular and Molecular Physiology
SASSANI, J. W., Ophthalmology and Pathology
Pharmacology:
BERLIN, C. M., Jr, Paediatrics and Pharmacology
BILLINGSLEY, M. L., Pharmacology
BURKHART, K. K., Emergency Medicine and Pharmacology
JONES, B. C., Biobehavioural Health and Pharmacology
KESTER, M., Pharmacology
LAKOSKI, J. M., Pharmacology and Anaesthesiology
LEVENSON, R., Pharmacology
LLOYD, T. A., Health Evaluation Sciences
MULDER, K. M., Pharmacology
NAIDES, S. J., Medicine, Microbiology and Immunology, Pharmacology
PEGG, A. E., Cellular and Molecular Physiology and Pharmacology
SMITH, C. D., Pharmacology
SUMMY-LONG, J. Y., Pharmacology
VESELL, E. S., Pharmacology, Medicine, Genetics

The Eberly College of Science (Office of Public Information, 427 Thomas Bldg, University Park, PA 16802-2112; fax (814) 863-2246; internet www.science.psu.edu):
Astronomy and Astrophysics:
BEATTY, J. J.
FEIGELSON, E. D.
GARMIRE, G. P.
LAGUNA, P.
MESZAROS, P. I.
RAMSEY, L. W.
RICHARDS, M.
SCHNEIDER, D. P.
WOLSZCZAN, A.
Biochemistry and Molecular Biology:
BRENCHLEY, J. E., Microbiology and Biotechnology
BRYANT, D. A., Biotechnology
FERRY, J. G., Biochemistry and Molecular Biology
FRISQUE, R. J., Molecular Virology
GAY, C. V., Cell Biology and Poultry Science
GOLBECK, J. H., Biochemistry and Biophysics
HARDISON, R. C., Biochemistry
KAO, T.-H., Biochemistry and Molecular Biology
MASTRO, A. M., Microbiology and Cell Biology
SCHLEGEL, R. A., Biochemistry and Molecular Biology
SIMPSON, R. T., Biochemistry and Molecular Biology
TIEN, M., Biochemistry
TU, C.-P. D., Biochemistry and Molecular Biology
Biology:
ASSMANN, S. M.
CAVENER, D. R.
COSGROVE, D. J.
CYR, R. J.
FEDOROFF, N. V.
FISHER, C. R.
HEDGES, B.
MA, H.
MITCHELL, R. B.
NEI, M.
STEPHENSON, A. G.
UHL, C.
WALKER, A., Anthropology and Biology
Chemistry:
ALLARA, D. L., Polymer Science and Chemistry
ALLCOCK, H. R.
ANDERSON, J. B.
BENKOVIC, S. J.
CASTLEMAN, A. W., Jr
ERNST, W. E., Physics and Chemistry
EWING, A. G.
FELDMAN, K.
FUNK, R. L.
GARRISON, B. J.
JURS, P. C.
MALLOUK, T. E.
MARONCELLI, M.
MERZ, K. M., Jr
SEN, A.
WEINREB, S. M., Natural Products Chemistry
WEISS, P. S.
WINOGRAD, N.
Mathematics:
ANDERSON, J. H.
ANDREWS, G. E.
BANYAGA, A.
BAUM, P.
BROWNAWELL, D.
DU, Q.
FORMANEK, E.
HAMMACK, J.
HUNTER, R. P.
JAMES, D. G.
KATOK, A.
KATOK, S.
LALLEMENT, G. J.
LEVI, M.
LI, W.-C.
MULLEN, G. L.
NISTOR, V.
NOURI, M.
OCNEANU, A.
PESIN, Y. B.
ROE, J.
SIMPSON, S.
SWIATEK, G.
VASERSTEIN, L.
VAUGHAN, R.
WARE, R. P.
WATERHOUSE, W. C.
XU, J.
ZARHIN, Y.
ZHENG, Y.
Physics:
BANAVAR, J. R.
CASTLEMAN, W., Jr,
CHAN, M. H. W.
COLE, M. W.
COLLINS, J. C.
COLLINS, R. W.
DIEHL, R.
ERNST, W. E.
FREED, N.
GUNAYDIN, M.
JAIN, J.
MAYNARD, J. D.
OH, B.
SOKOL, P. E.

STRIKMAN, M.
WEISS, D. S.
WHITMORE, J. J.

Statistics:

AKRITAS, M. G.
ARNOLD, S. F.
BABU, G. J.
CHINCHILLI, V., Biostatistics
FONG, D., Management Science and Statistics
HARKNESS, W. L.
HETTMANSPERGER, T. P.
LIN, D. K. J., Management Science and Statistics
LINDSAY, B. G.
PATIL, G. P.
RAO, C. R.
ROSENBERGER, J. L.
TEMPELMAN, A.

The Mary Jean and Frank P. Smeal College of Business Administration (Dean's Office, 801 H Business Admin. Bldg, University Park, PA 16802-3009; tel. (814) 867-0448; fax (814) 865-7064; e-mail deansoffice@smeal.psu.edu; internet www.smeal.psu.edu):

Accounting:

DIRSMITH, M. W.
GIVOLY, D.
MCKEOWN, J. C.
SMITH, C. H.

Business Logistics:

SPYCHALSKI, J. C., Business Logistics
STENGER, A. J., Business Logistics
TYWORTH, J. E., Business Logistics

Finance:

EZZELL, J. R.
GHADAR, F.
KRACAW, W. A.
MILES, J. A.
MUSCARELLA, C.
WOOLRIDGE, J. R.

Insurance and Real Estate:

BAGBY, J. W., Business Law
JAFFE, A. J., Business Admin.
LUSHT, K. M., Business Admin.
SHAPIRO, A. F., Business Admin.
YAVAS, A., Business Admin.

Management and Organization:

GIOIA, D. A., Organizational Behaviour
GRAY, B. L., Organizational Behaviour
HAMBRICK, D., Management
HARRISON, D. A., Management
KILDUFF, M., Organizational Behaviour
SNOW, C. C., Business Admin.
STEVENS, J. M.
SUSMAN, G. I., Management
TREVINO, L. K., Management

Management Science and Information Systems:

BALAKRISHNAN, A.
BARTON, R., Management Science
BHARGAVA, H., Management Information Systems
BOLTON, G. E., Management Science
CHATTERJEE, K., Management Science
FONG, D. K. H., Management Science and Statistics
HARRISON, T. P., Management Science
KELTON, W. D., Management Science and Information Systems
LILIEN, G. L., Management Science
LIN, D. K., Management Science
XU, S., Management Science

Marketing:

BAUMGARTNER, J.
DESARBO, W. S., Marketing
GOLDBERG, M. E., Marketing
OLIVA, R. A., Marketing
OLSON, J. C., Marketing
RANGASWANY, A., Marketing

Dickinson School of Law, Carlisle (150 South College St, Carlisle, PA 17013; tel. (717) 240-5000; internet www.dsl.psu.edu):

ACKERMAN, R. M.
ALEXANDER, P. C.
BACKER, L. C.
BARKER, W. B.
DEL DUCA, L. F.
FARMER, S. B.
FARRIOR, S. T.
FELDMAN, H. A.
FOX, J. R.
GILDIN, G. S.
GLENN, P. G.
HAUGHNEY, E. W.
KEATING, W. J.
KELLETT, C. H.
MACRAE, L. M.
MARION, C.
MOGILL, M. A.
MOOTZ, F. J., III
MULLER-PETERSON, J.
NAIDES, P. H.
NAVIN, M. J.
PEARSON, K.
PLACE, T. M.
POLACHEK, M. K.
RAINS, R. E.
RIGLER, J.
ROMERO, V.
SCOTT, G. R.
TERRY, L. S.

School of Graduate Professional Studies, Penn State Great Valley (30 East Swedesford Rd, Malvern, PA 19355-1443; tel. (610) 648-3200; e-mail gvinfo@psu.edu; internet www.gv.psu.edu):

Education:

MILHEIM, W., Education

Engineering:

MCCOOL, J., Systems Engineering
RUSSELL, D., Electrical Engineering

Information Sciences:

RUSSELL, D., Electrical Engineering

Management:

FRITZSCHE, D. J., Management and Organization

School of Information Sciences and Technology (504 Rider I Bldg, 120 South Burrowes St, University Park, PA 16801-3857; tel. (814) 865-3528; fax (814) 865-5604; internet ist.psu.edu):

BAGBY, J. W., Information Sciences and Technology
GILES, C. L., Information Sciences and Technology, Computer Science and Engineering
TRAUTH, E. M., Information Sciences and Technology
YEN, J., Information Sciences and Technology, Computer Science and Engineering

ATTACHED RESEARCH INSTITUTES

Applied Research Laboratory: POB 30, State College, PA 16804;N Atherton St, State College, PA 16801; tel. (814) 865-6343; internet www.arl.psu.edu; f. 1945 by the US Navy; research and devt in technical fields, especially underwater systems; Dir Dr EDWARD G. LISZKA.

Biotechnology Institute: internet www.lsc.psu.edu/biotech.html; f. 1984.

Center for Applied Behavioural Sciences.

Center for Developmental and Health Genetics: Amy Gardner House, University Park, PA 16802-2317; tel. (814) 865-1717; fax (814) 863-4768; e-mail pvq@psu.edu; internet www.hhdev.psu.edu/old/centers/genetics.htm; f. 1988.

Center for the Study of Higher Education: 400 Rackley Bldg, University Park, PA 16802; tel. (814) 865-6346; fax (814) 865-3638; e-mail cshe@psu.edu; internet www.ed.psu.edu/cshe; f. 1969; Dir Prof. DONALD E. HELLER.

Institute for the Arts and Humanistic Studies: 101 Ihlseng Cottage, University Park, PA 16802; tel. (814) 865-0495; fax (814) 863-8349; e-mail arts-humanities@psu.edu; internet www.research.psu.edu/iah; attached to the Office of the Vice-Pres. for Research; Dir Dr MARICA S. TACCONI.

Materials Research Institute: 199 MRI Bldg, University Park, PA 16802-7003; tel. (814) 863-8407; fax (814) 863-8561; internet www.mri.psu.edu; established to coordinate activities and provide leadership for interdisciplinary materials research throughout the Pennsylvania State University; Dir Prof. CARLO PANTANO.

Particulate Materials Center: 249 Materials Research Center, University Park, PA 16802; internet www.mri.psu.edu/centers/pmc; Dir Dr JAMES H. ADAIR.

Pennsylvania Transportation Institute: Dir Dr JOHN M. MASON, Jr.

Population Research Institute: 601 Oswald Tower, University Park, PA 16802-6211; tel. (814) 865-0486; fax (814) 863-8342; internet www.pop.psu.edu; Dir Prof. NANCY LANDALE.

PHILADELPHIA BIBLICAL UNIVERSITY

200 Manor Ave, Langhorne, PA 19047
Telephone: (215) 752-5800
E-mail: admissions@pbu.edu
Internet: www.pbu.edu

Founded 1913 as Bible Institute of Pennsylvania, present name 2000
Private control
Academic year: August to May
Pres.: Dr TODD J. WILLIAMS
Sr Vice-Pres. for Finance and Admin.: JAN M. HAAS
Provost: Dr BRIAN TOEWS
Sr Vice-Pres. for Univ. Advancement: SCOTT A. KEATING
Vice-Pres. for Research and Planning: MAE E. STEWART

Library of 132,778 vols
Number of teachers: 130
Number of students: 1,311 (1,015 undergraduate, 296 postgraduate)

PHILADELPHIA COLLEGE OF OSTEOPATHIC MEDICINE

4170 City Ave, Philadelphia, PA 19131
Telephone: (215) 871-6100
E-mail: admissions@pcom.edu
Internet: www.pcom.edu

Pres.: Dr MATTHEW SCHURE
Vice-Pres. for Academic Affairs and Dean: Dr KENNETH J. VEIT
Vice-Pres. for Alumni Relations and Devt: FLORENCE D. ZELLER
Vice-Pres. for Finance: PETER DOULIS
Number of students: 1,410

PHILADELPHIA UNIVERSITY

4201 Henry Ave, Philadelphia, PA 19144-5497
Telephone: (215) 951-2700
Fax: (215) 951-2615
E-mail: pr@philau.edu
Internet: www.philau.edu

Founded 1884
Academic year: September to August
Pres.: Dr STEPHEN SPINELLI, Jr

Vice-Pres. for Academic Affairs: CAROL S. FIXMAN
Vice-Pres. for Business and Finance: RANDALL D. GENTZLER
Vice-Pres. for Enrollment and Student Affairs: JANE H. ANTHEIL
Library of 88,000 vols, 16,000 periodicals, 5,500 microforms
Number of teachers: 90
Number of students: 3,600

PITTSBURGH THEOLOGICAL SEMINARY

616 North Highland Ave, Pittsburgh, PA 15206-2525
Telephone: (412) 362-5610
Fax: (412) 363-3260
Internet: www.pts.edu
Founded 1794 by the merger of Pittsburgh-Xenia Theological Seminary and Western Theological Seminary
Private control
Pres.: WILLIAM CARL, III
Vice-Pres. for Academic Affairs: BRIAN JACKSON
Vice-Pres. for Finance and Admin.: PATRICK J. CUNNINGHAM
Library Dir: SHARON TAYLOR
Number of teachers: 30
Number of students: 385

POINT PARK UNIVERSITY

201 Wood St, Pittsburgh, PA 15222
Telephone: (412) 391-4100
E-mail: enroll@ppc.edu
Internet: www.ppc.edu
Private control
Academic year: August to May
Fmrly Point Park College
Pres.: Dr PAUL HENNIGAN
Provost and Vice-Pres. for Academic Affairs: Dr CHARLES A. PERKINS
Vice-Pres. for Finance and Admin.: BRIDGET MANCOSH
Registrar: JENNIFER FEDELE
Number of teachers: 70
Number of students: 3,123 (2,743 undergraduate, 380 postgraduate)

DEANS

School of Arts and Sciences: Dr STEPHEN FRITZ
School of Business: Dr BRUCE MURPHY
Conservatory of Performing Arts: RONALD LINDBLOM

ROBERT MORRIS UNIVERSITY

6001 University Blvd, Moon Township, PA 15108
Telephone: (412) 262-8200
E-mail: admissions@rmu.edu
Internet: www.rmu.edu
Founded 1921
Private control
Academic year: August to May
Pres.: Dr GREGORY G. DELL'OMO
Provost and Sr Vice-Pres. for Academic Affairs: DAVID L. JAMISON
Sr Vice-Pres. for Business Affairs: DAN KIENER
Vice-Pres. and Gen. Counsel: SIDNEY ZONN
Vice-Pres. for Financial Operations: JEFFREY A. LISTWAK
Vice-Pres. for Institutional Advancement: JAY T. CARSON
Registrar: FRANCIS E. PERRY
Dean of Libraries: Dr FRANCES J. CAPLAN
Library of 119,203 vols
Number of teachers: 411
Number of students: 4,967

DEANS

School of Business: Dr DERYA A. JACOBS
School of Communications and Information Systems: Dr BARBARA J. LEVINE
School of Education and Social Sciences: Dr JOHN E. GRAHAM
School of English, Mathematics and Science: Dr MARIA KALEVITCH
School of Nursing and Health Services: Dr LYNDA J. DAVIDSON

ROSEMONT COLLEGE

1400 Montgomery Ave, Rosemont, PA 19010
Telephone: (610) 527-0200
Fax: (610) 527-1041
E-mail: webinfo@rosemont.edu
Internet: www.rosemont.edu
Founded 1921
Catholic liberal arts college
Pres.: SHARON LATCHAW HIRSH
Vice-Pres. for Academic Affairs: DEBRA G. KLINMAN
Vice-Pres. for Information Services: CATHERINE M. FENNELL
Vice-Pres. for Institutional Advancement: MADONNA MARION-LANDAIS
Vice-Pres. for Student Affairs: MARILYN A. MOLLER
Registrar: JOSEPH T. ROGERS
Library of 157,000 vols
Number of teachers: 141
Number of students: 947 (361 full-time, 434 part-time, 152 graduate)

SAINT CHARLES BORROMEO SEMINARY

100 Wynnewood Rd, Wynnewood, PA 19096
Telephone: (610) 667-3394
Fax: (610) 617-9267
E-mail: developmentscs@adphila.org
Internet: www.scs.edu
Founded 1832
Private control
Academic year: September to May
Rector: Rev. JOSEPH G. PRIOR
Vice-Rector: Rev. CHRISTOPHER J. SCHRECK
Vice-Pres. for Finance and Operations: ELAINE K. RICE
Registrar: LAWRENCE A. HEYMAN
Library Dir: CAIT KOKOLUS
Number of teachers: 32
Number of students: 160 (full-time)

SAINT FRANCIS UNIVERSITY

POB 600, Loretto, PA 15940
Telephone: (814) 472-3000
E-mail: admissions@francis.edu
Internet: www.francis.edu
Founded 1847
Academic year: August to May
Pres.: Rev. CHRISTIAN ORAVEC
Asst to the Pres.: RICHARD CRAWFORD
Vice-Pres. for Academic Affairs: Rev. ANTHONY DE CONCILIIS
Vice-Pres. for Finance: KEVIN O'FLAHERTY
Vice-Pres. for Student Affairs: DENNIS RIEGELNEGG
Dir of Devt: RAYMOND PONCHIONE
Dir of Library: SANDRA A. BALOUGH
Library of 199,000 vols
Number of teachers: 172
Number of students: 2,090

SAINT JOSEPH'S UNIVERSITY

5600 City Ave, Philadelphia, PA 19131
Telephone: (610) 660-1000
Fax: (610) 660-3300
Internet: www.sju.edu
Founded 1851
Pres.: TIMOTHY R. LANNON
Vice-Pres. for Academic Affairs: DANIEL J. CURRAN
Asst Vice-Pres. for Enrollment Management: DAVID CONWAY
Registrar: GERARD DONAHUE
Librarian: EVELYN MINICK
Library of 335,000 vols
Number of teachers: 428 (189 full-time; 239 part-time)
Number of students: 7,027 (3,076 day, 1,128 evening, 2,823 graduate)
Degree courses in business admin., computer sciences, liberal arts, science.

SAINT VINCENT COLLEGE

300 Fraser Purchase Rd, Latrobe, PA 15650-2690
Telephone: (724) 539-9761
E-mail: pr@stvincent.edu
Internet: www.stvincent.edu
Founded 1846
Pres.: H. JAMES TOWEY
Exec. Vice-Pres.: Bro. NORMAN W. HIPPS
Vice-Pres. for Finance and Admin.: DENNIS THIMONS (acting)
Vice-Pres. for Institutional Advancement: PAUL R. TAYLOR
Vice-Pres. for Student Affairs: ALICE KAYLOR
Registrar: CELINE R. HAAS
Librarian: Rev. CHRYSOSTOM V. SCHLIMM
Library of 340,000 vols
Number of teachers: 100
Number of students: 1,200
Publication: *Saint Vincent Magazine* (4 a year).

SALUS UNIVERSITY

8360 Old York Rd, Elkins Park, PA 19027-1516
Telephone: (215) 780-1400
Fax: (215) 780-1336
Internet: www.salus.edu
Founded 1919
Academic year: August to May
Pres.: THOMAS L. LEWIS
Vice-Pres. for Academic Affairs: ANTHONY F. DI STEFANO
Vice-Pres. for Finance: DONALD C. KATES
Vice-Pres. and Dean of Student Affairs: ROBERT E. HORNE
Dir of Devt: LYNNE C. CORBOY
Dir of Library: KEITH LAMMERS
Library of 21,000 vols
Number of teachers: 70 (46 full-time, 24 part-time)
Number of students: 850

SETON HILL COLLEGE

1 Seton Hill Dr., Greensburg, PA 15601
Telephone: (724) 834-2200
Fax: (724) 830-1294
Internet: www.setonhill.edu
Founded 1883
Academic year: August to May
Pres.: JOANNE W. BOYLE
Vice-Pres. for Enrollment Services: BARBARA HINKLE
Dir of Library: DAVID STANLEY
Library of 119,000 vols
Number of teachers: 114 (58 full-time, 56 part-time)
Number of students: 1,200

SUSQUEHANNA UNIVERSITY

51 University Ave, Selinsgrove, PA 17870
Telephone: (574) 374-0101

Fax: (574) 372-4040
Internet: www.susqu.edu

Founded 1858

Pres.: L. JAY LEMONS
Provost and Dean of Faculty: Dr LINDA McMILLIN
Dir of Library: KATHLEEN GUNNING

Library of 244,000 vols
Number of teachers: 123
Number of students: 1,900

Publication: *Susquehanna University Studies.*

SWARTHMORE COLLEGE

500 College Ave, Swarthmore, PA 19081-1397

Telephone: (610) 328-8000
Fax: (610) 328-8673
E-mail: admissions@swarthmore.edu
Internet: www.swarthmore.edu

Founded 1864 by mems of the Religious Soc. of Friends
Private control
Academic year: September to May

Pres.: REBECCA CHOPP
Vice-Pres.: MAURICE G. ELDRIDGE
Registrar: MARTIN O. WARNER
Provost: THOMAS STEPHENSON
Dean of Admissions and Financial Aid: JAMES L. BOCK
Dean of Students: H. ELIZABETH BRAUN
Librarian: PEGGY SEIDEN

Library of 860,000 vols, 15,164 online journals, 501,811 electronic books
Number of teachers: 166
Number of students: 1,524

TEMPLE UNIVERSITY

1801 North Broad St, Philadelphia, PA 19122

Telephone: (215) 204-7000
Internet: www.temple.edu

Founded 1884

Pres.: ANN WEAVER HART
Provost: LISA STAIANO-COICO
Vice-Pres. for Research and Graduate Studies: Dr KENNETH SOPRANO
Vice-Provost for Faculty Affairs: Dr RON J. TALLARIDA (acting)
Vice-Provost for Libraries: LARRY ALFORD
Vice-Provost for Undergraduate Studies: STEPHEN ZELNICK
Sec.: WILLIAM C. SEYLER

Library of 2,400,000 vols, 16,000 periodicals
Number of teachers: 2,600
Number of students: 33,286

Publications: *Journal of Economics and Business, Law Quarterly, Temple Review, The American Journal of Legal History*

DEANS

Ambler Campus: SOPHIA WISNIEWSKA
College of Allied Health: RONALD BROWN
College of Education: KENT McGUIRE
College of Engineering: KEYA SADEGHIPOUR
College of Liberal Arts: SUSAN HERBST
College of Science and Technology: ALLEN NICHOLSON (acting)
Esther Boyer College of Music and Department of Dance: ROBERT STROKER
School of Communications and Theatre: CONCETTA STEWART
School of Dentistry: F. MARTIN TANSY
School of Medicine: JOHN M. DALY
School of Pharmacy: PETER DOUKAS
School of Podiatric Medicine: JOHN MATTIACCI
School of Social Administration and Department of Health Studies: LARRY ICARD
School of Tourism and Hospitality Management: MOSHE PORAT
Beasley School of Law: ROBERT REINSTEIN
Fox School of Business and Management: MOSHE PORAT
Graduate School: AQUILES IGLESIAS
Tyler School of Art: HESTER STINNETT (acting)

THIEL COLLEGE

Greenville, PA 16125

Telephone: (412) 589-2000
Internet: www.thiel.edu

Founded 1866

Pres.: ROBERT C. OLSON
Sr Vice-Pres.: GARY J. WITOSKY
Vice-Pres. for College Advancement: DAVID J. GROBER
Vice-Pres. for Finance: M. SCOTT HARTLE
Vice-Pres. for Student Life and Dean of Students: ROSEANNE GILL JACOBSON
Dir of Admissions: SONYA LAPIKAS
Dir of Library: ALLEN S. MORRILL
Dean of the Faculty: MERVIN E. NEWTON

Library of 135,000 vols
Number of teachers: 57
Number of students: 965

THOMAS JEFFERSON UNIVERSITY

1020 Walnut St, Philadelphia, PA 19107

Telephone: (215) 955-6000
Internet: www.jefferson.edu

Founded 1824

Pres.: ROBERT L. BARCHI
Librarian: EDWARD N. TAWYEA

Library of 167,504 vols
Number of teachers: 761
Number of students: 2,596

DEANS

College of Allied Health Sciences: LAWRENCE ABRAMS
College of Graduate Studies: JUSSI J. SAUKKONEN
Jefferson Medical College: JOSEPH S. GONNELLA

TRINITY EPISCOPAL SCHOOL FOR MINISTRY

311 Eleventh St, Ambridge, PA 15003

Telephone: (724) 266-3838
Fax: (724) 266-4617
Internet: www.tesm.edu

Founded 1976
Private control

Dean and Pres.: PAUL ZAHL
Academic Dean: Rev. Dr GAVIN J. McGRATH
Registrar: SHIRLEY BRUCE
Library Dir: SUSANAH HANSON

Number of teachers: 40
Number of students: 110 (full-time)

UNIVERSITY OF PENNSYLVANIA

3451 Walnut St, Philadelphia, PA 19104

Telephone: (215) 898-5000
Internet: www.upenn.edu

Founded 1740
Private control
Academic year: September to May, and two six-week summer terms

Pres.: AMY GUTMANN
Provost: VINCENT PRICE
Vice-Provost and Dir of Libraries: CARTON ROGERS
Exec. Vice-Pres.: CRAIG CARNAROLI
Exec. Vice-Pres. for Univ. of Pennsylvania Health System: ARTHUR H. RUBENSTEIN
Sr Vice-Pres. and Gen. Counsel: WENDY WHITE
Vice-Pres. for Budget and Management Analysis: BONNIE GIBSON
Vice-Pres. for Business Services: MARIE WITT
Vice-Pres. and Chief of Staff: GREGORY S. ROST
Vice-Pres. for Devt and Alumni Relations: JOHN H. ZELLER
Vice-Pres. for Division of Public Safety: MAUREEN RUSH
Vice-Pres. for Facilities and Real Estate Services: ANNE PAPAGEORGE
Vice-Pres. for Finance and Treas.: STEPHEN D. GOLDING
Vice-Pres. for Govt and Community Affairs: JEFFREY COOPER
Vice-Pres. of Human Resources: JOHN J. HEUER
Vice-Pres. for Information Systems and Computing: ROBIN BECK
Vice-Pres. for Institutional Affairs: JOANN MITCHELL
Vice-Pres. for Univ. Communications: LORI DOYLE
Comptroller: JOHN F. HORN
Sec.: LESLIE LAIRD KRUHLY
CEO for Univ. of Pennsylvania Health System: RALPH W. MULLER
Registrar: RONALD SANDERS
Dean of Admissions: ERIC J. FURDA

Library: see Libraries and Archives
Number of teachers: 4,127
Number of students: 24,599

Publications: *Almanac* (journal of record), *Arts at Penn, PENN Current, Red and Blue, Research at PENN* (online)

DEANS AND DIRECTORS

Annenberg School for Communication: MICHAEL DELLI CARPINI
Graduate School of Education: ANDREW PORTER
Law School: MICHAEL FITTS
School of Arts and Sciences: REBECCA BUSHNELL
School of Dental Medicine: DENIS KINANE
School of Design: MARILYN JORDAN TAYLOR
School of Engineering and Applied Science: EDUARDO GLANDT
School of Medicine: ARTHUR RUBENSTEIN
School of Nursing: AFAF MELEIS
School of Social Policy and Practice: RICHARD GELLES
School of Veterinary Medicine: JOAN HENDRICKS
Wharton School: THOMAS ROBERTSON

PROFESSORS

Annenberg School for Communication

Communications:

CAPPELLA, J.
DELLI CARPINI, M.
FISHBEIN, M.
GANDY, O. H.
GROSS, L.
HORNIK, R.
JAMIESON, K. H.
JEMMOTT, J.
KATZ, E.
KRIPPENDORFF, K.
LINEBARGER, D.
MARVIN, C.
MESSARIS, P.
PRICE, V.
TUROW, J.
ZELIZER, B.

Law School:

ADLER, M.
ALLEN-CASTELLITO, A.
AUSTIN, R.
BAKER, C. E.
BURBANK, S.
CHANG, H.
DELISLE, J.
EWALD, W.
FINKELSTEIN, C.
FITTS, M.
GOODMAN, F.

GORDON, S.
JOHNSTON, J.
KATZ, L.
KNOLL, M.
KREIMER, S.
KUBLER, F.
LESNICK, H.
MANN, B.
MOONEY, C.
MORSE, S.
PARCHOMOVSKY, G.
PERRY, S.
REITZ, C.
ROBINSON, P.
ROCK, E.
RUBIN, E.
SANCHIRICO, C.
SCHEPPLE, K. L.
SHULDINER, R.
SKEEL, D.
WACHTER, M.
WAX, A.

Wharton School

Accounting:

BAIMAN, S.
GONEDES, N.
HOLTHAUSEN, R.
ITTNER, C.
LAMBERT, R. A.
LARCKER, D.
VERRECCHIA, R.

Business and Public Policy:

ALLEN, W. B.
BAILEY, E.
FAULHABER, G.
PACK, H.
PACK, J.
WALDFOGEL, J.

Finance:

ABEL, A.
ALLEN, H. F.
BLUME, M.
GIBBONS, M.
GORTON, G.
HERRING, R.
INMAN, R.
KEIM, D.
KIHLSTROM, R.
LEWIS, K. K.
MACKINLAY, A. C.
MARSTON, R.
RAMASWAMY, K.
SIEGEL, J.
STAMBAUGH, R.

Health Care Systems:

BURNS, L.
DANZON, P.
HARRINGTON, S.
PAULY, M.

Insurance and Risk Management:

BABBEL, D.
CUMMINS, J. D.
DOHERTY, N.
LEMAIRE, J.
MITCHELL, O.
ROSENBLOOM, J.

Legal Studies:

BELLACE, J.
DONALDSON, T.
DUNFEE, T.
ORTS, E.
ROSOFF, A.
SHELL, G. R.
SHROPSHIRE, K.

Management:

AMIT, R.
CAPPELI, P.
GERRITY, T.
GULLEN, M.
HAMILTON, W. F.
HOUSE, R.
KIMBERLY, J.
KLEIN, K.
KOBRIN, S.
LEVINTHAL, D.
MACMILLAN, I.
MEYER, M.
PENNINGS, J.
SINGH, H.
SINGH, J.
USEEM, M.
WEIGELT, K.
WINTER, S.

Marketing:

ARMSTRONG, J. S.
DAY, G.
ELIASHBERG, J.
FADER, P.
HOCH, S.
HUTCHISON, J.
IANOBUCCI, D.
KAHN, B.
LODISH, L.
MEYER, R.
RAJU, J. S.
REIBSTEIN, D.
SCHMITTLEIN, D.
WARD, S.
WIND, Y.

Operations and Information Management:

CLEMONS, E.
COHEN, M.
FISHER, M.
GUIGNARD-SPIELBERG, M.
HARKER, P.
HERSHEY, J.
KIMBROUGH, S.
KLEINDORFER, P.
KUNREUTHER, H.
ULRICH, K.
ZHENG, Y.

Real Estate:

GYOURKO, J.
LINNEMAN, P.
POINDEXTER, G.
WACHTER, S.

Statistics:

BROWN, L.
BUJA, A.
GEORGE, E.
KRIEGER, A.
LOW, M.
ROSENBAUM, P.
SHAMAN, P.
STEELE, J. M.
STINE, R.

School of Arts and Sciences

Anthropology:

DIBBLE, H. L.
KOPYTOFF, I.
LEVENTHAL, R.
POSSEHL, G.
SABLOFF, J.
SANDAY, P.
SHARER, R.
SILVERSTEIN, M.
SPOONER, B.
URBAN, G.

Biology:

BINNS, A.
CASHMORE, A.
CASPER, B.
CEBRA, J.
CHENEY, D.
DALDAL, M. F.
DUNHAM, A. E.
EWENS, W.
GUILD, G.
JANZEN, D.
KIM, J.
PETRAITIS, P.
POETHIG, R. S.
REA, P. A.
ROME, L.
ROOS, D. S.
SCHULTZ, R.
WALDRON, I.
WEINBERG, E.
ZIGMOND, S.

Chemistry:

BERRY, D.
BLASIE, J. K.
CHRISTIANSON, D.
COOPERMAN, B.
DAI, H.-L.
FITTS, D.
HOCHSTRASSER, R.
JOULLIE, M.
KLEIN, M.
LESTER, M. I.
LU, P.
MACDIARMID, A.
MOLANDER, G.
PERCEC, V.
SMITH, A. B.
SNEDDON, L.
THERIEN, M.
THORNTON, E.
TOPP, M. R.
WAYLAND, B.
WINKLER, J.

Classical Studies:

COPELAND, R.
FARRELL, J., Jr
MURNAGHAN, S.
ROSEN, R.

Criminology:

SHERMAN, L.

Earth and Environmental Science:

GIEGENGACK, R.
JOHNSON, A.
PFEFFERKORN, H.
SCATENA, F.

East Asian Languages and Civilizations:

HURST, G.
LAFLEUR, W.
MAIR, V.
STEINHARDT, N.

Economics:

BEHRMAN, J. R.
BURDETT, K.
CASS, D.
DIEBOLD, F.
ETHIER, W.
LEVINE, H.
MAILATH, G.
MATTHEWS, S.
MERLO, A.
POSTLEWAITE, A.
RIOS-RULL, J.-V.
ROB, R.
WOLPIN, K.
WRIGHT, R.

English:

AUERBACH, N.
BERNSTEIN, C.
BUSHNELL, R.
CONN, P.
CORRIGAN, T.
CURRAN, S.
DAVIS, T.
DE GRAZIA, M.
ENGLISH, J.
FILREIS, A.
KAPLAN, A.
KAUL, S.
LOOMBA, A.
MAHAFFEY, V.
PERELMAN, R.
QUILLIGAN, M.
RABATE, J.
RICHETTI, J.
STALLYBRASS, P.
STEINER, W.
STEWART, S.
WALLACE, D.

Germanic Languages and Literatures:
TROMMLER, F.
WEISSBERG, L.

History:
BEEMAN, R.
BERRY, M. F.
CHILDERS, T.
ENGS, R. F.
FARRISS, N.
HACKNEY, S.
HAHN, S.
KATZ, M.
KORS, A.
KUKLICK, B.
LEES, L. H.
LICHT, W.
LUDDEN, D.
MCDOUGALL, W.
PEISS, K.
PETERS, E.
RICHTER, D.
RUDERMAN, D.
SAVAGE, B.
STEINBERG, J.
SUGRUE, T. J.
TODD, M.
WALDRON, A.
ZUCKERMAN, M.

History and Sociology of Science:
COWAN, R.
FEIERMAN, S.
KOHLER, R.
KUKLICK, H.
LINDEE, M.
SIVIN, N.

History of Art:
BROWNLEE, D.
HOLOD, R.
MEISTER, M.
PITTMAN, H.
SILVER, L.

Linguistics:
CARDONA, G.
KROCH, A.
LABOV, W.
LIBERMAN, M
PRINCE, E.
RINGE, D.
SANKOFF, G.

Mathematics:
CHAI, C.
CHINBURG, T.
CROKE, C.
DETURCK, D.
DONAGI, R.
EPSTEIN, C.
FREYD, P.
GERSTENHABER, M.
GLUCK, H.
HARBATER, D.
KADISON, R. V.
KAZDAN, J.
KIRILLOV, A.
MINSKY, Y.
PEMANTLE, R.
PIMSNER, M.
POP, F.
PORTER, G.
POWERS, R.
SCEDROV, A.
SHANESON, J.
SHATZ, S.
WILF, H.
ZILLER, W.

Music:
BERNSTEIN, L.
KALLBERG, J.
NARMOUR, E.
PRIMOSCH, J.
REISE, J.
TOMLINSON, G.

Near Eastern Languages and Civilizations:
ALLEN, R.
BEN-AMOS, D.
SILVERMAN, D.
STERN, D.
TIGAY, J. H.

Philosophy:
BICCHIERI, C.
DOMOTOR, Z.
FREEMAN, S.
GUYER, P.
HATFIELD, G.
KAHN, C.
ROSS, J.
WEINSTEIN, S.

Physics and Astronomy:
BALAMUTH, D.
BEIER, E.
CVETIC, M.
DURIAN, D.
FORTUNE, H.
HEINEY, P.
HOLLEBEEK, R.
KAMIEN, R.
LANDE, K.
LANGACKER, P. G.
LIU, A.
LOCKYER, N.
LUBENSKY, T.
MELE, E.
NELSON, P.
OVRUT, B.
SEGRE, G.
SOVEN, P.
WILLIAMS, H.
YODH, A.

Political Science:
CALLAGHY, T.
DIIULIO, J.
FRANKEL, F.
GOLDSTEIN, A.
GUMANN, A.
KENNEDY, E.
KETTI, D.
LUSTICK, I. S.
MANSFIELD, E.
MUTZ, D.
NAGEL, J.
NORTON, A.
O'LEARY, B.
REED, A.
SMITH, R.
TEUNE, H.

Psychology:
BARON, J.
BRAINARD, D.
CHAMBLESS, D.
DERUBEIS, R.
FARAH, M.
GRILL, H.
KAHANA, M.
NORMAN, M. F.
RESCORLA, R.
RICHARDS, V.
RODIN, J.
ROZIN, P.
SABINI, J. P.
SELIGMAN, M.
SEYFARTH, R.

Religious Studies:
DUNNING, S.
DYSON, M.
MATTER, E. A.

Romance Languages:
ALONSO, C.
BROWNLEE, K.
DEJEAN, J.
DONALDSON-EVANS, L.
KIRKHAM, V.
LOPEZ, I.
MARCUS, M.
PRINCE, G.

Slavic Languages:
STEINER, P.

Sociology:
ALLISON, P.
ANDERSON, E.
BERG, I.
BIELBY, W.
BOSK, C.
COLLINS, R.
ENGLAND, P.
FURSTENBERG, F.
JACOBS, J.
MADDEN, J. F.
PRESTON, S.
SMITH, H.
WATKINS, S.
ZUBERI, T.

South Asian Regional Studies:
ROCHER, R.
SCHIFFMAN, H.

School of Dental Medicine

Anatomy/Cell Biology:
MACARAK, E.
GIBSON, C.

Biochemistry:
ADAMS, S.
GOLUB, E. E.
LEBOY, P.
MALAMUD, D.

Endodontics.
KIM, S.

Microbiology:
COHEN, G.
DIRIENZO, J.
RICCIARDI, R.

Oral Medicine:
GREENBERG, M.

Oral Surgery:
FONSECA, R.
HERSH, E.
QUINN, P.

Orthodontics:
KATZ, S.
VANARSDALL, R.

Pathology:
LALLY, E.
SHENKER, B.

Periodontics:
EVIANS, C.
JEFFCOAT, M.
POLSON, A.

School of Education:
BOE, E.
BORUCH, R.
FANTUZZO, J.
FUHRMAN, S.
GOERTZ, M.
GOODMAN, J.
HORNBERGER, N.
INGERSOLL, R.
KURILOFF, P.
LAZERSON, M.
MCDERMOTT, P.
MAYNARD, R.
PICA, T.
SLAUGHTER-DEFOE, D.
SPENCER, M. B.
WAGNER, D.
WORTHAM, S.
ZEMSKY, R. M.

School of Engineering and Applied Science:
ALUR, R.
AYYASWAMY, P.
BADLER, N.
BASSANI, J.
BAU, H.
BONNELL, D.
BORDOGNA, J.
BUCHSBAUM, G.

CASSEL, T.
CHEN, I.-W.
COHEN, I.
DAVIDSON, S.
DAVIES, P.
DIAMOND, S.
DUCHEYNE, P.
EGAMI, T.
ENGHETA, N.
FARHAT, N.
FINKEL, L.
FISCHER, J.
FOSTER, K.
GALLIER, J. H.
GIRIFALCO, L.
GLANDT, E.
GORTE, R.
GRAHAM, W.
GUERIN, R.
HAMMER, D.
JAGGARD, D.
JOSHI, A.
KANNAN, S.
KASSAM, S.
KEARNS, M.
KEENAN, J.
KUMAR, V.
LAIRD, C.
LAKER, K.
LEE, I.
LIOR, N.
LUZZI, D.
MACARAK, E.
MARCUS, M. P.
MARGULIES, S.
MEANEY, D.
MINTZ, M.
PEREIRA, F.
PIERCE, B.
PONTE-CASTANEDA, P.
POPE, D.
RABII, S.
SCHERER, P.
SEIDER, W.
SHIEH, W.
SILVERMAN, B.
SMITH, J. M.
SMITH, T.
SOSLOWSKY, L.
TANNEN, V. B.
ULRICH, K.
VAN DER SPEIGEL, J.
VITEK, V.
VOHS, J.
VUCHIC, V.

School of Medicine (295 John Morgan, Philadelphia, PA 19104-6055; internet www.med.upenn.edu):

Anaesthesia:

DEUTSCHMANN, C.
ECKENDOFF, R.
FLEISHER, L.
LONGNECKER, D.

Biochemistry and Biophysics:

DEGRADO, W.
DREYFUSS, G.
DUTTON, P. L.
ENGLANDER, S. W.
KALLEN, R.
LEMMON, M.
LEWIS, M.
LIEBMAN, P.
MATSCHINSKY, F.
OHNISHI, T.
VAN DUYNE, G.
VANDERKOOI, J.
WAND, A. J.
WILSON, D.
YONETANI, T.

Biostatistics and Epidemiology:

HEITJAN, D.
KUMANYIKA, S.
LANDIS, J. R.
LEE, H.
REBBECK, T.
STROM, B.
TEN HAVE, T.

Cancer Biology:

ALWINE, J.

Cell and Developmental Biology:

DINARDO, S.
FRANZINI-ARMSTRONG, C.
SANGER, J.
SIMON, M.
WEISEL, J.

Dermatology:

ROOK, A.
STANLEY, J.

Emergency Medicine:

BAXT, W. G.
THORN, S.

Family Practice and Community Medicine:

BOWMAN, M.

Genetics:

BUCAN, M.
GASSER, D.
KADESCH, T.
KAZAZIAN, H.
LIEBHABER, S.
SPIELMAN, R.

Medical Ethics:

CAPLAN, A.

Medicine:

ALBELDA, S.
ASCH, D.
BENNETT, J.
BIRNBAUM, M.
BLUMBERG, B.
BRASS, L.
COHEN, P.
COLLMAN, R.
COOKE, N.
DANIELE, R.
EISENBERG, R.
EMERSON, S. G.
EPSTEIN, J.
FELDMAN, H.
FITZGERALD, G.
FRIEDMAN, H. M.
GEWIRTZ, A.
GLICK, J.
HILLMAN, A.
HOXIE, J.
KELLEY, W.
LAZAR, M.
LEVINSON, A.
MACGREGOR, R. R.
MADAIO, M.
PACK, A.
PANETTIERI, R.
PARMACEK, M.
PHILLIPS, S.
PYERITZ, R.
RUBENSTEIN, A.
RUBIN, H.
RUSTGI, A.
SCHAFER, A.
SCHREIBER, A.
SCHUMACHER, H.
SCHWARTZ, J.
SNYDER, P.
TANNEN, R.
THOMPSON, C.
TURKA, L.
TURNER, B.
WEBER, B.
WILSON, J.
ZIYADEH, F.

Microbiology:

BOETTIGER, D.
BUSHMAN, F.
DAVIES, H. C.
FRANKEL, F.
FRASER, N.
GOLDFINE, H.
KAJI, A.
PATERSON, Y.
ROSS, S.
WEISS, S.

Neurology:

BARCHI, R.
BERMAN, P.
BROWN, M.
COSLETT, H. B.
DICHTER, M.
GONZALEZ-SCARANO, F.
PLEASURE, D.
SCHERER, S.
SELZER, M.
TENNEKOON, G. I.

Neuroscience:

HAYDON, P.
LEVITAN, I.
LINDSTROM, J.
NUSBAUM, M.
PALMER, L.
RAPER, J.
ROSENQUIST, A.
SALZBERG, B.
SEHGAL FIELD, A.
STERLING, P.

Neurosurgery:

GRADY, M. S.
WELSH, F.

Obstetrics and Gynaecology:

HECHT, N.
MASTROIANNI, L.
MENNUTI, M.
RUBIN, S.
STRAUSS, J.

Ophthalmology:

BENNETT, J.
FINE, S.
JACOBSON, S.
LATIES, A.
PUGH, E.
STONE, R.

Orthopaedic Surgery:

FITZGERALD, R.
HEPPENSTALL, R.
KAPLAN, F.
SOSLOWSKY, L.

Otorhinolaryngology:

DOTY, R.
KENNEDY, D.
O'MALLEY, B.
SAUNDERS, J.

Paediatrics:

ASAKURA, T.
BALLARD, P. L.
BRODEUR, G.
DOUGLAS, S.
EMANUEL, B.
FOX, W.
GRUNSTEIN, M.
HIGH, K.
HONIG, P.
HOYER, J.
JOHNSON, P.
LEVY, R.
OFFIT, P.
PONCZ, M.
SEGAL, S.
SILBER, J.
YUDKOFF, M.

Pathology and Laboratory Medicine:

ARGON, Y.
CANCRO, M.
CHOI, Y.
CINES, D.
DAVIES, P.
DOMS, R.
GAULTON, G.
GONATAS, N.
GREENE, M.
HANCOCK, W.

JARETT, L.
JUNE, C. H.
KAMOUN, M.
KORETZKY, G. A.
LAMBRIS, J.
LEE, V. M.-Y.
LIVOLSI, V.
MONROE, J.
MUSCHEL, R.
NOWELL, P.
SCHLAEPFER, W.
SHAW, L.
TROJANOWSKI, J.
TYKOCINSKI, M.
WOLF, B.
YOUNG, D.

Pharmacology:

ASSOIAN, R.
BLAIR, I.
EBERWINE, J.
MANNING, D.
PENNING, T.
PITTMAN, R.
WHITEHEAD, A. S.

Physiology:

BAYLOR, S. M.
CIVAN, M.
COBURN, R.
DE WEER, P.
DEUTSCH, C.
FISHER, A.
FOSKETT, J. K.
GOLDMAN, Y.
HOLZBAUR-HOWARD, E.
JAMMEY, P.
LAHIRI, S.
LU, Z.
SWEENEY, H. L.
WINEGRAD, S.

Psychiatry:

ASTON-JONES, G.
BERRETTINI, W.
COYNE, J.
CRITS-CHRISTOPH, P.
DINGES, D. F.
EVANS, D.
FOA, E.
GUR, R.
KATZ, I.
LERMAN, C.
LUCKI, I.
NICHOLLS, R.
O'BRIEN, C.
PRICE, R.
RICKELS, K.
WADDEN, T.
WELLER, E.

Radiation Oncology:

BIAGLOW, J.
BLOCH, P.
GLATSTEIN, E.
KENNEDY, A.
KOCH, C.
MCKENNA, W.

Radiology:

BAUM, S.
BRYAN, R. N.
JOSEPH, P.
KARP, J.
KUNG, H.
LEIGH, J.
SCHNALL, M.
UDUPA, J.
WEHRLI, F.

Surgery:

ADZICK, N. S.
BARKER, C. F.
DREBIN, J.
EDMUNDS, L.
FLAKE, A.
KAISER, L.
NAJI, A.
NUSBAUM, M.
ROMBEAU, J.
ROSATO, E.
SHAKED, A.
SPRAY, T.
WEIN, A.
WHITAKER, L.

School of Nursing:

AIKEN, L.
BARNSTEINER, J.
BROWN, L. P.
BUHLER-WILKERSON, K.
EVANS, L.
GENNARO, S.
JEMMOTT, L.
LANG, N.
MCCAULEY, L.
MEDOFF-COOPER, B.
MELEIS, A.
NAYLOR, M.
O'SULLIVAN, A.
STRUMPF, N.

School of Social Work

Social Work:

CNAAN, R.
ESTES, R.
SANDS, R.
SELTZER, V.
SOLOMON, P.
SPIGNER, C.
STERN, M.

School of Veterinary Medicine:

AQUIRRE, G.
ATCHISON, M.
AVADHANI, N.
BEECH, J.
BELLO, L.
BENSON, C.
BOSTON, R.
BRINSTER, R.
CHACKO, S.
CHALUPA, W.
DAVIES, R.
DODSON, P.
DROBATZ, K.
EISENBERG, R.
FARRELL, J.
FERGUSON, J.
FERRER, J.
FLUHARTY, S.
GIGER, U.
GOLDSCHMIDT, M. H.
HARVEY, C.
HASKINS, M.
HENDRICKS, J. C.
KELLY, A.
KING, L.
KLIDE, A.
LASTER, L.
MISELIS, R.
NEWTON, C.
NUNAMAKER, D.
RAMBERG, C.
REEF, V.
RICHARDSON, D.
ROSS, M.
ROZMIAREK, H.
SCHAD, G.
SCOTT, P.
SERPELL, J.
SHAPIRO, B.
SMITH, G.
SOMA, L.
SPEAR, J.
SWEENEY, C.
WEBER, W.
WEISS, L.
WOLFE, J. H.

PennDesign:

GYOURKO, J.
LINNEMAN, P.
POINDEXTER, G.
RYBCZYNSKI, W.
SAGALYN, L.

UNIVERSITY OF PITTSBURGH

Pittsburgh, PA 15260
Telephone: (412) 624-4141
Internet: www.pitt.edu

Founded 1787 as Pittsburgh Acad., became Western Univ. of Pennsylvania 1819, present name and status 1908
State control
Academic year: August to April (two semesters)

Chancellor: MARK A. NORDENBERG
Assoc. Chancellor: VIJAI SINGH
Exec. Vice-Chancellor and Gen. Counsel: JEROME COCHRAN
Sr Vice-Chancellor and Provost: PATRICIA BEESON
Sr Vice-Chancellor for Health Sciences and Dean, School of Medicine: ARTHUR S. LEVINE
Chief Financial Officer: ARTHUR G. RAMICONE
Vice-Chancellor for Community Initiatives and Chief of Staff: G. REYNOLDS CLARK
Vice-Chancellor for Govt Relations: PAUL SUPOWITZ
Vice-Chancellor for Health Sciences Devt: CLYDE B. JONES, III
Vice-Chancellor for Institutional Advancement: ALBERT J. NOVAK, Jr
Vice-Chancellor for Public Affairs: ROBERT HILL
Vice-Chancellor for Research Conduct and Compliance: RANDY JUHL
Vice-Provost and Dean of Students: KATHY W. HUMPHREY
Sec. of the Board of Trustees and Asst Chancellor: B. JEAN FERKETISH
Athletic Dir: STEVEN PEDERSON
Dir of Internal Audit: JOHN ELLIOTT
Dir of Univ. Library System: RUSH G. MILLER
Univ. Registrar: RALPH E. HERTEL

Library: see Libraries and Archives
Number of teachers: 4,807
Number of students: 28,823

DEANS

College of Gen. Studies: KELLY OTTER (Assoc. Dean)
Graduate School of Public and Int. Affairs: JOHN T. S. KEELER
Graduate School of Public Health: D. BURKE
Joseph M. Katz Graduate School of Business and College of Business Admin.: JOHN T. DELANEY
School of Arts and Sciences: N. JOHN COOPER
School of Dental Medicine: THOMAS W. BRAUN
School of Education: ALAN LESGOLD
Swanson School of Engineering: GERALD D. HOLDER
School of Health and Rehabilitation Sciences: CLIFFORD E. BRUBAKER
School of Information Sciences: RONALD L. LARSEN
School of Law: MARY CROSSLEY
School of Medicine: ARTHUR S. LEVINE
School of Nursing: JACQUELINE DUNBAR-JACOB
School of Pharmacy: PATRICIA D. KROBOTH
School of Social Work: LARRY DAVIS
Univ. Honors College: STEVEN HUSTED

REGIONAL CAMPUSES

University of Pittsburgh at Bradford: 300 Campus Dr., Bradford, PA 16701; tel. (800) 872-1787; internet www.upb.pitt.edu; academic year August to April; Pres. LIVINGSTON ALEXANDER; 92 teachers; 1,629 students (1,438 full-time, 191 part-time).

University of Pittsburgh at Greensburg: 150 Finoli Dr., Greensburg, PA 15601; tel. (724) 837-7040; internet www.greensburg.pitt.edu; academic year August to April; President SHARON P. SMITH; 92 teachers; 1,803 students.

University of Pittsburgh at Johnstown: 450 Schoolhouse Rd, Johnstown, PA 15904; tel. (814) 269-7000; internet www.upj.pitt.edu; academic year August to April; Pres. JEM M. SPECTAR; 154 teachers; 2,965 students.

University of Pittsburgh at Titusville: 504 E Main St, Titusville, PA 16454; internet www.upt.pitt.edu; academic year August to April; Pres. WILLIAM A. SHIELDS; 65 teachers; 514 students (422 full-time, 72 part-time).

UNIVERSITY OF SCRANTON

Scranton, PA 18510
Telephone: (570) 941-7400
Fax: (570) 941-6369
E-mail: admissions@scranton.edu
Internet: www.scranton.edu

Founded 1888
Academic year: August to May

Pres.: Fr KEVIN QUINN
Provost and Vice-Pres. for Academic Affairs: HAROLD W. BAILLIE
Vice-Pres. for Finance and Treas.: ED STEINMETZ
Vice-Pres. for Student Affairs: VINCENT CARILLI
Dean of Library: CHARLES E. KRATZ

Number of teachers: 267
Number of students: 6,070

Publications: *Aquinas* (student newspaper), *Diakonia* (eastern Christian studies), *The Scranton Journal* (alumni magazine, 4 a year), *Windhover* (1 a year)

DEANS

Arthur J. Kania School of Management: Dr MICHAEL MENSAH
College of Arts and Sciences: Dr BRIAN CONIFF
College of Graduate and Continuing Education: Dr WILLIAM JEFF WELSH
Panuska College of Professional Studies: Dr DEBRA PELLIGRINO

UNIVERSITY OF THE ARTS

320 South Broad St, Philadelphia, PA 19102
Telephone: (215) 717-6000
Fax: (215) 717-6045
E-mail: admissions@uarts.edu
Internet: www.uarts.edu

Founded 1987 by merger of Philadelphia College of Art and Design (f. 1876) and Philadelphia College of Performing Arts (f. 1870)
Academic year: September to May

Pres.: MIGUEL ANGEL CORZO
Provost: Dr TERRY APPLEBAUM
Dean of Admissions: BARBARA ELLIOTT
Dean of Students: ALLEN LEFFERS
Dir of Libraries: CAROL GRANEY

Number of teachers: 534 (114 full-time, 420 part-time)
Number of students: 2,300

DEANS

College of Art and Design: STEPHEN TARANTAL
College of Media and Communications: NEIL KLEINMAN
College of Performing Arts: RICHARD LAWN
Liberal Arts: PETER STAMBLER

UNIVERSITY OF THE SCIENCES IN PHILADELPHIA

600 South 43rd St, Philadelphia, PA 19104
Telephone: (215) 596-8800
Internet: www.pcps.edu

Founded 1821

Pres.: Dr PHILIP P. GERBINO
Vice-Pres. for Academic Affairs: BARBARA BYRNE
Dean of Arts and Sciences: CHARLES W. GIBLEY, Jr
Dean of Pharmacy: GEORGE DOWNS
Dean of Students and Academic Support Services: JUANA REINA-LEWIS
Financial Aid Officer: MICHAEL COLAHAN
Registrar: M. THERESE SCANLON
Librarian: MIGNON ADAMS

Library of 76,000 vols
Number of teachers: 145
Number of students: 2,970

Publication: *American Journal of Pharmacy* (4 a year)

DIRECTORS

Biological Sciences: MARGARET KASSCHAU
Biomedical Writing: LILI FOX VELEZ
Chemistry: EDWARD BIRNBAUM
Humanities: BEVERLEY ALMGREN (acting)
Mathematics, Physics and Computer Science: BERNARD BRUNNER
Medical Technology: MARGARET REINHART
Occupational Therapy: RUTH SCHEMM
Pharmaceutical Sciences: EDWIN T. SUGITA
Pharmacy Practice and Administration: REBECCA FINLEY
Physical Education: ROBERT MORGAN
Physical Therapy: ANNETTE IGLARSH
Physician Assistants: KENNETH HARBERT
Social Sciences: JOSEPH LAMBERT

URSINUS COLLEGE

POB 1000, Collegeville, PA 19426-1000
Telephone: (610) 409-3000
Internet: www.ursinus.edu

Founded 1869

Pres.: Dr JOHN STRASSBURGER
Vice-Pres. for Enrollment: RICK DIFELICIANTONIO
Librarian: CHARLIE JAMISON

Library of 200,000 vols
Number of teachers: 165
Number of students: 1,184 day, 1,300 evening

VALLEY FORGE CHRISTIAN COLLEGE

1401 Charlestown Rd, Phoenixville, PA 19460
Telephone: (610) 935-0450
Fax: (610) 917-2069
E-mail: admissions@vfcc.edu
Internet: www.vfcc.edu

Founded 1932 as Maranatha Summer Bible School; present name 1977
Private control
Academic year: August to May

Pres.: Dr DONALD G. MEYER
Provost and Vice-Pres. for Academic Affairs: Dr PHILIP MCLEOD
Vice-Pres. for Finance: Dr DANIEL MORTENSEN
Vice-Pres. for Institutional Advancement: CHARLES COLES
Vice-Pres. for Student Life: Rev. JENNIFER DUNCAN
Head Librarian: PAUL MATHIAS

Number of teachers: 75
Number of students: 856

VILLANOVA UNIVERSITY

Villanova, PA 19085
Telephone: (610) 519-4500
Fax: (610) 519-5000
Internet: www.villanova.edu

Founded 1842
Academic year: August to May

Pres.: Rev. EDMUND J. DOBBIN
Sr Vice-Pres. for Admin.: Rev. WILLIAM MCGUIRE
Univ. Vice-Pres.: Dr HELEN K. LAFFERTY
Vice-Pres. for Academic Affairs: Dr JOHN JOHANNES
Vice-Pres. and Gen. Counsel: DOROTHY MOLLOY
Vice-Pres. for Institutional Advancement: JOHN M. ELIZANDRO
Vice-Pres. for Student Life: Rev. JOHN STACK
Librarian: JOSEPH LUCIA

Library of 1,010,421 vols, 2,998 periodicals, 1,789,816 microforms
Number of teachers: 820 (511 full-time, 309 part-time)
Number of students: 9,833

Publications: *American Catholic Studies* (4 a year), *Augustinian Studies* (2 a year), *Concept* (2 a year), *Concept: Graduate Journal of Interdisciplinary Research* (1 a year), *Horizons* (2 a year), *Journal of Catholic Social Thought* (2 a year), *Journal of Financial Education* (2 a year), *Journal for Peace and Justice Studies* (2 a year), *Journal of South Asian and Middle Eastern Studies* (4 a year), *The Theology Institute Proceedings* (1 a year), *Villanova Law Review* (4 a year)

DEANS

Arts and Science: Rev. KAIL C. ELLIS
Commerce and Finance: Dr EDWARD MATHIS
Engineering: BARRY C. JOHNSON
Enrollment Management: STEPHEN MERRITT
Law: (vacant)
Nursing: Dr M. LOUISE FITZPATRICK
Graduate Studies for the College of Liberal Arts and Sciences: Dr GERALD LONG

WASHINGTON & JEFFERSON COLLEGE

60 S Lincoln St Washington, PA 15301
Telephone: (724) 222-4400
Fax: (724) 223-6534
Internet: www.washjeff.edu

Private control

Accredited to Middle States Asscn of Colleges and Schools (MSACS) and American Chemical Soc. (ACS)
Language of instruction: English

Founded 1781
Academic year: September to May

Pres.: TORI HARING-SMITH
Vice-Pres. for Academic Affairs and Dean of the Faculty: JAMES WHITE
Vice-Pres. for Business and Finance: DENNIS MCMASTER
Vice-Pres. for Devt and Alumni Relations: MICHAEL GRZESIAK
Vice-Pres. for Enrollment: ALTON E. NEWELL
Vice-Pres. and Dean of Student Life: BYRON MCCRAE
Assoc. Vice-Pres. for Business and Finance: THOMAS SZEJKO
Exec. Dir of Communications and Corporate Relations: MARY BETH FORD
Dir of Academic Advising: CATHERINE SHERMAN
Dir of Admissions: ROBERT ADKINS
Dir of Alumni Relations: MICHELE HUFNAGEL
Dir of Athletics: WILLIAM DUKETT
Dir of Career Services: ROBERTA CROSS
Dir of Confs and Events: MAUREEN VALENTINE
Dir of Counselling Services: LISA HAMILTON
Dir of Financial Aid: MICHELLE ANDERSON
Dir of Global Education: TRACI FRUEHAUF
Dir of Human Resources: SUSAN MEHALIK
Dir of Information and Technology Services: DANIEL FAULK
Dir of Information Systems: NANCY BRYANT
Dir of Library Services: ALEXIS RITTENBERGER
Dir of Prospect Research: DAVID KOLSKI
Dir of Protection Service: EDWARD COCHRAN

Dir of Student Activities: Billie Eaves
Registrar: Leslie Maxin
Library of 185,906 vols, 412 current serial subscriptions, 15,458 microforms, 10,469 audiovisual materials and 35,286 periodicals
Number of teachers: 168 (113 full-time, 55 part-time)
Number of students: 1,460 (1,443 full-time, 17 part-time)
Publications: *Topics*, *Washington & Jefferson College Review* (1 a year), *Wooden Tooth Review* (1 a year)

PROFESSORS

Benze, J., Jr, Political Science
Brletic, P., Chemistry
Cameron, W., Theatre and Communications
Cavoti, N., Psychology
Crabtree, M., Psychology
DiSarro, J., Political Science
Dodge, R., History
Drew-Bear, A., English
Dryden, R., Biology
Easton, R., English
Gormly, J., History
Greb, E., Sociology
Gregor, J., Economics and Business
Kuhn, S., Economics and Business
Kyler, C., English
Lee, A., Biology
List, V., History
Longo, J., Education
Mainwaring, W., History
Maloney, P., Art
Miller, S., Sociology
Morrow, D., Mathematics
Myers, S., Psychology
Robison, K., Economics and Business
Scott, J., Jr, Modern Languages
Sheers, W., Physics
Staton, V., Physical Education
Trelka, D., Biology
Troost, L., English
Van de Kappelle, R., Religion
West, J., Economics and Business
Woltermann, M., Mathematics
Wong, R., Mathematics
Woodard, S., Music

WAYNESBURG COLLEGE

51 West College St, Waynesburg, PA 15370
Telephone: (724) 627-8191
E-mail: admissions@waynesburg.edu
Internet: www.waynesburg.edu
Founded 1849
Liberal arts and sciences
Pres.: Timothy R. Thyreen
Sr Vice-Pres. for Institutional Planning, Research and Educational Services: Richard L. Noftzger, Jr
Vice-Pres. for Academic Affairs: A. J. Anglin
Vice-Pres. for Business and Finance: Roy R. Barnhart
Vice-Pres. of Student Devt: Gerald Wood
Assoc. Vice-Pres. for Institutional Advancement: Karen E. Galentine
Dir of College Relations: Bethany Doyle
Registrar: Ronald D. Coltrane
Library Dir: Suzanne Wylie
Library of 126,098 vols
Number of teachers: 114 (66 full-time and 48 part-time
Number of students: 1,351

WESTMINSTER COLLEGE

New Wilmington, PA 16172
Telephone: (724) 946-8761
Fax: (724) 946-7171
Internet: www.westminster.edu
Founded 1852
Academic year: August to May
Related to the Presbyterian Church (USA)
Pres.: R. Thomas Williamson
Vice-Pres. for Academic Affairs and Dean of the College: Jesse T. Mann
Vice-Pres. for Finance: Kenneth J. Romig
Dean of Admissions: Bradley P. Tokar
Dean of Students: Neal A. Edman
Registrar: June G. Pierce
Head Librarian: Dorita F. Bolger
Library of 224,000 vols
Number of teachers: 96
Number of students: 1,650 (1,450 undergraduate, 200 postgraduate)
Publications: *Scrawl* (literary), *Westminster Magazine* (4 a year).

WESTMINSTER THEOLOGICAL SEMINARY

2960 W Church Rd, Glenside, PA 19038
Telephone: (215) 887-5511
Fax: (215) 887-5404
E-mail: admissions@wts.edu
Internet: www.wts.edu
Founded 1929
Private control
Academic year: June to May
Pres.: Peter A. Lillback
Chief Operating Officer: A. D. Dabney
Vice-Pres. and Dean of Texas Campus: Steven T. Vanderhill
Vice Pres. for Finance: Erik V. Davis
Vice-Pres. for Institutional Advancement: David B. Garner
Registrar and Dir of Financial Aid: Melinda E. G. Dugan
Library Dir: Alexander Finlayson
Number of teachers: 50
Number of students: 450 (full-time)

WIDENER UNIVERSITY

1 University Pl., Chester, PA 19013-5792
Telephone: (610) 499-4000
Fax: (610) 876-9751
Internet: www.widener.edu
Founded 1821; fmrly Widener College
Pres: Dr Robert J. Bruce, Dr James T. Harris, III
Sr Vice-Pres. and Provost: Jo Allen
Library of 845,762 vols
Number of teachers: 704 (310 full-time, 394 part-time)
Number of students: 7,355 (3,823 full-time, 3,532 part-time)
Publications: *Corporate Law Journal*, *Law Review*, *Widener Law Symposium Journal*

DEANS

College of Arts and Sciences: Dr Lawrence W. Panek
School of Business Administration: Dr Joseph A. DiAngelo, Jr
School of Engineering: Dr Fred A. Akl
School of Hospitality Management: Nicholas J. Hadgis
School of Human Service Professions: Dr Stephen C. Wilhite
School of Law: Douglas E. Ray
School of Nursing: Dr Marguerite M. Barbiere
University College: Dr Arlene DeCosmo

WILKES UNIVERSITY

84 West South St, Wilkes-Barre, PA 18766
Telephone: (570) 408-5000
Fax: (570) 408-7800
E-mail: info@wilkes.edu
Internet: www.wilkes.edu
Founded 1933
Academic year: August to May
Pres.: Tim Gilmore
Provost: Bernard Graham
Vice-Pres. for Devt: Marty Williams
Vice-Pres. for Enrollment Services: Michael J. Frantz
Vice-Pres. for Human Resources: Maggie Lund
Registrar: Susan A. Hritzak
Library Dir: Jon Lindgren
Library of 233,709 vols
Number of teachers: 122 full-time
Number of students: 2,157 full-time

DEANS

College of Arts, Humanities and Social Sciences: Dr Darin E. Fields
College of Science and Engineering: Dr Dale A. Burns
Jay S. Sidhu School of Business and Leadership: Dr Paul C. Browne
Nesbit College of Pharmacy of Nursing: Dr Bernard W. Graham

WILSON COLLEGE

Chambersburg, PA 17201-1285
Telephone: (717) 264-4141
Fax: (717) 264-1578
E-mail: admissions@wilson.edu
Internet: www.wilson.edu
Founded 1869
Private liberal arts college for women
Academic year: August to May
Pres.: Dr Lorna Duphiney Edmundson
Dir of Admissions: Mary Ann Naso
Librarian: Kathleen Murphy
Library of 177,491 vols, 450 periodicals
Number of teachers: 77 (38 full-time, 39 part-time)
Number of students: 776 (370 full-time, 406 part-time)

YORK COLLEGE OF PENNSYLVANIA

York, PA 17405-7199
Telephone: (717) 846-7788
Fax: (717) 846-1607
E-mail: admissions@ycp.edu
Internet: www.ycp.edu
Founded 1787 as York County Acad.; present name 1968
Private control
Academic year: August to May
Pres.: Dr George W. Waldner
Dean of Academic Affairs: Dr William T. Bogart (acting)
Dean of Student Affairs: Joseph F. Merkle
Library Dir: Susan M. Campbell
Number of teachers: 370
Number of students: 5,900 (4,400 full-time undergraduate, 1,500 part-time and postgraduate)

RHODE ISLAND

BROWN UNIVERSITY

POB 1920, Providence, RI 02912
Telephone: (401) 863-1000
Fax: (401) 863-7737
E-mail: postmaster@brown.edu
Internet: www.brown.edu
Founded 1764
Private
Academic year: September to May
Chancellor: Thomas J. Tisch
Pres.: Ruth J. Simmons
Provost: David Kertzer
Sr Vice-Pres. for Corporation Affairs and Governance: Russell Carey
Sr Vice-Pres. for Univ. Advancement: Steven King

Exec. Vice-Pres. for Finance and Admin.: ELIZABETH HUIDEKOPER
Exec. Vice-Pres. for Planning: RICHARD R. SPIES
Vice-Pres. and Chief Investment Officer: CYNTHIA E. FROST
Vice-Pres. and Gen. Counsel: BEVERLY E. LEDBETTER
Vice-Pres. for Admin.: WALTER C. HUNTER
Vice-Pres. for Alumni Relations: TODD ANDREWS
Vice-Pres. for Campus Life and Student Services: MARGARET KLAWUNN
Vice-Pres. for Computing and Information Services: TERRI-LYNN THAYER (acting)
Vice-Pres. for Devt: KRISTIN DAVITT
Vice-Pres. for Facilities Management: STEPHEN MAIORISI
Vice-Pres. for Human Resources: KAREN DAVIS
Vice-Pres. for Int. Advancement: RONALD MARGOLIN
Vice-Pres. for Int. Affairs: MATTHEW GUTMANN
Vice-Pres. for Public Affairs and Univ. Relations: MARISA QUINN
Vice-Pres. for Research: CLYDE BRIANT
Vice-Pres. and Chief Information Officer: MICHAEL PICKETT
Dean of Admission: JAMES MILLER
Univ. Registrar: ROBERT FITZGERALD
Univ. Librarian: HARRIETTE HEMMASI

Library: 6m. vols
Number of teachers: 681
Number of students: 8,261

DEANS

College: KATHERINE BERGERON
Faculty: RAJIV VOHRA
Graduate School: PETER WEBER
Medicine and Biological Sciences: EDWARD WING

BRYANT COLLEGE

1150 Douglas Pike, Smithfield, RI 02917-1284
Telephone: (401) 232-6000
Fax: (401) 232-6319
E-mail: www@bryant.edu
Internet: www.bryant.edu

Founded 1863

Pres.: RONALD K. MACHTLEY
Vice-Pres. for Academic Affairs: V. K. UNNI
Vice-Pres. for Business Affairs: BARRY MORRISON
Vice-Pres. for Enrollment Management: LORNA J. HUNTER
Vice-Pres. for Information Services: ART GLOSTER
Vice-Pres. for Student Affairs: TOM EAKIN
Vice-Pres. for Univ. Advancement: JAMES DAMRON
Dir of Graduate Programmes: W. DAYLE NATTRESS
Dir of Undergraduate Programmes: ELIZABETH A. POWERS
Dir of Library Services: MARY F. MORONEY

Library: over 150,000 vols, 25,000 journals
Number of students: 3,200

DEANS

College of Arts and Sciences: DAVID LUX
College of Business: JACK TRIFTS

JOHNSON AND WALES UNIVERSITY

8 Abbott Park Pl., Providence, RI 02903
Telephone: (401) 598-1000
E-mail: admissions@jwu.edu
Internet: www.jwu.edu

Founded 1914
Private control
Language of instruction: English
Academic year: September to August
Campuses at Providence (RI), Charleston (SC), Norfolk (VA), North Miami (FL), Denver (CO)

Pres.: Dr JOHN J. BOWEN
Exec. Vice-Pres. and Chief Financial Officer: THOMAS L. G. DWYER
Provost: Dr RICHARD J. KOSH
Sr Vice-Pres. and Treas.: WILLIAM F. MCARDLE
Sr Vice-Pres. of Advancement: VINCENT F. SAELE
Dean of Libraries: Dr HELENA RODRIGUES
Number of students: 9,635

DEANS

College of Business: Dr DAVID MITCHELL
College of Culinary Arts: KARL GUGGENMOS
Graduate School: Dr FRANK PONTARELLI
Hospitality College: RICHARD L. BRUSH
School of Arts and Sciences: Dr ANGELA R. RENAUD
School of Education: Dr CLIFTON BOYLE
School of Technology: FRANCIS X. TWEEDIE

PROVIDENCE COLLEGE

549 River Ave, Providence, RI 02918-0001
Telephone: (401) 865-1000
Internet: www.providence.edu

Founded 1917

Pres.: Rev. BRIAN J. SHANLEY
Exec. Vice-Pres. and Treas.: Rev. KENNETH SICARD
Vice-Pres. for Academic Affairs: Dr HUGH LENA
Vice-Pres. for College Relations and Planning: EDWARD CARON
Vice-Pres. for Finance and Business: MICHAEL FRAZIER
Vice-Pres. and Gen. Counsel: MARIFRANCES MCGINN
Vice-Pres. for Institutional Advancement: DAVID WEGRZYN
Vice-Pres. for Mission and Min.: Rev. JOSEPH J. GUIDO
Vice-Pres. for Student Affairs Admin.: Rev. BRENDAN MURPHY
Librarian: Dr RUSSELL BAILEY

Library of 342,000 vols
Number of teachers: 338
Number of students: 3,998 undergraduate, 837 graduate, 596 in School of Continuing Education

DEANS

Graduate Studies: Dr THOMAS FLAHERTY
Int. Studies: ADRIAN BEAULIEU
Multicultural Affairs: Dr EDWARD TWYMAN
School of Business: Dr FRANCINE NEWTH (acting)
School of Continuing Education: MADELEINE METZLER

RHODE ISLAND COLLEGE

600 Mount Pleasant Ave, Providence, RI 02908-1991
Telephone: (401) 456-8000
Fax: (401) 456-8379
E-mail: theweb@ric.edu
Internet: www.ric.edu

Founded 1854

Pres.: JOHN NAZARIAN
Vice-Pres. for Academic Affairs: NANCY CARRIUOLO
Vice-Pres. for Admin. and Finance: IVY DENISE LOCKE
Vice-Pres. for Devt and College Relations: MARGUERITE BROWN
Vice-Pres. for Student Affairs: GARY M. PENFIELD
Dir of Admissions: HOLLY L. SHADOIAN
Librarian: CAROL HRYCIW-WING

Library of 360,000 vols
Number of teachers: 375
Number of students: 7,214 undergraduate, 1,852 graduate

DEANS

Faculty of Arts and Sciences: RICHARD WEINER
School of Education and Human Devt: ROGER ELDRIDGE
School of Management: JAMES A. SCHWEIKART
School of Nursing: JANE WILLIAMS
School of Social Work: CAROL BENNETT-SPEIGHT

RHODE ISLAND SCHOOL OF DESIGN

Providence, RI 02903
Telephone: (401) 454-6100
Fax: (401) 454-6420
E-mail: admissions@risd.edu
Internet: www.risd.edu

Founded 1877
Academic year: September to May

Pres.: ROGER MANDLE
Exec. Vice-Pres. for Communications and Design: ELIZABETH O'NEIL
Exec. Vice-Pres. for Finance and Admin.: W. ARNOLD YASINSKI
Provost: JAY COOGAN
Assoc. Provost for Student Affairs: EDWARD DWYER
Dir for Instn Research and Planning: FELICE BILLUPS
Dir of Admissions: EDWARD NEWHALL
Librarian: CAROL TERRY

Library of 107,000 vols
Number of teachers: 350
Number of students: 2,294

DEANS

Architecture and Design: DAWN BARRETT
Fine Arts: JOHN TERRY
Foundation Studies: JOANNE STRYKER
Graduate Studies: JESSIE SHEFRIN
Liberal Arts: BARBARA VON ECKARDT

ATTACHED INSTITUTE

RISD Museum: 224 Benefit St, Providence, RI 02903; tel. (401) 454-6500; fax (480) 945-4199; internet www.risd.edu/museum.cfm; 75,000 items; Dir HOPE ALSWANG.

ROGER WILLIAMS UNIVERSITY

1 Old Ferry Rd, Bristol, RI 02809
Telephone: (401) 253-1040
E-mail: admit@rwu.edu
Internet: www.rwu.edu
Private control
Academic year: September to May

Pres.: Dr ROY J. NIRSCHEL
Provost and Sr Vice-Pres.: Dr LAURA NIESEN DE ABRUNA
Vice-Pres. and Chief Information Officer: JOSEPH PANGBORN
Vice-Pres. for Advancement: KASSANDRA JOLLEY
Vice-Pres. for Enrollment Management and Retention: LYNN FAWTHROP
Vice-Pres. for Finance and Chief Financial Officer: JAMES C. NOONAN
Vice-Pres. for Strategic Planning and Community Relations: PETER WILBUR
Vice-Pres. for Student Affairs: JOHN J. KING
Gen. Counsel and Vice-Pres. for Legal Affairs: RICHARD H. AVERY
Registrar: DANIEL P. VILENSKI (acting)
Dean of Libraries: PETER DEEKLE

Number of teachers: 315
Number of students: 3,840 full-time undergraduate, 823 postgraduate and professional, 506 continuing studies

DEANS

College of Arts and Sciences: Dr ROBERT A. COLE
School of Architecture, Art and Historic Preservation: STEPHEN WHITE
School of Business: Dr MALING EBRAHIMPOUR
School of Continuing Studies: Dr JOHN W. STOUT
School of Education: Dr MIEKO KAMII
School of Engineering, Computing and Construction Management: ROBERT A. POTTER, Jr
School of Justice Studies: Dr STEPHANIE PICOLO MANZI
School of Law: (vacant)

RESEARCH INSTITUTE

Justice System Training and Research Institute: internet www.rwu.edu/academics/schools/sjs/jstri; Dir ROBERT MCKENNA.

SALVE REGINA UNIVERSITY

100 Ochre Point Ave, Newport, RI 02840-4129
Telephone: (401) 847-6650
Fax: (401) 341-2916
Internet: www.salve.edu

Founded 1934 as Salve Regina College; present name 1991
Private control (Religious Sisters of Mercy)

Pres.: Dr JANE GERETY
Vice-Pres. for Academic Affairs: Dr DEAN DE LA MOTTE
Vice-Pres. for Admin. and Chief Financial Officer: WILLIAM B. HALL
Vice-Pres. for Enrollment and Dean of Admissions: LAURA MCPHIE OLIVEIRA
Vice-Pres. for Mission Integration and Planning: Dr LEONA MISTO
Vice-Pres. for Student Life: JOHN J. ROK
Vice-Pres. for Univ. Relations and Advancement: MICHAEL SEMENZA
Registrar: Dr JAMES H. TERRY
Dean of Arts and Sciences: Dr LAURA O' TOOLE
Dean of Professional Studies: Dr TRACI WARRINGTON
Dean of Students: JOHN QUINN
Dir of Library Services: KATHLEEN BOYD

Library of 116,000 vols
Number of teachers: 120
Number of students: 2,500

Depts of admin. of justice, art, biology and biomedical science, business studies and economics, chemistry, cultural and historic preservation, education, English, history, mathematical sciences, modern languages, music, nursing, philosophy, politics, psychology, religious studies, social work, sociology and anthropology, theatre arts.

UNIVERSITY OF RHODE ISLAND

Kingston, RI 02881
Telephone: (401) 874-1000
E-mail: admissions@uri.edu
Internet: www.uri.edu

Founded 1892 as Rhode Island College of Agriculture and Mechanic Arts; attained univ. status 1951

Pres.: DAVID M. DOOLEY
Provost and Vice-Pres. for Academic Affairs: M. BEVERLY SWAN
Vice-Pres. for Admin.: ROBERT A. WEYGAND
Vice-Pres. for Student Affairs: Dr THOMAS R. DOUGAN
Vice-Pres. for Univ. Advancement: ROBERT L. BEAGLE
Registrar: ROBERT STROBEL
Dean of Univ. Libraries: DAVID MASLYN

Library: 1m. vols
Number of teachers: 721
Number of students: 13,698

Publication: *Maritimes* (4 a year)

DEANS

College of Arts and Sciences: WINIFRED BROWNELL
College of Business Administration: MARK HIGGINS
College of Engineering: BAHRAM NASSER-SHARIF
College of Environment and Life Sciences: NANCY L. FEY-YENSAN
College of Human Science and Services: W. LYNN MCKINNEY
College of Nursing: DAYLE JOSEPH
College of Pharmacy: RONALD P. JORDAN
Graduate School of Oceanography: DAVID M. FARMER
University College: DIANE W. STROMMER

BRANCH CAMPUSES

Feinstein Providence Campus: 80 Washington St, Providence, RI 02903; tel. (401) 277-5000; internet www.uri.edu/prov.

Narragansett Bay Campus: South Ferry Rd, Narragansett, RI 02882-1197; tel. (401) 874-6222; fax (401) 874-6889; e-mail thedean@gso.uri.edu.

W. Alton Jones Campus: 401 Victory Highway, West Greenwich, RI 02817; tel. (401) 397-3302; fax (401) 397-3293; internet www.uri.edu/ajc; Dir THOMAS H. MITCHEL.

ATTACHED RESEARCH PROGRAMMES

Agricultural Experiment Station: tel. (401) 874-5493; fax (401) 874-4017; internet riaes.cels.uri.edu; Dir JEFFERY R. SEEMANN.

Biotechnology Center.

Center for Atmospheric Chemistry Studies: tel. (401) 874-6834; fax (401) 874-6898; e-mail www@euros.gso.uri.edu; internet euros.gso.uri.edu/index.html.

Coastal Institute: tel. (401) 874-6513; fax (401) 874-6869; e-mail ci@edc.uri.edu; internet www.ci.uri.edu.

Coastal Resources Center: tel. (401) 874-6224; fax (401) 874-4670; e-mail info@crc.uri.edu; internet www.crc.uri.edu; Dir PETER AUGUST.

Institute for International Sport: tel. (401) 874-2375; fax (401) 874-2429; e-mail info@internationalsport.com; internet www.internationalsport.com; f. 1986; Dir DANIEL E. DOYLE.

Institute for the Study of International Aspects of Competition: tel. (401) 874-9195; fax (401) 874-2858; internet www.uri.edu/research/isiac; Dir JOHN P. BURKETT.

National Sea Grant Depository.

Research Institute for Telecommunicatons Marketing (RITIM): tel. (401) 874-5065; fax (401) 874-4312; e-mail ritim@etal.uri.edu; internet ritim.cba.uri.edu; Dir RUBY ROY DHOLAKIA.

Rhode Island Sea Grant: tel. (401) 874-6842; fax (401) 874-6817; e-mail allard@gso.uri.edu; internet seagrant.gso.uri.edu; Dir BARRY A. COSTA-PIERCE.

Robotics Research Center.

SOUTH CAROLINA

ALLEN UNIVERSITY

1530 Harden St, Columbia, SC 29204
Telephone: (803) 375-5700
Fax: (803) 375-5733
E-mail: admissions@allenuniversity.edu
Internet: www.allenuniversity.edu

Founded 1870
Private control

Pres.: Dr CHARLES E. YOUNG
Vice-Pres. for Academic Affairs: Dr WALTER C. HOWARD

Number of teachers: 35
Number of students: 350

ANDERSON UNIVERSITY

316 Boulevard, Anderson, SC 29621-40350
Telephone: (864) 231-2030
Fax: (864) 231-2033
E-mail: admissions@andersonuniversity.edu
Internet: www.andersonuniversity.edu

Founded 1911
Private control
Academic year: August to May

Pres.: Dr EVANS P. WHITAKER
Vice-Pres. for Academic Affairs and Academic Dean: Dr DANNY PARKER
Vice-Pres. for Enrollment Services and Quality Initiatives: R. MARK HUGHES
Vice-Pres. for Finance and Admin.: JOHN M. KUNST
Vice-Pres. for Institutional Advancement: R. DEAN WOODS
Vice-Pres. for Student Services: Dr BOB L. HANLEY
Registrar: LISA M. THOMPSON
Library Dir: KENT MILLWOOD

Number of teachers: 151
Number of students: 1,664

BENEDICT COLLEGE

1600 Harden St, Columbia, SC 29204
Telephone: (803) 253-5143
Fax: (803) 253-5215
Internet: www.benedict.edu

Founded 1870 as Benedict Institute; present name 1894
Private control
Academic year: August to May

Pres.: Dr DAVID H. SWINTON
Exec. Vice-Pres.: Dr RUBY W. WATTS
Sr Vice-Pres. for Academic Affairs: Dr RICHARD C. MILLER
Vice-Pres. for Business Affairs: CLAUDINE GEE
Vice-Pres. for Community Devt: JABARI SIMAMA
Vice-Pres. for Institutional Advancement: BARBARA C. MOORE
Vice-Pres. for Institutional Effectiveness: GARY E. KNIGHT
Vice-Pres. for Student Affairs: Dr DAVID B. WHALEY
Library Dir: DARLENE ZINNERMAN-BETHEA

Number of teachers: 159 (126 full-time, 33 part-time)
Number of students: 2,770

DEANS

School of Business: Dr JOHN COLE
School of Education: Dr JANEEN WITTY
School of Humanities, Arts and Social Sciences: CHARLES AUSTIN
School of Science, Technology, Engineering and Mathematics: Dr STACEY JONES

CHARLESTON SOUTHERN UNIVERSITY

9200 University Blvd, POB 118087, Charleston, SC 29406
Telephone: (843) 863-7000
Fax: (843) 863-8074
Internet: www.csuniv.edu

Founded 1964
Private control
Academic year: August to April

Pres.: Dr JAIRY C. HUNTER, Jr
Provost: Dr A. KENNERLEY BONNETTE

Vice-Pres. for Advancement and Marketing: JIM BRADLEY
Vice-Pres. for Business Affairs: KENT BRASHER
Vice-Pres. for Enrollment Management: DEBBIE WILLIAMSON
Vice-Pres. for Planning and Student Affairs: Dr RICK BREWER
Registrar: REX NESTOR
Library Dir: Dr ENID RUTHERFORTH CAUSEY
Number of teachers: 80
Number of students: 2,800

DEANS

College of Human and Social Sciences: Dr DON DOWLESS
College of Science and Mathematics: Dr JERYL JOHNSON
School of Business: Dr JOHN B. DUNCAN
School of Education: Dr SANDRA BOWDEN
School of Nursing: Dr MARIAN M. LARISEY

THE CITADEL

171 Moultrie St, Charleston, SC 29409
Telephone: (843) 225-3294
Internet: www.citadel.edu

Founded 1842
Controlled by state of South Carolina

Pres.: Lt-Gen. JOHN W. ROSA
Exec. Vice-Pres. and Dean of the College: Brig.-Gen. R. CLIFTON POOLE
Vice-Pres. for Facilities and Admin.: Col DONALD M. TOMASIK
Vice-Pres. for Finance and Business Affairs: Col CALVIN G. LYONS
Commandant of Cadets: Col JOSEPH W. TREZ
Dir of Libraries: Lt-Col ANGIE S. W. LE CLERCQ
Registrar: Col ISAAC S. METTS, Jr (acting)

Library of 182,000 vols
Number of teachers: 163 full-time, 53 part-time, 28 ROTC
Number of students: 7,500

Publications: *Brigadier*, *Citadel Monograph Series*, *Citadel Review*, *Guidon*, *Shako*, *Sphinx*.

CLAFLIN UNIVERSITY

400 Magnolia St, Orangeburg, SC 29115
Telephone: (803) 535-5000
E-mail: mzeigler@claflin.edu
Internet: www.claflin.edu

Founded 1869
Private control
Academic year: August to May

Pres.: Dr HENRY N. TISDALE
Vice-Pres. for Academic Affairs: Dr HOWARD D. HILL
Vice-Pres. for Devt and Alumni Affairs: Rev. W. V. MIDDLETON
Vice-Pres. for Student Devt and Services: Dr LEROY A. DURANT
Head Librarian: MARILYN PRINGLE

Number of teachers: 50
Number of students: 965

CLEMSON UNIVERSITY

Clemson, SC 29634
Telephone: (864) 656-3311
Fax: (864) 656-4676
Internet: www.clemson.edu

Founded 1889 as Clemson Agricultural College
Language of instruction: English
Academic year: August to May

Pres.: JAMES F. BARKER
Provost and Vice-Pres. for Academic Affairs: DORIS R. HELMS
Vice-Pres. for Advancement: NEILL CAMERON, Jr
Vice-Pres. for Public Service and Agriculture: JOHN W. KELLY
Vice-Pres. for Research: CHRISTIAN E. G. PRZIREMBEL
Vice-Pres. for Student Affairs: ALMEDA R. JACKS
Exec. Sec. of the Board: J. THORNTON KIRBY
Librarian: J. F. BOYKIN

Library of 1,437,333 vols
Number of teachers: 1,204 (1,057 full-time, 147 part-time)
Number of students: 16,980

DEANS

Vice-Provost and Dean of Graduate School: BONNIE HOLADAY
Vice-Provost and Dean of Undergraduate Studies: JEROME REEL
College of Agriculture, Forestry and Life Sciences: CALVIN SCHOUTTIES
College of Architecture, Arts and Humanities: JANICE SCHACH
College of Business and Public Affairs: JERRY TRAPNELL
College of Engineering and Science: THOMAS M. KEINATH
College of Health, Education and Human Development: LAWRENCE R. ALLEN

COASTAL CAROLINA UNIVERSITY

POB 261954, Conway, SC 29528-6054
Telephone: (843) 347-3161
E-mail: admissions@coastal.edu
Internet: www.coastal.edu

Founded 1954 as Coastal Carolina Junior College; present name 1993
Academic year: August to May

President: DAVID A. DECENZO
Exec. Dir of Library and Instructional Technologies: BARBARA BURD

Number of teachers: 353
Number of students: 5,980

DEANS

College of Business Administration: DAVID A. DECENZO
College of Education: GILBERT H. HUNT
College of Humanities and Fine Art: LYNN FRANKEN
College of Natural and Applied Sciences: (vacant)
School of Continuing Studies: PETER B. BALSAMO

COKER COLLEGE

300 East College Ave, Hartsville, SC 29550
Telephone: (843) 383-8000
Internet: www.coker.edu

Founded 1908
Academic year: September to May

Pres.: Dr B. JAMES DAWSON
Dean of the Faculty and College Provost: RONALD L. CARTER
Vice-Pres. for Enrollment Management: Dr STEPHEN B. TERRY
Dir of Financial Aid: BETTY WILLIAMS
Librarian: MINOO MONAKES

Library of 70,000 vols
Number of teachers: 51
Number of students: 975

COLLEGE OF CHARLESTON

66 George St, Charleston, SC 29424
Telephone: (803) 953-5500
Fax: (843) 953-5811
Internet: www.cofc.edu

Founded 1770, chartered 1785
Public control
Language of instruction: English
Academic year: August to July

Pres.: P. GEORGE BENSON
Provost and Sr Vice-Pres. for Academic Affairs: GEORGE W. HYND
Registrar: CATHERINE C. BOYD
Librarian: DAVID J. COHEN

Library of 797,550 vols
Number of teachers: 529
Number of students: 11,532

Publications: *Chrestomathy* (undergraduate research in the humanities and social sciences, 1 a year), *Crazyhorse* (literary journal, 2 a year)

DEANS

School of Arts: VALERIE MORRIS
School of Business: ALAN T. SHAO
School of Education, Health and Human Performance: FRANCES C. WELCH
School of Humanities and Social Sciences: CYNTHIA J. LOWENTHAL
School of Languages, Cultures and World Affairs: DAVID J. COHEN
School of Sciences and Mathematics: MIKE AUERBACH

COLUMBIA COLLEGE

Columbia, SC 29203
Telephone: (803) 754-3178
Internet: www.columbiacollegesc.edu

Founded 1854

Pres.: Dr CAROLINE WHITSON
Provost: Dr LAURIE B. HOPKINS
Registrar: JACK HAMILTON
Librarian: JOHN C. PRITCHETT

Library of 176,018 vols
Number of teachers: 105
Number of students: 1,453

COLUMBIA INTERNATIONAL UNIVERSITY

7435 Monticello Rd, Columbia, SC 29203
Telephone: (803) 754-4100
Fax: (803) 786-4209
E-mail: yesciu@ciu.edu
Internet: www.ciu.edu

Founded 1923 as Columbia Bible School, present name 1994
Private control
Academic year: August to May

Pres.: Dr WILLIAM H. JONES
Vice-Pres. for Development: KEITH MARION
Vice-Pres. for Enrollment: MIKE BLACKWELL
Vice-Pres. for Institutional Assessment: BOB KALLGREN
Provost: JAMES LANPHER
Registrar: JIM ROCHE
Dean of Information Sources and Services: DAVID MASH
Library Dir: JO ANN RHODES

Library of 142,238 vols
Number of teachers: 75
Number of students: 975

CONVERSE COLLEGE

580 East Main St, Spartanburg, SC 29302
Telephone: (864) 596-9000
Fax: (864) 596-9225
E-mail: info@converse.edu
Internet: www.converse.edu

Founded 1889
Academic year: September to May

Pres.: Dr ELIZABETH A. FLEMING
Dir of Admissions: WANDA MOORE MCDOWELL
Librarian: WADE WOODWARD

Library of 200,000 vols
Number of teachers: 85
Number of students: 1,200

Arts, music, sciences.

ERSKINE COLLEGE

POB 338, Due West, SC 29639
2 Washington St, Due West, SC 29639
Telephone: (864) 379-2131
Fax: (864) 379-2167
E-mail: admissions@erskine.edu
Internet: www.erskine.edu
Founded 1839
Pres.: Dr RANDALL T. RUBLE
Dir of Admissions: WOODY O'CAIN
Librarian: JOHN F. KENNERLY
Library of 150,000 vols
Number of teachers: 62
Number of students: 600

FRANCIS MARION UNIVERSITY

POB 100547, Florence, SC 29502
Telephone: (843) 661-1231
E-mail: admissions@fmarion.edu
Internet: www.fmarion.edu
Founded 1970
State control
Academic year: August to May
Pres.: Dr LUTHER F. CARTER
Provost: Dr RICHARD N. CHAPMAN
Vice-Pres. for Admin.: Dr GARY W. HANSON
Vice-Pres. for Business Affairs: JOHN J. KISPERT
Vice-Pres. for Student Affairs: Dr JOSEPH E. HEYWARD
Dir of Alumni Affairs: JULIAN YOUNG
Registrar: H. ELIZABETH MCLEAN
Dean of Library: H. PAUL DOVE, Jr
Number of teachers: 210
Number of students: 3,360 (2,940 undergraduate, 420 postgraduate)

DEANS
College of Liberal Arts: Dr RICHARD N. CHAPMAN
School of Business: Dr M. BARRY O'BRIEN
School of Education: (vacant)

FURMAN UNIVERSITY

3300 Poinsett Highway, Greenville, SC 29613
Telephone: (864) 294-2000
Internet: www.furman.edu
Founded 1826
Pres.: Dr DAVID E. SHI
Vice-Pres. for Academic Affairs and Dean: A. V. HUFF
Vice-Pres. for Business Affairs: WENDY LIBBY
Vice-Pres. for Devt: DONALD J. LINEBACK
Vice-Pres. for Enrollment: BILL BERG
Vice-Pres. for Intercollegiate Athletics: JOHN BLOCK
Vice-Pres. for Marketing and Public Relations: GREGORY A. CARROLL
Vice-Pres. for Student Services: HARRY B. SHUCKER
Registrar: PAUL H. ANDERSON
Librarian: JANIS BANDELIN
Library of 390,000 vols
Number of teachers: 200
Number of students: 2,840
Publications: *Furman Magazine* (1 a year), *Furman Reports* (4 a year), *Humanities Review* (1 a year), *Paladin* (52 a year), *Studies* (2 a year), *The Echo* (literary, 2 a year)

DEANS
Continuing Education: JOHN H. DICKEY
Graduate Studies: HAZEL W. HARRIS

LANDER UNIVERSITY

Greenwood, SC 29649
Telephone: (864) 388-8000
Fax: (864) 388-8890
Internet: www.lander.edu
Founded 1872
State control
Pres.: Dr DANIEL W. BALL
Vice-Pres. for Academic Affairs: DANNY MCKENZIE
Vice-Pres. for Business and Admin.: JAMES THOMAS COVAR
Vice-Pres. for Student Affairs: RANDY BOUKNIGHT
Vice-Pres. for Univ. Advancement: ADAM TAYLOR
Dean of Enrollment Services: R. THOMAS NELSON, III
Dir for Library: DAVID MASH
Library of 379,300 vols
Number of teachers: 164
Number of students: 2,625

LIMESTONE COLLEGE

Gaffney, SC 29340-3799
Telephone: (864) 489-7151
Fax: (864) 487-8706
E-mail: admiss@limestone.edu
Internet: www.limestone.edu
Founded 1845
Academic year: August to May
Pres.: Dr WALT GRIFFIN
Vice-Pres. for Academic Affairs: Dr KAREN W. GAINEY
Vice-Pres. for Enrollment Services: CHRISTOPHER N. PHENICIE
Vice-Pres. for Financial Affairs: DAVID S. RILLING
Vice-Pres. for Information Technology: CARNEGIE R. HORTON
Vice-Pres. for Institutional Advancement: Dr WILLIAM H. BAKER
Vice-Pres. for Student Services: (vacant)
Librarian: CAROLYN T. HAYWARD
Library of 151,677 vols, 2,873 microforms, 2,900 audio and video cassettes
Number of teachers: 80 (full-time)
Number of students: 3,119 (859 main campus, 2,260 off-campus)

LUTHERAN THEOLOGICAL SOUTHERN SEMINARY

4201 N Main St, Columbia, SC 29203
Telephone: (803) 786-5150
Fax: (803) 786-6499
E-mail: dlondon@ltss.edu
Internet: www.ltss.edu
Private control
Pres.: Rev. Dr MARCUS J. MILLER
Vice-Pres. for Academic Affairs and Dean: Rev. Dr GINGER BARFIELD
Vice-Pres. for Devt and Seminary Relations: RON WALRATH
Registrar: Dr GINGER BARFIELD
Library Dir: Dr LYNN A. FEIDER
Number of teachers: 17
Number of students: 152 (full-time)

MEDICAL UNIVERSITY OF SOUTH CAROLINA

171 Ashley Ave, Charleston, SC 29425
Telephone: (803) 792-2300
Fax: (803) 792-0392
Internet: www.musc.edu
Founded 1824
Language of instruction: English
Academic year: September to June
Pres.: Dr RAYMOND S. GREENBERG
Vice-Pres. for Academic Affairs: Dr JOHN R. RAYMOND
Vice-Pres. for Finance and Admin.: Dr LISA MONTGOMERY
Vice-Pres. for Information Technology: Dr FRANK C. CLARK
Vice-Pres. for Medical Affairs: Dr JOSEPH G. REVES
Librarian: Dr THOMAS P. BASLER
Number of teachers: 1,281
Number of students: 2,339
Publication: *Humanitas* (1 a year)

DEANS
College of Dental Medicine: JACK SANDERS
College of Graduate Studies and University Research: Dr PERRY V. HALUSHKA
College of Health Professions: Dr DANIELLE RIPICH
College of Medicine: Dr JOSEPH G. REVES
College of Nursing: Dr GAIL W. STUART
College of Pharmacy: Dr JOSEPH DIPERO

MORRIS COLLEGE

100 W College St, Sumter, SC 29150-3599
Telephone: (803) 934-3200
Fax: (803) 773-3687
E-mail: webcomment@morris.edu
Internet: www.morris.edu
Founded 1908
Private control
Pres.: LUNS C. RICHARDSON
Dean of Student Affairs: MARION R. SANFORD
Number of teachers: 70
Number of students: 880

NEWBERRY COLLEGE

2100 College St, Newberry, SC 29108
Telephone: (803) 276-5010
Fax: (803) 321-5627
E-mail: admissions@newberry.edu
Internet: www.newberry.edu
Founded 1856
Private control (affiliated with the Evangelical Lutheran Church in America: South Carolina, Southeastern, Florida-Bahamas, and Caribbean Synods)
Academic year: August to May
Pres.: Dr MITCHELL M. ZAIS
Dean of Academic Affairs: Dr L. FRANK MCCOY
Librarian: LAWRENCE ELLIS
Library of 79,899 vols
Number of teachers: 70
Number of students: 760
Publications: *Eklekta* (1 a year), *Dimensions* (2 a year), *Kinnikinnick* (1 a year), *The Indian* (24 a year), *The Newberrian* (1 a year).

NORTH GREENVILLE UNIVERSITY

POB 1892, Tigerville, SC 29688
Telephone: (864) 977-7000
Internet: www.ngu.edu
Founded 1892 as North Greenville High School; present name 1972
Private control
Academic year: August to May
Pres.: Dr JAMES B. EPTING
Number of teachers: 35
Number of students: 1,300

PRESBYTERIAN COLLEGE

Clinton, SC 29325
Telephone: (864) 833-2820
Fax: (864) 833-8481
Internet: www.presby.edu
Founded 1880
Academic year: August to May
Pres.: Dr JOHN V. GRIFFITH
Vice-Pres. for Academic Affairs: Dr J. DAVID GILLESPIE

Vice-Pres. for Enrollment: R. DANA PAUL
Dean of Students: TELESIA DAVIS
Dir of Library: DAVID CHATHAM

Library of 166,110 vols
Number of teachers: 111 (79 full-time, 32 part-time)
Number of students: 1,182

SOUTH CAROLINA STATE UNIVERSITY

Orangeburg, SC 29117
Telephone: (803) 536-7000
Fax: (803) 533-3622
Internet: www.scsu.edu

Founded 1896
Academic year: August to May

Pres.: Dr LEROY DAVIS
Dir of Admissions: LILLIAN ADDERSON (acting)
Library Dir: MARY L. SMALLS

Library of 298,051 vols
Number of teachers: 311
Number of students: 4,500

SOUTHERN WESLEYAN UNIVERSITY

POB 1020, 907 Wesleyan Drive, Central, SC 29630-1020
Telephone: (864) 644-5000
Internet: www.swu.edu

Founded 1906
Private control
Academic year: August to May

Pres.: Dr DAVID J. SPITTAL

Number of teachers: 130
Number of students: 1,360 (1,310 undergraduate, 50 postgraduate)

UNIVERSITY OF SOUTH CAROLINA

Columbia, SC 29208
Telephone: (803) 777-7000
Fax: (803) 777-0101
E-mail: info@sc.edu
Internet: www.sc.edu

Chartered 1801; opened 1805

Pres.: Dr HARRIS PASTIDES
Exec. Vice-Pres. for Academic Affairs and Provost: Dr WILLIAM T. MOORE
Vice-Provost for Academic Affairs and Dean of Undergraduate Studies: Dr HELEN I. DOERPINGHAUS
Vice-Provost for Faculty Devt: Dr CHRISTINE W. CURTIS
Vice-Provost for Health Sciences: Dr RUSS PATE
Vice-Provost for System Affairs and Exec. Dean for Extended Univ.: Dr CHRIS P. PLYLER
Vice-Pres. for Human Resources: JANE M. JAMESON
Vice-Pres. for Information Technology and Chief Information Officer: Dr WILLIAM F. HOGUE
Vice-Pres. for Research and Economic Devt: Dr . ROSEMARIE BOOZE
Vice-Pres. for Student Affairs and Vice-Provost for Academic Support: Dr DENNIS A. PRUITT
Vice-Pres. for Univ. Advancement: JOHN J. DUFFY
Registrar: BARBARA R. BLANEY
Chancellor of USC Aiken: Dr THOMAS L. HALLMAN
Chancellor of USC Beaufort: Dr JANE T. UPSHAW
Chancellor of USC Upstate: JOHN C. STOCKWELL
Dean of Libraries: Dr TOM MCNALLY

Library of over 9m. vols
Number of teachers: 1,709 full-time at Univ. of SC Columbia campus only
Number of students: 41,581 (8 campuses)

DEANS

College of Arts and Sciences: Dr MARY ANNE FITZPATRICK
College of Education: Dr LES STERNBERG (acting)
College of Engineering and Computing: CRAIG A. ROGERS
College of Hospitality, Retail and Sport Management: Dr SHERYL KLINE (acting)
College of Mass Communications and Information Studies: JUDY VANSLYKE TURK
College of Nursing: Dr PEGGY HEWLETT
College of Pharmacy: Dr RANDALL ROWEN (acting)
College of Social Work: Dr DENNIS POOLE
South Carolina Honors College: Dr DAVIS BAIRD
School of Law: WALTER PRATT
School of Medicine: Dr DONALD J. DIPETTE
School of Music: Dr TAYLOE HARDING
School of Public Health: Dr G. THOMAS CHANDLER
Moore School of Business: Dr HILDY TEEGEN
Graduate School: Dr JAMES BUGGY
USC Lancaster: Dr JOHN CATALANO
USC Salkehatchie: Dr ANN C. CARMICHAEL
USC Sumter: Dr C. LESLIE CARPENTER
USC Union: Dr HUGH C. ROWLAND

VOORHEES COLLEGE

POB 678, Denmark, SC 29042
Telephone: (803) 780-1234
Internet: www.voorhees.edu

Founded 1897
Private control
Academic year: August to May

Pres.: Dr CLEVELAND L. SELLERS, Jr
Vice-Pres. for Academic Affairs: Dr JUDY CARTER
Vice-Pres. for Business Affairs: GERALDINE JONES
Vice-Pres. for Institutional Advancement: GLORIA A. RICHARD
Vice-Pres. for Planning and Information Management: SAMUEL BLACKWELL
Vice-Pres. for Student Affairs: WILLIE JEFFERSON
Registrar: FELICIA MAYES
Library Dir: MARIE MARTIN

Number of teachers: 25
Number of students: 700

DEANS

Division of Arts and Sciences: Dr CASSANDRA SMITH
Division of Business and Professional Studies: Dr CHEULHO LEE
Division of Education: COSTA LEMPESIS

WINTHROP UNIVERSITY

Rock Hill, SC 29733
Telephone: (803) 323-2211
Internet: www.winthrop.edu

Founded 1886

Pres.: Dr ANTHONY J. DIGIORGIO
Vice-Pres. for Academic Affairs: PATRICIA CORMIER
Vice-Pres. for External Relations: BECKY MCMILLAN
Vice-Pres. for Finance and Business: J. P. MCKEE
Vice-Pres. for Student Life: FRANK P. ARDAIOLO
Registrar: KAREN C. JONES
Dir of Admissions: DEBI BARBER

Library of 357,110 vols
Number of teachers: 401
Number of students: 5,107

Publications: *The Johnsonian* (52 a year), *The Tatler*, *The Winthrop Anthology* (1 a year)

DEANS

Admissions: JIM BLACK
Arts and Sciences: BETSY BROWN (acting)
Business Administration: JERRY H. PADGETT
Education: TOM POWELL
Library Services: PAUL DUBOIS
Visual and Performing Arts: BENNETT LENTCZNER

WOFFORD COLLEGE

429 North Church St, Spartanburg, SC 29303-3663
Telephone: (864) 597-4000
Fax: (864) 597-4019
Internet: www.wofford.edu

Founded 1854

Pres.: Dr BENJAMIN BERNARD DUNLAP
Sr Vice-Pres. for Devt: MARION B. PEAVEY
Sr Vice-Pres. for Operations and Finance: ROBERT L. KEASLER
Vice-Pres: LARRY MCGEHEE, B. G. STEPHENS
Vice-Pres. for Academic Affairs and Dean: DAVID S. WOOD
Vice-Pres. for Academic Admin. and Planning: BOYCE M. LAWTON
Vice-Pres. for Admin.: DAVID M. BEACHAM
Vice-Pres. for Business: EDWARD E. GREENE
Vice Pres. for Enrollment: BRAND R. STILLE
Vice-Pres. for Student Affairs and Dean of Students: ROBERTA R. BIGGER
Vice-Pres. for Technology and Information Management: JASON H. WOMICK
Dean of Int. Programmes: ANA MARIÁ WISEMAN
Dir of Admissions: BRAND STILLE
Exec. Dir of Devt: DAVID BEACHAM
Registrar: LUCY B. QUINN
Librarian: OAKLEY HERMAN COBURN

Library of 360,434 items
Number of teachers: 127 (full-time)
Number of students: 1,439

SOUTH DAKOTA

AUGUSTANA COLLEGE

2001 South Summit Ave, Sioux Falls, SD 57197
Telephone: (605) 274-0770
Fax: (605) 274-5299
E-mail: admission@augie.edu
Internet: www.augie.edu

Founded 1860

Depts of art/anthropology, biology, business admin., chemistry, communication, computer science, economics, education, English, govt and int. affairs, health, history, int. studies, mathematics, modern foreign languages, music, nursing, philosophy and classics, physical education and recreation, physics, psychology, religion, sociology, theatre

Pres.: ROBERT C. OLIVER
Vice-Pres. for Academic Affairs and Dean: Dr MARK BRAUN
Vice-Pres. for Devt: JON HENKES
Vice-Pres. for Enrollment: NANCY DAVIDSON
Vice-Pres. for Finance and Admin.: THOMAS MEYER
Vice-Pres. for Marketing and Communications: ROBERT PRELOGER
Vice-Pres. for Student Services: JAMES BIES
Registrar: JONI KRUEGER
Dir for Mikkelsen Library: RONELLE THOMPSON

Library of 228,000 vols
Number of teachers: 138
Number of students: 1,790

BLACK HILLS STATE UNIVERSITY

1200 University St, Spearfish, SD 57799
Telephone: (605) 642-6011
Fax: (605) 642-6214
Internet: www.bhsu.edu

Founded 1883
Academic year: August to May

Pres.: Dr KAY SCHALLENKAMP
Provost and Vice-Pres. for Academic Affairs: DEAN MYERS
Vice-Pres. for Finance and Admin.: KATHY JOHNSON
Vice-Pres. for Institutional Advancement: STEVE MEEKER
Vice-Pres. for Student Life: LOIS FLAGSTAD
Dir of Admissions: BETH AZEVEDO
Library Dir: RAJEEV BUKRALIA

Library of 235,000 vols
Number of teachers: 183
Number of students: 4,004

Colleges of arts and sciences, business and technology, education.

DAKOTA STATE UNIVERSITY

Madison, SD 57042
Telephone: (605) 256-5111
Fax: (605) 256-5316
E-mail: dsuinfo@pluto.dsu.edu
Internet: www.dsu.edu

Founded 1881
Academic year: September to May

Pres.: Dr DOUGLAS KNOWLTON
Vice-Pres. for Academic Affairs: Dr CECELIA M. WITTMAYER
Vice-Pres. for Business and Admin. Services: STACY KRUSEMARK
Vice-Pres. for Student Affairs: STEVEN W. SHIRLEY
Registrar: SANDRA A. ANDERSON
Dir of Admissions: AMY CRISSINGER
Librarian: ETHELLE BEAN

Library of 133,371 vols
Number of teachers: 110
Number of students: 2,570

DEANS

College of Arts and Sciences: Dr KARI FORBES-BOYTE
College of Business and Information Systems: Dr TOM HALVERSON
College of Education: Dr JUDY DITTMAN

DAKOTA WESLEYAN UNIVERSITY

1200 West University Ave, Mitchell, SD 57301
Telephone: (605) 995-2600
Fax: (605) 995-2699
Internet: www.dwu.edu

Founded 1885

Pres.: Dr ROBERT G. DUFFETT
Vice-Pres. for Academic Affairs: Dr DONALD WATT
Vice-Pres. for Campus Life: GWENDA L. KOCH
Vice-Pres. for Instn Advancement: GREGORY CHRISTY
Vice-Pres. for Enrollment Management: AMY C. NOVAK
Vice-Pres. for Univ. Relations: LORI ESSIG
Registrar: SARA JORGENSEN
Dir of Learning Resources: KEVIN KENKEL

Library of 66,000 vols
Number of teachers: 49
Number of students: 788

Depts of art, athletic training, biology, business admin., communications/theatre, computers and multimedia, criminal justice, education, English/foreign languages, history/political science, human services, Kelley Center for Entrepreneurship, McGovern Center, mathematics, music, nursing, physical education, psychology, religion/philosophy, sports management

PROFESSORS

ALMJELD, P., Music
CATALANO, M., Mathematics
DITTA, J., English
FARNEY, M. N., Mathematics
MCGREEVY, M. J., Criminal Justice
MILLER, M. H., Religion and Philosophy
MITCHELL, D. B., Business Admin. and Economics
MULLICAN, T. R., Biology
NIELSON, G. E., Sociology
TATINA, R. E., Biology

MOUNT MARTY COLLEGE

1105 West Eighth St, Yankton, SD 57078
Telephone: (605) 668-1545
Fax: (605) 668-1508
E-mail: mmcadmit@mtmc.edu
Internet: www.mtmc.edu

Founded 1936
Private control (Benedictine)

Pres.: Dr JAMES T. BARRY
Vice-Pres. and Dean for Academic Affairs: Dr JAMES T. BARRY
Registrar: JONNA SUPURGECI
Librarian: SANDY BROWN

Library of 76,000 vols
Number of teachers: 65
Number of students: 1,100

Business and social sciences, humanities, natural sciences, nursing, teacher education.

NORTHERN STATE UNIVERSITY

Aberdeen, SD 57401
Telephone: (605) 626-3011
Fax: (605) 626-3022
E-mail: info@northern.edu
Internet: www.northern.edu

Founded 1901

Pres.: PATRICK SCHLOSS
Provost and Vice-Pres. for Academic Affairs: CLYDE ARNOLD
Vice-Pres. for Finance and Admin.: DON ERLENBUSCH
Registrar: STEPHANIE BITTERMAN
Dir of Libraries: J. PHILIP MULVANEY

Library of 250,000 vols
Number of teachers: 150
Number of students: 2,200

DEANS

College of Arts and Sciences: Dr DAVID GRETTLER
School of Business: Dr DAVID CHOWN
School of Education: Dr TOM HAWLEY
School of Fine Arts: Dr ALAN D. LAFAVE

OGLALA LAKOTA COLLEGE

Piya Wiconi, POB 490, Kyle, SD 57752
Telephone: (605) 455-6000
Fax: (605) 455-2787
Internet: www.olc.edu

Founded 1971
Private control
Academic year: August to May

Pres.: THOMAS SHORT BULL
Vice-Pres. for Business: ARLENE QUIST
Vice-Pres. for Instruction: Dr GERALD GIRAUD
Registrar: LESLIE MESTETH
Library Dir: MICHELE MAY

Library of 20,000 vols
Number of teachers: 15
Number of students: 900 (full-time)

PRESENTATION COLLEGE

1500 North Main St, Aberdeen, SD 57401
Telephone: (605) 229-84244
Fax: (605) 229-8537
E-mail: admit@presentation.edu
Internet: www.presentation.edu

Campuses at Aberdeen and Eagle Butte (SD), and Fairmont (MN)

Founded 1922 as Notre Dame Junior College; present name 1965
Private control
Academic year: August to May

Pres.: Sr LORRAINE HALE
Registrar: MAUREEN SCHUCHARDT
Library Dir: LEA BRIGGS

Number of teachers: 47
Number of students: 642

Degrees in biology, business, nursing, radiologic technology, recreation, social work.

SINTE GLESKA UNIVERSITY

POB 105, Mission, SD 57555
Telephone: (605) 856-8100
E-mail: admin@sinte.edu
Internet: www.sintegleska.edu

Founded 1970 as Sinte Gleska College; present name 1992
Private control
Academic year: August to May

Pres.: LIONEL R. BORDEAUX
Vice-Pres. for Admin. and Academic Affairs: LELAND BORDEAUX
Vice-Pres. for Education: MIKE BENGE
Vice-Pres. for Institutional Relations and Devt: GEORGIA HACKETT
Registrar: JACK HERMAN
Library Dir: RACHEL LINDVALL

Number of teachers: 36
Number of students: 1,080 (960 undergraduate, 120 postgraduate)

Depts of art and sciences, business admin. and management, education, human services.

SIOUX FALLS SEMINARY

2100 S Summit Ave, Sioux Falls, SD 57105
Telephone: (605) 336-6588
Fax: (605) 335-9090
E-mail: info@sfseminary.edu
Internet: www.sfseminary.edu
Private control
Academic year: September to May

Fmrly N American Baptist Seminary

Pres.: Dr G. MICHAEL HAGAN
Academic Vice-Pres. and Dean: Dr RONALD D. SISK
Registrar: BRENDA MEDALEN

Library of 72,500 vols, 300 periodicals
Number of teachers: 13
Number of students: 250

SOUTH DAKOTA SCHOOL OF MINES AND TECHNOLOGY

501 East St Joseph St, Rapid City, SD 57701
Telephone: (605) 394-2511
Fax: (605) 394-3388
E-mail: info@sdsmt.edu
Internet: www.sdsmt.edu

Founded 1885
Academic year: September to May

Pres.: CHARLES P. RUCH
Provost and Vice-Pres. for Academic Affairs: KAREN L. WHITEHEAD
Vice-Pres. for Business and Admin.: TIMOTHY G. HENDERSON
Vice-Pres. for Student Affairs and Dean of Students: PATRICIA G. MAHON
Dir of Library: PATRICIA M. ANDERSEN

Library of 220,224 vols
Number of teachers: 110 (full-time)
Number of students: 2,275

Depts in college of engineering: chemical and biological engineering, civil and environmental engineering, electrical and computer engineering, geology and geological engineering, industrial engineering, materials and metallurgical engineering, mechanical engineering, mining engineering; depts in college of science and letters: atmospheric sciences, chemistry, humanities, mathematics and computer science, military science, physical education, physics, social sciences.

SOUTH DAKOTA STATE UNIVERSITY

Box 2201, Brookings, SD 57007
Telephone: (605) 688-4121
Fax: (605) 688-6891
E-mail: sdsu.admissions@sdstate.edu
Internet: www.sdstate.edu

Founded 1881 as Dakota Agricultural College; univ. status in 1964
Academic year: August to May

Pres.: Dr DAVID L. CHICOINE
Provost and Vice-Pres. for Academic Affairs: CAROL J. PETERSON
Exec. Vice-Pres. for Admin.: Dr MICHAEL REGER
Vice-Pres. for Information Technology: Dr MICHAEL F. ADELAINE
Vice-Pres. for Research: Dr KEVIN KEPHART
Vice-Pres. of Student Affairs: Dr MARYSZ RAMES
Dean of Libraries: DAVID GLEIM

Library of 617,767 vols
Number of teachers: 657 (515 full-time, 142 part-time)
Number of students: 10,954

DEANS

College of Agriculture and Biological Sciences: Dr GARY LEMME
College of Arts and Sciences: Dr JERRY D. JORGENSEN
College of Education and Counselling: Dr HOWARD SMITH
College of Engineering: Dr LEWIS F. BROWN
College of Family and Consumer Sciences: Dr LAURIE NICHOLS
College of General Studies: Dr KEITH CORBETT
College of Nursing: Dr ROBERTA K. OLSON
College of Pharmacy: Dr BRIAN KAATZ
Continuing and Extended Education: Dr GAIL DOBBS TIDEMANN
Graduate School: Dr KEVIN KEPHART

UNIVERSITY OF SIOUX FALLS

1101 West 22nd St, Sioux Falls, SD 57105
Telephone: (605) 331-6600
Fax: (605) 331-6615
E-mail: admissions@usiouxfalls.edu
Internet: www.usiouxfalls.edu

Founded 1883
Private (American Baptist)
Pre-professional liberal arts univ.

Pres.: MARK BENEDETTO
Vice-Pres. and Dean of Academic Affairs: BRETT BRADFIELD
Vice-Pres. for Business and Finance: AMY WARWICK
Vice-Pres. for Enrollment Management and Marketing: GREG A. FRITZ
Vice-Pres. for Instn Advancement: DENNIS HOFFMAN
Registrar: PHYLLIS THOMPSON
Dir of Library Services: JUDY CLAUSON KRULL

Library of 75,000 vols
Number of teachers: 65 (37 full-time; 28 part-time)
Number of students: 1,674

UNIVERSITY OF SOUTH DAKOTA

Vermillion, SD 57069-2390
Telephone: (605) 677-5011
Fax: (605) 677-5073
Internet: www.usd.edu

Founded 1862
Academic year: August to May

Pres.: JAMES W. ABBOTT (acting)
Provost and Vice-Pres. for Academic Affairs: MATTHEW MOEN (acting)
Vice-Pres. for Finance and Admin.: RICHARD D. VAN DEN HUL
Vice-Pres. for Information Technology: ROBERTA AMBUR
Vice-Pres. for Marketing: TEDDI JOYCE
Vice-Pres. for Research: LAURA JENSKI
Registrar: JENNIFER JOST (acting)
Dir of Libraries: DAVID HULKONEN

Library of 488,000 vols
Number of teachers: 463
Number of students: 7,317

DEANS

College of Arts and Sciences: MATTHEW MOEN
College of Fine Arts: DANIEL GUYETTE
School of Business: MICHAEL KELLER
School of Education: LINDA REETZ
School of Law: BARRY VICKREY
Graduate School: KAREN OLMSTED

TENNESSEE

AMERICAN BAPTIST COLLEGE

1800 Baptist World Centre Dr., Nashville, TN 37207-4952
Telephone: (615) 256-1463
Fax: (615) 226-7855
Internet: www.abcnash.edu

Pres.: Dr FORREST ELLIOTT HARRIS, Sr
Vice-Pres. of Campus Operations: JOHN K. WRIGHT
Academic Dean: DOREEN W. MCCALLA
Librarian: (vacant).

AQUINAS COLLEGE

4210 Harding Rd, Nashville, TN 37205
Telephone: (615) 297-7545
E-mail: president@aquinas-tn.edu
Internet: www.aquinas-tn.edu

Founded 1961
Academic year: August to May

Pres.: Sis. THOMAS AQUINAS
Head Librarian: J. MARK HALL.

AUSTIN PEAY STATE UNIVERSITY

601 College St, Clarksville, TN 37044
Telephone: (931) 221-7566
Fax: (931) 221-7297
E-mail: gov@apsu.edu
Internet: www.apsu.edu

Founded 1927
Academic year: August to May

Pres.: SHERRY L. HOPPE
Provost and Vice-Pres. for Academic and Student Services: Dr BRUCE SPECK
Vice-Pres. for Admin. and Finance: MITCH ROBINSON
Vice-Pres. for Legal Affairs: RICHARD E. JACKSON
Exec. Dir for Devt: ROY GREGORY
Registrar: TELAINA WRIGLEY
Dir of Library: JOE WEBER

Library of 328,523 vols
Number of teachers: 276
Number of students: 7,033

BELMONT UNIVERSITY

1900 Belmont Blvd, Nashville, TN 37212-3757
Telephone: (615) 383-7001
Fax: (615) 385-6446
Internet: www.belmont.edu

Founded 1951

Pres.: BOB FISHER
Provost: MARCIA MCDONALD
Registrar: STEVEN REED
Library Dir: Dr ERNEST WILLIAM HEARD

Library of 127,688 vols
Number of teachers: 280 (141 full-time; 139 part-time)
Number of students: 4,500

Publications: *Belmont Circle* (4 a year), *The Tower* (1 a year), *Vision* (6 a year)

DEANS

Academic: JERRY WARREN
Admissions: CLAUDE PRESSNELL
Students: SUZANNE MATHENY

BETHEL COLLEGE

325 Cherry Ave, McKenzie, TN 38201
Telephone: (731) 352-4000
Internet: www.bethel-college.edu

Founded 1842

Pres.: ROBERT PROSSER
Academic Dean: MARIBETH MCGUIRE
Registrar: SHIRLEY MARTIN
Dir of Library: HAROLD KELLY

Library of 53,000 vols
Number of teachers: 36
Number of students: 843

Publications: *Bethel Beacon* (52 a year), *Bethel Captions* (4 a year), *Log Cabin* (1 a year).

CARSON-NEWMAN COLLEGE

1646 Russell Ave, Jefferson City, TN 37760
Telephone: (865) 471-2000
Fax: (865) 471-3502
Internet: www.cn.edu

Founded 1851
Academic year: August to May

Pres.: JOE BILL SLOAN
Vice-Pres. for Finance: ROBERT DRINNEN

Library of 200,000 vols
Number of teachers: 125
Number of students: 2,200

Publications: *Baptist History and Heritage*, *CN Studies*, *Mossy Creek Reader*, *NUA—Studies in Contemporary Irish Writing*.

CHRISTIAN BROTHERS UNIVERSITY

650 E Parkway, S, Memphis, TN 38104
Telephone: (901) 321-3000
Internet: www.cbu.edu

Founded 1871; attached to Southern Asscn of Colleges and Schools (COC-SACS); Accreditation Board for Engineering and Technology (ABET); Nat. Ccl for Accreditation of Teacher Education (NCATE)
Private control
Language of instruction: English

Pres.: Dr JOHN SMARRELLI (acting)
Vice-Pres. for Academic Affairs: Dr FRANK BUSCHER (acting)
Vice-Pres. for Advancement: ANDREW PRISLOVSKY
Vice-Pres. for Finance and Admin.: DAN WORTHAM
Vice-Pres. for Mission and Identity: Dr EVELYN MCDONALD
Registrar: MELODY NABORS
Librarian: KAY CUNNINGHAM

Library of 97,000 vols, 300 print periodicals, 60,000 electronic books, 1,800 DVDs, CDs and video cassettes
Number of teachers: 101 full-time
Number of students: 1,521 F.t.e. (1,731 total undergraduate and graduate student headcount)
Publication: *Catalog* (1 a year)

DEANS

School of Arts: Dr PAUL HAUGHT
School of Business: Dr SARAH PITTS
School of Business: Dr KRISTEN PRIEN
School of Engineering: Dr ERIC WELCH
School of Sciences: Dr JOHNNY HOLMES

CRICHTON COLLEGE

255 North Highland, Memphis, TN 38111
Telephone: (901) 320-9725
Fax: (901) 320-9700
E-mail: info@crichton.edu
Internet: www.crichton.edu

Founded 1960 as Mid-South Bible College, present name 1987

Pres.: (vacant): LARRY L. LLOYD
Vice-Pres. for Academic Affairs: ROBERT M. BRIAN
Vice-Pres. for Admissions: CAROLYN S. CATES

DEANS

Arts and Sciences: KEITH CALLIS
Business Faculty: BOB WHARTON
Education and Behavioural Studies: (vacant)
School of Bible and Theology: JAMES THORNE

CUMBERLAND UNIVERSITY

1 Cumberland Sq., Lebanon, TN 37087-3408
Telephone: (615) 444-2562
Fax: (615) 444-2569
Internet: www.cumberland.edu

Founded 1842
Academic year: August to May

Pres.: Dr HARVILL C. EATON
Vice-Pres. for Academic Affairs: WILBUR PETERSON

Number of teachers: 127
Number of students: 1,420

DIRECTORS OF SCHOOLS

Arts and Humanities: Dr STEPHEN FARNSLEY
Business and Economics: Dr WILLIAM B. FOX
Educational Studies: Dr K. CHARLES COLLIER
Mathematics, Natural and Social Sciences: Dr WILBUR L. PETERSON
Nursing: Dr LEANNE C. BUSBY

EAST TENNESSEE STATE UNIVERSITY

807 University Pkwy, Box 70267, Johnson City, TN 37614-1700
Telephone: (423) 439-1000
Fax: (423) 439-5710
E-mail: webmaster@mail.etsu.edu
Internet: www.etsu.edu

Founded 1911
Academic year: August to May

Pres.: Dr PAUL E. STANTON, Jr
Assoc. Vice-Pres. for Admissions, Retention and Enrollment Management: (vacant)
Assoc. Registrar: PAUL HAYES
Provost and Vice-Pres. for Academic Affairs: Dr BERT C. BACH
Vice-Pres. for Admin. and Student Affairs: Dr WAYNE ANDREWS
Vice-Pres. for Business and Finance: JAMES BOWMAN
Vice-Pres. for Health Affairs: Dr RONALD D. FRANKS
Vice-Pres. for Univ. Advancement: Dr RICHARD MANAHAN
Dean of Univ. Libraries: RITA SCHER

Library of 456,000 vols
Number of teachers: 650
Number of students: 12,000

Publications: *Aethlon: Journal of Sport Literature* (2 a year), *Science Educator* (2 a year), *Storytelling World* (2 a year), *The Tennessee Reading Educator* (2 a year)

DEANS

College of Applied Science and Technology: Dr JAMES HALES
College of Arts and Sciences: Dr DONALD R. JOHNSON
College of Business: Dr GLEN RIECKEN
College of Education: Dr MARTHA COLLINS
College of Nursing: Dr JOELLEN EDWARDS
College of Public and Allied Health: Dr WILSIE BISHOP
James H. Quillen College of Medicine: Dr RONALD D. FRANKS
School of Continuing Studies: Dr GLENN BETTIS
School of Graduate Studies: Dr WESLEY BROWN

FISK UNIVERSITY

17th Ave, N, Nashville, TN 37208-3051
Telephone: (615) 329-8500
Fax: (615) 329-8576
Internet: www.fisk.edu

Founded 1866 as Fisk School; univ. charter 1867
Academic year: August to May

Pres.: HAZEL R. O'LEARY
Provost: KOFI LOMOTEY
Librarian: JESSIE C. SMITH

Library of 210,000 vols
Number of teachers: 85 (63 full-time, 22 part-time)
Number of students: 845

Publications: *Fisk Herald* (2 a year), *Fisk News* (1 a year), *Fisk Reports* (4 a year), *Fisk University Bulletin* (every 2 years).

FREE WILL BAPTIST BIBLE COLLEGE

3606 West End College, Nashville, TN 37205
Telephone: (800) 763-9222
Fax: (615) 269-6028
Internet: www.fwbbc.edu

Pres.: J. MATHEW PINSON
Chancellor: Dr TOM MALONE
Registrar: Dr MILTON FIELDS
Librarian: CAROL REID (acting).

FREED-HARDEMAN UNIVERSITY

158 E Main St, Henderson, TN 38340
Telephone: (800) 348-3481
Internet: www.fhu.edu

Pres.: Dr JOE A. WILEY
Vice-Pres. for Academics and Enrollment Management: Dr SAMUEL T. JONES

DEANS

School of Arts and Humanities: Dr W. STEPHEN JOHNSON
School of Biblical Studies: Dr BILLY R. SMITH
School of Business: Dr KEITH SMITH
School of Education: Dr JOHN SWEENEY
School of Sciences and Mathematics: Dr LEANN SELF-DAVIS
Honours College: Dr JENNIFER JOHNSON

HARDING UNIVERSITY GRADUATE SCHOOL OF RELIGION

1000 Cherry Rd, Memphis, TN 38117-5499
Telephone: (901) 761-1356
Fax: (901) 761-1358
E-mail: mparker@hugsr.edu
Internet: www.hugsr.edu

Dean and Exec. Dir: Dr EVERTT W. HUFFARD.

JOHNSON BIBLE COLLEGE

7900 Johnson Dr., Knoxville, TN 37998
Telephone: (865) 573-4517
Fax: (865) 251-2337
E-mail: jbc@jbc.edu
Internet: www.jbc.edu
Academic year: August to May

Pres.: Dr GARY E. WEEDMAN
Vice-Pres. for Academics: RICHARD BEAM
Vice-Pres. for Business: BEN LUTZ, Sr
Vice-Pres. for Devt: PHILIP EUBANKS
Vice-Pres. for Student Services: DAVID LEGG

Number of teachers: 55
Number of students: 850

KING COLLEGE

1350 King College Rd, Bristol, TN 37620
Telephone: (423) 652-4861
Fax: (423) 968-4456
E-mail: admissions@king.edu
Internet: www.king.edu
Founded 1867
Academic year: August to May

Pres.: GREGORY D. JORDAN
Dean of Academic Affairs: MATTHEW S. PELTIER
Vice-Pres. for Business Operations: JAMES P. DONAHUE
Vice-Pres. for Enrollment Management: MELINDA S. CLARK
Vice-Pres. for Institutional Advancement: WILLIAM M. MCELROY
Vice-Pres. for Student Affairs: ROBERT A. LITTLETON
Librarian: MATTHEW S. PELTIER

Library of 98,000 vols
Number of teachers: 70
Number of students: 608
Publication: *Tornado*.

KNOXVILLE COLLEGE

901 Knoxville College Dr., Knoxville, TN 37921
Telephone: (615) 524-6500
E-mail: admissions@knoxvillecollege.edu
Internet: www.knoxvillecollege.edu

Founded 1875

Liberal arts college

Pres.: Dr ROBERT H. HARVEY
Dean: Dr EVELYN HALLMAN
Registrar: BARBARA BOOKER
Librarian: PATTY COOPER

Library of 78,445 vols
Number of teachers: 51
Number of students: 633

LAMBUTH UNIVERSITY

705 Lambuth Blvd, Jackson, TN 38301
Telephone: (731) 425-2500
Fax: (731) 988-7000
Internet: www.lambuth.edu

Founded 1843
Academic year: August to April

Pres.: BILL SEYMOUR
Vice-Pres. for Academic Affairs and Dean of the College: Dr LEE WEIMER
Vice-Pres. for Business Affairs: JOEY STONER
Vice-Pres. for Devt: RUSS ELLIS
Vice-Pres. for Enrollment Management: LISA WARMATH
Library Dir: JONATHAN ORR

Library of 155,554 vols
Number of teachers: 65 (38 full-time; 27 part-time)

Number of students: 459

DEANS

Arts and Communication: Prof. LENDON NOE
Business and Economics: Asst Prof. AMY HALTERS
Education and Health and Human Performance: Asst Prof. PAULA BROWNYARD
Humanities: Prof. Dr JOY AUSTIN
Mathematical and Natural Sciences: Assoc. Prof. Dr REBECCA COOK
Social Sciences: Assoc. Prof. Dr PAUL MEGO

LANE COLLEGE

545 Lane Ave, Jackson, TN 38301-4598
Telephone: (901) 426-7500
Fax: (901) 427-3987
Internet: www.lanecollege.edu

Founded 1882
Academic year: August to June

Pres.: WESLEY MCCLURE
Registrar: TERRY BLACKMON
Vice-Pres.: MELVIN R. HAMLETT
Vice-Pres. for Academic Affairs: Dr VICKI VERNON LOTT
Vice-Pres. for Admin.: NICOL EDWARDS
Exec. Vice-Pres.: SHARRON BURNETT
Librarian: SHIRLEY HUDSON

Library of 130,000 vols
Number of teachers: 42
Number of students: 627

LEE UNIVERSITY

1120 North Ocoee St, Cleveland, TN 37320-3450
Internet: www.leeuniversity.edu

Pres.: Dr CHARLES PAUL CONN
Vice-Pres. for Academics: CAROLYN DIRKSEN
Vice-Pres. for Business and Finance: DAVID PAINTER
Vice-Pres. of Enrollment Management: GARY RAY
Vice-Pres. for Institutional Advancement: DALE GOFF
Vice-Pres. for Student Life: WALT MAULDIN.

LE MOYNE-OWEN COLLEGE

807 Walker Ave, Memphis, TN 38126
Telephone: (901) 774-9090
E-mail: contact@nile.loc.edu
Internet: www.loc.edu

Founded 1862

Pres.: JOHNNIE B. WATSON
Dean of Academic Affairs: BARBARA FRANKLE
Librarian: ANNETTE BERHA

Library of 82,043 vols
Number of teachers: 41
Number of students: 1,212

LINCOLN MEMORIAL UNIVERSITY

6965 Cumberland Gap Parkway, Harrogate, TN 37752
Telephone: (423) 869-3611
Fax: (423) 869-6250
E-mail: presidentsoffice@lmunet.edu
Internet: www.lmunet.edu

Founded 1897
Academic year: August to May

Pres.: Dr C. WARREN NEEL
Vice-Pres. and Dean of the Faculty: Dr RAY E. STOWERS
Vice-Pres. for Academic Affairs: Dr SHERILYN EMBERTON
Vice-Pres. for Enrollment Management and Student Services: Dr JUDY BEAL
Vice-Pres. for Finance: RANDY ELDRIDGE
Vice-Pres. for Univ. Advancement: CYNTHIA WHITT
Dir of Admissions: CONRAD DANIELS
Head Librarian: RHONDA ARMSTRONG

Library of 199,892 vols, 334 current serial subscriptions, 101,745 microforms, 4,064 audio and video units
Number of teachers: 247
Number of students: 3,365

Publication: *The Lincoln Herald* (4 a year)

DEANS

School of Allied Health: RANDY EVANS
School of Business: Dr JACK MCCANN
Carter and Moyers School of Education: Dr FRED BEDELLE
Caylor School of Nursing: Dr MARY ANNE MODRCIN
Paul V. Hamilton School of Arts and Sciences: Dr AGGY VANDERPOOL

LIPSCOMB UNIVERSITY

3901 Granny White Pike, Nashville, TN 37204-3951
Telephone: (615) 269-1000
Internet: www.lipscomb.edu

Founded 1891

Four-year liberal arts college

Pres.: L. RANDOLPH LOWDRY
Exec. Vice-Pres.: WILLIAM TUCKER
Provost: Dr W. CRAIG BLEDSOE
Vice-Pres. for Univ. Relations: WALT LEAVER
Library Dir: CAROLYN T. WILSON

Library of 216,300 vols
Number of teachers: 194
Number of students: 2,555

DEANS

College of Arts and Humanities: Dr VALERY A. PRILL
College of Bible and Ministry: Dr TERRY BRILEY
College of Education and Professional Studies: JIM L. THOMAS
College of Natural and Applied Sciences: Dr LINDA ROBERSON

MARTIN METHODIST COLLEGE

433 West Madison St, Pulaski, TN 38478-2799
Telephone: (931) 363-9868
Fax: (931) 363-9811
E-mail: admit@martinmethodist.edu
Internet: www.martinmethodist.edu

Pres.: TED BROWN
Vice-Pres. for Enrollment Management: ROBBY SHELTON
Vice-Pres. for Finance and Admin.: RON DOWDY
Academic Dean: JAMES T. MURRELL
Registrar: SHERRY YOKLEY
Library Dir: RICHARD MADDEN.

MARYVILLE COLLEGE

Maryville, TN 37804
Telephone: (865) 981-8000
Fax: (865) 981-8136
Internet: www.maryvillecollege.edu

Founded 1819
Academic year: September to May

Pres.: Dr GERALD W. GIBSON
Vice-Pres. and Dean of College: Dr JEFFREY FAGER
Vice-Pres. and Dean of Students: VANDY KEMP
Vice-Pres. for Advancement and Community Relations: JASON MCNEAL
Vice-Pres. for Enrollment: BILL SILWA
Vice-Pres. and Treas.: DANA SMITH
Library Dir: ANGELA QUICK

Library of 128,022 vols
Number of teachers: 112 (72 full-time, 40 part-time)
Number of students: 1,080

Publications: *Impressions* (2 a year), *Laurels* (2 a year).

MEHARRY MEDICAL COLLEGE

1005 Dr D. B. Todd, Jr Boulevard, Nashville, TN 37208
Telephone: (615) 327-6000
Internet: www.mmc.edu

Pres.: WAYNE J. RILEY
Sr Vice-Pres. of Health Affairs: VALERIE MONTGOMERY RICE
Vice-Pres. of Finance: LAMEL BANDY-NEAL
Vice-Pres. for Student and Academic Affairs: PAMELA WILLIAMS

DEANS

School of Allied Health: KATHLEEN MCENERNEY (acting)
School of Dentistry: WILLIAM B. BUTLER (acting)
School of Graduate Studies and Research: MARIA FATIMA LIMA (acting)
School of Medicine: PON JOLA CONEY (acting)

MEMPHIS COLLEGE OF ART

Overton Park, 1930 Poplar Ave, Memphis, TN 38104-2764
Telephone: (901) 272-5100
Fax: (901) 272-5104
E-mail: info@mca.edu
Internet: www.mca.edu

Founded 1936
Academic year: August to May

Pres.: JEFFREY D. NASIN
Vice Pres. for Academic Affairs: KEN STRICKLAND
Vice-Pres. for College Advancement: KIM WILLIAMS
Vice-Pres. for Enrollment and Student Services: SUSAN MILLER

Library of 19,000 vols
Number of teachers: 34 (19 full-time, 15 part-time)
Number of students: 297

MEMPHIS THEOLOGICAL SEMINARY

168 East Parkway, S, Memphis, TN 38104
Telephone: (901) 458-8232
Fax: (901) 452-4051
E-mail: admissions@memphisseminary.edu
Internet: www.memphisseminary.edu

Pres.: Dr DANIEL J. EARHEART-BROWN
Vice-Pres. for Academic Affairs and Dean: Dr BARBARA HOLMES
Library Dir: STEVE EDSCORN (acting).

MID-AMERICA BAPTIST THEOLOGICAL SEMINARY

2095 Appling Rd, Cordova, TN 38016
Telephone: (901) 751-8453
Fax: (901) 751-8454
E-mail: info@mabts.edu
Internet: www.mabts.edu

Pres.: Dr MICHAEL R. SPRADLIN
Exec. Vice-Pres.: BRAD THOMPSON
Vice-Pres. for Institutional Advancement: Dr GARY REDDING.

MIDDLE TENNESSEE STATE UNIVERSITY

Murfreesboro, TN 37132
Telephone: (615) 898-2300
Fax: (615) 898-5906
Internet: www.mtsu.edu

Founded 1911
Academic year: August to May

Pres.: Dr SIDNEY A. MCPHEE

Sr Vice-Pres.: JOHN W. COTHERN
Provost and Exec. Vice-Pres.: Dr KAYLENE GEBERT
Vice-Pres. for Devt and Univ. Relations: WILLIAM J. BALES
Vice-Pres. for Finance and Admin.: DUANE STUCKY
Vice-Pres. for Student Affairs: Dr ROBERT K. GLENN
Librarian: DON CRAIG

Library of 564,000 vols
Number of teachers: 642
Number of students: 17,000

DEANS

College of Basic and Applied Sciences: EARL KEESE
College of Business: DWIGHT BULLARD (acting)
College of Education: ROBERT EAKER
College of Liberal Arts: JOHN MCDANIEL
College of Mass Communication: DERYL LEAMING
Graduate School: DONALD CURRY

MILLIGAN COLLEGE

Milligan College, TN 37682
Telephone: (615) 929-0116
E-mail: admissions@milligan.edu
Internet: www.milligan.edu

Founded 1866 (reorganized 1881)

Pres.: DONALD R. JEANES
Academic Dean: GARY E. WEEDMAN
Library Dir: STEVEN L. PRESTON

Library of 108,500 vols
Number of teachers: 46
Number of students: 811

O'MORE COLLEGE OF DESIGN

423 South Margin St, Franklin, TN 37064
Telephone: (615) 794-4254
Fax: (615) 790-1662
E-mail: admissions@omorecollege.edu
Internet: www.omorecollege.edu

Pres.: Dr MARK HILLIARD.

RHODES COLLEGE

2000 N Parkway, Memphis, TN 38112
Telephone: (901) 843-3000
Fax: (901) 843-3718
Internet: www.rhodes.edu

Liberal arts college

Founded 1848
Academic year: August to May

Pres.: WILLIAM E. TROUTT
Provost: CHARLOTTE G. BORST
Dean of Academic Affairs: JOHN S. OLSEN (acting)
Dean of Admissions: DAVID J. WOTTLE
Dean of Students: CAROL E. CASEY
Vice-Pres. for College Relations: RUSSELL T. WIGGINTON
Vice-Pres. for Finance and Admin.: JAMES ALLEN BOONE, Jr
Vice-Pres. for Information Services: ROBERT M. JOHNSON, Jr
Registrar: GLENN W. MUNSON
Dir of Library: LYNNE M. BLAIR

Library of 338,950 vols, incl. 287,950 print publs and 51,000 e-books
Number of teachers: 167 full-time
Number of students: 1,698

SOUTHERN ADVENTIST UNIVERSITY

POB 370, Collegedale, TN 37315-0370
Telephone: (423) 238-2111
Fax: (423) 238-3001
E-mail: postmaster@southern.edu
Internet: www.southern.edu

Founded 1892
Academic year: August to May

Pres.: GORDON BIETZ
Registrar: JONI ZIER
Librarian: GENEVIEVE STEYN

Library of 127,186 vols, 11,163 periodical subscriptions, 587,809 microforms
Number of teachers: 111 (108 full-time, 3 part-time)
Number of students: 2,200

SOUTHERN COLLEGE OF OPTOMETRY

1245 Madison Ave, Memphis, TN 38104-2222
Telephone: (901) 722-3200
Internet: www.sco.edu

Pres.: RICHARD W. PHILLIPS
Vice-Pres. for Academic Affairs: CHARLES L. HAINE
Vice-Pres. for Clinical Programmes: FRANK S. GIBSON
Vice-Pres. for Finance and Admin.: EUGENE J. BAGAGLIO
Vice-Pres. for Institutional Advancement: LISA R. WADE
Librarian: NANCY GATLIN.

TENNESSEE STATE UNIVERSITY

3500 John A. Merritt Blvd, Nashville, TN 37209-1561
Telephone: (615) 963-5000
Internet: www.tnstate.edu

Founded 1912

Pres.: MALVIN N. JOHNSON
Provost and Exec. Vice-Pres.: Dr ROBERT L. HAMPTON
Registrar: VICKIE HOLMES
Librarian: Dr YILDIZ BINKLEY

Library of 565,400 vols
Number of teachers: 518
Number of students: 8,625

TENNESSEE TECHNOLOGICAL UNIVERSITY

Cookeville, TN 38505
Telephone: (615) 372-3101
Fax: (615) 372-3898
Internet: www.tntech.edu

Founded 1915
Academic year: August to May

Pres.: Dr ROBERT R. BELL
Provost: Dr JACK ARMISTEAD
Vice-Pres. for Business and Fiscal Affairs: CLAIRE STINSON
Vice-Pres. for Student Affairs: MARC BURNETT
Vice-Pres. for Univ. Advancement: MARK HUTCHINS
Dir of Library Services: DEANNE NIPP-KIENTZ

Library of 981,761 vols
Number of teachers: 400
Number of students: 10,321

TENNESSEE TEMPLE UNIVERSITY

1815 Union Ave, Chattanooga, TN 37404-3587
Telephone: (423) 493-4378
Fax: (423) 493-4497
E-mail: ttuinfo@tntemple.edu
Internet: www.tntemple.edu

Pres.: Dr DANNY LOVETT
Chancellor: Dr LEE ROBERSON
Exec. Vice-Pres.: ROGER H. STILES
Sec. and Treas.: JIMMY WILSON.

TENNESSEE WESLEYAN COLLEGE

POB 40, Athens, TN 37371-0040
Telephone: (423) 745-7504
Internet: www.twcnet.edu

Founded 1857

Pres.: Dr STEPHEN CONDON
Vice-Pres. for Academics: Dr SUZANNE HINE
Vice-Pres. for Student Life and Enrollment Management: Dr SCOTT MASHBURN

Library of 75,000 vols
Number of teachers: 29
Number of students: 633

TREVECCA NAZARENE UNIVERSITY

333 Murfreesboro Rd, Nashville, TN 37210
Telephone: (615) 248-1200
Fax: (615) 248-1432
E-mail: admissions_und@trevecca.edu
Internet: www.trevecca.edu

Founded 1901 as Literary and Bible Training School for Christian Workers; became Trevecca College 1911 and Trevecca Nazarene College 1917; present name 1995
Private control

Pres.: DAN BOONE
Provost: STEPHEN M. PUSEY
Exec. Vice-Pres. for Financial Services and Admin.: MARK MYERS
Vice-Pres. for Church Relations: JIM MAHAN
Vice-Pres. for External Relations: PEGGY COONING
Dean of Enrollment Management: SAM GREEN
Dean of Student Devt: STEPHEN HARRIS
Dir of Library Services: RUTH KINNERSLEY

Library of 103,571 vols, 507 print periodicals, 3,632 audiovisual items, 295,265 microforms, electronic periodicals
Number of teachers: 77
Number of students: 1,911

DEANS

School of Arts and Sciences: Div. of Communication, Language and Literature: Dr J. DOUGLAS LEPTER
School of Arts and Sciences: Div. of Music: Dr SAM GREEN
School of Arts and Sciences: Div. of Natural and Applied Sciences: Dr G. MICHAEL MOREDOCK
School of Arts and Sciences: Div. of Social and Behavioural Sciences: Dr PETER WILSON
School of Business and Management: Dr JAMES HIATT
School of Education: Dr ESTHER SWINK
School of Religion: Dr TIM GREEN

TUSCULUM COLLEGE

60 Shiloh Rd, Greeneville, TN 37743
Telephone: (423) 636-7300
Fax: (423) 798-1622
E-mail: admissions@tusculum.edu
Internet: www.tusculum.edu

Founded 1794
Academic year: August to May

Pres.: Dr RUSSELL L. NICHOLS
Provost and Academic Vice-Pres.: Dr KIMBERLY K. ESTEP
Vice-Pres. and Chief Financial Officer: FRANK G. WILLIAMS
Vice-Pres. for Admin.: MARK A. STOKES
Vice-Pres. for Enrollment Management: GEORGE WOLF
Dir of Admissions: TONY S. ENGLAND

Library of 192,000 vols
Number of teachers: 130
Number of students: 2,000

UNION UNIVERSITY

1050 Union University Dr., Jackson, TN 38305
Telephone: (901) 668-1818
Fax: (901) 661-5187
E-mail: info@uu.edu
Internet: www.uu.edu
Founded 1823
Academic year: September to May
Pres.: Dr DAVID S. DOCKERY
Provost: STEVE BAKER
Vice-Pres. of Information Services and Academic Resources: Dr HAL POE
Dir of Student Enlistment: CARROLL GRIFFIN
Library of 167,629 vols
Number of teachers: 197
Number of students: 2,783

UNIVERSITY OF MEMPHIS

Memphis, TN 38152
Telephone: (901) 678-2000
Fax: (901) 678-3299
Internet: www.memphis.edu
Founded 1912
Pres.: Dr SHIRLEY RAINES
Provost: Dr RALPH FAUDREE
Vice-Pres. for Advancement: JULIE JOHNSON
Vice-Pres. for Business and Finance: CHARLES SMITH
Vice-Pres. for Information Technology: Dr DOUGLAS HURLEY
Vice-Pres. for Student Affairs: Dr ROSIE PHILLIPS BINGHAM
Dean of Libraries: Dr SYLVERNA V. FORD
Library of 1,051,000 vols
Number of teachers: 1,207 (full-time and part-time)
Number of students: 20,100
Publications: *Bulletin of the University of Memphis* (4 a year), *Law Review*, *Mid-South Business Journal*, *Memphis Economy*, *The Southern Journal of Philosophy* (4 a year), *The University of Memphis Magazine* (4 a year).

UNIVERSITY OF TENNESSEE SYSTEM

Knoxville, TN 37996
Telephone: (615) 974-1000
Internet: www.tennessee.edu/system
Chartered 1794 as Blount College; name changed by legislature 1840 to E Tennessee Univ., and in 1879 to The Univ. of Tennessee
Major campuses at Chattanooga, Knoxville, Martin and Memphis
State control
Academic year: September to August
Pres.: Dr JOHN D. PETERSEN
Gen. Counsel and Sec. of Board of Trustees: BEAUCHAMP E. BROGAN
Sr Vice-Pres. and Chief Financial Officer: Dr GARY W. ROGERS
Vice-Pres., Gen. Counsel and Sec.: CATHERINE S. MEZILL
Vice-Pres. for Academic Affairs: Dr ROBERT LEVY
Vice-Pres. for Agriculture: Dr JOSEPH A. DIPIETRO
Vice Pres. for Devt: HENRY NEMCIK
Vice-Pres for Public and Govt Relations: SAMMIE LYNN PUETT HANK DYE
Library: see Libraries
Number of teachers: 3,189
Number of students: 41,927
Publications: *Extension Series* (4 to 6 a year), *Horizons* (4 a year), *Tennessee Alumnus* (4 a year), *The University Record*.

MAJOR CAMPUSES

University of Tennessee at Chattanooga

Chattanooga, TN 37401
Telephone: (615) 755-4141
Internet: www.utc.edu
Chancellor: FREDERICK W. OBEAR
Asst to the Chancellor: SUSAN CARDWELL
Provost: GRAYSON H. WALKER
Assoc. Provost for Academic Admin.: WILLIAM AIKEN
Assoc. Provost for Academic Services: JANE W. HARBAUGH
Vice-Chancellor for Business and Finance: RALPH W. MOSER (acting)
Vice-Chancellor for Devt: VINCENT M. PELLEGRINO
Vice-Chancellor for Student Affairs: CHARLES RENNEISEN
Asst Vice-Chancellor for Admin.: RICHARD L. BROWN (acting)

DEANS

College of Arts and Sciences: CHARLES T. SUMMERLIN
College of Health and Human Services: RANDY WALKER (acting)
Continuing Education: MARILYN WILLIS
School of Business Administration: LINDA P. FLETCHER
School of Education: MARY N. TANNER (acting)
School of Engineering: RONALD B. COX
Library: SHEILA DELACROIX

University of Tennessee Health Science Center

Memphis, TN 38163
Telephone: (902) 448-5000
Internet: www.uthsc.edu
Chancellor: STEVE J. SCHWAB
Exec. Chancellor: KENNARD D. BROWN
Vice-Chancellor for Admin.: RAYMOND H. COLSON
Vice-Chancellor for Finance and Operations: ANTHONY A. FERRARA
Vice-Chancellor for Devt and Alumini Affairs: Dr KEITH CARVER
Vice-Chancellor for Research: Dr LEONARD R. JOHNSON
Vice-Chancellor for Student Affairs: Dr CHERYL R. SCHEID
Vice-Chancellor for Univ. Relations: JESSE F. MCCLURE

DEANS

College of Allied Health Sciences: BARBARA H. CONNOLLY
College of Dentistry: TIMOTHY L. HOTTEL
College of Graduate Health Sciences: CHERYL R. SCHEID
College of Medicine: STEVE J. SCHWAB
College of Nursing: DONNA HATHAWAY
College of Pharmacy: DICK R. GOURLEY

University of Tennessee at Knoxville

Knoxville, TN 37996
Telephone: (615) 974-1000
Internet: www.utk.edu
Chancellor: Dr WILLIAM T. SNYDER
Exec. Asst to the Chancellor: MARIANNE R. WOODSIDE
Vice-Chancellor for Business and Finance: RAYMOND L. HAMILTON
Vice-Chancellor for Computing and Telecommunications (vacant)
Vice-Chancellor for Devt and Alumni Affairs: JACK E. WILLIAMS
Vice-Chancellor for Student Affairs: PHILIP A. SCHEURER

DEANS

College of Agriculture: GERHARDT SCHNEIDER (acting)
College of Business Administration: C. WARREN NEEL
College of Communications: DWIGHT L. TEETER, Jr
College of Education: RICHARD WISNIEWSKI
College of Engineering: JERRY E. STONEKING
College of Human Ecology: JACQUELYN O. DEJONGE
College of Law: RICHARD S. WIRTZ
College of Liberal Arts: LORMAN A. RATNER
College of Veterinary Medicine: MICHAEL H. SHIRES
School of Architecture: MARLEEN K. DAVIS
School of Nursing: (vacant)
Division of Continuing Education: LAVERNE B. LINDSEY
Graduate School of Library and Information Science: (vacant)
Graduate School of Social Work: EUNICE O. SHATZ
Graduate Studies: CLARENCE W. MINKEL
Institute of Agriculture: DON O. RICHARDSON (Agricultural Experiment Stations: BILLY G. HICKS (Admin.)
Space Institute: JOEL W. MUELHAUSER (Admin.: KAPULURU C. REDDY (Academic Affairs)
Admissions and Records: SUSIE COLEMAN ARCHER
Library: PAULA T. KAUFMAN
Research: LEO RIEDINGER
Students: W. TIMOTHY ROGERS

PROFESSORS

College of Agriculture:

ALLEN, F. L., Plant and Soil Science
ASHBURN, E. L., Plant and Soil Science
BERNARD, E. C., Entomology and Plant Pathology
BLEDSOE, B. L., Agricultural Engineering
BOST, S. C., Entomology and Plant Pathology
BREKKE, C. J., Food Science and Technology
BROOKER, J. R., Agricultural Economics
BUCKNER, E. R., Forestry
BURGESS, E. E., Entomology and Plant Pathology
CALLAHAN, L. M., Ornamental Horticulture and Landscape Design
CARTER, C. E., Jr, Agricultural Extension Education
CHAMBERS, A. Y., Entomology and Plant Pathology
CLELAND, C. L., Agricultural Economics
COFFEY, D. L., Plant and Soil Science
COLLINS, J. L., Food Technology and Science
CONATSER, G. E., Animal Science
CONGER, B. V., Plant and Soil Science
COOK, O. F., Four-H Club
CRATER, G. D., Ornamental Horticulture and Landscape Design
DALY, R. T., Home Economics
DEARDEN, B. L., Forestry
DIMMICK, R. W., Forestry
DRAUGHON, F. A., Food Science and Technology
EASTWOOD, D. B., Agricultural Economics
ENGLISH, B. C., Agricultural Economics
FARMER, C. M., Agricultural Economics
FLINCHUM, W. T., Plant and Soil Science
FOSS, J. E., Plant and Soil Science
FRIBOURG, H. A., Plant and Soil Science
GARLAND, C. D., Agricultural Economics
GERHARDT, R. R., Entomology and Plant Pathology
GILL, W. W., Animal Science
GOAN, H. C., Animal Science
GODKIN, J. D., Animal Science
GRAHAM, E. T., Ornamental Horticulture and Landscape Design

GRAVES, C. R., Plant and Soil Science
GRESSHOFF, P. M., Ornamental Horticulture, Center of Excellence
HADDEN, C. H., Entomology and Plant Pathology
HALL, R. F., Extension Veterinary Medicine
HAYES, R. M., Plant and Soil Science
HENRY, Z. A., Agricultural Engineering
HILL, T. K., Forestry
HOPPER, G. M., Forestry
HOWARD, D. D., Plant and Soil Science
HUNTER, D. L., Agricultural Economics
JENKINS, R. P., Agricultural Economics
KIRKPATRICK, F. D., Animal Science
LAMBDIN, P. L., Entomology and Plant Pathology
LANE, C. D., Jr, Animal Science
LESSLY, R. R., Agricultural Extension Education
LEUTHOLD, F. O., Agricultural Economics
LITTLE, R. L., Forestry
LOCKWOOD, D. W., Plant and Soil Science
McDANIEL, G. L., Ornamental Horticulture and Landscape Design
McLEMORE, D. L., Agricultural Economics
MAYS, G. C., Communication
MEADOWS, D. G., Animal Science (Beef)
MELTON, C. C., Food Technology
MELTON, S. L., Food Technology and Science
MILLER, J. K., Animal Science
MILLER, R. D., Plant and Soil Science
MONTGOMERY, M. J., Animal Science
MORRIS, W. C., Food Science and Technology
MOTE, C. R., Agricultural Engineering
MULLINS, C. A., Plant and Soil Science
MUNDY, S. D., Agricultural Economics
NEEL, J. B., Animal Science
NEWMAN, M. A., Entomology and Plant Pathology
OLIVER, S. P., Animal Science
OSTERMEIER, D. M., Forestry
PARK, W. M., Agricultural Economics
PATRICK, C. R., Entomology and Plant Pathology
PELTON, M. R., Forestry
PENFIELD, M. P., Food Technology and Science
PLESS, C. D., Entomology and Plant Pathology
POWELL, B. T., Four-H
RAWLS, E. L., Agricultural Economics
RAY, D. E., Agricultural Economics
REINHARDT, C. A., Communication
RENNIE, J. C., Forestry
REYNOLDS, J. H., Plant and Soil Science
ROBBINS, K. R., Animal Science
ROBERTS, R. K., Agricultural Economics
RUTLEDGE, A. D., Plant and Soil
SAMS, C. E., Plant and Soil Science
SAMS, D. W., Plant and Soil Science
SANDERS, W. L., Statistics
SAXTON, A. M., Statistics
SIMMS, R. H., Animal Science
SMITH, G. F., Agricultural Economics
SOUTHARDS, C. J., Entomology and Plant Pathology
STRANGE, R. J., Forestry
TODD, J. D., Agricultural Extension and Education
TYLER, D. D., Plant and Soil Science
WEST, D. R., Plant and Soil Science
WESTBROOK, E. M., Home Economics and Family Economy
WILHELM, L. R., Agricultural Engineering
WILLIAMS, D. B., Ornamental Horticulture and Landscape Design
WILLIAMSON, H., Agricultural Economics
WILLS, J. B., Agricultural Engineering
WILSON, J. L., Forestry

College of Business Administration:

BARNABY, D. J., Marketing and Transportation
BLACK, H. A., Finance
BOEHM, T. P., Finance
BOHM, R. A., Economics
BOWLBY, R. L., Economics
CADOTTE, E. R., Marketing and Transportation
CARROLL, S. L., Economics
CHANG, H., Economics
CLARK, D. P., Economics
COLE, W. E., Economics
DAVIDSON, P., Economics
DAVIS, F. W., Jr, Marketing and Transportation
DEWHIRST, H. D., Management
DICER, G. N., Marketing and Transportation
FISHER, B. D., Accounting
FOX, W. F., Economics
GARRISON, C. B., Economics
HERRING, H. C., Accounting
HERZOG, H. W., Economics
JAMES, L. R., Management
KIGER, J. E., Accounting
LANGLEY, C. J., Jr, Marketing and Transportation
LEE, F.-Y., Economics
MAYHEW, A., Economics
MAYO, J. W., Economics
MENTZER, J. T., Marketing Logistics and Transportation
MUNDY, R. A., Marketing and Transportation
PARR, W. C., Statistics
PATTON, E. P., Marketing and Transportation
PHILIPPATOS, G. C., Finance
PHILPOT, J. W., Statistics
REEVE, J. M., Accounting
ROTH, H. P., Accounting
RUSH, M. C., Management
SANDERS, R. D., Statistics
SCHLOTTMANN, A., Economics
SHRIEVES, R. E., Finance
STAHL, M. J., Business Admin.
STANGA, K. G., Accounting
SYLWESTER, D. L., Statistics
WACHOWICZ, J. M., Finance
WANSLEY, J. W., Finance
WILLIAMS, J. R., Accounting
WOODRUFF, R. B., Marketing Logistics and Transportation

College of Communications:

ASHDOWN, P. G., Journalism
BOWLES, D. A., Journalism
CROOK, J. A., Journalism
EVERETT, G. A., Journalism
HOWARD, H. H., Broadcasting
LITTMANN, M. E., Journalism
MILLER, M. M., Journalism
MOORE, B. A., Broadcasting
SINGLETARY, M. W., Journalism
SMYSER, R. D., Journalism
STANKEY, M. J., Advertising
SWAN, N. R., Jr, Broadcasting
TAYLOR, R. E., Advertising

College of Education:

ALEXANDER, J. E., Holistic Teaching and Learning
ALLISON, C. B., Cultural Studies in Education
BENNER, S. M., Inclusive Early Childhood Education
BLANK, K. J., Inclusive Early Childhood Education
BOGUE, E. G., Leadership Studies
BUTEFISH, W. L., Education in Science and Mathematics
CAMERON, W., Psychoeducational Studies
COLEMAN, L. J., Inclusive Early Childhood Education
DAVIS, A. R., Holistic Teaching and Learning
DAVIS, K. L., Counselor Education and Counseling Psychology
DESSART, D. J., Curriculum and Instruction
DICKINSON, D. J., Education in Science and Mathematics
DOAK, E. D., Education in Science and Mathematics
FRENCH, R. L., Education in Science and Mathematics
GEORGE, T. W., Educational Administration
HARGIS, C. H., Holistic Teaching and Learning
HARRIS, G., Leadership Studies
HECTOR, M. A., Counselor Education and Counseling Psychology
HIPPLE, T. W., Holistic Teaching and Learning
HOWLEY, E. T., Exercise Science
HUCK, S. W., Counselor Education and Counseling Psychology
HUFF, P. E., Holistic Teaching and Learning
HULL, H. N., Language Communication and Humanities Education
JOST, K. J., Holistic Teaching and Learning
KASWORM, C. E., Bureau of Educational Research and Services
KNIGHT, L. N., Holistic Teaching and Learning
KOZAR, A. J., Exercise Science
KRONICK, R. F., Holistic Teaching and Learning
LIEMOHN, W. P., Exercise Science
McCALLUM, R. S., Psychoeducational Studies
McINTYRE, L. D., Education in Science and Mathematics
MALIK, A., Cultural Studies in Education
MEAD, B. J., Cultural Studies in Education
MERTZ, N. T., Leadership Studies
MILLER, J. H., Rehabilitation and Deafness Programmes
MORGAN, W. J., Cultural Studies in Education
MYER, M. E., Jr, Education in Science and Mathematics
PAUL, M. J., Cultural Studies in Education
PETERS, J. M., Psychoeducational Studies
PETERSON, M. P., Counselor Education and Counseling Psychology
POPPEN, W. A., Counselor Education and Counseling Psychology
RAY, J. R., Education in Science and Mathematics
ROCKETT, I. R. H., Exercise Science
ROESKE, C. E., Education in Science and Mathematics
ROWELL, C. G., Educational Administration
SCHINDLER, W. J., Holistic Teaching and Learning
THOMPSON, C. L., Counselor Education and Counseling Psychology
TURNER, T. N., Holistic Teaching and Learning
UBBEN, G. C., Leadership Studies
WELCH, O. M., Rehabilitation and Deafness Programmes
WILEY, P. D., Language Communication and Humanities Education
WILLIAMS, R. L., Psychoeducational Studies
WOODRICK, W. E., Rehabilitation and Deafness Programmes
WRISBERG, C. A., Cultural Studies in Education

College of Engineering:

ALEXEFF, I., Electrical Engineering
ARIMILLI, R. V., Mechanical and Aerospace Engineering
BAILEY, J. M., Electrical Engineering
BAKER, A. J., Engineering Science and Mechanics
BENNETT, R. M., Civil and Environmental Engineering
BIENKOWSKI, P. R., Chemical Engineering
BIRDWELL, J. D., Electrical Engineering
BISHOP, A. O., Jr, Electrical Engineering
BLALOCK, T. V., Electrical Engineering

BODENHEIMER, R. E., Electrical Engineering
BOGUE, D. C., Chemical Engineering
BONTADELLI, J. A., Industrial Engineering
BOSE, B. K., Electrical Engineering
BOULDIN, D. W., Electrical Engineering
BROOKS, C. R., Jr, Materials Science and Engineering
BUCHANAN, R. A., Materials Science and Engineering
BURDETTE, E. G., Civil and Environmental Engineering
CARLEY, T. G., Engineering Science and Mechanics
CHATTERJEE, A., Civil and Environmental Engineering
CLARK, E. S., Materials Science and Engineering
CLAYCOMBE, W. W., Industrial Engineering
COUNCE, R. M., Chemical Engineering
CUMMINGS, P. T., Chemical Engineering
DAVIS, W. T., Civil and Environmental Engineering
DEPORTER, E. L., Industrial Engineering
DODDS, H. L., Nuclear Engineering
DRUMM, E. C., Civil and Environmental Engineering
EDMONDSON, A. J., Mechanical and Aerospace Engineering
FELLERS, J. F., Materials Science and Engineering
FORRESTER, J. H., Engineering Science and Mechanics
FRAZIER, G. C., Chemical Engineering
GHOSH, M. M., Civil and Environmental Engineering
GONZALEZ, R. C., Electrical Engineering
GOODPASTURE, D. W., Civil and Environmental Engineering
GREEN, W. L., Electrical Engineering
HANSEN, M. G., Chemical Engineering
HODGSON, J. W., Mechanical and Aerospace Engineering
HOFFMAN, G. W., Electrical Engineering
HUNG, J. C., Electrical Engineering
JENDRUCKO, R. J., Engineering Science and Mechanics
JOHNSON, W. S., Mechanical and Aerospace Engineering
KENNEDY, E. J., Electrical Engineering
KERLIN, T. W., Jr, Nuclear Engineering
KIM, K. H., Engineering Science and Mechanics
KRANE, R. J., Mechanical and Aerospace Engineering
KRIEG, R. D., Engineering Science and Mechanics
LANDES, J. D., Engineering Science and Mechanics
LAWLER, J. S., Electrical Engineering
LIAW, P. K., Materials Science and Engineering
LUNDIN, C. D., Materials Science and Engineering
MILLER, L. F., Nuclear Engineering
MILLER, W. A., Civil and Environmental Engineering
MILLIGAN, M. W., Mechanical and Aerospace Engineering
MOORE, C. F., Chemical Engineering
NEFF, H. P., Jr, Electrical Engineering
OLIVER, B. F., Materials Science and Engineering
PACE, M. O., Electrical Engineering
PARANG, M., Mechanical and Aerospace Engineering
PARSONS, J. R., Mechanical and Aerospace Engineering
PEDRAZA, A. J., Materials Science and Engineering
PERONA, J. J., Chemical Engineering
PHILLIPS, P. J., Materials Science and Engineering
PITTS, D. R., Engineering—Admin.
PRADOS, J. W., Chemical Engineering
REED, G. D., Civil and Environmental Engineering
ROBERTS, M. J., Electrical Engineering
ROBINSON, R. B., Civil and Environmental Engineering
ROTH, J. R., Electrical Engineering
SCHMITT, H. W., Industrial Engineering
SCOTT, W. E., Engineering Science and Mechanics
SHANNON, T. E., Nuclear Engineering
SMITH, G. V., Mechanical and Aerospace Engineering
SNIDER, J. N., Industrial Engineering
SOLIMAN, O., Engineering Science and Mechanics
SPECKHART, F. H., Mechanical and Aerospace Engineering
SPRUIELL, J. E., Materials Science and Engineering
SYMONDS, F. W., Electrical Engineering
TOMPKINS, F. D., Engineering Academic
TRIVEDI, M. M., Electrical Engineering
TSCHANTZ, B. A., Civil and Environmental Engineering
UHRIG, R. E., Nuclear Engineering
UPADHYAYA, B. R., Nuclear Engineering
WASSERMAN, J. F., Engineering Science and Mechanics
WEGMANN, F. J., Civil and Environmental Engineering
WEITSMAN, Y. J., Center of Excellence
WILKERSON, H. J., Mechanical and Aerospace Engineering
WILSON, C. C., Mechanical and Aerospace Engineering

College of Human Ecology:

BLANTON, P. W., Child and Family Studies
CAMPBELL, C. P., Human Resources Devt
CARRUTH, B. R., Nutrition
CHEEK, G. D., Human Resources Devt
COAXLEY, C. B., Human Resources Devt
CRAIG, D. G., Human Resources Devt
CUNNINGHAM, J. L., Child and Family Studies
DELONG, A. J., Textiles, Retailing and Interior Design
DRAKE, M. F., Textiles, Retailing and Interior Design
DUCKETT, K. E., Textiles, Retailing and Interior Design
FOX, G. L., Child and Family Studies
GORSKI, J. D., Health, Leisure and Safety Sciences
HAMILTON, C. B., Health, Leisure and Safety Sciences
HANSON, R. R., Human Resources Devt
HASKELL, R. W., Human Resources Devt
HAYES, G. A., Health, Leisure and Safety Sciences
KIRK, R. H., Health, Leisure and Safety Sciences
MORAN, J. D., Admin.
NORDQUIST, V. M., Child and Family Studies
SACHAN, D. S., Nutrition
SKINNER, J. D., Nutrition
STEELE, C., Child and Family Studies
TWARDOSZ, S. L., Child and Family Studies
WADSWORTH, L. C., Textiles, Retailing and Interior Design
WALLACE, B. C., Health, Leisure and Safety Sciences
ZEMEL, M. B., Nutrition

College of Law:

BLAZE, D. A.
COHEN, N. P.
COOK, J. G.
DESSEM, R. L.
HARDIN, P.
HESS, A. M.
KING, J. H., Jr
LECLERQ, F. S.
LLOYD, R. M.
PHILLIPS, J. J.
RIVKIN, D. H.
SOBIESKI, J. L., Jr

College of Liberal Arts:

ADCOCK, J. L., Chemistry
AIKEN, C. S., Geography
ALEXANDRATOS, S. D., Chemistry
ALEXIADES, V., Mathematics
ALIKAKOS, N., Mathematics
ANDERSON, D. F., Mathematics
AQUILA, R. E., Philosophy
ASP, C. W., Audiology and Speech Pathology
BAGBY, R. M., Zoology
BAKER, D. C., Chemistry
BAKER, G. A., Mathematics
BALL, C. H., Music
BARRETTE, P., Romance and Asian Languages
BARTMESS, J. E., Chemistry
BECKER, J. M., Microbiology
BELL, T. L., Geography
BERGERON, P. H., History
BETZ, M., Sociology
BINGHAM, C. R., Physics
BITZAS, G. C., Music
BLACK, J. A., Sociology
BLAIN, S. J., Arts
BLASS, W. E., Physics
BRADY, P. S., Romance and Asian Languages
BRAKKE, P. M., Arts
BRATTON, E. W., English
BREINIG, M., Physics
BRENKERT, G. G., Philosophy
BROADHEAD, T., Geological Sciences
BROCK, J. P., Jr, Music
BUGG, W. M., Physics
BUHITE, R. D., History
BULL, W. E., Chemistry
BUNTING, D. L., II, Ecology
BURGDOERFER, J. E., Physics
BURGHARDT, G. M., Psychology
BURSTEIN, A. G., Psychology
CALHOUN, W. H., Psychology
CALLCOTT, T. A., Physics
CAPONETTI, J. D., Botany
CARNEY, P. J., Audiology and Speech Pathology
CARROLL, D. A., English
CARRUTH, J. H., Mathematics
CEBIK, L. B., Philosophy
CHAMBERS, J. Q., Chemistry
CHEN, T. T., Zoology
CHILDERS, R. W., Physics
CHMIELEWSKI, E. V., History
CHURCHICH, J. E., Biochemistry
CLARK, C. E., Mathematics
COBB, C. W., Romance and Asian Languages
COBB, J. C., History
COHEN, C. P., Psychology
COHN, H. O., Physics
COKER, J., Music
COMBS, F. M., Music
CONDO, G. T., Physics
CONWAY, J. B., Mathematics
COOK, K. D., Chemistry
COOKE, T. P., Theatre
COTHRAN, R. M., Jr, Theatre
COX, D. R., English
CUNNINGHAM, R. B., Political Science
CUSTER, M., Theatre
CUTLER, E. W., History
DAEHNERT, R. H., Arts
DAVERMAN, R. J., Mathematics
DOBBS, D. E., Mathematics
DONGARRA, J., Computer Science
DRAKE, R. Y., Jr, English
DUNGAN, D. L., Religious Studies
DYDAK, J., Mathematics
ECHTERNACHT, A. C., Zoology
EDWARDS, R. B., Philosophy
EGUILUZ, A. G., Physics
ELSTON, S. B., Physics
ENSOR, A. R., English
ETNIER, D. A., Zoology

FALSETTI, J. S., Arts
FARRIS, W. W., History
FAULKNER, C. H., Anthropology
FIELD, R. C., Theatre
FINGER, J. R., History
FINNERAN, R. J., English
FITZGERALD, M. R., Political Science
FORESTA, R., Geography
FOX, K., Physics
FRANDSEN, H., Mathematics
GANT, M. M., Political Science
GEORGHIOU, S., Physics
GESELL, G. C., Classics
GOLDENSTEIN, M. B., Arts
GORMAN, R., Political Science
GOSLEE, N. M., English
GRABER, G. C., Philosophy
GRIMM, F. A., Chemistry
GROSS, L. J., Mathematics
GUIDRY, M. W., Physics
GUIOCHON, G. A., Chemistry
HAAS, A. G., History
HALLAM, T. G., Mathematics
HANDEL, M. A., Zoology
HANDEL, S. J., Psychology
HANDELSMAN, M. H., Romance and Asian Languages
HANDLER, L., Psychology
HANDLER, T., Physics
HAO, YEN-PING, History
HARRIS, W. F., Biology
HART, E. L., Physics
HASTINGS, D. W., Sociology
HATCHER, R. D., Zoology
HEFFERNAN, T. J., English
HEFLIN, W. H., Romance and Asian Languages
HICKOK, L. G., Botany
HINTON, D. B., Mathematics
HOLTON, R. W., Botany
HOOD, T. C., Sociology
HUGHES, K. W., Botany
HUSCH, L. S., Mathematics
JACKSON, C. O., Admin.
JACOBS, K. A., Music
JACOBSON, H. C., Admin.
JANTZ, R. L., Anthropology
JEON, K. W., Zoology
JOHANNSON, K., Mathematics
JONES, W. H., Psychology
JORDAN, G. S., Mathematics
JOSHI, J. G., Biochemistry
JOY, D. C., Zoology
JUMPER, S. R., Geography
KABALKA, G. W., Chemistry
KALLET, M., English
KAMYCHKOV, I. A., Physics
KARAKASHIAN, O., Mathematics
KEELING, K. A., Music
KEENE, M. L., English
KELLY, R. M., English
KENNEDY, J. R., Zoology
KENNEDY, W. C., Arts
KLEINFELTER, D. C., Chemistry
KLIPPEL, W. E., Anthropology
KOPP, O. C., Geology
KOVAC, J. D., Chemistry
LABOTKA, T. C., Geological Sciences
LANGSTON, M. A., Computer Science
LAWLER, J. E., Psychology
LAWLER, K., Psychology
LEE, B. S., Arts
LEGGETT, B. J., English
LEKI, I., English
LELAND, W. E., Arts
LENHART, S. M., Mathematics
LESTER, L. W., Admin.
LEVY, K. D., Romance and Asian Languages
LINGE, D. E., Religious Studies
LIVINGSTON, P. R., Arts
LOFARO, M. A., English
LUBAR, J., Psychology
LYONS, W., Political Science
MACCABE, J. A., Zoology
MCCLELLAND, D. K., Music
MCCONNEL, R. M., Mathematics
MCCORMICK, J. F., Ecology
MCCRACKEN, G. F., Zoology
MACEK, J. H., Physics
MCSWEEN, H. Y., Geological Sciences
MAGDEN, N. E., Arts
MAGID, L. J., Chemistry
MAGID, R. M., Chemistry
MAHAN, G. D., Physics
MALAND, C., English
MALONE, J. C., Jr, Psychology
MARSH, F. H., Arts
MARTINSON, F. H., Arts
MASHBURN, R. R., Speech and Theatre
MATHEWS, H. T., Mathematics
MISRA, K. C., Geology
MONTIE, T. C., Microbiology
MONTY, K. J., Biochemistry
MOORE, M. C., Music
MOORE, R. N., Microbiology
MOSER, H. D., History
MULLIN, B. C., Botany
NABELEK, A. K., Audiology and Speech Pathology
NAZAREWICZ, W., Physics
NORMAN, R. V., Religious Studies
NORTHINGTON, D. B., Music
PAGNI, R. M., Chemistry
PAINTER, L. R., Physics
PEACOCK, D., Arts
PEDERSON, D. M., Music
PEGG, D. J., Physics
PENNER, A. R., English
PETERSEN, R. H., Botany
PETERSON, H. A., Audiology and Speech Pathology
PETERSON, J. R., Chemistry
PIMM, S. L., Zoology
PLAAS, H., Political Science
PLOCH, D. R., Sociology
PLUMMER, E. W., Physics
POLLIO, H. R., Psychology
POORE, J. H., Computer Science
POSTOW, B. C., Philosophy
PULSIPHER, L. M., Geography
QUINN, J. J., Physics
RAJPUT, B. S., Mathematics
RALSTON, B. A., Geography
REESE, J. E., English
REYNOLDS, C. H., Religious Studies
RIECHERT, S. E., Zoology
RIESING, T. J., Arts
RIGGSBY, W. S., Microbiology
RIVERA-RODAS, O, Romance and Asian Languages
ROMEISER, J. B., Romance and Asian Languages
ROSINSKI, J., Mathematics
ROTH, L. E., Zoology
RUTLEDGE, H. C., Classics
SAMEJIMA, F., Psychology
SANDERS, N. J., English
SAUDARGAS, R. S., Psychology
SAVAGE, D. C., Psychology
SAYLER, G. S., Microbiology
SCHAEFER, P. W., Mathematics
SCHEB, J. M., Political Science
SCHILLING, E., Botany
SCHMUDDE, T. H., Geography
SCHWEITZER, G. K., Chemistry
SCURA, D. M., English
SELLIN, I. A., Physics
SEPANIAK, M. J., Chemistry
SERBIN, S. M., Mathematics
SHIH, C. C., Physics
SHIVERS, C. A., Zoology
SHOVER, N. E., Sociology
SHURR, W. H., English
SILVERSTEIN, B., Audiology and Speech Pathology
SIMPSON, H. C., Mathematics
SMITH, T. A., Political Science
SMITH, W. O., Botany
SONI, K., Mathematics
SONI, R. P., Mathematics
SORENSEN, S. P., Physics
STACEY, G., Microbiology
STEPHENS, O. H., Jr, Political Science
STEPHENSON, K., Mathematics
STEWART, F. C., Arts
STUTZENBERGER, D. R., Music
SUNDBERG, C., Mathematics
SUNDELL, S. E., Physics
SUNDSTROM, E. D., Psychology
TAYLOR, L. A., Geology
THISTLETHWAITE, M. B., Mathematics
THOMAS, J. C., English
THOMASON, M. G., Computer Science
THOMPSON, J. R., Jr, Physics
THONNARD, N., Science Alliance
TIPPS, A. W., Music
TRAHERN, J. B., English
TRAVIS, C. B., Psychology
UNGS, T. D., Political Science
VAN DE VATE, D., Jr, Philosophy
VANHOOK, A., Chemistry
VAUGHN, G. L., Zoology
WADE, W. R., II, Mathematics
WAGNER, C. G., Mathematics
WAHLER, R. G., Psychology
WALKER, K. R., Geology
WALLACE, S. E., Sociology
WALNE, P. L., Botany
WARD, B. F. L., Physics
WARD, R. C., Computer Science
WASHBURN, Y. M., Romance and Asian Languages
WEHRY, E. L., Chemistry
WEIR, A., English
WELBORN, D. M., Political Science
WHEELER, T. V., English
WHEELER, W. B., History
WHITE, D. C., Microbiology
WHITSON, G. L., Zoology
WICKS, W. D., Biochemistry
WILLIAMS, T. F., Chemistry
WOODS, C., Chemistry
WUNDERLICH, B., Chemistry
YATES, S. A., Arts
ZAK, T., Mathematics
ZHANG, J. Y., Physics

College of Veterinary Medicine:

BRACE, J. J., Administration
BRIAN, D. A., Microbiology and Veterinary Medicine
BRIGHT, R. M., Small Animal Clinical Sciences
DORN, A. S., Small Animal Clinical Sciences
EDWARDS, D. F., Pathology
FARKAS, W. R., Comparative Medicine
GREEN, E. M., Large Animal Clinical Sciences
HENRY, R. W., Animal Science
HOPKINS, F. M., Large Animal Clinical Sciences
KRAHWINKEL, D. J., Jr, Small Animal Clinical Sciences
LEGENDRE, A. M., Small Animal Clinical Sciences
MCCORD, S. P., Comparative Medicine
MCDONALD, T. P., Animal Science and Veterinary Medicine
MCGAVIN, M. D., Pathology
OLIVER, J. W., Comparative Medicine
PATTON, C. S., Pathology
POTGIETER, L. N. D., Comparative Medicine
ROUSE, B. T., Microbiology and Veterinary Medicine
SCHULLER, H. M., Pathology
SHULL, R. M., Pathology
SHULTZ, T. W., Animal Science and Veterinary Medicine
SIMS, M. H., Animal Science and Veterinary Medicine
SLAUSON, D. O., Pathology

School of Architecture:

ANDERSON, G.
GRIEGER, F.
KELSO, R. M.
KERSAVAGE, J. A.

KINZY, S. A.
LAUER, W. J.
LESTER, A. J.
LIZON, P.
ROBINSON, M. A.
RUDD, J. W.
SHELL, W. S.
WATSON, J. S.
WODEHOUSE, L. M.

School of Nursing:
ALLIGOOD, M. R.
GOODFELLOW, D. H.
MOZINGO, J.
THOMAS, S. P.

Graduate School of Bio-medical Sciences:
OLINS, A. L.
OLINS, D. E.
POPP, R. A.

Graduate School of Library and Information Science:
ESTES, G. E.
TENOPIR, C.

Graduate School of Planning:
JOHNSON, D. A.
PROCHASKA, J. M.
SPENCER, J. A.

Graduate School of Social Work:
CETINGOK, M.
FAVER, C. A.
GLISSON, C. A.
HIRAYAMA, H.
NOOE, R. M.
RUBINSTEIN, H.

Space Institute:
ANTAR, B. N.
COLLINS, F. G.
CRATER, H. W.
CRAWFORD, L. W.
CRAWFORD, R. A.
FLANDRO, G. A.
GARRISON, G. W.
KEEFER, D. R.
KUPERSCHMIDT, B. A.
LEWIS, J. W.
LO, C.
MCCAY, M. H.
PALUDAN, C. T. N.
PETERS, C. E.
PUJOL, A.
SCHULZ, R. J.
SHAHROKHI, F.
SHETH, A. C.
WU, J. M.

Center for Assessment Research:
MCGLASSON, N.

Energy, Environment and Resources Center:
COLGLAZIER, E. M.

Learning Research Center:
HUMPHREYS, WALTER L.

Library:
BAYNE, P. S.
BEST, R. A., Law
CRAWFORD, M. F.
FELDER-HOEHNE, F. H.
GRADY, A. M.
LECLERCQ, A. W.
PHILLIPS, L. L.
PIQUET, D. C., Law
RADER, J. C.

University of Tennessee at Martin

Martin, TN 38328
Telephone: (901) 587-7000
Internet: www.utm.edu

Chancellor: MARGARET N. PERRY
Exec. Vice-Chancellor for Devt: NICK DUNAGAN
Vice-Chancellor for Academic Affairs: FRANK S. BLACK
Vice-Chancellor for Financial Affairs: PHILLIP W. DANE
Vice-Chancellor for Student Affairs: PHILIP W. WATKINS

DEANS

Intensive English Language Programmes: JOHN A. EISTERHOLD
School of Agriculture and Home Economics: JAMES L. BYFORD
School of Arts and Sciences: ROBERT M. SMITH
School of Business Administration: GARY F. YOUNG
School of Education: GARY RUSH
School of Engineering: TROY F. HENSON
Student Affairs: DONALD G. SEXTON

UNIVERSITY OF THE SOUTH

Sewanee, TN 37383-1000
Telephone: (931) 598-1000
Internet: www.sewanee.edu

Founded 1858
Private control (Protestant Episcopal Church)
Language of instruction: English
Academic year: August to May

Pres.: Dr JOEL L. CUNNINGHAM
Provost: LINDA B. LANKEWICZ
Dean of Graduate School of Theology: WILLIAM STAFFORD
Dir of Admissions: DAVID LESESNE
Dir of Summer College: JESSE SPAULDING
Registrar: PAUL G. WILEY, II
Librarian: VICKI SELLS

Library of 469,000 vols
Number of teachers: 156 (127 full-time, 29 part-time)
Number of students: 1,559 (1,467 college, 92 seminary)
Publications: *Sewanee Review*, *Sewanee Theological Review*

DEANS

College of Arts and Sciences: THOMAS A. KAZEE
School of Theology: Very Rev. Dr GUY F. LYTLE, III

VANDERBILT UNIVERSITY

211 Kirkland Hall, Nashville, TN 37240
Telephone: (615) 322-7311
Fax: (615) 343-7765
E-mail: admissions@vanderbilt.edu
Internet: www.vanderbilt.edu

Founded 1873
Private control
Academic year: August to April

Chancellor: NICHOLAS ZEPPOS
Provost and Vice-Chancellor for Academic Affairs: RICHARD MCCARTY
Vice-Chancellor for Admin.: JERRY FIFE
Vice-Chancellor for Devt and Alumni Relations: SUSIE STALCUP
Vice-Chancellor for Finance and Chief Financial Officer: BRETT SWEET
Vice-Chancellor for Health Affairs and Dean of the School of Medicine: JEFFREY BALSER
Vice-Chancellor for Investments: MATTHEW WRIGHT
Vice-Chancellor for Public Affairs: BETH FORTUNE
Vice-Chancellor for Univ. Affairs and Athletics, Gen. Counsel, and Sec. of the Univ.: DAVID WILLIAMS, II
Dean of Libraries: CONNIE DOWELL

Number of teachers: 3,844 (3,448 full-time, 396 part-time)
Number of students: 12,714
Publications: *Peabody Reflector* (College of Education and Continuing Development, 2 a year), *The Cornerstone* (College of Arts and Science, 3 a year), *The Engineer* (2 a year), *The Graduate Post* (1 a year), *The Lawyer* (2 a year), *The Nurse* (2 a year), *The Spire* (Divinity School, 3 a year), *Vanderbilt Business* (Graduate School of Management, 2 a year)

DEANS

Blair School of Music: MARK WAIT
College of Arts and Science: CAROLYN DENVER
Divinity School: JAMES HUDNUT-BEUMLER
George Peabody College: CAMILLA BENBOW
Graduate School: DENNIS HALL
Law School: CHRIS GUTHRIE
Owen Graduate School of Management: JIM BRADFORD
School of Engineering: KENNETH GALLOWAY
School of Medicine: JEFFREY R. BALSER
School of Nursing: COLLEEN CONWAY-WELCH

PROFESSORS

ABKOWITZ, M. D., Civil and Environmental Engineering
ABUMRAD, N. N., Surgery
AHNER, J., Mathematics
ALBRIDGE, R. G., Physics and Astronomy
ALDROUBI, A., Mathematics
ALLEN, G. S., Neurological Surgery
ARMSTRONG, R. N., Biochemistry
ARTEAGA, C. L., Medicine
ATACK, J., Economics
ATKINSON, J. B., III, Pathology
AURBACH, M. L., Art and Art History
AVISON, M. J., Radiology and Radiological Sciences
BADER, D. M., Medicine
BALDWIN, H. S., Paediatrics
BALDWIN, L. V., Religious Studies
BALL, C. A., Management
BALLARD, D. W., Microbiology and Immunology
BALSER, J. R., Anaesthesiology
BARRY, B., Management
BARSKY, R. F., French and Italian
BASU, P. K., Civil and Environmental Engineering
BEAUCHAMP, R. D., Surgery
BELL, V. M., English
BELTON, R., Law
BENBOW, C. P., Psychology and Human Devt
BERNARD, G. R., Medicine
BESS, F. H., Hearing and Speech Sciences
BETH, A. H., Molecular Physiology and Biophysics
BIAGGIONI, I. O., Medicine
BICKMAN, L., Psychology and Human Devt
BISCH, D., Mathematics
BLACKBURN, J. O., Management
BLACKETT, R., History
BLAKE, R., Psychology
BLAKELY, R. D., Pharmacology
BLANNING, R. W., Management
BLOCH, F. S., Law
BOEHM, F. H., Obstetrics and Gynaecology
BÖER, G. B., Management
BOLTON, R., Management
BOND, E., Economics
BONDS, A. B., III, Electrical Engineering and Computer Science
BOOTH, W. J., Political Science
BORNHOP, D. J., Chemistry
BOYD, S. B., Oral and Maxillofacial Surgery
BRANDON, M. E., Law
BRANDT, S. J., Medicine
BRASH, A. R., Pharmacology
BRAU, C. A., Physics and Astronomy
BRAXTON, J., Leadership, Policy and Organizations
BRESSMAN, L. S., Law
BREYER, M. D., Medicine
BROADIE, K., Biological Sciences
BROWN, R. L., Law
BRUCE, J. W., Law
BUERHAUS, P. I., Nursing
BURK, R. F., Medicine

BURNETT, L. S., Obstetrics and Gynaecology
BURNS, J. P., Divinity
BURR, I. M., Paediatrics
BYRD, B. F., III, Medicine
CADZOW, J. A., Electrical Engineering and Computer Science
CAMARATA, S. M., Hearing and Speech Sciences
CAPDEVILA, J. H., Medicine
CAPRIOLI, R. M., Biochemistry
CARBONE, D. P., Medicine
CARPENTER, G. F., Biochemistry
CARROLL, F. E., Jr, Radiology and Radiological Sciences
CARTER, C. E., Biological Sciences
CASAGRANDE, V. A., Cell Biology
CHALKLEY, G. R., Molecular Physiology and Biophysics
CHANEY, P. K., Management
CHAZIN, W. J., Biochemistry
CHERRINGTON, A. D., Molecular Physiology and Biophysics
CHRISTIE, W. G., Management
CHRISTMAN, J. W., Medicine
CHURCHILL, L. R., Medicine
CLAYTON, E., Paediatrics
CLAYTON, J. B., English
COBB, P. A., Teaching and Learning
COFFEY, R. J., Jr, Medicine
COLE, D. A., Psychology and Human Devt
COLLINS, R. D., Pathology
COMPAS, B., Psychology and Human Devt
CONLEY, J., Economics
CONN, P. J., Pharmacology
CONTURE, E. G., Hearing and Speech Sciences
CONWAY-WELCH, C. M., Nursing
COOK, G. E., Electrical Engineering and Computer Science
CORBIN, J. D., Molecular Physiology and Biophysics
CORDRAY, D. S., Psychology and Human Devt
CORN, A. L., Special Education
CORNFIELD, D. B., Sociology
COTTON, R. B., Paediatrics
COVINGTON, R. N., Law
CROOKE, P. S., III, Mathematics
CROWSON, R., Leadership, Policy and Organizations
CUMMINGS, P., Chemical Engineering
D'AQUILA, R. T., Medicine
DAFT, R. L., Management
DALLEY, A. F., Cell Biology
DAMON, W. W., Economics
DANZO, B. J., Obstetrics and Gynaecology
DAUGHETY, A. F., Economics
DAVIDSON, J. L., Electrical Engineering and Computer Science
DAVIDSON, J. M., Pathology
DAVIS, S. N., Medicine
DAVIS, T. M., English
DEFELICE, L. J., Pharmacology
DELBEKE, D., Radiology and Radiation Sciences
DEMAREST, A. A., Anthropology
DERMODY, T. S., Paediatrics
DESHPANDE, J. K., Paediatrics
DESPREZ, R. M., Nursing
DEUTCH, A. Y., Psychiatry
DEY, S. K., Paediatrics
DIBENEDETTO, E., Mathematics
DICKERSON, D. C., History
DILLEHAY, T. D., Anthropology
DILTS, D., Electrical Engineering and Computer Science
DITTUS, R. S., Medicine
DOKECKI, P. R., Human and Organizational Devt
DOWDY, L. W., Electrical Engineering and Computer Science
DOWNING, J. W., Anaesthesiology
DOYLE, D. H., History
DREWS, R., Classical Studies
DRINKWATER, D. C., Jr, Cardiac and Thoracic Surgery
DRISKILL, R. A., Economics
DUBOIS, R. N., Jr, Medicine
DUNCAVAGE, J. A., Otolaryngology
DUPONT, W. D., Preventative Medicine
DYKENS, E. A., Psychology and Human Devt
EAKIN, M. C., History
EBNER, F. F., Psychology
EDELMAN, P. H., Mathematics
EDEN, B., Economics
EDWARDS, K. M., Paediatrics
ELLEDGE, W. P., English
ELLIOTT, S. N., Special Education
ELY, J. W., History
ELY, J. W., Law
ENTERLINE, L., English
ENTMAN, S. S., Obstetrics and Gynaecology
EPSTEIN, J. A., History
ERNST, D. J., Physics and Astronomy
EXTON, J. H., Molecular Physiology and Biophysics
FAN, Y., Economics
FANNING, E. H., Biological Sciences
FARRAN, D., Teaching and Learning
FAZIO, S., Medicine
FELZMAN, L. C., Physics and Astronomy
FENICHEL, G. M., Neurology
FITZ, E. E., Spanish and Portuguese
FITZPATRICK, J. M., Electrical Engineering and Computer Science
FLEETWOOD, D. M., Electrical Engineering and Computer Science
FLEISCHER, A. C., Radiology and Radiological Sciences
FLEXNER, J. M., Medicine
FOGO, A. B., Pathology
FOLGARAIT, L., Art and Art History
FOSTER, J. E., Economics
FOX, R., Psychology
FRANKS, J. J., Psychology
FREEMAN, M. L., Radiation Oncology
FREEMON, F. R., Neurology
FRIEDMAN, E. H., Spanish and Portuguese
FRIEDMAN, R. A., Management
FROMENT-MEURICE, M., French and Italian
FRYD, V. G., Art and Art History
FUCHS, D. H., Special Education
FUCHS, L. S., Special Education
FURBISH, D. J., Geology
GABBE, S. G., Obstetrics and Gynaecology
GAFFNEY, F. A., Medical Admin.
GALLOWAY, K. F., Electrical Engineering and Computer Science
GALLOWAY, R. L., Jr, Biomedical Engineering
GARBER, J., Psychology and Human Devt
GAY, V. P., Religious Studies
GEE, E. G., Law
GEER, J., Political Science
GEORGE, A. L., Jr, Medicine
GIRGUS, S. B., English
GIUSE, N. B., Biomedical Informatics
GOLDBERG, J. C., Law
GOLDENRING, J. R., Surgery
GOLDRING, E., Leadership, Policy and Organizations
GOODMAN, L. E., Philosophy
GORDON, J., Nursing
GORE, J. C., Radiology and Radiological Sciences
GOTTFRIED, R. K., English
GOULD, K. L., Cell and Developmental Biology
GOULD, M. I., Mathematics
GRAHAM, G. J., Jr, Political Science
GRAHAM, T. P., Jr, Paediatrics
GRANNER, D. K., Molecular Physiology and Biophysics
GRANTHAM, D. W., Hearing and Speech Sciences
GREEN, N. E., Orthopaedics and Rehabilitation
GREENE, J. W., Paediatrics
GREER, J. P., Medicine
GREGOR, T. A., Anthropology
GRIFFIN, L. J., Sociology and Political Science
GRIFFIN, M. R., Preventive Medicine
GUENGERICH, F. P., Biochemistry
GUTHRIE, C. P., Law
GUTHRIE, J. W., Leadership, Policy and Organizations
HAGLUND, R. F., Physics and Astronomy
HAHN, B., German and Slavic Language
HAINES, J. L., Molecular Physiology and Biophysics
HALL, D., Physics and Astronomy
HALL, D. J., Law
HALL, R., Teaching and Learning
HALLAHAN, D., Radiation Oncology
HALPERIN, J., English
HAMILTON, J. H., Physics and Astronomy
HAMM, H. E., Pharmacology
HANCOCK, M. D., Political Science
HANDE, K. R., Medicine
HANKS, S. K., Cell Biology
HANN, S. R., Cell Biology
HARRIS, R. C., Jr, Medicine
HARRIS, T. R., Biomedical Engineering
HAWIGER, J., Microbiology and Immunology
HAZINSKI, T. A., Paediatrics
HEAD, D. R., Pathology
HEARN, J., Leadership, Policy and Organizations
HELDERMAN, J. H., Medicine
HELFER, L. R., Law School
HELLER, R. M., Jr, Radiology and Radiological Sciences
HELLERQVIST, C. G., Biochemistry
HERCULES, D. M., Chemistry
HERNANZ-SCHULMAN, M., Radiology and Radiological Sciences
HESS, B. A., Jr, Chemistry
HETCHER, S. A., Law
HEYNEMAN, S., Leadership, Policy and Organizations
HICKSON, G. B., Paediatrics
HIEBERT, S. W., Biochemistry
HILL, G. C., Medical Admin.
HODAPP, R., Special Education
HODGES, M., Philosophy
HOFFMAN, D. L., Management
HOGGE, J. H., Psychology and Human Devt
HOLLON, S. D., Psychology
HOOVER, R. L., Pathology
HUDNET-BEUMLER, J., Divinity
HUDSON, B. G., Medicine
HUFFMAN, G. W., Economics
HUGHES, C. B., Mathematics
ICHIKAWA, I., Paediatrics
INAGAMI, T., Biochemistry
ISAAC, L. W., Sociology
JACOBSON, G. P., Hearing and Speech Sciences
JACOBSON, H. R., Medicine
JARMAN, M. F., English
JENSEN, G. F., Sociology
JENSEN, R. M., Divinity
JOHNS, C. M. S., Art and Art History
JOHNSON, C. H., Biological Sciences
JOHNSON, D. A., Divinity
JOHNSON, D. H., Nursing
JONES, H. W., III, Obstetrics and Gynaecology
JRADE, C. L., Spanish and Portuguese
KAAS, J. H., Psychology
KAISER, A. B., Medicine
KAISER, A. P., Special Education
KANG, W. P., Electrical Engineering and Computer Science
KASPAROV, G., Mathematics
KAWAMURA, K., Electrical Engineering and Computer Science
KAYE, J. J., Radiology and Radiological Sciences
KESSLER, R. M., Radiology and Radiological Sciences
KING, L. E., Jr, Medicine
KING, N. J., Law
KINSER, D. L., Mechanical Engineering
KIRSHNER, H. S., Neurology
KNIGHT, D. A., Divinity
KOSSON, D. S., Civil and Environmental Engineering
KOURY, M. J., Medicine
KOVACS, W. J., Medicine
KREYLING, M. P., English

KUTZINSKI, V. M., Dean's Office
LACHS, J., Philosophy
LAMB, J., English
LAMONTAGNE, L. L., Nursing
LANCASTER, L. E., Nursing
LAPPIN, J. S., Psychology
LAWTON, A. R., III, Paediatrics
LEBLANC, L. J., Management
LEGAN, H. L., Oral and Maxillofacial Surgery
LEHRER, R., Teaching and Learning
LESTOURGEON, W. M., Biological Sciences
LEVAN, D. M., Chemical Engineering
LEVINE, A.-J., Divinity
LEVITT, P. R., Pharmacology
LEWIS, J. G., Medicine
LIEBLER, D. C., Biochemistry
LIGHT, R. W., Medicine
LIMBIRD, L. E., Pharmacology
LINTON, M. F., Medicine
LOGAN, G. D., Psychology
LOOSEN, P. T., Psychiatry
LORENZI, N. M., Biomedical Informatics
LOYD, J. E., Medicine
LUBINSKI, D., Psychology and Human Devt
LUIS, W., Spanish and Portuguese
LUKEHART, C. M., Chemistry
LYBRAND, T. P., Chemistry
MCCARTHY, J. A., German and Slavic Languages
MCCARTY, R., Psychology
MCCAULEY, D. E., Biological Sciences
MCCLURE, J. S., Divinity
MCCOY, T. R., Law
MACDONALD, R. L., Neurology
MCKENNA, S. J., Oral and Maxillofacial Surgery
MCKENZIE, R. N., Mathematics
MCLOED, R., Nursing
MCMAHON, D. G., Biological Sciences
MCNAMARA, T. P., Psychology
MCWILLIAM, R. A., Paediatrics
MAGNUSON, M. A., Molecular Physiology and Biophysics
MAGUIRE, C. F., Physics and Astronomy
MAHADEVAN, S., Civil and Environmental Engineering
MAIER, H. G., Law
MANESCHI, A. E., Economics
MARCH, S. T., Management
MARCUS, L. S., English
MARGO, R. A., Economics
MARNETT, L. J., Biochemistry
MARTIN, P. R., Psychiatry
MASSENGILL, L.W., Electrical Engineering and Computer Science
MASULIS, R. W., Management
MATRISIAN, L. M., Cancer Biology
MATUSIK, R. J., Urologic Surgery
MAY, J. M., Medicine
MEEKS, M. D., Divinity
MEGIBBEN, C. K., Mathematics
MELLOR, A. M., Mechanical Engineering
MELNER, M. H., Obstetrics and Gynaecology
MELTZER, H. Y., Psychiatry
MEYRICK-CLARRY, B. O., Pathology
MIHALIK, M. L., Mathematics
MILLER, C. F., Geology
MILLER, G. G., Medicine
MILLER, M. F., Geology
MILLER, R. A., Biomedical Informatics
MILLER-MCLEMORE, B. J., Divinity
MITCHELL, W. M., Pathology
MONGA, L., French and Italian
MOORE, R. A., Nursing
MORAN, B. I., Law
MORRIS, J. A., Jr, Surgery
MORROW, J. D., Medicine
MOSES, H. L., Cancer Biology
MURPHY, J. F., Leadership and Organizations
MURPHY, M. L., Art and Art History
NAGAREDA, R. A., Law
NANNEY, L. B., Plastic Surgery
NEILSON, E. G., Medicine
NELSON, D., Dean's Office
NETTERVILLE, J. L., Otolaryngology
NEWBROUGH, J. R., Human and Organization Devt
NEWMAN, J. H., Medicine
NORDEN, J. J., Cell and Devt Biology
NOVAK, T. P., Management
OATES, J. A., Medicine
OBERACKER, V. E., Physics and Astronomy
O'DAY, D. M., Ophthalmology and Visual Sciences
O'HARA, E. A., Law
OHDE, R. N., Hearing and Speech Sciences
OLIVER, K., Philosophy
OLIVER, R. L., Management
OLSEN, N. J., Medicine
OLSON, G. E., Cell and Developmental Biology
ONG, D. E., Biochemistry
OPPENHEIMER, B. I., Political Science
ORGEBIN-CRIST, M. C., Obstetrics and Gynaecology
OSHEROFF, N., Biochemistry
OSSOFF, R. H., Otolaryngology
OSTEEN, K. G., Obstetrics and Gynaecology
OUTLAW, L. T., Philosophy
OVERHOLSER, K. A., Biomedical Engineering
OZBOLT, J. G., Nursing
PACE, J., Nursing
PAGE, D. L., Pathology
PAGE, T. L., Biological Sciences
PANTELIDES, S. T., Physics and Astronomy
PARK, J. H., Molecular Physiology and Biophysics
PARKER, F. L., Civil and Environmental Engineering
PARL, F. F., Pathology
PARTAIN, C. L., Radiology and Radiological Sciences
PARTRIDGE, W., Human and Organizational Devt
PATTE, D. M., Religious Studies
PATTON, J. A., Radiology and Radiological Sciences
PENN, J. S., Ophthalmology and Visual Sciences
PHILLIPS, J. A., III, Paediatrics
PIETENPOL, J. A., Biochemistry
PILON, B. A., Nursing
PINCUS, T., Medicine
PISTON, D. W., Molecular Physiology and Biophysics
PITZ, R. W., Mechanical Engineering
PLUMMER, J. F., English
PLUMMER, M. D., Mathematics
POLAVARAPU, P. L., Chemistry
PORTER, A. C., Leadership and Organizations
PORTER, N. A., Chemistry
PRICE, R. R., Radiology and Radiological Sciences
PRIETO, R., Spanish and Portuguese
PRILLELTENSKY, I., Human and Organizational Devt
PUTNAM, J. B., Jr, Thoracic Surgery
QUARANTA, V., Cancer Biology
RAMAYYA, A. V., Physics and Astronomy
RASCH, R. F. R., Nursing
RASICO, P. D., Spanish and Portuguese
RASMUSSEN, R. K., Law
RATCLIFFE, J. G., Mathematics
RAY, J. L., Political Science
RAY, W. A., Preventive Medicine
REINGANUM, J. F., Economics
RESCHLY, D. J., Special Education
REYNOLDS, A. B., Cancer Biology
RICHARDS, W. O., Surgery
RICHMOND, J. A., Cancer Biology
RIESER, J. J., Psychology and Human Devt
RISKO, V. J., Teaching and Learning
ROBACK, H. B., Psychiatry
ROBERTS, L. J., II, Pharmacology
ROBERTSON, D. H., Medicine
ROBERTSON, R. M., Medicine
RODEN, D. M., Medicine
ROSELLI, R. J., Biomedical Engineering
ROTH, B. J., Medicine
ROTH, J. A., Chemical Engineering
ROTHENBERG, M. L., Medicine
RUBIN, C. A., Mechanical Engineering
RUBIN, D. H., Medicine
RULEY, H. E., Microbiology and Immunology
SAFF, E. B., Mathematics
SANDERS-BUSH, E., Pharmacology
SANDLER, H. M., Psychology and Human Devt
SANDLER, M. P., Radiology and Radiological Sciences
SAPIR, M., Mathematics
SASSON, J., Divinity
SCHAFFNER, W., Preventative Medicine
SCHALL, J. D., Psychology
SCHAUBLE, L., Teaching and Learning
SCHERRER, R. J., Physics and Astronomy
SCHLUNK, H. J., Law
SCHMIDT, D., Electrical Engineering and Computer Science
SCHNELLE, K. B., Chemical Engineering
SCHOENBLUM, J. A., Law
SCHRIMPF, R., Electrical Engineering and Computer Science
SCHUENING, F. G., Medicine
SCHULMAN, G., Medicine
SCHUMAKER, L. L., Mathematics
SCHWARTZ, H. S., Orthopaedics and Rehabilitation
SCHWARTZ, T. A., History
SCUDDER, G. D., Management
SEGOVIA, F. F., Divinity
SELIGSON, M. A., Political Science
SERGENT, J. S., Medicine
SEVIN, D. H. O., German and Slavic Languages
SHACK, R. B., Plastic Surgery
SHELTON, R. C., Psychiatry
SHENAI, J., Paediatrics
SHEPHERD, V. L., Pathology
SHERRY, S., Law
SHIAVI, R. G., Biomedical Engineering
SHU, X. O., Medicine
SHYR, Y., Preventative Medicine
SIAMI, G., Medicine
SIEGFRIED, J. J., Economics
SINGLETON, C. K., Biological Sciences
SLOVIS, C. M., Emergency Medicine
SMITH, H. W., History
SMITH, J. A., Jr, Urologic Surgery
SMITH, W. P., Psychology
SNELL, J. D., Jr, Medicine
SODERQUIST, L. D., Law
SOSMAN, J. A., Medicine
SPENGLER, D. M., Orthopaedics and Rehabilitation
SPICKARD, W. A., Jr, Medicine
SPINDLER, K. P., Orthopaedics and Rehabilitation
SRIRAM, S., Neurology
STAHLMAN, M. T., Paediatrics
STEAD, W. W., Medicine
STEIGER, J. H., Psychology and Human Devt
STEIN, R. W., Molecular Physiology and Biophysics
STEINBERG, R., Sociology
STERNBERG, P., Ophthalmology and Visual Sciences
STOLL, H. R., Management
STONE, M. P., Chemistry
STONE, W. J., Medicine
STONE, W. L., Paediatrics
STRANGE, K., Anaesthesiology
STRAUSS, A. M., Mechanical Engineering
STRAUSS, A. W., Paediatrics
STRICKLIN, G. P., Medicine
STUBBS, G. J., Biological Sciences
STUHR, J. J., Philosophy
SUNDELL, H. W., Paediatrics
SWAIN, C. M., Law
SWIFT, L. L., Pathology
SYVERUD, J., Electrical Engineering and Computer Science
SZTIPANOVITS, J., Electrical and Computer Engineering
TAM, J. P., Microbiology and Immunology
TANNER, R. D., Chemical Engineering
TATE, C. N., Political Science

TELLINGHUISEN, J., Chemistry
TELOH, H. A., Philosophy
THOITS, P. A., Sociology
THOMAS, J. W., II, Medicine
THOMAS, R. S., Law
THOMPSON, P. W., Teaching and Learning
THOMPSON, R. B., Law
TICHI, C., English
TOLK, N. H., Physics and Astronomy
TRANGENSTEIN, P., Nursing
TULIPAN, N. B., Neurological Surgery
UMAR, S. A., Physics and Astronomy
USNER, D. H., History
VAN KAER, L., Microbiology and Immunology
VAUGHAN, D. E., Medicine
VICTOR, B., Management
WAGNER, C., Biochemistry
WALDEN, T. A., Psychology and Human Devt
WALKER, L. S., Paediatrics
WALLER, N., Psychology and Human Devt
WALLSTON, K. A., Nursing
WANG, P., Economics
WANG, T. G., Mechanical Engineering
WARD, P. A., French and Italian
WASHINGTON, M. K., Pathology
WASSERMAN, D. H., Molecular Physiology and Biophysics
WASSERSTEIN, D. J., History
WATERMAN, M. R., Biochemistry
WEBB, G. F., Mathematics
WEBSTER, M. S., Physics and Astronomy
WEIL, P. A., Molecular Physiology and Biophysics
WEILER, T. J., Physics and Astronomy
WEINER, E. E., Nursing
WELLER, R. A., Electrical Engineering and Computer Science
WENTE, S. R., Cell and Devt Biology
WEYMARK, J. A., Economics
WIKSWO, J. P., Physics and Astronomy, Molecular Physiology and Biophysics
WILEY, R. G., Neurology
WILKINSON, G. R., Pharmacology
WILSON, J. R., Medicine
WILTSHIRE, S. F., Classical Studies
WOLERY, M., Special Education
WONG, K. K., Leadership, Policy and Organizations
WOOD, A. J., Medicine
WOOD, D. C., Philosophy
WRENN, K. D., Emergency Medicine
WRIGHT, C. V., Cell and Developmental Biology
WRIGHT, P. F., Paediatrics
XIA, D., Mathematics
YODER, P. J., Special Education
YU, G., Mathematics
ZEPPOS, N. S., Jr, Law
ZHENG, W., Medicine
ZUTTER, M. M., Pathology

TEXAS

ABILENE CHRISTIAN UNIVERSITY

ACU Box 29100, Abilene, TX 79699-9105
Telephone: (325) 674-2000
Fax: (325) 674-2958
Internet: www.acu.edu

Founded 1906
Private (Church of Christ) liberal arts
Language of instruction: English
Academic year: August to May; attached to Comm. on College of the Southern Assn of Colleges and Schools

Pres.: Dr PHIL SCHUBERT
Vice-Pres.: Dr GARY MCCALEB
Provost: Dr JEANINE VARNER
Dean of Library and Information Services: Dr GARY TUCKER

Library of 530,254 vols, 1,195 periodical titles
Number of teachers: 275
Number of students: 4,728

DEANS
College of Arts and Sciences: CHARLES MATTIS
College of Biblical Studies: JACK REESE
College of Business Administration: RICK LYTLE
College of Education and Human Services: MALESA BREEDING
Graduate School: CARLEY DODD

ARLINGTON BAPTIST COLLEGE

3001 W Division St, Arlington, TX 76012
Telephone: (817) 461-8741
Fax: (817) 274-1138
E-mail: info@abconline.org
Internet: www.abconline.edu

Pres.: Dr DAVID BRYANT.

AUSTIN COLLEGE

900 North Grand Ave, Sherman, TX 75090-4400
Telephone: (903) 813-2000
Fax: (903) 813-3199
E-mail: admission@austincollege.edu
Internet: www.austincollege.edu

Founded 1849
Private control, affiliated to Presbyterian Church (USA)
Academic year: September to June

Pres.: MARJORIE HASS
Treas. and Vice-Pres. for Business Affairs: HEIDI ELLIS
Vice-Pres. for Academic Affairs and Dean of the Faculty: MICHAEL IMHOFF
Vice-Pres. for Institutional Advancement: JERRY HOLBERT
Vice-Pres. for Institutional Enrollment: NAN DAVIS
Vice-Pres. for Student Affairs: TIMOTHY P. MILLERICK

Library of 206,324 vols
Number of teachers: 122 (92 full-time, 30 part-time)
Number of students: 1,300

Four-year liberal arts coeducational Christian college.

AUSTIN PRESBYTERIAN THEOLOGICAL SEMINARY

100 E 27th St, Austin, TX 78705
Telephone: (512) 472-6736
Fax: (512) 479-0738
Internet: www.austinseminary.edu

Founded 1902

Pres.: THEODORE J. WARDLAW
Vice-Pres. for Business and Finance: KURT GABBARD
Vice-Pres. for Institutional Advancement: DONNA SCOTT
Vice-Pres. for Student Affairs: JACQULINE SAXON
Academic Dean: MICHAEL JINKINS
Registrar: JACQUELINE D. HEFLEY

Publications: *Horizons in Biblical Theology* (2 a year), *Insights* (2 a year).

BAPTIST MISSIONARY ASSOCIATION THEOLOGICAL SEMINARY

1530 East Pine St, Jacksonville, TX 75766-5407
Telephone: (903) 586-2501
Fax: (903) 586-0378
E-mail: bmatsem@bmats.edu
Internet: www.bmats.edu

Pres.: Dr CHARLEY HOLMES
Dean and Registrar: PHILIP ATTEBERY
Librarian: JAMES C. BLAYLOCK.

BAYLOR COLLEGE OF MEDICINE

1 Baylor Plaza, Houston, TX 77030
Telephone: (713) 798-4951
Fax: (713) 798-4951
E-mail: admissions@bcm.edu
Internet: www.bcm.edu

Founded 1900

Pres.: Dr WILLIAM T. BUTLER
Vice-Pres. and Dean of Medicine: BOBBY R. ALFORD
Vice-Pres. and Dean of Research: JAMES W. PATRICK
Vice-Pres. for Graduate Sciences and Dean of Graduate School of Biomedical Sciences: WILLIAM R. BRINKLEY.

BAYLOR UNIVERSITY

One Bear Place, Waco, TX 76798
Telephone: (254) 710-1011
Internet: www.baylor.edu

Chartered 1845 under Republic of Texas by Texas Baptist Educational Society at Independence, Texas; consolidated 1886 with Waco University and affiliated with Baptist Gen. Convention of Texas
Academic year: August to May

Pres.: Dr ROBERT B. SLOAN, Jr
Sec.: PAM EDENS
Dir of Admissions: DIANA RAMEY
Librarian: Dr REAGAN M. RAMSOWER

Number of teachers: 775
Number of students: 14,000

Publications: *Baylor Business Review*, *Baylor Geological Studies*, *Baylor Line*, *Baylor Magazine* (6 a year), *Baylor News*, *Journal of Church and State*, *Law Review*, *The Lariat*.

CONCORDIA UNIVERSITY, AUSTIN

3400 IH 35 North, Austin, TX 78705
Telephone: (512) 486-2000
Fax: (512) 459-8517
E-mail: admissions@concordia.edu
Internet: www.concordia.edu

Founded 1926
Academic year: July to June

Pres.: Dr THOMAS CEDEL
Vice-Pres. for Academic Services: JOEL HECK
Vice-Pres. for Advancement: JOHN SCHOEDEL
Vice-Pres. for Business and Finance: PAMELA LEE
Vice-Pres. for Univ. Services: DAVID KLUTH
Vice-Pres. for Student Services: WILLIAM DRISKILL

Number of students: 1,160

DEANS
Adult Education: Dr VICTORIA SCHOEDEL
Business: DAVID WHITE
Education: Dr SANDRA DOERING
Liberal Arts and Sciences: Dr MICHAEL MOYER

CRISWELL COLLEGE

4010 Gaston Ave, Dallas, TX 75246
Telephone: (214) 821-5433
Fax: (214) 818-1310
Internet: www.criswell.edu

Founded 1970
Academic year: August to July

Chancellor: D. MCCALL BRUNSON
Exec. Vice-Pres. and Provost: LAMAR E. COOPER, SR
Vice-Pres. for Devt: MARK M. OVERSTREET
Vice-Pres. for Enrollment and Academic Services: KATE FINLEY
Registrar: PATRICIA MCCLUNG

Library of 100,000 vols
Number of teachers: 18

Number of students: 460
Publication: *Criswell Theological Review* (2 a year).

DALLAS BAPTIST UNIVERSITY

3000 Mountain Creek Parkway, Dallas, TX 75211-9299
Telephone: (214) 333-7100
Fax: (214) 333-5447
E-mail: admiss@dbu.edu
Internet: www.dbu.edu
Founded 1898
Private control
Pres.: Dr GARY COOK
Exec. Vice-Pres.: J. BLAIR BLACKBURN
Provost: Dr GAIL LINAM
Vice-Pres.: Dr RICK GREGORY
Vice-Pres. for Financial Affairs: ERIC BRUNTMYER
Vice-Pres. for Graduate Affairs and Sr Assoc. Provost: Dr DENNY DOWD
Vice-Pres. for Technology: MATT MURRAH
Librarian: DEBRA Y. COLLINS
Library of 810,447 vols, 1,119 periodicals
Number of teachers: 532 (123 full-time, 409 part-time)
Number of students: 4,189 (F.t.e.)

DEANS
College of Adult Education: Dr DONOVAN FREDRICKSEN
College of Business: CHARLENE CONNER
College of Christian Faith: STEVEN MULLEN
College of Fine Arts: RONALD BOWLES
College of Humanities and Social Sciences: Dr MICHAEL WILLIAMS
College of Natural Sciences and Mathematics: Dr BEVERLY GILTNER
Dorothy M. Bush College of Education: CHARLES CARONA
Graduate School of Leadership: Dr RICK GREGORY

DALLAS CHRISTIAN COLLEGE

2700 Christian Parkway, Dallas, TX 75234-7299
Telephone: (972) 241-3371
E-mail: admin@dallas.edu
Internet: www.dallas.edu
Founded 1950
Pres.: DUSTIN D. RUBECK
Vice-Pres. for Academic Affairs: Dr RAY KELLEY
Registrar: CRYSTAL LAIDACKER
Library Dir: SUSAN SPRINGER.

DALLAS THEOLOGICAL SEMINARY

3909 Swiss Ave, Dallas, TX 75204
Telephone: (214) 824-3094
Fax: (214) 841-3664
Internet: www.dts.edu
Pres.: Dr MARK L. BAILEY
Number of students: 2,050

EAST TEXAS BAPTIST UNIVERSITY

1209 N Grove St, Marshall, TX 75670
Telephone: (903) 935-7963
Fax: (903) 938-1705
E-mail: admissions@etbu.edu
Internet: www.etbu.edu
Founded 1912
Pres.: Dr BOB E. RILEY
Registrar: DAVID MOHN
Librarian: Dr ROSE MARY MAGRILL
Library of 100,000 vols
Number of teachers: 55
Number of students: 1,200
Courses in the liberal arts.

HARDIN-SIMMONS UNIVERSITY

2200 Hickory, Abilene, TX 79698
Telephone: (325) 670-1000
Fax: (325) 671-2157
Internet: www.hsutx.edu
Founded 1891
Academic year: August to May
Pres.: JESSE FLETCHER
Exec. Vice-Pres. and Chief Academic Officer: Dr CRAIG TURNER
Assoc. Vice-Pres. for Enrollment Services: SHANE DAVIDSON
Registrar: DOROTHY KISER
Dir of University Libraries: ALICE W. SPECHT
Library of 415,752 vols
Number of teachers: 140
Number of students: 2,392

HOUSTON BAPTIST UNIVERSITY

7502 Fondren Rd, Houston, TX 77074
Telephone: (281) 649-3000
E-mail: admissions@hbu.edu
Internet: www.hbu.edu
Pres.: Dr ROBERT B. SLOAN, Jr
Vice-Pres. for Academic Affairs: DONALD W. LOOSER
Vice-Pres. for Devt: DON ANDERSON
Vice-Pres. for Financial Affairs: RICHARD D. PARKER
Vice-Pres. for Marketing: SHARON SAUNDERS
Vice-Pres. for Student Affairs: JACK PURCELL.

HOWARD PAYNE UNIVERSITY

Brownwood, TX 76801
Telephone: (325) 646-2502
Fax: (325) 649-8901
E-mail: enroll@hputx.edu
Internet: www.hputx.edu
Founded 1889
Private control
Academic year: August to May
Pres.: Dr WILLIAM N. ELLIS
Provost: Dr WILLIAM MARK TEW
Sr Vice-Pres. for Finance and Administration: BRENDA J. MCLENDON
Sr Vice-Pres. for Institutional Advancement: Dr BRAD JOHNSON
Registrar: LANA WAGNER
Librarian: NANCY ANDERSON
Library of 116,667 vols
Number of teachers: 123
Number of students: 1,290

DEANS
Developmental Studies: Dr WENDY MCNEELEY
School of Business: Dr LES PLAGENS
School of Christian Studies: Dr DONNIE AUVENSHINE
School of Education: Dr MICHAEL ROSATO
School of Humanities: Dr JUSTIN MURPHY
School of Music and Fine Arts: Dr ROBERT TUCKER
School of Science and Mathematics: Dr LYNN LITTLE

HUSTON-TILLOTSON UNIVERSITY

900 Chicon St, Austin, TX 78702
Telephone: (512) 505-3000
Fax: (512) 505-3190
E-mail: admission@htu.edu
Internet: www.htu.edu
Founded 1875
Academic year: August to May
Pres.: Dr LARRY L. EARVIN
Provost and Vice-Pres. for Academic and Student Affairs: Dr VICKI LOTT
Dean of Enrollment Management: ROBERT SHINDELL
Dean of Student Affairs: YVONNE ORTIZ-PRINCE
Registrar: EARNESTINE STRICKLAND
Librarian: PATRICIA WILKINS
Library of 88,000 vols
Number of teachers: 75
Number of students: 950

DEANS
College of Arts and Sciences: Dr JOSEPH JONES
School of Business and Technology: Dr STEVEN EDMOND

JARVIS CHRISTIAN COLLEGE

POB 1470, Highway 80 East, Private Rd 7631, Hawkins, TX 75765
Telephone: (903) 769-5700
Fax: (903) 769-1282
E-mail: webmaster@jarvis.edu
Internet: www.jarvis.edu
Pres.: Dr SEBETHA JENKINS
Chair. of the Admin. Ccl: JOHN GLOVER.

LETOURNEAU UNIVERSITY

POB 7001, Longview, TX 75607-7001
Located at: 2100 S Mobberly Ave, Longview, TX 75602
Telephone: (903) 233-4300
Fax: (903) 233-4301
E-mail: admissions@letu.edu
Internet: www.letu.edu
Pres.: Dr DALE A. LUNSFORD
Exec. Vice-Pres. for Academic Affairs: Dr ROBERT HUDSON
Exec. Vice-Pres. for Business and Admin.: Dr WILLIAM MCDOWELL
Exec. Vice-Pres. for External Relations: (vacant)
Vice-Pres. for Enrollment Services: LINDA FITZHUGH
Vice-Pres. for Financial Affairs: MIKE HOOD
Vice-Pres. for Graduate and Professional Studies: Dr CAROL GREEN
Vice-Pres. for Univ. Devt: BEN MARCH
Registrar: TEXAS RÜEGG
Number of students: 3,663

LUBBOCK CHRISTIAN UNIVERSITY

5601 19th St, Lubbock, TX 79407
Telephone: (806) 796-8800
Fax: (806) 796-8917
E-mail: admissions@lcu.edu
Internet: www.lcu.edu
Founded 1957
Pres.: Dr L. KEN JONES
Exec. Vice-Pres.: ROD BLACKWOOD
Vice-Pres. for Academic Affairs: DOYLE CARTER
Vice-Pres. for Admissions: KEVIN ELMORE
Vice-Pres. for Enrollment Management: RANDY SELLERS
Vice-Pres. for Global Affairs: NAT COOPER.

MCMURRY UNIVERSITY

14th & Sayles Blvd, McMurry Station, Box 278, Abilene, TX 79697
Telephone: (325) 793-4700
E-mail: admissions@mcm.edu
Internet: www.mcm.edu
Founded 1923
Pres.: Dr JOHN H. RUSSELL
Vice-Pres. for Academic Affairs: PAUL LACK
Vice-Pres. for Enrollment Management and Student Relations: RUSSELL WATJEN
Vice-Pres. for Financial Affairs: CARL BROWN
Vice-Pres. for Institutional Advancement: JAMES DOTHEROW
Dir of Library: JOE W. SPECHT

Library of 200,000 vols
Number of teachers: 119
Number of students: 1,400

MIDWESTERN STATE UNIVERSITY

3410 Taft Boulevard, Wichita Falls, TX 76308
Telephone: (940) 397-4000
Fax: (940) 397-4302
E-mail: information@mwsu.edu
Internet: www.mwsu.edu

Founded 1922
Academic year: September to August

Pres.: Dr JESSE W. ROGERS
Provost: FRIEDERIKE WIEDEMANN
Vice-Pres. for Business Affairs: JOHN H. ALEXANDER
Vice-Pres. for Univ. Devt and Student Affairs: Dr HOWARD FARRELL
Registrar: DARLA INGLISH
Librarian: CLARA LATHAM

Number of teachers: 172
Number of students: 6,500

Publications: *Faculty Forum Papers* (1 a year), *The Wai-Kun* (1 a year), *The Wichitan* (52 a year), *Voices* (1 a year).

OBLATE SCHOOL OF THEOLOGY

285 Oblate Drive, San Antonio, TX 78216-6693
Telephone: (210) 341-1366
Fax: (210) 341-4519
E-mail: info@ost.edu
Internet: www.ost.edu

Founded 1903

Pres.: Fr RONALD ROLHEISER
Academic Dean: ELAINE BROTHERS.

OUR LADY OF THE LAKE UNIVERSITY

411 SW 24th St, San Antonio, TX 78207
Telephone: (210) 434-6711
Fax: (210) 431-4036
E-mail: webmaster@lake.ollusa.edu
Internet: www.ollusa.edu

Founded 1883
Academic year: August to May

Pres.: Dr TESSA MARTINEZ POLLACK
Provost: JAMES L. GEARITY
Vice-Pres. and Dean of Student Life: MARY ELLEN SMITH
Vice-Pres. for Finance and Facilities: ALLEN R. KLAUS
Vice-Pres. for Institutional Advancement: MICHAEL MULNIX
Dean of Enrollment and Management: LORETTA A. SCHLEGEL
Institutional Research Officer: FRED D. SCOTT

Library of 254,419 vols
Number of teachers: 140
Number of students: 3,564

PAUL QUINN COLLEGE

3837 Simpson-Stuart Rd, Dallas, TX 75241
Telephone: (214) 376-1000
E-mail: admissions@pqc.edu
Internet: www.pqc.edu

Founded 1872

Pres.: MICHAEL J. SORRELL
Vice-Pres. for Academic Affairs: Dr CHARLES HUMPHREY
Registrar: J. D. HURD
Librarian: MACHIE

Number of teachers: 48
Number of students: 780

Publication: *Paul Quinn Gazette*.

RICE UNIVERSITY

POB 1892, Houston, TX 77251-1892
Telephone: (713) 348-0000
E-mail: info@rice.edu
Internet: www.rice.edu

Founded 1891
Private control
Language of instruction: English

Pres.: DAVID W. LEEBRON
Provost: GEORGE L. MCLENDON
Vice-Pres. for Admin.: KEVIN E. KIRBY
Vice-Pres. for Enrollment: CHRIS MUÑOZ
Vice-Pres. for Finance: KATHY COLLINS
Vice-Pres. for Investments and Treas.: SCOTT W. WISE
Vice-Pres. for Public Affairs: LINDA L. THRANE
Vice-Pres. for Resource Devt: DARROW ZEIDENSTEIN
Vice-Provost and Univ. Librarian: SARA LOWMAN

Library of 1,400,000 vols
Number of teachers: 831 (644 full-time, 143 part-time, 44 adjunct)
Number of students: 5,556 (3,279 undergraduate, 2,277 graduate)

Publications: *Baker Institute Report*, *Houston Area Survey* (1 a year), *Journal of Southern History*, *Rice University Studies* (4 a year), *Studies in English Literature 1500–1900*, journals on chemistry, environmental toxicology and feminist economics

DEANS

Jesse H. Jones Graduate School of Management: WILLIAM GLICK
School of Architecture: SARAH WHITING
George R. Brown School of Engineering: SALLIE KELLER
School of Humanities: ALLEN MATUSOW
Shepherd School of Music: ROBERT YEKOVICH
Wiess School of Natural Sciences: DANIEL D. CARSON
School of Social Sciences: LYN RAGSDALE
Glasscock School of Continuing Studies: MARY B. MCINTIRE

PROFESSORS

AAZHANG, B., Electrical and Computer Engineering
AKIN, J. E., Mechanical Engineering
ALCOVER, M., French
ALFORD, J. R., Political Science
AMBLER, J. S., Political Science
ANDERSON, J. B., Earth Science
ANTOULAS, A. C., Electrical and Computer Engineering
ARESU, B., French Studies
ARMENIADES, C. D., Chemical Engineering
ATHANASIOU, A., Bioengineering
AVE-LALLEMANT, H. G., Earth Science
BAGOZZI, R., Management
BAKER, S. D., Physics and Astronomy
BARRON, A., Chemistry
BAYAZITOGLU, Y., Mechanical Engineering and Materials Science
BECKINGHAM, K., Biochemistry and Cell Biology
BEDIENT, P. B., Civil and Environmental Engineering
BENNETT, G., Biochemistry and Cell Biology
BILLUPS, W. E., Chemistry
BLACK, E., Political Science
BOLES, J. B., History
BONNER, B. E., Physics and Astronomy
BOSHERNITZAN, M., Mathematics
BRACE, P., Political Science
BRITO, D. L., Economics
BRODY, B. A., Philosophy
BROKER, K. L., Art and Art History
BROOKS, P. R., Chemistry
BROWN, B. W., Economics and Statistics
BROWN, J. N., Economics
BRYANT, J., Economics
BURRUS, C. S., Electrical and Computer Engineering
BUYSE, L., Music
CAMFIELD, W. A., Art and Art History
CANNADY, W. T., Architecture
CARROLL, M. M., Computational and Applied Mathematics
CARTWRIGHT, R. S., Computer Science
CASBARIAN, J. J., Architecture
CASTAÑEDA, J. A., Hispanic and Classical Studies
CHANCE, J., English
CHAPMAN, W. G., Chemical Engineering
CITRON, M., Music
CLARK, J. W., Jr, Electrical and Computer Engineering
CLOUTIER, P. A., Physics and Astronomy
COCHRAN, T., Mathematics
COOPER, K. D., Computer Science
CORCORAN, M., Physics and Astronomy
COX, D., Statistics
COX, S. G., Philosophy
COX, S. J., Computational and Applied Mathematics
CROWELL, S. G., Philosophy
CURL, R. F., Jr, Chemistry
CUTHBERTSON, G. M., Political Science
DAVIDSON, C., Sociology
DAVIS, P. W., Linguistics
DHARAN, B. G., Management
DIPBOYE, R., Psychology
DOODY, T., English
DRISKILL, L., English
DUCK, I., Physics and Astronomy
DUFOUR, R. J., Physics and Astronomy
DUNHAM, J. F., Music
DUNNING, F. B., Physics and Astronomy
DURRANI, A. J., Civil and Environmental Engineering
EIFLER, M., German and Slavic Studies
EL-GAMAL, M., Economics
ELLISON, P., Music
ENGEL, P. S., Chemistry
ENGELHARDT, T., Philosophy
ENSOR, K. B., Statistics
FARWELL, J., Music
FELLEISEN, M., Computer Science
FEW, A., Physics and Astronomy
FISCHER, N., Music
FISHER, F. M., Jr, Ecology and Evolutionary Biology
FORMAN, R., Mathematics
GEORGE, J., Management
GLANTZ, R. M., Biochemistry and Cell Biology
GLASS, G. P., Chemistry
GOLDMAN, R. N., Computer Science
GOLDSMITH, K., Music
GOMER, R. H., Biochemistry and Cell Biology
GONZÁLEZ-STEPHEN, B., Hispanic and Classical Studies
GORDON, R., Earth Science
GORRY, G. A., Management
GOTTSCHALK, A. W., Music
GOUX, J., French
GRANDY, R. E., Philosophy
GROB, A., English
GRUBER, I. D., History
HALAS, N., Electrical and Computer Engineering
HAMM, K. E., Political Science
HANNON, J. P., Physics and Astronomy
HARCOMBE, P., Ecology and Environmental Biology
HARDT, R. M., Mathematics
HARTLEY, P. R., Economics
HARVEY, F. R., Mathematics
HASKELL, T., History
HEMPEL, J., Mathematics
HIGHTOWER, J. W., Chemical Engineering
HILL, T. W., Physics and Astronomy
HIRASAKI, G., Chemical Engineering
HOLLOWAY, C., Music
HUANG, H. W., Physics and Astronomy
HUFFER, L., French Studies

HUGHES, J. B., Civil and Environmental Engineering
HULET, R., Physics and Astronomy
HUSTON, J. D., English
HUTCHINSON, J. S., Chemistry
IAMMARINO, N., Kinesiology
ISLE, W., English
JOHNSON, D. H., Electrical and Computer Engineering
JONES, B. F., Mathematics
JUMP, J. R., Electrical and Computer Engineering
KANATAS, G., Administrative Science
KAUN, K., Music
KELBER, W. H., Religious Studies
KENNEDY, K. W., Jr, Computer Science
KIMMEL, M., Statistics
KINSEY, J. L., Chemistry
KLEIN, A., Religious Studies
KLINEBERG, S. L., Sociology
KONISKY, J., Biochemistry and Cell Biology
KULSTAD, M., Philosophy
LANE, N., Physics and Astronomy
LEE, B., Anthropology
LEEMAN, W. P., Earth Science
LEVANDA, R. A., Music
LEVANDER, A. R., Earth Science
LIANG, E., Physics and Astronomy
LUCA, S., Music
MCINTIRE, L. V., Chemical Engineering
MCINTOSH, R. J., Anthropology
MCINTOSH, S. K., Anthropology
MCLELLAN, R. B., Materials Science
MANCA, J., Art and Art History
MARCUS, G. E., Anthropology
MARGRAVE, J. L., Chemistry
MARTIN, R. C., Psychology
MARTIN, W. C., Sociology
MATUSOW, A., History
MICHIE, H., English
MIESZKOWSKI, P., Economics
MIETTINEN, H. E., Physics and Astronomy
MIKOS, A., Bioengineering
MILLER, C. A., Chemical Engineering
MORGAN, T. C., Political Science
MORRIS, W. A., English
MORRISON, D. R., Philosophy
MOULIN, H. M., Economics
MUTCHLER, G. S., Physics and Astronomy
NAPIER, H. A., Management
NELSON, D., French Studies
NORDLANDER, P., Physics and Astronomy
ODHIAMBO, A., History
OLSON, J. S., Biochemistry
ORCHARD, M. T., Electrical and Computer Engineering
OSHERSON, D., Psychology
PARKER, J. K., Music
PARRY, R. J., Chemistry
PATTEN, R. L., English
POLKING, J. C., Mathematics
POULOS, B., Art and Art History
QUELLER, D. C., Ecology and Evolutionary Biology
RACHLEFF, L., Music
RAU, C., Physics and Astronomy
REIFF, P., Physics and Astronomy
ROBERT, M., Chemical Engineering
ROBERTS, J. B., Physics and Astronomy
ROJO, J., Statistics
ROUX, R., Music
RUDOLPH, F. B., Biochemistry and Cell Biology
SAN, K. Y., Bioengineering
SASS, R. L., Ecology and Evolutionary Biology
SAWYER, D., Earth Science
SCHNEIDER, D. J., Psychology
SCHNOEBELEN, A. M., Music
SCOTT, D. W., Statistics
SCUSERIA, G., Chemistry
SEED, P., History
SEMMES, S. W., Mathematics
SHER, G., Philosophy
SHIBATANI, M., Linguistics
SICKLES, R., Economics
SKURA, M., English
SMALLEY, R. E., Chemistry
SMITH, G., Art and Art History
SMITH, G. W., Economics
SMITH, R. J., History
SNOW, E. A., English
SOLIGO, R., Economics
SORENSEN, D. C., Computational and Applied Mathematics
SPANOS, P. D., Mechanical Engineering and Materials Science
SPENCE, D. W., Kinesiology
STEIN, R., Political Science
STEVENSON, P. M., Physics and Astronomy
STEWART, C. R., Biochemistry and Cell Biology
STOKES, G., History
STOLL, R. J., Political Science
STRASSMAN, J., Ecology and Evolutionary Biology
STRONG, R., Mathematics
STROUP, J. M., Religious Studies
SYMES, W. W., Computational and Applied Mathematics
TALWANI, M., Earth Science
TAPIA, R. A., Computational and Applied Mathematics
TAYLOR, J., Anthropology
TAYLOR, R. N., Management
TEZDUYAR, T. E., Mechanical Engineering and Materials Science
THOMPSON, E. M., German and Slavic Studies
THOMPSON, J. R., Statistics
TITTEL, F., Electrical and Computer Engineering
TOMSON, M. B., Civil and Environmental Engineering
TOUR, J., Chemistry
TYLER, S. A., Anthropology
UECKER, W. C., Management
VARDI, M. Y., Computer Science
VEECH, W. A., Mathematics
VELETSOS, A. S., Civil and Environmental Engineering
WARD, C. H., Civil and Environmental Engineering
WARREN, J. D., Computer Science
WATKINS, M. J., Psychology
WEISMAN, R. B., Chemistry
WEISSENBERGER, K. H., German and Slavic Studies
WESTBROOK, R. A., Management
WHITAKER, G., Management
WHITMIRE, K. H., Chemistry
WIENER, M. J., History
WIESNER, M., Civil and Environmental Engineering
WILLIAMS, E. E., Management
WILSON, L. J., Chemistry
WILSON, R. K., Political Science
WILSON, W. L., Electrical and Computer Engineering
WINDSOR, D., Management
WINKLER, K., Music
WINNINGHAM, G. L., Art and Art History
WITTENBERG, G., Architecture
WOLF, M., Mathematics
WOLF, R. A., Physics and Astronomy
WOOD, S., English
WYSCHOGROD, E., Religious Studies
YOUNG, J. F., Electrical and Computer Engineering
YUNIS, H., Hispanic and Classical Studies
ZAMMITO, J. H., History
ZEFF, S. A., Management
ZODROW, G., Economics
ZWAENEPOEL, W., Computer Science
ZYGOURAKIS, K., Chemical Engineering

ST EDWARD'S UNIVERSITY

3001 South Congress Ave, Austin, TX 78704
Telephone: (512) 448-8400
Fax: (512) 448-8492
E-mail: seu.admit@admin.stedwards.edu
Internet: www.stedwards.edu

Founded 1885
Academic year: August to May

Pres.: Dr GEORGE E. MARTIN
Exec. Vice-Pres.: Sr DONNA M. JURICK
Vice-Pres. for Financial Affairs: DAVID A. DICKSON, Jr
Vice-Pres. for Information Technology: BILL CAHILL
Vice-Pres. for Marketing: PAIGE BOOTH
Vice-Pres. for Student Affairs: Dr SANDRA PACHECO
Vice-Pres. for Univ. Advancement: MICHAEL LARKIN
Dean of Academic Standing: Dr MOLLY E. MINUS
Dean of Admissions: TRACY MANIER
Dean of Graduate and Adult Services: Dr THOMAS M. EVANS
Dean of Students: LISA KIRKPATRICK
Dir of Student Financial Services: DORIS F. CONSTANTINE
Dir of Campus Min.: Fr RICHARD WILKINSON
Controller: PAUL R. SINTEF
Registrar: Dr LANCE HAYES
Dir of Scarborough-Phillips Library: THOMAS LEONHARDT

Library of 122,403 titles
Number of teachers: 435
Number of students: 4,651

Private, co-educational; four-year liberal arts; graduate courses in business, counselling, computer information science, human services, liberal studies, organizational leadership and ethics; also New College (non-traditional undergraduate courses)

DEANS

School of Behavioural and Social Sciences: BRENDA VALLENCE
School of Business and Management: MARSHA KELLIHER
School of Education: KAREN JENLINK
School of Humanities: Fr LOUIS BRUSATTI
School of Natural Sciences: CHARLES BICAK
New College: Dr RAMSEY FOWLER

ST MARY'S UNIVERSITY OF SAN ANTONIO

San Antonio, TX 78228-8572
Telephone: (210) 436-3011
Fax: (210) 436-3500
Internet: www.stmarytx.edu

Founded 1852
Academic year: August to May

Pres.: Dr CHARLES L. COTRELL
Academic Vice-Pres.: Dr DAVID MANUEL (acting)
Vice-Pres. for Financial Admin.: DAVID SIMPSON
Vice-Pres. for Student Devt: KATHERINE SISOIAN
Vice-Pres. for Univ. Advancement: THOMAS B. GALVIN
Asst to Pres. for Planning: Dr GERARD DIZINNO
Registrar: LOUISA AVITUA-TREVINO
Librarian: H. PALMER HALL

Library of 324,000 vols
Number of students: 4,166

DEANS

School of Business Administration: Dr SUZANNE CORY (acting)
School of Humanities and Social Sciences: Dr JANET B. DIZINNO
School of Science, Engineering and Technology: Dr ANTHONY KAUFMANN
Graduate School: Dr RON MERRELL
Law School: ROBERT WILLIAM PIATT

SCHREINER UNIVERSITY

2100 Memorial Bd, Kerrville, TX 78028
Telephone: (830) 896-5411
Fax: (830) 792-7226
Internet: www.schreiner.edu

Pres.: TIM SUMMERLIN
Provost and Vice-Pres. for Academic Affairs: Dr MICHAEL LOONEY
Vice-Pres. for Admin.: FRED GAMBLE
Vice-Pres. for Advancement and Public Affairs: MARK TUSCHAK
Vice-Pres. for Enrollment and Student Services: PEG LAYTON
Dean of Admissions and Financial Aid: SANDY SPEED

DEANS

Cailloux School of Professional Studies: Prof. JOHN JONES
School of Liberal Arts: Dr JOHN HUDDLESTON
The Trull School of Science and Mathematics: Dr DIANA COMUZZIE

SEMINARY OF THE SOUTHWEST

POB 2247, Austin, TX 78768
501 East 32nd, Austin, TX 78705
Telephone: (512) 472-4133
Fax: (512) 472-3098
E-mail: seminary@etss.edu
Internet: www.etss.edu

Pres. and Dean: Very Rev. Dr DOUGLAS TRAVIS
Vice-Pres. of Admin.: JOHN BENNET WATERS
Vice-Pres. of Devt: NANCY SPRINGER-BALDWIN.

SOUTH TEXAS COLLEGE OF LAW

1303 San Jacinto St, Houston, TX 77002
Telephone: (713) 659-8040
Fax: (713) 646-2909
Internet: www.stcl.edu

Library of 400,000 vols

Pres. and Dean: DONALD J. GUTER.

SOUTHERN METHODIST UNIVERSITY

6425 Boaz, Dallas, TX 75275
Telephone: (214) 768-2000
Fax: (214) 768-1001
E-mail: enrol_serv@mail.smu.edu
Internet: www.smu.edu

Founded 1911
Language of instruction: English
Academic year: August to May

Pres.: Dr R. GERALD TURNER
Provost: Dr ROSS C. MURFIN
Vice-Pres. for Business and Finance, and Treas.: Dr MORGAN OLSEN
Vice-Pres. for Devt and External Affairs: JEANNE WHITMAN
Vice-Pres. for Exec. Affairs: Dr THOMAS BARRY
Vice-Pres. for Legal Affairs and Govt Relations, Gen. Counsel and Univ. Sec.: S. LEON BENNETT
Vice-Pres. for Student Affairs: Dr JAMES E. CASWELL
Admissions: RON MOSS
Registrar: JOHN A. HALL
Library of 4,111,460 vols
Number of teachers: 732 (520 full-time, 212 part-time)
Number of students: 10,266
Publications: *Journal of Air Law and Commerce* (4 a year), *SMU Law Review* (4 a year), *Southwest Review* (4 a year), *The International Lawyer* (4 a year)

DEANS

Arts: Dr CAROLE BRANDT
Business: Dr ALBERT W. NIEMI, Jr
Engineering: Dr STEPHEN SZYGENDA
Law: JOHN B. ATTANASIO
Theology: Dr ROBIN W. LOVIN
Dedman College: Dr JASPER NEEL

SOUTHWESTERN ADVENTIST UNIVERSITY

POB 567, Keene, TX 76059-0567
100 W Hillcrest, Keene, TX 76059
Telephone: (817) 645-3921
Fax: (817) 556-4744
E-mail: admissions@swau.edu
Internet: www.swau.edu

Pres.: ERIC ANDERSON
Sec. to the Pres.: DICKIE MARTIN
Vice-Pres. for Academics: Dr TOM BUNCH
Vice-Pres. for Finance: LARRY GARRETT
Vice-Pres. for Student Services: DAVID KNIGHT.

SOUTHWESTERN ASSEMBLIES OF GOD UNIVERSITY

1200 Sycamore St, Waxahachie, TX 75165
Telephone: (972) 937-4010
Fax: (972) 923-0488
E-mail: info@sagu.edu
Internet: www.sagu.edu

Pres.: KERMIT S. BRIDGES
Vice-Pres. for Academics: PAUL BROOKS
Vice-Pres. for Student Services: TERRY PHIPPS
Asst to the Pres.: EDDIE DAVIS.

SOUTHWESTERN BAPTIST THEOLOGICAL SEMINARY

POB 22000, Fort Worth, TX 76122
2001 W Seminary Drive, Fort Worth, TX 76115
Telephone: (817) 923-1921
Fax: (817) 921-8761
Internet: www.swbts.edu

Founded 1908

Pres.: PAIGE PATTERSON
Exec. Vice-Pres. and Provost: CRAIG BLAISING
Vice-Pres. for Business Affairs: HUBERT MARTIN
Vice-Pres. for Institutional Advancement: JACK TERRY
Vice-Pres. for Student Services: RUDY GONZALEZ

Publication: *Southwestern Journal of Theology* (4 a year).

SOUTHWESTERN CHRISTIAN COLLEGE

200 Bowser Circle, Terrell, TX 75160
Telephone: (972) 524-3341 ext. 142
Fax: (972) 563-7133
Internet: www.swcc.edu
Private control
Academic year: August to May

Pres.: Dr JACK EVANS, Sr
Vice-Pres. of Academic Affairs: ZOAANN TURNER
Vice-Pres. of Fiscal Affairs: DOUGLAS HOWIE
Vice-Pres. for Institutional Advancement: Dr JAMES MAXWELL
Vice-Pres. of Student Affairs: Dr BEN FOSTER
Comptroller: JOYCE CATHEY
Asst to the Pres. for Devt: GERALD LEE
Librarian: DORIS JOHNSON

Library of 30,870 books, 158 periodicals
Number of teachers: 21
Number of students: 220

SOUTHWESTERN UNIVERSITY

Telephone: (512) 863-6511
Fax: (512) 863-5788
Internet: www.southwestern.edu

Founded 1873 by merging of Rutersville College (chartered 1840), Wesleyan College (1844), McKenzie College (1848), and Soule Univ. (1856)
Academic year: August to May

Pres.: JAKE B. SCHRUM
Vice-Pres. for Enrollment Services: THOMAS J. OLIVER
Vice-Pres. for Fiscal Affairs: RICHARD L. ANDERSON
Vice-Pres. for Institutional Advancement: C. RICHARD MCKELVEY
Assoc. Vice-Pres. for Univ. Relations: CINDY LOCKE
Provost and Dean of the Faculty: JAMES W. HUNT
Dean of the Sarofin School of Fine Arts: Dr PAUL GAFFNEY
Registrar: DAVID STONES
Dean of Library Services: LYNNE M. BRODY
Library of 292,756 vols
Number of teachers: 116
Number of students: 1,309
Publications: *Bulletin* (12 a year), *The Megaphone* (52 a year), *Southwestern Magazine* (4 a year), *The Sou' Wester* (1 a year).

STEPHEN F. AUSTIN STATE UNIVERSITY

1936 North St, Nacogdoches, TX 75962
Telephone: (936) 468-2011
Internet: www.sfasu.edu

Founded 1923

Pres.: Dr BAKER PATTILLO
Provost and Vice-Pres. for Academic Affairs: Dr RICHARD BERRY
Vice-Pres. for Finance and Admin.: DANNY GALLANT
Vice-Pres. for Univ. Affairs: STEVE WESTBROOK
Vice-Pres. for Univ. Devt: Dr JOHN LEWIS
Library Dir: ALVIN CAGE
Library of 1,465,322 vols
Number of teachers: 599
Number of students: 12,500 full-time

DEANS

College of Applied Arts and Sciences: JAMES STANDLEY
College of Business: MARLIN YOUNG
College of Education: THOMAS FRANKS
College of Fine Arts: RON JONES
College of Forestry: SCOTT BEASLEY
College of Liberal Arts: JIM SPEER (acting)
College of Sciences and Mathematics: THOMAS ATCHISON

TEXAS A&M UNIVERSITY SYSTEM

200 Technology Way, Suite 2043, College Station, TX 77845
Telephone: (979) 458-6023
Fax: (979) 458-6025
E-mail: syscomm@tamu.edu
Internet: www.tamus.edu

Founded 1876
Academic year: September to August

Chancellor: Dr BARRY B. THOMPSON
Deputy Chancellor for Academic Institutions and Agencies: Dr LEO SAYAVEDRA
Deputy Chancellor for Finance and Operations: RICHARD LINDSAY
Vice-Chancellor for Agriculture: Dr EDWARD HILER
Vice-Chancellor for Business Services: TOM KALE
Vice-Chancellor for Engineering: Dr C. ROLAND HADEN
Vice-Chancellor for Facilities Planning and Construction: Gen. WESLEY PEEL

Vice-Chancellor for Research, Planning and Continuing Education: Dr J. CHARLES LEE.

CONSTITUENT UNIVERSITIES

Prairie View A&M University

POB 519, Prairie View, TX 77446-0519
FM 1098 Rd and University Dr., Prairie View, TX 77446
Telephone: (936) 261-3311
Fax: (409) 857-3928
Internet: www.pvamu.edu
Founded 1876, univ. status 1973
Pres.: GEORGE C. WRIGHT
Registrar: ROBERT FORD
Provost and Vice-Pres. for Academic Affairs: FLOSSIE M. BYRD
Vice-Pres. for Admin. and Finance: HAROLD S. BONNER
Vice-Pres. for Student Affairs: JILES P. DANIELS
Dir of Institutional Devt: HARVEY G. DICKERSON
Dir for Library: DUDLEY YATES
Dir for Public Information Services: BRYAN BARROWS
Library of 260,000 vols
Number of teachers: 315
Number of students: 5,600

DEANS

Banneker Honors College: JEWEL L. PRESTAGE
College of Applied Sciences and Engineering Technology: HAKUMAT ISRANI
College of Arts and Sciences: EDWARD W. MARTIN
College of Business: BARBARA A. JONES
College of Education: M. PAUL MEHTA
College of Engineering and Architecture: JOHN FOSTER
College of Nursing: DOLLIE BRATHWAITE
Graduate School: WILLIE F. TROTTY

Tarleton State University

Stephenville, TX 76402
Telephone: (254) 968-9000
Fax: (254) 968-9920
E-mail: info@tarleton.edu
Internet: www.tarleton.edu
Founded 1899, Univ. 1973
Academic year: September to August
Pres.: Dr F. DOMINIC DOTTAVIO
Provost and Vice-Pres. for Academic Affairs (vacant)
Vice-Pres. for Finance and Admin.: JERRY GRAHAM
Vice-Pres. for Student Services: RUSTY JERGINS
Vice-Pres. for Enrollment and Information Management: Dr BRAD CHILTON
Exec. Dir for TIAER: DAN HUNTER
Dir for Admissions: CYNTHIA HESS
Registrar: DENISE GROVES
Librarian: DONNA SAVAGE
Library: 1m. items
Number of teachers: 942
Number of students: 9,465

DEANS

College of Agriculture and Human Sciences: Dr DON CAWTHON
College of Business Administration: Dr ADOLFO BENEVIDAS
College of Education: Dr JILL BURK
College of Graduate Studies: Dr LINDA JONES
College of Liberal and Fine Arts: Dr DEAN MINIX
College of Science and Technology: Dr JAMES PIERCE

Texas A&M International University

5201 University Blvd, Laredo, TX 78041-1900
Telephone: (956) 326-2001
Fax: (956) 326-2346
Internet: www.tamiu.edu
Founded 1969 as part of Texas A&I Univ.
State control
Languages of instruction: English, Spanish
Academic year: August to DecemberJanuary to MayMay to August (3 semesters)
Upper level college, junior, senior and graduate courses
Pres.: Dr RAY M. KECK
Dir for Admissions: ROSIE A. DICKINSON
Vice-Pres. for Academic Affairs and Provost: Dr PABLO ARENAZ
Vice-Pres. for Finance and Admin.: JUAN J. CASTILLO
Vice-Pres. for Institutional Advancement: CANDY WEIN
Dean of Student Affairs: Dr MINITA RAMÍREZ
Registrar: OSCAR REYNA
Librarian: RODNEY WEBB
Library of 259,086 vols, 1,079,218 microfiche and microfilm and over 51,298 state and fed. documents, 1,464 print subscriptions and approximately 28,895 e-journals, 46,000 e-books
Number of teachers: 185
Number of students: 6,100
Publications: *International Trade Journal*, *Journal of Border Education Research*, *Journal of Social and Ecological Boundaries*, *Western Hemispheric Trade Digest*

DEANS

A. R. Sanchez, Jr School of Business Admin.: Dr STEVEN SEARS
College of Arts and Sciences: Dr TOM MITCHELL
College of Education: Dr HUMBERTO GONZÁLEZ
College of Nursing and Health Sciences: Dr REGINA AUNE

Texas A&M University

College Station, TX 77843
Telephone: (979) 845-3211
Internet: www.tamu.edu
Founded 1876, univ. status 1963
Pres.: Dr R. BOWEN LOFTIN
Provost and Exec. Vice-Pres. for Academic Affairs: Dr KARAN L. WATSON
Vice-Pres. for Administration: Dr RODNEY P. MCCLENDON
Vice-Pres. and Assoc. Provost for Diversity: Dr CHRISTINE A. STANLEY
Vice-Pres. for Finance and Admin.: TERRY SPANG
Vice-Pres. for Global Initiatives: ERIC BOST
Vice-Pres. for Govt Relations: MICHAEL G. O'QUINN
Vice-Pres. for Information Technology: Dr PIERCE E. CANTRELL, Jr
Vice-Pres. for Marketing and Communications: JASON D. COOK
Vice-Pres. for Research and Graduate Studies: Dr JEFFREY R. SEEMANN
Vice-Pres. for Student Affairs: Lt-Gen. JOSEPH F. WEBER
Dean of Univ. Libraries: Dr CHARLES GILREATH
Library: 2.5m. vols
Number of teachers: 2,900
Number of students: 49,000

DEANS

College of Agriculture and Life Sciences: Dr MARK HUSSEY
College of Architecture: Prof. JORGE VANEGAS
College of Education and Human Devt: Dr DOUGLAS J. PALMER
College of Geosciences: Dr KATE C. MILLER
Bush School of Govt and Public Service: RYAN C. CROCKER
College of Liberal Arts: Dr JOSÉ LUIS BERMÚDEZ Jr
College of Medicine: Dr T. SAM SHOMAKER
College of Science: Dr H. JOSEPH NEWTON
College of Veterinary Medicine and Biomedical Sciences: Dr ELEANOR M. GREEN
Dwight Look College of Engineering: Dr G. KEMBLE BENNETT
Mays Business School: Dr JERRY R. STRAWSER

Texas A&M University—Commerce

POB 3011, Commerce, TX 75429
Telephone: (903) 886-5014
Internet: www.tamu-commerce.edu
Founded 1889
Pres.: DAN R. JONES
Vice-Pres. for Academic Affairs: Dr DONNA ARLTON
Vice-Pres. for Student and Univ. Services: GENE LOCKHART
Library: 2m. vols and microfilms
Number of teachers: 450 full-time
Number of students: 8,900

Texas A&M University—Corpus Christi

6300 Ocean Dr., Corpus Christi, TX 78412
Telephone: (361) 825-5700
Fax: (361) 825-5810
Internet: www.tamucc.edu
Founded 1971, part of Univ. System of South Texas since 1989
State control
Academic year: August to DecemberJanuary to MayJune to August
Pres.: Dr FLAVIUS KILLEBREW
Vice-Pres.: Dr ANANTHA BABBILI
Provost/Vice-Pres. for Academic Affairs: SANDRA S. HARPER
Exec. Vice-Pres. for Finance and Admin.: JODI NELSEN
Vice-Pres. for Institutional Advancement: S. TRENT HILL
Librarian: CHRISTINE SHUPALA

DEANS

Business Administration: MOUSTAFA ABDELSAMAD
Liberal Arts: KELLY QUINTANILLA
Science and Technology: FRANK PEZOLD
Teacher Education: ART HERNANDEZ

Texas A&M University - Galveston

POB 1675, Galveston, TX 77553-1675
Telephone: (409) 740-4403
Fax: (409) 740-5005
Internet: www.tamug.edu
Pres.: Dr R. BOWEN LOFTIN
Vice-Pres. for Research and Academic Affairs: Dr JAMES M. MCCLOY
Vice-Pres. for Student Affairs and Admin.: WILLIAM C. HEARN.

Texas A&M University—Kingsville

700 University Blvd, MSC101, Kingsville, TX 78363
Telephone: (361) 593-2111
Internet: www.tamuk.edu
Founded 1917 as South Texas Normal School; name changed to South Texas State Teachers' College in 1923, to Texas College of Arts and Industries in 1929, to Texas A&I University by law in 1967, and to Texas A&M Univ.—Kingsville in 1993
Pres.: RUMALDO Z. JUAREZ
Vice-Pres. for Academic Affairs and Provost: KAY CLAYTON
Vice-Pres. for Finance and Admin.: STEVE CRANDALL

Vice-Pres. for Institutional Advancement: J. RANDY HUGHES
Vice-Pres. for Student Affairs: TOM JACKSON, Jr
Dir of Research: SANDRA REXROAT
Dir of Continuing Education: TADEO REYNA
Registrar: MAGGIE WILLIAMS
Librarian: GILDEO B. ORTEGO

Library of 748,000 vols, 2,122 periodicals
Number of teachers: 329
Number of students: 5,876

DEANS

Agriculture: RON ROSATI
Arts and Sciences: RONN HY
Business Administration: ROBERT DIERSING
Education: MIKE DANIEL
Engineering: WILLIAM HEENAN
Graduate Studies: ALBERTO M. OLIVARES
King Ranch Institute of Range Management: BARRY DUNN
Pharmacy: INDRA REDDY
University College: GLADYS HINES

ATTACHED INSTITUTES

Caesar Kleberg Wildlife Research Institute: Kingsville, Texas; Dir Dr FRED BRYANT.

System Center: Palo Alto, San Antonio, Texas; Dir GARRY ROSS.

Texas A&M University Kingsville Citrus Center: Weslaco, Texas; Dir JOHN DA GRACA.

Texas A&M University System Health Science Center

MS 1361, John B. Connally Bldg, 301 Tarrow, College Station, TX 77840-7896
Telephone: (979) 458-7200
Fax: (979) 458-7202
E-mail: hsccomm@tamu.edu
Internet: tamushsc.tamu.edu

Pres.: Dr NANCY W. DICKEY
Exec. Vice-Pres.: Dr ELVIN E. SMITH
Vice-Pres. for Academic Affairs: Dr WILLIAM H. BINNIE
Vice-Pres. of Finance and Admin.: Dr BARRY C. NELSON
Vice-Pres. for Governmental Affairs: Dr LAURA R. SMITH
Vice-Pres. for Research and Graduate Studies: Dr DAVID S. CARLSON
Dir for Medical Sciences Library: MARTHA BEDARD

DEANS

Baylor College of Dentistry: Dr JAMES S. COLE
Coastal Bend Health Education Center: Dr JUAN F. CASTRO (Dir)
College of Medicine
Institute of Biosciences and Technology: Dr RICHARD H. FINNELL (Dir)
School of Rural Public Health: Dr CIRO V. SUMAYA

Texas A&M University – Texarkana

2600 N Robison Rd, Texarkana, TX 75501
Internet: www.tamut.edu

Founded 1971 as E Texas State Univ. at Texarkana; joined Texas A&M Univ. System 1996
Academic year: August to May

Pres.: Dr C. B. (BIX) RATHBURN

Number of teachers: 53 full-time
Number of students: 1,738

DEANS

College of Arts and Sciences, and Education: Dr GLENDA BALLARD
College of Business: Dr ED BASHAW
College of Health and Behavioral Sciences: Dr JO KAHLER
Department of Nursing: Dr JO KAHLER (Dir)

West Texas A&M University

WTAMU, POB 61001, Canyon, TX 79016-0001
Telephone: (806) 651-0000
Fax: (806) 651-2126
E-mail: cbarnes@wtamu.edu
Internet: www.wtamu.edu

Founded 1920
Academic year: August to May

Pres.: Dr J. PATRICK O'BRIEN
Provost and Vice-Pres. for Academic Affairs: Dr JAMES HALLMARK

Library of 1,086,936 vols
Number of teachers: 301
Number of students: 7,535

TEXAS CHIROPRACTIC COLLEGE

5912 Spencer Highway, Pasadena, TX 77505-1170
Telephone: (281) 487-1170
Fax: (281) 991-4871
Internet: www.txchiro.edu

Founded 1908

Pres.: Dr RICHARD G. BRASSARD

Number of teachers: 36
Number of students: 517

TEXAS CHRISTIAN UNIVERSITY

2800 S University Dr., Fort Worth, TX 76129
Telephone: (817) 257-7000
Fax: (817) 257-7333
E-mail: frogmail@tcu.edu
Internet: www.tcu.edu

Founded 1873
Private control
Academic year: September to May

Chancellor: VICTOR BOSCHINI, Jr
Provost and Vice-Chancellor for Academic Affairs: R. NOWELL DONOVAN
Vice-Chancellor for Finance and Administration: BRIAN GUTIERREZ
Vice-Chancellor for Student Affairs: DONALD B. MILLS
Vice-Chancellor for Univ. Advancement: DONALD WHELAN
Registrar: PATRICK MILLER
Librarian: JUNE KOELKER

Library of 2,206,698 vols, incl. 69,078 periodicals titles
Number of teachers: 609
Number of students: 8,700

DEANS

Addran College of Liberal Arts: ANDREW SCHOOLMASTER
College of Communication: DAVID WHILLOCK
College of Education: MARY MARTIN PATTON
College of Fine Arts: SCOTT A. SULLIVAN
College of Science and Engineering: DEMITRIS KOURIS
Harris College of Nursing & Health Sciences: PAULETTE BURNS
John V. Roach Honors College: PEGGY WATSON
M. J. Neeley School of Business: O. HOMER EREKSON

TEXAS COLLEGE

2404 North Grand Avenue, Tyler, TX 75702
Telephone: (903) 593-8311
Internet: www.texascollege.edu

Founded 1894
Academic year: August to May

Pres.: DWIGHT J. FENNELL
Vice-Pres. for Academic Affairs: Dr JEAN FITTS
Vice-Pres. for Business and Finance: JAMES HARRIS
Vice-Pres. for Student Affairs: Dr NEVILLE MORGAN

Number of teachers: 63
Number of students: 740

TEXAS LUTHERAN UNIVERSITY

1000 W Court St, Seguin, TX 78155
Telephone: (830) 372-8000
Fax: (830) 372-8096
E-mail: admissions@tlu.edu
Internet: www.tlu.edu

Founded 1891

A church-related, co-educational, liberal arts, undergraduate college with programmes in business admin., computer science, health-related fields, teacher education

Pres.: ANN M. SVENNUNGSEN
Academic Dean: Dr LEONARD G. SCHULZE
Registrar: KRISTIN PLAEHIN
Librarian: PATRICK HSU

Library of 151,402 vols
Number of teachers: 77 (full-time)
Number of students: 1,400

TEXAS SOUTHERN UNIVERSITY

3100 Cleburne Ave, Houston, TX 77004
Telephone: (713) 313-7011
Fax: (713) 313-1092
Internet: www.tsu.edu

Founded 1947
State control
Academic year: September to August

Pres.: Dr PRISCILLA SLADE
Exec. Vice-Pres.: Dr CHARLENE EVANS
Provost/Vice-Pres. for Academic Affairs: Dr BOBBY WILSON
Sr Vice-Pres. for Admin.: BRUCE WILSON
Sr Vice-Pres. for Business and Finance: QUINTIN WIGGINS
Sr Vice-Pres. for Enrollment Management and Planning: Dr GAYLA THOMAS
Vice-Pres. for Architectural Engineering and Construction Services: WILLIAM BECKHAM
Registrar: NORMA ROBINSON
Dir of Libraries: Dr OBIDIKE KAMAU

Library: Libraries with 729,568 vols
Number of teachers: 509
Number of students: 10,567

Publications: *Ex-Press* (4 a year), *Inside TSU* (12 a year), *Urban Notebook* (4 a year)

DEANS

School of Business: Dr JOSEPH BOYD
School of Education: Dr JAY CUMMINGS
School of Law: McKEN CARRINGTON
School of Public Affairs: Dr ANTHONY WOODS
School of Science and Technology: Dr MITCHELL ALLEN
Graduate School: Dr RICHARD PITRE
College of Liberal Arts and Behavioural Sciences: Dr MERLINE PITRE
College of Pharmacy and Health Sciences: Dr BARBARA HAYES

TEXAS STATE UNIVERSITY SYSTEM

Thomas J. Rusk Bldg, 200 E 10th St, Suite 600, Austin, TX 78701-2407
Telephone: (512) 463-1808
Fax: (512) 463-1816
E-mail: chancellor@tsus.edu
Internet: www.tsus.edu

Number of students: 70,000 at 9 univs and colleges

Chancellor: CHARLES R. MATTHEWS.

CONSTITUENT UNIVERSITIES

Angelo State University

POB 11007, ASU Station, San Angelo, TX 76909-1007

Telephone: (325) 942-2073
Fax: (325) 942-2038
Internet: www.angelo.edu

Founded 1928
State control
Language of instruction: English
Academic year: September to August

Pres.: Dr JOSEPH C. RALLO
Provost and Vice-Pres. for Academic Affairs: Dr ANTHONY P. BLOSE
Vice-Pres. for Finance and Admin.: SHARON MEYER
Vice-Pres. for Strategy, Planning and Policy: Dr JAMES M. LIMBAUGH
Dir of Admissions: STEVE KLEIN
Dir of Athletics: KATHLEEN L. BRASFIELD
Dir of Communications and Marketing: PRESTON LEWIS
Dir of Devt: Dr JASON PENRY
Dir of Financial Aid: MICHELLE BENNETT
Registrar: CYNTHIA D. WEEAKS
Librarian: Dr MAURICE G. FORTIN

Library of 1,705,900 items
Number of teachers: 321
Number of students: 6,387

DEANS

Business: Dr CORBETT F. GAULDEN, Jr
Education: Dr JOHN J. MIAZGA, Jr
Graduate Studies: Dr BRIAN J. MAY
Liberal and Fine Arts: Dr KEVIN J. LAMBERT
Nursing and Allied Health: Dr LESLIE M. MAYRAND
Sciences: Dr GRADY PRICE BLOUNT

Lamar University

POB 10001, Beaumont, TX 77710

Telephone: (409) 880-7011
Fax: (409) 880-8404
Internet: www.lamar.edu

Founded 1923 as South Park Junior College

Chancellor: LAMAR URBANOVSKY
Pres.: Dr JAMES M. SIMMONS
Exec. Vice-Pres. for Academic Affairs: Dr STEPHEN DOBLIN
Vice-Pres. for Finance and Operations: ROBERT LOVITT
Registrar: KEITH CAPPS
Dir of Library: LINDA DUGGER

Library of 964,543 vols
Number of teachers: 507
Number of students: 8,235

DEANS

Graduate Studies: Dr JERRY BRADLEY
College of Arts and Sciences: Dr BRENDA NICHOLS
College of Business: (vacant)
College of Education: Dr CARL WESTERFIELD
College of Engineering: Dr JACK HOPPER
College of Fine and Applied Arts: Dr RUSS SCHULTZ

Sam Houston State University

POB 2026, Huntsville, TX 77341

Telephone: (409) 294-1111
E-mail: adm_smm@shsu.edu
Internet: www.shsu.edu

Founded 1879 as Sam Houston Normal Institute

Academic year: August to May

Pres.: JAMES F. GAETNER
Vice-Pres. for Academic Affairs: DAVID E. PAYNE
Vice-Pres. for Finance: JACK PARKER
Vice-Pres. for Student Services: THELMA DOUGLASS
Vice-Pres. for Univ. Advancement: FRANK HOLMES
Dir of Admissions: JOEY CHANDLER
Registrar: ROBERT DUNNING
Dir of Libraries: ANN HOLDER

Library of 1,379,682 vols, 3,556 periodicals, 1,379,682 microforms, 629,489 records and tapes
Number of teachers: 551
Number of students: 13,091

Publications: *Advancing Women in Leadership*, *Crime and Justice International*, *Ed Leadership Review*, *Journal of Business Strategies*, *Texas Review* (2 a year), *The Texas Crime Pole*

DEANS

College of Arts and Sciences: BRIAN CHAPMAN
College of Business Administration: R. DEAN LEWIS
College of Criminal Justice: RICHARD WARD
College of Education and Applied Science: GENEVIEVE BROWN

Sul Ross State University

Alpine, TX 79832

Telephone: (432) 837-8032
Fax: (432) 837-8334
E-mail: rvmorgan@sulross.edu
Internet: www.sulross.edu

Founded 1917
Academic year: September to August

Pres.: Dr R. VIC MORGAN, Jr
Vice-Pres. for Academic Affairs: Dr DAVE COCKRUM
Vice-Pres. for Enrollment Management and Student Services: Dr NADINE F. JENKINS
Librarian: DON DOWDY

Library of 760,700 vols
Number of teachers: 117
Number of students: 3,144

DEANS

Agricultural and Natural Resource Sciences: Dr ROB KINUCAN
Arts and Sciences: (vacant)
Professional Studies: Dr CHET SAMPLE
Rio Grande College: Dr FRANK ABBOTT

ATTACHED COLLEGE

Rio Grande College: 205 Wildcat Dr., Del Rio, TX 78840; tel. (830) 703-4832; internet rgc.sulross.edu; Vice-Pres. Dr JOEL E. VELA; 3 campuses located at Del Rio, Eagle Pass and Uvalde.

Texas State University–San Marcos

601 University Dr., JCK 883, San Marcos, TX 78666

Telephone: (512) 245-2386
Fax: (512) 245-8446
Internet: www.txstate.edu

Founded 1899
State control
Academic year: August to May
Language of instruction: English

Pres.: Dr DENISE TRAUTH
Provost and Vice-Pres. for Academic Affairs: Dr PERRY MOORE
Vice-Pres. for Finance and Support Services: BILL NANCE
Vice-Pres. for Information Technology: Dr CARL VAN WYATT
Vice-Pres. for Student Affairs: Dr JOANN SMITH (acting)
Vice-Pres. for Univ. Advancement: TED MCKINNON (acting)
Dir of Alumni Relations: KIM GANNON
Librarian: JOAN HEATH

Library of 1,543,562 vols, 1,353,581 microforms, 14,764 serials, 276,062 audiovisual items, 227,959 ebooks
Number of teachers: 1,546
Number of students: 32,572

Publications: *Electronic Journal of Differential Equations*, *Persona* (student literary journal, 1 a year), *Southwestern American Literature* (2 a year), *Texas Books in Review* (4 a year), *The Journal of Texas Music History* (2 a year)

DEANS

College of Applied Arts: Dr JAIME CHAHIN
College of Business: Dr DENISE SMART
College of Education: Dr STAN CARPENTER
College of Fine Arts: Dr RICHARD CHEATHAM
College of Health Professions: Dr RUTH WELBORN
College of Liberal Arts: Dr MICHAEL HENNESSY
College of Science: Dr STEPHEN SEIDMAN
Graduate College: Dr J. MICHAEL WILLOUGHBY
University College: Dr RONALD C. BROWN

PROFESSORS

ABBASIAN, R., Mathematics
ALI, M., Computer Science
ALLEN, J., Consumer Science
ANDREWS, G., History
ANGIRASSA, A., Agribusiness
ARCHER, R., Psychology
ARON, G., Biology
AUGUSTIN, B., Geography
BACCUS, J., Biology
BALANOFF, H., Political Science
BANDY, C., Mathematics
BECK, J., Education Administration
BEEBE, S., Communication Studies
BELL, J., Management
BELL-METEREAU, R., English
BIBLE, J., Business Law
BLAIR, J., English
BLANCHARD-BOEHM, D., Geography
BLANDA, M., Chemistry and Biochemistry
BLANKMEYER, E., Economics
BOEHM, R., Geography
BOONE, M., Education Administration
BURKE, G., Health Administration
BUTLER, D., Geography
BYNUM, V., History
CASSIDY, P., Chemistry and Biochemistry
CAVERLY, D., Curriculum and Instruction
CHAMPION, J., Spanish
CHATFIELD, J., Mathematics
CHAVKIN, A., English
CHAVKIN, N., Social Work
CHIODO, B., Management
COHEN, P., English
COOK, J., Computer Information Systems
DAVIS, J., Psychology
DAVIS, W., Computer Science
DAY, F., Geography
DAY, S., Sociology
DE LA TEJA, J., History
DIX, J., Mathematics
DOLEZAL, C., Curriculum and Instruction
DONNELLY, D., Physics
ECHEVERRIA, M., Spanish
EDGELL, J., Mathematics
EIKNER, E., Accounting
ESTAVILLE, L., Geography
FITE, K., Curriculum and Instruction
FLAHERTY, D., Accounting
FLAMMANG, R., Economics
FLING, S., Psychology
FORREST, J., French
FRIEDMAN, B. J., Nutrition and Foods
FULMER, G., Philosophy
FURNEY, S., Health Education
GARBER, J., Anthropology
GAROFALO, C., Political Science
GEURAS, D., Philosophy
GILLIS, M., Curriculum and Instruction
GINSBURG, H., Psychology
GLASSMAN, D., Anthropology
GORDAN, S., Educational Administration

GORDON, J., Philosophy
GORMAN, R., Political Science
GOWENS, P., Economics
GRASSO, K., Political Science
GRAYSON, N., English
GREEN, D., Respiratory Care
GROSS, D., English
GU, W., Mathematics
GUTIERREZ, C., Physics
HABINGREITHER, R., Technology
HATCHER, B., Curriculum and Instruction
HAWKINS, C., Social Work
HAZELWOOD, D., Mathematics
HEABERLIN, D., English
HENNESSY, M., English
HILL, J., English
HOFER, M., Political Science
HOLT, E., English
HORNE, F., Biology
HUFFMAN, D., Biology
HULING, L., Curriculum and Instruction
HUMPHREY, J., Accounting
HUNNICUTT, G., Management
HUSTON, M., Biology
HUTCHESON, P., Philosophy
INGRAM, A., English
JAFFE, C., Spanish
JAGER, R., History
JAMES, S. G., Health Education
JAMIESON, J., Criminal Justice
JIA, X.-D., Mathematics
JOHNSON, M., Physical Education
JOHNSTON, W., Computer Information Systems
JORGENSON, C., School Psychology
JOY, G., Philosophy
KENS, P., Political Science
KISHAN, R., Economics
KOKE, J., Biology
LAIRD, E., English
LARSEN, R., Geography
LEDER, P., English
LEMKE, D., Biology
LOCHMAN, D., English
LONGLEY, G., Biology
MCGEE, JOHN, Business Law
MCGEE, JON, Anthropology
MANDZIUK, R., Communication Studies
MARGERISON, K., History
MARTIN, G., Curriculum and Instruction
MARTIN, R., Computer Information Systems
MEIXNER, W., Accounting
MELZER, B., Physical Therapy
MENDEZ, R., Psychology
MICHALK, V., Physics
MIDDLEBROOK, B., Management
MIJARES, T., Criminal Justice
MINIFIE, J., Management
MOGAB, J., Economics
MONROE, D., English
MONTODON, L., Accounting
MURRAY, T., Physical Education
NEELY, J., Music
NELSON, D., Mass Communication
NEWSOM, R., Sociology
NIELSON, E., Art and Design
NOWICKI, M., Health Administration
OGLETREE, S., Psychology
OLNEY, R., Management
OLSON, D., Physics
OLSON, M., English
OPHEIM, C., Political Science
PAESE, P., Physical Education
PANKEY, R., Physical Education
PARKIN, D., English
PASCOE, C., Theatre
PASSTY, G., Mathematics
PEIRCE, K., Mass Communication
PETERSEN, J., Geography
PETOFF, P., Respiratory Care
PINO, D., Music
POHL, J., History
POLLOCK, J., Criminal Justice
RAHE, H., Agriculture
RANSOME, J., Physical Education
RENFRO, P., Mass Communication
RIEPE, R., Music
RONAN, C., English
ROSSMO, K., Criminal Justice
RUDZINSKI, W., Chemistry and Biochemistry
SALEM, P., Communication Studies
SHAH, V., Computer Information Systems
SINGH, S., Mathematics
SKERPAN-WHEELER, E., English
SMITH, B., Mass Communication
SODDERS, R., Theatre
SPELLMANN, J., Mathematics
STEA, D., Geography
STEPHENSON, S., Quantitative Methods
STIMMEL, D., Psychology
STONE, W., Criminal Justice
STOUFFER, W., Political Science
STUTTS, M., Marketing
STUTZMAN, J., Finance
SULLIVAN, A., Political Science
SUMMERS, J., Health Administration
TAYLOR, R., Marketing
THICKSTUN, T., Mathematics
THOMAS, N., Music
TORREJON, R., Mathematics
UGALDE, S., Spanish
WAITE, D., Educational Administration
WALTER, R., Chemistry and Biochemistry
WANG, C. J., Computer Science
WARMS, R., Anthropology
WARSHAUER, M., Mathematics
WATKINS, T., Social Work
WAYMAN, M., Criminal Justice
WEBBER, J. A., Curriculum and Instruction
WEINBERGER, G., Political Science
WELSH, S., Mathematics
WHEELER, L., Curriculum and Instruction
WHEELER, R., Psychology
WILLIAMS, M. L., Communication Studies
WILLIAMSON, P., Biology
WILSON, J., History
WINEK, G., Technology
WINKING, K., Music
WOOSLEY, T., Music
WRIGHT, L., Psychology
YAGER, B., Chemistry and Biochemistry
YICK, J., History

Other constituent institutions awarding Associate-level degrees include: Lamar Institute of Technology, Lamar State College-Orange and Lamar State College-Port Arthur.

TEXAS TECH UNIVERSITY

Box 42005, Lubbock, TX 79409-2005
Telephone: (806) 742-2121
Internet: www.ttu.edu

Founded 1923

Pres.: DAVID J. SCHMIDLY
Registrar: DON WICKARD
Dir of Libraries: E. DALE CLUFF

Library of 1,614,148 vols
Number of teachers: 1,574
Number of students: 24,007

DEANS

College of Agricultural Sciences and Natural Resources: Dr JOHN ABERNATHY
College of Architecture: JAMES WHITE
College of Arts and Sciences: Dr JANE WINER
College of Business Administration: Dr ALLAN MCINNIS
College of Education: Dr GREGORY BOWES
College of Engineering: Dr WILLIAM MARCY
College of Human Sciences: Dr LINDA HOOVER
Graduate School: Dr RON ANDERSON
School of Law: FRANK NEWTON

ATTACHED INSTITUTES AND CENTRES

Institute for Banking and Financial Studies: Dir STEVE SEARS.

Institute for Biotechnology: Dir DAVID KNAFF.

Institute for Child and Family Studies: Dir MARY TOM RILEY.

Institute for Communications Research: Dir JERRY HUDSON.

Institute for Design and Advanced Technology: Dir A. ERTAS.

Institute for Disaster Research: Dir JAMES R. MCDONALD.

Institute for Environmental and Human Health: Dir Dr RON KENDALL.

Institute for Environmental Sciences: Dir MICHAEL WILLIG.

Institute for Ergonomics Research: Dir M. M. AYOUB.

Institute for Management and Leadership Research: Dir ROBERT L. PHILLIPS.

Institute for Marketing Studies: Dir ROY D. HOWELL.

Institute for Multicomputer Processing and Controls: Dir WILLIAM J. B. OLDHAM.

Institute for Multidisciplinary Research on Adolescent and Adult Risk-taking Behaviour: Dir NANCY BELL.

Institute for Research in Plant Stress: Dir ROBERT ALBIN.

Institute for Studies in Organizational Automation: Dir KATHLEEN HENNESSEY.

Institute for Studies in Pragmaticism: Dir KENNETH KETNER.

Institute for the Gifted: Dir MARTHA HISE.

Agricultural Finance Institute: Dir PHILLIP N. JOHNSON.

Leather Research Institute: Dir JINGER EBERSPACHER.

Pork Industry Institute for Research and Education: Dir JOHN MCGLONE.

Small Business Institute: Dir ALEX STEWART.

Texas Wine Marketing Research Institute: Dir TIM H. DODD.

Wildlife and Fisheries Management Institute: Dir RON SOSEBEE.

Center for Agricultural Technology Transfer: Dir PAUL VAUGHN.

Center for Applied International Development Studies: Dir GARY S. ELBOW.

Center for Applied Petrophysical Studies: Dirs GEORGE ASQUITH, MARION ARNOLD.

Center for Applied Research in Industrial Automation and Robotics: Dir WILLIAM KOLARIK.

Center for Applied Systems Analysis: Dir CLYDE F. MARTIN.

Center for Energy Research: Dir WALT J. OLER.

Center for Excellence in Education: Dir BILL SPARKMAN.

Center for Feed and Industry Research and Education: Dir REED RICHARDSON.

Center for Forensic Studies: Dir E. ROLAND MENZEL.

Center for Hazardous and Toxic Waste Studies: Dir RAGHU NARAYAN.

Center for Historic Preservation and Technology: Dir JOE KING.

Center for Improvement of Teaching Effectiveness: Dir A. L. SMITH.

Center for Petroleum Mathematics: Dir WAYNE FORD.

Center for Professional Development: Dir DAVID ANDERSON.

Center for Public Service: Dir CHARLES FOX.

Center of Sports Health and Human Performance: Chair. GIL REAVES.

Center for Study of Addiction: Dir CARL ANDERSEN.

Center for the Study of the Vietnam Conflict: Dir JAMES R. RECKNER.

Child Development Research Center: Dir CATHY NATHAN.

Home Economics Instructional Curriculum Center: Dir MARILYN WRAGG.

International Center for Arid and Semiarid Land Studies: Dir KARY MATHIS.

International Center for Textile Research and Development: Dir DEAN ETHRIDGE.

Murdough Center for Engineering Professionalism: Dir JIMMY SMITH.

Science and Mathematics Education Center: Dir GERALD SKOOG.

Small Business Development Center: Dir CRAIG BEAN.

Southwest Center for German Studies: Dir MEREDITH MCCLAIN.

State Affiliate Census Data Center: Dir EVANS W. CURRY.

Texas Center for Productivity and Quality of Work Life: Dir BARRY MACY.

Water Resources Center: Dir LLOYD V. URBAN.

Wind Engineering Research Center: Dir KISHOR C. MEHTA.

HEALTH SCIENCES CENTRE

Texas Tech University Health Sciences Center

3601 4th St, Lubbock, TX 79430

Telephone: (806) 743-3111
Internet: www.ttuhsc.edu

Pres.: Dr DAVID SMITH

DEANS

School of Allied Health: (vacant)
School of Medicine: Dr JOEL KUPPERSMITH
School of Nursing: (vacant)
School of Pharmacy: ARTHUR NELSON

TEXAS WESLEYAN UNIVERSITY

Fort Worth, TX 76105-1536

Telephone: (817) 531-4444
Fax: (817) 531-4425
E-mail: info@txwesleyan.edu
Internet: www.txwesleyan.edu

Founded 1890
Academic year: September to May

President: HAROLD G. JEFFCOAT
Provost: ALLEN HENDERSON
Vice-Presidents: BILL BLEIBDREY, GARY CUMBIE, PATI ALEXANDER
Registrar: KAHLA VAN TOORN
Librarian: CINDY SWIGGER

Library of 219,053 vols
Number of teachers: 140

TEXAS WOMAN'S UNIVERSITY

304 Administration Dr., POB 425589, Denton, TX 76204

Telephone: (940) 898-2000
Fax: (940) 898-3198
E-mail: info@twu.edu
Internet: www.twu.edu

Founded 1901
Academic year: August to May

Chancellor and Pres.: Dr ANN STUART
Vice-Pres. for Academic Affairs: Dr LOIS SMITH
Vice-Pres. for Finance and Admin.: Dr BRENDA FLOYD
Vice-Pres. for Institutional Advancement: (vacant)
Vice-Pres. for Student Life: Dr RICHARD NICHOLAS
Librarian: ELIZABETH SNAPP

Library of 788,271 vols
Number of teachers: 500
Number of students: 8,690

TRINITY UNIVERSITY

1 Trinity Pl., San Antonio, TX 78212

Telephone: (210) 999-7011
Fax: (210) 999-7696
E-mail: admissions@trinity.edu
Internet: www.trinity.edu

Founded 1869
Academic year: August to May

Pres.: Dr DENNIS AHLBURG
Vice-Pres. for Academic Affairs: Dr MICHAEL FISCHER
Dean of Admissions: CHRISTOPHER ELLERTSON
Dean of Students and Dir of Residential Life: DAVID TUTTLE
Registrar: ALFRED RODRIGUEZ
Librarian: DIANE GRAVES

Library of 937,000 vols
Number of teachers: 242
Number of students: 2,686

Liberal arts and sciences.

UNIVERSITY OF DALLAS

1845 E Northgate Dr., Irving, TX 75062-4736

Telephone: (972) 721-5000
Fax: (972) 721-5017
E-mail: nettie@udallas.edu
Internet: www.udallas.edu

Founded 1956

Pres.: THOMAS W. KEEFE (acting)
Exec. Vice-Pres.: ROBERT M. GALECKE
Exec. Vice-Pres. and Provost: Dr J. WILLIAM BERRY
Provost and Dean of the College: Dr GLEN THUROW
Registrar: JANET BURK
Dir of Research: Dr ROBERT S. DUPREE
Librarian: SUE KENDALL (acting)

Library of 365,852 vols, 502 serials
Number of teachers: 188 , (132 full time)
Number of students: 2,977

UNIVERSITY OF HOUSTON SYSTEM

4800 Calhoun, Houston, TX 7704

Telephone: (713) 743-8189
Fax: (713) 743-0946
Internet: www.uhsa.uh.edu

Chancellor: JAY GOGUE.

CONSTITUENT INSTITUTIONS

University of Houston

Houston, TX 77204-2018

Telephone: (713) 743-1000
Internet: www.uh.edu

Founded 1927
State control
Language of instruction: English
Academic year: September to August

Pres.: RENU KHATOR
Sr Vice-Pres. for Academic Affairs and Provost: JOHN ANTEL
Vice-Pres. for Admin. and Finance: CARL CARLUCCI
Vice-Pres. for Community Relations and Institutional Access: ELWYN LEE
Vice-Pres. for Govt Relations: GROVER CAMPBELL
Vice-Pres. for Legal Affairs and Gen. Counsel: DONA H. CORNELL
Vice-Pres. for Research: RATHINDRA BOSE
Vice-Pres. for Student Affairs: MICHAEL LAWRENCE
Vice-Pres. for Univ. Advancement (vacant)
Univ. Librarian: DANA ROOKS

Library of 2,000,000 vols
Number of teachers: 3,364
Number of students: 38,782

Publications: *Experts Directory*, *UHouston*

DEANS

College of Architecture: JOSEPH L. MASHBURN
College of Education: ROBERT MCPHERSON
College of Liberal Arts and Social Sciences: JOHN ROBERTS
College of Natural Sciences and Mathematics: MARK SMITH
College of Optometry: EARL L. SMITH
College of Pharmacy: LAMAR PRITCHARD
College of Technology: WILLIAM FITZGIBBON
Conrad N. Hilton College of Hotel and Restaurant Management: JOHN BOWEN
C. T. Bauer College of Business Administration: LATHA RAMCHAND
Cullen College of Engineering: JOSEPH TEDESCO
Gerald D. Hines College of Architecture: PATRICIA OLIVER
Graduate College of Social Work: IRA COLBY
Honors College: WILLIAM MONROE
Law Centre: RAYMOND NIMMER

ATTACHED INSTITUTIONS

A. A. White Dispute Resolution Institute: Dir (vacant).

Allied Geophysical Laboratories: Dir KURT MARFURT.

CBA Energy Institute: Dir MICHELLE FOSS.

Center for Entrepreneurship and Innovation: Dir BILL SHERRILL.

Center for Immigration Research: Dirs J. HAGAN, N. RODRIGUEZ.

Center for Public Policy: Dir RICHARD MURRAY.

Center for the Americas: Dir RODOLFO CORTINO.

Composites Engineering and Applications Center: Dir SU SU WANG.

Environmental Institute of Houston: Dir GLENN AUMANN.

Health Law and Policy Institute: Dir MARY ANNE BOBINSKI.

Institute for Beam Particle Dynamics: Dir ROY WEINSTEIN.

Institute for Cardiovascular Studies: Dir BHAGAVAN JANDHYALA.

Institute for Drug Education and Research: Dir DIANA CHOW.

Institute for Energy Studies: Dir MICHELLE FOSS.

Institute for Fluid Dynamics and Turbulence: Dir FAZIE HUSSAIN.

Institute for Higher Education Law and Governance: Dir MICHAEL OLIVAS.

Institute for Intellectual Property and Information Law: Dir (vacant).

Institute for Molecular Biology: Dir MICHAEL BENEDIK.

Institute for Molecular Design: Dir MONTY PETTITT.

Institute for Regional Forecasting: Dir BARTON SMITH.

Institute for Space Systems Operations: Dir DAVID CRISWELL.

Institute for the Study of Political Economy: Dir STEPHEN CRAIG.

Institute for Theoretical Engineering Sciences: Dir MARTIN GOLUBITSKY.

Institute for Urban Education: Dir ROBERT HOUSTON.

International Law Institute: Dirs SANFORD GAINES, STEPHEN ZAMORA.

Materials Research Science and Engineering Center: Dir ALLAN JACOBSON.

Space Vacuum Epitaxy Center: Dir ALEX IGNATIEV.

Texas Center for Superconductivity: Dir C. W. PAUL CHU.

UH—North Houston Institute: Dir JOEL HAMMETT.

UH—West Houston Institute: Dir KURT CZUPRYN.

UHS at Fort Bend: Dir SHARON BACA.

University Center at The Woodlands: Dir PENNY WESTERFELD.

University Eye Institute: Dir NICK HOLDEMAN.

University of Houston–Clear Lake

2700 Bay Area Blvd, Houston, TX 77058-1098
Telephone: (281) 283-7600
Fax: (281) 283-2010
E-mail: president@cl.uh.edu
Internet: www.uhcl.edu

Founded 1974
Academic year: September to August

Pres.: Dr WILLIAM A. STAPLES
Sr Vice-Pres. and Provost: Dr EDWARD J. HAYES
Vice-Pres. for Admin. and Finance: MICHELLE DOTTER
Librarian: KAREN WEILHORSKI

Library of 2,222,020 vols
Number of teachers: 554 (227 full-time, 327 part-time)
Number of students: 7,753

DEANS

School of Business and Public Administration: Dr WILLIAM T. CUMMINGS
School of Education: Dr DENNIS W. SPUCK
School of Human Sciences and Humanities: Dr BRUCE PALMER
School of Natural and Applied Sciences: Dr CHARLES W. MCKAY

University of Houston—Downtown

One Main St, Houston, TX 77002
Telephone: (713) 221-8000
Fax: (713) 221-8157
Internet: www.uhd.edu

Founded 1974; adopted present name in 1983

Pres.: Dr MAX CASTILLO
Vice-Pres. for Academic Affairs and Provost: Dr MOLLY R. WOODS
Vice-Pres. for Admin.: CHANEY ANDERSON
Exec. Asst to the Pres. and Dir of Constituent Relations: IVONNE MONTALBANO
Exec. Dir of Institutional Advancement: Dr MICHELE SABINO
Dean of Student Affairs (vacant)
Library Dir: PAT ENSOR

Library of 230,000 vols
Number of teachers: 528
Number of students: 10,528

DEANS

College of Business: Dr BOBBY BIZZELL
College of Humanities and Social Sciences: Dr MICHAEL DRESSMAN
College of Sciences and Technology: Dr GEORGE PINCUS
University College: Dr CHRIS BIRCHAK

University of Houston—Victoria

3007 N Ben Wilson, Victoria, TX 77901
Telephone: (877) 970-4848
Fax: (361) 580-5506
E-mail: webmaster@uhv.edu
Internet: www.uhv.edu

Founded 1973

Pres.: Dr TIM HUDSON
Provost and Vice-Pres. for Academic Affairs: Dr DON SMITH
Chief of Staff: Dr MARGARET RICE
Provost and Vice-Pres. for Academic Affairs: Dr SUZANNE LABRECQUE
Vice-Pres. for Admin. and Finance: WAYNE B. BERAN
Assoc. Vice-Pres. of Student Services: RICHARD D. PHILLIPS
Exec. Dir of Institutional Advancement: CAROLE OLIPHANT
Sr Dir for Information Technology: JOSEPH S. FERGUSON
Sr Dir for Library: Dr JOE F. DAHLSTROM

Library of 177,815 vols
Number of teachers: 176
Number of students: 3,655

School of Arts and Sciences: Dr JEFFREY R. DILEO
School of Business Administration: Dr FARHANG NIROOMAND
School of Education and Human Development: Dr LAWRENCE F. ROSSOW
School of Nursing: Dr KATHRYN TART

CHAIRMEN

Division of Arts and Sciences: Dr DAN JAECKLE
Division of Business Administration: Dr CHARLES BULLOCK
Division of Education: Dr MARY NATIVIDAD

UNIVERSITY OF MARY HARDIN-BAYLOR

Belton, TX 76513
Telephone: (254) 295-8642
Fax: (254) 295-4535
Internet: www.umhb.edu

Founded 1845

Pres.: Dr RANDY G. O'REAR
Provost and Vice-Pres. for Academic Affairs: Dr STEVE OLDHAM
Registrar: AMY MCGILVRAY
Dir of Admissions: BRENT BURKS
Librarian: DENISE KARIM KHAN

Library of 208,353
Number of teachers: 148
Number of students: 2,768

UNIVERSITY OF NORTH TEXAS

1155 Union Circle 311277, Denton, TX 76203-5017
Telephone: (940) 565-2000
E-mail: ugrd@unt.edu
Internet: www.unt.edu

Founded 1890

Pres.: GRETCHEN M. BATAILLE
Provost and Vice-Pres. for Academic Affairs: Dr BLAINE A. BROWNELL
Vice-Pres. and Gen. Counsel: Dr RICHARD RAFES
Vice-Pres. for Admin. Affairs: FREDERICK R. POLE
Vice-Pres. for Devt: Dr PETER LANE
Vice-Pres. for External Affairs: WALTER E. PARKER
Vice-Pres. for Fiscal Affairs: PHILIP C. DIEBEL
Vice-Pres. for Student Affairs: Dr JOE G. STEWART
Dir of Admissions: MARCILLA COLLINSWORTH
Registrar: JONEEL J. HARRIS
Librarian: Dr B. DONALD GROSE

Library of 2,164,427 vols, 2,190,831 microforms
Number of teachers: 800 full-time, 540 teaching assistants and teaching fellows
Number of students: 25,605

DEANS

Arts and Sciences: Dr NORA KIZER BELL
Business Administration: (vacant)
Community Service: Dr DANIEL M. JOHNSON
Education: Dr PAUL DIXON
Library Science: (vacant)
Merchandising and Hospitality Management: Dr SUZANNE LA BRECQUE
Music: Dr DAVID SHRADER
Graduate School: Dr ROLLIE SCHAFER
School of Visual Arts: Dr D. JACK DAVIS

HEALTH SCIENCES CENTRE

University of North Texas Health Science Center at Fort Worth

3500 Camp Bowie Blvd, Fort Worth, TX 76107
Telephone: (817) 735-2000
Internet: www.hsc.unt.edu

Pres.: RONALD R. BLANCK
Sr Vice-Pres.: STEVE R. RUSSELL
Sr Vice-Pres. for Academic Affairs: GREG MCQUEEN
Vice-Pres. for Advancement: CHERYL GRAY KIMBERLING
Vice-Pres. for Governmental Affairs: DANIEL M. JENSEN
Vice-Pres. for Institutional Coordination: GREG UPP
Vice-Pres. for Strategic and Institutional Affairs: ADELA N. GONZALEZ

UNIVERSITY OF ST THOMAS

3800 Montrose Blvd, Houston, TX 77006-4626
Telephone: (713) 522-7911
Internet: www.stthom.edu

Founded 1947
Private control
Academic year: August to May

Pres.: Dr ROBERT R. IVANY
Vice-Pres. for Academic Affairs: Dr DOMINIC AQUILA
Vice-Pres. for Finance: JAMES BOOTH
Vice-Pres. for Information Technology: GARY MCCORMACK
Vice-Pres. for Institutional Advancement: H. KEN DEDOMINICIS
Vice-Pres. for Marketing Communications and Enrollment Management: VICKIE ALLEMAN
Vice-Pres. for Student Affairs: PATRICIA MCKINLEY
Registrar: KIMBERLY SANDERS
Librarian: JAMES PICCININNI

Library of 203,000 vols
Number of teachers: 215
Number of students: 2,696

Publications: *Cauldron* (12 a year), *St Thomas Magazine* (2 a year), *UST Insider* (3 a year)

DEANS

Cameron School of Business: Dr BAHMAN MIRSHAB
Extended Programmes: Dr RAVI SRINIVAS
School of Arts and Sciences: Rev. JOSEPH PILSNER
School of Education: Dr NORA HUTTO
School of Theology: Dr SANDRA MAGIE

UNIVERSITY OF TEXAS SYSTEM

601 Colorado St, Austin, TX 78701
Telephone: (512) 499-4201
Internet: www.utsystem.edu

Founded 1883

Chancellor: MARK G. YUDOF
Exec. Vice-Chancellor for Academic Affairs: TERESA A. SULLIVAN

Exec. Vice-Chancellor for Business Affairs: SCOTT C. KELLEY
Exec. Vice-Chancellor for Health Affairs: KENNETH I. SHINE (acting)
Vice-Chancellor for Admin.: TONYA MOTEN BROWN
Vice-Chancellor for Community and Business Relations: JOHN DE LA GARZA, Jr
Vice-Chancellor for External Relations: RANDA S. SAFADY
Vice-Chancellor for Federal Relations: WILLIAM H. SHUTE
Vice-Chancellor and Gen. Counsel: BARRY D. BURGDORF
Vice-Chancellor for Governmental Relations and Policy: E. ASHLEY SMITH
Vice-Chancellor for Research and Technology Transfer: ROBERT E. BARNHILL
Counsel and Sec. to the Board of Regents: FRANCIE A. FREDERICK.

CONSTITUENT INSTITUTIONS

University of Texas at Austin

Austin, TX 78712
Telephone: (512) 471-3434
E-mail: utopa@www.utexas.edu
Internet: www.utexas.edu

Founded 1883, fmrly Univ. of Texas, Main Univ.
State control
Academic year: September to May (two terms) with two summer sessions

Pres.: WILLIAM POWERS, Jr
Exec. Vice-Pres. and Provost: STEVEN LESLIE
Vice-Pres. and Chief Financial Officer: KEVIN P. HEGARTY
Vice-Pres. for Diversity and Community Engagement: GREGORY VINCENT
Vice-Pres. for Legal Affairs: PATRICIA C. OHLENDORF
Vice-Pres. for Public Affairs: DONALD A. HALE
Vice-Pres. for Research: JUAN M. SANCHEZ
Vice-Pres. for Student Affairs: JUAN C. GONZÁLEZ
Vice-Pres. for Univ. Operations: PATRICIA L. CLUBB
Chief Information Officer: BRAD ENGLERT
Vice Provost and Dir of Libraries: FRED HEATH

Library: see Libraries and Archives
Number of teachers: 2,500
Number of students: 50,000

DEANS

Cockrell College of Engineering: GREGORY L. FENVES
College of Communication: RODERICK P. HART
College of Education: MANUEL J. JUSTIZ
College of Fine Arts: DOUGLAS DEMPSTER
College of Liberal Arts: RANDY L. DIEHL
College of Natural Sciences: MARY ANN RANKIN
College of Pharmacy: M. LYNN CRISMON
Continuing and Innovative Education: JUDY ASHCROFT
Graduate School: VICTORIA RODRÍGUEZ
Jackson School of Geosciences: SHARON MOSHER
LBJ School of Public Affairs: ROBERT HUTCHINGS
McCombs School of Business: THOMAS W. GILLIGAN
School of Architecture: FREDERICK R. STEINER
School of Information: ANDREW P. DILLON
School of Law: LAWRENCE G. SAGER
School of Nursing: ALEXA K. STUIFBERGEN
School of Social Work: BARBARA W. WHITE
School of Undergraduate Studies: PAUL WOODRUFF

PROFESSORS

School of Architecture:

ALOFSIN, A.
ARUMI, F. N.
ATKINSON, S. D.
BENEDIKT, M. L.
BLACK, J. S.
GARRISON, M. L.
KAHN, T. D.
KWALLEK, N. P.
LEIDING, G.
SPECK, L. W.
SWALLOW, R. P.
WILSON, P. A.

School of Information:

DAVIS, D. G., Jr
GRACY, II, D. B.
HALLMARK, J.
HARMON, E. G.
IMMROTH, B. F.
LUKENBILL, W. B.
MIKSA, F. L.
ROY, L.

School of Law:

ANDERSON, D. A.
ASCHER, M. L.
BAKER, L. A.
BERMAN, M. N.
BLACK, B. S.
BLAIS, L. E.
BOBBITT, P. C.
CARSON II, L. C.
CHURGIN, M. J.
CLEVELAND, S. H.
COHEN, J. M.
DAWSON, R. O.
DIX, G. E.
DZIENKOWSKI, J. S.
ENGLE, K. L.
FORBATH, W. E.
GERGEN, M. P.
GETMAN, J. G.
GOODE, S. J.
GRAGLIA, L. A.
HANSEN, P. I.
HU, H. T. C.
JOHANSON, S. M.
JOHNSON, C. H.
KLEIN, S. R.
LAYCOCK, H. D.
LEITER, B. R.
LEVINSON, S. V.
MCGARITY, T. O.
MANN, R. J.
MARKESINIS, B. S.
MARKOVITS, I.
MARKOVITS, R. S.
MULLENIX, L. S.
PERONI, R. J.
POWE, L. A., Jr
RABBAN, D. M.
RAU, A. S.
REESE, R. A.
ROBERTSON, D. W.
ROBERTSON, J. A.
SAGER, L.
SAMPSON, J. J.
SHARLOT, M. M.
SILVER, C. M.
SMITH, E. E.
STEIKER, J. M.
STURLEY, M. F.
TORRES, G.
WAGNER, W. E.
WEINBERG, L.
WELLBORN, O. G.
WESTBROOK, J. L.
WOOLLEY, P.
YOUNG, E. A.

School of Nursing:

GROBE, S. J.
HOUSTON, L. S.
PENTICUFF, J. H.
REW, D. L.
STUIFBERGEN, A. M.
WALKER, L. O.

School of Social Work:

CHOI, N.
DINITTO, D. M.
FONG, R.
FRANKLIN, C. G. S.
GREENE, R. R.
LAUDERDALE, M. L.
LEIN, L.
MCROY, R. G.
POOLE, D. L.
RUBIN, A.
SCHWAB, A. J., Jr
SHORKEY, C. T.
STREETER, C. L.

LBJ School of Public Affairs:

APFEL, K. S.
AUERBACH, R. D.
BOSKE, L. B.
EATON, D. J.
FLAMM, K.
GALBRAITH, J. K.
HAMILTON, D. S.
INMAN, B. R.
RHODES, L.
SCHOTT, R. L.
SPELMAN, W. G.
WARNER, D. C.
WILSON, R. H.

McCombs School of Business:

ALLISON, J. R., Management Science and Information Systems
ALPERT, M. I., Marketing Admin.
ANDERSON, U. L., Accounting
ATIASE, R., Accounting
BAGCHI, U., Management
BALAKRISHNAN, A., Management Science and Information Systems
BARUA, A., Management Science and Information Systems
BROCKETT, P. L., Management Science and Information Systems
BRONIARCZYK, S. M., Marketing Admin.
BROWN, K. C., Finance
BUTLER, J. S., Management
COX III, E. P., Marketing Admin.
CROSS, F. B., Management Science and Information Systems
CUNNINGHAM, W. H., Marketing Admin.
DAMIEN, P., Management Science and Information Systems
DAVIS-BLAKE, A., Management
DEITRICK, J. W., Accounting
DUKERICH, J. M., Management
DYER, J. S., Management Science and Information Systems
FITZSIMMONS, J. A., Management
FREDRICKSON, J. W., Management
FREEMAN, R. N., Accounting
GOLDEN, L. L., Marketing Admin.
GRANOF, M. H., Accounting
HENION II, K. E., Marketing Admin.
HIRST, D. E., Accounting
HOYER, W. D., Marketing Admin.
HUBER, G. P., Management
HUFF, D. L., Marketing Admin.
JARVENPAA, S. L., Management Science and Information Systems
JEMISON, D. B., Management
JENNINGS, R. G., Accounting
KACHELMEIER, S. J., Accounting
KINNEY, W. R., Jr, Accounting
KOEHLER, J. J., Management Science and Information Systems
KOONCE, L. L., Accounting
LASDON, L. S., Management Science and Information Systems
LIMBERG, S. T., Accounting
MCALISTER, L. M., Marketing Admin.
MCDANIEL, R. R., Jr, Management Science and Information Systems
MAGEE, S. P., Finance
MAHAJAN, V., Marketing Admin.
MAY, R. G., Accounting
METTLEN, R. D., Finance

MORRICE, D. J., Management
MURRAY, P. C., Management Science and Information Systems
NEWMAN, D. P., Accounting
PETERSON, R. A., Marketing Admin.
PRENTICE, R. A., Management Science and Information Systems
RAO, R. K. S., Finance
ROBINSON, J. R., Accounting
RONN, E. I., Finance
RUEFLI, T. W., Management Science and Information Systems
SAGER, T. W., Management Science and Information Systems
SALBU, S. R., Management Science and Information Systems
SHAW, B. M., Management Science and Information Systems
SHIVELY, T. S., Management Science and Information Systems
SPELLMAN, L. J., Finance
STARKS, L. T., Finance
TITMAN, S., Finance
WESTPHAL, J. D., Management
WHINSTON, A. B., Management Science and Information Systems
YU, G., Management Science and Information Systems

College of Communication:
ALVES, R. C., Journalism
BERG, C. E., Radio, Television, Film
BRANHAM, L. E., Journalism
BROWNING, L. D., Communication Studies
BRUMMETT, B., Communication Studies
BURNS, N. M., Advertising
CHAMPLIN, C. A., Communication Sciences and Disorders
CHERWITZ, R. A., Communication Studies
CUNNINGHAM, I. C., Advertising
DALY, J. A., Communication Studies
DARLING, D. C., Journalism
DAVIS, B. L., Communication Sciences and Disorders
GILLAM, R. B., Communication Sciences and Disorders
KNAPP, M. L., Communication Studies
LECKENBY, J. D., Advertising
MCCOMBS, M. E., Journalism
MARQUARDT, T. P., Communication Sciences and Disorders
MARTIN, F. N., Communication Sciences and Disorders
MAXWELL, M. M., Communication Studies
MORRISON, D. K., Advertising
MURPHY, J. H., Advertising
OLASKY, M. N., Journalism
REESE, S. D., Journalism
RICHARDS, J. I., Advertising
SCHATZ, T. G., Radio-Television-Film
STAIGER, J., Radio-Television-Film
STEKLER, P. J., Radio-Television-Film
STOUT, P. A., Advertising
STRAUBHAAR, J., Radio-Television-Film
STROVER, S. L., Radio-Television-Film
TODD, R. G., Journalism
VANGELISTI, A. L., Communication Studies
WILCOX, G. B., Advertising
WILLIAMS, J. D., Advertising

College of Education:
ABRAHAM, L. D., Curriculum and Instruction
AINSLIE, R. C., Educational Psychology
BARUFALDI, J. P., Curriculum and Instruction
BETHEL, L. J., Curriculum and Instruction
BORICH, G. D., Educational Psychology
BRYANT, D. P., Special Education
CANTU, N. V., Educational Admin.
CARLSON, C. I., Educational Psychology
CHALIP, L. H., Kinesiology and Health Education
COYLE, E. F., Kinesiology and Health Education
DAVIS, O. L., Jr, Curriculum and Instruction
DODD, B. G., Educational Psychology
DUNCAN, J. P., Educational Adminstration
EMMER, E. T., Educational Psychology
FALBO, T. L., Educational Psychology
FARRAR, R. P., Kinesiology and Health Education
FIELD, S. L., Curriculum and Instruction
FOLEY, D. E., Curriculum and Instruction
GOTTLIEB, N. H., Kinesiology and Health Education
GUSZAK, F. J., Curriculum and Instruction
HOFFMAN, J. V., Curriculum and Instruction
HOLAHAN, C. K., Kinesiology and Health Education
HORWITZ, E. K., Curriculum and Instruction
IVY, J. L., Kinesiology and Health Education
KAMEEN, M. C., Educational Admin.
KEITH, T. Z., Educational Psychology
KOCH, W. R., Educational Psychology
LASHER, W. F., Educational Adminstration
MANASTER, G. J., Educational Psychology
MOORE, W., Educational Admin.
ORTIZ, A. A., Special Education
OVANDO, M. N., Educational Admin.
PARKER, R. M., Special Education
REIFEL, S., Curriculum and Instruction
RESTA, P. E., Curriculum and Instruction
RICHARDSON, F. C., Educational Psychology
RIETH, H. J., Special Education
ROSER, N. L., Curriculum and Instruction
ROUECHE, J. E., Jr, Educational Admin.
SCHALLERT, D. L., Educational Psychology
SCRIBNER, J. D., Educational Admin.
SEMRUD-CLIKEMAN, M., Educational Psychology
SIGAFOOS, J., Special Education
SPIRDUSO, W. W., Kinesiology and Health Education
STARK, K. D., Educational Psychology
STARNES, J. W., Kinesiology and Health Education
STEINHARDT, M. A., Kinesiology and Health Education
THOMAS, M. P., Jr, Educational Admin.
VALENCIA, R., Educational Psychology
VAUGHN, S., Special Education
WEINSTEIN, C. E., Educational Psychology
WICKER, F. W., Educational Psychology
YATES, J. R., Educational Admin.

College of Engineering:
ABRAHAM, J. A., Electrical and Computer Engineering
AGGARWAL, J. K., Electrical and Computer Engineering
ALLEN, D. T., Chemical Engineering
AMBLER, A. P., Electrical and Computer Engineering
ARAPOSTATHIS, A., Electrical and Computer Engineering
BABUSKA, I. M., Aerospace Engineering
BALDICK, R., Electrical and Computer Engineering
BANERJEE, S. K., Electrical and Computer Engineering
BARBER, K. S., Electrical and Computer Engineering
BARD, J. F., Mechanical Engineering
BARNES, J. W., Mechanical Engineering
BARR, R. E., Mechanical Engineering
BEAMAN, J. J., Jr, Mechanical Engineering
BECKER, E. B., Aerospace Engineering
BECKER, M. F., Electrical and Computer Engineering
BENNIGHOF, J. K., Aerospace Engineering
BISHOP, R. H., Aerospace Engineering
BOGARD, D. G., Mechanical Engineering
BONNECAZE, R. T., Chemical Engineering
BOSTICK, F. X., Jr, Electrical and Computer Engineering
BOURELL, D. L., Mechanical Engineering
BOVIK, A. C., Electrical and Computer Engineering
BREEN, J. E., Civil Engineering
BRYANT, M. D., Mechanical Engineering
BUCKMAN, A. B., Electrical and Computer Engineering
CAMPBELL, J. C., Electrical and Computer Engineering
CAREY, G. F., Aerospace Engineering
CHARBENEAU, R. J., Civil Engineering
CHEN, R. T., Electrical and Computer Engineering
COGDELL, J. R., Electrical and Computer Engineering
CORSI, R. L., Civil Engineering
CRAWFORD, M. E., Mechanical Engineering
CRAWFORD, M. M., Mechanical Engineering
CRAWFORD, R. H., Mechanical Engineering
DAWSON, C. N., Aerospace Engineering
DE VECIANA, G. A., Electrical and Computer Engineering
DEMKOWICZ, L. F., Aerospace Engineering
DEPPE, D. G., Electrical and Computer Engineering
DILLER, K. R., Biomedical Engineering
DODABALAPUR, A., Electrical and Computer Engineering
DOLLING, D. S., Aerospace Engineering
DRIGA, M. D., Electrical and Computer Engineering
EDGAR, T. F., Chemical Engineering
EKERDT, J. G., Chemical Engineering
ELLZEY, J. L., Mechanical Engineering
ENGELHARDT, M. D., Civil Engineering
FAHRENTHOLD, E. P., Mechanical Engineering
FLAKE, R. H., Electrical and Computer Engineering
FOWLER, D. W., Civil Engineering
FOWLER, W. T., Aerospace Engineering
FRANK, K. H., Civil Engineering
FREEMAN, B. D., Chemical Engineering
GARG, V. K., Electrical and Computer Engineering
GEORGIOU, G., Chemical Engineering
GHOSH, J., Electrical and Computer Engineering
GIBSON, G. E., Jr, Civil Engineering
GOODENOUGH, J. B., Mechanical Engineering
GRADY, W. M., Electrical and Computer Engineering
GRAY, K. E., Petroleum and Geosystems Engineering
GREEN, P. F., Chemical Engineering
HAAS, C. T., Civil Engineering
HALL, M. J., Mechanical Engineering
HALLOCK, G. A., Electrical and Computer Engineering
HAMILTON, M. F., Mechanical Engineering
HAYES, L. J., Aerospace Engineering
HO, P. S., Mechanical Engineering
HOWELL, J. R., Mechanical Engineering
HUGHES, T. J., Aerospace Engineering
HULL, D. G., Aerospace Engineering
JIRSA, J. O., Civil Engineering
JOHNSTON, K. P., Chemical Engineering
JOSE-YACAMAN, M., Chemical Engineering
KINNAS, S. A., Civil Engineering
KLINGNER, R. E., Civil Engineering
KOEN, B. V., Mechanical Engineering
KWONG, D.-L., Electrical and Computer Engineering
KYRIAKIDES, S., Aerospace Engineering
LAKE, L. W., Petroleum and Geosystems Engineering
LANDSBERGER, S., Mechanical Engineering
LAWLER, D. F., Civil Engineering
LEE, J. C., Electrical and Computer Engineering
LIECHTI, K. M., Aerospace Engineering
LILJESTRAND, H. M., Civil Engineering
LING, H., Electrical and Computer Engineering
LIPOVSKI, G. J., Electrical and Computer Engineering
LLOYD, D. R., Chemical Engineering
MACHEMEHL, R. B., Civil Engineering

McKinney, D. C., Civil Engineering
Maidment, D. R., Civil Engineering
Malina, J. F., Jr, Civil Engineering
Manthiram, A., Mechanical Engineering
Mark, H. M., Aerospace Engineering
Masada, G. Y., Mechanical Engineering
Matthews, R. D., Mechanical Engineering
Mear, M. E., Aerospace Engineering
Moon, T. J., Mechanical Engineering
Mullins, C. B., Chemical Engineering
Neikirk, D. P., Electrical and Computer Engineering
Nichols, S. P., Mechanical Engineering
O'Connor, J. T., Civil Engineering
Oden, J. T., Aerospace Engineering
Pandy, M. G., Biomedical Engineering
Panton, R. L., Mechanical Engineering
Patt, Y. N., Electrical and Computer Engineering
Paul, D. R., Chemical Engineering
Pearce, J. A., Electrical and Computer Engineering
Peppas, N. A., Biomedical Engineering
Perry, D. E., Electrical and Computer Engineering
Peters, E. J., Petroleum and Geosystems Engineering
Pope, G. A., Petroleum and Geosystems Engineering
Powers, E. J., Jr, Electrical and Computer Engineering
Qin, S. Z. J., Chemical Engineering
Ralls, K. M., Mechanical Engineering
Rappaport, T. S., Electrical and Computer Engineering
Ravi-Chandar, K. A., Aerospace Engineering
Reible, D. D., Civil Engineering
Richards Kortum, R. R., Biomedical Engineering
Rochelle, G. T., Chemical Engineering
Rodin, G. J., Aerospace Engineering
Rossen, W. R., Petroleum and Geosystems Engineering
Rylander III, H. G., Biomedical Engineering
Sanchez, I. C., Chemical Engineering
Sandberg, I. W., Electrical and Computer Engineering
Schmidt, P. S., Mechanical Engineering
Schutz, B. E., Aerospace Engineering
Sepehrnoori, K., Petroleum and Geosystems Engineering
Sharma, M. M., Petroleum and Geosystems Engineering
Sorber, C. A., Civil Engineering
Speitel, G. E., Jr, Civil Engineering
Stearman, R. O., Aerospace Engineering
Stokoe II, K. H., Civil Engineering
Swartzlander, E. E., Jr, Electrical and Computer Engineering
Tapley, B. D., Aerospace Engineering
Tassoulas, J. L., Civil Engineering
Tesar, D., Mechanical Engineering
Valvano, J. W., Electrical and Computer Engineering
VanRensburg, W. C. J., Petroleum and Geosystems Engineering
Varghese, P. L., Aerospace Engineering
Vliet, G. C., Mechanical Engineering
Wagner, T. J., Electrical and Computer Engineering
Walser, R. M., Electrical and Computer Engineering
Walton, C. M., Civil Engineering
Welch, A. J., Biomedical Engineering
Wheeler, M. F., Aerospace Engineering
Willson, C. G., Chemical Engineering
Womack, B. F., Electrical and Computer Engineering
Wood, K. L., Mechanical Engineering
Wood, S. L., Civil Engineering
Wright, S. G., Civil Engineering
Yura, J. A., Civil Engineering

College of Fine Arts:

Allen, G. D., Music
Antokeletz, E. M., Music
Baltzer, R. A., Music
Barnitz, J. E., Art and Art History
Behague, G. H., Music
Bloom, M., Theatre and Dance
Bolin, P. E., Art and Art History
Brickens, N. O., Music
Brockett, O. G., Theatre and Dance
Brooks, R. L., Art and Art History
Chandler, B. G., Music
Clarke, J. R., Art and Art History
Coles, T. R., Art and Art History
Daly, S. J., Art and Art History
Dempster, D. J., Theatre and Dance
DeSimone, R. A., Music
Dolan, J. S., Theatre and Dance
Dorn, F., Theatre and Dance
Duke, R. A., Music
Erlmann, V. F., Music
Garrett, N. B., Music
Glavan, J. J., Theatre and Dance
Goodman, M. K., Art and Art History
Grantham, D. J., Music
Guerra, L. A., Music
Hale, K. J., Art and Art History
Hellmer, J. L., Music
Henderson, L. D., Art and Art History
Hilley, M. F., Music
Holladay, J. A., Art and Art History
Holzman, A., Music
Isackes, R. M., Theatre and Dance
Jellison, J. A., Music
Jennings, C. A., Theatre and Dance
Junkin, J. F., Music
Lewis, W. L., Music
Lucero, A. L., Theatre and Dance
Lundberg, W. A., Art and Art History
McFarland, L. D., Art and Art History
March, H. C., Music
Mariani, V. A., Art and Art History
Miller, L. C., Theatre and Dance
Milliken, G., Art and Art History
Nel, A., Music
Neubert, B. D., Music
Neumeyer, D. P., Music
Pinkston, R. F., Music
Pittel, H. C., Music
Richter, G. A., Music
Sasaki, R. K., Music
Sawyer, M. L., Art and Art History
Schmidt, R. N., Theatre and Dance
Shiff, R. A., Art and Art History
Slawek, S. M., Music
Smith, J. C., Art and Art History
Stuart, D. S., Art and Art History
Taylor, R. A., Music
Tusa, M. C., Music
Ulbricht, J. W., Art and Art History
Welcher, D. E., Music
Wiley, D. C., Music
Wiman, L. R., Art and Art History
Young, P. C., Music
Zeder, S. L., Theatre and Dance

College of Liberal Arts:

Abboud, P. F., Middle Eastern Studies
Abzug, R. H., History
Albrecht, D. G., Psychology
Allaire, E. B., Philosophy
Angel, R. J., Sociology
Angelelli, I. A., Philosophy
Arens, K. M., Germanic Studies
Armstrong, D., Classics
Asher, N. M., Philosophy
Ayres, J. B., English
Baker, M.-F. J., French and Italian
Bar-Adon, A., Middle Eastern Studies
Barany, Z. D., Government
Barnouw, J., English
Bealer, G., Philosophy
Bernucci, L. M., Spanish and Portuguese
Bertelsen, L., English
Bini, D., French and Italian
Biow, D. G., French and Italian
Birdsong, D. P., French and Italian
Blockley, M. E., English
Bonevac, D. A., Philosophy
Braybrooke, D., Government
Bronars, S. G., Economics
Brow, J. B., Anthropology
Brown, J. C., History
Brown, N. D., History
Buchanan II, B., Government
Budziszewski, J., Government
Bump, J. F., English
Buss, A. H., Psychology
Buss, D. M., Psychology
Butzer, K. W., Geography
Cable, T. M., English
Carlson, C. L., Psychology
Carter, J. C., Classics
Carton, E. B., English
Carver, L. D., English
Causey, R. L., Philosophy
Cauvin, J.-P. B., French and Italian
Chang, S.-S., Asian Studies
Charney, D. H., Rhetoric and Composition
Cohen, L. B., Psychology
Cooper, R. W., Economics
Corbae, P. D., Economics
Crew, D. F., History
Cullingford, E., English
Cvetkovich, A., English
Dacy, D. C., Economics
Davies, C. S., Geography
Dawson, R. L., French and Italian
Deigh, J., Philosophy
Diehl, R. L., Psychology
Dietz, H. A., Government
Domjan, M. P., Psychology
Donahue, F. E., Germanic Studies
Donald, S., Economics
Doolittle, W., Geography
Doughty, R. W., Geography
Dulles, J. W. F., American Studies
Dusansky, R., Economics
Edlund-Berry, I. M., Classics
Edwards, D. V., Government
Ellison, C. G., Sociology
Enelow, J. M., Government
England, N. C., Linguistics
Faigley, L. L., English
Falola, O. O., History
Farrell, J. P., English
Flores, R. R., Anthropology
Freeman, G. P., Government
Friedman, A. W., English
Frisbie, W. P., Sociology
Fullerton, D., Economics
Furman, L. J., English
Gagarin, M., Classics
Galinsky, G. K., Classics
Galle, O. R., Sociology
Garrison, J. D., English
Geisler III, W. S., Psychology
Geraci, V. J., Economics
Ghanoonparvar, M., Middle Eastern Studies
Ghose, Z. A., English
Gilden, D. L., Psychology
Glade, W. P., Economics
Glenn, N. D., Sociology
Goetzmann, W. H., History
Gonzalez-Gerth, M., Spanish and Portuguese
Gonzalez-Lima, F., Psychology
Graham, D. B., English
Hake, S., Germanic Studies
Hamermesh, D. S., Economics
Hancock, I. F., Linguistics
Hankinson, R. J., Philosophy
Hansen, K. G., Asian Studies
Harlow, B. J., English
Harms, R. T., Linguistics
Heinzelman, K. O., English
Helmreich, R. L., Psychology
Hendricks, K., Economics
Henry, C. M., Government
Hensey, F. G., Spanish and Portuguese
Higgins, K. M., Philosophy

HIGLEY, J. C., Government
HILFER, A. C., English
HILLMANN, M. C., Middle Eastern Studies
HINICH, M. J., Government
HINOJOSASMITH, R., English
HOBERMAN, J. M., Germanic Studies
HOCHBERG, H. I., Philosophy
HOLAHAN, C. J., Psychology
HOLDEN, G. W., Psychology
HOPKINS, A. G., History
HORN, J. M., Psychology
HUBBARD, T. K., Classics
HUMMER, R. A., Sociology
JACOBSOHN, G. J., Government
KALLET, L., Classics
KANE, R. H., Philosophy
KAPPELMAN, J. W., Jr, Anthropology
KAULBACH, E. N., English
KELLY, W. R., Sociology
KENDRICK, D. A., Economics
KING, R. D., Linguistics
KOLSTI, J. S., Slavic Languages and Literatures
KOONS, R. C., Philosophy
KROLL, J. H., Classics
KRONZ, F. M., Philosophy
KRUPPA, J. E., English
KURTZ, L. R., Sociology
LAMBRECHT, K. P., French and Italian
LAMPHEAR, J. E., History
LANGLOIS, J. H., Psychology
LASALLE, P. N., English
LEVACK, B. P., History
LIEBOWITZ, H. A., Middle Eastern Studies
LIMON, J. E., English
LINDSTROM, N. E., Spanish and Portuguese
LIPPMANN, J. N., French and Italian
LITVAK, L., Spanish and Portuguese
LOUIS, W. R., History
LUJAN, M. E., Spanish and Portuguese
MCFADDEN, D., Psychology
MACKAY, C. H., English
MACNEILAGE, P. F., Psychology
MAGNUSON, J. L., English
MANNERS, I. R., Geography
MARKMAN, A. B., Psychology
MARSHALL, S. E., Sociology
MARTINICH, A. P., Philosophy
MEIER, R. P., Linguistics
MEIKLE, J. L., American Studies
MENCHACA, M., Anthropology
MINAULT, G., History
MIROWSKY, J., Sociology
MONTREUIL, J.-P., French and Italian
MORGAN, M. G., Classics
MOURELATOS, A., Philosophy
MULLIN, J. A., Rhetoric and Composition
NAPIER, S. J., Asian Studies
NETHERCUT, W. R., Classics
NEWTON, A. Z., English
NORMAN, A. L., Economics
OLIVELLE, J. P., Asian Studies
OSHINSKY, D. A., History
PALAIMA, T. G., Classics
PANGLE, T. L., Government
PARKER, D. S., Classics
PELLS, R. H., History
PENNEBAKER, J. W., Psychology
PEREZ, F. L., Geography
PHILLIPS, S. H., Philosophy
POTTER, J. E., Sociology
PRINDLE, D. F., Government
PULLUM, T. W., Sociology
RAMIREZ III, M., Psychology
RAPPAPORT, G. C., Slavic Languages and Literature
REBHORN, W. A., Jr, English
RENWICK, R. D., English
ROBERTS, B. E., Government
ROBERTS, B. R., Sociology
ROSS, C. E., Sociology
ROSSMAN, C. R., English
RUMRICH, J. P., English
RUSZKIEWICZ, J. J., Rhetoric and Composition
SAINSBURY, R. M., Philosophy
SARKAR, S., Philosophy
SCHALLERT, T. J., Psychology
SCHEICK, W. J., English
SEUNG, T. K., Philosophy
SHELMERDINE, C. W., Classics
SHERZER, D. M., French and Italian
SHERZER, J. F., Anthropology
SHUMWAY, N., Spanish and Portuguese
SINGH, D., Psychology
SJOBERG, G. A., Sociology
SLESNICK, D. T., Economics
SMITH, C. S., Linguistics
SOLE, C. A., Spanish and Portuguese
SOLOMON, R. C., Philosophy
STAFFORD, M. C., Sociology
STAHL II, D. O., Economics
STINCHCOMBE, M. B., Economics
STROSS, B. M., Anthropology
SUSSMAN, H. M., Linguistics
SWAFFAR, J. K., Germanic Studies
SWANN, W. B., Jr, Psychology
TELCH, M. J., Psychology
TRIMBLE, J. R., English
TULLY, W. A., History
TWINAM, A., History
TYE, M., Philosophy
TYLER, R. C., History
UMBERSON, D. J., Sociology
VAN OLPHEN, H. H., Asian Studies
WAGNER, R. H., Government
WALKER, J., Rhetoric and Composition
WALKER, J. E., History
WALKER, S. S., Anthropology
WALTERS, S. K., Linguistics
WARD, P., Sociology
WARR, E. M., Sociology
WEINSTOCK, J. M., Germanic Studies
WEVILL, D. A., English
WEYLAND, K. G., Government
WHIGHAM, F. F., Jr, English
WHITBREAD, T. B., English
WHITE, L. M., Classics
WILCZYNSKI, W., Psychology
WILLIAMS, C. L., Sociology
WILSON, P. W., Economics
WILSON, S. M., Anthropology
WINSHIP, M. B., English
WOLITZ, S. L., French and Italian
WOODBURY, A. C., Linguistics
WOODRUFF, P. B., Philosophy
ZIMIC, S., Spanish and Portuguese
ZONN, L. E., Geography

College of Natural Sciences:

ANSLYN, E. V., Chemistry and Biochemistry
ANTONIEWICZ, P. R., Physics
APPLING, D. R., Chemistry and Biochemistry
ARBOGAST, T. J., Mathematics
ARMENDARIZ, E. P., Mathematics
ARTZT, K. J., Molecular Genetics and Microbiology
BAJAJ, C. L., Computer Sciences
BANNER, J. L., Geological Sciences
BARBARA, P. F., Chemistry and Biochemistry
BARD, A. J., Chemistry and Biochemistry
BASH, F. N., Astronomy
BATORY, D. S., Computer Sciences
BAULD, N. L., Chemistry and Biochemistry
BECKNER, W., Mathematics
BENGTSON, R. D., Physics
BENNETT, P. C., Geological Sciences
BERK, H. L., Physics
BICHTELER, K. R., Mathematics
BITTNER, G. D., Neurobiology
BOHM, A. R., Physics
BOSE, H. R., Molecular Genetics and Microbiology
BOYER, R. S., Computer Sciences
BRAND, J. J., Molecular Cell and Development Biology
BRILEY, M. E., Human Ecology
BRODBELT, J. S., Chemistry and Biochemistry
BRONSON, F. H., Integrative Biology
BROWN, R. M., Jr, Molecular Genetics and Microbiology
BROWNE, J. C., Computer Sciences
BULL, J. J., Integrative Biology
BUSKEY, E. J., Marine Science
CAFFARELLI, L. A., Mathematics
CAMPION, A., Chemistry and Biochemistry
CARLSON, W. D., Geological Sciences
CHENEY, E. W., Mathematics
CHIU, C. B., Physics
CLINE, A. K., Computer Sciences
CLOOS, M. P., Geological Sciences
COKER, W. R., Physics
COWLEY, A. H., Chemistry and Biochemistry
CREWS, D. P., Integrative Biology
DANIEL, J. W., Mathematics
DAVIS, R. E., Chemistry and Biochemistry
DE LA LLAVE, R., Mathematics
DE LOZANNE, A. L., Physics
DICUS, D. A., Physics
DINERSTEIN, H. L., Astronomy
DISTLER, J., Physics
DOWNER, M. W., Physics
DRUMMOND, W. E., Physics
DUDLEY, J. P., Molecular Genetics and Microbiology
DUNTON, K. H., Marine Science
DURBIN, J. R., Mathematics
EARHART, C. F., Molecular Genetics and Microbiology
ELLINGTON, A., Chemistry and Biochemistry
EMERSON II, E. A., Computer Sciences
ENGQUIST, B., Mathematics
ERSKINE, J. L., Physics
EVANS II, N. J., Astronomy
FINK, M., Physics
FISCHLER, W., Physics
FISHER, W. L., Geological Sciences
FOWLER, N. L., Integrative Biology
FREED, D. S., Mathematics
FREELAND, J. H., Human Ecology
FREEMAN, G. L., Integrative Biology
FROMMHOLD, L. W., Physics
FUSSELL, D. S., Computer Sciences
GAMBA, I. M., Mathematics
GARDNER, W. S., Marine Science
GENTLE, K. W., Physics
GERTH III, F. E., Mathematics
GILBERT, J. C., Chemistry and Biochemistry
GILBERT, J. E., Mathematics
GILBERT, L. E., Integrative Biology
GLEESON, A. M., Physics
GOMPF, R. E., Mathematics
GORDON, C. M., Mathematics
GOUDA, M. G., Computer Sciences
GRAND, S. P., Geological Sciences
GUY, W. T., Jr, Mathematics
HACKERT, M. L., Chemistry and Biochemistry
HAMRICK, G. C., Mathematics
HARRIS, R. A., Neurobiology
HARSHEY, R. M., Molecular Genetics and Microbiology
HARVEY, P. M., Astronomy
HAZELTINE, R. D., Physics
HEINZEN, D. J., Physics
HEITMANN, R. C., Mathematics
HERRIN, D. L., Molecular Cell and Development Biology
HILLIS, D. M., Integrative Biology
HOFFMANN, G. W., Physics
HOLCOMBE, J. A., Chemistry and Biochemistry
HORTON, C. W., Jr, Physics
HUNT, W. A., Jr, Computer Sciences
HUSTON, A. C., Human Ecology
HUSTON, T. L., Human Ecology
IVERSON, B. L., Chemistry and Biochemistry
JACOBVITZ, D. B., Human Ecology
JAFFE, D. T., Astronomy
JANSEN, R. K., Integrative Biology

JAYARAM, M., Molecular Genetics and Microbiology
JOHNSON, K., Chemistry and Biochemistry
JOHNSTON, D., Neurobiology
JONES, R. A., Chemistry and Biochemistry
KALTHOFF, K. O., Molecular Cell and Development Biology
KAPLUNOVSKY, V., Physics
KEEL, S. M., Mathematics
KETO, J. W., Physics
KIRKPATRICK, M. A., Integrative Biology
KITTO, G. B., Chemistry and Biochemistry
KLEINMAN, L., Physics
KLINE, K., Human Ecology
KOCH, H. A., Mathematics
KOCUREK, G. A., Geological Sciences
KORMENDY, J., Astronomy
KRISCHE, M. J., Chemistry and Biochemistry
KRUG, R. M., Molecular Genetics and Microbiology
KUIPERS, B. J., Computer Sciences
KUMAR, P., Astronomy
KYLE, J. R., Geological Sciences
LA CLAIRE II, J. W., Molecular Cell and Development Biology
LACY, J. H., Astronomy
LAGOW, R. J., Chemistry and Biochemistry
LAGOWSKI, J. J., Chemistry and Biochemistry
LAGOWSKI, J. M., Neurobiology
LAM, S. S., Computer Sciences
LAMBOWITZ, A., Molecular Genetics and Microbiology
LANG, K., Physics
LARIMER, J. L., Neurobiology
LAUDE, D. A., Chemistry and Biochemistry
LEVIN, D. A., Integrative Biology
LIFSCHITZ, V., Computer Sciences
LONG, L. E., Geological Sciences
LOOP, R., Human Ecology
LUECKE, J. E., Mathematics
MABRY, T. J., Molecular Cell and Development Biology
MCADAM, S. J., Mathematics
MCBRIDE, E. F., Geological Sciences
MCDEVITT, J. T., Chemistry and Biochemistry
MACDONALD, A. H., Physics
MACDONALD, P. M., Molecular Cell and Development Biology
MAGNUS, P. D., Chemistry and Biochemistry
MARDER, M. P., Physics
MARKERT, J. T., Physics
MARTIN, S. F., Chemistry and Biochemistry
MATZNER, R. A., Physics
MAUSETH, J. D., Integrative Biology
MEYER, R. J., Molecular Genetics and Microbiology
MIIKKULAINEN, R. P., Computer Sciences
MISRA, J., Computer Sciences
MOK, A. K., Computer Sciences
MOLINEUX, I. J., Molecular Genetics and Microbiology
MONTAGNA, P. A., Marine Science
MOONEY, R. J., Computer Sciences
MOORE, C. F., Physics
MOORE II, J. S., Computer Sciences
MORRISON, P. J., Physics
MOSHER, S., Geological Sciences
NAKAMURA, Y., Geological Sciences
NIU, Q., Physics
NOVAK, G. S., Jr, Computer Sciences
OAKES, M. E. L., Physics
ODELL, E. W., Mathematics
PALKA, B. P., Mathematics
PAYNE, S. M., Molecular Genetics and Microbiology
PIANKA, E. R., Integrative Biology
PLAXTON, C. G., Computer Sciences
POLLAK, G. D., Neurobiology
PORTER, B. W., Computer Sciences
RADIN, C. L., Mathematics
RAIZEN, M. G., Physics
RAMACHANDRAN, V., Computer Sciences
REICHL, L. E., Physics
REID, A. W., Mathematics
RICHARDSON, R. H., Integrative Biology
RIGGS II, A. F., Neurobiology
RILEY, P. J., Physics
RITCHIE, J. L., Physics
ROBERTUS, J. D., Chemistry and Biochemistry
ROBINSON, E. L., Astronomy
ROSENTHAL, H. P., Mathematics
ROSSKY, P. J., Chemistry and Biochemistry
ROUX, S. J., Jr, Molecular Cell and Development Biology
ROWE, T. B., Geological Sciences
RYAN, M. J., Integrative Biology
SADUN, L. A., Mathematics
SALTMAN, D. J., Mathematics
SANDERS, B. G., Molecular Genetics and Microbiology
SCALO, J. M., Astronomy
SCHIEVE, W. C., Physics
SCHWITTERS, R. F., Physics
SEN, M. K., Geological Sciences
SESSLER, J. L., Chemistry and Biochemistry
SHANKLAND, S. M., Molecular, Cellular and Developmental Biology
SHAPIRO, P. R., Astronomy
SHARP, J. M., Jr, Geological Sciences
SHIELDS, G. A., Astronomy
SHIH, C.-K., Physics
SIMPSON, B. B., Integrative Biology
SINGER, M. C., Integrative Biology
SITZ, G. O., Physics
SMITH, M. K., Mathematics
SNEDEN, C. A., Astronomy
SOUGDANIDIS, P. E., Mathematics
SPRINKLE, J. T., Geological Sciences
STANTON, J. F., Chemistry and Biochemistry
STARBIRD, M. P., Mathematics
STEEL, R. J., Geological Sciences
SUDARSHAN, G., Physics
SURRA, C. A., Human Ecology
SWIFT, J. B., Physics
SWINNEY, H. L., Physics
SZANISZLO, P. J., Molecular Genetics and Microbiology
TATE, J. T., Mathematics
TATHAM, R. H., Geological Sciences
THOMAS, P., Marine Science
THOMPSON, W. J., Neurobiology
TREISMAN, P. U., Mathematics
TUCKER, P. W., Molecular Genetics and Microbiology
UDAGAWA, T., Physics
UHLENBECK, K., Mathematics
VAALER, J. D., Mathematics
VAN DE GEIJN, R. A., Computer Sciences
VIN, H. M., Computer Sciences
VISHIK, M. M., Mathematics
VOLOCH, J. F., Mathematics
WALKER, J. R., Molecular Genetics and Microbiology
WARNOW, T., Computer Sciences
WEBBER, S. E., Chemistry and Biochemistry
WEINBERG, S., Physics
WHEELER, J. C., Astronomy
WHITE, J. M., Chemistry and Biochemistry
WILLIS, R. A., Human Ecology
WILLS, D., Astronomy
WILSON, C. R., Geological Sciences
WINGET, D. E., Astronomy
WYATT, R. E., Chemistry and Biochemistry
XIN, J., Mathematics
XU, B., Human Ecology
ZAKON, H. H., Neurobiology
ZARIPHOPOULOU, T., Mathematics
ZUCKERMAN, D. I., Computer Sciences

College of Pharmacy:

ABELL, C. W.
BUSSEY, H. I.
COMBS, A. B.
CRISMON, M. L.
DAVIS, P. J.
ERICKSON, C. K.
GONZALES, R. A.
KEHRER, J. P.
KOELLER, J. M.
KUHN, J. G.
LITTLEFIELD, L. C.
LIU, H.-W.
MCGINITY, J. W.
PEARLMAN, R.
RASCATI, K. L.
SHEPHERD, M. D.
STAVCHANSKY, S. A.
TALBERT, R. L., Jr
WHITMAN, C. P.
WILCOX, R. E.

University of Texas at Arlington

POB 19125, Arlington, TX 76019
Telephone: (817) 272-2101
E-mail: public.affairs@uta.edu
Internet: www.uta.edu

Founded 1895 as Arlington College, reorganized as a component of the Univ. of Texas 1965

Pres.: Dr ROBERT E. WITT
Provost: Dr GEORGE C. WRIGHT
Sr Vice-Pres. for Finance and Admin.: M. DAN WILLIAMS
Vice-Pres. for Devt: ANNE ABBE
Vice-Pres. for Student Enrollment Services: SHIRLEY BINDER
Vice-Pres. for Undergraduate Academic and Student Affairs: Dr MARY RIDGWAY
Librarian: THOMAS WILDING

Library: 1m. vols
Number of teachers: 997
Number of students: 21,200

DEANS

Architecture: EDWARD BAUM
Business: Dr DAN WORRELL (acting)
Center for Professional Teacher Education: Dr JEANNE GERLACH
Engineering: Dr RON BAILEY
Graduate School: Dr DALE ANDERSON
Liberal Arts: Dr RUTH GROSS (acting)
Nursing: Dr ELIZABETH POSTER
School of Social Work: Dr SANTOS HERNANDEZ
School of Urban and Public Affairs: Dr RICHARD L. COLE
Science: Dr NEAL SMATRESK

University of Texas at Brownsville and Texas Southernmost College

80 Fort Brown, Brownsville, TX 78520
Telephone: (956) 5448200
Fax: (956) 5448832
E-mail: admissions@utb.edu
Internet: www.utb.edu

Founded 1991 as partnership between Univ. of Texas at Brownsville (f. 1973) and Texas Southernmost College (f. 1926)

Pres.: Dr JULIET V. GARCÍA
Provost: Dr ALAN F. J. ARTIBISE
Vice-Pres. for Admin. and Partnership Affairs: Dr JOHN RONNAU
Vice-Pres. for Business Affairs: ROSEMARY MARTÍNEZ
Vice-Pres. for External Affairs: Dr TONY ZAVALETA
Vice-Pres. for Institutional Advancement: Dr WILLIAM STRONG
Vice-Pres. for Research: LUIS V. COLOM
Vice-Pres. for Student Affairs: Dr HILDA SILVA
Registrar: AL BARREDA
Library Dir: DOUGLAS FERRIER

Library of 170,000 vols
Number of teachers: 357
Number of students: 9,974

DEANS

College of Liberal Arts: Dr FARHAT IFTEKHARUDDIN
College of Science, Mathematics and Technology: Dr DIMITRIOS A. SOTIROPOULOS
School of Business: Dr BETSY BOZE
School of Education: Dr SYLVIA PEÑA
School of Health Sciences: Dr ELDON NELSON

University of Texas at Dallas

800 W Campbell Rd, Richardson, TX 75080
Telephone: (972) 883-2111
Fax: (972) 883-2237
E-mail: utdallas@utdallas.edu
Internet: www.utdallas.edu
State control
Language of instruction: English
Founded 1969, fmrly Southwest Center for Advanced Studies
Academic year: September to August
Pres.: Dr DAVID DANIEL
Exec. Vice-Pres. and Provost: Dr B. HOBSON WILDENTHAL
Vice-Pres. for Business Affairs: Dr CALVIN JAMISON
Vice-Pres. for Research Devt: Dr. BRUCE GNADE
Vice-Pres. for Student Affairs: Dr DARRELENE RACHAVONG
Assoc. Vice-Pres. for Budget: DAVID GAARDER
Dir of Enrollment Services: CURT ELY
Dir of Admissions (vacant)
Registrar: KAREN JARRELL
Dir of Libraries: Dr SHEILA AMIN GUTIERREZ DE PINERES
Library of 2,439,847 vols, serial backfiles and other paper materials
Number of teachers: 898
Number of students: 17,128
Publications: *Issues in Science and Technology* (4 a year), *Political Research Quarterly*, *Public Administration Review* (6 a year), *Translation Review* (3 a year)

DEANS

Graduate Studies: Dr AUSTIN CUNNINGHAM
Jonsson School of Engineering and Computer Science: Dr MARK SPONG
School of Arts and Humanities: Dr DENNIS M. KRATZ
School of Behavioural and Brain Sciences: Dr BERT MOORE
School of Economic, Political and Policy Sciences: Dr JAMES W. MARQUART
School of Interdisciplinary Studies: Dr GEORGE W. FAIR
School of Management: Dr HASAN PIRKUL
School of Natural Sciences and Mathematics: Dr MYRON SALAMON
Undergraduate Education: Dr SHEILA AMIN GUTIERREZ DE PINERES

PROFESSORS

ABDI, H.
AIKEN, C.
ALI, A.
AMMANN, L.
ARGYROS, A.
ASSMANN, P.
BALKUS, K.
BALSARA, P.
BAMBACH, C.
BARON, M.
BARTLETT, J.
BASTANI, F.
BAUGHMAN, R.
BERON, K.
BLANCHARD, A.
BOWER, T.
BRETTELL, R.
BRIGGS, R.
BUHRMESTER, D.
BULLA, L.
BUTTS, T.
CALDWELL, R.
CANTRELL, C.
CHAMPAGNE, A.
CHANDRASEKARAN, R.
CHANEY, R.
CHANNELL, D.
CHAPMAN, S.
CLARKE, H.
COHEN, M.
COLLINS, C.
CREADY, W.
CURCHACK, F.
DAY, T.
DESS, G.
D'MELLO, S.
DOLLAGHAN, C.
DOWLING, W.
DRAPER, R.
DUMAS, L.
ECKEL, C.
EDMUNDS, R.
EFROMOVICH, S.
ELLIOTT, E.
ENTHOVEN, A.
FARAGO, A.
FENYVES, E.
FERRARIS, J.
FONSEKA, J.
FORD, D.
FRENSLEY, W.
FUMAGALLI, A.
GLOSSER, R.
GNADE, B.
GOLDEN, R.
GOODMAN, S.
GRAY, D.
GRIFFITH, D.
GUPTA, G.
HAMBLY, G.
HANSEN, J.
HARPHAM, E.
HEELIS, R.
HICKS, D.
HOFFMAN, J.
HOOSHYAR, M.
HULSE, R.
HUNT, L.
HUYNH, D.
IZEN, J.
JACOB, V.
JERGER, S.
KEHTARNAVAZ, N.
KEMPF-LEONARD, K.
KIASALEH, K.
KIEL, L.
KIM, M.
KONSTANS, C.
LEAF, M.
LEE, G.
LIEBOWITZ, S.
LINEHAN, T.
LOIZOU, P.
LOU, X.
LOWRY, R.
MACFARLANE, D.
MCMECHAN, G.
MADRIGUERA, E.
MAJUMDAR, S.
MANTON, W.
MARQUART, J.
MELTON, L.
MOLDOVAN, D.
MOLLER, A.
MOOKERJEE, V.
NADIN, M.
NIU, S.
NTAFOS, S.
OBER, R.
O'TOOLE, A.
OVERZET, L.
OWEN, M.
OZSVATH, I.
OZSVATH, Z.
PACE, B.
PENG, M.
PERVIN, W.
PRAGER, K.
RABE, S.
RADHAKRISHNAN, S.
RAGHAVACHARI, B.
RAO, R.
REDLINGER, L.
REDMAN, T.
REITZER, L.
REYNOLDS, R.
RICCIO, T.
RINDLER, W.
RODRIGUEZ, R.
ROESER, R.
SANDLER, T.
SANTROCK, J.
SARKAR, S.
SCHULTE, R.
SCOTCH, R.
SELDON, B.
SERFLING, R.
SETHI, S.
SHA, H.
SHERRY, A.
SRISKANDARAJAH, C.
STECKE, K.
STERN, R.
STEWART, M.
STILLMAN, R.
SUDBOROUGH, I.
TAMIL, L.
THIBODEAU, L.
THURAISINGHAM, B.
TINSLEY, B.
TOBEY, E.
TRACY, P.
TRUEMPER, K.
TURI, J.
TURNER, F.
ULATOWSKA, H.
UNDERWOOD, M.
VAN KLEECK, A.
VIJVERBERG, W.
WATSON, D.
WIORKOWSKI, J.
ZAKHIDOV, A.
ZHANG, K.
ZHENG, S.
ZHOU, D.

University of Texas at El Paso

El Paso, TX 79968 0500
Telephone: (915) 747-5000
E-mail: uc@utep.edu
Internet: www.utep.edu
Founded 1913 as Texas School of Mines and Metallurgy, name changed to Texas Western College 1949, present name 1967
Pres.: Dr DIANA NATALICIO
Vice-Pres. for Academic Affairs: Dr STEPHEN RITER
Vice-Pres. for Finance and Admin.: JUAN SANDOVAL
Dean of Students: Dr WILLIAM SCHAFER
Dir of Admissions: IRMA RUBIO
Librarian: PATRICIA A. PHILLIPS
Library: see Libraries
Number of teachers: 923
Number of students: 16,220
Publications: *Horizons*, *Nova* (9 a year, September to May), *Shangri-La*, *Southwestern Studies* (irregular), *Southwest Journal of Business and Economics* (irregular), *The Prospector* (2 a week)

DEANS

Business Admin.: Dr CHARLES CRESPY
Education: Dr ARTURO PACHECO
Engineering: Dr ANDREW H. SWIFT
Liberal Arts: Dr HOWARD DAUDISTEL
Nursing: Dr JOHN CONWAY
Sciences: Dr THOMAS E. BRADY
Graduate School: Dr CHARLES AMBLER

University of Texas at San Antonio

6900 N Loop 1604W, San Antonio, TX 782490619

Telephone: (210) 4584011
Fax: (210) 4584117
E-mail: prospects@utsa.edu
Internet: www.utsa.edu

Founded 1969

Pres.: Dr RICARDO ROMO
Provost and Vice-Pres. for Academic Affairs: Dr GUY H. BAILEY
Vice-Pres. for Admin. and Interim Vice-Pres. for Univ. Advancement: GERARD H. BARLOCO
Vice-Pres. for Business Affairs: DAVID R. LARSON
Vice-Pres. for Extended Services: Dr JUDE VALDEZ
Vice-Pres. for Student Affairs: Dr ROSALIE AMBROSINO
Dean of Libraries: Dr MICHAEL KELLY

Number of teachers: 389
Number of students: 18,606 (15,795 undergraduate, 2,811 graduate)

DEANS

College of Business: Dr BRUCE BUBLITZ
College of Education and Human Development: Dr BLANDINA CARDENAS
College of Engineering: Dr ZORICA PANTIC-TANNER
College of Liberal and Fine Arts: Dr DANIEL J. GELO
College of Public Policy: Dr JESSE T. ZAPATA
College of Sciences: Dr WILLIAM SCOUTEN
School of Architecture: JULIUS M. GRIBOU

University of Texas at Tyler

3900 University Blvd, Tyler, TX 75799

Telephone: (903) 5667000
Fax: (903) 5667068
E-mail: info@mail.uttyler.edu
Internet: www.uttyler.edu

Founded 1971 as Tyler State College, present name 1979

Academic year: August to May

Pres.: Dr RODNEY H. MABRY
Provost and Vice-Pres. for Academic Affairs: Dr RICHARD OSBURN
Vice-Pres. for Business Affairs: Dr JIM FERGUSON
Vice-Pres. for Student Affairs and External Relations: Dr DALE LUNSFORD
Vice-Pres. for Univ. Advancement: NANCY LAMAR
Registrar: NINA ROGERS
Library Dir: JEANNE PYLE

Library of 215,000 vols
Number of teachers: 267 , incl. 180 full-time instructional
Number of students: 4,760 (3,593 undergraduate, 1,167 graduate)

DEANS

College of Arts and Sciences: Dr DONNA DICKERSON
College of Business and Technology: Dr JIM TARTER
College of Education and Psychology: Dr WILLIAM GEIGER
College of Engineering and Computer Science: Dr TROY HENSON
College of Nursing and Health Sciences: Dr LINDA KLOTZ

University of Texas of the Permian Basin

Odessa, TX 79762

Telephone: (915) 552-2000
Internet: www.utpb.edu

Founded 1969

Pres.: CHARLES A. SORBER

Library of 763,000 vols
Number of students: 2,217

DEANS

College of Arts and Sciences: Dr JAMES OLSON
School of Business: Dr GARY KLEIN
School of Education: Dr PETE IENATSCH

University of Texas Pan American

Edinburg, TX 78539

Telephone: (956) 381-2100
Fax: (956) 381-2150
E-mail: info@panam.edu
Internet: www.panam.edu

Founded 1927 as Edinburg College, became Edinburg Junior College 1933, Edinburg Regional College 1948, Pan American College 1952, Pan American University 1971, present name 1989

Academic year: September to August

Pres.: Dr ROBERT S. NELSON
Dir of Admissions: DAVID ZUNIGA
Dir of Financial Aid: MICHELLE ALVARADO
Dir of Library: LAWRENCE CAYLOR

Library of 536,204 vols
Number of teachers: 601
Number of students: 14,399

University of Texas Southwestern Medical Center at Dallas

5323 Harry Hines Blvd, Dallas, TX 75235

Telephone: (214) 648-3111
Fax: (214) 648-8690
Internet: www3.utsouthwestern.edu

Founded 1949, fmrly Southwestern Medical School (f. 1943)

Pres.: KERN WILDENTHAL
Exec. Vice-Pres. for Academic Affairs: WILLIAM B. NEAVES
Exec. Vice-Pres. for Business Affairs: PETER H. FITZGERALD
Exec. Vice-Pres. for Clinical Affairs: WILLIS C. MADDREY
Dean of Graduate School of Biomedical Sciences: JOHN P. PERKINS
Dean of Southwestern Medical School: ROBERT J. ALPERN
Dean of School of Allied Health Sciences: H. GORDON GREEN
Assoc. Dean for Academic Affairs: Dr JAMES GRIFFIN
Assoc. Dean for Student Affairs: BARBARA WALLER
Assoc. Vice-Pres. of Student Services: J. WESLEY NORRED
Librarian: MARTY ADAMSON

Number of teachers: 1,149
Number of students: 800 medical, 499 graduates, 397 allied health

University of Texas Medical Branch at Galveston

301 University Blvd, Galveston, TX 77555-0144

Telephone: (409) 772-2618
Fax: (409) 772-6216
E-mail: public.affairs@utmb.edu
Internet: www.utmb.edu

Founded 1891, fmrly Medical Br., Galveston

Pres.: THOMAS N. JAMES
Exec. Vice-Pres. for Admin. and Business Affairs: E. J. PEDERSON
Dir of Library: EMIL FREY

Number of teachers: 873
Number of students: 1,692

DEANS

Graduate School of Biomedical Sciences: K. LEMONE YIELDING
Medicine: GEORGE T. BRYAN
School of Allied Health Sciences: JOHN G. BRUHN
School of Nursing: MARY V. FENTON

University of Texas Health Science Center at Houston, School of Public Health

POB 20186, Houston, TX 77225

Telephone: (713) 500-9050
Fax: (713) 500-9020
E-mail: sphdean@uth.tmc.edu
Internet: www.sph.uth.tmc.edu

Founded 1967

Academic year: August

Pres.: Dr LARRY R. KAISER
Dean: Dr ROBERTA B. NESS

Number of teachers: 165
Number of students: 1,300

University of Texas Health Science Center at San Antonio

7703 Floyd Curl Dr., San Antonio, TX 78284

Telephone: (210) 567-7000
Internet: www.uthscsa.edu

Founded 1959 as South Texas Medical School, a part of The Univ. of Texas System, name changed to Univ. of Texas Medical School at San Antonio 1967, present name 1972

Pres.: Dr JOHN P. HOWE, III
Exec. Vice-Pres. for Admin. and Business Affairs: ROBERT B. PRICE
Vice-Pres. for Academic Services: Dr JOHN A. THOMAS
Vice-Pres. for Univ. Relations: JUDY P. WOLF
Exec. Assistant to the Pres.: MARY G. ETTLINGER
Pres. and Chief Exec. Officer for Univ. Health System: JOHN A. GUEST
Dir of Student Services (vacant)

Library of 192,576 vols

DEANS

Dental School: KENNETH L. KALKWARF
Graduate School of Biomedical Sciences: Dr SANFORD A. MILLER
Medical School: Dr JAMES J. YOUNG
School of Allied Health Sciences: Dr JAMES G. VAN STRATEN
School of Nursing: Dr ROBIN D. FROMAN

University of Texas M. D. Anderson Cancer Center

1515 Holcombe Blvd, Houston, TX 77030

Telephone: (713) 7926161
Internet: www.mdanderson.org

Founded 1941

Academic year: August to July

Pres.: Dr JOHN MENDELSOHN
Exec. Vice-Pres.: LEON J. LEACH
Exec. Vice-Pres. and Chief Academic Officer: Dr MARGARET L. KRIPKE
Exec. Vice-Pres. and Chief Operating Officer: Dr DAVID L. CALLENDER
Dean of School of Health Sciences: Dr MICHAEL J. AHEARN
Exec. Dir of Library: KATHY HOFFMAN

Library of 19,611 vols
Number of teachers: 900

DIRECTORS

Clinical Laboratory Science (Medical Technology): KAREN MCCLURE
Cytogenetic Technology: VICKI L. HOPWOOD
Cytotechnology: CHRISTINA M. ALAPAT
Histotechnology: HAZEL V. DALTON
Medical Dosimetry: MELISSA JANE CHAPMAN
Radiation Therapy: SHAUN T. CALDWELL

UNIVERSITY OF THE INCARNATE WORD

4301 Broadway, San Antonio, TX 78209-6397

Telephone: (210) 829-6000

Fax: (210) 829-6096
E-mail: admis@uiwtx.edu
Internet: www.uiw.edu

Founded 1881
Private control
Academic year: August to June

Chancellor: HELENA MONAHAN
Pres.: Dr LOUIS J. AGNESE, Jr
Provost: Dr DENIS DOYLE
Vice-Pres. for Enrollment Management and Student Services: Dr DAVID JURENOVICH
Vice-Pres. for Finance and Technology: Dr DOUG ENDLSEY
Vice-Pres. for Institutional Advancement: Sister KATHLEEN COUGHLIN
Vice-Pres. for Int. Programmes: Dr MARCOS FRAGOSO
Registrar: Dr BOBBYE G. FRY
Dean of Enrollment: ANDREA CYTERSKI-ACOSTA
Dean of Library Services: CHERYL ANDERSON

Library of 271,657 books, serial backfiles, govt douments, 46,637 current serial subscriptions incl. periodicals, newspapers and govt documents
Number of teachers: 524
Number of students: 7,214

Publications: *Illuminatus*, *Journal of the Life and Culture of San Antonio*, *Quirk* (UIW Journal of Literature and Art), *Verbum Incarnatum* (Journal of Multidisciplinary Studies)

DEANS

College of Humanities, Arts and Social Sciences: Dr ROBERT CONNELLY
Dreeben School of Education: Dr DENISE STAUDT
Feik School of Pharmacy: Dr ARCELIA JOHNSON-FANNIN
H. E. B. School of Business and Administration: Dr SHAWN DALY
School of Graduate Studies and Research: Dr KEVIN VICHCALES
School of Interactive Media and Design: Dr SHARON WELKEY
School of Mathematics, Science and Engineering: Dr GLENN JAMES
School of Nursing and Health Professions: Dr KATHI LIGHT
School of Optometry: Dr HANI GHAZI-BIRRY

WAYLAND BAPTIST UNIVERSITY

Plainview, TX 79072
Telephone: (806) 291-1000
Fax: (806) 291-1960
E-mail: admityou@wbu.edu
Internet: www.wbu.edu

Founded 1906, chartered 1908
Private control
Academic year: June to May

Pres.: Dr PAUL ARMES
Exec. Vice-Pres. and Provost: Dr BOBBY HALL
Assoc. Vice-Pres. of External Campuses: Dr ELANE SEEBO
Asst Vice-Pres. for Academic Affairs: STANLEY DEMERRITT
Vice-Pres. for Enrollment Management: Dr CLAUDE LUSK
Chief Financial Officer: JIM SMITH
Registrar: JULIE BOWEN
Librarian: Dr POLLY LACKEY

Library of 130,044 vols
Number of teachers: 95
Number of students: 1,430

Publications: *Footprints* (24 a year), *The Traveler* (yearbook, 1 a year)

DEANS

Don Williams School of Education and Exercise and Sport Science: Dr JAMES TODD
School of Behavioural and Social Sciences: Dr ESTELLE OWENS
School of Business: Dr OTTO B. SCHACHT
School of Fine Arts: Dr MARTI RUNNELS
School of Languages and Literature: Dr CINDY MCCLENAGAN
School of Mathematics and Sciences: Dr HERBERT GROVER
School of Music: Dr ANN STUTES
School of Religion and Philosophy: Dr PAUL SADLER

WILEY COLLEGE

Marshall, TX 75670
Telephone: (903) 927-3300
Fax: (903) 938-8100
Internet: www.wileyc.edu

Founded 1873
Academic year: August to May

Pres.: Dr HAYWOOD L. STRICKLAND
Exec. Vice-Pres.: Dr GLENDA F. CARTER
Vice-Pres. for Academic Affairs: Dr MARION ELBERT
Vice-Pres. for Student Affairs: Dr JOSEPH L. MORALE
Librarian: FRANK FRANCIS

Library of 85,000 vols
Number of teachers: 45
Number of students: 552

DIVISION CHAIRS

Chair. of Education: Dr WILLIAM A. BROWN
Chair. of Humanities: Dr SOLOMON MASENDA
Chair. of Natural and Computational Sciences: Dr OBADIAH NJUE
Chair. of Social and Behavioural Sciences: Dr LLOYD THOMPSON

UTAH

BRIGHAM YOUNG UNIVERSITY

Provo, UT 84602
Telephone: (801) 378-4636
E-mail: admissions@byu.edu
Internet: www.byu.edu

Founded 1875 by Pres. Brigham Young of the Church of Jesus Christ of Latter-day Saints
Academic year: August to April

Pres.: CECIL O. SAMUELSON
Chief Financial Officer and Vice-Pres. for Admin.: BRIAN K. EVANS
Vice-Pres. for Academic Affairs: JOHN S. TANNER
Vice-Pres. for Advancement: K. FRED SKOUSEN
Vice-Pres. for Student Life: JANET S. SCHARMAN
Gen. Counsel: THOMAS B. GRIFFITH
Dean of Admissions and Records: ERLEND D. PETERSON
Univ. Librarian: RANDY J. OLSEN

Library of 3,570,930 vols, pamphlets and bulletins
Number of teachers: 1,857 (1,517 full-time, 340 part-time)
Number of students: 39,577

DEANS

School of Education: ROBERT S. PATTERSON
School of Law: H. REESE HANSEN
School of Management: NED C. HILL
College of Biology and Agriculture: R. KENT CROOKSTON
College of Engineering and Technology: DOUGLAS M. CHABRIES
College of Family, Home and Social Sciences: DAVID B. MAGLEBY
College of Fine Arts and Communications: K. NEWELL DAYLEY
College of Health and Human Performance: ROBERT CONLEE
College of Humanities: VAN C. GESSEL
College of Nursing: ELAINE MARSHALL
College of Physical and Mathematical Sciences: EARL M. WOOLLEY
Continuing Education: RICHARD C. EDDY
Graduate Studies: BONNIE BRINTON
Honours and General Education: GEORGE S. TATE
Religious Education: ANDREW C. SKINNER

ITT TECHNICAL INSTITUTE

920 West LeVoy Dr., Murray, UT 84123
Telephone: (801) 263-3313
Fax: (801) 263-3497
Internet: www.itt-tech.edu

Exec. Sec.: NORMA JEAN SEGER.

UNIVERSITY OF UTAH

201 President's Circle, Salt Lake City, UT 84112-9009
Telephone: (801) 581-7200
Fax: (801) 581-3007
Internet: www.utah.edu

Founded 1850 as Univ. of Deseret, present name 1892
Academic year: August to May

Pres.: MICHAEL K. YOUNG
Sr Vice-Pres. for Academic Affairs: DAVID W. PERSHING
Sr Vice-Pres. for Health Sciences: A. LORRIS BETZ
Vice-Pres. for Admin. Services: ARNOLD B. COMBE
Vice-Pres. for Human Resources: LORETTA HARPER
Vice-Pres. for Institutional Advancement: FRED C. ESPLIN
Vice-Pres. for Research: THOMAS PARKS
Vice-Pres. for Student Affairs: BARBARA H. SNYDER
Exec. Asst to the Pres.: LIZ MCCOY
Gen. Counsel: JOHN K. MORRIS
Registrar: TIM EBNER
Dir of Library: JOYCE L. OGBURN

Number of teachers: 3,274
Number of students: 28,025

Publications: *Hinckley Journal of Politics*, *Journal of Land Resources and Environmental Law*, *Journal of Law and Family Studies*, *Political Research Quarterly*, *Quarterly West* (creative writing journal), *Tanner Lectures on Human Values* (cumulative volume of transcripts), *Undergraduate Research Abstracts*, *Utah Foreign Language Abstracts*, *Utah Law Review* (4 a year), *Western Humanities* (4 a year)

DEANS

Architecture: BRENDA C. SCHEER
Business: JACK BRITTAIN
Education: MICHAEL L. HARDMAN
Engineering: RICHARD B. BROWN
Fine Arts: RAYMOND TYMAS-JONES
Health: JAMES E. GRAVES
Humanities: ROBERT NEWMAN
Law: HIRAM CHODOSH
Medicine: DAVID J. BJORKMAN
Mines and Earth Sciences: FRANCIS H. BROWN
Nursing: MAUREEN R. KEEFE
Pharmacy: JOHN W. MAUGER
Science: PIERRE V. SOKOLSKY
Social and Behavioural Science: M. DAVID RUDD
Social Work: JANNAH MATHER
Continuing Education: CHUCK WIGHT
Graduate School: DAVID S. CHAPMAN

CHAIRMEN OF DEPARTMENTS

Business (Kendall Garff Bldg, 1645 East Campus Centre Dr., Salt Lake City, UT 84112; tel. (801) 581-7347; fax (801) 581-7214; e-mail dean@business.utah.edu; internet www.business.utah.edu):

Accounting: BOB ALLEN
Finance: URI LOEWENSTEIN
Management: DON WARDELL
Marketing: BILL MOORE

Education (Milton Bennion Hall, 1705 East Campus Center Dr., Salt Lake City, UT 84112; tel. (801) 581-8221; fax (801) 581-5223; e-mail sperry@ed.utah.edu; internet www.gse.utah.edu):

Education, Culture and Society: HARVEY KANTOR
Education, Leadership and Policy: DIANA POUNDER
Educational Psychology: ELAINE CLARK
Special Education: ANDREA MCDONNELL
Teaching and Learning: MICHAEL HARDMAN

Engineering (Kennecott Research Center, 1515 Mineral Sq., Salt Lake City, UT 84112; tel. (801) 581-6912; fax (801) 581-8692; e-mail stringfellow@coe.utah.edu):

Bioengineering: VLADIMIR HLADY
Chemical Engineering: PHIL SMITH
Civil and Environmental Engineering: LAWRENCE REAVELEY
EGI: RAY LEVY
Electrical and Computer Engineering: MARC BODSON
Materials Science and Engineering: ANIL VIRKAR
Mechanical Engineering: JOSEPH C. KLEWICKI
School of Computing: CHRIS JOHNSON

Fine Arts (Art Bldg, 375 South 1530E, Rm 250, Salt Lake City, UT 84112; tel. (801) 581-6764; fax (801) 585-3066; e-mail phyllis.haskell@finearts.utah.edu; internet www.finearts.utah.edu):

Art and Art History: ELIZABETH PETERSON
Ballet: CAROL IWASAKI
Film Studies: KEVIN HANSON
Modern Dance: DONNA WHITE
Music: ROBERT WALZEL
Theatre: BOB NELSON

Health (Hyper-North, 250 South 1850E, Salt Lake City, UT 84112; tel. (801) 581-8537; fax (801) 581-5580; e-mail cheri.curtis@health.utah.edu; internet www.health.utah.edu):

Communication Disorders: BRUCE L. SMITH
Exercise and Sport Science: BARRY SHULTZ
Foods and Nutrition: WAYNE ASKEW
Health Promotion and Education: LES CHATELAIN
Occupational Therapy: JOANNE WRIGHT
Parks, Recreation and Tourism: DAN DUSTIN
Physical Therapy: SCOTT WARD

Humanities (LNCO, 255 South Central Campus Dr., Rm 2100, Salt Lake City, UT 84112; tel. (801) 581-6214; fax (801) 585-5190; e-mail robert.newman@hum.utah.edu; internet www.hum.utah.edu):

Communication: ANN DARLING
English: VINCENT PECORA
History: JIM LEHNING
Languages and Literature: JANE HACKING
Linguistics: ED RUBIM
Middle East Centre: FERNANDO RUBIO
Philosophy: LESLIE FRANCIS
Tanner Humanities Centre: BOB GOLDBERG
Writing Programme: MAUREEN MATHISON

Medicine (Moran Eye Center, 50 North Medical Dr., Moran 5th Fl., Salt Lake City, UT 84112; tel. (801) 581-5619; fax (801) 585-3109; e-mail lorris.betz@hsc.utah.edu; internet www.med.utah.edu/som):

Anaesthesiology: MICHAEL CAHALAN
Biochemistry: DANA CARROLL
Dermatology: JOHN ZONE
Family and Preventive Medicine: MICHAEL MAGILL
Human Genetics: MARK F. LEPPERT, MARIO CAPECCHI
Huntsman Cancer Institute: MARY BECKERLY
Internal Medicine: JOHN R. HOIDAL
Medical Informatics: JOYCE MITCHEL
Neurobiology and Anatomy: MONICA VETTER
Neurology: STEFAN PULST
Neurosurgery: WILLIAM T. COULDWELL
Obstetrics and Gynaecology: MATT PETTERSON
Oneological Sciences: BARBARA J. GRAVES
Ophthalmology with Visual Sciences: R. J. OLSON
Orthopaedics: CHARLES SALTZMAN
Paediatrics: EDWARD B. CLARK
Pathology: PETER JENSEN
Pharmacy and Toxicology: WILLIAM R. CROWLEY
Physical Medicine and Rehabilitation Division: JOSEPH WEBSTER
Physiology: ED DUDEK (acting)
Psychiatry: WILLIAM MCMANN
Radiation Oncology: DENNIS C. SHRIEVE
Radiology: EDWIN A. STEVENS
Surgery: SEAN MULVIHILL

Mines and Earth Sciences (Browning Bldg, 135 South 1460E, Rm 209, Salt Lake City, UT 84112; tel. (801) 581-8767; fax (801) 581-5560; e-mail fbrown@mines.utah.edu; internet www.mines.utah.edu):

Geology and Geophysics: ERIK PETERSON
Metallurgical Engineering: JAN MILLER
Meteorology: JAMES SPEENDURGH
Mining Engineering: MICHAEL K. MCCARTER
Seismograph Stations: WALTER J. ARABASZ

Pharmacy (Skaggs Pharmacy Bldg, 30 S 1990E, Salt Lake City, UT 84112; tel. (801) 581-3402; fax (801) 581-3716; e-mail jmauger@deans.pharm.utah.edu; internet www.pharmacy.utah.edu):

Medicinal Chemistry: CHRIS IRELAND
Pharmaceutics and Pharmaceutical Chemistry: DAVID GRANGER
Pharmacology and Toxicology: WILLIAM R. CROWLEY
Pharmacy Therapy: DIANE BRIXNER

Science (James Talmage Bldg, 1430 E President's Circle, Salt Lake City, UT 84112; tel. (801) 581-6958; fax (801) 585-3169; e-mail stang@chemistry.utah.edu; internet www.science.utah.edu):

Biology: NEIL J. VICKERS
Chemistry: HENRY S. WHITE
Mathematics: AARON BETRTRAM
Physics: DAVID B. KIEDA

Social and Behavioural Science (Orson Spencer Hall, 260 S Central Campus Dr., Salt Lake City, UT 84112; tel. (801) 581-8620; fax (801) 585-5081; e-mail jsott@cppa.utah.edu; internet www.csbs.utah.edu):

Aerospace Studies: Lt Col KENT WONG
Anthropology: ELIZABETH CASHDIN
Economics: KORKUK ERTURK
Family and Consumer Studies: SHERYL WRIGHT
Geography: HARVEY MILLER
Military Science: Lt Col JACK E. STURGEON
Naval Science: Capt. TIMOTHY LAWRENCE
Political Science: MATHEW BERBANK
Psychology: FRANCES J. FRIEDERICH
Sociology: MICHAEL TIMBERLAKE

UTAH STATE UNIVERSITY

Office of the Pres., 1400 Old Main Hill, Logan, UT 84322-1400
Telephone: (435) 797-1000
Fax: (435) 797-1173
E-mail: prm@usu.edu
Internet: www.usu.edu
Founded 1888
Academic year: August to May
Pres.: STAN L. ALBRECHT
Exec. Vice-Pres. and Provost: RAYMOND T. COWARD
Vice-Pres. for Business and Finance: FRED R. HUNSAKER
Vice-Pres. for Extension and Agriculture: NOELLE COCKETT
Vice-Pres. for Information Technology: M. K. JEPPESEN
Vice-Pres. for Research: BRENT C. MILLER
Vice-Pres. for Strategic Ventures: NED M. WEINSHENKER
Vice-Pres. for Student Services: JAMES D. MORALES
Vice-Pres. for Univ. Advancement: F. ROSS PETERSON
Number of teachers: 803
Number of students: 23,925
Publications: *Outlook* (6 a year), *Outreach* (12 a year), *Utah Science* (4 a year), *Western American Literary Journal* (4 a year), *Western Historical Quarterly*

DEANS

Caine College of the Arts: CRAIG JESSOP
College of Agriculture: NOELLE COCKETT
College of Engineering: H. SCOTT HINTON
College of Humanities and Social Sciences: JOHN ALLEN
College of Natural Resources: NAT B. FRAZER
College of Science: MARY S. HUBBARD
Emma Eccles Jones College of Education and Human Services: BETH FOLEY
Extension: NOELLE COCKETT
John M. Huntsman School of Business: DOUGLAS D. ANDERSON
School of Graduate Studies: BYRON R. BURNHAM

UTAH VALLEY STATE COLLEGE

800 West University Parkway, Orem, UT 84058
Telephone: (801) 222-8000
Fax: (801) 226-5207
E-mail: info@uvsc.edu
Internet: www.uvsc.edu
Pres.: Dr WILLIAM A. SEDERBURG.

WEBER STATE UNIVERSITY

3850 University Circle, Ogden, UT 84408
Telephone: (801) 626-6000
Fax: (801) 626-7922
E-mail: mediarelations@weber.edu
Internet: www.weber.edu
Founded 1889
Academic year: August to August
Pres.: F. ANN MILNER
Provost: MICHAEL B. VAUGHAN
Vice-Pres. for Admin. Services: NORM TARBOX
Vice-Pres. for Student Affairs: Dr JAN WINNIFORD
Registrar: Dr WINSLOW L. HURST
Dir of Library: JOAN G. HUBBARD
Library of 580,000 vols
Number of teachers: 442
Number of students: 14,000
Publications: *Legacy* (2 a year), *Metaphor* (1 a year), *U-News* (12 a year), *Vista* (2 a year), *Weber Studies* (4 a year)
Courses in arts and humanities, applied science and technology, business and eco-

nomics, education, science, social and behavioural science and the health professions.

WESTMINSTER COLLEGE

1840 South 1300 East St, Salt Lake City, UT 84105
Telephone: (801) 484-7651
Fax: (801) 466-6916
E-mail: admissions@wcslc.edu
Internet: www.wcslc.edu

Founded 1875

Pres.: Dr MICHAEL S. BASSIS
Exec. Vice-Pres. and Treas.: STEPHEN MORGAN
Vice-Pres. for Academic Affairs and Dean of the Faculty: Dr STEPHEN R. BAAR
Vice-Pres. for Information Technology: Dr SHERYL PHILLIPS
Vice-Pres. for Institutional Advancement: NANCY MICHAEKO
Vice-Pres. for Student Devt and Enrollment Planning: PHIL ALLETTO
Dean of Students: MARK FERNE
Librarian: DAVID HALES

Library of 84,000 vols
Number of teachers: 216
Number of students: 2,140

DEANS

School of Arts and Sciences: Dr MARY JANE CHASE
School of Business: Dr JAMES SIEDELAMN
School of Education: Dr JANET DYNAK
School of Nursing and Health Sciences: (vacant)

VERMONT

BENNINGTON COLLEGE

1 College Dr., Bennington, VT 05201
Telephone: (802) 442-5401
Fax: (802) 442-4320
E-mail: admissions@bennington.edu
Internet: www.bennington.edu

Founded 1932
Private control; attached to New England Assen of Schools and Colleges (NEASC)
Academic year: September to June

Pres.: ELIZABETH COLEMAN
Exec. Vice-Pres. for Finance and Admin.: WILLIAM MORGAN
Vice-Pres. for External Relations: PAIGE BARTELS
Vice-Pres. for Planning and Spec. Projects: JOAN GOODRICH
Vice-Pres. and Chief Information Officer: ALAN USAS
Provost and Dean of the College: ELISSA TENNEY
Dean of Admissions and Financial Aid: KEN HIMMELMAN
Dean of Students: EVA CHATTERJEE-SUTTON
Registrar: KATHY POSEY
Dir of Library and Information Services: OCEANA WILSON

Library of 108,000 vols
Number of teachers: 70
Number of students: 732

Courses in anthropology, architecture, art history, astronomy, biology, ceramics, chemistry, Chinese, computer science, dance, design, digital arts, directing, drama, drawing, economics, education, environmental science, film and video, French, history, int. relations, Italian, Japanese, literature, mathematics, music, painting, philosophy, photography, physics, playwriting, political science, printmaking, psychology, religion, sculpture, Spanish, teaching.

BURLINGTON COLLEGE

95 North Ave, Burlington, VT 05401
Telephone: (802) 862-9616
Fax: (802) 660-4331
E-mail: admissions@burlington.edu
Internet: www.burlington.edu

Pres.: JANE O'MEARA SANDERS (acting)
Academic Dean: MICHAEL SHERMAN
Dir of Admissions: JOSH DOYLE
Dir of Communications: MARIA ZAMORA-CROSBY
Dir of Devt: SARAH JUDD
Dir of Library and Information Services: JESSICA ALLARD
Dir of Student Services: SARAH MELL
Chief Financial Officer: LARRY VELADOTA
Registrar: MELISSA HOWANITZ

Library of 13,000 vols, 1,000 video cassettes and 500 sound recordings

Depts of cinema studies, humanities, int. studies, photography, psychology/gender studies, writing.

CASTLETON STATE COLLEGE

86 Seminary St, Castleton, VT 05735
Telephone: (802) 468-5611
Fax: (802) 468-6470
E-mail: info@castleton.edu
Internet: www.csc.vsc.edu

Founded 1787
Liberal arts, career education
Academic year: August to May

Pres.: DAVID S. WOLK
Dean of Academics: Dr JOSEPH T. MARK
Dean of Admin.: WILLIAM ALLEN
Dean of Students: GREGORY STONE
Dir of Communications: ENNIS DULING
Dir of Devt: GEORGE MCGURL
Dir of Human Resources: LYN SAWYER
Registrar: LORI PATTEN
Dir of the Library: SANDRA DULING

Library of 160,000 vols
Number of teachers: 89
Number of students: 1,700

Depts of art, business admin., communication, economics and politics, education, English, history, geography, mathematics, music, natural science, nursing, physical education, psychology, sociology, social work and criminal justice, Spanish, theatre arts.

CHAMPLAIN COLLEGE

163 South Willard St, Burlington, VT 05401
Telephone: (802) 860-2700
Fax: (802) 862-2772
E-mail: admission@champlain.edu
Internet: www.champlain.edu

Founded 1878
Private

Pres.: DAVID F. FINNY
Registrar: BECKY PETERSON
Library Dir: JANET COTTRELL

Number of teachers: 112
Number of students: 1,950

Divs of business, communication and creative media, education and human studies, information technology and sciences.

COLLEGE OF ST JOSEPH

71 Clement Rd, Rutland, VT 05701
Telephone: (802) 773-5900
E-mail: info@csj.edu
Internet: www.csj.edu
Catholic, liberal arts

Founded 1956 by Sisters of St Joseph
Language of instruction: English
Academic year: September to May

Divs of arts and sciences, business, education, psychology and human services

Pres.: FRANK G. MIGLORIE
Vice-Pres. for Academic Affairs: LUIS GARCIA
Vice-Pres. for External Affairs: SUSAN ENGLESE
Registrar: PATRICIA C. MIGLORIE
Librarian: DOREEN J. MCCULLOUGH

Library of 54,000
Number of students: 500

GODDARD COLLEGE

123 Pitkin Rd, Plainfield, VT 05667
Telephone: (802) 454-8311
Fax: (802) 454-8017
E-mail: admissions@goddard.edu
Internet: www.goddard.edu

Founded 1938

Pres.: MARK SCHULMAN
Vice-Pres. for Academic Affairs and Dean of College: KABBA COLLEY
Vice-Pres. for Finance and Admin.: DARYL CAMPBELL
Dean of Enrollment Management: PETER BURNS
Registrar: JOHN CASTLE
Chief Information and Technology Officer: CHRIS RIDDELL

Library of 72,000 vols
Number of teachers: 32 (24 full-time, 8 part-time)
Number of students: 500

GREEN MOUNTAIN COLLEGE

1 Brennan Circle, Poultney, VT 05764
Telephone: (802) 287-8000
Fax: (802) 287-8099
Internet: www.greenmtn.edu

Founded 1834 as Troy Conf. Acad.
Private control
Academic year: September to May

Pres.: PAUL J. FONTEYN
Provost and Vice-Pres. of Academic Affairs: WILLIAM THROPP
Vice Pres. for Devt: RICHARD J. DONOVAN
Vice-Pres. for Finance and Admin.: JOSEPH MANNING
Dir of Communications: KEVIN COBURN
Dean of Faculty: THOMAS J. MAUHS-PUGH
Registrar: SHARON L. HOFFMAN
Dir of Library, IT Services and Learning Support: PAUL MILLETTE

Number of teachers: 82
Number of students: 750

Depts of business and economics, education, English and communications, environmental liberal arts, environmental studies, liberal studies, Masters programmes, natural and mathematical sciences, natural resource management, philosophy, recreation and outdoor studies, resort and hospitality management, social and behavioural science, visual and performing arts.

JOHNSON STATE COLLEGE

Johnson, VT 05656
Telephone: (802) 635-2356
Fax: (802) 635-9745
Internet: www.jsc.vsc.edu

Founded 1828

Pres.: BARBARA E. MURPHY
Dean of Academic Affairs: DAN REGAN
Dean of Admin.: SHARRON SCOTT
Dean of Students: DAVE BERGH
Registrar: DOUGLAS EASTMAN
Librarian: PAM GELINEAU

Library of 106,000 vols, 601 journals
Number of teachers: 137 (54 full-time, 83 part-time)

Number of students: 1,934

Depts of behavioural sciences, business and economics, education, environmental and health sciences, fine and performing arts, humanities, mathematics, writing and literature.

LYNDON STATE COLLEGE

Lyndonville, VT 05851

Telephone: (802) 626-6413
Fax: (802) 626-6335
E-mail: admissions@lyndonstate.edu
Internet: www.lyndonstate.edu

Founded 1911

College of the liberal arts and professional programmes; depts of arts, atmospheric sciences, business admin., education, electronic journalism arts, English, exercise science, film studies, general studies, liberal studies, music and performing arts, mountain recreation management, mathematics and computer science, natural sciences, philosophy, psychology, social sciences, visual arts

Pres.: Dr Carol A. Moore
Dean of Academic and Student Affairs: Donna Dalton
Dean of Admin.: Wayne T. Hamilton
Dean of Institutional Advancement: Robert E. Whittaker
Registrar and Asst Academic Dean: Debra A. Hale
Librarian: Garet Nelson

Library of 113,000 vols
Number of teachers: 59 full-time, 103 part-time
Number of students: 1,521

MARLBORO COLLEGE

Marlboro, VT 05344

Telephone: (802) 257-4333
Fax: (802) 257-4154
E-mail: admissions@marlboro.edu
Internet: www.marlboro.edu

Founded 1946

Pres.: Ellen McCulloch-Lovell
Dean of Faculty: Felicity Ratté
Dean of Students: Ken Schneck
Admissions Dir: Kirsten Camp
Registrar: Hilly van Loon
Librarian: Radka Ballada

Library of 75,000 vols, 17,000 periodicals
Number of teachers: 41
Number of students: 330

Divs of arts, humanities, natural sciences, social sciences, world studies.

MIDDLEBURY COLLEGE

Middlebury, VT 05753

Telephone: (802) 443-5000
E-mail: mpaine@middlebury.edu
Internet: www.middlebury.edu

Founded 1800

Pres.: Ronald D. Liebowitz
Exec. Vice-Pres. and Provost: Alison Byerly
Vice-Pres. for Language Schools, Schools Abroad and Graduate Programmes: Michael Geisler
Dean of Faculty: Susan Campbell
Dean of Faculty Devt and Research: Sunder Ramaswamy
Dean of Library and Information Services: Barbara Doyle-Wilch

Library of 852,000 vols
Number of teachers: 281
Number of students: 2,350

Divs of arts, foreign languages, humanities, literature, natural sciences, social sciences

Publication: *New England Review* (4 a year).

NORWICH UNIVERSITY

158 Harmon Dr., Northfield, VT 05663

Telephone: (802) 485-2000
Fax: (802) 485-2032
E-mail: nuadm@norwich.edu
Internet: www.norwich.edu

Founded 1819
Private, military

Pres.: Richard W. Schneider
Vice-Pres. for Academic Affairs and Dean of Faculty: Bjong Wolf Yeigh
Vice-Pres. for Devt and Alumni Relations: David J. Whaley
Vice-Pres. for Enrollment and Communication: Karen P. McGrath
Vice-Pres. for Strategic Partnerships: Phil Susmann
Vice-Pres. for Student Affairs: Michael B. Kelley
Chief Admin. Officer: David Magida
Treas.: Richard E. Rebmann
Library Dir: Ellen Hall

Library of 240,000 vols and microfilms; military history colln
Number of teachers: 112
Number of students: 1,900

SAINT MICHAEL'S COLLEGE

1 Winooski Park, Colchester, VT 05439

Telephone: (802) 654-2000
Fax: (802) 654-2297
E-mail: admission@smcvt.edu
Internet: www.smcvt.edu

Founded 1904
Academic year: August to May

Pres.: Jack Neuhauser
Provost and Vice-Pres. of Academic Affairs: Karen Talentino
Vice-Pres. for Finance and Treas.: Nancy Brock
Vice-Pres. for Instn Advancement: Patrick Gallivan
Vice-Pres. for Student Life and Dean of Students: Michael Samara
Dean of the College: Dr Jeffrey Trumbower
Registrar: John D. Sheehey
Dir of Library and Information Services: John K. Payne

Library of 369,000 units
Number of teachers: 144 full-time
Number of students: 2,000 undergraduates, 500 graduates

Majors in accounting, American studies, art, biochemistry, biology, business, chemistry, classics, computer science, East Asian studies, economics, education, engineering, English, environmental science, environmental studies, finance, fine arts, French, gender/women's studies, geography, global studies, history, information systems, int. business, Italian, journalism and mass communication, language and linguistics, management, marketing, mathematics, medieval studies, modern languages and literature, music, peace and justice, philosophy, physical science, physics, political science, psychology, religious studies, sociology/anthropology, Spanish, theatre.

SIT GRADUATE INSTITUTE

Kipling Rd, POB 676, Brattleboro, VT 05302-0676

Telephone: (802) 257-7751
Fax: (802) 258-3248
E-mail: info@sit.edu
Internet: www.sit.edu

Pres.: Adam S Weinberg.

SOUTHERN VERMONT COLLEGE

982 Mansion Dr., Bennington, VT 05201-6002

Telephone: (802) 442-5427
Fax: (802) 447-4695
E-mail: info@svc.edu
Internet: www.svc.edu

Founded 1926
Academic year: September to August

Pres.: Karen Gross
Dean of Academics: Rebecca M. DiLiddo
Dean of Advancement: Karen Trubritt
Dean of Enrolment: Joel Wincowski
Dean of Students: Anne Hopkins Gross
Registrar: James Frederick
Dir of Library: Sarah Sanfilippo

Number of teachers: 40
Number of students: 400

Divs of business, humanities, nursing, science and technology, social sciences.

UNIVERSITY OF VERMONT

Burlington, VT 05405

Telephone: (802) 656-3131
Internet: www.uvm.edu

Founded 1791
Public control
Language of instruction: English
Academic year: September to May

Pres.: Daniel M. Fogel
Sr Vice-Pres. and Provost: Jane E. Knodell
Vice-Pres. for Devt and Alumni Relations: Richard Bundy
Vice-Pres. for Enrollment Management: Christopher H. Lucier
Vice-Pres. for Finance and Admin.: Richard Cate
Vice-Pres. for Legal Affairs and Gen. Counsel: Francine T. Bazluke
Vice-Pres. for Research and Dean of Graduate Studies: Domenico Grasso
Vice-Pres. for State, Community and Federal Relations: Karen M. Meyer
Vice-Pres. for Student and Campus Life: Thomas J. Gustafson
Registrar: Keith P. Williams
Librarian: Mara R. Saule

Library: 2.6m. vols, 20,000 periodicals
Number of teachers: 1,316
Number of students: 11,593 undergraduates, 1,961 graduates

DEANS

College of Agriculture and Life Sciences: Thomas C. Vogelmann
College of Arts and Sciences: Joel Goldberg
College of Education and Social Services: Fayneese Miller
College of Engineering and Mathematics: Bernard F. Cole
College of Medicine: Frederick C. Morin
College of Nursing and Health Sciences: Patricia Prelock
Continuing Education: Cynthia L. Belliveau
Graduate Studies: Domenico Grasso
Honors College: S. Abu Rizvi
School of Business Administration: Sanjay Sharma
School of the Environment and Natural Resources: Mary Watzin

VERMONT LAW SCHOOL

POB 96, Chelsea St, South Royalton, VT 05068

Telephone: (802) 831-1000
Fax: (802) 763-2663
E-mail: admiss@vermontlaw.edu
Internet: www.vermontlaw.edu

Founded 1972
Private control
Language of instruction: English

Library of 230,000 vols, 2,300 periodicals and serial titles
Number of teachers: 44 regular, 7 visiting, 36 adjunct

Pres. and Dean: GEOFFREY B. SHIELDS
Chair. of Board: EDWARD C. MATTES
Vice-Pres. for Finance and Admin.: LORRAINE ATWOOD
Vice-Pres. for Institutional Advancement: DOROTHY BEHLEN HEINRICHS
Vice-Pres. for Interdepartmental Coordination: DENNIS STERN
Asst Vice-Pres. for Foundation and Corporate Relations: MICHAEL HEALY
Dir of Academic Procedures and Registrar: KATHRYN MAIELI
Dir of Communications: CAROL WESTBERG
Dir of Human Resources: DIANE HAYES
Dir of Library: CARL A. YIRKA
Dir of Media Relations: DIANE DERBY

Publications: *Vermont Journal of Environmental Law* (online), *Vermont Law Review* (4 a year).

VERMONT TECHNICAL COLLEGE

POB 500, Randolph Center, VT 05061-0500
Telephone: (802) 728-1000
Fax: (802) 728-1597
E-mail: admissions@vtc.edu
Internet: www.vtc.edu

Pres.: TY HANDY
Dean of Academic Affairs: PATRICIA MENCHINI
Dean of Admin.: JOHN DANIELS
Dean of College: MICHAEL VAN DYKE
Number of students: 1,453

Bachelors and Assoc. degrees in aeronautical engineering technology, agribusiness management technology, applied technology, architectural and building engineering technology, architectural engineering technology, automotive technology, business technology and management, civil and environmental engineering, computer engineering technology, construction practice and management, dairy farm management technology, dental hygiene, diesel power technology, electrical engineering technology, electromechanical engineering technology, equine studies, fire science, general engineering technology, information technology, landscape devt and ornamental horticulture, mechanical engineering technology, nursing, respiratory therapy, software engineering, sustainable design and technology, veterinary technology.

VIRGINIA

AVERETT UNIVERSITY

420 West Main St, Danville, VA 24541
Telephone: (434) 791-5600
E-mail: admit@averett.edu
Internet: www.averett.edu

Pres.: Dr TIFFANY MCKILLIP FRANKS.

BAPTIST THEOLOGICAL SEMINARY AT RICHMOND

3400 Brook Rd, Richmond, VA 23227
Telephone: (804) 355-8135
Fax: (804) 355-8182
Internet: www.btsr.edu

Pres.: RONALD CRAWFORD.

BLUEFIELD COLLEGE

3000 College Drive, Bluefield, VA 24605
Telephone: (276) 326-3682
Fax: (276) 326-4288
E-mail: bluefield@bluefield.edu
Internet: www.bluefield.edu
Founded 1922

Pres.: DANIEL G. MACMILLAN.

BRIDGEWATER COLLEGE

Bridgewater, VA 22812
Telephone: (540) 828-8000
Fax: (540) 828-5481
E-mail: admissions@bridgewater.edu
Internet: www.bridgewater.edu
Founded 1880
Liberal arts college
Academic year: August to May

Pres.: Dr PHILLIP C. STONE
Exec. Asst to the Pres.: ROY W. FERGUSON, Jr
Dean of the College: ART HESSLER
Librarian: DONNA S. BIBLE

Library of 184,160 vols
Number of teachers: 126 (96 full-time, 30 part-time)
Number of students: 1,500

Publication: *The Philomathean* (1 a year).

CHRISTENDOM COLLEGE

134 Christendom Drive, Front Royal, VA 22630
Telephone: (540) 636-2900
Fax: (540) 636-1655
E-mail: info@christendom.edu
Internet: www.christendom.edu

Pres.: Dr TIMOTHY T. O'DONNELL
Head of Academic Affairs: JONATHAN J. REYES
Registrar: WALTER JANARO.

CHRISTOPHER NEWPORT UNIVERSITY

1 University Place, Newport News, VA 23606
Telephone: (757) 594-7000
Fax: (757) 594-7333
E-mail: www@cnu.edu
Internet: www.cnu.edu

Pres.: PAUL S. TRIBLE, Jr.

COLLEGE OF WILLIAM AND MARY IN VIRGINIA

Williamsburg, VA 23187-8795
Telephone: (757) 253-4000
E-mail: admiss@wm.edu
Internet: www.wm.edu
Founded 1693
Academic year: September to May

Pres.: DENE R. NICHOL
Provost: P. GEOFFREY FEISS
Vice-Pres. for Admin.: ANNA K. MARTIN
Vice-Pres. for Devt: DENNIS CROSS
Vice-Pres. for Finance: SAMUEL E. JONES
Vice-Pres. for Public Relations: STEWART GAMAGE
Vice-Pres. for Student Affairs: SAMUEL SADLER
Registrar: CAROLINE BOGGS
Librarian: CONNIE K. MCCARTHY

Library: Libraries with 2,128,645 vols
Number of teachers: 736 (576 full-time, 160 part-time)
Number of students: 7,575

Publications: *Business Review*, *Environmental Law and Policy Review*, *Law Review*, *The William and Mary Quarterly*

DEANS

Faculty of Arts and Sciences: CARL STRIKWERDA
School of Business Administration: LAWRENCE PULLEY
School of Education: VIRGINIA MCLAUGHLIN
School of Marine Science: L. DONELSON WRIGHT
William and Mary School of Law: W. TAYLOR REVELEY, III
Research and Graduate Studies: DAVID FINIFTER

EASTERN MENNONITE UNIVERSITY

1200 Park Rd, Harrisonburg, VA 22802-2462
Telephone: (540) 432-4000
Fax: (540) 432-4444
E-mail: admiss@emu.edu
Internet: www.emu.edu
Founded 1917

Liberal arts college affiliated with the Mennonite Church, with programmes in 50 subject areas; emphasis on international education

Pres.: LOREN SWARTZENDRUBER
Dir for Admissions: STEPHANIE SHAFER
Registrar: DAVID A. DETROW
Librarian: BERYL BRUBAKER

Library of 149,000 vols
Number of teachers: 90
Number of students: 1,600

Publication: *Crossroads Magazine*.

EMORY AND HENRY COLLEGE

POB 947, Emory, VA 24327
Telephone: (276) 944-4121
E-mail: ehadmiss@ehc.edu
Internet: www.ehc.edu
Founded 1836

Pres.: Dr ROSALIND REICHARD
Number of students: 1,000

FERRUM COLLEGE

POB 1000, Ferrum, VA 24088
Telephone: (540) 365-2121
Fax: (540) 365-4266
E-mail: ferrumcollege@mac.com
Internet: www.ferrum.edu
Founded 1913

Pres.: Dr JENNIFER L. BRAATEN.

GEORGE MASON UNIVERSITY

4400 University Dr., Fairfax, VA 22030-4444
Telephone: (703) 993-1000
Internet: www.gmu.edu
Founded 1957

Pres.: Dr ALAN G. MERTEN
Sr Vice-Pres. for Finance and Planning: MAURICE W. SCHERRENS
Vice-Pres. for Univ. Life: Dr KAREN ROSENBLUM
Provost: Dr PETER N. STEARNS

Library of 2,846,733 vols
Number of teachers: 1,658 (965 full-time, 693 part-time)
Number of students: 24,897

Publication: *Faculty Bibliography* (1 a year).

HAMPDEN-SYDNEY COLLEGE

Hampden-Sydney, VA 23943
Telephone: (434) 223-6000
Fax: (434) 223-6346
E-mail: hsapp@hsc.edu
Internet: www.hsc.edu
Founded 1776
Academic year: August to May

Men's college of the liberal arts and sciences

Pres.: CHRISTOPHER B. HOWARD
Vice-Pres. for Admin.: PAUL S. BAKER
Vice-Pres. for Business Affairs: C. NORMAN KRUEGER
Dean of Admissions: ANITA H. GARLAND
Dean of the Faculty: ROBERT T. HERDEGEN, III
Registrar: DAWN L. CONGLETON

Librarian: CYRUS I. DILLON, III
Library of 250,000 vols
Number of teachers: 106
Number of students: 1,058

HAMPTON UNIVERSITY

Hampton, VA 23668
Telephone: (757) 727-5000
Fax: (757) 727-5746
Internet: www.hamptonu.edu
Founded 1868
Pres.: Dr WILLIAM R. HARVEY
Provost: Dr PAMELA HAMMOND
Vice-Pres. for Business Affairs and Treas.: DORETHA J. SPELLS
Vice-Pres. for Devt: LARON J. CLARK
Dir for Admissions: ANGELA BOYD
Registrar: JORSENE COOPER
Library of 331,727 vols
Number of students: 5,400

HOLLINS UNIVERSITY

POB 9625, Roanoke, VA 24020
Telephone: (540) 362-6401
Fax: (540) 362-6218
E-mail: huadm@hollins.edu
Internet: www.hollins.edu
Founded 1842
Independent liberal arts university with 29 major field of study; undergraduate programmes for women, selected graduate programmes for both men and women
Pres.: NANCY OLIVER GRAY (acting)
Provost: L. WAYNE MARKERT
Dean of Admissions: CELIA MCCORMICK
Dir of Scholarships and Financial Assistance: REBECCA ECKSTEIN
Univ. Registrar: THOMAS MESNER
Univ. Librarian: JOAN RUELLE
Library of 212,000 vols
Number of teachers: 111 (76 full-time, 35 part-time)
Number of students: 1,057
Publications: *Hollins Magazine* (3 a year), *The Hollins Critic* (4 a year).

JAMES MADISON UNIVERSITY

Harrisonburg, VA 22807
Telephone: (540) 568-6211
Fax: (540) 568-3634
E-mail: got@jmu.edu
Internet: www.jmu.edu
Founded 1908, name changed from Madison College 1977
Academic year: August to May
Pres.: Dr LINWOOD H. ROSE
Exec. Vice-Pres.: (vacant)
Vice-Pres. for Academic Affairs: Dr DOUGLAS BROW
Vice-Pres. for Student Affairs: Dr MARK WARNER
Univ. Librarian: RALPH ALBERICO
Library of 700,000 vols
Number of teachers: 700 (full-time)
Number of students: 15,000
Colleges of arts and letters, business education and psychology, integrated science and technology, science and mathematics, graduate school.

LIBERTY UNIVERSITY

1971 University Blvd, Lynchburg, VA 24502
Telephone: (434) 582-2000
Fax: (434) 582-2304
E-mail: admissions@liberty.edu
Internet: www.liberty.edu
Founded 1971
Chancellor and Pres.: JERRY FALWELL, Jr
Number of teachers: 341
Number of students: 35,300 (11,300 residential, 24,000 distance learning)

LONGWOOD COLLEGE

201 High St, Farmville, VA 23909
Telephone: (434) 395-2000
Fax: (434) 395-2635
E-mail: lcadmit@longwood.edu
Internet: www.longwood.edu
Founded 1839 as comprehensive college
Academic year: August to May
Pres.: Dr PATRICIA P. CORMIER
Vice-Pres. for Academic Affairs: NORMAN BREGMAN
Vice-Pres. for Business Affairs: DAVID HARNAGE
Vice-Pres. for Institutional Advancement: BOBBIE BURTON
Vice-Pres. for Student Affairs: PHYLLIS L. MABLE
Dir of Public Relations: DENNIS SERCOMBE
Assoc. Vice-Pres. for Research and Information Systems: RICHARD BRATCHER
Dir of Financial Aid: JEFF SCOFIELD
Registrar: ALECIA KNOX
Library of 288,175 vols
Number of teachers: 258 (168 full-time, 90 adjunct)
Number of students: 4,700

LYNCHBURG COLLEGE

1501 Lakeside Drive, Lynchburg, VA 24501
Telephone: (434) 544-8100
E-mail: president@lynchburg.edu
Internet: www.lynchburg.edu
Founded 1903
Pres.: Dr KENNETH R. GARREN
Registrar: JAY WEBB
Vice-Pres. for Enrollment Management: Dr DAVID BEHRS
Dean of the College: Dr JACQUELINE W. ASBURY
Librarian: CHRISTOPHER MILLSON-MARTULA
Library of 243,300 vols
Number of teachers: 161 (full-time)
Number of students: 2,500

MARY BALDWIN COLLEGE

Staunton, VA 24401
Telephone: (540) 887-7000
Fax: (540) 887-7292
E-mail: admit@mbc.edu
Internet: www.mbc.edu
Founded 1842
Private control
Academic year: August to May
Pres.: PAMELA FOX
Vice-Pres. for Academic Affairs and Dean: CATHARINE O'CONNELL
Registrar: LEWIS D. ASKEGAARD
Librarian: CAROL CREAGER
Library of 150,205 vols; 24,982 serial subscriptions, 61,761 microforms, 7,907 audiovisual items, 25,848 e-books
Number of teachers: 138
Number of students: 1,825 (1,537 undergraduates, 288 graduates)

MARYMOUNT UNIVERSITY

2807 North Glebe Rd, Arlington, VA 22207
Telephone: (703) 522-5600
Fax: (703) 284-1637
E-mail: admissions@marymount.edu
Internet: www.marymount.edu
Pres.: Dr JAMES E. BUNDSCHUH

DEANS
School of Arts and Humanities: Dr ROSEMARY HUBBARD
School of Business Administration: RONALD P. HUDAK
School of Education and Human Services: LESKO
School of Health Professions: THERESA CAPPELLO

NORFOLK STATE UNIVERSITY

700 Park Ave, Norfolk, VA 23504
Telephone: (757) 823-8600
Fax: (757) 823-2342
Internet: www.nsu.edu
Founded 1935
Pres.: Dr CAROLYN W. MEYERS.

OLD DOMINION UNIVERSITY

Norfolk, VA 23529
Telephone: (757) 683-3000
Fax: (757) 683-4505
Internet: www.odu.edu
Founded 1930 as a college
Pres.: ROSEANN RUNTE
Registrar: MARY SWARTZ
Librarian: VIRGINIA S. O'HERRON (acting)
Library of 2,870,692 items
Number of teachers: 632
Number of students: 20,656

RADFORD UNIVERSITY

Radford, VA 24142
Telephone: (540) 831-5000
Fax: (540) 831-5142
Internet: www.radford.edu
Founded 1910
Academic year: August to May
Pres.: Dr DOUGLAS COVINGTON
Vice-Pres. for Academic Affairs: WARREN P. SELF
Vice-Pres. for Business Affairs: DAVID A. BURDETTE
Vice-Pres. for Student Affairs: NORLEEN K. POMERANTZ
Vice-Pres. for Univ. Advancement: CHARLES A. WOOD
Library of 552,687 vols
Number of teachers: 551 (358 full-time, 193 part-time)
Number of students: 9,142

RANDOLPH COLLEGE

Lynchburg, VA 24503-1526
Telephone: (434) 947-8000
Fax: (434) 947-8138
Internet: www.randolphcollege.edu
Founded 1891
Academic year: August to May
Pres.: JOHN KLEIN
Vice-Pres. for Academic Affairs: DENNIS STEVENS
Vice-Pres. for Devt: JAMES C. KUGHN, Jr
Vice-Pres. for Enrollment: JOHN W. WHITE
Vice-Pres. for Finance and Admin.: CHRISTOPHER BURNLEY
Vice-Pres. for Institutional Advancement: JAN MERIWETHER
Vice-Pres. for Student Affairs: SARAH L. SWAGER
Librarian: THEODORE J. HOSTETLER
Library of 150,000 vols
Number of teachers: 96
Number of students: 764
Publications: *Hail, Muse!* (1 a year), *Randolph-Macon Alumnae Bulletin* (4 a year).

RANDOLPH-MACON COLLEGE

POB 5005, Ashland, VA 23005-5505
Telephone: (804) 752-7200
Fax: (804) 752-7231
Internet: www.rmc.edu

Founded 1830
Academic year: September to May

Pres.: Dr ROGER H. MARTIN
Registrar: Dr MARILYN J. GIBBS
Dean of Admissions: JOHN C. CONKRIGHT
Librarian: Dr VIRGINIA E. YOUNG

Library of 182,368 vols
Number of teachers: 88 full-time
Number of students: 1,126

REGENT UNIVERSITY

1000 Regent University Drive, Virginia Beach, VA 23464
Telephone: (757) 226-4127
E-mail: admissions@regent.edu
Internet: www.regent.edu

Pres.: PAT ROBERTSON
Chief Financial Officer: LARRY DANTZLER
Vice-Pres. for Academic Affairs: BARRY RYAN
Vice-Pres. for Devt and Communications: MAUREEN MCDONNELL
Vice-Pres. of Information Technology: TRACY STEWART
Vice-Pres. for Student Services: JEFF PITTMAN.

ROANOKE COLLEGE

221 College Lane, Salem, VA 24153
Telephone: (540) 375-2500
E-mail: admissions@roanoke.edu
Internet: roanoke.edu

Founded 1842

Pres.: MICHAEL C. MAXEY
Vice-Pres. and Dean: KENNETH R. GARREN
Vice-Pres. for Admissions Services: MICHAEL C. MAXEY
Vice-Pres. for Business Affairs: RICHARD C. HEMBERGER
Vice-Pres. for Resource Devt: JUDITH L. NELSON
Vice-Pres. for Student Affairs: MCMILLAN JOHNSON
Librarian: STANLEY F. UMBERGER

Library of 170,000 vols
Number of teachers: 150
Number of students: 1,700

SAINT PAUL'S COLLEGE

115 College Dr., Lawrenceville, VA 23868
Telephone: (434) 848-3111
Internet: www.saintpauls.edu

Founded 1888

Pres.: Dr ROBERT L. SATCHER, Sr
Provost and Vice-Pres. for Academic Affairs: Dr RAYMOND F. HOLMES
Vice-Pres. for Institutional Advancement: WILLIAM HERRINGTON
Vice-Pres. for Student Affairs: ROSEMARY LEWIS
Man. and Admin.: RYAN SPENCER (acting).

SHENANDOAH UNIVERSITY

1460 University Drive, Winchester, VA 22601
Telephone: (540) 665-4500
Fax: (540) 678-4331
E-mail: pr@su.edu
Internet: www.su.edu

Founded 1875

Pres.: TRACY FITZSIMMONS

Number of teachers: 348 (185 full-time, 163 part-time)
Number of students: 3,000

DEANS

Conservatory: CHARLOTTE A. COLLINS
School of Arts and Sciences: Dr CALVIN ALLEN
School of Health Professions: (vacant)
Bernard J. Dunn School of Pharmacy: (vacant)
Harry F. Byrd School of Business: STAN HARRISON

SWEET BRIAR COLLEGE

Sweet Briar, VA 24595
Telephone: (804) 381-6100
Fax: (804) 381-6173
E-mail: admissions@sbc.edu
Internet: www.sbc.edu

Liberal arts and sciences college

Founded 1901
Academic year: August to May

Pres.: Dr JO ELLEN JOHNSON PARKER
Vice-Pres. for College Relations: IVANA PELNAR-ZAIKO
Dean: Dr GEORGE H. LENZ
Assoc. Dean of Academic Affairs: Dr ALIX S. INGBER
Dean of Co-Curricular Life: Dr VALDRIE N. WALKER
Dir of Admissions: MARGARET WILLIAMS BLOUNT
Dir of Alumnae Affairs: LOUISE S. ZINGARO
Registrar: DEBBIE POWELL
Librarian: JOHN JAFFE

Library of 240,000 vols
Number of teachers: 109 (69 full-time, 40 part-time)
Number of students: 710

Publications: *Admissions Newsletter* (2 a year), *Alumnae Magazine* (3 a year), *Catalog* (1 a year), *President's Letter* (3 a year).

UNION THEOLOGICAL SEMINARY AND PRESBYTERIAN SCHOOL OF CHRISTIAN EDUCATION

3401 Brook Rd, Richmond, VA 23227
Telephone: (804) 355-0671
Fax: (804) 355-3919
Internet: www.union-psce.edu

Founded 1914

Pres.: Dr BRIAN K. BLOUNT
Registrar: BRENDA C. BARROWS
Librarian: JOHN TROTTI

Library of 260,000 vols
Number of teachers: 32
Number of students: 139

UNIVERSITY OF MARY WASHINGTON

1301 College Ave, Fredericksburg, VA 22401
Telephone: (540) 654-1000
Fax: (540) 654-1073
Internet: www.umw.edu

Founded 1908

Pres.: RICHARD V. HURLEY
Vice-Pres. for Academic Affairs and Dean of the Faculty: Dr JAY HARPER
Librarian: ROSEMARY HUFF ARNESON

Number of teachers: 177
Number of students: 5,000

DEANS

College of Arts and Sciences: Dr RICHARD FINKLESTEIN
College of Business: Dr LARRY PENWELL
College of Education: Dr MARY GENDERNALIK-COOPER

UNIVERSITY OF RICHMOND

28 Westhampton Way, University of Richmond, VA 23173
Telephone: (804) 289-8000
E-mail: admissions@richmond.edu
Internet: www.richmond.edu

Chartered as Richmond College 1830; as Univ. of Richmond 1920

Pres.: EDWARD L. AYERS
Chancellor: E. BRUCE HEILMAN
Vice-Pres. for Business and Finance: L. W. MOELCHERT
Vice-Pres. and Provost: ZEDDIE P. BOWEN
Vice-Pres. for Student Affairs: LEONARD S. GOLDBERG
Vice-Pres. for Univ. Relations: H. G. QUIGG
Registrar: W. VON KLEIN
Librarian: (vacant)

Library of 421,000 vols
Number of teachers: 529 (350 full-time, 179 part-time)
Number of students: 4,250

DEANS

Business Administration: T. L. REUSCHLING
Faculty of Arts and Sciences: F. SHELDON WETTACK
Graduate: JOHN L. GORDON, Jr
Law: JOSEPH D. HARBAUGH
Richmond College (Men): R. A. MATEER
University College, Summer School, Continuing Education: M. C. GRAEBER
Westhampton College (Women): PATRICIA C. HARWOOD

UNIVERSITY OF VIRGINIA

POB 400229, Charlottesville, VA 22904-4229
Telephone: (434) 924-0311
Fax: (434) 924-0938
Internet: www.virginia.edu

Founded 1819
Public control
Academic year: September to May

Pres.: TERESA SULLIVAN
Exec. Vice-Pres. and Chief Operating Officer: LEONARD W. SANDRIDGE, Jr
Exec. Vice-Pres. and Provost: ARTHUR GARSON, Jr
Dean of Admissions (Undergraduate): GREGORY ROBERTS
Dean of Students: ALLEN GROVES
Librarian: KARIN WITTENBORG

Library: see Libraries and Archives
Number of teachers: 1,309
Number of students: 24,391

Publications: *Virginia Law Review*, *Virginia Law Weekly*, *Virginia Quarterly Review*

DEANS

College and Graduate School of Arts and Sciences: MEREDITH JUNG-EN WOO
Curry School of Education: ROBERT C. PIANTA
Darden School of Business: ROBERT F. BRUNER
Frank Batten School of Leadership and Public Policy: HARRY HARDING
McIntire School of Commerce: CARL P. ZEITHAML
School of Architecture: KIM TANZER
School of Continuing and Professional Studies: BILLY CANNADAY, Jr
School of Engineering and Applied Science: JAMES H. AYLOR
School of Law: PAUL MAHONEY
School of Medicine: STEVEN T. DEKOSKY
School of Nursing: DORRIE FONTAINE

PROFESSORS

Curry School of Education (POB 400260, Charlottesville, VA 22904-4260; tel. (434) 924-3334; fax (434) 924-0747; e-mail curry@

virginia.edu; internet curry.edschool.virginia .edu):

BREDO, E., Leadership, Foundations and Policy Studies
BRENEMAN, D., Education
BULL, G., Leadership, Foundations and Policy Studies
BURBACH, H., Leadership, Foundations and Policy Studies
BUTLER, A., Leadership, Foundations and Policy Studies
CALLAHAN, C., Leadership, Foundations and Policy Studies
COHEN, S., Curriculum, Instruction and Special Education
CORNELL, D., Human Services
DUKE, D., Leadership, Foundations and Policy Studies
FAN, X., Leadership, Foundations and Policy Studies
GAESSER, G., Human Services
GANSNEDER, B., Leadership, Foundations and Policy Studies
HALLAHAN, D., Curriculum, Instruction and Special Education
HANSEN, J., Education
INGERSOLL, C., Human Services
INVERNIZZI, M., Curriculum, Instruction and Special Education
KELLY, L., Human Services
KNEEDLER, R., Education
LAWRENCE, E., Human Services
LLOYD, J., Education
LOPER, A., Human Services
MCKENNA, M., Curriculum, Instruction and Special Education
MCNERGNEY, J., Education
MCNERGNEY, R., Leadership, Foundations and Policy Studies
MILLER, M., Leadership, Foundations and Policy Studies
PATE, R., Education
REEVE, R., Human Services
RICHARDS, H., Leadership, Foundations and Policy Studies
SHERAS, P., Human Services
SHORT, J., Leadership, Foundations and Policy Studies
SMOLKIN, L., Curriculum, Instruction and Special Education
SNELL, M., Curriculum, Instruction and Special Education
STRANG, H., Leadership, Foundations and Policy Studies
TOMLINSON, C., Leadership, Foundations and Policy Studies
WELTMAN, A., Human Services

Darden School (Graduate School of Business Administration) (POB 400321, Charlottesville, VA 22904-4321; tel. (434) 924-3900; fax (434) 924-4859; internet www.darden .edu):

ALLEN, B., Business Admin.
BECKENSTEIN, A., Business Admin.
BODILY, S., Business Admin.
BOURGEOIS, L., Business Admin.
BROWNLEE, E., Business Admin.
CHAPLINSKY, S., Business Admin.
CHEN, M., Business Admin.
CLAWSON, J., Business Admin.
COLLEY, J., Business Admin.
DAVIS, E., Business Admin.
DOYLE, J., Business Admin.
EADES, K., Business Admin.
EAKER, M., Business Admin.
FARRIS, P., Business Admin.
FREEMAN, R., Business Admin.
FREY, S., Business Admin.
GLYNN, J., Business Admin.
HARRIS, R., Business Admin.
HASKINS, M., Business Admin.
HESS, E., Business Admin.
HORNIMAN, A., Business Admin.
LANDEL, R., Business Admin.
LIEDTKA, J., Business Admin.
MOORE, M., Business Admin.
PFEIFER, P., Business Admin.
SIHLER, W., Business Admin.
SNELL, S., Business Admin.
SPEKMAN, R., Business Admin.
VENKATARAMAN, S., Business Admin.
WEISS, E., Business Admin.
WERHANE, P., Business Admin.

McIntire School of Commerce (POB 400173, Charlottesville, VA 22904-4173; tel. (434) 924-3257; internet www.commerce.virginia .edu):

ATCHISON, M., Commerce
BATEMAN, T., Commerce
BROOME, O., Commerce
DE MONG, R., Commerce
KEHOE, W., Commerce
KEMP, R., Commerce
LINDGREN, J., Commerce
MALONEY, D., Commerce
MARSTON, F., Commerce
MICK, D., Commerce
NELSON, R., Commerce
NETEMEYER, R., Commerce
OVERSTREET, G., Commerce
SMITH, D., Commerce
WEBB, R., Commerce
WILHELM, W., Commerce
WILLIAMS, S., Commerce

School of Architecture (POB 400122, Charlottesville, VA 22904-4122; tel. (434) 924-3715; fax (434) 982-2678; internet www .virginia.edu/arch):

BEATLEY, T., Planning
BEDNAR, M., Architecture
BOESCHENSTEIN, W., Architecture
CLARK, W., Architecture
DRIPPS, R., Architecture
FORD, E., Architecture
LUCY, W., Planning
MORRISH, W., Architecture
SCHWARTZ, K., Architecture
SPAIN, D., Planning
WALDMAN, P., Architecture
WILSON, R., Architectural History

School of Arts and Sciences (POB 400772, Charlottesville, VA 22904-4772; tel. (434) 924-3389; fax (434) 924-1317; e-mail grad-a-s@virginia.edu; internet artsandsciences.virginia.edu):

ADLER, P., Biology
ALLEN, J., Psychology
ALLEN, R., Chemistry
ANDERSON, A., Spanish, Italian and Portuguese
ANDERSON, S., Economics
ANDREWS, L., Chemistry
ANTONOVICS, J., Biology
ARNOLD, A., French Literature and General Linguistics
ARNOLD, K., Music
ARNOLD, P., Physics
ARON, M., History
ARRAS, J., Philosophy
BAKER, P., English
BAROLSKY, P., Art
BEATTIE, A., Creative Writing
BELANGER, T., Book Arts Press
BELL, M., Art
BENNETT, B., German Literature
BERLANSTEIN, L., History
BEST, T., German Literature
BLACK, D., Sociology
BLOOM, G., Biology
BLOOMFIELD, L., Physics
BLUMBERG, R., Sociology
BOND, H., History
BOOTH, A., English
BRADEN, G., English
BRODIE, E., Biology
BRUNJES, P., Psychology
BRYANT, R., Chemistry
BURNETT, R., Chemistry
BURTON, E., Economics
CAFISO, D., Chemistry
CANTOR, P., English
CARGILE, J., Philosophy
CASEY, J., Creative Writing
CATES, G., Physics
CEASER, J., Government and Foreign Affairs
CHANG, T., Statistics
CHAPEL, R., Drama Operations
CHASE LEVENSON, K., English
CHEN, J., History
CHEVALIER, R., Astronomy
CHILDRESS, J., Religious Studies
CLAY, J., Classics
CLORE, G., Psychology
COLOMB, G., English
CONETTI, S., Physics
CONFINO, A., History
CONNOLLY, J., Slavic Languages and Literature
CONTINI-MORAVA, E., Anthropology
COX, B., Physics
CRABB, D., Nuclear and Particle Physics
CRACKEL, T., Editing Wash Papers
CRAWFORD, J., Classics
CRONMILLER, C., Biology
CROSBY, E., History
CROZIER, R., Art
CUSHMAN, S., English
DAMON, F., Anthropology
DASS, D., Art
DAVIS, R., Environmental Sciences
DAY, D., Nuclear and Particle Physics
DEAVER, B., Physics
DELLA COLETTA, C., Spanish, Italian and Portuguese
DELOACHE, J., Psychology
DEMAS, J., Chemistry
DEVEREUX, D., Philosophy
DOBBINS, J., Art
DOLAN, R., Environmental Sciences
DOVE, R., Creative Writing
DRUCKER, J., Media Studies
DUKES, E., Physics
EDMUNDSON, M., English
EISENBERG, D., Creative Writing
ELSON, M., Slavic Languages and Literature
ELZINGA, K., Economics
EMERY, R., Psychology
ENGERS, M., Economics
FATTON, R., Government and Foreign Affairs
FELDMAN, J., English
FELSKI, R., English
FENDLEY, P., Physics
FERREIRA, M., Religious Studies
FISHBANE, P., Physics
FOGARTY, G., Religious Studies
FOWLER, M., Physics
FRAIMAN, S., English
FRASER, C., Chemistry
FREEMAN, J., Psychology
FRICK, J., Drama Operations
FRIESEN, W., Biology
FUCHS, S., Sociology
FUENTES, J., Environmental Sciences
GALLAGHER, G., History
GALLAGHER, T., Physics
GALLOWAY, J., Environmental Sciences
GAMBLE, H., Religious Studies
GARRETT, R., Biology
GEIGER, P., Art
GERLI, E., Spanish, Italian and Portuguese
GERRANS, G., Chemistry
GEYSEN, H., Chemistry
GIES, D., Spanish, Italian and Portuguese
GOEDDE, L., Art
GRAINGER, R., Biology
GREEN, C., Biology
GRISHAM, C., Chemistry
GRONER, P., Religious Studies
GUTERBOCK, T., Sociology
HABERLY, D., Spanish, Italian and Portuguese
HANDLER, R., Anthropology

HARMAN, W., Chemistry
HARRISON, A., Chemistry
HART, K., Religious Studies
HAWLEY, J., Astronomy
HAYDEN, B., Environmental Sciences
HECHT, S., Chemistry
HERBST, I., Mathematics
HERMAN, J., Environmental Sciences
HESS, G., Physics
HILL, D., Psychology
HILL, R., Spanish, Italian and Portuguese
HIRSH, J., Biology
HOH, L., Drama Operations
HOLSINGER, B., Music
HOLT, C., Economics
HOLT, M., History
HORNBERGER, G., Environmental Sciences
HOWARD, A., Environmental Sciences
HUECKSTEDT, R., Middle Eastern and South Asian Languages and Culture
HUMPHREYS, P., Philosophy
HUNT, D., Chemistry
HUNTER, J., English
HUNTER, J., Sociology
IMBRIE, J., Mathematics
JAMES, J., Economics
JOHNSON, W., Economics
JONES, R., Physics
JORDAN, D., Government and Foreign Affairs
JOST, W., English
KAWASAKI, M., Biology
KEEN, R., Psychology
KEENAN, D., Statistics
KEENE, W., Environmental Sciences
KELLER, R., Biology
KETT, J., History
KHARE, R., Anthropology
KINGSTON, P., Sociology
KINNEY, A., East Asian Languages, Literature and Cultures
KINNEY, J., English
KLOSKO, G., Government and Foreign Affairs
KOVACS, P., Classics
KRETSINGER, R., Biology
KRIETE, T., Mathematics
KUBOVY, M., Psychology
KUHN, N., Mathematics
KUMAR, J., Sociology
LAGOS, M., Spanish, Italian and Portuguese
LANDERS, J., Chemistry
LANE, A., History
LANG, K., Religious Studies
LASIECKA, I., Mathematics
LEFFLER, M., History
LEFFLER, P., History
LEGRO, J., Government and Foreign Affairs
LEHMANN, K., Chemistry
LENDON, J., History
LERDAU, M., Environmental Sciences
LEVENSON, M., English
LILLARD, A., Psychology
LINDGREN, R., Nuclear and Particle Physics
LLEWELLYN, P., Psychology
LOMASKY, L., Philosophy
LOTT, E., English
LYNCH, A., Government and Foreign Affairs
LYONS, J., French Literature and General Linguistics
MACCLUER, B., Mathematics
MCCRIMMON, K., Mathematics
MCCURDY, C., History
MACDONALD, T., Chemistry
MCDONALD, W., German Literature
MCDOWELL, D., English
MCGANN, J., English
MCKINLEY, M., French Literature and General Linguistics
MCKINNON, S., Anthropology
MCLAREN, J., Economics
MACKO, S., Environmental Sciences
MAJEWSKI, S., Astronomy
MARLATT, M., Art
MARSH, C., Religious Studies
MARSHALL, J., Chemistry
MARTENS, L., German Literature
MATTERN, D., Editing Madison Papers
MAUS, K., English
MEGILL, A., History
MELLON, D., Biology
MENAKER, M., Biology
MERRICKS, T., Philosophy
METCALF, P., Anthropology
MICHAELS, P., Environmental Sciences
MIDELFORT, H., History
MIKALSON, J., Classics
MILANI, F., Middle Eastern and South Asian Languages and Culture
MILKIS, S., Government and Foreign Affairs
MILLER, J., Classics
MILLER, J., History
MILLS, A., Environmental Sciences
MILLS, D., Economics
MIRMAN, L., Economics
MOST, R., Undergraduate College Operations
NELSON, R., English
NESSELROADE, J., Psychology
NIMA, T., Religious Studies
NOCK, S., Sociology
NOHRNBERG, J., English
NOLAN, B., English
NORUM, B., Physics
O'BRIEN, D., Government and Foreign Affairs
O'CONNELL, R., Astronomy
OCHS, P., Religious Studies
OLICK, J., Sociology
OLSEN, E., Economics
ONUF, P., History
OPERE, F., Spanish, Italian and Portuguese
ORR, G., Creative Writing
OSHEIM, D., History
PAPOVICH, J., Undergraduate College Operations
PARKER, D., Spanish, Italian and Portuguese
PARSHALL, B., Mathematics
PARSHALL, K., Mathematics
PATE, B., Chemistry
PATTERSON, C., Psychology
PERIASAMY, A., Biology
PERKOWSKI, J., Slavic Languages and Literature
PHAM, H., Physics
PLOG, S., Anthropology
POCANIC, D., Physics
POON, J., Physics
POPE, R., Spanish, Italian and Portuguese
PRESS, A., Sociology
PROFFITT, D., Psychology
PU, L., Chemistry
QUANDT, W., Government and Foreign Affairs
RAILTON, S., English
RAMAZANI, R., English
RAMIREZ, D., Mathematics
RAPINCHUK, A., Mathematics
RAY, B., Religious Studies
REPPUCCI, N., Psychology
REYNOLDS, B., Economics
RHOADS, S., Government and Foreign Affairs
RINI, J., Spanish, Italian and Portuguese
ROBERTS, M., Art
ROGER, P., French Literature and General Linguistics
ROOD, R., Astronomy
ROSS, M., English
SACHEDINA, A., Religious Studies
SALTHOUSE, T., Psychology
SARAZIN, C., Astronomy
SASLAW, W., Astronomy
SAVAGE, J., Government and Foreign Affairs
SAWAIE, M., Middle Eastern and South Asian Language and Culture
SCHOPPA, L., Government and Foreign Affairs
SCHUKER, S., History
SCHWARTZ, H., Government and Foreign Affairs
SCOTT, D., Philosophy
SCOTT, L., Mathematics
SENEVIRATNE, H., Anthropology
SHATIN, J., Music
SHAW, D., Spanish, Italian and Portuguese
SHUGART, H., Environmental Sciences
SIMMONS, A., Philosophy
SKRUTSKIE, M., Astronomy
SMITH, D., Environmental Sciences
SPEARING, A., English
SPELLMAN, B., Psychology
STAGG, J., Editing Madison Papers
STERN, S., Economics
STEWART, G., Undergraduate College Options
SUMMERS, J., Art
SUNDBERG, R., Chemistry
TAYLOR, D., Biology
THACKER, H., Physics
THOMAS, L., Mathematics
THOMAS, M., History
THOMPSON, A., Religious Studies
THORNTON, S., Physics
THUAN, T., Astronomy
TILGHMAN, C., Creative Writing
TIMKO, M., Biology
TOLBERT, C., Astronomy
TRIGGIANI, R., Mathematics
TRINDLE, C., Chemistry
TUCKER, H., English
TURKHEIMER, E., Psychology
TURNER, E., Art
UPTON, D., Art
VAN WINCOOP, E., Economics
VANDER MEULEN, D., English
VORIS, R., German Literature
WAGNER, R., Anthropology
WALKER, K., Psychology
WALL, C., English
WANG, W., Mathematics
WARNER, R., Drama Operations
WEBER, A., Spanish, Italian and Portuguese
WEST, G., Drama Operations
WHITE, S., Government and Foreign Affairs
WHITTLE, D., Astronomy
WIBERG, P., Environmental Sciences
WICKE, J., English
WILBUR, H., Biology
WILKEN, R., Religious Studies
WILLIAMS, B., Sociology
WILLINGHAM, D., Psychology
WILSON, M., East Asian Languages, Literature and Cultures
WILSON, M., Psychology
WILSON, T., Psychology
WOMACK, B., Government and Foreign Affairs
WOODMAN, A., Classics
WRIGHT, C., Creative Writing
ZELIKOW, P., History
ZIEMAN, J., Environmental Sciences
ZUNZ, O., History

School of Continuing and Professional Studies:

ABOUZEID, M., TEMPO Reading Programme
HARRISON, E., N Virginia Center
ROBERSON, S., Lynchburg Center

School of Engineering and Applied Science (POB 400246, Charlottesville, VA 22904-4246; tel. (434) 924-3072; fax (434) 924-3555; internet www.seas.virginia.edu):

ACTON, S., Electrical and Computer Engineering
ALLAIRE, P., Mechanical and Aerospace Engineering
BAILEY, M., Computer Science

BARAGIOLA, R., Materials Science and Engineering
BARRETT, L., Mechanical and Aerospace Engineering
BEAN, J., Electrical and Computer Engineering
BERGER, T., Electrical and Computer Engineering
BROWN, D., Systems and Information Engineering
CAHEN, G., Materials Science and Engineering
CAMPBELL, J., Electrical and Computer Engineering
CARLSON, W., Science, Technology and Society
CARTA, G., Chemical Engineering
CRANDALL, J., Mechanical and Aerospace Engineering
DAVIDSON, J., Computer Science
DAVIS, R., Chemical Engineering
DEMETSKY, M., Civil and Environmental Engineering
DORNING, J., Materials Science and Engineering
DUGAN, J., Electrical and Computer Engineering
FERNANDEZ, E., Chemical Engineering
FORD, R., Chemical Engineering
GANGLOFF, R., Materials Science and Engineering
GARBER, N., Civil and Environmental Engineering
GILLIES, G., Mechanical and Aerospace Engineering
GORMAN, M., Science, Technology and Society
GRIMSHAW, A., Computer Science
GUPTA, M., Electrical and Computer Engineering
HAIMES, Y., Systems and Information Engineering
HAJ-HARIRI, H., Mechanical and Aerospace Engineering
HARRIOTT, L., Electrical and Computer Engineering
HOEL, L., Civil and Environmental Engineering
HOLMES, A., Electrical and Computer Engineering
HORGAN, C., Civil and Environmental Engineering
HOROWITZ, B., Systems and Information Engineering
HOWE, J., Materials Science and Engineering
HUDSON, J., Chemical Engineering
HULL, R., Materials Science and Engineering
HUMPHREY, J., Mechanical and Aerospace Engineering
HUMPHREY, M., Computer Science
IWASAKI, T., Mechanical and Aerospace Engineering
JESSER, W., Materials Science and Engineering
JOHNSON, B., Electrical and Computer Engineering
JOHNSON, D., Science, Technology and Society
JOHNSON, R., Materials Science and Engineering
JOHNSON, W., Materials Science and Engineering
JONES, A., Computer Science
KELLY, R., Materials Science and Engineering
KENT, R., Mechanical and Aerospace Engineering
KING, M., Chemical Engineering
KIRWAN, D., Chemical Engineering
KNIGHT, J., Computer Science
KRZYSZTOFOWICZ, R., Systems and Information Engineering
LIN, Z., Electrical and Computer Engineering
LUNG, W., Civil and Environmental Engineering
MCDANIEL, J., Mechanical and Aerospace Engineering
MARSHALL, P., Electrical and Computer Engineering
MASLEN, E., Mechanical and Aerospace Engineering
MIKSAD, R., Civil and Environmental Engineering
NEUROCK, M., Chemical Engineering
NORRIS, P., Mechanical and Aerospace Engineering
O'CONNELL, J., Chemical Engineering
PINDERA, M., Civil and Environmental Engineering
REED, M., Electrical and Computer Engineering
REYNOLDS, P., Computer Science
RICHARDS, L., Mechanical and Aerospace Engineering
ROBERTS, W., Mechanical and Aerospace Engineering
ROBINS, G., Computer Science
SCHERER, W., Systems and Information Engineering
SCULLY, J., Materials Science and Engineering
SHIFLET, G., Materials Science and Engineering
SKALAK, T., Biomedical Engineering Department
SMITH, J., Civil and Environmental Engineering
SOFFA, M., Computer Science
SOFFA, W., Materials Science and Engineering
SON, S., Computer Science
STANKOVIC, J., Computer Science
STARKE, E., Materials Science and Engineering
TAO, G., Electrical and Computer Engineering
THACKER, J., Mechanical and Aerospace Engineering
THORNTON, K., Science, Technology and Society
TOWNSEND, I., Science, Technology and Society
VEERARAGHAVAN, M., Electrical and Computer Engineering
WADLEY, H., Materials Science and Engineering
WEAVER, A., Computer Science
WEIKLE, R., Electrical and Computer Engineering
WHITE, K., Systems and Information Engineering
WILSON, S., Electrical and Computer Engineering
WOLF, S., Materials Science and Engineering
WOOD, H., Mechanical and Aerospace Engineering
WULF, W., Computer Science

School of Law (POB 400405, Charlottesville, VA 22904-4405; tel. (434) 924-7354; fax (434) 924-7536; internet www.law.virginia.edu):

ABRAHAM, K., Law
ARMACOST, B., Law
BAGLEY, M., Law
BALNAVE, R., Law
BEVIER, L., Law
BLASI, V., Law
BONNIE, R., Law
BROWN, D., Law
BROWN-NAGIN, T., Law
BUCK, D., Law
CANNON, J., Law
COHEN, G., Law
COLLINS, M., Law
COUGHLIN, A., Law
CUSHMAN, B., Law
DOOLEY, M., Law
DUDLEY, E., Law
FORDE-MAZRUI, K., Law
GOLUBOFF, R., Law
HARRISON, J., Law
HOWARD, A., Law
HYNES, R., Law
IBBEKEN, D., Law
JOHNSON, A., Law
KITCH, E., Law
KLARMAN, M., Law
KORDANA, K., Law
KRAUS, J., Law
LESLIE, D., Law
LOW, P., Law
MAGILL, M., Law
MAHONEY, J., Law
MAHONEY, P., Law
MARTIN, D., Law
MITCHELL, P., Law
MONAHAN, J., Law
MOORE, J., Law
NACHBAR, T., Law
NELSON, C., Law
O'CONNELL, J., Law
ORTIZ, D., Law
RILEY, M., Law
ROBINSON, G., Law
ROBINSON, M., Law
RUTHERGLEN, G., Law
RYAN, J., Law
SAYLER, R., Law
SCHRAGGER, R., Law
SETEAR, J., Law
SINCLAIR, K., Law
SMITH, S., Law
STEPHAN, P., Law
TURNER, R., Law
VERKERKE, J., Law
WALKER, W., Law
WALT, S., Law
WHITE, G., Law
WHITE, T., Law
WOOLHANDLER, N., Law
YIN, G., Law

School of Medicine (POB 800793, Charlottesville, VA 22908-0793; tel. (434) 924-5118; internet www.healthsystem.virginia.edu/internet/som/home.cfm):

ABEL, M., Paediatric Orthotics
ALFORD, B., Musculoskeletal Medicine
APPREY, M., Psychiatry
ARLET, V., Orthopaedics (Spine)
AYERS, C., Cardiovascular Medicine
BALIAN, G., Orthopedic Research
BARRETT, E., Endocrinology
BARRETT, P., Pharmacology
BARTH, J., Psychiatry
BAUM, V., Anaesthesiology
BAYLISS, D., Pharmacology
BECKER, D., Medicine
BELLER, G., Cardiovascular Medicine
BENDER, T., Microbiology
BENNETT, J., Neurology
BERGIN, J., Cardiovascular Medicine
BERTRAM, E., Neurology
BEYER, A., Microbiology
BLOODGOOD, R., Cell Biology
BOLTON, W., Nephrology
BORISH, L., Allergy
BOUTON, A., Microbiology
BRADDOCK, S., Genetics
BRADY, W., Emergency Medicine
BRANT, W., Thoracoabdominal Radiology
BRAUTIGAN, D., Cell Signalling
BROOKEMAN, J., Radiological Research
BROWN, J., Microbiology
BURKE, D., Biochemistry and Molecular Genetics
BUSHWELLER, J., Molecular Physics and Biophysics
CANTERBURY, R., Psychiatry
CAREY, R., Endocrinology
CASANOVA, J., Cell Biology
CASTLE, J., Cell Biology
CHIRGWIN, J., Endocrinology
CLAYTON, A., Psychiatry

COHEN, M., Breast Imaging
COMINELLI, F., Gastroenterology
CONCANNON, P., Biochemistry and Molecular Genetics
CONNELLY, J., Medicine
CONWAY, B., Ophthalmology
CORBETT, E., Medicine
CORWIN, J., Neuroscience
COUSAR, J., Clinical Pathology
COX, D., Psychiatry
CREUTZ, C., Pharmacology
DALKIN, A., Endocrinology
DEREWENDA, Z., Molecular Physics and Biophysics
DESIMONE, D., Cell Biology
DIDUCH, D., Sports Medicine
DIMARCO, J., Cardiovascular Medicine
DONOWITZ, G., Infectious Diseases
DULING, B., Molecular Physics and Biophysics
DURBIN, C., Anaesthesiology
DURIEUX, M., Anaesthesiology
DUTTA, A., Biochemistry and Molecular Genetics
EGELMAN, E., Biochemistry and Molecular Genetics
ENGELHARD, V., Microbiology
ERNST, P., Gastroenterology
EVANS, W., Endocrinology
FOX, J., Microbiology
FRACASSO, P., Haematology and Oncology
FRYSINGER, R., Multiple Neuralgia
FU, S., Rheumatology
GAL, T., Anaesthesiology
GALAZKA, S., Family Medicine
GARRISON, J., Pharmacology
GASKIN, F., Psychiatry
GEAR, A., Biochemistry and Molecular Genetics
GIBSON, R., Cardiovascular Medicine
GIMPLE, L., Cardiovascular Medicine
GOLDBERG, J., Microbiology
GREER, K., Dermatology
GREYSON, C., Psychiatry
GUERRANT, R., Infectious Diseases
GUISE, T., Endocrinology
GUMBINER, B., Cell Biology
GUYENET, P., Pharmacology
HACKETT, J., Molecular Physics and Biophysics
HAGSPIEL, K., Radiology
HALEY, E., Neurology
HAMLIN, J., Biochemistry and Molecular Genetics
HAMMARSKJOLD, M., Microbiology
HARRISON, M., Neurology
HARVEY, J., Breast Imaging
HAYDEN, F., Epidemiology
HERR, J., Cell Biology
HESS, C., Haematology and Oncology
HEWLETT, E., Clinical Pharmacy
HINTON, B., Cell Biology
HOFFMAN, P., Infectious Diseases
HOLROYD, S., Psychiatry
HORWITZ, A., Cell Biology
HOWARDS, S., Urology
JAGGER, J., Infectious Diseases
JEVTOVIC-TODOROVIC, V., Anaesthesiology
JOHNSON, B., Psychiatry
JOHNSON, M., Pharmacology
JOHNSTON, K., Neurology
JU, S., Rheumatology
KAPUR, J., Neurology
KASSELL, N., Cardiovascular Disease
KERRIGAN, D., Physical Medicine and Rehabilitation
KIM, Y., Biomedical Engineering
KOENIG, S., Pulmonary Medicine
KRAMER, C., Radiological Research
KUTCHAI, H., Molecular Physics and Biophysics
LARNER, J., Radiation Oncology
LAURENCIN, C., Sports Medicine
LEE, K., Neuroscience
LEY, K., Biomedical Engineering
LI, M., Psychiatry
LIN, K., Plastic Surgery
LINDEN, J., Cardiovascular Medicine
LOGIN, I., Neurology
LYNCH, C., Anaesthesiology
LYNCH, K., Pharmacology
MCCALL, A., Endocrinology
MCDUFFIE, M., Microbiology
MCNAMARA, C., Cardiovascular Medicine
MACARA, I., Cell Signalling
MARSHALL, J., Endocrinology
MARTIN, M., Emergency Medicine
MILLER, M., Sports Medicine
MINOR, W., Molecular Physics and Biophysics
MOENTER, S., Endocrinology
MOORMAN, J., Cardiovascular Medicine
MORGAN, R., Plastic Surgery
MUGLER, J., Radiological Research
NADLER, J., Endocrinology
NAKAMOTO, R., Molecular Physics and Biophysics
NEWMAN, S., Ophthalmology
OBRIG, T., Nephrology
O'CONNOR, R., Emergency Medicine
OKUSA, M., Nephrology
OLDFIELD, E., Neuroendocrinology
OWENS, G., Molecular Physics and Biophysics
PARKER, W., Neurology
PARSONS, J., Microbiology
PARSONS, S., Microbiology
PEARSON, R., Geographic Medicine
PEARSON, W., Biochemistry and Molecular Genetics
PEREZ-REYES, E., Pharmacology
PETERS, C., Urology
PETRI, W., Infectious Diseases
PEURA, D., Gastroenterology
PHILBRICK, J., Medicine
PHILLIPS, L., Neurology
PLATTS-MILLS, T., Allergy
PORTERFIELD, P., Psychiatry
POWERS, R., Medicine
RAVICHANDRAN, K., Microbiology
REIN, M., Infectious Diseases
REKOSH, D., Microbiology
REMBOLD, C., Cardiovascular Medicine
REYNOLDS, P., Medicine
RICH, G., Anaesthesiology
RICH, T., Radiation Oncology
RISSMAN, E., Biochemistry and Molecular Genetics
RODEHEAVER, G., Plastic Surgery
ROSE, C., Pulmonary Medicine
ROWLINGSON, J., Anaesthesiology
RUST, R., Neurology
SALEH, K., Adult Reconstruction
SALLER, D., Maternal Fetal Medicine
SANDO, J., Anaesthesiology
SANTEN, R., Endocrinology
SCHELD, W., Infectious Diseases
SCHIFF, D., Neurology
SCHLAGER, T., Emergency Medicine
SCHORLING, J., Medicine
SCHWARTZ, M., Microbiology
SHAFFREY, C., Neuro-Oncology
SHAFFREY, M., Neuro-Oncology
SHAO, Z., Molecular Physics and Biophysics
SHUPNIK, M., Endocrinology
SILVERMAN, L., Clinical Pathology
SINKIN, R., Neonatology
SIRAGY, H., Endocrinology
SLAWSON, D., Family Medicine
SMITH, M., Microbiology
SOMLYO, A., Molecular Physics and Biophysics
STEERS, W., Urology
STEINER, L., Gamma Knife
STOLER, M., Surgical Pathology
STOVALL, D., Reproductive Endocrinology and Infertility
STURGILL, T., Pharmacology
SURATT, P., Pulmonary Medicine
SUTHERLAND, W., Cell Biology
SYVERUD, S., Emergency Medicine
SZABO, G., Molecular Physics and Biophysics
TAMM, L., Molecular Physics and Biophysics
TAYLOR, R., Biochemistry and Molecular Genetics
THEODORESCU, D., Urology
THISSE, B., Cell Biology
THISSE, C., Cell Biology
THORNER, M., Endocrinology
TIEDEMAN, J., Ophthalmology
TRUWIT, J., Pulmonary Medicine
TURNER, T., Urology
TUTTLE, J., Neuroscience
VANCE, M., Endocrinology
WARREN, J., Psychiatry
WATERS, D., Family Medicine
WATSON, D., Radiological Research
WEBER, M., Microbiology
WEISS, G., Haematology and Oncology
WHITE, J., Cell Biology
WHITEHILL, R., Orthopaedics (Spine)
WILLIAMS, M., Haematology and Oncology
WILLIAMS, M., Medicine
WILLIAMSON, B., Nuclear Medicine
WISPELWEY, B., Infectious Diseases
WOOTEN, G., Neurology
YEAGER, M., Molecular Physics and Biophysics

School of Nursing (POB 800782, Charlottesville, VA 22908-0782; tel. (434) 924-0141; e-mail nur-osa@virginia.edu; internet www.nursing.virginia.edu):

BRASHERS, V., Nursing
HAUENSTEIN, E., Nursing
HOLLEN, P., Nursing
KEELING, A., Nursing
LYDER, C., Nursing
MERWIN, E., Nursing
PARKER, B., Nursing
STEEVES, R., Nursing
TAYLOR, A., Nursing

AFFILIATED COLLEGE

University of Virginia's College at Wise: Wise, VA 24293; Chancellor DAVID J. PRIOR; Provost and Sr Vice-Chancellor GILMER W. BLACKBURN; Vice-Chancellor for Admin. GARY W. JUHAN; Vice-Chancellor for Devt and College Relations JAMES (JIM) A. KNIGHT; Vice-Chancellor for Enrollment Management RUSSELL D. NECESSARY; Vice-Chancellor for Finance and Govt Relations SIMEON E. EWING; Vice-Chancellor for Information Technology and CIO KEITH FOWLKES; 140 teachers; 1,911 students

PROFESSORS

ACHUA, C.
ADAMS-RAMSEY, K.
CANTRELL, R.
COSTA, T.
DANIEL, V.
DIN, F.
KENDALL, D.
RICHARDSON, S.
ROUSE, D.
SHELDON, G.
TUCKER, M.
TURNER, C.
WHEATLEY, F.
WILLS, B.
ZYLAWY, R.

VIRGINIA COMMONWEALTH UNIVERSITY

910 West Franklin St, Richmond, VA 23284
Telephone: (804) 828-0100
E-mail: cipia@vcu.edu
Internet: www.vcu.edu

Founded 1838 as the medical dept of Hampden-Sydney College; Richmond Professional Institute and Medical College of Virginia merged in 1968 to form this univ.

State control
Academic year: August to May
Pres.: Dr EUGENE P. TRANI
Provost and Vice-Pres. for Academic Affairs: RODERICK J. MCDAVIS
Vice-Pres. for Advancement: PETER L. WYETH
Vice-Pres. for Finance and Admin.: PAUL W. TIMMRECK
Vice-Pres. for Govt and Community Relations: DONALD C. GEHRING
Vice-Pres. for Health Sciences and Chief Exec. Officer of the VCU Health System: HERMES A. KONTOS
Vice-Pres. for Research: MARSHA R. TORR
Vice-Pres. for Univ. Outreach: SUE A. MESSMER
Library of 1,680,393 vols, 3,007,035 microforms, 9,188 printed journals, 17,441 electronic journals
Number of teachers: 1,660 full-time
Number of students: 25,001

DEANS

College of the Humanities and Sciences: STEPHEN D. GOTTFREDSON
School of Allied Health Professions: CECIL B. DRAIN
School of the Arts: RICHARD E. TOSCAN
School of Business: MICHAEL SEZNOWITZ
School of Dentistry: RONALD J. HUNT
School of Education: RICHARD J. REZBA
School of Engineering: ROBERT J. MATTAUCH
School of Graduate Studies: ALBERT T. SNEDEN
School of Medicine: HEBER H. NEWSOME, JR.
School of Nursing: NANCY F. LANGSTON
School of Pharmacy: VICTOR A. YANCHICK
School of Social Work: FRANK R. BASKIND

VIRGINIA INTERMONT COLLEGE

1013 Moore St, Bristol, VA 24201
Telephone: (540) 669-6101
Fax: (540) 669-5763
E-mail: vicadmit@vic.edu
Internet: www.vic.edu
Founded 1884
Pres.: Dr STEPHEN G. GREINER
Number of teachers: 73
Number of students: 555

VIRGINIA MILITARY INSTITUTE

Lexington, VA 24450
Telephone: (540) 464-7207
Internet: www.vmi.edu
Founded 1839
Academic year: August to May
Superintendent: Gen. J. H. BINFORD PEAY, III
Dean: Brig. Gen. R. WANE SCHNEITER
Business Exec.: Brig. Gen. ROBERT GREEN
Commandant: Col THOMAS TRUMPS
Treas.: Col GARY R. KNICK
Librarian: Col DONALD H. SAMDAHL, Jr (acting)
Library of 300,000 vols
Number of teachers: 119 full-time, 61 part-time, 26 military
Number of students: 1,500
Publication: *Catalogue*.

VIRGINIA POLYTECHNIC INSTITUTE AND STATE UNIVERSITY

Blacksburg, VA 24061
Telephone: (540) 231-6000
E-mail: vtadmiss@vt.edu
Internet: www.vt.edu
Founded 1872
State control
Academic year: August to May
Pres.: Dr CHARLES W. STEGER
Provost: MARK G. MCNAMEE
Exec. Vice-Pres. and Chief Operating Officer: JAMES HYATT
Vice-Provost for Academic Affairs: DAVID FORD
Vice-Pres. for Devt: ELIZABETH A. FLANAGAN
Vice-Pres. for Information Technology: EARVING BLYTHE
Vice-Pres. for Student Affairs: ZENOBIA HIKES
Dir of Admissions: NORRINE BAILEY SPENCER
Librarian: EILEEN HITCHINGHAM
Number of teachers: 1,586
Number of students: 28,470
Publications: *Research Magazine*, *Virginia Tech Magazine*

DEANS

Agriculture and Life Sciences: SHARRON QUISENBERRY
Architecture and Urban Studies: JACK DAVIS
Business: RICHARD E. SORENSEN
Engineering: RICHARD BENSON
Graduate: KAREN DEPAUW
Liberal Arts and Human Sciences: SUSAN ROWLANDS
Natural Resources: J. MICHAEL KELLY
Research: BRADLEY FENWICK
Science: LAY NAM CHANG
Veterinary Medicine: GERHARDT SCHURIG

VIRGINIA STATE UNIVERSITY

1 Hayden Dr., Petersburg, VA 23806
Telephone: (804) 524-5000
Fax: (804) 524-6505
E-mail: admiss@vsu.edu
Internet: www.vsu.edu
Founded by State of Virginia as Virginia Normal and Collegiate Institute 1882; opened 1883; name changed to Virginia Normal and Industrial Institute 1902; to Virginia State College for Negroes 1930; to Virginia State College 1946; to Virginia State Univ. 1979
Pres.: EDDIE N. MOORE, Jr
Library of 245,731 vols
Number of teachers: 191
Number of students: 4,007

DEANS

School of Agriculture Sciences and Technology: Dr LORENZA W. LYONS
School of Business: Dr SADIE R. GREGORY
School of Continuing Education and Graduate Studies: Dr WAYNE F. VIRAG
School of Liberal Arts and Education: Dr SAMUEL L. CREIGHTON

VIRGINIA THEOLOGICAL SEMINARY

3737 Seminary Rd, Alexandria, VA 22304
Telephone: (703) 370-6600
Fax: (703) 370-6234
E-mail: admissions@vts.edu
Internet: www.vts.edu
Founded 1823
Dean and Pres.: Very Rev. IAN MARKHAM
Vice-Pres. for Academic Affairs: Very Rev. MARTHA J. HORNE
Vice-Pres. for Admin. and Finance: MARY LEWIS HIX
Vice-Pres. for Institutional Advancement: EDWIN KING HALL
Librarian: MITZI JARRETT BUDDE
Number of students: 232

VIRGINIA UNION UNIVERSITY

1500 North Lombardy St, Richmond, VA 23220
Telephone: (804) 257-5600
Fax: (804) 257-5818
Internet: www.vuu.edu
Founded 1865
Academic year: August to May
Pres.: Dr CLAUDE PERKINS (acting)
Vice-Pres. for Academic Affairs: Dr W. WELDON HILL
Vice-Pres. for Financial Affairs: ROBERT BUSCH
Vice-Pres. for Student Affairs: WILBERT D. TALLEY
Dir of Univ. Services: GILBERT L. CARTER
Registrar: JANICE D. BAILEY
Librarian: Dr VONITA W. FOSTER
Library of 162,000 vols
Number of teachers: 105 (85 full-time, 20 part-time)
Number of students: 1,500

DEANS

School of Arts and Sciences: Dr RAMSEY KLEFF
School of Theology: Dr JOHN W. KINNEY
Sydney Lewis School of Business: Dr PHILIP UMANSKY

VIRGINIA WESLEYAN COLLEGE

1584 Wesleyan Drive, Norfolk, VA 23502
Telephone: (757) 455-3200
Fax: (757) 461-5238
Internet: www.vwc.edu
Founded 1961
Pres.: WILLIAM T. GREER, Jr
Library of 129,000 vols
Number of teachers: 82
Number of students: 1,417

WASHINGTON AND LEE UNIVERSITY

204 West Washington St, Lexington, VA 24450-2116
Telephone: (540) 458-8400
Internet: www.wlu.edu
Founded as Augusta Acad. 1749, chartered as Liberty Hall Acad. 1782, name changed to Washington Acad. 1798, to Washington College 1813, and to present name 1871
Pres.: Dr KENNETH P. RUSCIO
Treas.: STEVEN MCALLISTER
Registrar: D. SCOTT DITTMAN
Librarian: MERRILY TAYLOR
Library: undergraduate library of 950,000 vols; law library of 350,000 vols
Number of teachers: 198 (full-time)
Number of students: 2,155
Publications: *Journal of Science*, *Political Review*, *Shenandoah* (literary quarterly), *Washington and Lee Law Review*

DEANS

Arts and Sciences: HANK DOBIN
Commerce, Economics and Politics: LARRY C. PEPPERS
Law: RODNEY A. SMOLLA

WASHINGTON

BASTYR UNIVERSITY

14500 Juanita Dr., NE, Kenmore, WA 98028-4966
Telephone: (425) 823-1300
Fax: (425) 823-6222
E-mail: admissions@bastyr.edu
Internet: www.bastyr.edu
Founded 1978
Pres.: Dr DANIEL L. CHURCH
Number of teachers: 142 (51 full-time, 91 part-time)
Number of students: 1,101
Degree programmes in the natural health sciences.

CENTRAL WASHINGTON UNIVERSITY

Ellensburg, WA 98926

Telephone: (509) 963-2111
Internet: www.cwu.edu

Founded 1891

Pres.: Jerilyn S. McIntyre
Registrar: Carolyn L. Wells
Librarian: David Kaufman
Provost and Vice-Pres. for Academic Affairs: David Soltz
Vice-Pres. for Business Affairs: Abdul Nasser
Vice-Pres. for Student Affairs and Enrollment Management: Charlotte Tullos
Vice-Pres. for Univ. Relations: Jen Gray

Library of 485,417 vols
Number of teachers: 370
Number of students: 7,471 (full-time)

CITY UNIVERSITY

11900 NE First St, Bellevue, WA 98005

Telephone: (425) 637-1010
Fax: (425) 637-9689
E-mail: info@cityu.edu
Internet: www.cityu.edu

Founded 1973 as City College; present name 1982
Private control

Sites in states of Washington and California, and in Canada, Denmark, Germany, Slovakia, Spain and Switzerland

Pres.: Dr W. Michael Easton
Exec. Vice-Pres. for Academic Affairs: Dr Fernando Leon Garcia
Exec. Vice-Pres. for Finance and Operations: James R. Ladd
Vice-Pres. for Academic and Institutional Assessment: Chris J. Rigos
Vice-Pres. for Admissions and Student Services: Melissa Mecham
Vice-Pres. for the Business Office and Controller: Marieta C. Johnson
Vice-Pres. for European Operations: Ing. Jan Rebro
Vice-Pres. for External Relations: Dr Winston C. Addis
Assoc. Vice-Pres. for Human Resources: Nancy J. Johnston
Chief Information Officer: Greg Foy
Registrar: Mary R. Belknap

Number of teachers: 1,300
Number of students: 6,840 worldwide

CORNISH COLLEGE OF THE ARTS

1000 Lenora St, Seattle, WA 98121

Telephone: (206) 726-5151
E-mail: admission@cornish.edu
Internet: www.cornish.edu

Founded 1914

Pres.: Sergei P. Tschernisch
Provost: Lois Harris
Vice-Pres. of Institutional Advancement: Jane Ewing

Number of teachers: 145
Number of students: 800

EASTERN WASHINGTON UNIVERSITY

115 Showalter Hall, Cheney, WA 99004

Telephone: (509) 359-6200
Fax: (509) 359-6946
E-mail: universityre@ewu.edu
Internet: www.ewu.edu

Founded 1882
Language of instruction: English
Academic year: September to June

Pres.: Dr Rodolfo Arévalo
Registrar: Erin Morgan
Dir of Enrollment Management: Larry Briggs
Dir of Libraries: Richard Wilson

Library of 483,152 vols
Number of teachers: 365
Number of students: 10,500

DEANS

Social and Behavioral Sciences and Social Work: Vickie Shields

EVERGREEN STATE COLLEGE

2700 Evergreen Parkway NW, Olympia, WA 98505

Telephone: (360) 867-6310*Tacoma Campus*, 1210 6th Ave, Tacoma, WA 98405

Telephone: (360) 867-3000
E-mail: admissions@evergreen.edu
Internet: www.evergreen.edu

Pres.: Dr Thomas L. (Les) Purce
Exec. Dir of Tacoma Campus: Dr Artee F. Young

Library of 35,000 journals, spec. collns, rare books, archival material and govt docs
Number of teachers: 243
Number of students: 4,616

GONZAGA UNIVERSITY

502 E. Boone Ave, Spokane, WA 99258-0102

Telephone: (509) 328-4220
Fax: (509) 484-2818
Internet: www.gonzaga.edu

Founded 1887
Private control
Academic year: September to May, and summer session

Chancellor: Rev. Bernard J. Coughlin
Pres.: Rev. Robert J. Spitzer
Vice-Pres.: Rev. Frank Costello
Vice-Pres. for Academic Affairs: Rev. Patrick Ford
Vice-Pres. for Admin. and Planning: Harry H. Sladich
Vice-Pres. for Finance: Charles J. Murphy
Vice-Pres. for Student Life: Sue Weitz
Vice-Pres. for Univ. Relations: Margot Stanfield
Dean of Admissions: Phillip Ballinger
Librarian: Eileen Bell-Garrison

Library of 425,000 vols
Number of teachers: 275
Number of students: 6,923

Publications: *Charter* (1 a year), *Gonzaga Bulletin* (52 a year), *Reflections* (1 a year), *Signum* (4 a year), *Spires* (1 a year)

DEANS

Arts and Sciences: Robert Prusch
Business Administration: Clarence Barnes
Education: Richard Wolfe
Engineering: Dennis Horn
Graduate School: Leonard Doohan
Law: John E. Clute
Professional Studies: Mary McFarland
Students: Sue Weitz

HENRY COGSWELL COLLEGE

3002 Colby Avenue, Everett, WA 98201

Telephone: (425) 258-3351
E-mail: information@henrycogswell.edu
Internet: www.henrycogswell.edu

Pres.: Ronnie Hundley

DEANS

Business: Dr Jerry Knutson
Digital Arts: Ken Rowe
Engineering and Science: El-Hadi Aggoune

HERITAGE UNIVERSITY

3240 Fort Rd, Toppenish, WA 94563

Telephone: (509) 865-8500
Fax: (509) 865-7976
Internet: www.heritage.edu

Founded 1907; univ. status 2004
Private control; non-profit making

Liberal arts univ.

Pres.: Dr Kathleen Ross
Vice-Pres. for Academic Affairs: Dr Sneh Veena
Vice-Pres. for Advancement: Michael P. Moore
Vice-Pres. for Support Services, and Chief Financial Officer: Rick R. Gagnier
Dean of Enrollment Management Services: Norberto T. Espindola

Library of 55,000 vols (main campus)
Number of teachers: 170 (45 full-time, 125 part-time)
Number of students: 1,355

DEANS

Arts and Sciences: James Falco
Education and Psychology: Karen Garrison

NORTHWEST UNIVERSITY

POB 579, Kirkland, WA 98083-0579
5520 108th Ave NE, Kirkland, WA 98033

Telephone: (425) 822-8266
Fax: (425) 889-5224
E-mail: recpt@northwestu.edu
Internet: www.northwestu.edu

Founded 1934; present name 2005
Private control

Liberal arts univ.; Accredited by Northwest Comm. on Colleges and Univs (NWCCU)
Language of instruction: English
Academic year: August to May

Pres.: Dr Joseph Castleberry
Chancellor: Dr Don Argue
Exec. Vice-Pres.: Dan Neary
Provost: Jim Heugel
Sr Vice-Pres. for Finance: Dan Schimelpfenig
Vice-Pres. for Campus Ministries: Phil Rasmussen
Vice-Pres. for Student Devt: Paul Banas
Asst Vice-Pres. for Devt: Jeff Lockhart
Asst Vice-Pres. for Enrollment: Rose-Mary Smith
Assoc. Vice-Pres. for Marketing: Merlin Quiggle
Librarian: Charles Diede

Library of 88,794 vols, 12,458 periodicals
Number of teachers: 53
Number of students: 11,736

DEANS

College of Arts and Sciences: Darrel Hobson
College of Ministry: Kent Ingle
College of Social and Behavioural Sciences: William Herkelrath
School of Business and Management: Teresa Gillespie
School of Education: Gary Newbill
School of Nursing: Carl Christensen

PROFESSORS

Charette, Blaine, Bible, Greek
Harris, Moses, Education, Modern Languages
Johnson, LeRoy, History, Interdisciplinary Studies, Political Science
JungJin, Doo, Chemistry
Leach, Kevin, Psychology
Kowalski, Waldemar, Bible, Theology
Kress, Paul, Education
Mestre, Michel, Business
Stallman, Robert, Bible, Hebrew
Thompson, Michael, Christian Education, Youth Ministries

PACIFIC LUTHERAN UNIVERSITY

Tacoma, WA 98447
Telephone: (206) 531-6900
Fax: (206) 535-8320
Internet: www.plu.edu

Founded 1890

Pres.: LOREN J. ANDERSON
Provost: PAUL T. MENZEL
Dean of Information Resources: CHRIS D. FERGUSON

Library of 363,580 vols
Number of teachers: 250
Number of students: 3,600

PUGET SOUND CHRISTIAN COLLEGE

POB 13108, Everett, WA 98206
2610 Wetmore Ave, Everett, WA 98201

Telephone: (425) 257-3090
Fax: (425) 258-1488
E-mail: president@pscc.edu
Internet: www.pscc.edu

Pres.: Dr RANDY BRIDGES.

SAINT MARTIN'S COLLEGE

5300 Pacific Ave SE, Lacey, WA 98503

Telephone: (206) 491-4700
Fax: (206) 459-4124
E-mail: information@stmartin.edu
Internet: www.stmartin.edu

Founded 1895
Academic year: September to May

Pres.: Dr DAVID R. SPANGLER
Vice-Pres. for Academic Affairs: (vacant)
Vice-Pres. of Finance: MARY SIGMEN
Registrar: MARY LAW
Librarian: DALIA HAGAN

Library of 85,000 vols
Number of teachers: 70
Number of students: 978

SEATTLE PACIFIC UNIVERSITY

3307 Third Ave W, Seattle, WA 98119

Telephone: (206) 281-2111
Fax: (206) 281-2115
Internet: www.spu.edu

Founded 1891
Academic year: September to June

Pres.: PHILIP W. EATON
Vice-Pres. for Academic Affairs: LES L. STEELE
Vice-Pres. for Business and Planning: DONALD W. MORTENSON
Vice-Pres. for Univ. Advancement: THOMAS W. BOX
Vice-Pres. for Univ. Relations: MARJORIE R. JOHNSON
Asst Vice-Pres. and Dean for Enrollment Management: JANET L. WARD
Assoc. Vice-Pres. and Dean of Student Life: JEFFREY JORDAN
Dir of Student Academic Services and Univ. Registrar: RUTH ADAMS
Univ. Librarian: BRYCE NELSON

Library of 169,527 vols
Number of teachers: 343
Number of students: 3,891

SEATTLE UNIVERSITY

Seattle, WA 98122

Telephone: (206) 296-6000
Fax: (206) 296-6200
Internet: www.seattleu.edu

Founded 1891
Academic year: October to July

Pres.: STEPHEN V. SUNDBORG
Provost: Dr JOHN D. ESHELMAN
Vice-Pres. of Planning and Assoc. Provost: SUSAN SECKER
Asst Provost for Academic Admin.: ROBERT DULLEA
Dean of Admissions: MICHAEL MCKEON
Controller: BINH LE
Librarian: JOHN POPKO

Library of 234,978 vols
Number of teachers: 440
Number of students: 6,337 (3,561 undergraduate, 1,735 postgraduate, 1,041 law)

DEANS

College of Arts and Sciences: Dr WALLACE LOH
Matteo Ricci College: Dr ARTHUR FISHER
School of Business: Dr JOSEPH PHILLIPS
School of Education: Dr SUSAN SCHMITT
School of Law: Dr RUDOLPH HASL
School of Nursing: Dr MARY WALKER
School of Science and Engineering: Dr GEORGE SIMMONS
School of Theology and Ministry: Rev. PATRICK HOWELL

TRINITY LUTHERAN COLLEGE

2802 Wetmore Ave, Everett, WA 98201

Telephone: (425) 249-4800
Fax: (425) 249-4801
E-mail: info@tlc.edu
Internet: tlc.edu

Pres.: Dr JOHN M. STAMM.

UNIVERSITY OF PUGET SOUND

Tacoma, WA 98416

Telephone: (253) 879-3100
Internet: www.ups.edu

Founded 1888
Private control

Pres.: RONALD R. THOMAS
Dean of Students: (vacant)
Vice-Pres. for Academics: KRISTINE M. BARTANEN
Vice-Pres. for Enrollment: GEORGE H. MILLS
Vice-Pres. for Finance: (vacant)
Registrar: JOHN FINNEY
Librarian: KAREN FISCHER

Number of teachers: 220
Number of students: 2,600 full-time

UNIVERSITY OF WASHINGTON

POB 351270, Seattle, WA 98195-1270

Telephone: (206) 543-2100
Fax: (206) 221-4622
E-mail: acadpers@u.washington.edu
Internet: www.washington.edu

Founded 1861

Pres.: PHYLLIS WISE
Provost: MARY LIDSTROM
Exec. Vice-Pres. for Medical Affairs: PAUL RAMSEY
Vice-Pres. for External Affairs: RANDY HODGINS
Vice-Pres. for Finance and Facilities: V'ELLA WARREN
Vice-Pres. for Human Resources: MINDY KORNBERG
Vice-Pres. for Minority Affairs and Diversity: SHEILA EDWARDS LANGE (acting)
Vice-Pres. for Student Affairs: ERIC GODFREY
Vice-Pres. for Univ. Advancement: CONNIE KRAVAS
Exec. Vice-Provost: DOUG WADDEN (acting)
Vice-Provost for Academic Personnel: CHERYL CAMERON (acting)
Vice-Provost for Educational Outreach: DAVID SZATMARY
Vice-Provost for Global Affairs: STEPHEN E. HANSON
Vice-Provost for the Graduate School: GERALD BALDASTY
Vice-Provost for Minority Affairs and Diversity: SHEILA EDWARDS LANGE
Vice-Provost for Planning and Budgeting: PAUL JENNY
Vice-Provost for Research: MARY LIDSTROM
Vice-Provost for Special Programs: GUS KRAVAS
Vice-Provost for Undergraduate Academic Affairs: ED TAYLOR
Dir of Fed. Relations: CHRISTY GULLION
Dir of State Relations: MARGARET SHEPHERD
Dean of Undergraduate Academic Affairs: ED TAYLOR (acting)
Dir of Libraries: LIZABETH WILSON

Library: see Libraries
Number of teachers: 3,884 (f.t.e.)
Number of students: 47,361 (42,098 on Seattle campus)

Publications: *American Journal of Human Genetics*, *Biochemistry*, *Journal of Financial and Quantitative Analysis*, *Journal of Limnology and Oceanography*, *Modern Language Quarterly*, *Pacific Northwest Quarterly*, *Papers of Regional Science Association*, *Poetry Northwest*, *Trends in Engineering*, *Washington Law Review*

DEANS

College of Arts and Sciences: ANA MARI CAUCE
College of Built Environments: DANIEL FRIEDMAN
College of Education: PATRICIA WASLEY
College of Engineering: MATTHEW O'DONNELL (acting)
College of the Environment: LISA GRAUMLICH (acting)
College of Ocean and Fishery Sciences: ARTHUR NOWELL
Graduate School: JERRY BALDASTY (acting)
Information School: HARRY BRUCE
Foster School of Business: JAMES JIAMBALVO (acting)
School of Dentistry: MARTHA SOMERMAN
School of Law: KELLYE TESTY
School of Medicine: PAUL RAMSEY
School of Nursing: MARLA SALMON
School of Pharmacy: THOMAS BAILLIE
School of Public Health: PATRICIA WAHL
School of Social Work: EDWINA UEHARA (acting)
Evans School of Public Affairs: SANDRA ARCHIBALD
University of Washington, Bothell: KENYON CHAN (Chancellor)
University of Washington, Tacoma: PATRICIA SPAKES (Chancellor)

DIRECTORS

Alcoholism and Drug Abuse Institute: H. H. SAMSON
Applied Physics Laboratory: R. C. SPINDEL
Friday Harbor Laboratories: A. O. D. WILLOWS
Center for Bioengineering: L. HUNTSMAN
Center for Inherited Diseases: A. G. MOTULSKY
Center for Law and Justice: J. G. WEIS
Center for Research in Oral Biology: R. C. PAGE
Center for Studies in Demography and Ecology: C. HIRSCHMAN
Child Development and Mental Retardation Center: M. J. GURALNICK
Quaternary Research Center: S. C. PORTER
Regional Primate Center: D. M. BOWDEN
Institute on Aging: I. B. ABRASS (acting)
Institute for Environmental Studies: C. B. LEOVY
Institute for Marine Studies: E. L. MILES
Fisheries Research Institute: R. C. FRANCIS

PROFESSORS

College of Architecture and Urban Planning (Box 355726, Seattle, WA 98195; tel. (206) 543-7679; fax (206) 543-2463; internet www.caup.washington.edu):

BADANES, S. P., Architecture
BLANCO, H. J., Urban Design and Planning
CHING, F. D. K., Architecture
DANIALI, S., Construction Management
FINROW, J. V., Architecture
MILLER, D. E., Architecture
MILLER, D. H., Urban Design and Planning
MUGERAUER, R., Architecture
OCHSNER, J. K., Architecture
PYATOK, M., Architecture
STREATFIELD, D. C., Landscape Architecture
SUTTON, S. E., Architecture
VERNEZ-MOUDON, A., Urban Design and Planning

College of Arts and Sciences (Box 353765, Seattle, WA 98195; tel. (206) 543-5340; fax (206) 543-5462; internet www.artsci.washington.edu):

ADELBERGER, E. G., Physics
ALEXANDER, E., English
ALLEN, C., English
AMMERLAHN, H., German
AMMIRATI, J. F., Biology
ANDERSEN, N. H., Chemistry
ANDERSON, S., Astronomy
BACHMAN, D. M., International Studies
BALDASTY, G. J., Communication
BALICK, B., Astronomy
BARASH, D. P., Psychology
BARDEEN, J. M., Physics
BARLOW, T. E., Women Studies
BARRACK, C. M., German
BARZEL, Y., Economics
BATTISTI, D. S., Atmospheric Science
BEECHER, M. D., Psychology
BEHLER, D. I., German
BEHLMER, G. K., History
BENDICH, A. K., Biology
BENNETT, W. L., Political Science
BERGANTZ, G. W., Earth and Space Sciences
BERGER, P. E., Art
BERNARD, J. W., Music
BERNSTEIN, I. L., Psychology
BERTSCH, G. F., Physics
BESAG, J. E., Statistics
BEYERS, W. B., Geography
BIERDS, L. L., English
BLAKE, K., English
BLAU, H., English
BLIQUEZ, L. J., Classics
BLONDELL, R., Classics
BOARCH-JACOBSEN, M., Comparative Literature
BOERSMA, P. D., Biology
BOLTZ, W., Asian Languages and Literatures
BONJOUR, L. A., Philosophy
BOOKER, J. R., Earth and Space Sciences
BORDEN, W. T., Chemistry
BOULWARE, D. G., Physics
BOURGEOIS, J., Earth and Space Sciences
BOYNTON, P., Physics
BOZARTH, G. S., Music
BRADSHAW, H. D., Biology
BRAME, M. K., Linguistics
BRAVMANN, R. A., Art
BRENOWITZ, E. A., Psychology
BRETHERTON, C. S., Atmospheric Science
BROWN, J. K., German
BROWN, J. M., Earth and Space Sciences
BROWN, M. J., English
BROWNLEE, D. E., Astronomy
BRUCE, N., Economics
BUBE, K. P., Mathematics
BUCK, S. L., Psychology
BULGAC, A., Physics
BURDZY, K., Mathematics
BURKE, J. V., Mathematics
BURNETT, T. H., Physics
BURSTEIN, P., Sociology
BUTLER, J. E., American Ethnic Studies
CALLIS, J. B., Chemistry
CAMPBELL, C. T., Chemistry
CAMPBELL, P. S., Music
CAPORASO, J. A., Political Science
CASTERAS, S. P., Art
CATTOLICO, R. A., Biology
CAUCE, A. M., Psychology
CHALOUPKA, V., Physics
CHAN, K. W., Geography
CHEN, Z., Mathematics
CHENEY, E. S., Earth and Space Sciences
CHIROT, D., International Studies
CIRTAUTAS, I. D., Near Eastern Languages and Literatures
CLATTERBAUGH, K. C., Philosophy
CLAUSEN, M. L., Art
CLAUSS, J. J., Classics
CLOSE, A. E., Anthropology
COBURN, R. C., Philosophy
COHEN, S. M., Philosophy
COLDEWEY, J. C., English
COLLINGWOOD, D., Mathematics
COMAI, L., Biology
COVEY, E., Psychology
COWAN, D. S., Earth and Space Sciences
COX, C. D., Asian Languages and Literatures
CRAMER, J. G., Jr, Physics
CREAGER, K. C., Earth and Space Sciences
CRIMINALE, W. O., Jr, Applied Mathematics
CRUTCHFIELD, R. D., Sociology
CURTIS, E. B., Mathematics
DAHLSTROM, R. A., Drama
DALTON, L. R., Chemistry
DANIEL, T. L., Sociology
DAWSON, G., Psychology
DEL MORAL, R., Biology
DEN NIJS, M. P., Physics
DIAZ, F. L., Psychology
DILLON, G. L., English
DOVICHI, N. J., Chemistry
DROBNY, G. P., Chemistry
DUCHAMP, T. E., Mathematics
DUNN, R. J., English
DURAND, J., Music
DURRAN, D. R., Atmospheric Science
EBREY, P. B., History
ELLINGSON, T. J., Music
ELLIS, J. M., Geography
ELLIS, S. D., Physics
ENGEL, T., Chemistry
EPIOTIS, N., Chemistry
ERICKSON, K. B., Mathematics
EROS, P. S., Music
FAILING, P. A., Art
FAIN, S. C., Physics
FINDLEY, J. M., History
FINE, A. I., Philosophy
FLORES, L. H., American Ethnic Studies
FOLLAND, G. B., Mathematics
FOLSOM, R. C., Speech and Hearing Sciences
FORTSON, E. N., II, Physics
FREY, C. H., English
GAMMON, R. H., Chemistry
GARCIA, A., Physics
GATES, S. N., Drama
GEIST, A. L., Romance Languages and Literatures
GELB, M. H., Chemistry
GHOSE, S., Earth and Space Sciences
GIFFARD, C. A., Communications
GOLDE, H., Computer Science
GOLDSTEIN, A. A., Mathematics
GORE, W. J., Political Science
GOTTMAN, J. M., Psychology
GOUTERMAN, M. P., Chemistry
GRAYSON, D. K., Anthropology
GREENBERG, R., Mathematics
GREENWALD, A. G., Psychology
GREGORY, N. W., Chemistry
GROSSMAN, A. J., Music
GRUNBAUM, B., Mathematics
GUARRERA, F. P., Music
GUEST, A. M., Sociology
GURALNIK, M. J., Psychology and Paediatrics
HALL, B. D., Genetics
HALLET, B., Geological Sciences
HALPERIN, C. S., Botany
HALPERN, I., Physics
HALSEY, G. D., Jr, Chemistry
HALVORSEN, R., Economics
HANEY, J. V., Slavic Languages and Literatures and International Studies
HANKINS, T. L., History
HANLEY, S. B., International Studies
HARMON, D. P., Classics and Comparative Literature
HARRELL, C. S., Anthropology and International Studies
HARTMANN, D., Atmospheric Sciences
HARTWELL, L. H., Genetics
HASKINS, E. F., Botany
HEER, N. L., Near Eastern Languages and Literature
HELLER, E. J., Chemistry and Physics
HELLMANN, D. C., Political Science and School of International Studies
HENLEY, E. M., Physics
HERTLING, G. H., Germanics
HILDEBRAND, G., Art History and Architecture
HIRSCHMAN, C., Sociology
HIXSON, W. J., Art
HOBBS, P. V., Atmospheric Sciences
HODGE, P. W., Astronomy
HOLTON, J. R., Atmospheric Sciences
HOSTETLER, P. S., Drama
HOUZE, R. A., Atmospheric Physics
HU, M., Art
HUEY, R. B., Zoology
HUNN, E. S., Anthropology
HUNT, E. B., Psychology
HUTTON, R. S., Psychology
INGALLS, R. L., Physics
IRVING, R., Mathematics
JACKSON, W. A. D., Geography and School of International Studies
JACOBSON, N., Psychology
JAEGER, C. S., German
JANS, J. P., Mathematics
JOHNSON, C. R., English
JONES, R. C., Art
KAPETANIC, D., Slavic Languages and Literature, and International Studies
KAPLAN, A., Music
KARTIGANER, D. M., English
KENAGY, G. J., Zoology
KEYES, C. F., Anthropology
KEYT, D., Philosophy
KINGSBURY, M., Art History
KLAUSENBURGER, J., Romance Languages and Literature
KLEE, V. M., Jr, Mathematics
KNAPP, J. S., Dance
KNECHTGES, D. R., Asian Languages and Literature
KOBLITZ, N., Mathematics
KOHN, A. J., Zoology
KORG, J., English
KOTTLER, H. W., Art
KOTTWITZ, R., Mathematics
KOWALSKI, B. R., Chemistry
KRUMME, G., Geography
KUHL, P. K., Speech and Hearing
KWIRAM, A. L., Chemistry
LADNER, R. E., Computer Science
LAIRD, C. D., Zoology
LANG, G. E., Communications, Political Science and Sociology
LANG, K., Communications
LARDY, N., International Studies
LAZOWSKA, E., Computer Science
LEGTERS, L. H., School of International Studies
LEOPOLD, E. B., Botany and Forest Resources

LEOVY, C. B., Atmospheric Sciences and Geophysics
LEV, D. S., Political Science
LEVI, M. A., Political Science
LEVY, F. J., History
LEWIS, B., Geophysics and Oceanography
LIND, D. A., Mathematics
LISTER, C. R. B., Geophysics and Oceanography
LOCKARD, J. S., Psychology and Neurosurgery
LOCKWOOD, T. F., English
LOFTUS, E. J., Psychology
LOFTUS, G. R., Psychology
LOPER, R. B., Drama
LORD, J. J., Physics
LUBATTI, H. J., Physics
LUJAN, H. D., Political Science
LUNDIN, N. K., Art
LUNDQUIST, B. R., Music
LUNNEBORG, C., Psychology and Statistics
MCCALLUM, I. S., Geological Sciences
MCCOLL, W. D., Music
MCCRACKEN, J. D., English
MCCRONE, D. J., Political Science
MCDERMOTT, L. C., Physics
MCDERMOTT, M. N., Physics
MCELROY, C. W., English
MCGEE, J. S., Economics
MCHUGH, H., English
MACKAY, P. A., Classics, Comparative Literature, Near Eastern Language and Civilization
MARGON, B., Astronomy
MARKS, C. E., Philosophy
MARLATT, G. A., Psychology
MARSHALL, D., Mathematics
MARSHALL, J. C., Art
MARTIN, R. D., Statistics
MATTHEWS, D. R., Political Science
MAYER, J., Geography
MELTZOFF, A., Psychology
MERRILL, R. T., Geophysics and Geological Sciences
MICHAEL, E. A., Mathematics
MICKLESEN, L. R., Slavic Languages and Literature, Linguistics and International Studies
MIGDAL, J. S., International Studies
MILLER, G., Physics
MILLER, R. A., Asian Languages and Literature
MINIFIE, F. D., Speech and Hearing Sciences
MITCHELL, T. R., Management and Organization and Psychology
MODELSKI, G., Political Science
MODIANO, R., English and Comparative Literature
MORRILL, R. L., Geography and Environmental Studies
MORROW, J. A., Mathematics
MOSELEY, S., Art
NAMIOKA, I., Mathematics
NASON, J. D., Anthropology
NELSON, C. R., Economics
NELSON, T. O., Psychology
NEUMAN, D. M., Art
NEWELL, L. L., Anthropology
NEWMEYER, F. J., Linguistics
NOE, J. D., Computer Science
NORMAN, J. G., Chemistry
NORMAN, J. L., Asian Languages and Literatures
NUNKE, R. J., Mathematics
NUTE, P. E., Anthropology
ODELL, G. M., Zoology
O'DOAN, N. D., Music
OLSON, D. J., Political Science
OPPERMAN, H. N., Art
ORIANS, G. H., Zoology and Environmental Studies
OSBORNE, M. S., Mathematics
OTTENBERG, S., Anthropology
PAINE, R. T., Jr, Zoology
PALAIS, J. B., International Studies and History
PALKA, J. M., Zoology
PALMER, J. M., Prosthodontics and Speech and Hearing Sciences
PARKS, G. K., Geophysics
PARKS, R. W., Economics
PASCAL, P., Classics
PEASE, O. A., History
PEMBER, D. R., Communication
PERLMAN, M. D., Statistics
PERRY, E., International Studies
PETERS, P. C., Physics
PHELPS, R. R., Mathematics
PIZZUTO, E., Art
POCKER, Y., Chemistry
PORTER, S. C., Geological Sciences
POTTER, K. H., International Studies and Philosophy
PRINS, D., Speech and Hearing Sciences
PUFF, R. D., Physics
PUNDT, G. H., Art and Architecture
PYKE, R., Mathematics
PYLE, K. B., International Studies and History
RAGOZIN, D., Mathematics
RAHN, J., Music
RAYMOND, C. F., Geophysics
REED, R., Atmospheric Sciences
REHR, J. J., Physics
REID, B. R., Chemistry
REINERT, O., English and Comparative Literature
RENSBERGER, J. M., Geological Sciences
RESHETAR, J. S., Jr, Political Science
RICHMAN, R. J., Philosophy
RIDDIFORD, L. M., Zoology
RIEDEL, E. K., Physics
ROCKAFELLAR, R. T., Mathematics
ROHWER, S. A., Zoology
RORABAUGH, W. J., History
ROSE, N. J., Chemistry
ROSSEL, S. H., Scandinavian Languages and Literatures
ROTHBERG, J. E., Physics
RUBIN, J., Asian Languages and Literatures
RUSS, J., English
RUTHERFOORD, J. P., Physics
RUZICKA, J., Chemistry
SACKETT, G. P., Psychology
SALE, R. H., English
SAPORTA, S., Linguistics and Romance Languages
SARASON, I. G., Psychology
SARASON, L., Mathematics
SAUM, L. O., History
SAX, G., Education
SCHEIDEL, T. M., Speech
SCHEINGOLD, S. A., Political Science
SCHICK, M., Physics
SCHIFFMAN, H. F., Asian Languages and Literatures
SCHMITT, D. R., Sociology
SCHOMAKER, V., Chemistry
SCHUBERT, W. M., Chemistry
SCHUBIGER, G. A., Zoology
SCHURR, J. M., Chemistry
SCHWARTZ, P., Sociology
SCOTT, J. W., American Ethnic Studies, Sociology
SEGAL, J., Mathematics
SHAW, A. C., Computer Science
SHORACK, G. R., Statistics
SHULMAN, R., English
SIKI, B., Music
SILBERBERG, E., Economics
SILBERGELD, J. L., Art
SIMONSON, H. P., English
SIMPSON, J. B., Psychology
SKOWRONEK, F. E., Music
SLUTSKY, L. J., Chemistry
SMITH, C. W., Art
SMITH, J. D., Oceanography, Geophysics and Geological Sciences
SMITH, R. E., Psychology
SMITH, S. W., Geophysics
SMITH, W. O., Music
SNYDER, L., Computer Science
SNYDER, R., Zoology
SPAFFORD, M. C., Art
STADLER, D. R., Genetics
STAMM, K., Communications
STARK, R., Sociology
STARYK, S. S., Music
STEELE, C. M., Psychology
STEENE, B., Scandinavian Languages and Literature and Comparative Literature
STERN, E. A., Physics
STEVICK, R. D., English
STORCH, L., Music
STOUT, E. L., Mathematics
STRATHMANN, R. R., Zoology
STREITBERGER, W., English
STUIVER, M., Geological Sciences
SUGAR, P. F., History and International Studies
SULLIVAN, J. B., Mathematics
SULLIVAN, W., Astronomy
SWINDLER, D. R., Anthropology
TANIMOTO, S. L., Computer Science
TAYLOR, M. J., Political Science
TELLER, D. Y., Psychology and Physiology
THOMAS, C. S., History
THOMAS, M. D., Geography
THOMPSON, E. A., Statistics
THOMPSON, G., Speech and Hearing Sciences
THORNTON, J., Economics
THOULESS, D. J., Physics
TOWNSEND, J. R., International Studies and Political Science
TREADGOLD, D. W., International Studies and History
TRUMAN, J. W., Zoology
TSUKADA, M., Botany
TUFTS, P. D., Music
UHLMANN, G. A., Mathematics
ULLMAN, J. C., History
UNTERSTEINER, N., Atmospheric Sciences and Geophysics
VAN DEN BERGHE, P. L., Sociology
VANDENBOSCH, R., Chemistry
VANDYCK, R. S., Physics
VELIKONJA, J., Geography
VILCHES, O. E., Physics
VOYLES, J. B., Germanics
WAALAND, J. R., Botany
WADDEN, D. J., Art
WAGER, L. W., Sociology
WAGONER, D. R., English
WALLACE, J. M., Atmospheric Sciences
WALLERSTEIN, G., Astronomy
WAN, F. Y., Applied Mathematics
WANG, C. H., Asian Languages and Literature and Comparative Literature
WARASHINA, P. B., Art
WARD, P., Geological Sciences
WARFIELD, R. B., Mathematics
WARNER, G. W., Jr, Mathematics
WATTS, R. O., Chemistry
WEBB, E., International Studies and Comparative Literature
WEIS, J. G., Sociology
WELLNER, J. A., Statistics
WESTWATER, M. J., Mathematics
WHISLER, H. C., Botany
WHITEHILL-WARD, J., Art
WILETS, L., Physics
WILEY, H., Dance
WILLEFORD, W., English and Comparative Literature
WILLIAMS, R. W., Physics
WILLOWS, A. O. D., Zoology
WILSON, W. R., Speech and Hearing Sciences
WINANS, E. V., Anthropology
WINGFIELD, J., Zoology
WITHERSPOON, G., Anthropology
WOODS, S. C., Psychology
YAMAMURA, K., International Studies
YANTIS, P. A., Speech and Hearing Sciences

YOUNG, K. K., Physics
YOUNG, P. R., Computer Science
ZOLLER, W. H., Chemistry

College of Education:

ABBOTT, R. D.
AFFLECK, J. Q.
ANDERSON, R.
ANDREWS, R. L.
BANKS, J. A.
BILLINGSLEY, F. F.
BOLTON, D. L.
BRAMMER, L. M.
BURGESS, C. O.
BUTTERFIELD, E. C.
DOI, J. I.
EDGAR, E. B.
EVANS, E. D.
GOODLAD, J. I.
HARING, N. G.
HUNKINS, F. P.
JENKINS, J. R.
KALTSOUNIS, T.
KERR, D. H.
KERR, S. T.
KLOCKARS, A. J.
LIEBERMAN, A.
LOVITT, T. C.
LOWENBRAUN, S.
MCCARTIN, R. E.
MADSEN, D. L.
MORISHIMA, J. K.
NEEL, R. S.
OLSTAD, R. G.
PECKHAM, P. D.
RYCKMAN, D. B.
SAX, G.
SCHILL, W. J.
SEBESTA, S. L.
THOMPSON, M. D.
TOSTBERG, R. E.
WHITE, O.
WINN, W. D.

College of Engineering:

AKSAY, I. A., Materials Science Engineering
ALBRECHT, R. W., Electrical and Nuclear Engineering
ALEXANDER, D. E., Mechanical Engineering
ALEXANDRO, F., Electrical Engineering
ALLAN, G. G., Forest Resources and Chemical Engineering
ANDERSEN, J., Electrical Engineering
ARCHBOLD, T. F., Mining, Metallurgical and Ceramic Engineering
BABB, A. L., Chemical and Nuclear Engineering
BALISE, P. L., Mechanical Engineering
BEREANO, P., Interdepartmental Curricular Programme
BERG, J. C., Chemical Engineering
BOGAN, R. H., Civil Engineering
BOLLARD, R. J. H., Aeronautics and Astronautics
BOWEN, J. R., Chemical Engineering
BRADT, R. C., Mining, Metallurgical and Ceramic Engineering
BROWN, C. B., Civil Engineering
BURGES, S. J., Civil Engineering
CHALUPNIK, J. D., Mechanical Engineering
CHEUNG, P. W., Electrical Engineering and Bioengineering
CHRISTIANSEN, W. H., Aeronautics and Astronautics
CLARK, R. N., Electrical Engineering
COLCORD, J. E., Civil Engineering
CORLETT, R. C., Mechanical Engineering
DALY, C. H., Mechanical Engineering
DAVIS, E. J., Chemical Engineering
DECHER, R., Aeronautics and Astronautics
DEPEW, C. A., Mechanical Engineering
DOW, D. G., Electrical Engineering
ELIAS, Z. M., Civil Engineering
EMERY, A. F., Mechanical Engineering
EVANS, R. J., Civil Engineering
FERGUSON, J. F., Civil Engineering
FINLAYSON, B. A., Chemical Engineering
FISCHBACH, D. B., Materials Science and Engineering
FYFE, I. M., Aeronautics and Astronautics
GARLID, K. L., Chemical and Nuclear Engineering
GESSNER, F., Mechanical Engineering
HARALICK, R. M., Electrical Engineering
HAWKINS, N. M., Civil Engineering
HEIDEGER, W. J., Chemical Engineering
HERTZBERG, A., Aeronautics and Astronautics
HOFFMAN, A. S., Chemical Engineering and Bioengineering
HOLDEN, A., Electrical Engineering
HOLSAPPLE, K. A., Aeronautics and Astronautics
HSU, C.-C., Electrical Engineering
ISHIMARU, A., Electrical Engineering
JOHNSON, D. E., Bioengineering
JOHNSON, D. L., Electrical Engineering
JOPPA, R. G., Aeronautics and Astronautics
JORGENSEN, J. E., Mechanical Engineering
KEVORKIAN, J. K., Aeronautics and Astronautics
KIPPENHAM, C. J., Mechanical Engineering
KOBAYASHI, A. S., Mechanical Engineering
KOSALY, G., Nuclear and Mechanical Engineering
KUROSAKA, M., Aeronautics and Astronautics
LAURITZEN, P. O., Electrical Engineering
LYTLE, D. W., Electrical Engineering
MCCORMICK, N. J., Nuclear Engineering
MCKEAN, W. T., Chemical Engineering and Forest Resources
MALTE, P. C., Mechanical Engineering
MAR, B. W., Civil Engineering
MARKS, R. J., Electrical Engineering
MATTOCK, A. H., Civil Engineering
MEDITCH, J. S., Electrical Engineering
MONTGOMERY, D. C., Industrial Engineering
MORITZ, W. E., Electrical Engineering
NECE, R. E., Civil Engineering
NIHAN, N. L., Civil Engineering
NOGES, E., Electrical Engineering
PARMETER, R. R., Aeronautics and Astronautics
PEARSON, C. E., Aeronautics and Astronautics, Applied Mathematics
PEDEN, I., Electrical Engineering
PILAT, M. J., Civil Engineering
PINTER, R. E., Electrical Engineering
POLONIS, D. H., Mining, Metallurgical and Ceramic Engineering
PORTER, R. P., Electrical Engineering
PRATT, D. T., Mechanical Engineering
RAO, Y. K., Mining, Metallurgical and Ceramics Engineering
RATNER, B., Bioengineering and Chemical Engineering
RIBE, F. L., Nuclear Engineering
RILEY, J., Mechanical Engineering
ROBKIN, M. A., Nuclear Engineering
ROEDER, C. W., Civil Engineering
RUSSELL, D. A., Aeronautics and Astronautics
SCHNEIDER, J. B., Urban Planning and Civil Engineering
SCOTT, W. D., Mining, Metallurgical and Ceramic Engineering
SEFERIS, J. C., Chemical Engineering
SIGELMANN, R. A., Electrical Engineering
SLEICHER, C. A., Jr, Chemical Engineering
SPINDEL, R. C., Electrical Engineering
STEAR, E. B., Electrical Engineering
STENSEL, H. D., Civil Engineering
STOEBE, T. G., Mining, Metallurgical and Ceramic Engineering
TAGGART, R., Mechanical Engineering
TSANG, L., Electrical Engineering
VAGNERS, J., Aeronautics and Astronautics
VENKATA, S. S., Electrical Engineering
VERESS, S. A., Civil Engineering
VESPER, K. H., Mechanical Engineering and Management and Organization, Marine Studies
VLASES, G. C., Nuclear Engineering
WELCH, E. B., Civil Engineering
WOLAK, J., Mechanical Engineering
WOODRUFF, G. L., Nuclear Engineering
YEE, S. S., Electrical Engineering
ZICK, G. L., Electrical Engineering

College of Forest Resources:

ADAMS, D. M.
AGEE, J. K.
ALLAN, G. G., Forest Resources and Chemical Engineering
BARE, B. B.
BETHEL, J. S.
BRUBAKER, L. B.
COLE, D. W.
DOWDLE, B.
EDMONDS, R. L.
FIELD, D. R.
FRITSCHEN, L. J.
GARA, R. I.
HATHEWAY, W. H.
HINCKLEY, T. M.
HRUTFIORD, B. F.
LEE, R. G.
MANUWAL, D. A.
OLIVER, C.
PICKFORD, S. G.
SARKENEN, K., Forest Resources and Chemical Engineering
SCHREUDER, G. F.
SHARPE, G. W.
STETTLER, R. F.
THORUD, D. B.
TUKEY, H. B.
UGOLINI, F. C.
WAGGENER, T. R.
WOTT, J. A.

College of Ocean and Fishery Science

School of Oceanography:

BANSE, K.
CARPENTER, R.
COACHMAN, L.
CREAGER, H. S.
DELANEY, J.
EMERSON, S.
ERIKSEN, C.
FROST, B. W.
HEATH, G. R.
HEDGES, J.
HERSHMAN, M. J.
JUMARS, P. A.
LEWIS, B.
LISTER, C. R. B.
MCMANUS, D. A.
MERRILL, R. T.
MILES, E. L.
MURPHY, S. R.
MURRAY, J.
NOWELL, A. R. M.
RHINES, P. B.
RICHARDS, F. A.
SMITH, J. D.
STERNBERG, R. W.
WELANDER, P.
WINTER, D. R.
WOOSTER, W. S.

School of Fisheries:

BRANNON, E. L.
BROWN, G. W.
CHEW, K. K.
FORD, E. D.
FRANCIS, R. C.
GALLUCCI, V. F.
HALVER, J. D.
HILBORN, R. W.
LANDOLT, M.
LISTON, J.
MATCHES, J. R.
MATHEWS, S. B.
MILLER, B. S.
PIETSCH, T. W.

PIGOTT, G. M.
SCHELL, W. R.
SMITH, L. S.
STICKNEY, R. R.
TAUB, F.
WHITNEY, R. R.

Graduate School of Library and Information Science:

CHISHOLM, M. E., Library and Information Science

Graduate School of Public Affairs:

DENNY, B. C.
KROLL, M., Public Affairs and Political Science
LOCKE, H. G.
LYDEN, F. J.
WILLIAMS, W.
ZERBE, R. O.

School of Business:

ALBERTS, W. W., Finance, Business Economics and Quantitative Methods
BOURQUE, P. J., Finance, Business Economics and Quantitative Methods
CHIU, J. S. Y., Management Science
D'AMBROSIO, C. A., Finance, Business Economics
DUKES, R. E., Accounting
ETCHESON, W. W., Marketing
FAALAND, B. H., Finance, Business Economics and Quantitative Methods
FROST, P. A., Finance, Business Economics and Quantitative Methods
HALEY, C. W., Finance, Business Economics and Quantitative Methods
HEATH, L. C., Accounting
HENNING, D. A., Management and Organization
HESS, A. C., Finance, Business Economics and Quantitative Methods
HIGGINS, R. C., Finance, Business Economics and Quantitative Methods
INGENE, C., Marketing and International Business
JACOB, N. L., Finance, Business Economics and Quantitative Methods
JIAMBALVO, J., Accounting
JOHANSSON, J. K., Marketing, Transportation, and International Business
JOHNSON, D. W., Finance, Business Economics and Quantitative Methods
KLASTORIN, T., Management Science
KNUDSON, H. R., Management and Organization
LATHAM, G., Management and Organization
MACLACHLAN, D. L., Marketing
MITCHELL, T. R., Management and Organization
MOINPOUR, R., Marketing, Transportation and International Business
MUELLER, G. G., Accounting
NARVER, J. C., Marketing, Transportation and International Business
NEWELL, W. T., Management and Organization, Management Science
NOREEN, E. W., Accounting
PAGE, A. N., Finance, Business Economics and Quantitative Methods
PETERSON, R. B., Finance, Business Economics and Quantitative Methods
RAMANATHAN, K. V., Accounting
ROLEY, V. V., Finance and Business Economics
SAXBERG, B. O., Management and Organization
SCHALL, L. D., Finance, Business Economics and Quantitative Methods
SCOTT, W. G., Management and Organization
SPRATLEN, T. H., Marketing, Transportation and International Business
SUMMER, C. E., Management and Organization
SUNDEM, G. L., Accounting
WHEATLEY, J. J., Marketing, Transportation and International Business
YALCH, R., Marketing

School of Dentistry:

AMMONS, W. F., Periodontics
BOLENDER, C. L., Prosthodontics
BRUDVIK, J. S., Prosthodontics
CANFIELD, R. C., Restorative Dentistry
CLAGETT, J. A., Periodontics and Microbiology
CONRAD, D. A., Dental Public Health Sciences and Health Services
DERONEN, T. A., Dental Public Health Services, Biostatistics
DWORKIN, S. F., Oral Surgery
ENGEL, D., Periodontics
FRANK, R. P., Prosthodontics
GEHRIG, J. D., Oral Surgery
HARRINGTON, G. W., Endodontics
JOHNSON, R. H., Periodontics
KOKICH, V., Orthodontics
LEWIS, T. M., Restorative Dentistry
LITTLE, R. M., Orthodontics
MILGROM, P. M., Dental Public Health Services
MOFFETT, B. C., Orthodontics
MYALL, R. W., Oral Surgery
NATKIN, E., Endodontics
NICHOLLS, J. I., Restorative Dentistry
OMNELL, K.-A., Oral Medicine
PAGE, R. C., Pathology and Periodontics
PALMER, J. M., Speech and Hearing Sciences and Prosthodontics
ROBINOVITCH, M. R., Oral Biology
SHAPIRO, P., Orthodontics
SMITH, D. E., Prosthodontics
TAMARIN, A., Oral Biology
WARNICK, M. E., Restorative Dentistry
WORTHINGTON, P., Oral and Maxillofacial Surgery
YUODELIS, R. A., Restorative Dentistry

School of Law:

ANDERSON, W. R.
ARONSON, R. H.
BURKE, W. T.
CHISUM, D. S.
FITZPATRICK, J. F.
FLETCHER, R. L.
HALEY, J. O.
HARDISTY, J. H.
HAZELTON, P. A.
HENDERSON, D. F.
HJORTH, R. L.
HUME, L. S.
HUSTON, J. C.
JAY, S. M.
JOHNSON, R. W.
JUNKER, J. M.
KUMMERT, R. O.
LOH, W. D.
MORRIS, A.
PECK, C. J.
PRICE, J. R.
PROSTERMAN, R. L.
RODDIS, R. S.
RODGERS, W. H.
ROMBAUER, M.
SMITH, F. W., Jr
STOEBUCK, W. B.
TRAUTMAN, P. A.

School of Medicine:

ABELSON, H. T., Paediatrics
ABRASS, I., Medicine
ADAMSON, J. W., Medicine
ALBERT, R., Medicine
ALMERS, W., Physiology and Biophysics
ALVORD, E. C., Pathology
ANDERSON, M. E., Rehabilitation Medicine and Physiology
ANSELL, J. S., Urology
APPELBAUM, F., Medicine
BARNES, G. W., Urology
BASSINGTHWAIGHTE, J. B., Bioengineering
BEAVO, J., Pharmacology
BECKER, J., Psychiatry, Psychology
BELKNAP, B. H., Medicine
BENEDETTI, T. J., Obstetrics and Gynaecology
BEN-MENACHEM, Y., Radiology
BERGER, A. J., Physiology and Biophysics
BERGMAN, A. B., Paediatrics
BERNSTEIN, I. D., Paediatrics
BIERMAN, E. L., Medicine
BINDER, M., Physiology and Biophysics
BIRD, T., Medicine
BLACKMON, J. R., Medicine
BLAGG, C. R., Medicine
BLEYER, W. A., Paediatrics
BORNSTEIN, P., Medicine and Biochemistry
BOWDEN, D. M., Psychiatry
BREMNER, W. J., Medicine
BRENGELMANN, G., Physiology and Biophysics
BROWN, B. G., Medicine
BRUNZELL, J. D., Medicine
BUCHANAN, T. M., Medicine and Pathobiology
BUCKNER, C. D., Medicine
BUNT-MILAM, A. H., Ophthalmology
BUTLER, J., Medicine
BYERS, P., Medicine and Pathology
CARR, J. E., Psychiatry and Psychology
CARRICO, C. J., Surgery
CATTERALL, W. A., Pharmacology
CHAIT, A., Medicine
CHAMPOUX, J. J., Microbiology
CHAPMAN, C. R., Anaesthesiology and Psychiatry
CHAPMAN, W. H., Urology
CHATRIAN, G. E., Laboratory Medicine and Neurological Surgery
CHEEVER, M. A., Medicine
CHENEY, F. W., Anaesthesiology
CHESNUT, C. H., Radiology and Medicine
CLARREN, S., Paediatrics
COBB, L. A., Medicine
COPASS, M. K., Medicine
COREY, L., Laboratory Medicine and Microbiology
COUNTS, G. W., Medicine
COUSER, W. G., Medicine
CRILL, W. E., Medicine, Physiology and Biophysics
CROAKE, J. S., Psychiatry
CULLEN, B. F., Anaesthesiology
CUMMINGS, C. W., Otolaryngology
DALE, D. C., Medicine
DAVIE, E. W., Biochemistry
DEISHER, R. W., Paediatrics
DELATEUR, B. J., Rehabilitation Medicine
DETTER, J. C., Laboratory Medicine
DETWILER, P., Physiology and Biophysics
DILLARD, D. H., Surgery
DOBIE, R. A., Otolaryngology
DODGE, H. T., Medicine
DODRILL, C. B., Neurological Surgery
DOERR, H. O., Psychiatry and Psychology
DOHNER, C. W., Medicine and Education
DONALDSON, J. A., Otolaryngology
DUNNER, D. L., Psychiatry
EISENBERG, M., Medicine
EMANUEL, I., Epidemiology and International Health and Paediatrics
ENSINCK, J. W., Medicine
ESCHENBACH, D., Obstetrics and Gynaecology
EYRE, D. R., Orthopaedics
FARRELL, D. F., Medicine
FEFER, A., Medicine
FEIGL, E., Physiology and Biophysics
FETZ, E. E., Physiology and Biophysics
FIALKOW, P. J., Medicine and Genetics
FIGGE, D. C., Obstetrics and Gynaecology
FIGLEY, M. M., Radiology
FISCHER, E. H., Biochemistry
FRENCH, J. W., Paediatrics
FUCHS, A., Physiology and Biophysics
FUJIMOTO, W. Y., Medicine
GARTLER, S. M., Medicine and Genetics
GEYMAN, J. P., Family Medicine

GILLILAND, B., Laboratory Medicine and Medicine
GLOMSET, J. A., Medicine and Biochemistry
GODWIN, J. D., Radiology
GOLDMAN, M. L., Radiology
GOODNER, C. J., Medicine
GORDON, A. M., Physiology and Biophysics
GORDON, M., Biochemistry
GRAHAM, C. B., Radiology and Paediatrics
GREENBERG, P., Medicine
GREENE, H. L., Medicine
GREER, B. E., Obstetrics and Gynaecology
GRIFFIN, T. W., Radiation Oncology
GROMAN, N. B., Microbiology
GROUDINE, M., Radiation Oncology
GUNTHEROTH, W. G., Paediatrics
GUY, A., Rehabilitation Medicine and Bioengineering
HAGGITT, R. C., Pathology
HAKOMORI, S., Pathobiology and Microbiology
HALAR, E. M., Rehabilitation Medicine
HANDSFIELD, H. H., Medicine
HANSEN, J. A., Medicine
HANSEN, S., Orthopaedics
HARLEY, J. D., Radiology
HARRIS, A. B., Neurological Surgery
HAUSCHKA, S. D., Biochemistry
HAYDEN, P., Paediatrics
HEIMAN, J., Psychiatry and Behavioural Sciences
HEIMBACH, D. M., Surgery
HELLSTROM, I. E., Microbiology
HELLSTROM, K. E., Pathology
HENDERSON, M., Medicine and Epidemiology
HENDRICKSON, A. E., Ophthalmology and Biological Structure
HERMAN, C. M., Surgery
HILDEBRANDT, J., Physiology and Medicine
HILLE, B., Physiology and Biophysics
HLASTALA, M. P., Physiology and Biophysics and Medicine
HODSON, W. A., Paediatrics
HOLBROOK, K. A., Biological Structure
HOLMES, K. K., Medicine
HORITA, A., Pharmacology
HORNBEIN, T. F., Anaesthesiology, Physiology and Biophysics
HUDSON, L. D., Medicine
HUNTSMAN, L. L., Bioengineering
INUI, T. S., Medicine and Health Services
IVEY, T. D., Surgery
JOHANSEN, K. H., Surgery
JOHNSON, M. H., Psychiatry
JONES, R. F., Surgery
JONSEN, A. R., Medical History and Ethics
JUCHAU, M. R., Pharmacology
KALINA, R. E., Ophthalmology
KEHL, T. H., Physiology, Biophysics and Computer Science
KELLY, W. A., Neurological Surgery
KENNEDY, J. W., Medicine
KENNY, M. A., Laboratory Medicine
KLEBANOFF, S. J., Medicine
KNOPP, R. H., Medicine
KOEHLER, J. K., Biological Structure
KOERKER, D. J., Physiology and Biophysics and Medicine
KRAFT, G. H., Rehabilitation Medicine
KREBS, E. G., Pharmacology and Biochemistry
KROHN, K., Radiology
LABBE, R. F., Laboratory Medicine
LAKSHMINARAYAN, S., Medicine
LANDESMAN, S., Psychiatry
LARAMORE, G., Radiation Oncology
LARSON, E., Medicine
LEHMANN, J. F., Rehabilitation Medicine
LEIN, J. N., Obstetrics and Gynaecology
LEMIRE, R. J., Paediatrics
LIVINGSTON, R. B., Medicine
LOCKARD, J. S., Neurological Surgery
LOEB, L. A., Pathology
LOESER, J. B., Neurological Surgery
LOGERFO, J. P., Medicine and Health Services
LOOP, J. W., Radiology
LUFT, J. H., Biological Structure
MCARTHUR, J. R., Medicine
MCDONALD, G. B., Medicine
MACK, L. A., Radiology
MACKLER, B., Paediatrics
MANNIK, M., Medicine
MARAVILLA, K. R., Radiology and Neurological Surgery
MARCHIORO, T. L., Surgery
MARTIN, G. M., Pathology
MARTIN, J. C., Psychiatry
MATSEN, F. A., Orthopaedics
MAYO, M. E., Urology
MEYERS, J., Medicine
MILLS, R. P., Ophthalmology
MONSEN, E. R., Medicine
MORRIS, D. R., Biochemistry
MOSS, A. A., Radiology
MOTTET, N. K., Pathology and Environmental Health
MOTULSKY, A., Genetics and Medicine
MURPHY, T. M., Anaesthesiology
NEFF, J. M., Paediatrics
NEIMAN, P. E., Medicine
NELP, W. B., Medicine and Radiology
NELSON, J. A., Radiology
NESTER, E. W., Microbiology
NORWOOD, T., Pathology
NOVACK, A. H., Paediatrics
OCHS, H. D., Paediatrics
ODLAND, G. F., Medicine, Biological Structure
OJEMANN, G. A., Neurological Surgery
OMENN, G. S., Medicine and Environmental Health
PAGE, R. C., Pathology and Periodontics
PALMER, J., Medicine
PALMITER, R. D., Biochemistry
PAPAYANNOPOULOU, T., Medicine
PARSON, W. W., Biochemistry
PAULSEN, C. A., Medicine
PETRA, P. H., Obstetrics and Gynaecology and Biochemistry
PHILLIPS, T. J., Family Medicine
PIERSON, D., Medicine
PIOUS, D. A., Paediatrics
PLORDE, J. J., Laboratory Medicine
POLLACK, G. H., Bioengineering
POPE, C. E., Medicine
PORTE, D., Medicine
PRESTON, T. A., Medicine
PRINZ, P., Psychiatry
RAISYS, V., Laboratory Medicine
RASEY, J. S., Radiation Oncology
RASKIND, M. A., Psychiatry
RAUSCH, R. L., Animal Medicine and Pathobiology
REICHENBACH, D. D., Pathology
REICHLER, R. J., Psychiatry
REID, B. R., Biochemistry and Chemistry
RICE, C. L., Surgery
RITCHIE, J. L., Medicine
ROBERTS, T. S., Neurological Surgery
ROBERTSON, W. O., Paediatrics
ROBINSON, N. L., Psychiatry
RODIECK, R. W., Ophthalmology
ROHRMAN, C. A., Radiology
ROOS, B. A., Medicine
ROSENBLATT, R. A., Family Medicine
ROSS, R., Pathology
ROSSE, C., Biological Structure
ROWELL, L. B., Physiology and Biophysics
RUBELL, E. W., Otolaryngology
RUBIN, C. E., Medicine
RUVALCABA, R., Paediatrics
SAARI, J. C., Ophthalmology and Biochemistry
SALE, G., Pathology
SAUNDERS, D. R., Medicine
SCHER, A. M., Physiology and Biophysics
SCHMER, G., Laboratory Medicine
SCHOENKNECHT, F. D., Laboratory Medicine and Microbiology
SCHUFFLER, M., Medicine
SCHWARTZ, S. M., Pathology
SCHWARTZKROIN, P., Neurological Surgery and Physiology, Biophysics
SCHWINDT, P. C., Physiology and Biophysics
SCOTT, C. R., Paediatrics
SCRIBNER, B. H., Medicine
SELLS, C. J., Paediatrics
SHAPIRO, B. M., Biochemistry
SHAW, C., Pathology
SHEPARD, T. H., Paediatrics
SHERRARD, D. J., Medicine
SHERRIS, J. C., Microbiology
SHURTLEFF, D. B., Paediatrics
SILVERSTEIN, F., Medicine
SIMKIN, P. A., Medicine
SINGER, J., Medicine
SLICHTER, S., Medicine
SMITH, A. L., Paediatrics
SMITH, O. A., Jr, Physiology and Biophysics
SNYDER, J. M., Otolaryngology
SOULES, M. R., Obstetrics and Gynaecology
SPADONI, L. R., Obstetrics and Gynaecology
SPENCE, A. M., Medicine
STAHELI, L. T., Orthopaedics
STAHL, W., Medicine, Physiology and Biophysics
STALEY, J. T., Microbiology
STAMATOYANNOPOULOS, G., Medicine
STAMM, W., Medicine
STEINER, R., Obstetrics and Gynaecology, Physiology and Biophysics
STENCHEVER, M. A., Obstetrics and Gynaecology
STEVENSON, J. G., Paediatrics
STIRLING, C. E., Physiology and Biophysics
STOLOV, W. C., Rehabilitation Medicine
STORM, D. R., Pharmacology
STRANDJORD, P. E., Laboratory Medicine
STRANDNESS, D. E., Surgery
STREISSGUTH, A. P., Psychiatry
SUMI, S. M., Medicine and Pathology
SWANSON, P. D., Medicine
TAPPER, D., Surgery
TELLER, D. C., Biochemistry
TELLER, D. Y., Physiology and Psychology
THOMAS, E. D., Medicine
THOMPSON, A. R., Medicine
TOWE, A. L., Physiology and Biophysics
TOWNES, B. D., Psychiatry
TRIER, W. C., Surgery
TRUOG, W. E., Paediatrics
TUCKER, G. J., Psychiatry
TURCK, M., Medicine
VANARSDEL, P. P., Medicine
VANCITTERS, R. L., Physiology and Biophysics, Medicine
VANHOOSIER, G. L., Animal Medicine
VESTAL, R., Medicine
VINCENZI, F. F., Pharmacology
VONTVER, L., Obstetrics and Gynaecology
VRACKO, R., Pathology
WALKER, R. D., Psychiatry and Behavioural Science
WALLACE, J. F., Medicine
WALSH, K. A., Biochemistry
WARD, R. J., Anaesthesiology
WEDGWOOD, R. J., Paediatrics
WESTRUM, L. E., Neurological Surgery and Biological Structure
WEYMULLER, E. A., Otolaryngology
WHITELEY, H. R., Microbiology
WHORTON, J. C., Biomedical History
WIGHT, T., Pathology
WINN, H. R., Neurological Surgery
WINTERSCHEID, L. C., Surgery
WOODRUM, D. E., Paediatrics
WOOTON, P., Radiation Oncology
YOUNG, E. T., Biochemistry
ZAGER, R., Medicine

School of Nursing:

BARNARD, K. E., Parent and Child Nursing
BATEY, M. V., Community Health Care Systems

BENOLIEL, J. Q., Community Health Care Systems
CHRISMAN, N. J., Community Health Care Systems
DE TORNYAY, R., Community Health Care Systems
EYRES, S. J., Parent and Child Nursing
GALLUCCI, B. J., Physiological Nursing
GOERTZEN, I. E., Community Health Care Systems
HORN, B. J., Community Health Care Systems
HEGYVARY, S. T., Community Health Care Systems
KOGAN, H., Psychosocial Nursing
KURAMOTO, A., Physiological Nursing
LEWIS, F. M., Community Health Care Systems
MITCHELL, P. H., Physiological Nursing
OSBORNE, O. H., Psychosocial Nursing
PATRICK, M. I., Physiological Nursing
ROSE, M. H., Parent and Child Nursing
WOLF-WILETS, V. C., Psychosocial Nursing
WOODS, N. A., Physiological Nursing

School of Pharmacy:

BAILLIE, T., Medicinal Chemistry
BRADY, L. R., Medicinal Chemistry
CAMPBELL, W. H., Pharmacy Practice
GIBALDI, M., Pharmaceutics
KRADJAN, W., Pharmacy Practice
LEVY, R. H., Pharmaceutics
NELSON, S. D., Medicinal Chemistry
NELSON, W. L., Medicinal Chemistry
PLEIN, J. B., Pharmacy Practice
TRAGER, W. F., Medicinal Chemistry

School of Public Health and Community Medicine:

BRESLOW, N. E., Biostatistics
BUCHANAN, T. L., Pathobiology and Medicine
CROWLEY, J. J., Biostatistics
DALING, J. R., Epidemiology
DAVIS, K. A., Biostatistics
DAY, R. W., Health Services
DE ROUEN, T., Biostatistics
DIEHR, P. K., Biostatistics
EMANUEL, I., Epidemiology and Paediatrics
FEIGL, P., Biostatistics
FISHER, L. D., Biostatistics
FLEMING, T. R., Biostatistics
FOY, H. M., Epidemiology
GALE, J. I., Epidemiology
GRAYSTON, J. T., Epidemiology
HAKOMORI, S., Pathobiology and Microbiology
HENDERSON, M. M., Epidemiology and Medicine
INUI, T. S., Health Services and Medicine
JACKSON, K. L., Environmental Health
KENNY, G. E., Pathobiology
KOEPSELL, T., Health Services, Epidemiology
KRONMAL, R. A., Biostatistics
KUO, C.-C., Pathobiology
LEE, J. A., Environmental Health
LOGERFO, J. P., Health Services and Medicine
MARTIN, D. C., Biostatistics
MOOLGAVKAR, S. H., Epidemiology
MOTTET, N. K., Environmental Health and Pathology
MURPHY, S. D., Environmental Health
OMENN, G. S., Environmental Health and Medicine
PATRICK, D. L., Health Services
PERINE, P. L., Epidemiology
PERRIN, E. B., Health Services
PETERSON, A. V., Biostatistics
PRENTICE, R. L., Biostatistics
RAUSCH, R. L., Pathobiology
ROBKIN, M. A., Environmental Health and Nuclear Engineering
THOMAS, D. B., Epidemiology
VAN BELLE, G., Biostatistics
WAGNER, E. H., Health Services
WAHL, P. W., Biostatistics
WANG, S., Pathobiology
WEISS, N. S., Epidemiology
WILSON, J. T., Environmental Health
WORTHINGTON-ROBERTS, B., Epidemiology

School of Social Work:

BRIAR, S.
GOTTLIEB, N. R.
HAWKINS, J. D.
JAFFEE, B.
LEVY, R. L.
PATTI, R. J.
RESNICK, H.
TAKAGI, C. Y.
WHITTAKER, J. K.

WALLA WALLA COLLEGE

204 South College Avenue, College Place, WA 99324
Telephone: (509) 527-2615
Fax: (509) 527-2253
Internet: www.wwc.edu

Founded 1892
Academic year: September to June

Pres.: (vacant)
Vice-Pres. for Academic Admin.: JOHN BRUNT
Vice-Pres. for Admissions and Marketing: VICTOR BROWN
Vice-Pres. for College Advancement: KAREN JOHNSON
Vice-Pres. for Financial Admin.: MANFORD SIMCOCK
Vice-Pres. for Student Admin.: NELSON THOMAS
Registrar: CAROLYN DENNEY
Dir of Libraries: CAROLYN GASKELL

Library of 170,000 vols
Number of teachers: 125
Number of students: 1,650

WASHINGTON STATE UNIVERSITY

Pullman, WA 99164-5910
Telephone: (509) 335-3564
E-mail: admissions@wsu.edu
Internet: www.wsu.edu

Founded 1890 as college, univ. status 1959
Public control
Accredited by NWCCU
Academic year: August to May

Pres.: ELSON S. FLOYD
Provost and Exec. Vice-Pres.: WARWICK BAYLY
Vice-Pres. for Business and Finance: ROGER PATTERSON
Vice-Pres. for Information Services and Chief Information Officer: VIJI MURALI
Vice-Pres. for Student Affairs and Enrollment Management: JOHN FRAIRE
Chancellor of Spokane Campus: BRIAN PITCHER
Chancellor of Tri-Cities Campus: VICKY CARWEIN
Chancellor of Vancouver Campus: HAROLD DENGERINK
Registrar: JULIA POMERENK
Dean of Libraries: JAY STARRATT

Library of 2,178,040 vols
Number of teachers: 1,640
Number of students: 26,301

Publications: *ESQ: A Journal of the American Renaissance* (3 a year), *LandEscapes*, *Western Journal of Black Studies* (4 a year)

DEANS

College of Agriculture, Human and Natural Resource Sciences: DANIEL BERNARDO
College of Business: ERIC SPANGENBERG
College of Education: A. G. RUD
College of Engineering and Architecture: CANDIS CLAIBORN
College of Liberal Arts: DOUG EPPERSON
College of Pharmacy: GARY POLLACK
College of Sciences: DARYLL DEWALD
College of Veterinary Medicine: BRYAN SLINKER
Distance and Professional Education: DAVE CILLAY (Dir)
Edward R. Murrow College of Communication: LAWRENCE PINTAK
Graduate School: HOWARD GRIMES
Honours College: LIBBY WALKER
Intercollegiate College of Nursing, Spokane: PATRICIA BUTTERFIELD

WESTERN WASHINGTON UNIVERSITY

Bellingham, WA 98225
Telephone: (360) 650-3000
E-mail: admit@cc.wwu.edu
Internet: www.wwu.edu

Founded 1893 as Bellingham Normal School, name changed to Western Washington College of Education 1937, finally Western Washington Univ. 1977
Academic year: September to June

Pres.: Dr KAREN W. MORSE
Provost/Vice-Pres. for Academic Affairs: Dr ANDREW BODMAN
Vice-Pres. for Business and Financial Affairs: Dr GEORGE A. PIERCE
Vice-Pres. for External Affairs: ROBERT EDIE
Vice-Pres. for Student Affairs: Dr EILEEN V. COUGHLIN
Librarian: BÉLA FOLTIN, Jr

Library: 1.9m. vols
Number of teachers: 615
Number of students: 11,708

Publications: *Bellingham Review* (literary, 2 a year), *Journal of Cross-Cultural Psychology* (international, 1 a year), *Journal of Rural Sociology* (1 a year), *Northwest Journal of Business and Economics* (1 a year), *Studies in American Indian Literature* (4 a year).

WHITMAN COLLEGE

345 Boyer Ave, Walla Walla, WA 99362
Telephone: (509) 527-5111
E-mail: communication@whitman.edu
Internet: www.whitman.edu

Founded 1859

Pres.: Dr GEORGE BRIDGES
Vice-Pres. for Devt: STEPHEN BECKER
Dean of Faculty: PATRICK KEEF
Dean of Students: CHARLES CLEVELAND
Registrar: RONALD URBAN
Librarian: HENRY YAPLE

Library of 325,000 vols
Number of teachers: 101 full-time
Number of students: 1,434

WHITWORTH UNIVERSITY

300 W Hawthorne Rd, Spokane, WA 99251
Telephone: (509) 777-1000
Fax: (509) 777-4763
Internet: www.whitworth.edu

Founded 1890
Liberal arts univ. affiliated with the Presbyterian Church (USA)

Pres.: Dr BECK A. TAYLOR
Vice-Pres. of Academic Affairs: Dr MICHAEL K. LEROY
Library Dir: Dr HANS BYNAGLE

Library of 188,000 vols
Number of teachers: 180 (full-time)
Number of students: 2,800

WEST VIRGINIA

ALDERSON-BROADDUS COLLEGE

101 College Hill Dr., Philippi, WV 26416
Telephone: (304) 457-1700
Fax: (304) 457-6239
Internet: www.ab.edu

Founded 1871

Pres.: Dr J. MICHAEL CLYBURN
Provost and Vice-Pres. for Academic Affairs: Dr DENNIS H. STULL
Dir of Admissions: KIMBERLY N. KLAUS
Dir of Annual Giving and Alumni Relations: JAMIE COOPER
Dir of Communications: MENDI SIMON
Dir of Devt: ANNETTE FETTY
Dir of Financial Aid: BRIAN WEINGART
Dir of Information and Research: JULIA MORRIS
Vice-Pres. for Advancement: TANYA L. SHELTON
Vice-Pres. for Assessment, Planning and Technology: BRUCE BLANKENSHIP
Vice-Pres. for Business and Finance: MARSHA DENNISTON
Vice-Pres. for Student Services and Enrollment Management: Dr ALLEN B. WITHERS
Registrar: SAUNDRA HOXIE
Librarian: DAVID E. HOXIE

Library of 100,000 vols
Number of teachers: 76 (60 full-time, 16 part-time)
Number of students: 780

4-Year liberal arts college.

APPALACHIAN BIBLE COLLEGE

POB ABC, Bradley, WV 25818
161 College Dr., Mount Hope, WV 25880
Telephone: (304) 877-6428
Fax: (304) 877-5082
E-mail: abc@abc.edu
Internet: www.abc.edu

Founded 1950
Number of students: 300

Pres.: Dr DANIEL ANDERSON

Ind., non-denominational.

BETHANY COLLEGE

Bethany, WV 26032
Telephone: (304) 829-7000
Fax: (304) 829-7108
Internet. www.bethanywv.edu

Founded 1840
Private control
Academic year: August to May

Pres.: G. T. SMITH
Provost and Dean of Faculty: MICHAEL MIHALYO
Sr Vice-Pres.: JOHN S. CUNNINGHAM
Spec. Counsel to the Pres.: JOSEPH M. KUREY
Exec. Vice-Pres.: PATRICIA MLODZIK
Exec. Vice-Pres. and Treas.: WILLIAM KIEFER
Vice-Pres. for Admission and Institutional Advancement: SVEN DE JONG
Assoc. Vice-Pres. for Student Services: SANDRA NEEL
Provost: KATHLEEN C. GODINA
Librarian: MARY-BESS HALFORD

Library of 275,340 vols
Number of teachers: 65 (56 full-time, 9 part-time)
Number of students: 830

4-Year liberal arts college; depts of biology, chemistry, communication, economics and business, English, equine studies, fine arts, fundamental science, gen. science, history and political science, interdisciplinary studies, mathematics and computer science, philosophy, physical education and sports studies, physics, psychology, religious studies, social science, teaching and social services, world languages and cultures.

BLUEFIELD STATE COLLEGE

219 Rock St, Bluefield, WV 24701
Telephone: (304) 327-4000
Fax: (304) 325-7747
E-mail: bscadmit@bluefieldstate.edu
Internet: www.bluefieldstate.edu

Founded 1895
Academic year: August to May

Pres.: ALBERT L. WALKER
Vice-Pres. for Academic Affairs and Provost: DONALD H. SMITH
Vice-Pres. for Financial and Admin. Affairs: SHELIA JOHNSON
Dir of Enrollment Management and Vice-Pres. for Student Affairs: JOHN C. CARDWELL
Dir of Library Services: JOANNA THOMPSON

Library of 75,700 vols
Number of teachers: 90
Number of students: 3,600

4-Year state-supported college; offers liberal arts and professional programmes.

CONCORD UNIVERSITY

Vermillion St, POB 1000, Athens, WV 24712-1000
Telephone: (304) 384-5249
Fax: (304) 384-3218
E-mail: info@concord.edu
Internet: www.concord.edu

Founded 1872
Academic year: September to May
4-Year public liberal arts college

Pres.: Dr GREGORY F. ALOIA
Vice-Pres. and Academic Dean: Dr JOHN DAVID SMITH
Vice-Pres. for Business and Finance: CHARLES BECKER
Vice-Pres. for Student Affairs and Dir for Retention: MARJIE FLANIGAN
Assoc. Vice-Pres. for Devt: LORETTA YOUNG
Dir for Admissions and Financial Aid: KENT J. GAMBLE
Dean of Students: RICK DILLON
Librarian: Dr STEPHEN ROWE

Library of 145,000 vols, 5,000 periodicals
Number of teachers: 95
Number of students: 2,900

DAVIS AND ELKINS COLLEGE

100 Campus Dr., Elkins, WV 26241
Telephone: (304) 637-1900
Internet: www.davisandelkins.edu

Founded 1904
Academic year: August to May

Pres.: Dr G. THOMAS MANN
Vice-Pres. and Dean of the Faculty: Dr LAURENCE B. MCARTHUR
Vice-Pres. for College Advancement: PATRICIA J. SCHUMANN
Vice-Pres. for Student Life and Dean of Students: DAVID SNEED
Dir of the Library: JACKIE SCHNEIDER

Library of 116,000 vols
Number of students: 635

Liberal arts college; depts of biology and environmental science, business admin. and economics, chemistry, communications and foreign languages, computer science and physics, education, English, fine and performing arts, health, history and political science, mathematics, nursing, psychology and human services, religion and philosophy, sociology and criminology, sport and movement sciences.

FAIRMONT STATE UNIVERSITY

1201 Locust Ave, Fairmont, WV 26554
Telephone: (304) 367-4892
Fax: (304) 366-4870
E-mail: admit@fairmontstate.edu
Internet: www.fscwv.edu

Founded 1867

Pres.: Dr DANIEL BRADLEY
Pres. of Pierpont Community and Technical College: BLAIR MONTGOMERY
Provost and Vice-Pres. for Academic Affairs: ANNE L. PATTERSON
Vice-Pres. for Academic Services and Dir of Retention: Dr MARIA ROSE
Vice-Pres. for Admin. and Fiscal Affairs: ENRICO PORTO
Vice-Pres. and Chief Information Officer: MICHAEL BESTUL
Vice-Pres. for Institutional Advancement: K. JEAN AHWESH
Vice-Pres. for Research and Graduate Studies: Dr PHILLIP MASON
Vice-Pres. for Student Services: MICHAEL BELMEAR
Dir of Communications: SARAH HENSLEY
Dir of Library Services: THELMA HUTCHINS

Library of 265,000 vols
Number of teachers: 190
Number of students: 7,740

Incl. Pierpont Community and Technical College.

GLENVILLE STATE COLLEGE

200 High St, Glenville, WV 26351
Telephone: (304) 462-7361
E-mail: admissions@glenville.edu
Internet: www.glenville.edu

Founded 1872
Academic year: August to May

Pres.: Dr PETER BARR
Dean of Academic Affairs: Dr KATHY BUTLER
Librarian: GAIL WESTBROOK

Library of 110,000 vols, 483 microforms, 625 hard-copy periodical titles, 18 newspaper titles
Number of teachers: 52 full-time, 30 part-time
Number of students: 1,400

Depts of business, education, English, fine arts, land resources, science and mathematics, social science.

MARSHALL UNIVERSITY

1 John Marshall Dr., Huntington, WV 25755
Telephone: (304) 696-3170
Fax: (304) 696-3135
Internet: www.marshall.edu

Founded 1837
Academic year: August to May

Pres.: Dr STEPHEN J. KOPP
Chief of Staff and Sr Vice-Pres. for Communications: BILL BISSETT
Provost and Sr Vice-Pres. for Academic Affairs: Dr SARAH DENMAN
Assoc. Vice-Pres. for Academic Affairs: Dr FRANCES HENSLEY
Gen. Counsel and Vice-Pres. for External Affairs: LAYTON COTTRILL
Dean of Libraries: BARBARA WINTERS

Library of 1,411,480 vols, documents, journal subscriptions, microforms and audiovisual items
Number of teachers: 666 full-time
Number of students: 14,000

DEANS

College of Education and Human Services: Dr ROSALYN ANSTINE TEMPLETON
College of Fine Arts: DONALD VAN HORN

College of Health Professions: Dr SHORTIE McKINNEHY
College of Information Technology and Engineering: Dr TONY B. SZWILSKI
College of Liberal Arts: Dr CHRISTINA MURPHY
College of Science: Dr ANDREW ROGERSON
Lewis College of Business: Dr PAUL USELDING
Marshall Community and Technical College: JANET AMOS
School of Extended Education: DON COMBS
School of Journalism and Mass Communications: Dr CORLEY DENNISON
Graduate School: Dr LEONARD J. DEUTSCH
Joan C. Edwards School of Medicine: Dr CHARLES H. McKOWN, Jr

MOUNTAIN STATE UNIVERSITY

POB 9003, Beckley, WV 25802
Telephone: (304) 929-1300
E-mail: gomsu@mountainstate.edu
Internet: www.mountainstate.edu

Pres.: CHARLES H. POLK
Exec. Vice-Pres. and Chief Academic Officer: JAMES G. SILOSKY
Vice-Pres. and Chief of Staff: CINDY ALEXANDER
Vice-Pres. for Finance and Chief Financial Officer: MICHELE SARRETT
Vice-Pres. for Legal Affairs: JOHN REED
Vice-Pres. for Operations: RON WARD
Assoc. Vice-Pres. and Dean of PLA: JILL HOPKINS
Registrar: REBECCA HALL
Dir of Library and Technology Resources: JUDY ALTIS

Number of teachers: 368 (87 full-time, 281 part-time)
Number of students: 4,422

OHIO VALLEY UNIVERSITY

1 Campus View Dr., Vienna, WV 26105-8000
Telephone: (304) 865-6000
Fax: (304) 865-6001
E-mail: admissions@ovu.edu
Internet: www.ovu.edu

Founded 1958
Private, religiously affiliated
Accredited by Higher Learning Comm. of the N Central Asscn of Colleges and Schools

Pres.: Dr E. KEITH STOTTS
Chief Financial Officer: Dr JOY JONES
Vice-Pres. for Academic Affairs: Dr JIM BULLOCK
Dir of Admissions: AMY BORTELL
Librarian: AMANDA SHOCKEY

Library of 34,000 vols, 142 print periodical subscriptions, 60,203 microforms, 6,779 audiovisual materials; 30 electronic databases for periodicals, reference sources and 93,763 e-book titles
Number of students: 560

SALEM INTERNATIONAL UNIVERSITY

223 West Main St, Salem, WV 26426
Telephone: (304) 782-5011
Fax: (304) 782-5395
E-mail: admissions@salemu.edu
Internet: www.salemu.edu

Founded 1888

Pres.: Dr RONALD E. OHL
Vice-Pres. for Academic Affairs and Provost: Dr WAYNE H. ENGLAND
Registrar: CYNTHIA J. CALISE
Librarian: Dr PHYLLIS D. FREEDMAN

Library of 200,000 vols
Number of teachers: 55
Number of students: 810

SHEPHERD UNIVERSITY

POB 5000, Shepherdstown, WV 25443
Telephone: (304) 876-5000
Fax: (304) 876-3101
Internet: www.shepherd.edu

Founded 1871
Academic year: August to May

Pres.: Dr SUZANNE SHIPLEY
Vice-Pres. for Academic Affairs: Dr RICHARD HELLDOBLER
Vice-Pres. for Admin. and Finance: Dr ED MAGEE
Vice-Pres. for Advancement: Dr DIANE MELBY
Librarians: JEAN ELLIOTT, JOHN SHERIDAN

Library of 185,849 vols
Number of teachers: 327 (119 full-time, 208 part-time)
Number of students: 4,185

UNIVERSITY OF CHARLESTON

2300 MacCorkle Ave, SE, Charleston, WV 25304
Telephone: (304) 357-4800
Fax: (304) 357-4715
E-mail: admissions@ucwv.edu
Internet: www.ucwv.edu

Founded 1888 as Morris Harvey College, present name 1979
Academic year: August to April

Pres.: Dr EDWIN H. WELCH
Provost and Dean of Faculty: Dr CHARLES STEBBINS
Vice-Pres. for Admin. and Finance: CLETA M. HARLESS
Vice-Pres. for Enrollment and Student Life: BRAD PARRISH
Dir of Library Services: LYNN SHEEHAN

Library of 106,000 vols
Number of teachers: 65 full-time
Number of students: 1,200

Divs of arts and sciences, business, health sciences; center for pharmacy education.

WEST LIBERTY STATE COLLEGE

West Liberty, WV 26074
Telephone: (304) 336-5000
Fax: (304) 336-8403
Internet: www.westliberty.edu

Founded 1837
Academic year: August to May

Pres.: Dr JOHN P. McCULLOUGH
Vice-Pres. for Student Affairs and Enrollment Management: J. D. CARPENTER
Provost and Vice-Pres. for Academic Affairs: Dr DONNA J. LUKICH (acting)
Registrar: SCOTT A. COOK
Librarian: CHERYL HARSHMAN

Library of 194,711 vols
Number of teachers: 166 (112 full-time, 54 part-time)
Number of students: 2,654

WEST VIRGINIA SCHOOL OF OSTEOPATHIC MEDICINE

Office of Communications, 400 North Lee St, Lewisburg, WV 24901
Telephone: (304) 647-6238
E-mail: jmanchester@wvsom.edu
Internet: www.wvsom.edu

Pres.: OLEN E. JONES
Vice-Pres. for Academic Affairs and Dean: Dr MICHAEL D. O. ADELMAN
Vice-Pres. for Finance and Facilities: LAWRENCE KELLEY

Library of 17,000 vols, 450 journals, 2,000 multimedia titles
Number of teachers: 49
Number of students: 503

WEST VIRGINIA STATE UNIVERSITY

POB 1000, Institute, WV 25112
Telephone: (304) 766-3000
E-mail: admissions@wvstateu.edu
Internet: www.wvstateu.edu

Founded 1891 as a land-grant college by West Virginia Legislature

Pres.: Dr HAZO W. CARTER, Jr
Vice-Pres. for Academic Affairs: Dr R. CHARLES BYERS
Vice-Pres. for Admin. Services: Dr CASSANDRA B. WHYTE
Vice-Pres. for Finance: ROBERT PARKER
Vice-Pres. for Planning and Advancement: Dr R. CHARLES BYERS
Vice-Pres. for Student Affairs: BRYCE CASTO
Dir of Library Resources: PATRICK HALL

Library of 200,000 vols, 300 periodical subscriptions
Number of teachers: 253 (137 full-time, 16 part-time)
Number of students: 3,344

Depts of art, biology, business admin., chemistry, communications, criminal justice, economics, education, English, health and human performance, history, mathematics, modern foreign languages, music, physics, political science, psychology, social work, sociology.

WEST VIRGINIA UNIVERSITY

POB 6201, Morgantown, WV 26506-6201
Telephone: (304) 293-0111
Fax: (304) 293-3080
E-mail: wvuadmissions@arc.wvu.edu
Internet: www.wvu.edu

Founded 1867
State control
Academic year: August to May
Accredited by Higher Learning Comm., N Central Asscn of Colleges and Schools

Pres.: Dr JAMES CLEMENTS
Provost and Vice-Pres.: Dr MICHELE G. WHEATLY
Chancellor for Robert C. Byrd Health Sciences Center: CHRISTOPHER C. COLENDA
Vice-Pres. for Admin. and Finance: NARVEL G. WEESE, Jr
Vice-Pres. for Human Resources: MARGARET R. PHILLIPS
Vice-Pres. for Legal Affairs: WILLIAM HUTCHENS
Vice-Pres. for Research and Economic Devt: Dr CURT M. PETERSON
Vice-Pres. for Student Affairs: KENNETH D. GRAY
Vice-Pres. for Univ. Relations: CHRISTINE MARTIN

Library: see Libraries and Archives
Number of teachers: 2,239
Number of students: 29,306

DEANS

College of Business and Economics: Dr JOSE SARTARELLI
College of Creative Arts: Dr J. BERNARD SCHULTZ
College of Engineering and Mineral Resources: Dr EUGENE V. CILENTO
College of Human Resources and Education: Dr DEE HOPKINS
College of Law: JOYCE E. McCONNELL
David College of Agriculture, Forestry and Consumer Sciences: CAMERON HACKNEY
Eberly College of Arts and Sciences: Dr ROBERT JONES
Perley Isaac Reed School of Journalism: MARYANNE REED
Potomac State College: KERRY S. O'DELL
School of Dentistry: Dr LOUISE VESELICKY
School of Medicine: Dr ARTHUR ROSS
School of Nursing: GEORGIA L. NARSAVAGE

School of Pharmacy: PATRICIA A. CHASE
School of Physical Activity and Sports Science: Dr DANA D. BROOKS
WVU Institute of Technology: Dr SCOTT M. HURST

WEST VIRGINIA UNIVERSITY INSTITUTE OF TECHNOLOGY

405 Fayette Pike, Montgomery, WV 25136
Telephone: (304) 442-3071
Fax: (304) 442-3059
E-mail: admissions@wvutech.edu
Internet: www.wvutech.edu
Founded 1895
Pres.: CHARLES E. BAYLESS
Provost and Vice-Pres. for Academic and Student Affairs: Dr GALAN JANEKSELA
Campus Provost: Dr SCOTT HURST
Dir for Relations and Communications: MARY E. HOLLISTER
Dir of Library: Dr JEWEL RUCKER
Library of 153,056 vols, 360,000 microtexts, 111 periodical subscriptions
Number of teachers: 112 (89 full-time, 23 part-time)
Number of students: 1,224

WEST VIRGINIA WESLEYAN COLLEGE

59 College Ave, Buckhannon, WV 26201
Telephone: (304) 473-8000
Fax: (304) 473-8187
Internet: www.wvwc.edu
Founded 1890
Pres.: PAMELA BALCH
Dean of the College: LARRY R. PARSONS
Vice-Pres. for Admin. and Finance: BARRY R. PRITTS
Vice-Pres. for Information Technology: R. DUWANE SQUIRES
Vice-Pres. for Institutional Advancement: BRENT A. BUSH
Vice-Pres. for Student Affairs and Enrollment Management: JULIA KEEHNER
Dir of Library Services: PAULA L. MCGREW
Dir of Marketing and Communication: ROBERT N. SKINNER, II
Dir of Undergraduate Admission: JOHN R. WALTZ
Coordinator of Graduate Studies and Extended Learning: KATHLEEN M. LONG
Library of 149,085 vols
Number of teachers: 160 (80 full-time, 80 part-time)
Number of students: 1,405 (undergraduate)

WHEELING JESUIT UNIVERSITY

316 Washington Ave, Wheeling, WV 26003-6295
Telephone: (304) 243-2000
Fax: (304) 243-2243
E-mail: news@wju.edu
Internet: www.wju.edu
Founded 1954
Jesuit liberal arts univ.
Academic year: August to May
Pres.: Rev. JULIO GIULIETTI
Controller: MICHAEL LEO
Vice-Pres. for Institutional Advancement: BRENT BUSH
Dean for Student Devt: CORY KING
Assoc. Dir of Admissions: BETH LOY
Registrar: CHAD CARTER
Librarian: KELLY MUMMERT (acting)
Library of 139,000 vols
Number of teachers: 97
Number of students: 1,527

WISCONSIN

ALVERNO COLLEGE

3400 South 43 St, POB 343922, Milwaukee, WI 53234-3922
Telephone: (414) 382-6000
Fax: (414) 382-6354
Internet: www.alverno.edu
Founded 1887
Academic year: August to May
Pres.: Dr MARY MEEHAN
Vice-Pres. for Academic Affairs: KATHLEEN O'BRIEN
Vice-Pres. for Devt: JULIE LANDES
Vice-Pres. for Finance and Management Services: JAMES OPPERMANN
Registrar: PATRICIA HARTMAN
Dir of Library: CAROL BRILL
Library of 82,416 vols, 1,382 periodicals, 287,726 microforms, 15,728 audiovisual items
Number of teachers: 107 full-time
Number of students: 2,480

BELLIN COLLEGE OF NURSING

725 South Webster Ave, POB 23400, Green Bay, WI 54305-3400
Telephone: (920) 433-3560
Fax: (920) 433-7416
E-mail: admissions@bcon.edu
Internet: www.bcon.edu
Founded 1909 as Bellin Hospital School of Nursing, adopted current name in 1988
Pres.: JANE MUHL
Vice-Pres. and Dir of Business: JOSEPH KEEBAUGH
Vice-Pres. for Student Services: JO WOELFEL
Dir of Admissions: PENELOPE CROGHAN
Dir of Financial Aid: LENA GOODMAN
Dir of Grants: DALE WHEELOCK
Registrar: VICKY SCHAULAND
Number of teachers: 19
Number of students: 290

BELOIT COLLEGE

700 College St, Beloit, WI 53511
Telephone: (608) 363-2000
Fax: (608) 363-2717
E-mail: pubaff@www.beloit.edu
Internet: www.beloit.edu
Founded 1846
Academic year: June to May
Pres.: JOHN E. BURRIS
Vice-Pres. for Academic Affairs and Dean of the College: LYNN FRANKEN
Vice-Pres. for Admin. and Treas.: JOHN M. NICHOLAS
Vice-Pres. for Enrollment Services: NANCY BENEDICT
Vice-Pres. for Student Affairs and Dean of Students: WILLIAM J. FLANAGAN
Registrar: MARY BOROS-KAZAI
Library of 240,000 vols, 1,100 periodical and newspaper titles
Number of teachers: 90
Number of students: 1,200
Publications: *Avatar* (1 a year), *Beloit Magazine* (3 a year), *The Round Table* (52 a year).

CARDINAL STRITCH UNIVERSITY

6801 North Yates Rd, Milwaukee, WI 53217
Telephone: (414) 410-4000
Internet: www.stritch.edu
Founded 1937
Provost: DAN BLANKENSHIP
Pres.: KENT BERGMANN
Exec. Vice-Pres. and Chief Operating Officer: PETER HOLBROOK
Vice-Pres. for Academic Affairs: Dr MARNA BOYLE
Vice-Pres. for Business and Finance: KAREN WALRATH
Vice-Pres. for Facilities: JACK GLYNN
Vice-Pres. for Information Technology: LINDA CABOT
Vice-Pres. for Public Relations and Communications: LINDA STEINER
Vice-Pres. for Student Devt and Dean of Students: CHRISTINE ROBINSON
Vice-Pres. for Univ. Advancement: MICHAEL BRAUER
Library Dir: DAVID WEINBERG-KINSEY
Library of 139,000 vols
Number of teachers: 98
Number of students: 6,900
Ind., Franciscan institution; comprises College of Arts and Sciences, College of Business, College of Education and Leadership, and the Ruth S. Coleman College of Learning.

CARROLL COLLEGE

100 North East Ave, Waukesha, WI 53186
Telephone: (414) 547-1211
Fax: (414) 524-7139
E-mail: ccinfo@carroll1.cc.edu
Internet: www.cc.edu
Founded 1846
Pres.: Dr DOUGLAS N. HASTAD
Dean of Students: PATRICK PEYER (acting)
Dir of Library: LELAN MCLEMORE
Library of 196,000 vols
Number of teachers: 286 (111 full-time, 175 part-time)
Number of students: 3,292 full-time

CONCORDIA UNIVERSITY WISCONSIN

12800 North Lake Shore Dr., Mequon, WI 53097
Telephone: (262) 243-5700
Fax: (262) 243-4351
E-mail: admissions@cuw.edu
Internet: www.cuw.edu
4-Year, Lutheran liberal arts college
Founded 1881
Pres.: Dr PATRICK T. FERRY
Number of students: 5,574

EDGEWOOD COLLEGE

1000 Edgewood College Dr., Madison, WI 53711
Telephone: (608) 663-2294
Fax: (608) 663-3291
Internet: www.edgewood.edu
4-Year liberal arts college; coeducational
Founded 1927
Academic year: September to May
Pres.: Dr DANIEL J. CAREY
Vice-Pres. for Academic Affairs and Academic Dean: MARY KELLY-POWELL
Vice-Pres. for Student Devt and Dean of Students: MAGGIE BALISTRERI-CLARKE
Registrar: ELLEN FEHRING
Dir of Library: SYLVIA CONTRERAS
Library of 93,000 vols
Number of teachers: 159 (72 full-time, 87 part-time)
Number of students: 2,400

LAKELAND COLLEGE

POB 359, Sheboygan, WI 53082-0359
Telephone: (414) 565-2111
Fax: (414) 565-1206

Internet: www.lakeland.edu
4-Year liberal arts college
Founded 1862
Pres.: Dr STEPHEN A. GOULD
Vice-Pres. for Academic Affairs and Dean of the College: Dr TIMOTHY E. FULOP
Vice-Pres. for Advancement: JAMES C. CAPE
Vice-Pres. for Enrollment Management: ALLAN D. MITCHLER
Vice-Pres. for Finance: JOSEPH D. BOTANA, II
Gen. Counsel and Vice-Pres. for Int. Programs: E. ANTHONY FESSLER
Dean of Students and Vice-Pres. for Student Affairs: SANDRA GIBBONS-VOLLBRECHT
Librarian: ANN PENKE
Library of 70,000 vols
Number of teachers: 41
Number of students: 954

LAWRENCE UNIVERSITY

711 E Boldt Way, SPC 29 Appleton, WI 54911
115 South Drew St, Appleton, WI 54911
Telephone: (920) 832-6500
Fax: (920) 832-6782
E-mail: excel@lawrence.edu
Internet: www.lawrence.edu
Founded 1847
Private control
Academic year: September to June
Languages of instruction: Arabic, Chinese, English, French, German, Japanese, Russian, Spanish
Private college of the liberal arts and sciences with conservatory of music
Pres.: JILL BECK
Dean for Admissions and Financial Aid: KEN ANSELMENT
Provost and Dean of the Faculty: DAVID BURROWS
Library Dir: PETE GILBERT
Library of 400,000 vols
Number of teachers: 165 full-time
Number of students: 1,500

MARANATHA BAPTIST BIBLE COLLEGE

745 West Main St, Watertown, WI 53094
Telephone: (920) 261-9300
Fax: (920) 261-9109
E-mail: webmaster@mbbc.edu
Internet: www.mbbc.edu
Founded 1968
Academic year: September to May
Pres.: MARTIN MARRIOTT
Vice-Pres. for Academic Affairs: JOHN BROCK
Vice-Pres. for Business Affairs: MARK STEVENS
Vice-Pres. for Institutional Advancement: JIM HARRISON
Dean of Students: DOUG RICHARDS
Registrar: DAVID HERSHBERGER
Number of teachers: 40
Number of students: 862

MARIAN COLLEGE OF FOND DU LAC

45 S National Ave, Fond du Lac, WI 54935
Telephone: (920) 923-7600
Fax: (920) 923-7154
E-mail: admissions@mariancollege.edu
Internet: www.mariancollege.edu
Catholic liberal arts college
Founded 1936
Academic year: August to May
Pres.: Dr JOSEFINA CASTILLO BALTODANO
Vice-Pres. for Enrollment Management: STACEY AKEY
Vice-Pres. of Student Life: Dr JAMES MOORE
Academic Dean: SHERYL AYALA
Librarian: MARY ELLEN GORMICAN
Library of 92,000 vols
Number of teachers: 92 full-time, 3 part-time
Number of students: 1,330 full-time

DEANS

Arts and Humanities: Dr BRANDON CLAYCOMB
Social and Behavioural Sciences: Dr LARRY REYNOLDS

MARQUETTE UNIVERSITY

POB 1881, Milwaukee, WI 53201-1881
Telephone: (414) 288-7250
Fax: (414) 288-7197
E-mail: admissions@marquette.edu
Internet: www.marquette.edu
Private control (Jesuit)
Founded 1881 as Marquette College; chartered as univ. in 1907
Pres.: Rev. ROBERT A. WILD
Provost: MADELINE WAKE
Sr Vice-Pres.: GREG KLIEBHAN
Vice-Pres. and Gen. Counsel: CYNTHIA M. BAUER
Vice-Pres. for Admin.: ARTHUR F. SCHEUBER
Vice-Pres. for Finance: JOHN C. LAMB
Vice-Pres. for Marketing and Communication: TRICIA GERAGHTY
Vice-Pres. for Public Affairs: RANA H. ALTENBURG
Vice-Pres. for Student Affairs: Rev. ANDREW J. THON
Vice-Pres. for Univ. Advancement: JULIE TOLAN
Dean of Univ. Library: JANICE SIMMONS-WELBURN
Library: 1.5m. vols
Number of teachers: 1,057
Number of students: 10,892

DEANS AND DIRECTORS

College of Arts and Sciences: Dr MICHAEL A. MCKINNEY
College of Business Administration and Graduate School of Management: Dr DAVID L. SHROCK
College of Communication: Dr JOHN J. PAULY
College of Health Sciences: Dr JACK C. BROOKS
College of Nursing: Dr LEA T. ACORD
College of Professional Studies: Dr ROBERT J. DEAHL
School of Dentistry: Dr WILLIAM K. LOBB
School of Education: Dr WILLIAM A. HENK
School of Engineering: Dr STANLEY V. JASKOLSKI
Law School: JOSEPH D. KEARNEY

MEDICAL COLLEGE OF WISCONSIN

8701 Watertown Plank Rd, Milwaukee, WI 53226
Telephone: (414) 456-8296
Fax: (414) 456-6550
Internet: www.mcw.edu
Founded 1893
Pres. and CEO: T. MICHAEL BOLGER
Dean and Exec. Vice-Pres.: MICHAEL J. DUNN
Number of teachers: 900 faculty physicians
Number of students: 1,365

MILWAUKEE INSTITUTE OF ART AND DESIGN

273 East Erie St, Milwaukee, WI 53202
Telephone: (414) 276-7889
Fax: (414) 291-8077
E-mail: miadadm@miad.edu
Internet: www.miad.edu
Provost: DAVID MARTIN (acting).

MILWAUKEE SCHOOL OF ENGINEERING

1025 North Broadway, Milwaukee, WI 53202-3109
Telephone: (414) 277-7300
Internet: www.msoe.edu
Pres.: HERMANN VIETS
Vice-Pres. of Academics: Dr ROGER FRANKOWSKI
Vice-Pres. of Devt: FRANK HABIB
Vice-Pres. of Finance and Chief Financial Officer: ARMUND JANTO
Vice-Pres. for Student Life and Dean of Students: PATRICK J. COFFEY
Dir of the Library: GARY SHIMEK.

MOUNT MARY COLLEGE

2900 North Menomonee River Parkway, Milwaukee, WI 53222
Telephone: (414) 258-4810
Internet: www.mtmary.edu
Catholic women's college
Founded 1913
Pres.: Dr LINDA TIMM
Library Dir: VOLKER H. KRIEGISCH
Library of 111,000 vols
Number of teachers: 144
Number of students: 1,700

NASHOTAH HOUSE

2777 Mission Rd, Nashotah, WI 53058
Telephone: (262) 646-6500
E-mail: nashotah@nashotah.edu
Internet: www.nashotah.edu
Founded 1842
Seminary of the Episcopal Church in the Anglican Communion of Churches
Dean and Pres.: Very Rev. ROBERT S. MUNDAY
Associate Dean for Academic Affairs: Dr GARWOOD P. ANDERSON
Provost: Rev. Dr RICHARD LONGABAUGH
Registrar and Dir of Admissions: Dr CAROL KLUKAS
Dir of Library: DAVID SHERWOOD
Publication: *The Missioner*.

NORTHLAND COLLEGE

1411 Ellis Ave, Ashland, WI 54806
Telephone: (715) 682-1699
Fax: (715) 682-1308
E-mail: admit@northland.edu
Internet: www.northland.edu
Founded 1892
Private control
Accredited by Higher Learning Comm. of the N Central Assen of Colleges and Schools
Academic year: September to May
Language of instruction: English
Pres.: MICHAEL MILLER
Vice-Pres. of Academic Affairs and Provost: ALAN BREW
Vice-Pres. for Finance and Admin.: ROBERT JACKSON
Vice-Pres. for Institutional Advancement: MARC BARBEAU
Vice-Pres. for Enrollment Management: RICK SMITH
Vice-Pres. for Marketing: DAVID WAHLBERG
Dir of Sigurd Olson Environmental Institute: MARK LEACH
Library Dir: JULIA TROJANOWSKI
Library of 76,640 vols and 250 print periodical subscriptions, excl. electronic access
Number of teachers: 45 full-time
Number of students: 700

Publications: *Eco-Vision* (1 a year), *Northland College Magazine* (2 a year), *The Drifts* (student paper, print and online)

PROFESSORS

ALLDRITT, L., Religion
DAMRELL, J., Sociology and Anthropology
DILLENSCHNEIDER, C., Outdoor Education
GLICKMAN, J., Music
GOETZ, B., Geoscience
GORMAN, W., Biology
GOYKE, A., Biology
JOYAL, R., Business Administration and Economics
KIM, Y., Mathematics and Computer Information Systems
SMALL, M., English and Modern Languages

RIPON COLLEGE

POB 248, Ripon, WI 54971
Telephone: (920) 748-8115
E-mail: adminfo@ripon.edu
Internet: www.ripon.edu

4-Year private liberal arts and sciences college

Founded 1851

Pres.: Rev. Dr DAVID C. JOYCE
Vice-Pres. and Dean of Admission and Financial Aid: STEVE SCHUETZ
Vice-Pres. and Dean of Faculty: GERALD SEAMAN
Vice-Pres. and Dean of Students: CHRISTOPHER M. OGLE
Vice-Pres. for Advancement: LINDA J. CARTER
Vice-Pres. for Finance: MARY DEREGNIER
Chair. of Library Dept: VALERIE VIERS

Library of 150,000 vols
Number of teachers: 75
Number of students: 750

SACRED HEART SCHOOL OF THEOLOGY

7335 South Highway 100, POB 429, Hales Corners, WI 53130-0429
Telephone: (414) 425-8300
Fax: (414) 529-6999
Internet: www.shst.edu

Founded 1929
Roman Catholic seminary
Academic year: September to June
Language of instruction: English

Library of 100,000 vols, 450 periodicals

Pres.-Rector: Very Rev. JAN DE JONG
Vice-Rector: Rev. THOMAS L. KNOEBEL
Vice-Pres. for Finance: SALLY A. SMITS
Academic Dean: Rev. RAUL GOMEZ
Dir for Pastoral Education: Rev. ROBERT SCHIAVONE
Dir for Spiritual Formation: Rev. PETER SCHUESSLER
Registrar: ROSE M. STINEFAST
Dir for Library: EUGENE ENGELDINGER

Number of teachers: 35
Number of students: 175

ST FRANCIS SEMINARY

3257 South Lake Dr., St Francis, WI 53235
Telephone: (414) 747-6400
E-mail: mkarr@sfs.edu
Internet: www.sfs.edu

Founded 1845

Rector: Rev. DONALD J. HYING
Dirs of Library: MARY CARIAN, KATHY FRYMARK

Library of 80,000 vols.

ST NORBERT COLLEGE

100 Grant St, De Pere, WI 54115
Telephone: (920) 403-3557
Fax: (920) 403-4010
Internet: www.snc.edu

Catholic liberal arts college

Founded 1898

Pres.: WILLIAM J. HYNES
Dean of the College and Academic Vice-Pres.: MICHAEL MARSDEN
Vice-Pres. for College Advancement: MARK W. JONES
Registrar: RICHARD GUILD
Dir of Library: FELICE E. MACIEJEWSKI

Library of 175,000 vols
Number of teachers: 140 (115 full-time, 25 part-time)
Number of students: 1,987

Publication: *The Chronicle* (online).

SILVER LAKE COLLEGE

2406 South Alverno Rd, Manitowoc, WI 54220-9319
Telephone: (920) 684-6691
Fax: (920) 684-7082
Internet: www.sl.edu

Founded 1935
Academic year: August to May

Accredited by North Central, NCATE (National Council for Accred. of Teacher Education), DPI (Dept. of Public Instruction, NASN (National Assoc. of Schools of Music)

Pres.: Dr GEORGE ARNOLD
Academic Dean: Dr GEORGE GRINDE
Registrar: Sister JANICE STINGLE
Librarian: Sister RITA ROSE STAHL

Library of 62,465 vols, 295 current periodicals
Number of teachers: 122 (42 full-time, 80 part-time)
Number of students: 850 (467 F.t.e.)

Publications: *New Directions* (4 a year), *Silver Reflections* (1 a year), *SLC Update* (52 a year)

Depts of art, English and world languages, mathematics and computer sciences, music, natural science, nursing, religious studies and philosophy, social science and history.

UNIVERSITY OF WISCONSIN SYSTEM

1220 Linden Dr., 1720 Van Hise Hall, Madison, WI 53706-1559
Telephone: (608) 262-2321
Fax: (608) 262-3985
Internet: www.wisconsin.edu

Founded 1848, merged with the Wisconsin State Univs system 1971

13 Instns offering 4-year courses (constituent univs), and 2 other instns offering 2-year courses (other constituent institutions)

Pres.: KEVIN P. REILLY
Exec. Sr Vice-Pres.: DON MASH
Sr Vice-Pres. for Academic Affairs: REBECCA MARTIN
Vice-Pres. for Finance: DEBORAH A. DURCAN
Gen. Counsel: PATRICIA BRADY
Assoc. Vice-Pres. for Budget and Planning: FREDA HARRIS
Assoc. Vice-Pres. for Human Resources: ALAN CRIST
Number of students: 160,000 (26 campuses).

CONSTITUENT UNIVERSITIES

University of Wisconsin–Eau Claire

105 Garfield Ave, POB 4004, Eau Claire, WI 54702-4004
Telephone: (715) 836-2637
Fax: (715) 836-2902
Internet: www.uwec.edu

Founded 1916
Academic year: September to May

Chancellor: BRIAN LEVIN-STANKEVICH
Provost and Vice-Chancellor for Academic Affairs: STEVEN TALLANT
Vice-Chancellor for Business and Student Services: ANDREW SOLL
Assoc. Vice-Chancellor for Academic Affairs: ANDREW PHILLIPS
Assoc. Vice-Chancellor for Student Devt and Diversity: KIMBERLY BARRETT
Registrar: SUE MOORE
Librarian: ROBERT ROSE

Library of 574,000 vols
Number of teachers: 700
Number of students: 10,500

DEANS

College of Arts and Sciences: DONALD CHRISTIAN
College of Business: V. THOMAS DOCK
College of Education and Human Sciences: KATHERINE A. RHOADES
College of Nursing and Health Sciences: Dr L. ELAINE WENDT

University of Wisconsin—Green Bay

2420 Nicolet Dr., Green Bay, WI 54311-7001
Telephone: (920) 465-2000
Fax: (920) 465-2032
E-mail: uwgb@uwgb.edu
Internet: www.uwgb.edu

Founded 1965
Academic year: September to May

Chancellor: Dr THOMAS HARDEN
Provost and Vice-Chancellor for Academic Affairs: Dr JULIA A. WALLACE
Vice-Chancellor for Business and Finance: THOMAS D. MAKI
Vice-Chancellor for Planning and Budget: Dr DEAN RODEHEAVER
Library Dir: PAULA GANYARD

Library: 1m. bibliographic items
Number of teachers: 356
Number of students: 6,636

Liberal arts, performing arts and professional programmes.

University of Wisconsin—La Crosse

1725 State St, La Crosse, WI 54601
Telephone: (608) 785-8000
Fax: (608) 785-8809
Internet: www.uwlax.edu

Founded 1909

Chancellor: JOE GOW
Provost and Vice-Chancellor for Academic Affairs: KATHLEEN ENZ FINKEN
Vice-Chancellor for Admin. and Finance: BOB HETZEL
Dean of Student Devt and Academic Services: Dr PAULA M. KNUDSON
Dir of Library: ANITA EVANS

Library of 546,766 vols
Number of teachers: 531
Number of students: 9,890

University of Wisconsin—Madison

Madison, WI 53706
Telephone: (608) 263-2400
Fax: (608) 262-8333
Internet: www.wisc.edu

Founded 1848
Public control
Academic year: September to May

Chancellor: CAROLYN BIDDY MARTIN
Provost and Vice-Chancellor for Academic Affairs: PAUL DELUCA, Jr
Vice-Chancellor for Admin.: DARRELL BAZZELL

Vice-Chancellor for Medical Affairs: ROBERT GOLDEN
Vice-Chancellor for Research and Dean of Graduate School: MARTIN CADWALLADER
Vice-Chancellor for Univ. Relations: VINCE SWEENEY
Registrar: SCOTT OWCZAREK
Dir of Admissions: ADELE C. BRUMIELD
Sec. of the Faculty: DAVID MUSOLF
Dir-Gen. of Library System: KENNETH FRAZIER
Library: see Libraries and Archives
Number of teachers: 2,177
Number of students: 42,595

DEANS

College of Agricultural and Life Sciences: WILLIAM TRACY
College of Engineering: PAUL PEERCY
College of Letters and Science: GARY SANDEFUR
Division of Continuing Studies: JAMES CAMPBELL
Int. Studies and Programs: GILLES BOUSQUET
Law School: KENNETH DAVIS, Jr
School of Business: JOAN SCHMIT
School of Education: JULIE UNDERWOOD
School of Human Ecology: ROBIN DOUTHITT
School of Medicine and Public Health: Dr ROBERT GOLDEN
School of Nursing: KATHARYN A. MAY
School of Pharmacy: JEANETTE ROBERTS
School of Veterinary Medicine: Dr DARYL D. BUSS

PROFESSORS

Some professors serve in more than one college or school

College of Agriculture and Life Sciences (116 Agricultural Hall, 1450 Linden Dr., Madison, WI 53704; tel. (608) 262-3003; fax (608) 265-5905; e-mail asa@cals.wisc.edu; internet www.cals.wisc.edu):

ALANEN, A. R., Landscape Architecture
ALBRECHT, K. A., Agronomy
ALBRECHT, R. M., Animal Science
AMASINO, R. M., Biochemistry
ANDERSON, P., Genetics
ANDREWS, J. H., Plant Pathology
ARMENTANO, L. E., Dairy Science
ATKINSON, R. L., Nutritional Sciences, Medicine
ATTIE, A. D., Biochemistry
BALKE, N. E., Agronomy
BARHAM, B. L., Programme on Agricultural Technology Studies
BISHOP, J. R., Food Science
BISHOP, R. C., Agricultural and Applied Economics
BLAND, W. L., Soil Science
BLATTNER, F. R., Genetics
BLEAM, W. F., Soil Science
BOCKHEIM, J. G., Soil Science
BOERBOOM, C. M., Agronomy
BOHNHOFF, D. R., Biological Systems Engineering
BROMLEY, D. W., Agricultural and Applied Economics
BROWN, M. R., Life Sciences Communication
BUEGE, D. R., Animal Science
BUNDY, L. G., Soil Science
BUONGIORNO, J., Forest Ecology and Management
BUTTEL, F. H., Rural Sociology
CAMPBELL, G. R., Agricultural and Applied Economics
CARROLL, S. B., Genetics
CARTER, M. R., Agricultural and Applied Economics
CHAMBLISS, G. H., Bacteriology
CHENOWETH, R. E., Urban and Regional Planning
CLAGETT-DAME, M., Biochemistry
CLAYTON, M. K., Statistics
CLELAND, W. W., Biochemistry
COLLINS, J. L., Rural Sociology, Women's Studies Programme
COMBS, D. K., Dairy Science
CONVERSE, J. C., Biological Systems Engineering
COOK, M. E., Animal Science
COORS, J. G., Agronomy
COX, M. M., Biochemistry
COX, T. L., Agricultural and Applied Economics
COXHEAD, I. A., Agricultural and Applied Economics
CRAIG, E. A., Biochemistry
CRAVEN, S. R., Wildlife Ecology
CRENSHAW, T. D., Animal Science
DAMODARAN, S., Food Science
DELLER, S. C., Agricultural and Applied Economics
DELUCA, H. F., Biochemistry
DOEBLEY, J., Genetics
DOLL, J. D., Agronomy
DONOHUE, T. J., Bacteriology
DOWNS, D. M., Bacteriology
DUKE, S. H., Agronomy
EIDE, D. J., Nutritional Sciences
ENGELS, W. R., Genetics
ESCALANTE, J. C., Bacteriology
ETZEL, M. R., Food Science
FIELD, D. R., Forest Ecology and Management
FILUTOWICZ, M. S., Bacteriology
FIRST, N. L., Animal Science
FOX, B. G., Biochemistry, Enzyme Institute
FREY, P. A., Biochemistry
FRIESEN, P. D., Biochemistry, Institute for Molecular Virology
GANETZKY, B. S., Genetics
GERMAN, T. L., Entomology
GIANOLA, D., Animal Science
GILBERT, J. C., Rural Sociology
GOLDMAN, I. L., Horticulture
GOODMAN, R. M., Plant Pathology
GOODMAN, W. G., Entomology
GOURSE, R. L., Bacteriology
GOWER, S. T., Forest Ecology and Management
GRAU, C. R., Plant Pathology
GREASER, M. L., Animal Science
GREEN, G. P., Rural Sociology
GRUMMER, R. R., Dairy Science
GUNASEKARAN, S., Biological Systems Engineering
GUNTHER, A. C., Life Sciences Communication
GURIES, R. P., Forest Ecology and Management
HANDELSMAN, J., Plant Pathology
HARRINGTON, J. A., Landscape Architecture
HARRIS, P. E., Agricultural and Applied Economics
HARTEL, R. W., Food Science
HAYES, C. E., Biochemistry
HELMKE, P. A., Soil Science
HICKEY, W. J., Soil Science
HITCHON, J. C., Life Sciences Communication
HOLDEN, H. M., Biochemistry
HOLMES, B. J., Biological Systems Engineering
HOWELL, E. A., Landscape Architecture
INGHAM, S. C., Food Science
INMAN, R. B., Biochemistry
INMAN, R. B., Institute for Molecular Virology
JEANNE, R. L., Entomology
JESSE, E. V., Agricultural and Applied Economics
JIANG, J., Horticulture
JOHNSON, E. A., Food Microbiology and Toxicology
JOHNSON, M. B., Agricultural and Applied Economics
JONES, B. L., Agricultural Database for Decision Support
KAEPPLER, S. M., Agronomy
KAMMEL, D. W., Biological Systems Engineering
KARASOV, W. H., Wildlife Ecology
KASPAR, C. W., Food Microbiology and Toxicology
KELLER, N. P., Food Microbiology and Toxicology, Plant Pathology
KIMBLE, J. E., Biochemistry
KIRKPATRICK, B. W., Animal Science
KLOPPENBURG, J. R., Rural Sociology
KRUGER, E. L., Forest Ecology and Management
KUNG, C., Genetics, Molecular Biology
KUNG, K.-J. S., Soil Science
KUSSOW, W. R., Soil Science
LAGRO, J. A., Jr, Urban and Regional Planning
LANDICK, R. C., Bacteriology
LAUER, J. G., Agronomy
LAUGHON, A. S., Genetics
LINDROTH, R. L., Entomology
LINDSAY, R. C., Food Science
LORIMER, C. G., Forest Ecology and Management
LOWERY, B., Soil Science
MCCLAIN, W. H., Bacteriology
MCCOWN, B. H., Horticulture
MACGUIDWIN, A. E., Plant Pathology
MADISON, F. W., Soil Science
MAHR, D. L., Entomology
MANSFIELD, J. M., Bacteriology
MARKLEY, J. L., Biochemistry
MARTIN, T. F. J., Biochemistry
MASSON, P. H., Genetics
MENON, A. K., Biochemistry
MLADENOFF, D. J., Forest Ecology and Management, Statistics
NELSON, D. L., Biochemistry
NEY, D. M., Nutritional Sciences
NIENHUIS, J., Horticulture
NITZKE, S. A., Nutritional Sciences
NORBACK, J. P., Food Science
NORDHEIM, E. V., Statistics
NORMAN, J. M., Soil Science
NOWAK, P., Soil and Water Conservation
NTAMBI, J. M., Biochemistry, Nutritional Sciences
OSBORN, T. C., Agronomy
PALMENBERG, A. C., Biochemistry
PALTA, J. P., Horticulture
PARIZA, M. W., Food Microbiology and Toxicology
PARKIN, K. L., Food Science
PARRISH, J. J., Animal Science
PASKEWITZ, S. M., Entomology
PETERSON, J. O., Environmental Resources Center
PHILLIPS, G. N., Jr, Biochemistry
PIKE, J. W., Biochemistry
PINGREE, S., Life Sciences Communication
POSNER, J. L., Agronomy
RAFFA, K. F., Entomology
RAINES, R. T., Biochemistry
RAYMENT, I., Biochemistry, Enzyme Institute
REED, G. H., Biochemistry
REINEMANN, D. J., Biological Systems Engineering
REZNIKOFF, W. S., Biochemistry
ROBERTS, G. P., Bacteriology
ROPER, T. R., Horticulture
ROUSE, D. I., Plant Pathology
RUTLEDGE, J. J., Animal Science
SCHAEFER, D. M., Animal Science
SCHOELLER, D. A., Nutritional Sciences
SCHULER, R. T., Biological Systems Engineering
SHAVER, R. D., Dairy Science
SHEFFIELD, L. G., Dairy Science
SHINNERS, K. J., Biological Systems Engineering
SHOOK, G. E., Dairy Science
SMITH, S. M., Nutritional Sciences
STANOSZ, G. R., Plant Pathology
STEELE, J. L., Food Science
STEVENSON, W. R., Plant Pathology

STIER, J. C., Forest Ecology and Management
STIMART, D. P., Horticulture
STOLTENBERG, D. E., Agronomy
SUNDE, R. A., Nutritional Sciences
SUSSMAN, M. R., Biochemistry
TEMPLE, S. A., Wildlife Ecology
THOMAS, D. L., Animal Science
TIGGES, L. M., Rural Sociology
TRACY, W. F., Agronomy
TYLER, E. J., Small-scale Waste, Soil Science
UNDERSANDER, D. J., Agronomy
VIERSTRA, R. D., Genetics
VOSS, P. R., Rural Sociology
WALSH, P. W., Biological Systems Engineering
WENDORFF, W. J., Food Science
WENTWORTH, B. C., Animal Science
WICKENS, M. P., Biochemistry
WILTBANK, M. C., Dairy Science
WONG, A. C., Food Microbiology and Toxicology
WYMAN, J. A., Entomology
YOUNG, D. K., Entomology

College of Engineering (2640 Engineering Hall, 1415 Engineering Dr., Madison, WI 53706; tel. (608) 262-3484; internet www.engr.wisc.edu):

ABBOTT, N. L., Chemical Engineering
ADAMS, T. M., Civil and Environmental Engineering
ANDERSON, D. T., Electrical and Computer Engineering
ANDERSON, M. A., Civil and Environmental Engineering
ARMSTRONG, D. E., Civil and Environmental Engineering
BABCOCK, S. E., Materials Science and Engineering
BANK, L., Civil and Environmental Engineering
BARMISH, B. R., Electrical and Computer Engineering
BENSON, C. H., Civil and Environmental Engineering
BIER, V. M., Industrial Engineering
BISOGNANO, J. J., Synchrotron Radiation Center
BLANCHARD, J. P., Engineering Physics
BOOSKE, J. H., Electrical and Computer Engineering
BOSSCHER, P. J., Civil and Environmental Engineering
BOTEZ, D., Electrical and Computer Engineering
BUCKLEW, J. A., Electrical and Computer Engineering
CARAYON, P., Industrial Engineering
CERRINA, F., Electrical and Computer Engineering
CHANG, Y. A., Materials Science and Engineering
CORRADINI, M. L., Engineering Physics
CRAMER, S. M., Civil and Environmental Engineering
DAVIS, J. L., Engineering Outreach Technical Japanese, Technical Communications
DEMARCO, C., Electrical and Computer Engineering
DEPABLO, J. J., Chemical Engineering
DEVRIES, M. F., Mechanical Engineering
DOBSON, I., Electrical and Computer Engineering
DRUGAN, W. J., Engineering Physics
DUFFIE, N. A., Mechanical Engineering
DUMESIC, J. A., Chemical Engineering
EDIL, T. B., Civil and Environmental Engineering
ENGELSTAD, R. L., Mechanical Engineering
EOM, C.-B., Materials Science and Engineering
FARRELL, P. V., Mechanical Engineering
FONCK, R. J., Engineering Physics
FOSTER, D. E., Mechanical Engineering
FRONCZAK, F. J., Mechanical Engineering
GIACOMIN, A. J., Mechanical Engineering
GRAHAM, M. D., Chemical Engineering
HAIMSON, B. C., Materials Science and Engineering
HANNA, A. S., Civil and Environmental Engineering
HELLSTROM, E. E., Materials Science and Engineering
HENDERSON, D. L., Engineering Physics
HERSHKOWITZ, N., Engineering Physics
HILL, C. G., Jr, Chemical Engineering
HITCHON, W. N., Electrical and Computer Engineering
HOOPES, J. A., Civil and Environmental Engineering
HU, Y. H., Electrical and Computer Engineering
JAHNS, T., Electrical and Computer Engineering
KAMMER, D. C., Engineering Physics
KLEIN, S. A., Mechanical Engineering
KOU, S., Materials Science and Engineering
KUECH, T. F., Chemical Engineering
LAGALLY, M. G., Materials Science and Engineering
LAKES, R. C., Engineering Physics
LARBALESTIER, D. C., Materials Science and Engineering
LIPO, T. A., Electrical and Computer Engineering
LORENZ, R. D., Mechanical Engineering
LOVELL, E. G., Mechanical Engineering
LUMELSKY, V. J., Mechanical Engineering
MCCAUGHAN, L., Electrical and Computer Engineering
MARTIN, J. K., Mechanical Engineering
MOSES, G. A., Engineering Physics
MOSKWA, J. J., Mechanical Engineering
MURPHY, R. M., Chemical Engineering
OLEARY, P. R., Engineering Professional Devt
OSSWALD, T. A., Mechanical Engineering
PARK, J. K., Civil and Environmental Engineering
PEREPEZKO, J. H., Materials Science and Engineering
PLESHA, M. E., Engineering Physics
POTTER, K. W., Civil and Environmental Engineering
RADWIN, R. G., Biomedical Engineering
RAMANATHAN, P., Electrical and Computer Engineering
RAWLINGS, J. B., Chemical Engineering
REITZ, R. D., Mechanical Engineering
ROBINSON, S. M., Industrial Engineering
ROWLANDS, R. E., Mechanical Engineering
RUSSELL, J. S., Civil and Environmental Engineering
RUTLAND, C. J., Mechanical Engineering
SALUJA, K. K., Electrical and Computer Engineering
SCHARER, J. E., Electrical and Computer Engineering
SETHARES, W. A., Electrical and Computer Engineering
SHAPIRO, V., Mechanical Engineering
SHI, L., Industrial Engineering
SHOHET, J. L., Electrical and Computer Engineering
SMITH, J. E., Electrical and Computer Engineering
SMITH, M. J., Industrial Engineering
STEUDEL, H. J., Industrial Engineering
SURI, R., Industrial Engineering, Manufacturing Systems Engineering
TOMPKINS, W. J., Biomedical Engineering
UICKER, J. J., Jr, Mechanical Engineering
VANDERHEIDEN, G. C., Industrial Engineering
VANDERWEIDE, D. W., Electrical and Computer Engineering
VAN VEEN, B. D., Electrical and Computer Engineering
VEERAMANI, D., Industrial Engineering
VONDEROHE, A. P., Civil and Environmental Engineering
WENDT, A. E., Electrical and Computer Engineering
YIN, J., Chemical Engineering
ZIMMERMANN, D. R., Industrial Engineering

College of Letters and Science (500 Lincoln Dr., Room B12, Madison, WI 53706; tel. (608) 262-2644; fax (608) 262-5093; internet www.ls.wisc.edu):

ABRAMSON, L. Y., Psychology
ACKERMAN, S. A., Space Science and Engineering Center
ADELL, S. A., Afro-American Studies
ADEM, A., Mathematics
ADLER, H., German
AHERN, P. R., Mathematics
ALBUQUERQUE, S. J., Spanish and Portuguese
ALEY, J. E., School of Music
ALIBALI, M. W., Psychology
ALLEN, T. F., Botany
ANDERSON, L. A., School of Music
ANDERSON, M. P., Geology and Geophysics
ANDREONI, J., Economics
ANGENENT, S. B., Mathematics
ARCHDEACON, T. J., History
ASSADI, A. H., Mathematics
ATIS, S. G., Languages and Cultures of Asia
BACH, C. E., Computer Sciences
BAHR, J. M., Geology and Geophysics
BAKER, T. B., Gen. Internal Medicine
BALANTEKIN, A. B., Physics
BARGER, V. D., Physics
BARTLEY, L. L., School of Music
BATES, D. M., Statistics
BAUGHMAN, J. L., Journalism and Mass Communication
BAUM, D. A., Botany
BECK, A., Mathematics
BECKER, D. E., School of Music
BEISSINGER, M., Political Science
BENDER, T. K., English
BENKART, G. M., Mathematics
BERG, W. J., French and Italian
BERGHAHN, K. L., German
BERNARD-DONALS, M. F., English
BERNAULT, F., History
BERNSTEIN, S. D., English
BERRIDGE, C. W., Psychology
BERRY, P. E., Botany
BETHEA, D. M., Slavic Languages
BICKNER, R. J., Languages and Cultures of Asia
BILBIJA, K., Spanish and Portuguese
BLAIR, S. S., Zoology
BLANCO, A., Spanish and Portuguese
BLEECKER, A. B., Botany
BLESS, D. M., Communicative Disorders
BLUM, D. L., Journalism and Mass Communication
BOLOTIN, S. V., Mathematics
BORN, S. M., Urban and Regional Planning
BOSTON, N., Mathematics
BOWIE, K. A., Anthropology
BOYDSTON, J., History
BOYETTE, P. J., Theatre and Drama
BRANDT, D. L., English
BRANTLY, S. C., Scandinavian Studies
BRENNER, R. F., Hebrew and Semitic Studies
BRIGHOUSE, M. H., Philosophy
BROCK, W. A., Economics
BROWER, A. M., Social Work
BROWN, P. E., Geology and Geophysics
BRUALDI, R. A., Mathematics
BRUCH, L. W., Physics
BUCCINI, S., French and Italian
BUENGER, B. C., Art History
BÜHNEMANN, G., Languages and Cultures of Asia
BUNKER, S. G., Sociology

BUNN, H. T., Anthropology
BURKE, S. D., Chemistry
BURSTYN, J. N., Chemistry
BURT, J. E., Geography
BUSBY, K. R., French and Italian
BYERS, C. W., Geology and Geophysics
CAI, J.-Y., Computer Sciences
CALDERON, J. F., School of Music
CAMIC, C., Sociology
CANCIAN, M., Institute for Research on Poverty
CANON, D. T., Political Science
CARD, C. F., Philosophy
CARLSMITH, D. L., Physics
CARPENTER, S. R., Zoology
CARROLL, A. R., Geology and Geophysics
CARROLL, N., Philosophy
CASEY, C. P., Chemistry
CASPI, A., Psychology
CASSINELLI, J. P., Astronomy
CASTRONOVO, R., English
CAULKINS, J. H., French and Italian
CHAPPELL, R. J., Biostatistics and Medical Informatics
CHAVEZ, M. M. T., German
CHE, Y.-K., Economics
CHENG, T. F., East Asian Languages and Literature
CHIAL, M. R., Communicative Disorders
CHINN, M. D., Economics
CHISHOLM, S. L., School of Music
CHUBUKOV, A. V., Physics
CHURCHWELL, E. B., Astronomy
COE, C. L., Psychology
COHEN, C. L., History
COHEN, L. K., Comparative Literature
COLEMAN, J. J., Political Science
COOK, S. C., School of Music
COOPER, J. M., Jr, History
COPPERSMITH, S. N., Physics
CORFIS, I. A., Spanish and Portuguese
CORN, R. M., Chemistry
CORTEZ, E. M., Library and Information Studies
COURTENAY, W. J., History
COWELL, D. C., African Languages and Literature
COX, D. P., Physics
CRAVENS, T. D., French and Italian
CRIM, F. F., Jr, Chemistry
CRONON, W., History
CROOK, D., School of Music
CURTIN, M. J., Communication Arts
CUTTER, R. J., East Asian Languages and Literature
D'ACCI, J., Communication Arts
DAHL, L. F., Chemistry
DANNEMILLER, J. L., Psychology
DAVIDSON, R. J., Psychology
DAVIS, R., School of Music
DE STASIO, G., Physics
DEBAISIEUX, M. M., French and Italian
DELAMATER, J. D., Sociology
DEMBSKI, S., School of Music
DEMETS, D. C., Geology and Geophysics
DENECKERE, R. J., Economics
DESAN, S. M., History
DESAUTELS, E. J., Computer Sciences
DEVINE, P. G., Psychology
DEWITT, D. J., Computer Sciences
DICKEY, L. W., History
DICKEY, R. W., Mathematics
DILL, C. W., School of Music
DOANE, A. N., English
DODSON, S. I., Zoology
DOKSUM, K. A., Statistics
DOLININ, A. A., Slavic Languages
DONNELLY, J. S., Jr, History
DORN, D. L., Theatre and Drama
DOWNS, D. A., Political Science
DRAINE, B., English
DRECHSEL, R. E., Journalism and Mass Communication
DRESANG, D. L., Political Science
DREWAL, H. J., Art History
DUBOIS, T. A., Scandinavian Studies
DUBROW, H., English
DUNLAVY, C. A., History
DUNWOODY, S. L., Journalism and Mass Communication
DURAND, B., Physics
DURLAUF, S. N., Economics
DYER, C. R., Computer Sciences
EARP, L. M., School of Music
EDIGER, M. D., Chemistry
EELLS, E. T., Philosophy
ELDER, J. W., Languages and Cultures of Asia
ELLIS, A. B., Chemistry
ELLIS WEISMER, S., Communicative Disorders
ENC, M., Linguistics
ENGEL, C. M., Economics
ERWIN, A. R., Physics
ESSIG, L., Theatre and Drama
FAIR, J. E., Journalism and Mass Communication
FERNANDEZ, D. E., Botany
FERREE, M. M., Sociology
FERRIS, M. C., Computer Sciences
FILIPOWICZ, H., Slavic Languages
FINK, M. D., School of Music
FISCHER, C. N., Computer Sciences
FITZPATRICK, M. A., Communication Arts
FOLEY, J. A., Sustainability and Global Environment
FORD, C. E., English
FORSTER, M. R., Philosophy
FOWLER, C. G., Communicative Disorders
FOX, M. V., Hebrew and Semitic Studies
FRANKLIN, C. H., Political Science
FRIEDLAND, L. A., Journalism and Mass Communication
FRIEDMAN, E., Political Science
FRIEDMAN, S. S., English
FUJIMURA, J., Sociology
FULMER, M. K., School of Music
GALLAGHER, J. S., III, Astronomy
GAMORAN, A., Center for Education Research
GEARY, D. H., Geology and Geophysics
GEIGER, G. L., Art History
GELLMAN, S. H., Chemistry
GEORGE, K. M., Anthropology
GERNSBACHER, M. A., Psychology
GIVNISH, T. J., Botany
GLENBERG, A. M., Psychology
GOLDSMITH, H. H., Psychology
GOLDSTEIN, K. M., Political Science
GOODKIN, R. E., French and Italian
GOODMAN, J. R., Computer Sciences
GORSKI, P. S., Sociology
GOTTLIEB, P. L., Philosophy
GRAHAM, L. K., Botany
GREENBERG, J., Social Work
GREIVE, T. D., School of Music
GRIFFEATH, D. S., Mathematics
GROSS, S. D., German
GUERIN GONZALES, C., Chicano Studies
HAEBERLI, W., Physics
HALZEN, F. L., Physics
HAMERS, R. J., Chemistry
HAN, T., Physics
HANSEN, B. E., Economics
HARACKIEWICZ, J. M., Psychology
HARDIN, J. D., Zoology
HARRIS, R. A., Spanish and Portuguese
HAUSER, R. M., Sociology
HAUSMAN, D., Philosophy
HAWKINS, R. P., Journalism and Mass Communication
HENDEL, I. E., Economics
HILDNER, D. J., Spanish and Portuguese
HILL, D. D., School of Music
HILL, M. D., Computer Sciences
HILL, R. J., English
HILMES, M., Communication Arts
HILTS, V. L, History of Science
HIMPSEL, F. J., Physics
HINDEN, M. C., English
HITCHMAN, M. H., Atmospheric and Oceanic Sciences
HOESSEL, J. G., Astronomy
HORWITZ, S. B., Computer Sciences
HOWELL, R. B., German
HUBER, D. L., Physics
HUDDLESTON, J. R., Urban and Regional Planning
HUNT, L. H., Philosophy
HUNTER, L., African Languages and Literature
HUTCHINSON, S. E., Anthropology
HUTCHISON, J. C., Art History
HUTCHINSON, S., Spanish and Portuguese
HYDE, J. S., Women's Studies Research Center
HYER, B., School of Music
IONEL, E.-N., Mathematics
ISAACS, I. M., Mathematics
IVES, A. R., Zoology
JACOBS, H. M., Urban and Regional Planning
JACOBS, L., Communication Arts
JAMES, C. J., German
JAMES, S. M., Afro-American Studies
JENISON, R. L., Psychology
JENSEN, J. L., School of Music
JIN, S., Mathematics
JOHNSON, A. A., Mathematics
JOHNSON, C. M., Geology and Geophysics
JOHNSON, R. A., Statistics
JOYNT, R. J., Physics
KAISER, N. A., German
KAISER, N. A., Women's Studies Programme
KAISER, R. J., Geography
KARP, P. D., School of Music
KAUTSKY, C. C., School of Music
KEENE, N., Communication Arts
KELLER, L., English
KELLEY, T. M., English
KENNAN, J. F., Economics
KENOYER, J. M., Anthropology
KENT, R. D., Waisman Center for Mentally Retarded People and Human Devt
KEPLEY, V. I., Communication Arts
KERCHEVAL, J. L., English
KHAZANOV, A., Anthropology
KIESSLING, L. L., Biochemistry
KIRSCH, J. A. W., Zoology
KITCHELL, J. F., Zoology
KLEINHENZ, C., French and Italian
KLUENDER, K. R., Psychology
KLUGE, C. L., German
KNOWLES, R. A. J., English
KNOX, J. C., Geography
KNUTSON, L. D., Physics
KOSHAR, R. J., History
KOSOROK, M. R., Biostatistics and Medical Informatics
KRAVETZ, D., Social Work
KRITZER, H. M., Political Science
KUELBS, J. D., Mathematics
KUNEN, K., Mathematics
KURTZ, T. G., Mathematics
KURTZ, T. G., Statistics
LANDIS, C. R., Chemistry
LANGER, U. G., French and Italian
LAWLER, J. E., Physics
LAYOUN, M. N., Comparative Literature
LEARY, J. P., Folklore
LECKRONE, M. E., School of Music
LEE, J. B., History
LEMPP, S., Mathematics
LEPOWSKY, M. A., Anthropology
LEZRA, J., English
LI, Y., Linguistics
LIN, C. C., Physics
LINDSTROM, D. L., History
LIU, Z.-U., Atmospheric and Oceanic Sciences
LIVNY, M., Computer Sciences
LOEWENSTEIN, D. A., English
LOH, W.-Y., Statistics
LONGINOVIC, T., Slavic Languages
LOUDEN, M. L., German
LUCAS, S. E., Communication Arts

LUNDIN, A. H., Library and Information Studies
LUTFI, R. A., Communicative Disorders
MACAULAY, M. A., Linguistics
MCCAMMON, D., Physics
MCCLINTOCK, A. P., English
MCCLURE, L. K., Integrated Liberal Studies
MCCOY, A. W., History
MCDONALD, D. M., History
MACDONALD, M. C., Psychology
MCGLOIN, N. H., East Asian Languages and Literature
MCKAY, N. Y., Afro-American Studies
MCKAY, N. Y., English
MCKEOWN, J. C., Classics
MCLEOD, D. M., Journalism and Mass Communication
MCMAHON, R. J., Chemistry
MACKEN, M. A., Linguistics
MAGNAN, S. S., French and Italian
MALLON, F. E., History
MANION, M., Political Science
MANOOGIAN, V. I., School of Music
MANUELLI, R. E., Economics
MARCOUILLER, D. W., Urban and Regional Planning
MARLER, C. A., Psychology
MARQUEZ, B., Political Science
MARTIN, J. E., Atmospheric and Oceanic Sciences
MATHIEU, R. D., Astronomy
MAYER, K. R., Political Science
MAYNARD, D. W., Sociology
MAZZAOUI, M. F., History
MEMON, M. U., Languages and Cultures of Asia
MENOCAL, N. G., Art History
MEYER, D. R., Social Work
MEYER, R. R., Computer Sciences
MICKELSON, D. M., Geology and Geophysics
MIERNOWSKI, J., French and Italian
MILEWSKI, P. A., Mathematics
MILLER, A. W., Mathematics
MILLER, B. P., Computer Sciences
MILLER, J. F., Communicative Disorders
MITMAN, G. A., History of Science
MOFFITT, T. E., Psychology
MOORE, C. F., Psychology
MOORE, J. W., Chemistry
MOORE, M. L., English
MORAHG, G., Hebrew and Semitic Studies
MORGAN, D. O., Institute for Humanities Research
MORSE, R. M., Physics
MORTENSEN, C. D., Communication Arts
MURPHY, J. J., Communication Arts
MURRAY, J. K., Art History
NADLER, S. M., Philosophy
NARAYAN, K., Anthropology
NATHANSON, G. M., Chemistry
NAUGHTON, J. F., Computer Sciences
NELSEN, S. F., Chemistry
NEWLANDS, C., Classics
NEWMAN, J. P., Psychology
NICHOLS, D. A., Lafollette School of Public Affairs
NIENHAUSER, W. H., East Asian Languages and Literature
NILES, J. D., English, Institute for Humanities Research
NIXON, R. D., English
NORDSIECK, K. H., Astronomy
NYSTRAND, P. M., English
OGELMAN, H. B., Physics
OH, Y.-G., Mathematics
OHNUKI-TIERNEY, E., Anthropology
OLANIYAN, T., African Languages and Literature
OLIVER, P. E., Sociology
OLSSON, M. G., Physics
ONELLION, M. F., Physics
ONO, K., Mathematics
ORLIK, P. P., Mathematics
OSTERGREN, R. C., Geography
PALLONI, A., Sociology
PAN, Z., Communication Arts
PASSMAN, D. S., Mathematics
PAWLEY, J. B., Zoology
PAYNE, L. A., Political Science
PAYNE, S. G., History
PECK, J. A., Geography
PERRY, D., School of Music
PETTY, G. W., Atmospheric and Oceanic Sciences
PHILLIPS, Q. E., Art History
PILIAVIN, J. A., Sociology
PLUMMER, B. G., Afro-American Studies
PODESTA, G. A., Spanish and Portuguese
PONDROM, C. N., English
PONDROM, L. G., Physics
PORTER, W. P., Zoology
POWELL, B. B., Classics
PRAGER, S. C., Physics
PREPOST, R., Physics
PRICE, T. D., Anthropology
RABINOWITZ, P. H., Mathematics
RADANO, R. M., School of Music
RAFFERTY, E. M., Languages and Cultures of Asia
RAM, A., Mathematics
RAMAKRISHNAN, R., Computer Sciences
RAND, N. T., French and Italian
RAO, V. N., Languages and Cultures of Asia
REAMES, S. L., English
RECORD, M. T., Jr, Biochemistry
REEDER, D. D., Physics
REICH, H. J., Chemistry
REPS, T. W., Computer Sciences
RESCHOVSKY, A. M., Lafollette School of Public Affairs
REYNOLDS, A. J., Waisman Center for Mentally Retarded People and Human Devt
REYNOLDS, R. J., Astronomy
RICHARDSON, N. R., Political Science
RICHARDSON, W. W., Music
RIFKIN, B., Slavic Languages
RILEY, P. T., Political Science
RISLEY, W. R., Spanish and Portuguese
ROBBIN, J. W., Mathematics
ROBBINS, L. S., Library and Information Studies
ROBERTS, M. L., History
ROESLER, F. L., Physics
RON, A., Computer Sciences
ROSAY, J.-P., Mathematics
ROSENMEYER, P., Classics
ROTHSTEIN, E., English
RUAN, Y., Mathematics
RZCHOWSKI, M. S., Physics
SACK, R. D., Geography
SAIZ, P., Comparative Literature
SALMONS, J. C., German
SALOMON, F. L., Anthropology
SAMUELSON, L. W., Economics
SAPIRO, V., Academic Affairs
SAVAGE, B. D., Astronomy
SCARANO, F. A., History
SCHAEFFER, N. C., Sociology
SCHAFER, B. E., Political Science
SCHAFER-LANDAU, R. S., Philosophy
SCHAFFER, J. W., School of Music
SCHAMILOGLU, U., Languages and Cultures of Asia
SCHAPIRO, L. A., Philosophy
SCHATZBERG, M. G., Political Science
SCHAUB, T. H., English
SCHEUB, H. E., African Languages and Literature
SCHEUFELE, D. A., Journalism and Mass Communication
SCHLEICHER, A. Y., African Languages and Literature
SCHOLZ, J. K., Economics
SCHULTZ, S. K., History
SCHWARTZ, D. C., Chemistry
SEEGER, A., Mathematics
SEIDENBERG, M. S., Psychology
SEIDMAN, G. W., Sociology
SHAH, D. V., Journalism and Mass Communication
SHAH, H. G., Journalism and Mass Communication
SHAKHASHIRI, B. Z., Chemistry
SHANK, M. H., History of Science
SHAO, J., Statistics
SHARKEY, T. D., Botany
SHARPLESS, J. B., History
SHAVLIK, J. W., Computer Sciences
SHCHEGLOV, Y. K., Slavic Languages
SIBERT, E. L., Chemistry
SIDELLE, A. G., Philosophy
SILBERMAN, M. D., German
SIMO, J. A., Geology and Geophysics
SKINNER, J. L., Chemistry
SKLOOT, R., Theatre and Drama
SLEMROD, M., Mathematics
SMITH, J. R., School of Music
SMITH, LESLIE M., Mathematics
SMITH, LLOYD M., Chemistry
SMITH, W. H., Physics
SNOWDON, C. T., Psychology
SOBER, E. R., Philosophy
SOHI, G. S., Computer Sciences
SOLL, A. I., Philosophy
SOLOMON, M. H., Computer Sciences
SOMMERVILLE, J. P., History
SORKIN, D. J., Institute for Humanities Research
SPALDING, E. P., Botany
SPARKE, L. S., Astronomy
SPROTT, J. C., Physics
STAIGER, R. W., Economics
STAMPE, D. W., Philosophy
STEAKLEY, J. D., German
STEELE, J. A., English
STERN, S. J., History
STEUDEL, K. L., Zoology
STEVENS, J. D., School of Music
STOWE, J. C., School of Music
STRETTON, A. O., Zoology
STRIER, K. B., Anthropology
STRIKWERDA, J. C., Computer Sciences
SUCHMAN, M. C., Sociology
SUTTON, R. A., School of Music
SWACK, J. R., School of Music
SWEENEY, S. R., Theatre and Drama
SYTSMA, K. J., Botany
TAYLOR, M. S., Economics
TEMPRANO, J. C., Spanish and Portuguese
TERRY, P. W., Physics
TERWILLIGER, P. M., Mathematics
TESFAGIORGIS, F. H. W., Afro-American Studies
THIMMIG, L. L., School of Music
THOMSON, E. J., Sociology
THORNTON, M. C., Afro-American Studies
THURBER, C. H., Geology and Geophysics
TIMBIE, P. T., Physics
TREICHEL, P. M., Chemistry
TRIPOLI, A., Political Science
TRIPP, G. J., Atmospheric and Oceanic Sciences
TSUI, K.-W., Statistics
TURNER, M. G., Zoology
TZAVARAS, A., Mathematics
UHLENBROCK, D., Mathematics
VALLEY, J. W., Geology and Geophysics
VAN DEBURG, W. L., Afro-American Studies
VANDENHEUVEL, M. J., Theatre and Drama
VARDI, U., School of Music
VAUGHN, S. L., Journalism and Mass Communication
VERNON, M. K., Computer Sciences
WAHBA, G. G., Statistics
WAINGER, S., Mathematics
WALEFFE, F., Mathematics
WALKER, J. R., Economics
WALKER, T. G., Physics
WALLACE, R. W., English
WALLER, D. M., Botany
WANDEL, L. P., History
WANDEL, L. P., Institute for Humanities Research

WANG, P.-K., Atmospheric and Oceanic Sciences
WARDROP, R. L., Statistics
WEIMER, D., Political Science
WEINBROT, H. D., English
WEINHOLD, F. A., Chemistry
WEISMER, G. G., Communicative Disorders
WEISSHAAR, J. C., Chemistry
WELBOURNE, T. G., School of Music
WERNER, C., Afro-American Studies
WEST, K. D., Economics
WHITEHEAD, N. L., Anthropology
WHITLOCK, H. W., Jr, Chemistry
WILSON, F. D., Sociology
WILSON, G. K., Political Science
WILSON, R. L., Mathematics
WINICHAKUL, T., History
WINK, A., History
WINOKUR, M. J., Physics
WINSPUR, S., French and Italian
WITTE, J. F., Political Science
WOFFORD, S., English
WOLF, K., Scandinavian Studies
WOOD, D. A., Computer Sciences
WOODS, R. C., Chemistry
WORCESTER, N. A., Women's Studies Programme
WRIGHT, E. O., Sociology
WRIGHT, J. C., Chemistry
WRIGHT, S. J., Computer Science
WU, S. L. Y., Physics
YANDELL, K. E., Philosophy
YETHIRAJ, A., Chemistry
YOUNG, J. A., Atmospheric and Oceanic Sciences
YOUNG, R. F., English
ZAMORA, M. M., Spanish and Portuguese
ZEDLER, J. B., Arboretum: Tours
ZEDLER, J. B., Botany
ZEITLIN, J., Sociology
ZEPPENFELD, D., Physics
ZIMMERER, K. S., Geography
ZIMMERMAN, H. E., Chemistry
ZUENGLER, J, English
ZWEIBEL, E. G., Physics

School of Business (2265 Grainger Hall, 975 University Ave, Madison, WI 53706; tel. (608) 262-0471; fax (608) 265-6041; e-mail busundergrads@bus.wisc.edu; internet www.bus.wisc.edu):

ALDAG, R. J., School of Business
ANDERSON, D. R., School of Business
ANTONIONI, D. T., School of Business
BROWN, D. P., School of Business
BROWNE, M. J., School of Business
COVALESKI, M. A., School of Business
DAVIS, J. S., School of Business
DUNHAM, R. B., School of Business
EICHENSEHER, J. W., School of Business
FREES, E. W., ASchool of Business
GERHART, B. A., School of Business
HARMATUCK, D. J., School of Business
HAUSCH, D. B., School of Business
HEIDE, J. B., School of Business
HODDER, J. E., School of Business
JOHANNES, J. M., School of Business
KRAINER, R. E., School of Business
MALPEZZI, S., School of Business
MARIEN, E. J., School of Business
MILLER, R. B., School of Business
MINER, A. S., School of Business
MORRIS, J. G., School of Business
NAIR, R. D., School of Business
NEVIN, J. R., School of Business
PETER, J. P., School of Business
RIDDIOUGH, T. J., School of Business
RITTENBERG, L. E., School of Business
SCHMIT, J. T., School of Business
SHILLING, J. D., Real Estate
STEVENSON, R. E., School of Business
THOMPSON, J. C., Marketing
VANDELL, K. D., School of Business
WEMMERLÖV, U., School of Business
WEYGANDT, J. J., School of Business
WILD, J. J., School of Business

School of Education (Dean's Office, 123 Education, 1000 Bascom Hall, Madison, WI 53706; tel. (608) 262-1763; fax (608) 265-3284; e-mail easinfo@education.wisc.edu; internet www.education.wisc.edu):

ABBEDUTO, L. J., Educational Psychology
APPLE, M. W., Curriculum and Instruction
BECKER, D. H., Art
BERVEN, N. L., Rehabilitation Psychology and Spec. Education
BLOCH, M., Curriculum and Instruction
BRECKENRIDGE, B. M., Art
BREDESON, P. V., Gen. Education
BROWN, B. B., Educational Psychology
CABRERA, A. F., Gen. Education
CAPPER, C. A., Gen. Education
CHAN, F., Rehabilitation Psychology and Spec. Education
COLEMAN, H. L. K., Counseling Psychology
CONRAD, C. F., Gen. Education
DAMER, J. F., Art
DERRY, S. J., Educational Psychology
ENRIGHT, R. D., Educational Psychology
ESCALANTE, J. A., Art
FENNELL, P., Art
FENSTER, F., Art
FEREN, S. F., Art
FULTZ, M., Educational Policy Studies
GEE, J. P., Curriculum and Instruction
GETTINGER, M., Educational Psychology
GLORIA, A. M., Counseling Psychology
GOMEZ, M. L., Curriculum and Instruction
GRANT, C. A., Curriculum and Instruction
GRAUE, M. E., Center for Education Research
HANLEY-MAXWELL, C. D., Rehabilitation Psychology and Spec. Education
HAYES, E. R., Curriculum and Instruction
HEWSON, P. W., Curriculum and Instruction
JI, L.-L., Kinesiology
KALISH, C. W., Educational Psychology
KAZAMIAS, A. M., Educational Policy Studies
KETCHUM, C. G., Art
KNOX, A. B., Gen. Education
KOYKKAR, J. N., Dance
KOZA, J. E., Curriculum and Instruction
KRATOCHWILL, T. R., Center for Education Research, Educational Psychology
LADSON-BILLINGS, G. J., Curriculum and Instruction
LEE, S. J., Educational Policy Studies
LI, C.-P., Dance
LOCKWOOD, A. L., Curriculum and Instruction
LOESER, T., Art
LONG, R. L., Art
LOWE, T. T., Art
LYNCH, R. T., Rehabilitation Psychology and Spec. Education
MARSCHALEK, D. G., Art
MELROSE, C. A., Dance
METZ, M. H., Educational Policy Studies
MORGAN, W. P., Kinesiology
MYERS, F. J., Art
ODDEN, A. R., Center for Education Research
OLNECK, M. R., Educational Policy Studies
PEKARSKY, D. N., Educational Policy Studies
PETERSON, K. D., Gen. Education
PHELPS, L. A., Center on Education and Work
POPKEWITZ, T. S., Curriculum and Instruction
PRICE, G. G., Curriculum and Instruction
PYLANT, C. S., Art
QUINTANA, S. M., Counseling Psychology
REESE, W. J., Educational Policy Studies
RIEBEN, J. R., Art
SCHEER, J. M., Art
SCHNEIDER, M. L., Kinesiology
SCHRAG, F. K., Educational Policy Studies
SERLIN, R. C., Educational Psychology
STEWART, J. H., Curriculum and Instruction
STREIBEL, M. J., Curriculum and Instruction
SUBKOVIAK, M. J., Educational Psychology
TARVER, S. G., Rehabilitation Psychology and Spec. Education
TOCHON, F. V., Curriculum and Instruction
VANDELL, D. L., Educational Psychology
WAMPOLD, B. E., Counseling Psychology
ZEICHNER, K. M., Curriculum and Instruction

School of Human Ecology (1300 Linden Dr., Madison, WI 53706; tel. (608) 262-2608; fax (608) 265-4969; internet www.sohe.wisc.edu):

APPLE, R. D., Consumer Science
AQUILINO, W. S., Human Devt and Family Studies
BOGENSCHNEIDER, K. P., Human Devt and Family Studies
BOYD, V. T., Environment, Textiles and Design
DOHR, J. H., Environment, Textiles and Design
DONG, W., Environment, Textiles and Design
GOEBEL, K. P., Consumer Science
GORDON, B., Environment, Textiles and Design
HOLDEN, K. C., Lafollette School of Public Affairs
HOYT, A. A., Consumer Science
HUNT, M. E., Environment, Textiles and Design
JASPER, C. R., Consumer Science
MARKS, N. F., Human Devt and Family Studies
RILEY, D. A., Human Devt and Family Studies
ROSSING, B. E., Interdisciplinary Studies
SARMADI, M., Environment, Textiles and Design
SHEEHAN, D., Environment, Textiles and Design
SMALL, S. A., Human Devt and Family Studies
WAY, W. L., Gen. Science
ZEPEDA, L., Consumer Science

School of Nursing (600 Highland Ave, H6/150, Madison, WI 53792; tel. (608) 263-5155; fax (608) 263-5323; e-mail clangsdo@facstaff.wisc.edu; internet www.son.wisc.edu):

BAUMANN, L. J.
BOWERS, B. J.
BRENNAN, P.
BROWN, R. L.
DIEKELMANN, N. L.
DIEMER, G. A.
ESSER-ANDERSON, J. J.
GALAROWICZ, L. R. B.
KIRCHHOFF, K.
LASKY, P. A.
LITTLEFIELD, V. M.
MCCARTHY, D. O.
MCCUBBIN, M. A.
MAY, K. A.
OWEN, B. D.
RATHER, M. L.
RIESCH, S.
WARD, S. E.
WELLS, T.

School of Pharmacy (Renn & Bohm Hall, 777 Highland Ave, Madison, WI 53705; tel. (608) 262-1416; fax (608) 262-3397; internet www.pharmacy.wisc.edu):

DEMUTH, J. E., Pharmacy Outreach
HANSON, A. L., Pharmacy Outreach
HEIDEMAN, W., Pharmacy
HORNEMANN, U., Pharmacy
KRELING, D. H., Pharmacy
MELLON, W. S., Pharmacy
NORTHROP, D. B., Pharmacy
PETERSON, R. E., Pharmacy

RICH, D. H., Pharmacy
ROBINSON, J. R., Pharmacy
RUDY, T. A., Pharmacy
SCARBOROUGH, J., Pharmacy
SHEN, B., Pharmacy
THORSON, J. S., Pharmacy

School of Veterinary Medicine (2015 Linden Dr., Madison, WI 53706; tel. (608) 263-6716; internet www.vetmed.wisc.edu):

AIKEN, J. M.
BEHAN, M., Comparative Biosciences
BJORLING, D. E., Surgical Sciences
BOSU, W. T., Medical Sciences
CAREY, H. V., Comparative Biosciences
CHRISTENSEN, B. M.
COLLINS, M.
CZUPRYNSKI, C. J
DUBIELZIG, R. R.
DUNCAN, I. D., Medical Sciences
ELFARRA, A. A., Comparative Biosciences
GINTHER, O. J.
HELLEKANT, G.
KAWAOKA, Y.
MCGUIRK, S. M., Medical Sciences
MACWILLIAMS, P. S.
MANLEY, P. A., Surgical Sciences
MARKEL, M. D., Medical Sciences
MESSING, A.
MILETIC, V., Comparative Biosciences
MITCHELL, G. S., Comparative Biosciences
MURPHY, C. J., Surgical Sciences
OAKS, J. A., Comparative Biosciences
OLSEN, C. W.
SCHULER, L. A., Comparative Biosciences
SCHULTZ, R. D.
SPLITTER, G. A.
WILSMAN, N. J., Comparative Biosciences
YOSHINO, T. P.

Law School (975 Bascom Hall, Madison, WI 53706; tel. (608) 262-2240; fax (608) 262-5485; e-mail deansoffice@law.wisc.edu; internet www.law.wisc.edu):

ALTHOUSE, A.
BRITO, T. L.
CARSTENSEN, P. C.
CHARO, R. A.
CHURCH, W. L.
CLAUSS, C. A.
DICKEY, W. J.
ERLANGER, H. S.
GREENE, L. S.
IRISH, C. R.
KAPLAN, L. V.
KIDWELL, J. A.
KLUG, H. J.
KOMESAR, N. K.
LARSON, J. E.
MACAULAY, S.
MCEVOY, A. F.
MERTZ, E. E.
MORAN, B. I.
NOURSE, V. F.
PALAY, T. M.
SCHACTER, J. S.
SCHULTZ, D. E.
SHAFFER, G. C.
SMITH, D. G.
SMITH, M. E.
THOMPSON, C. F.
TRUBEK, D. M.

Medical School (1300 University Ave, Madison, WI 53706; tel. (608) 263-4900; fax (608) 262-2327; internet www.med.wisc.edu):

ABBOTT, D. H., Primate Research Center
ABBS, J. H., Neurology
ALBANESE, M. A., Population Health Sciences
ALBERT, D. M., Ophthalmology and Visual Sciences
ALLEN-HOFFMANN, B. L., Anatomic Pathology
ANDERSON, R. A., Pharmacology
ANDERSON, W. H., History of Medicine
BACH-Y-RITA, P., Rehabilitation Medicine
BANGS, J. D., Medical Microbiology
BENCA, R. M., Psychiatry
BENTZ, M. L., Dental and Plastic Surgery
BERSU, E. T., Anatomy
BERTICS, P. J., Biomolecular Chemistry
BIANCO, J. A., Nuclear Medicine
BIRD, I. M., Obstetrics and Gynaecology
BRADFIELD, C. A., Oncology
BRANDT, C. R., Ophthalmology and Visual Sciences
BRESNICK, E. H., Pharmacology
BROOKS, B. R., Neurology
BROW, D. A., Biomolecular Chemistry
BRUSKEWITZ, R. C., Urology
BURGESS, R. R., Oncology
CARNES, M. L., Geriatrics and Adult Devt
CHIU, S.-Y., Physiology
COMPTON, T., Oncology
CORONADO, R., Physiology
CRAIG, W. A., Infectious Disease
CRUICKSHANKS, K. J., Ophthalmology and Visual Sciences
DAHL, J. L., Pharmacology
DAHLBERG, J. E., Biomolecular Chemistry
DALESSANDRO, A., Transplant Research and Devt
DEJESUS, O. T., Medical Physics
DELUCA, P. M., Jr, Medical Physics
DEMETS, D. L., Biostatistics and Medical Informatics
DEMPSEY, J. A., Population Health Sciences
DEMPSEY, R. J., Neurological Surgery
DENNISTON, C., Genetics
DESMET, A. A., Diagnostic
DIAMOND, R. J., Psychiatry
DOVE, W. F., Sr, Oncology
DREZNER, M. K., Endocrinology
DRINKWATER, N. R., Oncology
EHRMEYER, S. L., Clinical Laboratory Science Programme
EPSTEIN, M. L., Anatomy
ERVASTI, J. M., Physiology
FAHL, W. E., Oncology
FALLON, J. F., Anatomy
FETTIPLACE, R., Physiology
FILLINGAME, R. H., Biomolecular Chemistry
FIORE, M. C., Gen. Internal Medicine
FLEMING, J. O., Neurology
FLEMING, M. F., Research Grants
FOLTS, J. D., Cardiology
FORD, C. N., Otolaryngology
FOST, N. C., Paediatrics
FREY, J. J., Family Medicine
FRYBACK, D. G., Population Health Sciences
GENTRY, L. R., Diagnostic
GERN, J. E., Paediatrics
GJERDE, C. L., Education Research and Devt
GLASSROTH, J. L., Medicine
GOLOS, T. G., Obstetrics and Gynaecology
GOULD, M. N., Oncology
GRAZIANO, F. M., Rheumatology
GREENSPAN, D. S., Anatomic Pathology
GREER, F. R., Paediatrics
GRIEP, A. E., Anatomy
GRIST, T. M., Diagnostic
GURMAN, A. S., Psychiatry
GUSTAFSON, J. P., Psychiatry
HABERLY, L. B., Anatomy
HACKNEY, C. M., Anatomy
HALL, T. J., Medical Physics
HARMS, B. A., Gen. Surgery
HART, M. N., Anatomic Pathology
HARTING, J. K., Anatomy
HAUGHTON, V. M., Diagnostic
HERMANN, B. P., Neurology
HOFFMANN, F. M., Oncology
HOLDEN, J. E., Medical Physics
JACKSON, M. B., Physiology
JANUARY, C. T., Cardiology
JARJOUR, N. N., Pulmonary Medicine
JEFCOATE, C. R., Pharmacology
KAHAN, L., Biomolecular Chemistry
KALAYOGLU, M., Transplant Research and Devt
KALIL, K., Anatomy
KALIL, R. E., Center for Neuroscience
KALIN, N. H., Psychiatry
KANAREK, M. S., Population Health Sciences
KAUFMAN, P. L., Ophthalmology and Visual Sciences
KEENE, J. S., Orthopaedics
KELLEY, A. E., Psychiatry
KILEY, P. J., Biomolecular Medicine
KIM, K.-M., Biostatistics and Medical Informatics
KLEIN, B. E. K., Ophthalmology and Visual Sciences
KLEIN, B. S., Paediatrics
KLEIN, M. H., Psychiatry
KLEIN, R., Ophthalmology and Visual Sciences
KLIEWER, M. A., Diagnostic
KNECHTLE, M. J., Transplant Research and Devt
KUDSK, K. A., Gen. Surgery
KUHLMAN, J. E., Diagnostic
LALLEY, P. M., Physiology
LAMBERT, P. F., Oncology
LAUBE, D. W., Obstetrics and Gynaecology
LEAVITT, J. W., History of Medicine
LEAVITT, L. A., Paediatrics
LEMANSKE, R. F., Paediatrics
LINZER, M., Gen. Internal Medicine
LIPTON, P., Physiology
LOEB, D. D., Oncology
LONGLEY, B. J., Dept of Dermatology
LOVE, R. R., Clinical Oncology
LUCEY, M. R., Gastroenterology
MCBRIDE, P. E., Cardiology
MACDONALD, M. J., Paediatrics
MACK, E. A., Gen. Surgery
MACKIE, T. R., Medical Physics
MAGNESS, R. R., Obstetrics and Gynaecology
MAKI, D. G., Infectious Disease
MAKIELSKI, J. C., Cardiology
MALKOVSKY, M., Medical Microbiology
MALTER, J. S., Anatomic Pathology
MARES, J. A., Ophthalmology and Visual Sciences
MARSHALL, J. R., Psychiatry
MEHTA, M. P., Human Oncology
MEISNER, L. F., Population Health Sciences
MERTZ, J. E., Oncology
MEYER, K. C., Pulmonary Medicine
MISTRETTA, C. A., Medical Physics
MONTERO, V. M., Physiology
MOSHER, D. F., Haematology
MOSS, R. L., Physiology
MUKHTAR, H., Dept of Dermatology
MULLAHY, J., Population Health Sciences
NICKLES, R. J., Medical Physics
NIEDERHUBER, J. E., Comprehensive Cancer Center
NIETO, F. J., Population Health Sciences
NUMBERS, R. L., History of Medicine
OBERLEY, T. D., Anatomic Pathology, Medicine
OERTEL, D., Physiology
OLIVE, D. L., Obstetrics and Gynaecology
PALIWAL, B. R., Human Oncology
PALTA, M., Population Health Sciences
PAULI, R. M., Genetics
PAULNOCK, D. M., Medical Microbiology
PEARCE, R. A., Anaesthesiology
PROCTOR, R. A., Infectious Disease, Medical Microbiology
RAPRAEGER, A. C., Anatomic Pathology
REMINGTON, P. L., Population Health Sciences
RHODE, W. S., Physiology
RIKKERS, L., Dept of Surgery
ROBBINS, J., Gastroenterology
ROBINS, H. I., Clinical Oncology
ROSS, J., Oncology
RUOHO, A. E., Pharmacology
RUTECKI, P. A., Neurology

SANDOR, M., Anatomic Pathology
SCHILLER, J. H., Clinical Oncology
SCHULTZ, E., Anatomy
SKATRUD, J. B., Pulmonary Medicine
SKOCHELAK, S. E., Family Medicine
SOBKOWICZ, H. M., Neurology
SOLLINGER, H. W., Transplant Research and Devt
SONDEL, P. M., Paediatrics
SONZOGNI, W. C., Environmental Health Admin.
STAFSTROM, C. E., Neurology
STARLING, J. R., Gen. Surgery
STEELE, T. H., Nephrology
SUGDEN, W. M., Oncology
SUTULA, T. P., Neurology
SVENDSEN, C. N., Anatomy
TERASAWA-GRILLEY, E. I., Primate Research Center
THOMSON, J. A., Anatomy
TONONI, G., Psychiatry
TURNIPSEED, W. D., Gen. Surgery
TURSKI, P. A., Diagnostic
UEHLING, D. T., Urology
VALDIVIA, H. H., Physiology
VANDERBY, R., Jr, Orthopaedics
VERMA, A. K., Human Oncology
WAKAI, R. T., Medical Physics
WALKER, J. W., Physiology
WATKINS, D. I., Anatomic Pathology
WEIDANZ, W. P., Medical Microbiology
WEINDRUCH, R. H., Geriatrics and Adult Devt
WEISBLUM, B., Pharmacology
WELCH, R. A., Medical Microbiology
WESTGARD, J. O., Anatomic Pathology
WHITE, J. G., Molecular Biology
WOLFE, B. L., Population Health Sciences
WOLFF, J. A., Paediatrics
WOOD, G. S., Dept of Dermatology
YIN, T. C. T., Physiology
YOUNG, J. A. T., Oncology
YOUNG, T. B., Population Health Sciences
ZAGZEBSKI, J. A., Medical Physics
ZDEBLICK, T. A., Orthopaedics
ZISKIND-CONHAIM, L., Physiology

Division of Continuing Studies (tel. (608) 262-1156; fax (608) 265-4555; e-mail info@dcs.wisc.edu; internet www.dcs.wisc.edu):

AUERBACH, E. K., Liberal Studies and the Arts
CAMPBELL, J. A., Professional Devt and Applied Studies
COOK, M. J., Liberal Studies and the Arts
KESSEL, R., Professional Devt and Applied Studies
NELSON, L. J., Liberal Studies and the Arts
ORTON, B. M., Professional Devt and Applied Studies
PADDOCK, S. C., Professional Devt and Applied Studies
SCHULENBURG, J. A., Liberal Studies and the Arts
WILLIAMS, R. T., Professional Devt and Applied Studies

Institute for Environmental Studies (Science Hall, 550 N Park St, Madison, WI 53706; tel. (608) 263-1796; internet www.ies.wisc.edu):

ADAMS, M. S., Botany
ALANEN, A. R., Landscape Architecture
ALBRECHT, K. A., Agronomy
ALLEN, T. F., Botany, Integrated Liberal Studies
ALVARADO, F. L., Electrical and Computer Engineering
ANDERSON, D. R., Business
ANDERSON, M. P., Geology and Geophysics
ANDREN, A. W., Civil and Environmental Engineering
ANDREWS, J. H., Plant Pathology
ARMSTRONG, D. E., Civil and Environmental Engineering
BAHR, J. M., Geology and Geophysics, Geological Engineering
BARROWS, R. L., Agricultural and Applied Economics
BAYLIS, J. R., Zoology
BERRY, P. E., Botany
BISHOP, R. C., Agricultural and Applied Economics
BLEAM, W. F., Soil Science
BOCKHEIM, J. G., Soil Science
BORN, S. M., Urban and Regional Planning
BRETHERTON, F. P., Atmospheric and Oceanic Sciences
BRINKMANN, W. A. R., Geography
BROWN, M. R., Agricultural Journalism
BUBENZER, G. D., Biological Systems Engineering
BUONGIORNO, J., Forest Ecology and Management
BUTTEL, F. H., Rural Sociology
CAMPBELL, G. R., Agricultural and Applied Economics
CARD, C. F., Philosophy, Women's Studies
CARPENTER, S. R., Zoology
CHENOWETH, R. E., Urban and Regional Planning
COLLINS, J. L., Sociology, Women's Studies
COMPTON, J. L., Forest Ecology and Management
CONVERSE, J. C., Biological Systems Engineering
CORRADINI, M. L., Engineering Physics, Mechanical Engineering
CRONON, W., History, Geography
DEWITT, C. B., Environmental Studies
DODSON, S., Zoology
DUNWOODY, S. L., Journalism and Mass Communication
ELDER, J. W., Sociology, Languages and Cultures of Asia
FELSTEHAUSEN, H. H., Urban and Regional Planning
FELTSKOG, E. N., English
FIELD, D. R., Forest Ecology and Management, Rural Sociology
FREUDENBURG, W. R., Rural Sociology
FRIEDMAN, E., Political Science
GIVNISH, T. J., Botany
GOODMAN, R. M., Plant Pathology
GRAHAM, L. K., Botany
GURIES, R. P., Forest Ecology and Management
HAMERS, R. J., Chemistry
HARRINGTON, J. A., Landscape Architecture
HAVEMAN, R. H., Economics
HEBERLEIN, T. A., Rural Sociology
HILL, R. J., English, American Indian Studies
HOOPES, J. A., Civil and Environmental Engineering
HOWELL, E. A., Landscape Architecture
HUDDLESTON, J. R., Urban and Regional Planning
IRISH, C. R., Law
JACOBS, H. M., Urban and Regional Planning
JEANNE, R. L., Entomology
JEFFRIES, T. W., Bacteriology
JOERES, E. F., Civil and Environmental Engineering
KANAREK, M. S., Preventive Medicine
KARASOV, W. H., Wildlife Ecology, Zoology
KITCHELL, J. F., Zoology
KNOX, J. C., Geography
KOEGEL, R. C., Biological Systems Engineering, Mechanical Engineering
KULCINSKI, G. L., Engineering Physics
KUTZBACH, J. E., Atmospheric and Oceanic Sciences
LEPOWSKY, M., Anthropology, Women's Studies
LILLESAND, T. M., Forest Ecology and Management, Civil and Environmental Engineering
LINDROTH, R. L., Entomology
LONG, W. F., Electrical and Computer Engineering
LOWERY, B., Soil Science
MCCOWN, B. H., Horticulture
MCEVOY, A. F., Law, History
MCSWEENEY, K., Soil Science
MADISON, F. W., Soil Science
MARIEN, E. J., Business
MICKELSON, D. M., Geology and Geophysics
MITCHELL, J. W., Mechanical Engineering
MOERMOND, T. C., Zoology
NIEMANN, B. J., Jr, Urban and Regional Planning
NORMAN, J. M., Soil Science, Atmospheric and Oceanic Sciences
NOWAK, P., Rural Sociology
O'KEEFE, G. J., Life Sciences Communication
O'LEARY, P. R., Biological Systems Engineering
PALLONI, A., Sociology
PINGREE, S., Life Sciences Communication, Human Ecology
PORTER, W. P., Zoology
POSNER, J. L., Agronomy
POTTER, K. W., Civil and Environmental Engineering
RAY, R. O., Forest Ecology and Management
REED, J. D., Animal Sciences, Dairy Science
RICHARDSON, N. R., Political Science
RUTLEDGE, J. J., Animal Sciences, Genetics
SCARPACE, F. L., Civil and Environmental Engineering
SCHMIT, J. T., Business
SCHULER, R. T., Biological Systems Engineering
SNOWDON, C. T., Psychology, Zoology
SONZOGNI, W. C., Civil and Environmental Engineering
STEVENSON, R. E., Business
STEVENSON, W. R., Plant Pathology
STEWART, J. H., Curriculum and Instruction
STIER, J. C., Forest Ecology and Management
STRAUB, R. J., Biological Systems Engineering
STRIER, K. B., Anthropology, Zoology
TAYLOR, M. S., Economics
TEMPLE, S. A., Wildlife Ecology
TISHLER, W. H., Landscape Architecture
TRIPLETT, E. W., Agronomy
VALE, T. R., Geography
VANDELL, K. D., Business
VENTURA, S. J., Soil Science
VONDEROHE, A. P., Civil and Environmental Engineering
WALLER, D. M., Botany
WANG, P. K., Atmospheric and Oceanic Sciences
YANDELL, B. S., Statistics, Horticulture
YUILL, T. M., Animal Health and Biomedical Sciences, Pathobiological Sciences, Wildlife Ecology
ZEDLER, J. B., Botany, Arboretum
ZEDLER, P. H., Arboretum
ZIMMERER, K. S., Geography

University of Wisconsin—Milwaukee

POB 413, Milwaukee, WI 53201-0413

Telephone: (414) 229-1122

Internet: www4.uwm.edu

Founded 1885

Academic year: September to May

Chancellor: CARLOS E. SANTIAGO

Provost and Vice-Chancellor for Academic Affairs: RITA CHENG

Vice-Chancellor for Finance and Admin. Affairs: SHERWOOD G. WILSON

Secretary of the University: RANDALL J. RYDER

Number of teachers: 1,381 (817 full-time, 564 part-time)

Number of students: 28,356

DEANS

College of Engineering and Applied Science: Dr RONALD PEREZ
College of Health Sciences: RANDALL LAMBRECHT
College of Letters and Science: G. RICHARD MEADOWS
College of Nursing: SALLY LUNDEEN
Graduate School: WILLIAM REED RAYBURN
School of Architecture and Urban Planning: ROBERT C. GREENSTREET
School of Business: Dr V. KANTI PRASAD
School of Continuing Education: MARK KRUEGER
School of Education: ALFONZO THURMAN
School of Information Studies: Dr JOHANNES BRITZ
School of Social Welfare: Dr STAN STOJKOVIĆ
School of the Arts: ROBERT BUCKER

CHAIRS OF DEPARTMENT

College of Engineering and Applied Science (3200 North Cramer St, Milwaukee, WI 53211; tel. (414) 229-4768; fax (414) 229-6958; internet www.uwm.edu/ceas):

Civil Engineering and Mechanics: FATTAH SHAIKH
Computer Science: Prof. K. VAIRAVAN
Electrical Engineering: Prof. DEVENDRA MISRA
Industrial and Manufacturing Engineering: MINNIE PATEL
Materials Engineering: HUGO LOPEZ
Mechanical Engineering: RYOICHI AMANO

College of Letters and Science (POB 413, Milwaukee, WI 53201; tel. (414) 229-4654; fax (414) 229-6827; internet www.uwm.edu/letsci):

Africology: BARTHOLEMEW ARMAH
Anthropology: JOSEPH PATRICK GRAY
Art History: BARRY WIND
Biological Sciences: JAMES COGGINS
Chemistry: DENNIS BENNETT
Communication: RENEE MEYERS
Economics: WILLIAM HOLAHAN
English: JAMES SAPPENFIELD
Foreign Languages and Linguistics: GARRY DAVIS
French, Italian and Comparative Literature: RACHEL SKALITZKY
Geography: MICHAEL DAY
Geosciences: NORMAN LASCA
History: Prof. JEFFREY MERRICK
Mass Communication: Prof. DAVID PRITCHARD
Mathematical Sciences: KAREN BRUCKS
Philosophy: MICHAEL LISTON
Physics: MARIJA GAJDARDZISKA-JOSIFOV
Political Science: Prof. MARCUS ETHRIDGE
Psychology: Prof. RAYMOND FLEMING
Sociology: STACEY OLIKER
Spanish and Portuguese: Prof. JULIO RODRIGUEZ-LUIS

School of Allied Health Professions (POB 413, Milwaukee, WI 53201; tel. (414) 229-5981; fax (414) 906-3920; internet www.uwm.edu/sahp):

Communication Sciences and Disorders: MARYLOU GELFER
Health Sciences: MARY K. MADSEN
Human Kinetics: CYNTHIA HASBROOK

School of Architecture and Urban Planning (POB 413, Milwaukee, WI 53201; tel. (414) 229-4014; fax (414) 229-6976; internet www.uwm.edu/sarup):

Architecture: DONALD HANLON
Urban Planning: NANCY FRANK

School of Education (POB 413, Milwaukee, WI 53201; tel. (414) 229-4725; internet www.uwm.edu/soe):

Admin. Leadership: Prof. LARRY MARTIN
Curriculum and Instruction: Prof. LINDA POST
Educational Policy and Community Studies: IAN HARRIS
Educational Psychology: Prof. DOUG MICKELSON
Exceptional Education: ALISON FORD

School of Fine Arts (POB 413, Milwaukee, WI 53201; tel. (414) 229-4762; fax (414) 229-6154; internet www.uwm.edu/soa):

Art: LESLIE VANSEN
Film: ROB YEO
Music: SCOTT EMMONS
Theatre and Dance: LEROY STONER

School of Nursing (POB 413, Milwaukee, WI 53201; tel. (414) 229-4801; fax (414) 229-6474; internet www.umw.edu/dept/nursing):

Foundations of Nursing: BETH ROGERS
Health Maintenance: EILEN SHEIL
Health Restoration: MARY WIERENGA

University of Wisconsin—Oshkosh

800 Algoma Blvd, Oshkosh, WI 54901

Telephone: (920) 424-1234
Fax: (920) 424-7317
Internet: www.uwosh.edu

Founded 1871

Chancellor: RICHARD H. WELLS
Provost and Vice-Chancellor for Academic Affairs: Dr LANE EARNS
Vice-Chancellor for Student Affairs: PETRA ROTA
Dean of Students: Dr JAMES M. CHITWOOD
Dir of Library: PATRICK WILKINSON

Library of 1,140,000 vols
Number of teachers: 535
Number of students: 10,619

DEANS

College of Business Administration: Dr E. ALAN HARTMAN
College of Education and Human Services: Dr FREDERICK YEO
College of Letters and Science: JOHN KOKER
College of Nursing: ROSEMARY SMITH

University of Wisconsin—Parkside

Box 2000, 900 Wood Rd, Kenosha, WI 53141-2000

Telephone: (262) 595-2345
Internet: www.uwp.edu

Founded 1968

Academic year: September to May

Chancellor: JOHN P. KEATING
Provost: GERALD GREENFIELD
Registrar: RHONDA HOLLAND
Library Dir: VANAJA MENON

Library of 395,000 vols
Number of students: 5,000

University of Wisconsin—Platteville

1 University Plaza, Platteville, WI 53818

Telephone: (608) 342-1491
Fax: (608) 342-1232
E-mail: web@uwplatt.edu
Internet: www.uwplatt.edu

Founded 1866

Chancellor: DAVID J. MARKEE
Provost and Vice-Chancellor: CAROL SUE BUTTS
Assoc. Vice-Chancellor: DAVID VAN BUREN
Assoc. Vice-Chancellor for Information Services: JOHN KROGMAN
Asst Chancellor for Admin. Services: JIM MUELLER
Asst Chancellor for Student Affairs: MICK VIREY

Library of 195,000 vols
Number of teachers: 270
Number of students: 5,100

DEANS

College of Business, Industry, Life Science and Agriculture: DUANE MERLIN FORD
College of Engineering, Mathematics and Science: RICHARD SHULTZ
College of Liberal Arts and Education: MITTIE NIMOCKS

University of Wisconsin—River Falls

410 South Third Street, River Falls, WI 54022

Telephone: (715) 425-3911
Fax: (715) 425-4487
Internet: www.uwrf.edu

Founded 1874
State control
Academic year: August to May

Chancellor: Dr DEAN VAN GALEN
Provost and Vice-Chancellor for Academic Affairs: Dr CHARLES D. HURT
Vice-Chancellor for Administration and Finance: MARY L. HALADA

Library of 260,000 vols
Number of teachers: 222
Number of students: 6,000

DEANS

College of Agriculture, Food and Environmental Sciences: DALE GALLENBERG
College of Arts and Sciences: TERRY BROWN
College of Business and Economics: GLENN POTTS
College of Education and Professional Studies: CONNIE FOSTER
Outreach and Graduate Studies: Dr DOUG JOHNSON

University of Wisconsin—Stevens Point

2100 Main St, Stevens Point, WI 54481

Telephone: (715) 346-0123
Fax: (715) 346-2561
Internet: www.uwsp.edu

Founded 1894
Academic year: September to May

Chancellor: LINDA BUNNELL
Provost and Vice-Chancellor: VIRGINIA HELM
Vice-Chancellors for Business Affairs: BOB TOMLINSON, GREG DIEMER

Library: 1,025,000 items
Number of teachers: 400
Number of students: 8,800

Publication: *Issues in Writing* (2 a year).

University of Wisconsin—Stout

Menomonie, WI 54751

Telephone: (715) 232-1122
Fax: (715) 232-1667
Internet: www.uwstout.edu

Founded 1891
State control
Academic year: September to May

Chancellor: Dr CHARLES W. SORENSON
Provost and Vice-Chancellor for Academic and Student Affairs: JULIE FURST-BOWE
Dir of Library Learning Center: PAUL ROBERTS

Library of 221,392 vols
Number of teachers: 453
Number of students: 9,300

Publication: *Stoutonia* (104 a year)

DEANS

College of Arts, Humanities, and Social Sciences: RAY HAYES
College of Management: DONNA HILTON STEWART
College of Science, Technology, Engineering and Mathematics: JEFFREY ANDERSON
School of Education, Health and Human Sciences: Dr MARY HOPKINS-BEST

University of Wisconsin—Superior
POB 2000, Superior, WI 54880-4500
Telephone: (715) 394-8101
E-mail: relations@uwsuper.edu
Internet: www.uwsuper.edu
Founded 1893
Chancellor: JULIUS E. ERLENBACH
Registrar: BARB ERICKSON
Librarian: FELIX UNAEZE
Library of 240,000 vols
Number of teachers: 135
Number of students: 2,800

University of Wisconsin—Whitewater
800 West Main St, Whitewater, WI 53190-1790
Telephone: (262) 472-1918
Fax: (262) 472-1518
Internet: www.uww.edu
Founded 1868
Academic year: August to May
Chancellor: MARTHA SAUNDERS
Provost and Vice-Chancellor for Academic Affairs: JOHN HEYER
Vice-Chancellor for Admin. Affairs: JAMES W. FREER
Library of 1,970,600 vols
Number of teachers: 331
Number of students: 10,502

OTHER CONSTITUENT INSTITUTIONS

University of Wisconsin Colleges
Central Administrative Offices, 780 Regent St, Suite 130, Madison, WI 53715-2635
Telephone: (608) 262-1783
Internet: www.uwc.edu
Chancellor: Dr DAVID WILSON
2-Year courses
Number of students: 12,261
Colleges at Barron County, Baraboo/Sauk County, Fox Valley, Fond du Lac, Manitowoc, Marathon County, Marshfield/Wood County, Marinette, Richland, Rock County, Sheboygan, Washington County, Waukesha.

University of Wisconsin Extension
Madison, WI 53706
Internet: www.uwex.edu
Chancellor: Dr DAVID WILSON
Provost and Vice-Chancellor: MARV VAN KEKERIX.

VITERBO UNIVERSITY
900 Viterbo Dr., La Crosse, WI 54601
Telephone: (608) 796-3000
E-mail: communication@viterbo.edu
Internet: www.viterbo.edu
Founded 1890
Academic year: August to May
Roman Catholic (Franciscan) liberal arts college
Pres.: Dr RICK ARTMAN
Vice-Pres. for Academic Affairs: JACK HAVERTAPE
Vice-Pres. for Admin. and Finance: TODD ERICSON
Vice-Pres. for Admission: ROLAND NELSON
Vice-Pres. for Communications and Marketing: PATRICK KERRIGAN
Vice-Pres. for Institutional Advancement: GARY KLEIN
Vice-Pres. for Mission and Ministry: Father TOM O'NEILL
Vice-Pres. for Student Devt: DIANE BRIMMER
Library Dir: RITA MAGNO
Library of 90,000 vols
Number of teachers: 176 (92 full-time, 84 part-time)
Number of students: 4,311
Schools of adult learning, business, education, fine arts, letters and sciences, nursing.

WYOMING

UNIVERSITY OF WYOMING
1000 East University Ave, Laramie, WY 82071
Telephone: (307) 766-1121
Internet: www.uwyo.edu
Founded 1886
State control
Language of instruction: English
Academic year: September to May
Pres.: THOMAS BUCHANAN
Vice-Pres. for Academic Affairs: MYRON ALLEN
Vice-Pres. for Admin.: DOUGLAS H. VINZANT
Vice-Pres. for Govt, Community and Legal Affairs: RICK MILLER
Vice-Pres. for Information Technology: ROBERT AYLWARD
Vice-Pres. for Institutional Advancement: BEN BLALOCK
Vice-Pres. for Research: WILLIAM GERN
Vice-Pres. for Student Affairs: SARA AXELSON
Assoc. Vice-Pres. for Academic Affairs and Dean of the Outreach School: MAGGI MURDOCK
Athletics Dir for Intercollegiate Athletics: TOM BURMAN
Librarian: MAGGIE FARREL
Library of 1,274,830 vols
Number of teachers: 685
Number of students: 13,000

DEANS
College of Agriculture: FRANK GALEY
College of Arts and Sciences: B. OLIVER WALTER
College of Business: BRENT HATHAWAY
College of Education: PATRICIA MCCLURG
College of Engineering: GUS PLUMB
College of Health Sciences: ROBERT O. KELLEY
College of Law: JERRY PARKINSON
Graduate School: DON ROTH
Outreach School: MAGGI MURDOCK

GUAM

Regulatory Body

GOVERNMENT

Guam Department of Education: POB DE, Hagåtña GU 96932; tel. 671-475-0457; fax 671-472-5003; e-mail geis@teleguam.net; internet www.gdoe.net; Superintendent NERISSA BRETANIA UNDERWOOD.

Learned Societies

BIBLIOGRAPHY, LIBRARY SCIENCE AND MUSEOLOGY

Guam Library Association: POB 22515 GMF, Barrigada GU 96921; tel. 671-475-4753; fax 671-477-9777; e-mail guam.library.association@gmail.com; internet sites.google.com/site/guamlibraryassociation/home; promotes knowledge; develops and improves library services, resources on the island; provides continuing library-related education; Pres. R. A. MEYER; Pres.-Elect CHRISTINE B. MATSON; Vice-Pres. for Membership ROSE UNPINGCO; Vice-Pres. for Programmes ANNA SLOAN; Sec. ALICE HADLEY; Treas. CYNDY PRUSKI.

FINE AND PERFORMING ARTS

Guam Preservation Trust/Inangokkon Inadahi Guahan: POB 3036, Hagåtña GU 96932; Suite 211, 2nd Floor, 194 Hernan Cortes Ave, Hagatna GU 96910; tel. 671-472-9439; fax 671-477-2047; e-mail jqpreservation@guam.net; internet www.guampreservationtrust.com; f. 1990; acquires for preservation threatened historical sites; supports activities related to public appreciation of historic places; awards grants for property documentation, protection through stablization, rehabilitation, reconstruction and restoration; archival and archaeological research; Chief Programme Officer JOSEPH E. QUINATA; Programme Officer ROSANNA BARCINAS.

Guam Symphony Society: POB 4069, Hagåtña GU 96932; tel. 671-477-1959; e-mail guamsymphony@yahoo.com; internet www.guamsymphony.com; f. 1967; non-profit org.; promotes classical music; develops local musical talent; conducts spec. orchestral performances; 50 volunteer musicians; Dir for Music and Conductor STEPHEN C. BEDNARZYK; Pres. DONNA KLOPPENBURG; Vice-Pres. LOUISE LIPPERT; Sec. APRIL BRIGGS; Treas. KAREN CARPENTER.

MEDICINE

Guam Medical Association:tel. 671-483-6600; e-mail guammedicalassociation@gmail.com; internet www.gma-assn.org; non-profit org.; devt of medical science; advocacy for community and public health issues; Pres. Dr PATRICK SANTOS; Pres.-Elect Dr THOMAS SHIEH; Exec. Dir PRAM SULLIVAN; Sec. Dr BEVAN GESLANI; Treas. Dr CHRIS BIELING; publ. *GMA Medical Journal*.

Research Institutes

HISTORY, GEOGRAPHY AND ARCHAEOLOGY

WERI–Water and Environmental Research Institute of the Western Pacific: UOG Station, Mangilao GU 96923; e-mail gdenton@uguam.uog.edu; internet weriguam.org; f. 1975, fmrly the Water and Energy Research Institute of the Western Pacific, present name 1998; attached to Univ. of Guam; research on water problems and water-related phenomena, incl. engineering, environmental toxicology, environmental chemistry, geology, geohydrology, hydrology, mapping and modelling, meteorology; production, distribution and management of freshwater resources; teaching and outreach programmes; Dir Prof. Dr GARY DENTON; Sec. NORMA BLAS.

LANGUAGE AND LITERATURE

Richard F. Taitano Micronesia Area Research Center (MARC): UOG Station, Mangilao GU 96923; tel. 671-735-2150; fax 671-734-7403; e-mail mstorie@guam.uog.edu; internet www.uog.edu/marc; attached to Univ. of Guam; preserves and provides access to collns of archival maps, photographs, texts and cultural materials related to the Micronesian geographical region; offers a programme in archaeological studies; instns: Micronesian Language Institute, Chamorro Language and Culture Centre; 200 titles in separate series; library of 40,000 vols on Guam, Micronesia and the Pacific; 800 dissertations and theses, news clippings and brochures; Dir Dr JOHN A. PETERSON; Dir for Chamorro Language and Culture Centre Dr MARILYN SALAS (acting).

MEDICINE

Cancer Research Center: UOG Station, Mangilao GU 96923; tel. 671-735-2994; fax 671-734-3636; internet www.uog.edu/dynamicdata/cancerresearchcenterhome.aspx; f. 2004; attached to Univ. of Guam; promotes improvement in cancer research capabilities; undergraduate and postgraduate education and training; Admin. HELEN J. D. WHIPPY.

NATURAL SCIENCES

Western Pacific Tropical Research Center: UOG Station, Mangilao GU 96923; tel. 671-735-2684; fax 671-734-0485; internet www.wptrc.org; attached to Univ. of Guam; research in agricultural profitability, economic devt using natural resources, improvement in quality and safety of food products, protection of environment; offers Masters programmes in biology and environmental science; field stations in Ija, Inarajan and Yigo; soil testing laboratory; Dir LEE S. YUDIN; Assoc. Dir GREG WIECKO; Assoc. Dean HENRY TAIJERON; publ. *WPTRC Impact Report* (1 a year).

Libraries and Archives

Hagåtña

Guam Law Library: 141 San Ramon St, Hagåtña GU 96910-4333; tel. 671-477-7623; fax 671-472-1246; e-mail gll@teleguam.net; internet www.guamlawlibrary.org; f. 1978; maintains the Judicial Centre br. libraries serving judges and law clerks of the Guam Supreme and Superior courts; serves as depository for all public laws, exec. orders, legislative materials and decisions of the courts; 52,000 vols; Exec. Dir and Librarian ANDREW S. QUENGA; Pres. VERNON PEREZ; Vice-Pres. BRIDGET ANN KEITH; Sec. JUDITH HATTORI; Treas. MITCHELL THOMPSON.

Guam Public Library System: 254 Martyr St, Hagåtña GU 96910-5141; tel. 671-475-4751; fax 671-477-9777; e-mail gpls@gpls.guam.gov; internet gpls.guam.gov; f. 1949; promotes literacy and lifelong learning; maintains materials of cultural significance on the island; cooperates with libraries on other islands; local govt document depository; br. libraries in Agat, Barrigada, Dededo, Merizo, Yona; one bookmobile; Dir (Acting Territorial Librarian) TERESITA KENNIMER; Sec. BERTHA GUERRERO.

Branch Libraries:

Barrigada Public Library: 177 San Roque Dr., Barrigada; tel. 671-734-5007; fax 671-734-5008.

Dededo Public Library: 283 West Santa Barbara Ave, Dededo; tel. 671-632-5503; fax 671-632-1046.

Maria R. Aguigui Memorial Library—Agat Public Library: 165 Follard St, Agat; tel. 671-565-5006; fax 671-565-5007.

Rosa Aguigui Reyes Memorial Library—Merizo Public Library: 376 Cruz Ave, Merizo; tel. 671-828-5008; fax 671-828-5009.

Yona Public Library: 265 Sister Mary Eucharita Dr., Yona; tel. 671-789-5010; fax 671-789-5011.

Mangilao

University of Guam, Robert F. Kennedy Memorial Library: Tan Siu Lin Bldg, UOG Station, Mangilao GU 96923; tel. 671-735-2331; fax 671-734-6882; e-mail csctsmth@uguam.uog.edu; internet www.uog.edu/library; f. 1963; central library facility at the Univ. of Guam; largest library in Micronesia; 124,684 vols, 1,527 print serial titles, 899,748 microfilm units, 47,481 online journals, 27,318 unique titles, 52 online databases; Dir CHRISTINE K. SCOTT-SMITH; Admin. Officer CONNIE QUINATA.

Museums and Art Galleries

Hagåtña

Guam Gallery of Arts: 138A–139B, Chamorro Village, Hagåtña; tel. 671-472-9659; e-mail guamarts@ite.net; f. 1994; display and sale of original artwork and reproductions by local artists; seasonal exhibits and art events; Dir FILAMORE PALOMO ALCON.

Guam Museum of Culture, Art and History: POB 518, Hagåtña GU 96932; 238 Archbishop Felixberto Flores St, DNA Bldg, 4th Floor, Suite 405A, Hagåtña GU 96910; tel. 671-475-4634; fax 671-475-4636; e-mail leona@guammuseum.com; internet www.guammuseum.com; attached to Guam Museum Foundation Inc.; represents Guam and Chamorro cultures; holds artefacts and remnants destroyed during the Second World War; Dir ANTHONY RAMIREZ (acting).

Kahan i Kutturan Guahan–The Gallery: c/o Guam Ccl on Arts and Humanities Agency, POB 2950, Hagåtña GU 96932; Dos Amantes Complex, Two Lovers' Leap, Tamuning; tel. 671-475-2781; fax 671-477-2786; e-mail kahal@teleguam.net; internet www.guamcaha.org; f. 1972 as the Insular Arts Ccl Gallery; attached to Guam Ccl on the Arts and Humanities Agency; local art exhibits; fellowship programmes; grants and services to local artists; Dir PATRICK BAMBA.

National Museum of the Dulce Nombre de Maria Cathedral Basilica: Cathedral-Basilica Pastoral Centre, 207 Archbishop Felixberto C. Flores St, Hagåtña GU 96910; above the Chapel of St Therese of Lisieux; tel. 671-477-1842; fax 671-472-1729; e-mail info@aganacathedral.org; internet aganacathedral.org; f. 2006; attached to Dulce Nombre de Maria Cathedral Basilica; displays frame views of the *Plaza de España*, inspirational art by local artists; Rector Mgr JAMES L. G. BENAVENTE.

Pacific War Museum: POB 2037, Hagåtña GU 96932; tel. 671-477-8355; fax 671-472-6070; internet www.guammuseum.com/pacific-war.htm; f. 2008; dedicated to US and Japanese armed forces who fought during the liberation of Guam; displays 15 military vehicles and 3 motorcycles; Chair. JOHN GERBER; Admin. Dir MELA L. GOMEZ.

War in the Pacific National Historical Park: 135 Murray Blvd, Suite 100, Hagåtña GU 96910; tel. 671-477-7278; fax 671-477-7281; internet www.nps.gov/wapa; attached to Nat. Park Service (USA); battlefields, gun emplacements, trenches and historic structures recreate life in Guam during the Second World War; Memorial Wall: displays 16,142 names of Chamorro and US casualties; Liberator's Memorial: honours the armed forces of the 1944 landing on Guam; tropical resources incl. 3,500 marine species and 200 coral species.

Mangilao

Isla Center for the Arts: House 15, Dean's Circle, Univ. of Guam, Mangilao GU 96923; tel. 671-735-2965; fax 671-735-2967; e-mail islacenter@gmail.com; internet www.uog.edu/isla; f. 1980; attached to Univ. of Guam; conducts exhibitions, workshops, lectures; promotes appreciation and awareness of cultures of the Western Pacific; permanent colln: preserves indigenous arts and crafts from Micronesia, Europe and Philippines, items of contemporary Western fine art, sculpture and Pre-Columbian art; Isla colln: 492 2-d and 3-d objects of folk art (produced for decorative purposes), ceremonial art (used by specific cultures in ceremonies and rituals), utilitarian crafts; other 2-d and 3-d works produced in Asian or Western cultures; Dir VELMA YAMASHITA.

Universities

PACIFIC ISLANDS UNIVERSITY

POB 22619 GMF, Mangilao GU 96921-2619
172 Kinney's Rd, off Route 15, 2 miles north of Route 10, Mangilao
Telephone: 671-734-1812
Fax: 671-734-1813
E-mail: guamcampus@piu.edu
Internet: www.piu.edu

Founded 1976 as Micronesian Institute of Biblical Studies, renamed Pacific Islands Bible College 1991, present name and status 2009

Private control

Christian liberal arts education; accredited by Transnational Assen of Christian Colleges and Schools (TRACS)

Chair.: Rev. BILL SCHUIT
Sec. and Treas.: Rev. HARALD GORGES
Pres.: Dr DAVID L. OWEN
Vice-Pres. for Academics: MELODY PAXTON
Vice-Pres. for Advancement: STEVE STINNETTE
Vice-Pres. for Finance: HARUMI ELIASON
Vice-Pres. for Operations: (vacant)
Vice-Pres. for Student Life: ROBERT WATT
Registrar: URTE SCHERER
Dir of Libraries: LISA COLLINS

Library of 13,500 vols
Number of teachers: 30
Number of students: 225

UNIVERSITY OF GUAM/ UNIBETSEDÅT GUAHAN

UOG Station, Mangilao GU 96923
Telephone: 671-735-2990
Fax: 671-734-2296
E-mail: admitme@uguam.uog.edu
Internet: www.uog.edu

Founded 1952 as the Territorial College of Guam, present campus 1960, accredited 1963 and 1965, present name 1968, present status 1984
Public control
Language of instruction: English
Academic year: August to May

Chair., Board of Regents: PETER ADA
Vice-Chair., Board of Regents: Dr W. CHRIS PEREZ
Treas., Board of Regents: CYNTHIA HENSON
Pres.: Dr ROBERT A. UNDERWOOD
Sr Vice-Pres. for Academic and Student Affairs: Dr HELEN J. D. WHIPPY
Vice-Pres. for Admin. and Finance: DAVID M. O'BRIEN
Registrar: REMY B. CRISTOBAL
Library: see Libraries and Archives

Number of teachers: 260
Number of students: 3,639

Publications: *Isla* (2 a year), *Micronesian Educator* (1 a year), *Micronesica* (2 a year), *Storyboard: A Journal of Pacific Imagery*, *University Magazine* (1 a year)

DEANS

College of Liberal Arts and Social Sciences: Dr JAMES SELLMANN
College of Natural and Applied Sciences: Dr LEE S. YUDIN
Enrolment Management and Student Services: Dr JULIE ULLOA-HEATH
Learning Resources: CHRISTINE SCOTT-SMITH
School of Business and Public Administration: Dr ANITA BORJA-ENRIQUEZ
School of Education: Dr ELIZABETH HAWTHORNE
School of Nursing and Health Sciences: Dr MARIA SALOMON

PUERTO RICO

Regulatory and Representative Bodies

GOVERNMENT

Consejo de Educación Superior de Puerto Rico (Puerto Rico Council on Higher Education): POB 19900, San Juan PR 00910-190; Ave Ponce de León 268, Edif. Hato Rey Centre, Suite 1500, San Juan PR 00918; tel. (787) 641-7100; fax (787) 641-2573; e-mail vi_abreu@ces.gobierno.pr; internet www.gobierno.pr/cespr; f. 1993; 8 mems; Pres. Dr JOSÉ LEMA MOYÁ; Exec. Dir. Prof. DAVID DÁVILA BÁEZ.

Department of Education: POB 190759, Hato Rey PR 00917; Avda Teniente César González, esq. Calle Juan Calaf, Urb. Industrial Tres Monjitas, San Juan PR 00919-0759; tel. (787) 759-2000; fax (787) 250-0275; internet www.de.gobierno.pr; Sec. RAFAEL ARAGUNDE TORRES.

Learned Societies

GENERAL

Ateneo de Ponce: POB 32144, Ponce PR 00732-2144; e-mail ateneodeponce@yahoo.com; internet www.pucpr.edu/alianzas/ateneodeponce; f. 1956; lectures, competitions, conferences and concerts; publs; five divs of fine arts, history, literature, moral and political sciences, physics and mathematics; Pres. Dr JOSÉ R. ESCABÍ; Vice-Pres. Profa ADA HILDA MARTÍNEZ DE ALICEA; Sec. Profa MARÍA ISABEL CHAPARRO DE ESCABÍ; Treas. Profa LESBIA CRUZ; publ. *Pergamino* (12 a year).

Ateneo Puertorriqueño (Puerto Rican Athenaeum): Apdo 9021180, San Juan PR 00902-1180; Avda Ponce de León, Pda 2, Edif. Histórico III, San Juan PR 00902; tel. (787) 721-3877; fax (787) 725-3873; e-mail ateneopr@caribe.net; internet www.puertadetierra.info/edificios/ateneo/ateneo.htm; f. 1876; literature, theatre, arts and sciences; art gallery: holds 450 works of art; 600 mems; library of 30,000 vols, periodicals, old newspapers and microfilm copies; Pres. Lic. EDUARDO MORALES COLL; Vice-Pres. Dr JOSÉ MILTON SOLTERO; Sec. Dr INÉS QUILES; Treas. Dr OSIRIS DELGADO; publ. *Revista* (2 a year).

BIBLIOGRAPHY, LIBRARY SCIENCE AND MUSEOLOGY

Sociedad de Bibliotecarios de Puerto Rico (Library Society of Puerto Rico): Apdo 22898, San Juan PR 00931-2898; tel. (787) 831-0000; e-mail mzavala@rrpac.upr.clu.edu; internet www.sociedadbibliotecarios.org; f. 1961; non-profit org. for the promotion of librarianship; organizes conferences, continuing education activities; promotes Library Week; 280 mems; Pres. IVÁN CALIMANO; Vice-Pres. VICTOR M. MALDONADO; Sec. CARMEN RÍOS PORTO; Treas. LUIS CASIANO; publs *Acceso: revista puertorriqueña de bibliotecología y documentación* (1 a year), *Informa* (4 a year).

FINE AND PERFORMING ARTS

Sociedad Mayagüezana Pro Bellas Artes: POB 5004, Mayagüez PR 00709; f. 1977; ballet, opera, concerts, lectures, symphonies, art and sculpture exhibitions; 300 mems; Pres. Dr LUIS E. BACÓ RODRÍGUEZ.

HISTORY, GEOGRAPHY AND ARCHAEOLOGY

Academia Puertorriqueña de la Historia: Apdo 1447, San Juan; Del Cristo 52, San Juan PR 00901-1308; tel. (787) 721-5200; f. 1932; 40 mems; Pres. LUIS E. GONZÁLEZ VALES; publ. *Boletín*.

LANGUAGE AND LITERATURE

Academia Puertorriqueña de la Lengua Española (Puerto Rican Academy of the Spanish Language): Apdo 36 4008, San Juan PR 00936-4008; Ballajá Barracks 3rd Fl., San Juan PR 00906; tel. (787) 721-6070; fax (787) 724-6463; e-mail info@academiapr.org; internet www.academiapr.org; f. 1955; attached to Asociación de Academias de la Lengua Española; research; literary criticism, linguistics and poetic creation; 28 mems; Dir Dr JOSÉ LUIS VEGA; Vice-Dir LUCE LÓPEZ BARALT; Sec. AMPARO MORALES (acting); Treas. GERVASIO LUIS GARCÍA; publs *Boletín* (4 a year), *DILO* (4 a year).

PEN Club de Puerto Rico: 6 Mariano Ramírez Bages, Apt 4B, San Juan PR 00907; tel. (787) 645-9533; e-mail mairymcb@hotmail.com; internet www.internationalpen.org.uk/go/centres/find-a--centre/latin-america-and-the-caribbean; f. 1966; 40 mems; Pres. MAIRYM CRUZ-BERNALL; Sec. ANA MARÍA FUSTER.

Research Institutes

GENERAL

Instituto de Cultura Puertorriqueña (Institute of Puerto Rican Culture): POB 9024184, San Juan PR 00902-4184; tel. (787) 724-0700; fax (787) 724-8393; e-mail webicp@icp.gobierno.pr; internet www.icp.gobierno.pr; f. 1955; studies and preserves Puerto Rican historical and cultural patrimony; promotes study of Puerto Rican culture; Exec. Dir MERCEDES GÓMEZ MARRERO; Sub-Dir FREDDY VÉLEZ GARCIA.

AGRICULTURE, FISHERIES AND VETERINARY SCIENCE

International Institute of Tropical Forestry: USDA Forest Service, Jardín Botánico Sur, 1201 Calle Ceiba, San Juan PR 00926-1119; tel. (787) 766-5335; fax (787) 766-6302; e-mail alugo@fs.fed.us; internet www.fs.fed.us/global/iitf; f. 1939; research in timber management, tropical ecosystem, plantation forestry, wildlife management, watershed management and global change research; cooperative assistance to state and private forest landowners, timber processors; cooperative research with univs and US and foreign governmental agencies; trains foreign forestry students in cooperation with FAO and USAID; library of 15,000 vols; Dir Dr ARIEL E. LUGO.

Tropical Agriculture Research Station: 2200 Pedro Albizu Campos Ave, Suite 201, Mayagüez PR 00680-5470; tel. (787) 831-

3435; fax (787) 831-3386; e-mail ricardo .goenaga@ars.usda.gov; internet www.ars .usda.gov/saa/tars; f. 1901; attached to Agricultural Research Service of US Dept of Agriculture; conducts research to develop solutions to agricultural problems of high nat. priority; protects human health and the environment; Coordinator Dr RICARDO GOENAGA.

NATURAL SCIENCES

Arecibo Observatory: HC03, POB 53995, Arecibo PR 00612; tel. (787) 878-2612; fax (787) 878-1861; e-mail mrodrigu@naic.edu; internet www.naic.edu; f. 1960; attached to Nat. Astronomy and Ionosphere Centre (operated by Cornell Univ. under a cooperative agreement with the Nat. Science Foundation); world's largest radio/radar telescope, for use by scientists from all over the world; 1,000-ft diameter fixed spherical reflector with movable feeds; for use in the radar study of planets and the properties of the earth's upper atmosphere and reception of natural radio emissions from celestial objects incl. pulsars and quasars; reflector surface upgraded to work at higher frequencies; library of 2,300 vols, 845 periodicals; Dir DON CAMPBELL.

Institute for Tropical Ecosystem Studies: POB 70377, San Juan PR 00936-8377; 207 Anexo Facundo Bueso, Univ. of Puerto Rico, Rio Piedras campus, San Juan PR 00931; tel. (787) 764-0000; fax (787) 772-1481; e-mail elmelend@uprrp.edu; internet ites.upr.edu; f. 1957 as PR Nuclear Centre; attached to Univ. of Puerto Rico; research, and devt of tropical terrestrial ecological studies; graduate-level research and training centre in basic ecological principles, primarily for minorities; Dir Dr ELVIA MELÉNDEZ-ACKERMAN; Sec. EVA CORTÉS.

Libraries and Archives

Mayagüez

Biblioteca General Recinto Universitario de Mayagüez (General Library Mayagüez Campus): Univ. of Puerto Rico, Mayagüez Campus, POB 9000, Mayagüez PR 00681; tel. (787) 265-3810; fax (787) 265-5483; e-mail library@uprm.edu; internet www.uprm.edu/library; f. 1911; attached to Univ. of Puerto Rico; 164,068 vols of books, 5,259 journals, 263,982 microfiches, 12,719 micro cards, 19,486 microfilms, 561,641 govt documents, 949 films, 8,149 maps, 8,458 sound recordings, 606 musical scores, 917 sound magnetic tapes, 24,810 slides, 4,550 videocassettes, 687 film strips, 3,585 theses and dissertations, 7m. US patents and 3m. US issues trademarks; Dir Prof. WANDA PÉREZ (acting); Assoc. Dir Prof. NORMA I. SOJO (acting); publs *Bibliorum* (4 a year), *Conoce Tu Biblioteca* (1 a year), *List of Publications on Agriculture and Related Sciences* (12 a year), *Serials Holdings in the Mayagüez Library* (every 2 years).

Ponce

Biblioteca Valdés (Encarnación Valdés Library): Ponce PR 00717-0777; tel. (787) 841-2000; fax (787) 284-0235; internet www .pucpr.edu; f. 1948; attached to Pontifical Catholic Univ. of Puerto Rico; spec. collns: Puerto Rican materials, Murga Colln; 269,000 vols, 46,000 periodicals, 4,600 microfilms, 2,600 CDs; Dir ESTHER IRIZARRY VÁZQUEZ; Exec. Sec. CECILIA LUGO CASIANO.

Law Library: 2250 Avda Las Américas, Suite 544, Ponce PR 00717-9997; tel. (787) 841-2000; fax (787) 841-5354; e-mail bib-derecho@pucpr.edu; internet www.pucpr .edu/derecho/nbiblioteca/index.html; f. 1961; attached to Pontifical Catholic Univ. of Puerto Rico; part of Centre for Legal Research and Information; spec. collns: US and UN documents, Puerto Rico; 235,945 vols; Dir NOELIA PADUA; publ. *Revista de Derecho Puertorriqueño* (4 a year).

Ponce Public Library: POB 7477, Ponce PR 00732; Calle Reina, Esquina Fogos, Ponce PR 00731; f. 1937; 9,516 mems; 20,000 vols; Librarian M. MADERA.

San Juan

Archivo General de Puerto Rico: Instituto de Cultura Puertorriqueña, Apdo 9024184, San Juan PR 00902-4184; Avda Constitución 500, Puerta de Tierra, San Juan; tel. (787) 725-1060; fax (787) 725-1685; e-mail archivogeneral@icp.gobierno .pr; internet www.icp.gobierno.pr/agp; f. 1955; attached to Instituto de Cultura Puertorriqueña; 80,000 cubic ft of documents, incl. text, graphics (drawings, maps), print (newspapers, journals), films and recordings in various formats; Dir JOSÉ A. FLORES (acting).

Biblioteca del Departamento de Justicia: POB 9020192, San Juan PR 00902-0192; tel. (787) 724-6869; fax (787) 721-3977; e-mail webmail@justicia.gobierno.pr; internet www.justicia.gobierno.pr/ rs_template/v2/secauxase/secauxase_biblo .html; f. 1950; attached to Dept of Justice of Puerto Rico; provides and manages bibliographic and reference services required by the Office of the Atty Gen.; allocates library resources to lawyers and specialized divs of the Dept of Justice; 75,000 vols; Dir of the Law Library Atty SHEILA MIRANDA RIVERA; publs *Anuario Estadístico*, *Informe Anual del Secretario de Justicia de Puerto Rico*, *Opiniones del Secretario de Justicia de Puerto Rico*.

Attached Library:

Supreme Court of Puerto Rico Library: Avda Ponce de León Pda 8, Apdo 2392, San Juan PR 00903; tel. (787) 723-3863; f. 1953; law library with spec. collns of Puerto Rican law, common law, Spanish and French civil law; 75,243 vols; Librarian (vacant); publ. *Nuevas Adquisiciones* (12 a year).

Biblioteca Madre María Teresa Guevara: Apdo 12383, San Juan PR 00914-12383; tel. (787) 728-1515; fax (787) 268-8868; internet biblioteca.sagrado.edu; f. 1935; attached to Univ. del Sagrado Corazón; 130,000 vols, 1,375 periodicals; Dir SONIA DÍAZ LATORRE; Admin. Sec. MARITZA NIEVES; publs *Delfilinea* (Library News, 3 a year), *Lista de Publicaciones Periódicas* (1 a year).

Biblioteca Nacional: Instituto de Cultura Puertorriqueña, Apdo 9024184, San Juan PR 00902-4184; Ave Ponce de León 500, Puerta de Tierra, San Juan; tel. (787) 725-1060; fax (787) 723-5006; e-mail biblioteca@icp .gobierno.pr; internet www.icp.gobierno.pr/ bge; f. 2003; attached to Instituto de Cultura Puertorriqueña; acquires, preserves and disseminates the literature written and published in Puerto Rico; Dir JOSEFINA GÓMEZ DE HILLYER.

Caribbean and Latin American Studies Library: POB 21927, San Juan PR 00931-1927; tel. (787) 764-0000; fax (787) 763-5685; e-mail afiguer@upracd.upr.clu.edu; f. 1946 in Trinidad, present location 1961; specializes in humanities and social sciences in Latin America and the Caribbean; 50,000 vols, spec. colln of Caribbean Comm. documents; Librarian Prof. ALMALUCES FIGUEROA.

Carnegie Public Library: 7 Avda Ponce de León, Puerta de Tierra, San Juan PR 00901-2010; tel. (787) 722-4753; fax (787) 725-0261; f. 1903 as Island Library, present name and bldg 1918; attached to Dept of Education of Puerto Rico; 50,000 vols; Dir MARY JEAN HAVER.

Programa de Servicios Bibliotecarios y de Información (Programme Library and Information Services): POB 190759, San Juan PR 00919-0759; tel. (787) 759-2000; internet www.de.gobierno.pr/tags/ bibliotecas; attached to Dept of Education of Puerto Rico; 1,500,000 vols; Dir MARIA LUGO.

Sistema de Bibliotecas: POB 23302, San Juan PR 00931-3302; tel. (787) 764-0000; fax (787) 772-1479; internet biblioteca.rrp.upr .edu; f. 1903; attached to Univ. of Puerto Rico; main library and 11 deptl libraries; 33,777 titles of printed books, 359 print journals titles, 731 masters theses, 1,341 reference books, govt and corporate documents; Dir Dra SNEJANKA PENKOVA; Assoc. Dir Prof. AMÍLCAR TIRADO (acting); publs *Al Día* (4 a year), *Biblionotas* (12 a year), *Boletines de Divulgación* (irregular), *Entorno* (2 a year), *Lumbre* (6 a year), *Perspectiva* (2 a year), *Servicio de Alerta* (irregular).

University of Puerto Rico Law Library: Univ. of Puerto Rico, POB 23310, San Juan PR 00931-3310; tel. (787) 999-9684; fax (787) 999-9680; e-mail motero@upracd.upr.clu .edu; internet ls-po.law.upr.edu; f. 1913; Caribbean Basin legal colln, judicial archives; 382,000 vols; Dir Licda MARÍA M. OTERO; publ. *Lista Selectiva de Nuevas Adquisiciones*.

Museums and Art Galleries

Ponce

Museo de Arte de Ponce: 2325 Ave Las Américas, Ponce PR 00732-9027; tel. (787) 848-0505; fax (787) 841-7309; e-mail map@ museoarteponce.org; internet www .museoarteponce.org; f. 1959; attached to Fundación Luis A. Ferré, Inc.; European, American and Hispanic American paintings and sculptures; library of 7,000 vols; Exec. Dir AGUSTÍN ARTEAGA.

Museo de la Historia de Ponce (Museum of Ponce History): Calle 53 Isabel, Ponce; tel. (787) 844-7071; f. 1992; promotes research and preservation of Ponce's heritage for the devt of the Puerto Rican culture; 10 galleries display colln of 3,000 Ponce historical relics, photos and documents.

Museo de la Música Puertorriqueña: Calle Isabel, esquina Salud, Ponce; tel. (787) 290-6617; internet www.icp.gobierno .pr/myp/museos/m15.htm; f. 1990; attached to Instituto de Cultura Puertorriqueña; neoclassical residence that displays the history of indigenous Puerto Rican music from pre-Columbian times to the present.

San Germán

Museo de Arte Religioso Santo Domingo de Porta Coeli: Apdo 1160, San Germán PR 00683; Frente a la Plaza Santo Domingo, San Germán; tel. (787) 892-5845; internet www .icp.gobierno.pr/myp/museos/m12.htm; attached to Museos y Parques, Instituto de Cultura Puertorriqueña; 17th-century church of Porta Coeli; constructed as a chapel for convent of Dominican Friars in San Germán; restored and converted into museum of religious art (paintings, pictures, sculptures, ornaments and ritual objects) in 1960; Admin. GUIDO BARLETTA.

San Juan

La Casa del Libro: Amigos de Calle del Cristo 255, Inc., POB 9023544, San Juan PR 00902-3544; tel. and fax (787) 723-0354; e-mail lcdl@prw.net; internet www.lacasadellibro.org; f. 1955; devoted to the art and history of the book; colln of 6,000 books incl. rare vols 500 years old; displays antique printing tools; library of 7,000 vols; Dir MARIA TERESA ARRARÁS; Librarian JOSE M. ESTRADA-BOLIVAR.

Museo de Arte Contemporáneo de Puerto Rico (Puerto Rico Museum of Contemporary Art): POB 362377, San Juan PR 00936-2377; Edif. Histórico Rafael M. de Labra, Ave Juan Ponce de León, esquina Ave Roberto H. Todd Parada 18, Santurce, San Juan; tel. (787) 977-4030; fax (787) 977-4036; e-mail adm1@museocontemporaneopr.org; internet www.museocontemporaneopr.org; f. 1984; collects, preserves, documents and disseminates art produced in Puerto Rico, the Caribbean and Latin America from the 1940s to present; Pres. SALVADOR ALEMAÑY; Vice-Pres. Ing. WILLIAM DÍAZ; Sec. HÉCTOR SALDAÑA EGOZCUE; Treas. MANUEL FELICIANO; Exec. Dir MARIANNE RAMÍREZ APONTE; Curator Dr LILLIANA RAMOS-COLLADO.

Museo de Arte de Puerto Rico (Museum of Art of Puerto Rico): Ave De Diego 299, Santurce, San Juan PR 00909; tel. (787) 977-6277; fax (787) 977-4446; e-mail infoproa@mapr.org; internet www.mapr.org; f. 2000; colln of works from 17th century to present; 1,100 artworks incl. drawings, prints, photography, sculpture and new media; Pres. ZOILA LEVIS; Vice-Pres. ARTURO GARCÍA-SOLÁ; Sec. MELBA ACOSTA; Treas. MABEL BURCKHART.

Museo de Arte e Historia de San Juan (Museum of Art and History in San Juan): Calle Norzagaray 150, San Juan; tel. (787) 724-1875; f. 1979; museum bldg reflects Spanish colonial architecture; showcases history of San Juan from 1521 to the present; displays artworks by local artists.

Museo de Historia Militar: c/o Instituto de Cultura Puertorriqueña, POB 9024184, San Juan PR 00902-4184; tel. (787) 723-7837; e-mail info@icp.gobierno.pr; internet www.icp.gobierno.pr; small Spanish fort from 16th century.

Universities

BAYAMÓN CENTRAL UNIVERSITY

POB 1725, Bayamón PR 00960-1725
Telephone: (787) 786-3030
Fax: (787) 740-2200
Internet: www.ucb.edu.pr

Founded 1961 as a regional school at the Catholic Univ. of Puerto Rico, present name and status 1970
Private control
Language of instruction: Spanish
Academic year: August to May and long-vacation courses

Pres.: Prof. NILDA NADAL CARRERAS
Academic Dean: Dra MARITZA ORTIZ
Registrar: VICTOR COLÓN-RODRÍGUEZ
Librarian: Prof. WANDA OCASIO

Library of 51,011 vols
Number of teachers: 57 (full-time)
Number of students: 3,228

Publications: *Cruz Ansata* (1 a year), *Familia y Escuela* (12 a year), *Hawk Magazine*, *President's Letter* (4 a year)

DEANS

College of Business and Technology Development: Dra NIDIA COLÓN QUINTANA
College of Education and Professional Conduct: Dra PURA ECHANDI
College of Liberal Arts, Sciences and Health Professions: Dr LUIS A. SÁNCHEZ GÓMEZ

UNIVERSIDAD INTERAMERICANA DE PUERTO RICO (InterAmerican University of Puerto Rico)

POB 363255, San Juan PR 00936-3255
Telephone: (787) 766-1912
Internet: www.inter.edu

Founded 1912 as Polytechnic Institute of Puerto Rico
Private control
Languages of instruction: Spanish, English
Academic year: August to May (2 semesters)

Pres.: MANUEL J. FERNÓS
Pres. for Board of Trustees: LUIS A. PLAZA MARIOTA

Number of teachers: 2,548
Number of students: 40,000

Publications: *Homines*, *Interamericana Newspaper*.

PONTIFICAL CATHOLIC UNIVERSITY OF PUERTO RICO

2250 Ave Las Americas, Ponce PR 00717-0777
Telephone: (787) 651-2000
Fax: (787) 840-4295
Internet: www.pucpr.edu

Founded 1948 as Santa María
Languages of instruction: Spanish, English
Private control
Academic year: August to May (2 semesters and 2 summer sessions)

Campuses at Arecibo and Mayagüez

Chancellor: Most Rev. RICARDO SURIÑACH
Vice-Chancellor: Most Rev. FÉLIZ LÁZARO
Pres.: Prof. MARCELINA VÉLEZ DE SANTIAGO (acting)
Vice-Pres. for Academics: Prof. CARL SAUDER
Vice-Pres. for Finance: Prof. IRMA RODRÍGUEZ
Vice-Pres. for Institutional Mission: Prof. CARL SAUDER
Vice-Pres. for Students: Prof. CARILIN FRAU
Registrar: Prof. IVÁN DÁVILA
Librarian: ESTHER IRIZARRY

Number of teachers: 702
Number of students: 9,862

Publications: *Horizontes*, *La Nao*, *Revista de Derecho Puertorriqueño*

DEANS

College of Arts and Humanities: Prof. ALFONSO SANTIAGO
College of Business Administration: Dr JAIME L. SANTIAGO CANET
College of Education: Dr LILLIAN NEGRÓN COLON
College of Graduate Studies in Behavioural Sciences and Community Affairs: Dr HERNÁN A. VERA RODRÍGUEZ
College of Law: ANGEL GONZÁLEZ ROMÁN
College of Science: Prof. CARMEN C. VELÁZQUEZ

UNIVERSIDAD DE PUERTO RICO (University of Puerto Rico)

POB 364984, San Juan PR 00936-4984
Telephone: (787) 250-0000
Fax: (787) 759-6917
Internet: www.upr.edu

Founded 1903, present status 1998
State control
Languages of instruction: Spanish, English
Academic year: August to May

Pres.: Dr JORGE L. SÁNCHEZ (acting)
Dir for Academic Affairs: MANUEL GÓMEZ
Dir for Budget: BASILIO RIVERA (acting)
Dir for Finance: NAZEERAH ELMADAH (acting)
Dir for Financial Aid: HERNÁN VAZQUEZTELL
Dir for Information Systems: SANDRA SANTOS (acting)
Dir for Planning and Devt: IRVING JIMÉNEZ (acting)
Dir for Public Relations: (vacant)

Number of teachers: 5,287
Number of students: 62,292

Publications: *La Torre*, *RIE* (4 a year).

ATTACHED CAMPUSES

Universidad de Puerto Rico en Aguadilla (University of Puerto Rico at Aguadilla): POB 6150, Aguadilla PR 00604-6150; tel. (787) 890-2681; fax (787) 891-3455; internet www.uprag.edu; f. 1972; programmes in biology with an emphasis on bioinformatics, biomedical quality systems assessment process industries, environmental technology, education (concentration on English) and multimedia technology, quality control in manufacturing; 167 teachers; 3,218 students; Chancellor IVELICE CARDONA; Exec. Sec. CRISTINA DÍAZ VEGA; Dean for Academic Affairs Dr JOSEPH M. PLANAS RIVERA.

Universidad de Puerto Rico en Arecibo (University of Puerto Rico at Arecibo): POB 4010, Arecibo PR 00614-4010; tel. (787) 815-0000; internet www.upra.edu; f. 1967; depts of biology, business administration, chemical physics, computer science, counselling and guidance, education, English, humanities, mathematics, nursing, social sciences, Spanish, tele-radio communication; 270 teachers; 4,041 students; Chancellor JOSEFA GARCÍA FIRPI; Registrar NEREIDA GONZÁLEZ; Library Dir VICTOR MALDONADO MALDONADO (acting).

Universidad de Puerto Rico en Bayamón (University of Puerto Rico at Bayamón): 170 Industrial Minillas Carr 174, Bayamón PR 00959-1919; tel. (787) 993-8850; fax (787) 993-8900; internet www.uprb.edu; f. 1971; depts of early childhood education, electronics, materials engineering, natural science, physical education; 300 teachers; 4,565 students; Rector Dr ARTURO AVILÉS GONZÁLEZ (acting); Registrar WANDA RIVERA.

Universidad de Puerto Rico en Carolina (University of Puerto Rico at Carolina): POB 4800, Carolina PR 00984-4800; tel. (787) 257-0000; fax (787) 750-7940; internet www.uprc.edu; f. 1974; programmes in automotive technology, cultural tourism, hotel and restaurant administration, industrial automation, interior design, mechanical engineering, physical education and recreation for people with disabilities; 200 teachers; 3,930 students; Rector TRINIDAD FERNÁNDEZ MIRANDA.

Universidad de Puerto Rico en Cayey: Antonio R. Barceló 205, Cayey PR 00736; tel. (787) 738-2161; internet www.upr.edu; f. 1967; programmes in business administration, biology, chemistry, humanities, Hispanic studies, mathematics and physics, natural sciences, social sciences, pedagogy; promotes student participation in scientific research in univ. laboratories outside Puerto Rico; attached centres: Environmental Education Centre, Institute for Interdisciplinary Research; 224 teachers; 3,626 students; Chancellor RAFAEL RIVERA-LEHMAN; Registrar ANGEL L. MATOS.

Universidad de Puerto Rico en Humacao (University of Puerto Rico at Humacao): Estación Postal CUH 100 Carr. 908, Humacao PR 00791-4300; tel. (787) 850-0000;

e-mail marisol.benitez@upr.edu; internet www.uprh.edu; f. 1962; programmes in applied physical electronics, business administration, coastal marine biology, computational mathematics, education, industrial chemistry, microbiology and general biology, nursing sciences, social sciences, social work, wildlife management; 340 teachers; 4,294 students; Chancellor ENRIQUE ALVARADO (acting); Registrar JORGE ACEVEDO; Library Dir Prof. FELIX NERIS BAEZ.

Universidad de Puerto Rico Recinto de Mayagüez (Mayagüez Campus): Apdo 9000, Mayagüez PR 00681-9000; tel. (787) 832-4040; fax (787) 834-3031; e-mail rectoria@uprm.edu; internet www.uprm.edu; f. 1911 as College of Agriculture at Mayagüez, present status 1966; 4 academic units: colleges of agricultural sciences, arts and sciences, business administration, engineering; 800 teachers; 12,264 students; Pres. JORGE I. VÉLEZ AROCHO (acting); Dean for Academic Affairs MILDRED CHAPARRO; Dean for Students VÍCTOR SIBERIO TORRES; Sec. JOANNE R. SAVINO.

Universidad de Puerto Rico en Ponce (University of Puerto Rico at Ponce): POB 7186, Ponce PR 00732-7186; tel. (787) 844-8181; fax (787) 840-8679; internet www.uprp.edu; f. 1970; programmes in civil engineering (architectural delineation and technology construction), industrial engineering, natural science (biodiversity assessment, biotechnology, coastal marine environment assessment), physical therapy; 204 teachers; 3,265 students; Chancellor IRMA RODRÍGUEZ-VEGA; Registrar AIDA HERNÁNDEZ.

Universidad de Puerto Rico en Río Piedras (University of Puerto Rico at Rio Piedras): POB 21907, San Juan PR 00931-1907; tel. (787) 764-0000; fax (787) 764-3680; e-mail amaortiz@uprrp.edu; internet www.uprrp.edu; f. 1903; colleges and schools of architecture, business administration, communication, education, general studies, humanities, law, natural sciences, planning, school of sciences and information technology, social sciences; system of 29 libraries; 19,000 students; Rector ANA R. GUADALUPE; Dean for Academic Affairs Dra SONIA BALET; Dean for Admin. JOSEPH J. ESTRADA PEÑA.

Recinto de Ciencias Médicas (Medical Sciences Campus): Apdo 365067, San Juan PR 00936-5067; tel. (787) 758-2525; internet www.upr.edu/frames/rcm/index.htm; f. 1926; promotes education integrated with practice and experimentation; offers multiple programmes of study in the health field incl. assoc. degrees, bachelor degrees, post-baccalaureate certificates, masters, doctoral, residences, post-doctoral degrees; 762 teachers; 2,365 students; Chancellor JOSÉ R. CARLO (acting); Registrar ELIZABETH SÁNCHEZ; Librarian FRANCISCA CORRADA.

UNIVERSIDAD DEL SAGRADO CORAZÓN (University of Sacred Heart)

POB 12383, San Juan PR 00914-0383
Telephone: (787) 728-1515
Fax: (787) 728-1692
E-mail: admision@sagrado.edu
Internet: www.sagrado.edu

Founded 1935
Private control
Language of instruction: Spanish

Pres.: Dr JOSÉ JAIME RIVERA
Dean of Academic and Student Affairs: Dr CÉSAR REY
Dean of Admin.: LOURDES BERTRÁN
Library Dir: SONIA DÍAZ LATORRE

Number of teachers: 151 (full-time), 225 (part-time)
Number of students: 4,943

DIRECTORS

Department of Business Administration: Prof. YEZMIN HERNÁNDEZ
Department of Communications: Prof. MARÍA T. MARTÍNEZ
Department of Continuing Education: ELVIA AGOSTO
Department of Education: Prof. FERNANDO PIERAS
Department of Humanities: Prof. IRMA HERNÁNDEZ
Department of Natural Sciences: Dr CARMEN PADIAL
Department of Social Sciences: Lic. ROSA RAQUEL RUIZ
Evening Programmes: NOEMÍ TORRES

Colleges

Conservatorio de Música de Puerto Rico (Conservatory of Music of Puerto Rico): 350 Calle Rafael Lamar, San Juan, PR 00918; tel. (787) 751-0160; fax (787) 766-1216; e-mail rectoria@cmpr.gobierno.pr; internet www.cmpr.edu; f. 1959; performance, composition, jazz and teacher training; library: 40,000 items; 140 teachers; 1,600 students; Pres. MARIA CRISTINA FIRPI; Vice-Pres. RAFAEL IRIZARRY CUEBAS; Rector MARIA DEL CARMEN GIL; Library Dir DAMARIS CORDERO.

Facultad de Derecho (Faculty of Law): Apdo 70351, San Juan PR 00936-8351; tel. (787) 751-1912; fax (787) 751-2975; e-mail oicruz@inter.edu; internet www.derecho.inter.edu; f. 1961 as a night school; attached to InterAmerican Univ. of Puerto Rico; language of instruction: Spanish; library: 170,000 vols; 610 students; 28 full-time and 22 part-time teachers; Dean Prof. LUIS MARIANO NEGRÓN PORTILLO.

Recinto de Aguadilla (Aguadilla Campus): POB 20000, Aguadilla PR 00605-2000; tel. (787) 891-0925; fax (787) 882-3020; internet www.aguadilla.inter.edu; f. 1957, present status 1991; attached to InterAmerican Univ. of Puerto Rico; graduate-level programmes; promotes social commitment, cultural appreciation, environmental awareness, critical thinking, handling of multi-manner communication skills, skilful use of technology; Chancellor Dr JUAN A. APONTE; Rector Dr ELIE E. AGÉSILAS; Registrar MIRIAM MARCIAL.

Recinto de Arecibo (Arecibo Campus): POB 4050, Arecibo PR 00614-4050; tel. (787) 878-5475; fax (787) 880-1624; internet www.arecibo.inter.edu; f. 1957; non-univ. post-secondary academic programmes; undergraduate and graduate studies; research; 4,700 students (postgraduate); Chancellor Dra JEAN MARIE GONZÁLEZ; Rector RAFAEL RAMÍREZ RIVERA; Dean of Studies Dra KAREN WOOLWOCK; Registrar CARMEN RODRÍGUEZ; Dir for Information Centre SARA ABREU.

Recinto de Barranquitas (Barranquitas Campus): POB 517, Barranquitas PR 00794; tel. (787) 857-3600; fax (787) 857-2244; internet www.br.inter.edu; f. 1957; attached to InterAmerican Univ. of Puerto Rico; offers programmes in education, social sciences and the humanities which foster the devt of competent professionals, efficient and equipped with knowledge, skills and attitudes; stimulates interest in the natural sciences, mathematics, technology and health sciences; develops professionals in the field of business administration and related brs; 1,700 students; Rector IRENE FERNÁNDEZ; Dean of Studies Dr PATRICIA ALVAREZ SWIHART; Registrar MARIBEL DÍAZ PEÑA; Dir for the Information Centre MARIBEL LÓPEZ.

Recinto de Bayamón (Bayamón Campus): 500 Carretera Dr John Will Harris, Bayamón PR 00957-6257; tel. (787) 279-1912; fax (787) 279-2205; e-mail interbcinfo@bc.inter.edu; internet bc.inter.edu; f. 1956, present name and status 1991; attached to InterAmerican Univ. of Puerto Rico; programmes with emphasis on technology, engineering, aviation, computing, communications, science and business administration; 5,000 students; Chancellor Prof. MARILINA WAYLAND; Rector JUAN MARTÍNEZ; Dean of Studies Dr OMAR CUETO; Registrar EDDIE AYALA; Dir for Information Centre EDUARDO ORTIZ.

Recinto de Fajardo (Fajardo Campus): POB 70003, Fajardo PR 00738-7003; tel. (787) 863-2390; fax (787) 860-3470; internet fajardo.inter.edu; f. 1912; attached to InterAmerican Univ. of Puerto Rico; Pres. MANUEL J. FERNÓS.

Recinto de Guayama (Guayama Campus): POB 10004, Guayama PR 00784-4004; tel. (787) 864-2222; fax (787) 866-1176; e-mail ccolon@inter.edu; internet guayama.inter.edu; f. 1956, present status 1993; attached to InterAmerican Univ. of Puerto Rico; depts of business administration, education and social sciences, health sciences, humanities, natural and applied sciences; Rector CARLOS E. COLÓN RAMOS; Dean of Students RIOS-ESTRELLA MENDEZ.

Recinto Metro (Metropolitan Campus): Apdo 191293, San Juan PR 00936-1293; tel. (787) 250-1912; fax (787) 250-0782; e-mail webmaster.metro@inter.edu; internet www.metro.inter.edu; f. 1912; attached to InterAmerican Univ. of Puerto Rico; faculties of economics and administrative sciences, education and professional conduct, humanistic studies, science and technology; 626 teachers; 10,613 students; Pres. Atty J. MANUEL FERNÓS; Rector Prof. MARILINA LUCCA WAYLAND.

Recinto de Ponce (Ponce Campus): 104 Turpeaux Ind Park, Ponce PR 00715-1602; tel. (787) 284-1912; fax (787) 841-0103; internet ponce.inter.edu; f. 1962; attached to InterAmerican Univ. of Puerto Rico; depts of business administration, graduate studies, health sciences, humanistic studies, pedagogical studies, science and technology, social and behavioural sciences; 5,000 students; Rector Dra VILMA E. COLÓN ACOSTA.

Recinto de San Germán (San Germán Campus): POB 5100, San Germán PR 00683; tel. (787) 264-1912; fax (787) 892-6350; e-mail eberroca@sg.inter.edu; internet www.sg.inter.edu; attached to InterAmerican Univ. of Puerto Rico; depts of biology, chemistry and environmental sciences, business and management, education and physical education, fine arts, health sciences, languages and literature, mathematics and applied sciences, social sciences and liberal arts; Rector Prof. AGNES MOJICA.

School of Optometry: 500 John Will Harris Ave, Rd 830, Bayamón PR 00957-6257; tel. (787) 765-1915; fax (787) 756-7351; e-mail admissions@inter.edu; internet www.optonet.inter.edu; f. 1981, present status 1992; f. 1981; attached to InterAmerican Univ. of Puerto Rico; language of instruction: Spanish; offers a four-year professional programme leading to the degree of Dr of Optometry; Dean Dr HÉCTOR SANTIAGO; Dean for Admin. Dr FRANCISCO RIVERA MEDINA; Dir for Information Centre ROSA M. ROSARIO.

UNITED STATES VIRGIN ISLANDS

Regulatory Body

GOVERNMENT

Department of Education: 1834 Kongens Gade, St Thomas VI 00802; tel. (340) 774-0100; fax (340) 779-7153; e-mail llarsen@sttj.k12.vi; internet www.doe.vi; Commr Dr LAVERNE TERRY.

Learned Societies

BIBLIOGRAPHY, LIBRARY SCIENCE AND MUSEOLOGY

Virgin Islands Library Association: POB 446, Kingshill VI 00851-0446; tel. (340) 692-4132; fax (340) 692-4135.

HISTORY, GEOGRAPHY AND ARCHAEOLOGY

St Croix Landmarks Society: 52 Estate Whim, Frederiksted, St Croix VI 00840; tel. (340) 772-0598; fax (340) 772-9446; e-mail info@stcroixlandmarks.org; internet www.stcroixlandmarks.org; f. 1948; preserves heritage sites in St Croix; attached museums: Christiansted Apothecary Hall, Lawaetz Museum and the Whim Plantation Museum; library of 6,000 vols of books, holdings incl. traditional research resources such as artwork, collns of photographs, maps and MSS, drawings of the Virgin Islands by Henry Morton (1843–44) and Dr Allen Voorhees Lesley (1856), extensive photographic colln from Axel Ovesen (1902–72), street scenes from Christiansted and Frederiksted and images of bldgs from both the towns and country estates in the 19th and 20th centuries; Exec. Dir SONIA JACOBS DOW.

St Thomas Historical Trust: POB 6707, St Thomas VI 00804; tel. (340) 774-5541; e-mail info@stthomashistoricaltrust.org; internet www.stthomashistoricaltrust.org; advocacy and education; identifies, protects and preserves historical sites, structures and cultural heritage of St Thomas; Pres. RONALD S. LOCKHART; Vice-Pres. JOANN BOZZUTO; Sec. CAROL FAVA; Treas. FRANK MCCONNELL.

MEDICINE

US Virgin Islands Medical Society (VIMS): POB 5986, Sunny Isle, St Croix; tel. (340) 712-2402; fax (340) 712-2449; e-mail vimedicalsociety@hotmail.com; internet www.vimipro.org/links/vims.html; f. 1955; represents physicians of the Virgin Islands; affiliated to American Medical Assn and Nat. Medical Assn; Pres. RONALD C. NIMMO; Pres.-Elect RAYMOND CINTRON; Exec. Sec. and Treas. CORA L. E. CHRISTIAN; Sec. GILBERT COMMISSIONG; Treas. ALFRED O. HEATH.

NATURAL SCIENCES

St Croix Environmental Association: 5032 Anchor Way, Suite 3, Christiansted, St Croix VI 00820; tel. (340) 773-1989; fax (340) 773-7545; e-mail info.atsea@gmail.com; internet www.stxenvironmental.org; f. 1986; advocacy, research and programmes in conservation and education for a sustainable environment; 500 mems; Chair. ROGER HOSS; Vice-Chair. RYAN SMITH; Exec. Dir PAUL CHAKROFF; Programme Dir CAROL CRAMER-BURKE; Sec. JENNIFER MARTIN; Treas. JAMES NEALON.

Research Institutes

GENERAL

Virgin Islands Sustainable Farm Institute (VISFI): St Croix; e-mail rebecca@visfi.org; internet www.visfi.org; f. 2003; community education in environmental sustainability; promotes agroecology and creation of sustainable life systems; Founder and Exec. Dir BEN JONES; Dir of Operations DAN GLENN.

MEDICINE

Virgin Islands Medical Institute, Inc.: 1AD Diamond Ruby, POB 5989, Sunny Isle, Christiansted VI 00823-5989; tel. (340) 712-2400; fax (340) 712-2449; e-mail askvimi@viqio.sdps.org; internet www.vimipro.org; researches and documents areas of devt and improvement in health care; monitors the quality of the health care system on the Islands; non-profit org; Pres. KENDALL GRIFFITH; Vice-Pres. DEREK BURNETT; Sec. LEONARD W. BONELLI SR; Treas. ALFRED O. HEATH; Medical Dir CORA L. E. CHRISTIAN; publ. *Medicare Watch* (1 a year).

NATURAL SCIENCES

Water Resources Research Institute: 2 John Brewer's Bay, St Thomas VI 00802-9990; tel. (340) 693-1021; fax (340) 693-1025; e-mail hsmith@uvi.edu; internet www.uvi.edu/sites/uvi/pages/wrri-home.aspx; f. 1973; attached to Univ. of the Virgin Islands; research, information dissemination and training on water resources and related areas; Dir Dr HENRY H. SMITH.

Libraries and Archives

St Croix

Virgin Islands Public Library System: 1122 King St, Christiansted, St Croix VI 00820; tel. (340) 773-5715; fax (340) 773-5327 23 Dronningens Gade, St. Thomas VI 00802; tel. (340) 774-3407; fax (340) 775-1887; e-mail dlmdir@vipowernet.net; internet www.virginislandspubliclibraries.org; attached to Dept of Planning and Natural Resources—Div. of Libraries, Archives and Museums; depository of govt records; preserves historical and public records; spec. colins: Von Scholten Colln, located at the Enid; Baa Public Library and Archives in St Thomas, Caribbean Colln of the Florence Williams Public Library in St Croix; houses books, MSS, pamphlets; newspapers on microfilm; church records incl. birth and death certificates, other archival materials; Territorial Dir INGRID A. BOUGH; Asst Dir DONALD G. COLE.

Public Libraries:

Athalie McFarlane Petersen Public Library: Strand St, Frederiksted, St Croix VI 00840; tel. (340) 772-0315; f. 1803; fmr private residence; Victorian architecture.

Elaine I. Sprauve Public Library: POB 30, Enighed Estate, St John VI 00831; tel. (340) 776-6359; f. 1980; temporarily closed for renovation; Head Librarian CAROL MCGUINNESS.

Enid M. Baa Public Library: 20 Dronningens Gade, St. Thomas VI 00802; tel. (340) 774-0630; f. 1920 fmrly the St Thomas library, renamed after Enid Baa 1978.

Florence Williams Public Library: 1122 King St, Christiansted, St Croix VI 00820; tel. (340) 773-5715; 30,000 vols.

VI Regional Library for the Blind & Physically Handicapped (Talking Books Library): 3012 Golden Rock, Christiansted, St Croix VI 00820; tel. (340) 772-2250; free service available to people of all ages with low vision, blindness or physical handicaps; Head Librarian LETITIA GITTENS.

Museums and Art Galleries

St Croix

Fort Frederik–Frederiksfort: Waterfront, Frederiksted, St Croix VI 00840; tel. (340) 772-2021; f. in the 18th century (1752–1760) by the Danish govt to protect St Croix against invasion of pirates, smugglers and European invaders; named after Frederik V of Denmark; deep red rubble and masonry fort represents classic Danish military architecture of the period; indoor exhibits display colonial military life; listed in the Nat. Register for Historic Places in 1996 and Nat. Historic Landmark in 1997.

St John

Bajo el Sol Gallery: Mongoose Junction, Cruz Bay; tel. (340) 693-7070; fax (340) 715-4841; e-mail bajoelsol@pennswoods.net; internet www.bajoelsolgallery.com; f. 1993; ceramics, jewellery, painting, sculpture and works by local artists.

Galeria del Mar: Wharfside Village, Cruz Bay; tel. (340) 693-9399; fax (340) 693-9599; Caribbean fine arts and crafts gallery featuring original works and ltd edn prints by local artists, glasswork, pottery and wood sculptures.

Ivan Jadan Museum: 251 Contant, POB 84, Cruz Bay, St John VI 00831; tel. (340) 776-6423; fax (340) 779-4323; e-mail ijadan@islands.vi; internet www.ijadan.vi; 5,000 artefacts relating to the life of Russian tenor Ivan Jadan; colins incl. books, historical documents, photographs and videos; Curator DORIS JADAN.

St Thomas

American Caribbean Historical Museum: 32 Raadets Gade, Charlotte Amalie, St Thomas; tel. (340) 714-5150; history of the Virgin Islands since 15th century; exhibits incl. artefacts, documents, historic costumes, photographs.

Fort Christian and Virgin Islands Museum: Waterfront, Charlotte Amalie, St Thomas; tel. (340) 776-4566; historic museum housed within Fort Christian, the oldest standing structure in St Thomas (built in 1672); exhibits incl. antique maps, handmade West Indian furnishings, military hardware, natural history colln, period furniture; attached art gallery; added to Nat. Register of Historic Places in 1977.

University

UNIVERSITY OF THE VIRGIN ISLANDS

St Croix Campus: RR 1, POB 10000, Kingshill VI 00850-9781

Telephone: (340) 692-4158*St Thomas Campus*: 2 John Brewer's Bay, St Thomas VI 00802-9990

Telephone: (340) 693-150

E-mail: pr@uvi.edu

Internet: www.uvi.edu

Founded 1962 as College of the Virgin Islands, present name and status 1986

Pres.: Dr LaVerne E. Ragster

Vice-Pres. for Admin. and Finance: Vincent O. Paul

Vice-Pres. for Institutional Advancement: Dr Henry H. Smith

Provost: Dr Al Hassan I. Musah

Vice-Provost for Access and Enrolment: Dr Judith Edwin

Vice-Provost for Research and Public Service: Dr Henry H. Smith

Dir of Libraries: Jennifer Jackson

Library: St Croix Campus: 53,000 vols, 167 periodicals; St Thomas campus: 80,500 vols, 690 periodicals, 590,000 microforms, 15,000 US govt documents, 20,000 other items; spec. collns: Virgin Islands Digital Colln, Ralph D. DeChabert Spec. Colln

Number of teachers: 270

Number of students: 2,500

Publications: *Graduate Bulletin* (1 a year), *The Caribbean Writer* (1 a year), *UVI Magazine* (1 a year)

DEANS

Division of Business Administration: Michael Vineyard

Division of Education: Dr Joane W. McKay

Division of Humanities and Social Sciences: George Lord

Division of Nursing: Dr Cheryl Franklin

Division of Science and Mathematics: Dr Camille McKayle

URUGUAY

The Higher Education System

Institutions of higher education date from after Uruguay's independence from Spain in 1825, the oldest being Universidad de la República, which was founded in 1849. The next oldest institution is Universidad del Trabajo de Uruguay, which was founded in 1878. All education, including university tuition, is provided free of charge. Higher education is provided by public universities (universidades públicas), private universities (universidades privadas), university institutes (institutos universitarios), public non-university higher institutions (institutos terciarios no universitario públicos) and private non-university higher institutions (institutos terciarios no universitario privados). There were six public universities and their equivalents in 2005 with 72,100 students. In 2006 there were four private universities, 11 university institutes (private), 12 public non-university institutes and five private non-university institutes.

The main requirement for admission to higher education is the main secondary school award, the Bachillerato Diversificado, with specialization depending on the degree applied for. Intermediate degrees (carreras intermedios) last two-and-a-half to three years and often culminate with the award of a professional title; students may then graduate to full undergraduate degrees. Undergraduate degrees (carreras de grado) usually last four years and lead to the award of Título de Licenciado in the subject studied. Professional degrees, such as Licenciado en Enfermería (nursing), Licenciado en Nutrición (nutrition) and Licenciado en Psicología (psychology) last upwards of five years. Medical degrees last eight years, and students receive the title Doctor en Medicina. The first postgraduate degree is the especialización (specialist course), a course lasting one year, which leads to the titles Título de Especialista or the Título de Diplomado. The Masters (Título de Maestría) is a two-year programme of study; students are required to submit a thesis in the second year to complete the degree. Finally, the highest level of postgraduate study is at doctoral level, where students work for three years to achieve the Doctorate (Doctorado).

The Consejo de Educación Técnico y Professional—Universidad de Trabajo is responsible for providing post-secondary technical and vocational education (although, despite what its name might suggest, it does not offer degree-level qualifications). The primary qualification awarded at this level is the Título Técnico in the subject studied.

Uruguay is a Mercosur state and therefore participates in the El Mecanismo Experimental de Acreditación de Carreras del Mercosur, which has so far accredited programmes in agronomy, medicine and engineering. However, Uruguay is the only member of Mercosur that does not have a national accreditation or quality assurance agency.

Regulatory Body

GOVERNMENT

Ministry of Education and Culture: Reconquista 535, 11000 Montevideo; tel. and fax (2) 9161016; e-mail rpi@mec.gub.uy; internet www.mec.gub.uy; Min. RICARDO EHRLICH; Gen. Dir Dr JAIME RUBEN SAPOLINSKI.

Learned Societies

AGRICULTURE, FISHERIES AND VETERINARY SCIENCE

Asociación Rural del Uruguay (Rural Association): Avda Uruguay 864, Montevideo; tel. (2) 902-04-84; fax (2) 902-04-89; internet www.aru.org.uy; f. 1871; 3,000 mems; library of 3,000 vols; Pres. Dr FERNANDO ALFONSO; publ. *Revista* (12 a year).

ARCHITECTURE AND TOWN PLANNING

Sociedad de Arquitectos del Uruguay (Society of Architects): Gonzalo Ramírez 2030, 11200 Montevideo; tel. (2) 419-34-63; e-mail sau@sau.org.uy; internet www.sau.org.uy; f. 1914; 2,000 mems; library of 2,000 vols; Pres. Arq. JOSÉ OLIVER; Exec. Sec. Arq. GRICELDA BARRIOS; publ. *Boletín de Arquitectura* (6 a year).

BIBLIOGRAPHY, LIBRARY SCIENCE AND MUSEOLOGY

Agrupación Bibliotecológica del Uruguay (Library Association): Cerro Largo 1666, 11200 Montevideo; tel. (2) 400-57-40; f. 1960; activities incl. library science, archives, documentation, bibliography, history and numismatics; 238 mems; Pres. LUIS ALBERTO MUSSO; publs *Anales del Senado del Uruguay-Cronología* (2nd edition), *Aportes para la historia de la bibliotecología en el Uruguay*, *Archivos del Uruguay*, *Artigas en la medalla Inventario de una colección*, *Bibliografía básica de la historia de la República Oriental del Uruguay*, *Bibliografía bibliográfica y bibliotecología*, *Bibliografía de Bibliografías uruguayas*, *Bibliografía de Luis Alberto Musso*, *Bibliografía del Poder Legislativo desde sus comienzos hasta el año 1965*, *Bibliografía uruguaya sobre Brasil*, *Bibliografía Uruguaya sobre Historia Argentina*, *Bibliografía y documentación en el Uruguay*, *Breves apuntes para la historia del microfilm*, *Canarios en el Uruguay*, *Colonización canaria en la Banda Oriental*, *De Libros y Lectores*, *Documentalistas Uruguayos*, *El Río de la Plata en el Archivo de Indias*, *Fernández Saldaña. Obra bibliográfica*, *Historiografía y Bibliografía sobre los canarios en el Uruguay*, *Indice de la Revista Jurídica 'Los Debates'*, *Indice de la Revista Jurídica 'La Revista Nueva'*, *Indice Suplemento Diario 'El Día'*, *La Estrella del Sur*, *La Revista Nueva*, *Legislación Uruguaya sobre Brasil*, *Los cabildantes canarios de Montevideo*, *Uruguay, Brasil y sus Medallas*.

Asociación de Bibliotecólogos del Uruguay (Uruguayan Librarians' Association): Eduardo V. Haedo 2255, 11200 Montevideo; tel. (2) 409-99-89; fax (2) 409-99-89; e-mail abu@adinet.com.uy; f. 1978; 300 mems; Pres. Lic. ALICIA OCASO FERREIRA; publ. *Panel de Noticias*.

HISTORY, GEOGRAPHY AND ARCHAEOLOGY

Instituto Histórico y Geográfico del Uruguay: Río Negro 1495/a. 202, Montevideo; e-mail histogeo@adinet.com.uy; f. 1843; 40 academicians; Pres. Prof. EDMUNDO M. NARANCIO; publ. *Revista*.

LANGUAGE AND LITERATURE

Academia Nacional de Letras (National Academy of Literature): Ituzaingó 1255, 11000 Montevideo; tel. (2) 915-23-74; fax (2) 916-74-60; e-mail academia@montevideo.com.uy; internet www.mec.gub.uy/academiadeletras; f. 1943; researches in Spanish language, mainly lexicography, especially Uruguayan spoken Spanish; also Uruguayan literature; organizes lectures, readings of Uruguayan literature, workshops; contributes to comprehensive works elaborated within the ASALE (Asociación de Academias de la Lengua Española) such as the Nueva Gramática de la lengua española, Diccionario de Americanismos, Ortografía de la lengua española, etc.; 19 mems, 33 corresp. mems; Pres. Dr WILFREDO PENCO; Sec. Dr ADOLFO ELIZAINCÍN; publs *Boletín*, *Ensayos Literarios*, *Revista de la Academia Nacional de Letras*.

Alliance Française: Bulevar Artigas 1229, Montevideo; tel. (2) 400-05-05; fax (2) 400-05-05 ext. 220; e-mail info@alliancefrancaise.edu.uy; internet www.alliancefrancaise.edu.uy; f. 1923; offers courses and examinations in French language and culture and promotes cultural exchange with France; attached teaching centres in Artigas, Colonia, Florida, Maldonado, Melo, Mercedes, Montevideo, Paysandú, Rocha, Salto, San José, Tacuarembó and Trinidad; Pres. PEDRO NICOLÁS BARIDON; Dir YVES MAHÉ.

Goethe-Institut: Canelones 1524, 11200 Montevideo; tel. (2) 410-58-13; fax (2) 410-44-32; e-mail info@montevideo.goethe.org; internet www.goethe.de/montevideo; offers courses and examinations in German language and culture and promotes cultural exchange with Germany; library of 8,000 vols, 23 periodicals; Dir MIKKO FRITZE.

MEDICINE

Academia Nacional de Medicina del Uruguay: 18 de Julio 2175, 5° piso, Montevideo; tel. (2) 408-41-03; fax (2) 401-60-58; e-mail academiamed@adinet.com.uy; f. 1976; 26 mems; Dir Dr ROBERTO DE BELLIS; publ. *Boletín* (1 a year).

Asociación Odontológica Uruguaya (Odontological Association): Avda Durazno 937-39, Montevideo; tel. and fax (2) 900-15-72; e-mail aou@adinet.com.uy; internet www.aou.org.uy; f. 1946; 3,000 mems; comprises 8 depts and 6 sections; museum; library of 6,000 vols; Pres. Dr ALVARO RODA; Sec. Dr RAFAEL PÉREZ; publs *Boletín Informativo* (12 a year), *Odontología Uruguaya* (2 a year).

Sociedad de Cirugía del Uruguay (Surgical Society): Canelones 2280, Montevideo CP 11200; tel. (2) 402-68-20; fax (2) 403-05-32; e-mail scu@cirugia-uy.com; internet cirugia-uy.com; f. 1920; scientific sessions, meetings, continuous education, annual Uruguayan congress of surgery; 443 mems; library of 2,800 vols; Pres. Dr MARIO BOUNOUS; Vice-Pres. Dr MARIO BURGER; Sec.-Gen. Dra MONICA CARABALLO; publ. *Cirugía del Uruguay* (3 a year).

Sociedad de Radiología e Imagenología del Uruguay: Julio César 1460 bis, Montevideo; tel. and fax (2) 481-17-14; e-mail sriu@adinet.com.uy; internet www.sriu.org.uy; f. 1923; scientific activity linked to the Médicos Imagenólogos; holds conferences and seminars; 150 mems; Pres. Dr IVONNE MARTINEZ; Sec. Dr LUIS DIBARBOURE; publ. *Revista de Imagenología del Uruguay*.

Attached Institutes:

Gremial Uruguaya de Médicos Radiólogos: Montevideo; f. 1972; 70 mems; Pres. Dr ERNESTO H. CIBILS.

Sociedad Uruguaya de Historia de la Medicina: Casilla de Correo 157, Montevideo; tel. (2) 401-47-01; fax (2) 409-16-03; e-mail histmed@fmed.edu.uy; f. 1971; research on history of medicine and allied sciences; 80 mems; Pres. Prof. Dr FERNANDO MAÑÉ GARZÓN; Sec. Dr JUAN I. GIL; publ. *Sesiones de la Sociedad Uruguaya* (1 a year).

Sociedad Uruguaya de Pediatría (Paediatrics Society): Centro Hospitalario Pereira Rossell, Bulevar Artigas 1550, Montevideo; tel. (2) 709-18-01; fax (2) 708-52-13; e-mail pedsoc@adinet.com.uy; internet www.sup.org.uy; f. 1915, 500 mems, affiliated to the Asociación Latino Americana de Pediatría; library of 3,500 vols, 6,500 periodicals; Pres. Dr ÁLVARO GALIANA; Sec. Dr DANIEL BORBONET; publ. *Archivos de Pediatría del Uruguay* (4 a year).

NATURAL SCIENCES

Biological Sciences

Sociedad Malacológica del Uruguay (Malacological Society): Casilla 1401, 11000 Montevideo; e-mail smu@adinet.com.uy; internet moluscos.net/smu; f. 1957; 210 mems; Pres. JORGE BROGGI; Sec. JUAN CARLOS ZAFFARONI; publ. *Comunicaciones* (2 a year).

Sociedad Zoológica del Uruguay: Casilla 10739, 11200, Montevideo; tel. (2) 525-86-18; fax (2) 525-86-17; internet www.serpentario.edu.uy/szu; f. 1961; 200 mems; Pres. RAÚL MANEYRO; Sec. FEDERICO ACHAVAL; publ. *Boletín* (irregular, online).

TECHNOLOGY

Academia Nacional de Ingeniería: Cuareim 1492, Montevideo; tel. (2) 901-17-62; fax (2) 900-89-51; e-mail cutinella@redfacil.com.uy; internet www.artech.com.uy/aniu; f. 1965; 40 full mems; Pres. Ing. ALVARO CUTINELLA; Sec. Ing. EDISON GARCÍA REGUEIRO.

Asociación de Ingenieros del Uruguay (Association of Uruguayan Engineers): Cuareim 1492, Montevideo; tel. (2) 901-17-62; fax (2) 900-89-51; e-mail asocing@adinet.com.uy; internet www.aiu.org.uy; f. 1905; 1,400 mems, also hon. and corresp. mems abroad; Pres. Ing. EDUARDO ALVAREZ MAZZA; Sec. Ing. CARLOS MALCUORI; affiliated to the Unión Panamericana de Asociaciones de Ingenieros; library of 2,000 vols; publ. *Revista de Ingeniería*.

Research Institutes

GENERAL

Dirección Nacional de Ciencia, Tecnología y Innovación (DINACYT): Paraguay 1470, Piso 2, 11100 Montevideo; tel. (2) 901-42-85; fax (2) 902-48-70; e-mail webmaster@dicyt.gub.uy; internet www.dicyt.gub.uy; f. 1961 to encourage research in all branches of knowledge, especially scientific, technological and innovation policies; fmrly Consejo Nacional de Investigaciones Científicas y Técnicas (CONICYT); 14 council mems; library of 7,000 vols, 275 periodicals; Gen. Dir Dr AMILCAR DAVYT; publs *Boletín electrónico* (52 a year), *Claro Que Se Puede* (irregular), *El Proceso de Innovación en la Industria Uruguaya* (every 2 years), *Indicadores de Ciencia y Tecnología* (irregular).

UNESCO Office Montevideo and Regional Office for Science in Latin America and the Caribbean: Casilla de correo 859, Montevideo; Edificio del MERCOSUR (ex Parque Hotel), Calle Dr Luis Piera 1992 (2° piso), 11200 Montevideo; tel. (2) 413-20-75; fax (2) 413-20-94; e-mail montevideo@unesco.org.uy; internet www.unesco.org.uy; f. 1949; designated Cluster Office for Argentina, Brazil, Paraguay, Uruguay; coordinates UNESCO's programmes in the region, particularly: basic sciences, environmental and water sciences, science, technology and society, earth sciences and natural hazards, marine sciences, information and communication, education, culture and world heritage; Dir JORGE GRANDI.

AGRICULTURE, FISHERIES AND VETERINARY SCIENCE

Centro de Investigaciones Pesqueras y Piscicultura (Fisheries and Fish-farming Research Institute): c/o DINARA, Villa Constitución, Salto; internet www.dinara.gub.uy; attached to State Office for Aquatic Resources; Nat. Dir for Aquatic Resources DANIEL MONTIEL.

Instituto Nacional de Investigación Agropecuaria (National Agricultural Research Institute): Andes 1365, Piso 12 CP, 11100 Montevideo; tel. (2) 902-05-50; fax (2) 902-36-33; internet www.inia.org.uy; f. 1914; library of 12,000 vols, 1,000 periodicals; Dir MARIO ALLEGRI; publs *Boletín de Divulgación*, *Hojas de Divulgación*, *Serie Actividades de Difusión*, *Serie Técnica*.

ECONOMICS, LAW AND POLITICS

Centro de Estadísticas Nacionales y Comercio Internacional del Uruguay (CENCI Uruguay): Juncal 1327D, Oficina 1603, Montevideo; tel. (2) 915-29-30; fax (2) 915-45-78; e-mail cenci@cenci.com.uy; internet www.cenci.com.uy; f. 1956; provides economic and statistical information on all American countries; operates computer programmes handling the import tariffs on commodities; library of 900 vols; Dir KENNETH BRUNNER; publs *Anuario estadístico sobre el intercambio comercial* (1 a year), *Boletines: Noticias Latinoamericanas*, *Dictámenes de Clasificación Arancelaria—MERCOSUR*, *Estudios del Mercado*, *Industrias por sectores de actividad*, *Manual práctico Aduanero* (52 a year), *Manual práctico del Contribuyente* (52 a year), *Manual práctico del Exportador* (52 a year), *Manual práctico del Importador* (52 a year), *Régimen de Origen–ALADI y MERCOSUR*.

Instituto Nacional de Estadística (Statistical Office): Río Negro 1520, 11100 Montevideo; tel. (2) 902-73-03; fax (2) 903-28-81; e-mail difusion@ine.gub.uy; internet www.ine.gub.uy; f. 1852; library of 4,000 vols; Technical Dir Ec. ALICIA MELGAR; publs *Anuario Estadístico*, *Boletín Trimestral* (4 a year), *Encuesta Continua de Hogares*, *Síntesis Estadística*.

HISTORY, GEOGRAPHY AND ARCHAEOLOGY

Servicio Geográfico Militar (Military Geographical Institute): Avda 8 de Octubre 3255, 11600 Montevideo; tel. (2) 487-18-10; fax (2) 487-08-68; e-mail sgm@iau.gub.uy; f. 1913; geodesy, photogrammetry, geophysics and cartography; library of 3,500 vols; Dir Col ARTIGAS P. BACCI; publs *Boletín*, scale aeronautic and aerial maps.

MEDICINE

Instituto Nacional del Cáncer: Av. 8 de Octubre 3265 y Abreu, Montevideo; tel. (2) 481-36-25; f. 1960; Dir Dr ALBERTO VIOLA.

Liga Uruguaya contra la Tuberculosis (Anti-Tuberculosis League): Magallanes 1320, 11200 Montevideo; tel. (2) 408-35-70; fax (2) 400-55-75; e-mail ligatub@adinet.com.uy; f. 1902; specializes in combating tuberculosis in children and the elderly; library of 3,000 vols; Pres. MÁXIMO A. SAAVEDRA; Sec. Dr LORENZO PÍRIZ LOSTAO.

NATURAL SCIENCES

Biological Sciences

Instituto de Investigaciones Biológicas Clemente Estable: Avda Italia 3318, 11600 Montevideo; tel. (2) 487-16-16; fax (2) 487-55-48; e-mail asistentes@iibce.edu.uy; internet www.iibce.edu.uy; f. 1927; 12 divs, 3 depts; biological research; library of 12,000 vols; Pres. Dr GUSTAVO FOLLE.

Physical Sciences

Dirección Nacional de Meteorología del Uruguay (National Meteorological Directorate): Javier Barrios Amorín 1488, Casilla de Correo 64, 11200 Montevideo; tel. (2) 400-56-55; fax (2) 409-73-91; e-mail dnm25255@adinet.com.uy; internet www.meteorologia.com.uy; f. 1895; library of 6,000 vols, 13,800 documents; Dir RAUL MICHELINI; publs *Anuario Climatológico*, *Boletín Agrometeorológico*, *Boletín Pluviométrico*, *Notas Técnicas*.

Observatorio Astronómico de Montevideo (Montevideo Astronomical Observatory): Liceo No. 35 IAVA, J. E. Rodó y E. Acevedo, Montevideo; tel. (2) 408-58-25; f. 1927; library of 5,000 vols; Dir (vacant).

RELIGION, SOCIOLOGY AND ANTHROPOLOGY

Instituto Interamericano del Niño (Inter-American Children's Institute): Avda 8 de Octubre 2904, 11600 Montevideo; tel. (2) 487-21-50; fax (2) 487-32-42; e-mail iin@oas.org; internet www.iin.oea.org; f. 1927; specialized institute of the Organization of American States (OAS); library: specialized library of 50,000 vols, open to the public; computerized information centre; Pres. CAR-

MEN BERGÉS DE AMARO; Dir-Gen. ALEJANDRO BONASSO; publ. *Boletín*.

TECHNOLOGY

Dirección Nacional de Minería y Geología: Calle Hervidero 2861, CP 11800, Montevideo; tel. (2) 200-19-51; fax (2) 209-49-05; e-mail secretaria@dinamige.miem.gub.uy; internet www.dinamige.gub.uy; f. 1912; library of 3,000 vols; Dir Prof. PIER ROSSI; publ. *Industria Extractiva del Uruguay* (1 a year).

Dirección Nacional de Tecnología Nuclear: Mercedes 1041, 11100 Montevideo; tel. (2) 900-69-19; fax (2) 902-16-19; f. 1955 as Comisión Nacional de Energía Atómica; controls activities involving the use of radioactive materials or equipment producing ionizing radiation; prepares technical and safety rules for activities involving nuclear technology; liaises with national and international institutions on procedural aspects of nuclear technology; library of 3,500 vols; collection of microfiches; Dir ROSARIO ODINO; publs *Memoria* (1 a year), *Revista* (1 a year).

Instituto Uruguayo de Normas Técnicas (Uruguayan Standards Institution): Plaza Independencia 812, (2ºpiso), Montevideo; tel. (2) 901-20-48; fax (2) 902-16-81; e-mail unit-iso@unit.org.uy; internet www.unit.org.uy; f. 1939; standardization, certification, information on standards, training in high-level management; library of 250,000 vols; Dir Eng. PABLO BENIA; publ. *UNIT Standards*.

Libraries and Archives

Florida

Biblioteca Municipal: C/Barreiro 420, 94000 Florida; tel. and fax (35) 2-21-02; f. 1889; 42,000 vols; Dir FERNANDO GABRIEL GIORDANO FOLIGNO.

Montevideo

Archivo General de la Nación (National Archives): Calle Convención 1474, Montevideo; tel. (2) 900-72-32; fax (2) 908-13-30; e-mail agn@adinet.com.uy; internet www.mec.gub.uy/agn; f. 1926; 14,000 vols; Dir ABELARDO MANUAL GARCIA VIERA; publ. *Revista*.

Biblioteca Central y Publicaciones del Consejo de Educación Secundaria: Eduardo Acevedo 1427, 11200 Montevideo; tel. (2) 408-42-73; fax (2) 408-12-52; e-mail biblos@adinet.com.uy; internet www.ces.edu.uy/bibliotecacentral/bicentral.htm; f. 1885; secondary and higher education; 74,000 vols; collection of rare books.

Biblioteca del Museo Histórico Nacional (Library of the National Historical Museum): Rincón 437, 1000, Montevideo; f. 1940; 150,000 vols, 4,000 vols of MSS; specialization in the history of America and history of art; iconography, engravings, maps, numismatics; the entire library and Uruguayan collections of Dr Pablo Blanco Acevedo; Dir ELISA SILVA CAZET.

Biblioteca del Palacio Legislativo: Avda Libertador Brigadier Gral Lavalleja y Avda Gral Flores, Montevideo; f. 1929; legal deposit library in conjunction with National Library; 322,000 vols; specializes in jurisprudence; Dir LUIS H. BOIONS POMBO; publs *Bibliografía Uruguaya*, *Boletín Bibliográfico* (12 a year).

Biblioteca Municipal 'Dr Francisco Albero Schinca': 8 de Octubre 4210, Montevideo; tel. (2) 508-81-52; f. 1929; 14,000 vols; Dir GRACIELA NAVARRO.

Biblioteca Municipal 'Joaquín de Salterain': Solis 1456 e/ 25 de Mayo y Cerrito, Montevideo; tel. (2) 915-62-82; 36,000 vols; includes a slide library; Librarian GRACIELA FERNÁNDEZ RIBEIRO.

Biblioteca Nacional del Uruguay (National Library): Avda 18 de Julio 1790, Montevideo; tel. (2) 400-63-85; fax (2) 409-69-02; e-mail bibna@adinet.com.uy; internet www.bibna.gub.uy; f. 1816; 900,000 vols, 20,000 periodicals; comprises reference service, copyright office, legal deposit, Uruguayan and special materials, restoration of printed works, National Information System project, cultural extension; Dir-Gen. RAÚL RICARDO VALLARINO; publ. *Revista de la Biblioteca Nacional*.

Attached Institute:

Centro Nacional de Documentación Científica, Técnica y Económica: 18 de Julio 1790, Montevideo; tel. (2) 408-41-72; fax (2) 409-69-02; f. 1953; part of National Library; Dir ELENA CASTRO.

Biblioteca Pedagógica Central 'Mtro. Sebastián Morey Otero' (Pedagogic Library): Plaza de Cagancha 1175, Montevideo; tel. (2) 902-09-15; fax (2) 908-41-31; e-mail bepece@adinet.com.uy; f. 1889; 120,000 vols; Dir ANAIR MARTINOL; publs *Bibliografía Uruguaya sobre Educación*, *Información Bibliográfica* (2 a year), *Temas*, *Traducciones*.

Museums and Art Galleries

Montevideo

Museo de Descubrimiento: Zabala 1583 y Piedras, 11000 Montevideo; evokes the journeys of Cristóbal Colón, the meeting of the two worlds; maps, dioramas and photographs.

Museo Histórico Nacional (National Historical Museum): Casa Rivera, Calle Rincón 437, 11000 Montevideo; tel. (2) 915-10-51; fax (2) 915-68-63; e-mail mhistoricnac@mixmail.com; f. 1900; sectional collections of local Indian cultures (prehistoric, colonial epoch, development and political history of the country); portraits, relics, arms, documents, coins, medals, etc., relating to the Wars of Independence, British invasion, early revolutions, etc.; Dir Prof. ENRIQUE MENA SAGARRA; publ. *Revista Histórica*.

Museo Municipal de Bellas Artes 'Juan Manuel Blanes': Avda Millán 4015, 11700 Montevideo; tel. (2) 336-22-48; fax (2) 336-71-34; e-mail blanes@internet.com.uy; internet www.montevideo.gub.uy/museoblanes; f. 1928; paintings, drawings, wood-carvings, sculptures; Coordinator Arq. GABRIEL PELUFFO.

Museo Nacional de Artes Visuales (National Museum of Visual Arts): Julio Herrera y Reissig esq. Tomás Giribaldi s/n, Parque Rodó, 11300 Montevideo; tel. (2) 711-60-54; fax (2) 711-61-27; e-mail secretariamnav@gmail.com; internet www.mnav.gub.uy; f. 1911; 6,200 paintings, engravings, drawings, sculptures, ceramics; Dir Lic. JACQUELINE LACASA.

Museo Nacional de Historia Natural y Antropología (National Museum of Natural History and Anthropology): Casilla 399, 11000 Montevideo; tel. (2) 916-09-08; fax (2) 917-02-13; e-mail mnhn@internet.com.uy; internet www.mec.gub.uy/natura; f. 1837 as National Museum; zoology, botany, palaeontology, archaeology, ethnography, history of natural sciences; library of 250,000 vols; Dir ALVARO MONES; publs *Anales* (irregular), *Comunicaciones Antropológicas* (irregular), *Comunicaciones Botánicas* (irregular), *Comunicaciones Paleontológicas* (irregular), *Comunicaciones Zoológicas* (irregular), *Publicación Extra* (irregular).

Museo Pedagógico 'José Pedro Varela' (Pedagogic Museum): Plaza Cagancha 1175, Montevideo; tel. (2) 900-4744; fax (2) 908-4131; e-mail museopedagogico@gmail.com; internet www.cep.edu.uy; f. 1888; contains 5,000 exhibits, 2,000 photographs; library of 6,500 vols and periodicals; Dir SUSANA LUZARDO BRIANO; publ. *Boletín* (52 a year).

Museo y Archivo Histórico Municipal: Palacio del Cabildo, Calle Juan Carlos Gómez 1362, 11100 Montevideo; tel. (2) 915-96-85; fax (2) 915-96-85; e-mail museocabildo@correo.imm.gub.uy; f. 1915; permanent exhibition of the history of Montevideo from 1726; furniture, icons, paintings, jewellery and maps; library of 9,000 vols; Hon. Dir JORGE R. DELUCCHI; publ. *Anales*.

Museo y Jardin Botánico de Montevideo 'Prof. Atilio Lombardo': Avda 19 de Abril 1181, 11700 Montevideo; tel. (2) 336-40-05; fax (2) 336-64-88; e-mail botanico@adinet.com.uy; f. 1902; Dir Ing. Agr. PABLO B. ROSS.

Museo Zoológico 'Dámaso Antonio Larrañaga': Rambla República de Chile 4215, Montevideo; tel. (2) 622-02-58; f. 1956; instruction on national and exotic fauna; library of 2,000 specialized vols; 2,000 species of fauna and molluscs, etc.; Dir JUAN PABLO CUELLO.

San José de Mayo

Museo de Bellas Artes Departamental de San José: Calle Dr Julián Becerro de Bengoa 493, 80000 San José de Mayo; tel. 3642; paintings, drawings, sculptures, ceramics; f. 1947; school of art; library of 3,000 vols; Dir CÉSAR BERNESCONI; publ. *Notimuseo* (12 a year).

Tacuarembó

Museo del Indio y del Gaucho: General Artigas 256, Tacuarembó; affilated to the Museo Histórico de Montevideo; large collection representing ancient native crafts, weapons and other implements of the aboriginal Indians and gauchos; Founder and Dir WASHINGTON ESCOBAR.

Universities

UNIVERSIDAD CATÓLICA DEL URUGUAY

Avda 8 de Octubre 2738, 11600 Montevideo
Telephone: (2) 487-27-17
Fax: (2) 480-81-24
E-mail: relinter@ucu.edu.uy
Internet: www.ucu.edu.uy

Founded 1985
Private control
Academic year: March to November

Chancellor: Mgr NICOLÁS COTUGNO
Vice-Chancellor: Fr JOSÉ LUIS MOSCA
Rector: Fr EDUARDO CASAROTTI
Vice-Pres. for Academic: Dr ARIEL CUADRO
Vice-Pres. for Administrative: Cr. AUGUSTO BAYLEY
Vice-Pres. for Devt: Fr MARCELO COPPETTI
Vice-Pres. for Univ. Environment: Fr MARCELO COPPETTI
Librarian: Dra. SUSANA MONREAL

Number of teachers: 607
Number of students: 5,000

Publications: *Cuadernos de Negocios Internacionales e Integración*, *Prisma*, *Relaciones Laborales en el Uruguay*, *Revista de Derecho*, *Revista FCE (Facultad de*

Ciencias Empresariales), Revista Lazos, Revista Páginas del Área Educación

DEANS

Faculty of Business Administration: JOHN
Faculty of Dentistry: Dr WALTER LIEBER
Faculty of Engineering and Technology: Ing. OMAR PAGANINI
Faculty of Human Sciences: ADRIANA ARISTIMUÑO
Faculty of Law: Dr CARLOS BARBÉ
Faculty of Psychology: Mag. MARA GONZÁLEZ
Postgraduate Centre: Dr CARONLINA GREISING (Dir)

UNIVERSIDAD DE LA REPÚBLICA

Avda 18 de Julio 1968 (2° piso), 11200 Montevideo
Telephone: (2) 408-49-01
Fax: (2) 408-03-03
E-mail: secretar@oce.edu.uy
Internet: www.universidad.edu.uy
Founded 1849
State control
Language of instruction: Spanish
Academic year: March to December

Rector: Dr RODRIGO AROCENA
Vice-Rector: Dr ÁLVARO MAGLIA
Pro-Rector for Academic Affairs: Dr LUIS CALEGARI
Pro-Rector for Admin. Management: Dr RICARDO ROCA
Pro-Rector for Extension: Dr HUMBERTO TOMMASINO
Pro-Rector for Research: Dr GREGORY RANDALL
Sec.: MANUEL FLORES

Number of teachers: 6,130
Number of students: 81,774

Libraries with 1m. vols

DEANS

Faculty of Agronomy: Ing. Agr. FERNANDO GARCÍA PRÉCHAC
Faculty of Architecture: Arq. GUSTAVO SCHEPS
Faculty of Chemistry: Dr EDUARDO MANTA
Faculty of Dentistry: Dr HUGO CALABRIA
Faculty of Economics and Administration: Cr. WALTER ROSSI
Faculty of Engineering: Ing. ISMAEL PIEDRA CUEVA
Faculty of Humanities and Education: Prof. Dr JOSÉ SEOANE
Faculty of Law: DORA BAGDASSARIAN
Faculty of Medicine: Dr FELIPE SCHELOTTO
Faculty of Nursing: Prof. Mag. ALICIA CABRERA
Faculty of Psychology: Prof. Lic. LUIS LEOPOLD
Faculty of Science: Dr JULIO FERNÁNDEZ
Faculty of Social Sciences: Mag. DIEGO PIÑEIRO
Faculty of Veterinary Medicine: Dra PERLA A. CABRERA

DIRECTORS

Dr Manuel Quintela Clinical Hospital: Dra GRACIELA UBACH
School of Administration: JORGE XAVIER
School of Dental Technology: Prof. Dra ESTHER SZWARC
School of Librarianship and Related Sciences: Lic. GLADYS CERETTA (see Escuela Universitaria de Bibliotecología y Ciencias Afines 'Ing. Federico E. Capurro')
School of Medical Technology: Prof. Lic. JUAN MILA
School of Music: Prof. MARITA FORNARO
School of Nutrition and Dietetics: Nutr. EMA LEITES
National Institute of Fine Arts: Prof. SAMUEL SZTERN
Institute of Hygiene: Dra GABRIELA ALGORTA
Higher Institute of Physical Education: Prof.Lic. MARÍA CECILIA RUEGGER
Licentiate in Communication Sciences: Dr GABRIEL KAPLÚN
Food Engineering Career: Ing. PATRICIA LEMA
University Centre in Paysandú: Ing. Agr. MARGARITA HEINZEN
University Centre in Rivera: Lic. MARIO CLARA
Northern Regional Centre: Dr ALEJANDRO NOBOA

Colleges

Escuela Universitaria de Bibliotecología y Ciencias Afines 'Ing. Federico E. Capurro': Emilio Frugoni 1427, 11200 Montevideo; tel. (2) 400-58-10; fax (2) 400-58-10; e-mail eubca@adinet.com.uy; f. 1945; attached to Univ. de la República; 4-year courses in library and information science, 3-year courses in archive studies; library: 13,150 books and monographs, 200 periodicals; 50 teachers; 500 students; Dir Lic. MARÍA GLADYS CERETTA; publ. *Informatio* (1 a year).

Universidad del Trabajo del Uruguay: Calle San Salvador 1674, Montevideo; e-mail web.utu@anep.edu.uy; internet www.utu.edu.uy; f. 1878; offers 220 different courses at 81 colleges in agriculture, handicrafts, industry and commerce; lower- and intermediate-level education and training; 4,500 full-time teachers; 50,000 students; Dir Prof. WILSON NETTO MARTURET; publs *Boletín UTU* (irregular), *Serie Estadística* (1 a year, online).

UZBEKISTAN

The Higher Education System

Institutions of higher education predate Uzbekistan (formerly Uzbek SSR)'s independence from the USSR in 1991, the oldest being the Uzbek National University, Tashkent State Medical Institute and Tashkent Institute of Irrigation and Melioration, which were all founded in 1920. The main laws governing education in Uzbekistan are the Law on Education (1990) and the Law on Education (1997). In 1997 major reforms of the education system at all levels commenced under the National Programme for Personnel Training (NPPT). Reforms specific to the higher education sector include the re-modelling of the degree system, particularly the abolition of the old-style Soviet-era degrees and introduction of two-tier Bachelors and Masters degrees; institutional restructuring; strengthening of links between universities and industries; and improvements to part-time and distance education programmes. Higher education is mostly the responsibility of the Ministry of Higher and Specialized Secondary Education although other Ministries administer the relevant specialist schools. In 2004 higher education was provided in 63 institutes, of which 23 were universities, with a total enrolment of 263,600 students. There are also five foreign universities operating in Uzbekistan: the Tashkent branches of the Westminster International University, the Russian Academy of Economics, the Moscow State University, the Russian University of Oil and Gas, and the Singapore Institute of Management.

The main requirements for admission to higher education are the certificate for completion of secondary education and results achieved in the national university entrance examination (Kirish Imtakhoni), which is administered by the State Testing Centre (Devlet Test Markazi). The old-style Soviet degree system consisted primarily of a single five-year Specialist Diploma followed by doctoral-level studies. Since the implementation of the NPPT students are required to gain both the Bachelors and Masters degrees before pursuing doctoral studies. The Bachelors degree (Bakalavr Diplomi) lasts four years divided into two phases of two years each. In the first phase students undertake a general programme of study before, in the second phase, focusing on a 'major' subject. The Bachelors is a first degree, which may last longer in other (usually professional) fields of study, such as medicine, dentistry and veterinary medicine (upwards of six years). Graduates who have been awarded the Bachelors are eligible for the Masters (Magistr Diplomi), which is a two-year course, often in the same subject as the undergraduate degree. At the doctoral level, the Soviet distinction between the titles of Candidate of Science and Doctor of Science has been retained, albeit under their Uzbek names of, respectively, Fanlari Nomzodi and Fanlari Doctori. The Candidate of Science is a three-year period of study consisting of independent research leading to the submission of a thesis. Students intending to a career in research or academia then work towards the title of Doctor of Science, which is awarded after an unspecified period of study and research.

Post-secondary technical and vocational education takes the form of two- to four-year courses in 260 areas of specialization, resulting in the award of the Diploma of Post Secondary Vocational Education (O'rta Maxsus Ta'lim To'g'risidagi Diplom). The Monitoring Department of the Ministry of Higher and Specialized Secondary Education is responsible for accreditation and quality assurance at the tertiary level, standards for which are defined by the Ministry.

Regulatory Bodies

GOVERNMENT

Ministry of Culture and Sport: 100017 Tashkent, Mustaqillik ko'ch. 5; tel. (71) 139-83-31; fax (71) 139-46-11; e-mail madaniyat@sport.uz; internet www.madaniyat.sport.uz; Minister RUSTAM J. QURBONOV.

Ministry of Higher and Specialized Secondary Education: 100090 Tashkent, Bobrus ko'ch. 55; tel. (71) 152-77-64; e-mail mhsse@edu.uz; internet www.edu.uz; Minister AZIMJON P. PARPIYEV.

Ministry of National Education: 100078 Tashkent, O'zbekiston ko'ch. 80; tel. (71) 139-17-35; fax (71) 139-42-14; e-mail info@uzedu.uz; internet www.uzedu.uz; Minister TUROBJON I. JO'RAYEV.

Learned Societies

GENERAL

UNESCO Office Toshkent (Tashkent): 100084 Tashkent, Ergashev str. 9; tel. (71) 120-71-16; fax (71) 120-71-59; e-mail tashkent@unesco.org; f. 1996; Head JORGE IVAN ESPINAL.

Uzbekistan Academy of Sciences: 100047 Tashkent, Ya Gulomov Str. 70; tel. (71) 233-68-47; fax (71) 233-74-82; e-mail academy@uznet.net; internet www.academy.uz; f. 1943; divs of Physical-Mathematical and Technical Sciences (Chair. Prof. S. LUTPULLAEV), Natural Sciences (Chair. Acad. T. F. ARIPOV), Social and Humanitarian Sciences (Chair. Acad. S.GULYAMOV) 3 regional brs and 48 attached research institutes: see under Research Institutes; library: see under Libraries and Archives; 156 mems (71 ordinary, 85 corresp.); Pres. Acad. SHAVKAT SALIKHOV; Sec.-Gen. Dr BAKHTIER IBRAGIMOV; publs *Doklady* (Reports), *Obshchestvennye Nauki v Uzbekistane* (Social Sciences in Uzbekistan), *Science and Life*, *Uzbek Geological Journal*, *Uzbekskii Fizicheskii Zhurnal* (Uzbek Journal of Physics), *Uzbekskii Khimicheskii Zhurnal* (Uzbek Chemical Journal), *Uzbekskii Matematicheskii Zhurnal* (Uzbek Journal of Mathematics), *Uzbekskii Zhurnal—Problemy Informatiki i Energetiki* (Uzbek Journal—Problems in Informatics and Energetics), *Uzbekskii Zhurnal—Problemy Mekhaniki* (Uzbek Journal—Problems in Mechanics), *Uzbeksky Biologichesky Zhurnal* (Uzbek Biological Journal), *Uzbeksky Yazik i Literatura* (Uzbek Language and Literature).

LANGUAGE AND LITERATURE

Alliance Française: 140104 Samarqand, Ul. Baraka 26; tel. and fax (66) 33-66-27; offers courses and examinations in French language and culture and promotes cultural exchange with France.

British Council: 100031 Tashkent, University of World Languages Bldg, Kunayev ko'chasi 11; tel. (71) 120-67-52; fax (71) 120-63-71; e-mail bc-tashkent@britishcouncil.uz; internet www.britishcouncil.org/uzbekistan; offers courses and examinations in English language and British culture and promotes cultural exchange with the UK; library of 5,000 vols; Dir NEVILLE MCBAIN.

Goethe-Institut: 100031 Tashkent, Kunayev ko'chasi 11; tel. (71) 152-70-23; fax (71) 152-70-24; internet www.goethe.de/oe/tas/deindex.htm; offers courses and examinations in German language and culture and promotes cultural exchange with Germany; Dir Dr CHRISTIANE GÜNTHER.

Research Institutes

GENERAL

Buxoro Scientific Centre: 200109 Buxoro, Naqshbandi 153; tel. (65) 225-02-41; fax (65) 225-42-30; e-mail alexz@uzpak.uz; attached to Uzbek Acad. of Sciences; Dir I. SAFAROV.

Karakalpak Branch of the Uzbek Academy of Sciences: 230100 Qoraqalpog'iston, Nukus, Berdakh gazari 41; tel. (61) 222-17-44; fax (61) 222-17-56; e-mail nukus@aknuk.uzsci.net; internet www.aknuk.uzsci.net; Pres. AIMBETOV NAGMET KALLIEVICH.

Khorezm Academy of Mamun: 220900 Khiva, Markaz-1; tel. and fax (62) 375-51-43; e-mail mamun@dri.uz; attached to Uzbek Acad. of Sciences; Dir A. SADULLAYEV.

Research Institute of Regional Problems: 140100 Samarqand, Temur Malik 3; tel. (662) 33-19-94; fax (662) 31-00-39; e-mail samacdem@online.ru; attached to Uzbek Acad. of Sciences; Dir B. KHUJAYOROV.

Samarqand Branch of the Uzbek Academy of Sciences: 140100 Samarqand,

Temur Malik 3; tel. (662) 33-39-50; fax (662) 31-00-39; e-mail samacdem@online.ru; Chair. T. SHIRINOV.

AGRICULTURE, FISHERIES AND VETERINARY SCIENCE

Research Institute of Karakul Sheep Breeding and Ecology of Deserts: 140100 Samarqand, Mirzo Ulugbek ko'chasi 47; tel. (662) 33-32-79; fax (662) 33-34-81; e-mail ecokar@rol.uz; f. 1930; 100 mems; library of 56,000 vols; Dir Dr SURATBEK YUNUSOVICH YUSUPOV; publ. *Collection of Contributions Concerning Karakul Sheep Breeding and Arid Fodder Production* (every 2 years).

State Research Institute of Soil Science and Agrochemistry: 100179 Tashkent, Kamarniso ko'chasi 3; tel. (71) 246-09-50; fax (71) 246-76-00; e-mail gosniipa@rambler .ru; Dir D. S. SATTAROV.

ECONOMICS, LAW AND POLITICS

Abu Rayhan Biruni Institute of Oriental Studies: 100170 Tashkent, 81 Mirzo Ulugbek str.; tel. (71) 262-54-61; fax (71) 262-52-77; e-mail beruni@globalnet.uz; f. 1943; attached to Uzbek Acad. of Sciences; research activity in the sphere of medieval oriental MSS, and in the field of medieval and modern history of Central Asia; Dir B. A. ABDUKHALIMOV; publ. *Sharqshunoslik* (1 a year).

Institute of Economics: 100060 Tashkent, Borovskogo ko'chasi 5; tel. and fax (71) 133-14-78; e-mail econ@uzsci.net; f. 1943; attached to Uzbek Acad. of Sciences; Dir O. KHIKMATOV.

Muminov, I., Institute of Philosophy and Law: 100170 Tashkent, Muminov ko'chasi 9; tel. (71) 262-38-87; e-mail ifpanuz@yahoo .com; attached to Uzbek Acad. of Sciences; Dir Prof. R. D. RUZIEV.

EDUCATION

Scientific-Training Centre 'Fanum': 100170 Tashkent, Muminov ko'chasi 9; tel. (71) 162-93-31; fax (71) 269-13-78; e-mail fanum@uzsci.net; attached to Uzbek Acad. of Sciences; conducts lessons for postgraduate students and research workers with scientific degrees on the programmes established by VAK (Higher Appraisal Commission) under the Cabinet of the Ministries of the Republic of Uzbekistan; organizes translation activities; promotes public education; Dir N. Y. TURAEV; publs *Philosophy and Law*, *Uzbek Physics Journal*.

HISTORY, GEOGRAPHY AND ARCHAEOLOGY

Institute of Archaeology: 140151 Samarqand, Abdullayev ko'chasi 3; tel. (662) 32-15-13; fax (662) 31-12-90; e-mail archaeo@online .ru; f. 1970; attached to Uzbek Acad. of Sciences; Dir T. SHIRINOV.

Institute of History: 100170 Tashkent, Muminov ko'chasi 9; tel. (71) 162-38-73; fax (71) 162-93-51; e-mail tarih@uzsci.net; internet www.history.uzsci.net; f. 1943; attached to Uzbek Acad. of Sciences; Dir DILOROM AGZAMOVNA ALIMOVA; publ. *Uzbekiston Tarihi* (4 a year).

Institute of History, Archaeology and Ethnography: 230100 Qoraqalpog'istan, Nukus, Amir Temur 179A; tel. (61) 224-05-98; fax (61) 217-72-28; e-mail vyagodin@ online.ru; attached to Uzbek Acad. of Sciences; Dir V. YAGODIN.

LANGUAGE AND LITERATURE

Institute of Language and Literature: 230100 Qoraqalpog'istan, Nukus, Amir Temur 199A; tel. (61) 217-21-61; attached to Uzbek Acad. of Sciences; Dir S. BAHADIROVA.

Navoi Institute of Language and Literature: 100170 Tashkent, Muminov ko'chasi 9; tel. (71) 162-42-64; attached to Uzbek Acad. of Sciences; Dir T. M. MIRZAEV.

MEDICINE

Institute for Dermatology and Venereology: 100109 Tashkent, Farabi 3; tel. (71) 246-08-07; f. 1932; attached to Min. of Health; library of 14,000 vols; Dir Prof. V. A. AKOVBAYAN; publ. *Pathogenesis and Therapy for Skin and Venereal Diseases* (1 a year).

Institute of Haematology and Blood Transfusion: 100059 Tashkent, Druzhba Narodov 42; tel. (71) 279-79-35; fax (71) 279-95-26.

Institute of Immunology: 100060 Tashkent, Ya. Gulamov 74; tel. (71) 133-08-05; fax (71) 133-08-55; e-mail immuno@uzsci.net; attached to Uzbek Acad. of Sciences; Dir R. RUZIBAKIYEV.

Institute of Vaccines and Sera: 100084 Tashkent, Abdurashidov 37; tel. (71) 243-79-53; fax (71) 234-77-22; Dir B. A. SHEVCHENKO.

Isaev, L. M., Research Institute of Medical Parasitology: 140105 Samarqand, Isaeva 38; tel. (662) 37-42-42; f. 1923; library of 45,000 vols; Dir SH. A. RAZAKOV; publ. *Current Problems in Medical Parasitology* (1 a year).

Republic Specialized Centre of Cardiology: 100052 Tashkent, Osio 4; tel. (71) 236-08-16; e-mail cardio@sarkor.com; f. 1976; library of 30,000 vols; Dir Prof. RAVSHANBEK KURBANOV.

Research Institute of Clinical and Experimental Medicine: 230100 Qoraqalpog'istan, Nukus, M. Gorkogo ko'chasi 185; tel. (612) 24-50-41.

Research Institute of Epidemiology, Microbiology and Infectious Diseases: 100133 Tashkent, Reshetova 2; tel. (71) 243-36-05; f. 1961; Dir SH. SH. SHAVAKHABOV.

Uzbek Institute of Rehabilitation and Physiotherapy (Semashko Institute): 100084 Tashkent, Khurshida 4; tel. (71) 234-55-00, fax (71) 235-30-63; f. 1919; physiotherapy in cardiology, arthropology, neurology and pulmonology, oriental medicine, phytotherapy; library of 16,210 vols; Dir Prof. KARIM U. ULDASHEV; publ. *Collection of Scientific Works* (1 a year).

Uzbek Research Institute of Traumatology and Orthopaedics: 100047 Tashkent, Pakhlavon Makhmud Str. 78; tel. (371) 233-10-30; f. 1932; library of 30,000 vols; Dir Prof. M. AZIMOV.

NATURAL SCIENCES

General

Institute for Natural Sciences: 230100 Qoraqalpog'istan, Nukus, Berdakh gazari 41; tel. (612) 22-17-45; fax (612) 22-17-45; f. 1996; attached to Uzbek Acad. of Sciences; Dir BAKHYT NARYMBETOV.

Biological Sciences

Institute of Biochemistry: 100143 Tashkent, Abdullayev ko'chasi 56; tel. (71) 162-25-66; fax (71) 162-24-41; e-mail saatov@uzsci .net; attached to Uzbek Acad. of Sciences; Dir T. S. SAATOV.

Institute of Bioecology: 230100 Qoraqalpog'istan, Nukus, Berdakh gazari 1; tel. (612) 17-17-13; fax (612) 17-72-28; e-mail ecol@ online.ru; attached to Uzbek Acad. of Sciences; Dir A. BAKHIYEV.

Institute of Botany: 100143 Tashkent, Khodzhayev ko'chasi 32; tel. (71) 162-70-65; fax (71) 162-79-38; e-mail botany@uzsci.net; attached to Uzbek Acad. of Sciences; Dir Prof. Dr OZODBEK A. ASHURMETOV.

Institute of Genetics and Plant Experimental Biology: 111226 Tashkent, Kibray Dist., Yukori-Yuz; tel. (71) 264-23-90; fax (71) 264-22-30; e-mail inst@gen.org.uz; attached to Uzbek Acad. of Sciences; Dir A. ABDUKARIMOV.

Institute of Microbiology: 100128 Tashkent, Abdulla Kadiri gazari 7B; tel. (71) 144-25-19; fax (71) 144-25-82; e-mail imbasru@ uzsci.net; f. 1965; attached to Uzbek Acad. of Sciences; Dir K. DAVRANOV; publ. *Uzbeksky Biologichesky Zhurnal*.

Institute of Physiology and Biophysics: 100095 Tashkent, A. Niyazov str. 1; tel. (71) 246-95-17; fax (71) 246-92-54; e-mail pusman@uzsci.net; internet biophys.fan.uz; f. 1975; attached to Uzbek Acad. of Sciences; Dir Prof. P. B. USMANOV.

Institute of the Chemistry of Plant Substances: 100170 Tashkent, Mirzo Ulugbek St 77; tel. (71) 262-70-00; fax (71) 262-74-76; e-mail shakhidoyatov@yahoo.com; internet www.icps.org.uz; attached to Uzbek Acad. of Sciences; organic synthesis, nature chemistry, physical chemistry; Dir Prof. Dr KHUSNUTDIN SHAKHIDOYATOV; publ. *Chemistry of Natural Compounds*.

Institute of Zoology: 100095 Tashkent, A. Niyazov ko'chasi 1; tel. (71) 246-07-18; fax (71) 120-67-91; e-mail uzzool@uzsci.net; f. 1950; attached to Uzbek Acad. of Sciences; Dir J. AZIMOV.

Acad. A.Sadikov Institute of Bioorganic Chemistry: 100143 Tashkent, Abdullayev ko'chasi 83; tel. (71) 262-35-40; fax (71) 262-70-63; e-mail ibchem@uzsci.net; f. 1977; attached to Uzbek Acad. of Sciences; bioorganic chemistry, chemistry of natural physiologic active compounds; Dir Prof. A. S. TURAEV.

Mathematical Sciences

Institute of Mathematics and Information Technologies: 100125 Tashkent, Akademgorodok, Dormon Yoli 29; tel. (71) 262-56-94; fax (71) 262-73-57; e-mail mathinst@ uznet.net; f. 1943, fmrly Romanovsky, V. I., Institute of Mathematics, present name and status 2007; attached to Uzbek Acad. of Sciences; research in pure and applied mathematics, mathematical modelling, informatics; 180 mems; library of 112,000 vols; Dir Prof. Acad. SHAVKAT AYUPOV; publ. *Uzbek Mathematical Journal* (4 a year).

Physical Sciences

Abdullaev, Kh. M., Institute of Geology and Geophysics: 100041 Tashkent, N. Khodjibaeva 49; tel. (71) 262-65-16; fax (71) 262-63-81; e-mail ingeo@ingeo.uz; internet www.ingeo.uz; f. 1939; attached to Uzbek Acad. of Sciences; study of the structure, composition, and evolution of the lithosphere; devt of the fundamentals of expansion of mineral raw materials in Uzbekistan and effective exploitation of mineral deposits; Dir Dr SOBIT MAKSUDOV; publ. *Geology and Mineral Resources* (6 a year).

Heat Physics Department of the Uzbek Academy of Sciences: 100135 Tashkent; tel. (71) 276-44-57; fax (71) 276-90-53; e-mail hpd@uzsci.net; f. 1977; Dir P. KHABIBULLAYEV.

Institute of General and Inorganic Chemistry: 100170 Tashkent, Amir Temur ko'chasi 77A; tel. (71) 162-56-60; fax (71) 162-79-90; e-mail ionxanruz@mail.ru; internet www.igic.uzsci.net; f. 1933; attached to Uzbek Acad. of Sciences; researches colloidal, inorganic and petroleum chemistry, involved in localization of new fertilizers, defoliants for agriculture, materials of construction, flocculating agents, oil additives, depressors, corrosion inhibitors for domestic industry; library of 50,000 vols; Dir Prof. ZAKIRJAN SALIMOV; Deputy Dir Prof. BAHTYER ZAKIROV; publs *Reports of Uzbekistan Academy of Sciences–Joint Academic Institutes Journal* (6 a year), *Uzbekistan Journal of Chemistry* (6 a year).

Institute of Mineral Resources: 100060 Tashkent, T. Shevchenko ko'chasi 11A; tel. (712) 56-13-49; fax (71) 120-68-12; e-mail mineral@cu.uz; internet www.geology.uz; f. 1957; Dir B. A. ISAKHODJAYEV; publ. *Geology and Mineral Resources* (6 a year).

Institute of Nuclear Physics: 100214 Tashkent, Ulugbek; tel. and fax (71) 264-25-90; e-mail yuldashev@iae.tashkent.su; f. 1956; attached to Uzbek Acad. of Sciences; Dir B. S. YULDASHEV.

Institute of Seismology: 100128 Tashkent, Zulfiyakhonim ko'chasi 3; tel. (71) 241-51-70; fax (71) 241-53-14; e-mail akhror@uzsci.net; f. 1966; attached to Uzbek Acad. of Sciences; library of 43,000 vols; Dir Prof. K. N. ABDULLABEKOV; publ. *Uzbek Geological Journal* (6 a year).

Institute of the Chemistry and Physics of Polymers: 100128 Tashkent, A. Kadiri ko'chasi 7B; tel. (71) 241-70-80; fax (71) 244-26-61; e-mail carbon@uzsci.net; attached to Uzbek Acad. of Sciences; Dir S. SH. RASHIDOVA.

Physical–Technical Institute: 100084 Tashkent, G. Mavlyanov 2B; tel. (71) 133-12-71; fax (71) 235-42-91; e-mail lutp@physic.uzsci.net; attached to Uzbek Acad. of Sciences; Dir S. LUTPULLAYEV; publ. *Applied Solar Engineering*.

Ulugh Beg Astronomical Institute: 100052 Tashkent, Astronomicheskaya ko'chasi 33; tel. (71) 235-81-02; fax (71) 136-00-37; e-mail admin@astrin.uzsci.net; internet www.astrin.uzsci.net; attached to Uzbek Acad. of Sciences; Dir SH. A. EHGAMBERDIEV.

RELIGION, SOCIOLOGY AND ANTHROPOLOGY

Institute for Socio-Economic Problems of the Aral Sea Region: 742000 Qoraqalpog'istan, Nukus, Berdaha pr. 41; tel. (61) 222-17-44; fax (61) 222-17-56; e-mail nagmet@aknuk.uzsci.net; internet www.aknuk.uzsci.net; attached to Uzbek Acad. of Sciences; Dir N. AIMBETOV.

TECHNOLOGY

Arifov Institute of Electronics: 100125 Tashkent, F. Khodjaev 33; tel. (71) 262-79-40; fax (71) 262-87-67; e-mail aie@aie.uz; f. 1967; attached to Uzbek Acad. of Sciences; Dir U. KH. RASULEV.

Institute of Cybernetics: 700125 Tashkent, Khodzhayev ko'chasi 34; tel. (71) 162-72-47; fax (71) 162-73-21; e-mail uzkiber@cyber.ccc.uz; f. 1966; attached to Uzbek Acad. of Sciences; library of 100,000 vols; Dir F. SHAVKAT; publs *Problemy Informatiki i Energetiki* (6 a year), *Voprosy Kibernetiki* (3 a year), *Voprosy Vychislitelnoi i Prikladnoi Matematiki* (3 a year), *Algoritmy* (3 a year), *Voprosy Modelirovaniya i Informatizatsii Ekonomiki* (3 a year).

Institute of Hydrogeology and Engineering Geology: 100041 Tashkent, Olimlar st, 64; tel. and fax (71) 262-75-90; fax (71) 262-62-15; e-mail hydrouz@rambler.ru; f. 1960; attached to Int. Consortium of Landslides, Int. Union of Geological Sciences; research into hydrogeology, petroleum, geoecology, landslides and remote-sensing; library of 18,000 vols; Dir Dr ASLON A. MAVLONOV; publs *Geology and Mineral Resources* (6 a year), *Hydrogeology and Engineering Geology Problems in Uzbekistan* (1 a year).

Institute of Materials Science: 100084 Tashkent, Bodomzor yo'li 2B; tel. (71) 235-75-06; fax (71) 233-95-64; e-mail jabbar@uzsci.net; attached to Uzbek Acad. of Sciences; Dir Dr ABDUJABBAR ABDURAKHMANOV.

Institute of Mechanics and Seismic Stability of Structures: 100125 Tashkent, Akademia Shaharchasi, Dormon yoli 31; tel. (71) 162-72-97; fax (71) 162-71-52; e-mail instmech@uzsci.net; internet www.instmech.fan.uz; f. 1959; attached to Uzbek Acad. of Sciences; Dir Prof. A. A. RIZAEV; publ. *Problems in Mechanics* (6 a year).

Institute of Power Engineering and Automation: 100143 Tashkent, Akademgorodok; tel. (71) 162-05-22; fax (71) 162-09-19; e-mail ipea@uzsci.net; f. 1941; attached to Uzbek Acad. of Sciences; Dir R. A. ZAKHIDOV.

Institute of Water Problems: 100187 Tashkent, Khodjayev ko'chasi 25A; tel. and fax (71) 169-12-70; e-mail root@pwater.tashkent.su; f. 1992; attached to Uzbek Acad. of Sciences; Dir ERNAZAR J. MAKHMUDOV.

Scientific and Production Association 'Akadempribor': 100125 Tashkent, Akademia Shaharchasi; tel. (71) 262-72-73; fax (712) 69-01-24; e-mail bahramov@mail.ru; f. 1962; attached to Uzbek Acad. of Sciences; research, design and production the instruments and equipment for scientific orgs, agriculture, medicine and industry; Dir-Gen. Prof. SAGDILLA A. BAKHRAMOV.

Scientific Production Centre 'Modern Information Technologies': 100143 Tashkent, Khodzhayev ko'chasi 34; tel. (71) 162-72-47; fax (71) 162-73-12; e-mail shavkat@cyber.uzsci.net; attached to Uzbek Acad. of Sciences; Dir O. NABIYEV.

Uzbek Research Institute of Sericulture: 111812 Jar-Arik, Tashkent Viloyat, Zangyata; f. 1927; attached to Min. of Agriculture and Water; Dir SH. YULDASHEV; publ. *Silk*.

UzLITIneftgaz (Uzbekistan Research and Design Institute of the Gas and Oil Industry): 100029 Tashkent, T. Shevchenko ko'chasi 2; tel. (71) 256-74-17; fax (71) 256-66-48; Dir U. S. NAZAROV; publ. *Uzbek Journal of Oil and Gas* (4 a year).

Libraries and Archives

Samarqand

Samarqand State University Central Library: 140100 Samarqand, Pl. Navoi 15; tel. (662) 35-19-38; fax (662) 35-64-90; e-mail soleev@samuni.silk.org; 1,632,000 vols; spec. collns incl. ancient oriental literature; Dir R. KHOLMURODOV.

Tashkent

Alisher Navoi National Library of Uzbekistan: 100047 Tashkent, Milliy kutubxonasi, Xorazm ko'chasi 51; tel. (71) 239-47-09; fax (71) 233-09-08; e-mail navoi@tshtt.uz; internet www.natlib.uz; f. 1870, incorporates Republican Library for Science and Technology since 2002; 10,000,000 vols; Dir ZUHRIDDIN ISAMIDDINOV.

Central State Archive of Uzbekistan: 100043 Tashkent, Chilonzar ko'chasi 2; tel. (712) 77-04-08; e-mail csa@archive.uz; internet central.archive.uz; Dir SHUHRATBAY KHODJIBAEV.

Foundation Library of the Uzbek Academy of Sciences: 100170 Tashkent, Muminov ko'chasi 13; tel. (71) 262-74-56; fax (71) 262-74-58; e-mail acadlib@acadlib.uzsci.net; internet www.acadlib.uzsci.net; f. 1934; Uzbek Academy of Sciences library system incl. 31 other research institute libraries; 5,000,000 vols; Dir SH. N. NURITDINOV.

Mirzo Ulugbek Library of the National University of Uzbekistan: 100095 Tashkent, Vozgorodok, Universitet ko'chasi 95; tel. (371) 2466771; fax (371) 2460224; e-mail info@nuu.uz; internet www.nuu.uz; 18 brs; 350,000 vols, 45,000 journals, 2,600 govt documents, 4,000 maps; Dir IRINA LVOVNA KISLITSINA.

Museums and Art Galleries

Nukus

Botanical Garden: 230100 Qoraqalpog'istan, Nukus, Chimbay ko'chasi; tel. (612) 22-30-47; fax (612) 17-72-28; attached to Uzbek Acad. of Sciences; Dir T. OTENOV.

Karakalpak State Museum of Arts 'I.V.Savitsky': 230100 Karakalpakstan, Nukus, K. Rzaev b/n; tel. and fax (61) 222-25-56; e-mail museum_savitsky@intal.uz; internet www.museum.kr.uz; f. 1966 by the archaeologist and ethnographer Igor Savitsky; archaeology of ancient Khorezym, Karakalpak folk art, Russian and Central Asian avant-garde art 1910–1935; library of 10,500 vols; Dir MARINIKA BABANAZAROVA; Chief Curator VALENTINA SYCHEVA.

Kara-Kalpak Historical Museum: 230100 Qoraqalpog'istan, Nukus, Rakhmatov ko'chasi 3; illustrates the part played by the Uzbek people in the October Socialist Revolution, the Civil War and the Second World War.

Samarqand

Samarqand State United Historical-Architectural and Art Museum Preserve: 140100 Samarqand, Registan ko'chasi 1; tel. (66) 35-38-96; f. 1982; comprises 9 museums in Samarqand city and Viloyat, containing more than 182,000 exhibits in total.

Tashkent

Alisher Navoi State Museum of Literature: 100011 Tashkent, Navoi str. 69; tel. (71) 241-02-75; fax (71) 244-00-61; e-mail a_navoi@uzsci.net; internet www.navoimuseum.uz; f. 1936; attached to Uzbek Acad. of Sciences; collects, investigates, maintains and displays the history of Uzbek literature, incl. MSS, documents, pictures, archives and photographic materials; Dir Prof. SAIDBEK KHASANOV; publ. *Adabiyot kozgusi* (12 a year).

Museum of Uzbek History: 100000 Tashkent, Sharaf Rashidov ko'chasi 3; tel. (71) 139-10-83; f. 1992 by merger of the Museum of the History of the People of Uzbekistan and the Lenin Central Museums; more than 300,000 exhibits; Dir G. R. RASHIDOV.

Oibek, M. T., Historical Museum of Uzbekistan: 100047 Tashkent, Sh. Rashidov ko'chasi 3; tel. (71) 139-10-83; fax (71) 139-44-25; attached to Uzbek Acad. of Sciences; Dir K. INOYATOV.

State Museum of Timurid History: 700000 Tashkent, Amir Temur 1; tel. and fax (71) 132-02-13; e-mail timurid@uzsci.net; attached to Uzbek Acad. of Sciences; Dir N. KHABIBULLAYEV.

Uzbek State Museum of Art: 100060 Tashkent, Movarounnakhr 16; tel. (71) 136-74-36; fax (71) 136-77-40; f. 1918; library of 22,700 vols; Dir D. S. RUSIBAYEV.

Universities

ACADEMY OF STATE AND SOCIAL CONSTRUCTION

100029 Tashkent, Uzbekistan ko'chasi 45
Telephone: (71) 245-69-51
Founded 1995
State control
Languages of instruction: Uzbek, Russian
Rector: ALISHER AZIZHOJAYEV.

ANDIJON STATE UNIVERSITY

170100 Andijon, Namangan 129
Telephone: (742) 25-05-09
Fax: (742) 22-18-63
E-mail: asu2001@rambler.ru
Founded 1931
State control
Languages of instruction: Uzbek, Russian
Academic year: September to June
Rector: SIROJIDDIN ZAYNOBBIDINOV
Vice-Rector: TOLIB MADUMAROV
Library of 320,314 vols
Number of teachers: 434
Number of students: 5,021

DEANS

Faculty of Biology: ALIJON DADAMIRZAYEV
Faculty of Chemistry: MIRAHMAD KHOJIMATOV
Faculty of History: ZOKIR KUTIBOYEV
Faculty of Mathematics: ABDUVAHOB MILADJONOV
Faculty of Philology: DILMUROD QURONOV
Faculty of Physical Training: NOIB YULDASHEV
Faculty of Physics: ABDULQAHOR ORTIQOV
Faculty of Physical Education: DEHQONBOY MAMATISAQOV
Faculty of Teacher Training: MUHTOR VOHIDOV

BUXORO STATE UNIVERSITY

200118 Buxoro, Muhammad Ikbol ko'chasi 11
Telephone: (65) 223-23-14
Fax: (65) 223-12-54
E-mail: bukhsu-monitor@mail.ru
Internet: www.bukhsu.uzsci.net
Founded 1930
State control
Academic year: September to June
Rector: K. M. MUQIMOV
Vice-Rector: O. M. EYRIYEV
Number of teachers: 361
Number of students: 5,577
Publications: *Marifat Nuri* (12 a year), *University Review* (12 a year)
Faculties of agriculture, biology and chemistry, economics, education, foreign philosophy, graphic arts, history and geography, physics and mathematics, sociology and Uzbek-Tajik philology.

FERGHANA STATE UNIVERSITY

150100 Farg'ona, Usmanhojayev 19
Telephone: (732) 24-28-71
Fax: (732) 24-35-32
E-mail: fdu@fdu.vodiy.uz
Founded 1991
State control
Languages of instruction: Uzbek, Russian
Rector: AHMADJON URINOV
Vice-Rector: MADAMIN AKHMEDOV
Library of 757,461 vols
Number of teachers: 459
Number of students: 5,639

GULISTAN STATE UNIVERSITY

120100 Gulistan, Microraion 4
Telephone: (672) 25-45-72
Fax: (672) 25-02-72
E-mail: gdu@intal.uz
Founded 1966
State control
Languages of instruction: Uzbek, Russian
Rector: AZIMJON P. RARPIYEV
Library of 195,000 vols
Faculties of economics and engineering, education, foreign languages, history and Uzbek philology, Kazakh philology, natural sciences, physics and mathematics.

KARA-KALPAK STATE UNIVERSITY

230112 Qoraqalpog'istan, Nukus, Ch. Abidov 1
Telephone: (612) 23-60-47
Fax: (612) 23-60-78
E-mail: korun@korun.silk.org
Founded 1979
State control
Rector: Prof. K. ATENIYAZOV
Number of students: 7,000
Faculties of agriculture, chemistry, construction, engineering, economics, law and history, natural sciences, philology, physics and mathematics.

KARSHI STATE UNIVERSITY

140103 Karshi, Kuchabog 17
Telephone: (752) 25-34-13
Fax: (752) 25-57-01
E-mail: kardu@mail.ru
Internet: www.kasu.uz
Founded 1956
State control
Languages of instruction: Uzbek, Russian
Academic year: September to June
Rector: Prof. MURADULLA NORMURADOV
Library of 10,000 vols.

NAMANGAN STATE UNIVERSITY

160119 Namangan, Uychi 316
Telephone: (692) 26-55-01
Fax: (692) 26-61-07
E-mail: pulathon2001@yahoo.com
Internet: www.namsu.uz
Founded 1942
Public control
Languages of instruction: Uzbek, Russian, English
Academic year: September to June
Rector: Dr YULDOSHALI RAHIMOV
Library of 1,000,000 vols
Number of teachers: 420
Number of students: 7,500
Publication: *Periodical of Namangan State University*

DEANS

Faculty of Art and Drawing: BOTIRSHER JABBOROV
Faculty of Biology and Chemistry: YOLDOSHALI TOSHMATOV
Faculty of Education: MUNOJATHON MIRABDULLAYEVA
Faculty of Geography and Economics: MUHAMMADSOLI MUMINOV
Faculty of Graduate Studies: SHAVKAT ABDULLAYEV
Faculty of History: RUZIMAT JURAYEV
Faculty of Law: YULDOSHALI RHIMOV
Faculty of Mathematics: SOBIRJON ALIHANOV
Faculty of Physical Education and Sport: SOBITHON AZIZOV
Faculty of Physics and Labour Education: TOSHKINBOY UMARALIYEV
Faculty of Uzbek Philology: TOHIRJON RAHMONOV
Faculty of World Languages: SAIDUMOR SAIDALIYEV

SAMARQAND STATE UNIVERSITY

140104 Samarqand, Universitet ko'chasi 15
Telephone: (662) 33-54-83
Fax: (662) 33-27-24
E-mail: safarovsh@rambler.ru
Internet: www.samdu.uz
Founded 1927
State control
Languages of instruction: Uzbek, Russian, Tajik
Academic year: September to June
Rector: Dr T. SH. SHIRINOV
Vice-Rector: Prof. M. K. MHIDDINOV
Number of teachers: 800
Number of students: 13,000
Publication: *Samarqand Davlat Universiteti* (52 a year)
Faculties of applied mathematics, biology, chemistry, economics, foreign languages, geography, history, law, management, mathematics, musical education, physical training, physics, pre-school and primary education, sociology, Uzbek, Tajik and Russian philology.

TASHKENT ISLAMIC UNIVERSITY

100006 Tashkent, Abdullah Qodiriy 11
Telephone: (71) 139-52-15
Fax: (71) 139-82-15
Founded 1999
State control
Languages of instruction: Uzbek, Arabic
Academic year: September to June
Rector: HAMIDULLA KAROMATOV
Vice-Rector: ABDULHAY ABDULLAYEV
Number of students: 100
Faculties of Islamic history and natural sciences.

TASHKENT NIZAMI STATE PEDAGOGICAL UNIVERSITY

100100 Tashkent, Yusuf Has Hajib 103
Telephone: (71) 254-92-02
Fax: (71) 254-92-17
E-mail: tdpu@albatros.uz
Founded 1935
State control
Languages of instruction: Uzbek, Russian, Kazakh, Korean, German, English
Academic year: September to June
Rector: BAHRAM G. KADIROV
Number of teachers: 932
Number of students: 10,380
Faculties:

DEANS

Faculty of Applied Physiologists Training: FAZLIDDIN KHAYDAROV
Faculty of Drawing and Applied Art: BOTOR BOYMETOV
Faculty of Foreign Languages: QURBON SHODMONOV
Faculty of Handicrafts Education: NARZULLA MUSLIMOV
Faculty of History: SAMAD TORAYEV
Faculty of Military Physical Training: ILHOM IKROMOV

Faculty of Music: HAMIDULLA NURMATOV
Faculty of Natural Sciences: FARIDA MURHAMIDOVA
Faculty of Pedagogics and Defectology: MAMAD KHAYDAROV
Faculty of Physics and Mathematics: ERKIN SAYDAMATOV
Faculty of Russian and Korean Philology: RUSTAM KOBILOV
Faculty of Teaching Skills Enhancement: NURIDDIN DOSANOV
Faculty of Uzbek and Kazakh Language and Literature: IBROHIM YULDASHEV

TASHKENT STATE UNIVERSITY OF ECONOMICS

100003 Tashkent, Uzbekistanskaya 49
Telephone: (71) 132-64-21
Fax: (71) 139-41-23
E-mail: info@tsue.uz
Internet: www.tsue.uz
Founded 1931
Rector: Prof. RAIMJON KH. ALIMOV
Library of 300,000 vols
Number of teachers: 600
Number of students: 11,000

Faculties of accounting, agricultural economics, economic cybernetics, economic planning, financial economics, trade economics; br. in Andizhan.

TERMIZ STATE UNIVERSITY

190111 Termiz, F. Hodjayev 43
Telephone: (762) 23-19-08
Fax: (762) 24-25-36
Founded 1992
State control
Languages of instruction: Uzbek, Russian
Rector: SAYFULLO T. TURSUNOV
Library of 183,000
Number of students: 47,000

Faculties of chemistry, economics, education, education and psychology, finance and management, foreign languages, history, industrial education, natural sciences and geography, physical education, physics and mathematics, Russian philology, technology and engineering, training of specialists and retraining.

URGENCH AL-KHARAZMI STATE UNIVERSITY

220100 Urgench, H. Alimjan 14
Telephone: (622) 26-61-66
Fax: (622) 26-35-44
E-mail: ayus@khorsu.silk.org
Internet: urdu.freenet.uz
Founded 1992
State control
Languages of instruction: Uzbek, Russian
Rector: AZIMBAY S. SAGDULLAYEV
Number of students: 34,000

Faculties of economics, engineering and technology, natural sciences, physics and mathematics, Uzbek philology and history, world languages.

UZBEK NATIONAL UNIVERSITY

100014 Tashkent, Vozgorodok, Universitet ko'chasi 95
Telephone: (71) 246-02-24
Fax: (71) 144-73-12
E-mail: oms@tsu.silk.org
Internet: www.nuu.uz
Founded 1920
State control
Rector: Dr T. N. DALIMOV
Vice-Rector: R. MURAZAYEVA
Library Dir: L. S. YUGAI
Number of teachers: 1,480
Number of students: 19,300

Faculties of applied mathematics, biology and soil science, chemistry, geology and geography, history, journalism, law, mathematics, Oriental studies, philosophy and economics, physics, Russian philology, Uzbek philology.

Other Higher Educational Institutes

Academy of Arts of Uzbekistan: 100029 Tashkent, Sharif Rashidov gazari 40; tel. (71) 256-50-47; fax (71) 256-50-46; e-mail acart@umid.uz; internet www.arts-academy.uz; f. 1997 by merger of existing instns; 190 teachers; 900 students; Rector TURSUNALI KUZIYEV.

Andijon Cotton Institute: 170600 Andijon, Selo Kuigan-Yar; tel. (742) 24-54-34.

Andijon State Medical Institute: 170100 Andijon, Atabekova 1; tel. (742) 37-93-53; fax (742) 22-19-41; e-mail agmi@online.ru; internet www.andmi.uz; library: 105,000 vols; Rector Prof. MAMAZAIR A. KHUJAMBERDIEV.

Andijon State Pedagogical Institute of Languages: 170111 Andijon, Babur ko'chasi 5; tel. (742) 24-75-15; fax (742) 24-75-26; e-mail adtpi@online.ru; f. 1966; faculties of Russian language and literature, foreign languages (English, German, French); Rector RASHID G. BARATOV; publ. *Scientific Proceedings*.

Buxoro State Medical Institute: 200118 Buxoro, Navoi ko'chasi 1; tel. (65) 223-00-50; fax (65) 223-49-43; e-mail buhme@rambler.ru; internet www.buhmi.uz; f. 1990; library: 90,000 vols; 240 teachers; 1,728 students; Rector Prof. RAKHMAT M. AKHMEDOV.

Buxoro Technological Institute of Food and Light Industry: 200117 Buxoro, K. Murtazoyev 15; tel. (65) 223-61-97; fax (65) 223-78-84; e-mail javlonbek@intal.uz; f. 1976; faculties of oil and gas, mechanical engineering, light industry, professional education, food technology, business and management; 320 teachers; 4,800 students; Rector Prof. MUHSIN T. HODJIEV.

Farg'ona Polytechnic Institute: 150100 Farg'ona, Ferganskaya ko'chasi 86; tel. (732) 22-13-50; fax (732) 22-13-33; e-mail monitoring@farpi.uz; internet www.farpi.uz; f. 1967; faculties of chemical technology, power, mechanics, construction, economics; device building centre; library: 290,000 vols; 234 teachers; 3,239 students; Rector RASUL J. TOJIYEV; publ. *Scientific-Technical Journal* (4 a year).

Samarqand Agricultural Institute: 140103 Samarqand, M. Ulugbek 77; tel. (662) 34-33-20; fax (662) 34-07-86; e-mail samsi@uzpak.uz; f. 1929; faculties of agronomics, agro-engineering, animal husbandry, economics and accounting, karakul (sheep-breeding), veterinary science, zootechnics; library: 533,777 vols; 274 teachers; 3,500 students (2,000 full-time, 1,500 correspondence); Rector Prof. ABDI-KADIR ERGASHEV.

Samarqand Cooperative Institute: 140100 Samarqand, A. Temur 9; tel. (662) 33-38-72; fax (662) 31-12-53; e-mail samki@intal.uz; f. 1931; faculties of engineering technology, trade economics, trade, accounting; library: 205,718 vols; 210 teachers; 7,000 students; Rector AKBARALI N. JABRIYEV.

Samarqand State Architectural and Civil Engineering Institute: 140147 Samarqand, Lolazor 70; tel. (662) 37-15-93; fax (662) 31-04-52; e-mail unesco_aliance@rambler.ru; f. 1966; depts of architecture, economics, building, building technology, engineering, professional education, building engineering and ecology, machine construction and land cadastre; library: 400,000 vols; 266 teachers; 2,000 students; Rector SOBIR M. BOBOEV.

Samarqand State Institute of Foreign Languages: 140104 Samarqand, Akhunbabayev 93; tel. (662) 33-78-43; fax (662) 35-66-19; e-mail samdchti@online.ru; internet sifl.50megs.com; f. 1994; library: 91,000 vols; 225 teachers; 2,165 students (1,387 undergraduate, 778 postgraduate); Rector Prof. M. SH. MAMATOV.

Samarqand State Medical Institute: 140100 Samarqand, Amir Temur 18; tel. and fax (662) 33-54-21; e-mail info@sammi.samuni.silk.org; internet www.sammi.da.ru; f. 1930; faculties of general practice and paediatrics; library: 330,000 vols; Rector B. U. SOBIROV.

Tashkent Abu Reihan Beruni State Technical University: 100095 Tashkent, Universitetskaya 2; tel. (71) 246-46-00; fax (71) 229-48-96; e-mail intdep@online.ru; internet www.tstu.re.uz; f. 1929; faculties of oil and gas, electronics, automation and computer hardware, power engineering, mechanical engineering and machine building, mining and geology, humanities; 2,000 teachers; 20,000 students; Rector KAKHRAMON R. ALLAYEV.

Tashkent Automobile and Road Construction Institute: 100060 Tashkent, Mavoraunnakhr 20A; tel. (71) 133-08-27; fax (71) 132-14-80; e-mail tayi.admin@mail.ru; f. 1972; faculties of road building machinery, roads, road transport, road transport management, engineering economics; br. in Termez; Rector S. M. KADIROV.

Tashkent Institute of Architecture and Construction: 100011 Tashkent, Navoi 13; tel. (71) 241-15-01; fax (71) 241-80-00; e-mail ismoil_i@mail.ru; internet www.tasi.uzsci.net; 200 teachers; 2,400 students; Rector BAKHTIYAR A. ASKAROV.

Tashkent Institute of Finance: 100084 Tashkent, Asomova 7; tel. (71) 234-55-37; fax (71) 235-77-04; e-mail tfi@online.ru; 4,200 students; Rector M. SHARIFKHOJAYEV.

Tashkent Institute of Irrigation and Melioration: 100000 Tashkent, Qari-Niyazov ko'chasi 39; tel. (71) 137-46-68; fax (71) 133-14-39; e-mail tiiame@freenet.uz; internet www.tiiame.uzsci.net; f. 1920; faculties of agricultural mechanization, electrical energetic of agriculture and water management, education science, economics, hydromelioration, irrigation and land improvement of hydromeliorative works, land management, magistracy, management and marketing, natural resources management; library: 864,000 vols; 484 teachers; 5,371 students; Rector Prof. T. S. HUDOYBERDIYEV; Vice-Rector UKTAM PARDAYEVICH UMURZAKOV.

Tashkent Institute of Railway Transport Engineers: 100167 Tashkent, Adilkhodjayeva 1; tel. (71) 191-14-40; fax (71) 191-10-73; f. 1931; faculties of automation, engineering, construction, economics, industrial and civil construction, telemechanics and communication, traffic management; f. 1931; library: 500,000 vols; 400 teachers; 12,000 students; Rector ANVAR E. ODILKHUJAYEV.

Tashkent Institute of Textile and Light Industry: 100100 Tashkent, Shokhyahon 5; tel. (71) 253-06-06; fax (71) 253-36-17; e-mail titlp@buzton.com; f. 1932; faculties of chemical technology, cotton technology, engineering economics, mechanical technology, technology for light industry; library: 644,000 vols; 242 teachers; 2,214 students; Rector Prof. KH. ALIMOVA.

Tashkent Law Institute: 100047 Tashkent, Sayilgokh 3; tel. (71) 133-41-09; fax (71) 133-37-46; e-mail interlaw1@uzsci.net; Rector M. KH. RUSTAMBAYEV.

Tashkent Paediatric Medical Institute: 100140 Tashkent, Obidova 223; tel. (71) 162-28-71; fax (71) 162-33-14; e-mail tpmi@uzsci.net; Rector ANVAR V. ALIMOV.

Tashkent Pharmaceutical Institute: 100015 Tashkent, Oibek ko'chasi 45; tel. (71) 256-37-38; fax (71) 256-45-04; e-mail pharmi@bcc.com.uz; internet www.pharmi.re.uz; f. 1937; library: 423,420 vols; 212 teachers; 1,323 students; Dir Dr A. N. YUNUSKHOJAYEV.

Tashkent State Agrarian University: 100140 Tashkent, Kibray District, Universitetskaya 5; tel. and fax (71) 263-76-00; e-mail gulumov@atabah.silk.org; f. 1930; depts of accounting, agrochemistry and soil science, agronomy, economics and management, forestry, fruit and vegetable growing, plant protection, silkworm breeding, viticulture,; library: 196,000 vols; 320 teachers; 7,200 students; Rector H. C. H. BURIYEV.

Tashkent State Conservatoire: 100000 Tashkent, Pushkin ko'chasi 31; tel. (71) 133-52-74; fax (71) 133-10-35; f. 1936; piano, orchestral, Uzbek folk instruments, singing, choral conducting, composition, musicology, sound production; library: 243,000 vols; 288 teachers; 548 students; Rector R. Y. YUNUSOV.

Tashkent State Institute of Culture: 100164 Tashkent, Yalangach 127A; tel. and fax (71) 162-03-23; e-mail bbdjuraev@yahoo.com; librarianship, educational and cultural work; br. in Namangan; Rector AZIZ A. TURAYEV.

Tashkent State Medical Institute: 100048 Tashkent, Khamz ko'chasi 03; tel. (71) 267-63-05; fax (71) 233-62-26; e-mail tashmi@mail.ru; f. 1920; trains general practitioners and stomatologists; library: 600,000 vols; 450 teachers; 3,000 students; Rector Prof. T. A. DAMINOV.

Tashkent University of Information Technology: 100084 Tashkent, Amir Temur 108; tel. (71) 138-64-20; fax (71) 135-10-40; e-mail teic@uzpak.uz; f. 1955; faculties of economics, radio communication, special communication, telecommunication networks and switching systems, telecommunication transmission systems, television and broadcasting; library: 500,000 vols; 271 teachers; 3,100 students; Rector Prof. Dr S. S. KASIMOV.

University of World Economics and Diplomacy: 100045 Tashkent, Buyuk Ipak Yuli 54; tel. (71) 267-67-69; fax (71) 267-09-13; e-mail uwed@list.ru; internet www.uwed.uz; f. 1992; 350 teachers; 1,200 students; First Vice-Rector Dr A. FAYZULLAEV.

Uzbek State World Languages University: 100015 Tashkent, Sobir Yusupov ko'chasi 21A, Block G9A; tel. (71) 275-77-95; fax (71) 275-55-57; internet uswlu.freenet.uz; f. 1992 by merger of Tashkent State Pedagogical Institute of Foreign Languages and Republican Russian Language and Literature Pedagogic Institute; faculties of English, German, Spanish, Romance, Russian, translation, international journalism; Rector GAYRAT B. SHOUMAROV.

VANUATU

The Higher Education System

Higher education in Vanuatu is limited, the only institution being a campus of the University of the South Pacific, which opened in 1989. It offers courses leading to certificates, diplomas, degrees and postgraduate qualifications. The campus in Port Vila, known as the Emalus Campus, houses the University's law school. In 2002 there were 2,124 students enrolled in tertiary education. Gross enrolment at tertiary level was just 5% in 2005.

Regulatory Body

GOVERNMENT

Ministry of Education, Youth and Sports: PMB 028, Port Vila; tel. (678) 22309; fax (678) 24569; Minister of Education THOMPSON SEINAVAO TASSO.

Learned Societies

BIBLIOGRAPHY, LIBRARY SCIENCE AND MUSEOLOGY

Pacific Islands Museums Association (PIMA): Vanuatu Cultural Centre, Port Vila; tel. (678) 28063; fax (678) 26590; e-mail pima@vanuatu.com.vu; internet www.culturepacific.org; f. 1994; regional, multilingual, multicultural, non-profit org. to preserve, celebrate and nurture the heritage of the peoples of the Pacific Islands; Sec.-Gen. Dr KIM SELLING.

Vanuatu Library Association: Port Vila; tel. (678) 22888; fax (678) 24494; internet www.vanuatu.usp.ac.fj/library/vla/homepage.htm; to develop and improve library services in Vanuatu; support and encourage devt of libraries, archives and associated professions; Pres. FLORA DIXON; Sec. PAULINE KALO.

Research Institute

NATURAL SCIENCES

Biological Sciences

Environment Unit: Pompidou Complex, Port Vila; e-mail environ@vanuatu.com.vu; internet www.biodiversity.com.vu; govt agency; programmes for devt, conservation and management of natural resources; Dir ERNEST BANI.

Libraries and Archives

Port Vila

National Library: Nat. Museum Bldg, Port Vila; tel. (678) 22129; fax (678) 26590; e-mail nasonal.laebri@vanuatuculture.org; internet www.vanuatuculture.org; 2 spec. collns, Pacific and Vanuatu in English, French and Bislama; linguistics section on the 113 vernacular languages; anthropological and archaeological materials, art and arts references, autobiographical records and biographies, large section of works on the languages of Vanuatu, mission histories, oral traditions, cultural, historical and political records; Librarians ANNE NAUPA, JUNE NORMAN.

National Photo, Film and Sound Archive: POB 184, Port Vila; tel. (678) 23197; fax (678) 26590; internet www.vanuatuculture.org; f. to preserve information about custom, culture and tradition; 3,000 hours of footage (8mm films, Video 8 and VHS ½-inch video) and photographs of oral traditions and rituals.

Port Vila Public Library: Cultural Centre, Port Vila; tel. (678) 23837; fax (678) 27837; internet www.vanuatuculture.org; f. 1960; only public library in Vanuatu; Librarian NAOMI ANIEL.

Museum

Port Vila

Vanuatu Cultural Centre and National Museum (Vanuatu Kaljoral Senta): POB 184, Port Vila; tel. (678) 23197; fax (678) 26590; e-mail vks@vanuatu.com.vu; internet www.vanuatuculture.org; f. 1960 as Port Vila Library; Museum opened in 1995; incl. Malakula Cultural Centre in Lakatoro; houses Vanuatu Cultural and Historic Sites Survey (VCHSS), Young People's Project, Women's Cultural Project; collns of traditional artefacts (masks, slit gongs, outrigger canoes), daily screenings of cultural documentaries; Dir RALPH REGENVANU.

University

UNIVERSITY OF THE SOUTH PACIFIC, EMALUS CAMPUS

POB 9072, Port Vila

Telephone: (678) 22748
Fax: (678) 22633
E-mail: ngwele_a@vanuatu.usp.ac.fj
Internet: www.vanuatu.usp.ac.fj

Dir: JOHN LYNCH
Librarian: MARGARET AUSTRAI-KAILO

Pacific Languages Unit, School of Early Childhood Education, School of Law.

VATICAN CITY

The Higher Education System

The State of the Vatican City is situated entirely within the Italian capital, Rome. In 1929 the Lateran Treaty was concluded between the Italian Government and the Holy See (a term designating the papacy, i.e. the office of the Pope, and thus the central governing body of the Roman Catholic Church). Higher education principally consists of Pontificial universities and institutes offering training for the priesthood and conducting research relating to the Roman Catholic Church, the oldest being the Pontificia Universitas Gregoriana, which was founded in 1553. The majority of institutions are located in Rome outside the boundaries of the Vatican City itself.

Regulatory and Representative Bodies

GOVERNMENT

Congregation for Catholic Education: Palazzo delle Congregazioni, Piazza Pio XII 3, 00193 Rome; tel. (6) 69884167; fax (6) 69884172; e-mail cec@cec.va; f. 1588; concerned with the direction, temporal admin. and studies of Catholic univs, seminaries, schools and colleges; Prefect Cardinal ZENON GROCHOLEWSKI; Sec. Most Rev. JEAN-LOUIS BRUGUÈS.

Pontifical Commission for the Cultural Patrimony of the Church: Via della Conciliazione 5, 00193 Rome; Città del Vaticano, 00120 Rome; tel. (6) 69885640; fax (6) 69884621; e-mail beniculturali@beniculturali.va; f. 1988; acts as curator for the artistic and historical patrimony of the whole Church; library of 6,500 vols; Pres. GIANFRANCO RAVASI.

ACCREDITATION

ENIC/NARIC Holy See: Congregation for Catholic Education, 00120 Vatican City; tel. (6) 69884167; fax (6) 69884172; e-mail educatt@ccatheduc.va; internet www.vatican.va; Contact Rev. PASCALE IDE.

Learned Societies

GENERAL

Pontificia Academia Sancti Thomae Aquinatis (Pontifical Academy of St Thomas Aquinas): 00120 Vatican City; tel. (6) 69881441; fax (6) 69885218; e-mail past@acdscience.va; f. 1879; theological, philosophical and juridico-economic sections; 51 mems; Pres. LLUÍS CLAVELL; Sec. HE Mgr MARCELO SÁNCHEZ SORONDO; publ. *Doctor Communis* (irregular).

ECONOMICS, LAW AND POLITICS

Pontificia Accademia Scientiarum Socialium (Pontifical Academy of Social Sciences): Casina Pio IV, 00120 Vatican City; tel. (6) 69881441; fax (6) 69885218; e-mail social.sciences@acdscience.va; internet www.vatican.va/roman_curia/pontifical_academies/acdscience; f. 1994; social, economic, political and juridical sciences; 37 mems; Pres. Prof. MARY ANN GLENDON; Chancellor Prof. HE MARCELO SÁNCHEZ SORONDO; publs *Acta, Miscellanea*.

FINE AND PERFORMING ARTS

Pontificia Insigne Accademia di Belle Arti e Lettere dei Virtuosi al Pantheon: Via della Conciliazione, 5, 00193 Rome, Italy; tel. (6) 69882232; f. 1542; 90 mems; Pres. Dott. VITALIANO TIBERIA; Sec. Dott. VITTORIO DI GIACOMO; publ. *Annali* (1 a year).

HISTORY, GEOGRAPHY AND ARCHAEOLOGY

Pontificia Accademia Romana di Archeologia (Pontifical Roman Academy of Archaeology): Via della Conciliazione 5, 00193 Rome, Italy; f. 1810; 109 mems; Pres. LETIZIA PANI ERMINI; Sec. VINCENZO FIOCCHI NICOLAI; publs *Memorie, Rendiconti*.

NATURAL SCIENCES

General

Pontificia Academia Scientiarum (Pontifical Academy of Sciences): Casina Pio IV, 00120 Vatican City; tel. (6) 69883451; fax (6) 69885218; e-mail academy.sciences@acdscience.va; internet www.vatican.va/roman_curia/pontifical_academies/acdscience; f. 1603; promotes the mathematical, physical and natural sciences and the study of related epistemological problems; 80 mems; Pres. (vacant) Prof. WERNER ARBER; Chancellor Prof. Mgr MARCELO SÁNCHEZ SORONDO; publs *Acta, Commentari, Documenta, Scripta Varia*.

RELIGION, SOCIOLOGY AND ANTHROPOLOGY

Collegium Cultorum Martyrum: Via Napoleone III 1, 00185 Rome, Italy; f. 1879; 750 mems; Master Mgr EMANUELE CLARIZIO; Sec. LUIGI CIOTTI.

Pontificia Accademia Mariana Internationalis (Pontifical International Marian Academy): Via Merulana 124, 00185 Rome, Italy; premises in Vatican City; tel. (6) 70373235; fax (6) 70373234; e-mail accademiamariana@libero.it; f. 1946, Pontifical since 1959; studies on Our Lady; 75 mems; 155 corresp. mems; 134 hon. mems; Pres. VINCENZO BATTAGLIA; Sec. STEFANO CECCHIN; publ. Scientific collections.

Pontificia Accademia dell'Immacolata (Academy of the Immaculate Conception): Via del Serafico 1, 00142 Rome, Italy; f. 1835; 15 mems; promotes Marian studies and culture, especially the doctrine of the Immaculate Conception in the fields of theology, literature and art; Pres. Cardinal ANDREA M. DESKUR; Sec. and Archivist Fr ZDZISLAW J. KIJAS.

Pontificia Accademia di Teologia: Piazza St Giovanni in Laterano 4, 00120 Vatican City; tel. 06-69895513; e-mail path@pul.it; f. 1718; 7 emeritus mems; 39 ordinary mems; 25 normally resident in Rome, 6 in the rest of Italy and 8 in other countries; 16 corresp. mems; Pres. MARCELLO BORDONI; Sec. Prof. PIERO CODA; publ. *PATH*.

Research Institute

NATURAL SCIENCES

Physical Sciences

Vatican Observatory: 00120 Vatican City; tel. (6) 69885266; f. 1889; carries out research into dark matter and energy in the cosmos, the acceleration of the universe, quasars, globular clusters; library of 33,000 vols; Dir Fr JOSÉ GABRIEL FUNES.

Attached Centre:

Vatican Observatory Research Group (VORG): see entry for Mount Graham International Observatory in USA chapter.

Libraries and Archives

Vatican City

Archivio Segreto Vaticano (Papal Archives): 00120 Vatican City; internet asv.vatican.va; f. 1611; attached school: see Schools; Prefect HE SERGIO PAGANO; publs *Collectanea Archivi Vaticani, Varia*.

Biblioteca Apostolica Vaticana (Vatican Library): 00120 Vatican City; tel. (6) 69879400; fax (6) 69885327; e-mail bav@vatlib.it; internet www.vaticanlibrary.va; f. 1451 as a public library by Pope Nicholas V, and provided with staff and a structure by Sixtus IV in 1475; at the present time it contains 75,000 MSS, 80,000 archival files, 1.6m. engravings, 8,000 incunabula, and 1m. other vols; collns include those of the Dukes of Urbino (1657), of Queen Christina of Sweden (1690), of the Florentine Marquis Capponi (1745), of Barberini (1902), of Chigi (1923), and the Borghese colln, which included many items housed in the Papal Library at Avignon; the Sistine Chapel colln is of importance to historians of music; the Library holds a 4th–century Greek Bible, Vergils from the 4th–6th centuries, a 4th–5th century palimpsest of Cicero's *Republic*, autographs of St Thomas Aquinas, Tasso, Petrarch, Boccaccio, Poliziano, Michelangelo, and Luther; houses numismatic colln; attached museums: see Museums and Art Galleries; attached school: see Schools; Protector Cardinal JEAN-LOUIS TAURAN; Prefect Prof. Don RAFFAELE FARINA; Vice-Prefect Dr AMBROGIO M. PIAZZONI.

Museums and Art Galleries

Vatican City

Museo Profano: Vatican City; f. 1767 by Pope Clement XIII; administered by Vatican Apostolic Library; bronze sculptures and minor arts of the classical era; Curator Dr GIOVANNI MORELLO.

Museo Sacro: Vatican City; f. 1756 by Pope Benedict XIV; administered by Vatican Apostolic Library; contains objects of liturgical art, historical relics and curios from the Lateran, objects of palaeolithic, medieval and Renaissance minor arts, paintings of the Roman era; Curator Dr GIOVANNI MORELLO.

Vatican Museums and Galleries: 00120 Vatican City; tel. (6) 69883333; fax (6) 69885061; internet mv.vatican.va/startnew_en.html; Dir-Gen. Dr FRANCESCO BURANELLI; Administrator Dr FRANCESCO RICCARDI; Sec. Dr EDITH CICERCHIA; publs *Bollettino dei Monumenti, Musei e Gallerie Pontificie*.

Constituent Museums:

Collezione d'Arte Religiosa Moderna (Collection of Modern Religious Art): 00120 Vatican City; f. 1973 by Pope Paul VI; paintings, sculptures and drawings offered to the Pope by over 200 artists and donors; Curator Dott. MARIO FERRAZZA.

Padiglione delle Carrozze (Carriage Pavilion): 00120 Vatican City; f. 1973 by Pope Paul VI; located in the Vatican gardens, containing carriages, berlins and the first cars used by the Popes; Dir Asst Mons. PIETRO AMATO.

Museo Chiaramonti e Braccio Nuovo (Chiaramonti Museum and 'New Side'): 00120 Vatican City; f. by Pope Pius VII at the beginning of the 19th century; house the many new findings excavated in the 19th century; exhibits incl. the statues of the Nile, of Demosthenes and of the Augustus 'of Prima Porta'; Curator Dott. PAOLO LIVERANI.

Museo Gregoriano Egizio (Gregorian Egyptian Museum): 00120 Vatican City; internet mv.vatican.va/3_en/pages/mez/mez_main.html; f. 1839 by Pope Gregory XVI; contains artefacts from Ancient Egypt; 9 exhibition rooms dating from 2600BC to 8th century AD incl. hieroglyphic stelae and statues, finds from Ancient Mesopotamia and Syria–Palestine, Hellenistic and Roman Egypt; Curator Dr ALESSIA AMENTA.

Museo Gregoriano Etrusco (Gregorian Etruscan Museum): 00120 Vatican City; tel. (6) 69883041; fax (6) 69885061; e-mail aei.musei@scv.va; internet mv.vatican.va/3_en/pages/mge/mge_main.html; f. 1837 by Pope Gregory XVI; objects from the Tomba Regolini Galassi of Cerveteri, the Mars of Todi, bronzes, terracottas and jewellery, and Greek vases from Etruscan tombs; Curator Dott. MAURIZIO SANNIBALE.

Museo Gregoriano Profano (Gregorian Museum of Profane Art): 00120 Vatican City; f. by Gregory XVI in 1844 and housed in the Lateran Palace; transferred from fmr site in the Vatican and opened to the public in 1970; Roman sculptures from the Pontifical States; portrait-statue of Sophocles, the Marsyas of the Myronian group of Athena and Marsyas, the Flavian reliefs from the Palace of the Apostolic Chancery; Curator Dott. GIANDOMENICO SPINOLA.

Museo Missionario Etnologico (Ethnological Missionary Museum): 00120 Vatican City; internet mv.vatican.va/3_en/pages/met/met_main.html; f. by Pius XI in 1926 and housed in the Lateran Palace; transferred from fmr site in the Vatican and opened to the public in 1973; ethnographical collns from all over the world; Curator Rev. ROBERTO ZAGNOLI.

Museo Pio Clementino (Museum of Popes Clement XIV and Pius VI): 00120 Vatican City; f. by Pope Clement XIV (1769–74), and enlarged by his successor, Pius VI (1775–1799); exhibits include the Apollo of Belvedere, Roman copies of the Apoxyomenos by Lysippus, of the Meleager by Skopas and of the Apollo Sauroktonous by Praxiteles; the original Vatican Colln was begun with the Apollo—already in possession of Pope Julius II when he was still a Cardinal, at the end of the 15th century—and the Laocoon Group, found in 1506; Curator Dott. PAOLO LIVERANI.

Museo Pio Cristiano (Early Christian Art Museum): 00120 Vatican City; tel. (6) 69881349; fax (6) 69885061; e-mail ap.musei@scv.va; f. 1854 by Pius IX, housed in the Lateran Palace; transferred from fmr site in the Vatican and opened to the public in 1970; largest colln in the world of early Christian sarcophagi; Latin and Greek inscriptions from Christian cemeteries and basilicas; the Good Shepherd; inscriptions from Jewish catacombs; Curator Prof. Dr UMBERTO UTRO.

Pinacoteca Vaticana (Vatican Picture Gallery): 00120 Vatican City; internet mv.vatican.va/3_en/pages/pin/pin_main.html; inaugurated by Pope Pius XI in 1932; incl. paintings by Giotto, Fra Angelico, Raphael, Leonardo da Vinci, Titian and Caravaggio, and the Raphael Tapestries; Curator Dott. ARNOLD NESSELRATH.

Vatican Palaces: 00120 Vatican City; Nicoline Chapel decorated by Beato Angelico (1448–1450); Sistine Chapel restructured by Sixtus IV (1477–1483): frescoes by Perugino, Botticelli, Cosimo Rosselli, Ghirlandaio, Luca Signorelli, Michelangelo; Borgia Apartment: decorated by Pinturicchio and his workshop; Chapel of Urban VIII (1631–1635); Raphael Stanze and loggias decorated by Raphael and his assistants; Gallery of Maps (1580–83), Gallery of Tapestries, etc.; Curator Dott. ARNOLD NESSELRATH.

Universities

PONTIFICIA UNIVERSITAS GREGORIANA
(Pontifical Gregorian University)

Piazza della Pilotta 4, 00187 Rome, Italy
Telephone: (6) 67011
Fax: (6) 67015413
E-mail: segreteria@unigre.it
Internet: www.unigre.it

Founded by St Ignatius Loyola and St Francis Borgia, and constituted by Pope Julius III in 1553; confirmed and established by Pope Gregory XIII in 1582

The central university for ecclesiastical studies is under the direction of the Jesuit Order; Pontificium Institutum Biblicum and Pontificium Institutum Orientalium Studiorum are autonomous colleges associated with the Univ.

Languages of instruction: Italian, English, German, French, Spanish, Portuguese

Academic year: October to June (two terms)

Grand Chancellor: HE Card. ZENON GROCHOLEWSKI

Vice-Grand Chancellor: Rev. PETER-HANS KOLVENBACH

Rector Magnificus: Rev. GIANFRANCO GHIRLANDA

Vice-Rector: Rev. FRANCISCO J. EGAÑA

Academic Vice-Rector: Rev. SERGIO BASTIANEL

Admin. Vice-Rector: Rev. VITALE SAVIO

Sec.-Gen.: LUIGI ALLENA

Librarian: Dr MARTA GIORGI DEBANNE

Library of 900,000 vols

Number of teachers: 423

Number of students: 2,949

Publications: *Acta Nuntiaturae Gallicae, Analecta Gregoriana, Archivum Historiae Pontificiae, Documenta Missionalia, Gregorianum, Inculturation, Miscellanea Historiae Pontificiae, Periodica de re morali canonica liturgica, Saggi ISR, Studia Missionalia, Studia Socialia, Tesi Gregoriana*

DEANS AND DIRECTORS

Cultural Heritage of the Church: J. JANSSEN
Faculty of Canon Law: M. HILBERT
Faculty of Ecclesiastical History: M. INGLOT
Faculty of Missionary Work: A. WOLANIN
Faculty of Philosophy: K. FLANNERY
Faculty of Social Sciences: J. JELENIC
Faculty of Theology: L. LADARIA
Institute of Psychology: T. HEALY
Institute of Religious Sciences: S. BARLONE
Institute of Spirituality: M. SZENTMÁRTONI
Interdisciplinary Centre of Social Communication: J. SRAMPICKAL

PROFESSORS

Cultural Heritage of the Church (tel. (6) 67015114; e-mail segrbcc@unigre.it):

JANSSENS, J., Church History
PFEIFFER, H., Art History

Faculty of Canon Law (tel. 6 67015123; e-mail hilbert@unigre.it):

ASTIGUETA, D., Text of Canon Law
CONN, J., Text of Canon Law
GHIRLANDA, G., Canon Law and Theology of Church Law
HILBERT, M., Text of Canon Law
KOWAL, J., Canon Law and Sacraments
SUGAWARA, Y., Text of Canon Law

Faculty of Ecclesiastical History (tel. (6) 67015410; e-mail inglot@unigre.it):

BENITEZ, J. M., Modern Church History
DE LASALA CLAVER, F., History of the Roman Curia
GUTIERREZ, A., Church History of Latin America
INGLOT, M., History of the Roman Curia
JANSSENS, J., Christian Archaeology – Historical Methodology
MEZZADRI, L., Modern Church History
PFEIFFER, H., Christian Art

Faculty of Missionary Work (tel. (6) 67015240; e-mail wolanin@unigre.it):

FARAHIAN, E., Missionary Biblical Theology
FUSS, M., Buddhism
SHELKE, C., Comparative Study of Religions
WOLANIN, A., Mission Dogmatics

Faculty of Philosophy (tel. and fax (6) 67015441; e-mail filosofia@unigre.it):

BABOLIN, S., Aesthetics and Philosophy of Human Culture
CARUANA, L., Philosophy of Science and Nature
DI MAIO, A., Medieval Philosophy
FLANNERY, K., Greek Philosophy
GILBERT, P., Metaphysics
GORCZYCA, J., Ethics
LECLERC, M., History of Modern Philosophy
LUCAS, R., Philosophical Anthropology
NKERAMIHIGO, T., Philosophy of Theology
PANGALLO, M., History of Medieval Philosophy

Faculty of Social Sciences (tel. (6) 67015316; e-mail scienzesoc@unigre.it):

BAUGH, L., Film and Television Language
JELENIC, J., Social Sciences
SCARVAGLIERI, G., General Religious Sociology

Faculty of Theology (tel. and fax (6) 67015262; e-mail teologia@unigre.it):

ATTARD, M., Moral Theology

BASTIANEL, S., Moral Theology
CALDUCH BENAGES, N., Old Testament Exegesis
CHAPPIN, M., Church History
CONROY, C., Old Testament Exegesis
COSTACURTA, B., Exegesis
FARRUGIA, M., Dogmatic Theology
GALLAGHER, M. P., Fundamental Theology
GRILLI, M., New Testament Exegesis
HENN, W., Dogmatic Theology
LADÁRIA, L., Dogmatic Theology
MEYNET, R., New Testament Exegesis
MILLÁS, J. M., Dogmatic Theology
PASTOR, F., Dogmatic Theology
PECKLERS, K., Liturgy
SCHMITZ, P., Moral Theology
TANNER, N., Patristic Theology
VITALI, D., Dogmatic Theology

Institute of Psychology (tel. (6) 67015299; e-mail psicologia@unigre.it):
HEALY, T., Psychology and Statistics
IMODA, F., Psychology
KIELY, B., Psychopathology
VERSALDI, G., Psychology and Psychotherapy

Institute of Religious Sciences (tel. and fax (6) 67015405; e-mail segrsr@unigre.it):
BARLONE, S., Fundamental Theology
FINAMORE, R., Education
SALATIELLO, G., Anthropology

Institute of Spirituality (tel. (6) 67015532; e-mail szentmartoni@unigre.it):
COSTA, M., Spiritual Theology
GARCÍA MATEO, R., Spiritual Theology
SECONDIN, B., Pastoral Theology
SZENTMÁRTONI, M., Pastoral Psychology

Interdisciplinary Centre on Social Communication (tel. (6) 67015393; fax (6) 67015124; e-mail comunicazione@unigre.it):
BABOLIN, S., Symbology
BAUGH, L., Film and Television Language

AFFILIATED INSTITUTES

Filozofsko-Teološki Institut Družbe Isusove: Jordanovac 110, 41001 Zagreb, Croatia; Dir M. STEINER.

Institut de Philosophie St Pierre Canisius: Kimwenza, BP 3724, Kinshasa-Gombe, Democratic Republic of the Congo; Rector R. DE HAES; Sec. E. STIENNON.

Instituto Superior de Direito Canônico do Brasil: Rua Benjamin Constant 23, 20241 Rio de Janeiro, Brazil; Dir L. MADERO LOPEZ.

Istituto Superiore per i Formatori: Seminario Vescovile, c/o Almo Collegio Capranica 98, 00186 Rome, Italy; Dir A. RAVAGLIOLI.

Istituto Superiore di Scienze Religiose 'Giuseppe Toniolo': Via S. Benedetto da Norcia 2, 65127 Pescara, Italy; Pres. G. CILLI.

Istituto di Filosofia 'Aloisianum': Via Donatello 24, 35123 Padua, Italy; Dir S. BONGIOVANNI.

Jesuit School of Philosophy and Theology 'Arrupe College': POB MP320, Mount Pleasant, Harare, Zimbabwe; Pres. A. L. SHIRIMA.

Pontificio Istituto 'Regina Mundi': Lungotevere Tor di Nona 7, 00186 Rome, Italy; Rector C. MCGOVERN.

Priesterseminar Redemptoris Mater des Erzbistum Berlin: Fortunaallee 29, 12683 Berlin, Germany; Rector S. LATINI.

PONTIFICIA UNIVERSITAS LATERANENSIS
(Pontifical Lateran University)

Piazza S. Giovanni in Laterano, 400120 Vatican City
Telephone: (6) 69895599
Fax: (6) 69886508
E-mail: info@pul.it
Internet: www.pul.it

Founded 1773
Language of instruction: Italian
Academic year: October to June

Grand Chancellor: HE Card. AGOSTINO VALLINI
Rector: HE Bishop RINO FISICHELLA
Vice Rector: Rev. Mgr GAETANO DE SIMONE
Gen. Sec. and Registrar: Dr ULDERICO CONTI
Chief Bursar: Ing. FLAMINIA SACERDOTI

Library of 700,000 vols
Number of teachers: 199 199
Number of students: 4,146

Publications: *Apollinaris* (Questions in Canon and Comparative Law, 2 a year), *Aquinas* (Philosophy, 4 a year), *Lateranum* (Theology, 4 a year), *Nuntium* (Cultural Journal, 43 a year), *Storia et Documenta Historiae et Iuris* (Roman Law, 1 a year)

DEANS

Faculty of Canon Law: Rev. Prof. LUIS BOMBIN BOMBIN
Faculty of Civil Law: Prof. VINCENZO BUONOMO
Faculty of Philosophy: Rev. Prof. GIANFRANCO BASTI
Faculty of Theology: Rev. Prof. RENZO GERARDI

INCORPORATED INSTITUTES

Istituto Patristico 'Augustinianum': Via Paolo VI 25, 00193 Rome, Italy; Pres. Rev. Fr ROBERT J. DODARO.

Istituto Superiore di Teologia Morale 'Accademia Alfonsiana': Via Merulana 31, 00185 Rome, Italy; Pres. Rev. Fr MARTIN MCKEEVER.

Istituto di Teologia della Vita Consacrata 'Claretianum': Largo Lorenzo Mossa 4, 00165 Rome, Italy; Pres. Fr JOSU MIRENA ALDAY.

AGGREGATED INSTITUTES

Instituto Diocesano de Estudios Canónicos: C/ Corona 34, 46003 Valencia, Spain; Pres. Rev. ANTONIO CORBÍ COPOVÍ.

Instituto di Direito Canônico 'Pe. Dr Giuseppe Beinto Pegoraro': Av. Nazaré 993, Ipiranga, 04263-100 São Paulo, Brazil; Dir Mgr MARTIN SEGÚ GIRONA.

Istituto Superiore per l'insegnamento del Diritto 'Université St Paul la Sagesse' de Beyrouth: POB 50-501, Furn El Chebbak, Baada 1011 2050, Lebanon; teaching of law; Pres. Mgr JOSEPH MERHEJ.

Istituto Teologico di Assisi: Piazza S. Francesco 2, 06081 Assisi Santuario, Italy; Pres. Mgr GIOVANNI CAPPELLI.

Istituto Teologico Marchigiano: Via Monte Dago 87, 60131 Ancona, Italy; Pres. Mgr MARIO FLORIO.

AFFILIATED INSTITUTES

Istituto Filosofico della Facoltá di Teologia di Lugano: Via Buffi 13, CP 4663, 69004 Lugano, Switzerland; Rector Prof. LIBERO GEROSA.

Istituto Teologico Abruzzese-Molisano di Chieti: Via Nicoletto Vernia 1, 66100 Chieti, Italy; Prefect of Studies Rev. GIOVANNI GIORGIO.

Istituto Teologico-Cattolico per l'Oceania 'Blessed Diego Luis de San Vitores' di Guam: Catholic Theological Institute for Oceania, 130 Chalan Seminariu, Yona, 96915 Guam, USA; Prefect of Studies Mgr DAVID C. QUITUGUA.

Istituto Teologico della Comunità 'Saint Martin': BP 34, 41120 Candé sur Beuvron, France; Prefect of Studies Rev. Fr FRANÇOIS-REGIS MOREAU.

Istituto Teologico del Seminario di Denver: St John Vianney Theological Seminary, 1300 S Steele St, Denver, CO 80210-2599, USA; Prefect of Studies Dr ANTHONY LILLES.

Istituto Teologico del Seminario di Guadalajara: Seminario Mayor, Santo Domingo 1120, Col. Chapalita, 45040 Guadalajara, Jal., Mexico; Prefect of Studies Rev. FRANCISCO GARCÍA VELARDE.

Istituto Teologico del Seminario di Györ: R. K. Hittudományi Főiskola, Káptalandomb 7, 9021 Györ, Hungary; Prefect of Studies Rev. GÁBOR NÉMETH.

Istituto Teologico del Seminario di Kamyanets-Podilskyi 'Seminarium Maius S. Spiritus': Provulok O. Wanagsa 14, 32000 Gorodok, Khmelnystka obl., Ukraine; Prefect of Studies Rev. JERZY KURCEK.

Istituto Teologico del Seminario di Montréal: Institut de formation théologique, 2065 rue Sherbrooke Ouest, Montréal, QB H3H 1G6, Canada; Prefect of Studies Prof. THUY-LINH NGUYEN.

Istituto Teologico del Seminario di Rīga: Rigas Teologijas Instituts, Katolu iela 16, 1003 Rīga, Latvia; Pro-Prefect of Studies Rev. EDGAR CAKULS.

Istituto Teologico del Seminario Roermond: Groot-Seminarie Rolduc, Heyendallaan 82, 6464 EP Kerkrade, Netherlands; Prefect of Studies Prof. HENDRIK M. G. KRETZERS.

Istituto Teologico del Seminario di Alba Iulia: Str. Bibliotecii 3, 510009 Alba Iulia, Romania; Prefect of Studies Fr ZSOLT F. KOVACS.

Istituto Teologico del Seminario di Iaši: Str. Vâscâuteanu 6, 700462 Iași, Romania; Prefect of Studies Rev. MIHAI PATRASCU.

Istituto Teologico del Seminario San Giuseppe di Vilnius: Juozapo Kunigu Seminarija, Kalvariju 325, 2021 Vilnius, Latvia; Prefect of Studies Rev. HANS FRIEDRICH FISCHER.

Istituto Teologico 'Josephinum' di Columbus: Pontifical College Josephinum, 7625 N High St, Columbus, OH 80210-2599, USA; Prefect of Studies Rev. Fr MICHAEL ROSS.

Istituto Teologico 'St Giovanni Crisostomo' del Seminario di St Pietroburgo: Vysshaya Dukhovnaya Seminariya 'Maria-Tsaritsa Apostolov', Ul. 1-aya Krasnoarmeiskaya 11, 198005 St Petersburg, Russia; Prefect of Studies Rev. JAKUB BLASZCZYSZYN.

Istituto Teologico 'Willibrordhuis' della Diocesi di Haarlem: Willibrordhuis, Zilkerduinweg 375, 2114 Vogelenzang, Netherlands; Prefect of Studies Fr J. MANUEL TERCERO SIMÓN.

Studio Filosofico dell' 'Oratorio di San Filippo Neri': 1372 King St, W, Toronto, ON MGK 1H3, Canada.

Studio Teologico del Seminario di Gerusalemme: Séminaire Patriarcal Latin, POB 14152, Jerusalem, Israel; Prefect of Studies Mgr WILLIAM SHOMALI.

Studio Filosofico del Seminario di Montreal: Institut de Formation Théologique de Montréal, 2065 rue Sherbrooke Ouest, Montréal, QC H3H 1G6, Canada; Prefect of Studies Prof. . THUY-LINH NGUYEN.

Studio Filosofico del Seminario Patriarcale Latino di Gerusalemme: Séminaire Patriarchal Latin, POB 14152, Jerusalem, Israel; Rector Mgr WILLIAM SHOMALI.

Studio Teologico 'Studium Theologicum': CP 153, 80001-970 Curitiba, PR,

Brazil;Ave. Presidente Getúlio Vargas 1193, 80250-180 Curitiba, PR, Brazil; Dir Rev. Fr JAIME SANCHEZ BOSCH.

INSTITUTES WITHIN THE PREMISES

Pontifical John Paul II Institute for Studies on Marriage and Family: Pres. HE Bishop RINO FISICHELLA.

Pontifical Pastoral Institute 'Redemptor Hominis': Piazza St Giovanni in Laterano 4, 00120 Rome, Italy; Pres. Mgr DARIO E. VIGANÒ.

PONTIFICIA UNIVERSITÀ DELLA SANTA CROCE
(Pontifical University of the Holy Cross)

Piazza di Sant'Apollinare 49, 00186 Rome

Telephone: (6) 681641
Fax: (6) 68164400
E-mail: santacroce@pusc.it
Internet: www.pusc.it

Founded 1984; univ. status 1998
Private control (erected by the Holy See)
Chancellor: Rev. Bishop JAVIER ECHEVARRÍA
Vice-Chancellor: Mgr Prof. FERNANDO OCÁRIZ
Rector: Mgr. Prof. LUIS ROMERA
Vice-Rector: Rev. Prof. HÉCTOR FRANCESCHI
Gen.-Sec.: Rev. MANUEL MIEDES
Dir of Academic Affairs: Rev. Prof. FRANCISCO FERNÁNDEZ
Dir of Communications: Prof. NORBERTO GONZÁLEZ GAITANO
Dir of Devt: Dr JOAQUÍN GÓMEZ-BLANES
Librarian: Dott. JUAN DIEGO RAMÍREZ

Number of teachers: 163 ((126 permanent profs, 28 visiting profs in four faculties); 46 permanent profs, 8 visiting professors in the Higher Institute for Religious Studies)
Number of students: 1,470 (1003 students in the 4 faculties; 467 students in the Higher Institute for Religious Studies)

Publications: *International Canon Lawjournal: 'IUS Ecclesiae', International Theology journal: 'Annales Theologici', International Philosophy journal: 'Acta Philosophica'*

HEADS OF SCHOOLS

Higher Institute for Religious Studies: Rev. Prof. MARCO PORTA
School of Canon Law: Rev. Prof. LUIS NAVARRO
School of Philosophy: Rev. Prof. RAFAEL MARTÍNEZ
School of Social Institutional Communications: Dr DIEGO CONTRERAS
School of Theology: Rev. Prof. ÁNGEL RODRÍGUEZ LUÑO

PROFESSORS

Faculty of Church Communications:

ARASA, D.
BAILLY-BAILLIÉRE, A.
BARILLARI, A.
BÜHREN, R. V.
CALOGERO, F.
CANTONI, L.
CARROGGIO, M.
CONTRERAS, D.
DE LA CIERVA, Y.
DOLZ, M.
ESPOZ,, C.
FUSTER, E.
GAGLIARDI, F.
GARCÍA-NOBLEJAS, J. J.
GONZÁLEZ GAITANO, N.
GRAZIANI, N.
GRONOWSKI, D.
JIMÉNEZ, A.
JIMÉNEZ CATAÑO, R.
LA PORTE, J. M.
MACCARINI, A.
MASTROIANNI, B.
MILÁN, J.
MORA, J. M.
PILAVAKIS, M.
POLENGHI, G.
ROMOLO, R.
RUIZ LUCIO, A.
RUSSO, M.
SHAW, R.
TAPIA, S.
TRIDENTE, G.
WAUCK, J.

Faculty of Theology:

AGULLES, P.
AREITIO, J. R.
ARROYO, J. M.
BELDA, M.
BOSCH, V.
CHACÓN, A.
COLOM, E.
DE SALIS AMARAL, M.
DE VIRGILIO, G.
DÍAZ DORRONSORO, R.
DIÉGUEZ, J.
DUCAY, A.
ESTRADA, B.
FABBRI, M. V.
GALVÁN, J. M.
GARCÍA IBÁÑEZ, A.
GONZÁLEZ, E.
GOYRET, P.
GRANADOS, A.
GROHE, J.
JÓDAR, C.
LAMERI, A.
LEAL, J.
LIMBURG, K.
LÓPEZ DÍAZ, J.
MARTÍNEZ-FERRER, L.
MASPERO, G.
MIRA, M.
MIRALLES, A.
NIN, M.
O'CALLAGHAN, P.
OSSANDÓN, J. C.
PIOPPI, C.
PORRAS, A.
REALE, V.
REQUENA, F.
REQUENA, P.
RIESTRA, J. A.
RIO GARCÍA, M.
RODRÍGUEZ LUÑO, A.
ROSSI ESPAGNET, C.
SANZ, S.
SCHLAG, M.
SILVESTRE, J. J.
TÁBET, M.
TANZELLA-NITTI, G.
TORRES, E.
TOUZE, L.
VIAL, W.
WIELOCKX, R.

School Of Canon Law:

ÁLVAREZ DE LAS ASTURIAS, N.
ARAÑA, J. A.
ARRIETA, J. I.
BACCARI, M. P.
BAURA, E.
CANOSA, J.
CITO, D.
DEL POZZO, M.
EISENRING, G.
ERRÁZURIZ M., C. J.
FRANCESCHI, H.
GEFAELL, P.
GÓMEZ-IGLESIAS, V.
GUTIÉRREZ, J. L.
LLOBELL, J.
MARTÍN DE AGAR, J. T.
MIÑAMBRES, J.
NAVARRO, L.
ORTIZ, M. A.
PUIG, F.
SÁNCHEZ-GIL, A. S.
SCHOUPPE, J.-P.

School Of Philosophy:

ACERBI, A.
AIELLO, A.
BERGAMINO, F.
BROCK, S. L.
CHIRINOS, M. A.
CLAVELL, L.
DALLEUR, P.
D'AVENIA, M.
FARO, G.
FERNÁNDEZ LABASTIDA, F.
FERRARI, M. A.
GAHL, R. A.
IPPOLITO, B.
ITURBE, M.
LOMBO, J. A.
MALO, A.
MARTÍNEZ, R.
MERCADO, J. A.
PÉREZ DE LABORDA, M.
PORTA, M.
QUINTILIANI, M.
REYES, C.
RHONHEIMER, M.
ROMERA, L.
RUSSO, F.
SANGUINETI, J. J.
VITORIA, M. A.
YARZA, I.

PONTIFICIA UNIVERSITÀ SAN TOMMASO D'AQUINO
(St Thomas Aquinas Pontifical University)

Largo Angelicum 1, 00184 Rome, Italy

Telephone: (6) 67021
Fax: (6) 6790407
E-mail: segreteria@pust.urbe.it
Internet: www.angelicum.org

Founded 1580 as college, became Univ. 1909; present title conferred 1963
Languages of instruction: Italian, English
Academic year: October to June

Grand Chancellor: Rev. CARLOS AZPIROZ COSTA
Rector Magnificus: Rev. CHARLES MOREROD
Administrator: Rev. VIRGILIO AMBROSINI
Sec.-Gen.: Rev. GLENN MORRIS
Librarian: Rev. MIGUEL ITZA

Library of 200,000 vols
Number of teachers: 125
Number of students: 1,300

Publications: *Angelicum, Istituto S. Tommaso: Studi, Oikonomia* (ethics and social sciences, 3 a year), *Rassegna di Letteratura Tomistica, Studia Univ. S. Thomae In Urbe*

DEANS

Faculty of Canon Law: Rev. MIROSLAV KONSTANC ADAM
Faculty of Philosophy: Rev. PHILIPPE-ANDRE HOLZER
Faculty of Social Sciences: Rev. Sr HELEN ALFORD
Faculty of Theology: JOSEPH PHANTAN THAN

DIRECTORS

Institute of St Thomas: Rev. WALTER SENNER
Institute of Spirituality: Rev. PAUL MURRAY
'Mater Ecclesiae' Institute: S. JURIC

PONTIFICIA UNIVERSITAS URBANIANA
(Pontifical Urbanian University)

Via Urbano VIII 16, 00165 Rome, Italy

Telephone: (6) 69889611
Fax: (6) 69881871
E-mail: segreteria@urbaniana.edu
Internet: www.urbaniana.edu

Founded 1627 by Pope Urban VIII

Language of instruction: Italian
Academic year: October to June

Chancellor: Cardinal IVAN DAS
Vice-Chancellor: Mgr SAVIO HON TAI-FAI
Rector Magnificus: Rev. CATALDO ZUCCARO
Vice-Rector: Rev. L. GODFREY ONAH
Sec.-Gen.: Rev. DON ROBERTO CHERUBINI,
Librarian: Rev. Fr MAREK ROSTKOWSKI

Number of teachers: 158 (incl. 40 full-time)
Number of students: 1,450

Publications: *Annales*, *Bibliografia Missionaria*, *Euntes Docete*, *Urbaniana*, *IUS*, *Missionale*

DEANS

Faculty of Canon Law: Rev. Prof. ANDREA D'AURIA
Faculty of Missiology: Rev. Prof. BENEDICT KANAKAPALLY
Faculty of Philosophy: Rev. Prof. GUIDO MAZZOTTA
Faculty of Theology: Rev. Prof. FRANCESCO CICCIMARRA

PROFESSORS

Faculty of Canon Law:
- D'AURIA, A., General Norms
- MOSCA, V., Matrimony and Canon Law
- PAPALE, C., Oriental Canon Law
- SABBARESE, L., Matrimony and Canon Law

Faculty of Missiology:
- BARREDA, J., Ecumenism
- COLZANI, G., Missionary Systematic Theology
- DOTOLO, C., History and Phenomenology of Religions
- MAZZOLINI, S., Ecclesiology
- SCAIOLA, D., Scriptures
- TREVISIOL, A., History of Missions

Faculty of Philosophy:
- CONGIUNTI, L., Hermeneutics
- MAZZOTTA, G., Metaphysics
- NORECA, A., Logic, Philosophy of Knowledge
- ONAH, I. G., Methodology, Anthropology
- VENDEMIATI, A., General Ethics

Faculty of Theology:
- BIGUZZI, G., New Testament Exegesis
- CICCIMARRA, F., Canon Law
- COLOMBO, G., Moral Theology
- DEIANA, G., Biblical Languages and Scriptures
- EGBULEFU, J., Sacramental Theology
- GONZALEZ FERNANDEZ, F., Church History
- PIRC, J., Ecclesiology
- RIZZI, G., Old Testament Exegesis
- SCHMID, E., Moral Theology
- ZUCCARO, C., Special Moral Theology

DIRECTORS

Affiliated Institutes: Rev. P. GIUSEPPE IULIANO
Chinese Study Centre: Rev. P. ALESSANDRO DELL'ORTO
Department of Languages: Rev. P. ANDREJ GIENIUSZ
Department of Social Communication: LUCA PANDOLFI
Institute for Missionary Catechesis and Spirituality: Fr POMBO KYPOI
Institute for the Study of Atheism: Prof. ADRIAN NORECA

UNIVERSITÀ PONTIFICIA SALESIANA
(Salesian Pontifical University)

Piazza Ateneo Salesiano 1, 00139 Rome, Italy
Telephone: (6) 872901
Fax: (6) 87290318
E-mail: segreteria@unisal.it
Internet: www.unisal.it

Founded 1940, univ. status granted by Pope Paul VI 1973
Language of instruction: Italian
Academic year: October to June (2 semesters)

Chancellor: Very Rev. PASCUAL CHÁVEZ VILLANUEVA
Rector: Very Rev. CARLO NANNI
Vice-Rector: Very Rev. MAURO MANTOVANI
Vice-Rector: Very Rev. VITO ORLANDO
Vice-Rector: Very Rev. GIANFRANCO COFFELE
Admin.: Very Rev. TULLIO ORLER
Sec.-Gen.: Very Rev. JAROSŁAW ROCHOWIAK
Librarian: Very Rev. GIUSEPPE TABARELLI

Library of 750,000 vols
Number of teachers: 224
Number of students: 3,963

Publications: *Orientamenti Pedagogici* (6 a year), *Salesianum* (4 a year)

DEANS

Department of Youth, Pastoral Theology and Catechetics: Very Rev. CYRIL DE SOUZA
Faculty of Canon Law: Very Rev. DAVID ALBORNOZ
Faculty of Education: Very Rev. FRANCESCO CASELLA
Faculty of Letters (Christian and Classics): Very Rev. MARIO MARITANO
Faculty of Philosophy: Very Rev. MAURO MANTOVANI
Faculty of Social Communication Sciences: Very Rev. FRANCO LEVER
Faculty of Theology: Very Rev. GIORGIO ZEVINI
Postgraduate School of Clinical Psychology: Prof. CARLA DE NITTO

PROFESSORS

Faculty of Canon Law (tel. (6) 87290639; fax (6) 87290258; e-mail diritto@unisal.it):
- ALBORNOZ, D., Text of Canon Law
- ARDITO, S., Text of Canon Law
- GRAULICH, M., Foundation and History of Canon Law
- PUDUMAI DOSS, M. J., Canon Law
- URÍA, J., Text of Canon Law

Faculty of Education (tel. (6) 87290426; fax (6) 87290656; e-mail fse@unisal.it;):
- BAJZEK, J., Sociology of Religion
- BAY, M., Methodology of Research
- CASELLA, F., History of Pedagogy
- COMOGLIO, M., Didactics
- DESBOUTS, C., Didactics
- DE SOUZA, C., Anthropology and Catechesis
- FORMELLA, Z., Psychology of Education
- GAMBINI, P., General Psychology and Dynamic
- GRZADZIEL, D., General Pedagogy
- LLANOS, M., Vocational Pastoral
- MONTISCI, U., Theology of Education
- NANNI, C., Philosophy of Education
- ORLANDO, V., Social Pedagogy
- PASTORE, C., Bible and Catechesis
- ROGGIA, G., Pedagogic Methodology
- VALLABARAJ, J., Catechesis
- VETTORATO, G., Sociology of Deviance
- ZANNI, N., Didactics

Faculty of Letters (Christian and Classics) (tel. (6) 87290304; fax (6) 87290641; e-mail lettere@ups.urbe.it):
- BRACCHI, R., History of the Greek and Latin Languages
- DAL COVOLO, E., Ancient Christian Greek Literature
- MARITANO, M., Patristic
- MAZEWSKI, A., History of Latin Classic Literature
- SAJOVIC, M., Ancient Christian Latin Literature

Faculty of Philosophy (tel. (6) 87290625; fax (6) 87290640; e-mail filosofia@unisal.it):
- ABBÀ, G., Ethics
- ALESSI, A., Metaphysics
- KUREETHADAM, J., Philosophy of Science
- MANTOVANI, M., Metaphysics
- MARIN, M., History of Philosophy
- ROSON GALACHE, L., Philosophical Anthropology
- THURUTHIYIL, S., History of Philosophy
- TOSO, M., Social and Political Philosophy

Faculty of Social Communication Sciences (tel. (6) 87290331; fax (6) 87290536; e-mail fsc@unisal.it; internet fscs.ups.urbe.it):
- CEPEDA, E., Theory and Research of Social Communication
- DEVADOSS, J., Sciences of Social Communication
- GONSALVES, P., Theory and History of Communication
- LEVER, F., Theory and Technics of Television/Mass Media and Catechesis
- LEWICKI, T., Theory and Technics of Theatre
- PASQUALETTI, F., Theory and Technics of Radio
- PRESERN, V. A., Theory and Research of Social Communication

Faculty of Theology (tel. (6) 87290297; fax (6) 87290556; e-mail teologia@unisal.it):
- ANTHONY, F., Pastoral Theology
- BALDERAS, R., Spiritual Theology
- BOZZOLO, A., Dogmatics
- CARLOTTI, P., Moral Theology
- CASTELLANO, A., Dogmatic
- CHUNKAPURA, J., Missiology
- CIMOSA, M., Old Testament
- COFFELE, G., Fundamental Theology
- ESCUDERO, A., Dogmatic
- GARCÍA, J., Spiritual Theology
- GIRAUDO, A., Spiritual Theology
- KRASON, F., Liturgy
- MARITANO, M., Ancient Church History and Patrology
- MEDEIROS, D. R., Systematic Theology of Sacraments
- MORAL DE LA PARTE, J. L., Youth Pastoral
- MERLO, P., Moral Theology
- MUSONI, A., Systematic Theology: Ecclesiology and Ecumenism
- PALOMBELLA, M., Dogmatic
- PERRENCHIO, F., Old Testament
- PLASCENCIA, J., Systematic Theology II: Theological Anthropology
- SODI, M., Liturgy
- VICENT, R., Old Testament
- ZEVINI, G., New Testament

SALESIAN HOUSE THEOLOGICAL STUDIES, VIETNAM

Centre Saint-Augustin: Villa Contiguë au Village S.O.S., BP 15222, Dakar-Fann, Senegal; Dean Very Rev. CHRISTIAN CARLIER.

Département de Philosophie de l'Institut Catholique de l'Afrique Centrale: BP 11628, Yaoundé, Cameroon; Dean Rev. KIZITO FORBI.

Departamento de Filosofía del Instituto de Teología para Religiosos: 3A Avda con 6A Transversal (H. B. Pinto), Apdo 68865 Altamira, Caracas 1062-A, Venezuela; Dean Rev. CARLOS LUIS SUÁREZ CODORNIÚ.

Institut de Philosophie 'Saint-Joseph-Mukasa': Nkol-Bisson, BP 185, Yaoundé, Cameroon; Dean Rev. KRZYSZTOF ZIELENDA.

Institut de Theologie Saint François de Sales Lubumbashi: Congo; tel. and fax (243) 970-176-94; e-mail theosdb_lubum@yahoo.com; Pres. Prof. JEAN-LUC VANDE KERKHOVE.

Instituto Superior de Estudios Teologicos 'Cristo Buen Pastor' (ISET): Hipólito Yrigoyen 3951, 1208 Buenos Aires, Argentinia; Dir Very Rev. JUAN PICCA.

Instituto 'Santo Tomás de Aquino': Rua Itutinga 300-B, Minas Brasil, 30535-640 Belo Horizonte, MG, Brazil; Dean Very Rev. PAULO ROBERTO GOMES.

Instituto Superior de Ciencias Religiosos 'Don Bosco': Avda Card. Vidal i Barraquer 1, 08035 Barcelona, Spain; Dean Very Rev. JORDI LA TORRE I CASTILLO.

Instituto de Teología para Religiosos–ITER: 3A Avda con 6A Transversal (H. B. Pinto), Apdo 68865 Altamira, Caracas 1062-A, Venezuela; Dean Rev. CARLOS LUIS SUÁREZ CODORNIÚ.

Instituto Teológico Pio XI: Rua Pio XI, 1100–Alto da Lapa, 05060-001 São Paulo, Brazil; tel. (11) 364-902-00; fax (11) 383-185-74; e-mail secretaria@institutoteologico.org .br; Pres. Prof. RONALDO ZACHARIAS.

Instituto Teológico Salesiano 'Cristo Resucitado' Tlaquepaque: Apdo. POB 66, 45500, San Pedro Tlaquepaque, Messico; tel. (3) 657-45-55; fax (3) 635-54-54; e-mail teologia_its@yahoo.com.mx; Pres. SERGIO DE LA CRUZ LOERA.

Instituto Universitario Salesiano 'Padre Ojeda': Avda El Liceo, Apdo 43, Los Teques, 1201-A Venezuela; Dean Very Rev. JULIÁN RODRÍGUEZ V.

Philosophische-Theologische Hochschule der Salesianer: Don Bosco-Str. 1, 83671 Benediktbeuern, Germany; Rector Very Rev. LOTHAR BILY.

Salesian House Philosophical Studies, Nave: Centro di Studi 'Paolo VI', Via S. Giovanni Bosco 1, 25075 Nave, Italy; Dean Very Rev. PAOLO ZINI.

Salesian House Philosophical Studies, Santiago: Avda Lo Cañas 3636, Casilla 53, La Florida, Santiago, Chile; Dean Very Rev. NILO DAMIÁN ZÁRATE LÓPEZ.

Salesian House Theological Studies, Bangalore: Kristu Jyoti College, Bosco Nagar, Krishnarajapuram, Bangalore 560036, India; Dean Very Rev. ANTON PAUL PADINJARATHALA.

Salesian House Theological Studies, Guatemala: 20 Avda 13–45, Zona 11, Guatemala City, Guatemala 01011, CA; Dean Very Rev. FÉLIX VALLEJOS.

Salesian House Theological Studies, 'Saints Peter and Paul', Jerusalem: St Paul, 26 Rehov Shmuel Hanagid St, POB 7336, 91072 Jerusalem, Israel; Dean Very Rev. ROBERTO SPATARO.

Salesian House Theological Studies 'Don Bosco', Manila: POB 8206, CPO 1700, Parañaque City, Metro Manila, Philippines; Dean Very Rev. RAFAEL DELA CRUZ.

Salesian House Theological Studies, Meghalaya: Sacred Heart Theological College, Mawlai, Shillong 793008, Meghalaya, India; Dean Very Rev. JOSEPH PUYKUNNEL.

Salesian House for Theological Studies 'S. Tommaso d'Aquino', Messina: Via del Pozzo 43–CP 28, 98121 Messina, Italy; Dean Very Rev. GIOVANNI RUSSO.

Salesian Institute of Philosophy: Divya Daan, Don Bosco Marg, College Rd, Nasik 422005, India; Dean Very Rev. ROBERT PEN.

Colleges

ATHENAEUM PONTIFICIUM REGINA APOSTOLORUM

Via degli Aldobrandeschi 190, 00163 Rome, Italy
Telephone: (6) 66527800
Fax: (6) 66527814
E-mail: segreteria@upra.org
Internet: www.upra.org

Founded 1993

Rector: Fr PAOLO SCARAFONI
Sec.-Gen.: Fr LUCA MARIA GALLIZIA

DEANS

Faculty of Bioethics: Fr GONZALO MIRANDA
Faculty of Philosophy: Fr MICHAEL RYAN
Faculty of Theology: Fr THOMAS WILLIAMS

PONTIFICIA FACOLTÀ DI SCIENZE DELL'EDUCAZIONE 'AUXILIUM'

Via Cremolino 141, 00166 Rome, Italy
Telephone: (6) 6157201
Fax: (6) 61564640
E-mail: segreteria@pfse-auxilium.org
Internet: www.pfse-auxilium.org

Founded 1954

Academic year: October to July

Grand Chancellor: Rev. PASCUAL CHAVEZ VILLANUEVA
Vice-Grand Chancellor: YVONNE REUNGOAT
Pres.: GIUSEPPINA DEL CORE
Sec.: M. GIOVANNA CERUTI
Librarian: MARIA ANTONIETTA VALENTINO

Library of 106,330 vols, 570 periodicals
Number of teachers: 55
Number of students: 400

Publication: *Rivista di Scienze dell' Educazione* (3 a year).

PONTIFICIA FACOLTÀ TEOLOGICA DI S. BONAVENTURA

Via del Serafico 1, 00142 Rome, Italy
Telephone: (6) 51503206
Fax: (6) 5192067
E-mail: seraphicum1@ofmconv.org
Internet: www.bon.ofmconv.org

Founded 1587, re-founded 1905

Grand Chancellor: Most Rev. AGOSTINO GARDIN
Pres.: Rev. Fr GIOVANNI IAMMARRONE
Vice-Pres.: Rev. Fr MAURIZIO WSZOLEK
Sec.: Rev. Fr JULIAN ZAMBANINI
Librarian: Rev. Fr BONAVENTURA DANZA

Library of 210,000 vols
Number of teachers: 41
Number of students: 130

Publication: *Miscellanea Francescana* (4 a year).

PONTIFICIA FACOLTÀ TEOLOGICA 'MARIANUM'

Viale Trenta Aprile 6, 00153 Rome, Italy
Telephone: (6) 58391601
Fax: (6) 5880292
E-mail: marianum@marianum.it
Internet: www.marianum.it

Founded 1950

Academic year: October to July

Grand Chancellor: Rev. Fr ANGEL M. RUIZ GORNICA
Pres.: Rev. Fr SILVANO M. MAGGIANI
Sec.: Sis. ORNELLA DI ANGELO

Library of 109,000 vols on Mariological studies
Number of teachers: 55
Number of students: 318

Publication: *Marianum* (2 a year).

PONTIFICIA FACOLTÀ TEOLOGICA TERESIANUM

Piazza San Pancrazio 5A, 00152 Rome, Italy
Telephone: (6) 58540248
Fax: (6) 58540243
E-mail: segreteria@teresianum.org
Internet: www.teresianum.org

Founded 1935

Academic year: October to June

Grand Chancellor: Most Rev. Fr LUIS AROSTEGUI GAMBOA
Pres.: Fr VIRGILIO PASQUETTO
Sec.-Gen.: Fr ADRIAN ATTARD
Librarian: Fr ARTURO BELTRAN

Library of 500,000 vols (open to the public)
Number of teachers: 51
Number of students: 450

Publications: *Bibliographia Internationalis Spiritualitatis*, *Studia Theologica*, *Teresianum* (specialist review, 2 a year).

ATTACHED INSTITUTE

Pontificio Istituto di Spiritualità: f. 1957; 30 teachers; 300 students; centre for bibliographical research in field of spiritual theology; Moderator Fr BENITO GOYA.

PONTIFICIO ATENEO ST ANSELMO

Piazza Cavalieri di Malta 5, 00153 Rome, Italy
Telephone: (6) 5791401
Fax: (6) 5791402
E-mail: segreteria@santanselmo.org
Internet: www.santanselmo.org

Founded 1687

Language of instruction: Italian

Academic year: October to June

Grand Chancellor: Most Rev. Fr NOTKER WOLF
Rector Magnificus: Rev. Fr MARK SHERIDAN
Registrar: Rev. Fr STEFANO VISINTIN
Librarian: Rev. Fr JAMES LEACHMAN
Treas.: Rev. Fr GERARDO GAREGNANI

Library of 131,000 vols
Number of teachers: 78
Number of students: 423

Publications: *Corpus Consuetudinum Monasticarum*, *Ecclesia Orans* (Liturgical Inst. Review), *Rerum Ecclesiasticarum Documenta* (Critical Editions of Liturgical Texts), *Studia Anselmiana*

DEANS

Faculty of Philosophy: Rev. Mons. ANICETO MOLINARO
Faculty of Theology: Rev. Fr DANIEL HOMBERGEN
Pontifical Liturgical Institute: Rev. Fr JUAN JAVIER FLORES ARCAS

PONTIFICIO ATENEO ANTONIA

Via Merulana 124, 00185 Rome, Italy
Telephone: (6) 70373502
Fax: (6) 70373604
E-mail: segreteriapaa@ofm.org
Internet: www.antonianum.ofm.org

Founded 1933

Franciscan Int. Univ.

Grand Chancellor: Most Rev. J. RODRÍGUEZ CARBALLO
Rector Magnificus: Rev. Fr JOHANNES B. FREYER
Vice-Rector: Rev. P. MANUEL BLANCO
Sec.-Gen.: Rev. Fr JORGE HORTA
Librarian: Rev. Fr MARCELLO SARDELLI

Library of 500,000 vols
Number of professors: 145

Publication: *Antonianum*

DEANS

Faculty of Biblical Science and Archaeology: Rev. Fr GIOVANNI C. BOTTINI
Faculty of Canon Law: Rev. Fr PRIAMO ETZI
Faculty of Philosophy: Rev. Fr STÉPHANE OPPES
Faculty of Theology: Rev. Fr VINCENZO BATTAGLIA

DIRECTORS

Higher Institute of Religious Studies: Sr M. MELONE

Higher School of Medieval and Franciscan Studies: Rev. Fr A. CACCIOTTI
Institute of Ecumenical Studies: Rev. Fr R. GIRALDO
Institute of Spirituality: Rev. Fr P. MARTINELLI

PONTIFICIO ISTITUTO DI ARCHEOLOGIA CRISTIANA

Via Napoleone III 1, 00185 Rome, Italy
Telephone: (6) 4465574
Fax: (6) 4469197
E-mail: piac@piac.it
Internet: www.piac.it

Founded 1925 by Pope Pius XI
Academic year: November to May

Grand Chancellor: Bishop ZENON GROCHOLEWSKI
Rector: Prof. VINCENZO FIOCCHI NICOLAI
Sec.: Dr OLOF BRANDT
Librarian and Prefect of Collns: Dr GIORGIO NESTORI

Library of 60,000 vols
Number of teachers: 8
Number of students: 80

Publications: *Inscriptiones Christianae Urbis Romae, Monumenti di Antichità Cristiana, Rivista di Archeologia Cristiana, Roma Sotterranea Cristiana, Studi di Antichità Cristiana, Sussidi allo Studio delle Antichità Cristiane*

PROFESSORS

BISCONTI, F., Christian Iconography
DATTRINO, L., Patristics
FIOCCHI NICOLAI, V., Christian Cemeteries and Topography of Ancient Rome
GUIDOBALDI, F., Ancient Sacred Architecture
HEID, S., Hagiography and Liturgy of the Early Church
MAZZOLENI, D., Classical and Christian Epigraphy
PERGOLA, PH., 'Orbis Christianus' and Classical Topography
RAMIERI, A. M., Art History
SPERA, L., Christian Topography of Rome

PONTIFICIO ISTITUTO DI MUSICA SACRA

Via di Torre Rossa 21, 00165 Rome, Italy
Telephone: (6) 6638792
Fax: (6) 6622453
E-mail: pims@musica-sacra.va
Internet: www.vatican.va

Founded 1911 by Pope Pius X
Language of instruction: Italian
Academic year: October to June

Grand Chancellor: HE Rev. Mgr ZENON GROCHOLEWSKI
Pres.: Mgr VALENTINO MISERACHS GRAU
Sec.: Dott. GIUSEPPE MORETTI
Librarian: Dott. ANTONIO ADDAMIANO

Library of 40,000 vols
Number of teachers: 18
Number of students: 141

Publication: *Calendar* (1 a year).

PONTIFICIO ISTITUTO ORIENTALE (Pontifical Oriental Institute)

Piazza Santa Maria Maggiore 7, 00185 Rome, Italy
Telephone: (6) 4474170
Fax: (6) 4465576
E-mail: piosgr@pio.urbe.it
Internet: www.pio.urbe.it

Founded 1917 by Pope Benedict XV for the benefit of Eastern and Western scholars both Catholic and non-Catholic, interested in Oriental ecclesiastical questions

Associated with the Pontifical Gregorian University (see above)

Rector: Rev. Prof. HÈCTOR VALL VILARDELL
Pro-Rector: Rev. Prof. SUNNY T. KOKKARAVALAYIL
Vice-Rector: Rev. Prof. CONSTANTIN SIMON
Gen. Sec.: MAURIZIO DOMENICUCCI
Librarian: Rev. FRANÇOIS GICK

Library of 185,000 vols
Number of teachers: 73
Number of students: 355

Publications: *Anaphorae Orientales, Kanonika, Orientalia Christiana Analecta, Orientalia Christiana Periodica*

DEANS

Faculty of Oriental Canon Law: Rev. Prof. MICHAEL J. KUCHERA
Faculty of Oriental Ecclesiastical Studies: Rev. Prof. EDWARD G. FARRUGIA

PROFESSORS

ARRANZ, L. M., Oriental Liturgy
CECCARELLI MOROLLI, D., Oriental Canon Law
FARRUGIA, E., Oriental Theology
GARGANO, G., Oriental Patrology
GIRAUDO, C., Liturgy and Dogmatic Theology
LUISIER, P., Coptic Patrology and Language
NEDUNGATT, G., Oriental Canon Law
RUGGERI, V., Byzantine History and Archaeology
SENYK, S., Ukrainian Church History
SIMON, C., Slavic History
TAFT, R., Byzantine Liturgy
VALL VILARDELL, H., Ecumenism
VASIL, C., Oriental Canon Law
YOUSSIF, P., Syriac Patrology
ŽUŽEK, I., Oriental Canon Law

PONTIFICIO ISTITUTO DI STUDI ARABI E D'ISLAMISTICA

Viale di Trastevere 89, 00153 Rome, Italy
Telephone: (6) 58392611
Fax: (6) 5882595
E-mail: info@pisai.it

Founded 1949
Academic year: October to June

Dir: Fr MIGUEL ÁNGEL AYUSO GUIXOT
Librarian: Fr PIET HORSTEN

Library of 32,500 vols
Number of teachers: 10
Number of students: 52

Publications: *Encounter* (Documents for Christian–Muslim Understanding, 10 a year), *Etudes Arabes* (1 a year), *Islamochristiana* (1 a year).

PONTIFICIUM INSTITUTUM BIBLICUM

Via della Pilotta 25, 00187 Rome, Italy
Telephone: (6) 695261
Fax: (6) 695266211
E-mail: pibsegr@biblico.it
Internet: www.biblico.it

Founded 1909 by Pope Pius X for scriptural studies, Faculty of Ancient Oriental Studies added 1932, Pontifical Biblical Institute of Jerusalem (f. 1927), br. of Roman Institute

Associated with the Pontifical Gregorian Univ. (see above)
Languages of instruction: Italian, English
Academic year: October to June

Rector: Rev. JOSÉ MARIA ABREGO DE LACY
Sec.: CARLO VALENTINO
Librarian: Rev. J. JANSSENS

Number of teachers: 40
Number of students: 300
Library of 165,000 vols

Publications: *Acta Pont. Inst. Biblici* (1 a year), *Analecta Biblica, Analecta Orientalia, Biblica* (4 a year), *Biblica et Orientalia, Elenchus of Biblica* (1 a year), *Orientalia* (4 a year), *Studia Pohl, Subsidia Biblica*

DEANS

Faculty of Ancient Oriental Studies: Rev. A. GIANTO
Faculty of Biblical Studies: Rev. S. PISANO

PROFESSORS

Faculty of Ancient Oriental Studies:

ALTHANN, R., Languages and Literature of Ancient Israel
GIANTO, A., Semitic Philology and Linguistics
MAYER, W., Accadian Language and Literature
MORRISON, C., Syriac and Targumic-Aramaic Languages

Faculty of Biblical Studies:

ALETTI, J.-N., New Testament Exegesis
BARBIERO, G., Old Testament Exegesis
BECHARD, D., New Testament Exegesis
BOVATI, P., Old Testament Exegesis
LUZARRAGA, J., New Testament Exegesis
NEUDECKER, R., Rabbinic Literature
PISANO, S., Textual Criticism
SIEVERS, J., History and Literature of the Intertestamental Period
SKA, J. L., Old Testament Exegesis

Schools

Scuola Vaticana di Biblioteconomia (Vatican School of Library Services): 00120 Vatican City; tel. (6) 69879526; fax (6) 69879525; e-mail scuola@vatlib.it; internet www-urbs.vatlib.it/scuola; f. 1934; attached to Vatican Apostolic Library; 6 teachers; 48 students a year; Dir Prof. Don RAFFAELE FARINA.

Scuola Vaticana di Paleografia, Diplomatica e Archivistica (Vatican School of Paleography, Diplomacy and Archive Science): 00120 Vatican City; tel. (6) 69883595; fax (6) 69881377; e-mail asv@asv.va; attached to Papal Archives; Dir SERGIO PAGANO; publ. *Littera Antiqua*.

VENEZUELA

The Higher Education System

Institutions of higher education predate Venezuela's independence from Spain in 1830, the oldest being Universidad Central de Venezuela, which was founded in 1721. The next oldest institution is Universidad de los Andes, which was founded in 1785 (current status 1810). The Ministry of Higher Education has supreme authority over higher education, which consists of public and private universities, polytechnic institutes and an 'open' university (for distance-learning and continuing education). In 2003/04 there were 48 universities with 626,837 students.

The main requirement for admission to higher education is the Bachillerato, the secondary school certificate. In 2009 the government passed a law to establish a national standardized university entrance examination system, replacing public universities' internal entrance examinations. However, some universities have rejected the new system. The undergraduate degree is the Licenciado, which lasts four to five years. (Alternatively, a professional title may be awarded.) Following the award of the Licenciado, graduates may study for a further year for the award of the Especialización, which indicates specialization in a particular area or subject. Alternatively, graduates study for two years after the Licenciado for the Masters (Maestría) degree, which culminates with the submission of a thesis. Finally, the highest university degree is the Doctorado, a research-based degree lasting three years following the award of either the Maestría or Especialización.

Post-secondary technical and vocational education is offered by technological institutes (institutos universitarios de tecnología) and university colleges (colegios universitarios), but the qualifications are regarded as sub-degree level. The main qualification is the Técnico Superior, a three-year course comprising mostly of practical study.

There is currently no external agency that accredits undergraduate programmes, although the National Council of Universities maintains a register of authorized degree programmes. All postgraduate programmes are subject to accreditation by the Consejo Consultivo Nacional de Postgrado, an independent accreditation body established by the Ministry of Education.

Regulatory and Representative Bodies

GOVERNMENT

Ministry of Culture: Edif. Archivo General de la Nación, Avda Panteón, Foro Libertador, Caracas; tel. (212) 509-56-00; e-mail mppc@ministeriodelacultura.gob.ve; internet www.ministeriodelacultura.gob.ve; Minister FRANCISCO SESTO.

Ministry of Education: Edif. Ministerio de Educación, Mezzanina, esq. de Salas, Parroquia Altagracia, Caracas, 1010; tel. (212) 506-8211; e-mail atencion_al_publico@me.gob.ve; internet www.me.gov.ve; Minister HÉCTOR NAVARRO.

Ministry of Higher Education: Torre MCT, 6°, Avda Universidad, esq. el Chorro, Caracas 1010; tel. (212) 596-5293; e-mail enlacesmes@mes.gov.ve; internet www.mes.gov.ve; Minister LUIS AUGUSTO ACUÑA CEDEÑO.

NATIONAL BODIES

Asociación Venezolana de Rectores Universitarios (AVERU) (Venezuelan Association of University Rectors): Avda Santa Fe Sur, Edif. 'Araucaria', Piso 4°-43, Urb. Santa Fe, Caracas; tel. (212) 975-14-62; fax (212) 979-92-63; Pres. RITA AÑEZ.

Consejo Nacional de Universidades (National Council of Universities): Avda La Salle, Centro Capriles P.B., Caracas; tel. (212) 709-1200; e-mail webmaster@cnu.gov.ve; internet www.cnu.gov.ve/informacion/cnu.php; f. 1946; consists of staff and student reps of all univs and reps from the Ministry of Finance and the Science Council; coordinates academic relations within the higher education system and fosters links between the univs and the remainder of the nat. educational system; establishes academic, cultural and scientific policies in the higher education sector and stipulates its devt; suggests to the Nat. Exec. regulations concerning the recognition of studies and qualifications; proposes to the Nat. Exec. the annual univ. budget and distributes funding to nat. univs; library of 2,000 vols; Pres. THE MINISTER OF HIGHER EDUCATION; Perm. Sec. ASALIA VENEGAS SIMANCAS; publ. *Boletín Informativo* (4 a year).

Learned Societies

GENERAL

Academia Venezolana de la Lengua (Venezuelian Academy of Language): Apdo 1421, Caracas; Palacio de las Academias, Av. Universidad, Caracas 1010-A; tel. (212) 481-2890; fax (212) 481-2890; e-mail acadlengv@cantv.net; f. 1883; corresp. of the Real Academia Española (Madrid, Spain); 24 mems; library: see Libraries and Archives; Pres. ÓSCAR SAMBRANO URDANETA; Sec. HORACIO BIORD CASTILLO; publs *Boletín* (4 a year), *Clásicos Venezolanos*.

ARCHITECTURE AND TOWN PLANNING

Asociación de Agrimensores de Venezuela (Surveyors' Association): c/o Colegio de Ingenieros de Venezuela, Apdo 2006, Bosque Los Caobos, Caracas 1010; Pres. Agm. GERMÁN AÑEZ OTERO; Sec. Agm. RAFAEL ELSTER NODA.

Colegio de Arquitectos de Venezuela (Venezuela Architects' Association): C.C. Casa Mall en Los Naranjos, El Cafetal, Caracas; tel. (212) 988-1331; internet cav.org.ve; f. 1945 as Sociedad Venezolana de Arquitectos; 3,600 mems; Pres. Arq. ITALO BALBI; Sec. Arq. HENRY SAAD; publ. *Revista del CAV*.

BIBLIOGRAPHY, LIBRARY SCIENCE AND MUSEOLOGY

Colegio de Bibliotecólogos y Archivólogos de Venezuela (Venezuelan Librarians' and Archivists' Association): Parroquia Altagracia, Avda Panteón, Foro Libertador, Biblioteca Nacional, Cuerpo 2, S1, Caracas; tel. (212) 564-1203; fax (212) 564-1203; e-mail cbiarchiv@hotmail.com; internet personales.com/venezuela/caracas/cbav; f. 1989; 419 mems; Pres. Lic. ELSI JIMENEZ DE DÍAZ; Vice-Pres. Lic. FLOR MARINA LUNA; publs *AB Te Informa* (4 a year), *CBActualidad* (irregular).

ECONOMICS, LAW AND POLITICS

Academia de Ciencias Políticas y Sociales (Academy of Political and Social Sciences): Palacio de las Academias, Bolsa a San Francisco, Caracas 1010; tel. (212) 481-6035; fax (212) 483-2674; e-mail acienpol@cantv.net; internet www.acienpol.org.ve; f. 1915; 35 mems; Pres. Dr ENRIQUE LAGRANGE; Sec. GABRIEL RUAN SANTOS; Chief Librarian BEATRIZ MARTÍNEZ; publ. *Boletín de la Academia*.

Colegio de Abogados del Distrito Capital (Lawyers' Association): Apdo Postal 1060, Caracas; Av. Veracruz, Edif. Keope, Piso 1, Of. 15-B, Las Mercedes, Caracas; tel. (212) 991-98-45; e-mail secretaria@justicia.net; internet www.justicia.net; f. 1788; 2,000 mems; Pres. Abog. RAFAEL VELOZ GARCIA; Sec. Abog. ROSAURA SÁNCHEZ; publ. *Revista*.

EDUCATION

Grupo Universitario Latinoamericano de Estudio para la Reforma y el Perfeccionamiento de la Educación (GULERPE) (Latin American University Group for Reform and Improvement in Education): Residencias Araucaria, Apdo 43, Santa Fe Sur, Caracas 1080-150; Piso 4, Avda Santa Fe Sur, Santa Fe, Caracas 1080-150; tel. (212) 979-9263; fax (212) 979-9263; internet www.universitas2000.usb.ve; f. 1965; higher education, research, and educational policy, administration and planning; 150 mems; Pres. Dra ELIZABETH Y. DE CALDERA; Exec. Sec. Prof. FELIPE BEZARA; publ. *Universitas 2000* (in single or double editions, 4 a year).

FINE AND PERFORMING ARTS

Asociación Venezolana Amigos del Arte Colonial (Venezuelan Association of Friends of Colonial Art): Museo de Arte Colonial,

Quinta de 'Anauco', Avda Panteón, San Bernardino, Caracas 1011; tel. (212) 551-8517; fax (212) 551-8517; e-mail artecolonialanauco@cantv.net; internet www.quintadeanauco.org.ve; f. 1942; preservation and collection of architectural forms, bronze, ceramics, glass, iron, music, period furniture, paintings, porcelain, silver, sculpture, textiles from the 16th–18th centuries; Pres. JUAN CARLOS SOSA; Dir CARLOS F. DUARTE; publ. *Revista*.

Consejo Nacional de la Cultura (CONAC) (National Cultural Council): Torre Norte, Pisos 12–16, Centro Simón Bolívar, Apdo 50995, Caracas; tel. (212) 483-4980; e-mail directorgeneral@conac.gov.ve; internet www.conac.gov.ve; f. 1990 for the planning, promotion, dissemination and formation of human resources in the fields of cinema and folklore music, dancing, historic and artistic resources, literature, libraries, museums, plastic arts, theatre; Pres. Dr FRANCISCO SESTO NOVAS; Dir-Gen. SILVIA DÍAZ ALVARADO; Sec. GUSTAVO ARNSTEIN; publs *Revista de Cine 'ENCUADRE'* (4 a year), *Revista 'IMAGEN'* (12 a year), *Revista Nacional de Cultura* (4 a year).

Attached Foundation:

Fundación de Etnomusicología y Folklore del CONAC (Foundation for Ethnomusicology and Folklore): Apdo 81015, Caracas 1080; f. 1990; consists of: Instituto Nacional de Folklore (INAF, f. 1950), Instituto Interamericano de Etnomusicología y Folklore (INIDEF, f. 1970), Museo Nacional de Folklore (f. 1971), Centro Interamericano de Etnomusicología y Folklore (CIDEF, f. 1973) for the OAS Regional Development Programme; aims to preserve and protect the American cultural heritage; annual courses in ethnomusicology, folklore, handicrafts, ethnohistory, anthropolinguistic studies; PRA/OAS scholarships; archive of ethnomusic, slides and photographs; library of 2,700 vols, 308 periodicals; Dir Dra ISABEL ARETZ; publ. *Anuario FUNDEF*.

Instituto Zuliano de la Cultura 'Andrés E. Blanco': Gobernación del Estado Zulia, Academia de Bellas Artes 'Neptali Rincón', Maracaibo; f. 1972; administers all the cultural institutes in the state; Dir CARMEN DELGADO PEÑA; Administrator DOMINGO GUZMÁN RAMOS.

HISTORY, GEOGRAPHY AND ARCHAEOLOGY

Academia de Historia del Táchira: Casa Bolivariana, Calle 4 entre carreras 3 y 4, San Cristóbal, Estado Táchira; f. 1942; Pres. Dr ROBERTO ESTEBAN AVENDAÑO; Sec. Lic. JOSÉ ERNESTO BECERRA GOLINDANO; publ. *Boletín*.

Academia de Historia del Zulia: Calle 95 esquina con Av. 5, Sector Plaza Bolívar, al lado del Palacio de Gobierno del Zulia, Maracaibo, Estado Zulia; tel. (261) 725-1194; internet www.academiahistoriazulia.com; f. 1940; 12 mems; Pres. ABRAHÁN BELLOSO; Sec.-Gen. ANICETO RAMÍREZ Y ASTIER; Librarian JOSÉ A. BUTRÓN OLIVARES; publ. *Boletín*.

Academia Nacional de la Historia (National Academy of History): Palacio de las Academias, Bolsa a San Francisco, Caracas 1010; tel. (212) 482-6720; fax (212) 482-6720; e-mail anhistoria@cantv.net; internet www.acadnachistoria.org; f. 1888; library: see Libraries and Archives; Dir RAFAEL FERNÁNDEZ HERES; Sec. MARIANELA PONCE; publs *Boletín*, *Memorias*.

Centro de Historia Larense (Lara Historical Centre): Carrera 17 frente a la Plaza Lara, Barquisimeto, Distrito Iribarren; f. 1941; 12 mems; library of 1,000 vols; publ. *Boletín*.

Centro Histórico Sucrense (Historical Centre): Cumaná; f. 1945; 24 national and 14 foreign corresp. mems; Dir R. P. Fray CAYETANO DE CARROCERA; Sec.-Gen. Br. ALBERTO SANABRIA; publ. *Boletín*.

Junta Nacional Protectora y Conservadora del Patrimonio Histórico y Artístico de la Nación (Commission for the Protection and Preservation of the Historical and Artistic Heritage of the Nation): Palacio de Miraflores, Avda Urdaneta, Caracas; there is a subsidiary office in each State; authorizes exploration and excavation of sites; mems are nominated by the Government for 5-year terms, and may be re-elected; Dir Dr RAFAEL ARMANDO ROJAS.

Sociedad Bolivariana de Venezuela (Bolivar Society): San Jacinto a Traposos, Urb. Catedral, Caracas; tel. (212) 545-7271; f. 1938; to promote by all available media the knowledge of Simón Bolívar's life and works, as well as his political, cultural and social ideas; publishes about 15,000 volumes of historical works per year; 300 mems; library of 6,000 vols; Pres. Gral CANDIDO PEREZ MENDEZ; Sec. Gral ADOLFO ROMERO LUENGO; publ. *Revista*.

LANGUAGE AND LITERATURE

Alliance Française: Av. Mohedano entre 1A y 2A Transversal, Quinta Wilmarú, Urb La Castellana, Caracas; tel. (212) 264-4611; fax (212) 267-3470; e-mail castellana@afcaracas.org; internet www.afcaracas.org; offers courses and exams in French language and culture and promotes cultural exchange with France; attached teaching centres in Barquisimeto, Maracaibo, Margarita, Mérida and Valencia.

British Council: Torre Credicard, Piso 3, Avda Principal de El Bosque, Chacaíto, Caracas 1050; tel. (212) 952-9965; fax (212) 952-9691; e-mail information@britishcouncil.org.ve; internet www.britishcouncil.org/es/venezuela; teaching centre; offers courses and exams in English language and British culture and promotes cultural exchange with the UK; Dir BARBARA WICKHAM.

Goethe-Institut: Avda Juan Germán Roscio, cruce con Avda Jorge Washington, Qta. 'Asociación Cultural Humboldt', San Bernardino, Apdo 60501, Caracas 1060; tel. (212) 552-6445; fax (212) 552-5621; e-mail sekr@caracas.goethe.org; internet www.goethe.de/hn/car; offers courses and exams in German language and culture and promotes cultural exchange with Germany; library of 4,000 vols; Dir Dr ULRICH GMÜNDER.

MEDICINE

Academia de Medicina del Zulia: Apdo 1725, Maracaibo, Zulia 4001A; tel. (61) 42-34-42; fax (61) 42-34-42; f. 1927; 150 mems; library of 950 vols; Pres. Dr GILBERTO OLIVARES; Sec. Dr JOSÉ A. COLINA-CHOURIO; publ. *Revista*.

Academia Nacional de Medicina (National Academy of Medicine): Bolsa a San Francisco, Apdo 804, Caracas 1010; tel. (212) 42-18-68; internet www.anm.org.ve; f. 1904; 40 mems; 50 nat. corresp. mems; 30 foreign corresp. mems; library: see Libraries and Archives; Pres. Dr AUGUSTO LEÓN C.; Sec. Dr JULIAN MORALES R.; publs *Boletín*, *Gaceta Médica de Caracas* (4 a year).

Colegio de Farmacéuticos del Distrito Federal y Estado Miranda (Association of Pharmacists): Urbanización Las Mercedes, Caracas 1060; deals with all aspects of the pharmaceutical industry; 1,200 mems; library of 600 vols; Pres. Dr PEDRO RODRÍGUEZ MURILLO; Sec. Dra ESTHER VALERA DE PÉREZ B.; Librarian Dra CARMEN ELENA GARCIA; publ. *Revista 'Colfar'*.

Colegio de Médicos del Distrito Metropolitano de Caracas (Doctors' Association): Plaza de Bellas Artes, Avda Bellas Artes, Los Chaguaramos, Caracas; tel. (212) 979-9846; fax (212) 979-2986; e-mail presidencia@cmdmc.com.ve; internet www.cmdmc.com.ve; f. 1942; 2,800 mems; Pres. Dr FERNANDO JOSE BIANCO COLMENARES; Sec. Dra TAHIRI MARIÑEZ; publ. *Acta Médica Venezolana*.

Colegio de Médicos del Estado Miranda (Doctors' Association): Av. El Golf, Qta La Setentiseis, Urb. El Bosque, Caracas 1041-A; f. 1944; 3,100 mems; professional and scientific association; Pres. Dr HERNÁN VÁSQUEZ RIGUAL; Gen. Sec. Dr RUBEN HERNÁNDEZ SERRANO; publ. *Cuadernos Medicos*.

Instituto J. I. Baldó: El Algodonal, Antímano, Caracas; f. 1937; lung diseases; Pres. Dr MANUEL ADRIANZA.

Sociedad de Obstetricia y Ginecología de Venezuela (Society of Obstetrics and Gynaecology): Maternidad Concepción Palacios, Avda San Martín, Apdo 20081, Caracas 1020-A; tel. (212) 451-0895; fax (212) 451-0895; e-mail sogvzla01@gmail.com; internet www.sogvzla.org; f. 1940; 1,200 mems; Pres. Dr ROGELIO PEREZ D'GREGORIO; publ. *Revista de Obstetricia y Ginecología de Venezuela* (4 a year).

Sociedad Venezolana de Anestesiología (Society of Anaesthesiology): Final Av. Guaicaipuro, Edificio Edicentro, Piso 4, Oficina 4-B, diagonal a la entrada principal del Centro Médico de Caracas, Urb. San Bernardino, Caracas; tel. (212) 552-8788; fax (212) 552-8520; e-mail svanestesiologia@cantv.net; internet www.sva.org.ve; f. 1954; Pres. OSCAR LOYNAZ-REVERÓN.

Sociedad Venezolana de Cardiología (Society of Cardiology): Oficina B-1, Piso 2, Torre Colegio de Médicos, Av. José María Vargas, Urb. Santa Fe Norte, Caracas 1080; tel. (212) 263-5787; e-mail editorweb@svcardiologia.org; internet www.svcardiologia.org; f. 1954; 196 mems; Pres. Dr JOSÉ ANTONIO CANDADO R.; Sec.-Gen. Dr GUILLERMO VILLORIA.

Sociedad Venezolana de Cirugía (Society of Surgery): Av. Sucre, Los Dos Caminos, Edif. Centro, Parque Boyacá, Torre Centro, Piso 17, Oficina 173, Caracas; tel. (212) 286-8106; e-mail sv_cirugia@cantv.net; internet www.sociedadvenezolanadecirugia.org; f. 1945; Pres. Dr AUGUSTO DIEZ; Sec.-Gen. Dr ISMAEL J. SALAS M.

Sociedad Venezolana de Cirugía Ortopédica y Traumatología (Society of Orthopaedics and Traumatological Surgery): Av. José María Vargas, Torre Colegio de Médicos, Piso 3 Oficina N° 3, Santa Fe Norte, Caracas; e-mail info@svcot.web.ve; internet www.svcot.web.ve; f. 1949; 197 mems; Pres. Dr RAFAEL HERRERA; publ. *Boletín de Ortopedia y Traumatología* (4 a year).

Sociedad Venezolana de Dermatología y Cirugía Dermatología (Society of Dermatology and Dermatological Surgery): Avda. Francisco de Miranda, Edif. Menegrande, Piso 6, Ofic. 6-4, Urb. Los Palos Grandes, Caracas 1080; tel. (212) 285-5284; fax (212) 285-0896; e-mail derma@svdcd.org.ve; internet www.svdcd.org.ve; f. 1946; promotes dermatological education and dermatological science in Venezuela; organizes monthly meetings, annual journals and congress; Pres. Dr ELDA GIANSANTE DE MARINUCCI; Vice-Pres. Dr NAHIR LOYO; Gen. Sec. Dr ROSANELLY ROYE.

Sociedad Venezolana de Gastroenterología (Venezuelan Society of Gastroenterology): Paseo Enrique Eraso, Torre La Noria, piso 5, Oficina 5-B3, Urb. Las Mercedes, Caracas 1061; tel. (212) 991-2660; fax (212) 992-7879; e-mail paginawebsovegastro@gmail.com; internet www.sovegastro.com; f. 1945; 606 mems; Pres. Dr SATURNINO FERNÁNDEZ; Sec. Dra MARIA LUISA CLAVO; publ. *GEN* (4 a year).

Sociedad Venezolana de Hematología (Society of Haematology): Avda José María Vargas, Edif. Torre del Colegio, Piso 2, Local E–2 Urb. Santa Fé Norte, Caracas 1080; tel. (212) 979-5664; f. 1959; library of 527 vols, 14 periodicals; Pres. Dr CARLOS GOLDSTEIN.

Sociedad Venezolana de Historia de la Medicina (History of Medicine Society): Palacio de las Academias, Bolsa a San Francisco, Caracas 1010; tel. (212) 483-4361; fax (212) 483-4361; e-mail migongue@yahoo.com; f. 1944; 75 mems; Pres. Dr MIGUEL GONZÁLEZ GUERRA; publ. *Revista* (2 a year).

Sociedad Venezolana de Medicina Interna (Society of Internal Medicine): Av. Francisco de Miranda, Edificio Mene Grande, Piso 6, Oficina 6-4, Los Palos Grandes, Caracas 1010; tel. (212) 285-0237; fax (212) 285-4026; e-mail socvmi@cantv.net; internet www.svmi.web.ve; f. 1956; Pres. Dr MARIO PATIÑO TORRES; Gen. Sec. Dra MARÍA EVELYN MONSALVE.

Sociedad Venezolana de Oftalmología (Society of Ophthalmology): Avda Principal de Los Ruices, Centro Empresarial Los Ruices (Piso 05, Oficina 507), Caracas; tel. (212) 239-8127; fax (212) 239-4384; e-mail svo@reacciun.ve; internet www.svo.org.ve; f. 1953; 600 mems; Pres. Dra SILVIA SALINAS; Sec.-Gen. Dr ROSEADO CASTELLANOS; publ. *Revista Oftalmológica Venezolana* (4 a year).

Sociedad Venezolana de Otorrinolaringología (Society of Otorhinolaryngology): Av. Principal de Santa Fe (Av. José María Vargas), Edificio Colegio de Médicos del Distrito Capital, Piso 2, Oficina 10, Santa Fe Norte, Caracas; tel. (212) 978-3311; internet www.svorl.org.ve; Pres. Dr FRANÇOIS CONDE JAHN; Sec. Dr GERMÁN TOVAR BUSTAMANTE; publ. *Acta Venezolana de ORL* (1 a year).

Sociedad Venezolana de Psiquiatría (Society of Psychiatry): Apdo 3380, Caracas 1010A; tel. (212) 731-2024; fax (212) 731-2024; f. 1942; 600 mems; library of 1,650 vols; Pres. Dr MANUEL MATUTE; Sec.-Gen. Dr EDGARD BELFORT; publ. *Archivos Venezolanos de Psiquiatría y Neurología* (2 a year).

Sociedad Venezolana de Puericultura y Pediatría (Society of Puericulture and Paediatrics): Apdo 3122, Caracas 1010A; Urb. La Castellana, Av. San Felipe, entre 2da Transversal y Calle José Angel Lamas, Centro Coinasa, Mezzanina 6, Caracas; tel. (212) 263-7378; fax (212) 267-6078; internet www.pediatria.org; Pres. Dra MICHELLE LÓPEZ.

Sociedad Venezolana de Radiología y Diagnóstico por Imágenes (Society of Radiology and Diagnostic Imaging): Hospital de Clínicas Caracas, Av. Panteón, San Bernardino, Caracas; tel. (212) 574-8210; fax (212) 575-2310; e-mail uribvictor@gmail.com; internet www.soveradi.org.ve; Pres. Dr RODRIGO SOCARRAS; Pres. Dr ANIBAL RIVERO.

NATURAL SCIENCES

General

Academia de Ciencias Físicas, Matemáticas y Naturales (Academy of Physical, Mathematical and Natural Sciences): Bolsa a San Francisco, Avda Universidad, Apdo 1421, Caracas 1010; tel. (212) 482-2954; fax (212) 484-6611; e-mail acfiman@cantv.net; internet www.acfiman.org.ve; f. 1917; 80 mems (30 ordinary, 20 Venezuelan corresp., 30 foreign corresp.); Pres. LUIS MANUEL CARBONELL; Sec. JOSÉ M. CARRILLO; publ. *Boletín* (4 a year).

Asociación Venezolana para el Avance de la Ciencia (ASOVAC) (Venezuelan Association for the Advancement of Science): Edificio Fundavac–Asovac, Calle Neverí, Colinas de Bello Monte, Caracas; internet www.asovac.org.ve; f. 1950; 3,000 mems; Pres. FRANCISCO EMIRO DURÁN; Sec.-Gen. YOLANDA SEVILLA; publ. *Acta Científica Venezolana* (6 a year).

Fundación La Salle de Ciencias Naturales (La Salle Foundation of Natural Sciences): Edificio Fundación La Salle, Avda Boyacá, Apdo 1930, Caracas 1010-A; tel. (212) 709-5811; fax (212) 793-7493; internet www.fundacionlasalle.org.ve; f. 1957; anthropology, aquaculture, agronomy, limnology, mining and forestry, oceanography; runs stations for marine, agricultural and hydrobiological research, the *Instituto Universitario de Tecnología del Mar* on the island of Margarita, *Instituto de Tecnología Agropecuaria* at San Carlos and at Boconó, *Instituto de Tecnología Industrial* at San Félix, *Instituto Universitario de Technología* at Tumeremo and *Instituto Universitario de Technología Amazonas* in Amazonas State; library: (see under Libraries); 1,300 mems; Pres. Hno. GINÉS; publs *Antropológica* (review, 4 a year), *Memoria* (oceanography and natural science studies, 2 a year), *Natura* (3 a year).

Biological Sciences

Sociedad de Ciencias Naturales 'La Salle' ('La Salle' Society of Natural Sciences): Edificio Fundación La Salle, Avda Boyacá, Apdo 1930, Caracas 1010A; tel. (212) 21-76-53; fax (212) 22-48-12; f. 1940; 504 mems; 17 hon., 42 national and 30 foreign corresps, 500 associates; comprises 3 depts: Botany, Zoology and Publications; the Museum contains more than 100,000 exhibits; Dir Lic. JESÚS HOYOS; Pres. Dr LUIS RIVAS L.; Sec. Dr CARLOS ACEVEDO; publs *Memoria* (2 a year), *Natura* (4 a year).

Sociedad Venezolana de Ciencias Naturales (Venezuelan Society of Natural Sciences): Calle Arichuna y Cumaco, El Marqués, Apdo 1521, Caracas 1010A; tel. (212) 21-76-53; fax (212) 22-48-12; f. 1931; 1,100 mems; library of 12,000 vols, 400 periodicals; annual exhibitions, lectures, films on nature conservation; department of speleology for study and exploration of caves throughout the country; biological station for research on flora and fauna, soil science and crop studies, ecology of neo-tropical savannas; dept for education on environmental protection; depts for the study of tropical orchids, bromeliads and astronomy; studies in environmental pollution; Pres. R. AVELEDO HOSTOS; Gen. Sec. Dr RICARDO MUÑOZ TÉBAR; publs *Boletín de la SVCN*, *Boletín Informativo*.

Physical Sciences

Sociedad Venezolana de Geólogos (Venezuelan Geological Society): Apdo 17493, Parque Central, Caracas, 1015-A; located at: Avda A, Quinta Mercedes 13-10, Urbanización, La Carlota, Caracas; tel. (212) 234-4085; fax (212) 234-0716; e-mail svg@mailser.reacciun.ve; internet www.socvengeo.org; f. 1955; 1,050 mems; Pres. DANIEL LOUREIRO; Sec. FRANCISCO BARRIOS; publs *Boletín* (3 a year), *Geologia de Venezuela*.

TECHNOLOGY

Asociación Venezolana de Ingeniería Sanitaria y Ambiental (Sanitary and Environmental Engineering Association): El Trigal Centro, Calle Pocaterra 88-20, Quinta los Corales, Valencia 2002, Carabobo; tel. (41) 421-435; fax (41) 428-028; e-mail avisa@eldish.net; Pres. Ing. RAFAEL DAUTANT.

Colegio de Ingenieros de Venezuela (Engineers' Association): Av. Principal de Quebrada Honda, Los Caobos, Caracas 1050; tel. (212) 575-3532; internet www.civ.net.ve; f. 1861; 7,000 mems; library of 4,000 vols; Pres. DARÍO BRILLEMBOURG; Sec. JULIO URBINA; publ. *Boletín* (12 a year).

Sociedad Venezolana de Ingeniería Hidráulica (Society of Hydraulic Engineering): c/o Colegio de Ingenieros de Venezuela, Los Caobos, Caracas; tel. (414) 868-2570; internet www.svihvenezuela.org.ve; f. 1960; Pres. ARTURO MARCANO.

Sociedad Venezolana de Ingenieros Agrónomos (Society of Agricultural Engineers): c/o Colegio de Ingenieros de Venezuela, Av. Principal de Quebrada Honda, Los Caobos, Caracas 1050; f. 1944; Pres. Ing. Agr. HUMBERTO FONTANA.

Sociedad Venezolana de Ingenieros Civiles (Society of Civil Engineers): c/o Colegio de Ingenieros de Venezuela, v. Principal de Quebrada Honda, Los Caobos, Caracas 1050; tel. (212) 368-6077; e-mail sovinciv@sovinciv.com; internet www.sovinciv.com; f. 1995; Pres. MANUEL FERNANDO MEJÍAS.

Sociedad Venezolana de Ingenieros de Petróleo (Society of Petroleum Engineers): Calle Negrín con calle Las Flores, Torre Negrín, piso 5, oficina 5A, Sabana Grande, Caracas 1050; tel. (212) 761-4497; fax (212) 761-4223; e-mail soveip@cantv.net; internet www.svip.org; f. 1958; Pres. FERNANDO SÁNCHEZ.

Sociedad Venezolana de Ingenieros Forestales (Society of Forestry Engineers): c/o Colegio de Ingenieros de Venezuela, Av. Principal de Quebrada Honda, Los Caobos, Caracas 1050; internet www.civ.net.ve; f. 1960; 1,122 mems; library of 8,000 vols; Pres. Ing. For. LOURDES ALTUVE; Sec. Ing. For. SONIA RIVAS; publ. *Revista Forestal* (4 a year).

Sociedad Venezolana de Ingenieros Químicos (Society of Chemical Engineers): c/o Colegio de Ingenieros de Venezuela; Av. Principal de Quebrada Honda, Los Caobos, Caracas 1050; f. 1958 to promote the chemical engineering profession and exchange information with similar orgs in Venezuela and abroad; 1,000 mems; Exec. Dir YOLANDA DE OSORIO; publ. *Boletín* (4 a year).

Research Institutes

GENERAL

Consejo Nacional de Investigaciones Científicas y Tecnológicas (CONICIT) (National Council for Scientific and Technological Research): Apdo 70617, Los Ruices, Caracas; fax (212) 239-8677; f. 1967 for the promotion of scientific and technological research, and for coordinating the activities of organizations involved in the science and technology sector, and of organizations of the national executive; Pres. Dr IGNACIO AVALOS GUTIERREZ; Vice-Pres. Dr MICHAEL SUAREZ F.

Instituto Venezolano de Investigaciones Científicas (IVIC) (Venezuelan Scientific Research Institute): Apdo 21827, Caracas 1020A; tel. (212) 504-1122; fax (212) 504-1428; e-mail webmaster@ivic.ve; internet www.ivic.ve; f. 1959; research in atomic research, archaeology, anthropology, biology, chemistry, medicine, mathematics and technology, physics, sociology of science; postgraduate studies; library: see Libraries and Archives; Dir MAXIMO GARCIO SUCRE.

AGRICULTURE, FISHERIES AND VETERINARY SCIENCE

Centro Nacional de Investigaciones Agropecuarias (Agricultural Research Centre): Avda Casanova Godoy, Maracay 2103, Estado Aragua; tel. (243) 245-3075; fax (243) 245-4320; internet www.ceniap.gov.ve; f. 1937; attached to the Instituto Nacional de Investigaciones Agrícolas de Venezuela; Dir Dra SUSMIRA GODOY; publs *Agronomía Tropical*, *Veterinaria Tropical*, *Zootecnia Tropical*.

Estación Experimental Táchira: Bramón, Rubio 6070, Edo Táchira; tel. (76) 66783; f. 1953; agricultural research; library of 1,100 vols; Dir JOSÉ ROSARIO MANRIQUE.

Instituto de Investigaciones Veterinarias (Veterinary Research Institute): Apdo 70, Maracay, Estado Aragua; Av. Las Delicias, Maracay, Estado Aragua; tel. (243) 414-365; f. 1940; small specialized library; 55 mems; Dir Dr CLAUDIO FUENMAYOR F.

Instituto Nacional de Investigaciones Agrícolas de Venezuela (National Institute for Agricultural Research): Via El Limon, Maracay, Estado Aragua; fax (243) 283-6978; e-mail ger_inia@impsat.com.ve; internet www.inia.gov.ve; f. 1961 as Fondo Nacional de Investigaciones Agropecuarias, 2000 re-named; centres and experimental stations: Amazonas, Anzoátegui, Apure, Barinas, CENIAP, Delta Amacuro, Falcón, Guárico, Lara, Mérida, Miranda, Monagas, Portuguesa, Sucre, Táchira, Trujillo, Yaracuy, Zulia; Pres. PRUDENCIO CHACÓN; Gen.-Man. ALICIA LEÓN.

Instituto Nacional de Tierras (National Land Institute): Calle San Carlos, Urb. Vista Alegre, Qta. La Barranca, Caracas; internet www.inti.gob.ve; f. 1949; concerned with agrarian reform activities; Pres. JUAN CARLOS LOYO; publ. *Memoria y Cuenta*.

ARCHITECTURE AND TOWN PLANNING

Dirección General de Ordenación del Territorio Urbanístico del Ministerio del Poder Popular para las Obras Públicas y Vivienda (Bureau of Urban Development of the Ministry for Public Works and Housing): Av. Francisco de Miranda, Torre Minfra, Piso 10, Chacao, Caracas; f. 1946; 350 mems; library of 20,000 vols; Dir MARIBEL CHELLINI AROCHA.

ECONOMICS, LAW AND POLITICS

Centro de Estudios del Desarrollo Universidad Central de Venezuela (Centre for Development Studies): Av. Neverì, Edif. Fundavac-Asovac, Colinas de Bello Monte, POB 47604, Caracas 1041; tel. (212) 753-3475; fax (212) 751-2691; e-mail cendesdir@ucv.ve; internet www.cendes-ucv.edu.ve; f. 1961; centre for research and graduate studies on problems relating to economic, social, educational, regional, political, ecological, environmental and scientific-technological devt of Venezuela and Latin America; library of 12,011 vols, 35,141 documents, 915 periodicals and 578 thesis; Dir Dr CARLOS WALTER; publs *Cuadernos del CENDES* (3 a year), *Revista Cuadernos del CENDES*.

Instituto Iberoamericano de Derecho Agrario y Reforma Agraria: Facultad de Ciencias Jurídicas y Políticas, Universidad de los Andes, Mérida; tel. (275) 402646; fax (275) 402644; f. 1973; 12 mem. countries; training and research in agrarian law, agricultural economics, rural sociology; postgraduate courses; library of 4,000 vols; Pres. RAMÓN VICENTE CASANOVA; publ. *Revista de Derecho Agrario y Reforma Agraria*.

Oficina Central de Estadística e Informática (Central Office of Statistics and Informatics): Apdo 4593, Caracas 1010; tel. (212) 782-1133; e-mail ocei@platino.gov.ve; internet www.ocei.gov.ve; f. 1978; Dir Dr GUSTAVO MÉNDEZ; publs *Anuario del Comercio Exterior de Venezuela*, *Anuario Estadístico de Venezuela*.

EDUCATION

Instituto Latinoamericano de Investigaciones Científicas en Educación a Distancia (Latin American Institute of Scientific Research on Distance Education): Calle California, Qta. Las Churrucas, Apdo 69680, Las Mercedes 1060A, Caracas; f. 1980; research, teaching and planning in distance and open education; library of 8,000 vols; Pres. MIGUEL A. ESCOTET.

HISTORY, GEOGRAPHY AND ARCHAEOLOGY

Centro de Historia del Estado Carabobo: Valencia, Edo de Carabobo; f. 1979 to conduct research into national and regional history, preserve and improve regional archives, conserve monuments, encourage and publicize celebrations of national historic events, and establish cultural relations with similar Venezuelan and foreign organizations; 24 mems; Pres. Lic. LUIS CUBILLÁN; Sec. Dr MARCO TULIO MÉRIDA; publ. *Boletín*.

Instituto de Geografía y Conservación de Recursos Naturales (Institute of Geography and Conservation of Natural Resources): Vía Chorros de Milla, Mérida; tel. (275) 401603; fax (275) 401603; e-mail regeoven@forest.ula.ve; f. 1959; library of 20,236 vols and 44,555 periodicals; research in theoretical geography, applied geography and geographical techniques; committees for research and teaching technical coordination; documentation and information; Dir Prof. RICARDO PONTE R.; publs *Cuadernos Geográficos* (irregular), *Revista Geográfica Venezoluna* (2 a year).

Ministerio del Ambiente y de los Recursos Naturales Renovables, Servicio Autónomo del Geografía y Cartografía Nacional: Avda Este 6, Esquina de Camejo, Edificio Camejo (Piso 2-220), Centro Simón Bolívar, Caracas; tel. (212) 482-2218; fax (212) 542-0374; f. 1935; Dir-Gen. Lic. ALICIA MOREAU D.

MEDICINE

Instituto de Medicina Experimental (Institute of Experimental Medicine): Apdo 50587, Sabana Grande, Ciudad Universitaria, Caracas 1051; tel. (212) 693-1862; fax (212) 693-1260; f. 1940; research in biochemistry, general and applied pathology, neurology, pharmacology, physiology; 130 staff; library of 30,176 vols, 4,100 periodicals; Dir Dra ITALA LIPPO DE BECEMBERG; Librarian Lic. TRINA YANES DE RAMÍREZ; publ. *Boletín Informativo Sistema Nacional de Documentación e Información Biomédica*; (see also under the Universidad Central de Venezuela).

Instituto Nacional de Nutrición (Institute of Nutrition): Av. Baralt, Esquina El Carmen, Edif. INN, Quinta Crespo, Municipio Libertador, Caracas; tel. (212) 483-3378; e-mail amogollon@inn.gob.ve; internet www.inn.gob.ve; f. 1949; library of 10,000 vols; Dir Dr LUIS BERMÚDEZ CHAURIO; publ. *Archivos Latinoamericanos de Nutrición*.

NATURAL SCIENCES

General

Estación de Investigaciones Marinas (EDIMAR): Apdo 144, Porlamar, Punta de Piedras, Isla de Margarita, Edo Nueva Esparta; tel. (295) 239-8051; fax (295) 239-8051; e-mail marllano@edimar.org; internet www.edimar.org; affiliated to the Fundación La Salle de Ciencias Naturales (see under Learned Societies); f. 1958; aquaculture, fisheries, marine biology, marine geology, marine food processing, oceanography; library: library 'H. Ginés' of 18,000 vols, 1,200 periodicals; Dir Dr MARTÍN LLANO GARCÍA; publ. *Memoria de la Sociedad La Salle de Ciencias Naturales*.

Biological Sciences

Estación Biológica de los Llanos (Biological Station): Calabozo, Estado Guárico; f. 1961; library of 3,200 vols; Dirs F. TAMAYO, R. A. HOSTOS, L. ARISTEGUIETA.

Fundación Instituto Botánico de Venezuela (Botanical Institute): Apdo 2156, Jardín Botánico de Caracas, Avda Salvador Allende, Caracas 1010-A; tel. (212) 605-3989; fax (212) 605-3994; e-mail unidad.educacion.fibv@gmail.com; internet www.fibv.org.ve; f. 1991; library of 14,000 vols, 1,300 periodicals; Pres. Dr ANÍBAL CASTILLO SUÁREZ; publs *Acta Botanica Venezuelica* (2 a year), *Flora de Venezuela*.

Physical Sciences

Dirección de Geología del Ministerio de Energía y Minas (Department of Geology of the Ministry of Energy and Mines): Torre Oeste, 4° piso, Parque Central, Caracas 1010; f. 1936; conducts national geological surveys, and research in geotechnics, marine geology and mineralogy; library of 120,000 vols; Dir SIMÓN E. RODRIGUEZ; publs *Boletín de Geología* (2 a year), *Boletín Informativo del Centro de Análisis de Información Geológica-Minera (CAIGEOMIN) (2 a year)*, *Cuadernos Geológicos* (3 a year), research bulletins, statistical and other data (1 a year).

Estación Meteorológica (Meteorological Station): Ciudad Bolívar; f. 1940; undertakes meteorological research and hydrographical surveys of the River Orinoco and its tributaries; Dir E. SIFONTES; numerous publications on meteorology and climatology of Venezuela.

Observatorio Naval 'Juan Manuel Cagigal' (Juan Manuel Cagigal Naval Observatory): Apdo 6745, La Planicie, 23 Enero, Caracas; tel. (212) 481-2266; fax (212) 483-5878; e-mail dhn@truevision.net; f. 1888; astronomy, hydrography, meteorology, oceanography, planetarium; Dir GREGORIO PÉREZ MORENO; publs *Almanaque Astronómico Venezolano*, *Boletín Avisos a los Navegantes*, *Boletín Climatológico Anual*, *Boletín Meteorologico* (1 a year).

RELIGION, SOCIOLOGY AND ANTHROPOLOGY

Fundación Lisandro Alvarado: Casa de Los Celis, Av. Soublette c/o Calle Comercio, Valencia; tel. (41) 421245; e-mail casacelis@cantv.net; internet mipagina.cantv.net/casacelis; f. 1965; museums of art, history, anthropology, historical archives); brs in Maracay (archaeological and historical research; museums of history and anthropology; specialized library (in preparation)) and Puerto Cabello (museum of art and history); 40 mems; Pres. Dra HENRIQUETA PEÑALVER GÓMEZ; Dir Tec. CESAR A. VARELA H.

Instituto Caribe de Antropología y Sociología: Av. Boyacá (Cota Mil) con Maripérez, al lado de la Estación del Teleférico 'Avila Mágica', Caracas; tel. (212) 709-5845; e-mail info@fundacionlasalle.org.ve; internet www.fundacionlasalle.org.ve; f. 1962; anthropological research and devt programmes among Indian populations of Venezuela; dept of the Fundación La Salle de Ciencias Naturales (see under Learned Societies); library of 40,000 vols; Pres. JUAN BOSCO CHACON; Dir MIGUEL ANGEL PERERA; publ. *Antropológica* (2 a year).

TECHNOLOGY

Dirección de Minas del Ministerio de Minas e Hidrocarburos (Department of Mining of the Ministry of Mines and Hydrocarbons): Torre Norte, 20° piso, Caracas 101; f. 1936; Dir BRÍGIDO R. NATERA.

PDUSA-INTEVEP, Centro de Investigación y Apoyo Tecnológico: Apdo 76343, Caracas 1070A; tel. (212) 908-6111; fax (212) 908-6447; f. 1974; research and development branch of Petróleos de Venezuela, concerned with hydrocarbons and petrochemicals; Information Centre of 30,000 publs, 1,600 periodicals, connected to int. online systems; Pres. FRANCISCO PRADAS; publ. *Visión Tecnológica* (2 a year).

Libraries and Archives

Barquisimeto

Biblioteca Pública 'Pio Tamayo' (Public Library): Calle 26, entre Carreras 20 y 21, Barquisimeto; f. 1911; 21,943 vols; Librarian GERMÁN HURTADO REYES.

Biblioteca Técnica Científica Centralizada 'Froilan Alvarez Yepez' (Central Scientific and Technical Library): Apdo 254, Barquisimeto; fax (251) 544394; f. 1966; specializes in social sciences, economic development and technology; 50,000 vols, 800 periodicals; Librarian Lic. CECILIA VEGA F.; publ. *Indice Bibliográfico de los estudios de FUDECO*.

Caracas

Archivo de Música Colonial Venezolano (Archives of Colonial Music): Escuela Superior de Música, esquinas de Veroes a Santa Capilla de la Av. Urdaneta, Caracas; Librarian GARCÍA LAZO.

Archivo General de la Nación (National Archives): Av. Panteón, Foro Libertador, Edif. Archivo General de la Nación, Caracas 1010; tel. (212) 509-5600; e-mail mppc@ministeriodelacultura.gob.ve; f. 1910; sections: La Colonia (1498–1810), La Revolución (1810–21), La Gran Colombia (1821–30), La República (1830 to present day); comprises Seminario de Investigación Archivística and courses on palaeography; Dir CARMEN ALIDA SOTO; publs *Biblioteca Venezolana de Historia* (2 a year), *Boletín* (2 a year).

Biblioteca Central de la Universidad Católica 'Andrés Bello' (Central Library of the 'Andrés Bello' Catholic University): Edificio de Biblioteca, piso 1, Urb. Montalbán, La Vega, Caracas; tel. (212) 407-4172; fax (212) 471-3307; e-mail tbalza@ucab.edu.ve; f. 1953; 111,558 vols; Librarian TAIDÉ BALZA; publ. *Montalbán*.

Biblioteca Central de la Universidad Central de Venezuela (Central University Library): Apdo 1050, Caracas; Edif. Biblioteca Central, Ciudad Universitaria, Los Chaguaramos, Caracas; tel. (212) 605-4190; fax (212) 605-0861; internet www.sicht.ucv.ve:8080/bc; f. 1850; sections on social science, the humanities, pure science and technology; official publications; reference section; 280,000 vols; 3,500 periodicals; Dir Prof. MANUEL RODRIGUEZ CAMPOS.

Biblioteca Central del Ministerio de Agricultura y Cría (Library of the Ministry of Agriculture): Avda Lecuna, Parque Central, Torre Este, 1° piso, Caracas; f. 1936; 70,000 vols; Librarian TUSNELDA CRESPO PIETRI.

Biblioteca Central del Ministerio del Trabajo (Library of the Ministry of Labour): Centro Simón Bolívar, Edificio Sur, 5° piso, Caracas; f. 1988; 3,200 vols; Librarian MARCELA GARCÍA JORDAN; publ. *Boletín Legislativo*.

Biblioteca de la Academia Nacional de la Historia (Library of the National Academy of History): Palacio de las Academias, Avda Universidad, Bolsa a San Francisco, Caracas; tel. (212) 482-3849; fax (212) 482-6720; f. 1888; 120,000 vols; Dir Dr RAFAEL FERNÁNDEZ HERES; publ. *Boletín de la Academia Nacional de la Historia*.

Biblioteca de la Academia Nacional de Medicina (Library of the National Academy of Medicine): Apdo 1121-A, Caracas; Palacio de las Academias, Av. Universidad, Bolsa a San Francisco, Caracas; tel. (212) 481-8939; fax (212) 481-8939; e-mail bibliotanm@yahoo.es; internet www.msinfo.info/default/anm; f. 1893; 4,000 vols; Librarian Dr TULIO BRICEÑO MAAZ; publ. *Gaceta Médica de Caracas*.

Biblioteca de la Academia Venezolana de la Lengua (Library of the Venezuelan Academy of Language): Apdo 1421, Caracas; Palacio de las Academias, Av. Universidad, Caracas 1010-A; e-mail acadlengv@cantv.net; f. 1883; 25,000 vols; special collections: Venezuelan classics, dictionaries, Ayacucho collection, 'El Coyo Ilustrado'; Librarian FRANCISCO JAVIER PÉREZ.

Biblioteca del Ministerio de Fomento (Library of the Ministry of Development): Centro Simón Bolívar, Edificio Sur, 5° piso, Oficina 535, Caracas; f. 1953; 6,000 vols; Librarian ROSARIO BARNOLA.

Biblioteca del Ministerio de Obras Públicas (Library of the Ministry of Public Works): Centro Simón Bolívar, Edificio Camejo, Mezzanina, Caracas; f. 1948; 4,312 vols; Dir CARLOS A. ARREAZA F.

Biblioteca del Ministerio de Relaciones Interiores (Library of the Ministry of the Interior): Esquina de Carmelitas, 2° piso, Caracas; 3,585 vols; Librarian Dr RUIZ LANDER.

Biblioteca del Ministerio de Sanidad y Asistencia Social (Library of the Ministry of Health): c/o Ministerio de Salud y Desarrollo Social, Parque Central, Torre Oeste Piso 30-41 Distrito Federal, Caracas; f. 1936; 9,411 vols; Librarian ESPERANZA REYES BAENA; publs *Memorias del MSAS*, *Revista Venezolana de Sanidad y Asistencia Social*.

Biblioteca del Ministerio del Poder Popular para Relaciones Exteriores (Library of the Ministry of Foreign Affairs): Av. Urdaneta, Torre MRE, al lado del Correo de Carmelitas, Caracas; e-mail dgab.divisionbiblioteca@mre.gob.ve; 7,450 items; specializes in international law; Librarian Lic. MIGUEL ABELLO.

Biblioteca del Tribunal Supremo de Justicia (Library of the Supreme Tribunal of Justice): Edificio del Tribunal Supremo de Justicia, Mezanina, final de la Av. Baralt, esquina dos pilitas, Caracas; tel. (212) 801-9051; e-mail biblioteca@tsj.gov.ve; internet www.tsj.gov.ve/index.shtml; f. 1942; 4,500 vols; Dir Br FERNANDO ARAUJO M.

Biblioteca 'Dr M. A. Sánchez Carvajal' de la Sociedad de Obstetricia y Ginecología de Venezuela (Dr M. A. Sánchez Carvajal Library of the Society for Obstetrics and Gynaecology of Venezuela): Maternidad Concepción Palacios, Avda San Martín, Apdo 20081, Caracas 1020A; tel. (212) 451-0895; fax (212) 451-0895; e-mail sogvzla@cantv.net; internet www.sogvzla.org; f. 1940; 8,500 vols, 113 periodicals, also MSS and medical history collection; Librarian Dra FANNY FLEITAS.

Biblioteca Ernesto Peltzer del Banco Central de Venezuela: Apdo 2017, Caracas; Esquina de Mijares, Plaza Juan Pedro López, Mezzanina 2, Altagracia, Caracas 1010; tel. (212) 801-8617; fax (212) 861-0048; internet www.bcv.org.ve//biblioteca/biblioep.htm; f. 1940; economics and finance; 100,000 vols, 862 periodicals; Dir SILVIO CASTELLANOS.

Biblioteca Juan Pablo Pérez Alfonzo (Library of the Ministry of Energy and Petroleum): Av. Lecuna, Parque Central, Torre Oeste, 2° piso, Caracas; tel. (212) 507-5206; fax (212) 575-4386; f. 1950; specializes in mines, petroleum, gas, geology, refinement, petrochemicals; 20,000 vols; Librarian Lic. SILVIA PERNIA C.; publs *Anuario Estadísticos Mineros*, *Boletín de Geología*, *Carta Semanal*, *Compendia Estadística del Sector Eléctrico*, *Memoria y Cuenta del Ministerio de Energía y Minas*, *Petróleo y otros Datos Estadísticos*.

Biblioteca Luís Beltrán Prieto Figueroa (Library of the National Assembly): Monjas a San Francisco, Palacio Federal Legislativo, El Silencio, Caracas; internet www.bibliotecalbpf.an.gob.ve; f. 1915; 9,000 vols; Librarian Lic. LUÍS PÉREZ PESCADOR.

Biblioteca 'Marcel Roche' del Instituto Venezolano de Investigaciones Científicas (Library of the Venezuelan Institute of Scientific Research): Altos de Pipe, Km 11, Carretera Panamericana, Apdo 21827, Caracas 1020A; tel. (212) 504-1515; fax (212) 504-1423; internet www.zeus.ivic.ve/biblioteca; f. 1959; 500,000 vols, 5,817 periodicals; Dir Dr EGIDIO ROMANO; Librarian XIOMARA JAYARO Y.

Biblioteca Nacional de Venezuela (National Library of Venezuela): Parroquia Altagracia, Final Avda Panteón, Esquina Fe a Remedios, Caracas 1010; tel. (212) 505-9254; fax (212) 505-9175; internet www.bibliotecanacional.bib.ve; f. 1883; 6.5m. books, newspapers, MSS and audiovisual items, 2.5m. records on database; Dir SAÉL IBÁÑEZ; publ. *Revista Bibliotecas Públicas* (4 a year).

Biblioteca Pública Mariano Picón Salas (Public Library): Av. Andrés Bello, cruce con Av. Principal de Maripérez, Parque Arístides Rojas, Maripérez, Caracas; f. 1965; 23,689 vols; Dir Lic. ROMULO NAVEA SOTO.

Centro de Documentación e Información Fundación La Salle de Ciencias Naturales (Documentation and Information Centre, 'La Salle' Foundation for Natural Sciences): Avda Boyacá, Cota Mil., Edif. Fundación La Salle, Apdo 1930, Caracas 1010A; tel. (212)709-5845; fax (212) 793-7493; f. 1942; 40,000 vols; spec. colln: botany, cultural anthropology, local languages, natural resources contamination, zoology, Venezuelan Indians; Librarian MIREYA VILORIA.

Cumaná

Biblioteca General de la Universidad de Oriente (General Library of the Universidad de Oriente): Av Universidad, Cerro Colorado, 6101 Cumaná; e-mail bashiru@udo.edu.ve; internet bibliotecadigital.udo.edu.ve; 154,000 vols; Librarian Lic. ROSA GONZÁLEZ DE LÓPEZ.

Maracaibo

Biblioteca Central 'General Rafael Urdaneta': Apartado Postal 526, Maracaibo

4001-A; tel. (261) 759-6700; fax (261) 759-6703; e-mail bibcentral.serbi@luz.edu.ve; internet www1.serbi.luz.edu.ve; f. 1946; 19,000 vols; Librarian Lic. EGLA ORTEGA.

Biblioteca Pública del Estado Zulia: Maracaibo; administered by the Instituto Zuliano de la Cultura (*q.v.*); Dir FERNANDO GUERRERO MATHEUS.

Maracay

Biblioteca Central del Centro Nacional de Investigaciones Agropecuarias (Library of the National Agricultural Research Centre): Av. Casanova Godoy, Zona Universitaria, Maracay 2103, Estado Aragua; tel. (243) 245-2491; fax (243) 245-4320; f. 1937; 200,000 vols; Library Asst NANCY GARCÉS DE HERNÁNDEZ.

Mérida

Servicios Bibliotecarios Universidad de los Andes (Los Andes University Library Services): Edificio Administrativo de la Universidad de los Andes, 2° piso, Mérida 5101; tel. (275) 402731; fax (275) 402507; f. 1889; 250,000 vols, 7,817 periodical titles; reference books for all subjects taught in the University; small collection of 16th- and 17th-century books; Coordinator Lic. MARÍA E. CHÁVEZ DE BURGOS.

Trujillo

Biblioteca '24 de Julio' (Public Library): Trujillo; f. 1930; 12,000 vols; Librarian ITALA BRICEÑO RUMBOS.

Valencia

Biblioteca Central de la Universidad de Carabobo: Urb. Prebo, Av. Andrés Eloy Blanco c/c 137-20, Edif. Centro Escorpio, pisos 2 y 3, Valencia; tel. (241) 822-2606; fax (241) 821-2121; internet www.cid.uc.edu.ve; 11,000 vols; Librarian ANTONIETA PINTO DE KATZ.

Museums and Art Galleries

Caracas

Casa Natal del Libertador Simón Bolívar (Simón Bolívar's Birthplace): San Jacinto a Traposos, Caracas; tel. (212) 541-2563; murals by Tito Salas depicting the life of Bolívar and events of the Independence Movement; Curator JOSEFINA DE SANDOVAL.

Colección Ornitológica Phelps (Phelps Ornithological Collection): c/o Robin Restall, POB 025304, Miami, FL 33102-5304, USA; located at: Blvd Sabana Grande, Edif. Gran Sabana, 3° piso, Apdo 2009, Caracas, 1001A; tel. (212) 719-238; fax (212) 762-5921; f. 1938; library of 10,000 vols; Pres. KATHLEEN PHELPS; Curator M. LENTINO R.

Fundación Museo de Ciencias: Avda Mexico, Plaza de los Museos, Parque Los Caobos, Apdo Postal 5883, Caracas 1010; tel. (212) 577-5094; fax (212) 571-1265; e-mail mciencia@reacciun.ve; internet www.museo-de-ciencias.org; f. 1875 as Museo Nacional, subsequently Museo de Ciencias Naturales; archaeology, anthropology, entomology, ethnology, geology, palaeontology, zoology; library of 2,100 vols; Pres. Ing. SERGIO ANTILLANO ARMAS.

Galería de Arte Nacional: Plaza de los Museos, Los Caobos, Apdo 6729, Caracas 1010; tel. (212) 578-1818; fax (212) 578-1661; internet www.wtfe.com/gan; f. 1976; Venezuelan visual art from pre-Hispanic time to the present; Pres. CLEMENTINA VAAMONDE B.; Exec. Dir RAFAEL SANTANA.

Museo Bolivariano (Bolívar Museum): Esquina San Jacinto a Traposos, Caracas; f. 1911 and inaugurated in present building 1960; contains 1,546 exhibits; mementos, portraits, personal relics and historical paintings of Simón Bolívar and his fellow-workers in the Independence Movement; library of 1,200 vols; Dir ANITA TAPIAS.

Museo de Arte Colonial (Museum of Colonial Art): Quinta de Anauco, Avda Panteón, San Bernardino, Caracas 1011; tel. (212) 551-8650; fax (212) 551-8517; e-mail artecolonialanauco@cantv.net; internet www.quintadeanauco.org.ve; f. 1942; painting, sculpture, decorative arts; library; under the supervision of the Asociación Venezolana de Amigos del Arte Colonial (*q.v.*); Dir CARLOS F. DUARTE.

Museo de Arte Contemporáneo de Caracas Sofía Imber (Sofía Imber Museum of Contemporary Art in Caracas): Zona Cultural, Parque Central, Apdo 17093, Caracas 1010; tel. (212) 577-0075; fax (212) 577-1883; internet www.maccsi.org.ve; f. 1973; incl. works by Picasso, Braque, Chagall, Bacon, Matisse, Kandinsky and Miró; Dir RITA SALVESTRINI.

Museo de Bellas Artes de Caracas (Museum of Fine Arts): Plaza Morelos, Parque Los Caobos, Caracas 105; tel. (212) 578-2197; fax (212) 571-0169; e-mail fmba@reacciun.ve; internet www.museodebellasartes.org; f. 1917; paintings and sculpture by national and foreign artists; library of 6,000 vols; Dir MARÍA ELENA RAMOS.

Ciudad Bolívar

Museo 'Talavera: Quinta San Isidro, Ciudad Bolívar; f. 1940; pre-Columbian and Colonial period exhibits, religious art, natural science, numismatics; Dir Dr J. GABRIEL MACHADO; publ. *Museo Talavera*.

El Tocuyo

Museo Colonial (Historical Museum): El Tocuyo; f. 1945.

Maracaibo

Museo Histórico 'General Rafael Urdaneta' (Museum of Military History): Calle 91A No. 7A-70, Sector Veritas, Maracaibo; tel. (261) 721-3414; f. 1936; colln of art, arms, sculpture, numismatic and philatelic items, photographs; Dir Prof. J. C. BORGES ROSALES.

Trujillo

Museo 'Cristóbal Mendoza' (Historical Museum): Trujillo.

Universities

UNIVERSIDAD DE CARABOBO

Av. Bolívar Norte, Sede del Rectorado U.C., Valencia, Edo. Carabobo
Telephone: (241) 821-5044
E-mail: di@uc.edu.ve
Internet: www.uc.edu.ve

Founded 1852
State control
Academic year: September to February, March to July

Rector: Dr GUSTAVO HIDALGO-VITALE
Academic Vice-Rector: Dr ELIS MERCADO MATUTE
Admin. Vice-Rector: Ing. JOSÉ BOTELLO WILSON
Sec.: Dr RUBÉN BALLESTEROS
Librarian: ANTONIETA PINTO DE KATZ

Library: see Libraries and Archives
Number of teachers: 2,585
Number of students: 44,654
Publications: *Boletín Universitario*, *Utopia y Praxis*

DEANS

Faculty of Economics and Social Sciences: Econ. LIONEL AGUDO
Faculty of Education: Lic. CARLOS HERRERA
Faculty of Engineering: Ing. GIOVANNI NANI
Faculty of Health Sciences: Dr CLAUDIO ROMANO
Faculty of Law: Abog. ELOY RUTMAN CISNEROS
Postgraduate Studies: Dr ALEJANDRO SUE MACHADO

UNIVERSIDAD CATÓLICA 'ANDRÉS BELLO'

Urb. Montalbán, La Vega, Apdo 1020, Caracas 1020
Telephone: (212) 407-4444
Fax: (212) 407-4349
E-mail: webmaster@ucab.edu.ve
Internet: www.ucab.edu.ve

Founded 1953
Private control (Society of Jesus)
Academic year: October to July

Campuses in San Cristóbal, Táchira

Chancellor: Rev. Fr PEDRO NICOLÁS BERMÚDEZ
Vice-Chancellor: Rev. Fr JESUS MARÍA ORBEGOZO EGUIGUREN
Rector: Rev. Fr LUIS UGALDE
Academic Vice-Rector: Dra MIRIAM LÓPEZ DE VALDIVIESO
Admin. Vice-Rector: Ing. LORENZO CALDENTEY LUQUE
Dean of Student Devt: Dr RUBÉN ANGEL PEÑALVER GODINES
Sec.-Gen.: Rev. Fr GUSTAVO SUCRE
Librarian: Lic. EMILIO PÍRIZ PÉREZ

Library: see Libraries and Archives
Number of teachers: 1,225
Number of students: 14,131
Publications: *Analogías del Comportamiento*, *Cuadernos Venezolanos de Filosofía*, *Encuentro EAC y Cuadernos UCAB-Educación*, *Espacios*, *Pensamiento Agustiniano*, *Revista de la Facultad de Derecho*, *Revista Montalbán*, *Revista de Relaciones Industriales y Laborales*, *Revista Tekhne de la Facultad de Ingeniería*, *Temas de Comunicación Social*, *Temas de Coyuntura*

DEANS

Faculty of Engineering: Ing. RAFAEL HERNÁNDEZ SÁNCHEZ-OCAÑA
Faculty of Humanities and Education: Dra SILVANA CAMPAGNARO
Faculty of Law: Dr JESÚS MARÍA CASAL
Faculty of Social and Economic Sciences: Dr EDUARDO OTIZ
Faculty of Theology: Rev. Fr GIAN PAOLO PERÓN

DIRECTORS

School of Business Administration and Accounting: Lic. FREDDY MARTÍN
School of Civil Engineering: Ing. JOSÉ OCHOA ITURBE
School of Economics: Econ. MARÍA ISABEL MARTÍNEZ ABAL
School of Education: Dra MARÍA ELENA FEBRES-CORDERO BRICEÑO
School of Engineering: Ing. MILAGROS BOSCHETTI
School of Industrial Engineering: Ing. VICENTE NAPOLITANO CASTALDO
School of Informatics: Ing. SUSANA GARCÍA MARTÍNEZ
School of Law: Abga AURA JANESKY LEHMANN
School of Letters: Lic. MARÍA DE LOS ANGELES PEÑA

School of Philosophy: Lic. JESÚS HERNÁEZ
School of Psychology: Dr GUSTAVO PEÑA
School of Social Sciences: Lic. INGRID OCHOA DE PÉREZ
School of Telecommunications Engineering: Ing. MAYRA NARVÁEZ
School of Theology: Rev. Fr RAFAEL SERRANO
Institute of Economic and Social Research: Lic. LUIS PEDRO ESPAÑA NAVARRO
Institute of Historical Research: Dr ELÍAS PINO ITURRIETA
Centre of Advice and Human Development: Lic. ALCIRA TEXEIRA DE CERRADA
Centre of Behavioural Studies: Dra SILVANA CAMPAGNARO
Centre of Communication Research: Lic. ERCILIA VÁSQUEZ
Centre of Engineering Research: Ing. LOURDES ORTIZ
Centre of Human Rights: Abga LIGIA BOLÍVAR
Centre of Legal Research: Dra MARÍA GRACIA MORAIS DIAZ
Centre of Philosophical Studies: Dra SILVANA CAMPAGNARO
Centre of Religious Studies: Dra SILVANA CAMPAGNARO
Engineering Laboratories: Ing. FRANCISCO MORERA

UNIVERSIDAD CATÓLICA DEL TÁCHIRA

Barrio Obrero, Calle 14 con Carrera 14, San Cristóbal, Edo. Táchira
Telephone: (276) 342-1614
E-mail: asosa@ucat.edu.ve
Internet: www.ucat.edu.ve

Founded 1982

Rector: Dr ARTURO SOSA ABASCAL
Vice-Rector: ASTRID RICO DE MÉNDEZ
Chief Admin. Officer: FÉLIDA ROA DE ROA
Librarian: EMILIO J. URBINA MENDOZA

Number of teachers: 336
Number of students: 5,000

Publications: *Paramillo* (1 a year), *Revista Tachirense de Derecho* (1 a year), *Siglo XXI* (1 a year), *Tributum* (1 a year)

DEANS

Faculty of Economics and Social Sciences: MARINÉS SÁNCHEZ
Faculty of Humanities and Education: EDUARDO FAJARDO RUEDA
Faculty of Law and Political Science: JESÚS ALBERTO LABRADOR SUÁREZ
Faculty of Religion: EDUARDO FAJARDO RUEDA

UNIVERSIDAD CENTRAL DE VENEZUELA

Apdo Postal 1050, Ciudad Universitaria, Los Chaguaramos, Caracas 1051
Telephone: (212) 605-4050
Fax: (212) 605-4086
Internet: www.ucv.ve

Founded 1721
State control
Language of instruction: Spanish
Academic year: January to December

Rector: GIUSEPPE GIANNETTO
Academic Vice-Rector: ERNESTO GONZÁLEZ
Admin. Vice-Rector: MANUEL MARIÑA
Registrar: Dr ANTONIO DEL NOGAL
Gen. Coordinator: JEANETTE BLANCO DE MÉNDEZ
Sec.: ELIZABETH MARVAL
Librarian: Dr EUDIS BORRA

Number of teachers: 6,987
Number of students: 45,000

Publications: *Acta Odontologica*, *Akademos* (2 a year), *Aula Magna*, *Boletín del Archivo Histórico*, *Boletín de Lingüística*, *Correo Ucevista*, *Gaceta Universitaria*, *Revista Alcance 57* (organic soil science, 2 a year), *Revista del Centro de Información y Documentación* (6 a year), *Revista Escuela de Metalurgia*, *Revista de la Facultad de Agronomía* (2 a year), *Revista de la Facultad de Ciencias Jurídicas y Políticas* (4 a year), *Revista de la Facultad de Ciencias Veterinarias*, *Revista de la Facultad de Farmacia* (4 a year), *Revista de la Facultad de Ingeniería* (6 a year), *Revista de la Facultad de Medicina*, *Revista Latinoamericana de Estudios Avanzados*, *Revista Tecnología y Construcción* (3 a year), *Revista Tharsis*, *Revista Urbana* (town planning, 2 a year), *Revista Venezolana de Economía y Ciencias Sociales*, *Revista Venezolana de Estudios Internacionales*

DEANS

Faculty of Agriculture: FRANKLÍN CHACÍN LUGO
Faculty of Architecture and Town Planning: ABNER COLMENARES
Faculty of Dentistry: CECILIA GARCÍA AROCHA
Faculty of Economic and Social Sciences: VÍCTOR RAGO
Faculty of Engineering: RAFAEL ROCA
Faculty of Humanities and Education: BENJAMÍN SÁNCHEZ
Faculty of Law and Political Science: PEDRO GUEVARA
Faculty of Medicine: MIGUEL REQUENA
Faculty of Pharmacy: ORLANDO VIZCARRONDO
Faculty of Science: MASSIMO CANESTRARI
Faculty of Veterinary Science: RAFAEL INFANTES

UNIVERSIDAD CENTRO-OCCIDENTAL 'LISANDRO ALVARADO'

Apdo 400, Barquisimeto, Lara
Telephone: (251) 259-1061
Fax: (251) 259-1064
Internet: www.ucla.edu.ve

Founded 1963 as Experimental Centre of Higher Education; univ. status 1968
State control
Language of instruction: Spanish
Academic year: January to December

Rector: Dr RICARDO GARCÍA DE LONGORIA
Academic Vice-Rector: Dra GADRA SÁNCHEZ DE PÉREZ
Admin. Vice-Rector: Dr GUÉDEZ CORTEZ
Sec.-Gen.: Dr RICARDO GÁSPERI MAGO
Librarian: Lic. MORELLA BARRANCOS

Number of teachers: 930
Number of students: 9,665

Publications: *Boletín Científico*, *Boletín Informativo*, *El Veterinario* (12 a year), *Escuela de Administración*, *Escuela de Agronomía*, *Memoria y Cuenta* (1 a year), *Tarea Común* (4 a year)

DEANS

Faculty of Administration and Accountancy: Lic. CÉSAR MORENO
Faculty of Agronomy: Ing. JOSÉ PASTOR GUTIÉRREZ
Faculty of Civil Engineering: Ing. HERMES ESPINOZA
Faculty of Medicine: Dr RÉGULO CARPIO
Faculty of Sciences: Dr JOSÉ BETHELMY
Faculty of Veterinary Medicine: Dr RAMÓN SALCEDO

ATTACHED INSTITUTES

Consejo Asesor de Investigación y Servicios (Advisory Council on Research and Services): assessment and consultation on the planning of research; Pres. Dr FRANCISCO MONTES DE OCA.

Instituto de la Uva (Institute for Research on Grapes): research on grape cultivation and advisory service to wine growers; Dir MARIA LUISA DE PIRE.

UNIVERSIDAD DE LOS ANDES

Avda 3, Independencia, Edif. Rectorado, Mérida 5101
Telephone: (275) 240-1111
Fax: (275) 240-1998
E-mail: dsia@ula.ve
Internet: www.ula.ve

Founded 1785 as the Real Colegio Seminario de San Buenaventura de Mérida, became Univ. 1810

Campuses at Trujillo and Táchira
State control
Language of instruction: Spanish
Academic year: January to December

Rector: GENRY VARGAS
Academic Vice-Rector: MANUEL HERNÁNDEZ
Admin. Vice-Rector: JULIO FLORES MENESINI
Sec.: GLADYS BECERRA DEPABLOS
Registrar: (vacant)
Librarian: NILZA GONZÁLEZ DE GUTIÉRREZ

Library: see Libraries and Archives
Number of teachers: 2,947
Number of students: 34,294

DEANS

Faculty of Architecture: Arq. INÉS BENAVIDES
Faculty of Economic and Social Sciences: MANUEL ARANGUREN
Faculty of Engineering: Ing. RUBÉN AÑEZ
Faculty of Forestry: Prof. CERES BOADA
Faculty of Humanities and Education: FRANCISCO GAVIDIA
Faculty of Law and Political Science: ANDREY GROMIKO URDANETA
Faculty of Medicine: Dr JOSÉ FREYTEZ O'CALLAGHAN
Faculty of Odontology: Dr PATRICIO JARPA
Faculty of Pharmacy: Dr ALFREDO CARABOT CUERVO
Faculty of Sciences: CARLOS ALVAREZ
Rafael Rangel Campus: Dr CONRADO DABOÍN VÁSQUEZ
Táchira Campus: Dr RAMÓN GONZÁLEZ E.

UNIVERSIDAD METROPOLITANA

Apdo 76819, Caracas 1070
Telephone: (212) 242-2958
Fax: (212) 242-5450
E-mail: cvicentini@unimet.edu.ve
Internet: www.unimet.edu.ve

Founded 1970
Private control
Language of instruction: Spanish
Academic year: October to September

Pres.: Ing. HERNAN ANZOLA
Rector: Ing. JOSÉ IGNACIO MORENO LEÓN
Academic Vice-Rector: Ing. JOSÉ ROBERTO BELLO
Admin. Vice-Rector: Ing. ANTINIO IZSAK
Registrar: Prof. MARÍA DE LOURDES ACEDO DE SUCRE
Librarian: Dr ELEIDA GARCÍA

Number of teachers: 438
Number of students: 4,670

Publications: *Anales de la Universidad Metropolitana* (2 a year), *Revista UNIMET* (12 a year)

DEANS

Arts and Sciences: Prof. JAVIER RÍOS
Economics and Social Sciences: Prof. JOSÉ ANGEL VELÁZQUEZ
Engineering: Ing. MARIA BLANCA FERNÁNDEZ

UNIVERSIDAD NACIONAL ABIERTA (Open University)

Apdo 2096, Caracas 1010A
Telephone: (212) 574-1322
Fax: (212) 574-4075
E-mail: mromero@reacciun.ve
Internet: www.una.edu.ve

Founded 1977 on the 'open university' principle, using modern methods of communication and educational technology. One national centre in Caracas and 20 regional centres
State control
Language of instruction: Spanish
Academic year: October to July

Rector: Dr MANUEL CASTRO PEREIRA
Academic Vice-Rector: Dr NÉSTOR LEAL ORTIZ
Admin. Vice-Rector: Prof. ARNALDO ESCALONA PEÑUELA
Sec.: Prof. ARELIS COROMOTO SAAVEDRA
Librarian: Lic. CARMEN IBARRA

Number of teachers: 831
Number of students: 61,648

Publications: *Informe de Investigaciones Educativas, Una Documenta*

COURSE COORDINATORS

Academic Areas and Courses: Prof. MARÍA J. BERMÚDEZ
Academic Coordinator: Dr MANUEL CASTRO PEREIRA
Academic Evaluation: Prof. ISALIV MATHEUS
Accountancy: Prof. FRANCISCO EGAÑEZ
Administration and Accountancy: Dr PEDRO RUIZ
Education: Dra ERICKA NAVEDA
General Studies: Dra MARÍA CLARA SALAS
Industrial Engineering: Prof. MARTHA URBINA
Mathematics: Prof. SERGIO RIVAS
Planning and Evaluation: Dra ARLETTE URGELLES
Regional and Local Centres: Prof. MIRIAM PÉREZ
Student Services: Prof. OMAIRA CORDERO
Systems Engineering: Prof. JUDIT CARVALLO
University Extension: Prof. TERESITA PÉREZ DE MAZA

LOCAL CENTRES

Anzoátegui: Dir Prof. LUIS RIVAS.
Apure: Dir Prof. JOSÉ GREGORIO FIGUEROA.
Aragua: Dir Prof. NELSON GUARDIA.
Barinas: Dir Prof. RAMÓN CHACÓN.
Bolivar: Dir Prof. ELMES PÉREZ.
Carabobo: Dir Prof. LUCILA CABRICES.
Cojedes: Dir (vacant).
Falcón: Dir Prof. NOÉ JIMENEZ.
Guárico: Dir Prof. DUNIA SISO.
Lara: Dir Prof. MILAGROS BARTOLOMÉ.
Mérida: Dir Prof. NAPOLEÓN SÁNCHEZ.
Metropolitano: Dir Prof. OSCAR ODÓN.
Monagas: Dir Prof. LUIS BALBAS.
Nueva Esparta: Dir Prof. AQUILES ROJAS.
Portuguesa: Dir Prof. NANCY CONTRERAS.
Sucre: Dir Prof. FREDDY PÉREZ.
Táchira: Dir MARÍA LOURDES RINCÓN.
T. F. Delta Amacuro: Dir Prof. JUANA LUGO.
Trujillo: Dir Prof. EVELYN HACKETT.
Yaracuy: Dir Prof. JORGE MILLA.
Zulia: Dir Prof. ANA YSOLINA SOTO.

UNIVERSIDAD NACIONAL EXPERIMENTAL FRANCISCO DE MIRANDA

Edif. Rectorado, Calle Norte, Santa Ana de Coro, Estado Falcón
Telephone: (293) 250-2406
Fax: (293) 250-2429
E-mail: webmaster@unefm.edu.ve
Internet: www.unefm.edu.ve

Founded 1977
Academic year: January to December (two semesters)

Chancellor: SIMON ALBERTO CONSALVI
Rector: Dr PEDRO BORREGALES P.
Academic Vice-Rector: Dr OSCAR ABREU
Admin. Vice-Rector: Dr JULIO LÓPEZ P.
Administrator: Lic. CESAR VELÁSQUEZ
Librarian: Lic. NIDYA PETIT DE MOTTA

Number of teachers: 350
Number of students: 3,000

Publications: *Boletín* (weekly), *Cultura Falconiana* (4 a year), *Gaceta Universitaria* (4 a year)

DEANS

Faculty of Civil and Industrial Engineering: Ing. ORANGEL NUÑEZ
Faculty of Medicine: Dr ROBERTO GRAND L.
Faculty of Veterinary Medicine and Agriculture: Dr DIOGENES RODRÍGUEZ

UNIVERSIDAD NACIONAL EXPERIMENTAL DE GUAYANA

Avda Las Américas, Edificio General de Seguros, Puerto Ordaz, Estado Bolívar
Telephone: (286) 923-2423
Fax: (286) 922-5673
E-mail: secretaria@uneg.edu.ve
Internet: www.uneg.edu.ve

Founded 1982
State control

Rector: JOSÉ TARAZONA
Vice-Rector for Academic Affairs: Dr LUIS ALEXIS VELÁSQUEZ
Vice-Rector for Admin.: Dra MARÍA ELENA LATUFF
Sec.-Gen.: Dra MYRIAN ARLENY ZAMBRANO DE GUERRERO

Publications: *Copérnico*, *Gaceta Universitaria* (1 a year), *Kaleidoscopio* (4 a year)

Depts of Education, Humanities and Arts, Man and the Environment, Management and Science and Technology.

UNIVERSIDAD NACIONAL EXPERIMENTAL DE LOS LLANOS CENTRALES 'ROMULO GALLEGOS'

Ciudad Universitaria, Avenida Universitaria, vía El Castrero, San Juan de los Morros, Estado Guárico
Telephone: (246) 431-0584
Fax: (246) 431-2670
E-mail: webmaster@unerg.edu.ve
Internet: www.unerg.edu.ve

Founded 1977
State control
Language of instruction: Spanish
Academic year: March to December (two semesters)

Pres. and Rector: Ing. GIOVANNI NANI R.
Academic Vice-Rector: Ing. ENRIQUE MUJICA ALVÁREZ
Admin. Vice-Rector: Lic. GHENRY J. NAVARRO U.
Librarian: Lic. RHAIZA MARQUEZ

Number of teachers: 367
Number of students: 5,306

Publication: *Horizontes Universitarios*

DEANS

Continuing Education: Lic. YOLANDA VILLASMIL
Faculty of Economics: Lic. CARLOS HERRERA
Faculty of Education: Lic. CECILIA REQUENA R.
Faculty of Engineering: Ing. NELSON MARTE
Faculty of Health: Dra MARTHA CANTAVELLA
Faculty of Odontology: Dr OMAR SCOVINO
Faculty of Veterinary Medicine: Méd. Vet. SALVADOR DE J. PÉREZ ALEMÁN
Postgraduate Studies: Lic. GLADYS MORENO V.
Research and Extension: Prof. GEOMAIRA MONTENEGRO

ATTACHED INSTITUTE

Centre for Legal Studies: Dir Abog. GLADYS BOYER.

UNIVERSIDAD NACIONAL EXPERIMENTAL DE LOS LLANOS OCCIDENTALES 'EZEQUIEL ZAMORA'

Av. 23 de Enero, Redoma de Punto Fresco, Barinas
Telephone: (73) 41201
Fax: (73) 41858
Internet: www.unellez.edu.ve

Founded 1975
Language of instruction: Spanish
Academic year: January to December (two semesters)

Rector: Prof. MIGUEL ÁNGEL HENRÍQUEZ MARCANO
Vice-Rector: Dr JOSÉ ALFREDO GUERRERO SOSA
Sec.: Dr LUIS A. SUÁREZ CORDERO
Librarian: Dra MIGDALIA DE LARA

Number of teachers: 600
Number of students: 8,000

Publications: *Biollania*, *Revista UNELLEZ de Ciencia y Tecnología*

Experimental govt-sponsored institute of higher education, serving the Los Llanos Occidentales region, and the States of Apure, Barinas, Cojedes and Portuguesa

Courses in Agriculture and Mechanization, Economics, Social Development, Regional Planning, Human Ecology.

UNIVERSIDAD NACIONAL EXPERIMENTAL MARÍTIMA DEL CARIBE

Calle El Ejército, Catia la Mar, Vargas, Caracas
Telephone: (212) 351-0834
Fax: (212) 351-0834
Internet: www.umc.edu.ve

Founded 2000
State control

Rector: MIGUEL LÓPEZ
Vice-Rector (for Academic Affairs: REYNALDO MONTES DE OCA
Vice-Rector for Admin.: MANUEL PÉREZ ALVAREZ.

UNIVERSIDAD NACIONAL EXPERIMENTAL POLITECNICA 'ANTONIO JOSÉ DE SUCRE'

Apdo Postal 539, Barquisimeto, Edo Lara
Telephone: (251) 420133
Fax: (251) 413880
Internet: www.unellez.edu.ve

Founded 1962
Private control

Rector: Dr IVÁN OLAIZOLA D'ALESSANDRO
Vice-Rector for Secretariat: Dr RAMÓN VIELMA
Vice-Rector for Barquisimeto Campus: Ing. AMAEL CASTELLANO
Vice-Rector for Caracas Campus: Ing. ILDELFONSO MEJÍA ZAMBRANO
Vice-Rector for Ordaz Campus: Ing. LUIS CÁRDENAS CASTILLO
Academic Admin. Coordinator: Ing. EDUARDO CABRÉ TRUJILLO
Coordinator: Lic. XIOMARA DE BARRA

Library of 19,200 vols, 9,000 periodicals
Number of teachers: 900
Number of students: 10,000
Publications: *Avance Universitario* (2 a year), *Boletín Bibliográfico de Publicaciones Recibidas* (2 a year), *Información General de la Universidad* (1 a year)
Faculties of chemistry and industrial engineering, electrical engineering, electronic engineering, mechanical engineering, metallurgy, systems.

UNIVERSIDAD NACIONAL EXPERIMENTAL RAFAEL MARÍA BARALT

Avda El Rosario, Parroquia Carmen Herrera, Cabimas, Estado Zulia
Telephone: (264) 241-5306
E-mail: rectorado@unermb.edu.ve
Internet: www.unermb.edu.ve
Founded 1982
State control
Rector: Dr VICTOR HUGO MERIÑO CÓRDOBA
Vice-Rector for Academic Affairs: BOLÍVAR SÁENZ TRAÑA
Vice-Rector for Admin.: AÍDA CÓRTES DE VERBEL
Sec.-Gen.: ODA GONZÁLEZ RINCÓN.

UNIVERSIDAD NACIONAL EXPERIMENTAL SIMÓN RODRÍGUEZ

Calle 1, Zona Industrial Urb. Palo Verde, Caracas
Telephone: (212) 251-3684
Internet: www.unesr.edu.ve
Founded 1974
Regional centres in 13 towns
Pres.: Dr GUSTAVO GONZÁLEZ ERASO
Rector: Dr MANUEL MARIÑAS
Academic Vice-Rector: JUDITH SOSA DE VÁZQUEZ
Admin. Vice-Rector: ASDRÚBAL LOZANO FERNÁNDEZ
Sec.: MARÍA SILVA VIVANCO
Number of teachers: 387
Number of students: 12,859
Publications: *Gaceta Universitaria* (4 a year), *Memoria y Cuenta de la Universidad* (1 a year), *Revista de Cultura* (4 a year)
Faculties of administration, education and food technology.

UNIVERSIDAD NACIONAL EXPERIMENTAL DEL TÁCHIRA

Apdo 436, Avda Universidad, Paramillo, San Cristóbal, Táchira
Telephone: (276) 353-0422
Fax: (276) 353-2896
E-mail: rectorad@unet.edu.ve
Internet: www.unet.edu.ve
Founded 1974
State control
Language of instruction: Spanish
Academic year: February to December
Rector: Lic. JOSÉ VICENTE SÁNCHEZ FRANK
Academic Vice-Rector: Ing. CARLOS CHACÓN LABRADOR
Admin. Vice-Rector: Ing. MARTÍN PAZ
Sec.: Arq. OSCAR MEDINA HERNÁNDEZ
Dean of Extension: Ing. SALVADOR GALEANO
Dean of Graduate Studies: Ing. JESÚS WILFREDO BOLÍVAR
Dean of Research: Ing. RAÚL CASANOVA
Dean of Teaching: Ing. JOSÉ BECERRA
Dean of Undergraduate Studies: Ing. LUIS VERGARA
Librarian: Ing. ERLAND MARTÍNEZ
Number of teachers: 530
Number of students: 10,500 (6,000 undergraduate, 1,500 propaedeutic, 3,000 graduate)
Publications: *Aleph sub cero*, *Boletín*, *Boletín Estadístico*, *Gaceta*, *Revista Científica UNET*, *Vocero Universitario*.

UNIVERSIDAD NACIONAL EXPERIMENTAL DEL YARACUY

Zona Industrial Agustín Rivero, Edificio Fundación CIEPE, San Felipe, Estado Yaracuy
Telephone: (254) 232-2441
Fax: (254) 232-1351
E-mail: rectorado@uney.edu.ve
Internet: www.uney.edu.ve
Founded 1999
State control
Rector: Dr FREDDY CASTILLO CASTELLANOS
Vice-Rector: Ing. JOSÉ LUIS NAJUL SALDIVIA
Sec.-Gen.: Ing. RAMÓN G. SÁNCHEZ SIVIRA
Courses in food science and sport.

UNIVERSIDAD DE ORIENTE

Edificio Rectorado, Apdo 094, Cumaná, Estado Sucre
Telephone: (93) 23366
Internet: www.udo.edu.ve
Founded 1958
State control
Academic year: February to December
Rector: Dr ANDRÉS PASTRANA VÁSQUEZ
Academic Vice-Rector: Dr OSWALDO BETANCOURT
Admin. Vice-Rector: Dr DIOGENES FIGUEROA LUGO
Sec.-Gen.: Dr CESAR A. BOADA SALAZAR
Library: see Libraries and Archives
Number of teachers: 1,382
Number of students: 23,084
Publications: *Boletín del Instituto Oceanográfico*, *Catálogo de la UDO* (1 a year), *Directorio del Personal Docente e Investigación* (1 a year), *Lagena*, *La UDO Investiga*, *Oriente Agropecuario*, *Oriente Universitario* (12 a year, bulletin).

CONSTITUENT CAMPUSES

Universidad de Oriente, Nucleo Anzoátegui

Apdo postal 4327, Puerto La Cruz, Anzoátegui
Telephone: (281) 420-3402
Internet: www.anz.udo.edu.ve
Founded 1965
Dean: Prof. MANUEL LÓPEZ FARÍAS
Number of teachers: 418
Number of students: 9,000

HEADS OF SCHOOLS

Administrative Sciences: Prof. JUAN D. GUAICAIN
Basic Courses: Prof. PEDRO JIMÉNEZ
Engineering and Applied Science: Prof. RUBÉN AULAR

Universidad de Oriente, Nucleo Bolívar

La Sabanita, Ciudad Bolívar
Internet: www.bolivar.udo.edu.ve
Dean: Dr ARTURO RAUL LARA ROJAS

DIRECTORS

Basic Courses: Prof. MARGOTH SISO DE SAN MARTIN
Geology and Mines: Prof. OSCAR GARCÍA CACHAZO
Medicine: Prof. VICTOR ESPINOZA LEÓN

Universidad de Oriente, Nucleo de Monagas

Avda Universidad, Maturín, Edo Monagas
Internet: www.monagas.udo.edu.ve
Founded 1961
Dean: Dr JOSÉ JIMÉNEZ TIAMO
Academic Coordinator: Ing. LUIS ARISMENDI
Admin. Coordinator: Ing. MARCIAL VIÑAS DE LA HOZ
Librarian: Lic. RAMÓN JOSÉ NÚÑEZ
Publication: *Oriente Agropecuario* (2 a year)

HEADS OF SCHOOLS

Basic Courses: Prof. JOSÉ VICENTE ANDÉRICO
Programme of Administrative Science: Prof. ARNALDO ROJAS
Programme of Human Resources: Prof. LUIS MÁRQUEZ
School of Agricultural Engineering: NILDA ALCORCES DE GUERRA

Universidad de Oriente, Nucleo Nueva Esparta

Apdo Postal 147, Guatamare, Nueva Esparta
Telephone: (95) 610131
Fax: (95) 610131
Internet: www.ne.udo.edu.ve
Founded 1958
State control
Dean: Ing. CASTO GONZÁLEZ M.
Academic Coordinator: Prof. JOSÉ G. MARCANO
Admin. Coordinator: Ing. LUIS MARCANO

HEADS OF SCHOOLS

Applied Ocean Sciences: Prof. JOSÉ LUIS FUENTES
Basic Courses: Prof. ESTEBAN OBANDO
Hotel and Tourism: Prof. JOSÉ M. VELÁSQUEZ

Universidad de Oriente, Nucleo de Sucre

Cumaná
Internet: www.sucre.udo.edu.ve
Dean: Prof. FRANCIA PADILLA DE KORCHOFF

HEADS OF SCHOOLS

Administration and Accountancy: Prof. JOSÉ ANTONIO ARISTIMUÑO
Basic Courses: Prof. FORTUNATO MALAN
Humanities and Education: Prof. EZEQUIEL SALAZAR
Sciences: Prof. ELSIE ROMERO DE BELLORIN
Social Sciences: Prof. MARÍA ELENA ZAJÍA

UNIVERSIDAD PEDAGÓGICA EXPERIMENTAL LIBERTADOR

Avda Sucre, Parque del Oeste, Catia, 1030 Caracas
Telephone: (212) 864-7511
Fax: (212) 864-7977
Internet: www.upel.edu.ve
Founded 1983
State control
Academic year: September to July
Rector: Prof. ÁNGEL ARÍSTIDES HERNÁNDEZ ABREU
Vice-Rector for Extension: Prof. LUIS MARÍN
Vice-Rector for Research and Postgraduate Studies: Prof. MAXIMILIANO BEZADA
Vice-Rector for Teaching: Prof. JESÚS RODRÍGUEZ
Sec.: Prof. FRANCIA CELIS.

CONSTITUENT INSTITUTES

Instituto de Mejoramiento Profesional del Magisterio

Avda Rómulo Gallegos, Segunda Transversal de Montecristo, Caracas 1071
Telephone: (212) 234-6640

Fax: (212) 234-6608
E-mail: pontivero@impm.upel.edu.ve
Internet: www.impm.upel.edu.ve.

Institutio Pedagógico de Barquisimeto

Avda Los Horcones con Calle 64, Barquisimeto, Estado Lara
Telephone: (251) 442-5333
Fax: (251) 423-887
E-mail: r.valera@ipb.upel.edu.ve
Internet: www.ipb.upel.edu.ve
Dir: RAFAEL VALERA.

Instituto Pedagógico de Caracas

Avda Páez, El Paraíso, Caracas 1020
Telephone: (212) 461-6121
Fax: (212) 462-2760
E-mail: webmaster@ipc.upel.edu.ve
Internet: www.ipc.upel.edu.ve
Founded 1936 as Instituto Pedagógico Nacional; present status 1987
Academic year: May to February (two semesters)
Dir: Prof. CRISTIAN SÁNCHEZ
Sub-Dir for Extension: Prof. ÁNGEL FLORES
Sub-Dir for Research and Postgraduate Studies: Prof. SILVANA MESSORI DE NEGRETE
Sub-Dir for Teaching: Prof. HEAGDLINE ARIAS
Librarian: Lic. MELVIS PIRE
Publications: *Candidus Infantil* (4 a year), *Lingvo & Internacia Komunikado*, *Revista de Investigación*, *Tiempo y Espacio*.

Instituto Pedagógico de Maturín

Carretera Sur, Maturín 6263, Estado Monagas
Telephone: (291) 641-6863
Fax: (291) 641-7750
E-mail: carzolay@ipm.upel.edu.ve
Internet: www.ipm.upel.edu.ve
Dir: COSME ALZOLAY.

Instituto Pedagógico de Miranda

Calle 6, Edificio Papeca Modulo 2, Urbanización La Urbina, Caracas 1070
Telephone: (212) 461-6472
Fax: (212) 462-2760
E-mail: nbarreto@ipmjmsm.upel.edu.ve
Internet: www.ipmjmsm.upel.edu.ve
Dir: NANCY BARRETO.

Instituto Pedagógico Rural 'El Mácaro'

Carretera Nacional Maracay/Turmero, Maracay 2115, Estado Aragua
Telephone: (244) 631294
Fax: (244) 61380
E-mail: aperales@iprm.upel.edu.ve
Internet: www.iprm.upel.edu.ve
Dir: AURA DÍAZ DE PERALES.

Instituto Pedagógico Rural 'Gervasio Rubio'

Final Avda Dr 'Manuel Pulido Méndez', Vía Bramón, Rubio, Estado Táchira
Telephone: (276) 762-1746
Fax: (276) 762-4041
E-mail: fespinel@iprgr.upel.edu.ve
Internet: www.iprgr.upel.edu.ve
Dir: FRANCISCO ESPINEL.

UNIVERSIDAD SIMÓN BOLÍVAR

Carretera Hoyo de la Puerta, Valle de Sartenejas Baruta Estado Miranda
Telephone: (212) 906-3111
Fax: (212) 962-1615
Internet: www.usb.ve
Founded 1970
State control
Language of instruction: Spanish
Academic year: September to July
Rector: Ing. PEDRO ASO
Academic Vice-Rector: Dr OSMAR ISSA
Admin. Vice-Rector: Ing. JUAN LEON
Gen.-Sec.: Dr PEDRO MARÍA ASO
Librarian: Dra ROSARIO GASSOL DE HOROWITZ
Number of teachers: 850
Number of students: 10,000
Publications: *Argos*, *Atlántida*, *Perfiles*

DEANS

General Studies: JUAN CARLOS RODRÍGUEZ
Postgraduate Studies: CARLOS PÉREZ
Professional Studies: RAUL GONCALVES
Research: BENJAMÍN SCHARIFKER

DIVISION DIRECTORS

Biological Sciences: DAISY PÉREZ DE ACOSTA
Humanities and Social Sciences: ANA MARÍA RAJKAY
Physics and Mathematics: ROBERTO RÉQUIZ
Technological Studies (Núcleo Universitario del Litoral): ENRIQUE LÓPEZ CONTRERAS

UNIVERSIDAD DEL ZULIA

Av. 16 con calle 67B, Maracaibo, Estado Zulia
Telephone: (261) 759-8441
E-mail: webmaster@luz.edu.ve
Internet: www.luz.edu.ve
Founded 1891, closed 1904, reopened 1946
State control
Academic year: September to July
Rector: Dr ANGEL LOMBARDI LOMBARDI
Academic Vice-Rector: Lic. ANTONIO CASTEJÓN
Admin. Vice-Rector: Econ. NEURO VILLALOBOS
Sec.: Ing. ANGEL LARREAL
Librarian: Lic. EGLA ORTEGA
Library: see Libraries and Archives
Number of teachers: 3,652
Number of students: 47,590
Publications: *Gaceta* (4 a year), *Memoria y Cuenta de LUZ* (1 a year), *Publicaciones de la Unidad de Estadísticas*

DEANS

Faculty of Agriculture: Prof. ALONSO FERNÁNDEZ
Faculty of Architecture: Prof. IGNACIO DE OTEIZA
Faculty of Dentistry: Prof. EXEQUIADES PAZ A.
Faculty of Economic and Social Sciences: Prof. JULIANA FERRER
Faculty of Engineering: Prof. NELSON MOLERO
Faculty of Experimental Sciences: Prof. TERESITA ALVAREZ DE FERNANDEZ
Faculty of Humanities and Education: Prof. NERIO VÍLCHEZ
Faculty of Law: Dr HERMANN PETZOLD PERNÍA
Faculty of Medicine: Dr RAFAEL MARTÍNEZ
Faculty of Veterinary Sciences: Prof. GUSTAVO SOTO

Polytechnic Institute

INSTITUTO UNIVERSITARIO POLITÉCNICO 'LUIS CABALLERO MEJÍAS'

Apdo 20955, San Martin, Caracas 1020A
Telephone: (212) 498917
Founded 1974
Dir: Ing. RAFAEL DUQUE SALINAS
Deputy Dir of Academic Affairs: Ing. IDELFONSO MEJÍAS
Deputy Dir of Admin. Affairs: Lic. RAMÓN PELLES
Librarian: Lic. MYRIAM LÓPEZ ACOSTA
Number of teachers: 216
Number of students: 2,017

College

Instituto de Estudios Superiores de Administración (IESA) (Institute for Advanced Studies in Administration): Edificio IESA, Avda IESA, San Bernardino, Caracas 1010; tel. (212) 552-2055; e-mail relinsti@iesa.edu.ve; internet www.iesa.edu.ve; f. 1965; private non-profit business school; Pres. RAMÓN PIÑANGO.

Schools of Art and Music

Centro de Bellas Artes (Center for Fine Arts): Avenida 3F Nº 67-217, Colonia Bella Vista, Sector La Lago, Maracaibo; tel. (261) 912950; fax (261) 912239; e-mail centrobellasartes@iamnet.com; f. 1954 to promote cultural activities; theatre, 2 art galleries, school of ballet and modern dance, Maracaibo Contemporary Dance Troupe, Maracaibo Symphony Orchestra, National Youth Theatre, Goajiro Indian workshop, *Colegio Bellas Artes*, library; Dir OSCAR D'EMPAIRE.

Conservatorio de Música José Luis Paz: Av. 2 El Milagro, Edif. Secretaría de Cultura, 2° piso, Maracaibo; tel. (261) 808-6231; internet conservatoriojlp.com.ve; f. 1943; Dir Prof. OSCAR FACCIO.

Escuela de Artes Visuales 'Cristóbal Rojas' (Cristóbal Rojas School of Visual Arts): Esquina Ño Pastor, frente a la Plaza Parque Carabobo, La Candelaria, Caracas 1010; tel. (212) 621-0940; f. 1936; Dir EMILY HERNÁNDEZ DE VILLAROEL.

Escuela Superior de Arte 'Neptali Rincón': Centro Vocacional Dr O. Hernández, Avda El Milagro Diagonal al Hospital Central, Maracaibo; tel. (261) 223868; f. 1957; courses in painting, sculpture, ceramics, etc.; 12 teachers; 300 students; Dir CONSUELO BUSTOS.

Escuela Superior de Música 'José Angel Lamas' (Lamas High School of Music): Av. Urdaneta, Esq. de Santa Capilla, Caracas; tel. (212) 864-1618; f. 1887; Dir VICENTE EMILIO SOJO.

Fundación Teresa Carreño: Teatro Teresa Carreño, Final Paseo Colón, Caracas; tel. (212) 574-9122; e-mail webmaster@teatroteresacarreno.com; internet www.teatroteresacarreno.com; f. 1983; concerts, opera, ballet, master classes and courses for opera singers; Dir-Gen. BEATRICE RANGEL MANTILLA.

VIET NAM

The Higher Education System

Institutions of higher education predate Viet Nam's partition in 1954 (it was reunified as the Socialist Republic of Viet Nam in 1976), the oldest being Hanoi Medical University, which was founded in 1902 when Viet Nam was under French colonial rule. Over 30 institutions were founded during the period of partition (1954–76), including major universities in Hanoi and Ho Chi Minh City (formerly Saigon). In 1989 Viet Nam's first private college since 1954 was opened in Hanoi; Thang Long College was to cater for university students. The presence of foreign universities is increasing with universities such as Royal Melbourne Institute of Technology and University of Hawaii offering degrees in fields such as business, English as a Second Language and Information Technology. The Ministry of Education and Training is responsible for higher education, although institutions of health education and military or security training come under the appropriate Ministries. In 2007/08 there were 322 universities and colleges of higher education, with a total enrolment of 1.5m. students.

Since academic year 2003/04 a national university entrance examination has been the determining factor in university admissions. Students sit examinations in one of four subject streams, depending on the course of study for which the student has applied. A College Diploma or Associate degree (Tot nghiep dai hoc) is a three-year course that can be upgraded to a Bachelors degree after one year. The Bachelors degree (Bang tot nghiep dai hoc) is the main undergraduate qualification and often lasts four years, although degrees in veterinary medicine (five years) and medicine (six years) are longer in duration. Graduates who have been awarded the Bachelors degree are eligible to sit the entrance examination for admission to the Masters degree (Thac si), a two-year taught or research-based course. The Doctorate (Tien si) is open to students who hold either the Bachelors or the Masters degree and admission is again based on competitive examination. However, students with Bachelors degrees must study for four to five years to gain the Doctorate (and usually earn a Masters 'in passing') while students with the Masters are awarded the Doctorate after two or three years. Technical and vocational education at the post-secondary level is offered by universities through professional programmes of study (see above). The Division of Quality Accreditation was established in 2002 to administer accreditation of institutions and quality assurance.

In 2009 the World Bank approved a US $50m. loan for its higher education development policy programme in Viet Nam; in return, the bank is expecting a 40% increase in student enrolments by 2020. The Government is also working on its own education strategy plan covering the period from 2006–2010.

Regulatory Bodies

GOVERNMENT

Ministry of Culture, Sports and Tourism: 51–53 Ngo Quyen, Hoan Kiem District, Hanoi; tel. (4) 9438231; fax (4) 9439009; internet www.cinet.gov.vn; Minister of Culture, Sports and Tourism HOANG TUAN ANH.

Ministry of Education and Training: 49 Dai Co Viet, Hai Ba Trung District, Hanoi; tel. (4) 8694904; fax (4) 8694085; e-mail intlaff@iupui.edu; internet www.edu.net.vn; Minister NGUYEN THIEN NHAN.

Learned Societies

GENERAL

UNESCO Office Hanoi: 23 Cao Ba Quat St, Hanoi; tel. (4) 7470275; fax (4) 7470274; e-mail registry@unesco.org.vn; internet www.unesco.org.vn; gender equality, HIV/AIDS prevention, youth devt, and poverty reduction; Dir DUNG DOAN THI.

Viet Nam Union of Literary and Arts Associations: 51 Tran Hung Dao St, Hanoi; tel. (4) 8682608; fax (4) 9437431; f. 1957; 10 mem. orgs (assocs of writers, cinematographers, fine arts, composers and musicologists, theatre artists, photographers, folklorists, dancers, architects, and minority writers and artists), with a total of 10,000 mems; Pres. NGUYEN DINH THI; Sec.-Gen. THANH TO NGOC; publ. *Dien dan van nghe Viet Nam* (Forum of Vietnamese Literature and Arts, 4 a year).

Viet Nam Union of Science and Technology Associations: 53 Nguyen Du St, Hanoi; tel. (4) 9432206; fax (4) 8227593; e-mail thongtin@vusta.vn; internet www.vusta.org.vn; f. 1983; 114 mem. socs; Chair. Prof. Dr HO UY LIEM (acting).

AGRICULTURE, FISHERIES AND VETERINARY SCIENCE

National Association of Vietnamese Gardeners: 15 Thanh Cong St, Hanoi; tel. (4) 8345216; f. 1985; Pres NGUYEN NGOC TRIU.

Viet Nam Forestry Association: 114 Hoang Quoc Viet St, Cau Giay District, Hanoi; tel. (4) 7541311; Pres. NGUYEN NGOC LUNG; Sec.-Gen. NGO DUC MINH.

ARCHITECTURE AND TOWN PLANNING

Builders' Association: 34 Hang Chuoi St, Hanoi; Pres. VU KHOA.

ECONOMICS, LAW AND POLITICS

Economics Association: 1B Cam Hoi St, Hai Ba Trung Dist., Hanoi; tel. (4) 9712899; e-mail vie-lam@fpt.vn; f. 1974, recognized by Govt. 1975; attached to Viet Nam Union of Scientific and Technological Associations (VUSTA), International Economics Association, ASEAN Federation of Economics Associations; 2,000 mems.

Viet Nam Lawyers Association: A2-261 Thuy Khue St, Tay Ho District, Hanoi; tel. (4) 8474826; fax (4) 8474831; e-mail vla@fpt.vn; attached to ASEAN Law Association; Sec.-Gen. (vacant).

HISTORY, GEOGRAPHY AND ARCHAEOLOGY

Vietnamese Association of Historians: 25 Tong Dan St, Hanoi; tel. (4) 8256588; Pres. PHAN HUY LE; Sec.-Gen. DUONG TRUNG QUOC.

LANGUAGE AND LITERATURE

British Council: 40 Cat Linh St, Dong Da District, Hanoi; tel. (4) 8436780; fax (4) 8434962; e-mail bchanoi@britishcouncil.org.vn; internet www.britishcouncil.org/vietnam; f. 1993; offers courses and exams in English language and British culture and promotes cultural exchange with the UK; attached teaching centre in Ho Chi Minh City; Dir KEITH DAVIES; Training Centre Man. TIM HOOD.

Goethe-Institut: Nguyen Thai Hoc St 56–58, Ba Dinh District, Hanoi; tel. (4) 7342251; fax (4) 7342254; e-mail gihanoi-il@fpt.vn; internet www.goethe.de/so/han/deindex.htm; offers courses and exams in German language and culture and promotes cultural exchange with Germany; Dir FRANZ XAVER AUGUSTIN.

MEDICINE

Traditional Medicine Association of Viet Nam: 19 Tong Dan St, Hanoi; tel. (4) 8253006; Pres. NGUYEN XUAN HUONG.

Viet Nam General Association: 68A Ba Trieu St, Hanoi; tel. and fax (4) 39439323; e-mail vgamp@hn.vnn.vn; internet tonghoiyhoc.org.vn; f. 1955; 21 mem. socs; Pres. Prof. PHAM SONG; Sec.-Gen. TRAN HUU THANG; publ. *Y hoc Viet Nam* (magazine).

NATURAL SCIENCES

Biological Sciences

Viet Nam Association of Biological Science Societies: Biological Experiment Centre, Ha Noi Pedagogical Institute, Hanoi; tel. (4) 8347654; Pres. VU TUYEN HOANG; Sec.-Gen. NGUYEN LAN HUNG.

Mathematical Sciences

Viet Nam Mathematical Society: 46 Lieu Giai St, Hanoi; tel. (4) 8682414; President DO LONG VAN; Sec.-Gen. TONG DINH QUY.

Physical Sciences

Geological Society of Viet Nam: 6 Pham Ngu Lao St, Hanoi; tel. (4) 8260752; fax (4)

8254734; e-mail gsv@hn.vnn.vn; f. 1983; 5,000 mems; Sec.-Gen. NGUYEN TIEN THANH.

Viet Nam Physical Society: P104-46 Nguyen Van Ngoc St, Hanoi; tel. (4) 8349209; fax (4) 8349050; Pres. PHAN HONG KHOI.

TECHNOLOGY

Mining Association: 54 Hai Ba Trung St, Hanoi; tel. (4) 9342723; fax (4) 5654995; Pres. NGUYEN VAN LONG; Sec.-Gen. DINH NGOC DANG.

Viet Nam Foundry and Metallurgical Association: 54 Hai Ba Trung St, Hanoi; tel. (4) 8262052; Pres. PHAN TU PHUNG.

Vietnamese Association of Mechanics: 264 Doi Can, Badinh, Hanoi; tel. (4) 7625804; fax (4) 8683280; e-mail phong@mail.hut.edu.vn; internet www.cohocvietnam.org.vn; Pres. NGUYEN HOA THINH; Sec.-Gen. DINH VAN PHONG.

Research Institutes

GENERAL

Viet Nam Institute of Culture and Arts: 32 Pho Hao Nam, La Thanh, Phuong O Cho Dua, Quan Dong Da, Hanoi; tel. (4) 8569160; fax (4) 8516415; e-mail vncvhnt@fpt.vn; f. 1971; attached to Min. of Culture, Sports and Tourism; 50 staff; study of Vietnamese culture in all its aspects and relations with other countries; library of 5,000 vols; Dir-Gen. Prof. NGUYEN CHI BEN; publ. *Culture Research Information*.

AGRICULTURE, FISHERIES AND VETERINARY SCIENCE

Centre for Applied Research in Agricultural Engineering: 10A Tran Nhat Duat St, 1st District, Ho Chi Minh City; tel. (8) 8442947; fax (8) 8438842; f. 1976; 100 mems; library of 3,000 vols; Head of Administration PHAM VAN TAN; publ. *Agricultural Engineering* (1 a year).

Food Crops Research Institute: Lien Hong, Gia Loc, Hai Duong Province; tel. (320) 3716463; fax (320) 3716385; e-mail vcltctp@fpt.vn; f. 1968; research on varietal and technological improvement of rice, root and tuber crops, legumes, vegetables and fruit-tree crops; library of 1,950 vols, 170 journals; Dir Prof. Dr HOAN NGUENTRI (acting); publ. *Research Bulletin of Field Crops* (every 2–3 years).

Forest Science Institute of Viet Nam (FSIV): Chem, Tu Liem District, Hanoi; tel. (4) 8389031; fax (4) 8389722; internet www.fsiv.org.vn; f. 1988; Dir-Gen. Prof. Dr TRIEU VAN HUNG; publ. *Vietnam Forestry Review* (4 a year).

Fruits and Vegetables Research Institute: Thi Tran Trau Quy, Huyen Gia Lam, Thanh pho, Hanoi; tel. (4) 8276254; fax (4) 8276148; e-mail vrqhnvn@hn.vnn.vn; f. 1969; attached to Viet Nam Acad. of Agricultural Sciences; responsible for scientific research and technology transfer on vegetables, fruits, flowers, landscape plants, mulberry silk.

Institute of Agricultural Science of South Viet Nam: 121 Nguyen Binh Khiem St, 1st District, Ho Chi Minh City; tel. (8) 38291746; fax (8) 38297650; e-mail iasvn@vnn.vn; internet iasvn.org; f. 1925; research on pedology, crop sciences and animal sciences, agricultural system, agricultural and development economics; library of 10,000 vols; collection of insects; Dir Prof. BUI CHI BUU.

Institute of Soil and Fertilizer Research: East Ngac, Tu Liem Dist., Hanoi; tel. (4) 8362379; fax (4) 8389924; e-mail khkh_tnnh@hn.vnn.vn; f. 1968; attached to Viet Nam Acad. of Agricultural Sciences; Dir Dr. BUI HUY HIEN.

National Institute of Animal Husbandry: Chem Thuy Phuong, Hanoi; tel. (4) 385022; fax (4) 389775; f. 1969; research on domestic animals; extension service; Dir Dr LE VIET LY; publ. *Scientific and Technical Journal on Animal Husbandry*.

National Institute of Veterinary Research: 86 Truong Chinh Rd, Dong Da Precinct, Hanoi; tel. (4) 8686817; fax (4) 8686615; e-mail longlinh5@yahoo.com; f. 1968.

Plant Protection Research Institute: Dongngac, Tu Liem District, Hanoi; tel. (4) 38389724; fax (4) 38363563; e-mail nipp-tonghop@hn.vnn.vn; internet www.vaas.org.vn; f. 1968; attached to Viet Nam Acad. of Agricultural Sciences; plant protection research and development with emphasis on biological and genetic control, integrated pest management of food and vegetable and specific tropical crops; library of 700 vols; Dir Dr NGO VINH VIEN; publ. *Plant Protection Bulletin* (6 a year).

Research Institute for Aquaculture: Dinh Bang, Tu Son, Bac Ninh; tel. (4) 271368; fax (4) 273070; internet vanphong@ria1.org; internet www.ria1.org; f. 1975.

Research Institute of Marine Fisheries: 170 Le Lai St, Haiphong; tel. (31) 3836656; fax (31) 3836812; e-mail vhs@rimf.org.vn; f. 1961; study, training and research in fisheries biology, stock assessment, brackish water aquaculture, mariculture, oceanography, technology of fishing and processing; library of 12,000 vols; Dir Prof. Dr DO VAN KHUONG; publs *Aquaculture*, *Aquaculture Asia*, *Aquaculture International*, *Aquaculture Research*, *Infofish International*, *Journal of Fish Disease*, *World Fishing*.

Rubber Research Institute of Viet Nam: 177 Hai Ba Trung St, Ho Chi Minh City; tel. (8) 8294139; fax (8) 8298599; e-mail rriv@hcm.vnn.vn; f. 1975; library of 3,000 vols; Gen. Dir MAI VAN SON.

Viet Nam Institute of Agricultural Engineering: A2 Phuong Mai, Dong Da, Hanoi; tel. (4) 8523187; fax (4) 8521131; f. 1968; research machinery for agricultural production and food processing; library of 3,000 vols; Dir Prof. Dr PHAM VAN LANG; publ. *Agricultural and Food Industries* (12 a year, in Vietnamese with a summary in English).

Viet Nam Institute of Agricultural Science and Technology: Thanh Tri District, Hanoi; f. 1978; Dir Prof. DAO THE TUAN.

ECONOMICS, LAW AND POLITICS

Central Institute of Economic Management: 68 Phan Dinh Phung, Ba Dinh, Hanoi; tel. (4) 7338930; fax (4) 7338930; internet www.ciem.org.vn; f. 1978.

Institute of Economics: 27 Tran Xuan Soan St, Hanoi; tel. (4) 8261633; fax (4) 8261632; f. 1960; library of 16,000 vols; attached to Viet Nam National Centre for Social Sciences and Humanities; Dir DO HOAI NAM; publs *Nghien Cuu Kinh Te* (Economic Studies Review, 12 a year in Vietnamese), *Viet Nam's Socio-Economic Development* (4 a year).

Institute of Finance: 7 Ly Thuong Kiet St, Hoan Kiem District, Hanoi; tel. (4) 9331872; fax (4) 9331865; e-mail hvtc@hn.vnn.vn; f. 1961.

Institute for International Relations: 69 Chua Lang St, Dong Da District, Hanoi; tel. (4) 8344540; fax (4) 8343543; e-mail iirmofa@hn.vnn.vn; f. 1959; library of 25,000 vols; publ. *International Studies* (6 a year in Vietnamese, 2 a year in English).

Institute of Labour Science and Social Affairs: 2 Dinh Le St, Hanoi; tel. (4) 8258801; fax (4) 8269733; f. 1978; labour relations, working conditions, wages and living standards, levels of skill, social security; Dir Dr DO MINH CUONG.

Institute of Social Sciences: 49 Nguyen Thi Minh Khai St, District 1, Ho Chi Minh City; tel. (8) 8223995; fax (8) 8223735; f. 1978; Dir Dr NGUYEN THE NGHIA; publ. *Journal of Social Sciences* (6 a year).

Institute of State and Law: 27 Tran Xuan Soan St, Hai Ba Trung, Hanoi; tel. (4) 39784637; fax (4) 39713136; f. 1960; attached to Viet Nam Acad. of Social Sciences; Dep. Dir NGUYEN NHU THE.

Institute of Statistical Science: 48A Lang Trung, Dong Da, Hanoi; tel. (4) 8244234; fax (4) 8243763; f. 1976; library of 3,700 vols (2,600 foreign books, 1,100 Vietnamese); spec. colln in field of statistics; Dir NGUYEN VIET CUONG; publs *Bulletin of Statistical Science*, Selection of Information Dissemination Periodicals.

Research Institute of Trade: 46 Ngo Quyen St, Hoan Kiem District, Hanoi; tel. (4) 8262720; fax (4) 8248279; f. 1995 following merger of Research Institute for Foreign Economic Relations and Institute of Economic and Technological Research on Trade.

EDUCATION

Centre for Information and Library Educational Science: 101 Tran Hung Dao St, Hanoi; tel. (4) 8220911; fax (4) 8223213; e-mail dinhphuong@bdvn.vnmail.vnd.net; f. 1961 as National Institute for Educational Science; library of 5,000 vols and 1,500 periodicals; Dir Assoc. Prof. Dr DANG THANH HUNG; publ. *Information on Educational Sciences* (6 a year).

Research Centre for Vocational and Higher Education: 101 Tran Hung Dao St, Hanoi; tel. (4) 9423108; fax (4) 8221521; e-mail vkhgd.qhqt@bdvn.vnd.net; f. 1977; attached to National Institute for Education Strategy and Curriculum Development; Dir Assoc. Prof. Dr NGUYEN HUU CHAU.

Viet Nam Sports Science Institute: 141 Nguyen Thai Hoc St, Ba Dinh, Hanoi; tel. (4) 7330286; e-mail vkh-tt@fpt.vn; f. 1979; 5,000 mems; library of 10,000 vols on sports science; publ. *Bulletin* (16 a year).

FINE AND PERFORMING ARTS

Ha Noi Institute of Stage and Cinematography: Tu Liem, Hanoi; tel. (4) 8243397; f. 1978.

Vietnamese Institute for Musicology: 32 Nguyen Thai Hoc St, Ba Dinh District, Hanoi; tel. (4) 8457368; fax (4) 8434953; e-mail musicology@hn.vnn.vn; f. 1976; research in the national heritage of music, song, dance; Dir Prof. NGUYEN PHUC LINH; publ. *Bulletin* (in English and Vietnamese, 3 a year).

HISTORY, GEOGRAPHY AND ARCHAEOLOGY

Institute of Archaeology: 61 Phan Chu Trinh, Quan Hoan Kiem, Hanoi; tel. (4) 8255449; fax (4) 9331607; f. 1968; Dir and Editor-in-Chief HA VAN TAN; Dep. Dirs HA VAN PHUNG, TONG TRUNG TIN.

Institute of History: 38 Hang Chuoi, Quan Hai Ba Trung, Hanoi; tel. (4) 9711682; fax (4) 9717615; f. 1960; attached to Viet Nam Acad. of Social Sciences; library of 70,000 vols from fmr library of École Français d'Extrême-

Orient; Dir NGUYEN VAN NHAT; publ. *Nghien cuu Lich su (Historical Studies) Review*.

Viet Nam Research Institute of Land Administration: Hoang Quoc Viet St, Cau Giay, Hanoi; tel. (4) 7561154; fax (4) 7540186; e-mail vgcr@hn.vnn.vn; internet www.virila.ac.vn; f. 1994; attached to Min. of Natural Resources and the Environment; scientific research and technological development in geodesy, cartography, and land administration; dependent centres: GIS and databases, geodynamics, spatial images and aerial photography; 240 staff; Dir Dr NGUYEN DUNG TIEN.

LANGUAGE AND LITERATURE

Institute of Linguistics: 36 Hang Chuoi St, Hanoi; tel. (4) 9710968; fax (4) 9712247; e-mail lytoanthang@yahoo.com; f. 1968; library of 12,000 vols; Dir Dr LY TOAN CHANG; publ. *Ngon Ngu* (4 a year).

Institute of Literary Studies: 20 Ly Thai To St, Hanoi; tel. (4) 8253548; fax (4) 8250385; f. 1959; library of 150,000 vols; Dir Prof. Dr PHAN TRONG THUONG; publ. *Tap chi Nghien cuu Van hoc* (Literary Studies Review, 12 a year).

Institute of Research on Chinese and Demotic Characters: 26 Ly Thuong Kiet St, Hanoi; f. 1970.

MEDICINE

Central Institute of Ophthalmology: 85 Ba Trieu St, Hanoi; tel. and fax (4) 9438004; e-mail tonthi.kimthanh@hn.vnn.vn; f. 1957.

Ho Chi Minh City Institute of Hygiene and Epidemiology: 167 Nguyen Thi Minh Khai St, Ho Chi Minh City; f. 1977.

Ho Chi Minh City Institute of Hygiene and Public Health: 159 Hung Phu St, District 8, Ho Chi Minh City; tel. (8) 8559503; fax (8) 8563164; e-mail vienvsytcc@hcm.vnn.vn; f. 1977; Dir Prof. LE THE THU.

Institute of Traditional Medicine in Ho Chi Minh City: 273 Nam Ky Khoi Nghia St, Phu Nhuan Dist., Ho Chi Minh City; tel. (8) 38443047; fax (8) 38444769; e-mail v.ydhdt@tphcm.gov.vn; internet www.vienydhdt.com.vn; f. 1975; short-term courses in health: acupuncture, acupressure, massage (foot and body), yoga.

Institute for the Protection of the Mother and Newborn Child: 43 Trang Thi St, 08-4 Hanoi; tel. (4) 8252161; fax (4) 8254638; e-mail ipmn@hn.vnn.vn; f. 1966; obstetrics, gynaecology, care of the newborn child and family planning, invitro fertilization; library of 5,000 vols; Dir Dr NGUYEN DUC VY; publs *Nôi san Šan Phu Khoa* (internal journal of obstetrics and gynaecology, 1 a year), *Tông kêt công trinh nghiên cúu khoa hoc* (review of scientific studies, 1 a year).

Institute of Malariology, Parasitology and Entomology: Luong The Vinh St, Hanoi; tel. (4) 8543035; fax (4) 8543015; e-mail nimpe@netnam.org.vn; f. 1957.

Institute of Traditional Medicine in Ho Chi Minh City: 273 Nam Ky Khoi Nghia St, Phu Nhuan Dist., Ho Chi Minh City; tel. (8) 38443047; fax (8) 38444769; e-mail v.ydhdt@tphcm.gov.vn; internet www.vienydhdt.com.vn; f. 1975; short-term courses in health: acupuncture, acupressure, massage (foot and body), yoga.

Institute of Vaccines and Medical Biologicals: 9 Pasteur St, Nha Trang, Khanh Hoa; e-mail ivac@dng.vnn.vn; f. 1979.

National Institute of Drug Quality Control: 48 Hai Ba Trung St, Hoan Kiem Dist., Hanoi; tel. (4) 38255742; fax (4) 38256911; e-mail tvlauvkn@hotmail.com; f. 1957 as Drug Quality Control Laboratory; drug quality control analysis and specification evaluation, devt of standards and reference substances, scientific research and training, participating in devt of Vietnamese pharmacopoeia; library of 1,450 vols; Dir Prof. Dr THAO NGUYEN THI PHUONG; publ. *Journal of Drug Quality Control* (4 a year).

National Institute of Hygiene and Epidemiology: 1 Yersin St, 10000 Hanoi; tel. (4) 8212416; fax (4) 9723130; e-mail nihe@netnam.org.vn; f. 1924; epidemiology of communicable diseases, vaccine development; library of 12,000 vols; Dir Prof. NGUYEN TRAN HIEN; publ. *Tap Chi Ve Sinh Phong Dich* (Journal, in Vietnamese with abstract in English, 4 a year).

National Institute of Medicinal Materials: 3B Quang Trung St, Hoan Kiem District, Hanoi; tel. (4) 8252644; fax (4) 9349072; e-mail htqt-imm@hn.vnn.vn; internet www.nimm.org.vn; f. 1961; multidisciplinary research on pharmaceutical materials, mainly medicinal plants; postgraduate training; library of 6,000 vols; Dir Prof. NGUYEN GIA CHAN; publ. *Materia Medica Bulletin* (4 a year).

National Institute of Nutrition: 48B Tang Bat Ho St, Hanoi; tel. (4) 39717090; fax (4) 39717885; e-mail ninvietnam@viendinhduong.vn; internet www.viendinhduong.vn; f. 1980; depts of basic nutrition, community nutrition, applied nutrition, clinical nutrition, food science, food safety, dietetics, experiment workshop, library; Dir Assoc. Prof. LE THI HOP; publs *Journal of Food and Nutrition Sciences*, *Nutrition, Health and Life*.

National Institute of Occupational and Environmental Health Research: c/o Ministry of Health, Ib pho Yersin, Hanoi; tel. (4) 9713649; fax (4) 8212894; e-mail byt@moh.gov.vn; Dir Prof. Dr LE VAN TRUNG.

National Institute of Otolaryngology: Bachmai Hospital Centre, 78 Giai Phong St, Phuong Mai, Hanoi; tel. (4) 8693731; fax (4) 8691607; f. 1969; 200 staff; library of 1,000 vols; Dir Prof. LUONG SY CAN; publs *Noi San Tai Mui Hong* (1 a year), *Thong Tin Tai Mui Hong* (1 a year).

National Institute of Paediatrics: 18/8779 La Thanh, Dong Da, Hanoi; tel. (4) 8343700; fax (4) 7754448; e-mail nip_vn@hn.vnn.vn; internet www.benhviennhitu.org.vn; f. 1969 as the Institute of Child Care, renamed Viet Nam–Sweden Children's Hospital and the Olof Palme Paediatric Institute, present name since 1997; Dir Assoc. Prof NGUYEN THANH LIEM.

National Institute of Traditional Medicine: The National Hospital of Traditional Medicine, 29 Nguyen Binh Khiem, Hanoi; tel. (4) 9432442; fax (4) 8229353; e-mail yhcotruyen@hn.vnn.vn; internet www.natiotradimedhos.org.vn; f. 1957; traditional medicine; library of 19,343 vols, special collection of books on Chinese medicine and medicine in Viet Nam since 15th century; Dir Prof. Dr CHU QUOC TRUONG; publ. *Journal of Research in Vietnamese Traditional Medicine and Pharmacy* (4 a year).

National Institute of Tuberculosis and Respiratory Diseases: 120 Hoang Hoa Tham St, Hanoi; tel. (4) 8326249; fax (4) 8326162; f. 1957; research on asthma, chronic bronchitis, lung cancer, occupational lung diseases, tuberculosis; operates two national programmes: Acute Respiratory Infections in Children, National Tuberculosis Control Programme; library of 10,000 vols; Dir Prof. N. V. CO; publ. *Lao và bênh phôi* (4 a year).

Nha Trang Institute of Hygiene and Epidemiology: 10 Tran Phu St, Nha Trang, Phu Khanh Province; f. 1976.

Odonto Stomato Maxillo Facial Surgery Institute (Vien Rang Ham Mat Hanoi): 40B Trang Thi St, Hanoi; tel. (4) 8269723; e-mail vienrhm@hn.vnn.vn; internet www.toancausoft.com.vn/vienrhm/default.asp; f. 2002 by merger of Odonto-Maxillofacial dept of Hanoi Medical University and Hanoi Odonto-Maxillo-Facial Institute; attached to Min. of Health; Dir Prof. TRAN VAN TRUONG.

Tay Nguyen Institute of Hygiene and Epidemiology: Buon Ma Thuoc, Dak Lak Province; f. 1976; Man. for Planning and Science HAU VAN PHAM; Vice-Man. HAU PHAM VAN.

NATURAL SCIENCES

General

National Centre for Scientific Research of Viet Nam, Ho Chi Minh City Branch: 1 Mac Dinh Chi St, Dist. 1, Ho Chi Minh City; tel. (8) 222246; fax (8) 222068; f. 1975; chemistry, fundamental and applied research in biology, geoscience, mathematics, physics; Pres. Prof. Dr HO SI THOANG; Sec. Prof. Dr NGUYEN VAN TRONG.

Biological Sciences

Dalat Institute of Biology: 116 Xo Viet Nghe Tinh, Dalat, Lam Dong; tel. (63) 822078; fax (63) 831028; e-mail sdhl@vnn.vn; internet www.vast.ac.vn; f. 1975; attached to Viet Nam Acad. of Science and Technology; biochemistry and molecular biology of nitrogen fixation; plant genetics; Dir Prof. LE XUAN TU; publ. *Journal of Biology*.

Mathematical Sciences

Institute of Mathematics: Vietnamese Acad. of Science and Technology, 18 Hoang Quoc Viet, 10307 Hanoi; tel. (4) 7563474; fax (4) 7564303; e-mail vientruong@math.ac.vn; internet www.math.ac.vn; f. 1969; attached to Vietnamese Acad. of Science and Technology; algebra, dynamic systems, discrete mathematics, functional analysis, geometry and topology, methods of mathematical physics, numerical analysis, operations research, optimal control theory, partial differential equations, probability and mathematical statistics; library of 12,000 vols, 350 periodicals; Dir Prof. HA HUY KHOAI, Prof. Dr NGO VIET TRUNG; publ. *Acta Mathematica Vietnamica* (3 a year).

Physical Sciences

Institute of Chemistry: 18 Hoang Quoc Viet Rd, Cau Giay District, Hanoi; tel. (4) 7564312; fax (4) 8361283; e-mail info@vienhoahoc.ac.vn; internet www.vienhoahoc.ac.vn; f. 1978; attached to Vietnamese Acad. of Science and Technology; basic and applied research and engineering in organic, inorganic, physicochemical and analytical chemistry; chemistry of natural products and polymers; library of 6,000 vols; Dir Prof. Dr TRAN VAN SUNG; publs *Collection of Selected Scientific Works* (1 a year), *Tap chí Hóa hoc* (Journal of Chemistry, 6 a year).

Institute of Geological Sciences: 84 Chua Lang St, Dong Da, Hanoi; tel. (4) 37754798; fax (4) 37754797; e-mail info@igsvn.ac.vn; internet www.igsvn.ac.vn; f. 1967; Dir Dr TRONG-HUE TRAN.

Institute of Meteorology and Hydrology: Gate 62/5, Nguyen Chi Thanh, Dong Da, Hanoi; tel. (4) 7733090; fax (4) 8355993; e-mail mandt@vkttv.edu.vn; internet www.imh.ac.vn; f. 1977; Dir Dr TRAN THUC.

Institute of Oceanography: 01 Cau Da, Nha Trang, Khanh Hoa Province; tel. (58) 590036; fax (58) 590034; e-mail haiduong@

dng.vnn.vn; internet www.vnio.org.vn; f. 1923; library of 60,000 vols; incorporates National Oceanographic Museum and Aquarium; Dir Dr NGUYEN TAC AN; publs *Collection of Marine Research Works* (1 a year), *Journal of Marine Science and Technology* (4 a year).

Institute of Physics: 10 Dao Tan, Thu Le, Ba Dinh, Hanoi; tel. (4) 22123631; fax (4) 37669050; e-mail office@iop.vast.ac.vn; internet iop.vast.ac.vn; f. 1969; attached to Viet Nam Acad. of Science and Technology; Deputy Dir Assoc. Prof. Dr NGUYEN HONG QUANG.

Viet Nam Institute of Geosciences and Mineral Resources: Ministry of Natural Resources and Environment, Thanh Xuan, Hanoi; tel. (4) 8547335; fax (4) 8542125; e-mail van@vigmr.vn; f. 1976; Dir Assoc. Prof. NGUYEN XUAN KHIEN; publ. *Geology and Mineral Resources* (irregular).

PHILOSOPHY AND PSYCHOLOGY

Institute of Philosophy: 59 Lang Ha St, Ba Dinh District, Hanoi; tel. (4) 5143338; fax (4) 5141935; e-mail ducphilosophy@yahoo.com; internet www.vientriethoc.com.vn; f. 1962; research on theoretical and practical issues of the devt of Viet Nam; scientific foundation for the planning of the Party and govt's policies and guidelines in Viet Nam; research on philosophical issues and practice of devt of philosophy in Viet Nam, devts and achievements of philosophical research both in Viet Nam and abroad; other research and teaching activities incl. training MA and PhD students, organizing nat. and int. seminars and conferences; library of 50,000 vols; Dir Prof. PHAM VAN DUC; publ. *Philosophy* (12 a year, in Vietnamese; English edn 4 a year).

RELIGION, SOCIOLOGY AND ANTHROPOLOGY

Institute of Ethnology: 27 Tran Xuan Soan, Quan Hai Ba Trung, Hanoi; tel. (4) 9784867; fax (4) 9711435; e-mail khongdienvdt@hn.vnn.vn; f. 1968; research in cultural history and social structure of the nationalities in Viet Nam and Southeast Asia; 62 staff; library of 10,000 vols; attached to Viet Nam Acad. of Social Sciences; Dir PHAM QUANG HOAN; publ. *Ethnographical Studies* (4 a year).

TECHNOLOGY

Broadcast Research and Application Center: 171 Ly Chinh Thang St, Dist. 3, Ho Chi Minh City; tel. (8) 8298427; fax (8) 8293487; f. 1978; 150 staff; library of 3,000 vols; Dir Prof. NGUYEN KIM SACH.

Hydraulic Engineering Consultants Corporation No. 1: 95/2 Chùa Bộc, Dong Da, Hanoi; tel. (4) 8534162; fax (4) 5632169; e-mail hec1@hn.vnn.vn; f. 1956; library of 9,000 vols; Dir-Gen. HOANG MINH DZUNG; publ. *Hydraulic Engineering* (1 a year).

Institute for Building Science and Technology: Tran Cung St, Nghia Tan Ward, Cau Giay District, Hanoi; tel. (4) 7544196; fax (4) 8361197; e-mail ibst_vn@fpt.vn; internet www.ibst.vn; f. 1963; concrete and concrete technology, construction chemistry, corrosive research and structural protection, construction technology, environmental engineering, fire safety for houses and engineering works, geotechnical and foundation engineering, geodesy and engineering surveying, structural engineering, structural testing, water supply and drainage technology; 370 mems; library of 22,000 vols; Dir Assoc. Prof. Dr CAO DUY TIEN; publ. *Building Science and Technology Journal* (4 a year).

Institute for Standardization in Construction: 303 Doi Can St, Hanoi; tel. 343689; f. 1979; library of 5,000 vols; Dir Dr PHAM KINH CUONG; publs *National Typification Design in Construction*, *Vietnamese Standards* (TCVN).

Institute for Tropical Technology: 18 Hoang Quoc Viet, Cau Giay, Hanoi; tel. (4) 8360376; fax (4) 7564696; e-mail hien-vktnd@hn.vnn.vn; f. 1980; corrosion testing and metal protection, concrete protection, testing of non-metallic materials, their resistance to tropical climates and lifetime prediction, development of new materials, new coatings (organic and inorganic), tropic-proofing of electrical and electronic equipment; small library; Dir Dr LE XUAN HIEN.

Institute of Cybernetics and Computing Technology: Tu Liem District, Hanoi; f. 1976.

Institute of Electronics, Informatics and Automation: 156A, Quan Thanh St, Hanoi; tel. (4) 37164855; fax (4) 37164842; e-mail vielina@hn.vnn.vn; internet www.vielina.com.vn; f. 1985 as Viet Nam Institute of Research and Development in Electronics; informatics and automation, research and application of new technologies, techniques and products concerned with electronics; centers and laboratories: Automatic Control Center, High-Tech Center, Hydrodynamics and Automation, Information Technology Center, Information Technology Support Center, Quality Measurement Center, Robotics Laboratory, High Quality Printed Circuit Laboratory, Special Laboratory of PLC; 81 researchers and employees; Dir Prof. Dr NGUYEN XUAN QUYNH.

Branch Office:

Branch Institute of Electronics, Informatics and Automation: 138 To Thien Thanh St, 10th District, Ho Chi Minh City; tel. (8) 8652126; fax (8) 8652126; juridicial basics.

Institute of Energy: Ton That Tung St, Khuong Thuong, Dong Da, Hanoi; tel. (4) 8523741; fax (4) 8523311; f. 1988; research, programmes and projects concerning energy development in Viet Nam; departments: science and technology; nuclear, thermal power and the environment; electrical design; computers; electrical power systems development; energy demand forecasting and management; energy economics; high voltage electrical techniques; Gia Sang Research Station for the Protection of Electrical Lines from Lightning; hydropower; electrical network planning; biogas energy; rural energy planning and fuel; solar and wind energy; basic construction projects; production; 193 staff; Dir Dr TRAN QUOC CUONG.

Institute of Industrial Chemistry: 2 Pham Ngu Lao St, Hoan Kiem District, Hanoi; tel. (4) 8253930; fax (4) 8257383; e-mail vienhoacn@hn.vnn.vn; internet www.vinachem.com.vn/english/companydetail.asp?comid=43; f. 1959; Dir Prof. Dr MAI NGOC CHUC.

Institute of Machinery and Industrial Instruments: 34 Lang Ha St, Dong Da Dist., Hanoi; tel. (4) 8344372; fax (4) 8344975; f. 1973; library of 10,000 vols; Dir Dr TRAN VIET HUNG.

Institute of Mechanics: 264 Doi Can St, Ba Dinh, Hanoi; tel. (4) 8325541; fax (4) 8333039; f. 1979; basic and applied research in the fields of fluids, deformable solids and vibration mechanics; library of 14,182 vols; Dir Prof. NGUYEN TIEN KHIEM; publ. *Journal of Mechanics* (4 a year).

Institute of Mining Science and Technology: Phuong Lien St, Dong Da Dist, Hanoi; tel. (4) 8642024; fax (4) 8641564; e-mail ttthan@hn.vnn.vn; f. 1979; research on underground and opencast mining, mine development and construction, excavating and tunnelling, environmental mine safety, ventilation, electro-mechanization, transport, coal preparation and processing; library of 9,000 vols; Dir Dr PHUNG MANH DAC; publs *Mining Technology Information* (6 a year), *Works Collection* (every 5 years), *Mining Management* (12 a year).

Institute of Paper and Cellulose Research: Thanh Xuan District, Hanoi, Vinh Phu Province; tel. (4) 8581072; fax (4) 8581070; f. 1970.

Institute of Transport Science and Technology: 80 Tran Hung Dao St, Hoan Kiem, Hanoi; tel. (4) 38224464; fax (4) 38222979; e-mail itc-mot@mt.gov.vn; f. 1978; attached to Ministry of Transport.

Food Industry Research Institute: Km. 8 Nguyen Trai Rd, Thanh Xuan, Hanoi; tel. (4) 8584318; fax (4) 8584554; e-mail vu@fii.ac.vn; f. 1967; carries out research in biotechnology, food processing technology using local raw materials, and other areas connected with food; Dir Prof. Dr LE DUC MANH.

National Institute for Urban and Rural Planning: 37 Le Dai Hanh St, Hanoi; tel. (4) 9760691; fax (4) 9764339; f. 1956, current name 1990; research and establishment of construction planning projects, and environmental and landscape organization in the territorial regions, urban and rural settlements; 8 research, design and planning divisions, 4 administrative divisions; centers: Center for Research on Urban and Rural Environmental Planning, Center for Rural Planning and Development, Center for Urban and Rural Planning in the Middle Regions; 290 staff; Dir Prof. Dr LE HONG KE.

National Research Institute for Mechanical Engineering: Thang Long St, Caugiay, Hanoi; tel. (4) 8344225; fax (4) 8347883; f. 1962 as the Institute of Mechanical Design and Manufacture; 4 professional depts: economic planning, scientific management, finance, administration and personnel; research depts: dynamics, mechanical design, hydromechanical and hydroelectrical heavy mechanics, technology, 'cold' welding; 265 staff; Dir Prof. Dr HAN DUC KIM.

National Research Institute of Mining and Metallurgy: 30B Doan Thi Diem St, Hanoi; tel. (4) 8233775; fax (4) 8456983; e-mail vimluki@netnam.org.vn; f. 1967; library of 10,000 vols; Dir Dr NGUYEN ANH.

Research Institute for Agricultural Machinery: Km 9 Nguyen Trai St, Thanh Xuan, Dong Da, Hanoi; tel. (4) 8544429; fax (4) 8547366; f. 1970; research, machinery design; library of 5,500 vols; Dir NGUYEN VAN HOI.

Research Institute of Posts and Telecommunications: 122 Hoang Quoc Viet Rd, Nghia Tan, Cau Giay Dist., Hanoi; tel. (4) 7562037; fax (4) 7562036; e-mail vkhktbdld@hn.vnn.vn; internet www.ptit.edu.vn/ptit_english.asp; Dir Prof. Dr NGUYEN CANH TUAN; publ. *Ket Qua Nghien Cuu Khoa Hoc* (1 a year).

Scientific and Technological Institute for Communications and Transport: 80 Tran Hung Dao St, Hoan Kiem, Hanoi; tel. (4) 38224464; fax (4) 38222979; e-mail vukhcn@mt.gov.vn; internet khcn.mt.gov.vn; f. 1956.

Shipbuilding Science and Technology Institute–SHIPSCITECH: 80B Tran Hung Dao St, Hanoi; tel. (4) 8257070; fax (4) 8258672; f. 1983; development and application of new technologies in shipbuilding, design, building and modernization of marine facilities, consultancy services, training of staff and development of standards; units and facilities: professional design department, Centre for Research and Testing of Models, pilot production workshops, testing tank; Dir Dr NGO CAN (acting).

Textile Research Institute: 478 Minhkhai St, Hanoi; tel. (4) 8624025; fax (4) 8622867; e-mail viendetmay@hn.vnn.vn; f. 1969; research in material technology, machinery for spinning, weaving and finishing; inspection of quality of material and finished products, fashion design; library of 3,500 vols; Dir Dr NGUYEN VAN THONG; publs *Textiles Magazine* (6 a year), *Textile Research Journal* (1 a year).

Viet Nam Atomic Energy Commission: 59 Ly Thuong Kiet St, Hanoi; tel. (4) 9423479; fax (4) 9424133; e-mail hg.vaec@hn.vn.vnn; internet www.vaec.gov.vn; f. 1979; nuclear science and technology; Chair. TRAN HUU PHAT; publ. *Nuclear Science and Technology*.

Viet Nam Institute for Building Materials: 235 Nguyen Trai St, Thanh Xuan, Hanoi; tel. (4) 8581111; fax (4) 8581112; e-mail vienvlxd@hn.vnn.vn; internet www.vibm.vn; f. 1975; Pres. THAI DUY SAM.

Viet Nam Institute of Water Conservation: 299 Tayson St, Dong Da District, Hanoi; tel. (4) 8522086; fax (4) 8536290; f. 1959; units: Centre for Termite Prevention, Centre for Irrigation, Centre for Water Treatment and Environmental Research, Centre for Research in River and Marine Dynamics, Centre for Hydraulic Research, Centre for Structures and Materials, Centre for Small-Scale Hydroelectric Research, Geotechnics Division, Hydraulic Research Division, Irrigation Systems Management Division, Pump Research Division; 236 staff; Dir Dr NGUYEN TUAN ANH.

Libraries and Archives

Hanoi

Central Library for Science and Technology: 24 Lý Thuòng Kiêt, Hanoi; tel. (4) 9349111; fax (4) 8246325; e-mail thutt@vista.gov.vn; internet www.clst.ac.vn; f. 1960; attached to the National Centre for Scientific and Technological Information and Documentation; 230,000 vols, 4,500 periodicals; Dir VU VAN SON.

Institute of Social Sciences Information–National Social Sciences Library: 26 Ly Thuong Kiet, Hanoi; tel. and fax (4) 8253074; f. 1975 by amalgamation of Dept. of Social Sciences Information and Central Social Sciences Library; attached to Viet Nam Academy of Social Sciences; 1m. vols; Dir Prof. HO SI QUY; publs *Bibliography of Social Sciences* (1 a year), *Review of Social Sciences Information* (12 a year).

National Centre for Scientific and Technical Information: 24 Ly Thuong Kiet St, Hanoi; tel. (4) 9342945; fax (4) 8249874; e-mail techmart@vista.gov.vn; internet vista.gov.vn; f. 1990 by merger of the Central Institute for Scientific and Technical Information and the Central Library; formulation and implementation of Science and Technology programmes; national databank, documentation sources and publications; publs *Information and Documentation* (4 a year), *KCM—S&T Information* (12 a year), *Vietnam S&T Abstracts* (6 a year).

Central Health Information and Technology Institute: 15 Le Thanh Tong, và 135 Nui Truc, Ba Dinh, Hanoi; tel. (4) 37368315; fax (4) 37368319; e-mail cimsi@cimsi.org.vn; internet www.cimsi.org.vn; f. 1979 by merger of Central Library for Medical Sciences (1964) and Central Institute for Medical Sciences Information (1979); attached to Min. of Health of Socialist Republic of Viet Nam; specialized in medical information and technology services to all orgs of health sector in Viet Nam; 50,000 vols; Gen. Dir Dr LUONG CHI THANH; publs *Bibliography of Vietnamese Medical Literature* (1 a year), *Health Newsweek from Internet* (48 a year), *Vietnam Medical and Pharmaceutical Information Journal* (12 a year).

National Library of Viet Nam: 31 Trang Thi, 10000 Hanoi; tel. (4) 8253040; fax (4) 8253357; e-mail ptkhang@nlv.gov.vn; f. 1917; attached to Ministry of Culture and Information; 1.2m. vols, 8,000 periodical titles; Dir PHAM THE KHANG; publs *Information on Culture and Arts, Library and Bibliographical Work* (4 a year), *Library Magazine* (4 a year), *National Bibliography* (12 a year and 1 a year).

Ho Chi Minh City

General Sciences Library of Ho Chi Minh City: 69 Ly Tu Trong, Dist. 1, Ho Chi Minh City; tel. (8) 8225055; fax (8) 8299318; e-mail gsl.hcmc@hcm.vnn.vn; internet www.gslhcm.org.vn; f. 1976; attached to Service of Culture, Sports and Tourism of Ho Chi Minh City; 700,000 vols, 4,500 periodical titles, databases; Dir BUI XUAN DUC.

Social Sciences Library: 49 Nguyen Thi Minh Khai, Dist. 3, Ho Chi Minh City; tel. (8) 8228934; fax (8) 8223735; e-mail siss@hcm.vnn.vn; f. 1975; attached to Institute of Social Sciences; the collections of the fmr Archaeological Research Institute have been added to the library; provides facilities for research in archaeology, economics, ethnology, history, law, literature, linguistics, philosophy, sociology; 145,000 vols; Dir TRAN MINH DUC.

Museums and Art Galleries

Haiphong

Haiphong Museum: c/o Dept. of Tourism, 44 Lach Tray, Haiphong; 65 Dien Bien Phu St, Haiphong; tel. (31) 852720; f. 1919; local history.

Hanoi

Bao tàng Cách mang Viêt Nam (National Museum of Vietnamese Revolution): 25 Tong Dan St, 216 Tran Quang Khai, Hoan Kiem District, Hanoi; tel. (4) 8254323; fax (4) 9342064; e-mail baotangcmvn@hn.vnn.vn; internet www.baotangcm.gov.vn; f. 1959; study of revolutionary history of Viet Nam; library of 21,000 vols and historical documents, 17,900 documentary photographs; Dir Prof. Dr TRIEU VAN HIEN.

Ho Chi Minh Museum: 19 Ngoc Ha St, Ba Dinh Dist., Hanoi; tel. (4) 8463572; fax (4) 8439837; f. 1990 1977; study of Ho Chi Minh's life and work; Dir HA HUY GIAP.

Viet Nam Fine Arts Museum: 66 Nguyên Thai Hoduc St, Ba Dinh Dist, Hanoi; tel. (4) 38233084; fax (4) 37341427; e-mail binhtruong451@hn.vnn.vn; f. 1966; preservation and presentation of nat. cultural heritage; research on ancient and modern fine arts, ceramics, handicrafts, folk arts; exhibitions of foreign art; library of 1,100 vols; Dir TRUONG QUOC BINH.

Viet Nam History Museum: 1 Trang Tien, Hanoi; tel. (4) 8253518; fax (4) 8252853; f. 1958; research and conservation, history of Viet Nam from palaeolithic period to 1945; Dir Dr PHAM QUOC QUÂN; publ. *Bulletin* (1 a year).

Viet Nam Military History Museum: 28A Dien Bien Phu St, Ba Dinh, Hanoi; tel. (4) 7334682; fax (4) 7334692; e-mail btqsvn@bt.vnn.vn; internet www.btlsqsvn.org.vn; f. 1959; fmrly People's Army Museum; exhibits Viet Nam's military history since the founding of the country to the Ho Chi Minh era; 4,000 of 160,000 objects on display; Dir LE CHIEU.

Ho Chi Minh City

Ho Chi Minh City Museum: 65 Ly Tu Trong, Ward Dist. 1 Ho Chi Minh City; tel. (8) 8299741; fax (8) 8298250; e-mail bttphcm@hcm.vnn.vn; internet www.hcmc-museum.edu.vn; f. 1977; 2 sections: 1 devoted to the revolution, the other to ancient arts.

Hue

Hue Royal Antiquities Museum: 3 Le Truc St, Hue; tel. (54) 3524429; fax (54) 3522879; e-mail hueroyalmuseum@yahoo.com.vn; f. 1923; history of the old capital; administered by the Hue Monuments Conservation Centre; library of 1,345 vols; Man. NGUYEN PHUOC HAI TRUNG; Head of Exhibition Dept HOANG NGOC SON; publ. *Hue Royal Antiquities Museum*.

Thai Nguyen

Museum of the Cultures of Ethnic Groups in Viet Nam: Doi Can Rd, Thai Nguyen 84, Thai Nguyen province; tel. (280) 855781; fax (280) 752940; e-mail baotangvh@hn.vnn.vn; f. 1960; conserves and publicizes the cultural heritage of Viet Nam's ethnic groups; Dir HA THI NU.

Vinh

Nghe-Tinh Museum: 10 Dao Tan, Khoi 3, Cong Vien Thanh Co, Phuong Cua Nam, Thanh Pho Vinh, Nghe Tinh Province; tel. (38) 841890; f. 1960; study of the Nghe-Tinh 'Soviet' Uprising, 1930–31; artefacts on view incl. photographs and documents related to the uprising, weapons and equipment used, including the personal possessions of leading revolutionaries Nguyen Phong Sac, Nguyen Tiem and Nguyen Chau; Man. PHAN XUAN THANH.

Universities

CAN THO UNIVERSITY

3/2 Street, Cantho City, Cantho Province
Telephone: (710) 3838237
Fax: (710) 3838474
E-mail: ductri@ctu.edu.vn
Internet: www.ctu.edu.vn

Founded 1966
State control
Academic year: September to July

Rector: TRAN THUONG TUAN
Vice-Rectors: CHAU VAN LUC, Dr LE QUANG MINH

Library of 30,000 vols
Number of teachers: 752
Number of students: 14,000

Publication: annual scientific and technology reports

DEANS

College of Information Technology: VO VAN CHIN
School of Agriculture: Prof. TRAN THUONG TUAN
School of Economics and Business Administration: NGUYEN TAN NHAN

School of Education: Dr LE PHUOC LOC
School of Law: Dr NGUYEN NGOC DIEN
School of Medicine, Dentistry and Pharmacy: PHAM HUNG LUC
School of Sciences: NGUYEN XUAN TRANH
School of Technology: LE QUANG MINH

DA NANG UNIVERSITY OF TECHNOLOGY

54 Nguyen Luong Bang Hoa Khanh, Lien Chieu, Da Nang City
Telephone: (511) 842308
Fax: (511) 842771
E-mail: dhbk@ud.edu.vn
Internet: www.dut.edu.vn

Founded 1975, fmrly Univ. Polytechnic Da Nang.

DUY TAN UNIVERSITY

184 Nguyen Van Linh St, Thank Khe Dist., Da Nang City
Telephone: (511) 3650403
Fax: (511) 3650443
E-mail: webmaster@dtu.edu.vn
Internet: www.dtu.edu.vn

Founded 1994

Pres.: LE CONG CO

Faculties of accountancy and finance, business, engineering, languages, technology.

FOREIGN TRADE UNIVERSITY

91 Chua Lang, Lang Thuong, Dong Da, Hanoi
Telephone: (4) 32595168
Fax: (4) 38343605
E-mail: qhqt@ftu.edu.vn
Internet: www.ftu.edu.vn

Founded 1960

Chair. of Board of Trustees: Prof. Dr VU CHI LOC
Pres: Prof. Dr HOANG VAN CHAU
Vice-Pres.: Prof. Dr NGUYEN VAN HONG
Vice-Pres.: Prof. Dr BUI NGOC SON
Vice-Pres.: Assoc. Prof. Dr NGUYEN DINH THO
Vice-Pres.: Assoc. Prof. Dr DAO THI THU GIANG
Rector: Prof. Dr NGUYEN THI MO
Vice-Rectors: Prof. Dr HOANG VAN CHAU, Prof. Dr HOANG NGOC THIET, Prof. Dr NGUYEN PHUC KHANH
Number of teachers: 193
Number of students: 10,720
Publication: *External Economics Review* (4 a year)

DEANS
Faculty of Basic and Fundamental Studies: Prof. Dr LE THANH CUONG
Faculty of Business Administration: Dr BU NGOC SON
Faculty of Business English: Dr NGUYEN DUC HOAT
Faculty of Foreign Trade Economics: Dr VU SY TUAN
Faculty of In-Service Training: NGUYEN THI MO
Faculty of Marxism and Leninism Studies: Dr DOAN VAN KHAI
Faculty of Postgraduate Studies: Prof. Dr VU CHI LOC

HAIPHONG UNIVERSITY OF MEDICINE

213 Tran Quoc Toan (Lach Tray), Ngo Quyen, Haiphong
Telephone: (31) 731907
Fax: (31) 731224
E-mail: dhyhp@hn.vnn.vn
Rector: HUU CHINH NGUYEN.

HANOI AGRICULTURAL UNIVERSITY

Trau Quy, Gia Lam, Hanoi
Telephone: (4) 62617586
Fax: (4) 38276554
E-mail: raico@hua.edu.vn
Internet: www.hau.edu.vn/en

Founded 1956
Public control
Languages of instruction: English, Vietnamese
Academic year: August to June

Faculties of Agronomy and Agricultural Resources Environment Management, Animal Husbandry and Veterinary Medicine, Economics and Rural Development, Farm Engineering and Rural Electricity, Land Resources and Environment, Post-Harvest Technology and Food Processing, Postgraduate Studies and Technical Teachers Training; Institute of Agricultural Biology; Experimental and Demonstration Station, Viet Nam Agricultural College Training, Research and Development Center, Center for Sustainable Agriculture Research and Development, Professional Dogs Research Center, Botanical Garden and Germplasm Conservation, Center for Agricultural Research and Environmental Studies, Cadastral Center

Rector: DUC VIEN TRAN
Number of teachers: 850
Number of students: 12,900
Publication: *Journal of Scientific and Development.*

HANOI ARCHITECTURAL UNIVERSITY

Km 10, Nguyen Trai Rd, Thanh Xuan, Hanoi
Telephone: (4) 8544346
Fax: (4) 8541616
E-mail: pth@hn.vnn.vn
Internet: www.hau.edu.vn

Founded 1969

Rector: Prof. Dr Arch. TRONG HAN TRAN
Vice-Rectors: Prof. Dr Arch. CHE DINH HOANG, Dr. DO DINH DUC, Prof. Dr Arch. DO HAU
Dir for Centre of Information and Library: PHAM VAN THINH

DEANS
Dept of Political Theory: PHAM KHOAN
Faculty of Architecture: Dr Arch. LE QUAN
Faculty of Civil Engineering: Asst Prof. Dr NGUYEN TAI TRUNG
Faculty of Infrastructure Techniques and Urban Environment: Asst Prof. HOANG VAN HUE
Faculty of Rural and Urban Planning: Asst Prof. Dr Arch. LE DUC THANG
Faculty of Urban Management: Asst Prof. Dr Arch. NGUYEN TO LANG
In-Service Faculty: Asst Prof. Dr VUONG VAN THANH
Postgraduate Faculty: Asst Prof. Dr Arch. DANG DUC QUANG

HANOI LAW UNIVERSITY

87 Nguyen Chi Thanh, Duong Lang, Hanoi
Telephone: (4) 8352630
Fax: (4) 8343226
E-mail: info@hlu.edu.vn
Internet: www.hlu.edu.vn

Founded 1979

Rector: LE MINH TAM

Faculties of administrative and state law, economic law, international law, justice, part-time learning, postgraduate training.

HANOI NATIONAL ECONOMICS UNIVERSITY

207 Duong Giai Phong, Quan Hai Ba Trung, Hanoi
Telephone: (4) 36280280
E-mail: nghind@neu.edu.vn
Internet: www.neu.edu.vn

Founded 1956
Languages of instruction: English, French
Number of teachers: 1,000
Number of students: 32,000
Publication: *Economics and Development Review* (12 a year)

Faculties of accountancy and auditing, agricultural economics, banking and finance, industrial economics, labour economics, planning and statistics.

HANOI OPEN UNIVERSITY

Nha B-101 Phuong Bach Khoa, Quan Hai Ba Trung, Hanoi
Telephone: (4) 8694821
Fax: (4) 8691587
E-mail: dhm-hou@hn.vnn.vn
Internet: www.hou.edu.vn

Founded 1990, univ. status since 1993
Language of instruction: Vietnamese
Academic year: August to June
Number of teachers: 470
Number of students: 19,000

Faculties of Biological Technology, Education and Training, Foreign Languages, Industrial Design, Information Systems, Law, Management Training, Telecommunication Technology; Multimedia Centre; Research Centre of Distance Education.

HANOI UNIVERSITY OF CIVIL ENGINEERING

5 Giai Phong Rd, Hanoi
Telephone: (4) 8691302
Fax: (4) 8691684
E-mail: dngoaidhxd@hn.vnn.vn
Internet: www.dhxd.edu.vn

Founded 1956, univ. status since 1966
Language of instruction: Vietnamese
Academic year: August to June
Number of teachers: 700
Number of students: 14,000
Publication: *Science-Technology*

Rector: LE NINH NGUYEN

Faculties of architecture, civil and industrial engineering, construction engineering, environmental engineering, highway and bridge construction, hydraulic engineering, industrial economics, information technology, mechanical engineering, postgraduate studies; institute of offshore engineering; centre for continuing education.

HANOI UNIVERSITY OF CULTURE

418 De La Thanh, Dong Da Dist., Hanoi
Telephone: (4) 8511971
Fax: (4) 5141629
E-mail: daihocvanhoahanoi@gmail.com
Internet: www.huc.edu.vn

Founded 1977
Number of teachers: 125
Number of students: 2,514

Rector: Prof. Dr TRAN DUC NGON

Faculty of Cultural Studies, Library and Information, Tourism, Postgraduate Training.

HANOI NATIONAL UNIVERSITY OF EDUCATION

136 Duong Xuan Thuy, Quan Hoa Cau Giay, Tu Liem, Hanoi
Telephone: (4) 7547823
Fax: (4) 7547971
E-mail: p.qhqt@hnue.edu.vn
Internet: www.hnue.edu.vn

Founded 1951

Faculties of foreign languages education, teacher training.

HANOI UNIVERSITY OF FINE ARTS

42 Yet kien, Quan Hoan Kiem, Hanoi
Telephone: (4) 8224013
Fax: (4) 8226418
E-mail: dhmythuathn@hn.vnn.vn

Founded 1957 as the Hanoi College of Fine Art, univ. status 1981

Dir: NGUYEN LUONG TIEU BACH
Dept Dir: LE ANH VAN

Offers 5-year BFA programmes, 2- and 3-year full and part-time MA programmes in painting, graphic art, sculpture.

HANOI UNIVERSITY OF FOREIGN STUDIES

Km 9, Nguyen Trai St, Thanh Xuan, Hanoi
Telephone: (4) 38544338
Fax: (4) 38544550
E-mail: hanu@hanu.vn
Internet: www.hunu.edu.vn

Founded 1959

Depts of Accountancy, Business, Commerce, Economics, Human Resource Management, International Studies, Languages and Tourism

Pres.: NGUYEN DINH LUAN.

HANOI UNIVERSITY OF FOREIGN TRADE

91 Chua Lang St, Dong Da Dist., Hanoi
Telephone: (4) 8356800
Fax: (4) 8343605
E-mail: qhqt@ftu.edu.vn
Internet: www.ftu.edu.vn

Founded 1965

Pres: Prof. Dr HOANG VAN CHAU
Rector: Prof Dr THI MO NGUYEN
Vice-Rectors: Prof. Dr NGUYEN HONG DAM, HOANG NGOC THIET

Faculties of international business, business administration, commercial English.

HANOI UNIVERSITY OF INDUSTRIAL FINE ARTS

360 La Thanh, O Cho Dua, Dong Da, Hanoi
Telephone: (4) 8517364
Fax: (4) 8517390
E-mail: pkhmtcn@fpt.vn

Founded 1965

Rector: LE HUYEN

Dept of industrial art.

HANOI MEDICAL UNIVERSITY

1 Ton That Tung St, Dong Da, Hanoi
Telephone: (4) 8523798
Fax: (4) 8525115
E-mail: daihocyhn@hmu.edu.vn
Internet: www.hmu.edu.vn

Founded 1902

Dir.: Prof. NGUYEN LAN VIET
Prin.: Prof. NGUYEN DUC HINH
Vice-Rector for Finance: LUU NGOC HOAT
Vice-Rector for Postgraduate Training: PHAM NHAT AN
Vice-Rector for Scientific Research: DOAN LOI
Vice-Rector for Undergraduate Training: DAO VAN LONG

Number of teachers: 508
Number of students: 2,419

Publication: *Journal of Medical Research* (1 a year)

DEANS

Faculty of Public Health: Dr. TRUONG VIET DUNG
Faculty of Traditional Medicine: Dr. NGUYEN KIM NHUOC

HANOI UNIVERSITY OF MINING AND GEOLOGY

Dong Ngac Commune, Tu Liem Dist., Hanoi
Telephone: (4) 8389633
Fax: (4) 8389633
E-mail: thdn@hn.vnn.vn
Internet: www.humg.edu.vn

Founded 1966

Prin.: Dr TRAN DINH KIEN
Deputy-Prins: Dr NGUYEN PHU VU, Dr NGUYEN XUAN TRUONG, Dr TA DUC THINH
Dir of Univ. Library: PHAM MINH KHOI

Library of 100,000 vols, 900 periodicals
Number of students: 5,338

DEANS

Dept of Defence Education: Col DO KIM CHIEN
Dept of General Education: NGUYEN MINH MAN
Dept of Graduate and Postgraduate Training: TRAN HONG HAI
Dept of Open Science: VO TRONG HUNG
Dept of Science and Technology: NGUYEN QUANG LUAT
Faculty of Economics and Business Administration: DO HUU TUNG
Faculty of Electrical Engineering: NGUYEN CHI TINH
Faculty of Geodesy: NAM DANG CHINH
Faculty of Geology: NGUYEN VAN LAM
Faculty of Information Technology: NGUYEN TRUONG XUAN
Faculty of Oil: LE HAI AN
Faculty of Political Theory: NGUYEN BINH YEN

HANOI UNIVERSITY OF TECHNOLOGY

1 Dai Co Viet Rd, Hanoi
Telephone: (4) 8693796
Fax: (4) 8696720
E-mail: qhqt@mail.hut.edu.vn
Internet: www.hut.edu.vn

Founded 1956
Language of instruction: Vietnamese
Academic year: August to July

Rector: QUOC THANG TRAN
Vice-Rectors: Prof. Dr CONG HOA LE
Chief Admin. Officer: DUONG VAN NGHI
Librarian: GIAN HUU CAN

Library of 700,000 vols
Number of teachers: 1,500
Number of students: 35,650

Publication: *Sciences et Techniques* (4 a year)

DEANS

Applied Mathematics: Dr NGUYEN CANH LUONG
Chemical Technology: Dr VU DAO THANG
Economics and Management: Dr TRAN VAN BINH
Electronics and Telecommunications: Dr PHAM MINH VIET
Engineering Education: Prof. NGUYEN HOA TOAN
Foreign Languages: DO VAN MOC
General Chemistry: LE CONG HOA
Hydraulic Machinery and Automation: NGUYEN PHU VINH
Industrial Management: NGUYEN MINH DUE
Information Technology: Prof. NGUYEN THUC HAI
Mechanical Engineering: Prof. TANG HUY
Metallurgy and Materials Technology: Prof. DO MINH NGHIEP
Physical Education: LE VAN LINH
Social Sciences: Prof. NGO MINH KHANG
Textile Engineering: Dr TRAN MINH NAM

HANOI WATER RESOURCES UNIVERSITY

175 Tay Son St, Dong Da, Hanoi
Telephone: (4) 8522201
Fax: (4) 5633351
E-mail: wru@wru.edu.vn
Internet: www.wru.edu.vn

Founded 1959

Rectors: Assoc. Prof. Dr DO VAN HUA, Prof. Dr LE KIM TRUYEN
Vice-Rectors: Prof. Dr DAO XUAN HOC, Assoc. Prof. Dr PHAM NGOC QUY
Chief Librarian: Dr NGUYEN HUU THAI

Number of teachers: 520
Number of students: 6,930

DEANS

Department of Foreign Languages: LE VAN KHANG (Head)
Department of Marxist-Leninist Philosophy and Sociology: Dr NGUYEN QUOC LUAT (Head)
Department of Military and Physical Education: Sr Lt-Col NGUYEN SY HOI (Head)
Faculty of Hydraulic Construction: Assoc. Dr NGUYEN VAN MAO
Faculty of Hydraulic Machinery and Equipment: Dr NGUYEN DANG CUONG
Faculty of Hydrology and Environment: Assoc. Prof. Dr DO TAT TUC
Faculty of Hydrology Power: Assoc. Prof. Dr HO SY DU
Faculty of Information Technology: Prof. Dr NGUYEN VAN LE
Faculty of In-Service Training: TRAN NGU PHUC
Faculty of Planning and Management of Water Resources Systems: Dr PHAM NGOC HAI
Faculty of Postgraduate Studies: Assoc. Prof. Dr DUONG VAN TIEN
Faculty of Water Resources Economics: Dr NGUYEN XUAN PHU

HO CHI MINH CITY OPEN UNIVERSITY

97 Vo Van Tan, Ward 6, Dist. 3, Ho Chi Minh City
Telephone: (8) 9300210
Fax: (8) 9300085
E-mail: international@ou.edu.vn
Internet: www.ou.edu.vn

Founded 1990, univ. status since 1993
Language of instruction: Vietnamese
Academic year: September to July

Rector: Assoc. Prof. Dr LE BAO DONG
Vice-Rector: Dr NGUYEN THUAN

Library of 12,000
Number of teachers: 530
Number of students: 14,000

Faculties of Biotechnology, Computer Science, Economics and Business Administration, Engineering and Technology, Foreign Languages, Southeast Asian Studies and Sociology; Centres of Applied Computer Science, Distance Training, Foreign Languages and Overseas Studies, Professional Accounting.

HO CHI MINH CITY UNIVERSITY OF ARCHITECTURE

196 rue Pasteur, Q. 3, Ho Chi Minh City
Telephone: (83) 8222748
Fax: (83) 8244678
E-mail: pnckh@hcmuarc.edu.vn
Internet: www.hcmuarc.edu.vn
Founded 1976
State control
Languages of instruction: Vietnamese, English(for Urban Design programme only)
Accredited by Min. of Construction of Viet Nam
Rector: Dr Pham Tu
Vice-Rector: Le van Thuong
Vice-Rector: Le Quang Quy
Vice-Rector: Nguyen Thanh Nghi
Vice-Rector: Truong Ngoc An
Librarian: Nguyen Thi Thanh Thuy
Number of students: 6,000

DEANS

Architecture: Dr Trinh Duy Anh
Civil Engineering: Dr Nguyen Khac Man
Industrial Art: Dr Nguyen Duc Anh
Interior Design: (vacant)
Urban Infrastructure: Dr Pham Anh Dung
Urban Planning: Dr Nguyen Thanh Ha

HO CHI MINH CITY UNIVERSITY OF ECONOMICS

59c, Nguyen Dinh Chieu, Dist. 3, Ho Chi Minh City
Telephone: (8) 8295299
Fax: (8) 8241186
E-mail: tchc@ueh.edu.vn
Internet: www.ueh.edu.vn
Founded 1976
Public control
Languages of instruction: Vietnamese, English, French
Academic year: January to December
Rector: Pham Van Nang
Vice-Rector: Prof. Dr Minh Duong Thi Binh
Vice-Rector: Assoc. Prof. Dr Te Nguyen Quoc
Vice-Rector: Assoc. Prof. Dr Nguyen Viet
Vice-Rector: Prof. Dr. Phong Nguyen Dong
Vice-Rector: Assoc. Prof. Dr. Dinh Nguyen Ngoc
Vice-Rector: Assoc. Prof. Dr. Ngan Tran Hoang
Dir of Univ. Library: Thuy Doan Thi
Library of 60,000 vols
Number of teachers: 700
Number of students: 50,000
Publication: *Economic Development Review* (12 a year)

DEANS

Dept of Foreign Languages: Prof. Phuoc Vo Dinh
Dept of Political Studies: Dr Tuan Nguyen Minh
Faculty of Accounting and Auditing: Assoc. Prof. Dr Duoc Pham Van
Faculty of Business Administration: Assoc. Prof. Dr Dung Ho Tien
Faculty of Commerce, Tourism and Marketing: Dr Buu Le Tan
Faculty of Corporate Finance: Prof. Dr Tho Tran Ngoc
Faculty of Development Economics: Assoc. Prof. Dr Hoai Trong Hoai
Faculty of Economical Mathematics and Statistics: Dr Trung Bui Phuc
Faculty of Economics Law: Dr Hung Le Van
Faculty of Management Information System: Huong Vu Thi Lien
Faculty of Public Finance: Assoc. Prof. Dr Thanh Su Dinh

ATTACHED INSTITUTES

Centre for Economic Studies and Application (CESAIS): 59c Nguyen Dinh Chieu, Dist. 3, Ho Chi Minh; tel. (8) 8223408.

Centre for Excellence in Management Development: 196 Tran Quang Khai St, Dist. 1, Ho Chi Minh City; tel. (8) 38483107; fax (8) 38483252; e-mail cemd@ueh.edu.vn; internet www.cemd.ueh.edu.vn.

Institute of Development Economics Research: 279 Nguyen Tri Phuong, Dist. 10, Ho Chi Minh City; tel. and fax (8) 8561250; e-mail vnckt@idr.edu.vn; internet www.idr.edu.vn; Dir Ho Duc Hung.

International Centre for Informatics Training (KOVIT): 279 Nguyen Tri Phuong, Dist. 10, Ho Chi Minh City; tel. (8) 8549352.

International Commerce Training Centre: 54 Nguyen Van Thu, Dist 1, Ho Chi Minh City; tel. (8) 8297233; fax (8) 8221210; e-mail ict@ueh.edu.vn; internet www.ueh.edu.vn/ict/default.htm; Dir Dong Nguyen Phong.

HO CHI MINH CITY UNIVERSITY OF FINE ARTS

5 Phan Dang Luu, Ho Chi Minh City
Telephone: (8) 84126010
Fax: (8) 8412695
E-mail: dhmt@hcm.vnn.vn
Founded 1913
Dir: Prof. Nguyen Huy Long
Number of teachers: 58
Number of students: 700
Publication: *Fine Arts Information*
Courses taught incl. Graphic Arts and Graphic Design, Painting, Sculpture; Depts of Applied Arts, Basic Knowledge, Fine Arts Pedagogy, Fine Arts Critique, Fine Art Higher Education.

HO CHI MINH CITY UNIVERSITY OF FOREIGN LANGUAGES AND INFORMATION TECHNOLOGY

155 Su Van Hanh St (Extension), Ward 13, Dist. 10, Ho Chi Minh City
Telephone: (8) 8632052
Fax: (8) 8650991
E-mail: daotaohuflit@hcm.vnn.vn
Internet: www.huflit.vnn.vn
Founded 1994
Chair.: Huynh The Cuoc
Number of teachers: 100
Number of students: 1,200
Schools of Computer Sciences and Eastern Cultures and Languages, Foreign Languages.

HO CHI MINH CITY UNIVERSITY OF LAW

2 Nguyen tat Thanh, Phuong 12, Q4, Ho Chi Minh City
Telephone: (8) 9400989
Fax: (8) 8265291
E-mail: quantrimang@hcmulaw.edu.vn
Internet: www.hcmulaw.edu.vn
Founded 1996
Rector: Van Luyen Nguyen
Faculties of administrative and state law, business law, civil law, criminal law, international law, part-time training, postgraduate training.

HO CHI MINH CITY UNIVERSITY OF MEDICINE AND PHARMACY

217 Hong Bang, Q. 5, Ho Chi Minh City
Telephone: (8) 8558411
Fax: (8) 8552304
E-mail: info@yds.edu.vn
Internet: www.yds.edu.vn
Founded 1947 as Saigon Univ. of Medicine and Pharmacy, present name since 1976
Rector: Dinh Hoi Nguyen
Number of teachers: 982
Number of students: 7,966
Library of 30,000 vols, 700 periodicals
Publication: *Journal of Medicine of Ho Chi Minh City* (4 a year)
Faculties of fundamental sciences, medicine, odonto-stomatology, traditional medicine, pharmacy, nursing medical techniques, public health; University medical center; advanced medical technology center; biomedical laboratory; pharma technology center, medical skills lab unit.

HO CHI MINH CITY UNIVERSITY OF PEDAGOGY

280 An Duong Vuong, Quan 5, Ho Chi Minh City
Telephone: (8) 8352020
Fax: (8) 8398946
E-mail: nttrac@vol.vnn.vn
Internet: www.hcmupeda.edu.vn
Founded 1976
Rector: Manh Nhi Bui
Faculties of education, teacher training.

HO CHI MINH CITY UNIVERSITY OF TRANSPORT

2 D3 St, Binh Thanh District M, Ho Chi Minh City
Telephone: (8) 8992862
Fax: (8) 8980456
E-mail: ird@hcmutrans.edu.vn
Internet: www.hcmutrans.edu.vn
Founded 1962 as part of Viet Nam Maritime Univ., ind. status since 2001
Faculties of construction, information technology, marine electrical, marine engineering and electronic engineering, mechanics and transport economics, naval architecture and floating construction, navigation; departments of basic education, foreign languages, in-service training, political reasoning education, postgraduate studies; Merchant Marine Training Centre; Training Centre of Transport Vocation; Centre of Foreign Languages and Information Technology
Rector: Canh Vinh Tran
Vice-Rectors: Huu Khuong Nguyen, Van Thu Nguyen
Number of teachers: 298
Number of students: 8,062

HO CHI MINH UNIVERSITY OF TECHNICAL EDUCATION

1 Vo Van Ngan St, Thu Duc, Ho Chi Minh City
Telephone: (8) 37221223
Fax: (8) 38964922
E-mail: webmaster@hcmute.edu.vn
Internet: www.hcmute.edu.vn
Founded 1962 as Ho Chi Minh City Pedagogical Univ. of Technology; became College of Technical Teacher Training 1996; present name and status 2002
State control
Languages of instruction: Vietnamese, English
Academic year: September to May

Pres.: Assoc. Prof. Dr THAI BA CAN
Vice-Pres.: Assoc. Prof. Dr DO VAN DUNG
Vice-Pres.: Dr LAM MAI LONG
Vice-Pres.: NGUYEN VAN MINH
Librarian: VU TRONG LUAT

Library of 298,332 vols, 227 articles and journals
Number of teachers: 700
Number of students: 26,344

Publication: *Tap san Su Pham Ky Thuat* (4 a year)

DEANS

Faculty of Automotive Engineering: NGUYEN TAN QUOC
Faculty of Chemical and Food Technology: Assoc Prof. Dr NGUYEN VAN SUC
Faculty of Civil Engineering and Applied Mechanics: Assoc. Prof. Dr NGUYEN HOAI SON
Faculty of Economics: Dr TRAN DANG THINH
Faculty of Electrical and Electronic Engineering: Assoc. Prof. Dr QUYEN HUY ANN
Faculty of Foreign Languages: Dr NGUYEN DINH THU
Faculty of Foundation Sciences: Dr VO THANH TAN
Faculty of Garment Technology and Fashion Design: VU MINH HANH
Faculty of Graphic Arts and Media: Dr NGO ANH TUAN
Faculty of Information Technology: Dr DANG TRUONG SON
Faculty of Marxism-Leninism and Ho Chi Minh's Ideology: Assoc. Prof. DOAN DUC HIEU
Faculty of Mechanical Engineering: Dr NGUYEN NGOC PHUONG
Faculty of Technical Education: Dr NGUYEN VAN TUAN

HONG DUC UNIVERSITY

307 Duong Le Lai Rd, Phuong Dong Son, Thanh Hoa City

Telephone: (37) 910222
Fax: (37) 910475
Internet: www.hdu.edu.vn

Founded 1977 by amalgamation of 3 colleges

DEANS

Department of Foreign Languages: PHAM VAN CHU
Faculty of Agriculture and Forestry: Dr LE HUU CAN
Faculty of Economics and Business Administration: Dr NGUYEN HUU DIEN
Faculty of Medicine: NGUYEN THI TRUONG
Faculty of Natural Science: Dr DUONG DINH HOAN
Faculty of Nursery Teacher Training: NGUYEN THI TRUONG
Faculty of Primary Teacher Training: Dr NGUYEN DINH MAI
Faculty of Social Science: Dr NGUYEN VAN TRUONG
Faculty of Technology: Dr NGUYEN MANH AN

HUE UNIVERSITY

3 Le Loi, Hue City, Thua Thien Hue

Telephone: (54) 845658
Fax: (54) 845658
E-mail: bantin_dhh@hueuni.edu.vn
Internet: www.hueuni.edu.vn

Founded 1957
Language of instruction: Vietnamese
Academic year: November to July

Rector: VIEN THO NGUYEN

Library of 30,000
Number of teachers: 1,316
Number of students: 16,181 full-time, 19,387 part-time

Colleges of Agriculture and Forestry, Economics, Medicine, Pedagogy, Sciences.

HUE UNIVERSITY OF AGRICULTURE AND FORESTRY

102 Phung Hung, Hue

Telephone: (54) 3522535
Fax: (54) 3524923
E-mail: admin@huaf.edu.vn
Internet: www.huaf.edu.vn

Founded 1967
Language of instruction: Vietnamese
Academic year: September to July

Rector: Prof. Dr TRAN VAN MINH
Vice-Rector: Assoc. Prof. Dr. LE VAN AN
Vice-Rector: Assoc. Prof. Dr. LE DUC NGOAN
Vice-Rector: Assoc. Prof. Dr. LE THANH BON

Library of 200,000
Number of teachers: 411
Number of students: 6,800

DEANS

Central Research and Development in Agro-Forestry Technology: Dr LE VAN AN (Director)
Centre for Rural Development: Assoc. Prof. Dr LE VAN AN (Director)
Department of Sciences and International Relations: PHUNG THANG LONG (Director)
Faculty of Agricultural Engineering and Post-Harvest Technology: LE THANH LONG
Faculty of Agronomy: Dr TRAN DANG HOA
Faculty of Animal Sciences: Dr DAM VAN TIEN
Faculty of Forestry: DANG THAI DUONG

NHA TRANG UNIVERSITY

2 Nguyen Dinh Chieu, Nha Trang City, Khan Hoa Province

Telephone: (58) 831149
Fax: (58) 831147
E-mail: censtrad@ntu.edu.vn
Internet: www.ntu.edu.vn

Founded 1959

Rector: Assoc. Prof. Dr QUAC DINH LIEN
Vice-Rectors: Dr THAI VAN NGAN, Assoc. Prof. Dr TRAN THI LUYEN, VU VAN THUNG

Library of 18,000 vols, 500 periodicals
Number of teachers: 300
Number of students: 7,000

Publications: *Fisheries Journal* (4 a year), *Journal of Science and Technology* (4 a year)

Faculties of basic sciences, marine mechanics, navigation and marine exploitation, aquaculture, marine products processing, fishery economics.

NONG LAM UNIVERSITY

Khu Pho 6, Linh Trung Ward, Thu Duc Dist., Ho Chi Minh City

Telephone: (8) 8960711
Fax: (8) 8960713
E-mail: vp@hcmuaf.edu.vn
Internet: www.hcmuaf.edu.vn

Founded 1955, as Univ. of Forestry and Agriculture
Language of instruction: Vietnamese
Academic year: September to July

Rector: Dr BUI CACH TUYEN

Library of 60,000
Number of teachers: 400
Number of students: 11,000

Publication: *University Journal of Agricultural Sciences and Technology* (4 a year)

Faculties of agricultural energy and machinery research centre; agronomy, animal science and veterinary medicine, biotechnological research centre; fruit and vegetable processing research centre; centre for research and application of cadastral science and technology; chemical and biological analysis and experiment centre; computer centre; continuing education and placement service economics, engineering, fishery, environmental technology and management centre; environmental technology, experimental research and technology transfer centre; food science and technology, foreign language centre; foreign languages, forestry, information technology; science, veterinary clinic wood science and technology research centre; industrial crops centre.

RMIT INTERNATIONAL UNIVERSITY VIET NAM

21 Pham Ngoc Thach St, Dist. 3, Ho Chi Minh City

Telephone: (8) 8224992
Fax: (8) 8225039
E-mail: enquiries@rmit.edu.vn
Internet: www.rmit.edu.vn

Founded 2001 by RMIT Univ., Australia
Academic year: February to January

Pres.: MICHAEL MANN
Vice-Pres.: Prof. ROBERT SNOW
Campus Devt Man.: SUZANNE ARDAGH
Dir of Teaching and Learning: ROBERTA ABELL
Academic Registrar: TRISH CHAPMAN

Number of teachers: 70
Number of students: 800

Undergraduate programmes: university preparation, BSc (information technology for business, information technology and multimedia, applied science in software engineering, commerce); Postgraduate programmes: MEd Leadership, MBA and Management, Graduate Diploma in Tertiary Teaching and Learning; English programmes; CELTA courses.

THAI BINH MEDICAL UNIVERSITY

373 Ly Bon St, Thai Binh

Telephone: (36) 838545
Fax: (36) 847509
E-mail: dhytb@hn.vnn.vn
Internet: www.tbmc.edu.vn

Founded 1968
State control

Rector: Assoc. Prof. LUONG XUAN HIEN
Vice-Rectors: NGUYEN VAN SAI, Assoc. Prof. TRAN QUOC KHAM

Library of 30,000
Number of teachers: 305
Number of students: 2,500

DEANS

Faculty of Biology: LUONG XUAN HIEN
Faculty of Public Health: PHAM VAM TRONG
Faculty of Traditional Medicine: BUI THI NGUYET

THAI NGUYEN UNIVERSITY

Luong Ngoc Quyen St, Tan Thinh Ward, Thai Nguyen

Telephone: (280) 751681
Fax: (280) 852665
E-mail: bancntt@tnu.edu.vn
Internet: www.tnu.edu.vn

Founded 1994
State control
Academic year: September to June

Pres.: LE CAO THANG

Number of teachers: 1,400
Number of students: 39,000 (incl. 23,000 full-time)

DEANS

Faculty of Foreign Languages: (vacant)
Faculty of Information Technology: PHAM VIET BINH
Faculty of Natural and Social Sciences: (vacant)
Vocational School of Economics and Techniques: (vacant)

Learning Resource Centre: Tan Thinh Ward, Thai Nguyen; tel. (280) 3656600; e-mail vyhong@lrc-tnu.edu.vn; internet www.lrc-tnu.edu.vn; Librarian VU THI YEN HONG.

UNIVERSITY COLLEGES

College of Agriculture and Forestry

Telephone: (280) 855564
Fax: (280) 852921
E-mail: aitc@tuaf.edu.vn
Internet: www.tuaf.edu.vn

Rector: Assoc. Prof. DANG KIM VUI
Vice-Rectors: Assoc. Prof. NGUYEN QUANG TUYEN, Assoc. Prof. NGUYEN THI KIM LAN, Assoc. Prof. TRAN NGOC NGOAN

DEANS

Faculty of Agricultural Extension and Rural Development: Assoc. Prof. Dr NGUYEN DUY HOAN
Faculty of Agricultural Pedagogy: Dr NGUYEN THI LIEN
Faculty of Agricultural Sciences: Assoc. Prof. Dr LUAN THI DEP
Faculty of Animal Husbandry: Dr NGUYEN VAN QUANG
Faculty of Forestry: Dr. LE SY TRUNG
Faculty of Natural Resources and Environment Agriculture: Assoc. Prof. Dr NGUYEN NGOC NONG

College of Economics and Business Administration

Km 9, Duong 3/2 Tich Luong, Thai Nguyen
Telephone: (280) 647685
Fax: (280) 647684
E-mail: tueba@tueba.edu.vn
Internet: www.tueba.edu.vn

Rector: Assoc. Prof. Dr TRAN CHI THIEN

DEANS

Faculty of Accounting: Dr NGUYEN THI MINH THO
Faculty of Basic Science: Assoc. Prof. NGUYEN THI THU HUONG
Faculty of Business Administration: Assoc. Prof TRAN QUANG HUY
Faculty of Economics: Dr DO QUANG QUY
Postgraduate Studies: Dr TRAN DINH TUAN

College of Education

Duong Luong, Ngoc Quyen, Thai Nguyen
Telephone: (280) 856886
Fax: (280) 859521
E-mail: dhsupham.edu@hn.vnn.vn
Internet: www.dhsptn.edu.vn

Rector: NGUYEN VAN LOC
Vice-Rectors: PHAM HONG QUANG, PHAM HIEN BANG, DUONG DUY HUNG, PHAM VIET DUC

DEANS

Faculty of Chemistry: LE HUU THIENG
Faculty of Foreign Languages: NGUYEN VINH QUANG
Faculty of History: DAM THI UYEN
Faculty of Languages: NGUYEN HANG PHUONG
Faculty of Marxist-Leninist Political Theory: DONG VAN QUAN
Faculty of Mathematics: PHAM VIET DUC
Faculty of Physical Education: NGUYEN VAN LUC
Faculty of Physics: PHAM THAI CUONG
Faculty of Psychology: NGUYEN THI TINH

College of Industrial Technology

3–2 St, Thai Nguyen
Telephone: (2) 80847145
Fax: (2) 80847904
E-mail: tnut_office@tnut.edu.
Internet: www.tnut.edu.vn

Rector: Dr NGUYEN DANG BINH
Vice-Rectors: Assoc. Prof NGUYEN NHU HIEN, Assoc. Prof NGUYEN DANG HOE, Assoc. Prof. PHAN QUANG THE

DEANS

Faculty of Basic Science: NGUYEN VAN TUAN
Faculty of Electrical Engineering: TRAN XUAN MINH
Faculty of Electronics: NGUYEN HUU CONG
Faculty of Management & Industrial Environment: MAI VAN GU
Faculty of Mechanical Engineering: VU QUY DUC
Faculty of Pedagogy: DUONG PHUC TY

College of Medicine and Pharmacy

284 Duong Luong Ngoc, Quyen Thanh, Thai Nguyen
Telephone: (280) 852671
Fax: (280) 855710
E-mail: dhyktn@hn.vnn.vn
Internet: www.tnmc.edu.vn

Founded 1968

Rector: Assoc. Prof. Dr NGUYEN THANH TRUNG.

THAI NGUYEN UNIVERSITY OF AGRICULTURE AND FORESTRY

Quyet Thinhdan Commune, Thai Nguyen City, Thai Nguyen
Telephone: (280) 3855564
Fax: (280) 3852921
E-mail: tuaf@hn.vnn.vn
Internet: www.tuaf.edu.vn

Founded 1970

Faculties of agricultural economics, agricultural technology, agronomy, animal husbandry and veterinary science, forestry, graduate studies, land management, pedagogy, agro-forestry research and development centre for northern mountainous regions of Viet Nam; centre for mountainous natural resources and environment; experimental farm; life science research institute; centre for agricultural experiment and practices; mountainous resources and environment centre; centre for foreign language studies; centre for applied information technologies; centre for international training cooperation and consultancy

Rector: Prof. Dr DANG KIM VUI

Number of teachers: 300
Number of students: 10,000

UNIVERSITY OF DALAT

01 Phu Dong Thien, Vuong, Dalat, Lamdong
Telephone: (63) 3822246
Fax: (63) 3823380
E-mail: irdept@dlu.edu.vn
Internet: www.dlu.edu.vn

Founded 1958
State control
Languages of instruction: Vietnamese, English
Academic year: September to June

Faculties: agronomy, biology, business administration, chemistry, environmental studies, foreign languages, graduate studies history, information technology, law, mathematics, oriental philology, physics, social work and community development, studies, teacher training, tourism

Rector: Assoc. Prof. Dr LE BA DUNG
Vice-Rector: Dr NGUYEN DUC HOA
Vice-Rector: Dr MAI XUAN TRUNG
Vice-Rector: Dr NGUYEN DINH HAO

Number of teachers: 500
Number of students: 13,000

Publication: *Scientific Journal* (1 a year).

UNIVERSITY OF DANANG

41 Le Duan St, Da Nang
Telephone: (511) 822041
Fax: (511) 823683
E-mail: relint@dng.vnn.vn
Internet: www.ud.edu.vn

Founded 1994
State control

Library of 25,000 vols, 250 periodicals
Number of teachers: 889
Number of students: 35,000

President: Prof. Dr PHAN QUANG XUNG
Vice-Presidents: Prof. Dr BUI VAN GA, Dr LE THE GIOI

DIRECTORS

College of Economics and Business Administration: Dr VO XUAN TIEN
College of Education: NGUYEN KHAC SINH
College of Technology: Prof. Dr PHAM PHU LY
School of Technology: DANG VAN SON

VAN LANG UNIVERSITY

45 Nguyen Khac Nhu, Q 1, Ho Chi Minh City
Telephone: (8) 38367933
Fax: (8) 38369716
E-mail: tuyensinh@vanlangunni.edu.vn
Internet: www.vanlanguni.edu.vn

Rector: DUNG NGUYEN

Faculty of Foreign Languages.

VIET NAM FORESTRY UNIVERSITY

Main Campus, Xuan Mai, Chuong My, Hanoi
Second Campus, Trang Bom, Trang Bom, Dong Na
Telephone: (4) 33840441
Fax: (4) 33840540
E-mail: vfuhtqt@hn.vnn.vn
Internet: www.vfu.edu.vn

Founded 1964
Academic year: August to June

Rector: TRAN HUU VIEN

Library of 29,302 books, 15,696 periodicals
Number of teachers: 320
Number of students: 11,761

Research and production units: Centre for Experimental Research and Forest Industry Technology Transfer, Consulting Company for Forestry Investment and Development, Institute for Forest Ecology and Environment

Publications: *Forest Science and Technology Newsletter* (4 a year), *Scientific Research Periodical* (4 a year)

DEANS

Faculty of Economics and Business Administration: TRAN HUU DAO
Faculty of Engineering: LE TAN QUYNH
Faculty of Forest Products Technology: VU HUY DAI
Faculty of Forest Resources and Environmental Management: NGUYEN THE NHA
Faculty of Marx-Lenin: DOAN VAN HANH
Faculty of Postgraduate Training: NGUYEN PHAN THIET
Faculty of Silviculture: NGUYEN TRONG BINH
High School for Ethnic Students: NGUYEN QUANG CHUNG

PROFESSORS

HINH, V.
HUU VIEN, T.
PHAN THIET, N.
VAN CHU, T.
VAN CHUONG, P.
VAN TUAN, N.
XUAN HOAN, P.

VIET NAM MARITIME UNIVERSITY

19B/260, Thuy Khue, Tay Ho, Hanoi
Telephone: (4) 8470279
E-mail: duyluat@bigwall.com
Internet: www.vimaru.edu.vn

Founded 1956
Academic year: August to May

Rector: Dr DANG VAN UY
Vice-Rectors: Dr LUONG CONG NHO, Prof. Dr PHAM TIEN TINH, Prof. Dr PHAM VAN CUONG
Librarian: TRAN THI YEN

Number of teachers: 800
Number of students: 15,000

DEANS

Department of Postgraduate Studies: LE VIET LUONG
Faculty of Information Technology: LE QUOC DINH
Faculty of Marine Electrical and Electronic Engineering: PHAM NGOC TIEP
Faculty of Marine Engineering: NGUYEN DAI AN
Faculty of Navigation: DINH XUAN MANH
Faculty of Sea-Transport Economics: PHAM VAN CUONG
Faculty of Shipbuilding: NGUYEN VINH PHAT
Faculty of Waterway Construction: NGUYEN VAN NGOC

VIET NAM NATIONAL UNIVERSITY, HANOI

144 Xuan Thuy Rd, Cau Giay, Hanoi
Telephone: (4) 8332015
Fax: (4) 7680429
E-mail: vandao@vnu.ac.vn
Internet: www.vnu.edu.vn

Founded 1993 by amalgamation of Univ. of Hanoi and other instns of higher education in Hanoi
State control
Academic year: September to July

Faculties of general education, foreign languages, science, social sciences and humanities, teacher training; colleges of foreign languages, science, social sciences, humanities; school of business; institute of information technology training; centres of biotechnology, cooperation in mechanics training, education quality assurance and research development, natural resources management and environmental studies, systems development, teachers of political theory, Vietnamese and intercultural studies and women's studies; research centres in applied microbiology and Asian studies

Rector: Prof. Dr DAO TRONG THI
Vice-Rector: Prof. NGUYEN DUC CHINH
Librarian: NGUYEN HUY CHUONG

Library of 800,000 vols, 3,000 periodicals
Number of teachers: 1,320
Number of students: 22,761
Publication: *Tap Chi Khoa Hoc* (Scientific Journal).

VIET NAM NATIONAL UNIVERSITY, HO CHI MINH CITY

KP6, Linh-Trung, Thu Duc Dist., Ho Chi Minh City
Telephone: (84) 87242160
Fax: (84) 87242057
E-mail: hopthu_tuyensinh@vnuhcm.edu.vn
Internet: www.vnuhcm.edu.vn

Founded 1954, present structure since 1995
Dir: Dr PHAN THANH BINH.

CONSTITUENT UNIVERSITIES

University of Natural Sciences

227 Nguyen Van Cu, Dist. 5, Ho Chi Minh City
Telephone: (8) 8353193
Fax: (8) 8350096
Internet: www.hcmuns.edu.vn

Founded as a div. of the Indochina College of Sciences, Hanoi 1942, became Faculty of Sciences of Univ. of Saigon 1956; part of Ho Chi Minh Univ. 1977; current status since 1996

Rector: Assoc. Prof. Dr DUONG AI PHUONG
Vice-Rector: Assoc. Prof. Dr DONG THI BICH THUY
Vice-Rector: NGUYEN THANH HUONG
Vice-Rector: Assoc. Prof. Dr PHAM DINH HUNG
Library Dir: NGUYEN MINH HIEP

Library of 50,000 vols, 392 periodicals

DEANS

Department of Foreign Languages: NGUYEN HOANG TUAN (Head)
Department of Material Science: Prof. Dr LE KHAC BINH (Head)
Department of Physical Education: NGUYEN VAN HUNG
Faculty of Biology: Assoc. Prof. Dr TRAN LINH THUOC
Faculty of Chemistry: Assoc. Prof. Dr HA THUC HUY
Faculty of Environmental Science: Assoc. Prof. Dr LE MANH TAN
Faculty of Geology: TRAN PHU HUNG
Faculty of Information Technology: Dr DUONG ANH DUC
Faculty of Mathematics and Informatics: Dr TO ANH DUNG
Faculty of Physics: Dr DAV VAN LIET

University of Social Sciences and Humanities

10–12 Dinh Tien Hoang St, Ho Chi Minh City
E-mail: nckhhtqt@hcmc.netnam.vn
Internet: www.hcmussh.edu.vn

Founded 1996
Language of instruction: Vietnamese
Academic year: October to June

Faculties of Chinese linguistics and literature, English linguistics and literature, French linguistics and literature, geography, German linguistics and literature, history, linguistics and journalism, literature, oriental studies, philosophy, Russian linguistics and literature, sociology, Viet Nam studies and Vietnamese for foreigners; sections of culture studies, anthropology and physical education; Vietnamese and southeast asian research centre; centre for research in social development and poverty reduction; centre for foreign languages; centre for overseas studies; centre for informatics technology

Rector: VAN LE NGO
Librarian: Dr BUI LOAN THUY

Library of 87,784 vols, 375 periodicals.

University of Technology

268 Ly Thuong Kiet St, Dist. 10, Ho Chi Minh City
Telephone: (8) 8654087
Fax: (8) 8653823
Internet: www.hcmut.edu.vn

Faculties of chemical technology, civil engineering, electrical and electronic engineering, environmental management, geology and petroleum, industrial management, information technology, mechanical engineering, transportation engineering

Rector: TUOI PHAN THI.

VIET NAM UNIVERSITY OF COMMERCE

Mai Dich, Cau Giay, Hanoi
Telephone: (4) 7643219
Fax: (4) 7643228
E-mail: dhtm@vcu.edu.vn
Internet: www.vcu.edu.vn

Founded 1965

Rector: Prof. Dr PHAM VU LUAN
Vice-Rectors: NGUYEN THIEN DAT, Assoc. Prof. Dr TRAN THI DUNG, Assoc. Prof. Dr NGUYEN BACH KHOA
Library Dir: VU THI HUE

Library of 100,000 vols
Number of teachers: 267
Number of students: 7,600

DEANS

Faculty of Business Administration: VU THUY DUONG
Faculty of Economics: Dr THAN DANH PHUC
Faculty of Finance and Accounting: Dr DO MINH THANH
Faculty of Hospitality and Tourism: Dr BUI XUAN NHAN
Faculty of International Trade: Dr NGUYEN VAN THANH
Faculty of Part-Time Training: Assoc. Prof. Dr NGUYEN THI MINH NGUYET
Faculty of Postgraduate Training: Dr NGUYEN VAN MINH
Faculty of Trading Business: Dr DO THI NGOC
Section of Environment Economics: NGUYEN QUOC TIEN (Head)
Section of Foreign Languages: NGUYEN DUC CHAU (Head)
Section of the History of Viet Nam's Communist Party and Socialism: NGO XUAN DAU (Head)
Section of Mathematics: Dr HOANG VAN LAM (Head)
Section of Philosophy: Dr PHUONG KY SON (Head)
Section of Physical and Military Training: NGUYEN VAN KHANH (Head)
Section of Political Economy: Dr DINH THI THUY (Head)

VINH UNIVERSITY

182 Le Duan St, Vinh
Telephone: (38) 3855452
Fax: (38) 3855269
E-mail: lprvvinh@hn.vnn.vn

Rector: NGUYEN DINH HUAN
Vice-Rectors: NGUYEN NGOC HOI, TRAN NGOC GIAO

Number of students: 10,000

Colleges

ART AND SOCIAL ARTS AND CONSERVATOIRES

College of Law: Thuong Tin, Lang Ha Hanoi, Son Binh Province; tel. (4) 8343251.

Dong Nai College of Decorative Arts: 368 Quoc Lo 1, Thanh Pho Bien Hoa, Tinh Dong Nai; tel. (61) 822042; fax (61) 816170; e-mail mythuat.tung@gmail.com; internet dongnaiart.edu.vn; f. 1965; administered directly by the Min. of Culture, Sports and Tourism; specializes in art, ceramics, bronze-casting and natural and artificial stone sculpturing.

Hanoi College of Fine Arts: 42 Yet Kieu St, Hanoi; there are 3 faculties.

Hanoi Cultural College: 103 De La Thanh St, Hanoi; tel. (4) 8512606; there are 4 faculties.

Hanoi National Conservatory of Music: 77 Hao Nam, O Cho Dua, Dong Da Hanoi; fax (4) 8513545; e-mail nhacvienhn@netnam.vn; internet www.nhacvienhanoi.vn; Dir NGO THANH VAN.

Hanoi University of Drama and Cinematography: Mai Dich, Cau Giay, Hanoi; tel. (4) 7643397; fax (4) 8348732; e-mail skda@fpt.vn; f. 1980; undergraduate and postgraduate degrees in Theatre Direction, Screen Writing and Cinematography; Dir Prof. Dr NGUYEN MANH LAN.

Ho Chi Minh City College of Performing Arts and Cinema: 125 Cong Quynh St, Ho Chi Minh City; tel. (8) 8393658; f. 1995; Theatre, Costume Design, Pantomime and Mime, Film and Cinematography, Radio and Television.

Ho Chi Minh City Conservatory: 112 Nguyen Du St, Dist. 1, Thanh Po Ho Chi Minh City; tel. (8) 8225841; fax (8) 8220916; e-mail nhacvienhcm@hcm.vnn.vn; f. 1956; Theory, Composition, Conducting, Singing, National and Orchestral Instruments, Electric Instruments; 136 teachers; 758 students; Dir Prof. HOANG CUONG.

ECONOMICS AND PLANNING

Academy of Finance: 7 Ly Thuong Kiet St, Hoan Kiem Dist., Hanoi; tel. (4) 9331853; fax (4) 9331865; e-mail hvtc@hn.vnn.vn; internet www.hvtc.edu.vn; f. 2001; faculties of Accounting, Banking and Insurance, Business Administration, Continuing Education, Corporate Finance, Customs Taxation, Economic Information Systems, Foundation Studies, International Finance, Marx-Leninist-Ho Chi Minh Ideology, Postgraduate Training, Public Finance; institutes of Financial Science, and for Market and Price Research; library: 157,000 vols (16,500 titles), 162 current periodicals, 2,100 other publications; 350 teachers; 13,274 students; Dir-Gen. CHI NGO THE; publs *Finance and Accounting Research* (12 a year), *Financial Bulletin* (2 a month), *International Economics and Finance News* (52 a year), *Market Bulletin* (online, 365 a year), *Market and Price Bulletin* (in English, 52 a year), *Monography* (5 a year), *News for Leaders* (24 a year), *Scientific Research* (10 a year).

College of Commerce: Mai Dich, Tu Liem Dist., Hanoi; tel. (4) 8343207; there are 5 faculties.

College of Economics: 144, Xuan Thuy St, Hanoi; tel. (4) 7547506; fax (4) 7546765; e-mail kinhte@vnu.edu.vn; internet www.economics.vnu.edu.vn; attached to Viet Nam National Univ.; there are 12 faculties.

Ho Chi Minh City College of Finance and Accountancy: College Library, 279 Nguyen Tri Phuong St, Dist. 10, Ho Chi Minh City; tel. (8) 8550783; there are 3 faculties.

MEDICINE, PHYSICAL EDUCATION AND SPORTS

College of Physical Training and Sports: Tu Son Dist., Bac Ninh Province; tel. (241) 831609; fax (241) 832550; f. 1959; there are 6 faculties; 215 teachers; 2,500 students; Dir Prof. Dr TRAN DUC DUNG.

Hanoi College of Pharmacy: 13–15 Le Thanh Tong St, Hanoi; tel. (4) 8254539; fax (4) 9332332; e-mail dhduochn@netnam.org.vn; f. 1961; 160 teachers; 780 students; library: 20,000 vols; Dean Prof. Dr NGUYEN THANH DO.

TECHNICAL AND INDUSTRIAL

College of Water Conservancy: Dong Da Precinct, Hanoi; there are 6 faculties.

Posts and Telecommunications Training Centre No. 1: 10 Km, Nguyen Trai Rd, Hadong, Hatay, Hanoi; tel. (4) 8547795; fax (4) 5540587; e-mail pttci@hn.vnn.vn; internet www.ptit.edu.vn; f. 1953; library: 7,000 vols; Dir Dr CHU QUANG TOAN.

Road and Rail Transport College: Tu Liem Dist., Hanoi; there are 5 faculties.

YEMEN

The Higher Education System

Institutions of higher education predate Yemen's formation from a merger of the Yemen Arab Republic (YAR) and the People's Democratic Republic of Yemen (PDRY) in 1990, the oldest being San'a University, which was founded in 1970. In 1975 the University of Aden was founded and these remained the principal institutions of higher education until the 1990s. In 2004/05 some 188,124 students were enrolled at 16 institutions of higher education. The most recent legislation pertaining to higher education is the Universities, Colleges and Institutions of Higher Education Law (No. 14, 2005). The Ministry of Higher Education and Scientific Research (MHESR) is split into two main departments. The first is the University Affairs division, which is responsible for qualifications and certificates, equivalency, approval and recognition, with responsibility for both public and private universities. The second department is the National Accreditation Committee (NAC). In 2010 this section of the MHESR was not yet fully established; however it was implementing partial accreditation procedures and processes with regards to the monitoring of public and private universities. Therefore its work was largely limited to determining whether or not institutions should have the legal right to operate. The Law on Private Universities (2005) gives the ministry the power to shut down deficient programmes and courses. The NAC was also working towards the development of strategies for the accreditation of programmes offered at universities and this remains one of the Council's highest priorities.

The general secondary education certificate (thanawiya) is the principal requirement for admission to both public and private higher education. In 2001 the pass-mark in the thanawiya for entry to all undergraduate degrees was set at 70%; additionally, applicants to popular programmes such as engineering or medicine may have to sit a university entrance examination and attend a personal interview. Universities offer two-year, sub-degree Diplomas in professional and technical fields from which students can progress onto advanced degree programmes. Bachelors degrees must last at least four years, and students are required to accumulate a minimum of 132 'credits' for graduation. (The Bachelors of Medicine is a six-year programme of study.)

Traditionally, Yemeni graduate students travelled abroad to study for postgraduate degrees, however in recent years Yemeni institutions have begun awarding postgraduate degrees (although the range is still quite limited). The first postgraduate qualification is the postgraduate Diploma, which is a one-year course that is also regarded as a preparatory course for the Masters degree, which lasts two years. Finally, although Doctorates are now being offered by universities on an 'in-house' basis there is no uniform system for their award.

The Ministry of Technical Education and Vocational Training was established in 2001 and is the body responsible for technical and vocational education in Yemen. Post-secondary technical and vocational education is offered by a range of different professional and vocational institutes and is divided into Regular (or General), Parallel and Further (or Continuing) Education and Training. The Certificate in Technical Education is awarded after a two-year course at technical institutes and is open to students with either the thanawiya or the Certificate of Vocational Training. US-style 'community' colleges have been established and they specialize in three-year Diploma courses, admission to which requires the thanawiya.

Regulatory Bodies

GOVERNMENT

Ministry of Culture and Tourism: POB 129, San'a; tel. (1) 235114; fax (1) 235113; Minister of Culture MUHAMMAD ABU BAKR AL-MAFLAHI.

Ministry of Education: San'a; tel. (1) 274548; fax (1) 274555; e-mail moed@yemen.net.ye; Minister of Education ABD AS-SALAM AL-JAWFI; Minister of Higher Education and Scientific Research SALEH ALI BASORRA.

Learned Society

LANGUAGE AND LITERATURE

British Council: 3rd Fl., Administrative Tower, San'a Trade Centre, Algiers St, POB 2157, San'a; tel. (1) 448356; fax (1) 448360; e-mail information@ye.britishcouncil.org; internet www.britishcouncil.org/me-yemen.htm; offers courses and exams in English language and British culture and promotes cultural exchange with the UK; Asst Dir, Resources AZIZ AL-BAAR.

Libraries and Archives

Aden

Miswat Library: Aden; previously called Lake Library; administered by Aden Municipality; 30,000 vols, in English, Arabic and Urdu.

Teachers' Club Library: Aden; over 2,000 vols.

Travelling Library: Aden; ancillary to Miswat Library; administered by Aden Municipality; 9,500 vols, in English and Arabic.

San'a

British Council Library: Al-Sanabani Roundabout, Al Jame'a St, San'a; tel. (1) 373248; e-mail h.jailan@ust.edu.ye; internet www.britishcouncil.org/me-yemen-learning--centre-membership-details.htm; 10,000 vols, 36 periodicals; Dir RAJA'A BAZARA.

Library of the Great Mosque of San'a: San'a; f. 1925; the colln of 10,000 MSS and printed vols is not at present accessible to the public; Librarian ZAID BIN ALI ENAN.

Universities

UNIVERSITY OF ADEN

POB 6312, Khormaksar, Aden

Telephone: (2) 234428

Fax: (2) 234426

E-mail: rector@adenuniversity.edu.ye

Internet: www.adenuniversity.edu.ye

Founded 1975

State control

Languages of instruction: Arabic, English

Academic year: September to June

Rector: Prof. Dr ABDUL WAHAB RAWEH

Vice-Rector for Academic Affairs: Assoc. Prof. Dr SAEED ABDO GABALI

Vice-Rector for Scientific Research and Postgraduate Studies: Assoc. Prof. Dr AHMED ALI AL-HAMDANI

Vice-Rector for Students' Affairs: Asst Prof. Dr NASSER A. NASSER

Sec.-Gen.: Assoc. Prof. Dr AHMED SALEH MUNASSER

Number of teachers: 1,482

Number of students: 22,761

Publications: *Al-Tawassul* (2 a year), *Al-Yemen* (2 a year), *Journal of Natural and Applied Sciences* (2 a year), *Journal of Social Sciences and Humanities* (2 a year), *Saba* (2 a year), *Yemen Engineer* (3 a year), *Yemeni Journal for Agricultural Research* (2 a year)

DEANS

Faculty of Administration: Assoc. Prof. FUAD RASHED ABDO

Faculty of Agricultural Sciences: Assoc. Prof. Dr ABBAS BAWAZIR

Faculty of Arts: Assoc. Prof. Dr SULAIMAN FARAJ BIN AZOON

Faculty of Economics: Prof. Dr MOHAMED A WARET

Faculty of Education (Aden): Asst Prof. Dr YACOOB A. KASSEM

Faculty of Education (Dalea): Asst Prof. Dr MOHD S. OBADI

Faculty of Education (Loder): Asst Prof. Dr SALEH A AL BORKANI

Faculty of Education (Radfan): Asst Prof. Dr ABDULLA MOHAMMED

Faculty of Education (Sabr): Assoc. Prof. Dr ALI QASEM. AKLAN

Faculty of Education (Shabwa): Assoc. Prof. Dr NASER SALEH. HABTOOR
Faculty of Education (Tur Al-Baha): Asst Prof. Dr HAMID ABDUL MAGEED QUBATI
Faculty of Education (Yafai): Assoc. Prof. Dr ABDUL RAHMAN AL-WALI
Faculty of Education (Zingibar): Assoc. Prof. Dr MOHAMMED A. HOSEEN
Faculty of Engineering: Assoc. Prof. Dr ABDUL WALI HADI
Faculty of Law: Assoc. Prof. Dr SAAD M. SAAD
Faculty of Medicine: Assoc. Prof. Dr ABDULLA SAEED. HATAB
Faculty of Oil and Minerals: Asst Prof. Dr KHALED ALI. AL SHAMSI

UNIVERSITY OF DHAMAR

POB 87246, Dhamar
Telephone: (6) 509554
Fax: (6) 509556
Internet: www.thuniv.edu.ye
Founded 1996
Rector: AHMED AL-HADHRANI
Faculties of Admin. Sciences, Art, Dentistry, Education, Engineering, Law, Medicine, Nursing, Physical Sciences, Tourism, Veterinary Medicine.

HADHRAMOUT UNIVERSITY OF SCIENCE AND TECHNOLOGY

POB 50512–50511, Mukalla-Hadhramout Governate
Telephone: (5) 360865
Fax: (5) 360864
E-mail: hadhramout_univ@y.net.ye
Internet: www.hust.edu.ye
Founded 1993
State control
Vice Rector: SALEM AWAD RAMODHA
Faculties of Admin. Sciences, Applied Science, Arts, Engineering and Technology, Environment Science and Marine Biology, Nursing; College for Women, College of Education.

HODEIDAH UNIVERSITY

POB 3114, Hodeidah
Telephone: (3) 222703
Fax: (3) 222703
E-mail: info@hoduniv.edu.ye
Internet: www.hoduniv.edu.ye
State control
Chair.: Dr MOHAMMAD QASIM BERT
Faculties of Education, Management Systems and Marine Sciences.

IBB UNIVERSITY

POB 70270, Ibb
Telephone: (4) 408069
Fax: (4) 408068
E-mail: ibbunv@yemen.net.ye
Internet: www.ibbunv.com.ye
Founded 1996
State control
Rector: Prof. Dr AHMED M. SHUQ'A ALDEEN
Faculties of Agriculture and Veterinary Science, Arts, Dentistry, Economics and Management, Education, Engineering and Architecture and Science; Centres for Agricultural and Environmental Consultancy, Educational Technology and Engineering Consultancy.

QUEEN ARWA UNIVERSITY

POB 11586, San'a
Telephone: (1) 415991
Fax: (1) 449992
E-mail: arwa@arwauniversity.edu.ye
Internet: www.queenarwauniversity.edu.ye
Founded 1996
Vice-Rector: MUHAMMED A. ALKHAYYAT
Dean of Student Affairs: Dr HAZZA ABDO SALEM AL-HOMAIDI
Colleges of Arts and Human Science, Economics and Administration, Engineering and Computer Science, Law, Medicine and Pharmacy.

SAN'A UNIVERSITY

POB 1247, San'a
Telephone: (1) 464483
Fax: (1) 464483
E-mail: info@suye.ac
Internet: www.new.suye.ac/en
Founded 1970
State control; financial support from Kuwait
Languages of instruction: Arabic, English
Academic year: October to June
Pres.: Dr KHALID ABDULLAH TAMEM
Number of teachers: 332
Number of students: 10,715
Publication: Faculty research journals

DEANS

Faculty of Agriculture: Dr NASSER AULAQI (acting)
Faculty of Arts: Dr AHMED AL SAYDI
Faculty of Commerce and Economics: Dr NASSER AULAQI
Faculty of Education: Dr MOHAMED AL KHADER
Faculty of Engineering: Dr AWAD SALEH
Faculty of Law and Sharia: Dr ABDUL MUNIM AL BADRAWI
Faculty of Medicine and Health Sciences: Dr ABDALLAH AL-HURAYBI
Faculty of Science: Dr ALI AL SHUKAI

TAIZ UNIVERSITY

POB 6803, Taiz
Telephone: (4) 221378
Fax: (4) 221381
Internet: www.nationaluni.net
Founded 1995
State control
Languages of instruction: Arabic, English
Pres.: MOHAMED AL-SOOFI
Number of teachers: 629
Number of students: 27,266
Library of 95,139 vols, 5700 periodicals
Publications: *Journal of Educational and Academic Development* (1 a year), *Journal of Educational Sciences and Psychology* (1 a year), *Taiz University Research Journal* (1 a year)

DEANS

Faculty of Administration: Prof. MOHFOOZ ALLADITHI
Faculty of Arts: Prof. ABAS SOSWAH
Faculty of Education: Prof. NABEEL SUFIAN
Faculty of Engineering: Prof. FISAL IBRAHEEM
Faculty of Law: Prof. MOHAMED ALHUMAIDY
Faculty of Medicine: Prof. FAUD ALKHILY
Faculty of Science: Prof. ABDULRAHMAN ALZOBIRI

PROFESSORS

ADDULKARIM MOHARRAM, W., English Language Teaching
AHMAD ALTHAIFANY, A., Foundation of Education
ALI KAHTAN, M., Planning Management of National Economy
ALMEKHLAFY, S., Educational Management
ALSOOFI, M., Socio Psychology in Education
ALZOBIRI, A., Microbiology
HAIDER, A., Teaching Methods of Science
MOHAMED ALHAKIMY, A., Plant Physiology
MOHAMED TRBUSH, K., General Law
NASIR ALI, A., Geography
SAEED ALSHOAYBY, M., General International Law
SALEH SUFIAN, N., Psychology
SHARAF GHALEB, A., Geology (Minerals)
SOSWAH, A., Linguistics
TARESH, M., Educational Planning

College

High College of Koran Kareem: POB 11229, Riyadh Av., San'a; tel. (1) 216865; fax (1) 216869; e-mail high-kuraan@y.net; Sharia and Islamic Studies.

ZAMBIA

The Higher Education System

Institutions of higher education predate the independence of the Republic of Zambia (formerly Northern Rhodesia) from the United Kingdom in 1964, the oldest being Zambia College of Agriculture, which was founded in 1947. In 1965 the University of Zambia was founded and it remained the only university-level institution until the foundation of Copperbelt University in 1987. In 2008 the National College of Management and Development Studies was turned into a university by the government in a private–public partnership with Konkola Copper Mines. There are also 14 teacher training colleges. In 1999/2000 there were an estimated 24,553 students enrolled in tertiary education, which is administered by the Ministry of Education.

The standard administrative structure consists of the Chancellor, Vice-Chancellor, Registrar, Bursar, University Council, Senate, Boards of Studies, Deans and Heads of Department. The Chancellor is appointed by the Head of State while the Vice-Chancellors are appointed by the Minister of Education, who also appoints the University Council. The Registrar and Bursar are appointed by the University Council. Other than the State, the main source of university funding is students' tuition fees.

Students are required to obtain five credit-level passes on the Zambian School Certificate (Grade 12) for admission to university. The Bachelors is the main undergraduate degree and is generally four years in duration, except for degrees in agriculture, architecture, engineering (five years), veterinary science (six years) and medicine (seven years). The postgraduate Masters degree is open to students who have been awarded the Bachelors and is a two- to four-year programme of study. The PhD is the highest university degree in Zambia but is only available in a limited number of subjects; it requires four years of study.

The Ministry of Science, Technology and Vocational Training is responsible for providing post-secondary vocational and technical education. Within the Ministry, the Department of Technical Education and Vocational Training administers 11 institutions and 90 technical courses. The principal qualifications are (in ascending order) the Craft Certificate, Certificate, Advanced Certificate and Diploma.

Regulatory Bodies

GOVERNMENT

Ministry of Education: 15102 Ridgeway, POB RW50093, Lusaka; tel. (1) 227636; fax (1) 222396; Minister GEOFFREY LUNGWANGWA.

Ministry of Science, Technology and Vocational Training: POB 50464, Lusaka; tel. (1) 229673; fax (1) 252951; Minister PETER DAKA.

Learned Societies

BIBLIOGRAPHY, LIBRARY SCIENCE AND MUSEOLOGY

Zambia Library Association: POB 38636, Lusaka 10101; internet www.zla.co.zm; Chair. BENSON NJOBVU; Hon. Sec. MUTINTA NABUYANDA; publ. *Journal* (4 a year).

LANGUAGE AND LITERATURE

Alliance Française: Plot 22725, Alick Nkhata Ave, Longacres, POB 30948, 10101 Lusaka; tel. (1) 253467; fax (1) 254735; e-mail afl@microlink.zm; offers courses and exams in French language and culture and promotes cultural exchange with France; attached teaching centres in Kabwe, Kitwe, Livingstone and Ndola.

British Council: Heroes Place, Cairo Rd, POB 34571, Lusaka; tel. (1) 223602; fax (1) 224122; e-mail info@britishcouncil.org.zm; internet www.britishcouncil.org/zambia; offers courses and exams in English language and British culture and promotes cultural exchange with the UK; Dir JOHN MITCHELL.

MEDICINE

Zambia Medical Association: POB RW 148, Lusaka; Chair. Dr S. SIKANETA; Sec. Dr D. LEVITT; publ. *Medical Journal of Zambia* (6 a year).

NATURAL SCIENCES

Biological Sciences

Wildlife and Environmental Conservation Society of Zambia: POB 30255, Lusaka; tel. (1) 251630; fax (1) 251630; e-mail wecsz@zamnet.zm; internet www.conservationzambia.org; f. 1953; dedicated to promoting wildlife and natural resource conservation, environmental education; 2,000 mems; Pres. ADAM JONATHAN POPE; Programme Coordinator PATRICK SHAWA; publs *Black Lechwe* (4 a month), *Chongololo Magazine and Guide* (24 a year), *Chipembele Magazine and Guide* (24 a year).

TECHNOLOGY

Engineering Institution of Zambia: POB 34730, Lusaka; f. 1955; 2,600 mems; Pres. G. K. CHIBUYE; Vice-Pres. Dr K. AKAPELWA; publ. *Journal* (4 a year).

Research Institutes

GENERAL

National Institute for Scientific and Industrial Research: POB 310158, International Airport Rd, 15302 Lusaka; tel. (1) 281082; fax (1) 283533; e-mail directorate@nisir.org.zm; internet www.nisir.org.zm; f. 1967; statutory body to conduct scientific and industrial research and to collect and disseminate scientific information; incorporates Livestock and Pest Research Centre, Tree Improvement Research Centre, Radioisotopes Research Unit, Food Technology Research Unit, Water Resources Research Unit, Building and Industrial Minerals Research Unit, Information Services Unit, Technical Services Unit and Material Testing Unit; library of 9,200 vols, 100 periodicals; Exec. Dir Dr MWANANYANDA MBIKUSITA LEWANIKA; publs *Sci-Tech Newsletter* (4 a year), *Zambia Journal of Science and Technology* (irregular), *Zambia Science Abstracts* (1 a year).

AGRICULTURE, FISHERIES AND VETERINARY SCIENCE

Central Fisheries Research Institute: POB 350100, Chilanga; tel. (1) 278597; fax (1) 278173; e-mail piscator@zamnet.zm; f. 1965; hydrobiological research directed towards increasing fish production, co-management research directed towards sustainable fisheries management, fish-stock assessment, social and economic studies in fishing regions; library of 4,700 vols; Deputy Dir C. K. KAPASA; Chief Fisheries Research Officer P. NGALANDE; publs *Fisheries Statistics*, *Project Reports* (irregular).

Central Veterinary Research Station: POB 33980, Lusaka; tel. (1) 233444; e-mail cvri@zamnet.zm; f. 1926; directed by the Ministry of Lands and Agriculture; general veterinary diagnosis and research; Prin. Veterinary Research Officer Dr S. H. KABILIKA.

Division of Forest Products Research: POB 20388, Kitwe; tel. (2) 227088; f. 1963; controls research into wood utilization, timber properties preservation, engineering, forest products and wood composite studies; Chief Officer S. M. MUTEMWA; publ. *Records* (irregular).

Division of Forest Research: POB 22099, Kitwe; tel. (2) 220456; fax (2) 224110; f. 1956; ecological and botanical studies; soil and site assessment investigations; silvicultural research, exotic plantations and indigenous forests and woodlands; mensurational studies of plantation growth; tree breeding and selection; agroforestry and fuelwood projects; forest pathology and entomology; seed collection, processing, testing and low-temperature storage; staff of 24; library of 7,800 vols, 150 periodicals and 100 serials; Chief Forest Research Officer F. M. MALAYA; publs *Research Bulletins*, *Research Newsletter*, *Research Notes*, *Research Pamphlets*.

International Red Locust Control Organization for Central and Southern Africa: POB 240252, Ndola; tel. (2) 651251; fax (2) 650117; e-mail locust@zamnet.zm; f.

1970; to prevent plagues of red locust by controlling incipient outbreaks, to assist mem. countries in the management of army worm and grain-eating birds and to carry out research and training; member countries: Kenya, Malawi, Mozambique, Tanzania, Zambia, Zimbabwe; library of 3,000 vols, 35 periodicals; Dir A. D. GADABU; publ. *Scientific Papers*.

Mount Makulu Agricultural Research Station: Zambia Agriculture Research Institute, Private Bag 7, Chilanga; tel. and fax (1) 278130; internet www.zari.gov.zm/makuluresearchtest.php; f. 1952; Headquarters of Department of Research and Specialist Services, Ministry of Agriculture, Food and Fisheries, and 11 regional and specialist research stations; research on soils, soil classification, vegetation types and land classification; agronomy; chemistry; ecology; entomology; pasture research; phytosanitary services; plant breeding; plant pathology; Seeds Control and Certification Institute; stored products entomology; cotton entomology; main crops under investigation: maize, groundnuts, cotton, tobacco, pastures and pasture legumes, beans, wheat, sorghum, soyabeans; library of 30,000 vols, 20,000 reports, 15,000 reprints; Prin. Agricultural Research Officer BERNADETTE LUBOZUYA; publs *Accessions List* (6 a year), *Production Farming in Zambia* (12 a year), *Reprints of Articles by Staff Members*, *Research Branch Memoranda* (irregular).

ECONOMICS, LAW AND POLITICS

Pan-African Institute for Development, East and Southern Africa: POB 80448, Kabwe; tel. (5) 223651; fax (5) 223451; e-mail paidesa@zamnet.zm; f. 1979; training, research, surveys, follow-up action; library of 8,000 vols; Dir Dr LUTHER BANGA; publ. *Current Contents: Development Studies* (4 a year).

MEDICINE

National Food and Nutrition Commission: POB 32669, 10101 Lusaka; tel. (1) 227803; fax (1) 221426; e-mail nfnc@zamnet.zm; f. 1967; statutory body to improve the nutritional status of the people of Zambia; 98 mems; Chair. CRESTA KALUBA; Exec. Dir PRISCILLA N. LIKWASI.

Occupational Health Safety and Research Bureau: Independence Ave, POB 20205, Kitwe; tel. (2) 228977; fax (2) 222823; e-mail ohmb@zamnet.zm; internet www.geocities.com/ohsrb; f. 1950; research on pneumoconiosis and related chest diseases, assessment and advice on control of hazardous conditions in industrial workplaces; library of 300 vols; Dir Dr C. M. MUSOWE.

Tropical Diseases Research Centre: POB 71769, Ndola; tel. (2) 620737; fax (2) 620737; e-mail info@tdrc.org.zm; internet www.tdrc.org.zm; f. 1976; research in communicable diseases, support for disease control and primary health care programmes; trains Zambian scientists in the field of biomedical research, serves as int. research and training centre; epidemiological research, clinical trials, research in malaria, schistosomiasis, trypanosomiasis, diarrhoeal diseases, etc.; 28 researchers, 76 support staff; library of 3,300 vols, 219 periodicals; Dir Dr EMMANUEL KAFWEMBE.

NATURAL SCIENCES

Physical Sciences

Geological Survey of Zambia (Ministry of Mines and Minerals Development): POB 50135, Lusaka; tel. (1) 250174; fax (1) 250174; e-mail gsd@zamnet.zm; f. 1951; statutory depository for all mining and prospecting records and reports; responsible for geological mapping, economic mineral investigations, assisting the public on mineral matters, and advising the Ministry on all mineral and geological matters; library of 89,346 vols; Dir D. MULELA; publs *Records*, *Bulletins*, *Memoirs*, *Reports*, *Occasional Papers*, *Economic Reports*, *Annotated Bibliography and Index of the Geology of Zambia*, and maps.

Libraries and Archives

Kitwe

Hammarskjöld Memorial Library: POB 21493, Kitwe; tel. (2) 211488; fax (2) 211001; e-mail daglib@zamnet.zm; internet www.mindolo.org/dml; f. 1963; 26,000 vols; colln of films, filmstrips, slides, microfiche, video cassettes, tape-recordings on local history; rare book colln on the history of central Africa; specializes in social sciences; research library and archives of the Mindolo Ecumenical Foundation; colln on American society and culture; Librarian DUNSTAN CHIKONKA.

Kitwe Public Library: POB 20070, Kaunda Sq., Kitwe; tel. 213685; f. 1954; 33,000 vols; 1 br. library.

Lusaka

Lusaka City Libraries: POB 31304, Katondo Rd, Lusaka; tel. (1) 227282; f. 1943; 3 br. libraries and a mobile library; 145,000 vols, 200 periodicals, 320 maps; Librarian J. C. NKOLE; publ. *Library Bulletin* (4 a year).

National Archives of Zambia: POB 50010, Lusaka; tel. (1) 254081; fax (1) 254080; e-mail naz@zamnet.zm; f. 1947; covers national literature from 1890 to the present day in the forms of national archives, historical MSS, microfilms, cartographic, philatelic, currency, pictorial and printed publication collns; 18,000 linear metres of records; depository and reference library of 17,000 vols and 11,000 periodicals; the National Archives Library is a reference and legal deposit library for all printed publications published in Zambia; Dir CRISPIN HAMOOYA; Senior Archivist T. M. SUUYA; Senior Librarian H. K. NYENDWA; publs *Annual National Bibliography*, *Calendars of District Note Books, vols I and IV*, *Information About the National Archives of Zambia*, *List of Periodicals*.

Zambia Library Service: c/o Ministry of Education, POB 50093, Civic Center Area Plot 82, cnr Mogadishu and Chimanga Rd, 10101 Lusaka; tel. (1) 250855; fax (1) 250760; internet www.moe.gov.zm; f. 1962; 6 regional libraries, 18 branch libraries and a central library of 500,000 vols; aims to provide a countrywide free public library service; Chief Librarian ETHEL N. TEMBO; publ. *Zambia Library Service Newsletter* (irregular).

Ndola

Ndola Public Library: POB 70388, Independence Way, Ndola; tel. (2) 617173; f. 1934; 90,000 vols, 140 periodicals; public library services in Lusaka serving Ndola City Council Community; central library, 4 brs, 2 prison library centres; centre for American Circulating Library from American Cultural Center; Librarian Dr K. MUMBA CHISAKA; publ. *Copperbelt Library Bulletin* (irregular).

Museums and Art Galleries

Livingstone

Livingstone Museum: Mosi-oa-Tunya Rd, POB 60498, Livingstone; tel. (3) 321204; fax (3) 320991; e-mail livmus@zamnet.zm; f. 1934; ethnology of the peoples of Zambia; prehistory, history and natural history of Zambia; autograph, letters and relics of David Livingstone; library of 20,000 vols, 200 periodicals, including special collection of 2,000 vols on prehistory, history, ethnography and Africana; supporting depts of taxidermy, conservation and education; Dir V. K. KATANEKWA; publs *The Livingstone Museum Newsletter*, *Zambia Museum Journal*.

Mbala

Moto Moto Museum: POB 420230, Mbala; tel. and fax (4) 450243; e-mail motomoto@zamtel.zm; f. 1974; research in ethnography, prehistory and history; educational and exhibition programmes; library of 5,000 vols; Dir NKOLE E. SOSALA; publ. *Zambia Museums Journal* (irregular).

Ndola

Copperbelt Museum: 911 Buteko Ave, POB 71444, Ndola; tel. (2) 613591; fax (2) 617450; e-mail cbmus@zamnet.zm; f. 1962; colln, conservation, preservation, documentation and exhibit of geological and historical items, ethnography and natural history; Dir STANFORD MUDENDA SIACHOONO.

Universities

COPPERBELT UNIVERSITY

POB 21692, Kitwe
Telephone: (2) 225155
Fax: (2) 222218
E-mail: registrar@cbu.ac.zm
Internet: www.cbu.edu.zm

Founded 1979 as Ndola Campus of Univ. of Zambia; ind. univ. status 1987
State Control
Language of instruction: English
Academic year: March to December (3 terms)

Chancellor: Prof. MUYUNDA MWANALUSHI
Vice-Chancellor: Prof. MICHAEL MUSONDA
Deputy Vice-Chancellor: Dr ERNEST M. BEELE
Registrar: ALLAN M. ILLUNGA
Librarian: C. B. M. LUNGU

Number of teachers: 211
Number of students: 3,197

Publication: *Journal of Business* (4 a year)

DEANS

School of Built Environment: G. C. NGOMA
School of Business: Dr S. CHAMA
School of Natural Resources: EMMANUEL CHUNDA
School of Technology: Dr I. S. SINGH

PROFESSORS

BANDA, D., Civil Engineering and Construction
BANDA, F., Production Management
BANGILI, J., Electrical Engineering
CHULU, B. L., Mining
KANYMEBO, J. J., Chemical Engineering
LIBATI, H. M., Computer Science
MABO, B., Architecture
MALAMBO, F., Wildlife Management
MALAMBO, F., Wood Science and Technology
MULAMBYA, A., Business Administration
MUSOKWA, P. A. N., Accounting and Finance
NALUMINO, A., Land Economy

NJOVU, F., Forest Resource Management
OKRA, J. A., Urban and Regional Planning
SIMUSHI, S., Building Science
TAYLOR, T. K., Postgraduate Programme

CONSTITUENT SCHOOLS

School of Built Environment: tel. (2) 225086; e-mail deansbe@cbu.ac.zm.

School of Business: tel. (2) 227946; fax (2) 228346; e-mail deansb@cbu.ac.zm.

School of Natural Resources: tel. (2) 227946; e-mail forestry@cbu.ac.zm.

School of Technology: tel. (2) 228212; fax (2) 228212; e-mail deanst@cbu.ac.zm.

ATTACHED INSTITUTES

Centre for Lifelong Education: Dir Col (rtd) LLOYD MWILA.

Institute of Environmental Management: Dir M. NABUYANDA.

UNIVERSITY OF ZAMBIA

POB 32379, Lusaka
Telephone: (1) 291777
Fax: (1) 253952
E-mail: registrar@unza.zm
Internet: www.unza.zm

Founded 1965
State control
Language of instruction: English
Academic year: July to May

Chancellor: Dr JACOB M. MWANZA
Vice-Chancellor: Prof. STEPHEN SIMUKANGA
Deputy Vice-Chancellor: Dr WILSON MWENYA
Registrar: Dr ALVERT N'GANDU
Librarian: Dr V. CHIFWEPA

Number of teachers: 535
Number of students: 13,500

Publications: *African Social Research*, *Journal of Humanities*, *Journal of Medicine*, *Journal of Sciences and Technology*, *Zambia Law Journal*, *Zambian Papers*, *Zango*

DEANS

Agricultural Sciences: Dr MIKE MWALA
Distance Education: CHISHIMBA NKOSHA (Dir)
Education: W. CHAKANIKA
Engineering: Dr ZEBEDIAH PHIRI
Humanities and Social Sciences: Dr SIAMWIZA BENARD
Law: Dr M. MUNALULA
Medicine: Dr F. GOMA
Mines: Dr O. SIKAZWE
Natural Sciences: Dr HENRY M. SICHINGABULA
Research and Graduate Studies: Prof. S. NYAMBE (Dir)
Veterinary Medicine: Dr AARON MWEENE

PROFESSORS

BANDA, G. P. A., Geography
BANDA, S. F., Chemistry
BANDA, S. S., Medical Education
BHAT, G. J., Paediatrics and Child Health
CHAKANIKA, W., Adult Education and Extension Studies
CHISHIMBA, C. P., In-Service Education and Advisory Science Education
CHITAMBO, H., Paraclinical Studies
DILLON-MALONE, C., Philosophy
ERZINGATSIAN, K., Surgery
HAMBOKOMA, C., Mathematics and Science Education
HAWORTH, A., Psychiatry
KAELA, L. C. W., Political and Administrative Studies
KAFUMUKACHE, E. B., Anatomy
KAILE, T., Pathology and Microbiology
KALINDA, T., Agricultural Economics and Extension Education
KAMBANI, S., Mining Engineering
KASEBA, C., Obstetrics and Gynaecology
KWENDAKWEMA, N. J., Agricultural Engineering
LAMBWE, E., Post-Basic Nursing
LEMBA, M., Social Development Studies
LIPALITE, M., Development Studies
LUNGU, I. O., Soil Science
LUSWILI, J., Mathematics and Statistics
MANAKOV, A. K., Physiological Sciences
MATONDO, P., Internal Medicine
MILIMO, M. C., Gender Studies
MSANGO, H. J., Educational Administration and Policy Studies
MULENGA, F. E., History
MULENGA, M. N., Civil Engineering
MWALA, M. S., Crop Science
MWEENE, H. V., Physics
MWIKISA, C. N., Economics
NAMBOTA, A., Disease Control
NG'ANDU, A. N., Mechanical Engineering
NGANDU, S. K., Educational Psychology, Sociology and Special Education
NKHUWA, C. W., Geology
NSOMBO, P., Surveying
NYIRENDA, L. D., Electrical and Electronic Engineering
PHIRI, I. K., Clinical Studies
SIAKALIMA, D. (acting), Psychology
SIKULUMBA, J. K., Literature and Languages
SIULAPWA, J. N., Biomedical Sciences
SIZIYA, S., Community Medicine
TAMBULUKANI, G. (acting), Language and Social Sciences Education
WACHINGA, D. M., Biological Sciences
WITIKA, L. K., Metallurgy and Mineral Processing
YAMBAYAMBA, E. S. K., Animal Sciences
ZULU, S., Library and Information Studies

Colleges

Evelyn Hone College of Applied Arts and Commerce: POB 30029, Lusaka; tel. (1) 235344; fax (1) 225127; e-mail ehcbs@zamnet.zm; f. 1963; library: 14,000 vols; 145 teachers; 3,000 students (1,600 full-time, 1,400 part-time); Prin. MICHAEL TANDEO; Librarian SEBASTIAN NGWIRA.

National Institute of Public Administration: POB 31990, 10101 Lusaka; tel. (1) 228802; fax (1) 227213; e-mail nipa@zamnet.zm; f. 1963; trains govt administrators and accounting personnel for central and local govt; offers training and consultancy in the private sector in management, secretarial work, purchasing and supplies, and law and information technology; library: 28,000 vols; 50 teachers; 1,316 students; Exec. Dir Dr M. C. BWALYA; Registrar PAUL SIMUKOKO; Librarian N. MTANGA.

Natural Resources Development College: POB 310099, Lusaka; tel. (1) 284639; fax (1) 281941; f. 1964; 3-year diploma courses in agriculture, agricultural education and engineering, nutrition, fisheries, water engineering; library: 32,000 vols; 48 teachers; 430 students; Prin. T. F. F. MALUZA; Librarian M. M. MISENGO.

Northern Technical College: POB 250093, Ndola; tel. (2) 680141; fax (2) 680423; e-mail nortec@zamnet.zm; f. 1960; automotive, electrical, heavy duty and mechanical engineering, business studies and communication skills, refrigeration and air-conditioning; library: 20,000 vols; 96 teachers (68 full-time, 28 part-time); 1,300 students (800 full-time, 500 part-time); Prin. (vacant); Librarian NABOMBE PUMULO.

Zambia College of Agriculture: POB 660053, Monze; f. 1947; 2-year certificate course; 42 staff; library: 3,000 vols; 240 students; Prin. D. H. MCCLEERY.

ZIMBABWE

The Higher Education System

Institutions of higher education predate the independence of Zimbabwe (formerly Southern Rhodesia) from the United Kingdom in 1980, the oldest being Esigodini Agricultural Institute, which was founded in 1921. The oldest university-level institution is the University of Zimbabwe (formerly the University College of Rhodesia), which was founded in 1955 (present status since 1970 and present name since 1980) and is one of two state-run universities, the other being the University of Science and Technology at Bulawayo. There are also several private universities including Africa University in Mutare and Solusi University in Figtree. In 2002/03 a total of some 55,689 students were enrolled at institutions of higher education.

The Head of State is the Chancellor of the public universities while their day-to-day administration is overseen by a Vice-Chancellor. Both public and private universities are governed by University Councils.

Two grade 'E' passes at GCE A-level is the minimum requirement for admission to undergraduate studies; however, the strength of competition has effectively raised the bar for admission to grade 'C' in at least three subjects. Admission is also granted to applicants who hold the National Diploma. The principal undergraduate degree is the Bachelors, which may be classified either 'General' or 'Honours' (the distinction lies in the content of the course and not its length). On average, the Bachelors lasts three to four years, but in some subjects the period of study is longer, such as the Bachelors of Medicine and Bachelors of Surgery (both five years). Masters degrees are the first postgraduate-level qualifications, and vary in length from one to two years; they are usually a composite of coursework and research for dissertation, but the MPhil is a purely research degree. The main doctoral-level degree is the DPhil, which is three to four years in duration.

In 1990 the Government initiated wide-ranging reforms of technical and vocational education owing to the failure of the secondary and higher education sectors to match the expectations of both students and employers. Colleges, polytechnics and technical colleges, universities and university colleges all offer vocational training combining class-work and workplace experience. Vocational training centres were first established in 1998 to provide for a Government initiative known as the Skills Training programme. The principal technical and vocational awards are as follows: National Certificate, National Diploma and Higher National Diploma.

In 2008 a new law replacing the National Council for Higher Education Act was enacted amid much criticism. The Minister for Higher and Tertiary Education said the act had been promulgated to register and accredit institutions of higher education and to regulate quality assurance in them. Critics of President Mugabe's Government said it was an attempt to politicize education since the board that would exert control over institutions under the legislation would be appointed by the government.

Regulatory and Representative Bodies

GOVERNMENT

Ministry of Education, Sports and Culture: Ambassador House, Union Ave, POB CY 121, Causeway, Harare; tel. (4) 734051; fax (4) 707599; internet www.moesc.gov.zw; Minister AENEAS CHIGWEDERE.

Ministry of Higher Education and Technology: Government Composite Bldg, cnr Fourth St and Samora Machel Ave, Union Ave, POB UA 275, Harare; tel. (4) 796440; fax (4) 790923; e-mail thesecretary@mhet.ac.zw; internet www.mhet.ac.zw; Minister of Higher and Tertiary Education I. STANISLAUS GORERAZVO MUDENGE.

NATIONAL BODIES

Zimbabwe National Association for Distance and Open Learning: POB 2713, Harare; fax (4) 737640; e-mail college@speciss.co.zw; internet www.saide.org.za/worldbank/countries/zimbabwe/zinadol.htm; f. 1997; Chair. NARAN KALA; Sec. EVISON MUTI.

Learned Societies

GENERAL

UNESCO Office Harare: POB HG 435, Highlands, Harare; located at: 8 Kenilworth Rd, Newlands, Harare; tel. (4) 332222; fax (4) 332344; internet www.zimaids.co.zw/hae; designated Cluster Office for Botswana, Malawi, Mozambique, Zambia and Zimbabwe; Dir KO-CHIH TUNG.

AGRICULTURE, FISHERIES AND VETERINARY SCIENCE

Crop Science Society of Zimbabwe: POB UA 409, Union Ave, Harare; f. 1970; 200 mems.

Zimbabwe Agricultural Society: POB 442, Harare; tel. (4) 705641; fax (4) 705644; f. 1895; 3,500 mems; Gen. Man. J. R. PEARCE.

Zimbabwe Veterinary Association: POB 8397, Causeway, Harare; tel. (4) 303574; fax (4) 307349; f. 1920; 175 mems; Pres. Dr G. GELDART; publ. *Zimbabwe Veterinary Journal* (2 a year).

BIBLIOGRAPHY, LIBRARY SCIENCE AND MUSEOLOGY

Zimbabwe Library Association: POB BE 628, Belvedere, Harare; tel. (4) 792641; fax (4) 703050; e-mail harare.docu-center@unesco.org; f. 1959; 254 mems; Chair. DRIDEN KUNAKA; Sec. ALBERT MASHEKA; publ. *Zimbabwe Librarian.*

HISTORY, GEOGRAPHY AND ARCHAEOLOGY

Geographical Association of Zimbabwe: c/o Dept of Geography and Environmental Science, University of Zimbabwe, Box MP167, Mount Pleasant, Harare; tel. (4) 303211; fax (4) 883264; e-mail cumming@arts.uz.ac.zw; f. 1967; 500 mems; Chair. T. ZINYANDU; Sec. A. CHIKANDA; publs *Geographical Education Magazine* (2 a year), *Geographical Journal of Zimbabwe* (1 a year).

Prehistory Society of Zimbabwe: POB 876, Harare; tel. (4) 300516; f. 1958; promotion of the study of early history, prehistory and archaeology in Africa, with particular reference to Zimbabwe; 100 mems; library of 1,000 vols; Chair. (vacant); publ. *Zimbabwean Prehistory* (every 2 years).

LANGUAGE AND LITERATURE

Alliance Française: 328 Herbert Chitepo Ave, POB 2515, Harare; tel. (4) 704801; e-mail afharare@telco.co.zw; internet www.afzim.org/afharare/hre.html; offers courses and exams in French language and culture and promotes cultural exchange with France; attached teaching centre in Bulawayo.

British Council: Corner House, Samora Michel Ave, POB 664, Harare; tel. (4) 775313; fax (4) 756661; e-mail general.enquiries@britishcouncil.org.zw; internet www.britishcouncil.org.zw; offers courses and exams in English language and British culture and promotes cultural exchange with the UK; attached office in Bulawayo; Regional Dir, Central Africa DAVID MARTIN; Dir Operations, Zimbabwe RAJIV BENDRE.

Zimbabwe Writers Union: Gloag High School, POB 61, Turk Mine; Pres. CONT MHLANGA; Sec.-Gen. PATHISA NYATHI.

MEDICINE

Pharmaceutical Society of Zimbabwe: POB 1476, Harare; tel. (4) 706967; fax (4) 706967; Pres. G. N. MAHLANGY; Sec. Dr F. CHINYANGANYA.

Zimbabwe Dental Association: 1 Thorton Ave, POB 1268, Bulawayo; tel. (9) 72194; fax (9) 634589; e-mail musiyaw@netconnect.co.zw; f. 1939; affiliated to World Dental Fed.; 130 mems; Pres. Dr WEBSTER MUSIYA.

Zimbabwe Medical Association: POB 3671, Harare; tel. (4) 720731; Pres. B. G. MAUCHAZA; Sec. E. VUSHE.

NATURAL SCIENCES

General

Zimbabwe Scientific Association: POB CY 124, The Causeway, Harare; fax (4) 335143; f. 1899; 380 mems; Pres. Dr L. MHLANGA; Sec. Dr J. HUSSEIN; publs *Transactions* (1 a year), *Zimbabwe Science News* (2 a year).

Biological Sciences

BirdLife Zimbabwe: POB RV 100, Runiville, Harare; tel. (4) 481496; fax (4) 490208; e-mail birds@zol.co.zw; internet www.birdlifezimbabwe.co.zw; f. 1951; 480 mems; Dir CHIPANGURA CHIRARA; publs *Babbler* (6 a year), *Honeyguide* (2 a year).

Botanical Society of Zimbabwe: POB 461, Harare; tel. (4) 735163; f. 1934; Hon. Sec. J. R. JAMES.

Kirk Biological Society: Dept of Biological Sciences, University of Zimbabwe, POB MP 167, Mount Pleasant, Harare; tel. (4) 303211; fax (4) 333407; e-mail jmugodo@yahoo.com; f. 1969; botany, zoology, ecology, microbiology; Chair. JAMES MUGODO.

Lowveld Natural History Branch, Wildlife and Environment Zimbabwe: POB 81, Chiredzi; f. 1968; promotion of conservation and natural history education; 186 mems; Chair. G. DABBS; Sec. S. DE ROBILLARD; publs *Newsletter* (12 a year), *The Hartebeest* (1 a year).

Wildlife and Environment Zimbabwe: POB HG 996, Highlands, Harare; tel. (4) 747500/684; fax (4) 747174; e-mail zimwild@mweb.co.zw; internet www.zimwild.co.zw; f. 1927; all aspects of wildlife conservation and environmental awareness; 2,500 mems; Pres. ISAIAH NYAKUSENDWA; Dir Dr WILLIE K. NDUKU; publ. *Zimbabwe Wildlife* (4 a year, online).

Physical Sciences

Geological Society of Zimbabwe: POB CY 1719, Causeway, Harare; internet www.mining.co.zw/gsz.htm; f. 1981; 320 mems; Chair. M. L. VINYU; Sec. H. A. JELSMA.

Mennell Society: Dept of Geology, University of Zimbabwe, POB MP 167, Mount Pleasant, Harare; f. 1964; to promote the understanding of earth sciences through lectures, films, field trips; 40 mems; Pres. H. MUNYANYIWA; Chair. W. MOYCE; publ. *Detritus*.

TECHNOLOGY

Institution of Materials, Minerals and Mining (Zimbabwe Section): POB MP 791, Mount Pleasant, Harare; e-mail kirmir@zol.co.zw; f. 1931; Chair. J. L. NIXON; Hon. Sec. M. R. RICHARDSON.

Survey Institute of Zimbabwe: POB 3869, Harare; f. 1967; 80 mems; voluntary assen of surveyors in the fields of land, engineering, topographical and mine surveying; Pres. S. Z. ZHOU; Hon. Sec. J. BIRKETT.

Zimbabwe Institution of Engineers: POB 660, Harare; tel. (4) 746821; fax (4) 746652; e-mail zie@zarnet.ac.zw; internet www.zie.org.zw; f. 1944; 2,568 mems; Pres. Eng. DANIEL MACKENZIE NCUBE; Deputy Pres. Eng. D. Z. MAREYA; publs *Proceedings* (2 a year), *Zimbabwe Engineer* (12 a year).

Research Institutes

GENERAL

Research Council of Zimbabwe: POB CY 294, Causeway, Harare; tel. (4) 727562; fax (4) 726860; e-mail secretariat@zarnet.ac.zw; internet www.rcz.ac.zw; f. 1964, reconstituted 1984; advisory body to the Government on general scientific policy and official channel for exchange of national and international scientific and technical information; Chair. Dr F. P. GUDJANGA; Sec. S. MUZITE; publs *Directory of Organizations concerned with Scientific Research and Services in Zimbabwe* (every 2 years), *Zimbabwe Research Index* (1 a year), *Symposium Proceedings* (every 2 years).

AGRICULTURE, FISHERIES AND VETERINARY SCIENCE

Agricultural Research Council of Zimbabwe: POB CY 594, Causeway, Harare; internet www.arc.co.zw; f. 1970; advises on agricultural research policy and programmes in Zimbabwe; administers regional research institutes and stations through the Department of Research and Specialist Services (Dir Dr N. R. GATA); Chair. Prof. M. RUKUNI; publs *Kirkia – Journal of Botany of Zimbabwe* (1 a year), *Zimbabwe Agricultural Journal* (6 a year), *Zimbabwe Journal of Agricultural Research* (2 a year).

Research Institutes and Stations:

Agronomy Research Institute: POB CY 550, Causeway, Harare; tel. (4) 704531; fax (4) 728317; e-mail bmavankeni@gmail.com; f. 1975; research into crop agronomy, crop ecology and crop production; Head BUSISO MAVANKENI (acting).

Chemistry and Soil Research Institute: POB CY 550, Causeway, Harare; tel. (4) 704531; fax (4) 728317; f. 1905; research and advisory work on soils and agricultural chemistry; registration and regulation of fertilizers and foodstuffs; crop nutrition, chemistry, pedology, soil physics and soil productivity research sections; Head C. F. MUSHAMBI.

Coffee Research Station: POB 61, Chipinge; tel. (27) 2400; fax (27) 2951; f. 1964; research into all aspects of coffee management, growth, pest and disease control; tea research projects; Officer-in-Charge D. KUTYWAYO.

Cotton Research Institute: PMB 765, Kadoma; tel. (68) 23994; fax (68) 23996; e-mail zimcott@africaonline.co.zw; f. 1925; all aspects of cotton agronomy, breeding, pest and disease research; Head L. T. GONO (acting).

Crop Breeding Institute: POB CY 550, Causeway, Harare; tel. (4) 704531; fax (4) 728317; f. 1948; responsible for breeding programmes on maize, soya beans, groundnuts, wheat, barley, potatoes, sunflowers, cowpen, bambara, groundnut and foodbean; Head Dr A. MASHIRIGWANI.

Department of Research & Specialist Services, Division of Research Services: Fifth St Ext., POB Cy 550, Causeway, Harare; tel. (4) 704531; fax (4) 731133; e-mail rjkangai_biometrics@drss.org.zw; internet www.drss.gov.zw; f. 1967; attached to Biometrics Bureau; undertakes applied biometrical research, provides professional advice and training on experimental design, statistical problems and computer services for research workers; Head JOSEPHINE R. KANGAI.

Farming Systems Research Unit: POB 550, Causeway, Harare; f. 1983; responsible for adapting, developing and testing on farms improved crop and livestock production technologies and systems, and a model for farm systems research acceptable to the Department of Research and Specialist Services and suitable for widescale application in Zimbabwe; Team Leader B. MOMBESHORA.

Grasslands Research Station: PMB 3701, Marondera; tel. (79) 23526; fax (79) 23198; f. 1930; research on pasture, animal and crop production for the high-rainfall sandveld area; selection and testing of Rhizobium strains and commercial production of legume inoculants; Head G. MANYAN.

Henderson Research Station: PMB 2004, Mazowe; tel. (75) 2281; fax (75) 2284; f. 1948; pasture work on the introduction and screening of grasses and legumes for suitability as fertilized pastures; research in ruminant nutrition; herbicide and weed control research; Head Mr SCHAKEREDZA (acting).

Horticultural Research Centre: Grasslands Research Station, POB 810, Marondera; tel. (79) 24122; fax (79) 23198; f. 1975; responsible for all aspects of horticultural research; Officer-in-Charge N. NENGUWO.

Lowveld Research Station: POB 97, Chiredzi; tel. (31) 2397; f. 1967; research in irrigation agronomy in South-Eastern Lowveld; subtropical horticulture and vegetable crops; Head Dr P. NYAMUDEZA.

Matopos Research Station: PMB K 5137, Bulawayo; tel. (83) 8212; fax (83) 8289; f. 1903; research in veld management, ecology of regional soil types, bush encroachment, cattle breeding, and beef production; Head Dr S. MAYO.

Makoholi Experiment Station: PMB 9182, Masvingo; f. 1962; research into problems of animal and crop production for sandveld and medium rainfall districts of Zimbabwe; crop agronomy, cattle production (indigenous breeds) and natural grazing management; Head I. CHIGAMBA.

Nyanga Experimental Station: POB 2061, Nyanga; fax (31) 2739; f. 1911; Pome fruit research; Officer-in-Charge N. NAUBE.

Plant Protection Research Institute: POB CY 550, Causeway, Harare; tel. (4) 704531; fax (4) 728317; e-mail plantpro@ecoweb.co.zw; f. 1964; research and advisory work on plant pests and diseases; biological control, entomology, pathology and nematology sections; Head Dr S. Z. SITHOLE.

Agricultural Research Trust: POB MP 84, Mount Pleasant, Harare; tel. and fax (4) 2930359; e-mail artfarm@mweb.co.zw; internet www.artfarm.co.zw; f. 1980; research into cereals, grains, oilseed and horticultural crops and the provision of research field sites for crop breeders, agronomists and the crop chemical industry; Dir NICK BROOKE; Research Man. LANGTON T MUTEMERI; Financial Man. GORDON A. LIND.

Department of Veterinary Services; Tsetse Control Branch: POB CY 52, Causeway, Harare; tel. (4) 707381; fax (4) 722684; f. 1909; attached to Ministry of Lands and Agriculture; for the control of the tsetse fly population and the investigation of methods of control; laboratory at Harare and research station in the Zambezi Valley; Chief Research Officer W. SHERENI.

Attached Laboratory:

Central Veterinary Laboratory: POB CY551, Causeway, Harare; tel. (4) 705885; fax (4) 707952; e-mail vetlabs@africaonline.co.zw; f. 1906; diagnostic centre and research institute for animal diseases; 35 mems; library of 1,500 vols; Head of Veterinary Diagnostics and Research Branch Dr P. V. HAKAYA.

Forestry Commission: POB HG 139, Highlands, Harare; tel. (4) 498439; fax (4) 497070; f. 1954; state forest authority, responsible for formulating forest policy in Zimbabwe; engaged in large-scale plantation operations; research and advisory services, forestry extension and wildlife utilization.

Attached Centre:

Forest Research Centre: POB HG 595, Highlands, Harare; tel. (4) 498816; fax (4) 497070; conducts research into many aspects of forestry, principally high-yielding plantations, with special emphasis on tree genetics and the production of progressively improved pine and eucalypt seed, wood quality, general plantation management and fertilizer research; screening of multi-purpose tree species for use in fuelwood plantations and social forestry; Deputy Gen. Man. C. M. GUMBIE; publ. *Format* (4 a year).

Tobacco Research Board: POB 1909, Harare; tel. (4) 575289; fax (4) 575288; e-mail tobres@kutsaga.co.zw; f. 1950; conducts research into all types of tobacco, agronomy, breeding, engineering and pest control; operates 3 research stations; board mems, appointed by the Minister of Agriculture, represent growers, buyers, and Ministry of Agriculture; library of 12,000 vols, 250 periodicals; Chair. Dr R. M. MUPAWOSE; Dir A. J. MASUKA.

ECONOMICS, LAW AND POLITICS

Central Statistical Office: POB CY 342, Causeway, Harare; tel. (4) 703971; fax (4) 728529; f. 1927; coordinated statistical service for the Government; staff of 400; Dir L. MACHIROVI.

Institute of Development Studies: University of Zimbabwe, POB MP 167, Harare; tel. (4) 333341; fax (4) 333345; f. 1982 to undertake policy-oriented research, consultancy and training; three research departments: Agrarian and Labour Studies, Economics and Technology Studies and International Relations and Social Development Studies; Poverty Reduction Forum; library of 17,500 vols, 24,000 documents; Dir Dr DONALD P. CHIMANIKIRE.

MEDICINE

Public Health Laboratory: Box CY 430, Causeway, Harare; tel. and fax (4) 720746; e-mail maxhove@yahoo.com; f. 1909; Dir Dr M. G. M. HOVE; Pathologist Dr D. MADZIWA; Chief Medical Technologists Dr O. MAYO, L. ZAWAIRA.

NATURAL SCIENCES

Physical Sciences

Geological Survey of Zimbabwe: POB CY 210, Causeway, Harare; tel. (4) 726342; fax (4) 739601; e-mail zimgeosv@africaonline.co.zw; internet www.geosurvey.co.zw; f. 1910; geological mapping and survey of mineral resources; library of 1,400 vols, 800 symposia, 11,900 periodicals, 2,600 technical files; museum displaying Zimbabwean geology and economic minerals; Dir W. MAGALELA; publs *Bulletins*, *Mineral Resources Series* (irregular), short reports and maps.

Meteorological Service: POB BE 150, Belvedere, Harare; tel. (4) 778173; fax (4) 778161; e-mail jchifuna@weather.utande.co.zw; internet www.weather.utande.co.zw; f. 1897; part of the Ministry of Transport and Communications; Dir RUNGANO P. KARIMANZIRA; publs *Agromet Bulletin* (October–March), *Climate Handbook Supplements*, *Monthly Meteorological Summaries*, *Rainfall Handbook Supplements*, daily weather reports and forecasts, weekly rainfall maps during rainy season November–March.

Affiliated Institute:

Goetz Observatory: POB AC 65, Ascot, Bulawayo; tel. (9) 66197; fax (9) 77811; e-mail goetz@harare.iafrica.com; also seismology; publs *Seismological Bulletin*, *Agricultural Meteorological Bulletin* (12 a year).

TECHNOLOGY

Department of Metallurgy: Ministry of Mines, POB 1375, Causeway, Harare; tel. (4) 726629; fax (4) 793065; f. 1962; 88 staff; library of 280 vols; conducts investigations on methods of economic extraction from precious, base-metal and non-metallic ores and industrial minerals evaluation, also on physical metallurgy, e.g. non-destructive testing, impact testing, etc.; Dir T. I. NYATSANGA; publ. *Testwork Reports*.

Standards Association of Zimbabwe: POB 2259, Harare; tel. (4) 885511; fax (4) 882020; internet www.saz.org.zw; f. 1957; laboratory facilities for testing raw materials and manufactured goods and operates certification mark schemes; prepares and publishes Zimbabwean national standards; provides an information service on standards and a WTO/Technical Barriers to Trade enquiry point on standards and conformity assessment; provides training on standards; Chair. E. JINDA; Dir-Gen. M. P. MUTASA; publs *Catalogue of Zimbabwe Standards*, *Fulcrum* (official bulletin).

Libraries and Archives

Bulawayo

Bulawayo Public Library: 100 Fort St, Bulawayo; tel. (9) 60965; fax (9) 60966; e-mail bpl@graffiti.net; internet www.angelfire.com/ky/bpl; f. 1896; reference, lending, junior library; mobile library; postal service to rural readers; braille collection; African and Zimbabwe collections; Zimbabwe map collection; legal deposit library for Zimbabwe; video and audio cassette collns; 16,000 mems; 100,000 vols; Librarian and Sec. ROBIN WILLIAM DOUST.

National Library and Documentation Service, National Free Library of Zimbabwe: POB 1773, Bulawayo; tel. (9) 62359; fax (9) 77662; f. 1943 as national lending library for educational, scientific and technical books; national centre for inter-library loans; maintains National Union Catalogue; 100,000 vols; Librarian H. R. NCUBE.

Harare

Harare City Library: POB 1087, Harare; tel. (4) 751834; e-mail hararecitylibrary@yahoo.com; f. 1902; 150,000 vols; Public Subscription Library; Librarian and Sec. TRYMORE SIMANGO.

National Archives of Zimbabwe: Private Bag 7729, Causeway, Harare; tel. (4) 792741; fax (4) 792398; f. 1935 as the Government Archives of Southern Rhodesia; Dir. I. MURAMBIWA; incorp. archives of Northern Rhodesia and Nyasaland and designated the Central African Archives 1947; became National Archives of Rhodesia and Nyasaland 1958–63; reverted January 1964 to Rhodesian Government and responsibility for Northern Rhodesia and Nyasaland archives ceased; also serves Zimbabwean municipalities and some parastatal bodies and holds archives of Federation of Rhodesia and Nyasaland; comprises sections of Records Management, Research (Public Archives, Historical Manuscripts), Library (nat. historical reference colln, incl. photographic and map collns; legal deposit, depository for UNESCO publications) and Technical (Reprographic Unit, Conservation Unit, Oral History, Automation, Audio-Visual Archives Unit); exhibition gallery; four provincial records centres; Dir. I. MURAMBIWA; publs *Bibliographical Series*, *Current Periodicals*, *Directory of Libraries*, *Guide to the Public Archives of Rhodesia, Vol. 1, 1890–1923*, *Guide to the Historical Manuscripts in the National Archives*, *Oppenheimer Series*, *Report of the Director* (1 a year), *Zimbabwe National Bibliography* (1 a year).

University of Zimbabwe Library: POB MP 45, Mount Pleasant, Harare; tel. (4) 303211; fax (4) 335383; e-mail librarian@uzlib.uz.ac.zw; internet www.uz.ac.zw/library; f. 1956; c. 700,000 vols; more than 10,000 periodicals; Medical library; Mpilo Hospital library; Law library; Education library; Institute of Devt Studies Library; Lake Kariba Research Station library; Map library; Veterinary library; Africana (Zimbabweana) colln; colln of African languages; U. Z. Theses Colln; Librarian A. CHIKONZO; publ. *Newsletter* (12 a year).

Parliament of Zimbabwe Library: POB CY 298, Causeway, Harare; tel. (4) 700181 ext. 2187; fax (4) 795548; e-mail munatsir@parliament.gov.zw; internet www.parliament.gov.zw; f. 1923; wide range of parliamentary and govt documents obtained from Zimbabwe Parliament and from several Commonwealth countries; gen. colln specializing in political science, history, political biography, economics, sociology, public admin. and management, education, foreign relations; separate law colln, separate archival and reference colln and Zimbabwean publs; 115,000 vols; Prin. Librarian RONALD MUNATSI.

Zimbabwe National Library and Documentation Service: POB 758, Harare; tel. (4) 774943; f. 1972; co-ordinates all libraries in govt depts, colleges of education, agriculture and technology, public libraries; combined stock (100 libraries): 1m. vols; Dir S. R. DUBE; publs *Directory of Zimbabwean Libraries*, *Government Library Service Newsletter*.

Mutare

City of Mutare Public Libraries: POB 48, Mutare; tel. (20) 63412; fax (20) 67785; e-mail dmandowo@mutare.mweb.co.zw; f. 1902; incorporates Sakubva Public Library (f. 1972, 27,000 vols), Dangamvura Public Library (f. 1988, 18,000 vols), Turner Memorial Library (f. 1902, 40,000 vols), Chikanga Public Library (f. 2004, 5,000 vols); Head of Library Services D. MANDOWO.

Museums and Art Galleries

Bulawayo

Natural History Museum of Zimbabwe: Leopold Takawira Ave and Park Rd, POB 240, Bulawayo; tel. (9) 230046; fax (9) 234019; e-mail natmuse@acacia.samara.co.zw; f. 1901; geological, palaeontological, entomological and zoological; study collections and exhibits covering Ethiopian region, with special reference to southern Africa; historical, ethnographical and prehistorical exhibits appertaining to Zimbabwe and adjacent regions; Dir A. KUMIRAI; Curator of Mammals F. P. D. COTTERILL; Curator of Entomology R. SITHOLE; Curator of Arachnology M. FITZPATRICK; Curator of Ornithology A. MSIMANGA; Curator of Herpetology R. L. CHIDAVAENZI; Curator of Palaeontology D. MUNYIKWA; Curator of Ichthyology P.

MAKONI; publs *Arnoldia* (Zimbabwe), *Syntarsus*.

Gweru

Military Museum of Zimbabwe: Lobengula Ave, POB 1300, Gweru; tel. (54) 22816; fax (54) 20321; f. 1972; history of Zimbabwe Midlands and military history of Zimbabwe; Dir T. TSOMONDO.

Harare

National Gallery of Zimbabwe: 20 Julius Nyerere Way, POB CY 848, Causeway, Harare; tel. (4) 704666; fax (4) 704668; e-mail ngallery@harare.iafrica.com; internet www.nationalgallery.co.zw; f. 1957; national collection of sculpture, paintings, drawings, prints, ceramics and artefacts by Zimbabwean and other Southern African artists; also includes European works of art dating from 16th century, and traditional and contemporary African art; regular exhibition programme; education programme; BAT studio for emerging young artists; library of 6,500 vols; Dir Prof. GEORGE P. KAHARI.

National Herbarium and Botanic Garden: POB A 889, Avondale, Harare; tel. (4) 744170; fax (4) 708938; internet www.nationalherbarium.co.zw; f. 1909; attached to Department of Agricultural Research and Extension (AREX); maintains a comprehensive collection of 500,000 specimens, provides an identification service for workers in agriculture and related fields and contributes to knowledge of the flora of South-Central Africa; taxonomic and ecological research, and research on medicinal and poisonous plants; library of 544 vols; Head NOZIPO NOBANDA; publ. *Kirkia* (1 a year).

Zimbabwe Museum of Human Sciences: Civic Centre, POB CY 33, Causeway, Harare; tel. (4) 751797; fax (4) 774207; e-mail nmmz@pci.co.zw; internet www.zimheritage.co.zw/site/nr_museum.htm; f. 1902; zoological, ethnographical, archaeological and historical exhibits, study collections of archaeological and ethnographical material, and rock art appertaining to Zimbabwe and adjacent areas; Dir T. MASONA; publs *Zimbabwea*, *Cookeia*.

Masvingo

Great Zimbabwe National Monument: PB 1060, Masvingo; tel. (39) 62080; fax (39) 63310; e-mail greatzim@mweb.co.zw; internet www.zimheritage.co.zw; ruins of medieval dry-stone buildings representing the Zimbabwe culture; history and development of Great Zimbabwe shown in site museum; world heritage site; Dir E. MATENGA.

Mutare

Mutare Museum: Aerodrome Rd, POB 920, Mutare; tel. (20) 63672; fax (20) 61100; e-mail mutarmus@ecoweb.co.zw; internet www.zimheritage.co.zw; f. 1959; archaeological, zoological and historical exhibits, appertaining to the Eastern Districts in particular; national collection of road transport and firearms; aviary with 200 birds of 24 species; Dir TRAUDE ALLISON ROGERS.

Universities

BINDURA UNIVERSITY OF SCIENCE EDUCATION

Private Bag 1020, Bindura, Mashonaland Central

Telephone: (71) 7531

Fax: (71) 7534

E-mail: info@buse.ac.zw

Internet: www.buse.ac.zw

Founded 1996 as part of Univ. of Zimbabwe; univ. status 2000

State Control

Language of instruction: English

Academic year: August to July

Vice-Chancellor: CUTHBERT A. T. KATSVANGA (acting)

Registrar: TARIRO F. RUMHUMA (acting)

Librarian: A. MHALANGA

Library of 19,000 vols, 20 databases of e-journals

Number of teachers: 186

Number of students: 2,384

DEANS

Faculty of Agriculture and Environmental Science: CUTHBERT A. T. KATSVANGA

Faculty of Commerce: LANGTON RUNYOWA

Faculty of Science Education: A. ZENGAYA

MIDLANDS STATE UNIVERSITY

PMB 9055, Gweru

Telephone: (54) 260409

Fax: (54) 260233

E-mail: registrar@msu.ac.zw

Internet: www.msu.ac.zw

Founded 1999 by Act of Parliament

State control

Academic year: March to December

Vice-Chancellor: Prof. NGWABI BHEBE

Pro-Vice-Chancellor: Prof. RUNGANO J. ZVOBGO

Registrar: G. T. GUNIRA

Library of 50,850 vols

Number of teachers: 229

Number of students: 8,979

Publications: *Southern African Journal of Science and Agriculture and Technology* (4 a year), *The Dyke* (social sciences, 4 a year)

DEANS

Faculty of Arts: Prof. CAROLINE HARFORD

Faculty of Commerce: KATAZO C. MBETU

Faculty of Education: Dr O. P. NDAWI

Faculty of Natural Resources Management and Agriculture: FRANCIS MUGABE

Faculty of Science: A. CHAWANDA

Faculty of Social Sciences: C. N. GWATIDZO

NATIONAL UNIVERSITY OF SCIENCE AND TECHNOLOGY

POB AC 939, Ascot, Bulawayo

Telephone: (9) 282842

Fax: (9) 289057

E-mail: mtkariwo@nust.ac.zw

Internet: www.nust.ac.zw

Founded 1990

State control

Language of instruction: English

Academic year: August to May

Chancellor: Pres. of Zimbabwe R. G. MUGABE

Vice-Chancellor: (vacant)

Pro Vice-Chancellor: Prof. L. R. NDLOVU

Registrar: M. T. KARIWO

Librarian: K. MATSIKA

Number of teachers: 150 full-time

Number of students: 2,800

DEANS

Faculty of Applied Science: Dr M. M. BHALA

Faculty of Architecture and Quantity Surveying: Prof. S. IK-UMENNE

Faculty of Commerce: R. TADU

Faculty of Communication and Information Science: Prof. S. M. MADE

Faculty of Industrial Technology: Dr P. K. KUIPA

Depts of accounting, applied biology, applied chemistry, applied mathematics, applied physics, architecture, banking, business management, chemical engineering, computer science, civil and water engineering, electronic engineering, finance, industrial and manufacturing engineering, insurance and actuarial science, textile technology, business school, quantity surveying, environmental science and health, journalism and media studies, technical teacher education, sports science and coaching, and library, information science and archives; centre for continuing education, forestry resources and wildlife management; medical school

PROFESSORS

Faculty of Applied Sciences:

GHOLAP, A. V.
MUNDY, P.J.
READ, J. S.

Faculty of Architecture and Quantity Surveying:

HYLAND, A. D. C.

Faculty of Communication and Information Science:

MADE, S. M.

UNIVERSITY OF ZIMBABWE

POB MP 167, Mount Pleasant, Harare

Telephone: (4) 303212

Fax: (4) 333407

Internet: www.uz.ac.zw

Founded 1955 as Univ. College of Rhodesia; became Univ. of Rhodesia in 1970, present name 1980

Language of instruction: English

Academic year: August to June

Chancellor: HE THE PRES. OF THE REPUBLIC OF ZIMBABWE

Vice-Chancellor: Prof. LEVI NYAGURA

Registrar: SERGEANT CHEVO

Librarian: A. C. CHIKONZO

Number of teachers: 834

Number of students: 12,500

Publications: *Central African Journal of Medicine* (12 a year), *Journal of Applied Science in Southern Africa* (2 a year), *Zambezia* (2 a year)

DEANS

Faculty of Agriculture: Dr C. MUTISI

Faculty of Arts: Prof. P. MASHIRI

Faculty of Commerce: Dr I. CHANETA

Faculty of Education: Prof. R. MOYANA

Faculty of Engineering: W. NYEMBA

Faculty of Law: E. MAGADE

Faculty of Medicine: Prof. M. M. CHIDZONGA

Faculty of Science: Dr M. MUCHUWETI

Faculty of Social Studies: Prof. R. GAIDZANWA

Faculty of Veterinary Science: Prof. T. HOVE

ZIMBABWE OPEN UNIVERSITY

POB MP 1119, Mt Pleasant, Harare

Telephone: (4) 333452

Fax: (4) 303151

E-mail: kdzvimbo@icon.co.zw

Founded 1999

State control

Language of instruction: English

Chancellor: The President of the Republic of Zimbabwe

Vice-Chancellor: Prof. K. P. DZVIMBO

Registrar: R. E. MHASVI

Librarian: L. MAENZANISE

Library of 16,214 books, 16 periodicals

Number of teachers: 78 full-time

Number of students: 13,877 (13,443 undergraduate, 434 postgraduate)

DEANS

Faculty of Commerce and Law: C. J. MURombedzi

Faculty of Education and the Humanities: Prof. M. Izuagie

Faculty of Science and the Social Sciences: Dr R. Chimedza

Colleges

Bulawayo Polytechnic: Park Rd, 12th Ave, POB 1392, Bulawayo; tel. (9) 63181; f. 1927; tertiary education in technical, commercial, scientific, design and catering fields; library: 37,170 vols; 360 teachers (210 full-time, 150 part-time); 5,448 students; Prin. A. Mwadiwa.

Chibero College of Agriculture: Private Bag 901, Norton; tel. (62) 2238; f. 1960; 2-year national diploma in agriculture; library: 6,000 vols; 15 teachers; 120 students; Prin. M. E. Nyamangara; publ. *Agricultural Education.*

Esigodini Agricultural Institute: Private Bag 5808, Esigodini; tel. (88) 297; fax (88) 296; f. 1921; 18 teachers; 120 students; Prin. David Themba Mguni.

Gwebi College of Agriculture: Private Bag 376B, Harare; tel. (4) 304515; fax (4) 333850; e-mail gwebiagric@gta.gov.zw; f. 1950; 3-year diploma in agriculture, 15-month higher national diploma in horticulture; library: 2,300 vols; 15 teachers; 120 students; Prin. W. Matizha.

Harare Polytechnic: POB CY 407, Causeway, Harare; tel. (4) 752311; fax (4) 720955; f. 1927; full-time and sandwich courses for technicians and craftsmen; courses in printing and adult education; full-time and part-time courses in library and information science, computer studies, civil construction, mechanical engineering, mass communication, business studies, science and technology, automotive engineering, secretarial studies; library: 68,000 vols; 500 teachers (incl. part-time); 9,000 students; Prin. S. Raza.

Kushinga-Phikelela National Farmer Training Centre: Private Bag 3705, Marondera; tel. (79) 24329; fax (79) 23916; e-mail kushinga@africaonline.co.zw; f. 1982; 3-year certificate courses in commercial farming; short courses in animal production, crop production, farm machinery and farm and agri-business; library: 3,100 vols; 13 teachers; 120 students; Prin. B. Nleya.

Mlezu Institute of Agriculture: POB 8062, Kwekwe; f. 1982; 2-year course; Prin. J. K. D. Maripfonde (acting).

School of Social Work: University of Zimbabwe, Private Bag 66022, Kopje, Harare; tel. (4) 752965; fax (4) 751903; e-mail sswprinc@samara.co.zw; f. 1964; first degrees, certificate, Masters degree and diploma courses; library: 19,870 vols; 13 teachers; 250 students; Dir Prof. E. Kaseke.

Zimbabwe College of Music: Box 66352, Kopje, Harare; tel. and fax (4) 749077; e-mail zcmlib@zol.co.zw; f. 1948; library: 3,000 vols; 35 teachers; 500 students; Chair. Ben Zulu; Dir Christopher Timbe; Registrar Friday Mbirimi; Librarian Priscilla Chidohwe.

INDEX OF INSTITUTIONS

B

C

D

E

F

G

H

I

J

K

L

M

N

O

P

Q

R

S

T

U

V

W